PUBLIC LIBRARY CATALOG

TWELFTH EDITION

STANDARD CATALOG SERIES

JULIETTE YAAKOV, GENERAL EDITOR

CHILDREN'S CATALOG

MIDDLE AND JUNIOR HIGH SCHOOL
LIBRARY CATALOG

SENIOR HIGH SCHOOL LIBRARY CATALOG

FICTION CATALOG

PUBLIC LIBRARY CATALOG

PUBLIC LIBRARY CATALOG

Guide to Reference Books

and

Adult Nonfiction

TWELFTH EDITION

EDITED BY

JULIETTE YAAKOV

THE H. W. WILSON COMPANY
NEW YORK AND DUBLIN
2004

ISBN 0-8242-1039-5

Visit H.W. Wilson's Web site at: www://hwwilson.com

CONTENTS

Preface vii

Acknowledgments ix

Directions for Use of the Catalog x

Outline of Classification xi

Part 1. Classified Catalog 1

Part 2. Author, Title, Subject, and Analytical Index. 1007

CONTENTS

Preface vii

Acknowledgments xi

Directions for use of the Atlas xiii

Outline of Classification 1

Part I: Classical Concepts 7

Part 2: Author, Title, Subject, and Family Index 1007

PREFACE

PUBLIC LIBRARY CATALOG is a list of recommended reference and nonfiction books for adults, classified by subject. The Public Library Catalog service consists of this basic volume and three annual supplements for the years 2005-2007. They will be distributed on publication to purchasers of the twelfth edition without further charge. The Standard Catalogs are also available in electronic format on the Web.

History

PUBLIC LIBRARY CATALOG had its inception in the early 1900s when The H. W. Wilson Company considered ways to meet the needs of the general library user. The initial response was the publication in 1908 of a modest version of FICTION CATALOG. The first of several installments of the "Standard Catalog" for the general library was published in 1918. It was called Standard Catalog: Sociology Section and was considered a "test section," issued with the expectation that helpful criticism would be forthcoming from librarians before the full catalog was published. Additional installments of the test sections, covering Biography; Fiction; Fine Arts; History and Travel; Science and Useful Arts; Literature and Philology; and Philosophy, Religion and General Works, were issued over the next fourteen years. Finally, it was determined that the test sections had proven themselves, and a fully integrated first edition of the STANDARD CATALOG FOR PUBLIC LIBRARIES was assembled and published in 1934. The contents were displayed in classified order, according to the Dewey Decimal Classification. The name was changed to PUBLIC LIBRARY CATALOG with the publication of the fifth edition in 1969.

Although a Fiction Section was issued in 1923, followed by supplements in 1928 and 1931, fiction was omitted from the first edition of the complete Catalog in 1934, with the intention of developing an improved subject approach to works of fiction outside the classified Catalog. A new expanded edition of the Fiction Section was published as FICTION CATALOG in 1942. In its preface that Catalog was referred to as "a companion volume to the Standard Catalog for Public Libraries." This complementary relationship has continued to the present. Users of the latest edition of FICTION CATALOG and its supplements will find works of literary criticism and literary history and books about literary technique in generous measure in the PUBLIC LIBRARY CATALOG.

Scope and Purpose

The Catalog lists nonfiction books published in the United Sates, or published in Canada or the United Kingdom and distributed in the United States. It excludes non-print materials; periodicals; non-English items, with the exception of dictionaries, aids to language learning, and similar materials; and works that quickly become outdated, such as computer software user guides. All books were in print at the time of listing. Original paperback editions are included. Entries for hardcover editions provide information about the availability of paperback reprints. This volume comprises over 8,000 book titles with multiple subject access and some 1,500 analytical entries. The three annual supplements will expand the coverage by several thousand additional titles.

Satisfying the needs of a broad readership requires a catalog of extraordinary range. Each new edition of PUBLIC LIBRARY CATALOG is a mixture of the old and the new. Older titles, some in updated versions, are included if they remain the best titles in their field. Newer titles reflect new topics of interest and new interpretations of traditional knowledge. This edition of the catalog features extensive revision in the areas of health, science, and the environment, and ample coverage of cooking and gardening. Biography, drama, poetry, and literary criticism continue to receive comprehensive treatment. Reference materials in all subject fields have been updated. This edition has seen a large increase in the number of reference titles in all subject areas. Entries provide information about the availability of electronic versions and large print editions of books listed.

The catalog is intended to serve the needs of public and undergraduate libraries. Retention of useful material from the previous edition enables the librarian to make informed decisions about weeding a collection. The newer titles help in identifying areas that need to be updated or strengthened. With its classified arrangement, complete bibliographical data, and descriptive and critical annotations, the Catalog provides useful information for the acquisitions librarian, the reference librarian, and the cataloger. Analytical entries in the Index augment the local catalog by affording access to composite works and to topics for which whole books may not be available. This feature, which increases the usefulness of the library's resources by making the contents of the collection more accessible, should prove especially helpful to reader's advisers and reference librarians.

Preparation

Books included in this edition were elected by experienced librarians representing public library systems across the United States. The names of participating librarians and their affiliations are listed in the Acknowledgments.

Organization

The catalog is organized into two parts: the Classified Catalog; and an Author, Title, Subject, and Analytical Index.

Part 1. Classified Catalog. This is arranged according to the Dewey Decimal Classification. Within classes, arrangement is by main entry, with complete bibliographical and cataloging information given for each book. The classified arrangement, along with the descriptive and critical annotations, provides a useful guide to book selection. Entries include such information as price and ISBN to facilitate acquisitions.

Part 2. Author, Title, Subject, and Analytical Index. This is a comprehensive key to the Classified List. An important feature of this section is the detailed indexing given to composite works. These analytic entries are provided in order to exploit fully the contents of compilations.

For further information consult the Directions for Use of the Catalog.

ACKNOWLEDGMENTS

The H. W. Wilson Company is grateful to those publishers who supplied copies of their titles and information about prices and editions. The Company expresses its special appreciation to the following librarians who were instrumental in the selection of titles for this Catalog, in many cases with the participation of their colleagues:

Jacqueline Cooper
Providence Public Library
Providence, RI

James E. Bobick
Carnegie Library of Pittsburgh
Pittsburgh, PA

Pat Dempsey
Cuyahoga County Public Library
Parma, OH

Mary Griffin
Omaha Public Library
Omaha, NE

Nancy Pearl
Seattle Public Library
Seattle, WA

Lee Robinson
New York Public Library
New York, NY

Kate Sathi
St. Louis Public Library
St. Louis, MO

Catherine J. Willis
Boston Public Library
Boston, MA

Syma Zerkow
Houston Public Library
Houston, TX

DIRECTIONS FOR USE OF THE CATALOG

Part 1. Classified Catalog

The Classified Catalog is arranged by the Dewey Decimal Classification in numerical order from 000 to 999. Individual biographies are classed at 92 and follow the 920s (collective biography). Biographies of individual artists and musicians, found in class 709.2 and 780.92 respectively in previous editions of this Catalog, are now classed at 92 as well. An Outline of Classification, which serves as a table of contents for the Classified Catalog, is reproduced below. It should be noted that many topics can be classified in more than one discipline. If a particular title is not found where it might be expected, the Index should be consulted to determine if it is classified elsewhere.

Within classes, works are arranged alphabetically under main entry, usually the author. Works of individual biography are arranged alphabetically under the name of the person written about.

Each listing consists of a full bibliographical description. Prices, which are always subject to change, have been obtained from the publisher and are as current as possible. Entries include recommended subject headings derived from the *Sears List of Subject Headings*, a suggested classification number from the *Abridged Dewey Decimal Classification and Relative Index*, a brief description of the contents, and, whenever possible, an evaluation from a quoted source.

Part 2. Author, Title, Subject, and Analytical Index

The Index is a single alphabetical list of all the books entered in the Catalog. Each book is entered under author; title, if distinctive; and subject. Also included are author and title analytics for works contained in anthologies and collections, and subject analytics for parts of books not covered under the subject heading for the whole. The classification number, displayed in boldface type, is the key to the location of the main entry for the book in the Classified Catalog.

Appropriate added entries are made for joint authors and editors. "See" references are made from forms of names or subjects that are not used as headings. "See also" references are made to related or more specific headings.

Examples of analytical entries for author, title, and subject are as follows:

Wasserstein, Wendy
    Uncommon women and others
      In Wasserstein, W. The Heidi chronicles, and
        other plays   **812**

Uncommon women and others. Wasserstein, W.
    In Wasserstein, W. The Heidi chronicles, and
      other plays   **812**

Influenza
    See/See also pages in the following book(s);
    Oldstone, M. B. A. Viruses, plagues, and
    history   **614.4**

Outline of Classification

Reproduced below is the Second Summary of the Dewey Decimal Classification. * As Part 1 of this Catalog is arranged according to this classification, the outline will serve as a table of contents for it. Please note, however, that the inclusion of this outline is not to be considered a substitute for consulting the Dewey Decimal Classification itself.

000 Computer science, knowledge & systems
010   Bibliographies
020   Library & information sciences
030   Encyclopedias & books of facts
040   [Unassigned]
050   Magazines, journals & serials
060   Associations, organizations & museums
070   News media, journalism & publishing
080   Quotations
090   Manuscripts & rare books

100 Philosophy
110   Metaphysics
120   Epistemology
130   Parapsychology & occultism
140   Philosophical schools of thought
150   Psychology
160   Logic
170   Ethics
180   Ancient, medieval & eastern philosophy
190   Modern western philosophy

200 Religion
210   Philosophy & theory of religion
220   The Bible
230   Christianity & Christian theology
240   Christian practice & observance
250   Christian pastoral practice & religious orders
260   Christian organization, social work & worship
270   History of Christianity
280   Christian denominations
290   Other religions

300 Social sciences, sociology & anthropology
310   Statistics
320   Political science
330   Economics
340   Law
350   Public administration & military science
360   Social problems & social services
370   Education
380   Commerce, communications & transportation
390   Customs, etiquette & folklore

400 Language
410   Linguistics
420   English & Old English languages
430   German & related languages
440   French & related languages
450   Italian, Romanian & related languages
460   Spanish & Portuguese languages
470   Latin & Italic languages
480   Classical & modern Greek languages
490   Other languages

500 Science
510   Mathematics
520   Astronomy
530   Physics
540   Chemistry
550   Earth sciences & geology
560   Fossils & prehistoric life
570   Life sciences; biology
580   Plants (Botany)
590   Animals (Zoology)

600 Technology
610   Medicine & health
620   Engineering
630   Agriculture
640   Home & family management
650   Management & public relations
660   Chemical engineering
670   Manufacturing
680   Manufacture for specific uses
690   Building & construction

700 Arts
710   Landscaping & area planning
720   Architecture
730   Sculpture, ceramics & metalwork
740   Drawing & decorative arts
750   Painting
760   Graphic arts
770   Photography & computer art
780   Music
790   Sports, games & entertainment

800 Literature, rhetoric & criticism
810   American literature in English
820   English & Old English literatures
830   German & related literatures
840   French & related literatures
850   Italian, Romanian & related literatures
860   Spanish & Portuguese literatures
870   Latin & Italian literatures
880   Classical & modern Greek literatures
890   Other literatures

900 History
910   Geography & travel
920   Biography & genealogy
930   History of ancient world (to ca. 499)
940   History of Europe
950   History of Asia
960   History of Africa
970   History of North America
980   History of South America
990   History of other areas

PUBLIC LIBRARY CATALOG
TWELFTH EDITION
CLASSIFIED CATALOG

000 GENERALITIES

001.1 Intellectual life

Levine, Lawrence W.
The opening of the American mind; canons, culture, and history. Beacon Press 1996 xxiv, 212p hardcover o.p. paperback available $18 **001.1**
1. Higher education 2. United States—Intellectual life
ISBN 0-8070-3119-4 (pa)   LC 96-33866
The author "examines the current critique of higher education, the major debates over the curriculum and the canon over two centuries, and changes in the perceptions of the national culture. . . . Levine insists that there is no stable canon of writers; that universities have always mirrored dominant cultural attitudes toward gender, race, and ethnicity; and that diversity, pluralism, and multiculturalism have been present throughout American history." Choice
"Levine's presentation is eloquent, eminently reasonable, and gratifyingly optimistic." Booklist
Includes bibliographical references

Quick studies; the best of Lingua Franca; edited and introduced by Alexander Star. Farrar, Straus & Giroux 2002 xxvii, 514p il pa $15   **001.1**
1. United States—Intellectual life 2. Learning and scholarship
ISBN 0-374-52863-2   LC 2002-23061
A collection of pieces from Lingua Franca, selected by "LF editor Star, the reportage, essays and profiles include a poignant account of novelist Milan Kundera's fallings-out with his translators as he struggled hopelessly to find the perfect English translations of his work; a profile of Xanax-popping prankster Slavoj Zizek, the Slovenian philosopher who once slipped subversive messages into Communist propaganda; and a stinging self-denunciation by a former literary theorist who has turned against jargon-laden academic criticism." Publ Wkly

001.4 Research; statistical methods

Awards, honors, & prizes. Gale Res. 2v v1 $275, v2 $305, set $525   **001.4**
1. Awards
ISSN 0196-6316
First published 1969. (21st edition 2003) Frequently revised
Contents: v1 United States and Canada; v2 International and foreign

Volume one is an alphabetical directory of organizations in the United States and Canada sponsoring awards, honors and prizes in a wide range of endeavors from academic awards to prizes in sports. Volume two provides coverage of awards originating in other countries

Feldman, Burton
The Nobel Prize; a history of genius, controversy, and prestige. Arcade Pub. 2000 489p il $29.95; pa $15.95   **001.4**
1. Nobel Prizes
ISBN 1-55970-537-X; 1-55970-592-2 (pa)
LC 00-42002
The author provides a "history of the prizes awarded in the sciences, literature, social sciences, and humankind's . . . peace efforts. This is the first comprehensive critical history of the prizes to appear, and it's very good." Libr J

001.9 Controversial knowledge

Alschuler, William R.
The science of UFOs; edited by Howard Zimmerman. St. Martin's Press 2001 211p il $23.95; pa $13.95   **001.9**
1. Unidentified flying objects
ISBN 0-312-26225-6; 0-312-30071-9 (pa)
LC 00-45760
An "examination of UFO accounts through the lens of science—its method, presently accepted theory, and possible future directions." SLJ
"Although Alschuler's analysis seems at times like an introductory physics text as it delves into the quantum mechanics and physics of propective alien technologies, readers will appreciate his objective, fact-based analysis of a range of purported extraterrestrial phenomena." Publ Wkly
Includes bibliographical references

Boese, Alex
The museum of hoaxes; a collection of pranks, stunts, deceptions, and other wonderful stories contrived for the public from the Middle Ages to the new millennium. Dutton 2002 266p il $19.95   **001.9**
1. Impostors and imposture 2. Fraud
ISBN 0-525-94678-0   LC 2002-26780
A "catalog of tricks, pranks, publicity stunts, and outright scams that people have played on each other over the years. . . . Boese describes each trick's appearance, how the perpetrators did it, and its effect on the general public. . . . Whether it is picked for cover-to-cover reading or occasional browsing, readers are sure to find many laughs." Booklist
Includes bibliographical references

Clark, Jerome
Encyclopedia of strange and unexplained physical phenomena. Gale Res. 1993 xxvi, 395p il $85 **001.9**
1. Science 2. Curiosities and wonders
ISBN 0-8103-8843-X   LC 93-16958
This volume presents information about unusual physical phenomena. "About 150 entries are alphabetically arranged, ranging in length from one-half page (Fate Magazine) to six or seven pages (Fairies) or more (12 pages for Unidentified Flying Objects). . . . Articles begin with a description of the event, phenomenon, or researcher, as well as some historical background." Booklist

Eberhart, George M.
Mysterious creatures; a guide to cryptozoology. ABC-CLIO 2002 2v set $185 **001.9**
1. Mythical animals 2. Monsters 3. Parapsychology 4. Occultism
ISBN 1-57607-283-5   LC 2002-13785
Also available online
This is a study of "cryptids as distribution anomalies, unknown variations of known species, survivors thought to be extinct, mythical animals, paranormal creatures with animal-like characteristics, and hoaxes. More than 1,085 unknown animals are covered in field-guide format, some with pictures or drawings. . . . Useful as a biological guide, a folklore reference, and a study of paranormal creatures." Booklist

Ellis, Richard, 1938-
Imagining Atlantis. Knopf 1998 322p il maps hardcover o.p. paperback available $13 **001.9**
1. Atlantis
ISBN 0-375-70582-1 (pa)   LC 97-48432
"Chronicles the rarely examined history of the dream of Atlantis, a centuries-long quest for evidence of the existence of a lost continent that has involved philosophers, historians, scientists, and mystics." Booklist
"Engaging, lucid, and full of lore, Ellis's book makes a convincing case that Atlantis was merely a morality tale of Plato's, and along the way provides insight into our enduring preoccupation with things vanished and lost." New Yorker
Includes bibliographical references

Lewis, James R., 1949-
UFOs and popular culture; an encyclopedia of contemporary myth. ABC-CLIO 2000 393p il $75 **001.9**
1. Unidentified flying objects 2. Popular culture
ISBN 1-57607-265-7   LC 00-10925
This encyclopedia of ufology and its impact on contemporary American culture includes topics ranging from the radio broadcast War of the worlds and the X-Files to famous encounters and ufologists
Includes bibliographical references

McGuire, Bill, 1954-
A guide to the end of the world; everything you never wanted to know. Oxford Univ. Press 2002 191p il maps $25 **001.9**
1. Natural disasters
ISBN 0-19-280297-6   LC 2002-283522
The author discusses catastrophic events that are likely to take place and how they will effect our global society. Global warming, killer asteroids and super volcanoes are among the perils examined
Includes bibliographical references

Saler, Benson
UFO crash at Roswell; the genesis of a modern myth; [by] Benson Saler, Charles A. Ziegler, and Charles B. Moore. Smithsonian Institution Press 1997 198p il maps hardcover o.p. paperback available $15.95 **001.9**
1. Unidentified flying objects 2. Folklore
ISBN 1-58834-063-5 (pa)   LC 97-8674
This is a study of the 1947 sightings of UFOs near Roswell, New Mexico. The authors contend that the sightings "can be viewed as the evolution of a myth. . . . The chapters range from the historical development of the Roswell narratives, an analysis of the myth, the tie into the New York University balloon flights, and a comparison between the Roswell sightings and religion, to the images of these sightings from the perspective of the public, scholars, and believers." Choice
Includes bibliographical references

Shermer, Michael
Why people believe weird things; pseudoscience, superstition, and other confusions of our time; foreword by Stephen Jay Gould. rev and expanded. Freeman, W.H. 2002 xxvi, 349p il $16 **001.9**
1. Science 2. Belief and doubt 3. Parapsychology
ISBN 0-8050-7089-3   LC 2002-68784
First published 1997
Contents: Science and skepticism; Pseudoscience and superstition; Evolution and creationism; History and pseudohistory; Hope springs eternal
The author "explores the very human reasons people find otherworldly phenomena, conspiracy theories, and cults so appealing. In . . . [the] chapter, 'Why Smart People Believe in Weird Things' he takes on science luminaries like physicist Frank Tippler and others, who hide their spiritual beliefs behind the trappings of science." Publisher's note
Includes bibliographical references

Wilson, Colin, 1931-
The Atlantis blueprint; unlocking the ancient mysteries of a long-lost civilization; [by] Colin Wilson and Rand Flem-Ath. Delacorte Press 2001 xxv, 415p il maps $24.95 **001.9**
1. Atlantis
ISBN 0-385-33479-6   LC 00-47449
Also available in paperback from Delta
The authors "propose a single, geo-historical theory that links the Egyptian, Chinese and South American pyramids and other sacred sites. According to this argument, these civilizations received templates from Atlantis that contained crucial geodesic, geological and geometric information. Furthermore, Atlantean mariners, based in Antarctica, sailed the globe over 100,000 years ago and established more than 60 sacred sites around the world." Publ Wkly

002   The book

Basbanes, Nicholas A., 1943-
Patience & fortitude; a roving chronicle of book people, book places, and book culture. HarperCollins Pubs. 2001 636p il $35   **002**
1. Book collecting 2. Books and reading 3. Libraries
ISBN 0-06-019695-5   LC 2001-16935
The author "traces the crucial role that book collectors, librarians and scholars have played in the 'transmission and preservation of knowledge,' starting with the vast ancient library at Alexandria, Egypt, and ending with our current, not always book-friendly, era of computer technology." N Y Times Book Rev
"Basbanes's fund of stories will delight readers who value books for more than just a good story, have a yen for second-hand books plucked from dusty shops or look to book catalogs for suspense and excitement." Publ Wkly
Includes bibliographical references

002.075   Book collecting

Ahearn, Allen
Collected books; the guide to values; [by] Allen and Patricia Ahearn. 2002 ed. Putnam 2001 788p $75   **002.075**
1. Books—Prices 2. Book collecting
ISBN 0-399-14781-0   LC 2001-19518
First published 1991
The authors provide prices for the most widely collected modern first editions and first American printings of works in English. The Ahearns concentrate on fiction as well as Americana, children's books, natural history, belles lettres, and travel
Includes bibliographical references

004   Data processing. Computer science

Berry, Charles W.
Computer and Internet dictionary for ages 9 to 99; [by] Charles W. Berry and William H. Hawn, Jr.; illustrated by Yvette Santiago Banek and Denise Gilgannon. Barron's Educ. Ser. 2000 230p il $16.95   **004**
1. Internet—Dictionaries 2. Computers—Dictionaries
ISBN 0-7641-1520-0   LC 00-37852
Defines over eight hundred computer and Internet terms
"This is a beautifully and appropriately illustrated dictionary of computer and Internet-related terms." Sci Books Films

Computer sciences; Roger R. Flynn, editor in chief. Macmillan 2002 4v set $325   **004**
1. Computer science
ISBN 0-02-865566-4   LC 2002-754
Contents: v1 Foundations; v2 Software and hardware; v3 Social applications; v4 Electronic universe
This set "includes 286 signed entries written by more than 125 contributors. . . . Many articles are enhanced by sidebars, glossary definitions, black-and-white illustrations, cross-references, and bibliographic or Internet re-

sources. Additional features include time lines, a glossary, and an index to the set. Intended for general readers and high school students, this encyclopedia will appeal to anyone curious about this complex field or its impact on today's world." Choice
For a fuller review see: Booklist, Dec. 1, 2002

Downing, Douglas
Dictionary of computer and Internet terms; [by] Douglas A. Downing, Michael A. Covington, Melody Mauldin Covington. Barron's Educ. Ser. il pa $11.95   **004**
1. Computers—Dictionaries 2. Internet—Dictionaries
First published 1986 with title: Dictionary of computer terms. (8th edition 2003) Frequently revised
This work defines approximately 1,700 computer terms. Topics explained "include finding information with search tools on the Web, creating a home page with HTML, communicating via e-mail, tuning in to multimedia applications, and the technical details involved in connecting a computer with a modem to other computers and the Internet." Publisher's note

Encyclopedia of computer science. 4th ed, editors: Anthony Ralston, Edwin D. Reilly, David Hemmendinger. Grove's Dictionaries Inc. 2000 xxix, 2034p il $150   **004**
1. Computer science—Encyclopedias
ISBN 1-56159-248-X   LC 2002-319006
First published 1976 by Van Nostrand Reinhold & Co.
Alphabetically arranged and classified into subject areas, the entries cover: hardware, systems, information and data, software, mathematics, theory of computation, methodologies, applications, and computing milieux
For a review see: Booklist, Dec. 1, 2000

Encyclopedia of information systems; edited by Hossein Bidgoli. Academic Press 2003 4v il set $1,200   **004**
1. Data processing—Encyclopedias 2. Information technology—Encyclopedias
ISBN 0-12-227240-4
This encyclopedia offers both general and technical information about major elements, issues, opinions, and key studies {in information technology}, as well as cross-references to related subjects. Publisher's note
"In order to compile this unique resource--the first to examine comprehensively the core topics in the field--the editors reviewed current academic research in management information systems (MIS) and computer information systems (CIS) as recommended by their scholarly associations. They combined this with current practices in the MIS field carried out by leading IT corporations. The result is ten major topic areas, among them, hardware and software, AI, etc." Libr J

The **Facts** on File dictionary of computer science; edited by Valerie Illingworth and John Daintith. Facts on File 2001 249p (Facts on File science library) $44   **004**
1. Computer science—Dictionaries
ISBN 0-8160-4285-3   LC 00-55555
Based on the Minidictionary of computing, published 1986 by Oxford University Press
This dictionary contains 2300 headwords covering the terminology of modern computer science. Cross-references are included and the appendix provides mathematical symbols and notation, number conversions as well as organizational and geographic top-level domain names

From 0 to 1: an authoritative history of modern computing; edited by Atsushi Akera, Frederik Nebeker. Oxford Univ. Press 2002 228p il $39.95   **004**

1. Computers 2. Computer software

ISBN 0-19-514025-7   LC 2001-34058

This introduction to the history of computing provides an overview of information processing from the calculating machines and early computers to present day computer networks, interfaces, software and the computer industry

Gookin, Dan

PCs for dummies. Hungry Minds il pa $21.99   **004**

1. Microcomputers

First published 1992. (9th edition 2003) Frequently revised. Publisher varies

Starting with the assembly and plug-in operation the author goes on to outline how to use Windows XP. He explains concepts, procedures, (virus protection, spam blocking and digital imaging as well as Internet use)

Henderson, Harry, 1951-

Encyclopedia of computer science and technology. Facts on File 2003 450p il $82.50   **004**

1. Computers—Encyclopedias 2. Computer science—Encyclopedias

ISBN 0-8160-4373-6   LC 2002-6796

"In this A-to-Z resource, 400 mini essays . . . [offer] . . . an overview of the topic, a discussion of its significance, and a guide to further reading. An introduction ends with a list of subject groupings of related entries such as 'Computer Languages,' 'Business Applications,' and 'AI and Robotics.' Biographies of historical figures . . . and modern visionaries . . . are often accompanied by captioned photographs. . . . An illustration of the inner workings of a mouse and a simple graphic of computer animation are useful . . . More complex flowcharts explain database structure, HTML, and network systems. . . . This solid resource succeeds in explaining technical aspects of these subjects to general readers." SLJ

Ifrah, Georges

The universal history of computing; from the abacus to the quantum computer; translated from the French, and with notes by E.F. Harding, assisted by Sophie Wood [et al.] Wiley 2000 410p il $24.95; pa $16.95   **004**

1. Data processing—History 2. Computers—History

ISBN 0-471-39671-0; 0-471-44147-3 (pa)

LC 00-47771

The author covers "the history of computing from its earliest time to today's supercomputers. After extensive coverage of numbers and the calculating techniques of early history, he discusses in great detail modern calculating machines. . . . Ifrah's erudite book adds new and interesting findings to the topic." Libr J

Includes bibliographical references

Johnson, George, 1952-

A shortcut through time; the path to a quantum computer. Knopf 2003 204p il $24; pa $13   **004**

1. Quantum theory 2. Computers

ISBN 0-375-41193-3; 0-375-72618-7 (pa)

LC 2002-73013

The author "communicates some of the propositions offered by theorists about the virtually unlimited computing power that may follow certain practical triumphs that are not quite in sight." N Y Times Book Rev

"Johnson has presented the fascinating science of quantum computing and its future development in a down-to-earth style." Libr J

Includes bibliographical references

The **Macintosh** bible; edited by Clifford Colby [et al.] Peachpit Press il pa $34.99   **004**

1. Macintosh (Computer)

First published 1987 by Goldstein & Blair. (8th edition 2002) Frequently revised. Editors vary

This guide covers Macintosh hardware and software components and use of the Internet

White, Ron

How computers work; illustrated by Timothy Edward Downs. Que il pa $34.99   **004**

1. Microcomputers

First published 1993 by Ziff-Davis Press. (6th edition 2002 includes computer laser optical disc) Frequently revised

Captioned diagrams "conduct readers on a visual tour of PC terrain that begins with the bootstrap—the permanent coding that launches PC operations—and ends with explanations of how different kinds of printers handle the information PCs send. In between comes information about such things as RAM, a mouse, CD-ROM, and tape backup." Booklist

World of computer science; Brigham Narins, editor. Gale Group 2002 2v set $150 **004**

1. Computer science—Encyclopedias

ISBN 0-7876-4960-0   LC 2001-96880

This reference "presents approximately 800 alphabetically arranged entries covering computing concepts, hardware, software, programming terms and languages, and the biographies of important contributors to computer science." Libr J

"Writing is clear, with plentiful examples. . . . The bibliography lists many excellent Web sites on all facets of computers and also provides an excellent tool for updating this fast-moving part of the reference collection." Booklist

004.6   Interfacing and communications. Networks

History of the Internet; a chronology, 1843 to the present; [by] Christos J. P. Moschovitis [et al.] ABC-CLIO 1999 312p il $65   **004.6**

1. Internet 2. Telecommunication

ISBN 1-57607-118-9   LC 99-13275

A chronology of telecommunications from Charles Babbage's earliest theories of a "Difference Engine" to

History of the Internet—*Continued*

the impact of the Internet in 1998 to future trends

"This work can justifiably find a home in the reference collection or in the circulating collection, because an interested layperson could read it cover to cover. Public, academic, and secondary school libraries looking for a readable, nontechnical history of the Internet will want to purchase this volume." Booklist

Includes bibliographical references

Levine, John R.

The Internet for dummies; by John R. Levine, Carol Baroudi, and Margaret Levine Young; foreword by Paul McCloskey. Wiley il pa $21.99   **004.6**
1. Internet

First published 1993 by IDG Books. (9th edition 2003) Frequently revised

This guide to the Internet includes information on the Web, Internet service providers, sending e-mail as well as other benefits of electronic communication

Lowe, Doug

Networking for dummies. Wiley pa $24.99
    004.6
1. Computer networks

First published 1994 by IDG Books. (6th edition 2003) Frequently revised

This describes how to set up local area networks (LANs) enabling workers to share files, internet access, printers and other peripherals. Discusses operating systems, network architectures, cabling systems, and security issues

005   Computer programming, programs, data

Farrell, Mary

Learning computer programming; it's not about languages. Charles River Media 2002 xxiii, 374p il pa $34.95   **005**
1. Computer programming

ISBN 1-58450-061-1   LC 2002-259

Accompanied by CD-ROM

"This book is written for aspiring programmers, and teaches basic programming skills that can be . . . applied to any language including the key concepts of Loops, Strings, Array, Pointers, and more." Publisher's note

005.7   Data in computer systems

Godin, Seth

The big red fez; how to make any Web site better. Fireside 2002 111p il pa $11   **005.7**
1. Web sites

ISBN 0-7432-2790-5   LC 2001-54751

This "guide to making sites more attractive to browsers . . . offers simple but frequently overlooked design tips . . . that will keep impatient users from ditching your site before they buy whatever it is you're selling. Godin's primary mantra is to limit information on each page and offer clear incentives for clicking to the next screen." Publ Wkly

005.8   Data security

Jennings, Charles

The hundredth window; protecting your privacy and security in the age of the Internet; [by] Charles Jennings and Lori Fena; foreword by Esther Dyson. Free Press 2000 xxv, 278p $26   **005.8**
1. Computer security 2. Internet—Security measures

ISBN 0-684-83944-X   LC 00-22527

The authors "look at the typical day of a high-tech user, noting the myriad ways in which such an individual exposes information about personal income, health, buying preferences, and daily activities. They counsel online consumers on how to protect their privacy by encrypting e-mail, checking for security provisions on Web sites, and updating browsers." Booklist

Speed, Tim

The personal Internet security guidebook; keeping hackers and crackers out of your home; [by] Timothy Speed, Juanita Ellis, Steffano Korper. Academic Press 2002 xxiv, 202p il $44.95   **005.8**
1. Computer security 2. Internet

ISBN 0-12-656561-9   LC 2001-91437

This describes security for DSL, cable, and dial-up connections and networks, discussing virus protection, privacy protection and encryption and includes a list of vendors and services

006.3   Artificial intelligence

Kurzweil, Raymond

The age of spiritual machines; when computers exceed human intelligence; [by] Ray Kurzweil. Viking 1999 388p hardcover o.p. paperback available $14.95   **006.3**
1. Artificial intelligence 2. Computers

ISBN 0-14-028202-5 (pa)   LC 98-38804

"Kurzweil's contention is that artifical intelligence will surpass human intelligence by 2100, and this work outlines the incipient technical developments, such as quantum computing and nanobots (atom-sized robots), that will enable it." Booklist

"This superb work is a thoughtful melding of technology, philosophy, ethics, and humanism." Libr J

Includes bibliographical references

011   Bibliographies

American reference books annual. Libraries Unlimited $125   **011**
1. Reference books—Bibliography

ISSN 0065-9959

Cumulative indexes available 1990-1994; 1995-1999; 2000-2004

Annual. First published 1970

Editor: 1970-2001 Bohdan S. Wynar

"Each issue covers the reference book output (including reprints) of the previous year (i.e., the 1970 volume covers 1969 publications). Offers descriptive and evaluative notes (many of them signed by contributors), with references to selected reviews. Limited to titles in English. Classed arrangement; author-subject-title index." Guide to Ref Books. 11th edition

Bibliographic index; a cumulative bibliography of bibliographies. Wilson, H.W. service basis   **011**
1. Bibliography—Bibliography 2. Bibliography—Indexes
ISSN 0006-1255
Also available CD-ROM version and online
Published April and August with bound cumulation in December
This is a subject list of bibliographies, in both English and foreign languages. Bibliographies published separately as books and pamphlets or appearing as parts of books and pamphlets are included. In addition, approximately 2,800 periodicals are regularly examined for bibliographic material

Guide to reference books; edited by Robert Balay; associate editor, Vee Friesner Carrington; with special editorial assistance by Murray S. Martin. 11th ed. American Lib. Assn. 1996 xxvii, 2020p $275   **011**
1. Reference books—Bibliography
ISBN 0-8389-0669-9   LC 95-26322
First published 1902
Nearly 16,000 entries provide details on general reference works and on reference books in the humanities, social and behavioral sciences, history and area studies, and science, technology, and medicine. Electronic resources are included

Magazines for libraries; for the general reader and school, junior college, college, university, and public libraries; reviewing the best publications for all serials collections since 1969; edited by Cheryl LaGuardia with consulting editors Bill Katz and Linda Steinberg Katz. Bowker $199   **011**
1. Periodicals—Bibliography
ISSN 0000-0914
First published 1969. (12th edition 2003) Frequently revised
First-tenth edition edited by Bill Katz
"Annotated classified guide to recommended periodicals for the general reader and school, college, and public libraries. Provides comparative evaluations and grade- and age-level recommendations for all periodicals included." N Y Public Libr Book of How & Where to Look It Up

The **Reader's** adviser. Bowker 1994 6v set $529   **011**
1. Best books 2. Literature—Bio-bibliography 3. Reference books—Bibliography
ISBN 0-8352-3320-0
First published 1921 with title: The Bookman's manual
Contents: v1 The best in reference books, British literature, and American literature; v2 The best in world literature; v3 The best in social sciences, history, and the arts; v4 The best in philosophy and religion; v5 The best in science, technology, and medicine; v6 Indexes
"Reference works as well as nonreference titles from most fields of knowledge. An authoritative reference tool for background information and reading lists." Ref Sources for Small and Medium-sized Libr. 6th edition

Recommended reference books for small and medium-sized libraries and media centers. Libraries Unlimited $70   **011**
1. Reference books—Bibliography 2. Reference books—Reviews
ISSN 0277-5948
Annual. First published 1981
Editor: 1981-2001 Bohdan S. Wynar
Each annual volume includes reviews of about 550 titles chosen by the editor as the most valuable reference titles published during the previous year
"Where budget restrictions are a consideration, this is an invaluable asset; for small libraries, a superior selection/acquisitions tool. Highly recommended." Voice Youth Advocates

Reference sources for small and medium-sized libraries; Scott E. Kennedy, editor; compiled by Reference Sources for Small and Medium-sized Libraries Editorial Committee, Collection Development and Evaluation Section, Reference and User Services Association. 6th ed. American Lib. Assn. 1999 xxii, 368p pa $60   **011**
1. Reference books—Bibliography
ISBN 0-8389-3468-4   LC 98-52880
First published 1969 with title: Reference books for small and medium-sized libraries
"The sixth edition of this valuable resource . . . boasts many improvements: the inclusion of Dewey and LC numbers for every entry, expanded coverage of hobbies, sports, and music, and the elimination of children's reference books. The annotations are thorough and concise; slightly longer and more evaluative entires are included for works that are highly recommended or offer unique features." Libr J

The **Standard** periodical directory. Oxbridge Communications; [distributed by] Gale Res. $1,295   **011**
1. Periodicals—Bibliography 2. Periodicals—Directories
ISSN 0085-6630
Annual. First published 1964/1965
A guide to more than 75,000 publications published in the United States and Canada
"Alphabetical subject arrangement with index of titles and subjects. Information given includes name and address of publisher, editorial content and scope, year founded, frequency, subscription rate, total circulation, advertising rate, etc." Guide to Ref Books. 11th edition

Ulrich's periodicals directory. Bowker 5v set $749   **011**
1. Periodicals—Bibliography 2. Periodicals—Directories
ISSN 0000-2100
Also available CD-ROM version and online
Annual since 1980. First published 1932 with title: Periodicals directory. Variant title: Ulrich's international periodicals directory
"Arranged by subject classification, includes magazines, journals, newsletters, newspapers, annuals and irregular serials published worldwide. Separate indices list refereed serials, serials available on CD-ROM, CD-ROM producers, serials available online, online services, cessations, publications of international organizations, Interna-

Ulrich's periodicals directory—*Continued*
tional Standard Serial Numbers, and titles. Entries include title, circulation, frequency, complete publisher address, telephone, fax, email and URL, description, subscription price, with subscription and distribution addresses, telephone and fax information. Also includes bibliographic classification . . . abstracting and indexing information, document type notations, document delivery service availability, advertising rates and contact name, among other data." Publisher's note

011.6 General bibliographies of works for specific kinds of users

Best books for young adult readers; Stephen J. Calvert, editor. Bowker 1997 xx, 744p $63 **011.6**
1. Best books 2. Young adult literature—Bibliography
ISBN 0-8352-3832-6 LC 97-478
Combines and updates Best books for Junior high readers and Best books for senior high readers
This volume lists and annotates about 6,500 titles published between 1990 and 1996. Each entry provides bibliographic information, awards, review citations, etc.

Children's catalog. 18th ed, edited by Anne Price and Juliette Yaakov. Wilson, H.W. 2001 1265p (Standard catalog series) $165 **011.6**
1. Children's literature—Bibliography 2. Classified catalogs 3. School libraries—Catalogs
ISBN 0-8242-1009-3 LC 2001-46599
Replaces the seventeenth edition, published 1996
Also available online
First published 1909
Kept up to date by annual supplements included in the price of main volume
This collection of recommended materials includes approximately 7,000 entries of books for children from preschool to grade six. Entries contain full bibliographic information, Dewey Decimal Classification number, subject headings, reading level, descriptive, and when possible, critical annotations. A list of recommended Web resources is also included
"The most comprehensive bibliography in its field." Guide to Ref Books. 11th edition

Lipson, Eden Ross
The New York Times parent's guide to the best books for children. 3rd ed, fully rev & updated. Three Rivers Press (NY) 2000 530p il pa $18 **011.6**
1. Children's literature—Bibliography 2. Best books
ISBN 0-8129-3018-5 LC 00-37727
First published 1988
This title "cites the top 1,001 children's books of the 20th century. . . . The titles, divided by age range into six sections, progress from wordless books to 'middle reading books' classics . . . through young adult books." Publ Wkly
"Finely written and organized, this is a resource no library (or parent) should be without." Booklist
Includes bibliographical references

Middle and junior high school library catalog; edited by Anne Price and Juliette Yaakov; managing editor, Zaida Nidza Padró. 8th ed. Wilson, H.W. 2000 1021p (Standard catalog series) $235 **011.6**
1. Classified catalogs 2. School libraries—Catalogs
ISBN 0-8242-0996-6 LC 00-63316
Also available online
First published 1965 with title: Junior high school library catalog
Kept up to date by annual supplements which are included in price of main volume
This collection of recommended materials includes 4,520 titles and 4,492 analytical entries of books for grades five through nine. Entries contain full bibliographic information, Dewey Decimal Classification number, subject headings, descriptive, and when possible, critical annotations. A special section includes entries for a selection of CD-ROMs devoted to reference and educational materials

Senior high school library catalog. 16th ed, edited by Juliette Yaakov. Wilson, H.W. 2002 1243p (Standard catalog series) $200 **011.6**
1. Classified catalogs 2. High school libraries—Catalogs 3. Young adult literature—bibliography
ISBN 0-8242-1008-5 LC 2002-33133
Also available online
First published 1926-28 with title: Standard catalog for high school libraries
Kept up to date by annual supplements included in price of main volume
This collection of recommended materials includes 5,321 titles and 9,123 analytical entries of books for grades nine through twelve. Entries contain full bibliographic information, Abridged Dewey Decimal Classification number, subject headings, descriptive, and when available, critical annotations. Includes a list of recommended web resources

015.73 Bibliographies and catalogs of works issued or printed in the United States

Books in print. Bowker 9v set $769 **015.73**
1. Bibliography
ISSN 0068-0214
Also available CD-ROM version and online
Annual. First published 1948
Updated by Books in print Supplement (3v) published annually in Spring, available at $395 (ISSN 0000-0310)
Contents: v1-4 Authors; v5-8 Titles; v9 Publishers
Lists titles available during the current year from American publishers, supplying such information as authors, co-authors, title, price, publisher, year of publication, and International Standard Book Numbers of cooperating publishers

The Complete directory of large print books and serials. Bowker pa $245 **015.73**
1. Large print books—Bibliography
ISSN 0000-1120
Annual. First published 1970 with title: Large type books in print

The Complete directory of large print books and serials—*Continued*
This directory covers books, periodicals, and newspapers printed in 14 point type or larger. Books are indexed by subject, author and title, with complete bibliographic and ordering information

Forthcoming books. Bowker $299.95 per year   **015.73**
1. Bibliography
ISSN 0015-8119
Bimonthly. First published 1966
This supplement to Books in print, and Subject guide to Books in print, provides a cumulative author-title-subject index to books that are to appear in the next five-month period. Information includes price, publisher, ISBN and LC control numbers and expected publication date

Monthly catalog of United States Government publications; issued by the Superintendent of Documents. U.S. Govt. Ptg. Office apply to publisher for price   **015.73**
1. Government publications—United States—Bibliography
ISSN 0362-6830
Monthly. First published 1895. Title varies.
Also available CD-ROM version and online
"Each issue includes between 1500 and 3000 new documents, arranged by Superintendent of Documents classification number. Includes sales information and complete cataloging data. Utilizes Anglo-American cataloging rules and Library of Congress subject headings. Author, title, subject, and series/report index in each issue. Price includes twelve issues, serials supplement, semiannual index, and annual index." Ref Sources for Small & Medium-sized Libr. 6th edition

016.327   Bibliographies of foreign relations

American foreign relations since 1600; a guide to the literature; Robert L. Beisner, editor. 2nd ed. ABC-CLIO 2003 2v set $255   **016.327**
1. United States—Foreign relations—Bibliography
ISBN 1-57607-080-8   LC 2003-8684
Also available online
First published 1983 under the editorship of Richard Dean Burns with title: Guide to American foreign relations since 1700
"The arrangement is essentially chronological, with the first of 32 chapters covering reference works and bibliographies and the second chapter, overviews and synthesis. Individual chapter editors . . . include journal articles, essays in collections, and dissertations. . . . Each chapter begins with a brief statement of the editor's selection criteria. Works in related specialties are listed for their influence on foreign relations, including Native American relations, gender and ethnic issues, and religious groups. . . . This is an excellent book; imaginative users will find ways to apply these listings to a wide variety of projects." Libr J
Includes bibliographical references

016.3713   Bibliographies of instructional materials

El-hi textbooks and serials in print. Bowker $245   **016.3713**
1. Textbooks—Bibliography 2. Periodicals—Bibliography
ISSN 0000-0825
Annual. Title varies
"Index to textbooks, dictionaries, encyclopedias, maps, atlases, professional books, teaching aids and auxiliary AV materials for grades K-12, plus adult and special education. Subject index contains grade and reading level; also author and title indexes and series index. Lists information not in 'Books in Print.'" N Y Public Libr. Ref Books for Child Collect. 2d edition

016.381   Bibliographies of internal commerce (Domestic trade)

The **Directory** of mail order catalogs. Grey House Pub. pa $250   **016.381**
1. Mail-order business
ISSN 0899-5710
Also available online
Annual. First published 1981. Editors vary
"Lists companies by categories that sell directly to consumers; indexed by product and company name." Guide to Ref Books. 11th edition

016.39426   Bibliographies of holidays

World holiday, festival, and calendar books; edited by Tanya Gulevich. Omnigraphics 1998 477p $55   **016.39426**
1. Holidays—Bibliography 2. Festivals—Bibliography
ISBN 0-7808-0073-7   LC 97-37784
An annotated bibliography of English-language books organized into four sections: World holidays, Religious holidays, Ethnic and national holidays, and Calendar and time reckoning systems

016.613   Bibliographies of general and personal hygiene

Consumer health information source book; edited by Alan M. Rees. 7th ed. Greenwood Press 2003 325p pa $65   **016.613**
1. Health—Bibliography 2. Medicine—Bibliography 3. Health—Information services 4. Medicine—Information services
ISBN 1-57356-509-1   LC 2003-40871
"An Oryx book"
First published 1981 by Bowker
"The book contains more than 2,000 descriptive evaluations of 385 books, 165 popular health magazines and newsletters, 1,500 English-language pamphlets, 850 Spanish-language pamphlets, 215 toll-free information

Consumer health information source book—*Continued*

hotlines, 325 health resource and referral organizations, 31 online and fax-based information services and CD-ROMs, and 40 medical textbooks, monographs, and journals. . . . The *Consumer Health Information Source Book* remains a key resource for all libraries that provide health information to the general public." Booklist

016.8 Bibliographies of literature

Adamson, Lynda G.

World historical fiction; an annotated guide to novels for adults and young adults. Oryx Press 1999 719p $62.95 **016.8**

1. Historical fiction—Bibliography
ISBN 1-57356-066-9   LC 98-39981
Based on World historical fiction guide by Daniel D. McGarry and Sarah Harriman White published 1973 by Scarecrow Press
This title annotates "more than 6000 works. . . . Primary arrangement is by areas of the world, and then by time periods within each area." Booklist

Bleiler, Richard

Reference guide to mystery and detective fiction; [by] Richard J. Bleiler. Libraries Unlimited 1999 391p (Reference sources in the humanities series) $68.50 **016.8**

1. Mystery fiction—Bibliography
ISBN 1-56308-380-9   LC 99-19091
The 750 entries included in this volume "cover pre-1998 reader's guides, bibliographies, magazine and anthology indexes, guides to fictional characters, and bio-bibliographies. Core serials and professional organizations are listed, as are Web sites for authors of three or more novels. The titles cited . . . offer, besides complete bibliographic information, critical annotations that range in length from a paragraph to a page." Choice

Bouricius, Ann

The romance readers' advisory; the librarian's guide to love in the stacks. American Lib. Assn. 2000 107p pa $56 **016.8**

1. Love stories—Bibliography 2. Love stories—History and criticism
ISBN 0-8389-0779-2   LC 99-57295
The author provides "information about the highly popular romance genre and its diverse subgenres; addresses key issues regarding the establishment of a romance collection; and, in a series of reading lists, recommends outstanding romances of all flavors for avid fans and new converts." Booklist

Breen, Jon L., 1943-

Novel verdicts; a guide to courtroom fiction. 2nd ed. Scarecrow Press 1999 276p $65 **016.8**

1. Trials in literature—Bibliography 2. Law in literature—Bibliography
ISBN 0-8108-3674-2   LC 99-35315
First published 1984
Arranged alphabetically by author this is a guide to about 800 titles including works by John Grisham, Steve Martini and Scott Turow

Burgess, Michael, 1948-

Reference guide to science fiction, fantasy, and horror; [by] Michael Burgess, Lisa R. Bartle. 2nd ed. Libraries Unlimited 2002 605p (Reference sources in the humanities series) $75 **016.8**

1. Science fiction—Bibliography 2. Fantasy fiction—Bibliography 3. Horror fiction—Bibliography
ISBN 1-56308-548-8   LC 2002-151707
First published 1992
A guide to "amateur and professional reference materials in the related fields of science fiction, fantasy, and horror. . . . The book is divided into 32 sections . . . including 'Encyclopedias and Dictionaries,' 'Magazine and Anthology Indexes,' 'Subject Bibliographies,' 'Character Dictionaries and Author Cyclopedias,' and 'Film and Television Catalogs.' . . . Complete bibliographic citations are followed by literature and readable annotations that vary from a brief note to three or four lengthy paragraphs. The annotations consist of description and succinct analysis of the strengths and weaknesses of each item. . . . 'Major On-Line Resources,' is a particularly valuable examination of 20 Web sites." Booklist

Fantasy and horror; a critical and historical guide to literature, illustration, film, TV, radio, and the Internet; edited by Neil Barron. Scarecrow Press 1999 816p $85 **016.8**

1. Fantasy fiction—Bibliography 2. Fantasy fiction—History and criticism 3. Horror fiction—Bibliography 4. Horror fiction—History and criticism
ISBN 0-8108-3596-7   LC 98-46564
This is a "guide to more than 2,300 works of fiction and poetry from 1762 to 1998. Barron states in his preface that Fantasy and Horror 'is an extensive revision of two separate guides, Horror Literature and Fantasy Literature, both published . . . in 1990 and now out of print.' . . . The first half of his new book lists titles in chronological chapters such as 'Early and Later Gothic Traditions, 1762-1896' or 'Contemporary Fantasy, 1957-1998.' . . . The second half of the book focuses more on secondary material." Booklist
Includes bibliographical references

Fiction catalog. 14th ed, edited by Juliette Yaakov and John Greenfieldt; managing editor: Zaida Nidza Padró. Wilson, H.W. 2001 942p (Standard catalog series) $190 **016.8**

1. Fiction—Bibliography 2. Fiction—Indexes 3. Best books
ISBN 0-8242-1005-0   LC 00-054645
Also available online
First published 1908
Kept up to date by annual supplements included in price of main catalog
"A standard annotated bibliography of some 5000 works of classical and popular fiction. Serves both as a selection aid and as a source for identifying outstanding works of fiction. Entries, arranged alphabetically by author, contain full bibliographic information and brief descriptive summaries, along with excerpts from critical reviews. Includes out-of-print titles. . . . Title and subject indexes." Ref Sources for Small & Medium-sized Libr. 6th edition

Fonseca, Anthony J.

Hooked on horror; a guide to reading interests in horror fiction. 2nd ed. Libraries Unlimited 2003 xxiii, 464p il $55   **016.8**

1. Horror fiction—Bibliography 2. Horror films
ISBN 1-56308-904-1
First edition published 1999

"Although we . . . refer to this guide as a second edition . . . it is, for all practical purposes, volume 2 of Hooked on horror. This is because space constraints make it impossible for us to list most of the titles that are found in the first edition. Therefore, readers' advisors . . . who own the first edition are advised to use this guide as a supplement rather than as a stand-alone product." pxxii

"Focusing on titles published in the last decade and older classics that are currently in print or commonly available in libraries, the authors cover 13 popular subgenres of horror fiction, including vampires and werewolves, techno horror, ghosts and haunted houses, and small town horror. . . . Special features of this book . . . [include] the inclusion of graphic novels; indications of audio, e-book, and large print formats." Publisher's note

Heising, Willetta L.

Detecting women; a reader's guide and checklist for mystery series written by women. 3rd ed. Purple Moon Press 1999 478p $44.95; pa $34.95   **016.8**

1. Mystery fiction—Bibliography 2. Women authors—Bio-bibliography
ISBN 0-9644593-5-3; 0-9644593-6-1 (pa)
Also available Pocket guide pa $16.95 (ISBN 0-9644593-7-X)
Also available companion volume Detecting men pa $29.95 (ISBN 0-9644593-3-7)
First published 1994

This guide "covers approximately 4,000 titles in 815 mystery series written by 690 women. . . . Alphabetically arranged author entries are provided in the 'Master List,' each including a brief overview and a list of series characters and titles. . . . The Master List is followed by indexes of mystery types, characters, and settings." Booklist

Herald, Diana Tixier

Genreflecting; a guide to reading interests in genre fiction. 5th ed. Libraries Unlimited 2000 xxiii, 553p (Genreflecting advisory series) $52   **016.8**

1. Fiction—Bibliography 2. Fiction—History and criticism 3. Books and reading
ISBN 1-56308-638-7   LC 99-89778
First published 1982 under the authorship of Betty Rosenberg

A listing of recommended titles in such genres as crime, adventure, romance, science fiction, fantasy, horror, and their subgenres. Besides information on authors and titles, the volume provides information on anthologies, bibliographies, critical works, encyclopedias, organizations, and publishers

Jacob, Merle

To be continued; an annotated guide to sequels; by Merle Jacob and Hope Apple. 2nd ed. Oryx Press 2000 465p $67.95 **016.8**

1. Fiction—Bibliography
ISBN 1-57356-155-X   LC 00-42782
First published 1995

"This book contains 1,762 entries, which span every possible genre and era. A list of genres is provided, and each genre is described. . . . Following the main entry is a title index, a genre index, a subject and literary forms index, and a time and place index." Book Rep
Includes bibliographical references

Lesher, Linda Parent, 1947-

The best novels of the nineties; a reader's guide. McFarland & Co. 1999 482p pa $45   **016.8**

1. Fiction—Bibliography 2. Best books
ISBN 0-7864-0742-5   LC 99-44233
"A reader's guide to approximately one thousand novels written between 1990 and 1998. . . . Each title entry includes a short summary, as well as excerpts from the novels and/or reviews." Voice Youth Advocates

Pearl, Nancy

Now read this II; a guide to mainstream fiction, 1990-2001. Libraries Unlimited 2002 300p il $55   **016.8**

1. Fiction—Bibliography 2. Best books
ISBN 1-56038-867-3   LC 2002-274079
Also available Now read this, published 1999 covering the years 1978-1998

This is an annotated list of 500 books categorized by setting, story, characterization, or language. "New features include a YA designation for selected titles, a section on fiction trends, and two appendixes, one on genre bridges (books that share elements with genre fiction) and one on book groups. Like others in the Genreflecting series, this work is a truly useful tool." Booklist

Ramsdell, Kristin, 1940-

Romance fiction; a guide to the genre. Libraries Unlimited 1999 435p (Genreflecting advisory series) $47.50   **016.8**

1. Love stories—Bibliography 2. Love stories—History and criticism
ISBN 1-56308-335-3   LC 99-10207
First published 1987 with title: Happily ever after: a guide to reading interests in romance fiction

"Part 1 has several chapters that discuss the definition and appeal of romance and contain general information about advising readers and building collections. Part 2, 'The Literature,' has chapters devoted to 13 specific subgenres of romance, from contemporary to ethnic/multicultural. . . . Part 3, 'Research Aids,' surveys the secondary literature (histories and critical guides, dissertations, biographical sources, etc.), periodicals, organizations, awards, publishers, and other resources. . . . Libraries will want to hold on to their copies of *Happily Ever After*, which this new edition builds upon rather than supersedes." Booklist

Reginald, R., 1948-

Science fiction and fantasy literature, 1975-1991; a bibliography of science fiction, fantasy, and horror fiction books and nonfiction monographs; associate editors, Mary A. Burgess, Daryl F. Mallett; editorial assistants and advisors, Scott Alan Burgess [et al.] Gale Res. 1992 1512p $230 **016.8**

1. Science fiction—Bibliography 2. Fantasy fiction—Bibliography 3. Horror fiction—Bibliography
ISBN 0-8103-1825-3   LC 92-28219
Companion volume to the author's Science fiction and fantasy literature: a checklist, 1700-1974 (1979)

Reginald, R., 1948-—*Continued*
This is "an alphabetical listing of authors and their works. Excluded are stage plays, poetry, songs, and graphic novels and comic books, but nonfiction works about the field and compilations of sf art are included. Each author entry notes titles, place of publication, publisher, date, pagination, binding, type (novel, collection, anthology, television/movie adaptation, nonfiction), and series." Libr J

Richards, Phillip
Best literature by and about Blacks; by Phillip M. Richards and Neil Schlager. Gale Res. 2000 330p $115   **016.8**
1. American literature—African American authors—Bibliography 2. African Americans in literature
ISBN 0-7876-0507-7   LC 00-268988
This "compilation offers brief summaries of works of fiction, nonfiction, poetry, drama, and literary criticism by and about African Americans from 1750 to the present. The four chronological sections, subdivided into genres, are alphabetically arranged by author. Entries range from a few lines to a lengthy paragraph." SLJ
For a fuller review see: Booklist, Sept. 1, 2000

What do I read next? a reader's guide to current genre fiction, fantasy, western, romance, horror, mystery, science fiction; [by] Neil Barron [et al.] Gale Res. $155
016.8
1. Fiction—Bibliography
ISSN 1052-2212
Also available online
Also available volumes covering different genres of fiction
Annual. First published 1991 for 1989-1990
A guide to locating new fiction titles in specific genres. Arranged by author within six genre sections, each entry provides publisher and publication date, series name, major characters, time period, geographic setting, review citations, and related books

016.8093 Bibliographies of fiction history and criticism

Walker, Warren S., 1921-
Twentieth century short story explication: new series; with checklists of books and journals used. Shoe String Press 1993-2002 5v v1 $42.50; v2-5 ea $49.50   **016.8093**
1. Short stories—History and criticism—Bibliography
LC 92-22790
The third edition (1977) of the original series, its five supplements and index are still available
Volumes two-five by Wendell M. Aycock
Contents: v1 1989-1990 (ISBN 0-208-02340-2); v2 1991-1992 (ISBN 0-208-02370-4); v3 1993-1994 (ISBN 0-208-02419-0); v4 1995-1996 (ISBN 0-208-02493-X); v5 1997-1998 (ISBN 0-208-02508-1)
These volumes contain entries that provide a bibliography of interpretations for short stories published between 1989 and 1998

016.813 Bibliographies of American fiction

Adamson, Lynda G.
American historical fiction; an annotated guide to novels for adults and young adults. Oryx Press 1999 405p $62.95   **016.813**
1. Historical fiction—Bibliography 2. American fiction—Bibliography 3. United States—History—Fiction—Bibliography
ISBN 1-57356-067-7   LC 98-38044
Based on Dickinson's American historical fiction, 5th edition published 1986 by Scarecrow Press
"Organized by time period, the entries include author, title, date of publication, number of pages, content notes, setting, main characters, and, where applicable, genres, awards, and series/sequel information. . . . This work should be a boon to reader's advisory and collection development librarians needing to build specific areas of the collection." Libr J

018 Catalogs arranged by author and date

American book prices current. Bancroft-Parkman, Box 1236, Washington, CT 06793 price varies   **018**
1. Books—Prices 2. Autographs—Prices 3. Rare books
ISSN 0091-9357
Annual. First published 1894/95. Quadrennial indexes
"Arrangement and information given vary somewhat but usually include author, title, edition, place and date of publication, size, binding, condition, where sold, date of sale, catalog number of lot, and price. . . . Generally considered the most accurate of the auction record compilations." Guide to Ref Books. 11th edition

Bookman's price index; a guide to the values of rare and other out-of-print books. Gale Res. $415   **018**
1. Books—Prices 2. Rare books
ISSN 0068-0141
Irregular. First published 1964
This is "an index to both the prices and availability of antiquarian books in the United States, Canada and the British Isles. Each issue reports the prices and availability of more than 17,000 different antiquarian books that are important to collectors in the North Atlantic portion of the English-speaking community." Publisher's note

020 Library and information sciences

Library literature & information science index. Wilson, H.W. service basis   **020**
1. Library science—Bibliography 2. Library science—Periodicals—Indexes
ISSN 0024-2373
Also available CD-ROM version and online
Started publication 1921 as Library literature
Published bimonthly with bound annual cumulations

Library literature & information science index—*Continued*

This is a single-alphabet author and subject index to materials in library and information science published in the United States and abroad. Over 200 journals are indexed each year. Other materials indexed include selected state journals, conference proceedings, pamphlets, and library school theses. This index also includes monographs and book reviews

020.5 Library and information sciences—Serial publications

The **Bowker** annual library and book trade almanac. Information Today $199   **020.5**
1. Libraries 2. Book industry
ISSN 0068-0540

Annual. First published 1956 by Bowker. Title varies

"A compendium of statistical and directory information relating to most aspects of librarianship and the book trade. Professional reports from the field; international library news; library legislation; grants; survey articles of developments during the preceding year." Ref Sources for Small & Medium-sized Libr. 6th edition

Library Journal. Reed Business Information $134   **020.5**
1. Library science—Periodicals 2. Libraries—Periodicals
ISSN 0363-0277

Semimonthly February through June and September through November. Monthly January, July, August and December. First published 1876

"Each issue features commentary, technology news, timely articles, and hundreds of evaluative reviews of books, magazines, audio, video, and online products. Recent issues covered such topics as collection development, urban libraries, the automated system marketplace, pay equity, and medical librarianship. A required standard for all libraries." Mag. for Libr. 12th edition

021.7 Promotion of libraries, information centers

Wolfe, Lisa Ann
Library public relations, promotions, and communications; a how-to-do-it manual. Neal-Schuman 1997 208p (How-to-do-it manuals for librarians) pa $45   **021.7**
1. Libraries—Public relations
ISBN 1-55570-266-X   LC 97-1423

This volume "provides an introduction to the basic communications concepts, a step-by-step process for developing and implementing a library public relations/communications plan, and descriptions of effective library communications tools and strategies. The first three chapters focus on the theory and planning process for public relations and communications, the next ten chapters provide tools and strategies, and the final chapter will assist you in evaluating your efforts." Preface

Includes bibliographical references

023 Library personnel administration

Low, Kathleen
Recruiting library staff; a how-to-do-it manual for librarians. Neal-Schuman 1999 120p il (How-to-do-it manuals for libraries) pa $55   **023**
1. Librarians—Recruiting
ISBN 1-55570-355-0   LC 99-31281

"Low speaks to all library staffers involved in recruiting and selecting new staff members about such topics as current and future openings; the image the library wants to promote; which recruitment methods to employ; and the roles of advertisements, job fairs and similar events, and networking in publicizing staff needs." Booklist

Includes bibliographical references

025 Operations of libraries, information centers

Barclay, Donald A., 1958-
Managing public-access computers; a how-to-do-it manual for librarians. Neal-Schuman 2000 223p (How-to-do-it manuals for libraries) $59.95   **025**
1. Computers 2. Libraries
ISBN 1-55570-361-5   LC 99-89995

The author "first reviews the types of information about technology that a manager needs to know, then discusses the physical facilities for computer installations, hardware, software, CD-ROMs, and printers. Next, he turns to management issues (such as working with the systems department), security issues, issues relating to staffing public-access computer installations, staff training, and relations with end users." Booklist

Includes bibliographical references

025.04 Automated information storage and retrieval systems

Bolles, Richard Nelson
Job-hunting on the Internet. 3rd ed, rev. Ten Speed Press 2001 189p il (Parachute library) pa $9.95   **025.04**
1. Job hunting—Internet resources 2. Web sites
ISBN 1-58008-332-3   LC 2001-6447

First published 1997

"A desktop companion to the web site www.JobHuntersBible.com"

Contents: Counseling & testing sites; Sites to help your research; Sites where you can make contacts; Job posting sites; Resume sites on the Internet

This guide "comments on popular sites (arranged by subject) that list jobs, offer employment counseling, and address other career topics. The appendix introduces the Internet to novices." Libr J

Catron, Louis E.

Theatre sources dot com; a complete guide to online theatre and dance resources. Heinemann 2001 215p pa $18.95   **025.04**
1. Theater—Internet resources 2. Dance—Internet resources
ISBN 0-325-00382-3   LC 2001-39647
This is a "guide to the Internet for playwrights, actors, directors, designers, managers, and technicians. This thoroughly annotated bibliography of over 750 online resources based in the United States and Canada . . . includes chapters on all areas of theater interest, each beginning with an introductory discussion on the availability of online resources for that subject. . . . Also included are chapters on finding jobs, shopping, and copyright law." Libr J
Includes bibliographical references

Gale directory of databases. Gale Res. 2v in 4 parts pa v1 $335, v2 $210, set $490
025.04
1. Information systems—Directories
ISSN 1066-8934
Annual. First published 1993. Formed by the merger of Directory of online databases, Directory of portable databases, and Computer-readable databases
Contents: v1 Online databases; v2 CD-ROM, diskette, magnetic tape, handheld, and batch access database products
"Descriptive entries include such details as producer name and contact information, summary of content, database language, geographic coverage, year first available, time span, updating, availability, rates, and more." Publisher's note

Government online; one-click access to 3,400 federal and state Web sites; edited by John Maxymuk. Neal-Schuman 2001 xxi, 323p pa $75   **025.04**
1. Web sites 2. Government information
ISBN 1-55570-416-6   LC 2001-30180
This volume offers "articles on the history, status, and future of the depository library system, search engines for government information, and finding information on topics from legislation to education. . . . To facilitate access, a CD-ROM with links to significant URLs is included." Choice
"A valuable resource." SLJ

Hernon, Peter, 1944-

U.S. government on the Web; getting the information you need; [by] Peter Hernon, Robert E. Dugan, John A Shuler. 2nd ed. Libraries Unlimited 2001 xxv, 405p pa $47.50   **025.04**
1. Web sites 2. Government information
ISBN 1-56308-886-X   LC 01-29945
First published 1999
"The authors plan to revise this title every two years. . . . [This volume] covers the Bush administration and the 107th Congress. . . . [A] chapter on e-gov covers the policy, implementation, and politics of federal government information. . . . Comprehensiveness and breadth of the coverage are impressive." Choice
Includes bibliographical references

Kaufeld, John

AOL for dummies; foreword by Ted Leonsis. Wiley il pa $21.99   **025.04**
1. America Online Inc.
First published 1995 with title: America Online for dummies. (2003 edition) Frequently revised
This guide provides an introduction to what's available on AOL as well as tips on downloading, sending e-mail, and the "netiquette" you should follow when posting to newsgroups

Norlin, Elaina

Usability testing for library websites; a hands-on guide; [by] Elaina Norlin, CM! Winters. American Lib. Assn. 2002 69p il pa $35   **025.04**
1. Web sites
ISBN 0-8389-3511-7   LC 2001-33817
"Four goals are explored in improving library sites: usefulness, effectiveness, learn-ability, and user satisfaction. . . . Steps for recruitment of a testing team, development of sample questions and tasks, and evaluation of results are included." SLJ
Includes bibliographical references

Sauers, Michael

Using the Internet as a reference tool; a how to-do-it manual for librarians; [by] Michael P. Sauers; with contributions by Denice Adkins. Neal-Schuman 2001 143p il (Neal-Schuman netguide series) pa $59.95
025.04
1. Reference services (Libraries) 2. Internet searching 3. Computer networks
ISBN 1-55570-417-4   LC 2001-16419
"Chapters provide background on the impact of the new technology for reference solutions and offer an excellent comparison of print and Internet resources that will aid in justifying the need for both. Information on creating effective reference strategies and a discussion of search engines and directories are included." SLJ

Smith, J. Douglas, 1965-

World War II on the Web; a guide to the very best sites; [by] J. Douglas Smith and Richard Jensen. Scholarly Resources 2003 207p $65; pa $23.95   **025.04**
1. World War, 1939-1945—Internet resources 2. Web sites
ISBN 0-8420-5020-5; 0-8420-5021-3 (pa)
LC 2002-29236
"Provides descriptions and ratings for 'the top 100+' sites, plus listings for an additional 140 'sites worth a visit.' Arrangement is topical, and separate ratings are given for content, aesthetics, and navigation. Each topical chapter includes a fairly extensive list of suggested readings, a nice addition that we don't often find in Web site guides. A CD-ROM, included with the guide, links to all the sites that are listed." Booklist

025.2 Acquisitions and collection development

Baker, Nicholson

Double fold; libraries and the assault on paper. Random House 2001 370p il hardcover o.p. paperback available $14   **025.2**
1. Libraries—Special collections 2. Paper 3. Library resources—Conservation and restoration
ISBN 0-375-72621-7 (pa)   LC 00-59171
Baker criticizes libraries for discarding books, magazines and newspapers and disputes the arguments for doing so "that libraries are running out of space, and that paper, because of its acid content, is rapidly turning to dust. . . . What the Library of Congress spends in a year on microfilming would, (according to Baker), buy a storage facility 'the size of a Home Depot, which would hold a century of newsprint.' . . . Librarians, he says, 'have lied to us shamelessly about the extent of paper's fragility, and they continue to lie about it.'" N Y Times Book Rev
Includes bibliographical references

Foerstel, Herbert N.

Banned in the U.S.A; a reference guide to book censorship in schools and public libraries. rev and expanded ed. Greenwood Press 2002 xxvii, 296p $54.95   **025.2**
1. Books—Censorship 2. Libraries—Censorship
ISBN 0-313-31166-8   LC 2001-55620
First published 1994
This volume provides "a survey of major book-banning incidents in the United States, accessible background material on the legal history of book banning . . . interviews with banned writers, and a synopsis of the 50 most frequently challenged books from the period 1996-2000." Libr J
"Librarians and teachers need this book, but patrons who want to better understand the threats to their First Amendment rights should be led to it as well." SLJ
Includes bibliographical references

Jones, Barbara M.

Libraries, access, and intellectual freedom; developing policies for public and academic libraries. American Lib. Assn. 1999 266p pa $40   **025.2**
1. Libraries—Censorship 2. Freedom of information
ISBN 0-8389-0761-X   LC 99-20937
The author "discusses how libraries fit in the legal concept of the public forum, especially the *limited* public forum, then reviews intellectual freedom in the public forum. About half the book covers developing, preparing, and implementing intellectual freedom policies; and relevant policy statements from the ALA and other organizations are included." Booklist
Includes bibliographical references

Slote, Stanley J.

Weeding library collections; library weeding methods. 4th ed. Libraries Unlimited 1997 xxi, 240p il $69   **025.2**
1. Libraries—Collection development
ISBN 1-56308-511-9   LC 96-54865
First published 1975
"The author demonstrates how weeding strengthens a collection and increases circulation. . . . Four weeding methods are presented: the book card method, the spine-marking method, the historical reconstruction method, and the computer-assisted method. Slote gives precise instructions for each method, enhanced with illustrations." Book Rep
Includes bibliographical references

Symons, Ann K.

Protecting the right to read; a how-to-do-it manual for school and public librarians; [by] Ann K. Symons, Charles Harmon; illustrations by Pat Race. Neal-Schuman 1995 211p il (How-to-do-it manuals for librarians) pa $55   **025.2**
1. Libraries—Censorship 2. Intellectual freedom
ISBN 1-55570-216-3   LC 95-42444
"The authors take readers from discussion of the policies and principles of intellectual freedom to considerations specific to school and public libraries to the protection of freedom on the Internet. . . . Appendixes consist of reprints of documents put out by the ALA and the Minnesota Coalition Against Censorship." Book Rep
"Intellectual freedom issues and guiding principles get a thorough and comprehensive treatment. . . . An essential book." Voice Youth Advocates
Includes bibliographical references

025.3 Bibliographic analysis and control

Anglo-American cataloguing rules; prepared under the direction of the Joint Steering Committee for Revision of AACR, a committee of the American Library Association [et al.] 2nd ed, 2002 revision. American Lib. Assn. 2002 1v loose-leaf $62   **025.3**
1. Cataloging
ISBN 0-8389-3530-3   LC 2002-73596
Also available loose-leaf pages with binder and tabs
First published 1967
This volume provides rules that cover the description of, and the provision of access points for, library materials. Included are 1999 and 2001 amendments and revisions approved and finalized through 2002
Includes bibliographical references

CD-ROMs in print. Gale Res. $195   **025.3**
1. CD-ROMs—Directories
ISSN 0891-8198
Also available CD-ROM version
Annual. First published 1987 by Meckler
On cover: an international guide to CD-ROM. CD-1, 3DO, MMCD, CD32, Multimedia, Laserdisc, and Electronic Products
A listing of "more than 20,000 consumer and professional CDs worldwide." Publisher's note

Gorman, Michael, 1941-

The concise AACR2, 1998 revision; prepared by Michael Gorman. American Lib. Assn. 1999 168p pa $32   **025.3**
1. Anglo-American cataloguing rules 2. Cataloging
ISBN 0-8389-3494-3   LC 98-55150
This practical guide for beginning catalogers incorporates the 1993-1997 Amendments to the Anglo-American cataloguing rules

Intner, Sheila S., 1935-
Standard cataloging for school and public libraries; [by] Sheila S. Intner and Jean Weihs. 3rd ed. Libraries Unlimited 2001 346p il $47.50   **025.3**
1. Cataloging 2. Library classification
ISBN 1-56308-781-2   LC 2001-18615
First published 1990
This explains the Anglo-American Cataloging Rules (AACR2), Sears and Library of Congress subject headings, Dewey decimal and Library of Congress classification systems, MARC format, large computer networks, policy manuals, and how to manage a cataloging department
Includes bibliographical references

025.4   Subject analysis and control

Dewey, Melvil, 1851-1931
Abridged Dewey decimal classification and relative index; devised by Melvil Dewey. ed 14, edited by Joan S. Mitchell, Julianne Beall, Giles Martin, Winton E. Matthews, Jr., Gregory R. New. OCLC 2004 1050p $99
                                              025.4
1. Dewey Decimal Classification
ISBN 0-910608-73-3   LC 2003-542823
Also available online
First abridged edition published 1894
The 14th Abridged Edition is an abridgement of the four volume 22nd Edition. Adapted to the needs of small and growing libraries, the 14th Abridged Edition is designed primarily for school and public libraries with collections of up to 20,000 titles

Dewey decimal classification and relative index; devised by Melvil Dewey. ed 22, edited by Joan S. Mitchell, Julianne Beall, Giles Martin, Winton E. Matthews, Jr., Gregory R. New. OCLC 2003 4v set $375
                                              025.4
1. Dewey Decimal Classification
ISBN 0-910608-70-9   LC 2003-50872
Also available online
First published anonymously in 1876
Contents: v1 Manual, tables; v2 Schedules 000-599; v3 Schedules 600-999; v4 Relative index

Library of Congress. Cataloging Policy and Support Office
Library of Congress subject headings; prepared by the Cataloging Policy and Support Office, Library Sesrvices. Library of Congress 5v set $295   **025.4**
1. Subject headings
ISSN 1048-9711
Also available online
Annual. Variant title: Subject headings used in the dictionary catalogs of the Library of Congress. Issued previously by the Subject Cataloging Division and later by the Office for Subject Cataloging Policy
This work contains the headings and cross-references established and applied by the Library of Congress

Sears list of subject headings. 18th ed, Joseph Miller, editor; Joan Goodsell, associate editor. Wilson, H.W. 2004 864p $85   **025.4**
1. Subject headings
ISBN 0-8242-1040-9
Also available Canadian companion. 6th edition published 2001
First published 1923 with title: List of subject headings for small libraries, by Minnie Earl Sears
In addition to the inclusion of five hundred new subject headings, this edition has updated the suggested classification numbers to conform to the 14th edition of the *Abridged Dewey Decimal classification*. The new subject headings reflect developments in areas such as computers, technology, personal relations, politics, and popular culture

025.5   Services to users

Katz, William A., 1924-
Introduction to reference work. McGraw-Hill 2v v1 $58.75, v2 $60   **025.5**
1. Reference services (Libraries) 2. Reference books—Bibliography
First published 1969. (8th edition 2001) Periodically revised
Contents: v1 Basic information services; v2 Reference services and reference processes
Volume one opens with a general introduction to the reference process and online reference services. Types of services include: bibliographies; indexing and abstracting services; encyclopedias; ready-reference; biographies; government documents. Volume two covers community reference services; interviewing; online searching; and library and bibliographic instruction, as well as evaluation of reference services

Saricks, Joyce G.
The readers' advisory guide to genre fiction. American Lib. Assn. 2001 460p (ALA readers' advisory series) pa $38 **025.5**
1. Reference services (Libraries) 2. Fiction—Bibliography
ISBN 0-8389-0803-9   LC 2001-22750
The author explores popular fiction genres. "Each genre, from adventure to literary fiction, is given its own chapter in which the genre is defined, its characteristics and appeal to its fans are described, key authors and subgenres are discussed, the preparation needed to work with readers is detailed, and tips on the readers' advisory interview are offered." Voice Youth Advocates
Includes bibliographical references

Readers' advisory service in the public library; [by] Joyce G. Saricks and Nancy Brown. 2nd ed. American Lib. Assn. 1997 160p pa $28   **025.5**
1. Reference services (Libraries) 2. Fiction—Bibliography
ISBN 0-8389-0711-3   LC 97-14211
First published 1989
The authors discuss "history, reference sources, the advisory interview, background information that advisors in popular fiction need, and tips on promoting the service. . . . [They also include] electronic sources, detailed information on genre resources, and methods for the training of staff to be readers' advisors." Libr J
Includes bibliographical references

Willis, Mark R.
Dealing with difficult people in the library.
American Lib. Assn. 1999 195p pa $28

025.5

1. Public libraries
ISBN 0-8389-0760-1   LC 99-20426
"Besides the angry patron, [Willis] considers situations
including suspected child abuse, censorship, problems
with Internet users, homeless persons in the library, and
parents who treat the library as a convenient, free baby-
sitting service. In separate sections he focuses on communicating and preventing problems from occurring, and
he includes sample policy statements." Booklist
Includes bibliographical references

025.7 Physical preparation for storage of library materials

Lavender, Kenneth
Book repair; a how-to-do-it manual. 2nd
ed. Neal-Schuman 2001 xxiv, 269p il
(How-to-do-it manuals for libraries) pa $55

025.7

1. Books—Conservation and restoration
ISBN 1-55570-408-5   LC 00-48206
First published 1992
"Covering both basic book repair techniques and . . .
conservation practices, this . . . manual offers illustrated
sections on cleaning, mending, hinge and spine repair,
strengthening paperbacks, [etc.]. . . . Chapters cover: wet
and water-damaged books; mold and mildew; repair of
book linings and pamphlet bindings; using acid-free materials to repair damaged books; lining paper objects;
affordable repair tools and supplies. . . . A full discussion of when and how to make repairs, and alternative
conservation practices that enable each librarian to develop procedures appropriate to his or her library are also
provided." Publisher's note
Includes bibliographical references

Schechter, Abraham A.
Basic book repair methods; illustrated by
the author. Libraries Unlimited 1999 102p il
pa $37   **025.7**

1. Books—Conservation and restoration
ISBN 1-56308-700-6   LC 98-50950
Photographs accompany step-by-step instructions for
common preservation techniques, from the cleaning of
pages and their readhesion, to case reattachment and
rebacking
Includes bibliographical references

026 Libraries, information centers devoted to specific disciplines and subjects

Directory of special libraries and information
centers. Gale Res. v1 (pt.1-2) +
supplementary vol. $995, v2 $585   **026**

1. Special libraries—Directories
Annual. First published 1963. Volume one is kept up
to date by mid-year supplementary volume
Contents: v1 pt.1 A-M; v1 pt.2 N-Z; v2 Geographic
and personnel indexes

This is a guide to over "34,000 special libraries and
information centers associated with the general fields of
science and engineering, medicine, law, art, religion, the
social sciences and humanities, including nearly 15,000
international listings." Publisher's note

027 General libraries, information centers

American library directory. Information
Today 2v set $299   **027**

1. Libraries—Directories
ISSN 0065-910X
Also available CD-ROM version and online
Annual. First published 1923 by Bowker
"Includes U.S. and Canadian public, academic, and
special libraries arranged by state or province, city, and
institution. Gives personnel and statistical data, subject
interests, and special collections." Ref Sources for Small
& Medium-sized Libr. 6th edition

027.5 Government libraries

Conaway, James, 1941-
America's library; the story of the Library
of Congress, 1800-2000; foreword by James
Billington; introduction by Edmund Morris.
Yale Univ. Press; Library of Congress 2000
226p il $45   **027.5**

1. Library of Congress
ISBN 0-300-08308-4   LC 99-58751
This history of the Library of Congress is organized
"around that tiny, hardy band of men and women who
have used both political acumen and intellectual vision to
build the library's collections and establish those services
that make the LC library to both Congress and nation.
Richly supplemented with photographs, this history
reaches out to touch all who love libraries." Booklist
Includes bibliographical references

027.6 Libraries for special groups and organizations

Moller, Sharon Chickering
Library service to Spanish speaking
patrons; a practical guide. Libraries Unlimited
2001 207p pa $30   **027.6**

1. Libraries and Hispanic Americans 2. Public libraries
ISBN 1-56308-719-7   LC 00-45090
Chapters "cover the history of Spanish speakers in the
U.S., adult, children, and teen services; how to help access library resources; and helpful Internet sites. Some of
the chapters include examples of what other library systems or librarians have done to try and meet the needs
of Spanish-speaking patrons." SLJ
"Intended to stimulate discussion among library service planners and to offer counsel to service providers,
this book should become required reading in any juris-
diction with an underserved Latino population." Voice
Youth Advocates
Includes bibliographical references

027.62 Libraries for children and young people

Cullum, Carolyn N.
The storytime sourcebook; a compendium of ideas and resources for storytellers. 2nd ed. Neal-Schuman 1999 469p pa $49.95
027.62
1. Storytelling 2. Children's libraries
ISBN 0-55570-360-7   LC 99-46420
First published 1990
A guide to 146 topics and 2,200 picture books. Appropriate videos and CDs are discussed. A "Topical Calendar," arranged chronologically, suggests holidays or notable events that can be related to a storyhour theme
Includes bibliographical references

Steele, Anitra T.
Bare bones children's services; tips for public library generalists; [by] Anitra T. Steele [and] Association for Library Service to Children. American Lib. Assn. 2001 123p pa $32
027.62
1. Children's libraries 2. Libraries and students 3. Public libraries
ISBN 0-8389-0791-1   LC 00-48492
Partial contents: Storytime and storytelling; Summer reading programs; Collection development; Displays
"Covers children's services, programming, and promotion of books and the library, along the way pointing out practical differences between children and adult library users." Publisher's note
Includes bibliographical references

Vaillancourt, Renée J.
Bare bones young adult services; tips for public library generalists. American Lib. Assn. 2000 142p il pa $33
027.62
1. Young adults' libraries 2. Libraries and students 3. Public libraries
ISBN 0-8389-3497-8   LC 99-35643
The author "provides guidelines for forming Teen Advisory Boards and focus groups, dealing with unruly adolescent patrons, providing homework support, as well as some basic programming ideas. She also discusses collection development and suggests resources that specialize in reviewing teen-level materials." SLJ
Includes bibliographical references

028 Reading and use of other information media

Adler, Mortimer J., 1902-2001
How to read a book; revised and updated by Mortimer J. Adler and Charles Van Doren. Simon & Schuster 1972 hardcover o.p. paperback available $15
028
1. Books and reading 2. Reading
ISBN 0-671-21209-5 (pa)
First published 1940
This guide "is dedicated to the virtues of a disciplined and structured approach to reading. . . . The authors distinguish four levels: elementary reading; inspectional reading (e.g., skimming); analytical reading; and 'syntopical' reading, where complex ideas are pursued

through more than one book. . . . Appendix A is a recommended reading list. . . . Appendix B consists of exercises and tests. Recommended as stimulating and . . . provocative." Recomm Ref Books in Paperback. 2d edition

Bloom, Harold, 1930-
How to read and why. Scribner 2000 283p $25; pa $15
028
1. Books and reading 2. Literature—History and criticism
ISBN 0-684-85906-8; 0-684-85907-6 (pa)
LC 00-708611
This book "can be read most profitably as a series of short introductions to key novels, plays, and poems. Bloom provides pithy, memorable distillations of his lifetime of study." Natl Rev

Ellington, Elisabeth
A year of reading; a month-by-month guide to classics and crowd-pleasers for you and your book group; by H. Elisabeth Ellington and Jane Freimiller. Sourcebooks 2002 314p pa $14.95
028
1. Best books 2. Books and reading
ISBN 1-57071-935-7   LC 2002-6926
"Five titles designated as crowd pleasers, classics, challenges, memoirs, or potluck options are provided for each month. . . . There are brief descriptions of each book, thought-provoking discussion questions, information about the authors, video and Internet resources, and lists of related readings. Literary discussion groups will welcome this invaluable resource." Booklist

Fadiman, Clifton, 1904-1999
The new lifetime reading plan; [by] Clifton Fadiman and John S. Major. 4th ed. HarperCollins Pubs. 1997 xxi, 378p hardcover o.p. paperback available $14
028
1. Best books 2. Books and reading
ISBN 0-06-272073-2 (pa)   LC 97-4975
First published 1960 by Crowell
The author has selected a list of works ranging from the Koran and Confucius to Chinua Achebe and Gabriel García Márquez. An appendix profiling books by 100 important 20th-century authors is included
Includes bibliographical references

Lesser, Wendy
Nothing remains the same; rereading and remembering. Houghton Mifflin 2002 234p $24; pa $13
028
1. Books and reading
ISBN 0-618-08293-X; 0-618-34081-5 (pa)
LC 2001-51622
"Lesser decided to reread selected works to see how different her response is now than it was years ago. . . . This simple but amazingly fecund premise allows Lesser to reflect deeply and candidly on how a reader's life experiences alter her perceptions of literature, and she has truly fascinating and original things to say about a compelling assortment of writers." Booklist

Major, David C., 1938-

100 one-night reads; a book lover's guide; [by] David C. Major and John S. Major. Ballantine Bks. 2001 312p pa $12.95   **028**

1. Best books 2. Books and reading
ISBN 0-345-43994-5   LC 2001-16135

The authors "offer recommendations in nonfiction, general fiction, fantasy, humor, mystery, history, public affairs, memoirs, science, and travel. Most are by English or U.S. authors and were published in the 20th century. Each three-page entry includes a description of the book, information about the author, and an evaluation of what makes the book distinctive. Suggestions for additional writings by the author are often included." Libr J

Quindlen, Anna

How reading changed my life. Ballantine Pub. Group 1998 84p (Library of contemporary thought) pa $10   **028**

1. Books and reading
ISBN 0-345-42278-3   LC 98-30191

Quindlen argues "that books are not simply a means of imparting knowledge, but also a way to strenghten emotional connectedness, to lessen isolation, to explore alternate realities and to challenge the established order." Publ Wkly

"Technology's effect on publishing and attendant debates over the future of the book also engage Quindlen's nimble mind, and after a thorough assessment, she concludes that while computers are wonderfully useful, there's simply nothing like reading a real book. So ardent is Quindlen, she even compiled reading lists for book lovers of all ages." Booklist

Seymour-Smith, Martin

The 100 most influential books ever written; the history of thought from ancient times to today. Carol Pub. Group 1998 498p hardcover o.p. paperback available $24.95   **028**

1. Books and reading 2. Best books 3. Intellectual life
ISBN 0-8065-2192-9 (pa)   LC 98-10027

"A Citadel Press book"

"Arranged in chronological order from the *I Ching* to B.F. Skinner's *Beyond Freedom and Dignity*, the selection is admirably inclusive, setting Confucius's *Analects*, India's Upanishads, the Koran and the Zoroastrian *Avesta* alongside the Old and New Testaments, Plato's *Republic*, and works by Dante, Shakespeare, Spinoza, Gibbon, Copernicus, Voltaire, Marx, Thoreau, Einstein, Freud, Jung. . . . Seymour-Smith's compendium features concise, opinionated essays marked by intellectual depth and scope, and includes vivid biographical details of each book's author." Publ Wkly

028.1   Reviews of books and other media

Book review digest. Wilson, H.W. service basis   **028.1**

1. Books—Reviews
ISSN 0006-7326

Also available CD-ROM version and online
All annual cumulations 1905-to date available

Published monthly, except February and July. Quarterly cumulations. Permanent bound annual cumulations

This work provides excerpts from and citations to reviews of more than 8,000 books each year, gleaned from coverage of approximately 100 periodicals

Author/title index covering 1905-1974 (o.p.); Author/title index covering 1975-1984 available for $100 (ISBN 0-8242-0729-7); Author/title index covering 1985-1994 available for $125 (ISBN 0-8242-0907-9)

Booklist. American Lib. Assn. $79.95 per year   **028.1**

1. Books—Reviews 2. Best books
ISSN 0006-7385

Semimonthly September through June; monthly July and August. First published 1905 with title: A.L.A. Booklist. Merged with Subscription Books Bulletin in 1956

The Reference Books Bulletin section is also available separately in an annual cumulation pa $28.50

"Intended chiefly as a guide for librarians in public and school libraries, each issue covers titles in five major areas: advance reviews, adult books, books for youth, media, and reference books. . . . Because of its selectivity, its early reviews, and its broad coverage of popular non-print media, *Booklist* is essential reading for public, school, and many academic libraries." Mag for Libr. 12th edition

Carter, Betty, 1944-

Best books for young adults. 2nd ed, [by] Betty Carter, with Sally Estes and Linda Waddle; Young Adult Library Services Association. American Lib. Assn. 2000 229p pa $35   **028.1**

1. Young adult literature—Bibliography 2. Best books
ISBN 0-8389-3501-X   LC 00-35583

First published 1994

This volume lists over 1,800 titles that have been selected by the Best Books for Young Adults Committee of the American Library Association. "These titles are intended for classroom teachers, librarians, and parents who want to reach young adult or teenage readers. In part 1 there are detailed chapters on how the titles were selected and trends in young adult publishing. There is also a very useful and practical chapter that contains topical lists of titles arranged in a format that is easy to copy and distribute. Among the topics covered are adventure, animals, family, fantasy, friendship, historical fiction, romance, sports, survival, war, westerns, and youths in trouble. Part 2 consists of the book lists from 1966 through 1999." Am Ref Books Annu, 2001

Choice. Association of College & Res. Libs. $270 per year   **028.1**

1. Books—Reviews 2. Academic libraries—Periodicals
ISSN 0009-4978

Monthly with a combined July-August issue. First published 1964

Also available CD-ROM version and online

"*Choice* is a basic selection tool for academic librarians. Each issue includes a lengthy bibliographic essay that, in addition to listing key sources on the topic, provides a fine introduction to the subject under discussion. The remainder of the issue . . . is devoted to reviews. . . . Reviews of web sites and other electronic media supplement the reviews on general reference materials, and an occasional author interview looks at the people behind the books." Mag for Libr. 12th edition

Szymborska, Wisława, 1923-
Nonrequired reading; prose pieces; translated from the Polish by Clare Cavanagh. Harcourt 2002 233p $24   **028.1**
1. Books and reading
ISBN 0-15-100660-1   LC 2002-2440
The Nobel laureate's "essays are musings with unexpected twists on topics as diverse as Korean fairy tales, paleontology and the hygiene of the nobility." N Y Times Book Rev
"The skillful simplicity and lyric quality of these essays make them distinctive. With her poet's gift for compression, Szymborska captures large concepts and brilliantly reduces them to pithy, two-page essays." Libr J
Includes bibliographical references

028.5 Reading and use of other information media by children and young people

The **Cambridge** guide to children's books in English; [edited by] Victor Watson; advisory editors, Elizabeth L. Keyser, Juliet Partridge, Morag Styles. Cambridge Univ. Press 2001 814p il $75   **028.5**
1. Children's literature—Encyclopedias
ISBN 0-521-55064-5   LC 00-65163
This reference provides an "overview of historic and contemporary children's books published in English. The entries include authors, illustrators, and significant works primarily from Britain, the US, Canada, Australia, New Zealand, India, and Africa. . . . Major themes, such as fairy tales, fantasy, folktales, legends, mythology, and young adult fiction, are covered as well as less-expected entries on topics such as bias, the bush, disability, ecology, and nudity in children's books. Nonbook media are also covered by entries on animated cartoons, comics, superheroes, and television for children." Choice

The **Continuum** encyclopedia of children's literature; Bernice E. Cullinan and Diane G. Person, editors. Continuum 2001 861p $59.95   **028.5**
1. Children's literature—Encyclopedias 2. Children's literature—Bio-bibliography
ISBN 0-8264-1516-4   LC 00-59036
"A Giniger book"
This "encyclopedia contains 1,200 biographical-critical entries for international authors and illustrators of children's literature in English, and approximately 100 topical entries. The entries are arranged in alphabetical order and each is signed. Each author/illustrator entry briefly identifies the subject, gives birth and death date and place, awards received, further works, and bibliography. Entries vary in length." Choice
For a fuller review see: Booklist, Sept. 15, 2001

The **Coretta** Scott King Awards book, 1970-1999; edited by Henrietta M. Smith. American Lib. Assn. 1999 135p pa $40   **028.5**
1. Coretta Scott King Award 2. Children's literature—History and criticism 3. American literature—African American authors 4. African Americans in literature
ISBN 0-8389-3496-X   LC 99-25046
First published 1994

This work begins with discussions of the 1994-1999 award winners and honor books and then goes back year by year to 1969
"The text is broken up with quotes from the winning titles, and the book ends with photos and biographies of the authors and artists. An essential resource." Booklist

Gillespie, John Thomas, 1928-
The Newbery companion; booktalk and related materials for Newbery Medal and Honor books; [by] John T. Gillespie, Corinne J. Naden. 2nd ed. Libraries Unlimited 2001 465p $59   **028.5**
1. Newbery Medal 2. Children's literature—History and criticism 3. Authors
ISBN 1-56308-813-4   LC 00-45092
First published 1996
This "covers Newbery winners and honor books from 1922 through 2001. Each entry includes a plot summary, themes and subjects, incidents for booktalking, related titles, and a bibliography about the author. Honor books are each given only a plot summary. . . . This work supersedes the first edition and is essential for public, school, academic, and other libraries serving students of children's literature." Booklist
Includes bibliographical references

Helbig, Alethea
Dictionary of American children's fiction, 1995-1999; books of recognized merit; [by] Alethea K. Helbig and Agnes Regan Perkins. Greenwood Press 2002 614p $99.95   **028.5**
1. Children's literature—Dictionaries 2. Children's literature—Bio-bibliography 3. Best books
ISBN 0-313-30389-4   LC 2001-23871
Also available volumes in series covering the years 1859-1959, 1960-1984, 1985-1989 and 1990-1994
"This dictionary is arranged alphabetically by title entries, author entries, character entries, and miscellaneous entries. . . . Entries include award winning and notable books from 1995-1999, as well as a few from previous years. Descriptions of each book are concise and include an overview of the characters, plot, setting, and awards received." Book Rep
For a fuller review see: Booklist, April 15, 2002

Latrobe, Kathy Howard
The children's literature dictionary; definitions, resources, and teaching activities; [by] Kathy Latrobe, Carolyn S. Brodie, Maureen White. Neal-Schuman 2002 282p pa $59.95   **028.5**
1. Children's literature—Dictionaries
ISBN 1-55570-424-7   LC 2001-44434
"The first section is an alphabetical dictionary of 325 terms found in reviews, lesson plans, and other resources. Definitions of terms contain meanings and examples from popular children's literature and activities related to the term. The activities descriptions provide a starting point for teaching or demonstrating the term. This reference book supports resources and materials that librarians or teachers should have in their collection." Book Rep

Masterplots II, juvenile and young adult fiction series; edited by Frank N. Magill. Salem Press 1991 4v set $383 **028.5**
1. Children's literature—Stories, plots, etc. 2. Young adult literature—Stories, plots, etc.
ISBN 0-89356-579-2 LC 91-4509
Focusing "on fiction that is of interest to readers aged 10 to 18 . . . [this set] covers more than 500 titles. . . . The selection criteria are exceptionally broad, allowing for the inclusion of children's classics, works written for a general audience but of particular interest to children and young adults, those from past eras, and those of contemporary writers." Am Ref Books Annu, 1992
Includes bibliographical references

The **Newbery** & Caldecott medal books, 1986-2000; a comprehensive guide to the winners; [by] the Horn Book, Association for Library Service to Children. American Lib. Assn. 2001 368p il pa $47.50 **028.5**
1. Newbery Medal 2. Caldecott Medal 3. Children's literature—History and criticism 4. Authors 5. Illustrators
ISBN 0-8389-3505-2 LC 00-53430
This volume "chronologically presents the Newbery and Caldecott acceptance speeches, biographical essays on the authors and artists, and the original *Horn Book Magazine* and *Booklist* reviews of the award winners." Horn Book
Includes bibliographical references

Newbery and Caldecott Medal books, 1966-1975; with acceptance papers, biographies and related material chiefly from The Horn Book magazine; edited by Lee Kingman. Horn Bk. 1975 xx, 321p il $22.95 **028.5**
1. Newbery Medal 2. Caldecott Medal 3. Children's literature—History and criticism 4. Authors 5. Illustrators
ISBN 0-87675-003-X
Continues Newbery Medal books, 1922-1955, Caldecott Medal books, 1938-1957 (o.p.), and Newbery and Caldecott Medal books, 1956-1965 (o.p.)
"Gives for each Newbery or Caldecott award winner his acceptance speech, a biographical note, and a book note. An excerpt from each Newbery book gives an example of the writer's style; a sample illustration from each Caldecott book is supplemented by notes on size, medium, printing process, number of illustrations and type used." Choice

Newbery and Caldecott Medal books, 1976-1985; with acceptance papers, biographies, and related material chiefly from The Horn Book magazine; edited by Lee Kingman. Horn Bk. 1986 358p il $24.95 **028.5**
1. Newbery Medal 2. Caldecott Medal 3. Children's literature—History and criticism 4. Authors 5. Illustrators
ISBN 0-87675-004-8 LC 86-15223
This volume "compiles the winning speeches, biographies and book notes for the 1976 through 1985 awards. It includes essays by Barbara Bader, Ethel Heins and Zena Sutherland." Bookbird

Newbery Medal books, 1922-1955; with their authors' acceptance papers & related material chiefly from The Horn Book magazine; edited by Bertha Mahony Miller and Elinor Whitney Field. Horn Bk. 1955 458p il $22.95 **028.5**
1. Newbery Medal 2. Children's literature—History and criticism 3. Authors
ISBN 0-87675-000-5
Companion volume to Caldecott Medal books, 1938-1957
"Largely biographical notes about award recipients and the acceptance papers." Ref Sources for Small & Medium-sized Libr. 5th edition

Perrin, Noel
A child's delight. Dartmouth College; University Press of New England 1997 161p hardcover o.p. paperback available $15.95 **028.5**
1. Children's literature—History and criticism 2. Children—Books and reading 3. Books—Reviews
ISBN 1-58465-352-3 (pa) LC 97-28220
Analyzed in Essay and general literature index
Collection of essays originally appearing as columns in the Washington post and the Los Angeles times
Perrin offers thirty essays "on children's books he feels should be better known. Librarians will be familiar with the majority of the titles (ranging from *The Railway Children* to *Half Magic* to *Watership Down*), but many parents and other adults may not be . . . . His essays might well serve as booktalks for adults looking for time-honored literature they have forgotten or missed but would nonetheless like to share with their children." Bull Cent Child Books
Includes bibliographical references

Trelease, Jim
The read-aloud handbook. 5th ed. Penguin Bks. 2001 xxvi, 402p il pa $15 **028.5**
1. Books and reading 2. Children's literature—Bibliography
ISBN 0-14-100161-5 LC 2001-21012
First published 1982
This handbook explains the importance of reading aloud to children, offers guidance on how to set up a read-aloud atmosphere in the home or classroom, and "shows readers how to take full advantage of recent cultural and technological developments. A new chapter explores important lessons from Oprah, Harry Potter, and the Internet, and an updated appendix lists key Internet sites for children's literature and education." Publisher's note
Includes bibliographical references

031 American encyclopedias

Britannica concise encyclopedia. New ed. Encyclopaedia Britannica 2002 2067p il $59.95 **031**
1. Encyclopedias and dictionaries
ISBN 0-85229-832-3
"This one-volume desk reference, which is actually a condensed version of the massive 32-volume *Encyclopaedia Britannica*, includes about 28,000 clearly written entries covering various branches of human knowledge, such as science, history, business, art, culture, geography, and geology, as well as more contemporary issues, such as cloning, terrorism, and globalization." Libr J

The **Columbia** encyclopedia; edited by Paul Legassé. 6th ed. Columbia Univ. Press 2000 3156p $135 **031**

1. Encyclopedias and dictionaries
ISBN 0-7876-5015-3   LC 00-27927

First published 1935

This edition "presents information current to January [2001]. With an increase of 108 pages, the newly designed encyclopedia boasts more than 50,000 articles, 40,000 bibliographic citations, 80,000 cross-references, and 700 line drawings. . . . The strengths of this large one-volume encyclopedia lie in its authority and objectivity. . . . Given its currency and its wealth of factual information, this new edition should take its place on most library shelves next to its predecessors." Am Ref Books Annu, 2001

The **Encyclopedia** Americana. Grolier 30v il maps apply to publisher for price **031**

1. Encyclopedias and dictionaries

Also available online

First published 1829. Frequently revised

"An encyclopedia suitable for junior and senior high school students as well as adults and college-level students. Cross-references are plentiful throughout the 45,000 articles. The index is comprehensive and analytical. *Americana* contains an exceptionally large number of U.S. place-names and biographies. The sciences, mathematics, American history, and the social sciences are particularly well developed. There are bibliographies at the end of major articles, nearly 400 of which have been updated for this edition." Ref Sources for Small & Medium-sized Libr. 6th edition

For a review of 2002 edition see: Booklist, Sept. 15, 2003

Hirsch, E. D. (Eric Donald), 1928-

The new dictionary of cultural literacy; [by] E.D. Hirsch, Joseph F. Kett, James Trefil. Completely rev and updated, 3rd ed. Houghton Mifflin 2002 647p il maps $29.95 **031**

1. Civilization—Dictionaries 2. English language—Dictionaries 3. United States—Civilization—Dictionaries
ISBN 0-618-22647-8   LC 2002-27609

First published 1988 with title: The dictionary of cultural literacy

"The text is divided into sections by subject—e.g., fine arts, world politics, life sciences—each with a brief introduction; access is also aided by a thorough index. The entries themselves are complete, concise, and clearly written as well as extensively and effectively cross-referenced." Libr J

Merriam-Webster's collegiate encyclopedia. Merriam-Webster 2000 1792p il maps $34.95 **031**

1. Encyclopedias and dictionaries
ISBN 0-87779-017-5   LC 00-62189

"More than 25,000 brief articles range in length from 40 to 700 words. They are alphabetized letter by letter. Variant spellings or names are printed in bold type, and pronunciations are provided. Cross-references to other articles are indicated by bullets. More than 1,650 black-and-white photographs, maps, diagrams, and other illustrations enhance entries. . . . There is coverage of topics and people in art, business, geography, history, literature, medicine, music, religion, science, and more." Booklist

The **New** Encyclopaedia Britannica. Encyclopaedia Britannica 32v il maps apply to publisher for price **031**

1. Encyclopedias and dictionaries

Also available CD-ROM version and online

First published 1768 in England; in the United States 1902. Now published with the editorial advice of the University of Chicago. First published with current title with the fifteenth edition in 1974. Frequently revised

"In three sections: Propaedia, or outline of knowledge; Macropaedia, with longer in-depth articles covering major topics; and Micropaedia, with shorter A-to-Z ready reference entries. *Britannica's* reputation as the basic encyclopedia for all libraries and reference collections is based on the writing and knowledge of thousands of expert contributors and consultants. Updated between major editions by the Britannica *Book of the Year.*" NY Public Libr Book of How & Where to Look It Up

For a review of 2003 edition see: Booklist, Feb. 15, 2003

The **World** Book encyclopedia. World Bk. 22v il maps apply to publisher for price **031**

1. Encyclopedias and dictionaries

Also available CD-ROM version, The World Book multimedia encyclopedia, and online

First published 1917-1918 by Field Enterprises. Frequently revised

Supplemented by: World Book's year in review; another available annual supplement is World Book's science year in review

"Curriculum-oriented, this superior encyclopedia is well-edited and produced to meet the reference and informational needs of students from grade four through high school. Long standing tradition of excellence for readability, accuracy, authoritativeness, objectivity, judicious and extensive use of outstanding graphics and timeliness." N Y Public Libr. Ref Books for Child Collect

For a review of 2003 edition see: Booklist, Sept. 15, 2003

031.02 American books of miscellaneous facts

Cole, Sylvia

The Facts on File dictionary of cultural and historical allusions; [by] Sylvia Cole, Abraham H. Lass. Facts on File 2000 470p $45 **031.02**

1. Allusions
ISBN 0-8160-4057-5   LC 00-021995

First published 1990 with title: The Facts on File dictionary of 20th-century allusions

"This dictionary spans allusions of the past 1000 years, including more than 1500 terms, names, and words used as metaphors to crystallize moments within the larger context of history, culture, and literature." Libr J

Encyclopaedia Britannica almanac. Encyclopaedia Britannica $19.95; pa $10.95 **031.02**

1. Almanacs 2. Statistics 3. United States—Statistics

Annual. First published 2002

Encyclopaedia Britannica almanac—*Continued*

"Features include biographies of notable figures, from the past as well as the present; a lookup of thousands of facts covering various branches of knowledge (e.g., science, business, history, entertainment, sports, and the arts). . . . There are also entries for countries and their leaders, with maps, flags, and various statistics; for awards and award winners; for sporting events; and much more." Libr J

For a fuller review see: Booklist, May 15, 2003

The **Essential** desk reference. Oxford Univ. Press 2002 815p $30   **031.02**
1. Encyclopedias and dictionaries
ISBN 0-19-512873-7

This reference "is divided into about 50 chapters, each covering a specific field of human knowledge, e.g., world and U.S. geography, science and medicine, arts and leisure, sport, politics, religion, history, technology, literature, business, and finance." Libr J

For a fuller review see: Booklist, Sept. 1, 2002

Famous first facts, international edition; a record of first happenings, discoveries, and inventions in world history; [edited by] Steven Anzovin & Janet Podell. Wilson, H.W. 2000 837p $140   **031.02**
1. Encyclopedias and dictionaries
ISBN 0-8242-0958-3   LC 99-86869

This work "contains more than 5000 firsts from hundreds of countries and ranging in time from 3.5 billion years ago (the age of the oldest continental land discovered) to 2001 (the scheduled date of completion of the first building over 1500 feet tall). . . . [It] groups related entries under broad subject categories (arranged alphabetically) and sub-categories. Within each category or sub-category, entries are arranged chronologically." Publisher's note

Feldman, David, 1950-
When do fish sleep? and other imponderables of everyday life; illustrated by Kassie Schwan. Harper & Row 1989 260p il hardcover o.p. paperback available $12.95
          031.02
1. Questions and answers
ISBN 0-06-092011-4 (pa)   LC 89-45038

"Feldman offers answers to such 'imponderables' as Why are rented bowling shoes so ugly? and Why do doctors tap on our backs during physical exams? Delightful and informative browsing fare." Booklist

Why do clocks run clockwise? and other imponderables; mysteries of everyday life; explained by David Feldman; illustrated by Kas Schwan. Harper & Row 1987 251p il hardcover o.p. paperback available $12.95
          031.02
1. Questions and answers
ISBN 0-06-091515-3 (pa)   LC 87-45045

The author "answers such recurring questions as 'What causes the ringing sound in your ears?' 'Why do nurses wear white?' and 'Why doesn't a "two-by-four" measure two inches by four inches?' Feldman answers them as authoritatively and truthfully as he can, relying on as trustworthy sources as he can find and sometimes, when the query submits to no single answer, fielding several different probable responses." Booklist

Kane, Joseph Nathan, 1899-2002
Famous first facts; a record of first happenings, discoveries, and inventions in American history; by Joseph Nathan Kane, Steven Anzovin, Janet Podell. 5th ed. Wilson, H.W. 1997 xxix, 1122p $155   **031.02**
1. Encyclopedias and dictionaries 2. United States—History—Dictionaries
ISBN 0-8242-0930-3   LC 97-31252
Also available CD-ROM version and online
First published 1933

"Aims to establish the earliest date of various occurrences, achievements, inventions, etc. Dictionary arrangement with many cross-references. Gives brief description or explanation together with the date; some references to sources." Guide to Ref Books. 11th edition

The **New** York Public Library desk reference. 4th ed. Hyperion 2002 999p il maps $34.95
          031.02
1. Encyclopedias and dictionaries
ISBN 0-7868-6846-5   LC 2002-27480
"A Stonesong Press book"
First published 1989 by Webster's New World

Divided into chapters, this reference features charts, tables, lists, and illustrations providing information in such categories as signs and symbols, mathematics and science basics, the arts, grammar and punctuation, etiquette, personal finance, first aid, and household tips

The **New** York Times almanac. Penguin Ref. il maps pa $11.95   **031.02**
1. Almanacs 2. Statistics 3. United States—Statistics
Annual. First published 1997
Edited by John W. Wright

This almanac contains a "chronology of the year; major news stories of the year; U.S. history; U.S. presidential biographies; world history; world geography; economic and climate data; major awards in the arts, sciences, and sports; and a wide variety of U.S. demographic information. . . . It is well organized, the table layout is easy to read, and the typeface does not invite eye strain." Am Ref Books Annu, 1998

The **Time** almanac. Information Please il maps pa $10.99   **031.02**
1. Almanacs 2. Statistics 3. United States—Statistics
ISSN 1529-1154
Also available online

Annual. Time almanac began with 1998 edition; absorbed Information please in 1998

Also known as The Time almanac with Information please

Contains statistical and factual material with a general topical arrangement and subject index. Illustrated with news photos and maps

The **World** almanac and book of facts. World Almanac Educ. il maps $31.95; pa $11.95
          031.02
1. Almanacs 2. Statistics 3. United States—Statistics
ISSN 0084-1382
Annual. First published 1868. Publisher varies

"This is the most comprehensive and well-known of almanacs. . . . Contains a chronology of the year's events, consumer information, historical anniversaries, annual climatological data, and forecasts. Color section has flags and maps. Includes detailed index." N Y Public Libr Book of How & Where to Look It Up

032.02 English books of miscellaneous facts

Guinness book of records. Guinness Media il $27.95 **032.02**
1. Curiosities and wonders
ISSN 1057-4557

Also available in paperback from Bantam Bks.

Annual. First published 1955 in the United Kingdom; in the United States 1962. Variant titles: Guinness book of world records; Guinness world records

Editors and publisher vary

"Ready reference for current record holders in all fields, some esoteric. Index provides access to information arranged in broad subject categories. Must be replaced annually." N Y Public Libr. Ref Books for Child Collect

050 General serial publications

Humanities index. Wilson, H.W. service basis **050**
1. Humanities—Periodicals—Indexes
ISSN 0095-5981

Also available CD-ROM version and online

Quarterly with bound annual cumulations

Started publication in June 1974 as a result of the division of the Social sciences & humanities index to form the Humanities Index and the Social sciences index

A subject index to over 500 periodicals in a broad range of subject fields in the humanities. Author and subject entries are arranged in a single alphabet. Complete bibliographic information is given with each entry. Book reviews are indexed by author in a separate section

051 American general serial publications and their indexes

Readers' guide to periodical literature. Wilson, H.W. $345 per year **051**
1. Periodicals—Indexes
ISSN 0034-0464

Also available CD-ROM version and online

First published 1900. Monthly. Permanent bound annual cumulations

A free pamphlet: How to use the Reader's guide to periodical literature, is available upon request

A cumulative author and subject index to over 300 periodicals. Coverage includes computers, business, health, fashion, politics, education, science, sports, arts and literature with criticism of individual dramatic works, videodiscs and videotapes, operas, ballets, musicals, movies, phonograph records, dance, and television and radio programs

"This is a modern index of the best type." Sheehy. Guide to Ref Books. 10th edition

Yagoda, Ben
About town; the New Yorker and the world it made. Scribner 2000 478p il o.p.; Da Capo Press paperback available $18 **051**
1. New Yorker (Periodical)
ISBN 0-306-81023-9 (pa)   LC 99-58140

This history "not only scrutinizes the magazine's contents but also assesses its cultural impact. It does so with the kind of verve, insight, and elegance that would have had [the magazine's first editor Harold] Ross dancing a jig of delight. It is, furthermore, the most comprehensive and authoritative history of The New Yorker yet to appear." Columbia J Rev

Includes bibliographical references

060.25 General organizations— Directories

Directories in print. Gale Res. 3v set $590 **060.25**
1. Directories
ISSN 0899-353X

Also available online as part of Gale's ready reference shelf

Annual. First published 1980 by Information Enterprises with title: The Directory of directories. Beginning 1991 incorporates International directories in print

This work "describes approximately 15,500 active rosters, guides and other print and nonprint address lists published in the United States and worldwide. Hundreds of additional directories (defunct, suspended and directories that cannot be located) are cited, with status notes, in the title/keyword index." Publisher's note

The **World** of learning. Europa Publs.; [distributed by] Taylor & Francis $620 **060.25**
1. Societies—Directories 2. Colleges and universities—Directories
ISSN 0084-2117

Annual. First published 1947

"The standard international directory for the nations of the world, covering learned societies, research institutes, libraries, museums and art galleries, and universities and colleges. Includes for each institution address, officers, purpose, foundation date, publications, etc." Ref Sources for Small & Medium-sized Libr. 6th edition

060.4 General rules of order (Parliamentary procedure)

Robert, Henry Martyn, 1837-1923
Robert's rules of order. Perseus Bks. $35 **060.4**
1. Parliamentary practice

First published 1876 as Pocket manual of rules of order for deliberate assemblies. (10th edition 2000) Title and publisher vary

"A new and enlarged edition by Sarah Corbin Robert, Henry M. Robert III, William J. Evans, Daniel H. Honemann, Thomas J. Balch"

"Long the standard compendium of parliamentary law, explaining methods of organizing and conducting the business of societies, conventions, and other assemblies. Includes convenient charts and tables." Ref Sources for Small & Medium-sized Libr. 6th edition

Sturgis, Alice
The standard code of parliamentary procedure; original edition by Alice Sturgis. 4th ed, revised by the American Institute of Parliamentarians. McGraw-Hill 2001 xxiv, 285p pa $14.95 **060.4**
1. Parliamentary practice
ISBN 0-07-136513-3   LC 2001-265929
First published 1950

Sturgis, Alice—*Continued*

This guide to the rules of parliamentary procedure includes explanations of their purpose and examples of their use. Also considers ways the Internet and other technologies have rewritten rules of meetings
Includes bibliographical references

Webster's New World Robert's rules of order; simplified and applied; by Robert McConnell Productions. 2nd ed. Hungry Minds 2001 xx, 409p pa $10.99   **060.4**
1. Parliamentary practice
ISBN 0-7645-6399-8   LC 2001-92064
First Webster's New World edition published 1999
This explains the rules of parliamentary procedure, discussing the concepts behind each rule and including examples. This revised edition includes procedures for conducting meetings online, voting by mail and by e-mail, and adopting election procedures

061.025 American organizations—Directories

Encyclopedia of associations. Gale Res. 3v in 5   **061.025**
1. Societies—Directories 2. Trade and professional associations
ISSN 0071-0202
Also available online as part of Associations unlimited; Also available: International organizations 3v set $725 (ISSN 1041-0023); Regional, state, and local organizations 5v ea $170
Annual. First published 1956 with title: Encyclopedia of American associations
Contents: v1 pt 1-3 National organizations of the U.S.; v2 Geographic and executive indexes; v3 Supplement
This is a guide to more than 23,000 nonprofit American membership organizations of national scope

The **Foundation** directory; compiled by The Foundation Center. Foundation Center $215   **061.025**
1. Endowments—Directories 2. Charities—Directories
ISSN 0071-8092
Also available CD-ROM version and online
Annual. First published 1960 by Russell Sage. Replaces American foundations and their fields
"Provides detailed information concerning independent, corporate, community, and private foundations with assets of at least $2 million or annual giving of at least $200,000. Geographical arrangement. Entries give date founded; names of officers, contact, and donors; foundation type; financial data; fields of interest; types of support; limitations; application information; and number of staff. Six indexes: Donors, officers, and trustees; Geographic; Types of support; Subject; Foundations new to edition; Foundations name index." Guide to Ref Books. 11th edition

National trade and professional associations of the United States. Columbia Bks. pa $159   **061.025**
1. Trade and professional associations
Annual. First published 1966 with title: Directory of national trade and professional associations of the United States

"Includes nearly 6500 organizations arranged by subject. Indexed by title, key word, geographical location, size of budget, and executive officers. Particularly valuable for its data on the annual budget as well as such general information as date of establishment, address, headquarters staff, size of membership, publications, and telephone number." Ref Sources for Small & Medium-sized Libr. 6th edition

069 Museology

Mauriès, Patrick, 1952-
Cabinets of curiosities. Thames & Hudson 2002 256p il $65   **069**
1. Collectors and collecting 2. Curiosities and wonders—Collectors and collecting
ISBN 0-500-51091-1   LC 2002-100528
The author "presents the long history of cabinets of curiosities—grand accumulations of rare, exotic, or unusual objects either natural or human-made, displayed in decorative cases or entire rooms. The earliest documented case, from late 15th-century Italy, was a collection of books as well as a variety of botanical and zoological specimens (including a stuffed crocodile). Collections have also included textiles, scientific and musical instruments, ethnographic objects, automata, paintings, silverware, and mummified anatomical specimens. . . . In many ways, this book is a cabinet of curiosities in itself-crammed with fascinating images and information." Libr J
Includes bibliographical references

069.025 Museums—Directories

Museums of the world. Saur; [distributed by] Gale Group 2v set $450   **069.025**
1. Museums—Directories
First published 1973. (10th edition 2003) Periodically revised
"Lists over 41,600 museums in 199 countries. Museums are listed hierarchically by country and place, and within places, alphabetical by name." Publisher's note

The **Official** museum directory. National Register Pub. 2v pa set $305   **069.025**
1. Museums—Directories
ISSN 0090-6700
Annual. Supersedes the Museums directory of the United States and Canada, first published 1961 by The American Association of Museums and the Smithsonian Institution
This directory contains "listings on more than 8,100 museums operating in 87 different fields, ranging from science museums to zoos to historic homes to fine arts. It is one of the most trusted and accessible sources for museum professionals to identify vendors, access unique collections and exhibitions, and contact directors and curators. Volume 1 lists institutions by state, and contains a number of indexes: an alphabetic index to institutions, an index to personnel, an index to institutions by category, an index to institutions by collection, and new listings. Volume 2 is a guide to more than 2,100 vendors, their products, and their services, subdivided by category. . . . This product is one of the most useful and up-to-date reference works in the area of museums, especially in relation to current personnel and exhibitions." Recomm Ref Books for Small & Medium-sized Libr & Media Cent, 2003

070.025 Newspapers and journalism—Directories

Gale directory of publications and broadcast media. Gale Res. 5v maps set $815

070.025

1. Newspapers—Directories 2. Periodicals—Directories

ISSN 1048-7972

Price includes interedition supplement

Also available online as part of Gale's ready reference shelf

Annual. First published 1869. Variant titles: Gale directory of publications and Ayer directory of publications

"An annual guide to publications and broadcasting stations"

Contents: v1 U.S., Alabama-New Hampshire and Canada; v2 U.S., New Jersey-Wyoming and Canada; v3 U.S. and Canada Broadcast networks and News and Features Synicates, indexes and tables; v4 U.S. and Canada regional market index and maps; v5 International. International index and maps

Identifies specific print and broadcast sources of news and advertising for trade, business, labor, and professionals. Arrangement is geographic with a thumbnail description of each local market. Indexes are classified (by format and subject matter) and alphabetical (by name and keyword)

070.1 News media

Garner, Joe

We interrupt this broadcast; the events that stopped our lives—from the Hindenburg explosion to the attacks of September 11. Updated 3rd ed. Sourcebooks 2002 178p il + 2 sound discs $49.95 **070.1**

1. Television broadcasting of news 2. Broadcast journalism 3. Disasters

ISBN 1-57071-974-8   LC 2003-265013

First published 1998

"This book and double-CD set documents, in text, audio and black-and-white photographs, the moments when history, for better or for worse (though usually for worse), was made in an instant. . . . In addition to the CDs' reports and sound bites dramatically introduced and explained . . . each event gets about four pages of coverage, with an efficient summary and at least half a dozen photos. . . . These are the kinds of moments that still shock and amaze. This moving book is 'a tribute of sorts' to the events that defined eras, the journalists who reported on them and the media television, radio that made us all witnesses." Publ Wkly

070.4 Journalism

The **Best** business stories of the year. Vintage Bks. pa $15 **070.4**

1. Business

Annual. First published 2001

A comprehensive selection of articles on all aspects of the business world that have appeared in print media or online publications

"This carefully selected arrangement of interesting, well-written, and thought-provoking articles is a good choice for public and academic libraries." Libr J

Friedlander, Edward Jay

Feature writing for newspapers and magazines; the pursuit of excellence; [by] Edward Jay Friedlander, John Lee. 5th ed. Allyn & Bacon 2003 c2004 337p $57.33

070.4

1. Journalism

ISBN 0-205-38191-X   LC 2002-43729

First published 1988

Through suggestions and examples this guide for the novice writer provides tips from Pulitzer Prize-winning journalists and other magazine and newspaper feature writers

Howe, Peter

Shooting under fire; the world of the war photographer. Artisan 2002 223p il $35

070.4

1. Photojournalism 2. War—Pictorial works

ISBN 1-57965-215-8   LC 2002-74606

"An introduction and brief history of war photography precede individual observations by 'ten of the most famous living photographers,' male and female, that convey both the horrors and the highs associated with their profession. . . . More than 150 black-and-white and color photos taken in Vietnam, Nicaragua, Biafra, Beirut, Belfast, etc.—some that cannot be viewed without wincing—accompany the pieces." SLJ

Pearl, Daniel, 1963-2002

At home in the world; collected writings from the Wall Street Journal; edited by Helene Cooper; foreword by Mariane Pearl. Simon & Schuster 2002 278p $24 **070.4**

ISBN 0-7432-4317-X   LC 2002-66353

This "book comprises 50 stories by Pearl that appeared during his 12-year reporting career. Organized thematically, the book reveals Pearl's ability to cover diverse topics, ranging from the serious (war-ravaged Kosovo) to the mundane (Iran's pop music stars)." Libr J

Ross, Lillian, 1927-

Reporting back; notes on journalism. Counterpoint 2002 292p $25 **070.4**

1. Journalism 2. Reporters and reporting

ISBN 1-58243-109-4   LC 2002-3709

Ross "discusses her feelings about journalism, praising her *New Yorker* colleagues (notably the late editor William Shawn) and offering her definition of journalism. . . . The majority of the book is filled with Ross's deconstruction of some of her best-loved pieces." Publ Wkly

"A wonderful journalism handbook, memoir, and addition to books on the *New Yorker*." Booklist

070.5 Publishing

Appelbaum, Judith

How to get happily published. HarperCollins Pubs. pa $14 **070.5**

1. Authors and publishers 2. Publishers and publishing

First published 1978 with co-author Nancy Evans. (5th edition 1998) Periodically revised

Covers the mechanics of writing and manuscript preparation, selling the book to a publisher, stages of publication and the self-publishing option, promotional ideas, and possible markets such as poetry and children's books

Includes bibliographical references

The **Columbia** guide to digital publishing; edited by William E. Kasdorf. Columbia Univ. Press 2003 lxi, 750p $65; pa $34.95

070.5

1. Electronic publishing
ISBN 0-231-12498-8; 0-231-12499-6 (pa)
LC 2002-41462

Also available online

This volume begins with an introductory chapter on "the role of digital publishing in various facets of the publishing industry. . . . Other chapters address topics such as: the technical infrastructure, mark-up, content management, digital rights management, e-books, archiving issues, legal issues, accessibility, and international issues." The Indexer

"The editor and contributors . . . have exerted great effort to include all relevant information for beginners, yet they offer enough detail to capture the attention of advanced users without expanding to a multivolume work or becoming too long. . . . A superb opening gesture for creating a dialog on the scholarly communication process." Choice

Includes bibliographical references

Epstein, Jason
Book business; publishing past, present, and future. Norton 2001 188p $21.95; pa $13.95

070.5

1. Publishers and publishing
ISBN 0-393-04984-1; 0-393-32234-3 (pa)
LC 00-60079

"This memoir, adapted from a series of lectures given at the New York Public Library, looks back across Epstein's half century in the book business: he launched Anchor Books at Doubleday, helped found *The New York Review of Books*, and has worked at Random House since 1958." New Yorker

"Epstein's analysis of the dire straits in which publishing finds itself is well taken and convincingly argued; the effect that the Internet will have on the industry is not as well argued but explored interestingly." Booklist

Germano, William P., 1950-
Getting it published; a guide for scholars and anyone else serious about serious books; [by] William Germano. University of Chicago Press 2001 197p (Chicago guides to writing, editing, and publishing) $35; pa $15 **070.5**

1. Authors and publishers 2. Publishers and publishing
ISBN 0-226-28843-9; 0-226-28844-7 (pa)
LC 00-46715

The author "deconstructs and demystifies what publishers and editors actually do and what authors should look for in finding the right house for their subject and in putting the right words in their contract. He also does a lot of hand-holding through the review process and the production of the manuscript." Booklist

Includes bibliographical references

Guide to literary agents. Writer's Digest Bks. pa $23.99 **070.5**

1. Authors and publishers—Directories
ISSN 1078-6945

Annual. Supersedes in part Guide to literary agents & art/photo reps

"An invaluable tool for writers in search of an agent, this guide is indexed by agency, agent, format, subject, and geographic location. Submission procedures, fees, contracts and what to ask a prospective agent are covered." Libr J

Herman, Jeff, 1958-
Jeff Herman's guide to book publishers, editors, & literary agents. Writer Bks.; [distributed by] Kalmbach Pub. Co. pa $29.95

070.5

1. Authors and publishers 2. Publishers and publishing

Annual. First published 1992 by Prima Pub. with title: Insider's guide to book editors, publishers, and literary agents. Variant title: Writer's guide to book editors, publishers, and literary agents

Herman provides "portraits of more than 100 agents plus tips on writing query letters and nonfiction book proposals, dealing with rejections, ghostwriting, and self-publishing. With an excellent glossary and sample author-agent and collaboration agreements." Libr J

Poynter, Dan
The self-publishing manual; how to write, print and sell your own book. Para Pub. pa $19.95 **070.5**

1. Publishers and publishing

First published 1979. (14th edition 2003) Periodically revised

"Poynter gives the basics for producing a commercially successful manuscript, taking the reader step-by-step through printing a book, determining its value, promoting and advertising, fulfilling orders, and coping with being published. There are appendixes on printers, professional organizations, and fulfillment warehouses." Libr J

The **Publish-it-yourself** handbook. Pushcart Press 1998 pa $18 **070.5**

1. Publishers and publishing

First published 1973. (4th edition 1998) Periodically revised

An anthology of articles about how to publish without the assistance of commercial or vanity publishers

Rose, M. J.
How to publish and promote online; [by] M. J. Rose and Angela Adair-Hoy. St. Martin's Griffin 2001 266p pa $13.95 **070.5**

1. Publishers and publishing 2. Authorship—Internet resources
ISBN 0-312-27191-3
LC 00-45833

The authors "provide encouragement and tips for aspiring authors hoping to publish their works electronically." Booklist

070.5025   Publishing—Directories

American book trade directory. Information Today $285 **070.5025**

1. Book industry 2. Publishers and publishing—Directories 3. Book collecting
ISSN 0065-759X

Annual. First published 1915 by Bowker with title: American book trade manual

"Includes lists of booksellers, wholesalers, and publishers in the United States, with related information on the book trade in Canada, the United Kingdom, and Ireland. Bookstores are arranged under state and city with speciality of each noted. Separate lists include exporters, importers, and dealers in foreign books. Index of retailers and wholesalers in the United States and Canada." Ref Sources for Small & Medium-sized Libr. 6th edition

International literary market place: ILMP. Information Today pa $239 **070.5025**
1. Publishers and publishing—Directories
ISSN 0074-6827
Also available online
Annual. First published 1965 by Bowker
This directory of the international book publishing industry covers over 180 countries worldwide and profiles "more than 16,500 book-related concerns around the globe, including . . . 10,500 publishers and literary agents; 1,100 major booksellers and book clubs; 1,520 major libraries and library associations . . . and thousands of other book-related concerns—including trade organizations, distributors, dealers, literary associations, trade publications, book trade events, and other resources . . . organized in a country-by-country format." Publisher's note

Literary market place: LMP. Bowker 2v pa set $299 **070.5025**
1. Publishers and publishing—Directories
ISSN 0075-9899
Also available online
Annual. First published 1940. In 1972 absorbed Names & numbers. Subtitle varies
"Directory of U.S. and Canadian book publishers and related businesses such as book clubs, literary agents, translators, and manufacturers. Gives names of executives and addresses, telephone numbers, and fields of specialization for each publishing company." N Y Public Libr Book of How & Where to Look It Up

Publishers, distributors & wholesalers of the United States. Bowker 2v set $349
070.5025
1. Publishers and publishing—Directories
ISSN 0000-0671
Annual. First published 1979 with title: Publishers and distributors of the United States
This directory provides information on "more than 150,000 U.S. publishers, wholesalers, distributors, software firms, audiocassette producers, museum and association imprints, and trade organizations that publish." Publisher's note

071 Journalism and newspapers—North America

Downie, Leonard, 1942-
The news about the news; American journalism in peril; [by] Leonard Downie, Jr., and Robert G. Kaiser. Knopf 2002 292p $25; pa $14 **071**
1. Journalism
ISBN 0-375-40874-6; 0-375-71415-4 (pa)
LC 2001-37735
The authors "explore the developments of the past 20 years that have placed journalism at the crossroads—in need of a higher level of accountability and an examination of the values that drive the business of news gathering." Booklist
"This is an important, up-to-date study that should be required reading for journalism students and serious consumers of the news." Publ Wkly
Includes bibliographical references

The New York Times Index. New York Times Apply to publisher for price **071**
ISSN 0147-538X
Semimonthly with 3 quarterly cumulations and annual cumulation.
Also available CD-ROM version and online
"Summarizes and classifies news alphabetically by subjects, persons, and organizations. Helpful in locating articles not only in the *New York Times*, but also in other papers, as entries establish the date of events." Ref Sources for Small & Medium-sized Libr. 6th edition

Written into history; Pulitzer Prize reporting of the twentieth century from the New York times; edited and with an introduction by Anthony Lewis. Times Bks.; Holt & Co. 2001 xxv, 355p hardcover o.p. paperback available $17 **071**
1. Journalism 2. Pulitzer Prizes
ISBN 0-8050-7178-4 (pa)
LC 2001-35555
The award-winning articles "are sorted into the following categories: investigative reporting; dangerous stories that put reporters at risk; international news; public advocacy; criticism of the arts; science reporting; and biographical and human-interest stories. Among the topics are Russian slave-labor camps during the 1950s, the Pentagon Papers, the Vietnam War, and exploitation of illegal aliens in the U.S." Booklist
"For anyone interested in recent history or journalism at its best, this book will prove worthwhile." Publ Wkly

080 General collections

Adler, Mortimer J., 1902-2001
How to think about the great ideas; from the great books of Western civilization; [by] Mortimer J. Adler; edited by Max Weismann. Open Court 2000 xxiv, 530p pa $24.95 **080**
1. Great books of the Western world
ISBN 0-8126-9412-0
LC 99-45251
This volume contains the transcripts of 52 half-hour segments of Adler's 1953-1954 television program The great ideas
"The book showcases Adler's ideas about all the big categories—truth, beauty, freedom, love, sex, art, justice, rationality, humankind's nature, Darwinism, government." Publ Wkly

Essay and general literature index. Wilson, H.W. $265 per year **080**
1. Essays—Indexes 2. Literature—Indexes
ISSN 0014-083X
Also available CD-ROM version and online
Also available: Works indexed, 1900-1969 $75 (ISBN 0-8242-0503-0) which cites the 9,917 titles analyzed in the first seven permanent cumulations
Basic volume and permanent retrospective volumes available at $405 each
Continues the "A.L.A. index to general literature." The basic volume published 1934 covered the period 1900-1933. Kept up to date by semi-annual supplements, cumulating annually, with five year permanent cumulations
This subject-author index provides access to essays and articles in collections and anthologies published in English. Some 300 volumes are indexed annually plus more than 20 selected annuals and serials
"A boon to librarians. . . . A must for all academic and large public libraries." Am Ref Books Annu

Great treasury of Western thought; a compendium of important statements on man and his institutions by the great thinkers in Western history; edited by Mortimer J. Adler & Charles Van Doren. Bowker 1977 xxv, 1771p   **080**
1. Quotations   LC 77-154
Available from Libraries Unlimited $52 (ISBN 0-8352-0833-8)
"Quotations are often long ones, the average lengths being about 100 words. . . . Arranged in twenty chapters (Man, Family, Love, Emotion, Mind, Knowledge, etc.) with introductory notes for each chapter and subsection. Overall subject and proper name index." Sheehy. Guide to Ref Books. 10th edition

100 PHILOSOPHY & PSYCHOLOGY

Blackburn, Simon
Think: a compelling introduction to philosophy. Oxford Univ. Press 1999 312p $25   **100**
1. Philosophy
ISBN 0-19-210024-6   LC 00-265266
The author explores such areas as knowledge, mind, free will, identity, God, goodness and justice. "His method is to introduce what other philosophers—primarily Plato, Descartes, Locke, Berkeley, Leibniz, Hume, and Kant—have had to say about these themes. . . . Readers new to the subject could very well be captivated." Libr J
Includes bibliographical references

Masterpieces of world philosophy; edited by Frank N. Magill; selection by John K. Roth; with an introduction by John K. Roth. HarperCollins Pubs. 1990 684p $48
                                        100
1. Philosophy
ISBN 0-06-016430-1   LC 89-46545
This book "examines and summarizes nearly one hundred influential works through critical essays that focus on their themes and major points. Based on the . . . five-volume reference, *World Philosophy* [1982] each essay explains the historical background of the work, the life of its author, and its influence on modern thought. Alternate views of the philosopher's ideas are provided through reviews of important critical works." Publisher's note

Russell, Bertrand, 1872-1970
The problems of philosophy   **100**
1. Philosophy
Hardcover and paperback editions available from various publishers
First published 1912 by Holt
The author discusses: appearance and reality, matter, idealism, theories of knowledge, universals, intuition, and truth
"The work is concise, free from technical terms and perfectly clear to the general reader with no prior knowledge of the subject." Booklist

103 Philosophy—Encyclopedias and dictionaries

Blackburn, Simon
The Oxford dictionary of philosophy. Oxford Univ. Press 1994 408p il $49.95; pa $15.95   **103**
1. Philosophy—Dictionaries
ISBN 0-19-211694-0; 0-19-283134-8 (pa)
                                        LC 94-8832
"Almost 3000 entries—many extensively cross-referenced—cover Eastern and Western philosophy (with emphasis on the latter), all the main subdivisions of philosophy, terminology from other disciplines that is significant in philosophical discussion, and major historical figures." Libr J

The **Cambridge** dictionary of philosophy; edited by Robert Audi. 2nd ed. Cambridge Univ. Press 1999 xxxv, 1001p il $85; pa $30   **103**
1. Philosophy—Dictionaries
ISBN 0-521-63136-X; 0-521-63722-8 (pa)
                                        LC 99-12920
First published 1995
This work contains some 4,400 entries including 50 on major contemporary philosophers. Wide coverage of Western philosophy as well as non-Western and non-European philosophers is included. The rapidly growing fields of philosophy of mind and applied ethics are also covered

Concise Routledge encyclopedia of philosophy. Routledge 2000 xxxiv, 1030p $42.95   **103**
1. Philosophy—Encyclopedias
ISBN 0-415-22364-4   LC 99-52692
"This work consists of more than 2000 abbreviated entries culled from the ten-volume *Routledge Encyclopedia of Philosophy*. It has the same number of entries as the ten-volume set, whose lengthy essays each begin with a brief description of the subject; it is these descriptions that make up the content of the *Concise Encyclopedia*." Libr J
For a fuller review see: Booklist, Oct. 1, 2000

The **Encyclopedia** of philosophy; Paul Edwards, editor in chief. Free Press 1973 c1967 8v in 4 + supplement set $675
                                        103
1. Philosophy—Encyclopedias
ISBN 0-02-864651-7
Supplement published 1996 also available separately $135 (ISBN 0-02-864629-0)
A reissue of the title first published 1967 in eight volumes; supplement edited by Donald M. Borchert published 1996 by Macmillan
This is a "clear, readable compendium of articles by authorities in many areas; includes Eastern and Western thought." N Y Public Libr Book of How & Where to Look It Up
"*The Encyclopedia of Philosophy* . . . remains to this day the best and most comprehensive English-language reference source for philosophy. . . . The supplement includes a comprehensive index to both itself and the encyclopedia, and cross-referencing in the supplement is made to entries in both works. Libraries that own the en-

The Encyclopedia of philosophy—Continued

cyclopedia must acquire the supplement. Libraries that do not own the encyclopedia might want to mark the occasion of the publication of the supplement by purchasing both works." Booklist

The **Oxford** companion to philosophy; edited by Ted Honderich. Oxford Univ. Press 1995 1009p il $60 **103**
1. Philosophy—Dictionaries
ISBN 0-19-866132-0 LC 94-36914
This volume provides "brief entries on a wide range of persons, ideas, and schools. . . . The entries are arranged alphabetically, and each is followed by one or more bibliographic citations and/or cross-references. . . . Portraits of many famous philosophers . . . are included." Choice

Rohmann, Chris

A world of ideas; a dictionary of important theories, concepts, beliefs, and thinkers. Ballantine Pub. Group 1999 476p $24.95; pa $16.95 **103**
1. Philosophy—Dictionaries 2. Social sciences—Dictionaries 3. Religion—Dictionaries
ISBN 0-345-39059-8; 0-345-43706-3 (pa)
LC 98-39543
This "guide covers more than 400 theories, philosophies, ideologies, beliefs, and thinkers in the sciences, arts, and social sciences." Libr J

109 Philosophy—History

A **Companion** to world philosophies; edited by Eliot Deutsch and Ron Bontekoe; advisory editors, Tu Weiming [et al.] Blackwell 1997 587p (Blackwell companions to philosophy) hardcover o.p. paperback available $34.95 **109**
1. Philosophy
ISBN 0-631-21327-9 (pa) LC 96-36179
This volume "focuses on non-Western philosophies. . . . The editors have drawn together leading authors in the fields of Chinese, Indian, Buddhist, Islamic, Polynesian, and African philosophy to produce an excellent single-volume survey. . . . The essays are of a uniformly high quality and are accessible even to those with little background in non-Western philosophies." Libr J

Durant, William James, 1885-1981

The story of philosophy; the lives and opinions of the great philosophers; by Will Durant. [2nd ed] Simon & Schuster 1933 412p hardcover o.p. paperback available $15 **109**
1. Philosophy—History 2. Philosophers
ISBN 0-671-20159-X (pa)
First published 1926
A selective account of western thinkers from Socrates and Kant to Schopenhauer and Dewey
Includes bibliographical references

Jaspers, Karl, 1883-1969

The great philosophers. Harcourt Brace & Co. 1962-1994 4v v 1-3 op; v4 $29.95 **109**
1. Philosophy—History 2. Philosophers
Analyzed in Essay and general literature index

Originally published in German
v1-2 edited by Hannah Arendt; translated by Ralph Manheim; v3-4 edited by Michael Ermarth and Leonard H. Ehrlich; translated by Edith Ehrlich and Leonard H. Ehrlich
Contents: v1 The foundations: The paradigmatic individuals; Socrates; Buddha; Confucius; Jesus. The seminal founders of philosophical thought: Plato; Augustine; Kant; v2 The original thinkers: Anaximander; Heraclitus; Parmenides; Plotinus; Anselm; Nicholas of Cusa; Spinoza; Lao-Tzu; and Nagarjuna; v3 Xenophanes; Democritus; Empedocles; Bruno; Epicurus; Bohme; Schelling; Leibniz; Aristotle; Hegel; v4 The disturbers: Descartes; Pascal; Lessing; Kierkegaard; Nietzsche; philosophers in other realms: Einstein; Weber; Marx (ISBN 0-15-136943-7)
"Extracts the living essence of each philosopher's wisdom in these highly individualistic critiques." Publ Wkly
Includes bibliographical references

Russell, Bertrand, 1872-1970

A history of Western philosophy; and its connection with political and social circumstances from the earliest times to the present day. Simon & Schuster 1945 xxiii, 895p hardcover o.p. paperback available $24 **109**
1. Philosophy—History 2. Philosophers
ISBN 0-671-20158-1 (pa)
Analyzed in Essay and general literature index
Originally designed and partly delivered as lectures at the Barnes Foundation in Pennsylvania
Contents: Ancient philosophy; Catholic philosophy; Modern philosophy. A summary is given of the main contributions of each period
"My purpose is to exhibit philosophy as an integral part of social and political life; not as the isolated speculations of remarkable individuals." Preface

Solomon, Robert C.

A passion for wisdom; a very brief history of philosophy; [by] Robert C. Solomon, Kathleen M. Higgins. Oxford Univ. Press 1997 137p hardcover o.p. paperback available $12.95 **109**
1. Philosophy—History
ISBN 0-19-511209-1 (pa) LC 96-42034
Part one "examines the Greek roots of Western philosophy . . . [and] also looks at philosophical traditions in India, elsewhere in Asia, Africa, and the Americas. Part two covers the period from the origins of Christianity to the rise of Islam to Adam Smith; Part three begins with Kant and ends with a brief look at postmodernism." Libr J
The authors "provide a multicultural account of philosophical thought and developments across nearly 4000 years. The volume is necessarily simplified but not simplistic, and the thoughts themselves are given precedent over the biographies of the thinkers." SLJ
Includes bibliographical references

111 Ontology

Barrow, John D., 1952-
The book of nothing; vacuums, voids, and the latest ideas about the origins of the universe. Pantheon Bks. 2001 361p il hardcover o.p. paperback available $15 **111**
1. Zero (The number) 2. Science—History
ISBN 0-375-72609-8 (pa)   LC 00-58894
This volume traces the concept of nothing "from a Babylonian place holder, a Mayan decoration in the empty space where no number fell and an Indian dot signifying all the current aspects of zero, to one of the most essential elements in mathematics, physics and cosmology." Publ Wkly

Encyclopedia of aesthetics; editor in chief, Michael Kelly. Oxford Univ. Press 1998 4v set $495   **111**
1. Aesthetics—Encyclopedias
ISBN 0-19-511307-1   LC 98-18741
"Drawing from experts in the areas of philosophy, art, history, psychology, feminist theory, legal theory, and many more, the encyclopedia presents 600 signed essays alphabetically arranged. Most entries include a headnote clarifying the topic. Entries range from the philosophical essay on ugliness, to the more reality-based article on the impact of AIDS on the arts. Comprehensive coverage includes key figures, concepts, periods, theories, and movements in the history of aesthetics." Am Libr

Heidegger, Martin, 1889-1976
Being and time; translated by John Macquarrie & Edward Robinson. Harper & Row 1962 589p $29.95   **111**
1. Ontology 2. Phenomenology
ISBN 0-06-063850-8
Also available in paperback from State Univ. of New York Press
Original German edition, 1927
"All of Heidegger's work revolves around the essential inquiry: what is the nature of being? In his most important book, . . . he distinguishes between two types of being: human existence (*Dasein*) and nonhuman presence (*Vorhandensein*)." Reader's Ency. 4th edition
Includes bibliographical references

On time and being; translated by Joan Stambough. Harper & Row 1972 84p o.p.; University of Chicago Press paperback available $12   **111**
1. Ontology 2. Phenomenology
ISBN 0-226-32375-7 (pa)
Original German edition, 1969
This volume by the 20th Century philosopher "contains four items: a 1962 lecture, 'Time and Being,' and a seminar report on it by Alfred Guzzoni; a 1964 lecture, 'The End of Philosophy and the Task of Thinking'; and a 1963 Festschrift essay, 'My Way to Phenomenology.'" Libr J

Watson, Lyall
Dark nature; a natural history of evil. HarperCollins Pubs. 1996 c1995 318p hardcover o.p. paperback available $19 **111**
1. Good and evil 2. Human beings 3. Biology—Philosophy
ISBN 0-06-092790-9 (pa)   LC 96-1663
First published 1995 in the United Kingdom

The author "ranges through philosophy, psychology, anthropology, history, ecology and especially biology. . . . Watson believes that aggression is in our genes and examines such phenomena as war, rape and murder as manifestations of that aggression. But while he firmly believes that humans are made up of both good and evil and that natural selection is completely amoral, he is sanguine about humans as the world's first ethical animals with the capability of making moral decisions." Publ Wkly
Includes bibliographical references

113 Cosmology (Philosophy of nature)

Teilhard de Chardin, Pierre
The phenomenon of man; with an introduction by Julian Huxley. Harper & Row 1959 318p hardcover o.p. paperback available $14.95   **113**
1. Universe 2. Evolution 3. Human beings
ISBN 0-06-090495-X (pa)
Original French edition, 1955; this translation by Bernard Wall
The author integrates scientific findings with the tenets of Christian faith in this study of human evolution and destiny

Whitehead, Alfred North, 1861-1947
Process and reality; an essay in cosmology. corrected ed, edited by David Ray Griffin, Donald W. Sherburne. Free Press 1978 xxxi, 413p hardcover o.p. paperback available $18.95   **113**
1. Universe 2. Science—Philosophy
ISBN 0-02-934570-7 (pa)   LC 77-90011
First published 1929
Gifford lectures delivered in the University of Edinburgh during the session, 1927-28
This book presents a condensed scheme of cosmological ideas developed by confrontation with various topics of experience. The aesthetic, moral and religious interests are thus brought into relation with those elements of knowledge which have their origin in natural science
Includes bibliographical references

Wilson, Edward O., 1929-
In search of nature. Island Press 1996 214p il $22; pa $15   **113**
1. Philosophy of nature 2. Human beings 3. Human ecology
ISBN 1-55963-215-1; 1-55963-216-X (pa)
LC 96-11226
"A Shearwater book"
"A compilation of a dozen journal articles and book chapters published between 1975 and 1993, this collection is grouped into three thematic sections dealing with the importance of the preservation of biodiversity to our physical and emotional well-being, the deep-seated interconnectedness of animal nature and human nature . . . and the underlying genetic basis of human social behavior." Libr J
"Concerned people of all ages should enjoy the reasoning provided by the dedicated scientific writing presented in this attractive book." Sci Books Films
Includes bibliographical references

115 Time

Gorst, Martin, 1960-
Measuring eternity; the search for the beginning of time. Broadway Bks. 2002 338p il $23.95; pa $13.95 **115**
1. Time
ISBN 0-7679-0827-9; 0-7679-0844-9 (pa)
LC 2001-37556
The author "discusses how human understanding of time shifted throughout the centuries, as models of the universe became more accurate and instruments for gathering data grew more sophisticated." Publ Wkly
"For the most part Gorst avoids retrospective judgments on what now seem to be spectacular errors of calculation. Instead, he peppers his account with snippets and asides that bring the protagonists to life and make the story of time surprisingly easy to trace." New Sci
Includes bibliographical references

121 Epistemology (Theory of knowledge)

Locke, John, 1632-1704
An essay concerning human understanding **121**
1. Theory of knowledge 2. Thought and thinking
Hardcover and paperback editions available from various publishers
This essay first published 1690, deals "with the nature and scope of human knowledge. Its basic premise is the empirical origin of ideas, which can be described as the raw material with which the mind works. Locke's essay contributed greatly to the growth of 18th-century empiricism." Reader's Ency. 4th edition

Sartre, Jean Paul, 1905-1980
Truth and existence; original text established and annotated by Arlette Elkaïm-Sartre; translated by Adrian van den Hoven; edited and with an introduction by Ronald Aronson. University of Chicago Press 1992 xlix, 94p hardcover o.p. paperback available $11 **121**
1. Theory of knowledge
ISBN 0-226-73523-0 (pa)
LC 92-5889
Written in 1948; original French edition, 1989
This book "presents Sartre's ontology of truth in terms of his characteristic key moral questions of freedom, action, and bad faith. Here is Sartre the existentialist at his most original and most provocative." Univ Press Books for Public and Second Sch Libr
Includes bibliographical references

Wilson, Edward O., 1929-
Consilience; the unity of knowledge. Knopf 1998 332p $27.50; pa $15 **121**
1. Philosophy 2. Theory of knowledge 3. Science—Philosophy
ISBN 0-679-45077-7; 0-679-76867-X (pa)
LC 97-2816
"Wilson argues that there is a genetic and neurological basis for knowledge and that all subjects of human inquiry can be reunited under the umbrella of 'consilience.'" Libr J
The author's "extraordinarily clear, evocative imagery and elegant sentences make us see how a consilient world of knowledge might look. . . . Wilson's book of faith in the dream of reason and objective knowledge is a tour de force." Publ Wkly
Includes bibliographical references

128 Humankind

Abram, David
The spell of the sensuous; perception and language in a more-than-human world. Pantheon Bks. 1996 326p hardcover o.p. paperback available $14.95 **128**
1. Philosophy of nature 2. Mind and body 3. Perception 4. Language and languages
ISBN 0-679-77639-7 (pa)
LC 95-31466
This book grew out of Abram's "explorations of magic and sorcery in indigenous cultures and the relationship between magic and the natural world. Where he leads the reader after this is tough to summarize: Edmund Husserl, Maurice Merleau-Ponty, Balinese sorcerers, origins of the alphabet, Kant, Newton. Word by word this is readable and connected to a fascinating thesis: that our perceptions grew from the natural world around us, and we can 'return to our senses' and be reinvigorated, reformed, by the experience." Libr J
Includes bibliographical references

Bloom, Howard, 1943-
The Lucifer principle; a scientific expedition into the forces of history. Atlantic Monthly Press 1995 466p hardcover o.p. paperback available $16 **128**
1. Human beings 2. Evolution 3. History—Philosophy 4. Culture 5. Modern civilization 6. Good and evil
ISBN 0-87113-664-3 (pa)
LC 94-11464
The 'Lucifer principle' is the author's "theory that evil—which manifests in violence, destructiveness and war—is woven into our biological fabric. . . . [In this study] Bloom applies the ideas of sociobiology, ethology and the 'killer ape' school of anthropology to the broad canvas of history." Publ Wkly
"A disturbing book, but its broad generalities wear down the sharp edges of its arguments, leaving something that becomes food for thought rather than reason to despair." Booklist
Includes bibliographical references

Devlin, Keith J.
Goodbye, Descartes; the end of logic and the search for a new cosmology of the mind. Wiley 1997 301p $27.95; pa $14.95 **128**
1. Mind and body 2. Linguistics 3. Logic
ISBN 0-471-14216-6; 0-471-25186-0 (pa)
LC 96-25493
"Devlin traces the history of logic, particularly mathematical logic, over two-plus millennia and the shorter history of Chomsky's Cartesian linguistics to explain why at least some 'mathematicians and scientists have come to realize that the truly difficult problems of the information age . . . concern *ourselves*—what it is to think, to reason, and to engage in conversation.'" Booklist
"An excellent book that should be read by everyone who has ever wondered how we communicate with one another but find it so frustrating to interact with computers." Libr J
Includes bibliographical references

Terkel, Studs, 1912-
Will the circle be unbroken? reflections on death, rebirth, and a hunger for faith. New Press (NY) 2001 xxiv, 407p $25.95 **128**
1. Death 2. Faith
ISBN 1-56584-692-3
Also available in paperback from Ballantine Bks.
"Terkel talks to 60 people about their encounters with death. His subjects range from emergency room doctors and paramedics to public figures such as author Kurt Vonnegut and guitarist Doc Watson. A stirring celebration of life and exploration of death." Booklist

133 Parapsychology and occultism

Encyclopedia of occultism & parapsychology; edited by J. Gordon Melton. 5th ed. Gale Res. 2001 2v set $360 **133**
1. Occultism—Dictionaries 2. Parapsychology—Dictionaries
ISBN 0-8103-8570-8
First published 1978
Some 5,000 entries cover information on magic, demonology, superstitions, cults, spiritism, mysticism, metaphysics and psychical sciences

Goodman, Linda, 1925-1995
Linda Goodman's star signs; the secret codes of the universe: forgotten rainbows and forgotten melodies of ancient wisdom. St. Martin's Press 1987 xli, 477p il hardcover o.p. paperback available $7.99 **133**
1. Occultism 2. Parapsychology 3. Astrology 4. New Age movement
ISBN 0-312-95191-4 (pa) LC 87-28375
Also available in hardcover from Taplinger Pub.
"Goodman explains numerology, lexigrams (secret codes of words, names, and titles), the power of sound, and the power of color. . . . Along with explanations of karma and other modes of spiritual growth, she interweaves her own experiences with avatars and gurus, as well as common folk who are on their own spiritual path." Booklist

Guiley, Rosemary Ellen
Encyclopedia of the strange, mystical & unexplained; introduction by Marion Zimmer Bradley. Gramercy Bks. 2001 666p il $14.99 **133**
1. Occultism—Encyclopedias 2. Parapsychology—Encyclopedias 3. Supernatural—Encyclopedias
ISBN 0-517-16278-4 LC 2001-23879
A reissue of Harper's encyclopedia of mystical & paranormal experience published 1991
This work "provides 500 cross-referenced entries which emphasize major personalities, mystical techniques and traditions, locations of interest, and mystic and paranormal phenomena. While the coverage is not completely inclusive, Guiley manages to detail most areas and personalities paticulary well—albeit with a slight New Age bias. . . . This reference should prove useful to both serious researchers and curious browsers." Libr J
Includes bibliographical references

133.1 Apparitions

Guiley, Rosemary Ellen
The encyclopedia of ghosts and spirits. 2nd ed. Facts on File 2000 430p $65; pa $19.95 **133.1**
1. Ghosts—Encyclopedias 2. Parapsychology—Encyclopedias
ISBN 0-8160-4085-0; 0-8160-4086-9 (pa) LC 99-59617
This work examines famous hauntings, historical personages and happenings, and various legends and myths about ghosts and spirits throughout the world. Recent events, new findings about old myths and updated information on major figures in the field are covered

Norman, Michael, 1947-
Haunted America; [by] Michael Norman and Beth Scott. TOR Bks. 1994 411p maps hardcover o.p. paperback available $7.99 **133.1**
1. Ghosts
ISBN 0-8125-5054-4 (pa) LC 94-28984
"A Tom Doherty Associates book"
"This collection of chilling tales of the supernatural includes at least one story from each state and from the English-speaking Canadian provinces. The stories recount sightings of ghostly apparitions and mysterious happenings, and their history and evolution is documented." Libr J
Includes bibliographical references

Ramsland, Katherine M., 1953-
Ghost; investigating the other side; [by] Katherine Ramsland. St. Martin's Press 2001 322p il $25.95; pa $6.99 **133.1**
1. Ghosts
ISBN 0-312-26164-0; 0-312-98373-5 (pa) LC 2001-41725
"Cast as an adventure in 'participatory journalism,' the book begins with Ramsland's chance acquisition of a haunted silver ring. Determined to extract its secrets, she sets out on a quest that gradually turns into a full-blown investigation of psychic aberration in America." Publ Wkly
"Although prepared to dismiss many so-called paranormal occurrences in favor of natural explanations, [the author] nevertheless encounters, experiences, and investigates a variety of inexplicable visual, photographic, and verbal manifestations. Both skeptics and believers will be intrigued by this first-person exploration of ghostly visitations." Booklist
Includes bibliographical references

133.3 Divinatory arts

Ashe, Geoffrey
Encyclopedia of prophecy. ABC-CLIO 2001 291p il $90 **133.3**
1. Prophecies
ISBN 1-57607-079-4 LC 2001-1067
"This work brings together information on prophets, psychics, symbols, methods, and even a study of theories of prophecy." Booklist
"Entries are comprehensive, clearly written, entertaining . . . well indexed, and often include a brief list of further readings." Choice

133.4 Demonology and witchcraft

Adler, Margot
Drawing down the moon; witches, Druids, goddess-worshippers, and other pagans in America today. rev and expanded ed. Penguin Bks. 1997 584p il pa $16.95   133.4
1. Witchcraft
ISBN 0-14-019536-X   LC 97-145477
First published 1979 by Viking
A survey of goddess worship and witchcraft movements discussing their basic philosophies and practices
"Despite its clear anti-Judaic and anti-Christian bias, this book is recommended for general and college audiences interested in religion, the occult, and modern social phenomena." Choice [review of 1979 edition]
Includes bibliographical references

Carlson, Laurie M., 1952-
A fever in Salem; a new interpretation of the New England witch trials. Dee, I.R. 1999 197p hardcover o.p. paperback available $14.95   133.4
1. Witchcraft 2. Salem (Mass.)—History
ISBN 1-56663-309-5 (pa)   LC 99-27520
In this reading of the New England witch trials, Carlson argues that "the 'possessed' of Salem, and perhaps of many other places where witchcraft was suspected, were in thrall not to devilry but to a mysterious disease of the brain, encephalitis lethargica, popularly known as sleeping sickness." New Yorker
"Carlson's compelling narrative begs for assessment by medical experts. A valuable purchase for libraries seeking more than a basic summary of the witch trials." Libr J
Includes bibliographical references

Guiley, Rosemary Ellen
The encyclopedia of witches and witchcraft. 2nd ed. Facts on File 2000 417p il $82.50; pa $24.95   133.4
1. Witchcraft—Encyclopedias
ISBN 0-8160-3848-1; 0-8160-3849-X (pa)
          LC 98-54386
First published 1989
With more than 500 articles, this work delves into the subject from antiquity to the present. The entries vary in length from a paragraph to several pages and examine rituals, traditions, and events as well as people and places

Hutton, Ronald
The triumph of the moon; a history of modern pagan witchcraft. Oxford Univ. Press 1999 486p $55.50; pa $17.95   133.4
1. Witchcraft 2. Neopaganism
ISBN 0-19-820744-1; 0-19-285449-6 (pa)
          LC 99-31586
This "history of paganism in 19th- and 20th-century Britain centers on Wicca, the system of witchcraft Gerald B. Gardner introduced to a startled public in the 1950s. . . . Hutton's exceptional work is by far the most scholarly, comprehensive and judicious analysis of the subject yet published." Publ Wkly
Includes bibliographical references

Karlsen, Carol F., 1940-
The devil in the shape of a woman; witchcraft in colonial New England. Norton 1987 360p hardcover o.p. paperback available $15.95   133.4
1. Witchcraft 2. New England—History—1600-1775, Colonial period
ISBN 0-393-31759-5 (pa)   LC 87-16615
Also available in hardcover from P. Smith
The author presents a "social history of witchcraft in Puritan New England (1620-1725). She unearths detailed evidence which demonstrates that prosecuted and accused witches generally were older, married women who had violated the religious and/or economic Puritan social hierarchy. . . . A well-written, provocative addition to the . . . scholarship on New England witchcraft." Libr J
Includes bibliographical references

Lewis, James R., 1949-
Satanism today; an encyclopedia of religion, folklore, and popular culture. ABC-CLIO 2001 371p il $75   133.4
1. Satanism
ISBN 1-57607-292-4   LC 2001-5141
This "examines the role of Satan in modern popular culture by considering its roots in folklore, movies, books, theology, religious practices, etc. . . . The tone is scholarly and informative; each entry is clear and precise, and has *see* references and well-chosen citations for further reading." Choice

Norton, Mary Beth
In the devil's snare; the Salem witchcraft crisis of 1692. Knopf 2002 436p $30   133.4
1. Witchcraft 2. Salem (Mass.)—History
ISBN 0-375-40709-X   LC 2001-50500
This examination of the Salem witchcraft trials assigns "central importance to fears caused by the Second Indian War. Norton's 'dual narrative of war and witchcraft' examines the progress of threatening frontier disorders . . . links them to the development of the crisis, and considers the thought not only of the panicked accusers but of the judges as well." Libr J
"In her splendid re-creation of the notorious events of 1692, Cornell . . . offers fresh and provocative insights into the much-studied Salem witchcraft trials." Publ Wkly
Includes bibliographical references

Ogden, Tom
Wizards and sorcerers; from abracadabra to Zoroaster. Facts on File 1997 246p il $45; pa $18.95   133.4
1. Magic—Encyclopedias 2. Occultism—Encyclopedias
ISBN 0-8160-3151-7; 0-8160-3152-5 (pa)
          LC 96-52305
"This compilation attempts to define occult terms and identify significant people in magical fields. . . . The entries vary in length from a short paragraph to several pages, and are eclectic. There are detailed lists of films and musical theatre productions which have occult or magical themes." Book Rep

133.5 Astrology

Goodman, Linda, 1925-1995
Linda Goodman's sun signs. Taplinger 1968 xxiii, 549p $29.95   **133.5**
1. Astrology 2. Zodiac
ISBN 0-8008-4900-0
Also available in paperback from Bantam Bks.
The author tells how to identify and deal with people according to their astrological signs
"This book is part astrology, part psychology, and always entertaining." Libr J

Lewis, James R., 1949-
The astrology book; the encyclopedia of heavenly influences. 2nd ed. Visible Ink Press 2003 928p il pa $24.95   **133.5**
1. Astrology—Encyclopedias
ISBN 1-57859-144-9
First published 1994 by Gale Res. with title: The astrology encyclopedia
This "defines and explains more than 800 astrological terms and concepts from air signs to Zeus. . . . *The Astrology Book* includes a special section on casting a chart, plus a . . . chapter that explains and interprets every planet in every house and sign. The text also includes a table of astrological glyphs and abbreviations, and a list of organizations, books, periodicals, and Web sites." Publisher's note
"Although aimed at the believer, Lewis' work may be confidently consulted by the skeptic seeking basic information about astrology." Booklist

Miller, Susan
Planets and possibilities; explore the worlds beyond your sun sign. Warner Bks. 2001 418p il $30; pa $15.95   **133.5**
1. Astrology
ISBN 0-446-52434-4; 0-446-67806-6 (pa)
The author provides "character analysis of each sign. The cosmic gifts, relationship trends, financial tendencies, and career tendencies associated with each sign are all described in detail. The mythology of each sign is included as well, nicely rounding out the book." Libr J

Parker, Julia, 1932-
KISS guide to astrology; [by] Julia and Derek Parker; foreword by Eric Francis. Dorling Kindersley 2000 424p il (Keep it simple series) pa $20   **133.5**
1. Astrology
ISBN 0-7894-6044-0   LC 00-8797
This beginners guide explains the working of the planets and the symbolism and personality traits associated with each sign. Also provides instructions on creating and interpreting your horoscopes

Snodgrass, Mary Ellen
Signs of the zodiac; a reference guide to historical, mythological, and cultural associations; illustrated by Raymond Miller Barrett, Jr. Greenwood Press 1997 243p il $46.95   **133.5**
1. Zodiac 2. Astrology
ISBN 0-313-30276-6   LC 97-5598
"After brief descriptions of zodiacal variants from other parts of the world, plus chapters on the historical foundations of astrology and its pervasiveness in the arts and sciences, Snodgrass treats each sign to a full workover: major stars in each, mythological background and symbology, commonly accepted character traits of those born under its influence, and thumbnail biographies of select prominent people who exemplify those traits." SLJ
Includes bibliographical references

133.6 Palmistry

Reid, Lori
The art of hand reading. DK Pub. 1996 120p il hardcover o.p. paperback available $15   **133.6**
1. Palmistry
ISBN 0-7894-4837-8 (pa)   LC 96-15506
This volume uses color photographs of hands and handprints to analyze all the significant lines, mounts, and markings on hands. It shows how the different areas of the palm reveal the balance between instinctive desires and powers of intellect and reason

133.8 Psychic phenomena

Sheldrake, Rupert
Dogs that know when their owners are coming home; and other unexplained powers of animals. Crown 1999 352p il hardcover o.p. paperback available $14   **133.8**
1. Pets 2. Extrasensory perception
ISBN 0-609-80533-9 (pa)   LC 99-25439
"The author reports the results of five years of extensive research as he followed up on anecdotal accounts from pet owners on the homing abilities of lost pets, animals that show premonitions of earthquakes or epileptic seizures, and the fact that animals anticipate the arrival home of their owners." Booklist
Includes bibliographical references

141 Idealism and related systems and doctrines

Berlin, Sir Isaiah
The roots of romanticism; edited by Henry Hardy. Princeton Univ. Press 1999 171p (A.W. Mellon lectures in the fine arts, 1965) $29.95   **141**
1. Romanticism 2. Arts—Philosophy
ISBN 0-691-00713-6   LC 98-41657
Analyzed in Essay and general literature index
This is an edited transcript of the lectures "and the supporting bibliographic notes from which Berlin worked on his idea of romanticism. . . . Arguing that the concept flows from late 18th-century German thought and society, Berlin addresses romanticism's effect on the Enlightenment, the roles played by Hamann, Herder, and other early Romanticists in the codification of the movement, the more distilled approaches of Kant and Schiller, and romanticism's lingering effects on Western intellectual posture. . . . An excellent resource for both beginning researcher and seasoned scholar." Libr J
Includes bibliographical references

142 Critical philosophy

Barrett, William, 1913-1992
Irrational man; a study in existential philosophy. Doubleday 1958 278p hardcover o.p. paperback available $12.95   **142**
1. Existentialism
ISBN 0-385-03138-6 (pa)
This discussion of existentialism traces its origins and analyzes the contributions of chief exponents of existentialist thought—Nietzsche, Kierkegaard, Heidegger and Sartre

Existentialism from Dostoevsky to Sartre. rev and expanded, edited, with an introduction, prefaces, and new translations by Walter Kaufmann. New Am. Lib. 1975 384p pa $15.95   **142**
1. Existentialism
ISBN 0-452-00930-8
Also available in hardcover from P. Smith
"A Meridian book"
First published 1956 by World Pub.
This book contains selections from the basic writings of Dostoevsky, Kierkegaard, Nietzsche, Rilke, Ortega y Gasset, Jaspers, Heidegger, Sartre and Camus

Sartre, Jean Paul, 1905-1980
Being and nothingness; an essay on phenomenological ontology; translated and with an introduction by Hazel E. Barnes. Philosophical Lib. 1956 638p o.p.; Washington Sq. Press paperback available $17   **142**
1. Existentialism
ISBN 0-671-49606-9 (pa)
Also available in hardcover from P. Smith
Original French edition, 1943
This is "Sartre's major attempt to systematize his theoretical analysis of the human condition and human consciousness which underlies 'Existentialism.'" Reader's Ency. 4th edition

Existentialism and human emotions. Philosophical Lib. 1957 96p o.p.; Citadel Press paperback available $9.95   **142**
1. Existentialism
ISBN 0-8065-0902-3 (pa)
"The section on 'Existentialism' is taken from the book of that name; translated by Bernard Frechtman; all other selections are from 'Being and nothingness' translated by Hazel E. Barnes"
Contents: Existentialism; Freedom and responsibility; The desire to be God; Existentialist psychoanalysis; The hole; Ethical implications

146 Naturalism and related systems and doctrines

Dennett, Daniel Clement
Darwin's dangerous idea; evolution and the meanings of life; [by] Daniel C. Dennett. Simon & Schuster 1995 586p il hardcover o.p. paperback available $16   **146**
1. Natural selection 2. Evolution
ISBN 0-684-82471-X (pa)   LC 94-49158
"Current controversies associated with the origin of life, sociobiology, punctuated equilibrium, the evolution of culture and language, and evolutionary ethics are investigated rigorously within the context of Darwinian science and philosophy. Dennett challenges the ideas of several imminent scientists, including Roger Penrose and Stephen Jay Gould, who, Dennett asserts, tend to limit the power or implications of Darwin's dangerous ideas." Libr J
Includes bibliographical references

150 Psychology

Glasser, William, 1925-
Choice theory; a new psychology of personal freedom. HarperCollins Pubs. 1998 340p il $24; pa $13.95   **150**
1. Psychology
ISBN 0-06-019109-0; 0-06-093014-4 (pa)
          LC 97-36025
"Choice theory helps its users avoid confrontation and ask pertinent questions. It sees conscious or unconscious desire for external control as the main problem in the four major personal relationships: husband-wife, parent-child, teacher-student, and manager-worker. . . . Combining choice theory and reality therapy in his practice, Glasser has been able to shorten the durations of his treatment programs substantially. As he presents them here, his theories and approaches can be applied in education and business as well as for self-help." Booklist

Psychology. Grolier Educ. 2002 6v set $379   **150**
1. Psychology
ISBN 0-7172-5662-6   LC 2002-2494
Contents: v1 History of psychology; v2 The brain and the mind; v3 Thinking and knowing; v4 Developmental psychology; v5 Social psychology; v6 Abnormal psychology
"Color photographs and specially commissioned artworks accompany the chapters in this attractive and highly useful reference set that covers the entire spectrum of psychology. . . . This is the set to which high-school students would turn while attempting to understand psychology, and it is recommended for reference collections in high-school libraries and young adult departments of medium-sized and large public libraries." Booklist

150.19   Psychological systems, schools, viewpoints

Bettelheim, Bruno
Freud and man's soul. Knopf 1983 111p
hardcover o.p. paperback available $9
     150.19
1. Freud, Sigmund, 1856-1939 2. Psychoanalysis
ISBN 0-394-71036-3 (pa)   LC 82-47809
The author argues that Freud was a great humanist
and that mistranslation of his work has lead American
psychoanalysis astray

Blum, Deborah
Love at Goon Park; Harry Harlow and the
science of affection. Perseus Bks. 2002 336p
$26   **150.19**
1. Harlow, Harry F., 1905-1981 2. Love 3. Child development
ISBN 0-7382-0278-9   LC 2002-112387
The author "recounts Harlow's work while examining
the man himself. Harlow argued that mother-child bonding was crucial for normal development, and his experiments with monkeys showed that social organisms cannot survive isolation. But as Blum reveals, Harlow was
an enigma, brilliant but distant from his own children,
and his work raised ethical and controversial dilemmas
concerning the research treatment of animals." Libr J
Includes bibliographical references

Buhle, Mari Jo, 1943-
Feminism and its discontents; a century of
struggle with psychoanalysis. Harvard Univ.
Press 1998 432p $39.95; pa $21.50   **150.19**
1. Psychoanalysis 2. Feminism 3. Women—Psychology
ISBN 0-674-29868-3; 0-674-00403-5 (pa)
           LC 97-32397
Buhle bases her "historical study on the premise that
feminism and psychoanalytic theory, each in its own way
concerned with understanding the 'self,' developed in
continuous dialogue with each other. The author's captivating, energetic writing style reflects the often spirited,
surprisingly tenacious relationship of these two theories."
Booklist
Includes bibliographical references

Freud, Sigmund, 1856-1939
The basic writings of Sigmund Freud;
translated and edited by A.A. Brill. Modern
Lib. 1995 c1938 973p $24.95   **150.19**
1. Psychoanalysis
ISBN 0-679-60166-X   LC 95-13411
A reissue of the 1938 edition
Contents: Psychopathology of everyday life; The interpretation of dreams; Three contributions to the theory of
sex; Wit and its relations to the unconscious; Totem and
taboo; The history of the psychoanalytic movement

The Freud reader; edited by Peter Gay.
Norton 1989 832p hardcover o.p. paperback
available $21.95   **150.19**
1. Psychoanalysis
ISBN 0-393-31403-0 (pa)   LC 89-2949
This "work includes some 50 of Freud's texts, organized chronologically with headnotes. The selections
range from case studies and theoretical discussions about

dreams, anxiety and anal eroticism to essays on lay anal-
ysis and religion as humankind's obsessional neurosis."
Libr J
Includes bibliographical references

Freud: conflict and culture; edited by
Michael S. Roth. Knopf 1998 173p il
hardcover o.p. paperback available $14
     150.19
1. Freud, Sigmund, 1856-1939 2. Psychoanalysis
ISBN 0-679-77292-8 (pa)   LC 98-12373
Analyzed in Essay and general literature index
Published in conjunction with an exhibition at the Li-
brary of Congress this is a collection of essays by such
authors as Oliver Sacks, E. Ann Kaplan, Muriel Dimen,
Adolf Grunbaum, Hannah S. Decker, Peter Kramer, and
Robert Coles
"Mostly concerned with Freud's large themes and
their impact in history, these essays are pitched to a gen-
eralized intellectual audience." Libr J
Includes bibliographical references

Fromm, Erich, 1900-1980
On being human; foreword by Rainer Funk.
Continuum 1994 180p hardcover o.p.
paperback available $15.95   **150.19**
1. Humanism 2. Social psychology 3. Psychoanalysis
ISBN 0-8264-1005-7 (pa)   LC 93-9243
This volume includes the author's writings on humanism, social psychology, and psychoanalysis from the
1960s, based on Fromm's lectures, works written for specific occasions, and manuscripts intended as books
Includes bibliographical references

Gay, Peter, 1923-
A Godless Jew; Freud, atheism, and the
making of psychoanalysis. Yale Univ. Press
1987 182p $40; pa $17   **150.19**
1. Freud, Sigmund, 1856-1939 2. Psychoanalysis
3. Atheism
ISBN 0-300-04008-3; 0-300-04608-1 (pa)
           LC 87-8267
Based on lectures presented at Hebrew Union College,
Cincinnati, in 1986
The author "reviews the various claims for the Jewishness of psychoanalysis and finds them to be wholly without merit. Paradoxically, he argues that Freud's position
as an outsider—an atheist and Jew—enabled him to
pierce the taboo topics of sexuality and the unconscious
which led to his momentous discoveries." Publ Wkly
Includes bibliographical references

Horney, Karen, 1885-1952
New ways in psychoanalysis. Norton 1939
313p hardcover o.p. paperback available
$15.95   **150.19**
1. Psychoanalysis
ISBN 0-393-31230-5 (pa)
Also available hardcover from Routledge
"A critical re-evaluation of psychoanalysis, accepting
Freud's theories as a basis but showing how modern
practice is in some ways departing from the limitations
set by Freud's viewpoint, particularly in giving more importance to cultural factors." Booklist

Jung, C. G. (Carl Gustav), 1875-1961

The basic writings of C. G. Jung; edited with an introduction by Violet Staub de Laszlo. Modern Lib. 1993 c1959 xxxiii, 691p $21.95   **150.19**
1. Psychoanalysis
ISBN 0-679-60071-X   LC 93-17801
Also available in paperback from Princeton Univ. Press
This is a reissue of the 1959 edition
This volume contains excerpts from Symbols of transformation, On the nature of the psyche, Relations between the ego and the unconscious, Psychological types, Psychology of the transference, and Psychology and religion. It also includes Archetypes of the collective unconscious, Psychological aspects of the mother archetype, On the nature of dreams, On the psychogenesis of schizophrenia, Introduction to the religious and psychological problems of alchemy, and Marriage as a psychological relationship
Includes bibliographical references

The essential Jung; selected and introduced by Anthony Storr. Princeton Univ. Press 1983 447p hardcover o.p. paperback available $18.95   **150.19**
1. Psychoanalysis
ISBN 0-691-02935-0 (pa)   LC 82-61441
"This book is an attempt to distill the essential features of Jung's psychology as it developed during the course of his life by means of extracts from his own writings." Preface
Storr's "selections from Jung's writings are lucid and accessible; linked by skillful explanatory passages, they provide both interested laypersons and students with a perspective on Jung." Libr J
Includes bibliographical references

Man and his symbols; [by] Carl G. Jung [et al.] Doubleday 1964 320p il $30; pa $7.99   **150.19**
1. Symbolism 2. Psychology 3. Dreams
ISBN 0-385-05221-9; 0-440-35183-9 (pa)
Analyzed in Essay and general literature index
"The basic ideas of Jungian psychology are presented in popular language in six essays by Dr. Jung and [four] of his pupils; these are correlated to dreams and symbols and are shown in their archetypal relationships to ancient myths, present-day thought and art." Libr J
Includes bibliographical references

The portable Jung; edited with an introduction by Joseph Campbell; translated by R. F. C. Hull. Viking 1971 xli, 659p hardcover o.p. paperback available $17   **150.19**
1. Psychoanalysis
ISBN 0-14-015070-6 (pa)
"The Viking portable library"
A collection of writings spanning the career of the pioneering psychoanalyst. Includes a chronology and bibliography

May, Rollo

The discovery of being; writings in existential psychology. Norton 1983 192p hardcover o.p. paperback available $13.95   **150.19**
1. Existentialism 2. Psychotherapy
ISBN 0-393-31240-2 (pa)   LC 83-4282
Also available in hardcover from P. Smith
The author "provides the reader with principles of his existential psychotherapy; delineates his view of the cultural-historical context that gave rise to both psychoanalysis and existentialism; and sets forth what he considers to be the contributions to therapy of an existential approach." Choice
Includes bibliographical references

Menninger, Karl A. (Karl Augustus), 1893-1990

Love against hate; [by] Karl Menninger with the collaboration of Jeanetta Lyle Menninger. Harcourt Brace & Co. 1942 311p hardcover o.p. paperback available $10.95   **150.19**
1. Psychoanalysis 2. Sexual behavior 3. Love 4. Instinct
ISBN 0-15-653892-X (pa)
Analyzed in Essay and general literature index
The author "rehearses first the various frustrations which inhibit and misguide human energies, and then, in a series of chapters on Work, Play, Faith, Hope and Love considers how the destructive tendencies may be guided into creative channels." Wis Libr Bull
Includes bibliographical references

Mitchell, Stephen A., 1946-2000

Freud and beyond; a history of modern psychoanalytic thought; [by] Stephen A. Mitchell, Margaret Black. Basic Bks. 1995 293p hardcover o.p. paperback available $17.50   **150.19**
1. Freud, Sigmund, 1856-1939 2. Psychoanalysis
ISBN 0-465-01405-4 (pa)   LC 95-8972
The authors "concisely demythologize Sigmund Freud and engage themselves with a score of his key successors (including five women). Brief biographies and succinct theoretical summaries are fleshed out with clinical examples." Libr J
"Mitchell and Black's book establishes itself as the best single treatment of psychoanalytic theories, classical and current. Intended as an introduction, it will be of use to practicing clinicians as well, with virtues of coherent discussion of complex ideas, nonpolemical presentation, and clear, even humorous, writing." Choice
Includes bibliographical references

Rogers, Carl R. (Carl Ransom), 1902-1987

A way of being. Houghton Mifflin 1980 395p hardcover o.p. paperback available $15   **150.19**
1. Psychology 2. Humanism
ISBN 0-395-75530-1 (pa)   LC 80-20275
The author offers a "collection of papers, talks, autobiographical sketches and vignettes of patients' experiences in workshops and therapy." Publ Wkly
"This is a book rich in theoretical insights and experiential sharing, and full of invigorating optimism." Libr J
Includes bibliographical references

Skinner, B. F. (Burrhus Frederic), 1904-1990
About behaviorism. Knopf 1974 256p
hardcover o.p. paperback available $12
150.19
1. Behaviorism
ISBN 0-394-71618-3 (pa)
The author defines, analyzes and defends the science
of behaviorism with chapters exploring the causes of behavior, operant behavior, verbal behavior, thinking,
causes and reasons, knowledge, emotion and self
Includes bibliographical references

Thurschwell, Pamela, 1966-
Sigmund Freud. Routledge 2000 158p
(Routledge critical thinkers) $75; pa $16.95
150.19
1. Freud, Sigmund, 1856-1939 2. Psychoanalysis
ISBN 0-415-21520-X; 0-415-21521-8 (pa)
LC 00-32823
"The book contains chapters on early theories, interpretation, sexuality, case histories, maps of the mind, society and religion, and psychoanalysis's aftermath,
including feminist criticism and a remarkable summary
of Jacques Lacan's role." Booklist
Includes bibliographical references

Watson, John Broadus, 1878-1958
Behaviorism. rev ed. Norton 1930 308p il
o.p.; Transaction Pubs. paperback available
$21.95
150.19
1. Behaviorism
ISBN 1-56000-994-2 (pa)
First published 1925 by Peoples Institute, N.Y.
The author applies the concept of physiological stimuli
to the study of human behavior. He rejects conscious and
unconscious mental activity as bases of human behavior
and believes that man differs from other animals in terms
of the types of behavior he displays

150.3   Psychology—Encyclopedias and dictionaries

Colman, Andrew M.
A dictionary of psychology. Oxford Univ.
Press 2001 844p il $45; pa $16.95   **150.3**
1. Psychology—Dictionaries
ISBN 0-19-866211-4; 0-19-860761-X (pa)
LC 2001-133070
"The 10,500 entries range in length from one sentence
to half a column. . . . The vocabulary covers basic psy-
chology and psychiatry, along with psychoanalysis, psy-
chopharmacology, and neurophysiology, which all inform
psychological theory and practice. Colman is particularly
good at differentiating between closely related concepts."
Choice
For a fuller review see: Booklist, Dec. 15, 2001

The **Corsini** encyclopedia of psychology and
behavioral science; co-editors, W. Edward
Craighead, Charles B. Nemeroff. 3rd ed.
Wiley 2001 4v il set $800   **150.3**
1. Psychology—Encyclopedias
ISBN 0-471-23949-6   LC 99-58006
Also available in paperback ea $78
First published 1984 under the editorship of Raymond
J. Corsini with title: Encyclopedia of psychology

This work presents "more than 2,100 signed articles
on topics and persons (living and dead) in all areas of
psychology. Full citations for references are provided in
a general bibliography. An excellent general resource for
beginning and advanced students." Guide to Ref Books.
11th edition [entry for 2nd edition]
"Despite its poor indexing, this edition of *Corsini* is
an essential, solid, and important reference work in psychology and behavioral science." Choice

Encyclopedia of psychology; Alan E.
Kazdin, editor in chief. American
Psychological Assn.; Oxford Univ. Press
2000 8v set $750   **150.3**
1. Psychology—Encyclopedias
ISBN 1-55798-187-6   LC 99-55239
The 1500 articles survey behavioral, personal, interpersonal, social, developmental, cultural, pathological,
and therapeutic aspects of psychology. Includes nearly
400 biographical entries
For a review see: Booklist, Aug. 2000

The **Gale** encyclopedia of psychology;
Bonnie R. Strickland, executive editor. 2nd
ed. Gale Group 2001 701p il $191.50
150.3
1. Psychology—Encyclopedias
ISBN 0-7876-4786-1   LC 00-34736
First published 1996
Coverage includes noteworthy people, movements,
theories, and important case studies and experiments. The
articles, ranging from 25 to 1,500 words examine such
diverse topics as abnormal psychology, bipolar disorder,
Sigmund Freud and insomnia

152.1   Sensory perception

Ackerman, Diane
A natural history of the senses. Random
House 1990 331p hardcover o.p. paperback
available $14   **152.1**
1. Senses and sensation
ISBN 0-679-73566-6 (pa)   LC 89-43416
"Ackerman celebrates the senses by examining their
biological bases and the various and bizarre ways we
have come to indulge them. Her catalog of the senses is
itself a sensuous journey, with prose rich in imagery and
rhythm. Ackerman's book is a provocative and entertaining treat whose details will bestir the reader's imagination." Libr J
Includes bibliographical references

152.14   Visual perception

Hoffman, Donald D.
Visual intelligence; how we create what we
see. Norton 1998 294p il hardcover o.p.
paperback available $17.95   **152.14**
1. Perception 2. Vision
ISBN 0-393-31967-9 (pa)   LC 98-6181
The author "argues that the brain, via the eyes,
doesn't see what is 'really' in a scene being viewed but
rather constructs one image from 'countless possible interpretations' from the scene gathered at the retina."
Booklist
This book offers "wit, insight and charm. . . . An outstanding example of creative popular science." Publ
Wkly
Includes bibliographical references

152.3 Movements and motor functions

Coren, Stanley

The left-hander syndrome; the causes and consequences of left-handedness. Free Press 1992 308p o.p.; Vintage Bks. paperback available $15 **152.3**

1. Left- and right-handedness
ISBN 0-679-74468-1 (pa)   LC 91-26505

The author argues that left-handed people have a shorter life expectancy than right-handers. He maintains that "left-handedness is associated with birth and pregnancy complications—the likely cause of much left-handedness; greater risk for a variety of behavioural and medical problems; and an 89% higher rate of accidental injury, the result primarily of the world's functioning for the convenience of right-handers." Quill Quire

"The book is readable without oversimplifying the topic." Libr J

Includes bibliographical references

152.4 Emotions and feelings

Ackerman, Diane

A natural history of love. Random House 1994 xxiii, 358p hardcover o.p. paperback available $14 **152.4**

1. Love 2. Sexual behavior
ISBN 0-679-76183-7 (pa)   LC 94-171385

Companion volume to A natural history of the senses

"Ackerman sets out on her exploration by reviewing the lessons provided across time by such lovers as Antony and Cleopatra, Orpheus and Eurydice, Dido and Aeneas, Abelard and Heloise and Romeo and Juliet. During this journey, she explores the neurophysiology of love. . . . With dazzling poetic charm and insight, she uses history, literature, science, psychology, and personal experience as tools to illuminate the vigor and vehemence of the thrilling, devastating, and comforting phenomenon of love." Libr J

Allport, Gordon, 1897-1967

The nature of prejudice; [by] Gordon W. Allport; introduction by Kenneth Clark, foreword by Thomas Pettigrew. unabridged, 25th anniversary ed. Addison-Wesley 1979 xxxii, 537p il hardcover o.p. paperback available $18.50 **152.4**

1. Prejudices 2. Social psychology
ISBN 0-201-00179-9 (pa)   LC 79-112200

First published 1954

The author examines the roots of prejudice as well as its manifestations. The effects of prejudice on the "ingroup" and the "out-group" are discussed, as are the ways in which children form their perceptions of groups

Includes bibliographical references

Damasio, Antonio R.

Looking for Spinoza; joy, sorrow, and the feeling rain; [by] Antonio Damasio. Harcourt 2003 355p il $28; pa $15 **152.4**

1. Spinoza, Benedictus de, 1632-1677 2. Emotions
ISBN 0-15-100557-5; 0-15-602871-9 (pa)
LC 2002-11347

Contents: Enter feelings; Of appetites and emotions; Feelings; Ever since feelings; The body-minded brain; A visit to Spinoza; Who's there?

This is a "discussion of the difference between emotions (of the body) and feelings (of the mind), various sites in the brain that trigger these states, and the . . . synthesis of the homeostatic process, memory, sensory input, imagination, and foresight that links the unconscious to consciousness and feelings to reasoning." Booklist

Includes bibliographical references

Dozier, Rush W., Jr.

Fear itself; the origin and nature of the powerful emotion that shapes our lives and our world; [by] Rush W. Dozier, Jr. St. Martin's Press 1998 273p hardcover o.p. paperback available $13.95 **152.4**

1. Fear
ISBN 0-312-24724-9 (pa)   LC 98-21122

The author "summarizes recent neurological research and discusses current psychological and sociobiological theories on the nature of fear." Libr J

"Readers will learn much from Dozier's fascinating study." Booklist

Includes bibliographical references

Encyclopedia of human emotions; edited by David Levinson, James J. Ponzetti, Jr., Peter F. Jorgensen. Macmillan Ref. USA 1999 2v set $275 **152.4**

1. Emotions—Encyclopedias
ISBN 0-02-864766-1   LC 99-31198

This encyclopedia covers "specific emotions and their behavioral expressions (anxiety, envy, shame, zeal) . . . [as well as] theoretical issues that cut across emotions (cross-cultural patterns, psychoanalytic perspective, neurobiology of emotions, poetry) and biographies of individuals who have made significant contributions to the study of emotions." Libr J

Fromm, Erich, 1900-1980

The art of loving. Centennial ed. Continuum 2000 130p $18.95 **152.4**

1. Love
ISBN 0-8264-1260-2   LC 00-21030

Also available in paperback from HarperCollins Pubs.

A reissue of the title first published 1956

A study of all kinds of love, from narcissism to sex love and on to love of God. Dr. Fromm discusses the necessity of love, and the way to achieve maturity in love

"An astonishingly simple presentation of an abstract subject." Booklist

Gilligan, Carol, 1936-

The birth of pleasure. Knopf 2002 253p $24; pa $13 **152.4**

1. Love 2. Interpersonal relations
ISBN 0-679-44037-2; 0-679-75943-3 (pa)
LC 2001-50329

The author examines "why love between a man and a woman is so often burdened by a history of loss and how it can be freed and opened to the pursuit of happiness. Tracing a lineage from Greek mythology to our own most intimate relationships, she asks why we relive tragic stories of loss and betrayal; drawing on her own research, she offers a radical new map of love." Publisher's note

Gilligan's "mastery of literary sources and her intelligent but nonacademic writing style make this an enjoyable, challenging work." Publ Wkly

Includes bibliographical references

Goleman, Daniel

Emotional intelligence. Bantam Bks. 1995
352p $25.95; pa $16.95   **152.4**
1. Emotions 2. Intellect
ISBN 0-553-09503-X; 0-553-37506-7 (pa)
LC 95-16685
The author explains "how to develop our emotional
intelligence in ways that can improve our relationships,
our parenting, our classrooms, and our workplaces.
Goleman assures us that our temperaments may be determined by neurochemistry, but they can be altered."
Booklist
"Mr. Goleman, with an economy of style that serves
his reformer's convictions well, integrates a vast amount
of material on issues whose intricacy and problematic
character he reveals in an original and persuasive way."
N Y Times Book Rev
Includes bibliographical references

Jampolsky, Gerald G., 1925-

Love is the answer: creating positive
relationships; [by] Gerald G. Jampolsky and
Diane V. Cirincione. Bantam Bks. 1990 242p
il hardcover o.p. paperback available $14.95
152.4
1. Interpersonal relations 2. Love
ISBN 0-553-35268-7 (pa)   LC 89-18520
The authors suggest "moving past our illusions and
perceptions; transforming fear, blame, and guilt into love;
communicating with love in all our relationships; transforming relationships of control into relationships of freedom; finding peace, love, and happiness within ourselves; . . . forgiving ourselves and others; and achieving holy relationships. This is a 'New Age' book from
which all readers can benefit." Libr J

Jeffers, Susan J.

Feel the fear and do it anyway; [by] Susan
Jeffers. Harcourt Brace Jovanovich 1987
227p il o.p.; Fawcett Columbine paperback
available $14   **152.4**
1. Fear
ISBN 0-449-90292-7 (pa)   LC 86-18414
"By mixing positive thinking with situational exercises
that examine basic fear responses, psychologist Jeffers
shows that fear is what you make of it and that in most
cases it is unfounded." Libr J
Includes bibliographical references

Lewis, Thomas

A general theory of love; [by] Thomas
Lewis, Fari Amini, Richard Lannon. Random
House 2000 274p il hardcover o.p. paperback
available $13   **152.4**
1. Love
ISBN 0-375-70922-3 (pa)   LC 99-49930
The authors "aim to help physicians treat patients by
showing how the many and varied aspects of love,
including the lack and the warping of it, affect patients'
problems and strengths and by discussing what must,
therefore, be involved in treating patients." Booklist
Includes bibliographical references

Lutz, Tom

Crying; the natural and cultural history of
tears. Norton 1999 352p il hardcover o.p.
paperback available $14.95   **152.4**
1. Crying
ISBN 0-393-320103-7 (pa)   LC 99-21295
"Encompassing history, literature, the arts and the social sciences—Lutz explores how crying has been portrayed and perceived throughout history." Publ Wkly
"An affable, stimulating essay." Booklist
Includes bibliographical references

Tavris, Carol

Anger; the misunderstood emotion. rev ed.
Simon & Schuster 1989 383p pa $14 **152.4**
1. Anger
ISBN 0-671-67523-0   LC 89-33129
"A Touchstone book"
First published 1983
The author contends that anger is a complex, socially
learned response that is not necessarily cathartic
Includes bibliographical references

153   Imagination, imagery, creativity

Arendt, Hannah

The life of the mind. Harcourt Brace
Jovanovich 1981 2v in 1 pa $18   **153**
1. Intellect 2. Philosophy 3. Free will and determin-
ism
ISBN 0-15-651992-5
First published 1978 as two separate volumes with ti-
tles: v1 Thinking and v2 Willing
An exploration of the nature of mind and thought.
Among the concepts discussed are: appearance versus re-
ality, free will, determinism, and necessity
Includes bibliographical references

Baars, Bernard J.

In the theater of consciousness; the
workspace of the mind. Oxford Univ. Press
1997 193p il $35; pa $14.95   **153**
1. Consciousness 2. Intellect 3. Theory of knowledge
ISBN 0-19-510265-7; 0-19-514703-0 (pa)
LC 96-10379
"Baars offers the theater metaphor—inherited from
Aristotle, developed by William James and hotly contested by leading cognitive theorists such as Daniel
Dennett—as the best means of unifying the diverse mental phenomena and sensory experiences that make up
conscious life." Publ Wkly
The author "does a masterful job of explicating the issues and distinctions related to consciousness providing
representative charts, graphs, and figures to relate both
theory and data. . . . A most accessible and up-to-date
introduction to current ideas about consciousness, and a
valuable work for general readers." Choice
Includes bibliographical references

Carter, Rita

Exploring consciousness. University of
Calif. Press 2002 320p il $34.95   **153**
1. Consciousness
ISBN 0-520-23737-4   LC 2002-25900
This work explores the nature, origins, and purpose of
consciousness from philosophical, scientific, and experi-

Carter, Rita—*Continued*
ential perspectives
"A treasure trove of fact, argument and opinion, doing an excellent job of conveying both research and controversies. The general reader will find it filled with stimulating material." New Sci
Includes bibliographical references

Damasio, Antonio R.
The feeling of what happens; body and emotion in the making of consciousness. Harcourt Brace & Co. 1999 386p il $28; pa $15 **153**
1. Consciousness 2. Emotions
ISBN 0-15-100369-6; 0-15-601075-5 (pa)
LC 99-26357
The author contends "that consciousness arises from our ability to map relations between the self and others through our emotions. This bold attempt to mend the classical breach between emotion and reason is all the more compelling for its poetic expression." Publ Wkly
Includes bibliographical references

Pinker, Steven, 1954-
How the mind works. Norton 1997 660p il hardcover o.p. paperback available $17.95
153
1. Brain 2. Psychology 3. Evolution
ISBN 0-393-31848-6 (pa)
LC 97-1855
The author "explains what the mind is, how it evolved, and how it allows us to see, think, feel, laugh, interact, enjoy the arts, and ponder the mysteries of life." Publisher's note
Pinker "has a gift for making enormously complicated mechanisms—and human foibles—accessible." Publ Wkly
Includes bibliographical references

Sagan, Carl, 1934-1996
The dragons of Eden; speculations on the evolution of human intelligence. Random House 1977 263p il o.p.; Ballantine Bks. paperback available $7.50 **153**
1. Intellect 2. Brain 3. Genetics
ISBN 0-345-34629-7 (pa)
LC 76-53472
In this study of human intellect "Sagan is principally preoccupied with the neocortex, with its left hemisphere, responsible for language and logic, a right hemisphere in charge of intuition and spatial dimension, and a corpus callosum that mediates and synthesizes the two." Atl Mon
Includes bibliographical references

153.1 Memory and learning

Goldman, Bob, 1955-
Brain fitness; anti-aging strategies for achieving super mind power; [by] Robert M. Goldman with Ronald Klatz and Lisa Berger. Doubleday 1999 333p il hardcover o.p. paperback available $14.95 **153.1**
1. Aging 2. Memory 3. Sleep 4. Stress (Physiology)
ISBN 0-385-48869-6 (pa)
LC 98-18785
This is an "exploration of techniques—mental workouts, memory training, physical exercises, and nutrition and dietary supplements—that readers can use to maximize their concentration, memory, imagination, energy,

intelligence, and creativity while decreasing fatigue and stress and preventing Alzheimer's disease and other brain diseases." Libr J
Includes bibliographical references

Schacter, Daniel L.
Searching for memory; the brain, the mind, and the past. Basic Bks. 1996 398p il hardcover o.p. paperback available $17.50
153.1
1. Memory 2. Brain
ISBN 0-465-07552-5 (pa)
LC 96-19521
This book "describes how new technologies permit scientists to determine what brain centers control which memories. It also approaches subjects that have been sensationalized—hypnosis, multiple personality, and 'recovered' memories of sexual abuse." New Yorker
"This is an excellent book on an important topic: it is exceptionally well written; its examples of defects in memory are fascinating, as are the theories based on them; and its arguments are illustrated with opposite pictures, reproduced from works by many modern artists, and passages from novels." N Y Times Book Rev
Includes bibliographical references

The seven sins of memory; how the mind forgets and remembers. Houghton Mifflin 2001 272p il $25; pa $14 **153.1**
1. Memory
ISBN 0-618-04019-6; 0-618-21919-6 (pa)
LC 00-53885
The author discusses "the curious processes of memory by classifying its malfunctions into seven categories: transience, absent-mindedness, blocking, misattribution, suggestibility, bias, and persistence. Schacter illustrates each of these 'sins' with examples of routine misfortunes common to all." Libr J
Includes bibliographical references

Turkington, Carol
The encyclopedia of memory and memory disorders; [by] Carol Turkington and Joseph R. Harris. 2nd ed. Facts on File 2001 296p (Facts on File library of health and living) $66 **153.1**
1. Memory—Encyclopedias
ISBN 0-8160-4141-5
LC 00-52806
First published 1995
This volume includes over 70 entries describing: Alzheimer's disease; Football and memory loss; Huffing; Mad cow disease; Memory in infancy; Norepinephrine; "Punch drunk" syndrome; Social memory; Vitamins and memory

153.3 Imagination and imagery. Creativity

Csikszentmihalyi, Mihaly
Creativity; flow and the psychology of discovery and invention. HarperCollins Pubs. 1996 456p hardcover o.p. paperback available $15 **153.3**
1. Creative ability 2. Creative thinking
ISBN 0-06-092820-4 (pa)
LC 96-4116
"Utilizing the interviews garnered from 91 respondents (ranging from philosopher Mortimer Adler to biologist

Csikszentmihalyi, Mihaly—*Continued*
Edward O. Wilson to politician Eugene McCarthy), the
author . . . demonstrates the processes that these acknowledged creative thinkers and doers go through and
the characteristics that make them stand out. . . .
Csikszentmihalyi also deals with creativity and aging and
ways to enhance one's own personal creativity." Libr J
Includes bibliographical references

Gardner, Howard
Creating minds; an anatomy of creativity
seen through the lives of Freud, Einstein,
Picasso, Stravinsky, Eliot, Graham, and
Gandhi. Basic Bks. 1993 464p il hardcover
o.p. paperback available $22   **153.3**
1. Creative ability
ISBN 0-465-01454-2 (pa)   LC 92-56172
In seven "case studies, Gardner focuses on highly creative figures who lived in the same era but who exemplify different human intelligences. He postulates that each
of their major innovations involved an intersection of the
maturity and confidence of a master with the sensibilities
and impulsiveness of a child. This scholarly and
insightful study is highly recommended." Libr J
Includes bibliographical references

May, Rollo
The courage to create. Norton 1975 143p
hardcover o.p. paperback available $11.95
     153.3
1. Creative ability
ISBN 0-393-31106-6 (pa)
Also available in hardcover from P. Smith
The author argues that creativity is an act of encounter
and draws on examples from literature, art, and psycho-
analysis
Includes bibliographical references

153.6   Communication

Deacon, Terrence William
The symbolic species; the coevolution of
language and the brain; by Terrence W.
Deacon. Norton 1997 527p il hardcover o.p.
paperback available $16.95   **153.6**
1. Language and languages 2. Brain
ISBN 0-393-31754-4 (pa)   LC 96-31115
"Deacon proposes a challenging, holistic theory of
language that explains, among other things, how children
learn to speak and why there are grammatical similarities
across languages." Libr J
"Readers who savor the latest scientific research but
do not possess the esoteric vocabulary that allows for
easy penetration of such lofty thoughts should find Deacon's book both fascinating and accessible." Booklist
Includes bibliographical references

Fast, Julius, 1918-
Body language. Evans & Co. 1970 192p
o.p.; Pocket Bks. paperback available $6.50
     153.6
1. Nonverbal communication
ISBN 0-671-67325-4 (pa)
This book discusses the "science of kinesics, the use
of non-verbal communication through the means of body
movements which may support or contradict our verbal
expressions." Best Sellers
Includes bibliographical references

153.7   Perceptual processes

Jonsson, Erik, 1922-
Inner navigation; why we get lost and how
we find our way. Scribner 2002 347p il $25
     153.7
1. Direction sense 2. Navigation—Psychological aspects
ISBN 0-7432-2206-7   LC 2001-57693
"The author shows how we create cognitive maps—a
mental sense of how to navigate an area based on landmarks—and explains why such maps can work only if
we have both a good sense of direction ('direction
frame') and sense of location ('dead reckoning system')."
Publ Wkly
"An interesting, offbeat ramble." Booklist
Includes bibliographical references

153.8   Will (Volition)

Kohn, Alfie
Punished by rewards; the trouble with gold
stars, incentive plans, A's, praise, and other
bribes. Houghton Mifflin 1993 398p
hardcover o.p. paperback available $14
     153.8
1. Awards 2. Motivation (Psychology) 3. Behaviorism
ISBN 0-395-71090-1 (pa)   LC 93-21897
Also available in hardcover from Replica Bks.
The author "challenges the widely held assumption
that incentives lead to improved quality and increased
output in the workplace and in schools. . . . Kohn de-
rides rewards as bribes and offers instead the proposition
that collaboration (teamwork), content (meaningfulness),
and choice (autonomy) will serve to motivate both students and workers. He marshals impressive theoretical
support and, at the same time, uses humor disarmingly
to argue his case." Booklist
Includes bibliographical references

Spence, Gerry
How to argue and win every time; at home,
at work, in court, everywhere, every day. St.
Martin's Press 1995 307p hardcover o.p.
paperback available $14.95   **153.8**
1. Reasoning 2. International relations
ISBN 0-312-14477-6 (pa)   LC 94-43552
The author "distills his bar experience into the secrets
of his success and translates that into the plain language
of the real world of jobs, romance, and child rearing.
Spence exhorts readers to believe that the art of arguing
is verily the art of living, and aversion to
argumentativeness only hinders people from getting what
they want. . . . Though discursive in style, Spence's
prose is pointedly sharp in essence and displays unself-
consciously his own flamboyant personality." Booklist

153.9 Intelligence and aptitudes

Bloom, Harold, 1930-
Genius; a mosaic of one hundred exemplary creative minds. Warner Bks. 2002 814p il $35.95; pa $19.95 **153.9**
1. Genius 2. Authors 3. Literature—History and criticism
ISBN 0-446-52717-3; 0-446-69129-1 (pa)
LC 2002-16808
Bloom conducts an "inquiry into that elusive quality called genius, portraying 100 poets, dramatists, novelists, philosophers, and religious writers whose quests Bloom considers cosmic, their language transcendent, and their lives intriguing." Booklist
"Although the book is a delight to read, its real value lies in the author's ability to provoke the reader into thinking about literature, genius, and related topics. No similar work discusses literary genius in this way or covers this many writers." Libr J
Includes bibliographical references

Calvin, William H., 1939-
How brains think; evolving intelligence, then and now. Basic Bks. 1996 184p il (Science masters series) hardcover o.p. paperback available $14 **153.9**
1. Intellect 2. Thought and thinking 3. Brain 4. Comparative psychology
ISBN 0-465-07278-X (pa)
LC 96-21086
"Before making his argument that competitive processes in the cerebral cortex account for the content of people's thoughts, [Calvin seeks to] build a foundation by describing what intelligence is, how it might have evolved amid the ice ages of the past few million years, and the physiology of the brain's neurons and chemicals." Booklist
Calvin's book "offers an exquisite distillation of his key ideas. He's a member of that rare breed of scientists who can translate the arcana of their fields into lay language, and he's one of the best." N Y Times Book Rev
Includes bibliographical references

Gould, Stephen Jay, 1941-2002
The mismeasure of man. rev & expanded [ed] Norton 1996 444p il hardcover o.p. paperback available $15.95 **153.9**
1. Intelligence tests 2. Ability—Testing
ISBN 0-393-31425-1 (pa)
LC 95-44442
First published 1981
The author examines the history of various scientific methods used to measure intelligence. He demonstrates how the research was used to perpetuate the myth of the intellectual superiority of the white male
Includes bibliographical references

Sternberg, Robert J.
Successful intelligence; how practical and creative intelligence determine success in life. Simon & Schuster 1996 303p o.p.; Plume Bks. paperback available $14 **153.9**
1. Intellect 2. Intelligence tests 3. Creative thinking
ISBN 0-452-27906-2 (pa)
LC 96-25088
The author contends that society "is far too fixated on IQ. Such tests—and most other academic measures of achievement—typically gauge one's ability to memorize material. . . . According to Sternberg, people need to develop and nurture three types of intelligence for personal and professional success: analytical, creative, and practical. He defines each and provides commonsense ways for people to foster them." Booklist
"This insightful, savvy guide will help readers avoid self-sabotage and translate thought into action." Publ Wkly
Includes bibliographical references

154.2 The subconscious

Tallis, Frank
Hidden minds; a history of the unconscious. Arcade Pub. 2002 194p $25.95 **154.2**
1. Subconsciousness
ISBN 1-55970-643-0
LC 2002-74566
The author "presents the history of the unconscious from Leibniz to Pierre Janet and Freud to current experimentation, and he emphasizes that the unconscious is now at the heart of neuroscience. He describes historic medical and scientific advances and the individuals who made them, and he draws on Coleridge, DeQuincey, Moss Hart, and other writers to show how the literate public viewed the unconscious at various times." Booklist
"Highly readable and possessing a surprising degree of depth, this book manages to be both entertaining and informative." Libr J
Includes bibliographical references

154.6 Sleep phenomena

Alvarez, A. (Alfred), 1929-
Night; night life, night language, sleep, and dreams. Norton 1995 290p hardcover o.p. paperback available $13 **154.6**
1. Dreams 2. Sleep 3. Night 4. Psychoanalysis
ISBN 0-393-31434-0 (pa)
LC 94-35989
This work contains an "account of scientific and scholarly research on sleep and dreaming, . . . [some] chapters, in part autobiographical, about the dark and its attendant fears, and [others] centering on policework in New York and London." Times Lit Suppl
"Alvarez's superb variations on the theme of night enhance our appreciation of the miraculous intricacy and energy of our mind, an energy that produces everything from nightmares to poetry to lightbulbs." Booklist

Freud, Sigmund, 1856-1939
Interpretation of dreams **154.6**
1. Dreams 2. Psychoanalysis
Hardcover and paperback editions available from various publishers
Original German edition, 1900; first English translation published 1913
Groundbreaking analysis of dreams as manifestations of suppressed unconscious desires

Lewis, James R., 1949-
The dream encyclopedia. Gale Res. 1995 xxi, 416p il o.p.; Visible Ink Press paperback available $19.95 **154.6**
1. Dreams—Encyclopedias
ISBN 0-7876-0156-X (pa)
LC 95-10759
"This work presents brief articles on some 250 topics, from adaptive therapy and astral projections to Zulu and Zuni myths. . . . In addition to the main encyclopedia,

Lewis, James R., 1949-—*Continued*
a short introductory overview of dream and sleep research and a subject index are included. Also provided is a list of 'dream resources,' with the names and addresses of many of the organizations now focusing on the study of dreams and sleep research." Am Ref Books Annu, 1996

Parker, Julia, 1932-
Parkers' complete book of dreams; [by] Julia & Derek Parker. Dorling Kindersley 1995 208p il hardcover o.p. paperback available $15   **154.6**
    1. Dreams
    ISBN 0-7894-3295-1 (pa)   LC 94-27918
    This guide covers the history as well as theories concerning the meaning of dreaming. Advice is given on how to record and improve the ability to recall specific dreams

155.2 Individual psychology

Allport, Gordon, 1897-1967
Becoming; basic considerations for a psychology of personality. Yale Univ. Press 1955 106p hardcover o.p. paperback available $14   **155.2**
    1. Personality 2. Psychology
    ISBN 0-300-00002-2 (pa)
    "The Terry lectures"
    In this work Allport attempts "to correlate and interpret psychology's views on human welfare and religion." Booklist

Dimitrius, Jo-Ellan
Reading people; how to understand people and predict their behavior—anytime, anyplace; [by] Jo-Ellan Dimitrius and Mark Mazzarella. Random House 1998 281p hardcover o.p. paperback available $14.95
                                           155.2
    1. Personality 2. Nonverbal communication
    ISBN 0-345-42587-1 (pa)   LC 98-4934
    "Dimitrius shares the people-reading techniques she developed over 15 years as a jury consultant. In so doing, she provides a wealth of tips and strategies for ferreting out people's real viewpoints, motives and character traits." Publ Wkly

Hamer, Dean H.
Living with our genes; why they matter more than you think; [by] Dean Hamer and Peter Copeland. Doubleday 1998 355p hardcover o.p. paperback available $14.95
                                           155.2
    1. Temperament 2. Personality 3. Behavior genetics
    ISBN 0-385-48584-0 (pa)   LC 97-29818
    "The authors devote chapters to the most compelling of human behaviors and conditions: sex, worry, anger, thrill-seeking, addiction, intelligence, eating and aging. They explore the biochemistry underlying the characteristics in question, and ask how much of that biochemistry is under genetic control. . . . This thought-provoking book's explanations of how our genes 'express' themselves is sure to capture the imaginations of readers." Publ Wkly
    Includes bibliographical references

Lazear, Jonathon
The man who mistook his job for a life; a chronic overachiever finds the way home. Crown 2001 187p $17   **155.2**
    1. Men—Psychology 2. Workaholism
    ISBN 0-609-60846-0   LC 00-65967
    The author "outlines the causes and consequences of his chronic overachieving. Although he includes quizzes, exercises, and a nine-step plan to help others identify and change their job-related obsessions, the meat of this work is Lazear's own story of how he managed to become less and less productive by putting in more and more hours at the office." Libr J

Lunden, Joan
Wake-up calls; making the most out of every day. McGraw-Hill 2000 230p il $19.95; pa $12   **155.2**
    1. Conduct of life 2. Self-realization
    ISBN 0-07-136126-X; 0-07-137970-3 (pa)
    A collection of aphorisms and life principles the author feels may inspire readers faced with stress, change, and adversity

Maslow, Abraham Harold
Toward a psychology of being; [by] Abraham H. Maslow. 3rd ed. Wiley 1998 244p $45   **155.2**
    1. Personality 2. Motivation (Psychology)
    ISBN 0-471-29309-1   LC 98-3766
    First published 1962
    The author presents his theory of psychological health and motivation and explains his belief that human beings can be loving and creative, and capable of pursuing the highest values and aspirations
    Includes bibliographical references

Pinker, Steven, 1954-
The blank slate; the denial of human nature in modern intellectual life. Viking 2002 509p $27.95; pa $16   **155.2**
    1. Nature and nurture
    ISBN 0-670-03151-8; 0-14-2003344 (pa)
                                   LC 2002-22719
    The author "attacks the notion that an infant's mind is a blank slate, arguing instead that human beings have an inherited universal structure shaped by the demands made upon the species for survival, albeit with plenty of room for cultural and individual variation." Publ Wkly
    Includes bibliographical references

Steinem, Gloria
Revolution from within; a book of self-esteem. Little, Brown 1992 377p hardcover o.p. paperback available $14.95
                                           155.2
    1. Self-esteem 2. Feminism
    ISBN 0-316-81247-1 (pa)   LC 91-11356
    The author discusses the importance of self-esteem and offers practical advice on ways of acquiring it
    Steinem's "book unfolds like a flower: it offers literature, art, nature, meditation, and connectedness as ways of finding and exploring the self. . . . Her focus is women, but she is clear that what she has to say is for men, too, and she is neither strident nor dismissive." Libr J
    Includes bibliographical references

Weber, Robert J.

The created self; reinventing body, persona, spirit. Norton 2000 350p il hardcover o.p. paperback available $14.95 **155.2**

1. Self 2. Psychology
ISBN 0-393-32121-5 (pa)　　　LC 99-37480

The author contends that "having a self enables the individual to pursue creative endeavors, which though often adaptive from an evolutionary standpoint, actually extend beyond what can be explained in terms of biological, reproductive aims. Using the model of the self developed by William James . . . Weber attempts to show that the self is a constantly developing, 'unitary system', consisting of bodily awareness, persona and spirit, over which the individual has control." Publ Wkly

Includes bibliographical references

155.3　Sex psychology and psychology of the sexes

Lerner, Harriet Goldhor

The dance of deception; pretending and truth-telling in women's lives. HarperCollins Pubs. 1993 254p hardcover o.p. paperback available $14 **155.3**

1. Women—Psychology 2. Truthfulness and falsehood
ISBN 0-06-092463-2 (pa)　　　LC 92-53376

"Patriarchal culture teaches women to pretend and sometimes deceive, Lerner says, and in her study of the role this dissembling plays in women's lives, she shows how 'pretending reflects deep prohibitions, real and imagined, against a more direct and forthright assertion of self.' . . . She acknowledges that truth telling is not easy, yet her discussion of the many ways women lie and how lying affects them clearly shows the benefits of honesty and makes her prescription appealing." Booklist

Includes bibliographical references

Masters, William H.

Masters and Johnson on sex and human loving; [by] William H. Masters, Virginia E. Johnson, Robert C. Kolodny. Little, Brown 1986 598p il hardcover o.p. paperback available $29.99 **155.3**

1. Sexual behavior 2. Sex (Biology)
ISBN 0-316-50160-3 (pa)　　　LC 85-23950

"Provides complete coverage of the biological, psychological, and social aspects of human sexuality. Examines both cultural and historical trends and practices." NY Public Libr Book of How & Where to Look It Up

Includes bibliographical references

155.4　Child psychology

Barnet, Ann B.

The youngest minds; parenting and genes in the development of intellect and emotion; [by] Ann B. Barnet and Richard J. Barnet. Simon & Schuster 1998 352p il hardcover o.p. paperback available $21.95 **155.4**

1. Child psychology 2. Child development
ISBN 0-684-85440-6 (pa)　　　LC 98-13450

The authors debate "the relative importance of genetics vs. environment in shaping human personality. Explaining recent work in language acquisition and emotional development . . . they provide an accessible summary of our current state of knowledge of brain development and chemistry while placing significantly greater emphasis on the role played by environmental factors." Publ Wkly

Includes bibliographical references

Brazelton, T. Berry, 1918-

The earliest relationship; parents, infants, and the drama of early attachment; [by] T. Berry Brazelton, Bertrand G. Cramer. Addison-Wesley 1990 252p hardcover o.p. paperback available $17 **155.4**

1. Child psychology 2. Parent-child relationship
ISBN 0-201-56764-4 (pa)　　　LC 89-39839

"A Merloyd Lawrence book"

An examination of "the first bewildering stages of parent-infant interaction and development. Parents are warned about the natural roller coaster of responses they will undergo, from anxiety over the newborn through the resentment often felt when a child displays those first physical signs of independence." Booklist

Includes bibliographical references

The irreducible needs of children; what every child must have to grow, learn, and flourish; [by] T. Berry Brazelton, Stanley I. Greenspan. Perseus Bks. 2000 xx, 228p hardcover o.p. paperback available $14

155.4

1. Child development 2. Child psychology 3. Child rearing
ISBN 0-7382-0516-8 (pa)　　　LC 2001-2290

"Each chapter is devoted to the discussion of an 'irreducible' need, such as the Need for Ongoing Nurturing Relationships, the Need for Physical Protection, Safety and Regulation, the Need for Stable Supportive Communities and Cultural Continuity, and the Need to Protect the Future. After each discussion, the authors recommend ways to meet these needs." Publ Wkly

This is "a practical, well-organized volume, of value to parents, physicians, teachers, sociologists, and others who wish to improve children's lives locally and globally." Booklist

Includes bibliographical references

To listen to a child; understanding the normal problems of growing up; photographs by B.A. King. Addison-Wesley 1984 184p il hardcover o.p. paperback available $16

155.4

1. Child development 2. Child psychology 3. Emotionally disturbed children 4. Parent-child relationship
ISBN 0-201-63270-5 (pa)　　　LC 84-6174

"A Merloyd Lawrence book"

The author "advises parents on children's transient developmental problems such as fears, thumbsucking, eating and sleeping deviations, enuresis, and stomachaches." Libr J

"Brazelton's sensible, authoritative, clear approach provides parents with the kinds of information they need to relax over the long pull, and to understand and cope with day-to-day difficulties." Publ Wkly

Bruer, John T., 1949-

The myth of the first three years; a new understanding of early brain development and lifelong learning. Free Press 1999 244p il hardcover o.p. paperback available $18.95

155.4

1. Psychology of learning 2. Child development
ISBN 0-7432-4260-2 (pa)   LC 99-34934
Bruer offers a critique of recent thinking about early childhood development and learning. Specifically, he identifies as myth the notion that "a child's experiences and environment during his first three years play a crucial role in determining the course of his later life." Commentary
Includes bibliographical references

Coles, Robert

The moral intelligence of children. Random House 1997 218p o.p.; Plume Bks. paperback available $12.95   **155.4**

1. Child development 2. Moral education
ISBN 0-452-27937-2 (pa)   LC 96-20992
"Coles examines the nature of the moral imagination, what we mean when we distinguish between a good person and a not-so-good person, and the moral crossroads children as well as adults confront. The core of the book addresses 'The Moral Archaelogy of Childhood,' discussing children's moral development and particular dilemmas characteristic of different stages and suggesting appropriate adult responses to children in the early years, the elementary school years, and adolescence." Booklist
"Written with [Coles'] customary acute perceptiveness, this important inquiry will enlighten parents, teachers and caregivers concerned with children's moral intelligence." Publ Wkly

Gopnik, Alison

The scientist in the crib; minds, brains, and how children learn; [by] Alison Gopnik, Andrew N. Meltzoff, Patricia K. Kuhl. Morrow 1999 279p hardcover o.p. paperback available $14   **155.4**

1. Psychology of learning 2. Child development
ISBN 0-688-17788-3 (pa)   LC 99-24247
The authors examine "how children learn to understand and use language, control their emotions and arouse the emotions of others, and establish relationships. . . . Prospective and actual parents stand to learn much that may be helpful to them and their children from this lively book." Booklist
Includes bibliographical references

Montessori, Maria, 1870-1952

The absorbent mind; translated from the Italian by Claude A. Claremont. Holt, Rinehart & Winston 1967 304p il hardcover o.p. paperback available $17   **155.4**

1. Child development 2. Child psychology 3. Educational psychology
ISBN 0-8050-4156-7 (pa)
Also available in hardcover from Buccaneer Bks.
"In these lectures Dr. Montessori dwells, not so much on the techniques used in her schools, but on her insight into the development of children, physically and psychologically, from birth to adulthood." Publ Wkly

Piaget, Jean, 1896-1980

The moral judgment of the child; [translated by Marjorie Gabain] Free Press 1948 418p hardcover o.p. paperback available $15   **155.4**

1. Child psychology 2. Human behavior 3. Ethics
ISBN 0-684-83330-1 (pa)
Also available in paperback from Simon & Schuster
Original French edition, 1932
Piaget studies, not the moral behavior of children, but their ideas about right and wrong, the rules of a game, adult authority, and cooperation and justice

Segal, Nancy L., 1951-

Entwined lives; twins and what they tell us about human behavior. Dutton 1999 xx, 396p il o.p.; Plume Bks. paperback available $16   **155.4**

1. Twins
ISBN 0-452-28057-5 (pa)   LC 98-51460
"Segal describes twin types and elaborates on findings regarding the development of personality and intelligence. She also looks closely at twin relationships (including conjoined twins) to understand grief, competition, bonding, cooperation, and more." Libr J
"This elegantly written study cogently distills and makes available to the general reader a wealth of research from the fields of behavioral genetics, evolutionary psychology and social science." Publ Wkly
Includes bibliographical references

Seligman, Martin E. P.

The optimistic child; [by] Martin E.P. Seligman with Karen Reivich, Lisa Jaycox, and Jane Gillham. Houghton Mifflin 1995 336p il o.p.; HarperCollins Pubs. paperback available $14   **155.4**

1. Child psychology
ISBN 0-06-097709-4 (pa)   LC 95-12619
The author "discounts prevalent theory that children who are encouraged by others to feel good about themselves will do well. Instead, he proposes that self-esteem comes from mastering challenges, overcoming frustration and experiencing individual achievement. In clear, concise prose peppered with anecdotes, dialogues, cartoons and exercises, Seligman offers a concrete plan of action based on techniques of self-evaluation and social interaction." Publ Wkly
Includes bibliographical references

White, Burton L., 1929-

The new first three years of life. 20th anniversary ed. Fireside Bks. 1995 384p il pa $14   **155.4**

1. Infants—Development 2. Child psychology
ISBN 0-684-80419-0   LC 95-18297
First published 1975 with title: The first three years of life
"White describes the seven developmental phases of the first three years of life. He provides parents with a comprehensive treasury of techniques for enhancing development and establishing discipline that are refreshingly straight-forward and based on real-world experience." Publ Wkly

Wright, Lawrence

Twins; and what they tell us about who we are. Wiley 1997 202p $22.95; pa $14.95

155.4

1. Twins

ISBN 0-471-25220-4; 0-471-29644-9 (pa)

LC 97-38827

"Wright presents the conflicting, and often confounding results from twin studies done primarily over the last 50 years. . . . The book serves up questions such as: 'Do our genes determine our personality?' 'How much, if any, effect do parents have on the personalities of their children?'." SLJ

"Wright does an admirable job of sorting through the differing research in a well-reasoned, clearheaded manner." Publ Wkly

Includes bibliographical references

155.45 Exceptional children

Winner, Ellen

Gifted children; myths and realities. Basic Bks. 1996 449p il hardcover o.p. paperback available $21

155.45

1. Gifted children

ISBN 0-465-01759-2 (pa)

LC 95-49279

This study considers the following questions "are gifted children gifted in all subject areas? Are artistically gifted children gifted or talented? Does giftedness depend on IQ? What role do environment and biology play in giftedness? Are gifted children psychological and social misfits? In her analyses, Winner cites and explains a broad range of recent research, including extensive notes and references with each chapter. She then offers her recommendations for dealing with gifted children in America's educational systems." Libr J

155.5 Psychology of young people

Your adolescent; emotional, behavioral and cognitive development from early adolescence through the teen years; David B. Pruitt, editor-in-chief. HarperCollins Pubs. 1999 xxiii, 374p hardcover o.p. paperback available $18

155.5

1. Adolescent psychology 2. Parent-child relationship

ISBN 0-06-095676-3 (pa)

LC 98-34587

At head of title: The American Academy of Child and Adolescent Psychiatry

"In addition to discussing the milestones of normal development, common family, behavioral, physical, and emotional disorders are described and treatment options are discussed. . . . This is the most encyclopedic general treatment of the topic to be issued in years and will be a useful starting point for many parents." Libr J

155.6 Psychology of adults

Ackerman, Diane

Deep play; illustrations by Peter Sis. Random House 1999 235p il hardcover o.p. paperback available $13

155.6

1. Play—Psychological aspects

ISBN 0-679-77135-2 (pa)

LC 98-35067

The author contends that "deep play, 'ecstatic' play, transcends practical concerns and grants us passage to the sacred and the holy. Art is deep play, so is religion, the contemplation of nature, and playing sports; in short, pursuits that are all-consuming and inspire feelings of awe and a profound sense of connection with the universe. By turns anecdotal and philosophic, Ackerman vividly recounts her own 'deep play' experiences." Booklist

Includes bibliographical references

Estés, Clarissa Pinkola

Women who run with the wolves; myths and stories of the wild woman archetype. Ballantine Bks. 1992 520p hardcover o.p. paperback available $15

155.6

1. Women—Folklore 2. Women—Psychology

ISBN 0-345-39681-2 (pa)

LC 91-58630

In this "introduction to feminine psychology, a Jungian analyst . . . endeavors to define and describe the wild woman archetype. Arguing that it can be best elucidated through stories and myths, Estés examines traditional tales from various world cultures and explains their symbolism. By studying the meaning of these stories, she claims, a woman gains insight into her inner nature and can tap the wild woman within herself to bring forth new measures of self-determination and fresh expressions of creativity, thus achieving a state of greater empowerment and freedom. Written in a clear, richly evocative style." Libr J

Includes bibliographical references

Friday, Nancy

My mother/my self; the daughter's search for identity. Delacorte Press 1977 425p o.p.; Delta paperback available $14.95

155.6

1. Women—Psychology 2. Mothers 3. Parent-child relationship

ISBN 0-385-32015-9 (pa)

LC 77-23571

The author explores the psychological aspects of the mother-daughter relationship

Includes bibliographical references

Lerner, Harriet Goldhor

The dance of intimacy; a woman's guide to courageous acts of change in key relationships. Harper & Row 1989 255p hardcover o.p. paperback available $14

155.6

1. Women—Psychology 2. Interpersonal relations

ISBN 0-06-091646-X (pa)

LC 88-45519

The author explains "how to operate more effectively in key relationships—whether it be with a distant or unfaithful spouse, a depressed sister, a difficult mother, an alcoholic father, an uncommitted lover, a dying parent, or a family member that we have written off." Publisher's note

Includes bibliographical references

Levinson, Daniel J., 1920-1994
The seasons of a man's life; by Daniel J. Levinson [et al.] Knopf 1978 363p hardcover o.p. paperback available $15   **155.6**
1. Men—Psychology 2. Middle age
ISBN 0-394-533901-0 (pa)   LC 77-20978
The Levinson theory divides a man's "life cycle into five overlapping eras. . . . Each era is marked by periods of stability during which life structures are built. These stable periods alternate with transition periods during which life structures change." Saturday Rev
Includes bibliographical references

The seasons of a woman's life; in collaboration with Judy D. Levinson. Knopf 1996 438p hardcover o.p. paperback available $23   **155.6**
1. Women—Psychology 2. Middle age
ISBN 0-345-31174-4 (pa)   LC 95-20893
"This work asks whether there is a human life cycle and a process of adult growth similar to the process of child development, and how gender affects the lives of individual women and women in general. The Levinson team interviewed 15 homemakers, 15 women with corporate-financial careers, and 15 women with academic careers. Their stories are the core of Levinson's book." Booklist
Includes bibliographical references

155.67 Psychology of persons in late adulthood

Hillman, James
The force of character; and the lasting life. Random House 1999 xxx, 236p hardcover o.p. paperback available $14   **155.67**
1. Self-realization 2. Character 3. Aging
ISBN 0-345-42405-0 (pa)   LC 99-24097
"According to Hillman, aging is not a process that causes us to decline and become weaker; instead, the aging process strips us of the unimportant, thus exposing and confirming our true character." Libr J
"Perspicacity distinguishes the entire book, as Hillman quotes and cites poets and philosophers more than scientists, and the ancients as much as the moderns." Booklist
Includes bibliographical references

155.7 Evolutional psychology

Clark, William R., 1938-
Are we hardwired? the role of genes in human behavior; by William R. Clark & Michael Grunstein. Oxford Univ. Press 2000 322p il $30   **155.7**
1. Behavior genetics
ISBN 0-19-513826-0   LC 99-54699
The authors offer an "overview of the current evidence supporting genetic causes for general behavioral tendencies, such as aggression, consumption, sexual preferences, and, most controversial, intelligence. Case studies of identical twins separated as infants provide some of the most compelling proofs." Libr J
Includes bibliographical references

155.8 Ethnopsychology and national psychology

Lévi-Strauss, Claude
The savage mind. University of Chicago Press 1966 290p il (Nature of human society series) hardcover o.p. paperback available $18   **155.8**
1. Ethnopsychology 2. Anthropology
ISBN 0-226-47484-4 (pa)
Original French edition, 1962
"An anthropological study of the nature of thought, concepts and systems as they occur in various cultures." Chicago Public Libr
Includes bibliographical references

155.9 Environmental psychology

Attig, Thomas, 1945-
The heart of grief; death and the search for lasting love. Oxford Univ. Press 2000 xx, 289p $25; pa $15.95   **155.9**
1. Bereavement 2. Death 3. Loss (Psychology)
ISBN 0-19-511873-1; 0-19-515625-0 (pa)
    LC 99-49842
"The pain of loss can be overcome, says Attig . . . by survivors who keep alive in their hearts their love for the departed. He repeats his message in each of some 50 brief chapters, using numerous anecdotes gleaned from his experiences as a counselor to explain how he has helped people cope with the loss of loved ones." Publ Wkly
"A reassuring and useful book for those grieving or counseling those who grieve." Libr J

How we grieve; relearning the world. Oxford Univ. Press 1996 201p hardcover o.p. paperback available $24.95   **155.9**
1. Bereavement 2. Death 3. Loss (Psychology)
ISBN 0-19-507456-4 (pa)   LC 95-31907
"For Attig, grieving is a process of learning to live in a world disrupted by death and to accept the changes it brings. Sensible yet sensitive, this book helps both those who have suffered a loss and those who seek to comfort them." Libr J
Includes bibliographical references

Brehony, Kathleen A.
After the darkest hour; how suffering begins the journey to wisdom; [by] Kathleen Brehony. Holt & Co. 2000 274p il hardcover o.p. paperback available $14   **155.9**
1. Suffering 2. Adjustment (Psychology)
ISBN 0-8050-6436-2 (pa)   LC 00-29577
"Brehony provides stories and anecdotes throughout the book of people both known and unknown who have gotten through traumatic situations and have learned something from them. . . . Peppered throughout with inspirational quotations, this book teeters on the brink of self-help sentiment, but it succeeds where others might fail in its practicality." Booklist
Includes bibliographical references

Buchholz, Ester Schaler
The call of solitude; alonetime in a world of attachment. Simon & Schuster 1997 365p hardcover o.p. paperback available $22

155.9

1. Solitude
ISBN 0-684-87280-3 (pa)   LC 97-20698
The author contends "that today's culture overvalues attachment and neglects the importance of time alone. Using case studies, stories, poetry, and other sources, Buchholz shows how alonetime has always been important and that the lack of it in today's frenzied U.S. culture increases stress and depression." Libr J
"Buchholz's wide-ranging discussion, slanted toward professionals but accessible to interested general readers, may overreach on occasion, but she is often convincing in her timely and provocative advocacy of 'alonetime.'" Publ Wkly
Includes bibliographical references

Edelman, Hope
Motherless daughters; the legacy of loss. Addison-Wesley 1994 xxvii, 324p o.p.; Delta paperback available $15.95   **155.9**

1. Loss (Psychology) 2. Mother-daughter relationship 3. Bereavement
ISBN 0-385-31438-8 (pa)   LC 93-45048
"Writing of her own experiences of losing her mother when she was 17, and the grief of hundreds of women she interviewed who lost their mothers through death, abandonment or another form of separation . . . Edelman marshals a wealth of anecdotal evidence, supplemented with psychological research about bereavement, that indicates that one's longing for a mother never disappears." Publ Wkly
Includes bibliographical references

Emswiler, Mary Ann
Guiding your child through grief; [by] Mary Ann Emswiler and James P. Emswiler. Bantam Bks. 2000 286p il pa $13.95   **155.9**

1. Death 2. Bereavement 3. Child rearing
ISBN 0-553-38025-7   LC 00-23645
"Advice during difficult days to help a child grieve the death of a parent or sibling." Publisher's note
"Thoroughly researched and bolstered with the wisdom of bereavement experts nationwide, this fine guide does those working through the loss of loved ones an enormous service. It should rank amongst the first line of defense and support for those facing a death in the family." Publ Wkly
Includes bibliographical references

Finkbeiner, Ann K., 1943-
After the death of a child; living with loss through the years. Free Press 1996 273p o.p.; Johns Hopkins Univ. Press paperback available $17.95   **155.9**

1. Bereavement 2. Death 3. Loss (Psychology)
ISBN 0-8018-5914-X (pa)   LC 96-1358
The author "lost her 18-year-old son and only child in a train wreck in 1987. For her book she interviewed other parents who have lost children, and although she refers to psychological research, their experiences are the heart of the book." N Y Times Book Rev
"Those who have lost a child will find corroboration of many of their feelings in this enlightening and heart-rending study." Publ Wkly
Includes bibliographical references

Grosskopf, Barry, 1945-
Forgive your parents, heal yourself; how understanding your painful family legacy can transform your life. Free Press 1999 xxii, 279p $25   **155.9**

1. Forgiveness 2. Parent-child relationship
ISBN 0-684-82406-X   LC 99-11458
The author claims "that in order to understand our own problems and shortcomings, we must examine the lives of our parents as children. When we know their childhoods, we can begin to understand their behaviors as spouses and parents, which allows us to look at our own lives and relationships and begin to change our own behavior. Grosskopf writes simply and beautifully." Libr J
Includes bibliographical references

Kübler-Ross, Elisabeth
Living with death and dying. Macmillan 1981 181p il hardcover o.p. paperback available $10   **155.9**

1. Death 2. Terminal care
ISBN 0-684-83936-9 (pa)   LC 80-26984
The author argues that caring for, and living with the terminally ill need not be a solely negative experience

On children and death. Macmillan 1983 279p hardcover o.p. paperback available $12

155.9

1. Death 2. Child psychology
ISBN 0-684-83939-3 (pa)   LC 83-11252
A look at how one copes with a child's death by disease, accident or murder
Includes bibliographical references

On death and dying. Scribner Classics 1997 286p il $23; pa $13   **155.9**

1. Death 2. Terminal care
ISBN 0-684-84223-8; 0-684-83938-5 (pa)
LC 97-177294
A reissue of the title first published 1969 by Macmillan
A look at the psychological, sociological and theological issues faced by the terminally ill and their caregivers
Includes bibliographical references

Levy, Alexander
The orphaned adult; understanding and coping with grief and change after the death of our parents. Perseus Bks. 1999 190p hardcover o.p. paperback available $15.95

155.9

1. Death 2. Bereavement 3. Loss (Psychology)
ISBN 0-7382-0361-0 (pa)   LC 99-64773
"Incorporating his own personal experience with the accounts of others who have lost their parents, psychologist Levy examines this profound life-changing event with compassion and understanding." Libr J

Sife, Wallace
The loss of a pet. rev & expanded ed. Howell Bk. House 1998 194p il pa $14.99

155.9

1. Pets 2. Death 3. Bereavement
ISBN 0-87605-197-2   LC 97-41254
First published 1993

Sife, Wallace—Continued

The author "addresses the pet owner whose grief at a pet's death is largely misunderstood or even ridiculed by friends, associates and society in general. . . . Sife is to be commended for offering information that is not only compassionate but concise, wide-ranging and, above all, practical." Publ Wkly [review of 1993 edition]

Weenolsen, Patricia

The art of dying; how to leave this world with dignity and grace, at peace with yourself and your loved ones. St. Martin's Press 1996 299p hardcover o.p. paperback available $13.95　　　　　　　　　　　　　**155.9**
1. Death 2. Terminally ill 3. Loss (Psychology)
ISBN 0-312-16776-8 (pa)　　　　LC 96-1952
The author discusses "a variety of end-of-life concerns from the practical to the spiritual to help the dying make the most of the remainder of their lives and find meaning in death. Coming to terms with the disease itself, managing pain, planning funerals, making peace with loved ones, deciding about terminal care, and learning what the final experience of death is like are considered in a matter-of-fact way—a reassuring yet sensitive approach to difficult subjects." Libr J
Includes bibliographical references

156　Comparative psychology

Fouts, Roger

Next of kin; what chimpanzees have taught me about who we are; [by] Roger Fouts with Stephen Tukel Mills; introduction by Jane Goodall. Morrow 1997 420p il hardcover o.p. paperback available $14　　　　　　　**156**
1. Chimpanzees 2. Animal communication
ISBN 0-380-72822-2 (pa)　　　　LC 97-15144
"A Living planet book"
This is an account of a study known as Project Washoe where a female chimpanzee was taught American Sign Language
"What makes this book an exceptional popularization of scientific research is the authors' ability to charm with a fascinating story while also teaching why the story is so fascinating." Booklist
Includes bibliographical references

Waal, Frans de, 1948-

The ape and the sushi master; cultural reflections by a primatologist. Basic Bks. 2001 433p il $26; pa $18　　　　　　**156**
1. Animal behavior 2. Human behavior 3. Comparative psychology
ISBN 0-465-04175-2; 0-465-04176-0 (pa)
　　　　　　　　　　　　　　LC 00-57922
The author "argues that, because other animals, particularly other primates, create cultures—that is, add to their behavioral repertoire by nongenetic transmission (learning through innovation, demonstration, and imitation)—they are the same kinds of creatures as humans in all respects." Booklist
This is a "deftly written, deeply reflective work." N Y Times Book Rev
Includes bibliographical references

158　Applied psychology

Ban Breathnach, Sarah

A man's journey to simple abundance; [by] Sarah Ban Breathnach and friends; edited by Michael Segell. Scribner 2000 448p $22
　　　　　　　　　　　　　　　158
1. Men 2. Conduct of life
ISBN 0-7432-0061-6　　　　　LC 00-45012
"A Simple Abundance Press book"
"A collection of 50-plus pieces on men's experiences. . . . The book's sections cover family, emotional and moral concerns, men's roles and obligations, success and failure, amusements and obsessions, and the deepest values in life. . . . Contributors include respected novelists (Rick Bass, Jim Harrison, Reynolds Price), journalists (Roy Blount, Harold Evans), pop-culture figures (Sting, director Garry Marshall), and representatives of religious and spiritual movements." Booklist
Includes bibliographical references

Bloomfield, Harold H., 1944-

Making peace with your past; the six essential steps to enjoying a great future; [by] Harold H. Bloomfield with Philip Goldberg. HarperCollins Pubs. 2000 269p hardcover o.p. paperback available $13　　　**158**
1. Self-realization 2. Applied psychology
ISBN 0-06-093314-3 (pa)　　　　LC 99-89719
The author "addresses the syndrome Freud called 'repetition compulsion'—humans' tendency to re-create what they have not worked through. . . . With revealing exercises, Bloomfield shows readers how to rediscover 'the passion to live [their] highest destiny.'" Libr J
Includes bibliographical references

Browne, Joy

The nine fantasies that will ruin your life and the eight realities that will save you. Crown 1998 256p hardcover o.p. paperback available $13　　　　　　　　　　**158**
1. Conduct of life 2. Happiness
ISBN 0-609-80473-1 (pa)　　　　LC 98-36245
This is a "book of anti-romantic, practical advice about common life problems, cast largely as answers to readers' and listeners' questions. . . . Browne draws on her clinical expertise, her talk-show experience and her store of common sense." Publ Wkly

Burns, David D.

Feeling good; the new mood therapy; preface by Aaron T. Beck. Rev and updated. Avon Bks. 1999 xxxii, 706p il pa $15　**158**
1. Depression (Psychology) 2. Psychotherapy
ISBN 0-380-73176-2　　　　　LC 99-461798
First published 1980
"The author reports on results of treating depression (from mild blues to serious cases) with 'cognitive thinking.' . . . The therapy involves fighting automatic responses to disappointments by intelligent thinking that can put one's shortcomings into perspective." Publ Wkly [review of 1980 edition]
"The author . . . writes simply, clearly, and without any jargon; better yet, he has a sense of compassion and a sense of humor, and is aware of his own limitations." Libr J [review of 1980 edition]
Includes bibliographical references

Buscaglia, Leo F.

Loving each other; the challenge of human relationships. Slack 1984 208p o.p.; Fawcett Bks. paperback available $12 **158**
1. Love 2. Interpersonal relations
ISBN 0-449-90157-2 (pa) LC 84-50590
The author offers practical suggestions for improving human relationships
Includes bibliographical references

Carnegie, Dale, 1888-1955

How to win friends and influence people; editorial consultant, Dorothy Carnegie, editorial assistance, Arthur R. Pell. rev ed. Simon & Schuster 1981 299p o.p.; Dale Carnegie & Assocs. paperback available $7.50 **158**
1. Success 2. Applied psychology
ISBN 0-671-72365-0 (pa) LC 80-28759
First published 1936
An examination of the psychology of business and social success
Includes bibliographical references

Carter, Steve, 1956-

Men like women who like themselves; (and other secrets that the smartest women know about partnership and power); by Steven Carter & Julia Sokol. Delacorte Press 1996 259p hardcover o.p. paperback available $13.95 **158**
1. Interpersonal relations 2. Self-confidence 3. Dating (Social customs) 4. Women—Sexual behavior
ISBN 0-440-50615-8 (pa) LC 95-39450
The authors offer advice on male-female relationships and cover dating, self-esteem, abusive men, counseling, etc.

Covey, Stephen R.

First things first; to live, to love, to learn, to leave a legacy; [by] Stephen R. Covey, A. Roger Merrill, Rebecca R. Merrill. Simon & Schuster 1994 360p il hardcover o.p. paperback available $14 **158**
1. Conduct of life 2. Time management
ISBN 0-684-80203-1 (pa) LC 94-2305
The authors "offer a 'principle-centered' approach to time management that emphasizes what 'represents our vision, values, principles, mission, conscience, direction—what we feel is important and how we lead our lives.' The authors argue that central to our lives are 'four needs and capacities—to live, to love, to learn, to leave a legacy.' The ideas here are not only clearly explained but are reinforced by scenarios from the authors' lives and self-directed activities for the reader." Libr J
Includes bibliographical references

Foster, Rick, 1954-

How we choose to be happy; the 9 choices of extremely happy people: their secrets, their stories; [by] Rick Foster and Greg Hicks. Putnam 1999 xxi, 227p hardcover o.p. paperback available $12.95 **158**
1. Happiness
ISBN 0-399-52575-0 (pa) LC 98-37033
The authors "interviewed happy people from all walks of life, from the United States to Eastern Europe. The re-sulting personal stories, writing exercises, and quotes to-gether inform and instruct the reader in the nine princi-ples discovered by the authors in their travels." Libr J

Gegax, Tom

Winning in the game of life; self coaching secrets for success. Harmony Bks. 1999 318p il hardcover o.p. paperback available $19 **158**
1. Success 2. Self-realization
ISBN 0-609-80568-1 (pa) LC 99-13919
"For Gegax, creating a winning life plan requires de-fining a mission and taking steps that balances career, friends, community, and family into an integrated whole." Booklist
Includes bibliographical references

Goodman, Ellen

I know just what you mean; the power of friendship in women's lives; [by] Ellen Goodman, Patricia O'Brien. Simon & Schuster 2000 300p il $25; pa $14 **158**
1. Friendship 2. Women—Psychology
ISBN 0-684-84287-4; 0-7432-0171-X (pa)
LC 00-24859
Goodman and O'Brien "examine their friendship of more than 25 years and a host of other friendships among women, famous and unknown." Booklist
"Heavy on insight and light on psychological jargon, this book is an intelligent, observant read." Publ Wkly

Hallowell, Edward M.

Connect. Pantheon Bks. 1999 xx, 328p hardcover o.p. paperback available $13.95 **158**
1. Quality of life 2. Interpersonal relations
ISBN 0-7434-0621-4 (pa) LC 99-13082
The author "urges readers to 'make time for connect-edness,' which he alternately defines as having person-to-person interaction or being involved with something greater than oneself." Libr J

Harris, Thomas Anthony, 1913?-1995

I'm OK, you're OK; a practical guide to transactional analysis. Harper & Row 1969 278p il o.p.; Galahad Bks. paperback available $7.99 **158**
1. Transactional analysis
ISBN 1-57866-075-0 (pa)
This book describes the method of psychiatric group treatment, and applies the system to problems in mar-riage and child rearing, violence and revolution, racial prejudice, creativity, and international problems
Includes bibliographical references

July, William W., II

Understanding the tin man; why so many men avoid intimacy; [by] William July II. Doubleday 1999 201p $22.95; pa $12.95 **158**
1. Men—Psychology
ISBN 0-385-49663-X; 0-7679-0566-0 (pa)
LC 99-46434
The author addresses "the difficulties many men en-counter with commitment—to themselves and others. . . . [He] asserts that men need to acknowledge, under-stand and learn how to process their emotions in healthy ways." Publ Wkly
Includes bibliographical references

Kephart, Beth

Into the tangle of friendship; a memoir of the things that matter. Houghton Mifflin 2000 204p $23 **158**

1. Friendship
ISBN 0-618-03378-4   LC 00-38915

The author "meditates on circumstances that promote and encourage friends to find each other, stay together, or drift apart." Libr J

"Kephart's writing is luminous, filled with phrases so precise that they are worth committing to memory." Publ Wkly

Klauser, Henriette Anne

Write it down, make it happen; knowing what you want—and getting it! Scribner 2000 250p hardcover o.p. paperback available $12 **158**

1. Applied psychology
ISBN 0-684-85002-8 (pa)   LC 99-43551

The author "instructs her readers to write down their most extravagant wishes and, merely by the act of recording them, make them come true. . . . Her technique is intended to clarify goals, increase self-confidence, and dispel self-doubt, and she describes how it has dramatically improved her life and the lives of her friends and acquaintants." Libr J

Includes bibliographical references

May, Rollo

Freedom and destiny. Norton 1981 275p hardcover o.p. paperback available $14   **158**

1. Applied psychology 2. Free will and determinism 3. Fate and fatalism
ISBN 0-393-31842-7 (pa)   LC 81-4009

This book examines "the continuing tension in our lives between the possibilities freedom offers and the various limitations imposed upon us by our particular fate or destiny." America

Includes bibliographical references

McGraw, Phillip C., 1950-

Life strategies; doing what works, doing what matters. Hyperion 1999 282p il $21.95; pa $13.95   **158**

1. Success
ISBN 0-7868-6548-2; 0-7868-8459-2 (pa)
LC 98-46748

"McGraw claims that people in dire situations have serious problems, including denial and choosing initial assumptions without testing them for accuracy. To create a life strategy that works, McGraw lays out his ten 'Life Laws' along with checklists and 18 assignments." Libr J

Peck, M. Scott (Morgan Scott)

Further along the road less traveled; the unending journey toward spiritual growth: the edited lectures. Simon & Schuster 1993 255p hardcover o.p. paperback available $14   **158**

1. Self-realization 2. Applied psychology
ISBN 0-684-84723-X (pa)   LC 93-31322

The author "discusses 'growing up'—becoming self-aware, working through cycles of blame and toward wholesale forgiveness—and then the self-examination we each must undergo in order to groom ourselves for the most important step of all: the search for God." Booklist

The road less traveled; a new psychology of love, traditional values, and spiritual growth. 25th anniversary ed. Simon & Schuster 2002 315p $22.95   **158**

1. Applied psychology 2. Love
ISBN 0-7432-3825-7   LC 2002-75858

A reissue of the title first published 1978

This book attempts to bring together "psychology and religion. It is divided into four areas—discipline, love, religion and growth, and grace—and within each Peck tackles the . . . struggle between stagnation and progress which goes on in all of us throughout our lives." Libr J

The road less traveled and beyond; spiritual growth in an age of anxiety. Simon & Schuster 1997 314p $23; pa $14   **158**

1. Self-realization 2. Applied psychology
ISBN 0-684-81314-9; 0-684-83561-4 (pa)
LC 96-43391

In this volume Peck "continues his journey through the existential conflicts and baffling paradoxes on the meandering road of personal development. . . . Through copious detailed references from his previous books, he allows readers unfamiliar with them to understand and enjoy the present work, which completes his Road trilogy." Publ Wkly

Prager, Dennis, 1948-

Happiness is a serious problem; a human nature repair manual. ReganBooks 1998 179p hardcover o.p. paperback available $13   **158**

1. Happiness
ISBN 0-06-098735-1 (pa)   LC 97-35404

The author "uses the pursuit of happiness as a central motif but generally instructs in the modern art of self-improvement. The 31 short chapters . . . are cogent, complete, and preach a nonreligious yet morally guided moderation that should appeal across a wide range of patron groups." Libr J

Queen Latifah

Ladies first; revelations of a strong woman; [by] Queen Latifah with Karen Hunter; foreword by Rita Owens. Morrow 1999 xxvii, 173p il hardcover o.p. paperback available $13   **158**

1. Self-esteem 2. Women—Psychology
ISBN 0-688-17583-X (pa)   LC 98-41533

"This book attempts to impart the philosophy behind Latifah's image and, in so doing, 'let every woman know that she, too . . . is royalty. She does this by basing the narrative loosely around some of the major events in her life. . . . Also included are Latifah's views on drug use, God, romance and sex." Publ Wkly

Richardson, Brenda Lane, 1948-

What mama couldn't tell us about love; healing the emotional legacy of slavery; celebrating our light; [by] Brenda Lane Richardson and Brenda Wade. HarperCollins Pubs. 1999 xxviii, 241p hardcover o.p. paperback available $13.95   **158**

1. Love 2. African American women 3. Women—Psychology
ISBN 0-06-09379-9 (pa)   LC 99-12127

The authors present a "self-help guide on relationships and intimacy for African American women. What makes

Richardson, Brenda Lane, 1948-—*Continued*

this work unique is that it makes the direct connection between slavery and emotional health. . . . The resource sections on assistance for individual or group work, mental health organizations, and sisterly support are valuable additions." Booklist

Includes bibliographical references

Safer, Jeanne

The normal one; life with a difficult or damaged sibling. Free Press 2002 204p $24

158

1. Siblings 2. Emotionally disturbed children 3. Family life

ISBN 0-7432-1196-0   LC 2002-67529

This is an "examination of the considerable effect that 'damaged'—handicapped, troubled or otherwise impaired—brothers and sisters have upon their 'normal' siblings throughout life." N Y Times Book Rev

Includes bibliographical references

Siegel, Bernie S.

Prescriptions for living; inspirational lessons for a joyful, loving life. HarperCollins Pubs. 1998 xxiv, 210p hardcover o.p. paperback available $14   **158**

1. Spiritual life 2. Self-realization

ISBN 0-06-092936-7 (pa)   LC 98-39059

"Among the topics Siegel covers are how to find peace of mind; how to love, encourage, and forgive other people as well as yourself; and how to thrive in bad times and survive the good times. For those ready to be uplifted by the soothing repetition of time-tested homilies, Siegel delivers the goods." Booklist

Stone, Douglas

Difficult conversations; how to discuss what matters most; [by] Douglas Stone, Bruce Patton, Sheila Heen. Viking 1999 xxi, 250p il hardcover o.p. paperback available $14   **158**

1. Interpersonal relations 2. Communication

ISBN 0-14-028852-X (pa)   LC 98-33346

This is a "guide to the art of handling difficult conversations—e.g., firing an employee, ending a relationship, or discussing marital conflicts." Libr J

The authors "blend a daunting array of disciplines into highly readable and practical advice." Booklist

Ury, William

Getting past no; negotiating with difficult people; [by] William L. Ury. Bantam Bks. 1991 161p hardcover o.p. paperback available $14.95   **158**

1. Negotiation

ISBN 0-553-37131-2 (pa)   LC 91-10101

"Ury presents a five-step agenda to deal successfully with opponents, be they unruly teenagers, labor leaders, terrorists or international politicians. Strategies focus on self-discipline, or tactics for defusing the adversary's attacks, and suggestions for developing options designed to lead to a mutually satisfactory agreement." Publ Wkly

Includes bibliographical references

Viorst, Judith

Imperfect control; our lifelong struggles with power and surrender. Simon & Schuster 1998 446p hardcover o.p. paperback available $14   **158**

1. Psychology

ISBN 0-684-84814-7 (pa)   LC 97-37302

"Referring to the works of social scientists, psychologists, and philosophers as well as literary examples and personal experiences, Viorst shows how issues of power and surrender confront and affect us throughout our lives. . . . Her book is very readable, with traces of the author's special brand of humor woven throughout." Libr J

Includes bibliographical references

Viscott, David S., 1938-1996

Emotional resilience; simple truths for dealing with the unfinished business of your past; by David Viscott. Harmony Bks. 1996 358p il hardcover o.p. paperback available $15   **158**

1. Attitude (Psychology) 2. Human behavior

ISBN 0-517-88825-4 (pa)   LC 96-407

The author outlines his 10 step self help program. "His method, which includes truth telling, acceptance of self and others, letting go of the past and of false expectations, and taking responsibility for one's life, is for those trapped in emotionally confining situations, whether personal relationships, educational impasses, or financial situations." Booklist

160   Logic

Copi, Irving M.

Introduction to logic; Irving M. Copi, Carl Cohen. Prentice-Hall il $84   **160**

1. Logic   LC 89-37742

First published 1953 (11th edition 2002) Periodically revised

This introduction to logic covers language, fallacies, definitions, categories, arguments, deduction, probability and other areas of logical inquiry such as thought and reasoning

Includes bibliographical references

170   Ethics (Moral philosophy)

Aristotle, 384-322 B.C.

Ethics   **170**

1. Ethics

Hardcover and paperback editions available from various publishers

Variant titles: Ethica Nichomachea and Nichomachean ethics

According to Aristotle's ethical treatises, "happiness is the goal of life. Pleasure, fame, and wealth, however, will not bring one the highest happiness, which is achieved only through the contemplation of philosophic truth, because it exercises man's peculiar virtue, the rational principle." Reader's Ency. 3d edition

Carter, Stephen L.

Integrity. Basic Bks. 1996 277p hardcover
o.p. paperback available $14   **170**

1. Ethics 2. Conduct of life

ISBN 0-06-092807-7 (pa)   LC 95-44538

The author seeks to define "integrity in both personal
and political terms. . . . Mr. Carter divides true integrity
into three parts: discernment, steadfastness and forthright-
ness. Anyone who wants to act with integrity must first
think hard about what is right and wrong. . . . Once the
right course of action suggests itself, it should be acted
upon, even if doing so is risky or unpleasant. . . . People of integrity, finally, are willing to defend what they
do in public." N Y Times Book Rev

Includes bibliographical references

Cohen, Randy

The good, the bad & the difference; how to
tell right from wrong in everyday situations.
Doubleday 2002 277p $23.95   **170**

1. Ethics

ISBN 0-385-50273-7   LC 2001-42084

This is a "collection of columns that first appeared in
the *New York Times Magazine's* 'Ethicist' column. . . .
Although some of the columns touch on weighty moral
issues . . . most deal with everyday ethics." Booklist

Coles, Robert

Lives of moral leadership. Random House
2000 247p hardcover o.p. paperback available
$13.95   **170**

1. Ethics 2. Conduct of life 3. Leadership

ISBN 0-375-75835-6 (pa)   LC 00-27858

Drawing on interviews he conducted over the past
four decades with public and private figures, Coles reflects on the meaning of moral leadership in the United
States

Dewey, John, 1859-1952

Theory of the moral life; with an
introduction by Arnold Isenberg. Irvington
Pubs. 1980 c1960 179p pa $14.95   **170**

1. Ethics

ISBN 0-8290-3150-2   LC 80-18200

A reprint of the edition first published 1960 by Holt,
Rinehart & Winston

"A redaction . . . of part II of Dewey and Tufts' Ethics, from the revised edition of 1932"

This introduction to the study of moral philosophy is
a compact examination of basic moral theories and major
theorists, including Aristotle, Kant, Mill, Bentham, Spencer, and others. In addition, one of the aims of the book
is to provide the individual with a set of principles which
will help him follow a moral path

Includes bibliographical references

Edelman, Marian Wright

The measure of our success; a letter to my
children and yours. Beacon Press 1992 97p
o.p. HarperCollins paperback available $10
          170

1. Ethics 2. Human behavior 3. Child rearing
4. United States—Moral conditions

ISBN 0-06-097546-6 (pa)   LC 91-42743

The author presents her "beliefs on child rearing and
moral values. . . . She includes a personal letter to her
three sons, who were born into a family with a shared
African American and Jewish heritage, and offers 25 lessons, or 'road maps', for life." Libr J

Encyclopedia of applied ethics. Academic
Press 1998 4v set $790   **170**

1. Ethics—Encyclopedias

ISBN 0-12-227065-7   LC 97-74395

Editor-in-chief, Ruth Chadwick

"Arranged in an A-Z format, the set describes 282
topics in 5000- to 6000-word articles. Coverage includes
most of the 'hot topics' of our day from abortion and
adoption to zoos. Typical of the broad coverage, 'Aids
in the Developing World' includes a glossary description
of clinical research, a discussion of sex education, and
comments on resource allocation." Libr J

Encyclopedia of ethics; Susan Neiburg
Terkel, consulting editor; R. Shannon
Duval, editor. Facts on File 1999 302p
$71.50   **170**

1. Ethics—Encyclopedias

ISBN 0-8160-3311-0   LC 98-39932

This encyclopedia covers such topics as moral development, character, justice, self-realization, existentialism,
genetic engineering, the right to die, business, medical,
and sexual ethics, and includes the ideas of such thinkers
as Confucius, Hildegard von Bingen, and John Stuart
Mill

Encyclopedia of ethics; edited by Lawrence
C. Becker and Charlotte B. Becker. 2nd ed.
Routledge 2001 3v set $370   **170**

1. Ethics—Encyclopedias

ISBN 0-415-93672-1   LC 2001-19657

First published 1992 by Garland

"The coverage of ethical theory as pursued among English-speaking philosophers remains the scope of this set.
Entries are listed in word-by-word alphabetical order. A
list of entries gives a convenient overview of headwords
and *see* references. A subject index provides a guide to
subjects discussed in the text of the entries, including
persons; and a citation index provides an author-by-
author listing of writers, and some editors, cited in the
bibliographies of all 581 entries." Booklist

Gaines, Patrice

Moments of grace; meeting the challenge
to change. Crown 1997 206p hardcover o.p.
paperback available $15   **170**

1. Conversion 2. Conduct of life

ISBN 0-609-80171-6 (pa)   LC 96-25404

Companion volume to Laughing in the dark (1994)

The author focuses on the "process of personal
change. . . . She addresses in specific chapters friends,
family, work, dating, love and marriage, 'a higher power,' and perseverance." Libr J

"Gaines manifests an intelligent and mellow wisdom.
She treats her own insight into her travails as spiritual
awakenings, or gifts from God. Without preaching or
cheerleading, she points out the powerful, life-changing
lessons available in her experiences and in those of others." Publ Wkly

Kingwell, Mark, 1963-

In pursuit of happiness; better living from
Plato to prozac. Crown 2000 xx, 392p $25
          170

1. Happiness

ISBN 0-609-60535-6

First published 1998 in Canada with title: Better living

Kingwell, Mark, 1963-—*Continued*
The author "uses philosophical methods to examine . . . the idea of happiness. . . . [He] delves into how happiness, with all its variant definitions, is an element in every part of our lives." Libr J
Includes bibliographical references

Kübler-Ross, Elisabeth
Life lessons; two experts on death and dying teach us about the mysteries of life and living; [by] Elisabeth Kübler-Ross and David Kessler. Scribner 2000 224p $24; pa $13
170
1. Conduct of life 2. Death
ISBN 0-684-87074-6; 0-684-87075-4 (pa)
LC 00-57387
The authors argue that "there is a 'core self,' a real and eternal 'you,' who is not identified with actions, social roles or history. Happiness is its natural state. This self is good and pure but always learning; its experience is to be seen as 'lessons.'" Christ Century
"As in each of their previous individual works, the authors provide useful and accessible information." Libr J

Schlessinger, Laura C.
How could you do that?! the abdication of character, courage, and conscience; by Laura Schlessinger. HarperCollins Pubs. 1996 269p hardcover o.p. paperback available $13 **170**
1. Ethics 2. Conduct of life 3. Character
ISBN 0-06-092806-9 (pa)
LC 95-46266
The author's "premise is that character, courage, and conscience should be incorporated into our everyday living and decisions. With conversations from her radio show as the backdrop and biblical references throughout, she shows how this can be done. The problems are varied, and readers will surely find something they can relate to." Libr J

Wolfe, Alan
Moral freedom; the impossible idea that defines the way we live now. Norton 2001 256p $24.95; pa $14.95 **170**
1. Ethics 2. Public opinion 3. Values 4. United States—Moral conditions
ISBN 0-393-04843-8; 0-393-32302-1 (pa)
LC 00-51969
"Wolfe here discusses the results of a national public opinion poll he helped design on American beliefs about values, which he supplemented with detailed interviews of people from eight different U.S. communities. These ranged widely, from the Castro district of San Francisco to San Antonio." Libr J
Includes bibliographical references

Woodruff, Paul, 1943-
Reverence. Oxford Univ. Press 2002 248p $19.95 **170**
1. Ethics 2. Conduct of life
ISBN 0-19-514778-2
LC 2001-36135
The author "defines reverence and explains how it makes community life possible. Drawing on two classic traditions, ancient Greek philosophy and Confucianism, as well as the poetry of Tennyson, Yeats, and Larkin, Woodruff carefully separates reverence—the sense of a greater, transcendent force, the feeling of awe we feel in the presence of beauty—from faith, showing how tyranny occurs when reverence breaks down." Booklist
Includes bibliographical references

174   Occupational ethics

Barber, Nigel
Encyclopedia of ethics in science and technology. Facts on File 2002 386p il (Facts on File science library) $60 **174**
1. Science—Ethical aspects
ISBN 0-8160-4314-0
LC 2001-40832
"This work attempts to give a broad overview of the ethical issues surrounding the development of science and the deployment of technology. . . . The more than 400 entries range in length from 25 to more than 1,000 words and fall into five general categories: biography, legal aspects, specific technologies or theories, events, and movements and organizations. . . . The strength of the encyclopedia is its coverage of specific technologies and events and their controversial aspects. The author has done a good job of treating many of the technologies—such as contraception and genetic engineering—that we see in the daily news." Booklist

Clones and clones; facts and fantasies about human cloning; edited by Martha C. Nussbaum and Cass R. Sunstein. Norton 1998 351p $26.95; pa $15.95 **174**
1. Cloning 2. Reproductive technology 3. Bioethics
ISBN 0-393-04648-6; 0-393-32001-4 (pa)
LC 97-51781
This is a collection of essays and short stories on cloning. The contributors include Richard Dawkins; Eric A. Posner and Richard A. Posner; Andrea Dworkin; William N. Estridge and Edward Stein; and Richard A. Epstein
"The spectrum of authors and their varying perspectives in fact and fiction are assets to anyone who hopes to understand this broad issue and its vast cultural implications." Publ Wkly
Includes bibliographical references

The **Ethics** of organ transplants; the current debate; edited by Arthur L. Caplan and Daniel H. Coelho. Prometheus Bks. 1998 350p il pa $20 **174**
1. Transplantation of organs, tissues, etc. 2. Medical ethics
ISBN 1-57392-224-2
LC 98-31722
The editors "have selected 35 articles that are representative of the ethical issues surrounding organ transplantation. . . . In many cases, the editors have selected companion articles that illustrate contrasting viewpoints on a particular issue." Libr J
Includes bibliographical references

Flesh of my flesh; the ethics of cloning humans: a reader; edited by Gregory E. Pence. Rowman & Littlefield 1998 154p hardcover o.p. paperback available $12.95
174
1. Cloning 2. Reproductive technology 3. Medical genetics
ISBN 0-8476-8982-4 (pa)
LC 98-11287
"Written by distinguished scientists, law professors, theologians, and philosophers, these 13 provocative essays on the legal, medical, and moral implications of human cloning present a balanced view of the issues." Libr J
Includes bibliographical references

Fox, Michael W., 1937-
Beyond evolution; the genetically altered future of plants, animals, the earth—humans. Lyons Press 1999 256p $24.95 **174**
1. Genetic engineering 2. Bioethics
ISBN 1-55821-901-3 LC 99-12866
The author "argues that biotechnology—coupled with industrial, chemical-based agriculture—will only accelerate the adverse environmental and consumer-health consequences of factory farming." Publ Wkly
Includes bibliographical references

Fukuyama, Francis
Our posthuman future; consequences of the biotechnology revolution. Farrar, Straus & Giroux 2002 256p il $25 **174**
1. Biotechnology 2. Cloning 3. Genetic engineering 4. Bioethics
ISBN 0-374-23643-7 LC 2002-100914
The author contends "that there are sound nonreligious reasons to put limits on biotechnology, and that such limits can be enforced. Fukuyama argues that 'the most significant threat' from biotechnology is 'the possibility that it will alter human nature and thereby move us into a "posthuman" stage of history.'" Publ Wkly
"Fukuyama boldly parses complicated, controversial issues in order to instigate debate, pondering here, in rigorous detail, the ethical and social implications of biotechnologies." Booklist
Includes bibliographical references

Human cloning and human dignity; the report of the President's Council on bioethics; with a foreword by Leon R. Kass, chairman. PublicAffairs 2002 350p il pa $14 **174**
1. Cloning 2. Bioethics
ISBN 1-58648-176-2
This "report focuses on three major issues: cloning to produce children (reproductive uses), cloning for biomedical research (therapeutic uses), and various public policies that could be enacted. The council members were divided on their recommendations regarding human cloning, so both a majority and a minority opinion are presented here." Libr J
Includes bibliographical references

Kolata, Gina
Clone; the road to Dolly, and the path ahead. Morrow 1998 276p hardcover o.p. paperback available $14 **174**
1. Cloning
ISBN 0-688-16634-2 (pa) LC 97-29132
Kolata discusses the scientific work that led to the cloning of an adult sheep and examines the "ethical debate among scientists, theologians, reproductive rights activists, bioethicists, doctors, and politicians." Booklist
The author "brings keen insight to her analysis of the implications of cloning and makes the complex details of genetics and cell biology interesting and accessible." Publ Wkly
Includes bibliographical references

Moreno, Jonathan D.
Undue risk; secret state experiments on humans. Freeman, W.H. 1999 xx, 347p $24.95 **174**
1. Human experimentation in medicine 2. Medical ethics
ISBN 0-7167-3142-8 LC 99-16928
Also available in paperback from Routledge
"After reviewing Japanese experiments on human subjects in China, 1910-29, and on POWs during World War II, as well as the infamous Nazi research with human subjects, Moreno explores U.S. experimentation on members of its armed forces. . . . Clearly, he shows, experimenters did not inform research subjects adequately, sometimes deliberately misleading them." Booklist
Includes bibliographical references

Munson, Ronald, 1939-
Raising the dead; organ transplants, ethics, and society. Oxford Univ. Press 2002 288p $30 **174**
1. Transplantation of organs, tissues, etc. 2. Medical ethics
ISBN 0-19-513299-8 LC 2001-36119
This examination of the "variety of ethical issues surrounding organ transplantation . . . discusses the definition of death, methods for obtaining organs, recipient selection, xenotransplantation, and stem cell research." Libr J
"Lucid and compelling writing on a much-debated topic." Booklist
Includes bibliographical references

Wilmut, Ian
The second creation; Dolly and the age of biological control; [by] Ian Wilmut, Keith Campbell, Colin Tudge. Farrar, Straus & Giroux 2000 333p il $27 **174**
1. Cloning
ISBN 0-374-14123-1 LC 99-50032
Also available in paperback from Harvard Univ. Press
The scientists responsible for cloning the ewe Dolly "tell the full story of how they did it. . . . To demystify cloning (now called nuclear transfer by experts), the authors trace the history of cell biology and embryology, the linked sciences that made it possible, explaining in lucid terms the fundamental principles that brought Dolly and her successors to life." Booklist

176 Ethics of sex and reproduction

Stock, Gregory
Redesigning humans; our inevitable genetic future. Houghton Mifflin 2002 277p $24; pa $14 **176**
1. Genetics 2. Reproductive technology 3. Genetic engineering
ISBN 0-618-06026-X; 0-618-34083-1 (pa)
LC 2001-51890
The author gives an "overview of the new biotechnology that will allow scientists to delay aging and to insert genes that enhance physical and cognitive performance, combat disease or improve looks into embryos. Stock thoughtfully weighs the ethical dilemmas such advances present, arguing that the real threat is not frivolous abuse of technology but the fact that we don't know the long-term effects of these genetic changes." Publ Wkly
Includes bibliographical references

177   Ethics of social relations

Campbell, Jeremy, 1931-
The liar's tale; a history of falsehood. Norton 2001 363p $26.95; pa $15.95   **177**
1. Truthfulness and falsehood
ISBN 0-393-02559-4; 0-393-32361-7 (pa)
LC 2001-30286
Campbell discusses lying in history and in the writings of "philosophers and thinkers from the ancient Greeks to Darwin, Nietzsche, Marx, and Freud, down to . . . [the] postmodern deconstructionists." Christ Sci Monit
"This challenging romp through the underbelly of intellectual history . . . is fascinating and troublesome." NY Times Book Rev
Includes bibliographical references

Stengel, Richard
You're too kind; a brief history of flattery. Simon & Schuster 2000 315p $25; pa $14
177
1. Flattery
ISBN 0-684-85491-0; 0-684-85492-9 (pa)
"Charting the uses of flattery and the social contexts in which it is used from biblical times to the present, Stengel . . . illustrates that more than mere praise, flattery is praise with a motive, be it benign or grasping. . . . Enjoyable and informative." Libr J
Includes bibliographical references

Sullivan, Evelin E., 1947-
The concise book of lying; [by] Evelin Sullivan. Farrar, Straus & Giroux 2001 334p il $25; pa $15   **177**
1. Truthfulness and falsehood
ISBN 0-374-12868-5; 0-312-42047-1 (pa)
LC 2001-18760
The author discusses lying in history and literature. She examines what impels people to lie and what the results of lying might be
"Anyone interested in the history and philosophy of human nature will appreciate this compelling and cleverly written volume." Libr J
Includes bibliographical references

179   Other ethical norms

Blum, Deborah
The monkey wars. Oxford Univ. Press 1994 306p hardcover o.p. paperback available $19.95   **179**
1. Animal experimentation 2. Animal rights
ISBN 0-19-510109-X (pa)   LC 94-12439
"The 'wars' between scientific researchers and animal-rights activists have several aspects: fanaticism, propaganda, pragmatism, and idealism. Blum has written a beautifully balanced account of the major individuals and organizations involved. She points out the different shades of belief and approaches in the conflict and shows how these have developed over the years." Booklist
Includes bibliographical references

Coetzee, J. M., 1940-
The lives of animals; [by] J.M. Coetzee; [reflections by] Marjorie Garber [et al.]; edited and introduced by Amy Gutmann. Princeton Univ. Press 1999 127p (University Center for Human Values series) $29.95; pa $13.95   **179**
1. Animal rights 2. Animal welfare
ISBN 0-691-00443-9; 0-691-07089-X (pa)
LC 98-39591
"This hybrid collection of fiction and essays is a provocative version of Socratic philosophy. It begins with a story about a Doris Lessing-like author who visits her conflicted son and his antagonistic wife while lecturing at the university where they teach. The mother's hobby-horse, that Animals R Us, embarrasses the academic couple, and her suggestion that they are like Nazis because they eat meat infuriates them. Other distinguished academics carry on this dialogue in playful fiction and sober commentary, in which the most eloquent part may be the descriptions of communication with animals." New Yorker
Includes bibliographical references

Comte-Sponville, André
A small treatise on the great virtues; the uses of philosophy in everyday life; translated by Catherine Temerson. Metropolitan Bks. 2001 352p $27.50; pa $16   **179**
1. Ethics
ISBN 0-8050-4555-4; 0-8050-4556-2 (pa)
LC 2001-30299
Original French edition, 1995
"Dividing the book into 18 virtue-based chapters— "Politeness," "Fidelity," "Prudence," "Temperance," "Courage," "Mercy," "Gratitude," and so on—Comte-Sponville quotes a multitude of philosophers from the ancient Greeks through Spinoza, Hobbes and Nietzsche to modern Frenchmen like Vladimir Jankelevitch." Publ Wkly
"His subject demands a sober seriousness, but Comte-Sponville still manages to avoid taking himself too seriously: humility makes it into his litany of virtues, as does humor. A laudable renewal of the ancient quest for ethical wisdom." Booklist
Includes bibliographical references

Encyclopedia of animal rights and animal welfare; edited by Marc Bekoff with Carron A. Meaney; foreword by Jane Goodall. Greenwood Press 1998 xxi, 446p il $64.95   **179**
1. Animal rights—Encyclopedias 2. Animal welfare—Encyclopedias
ISBN 0-313-29977-3   LC 97-35098
This "work offers about 170 essays by well-known names in the animal industry who represent many fields. . . . The result is a welcome multidisciplinary approach that shows us the extensive roles nonhuman animals play in virtually all areas of our lives. The essays are well reasoned and often extensive." Libr J

Fox, Michael W., 1937-

Inhumane society; the American way of exploiting animals; introduction by Cleveland Amory. St. Martin's Press 1990 268p hardcover o.p. paperback available $18.95

179

1. Animal welfare
ISBN 0-312-30213-4 (pa)   LC 89-70299

The author "looks at the exploitative and inhumane treatment of domestic, agriculture, and laboratory animals." Booklist

This book "is very readable and takes a strong stance while presenting a creditably balanced treatment of the issues." Libr J

Includes bibliographical references

Greek, C. Ray

Sacred cows and golden geese; the human cost of experiments on animals; [by] C. Ray Greek and Jean Swingle Greek; foreword by Jane Goodall. Continuum 2000 256p $24.95; pa $18.95   **179**

1. Animal experimentation
ISBN 0-8264-1226-2; 0-8264-1402-8 (pa)
LC 99-57157

This "covers the history of animal experimentation, legislation that promulgates it, the real cost to humans, and alternatives. It is a well-written, if disturbing, book." Libr J

Includes bibliographical references

Rudacille, Deborah

The scalpel and the butterfly; the war between animal research and animal protection. Farrar, Straus & Giroux 2000 389p $25   **179**

1. Animal experimentation 2. Animal welfare
ISBN 0-374-25420-6   LC 00-28758

Also available in paperback from University of California Press

The author gives a "history of the conflict between anti-vivisectionists and research scientists. She begins with French physician Claude Bernard. . . . Rudacille then documents the rise of the animal welfare movement in Britain and the United States and legislation designed to govern the use of animals in research. . . . The author also discusses the Nazi 'science' of eugenics and explores the ethical implications of such new scientific developments as xenotransplantation." Libr J

Includes bibliographical references

Tillich, Paul, 1886-1965

The courage to be; with an introduction by Peter J. Gomes. 2nd ed. Yale Univ. Press 2000 197p (Yale Nota bene) pa $12.95 **179**

1. Courage 2. Ontology 3. Anxiety 4. Existentialism
ISBN 0-300-08471-4   LC 00-102364

First published 1952

Partial contents: Being and courage; Being, nonbeing and anxiety; Pathological anxiety, vitality, and courage; Courage and participation; Courage and individualization; Courage and transcendence

The author offers advice on how to conquer the anxiety caused by the loss of meaning in one's life

Wise, Steven M.

Drawing the line; science and the case for animal rights. Perseus Bks. 2002 322p $26; pa $18   **179**

1. Animal rights
ISBN 0-7382-0340-8; 0-7382-0810-8 (pa)
"A Merloyd Lawrence book"

Wise "sets out to determine whether animals ranging from dolphins to his family dog . . . have mental abilities meriting [legal] protection. . . . The key to granting any of them rights, Wise argues, is whether they possess 'practical autonomy'—desires and the ability to act to satisfy them." Christ Sci Monit

Includes bibliographical references

179.7   Respect and disrespect for human life

Durkheim, Émile, 1858-1917

Suicide, a study in sociology; translated by John A. Spaulding and George Simpson; edited with an introduction by George Simpson. Free Press 1951 405p maps hardcover o.p. paperback available $18.95

179.7

1. Suicide
ISBN 0-684-83632-7 (pa)
Original French edition, 1897

Durkheim's "Suicide is a major sociological classic, one that is still read today, not so much for its data, which are limited and out-of-date, but for the brilliance of his analysis of suicide rates and other data that had been initially obtained for administrative rather than scientific purposes." Reader's Adviser

Includes bibliographical references

Filene, Peter G.

In the arms of others; a cultural history of the right-to-die in America. Dee, I.R. 1998 282p il hardcover o.p. paperback available $15.95   **179.7**

1. Right to die 2. Euthanasia
ISBN 1-56663-268-4 (pa)   LC 97-42583

The author traces the history of euthanasia from the 19th century "through the present-day thicket of health-care issues, including the use (and removal) of life support, the question of whether a terminally sick person has the right to doctor-assisted suicide and the practical value of living wills." Publ Wkly

"A fine general overview of the right-to-die question." Libr J

Includes bibliographical references

Humphry, Derek, 1930-

Final exit; the practicalities of self-deliverance and assisted sucide for the dying. 3rd ed. Delta Trade Paperbacks 2002 xxviii, 220p pa $13.95   **179.7**

1. Suicide 2. Right to die
ISBN 0-385-33653-5   LC 2002-19403

First published 1991 by Hemlock Society

This offers information about how to commit suicide for the terminally ill and about the legality and ethics of assisted suicide and euthanasia

Includes bibliographical references

Humphry, Derek, 1930-— *Continued*

Freedom to die; people, politics, and the right-to-die movement; [by] Derek Humphry and Mary Clement. St. Martin's Press 1998 388p hardcover o.p. paperback available $14.95 **179.7**

1. Right to die

ISBN 0-312-25389-3 (pa)   LC 98-21127

This is "a history of the right-to-die debate. . . . Though obviously favoring the right to die, the authors present their opinions in a clear, low-key manner. All individuals interested in this question should read this work." Libr J

Includes bibliographical references

Marcus, Eric

Why suicide? answers to 200 of the most frequently asked questions about suicide, attempted suicide, and assisted suicide. HarperSanFrancisco 1996 240p pa $14

179.7

1. Suicide

ISBN 0-06-251166-1   LC 95-33431

The author's "questions range from 'Does everyone have thoughts of suicide?' to 'What are the arguments against legalizing doctor-assisted suicide?' His responses reflect not only a knowledgeable and well-informed consideration of suicidology but also empathetic treatment. The typical response aims to educate by giving factual information and/or practical advice as well as to console by providing personal stories from suicide survivors." Libr J

Includes bibliographical references

McKhann, Charles F., 1930-

A time to die; the place for physician assistance. Yale Univ. Press 1999 268p $42; pa $19   **179.7**

1. Euthanasia

ISBN 0-300-07631-2; 0-300-08698-9 (pa)

LC 98-22193

The author "believes that physician-assisted suicide is not only desirable but inevitable. Humanity is divided in two parts, he says: those who have seen a loved one die a miserable death and those who have not. . . . McKhann argues level-headedly about patients, doctors, and laws." Booklist

Includes bibliographical references

Peck, M. Scott (Morgan Scott)

Denial of the soul; spiritual and medical perspectives on euthanasia and mortality. Harmony Bks. 1997 242p hardcover o.p. paperback available $19   **179.7**

1. Euthanasia 2. Suicide 3. Right to die

ISBN 0-609-80134-1 (pa)   LC 97-157271

The author "argues against, with very few exceptions, euthanasia and physician-assisted suicide on demand." Publ Wkly

"Peck is a wonderful writer, engaging, intelligent, and full of stories from his long psychiatric practice; as usual, he takes on big issues with seriousness, sensitivity, and balance." Libr J

Wiesenthal, Simon

The sunflower; on the possibilities and limits of forgiveness; with a symposium edited by Harry James Cargas and Bonny V. Fetterman. rev & expanded ed. Schocken Bks. 1997 271p hardcover o.p. paperback available $13   **179.7**

1. Holocaust, 1933-1945—Personal narratives 2. Forgiveness

ISBN 0-8052-1060-1 (pa)   LC 96-36831

Original French edition, 1969

In this expanded version of a book first published in the United States in 1976 "Wiesenthal tackles the question of the possibilities and limits of forgiveness. The first part relates the story of how Wiesenthal, as a prisoner in a Nazi concentration camp, was brought before a dying SS trooper, who explained his actions and asked for forgiveness. . . . In the second section, Wiesenthal presents the story to an array of leading intellectuals and asks, 'What would you have done?' This edition contains all the original responses plus additional ones from Primo Levi, Cynthia Ozick, Albert Speer, and others." Libr J

"The responses to the author's question are as varied as their authors. The mystery of evil and atonement remain, and the reader is left challenged on these most basic issues of meaning in human life." Publ Wkly

180   Ancient, medieval, Oriental philosophy

Encyclopedia of classical philosophy; edited by Donald J. Zeyl; associate editors, Daniel T. Devereux and Phillip K. Mitsis. Greenwood Press 1997 614p $119.95   **180**

1. Ancient philosophy—Encyclopedias

ISBN 0-313-28775-9   LC 96-2562

"Covering Greek and Roman philosophy from the sixth century B.C. to the sixth century A.D., this encyclopedia boasts more than 270 signed articles from more than 90 contributors. . . . Entries range from a single paragraph (*Apollonius, Hecataeus, Theon*) to nearly 30 pages (*Aristotle*). While the majority of entries are for philosophers or other individuals, dozens of articles treat subjects such as the Academy, Cyrenaic philosophy, theories of medicine, tragic poets, and rhetoric." Booklist

"This encyclopedia fills a void in philosophical reference works that has existed for too long, and it will likely become a standard in the field." Libr J

Gottlieb, Anthony

The dream of reason; a history of western philosophy from the Greeks to the Renaissance. Norton 2000 468p $27.95; pa $17.95   **180**

1. Philosophy—History

ISBN 0-393-04951-5; 0-393-32365-X (pa)

LC 00-49012

"This book is the first installment of . . . a survey in two volumes of the whole of Western philosophy, from its origins in Greece in the sixth century B.C. to the present day." N Y Times Book Rev

"This eloquent book offers a lively chronicle of the evolution of Western philosophy." Publ Wkly

Includes bibliographical references

181   Oriental philosophy

Buber, Martin, 1878-1965
I and thou; translated by Ronald Gregor
Smith. Scribner 2000 c1986 126p $22; pa
$11   **181**
1. Jewish philosophy 2. God 3. Ontology
ISBN 0-7432-0133-7; 0-7432-0133-7 (pa)
Original German edition, 1923; first published in English 1958
In this book, the author "conceived the individual as in permanent relationship with all forms of life, finding his fulfillment in the reciprocity of the relationship—the 'Thou' being God." Reader's Adviser

Confucius
The analects of Confucius   **181**
1. Chinese philosophy 2. Chinese ethics
Hardcover and paperback editions available from various publishers
"One of the Chinese 'Four Books.' A brief, unsystematic collection of fragmentary writings attributed to Confucius and his school. . . . It is one of the most influential works in the history of Chinese thought." Reader's Ency

The wisdom of Confucius; edited and translated with notes by Lin Yutang. Modern Lib. 1938 290p   **181**
1. Chinese philosophy 2. Chinese ethics
Available in paperback from Citadel Press and Random House Value Pub.
A selection of writings by the Chinese political and ethical philosopher who advocated a form of rationalism based on humanity, reverence for ancient sages, and government by personal virtue

183   Sophistic, Socratic and related Greek philosophies

Stone, I. F. (Isidor Feinstein), 1907-1989
The trial of Socrates. Little, Brown 1988 282p o.p.; Anchor Bks. (NY) paperback available $13.95   **183**
1. Socrates
ISBN 0-385-26032-6 (pa)   LC 87-22855
The author attempts "to show that Athens was totally committed to free speech and did not normally place any check on it, and, therefore, that the trial of Socrates was a singular aberration which might be explicable, if finally not justifiable." Commentary

184   Platonic philosophy

Hare, R. M. (Richard Mervyn)
Plato. Oxford Univ. Press 1982 82p (Past masters series) hardcover o.p. paperback available $9.95   **184**
1. Plato
ISBN 0-19-287585-X (pa)   LC 83-159441
The author examines the chief Platonic concepts in their political and intellectual contexts
Includes bibliographical references

Plato
Complete works; edited, with introduction and notes, by John M. Cooper; associate editor, D.S. Hutchinson. Hackett 1997 xxx, 1808p $47   **184**
1. Ancient philosophy
ISBN 0-87220-349-2   LC 96-53280
"The translations are all relatively recent and thus reflect contemporary language use and terminology. The collection includes works such as the *Minos, Epinomis, Demodocus, Eryxias, and Axiochus*, which, though generally considered not to have been written by Plato, are 'Socratic' in form or style. The text itself is clearly printed and laid out, with useful notes, and Cooper's introduction and notes about the translations are helpful in setting the dialogs in context." Libr J
Includes bibliographical references

185   Aristotelian philosophy

Adler, Mortimer J., 1902-2001
Aristotle for everybody; difficult thought made easy. Macmillan 1978 206p hardcover o.p. paperback available $13   **185**
1. Aristotle, 384-322 B.C.
ISBN 0-684-83823-0 (pa)   LC 78-853
Adler traces "in the simplest language and with occasional modern analogues, the logic and growth of Aristotle's basic doctrines." Publ Wkly
Includes bibliographical references

188   Stoic philosophy

Marcus Aurelius, Emperor of Rome, 121-180
Meditations; a new translation, with an introduction, by Gregory Hays. Modern Lib. 2002 lvii, 191p $19.95   **188**
ISBN 0-679-64260-9   LC 2001-57947
Also available hardcover and paperback editions from other publishers including The emperor's handbook: a new translation of The meditations published 2002 by Scribner
"An emperor and Stoic philosopher records his thoughts as he struggles for composure and order in the face of national disaster." Good Read

189   Medieval Western philosophy

The **Renaissance** philosophy of man; [by] Petrarca [and others]; selections in translation, edited by Ernst Cassirer, Paul Oskar Kristeller, John Herman Randall, Jr. University of Chicago Press 1948 405p hardcover o.p. paperback available $17.50   **189**
1. Medieval philosophy
ISBN 0-226-09604-1 (pa)
Analyzed in Essay and general literature index
This book provides English translations from selected writings of six early Italian Renaissance philosophers from about the middle of the fourteenth century to the

The Renaissance philosophy of man—*Continued*
end of the sixteenth. Francesco Petrarca, Lorenzo Valla, Marsilio Ficino, Giovanni Pico della Mirandola, Pietro Pomponazzi, and Juan Luis Vives are represented. An introduction accompanies each of the translations
Includes bibliographical references

Rubenstein, Richard E.
Aristotle's children; how Christians, Muslims, and Jews rediscovered ancient wisdom and illuminated the Dark Ages. Harcourt 2003 368p $27   **189**
1. Aristotle, 384-322 B.C. 2. Medieval philosophy
ISBN 0-15-100720-9   LC 2003-6582
"In 12th-century Spain, a group of Muslim scholars, Jewish teachers, and Christian monks discovered Aristotle's De Anima (On the Soul). Until then, Aristotle's writings, like most of Greek culture, had been lost for centuries, following the fall of the Roman Empire around A.D. 480. . . . Aristotle's work, which was embraced enthusiastically by devotees of the three major religions, transformed the Dark Ages, reconciling faith and reason. Indeed, the impact of the Greek philosopher's new ideas (which focused on the material world, rather than the supernatural) was so far reaching that it created a revolution in thought that laid the foundation for the Renaissance and the 18th century's Age of Enlightenment." SLJ
"Although the book purports to trace Aristotle's influence on Christianity, Islam and Judaism, it devotes more attention to Christianity. Even so, Rubenstein's lively prose, his lucid insights and his crystal-clear historical analyses make this a first-rate study in the history of ideas." Publ Wkly
Includes bibliographical references

Thomas, Aquinas, Saint, 1225?-1274
Selected writings; edited and translated with an introduction and notes by Ralph McInerny. Penguin Bks. 1998 xxxviii, 841p pa $14.95   **189**
ISBN 0-14-043632-4
Arranged chronologically, this collection of theological and philosophical writings brings together sermons, commentaries, responses to criticism and lengthy extracts from the Summa theologia

190 Modern Western philosophy

The Columbia history of Western philosophy; edited by Richard H. Popkin. Columbia Univ. Press 1999 xxvi, 836p $64.50   **190**
1. Philosophy—History
ISBN 0-231-10128-7   LC 98-15219
This is an overview "of Western philosophy, from the pre-Socratics to 20th-century philosophy, both analytic and continental." Libr J
This survey's coverage of medieval Islamic, Jewish, and Christian philosophy is particularly strong. Choice
Includes bibliographical references

The Examined life; readings from Western philosophy from Plato to Kant; [edited by] Stanley Rosen. Random House 2000 628p $35   **190**
1. Philosophy
ISBN 0-375-40501-1   LC 99-59064
"While more than a third of the selections are from philosophers after Kant, at least a third of the material has nothing directly to do with the 'examined life.' But the collection is worthwhile because the material from Plato, Aristotle, Augustine, Descartes, Pascal, Machiavelli, Hobbes, Rousseau, and Hegel is carefully chosen and includes introductions by genuinely distinguished authors." Libr J
Includes bibliographical references

Gay, Peter, 1923-
The Enlightenment: an interpretation. Knopf 1966-1969 2v o.p.; Norton paperbacks available ea $19.95   **190**
1. Modern philosophy 2. Europe—Intellectual life 3. Enlightenment
(pa)
Also available in hardcover from P. Smith
Contents: v1 The rise of modern paganism (ISBN 0-393-31302-6); v2 The science of freedom (ISBN 0-393-31366-2)
Gay examines the ideas, experiences and impact of leading Enlightenment figures in 18th century Europe and America
Includes bibliographical references

Great thinkers of the Western world; edited by Ian P. McGreal. HarperCollins Pubs. 1992 572p $47   **190**
1. Philosophy 2. Theology 3. Science
ISBN 0-06-270026-X   LC 91-38362
"The major ideas and classic works of more than 100 outstanding Western philosophers, physical and social scientists, psychologists, religious writers, and theologians." Title page
"This guide to 116 selected authors . . . spans the ancient Greeks to the first half of the twentieth century. . . . The guide is arranged chronologically by the birthdate of the writer. Each entry contains birth and death dates, a list of the author's major ideas, an essay of three to five pages, and a short annotated list of secondary sources. . . . Its readable essays . . . are accessible to the layperson." Booklist

Magee, Bryan
The story of philosophy. DK Pub. 1998 240p il $29.95; pa $20   **190**
1. Philosophy
ISBN 0-7894-3511-X; 0-7894-7994-X (pa)
                    LC 98-3780
This "illustrated volume converts two-and-a-half millennia of Western philosophy into a colorful parade of provocative figures—from Heraclitus to Heidegger—who have enlarged the boundaries of thought." Booklist
"Writing with a clear and lively style, Magee provides an excellent introduction to the topic." SLJ
Includes bibliographical references

The **Oxford** history of Western philosophy; edited by Anthony Kenny. Oxford Univ. Press 1994 407p il maps $49.95; pa $15   **190**

1. Philosophy—History
ISBN 0-19-824278-6; 0-19-289329-7 (pa)
     LC 94-9858

Published in the United Kingdom with title: The Oxford illustrated history of Western philosophy

This volume covers "the ancients, the medievals, continental philosophers like Hegel, Nietzsche, and Sartre, and the English analyticals (Bentham and Mill), followed by a survey of political philosophies." Booklist

"The illustrations have been wisely chosen to show the constant play between art and idea. Some familiarity with analytic philosophy would be useful to gain the most from the text, but this is a significant addition to the literature." Libr J

Includes bibliographical references

Sedgwick, Peter
Descartes to Derrida; an introduction to European philosophy. Blackwell 2001 310p $76.95; pa $33.95   **190**
1. Modern philosophy
ISBN 0-631-20142-4; 0-631-20143-2 (pa)
     LC 00-57917

"This critical survey of issues in European philosophy offers . . . accounts of crucial texts by important thinkers. Sedgwick draws key ideas from these sources, analysing the various relationships between them and linking them to central themes in philosophical enquiry, such as the nature of subjectivity, reason and experience, anti-humanism and the nature of language." Publisher's note

"This book should take a place as one of the key texts in humanities programs throughout the English-speaking world." Choice

Includes bibliographical references

191   North American philosophy

Dewey, John, 1859-1952
The philosophy of John Dewey; edited with an introduction and commentary by John J. McDermott. University of Chicago Press 1981 2v in 1 pa $25   **191**
ISBN 0-226-14401-1   LC 80-39766
"Phoenix edition"

First published 1973 in two volumes by Putnam and analyzed in Essay and general literature index

Contents: v1 The structure of experience; v2 The lived experience

A digest of extracts from the American philosopher's most important works

Includes bibliographical references

Rand, Ayn, 1905-1982
The voice of reason; essays in objectivist thought; edited and with an introduction by Leonard Peikoff; and with additional essays by Leonard Peikoff and Peter Schwartz. New Am. Lib. 1989 c1988 353p hardcover o.p. paperback available $17   **191**
1. American philosophy
ISBN 0-452-01046-2 (pa)   LC 88-18192

The late author opposed liberalism and championed "capitalism, self-interest, and objective reality against collectivism, altruism, and mysticism. . . . These lectures, newspaper columns, and magazine articles are entirely characteristic of her—surprisingly emotional and dogmatic for a professed rationalist. Additional essays by editor Peikoff and disciple Peter Schwartz are of a piece." Booklist

Includes bibliographical references

192   British philosophy

Edmonds, David, 1964-
Wittgenstein's poker; the story of a ten-minute argument between two great philosophers; [by] David Edmonds and John Eidinow. Ecco Press 2001 340p il $24; pa $13.95   **192**
1. Wittgenstein, Ludwig, 1889-1951 2. Popper, Sir Karl Raimund, 1902-1994
ISBN 0-06-621244-8; 0-06-093664-9 (pa)
     LC 2002-276301

"On the Cambridge University campus in 1946, two of the twentieth-century's most notable philosophers, Ludwig Wittgenstein and Karl Popper, squared off in an intense 10-minute clash rumored to have culminated with Wittgenstein brandishing a red-hot poker. The authors explain what the fight was about and how it reflects the development of philosophy. Ivory-tower drama at its crackling best." Booklist

Includes bibliographical references

193   German and Austrian philosophy

Hegel, Georg Wilhelm Friedrich, 1770-1831
The philosophy of Hegel; edited with an introduction by Carl J. Friedrich. Modern Lib. 1954 552p o.p.; McGraw-Hill paperback available $8.55   **193**
ISBN 0-07-553655-2 (pa)
"Modern Library College editions"

Contents: The philosophy of history; The history of philosophy; The science of logic; Philosophy of right and law, or natural law and political science outlines; Lectures on aesthetics; The phenomenology of the spirit (1807); Political essays; Bibliography

Heidegger, Martin, 1889-1976
Basic writings; from Being and time (1927) to The task of thinking (1964); edited, with general introduction and introductions to each selection by David Farrell Krell. rev and expanded ed. HarperSanFrancisco 1993 452p pa $17.95   **193**
ISBN 0-06-063763-3   LC 91-58187
This anthology first published 1977 by Harper & Row

Heidegger, Martin, 1889-1976—*Continued*

Contents: Being and time: introduction; What is metaphysics?; On the essence of truth; The origin of the work of art; Letter on humanism; Modern science, metaphysics, and mathematics; The question concerning technology; Building dwelling thinking; What calls for thinking?; The way to language; The end of philosophy and the task of thinking
Includes bibliographical references

Kant, Immanuel, 1724-1804

Basic writings of Kant; edited and with an introduction by Allen W. Wood. Modern Lib. 2001 xxv, 478p pa $15.95 **193**
1. Philosophy
ISBN 0-375-75733-3   LC 2001-18303
First Modern Library edition published 1949 with title: The philosophy of Kant
This volume presents the essential works of the philosopher including "selected excerpts from his most frequently taught essays and book-length publications, including 'Critique of Pure Reason, Critique of Judgment,' and 'Eternal Peace.'" Publisher's note

Critique of pure reason   **193**
1. Theory of knowledge 2. Reason
Hardcover and paperback editions available from various publishers
Original German edition, 1781
In this philosophical work Kant "attempted to define the possibility and limits of our knowledge. He denied that we can ever know how the world 'really' is. However, he tried to show that science nevertheless has a sort of universal validity, insofar as it consists of sense experience, which comes from the world, coupled with the mind, which orders this sense experience according to the 'categories of the understanding' and the intuitions of space and time." Reader's Ency. 4th edition

Nietzsche, Friedrich Wilhelm, 1844-1900

Basic writings of Nietzsche; introduction by Peter Gay; translated and edited, with commentaries, by Walter Kaufmann. Modern Lib. 2000 xxiv, 862p pa $14.95 **193**
ISBN 0-679-78339-3   LC 00-64578
Also available hardcover 1992 edition; translated and edited by Walter Kaufmann
First Modern Library edition published 1968
"Gathers the complete texts of five of Nietzsche's most important works, from his first book to his last: The Birth of Tragedy, Beyond Good and Evil; On the Genealogy of Morals; The Case of Wagner; and Ecce Homo. . . . Included also are seventy-five aphorisms, selections from Nietzsche's correspondence, and variants from drafts for Ecce Homo." Publisher's note

The portable Nietzsche; selected and translated, with an introduction, prefaces, and notes, by Walter Kaufmann. Viking 1954 687p hardcover o.p. paperback available $17
193
ISBN 0-14-015062-5 (pa)
"The Viking portable library"
Includes the complete texts of Thus spake Zarathustra, Twilight of the idols, The antichrist, and Nietzsche contra Wagner. Selections from other works, notes and letters complete the volume

Thus spake Zarathustra   **193**
Hardcover and paperback editions available from various publishers
Written between 1883-1892
A philosophical narrative in which Nietzsche "transforms the ancient Persian philosopher Zarathustra . . . into a mouthpiece for his own views. Nietzsche develops his doctrine of the 'Übermensch' in a prophetic, quasi-biblical style. Nietzsche's Zarathustra announces the death of God, and preaches a new 'faithfulness to the earth,' which includes a new respect for the body . . . and attentiveness to this world rather than the next. He also attacks pity and virtue as weapons of weakness." Reader's Ency. 4th edition

The will to power; a new translation by Walter Kaufmann and R. J. Hollingdale; edited with commentary by Walter Kaufmann; with facsimiles of the original manuscript. Random House 1967 xxxii, 576p hardcover o.p. paperback available $16 **193**
ISBN 0-394-70437-1 (pa)
Partial contents: European nihilism: Critique of morality; The will to power as knowledge; The will to power as art; Discipline and breeding

Solomon, Robert C.

What Nietzsche really said; [by] Robert C. Solomon and Kathleen M. Higgins. Schocken Bks. 2000 263p hardcover o.p. paperback available $13   **193**
1. Nietzsche, Friedrich Wilhelm, 1844-1900
ISBN 0-8052-1094-6 (pa)   LC 99-33796
The authors offer an "overview of Friedrich Nietzsche's life, thought, and influence. . . . Particularly helpful are their brief annotations of Nietzsche's 14 books and short analyses of the thinkers who influenced him." Libr J
Includes bibliographical references

194   French philosophy

Descartes, René, 1596-1650

The philosophical writings of Descartes; translated by John Cottingham, Robert Stoothoff, Dugald Murdoch. Cambridge Univ. Press 1984-1991 3v il hardcover o.p. paperbacks available v1-2 $30; v3 $32   **194**
1. French philosophy   LC 84-9399
Also available one volume paperback edition published 1988 with title: Descartes: selected philosophical writings
Contents: v1: Early writings; Rules for the direction of the mind; The world; Treatise on man; Discourse on the method; Optics; Principles of philosophy; Comments on a certain broadsheet; Description of the human body; Passions of the soul (ISBN 0-521-28807-X); v2 Meditations; Objections and replies; Letter to Father Dinet; Search for truth (ISBN 0-521-28808-8); v3 Correspondence (ISBN 0-521-42350-3)
Includes bibliographical references

Teilhard de Chardin, Pierre

Toward the future; translated by René Hague. Harcourt Brace Jovanovich 1975 224p hardcover o.p. paperback available $13   **194**
ISBN 0-15-602819-0 (pa)
"A Helen and Kurt Wolff book"

Teilhard de Chardin, Pierre—*Continued*
Original French edition, 1973
A collection of essays written between 1929 and 1954 concerning the spiritual future of mankind. The function of art, Eastern mysticism and the concept of chastity are among the topics discussed
Includes bibliographical references

196 Spanish and Portuguese philosophy

Ortega y Gasset, José, 1883-1955
What is philosophy? translated from the Spanish by Mildred Adams. Norton 1961 c1960 252p hardcover o.p. paperback available $10.95   **196**
1. Philosophy
ISBN 0-393-00126-1 (pa)
This volume by the influential Spanish philosopher, essayist and critic "consists of a series of lectures begun in 1929 at the University of Madrid. Interrupted when the University was closed as a result of political troubles, they were resumed in a Madrid theatre. Part of the lectures had been given earlier in Buenos Aires." N Y Times Book Rev

200 RELIGION

Bowker, John, 1935-
World religions; contributing consultants: David Bowker [et al.] DK Pub. 1997 200p il maps $35   **200**
1. Religions 2. Religion
ISBN 0-7894-1439-2   LC 96-38277
Each chapter begins with an "introduction and is followed by one-or-two page sections that explain the basic tenets of the faith, symbols, events, people, buildings, works of art, and the differences and similarities to other religions. Hinduism, Buddhism, Judaism, Christianity, and Islam are included as are Jainism, Sikhism, Chinese and Japanese religions, and Native religions." SLJ

Encyclopedia of women and world religion; edited by Serinity Young. Macmillan Ref. USA 1999 2v il set $295   **200**
1. Women—Religious life—Encyclopedias
ISBN 0-02-864608-8   LC 98-39292
This work contains "more than 600 articles and more than 300 photographs with information about women in relation to most of the world's religions past and present, with emphasis on the major religions. . . . The articles are concise and evenhanded, providing brief critiques of scholarship and concluding with well-chosen bibliographies. Accessible to the general reader and a useful initial reference." Libr J

Williams, Juan
This far by faith; stories from the African-American religious experience; [by] Juan Williams and Quinton Dixie. Morrow 2003 326p il $29.95   **200**
1. African Americans—Religion 2. African Americans—History
ISBN 0-06-018863-4   LC 2002-71884
This study of African American worship "interweaves stories of individual spiritual journeys and accounts of church leaders and religious movements. The authors . . . [aim to] link blacks' faith to their ongoing fight for equality." Christ Sci Monit
"Brief topical articles and captioned illustrations supplement the main text, creating a balanced, readable, and nuanced introduction to the power of faith to sustain the African American community." Libr J

Wise women: over two thousand years of spiritual writing by women; edited by Susan Cahill. Norton 1996 xxiii, 395p hardcover o.p. paperback available $15.95   **200**
1. Spiritual life 2. Women—Religious life
ISBN 0-393-31679-3 (pa)   LC 95-40575
This anthology includes material "drawn from diverse traditions, genres, and places. . . . Each selection is prefaced by a brief biographical-historical introduction that locates the selection without presuming to tell readers how to interpret it. . . . More than half the book is devoted to material from the twentieth century." Booklist
"Cahill's collection of poems, stories, and essays is a rich and powerful testimony to the liberating power of divine love and justice in the lives of women." Libr J
Includes bibliographical references

200.3 Religion—Encyclopedias and dictionaries

The **encyclopedia** of cults, sects, and new religions; [edited by] James R. Lewis. 2nd ed. Prometheus Bks. 2002 951p il $180   **200.3**
1. Cults—Encyclopedias 2. Sects—Encyclopedias 3. United States—Religion—Encyclopedias
ISBN 1-57392-888-7   LC 2002-19180
First published 1998
This reference contains "information on approximately 1,000 religious groups, ranging from small churches with less than a hundred members (Chishti Order of America) to organizations such as the Assemblies of God that number in the millions. Most entries are relatively short. The more controversial religions, as well as religious groups that have had a high profile lately, receive more lengthy treatments. Also included are entries on broader religious movements such as the New Age and the Charismatic Movement. . . . Each article outlines the history of the group, its founders and leaders, its main teachings, and an approximate number of followers or congregations. The explanations are clearly written, interesting and understandable, without too much scholarly jargon." Booklist

The **Encyclopedia** of religion; Mircea Eliade, editor in chief. Complete and unabridged ed. Macmillan 1993 16v in 8 il set $1000
200.3
1. Religion—Encyclopedias
ISBN 0-02-897135-3   LC 93-37017
Also available CD-ROM version
First published 1987 in 16 volumes
"Treats theoretical (e.g., doctrines, myths, theologies, ethics), practical (e.g., cults, sacraments, meditations), and sociological (e.g., religious groups, ecclesiastical forms) aspects of religion; includes extensive coverage of non-Western religions. Signed articles by some 1,400 contributors worldwide end with bibliographies. Many composite entries treat two or more related topics. . . . Has quickly become the standard work." Guide to Ref Books. 11th edition

Merriam-Webster's encyclopedia of world religions; Wendy Doniger, consulting editor. Merriam-Webster 1999 1181p il $49.95   **200.3**
1. Religions—Encyclopedias
ISBN 0-87779-044-2   LC 99-33147
Arranged alphabetically this reference includes "entries for contemporary, historical, and legendary figures; movements; deities and supernatural characters; ritual implements; sacred scriptures; important religious places; and theological and philosophical concepts. Thirty . . . essays provide expanded coverage of major world religions, including Buddhism, Christianity, Hinduism, Islam, and Judaism. Tribal, primal, and ancient religions are also detailed." Booklist

The **Oxford** dictionary of world religions; edited by John Bowker. Oxford Univ. Press 1997 xxiv, 1111p $70   **200.3**
1. Religion—Dictionaries 2. Religions—Dictionaries
ISBN 0-19-213965-7   LC 97-166787
"World religions here include Christianity, Judaism, Islam, Buddhism, Hinduism, Sikhism, Zoroastrianism, various Chinese and Japanese religions, and what are defined as 'other' religions. The 8,200 entries focus on ideas, people, and texts important for each religion and are arranged alphabetically." Choice

200.9 Religion—Historical and geographic treatment

Balmer, Randall Herbert
Religion in twentieth century America; [by] Randall Balmer. Oxford Univ. Press 2001 142p il (Religion in American life) $22
200.9
1. United States—Religion
ISBN 0-19-511295-4   LC 00-60674
The author "traces the evolution of various movements, including the Pentecostal, Fundamentalist, Evangelical, and New Age movements, the emergence of the Religious Right, Promise Keepers, and televangelism." Booklist
"This title is accessible and reliable, brief and lively, and makes a fine addition to most libraries." SLJ
Includes bibliographical references

Bourne, Russell
Gods of war, gods of peace; how the meeting of native and colonial religions shaped early America. Harcourt 2002 425p il $28   **200.9**
1. United States—Religion
ISBN 0-15-100501-X   LC 2001-5952
The author "explores the religious interactions of Anglo Americans and Native Americans from 1635 through the 1830s and shows how their religions influenced each other in the shaping of the new nation. . . . This work offers a highly readable and valuable depiction of the possibilities and tragic failures of early American history as influenced and even created by religious faith." Libr J
Includes bibliographical references

Butler, Jon, 1940-
Religion in American life; a short history; [by] Jon Butler, Grant Wacker, and Randall Balmer. Oxford Univ. Press 2002 568p il $35
200.9
1. United States—Religion
ISBN 0-19-515824-5   LC 2002-14481
This volume begins by describing the state of religious affairs in the old and new worlds. The survey continues with a look at the religious landscape of 19th-century America and concludes with an examination of current religious beliefs and practices
Includes bibliographical references

The **Cambridge** illustrated history of religions; edited by John Bowker. Cambridge Univ. Press 2002 336p il (Cambridge illustrated history) $40   **200.9**
1. Religions
ISBN 0-521-81037-X   LC 2001-37866
"The major religions get thoroughgoing treatment, with short introductions also given to the Zoroastrianism; the religions of Greece, Rome, Egypt, and Mesopotamia; aboriginal religions; and new religious movements. . . . Christianity receives a separate chapter as well as substantial treatment in chapters on Chinese, Korean, and Japanese religions. . . . This volume presents a large amount of information in an engaging way, offering much scholarly insight for the lay reader." Libr J
Includes bibliographical references

Contemporary American religion; Wade Clark Roof, editor in chief. Macmillan Ref. USA 2000 2v set $275   **200.9**
1. United States—Religion—Encyclopedias
ISBN 0-02-864928-1   LC 99-46712
"This work describes various aspects of religious life in America from 1965 to the present. Each signed entry offers a . . . discussion of the topic followed by see-also references and a bibliography. Major religions and smaller and fringe groups are represented as are individual, symbols, traditions, beliefs, and practices." SLJ
For a fuller review see: Booklist, May 1, 2000

Corrigan, John
Religion in America; an historical account of the development of American religious life; [by] John Corrigan, Winthrop S. Hudson. Prentice-Hall pa $50.67   **200.9**
1. United States—Religion
First published 1965 with authors' names in reverse order. (7th edition 2003) Periodically revised

Corrigan, John—*Continued*

A survey of American religious life from 1607 to the present

Includes bibliographical references

Encyclopedia of African American religions; edited by Larry G. Murphy, J. Gordon Melton, Gary L. Ward. Garland 1993 lxxvi, 926p (Religious information systems series) $90   **200.9**

1. African Americans—Religion—Encyclopedias
2. United States—Religion—Encyclopedias

ISBN 0-8153-0500-1   LC 93-7224

This "encyclopedia includes three types of entries: biographical sketches of 773 African American religious leaders; 341 entries on African American denominations and religious organizations (including white churches with significant black memberships and educational institutions); and topical articles on . . . aspects of African American religious life." Booklist

Encyclopedia of fundamentalism; Brenda E. Brasher, editor. Routledge 2001 558p il (Religion and society) $125   **200.9**

1. Religious fundamentalism

ISBN 0-415-92244-5   LC 2001-19951

"A Berkshire Reference work"

This reference covers "fundamentalism, from definition, history, and beliefs to movements and churches, significant individuals, and expressions in various world religions. Creationism, fascism, rock music, and the Taliban are a sample of the topics covered. The contributors provide clear, readable explanations. . . . This beautifully laid-out work is the one to have." Libr J

For a fuller review see: Booklist, Feb. 15, 2002

Gaustad, Edwin Scott

New historical atlas of religion in America; by Edwin Scott Gaustad and Philip L. Barlow; with the special assistance of Richard W. Dishno. Oxford Univ. Press 2001 xxiii, 435p maps $160   **200.9**

1. United States—Church history 2. United States—Religion

ISBN 0-19-509168-X   LC 00-30001

First published 1976 with title: Historical atlas of religion in America

"A completely reorganized, updated, and expanded edition of Gaustad's 1962 original work and the 1976 revision, this beautifully illustrated atlas presents a historical narrative of America's rich and diverse religious past. Lively text along with 260 colorful, detailed maps and 200 other graphics provide the histories, migration, developments, and growths of religious communities in the United States."—"Outstanding Reference Sources." Am Libr

Gooch, Brad, 1952-

Godtalk: travels in spiritual America. Knopf 2002 xxiii, 388p $25   **200.9**

1. United States—Religion

ISBN 0-679-44709-1   LC 2001-38828

This report on the spiritual scenes in America includes "readers of the Urantia Book, followers of Deepak Chopra and Gurumayi Chidvilasananda, communities of Trappists and Trappistines, gay churches and Jerry Falwell's interaction with them and Muslims in New York City." Publ Wkly

"Gooch is a sophisticated spiritual tourist, and this travelogue is an engaging account of a journey driven, as he tells one person he interviews, by deep whim." Booklist

Includes bibliographical references

Hahn, Kristin

In search of grace; a religious outsider's journey across America's landscape of faith. Morrow 2002 302p $24.95   **200.9**

1. United States—Religion

ISBN 0-380-97701-X   LC 2001-44765

The author "made a journey through America's religious landscape to try to understand not so much theology as practice. She immersed herself in long interviews with believers of almost 20 different religions, from mainstream to alternative, and often joined them in some aspect of their ritual practices." Publ Wkly

"This absolutely fascinating account of one woman's search for spiritual fulfillment also serves as an enlightening overview of the positive power of religious diversity." Booklist

Includes bibliographical references

Jenkins, Philip, 1952-

Mystics and messiahs; cults and new religions in American history. Oxford Univ. Press 2000 294p $39; pa $15.95   **200.9**

1. Cults 2. United States—Religion

ISBN 0-19-512744-7; 0-19-514596-8 (pa)

LC 99-28732

"Jenkins argues that cults are . . . the cutting edge of religious development. Loaded with intriguing sketches of dozens of cults and distinguished by Jenkins' healthily nonjudgmental attitude, this is a superb historical primer." Booklist

Melton, J. Gordon

American religions; an illustrated history. ABC-CLIO 2000 316p il $99   **200.9**

1. United States—Religion

ISBN 1-57607-222-3   LC 00-11924

"Beginning with Native American religions, Melton traces American religious history from Colonial times to the present. . . . While the coverage is necessarily quite brief at each point, bibliographies are provided, and the text is highly readable and accurate. With its unbiased, even celebrative attitude toward religious diversity, this makes a good basic text or popular history." Libr J

The encyclopedia of American religions. Gale Res. $290   **200.9**

1. United States—Religion 2. Sects

First published 1978 by McGrath Publishing Company. (7th edition 2002) Periodically revised

"Presents coverage of more than 2,500 North American religious groups in the U.S. and Canada, from Adventists to Zen Buddhists. Entries contain essays and directory listings that describe the historical development of religious families and give . . . information about each group within those families, including, where available, headquarter location, membership figures, a listing of educational facilities and information on periodicals published by the group." Publisher's note

Moore, R. Laurence (Robert Laurence), 1940-

Selling God; American religion in the marketplace of culture. Oxford Univ. Press 1994 317p hardcover o.p. paperback available $19.95 **200.9**
1. United States—Religion
ISBN 0-19-509838-2 (pa)   LC 93-19624
"Moore traces the history of marketing techniques in American religion. The first amendment ban on state religion necessitated a competitive approach. Moore asserts that religion 'had to sell itself not only in the competitive church market, but also in a general market of other cultural commodities.'" Libr J
The author "is balanced and nonpedantic, treating religion as a cultural element of history." N Y Times Book Rev
Includes bibliographical references

Queen, Edward L.

The encyclopedia of American religious history; [by] Edward L. Queen II, Stephen R. Prothero, and Gardiner H. Shattuck, Jr.; foreword by Martin E. Marty, editorial advisor. rev ed. Facts on File 2001 2v set $137.50 **200.9**
1. United States—Religion—Encyclopedias
ISBN 0-8160-4335-3   LC 00-69512
First published 1995
This reference source presents over 500 articles, ranging from a few hundred words to approximately 9,000 examining different religions, religious leaders, events, and other topics that helped shape the history of religion in America. The coverage extends from Puritan America to the moral majority
This "is an excellent and readable resource for the study of the history of religion in the U.S." Booklist

Wilson, A. N. (Andrew Norman), 1950-

God's funeral. Norton 1999 402p il $27.95 **200.9**
1. Religion and science
ISBN 0-393-04745-8   LC 99-21306
"Wilson points out that the 19th century provided the context for various theories of God's demise. Wilson profiles some of the century's most famous intellectual challengers to faith, especially Darwin, George Eliot, James, Marx and Engels." Publ Wkly
"This is a stunning and provocative work, not necessarily in its scope but in its readability and its well-developed analysis." Libr J
Includes bibliographical references

Wuthnow, Robert

After heaven; spirituality in America since the 1950s. University of Calif. Press 1998 277p hardcover o.p. paperback available $18.95 **200.9**
1. United States—Religion
ISBN 0-520-22228-8 (pa)   LC 97-45121
The author "argues that American spirituality since the 1950s has shifted from a spirituality of dwelling to a spirituality of seeking. A spirituality of seeking centers on practices more than places and is marked by a loosening of attachments not only to geographical parishes but to territorially based denominations. . . . Wuthnow's cogent argument and his accessible narrative make appealing reading." Publ Wkly
Includes bibliographical references

210 Philosophy and theory of religion

Huxley, Aldous, 1894-1963

The perennial philosophy. Harper & Row 1945 312p hardcover o.p. paperback available $14 **210**
1. Philosophy and religion 2. Religion—Philosophy
ISBN 0-06-090191-8 (pa)
Analyzed in Essay and general literature index
An anthology of and commentary on Chinese, Latin, Greek, Catholic and Protestant mysticism
Includes bibliographical references

James, William, 1842-1910

The varieties of religious experience; study in human nature **210**
1. Religion—Philosophy 2. Psychology 3. Conversion
Hardcover and paperback editions available from various publishers
First published 1902 by Longman
"Based on material James had collected on the psychology and philosophy of religion for lectures at the University of Edinburgh in 1901 and 1902. *The varieties of religious experience* contains numerous descriptions of religious states of consciousness, which James presented from a pragmatic point of view." HarperCollins Reader's Ency of Am Lit. 2nd edition

Schweitzer, Albert, 1875-1965

The words of Albert Schweitzer; selected by Norman Cousins. Newmarket Press 1984 110p il $14.95 **210**
1. Quotations
ISBN 0-937858-41-2   LC 84-18890
Quotations from Schweitzer's speeches and writings on reverence for life, faith, music, civilization, peace, and other topics

211 Concepts of God

Turner, James, 1946-

Without God, without creed; the origins of unbelief in America. Johns Hopkins Univ. Press 1985 316p (New studies in American intellectual and cultural history) hardcover o.p. paperback available $20.95 **211**
1. Religion 2. Faith
ISBN 0-8018-3407-4 (pa)   LC 84-15397
The author traces the development of agnosticism and atheism in the United States
"Mr. Turner allows us to see clearly the decline of transcendental Christianity and its replacement by ever softer religions and ever harder systems of social metaphysics." N Y Times Book Rev
Includes bibliographical references

212 Existence, knowability, attributes of God

Adler, Mortimer J., 1902-2001
How to think about God; a guide for the 20th-century pagan. Macmillan 1980 175p hardcover o.p. paperback available $13   **212**
1. God
ISBN 0-02-016022-4 (pa)   LC 79-25098
"The central question to which the book addresses itself is whether or not God exists—whether or not there is anything in reality that corresponds to the notion we have of God. Dr. Adler examines and refutes several traditional arguments, proposing instead his own theory." Publisher's note
Includes bibliographical references

215 Science and religion

Johnson, George, 1952-
Fire in the mind; science, faith, and the search for order. Knopf 1995 379p maps hardcover o.p. paperback available $15   **215**
1. Religion and science 2. New Mexico—Description
ISBN 0-679-74021-X (pa)   LC 94-38382
"At New Mexico's Los Alamos National Laboratory and the Santa Fe Institute, cutting-edge scientists explore theories that . . . have resonances within the traditional cultures of the region's Native American and Spanish cultures. Johnson shows how both science and mythology strive to express the inexpressible." Libr J
"This complex and gracefully written book has much to say to both the general reader and the scientific specialist. It also reminds us of how the professional science writer has emerged as a 'cultural broker' for modern times." Choice
Includes bibliographical references

Schroeder, Gerald L.
The hidden face of God; how science reveals the ultimate truth. Free Press 2001 224p $26   **215**
1. Religion and science
ISBN 0-684-87059-2   LC 00-50363
Also available in paperback from Touchstone Bks.
The author contends that "from cosmology to neurology, the latest research makes sense only if viewed from a metaphysical perspective. The strict materialism that excludes all purpose, choice, and spirituality from the world simply cannot account for the data pouring in from labs and observatories." Booklist

Smith, Huston
Why religion matters; the fate of the human spirit in an age of disbelief. HarperSanFrancisco 2001 290p hardcover o.p. paperback available $14.95   **215**
1. Religion and science
ISBN 0-06-067102-5 (pa)   LC 00-58188
"Smith claims humanity is in the grip of a spiritual crisis. The cause: scientism, the modern belief, enforced by education and law, that the scientific method is the most reliable path to truth and that the material entities science deals with are the only things that exist. . . . What [Smith] opposes is the extension of scientific conclusions into areas of human experience about which, [he believes], science can tell us nothing." Chirst Sci Monit

220 Bible

The **Oxford** illustrated history of the Bible; edited by John Rogerson. Oxford Univ. Press 2001 395p il $40   **220**
1. Bible—History
ISBN 0-19-860118-2   LC 2001-272513
This volume offers an "overview of the origins of the Bible we know (consisting of the Old and New Testaments and the Apocrypha), the transmission and translation of the texts, and the historical and contemporary interpretation and influence of the Bible. Enhancing this overview are numerous color and black-and-white illustrations." Libr J

220.1 Bible—Origins and authenticity

Gomes, Peter John, 1942-
The good book; reading the Bible with mind and heart; [by] Peter J. Gomes. Morrow 1996 383p o.p.; HarperSanFrancisco paperback available $14.95   **220.1**
1. Bible—Criticism
ISBN 0-06-008830-3 (pa)   LC 96-32069
"The author begins by briefly explaining to the generalist the basics about the Bible's text, composition, canonicity, and the like. He then tackles what the Bible has to say or not say about 12 challenging topics including race, women, homosexuality, wealth, and science. Gomes succeeds in keeping the reader's attention with an approach that is honest, down-to-earth, personal, and thoughtful, and not preachy, pietistic, or fundamentalist." Libr J
Includes bibliographical references

Sheler, Jeffery L.
Is the Bible true? how modern debates and discoveries affirm the essence of the Scriptures. HarperSanFrancisco 1999 278p hardcover o.p. paperback available $15   **220.1**
1. Jesus Christ—Historicity 2. Bible—History of contemporary events 3. Bible—Antiquities
ISBN 0-06-0675420-X (pa)   LC 99-16882
The author explores the "reliability of the Bible as a historical source. Drawing on both the literature and personal interviews with leading scholars he describes the history of biblical interpretation and research, the evidence of archaeology, the nature and relevance of the Dead Sea Scrolls, and the three 'quests for the historical Jesus.'" Libr J
Includes bibliographical references

220.3 Bible—Encyclopedias and topical dictionaries

The **Anchor** Bible dictionary; David Noel Freedman, editor-in-chief; associate editors, Gary A. Herion, David F. Graf, John David Pleins; managing editor, Astrid B. Beck. Doubleday 1992 6v il maps set $360
220.3

1. Bible—Dictionaries
ISBN 0-385-42583-X   LC 91-8385
Contents: v1 A-C; v2 D-G; v3 H-J; v4 K-N; v5 O-Sh; v6 Si-Z
"The 6,000 separate subject entries reflect many of the changes that have taken place in biblical research over the last 30 years. . . . There are individual entries for all the different books of the Bible, major figures, places, names, and biblical terms. Substantial bibliographics and numerous cross references enhance the usefulness of this as a reference source." Am Libr
"With its sound scholarship, good organization, and readable prose, the ABD deserves a place in all academic and public libraries." Libr J

Eerdmans dictionary of the Bible; David Noel Freedman, editor-in-chief; Allen C. Myers, associate editor; Astrid B. Beck, managing editor. Eerdmans 2000 xxxiii, 1425p il maps $45   **220.3**
1. Bible—Dictionaries
ISBN 0-8028-2400-5   LC 00-56124
This "dictionary contains nearly 5,000 alphabetically ordered articles by 600 biblical scholars on the books, persons, places and significant terms found in the Bible." America
"Up-to-date, comprehensive, and well written, the *EDB* is highly recommended." Libr J

The **HarperCollins** Bible dictionary; general editor, Paul J. Achtemeier; associate editors, Roger S. Boraas [et al.] with the Society of Biblical Literature. HarperSanFrancisco 1996 xxiv, 1256p il $47   **220.3**
1. Bible—Dictionaries
ISBN 0-06-060037-3   LC 96-25424
First published 1985 with title: Harper's Bible dictionary
This volume features a "two-column format, with 16 single-column articles interspersed throughout (including 'Art in the Biblical Period,' 'Jesus Christ,' and 'The temple'), and it is well illustrated. Many of the longer articles include a brief bibliography. . . . Though not a flawless work (e.g., the article 'Manasseh' treats only the 14th king of Judah but neither the patriarch nor the tribe of Israel that also bear the name), it is outstanding in terms of scholarship and writing." Libr J

The **Interpreter's** dictionary of the Bible. Abingdon Press 1962-1976 5v il maps set $175   **220.3**
1. Bible—Encyclopedias
ISBN 0-687-19268-4
Volumes 1-4 edited by George Arthur Buttrick. Supplementary volume (v5) published 1976 and edited by Keith Crim, available separately for $45 (ISBN 0-687-19269-2)

"An illustrated encyclopedia identifying and explaining all proper names and significant terms and subjects in the Holy Scriptures, including the Apocrypha, with attention to archaeological discoveries and researches into the life and faith of ancient times." Subtitle
"A scholarly encyclopedic dictionary designed for the preacher, scholar, student, teacher, and general reader, referring to both the King James Version and the Revised Standard Version, to the Apocrypha, the Pseudepigrapha, the Dead Sea Scrolls, and other ancient manuscripts. . . . Important for modern biblical study." Guide to Ref Books. 11th edition

The **Oxford** companion to the Bible; edited by Bruce M. Metzger, Michael D. Coogan. Oxford Univ. Press 1993 xxi, 874p il maps $65   **220.3**
1. Bible—Dictionaries
ISBN 0-19-504645-5   LC 93-19315
This volume "contains more than 700 signed entries treating the formation, transmission, circulation, sociohistorical situation, interpretation, theology, uses, and influence of the Bible." Libr J
"The many contributors read as a veritable who's who among biblical scholars. Although this companion is not meant to be an exhaustive reference, it is a highly reliable guide." Booklist

The **Oxford** guide to ideas & issues of the Bible; edited by Bruce M. Metzger, Michael D. Coogan. Oxford Univ. Press 2001 xxi, 585p $35   **220.3**
1. Bible—Dictionaries
ISBN 0-19-514917-3   LC 2001-37039
This volume includes over "two hundred alphabetically-arranged entries that explore key aspects of the Bible and its teachings. The contributors examine what the Bible says about timeless issues such as adultery and abortion, divorce and drunkenness, marriage and murder, suffering and temptation; and they discuss religious concepts found in the Bible, ranging from incarnation, sin, and grace, to baptism, ethics, and the Holy Spirit." Publisher's note

220.5 Bible—Modern versions

Bible
The Anchor Bible. Doubleday 1964-2003 78v apply to publisher for price and availability   **220.5**
Contents: v1 Genesis; v2 Exodus 1-18; v3 Leviticus 1-16; v3A Leviticus 17-22; v3B Leviticus 23-27; v4 Numbers 1-20; v4A Numbers 21-36; v5 Deuteronomy 1-11; v6 Joshua; v6A Judges; v7 Ruth; v7A Lamentations, rev. ed; v7B Esther; v7C Song of songs; v8 I Samuel; v9 II Samuel; v10 I Kings; v11 II Kings; v12 I Chronicles; v13 II Chronicles; v14 Ezra & Nehemiah; v15 Job; v16 Psalms I: 1-50; v17 Psalms II: 51-100; v17A Psalms III: 101-150; v18A Proverbs 1-9; v18C Ecclesiastes; v19 Isaiah 1-39; v19A Isaiah 40-55; v20 II Isaiah; v21A Jeremiah 1-20; v21B Jeremiah 21-36; v22 Ezekiel 1-20; v22A Ezekiel 21-37; v23 The book of Daniel; v24 Hosea; v24A Amos; v24B Jonah; v24C Joel; v24D Obadiah; v24E Micah; v25 Habakkuk; v25A Zephaniah; v25B Haggai, Zechariah 1-8; v25C Zechariah 9-14; v25D Malachi; v26 Matthew; v27 Mark; v28 Luke 1-9; v28A Luke 10-24; v29 John 1-12; v29A John 13-21; v30 Epistles of John; v31 Acts of the Apostles; v32 I Corinthians; v32A

Bible—*Continued*

II Corinthians; v33 Romans; v33A Galatians; v34 Ephesians 1-3; v34A Ephesians 4-6; v34B Colossians; v34C The letter to Philemon; v35 The letter to Titus; v35A The first and second letters to Timothy; v36 Hebrews; v37A Letter of James; v37B 1 Peter; v37C 2 Peter, Jude; v38 Revelation; v39 The wisdom of Ben Sira; v40 Judith; v40A Tobit; v41 I Maccabees; v41A II Maccabees; v42 I and II Esdras; v43 The wisdom of Solomon; v46 Daniel, Esther and Jeremiah: the additions

"A project of Protestant, Catholic, and Jewish scholars. Offers new translations of the books of the Bible with extensive commentary." Guide to Ref Books. 11th edition

Good news Bible; today's English version. American Bible Soc. prices vary   **220.5**

Available in various bindings and editions

"Begun in 1964 with the Gospel of Mark, The New Testament was completed in 1966, with rev. eds. in 1971 and 1976. The whole Bible was published in 1976. An extremely popular, inexpensive translation using contemporary American English. . . . Especially useful for youth or lay Bible study as well as for private reading." Bollier. Lit of Theology

The HarperCollins study Bible; New Revised Standard Version, with the Apocraphal/Deuterocanonical books; general editor, Wayne A. Meeks; associate editors, Jouette M. Bassler [et al.] with the Society of Biblical Literature. HarperSanFrancisco 1993 xl, 2355p il maps $42   **220.5**

ISBN 0-06-065580-1   LC 92-56127

"This edition of the Bible—newly annotated by the Society of Biblical Studies—is definitely for a wide audience. It is interdenominational, incorporates the latest in biblical scholarship, and is sensitive to unnecessary gender specificity." Booklist

The Holy Bible; containing the Old and New Testaments; translated out of the original tongues; and with the former translations diligently compared and revised by King James's special command, 1611. Oxford Univ. Press prices vary   **220.5**

Available in various bindings and editions

The authorized or King James Version originally published 1611

The Holy Bible: new revised standard version; containing the Old and New Testaments with the Apocryphal/Deuterocanonical books. Nelson, T. prices vary   **220.5**

Available in various bindings and editions

This version first published 1989

"Intended for public reading, congregational worship, private study, instruction, and meditation, it attempts to be as literal as possible while following standard American English usage, avoids colloquialism, and prefers simple, direct terms and phrases." Sheehy. Guide to Ref Books. 10th edition. suppl

Holy Bible: the new King James Version; containing the Old and New Testaments. Nelson, T. prices vary   **220.5**

Available in various bindings and editions including large print edition

This version first published 1982

"Protestant. This edition replaces 17th Century verb forms and second person pronouns. Updates archaic terms. Psalms and Job appear as poetry." N Y Public Libr. Ref Books for Child Collect. 2d edition

The new American Bible; with revised New Testament; translated from the original languages, with critical use of all the ancient sources by members of the Catholic Biblical Association of America; sponsored by the Bishops' Committee of the Confraternity of Christian Doctrine.   **220.5**

Available in various bindings and editions from various publishers

First published 1970 by Kenedy

"Roman Catholic version based on modern English translations; replaces the Douay edition." N Y Public Libr Book of How & Where to Look It Up

New American standard Bible   **220.5**

Available in various bindings and editions from various publishers

This translation, completed 1971, is a modernization of the American Standard Version of 1901

The new Jerusalem Bible. Doubleday prices vary   **220.5**

Available in various bindings and editions

First published in this format 1966 with title: The Jerusalem Bible

General editor: Henry Wansbrough

"Derives from the French version edited at the Dominican Ecole Biblique de Jerusalem and known as 'La Bible de Jerusalem.' The introductions and notes are 'a direct translation from the French, though revised and brought up to date in some places' but translation of the Biblical text goes back to the original languages." Guide to Ref Books. 11th edition

The new Oxford annotated Bible; new revised standard version. Oxford Univ. Press prices vary   **220.5**

Available in various bindings with and without the Apocrypha

This study Bible incorporates the full text of the New revised standard version translation, with cross-referenced annotations, a collection of essays and introductions, and a section of maps

The revised English Bible. Oxford Univ. Press; Cambridge Univ. Press 1989 prices vary   **220.5**

Available in various bindings with and without the Apocrypha

A revised edition of The new English Bible, published 1970

This version is based upon a re-examination of the original Greek, Hebrew, and Aramaic texts, and is written in contemporary English

Bobrick, Benson, 1947-

Wide as the waters; the story of the English Bible and the revolution it inspired. Simon & Schuster 2001 379p il $26   **220.5**

1. Bible—History 2. Bible—Versions

ISBN 0-684-84747-7   LC 00-66174

"In surveying the translators and translations that paved the way for the King James Version, Bobrick rightly combines the history of translation with that of a political process that included key developments in the forging of Anglo-American democracy. The period under consideration runs from the end of the fourteenth century to the beginning of the seventeenth—that is, from Wycliffe to Tyndale and Coverdale to King James." Booklist

Includes bibliographical references

Cruden, Alexander, 1701-1770

Cruden's Complete concordance to the Old and New Testaments   **220.5**

1. Bible—Concordances

Hardcover and paperback editions available from various publishers

First edition 1737. Frequently revised

"The special value of this title is that Cruden provides an index to the Apocrypha. Note that some reprints of the work omit the Apocrypha in the concordance." Ref Sources for Small & Medium-sized Libr. 5th edition

McGrath, Alister E., 1953-

In the beginning; the story of the King James Bible. Doubleday 2001 340p il $24.95; pa $15   **220.5**

1. Bible—History 2. Bible—Versions

ISBN 0-385-49890-X; 0-385-572216-8 (pa)

LC 00-60348

The author recounts the production of the King James translation, "the forces that allowed for its genesis and its influence on modern English, the history of England and the faith of millions since its 1604 publication." Publ Wkly

Includes bibliographical references

Nicolson, Adam, 1957-

God's secretaries: the making of the King James Bible. HarperCollins Pubs. 2003 280p il $24.95   **220.5**

1. James I, King of Great Britain, 1566-1625 2. Bible—History 3. Bible—Versions

ISBN 0-06-018516-3

First published in the United Kingdom with title: Power and glory

"The English Bible that King James I commissioned in 1604 really was committee work. Each of six committees, or companies, as they were called, was charged with translating a different portion of the original Hebrew and Greek texts. . . . Their handiwork was to be the preferred pulpit Bible, so it had to be accessible in vocabulary and tonally. In that respect, the Translators succeeded so brilliantly that their style remains the quintessence of sacred prose to this day. . . . Nicolson tells the KJV's story so well that his book may prove to be the KJV's indispensable companion for years to come." Booklist

Includes bibliographical references

Strong, James, 1822-1894

The strongest Strong's exhaustive concordance of the Bible. 21st century ed, fully rev and corrected by John R. Kohlenberger III and James A. Swanson. Zondervan 2001 1742p maps $34.99   **220.5**

1. Bible—Concordances

ISBN 0-310-23343-7   LC 2001-26577

Also available large print edition $39.99 (ISBN 0-310-24697-0)

A version of Strong's exhaustive concordance of the Bible originally published 1894

"Kohlenberger has teamed with James A. Swanson to produce a volume that cross-indexes a . . . database with exhaustive Hebrew and Greek dictionaries and adds *Nave's Topical Bible Reference System* (essentially a Bible dictionary with subjects, persons, places, and biblical books in alphabetic order). . . . Charts plot the chronology of events in the Old and New Testament, miracles and parables of Jesus, and messianic prophecies. There is a harmony (parallels) of gospel stories, lists of biblical kings, weights and measures, Old Testament feasts, sacred days, sacrifices, and the major social concerns of the Mosaic Covenant. There is also a chart of the Hebrew Calendar. The work is based on the King James Version of the Bible and is generally conservative." Am Ref Books Annu, 2003

220.6 Bible—Interpretation and criticism

Bowker, John, 1935-

The complete Bible handbook; an illustrated companion. DK Pub. 1998 544p il maps $39.95; pa $25   **220.6**

1. Bible—Commentaries

ISBN 0-7894-3568-3; 0-7894-8154-5 (pa)

LC 98-4478

In this volume "every book of the Bible (including Jewish Apocrypha) has its own entry, and there are supplementary entries on specific stories, theological concerns, history (Routes of the Exodus), or background (Gods and Goddesses of the Ancient Near East). In his introduction, Bowker presents a well-balanced summary of the Bible as a piece of literature and as scripture in our time and in history. . . . One of the book's strengths is its abundance of pictures." Voice Youth Advocates

Davis, Kenneth C.

Don't know much about the Bible; everything you need to know about the Good Book but never learned. Eagle Brook 1998 xxiv, 533p $25   **220.6**

1. Bible—Study and teaching

ISBN 0-688-14884-0   LC 98-16744

Also available in paperback from Avon

"David analyzes the Bible book by book, asking and answering a succession of perplexing questions. . . . In addition, he also traces the actual evolution of the Good Book itself, placing many biblical stories more firmly in historical context. Brimming with fascinating facts and fresh interpretations." Booklist

Includes bibliographical references

220.7 Bible—Commentaries

The **HarperCollins** Bible commentary; general editor, James L. Mays; associate editors, Joseph Blenkinsopp [et al.]; with the Society of Biblical Literature. rev ed. HarperSanFrancisco 2000 xxvi, 1203p il $49.50 **220.7**
1. Bible—Commentaries
ISBN 0-06-065548-8 LC 00-20818

First published 1988 with title: Harper's Bible commentary

This "covers all of the Hebrew Bible, as well as the books of the Apocrypha and those of the New Testament. . . . [It includes] general essays setting the literary, cultural, and historical context for the entire Bible; articles introducing major sections of the Bible [and] commentaries on the individual books themselves." Publisher's note

This work is "outstanding in terms of scholarship and writing." Libr J

Includes bibliographical references

The **New** Interpreter's Bible; general articles & introduction, commentary, & reflections for each book of the Bible, including the Apocryphal/Deuterocanonical books. Abingdon Press 1994-2003 12v set $780 **220.7**
1. Bible—Commentaries
ISBN 0-687-06347-7 LC 94-21092

First published 1951-1957 with title: The Interpreter's Bible

Full texts and critical notes of the New International Version and the New Revised Standard Version of the Bible in parallel columns

Contents: v1 General and Old Testament articles; Genesis; Exodus; and Leviticus; v2 Numbers; Deuteronomy; Introduction to narrative literature; Joshua; Judges; Ruth; 1 & 2 Samuel; v3 1 & 2 Kings; 1 & 2 Chronicles; Ezra; Nehemiah; Esther; Tobit; Judith; v4 Introduction to Hebrew poetry;1 & 2 Maccabees; Psalms; Job; v5 Introduction to wisdom literature; Proverbs; Ecclesiastes; v6 Introduction to prophetic literature; Isaiah; Jeremiah; Baruch; Letter of Jeremiah; Lamentations; Ezekiel; v7 Introduction to apocalyptic literature; Daniel;the twelve prophets; v8 General articles on the New Testament; Matthew; Mark; v9 Luke; John; v10 Acts; Introduction to epistolary literature; Romans; 1 Corinthians; v11 2 Corinthians; Galatians; Ephesians; Philippians; Colossians; 1 & 2 Thessalonians; 1 & 2 Timothy; Titus; Philemon; v12 Hebrews; James; 1&2 Peter; 1, 2, & 3 John, Jude; Revelation

Oxford Bible commentary; edited by John Barton and John Muddiman. Oxford Univ. Press 2001 xxv, 1386p maps $65 **220.7**
1. Bible—Commentaries
ISBN 0-19-875500-7 LC 2001-21139

A team of scholars "examine the books of the Bible . . . taking a historical-critical approach that attempts to shed light on the scriptures by placing them in the context in which their first audiences would have encountered them, asking how they came to be composed and what were the purposes of their authors." Publisher's note

"An international, interfaith group of scholars is responsible for this rich, far-reaching commentary, which is most profitably studied alongside a copy of the New Revised Standard Version upon which it is based." Choice

Reader's digest complete guide to the Bible; an illustrated book-by-book companion to the Scriptures. Reader's Digest Assn. 1998 448p il maps $29.95 **220.7**
1. Bible—Commentaries
ISBN 0-7621-0073-7 LC 98-6836

This volume describes events, people, and themes of the Bible, and includes approximately 400 color illustrations and 25 maps and charts

220.8 Nonreligious subjects treated in Bible

Murphy, Cullen
The Word according to Eve; women and the Bible in ancient times and our own. Houghton Mifflin 1998 302p $24; pa $14 **220.8**
1. Bible—Criticism 2. Women in the Bible 3. Feminism
ISBN 0-395-70113-9; 0-618-00192-1 (pa)
LC 98-18015

"A Peter Davison book"

This is an examination of feminist Biblical scholarship. Murphy "divides his study into Old Testament scholarship and New Testament and early church history." N Y Times Book Rev

Includes bibliographical references

220.9 Bible—Geography, history, biography, stories

Calvocoressi, Peter
Who's who in the Bible. Viking 1987 xxxi, 269p maps hardcover o.p. paperback available $19.95 **220.9**
1. Bible—Biography
ISBN 0-14-051262-8 (pa) LC 87-50540

"This work provides profiles, ranging in length from a sentence to several pages, of some 450 biblical characters. It is unusual in discussing the literature, visual arts, and music associated with many of these characters." Libr J

The **Cambridge** companion to the Bible; [by] Howard Clark Kee [et al.] Cambridge Univ. Press 1997 616p il maps $60 **220.9**
1. Bible—History of Biblical events
ISBN 0-521-34369-0 LC 96-43914

"This work offers materials that are designed to give background to and interpretations of the canonical and apocryphal books of the Old and New Testaments as well as of selected pseudographical books. Four specialists present their ideas in four main subdivisions: introduction, Old Testament world, Jewish responses to Greco-Roman culture, and formation of the Christian community." Libr J

"This is an excellent, single-volume resource for serious students of the Bible. . . . The text is generally accessible; extensive maps and illustrations add to its popular appeal." Booklist

Deen, Edith

All of the women of the Bible. Harper & Row 1955 xxii, 410p hardcover o.p. paperback available $19 **220.9**

1. Bible—Biography 2. Women in the Bible
ISBN 0-06-061852-3 (pa)

"Good or bad, they are all here: three hundred and sixteen of them. They are not vague historical personages but living women whom we get to know well. Most of the portraits are preceded by the Bible chapters and verses which are the sources and by an outline sketch that establishes the background." Cincinnati Public Libr

The **HarperCollins** concise atlas of the Bible; edited by James B. Pritchard. HarperSanFrancisco 1997 c1991 151p il maps pa $25 **220.9**

1. Bible—Geography 2. Bible—History of biblical events
ISBN 0-06-251499-7

First published 1991 with title: The Harper concise atlas of the Bible

Based upon Harper atlas of the Bible (1987)

This atlas offers "access to the current knowledge of the historical geography of the Bible. . . . The arrangement is chronological, and uses maps, charts, and artwork to visually stimulate its multidisciplinary text." Libr J

The **Oxford** history of the biblical world; edited by Michael D. Coogan. Oxford Univ. Press 1998 643p il maps $60; pa $19.95 **220.9**

1. Bible—History of biblical events 2. Ancient civilization
ISBN 0-19-508707-0; 0-19-513937-2 (pa)
LC 98-16042

"Organized chronologically, the essays explore the many cultures of ancient Canaan, Israel, Judea, and Palestine from 10,000 B.C.E. to the rise of Islam in the seventh century C.E. Illustrations, maps, charts, chronologies, and bibliographies enhance the uniformly well-written essays. But the strengths of the work are its currency and breadth of coverage and perspective." Libr J

Women in scripture; a dictionary of named and unnamed women in the Hebrew Bible, the Apocryphal/Deuterocanonical books, and the New Testament; Carol L. Meyers, general editor; Toni Craven and Ross S. Kraemer, associate editors. Houghton Mifflin 2000 592p il $40 **220.9**

1. Bible—Biography 2. Women in the Bible
ISBN 0-395-70936-9
LC 99-89577

Also available in paperback from Eerdmans

This "reference describes every woman in Jewish and Christian scripture—with or without names—plus female dieties and personifications. . . . Frequent cross-referencing and bibliographical suggestions enrich the entries. Useful essays on biblical scholarship, biblical literature, and biblical naming enhance the volume." Libr J

221.5 Bible. Old Testament— Modern versions

Bible. O.T.

The Old Testament: King James Version; with an introduction by George Steiner. Knopf 1996 li, 1382p $35 **221.5**

ISBN 0-679-45102-1
LC 96-22789

"Everyman's library"

An edition of the classic translation of the Old Testament into the language of seventeenth-century England. Steiner's introduction provides a look at the historical, social, political, literary and philosophical impact of the King James version

Tanakh; a new translation of the Holy Scriptures according to the traditional Hebrew text. Jewish Publ. Soc. 1985 xxvi, 1624p prices vary **221.5**

LC 85-10006

Available in various bindings and editions

This volume represents a "collaboration between rabbis from the Orthodox, Conservative, and Reform branches of Judaism, and scholars in Semitic languages and biblical studies. The translators relied on the Hebrew tenth-century Masoretic text that is Judaism's standard. The Torah, Prophets, and Writings are here in a single volume." Publisher's note

221.6 Bible. Old Testament— Interpretation and criticism

Telushkin, Joseph, 1948-

Biblical literacy; the most important people, events, and ideas of the Hebrew Bible. Morrow 1997 xxviii, 628p $29.95 **221.6**

1. Bible. O.T.—Criticism 2. Jewish ethics
ISBN 0-688-14297-4
LC 97-6645

This volume is "intended as a reference work, to be used as an introduction to the weekly readings that are a part of Jewish Sabbath worship services. . . . The book is divided into three parts. . . . The first, titled 'People and Events,' takes up more than half the book. These are . . . chapter by chapter summaries of the Old Testament, in order of their appearance in the Jewish canon. Most of the summaries end with a short section titled 'Reflections.'" Christ Sci Monit

"Biblical truths that many a reader may have glossed over before stand out, thanks to this superb book, and, more important, misunderstandings are cleared up and previously mistranslated words correctly rendered." Booklist

Includes bibliographical references

222 Historical books of Old Testament

Armstrong, Karen

In the beginning; a new interpretation of Genesis. Knopf 1996 195p hardcover o.p. paperback available $14 **222**

1. Bible. O.T. Genesis—Criticism
ISBN 0-345-40604-4 (pa)
LC 96-26170

Armstrong "interprets selected accounts of Genesis using an archetypal approach to literature so as to offer in-

Armstrong, Karen—*Continued*

sights into the problematic nature of human religion, especially the problems of separation between humans and God. . . . The text of Genesis (NRSV) makes up a third of the book's volume." Libr J

Includes bibliographical references

Bible. O.T. Pentateuch

The book of J; translated from the Hebrew by David Rosenberg; interpreted by Harold Bloom. Grove Weidenfeld 1990 340p o.p.; Vintage Bks. paperback available $14.95

222

1. Bible. O.T.—Criticism

ISBN 0-679-73624-7 (pa)   LC 90-37391

This volume "contains three works: David Rosenberg's translation of those parts of the Pentateuch that have been attributed to the J Writer (most of Genesis and Exodus, parts of Numbers and Deuteronomy), Bloom's introduction, and, following the translation, his [commentary]." Voice Lit Suppl

The five books of Moses; Genesis, Exodus, Leviticus, Numbers, Deuteronomy; a new translation with introductions, notes, and commentary by Everett Fox. Schocken Bks. 1995 xxxi, 1024p hardcover o.p. paperback available $27.50   **222**

ISBN 0-8052-1119-5 (pa)   LC 95-10143

Fox's "introductions propose and outline a literary structure for each book, his commentary [addresses] . . . thematic and structural characteristics of the text, [and] his . . . notes point out linguistic features and cruxes and the interpretive issues that surround them." N Y Times Book Rev

This translation "captures the beautiful, majestic, and dynamic character of biblical Hebrew. . . . An essential purchase for all libraries." Libr J

The Torah: the five books of Moses; a new translation of the Holy Scriptures according to the Masoretic text; first section. Jewish Publ. Soc. 1963 393p $20   **222**

ISBN 0-8276-0015-1

This "translation of Genesis, Exodus, Leviticus, Numbers, and Deuteronomy was prepared . . . to present a version of the Bible that takes into account modern insights and knowledge of ancient times. . . . Of chief value to persons of the Jewish religion but of interest to Bible scholars of any religion." Booklist

Dershowitz, Alan M.

The Genesis of justice; ten stories of biblical injustice that led to the Ten Commandments and modern law. Warner Bks. 2000 273p $28; pa $14.95   **222**

1. Bible. O.T. Genesis—Criticism 2. Justice

ISBN 0-446-52479-4; 0-446-67677-2 (pa)

LC 99-50220

"The narratives deal with Adam and Eve, Cain and Abel, Abraham, Lot, Jacob, Dina, Tamar and Joseph. Dershowitz includes a translation of each story, recounts some theological commentaries and offers his own interpretations." Publ Wkly

"For believers of all faiths, as well as nonbelievers, this is an outstanding work." Libr J

Includes bibliographical references

Feiler, Bruce S.

Abraham; a journey to the heart of three faiths; [by] Bruce Feiler. Morrow 2002 224p $23.95; pa $12.95   **222**

1. Abraham (Biblical figure)

ISBN 0-380-97776-1; 0-06-052509-6 (pa)

LC 2002-70309

Also available large print edition $23.95 (ISBN 0-06-051863-4)

"Feiler explores how Christian, Judaic, and Islamic understandings of Abraham, a patriarch to all three faiths, express interfaith disagreements. On the way to a passionate, prayerful argument for interfaith peace, Feiler mixes theological meditation, adventurous travelogue, and sly wit." Booklist

Friedman, Richard Elliott

Who wrote the Bible? Prentice-Hall 1987 299p maps o.p.; HarperSanFrancisco paperback available $15   **222**

1. Bible. O.T. Pentateuch—Criticism

ISBN 0-06-063035-3 (pa)   LC 87-1978

The author describes the documentary hypothesis in Bible exegesis which ascribes the Torah to four sources: "J" (the Yahwist), "E" (the Elohist), "P" (the priestly writer), and "D" (the Deuteronomist). He then attempts to discover the authors of the four documents

Friedman "turns a potentially dry scholarly inquiry into a lively detective story. . . . This book is neither comprehensive nor unduly complex, making it a good introductory text for beginners and nonspecialists." Libr J

Kugel, James L.

The Bible as it was. Harvard Univ. Press 1997 680p il $37.50; pa $22.95   **222**

1. Bible. O.T. Pentateuch—Criticism

ISBN 0-674-06940-4; 0-674-06941-2 (pa)

LC 97-3299

"In this companion to the first five books of the Bible . . . each of the stories, the Creation, Cain and Abel, the Flood, Joseph and his brothers, and the Exodus saga, among others, is examined at face value. Then Kugel shows how various commentators, some known, some anonymous, scoured each line of the stories (and read between them) to shape what would become the standard interpretations." Booklist

"To cull material from these diverse sources requires no small expertise as a sleuth and a scholar. Kugel is equal to the task." N Y Times Book Rev

Includes bibliographical references

McKenzie, Steven L., 1953-

King David; a biography. Oxford Univ. Press 2000 232p il maps $41.50; pa $15.95   **222**

1. David, King of Israel

ISBN 0-19-513273-4; 0-19-514708-1 (pa)

LC 99-44315

McKenzie "views David as a ruthless, brutal usurper who would be well at home among many modern-day rulers. . . . Much of this portrait is inevitably speculation, and it is likely to outrage David's defenders . Still, given the limitations of written sources, McKenzie effectively coats his assertions with a veneer of credibility." Booklist

Includes bibliographical references

Moyers, Bill

Genesis: a living conversation. Doubleday 1996 361p il hardcover o.p. paperback available $22.95 **222**

1. Bible. O.T. Genesis—Criticism

ISBN 0-385-49043-7 (pa) LC 96-15318

Companion volume to the PBS series led by Bill Moyers in which writers and religious thinkers discussed episodes from the first book of the Bible. Among the participants are Burton Visotzky, a rabbi who initiated the conversations which gave rise to the series, "Elaine Pagels, Karen Armstrong, . . . John Barth, and Oscar Hijuelos. The book is divided by biblical tale (Adam and Eve, Cain and Abel, the blinding of Isaac) with five or six of the participants discussing the moral, literary, and personal meanings of the stories." Booklist

Satinover, Jeffrey, 1947-

Cracking the Bible code. Morrow 1997 346p il $23; pa $16.95 **222**

1. Bible. O.T. Pentateuch 2. Ciphers

ISBN 0-688-15463-8; 0-688-15994-X (pa)

LC 97-25280

"Satinover sets out to show how reading the Torah in a strict letter-by-letter sequence, as well as by applying the methods of the science of cryptology to the texts, decodes the Torah to yield startling information about contemporary events." Publ Wkly

This book "is the one to read if you really want to know about the Bible code." Booklist

Includes bibliographical references

223 Poetic books of Old Testament

Bible. O.T.

The Song of songs; a new translation with an introduction and commentary [by] Ariel Bloch and Chana Bloch; afterword by Robert Alter. Random House 1995 253p o.p.; University of Calif. Press paperback available $16.15 **223**

ISBN 0-520-21330-0 (pa) LC 93-33249

This book begins with an "introduction that establishes the context and date of the poem as well as the history of its incorporation into the canon of Hebrew scripture and its translation and interpretation in Jewish and Christian traditions. The translation and the Hebrew text are printed on facing pages, followed by Robert Alter's afterword and an extensive commentary accessible to laypersons as well as scholars, to readers who know Hebrew as well as those who don't." Booklist

Includes bibliographical references

224 Prophetic books of Old Testament

Heschel, Abraham Joshua, 1907-1972

The prophets; [by] Abraham J. Heschel. HarperPerennial 2001 xxix, 672p pa $19.95 **224**

1. Bible. O.T. Prophets—Criticism 2. Prophets

ISBN 0-06-093699-1 LC 2001-24817

A reissue of the two-volume edition published 1962 by Harper & Row

"Essays on the individual prophets—most of the pre-exilic, and of the post-exilic only the Second Isaiah—take up about a third of the book. The main effort . . . is to analyze the significance of prophecy in the history of religion, and the nature and meaning of prophetic inspiration." America

Includes bibliographical references

225 Bible. New Testament

Brown, Raymond Edward

An introduction to the New Testament; by Raymond E. Brown. Doubleday 1997 xxxviii, 878p maps (Anchor Bible reference library) $45 **225**

1. Bible. N.T.—Criticism

ISBN 0-385-24767-2 LC 96-37742

The author "focuses on the established 27-book New Testament canon. . . . He deemphasizes the prehistory of the documents (sources, editions, and so forth) and emphasizes the documents in their canonical form. He begins most chapters with a 'General Analysis of the Message' and addresses issues such as authorship, date, and composition afterward." Libr J

Brown's book "culminates his life's work and synthesizes the best of his generation's historical-critical scholarship clearly and cogently for beginners and advanced students alike." N Y Times Book Rev

Includes bibliographical references

225.9 Bible. New Testament— Geography, history, biography, stories

Crossan, John Dominic

Excavating Jesus; beneath the stones, behind the texts; [by] John Dominic Crossan & Jonathan L. Reed. HarperSanFrancisco 2001 298p il hardcover o.p. paperback available $19.95 **225.9**

1. Bible. N.T. Gospels—Criticism 2. Excavations (Archeology)—Israel

ISBN 0-06-061634-2 (pa) LC 2001-24960

The authors examine "what clues archaeology can offer about Jesus' life and times. . . . [They focus on] the 10 most significant archaeological digs in the towns of ancient Palestine (Nazareth, Tiberias, and Jerusalem) in context with 10 important textual discoveries, including the Dead Sea Scrolls and writings such as the Gnostic gospels of Thomas." Booklist

This "book provides a fascinating, beautifully illustrated and elegantly written account of the life and times of Jesus, providing readers with one of the richest glimpses into Jesus and his world now available." Publ Wkly

Includes bibliographical references

226 Gospels and Acts

Bible. N.T. Gospels
The five Gospels; the search for the authentic words of Jesus: new translation and commentary; by Robert W. Funk, Roy W. Hoover, and the Jesus Seminar. Macmillan 1993 xxii, 553p o.p.; HarperSanFrancisco paperback available $28   **226**
1. Jesus Christ—Historicity
ISBN 0-06-063040-X (pa)   LC 93-26451
"A Polebridge Press book"
"Based on the work of the Jesus Seminar, which brought together a group of biblical scholars, this new translation of and commentary on the five Gospels offers an answer to the perennial question, What did Jesus really say? The group not only surveyed all the surviving ancient texts for words attributed to Jesus, but also examined the Gnostic Gospel of Thomas." Booklist
Includes bibliographical references

The three Gospels; [by] Reynolds Price. Scribner 1996 288p $23; pa $13   **226**
1. Jesus Christ
ISBN 0-684-80336-4; 0-684-83281-X (pa)
     LC 95-39948
Contents: The good news according to Mark; The good news according to John; An honest account of a memorable life
"Of the four canonical Gospels, Mr. Price has chosen to translate the two that seem to him to express the strongest differing yet complementary perceptions of the life of Jesus—Mark and John. To these he has appended a third text, roughly the same length as each of the other two, which he calls 'An Honest Account of a Memorable Life: An Apocryphal Gospel.' . . . [The author also includes] a general preface, mainly devoted to the problems of translating New Testament Greek, and . . . prefatory interpretative essays for Mark and John and an explanatory introduction to the modern Apocryphal Gospel." N Y Times Book Rev
"Although there is so much to appreciate in these commentaries and in the translated texts, the best part of the book . . . is left to last: Price's own joyously written account of Jesus' life." Booklist

Bonhoeffer, Dietrich, 1906-1945
The cost of discipleship; containing material not previously translated. rev and unabridged ed. Macmillan 1959 hardcover o.p. paperback available $12   **226**
1. Bible. N.T. Gospels—Criticism 2. Sermon on the mount
ISBN 0-684-81500-1 (pa)
Also available in hardcover from P. Smith
Original German edition, 1937. This edition translated by R. H. Fuller with some revision by Irmgard Booth
The first part of the book "is an exposition of the conception of discipleship that is to be found in the Synoptic Gospels, together with an interpretation of the Sermon on the Mount. The second part consists of Bonhoeffer's attempt to show how the terminology used by the evangelists has been translated into the language of the Church of the Apostle Paul." Magill. Masterpieces of Christ Lit in Summary Form

Wroe, Ann
Pontius Pilate. Modern Library 2000 412p $26; pa $14.95   **226**
1. Pilate, Pontius, 1st cent.
ISBN 0-375-50305-6; 0-375-75397-4 (pa)
     LC 99-43000
First published 1999 in the United Kingdom with title: Pilate: the biography of an invented man
The author offers "a reconstructed life of the Roman official who, by ordering the execution of Jesus of Nazareth but otherwise serving with little distinction, managed to become simultaneously famous and obscure. Outside the Gospels, which each bring the governor on stage for a brief if highly charged cameo appearance, there are only a few references to Pilate in contemporary sources." Publ Wkly
"As long as readers don't take this as accurate history but enjoy it as a well-written, imaginative, and creative portrait of Pilate and his times, the book serves a useful purpose." Libr J
Includes bibliographical references

229 Apocrypha, pseudepigrapha, intertestamental works

Bible. O.T. Apocrypha
The Apocrypha   **229**
Available in various versions, including the New revised standard version, in hardcover and paperback from various publishers
"These books form part of the sacred literature of the Alexandrian Jews. . . . Some of them form an historical link between the Old and New Testament, others have a linguistic value in connexion with the Hellenistic phraseology of the latter. The narratives of Apocrypha are partly historical records, and partly allegorical." Oxford Univ. Press

Dead Sea scrolls
The Dead Sea scriptures; in English translation with introduction and notes by Theodor H. Gaster. 3rd ed rev and enl. Anchor Press; Doubleday 1976 580p pa $25   **229**
ISBN 0-385-08859-0
First published 1956
A translation, with commentary and notes, of the scrolls relating the life and faith of the Dead Sea sect
Includes bibliographical references

Pagels, Elaine H., 1943-
Beyond belief; the secret Gospel of Thomas; [by] Elaine Pagels. Random House 2003 241p $26.95   **229**
1. Gospel of Thomas 2. Bible. N.T. John 3. Christianity
ISBN 0-375-50156-8   LC 2002-36840
"Pagels discusses the early Christian writings known as the Gnostic Gospels that were discovered at Nag Hammadi, Egypt. She focuses particularly on the Gospel of Thomas. Pagels contends "that the Gospel of John is the only one in the New Testament that actually promotes the idea of Jesus as God in human form, and she argues . . . that it was written explicitly to counter the Gospel of Thomas, which said otherwise. Thomas's gospel, she writes, teaches 'that God's light shines not only in Jesus but, potentially at least, in everyone . . . and encourages the hearer . . . to seek to know God through

Pagels, Elaine H., 1943——_Continued_
one's own divinely given capacity, since all are created in the image of God.'" Christ Sci Monit
"Even those who possess only a nodding acquaintance with Gnostic writings will find themselves stimulated by the author's arguments and perhaps transformed by her conclusions. A fresh and exciting work of theology and spirituality." Booklist
Includes bibliographical references

230 Christianity. Christian theology

Bonhoeffer, Dietrich, 1906-1945
A testament to freedom; the essential writings of Dietrich Bonhoeffer; edited by Geffrey B. Kelly and F. Burton Nelson. HarperSanFrancisco 1990 xxii, 579p il hardcover o.p. paperback available $23   230
1. Theology
ISBN 0-06-064214-9 (pa)   LC 89-45514
"This book features previously untranslated writings, sermons, and selections from letters spanning [Bonhoeffer's] entire pastoral-theological career, including his prison letters." Publisher's note
This book will not "subsitute for the individual volumes of Bonhoeffer's best-known works. But as a single volume collection of Bonhoeffer's writings, however, there is none better." Christ Today
Includes bibliographical references

Davies, Brian, 1951-
The thought of Thomas Aquinas. Oxford Univ. Press 1992 391p hardcover o.p. paperback available $44.95   230
1. Thomas, Aquinas, Saint, 1225?-1274 2. Doctrinal theology
ISBN 0-19-826753-3 (pa)   LC 91-35671
This book on Aquinas "is arranged topically in 17 chapters with . . . [discussion of] the nature of God and creation, negative and positive theology, perfection, eternity, knowledge, justice, and providence. Chapters 10 through 16 treat the Trinity, human nature, and Christology. The final chapter treats Aquinas on the sacraments, particularly the Eucharist." Choice
"Davies aims to cover the whole programme of the Summa in 370 pages. This necessarily means that, though his writing is admirably clear and never cryptic, much of what he says is extremely concise, and some topics get less airing than others." Times Lit Suppl
Includes bibliographical references

Kierkegaard, Søren, 1813-1855
The present age, and Of the difference between a genius and an apostle; translated by Alexander Dru; introduction by Walter Kaufman. Harper & Row 1962 108p pa $12
          230
1. Theology
ISBN 0-06-130094-2
"Harper torchbooks. The Cloister library"
First published 1846. This translation "originally published, together with a third essay, by Oxford University Press under the title 'The Present Age and Two Minor Ethico-Religious Treatises in 1940'." Verso of title page
"Those who would know Kierkegaard, the intensely religious humorist, the irrepressibly witty critic of his age and ours, can do no better than to begin with this book." Introduction

Küng, Hans, 1928-
Great Christian thinkers. Continuum 1994 235p hardcover o.p. paperback available $19.95   230
1. Theology
ISBN 0-8264-0848-6 (pa)   LC 94-883
Analyzed in Essay and general literature index
The author "attempts a new approach to the introduction-to-theology genre by critically tracing the developing thought of key, usually 'paradigm-shifting,' theologians (Paul, Origen, Augustine, Aquinas, Luther, Schleiermacher, and Karl Barth) in relation to their social, intellectual, and religious environment. He explores the significance of their life and work for the Christian world in an interesting, quite understandable manner." Libr J
Includes bibliographical references

Lewis, C. S. (Clive Staples), 1898-1963
Mere Christianity; a revised and amplified edition, with a new introduction, of the three books, Broadcast talks, Christian behaviour, and Beyond personality. HarperSanFrancisco 2001 xx, 227p $19.95; pa $10   230
1. Christian philosophy
ISBN 0-06-065288-8; 0-06-065292-6 (pa)
          LC 00-49862
First published 1952
This omnibus edition includes most of C. S. Lewis' writings on Christian theology and moral philosophy
Includes bibliographical references

The world's last night, and other essays. Harcourt Brace & Co. 1960 113p hardcover o.p. paperback available $12   230
1. Christian philosophy
ISBN 0-15-602771-2 (pa)
Analyzed in Essay and general literature index
These seven essays cover topics such as culture, democracy, education, good works, prayers, the second coming of Christ, and space exploration

Teilhard de Chardin, Pierre
The divine milieu; an essay on the interior life. Harper & Row 1960 144p hardcover o.p. paperback available $13   230
1. Christian philosophy
ISBN 0-06-090487-9 (pa)
Original French edition, 1957
In this book Father de Chardin describes his spiritual philosophy

Tillich, Paul, 1886-1965
Theology of culture; edited by Robert C. Kimball. Oxford Univ. Press 1959 213p hardcover o.p. paperback available $13.95
          230
1. Christian philosophy 2. Culture
ISBN 0-19-500711-5 (pa)
Selected essays by the influential theologian focus on ethics, education, science, aesthetics, psychology, and existential philosophy

Ward, Keith, 1938-
Christianity; a short introduction. Oneworld
Publs. 2000 184p pa $14.95 **230**
1. Christianity
ISBN 1-85168-229-5
The author presents "the major elements of Christian
belief. Each motif is examined from three differing perspectives, treating each viewpoint fairly, with an apparent
sympathy for the feelings of those who hold to each
perspective. The result is an articulate presentation of diverse approaches to Christianity's central concerns." Libr
J

230.003 Christianity—
Encyclopedias and dictionaries

The **Encyclopedia** of Christianity; editors,
Erwin Fahlbusch [et al.]; translator and
English-language editor, Geoffrey W.
Bromiley; statistical editor, David B.
Barrett; foreword, Jaroslav Pelikan.
Eerdmans 1999-2002 3v il ea $100
230.003
1. Christianity—Encyclopedias   LC 98-45953
Contents: v1 A-D (ISBN 0-8028-2413-7); v2 E-I
(ISBN 0-8028-2414-5); v3 J-O (ISBN 0-8028-2415-3)
"*Evangelisches Kirchenlexikon* (3d ed.) is being pub-
lished in a five-volume expanded English translation ex-
pected to be completed over [a period of] five years. The
German editors have worked with the editors of the En-
glish edition to add significant content for American and
British audiences, and this first volume sets the standard
for reference works of this kind." Libr J [review of volume 1]

Encyclopedia of early Christianity; edited by
Everett Ferguson. 2nd ed. Garland 1997 2v
il maps (Garland reference library of the
humanities) set $245; pa set $55 **230.003**
1. Christianity—Encyclopedias 2. Church history—
Encyclopedias
ISBN 0-8153-1663-1; 0-8153-3319-6 (pa)
LC 96-36865
First published 1990
"Covers persons, places, doctrines, practices, art, liturgy, heresies, and schisms from the time of Jesus to approximately 600 CE. Articles by . . . specialists include
bibliographies and cross-references. Extensive subject index. Intended for general readers, students, and professionals in fields outside religion who want information
concerning early Christianity." Guide to Ref Books. 11th
edition [entry for 1990 edition]

Oxford companion to Christian thought;
edited by Adrian Hastings [et al.] Oxford
Univ. Press 2000 xxviii, 777p $75
230.003
1. Theology—Dictionaries
ISBN 0-19-860024-0   LC 2001-267818
This volume focuses "on the movement of ideas
among Christians. The articles (more than 500) by 268
scholars (mostly British) range in length from half a column . . . to seven pages. . . . They broadly cover the
themes . . . persons . . . places . . . and historical periods . . . that characterize Christian thought." Choice
For a fuller review see: Booklist, March 1, 2001

The **Oxford** dictionary of the Christian
Church; edited by F. L. Cross and E. A.
Livingstone. Oxford Univ. Press 1997 3rd
ed xxxvii, 1786p $125 **230.003**
1. Christianity—Dictionaries 2. Church history—Dictionaries
ISBN 0-19-211655-X
First published 1957
"The authoritative one-volume dictionary of the Christian Church. More than 6,000 entries presented in an alphabetical arrangement provide extensive information on
the history, beliefs, practices, people, and traditions of
the 2,000-year-old Christian world." Ref Sources for
Small & Medium-sized Libr. 6th edition

World Christian encyclopedia; a comparative
survey of churches and religions in the
modern world; [edited by] David B.
Barrett, George T. Kurian, Todd M.
Johnson. 2nd ed. Oxford Univ. Press 2001
2v il maps set $295 **230.003**
1. Christianity—Encyclopedias
ISBN 0-19-507963-9   LC 99-57323
First published 1982
Contents: v1 The world by countries: religionists,
churches, ministries; v2 The world by segments: religions, peoples, languages, cities, topics
"A rich compilation of demographic data about the
state of Christianity around the world. . . . Through the
15 parts of this 2-volume work, the reader is provided
with a country-by-country analysis of Christian and non-
Christian religious life, religious analyses of various ethnic groups (including evangelization efforts among
them), demographic data concerning various linguistic
groups, and so forth. Drawing on historical data and
present trends, the authors also interpolate the likely state
of the faith by 2025." Recomm Ref Books for Small &
Medium-sized Libr & Media Cent, 2003

231 God

Miles, Jack, 1942-
God: a biography. Knopf 1995 446p
$32.50; pa $15 **231**
1. Bible. O.T.—Criticism 2. God
ISBN 0-679-41833-4; 0-679-74368-5 (pa)
LC 94-30153
The author discusses "God's nature, character, motives
and designs through a close textual analysis of the Hebrew Bible, or Old Testament. He deduces that the God
of Judeo-Christian tradition is an amalgam of several ancient, divine personalities. Worshiped as the source of
mercy, wisdom, strength and love, God is also at times
an abrupt, unpredictable, wrathful being: a destroyer as
well as a creator." Publ Wkly
Miles "has produced a well-written, provocative
study." Choice
Includes bibliographical references

Price, Reynolds, 1933-
Letter to a man in the fire; does God exist
and does He care? Scribner 1999 108p $20;
pa $11 **231**
1. God 2. Suffering
ISBN 0-684-85626-3; 0-684-85627-1 (pa)
LC 98-54197
This book "consists of Price's response to a 1997 letter he received from a medical student stricken with can-

Price, Reynolds, 1933-—*Continued*
cer. Price telephoned and then followed up with this long, eloquent letter on the nature of suffering and the justice and righteousness of God." Publ Wkly

231.7 God's relation to the world

Harline, Craig E.
Miracles at the Jesus Oak; histories of the supernatural in Reformation Europe; by Craig Harline. Doubleday 2003 324p il map $22.95
231.7
1. Miracles 2. Belgium—Religion 3. Catholic Church
ISBN 0-385-50820-4   LC 2002-71622
"Having discovered in an ancient Belgian abbey library a 'miracle register' containing a series of accounts of miracle claims [Harline] presents them here as a collection of 'microhistories,' illuminating [in his words] 'the otherworld of Reformation Europe.' . . . Involved in each of these stories is a 'problem' concerning the miraculous." Commonweal
"Some of the tales seem bizarre, but they highlight universal contexts of miracle-making during the Reformation set against the variables of rival theologies, views on nature, and secular interests. Enjoyable reading." Libr J
Includes bibliographical references

Lewis, C. S. (Clive Staples), 1898-1963
Miracles; a preliminary study. Macmillan 1947 220 hardcover o.p.; HarperSanFrancisco paperback available $11   **231.7**
1. Miracles
ISBN 0-06-065301-9 (pa)
"Mr. Lewis casts his net fairly wide and, under the guise of a book on miracles, offers a rational justification both of theism and of doctrinal Christianity." Times Lit Suppl

Miller, Kenneth R. (Kenneth Raymond), 1948-
Finding Darwin's God; a scientist's search for common ground between God and evolution. Cliff St. Bks. 1999 338p il $25; pa $14   **231.7**
1. Evolution 2. Religion and science
ISBN 0-06-017593-1; 0-06-093049-7 (pa)
LC 99-16754
The author "explains the difference between evolution as validated scientific fact and as an evolving theory. He illustrates his contentions with examples from astronomy, geology, physics and molecular biology, confronting the illogic of creationists with persuasive reasons based on the known physical properties of the universe. . . . Then standing firmly on Darwinian ground, he turns to take on, with equal vigor, his outspoken colleagues in science who espouse a materialistic, agnostic or atheistic vision of reality." Publ Wkly
Includes bibliographical references

Teilhard de Chardin, Pierre
Christianity and evolution; translated by René Hague. Harcourt Brace Jovanovich 1971 255p hardcover o.p. paperback available $14   **231.7**
1. Theology
ISBN 0-15-617740-4 (pa)
"A Helen and Kurt Wolff book"

Original French edition, 1969
These essays "covering a wide expanse of Teilhard's thought . . . stimulate the reader to reflect seriously on the Christian dogma of creation, the role of Christ in evolution as a cosmic phenomenon, and on the relationship of the church to the modern world." Choice
Includes bibliographical references

232 Jesus Christ and his family. Christology

Cahill, Tom
Desire of the everlasting hills; the world before and after Jesus; [by] Thomas Cahill. Talese 1999 353p il maps $24.95; pa $14
232
1. Jesus Christ
ISBN 0-385-48251-5; 0-385-48372-4 (pa)
LC 99-16560
This is a "book on 'the historical Jesus' and the early church. Written from a conservative perspective, the work is a readable synthesis of Jesus scholarship." Libr J
Includes bibliographical references

Charlesworth, James H.
Jesus and the Dead Sea scrolls; [by] James H. Charlesworth, with internationally renowned experts. Doubleday 1992 xxxvii, 370p il maps (Anchor Bible reference library) hardcover o.p. paperback available $25   **232**
1. Jesus Christ 2. Dead Sea scrolls
ISBN 0-385-47844-5 (pa)   LC 92-2617
These essays "explore the question of Jesus' relationship to those who wrote the scrolls, and whether or not the scrolls' original scholars were hiding something profound or damaging to the Christian faith." Booklist
This book "will inform and challenge both scholars and lay readers." Libr J
Includes bibliographical references

Miles, Jack, 1942-
Christ: a crisis in the life of God. Knopf 2001 352p $26.95; pa $14   **232**
1. Jesus Christ 2. Bible. N.T.—Criticism
ISBN 0-375-40014-1; 0-679-78160-9 (pa)
LC 2001-33808
"Miles continues the literary analysis of the Bible that he began in . . . *God* (1995). Taking up the story of Jesus, he treats it as the record of God's sojourn on earth as a man. That is, unlike the hordes of scholars concerned with the historical Jesus, Miles takes the Gospels at face value, though he argues, with plenty of demonstration and reason, that in them Jesus is an ironist, who turns old messianic understandings, in particular, inside out and upside down." Booklist
"Weaving philosophy and literature into his reflections on the Bible, Miles offers literary perspectives on the life of Christ that are at once provocative and revelatory. After reading this book, one can never look at God, Jesus or the Bible in quite the same way." Publ Wkly
Includes bibliographical references

Vermès, Géza, 1924-
The changing faces of Jesus. Viking 2001
324p map hardcover o.p. paperback available
$15 **232**
1. Jesus Christ
ISBN 0-14-219602-9 (pa) LC 00-43897
The author examines "how the Jesus of history became the Church's divine figure. . . . Vermes calls his prologue 'From Christ to Jesus.' He traces the process of divinization backward, . . . according to the degree of 'evolution' of the Christological doctrine that Jesus was both entirely divine and entirely human." N Y Rev Books
"Vermes's vast knowledge of first century Judaism ensures that this work will become one of the most important works in historical Jesus studies, and his readable style makes it useful for both public and academic library patrons." Libr J
Includes bibliographical references

232.9 Family and life of Jesus

Allen, Charlotte, 1943-
The human Christ; the search for the historical Jesus. Free Press 1998 383p il $26 **232.9**
1. Jesus Christ—Biography 2. Jesus Christ—Historicity
ISBN 0-684-82725-5 LC 97-46463
"Allen surveys 'moments in the Western interpretation of the figure of Jesus from the second to the twentieth century. . . . [In each chapter she aims to] interweave a narrative of a given period's constructions of Jesus with a description of that period's key intellectual or political allegiances." Natl Rev
The author "writes with a breadth of perspective and a clarity of style that will be applauded. . . . A shrewd and reliable critique of more than 300 years of religious controversy." Booklist
Includes bibliographical references

Chilton, Bruce
Rabbi Jesus; an intimate biography.
Doubleday 2000 xxii, 330p il maps hardcover
o.p. paperback available $14.95 **232.9**
1. Jesus Christ—Biography
ISBN 0-385-49793-8 (pa) LC 00-31548
The author presents a "wonderfully fresh presentation of the implications of Jesus's being a Jewish male living in the context of first-century Judaism." Libr J
Includes bibliographical references

Crossan, John Dominic
Jesus; a revolutionary biography.
HarperSanFrancisco 1994 209p hardcover o.p.
paperback available $14 **232.9**
1. Jesus Christ—Biography 2. Jesus Christ—Historicity
ISBN 0-06-061662-8 (pa) LC 93-24685
This book is based on the author's The Historical Jesus. Using the Gospels and early Christian and Jewish sources as well as evidence from archeology and ancient history, Crossan attempts to discover what can be known about Jesus as a historical figure in the context of the society of his time
"Bound to disturb some people and stimulate others, this is recommended for all libraries where lay readers are likely to be interested in the issues raised." Libr J
Includes bibliographical references

Who killed Jesus? exposing the roots of anti-semitism in the Gospel story of the death of Jesus. HarperSanFrancisco 1995 238p hardcover o.p. paperback available $15
232.9
1. Jesus Christ—Resurrection 2. Bible. N.T. Gospels—Criticism
ISBN 0-06-061480-3 (pa) LC 94-40200
"The two main theses of this . . . book are that the roots of anti-Semitism spring from gospel narratives of the death of Jesus and that the Romans, not the Jews, killed Jesus as a revolutionary agitator inimical to their continued governance of Judea. Crossan . . . pleads for a reevaluation of the passion stories, which have caused such animus toward Jews for the past 2000 years." Libr J
"Well argued and highly readable, Who Killed Jesus? also includes an important epilogue stating Crossan's own faith perspectives on the divinity and resurrection of Christ." Publ Wkly
Includes bibliographical references

Fredriksen, Paula
Jesus of Nazareth, King of the Jews; a Jewish life and the emergence of Christianity.
Knopf 1999 327p hardcover o.p. paperback available $14 **232.9**
1. Jesus Christ
ISBN 0-679-76746-0 (pa) LC 99-31054
"To Fredriksen, Jesus was an observant Jew immersed in a context bounded by Galilee and Jerusalem. He was crucified as an imperial Roman deterrent to unruly inhabitants of a region prone to rebellion, and the emergence of Christianity is a work of creative theological reinterpretation as much as of historical memory." Booklist
Includes bibliographical references

Girzone, Joseph F.
A portrait of Jesus. Doubleday 1998 179p il hardcover o.p. paperback available $11.95
232.9
1. Jesus Christ—Biography 2. Christian life
ISBN 0-385-48477-1 (pa) LC 98-15618
The author "gives a simple narrative account of Jesus' life, envisioning facets of the person reflected in the gospel stories." Libr J
"This is popular liberal Catholic theology, more filled with forgiveness and fellowship than shaming and hierarchy. Many a non-Catholic and even non-Christian may embrace it, too." Booklist

Johnson, Luke Timothy
The real Jesus; the misguided quest for the historical Jesus and the truth of the traditional Gospels. HarperSanFrancisco 1996 182p hardcover o.p. paperback available $14
232.9
1. Jesus Christ—Biography 2. Jesus Christ—Historicity 3. Jesus Seminar 4. Bible. N.T.—Criticism
ISBN 0-06-064166-5 LC 95-19885
Johnson presents a critique "of the Jesus Seminar and of recent books allegedly describing the historical Jesus. . . . [He aims to] delineate the limitations of history, considers what is historical about Jesus, reflects on the 'real Jesus' and the Gospels and comments on the relation between critical scholarship and the church." America
"A passionately argued but fair response to the Jesus

Johnson, Luke Timothy—*Continued*
Seminar from an established scholar. . . . This book should be in any religious collection to help provide balance to the current historical Jesus literature." Libr J

Meier, John P.
A marginal Jew; rethinking the historical Jesus. Doubleday 1991-2001 3v maps (Anchor Bible reference library) v1 $45; v2 $42.50; v3 $45   **232.9**
1. Jesus Christ—Historicity
ISBN 0-385-26425-9 (v1); 0-385-46992-6 (v2); 0-385-46993-4 (v3)   LC 91-10538
Contents: v1 The roots of the problem and the person; v2 Mentor, message, and miracles; v3 Companions and competitors
The first three volumes in a projected series of four devoted to an examination of the historical Jesus and his Jewish environment
The author "summarizes the first two volumes of *A Marginal Jew* and forecasts the next while meticulously documenting his understanding of the relations between the historical Jesus, his historical companions, and his historical competitors—Pharisees, Sadduccees, Essenes, and others. . . . The only thing common about Meier's project is fascination with the character of Jesus. Those who share that will find this dense, academic work worth their effort." Booklist [review of volume 3]
Includes bibliographical references

Pelikan, Jaroslav Jan, 1923-
The illustrated Jesus through the centuries. Yale Univ. Press 1997 254p il $25   **232.9**
1. Jesus Christ—Historicity
ISBN 0-300-07268-6   LC 97-7360
Companion volume to Mary through the centuries
In this revision of Jesus through the centuries (1985) the author "has abridged the text and turns to illustrations to convey his interpretations. . . . Very beautiful and very appealing for the general reader, this edition by no means replaces the scholarship and documentation of the first; those notations and references are missing in the illustrated edition. However, the illustrations enhance this interesting and insightful text." Libr J

Sanders, E. P.
The historical figure of Jesus. Allen Lane/The Penguin Press 1994 c1993 337p map hardcover o.p. paperback available $14.95   **232.9**
1. Jesus Christ—Biography
ISBN 0-14-014499-4 (pa)   LC 94-136152
First published 1993 in the United Kingdom
Sanders gives "an account of Jesus' life and activity. . . . After discussing the context of Jesus in first-century Palestine and facing the problem of sources, he treats Jesus' ministry, miracles, preaching of God's kingdom, self-understanding and passion and death." America
"Highly readable, this is a key addition to literature on the historical Jesus." Libr J
Includes bibliographical references

Spoto, Donald, 1941-
The hidden Jesus; a new life. St. Martin's Press 1998 312p hardcover o.p. paperback available $14.95   **232.9**
1. Jesus Christ—Biography
ISBN 0-312-24333-2 (pa)   LC 98-18703
The author "relays Jesus' life as the Gospels tell it and . . . explains Jesus' context, interprets his meanings,

and ponders the implications. He also . . . mulls over the styles and uses of biography and history and in what ways those kinds of writing are factual." Booklist
This is "a probing work that examines its subject from the point of view of both a Christian apologist and a sympathetic and careful observer." Libr J
Includes bibliographical references

Wilson, A. N. (Andrew Norman), 1950-
Jesus. Norton 1992 269p $22.95   **232.9**
1. Jesus Christ—Biography 2. Jesus Christ—Historicity
ISBN 0-393-03087-3   LC 92-37046
Also available in paperback from Fawcett Columbine
The author attempts to understand Jesus as a historical figure and ethical teacher within the context of first-century Judaism
Includes bibliographical references

232.91   Mary, mother of Jesus

Harris, Ruth, 1958-
Lourdes; body and spirit in the secular age. Viking 1999 xxi, 473p il maps hardcover o.p. paperback available $17   **232.91**
1. Mary, Blessed Virgin, Saint 2. Bernadette, Saint, 1844-1879 3. Lourdes (France)
ISBN 0-14-019618-8 (pa)   LC 99-29779
Harris discusses Bernadette Soubirous's vision of the Virgin in a grotto at Lourdes, in the French Pyrenees, and how the site became a place of pilgrimage for the sick
Includes bibliographical references

Pelikan, Jaroslav Jan, 1923-
Mary through the centuries; her place in the history of culture. Yale Univ. Press 1996 267p il $40; pa $14.95   **232.91**
1. Mary, Blessed Virgin, Saint
ISBN 0-300-06951-0; 0-300-07661-4 (pa)
                             LC 96-24726
Companion volume to The illustrated Jesus through the centuries
Pelikan explores the history of Christian doctrine in regard to the Virgin Mary as well as representations of Mary in art and literature. "Each of Pelikan's 16 chapters is centered on a Marian title." Christ Century
"Although volumes have been written about the Virgin Mary from a wide variety of perspectives, it is rare to find a scholarly work that is easily accessible to the general, educated reader." Choice
Includes bibliographical references

234   Salvation and grace

Tillich, Paul, 1886-1965
Dynamics of faith. Harper & Row 1957 127p hardcover o.p. paperback available $14
                                      234
1. Faith
ISBN 0-06-093713-0 (pa)
"World perspectives"
"The author considers what faith is and is not, the symbols and types of faith and the truth and the life of faith. The discussion treats of history, science, the Bible, the individual and the community and the claims of Judaism, Mohammedanism, Protestantism and Catholicism." N Y Times Book Rev

235 Spiritual beings

Pagels, Elaine H., 1943-
The origin of Satan; [by] Elaine Pagels.
Random House 1995 214p hardcover o.p.
paperback available $12 **235**
1. Bible. N.T. Gospels—Criticism 2. Devil
ISBN 0-679-73118-0 (pa) LC 95-7983
The author "traces the development of Satan in the
Jewish community from a sort of roving agent acting on
God's behalf—always obstructing but not always evil—
to an increasingly evil force identified more and more
with intimate enemies, members of one's own communi-
ty with whom one is in conflict. That trend toward demonization of portions of the Jewish community intensified with the emergence of Christianity and became the
basis for demonization of heretics and centuries of anti-
Semitism." Booklist
Pagels "shows herself to be a masterful guide through
the risk-laden complexities of biblical studies." Publ
Wkly
Includes bibliographical references

236 Eschatology

McDannell, Colleen
Heaven; a history; [by] Colleen McDannell
and Bernhard Lang. 2nd ed. Yale Univ. Press
2001 xxv, 411p il pa $16.95 **236**
1. Heaven
ISBN 0-300-09107-9 LC 2001-90174
First published 1988
The authors "describe and interpret the ways in which
believers—from biblical authors to medieval mystics,
from Jesus to present-day religious thinkers—have pictured Heaven, not just in doctrine but also in poetry, art,
literature, and popular culture. In so doing, they shed
new light into both the private and public dimensions of
western culture." Univ Press Books for Public Libr [re-
view of 1988 edition]

Polkinghorne, John, 1930-
The God of hope and the end of the world.
Yale Univ. Press 2002 xxv, 154p $19.95
236
1. Eschatology
ISBN 0-300-09211-3 LC 2001-46577
"Theoretical physicist and Anglican priest
Polkinghorne sees in modern cosmology's grim predic-
tions of universal decay the absolute necessity for a theo-
logical affirmation of human hope. That hope, he insists,
depends upon the faithfulness of God, as revealed in the
Resurrection of Jesus Christ. . . . Though the casually
religious will find him too technical, thoughtful Christians will find much to praise in this modern Aquinas."
Booklist
Includes bibliographical references

241 Christian moral theology

Pagels, Elaine H., 1943-
Adam, Eve, and the serpent. Random
House 1988 xxviii, 189p hardcover o.p.
paperback available $12 **241**
1. Bible. O.T.—Criticism 2. Sexual behavior
ISBN 0-679-72232-7 (pa) LC 87-43227
The author "focuses on six schools of early Christian
opinion concerning sexuality, marriage, family, procre-
ation, celibacy, moral freedom, and human nature, as reflected in various interpretations of Genesis 1-3." Choice
"Pagels writes with a rare combination of formidable
knowledge and easy fluency. The old controversies she
discusses become, in her hands, matters of immediate interest." Economist
Includes bibliographical references

242 Devotional literature

The **African** prayer book; selected and with
an introduction by Desmond Tutu.
Doubleday 1995 xx, 139p $21 **242**
1. Prayers
ISBN 0-385-47730-9 LC 94-43444
Tutu "draws on the breadth and depth of African spirituality to assemble this little treasury of prayer and devotion. He has arranged material from throughout the
African continent and the African diaspora into a traditional pattern of adoration, contrition, thanksgiving, and
supplication." Booklist

Augustine, Saint, Bishop of Hippo
The confessions of St. Augustine **242**
Hardcover and paperback editions available from various publishers
"These confessions were written at the end of the
fourth century by the most distinguished of the Latin fathers as a revelation of his spiritual experience. They
have been a source of religious inspiration through the
centuries." Pratt Alcove

The **Doubleday** prayer collection; selected
and arranged by Mary Batchelor.
Doubleday 1997 509p il $22 **242**
1. Prayers
ISBN 0-385-48847-5 LC 97-12714
First published 1992 in the United Kingdom with title:
The Lion prayer collection
Batchelor "has compiled over 1300 prayers from many
eras, cultures, and sources. . . . An enormous variety of
themes are covered under 26 main headings, which are
further subdivided: grace before meals, prayers for animals, for the environment, for those dying of AIDS, and
for many other particular situations and needs. A beautiful collection of well-chosen Christian prayers." Libr J

Francis, of Assisi, Saint, 1182-1226
The little flowers of St. Francis. **242**
Paperback editions available from various publishers
These "simple anecdotes exemplify [St. Francis'] love
of nature, man and of God." Bookman's Manual

Imitation of Christ
The imitation of Christ; [by] Thomas à
Kempis **242**
Hardcover and paperback editions available from vari-
ous publishers

Imitation of Christ—*Continued*

This devotional classic originally written in Latin in the 15th century "traces in four books the gradual progress of the soul to Christian perfection, its detachment from the world, and its union with God." Oxford Companion to Engl Lit. Concise edition

248   Christian experience, practice, life

Girzone, Joseph F.

Never alone; a personal way to God. Doubleday 1994 115p il hardcover o.p. paperback available $10.95 **248**
1. Spiritual life
ISBN 0-385-47683-3 (pa)   LC 93-38725
Girzone's "empathy for the loneliness and insecurity of being human guides readers toward a more satisfying religious experience than that provided by organized religions, which he continues to criticize for not sufficiently following the living message of Jesus' life." Booklist

Lewis, C. S. (Clive Staples), 1898-1963

Letters to Malcolm: chiefly on prayer. Harcourt Brace & World 1964 124p hardcover o.p. paperback available $12   **248**
1. Christian life 2. Prayer
ISBN 0-15-650880-X (pa)
The author's "reflections on prayer are here set down in the form of thoughtful and engaging letters to his friend Malcolm." Cincinnati Public Libr

The Screwtape letters. Macmillan 1943
248
1. Christian life 2. Satire
Hardcover and paperback editions available from various publishers
"A popular work on Christian moral and theological problems. . . . It is in the form of a series of letters in which a devil, Screwtape, advises his nephew, Wormwood, on how to deal with his human 'patients.'" Reader's Ency. 4th edition

Merton, Thomas, 1915-1968

The Asian journal of Thomas Merton; edited from his original notebooks by Naomi Burton, Patrick Hart & James Laughlin; consulting editor: Amiya Chakravarty. New Directions 1973 xxviii, 445p il hardcover o.p. paperback available $16.95 **248**
1. Spiritual life
ISBN 0-8112-0570-3 (pa)
This volume is based on "notes written during [Merton's] last journey which took him to the monasteries of the Orient and ended with his accidental death in Bangkok." Libr J
Includes bibliographical references

Love and living; edited by Naomi Burton Stone & Patrick Hart. Farrar, Straus & Giroux 1979 232p o.p.; Harvest Bks. paperback available $13 **248**
1. Spiritual life
ISBN 0-15-602799-2 (pa)   LC 79-14717
These essays include "aspects of the perennial themes of love, death, life and the divine and also demonstrate the ease with which Merton assimilated the spiritual heritages of East and West." Publ Wkly

New seeds of contemplation. New Directions 1962 c1961 297p hardcover o.p. paperback available $12.95 **248**
1. Spiritual life
ISBN 0-8112-0099-X (pa)
First published 1949 with title: Seeds of contemplation and analyzed in Essay and general literature index
Meditations on integrity, fear, faith, liberty, love and renunciation

No man is an island. Harcourt Brace & Co. 1955 264p hardcover o.p. paperback available $14 **248**
1. Spiritual life 2. God
ISBN 0-15-665962-X (pa)
Analyzed in Essay and general literature index
This book contains "innumerable answers for those who have attempted a spiritual way of life in day-to-day living and are confronted with doubts about real love, the will of God, wisdom of charity, asceticism, conscience, and sincerity." Cincinnati Public Libr

Peale, Norman Vincent

The power of positive living. Doubleday 1990 398p o.p.; Fawcett Bks. paperback available $12.95 **248**
1. Pastoral psychology 2. Applied psychology 3. Success
ISBN 0-449-91166-7 (pa)   LC 90-36544
In this volume "Peale strings together dozens of personal success stories ('success' is always materialistic) that make readers feel good. Believing (in yourself, others, values, God) is all-important, and the stories of wealthy business executives who made it on their own grab center stage." Libr J

248.2   Religious experience

Armstrong, Karen

Visions of God; four medieval mystics and their writings. Bantam Bks. 1994 228p pa $19 **248.2**
1. Rolle, Richard, of Hampole, 1290?-1349 2. Hilton, Walter, 1340-1396 3. Julian, of Norwich, b. 1343 4. Mysticism
ISBN 0-553-35199-0   LC 94-20217
Contents: Richard Rolle of Hampole; Author of The cloud of unknowing; Walter Hilton; Dame Julian of Norwich
"The collection is eminently readable and should serve to make these important sources more accessible to a general audience. The selections are arranged chronologically, but Armstrong's reflections also place them in a 'developmental sequence.'" Booklist
Includes bibliographical references

Furlong, Monica

Visions & longings; medieval women mystics. Shambhala Publs. 1996 248p hardcover o.p. paperback available $24.95
248.2
1. Mysticism   2. Europe—History—476-1492 3. Women—Religious life
ISBN 1-57062-314-7 (pa)   LC 95-48804
This anthology contains a "range of material—from Heloise to Julian, from the eleventh century through the

Furlong, Monica—*Continued*
fourteenth. . . . These are not new translations, but readers—particularly those who are coming to some or all of these writings for the first time—will find it useful to have them gathered together with Furlong's introductions and biographical notes. The collection is a window into a medieval European world that is not widely known or understood." Booklist

248.4   Christian life and practice

Carter, Jimmy, 1924-
Sources of strength; meditations on scripture for a living faith. Times Bks. 1997 252p hardcover o.p. paperback available $14.99   **248.4**
1. Bible—Meditations 2. Christian life
ISBN 0-8129-3236-6 (pa)   LC 97-27501
Companion volume to Living faith
This "is a collection of 52 brief Bible lessons—one for each week of the year—written by former president Jimmy Carter. All were used in adult Sunday school classes he taught himself. Carter's lessons are open-minded and socially progressive while remaining unapologetically conservative and Christian theologically. . . . The lessons are grouped in nine categories, such as 'What We Believe' and 'Christians in the World,' but each lesson stands well on its own." Libr J

Dowrick, Stephanie
Forgiveness and other acts of love. Norton 1997 360p $23.95; pa $14   **248.4**
1. Spiritual life 2. Conduct of life
ISBN 0-393-04545-5; 0-393-31820-6 (pa)
       LC 97-17814
The paths to spirituality the author discusses are "courage, fidelity, restraint, generosity, tolerance and, especially, forgiveness." Publ Wkly
Includes bibliographical references

252   Texts of sermons

American sermons; the pilgrims to Martin Luther King, Jr. Library of Am. 1999 939p $40   **252**
1. Sermons
ISBN 1-88301-165-5   LC 98-34295
The contents of this "anthology appear chronologically according to publication or, because they were composed to be spoken, delivery dates. . . . [This is an] exceptionally rich collection." Booklist
Includes bibliographical references

King, Martin Luther, 1929-1968
Strength to love; [by] Martin Luther King, Jr. Harper & Row 1963 146p o.p.; Fortress Press paperback available $17   **252**
1. Sermons
ISBN 0-8006-1441-0 (pa)
Also available Walker & Co. large print edition
A collection of sermons addressing social injustice and racism
Includes bibliographical references

Tillich, Paul, 1886-1965
The eternal now. Scribner 1963 150p o.p.; SCM Press paperback available $14.95   **252**
1. Sermons
ISBN 0-334-02875-2 (pa)
"A collection of sixteen sermons on man's isolation, loneliness, and perplexity and on God's eternal Presence." Chicago Public Libr
"This is a very good place to begin an acquaintance with Tillich's thought." Libr J

253.5   Pastoral counseling and spiritual direction

Peale, Norman Vincent
The power of positive thinking   **253.5**
1. Pastoral psychology 2. Applied psychology 3. Success
Hardcover and paperback editions available from various publishers
First published 1952 by Prentice-Hall
The author argues that a positive attitude can change lives, win success and overcome obstacles

255   Religious congregations and orders

Norris, Kathleen, 1947-
The cloister walk. Riverhead Bks. 1996 384p hardcover o.p. paperback available $12.95   **255**
1. Monasticism and religious orders 2. Catholic Church—Liturgy 3. Spiritual life
ISBN 1-57322-584-3 (pa)   LC 96-863
Companion volume to Dakota: a spiritual geography (1993)
The author relates her experiences as a lay oblate at St. John's Abbey, a Benedictine monastery in Collegeville, Minnesota. The narrative is arranged chronologically according to the rhythm of the Catholic liturgical calendar
"Kathleen Norris knows about faith. She also knows a lot about doubt. . . . As a married Protestant woman, Norris appears to be an improbable candidate to live in a community of celibate men. Yet as she 'walks' with the Benedictine monks, spending days in continual reading, prayer, and singing, she gains new perspectives on their life and her own." Christ Sci Monit

261   Christian social theology and interreligious relations and attitudes

Armour-Hileman, Victoria, 1958-
Singing to the dead; a missioner's life among refugees from Burma. University of Ga. Press 2003 257p $27.95   **261**
1. Mon (Southeast Asian people) 2. Refugees 3. Christian missions
ISBN 0-8203-2358-6   LC 2001-8022
The author, a Catholic lay missionary relates her experiences working with the Mon ethnic minority refugees
"Armour-Hileman chronicles her unforgettable interlude with the enduring Mon with striking candor. . . .

Armour-Hileman, Victoria, 1958-—*Continued*

Observant, sweetly funny, modest, and compassionate, Armour-Hileman is a thought-provoking storyteller and an invaluable witness to what is both 'hideous and holy' in human nature." Booklist

Niebuhr, H. Richard (Helmut Richard), 1894-1962

Christ and culture. HarperSanFrancisco 2001 lv, 259p pa $15.95 **261**
1. Christian sociology 2. Christian civilization 3. Culture
ISBN 0-06-130003-9 LC 2002-284347
First published 1951
"Expanded edition, fiftieth anniversary." On cover
"Important, scholarly study presents five viewpoints of Christ and culture held over the centuries: (1) Christ against culture—and separation from 'the world'; (2) the Christ of culture—the identification of Christianity and civilization; (3) Christ above culture—the Thomist position; (4) Christ and culture in paradox—Luther's position; (5) Christ transforming culture—exemplified by Augustine and Calvin." Cincinnati Public Libr
Includes bibliographical references

261.2 Christianity and other systems of belief

Carroll, James

Constantine's sword; the church and the Jews: a history. Houghton Mifflin 2001 756p $28; pa $16 **261.2**
1. Catholic Church—Relations—Judaism 2. Christianity and other religions 3. Judaism
ISBN 0-395-77927-8; 0-6142-1908-0 (pa)
LC 00-61329
Carroll's thesis is "that the relationship with the Jews is not merely one issue among many for the modern church. It is the central issue in church history and inextricable from the core of what Christianity is about." NY Times Book Rev
"This magisterial work will satisfy Jewish and Christians readers alike, challenging both to a renewed conversation with one another." Publ Wkly
Includes bibliographical references

Cox, Harvey Gallagher

Many mansions; a Christian's encounter with other faiths; [by] Harvey Cox. Beacon Press 1988 216p hardcover o.p. paperback available $13 **261.2**
1. Christianity and other religions
ISBN 0-8070-1213-0 (pa) LC 88-47656
The author "here delineates his travels and explorations of how Jesus is perceived by adherents to Muslim, Buddhist, Hindu and Jewish faiths, as well as to the Catholic Church and Protestant denominations." Publ Wkly
"A warm and informative book that introduces some of the central issues confronting opponents of interfaith dialogue." N Y Times Book Rev
Includes bibliographical references

Kertzer, David I., 1948-

The Popes against the Jews; the Vatican's role in the rise of modern anti-semitism. Knopf 2001 355p $27.95; pa $15 **261.2**
1. Catholic Church—Relations—Judaism
2. Antisemitism
ISBN 0-375-40623-9; 0-375-70605-4 (pa)
LC 2001-33728
"Kertzer argues that the modern popes and their minions helped create and perpetuate an anti-Semitic Catholic culture that facilitated the eventual extermination of six million European Jews." Libr J
"This is a devastating indictment, and fair-minded critics will find flaws in Kertzer's methodology and sweeping conclusions. Nevertheless, he has opened a window that should be opened." Booklist
Includes bibliographical references

261.5 Christianity and secular disciplines

Davies, P. C. W., 1946-

God and the new physics. Simon & Schuster 1983 255p il hardcover o.p. paperback available $14 **261.5**
1. Physics 2. Religion and science
ISBN 0-671-52806-8 (pa) LC 83-14866
The author "outlines the physicist's view of the nature of time, space, and causality. He describes the way that natural processes can bring about things that were once thought to require the intervention of the Deity." Libr J
"The uninitiated reader will find in this volume brief presentations on quarks and black holes and a stimulating introduction to science as a helpful path in the search for God. Highly recommended for public and undergraduate libraries." Choice

Noble, David F.

The religion of technology; the divinity of man and the spirit of invention. Knopf 1997 273p hardcover o.p. paperback available $14.95 **261.5**
1. Technology and civilization 2. Religion and science 3. God
ISBN 0-14-027916-4 (pa) LC 96-48019
"Covering a period of a thousand years, Noble traces the evolution of the Western idea of technological development from the ninth century, when, [he argues], the useful arts became connected to the concept of redemption, up to the twentieth, when humans began to exercise God-like knowledge and powers." Publisher's note
"This is a dense, fascinating study of technology and Christianity." Libr J
Includes bibliographical references

Schroeder, Gerald L.

The science of God; the convergence of scientific and biblical wisdom; [by] Gerald Schroeder. Free Press 1997 226p il $25
261.5
1. Bible and science
ISBN 0-684-83736-6 LC 97-14978
Also available in paperback from Broadway Bks.
The author a physicist, "wants to show that modern study of the physical universe is really telling the same story of life and creation as the Hebrew Bible. To do this, Schroeder draws on . . . Jewish study of the Penta-

Schroeder, Gerald L.—*Continued*
teuch, the first five books of the Bible, and on his understanding of modern physics, cosmology, archeology, and the biology of evolution." Christ Sci Monit

This book contains "many interesting reflections and meaningful insights; and for those who need scientific backing to accept the pronouncements of ancient seers, this book may be highly recommended." Choice
Includes bibliographical references

261.8   Christianity and socioeconomic problems

Cone, James H.
A black theology of liberation. 20th anniversary ed. Orbis Bks. 1990 xx, 214p pa $17   **261.8**
1. Church and race relations 2. African Americans—Religion
ISBN 0-88344-685-5   LC 90-43041
First published 1970 by Lippincott
The author "takes as his theme the belief that 'Christian theology is a theology of liberation.' He then proceeds to relate the struggle for black liberation to the development of black theology in reaction to the indifference of white Christians to the plight of their fellow church members." Libr J
Includes bibliographical references

Martin, William C. (William Curtis), 1937-
With God on our side; the rise of the religious right in America; [by] William Martin. Broadway Bks. 1996 418p il $27.50; pa $15   **261.8**
1. Religion and politics 2. Religious fundamentalism 3. Conservatism 4. Christianity and politics
ISBN 0-553-06745-1; 0-553-06749-4 (pa)
           LC 96-2919
"Focusing on the modern era, the author analyzes the significance of church and clergy in the tradition of social action, from the civil rights movement through the growth of the Christian Coalition." Publ Wkly

"Unlike some companion volumes to television documentaries, Martin's well-written, superbly organized work stands on its own. . . . [It] is required reading for anyone seeking to understand the rise of the Religious Right. . . . Nothing has been published that can match Martin's book in sweep and substance." Christ Century
Includes bibliographical references

262   Ecclesiology

Chaves, Mark
Ordaining women; culture and conflict in religious organizations. Harvard Univ. Press 1997 237p hardcover o.p. paperback available $18.50   **262**
1. Ordination of women 2. Women in Christianity 3. Christian sociology 4. United States—Church history
ISBN 0-674-64146-9 (pa)   LC 97-12518
The author provides a "study of the 19th- and 20th-century ordination policies and practices of many Christian groups in the United States, including the Roman Catholic Church." Libr J
Includes bibliographical references

Wills, Garry, 1934-
Papal sin; structures of deceit. Doubleday 2000 326p $25; pa $15.95   **262**
1. Papacy 2. Catholic Church
ISBN 0-385-49410-6; 0-385-49411-4 (pa)
           LC 99-54851
The author "argues that the Church is not merely the clergy but the whole body of believers. His examination of papal policies on such topics as the Holocaust, clerical celibacy, and the role of women finds that the Church has often distorted history and Scripture in the attempt to bolster its authority. There's an undertone of grief to this rationally argued book, which ends with a wistful vision of the Church as it might be." New Yorker
Includes bibliographical references

264   Public worship

Episcopal Church
The book of common prayer prices vary
           264
Available in various bindings and editions
The official liturgy of the Episcopal Church

265   Sacraments, other rites and acts

Cuneo, Michael W.
American exorcism; expelling demons in the land of plenty. Doubleday 2001 314p $24.95   **265**
1. Exorcism 2. Demoniac possession 3. United States—Church history
ISBN 0-385-50176-5   LC 00-47439
Also available in paperback from Broadway Bks.
This is a sociological study of demonic possession and exorcisms. "Cuneo maintains that the demon-expulsion is a widespread and growing phenomenon among all types of Protestants and Roman Catholics." America

Cuneo's "descriptions of exorcisms, group and individual, are lively and well observed, as are his portraits of figures important in the recent history of exorcism in the United States." Libr J
Includes bibliographical references

270   History of Christianity and Christian church

Chadwick, Owen
A history of Christianity. St. Martin's Press 1996 304p il hardcover o.p. paperback available $21.95   **270**
1. Church history
ISBN 0-362-18723-8 (pa)   LC 96-2631
"A Thomas Dunne book"
This overview of Christianity is "illustrated, with the text and pictures working well together to give the reader a clear meaning of basic Christian concepts. . . . The facts are correct, the time lines are accurate, the voice is that of a lover of Christian history rather than a purely academic scholar." Libr J

Chidester, David

Christianity; a global history. HarperSanFrancisco 2000 627p il $32; pa $21 **270**

1. Church history 2. Christianity
ISBN 0-06-251708-2; 0-06-251770-8 (pa)
LC 00-37006

This volume is divided into three parts: "the emergence of Christian doctrine and ritual from the time of Jesus up until the year 600; the practices and personages of both the Roman and the Eastern churches up through the time of the Reformation; and, finally, the spread of Christianity around the globe beginning at the time of Columbus." Christ Sci Monit

"Highly recommended for religion and history collections looking for a work that anchors modern sensibilities to ancient ideas." Libr J

Includes bibliographical references

Jenkins, Philip, 1952-

The next Christendom; the coming of global Christianity. Oxford Univ. Press 2002 270p $28 **270**

1. Christianity 2. Forecasting
ISBN 0-19-514616-6
LC 2001-47554

The author "sketches the contours of a new Christendom emerging from the convergence of third-world demographic explosion, Muslim and Christian missionary zeal and the hunger of millions of newly urban poor for supernatural deliverance." N Y Times Book Rev

"A book everyone concerned about humanity's immediate future ought to read." Booklist

Includes bibliographical references

Riley, Gregory J. (Gregory John), 1947-

The river of God; a new history of Christian origins. HarperSanFrancisco 2001 252p $24; pa $14.95 **270**

1. Church history—30-600, Early church
ISBN 0-06-066979-9; 0-06-066980-2 (pa)
LC 2001-16888

The author "contends that Christianity originated from the tremendous theological diversity of Near Eastern religions and that its origins cannot be explained or understood adequately by simply emphasizing its roots in Judaism. . . . He proposes instead a threefold model of genealogy, punctuated equilibrium and the 'river of God' to investigate Christian origins." Publ Wkly

"This volume will become one of the most important books on the subject." Libr J

271 Religious orders in church history

Kiser, John W.

The monks of Tibhirine; faith, love, and terror in Algeria; [by] John W. Kiser III. St. Martin's Press 2002 335p il $25.95; pa $14.95 **271**

1. Trappists 2. Algeria—Church history 3. Terrorism
ISBN 0-312-25317-6; 0-312-30294-0 (pa)
LC 2001-57850

This is an account of the lives and deaths of seven French Trappist monks. In March 1996, they were killed by a group of Islamic fundamentalists who "broke through the gates and into the Cistercian Monastery of Our Lady of Atlas near the village of Tibhirine in Algeria. . . . This volume also includes the 'Testament' of [the superior, Father] Christian de Chergé." America

Includes bibliographical references

Lacouture, Jean

Jesuits; a multibiography; translated from the French by Jeremy Leggatt. Counterpoint Bks. 1995 550p il hardcover o.p. paperback available $30.95 **271**

1. Jesuits
ISBN 1-887178-60-0 (pa)
LC 95-34002

"A Cornelia and Michael Bessie book"
Original French edition, 1991

The author "presents a series of biographies of prominent Jesuits from the founder, Ignatius of Loyola, down to such modern disciples as Karl Rahner, Daniel Berrigan, and Robert Drinan." Libr J

This book "will appeal even to audiences that do not have a special interest in Jesuit history. . . . Insofar as particular stories of particular people and places are the best sources of global insight, this is an especially valuable work." Booklist

Includes bibliographical references

Read, Piers Paul, 1941-

The Templars. St. Martin's Press 2000 350p il $27.95 **271**

1. Templars 2. Crusades
ISBN 0-312-26658-8
LC 00-56144

Also available in paperback from DaCapo Press

The author provides a "chapter on the historical context that nurtured the growth of the order. He proceeds to describe, with chilling effect, the violence and thirst for power that led to the demise of the order in the fourteenth century. This is an engrossing and beautifully written work of popular history that unfolds like a well-structured crime novel." Booklist

Includes bibliographical references

272 Persecutions in church history

Foxe, John, 1516-1587

Foxe's Book of martyrs **272**

1. Martyrs 2. Persecution 3. Church history

Hardcover and paperback editions available from various publishers

First complete version published 1563 in England under title: Actes and monuments of these latter and perilous days

"The *Actes and Monuments* was tremendously influential, being used practically as a companion volume to the Bible in English churches and households for many years. The work is of interest historically for its many accounts of the deaths of contemporary Protestant martyrs." Reader's Ency. 4th edition

Kamen, Henry

The Spanish Inquisition; a historical revision. Yale Univ. Press 1998 369p il $45; pa $14.80 **272**

1. Inquisition 2. Spain—History
ISBN 0-300-07522-7; 0-300-07880-3 (pa)
LC 97-32451

First published 1965 in the United Kingdom; first United States edition 1966 by New Am. Lib.

In this revision of his 1965 study, the author "restates his original argument. . . . He reaffirms his contention that an all-powerful, torture-mad Inquisition is largely a 19th-century myth. In its place he portrays a poor, understaffed institution whose scattered tribunals had only a limited reach and whose methods were more hu-

Kamen, Henry—*Continued*
mane than those of most secular courts. . . . As for the Inquisition's much-vaunted role as Big Brother and its responsibility for intellectual decline, Kamen rejects this hypothesis out of hand. . . . [He] also dismisses the notion that the Inquisition enjoyed widespread popular support." N Y Times Book Rev
Includes bibliographical references

273 Doctrinal controversies and heresies in general church history

Rubenstein, Richard E.
When Jesus became God; the epic fight over Christ's divinity in the last days of Rome. Harcourt Brace & Co. 1999 267p map $26; pa $14 **273**
1. Jesus Christ—Divinity 2. Arius, d. 336 3. Athanasius, Saint, Patriarch of Alexandria, d. 373 4. Church history—30-600, Early church
ISBN 0-15-100368-8; 0-15-601315-0 (pa)
LC 98-52097
"Rubenstein examines the details of the fractious early period when Christianity was defining itself against other religious sects through a number of councils and creeds. He narrows his focus to the fiery fourth-century battle between Arius, who contended that Christ did not share God's nature, and Athanasius, the ferocious Alexandrian bishop who asserted that Christ was fully God. With a storyteller's verve, Rubenstein offers a panoramic view of early Christianity." Publ Wkly
Includes bibliographical references

277 Christian Church—North America

Yearbook of American and Canadian churches. Abingdon Press pa $29.95 **277**
1. Religious institutions—Directories
ISSN 0084-3644
Annual. First published 1916. Title and publisher vary
"Directory, statistical, and historical information on many religious and ecumenical organizations and service agencies, accredited seminaries, colleges and universities, and depositories of church history materials. Also a list of religious periodicals." Ref Sources for Small & Medium-sized Libr. 6th edition

277.3 Christian Church—United States

Bawer, Bruce, 1956-
Stealing Jesus; how fundamentalism betrays Christianity. Crown 1997 340p hardcover o.p. paperback available $14 **277.3**
1. Christian fundamentalism 2. Christianity 3. United States—Church history
ISBN 0-609-80222-4 (pa)
LC 97-20111
The author "contends that fundamentalist Christianity, what he calls the 'Church of Law,' has been preaching a message of wrath and judgment to modern American culture that Bawer believes is incompatible with Jesus' message of love. . . . [His] graceful prose and lucid insights make this a must-read book for anyone concerned with the relationship of Christianity to contemporary American culture." Publ Wkly

Lincoln, C. Eric (Charles Eric), 1924-2000
The black church in the African American experience; [by] C. Eric Lincoln and Lawrence H. Mamiya. Duke Univ. Press 1990 519p hardcover o.p. paperback available $26.95 **277.3**
1. African Americans—Religion 2. United States—Church history
ISBN 0-8223-1073-2 (pa)
LC 90-34050
This book was "developed from a ten-year field study that investigated the black church as it relates to the history of African Americans and to contemporary black culture. . . . [It considers] the church's relationships to politics, economics, women (attitudes of clergy as pastors), youth, music, civil rights, and trends for the next century." Libr J
Includes bibliographical references

Marty, Martin E., 1928-
Pilgrims in their own land; 500 years of religion in America. Little, Brown 1984 500p il o.p.; Penguin Bks. paperback available $15.95 **277.3**
1. United States—Church history 2. United States—Religion
ISBN 0-14-008268-9 (pa)
LC 84-821
This book examines "the force of religion in the United States since colonial times. Marty considers not only the religious beliefs and rituals brought to America by the various European settlers, but also those of native Americans. The clashes between Protestant, Catholic, Judaic, and other religious groups are perceived in light of their influence upon the development of this nation up to the present." Booklist

Utter, Glenn H.
The religious right; a reference handbook; [by] Glenn H. Utter and John W. Storey. 2nd ed. ABC-CLIO 2001 382p (Contemporary world issues) $45 **277.3**
1. Conservatism 2. Christianity and politics 3. United States—Politics and government 4. Christian fundamentalism
ISBN 1-57607-212-6
LC 2001-3625
First published 1995
The authors "'treat the religious Right as an essentially political movement that courts voters' and lobbies for conservative causes. . . . [The book discusses] the battlegrounds of evolution and creation, school prayer, and moral and sexuality issues. . . . [It includes] biographies of key figures, sociological survey data, a directory of organizations (both supporting and in opposition to the religious Right), and annotated bibliographies of print, video, audio, CD-ROM, and . . . Internet resources. . . . This is recommended for all public and academic libraries." Libr J

280 Christian denominations and sects

Mead, Frank Spencer, 1898-1982
Handbook of denominations in the United States; [by] Frank S. Mead, Samuel S. Hill. Abingdon Press $20 **280**
1. Sects 2. United States—Religion
First published 1951. (11th edition revised by Craig D. Atwood 2001) Periodically revised

Mead, Frank Spencer, 1898-1982—Continued

"History and present structure of Christian religious bodies in the United States. Reports on doctrines of different churches. Includes bibliography and index." NY Public Libr Book of How & Where to Look It Up

282   Roman Catholic Church

Carroll, James

Toward a new Catholic Church; the promise of reform. Houghton Mifflin 2002 130p pa $8.95   282

1. Catholic Church
ISBN 0-618-31337-0   LC 2002-27262

"A Mariner book"

The author "has a reform agenda . . . consisting of five proposals: expand the faithful's biblical literacy in sophistication and depth; purge the church's political pretensions and behavior; reformulate Christology to emphasize Jesus as revelator rather than savior; run the church democratically; and repent of anti-Semitism, sexism, homophobia, and other ills by admitting the church has sinned. . . . An important statement." Booklist
Includes bibliographical references

Catholic almanac. Our Sunday Visitor pa $24.95   282

1. Catholic Church—Directories 2. Almanacs
ISSN 0069-1208

Annual. First published 1904. Title varies

"Includes much miscellaneous information, e.g., annual survey of news, ecclesiastical calendar, glossary of terms in Catholic use, the Catholic church in various countries of the world, statistics, directory of information, etc." Guide to Ref Books. 11th edition

The **Catholic** encyclopedia; Robert C. Broderick, editor; Virginia Broderick, illustrator. rev and updated ed. Nelson, T. 1987 613p pa $24.99   282

1. Catholic Church—Encyclopedias
ISBN 0-8407-3175-2   LC 87-1529

First published 1976

"This work is best used to look up a broad range of traditional Catholic terms, such as the papacy, indulgences, and canonization, and its views on such things as Marxism, evolution, and euthanasia. New articles are added on such topics as liberation theology and the ordination of women, but the main thrust is historical." Recomm Ref Books in paperback. 2d edition

Collins, Paul

The modern Inquisition; seven prominent Catholics and their struggles with the Vatican. Overlook Press 2002 260p $29.95
                                                    282

1. Catholic Church
ISBN 1-58567-270-X   LC 2002-25223

This work is an "assessment of the Roman Catholic Church's treatment of its theologians who reflect contrary views from those of the Congregation for the Doctrine of the Faith (CDF). . . . In eight passionately written essays, [Collins] considers the lives, work, and trials of several priests and sisters whose ideas were reviewed by the CDF. . . . Among them Hans Kung, Lavinia Byrne, Charles Curran, Jeannine Gramick and Robert Nugent, Tissa Balusaria, and the author himself." Libr J
Includes bibliographical references

Cornwell, John, 1940-

Breaking faith; the Pope, the people, and the fate of Catholicism. Viking 2001 310p $24.95; pa $14   282

1. John Paul II, Pope, 1920- 2. Catholic Church
ISBN 0-670-03002-3; 0-14-219608-8 (pa)
                              LC 2001-26721

The author "takes a respectful yet critical look at the pontificate of John Paul II and the church he has created over the past 25 years. . . . A provocative, deeply personal, and intelligent book." Libr J
Includes bibliographical references

Donofrio, Beverly

Looking for Mary, or, The Blessed Mother and me. Viking 2000 246p il hardcover o.p. paperback available $14   282

1. Mary, Blessed Virgin, Saint
ISBN 0-14-019627-7 (pa)   LC 00-36790

The author "recounts her often painful spiritual odyssey from bitter nonbeliever to staunch devotee of the Virgin Mary." Booklist
"Deeply personal and wonderfully written, this book invites the reader to confront skeptical attitudes about religion." Libr J

Duffy, Eamon

Saints & sinners; a history of the Popes. Yale Univ. Press 1997 326p il maps $30; pa $17.95   282

1. Papacy 2. Catholic Church—History
ISBN 0-300-07332-1; 0-300-09165-6 (pa)
                              LC 97-60897

This illustrated volume is a companion piece to a six-part television series of the same name. The book offers an overview of the 2,000-year history of the papacy
"Duffy's task is to present a balanced and continuous narrative with as much personal and historical detail as possible. This he does admirably with an eye for lively anecdotes and apt quotations." Commonweal

Gillis, Chester, 1951-

Roman Catholicism in America. Columbia Univ. Press 1999 365p il (Columbia contemporary American religion series) $60; pa $20.50   282

1. Catholic Church—United States 2. United States—Church history
ISBN 0-231-10870-2; 0-231-10871-0 (pa)
                              LC 99-17945

The author "provides a broad overview of the history and practice of Catholicism in America at the end of the 20th century." Publ Wkly
This is "an excellent survey." Libr J
Includes bibliographical references

Greeley, Andrew M., 1928-

The Catholic myth; the behavior and beliefs of American Catholics. Scribner 1990 322p hardcover o.p. paperback available $13
                                                    282

1. Catholic Church—United States 2. Catholics—United States
ISBN 0-684-82682-8 (pa)   LC 89-39259

"Greeley debunks the popular myth that American Catholicism is virtually moribund. Employing . . . concrete sociological data to support his thesis, he asserts that Catholicism is thriving in the U.S. Though many American

Greeley, Andrew M., 1928-—*Continued*

Catholics have lost faith in the institutionalized hierarchy of the Church, they remain assiduously devoted to the essential poetry of their religion." Booklist

"This lively, readable assessment of contemporary Catholicism may affront some readers, but will likely stimulate and challenge others." Publ Wkly

The **HarperCollins** encyclopedia of Catholicism; general editor, Richard P. McBrien; associate editors, Harold W. Attridge [et al.] HarperSanFrancisco 1995 xxxviii, 1349p il maps $47.50   **282**
1. Catholic Church—Encyclopedias
ISBN 0-06-065338-8   LC 94-39972

"This encyclopedic dictionary contains 4700 entries by 277 experts. . . . Broad-ranging topics in Catholic theology, history, culture, art, canon law, literature, etc., are replete with cross references, photos, maps, tables, diagrams, and charts." Libr J

John Paul II, Pope, 1920-

Crossing the threshold of hope; edited by Vittorio Messori. Knopf 1994 244p hardcover o.p. paperback available $15   **282**
1. Apologetics 2. Catholic Church 3. Christian life 4. Faith
ISBN 0-679-76561-1 (pa)   LC 94-78675
Also available large print edition pa $15 (ISBN 0-679-75868-2)

In this book the Pope responds to written questions by an Italian Catholic journalist originally planned for a television interview which never took place. The questions addressed include: what is the papacy?; when and how should one pray?; is there proof of God's existence?; is Jesus the Son of God?; why is there so much evil in the world?; why does God tolerate suffering?; is only Rome right?; and what are human rights?

"This is a book to be read for insights, perspectives, connections, formulations that spark meditation and enrich our understanding." Commonweal

Küng, Hans, 1928-

The Catholic Church; a short history; translated by John Bowden. Modern Lib. 2001 xxv, 221p (Modern Library chronicles) $19.95; pa $9.95   **282**
1. Catholic Church—History
ISBN 0-679-64092-4; 0-8129-6762-3 (pa)
        LC 00-67568

The author "presents a summary of the major persons and movements that have formed the Catholic Church from its beginnings to the present." Libr J

"About as good a brief presentation of the 'liberal' view of church history as anyone could reasonably expect." Booklist

Maxwell-Stuart, P. G.

Chronicle of the popes; the reign-by-reign record of the papacy from St. Peter to the present. Thames & Hudson 1997 240p il maps $34.95   **282**
1. Papacy 2. Catholic Church—History
ISBN 0-500-01798-0   LC 97-60230
This survey examines the lives and deeds of the 264 popes from St. Peter to John Paul II

This history of the papacy "provides a good selection of illustrations with a lightweight text." N Y Times Book Rev

Includes bibliographical references

New Catholic encyclopedia. 2nd ed. Gale Group 2003 15v il maps set $1,295   **282**
1. Catholic Church—Encyclopedias
ISBN 0-7876-4004-2   LC 2002-924
First published 1967 as an update to the Catholic encyclopedia

This encyclopedia "covers the history of the eastern churches, the churches of the Protestant Reformation, and other ecclesial communities as well as the Christian roots based in ancient Israel and Judaism. No comprehensive resource on Catholicism can be complete without touching on other world religions as well, including Islam, Buddhism, and Hinduism. This resource provides entries not only on the doctrine, organization, and history of the church, but also on the people, institutions, and social changes that have affected the church over the years. Arranged alphabetically, the entries run in length from half a page to several pages in length. All entries provide the name of the contributor and a bibliography. Cross-references to related articles are located throughout the work. Adding to the usefulness of the set are more than 3,000 black-and-white photographs, maps, and charts that complement the scholarly articles." Am Ref Books Annu, 2003

New Catholic encyclopedia: jubilee volume, the Wojtyla years. Gale Group 2001 681p il $95   **282**
1. Catholic Church
ISBN 0-7876-4787-X   LC 00-60991
Published in association with the Catholic University of America

"Arranged into two parts, . . . [this volume] closely chronicles the life, teachings, and activities of Karol Wojtyla. First, 12 thematic essays review and critique the contributions of Pope John Paul II and his influence on the 20th century." Libr J

For a fuller review see: Booklist, March 1, 2001

The **Official** Catholic directory. National Register Pub. $245   **282**
1. Catholic Church—Directories
ISSN 0078-3854

Supplementary paperback volume published midyear included in price of subscription

Annual. First published 1886. Title and publisher vary

"Contains a large amount of useful and detailed directory, institutional, and statistical information about the organization, clergy, churches, missions, schools, religious orders, etc., of the Catholic church in the U.S. and its possessions. Coverage varies." Guide to Ref Books. 11th edition

Reese, Thomas J.

Inside the Vatican; the politics and organization of the Catholic Church. Harvard Univ. Press 1996 317p il $30; pa $16.95   **282**
1. Papacy 2. Vatican City 3. Catholic Church
ISBN 0-674-93260-9; 0-679-93261-7 (pa)
        LC 96-26641
The author examines "the internal workings of the Vatican both as city-state and the headquarters of the Roman Catholic Church. . . . With its wealth of information, historical background, and analysis, Reese's work should be an important addition for a variety of libraries." Libr J

Includes bibliographical references

Saints and sinners; the American Catholic experience through stories, memoirs, essays, and commentary; edited by Greg Tobin. Doubleday 1999 347p $25.95 **282**
1. Catholics—United States 2. Catholic Church—United States
ISBN 0-385-49331-2   LC 99-25167
This compilation of excerpts from books published since World War II "is divided into four sections: Politics and Protest, Witness and Dissent, Catholic Memories, Catholic Imagination. Because Tobin heavily emphasizes memoir and fiction, with smatterings of biography and sociology, the collection is a broad sample of American Catholic culture of the recent past." Publ Wkly
Includes bibliographical references

Wills, Garry, 1934-
Why I am a Catholic. Houghton Mifflin 2002 390p $26; pa $14   **282**
1. Papacy 2. Catholic Church
ISBN 0-618-13429-8; 0-618-38048-5 (pa)
    LC 2002-283644
The author "begins with a very personal, though brief, look at his life as a Catholic, which includes time spent as a Jesuit novice, then proceeds with a detailed defense of his views on the church and its papacy. He concludes with an explanation of the Apostles' Creed, which he regards as the true foundation of his faith." Publ Wkly
This book is "intellectually satisfying, and spiritually moving." Booklist

Woodward, Kenneth L.
Making saints; how the Catholic Church determines who becomes a saint, who doesn't, and why. Simon & Schuster 1990 461p il hardcover o.p. paperback available $21.50   **282**
1. Christian saints 2. Catholic Church
ISBN 0-684-81530-3 (pa)   LC 90-10117
A study of the politics and procedures of the modern process of canonization in the Roman Catholic church
This is "the most comprehensive, critical and up-to-date look at saint making so far written." N Y Times Book Rev
Includes bibliographical references

287.9 Salvation Army

Winston, Diane H., 1951-
Red-hot and righteous; the urban religion of the Salvation Army; [by] Diane Winston. Harvard Univ. Press 1999 290p il $31; pa $16.95   **287.9**
1. Salvation Army
ISBN 0-674-86706-8; 0-674-00396-9 (pa)
    LC 98-47842
"Winston traces the development of the Salvation Army from 1880, when it first arrived in New York, to 1950. . . . Winston's lively study is a must-read for anyone interested in the Salvation Army as a case study for the interrelationship of religion and culture." Publ Wkly
Includes bibliographical references

289   Other denominations and sects

Sprigg, June
Shaker—life, work, and art; [by] June Sprigg and David Larkin; photographs by Michael Freeman. Stewart, Tabori & Chang 1987 272p il o.p.; Abradale Press reprint available $19.98   **289**
1. Shakers
ISBN 0-8109-8214-5 (pa)   LC 87-9957
"A David Larkin book"
An illustrated look at Shaker's history, lifestyle, religious practices, and crafts
Includes bibliographical references

Stein, Stephen J., 1940-
The Shaker experience in America; a history of the United Society of Believers. Yale Univ. Press 1992 xx, 554p il $65; pa $21   **289**
1. Shakers
ISBN 0-300-05139-5; 0-300-05933-7 (pa)
    LC 91-30836
A historical look at the evolution of Shakerism focusing on the movement's cultural values, religion and artifacts
Includes bibliographical references

289.3   Latter-Day Saints (Mormons)

Abanes, Richard
One nation under gods; a history of the Mormon Church. Four Walls Eight Windows 2002 xxv, 651p il $32; pa $22   **289.3**
1. Church of Jesus Christ of Latter-day Saints
ISBN 1-56858-219-6; 1-56858-283-8 (pa)
    LC 2001-40430
The author "explains what Mormons believe, as well as how Mormonism came to be the religion that it is today. . . . [He also discusses the] origins of Mormonism, the socioeconomic factors that contributed to its growth, its ongoing political agenda, and its religious teachings." Publisher's note
"This well-researched and readable history will be of interest to anyone seeking an objective Mormon history." Libr J
Includes bibliographical references

Book of Mormon
The Book of Mormon. Herald House prices vary   **289.3**
1. Mormons
Available in various bindings and editions
First published 1830
"Based on golden plates which Joseph Smith claimed were revealed to him, and which he unearthed from Cumorah Hill, New York, this book is roughly similar in structure to the *Bible*. . . . Emphasized are the doctrines of pre-existence, perfection, the after-life, and Christ's second coming." Haydn. Thesaurus of Book Dig

Bushman, Richard L., 1931-
Joseph Smith and the beginnings of
Mormonism. University of Ill. Press 1984
262p maps hardcover o.p. paperback available
$16.95   **289.3**
1. Smith, Joseph, 1805-1844 2. Church of Jesus
Christ of Latter-day Saints
ISBN 0-252-06012-1 (pa)   LC 84-2451
The author surveys the historical background of the
Mormon church with particular emphasis on the spiritual
growth of its founder, Joseph Smith
"Resulting from many years of careful research and
reflections, this book will stand for decades as a major
contribution in the field." Choice
Includes bibliographical references

Givens, Terryl
By the hand of Mormon; the American
scripture that launched a new world religion;
[by] Terryl L. Givens. Oxford Univ. Press
2002 230p il maps $30; pa $16.95   **289.3**
1. Book of Mormon
ISBN 0-19-513818-X; 0-19-516888-7 (pa)
                                   LC 2001-53118
The author "investigates the history and theology of
the Book of Mormon, which he calls 'perhaps the most
religiously influential, hotly contested, and, in the secular
press at least, intellectually under-investigated book in
America.' Givens persuasively demonstrates how the
Book of Mormon was trumpeted by early Latter-day
Saints more for the fact of its existence . . . than for its
content per se." Publ Wkly
Includes bibliographical references

Ostling, Richard N.
Mormon America; the power and the
promise; [by] Richard N. Ostling and Joan K.
Ostling. HarperSanFrancisco 1999 xxvi, 454p
il $26; pa $17.95   **289.3**
1. Church of Jesus Christ of Latter-day Saints
ISBN 0-06-066371-5; 0-06-066372-3 (pa)
                                   LC 99-28516
The authors "look at the history, beliefs, and econom-
ic, social/cultural, and religious practices of the LDS, and
. . . the controversies facing the contemporary church,
such as issues of academic freedom at church-owned
Brigham Young University and the church's wealth.
Highly recommended for all libraries." Libr J
Includes bibliographical references

289.5 Church of Christ, Scientist (Christian Science)

Eddy, Mary Baker, 1821-1910
Science and health, with key to the
Scriptures; Trustees under the will of Mary
Baker G. Eddy. Christian Science Pub. Soc.
prices vary   **289.5**
1. Christian Science
Available in various bindings
First published 1875
This work is the foundation of the Christian Science
religion, setting forth Mrs. Baker's interpretations of the
Holy Scriptures and the method of healing. It has not
been revised since her death in 1910

Fraser, Caroline
God's perfect child; living and dying in the
Christian Science Church. Metropolitan Bks.
1999 561p il hardcover o.p. paperback
available $16   **289.5**
1. Eddy, Mary Baker, 1821-1910 2. Christian Science
ISBN 0-8050-4431-0 (pa)   LC 99-17535
This "history traces the roots of the Christian Science
church to nineteenth-century Calvinism, Emersonian self-
reliance, and the remarkable life of its grandiose, anxi-
ety-ridden founder, Mary Baker Eddy. . . . A work of
compelling skepticism and scholarship." New Yorker
Includes bibliographical references

Schoepflin, Rennie B.
Christian Science on trial; religious healing
in America. Johns Hopkins Univ. Press 2002
301p il (Medicine, science, and religion in
historical context) $39.95   **289.5**
1. Christian Science
ISBN 0-8018-7057-7   LC 2001-8512
"A historical examination of Christian Science's evolution during the late 19th and early 20th centuries and
the faith's struggle for existence and respectability in the
midst of organized American medicine's efforts to curtail
its influence." Libr J
Includes bibliographical references

289.6 Society of Friends (Quakers)

Hamm, Thomas D., 1957-
The Quakers in America. Columbia Univ.
Press 2003 304p (Columbia contemporary
American religion series) $40   **289.6**
1. Society of Friends
ISBN 0-231-12362-0   LC 2002-41422
The author provides an "introduction to Quaker origins abroad, their influences on American politics and
culture, as well as their beliefs and traditions as they are
played out on American soil. Though this is a serious
history with a glossary, chronology, and 40 pages of
notes, cartoons and anecdotes leaven the text. For both
public and academic libraries." Libr J
Includes bibliographical references

289.7 Mennonite churches

Amish roots; a treasury of history, wisdom,
and lore; [edited by] John A. Hostetler.
Johns Hopkins Univ. Press 1989 319p il
hardcover o.p. paperback available $19.95
                                    289.7
1. Amish
ISBN 0-8018-4402-9 (pa)   LC 88-31688
This is a compilation of "writing by and about the
Amish from journals and letters, family and farm records, newspaper stories, poems, songs and stories. Ranging from the observations of the first Anabaptist immigrants in the 1700s to the present, the over 150 entries—
commenting on church, family life, work, school and the
rich Amish agricultural heritage—form a remarkably
complete portrait." Publ Wkly
Includes bibliographical references

Hostetler, John A., 1918-

Amish society. 4th ed. Johns Hopkins Univ. Press 1993 435p il maps hardcover o.p. paperback available $13.37 **289.7**
1. Amish
ISBN 0-8018-4442-8 (pa)   LC 92-19304
First published 1963
This book discusses the sectarian origins of the Amish, immigration history, family and community life, population trends, farming practices, technological innovations, education, medicine and the effects of government regulation
Includes bibliographical references

Kraybill, Donald B.

On the backroad to heaven; Old Order Hutterites, Mennonites, Amish, and Brethren; [by] Donald B. Kraybill, Carl F. Bowman. Johns Hopkins Univ. Press 2001 330p il maps (Center books in Anabaptist studies) $57; pa $16.95 **289.7**
1. Mennonites 2. Amish 3. Hutterian Brethren
ISBN 0-8018-6565-4; 0-8018-7089-5 (pa)
LC 00-10406
"This look at the history, similarities and differences between four groups of Old Order faithful in North America—Hutterites, Mennonites, Amish and Brethren—is fascinating. . . . A book that, in one volume, tackles history, sociology and future trends—and does it well." Christ Century
Includes bibliographical references

The riddle of Amish culture. rev ed. Johns Hopkins Univ. Press 2001 397p il maps (Center books in Anabaptist studies) $65; pa $16.95 **289.7**
1. Amish
ISBN 0-8018-6771-1; 0-8018-6772-X (pa)
LC 00-13054

First published 1989
"Published in cooperation with the Center for American Places, Santa Fe, New Mexico, and Harrisonburg, Virginia"
The author examines the history and culture of the Amish, discussing such topics as the social structure of Amish society, rites of redemption and purification, recreation and social gatherings, work, technology, public relations, and social change
Includes bibliographical references

289.9   Other denominations and sects

Holden, Andrew, 1964-

Jehovah's Witnesses; portrait of a contemporary religious movement. Routledge 2002 206p $80; pa $23.95 **289.9**
1. Jehovah's Witnesses
ISBN 0-415-26609-2; 0-415-26610-6 (pa)
LC 2001-45726
"This ethnographic study, academic in tone and British in orientation, offers several chapters of general information about the faith and analyzes its relationship to the wider society." Libr J
Includes bibliographical references

291   Comparative religion and religious mythology

Anderson, Sherry Ruth

The feminine face of God; the unfolding of the sacred in women; [by] Sherry Ruth Anderson and Patricia Hopkins. Bantam Bks. 1991 253p hardcover o.p. paperback available $15.95 **291**
1. Women—Religious life 2. Femininity of God
ISBN 0-553-35266-0 (pa)   LC 91-6657
This book is "an attempt to see the divine face as mirrored on the faces of more than 100 women from all walks of life who were willing to describe their inner lives in open and intimate detail. . . . What these women have in common, the authors tell us, is that they were willing to trust their own essential natures and become their own teachers." N Y Times Book Rev
Includes bibliographical references

Armstrong, Karen

The battle for God; fundamentalism in Judaism, Christianity, and Islam. Knopf 2000 442p $29.95; pa $15 **291**
1. Religious fundamentalism
ISBN 0-679-43597-2; 0-345-39169-1 (pa)
LC 99-34022
This is a "study of fundamentalism among Jews (in Israel), Christians (American Protestants), and Muslims (Sunni Egyptians and Shiite Iranians). Armstrong argues that all strains of fundamentalism, despite their differences, are fearful defenses against modernity. . . . The author is sympathetic to the human need for spiritual meaning, but she points out that the intellectual flaws of fundamentalist beliefs are customarily accompanied by paranoia, anger, and aggression—which, in turn, frequently betray the message of the faith." New Yorker
Includes bibliographical references

A history of God; the 4000 year quest of Judaism, Christianity, and Islam. Knopf 1993 xxiii, 460p maps hardcover o.p. paperback available $15 **291**
1. God
ISBN 0-345-38456-3 (pa)   LC 92-38318
This is a study of ideas and experiences of God in Judaism, Christianity and Islam from Abraham to the twentieth century
"Public librarians should be aware that conservative readers may be offended by this book, and even religious scholars may find Armstrong's rather one-sided 'death of God' optimism about humanity a bit passé. Otherwise, this is an excellent and informative book." Libr J

The **Book** of heaven; an anthology of writings from ancient to modern times; edited by Carol Zaleski and Philip Zaleski. Oxford Univ. Press 2000 432p il music $30 **291**
1. Heaven
ISBN 0-19-511933-9   LC 99-56045
This anthology reflects the "diversity of opinion on the reality and experience of the blessed state of the afterlife, from the Bible to Pygmy hymns." Libr J
Includes bibliographical references

Eerdmans' handbook to the world's religions. rev ed. Eerdmans 1994 464p il maps pa $26 **291**

1. Religions 2. Religion
ISBN 0-8028-0853-0
First published 1982

This "volume has eight parts: religion as a phenomenon; ancient religions (e.g., those of ancient Egypt, Greece, and Rome); primal religions (e.g., those of sub-Saharan Africa, the Americas, and Oceania); Eastern religions (e.g., Hinduism, Buddhism); Judaism and Islam; Christianity; the context of modern religion (e.g., secularism, pluralism, and so on); and a 'rapid fact-finder'. . . . In these sections, the history, beliefs, and practices of religions are treated, and charts systematically present information on festivals, religious subdivisions, and pantheons. A general index concludes the handbook." Am Ref Books Annu, 1996

Eliade, Mircea, 1907-1986

A history of religious ideas; translated from the French by Willard R. Trask. University of Chicago Press 1978-1985 3v pa v1 $25; v2 $27.50; v3 $20 **291**

1. Religion 2. Religions   LC 77-16784
Contents: v1 From the Stone Age to the Eleusinian mysteries, original French edition 1976 (ISBN 0-226-20401-4); v2 From Gautama Buddha to the triumph of Christianity, original French edition 1978 (ISBN 0-226-20403-0); v3 From Muhammad to the Age of Reform, original French edition 1983 (ISBN 0-226-20405-7)

Eliade has chosen "to focus on moments and movements in which religious creativity has found expression. He gives attention not only to the major religions but also to less familiar religious creations. . . . [The author has] contributed immeasurably to our understanding of the nature and varieties of religious experience." Christ Century
Includes bibliographical references

Hopfe, Lewis M., d. 1992

Religions of the world; revised by Mark R. Woodward. Prentice-Hall il maps pa $57 **291**

1. Religions
First published 1976 by Glencoe. (8th edition 2000) Periodically revised

In exploring the major religions of the world, the author traces the historical development of each, its founders, teachings, and present status
Includes bibliographical references

The **Illustrated** guide to world religions; general editor, Michael D. Coogan. Oxford Univ. Press 1998 288p il maps $45 **291**

1. Religions
ISBN 0-19-521366-1   LC 98-6784

An introductory survey of seven major world religions: Judaism, Christianity, Islam, Hinduism, Buddhism, and Chinese and Japanese traditions

The information presented "is accurate and presented in lively prose, and the color photographs and maps greatly enhance reading pleasure." Libr J
Includes bibliographical references

Messadié, Gérald

A history of the devil; translated from the French by Marc Romano. Kodansha Int. 1996 377p hardcover o.p. paperback available $16 **291**

1. Devil 2. Demonology
ISBN 1-56836-198-X (pa)   LC 95-4949

"Using a comparative and phenomenological approach, the author traces the idea of the Devil from ancient Greece and India to contemporary Western culture. What emerges from Messadie's explorations is that the Devil is a very recent concept, arising primarily out of Zoroastrianism in Persia in the sixth century B.C." Publ Wkly

"Messadie's highly engaging and provocative cultural history is essential for most libraries." Libr J
Includes bibliographical references

Miller, Sukie

Finding hope when a child dies; what other cultures can teach us; [by] Sukie Miller with Doris Ober. Simon & Schuster 1999 206p $23; pa $12 **291**

1. Death 2. Religions
ISBN 0-684-84663-2; 0-684-86561-0 (pa)
                                        LC 99-21668

The author "outlines how non-Western spiritual beliefs concerning children can help Western parents deal with the loss of a child." Libr J
Includes bibliographical references

Religions of the world; a comprehensive encyclopedia of beliefs and practices; J. Gordon Melton, Martin Baumann, editors; David B. Barrett, world religious statistics; Donald Wiebe, introduction. ABC-CLIO 2002 4v il maps set $385 **291**

1. Religions—Encyclopedias
ISBN 1-57607-223-1   LC 2002-5617

This "work details the history, development, organization, current status, and contact information for major organizations associated with various living world faiths. Edited with the requisite authority by Melton . . . and Baumann . . . this unique encyclopedia is not concerned with defining and analyzing the major world religions but rather with presenting the constitutive communities, groups, and associations within each religion. The result is a sort of 'encyclopedia of associations' for world religions with superb commentary." Libr J

Turner, Alice K.

The history of hell. Harcourt Brace & Co. 1993 275p il hardcover o.p. paperback available $21 **291**

1. Hell
ISBN 0-15-600137-3 (pa)   LC 93-9909

"Belief in a hell or some sort of afterlife has been intrinsic to the religions of the world ever since the first stories were shared aloud and incised in clay tablets. Turner's richly illustrated history surveys the myriad forms hell has taken in the West from Sumer to Rome and beyond." Booklist

Weber, Eugen Joseph, 1925-

Apocalypses; prophesies, cults, and millennial beliefs through the ages; [by] Eugen Weber. Harvard Univ. Press 1999 294p $27; pa $16.95 **291**
1. End of the world 2. Millennium
ISBN 0-674-04080-5; 0-674-00395-0 (pa)
LC 99-18001
"Weber traces millennial beliefs as professed through the ages. From ancient and pre-Christian times to the present day, humankind has had an unshakable belief that the end is at hand. . . . Weber has an excellent grasp of his subject, an accessible style, and an understated sense of humor." Booklist
Includes bibliographical references

291.1 Religious mythology

Barbour, Ian G.

When science meets religion; enemies, strangers, or partners? HarperSanFrancisco 2000 205p pa $16 **291.1**
1. Religion and science
ISBN 0-06-060381-X
LC 99-55579
The author "guides readers through a four-fold typology of the science/religion relationship—Conflict, Independence, Dialogue and Integration. . . . Barbour's own sympathies are markedly on the side of dialogue and integration, but he makes an unusually sucessful effort to represent other perspectives in a fair light." Publ Wkly
Includes bibliographical references

Barlow, Connie C.

Green space, green time; the way of science; [by] Connie Barlow. Copernicus 1997 xxvii, 329p il $25 **291.1**
1. Nature 2. Ecology 3. Religion and science
ISBN 0-387-94794-9
LC 97-15704
"Religion and science are two different methods by which we can come to understand ourselves, the universe, and how we all fit into the scheme of things. Barlow [argues] . . . that to solve the complex ecological problems our planet faces today, we must reinvigorate our idea of the history of life on earth with the myth, metaphor, and meaning of religious experience." Booklist
"This book has the potential to be a key work for environmentalists and those interested in the relationship between science and religion." Libr J
Includes bibliographical references

Barr, Stephen M., 1953-

Modern physics and ancient faith. University of Notre Dame Press 2003 312p il $30 **291.1**
1. Physics 2. Religion and science
ISBN 0-268-03471-0
LC 2002-151565
The author "argues that the great discoveries of modern physics are more compatible with the central teachings of Christianity and Judaism about God, the cosmos, and the human soul than with the atheistic viewpoint of scientific materialism." Publ Wkly
"Neither religiously sectarian nor technically daunting, this is a book that invites the widest range of readers to ponder the deepest kind of questions." Booklist
Includes bibliographical references

Bulfinch, Thomas, 1796-1867

Bulfinch's mythology **291.1**
1. Mythology 2. Folklore—Europe 3. Chivalry
Hardcover and paperback editions available from various publishers
First combined edition published 1913 by Crowell. Originally published in three separate volumes 1855, 1858 and 1862 respectively
Contents: The age of fable; The age of chivalry; Legends of Charlemagne
"The classic work on mythology, Bulfinch's gives brief summations of Greek, Roman, Norse, Arthurian, and other miscellaneous myths and includes notes on the *Iliad*, the *Odyssey*, and the *Aeneid*." N Y Public Libr Book of How & Where to Look It Up

Campbell, Joseph, 1904-1987

The masks of God. Viking 1959-1968 4v hardcover o.p. paperbacks available ea $18 **291.1**
1. Mythology 2. Mythology in literature
Contents: v1 Primitive mythology (ISBN0-14-019443-6); v2 Oriental mythology (ISBN 0-14-019442-8); v3 Occidental mythology (ISBN 0-14-019441-X); v4 Creative mythology (ISBN 0-14-019440-1)
In the first three volumes the author deals "with the anonymous mythological past; in . . . [the final volume he shifts] the emphasis to individual creators of modern myths—from Dante to James Joyce, Thomas Mann, and T.S. Eliot." Libr J
Includes bibliographical references

The power of myth; [by] Joseph Campbell, with Bill Moyers; Betty Sue Flowers, editor. Doubleday 1988 231p il hardcover o.p. paperback available $29.95 **291.1**
1. Mythology 2. Religious art 3. Spiritual life
ISBN 0-385-24774-5 (pa)
LC 88-4218
Also available in paperback from Anchor Bks. $13.95 (ISBN 0-385-41886-8)
This companion to a public television series records conversations between Campbell and Bill Moyers. Campbell reflects on themes and symbols from world religions and mythologies and explores their relevance for his own spiritual journey
"Campbell is the hero on his own voyage of discovery. This well-bound book on lovely paper with helpful illustrations from art is highly recommended for all libraries." Choice

Transformations of myth through time. Perennial Lib. 1990 263p il hardcover o.p. paperback available $21.95 **291.1**
1. Mythology
ISBN 0-06-096463-4 (pa)
LC 89-45788
"This book consists of 13 chapters, each of which is a slightly edited version of one of the lectures in the PBS series of the same title. Drawing on his vast knowledge, Campbell explains in simple language, with copious examples from all times and cultures, how the same myths occur everywhere in slightly different forms." Libr J

Coles, Robert

The secular mind. Princeton Univ. Press 1999 189p $39.95; pa $13.95　　**291.1**
1. Secularism 2. Religion and science
ISBN 0-691-05805-9; 0-691-08862-4 (pa)
LC 98-39388
"In examining the nature of the secular and the sacred, Coles draws on his interviews with such notables as Paul Tillich, Dorothy Day, Anna Freud, and Walker Percy, as well as nuanced readings of the Bible and a range of great literature." Booklist
"This is a potent and powerful work readers will think about and return to again and again." Publ Wkly

Deloria, Vine

Evolution, creationism, and other modern myths; a critical inquiry; [by] Vine Deloria, Jr. Fulcrum 2002 274p $24.95　　**291.1**
1. Religion and science 2. Evolution 3. Creationism
ISBN 1-55591-159-5　　　　LC 2002-8171
Contents: Do we need a beginning?; The nature of science; The primacy of science; The logic of evolution; The nature of the present earth history; The nature of "religion"; The philosophy/science of other "religions"; The nature of history; Efforts at synthesis; The rocky road ahead
The author "argues that both sides in the evolution-versus-creationism debate are wrong. . . . This intellectual duel finds only mistaken orthodoxies in the field, for creationism has no scientific basis, but evolution is far from proven. . . . Certain to be controversial, likely to outrage the faithful of both camps, and a stunning good read." Booklist
Includes bibliographical references

Frazer, Sir James George, 1854-1941

The new golden bough; a new abridgment of the classic work; edited and with notes and foreword by Theodor H. Gaster. Phillips 1959 xxx, 738p $50.95　　**291.1**
1. Mythology 2. Religions 3. Superstition
ISBN 0-87599-036-3
First published with imprint Criterion Books
This edition is based on the 12 volumes of The golden bough and its supplements with revisions, commentary and annotations
"A comparative study of world religions, magic, vegetation and fertility beliefs and rites, kingship, taboos, totemism and the like." New Century Handb of Engl Lit
Includes bibliographical references

Gould, Stephen Jay, 1941-2002

Rocks of ages; science and religion in the fullness of life. Ballantine Pub. Group 1999 241p il $18.95; pa $12.95　　**291.1**
1. Religion and science
ISBN 0-345-43009-3; 0-345-45040-X (pa)
LC 98-31335
Gould discusses "the future relationship between scientists and religious believers. His aim is to resolve what he . . . terms 'the supposed conflict between science and religion.'" Commentary
Includes bibliographical references

The **History** of science and religion in the western tradition; an encyclopedia; Gary B. Ferngren, general editor; Edward J. Larson, Darrel W. Amundsen, co-editors; Anne-Marie E. Nakhla, assistant editor. Garland 2000 xxi, 586p (Garland reference library of the humanities) $160　　**291.1**
1. Religion and science
ISBN 0-8153-1656-9　　　　LC 00-25153
This is a collection of articles "grouped under ten headings covering everything from the relationship of science and religion to the approaches taken by specific religious traditions, from alchemy to chemistry to materialism to spiritualism. Ferngren . . . and his coeditors take the stand that the historical relationship between science and religion follows a complex model rather than the popularly understood model of unalterable conflict. The result is a work, well worth reading through or browsing, that is filled with respect for the roles and methodologies of both religion and science." Libr J

Juergensmeyer, Mark

Terror in the mind of God; the global rise of religious violence. University of Calif. Press 2000 316p (Comparative studies in religion and society) hardcover o.p. paperback available $16.95　　**291.1**
1. Terrorism 2. Religion and politics
ISBN 0-520-23206-2 (pa)　　　　LC 99-30466
"This comparative study of contemporary religious terrorism [seeks to] demonstrate that religious ideas and a sense of religious community have been a central part of many of the cultures of violence from which terrorism springs: [Juergensmeyer notes that] in contrast to politics, religion provides teleological moral justification and an enduring absolutism which generate intense commitment to transhistorical goals." MultiCult Rev
Includes bibliographical references

Koenig, Harold George

The healing power of faith; science explores medicine's last great frontier; [by] Harold G. Koenig; with additional research by Carol and Malcolm McConnell. Simon & Schuster 1999 331p $25; pa $14　　**291.1**
1. Health—Religious aspects
ISBN 0-684-85296-9; 0-684-85297-7 (pa)
LC 98-32079
The author "presents research in nine topical areas, including stress, depression, longevity, cardiovascular disease, and the immune system." Libr J
"Koenig's volume offers powerful examples of how religious faith has enabled some to endure and even triumph in the midst of woe." Publ Wkly
Includes bibliographical references

Leeming, David Adams, 1937-

The world of myth. Oxford Univ. Press 1990 362p il hardcover o.p. paperback available $17.95　　**291.1**
1. Mythology
ISBN 0-19-507475-0 (pa)　　　　LC 89-48070
This volume "is organized thematically, with sections on cosmic myths, myths of the gods, hero myths, and place and object myths. Modern myths, such as the idea of Earth as Gaia, intermingle . . . with their ancient counterparts." Booklist
Includes bibliographical references

Stark, Rodney

For the glory of God; how monotheism led to reformations, science, witch-hunts, and the end of slavery. Princeton Univ. Press 2003 488p il $35   **291.1**
1. Monotheism 2. Reformation 3. Religion and science 4. Witchcraft 5. Slavery
ISBN 0-691-11436-6   LC 2002-31746
"In this follow-up volume to . . . [One true God], Stark investigates the role of monotheistic religions in reformations, witch-hunts, slavery and science. Such efforts represent an attempt by monotheistic religions to preserve the idea of the One True God against corrupting influences inside and outside the religions themselves. Stark asserts that, contrary to traditional notions, no single religious reformation can be isolated in any monotheistic religion. Thus, Christianity has experienced not simply the Reformation of Luther but many and various reformations that resulted in a diversity of sectarian movements that practice the worship of the One True God in their own ways." Publ Wkly
A "provocative volume—lucid and tightly reasoned." Booklist
Includes bibliographical references

One true God; historical consequences of monotheism. Princeton Univ. Press 2001 319p il $45; pa $18.95   **291.1**
1. Monotheism 2. God
ISBN 0-691-08923-X; 0-691-11500-1 (pa)
                                       LC 2001-21128
Stark seeks "a theoretical understanding of monothetheism that will be . . . 'sociologically useful.' . . . Stark's theory has monotheism—the belief that there is just one God, just one giver of supernatural blessings and curses—as its object. He wants to explain monotheism's origins and development, to show its main effects upon the behavior and attitudes of social groups, and to account for the fact that monotheists are sometimes aggressively intolerant of those who do not share their beliefs and at other times civilly forebearing." Commonweal

Includes bibliographical references

Woodward, Kenneth L.

The book of miracles; the meaning of the miracle stories in Christianity, Judaism, Buddhism, Hinduism, Islam. Simon & Schuster 2000 429p hardcover o.p. paperback available $16   **291.1**
1. Miracles
ISBN 0-7432-0029-2 (pa)   LC 99-88083
The author "contends that miracles are found in all the major religions, and that one cannot understand or 'fully appreciate' any of the religions without some acquaintance with their miracle traditions." Publ Wkly
"A great resource for studies in comparative religions and interfaith dialog." Libr J
Includes bibliographical references

291.103 Religious mythology— Encyclopedias and dictionaries

Cotterell, Arthur

A dictionary of world mythology. [new ed rev & expanded] Oxford Univ. Press 1997 314p il maps pa $14.95   **291.103**
1. Mythology—Dictionaries
ISBN 0-19-217747-8
First published 1979 in the United Kingdom; first United States edition, 1980
"Contains some five hundred brief entries for mythic figures and themes, arranged according to the seven 'great traditions of world mythology' (West Asia, South and Central Asia, East Asia, Europe, America, Africa, and Oceania). For each tradition there is an overview article of several pages that discusses the historical background of the area's mythology." Wilson Libr Bull [review of 1980 edition]

Encyclopedia of science and religion; J. Wentzel Vrede van Huyssteen, editor in chief. Macmillan Ref. 2003 2v set $265
                                       291.103
1. Religion and science—Encyclopedias
ISBN 0-02-865704-7   LC 2002-152471
This reference "addresses the interactions, contradictions and tensions between science and religion, both historically and in contemporary life. The 2-vol. set examines technologies like in vitro fertilization, cloning, and continuing developments in neurophysiology against the backdrop of deeply-held religious beliefs. In addition, phenomena such as the Church of Scientology are also studied, along with more traditional issues, such as the origins of life, the nature of sin, and the philosophy of science and religion." Publisher's note
"Thousands of books have been written about the relationship between science and religion, but few can be characterized as reference resources. This two-volume set helps fill that niche with more than 400 scholarly articles written by experts from around the world." Libr J
Includes bibliographical references

Leeming, David Adams, 1937-

A dictionary of Asian mythology; [by] David Leeming. Oxford Univ. Press 2001 232p $35; pa $15.95   **291.103**
1. Asian mythology—Dictionaries 2. Asia—Religion—Dictionaries
ISBN 0-19-512052-3; 0-19-512053-1 (pa)
                                       LC 00-62389
"This concise dictionary references the mythologies of India, China, Tibet, Central and Southeast Asia, and Japan. The authoritative text is clearly written, thorough in coverage, and stylistically distinguished." Libr J

291.3 Public worship and other religious practices

Davidson, Linda Kay
Pilgrimage: from the Ganges to Graceland: an encyclopedia; [by] Linda Kay Davidson and David M. Gitlitz. ABC-CLIO 2002 2v il maps set $280   **291.3**
1. Pilgrims and pilgrimages
ISBN 1-57607-004-2   LC 2002-10119
"Defining a pilgrimage site by 'its ability to attract a transient population of devotees,' this . . . encyclopedia surveys the world's major destinations, from Delphi to Stonewall Inn. Entries are alphabetical and in addition to the sites also profile prominent figures, belief systems, activities, and institutions." Libr J
"This splendid encyclopedia is a delight to read and pleasing to view." Booklist
Includes bibliographical references

How to be a perfect stranger; the essential religious etiquette handbook; edited by Stuart M. Matlins & Arthur J. Magida. 3rd ed. SkyLight Paths Pub. 2002 c2003 399p pa $19.95   **291.3**
1. Etiquette 2. Rites and ceremonies
ISBN 1-89336-167-5   LC 2002-12994
First published 1996-1997 in two volumes by Jewish Lights Pub.
This guide "provides brief overviews of many religions: services, life-cycle events, home celebrations. It explains rituals so that those unfamiliar with them will know what to expect, how to dress, whether to bring a gift, and so on. It also has a glossary, explains various religious calendars, and lists religious festivals." Booklist [review of 1996-1997 edition]
Includes bibliographical references

Religious holidays and calendars; edited by Karen Bellenir. 3rd ed. Omnigraphics 2004 424p $84   **291.3**
1. Calendars 2. Religious holidays
ISBN 0-7808-0665-4   LC 2004-041500
First published 1993 under the editorship of Aidan A. Kelly, Peter Dresser, and Linda M. Ross
This handbook provides "information about the beliefs, practices, and history of more than 20 major religions. . . . Nearly 500 sacred feasts, fasts, festivals, and holidays are covered." Publisher's note

Wilson, Colin, 1931-
The atlas of holy places & sacred sites. DK Pub. 1996 192p il maps $29.95   **291.3**
1. Historic sites 2. Shrines
ISBN 0-7894-1051-6   LC 96-5632
"Brief accounts of more than 100 religious and ancient shrines are photographed, geographically mapped, and historically documented as to why and how the site became sacred." BAYA Book Rev

291.4 Religious experience, life, practice

Colegate, Isabel
A pelican in the wilderness; hermits and solitaries. Counterpoint 2002 284p il $25; pa $15.95   **291.4**
1. Hermits 2. Solitude
ISBN 1-58243-121-3; 1-58243-238-4 (pa)
LC 2001-47242
This "is a study of the soul that wants to be alone and knows how to do it; frequently met (so to say) in religion, the urge is also found in celebrities (J.D. Salinger, Howard Hughes)." N Y Times Book Rev

Coles, Robert
The spiritual life of children. Houghton Mifflin 1990 358p il hardcover o.p. paperback available $14   **291.4**
1. Children—Religious life
ISBN 0-395-59923-7 (pa)   LC 90-40097
"A Peter Davison book"
In this book the author presents "his research regarding children's understanding of and reflections on spiritual matters." Libr J
"One of the delights of his presentation is the combination of the children's searching comments and the struggle the author makes to hear beyond his own conceptions." J Youth Serv Libr
Includes bibliographical references

The **Oxford** book of prayer; general editor, George Appleton. Oxford Univ. Press 1985 397p hardcover o.p. paperback available $16.95   **291.4**
1. Prayers
ISBN 0-19-280374-3 (pa)   LC 85-176243
This collection contains "prayers from the Bible and other sacred texts and personal prayers of people as diverse as St. Thomas Aquinas, Dr. Johnson, and Solzhenitsyn. . . . While some are given in modern (often 'newspeak') translations, many are in their beautiful traditional forms. A welcome addition to general and academic collections." Libr J
Includes bibliographical references

Searching for your soul; writers of many faiths share their personal stories of spiritual discovery; edited and with an introduction by Katherine Kurs. Schocken Bks. 1999 xxix, 475p pa $15   **291.4**
1. Spiritual life
ISBN 0-8052-1111-X   LC 99-21266
This is a compilation "of writings in spiritual autobiography. Writers both contemporary and historical—ranging from Augustine, Thomas Merton and Mohandas Gandhi to Dan Wakefield, Dennis Covington and Kathleen Norris—reflect on questions of spiritual identity and heritage." Publ Wkly

Simmons, Philip

Learning to fall; the blessings of an imperfect life. Bantam Bks. 2002 157p $16.95; pa $12.95 **291.4**

1. Suffering 2. Spiritual life
ISBN 0-553-80266-6; 0-553-38158-X (pa)

"Since he was diagnosed with Lou Gehrig's disease, Simmons has had to master the art of living *and* the art of dying. By accepting failure and embracing imperfection, he has, and here he teaches not only how to fall *with* grace but also how to fall *to* grace." Booklist

291.9 Sects and reform movements

Belief beyond boundaries; Wicca, Celtic spirituality and the new age; edited by Joanne Pearson. Ashgate 2002 339p il maps (Religion today) $74.95; pa $29.95 **291.9**

1. Cults
ISBN 0-7546-0744-5; 0-7546-0820-4 (pa)
LC 2001-53654

This volume "explores 'religions' or forms of spirituality that tend to be marginal to the mainstream of British and North American religious expression. The book examines how alternative spiritualities traditionally classed as 'New Age' or new religious movements have grown exponentially in recent years. It progresses to detailed examination of Paganism, Celtic spirituality, Wicca, witchcraft, North American indigenous religion and New Age, considering the impact of the rise of science on religion and the emergence of new categories of spirituality." Publisher's note

"Though somewhat academic in tone, this is a solid overview of several New Age spiritual movements." Libr J

Includes bibliographical references

Lewis, James R., 1949-

Cults in America; a reference handbook. ABC-CLIO 1998 232p il map (Contemporary world issues) $50 **291.9**

1. Cults 2. Sects 3. United States—Religion
ISBN 0-585-05843-1
LC 98-29089

The author opens with a "discussion of minority religions and the public perception of them. Following is a detailed chronology of American religious conflicts from the late 18th century through the Heaven's Gate mass suicide in 1997. Lewis also discusses 47 sects and movements, including the Black Muslims, Hare Krishnas, the People's Temple, the Unification Church, and voodoo." Libr J

"This very readable book offers a balanced view of controversies centering on cults in America." Choice

Melton, J. Gordon

Encyclopedic handbook of cults in America. rev & updated ed. Garland 1992 407p (Religious information systems series) hardcover o.p. paperback available $35

291.9

1. Cults 2. Sects 3. United States—Religion
ISBN 0-8153-1140-0 (pa)
LC 92-11540
First published 1986

"A fascinating survey of cults that should provide answers to many questions on cult origins and founders, beliefs and practices, current status and controversies. The opening chapter surveys the topic of cults as alternative religion and is followed by sections reviewing thirty-seven movements active today. Counter-cult groups are discussed and an excellent section on violence and cults ends the book. Well written, thoroughly documented and indexed." Ref Sources for Small & Medium-sized Libr. 6th edition

Tabor, James D., 1946-

Why Waco? cults and the battle for religious freedom in America; [by] James D. Tabor and Eugene V. Gallagher. University of Calif. Press 1995 252p $39.95; pa $18.95 **291.9**

1. Koresh, David 2. Branch Davidians 3. Waco (Tex.) cult siege, 1993 4. Cults
ISBN 0-520-20186-8; 0-520-20899-4 (pa)
LC 95-3553

The authors argue that the Waco "confrontation was avoidable and could have been resolved peacefully. Attorney General Janet Reno made her decision to end the siege by force, they claim, against her better judgment under pressure from officials who gave her reports containing unsupported allegations of child abuse and sexual misconduct among the Branch Davidians. . . . Rejecting the label of 'cult,' the authors view the Branch Davidians and kindred groups as genuine, albeit unconventional, religious movements whose critics misunderstand the dynamics of charismatic leadership." Publ Wkly

Includes bibliographical references

292 Classical religion and religious mythology

Graves, Robert, 1895-1985

Greek myths **292**

1. Classical mythology
Hardcover and paperback editions available from various publishers
First published 1955 by Penguin Bks.

A collection of the author's interpretations of Greek myths based on anthropological and archaeological findings

Grimal, Pierre, 1912-

The dictionary of classical mythology; translated by A.R. Maxwell-Hyslop. Blackwell 1986 603p il hardcover o.p. paperback available $32.95 **292**

1. Classical mythology—Dictionaries
ISBN 0-631-20102-5 (pa)
LC 85-7387

Original French edition, 1951; this translation first published 1985 in the United Kingdom

"The dictionary is a comprehensive source dealing with every mythological creature and character, from Abas to Zeuxippe, and all the versions of the associated myths and legends. Articles are clear and readable, explain historical and literary allusions, and are attractively illustrated. . . . An essential purchase for both school and public libraries." Am Libr

Hamilton, Edith, 1867-1963

Mythology; illustrated by Steele Savage. Little, Brown 1942 497p il $27.95; pa $13.95   **292**

1. Classical mythology 2. Norse mythology
ISBN 0-316-34114-2; 0-316-34151-7 (pa)
A retelling of Greek, Roman and Norse myths

Vernant, Jean Pierre

The universe, the gods, and men; ancient Greek myths; told by Jean-Pierre Vernant; translated from the French by Linda Asher. HarperCollins Pubs. 2001 205p hardcover o.p. paperback available $13.95   **292**

1. Classical mythology
ISBN 0-06-095750-6 (pa)   LC 2001-16844
Vernant "explores the mythic foundations of the creation of the earth, the birth of the Titans, and the enduring momentum of human heritage. The casually arranged entries include readable accounts of Prometheus, Pandora, Odysseus, Dionysus, Oedipus, and other legendary figures whose narratives reveal a compelling path pertinent to our own civilization." Libr J

"Those seeking a first-rate account of the meanings and origins of the Greek myths, as well as a fresh and absorbing narrative, will find no better guide than Vernant." Publ Wkly

293   Germanic religion and religious mythology

Lindow, John

Handbook of Norse mythology. ABC-CLIO 2001 365p il (Handbooks of world mythology) $55   **293**

1. Norse mythology
ISBN 1-57607-217-7   LC 2001-1351
"Opening with a lengthy introduction followed by a chapter on the concept of time in Norse mythology, Lindow presents an overview of the history, literature, language, and culture of Scandinavia." Booklist

294.3   Buddhism

Armstrong, Karen

Buddha. Viking 2001 xxix, 205p map (Penguin lives series) $19.95   **294.3**

1. Gautama Buddha
ISBN 0-670-89193-2   LC 00-43808
"Armstrong interprets the mythologized story of the Buddha's abandonment of his life of comfort and privilege; commitment to practicing advanced forms of yoga and nearly fatal asceticism; enlightenment beneath a bodhi tree; and 45 years of wandering and teaching until his death in 483. And as she does so, she lucidly explains his revelations and influence." Booklist

Bernstein, Richard

Ultimate journey; retracing the path of an ancient Buddhist monk who crossed Asia in search of enlightenment. Knopf 2001 352p il maps hardcover o.p. paperback available $14   **294.3**

1. Hsüan-tsang, ca. 596-664 2. Buddhism
ISBN 0-679-78157-9 (pa)   LC 2001-267521
"In 629, a Buddhist monk named Hsuan Tsang set out from China, crossing Asia in search of Buddhist truth. Bernstein . . . decided to retrace the monk's journey over the silk road to Pakistan and India and back to China. In this entertaining and well-written account, more travel literature than religious study, he juxtaposes his account of Hsuan Tsang's experiences with descriptions of his own trials." Libr J

Breath sweeps mind; a first guide to meditation practice; edited by Jean Smith. Riverhead Bks. 1998 289p pa $14   **294.3**

1. Meditation 2. Buddhism
ISBN 1-57322-653-X   LC 97-28036
An "introduction to the practice and theory of meditation, including posture, breathing, and potential problems. All traditions are represented, with short pieces by a wide variety of teachers and ancient and contemporary texts—from the words of the Buddha to contemporary teachers such as Jon Kabat-Zinn and the Dalai Lama." Libr J

Buddhism: the illustrated guide; Kevin Trainor, general editor. Oxford Univ. Press 2001 256p il $39.95   **294.3**

1. Buddhism
ISBN 0-19-521849-3   LC 2001-36599
This introduction to the Buddhist world describes "the origins, principles, practices, holy writings, and current trends among the major schools and regional variations of this ancient belief." Libr J

"This illustrated guide to Buddhism skillfully embodies brains, brawn and beauty. With its 200 full-cover photos, maps and reproductions of art and architecture, it is a gorgeous coffee-table book that also succeeds in being both scholarly and lively." Publ Wkly

Crane, George

Bones of the master; a Buddhist monk's search for the lost heart of China. Bantam Bks. 2000 293p il maps hardcover o.p. paperback available $14.95   **294.3**

1. Tsung-tsai, 1925- 2. Buddhism 3. Mongolia
ISBN 0-553-37908-9 (pa)   LC 99-37868
This is an account of the friendship between Crane and Tsung Tsai, a Buddhist monk, and their journey to Mongolia to bury the bones of the monk's teacher

"Crane chronicles their perilous and miraculous adventures, the beauty of Mongolia's wilderness of wind and sand, and Tsung Tsai's transcendent determination with uncommon clarity, wit, vitality, and love." Booklist

Dalai Lama XIV, 1935-
Violence and compassion; [by] the Dalai Lama and Jean-Claude Carrière. Doubleday 1996 248p hardcover o.p. paperback available $11.50 **294.3**
1. Buddhism
ISBN 0-385-50144-7 (pa)   LC 95-30694
"This book records the conversation that screenwriter Carrière . . . held with the Dalai Lama, the exiled leader of Tibetan Buddhism, in 1993. The topics covered range from exile and reincarnation to education and science." Libr J
"This is a rich and invigorating volume, full of ponderable wisdom." Booklist

The way to freedom; by the Dalai Lama of Tibet; editor, Donald S. Lopez. HarperSanFrancisco 1994 181p il (Path to enlightenment series) $19   **294.3**
1. Buddhism
ISBN 0-06-061722-5   LC 94-31891
This book "presents the essence of Tibetan Buddhism. Coverage spans teaching, refuge, the guru, rebirth as continuity of consciousness, the nature of impermanence, suffering, freedom from delusion, and developing compassion." Libr J
"The Dalai Lama interprets these traditional teachings in contemporary terms, thus demonstrating the ongoing vitality of Buddhism." Booklist

The **Dalai** Lama; a policy of kindness: an anthology of writings by and about the Dalai Lama; foreword by Claiborne Pell; compiled and edited by Sidney Piburn. Snow Lion Publs. 1990 150p pa $10.95
294.3
1. Dalai Lama XIV, 1935-
ISBN 1-55939-022-0   LC 90-31752
This collection of writings includes "both biographical essays and the Dalai Lama's discussions of science and religion, human rights, the environment, and spiritual subjects." Antioch Rev
This book is "accessible to those who know nothing of Buddhism or of Tibet." Libr J
Includes bibliographical references

Essential Zen; edited by Kazuaki Tanahashi and Tensho David Schneider; brushwork by Kazuaki Tanahashi. HarperSanFrancisco 1994 174p hardcover o.p. paperback available $13   **294.3**
1. Zen Buddhism
ISBN 0-06-251046-0 (pa)   LC 94-10615
An anthology of Zen writings drawn from classic texts and contemporary masters and practitioners
Includes bibliographical references

Keown, Damien, 1951-
A dictionary of Buddhism; contributors, Stephen Hodge, Charles Jones, Paoli Tinti. Oxford Univ. Press 2003 357p il maps $35
294.3
1. Buddhism
ISBN 0-19-860560-9   LC 2003-276701
This dictionary covers Buddhist terms, biography, scriptures, important places and includes discussions of ethical issues and other matters

"The entries are short . . . but such accessibility is the very reason why this should be on the bookshelf of every student of Buddhism." Publ Wkly

Kerouac, Jack, 1922-1969
Some of the dharma. Viking 1997 419p hardcover o.p. paperback available $20
294.3
1. Buddhism
ISBN 0-14-028707-8 (pa)   LC 97-12870
"Begun in December 1951 as a notebook for his Buddhist studies, this work records Kerouac's reactions to a variety of Buddhist texts. Over the course of five years, it grew to include poems, prayers, dialogs, meditations, and notes on his reading, as well as commentary on family, friends, and meaningful concerns in his life. . . . Long anticipated by Kerouac scholars, this major work belongs in all literature collections." Libr J

Nhat Hanh, Thich
Living Buddha, living Christ; [by] Thich Nhat Hanh; introduction by Elaine Pagels; foreword by David Steindl-Rast. Riverhead Bks. 1995 xxvii, 208p $20; pa $12   **294.3**
ISBN 1-57322-018-3; 1-57322-568-1 (pa)
LC 95-24014
The author "offers insights into his own spiritual heritage and beckons readers to find meaning and peace within Buddhism—without abandoning their own belief system. . . . Nh'at Hanh observes many intersections of faith and belief between Buddhism and the Judeo-Christian faiths. . . . He does, however, clearly delineate differences." SLJ

Prebish, Charles S.
Historical dictionary of Buddhism. Scarecrow Press 1993 xxxiii, 387p (Historical dictionaries of religions, philosophies, and movements) $65   **294.3**
1. Buddhism—Dictionaries
ISBN 0-8108-2698-4   LC 93-4247
The author "narrows his dictionary topics to significant persons, places, texts, events, doctrines, practices, and movements within the Buddhist tradition. While he focuses on monastic and sectarian traditions, his concise introduction includes Buddha's life, the foothold of Buddhism in India, and its spread via Emperor Asoka's missionaries." Libr J

Ross, Nancy Wilson, 1905?-1986
Buddhism, a way of life and thought. Knopf 1980 208p il hardcover o.p. paperback available $12   **294.3**
1. Buddhism
ISBN 0-394-74754-2 (pa)   LC 80-7652
The author "presents the basic data of Buddha's life, his teachings, and Buddhist practice. . . . [She] describes Theravada Buddhism (of Southeast Asia), Tantra Buddhism (of Tibet), and Zen Buddhism (of Japan). . . . The book is a clear introduction to Buddhism, enthusiastically written and designed for the general public or beginning student." Choice
Includes bibliographical references

Smith, Huston

Buddhism: a concise introduction; [by] Hurston Smith and Philip Novak. HarperSanFrancisco 2003 242p $17.95 **294.3**

1. Buddhism

ISBN 0-06-050696-2 LC 2003-544630

This "book grew out of Smith's *The World's Religions*. . . . The first 12 chapters present his outstanding survey of the life and fundamental teachings of the 'Perfectly Enlightened One,' basic Buddhist concepts, and the major divisions of Buddhism (e.g., Mahayana, Theravada, Zen, and Tibetan). . . . Novak . . . is the primary author of the final six chapters, all-new sections on the migration of Buddhism to the West. Impressively, this informative portion with its emphasis on Buddhism in America lives up to the standards of lucidity so evident in earlier chapters." Libr J

Includes bibliographical references

Sogyal, Rinpoche

The Tibetan book of living and dying; edited by Patrick Gaffney and Andrew Harvey. rev and updated ed. HarperSanFrancisco 2002 441p il $28.95; pa $17.95 **294.3**

1. Buddhism 2. Death

ISBN 0-06-250793-1; 0-06-250834-2 (pa)

LC 2002-523084

First published 1992

This "modern reinterpretation of the classic *Tibetan Book of the Dead* is a manual on learning to accept death, on caring for the dying, and on spiritual growth. Rinpoche, . . . draws parallels between contemporary Western near-death experiences and the afterlife journey through *bardos*, or intermediate planes between death and rebirth, described in sacred Tibetan texts." Publ Wkly [review of 1992 edition]

The author "is well qualified to pass on his tradition. He does this beautifully, in limpid prose free of the scholastic list making that deadens many Tibetan Buddhist primers." N Y Times Book Rev [review of 1992 edition]

Includes bibliographical references

Suzuki, Daisetz Teitaro, 1870-1966

Manual of Zen Buddhism. Grove Press 1960 192p il pa $13 **294.3**

1. Zen Buddhism

ISBN 0-8021-3065-8

"An Evergreen original"

Fisrt published 1950 in the United Kingdom

In this volume, D. T. Suzuki has brought together some of Zen Buddhism's original sources. Included are the sutras or sermons of the Buddha: the gathas or hymns; the philosophical puzzles known as koan; and the dharanis or invocations to expel evil spirits. In addition to the written selections there are reproductions of Buddhist drawings and paintings, including religious statues found in Zen temples

Thondup, Tulku

Enlightened journey; Buddhist practice as daily life; edited by Harold Talbott. Shambhala Publs. 1995 268p pa $16.95

294.3

1. Buddhism

ISBN 1-57062-021-0 LC 94-36154

This is an "exposition on one of the more important sects of Tibetan Buddhism. As such, it comprises 15 talks and articles by Thondup, [a] leader and teacher of the Nyingma school of Tibetan Buddhism. His purpose here is to show how daily life can become the basis of Buddhist spiritual training, and each talk is an introduction to various aspects of Buddhism, covering such topics as meditation as a means to arouse compassion and the importance of suffering to reach enlightenment." Libr J

Includes bibliographical references

Tibetan book of the dead

The Tibetan book of the dead; or, The after-death experiences on the Bardo plane, according to Lāma Kazi Dawa-Samdup's English rendering; compiled and edited by W.Y. Evans-Wentz; with a new foreword and afterword by Donald S. Lopez, jr. Oxford Univ. Press 2000 lxxxiv, 264p il $40; pa $12.95 **294.3**

1. Buddhism 2. Death

ISBN 0-19-513311-0; 0-19-513312-9 (pa)

LC 00-22529

This translation first published 1927

A translation of the Bardo thödol, a Tibetan Buddhist scriptural work describing the mind's projections immediately after death. The accompanying commentary explains the symbolism and outlines applications of the teachings of the Bardo for living

Includes bibliographical references

Watts, Alan, 1915-1973

The way of Zen; by Alan W. Watts. Pantheon Bks. 1957 236p il hardcover o.p. paperback available $12 **294.3**

1. Zen Buddhism

ISBN 0-679-70510-4 (pa)

This is an historical and cultural survey of Zen, tracing its origins in Indian and Chinese thought. The author describes the Zen way of living and its techniques for overcoming the mind's conflict between symbolic thought and actual experience

Includes bibliographical references

294.5 Hinduism

Basham, Arthur Llewellyn

The origins and development of classical Hinduism; [by] A. L. Basham; edited and annotated by Kenneth G. Zysk. Beacon Press 1989 159p il o.p.; Oxford Univ. Press paperback available $15.95 **294.5**

1. Hinduism

ISBN 0-19-507349-5 (pa) LC 88-43314

This illustrated history "traces the spiritual life of India from the time of the Indus Culture (around 2700 B.C.E) through the crystallization of classical Hinduism in the first centuries of the common era. It chronicles as well the rise of other mystical and ascetic traditions, such as Buddhism and Jainism, and follows Hinduism's later incarnations in the West." Publisher's note

Includes bibliographical references

Klostermaier, Klaus K., 1933-
Hinduism; a short history. Oneworld Publs.
2000 342p pa $23.95 **294.5**
1. Hinduism
ISBN 1-85168-213-9
The author "addresses 'Hinduism' as a collection of
indigenous Indian religions, myths, and modes of worship that have mutually influenced one another for millennia. . . . Klostermaier deals with controversial interpretations of history in a frank and careful manner." Libr
J

Includes bibliographical references

Yoga, mind & body; [by] Sivananda Yoga
Vedanta Center. DK Pub. 1996 168p il
$24.95; pa $15 **294.5**
1. Yoga
ISBN 0-7894-0447-8; 0-7894-3301-X (pa)
LC 95-44387
"Five main principles of yoga based on the tenet of
'simple living and high thinking' are introduced. Each
one is explained and illustrated in a separate section of
the book. The chapter on proper exercise is the longest
section and goes through a complete workout session
with full-color photographs and drawings of each position. The mental and physical benefits of each position
are listed as well as possible problems, and variations for
different skill levels. The chapter on vegetarian diet has
20 pages of recipes." SLJ

295 Zoroastrianism (Mazdaism, Parseeism)

Kriwaczek, Paul
In search of Zarathustra; the first prophet
and the ideas that changed the world. Knopf
2003 248p il maps $25 **295**
1. Zoroaster, fl. 6th cent. B.C. 2. Zoroastrianism
ISBN 0-375-41528-9 LC 2002-73015
First published 2002 in the United Kingdom
The author contends "that Zoroastrianism, through its
prophet Zarathustra, greatly affected the three great monotheistic religions and gave them their common beliefs
of light and darkness, good and evil, heaven and hell, angels, and life after death. . . . An enthralling, sober, and
(sometimes) humorous exploration into the earliest roots
of Judaism, Christianity, and Islam." Libr J
Includes bibliographical references

296 Judaism

American Jewish year book. American
Jewish Com. $49.50 **296**
1. Jews—Periodicals 2. Jews—United States
ISSN 0065-8987

Annual. First published 1899

"An almanac of Jewish life and culture including population statistics, directories of Jewish organizations and
periodicals, a religious calendar, necrology, coverage of
international Jewish politics and communities, and periodicals." Ref Sources for Small & Medium-sized Libr.
6th edition

The **Cambridge** history of Judaism; edited by
W. D. Davies, Louis Finkelstein.
Cambridge Univ. Press 1984-1999 3v il
maps **296**
1. Judaism—History LC 77-85704
First three volumes of a projected four volume set

v3 edited by William Horbury, W. D. Davies, John
Sturdy
Contents: v1 Introduction; The Persian period $120
(ISBN 0-521-21880-2); v2 The Hellenistic age $140
(ISBN 0-521-21929-9); v3 The early Roman Period $150
(ISBN 0-521-24377-7)

The scope of this work is intended "to cover from the
Babylonian exile to the codification of the Mishnah, and
to include extensive background on the context in which
Judaism developed." Guide to Ref Books. 11th edition

Includes bibliographical references

Freedman, Samuel G.
Jew vs. Jew; the struggle for the soul of
American Jewry. Simon & Schuster 2000
397p $26; pa $14 **296**
1. Judaism 2. Jews—United States
ISBN 0-684-85944-0; 0-684-85945-9 (pa)
LC 00-33907
The author "describes the paradoxical situation faced
by today's American Jews, living in a country where re-
ligious freedom has yielded unreconcilable devisiveness.
. . . This is a helpful guide for anyone seeking an under-
standing of intra-Jewish conflicts in contemporary Ameri-
ca." Libr J
Includes bibliographical references

Glazer, Nathan
American Judaism. 2nd ed rev, with a new
introd. University of Chicago Press 1989
xxix, 214p (Chicago history of American
civilization) pa $21 **296**
1. Judaism 2. Jews—United States
ISBN 0-226-29843-4 LC 89-161422
First published 1957
Focusing upon Jews as a people and as a religious
group, the author surveys the history of Jews in the United States beginning with the first Jewish settlement in
New Amsterdam in 1654. Among the topics considered
are the German and East European immigrants, the Sephardic communities, and the Orthodox, Reform and
Conservative movements
Includes bibliographical references

Kushner, Harold S., 1935-
To life! a celebration of Jewish being and
thinking. Little, Brown 1993 304p o.p.;
Warner Bks. paperback available $14.99
296
1. Judaism
ISBN 0-446-67002-2 (pa) LC 92-36310
The author discusses the meaning of Jewish customs
and ceremonies and the purpose of prayer. Antisemitism,
Jewish-Christian relations, and the importance of Israel to
contemporary Jews are also examined
"This is a very easy book to read, to discuss, even to
argue about, and Kushner's celebration is everything his
many readers could have hoped it would be." Booklist

Robinson, George
Essential Judaism; a complete guide to
beliefs, customs and rituals. Pocket Bks. 2000
xxi, 644p hardcover o.p. paperback available
$18 **296**
1. Judaism
ISBN 0-671-03481-2 (pa) LC 99-55288
This book "attempts to provide the essentials of Judaism for novices, outsiders and those who, like Robinson,

Robinson, George—Continued
rediscovered their heritage as adults. It's an excellent introductory resource, vast but accessibly organized." Publ Wkly
Includes bibliographical references

Telushkin, Joseph, 1948-
Jewish wisdom; ethical, spiritual, and historical lessons from the great works and thinkers; [by] Rabbi Joseph Telushkin. Morrow 1994 xxiv, 663p $26   **296**
1. Judaism 2. Jewish ethics
ISBN 0-688-12958-7   LC 94-9186
Companion volume to Jewish literacy (1991)
"Organized by subject, this is a collection of teachings and quotations from the Talmud, the Bible, rabbinical commentaries, and ancient and modern religious and secular writings. Writers include Elie Wiesel, Isaac Bashevis Singer, Hebrew poet Hayim Bialik, Cynthia Ozick, Emile Zola, Albert Einstein, Bruno Bettelheim, Gertrude Stein, Irving Howe, and Maimonides. . . . Jews—and even non-Jews—will find the book a treasure." Booklist
Includes bibliographical references

Wouk, Herman, 1915-
This is my God: the Jewish way of life. Little, Brown 1987 345p hardcover o.p. paperback available $16.95   **296**
1. Judaism
ISBN 0-316-95514-0 (pa)   LC 87-3245
Reprint of the title first published 1959 by Doubleday
The author, an orthodox Jew, writes a personal declaration of faith. He also explains the holy days and the fasts and presents the historical background of Judaism, taking his readers back some five thousand years
Includes bibliographical references

The will to live on; this is our heritage. Cliff St. Bks. 2000 308p hardcover o.p. paperback available $15   **296**
1. Judaism 2. Holocaust, 1933-1945
ISBN 0-06-095562-7 (pa)   LC 99-49885
Wouk "explores the mystery of the survival of the Jewish people through the ages. The three main sections of this book cover the Holocaust, surveys of Jewish sacred and historical literature, and contemporary Jewish life in Israel and the United States. . . . Readers seeking an introduction to Judaism will be enlightened by the depth of knowledge here, as Wouk tells a complicated story so simply, and those who have read widely in Jewish literature will be entranced by his deeply felt and articulate sense of the importance of being a committed and believing Jew." Libr J

296.03 Judaism—Encyclopedias and dictionaries

The **Encyclopedia** of Judaism; edited by Jacob Neusner, Alan J. Avery-Peck, William Scott Green. Continuum 1999-2002 4v il maps set $255   **296.03**
1. Judaism—Encyclopedias
ISBN 0-8264-1178-9   LC 99-34729
Published in collaboration with the Museum of Jewish Heritage, New York

"The articles, which run from a few pages to 15 pages, touch on many contemporary issues, e.g., the article on medical ethics discusses the controversy surrounding 'test tube' babies. There is also in-depth discussion of concepts such as monotheism or creeds and modern Jewish movements such as Reform Judaism. Each article is signed and presents notes for further reading and research." Libr J
For a fuller review see: Booklist, April 15, 2000

The **New** encyclopedia of Judaism; editor-in-chief, Geoffrey Wigoder; coeditors, Fred Skolnik & Shmuel Himelstein. New York Univ. Press 2002 856p il $79.95   **296.03**
1. Judaism—Dictionaries
ISBN 0-8147-9388-6   LC 2002-16614
First published 1989 with title: The Encyclopedia of Judaism
This reference "seeks to present a balanced picture, offering current thinking among scholars in Reform, Conservative, and Orthodox movements and a roster of contributors hailing from Israel, England, and the United States. While the scholarship is solid, the material is readily accessible to a popular audience, and the work is magnificently illustrated." Libr J

The **Oxford** dictionary of the Jewish religion; editors in chief, R.J. Zwi Werblowsky, Geoffrey Wigoder. Oxford Univ. Press 1997 764p $110   **296.03**
1. Judaism—Dictionaries
ISBN 0-19-508605-8   LC 96-45517
"The 2400 entries in this dictionary include unsigned but revised articles from the editors' Encyclopedia of the Jewish Religion (1966), as well as . . . new signed articles covering [topics] . . . and biographies related to the Jewish religion and interfaith relations." Libr J

Reader's guide to Judaism; editor, Michael Terry. Fitzroy Dearborn Pubs. 2000 718p (Reader's guide) $135   **296.03**
1. Judaism—Encyclopedias
ISBN 1-57958-139-0   LC 2001-274119
This "work covers over 400 topics, including interfaith relations, historical periods, philosophical and mystical movements, important figures, and more. Preceding each essay is a bibliography of five to ten English-language titles. . . . Written by librarians and scholars . . . these 1000 to 2000-word essays include a descriptive and often analytical overview of each book. . . . This is an excellent tool for building Judaica collections in public and academic libraries." Libr J

296.1 Judaism—Sources

Cohen, A. (Abraham), b. 1887
Everyman's Talmud; with an introduction to the new American edition by Boaz Cohen. Dutton 1949 xli, 403p o.p.; Schocken Bks. paperback available $18   **296.1**
1. Talmud 2. Judaism
ISBN 0-8052-1032-6 (pa)
First published 1932 in the United Kingdom
"Its aim is to provide a summary of the teachings of the Talmud on Religion, Ethics, Folk-lore, and Jurisprudence. . . . All that is offered is a sufficient number of

Cohen, A. (Abraham), b. 1887—*Continued*
extracts to give [the] reader a general idea of the Talmudic doctrine." Preface
"A comprehensive and satisfactory summary of Talmudic doctrine . . . prefaced by an excellent introduction." Commonweal
Includes bibliographical references

Dead Sea scrolls
The complete Dead Sea scrolls in English;
[translated from the Hebrew and Aramaic and
edited by] Géza Vermès. Allen Lane/Penguin
Press 1997 648p hardcover o.p. paperback
available $18.95 **296.1**
ISBN 0-14-027807-9 (pa) LC 97-3722
This translation was first published 1962 with title:
The Dead Sea scrolls in English; the 1997 edition includes an introduction summarizing the 50-year history
of scrolls research
This "is an English version of the nonbiblical, sectarian and intertestamental Qumran writings. [Vermès's]
preface explains that he does not offer a translation of
'every fragment retrieved from the caves,' but of 'all the
texts sufficiently well preserved to be understandable in
English.'" N Y Times Book Rev
The "discussion of the Essene community, whom
Vermes believes created the scrolls, the scrolls' meanings
for early Christianity and other topics will be valuable to
anyone looking for accurate summaries of the fascinating
history of the discovery, translation and transmission of
the scrolls." Publ Wkly
Includes bibliographical references

The Dead Sea scrolls; a new translation;
[by] Michael Wise, Martin Abegg, Jr., and
Edward Cook. HarperSanFrancisco 1996 513p
hardcover o.p. paperback available $20.95
296.1
ISBN 0-06-069201-4 (pa) LC 96-28983
This translation captures "the nuances of the Hebrew,
and sometimes the Greek, of the scrolls, many of which
are merely fragments. Also contained here is a thorough
introduction to the history of the discovery of the scrolls
and a theory about the community that produced the
scrolls." Publ Wkly
"An engaging necessity for updating Dead Sea Scrolls
collections." Booklist
Includes bibliographical references

The Dead Sea scrolls uncovered; the first
complete translation and interpretation of 50
key documents withheld for over 35 years;
[edited by] Robert H. Eisenman and Michael
Wise. Element Bks. 1992 286p il o.p.;
Penguin Bks. paperback available $16 **296.1**
ISBN 0-14-023250-8 (pa) LC 93-108131
Text of scrolls in Aramaic and Hebrew with translation into English; introductions in English
"Eisenman and Wise have reconstructed fifty texts
from the scrolls found in Cave 4 near the Dead Sea.
They divide the documents into eight categories: messianic and visionary recitals; prophets and pseudo-prophets;
biblical interpretation; calendrical texts and priestly
courses; testaments and admonitions; works reckoned as
righteousness-legal texts; hymns and mysteries; and divination, magic and miscellaneous." Libr J
Includes bibliographical references

The **Encyclopedia** of the Dead Sea scrolls;
[edited by] Lawrence H. Schiffman and
James C. VanderKam. Oxford Univ. Press
2000 2v set $295 **296.1**
1. Dead Sea scrolls
ISBN 0-19-508450-0 LC 99-55300
"In addition to individual texts, coverage extends to
the archeological sites themselves; important historical
figures (Moses) and groups (Essenes, Pharisees) as they
are represented in the scrolls; scholars important to Dead
Sea scroll research . . . and methods employed both to
date and to preserve these ancient documents." Booklist

Frankel, Ellen, 1951-
The classic tales; 4,000 years of Jewish
lore. Aronson, J. 1989 659p hardcover o.p.
paperback available $40 **296.1**
1. Jewish legends 2. Hasidic legends
ISBN 1-56821-038-8 (pa) LC 88-35119
"Frankel selects and retells a wide selection of tales
arranged in broadly thematic sections. Biblical, hasidic,
and midrashic sources predominate, but the oral tradition
is also represented. Likewise, the balance between Ash-
kenazi and Sephardic stories aims for a broader geographical representation. Frankel also takes the opportunity to personalize the woman's role in many of these
tales and makes the references to God genderless."
Booklist
Includes bibliographical references

Golb, Norman
Who wrote the Dead Sea scrolls? the
search for the secret of Qumran. Scribner
1995 446p il maps hardcover o.p. paperback
available $22 **296.1**
1. Dead Sea scrolls 2. Judaism—History
ISBN 0-684-80692-4 (pa) LC 94-23295
Golb argues that "the Dead Sea Scrolls were the work
of individuals from many diverse groups and that they
were deposited in the caves near the Dead Sea (among
other locations) by Jews fleeing the Roman army during
the First Revolt (c.70 c.e.). He also claims that the Qumran complex served not as an Essene monastery but as
a fortress for Jews involved in the revolt." Libr J
"This is an archival book that should be considered
for any collection dealing with the Dead Sea Scrolls. It
is well written and can be read by the interested person
as well as by the professional scholar." Choice
Includes bibliographical references

Schiffman, Lawrence H.
Reclaiming the Dead Sea scrolls; the
history of Judaism, the background of
Christianity, the lost library of Qumran; with
a foreword by Chaim Potok. Jewish Publ.
Soc. 1994 xxvii, 529p il maps o.p.;
Doubleday paperback available $27.50 **296.1**
1. Dead Sea scrolls 2. Judaism—History
ISBN 0-385-48121-7 (pa) LC 94-26489
Schiffman provides a "description and evaluation of
the scrolls, the archeology of Qumran (the site near the
Dead Sea from which the scrolls originated), the history
and nature of the Jewish community that lived at Qumran and the setting of the scrolls in Jewish history and
thought from the second century B.C. through the first
century A.D." N Y Times Book Rev
Includes bibliographical references

Shanks, Hershel
The mystery and meaning of the Dead Sea scrolls. Random House 1998 xxi, 246p il maps hardcover o.p. paperback available $14

296.1

1. Dead Sea scrolls
ISBN 0-679-78089-0 (pa)   LC 97-29391
"Shanks looks at the key questions surrounding the Dead Sea Scrolls (who wrote them, what they say, and what they mean vis-à-vis Judaism and Christianity) and gives readers the most up-to-date information along with his own best guesses about what it all means, easily incorporating many divergent theories." Booklist
Includes bibliographical references

Understanding the Dead Sea scrolls; a reader from the Biblical archaeology review; edited by Hershel Shanks. Random House 1992 xxxviii, 336p il maps hardcover o.p. paperback available $14   **296.1**
1. Dead Sea scrolls
ISBN 0-679-74445-2 (pa)   LC 91-45727
This is a compilation of "22 articles from the pages of BAR and *Bible Review* dealing with the discovery of the Scrolls, the ancient community that stored them away, and their impact upon the study of the Bible, Rabbinic Judaism, and early Christianity. Three chapters on the controversy surrounding the publication (and in many cases non-publication) of the materials round out the volume. . . . The articles included are written by scholars but are easily accessible to laypersons. Coverage is balanced, including opposing viewpoints." Libr J
Includes bibliographical references

296.3 Judaism—Theology, ethics, views of social issues

Gager, John G.
The origins of anti-Semitism; attitudes toward Judaism in pagan and Christian antiquity. Oxford Univ. Press 1983 312p hardcover o.p. paperback available $26

296.3

1. Paul, the Apostle, Saint 2. Antisemitism 3. Christianity and other religions
ISBN 0-19-503607-7 (pa)   LC 82-24523
"Gager attempts to survey Greek and Roman attitudes toward Jews and Judaism, and to examine the bases of early Christian (especially Paul's) thinking about Jewish religion. He aims to show that Greek and Roman opinion about the Jews and their religion was divided." Choice
Includes bibliographical references

Kushner, Harold S., 1935-
When bad things happen to good people; with a new preface by the author. 20th anniversary ed. Schocken Bks. 2001 202p $21   **296.3**
1. Providence and government of God 2. Suffering
ISBN 0-8052-4193-0   LC 2001-531062
Also available in paperback from Avon Bks.
A reissue of the title first published 1981
"A bright and happy infant, Rabbi Kushner's firstborn son gradually succumbed to progeria, 'rapid aging': he never grew beyond three feet tall, looked like a hairless, wizened old man, and died in his teens. This book

is his father's attempt to make sense out of his son's fate, his own pain, and the pain of others enduring undeserved misfortunes." Libr J

296.4 Judaism—Traditions, rites, public services

Celebration & renewal; rites of passage in Judaism; edited by Rela M. Geffen. Jewish Publ. Soc. 1993 277p hardcover o.p. paperback available $19.95   **296.4**
1. Judaism—Customs and practices
ISBN 0-8276-0510-2 (pa)   LC 93-12493
Explains such life-cycle events as birth, marriage, midlife, sickness, religious conversion, and mourning as viewed, experienced, and treated from a Jewish perspective
"The book is not only practical to Jews, but useful to students of other religions and ethnic backgrounds who could benefit by comparing this book's portrayal of Jewish traditions with their own heritages." Booklist
Includes bibliographical references

Goldman, Ari L., 1949-
Being Jewish; the spiritual and cultural practice of Judaism today. Simon & Schuster 2000 286p $25   **296.4**
1. Judaism—Customs and practices
ISBN 0-684-82389-6   LC 00-44047
"The book's three sections cover life cycle events, holidays, and daily activities. Specific chapters include coming of age, mourning, Sukkot, Passover, Yom Ha'atzmaut, prayer, and study." Libr J
"An excellent resource." Booklist
Includes bibliographical references

Greenberg, Irving, 1933-
The Jewish way; living the holidays. Summit Bks. 1988 463p hardcover o.p. paperback available $15   **296.4**
1. Jewish holidays 2. Judaism—Customs and practices
ISBN 0-671-87303-2 (pa)   LC 88-20085
The author "explains and interprets each holiday's origin and background, ceremonial rituals, and religious significance. He shows how the holidays relate to one another and to Judaism's central themes and how they offer the individual the capacity to experience the full range of Judaism's and humankind's values." Publisher's note
Includes bibliographical references

Isaacs, Ronald H.
Sacred seasons; a sourcebook for the Jewish holidays. Aronson, J. 1997 163p $25

296.4

1. Jewish holidays 2. Jews—Folklore 3. Jewish legends
ISBN 0-7657-5963-2   LC 96-33635
Isaacs "notes in his introduction that the holidays and fast days in the Jewish calendar form an integral part of the body of ritual and social laws through which Jews relate both to society and to God. . . . Using basic rabbinic texts—the Talmud, Midrashim, the Zohar, etc.—as his source material, Isaacs presents a fascinating collection of folk tales and legends pertaining to these holidays." Libr J

Strassfeld, Michael

The Jewish holidays; a guide and commentary; illustrated by Betsy Platkin Teutsch; commentaries by Arnold Eisen [et al.] Harper & Row 1985 248p il hardcover o.p. paperback available $24   **296.4**
1. Jewish holidays 2. Judaism—Customs and practices
ISBN 0-06-272008-2 (pa)   LC 84-48196
This book examines the history and customs surrounding the major Jewish holidays

Wieseltier, Leon

Kaddish. Knopf 1998 588p $27.50; pa $16
    296.4
1. Kaddish 2. Judaism—Customs and practices 3. Funeral rites and ceremonies
ISBN 0-375-40389-2; 0-375-70362-4 (pa)
    LC 98-15881
"When his father died in 1996 . . . Wieseltier began to observe the Jewish rituals of the traditional year of mourning. His own mourning led him to an in-depth study of the history and meaning of Kaddish in Judaism. Wieseltier provides a work of history, philosophy and spiritual memoir that demonstrates how the practice of religion meets the needs of a troubled soul." Publ Wkly

296.7 Judaism—Religious experience, life, practice

Diamant, Anita, 1951-

Living a Jewish life; a guide for starting, learning, celebrating, and parenting; [by] Anita Diamant, Howard Cooper. HarperCollins Pubs. 1991 xx, 330p hardcover o.p. paperback available $15.95   **296.7**
1. Jews—Social life and customs
ISBN 0-06-273443-1 (pa)   LC 90-56092
This book "is written as a kind of handbook to help those who are perhaps new to the faith or rebuilding for themselves as adults the traditions with which they were (or were not) brought up. It would also make an excellent introduction for anyone unacquainted with Jewish customs." Booklist
Includes bibliographical references

Kaplan, Aryeh

Jewish meditation; a practical guide. Schocken Bks. 1985 165p hardcover o.p. paperback available $12   **296.7**
1. Meditation 2. Judaism—Customs and practices
ISBN 0-8052-1037-7 (pa)   LC 84-23589
The author "outlines various forms of meditation based on Jewish writings and practices. He discusses mantra meditation, visualization, and ways to contemplate God. With an eye toward traditional Judaism, Kaplan also explains how following the many commandments of the Bible is also a form of meditation. A profound book that is complex in subject matter yet simple in methodology." Booklist

Kushner, Harold S., 1935-

How good do we have to be? a new understanding of guilt and forgiveness. Little, Brown 1996 181p hardcover o.p. paperback available $11.95   **296.7**
1. Bible. O.T. Genesis—Criticism 2. Guilt 3. Good and evil
ISBN 0-316-51933-2 (pa)   LC 95-25350
The author "here retells the Genesis story of . . . [Adam and Eve to argue] that the imperfections of humankind do not merit the loss of God's love, nor should they foster the guilt and anxiety that they often do in a society driven by a misguided attachment to perfection. . . . [Kushner sees] acceptance and forgiveness as a means of overcoming the insidious consequences of a preoccupation with perfection." Libr J
"This is one psychological self-help book that deserves the popularity it is likely to achieve." Booklist

Who needs God. Summit Bks. 1989 208p o.p.; Fireside paperback available $13   **296.7**
1. God—Judaism
ISBN 0-7432-3477-4 (pa)   LC 89-35140
The author "believes that 'human life has meaning . . . but only in religious terms.' According to this crucial realization, it is religion that connects us to God and community." Libr J

Levy, Naomi

To begin again; a journey toward comfort, strength, and faith in difficult times. Knopf 1998 267p hardcover o.p. paperback available $12.95   **296.7**
1. Judaism—Customs and practices 2. Bereavement
ISBN 0-345-41383-0 (pa)   LC 98-16024
The author "offers a progressive Jewish approach to coping with life's darker moments. Having faced the murder of her father when she was 15, Levy joined the first class of women to study at the Jewish Theological Seminary. Drawing on her own suffering and her experience as a rabbi, she constructs a map for personal renewal." Publ Wkly
"A wise and practical guide for readers of any religious persuasion." Libr J

296.8 Judaism—Denominations and movements

Wiesel, Elie, 1928-

Souls on fire; portraits and legends of Hasidic masters; translated from the French by Marion Wiesel. Summit Bks. 1982 c1972 268p hardcover o.p. paperback available $14
    296.8
1. Hasidism 2. Hasidic legends
ISBN 0-671-44171-X (pa)   LC 82-5984
A reissue of the title first published 1972 by Random House
"A collection of legends and portraits of the founder of the Hasidic movement and his disciples. . . . Wiesel assumes the role of a storyteller, who simply transmits tales he heard as faithfully as his personal experience will allow." Publ Wkly

297 Islam, Babism, Bahai Faith

American jihad; Islam after Malcolm X; [edited by] Steven Barboza. Doubleday 1994 370p il hardcover o.p. paperback available $19 **297**
1. Black Muslims
ISBN 0-385-47694-9 (pa) LC 93-31469
A "collection of more than 50 brief interviews. While the interviews are not too deep, they do correct certain tabloid stereotypes of this rapidly growing religion. Some interviewees are famous: Kareem Abdul-Jabbar talks about how his conversion gave him credibility but not marketability, while Jamil Abdullah Al-Amin (the former H. Rap Brown) observes how Islam has enabled him to control his anger. A section on the separatist Nation of Islam fills out interesting history." Publ Wkly

Armstrong, Karen
Islam; a short history. Modern Lib. 2000 xxxiv, 222p maps $19.95; pa $11.95 **297**
1. Islam
ISBN 0-679-64040-1; 0-8129-6618-X (pa)
LC 00-25285
This history of the Islamic faith focuses on the religion's attitude toward politics
The author "does an admirable job of presenting Islamic history from an objective, unbiased point of view." Libr J
Includes bibliographical references

Ben Jelloun, Tahar, 1944-
Islam explained. New Press (NY) 2002 120p $19.95 **297**
1. Islam
ISBN 1-56584-781-4 LC 2002-30500
"Cast in the form of an extended conversation between Ben Jelloun and his young daughter. . . . Father and child discuss the history of Islam, what it means to be a Muslim today, the challenges facing the Islamic world, and terrorism. . . . Its openness and emotional honesty, particularly when discussing the tragedy of 9/11, make it a valuable addition to a growing public discourse. As an introduction to the religion, it is spotty, but as a liberal Muslim voice of reconciliation, heartbreak, and compassion, it is priceless." Booklist

Concise encyclopedia of Islam; edited on behalf of the Royal Netherlands Academy [by] H.A.R. Gibb and J.H. Kramers. Brill Academic Pubs. 2001 671p il map pa $39.95 **297**
1. Islam—Dictionaries
ISBN 0-391-04116-9 LC 2001-35754
First published 1953 with title: Shorter encyclopedia of Islam
This reference work "includes all the articles contained in the first edition and supplement of the *Encyclopedia of Islam* which are particularly related to the religion and law of Islam. . . . This volume has a vast geographical and historical scope which includes the old Arabo-Islamic Empire, the Islamic states of Iran, Central Asia, the Indian sub-continent and Indonesia, the Ottoman Empire and the various Muslim states and communities in Africa, Europe, and the former U.S.S.R." Publisher's note
Includes bibliographical references

Ernst, Carl W., 1950-
The Shambhala guide to sufism. Shambhala Publs. 1997 xxi, 264p il pa $18.95 **297**
1. Sufism
ISBN 1-57062-180-2 LC 97-10189
This guide to sufism "covers its beginnings, its basic philosophies, and its place in Islam." Libr J
Includes bibliographical references

Esposito, John L.
Islam; the straight path. 3rd ed. Oxford Univ. Press 1998 286p il map $30; pa $27.95 **297**
1. Islam
ISBN 0-19-511233-4; 0-19-511234-2 (pa)
LC 97-26850
First published 1988
The author discusses "Muslim origins, history, doctrine, and culture—generally in a Middle Eastern context. . . . Free of any evident anti-Muslim or anti-Christian bias, Esposito's scholarly prose is both straightforward and highly readable, with technical terms always clearly defined." Libr J
Includes bibliographical references

What everyone needs to know about Islam. Oxford Univ. Press 2002 204p $18.95 **297**
1. Islam
ISBN 0-19-515713-3 LC 2002-8387
In question-and-answer format the author presents information on a variety of aspects of Islam. The "format allows readers to skip ahead to areas that interest them, including hot-button issues such as 'Why are Muslims so violent?' or 'Why do Muslim women wear veils and long garments?' In his answers, which are anywhere from a paragraph to several pages long, Esposito elegantly educates the reader through what the Qur'an says, how Muslims are influenced by their local cultures, and how the unique politics of Islamic countries affects Muslims' views." Publ Wkly
Includes bibliographical references

Essential Sufism; edited by James Fadiman and Robert Frager. HarperSanFrancisco 1997 265p hardcover o.p. paperback available $13 **297**
1. Sufism
ISBN 0-06-251475-X (pa) LC 97-2555
This "volume offers sayings, religious quotes, poems, aphorisms, and prayers from many Sufi masters. . . . The book [also] includes the . . . discussions of the major Sufi teachers, history, culture, and beliefs." Libr J
Includes bibliographical references

Gardell, Mattias
In the name of Elijah Muhammad; Louis Farrakhan and the Nation of Islam. Duke Univ. Press 1996 482p (C. Eric Lincoln series on the black experience) $59.95; pa $23.95 **297**
1. Farrakhan, Louis 2. Elijah Muhammad, 1897-1975 3. Black Muslims
ISBN 0-8223-1852-0; 0-8223-1845-8 (pa)
LC 96-22666
The author presents a history of the Nation of Islam and "details the activities of the group and Farrakhan, covering their position on gangs, hip-hop, drugs, prisons, African American politics, public health, and black uni-

Gardell, Mattias—*Continued*

ty." Libr J

"Some will appreciate the author's brief critical airing of claims of pre-Columbian Africans in America and accounts of Muslims and the slave trade, but he is at his best when focusing on the leaders and on the changing theology of the Nation of Islam (NOI) and similar African American groups in the 20th-century US. The book is balanced and well researched." Choice

Includes bibliographical references

Gordon, Matthew

Islam; origins, practices, holy texts, sacred persons, sacred places; [by] Matthew S. Gordon. Oxford Univ. Press 2002 112p il $17.95   **297**

1. Islam

ISBN 0-19-521885-X   LC 2002-70371

The author "discusses the rise of Islam; the centrality of its sacred text, the Qur'an; the importance of the Prophet Muhammad; the major developments of both Sunni and Shi'i Islam . . . the ethical principles and 'Five Pillars' of the faith; the role of the mosque and of sacred sites such as Mecca; the concept of sacred time and the Islamic lunar calendar; Muslims' beliefs about death and the afterlife; and Islam in the modern world." Publ Wkly

Includes bibliographical references

Kepel, Gilles

Jihad; the trail of political Islam; translated by Anthony F. Roberts. Harvard Univ. Press 2002 454p $33.95; pa $15.95   **297**

1. Islam and politics

ISBN 0-674-00877-4; 0-674-01090-6 (pa)
                                      LC 2002-17181

Original French edition, 2000

"Kepel argues that the terrorism seen today throughout the world results from the failure of Islamic fundamentalism and not its success. . . . Fascinating despite its copious detail." Booklist

Lippman, Thomas W.

Understanding Islam; an introduction to the Muslim world. 2nd rev ed. Penguin Bks. 1995 198p pa $14   **297**

1. Islam

ISBN 0-452-01160-4   LC 95-24015

"A Meridian book"

First published 1982

The author explains fundamental Islamic beliefs and practices. The life and work of Mohammed is examined in depth

Includes bibliographical references

The **Many** faces of Islam; perspectives on a resurgent civilization; Nissim Rejwan [editor] University Press of Fla. 2000 282p $55   **297**

1. Islam 2. Islamic countries—Politics and government

ISBN 0-8130-1807-2   LC 00-32587

The editor offers "perspectives on modern Islamic culture and religious practice. Seeking to dispel the perception that Islamic fundmentalism and extremism represent Islam in its entirety, Rejwan surveys the issues and provides numerous excerpts from modern writers and scholars, Muslim and non-Muslim, summarizing the many problems and dilemmas facing contemporary Muslims." Univ. Press Books for Public and Second Sch Libr, 2001

Murphy, Caryle

Passion for Islam; shaping the modern Middle East: the Egyptian experience. Scribner 2002 359p $27   **297**

1. Islam and politics 2. Egypt—Politics and government 3. Egypt—Social conditions

ISBN 0-7432-3578-9   LC 2002-30290

"A Lisa Drew book"

The author "puts Egypt at the center of the growth of Islamic extremism. . . . Offering a vivid portrait of Egypt today, she attributes the spread of violent Islam to the interaction of three factors: a general reawakening of Islam, the reign of authoritarian governments in the Middle East and the Israeli-Palestinian conflict." Publ Wkly

Includes bibliographical references

The **Muslim** almanac; a reference work on the history, faith, culture, and peoples of Islam; Azim A. Nanji, editor. Gale Res. 1996 xxxv, 581p il map $120   **297**

1. Islam 2. Islamic countries

ISBN 0-8103-8924-X   LC 95-17324

This "basic reference on Islam contains 39 chapters, each contributed by a recognized scholar and each discussing a broad topic area of Islamic history, belief, or culture. Chapters conclude with useful topical bibliographies. A general bibliography, a chronology of Islamic history, and a glossary of Islamic terms also appear." Libr J

Naipaul, V. S. (Vidiadhar Surajprasad), 1932-

Among the believers; an Islamic journey. Knopf 1981 430p hardcover o.p. paperback available $16   **297**

1. Islam

ISBN 0-394-71195-5 (pa)   LC 81-47503

"Based on his seven-month journey across the Asian continent, Naipaul explores the life, the culture, the ferment inside the nations of Islam." Publisher's note

Beyond belief; Islamic excursions among the converted peoples. Random House 1998 408p hardcover o.p. paperback available $15
                                            297

1. Islam 2. Islamic countries—Description

ISBN 0-375-70648-8 (pa)   LC 97-37350

"Retracing a voyage he made in 1979, the novelist and essayist journeys through Indonesia, Iran, Pakistan and Malaya, using Islam as a window on the animism, nationalism, capitalism and other isms he encounters there." N Y Times Book Rev

Nasr, Seyyed Hossein

Islam: religion, history, and civilization. HarperSanFrancisco 2002 xx, 198p pa $12.95
                                            297

1. Islam 2. Islamic civilization

ISBN 0-06-050714-4   LC 2002-32810

This introduction to the world of Islam explores the following topics: What is Islam?; The doctrines and beliefs of Islam; Islamic practices and institutions; The history of Islam; Schools of Islamic thought; Islam in the contemporary world; Islam and other religions; The spiritual and religious significance of Islam

This introduction to Islamic faith and history provides "compelling analysis of contemporary Islam and its conflicts without overwhelming the reader with information." Booklist

Includes bibliographical references

The **Oxford** dictionary of Islam; John L. Esposito, editor in chief. Oxford Univ. Press 2003 359p $45 **297**

1. Islam—Dictionaries

ISBN 0-19-512558-4 LC 2002-30261

"Aimed at general readers with little knowledge of Islam, the dictionary focuses on 19th- and 20th-century topics, including many social, religious, and political aspects of modern Islam. Entries include hot topics (e.g., al-Qaeda, Osama Bin Laden, Afghanistan), various religious and political sects (Nation of Islam, Sevener Shiis, the Philippines' Moro National Liberation Front), and muslim views on a variety of issues (abortion, suicide, science, the treatment of women). Entries arranged alphabetically, use standard transliterations. Cross-references are listed at the end of entries, and attempts are made to link Arabic and English terms." Choice

"This is an excellent resource for ready-reference collections in any library." Libr J

The **Oxford** history of Islam; {edited by} John Esposito. Oxford Univ. Press 1999 749p il map $49.95 **297**

1. Islam

ISBN 0-19-510799-3 LC 99-13219

"Contributors treat, among other things, Muslim history, law, and society; art and architecture; and regional differences. Chapters on the @Globalization of Islam' and @Contemporary Islam' are particularly relevant to current events. . . . An ideal one-volume source." Libr J

Includes bibliographical references

Smith, Jane Idleman, 1937-

Islam in America; [by] Jane I. Smith. Columbia Univ. Press 1999 251p il (Columbia contemporary American religion series) $60; pa $20.50 **297**

1. Islam

ISBN 0-231-10966-0; 0-231-10967-9 (pa)

LC 98-31943

The author discusses "the basic tenets of the Muslim faith, surveys the history of Islam in this country, and profiles the lifestyles, religious practices, and worldviews of American Muslims. Sections of the book cover the role of women in American Islam, raising and educating children, the use of products acceptable to Muslims, appropriate dress and behavior, concerns about prejudice and unfair treatment, and other issues related to life in [America]." Univ Press Books for Public and Second Sch Libr, 2001

Includes bibliographical references

Wolfe, Michael, 1945-

One thousand roads to Mecca; ten centuries of travelers writing about the Muslim pilgrimage; edited and introduced by Michael Wolfe. Grove Press 1997 xxxi, 620p maps hardcover o.p. paperback available $17.50 **297**

1. Islam 2. Pilgrims and pilgrimages 3. Mecca (Saudi Arabia)

ISBN 0-8021-3599-4 (pa) LC 97-1329

Wolfe "has collected excerpts from the accounts of two dozen pilgrims to Mecca over a span of 1000 years. . . . The chosen excerpts give readers a sense of how the hajj has changed over time as well as how constant the central ceremonies have remained." Libr J

includes bibliographical references

297.1 Sources of Islam

Koran

The Koran **297.1**

Available in various bindings and editions

"The sacred scripture of Islam, regarded by Muslims as the Word of God, and except in sūra I.—which is a prayer to God—and some few passages in which Muhammad or the angels speak in the first person, the speaker throughout is God." Ency Britannica

299 Other religions

Blofeld, John Eaton Calthorpe, 1913-1987

Taoism: the road to immortality; [by] John Blofeld. Shambhala Publs. 1978 195p il o.p.; Random House paperback available $15.95 **299**

1. Taoism

ISBN 1-57062-89-1 (pa) LC 77-90882

The author seeks to explain the fundamental concepts of Taoism, tells stories of its masters and offers reflections on Taoist verse. In addition, he describes his visits to Taoist monasteries in China and discussions he had with contemporary masters

Castaneda, Carlos

The teachings of Don Juan; a Yaqui way of knowledge. University of Calif. Press 1968 196p $32.50; pa $16.95 **299**

1. Juan, Don 2. Yaqui Indians—Religion

ISBN 0-520-21755-1; 0-520-21757-8 (pa)

Available 30th anniversary edition with a new commentary by the author

Also available in paperback from Washington Square Press

"This book is the record of a young anthropologist's experiences as the apprentice of a [Yaqui] Indian sorcerer. Over a period of four years, Mr. Castaneda paid intermittant visits to Don Juan, first in Arizona, then in Sonora, Mexico." N Y Times Book Rev

Other titles about Don Juan are:

The active side of infinity (1999)

The art of dreaming (1993)

The eagle's gift (1981)

The fire from within (1984)

Journey to Ixtlan (1972)

Magical passes (1998)

The power of silence (1987)

The second ring of power (1977)

A separate reality (1971)

Tales of power (1974)

Chevannes, Barry

Rastafari: roots and ideology. Syracuse Univ. Press 1994 298p (Utopianism and communitarianism) hardcover o.p. paperback available $19.95 **299**

1. Rastafari movement 2. Jamaica—Religion

ISBN 0-8156-0296-0 (pa) LC 94-18608

"Chevannes begins by tracing the cultural roots of the Rastafari movement to the slave trade in Jamaica from the sixteenth through the nineteenth century, in reaction to which a foundation was laid for the spirit of resistance that was later a major factor in Rastafari's spread on the island. Chevannes also closely attends to the internal rifts and doctrinal disputes that caused denominational splits

Chevannes, Barry—*Continued*
within the movement." Booklist
"Vital for students of African American religions and Caribbean religions, but also of interest to anthropologists, sociologists, and historians." Choice
Includes bibliographical references

The **Encyclopedia** of African and African-American religions; Stephen D. Glazier, editor. Routledge 2000 xx, 452p il maps $125 **299**
1. African Americans—Religion—Encyclopedias 2. Blacks—Religion
ISBN 0-415-92245-3   LC 00-59136
"A Berkshire Reference work".
This encyclopedia presents "145 articles that explore the interaction of religion and culture and portray diversities of religious experience and research methodology. Religions outside North America, including lesser-known movements, receive the most coverage, and authors often present fruits of their own ethnographic studies." Choice
"This encyclopedia is a good starting point for understanding the complex interrelationships among African, African American, and European religious beliefs, practices, and traditions in a global context." Libr J

Gill, Sam D., 1943-
Dictionary of Native American mythology; [by] Sam D. Gill, Irene F. Sullivan. ABC-CLIO 1992 xxx, 425p il maps o.p.; Oxford Univ. Press paperback available $21.50 **299**
1. Native Americans—Religion—Dictionaries
ISBN 0-19-508602-3 (pa)   LC 92-27053
"The authors have included entries representing more than 150 Native American language groups. . . . For each of the alphabetically arranged entries, tribal source and culture area are included. A collection of vivid black-and-white illustrations is reprinted. A comprehensive bibliography and index by tribe complete this excellent reference work." Libr J

Glassman, Sallie Ann
Vodou visions; an encounter with divine mystery. Villard Bks. 2000 237p il $14.95 **299**
1. Voodooism
ISBN 0-375-75370-2   LC 99-88214
This is a guide to Voodoo's "history, practices, and creative applications. It describes the tools and techniques for developing the magical mind and honoring the soul, while revealing how Vodou can release creative spirituality and open doors to self-awareness." Publisher's note
Includes bibliographical references

Hirschfelder, Arlene B.
The encyclopedia of Native American religions; [by] Arlene Hirschfelder, Paulette Molin; foreword by Walter R. Echo-Hawk. updated ed. Facts on File 2000 390p il $71.50; pa $21.95 **299**
1. Native Americans—Religion—Encyclopedias
ISBN 0-8160-2017-5; 0-8160-4653-0 (pa)
    LC 99-21586
First published 1991
"The entries in this encyclopedia provide descriptions of religious ceremonies and terminology; biographies of native American religious leaders, missionaries, and others who have influenced the practice of these religions; summaries of major court cases affecting native religious practices; healing and other ceremonial practices that are spiritual rather than religious in nature; and some . . . mythology." Booklist [review of 1991 edition]
Includes bibliographical references

Hultkrantz, Åke
The religions of the American Indians; translated by Monica Setterwall. University of Calif. Press 1979 335p il hardcover o.p. paperback available $19.95 **299**
1. Native Americans—Religion
ISBN 0-520-04239-5 (pa)   LC 73-90661
Both sections of this book on North and South American Indians "provide fundamental knowledge and point to genetic connections between cultural areas. A well-researched work with a comprehensive bibliography, sure to be of interest to historians of religion and those interested in American culture." Libr J

I ching
The classic of changes; a new translation of the I Ching as interpreted by Wang Bi; translated by Richard John Lynn. Columbia Univ. Press 1994 602p (Translations from the Asian classics) $25.95 **299**
1. Divination
ISBN 0-231-08294-0   LC 93-43999
Also available CD-ROM version
"Most available editions of the I Ching are based on the James Legge translation, a work produced over 140 years ago and characterized by romanticized and idiomatic Victorian English. Although not more accurate or revealing than the Legge, this new translation is welcome because of its crisp usage of modern-day English." Libr J

Kebra Nagast
The Kebra Nagast; the last Bible of Rastafarian wisdom and faith from Ethiopia and Jamaica; edited by Gerald Hausman; introduction by Ziggy Marley. St. Martin's Press 1997 203p il $19.95 **299**
1. Rastafari movement
ISBN 0-312-16793-8   LC 97-18817
"The Kebra Nagast supports the claims to black presence in biblical lore through the lineage of King Solomon's Ethiopian children. Hausman augments the main text with a little compendium of parallel quotations from the Bible and the most famous Rastafarian . . . the late Bob Marley." Booklist
Includes bibliographical references

Lao-tzu, 6th cent. B.C.
Tao te ching **299**
Hardcover and paperback editions available from various publishers
"Chinese Taoist text attributed to Lao Tzu, supposedly an elder contemporary of Confucius (551?-479 BC). . . . A brief work in eighty-one-paragraphs in both verse and prose, it probably dates from the 4th or 3rd century BC, although some believe it may be as early as the 6th century BC. Because of its concise, poetic language, its meaning is subject to many interpretations. It is generally agreed that it is both a mystical book about union with the absolute, and a political handbook on how to rule and survive in chaotic times." Reader's Ency. 4th edition

Lifton, Robert Jay, 1926-

Destroying the world to save it; Aum Shinrikyo, apocalyptic violence, and the new global terrorism. Holt & Co. 1999 374p hardcover o.p. paperback available $16   **299**
1. Asahara, Shoko 2. Aum Shinrikyō 3. Cults
ISBN 0-8050-6511-3 (pa)   LC 99-23905
This is a "portrait of Aum Shinrikyo, the Japanese cult that became world-famous when it released a nerve gas called sarin into the Tokyo subway. . . . But the book is much more than a story of a single cult. It's an exploration of the idea of cults: how they grow, who joins them, who leads them. . . . Lifton places Aum in the broader context of world history, comparing it to Jim Jones' Peoples Temple and the Nazi movement." Booklist
Includes bibliographical references

MacKillop, James

Dictionary of Celtic mythology. Oxford Univ. Press 1998 xxix, 402p hardcover o.p. paperback available $15.95   **299**
1. Celtic mythology—Dictionaries
ISBN 0-19-280120-1 (pa)   LC 97-19398
"In addition to gods and goddesses, heroes and heroines, creatures, and other mythological figures, the approximately 4,000 entries cover real and imaginary places, archaeological sites, animals and plants, narrative cycles, and ideas. . . . This scholarly dictionary should be a valuable addition to academic and large public libraries." Booklist
Includes bibliographical references

Miller, Mary Ellen

The gods and symbols of ancient Mexico and the Maya; an illustrated dictionary of Mesoamerican religion; [by] Mary Ellen Miller and Karl Taube. Thames & Hudson 1993 216p il hardcover o.p. paperback available $16.95   **299**
1. Mayas—Religion 2. Aztecs—Religion
ISBN 0-500-27928-4 (pa)   LC 92-80338
"The authors give a brief history of the different Mesoamerican civilizations, explaining the rise and fall of each, and how one may have influenced the others. . . . The major portion of the work is the alphabetical dictionary section of approximately 300 terms. Most entries are between one-half column and one column in length, but some are more extensive; for example, *Calendar* is six pages with several illustrations and a chart of day names in Mayan and Aztec. The entries give etymologies where available, definitions, and commentary when appropriate." Booklist

Pagels, Elaine H., 1943-

The gnostic Gospels; by Elaine Pagels. Random House 1979 xxxvi, 182p hardcover o.p. paperback available $12   **299**
1. Gnosticism
ISBN 0-679-72453-2 (pa)   LC 79-4764
An examination of the origins of early Christianity based on Gnostic texts rediscovered in the 20th century
Pagels "writes for the layman, which is refreshing, and she does so lucidly, which is a challenge, especially when 'gnosticism' was regarded by its own adherents to be for the initiated only." Christ Sci Monit
Includes bibliographical references

Popol vuh

Popol vuh; the Mayan book of the dawn of life; translated by Dennis Tedlock; with commentary based on the ancient knowledge of the modern Quiché Maya. rev ed. Simon & Schuster 1996 388p il maps pa $15   **299**
1. Mayas—Religion 2. Native Americans—Religion
ISBN 0-684-81845-0   LC 95-46822
This translation first published 1985
A Touchstone book
A modern translation of the 16th century Mayan holy book
"Tedlock's translation splendidly combines scholarship, imagination, and literary sensitivity. His photographs (derived from field work in Guatemala) vividly illustrate the text, and the notes (based on his collaboration with a contemporary Quiché shaman) fascinate and inform." Libr J
Includes bibliographical references

Scheub, Harold

A dictionary of African mythology; the mythmaker as storyteller. Oxford Univ. Press 2000 368p il map $35; pa $16.95   **299**
1. African mythology—Dictionaries
ISBN 0-19-512456-1; 0-19-512457-X (pa)
                           LC 99-35035
"Along with commentary on 14 mythic themes, 400 tales from all over Africa are arranged alphabetically by name of the significant character." Booklist
Includes bibliographical references

Wilkinson, Richard H.

The complete gods and goddesses of ancient Egypt. Thames & Hudson 2003 256p il $39.95   **299**
1. Egyptian mythology 2. Egypt—Religion 3. Gods and goddesses
ISBN 0-500-05120-8   LC 2002-110321
A guide to "Egyptian deities—a complete catalogue of gods and goddesses supplemented by examinations of the history of Egyptian religion, the rise and fall of the gods, and the ways in which they were worshipped." Publ Wkly
"Wilkinson's gorgeously illustrated book adds new dimension to popular literature on ancient Egypt. . . . And once readers open the book to look at the pictures, they well may stay to read the well-organized, comprehensive, clearly written text." Booklist
Includes bibliographical references

300   SOCIAL SCIENCES

300.3   Social sciences— Encyclopedias and dictionaries

Dictionary of the social sciences; edited by Craig Calhoun. Oxford Univ. Press 2002 563p $75   **300.3**
1. Social sciences—Dictionaries
ISBN 0-19-512371-9   LC 00-68151
This dictionary provides "definitions of key terms, offering entries that also discuss the intellectual issues behind the terms' usage. The entries cover all the social sciences except for law, education, and public administration. . . . Some 275 biographies are included." Libr J

The **Social** science encyclopedia; edited by Adam Kuper and Jessica Kuper. 2nd ed. Routledge 1996 xxiv, 923p il $160; pa $41.94 **300.3**

1. Social sciences—Encyclopedias
ISBN 0-415-10829-2; 0-415-28560-7 (pa)
LC 97-166752
First published 1985

This encyclopedia presents some 600 articles, aiming to represent "current theory, practice, and policy in such disciplines as anthropology, economics, education, feminism, geography, government and politics, linguistics, philosophy, and sociology." Booklist

300.5   Social sciences—Serial publications

Social sciences index. Wilson, H.W. service basis **300.5**

1. Social sciences—Periodicals—Indexes
ISSN 0094-4920

Also available CD-ROM version and online

Quarterly with bound annual cumulations

"Author-subject index to over 400 periodicals in the social sciences. Specific subject headings and many cross-references aid research. Book reviews indexed by author in a separate section." Ref Sources for Small & Medium-sized Libr. 6th edition

301   Sociology and anthropology

Encyclopedia of sociology; Edgar F. Borgatta, editor-in-chief, Rhonda Montgomery, managing editor. 2nd ed. Macmillan Ref. USA 2000 5v set $575 **301**

1. Sociology—Encyclopedias
ISBN 0-02-864853-6
LC 00-28402
First published 1992

This set includes about 400 articles covering all fields and subfields of sociology: social psychology, social demography, social anthropology, social history, social geography, social ecology, certain branches of political science, political economy, and sociolinguistics. More recent studies include affirmative action, alernative lifestyles, genocide, information society, sexually transmitted diseases and terrorism

This work "is highly recommended for academic libraries and other institutions." Booklist

Required reading; sociology's most influential books; edited by Dan Clawson. University of Mass. Press 1998 221p hardcover o.p. paperback available $17.95 **301**

1. Sociology—Bibliography 2. Best books
ISBN 1-55849-153-8 (pa)
LC 98-11944

This volume "identifies and discusses 17 of the 'most influential' books in sociology written during the last 25 years. . . . The power of this book lies in reconsiderations by eminent sociologists of important titles in light of a quarter of a century's worth of political, social, and economic change." Libr J

Includes bibliographical references

World of sociology; Joseph M. Palmisano, editor. Gale Group 2001 2v il set $160 **301**

1. Sociology—Encyclopedias
ISBN 0-7876-4965-1
LC 00-48399

This is a "subject-specific guide to concepts, theories, discoveries, pioneers, issues and ethical questions associated with sociology. It includes approximately 1,000-1,500 alphabetically arranged topical essays, definitions and biographies." Publisher's note

302   Social interaction

Fromm, Erich, 1900-1980
To have or to be? Harper & Row 1976 xxiv, 215p o.p.; Continuum paperback available $17.95 **302**

1. Human behavior 2. Ontology 3. Civilization
ISBN 0-8264-0912-1 (pa)

"World perspectives"

The author maintains "that two modes of existence are struggling for the spirit of humankind: the *having* mode, which concentrates on material possession, acquisitiveness, power, and aggression . . . and the *being* mode, which is based in love." Publisher's note

Includes bibliographical references

302.2   Communication

Adler, Mortimer J., 1902-2001
How to speak, how to listen. Macmillan 1983 280p hardcover o.p. paperback available $12 **302.2**

1. Communication
ISBN 0-684-84647-0 (pa)
LC 82-25907

The author seeks to "describe various kinds of speeches—sales talks, lectures, courtroom arguments—with advice and examples from his own experiences and the classics. The second part of the book stresses active listening—taking notes during and after a speech, later reflection on what has been said, etc." Libr J

Biedermann, Hans, 1930-
Dictionary of symbolism; translated by James Hulbert. Facts on File 1992 465p il o.p.; Meridian Bks. paperback available $24 **302.2**

1. Signs and symbols
ISBN 0-452-01118-3 (pa)
LC 91-44933
Original German edition, 1989

This dictionary "incorporates symbols that originated in Asia, Africa, Europe and the 'New World'. There are almost 600 entries from mythology, fairy tale, psychology, religion, and sociology, plus historical and legendary figures. With 2000 black-and-white illustrations, the book is highly attractive. The symbols are accompanied by thorough interpretations based on various sources." SLJ

Dreyfuss, Henry, 1904-1979
Symbol sourcebook; an authoritative guide to international graphic symbols. McGraw-Hill 1972 292p il o.p.; Wiley paperback available $44.95   **302.2**
1. Signs and symbols
ISBN 0-471-28872-1 (pa)
"Approximately one-half of this . . . reference book is given over to graphic symbols, arranged by subject, from accommodations and travel, to engineering, to vehicle control. . . . The second half is a listing of basic graphic forms and how they are employed for a variety of duties. The first part is a ready reference aid, the second an inspiration to designers and artists." Libr J

Liungman, Carl G., 1938-
Dictionary of symbols. ABC-CLIO 1991 596p o.p.; Norton paperback available $21.95
302.2
1. Signs and symbols 2. Picture writing
ISBN 0-393-31236-4 (pa)   LC 91-36657
Original Swedish edition, 1974
This dictionary groups "icons according to their graphical style rather than their meaning. For example, all symbols based upon the cross are included in one chapter, those based upon the triangle in another, and those based upon the circle in yet another. Each symbol is succinctly defined and a source of origin (if known) is given. To enhance access, both name and form indexes are provided. This work will certainly become one of the key sources for tracing symbols and their meanings." Am Libr
Includes bibliographical references

Tannen, Deborah
You just don't understand; women and men in conversation. Morrow 1990 330p o.p.; Quill paperback available $14   **302.2**
1. Conversation 2. Sex differences (Psychology)
ISBN 0-06-095962-2 (pa)   LC 89-49000
The author "ponders gender-based differences that, she claims, define and distinguish male and female communication. . . . She asserts that for most women conversation is a way of connecting and negotiating. . . . Men, on the other hand, use conversation to achieve or maintain social status." Publ Wkly
"Aside from the vivid examples and lively prose, what makes this book particularly engaging is that the author makes linguistics . . . interesting and usable." N Y Times Book Rev
Includes bibliographical references

Tresidder, Jack, 1931-
Dictionary of symbols; an illustrated guide to traditional images, icons, and emblems. Chronicle Bks. 1998 c1997 240p il hardcover o.p. paperback available $16.95   **302.2**
1. Signs and symbols
ISBN 0-8118-1470-X (pa)   LC 97-27548
"A dictionary of symbolic and metaphoric meanings as found in religious, literary, and artistic traditions. Entries ranging from 'crow' to 'parasol' to 'wine' show a strong preference for myth or religion, but the author gives equal treatment to all major traditions and frequently notes meanings from lesser traditions and sects." Libr J

302.23   Media (Means of communication)

Bok, Sissela
Mayhem; violence as public entertainment. Addison-Wesley 1998 194p o.p.; Perseus Bks. paperback available $15   **302.23**
1. Violence 2. Mass media
ISBN 0-7382-0145-6 (pa)   LC 97-48620
"A Merloyd Lawrence book"
The author "examines the shallow debates surrounding violent entertainments, especially on television. She fleshes out both sides of the issue, offering a rigorous discussion of the ill effects of violent shows and of censorship, and then advances nongovernmental solutions to curbing exposure to violent media. . . . Packed with citations and rich in anecdote . . . this may be the best primer for a serious debate." Libr J
Includes bibliographical references

The **Encyclopedia** of new media; an essential reference to communication and technology; Steve Jones, editor. Sage Publs. 2003 532p il $125   **302.23**
1. Multimedia—Encyclopedias 2. Communication—Encyclopedias
ISBN 0-7619-2382-9   LC 2002-13229
This reference "examines artifacts, concepts, personalities, and contexts surrounding the history, adaptation, and growth of new media. The encyclopedia includes more than 250 entries on such topics as blog, cyborg, digital subscriber line, gaming, plug-ins, and telemedicine, as well as such personalities as Laurie Anderson, William Gibson, Jaron Lanier, and Steven Jobs. Each article includes a bibliography, suggestions for further reading, and 'see also' references. . . . [This is] a worthwhile and valuable addition to both science and technology and social science reference collections. It is suitable for high school, public and university library audiences." Ref & User Services Quarterly

History of the mass media in the United States; an encyclopedia; edited by Margaret A. Blanchard; commissioning editor Carol J. Burwash. Fitzroy Dearborn Pubs. 1998 xxxii, 752p il $150   **302.23**
1. Mass media 2. United States—Civilization
ISBN 1-57958-012-2   LC 98-233183
This volume examines the ways in which mass media affects and is affected by United States society. From the 1690s to 1990, the alphabetically arranged entries cover subjects ranging from newspaper history to media coverage of wars, court cases, legislation and interest groups
"Beautifully designed, with a nice clear typeface, this work is also enhanced by superb illustrations and well-chosen photographs. . . . This volume is outstanding." Booklist

Jones, Gerard
Killing monsters; why children need fantasy, super heroes, and make-believe violence; foreword by Lynn Ponton. Basic Bks. 2002 261p $25; pa $15   **302.23**
1. Mass media 2. Children 3. Fantasy 4. Violence
ISBN 0-465-03695-3; 0-465-03696-1 (pa)
LC 2001-52667
The author "argues that violent video games, movies, music and comics provide a safe fantasy world within

Jones, Gerard—_Continued_
which children learn to become familiar with and control the frightening emotions of anger, violence and sexuality." Publ Wkly
"Although not an academic, the author has done his homework. He presents his case convincingly, and the concluding notes provide support." SLJ
Includes bibliographical references

McLuhan, Marshall, 1911-1980
The global village; transformations in world life and media in the 21st century; [by] Marshall McLuhan and Bruce R. Powers. Oxford Univ. Press 1989 220p il (Communication and society) hardcover o.p. paperback available $14.95   **302.23**
1. Mass media 2. Technology and civilization
ISBN 0-19-507910-8 (pa)   LC 88-22718
This book "was written, according to Powers, between 1974 and 1980 . . . and 'put together' between 1976 and 1984. McLuhan's thesis has always been that electronic technologies have been altering and reconstituting people in ways they don't understand and causing them to lose their private identities. This book probes the same theme from different angles, but with the same McLuhanesque all-over-the-place reasoning." Libr J
Includes bibliographical references

Postman, Neil
Amusing ourselves to death; public discourse in the age of show business. Viking 1985 184p hardcover o.p. paperback available $14   **302.23**
1. Mass media 2. Television broadcasting 3. United States—Civilization
ISBN 0-14-009438-5 (pa)   LC 85-5335
"Elisabeth Sifton books"
The author argues that the constant exposure to television has contributed to a decline in America's intellectual life
"A sustained, withering and thought-provoking attack on television and what it is doing to us." Publ Wkly
Includes bibliographical references

302.3   Social interaction within groups

Ambrose, Stephen E.
Comrades; brothers, fathers, heroes, sons, pals; illustrations by Jon Friedman. Simon & Schuster 1999 139p il hardcover o.p. paperback available $11   **302.3**
1. Friendship 2. Men—Psychology 3. Father-son relationship 4. Brothers
ISBN 0-7432-0074-8 (pa)   LC 99-27400
The author "delves into male friendship through a reworking of selections from his own works that exemplify male bonding and adds reflections about his friends, starting with his family." Booklist

King, Larry, 1933-
How to talk to anyone, anytime, anywhere; the secrets of good communication; [by] Larry King with Bill Gilbert. Crown 1994 220p hardcover o.p. paperback available $12.95   **302.3**
1. Conversation 2. Communication
ISBN 0-517-88453-4 (pa)   LC 94-31458
King "shows you how to break the ice with strangers, what to say at a wedding or a funeral, and how to sell yourself to a prospective employer—or interview a prospective employee. He gives his secrets for how to survive if you have to appear on radio or television, and how to recover from making a blooper." Publisher's note

Locke, John L.
The de-voicing of society; why we don't talk to each other anymore. Simon & Schuster 1998 256p hardcover o.p. paperback available $18.95   **302.3**
1. Conversation 2. Communication
ISBN 0-684-85574-7 (pa)   LC 98-14921
"Locke offers a pointed diagnosis of the isolated society created by disembodied interaction. Ever more atomized and shackled to video screens, modern people watch and type, rather than talk. The loss, argues Locke, can be discerned in the purposes of talk, specifically gossip, in creating relationships and social networks. . . . An insightful lamentation about a palpable social pandemic." Booklist
Includes bibliographical references

302.4   Social interaction between groups

Maalouf, Amin
In the name of identity; violence and the need to belong; translated from the French by Barbara Bray. Arcade Pub. 2001 164p $22.95   **302.4**
1. Identity (Psychology) 2. Violence
ISBN 1-55970-593-0   LC 2001-24929
Also available in paperback from Penguin Bks.
"This meditation on identity asks why the Arab world increasingly looks like a stronghold of fanaticism. The author, a Lebanese-born Christian who is now a resident of France, points out that Islam is not, historically, any more violent than Christianity, and looks at the forces currently acting upon it. While noting the Middle East's poverty and instability, he also suggests that after the fall of the Soviet Union those who might once have turned to Communism as an agency of political change now turn to fanaticism, and its promise of salvation through action." New Yorker
"This is an important addition to contemporary literature on diversity, nationalism, race and international politics." Publ Wkly

303.3　Coordination and control

Cull, Nicholas John

Propaganda and mass persuasion; a historical encyclopedia, 1500 to the present; [by] Nicholas J. Cull, David Culbert, David Welch. ABC-CLIO 2003 xxi, 479p il $85

303.3

1. Propaganda—Encyclopedias
ISBN 1-57607-820-5　　　　LC 2003-9513
This is an "A-Z guide to five centuries of propaganda, in both wartime and peacetime, which covers key moments, techniques, concepts, and some of the most influential propagandists in history." Publisher's note
"This specialized encyclopedia does a good job of exploring the different uses of propaganda." Booklist
Includes bibliographical references

Harari, Oren

The leadership secrets of Colin Powell. McGraw-Hill 2002 278p $21.95; pa $14.95

303.3

1. Powell, Colin L. 2. Leadership
ISBN 0-07-138859-1; 0-07-141861-X (pa)
　　　　　　　　　　　LC 2002-277110
This book centers on Colin Powell's "leadership philosophy and is organized into 17 chapters of 'leadership secrets,' each one summarized into three or four of 'Powell's Principles.'" Booklist
"Harari has done an admirable job of distilling the essence of Powell's leadership style." Publ Wkly

Himmelfarb, Gertrude

The de-moralization of society; from Victorian virtues to modern values. Knopf 1995 314p hardcover o.p. paperback available $19

303.3

1. Social values 2. United States—Moral conditions 3. Great Britain—Moral conditions 4. United States—Social conditions
ISBN 0-679-76490-9 (pa)　　　　LC 94-12365
The author examines "post-industrial and post-modern society. Himmelfarb contends that if we can overcome our prejudices against Victorian society and . . . the so-called values—or disvalues—they bequeathed us, then maybe we can learn from the Victorians as we deal with crime, drug addiction, illiteracy, illegitimacy and welfare dependency in American society." America
"This is intellectual history and historically based argument as good as they get." Booklist
Includes bibliographical references

Huxley, Aldous, 1894-1963

Brave new world revisited. Harper & Row 1958 147p hardcover o.p. paperback available $10

303.3

1. Propaganda 2. Totalitarianism 3. Brainwashing 4. Culture
ISBN 0-06-095551-1 (pa)
Also available in hardcover from Amereon
In response to his 1932 novel Brave new world "Huxley reconsiders his prophecies and fears that some of these may be coming true much sooner than he thought." Oxford Companion to Engl Lit. 5th edition

Sowell, Thomas, 1930-

The quest for cosmic justice. Free Press 1999 214p $25; pa $14

303.3

1. Justice 2. Equality
ISBN 0-684-86462-2; 0-684-86463-0 (pa)
　　　　　　　　　　　LC 99-31470
"Thomas Sowell argues that government cannot afford to remedy, and should therefore ignore, a broad spectrum of . . . hardships caused by poverty, disability, geography, even race and nationality." N Y Times Book Rev
The author "presents his case in clear, convincing, and accessible language." Libr J
Includes bibliographical references

Wills, Garry, 1934-

Certain trumpets; the call of leaders. Simon & Schuster 1994 336p il hardcover o.p. paperback available $14

303.3

1. Leadership 2. Power (Social sciences)
ISBN 0-684-80138-8 (pa)　　　　LC 94-6526
The author "has chosen 16 figures who exemplify a distinctive leadership type—for example, military (Napoleon), charismatic (King David), saintly (Catholic worker activist Dorothy Day). Each leader is contrasted with an 'anti-type' who, in Wills's judgment, failed to capitalize on strengths similar to those of his or her successful counterpart. . . . Wills pairs Martha Graham with Madonna, Socrates with Ludwig Wittgenstein, Eleanor Roosevelt with Nancy Reagan in a wise, witty, entertaining look at the psychology of leaders and their followers." Publ Wkly
Includes bibliographical references

Young-Bruehl, Elisabeth

The anatomy of prejudices. Harvard Univ. Press 1996 632p hardcover o.p. paperback available $18.95

303.3

1. Prejudices
ISBN 0-674-03191-1 (pa)　　　　LC 95-43754
In this book the author "argues that anti-Semitism, racism, sexism and homophobia differ in their internal logic (or illogic) and, more important, that they are deeply rooted in character structure and the unconscious." NY Times Book Rev
"Clearly written and accessible to general as well as scholarly readers, this is a major work in personality and culture that asserts the plurality rather than the unity of prejudice." Libr J
Includes bibliographical references

303.4　Social change

Anderson, Terry H., 1946-

The movement and the sixties. Oxford Univ. Press 1995 500p il hardcover o.p. paperback available $19.95

303.4

1. Radicalism 2. Demonstrations 3. United States—Social conditions
ISBN 0-19-510457-9 (pa)　　　　LC 94-16344
This "book is a national study of U.S. social activism from 1960 to 1973, focusing on how 'the Movement' was experienced by participants and exploring why this activism arose when it did, how it developed, and what it accomplished." Booklist
Anderson's "sweeping study is a valuable, refreshingly unbiased reassessment of the '60s legacy." Publ Wkly
Includes bibliographical references

Diamond, Jared M.

Guns, germs, and steel; the fates of human societies. Norton 1997 480p il maps $27.50; pa $16.95 **303.4**
1. Technology and civilization 2. Social change 3. Environmental influence on humans
ISBN 0-393-03891-2; 0-393-31755-2 (pa)
LC 96-37068
"This book poses a simple but profound question about the distribution of wealth and power in the modern world: 'Why weren't Native Americans, Africans, and Aboriginal Australians the ones who decimated, subjugated, or exterminated Europeans and Asians?'. . . To explore the discrepancies in technological and cultural development he looks not at peoples but at places, and at the natural resources available to different indigenous populations since 11,000 B.C. The scope and the explanatory power of this book are astounding." New Yorker
Includes bibliographical references

Dyson, Freeman J., 1923-

The sun, the genome, & the Internet; tools of scientific revolutions. Oxford Univ. Press 1999 124p $22; pa $10.95 **303.4**
1. Forecasting 2. Social change 3. Technology and civilization
ISBN 0-19-512942-3; 0-19-513922-4 (pa)
LC 98-53830
This volume "is based on lectures given at the New York Public Library in 1997. . . . [The author] believes that solar energy, genetic engineering and the Internet have the potential to transform society profoundly in the next century." N Y Times Book Rev
"A wide-ranging, fascinating view of science and society's distant horizon." Booklist
Includes bibliographical references

Gould, Stephen Jay, 1941-2002

The hedgehog, the fox, and the magister's pox; mending the gap between science and the humanities. Harmony Bks. 2003 274p il $25.95 **303.4**
1. Science and the humanities
ISBN 0-609-60140-7
LC 2002-7807
"Gould's point of departure is the Greek soldier-poet Archilochus' proverb about the cunning fox versus the persistent hedgehog, which the author employs to exemplify what he asserts is the proper relationship between the sciences and the humanities—they are separate but equal players, he says, in the joint enterprise of wisdom. In his inimitable style, Gould mines rare and idiosyncratic sources to debunk the common notion of science and the humanities (which includes religion in Gould's taxonomy) as mortal foes. . . . This book is a fine read, rich with learning and insight." Publ Wkly

Hoffman, Abbie

The best of Abbie Hoffman; foreword by Norman Mailer; edited by Dan Simon with the author. Four Walls Eight Windows 1989 421p il $21.95; pa $18.95 **303.4**
1. Radicalism 2. United States—Civilization
ISBN 0-941423-27-1; 0-941423-42-5 (pa)
LC 89-23585
This volume contains selections from Revolution for the hell of it, Woodstock Nation, Steal this book, and New writings

Lewis, Michael

Next: the future just happened. Norton 2001 236p $23.95; pa $13.95 **303.4**
1. Internet—Social aspects
ISBN 0-393-02037-1; 0-393-32352-8 (pa)
LC 2001-32602
"Linked essays about the Internet as the universal solvent of the fundamental social order, best when the author personalizes change by exhibiting teenage prodigies who have out-run their elders and betters on the Information Highway." N Y Times Book Rev

Postman, Neil

Technopoly; the surrender of culture to technology. Knopf 1992 222p hardcover o.p. paperback available $12 **303.4**
1. Technology and civilization
ISBN 0-679-74540-8 (pa)
LC 91-53121
According to Postman, "the history of the world can be retold from the perspective of technological advances. In 'technopoly,' the present stage in Western culture, our tools, especially the computer, have committed a palace revolt, 'redefining what we mean by religion, by art, by family, by politics, by history, by privacy, by intelligence, so that our definitions fit its new requirements.'" Natl Rev
Postman's "style is comfortable, his exposition incisive, and his reasoning hard to ignore." Christ Sci Monit
Includes bibliographical references

Rifkin, Jeremy

The biotech century; harnessing the gene and remaking the world. Putnam 1998 271p hardcover o.p. paperback available $12.95 **303.4**
1. Biotechnology 2. Genetic engineering
ISBN 0-87477-953-7 (pa)
LC 97-44358
"A Jeremy P. Tarcher/Putnam book"
"Biotechnology has the capacity to deplete, rather than enhance, Earth's gene pool and irreparably damage ecological balance, according to Rifkin, and it may transform our conceptions of nature and of life itself. . . . [This is a] wide-ranging and deeply intelligent analysis." Publ Wkly

Stille, Alexander

The future of the past. Farrar, Straus & Giroux 2002 xxi, 339p $25; pa $15 **303.4**
1. Social change 2. Antiquities—Collection and preservation 3. Forecasting
ISBN 0-374-15977-7; 0-312-42094-3 (pa)
LC 2001-54348
The author presents a "report on cultural legacies that are in danger of disappearing." Booklist
"Stille consistently offers a powerful narrative, rich with anecdote, detailed description and lively dialogue. This is a must read for anyone interested in the preservation of our world's decaying treasures." Publ Wkly

Toffler, Alvin

Future shock. Random House 1970 505p o.p.; Bantam Bks. paperback available $7.99 **303.4**
1. Social change 2. Technology and civilization 3. Modern civilization—1950-
ISBN 0-553-27737-5 (pa)
According to the author, "future shock is 'the dizzying disorientation brought on by the premature arrival of the future.' . . . Toffler outlines some interesting strategies for survival, writing in a clear popular style." Publ Wkly
Includes bibliographical references

Toffler, Alvin—*Continued*

Powershift; knowledge, wealth, and violence at the edge of the 21st century. Bantam Bks. 1990 xxii, 585p hardcover o.p. paperback available $7.99 **303.4**
1. Social change 2. Power (Social sciences) 3. Modern civilization—1950-
ISBN 0-553-29215-3 (pa)   LC 90-1068
The author "argues that the control of knowledge has become the principal means to create wealth and power. Aided by the widespread use of computers and other communications technologies, this 'powershift,' Toffler predicts, will dramatically alter the world's political balance." Libr J
Includes bibliographical references

The third wave. Morrow 1980 544p o.p.; Bantam Bks. paperback available $7.99
303.4
1. Social change 2. Technology and civilization 3. Modern civilization—1950-
ISBN 0-553-24698-4 (pa)   LC 79-26690
Toffler argues that mankind, having already experienced the agricultural age and the industrial age, is on the verge of a new age characterized by "new technical systems, especially those in electronics, genetics and biology." N Y Times Book Rev
Includes bibliographical references

Whitaker, Reginald, 1943-
The end of privacy; how total surveillance is becoming a reality; [by] Reg Whitaker. New Press (NY) 1999 195p $25; pa $14.95
303.4
1. Right of privacy 2. Information society
ISBN 1-56584-378-9; 1-56584-569-2 (pa)
LC 98-27826
"With computers and other electronic devices playing an integral role in our lives, Whitaker argues that what now exists in developed countries is . . . a surveillance society. It's the private sector, not the government, that is eroding individual privacy." Publ Wkly
"Whitaker's potent portrayal shows that people don't have as much autonomy as they believe." Booklist
Includes bibliographical references

Wright, Robert
NonZero; the logic of human destiny. Pantheon Bks. 2000 435p $27.50; pa $15
303.4
1. Social change 2. Civilization 3. History
ISBN 0-679-44252-9; 0-679-75894-1 (pa)
LC 99-40859
This book "examines the sociocultural evolution of our species toward ever-greater complexity, advancing technology, and scientific information." Libr J
"A spritely, opinionated big-picture history of human civilization." Booklist
Includes bibliographical references

303.6   Conflict

Anderson, Sean, 1952-
Historical dictionary of terrorism; [by] Sean K. Anderson, Stephen Sloan. 2nd ed. Scarecrow Press 2002 588p (Historical dictionaries of religions, philosophies, and movements) $90 **303.6**
1. Terrorism—Dictionaries
ISBN 0-8108-4101-0   LC 2001-49656
First published 1995
The authors "investigate various underlying causes and motivations, providing insight into organizations, groups, and individuals directly involved or related to terrorism. They supply a typology of terrorists that will be valuable to researchers or others interested in penetrating the murkiness of terrorism." Choice
Includes bibliographical references

Arendt, Hannah
On revolution   **303.6**
1. Revolutions
Available in paperback from Penguin Bks. and in hardcover from Greenwood Press
First published 1963 by Viking
The author "believes that war and revolution are the central facts of our time. But while war may become obsolete through nuclear terror, revolution seems likely to persist as the order of the day, and those who understand revolution may well be the masters of the future." Atl Mon

Benjamin, Daniel, 1961-
The age of sacred terror; [by] Daniel Benjamin, Steven Simon. Random House 2002 490p $25.95; pa $15.95   **303.6**
1. Terrorism 2. Islam and politics
ISBN 0-375-50859-7; 0-8129-6984-7 (pa)
LC 2003-265413
"The authors, both staff members of the National Security Council in the Clinton administration, give an account of bureaucratic inertia in antiterrorist efforts before Sept. 11, with the F.B.I., the C.I.A. and the military reluctant to share information or work with one another." N Y Times Book Rev
Includes bibliographical references

Camus, Albert, 1913-1960
The rebel; an essay on man in revolt; with a foreword by Sir Herbert Read; a revised and complete translation of L'homme révolté by Anthony Bower. Vintage Bks. 1991 c1956 306p pa $12   **303.6**
1. Revolutions 2. Nihilism
ISBN 0-679-73384-1   LC 91-50022
Original French edition, 1951; this translation first published 1956 by Knopf
The author describes how the theories of philosophers have been used with disastrous effect by political leaders from the French Revolution through the nihilist revolutions of Russia and the governments of Lenin, Hitler and Stalin. The conclusion calls for a return to a political philosophy having as its aim the happiness and development of living human beings

Carr, Caleb, 1955-

The lessons of terror; a history of warfare against civilians: why it has always failed and why it will fail again. Random House 2002 272p hardcover o.p. paperback available $12.95 **303.6**
1. Terrorism
ISBN 0-375-76074-1 (pa)   LC 2002-280604
The author argues "that terrorism must be viewed in terms of 'military history, rather than political science or sociology,' and that the refusal to label terrorists as soldiers, rather than criminals, is a mistake. . . . This often fascinating, accessible tome skillfully contends that the terrorizing of civilians has a long and controversial history but, as an inferior method, is prone to failure." Publ Wkly
Includes bibliographical references

Combs, Cindy C.

Encyclopedia of terrorism; [by] Cindy C. Combs and Martin Slann. Facts on File 2002 339p il maps (Facts on File library of world history) $77 **303.6**
1. Terrorism—Encyclopedias
ISBN 0-8160-4455-4   LC 2001-23859
Alphabetically arranged entries cover "the events, people, organizations, and places that have figured prominently in international terrorism. Each entry is placed within its historical context to help readers understand the wide-ranging motivations behind terrorist actions." Publisher's note
For a review see: Booklist, Sept. 1, 2002

Confronting fear; a documentary history of terrorism; edited by Isaac Cronin. Thunder's Mouth Press 2002 561p pa $18.95 **303.6**
1. Terrorism
ISBN 1-56025-399-1   LC 2002-18005
Featuring essays by such authors as Simon Schama, Joseph Conrad, and V. S. Naipaul, this is "a compilation of writings on various forms of terrorism—political, religious, and 'fringe,' such as the Unabomber. . . . This is a good volume to have at hand in today's uncertain world as a quick reference to various instant newsmakers who populate our 'Breaking News' mindset." Booklist
"Cronin provides a rare overview for the public to understand this important and disturbing subject." Choice

Dershowitz, Alan M.

Why terrorism works; understanding the threat, responding to the challenge. Yale Univ. Press 2002 271p $24.95; pa $16 **303.6**
1. Terrorism
ISBN 0-300-09766-2; 0-300-10153-8 (pa)
LC 2002-6387
Contents: Deterring terrorism; The internalization of terrorism; How an amoral society could fight terrorism; Should the ticking bomb terrorist be tortured?: a case study in how a democracy should make tragic choices; Striking the right balance
The author "argues forcefully that the attacks of September 11 were largely of our own doing—the international community, Dershowitz says, repeatedly rewards terrorists with appeasement and legitimization, refusing to take the necessary steps to curtail attacks. . . . These penetrating arguments force readers to consider how we

got to September 11, how far we are willing to pursue terrorists and how much freedom we are willing to give up for our security." Publ Wkly
Includes bibliographical references

Herbst, Philip

Talking terrorism; a dictionary of the loaded language of political violence. Greenwood Press 2003 220p $49.95 **303.6**
1. Terrorism—Dictionaries
ISBN 0-313-32486-7   LC 2003-44071
"This is a dictionary with a social and political objective: to explore how supposedly civilized people, groups, and governments the world over use language to provide a moral justification for violence. . . .The 150 A-to-Z entries range from one half to several pages in length and include definitions, an examination of the charged use of a term both historically and in the present, and . . . cross references." Libr J
"This work is original, refreshing, and insightful. It attempts to discern the why of terrorism and political violence from the perspective of language." Choice
Includes bibliographical references

Kushner, Harvey W.

Encyclopedia of terrorism. Sage Publs. 2003 xxvii, 523p il maps $130 **303.6**
1. Terrorism—Encyclopedias
ISBN 0-7619-2408-6   LC 2002-15938
"This guide presents more than 300 article-length entries, arranged alphabetically and covering such topics as terrorist groups, key terrorists, types of terrorism, and terrorist events (including 9/11). . . . Kushner (along with a number of expert contributors) provides a solid powerful collection of timely data on the who, what, where, when, and why of international terrorism." Libr J
For a fuller review see: Booklist, Sept. 1, 2003

Laqueur, Walter, 1921-

No end to war; terrorism in the 21st century. Continuum 2002 288p $24.95 **303.6**
1. Terrorism 2. World politics—1991-
ISBN 0-8264-1435-4   LC 2002-151954
Contents: Roots of terrorism?; Origins of Islamic terrorism; Jihad; Suicide; Israel and the Palestinians; Intelligence failure?; The far right; Anti Americanism; Battlefields of the future 1: India and central Asia; Battlefields of the future 2: the international brigade; Conclusion: war against the West
"The author discusses what is (and what isn't) new about international terrorism, and predicts a long road ahead in dealing with aggressive fanaticism. Taking particular issue with the notion that terrorism can be dealt with by alleviating global economic disparity, Laqueur argues that the 'drain the swamp and the mosquitoes will disappear' strategy does not apply to wealthy internationally focused groups like al-Qaeda. . . . Laqueur's unabashedly conservative argument—ultimately based on the notion that being hated is a natural consequence of being great and powerful—is at heart a pointed critique of the postcolonialist sympathy for radicalism, made all the more compelling by the author's extensive background in terrorism studies." Booklist
Includes bibliographical references

Sontag, Susan, 1933-

Regarding the pain of others. Farrar, Straus & Giroux 2003 131p $20 **303.6**
1. War photography 2. Photojournalism 3. Documentary photography 4. Atrocities 5. Violence
ISBN 0-374-24858-3   LC 2002-192527
Companion volume to On photography (1977)

Sontag, Susan, 1933-—_Continued_

"In this long reflective essay, which examines photographs of calamities and the moral uses of looking at them, Sontag follows the trail of photojournalism from the Crimean War on and refines some of the observations of her 1977 book, 'On Photography.'" N Y Times Book Rev

"Academic libraries supporting programs in journalism (especially photojournalism), communications, psychology, sociology, military history, and art history will find this work invaluable, and it could also be useful in high schools to spark discussion in current events and history classes. All libraries, regardless of type, size, or demographics, should own this book." Libr J

Violence in America; an encyclopedia; Ronald Gottesman, editor; Richard Maxwell Brown, consulting editor [et al.] Scribner 1999 3v set $400   **303.6**

1. Violence—Encyclopedias

ISBN 0-684-80487-5   LC 99-52027

This reference "on the social, historical, biological, and cultural aspects of violence in the United States offers 600 entries on topics ranging from violence, homicide, and race and ethnicity to women, child abuse, labor and unions, sociobiology, 'ultimate fighting,' television, gun violence, and various events and persons." Libr J

Includes bibliographical references

304.2   Human ecology

Commoner, Barry, 1917-

Making peace with the planet. Pantheon Bks. 1990 292p o.p.; New Press (NY) paperback available $16.95   **304.2**

1. Pollution 2. Human influence on nature 3. Environmental protection 4. Nature conservation

ISBN 1-56584-012-7 (pa)   LC 89-43241

Also available in hardcover from P. Smith

The author offers an "analysis of our contemporary environmental crisis, using the metaphor of a war between the natural ecosphere and the human-made technosphere." Libr J

"Visionary yet specific, his urgent essay is a blueprint of our possible future and a beacon for the environmental struggles of the '90s." Publ Wkly

Includes bibliographical references

Gore, Albert, Jr.

Earth in the balance; ecology and the human spirit; [by] Al Gore. Houghton Mifflin 2000 xxiv, 407p il maps $26   **304.2**

1. Human ecology 2. Environmental protection

ISBN 0-618-05664-5   LC 00-38311

A reissue of the title first published 1992

In this discussion of the global environment and civilization the author "argues that only a radical rethinking of our relationship with nature can save the earth's ecology for future generations." Publisher's note

"The author exhibits little of the clichéd myopia of his profession and is aware of the political obstacles posed by such an integrated approach. He identifies the root of our current problems as spiritual. If civilization is to persist, he maintains, it must make the rescue of the environment its organizing principle." N Y Times Book Rev

Includes bibliographical references

Leakey, Richard E., 1944-

The sixth extinction; patterns of life and the future of humankind; [by] Richard Leakey and Roger Lewin. Doubleday 1995 271p il hardcover o.p. paperback available $14

304.2

1. Evolution 2. Human influence on nature 3. Mass extinction of species

ISBN 0-385-46809-1 (pa)   LC 95-18286

The authors contend that "human beings, by destroying tropical rain forests and driving tens of thousands of species into extinction, are dangerously reducing biodiversity, damaging ecosystems and possibly precipitating the next major mass extinction." Publ Wkly

Leakey and Lewin "present a powerful message based on years of observation and fieldwork." Libr J

Includes bibliographical references

Simpson, John W., 1952-

Yearning for the land; a search for the importance of place. Pantheon Bks. 2002 291p maps $24   **304.2**

1. Human geography

ISBN 0-375-42086-X   LC 2002-20692

The author "explores people's relationship with the landscape, defined in terms of all the physical and cultural events that have shaped it throughout history, including myths and folklore." Libr J

Simpson articulates "some keen insights into the tenuous ties we have to the places we live and the pleasure of giving in to a sense of belonging." Publ Wkly

Includes bibliographical references

304.5   Genetic factors

Taylor, Shelley E.

The tending instinct; how nurturing is essential for who we are and how we live. Times Bks. 2002 290p $25; pa $16   **304.5**

1. Sociobiology 2. Sex differences (Psychology) 3. Stress (Psychology)

ISBN 0-8050-6837-6; 0-8050-7289-6 (pa)

LC 2002-19879

The author "launched a series of innovative experiments that led her to believe that humans are biologically wired to nurture. She thus devised no less than a whole new psychology of women, presented in this accessible and well-grounded work." Libr J

Includes bibliographical references

304.6   Population

Encyclopedia of the U.S. Census; Margo J. Anderson, editor. CQ Press 2000 xxiv, 424p il $140   **304.6**

1. United States—Census

ISBN 1-56802-428-2   LC 00-30522

The alphabetically arranged articles "explain the history, methodology, and results of U.S. censuses since 1790. . . . Maps, tables, and charts show how the composition of the population has changed, where the center of population has moved over time, and how the address lists and census tracts are developed." Booklist

Includes bibliographical references

Power, Samantha

"A problem from hell"; America and the age of genocide. Basic Bks. 2002 xxi, 610p il $30 **304.6**

1. Genocide 2. United States—Foreign relations
ISBN 0-465-06150-8 LC 2001-52611
Also available in paperback from HarperCollins Pubs.

Power "concentrates on America's recent reluctance to intervene in the mass slaughter of civilians in Iraq, Bosnia, and Rwanda. She argues that had the U.S. done so—particularly in Bosnia and Rwanda—it could have averted the murder of tens or hundreds of thousands; instead, geopolitical considerations, indifference, and worries over domestic support trumped American ideals. Though clearly imbued with a sense of outrage, Power is judicious in her portraits of those who opposed intervention, and keenly aware of the perils and costs of military action. Her indictment of U.S. policy is therefore all the more damning." New Yorker
Includes bibliographical references

United Nations. Statistical Office

Demographic yearbook. U.N. Publs. $125 **304.6**

1. Population—Statistics
ISSN 0082-8041
Annual. First issue for 1948 published 1949. Text in English and French

"Official compilation of international demographic data in such fields as area and population, natality, mortality, marriage, divorce, and international migration. Each year some aspect of demographic statistics is treated intensively." Ref Sources for Small & Medium-sized Libr. 6th edition

304.8 Movement of people

Keneally, Thomas

The great shame; and the triumph of the Irish in the English-speaking world. Talese 1999 c1998 712p il maps $35; pa $18 **304.8**

1. Irish—History 2. Ireland—Civilization 3. Ireland—Immigration and emigration
ISBN 0-385-47697-3; 0-385-72026-2 (pa)
LC 99-24888
First published 1998 in the United Kingdom

The author "tells the story of the Irish diaspora in the 19th century, especially the thousands of men and women sent in chains to penal colonies in Australia, among them a core of political prisoners who continued to fight for an independent Ireland." N Y Times Book Rev
Includes bibliographical references

Sowell, Thomas, 1930-

Migrations and cultures; a world view. Basic Bks. 1996 516p hardcover o.p. paperback available $23 **304.8**

1. Immigration and emigration 2. Ethnic groups 3. Ethnic relations
ISBN 0-465-04589-8 (pa) LC 95-44316

In this book the author seeks "to determine how migrations across nations and continents over the course of human history. . . . He believes the habits and beliefs that migrants bring to a new homeland, what he calls their cultural capital, are far more important in determining their fate than the homeland's economy, culture or politics. . . . This is a lively and provocative

book that is important reading for anyone who thinks we have too many immigrants or too few, who favors affirmative action and multicultural programs or opposes them." N Y Times Book Rev
Includes bibliographical references

305.23 Young people

Adolescence in America; an encyclopedia; Jacqueline V. Lerner and Richard M. Lerner, editors; Jordan Finkelstein, advisory editor; foreword by Mark L. Rosenberg. ABC-CLIO 2001 2v il (American family) set $185 **305.23**

1. Adolescence—Encyclopedias
ISBN 1-57607-205-3 LC 2001-2276

This work is intended to "provide psychological, medical, sociological, ethical, biological, and medical information on aspects of adolescence." Choice
For a fuller review see: Booklist, Oct. 15, 2001

Canada, Geoffrey

Fist, stick, knife, gun; a personal history of violence in America. Beacon Press 1995 179p hardcover o.p. paperback available $12 **305.23**

1. Violence 2. Children 3. New York (N.Y.)—Social conditions
ISBN 0-8070-0423-5 (pa) LC 94-41357

The author explains "what is happening to poor, mostly black and brown youth in this country, as guns have replaced fist, stick, and knife as aggressive and protective weapons of choice. Canada's own battles for survival as a youth in the South Bronx punctuate and shape his argument." Libr J

"A more powerful depiction of the tragic life of urban children and a more compelling plea to end 'America's war against itself' cannot be imagined." Publ Wkly

Reaching up for manhood; transforming the lives of boys in America. Beacon Press 1998 160p hardcover o.p. paperback available $12.50 **305.23**

1. Boys—Psychology 2. African American children 3. Youth—United States
ISBN 0-8070-2316-7 (pa) LC 97-19919

The author "grew up on tough South Bronx streets, where he witnessed friends dying by the handful. Recounting his childhood at midlife, he powerfully depicts what children face in today's world, especially the crippling problems of African American boys." Libr J

Coles, Robert

Children of crisis; selections from the Pulitzer Prize-winning five-volume Children of crisis series; with a new introduction by the author. Little, Brown 2003 714p il $35; pa $22.45 **305.23**

1. Children—United States 2. Socially handicapped children
ISBN 0-316-15547-0; 0-316-15102-5 (pa)
LC 2003-47522

These are selections of Coles' social study of "African American children caught in the throes of the South's racial integration; the young children of impoverished sharecroppers, migrant workers, and mountaineers in Ap-

Coles, Robert—*Continued*

palachia; children whose families were transformed by the migration from South to North, from rural to urban communities; Latino, Native American, and Eskimo children in the poorest communities of the American West; the children of America's wealthiest families, wrestling with the burden of their own privilege." Publisher's note

Di Prisco, Joseph

Field guide to the American teenager; a parent's companion; by Joseph Di Prisco, Michael Riera. Perseus Bks. 2000 xxii, 309p hardcover o.p. paperback available $16.50　　　**305.23**

1. Teenagers 2. Parent-child relationship 3. Adolescent psychology

ISBN 0-7382-0519-2 (pa)

"The book discusses in separate chapters seventeen teen-related topics, including drinking and driving, date rape, drugs, race relations, eating disorders, divorce, being gay, making decisions, love relationship, depression, and death. Each chapter is divided into three elements: Narrative, Conversation, and Notes Home." Voice Youth Advocates

"This excellent work is to be thoroughly read, reread, and thought about." Libr J

Includes bibliographical references

Feig, Paul

Kick me; adventures in adolescence. Three Rivers Press (NY) 2002 278p pa $12.95

305.23

1. Adolescence 2. Boys

ISBN 0-609-80943-1　　　　　　LC 2002-18121

"These interlocking essays—on everything from a sadistic gym teacher and geeky after-class pastimes to obsessive romantic tendencies and a prom that wasn't the best night of the author's life—are terrifically entertaining, although undoubtedly imaginatively amped up for maximum readability." Publ Wkly

Gilbert, Susan

A field guide to boys and girls; cutting edge information every parent needs to know. HarperCollins Pubs. 2000 xx, 250p hardcover o.p. paperback available $13　　　**305.23**

1. Child development 2. Child rearing 3. Sex differences (Psychology)

ISBN 0-06-093192-2 (pa)　　　　　LC 00-27591

The author surveys "research that explores the differences between the sexes from birth to 12 years. . . . Each chapter ends with suggestions on how parents can use the research to help their sons and daughters to develop. This is an accessible book that provides a valuable resource to parents in raising sons and daughters." Booklist

Gurian, Michael

The wonder of girls; understanding the hidden nature of our daughters. Pocket Bks. 2002 xxii, 328p $26; pa $14　　　**305.23**

1. Girls 2. Sex differences (Psychology)

ISBN 0-7434-1702-X; 0-7434-1703-8 (pa)

LC 2001-51144

The author "challenges the cultural conventions regarding girls' development, explores girls' biological and personal maturation, and offers practical advice on how parents can help girls achieve their full potential. . . . Parents and teachers will find this an insightful resource." Booklist

Includes bibliographical references

Hine, Thomas, 1947-

The rise and fall of the American teenager. Bard 1999 322p $24; pa $14　　　**305.23**

1. Teenagers 2. Adolescence

ISBN 0-380-97358-8; 0-380-72853-2 (pa)

LC 99-24381

In this social history Hine "writes about ways the culture has affected what teenage has meant for youth and how youth have been perceived, as in World War II when teenagers readily took on roles supporting the war effort. Interesting, enjoyable, and multifaceted, Hine's work defies pigeonholing by covering anthropology, psychology, communications, and sociology." SLJ

Includes bibliographical references

Kozol, Jonathan

Ordinary resurrections; children in the years of hope. Crown 2000 388p $25　　　**305.23**

1. Children 2. Bronx (New York, N.Y.)—Social conditions

ISBN 0-517-70000-X　　　　　　LC 99-59808

Also available in paperback from HarperPerennial

"Kozol tells of his continued visits with the children who attend the after-school program at St. Ann's Episcopal Church in the racially segregated, impoverished South Bronx." SLJ

Lamb, Sharon

The secret lives of girls; what good girls really do—sex play, aggression, and their guilt. Free Press 2002 255p $24　　　**305.23**

1. Girls 2. Aggressiveness (Psychology)

ISBN 0-7432-0107-8　　　　　　LC 2001-54755

The author "challenges conventional notions about girls' sexuality and aggressive impulses. Based on interviews with more than 125 preteen girls, the sprawling text reveals girls' exploratory games, illustrated in explicit first-person accounts. In loosely organized chapters, Lamb defines types of games, discusses the line between play and abuse, explores the impact of trends, and always discusses how societal mores affect girls' experiences and self-image." Booklist

Includes bibliographical references

Medved, Michael

Saving childhood; protecting our children from the national assault on innocence; [by] Michael Medved and Diane Medved. HarperCollins Pubs. 1998 324p hardcover o.p. paperback available $13　　　**305.23**

1. Children—United States 2. Child rearing

ISBN 0-06-093224-4 (pa)　　　　　LC 98-11850

The authors "express their concerns about the climate of violence, sexuality, immorality, and activism that children encounter in America today." Libr J

This is a "lively, heartfelt book. . . . An honorable addition to the strain of child-advocacy literature." Booklist

Includes bibliographical references

Orme, Nicholas

Medieval children. Yale Univ. Press 2001 387p il $39.95; pa $19.95　　　**305.23**

1. Children—History 2. Middle Ages

ISBN 0-300-08541-9; 0-300-09754-9 (pa)

LC 2001-26172

This is an "examination of the daily lives of medieval children from diverse classes and backgrounds. . . . Orme's exacting research gives the book weight, and his

Orme, Nicholas—*Continued*
affectionate, eloquent prose carries its immediate manner
from history to sociology to philosophy and back again."
Booklist
Includes bibliographical references

Pollack, William S.
Real boys; rescuing our sons from the
myths of boyhood. Random House 1998 xxiv,
447p $25.95 **305.23**
1. Boys 2. Child rearing
ISBN 0-375-50131-2 LC 98-15282
Also available in paperback from Owl Bks.
Pollack "dismantles what he terms 'the Boy Code'—
society's image of boys as tough, cool, rambunctious and
obsessed with sports, cars and sex. These stereotypes, he
argues, thwart creativity and originality in boys. Linking
clinical insights to practical suggestions, Pollack advises
caregivers how to help boys repair their fragile self-
esteem, develop empathy and explore their sensitive
sides." Publ Wkly
Includes bibliographical references

Real boys' voices; [by] William S. Pollack
with Todd Shuster. Random House 2000
xxxv, 392p $25.95 **305.23**
1. Boys
ISBN 0-679-46299-6 LC 00-35318
Also available in paperback from Penguin Bks.
The author "talked with 11-to-20-year-old boys of all
races and economic backgrounds about sex, drugs, parents, religion, violence, emotions, and changes in the social expectations of boys and men. Here he presents the
boys not only through his interviews but also through
their poems, essays, and journals." Booklist

Simmons, Rachel, 1966-
Odd girl out; the hidden culture of
aggression in girls. Harcourt 2002 296p $25;
pa $14 **305.23**
1. Girls 2. Aggressiveness (Psychology)
ISBN 0-15-100604-0; 0-15-602734-8 (pa)
LC 2001-6864
"Why are girls inclined to relational rather than physical aggression? Simmons contends that girls are social-
ized into a psychological double bind. They are told that
they must be good, nice and quiet and that they should
value close and intimate relationships. . . . Trapped in a
constraining, stereotypical gender role, some girls craft
ways of expressing their anger covertly. . . . Odd Girl
Out explores this grim side of girlhood with {stories}
. . . about girls hurting other girls." Women Rev Books
The author "does an excellent job of articulating to
adults exactly the pain and subtle warfare that many teen
girls experience." Booklist
Includes bibliographical references

White, Emily, 1966-
Fast girls; teenage tribes and the myth of
the slut. Scribner 2002 219p $22 **305.23**
1. Teenagers 2. Girls—Sexual behavior 3. Promiscuity 4. Gossip
ISBN 0-684-86740-0 LC 2001-57562
The author "contacted over 150 mostly white women
and girls between ages 13 and 55. . . . White uses the
recollections of these women to piece together what she
calls the American slut archetype. . . . She examines
why these labels are ever present in the adolescent social
universe, and what they reveal about Americans' con-

flicted attitudes toward female sexuality. . . . The stories
of White's interviewees paint a textured, harrowing picture of high school life." Publ Wkly
Includes bibliographical references

305.24 Adults

Cohen, Gene D.
The creative age; awakening human
potential in the second half of life. Avon Bks.
2000 374p il hardcover o.p. paperback
available $15 **305.24**
1. Middle age 2. Creative ability
ISBN 0-380-80071-3 (pa) LC 99-58721
The author "outlines different ways in which people
can be creative and stimulating in the face of adversity,
in the context of relationships, or with changing opportunities as one ages." Libr J
"Cohen provides a wealth of information and a fresh,
timely perspective on aging." Publ Wkly
Includes bibliographical references

Sheehy, Gail
New passages; mapping your life across
time. Random House 1995 xxv, 498p
hardcover o.p. paperback available $15.95
305.24
1. Adulthood 2. Aging 3. Socialization 4. Middle age
5. United States—Social conditions
ISBN 0-345-40445-9 (pa) LC 94-43996
Companion volume to Passages (1976)
The author examines "what she calls 'second adulthood'—the period from what used to be thought of as
middle age into an ever-expanding 'age of integrity'—an
increasingly enjoyable, even serene old age. . . . Making
use of specially configured census data, extensive questionnaires and interviews with dozens of people, from celebrities to participants in middle-and lower-income discussion groups, she offers a broad picture of how they
can expect to experience the 'bonus years.'" Publ Wkly
This work is "grounded in the economic and psychological realities that make adult life so complex today.
The major themes of this book are accurate and important." N Y Times Book Rev
Includes bibliographical references

305.26 Late adulthood

Carter, Jimmy, 1924-
The virtues of aging. Ballantine Pub. Group
1998 140p (Library of contemporary thought)
$18.95; pa $11.95 **305.26**
1. Aging
ISBN 0-345-42826-9; 0-345-42592-8 (pa)
LC 98-25298
Also available large print edition $14.95 (0-375-
70460-4)
"Published in conjunction with Times Books"
"At age 56, Jimmy Carter 'involuntarily retired' when
he was defeated for a second term as president by
Ronald Reagan in 1980. . . . Carter sketches how he and
Rosalynn created new careers and new lives for themselves—as authors, educators, and senior family members
and as a couple growing old together. He adds statistics
about the aging population, makes suggestions for
healthy living, and defines successful aging." Libr J

Coles, Robert

Old and on their own; with photographs by Alex Harris, Thomas Roma. Norton 1998 184p hardcover o.p. paperback available $19.95   **305.26**

1. Elderly

ISBN 0-393-31912-1 (pa)   LC 97-36922

"A DoubleTake book"

Published by the Center for Documentary Studies in association with W.W. Norton

A series of interviews about aging with 11 men and women from 75 to nearly 100 years of age

Includes bibliographical references

Encyclopedia of aging; David J. Ekerdt, editor in chief. Macmillan Ref. USA 2002 4v set $450   **305.26**

1. Gerontology—Encyclopedias 2. Aging—Encyclopedias 3. Elderly—Encyclopedias

ISBN 0-02-865472-2   LC 2002-2596

"Topics represent the range of information in gerontology, covering biological, medical, psychological, and sociological topics as well as social and public policy issues. Articles range from very specific, for example, *Congregate housing* or *Fluid balance,* to more general essays, such as *Bereavement* or *Visual arts and aging.* About one-third to one-half of the articles focus on biological, medical, or psychological aspects of aging." Booklist

This includes "400-plus concise and readable entries that offer excellent introductions to important concepts." Libr J

The **Encyclopedia** of aging: a comprehensive resource in gerontology and geriatrics; George L. Maddox, editor-in-chief. 3rd ed. Springer Pub. 2001 2v set $275   **305.26**

1. Gerontology—Encyclopedias 2. Aging—Encyclopedias 3. Elderly—Encyclopedias

ISBN 0-8261-4842-5   LC 00-49663

First published 1987

This set includes nearly 600 articles on gerontology and geriatrics by scholars in the fields of biology, nursing, medicine, psychology, psychiatry, sociology, and social services

Facts about retiring in the United States; edited by Steven S. Shagrin; with contributions by Bryan Aubrey [et al.] Wilson, H.W. 2001 761p $105   **305.26**

1. Retirement

ISBN 0-8242-0969-9   LC 00-53423

"Part 1 delivers guidance in four major areas: housing, health care, and financial and legal concerns. Part 2, 'State-by-State Retirement Housing Options,' presents alternatives on a state-by-state basis, including facts about climate, cost of living, taxes, major transportation, and cultural attractions. Lists of elder hostels and other travel-related agencies, retirement counselors and consultants, and additional resources and organizations are listed in part 3. . . . This informative and practical guide is recommended in particular for public libraries." Booklist

Includes bibliographical references

Friedan, Betty

The fountain of age. Simon & Schuster 1993 671p hardcover o.p. paperback available $17   **305.26**

1. Old age 2. Women—United States

ISBN 0-671-89853-1 (pa)   LC 93-4090

The author "challenges our culture's pessimistic attitude toward aging. Friedan argues that we should view the years after 60 as a new stage of development, rather than as a time of decline and disease." Libr J

"Betty Friedan's metaphorical fountain of age spouts research, observation, conjecture, evangelical fervor, revolutionary rhetoric, and denial. The result is a pool of optimism in which the mother of the woman's movement examines the unlifted face of age and finds it lovable." New Repub

Includes bibliographical references

Kaplan, Lawrence J. (Lawrence Jay), 1915-

Retiring right; planning for a successful retirement. Square One Pubs. pa $17.95   **305.26**

First published 1986 (2003 edition) Periodically revised

The author "addresses lifestyle issues like continuing to work and housing; long-term funding vehicles like savings, investments, and pensions; day-to-day financial concerns such as credit, budgeting, and inflation; life, health, and medical insurance; and 'final facts' like estates, probate, and trusts. . . . [Includes] a section on retirement communities. . . . Given the difficulty in choosing among the many guide on retirement, the durability of Kaplan's manual makes an attractive option." Booklist

The **Practical** guide to aging; what everyone needs to know; editor Christine K. Cassel; developmental editor, George A. Vallasi. New York Univ. Press 1999 326p il $45; pa $17.95   **305.26**

1. Aging

ISBN 0-8147-1515-X; 0-8147-1516-8 (pa)

LC 97-21571

"The medical, legal, financial, psychological, social, and ethical aspects of aging are covered in this guide." Libr J

"Informative, comprehensive, and clearly written, this genuinely practical guide is the work of experts in a wide variety of fields." Booklist

Includes bibliographical references

Vaillant, George E.

Aging well; surprising guideposts to a happier life from the landmark Harvard study of adult development. Little, Brown 2002 373p $24.95; pa $14.95   **305.26**

1. Aging

ISBN 0-316-98936-3; 0-316-09007-7 (pa)

LC 2001-30651

"Vaillant posits that successful physical and emotional aging is most dependent on a lack of tobacco and alcohol abuse by subjects, an adaptive coping style, maintaining healthy weight with some exercise, a sustained loving (in most cases, marital) relationship and years of education." Publ Wkly

The author "offers much valuable information about aging, and his judgment calls (his term) are perceptive, understanding, and often tinged with delightful humor." Booklist

Includes bibliographical references

305.31 Men

Bly, Robert
Iron John; a book about men. Addison-Wesley 1990 268p o.p.; Vintage Bks. paperback available $13   **305.31**
1. Men—Psychology
ISBN 0-679-73119-9 (pa)   LC 90-37877
"Drawing vitally upon such diverse sources as ancient mythology, classic literature (including his own poetry), anthropology, psychology, and even the responses of the real-life men who have participated in his seminars ('gatherings'), Bly staunchly redefines male identity, emphasizing the importance of what he calls 'warrior energy' and all its positive implications." Booklist

Bordo, Susan, 1947-
The male body; a new look at men in public and in private. Farrar, Straus & Giroux 1999 358p il hardcover o.p. paperback available $16   **305.31**
1. Men
ISBN 0-374-52732-6 (pa)   LC 99-25386
"Bordo sets out to map the ambivalent attitudes that exist in the American cultural imagination toward male bodies and, in particular, toward the penis and its 'symbolic double,' the phallus. . . . Part memoir, part elegy, this feminist guided tour of the male body concludes with real hope for improved relations between the sexes." Publ Wkly
Includes bibliographical references

Faludi, Susan
Stiffed; the betrayal of the American man. Morrow 1999 662p il hardcover o.p. paperback available $16   **305.31**
1. Men
ISBN 0-380-72045-0 (pa)   LC 99-35504
"Men, Faludi argues, are actually suffering under the thumb of a cultural oppression similar to the one that inspired feminism's second wave." Libr J
Includes bibliographical references

Sheehy, Gail
Understanding men's passages; discovering the new map of men's lives. Random House 1998 xxvi, 292p hardcover o.p. paperback available $14   **305.31**
1. Men—Psychology 2. Middle age
ISBN 0-345-40690-7 (pa)   LC 98-9942
The author discusses the lives of "men over 35. . . . Sheehy interviewed 100 men . . . and the book is mostly made up of these 'case studies.' Another major part of the text is given over to a discussion of male sexual potency and how it affects men and the women in their lives." Booklist
"Sheehy's advice, bolstered with demographic research, group interviews, medical commentary and personal testimony, is tough and wise." N Y Times Book Rev
Includes bibliographical references

305.4 Women

Beauvoir, Simone de, 1908-1986
The second sex; translated and edited by H.M. Parshley; with an introduction by Margaret Crosland. Knopf 1993 lv, 786p $23; pa $17   **305.4**
1. Women
ISBN 0-679-42016-9; 0-679-72451-6 (pa)
LC 92-54303
"Everyman's library"
Original French edition, 1949; this translation first published 1953
This "thorough analysis of women's secondary status in society, became a classic of feminist literature." Reader's Ency. 3d edition

Brooks, Geraldine
Nine parts of desire; the hidden world of Islamic women. Anchor Bks. (NY) 1995 255p hardcover o.p. paperback available $14   **305.4**
1. Muslim women 2. Islamic countries
ISBN 0-385-47577-2 (pa)   LC 94-17496
"Taking on the *hijab* (the Muslim woman's black veil) herself, Brooks talked with women throughout the Islamic world, reexamined the Koran, spent time with fundamentalist and feminist alike, and emerged with a deeper understanding of the religion as one that once empowered but now cripples women." Booklist
"The author's revelations about these women's lives behind the veil are frank, enraging, and captivating." New Yorker
Includes bibliographical references

Brownmiller, Susan
In our time; memoir of a revolution. Dial Press (NY) 1999 360p hardcover o.p. paperback available $15.95   **305.4**
1. Women's movement 2. Feminism
ISBN 0-385-31831-6 (pa)   LC 99-39344
This book focuses on the women's movement between 1967 and 1977
"A riveting blend of eyewitness accounts and keen analysis, this is history at its most vital and a stirring testament to our ability to come together to combat social injustice, no matter how deeply entrenched it has become." Booklist

Cullen-DuPont, Kathryn
Encyclopedia of women's history in America. 2nd ed. Facts on File 2000 418p il $71.50   **305.4**
1. Women—United States—History 2. Feminism
ISBN 0-8160-4100-8   LC 99-87498
First published 1996
This work highlights the lives and contributions of women in American history ranging from Pocahontas to Hillary Clinton and Madeleine Albright. Entries cover individuals, movements, court cases and women's issues from Colonial times to the present
"Well-written and informative . . . . An excellent quick reference source . . . recommended . . . ." Choice

Encyclopedia of women in American history. Sharpe Ref. 2002 3v il set $299   **305.4**
1. Women—United States—History—Encyclopedias
ISBN 0-7656-8038-6   LC 2001-42025

Contents: v1 Colonization, revolution, and the new nation, 1585-1820, general editor, Joyce Appleby; v2 Civil War, western expansion, and industrialization, 1820-1900, general editor, Eileen K. Cheng; v3 Suffrage, world war, and modern times, 1900-present, general editor, Joanne Goodwin

The set "is divided into three chronologically arranged volumes. Each volume includes historical surveys and thematic essays on central issues and political changes affecting women's lives during the period. These are followed by A-Z entries on significant events and social movements, laws, court cases and more, as well as profiles of notable American women from all walks of life and all fields of endeavor. Primary sources and original documents are included throughout, and the set also features special highlights that appear next to the A-Z entries . . . and Charts and Graphs, which provide geographical and statistical data about women's history." Publisher's note

Includes bibliographical references

Fisher, Helen E.
The first sex; the natural talents of women and how they are changing the world; by Helen Fisher. Random House 1999 xx, 378p hardcover o.p. paperback available $16
305.4
1. Women—Psychology 2. Leadership 3. Sex differences (Psychology) 4. Ability
ISBN 0-449-91260-4 (pa)   LC 99-12545

"Fisher reviews the literature on the biological differences between the sexes and concludes that the genetically based tendencies of women to think in webs of interrelated factors, to operate best in nonhierarchical groups, and to prefer long-term committed relationships will give them the edge in most areas of endeavor in the future." Libr J

The author "offers a provocative overview of the latest bio-anthropological studies on gender and communication, menopause and romantic love." Publ Wkly

Fox-Genovese, Elizabeth, 1941-
Within the plantation household; black and white women of the Old South. University of N.C. Press 1988 544p il (Gender & American culture) $49.95; pa $19.95   **305.4**
1. Women—Southern States 2. Plantation life 3. Slavery—United States
ISBN 0-8078-1808-9; 0-8078-4232-X (pa)
LC 88-40139

"In this study, Fox-Genovese examines class, race, and gender in the antebellum South. . . . In her narrative, Fox-Genovese draws upon the letters, diaries, and journals of white women, and . . . the WPA slave narratives." Choice

"An illuminating and solid book of social history, with appeal to those who take a serious interest in historical research." Booklist

Includes bibliographical references

Franck, Irene M.
The Wilson chronology of women's achievements; a record of women's achievements from ancient times to present; by Irene M. Franck and David M. Brownstone. Wilson, H.W. 1998 507p $100
305.4
1. Women—History—Chronology
ISBN 0-8242-0936-2   LC 97-34394
First published 1995 by HarperPerennial with title: Women's world

This chronicle of women's history ranges "from the Egyptian queen Nefertiti and the Greek poet Sappho to Susan B. Anthony, Marie Curie, Eleanor Roosevelt, and Janet Reno." Publisher's note
Includes bibliographical references

Freedman, Estelle B., 1947-
No turning back; the history of feminism and the future of women. Ballantine Bks. 2002 446p hardcover o.p. paperback available $15.95   **305.4**
1. Feminism 2. Women—Social conditions
ISBN 0-345-45053-1 (pa)   LC 2002-280895
"Refuting a widespread misconception that feminism is either dead or irrelevant, Freedman presents a reflective history of the divergent roots of this essential yet controversial social movement." Booklist

This "work goes beyond previous studies in being interdisciplinary, international, and a pleasure to read." Libr J
Includes bibliographical references

Friedan, Betty
The feminine mystique; with a new introduction. Norton 1997 xlviii, 452p hardcover o.p. paperback available $14.95
305.4
1. Feminism 2. Women—United States
ISBN 0-393-32257-2 (pa)   LC 97-8877
A reissue of the title first published 1963

An "analysis of the dilemma facing the educated American woman; the post-war emphasis on the feminine image of the role as wife and mother has caused the American woman to lose her identity, says the author." Cincinnati Public Libr
Includes bibliographical references

Goodwin, Jan
Price of honor; Muslim women lift the veil of silence on the Islamic world. rev ed. Plume Bks. 2003 351p il pa $16   **305.4**
1. Muslim women 2. Islamic countries
ISBN 0-452-28377-9   LC 2002-28257
First published 1994 by Little, Brown

The author "examines the movement that is aggressively spreading a fundamentalist version of Islam throughout much of the world. Her interviews with Muslim women in ten countries both fascinate and disturb, for their candor reveals the movement's profound and often devastating effects on them. . . . A necessary purchase." Libr J [review of 1994 edition]

The **Greenwood** encyclopedia of women's issues worldwide; Lynn Walter, editor-in-chief. Greenwood Press 2003 6v il maps set $550 **305.4**

1. Women—Social conditions—Encyclopedias

ISBN 0-313-32787-4   LC 2004-695024

Volume editors include Manisha Desai; Amy Lind; Aili Mari Tripp; Bahira Sherif-Trask and Cheryl Toronto Kalny

Contents: {v1} Asia and Oceania; {v2} Central and South America; {v3} Europe; {v4} The Middle East and North Africa; {v5} North America and the Caribbean; {v6} Sub-Saharan Africa

This "reference set documents the achievements and current challenges for women in more than 130 countries. . . . Topics covered include education, employment, economy, family and sexuality, health, politics and law, religion, and violence." Lib Media Connect

"Readers looking for information on women's every day lives around the world will welcome this country-by-country survey." Booklist

Includes bibliographical references

Greer, Germaine, 1939-

The madwoman's underclothes; essays and occasional writings. Atlantic Monthly Press 1987 xxvii, 305p hardcover o.p. paperback available $12.95 **305.4**

1. Feminism 2. Women—Social conditions

ISBN 0-87113-308-3 (pa)   LC 87-11475

First published 1986 in the United Kingdom

A collection of the British feminist's nonfiction writings spanning her career from the 1960s to the 1980s

The whole woman. Knopf 1999 373p hardcover o.p. paperback available $14

305.4

1. Women—History 2. Women's rights 3. Women—Social conditions 4. Feminism 5. Sex role

ISBN 0-385-72003-3 (pa)   LC 99-18918

Greer argues that "women have come a long way in the past three decades but that innumerable forms of insidious discrimination and exploitation persist in every area of life." Publisher's note

"This is vintage Greer, profane and highly quotable." Time

Includes bibliographical references

Heymann, C. David (Clemens David), 1945-

The Georgetown ladies' social club; power, passion, and politics in the nation's capital. Atria Bks. 2003 389p il $26 **305.4**

1. Women in politics 2. Washington (D.C.)—Social life and customs

ISBN 0-7434-2856-0   LC 2004-266773

The author focuses on "a group of women whom Ronald Reagan dubbed the Georgetown Ladies' Social Club: Katharine Graham, Lorraine Cooper, Evangeline Bruce, Pamela Harriman, and Sally Quinn. These influential hostesses wielded political and social power from their Georgetown homes, where the politicking done behind the scenes was sometimes as important as what was happening on Capitol Hill." Booklist

This is "a captivating chronicle of the female power behind American politics in the latter half of the 20th century." Publ Wkly

Includes bibliographical references

A **History** of women in the United States: state-by-state reference; Doris Weatherford, general editor. Grolier Academic Reference 2003 4v il maps set $399 **305.4**

1. Women—United States—History

ISBN 0-7172-5805-X   LC 2003-49299

Contents: Introductory essays; v1 Alabama-Illinois; v2 Indiana-Nebraska; v3 Nevada-South Dakota; v4 Tennessee-Wyoming; appendices

"On the first page of each state entry both a map and a small box of statistical information appear, including such data as the percent of women in the state legislature. A literary epigraph introduces a brief history (18 pages for New York State, for example), beginning with a description of the place of women among the state's original Native American settlers. Subsequent sections divide the historical narrative into periods suitable to each state. . . . Each piece concludes with a time line as well as a handful of biographies of prominent women of the state . . . a directory of sites related to women within the state, and a listing of relevant books, web sites, and organizations. The encyclopedia ends with appendixes that include a chronology, several primary documents, a compendium of statistical tables, a small general bibliography, and an extensive index. . . . Reference librarians in public libraries will find this tool useful." Libr J

Jones, Jacqueline, 1948-

Labor of love, labor of sorrow; black women, work, and the family from slavery to the present. Basic Bks. 1985 432p il o.p.; Vintage Bks. paperback available $15 **305.4**

1. African American women

ISBN 0-394-74536-1 (pa)   LC 84-24310

"Jones examines the nature of employment and home life for the black woman through such socioeconomic eras as the period of bondage in the South, the so-called freedom that came with Reconstruction, the years between emancipation and the great migration to the North, the northern flight itself, the Depression, and the civil rights and feminist movements." Booklist

"Ambitious in scope, bold in interpretation, and comprehensive in its scholarship, Jones's book is a rare blend of seminal study and synthesis." Libr J

Includes bibliographical references

No small courage; a history of women in the United States; edited by Nancy Cott. Oxford Univ. Press 2000 646p il maps $45

305.4

1. Women—United States—History

ISBN 0-19-513946-1   LC 00-21130

This "book examines women's experiences in the New World since Columbus landed. . . . Its 10 chapters . . . look at 'work and leisure, family patterns, political activities, forms of organization and outstanding accomplishments.'" N Y Times Book Rev

"By examining the flow of American history as it has affected women [the authors] illuminate aspects of the past that have often been neglected." Booklist

Includes bibliographical references

Roberts, Cokie
We are our mothers' daughters. Morrow
1998 197p $19.95; pa $11　　　**305.4**
1. Women—United States—History 2. Sex discrimination 3. Feminism
ISBN 0-688-15198-1; 0-688-16967-8 (pa)
　　　　　　　　　　　　　　LC 98-14816
"Roberts uses the vantage point of mother, daughter and exasperated observer as she discusses the evolution of women's roles over the past few generations. . . . Although there's no sophisticated analysis or new material here, Roberts is at her best when describing the ambivalences and ambitions of a woman's life." N Y Times Book Rev

Rosen, Ruth
The world split open; how the modern women's movement changed America. Viking 2000 446p il $34.95; pa $15　　　**305.4**
1. Women's movement 2. Feminism
ISBN 0-670-81462-8; 0-14-009719-8 (pa)
　　　　　　　　　　　　　　LC 99-54439
"Rosen details the rebirth of feminism, from the liberalism of NOW through women's liberation, which grew out of the civil rights movement. Her focus is on the 'hidden injuries of sex' and how what had been construed as 'personal' problems—abortion, compulsory heterosexuality, rape and sexual violence, prostitution and pornography—became political issues." Publ Wkly
Includes bibliographical references

Salisbury, Joyce E.
Encyclopedia of women in the ancient world; foreword by Mary Lefkowitz. ABC-CLIO 2001 xxiii, 385p il map $85
　　　　　　　　　　　　　　305.4
1. Women—History—Encyclopedias 2. Women—Biography 3. Ancient civilization—Encyclopedias
ISBN 1-56707-092-1　　　　　　LC 00-13117
"Biographies of individual women from ancient Western civilization are interspersed with entries on topics such as clothing, work, and sexuality. The thematic discussions provide background and context." Booklist

Sommers, Christina Hoff
Who stole feminism? how women have betrayed women. Simon & Schuster 1994 320p il hardcover o.p. paperback available $14　　　　　　　　　　　　**305.4**
1. Feminism
ISBN 0-684-80156-6 (pa)　　　　LC 94-4734
The author's "critique of what she calls 'gender feminism' exposes numerous examples of distorted data and totalitarian methodology in the work of such feminist leaders as Susan Faludi, Catherine MacKinnon, and a cabal of like-minded academics. Controversial, to be sure, but objectively presented and impossible to dismiss." Booklist
Includes bibliographical references

Steinem, Gloria
Moving beyond words. Simon & Schuster 1994 319p hardcover o.p. paperback available $19.95　　　　　　　　　　　**305.4**
1. Feminism
ISBN 0-671-51052-5 (pa)　　　　LC 94-4839
"In these essays—some newly published, some reworked—Steinem surveys the women's movement." Libr

J
"Ms. Steinem's enduring contribution to the women's movement has been her ability to popularize feminist issues to a wide and often wary audience." N Y Times Book Rev
Includes bibliographical references

Outrageous acts and everyday rebellions. 2nd ed, with a new preface and notes by the author. Holt & Co. 1995 xxii, 406p pa $17
　　　　　　　　　　　　　　305.4
1. Feminism
ISBN 0-8050-4202-4　　　　　LC 95-31711
"An Owl book"
First published 1983
In addition to material addressing specific feminist issues, this collection includes personal accounts of political leaders and noted women
Includes bibliographical references

Wolf, Naomi
The beauty myth; how images of beauty are used against women. Perennial 2002 348p pa $14.95　　　　　　　　　**305.4**
1. Women 2. Sex role 3. Personal appearance
ISBN 0-06-051218-0　　　　　LC 2002-72516
First published 1991 by Morrow
A "book about the ways women enslave themselves—and their bank accounts—to an industry that promises physical perfection." N Y Times Book Rev
The author "presents a provocative and persuasive account of the pervasiveness of the beauty ideal in all facets of Western culture." Libr J
Includes bibliographical references

305.5　Social classes

Conniff, Richard
The natural history of the rich; a field guide. Norton 2002 344p il $26.95; pa $15.95
　　　　　　　　　　　　　　305.5
1. Wealth
ISBN 0-393-01965-9; 0-393-32488-5 (pa)
　　　　　　　　　　　　　　LC 2002-6899
The author "compares the super-rich to the animal kingdom in providing a frame of reference for their behaviors and actions. . . . A keen observer of both animal and human nature, Conniff . . . neither patronizes nor demeans his subjects. . . . He merely uses them and the natural world to illuminate a class of people and range of behaviors that few among us will ever have the opportunity to observe firsthand." Publ Wkly
Includes bibliographical references

Ehrenreich, Barbara
Nickel and dimed; on (not) getting by in boom-time America. Metropolitan Bks. 2001 221p $23; pa $13　　　　　　**305.5**
1. Minimum wage 2. Labor—United States 3. Poverty
ISBN 0-8050-6388-9; 0-8050-6389-7 (pa)
　　　　　　　　　　　　　　LC 00-52514
This is an exposé "of such abstractions as @living wage' and @affordable housing.' Ehrenreich worked, for a month at a time, at @unskilled' jobs—as a waitress and chambermaid in Florida, a housecleaner and nursing-home aide in Maine, a Wal-Mart clerk in Minnesota—to

Ehrenreich, Barbara—*Continued*
report on how people survive on wages of six or seven
dollars an hour." New Yorker
"No real answers to the problem but a compelling
sketch of its reality and pervasiveness." Libr J

Epstein, Joseph, 1937-
Snobbery: the American version. Houghton
Mifflin 2002 274p $25; pa $14 **305.5**
1. Snobs and snobbishness
ISBN 0-395-94417-1; 0-618-34073-4 (pa)
LC 2001-51623
This "work examines the nature and place of snobbery
and its various manifestations in America, from the
country's founding to the present." Libr J
"Every bracing page is a mirror in which readers can't
help but recognize themselves, and each offers a quot-
able quip . . . and much to think about." Booklist
Includes bibliographical references

Freeman, Joshua Benjamin
Working-class New York; life and labor
since World War II; {by} Joshua B. Freeman.
New Press (NY) 2000 409p il $35; pa $19.95
305.5
1. Working class 2. Labor unions 3. New York
(N.Y.)—Social conditions
ISBN 1-56584-575-7; 1-56584-712-1 (pa)
LC 99-87940
In this study the author "describes the social, political,
ethnic, racial, and numerical changes in New York's
working class over the years; the alterations in the city's
landscape that the working class effected; and the change
in how the working class itself has been viewed." Booklist
"Freeman charts the postwar rise and eventual fall of
Manhattan working-class life and culture. . . . Strong
narrative drive, attention to detail and historical insight
make this a superb addition to studies of postwar culture,
urbanology and labor history." Publ Wkly
Includes bibliographical references

Lubrano, Alfred
Limbo: blue-collar roots, white-collar
dreams. Wiley 2003 c2004 248p $27.95
305.5
1. Social classes 2. Working class
ISBN 0-4712-6376-1 LC 2003-273869
The author examines "the challenges that upwardly
mobile children of blue-collar families (he calls them
Straddlers) face in establishing themselves in white-collar
enclaves. . . . Lubrano's interviews with other Straddlers
have convinced him that ambition puts many of them in
positions fraught with . . . ambivalence and unexpected
culture shock." Publ Wkly
"This is an emotionally charged study of class values,
a subject even touchier than race or gender." Booklist

Mayle, Peter
Acquired tastes. Bantam Bks. 1992 229p
hardcover o.p. paperback available $13.95
305.5
1. Wealth
ISBN 0-553-37183-5 (pa) LC 92-3354
This is a collection of "articles on 'the spending habits
of the rich,' which . . . half poke fun at those habits but
at the same time assert the qualities of quality." Booklist
"This delightful celebration of the little (and not-so-
little) extravagances that make life worth living scintil-
lates with wit, brio and trenchant observations on the
best and the second-rate." Publ Wkly

Phillips, Kevin P.
Wealth and democracy; a political history
of the American rich; [by] Kevin Phillips.
Broadway Bks. 2002 xxii, 473p $29.95; pa
$16.95 **305.5**
1. Wealth 2. Political corruption 3. Representative
government and representation 4. United States—Politics and government
ISBN 0-7679-0533-4; 0-7679-0534-2 (pa)
LC 2001-52656
The author "relates how the disparity between rich and
poor correlates with our propensity for speculative excess
and technology manias and the corruption of government
throughout this nation's history." Booklist
"Phillips's astute analysis of the effects of wealth and
capital upon democracy is both eye-opening and disturbing." Publ Wkly
Includes bibliographical references

Posner, Richard A., 1939-
Public intellectuals; a study of decline.
Harvard Univ. Press 2001 408p $29.95; pa
$19.95 **305.5**
1. Intellectuals—United States
ISBN 0-674-00633-X; 0-674-01246-1 (pa)
LC 2001-39196
This is a critique of American intellectuals who ad-
dress issues of public policy. Among the thinkers Posner
discusses are David Riesman, Richard Rorty, Stephen Jay
Gould, Allan Bloom, Gertrude Himmelfard, Christopher
Lasch and Edward Luttwak
Includes bibliographical references

Veblen, Thorstein, 1857-1929
The theory of the leisure class **305.5**
1. Social classes
Hardcover and paperback editions available from various publishers
First published 1899 by Macmillan
In this economic treatise, "Veblen held that the feudal
subdivision of classes had continued into modern times,
the lords employing themselves uselessly . . . while the
lower classes labored at industrial pursuits to support the
whole of society. The leisure class, Veblen said, justifies
itself solely by practicing 'conspicuous leisure and conspicuous consumption'; he defined waste as any activity
not contributing to material productivity." Benet Reader's
Ency. 4th edition

305.8 Racial, ethnic, national groups

The **African** American almanac. Gale Res. il
$195 **305.8**
1. African Americans
ISSN 1071-8710
First edition under the editorship of Harry A. Ploski
published 1967 by Bellwether with title: The Negro almanac. (9th edition 2002) Periodically revised. Editors
vary
"Reference covering the cultural and political history
of Black Americans. Includes generous amount of statistical information and biographies of Black Americans,
both historical and contemporary." N Y Public Libr.
Book of How & Where to Look It Up

The **African** American encyclopedia. 2nd ed, managing editor, R. Kent Rasmussen. Marshall Cavendish 2001 10v il maps set $599.93   305.8
1. African Americans—Encyclopedias
ISBN 0-7614-7208-8   LC 00-31526
First published 1993
This source contains some 1,950 essays on many aspects of the African American experience such as religion, music, films, art, literature, dance, food, politics, the military, family life, and sports

American Jewish history; edited by Jeffrey S. Gurock. Routledge 1998 8v in 13 set $1,705   305.8
1. Jews—United States
ISBN 0-415-91933-9
Sponsored by the American Jewish Historical Society
Contents: v1 The colonial and early national periods, 1654-1840; v2 Central European Jews in America, 1840-1880; v3 pt 1-3 East European Jews in America, 1880-1920: immigration and adaptation; v4 American Jewish life, 1920-1990; v5 pt 1-3 The history of Judaism in America: transplantations, transformations, and reconciliations; v6 pt 1-2 Anti-semitism in America; v7 America, American Jews, and the Holocaust; v8 American Zionism: mission and politics

"This set is a compilation of 211 articles . . . chosen to relate the history of American Jews to that of other Americans or to that of Jews all over the world. . . . The wide range of issues discussed in the set includes anti-Semitism among the suffragettes, Jewish-black relations, the role of synagogue sisterhoods, and the political and cultural impact of Zionism. *American Jewish History* is a unique source." Booklist

Asante, Molefi K., 1942-
The African-American atlas; black history and culture—an illustrated reference; [by] Molefi K. Asante and Mark T. Mattson. Macmillan; Prentice-Hall 1998 251p il maps $135   305.8
1. African Americans—History
ISBN 0-02-864984-2   LC 98-25556
First published 1991 with title: The historical and cultural atlas of African Americans
"The authors introduce African-American history by interweaving information about the people and events that influenced our nation's development with maps, charts, reproductions, and photographs." SLJ

Avakian, Monique
Atlas of Asian-American history. Facts on File 2002 214p il maps (Facts on File library of American history) $85   305.8
1. Asian Americans—History
ISBN 0-8160-3699-3   LC 00-49509
This "overview of the political, social, and cultural history of Asian Americans opens with a discussion of the Asian heritage and ends with comments on Asian America today. Personal anecdotes throughout range from the Chinese miners in 19th-century California to modern day health-care workers from India. Sixty full-color maps, 100 historical photos, and 34 line drawings and graphs lead the reader through discussions of the people of China, Japan, Korea, India, the Philippines, and Southeast Asia." Libr J
Includes bibliographical references

Black firsts: 4,000 ground-breaking and pioneering historical events; [edited by] Jessie Carney Smith. 2nd ed rev and expanded. Visible Ink Press 2003 787p il $58; pa $24.95   305.8
1. African Americans—History
ISBN 1-57859-153-8; 1-57859-142-2 (pa)
                    LC 2002-154346
First published 1994 by Gale Research with title: Black firsts; 2,000 years of extraordinary achievement
"The chapters survey broad fields such as 'Arts and Entertainment,' 'Government: Local,' and 'Science and Medicine' and are broken down into more specific subject headings. 'Arts and Entertainment,' for example, encompasses 'Architecture,' 'Dance,' 'Music,' and 'Television,' among others. Under each of these headings, firsts are arranged chronologically. Each is described in an entry ranging from a line or two to half a page, and sources are always cited. . . . Many of the sidebars highlight achievements by women. . . . *Black firsts* remains an important part of the reference collection." Booklist
Includes bibliographical references

Chang, Iris
The Chinese in America; a narrative history. Viking 2003 496p il $29.95   305.8
1. Chinese Americans—History
ISBN 0-670-03123-2   LC 2002-44858
The author recounts "the immigration of Chinese people to the U.S. from the early nineteenth century to the end of the twentieth. . . . Chang threads personal stories of individuals she came across in her research into her book, making it a much more human account. . . . This is history at its most dramatic and relevant." Booklist
Includes bibliographical references

Cleaver, Eldridge, 1935-1998
Soul on ice; with an introduction by Maxwell Geismar. McGraw-Hill 1968 210p o.p.; Delta paperback available $13.95   305.8
1. African Americans
ISBN 0-385-33379-X (pa)
"A Ramparts book"
In a collection of essays and open letters written from California's Folsom State Prison, the author writes about the forces which shaped his life
There are sections "on the Watts riots, on Cleaver's religious conversion, on the black man's stake in the Vietnam War, on fellow-writers and white women." Saturday Rev

Cose, Ellis
Color-blind; seeing beyond race in a race-obsessed world. HarperCollins Pubs. 1997 260p hardcover o.p. paperback available $13   305.8
1. Race discrimination 2. Affirmative action programs 3. United States—Race relations
ISBN 0-06-092887-5 (pa)   LC 96-34433
Issues discussed include racial classification and discrimination, race and genetics, achieving educational parity, affirmative action in colleges and the workplace, and the concept of a color-blind society. The author concludes by proposing twelve steps toward a race-neutral nation
"Bolstered by research data and his own personal experience, Cose convincingly illuminates why race still remains a determining factor of success in America." Libr J
Includes bibliographical references

Cose, Ellis—*Continued*

The envy of the world; on being a Black man in America. Washington Sq. Press 2002 163p $22; pa $13 **305.8**

1. African Americans 2. United States—Race relations 3. United States—Social conditions

ISBN 0-7434-2715-7; 0-7434-2817-x (pa)

LC 2001-52073

"Cose's book is a journalist's report on the state of the black male (and black masculinity) at the start of the 21st century." N Y Times Book Rev

The author's "stated objective of opening a discussion on how racism affects individuals makes this book interesting reading for a broad range of readers." Booklist

Dash, Leon, 1944-

Rosa Lee; a mother and her family in urban America. Basic Bks. 1996 279p il o.p.; Plume Bks. paperback available $13.95

305.8

1. Cunningham, Rosa Lee 2. African Americans—Social conditions 3. Washington (D.C.)—Social conditions

ISBN 0-452-27896-1 (pa)

LC 96-19403

"Rosa Lee Cunningham, who died of AIDS in 1994, at the age of fifty-nine, was an illiterate thief, prostitute, and drug addict. She was also the mother of eight children (by assorted fathers), only two of whom escaped her pattern of crime and dependency on drugs and welfare, a pattern passed on to her grandchildren. . . . [This] is an attempt to understand the underclass that has grown up in our ghettos." New Yorker

"What makes Rosa Lee, Leon Dash's report on a particular Washington ghetto family, so convincing and so valuable is [Dash's] intimacy with his subjects, an intimacy that very few writers about the underclass have ever achieved." N Y Rev Books

Dershowitz, Alan M.

The vanishing American Jew; in search of Jewish identity for the next century. Little, Brown 1997 395p o.p.; Touchstone Bks. paperback available $14 **305.8**

1. Jews—United States 2. Judaism 3. Antisemitism

ISBN 0-684-84898-8 (pa)

LC 96-49292

Noting "that since 1988 the intermarriage rate has been over 50 percent, and adding to that figure the low birth rates of non-Orthodox Jews, Mr. Dershowitz . . . [argues] that 'if trends continue apace, American Jewry—indeed, Diaspora Jewry—may virtually vanish by the third quarter of the 21st century.'" N Y Times Book Rev

"Although this title is primarily of interest to Jews, Dershowitz's notoriety and lively writing style broaden its appeal." Booklist

Includes bibliographical references

Du Bois, W. E. B. (William Edward Burghardt), 1868-1963

The Oxford W. E. B. Du Bois reader; edited by Eric J. Sundquist. Oxford Univ. Press 1996 680p pa $34.95 **305.8**

1. African Americans 2. United States—Race relations

ISBN 0-19-509178-7

LC 95-21307

This reader covers Du Bois's "writing career, from the 1890s through the early 1960s. The volume selects key essays and longer works that portray the range of Du Bois's thought on such subjects as African American culture, the politics and sociology of American race relations, art and music, black leadership, gender and women's rights, Pan-Africanism and anti-colonialism, and Communism in the U.S. and abroad." Publisher's note

Includes bibliographical references

The souls of black folk; essays and sketches; by W.E. Burghardt Du Bois **305.8**

1. African Americans

Hardcover and paperback editions available from various publishers

First published 1903 by McClurg

"A collection of fifteen essays and sketches by W.E.B. Du Bois. In it he describes the lives of African American farmers, sketches the role of music in their churches, details the history of the Freedman's Bureau, discusses the career of Booker T. Washington, and advocates a commitment to higher education for the most talented African American youth." Benet's Reader's Ency of Am Lit

Dyson, Michael Eric

Race rules; navigating the color line. Addison-Wesley 1996 232p o.p.; Vintage Bks. paperback available $12 **305.8**

1. United States—Race relations

ISBN 0-679-78156-0 (pa)

LC 96-32592

"From the aftermath of the O.J. Simpson trial to the posturing of black leaders following the Million Man March, Dyson explores the social issues governed by race. . . . Dyson identifies three African American leaders—Jesse Jackson, Colin Powell, Louis Farrakhan—and how he believes they have aided or hindered justice for African Americans." Libr J

"Mr. Dyson has mapped out some valuable coordinates for the course the nation continues to steer." N Y Times Book Rev

Encyclopedia of African-American civil rights; from emancipation to the present; edited by Charles D. Lowery and John F. Marszalek; foreword by David J. Garrow. Greenwood Press 1992 xxv, 658p il $72.95

305.8

1. African Americans—Civil rights—Encyclopedias

ISBN 0-313-25011-1

LC 91-27814

This "compilation of information covering the general area of civil rights since the Emancipation Proclamation contains over 800 entries written by 157 experts in African American history. . . . In addition to people, also included are important laws, books, newspapers, journals, events, and landmark court cases. All entries provide bibliographies and are cross-referenced. . . . This is a fine work, unique in its focus and comprehensive in its coverage." Libr J

Encyclopedia of African-American culture and history; edited by Jack Salzman, David Lionel Smith, Cornel West. Macmillan 1996 5v il set $695 **305.8**

1. African Americans—Encyclopedias

ISBN 0-02-897345-3

LC 95-33607

Supplement I published 2000 $135 (ISBN 0-02-865441-2)

Also available CD-ROM version

With coverage beginning with the arrival in 1619 of the first slaves from Africa, this set provides a "survey

Encyclopedia of African-American culture and history—*Continued*

of both the contributions to and the problems of blacks in American society. The 2,300 signed entries treat North America only. . . . Two-thirds of the entries are biographies treating such important historical figures as Sojourner Truth and Frederick Douglass and such contemporary people as Marian Wright Edelman and Colin Powell." Booklist

Encyclopedia of multiculturalism; editor, Susan Auerbach. Marshall Cavendish 1993 6v il set $571.36 **305.8**

1. Multiculturalism—Encyclopedias 2. Minorities—Encyclopedias
ISBN 1-85435-670-4   LC 93-23405
Also available 2 volume supplement $214.21 (ISBN 0-7614-7096-4)

This encyclopedia "covers the ethnic groups of African Americans, American Indians, Inuets and Aluets, Asian and Pacific Islanders, European and Middle Eastern Americans, Jewish Americans, and Latinos. It also focuses on issues faced by groups such as women, gays and lesbians, the elderly, and the disabled. . . . Articles range from a few hundred words to several pages in length." Book Rep

The **Encyclopedia** of the Irish in America; Michael Glazier, editor. University of Notre Dame Press 1999 xxi, 988p $89.95 **305.8**

1. Irish Americans—Encyclopedias
ISBN 0-268-02755-2   LC 99-22389

The editor "devotes several dual-column pages of dense text to such well-known topics as emigration and the famine—but he also mentions Christopher Columbus because he visited Ireland and had an Irishman in his crew. Every state, including Hawaii, has had Irishmen in it, and so every state gets an entry. What may earn this title space on the shelves, however, is its exhaustive coverage of Irish American clerics, politicians, artists, actors, writers, and little-known businessmen. The entries, written by almost 250 contributors, cite scholarly books, other encyclopedias, magazines, and a couple of web pages." Libr J

Franklin, John Hope, 1915-

From slavery to freedom; a history of African Americans; [by] John Hope Franklin, Alfred A. Moss, Jr. Knopf il maps $49.95 **305.8**

1. African Americans—History 2. Slavery—United States
Also available in paperback from McGraw-Hill
First published 1947. (8th edition 2000) Periodically revised
A survey of African-Americans history from slavery to the present
Includes bibliographical references

Gale encyclopedia of multicultural America; contributing editor, Robert von Dassanowsky; author of introduction, Rudolph J. Vecoli; edited by Jeffrey Lehman. 2nd ed. Gale Group 2000 3v il set $215 **305.8**

1. Ethnic groups—Encyclopedias 2. Minorities—Encyclopedias
ISBN 0-7876-3986-9   LC 99-44226
First published 1995 in two volumes

Contents: v1 Acadians-Garifuna Americans; v2 Georgian Americans-Ojibwa; v3 Oneidas-Yupiat

Essays on approximately 150 culture groups of the U.S., from Acadians to Yupiats, covering their history, acculturation and assimilation, family and community dynamics, language and religion

Gates, Henry Louis

The future of the race; by Henry Louis Gates, Jr. and Cornel West. Knopf 1996 196p hardcover o.p. paperback available $12

305.8

1. Du Bois, W. E. B. (William Edward Burghardt), 1868-1963 2. African Americans—Social conditions 3. African Americans—Intellectual life 4. United States—Race relations
ISBN 0-679-76378-3 (pa)   LC 96-14450
"Gates and West explore the challenge of W.E.B. DuBois's famous essay 'The Talented Tenth' and consider the future of African American society in light of it. . . . The authors examine the responsibility of the successful and talented black middle and upper classes to uplift the impoverished. . . . The text includes DuBois's 'The Talented Tenth' and, reprinted for the first time, his 1948 critique of it." Libr J
Includes bibliographical references

Glazer, Nathan

Beyond the melting pot; the Negroes, Puerto Ricans, Jews, Italians, and Irish of New York City; by Nathan Glazer and Daniel Patrick Moynihan. 2nd ed. MIT Press 1970 xcviii, 363p hardcover o.p. paperback available $26.95 **305.8**

1. Minorities 2. New York (N.Y.)—Population
ISBN 0-262-57022-X (pa)
First published 1963
A study of the different levels of achievement of the five major ethnic groups of New York City in education, business, and politics
Includes bibliographical references

Graham, Lawrence Otis

Our kind of people; inside America's Black upper class. HarperCollins Pubs. 1999 418p il hardcover o.p. paperback available $14

305.8

1. African Americans—Social conditions 2. Elite (Social sciences) 3. United States—Race relations
ISBN 0-06-098438-4 (pa)   LC 98-34046
Graham presents a "study of the customs, social organizations, educational institutions, vacation enclaves and histories of wealthy African-American communities in a dozen cities across the country." N Y Times Book Rev
"This book is both a thorough work of social history and a thoughtful appraisal of [the author's] own place in the black social hierarchy." Publ Wkly

Griffin, John Howard, 1920-1980

Black like me. 2nd ed, with a new epilogue by the author. Houghton Mifflin 1977 208p o.p.; New Am. Lib. paperback available $6.99 **305.8**

1. African Americans—Southern States 2. Prejudices
ISBN 0-451-19203-6 (pa)   LC 76-47690
Also available in hardcover from Buccaneer Bks.
First published 1961

Griffin, John Howard, 1920-1980—*Continued*

The author, "who is white, a Catholic, and a Texan, conceived and carried out the unusual notion of blackening his skin with a newly developed pigment drug and traveling through the Deep South as a Negro. This book, part of which appeared in the Negro magazine Sepia, is a journal account of that experience." New Yorker

Harley, Sharon

The timetables of African-American history; a chronology of the most important people and events in African-American history. Simon & Schuster 1995 400p il hardcover o.p. paperback available $21

305.8

1. African Americans—History
ISBN 0-684-81578-8 (pa)   LC 94-22571
This work "is arranged by year; under each date events are listed across the page under such categories as *Education; Laws and Legal Actions; Religion; Arts; Science, Technology, and Medicine;* and *Sports.*" Booklist

"These timetables would be an excellent addition to any collection of African American studies as a ready reference source or a starting point for further research." Libr J

Harvard encyclopedia of American ethnic groups; Stephan Thernstrom, editor; Ann Orlov, managing editor, Oscar Handlin, consulting editor. Belknap Press 1980 xxv, 1076p maps $144   **305.8**
1. Ethnic groups—Encyclopedias 2. Minorities—Encyclopedias
ISBN 0-674-37512-2   LC 80-17756
"Defining *ethnic* in the widest possible way, this book contains substantial articles on American ethnic groups. Origins, migration and settlement, history in America, socioeconomic structure, religion and politics, and many other topics are addressed. Includes demographic information, individual bibliographies, and appendices." N Y Public Libr Book of How & Where to Look It up

Hendrickson, Paul

Sons of Mississippi; a story of race and its legacy. Knopf 2003 343p il map $26; pa $15

305.8

1. African Americans—Mississippi 2. Mississippi—Race relations 3. Police brutality
ISBN 0-375-40461-9; 0-375-70425-6 (pa)
LC 2002-29857
"Sons of Mississippi recounts the story of seven white Mississippi lawmen depicted in a . . . 1962 Life magazine photograph. . . . [In this photograph], the lawmen (six sheriffs and a deputy sheriff), . . . [are] preparing for the unrest they anticipate—and to which they clearly intend to contribute—in the wake of James Meredith's planned attempt to integrate the University of Mississippi. . . . [Hendrickson's] ultimate focus is on the part [their] legacy has played in the lives of their children and grandchildren." Publisher's note

"The number of telling quotes, interviews with friends and family, primary and secondary sources, allusions to art and history, and gut reactions Hendrickson offers are what really make the book. . . . He repeatedly comes up with electric interview material, and deftly places these men within the defining events of their times, when 'a 100-year-old way of life was cracking beneath them.'" Publ Wkly

Includes bibliographical references

The **Hispanic** American almanac; a reference work on Hispanics in the United States; edited by Sonia G. Benson. 3rd ed. Gale Group 2003 xxvii, 886p il maps $135

305.8

1. Hispanic Americans
ISBN 0-7876-2518-3   LC 2002-10070
First published 1993 under the editorship of Nicolás Kanellos

This is a "resource covering people of the U.S. whose ancestors come from Mexico, Cuba, Puerto Rico, and Central America. The book contains 25 subject chapters (e.g., 'Spanish Explorers and Colonizers'; 'Law, Government, and Military'; 'Art'. . . . A chronology offers a year-by-year outline of the migration of Hispanics to this country. . . . The 'Historical Overview' chapter details the evolution of three major Hispanic groups: Mexicans, Puerto Ricans, and Cubans. The 'Significant Documents' chapter provides the researcher with documents such as the Treaty of Guadalupe Hidalgo (1948), the NAFTA agreement, and California's Proposition 227. . . . The final chapter contains more than 500 biographies highlighting Hispanics. . . . Well organized and written at a reading level that is easily understood, this volume is an excellent resource for high-school and public libraries." Booklist

Includes bibliographical references

The **Jewish** people in America. Johns Hopkins Univ. Press 1992 5v set $145

305.8

1. Jews—United States
Edited by Henry L. Feingold

Contents: v1 A time for planting, by E. Faber (ISBN 0-8018-5120-3); v2 A time for gathering, by H. Diner (ISBN 0-8018-5121-1); v3 A time for building, by G. Sorin (ISBN 0-8018-5122-X); v4 A time for searching, by H. Feingold (ISBN 0-8018-5123-8); v5 A time for healing, by E. Shapiro (ISBN 0-8018-5124-6)

"The authors explore the roots of Jewish immigration, the experience of settling in America, economic and social adjustment, religious developments and educational aspirations, political involvements, and, above all, the experience from generation to generation of what it means to be at once Jewish and American." Univ Press Books for Public and Second Sch Libr

Kennedy, Randall

Nigger; the strange career of a troublesome word. Pantheon Bks. 2002 226p $22; pa $12

305.8

1. African Americans 2. Racism 3. United States—Race relations
ISBN 0-375-42172-6; 0-375-71371-9 (pa)
LC 2001-36442
Kennedy examines the history of the use of the racial epithet in American society by both African Americans and whites and its implications for race relations

"An insightful and highly provocative book that raises vital questions about the relationship between language, politics, social norms and how society and culture confront racism." Publ Wkly

Includes bibliographical references

Lasch-Quinn, Elisabeth
Race experts; how racial etiquette, sensitivity training, and New Age therapy hijacked the civil rights revolution. Norton 2001 267p $25.95 **305.8**
1. African Americans 2. United States—Race relations 3. Multiculturalism 4. Group relations training
ISBN 0-393-04873-X LC 2001-30913
Also available in paperback from Rowman & Littlefield
The author "probes the intersection of the civil rights struggle and modern social psychology, in particular the human potential movement. She highlights the 'overthrow of the social code of segregation' and the adoption of an etiquette of black assertiveness and white submissiveness that has produced a 'harangueflagellation' ritual that does not advance the goal of racial equality. . . . This is sure to be a controversial book among readers interested in race issues." Booklist
Includes bibliographical references

Loury, Glenn C.
The anatomy of racial inequality. Harvard Univ. Press 2001 226p il (W.E.B. Du Bois lectures) $22.95 **305.8**
1. African Americans—Social conditions 2. African Americans—Economic conditions 3. United States—Race relations
ISBN 0-674-00625-9 LC 2001-39192
"Loury argues that the image white Americans have of black Americans as less than full citizens influences policy far more than who African-Americans actually are. Although much of Loury's argument is theoretical . . . he grapples eloquently and vigorously with such concrete examples as affirmative action, arguments about racial IQ differences and racial profiling." Publ Wkly
Includes bibliographical references

Lukas, J. Anthony, 1933-1997
Common ground; a turbulent decade in the lives of three American families. Knopf 1985 659p il maps hardcover o.p. paperback available $18 **305.8**
1. Boston (Mass.)—Race relations 2. Busing (School integration) 3. School integration
ISBN 0-394-74616-3 (pa) LC 85-127
"By focusing on three families—one of them welfare black, one upper-middle-class white and one working-class Irish—a veteran journalist recreates the school-busing struggles of Boston in the 1970s, and delineates . . . the moral complexities of caste and class in America." Newsday

McWhorter, John H.
Losing the race; self-sabotage in Black America. Free Press 2000 285p $24 **305.8**
1. African Americans—Social conditions 2. African Americans—Education
ISBN 0-684-83669-6 LC 00-31655
Also available in paperback from HarperCollins Pub.
McWhorter discusses what he sees as "a cult of anti-intellectualism 'that has infected black America. . . . He concluded [black students] were held back by three defeatist thought patterns': the Cult of Victimology, which leads blacks to blame their problems on racism; the Cult of Separatism, which makes blacks think that whatever whites do, they should do the opposite; and the Cult of Anti-Intellectualism, which holds that scholastic excellence is a white thing." Time
Includes bibliographical references

Morales, Ed
Living in Spanglish; the search for a new Latino identity in America. St. Martin's Press 2002 310p $25.95; pa $14.95 **305.8**
1. Hispanic Americans 2. Racially mixed people 3. United States—Ethnic relations
ISBN 0-312-26232-9; 0-312-31000-5 (pa)
LC 2001-48867
"To the author, *Spanglish* isn't just . . . [an] increasingly common linguistic mélange. . . . It is the breakdown of the either/or of a black/white worldview through the inevitable mingling of race and culture. . . . The author meditates on his own coming to terms with Latino identity as well as positing the larger point that 'We have spent the last several centuries preparing for our role as the first wholly postmodern culture.'. . . . His ideas are provocative and engaging." Booklist

The **New** York Public Library African American desk reference. Wiley 1999 606p il $40 **305.8**
1. African Americans—Encyclopedias
ISBN 0-471-23924-0
"A Stonesong Press book"
This reference is "arranged into 19 chapters covering topics such as slavery, education, health, law, science and technology, the arts, and sports. Chapters include numerous tables, lists, photographs, and sidebars and end with sources for additional information. Quotations are sprinkled throughout." Booklist

Olmos, Edward James
Americanos; Latino life in the United States; [by] Edward James Olmos, Lea Ybarra, Manuel Monterrey; preface by Edward James Olmos; introduction by Carlos Fuentes. Little, Brown 1999 176p il $39; pa $25 **305.8**
1. Hispanic Americans
ISBN 0-316-64914-7; 0-316-64909-0 (pa)
LC 98-51930
This work includes essays, poetry, and commentary in English and Spanish by such authors as Carlos Fuentes and Maya Angelou and over 200 photographs of Latin Americans from many parts of the United States
"This is a beautiful, vibrant . . . book; it may also be one of the more socially important books to appear in some time." Booklist

Packard, Jerrold M.
American nightmare; the history of Jim Crow. St. Martin's Press 2002 291p $24.95; pa $14.95 **305.8**
1. African Americans—Segregation 2. Southern States—Race relations
ISBN 0-312-26122-5; 0-312-30241-X (pa)
LC 2001-41960
The author provides an "overview of the Jim Crow era, from Reconstruction through passage of the Voting Rights Act in 1965." Booklist
"This is a clear, concise, historical narrative of a draconian reality." Publ Wkly
Includes bibliographical references

Remembering Jim Crow; African Americans tell about life in the segregated South; edited by William H. Chafe [et al.] New Press (NY) 2001 xxxv, 346p il $55; pa $16.95 **305.8**

1. African Americans—Segregation 2. African Americans—Southern States 3. Southern States—Race relations

ISBN 1-56584-697-4; 1-56584-778-4 (pa)
LC 2001-31224

Companion volume to Remembering slavery

Recollections taken from interviews compiled by the Behind the Veil Project at the Center for Documentary Studies at Duke University

This work offers "views into the thoughts, activities, and anxieties of black Americans. . . . Included are two one-hour CDs of the radio documentary produced by American Radio Works, a transcript of the audio program, 50 rare segregation-era photographs, biographical information, and suggestions for further reading. This [is a] superb primary source." Libr J

Robeson, Paul, 1898-1976

Here I stand; with a preface by Lloyd L. Brown and a new introduction by Sterling Stuckey. Beacon Press 1988 c1958 xxxvi, 121p hardcover o.p. paperback available $14
305.8

1. African Americans—Civil rights

ISBN 0-8070-6445-9 (pa)
LC 87-47882

First published 1958 by Othello Associates

"Combining a narrative of his life and travels with commentary on history and the events of his time, [the author] relates the fight against segregation to social progress for all Americans, white and black, claiming that 'white supremacy' disenfranchises and impoverishes white workers and white farmers as well as black." Libr J

Rodriguez, Richard, 1944-

Brown: the last discovery of America. Viking 2002 232p $24.95; pa $14 **305.8**

1. Hispanic Americans 2. Racially mixed people 3. United States—Race relations

ISBN 0-670-03043-0; 0-14-200079-5 (pa)
LC 2001-57919

Rodriguez presents a "meditation on identity, racial and otherwise, in American culture. . . . This book draws upon . . . cultural figures and artifacts—e.g., Milton, James Baldwin, Ralph Waldo Emerson, Ralph Lauren advertisements, Leontyne Price in the opera *Cleopatra*, Edith Sitwell, *Showboat*, Carlos Fuentes, Francis Parkman's *Oregon Trail*—to make his case that our historical and contemporary conceptualization of race is rudimentary and psychologically and culturally damaging." Publ Wkly

Sachar, Howard Morley, 1928-

A history of the Jews in America; by Howard M. Sachar. Knopf 1992 1051p hardcover o.p. paperback available $24
305.8

1. Jews—United States

ISBN 0-679-74530-0 (pa)
LC 91-4261

The author examines "two different subjects. One is the rich, sometimes dark, ultimately triumphant story of Jews in the United States. The other is the relation between American Jews and Israel, a matter of the widest interest, for probably no other group in this country is so deeply committed to the success of a foreign state. That poses problems that Mr. Sachar confronts unflinchingly and in detail, making his narrative not only good history but a contribution to the current debate over American-Israeli relations." N Y Times Book Rev

Includes bibliographical references

Sowell, Thomas, 1930-

The economics and politics of race; an international perspective. Morrow 1983 324p hardcover o.p. paperback available $14
305.8

1. Race relations

ISBN 0-688-04832-3 (pa)
LC 83-715

"Through a comparative examination of migrants (Chinese, Germans, Italians, blacks, and others), each studied in a variety of overseas settings, the author seeks to discount the factor of race or racism as a lasting, or seriously disruptive, determinant in socioeconomic and political development." Choice

This book is "thoroughly, almost dauntingly, researched, yet it is as readable as a novel." Commentary

Includes bibliographical references

Ethnic America; a history. Basic Bks. 1981 353p hardcover o.p. paperback available $21
305.8

1. Minorities 2. Ethnic groups

ISBN 0-465-02075-5 (pa)
LC 80-68957

"Offering concise accounts of the Old World experiences of European groups (Irish, German, Jews, Italians) and Asians (Chinese, Japanese) as well as blacks, Puerto Ricans and Mexicans, the author examines the complexities and nuances of their American stories." Publ Wkly

"While bringing together the best of primary and secondary source materials from several vast fields, the book's extraordinary merit is its application of demographic and economic analysis to historical and social materials." New Repub

Takaki, Ronald T., 1939-

Strangers from a different shore; a history of Asian Americans; [by] Ronald Takaki. Updated and rev ed, 1st Back Bay ed. Little, Brown 1998 591p il pa $16.95 **305.8**

1. Asian Americans—History

ISBN 0-316-83130-1
LC 98-218270

First published 1989

This work discusses the Chinese transcontinental railroad workers, the plantation workers in the Hawaii canefields, the Japanese Americans in the U.S. internment camps during World War II, the Hmong refugees in Wisconsin and the stereotypical image of Asian American youth as model students

Includes bibliographical references

Tatum, Beverly Daniel, 1954-

"Why are all the Black kids sitting together in the cafeteria?" and other conversations about race. Basic Bks. 2003 294p pa $15.95
305.8

1. African Americans—Race identity 2. United States—Race relations

ISBN 0-465-08361-7

First published 1997

"Tatum explains the development of racial identity. To illustrate her point she uses anecdotes about her sons, excerpts from research interviews and essays written by her students." Libr J

Terkel, Studs, 1912-

Race; how blacks and whites think and feel about the American obsession. New Press (NY) 1992 403p o.p.; Anchor Bks. paperback available $15.95   **305.8**

1. United States—Race relations

ISBN 0-385-46889-X (pa)   LC 91-66864

"In this new oral history, Terkel explores Americans' inner feelings and values pertaining to the subject of race. . . . His study is primarily centered in Chicago, but the people chosen to be interviewed represent a broad spectrum of society. . . . Terkel demonstrates how very skilled he is at drawing out interviewees' intrinsic feelings pertaining to race." Libr J

West, Cornel

Race matters. Beacon Press 1993 105p o.p.; Vintage Bks. paperback available $12   **305.8**

1. United States—Race relations

ISBN 0-679-74986-1 (pa)   LC 92-35170

Analyzed in Essay and general literature index

In this collection of essays the author "addresses a number of issues of concern to black Americans: the Los Angeles riots after the Rodney King verdict; Malcolm X; Clarence Thomas and Anita Hill, and black street life. . . . West's essays have the feel of a fine sermon, with thought-provoking ideas and new ways of looking at the same old problems." Libr J

Restoring hope; conversations on the future of Black America; edited by Kelvin Shawn Sealey. Beacon Press 1997 xx, 226p il hardcover o.p. paperback available $13

     305.8

1. African Americans—Social conditions 2. United States—Social conditions

ISBN 0-8070-0943-1 (pa)   LC 97-21797

"A project of the Obsidian Society"

The author addresses "the topic of hope and meaning in the African American community by conducting a series of interviews with leading politicians, writers, musicians, journalists, and scholars, including Bill Bradley, Charlayne Hunter-Gault, Wynton Marsalis, and Maya Angelou. . . . The interviews—thoughtful, intimate, and intriguing—make the reader believe that hope in black America can indeed be restored." Libr J

When race becomes real; black and white writers confront their personal histories; edited by Bernestine Singley; epilogue by Derrick Bell. Hill Bks. 2002 335p $26.95

     305.8

1. United States—Race relations 2. Racism

ISBN 1-55652-448-X   LC 2002-2894

"This book of essays and commentaries from black and white people of various ages, economic status, and sexual orientations focuses on the social imposition of race as a reality. . . . The essays, while rich in individual insights, collectively reflect the complexity of how American ideals of equality fall prey to the blindness of a colored history." Booklist

Includes bibliographical references

Woodward, C. Vann (Comer Vann), 1908-1999

The strange career of Jim Crow. 3rd rev ed. Oxford Univ. Press 1974 233p hardcover o.p. paperback available $14.95   **305.8**

1. African Americans—Segregation

ISBN 0-19-501805-2 (pa)

First published 1955

An account of segregation in the South which analyzes events from 1877 to the Nixon administration

Includes bibliographical references

Wynter, Leon E.

American skin; pop culture, big business, and the end of white America. Crown 2002 296p $25   **305.8**

1. Popular culture—United States 2. United States—Race relations

ISBN 0-609-60489-9   LC 2002-19365

Making a "case for non-white influence on American culture, Wynter . . . here joins a chorus chronicling the dissolution of America's once-clear racial delineations into a 'transracial' culture." Publ Wkly

"Wynter brings cutting insights to this absorbing and refreshing look at American race relations and cultural diversity." Booklist

Includes bibliographical references

305.9   Occupational and miscellaneous groups

Kaiser, Charles

The gay metropolis; 1940-1996. Houghton Mifflin 1997 404p il o.p.; Harcourt paperback available $14   **305.9**

1. Gay men 2. New York (N.Y.)—History

ISBN 0-15-600617-0 (pa)   LC 97-25297

"Kaiser's history of American gay life and culture in the second half of the twentieth century centers on New York." Booklist

"Though Kaiser does not make a concerted or effective case for the existence of the borderless American gay metropolis that the title is meant to conjure, the decade-by-decade breakdown of people and events provides an excellent portrait of the urban gay community." Publ Wkly

Includes bibliographical references

Marcus, Eric

Is it a choice? answers to 300 of the most frequently asked questions about gay and lesbian people. 2nd ed. HarperSanFrancisco 1999 224p pa $13   **305.9**

1. Homosexuality 2. Gay men 3. Lesbians

ISBN 0-06-251623-X   LC 99-17799

First published 1993

"Straightforward answers for both straight and lesbian/gay readers to fundamental questions about definitions and origins of homosexuality and bisexuality, lesbian and gay life, and lesbians and gay men in American culture. Highly useful." Libr J [review of 1993 edition]

Includes bibliographical references

St. James Press gay & lesbian almanac; editor, Neil Schlager; with foreword by R. Ellen Greenblatt. St. James Press 1998 680p il $130 **305.9**
1. Gay men 2. Lesbians
ISBN 1-55862-358-2 LC 98-6156
This volume's "sections include a chronology, an annotated list of organizations, significant historical documents important to the gay and lesbian movement, and in-depth discussions of gay and lesbian involvement in such fields as politics, film, music, science, sports, travel, leisure, and visual and performing arts. Each section includes biographical profiles of prominent people in each field and extensive bibliographies of books, articles, and Web sites." Am Libr

306 Culture and institutions

Bok, Derek Curtis
The trouble with government; [by] Derek Bok. Harvard Univ. Press 2001 493p $36; pa $20.50 **306**
1. United States—Politics and government—1989-
2. Social policy—United States
ISBN 0-674-00448-5; 0-674-00832-4 (pa)
LC 00-63476
This "volume seeks to explain and propose remedies for government failings that affect the wide range of areas in which America lags. Bok first considers and largely rejects common diagnoses of what ails American government—politicians and parties, the media and special interests—then proposes his own theory of the four basic weaknesses that afflict this country: poorly designed legislation, burdensome regulation, the neglect of working-class interests and failed antipoverty policies." Publ Wkly

Bork, Robert H., 1927-
Slouching towards Gomorrah; modern liberalism and American decline. ReganBooks 1996 382p il hardcover o.p. paperback available $14 **306**
1. Liberalism 2. Social values 3. United States—Social conditions
ISBN 0-06-098719-7 (pa) LC 96-31277
The author claims that "with its emphasis on outcomes vs. opportunity and on personal gratification, liberalism is destroying the cultural fabric of America." Libr J
"Forthright and magisterial, this is a fine summary of 'social conservativism.'" Booklist
Includes bibliographical references

The **Dictionary** of anthropology; edited by Thomas Barfield. Blackwell 1997 626p il hardcover o.p. paperback available $34.95 **306**
1. Ethnology—Dictionaries
ISBN 0-57718-057-7 (pa) LC 96-37337
This work provides "both historical and contemporary definitions of anthropological terms. . . . Coverage is broad, touching on key concepts, theories, methodologies, and ethnographic and thematic research. . . . [It includes] more than 500 entries, including 42 biographies. . . . A handy ready-reference source." Libr J

Encyclopedia of social issues; editor, John K. Roth. Marshall Cavendish 1997 6v il maps set $459.95 **306**
1. United States—Social conditions—Encyclopedias
2. Canada—Social conditions—Encyclopedias
ISBN 0-7614-0568-2 LC 96-38361
Contents: v1 Abortion-Christopher, Warren; v2 Chronic fatigue syndrome-Esalin Institute; v3 Espionage, corporate-Juvenile Justice System, U.S.; v4 Karen Finley et al. v. NEA and John Frohnmayer-Politics and the media; v5 Poll tax-Supply-side economics; v6 Support groups-Zoos and wildlife refuges
"This encyclopedia on current U.S. and Canadian social issues covers topics in government and politics, social policy, information, economics, human rights, health, law, environment, religion, etc." Libr J

Freud, Sigmund, 1856-1939
Totem and taboo; some points of agreement between the mental lives of savages and neurotics **306**
1. Totems and totemism 2. Psychoanalysis 3. Taboo
Hardcover and paperback editions available from various publishers
Original German edition published 1912-1913 in Vienna
In the four essays in this volume Freud seeks to bridge the gap between psychoanalysis and such disciplines as social anthropology, philology and folklore
Includes bibliographical references

Lasch, Christopher
The revolt of the elites; and the betrayal of democracy. Norton 1995 276p $22; pa $14.95 **306**
1. Elite (Social sciences) 2. Democracy 3. United States—Social conditions
ISBN 0-393-03699-5; 0-393-31371-9 (pa)
LC 94-37270
Analyzed in Essay and general literature index
Lasch "argues that democracy today is threatened not by the masses, as José Ortega y Gasset (The Revolt of the Masses) had said, but by the elites. These elites—mobile and increasingly global in outlook—refuse to accept limits or ties to nation and place. Lasch contends that, as they isolate themselves in their networks and enclaves, they abandon the middle class, divide the nation, and betray the idea of a democracy for all America's citizens." Publisher's note
Includes bibliographical references

Mead, Margaret, 1901-1978
Coming of age in Samoa; a psychological study of primitive youth for Western civilisation; foreword by Franz Boas. Morrow 1928 297p il hardcover o.p. paperback available $14 **306**
1. Adolescence 2. Samoan Islands—Social life and customs 3. Sex differences (Psychology)
ISBN 0-688-05033-6 (pa)
An anthropological study of adolescent Samoan girls

Morgan, Peter W., 1951-
The appearance of impropriety; how ethics
wars have undermined American government,
business, and society; [by] Peter W. Morgan,
Glenn H. Reynolds. Free Press 1997 272p
hardcover o.p. paperback available $16.95
306
1. Political ethics 2. Business ethics 3. United
States—Moral conditions
ISBN 0-7432-4266-1 (pa)   LC 97-19251
"The authors recall how the press and public became
. . . aware of lies and cover-ups during Vietnam and
Watergate. Since then, . . . [they argue], the entire country has grown obsessed with ethics. Instead of paying attention to real transgressions, however, [they maintain],
government agencies and private businesses and institutions have concentrated on appearances." N Y Times
Book Rev
"Examples the authors give, concerning plagiarism and
election-posturing 'anti-crime' legislation, are so deliciously preposterous that the reader is well primed for
the concluding recommendations for reform." Booklist
Includes bibliographical references

Reich, Robert B.
The future of success. Knopf 2001 289p
$26; pa $14   **306**
1. Work 2. Information society 3. Quality of life
ISBN 0-375-41112-7; 0-375-72512-1 (pa)
    LC 00-40552
The author provides an "analysis of the new economy
and how it is affecting lives. . . . He argues that the current economic opportunities afforded by new communication, transportation, and information technologies have
produced a workforce that is unable to perform individual, family, and community roles effectively in a job market that is frenzied, economically divergent, and socially
stratified." Libr J
Includes bibliographical references

Savage, Dan
Skipping towards Gomorrah; the seven
deadly sins and the pursuit of happiness in
America. Dutton 2002 302p $23.95   **306**
1. United States—Moral conditions
ISBN 0-525-94675-6   LC 2002-21252
"Savage argues that whatever consenting adults want
to do in the privacy of their own homes is their own
business. . . . [He] organizes his book into seven chapters, each devoted to one of the deadly sins: greed, lust,
sloth, gluttony, envy, pride and anger." Publ Wkly
The author "uses humor to make a point. These are
not merely Keilloresque essays full of whimsy overload;
instead, they pack a political punch that will be repug-
nant to some." Libr J

Worldmark encyclopedia of cultures and
daily life. Gale Res. 1997 4v il maps set
$360   **306**
1. Ethnology—Encyclopedias 2. Manners and customs—Encyclopedias
ISBN 0-7876-0552-2   LC 97-3278
Contents: v1 Africa; v2 Americas; v3 Asia & Oceania;
v4 Europe
Provides information on 500 cultures of the world,
covering twenty different areas of daily life including
clothing, food, language, and religion

306.43   Education

Kozol, Jonathan
Death at an early age; the destruction of
the hearts and minds of Negro children in the
Boston public schools. Houghton Mifflin
1967 240p o.p.; New Am. Lib. paperback
available $13.95   **306.43**
1. Discrimination in education 2. Public schools—
Boston (Mass.) 3. African Americans—Education
ISBN 0-452-26292-5 (pa)
The author relates his experience as a fourth-grade
teacher in 1964 at a predominantly black Boston school,
emphasizing poorly trained teachers, biased text books,
overcrowded conditions, prejudiced school administrators,
and their effects upon the students
Includes bibliographical references

306.44   Language

Lepore, Jill, 1966-
A is for American; letters and other
characters in the newly United States. Knopf
2002 241p il $25; pa $13   **306.44**
1. English language—Social aspects 2. Americanisms
3. Sociolinguistics
ISBN 0-375-40449-X; 0-375-70408-6 (pa)
    LC 2001-38057
The author "explores the significant and occasionally
unsettling ways language was used to define national
character and boundaries in the early American republic.
Focusing on seven men—Noah Webster, Samuel F.B.
Morse, William Thornton, Sequoyah, Thomas Gallaudet,
Abd al-Rahman Ibrahima and Alexander Graham Bell—
Lepore offers a scholarly analysis of how they devised
alphabets, syllabaries, codes and signs." Publ Wkly
"Each man's story delivers a wealth of irony along
with valuable history. . . . Some familiar accounts, some
not well known, but all told with a fresh eye to their na-
tional significance." Booklist
Includes bibliographical references

McWhorter, John H.
Doing our own thing; the degradation of
language and music and why we should, like
care. Gotham Bks. 2003 xxiv, 279p $26
    306.44
1. English language—Social aspects 2. English language—Usage 3. Americanisms 4. Popular music
ISBN 1-5924-0016-7
Contents: People just talk: speech versus writing;
Mere rhetoric: the decline of oratory; "Got marjoram?' or
why I don't have any poetry; Rather too colloquial for
elegance: written English takes it light; What happened
to us? or play that funky music, white folks; La la la
through a new lens: music talks to America
The author "explores why American language and music are no longer crafted, honored or even well-regarded
means of expression. The expected social formality of an
earlier era, he argues, was eroded by the individualistic,
multicultural values of the *1960s*. . . . Laden with contemporary pop culture references and humorous asides,
this is an entertaining polemic that brings linguistics to
the people, while lamenting the populist mentality that
has made being cool more critical than being articulate."
Publ Wkly

306.7 Institutions pertaining to relations of the sexes

Bader, Michael J.
Arousal, the secret logic of sexual fantasies. Thomas Dunne Bks./St. Martin's Press 2002 293p $23.95; pa $14.95 **306.7**
1. Sexual behavior
ISBN 0-312-26933-1; 0-312-30242-8 (pa)
LC 2001-51290
"Bader covers how arousal works, how fantasies assist in arousal, the role of fantasies in therapy, and the social meaning of fantasies. Throughout, he gives numerous case studies, examples, and sensible and compassionate conjectures about particular fantasies and the fantasizing process. Bader is a clear, graceful writer, and he makes his points with rare facility in a way useful to both lay people and therapeutic professionals." Libr J
Includes bibliographical references

Barash, David P.
The myth of monogamy; fidelity and infidelity in animals and people; [by] David P. Barash, Judith Eve Lipton. Freeman, W.H. 2001 227p $24.95; pa $15 **306.7**
1. Sexual behavior 2. Marriage 3. Adultery
ISBN 0-7167-4004-4; 0-8050-7136-9 (pa)
The author offers "evidence that both sexes in supposedly monogamous species cheat, then segues into a . . . study of why faithless behavior is endemic. Ultimately, he concludes that cheating produces offspring of superior genetic quality and that genetic monogamy isn't 'natural,' not even for humans." Booklist
This is "guaranteed to entertain and may even pique thoughtful readers' interests." Sci Books Films
Includes bibliographical references

Encyclopedia of lesbian and gay histories and cultures. Garland 2000 2v il set $250 **306.7**
1. Lesbianism 2. Homosexuality
ISBN 0-8153-3354-4
Contents: v1 Lesbian histories and cultures, Bonnie Zimmerman, editor; v2 Gay histories and cultures, George E. Haggerty, editor
"The volumes consist of short, signed entries arranged alphabetically. This set, which should become the standard in its field, will be a useful addition to all public and academic libraries." Am Libr

Gray, John
Mars and Venus on a date; a guide for navigating the 5 stages of dating to create a loving and lasting relationship. HarperCollins Pubs. 1997 370p $25; pa $13 **306.7**
1. Dating (Social customs)
ISBN 0-06-017472-2; 0-06-093221-X (pa)
LC 97-19991
This offers advice to single men and women about dating, describing five stages: attraction, uncertainty, exclusivity, intimacy, and engagement

Mars and Venus starting over; a practical guide for finding love again after a painful breakup, divorce, or the loss of a loved one. HarperCollins Pubs. 1998 334p hardcover o.p. paperback available $13.95 **306.7**
1. Interpersonal relations 2. Remarriage 3. Love
ISBN 0-06-093027-6 (pa)
LC 98-175566
Also available large print edition pa $25 (ISBN 0-06-093303-8)
This is a guide to starting new relationships after a divorce, death, or other loss, with emphasis on the differing perspectives of men and women

Hooks, Bell
Salvation; Black people and love. Morrow 2001 xxiv, 225p hardcover o.p. paperback available $12.95 **306.7**
1. African Americans—Social life and customs 2. Interpersonal relations 3. Love
ISBN 0-06-095949-5 (pa)
LC 00-61648
The author contends "that there is a crisis of 'lovelessness' in the black community. . . . [In this exploration of love] she addresses its meaning in black experience today and offers a plan of action for 'black survival and self-determination.'" Libr J

Levine, Judith
Harmful to minors; the perils of protecting children from sex; foreword by Joycelyn Elders. University of Minn. Press 2002 xxxv, 299p $25.95 **306.7**
1. Sex education
ISBN 0-8166-4006-8
LC 2001-6553
Contents: Censorship: the sexual media and the ambivalence of knowing; Manhunt: the pedophile panic; Therapy: "children who molest" and the tyranny of the normal; Crimes of passion: statutory rape and the denial of female desire; No-sex education: from "chastity" to "abstinence"; Compulsory motherhood: the end of abortion; The expurgation of pleasure; The facts ... and truthful fictions; What is wanting? gender, equality, and desire; Good touch: a sensual education
"Levine argues that sex is not necessarily bad for minors, and that puritanical attitudes often backfire. . . . She notes the disturbing trend toward pathologizing young children's eroticized play and criticizes mainstream America for letting the Christian right steer sex education toward an emphasis on abstinence. Compounding that, she says, the right wing has expunged abortion discussions. . . . It's a good start to confronting some vital questions." Publ Wkly
Includes bibliographical references

Mondimore, Francis Mark, 1953-
A natural history of homosexuality. Johns Hopkins Univ. Press 1996 282p il hardcover o.p. paperback available $18.95 **306.7**
1. Homosexuality 2. Sex (Biology)
ISBN 0-8018-5440-7 (pa)
LC 96-16191
This is a "summary of history, biology, psychology, and social issues regarding homosexuality." Libr J
"The information in the book is basic, accurate, wide-ranging, up-to-date, and compassionate." Choice
Includes bibliographical references

Reinisch, June

The Kinsey Institute new report on sex;
what you must know to be sexually literate;
[by] June M. Reinisch with Ruth Beasley;
edited and compiled by Debra Kent. St.
Martin's Press 1990 xx, 540p il hardcover
o.p. paperback available $18.95   **306.7**
1. Sexual behavior
ISBN 0-312-06386-5 (pa)   LC 90-41444
This volume offers information about sexual matters,
divided into general areas, including "body image and
self esteem, problems with sexual functioning, sex and
aging, contraception, [and] sexually transmitted diseases."
Libr J

Williamson, Marvel L.

Great sex after 40; strategies for lifelong
fulfillment. Wiley 2000 246p pa $15.95
                                        306.7
1. Sex education 2. Aging 3. Sexual hygiene
ISBN 0-471-35153-9   LC 99-57415
The author provides "information on the sexual
changes brought about by aging and common mid- and
late-life health conditions—hysterectomy, prostate problems, cancer, heart disease, and Alzheimer's disease. She
also addresses how to achieve sexual fulfillment with
case studies that will help heterosexual couples understand their own sexuality." Libr J
Includes bibliographical references

Wolf, Naomi

Promiscuities; the secret struggle for
womanhood. Random House 1997 xxx, 286p
hardcover o.p. paperback available $15
                                        306.7
1. Girls—Sexual behavior 2. Women—Sexual behavior
ISBN 0-449-90764-3 (pa)   LC 96-46724
This "work centers on the way American culture of
the late Sixties and Seventies created a generation of females torn between the need to express their sensuality
and the desire to meet society's behavioral expectations.
To illustrate her position, Wolf relies . . . on the coming-of-age experiences of herself, her friends, and acquaintances in her hometown, San Francisco." Libr J
"Wolf offers some astute and eminently realizable
suggestions for a new approach to sexual education, even
healing." Booklist
Includes bibliographical references

306.8   Marriage and family

Caine, Lynn

Being a widow. Arbor House 1988 261p
o.p.; Penguin Bks. paperback available $14
                                        306.8
1. Widows
ISBN 0-14-013025-X (pa)   LC 88-15280
"An Eleanor Friede book"
The author discusses the emotional, practical, and
physical problems that arise when coping with terminal
illness and sudden death
"Caine's direct, articulate writing, full of compassion
and understanding, assure a large readership for this special book." Libr J
Includes bibliographical references

Cheever, Susan

As good as I could be; a memoir about
raising wonderful children in difficult times.
Simon & Schuster 2001 191p $23; pa $12
                                        306.8
1. Mothers 2. Parenting
ISBN 0-684-86341-3; 0-671-03498-7 (pa)
                                   LC 2001-20068
The author "reflects on the importance of motherhood
and tells us what having children has meant in her own
life. Although not a how-to manual for raising children,
Cheever's memoir will encourage readers in their efforts
to follow their own paths in parenting." Libr J

Cosby, Bill, 1937-

Fatherhood; introduction and afterword by
Alvin F. Poussaint. Doubleday 1986 178p
o.p.; Berkley Pub. Group paperback available
$12.95   **306.8**
1. Fathers
ISBN 0-425-09772-2 (pa)   LC 86-2100
"A Dolphin book"
Cosby's "advice on surviving the vagaries of one's
offspring consists of a succession of . . . [anecdotes and]
observations, all designed to encourage the application of
love and patience." Atl Mon
This volume "is like a prose version of a Cosby comedy performance—informal, commiserative anecdotes delivered in a sardonic style that's as likely to prompt a
smile of recognition as a belly laugh." Newsweek

Love and marriage; introduction by Alvin
F. Poussaint. Doubleday 1989 xxvi, 188p
hardcover o.p. paperback available $7.50
                                        306.8
1. Marriage
ISBN 0-553-28467-3 (pa)   LC 88-35242
The author "has produced a scrapbook of the happier
side of romance. . . . Though some of the dialogue
sounds as if it were part of a stand-up comedy routine—
meant to be said, not read—Mr. Cosby captures the give
and take of happy marriages." N Y Times Book Rev

Crittenden, Ann

The price of motherhood; why the most
important job in the world is still the least
valued. Metropolitan Bks. 2001 323p $25; pa
$15   **306.8**
1. Mothers 2. Women—United States
ISBN 0-8050-6618-7; 0-8050-06619-5 (pa)
                                   LC 00-53722
Crittenden argues that "the choice to become a mother
in America today imposes enormous costs on most wom-
en, including lower incomes and higher risks of poverty
than men or childless women face. And the remedies,
. . . [she suggests], raise some of the most difficult and
divisive questions about work, family life, law and social
policy." N Y Times Book Rev
"A wonderful resource for students of economics,
women's studies, politics, and for parents-to-be, this
book should be a wake-up call to America." Libr J
Includes bibliographical references

Cusk, Rachel, 1967-

A life's work; on becoming a mother. Picador 2002 c2001 213p $22; pa $13

306.8

1. Mothers 2. Parenting
ISBN 0-312-26987-0; 0-312-31130-3 (pa)
LC 2001-54894

First published 2001 in the United Kingdom

"Taking an unsentimental approach to one of the most dramatic changes in a woman's life, British novelist Cusk . . . dissects the process of new motherhood from a psychological and emotional perspective." Publ Wkly

"This is not a happy guide; instead, it is a penetrating, sometimes joyful and amusing, sometimes frightening and disturbing look at pregnancy and motherhood." Booklist

Engber, Andrea

The complete single mother; reassuring answers to your most challenging concerns; [by] Andrea Engber and Leah Klungness. 2nd ed. Adams Media Corp. 2000 426p il pa $12.95

306.8

1. Single parent family 2. Mother-child relationship 3. Parenting
ISBN 1-58062-302-6
LC 99-59671

First published 1995

This handbook for single mothers offers "practical advice on meeting the challenges of parenting without partners. In part 1, Engber and Klungness look for the various ways women become single mothers . . . and the special demands of each situation. In part 2, the authors focus on how single moms can handle pregnancy and birth, maintaining a household and maintaining their self-esteem alone, and in part 3, they talk . . . about the day-to-day difficulties of 'raising terrific kids.' They address in part 4 relations outside the family unit." Booklist [review of 1995 edition]

Includes bibliographical references

Gore, Albert, Jr.

Joined at the heart; the transformation of the American family; [by] Al and Tipper Gore. Holt & Co. 2002 417p il $26; pa $16

306.8

1. Family
ISBN 0-8050-6893-7; 0-8050-7450-3 (pa)
LC 2002-27252

The authors "examine subjects as diverse as the increased divorce rate, the parent-teen gap, dual-income households and the health problems associated with sleep deprivation. They divide the book into themes, including love, communication, work, play and community, and show how these factors influence one another, taking a holistic approach to the underlying problems affecting today's families." Publ Wkly

Includes bibliographical references

Hite, Shere

The Hite report on the family; growing up under patriarchy. Grove Press 1995 xxiv, 424p hardcover o.p. paperback available $14

306.8

1. Family 2. Parent-child relationship 3. Sexual behavior
ISBN 0-8021-3451-3 (pa)
LC 94-42157

First published 1994 in the United Kingdom

This study "based on some 3000 questionnaires completed by children and adults in 16 countries (50 from the U.S.), focuses on the child's developing psychosexual identity and the impact of this process on adulthood. . . . Her respondents' testimonies, organized around specific themes, touch on all manner of taboo subjects." Publ Wkly

Includes bibliographical references

Howey, Noelle

Dress codes of three girlhoods—my mother's, my father's, and mine. Picador 2002 332p $24; pa $14

306.8

1. Parent-child relationship 2. Transsexualism
ISBN 0-312-26921-8; 0-312-42220-2 (pa)
LC 2001-59060

This is a "look back at how teenager Howey and her mother struggled with her father's transformation from a bad-tempered dad to a loving transgendered woman." Libr J

"Howey manages to entertain, console, and enlighten readers. The book is impossible to ignore, and impossible to put down." SLJ

International encyclopedia of marriage and family; James J. Ponzetti, Jr., editor in chief. 2nd ed. Macmillan Ref. USA 2003 4v il set $495

306.8

1. Marriage—Encyclopedias 2. Family—Encyclopedias
ISBN 0-02-865672-5
LC 2002-14107

First published 1995 with title: Encyclopedia of marriage and the family

This set "surveys the patterns of family life from an interdisciplinary and multicultural perspective. . . . The authoritative, often lengthy essays consider topics such as 'Abortion,' 'Adoption,' 'Asian-American Families,' 'Assisted Reproductive Technologies,' 'Gay Parents,' 'Homeless Families,' 'Intimacy,' 'Surrogacy,' and 'War/Political Violence.'" SLJ

For a fuller review see: Booklist June 1 & 15, 2003

Miller, Alice

Paths of life; seven scenarios. Pantheon Bks. 1998 188p hardcover o.p. paperback available $12.95

306.8

1. Family
ISBN 0-375-70345-4 (pa)
LC 98-17578

The author provides "accounts of fictional characters, associating their childhood traumas with adult problems and abnormal relationships. . . . Miller suggests that only by confronting hidden truths can an individual be released from a cycle of interpersonal destructiveness. The final segments, 'Gurus and Cult Leaders' and 'What Is Hatred?,' summarize major concepts." Libr J

Includes bibliographical references

Parenthood in America; an encyclopedia; Lawrence Balter, editor; foreword by Robert B. McCall. ABC-CLIO 2000 2v il (American family) $185

306.8

1. Parenting—Encyclopedias 2. Family—Encyclopedias
ISBN 1-57607-213-4
LC 00-11782

This encyclopedia "covers a wide range of topics (e.g., spacing of children, prevention of physical abuse, language acquisition, night terrors, Latino parenting, bullies and victims, acculturation, divorce, sleep deprivation). Entries are informative, clear, detailed, and offer current coverage." Choice

Pipher, Mary Bray

Another country; navigating the emotional terrain of our elders; [by] Mary Pipher. Riverhead Bks. 1999 xx, 328p hardcover o.p. paperback available $13.95 **306.8**

1. Aging parents 2. Parent-child relationship
ISBN 1-57322-784-6 (pa)   LC 98-31877

The author is interested in studying "the aging process in order to promote meaningful connections between the generations and more cultural support for pursuing them. . . . Pipher describes strategies for dealing with illness, physical decline, the death of a husband or wife and the emotional problems that arise for both the elderly and their families. . . . One of the strengths of this excellent study is that Pipher includes examples of troubled as well as rewarding marital and parent/child relationships." Publ Wkly

Roiphe, Anne Richardson, 1935-

Married; a fine predicament; [by] Anne Roiphe. Basic Bks. 2002 285p $25; pa $14.95 **306.8**

1. Marriage
ISBN 0-465-07066-3; 0-465-07067-1 (pa)
                                 LC 2002-3506

The author writes "about how marriage and women's lives have changed since the 1950s, and about constants in human nature and the beleaguered but not yet improved upon institution of marriage. . . . Roiphe's rumination is a bit indulgent and soft with hearsay, yet it is timely, clever, candid, generous, and free of sentiment or trivialization." Booklist

Slater, Lauren

Love works like this; moving from one kind of life to another. Random House 2002 186p $21.95 **306.8**

1. Pregnancy 2. Depression (Psychology)
ISBN 0-375-50376-5   LC 2001-58911

"At the heart of this piercing memoir is Slater's struggle to become a mother in the face of bipolar disorder. At once sad and miraculous, the text reveals the quandary an expectant mother faces when she must take drugs that could harm the unborn child (she stopped taking Prozac during the first trimester but then resumed)." Libr J

Taffel, Ron

The second family; how adolescent power is challenging the American family; [by] Ron Taffel with Melinda Blau. St. Martin's Press 2001 204p $23.95; pa $12.95 **306.8**

1. Teenagers 2. Parenting 3. Popular culture
ISBN 0-312-26137-3; 0-312-28493-4 (pa)
                                 LC 00-45993

In this work the author "tracks adolescents' defection from the 'first family' (Mom, Dad, and siblings) for the 'second family' (the peer group and pop culture). This is not, he argues, an angry or rebellious culture but a comfort-seeking one—be it with sex, drugs, recreation, body sculpture, and consumer items." Libr J

This book is "required reading for anyone interacting with adolescents today." Voice Youth Advocates

Tannen, Deborah

I only say this because I love you; how the way we talk can make or break family relationships throughout our lives. Random House 2001 xxvii, 336p hardcover o.p. paperback available $15.95 **306.8**

1. Family 2. Communication
ISBN 0-345-40752-0 (pa)   LC 00-68851

The author "explores how caring and concern, connection and control are communicated between family members." Booklist

"With lively prose and genuine concern for people, Tannen brings linguistic concepts—metamessage, reframing, indirect request—to bear on dozens of situations to help lay readers strenghten family ties." Libr J
Includes bibliographical references

Waite, Linda J.

The case for marriage; [by] Linda J. Waite and Maggie Gallagher. Doubleday 2000 260p hardcover o.p. paperback available $14.95
                                            306.8

1. Marriage 2. Married people 3. Single people
ISBN 0-7679-0632-2 (pa)   LC 00-22672

The authors defend marriage and enumerate what they consider the benefits of the institution

"Waite and Gallagher overstate contemporary attacks on marriage, but they make a valid point that the revered institution has suffered stings lately." Booklist
Includes bibliographical references

Westheimer, Ruth

The value of family; a blueprint for the 21st century; [by] Ruth Wertheimer and Ben Yagoda. Warner Bks. 1996 211p hardcover o.p. paperback available $12.99 **306.8**

1. Family 2. Social values
ISBN 0-446-67336-6 (pa)   LC 96-15154

Westheimer "and Yagoda examine what constitutes a family, defined in the traditional sense of a household, and then recommend how the family can be helped by individuals, government, and business." Libr J

"A humane, levelheaded, eye-opening look at changing family dynamics." Publ Wkly
Includes bibliographical references

Wilson, James Q.

The marriage problem; how our culture has weakened families. HarperCollins Pubs. 2002 274p hardcover o.p. paperback available $13.95 **306.8**

1. Marriage 2. Family 3. United States—Social conditions
ISBN 0-06-093526-X (pa)   LC 2001-24495

"Wilson aims to explain not only how marriage has lost strength in modern America but also why that loss matters." Booklist

Winik, Marion

The lunch-box chronicles; notes from the parenting underground. Pantheon Bks. 1998 229p hardcover o.p. paperback available $15
                                            306.8

1. Single parent family 2. Parenting
ISBN 0-375-70170-2 (pa)   LC 97-26753

The author "covers death, bedtime stories, sexuality, God, team sports for geeks and other topics in this col-

Winik, Marion—*Continued*
lection of personal essays on raising children." N Y
Times Book Rev
"Winik brings together in winning fashion her decidedly nonmainstream attitude, laugh-out-loud humor, and
refreshing candor." Booklist

Yalom, Marilyn
A history of the wife. HarperCollins Pubs.
2001 441p il hardcover o.p. paperback
available $14.95   **306.8**
1. Marriage 2. Women—History
ISBN 0-06-093156-6 (pa)   LC 00-58153
The author examines the "history of women and marriage in the Western world." Publ Wkly
Yalom "has apparently written the first truly
comprehensive history of the Western female spousal experience; indeed, there are precious few long views of either marriage or the family to which this book can be
compared." Libr J

306.89 Separation and divorce

Gardner, Richard A., 1931-2003
The parents book about divorce. rev ed.
Creative Therapeutics 1991 xxi, 393p $31.43
                                                   306.89
1. Divorce 2. Parent-child relationship 3. Child psy-
chology
ISBN 0-933812-27-2   LC 91-21283
First published 1977 by Doubleday
Among the topics covered in this guide are when and
how to tell the children, dealing with guilt feelings, visi-
tation problems, and meeting children's emotional needs

Wallerstein, Judith S.
Second chances; men, women, and children
a decade after divorce; [by] Judith S.
Wallerstein and Sandra Blakeslee. Ticknor &
Fields 1989 xxi, 329p o.p.; Houghton Mifflin
paperback available $14   **306.89**
1. Divorce 2. Children of divorced parents
ISBN 0-395-73533-5 (pa)   LC 88-23320
In 1971 the author "began a study of 131 children and
adolescents from 60 families and their divorcing parents,
in Marin County, California. . . . The researchers
reinterviewed all family members 18 months later, again
5 years after divorce, and again 10 years after divorce.
. . . 'Second Chances' is Ms. Wallerstein's account of
the course and consequences of divorce for these parents
and children." N Y Times Book Rev
Includes bibliographical references

306.9 Institutions pertaining to death

Encyclopedia of death and dying; edited by
Glennys Howarth and Oliver Leaman.
Routledge 2001 xxii, 534p il $140 **306.9**
1. Death—Encyclopedias
ISBN 0-415-18825-3   LC 2001-19234
"In dictionary format, topics in historical, social, cultural, and technical areas are presented. . . . Biographical
entries and information on important associations and
journals are also included." Booklist
"This work will enrich all academic and public library
collections." Libr J

Macmillan encyclopedia of death and dying;
Robert Kastenbaum, editor in chief.
Macmillan Ref. USA 2002 c2003 2v set
$250   **306.9**
1. Death—Encyclopedias
ISBN 0-02-865689-X   LC 2002-5809
"The 327 signed entries . . . range in length from a
few paragraphs to several pages. . . . Types of entries
include causes of death . . . practices surrounding death
. . . individuals and events that have influenced the way
we think about death . . . and entries on the nature or
meaning of death from various multidisciplinary and
multicultural perspectives. . . . An appendix profiles and
gives contact information for 75 organizations active in
death-related education, research, advocacy, or other areas." Booklist

307 Communities

Etzioni, Amitai
The spirit of community; rights,
responsibilities, and the communitarian
agenda. Crown 1993 323p il o.p.; Simon &
Schuster paperback available $14   **307**
1. Community development 2. Social action 3. United States—Moral conditions
ISBN 0-671-88254-3 (pa)   LC 92-31527
"The book is divided into theoretical chapters, which
come at the beginning and the end, and a series of topical chapters in which social analysis is interspersed with
case studies and examples. The topics progress from the
family to the school, to a view of local institutions, . . .
including religious institutions, as the mainstay of communities, and then to policy issues such as safety and
health." Commonweal

307.7 Specific kinds of communities

Duany, Andres
Suburban nation; the rise of sprawl and the
decline of the American Dream; [by] Andres
Duany, Elizabeth Plater-Zyberk, and Jeff
Speck. North Point Press 2000 289p il $35;
pa $18   **307.7**
1. Urbanization 2. Cities and towns 3. City planning
4. Urban renewal
ISBN 0-86547-557-1; 0-86547-606-3 (pa)
                                     LC 99-52186
The authors, town planners associated with the New
Urbanism movement, argue that American suburbs have
failed on ecological, economic, aesthetic, and social levels. Drawing on their experiences with a variety of community development projects, they advocate a return to
more traditional planning principles
Includes bibliographical references

Encyclopedia of urban cultures; cities and
cultures around the world; edited by
Melvin Ember and Carol R. Ember. Grolier
2002 4v il maps set $399   **307.7**
1. Cities and towns—Encyclopedias 2. Urban sociology—Encyclopedias
ISBN 0-7172-5698-7   LC 2002-70034
Published under the auspices of the Human Relations
Area Files at Yale University

Encyclopedia of urban cultures—*Continued*

This reference work provides cultural and historical information on cities in all regions of the world. Each city article gives demographic, historical, social, economic, political, religions and cultural information

For a fuller review see: Booklist, March 1, 2003

Kunstler, James Howard

The city in mind; meditations on the urban condition. Free Press 2002 c2001 272p $25
307.7

1. Urban sociology 2. Cities and towns
ISBN 0-684-84591-1   LC 2001-40897
Also available in paperback from Touchstone Bks.

The author takes a "look at how eight cities (Paris, Atlanta, Mexico City, Berlin, Las Vegas, Rome, Boston, and London), either through inspired ideas or chaotic greed, became sublime expressions of the human spirit or of gigantic monstrosities and perversion." Libr J

This is an "excitable, funny, sometimes high-handed disquisition on the future of metropolitan life." New Yorker

Includes bibliographical references

Mumford, Lewis, 1895-1990

The city in history; its origins, its transformation, and its prospects. Harcourt Brace & World 1961 657p il hardcover o.p. paperback available $29   **307.7**

1. Cities and towns—History 2. City and town life 3. Civilization—History
ISBN 0-15-618035-9 (pa)
More than a history of the forms and functions of the city throughout the ages, this is a portrait of the development of man as a religious, a political, an economic, a cultural, and a sexual being

Includes bibliographical references

The culture of cities. Harcourt Brace & Co. 1938 586p il hardcover o.p. paperback available $24   **307.7**

1. Cities and towns 2. City planning 3. Regional planning
ISBN 0-15-623301-0 (pa)
Also available in hardcover from Greenwood Press

Traces the growth of cities from medieval times to the twentieth century

Includes bibliographical references

Savageau, David

Places rated almanac; [by] David Savageau with Ralph D'Agostino. IDG Bks. il maps pa $24.95   **307.7**

1. Cities and towns—United States 2. Quality of life
First published 1981 (millenium edition 1999) Periodically revised. Publisher varies

"Your guide to finding the best places to live in the United States and Canada"

This ranks "metropolitan areas as to factors that affect the quality of life: the arts, economics, education, crime, transportation, environment, housing, climate, and health care. Provides statistical information on American cities and towns. People planning to move will find it useful." Ref Sources for Small & Medium-sized Libr. 6th edition

Retirement places rated. Macmillan USA; [distributed by] Wiley il maps pa $21.95
307.7

1. Retirement communities
First published 1983 by Prentice Hall Press with title: Places rated retirement guide. (5th edition 1999) Periodically revised. Publisher varies

Retirement areas in the U.S. are "ranked and compared for cost of living, climate, health care, economic factors, crime, services, cultural life, and recreation. Included are climate graphs, maps of retirement regions, comparison charts, and demographic profiles of each area." Publisher's note

Includes bibliographical references

310.5   General statistics—Serial publications

The **Europa** world year book. Europa Publs.; [distributed by] Taylor & Francis 2v set $920   **310.5**

1. Statistics 2. Political science
ISSN 0956-2273
Annual. First published 1959 with title: The Europa year book

"The best annual directory of the nations of the world. For each country it includes demographic and economic statistics, and facts about constitution and government, political parties, press, trade and industry, publishers, etc. Also incorporates a substantive section with listings and information about international organizations." Ref Sources for Small & Medium-sized Libr. 6th edition

The **Statesman's** year-book; the politics, cultures, and economies of the world. St. Martin's Press $170   **310.5**

1. Statistics 2. Political science
ISSN 0081-4601
Also available online
Annual. First published 1864

"Descriptive and statistical information about international organizations and countries of the world—brief history, area, political status, economy, etc." N Y Public Libr. Ref Books for Child Collect. 2d edition

Statistical abstract of the world. Gale Res. maps $85   **310.5**

1. Statistics
ISSN 1077-1360
First published 1994. (3rd edition 1997) Periodically revised

"Topics include geography, population/demographics, health, ethnicity, crime, science and technology, government, finance, trade, economy, manufacturing, energy, military expenditures, and human rights observances. . . . The 30-page appendix explains the sources, definitions, and limitations of the data." Libr J

United Nations. Statistical Office

Statistical yearbook. U.N. Publs. $135
310.5

1. Statistics
Also available print and CD-ROM edition $269
First published 1948. Text in English and French

United Nations. Statistical Office—*Continued*

An annual giving statistics under the following headings: Population; Manpower; Production summary; Agriculture; Forestry; Fishing; Mining, quarrying; Manufacturing; Construction; Electricity, gas, consumption; Transport; Communications; Internal trade; External trade; Balance of payments; International economic aid; Wages and prices; National income; Public finance; Housing statistics; Education, culture

317.1 General statistics of Canada

Canadian almanac & directory. Micromedia; [distributed by] Information Handling Services $275   **317.1**
1. Canada—Directories 2. Almanacs
ISSN 0068-8193
Also available CD-ROM version and online
Annual. First published 1847. Publisher varies
"Contains reliable legal, commercial, governmental, statistical, astronomical, departmental, ecclesiastical, financial, educational, and general information." Guide to Ref Books. 11th edition

317.3 General statistics of the United States

County and city data book. U.S. Govt. Ptg. Office $68; pa $58   **317.3**
1. Cities and towns—United States 2. United States—Statistics
ISSN 0082-9455
Also available CD-ROM version and online
First published 1949. (2000 edition available) Periodically revised
"Presents the latest available census figures for each county, and for the larger cities in the United States. Also has summary figures for states, geographical regions, urbanized areas, standard metropolitan areas, and unincorporated places." Guide to Ref Books. 11th edition

CQ's state fact finder; rankings across America. CQ Press $99; pa $55   **317.3**
1. United States—Statistics
Annual. First published 1993 under the authorship of Victoria Van Son. Authors vary
"This guide provides data, state by state, under such headings as *Business and Economy, Education, Energy, Health, Population, Recreation, Social Services*, and *Transportation*. . . . A second section of the book rearranges the data by state, so that the user can go directly to a particular state and see where it ranks in each of 325 areas. . . . This is a must purchase for all academic, high-school, and public libraries, where information like this is sure to be in demand." Booklist
Includes bibliographical references

A **Statistical** portrait of the United States; social conditions and trends; edited by Patricia C. Becker. Bernan Assocs. il $147   **317.3**
1. United States—Statistics 2. United States—Social conditions
ISBN 0-89059-584-4
First published 1998. (2nd edition 2002) Periodically revised
"Offers twenty-five-year trends and international comparisons on American population; living arrangements; education; health; work; income; poverty and wealth; housing; crimes and victims; leisure, volunteerism, and religion; voting; the environment; and government. Offers data summaries and concise analysis; provides sources for additional information, including web site addresses." Ref Sources for Small & Medium-sized Libr. 6th edition
"Easy to use and well-organized, it assembles data for quick analysis and overview." Choice

United States. Bureau of the Census
Statistical abstract of the United States. U.S. Govt. Ptg. Office $39   **317.3**
1. United States—Statistics 2. Statistics
ISSN 0081-4741
Also available CD-ROM version and online
Annual. First published for the year 1878
"Compendium of statistics on the social, political and economic organization of the U.S. presented in tables. Lists other sources of such information." N Y Public Libr. Ref Books for Child Collect. 2d edition

320 Political science

Aristotle, 384-322 B.C.
Politics   **320**
1. Political science
Hardcover and paperback editions available from various publishers
"Discussion of public affairs by the most eminent of the Greek philosophers in terms applicable to many of the problems of modern political science." Pratt Alcove

Kaplan, Robert D.
Warrior politics; why leadership demands a pagan ethos. Random House 2002 xxii, 198p $22.95; pa $12   **320**
1. International relations 2. Leadership 3. Political ethics
ISBN 0-375-50563-6; 0-375-72627-6 (pa)
LC 2001-31862
"Integrating classic and contemporary scholarship, the author argues that the ills of the twentieth century are 'less unique than we think' and draws parallels between the complacency of Rome at its height and that of the U.S." Booklist
"This is a provocative, smart and polemical work that will stimulate lively discussion." Publ Wkly
Includes bibliographical references

Machiavelli, Niccolò, 1469-1527
The prince   **320**
1. Political science 2. Political ethics
Hardcover and paperback editions available from various publishers
Written in 1513
"A handbook of advice on the acquisition, use, and maintenance of political power, dedicated to Lorenzo de Medici." Haydn. Thesaurus of Book Dig

Paine, Thomas, 1737-1809
Common sense   **320**
1. United States—Politics and government—1775-1783, Revolution
Hardcover and paperback editions available from various publishers
"Published anonymously at Philadelphia (Jan. 10, 1776). At a time of rising passion against the British government, the work was the first unqualified argument for complete political independence, and helped turn colonial thought in the direction that, six months later, culminated in the Declaration of Independence. Over 100,000 copies were sold by the end of March, and it is generally considered the most important literary influence on the movement for independence." Oxford Companion to Am Lit. 6th edition

The rights of man   **320**
1. Political science 2. France—History—1789-1799, Revolution
Hardcover and paperback editions available from various publishers
First published 1791-1792
A political work "defending the French Revolution against attacks made on it by Edmund Burke. In it Paine argues that civil government exists only through a contract with a majority of the people for the safeguarding of the individual, and that if man's 'natural rights' are interfered with by the government, revolution is permissible." Benet's Reader's Ency. 4th edition

320.025 Political science— Directories

Government phone book USA; a comprehensive guide to federal, state, county, and local government offices in the United States; editorial data provided by Carroll Publishing Co. Omnigraphics $255   **320.025**
1. State governments—Directories 2. County government—Directories 3. Federal government—Directories 4. Municipal government—Directories
ISSN 1091-9643
Annual. First published 1992 with title: The Government directory of addresses and telephone numbers
This is a "compilation of more than 100,000 listings, giving names, mailing addresses, and telephone numbers for key offices and officials at every level of government. Each of the three sections (federal, state, and city and county) begins with quick reference listings of frequently called numbers, abbreviations, area codes, etc. Keyword indexes facilitate access to federal and states offices." Guide to Ref Books. 11th edition

Washington information directory.
Congressional Quarterly $110   **320.025**
1. Washington (D.C.)—Directories 2. Executive departments—United States—Directories
ISSN 0887-8064
Annual. First published 1975/76
"Lists names, telephone numbers, addresses, and responsibilities of 5,000 key personnel and agencies, both private and governmental, in the Washington, DC area; includes detailed indexes." N Y Public Libr Book of How & Where to Look It Up

320.03 Political science— Encyclopedias and dictionaries

The **Oxford** guide to the United States Government; edited by John J. Patrick, Richard M. Pious, Donald A. Ritchie. Oxford Univ. Press 2001 802p $35 **320.03**
1. United States—Politics and government—Encyclopedias
ISBN 0-19-514273-X   LC 00-51024
"In this alphabetical encyclopedia on topics relating to both the present activities and history of the U.S. government, entries include biographies of presidents and vice presidents, selected First Ladies and members of congress, and all Supreme Court justices who have ever served. Other types of biographical entries are those of unofficial groups of people who have played important roles in American government and history. . . . There are also articles on the various departments of the federal government; important historical events . . . issues and concepts . . . laws and decisions; and Supreme Court cases." Booklist
"This solid reference work is highly recommended for public, academic, and high school libraries." Libr J
Includes bibliographical references

320.1 The state

Hobbes, Thomas, 1588-1679
Leviathan   **320.1**
1. Political science 2. State, The
Hardcover and paperback editions available from various publishers
First published 1651
"A treatise on the origin and ends of government. . . . This work, a defense of secular monarchy, written while the Puritan Commonwealth ruled England, contains Hobbes's famous theory of the sovereign state." Benet's Reader's Ency. 4th edition

Locke, John, 1632-1704
Two treatises of government   **320.1**
1. Political science 2. State, The
Hardcover and paperback editions available from various publishers
First published 1690
Locke's Two treatises written in "defense of the Glorious Revolution, revealed his belief in the natural goodness and cooperative spirit of man and his theory that the state should operate according to natural laws of reason and tolerance. He advocated religious tolerance and rights to personal property." Benet's Reader's Ency. 4th edition

Rousseau, Jean-Jacques, 1712-1778
The social contract   **320.1**
1. Political science
Hardcover and paperback editions available from various publishers
First published 1762
"A treatise on the origins and organization of government and the rights of citizens. Rousseau's thesis states that, since no man has any natural authority over another, the social contract, freely entered into, creates natural reciprocal obligations between citizens." Benet's Reader's Ency. 4th edition

320.5 Political ideologies

Didion, Joan
Fixed ideas: America since 9.11; preface by
Frank Rich. New York Review of Bks. 2003
44p pa $7.95 **320.5**
1. Nationalism 2. September 11 terrorist attacks, 2001
3. United States—Politics and government—2001-
ISBN 1-590-17073-3 LC 2003-7251
The author contends that "after September 11, those
who initiated discussions regarding the causes of the
tragedy were instantly branded as traitors as the White
House simultaneously launched the war on terrorism and
a public relations campaign that blatantly oversimplified
the complex realities involved. . . . First published in the
New York Review of Books, this is an essential work of
clarity in a time of obfuscation." Booklist

Halstead, Ted
The radical center; the future of American
politics; [by] Ted Halstead and Michael Lind.
Doubleday 2001 264p $24.95; pa $13 **320.5**
1. United States—Politics and government—1989-
ISBN 0-385-50045-9; 0-385-72029-7 (pa)
LC 2001-28285
"According to the authors, the basic problem [in contemporary politics] is that the two dominant parties have
been captured by their extremes. 'Instead of expanding
their voter bases, both parties have allowed themselves to
be taken hostage by narrow pressure groups on certain
defining issues,' Republicans by 'social conservatives
and economic libertarians' and Democrats by 'a constellation of aggrieved minority groups and public employee
unions.' . . . Halstead and Lind propose a new 'center'
that's not halfway between right and left but outside the
standard range of political debate." N Y Times Book
Rev
"Sure to have its detractors across the political spectrum, this book adds many fresh insights to our currently
stale political discourse." Libr J
Includes bibliographical references

Pipes, Daniel, 1949-
Militant Islam reaches America. Norton
2002 309p $25.95; pa $15.95 **320.5**
1. Islamic fundamentalism 2. Muslims—United States
3. Islam and politics 4. Terrorism
ISBN 0-393-05204-4; 0-393-32531-8 (pa)
LC 2002-6482
"Pipes argues that Islam is not an inherent threat to
Western civilization, but that militant Islam . . . is the
greatest threat since the cold war. He goes on to explore
the threats posed to America by an influx of Muslim immigrants, extol the benefits of racial profiling, and argue
that the only viable form of Islamic belief is 'secularist'
Islam, which embraces Western values and eschews traditional Islamic ones. . . . It's controversial and often interesting stuff." Booklist
Includes bibliographical references

Podhoretz, Norman
My love affair with America; the
cautionary tale of a cheerful conservative.
Free Press 2000 248p $25 **320.5**
1. Conservatism 2. United States—Politics and gov-
ernment—20th century
ISBN 0-7432-0051-9 LC 99-462225
Also available in paperback from Encounter Bks.

The author "details his political metamorphosis from
liberal to neoconservative. . . . Podhoretz attributes the
gradual change in his political beliefs to a longstanding
'love affair with America' and a strong aversion to left-
wing (and extreme right-wing) anti-American statements
and activities." Libr J

321 Systems of governments and states

More, Sir Thomas, Saint, 1478-1535
Utopia **321**
1. Utopias
Hardcover and paperback editions available from various publishers
Originally published 1516 in Latin; 1551 in English
In his study of the ideal state, "More assigns the narrative to a Raphael Hythloday ('Hythloday' is Greek for
'talker of nonsense'). . . . Book I treats of the evils of
the world and asserts the need for an ideal commonwealth, which Book II describes." Haydn. Thesaurus of
Book Dig

Mumford, Lewis, 1895-1990
The story of utopias; with an introduction
by Hendrik Willem Van Loon. Boni and
Liveright 1922 315p o.p. **321**
1. Utopias
Available in hardcover from P. Smith and in paperback from Kessinger Pub.
The book "connects up the classic Utopias from Plato
onward with modern social myths and schemes for reform showing the contrasts as well as the points common
to all." Am J Sociol
Includes bibliographical references

321.9 Authoritarian government

Arendt, Hannah
Origins of totalitarianism. new ed with
added prefaces. Harcourt Brace Jovanovich
1973 xliii, 527p pa $19 **321.9**
1. Totalitarianism 2. Imperialism 3. Antisemitism
ISBN 0-15-670153-7
Also published as separate paperbacks with titles:
Antisemitism; Imperialism; Totalitarianism; the first and
third titles are available
"A Harvest book"
First published 1951 in the United Kingdom with title:
The burden of our time
In this book, the author documents her "belief that
Nazism and Communism had their roots in the anti-
Semitism and imperialism of the 19th century." Benet's
Reader's Ency. 4th edition
Includes bibliographical references

322 Relation of the state to organized groups and their members

Carter, Stephen L.
God's name in vain; how religion should and should not be involved in politics. Basic Bks. 2000 248p hardcover o.p. paperback available $15 **322**
1. Religion and politics 2. Church and state
ISBN 0-465-00887-9 (pa) LC 00-33741
The author "argues that religion mustn't and can't be walled out of politics but that church and clergy involvement in political parties only sullies religion. One of the most important books about freedom of religion of this, or perhaps any, era." Booklist
Includes bibliographical references

Djupe, Paul A.
Encyclopedia of American religion and politics; [by] Paul A. Djupe and Laura R. Olson. Facts on File 2003 512p il $85 **322**
1. Religion and politics 2. United States—Religion—Encyclopedias 3. United States—Politics and government—Encyclopedias
ISBN 0-8160-4582-8 LC 2002-33921
"Facts on File library of American history"
"An A-to-Z reference covering all facets of American politics and religion, from the early days of the American republic to the rise of the political power of the Christian Right. More than 600 entries cover key religious and political leaders, important historical events, descriptions of court cases, concepts, and religious denominations." Publisher's note
"The encyclopedia is timely and accessible. . . . Recommended for most reference collections in public libraries." Libr J
Includes bibliographical references

322.4 Political action groups

Alinsky, Saul
Rules for radicals; a practical primer for realistic radicals; by Saul D. Alinsky. Random House 1971 196p hardcover o.p. paperback available $12 **322.4**
1. Community organization 2. Radicalism
ISBN 0-679-72113-4 (pa)
The author discusses how radicals should organize and work within the system to effect social change
Includes bibliographical references

Atkins, Stephen E.
Encyclopedia of modern American extremists and extremist groups. Greenwood Press 2002 xxiv, 375p $74.95 **322.4**
1. Radicalism 2. Right and left (Political science)
ISBN 0-313-31502-7 LC 2001-57729
"An Oryx book"
This is "a reference source that lists 275 of the most influential and significant domestic extremists, organized groups, and extreme events. . . . Here they are divided into three categories: political, religious, and economic/social. While the book covers activities since the 1950s, three quarters of the entries focus on the period from 1980 to 2001." Libr J

"This is an excellent reference tool." Recomm Ref Books for Small & Medium-sized Libr & Media Cent, 2003
Includes bibliographical references

Bushart, Howard L.
Soldiers of God; white supremacists and their holy war for America; by Howard L. Bushart, John R. Craig, and Myra Barnes. Kensington Bks. 1998 308p il hardcover o.p. paperback available $15 **322.4**
1. White supremacy movements 2. Racism 3. United States—Race relations
ISBN 1-57566-659-6 (pa) LC 97-74364
"Through dozens of interviews with members involved in various supremacists organizations such as the Ku Klux Klan and Aryan Nation, the authors look at the motivations that drive individuals to support these extremist associations." Publ Wkly
"The authors should be commended for their evenhanded reporting of this inflammatory issue. . . . This book is a clear window into the mind of the white supremacist." Libr J
Includes bibliographical references

Chalmers, David Mark
Hooded Americanism: the history of the Ku Klux Klan. 3rd ed. Duke Univ. Press 1987 c1981 477p il hardcover o.p. paperback available $24.95 **322.4**
1. Ku Klux Klan
ISBN 0-8223-0772-3 (pa) LC 86-29133
First published 1965 by Doubleday; this is a reissue of the 1981 edition published by Watts
This book recounts the history of the Klan. It describes the sociological and psychological forces behind the Klan, and sets forth its dogmas
"The book is written in a breezy, journalistic style. . . . Especially instructive and sobering is Chalmers' account of the role of the Klan in politics." J Am Hist
Includes bibliographical references

Dees, Morris S., Jr.
Gathering storm; America's militia threat; [by] Morris Dees with James Corcoran. HarperCollins Pubs. 1996 254p il hardcover o.p. paperback available $13 **322.4**
1. Radicalism 2. Militia movements
ISBN 0-06-092789-5 (pa) LC 96-3846
This "exposé gets deep inside the paranoid mentality of antigovernment hate groups, documenting the growing links among paramilitary units, white supremacists and neo-Nazis who preach armed confrontation. Dees traces Oklahoma bombing suspect Timothy McVeigh's ties to the militia and super-patriot underground." Publ Wkly
Includes bibliographical references

Esposito, John L.
Unholy war; terror in the name of Islam. Oxford Univ. Press 2002 196p $26 **322.4**
1. Terrorism 2. Islam and politics 3. United States—Foreign opinion
ISBN 0-19-515435-5 LC 2001-58009
The author "explains the teachings of Islam—the Qur-an, the example of the Prophet, Islamic law—about jihad or holy war, the use of violence, and terrorism. He chronicles the rise of extremist groups and examines their frightening worldview and tactics." Publisher's note
"Engaging, evenhanded, and highly readable . . . this

Esposito, John L.—_Continued_
is essential reading for every concerned citizen and all those who wish to gain a deeper understanding of contemporary Islam and its internal struggles." Libr J
Includes bibliographical references

Ezekiel, Raphael S., 1931-
The racist mind; portraits of American Neo-Nazis and Klansmen. Viking 1995 xxxv, 330p hardcover o.p. paperback available $20
322.4
1. Ku Klux Klan 2. White Aryan Resistance 3. Racism 4. White supremacy movements 5. United States—Race relations
ISBN 0-14-023449-7 (pa)   LC 94-45177
"White supremacy groups are examined in this brutally honest portrait of hate and fear, based on personal interviews and interactions. A disturbingly provocative look at the frightening ignorance existing in the 1990s." Booklist
Includes bibliographical references

Gandhi, Mahatma, 1869-1948
Gandhi on non-violence; selected texts from Mohandas K. Gandhi's Non-violence in peace and war; edited with an introduction by Thomas Merton. New Directions 1965 82p pa $7.95
322.4
1. Passive resistance 2. India—Politics and government
ISBN 0-8112-0097-3
"A New Directions paperbook"
In an introductory essay Merton "considers Gandhi's ideas, not in relation to their Indian context, but in terms of their applicability to all men's lives. Brief quotations from Gandhi's writings make up most of the book." Asia: a Guide to Paperbacks

Ronson, Jon, 1967-
Them: adventures with extremists. Simon & Schuster 2002 c2001 330p $24; pa $13
322.4
1. Radicalism 2. Conspiracies
ISBN 0-7432-2707-7; 0-7432-3321-2 (pa)
LC 2001-47411
First published 2001 in the United Kingdom
"Ronson spent the last five years with extremists: religious fundamentalists in Great Britain, Texas, and Cameroon; white supremacists in Arkansas, Michigan, and Idaho; and New World Order conspiracy chasers in Portugal and California. Despite their differences, all seem to believe that the world is controlled by an elite group known as 'them.'" Libr J
This book "is at times funny, other times unsettling, but always astonishing. So difficult to accept are Ronson's narratives that any conclusions must be left up to the reader." Booklist

Stern, Kenneth S. (Kenneth Saul), 1953-
A force upon the plain; the American militia movement and the politics of hate. Simon & Schuster 1996 303p o.p.; University of Okla. Press paperback available $19.95
322.4
1. Militia movements 2. Resistance to government 3. Radicalism
ISBN 0-8061-2926-3 (pa)   LC 95-49228
This is a "survey of various right-wing militia groups, selected leaders, and members." Booklist

Stern "links militias to preexisting racist groups such as the Ku Klux Klan, Aryan Nations, and Posse Comitatus. . . . This book provides an excellent introduction to the latest incarnation of racist and paranoid politics." Libr J
Includes bibliographical references

323   Civil and political rights

Dershowitz, Alan M.
Shouting fire; civil liberties in a turbulent age. Little, Brown 2002 550p $26.95   **323**
1. Civil rights
ISBN 0-316-18141-2   LC 2001-34453
This book "contains 55 short essays on rights and their limitations, particularly in areas like free speech, church-state and the criminal process. . . . The earliest dates back 35 years; the latest include reflections on Sept. 11." N Y Times Book Rev
"Dershowitz's distinctive analysis of a rights framework will be an excellent addition to both public and academic libraries." Libr J
Includes bibliographical references

Devine, Carol
Human rights; the essential reference; [by] Carol Devine, Carol Rae Hansen, Ralph Wilde [et al.]; edited by Hilary Poole. Oryx Press 1999 311p il $73.95   **323**
1. United Nations. General Assembly. Universal Declaration of Human Rights 2. Human rights
ISBN 1-57356-205-X   LC 99-24395
"This volume is divided into four sections; the first 'traces the evolution of our modern concept of human rights' beginning with the ancient Greeks and continuing through World War II to the adoption of the Universal Declaration of Human Rights by the United Nations General Assembly in 1948. Part two is a thorough examination of this historical document, article by article. Part three provides a detailed overview of the contemporary human-rights movement. . . . The final section consists of short essays on 33 of the most pressing human-rights issues today." SLJ

Maddex, Robert L., 1942-
International encyclopedia of human rights; freedoms, abuses, and remedies. CQ Press 2000 xxxii, 404p il $156.25   **323**
1. Human rights—Encyclopedias
ISBN 1-56802-490-8   LC 00-42941
"Beginning its coverage with the 1948 Universal Declaration of Human Rights, the volume includes definitions of more than 150 important concepts . . . entries on decisions of national and international bodies; descriptions of well over 100 documents . . . information about agencies and organizations involved in human rights; and biographies of some key individuals." Booklist

Schulz, William F., Jr.
In our own best interest; how defending human rights benefits us all; foreword by Mary Robinson. Beacon Press 2001 235p $25; pa $15   **323**
1. Human rights
ISBN 0-8070-0226-7; 0-8070-0227-5 (pa)
LC 2001-392
According to the author, "defending human rights pays off not only in terms of justice, but also in ways

Schulz, William F., Jr.—*Continued*
that can include greater economic growth, a more protected environment, better public health, and a generally
less violent world." America
Includes bibliographical references

323.1   Civil and political rights of nondominant groups

Civil rights in the United States; Waldo E.
Martin, Jr., Patricia Sullivan, editors.
Macmillan Ref. USA 2000 2v set $260
323.1
1. Civil rights 2. African Americans—Civil rights
ISBN 0-02-864765-3   LC 99-57548
"Covering the period from 1865 to the present, the set
features more than 700 entries comprised of historical
and state surveys, biographies, entries on civil rights and
other organizations, political and social movements, legislation and government programs, court cases, overall
concepts, cultural and educational institutions, as well as
film, literature, music and art." Publisher's note
For a review see: Booklist, Aug. 2000

Egerton, John, 1935-
Speak now against the day; the generation
before the civil rights movement in the South.
Knopf 1994 704p il o.p.; University of N.C.
Press paperback available $19.95   **323.1**
1. African Americans—Civil rights 2. Southern
States—Race relations
ISBN 0-8078-4557-4 (pa)   LC 93-47491
Egerton presents a "historical narrative of black and
white Southerners opposing white supremacy during the
1930s and 1940s. . . . He explains why the South failed
to dismantle white supremacy when the possibility existed for voluntary, peaceful social reform." Libr J
This "book is a stunning achievement: a sprawling,
engrossing, deeply moving account." N Y Times Book
Rev

The **Eyes** on the prize civil rights reader;
documents, speeches, and firsthand
accounts from the black freedom struggle,
1954-1990; general editors, Clayborne
Carson [et al.] Penguin Bks. 1991 764p pa
$18   **323.1**
1. African Americans—Civil rights 2. United States—
Race relations
ISBN 0-14-015403-5   LC 91-9507
First published 1987 with title: Eyes on the prize:
America's civil rights years, a reader and guide
"An anthology of primary material important in the
historiography of this country's civil rights movement.
. . . Not simply for reference use, this compilation
makes provocative cover-to-cover reading and is ex-
tremely worthy of consideration by every library." Book-
list
Includes bibliographical references

Fairclough, Adam
Better day coming; Blacks and equality,
1890-2000. Viking 2001 384p il $26.95; pa
$16   **323.1**
1. African Americans—Civil rights 2. United States—
Race relations 3. Southern States—Race relations
ISBN 0-670-87592-9; 0-14-200129-5 (pa)
          LC 00-51342
This is a "history of black emancipation from 1890 to
the present." N Y Times Book Rev
"Although it adds little to what experts in the field al-
ready know, this well-written work is a fine general in-
troduction to the topic." Libr J
Includes bibliographical references

Guinier, Lani
The miner's canary; enlisting race, resisting
power, transforming democracy; [by] Lani
Guinier and Gerald Torres. Harvard Univ.
Press 2002 392p $28.95; pa $16.95   **323.1**
1. United States—Politics and government 2. Minorities 3. United States—Race relations
ISBN 0-674-00469-8; 0-674-01084-1 (pa)
         LC 2001-39629
"Guinier and Torres call for the building of grass-
roots, cross-racial coalitions to remake . . . structures of
power by fostering public participation in politics and re-
forming the process of democracy." Publisher's note
The authors "grapple intelligently and with passionate
wit with such explosive topics as racial profiling and the
elusiveness of racial identification and identity . . . making this one of the most provocative and challenging
books on race produced in years." Publ Wkly
Includes bibliographical references

Halberstam, David, 1934-
The children. Random House 1998 783p
o.p.; Ballantine Bks. paperback available
$17.95   **323.1**
1. African Americans—Civil rights 2. United States—
Race relations
ISBN 0-449-00439-2 (pa)   LC 97-19974
This is a "re-creation of the early days of the civil
rights movement. . . . [The author focuses] on a small
group of young African Americans who attended the
Reverend James Lawson's workshop for nonviolent dem-
onstrators in Nashville in 1959, then went on to play active roles in the movement. . . . A masterful achievement in reporting, research and understanding." Publ
Wkly
Includes bibliographical references

King, Martin Luther, 1929-1968
The papers of Martin Luther King, Jr.;
senior editor Clayborne Carson . University
of Calif. Press 1992-2000 4v ea $50   **323.1**
1. African Americans—Civil rights 2. United States—
Race relations   LC 91-42336
Contents: v1 Called to serve, January 1929-June 1951
(ISBN 0-520-07950-7); v2 Rediscovering precious
values, July 1951-November 1955 (ISBN 0-520-
07951-5); v3 Birth of a new age, December 1955-
December 1956 (ISBN 0-520-07952-3); v4 Symbol of
the movement, January 1957-December 1958 (ISBN 0-
520-22231-8)
The first four volumes of a projected 14 volume set,
this is a chronologically arranged collection of correspondence, speeches, and other primary documents by and related to the civil rights leader, with introductory biographical information

King, Martin Luther, 1929-1968—*Continued*

A testament of hope; the essential writings of Martin Luther King, Jr.; edited by James Melvin Washington. Harper & Row 1986 xxvi, 676p hardcover o.p. paperback available $23 **323.1**
1. African Americans—Civil rights 2. United States—Race relations
ISBN 0-06-064691-8 (pa)   LC 85-45370
"King's most important writings are gathered together in one source. The arrangement is topical: philosophy, sermons and public addresses, essays, interviews and excerpts of his books. The material within each of these categories is arranged chronologically. Included are Dr. King's writings on nonviolence, integration and politics." SLJ

Includes bibliographical references

Why we can't wait; [by] Martin Luther King, Jr. Harper & Row 1964 178p il o.p.; New Am. Lib. paperback available $6.95 **323.1**
1. African Americans—Civil rights 2. Birmingham (Ala.)—Race relations
ISBN 0-451-62754-7 (pa)

The author first reviews the background of the 1963 civil rights demands. He then describes the strategy of the Birmingham campaign and outlines future action

Olson, Lynne

Freedom's daughters; the unsung heroines of the civil rights movement from 1830 to 1970. Scribner 2001 460p il hardcover o.p. paperback available $16 **323.1**
1. African American women 2. African Americans—Civil rights
ISBN 0-684-85013-3 (pa)   LC 00-41306
Olson discusses the contribution of such women as Fannie Lou Hamer, Diane Nash, Rosa Parks and Ella Baker to the civil rights movement
This book "expertly mines oral history collections housed in Southern universities, biographies and testaments published in the last decade by Southern university presses and more general works by historians." N Y Times Book Rev

Reporting civil rights. Library of Am. 2003 2v ea $40 **323.1**
1. African Americans—Civil rights 2. Journalism 3. United States—Race relations
ISBN 1-931082-28-6 (v1); 1-931082-29-4 (v2)
                         LC 2002-27459
Contents: pt1 American journalism, 1941-1963; pt2 American journalism, 1963-1973
These "volumes present newspaper and magazine articles from the popular and African American press. . . . The 151 writers whose works are collected here include Ralph Ellison, Langston Hughes, John Hersey, Robert Penn Warren, David Halberstam, Jimmy Breslin, James Baldwin, Marshall Frady, and Tom Wolfe. . . . Each volume also contains a chronology and biographical sketches of the contributors." Libr J
"An important anthology for readers interested in the history of the civil rights movement." Booklist

Voices in our blood; America's best on the civil rights movement; edited by Jon Meacham. Random House 2001 561p hardcover o.p. paperback available $16.95 **323.1**
1. African Americans—Civil rights 2. United States—Race relations
ISBN 0-375-75881-X (pa)   LC 00-41474
A "collection of acclaimed 'voices' narrating the environment, origin, and progress of the Civil Rights movement, as told by reporters, artists, novelists, historians, and authors such as Maya Angelou, Eudora Welty, James Baldwin, Richard Wright, Willie Morris, Robert Penn Warren, Alice Walker, Murray Kempton, E. B. White, William Faulkner, Ralph Ellison, and Rebecca West." Libr J

Williams, Juan

Eyes on the prize: America's civil rights years, 1954-1965; [by] Juan Williams with the Eyes on the prize production team; introduction by Julian Bond. Viking 1987 300p il hardcover o.p. paperback available $18 **323.1**
1. African Americans—Civil rights 2. United States—Race relations
ISBN 0-14-009653-1 (pa)   LC 86-40271
"A Robert Lavelle book"
"This companion volume to the PBS TV series of the same name is an . . . account of black America's struggle for social and political equality, covering the civil rights battle from the landmark Brown v. Board of Education decision in 1954 to the Selma protest marches, and Voting Rights Act of 1965." Libr J
"Highly recommended both as a socio-historical document and as a heartfelt, poignant remembrance of a movement and its activists." Booklist
Includes bibliographical references

323.4 Specific civil rights; limitation and suspension of civil rights

Conroy, John, 1951-

Unspeakable acts, ordinary people; the dynamics of torture. Knopf 2000 304p $26 **323.4**
1. Torture
ISBN 0-679-41918-7   LC 99-28509
Also available in paperback from University of Calif. Press
The author "interviews torturers, torture victims, and government officials from such diverse locations as Israel, Northern Ireland, and a Chicago police interrogation room, focusing on how torture is performed and why." Booklist
Includes bibliographical references

Pipes, Richard

Property and freedom. Knopf 1999 328p hardcover o.p. paperback available $15
                         323.4
1. Freedom 2. Property
ISBN 0-375-70447-7 (pa)   LC 98-41728
This is a "survey of the Western philosophical stance toward property, primarily concerning its origins, justifi-

Pipes, Richard—*Continued*
cation of possession, and wisdom of redistribution. . . .
After rendering compact constitutional histories of England and Russia, Pipes usefully provides concrete, rather than theoretical, illustrations of the liberty-property nexus in action. An incisive essay." Booklist
Includes bibliographical references

Razac, Olivier
Barbed wire; a political history; translated from the French by Jonathan Kneight. New Press 2002 132p $22.95; pa $13.95   **323.4**
1. Barbed wire
ISBN 1-56584-735-0; 1-56584-812-8 (pa)
LC 2002-19536
"First introduced in 1874 as an inexpensive means of fencing off U.S. prairie land, barbed wire quickly became not only a way to manage livestock but a means to contain Native Americans on reservations. . . . Arguing that barbed wire is 'the political management of space,' Razac traces how it radicalized trench warfare during WWI . . . and, electrified, literally defined the space of Nazi concentration camps. . . . The simplicity and clarity of Razac's prose reinforces the enormous power and originality of his ideas, making this a vital work of cultural criticism." Publ Wkly
Includes bibliographical references

323.44   Freedom of action (Liberty)

Etzioni, Amitai
The limits of privacy. Basic Bks. 1999 280p hardcover o.p. paperback available $21
323.44
1. Right of privacy 2. Public interest
ISBN 0-465-04090-X (pa)   LC 98-47082
The author addresses the right to privacy and the common good. Topics discussed include HIV testing of infants, sex offender laws, deciphering encrypted messages, I.D. cards, and medical records
"Etzioni advocates rethinking privacy and placing it in the context of the common good. This book provides a valuable and informative analysis of a timely and interesting topic." Booklist

Foner, Eric
The story of American freedom. Norton 1998 422p il hardcover o.p. paperback available $16.95   **323.44**
1. Freedom 2. United States—History
ISBN 0-393-31962-8 (pa)   LC 98-3290
Foner offers a "survey of the various meanings—political, economic, personal, moral—that Americans have attached to freedom from the Revolution until today." Commentary
"The book's strongest claim to distinction lies . . . in its succinct, information-packed, wonderfully readable account of the twists and turns in 20th-century American history." N Y Times Book Rev
Includes bibliographical references

Henderson, Harry, 1951-
Privacy in the information age. Facts on File 1999 262p (Library in a book) $45
323.44
1. Right of privacy
ISBN 0-8160-3870-8   LC 99-21572
This book surveys the topic "by providing an overview of the issues, a survey of the applicable laws and court cases, a chronology, and an extensively annotated bibliography. . . . Librarians will like the section on organizations and agencies that directs users to associations with an interest in privacy rights." Libr J

Intellectual freedom manual; compiled by the Office for Intellectual Freedom of the American Library Association. American Lib. Assn. il pa $45   **323.44**
1. Intellectual freedom 2. Libraries—Censorship
First published 1974. (6th edition 2001) Periodically revised
This guide to preserving intellectual freedom includes: ALA interpretations to the Library Bill of Rights; recommendations for special libraries and specific situations; information about legal decisions affecting school and public libraries; a section on the ALA's Intellectual Freedom Action Network
"This manual details the professional standards to which librarians aspire and offers practical information about how to achieve those goals; it's a must for any librarian's professional library." Book Rep
Includes bibliographical references

324   The political process

American presidential campaigns and elections; William G. Shade, and Ballard C. Campbell, editors; Craig R. Coenen, documents editor. Sharpe Ref. 2002 3v set $325   **324**
1. Presidents—United States—Election 2. United States—Politics and government
ISBN 0-7656-8042-4   LC 2002-21185
This reference source covers "every presidential election from 1788-89 to 2000. Each election chapter offers a description of the issues, conventions, campaigns, and election results; a chronology; a 'highlight' sidebar focusing on an interesting aspect of the election; a vote analysis in chart and map form; a bibliography; and a collection of between five and seven documents. . . .
Also provided are more than 170 fact boxes presenting brief biographical summaries for each candidate, including place and date of birth, political party, parents' names, schooling, marriage, family, military service, career, and death information. . . . Although there are other reference sources that cover various aspects of U.S. presidential elections, none provide this kind of detailed election-by-election history. The text is both readable and informative, enhanced by good organization, well-chosen features, and attractive design." Booklist

Dershowitz, Alan M.
Supreme injustice; how the high court hijacked election 2000. Oxford Univ. Press 2001 275p il $25; pa $14.95 **324**
1. Bush, George W. 2. Gore, Albert, Jr. 3. Presidents—United States—Election—2000
ISBN 0-19-514827-4; 0-19-515807-5 (pa)
LC 2001-32193
Dershowitz evaluates the Supreme Court's final decision in the presidential election of 2000. He argues that the five majority justices "acted out of personal political preference, and therefore Bush v. Gore 'may be ranked as the single most corrupt decision in Supreme Court history.'" N Y Times Book Rev
"This well-reasoned and controversial book asks central questions about American democracy and the role of citizens and courts in our society." Libr J
Includes bibliographical references

Karabell, Zachary
The last campaign; how Harry Truman won the 1948 election. Knopf 2000 308p hardcover o.p. paperback available $14 **324**
1. Truman, Harry S., 1884-1972 2. Dewey, Thomas E. (Thomas Edmund), 1902-1971 3. Presidents—United States—Election
ISBN 0-375-70077-3 (pa)
LC 99-28567
This is an account of the presidential campaign which pitted Truman against Dewey
"The author is strongest discussing the impact of the press, polls, and radio and describing the importance of the convention, which was then 'a mix of high politics, low politics and entertainment.'" Libr J

Posner, Richard A., 1939-
Breaking the deadlock; the 2000 election, the constitution, and the courts. Princeton Univ. Press 2001 266p $26.95 **324**
1. Bush, George W. 2. Gore, Albert, Jr. 3. Presidents—United States—Election—2000 4. Elections—Florida
ISBN 0-691-09073-4
LC 2001-35078
The author offers an "examination of state and federal litigation concerning postelection ballot and constitutional controversies culminating in the U.S. Supreme Court decision in *Bush v. Gore* (2000). Posner offers precise insights and analysis of constitutional law and statutory provisions, criticizing both liberal and conservative constitutional scholars while exploring the complexities of Florida's voting processes." Libr J
Includes bibliographical references

Witcover, Jules
No way to pick a president. Farrar, Straus & Giroux 1999 303p o.p.; Routledge paperback available $17.95 **324**
1. Presidents—United States—Election 2. United States—Politics and government—20th century
ISBN 0-415-93031-6 (pa)
LC 99-34933
Witcover contends that "there is too much special-interest money distorting the [election] process. . . . The nominating conventions have become useless affairs. Political consultants, willing to do anything to win, have too much power. The press is at once shallow and relentlessly negative." N Y Times Book Rev
Includes bibliographical references

324.025 The political process— Directories

Political handbook of the world. CSA Publs. $175 **324.025**
1. Political science—Handbooks, manuals, etc. 2. Political parties
ISSN 0913-175X
Annual. First published 1927 with title: A political handbook of Europe
Edited by Arthur S. Banks et al.
"Provides data for each country on chief officials, government and politics, political parties, and news media. Sections devoted to intergovernmental organizations and to issues concerned with particular regions; e.g., Middle East, Latin America. Index to geographical, organizational, and personal names." Ref Sources for Small & Medium-sized Libr. 6th edition

324.5 Nomination of candidates

National party conventions, 1831-2000. CQ Press 2001 297p il $47.25 **324.5**
1. Political conventions 2. Political parties
ISBN 1-56802-563-7
LC 00-48648
First published 1995 with title: National party conventions, 1831-1992
This volume offers information about Republican and Democratic Party national conventions including sites, delegates, chief officers and keynote speakers, party organization and rules, credential fights, platform fights, ballots, and candidates
Includes bibliographical references

324.6 Election systems and procedures; suffrage

America votes; a handbook of contemporary American election statistics; compiled and edited [for] Governmental Affairs Institute. CQ Press maps $185 **324.6**
1. Elections—United States—Statistics
ISSN 0065-678X
Biennial. First volume published for the year 1954/55
"Presents statistics, alphabetical by state, for: (1) postwar, statewide vote for president, governor, and senator; (2) vote (by country and/or/city/town) in most recent election for president, governor, and senator: (3) vote (by congressional district) in elections for representatives since the last redistricting. Each state entry includes congressional district maps, a political profile, and general election/primary election data for the most recent election." Guide to Ref Books. 11th edition

Guide to U.S. elections. 4th ed. CQ Press 2001 2v set $295 **324.6**
1. Elections—United States—Statistics
ISBN 1-56802-603-X
LC 2001-37955
First published 1975
"An impressive compilation of data on presidential, gubernatorial, and congressional elections drawn from many sources, including 'Historical election returns file' of the Inter-University Consortium for Political and Social Research. Divided into sections covering political

Guide to U.S. elections—*Continued*
parties, presidential elections; gubernatorial elections; Senate elections; and House elections." Guide to Ref Books. 11th edition [entry for 3rd edition]

Includes bibliographical references

Moore, John Leo, 1927-
Elections A to Z; [by] John L. Moore. 2nd ed. CQ Press 2003 614p il map (CQ's American government A to Z series) $125
           324.6
   1. Elections—United States—Encyclopedias
ISBN 1-56802-801-6   LC 2003-11235
First published 1999
This "explains how campaigns and elections . . . are conducted in America and how voters, political parties and others participate in choosing their elected officials. . . . Entries range from short definitions of terms like 'front-runner' to in-depth essays exploring vital aspects of campaigns and elections such as the right to vote, turnout trends, and the history, evolution and current state of House, Senate, presidential, and some state-level elections." Publisher's note

Presidential elections, 1789-2000. CQ Press 2002 250p il maps $39.95   **324.6**
   1. Presidents—United States—Election
ISBN 1-56802-790-7   LC 2002-34814
First published 1995 with title: Presidential elections, 1789-1992
This offers information about the electoral college, electoral votes and popular votes in each presidential election, voter turn-out, primary returns, and Democratic and Republican Party conventions

White, Theodore H., 1915-1986
The making of the president, 1960. Atheneum Pubs. 1961 400p   **324.6**
   1. Nixon, Richard M. (Richard Milhous), 1913-1994 2. Kennedy, John F. (John Fitzgerald), 1917-1963 3. Presidents—United States—Election 4. United States—Politics and government—1953-1961
Available in hardcover from Buccaneer Bks.
A chronological account of the 1960 Presidential campaign "beginning with the first primaries in New Hampshire and Wisconsin and continuing through Inauguration Day, and into the White House." New Repub

324.7   Conduct of election campaigns

Morris, Dick
The new prince; Machiavelli updated for the twenty-first century. Renaissance Bks. (Los Angeles) 1999 252p hardcover o.p. paperback available $15.95   **324.7**
   1. Politics 2. United States—Politics and government
ISBN 1-58063-147-9 (pa)   LC 99-21767
This is a "guide for political success, loosely based on Machiavelli's *The Prince*. Dramatic technological improvements . . . have created a new breed of well-informed voters who are too sophisticated to fall for the hype and attack journalism of recent campaigns, Morris posits. Candidates must provide issue-oriented platforms that will benefit the 40 percent of the electorate who vote independent and ultimately decide who is elected." Libr J

"Regardless of whether readers agree with every point Morris makes, they will find him an entertaining and highly instructive guide to the mechanics of modern political life." Publ Wkly

325   International migration and colonization

Szulc, Tad, 1926-2001
The secret alliance; the extraordinary story of the rescue of the Jews since World War II. Farrar, Straus & Giroux 1991 327p il maps $24.95   **325**
   1. Beriḥah (Organization) 2. Jewish refugees 3. Palestine—Immigration and emigration 4. Israel—Immigration and emigration
ISBN 0-374-24946-6   LC 91-25542
"Szulc examines the covert movement of European, Middle Eastern, and North African Jews to an independent Palestine homeland following World War II." Booklist
"The story is updated with the saga of 'rescuing' the Jewish communities of Morocco, Yemen, Iraq, and most recently Ethiopa. Highlighted are the efforts of the American Jewish Joint Distribution Committee and the Hebrew Immigrant Aid Society, whose organizational talents essentially make it all happen. An excellent historical drama." Libr J

Includes bibliographical references

325.73   Immigration to the United States

Brownstone, David M.
Facts about American immigration; [by] David M. Brownstone and Irene M. Franck. Wilson, H.W. 2001 xxx, 818p il $105
           325.73
   1. United States—Immigration and emigration 2. Immigrants—United States
ISBN 0-8242-0959-1   LC 00-53422
"Coverage begins with the earliest Americans and continues to today's immigrants. An overview places the process of immigration in a wide historical context covering efforts to restrict immigration, a portrait of the immigrant journey over the centuries, and a chronology. The main section of the book covers emigration from Europe, Africa, Asia, the Americas, and Oceania." Publisher's note
For a review see: Booklist, June 1 & 15, 2002
Includes bibliographical references

Daniels, Roger
Coming to America; a history of immigration and ethnicity in American life. 2nd ed. Perennial 2002 515p il maps pa $17.95   **325.73**
   1. Minorities 2. United States—Immigration and emigration
ISBN 0-06-050577-X   LC 2002-72436
First published 1990
"After discussing the topic of immigration in general and sociological theories of why people migrate between countries, Daniel discusses each racial or national group that came to the United States during the various eras of the nation's history." SLJ [review of 1990 edition]
Includes bibliographical references

Handlin, Oscar, 1915-

The uprooted. 2nd ed. Little, Brown 1973
333p hardcover o.p. paperback available
$18.99 **325.73**
1. United States—Immigration and emigration 2. Acculturation
ISBN 0-316-34313-7 (pa)
"An Atlantic Monthly Press book"
First published 1951
This account of the American immigrant experience and the acculturation process describes employment, religion, ghetto life, benevolent societies, boss politics, family life, and social alienation

Pipher, Mary Bray

The middle of everywhere; the world's refugees come to our town; [by] Mary Pipher. Harcourt 2002 xxv, 390p $25; pa $14
325.73
1. Refugees
ISBN 0-15-100600-8; 0-15-602737-2 (pa)
LC 2001-5863
Contents: Cultural collisions on the Great Plains; The beautiful laughing sisters—an arrival story; Into the heart of the heartland; All that glitters...; Children of hope, children of tears; Adolescents—Mohammed meets Madonna; Young adults; "Who arranges marriages for us in Nebraska?"; Family—a bundle of sticks cannot be broken; African stories; Healing in all times and places; Home—a global positioning system for identity; Building a village of kindness
"Pipher explores the changing face of the U.S. as immigrants fan out from the coasts and inhabit more and more of the American heartland, changing the culture." Booklist
The author "writes in rich, empathetic language and with a keen, observant eye for detail and nuance." Publ Wkly
Includes bibliographical references

Yans-McLaughlin, Virginia, 1943-

Ellis Island and the peopling of America; the official guide; [by] Virginia Yans-McLaughlin and Marjorie Lightman, with the Statue of Liberty-Ellis Island Foundation. New Press (NY) 1997 209p il maps pa $19.95 **325.73**
1. Ellis Island Immigration Station 2. United States—Immigration and emigration
ISBN 1-56584-364-9 LC 96-54713
Photographs, time lines, charts and historical documents from the Ellis Island Museum accompany a text that places immigration policy in its historical context

326 Slavery and emancipation

Berlin, Ira, 1941-

Many thousands gone; the first two centuries of slavery in North America. Belknap Press 1998 497p il maps $31.50
326
1. Slavery—United States 2. United States—History—1600-1775, Colonial period 3. African Americans—Social conditions
ISBN 0-674-81092-9 LC 98-19336
This is an "account of American slavery from its origins at the beginning of the 17th century through the

Revolution. Focusing on regional differences [the author] examines African American life in the North, the Chesapeake, the Carolina low-country, and the lower Mississippi Valley." Libr J
"Throughout this fascinating book, Berlin deftly outlines the human negotiations that went on even in so unequal a relationship as master-slave." Booklist
Includes bibliographical references

Douglass, Frederick, 1817?-1895

Frederick Douglass; selected speeches and writings; edited by Philip S. Foner; abridged and adapted by Yuval Taylor. Hill Bks. 1999 789p hardcover o.p. paperback available $24
326
ISBN 1-55652-352-1 (pa) LC 99-23180
Based on Foner's five-volume The life and writings of Frederick Douglass (1950-1975), this volume "covers Douglass' speeches and writings over a 54-year period. The breadth and depth of his focus and concerns reflected in more than 2,000 speeches, editorials, articles, and letters provide a wellspring of knowledge about the man and his intellect." Booklist
Includes bibliographical references

Gallay, Alan

The Indian slave trade; the rise of the English empire in the American South, 1670-1717. Yale Univ. Press 2002 444p maps $35; pa $18 **326**
1. Native Americans—Southern States 2. Slave trade
ISBN 0-300-08754-3; 0-300-10193-7 (pa)
LC 2001-5270
The author "examines how Europeans and Native Americans together developed a trade in Native American slaves that proved critical in the development of plantation slavery." Libr J
"Powerfully argued and densely detailed. . . . Gallay's stunning and engrossing work, aimed especially at advanced students and scholars, seems to spur a renewed debate on the origins and meaning of racial slavery." Choice
Includes bibliographical references

Johnson, Charles Richard, 1948-

Africans in America: America's journey through slavery; [by] Charles Johnson, Patricia Smith, WGBH series Research Team. Harcourt Brace & Co. 1998 494p il $30; pa $15 **326**
1. Slavery—United States 2. African Americans—History
ISBN 0-15-100339-4; 0-15-600854-8 (pa)
LC 98-20829
Based on a television series produced by WGBH Television, in Boston, Massachusetts
This book is a "history of American slavery from the pre-Colonial era to the Civil War." Libr J
"This is an impressively researched book . . . that includes photographs, drawings, and posters." Booklist
Includes bibliographical references

Johnson, Walter
Soul by soul; life inside the antebellum slave market. Harvard Univ. Press 1999 283p il $28.50; pa $15.95   **326**
1. Slavery—United States 2. Slave trade 3. New Orleans (La.)—Race relations
ISBN 0-674-82148-3; 0-674-00539-2 (pa)
LC 99-46696
This is an examination of the antebellum slave market. "Using slave narratives, court records, planters' letters, and more, Johnson enters the slave pens and showrooms of the New Orleans slave market to observe how slavery turned men and women into merchandise and how slaves resisted such efforts to steal their humanity." Libr J
Includes bibliographical references

Macmillan encyclopedia of world slavery; edited by Paul Finkelman, Joseph C. Miller. Macmillan Ref. USA 1998 2v il maps set $250   **326**
1. Slavery—Encyclopedias
ISBN 0-02-864607-X   LC 98-30610
This "encyclopedia provides information on different kinds of human bondage—including serfdom, peonage, coolie status, and conscription under government corvee—throughout the world. It also covers the full array of antislavery movements within the context of a universal historical phenomenon." Libr J

Remembering slavery; African Americans talk about their personal experiences of slavery and emancipation; edited by Ira Berlin, Marc Favreau, and Steven F. Miller. New Press (NY) 1998 355p hardcover o.p. paperback available $16.95   **326**
1. Slavery—United States 2. African Americans—History—Sources
ISBN 1-56584-587-0 (pa)
This "book-and-tapes collection of slave narratives, drawn from slave narratives and audio recordings of former slaves collected by the Federal Writers' Project (FWP) during the 1930s and 1940s (some of which have been remastered and included in two 60-minute cassettes with the book), brings slavery to life as few recent books have done." Libr J
Includes bibliographical references

Schneider, Dorothy
Slavery in America; from colonial times to the Civil War; [by] Dorothy Schneider and Carl J. Schneider. Facts on File 2000 458p il maps (Eyewitness history series) $75   **326**
1. Slavery—United States
ISBN 0-8160-3863-5   LC 99-54779
"Chronologically and historically arranged, this is a comprehensive reference source on the events, people, writings, speeches, chronology, debates, and all other aspects related to slavery in America." Book Rep

Segal, Ronald, 1932-
Islam's Black slaves; the other Black diaspora. Farrar, Straus & Giroux 2001 273p maps $25; pa $14   **326**
1. Slavery 2. Slave trade
ISBN 0-374-22774-8; 0-374-52797-0 (pa)
LC 00-62256
This book presents "an overview of black slavery in the Islamic world from its beginnings to modern Sudan

and Morocco. . . . [It] explores Islamic slavery in China, India, the Middle East, and Africa and focuses on the differences between Islamic and Western slavery." Libr J
"The strength of this account is the meticulous documentation of what is fact and what is surmise. The dramatic narrative is sure to spark discussion and further research." Booklist

327   International relations

Bobbitt, Philip
The shield of Achilles; war, peace, and the course of history. Knopf 2002 xxxii, 919p $40; pa $19.95   **327**
1. State, The 2. International relations 3. Peace 4. War
ISBN 0-375-41292-1; 0-385-72138-2 (pa)
LC 2001-38085
In this volume, Bobbitt presents "a history of diplomacy from 1500 to 1990; a theory of the history of the state; [and] an analysis of globalization. As he moves from the past into our current embrace of free-market ideology, Bobbitt introduces what he calls the 'market-state'—a new kind of government. . . . In the new 'market-state,' citizens transcend terrestrial borders and adhere to economic allegiances, rendered ever more fluid by the Internet." Christ Sci Monit
"This work will be a valuable and intriguing look at where we have been and where we might be going." Booklist
Includes bibliographical references

Nolan, Cathal J.
The Greenwood encyclopedia of international relations. Greenwood Press 2002 4v maps set $475   **327**
1. International relations—Encyclopedias
ISBN 0-313-30743-1   LC 2002-19495
This alphabetically arranged set covers the history of international relations in over 6,000 entries
This "work dwells primarily on the deeds of the great powers since the 1648 Peace of Westphalia. . . . Lively, objective writing characterizes the first-rate historical essays. . . . This work belongs in all academic and large public libraries." Libr J

327.12   Espionage and subversion

Burrows, William E.
By any means necessary; America's secret air war in the Cold War. Farrar, Straus & Giroux 2001 398p il $26   **327.12**
1. Cold war 2. American espionage 3. Aerial reconnaissance
ISBN 0-374-11747-0   LC 2001-23622
Also available in paperback from Plume Bks.
The author "tells the story of Cold War air reconnaissance with emphasis on the individuals involved, the sacrifices they made, and the way the U.S. government turned a blind eye to those who served. A fascinating book that public and academic libraries will want to purchase." Libr J
Includes bibliographical references

Dorril, Stephen

MI6; inside the covert world of Her Majesty's secret intelligence service. Free Press 2000 907p $40; pa $22 **327.12**
1. Great Britain. MI6 2. Intelligence service—Great Britain
ISBN 0-7432-0379-8; 0-7432-1778-0 (pa)
LC 00-29385
This study of the British secret intelligence service "focuses on the years since World War II, when MI6 was dedicated to winning the cold war. . . . The book is invaluable for readers who want to separate spy fact from spy fiction." Booklist

Garton Ash, Timothy

The file; a personal history. Random House 1997 262p hardcover o.p. paperback available $14 **327.12**
1. Germany (East). Ministerium für Staatssicherheit 2. Intelligence service—Germany (East)
ISBN 0-679-77785-7 (pa)
"The author went to Berlin to study in 1978 and soon came under the scrutiny of the Stasi, the notorious East German secret police. In 1993, Garton Ash had the opportunity to examine the secret file kept on him. Comparing the file reports with his private diary of the time, he finds distortions, fabrications, and surprising omissions in the file. . . . This work makes an important contribution to the literature of the new Europe." Libr J

Grose, Peter, 1934-

Operation Rollback; America's secret war behind the Iron Curtain. Houghton Mifflin 2000 256p il map $25; pa $15 **327.12**
1. Kennan, George Frost, 1904- 2. Cold war 3. United States—Foreign relations—Soviet Union 4. Soviet Union—Foreign relations—United States
ISBN 0-395-51606-4; 0-618-15458-2 (pa)
LC 99-89830
The author chronicles American efforts, spearheaded by George F. Kennan, to undermine Communist power in the decades after World War II
"Thorough, thought-provoking and entertaining, this is a work that casts considerable light on a topic that has long lingered in the shadows." Publ Wkly
Includes bibliographical references

Gup, Ted, 1950-

Book of honor; covert lives and classified deaths at the CIA. Doubleday 2000 390p il hardcover o.p. paperback available $15
327.12
1. United States. Central Intelligence Agency 2. Spies
ISBN 0-385-49541-2 (pa) LC 99-89017
This exposé "reveals the names—and personal stories—of some three dozen CIA agents who died in the line of duty and whose identities have been kept secret—sometimes for decades. . . . Gup's sleuthing is a remarkable coup, full of high-level intrigue, cover-ups and drama." Publ Wkly

Haynes, John Earl

Venona; decoding Soviet espionage in America; [by] John Earl Haynes and Harvey Klehr. Yale Univ. Press 1999 487p $35; pa $14.95 **327.12**
1. Communist Party (U.S.) 2. Russian espionage 3. Communism—United States
ISBN 0-300-07771-8; 0-300-08462-5 (pa)
LC 98-51464
"The Venona Project, a U.S. secret revealed only in 1995, decrypted Soviet intelligence's wartime cable traffic. . . . The authors systematically recount Venona's references to approximately 350 Soviet spies in U.S. government and industry—some of them highly placed, most notoriously Alger Hiss. . . . Venona may open a fundamental revision of U.S. history." Booklist

Herrington, Stuart A., 1941-

Traitors among us; inside the spy catcher's world. Presidio Press 1999 409p il o.p.; Harvest paperback available $14 **327.12**
1. Intelligence service—United States 2. Russian espionage
ISBN 0-15-601117-4 (pa) LC 99-13408
"Herrington, former head of the U.S. Army Counterintelligence Unit . . . offers a fascinating view of life as a spy catcher in West Berlin during the height of the Cold War. His description of the search for and capture of Clyde Conrad and James Hall . . . (who for 13 years handed over America's secret war plans to the Soviets) surpasses any spy fiction." Libr J

Kessler, Ronald

Inside the CIA; revealing the secrets of the world's most powerful spy agency. Pocket Bks. 1992 xxiii, 283p il hardcover o.p. paperback available $7.99 **327.12**
1. United States. Central Intelligence Agency 2. Intelligence service—United States
ISBN 0-671-73458-X (pa) LC 92-11084
"Writing with the cooperation of active and retired personnel, Kessler offers a working portrait of the contemporary CIA. His background in journalistic study of intelligence, augmented by an unusual array of other resources, enables him to provide an account unique for balance, perspective, clarity of writing, and the large amount of factual material." Booklist

Laird, Thomas

Into Tibet; the CIA's first atomic spy and his secret expedition to Lhasa. Grove Press 2002 364p il $26; pa $15 **327.12**
1. American espionage 2. United States—Foreign relations—China 3. China—Foreign relations—United States 4. Tibet (China)
ISBN 0-8021-1714-7; 0-8021-3999-X (pa)
LC 2001-58459
The author "traces the story of two CIA agents, Douglas Mackiernan and Frank Bessac, sent on an intelligence expedition to Tibet in 1949-1950. . . . Focusing on the heart-stopping details of the expedition itself, Laird gives the now familiar story of callous CIA manipulation an absorbing twist." Publ Wkly

Prados, John

Presidents' secret wars; CIA and Pentagon covert operations from World War II through the Persian Gulf. rev & expanded ed. Dee, I.R. 1996 572p pa $18.95 **327.12**
1. United States. Central Intelligence Agency 2. Intelligence service—United States
ISBN 1-56663-108-4   LC 95-49737
"An Elephant paperback"
First published 1986
The author argues that presidents have too much freedom of action in covert operations, and discusses such operations with regard to the Cold War, Asia, Cuba, Vietnam, Angola, Afghanistan, Nicaragua, and the Persian Gulf
Includes bibliographical references

Richelson, Jeffrey

The wizards of Langley; inside the CIA's Directorate of Science and Technology; [by] Jeffrey T. Richelson. Westview Press 2001 386p il hardcover o.p. paperback available $17 **327.12**
1. United States. Central Intelligence Agency. Directorate of Science and Technology
ISBN 0-8133-4059-4 (pa)
One of the three main divisions of the CIA, "the Directorate of Science and Technology, was created in 1963, and Richelson offers this chronological narrative of its leaders and known activities. The text is peppered with code names as Richelson tracks the course of projects, such as the U-2 and its successors in the overhead reconnaissance role, spy satellites. Alongside stories of the CIA's fencing with the military over the years for operational control of these expensive spacecraft, Richelson relates specific international incidents in which satellite-gathered intelligence figured, as well as the stories of sundry eavesdropping technologies." Booklist
The author "provides a richly detailed account of the agency's work." Libr J

Stober, Dan

A convenient spy; Wen Ho Lee and the politics of nuclear espionage; [by] Dan Stober and Ian Hoffman. Simon & Schuster 2001 384p il $26 **327.12**
1. Lee, Wen Ho 2. Los Alamos National Laboratory 3. Espionage
ISBN 0-7432-2378-0   LC 2001-54945
The authors discuss the case of Wen Ho Lee, a computer scientist at the Los Alamos National Laboratory, who was suspected of spying for China and "was indicted on 59 charges. . . . [Eventually], Mr Lee pleaded guilty to a single count of using an unsecured computer to download a classified document. The sentence was cancelled out by the time he had already served." Economist
"The authors, in ably untangling a tale with endless twists and a dizzying cast of characters, illuminate issues far larger than the fate of the man at the center of this case." N Y Times Book Rev
Includes bibliographical references

Theoharis, Athan G.

Chasing spies; how the FBI failed in counterintelligence but promoted the politics of McCarthyism in the Cold War years; [by] Athan Theoharis. Dee, I.R. 2002 307p $27.50 **327.12**
1. United States. Federal Bureau of Investigation 2. Intelligence service—United States 3. United States—Politics and government—1945-
ISBN 1-56663-420-2   LC 2001-47399
The author "argues that Hoover's FBI was much more interested in promoting an anti-Communist agenda, which would enhance the credibility of the agency and its political influence, than in countering Soviet espionage. . . . Theoharis's book is an outstanding contribution to the growing historical literature on the Cold War and a potent warning to anyone who thinks we have heard the last word on the Cold War." Libr J
Includes bibliographical references

Trulock, Notra

Code name Kindred Spirit; inside the Chinese nuclear espionage scandal. Encounter Bks. 2002 xxi, 385p il $26.95 **327.12**
1. Lee, Wen Ho 2. Los Alamos National Laboratory—Security measures 3. Spies
ISBN 1-89355-451-1   LC 2002-67856
Trulock was the head of the Department of Energy's "intelligence office during the investigation into whether Los Alamos scientist Wen Ho Lee had given nuclear warhead secrets to China. . . . This detailed account reveals that the spy hunt didn't focus solely on Lee, or even on Los Alamos. . . . While he denies knowledge as to whether Lee 'did it,' the author drops hints that Lee and his wife may have been double agents. . . . He provides a unique look into the American intelligence community and an unsettling perspective on the lax attitude toward national security." Publ Wkly
Includes bibliographical references

Vise, David A.

The bureau and the mole; the unmasking of Robert Philip Hanssen, the most dangerous double agent in FBI history. Atlantic Monthly Press 2002 272p il $25; pa $14 **327.12**
1. Hanssen, Robert Philip 2. United States. Federal Bureau of Investigation 3. Espionage
ISBN 0-87113-834-4; 0-8021-3951-5 (pa)
          LC 2001-53872
"In February 2001, FBI special agent Bob Hanssen was arrested as a double agent for Russian intelligence in what turned out to be the biggest sellout of U.S. national security secrets in the long history of the bureau. . . . [The author] details how Hanssen did it and how he got caught." Booklist
Includes bibliographical references

Weinstein, Allen

The haunted wood; Soviet espionage in America—the Stalin era; [by] Allen Weinstein, Alexander Vassiliev. Random House 1999 xxviii, 402p il hardcover o.p. paperback available $23 **327.12**
1. Russian espionage 2. Spies 3. United States—History—1933-1945
ISBN 0-375-75536-5 (pa)   LC 98-11801
The authors examine "the espionage networks that Moscow created in the United States, especially after

Weinstein, Allen—*Continued*

Franklin Roosevelt's establishment of diplomatic relations with the USSR in 1934. From then until 1945, the Soviets amassed . . . information from agents and sources in a range of U.S. government agencies. . . . The information included diplomatic secrets and planning for the postwar period (particularly policy toward Germany and the USSR), U.S. industrial and military production, and, . . . the atom-bomb project." Natl Rev

"This is a relentlessly powerful book and an eye-openrer for all readers." Libr J

Includes bibliographical references

Wise, David, 1930-

Cassidy's run; the secret spy war over nerve gas. Random House 2000 228p il hardcover o.p. paperback available $15

327.12

1. Cassidy, Joseph Edward 2. United States. Federal Bureau of Investigation 3. Russian espionage

ISBN 0-8129-9263-6 (pa)   LC 99-15802

The "reconstruction of a hitherto unknown counterespionage case. Joseph Cassidy's double life began in August 1959. . . . For 20 years Cassidy, a master sergeant, worked for the United States during the day and pretended to work for the Soviet Union at night. . . . The F.B.I. decided to use this double agent to undermine the Soviet chemical weapons industry." N Y Times Book Rev

Spy: the inside story of how the FBI's Robert Hanssen betrayed America. Random House 2002 309p $24.95; pa $13.95 **327.12**

1. Hanssen, Robert Philip 2. United States. Federal Bureau of Investigation 3. Espionage

ISBN 0-375-50745-0; 0-375-75894-1 (pa)

LC 2002-31867

This book attempts to "unravel the mystery of how and why FBI staffer Robert Hanssen was able to sell secrets to the KGB for almost 22 years. . . . Wise presents a comprehensive portrait of Hanssen's life as a spy and the government's quest to uncover and prosecute him." Publ Wkly

"A relentless reporter and true expert on the world of spying, Wise recounts Hanssen's story and the hunt to catch him in precise, if sometimes overwhelming detail." N Y Times Book Rev

327.73   United States—Foreign relations

Bernstein, Richard

The coming conflict with China; [by] Richard Bernstein and Ross H. Munro. Knopf 1997 245p hardcover o.p. paperback available $13   **327.73**

1. United States—Foreign relations—China 2. China—Foreign relations—United States 3. China—Politics and government

ISBN 0-679-77662-1 (pa)   LC 96-44434

"The authors argue that China is no longer a strategic friend of the United States but a formidable enemy. China's intention to play a more active role in Asian affairs is presented here as a threat to U.S. political and economic interests." Libr J

"A controversial but effective critique." Booklist

Includes bibliographical references

Brands, H. W.

What America owes the world; the struggle for the soul of foreign policy. Cambridge Univ. Press 1998 335p $65; pa $23 **327.73**

1. United States—Foreign relations

ISBN 0-521-63031-2; 0-521-63968-9 (pa)

LC 97-38837

"With the end of the Cold War, a long time debate has been resumed between two schools of thought, the *exemplarists* and the *vindicators*. The former . . . contends that the US owes the world the example of a humane democratic and prosperous society. The vindicators go beyond example and, through active measures, coercion, and force, support what is right in the world. The literature offers examples of the two schools analyzed in Brands's intellectual history. . . . This is a valuable contribution to the intellectual history of American foreign policy." Choice

Includes bibliographical references

Cohen, Stephen F.

Failed crusade; America and the tragedy of post-Communist Russia. Norton 2000 304p hardcover o.p. paperback available $14.95

327.73

1. United States—Foreign relations—Russia 2. Russia (Federation)—Economic conditions

ISBN 0-393-32226-2 (pa)   LC 00-35501

"In part 1, Cohen describes the arrogant missionary crusade to impose U.S. political and economic institutions on the former Soviet Union. . . . Part 2 gathers 10 Cohen critiques of this American crusade published between 1992 and 1998. . . . In part 3, Cohen urges that the goal of U.S. policy should be to reduce the risk of nuclear disaster by stabilizing this giant nuclear power." Booklist

Encyclopedia of American foreign policy; studies of the principal movements and ideas; editors, Alexander DeConde [et al.] 2nd ed. Scribner 2002 3v set $400 **327.73**

1. United States—Foreign relations—Encyclopedias

ISBN 0-684-80657-6   LC 2001-49800

First published 1978

"General category coverage includes concepts and doctrines, policymaking, commerce and science, human rights and arms control. Specific articles cover topics ranging from anti-imperialism to environmental diplomacy, from refugee policies to terrorism and countermeasures." Publisher's note

For a review see: Booklist, May 15, 2002

Gates, Robert M.

From the shadows; the ultimate insider's story of five presidents and how they won the Cold War. Simon & Schuster 1996 604p il hardcover o.p. paperback available $16

327.73

1. Cold war 2. United States—Foreign relations—Soviet Union 3. Soviet Union—Foreign relations—United States

ISBN 0-684-83497-9 (pa)   LC 95-51704

"Gates chronicles the demise of Communism in Eastern Europe and the Soviet Union from the . . . perspective of someone who served during the Nixon through Bush administrations." Libr J

This is an "often entertaining, frequently self-serving but always thoughtful account of the United States' long

Gates, Robert M.—*Continued*
effort to contain the Soviet Union." N Y Times Book
Rev
Includes bibliographical references

Halberstam, David, 1934-
War in a time of peace; Bush, Clinton, and
the generals. Scribner 2001 543p $28; pa $16
327.73
1. Bush, George, 1924- 2. Clinton, Bill, 1946-
3. United States—Foreign relations 4. United States—
Politics and government—1989-
ISBN 0-7432-0212-0; 0-7432-2323-3 (pa)
LC 2001-38416
Halberstam examines "American foreign and military
policy in the 1990s—emphasizing the background, experience, and personalities of the key players." Christ Sci
Monit
"This is vintage Halberstam, combining sharp portraits
of the political players . . . with nuanced reportage of
the events they shape and are shaped by." Publ Wkly
Includes bibliographical references

Kagan, Robert
Of paradise and power; America and
Europe in the new world order. Knopf 2003
103p $18; pa $11   **327.73**
1. European Union 2. United States—Foreign relations—Europe 3. Europe—Foreign relations—United
States
ISBN 1-4000-4093-0; 1-4000-3418-3 (pa)
LC 2002-38549
Also available large print edition $20 (ISBN 0-375-
43291-4)
Published in the United Kingdom with title: Paradise
and power
"Kagan argues that the United States and Europe no
longer inhabit the same universe where power politics is
concerned. Power, then, lies at the heart of the transatlantic culture war. Americans have it—making them a
target and priming them to use it to address foreign
threats. Europeans don't have it, and, judging by their
trifling defense budgets, don't want it. Operating from a
@psychology of weakness,' says Kagan, Europeans place
their faith in diplomacy, international law, and international institutions—both to come to grips with the
Saddams of the world and to rein in what they see as the
excesses of the world's remaining superpower. It be-
hooves American officials to try to bridge this gap in
perspectives. This brilliant and controversial work belongs in all library collections." Libr J
Includes bibliographical references

Kissinger, Henry, 1923-
Diplomacy. Simon & Schuster 1994 912p
il maps hardcover o.p. paperback available
$22   **327.73**
1. Diplomacy 2. United States—Foreign relations
ISBN 0-671-51099-1 (pa)   LC 93-44001
Kissinger "draws lessons from the statecraft of Richelieu, Napoleon, Bismarck and Metternich, then . . . reap-
praises the foreign policy blunders and the failures of
moral nerve and vision that led in our century to the
mass carnage of two world wars, genocide, Cold War
and a nuclear arms race." Publ Wkly
"This is an important contribution to the theoretical
literature on foreign affairs and will also serve quite ably
as a one-volume synthesis of modern diplomatic history.
All libraries should have this impressive book." Libr J
Includes bibliographical references

Does America need a foreign policy?
towards a diplomacy for the 21st century.
Simon & Schuster 2001 318p maps $30; pa
$15   **327.73**
1. United States—Foreign relations
ISBN 0-684-85567-4; 0-684-85568-2 (pa)
LC 2001-20564
Also available large print edition $30 (ISBN 0-7432-
1227-4)
Kissinger "surveys Europe, Latin America, Asia, Africa and the Middle East, giving the historical context,
raising the issues in each region, and then searching out
some ideas on what a wise American policy would do
about them." Christ Sci Monit
Includes bibliographical references

LaFeber, Walter
The clash; a history of U.S.-Japan relations.
Norton 1997 xxii, 508p il maps hardcover
o.p. paperback available $16.95   **327.73**
1. United States—Foreign relations—Japan 2. Japan—Foreign relations—United States
ISBN 0-393-31837-0 (pa)   LC 96-48565
LaFeber presents an overview of U.S.-Japan relations
from the 1850s to the present. He argues that "amid all
the changes in the American-Japanese relationship, two
fundamental continuities persist: . . . different conceptions of capitalism and divergent approaches to China."
Booklist
Includes bibliographical references

Mann, Jim, 1946-
About face; a history of America's curious
relationship with China, from Nixon to
Clinton. Knopf 1999 433p il $30; pa $16
327.73
1. United States—Foreign relations—China 2. China—Foreign relations—United States
ISBN 0-679-45053-X; 0-679-76861-0 (pa)
LC 98-6285
The author contends that "the hallmark of the current
policy, which was originated by Richard Nixon and
reached its apogee under Jimmy Carter, is a preoccupation with the balance of power and . . . [a] lack of concern with China's domestic system or the human rights
of the Chinese people." New Repub
"Mann's descriptions of the behind-the-scenes jockey-
ing among U.S. policy makers—the micropolitics behind
the geopolitics—are so entertaining that his book will appeal to readers beyond foreign policy junkies." Publ
Wkly
Includes bibliographical references

Mead, Walter Russell
Special providence; American foreign
policy and how it changed the world. Knopf
2001 374p $30   **327.73**
1. United States—Foreign relations
ISBN 0-375-41230-1   LC 2001-33886
Also available in paperback from Routledge
"A Century Foundation book"
"Mead discerns several schools of thought that vie for
supremacy within the American diplomatic tradition:
Hamilton's preoccupation with commerce, Jefferson's
watchfulness over the Republic's founding principles,
Jackson's obsession with military strength, and Wilson's
pursuit of a just world order. The beneficial interplay of
these principles, says Mead, has yielded the most successful foreign policy in history. Largely celebratory and
sure to be controversial, this work belongs in all library
collections." Libr J

Moynihan, Daniel Patrick, 1927-2003
On the law of nations. Harvard Univ. Press
1990 211p $37; pa $10.95 **327.73**
1. International law 2. United States—Foreign relations
ISBN 0-674-63575-2; 0-674-63576-0 (pa)
LC 90-33227
"In the seven essays in this volume, Moynihan traces U.S. attitudes toward international law from the American Revolution to the current administration, and he makes a powerful argument for a return to the conventions of international behavior set out by Woodrow Wilson and the United Nations." Libr J

Nye, Joseph S., Jr.
The paradox of American power; why the world's only superpower can't go it alone; [by] Joseph S. Nye, Jr. Oxford Univ. Press 2002 222p $26; pa $13.95 **327.73**
1. Power (Social sciences) 2. United States—Foreign relations 3. International cooperation
ISBN 0-19-515088-0; 0-19-516110-6 (pa)
LC 2001-52369
The author "offers a prescription for America's new role in the world that calls for a broader, more responsible, and cooperative relationship with the rest of the world. . . . A very thoughtful look ahead at American power through this century." Booklist

Pillar, Paul R., 1947-
Terrorism and U.S. foreign policy. Brookings Institution Press 2001 272p $26.95 **327.73**
1. Terrorism 2. United States—Foreign relations
ISBN 0-8157-0004-0 LC 00-13070
This is an "analyses of current terrorist threats, the status of terrorism in world politics, counterterrorist tools available to the United States, state sponsors of terrorism, and how best to educate the public about terrorist threats and counterterrorism." Publisher's note
"Pillar is most useful when he shows that the disunity within the Muslim world indicates that any successful struggle against terrorism must include all kinds of dealmaking in order to play off groups and states against one another." N Y Times Book Rev
Includes bibliographical references

Schweizer, Peter, 1964-
Reagan's War; the epic story of his forty-year struggle and final triumph over Communism. Doubleday 2002 339p il $26 **327.73**
1. Cold war 2. United States—Foreign relations—Soviet Union 3. Soviet Union—Foreign relations—United States
ISBN 0-385-50471-3
Also available in paperback from Vintage Bks.
Schweizer examines "the origins of Ronald Reagan's vision of America, and [aims to] document his . . . belief in confronting the Soviet Union diplomatically, economically, and militarily. . . . Schweizer explores Reagan's involvement with anticommunist liberals in Hollywood and his role as a secret informer for the FBI. [He believes that] Reagan's outspoken criticism of détente in the late 1960s and his forceful advocacy for the overthrow of the USSR drew the attention of Soviet officials. . . . [Schweizer contends that as President, Reagan] mapped out and directed a campaign to bankrupt the Soviet Union and wage an economic and political war against Moscow." Publisher's note
Includes bibliographical references

Talbott, Strobe
The Russia hand; a memoir of presidential diplomacy. Random House 2002 478p il $29.95; pa $15.95 **327.73**
1. Clinton, Bill, 1946- 2. Yeltsin, Boris 3. United States—Foreign relations—Russia 4. Russia—Foreign relations—United States
ISBN 0-375-50714-0; 0-8129-6846-8 (pa)
LC 2001-48843
Talbott writes of his experiences as "President Bill Clinton's top adviser and operative for relations with the former Soviet Union. . . . 'The Russia Hand' recounts the major and minor crises over issues like the expansion of NATO, the removal of missiles from Ukraine, Western military action against the Bosnian Serbs, the . . . confrontation over Kosovo, the question of antimissile defense." N Y Times (Late N Y Ed)

Tuchman, Barbara Wertheim
Stilwell and the American experience in China, 1911-45; [by] Barbara W. Tuchman. Macmillan 1971 621p il maps o.p.; Grove Press paperback available $20 **327.73**
1. Stilwell, Joseph Warren, 1883-1946 2. United States—Foreign relations—China 3. China—Foreign relations—United States 4. World War, 1939-1945—China
ISBN 0-8021-3852-7 (pa)
Using the career of General "Vinegar Joe" Stilwell as a vehicle, this is a history of America's relations with China from the end of the Manchu Empire to the rise of Mao Tse-tung
Includes bibliographical references

328.73 The legislative process in the United States

Barone, Michael
The almanac of American politics; [by] Michael Barone and Grant Ujifusa. National Journal il maps $79.95; pa $59.95 **328.73**
1. United States. Congress 2. United States—Politics and government 3. Almanacs
ISSN 0362-076X
First published 1972 by Gambit. (2003 edition) Periodically revised
Subtitle and publisher vary
"The senators, the representatives and the governors; their records and elections results, their states and districts." Subtitle
"Provides essential data for the assessment of each representative and senator in Congress. Specifics include political background on the state or congressional district, biographies, voting records, group ratings (by such groups as Americans for Democratic Action and Americans for Constitutional Action), and recent election results. Provides information on the governor of each state. Arranged by state. Congressional district maps." Ref Sources for Small & Medium-sized Libr. 6th edition

Biographical directory of the American Congress, 1774-1996; the Continental Congress, September 5, 1774, to October 21, 1788, and the Congress of the United States, from the First through the 104th Congress, March 4, 1789, to January 3, 1997. CQ Staff Directories 1997 2108p il $295   **328.73**

1. United States. Congress 2. United States—Biography—Dictionaries
ISBN 0-87289-124-0

First published 1869 with title: Dictionary of the United States congress

This directory provides brief biographies of members of Congress from the Continental Congress through the 104th Congress. Each entry includes date and place of birth, education and employment, some entries also give additional biographical references

This edition "like its predecessors, will continue to be an indispensable reference tool for students and scholars of U.S. history and politics. . . . It is the most comprehensive biographical source on congressional members." Am Ref Books Annu, 1998

Broder, David S.
Democracy derailed; initiative campaigns and the power of money. Harcourt 2000 260p map hardcover o.p. paperback available $14   **328.73**

1. Referendum 2. Democracy 3. United States—Politics and government
ISBN 0-15-601410-6 (pa)   LC 99-54190
"A James H. Silberman book"

"The initiative process, available in half the states and hundreds of cities, allows for the placement on election ballots of legislative proposals that emanate directly from sources outside the legislative branch of government. . . . {The author explores how} lawyers, campaign consultants, signature-gathering firms, and other players sell their services to affluent interest groups or wealthy individuals who mask private policy and business agendas under the guise of political reform." Libr J

Includes bibliographical references

Congress A to Z; David R. Tarr, Ann O'Connor, editors. 4th ed. CQ Press 2003 605p il (CQ's American government A to Z series) $125   **328.73**

1. United States. Congress
ISBN 1-56802-800-8   LC 2003-14802
First published 1988

This work provides information on the structure and work of Congress in some 250 alphabetical entries. "Entries range from short definitions to a series of core essays exploring the legislative process, the seniority system, the committee system, the budget process, and other broad areas." Publisher's note

"This volume is an excellent example of . . . readable, accessible, comprehensive, and unbiased coverage of American politics. . . . This is perhaps the best one-volume reference work on the U.S. Congress." Am Ref Books Annu, 2000

Includes bibliographical references

Congress and the Nation; a review of government and politics. Congressional Quarterly 1965-2002 10v il maps v1-8 op; v9-10 ea $260   **328.73**

1. United States. Congress 2. Legislation 3. United States—Politics and government—20th century

Contents: v1 1945-1964 (ISBN 0-87187-294-3); v2 1965-1968 (ISBN 0-87187-004-5); v3 1969-1972 (ISBN 0-87187-055-X); v4 1973-1976 (ISBN 0-87187-112-2); v5 1977-1980 (ISBN 0-87187-216-1); v6 1981-1984 (ISBN 0-87187-334-6); v7 1985-1988 (ISBN 0-87187-532-2); v8 1989-1992 (ISBN 0-87187-789-9); v9 1993-1996 (ISBN 1-56802-240-9); v10 1997-2001 (ISBN 1-56808-624-2)

"Overview and detailed coverage of presidential, legislative, and political events in every major subject area." N Y Public Libr Book of How & Where to Look It Up

CQ almanac plus. CQ Press $370   **328.73**

1. United States. Congress 2. United States—Politics and government 3. Almanacs
ISSN 0095-6007

Annual. First published 1945. Variant titles: Congressional Quarterly almanac, CQ almanac

"Each volume offers a summary of congressional legislation for one session of Congress . . . . Divided into sections dealing with categories of legislation (e.g., economics and finance, law and judiciary, defense), each section subdivided by specific topics. Includes voting information on individual measures and several useful appendixes. . . . Bill number, roll-call vote, and general indexes." Guide to Ref Books. 11th edition

CQ's politics in America. CQ Press il maps $115; pa $75   **328.73**

1. United States. Congress 2. Elections—United States

Biennial. First published 1981

Current editors: David J. Hawkings and Brian Nutting; Hardcover edition includes free access to online versions and updates

Profiles each current member of Congress, providing political background, statistical information, committee assignments, etc.

Guide to Congress. CQ Press 2v il set $315   **328.73**

1. United States. Congress

First published 1971 with title: Congressional Quarterly's guide to the Congress of the United States. (5th edition 1999) Periodically revised

"Covers history and workings of Congress, with biographical data on all members." N Y Public Libr Book of How & Where to Look It Up

United States. Congress
Official Congressional directory. U.S. Govt. Ptg. Office $48, pa $36   **328.73**

1. United States. Congress
ISSN 0160-9890
Biennial

"Covers biographical information, committee assignments of members of Congress, and officers of Congress." N Y Public Libr Book of How & Where to Look It Up

Will, George F.

Restoration; Congress, term limits, and the recovery of deliberative democracy. Free Press 1992 260p maps hardcover o.p. paperback available $17.95   **328.73**
1. United States. Congress 2. Politics 3. United States—Politics and government
ISBN 0-02-934713-0 (pa)   LC 92-26005
In this book Will argues that "the tireless quest to hang on to office has left individual members of both parties dependent on pleasing special interests, which has all but robbed Congress of any larger notion of the public good. . . . Term limits, Will says, can help restore public faith, deliberative democracy, and congressional supremacy." New Repub
Includes bibliographical references

330   Economics

Galbraith, John Kenneth, 1908-

The affluent society. 4th ed. Houghton Mifflin 1984 xxxvii, 291p hardcover o.p. paperback available $14   **330**
1. Economics 2. United States—Economic conditions—20th century
ISBN 0-395-92500-2 (pa)   LC 84-12880
First published 1958
The author surveys the economic upheavals that have changed the economic climate of the world. He also discusses the proper goals and management of a modern society and the question of how the production and distribution of wealth should be organized
Includes bibliographical references

Sowell, Thomas, 1930-

Basic economics; a citizen's guide to the economy. Basic Bks. 2001 366p $32.50 **330**
1. Economics
ISBN 0-465-08138-X   LC 00-44420
"Sowell covers a broad range of topics, from scarcity, the balance of trade, and price controls to minimum-wage laws, competition, profits and losses, and the role of government." Libr J
Includes bibliographical references

Wheelan, Charles J.

Naked economics; undressing the dismal science; [by] Charles Wheelan; foreword by Burton G. Malkiel. Norton 2002 xxii, 260p $25.95; pa $15.95   **330**
1. Economics
ISBN 0-393-04982-5; 0-393-32486-9 (pa)
LC 2002-23580
The author explains the essentials of economics, defining "terms like GDP and inflation, explaining how they work and what the short- and long-term impact might be. . . . This is a thoughtful, well-written introduction to economics, with the author projecting a genuine excitement for his material." Libr J
Includes bibliographical references

330.1   Economic systems, schools, theories

Friedman, Milton, 1912-

Free to choose; a personal statement; [by] Milton & Rose Friedman. Harcourt Brace Jovanovich 1980 338p hardcover o.p. paperback available $15   **330.1**
1. Capitalism 2. United States—Economic conditions 3. Public welfare
ISBN 0-15-633460-7 (pa)   LC 79-1821
The authors "paint a picture in which a marketplace sensitive to the people's wants and needs is frustrated by governmental interference, extreme government costs, and governmentally induced inflation. . . . Citing sociological and economic laws, the Friedmans set out to prove that the harder a nation tries to control capitalism, the worse things get." Libr J
Includes bibliographical references

Greider, William

The soul of capitalism; opening paths to a moral economy. Simon & Schuster 2003 366p $28   **330.1**
1. Capitalism
ISBN 0-684-86219-0   LC 2003-53007
"The purpose of the book is to examine . . . how and why our brilliant economic system collides with society's broader aspirations as the author observes the lack of personal fulfillment in many people in spite of material affluence." Booklist
This is "a bold and ambitious attempt to remedy the lack of vision that has plagued the American left since the decline of New Deal liberalism. . . . For anyone interested in serious economic and social reform, his effort is worth reading." N Y Times Book Rev
Includes bibliographical references

Heilbroner, Robert L.

The worldly philosophers; the lives, times, and ideas of the great economic thinkers. Simon & Schuster pa $16   **330.1**
1. Economists 2. Economics
First published 1953. (7th edition 1999). Periodically revised
The author traces the story of economics and the great economists from Adam Smith, Malthus, Ricardo, the Utopians, Marx, Veblen and Keynes to those working with the problems of our contemporary world
Includes bibliographical references

Keynes, John Maynard, 1883-1946

The general theory of employment, interest and money. Harcourt Brace & Co. 1936 403p hardcover o.p. paperback available $15
330.1
1. Economics 2. Money 3. Interest (Economics)
ISBN 0-15-634711-3 (pa)
Also available in paperback from Prometheus Bks.
This work "revolutionized economic theory by showing how unemployment could occur 'involuntarily'. For 30 years after the Second World War governments of western nations pursued 'Keynesian' full-employment policies." Oxford Companion to Engl Lit. 5th edition

Marx, Karl, 1818-1883
Capital; a critique of political economy 3v
330.1
1. Capital 2. Economics
Hardcover and paperback editions available from various publishers
Edited by Friedrich Engels
Contents: v1 The process of capitalist production; v2 The process of circulation of capital; v3 The process of capitalist production as a whole
"A systematic critical study of capitalist economy by Karl Marx, based on the ideas which he formulated, with Friedrich Engels, in 'The Communist Manifesto,' the first volume appeared in 1867; The second and third volumes were completed by Engels from Marx's notes (1885-1894)." Benet's Reader's Ency. 4th edition

McMillan, John, 1951-
Reinventing the bazaar; a natural history of markets. Norton 2002 278p $25.95; pa $15.95
330.1
1. Capitalism
ISBN 0-393-05021-1; 0-393-32371-4 (pa)
LC 2002-521
The author "examines how markets in ancient times evolved and shows how countries experimented with markets, some successfully and some not. . . . He takes a refreshingly commonsense approach to his subject, doesn't talk down to his readers, and refrains from excessive economic jargon." Libr J
Includes bibliographical references

Smith, Adam, 1723-1790
The wealth of nations   **330.1**
1. Economics
Hardcover and paperback editions available from various publishers
First published 1776
Variant title: An inquiry into the nature and causes of the wealth of nations
This treatise "is the first comprehensive treatment of the whole subject of political economy, and is remarkable for its breadth of view. . . . [In it, the author presents an] attack on the mercantile system, and an advocacy of freedom of commerce and industry." Oxford Companion to Engl Lit. 6th edition

Soto, Hernando de
The mystery of capital; why captitalism triumphs in the West and fails everywhere else. Basic Bks. 2000 276p il $27.50; pa $17
330.1
1. Capitalism
ISBN 0-465-01614-6; 0-465-01615-4 (pa)
LC 00-34301
The author contends that "the poor do not really 'own' the property they work, because they are not registered as owning it, and because of this, they cannot turn it into capital. . . . The market is restricted and the growth of wealth retarded. His solution is simple: give the poor title to the property they own de facto, and their countries will become capital rich." N Y Times Book Rev

330.9 Economic situation and conditions

Fukuyama, Francis
Trust; the social virtues and the creation of prosperity. Free Press 1995 458p hardcover o.p. paperback available $16   **330.9**
1. Economics 2. International economic relations
ISBN 0-684-82525-2 (pa)   LC 95-19320
The author "compares how selected modern economies organize themselves, and he argues that these same societies depend on 'civil society' and the creation and maintenance of 'social capital' for their vitality and economic success. By social capital he means the set of intermediate institutions, such as businesses, unions, and voluntary organizations (churches, charities, clubs) that facilitate trust beyond the more traditional family oriented structures to socialize people into their culture and transmit both knowledge and values. . . . Fukuyama proposes that natural cultural laws are important determinants of a nation's wealth. This stimulating, well-documented volume will be widely read and discussed." Choice
Includes bibliographical references

331 Labor economics

Lichtenstein, Nelson
State of the Union: a century of American labor. Princeton Univ. Press 2002 336p il (Politics and society in twentieth-century America) hardcover o.p. paperback available $18.95   **331**
1. Labor—United States 2. Labor unions
ISBN 0-691-11654-7 (pa)   LC 2001-36863
The author "analyzes the history of the labor movement from the 1930's to the present in the context of U.S. economics, politics, and democracy and from this he formulates ideas about where labor may find opportunities in this new century." Libr J
Includes bibliographical references

Murolo, Priscilla, 1949-
From the folks who brought you the weekend; a short, illustrated history of labor in the United States; [by] Priscilla Murolo and A.B. Chitty; illustrations by Joe Sacco. New Press (NY) 2001 xx, 364p hardcover o.p. paperback available $17.95   **331**
1. Labor—United States 2. Working class 3. Labor movement
ISBN 1-56584-776-8 (pa)   LC 2001-30978
This is a "history of labor in America, starting with the arrival of Columbus in 1492 and ending with the election of George Walker Bush to be the 43rd President of the United States." Libr J
"Brandishing little-known facts, the authors reshape common views of social history." Publ Wkly
Includes bibliographical references

Murray, R. Emmett
The lexicon of labor; a glossary of more then 500 key terms, biographical sketches, and historical hightlights concering labor in America. New Press (NY) 1998 208p il pa $14.95 **331**
1. Labor—United States—Dictionaries
ISBN 1-56584-456-4   LC 98-12783
This is an "encyclopedia of 500 entries for terms, concepts, people, legislation, places, and events in U.S. labor history." Booklist
Includes bibliographical references

331.2   Conditions of employment

Shulman, Beth
The betrayal of work; how low-wage jobs fail 30 million Americans and their families. New Press (NY) 2003 255p $25.95   **331.2**
1. Minimum wage 2. Labor—United States 3. Work 4. United States—Economic conditions
ISBN 1-56584-733-4   LC 2003-43413
The author "analyzes one of the downsides of the 'new economy': the large number of American jobs that pay poverty-level wages, have few or no benefits, and create childcare nightmares." Libr J
Includes bibliographical references

Terkel, Studs, 1912-
Working; people talk about what they do all day and how they feel about what they do. Pantheon Bks. 1974 xlix, 589p o.p.; New Press (NY) paperback available $13   **331.2**
1. Labor—United States 2. Work 3. United States—Social conditions
ISBN 1-56584-342-8 (pa)
Based on interviews, this study describes the working lives and feelings of people engaged in occupations ranging from interstate truck driver to stockbroker to bookbinder to corporation president
This "is not a dry, academic treatise but a sensitive portrayal of the experience of working, with all its pain, tension, frustrations, and occasional satisfactions." Best Sellers

331.3   Workers by age group

Levine, Marvin J., 1930-
Children for hire; the perils of child labor in the United States. Praeger Pubs. 2003 233p $49.95   **331.3**
1. Child labor   2. Youth—Employment 3. Teenagers—Employment
ISBN 1-56720-433-3   LC 2002-29767
The author defines the problem of child labor and "analyzes the working conditions of people under 18, the legal context for their employment and exploitation, and the impact of such labor upon the education and development of America's young people. An important work about a hidden social problem." Libr J
Includes bibliographical references

331.4   Women workers

America's working women; a documentary history, 1600 to the present; edited by Rosalyn Baxandall and Linda Gordon, with Susan Reverby. rev and updated. Norton 1995 356p il hardcover o.p. paperback available $16.95   **331.4**
1. Women—Employment—History
ISBN 0-393-31262-3 (pa)   LC 94-32194
First published 1976 by Random House
"This chronologically arranged anthology presents an . . . overview of the changing roles and contributions of woman at home, in the fields, and in today's workplace." Booklist
Includes bibliographical references

Global woman; nannies, maids, and sex workers in the new economy; Barbara Ehrenreich and Arlie Russell Hochschild, editors. Metropolitan Bks. 2003 328p $25   **331.4**
1. Women—Employment 2. Women—Developing countries 3. Women—Social conditions
ISBN 0-8050-6995-X   LC 2002-71912
This is "a series of articles on the consequences of globalization on the lives of millions of women . . . as they leave the poverty of Third World countries to seek employment in domestic services for affluent women in First World countries. . . . Also considered is the enormous rise in the sex trade, both voluntary and coerced. While immigrant domestic labor is nothing new, the various authors from academia and some with personal experience shed new light on this reality." Booklist
Includes bibliographical references

Kessler-Harris, Alice
Out to work; a history of wage-earning women in the United States. 20th anniversary ed. Oxford Univ. Press 2003 414p il pa $19.95   **331.4**
1. Women—Employment—History
ISBN 0-19-515709-5   LC 2003-267644
First published 1982
"This work remains a landmark in the field of analyzing the history of women's work in the United States from Colonial times to the Reagan era." Libr J
Includes bibliographical references

331.7   Labor by industry and occupation

America's fastest growing jobs. Jist Works pa $15.95   **331.7**
1. Occupations 2. Vocational guidance
Biennial. First published 1997 to replace America's 50 fastest growing jobs
"Updated every two years with data from the Labor Department, this handy source focuses on 141 of the fastest-growing occupations in the country. Featuring an easier-to-use A-Z format, the edition also includes Farr's excellent 32-page 'Quick Job Search' section as well as a chapter outlining recent career trends." Libr J [review of 2002 edition]

Boldt, Laurence G.

Zen and the art of making a living; a practical guide to creative career design. 2nd rev ed. Penguin Bks. 1999 li, 640p il pa $17.95   **331.7**

1. Vocational guidance

ISBN 0-14-019599-8   LC 98-55070

First published 1992 by Lightning Press with title: Zen and the art of making a living in the post-modern world

This "career development guide helps the reader identify 'work purpose,' key talents, and objectives. . . . Boldt moves beyond the basics to address unusual practical and psychological issues such as starting a business, freelancing, founding a nonprofit corporation, maintaining a healthy self-esteem, and building marketing strategy." Libr J

Includes bibliographical references

Bolles, Richard Nelson

What color is your parachute? a practical manual for job-hunters & career changers. Ten Speed Press il $27.95; pa $17.95 **331.7**

1. Applications for positions 2. Vocational guidance

Annual. First published 1973

"With a supplemental web site (www.job-huntersbible.com), this perennial best seller remains a self-assessment favorite, identifying techniques to determine mission in life, interest, and skills; describing interview questions and answers and salary negotiation strategies; and advising on locating employment. Includes workbook exercises, listings of counseling firms, and tips for choosing a counselor." Libr J

The **Encyclopedia** of careers and vocational guidance. Ferguson, J.G. 4v il set $199.95 **331.7**

1. Occupations 2. Vocational guidance

First published 1967. (12th edition 2002) Periodically revised. Editors vary

The first volume of this "reference provides articles on career preparation, the job search process, and industries, the remaining three volumes offer lengthy essays on . . . occupations arranged within . . . industry fields." Libr J

Guide for occupational exploration; [edited by] J. Michael Farr, LaVerne L. Ludden, Laurence Shatkin. 3rd ed. Jist Works 2001 xxii, 532p $49.95; pa $39.95 **331.7**

1. Occupations 2. Vocational guidance

ISBN 1-56370-826-4; 1-56370-636-9 (pa)

LC 2001-29100

First published 1979 by U.S. Govt. Ptg. Office

"Based on an outstanding 1970s Labor Department system that matches general interest and skills to job characteristics and career options, this revised edition, used for initial occupational investigation, builds on the original strengths to update and simplify the structure, with new job groupings and descriptions for more than 1000 jobs." Libr J

Includes bibliographical references

Krantz, Les

Job finder's guide; the only book you need to get the job you want; foreword by Tony Lee. 4th ed. Barricade Bks. 2002 539p pa $18.95   **331.7**

1. Job hunting 2. Corporations—Directories

ISBN 1-56980-223-8   LC 2002-26065

First published 1999 by St. Martin's Griffin to replace The World almanac job finder's guide

This book includes information on 3,000 U.S. employers, including 1,000 of the largest corporations, their addresses, phone numbers, etc. plus ratings of how likely they are to be hiring. Also provides information about going on-line to find a job with facts on the Internet and tips on writing effective cover letters and resumes, as well as how to interview and negotiate your salary

Jobs rated almanac; the best and worst jobs—250 in all—ranked by more than a dozen vital factors, including salary, stress, benefits, and more. Barricade Bks. pa $14.95 **331.7**

1. Occupations 2. Vocational guidance

First published 1988 by World Almanac (6th edition 2002) Periodically revised. Title varies

This "describes and ranks 250 jobs on the basis of current salary and future prospects, stress factors, environmental conditions, career outlook, and safety and security issues." Libr J

O*NET dictionary of occupational titles. Jist Works 2001 pa $39.95 **331.7**

1. Occupations   LC 2001-38356

First published 1998 to replace Dictionary of occupational titles published by the government Printing Office. Frequently revised

"Based on information obtained from the U.S. Department of Labor, the U.S. Census Bureau, and other reliable sources"

"Developed under the direction of J. Michael Farr and LaVerne L. Ludden, Ed.D., with database work by Laurence Shatkin, Ph.D"

"This print version of the U.S. Department of Labor's O*NET OnLine (online.onetcenter.org) database is designed to replace the older and lengthier *Dictionary of Occupational Titles*. In addition to the standard occupational classification titles and codes, it offers detailed information on earnings, education, job growth, skills required, and related jobs." Libr J

United States. Bureau of Labor Statistics

Occupational outlook handbook. U.S. Govt. Ptg. Office il $57; pa $53 **331.7**

1. Occupations 2. Vocational guidance

Also available Occupational outlook handbook and Career guide to industries on CD-ROM

Biennial. First published 1949. Supplemented by Occupational Outlook Quarterly, subscription $15

"Gives information on employment trends and outlook in more than 800 occupations. Indicates nature of work, qualifications, earnings and working conditions, how to enter, where to go for more information, etc." Guide to Ref Books. 11th edition

VGM's careers encyclopedia; [by] the editors of VGM Career Books. 5th ed. VGM Career Bks. 2001 449p $39.95 **331.7**

1. Vocational guidance 2. Occupations

ISBN 0-658-01653-9   LC 2001-33252

First published 1980

This volume provides descriptions of over 200 careers. Each entry presents information on job outlook, educational requirements, training, income, work setting, opportunities for advancement and sources for further research

331.8 Labor unions and labor-management relations

Dubofsky, Melvyn, 1934-
Labor in America; a history; [by] Melvyn Dubofsky, Foster Rhea Dulles. Davidson, H. il pa $27.95   **331.8**
1. Labor—United States 2. Working class 3. Labor unions
First published 1949 by Crowell under the authorship of Foster Rhea Dulles. (6th edition 1999) Periodically revised
A study of the social and political impact of the American labor movement since colonial times
Includes bibliographical references

Historical encyclopedia of American labor; edited by Robert Weir and James P. Hanlan. Greenwood Press 2003 2v set $175   **331.8**
1. Labor—United States—Encyclopedias 2. Labor movement—Encyclopedias
ISBN 0-313-31840-9   LC 2003-52847
This "encyclopedia includes approximately 400 entries designed for the general researcher, students, and lay readers interested in learning more about such topics as unions, union leaders, union history, important laws and court cases, and labor terminology. An appendix contains excerpts from over 50 primary documents." Libr J

St. James encyclopedia of labor history worldwide; major events in labor history and their impact; with introductions by Willie Thompson and Daniel Nelson; Neil Schlager, editor; produced by Schlager Groups. St. James Press 2003 2v set $260   **331.8**
1. Labor movement—Encyclopedias
ISBN 1-558-62542-9   LC 2003-294
This set offers an "analysis of more than 300 key events in labor history over the last 200 years, focusing on the relevance of these events to both the labor movement as a whole and to societal changes around the world. Each entry . . . is three to five pages in length and includes a description of the event, information about the key players involved and discusses the event in historical context." Publisher's note
"This reference promises to fill an important niche for larger public and academic libraries." Libr J

Stepan-Norris, Judith, 1957-
Left out; Reds and America's industrial unions; [by] Judith Stepan-Norris, Maurice Zeitlin. Cambridge Univ. Press 2002 375p $75; pa $27   **331.8**
1. Labor unions—United States 2. Labor—United States
ISBN 0-521-79212-6; 0-521-79840-X (pa)
LC 2001-37655
"In 1947, ten 'Communist-dominated unions' were expelled from the CIO. The mythology that developed is that these unions sacrificed the interests of the American worker to the foreign policy dictates of the Statlin-era Soviet Union. The authors, both sociologists, use statistical analysis of contracts to argue that these unions actually had the most democracy, the most pro-labor contracts, and the best track record in fighting for gender and racial equality in the labor movement." Libr J
Includes bibliographical references

Zieger, Robert H.
American workers, American unions; the twentieth century; [by] Robert H. Zieger & Gilbert J. Gall. 3rd ed. Johns Hopkins Univ. Press 2002 292p (The American moment) pa $17.95   **331.8**
1. Labor unions 2. Labor—United States
ISBN 0-8018-7078-X   LC 2002-3250
First published 1986
This is a "history of American workers and their unions in twentieth-century America." Publisher's note
"This standard work of American labor history from the Gilded Age onward has been updated to almost the present, with the last paragraph discussing September 11. Zieger's strength lies in his striving for a balanced survey." Libr J
Includes bibliographical references

332.024 Personal finance

Glink, Ilyce R., 1964-
50 simple things you can do to improve your personal finances; how to spend less, save more, and make the most of what you have. Three Rivers Press (NY) 2001 222p pa $14   **332.024**
1. Personal finance
ISBN 0-8129-2742-7   LC 00-66675
The author gives advice on such topics as personal budgets and savings, credit and debt, investments, insurance, taxes, marriage, partnerships and children, and retirement planning

Miller, Ted
Kiplinger's practical guide to your money; keep more of it, make it grow, enjoy it, protect it, pass it on. Kiplinger Bks. 2002 567p il pa $18.95   **332.024**
1. Personal finance
ISBN 0-938721-93-3   LC 2002-16041
First published 1998
The author offers advice on such topics as budgets, cash-flow, savings, credit, banking, buying, selling, renting and insuring a home, buying and insuring a car, financial aspects of marriage and divorce, paying for college, funerals, and the care of aging parents, investments, taxes, insurance, retirement, and estate planning

Quinn, Jane Bryant
Making the most of your money. Simon & Schuster 1997 1066p il $30   **332.024**
1. Personal finance 2. Investments
ISBN 0-684-81176-6   LC 97-23183
First published 1991
"Completely revised and updated for the twenty-first century"
This guide includes information about investing, buying a home, life and health insurance, retirement planning, checklists for life changes, finding a financial advisor, and financing college

Schwab-Pomerantz, Carrie

It pays to talk; how to have the essential conversations with your family about money and investing; [by] Carrie Schwab-Pomerantz and Charles R. Schwab. Crown Business 2003 386p il $24.95; pa $14   **332.024**

1. Personal finance 2. Investments
ISBN 0-609-61028-7; 1-4000-4960-1 (pa)
     LC 2002-5994

The authors "share their insights on money, investing and the conversations that need to accompany these. Their focus is on the importance of conducting different lifestage conversations (e.g., how to financially approach being single, getting married, raising children, helping parents), and this . . . primer provides one-stop shopping for the many phases of financial understanding and planning. . . . This educational volume provides a useful framework that a family can refer to when approaching those often difficult but necessary conversations about finances." Publ Wkly

Includes bibliographical references

Tobias, Andrew P.

The only investment guide you'll ever need; [by] Andrew Tobias. Harcourt 2002 266p pa $14   **332.024**

1. Investments 2. Personal finance
ISBN 0-15-601107-7   LC 2002-279917
"A Harvest original"
First published 1987 by Simon & Schuster
"Expanded and updated throughout"
"How to manage your money in today's economy." Cover

This offers advice on such topics as personal investments, tax strategies, life insurance, stock market trading, college funds, real estate, and inheritance

Wolman, William

The great 401(k) hoax; why your family's financial security is at risk, and what you can do about it; [by] William Wolman and Anne Colamosca. Perseus Bks. 2002 246p il $26; pa $17.50   **332.024**

1. Personal finance 2. Retirement 3. 401(k) plan
ISBN 0-7382-0635-0; 0-7382-0852-3 (pa)
     LC 2002102640

This is a "critical examination of the 401(k) and its role in retirement funding. . . . The authors suggest that people should now pay less attention to Wall Street hype, consider the accounting practices used to compile financial reports, and diversify by investing in stock index funds, bonds, and government securities, and they offer other useful suggestions for improving their situations. This timely and thought-provoking book by a well-known and highly respected economist and journalist offers a concise overview of the financal times we live in." Libr J

Includes bibliographical references

332.1   Banks

Greider, William

Secrets of the temple; how the Federal Reserve runs the country. Simon & Schuster 1987 798p hardcover o.p. paperback available $19   **332.1**

1. Federal Reserve System (U.S.). Board of Governors 2. Banks and banking—United States 3. Monetary policy—United States
ISBN 0-671-67556-7 (pa)   LC 87-16712

An investigation of the structure and influence of the Federal Reserve System during the Reagan era

"This well-researched study, with its lively style, will certainly provide fuel for the conspiracy theorists but also sheds much-needed light on an often-baffling institution." Booklist

Includes bibliographical refernces

Mayer, Martin, 1928-

The Fed; the inside story of how the world's most powerful financial institution drives the market. Free Press 2001 350p $27.50; pa $15   **332.1**

1. Greenspan, Alan 2. Federal Reserve System (U.S.). Board of Governors 3. Monetary policy—United States
ISBN 0-684-84740-X; 0-452-28341-8 (pa)
     LC 2001-23250

The author "traces the evolution of the Federal Reserve from a sleepy regulatory agency to the most powerful economic institution in the world." Publ Wkly

"Mayer's well-written account helps to . . . demystify the Fed and makes us understand how important its role is in our lives." Libr J

Includes bibliographical references

Meltzer, Allan H.

A history of the Federal Reserve; with a foreword by Alan Greenspan. v1: 1913-1951. University of Chicago Press 2002 800p $75; pa $25   **332.1**

1. Federal Reserve System (U.S.). Board of Governors 2. Federal Reserve banks
ISBN 0-226-51999-6; 0-226-52000-5 (pa)
     LC 2002-72007

First volume of a projected two volume work

The author "provides a definitive history of the U.S. Federal Reserve from its founding in 1913 to its establishment as a separate, independent entity in 1951. Using meeting minutes, correspondence, and internal Federal Reserve documents, he traces the reasons behind Federal Reserves policy decisions, highlights the impact that individuals and events had on the Fed, and examines the Fed's influence on international affairs. . . . This well-written and thoroughgoing account is recommended for academic, business, and public libraries." Libr J

Includes bibliographical references

Woodward, Bob, 1943-

Maestro: Greenspan's Fed and the American boom. Simon & Schuster 2000 270p il $25; pa $14 **332.1**
1. Greenspan, Alan 2. Federal Reserve System (U.S.). Board of Governors 3. Monetary policy—United States
ISBN 0-7432-0412-3; 0-7432-0562-6 (pa)
LC 00-52627
The author discusses the influence exerted over the American economy by Alan Greenspan, chairman of the Federal Reserve Board
"In a surprisingly short book, Woodward lucidly explains the axes of intellectual and political disagreement over monetary policy, productivity growth, irrational exuberance and more, shedding new light on major conflicts of the Greenspan era and demystifying this most political of ostensibly technical institutions." N Y Times Book Rev
Includes bibliographical references

332.6 Investment and investments

Bernstein, William

The four pillars of investing; lessons for building a winning portfolio; [by] William J. Bernstein. McGraw-Hill 2002 316p il $27.95
332.6
1. Investments
ISBN 0-07-138529-0   LC 2002-726560
The author discusses "the four pillars—the theory of investing, the history of investing, the psychology of investing, and the business of investing. . . . Using humor, Bernstein advises readers to employ sound tenets of investing to manage risk while building a foundation of assests for the long term." Libr J
Includes bibliographical references

Carlson, Charles B.

The smart investor's survival guide; the nine laws of successful investing in a volatile market. Currency 2002 xxiii, 325p il $24.95; pa $14.95   **332.6**
1. Investments
ISBN 0-385-50387-3; 0-385-50402-0 (pa)
LC 2001-58289
"Carlson believes volatility or turbulence is here to stay and demonstrates to investors how to make it work to their advantage. . . The author discusses diversification within asset classes, across asset classes, and across time. A highlight of his work is the 'easy-hold' ratings on stocks and mutual funds." Booklist

Cramer, James J.

Confessions of a street addict. Simon & Schuster 2002 339p $26; pa $14   **332.6**
1. Wall Street (New York, N.Y.) 2. Stocks
ISBN 0-7432-2487-6; 0-7432-2488-4 (pa)
LC 2002-22902
The author "recounts his turbulent dual career as hedge fund manager and media pundit. . . . This is a lively, informative portrait of the highest levels of finance and media in the last decade." Publ Wkly

Downes, John

Barron's finance & investment handbook; {by} John Downes, Jordan Elliot Goodman. Barron's Educ. Ser. il $39.95   **332.6**
1. Personal finance 2. Investments   LC 98-36776
First published 1986. (6th edition 2003) Periodically revised
This handbook includes a "financial dictionary, an analysis of . . . key investment opportunities . . . explanations for laymen on how to read corporate reports and interpret financial news, and . . . {a} directory of . . . publicly traded corporations in the United States and Canada. Readers will also find the names and addresses of all brokerage and mutual funds firms, banks, savings and loan companies, insurance companies, federal and state regulations, and major investment publications." Publisher's note
Includes bibliographical references

Gardner, David

The Motley Fool's what to do with your money now; ten steps to staying up in a down market; [by] David and Tom Gardner. Simon & Schuster 2002 212p $23; pa $14
332.6
1. Investments 2. Personal finance
ISBN 0-7432-3378-6; 0-7432-3465-0 (pa)
LC 2002-21722
This title "focuses on how best to survive current economic uncertainty, secure personal finances, and fortify portfolios. . . . Throughout this relevant approach to financial management in today's down market, the crisp, upbeat narration . . . keeps listeners captivated." Libr J

Geisst, Charles R.

The last partnerships; inside the great Wall Street dynasties. McGraw-Hill 2001 338p $29.95; pa $16.95   **332.6**
1. Wall Street (New York, N.Y.)
ISBN 0-07-136999-6; 0-07-141317-0 (pa)
LC 2001-30374
A survey of the investment banking houses that helped finance America's growth with chapters on The Seligmans, Lehman Brothers, and Kuhn Loeb; Brown Brothers Harriman and August Belmont; Kidder Peabody and Dillon Read; J. P. Morgan and Morgan Stanley; Merrill Lynch and E. F. Hutton; Salomon Brothers and Drexel Burnham; and Goldman Sachs and Lazard Freres
Includes bibliographical references

Hagstrom, Robert G., 1956-

The Warren Buffett way; investment strategies of the world's greatest investor. Wiley 1994 274p il $24.95; pa $9.99 **332.6**
1. Buffett, Warren E. 2. Investments
ISBN 0-471-04460-1; 0-471-17750-4 (pa)
LC 94-20586
Hagstrom "describes the investment strategies and techniques used by Warren Buffett to realize . . . success as a professional investor. Aiming his analysis at the individual investor, Hagstrom reviews the influence of Buffett's mentors, Ben Graham and Philip Fisher, and . . . [discusses] Buffett's synthesis of their investment philosophies. Hagstrom provides case studies of Buffett's major investments, showing the qualities of the companies that had appeal." Libr J
Includes bibliographical references

Lewis, Michael

Liar's poker: rising through the wreckage on Wall Street. Norton 1989 249p o.p.; Penguin Bks. paperback available $14   **332.6**

1. Salomon Brothers Inc. 2. Wall Street (New York, N.Y.)

ISBN 0-14-014345-9 (pa)   LC 89-30819

"Lewis describes his four years with the Wall Street firm Salomon Brothers, from his bizarre hiring through the training program to his years as a successful bond trader." Libr J

"This is a story with much irony. Here is one of America's top investment banking and securities trading firms, an adviser to the largest corporations and money managers, unable to run itself. Its management style is one of warring individuals and factions." N Y Times Book Rev

Lutnick, Howard

On top of the world; Cantor Fitzgerald and 9/11: a story of loss and renewal; [by] Howard Lutnick and Tom Barbash. HarperCollins Pubs. 2002 282p il $25.95; pa $14.95   **332.6**

1. Cantor Fitzgerald LP 2. World Trade Center (New York, N.Y.) 3. September 11 terrorist attacks, 2001

ISBN 0-06-051029-3; 0-06-051030-7 (pa)

LC 2002-27550

The bond-trading firm Cantor Fitzgerald lost 658 employees on September 11, 2001. "'On Top of the World' sets out to tell the story of Cantor Fitzgerald's tragedy, and its survival, largely from its chairman's point of view; the book is interspersed with . . . passages in [Howard] Lutnick's own voice." N Y Times Book Rev

Lynch, Peter

One up on Wall Street; how to use what you already know to make money in the market; by Peter Lynch with John Rothchild. Simon & Schuster 1989 318p hardcover o.p. paperback available $14   **332.6**

1. Investments 2. Stocks 3. Speculation

ISBN 0-7432-0040-3 (pa)   LC 88-32741

The authors argue that "average investors can beat Wall Street professionals by using the information that they encounter in their everyday lives. . . . The book is also a primer on how the stock market works and is written in a light, entertaining style." Publ Wkly

Stern, Ken, 1965-

To hell and back; how I survived Wall Street's roller coaster and how you can too. Dearborn Trade 2002 231p pa $22   **332.6**

1. Investments 2. Stocks 3. Wall Street (New York, N.Y.)

ISBN 0-7931-4922-3   LC 2001-4680

The author "boils down the fundamentals of investing into nuggets of easy-to-grasp information. One example is a simple yet thorough explanation of the economy and the business cycle, along with key indicators. Another is his stock-picking tips, from comparisons (the right way) to classic mistakes." Booklist

332.7   Credit

Leonard, Robin

Credit repair; by Robin Leonard and Deanne Loonin; edited by Kathleen Michon. Nolo Press (Berkeley) pa $24.99   **332.7**

1. Consumer credit

First published 1996. (6th edition 2002) Periodically revised

This offers advice on assesssing your debt situation, avoiding overspending, handling existing debts, cleaning your credit file, how credit reports are used, and building and maintaining good credit

Includes bibliographical references

333.7   Natural resources and energy

Williams, Terry Tempest

Red: passion and patience in the desert. Pantheon Bks. 2001 258p $23   **333.7**

1. Natural history—Utah 2. Human ecology 3. Utah—Description

ISBN 0-375-42077-0   LC 2001-21456

This book is a "plea for preservation of the Colorado Plateau—the Four Corners region of Utah, Colorado, New Mexico, and Arizona—and more specifically the red rocks of Utah." Women's Rev Books

"Moving and provocative. William's compact book is essential for nature collections; also recommended for general collections." Libr J

333.79   Energy

Bryce, Robert

Pipe dreams; greed, ego, jealousy and the death of Enron. PublicAffairs 2002 394p il $27.50; pa $16   **333.79**

1. Enron Corp. 2. Business failures 3. Business—Corrupt practices

ISBN 1-58648-138-X; 1-58648-201-7 (pa)

LC 2002-31615

This is an account of the corrupt practices that led to the bankruptcy of the Enron Corporation

"All of the high-level players at Enron are profiled, and you get an excellent sense of their personalities and plenty of gossip. . . . Most importantly, Bryce unveils the intricate accounting schemes. . . . Bryce's account is a prime example of how greed, arrogance, and influence lead to corruption, deception, and ruin." Booklist

Includes bibliographical references

Cruver, Brian

Anatomy of greed; the unshredded truth from an Enron insider; foreword by Steve Salbu. Carroll & Graf Pubs. 2002 366p il $25; pa $14   **333.79**

1. Enron Corp. 2. Business failures 3. Business—Corrupt practices

ISBN 0-7867-1093-4; 0-7867-1205-8 (pa)

"Cruver was hired by Enron in late March 2001 to be part of a bankruptcy-trading group. Through Cruver, we see how a typical Enron employee viewed the company's dramatic collapse. . . . He writes with a wry sense of humor. . . . Cruver's fast-paced book puts a human face on the many employees hurt by the Enron and similar scandals." Libr J

Kryza, Frank, 1950-
The power of light; the epic story of man's quest to harness the sun. McGraw-Hill 2003 298p il map $24.95   **333.79**
1. Solar energy
ISBN 0-07-140021-4   LC 2003-545270
This is a history of solar energy technology from the 19th century to the present, discussing the work of such scientists as Frank Shuman, Augustin Mouchot, William Adams, and Aubrey Eneas
Includes bibliographical references

333.8   Subsurface resources

Rifkin, Jeremy
The hydrogen economy; the creation of the worldwide energy web and the redistribution of power on earth. Tarcher/Putnam 2002 294p $24.95   **333.8**
1. Hydrogen as fuel 2. Globalization
ISBN 1-58542-193-6   LC 2002-25370
The author's "basic premise is that the world must switch from a fossil-fuel economy to a hydrogen economy. . . . Detailing the shortcomings of traditional energy sources in light of possible terrorist attacks, Rifkin then covers the merits of hydrogen as a 'forever fuel' and offers his own vision of a social revolution that he calls worldwide hydrogen energy web (HEW). . . . This will be a welcome addition to most academic and larger public library collections." Libr J
Includes bibliographical references

333.91   Water

Barlow, Maude
Blue gold: the fight to stop the corporate theft of the world's water; [by] Maude Barlow, Tony Clarke. New Press 2002 278p hardcover o.p. paperback available $16.95   **333.91**
1. Water resources development 2. Water supply 3. Globalization
ISBN 1-56584-813-6 (pa)   LC 2003-389510
In this overview of the current water situation, the authors "warn readers that the time for taking water for granted is over, and that transnational corporations are privatizing drinking-water supplies, often charging the poorest citizens the most for this fundamental substance. Not to mention the bottled water industry, which is also wreaking havoc." Booklist
"This well-researched book provides a sobering, in-depth look at the growing scarcity of fresh water and the increasing privatization and corporate control of this non-renewable resource. . . . The proposals for corrective legislation, lobbying, and citizen environmental action make this book a highly recommended purchase for public and academic libraries." Libr J
Includes bibliographical references

De Villiers, Marq
Water: the fate of our most precious resource. Houghton Mifflin 2000 352p maps hardcover o.p. paperback available $15   **333.91**
1. Water supply 2. Water pollution 3. Water resources development
ISBN 0-618-12744-5 (pa)   LC 00-21224
First published 1999 in Canada

This book "depicts the current extent of world water scarcity, engineering efforts, and national and international water policies and briefly provides guidelines for dealing with the coming world water crisis." Libr J
De Villiers "presents a thoroughly researched and remarkably involving chronicle of the natural history, folklore, and politics of water, with stops in the Middle East, the U.S., and Russia, followed by a riveting assessment of the mistakes that have been made concerning water usage, and their perplexing consequences." Booklist
Includes bibliographical references

Dean, Cornelia
Against the tide; the battle for America's beaches. Columbia Univ. Press 1999 279p il $60; pa $18.95   **333.91**
1. Coasts 2. Beaches 3. Seashore ecology
ISBN 0-231-08418-8; 0-231-08419-6 (pa)
     LC 98-50755
Dean discusses the ecology of American beaches and contends that they are threatened by coastal development and erosion
"This thoroughly researched and thoughtful book is destined to become a classic of environmental science writing." Libr J
Includes bibliographical references

Reisner, Marc P.
Cadillac desert; the American West and its disappearing water; [by] Marc Reisner. rev and updated. Penguin Bks. 1993 582p il maps pa $17   **333.91**
1. Irrigation—West (U.S.) 2. Water resources development 3. Political corruption
ISBN 0-14-017824-4   LC 93-173272
First published 1986 by Viking
This "study of the economics, politics, and ecology of water covers more than a century of public and private desert reclamation in the American West." Publisher's note
"Reisner's groundbreaking history of water wheeling-and-dealing in the West helped launch the inquiry into water policy that has grown more urgent each year as the development of dry lands continues." Booklist
Includes bibliographical references

Rothfeder, Jeffrey
Every drop for sale; our desperate battle over water in a world about to run out. Tarcher/Putnam 2001 205p $24.95   **333.91**
1. Water supply
ISBN 1-58542-114-6   LC 2001-27903
The author "debunks the myth that dams solve water problems, decries the lack of an adequate method for large-scale desalinization, and condemns the commodification and privatization of clean water." Booklist
"Like the drip of water on stone, Rothfeder's steady exposition of horrors will wear down any reader's doubts that water is the next flashpoint of global politics, human rights and health issues." Publ Wkly
Includes bibliographical references

Ward, Diane Raines

Water wars; drought, flood, folly, and the politics of thirst. Riverhead Bks. 2002 280p $24.95; pa $14 **333.91**

1. Water supply 2. Hydraulic engineering 3. Water rights

ISBN 1-57322-229-1; 1-57322-995-4 (pa)

LC 2002-21301

The author considers the problems of "droughts, pollution, population growth, and climate change—which threaten to make water . . . the cause of war within our lifetime. . . . [She] tells the stories of those working to solve them: hydrologists, politicians, engineers, and everyday people." Publisher's note

"Ward writes with the sensibilities and concerns of an environmentalist. But unexpectedly, delightfully, she's an environmentalist who loves the scale, ingenuity and power of engineering." N Y Times Book Rev

Includes bibliographical references

333.95 Biological resources

Becher, Anne

Biodiversity; a reference handbook. ABC-CLIO 1998 275p il (Contemporary world issues) $50 **333.95**

1. Biological diversity

ISBN 0-87436-923-1 LC 97-42890

"The first 50 pages comprise a comprehensive overview, including definitions, history, and discussions of the importance of biodiversity, threats to maintaining it, and conservation efforts. Other chapters provide a chronology, biographical sketches, statistics and documents, a directory of organizations (including web-site addresses when available), print resources, nonprint resources, and a glossary. Each item receives a lengthy annotation. . . . One would have a hard time finding a better reference guide to an individual subject." Libr J

Encyclopedia of biodiversity; editor-in-chief, Simon Asher Levin. Academic Press 2001 5v il maps set $1,295 **333.95**

1. Biological diversity—Encyclopedias

ISBN 0-12-226865-2

This resource "consists of 313 signed, alphabetically arranged articles, prepared by international contributors. Each volume features a table of contents for the set plus a list of all articles arranged by 20 subject categories. . . . The final volume includes a subject index, list of authors, and glossary. Each entry follows a standard format consisting of an outline, glossary, statement of definition, the article, cross-references, and a bibliography. Volume 1 includes a 16-page section of color plates. Black-and-white illustrations . . . are integrated throughout the text. Limited online access time is included with purchase of the print set. Impressive in content and organization; highly recommended for all collections." Choice

Goodall, Jane, 1934-

The ten trusts; what we must do to care for the animals we love; [by] Jane Goodall and Marc Bekoff. HarperSanFrancisco 2002 xx, 200p $23.95 **333.95**

1. Animal rights 2. Animal welfare 3. Wildlife conservation 4. Human influence on nature

ISBN 0-06-251757-0 LC 2002-68717

The authors "offer a prescriptive conservation plan designed to protect animals as well as help educate people about the importance of saving both animals and the environment." Publ Wkly

"An accessible, compelling, and important exposé." Booklist

Includes bibliographical references

Life on earth; an encyclopedia of biodiversity, ecology, and evolution; edited by Niles Eldredge. ABC-CLIO 2002 2v set $185 **333.95**

1. Biological diversity—Encyclopedias 2. Ecology—Encyclopedias 3. Evolution—Encyclopedias

ISBN 1-57607-286-X LC 2002-15852

"Four introductory essays outline the definition, importance, and preservation of biodiversity. Many of the 194 articles are about specific phyla or species . . . or important concepts. . . . Others address issues that will appeal to students and general readers. . . . Articles are clearly written, usually define specialized terms, and include bibliographies of books and popular and scholarly periodical articles." Booklist

Sargent, William, 1946-

Crab wars; a tale of horseshoe crabs, bioterrorism, and human health. University Press of New England 2002 124p maps $24.95 **333.95**

1. Crabs 2. Drug industry

ISBN 1-584-65168-7 LC 2002-9946

The author relates how the horseshoe crab has become "the object of an intense legal and ethical struggle involving marine biologists, environmentalists, US government officials, biotechnologists, and international corporations. The source of this friction is the discovery 25 years ago that the blood of these ancient creatures serves as the basis for the most reliable test for the deadly and ubiquitous gram-negative bacteria. . . . Because every drug certified by the FDA must be tested using the horseshoe crab derivative known as Limulus lysate, a multimillion dollar industry has emerged involving the license to 'bleed' horseshoe crabs and the rights to their breeding grounds." Publisher's note

Sargent "is intimate with every aspect of the species' life and the lysate industry now irrevocably connected to it . . . a many-faceted story he illuminates by profiling fishermen, biotech entrepreneurs, politicians, and environmentalists." Booklist

Wilson, Edward O., 1929-

The future of life. Knopf 2002 xxiv, 229p il $22; pa $13 **333.95**

1. Endangered species 2. Nature conservation

ISBN 0-679-45078-5; 0-679-76811-4 (pa)

LC 2001-38316

Wilson "proposes that there is yet time to avoid a grand planetary environmental crash provided we get serious, acknowledge a duty of stewardship and recognize an emotional affiliation . . . with other kinds of life." NY Times Book Rev

335.4 Marxian systems

Marx, Karl, 1818-1883

The Communist manifesto of Karl Marx and Friedrich Engels **335.4**

1. Communism

Hardcover and paperback editions available from various publishers

First published 1848

Marx, Karl, 1818-1883—*Continued*
This document "analyzes history in terms of class conflict, predicts the imminent overthrow of the ruling bourgeoisie by the oppressed proletariat, and envisions a resulting classless society in which personal property would be abolished. The 'Manifesto' calls upon the proletariat of the world to unite and strengthen itself for this final revolution." Benet's Reader's Ency 4th edition

Pipes, Richard
Communism: a history. Modern Lib. 2001 175p $19.95; pa $10.95 **335.4**
1. Communism
ISBN 0-679-64050-9; 0-8129-6864-6 (pa)
LC 2001-275458
"This is a short history on the essentials of communism—as an ideal, as a program outlined by Marx, and as a state established by Lenin to implement the program." Booklist
"As a brief, polemical diatribe . . . this short account of communism should provoke and instruct." Libr J
Includes bibliographical references

336.2 Taxes and taxation

H & R Block income tax guide. Fireside Bks. pa $16 **336.2**
1. Income tax
Annual. First published 1967 by Macmillan with title: H & R Block income tax workbook
This is a line-by-line tax-preparation workbook and guide to specific situations. Tax tables and sample forms are appended

J.K. Lasser's your income tax; prepared by the J.K. Lasser Tax Institute. Wiley pa $16.95 **336.2**
1. Income tax
ISSN 0084-4314
Annual. First published by Simon & Schuster. Began publication with 1936 issue. Title varies. Early issues prepared by J.K. Lasser
A standard aid for filing income tax returns

Weisman, Steven R.
The great tax wars; Lincoln to Wilson: the fierce battles over money and power that transformed the nation. Simon & Schuster 2002 419p $27 **336.2**
1. Income tax 2. Taxation
ISBN 0-684-85068-0 LC 2002-70486
"Weisman uses the income tax as a spotlight to illuminate American political and economic history from Abraham Lincoln's Administration through Woodrow Wilson's." New Yorker
"This is an important, relevant and well-written story." Publ Wkly
Includes bibliographical references

337 International economics

Friedman, Thomas L.
The Lexus and the olive tree; understanding globalization. Farrar, Straus & Giroux 1999 416p il $30 **337**
1. International economic relations 2. Free trade 3. United States—Foreign economic relations
ISBN 0-374-19203-0 LC 99-10742
Also available in paperback from Anchor Bks.

Friedman "explains, with anecdotes as well as analyses, what the instant electronic global economy is and what it may take to live there." N Y Times Book Rev
Includes bibliographical references

Soros, George
George Soros on globalization. PublicAffairs 2002 191p $20 **337**
1. International economic relations 2. International finance 3. Globalization
ISBN 1-58648-125-8 LC 2001-58868
Soros presents his views on international finance and economic relations. He argues for reforms of international economic institutions such as the World Bank, the World Trade Organization and the International Monetary Fund. He concludes that "globalization has distorted the allocation of resources in favor of private goods at the expense of public goods." N Y Rev Books
"Though the subject matter is complicated, Soros' simplified treatment makes this a timely and necessary title for any basic economy collection." Booklist
Includes bibliographical references

Stiglitz, Joseph E.
Globalization and its discontents. Norton 2002 xxii, 282p $24.95; pa $15.95 **337**
1. International Monetary Fund 2. International economic relations 3. International finance 4. Developing countries—Economic conditions 5. Globalization
ISBN 0-393-05124-2; 0-393-32439-7 (pa)
LC 2002-23148
The author "posits that 'the level of pain in developing countries created in the process of globalization and development as it has been guided by the IMF and the international economic organizations has been far greater than necessary.'" Booklist
"This smart, provocative study contributes significantly to the ongoing globalization debate." Publ Wkly
Includes bibliographical references

338.1 Agriculture

Berry, Wendell, 1934-
Citizenship papers. Shoemaker & Hoard 2003 189p $24 **338.1**
1. Agriculture—Government policy 2. Agriculture—Environmental aspects 3. Economic policy—United States
ISBN 1-59376-000-0 LC 2003-13811
Analyzed in Essay and general literature index
Contents: A citizen's response; Thoughts in the presence of fear; The failure of war; Going to work; In distrust of movements; Twelve paragraphs on biotechnology; Let the farm judge; The total economy; A long job, too late to quit; Two minds; The prejudice against country people; The whole horse; Stupidity in concentration; Waterhed and commonwealth; The agrarian standard; Still standing; Conservationist and agrarian; Tuscany; Is life a mircle?
"Berry's recent essays may restate what he has said before—that agribusiness and the new globalism are inimical to human thriving—but they say it better, and through different immediate subjects, saliently including sound sheep raising and 9/11, than ever before." Booklist

338.2   Mineral industries

Yergin, Daniel
The prize; the epic quest for oil, money, and power. Simon & Schuster 1991 877, xxxiip il maps hardcover o.p. paperback available $22   **338.2**
1. Petroleum industry 2. World politics
ISBN 0-671-79932-0 (pa)   LC 90-47575
This is a "history of the oil industry, from the first oil well ever drilled (near Titusville, Pennsylvania, in 1859) to the Iraqi invasion of Kuwait. It recalls advances in technology, innovations in salesmanship, and wars and truces among corporations and nations." New Yorker
"A comprehensive careful book that pulls together reams of information." N Y Times Book Rev
Includes bibliographical references

338.5   General production economics

Galbraith, John Kenneth, 1908-
The Great Crash, 1929; with a new introduction by the author. Houghton Mifflin 1997 206p il pa $14   **338.5**
1. Great Depression, 1929-1939 2. United States—Economic conditions—1919-1933
ISBN 0-395-85999-9   LC 97-22051
"A Mariner book"
First published 1955
Beginning with the bull market of Coolidge and Hoover and continuing through the stock market crash, the author analyzes its causes and speculates about the chances of another crash
Includes bibliographical references

338.7   Business enterprises

Arden, Lynie, 1949-
Work-at-home sourcebook. Live Oak Publs. pa $19.95   **338.7**
1. Home-based business
First published 1987. (8th edition 2002) Frequently revised
"Arden lists over 1000 companies that either hire or contract with home workers. Categorized by types of work, home-based opportunities, markets for crafts, etc., entries include addresses, requirements, and provisions." Libr J

Brenner, Joël Glenn
The emperors of chocolate; inside the secret world of Hershey and Mars. Random House 1999 366p il hardcover o.p. paperback available $14.95   **338.7**
1. Hershey, Milton Snavely, 1857-1945 2. Mars, Forrest, Sr. 3. Hershey Foods Corp. 4. Mars, Inc. 5. Chocolate
ISBN 0-7679-0457-5 (pa)   LC 98-21610
"Brenner examines the candy industry, focusing on the rivalry between Hershey and Mars. Milton Hersey was and Forrest Mars is highly secretive and eccentric, and they both amassed huge fortunes. A wonderful inside look at successful businessmen." Booklist
Includes bibliographical references

Brinkley, Douglas
Wheels for the world; Henry Ford, his company, and a century of progress, 1903-2003. Viking 2003 xxii, 858p il $34.95   **338.7**
1. Ford, Henry, 1863-1947 2. Ford Motor Co. 3. Automobile industry
ISBN 0-670-03181-X   LC 2003-33066
This book is "about the people of Ford, including the Ford family, executives, workers, union organizers and others. . . . Brinkley's focus never strays far from Ford plants in Highland Park, River Rouge and Willow Run, Mich., yet he reflects events taking place in the outside world through the actions and feelings of people in nearby Dearborn, Mich." Publ Wkly
"Car lovers will appreciate this amazing account of the birth of the automobile industry, including funny anecdotes about the trusty Model T, the evolution of the V-8 engine, the artistic design of the Thunderbird, sophistication of the Lincoln Continental, and popularity of the Mustang." Booklist
Includes bibliographical references

Gerstner, Louis V., Jr.
Who says elephants can't dance? inside IBM's historic turnaround; [by] Louis V. Gerstner, Jr. HarperBusiness 2002 372p il $27.95   **338.7**
1. International Business Machines Corp. 2. Computer industry
ISBN 0-06-052379-4   LC 2002-27523
Also available Thorndike Press large print edition
This is the "tale of the rise, fall and rise of IBM. . . . [The author] became IBM's CEO in 1993, when the gargantuan company was near collapse. The book's opening section snappily reports Gerstner's decisions in his first 18 months on the job. . . . The following sections describe the marathon fight to make IBM once again 'a company that mattered.' . . . The book is a well-rendered self-portrait of a CEO who made spectacular change on the strength of personal leadership." Publ Wkly

Henry, Shannon
The Dinner Club; how the masters of the Internet universe rode the rise and fall of the greatest boom in history. Free Press 2002 288p $26   **338.7**
1. Executives 2. Internet 3. Stocks 4. Investments
ISBN 0-7432-2215-6   LC 2002-28833
Henry "tells the story of the Capital Investors, a Washington, D.C., social club and angel investor group comprising 26 technology wizards who gained fame and fortune in the late 1990s through 2000. Notable members include Steve Case, . . . James Kimsey, cofounder of America Online; and William Gorog, originator of Lexis." Booklist
"The book is riotous and riveting, but not flawless. Henry too often leaves readers hankering for more information. . . . Still, this brisk and incisive account combines the furtive thrill of restricted access with an outsider's detached reflection." Publ Wkly

Spector, Robert
Amazon.com; get big fast. HarperBusiness 2000 xxii, 263p hardcover o.p. paperback available $16   **338.7**
1. Amazon.com Inc. 2. Booksellers and bookselling 3. Internet
ISBN 0-06-662042-2 (pa)   LC 99-87599
"Spector looks at a Seattle company that has turned retailing and customer service upside down. Online bookseller Amazon.com almost instantly became a part of America's popular culture, but Amazon.com has yet to turn a profit." Booklist
Includes bibliographical references

Standard and Poor's register of corporations, directors, and executives. Standard & Poor's Corp. 3v set $1,075   **338.7**
1. Corporations—Directories 2. Executives—Directories
ISSN 0361-3623
Also available CD-ROM version and online
Annual. First published 1928
This "reference provides essential information on virtually all of the nation's corporations and their key people. Updated with supplements in April, July, and October. Volume 1: Profiles of more than 55,000 corporations in alphabetical order. Volume 2: Brief biographies of directors and executives. Volume 3: Indexes according to geography, industry, and other parameters." N Y Public Libr Book of How & Where to Look It Up

Zygmont, Jeffrey
Microchip: an idea, its genesis, and the revolution it created. Perseus Bks. 2003 xxii, 245p $25   **338.7**
1. Computer industry 2. Microelectronics
ISBN 0-7382-0561-3   LC 2002-112395
"Comparing the invention of the integrated circuit to that of steel, Zygmont tracks the incredible story of the microchip from the visionaries who conceived of it to the rapid-fire advances that have made this complex technology integral to everyday life." Booklist
Includes bibliographical references

338.8   Business combinations

Burrough, Bryan, 1961-
Barbarians at the gate: the fall of RJR Nabisco; [by] Bryan Burrough and John Helyar. Harper & Row 1990 528p il hardcover o.p. paperback available $16
338.8
1. RJR Nabisco Inc. 2. Conglomerate corporations
ISBN 0-06-092038-6 (pa)   LC 89-45635
The authors "describe the battle to control RJR Nabisco, providing a behind-the-scenes account of the deal through interviews with Wall Street power brokers and comments on the restructuring of corporations today." Publ Wkly
This book "contains enough individual examples of greed, egoism, conniving and sheer incompetence to stun even more jaundiced observers of the Wall Street madhouse. . . . [The authors] have done a solid job of American reportage; in other words, they tell a good story without getting bogged down in analysis." Economist

339.4   Factors affecting national product, wealth, income

Cohen, Lizabeth
A consumer's republic; the politics of mass consumption in postwar America. Knopf 2003 567p il $35; pa $16.95   **339.4**
1. Consumption (Economics) 2. Consumers 3. United States—Social conditions
ISBN 0-375-40750-2; 0-375-70737-9 (pa)
LC 2002-141599
Cohen contends that "the pursuit of prosperity [after World War II] defined much more than the nation's economy; it also became a basic component of American citizenship. . . . After a decade and a half of hard times resulting from the Great Depression and the war, the embrace of mass consumption, with its supposed far-reaching benefits—greater freedom, democracy, and equality—transformed American life. . . . [Cohen contends that consumption] has reshaped our relationship to government itself, with Americans increasingly judging public services—as if one more purchased good—by the personal benefits they derive from them." Publisher's note
"Without question, this is a difficult, demanding, and dense book—but it is also a greatly significant contribution to business literature. . . . Cohen submits a copiously researched, brilliantly conceived, and ultimately quite instructive study of American economics since the Depression." Booklist
Includes bibliographical references

340   Law

Feinman, Jay M.
Law 101; everything you need to know about the American legal system. Oxford Univ. Press 2000 353p $27.50   **340**
1. Law—United States
ISBN 0-19-513265-3   LC 99-28333
This is "an introduction to the laws in the U.S., providing background on the practical development and bases of the law from a layperson's perspective. Feinman asks basic questions and provides lengthy answers to the fundamental concerns a reader might have about how the law works." Booklist

Nolo's encyclopedia of everyday law; answers to your most frequently asked legal questions; edited by Shae Irving. Nolo Press (Berkeley) il pa $29.99   **340**
1. Law—United States
First published as a replacement of Nolo's everyday law book. (5th edition 2003) Frequently revised
This offers answers to frequently asked legal questions about such topics as credit and debt, workplace rights, wills, divorce, bankruptcy, social security, tenant's rights, child custody and visitation, patents and trademarks, travel, partnerships, healthcare directives and powers of attorney

340.03 Law—Encyclopedias and dictionaries

Black, Henry Campbell, 1860-1927
Black's law dictionary; Bryan A. Garner, editor in chief. West Pub. Co. $59.95
340.03
1. Law—Dictionaries
Also available in an abridged paperback edition
First published 1891 with title: A dictionary of law. (7th edition 1999) Periodically revised to bring terms up to date
"Definitions of the terms and phrases of American and English jurisprudence, ancient and modern." Subtitle
"This comprehensive work is the standard U.S. law dictionary. The 6th ed. includes more than 5,000 new or revised entries, as well as thousands of archaic or little-used legal terms. Many entries include references to cases or statutes. Appendixes include a table of abbreviations and the text of the U.S. Constitution." Guide to Ref Books. 11th edition

Legal systems of the world; a political, social, and cultural encyclopedia; edited by Herbert M. Kritzer. ABC-CLIO 2002 4v il maps set $385
340.03
1. Law—Encyclopedias
ISBN 1-57607-231-2   LC 2002-2659
"Written by an international team of more than 350 legal scholars, the more than 400 signed entries cover legal systems of countries from around the world, Australia, and the provinces of Canada; transnational systems (International Court of Justice); general systems (Islamlic law, indigenous, and folk legal systems); and key concepts. Each country profile includes a map with an inset of its location on the globe, general information about the country, its history, diagrams of its court structure, the evolution of its legal framework, its current structure, staffing or how judges are appointed, any specialized judicial bodies (i.e. military court), and the impact that the legal system has had on the country. Articles conclude with references and a bibliography. Academic and public libraries will find this source invaluable for comparative studies in legal and judicial systems."—"The Best of the Best Reference Sources." Am Libr

West's encyclopedia of American law. West Pub. Co.; [distributed by] Gale Res. 1997 12v set $995
340.03
1. Law—United States—Encyclopedias
ISBN 0-314-22770-9   LC 96-34350
First published 1983-1985 with title: The Guide to American law
New edition in preparation
Over 5,000 alphabetically arranged entries explain legal principles and concepts, landmark documents, laws, famous trials, historical movements, and notable persons
Includes bibliographical references

341.23 United Nations

Moore, John Allphin, 1940-
Encyclopedia of the United Nations; [by] John Allphin Moore, Jr., Jerry Pubantz. Facts on File 2002 xxvii, 484p il (Facts on File library of world history) $75
341.23
1. United Nations 2. International relations
ISBN 0-8160-4417-1   LC 2002-72222
"Over 400 articles cover people associated with the UN, the countries and regions where it has been involved, its agencies and institutions, its affiliated organizations, specific project names, and other issues that the UN has addressed over the past 55 years. Appendixes provide a chronology of major UN events, a selected bibliography, and a very useful list of web addresses to navigate the complex UN web site." Libr J

Osmańczyk, Edmund Jan, 1913-1989
Encyclopedia of the United Nations and international agreements; {by} Jan Edmund Osmancyzk; edited and revised by Anthony Mango. 3rd ed. Routledge 2002 4v set $550
341.23
1. United Nations 2. International relations—Encyclopedias
ISBN 0-415-93920-8   LC 2002-10761
Original Polish edition, 1975; first English language edition 1985
"An alphabetically arranged treasure trove of information on the United Nations, its specialized agencies, and many intergovernmental and non-governmental organizations. This especially valuable resource for smaller collections includes the full or partial texts of some 3,000 international agreements, conventions, and treaties as well as definitions of political, economic, military, geographical, and diplomatic terms. Analytical and agreements-conventions-treaties indexes." Ref Sources for Small & Medium-sized Libr. 6th edition {entry for 1990 edition}
For a review see: Booklist June 1 & 15, 2003

342 Constitutional and administrative law

Anosike, Benji O.
Immigration manual. Do-It-Yourself Legal Pubs. 2003 2v v1 $29.95; v2 $30.95   **342**
1. United States—Immigration and emigration
ISBN 0-932704-52-2 (v1); 0-932704-53-0 (v2)
LC 2002-41610
Contents: v1 How to obtain your U.S. immigration visa for a temporary stay; v2 How to obtain your U.S. immigration visa for a permanent stay
This "manual is extremely helpful in showing the step-by-step process for foreign nationals to qualify for a grant of entry visa into the U.S. . . . Possible problem areas are brought to light, and how the immigrant quota system works is carefully explained. . . . A handy and always timely reference." Booklist
Includes bibliographical references

Berkin, Carol
A brilliant solution; inventing the American Constitution. Harcourt 2002 310p $26; pa $14
342
1. United States. Constitutional Convention (1787) 2. Constitutional history—United States 3. United States—Politics and government—1783-1809
ISBN 0-15-100948-1; 0-15-602872-7 (pa)
LC 2002-5648
This history of the 1787 Constitutional Convention "emphasizes the importance of the delegates' anxieties, showing how they insinuated themselves into some of the compromises, such as the equality of the states in the Senate. Shrewd at integrating biographical detail on the delegates into their debates, Berkin fares well in comparison with previous historians on the topic." Booklist

Bingham, Clara
Class action; the story of Lois Jenson and the landmark case that changed sexual harassment law; [by] Clara Bingham & Laura Leedy Gansler. Doubleday 2002 390p $27.50
342
1. Jenson, Lois 2. Eveleth Mines (Firm) 3. Sexual harassment—Law and legislation
ISBN 0-385-49612-5
LC 2001-58158
"In 1975, Lois Jenson became one of the first women to work in the iron mines of Minnesota and the lead plaintiff in the lawsuit. Eveleth Mines was Jenson's employer. The center of the story is the 25-year ordeal Jenson and other women miners underwent." Publ Wkly
"This riveting, assiduously well-reported account follows the tortuous class-action lawsuit that finally improved working conditions at Eveleth and redefined sexual-harassment law." New Yorker

Carter, Stephen L.
Reflections of an affirmative action baby. Basic Bks. 1991 286p hardcover o.p. paperback available $20
342
1. Affirmative action programs 2. Race discrimination—Law and legislation
ISBN 0-465-06869-3 (pa)
LC 91-70054
The author begins by "discussing the positive and negative effects of affirmative action on his life. He then expands his study to include other topics such as the increase of racial incidents in America, dealing with political correctness and the conflicts between the mainstream liberal black community and the increasingly vocal so-called black conservatives." Libr J

The **Debate** on the Constitution; Federalist and Antifederalist speeches, articles, and letters during the struggle over ratification. Library of Am. 1993 2v ea $35
342
1. Constitutional history—United States 2. United States—Politics and government—1783-1809
ISBN 0-940450-81-X
LC 92-25449
Contents: v1. Debates in the press and in private correspondence, September 17, 1787-January 12, 1788; Debates in the state ratifying conventions: Pennsylvania, Connecticut, Massachusetts—v2. Debates in the press and in private correspondence, January 14, 1788-August 9, 1788; Debates in the state ratifying conventions: South Carolina, Virginia, New York, North Carolina
In addition to the documents themselves, these volumes contain "brief biographical notes on the various speakers and writers, a chronology of key events in American independence and the establishment of the new governmental system, notes on contemporary state constitutions, and notes explicating the text of the reprinted documents." Christ Sci Monit

Eisaguirre, Lynne, 1951-
Sexual harassment; a reference handbook. 2nd ed. ABC-CLIO 1997 285p il (Contemporary world issues) $45
342
1. Sexual harassment—Law and legislation 2. Sex discrimination
ISBN 0-87436-971-1
LC 97-35489
First published 1993
This handbook provides information on sexual harassment legislation and litigation from feminist, legal, management, male, and other perspectives
Includes bibliographical references

Encyclopedia of the American Constitution; edited by Leonard W. Levy and Kenneth L. Karst. 2nd ed, Adam Winkler, associate editor for the second ed. Macmillan Ref. USA 2000 6v set $595
342
1. Constitutional law—United States
ISBN 0-02-864880-3
LC 00-29203
First published 1986 in 4 volumes
This "reference contains approximately 3000 contributions from academics, lawyers, and judges concerning key constitutional law cases and legislative developments relating to constitutional issues (e.g., abortion, welfare rights, and affirmative action)." Libr J

The **Federalist**; edited, with introduction and notes, by Jacob E. Cooke. Wesleyan Univ. Press 1982 c1961 xxx, 672p pa $27.95
342
1. United States. Constitution
ISBN 0-8195-6077-4
LC 82-2815
A reissue of the 1961 edition
"From 27 Oct. 1787 to 2 April 1788, 77 essays were published in the semi-weekly 'Independent Journal' of New York, entitled 'The Federalist,' and signed first 'A Citizen of New York' then 'Publius.' Eight more were added when they were collected in book form [in 1789]. . . . They were so acute and massively learned in their exposition of the true intent of the Constitution, that even the courts have accepted them as authoritative comments in doubtful cases; and they are held by all the civilized world as among the noblest storehouses of political philosophy in existence. A classic textbook of political science." Ency Americana

Gelman, Robert B.
Protecting yourself online; the definitive resource on safety, freedom, and privacy in cyberspace; [by] Robert B. Gelman with Stanton McCandlish and members of the Electronic Frontier Foundation. HarperEdge 1998 xxiii, 198p il pa $15
342
1. Computer networks—Law and legislation 2. Right of privacy 3. Computer security
ISBN 0-06-251512-8
LC 97-32422
The authors seek "to provide the definitive source on maintaining safety in the electronic world. That lofty goal is realized fully with comprehensive ruminations on free expression and censorship; safeguarding privacy, anonymity, and sensitive personal and business data; treating viruses; spotting scams; and protecting intellectual property." Libr J

Lewis, Loida Nicolas

How to get a green card; legal ways to stay in the U.S.A; by Loida Nicolas Lewis and Len T. Madlansacay. Nolo Press (Berkeley) pa $29.99   **342**

1. Aliens—United States 2. United States—Immigration and emigration   LC 2002-190874

First published 1993. (5th edition 2003) Periodically revised

This book explains ways "to get a green card through parents, siblings and adult children; spouses and fiancees; employers; green card lotteries; political asylum or refugee status and more. {It also} provides a list of more than 400 immigration groups that help with paperwork and offer counseling and legal referrals." Publisher's note

Lively, Donald E., 1947-

Landmark Supreme Court cases; a reference guide. Greenwood Press 1999 374p $64.95   **342**

1. United States. Supreme Court 2. Constitutional law—United States

ISBN 0-313-30602-8   LC 98-44220

"This volume discusses 74 cases under four broad topics: the distribution of powers, the relationship between the nation and its states, concepts of equality, and individual rights. These are divided further into more specific topics. . . . The thematic approach combined with fairly detailed discussion of individual cases works well." Booklist

Includes bibliographical references

Maddex, Robert L., 1942-

The U.S. Constitution A to Z. CQ Press 2002 646p il map (CQ's ready reference encyclopedia of American government) $125
                                                        342

1. Constitutional law—United States 2. Constitutional history—United States

ISBN 1-56802-699-4   LC 2002-9230

"Maddex offers over 200 articles about issues (abortion, gun control), legal concepts (due process, privacy), landmark cases (*Roe v. Wade, Brown v. Board of Education*) and people (John Adams, Thurgood Marshall) related to the Constitution. . . . The unique feature of this work is its collection of source materials. . . . It is an excellent, concise reference." Choice

Includes bibliographical references

May it please the court: the First Amendment; edited by Peter Irons. New Press (NY) 1997 262p $59.95; pa $14.95
                                                        342

ISBN 1-56584-330-4; 1-56584-487-4 (pa)

Also available volume about the most important arguments made before the Supreme Court since 1955 on a range of issues including a volume dealing with reproductive rights and abortion cases

"Transcripts of the oral arguments made before the Supreme Court in sixteen key First Amendment cases." Title page

This book and accompanying 4 tapes cover sixteen cases dealing with issues of free speech, freedom of the press, and the right to assemble

"New Press' tapes-and-text combination offers a fascinating history lesson." Booklist

McDonald, Laughlin

The rights of racial minorities; the basic ACLU guide to racial minority rights; [by] Laughlin McDonald, John A. Powell. 2nd ed completely rev & updated. Southern Ill. Univ. Press 1993 288p (American Civil Liberties Union handbook) $36; pa $19.95   **342**

1. Race discrimination 2. African Americans—Civil rights

ISBN 0-8093-1899-7; 0-8093-1888-1 (pa)
                                            LC 93-15756

First published 1980 under the authorship of E. Richard Larson and Laughlin McDonald

"Individual chapters explain the federal civil laws and procedures protecting the rights of racial minorities in voting, employment, education, housing, public accommodations, federally assisted programs, and jury selection and trials. Relevant criminal statutes and the use of race-conscious remedies are covered as well." Publisher's note

Noonan, John Thomas, Jr.

Narrowing the nation's power: the Supreme Court sides with the states; [by] John T. Noonan, Jr. University of Calif. Press 2002 203p $34.95; pa $14.95   **342**

1. United States. Supreme Court 2. State governments

ISBN 0-520-23574-6; 0-520-24068-5 (pa)
                                            LC 2002-19473

The author "dissects an emerging trend in recent Supreme Court decisions bolstering the sovereign immunity of the 50 states—that is, saying the states and their many agencies . . . are immune from lawsuits by individuals for money damages." Publ Wkly

"In this highly recommended work, the author convincingly sounds the alarm." Libr J

Includes bibliographical references

O'Neil, Robert M.

The rights of public employees; the basic ACLU guide to the rights of public employees. 2nd ed completely rev & updated. Southern Ill. Univ. Press 1993 148p (American Civil Liberties Union handbook) hardcover o.p. paperback available $19.95
                                                        342

1. Employees—Civil rights 2. United States—Officials and employees

ISBN 0-8093-1928-4 (pa)   LC 93-17474

First published 1978 by Avon Books with title: The rights of government employees

Among the topics this legal guide for government employees addresses are wages, benefits, hiring and firing, discrimination, and job security

The **Oxford** guide to United States Supreme Court decisions; edited by Kermit L. Hall. Oxford Univ. Press 1999 428p $39.95; pa $19.95   **342**

1. United States. Supreme Court 2. Constitutional law—United States

ISBN 0-19-511883-9; 0-19-513924-0 (pa)
                                            LC 98-8747

This volume is a guide to approximately 400 Supreme Court decisions. "Each case entry typically provides background information on the case, explains the Court's decision, [and] explores any disagreement among the justices about the legal doctrines and societal values at

The Oxford guide to United States Supreme Court decisions—*Continued*

stake. . . . A glossary of terms, a copy of the U.S. Constitution, . . . appendixes charting the nominations and succession of Supreme Court justices, a case index, and a topical index complete the volume." Booklist

"An impressive accomplishment, this guide will be invaluable to all students of United States history and will also appeal to sophisticated readers." Libr J

Rabban, David M., 1949-

Free speech in its forgotten years. Cambridge Univ. Press 1997 404p il (Cambridge historical studies in American law and society) $60; pa $22 **342**

1. Freedom of speech 2. Constitutional law—United States

ISBN 0-521-62013-9; 0-521-65537-4 (pa)

LC 97-15281

The author "focuses on free speech issues between the Civil War and World War I. Through an impressive marshaling of controversies, cases, and litigants, he persuasively argues that libertarian radicalism and the Free Speech League . . . deserve much of the credit for pushing valuable First Amendment issues to the forefront of American social, political, and legal circles. . . . This enlightening work fills a void in First Amendment civil liberties studies." Libr J

Includes bibliographical references

Rehnquist, William H.

All the laws but one; civil liberties in wartime. Knopf 1998 254p il $27.50; pa $14 **342**

1. Civil rights 2. National security—United States

ISBN 0-679-44661-3; 0-679-76732-0 (pa)

LC 98-12641

This is "Supreme Court Chief Justice Rehnquist's narrative of the conflict between civil liberties and military necessity. . . . Fully two-thirds of the book covers Civil War issues. . . . One chapter discusses World War I espionage and draft resistance cases; three, the World War II internment of Japanese Americans and the imposition of martial law in Hawaii. . . . Far from a *complete* survey of wartime civil liberties—reviewing only cases that reached the Supreme Court before 1950—this is nonetheless both enlightening and entertaining." Booklist

Includes bibliographical references

Renstrom, Peter G., 1943-

Constitutional rights sourcebook. ABC-CLIO 1999 xxi, 770p $80 **342**

1. Constitutional law—United States

ISBN 1-57607-061-1

LC 99-13197

An "analysis of the individual rights and civil liberties guaranteed by the United States Constitution. Particular attention is focused on the Bill of Rights and the Fourteenth Amendment. . . . Each concept is fully developed and discussed at the adversarial level, and the discussion is replete with references and analysis drawn from applicable case law. The evolution of legal concepts is traced from one era to another." Libr J

Simon, James F.

What kind of nation; Thomas Jefferson, John Marshall, and the epic struggle to create a United States. Simon & Schuster 2002 348p $27.50; pa $14 **342**

1. Jefferson, Thomas, 1743-1826 2. Marshall, John, 1755-1835 3. United States. Supreme Court 4. Constitutional history—United States 5. Executive power 6. United States—Politics and government—1783-1809

ISBN 0-684-84870-8; 0-684-84871-6 (pa)

LC 2001-55027

The author "examines the decades of conflict between the states' rights views of Thomas Jefferson and the federalist beliefs of John Marshall." Publ Wkly

"Simon's enlivening account proves that writing about constitutional law needn't be the dry preserve of academics." Booklist

Includes bibliographical references

United States. Constitution

The Constitution of the United States of America; analysis and interpretation; prepared by the Congressional Research Service, Library of Congress. U.S. Govt. Ptg. Office $163 **342**

1. Constitutional law—United States

First published 1953. Periodically revised and kept up to date by supplements

"Sometimes known by its short title, the *Constitution Annotated* provides commentary on every article, section, and clause of the basic instrument, as well as the amendments, with citations to selected United States Supreme Court decisions construing these provisions." Introd to U.S. Govt Info Sources. 5th edition

Vile, John R.

Encyclopedia of constitutional amendments, proposed amendments, and amending issues, 1789-2002. 2nd ed. ABC-CLIO 2003 xxiv, 635p $85 **342**

1. Constitutional law—United States 2. Constitutional history—United States

ISBN 1-85109-428-8

LC 2003-1839

First published 1996, covering 1789-1995

"This title provides background historical material on successful and unsuccessful amendments and an overview of the thousands of failed amendments. . . . Over 425 alphabetically arranged entries explore everything from affirmative action, to balancing the budget, to victims' rights, to world government. . . . Five appendixes present the Constitution of the United States, dates amendments were proposed and ratified, number of amendments by decade, most popular amending proposals by year, and chronological list of proposals by individuals outside congress." Publisher's note

Includes bibliographical references

343   Military, tax, trade, industrial law

The **American** Bar Association legal guide for small business; everything a small-business person must know, from start-up employment laws to financing and selling a business. Three Rivers Press (NY) 2000 523p pa $17   **343**
1. Small business
ISBN 0-8129-3015-0   LC 99-86498
Topics covered "include legal forms of operating businesses, buying an existing business or a franchise, hiring and firing employees, managing temps and independent contractors, dealing with contracts and scams, taxes of all types, and, finally, closing, selling, or bequeathing the business." Libr J

344   Labor, social service, education, cultural law

The **American** Bar Association guide to workplace law; everything you need to know about your rights as an employee or employer. Times Bks. 1997 192p pa $14   **344**

1. Labor—Law and legislation
ISBN 0-8129-2928-4   LC 96-35913
This guide covers laws affecting hiring, sexual harassment, leave time, health insurance, ending an employment relationship, retirement, unions, government employment and workplace rights

Hull, N. E. H., 1949-
Roe v. Wade; the abortion rights controversy in American history; [by] N.E.H. Hull and Peter Charles Hoffer. University Press of Kan. 2001 315p (Landmark law cases & American society) $35; pa $15.95   **344**
1. McCorvey, Norma 2. Wade, Henry, 1914-2001 3. Roe v. Wade 4. Abortion—Law and legislation
ISBN 0-7006-1142-8; 0-7006-1143-6 (pa)   LC 2001-1785
This "study begins with three chapters on U.S. abortion history: its nineteenth-century criminalization; the effect of improving birth-control methods in the twentieth century; and state-level legal changes in the 1960s. The authors then analyze the decision itself and trace the continuing battles of the next three decades." Booklist
This volume "is crammed with information but remains very readable and a good source for student papers." Libr J

Irons, Peter H., 1940-
Jim Crow's children; the broken promise of the Brown decision; [by] Peter Irons. Viking 2002 376p $29.95   **344**
1. Brown v. Board of Education 2. Segregation in education—Law and legislation
ISBN 0-670-88918-0   LC 2002-19843
The author examines the 1954 Brown v. the Board of Education decision "and its cultural context—including jurist personalities and interests leading up to and subsequent to the Brown decision." Booklist
Includes bibliographical references

Joel, Lewin G.
Every employee's guide to the law; what you need to know about your rights in the workplace—and what to do if they are violated; [by] Lewin G. Joel III. 3rd ed, rev and updated. Pantheon Bks. 2001 431p pa $16   **344**
1. Employees—Civil rights 2. Labor—Law and legislation
ISBN 0-375-71445-6   LC 2001-21501
First published 1993
The author offers legal advice on such subjects as employee interviews, wages, hours, health and safety, sexual harassment, privacy, discrimination, and benefits

Outten, Wayne N.
The rights of employees and union members; the basic ACLU guide to the rights of employees and union members; [by] Wayne N. Outten, Robert J. Rabin, Lisa R. Lipman. 2nd ed completely rev & updated. Southern Ill. Univ. Press 1994 604p (American Civil Liberties Union handbook) hardcover o.p. paperback available $14.95   **344**
1. Employees—Civil rights 2. Labor unions—United States
ISBN 0-8093-1914-4 (pa)   LC 93-16895
A revised, combined edition of The rights of employees, by Wayne N. Outten, first published 1984 by Bantam Bks., and The rights of union members, by Clyde Summers and Robert J. Rabin, published 1979 by Avon Bks.
The authors use a "question-and-answer format to examine . . . such topics as the employment relationship, compensation and benefits, the union workplace, and workplace protections. They also answer questions about discrimination, including discrimination based on race, ethnicity, sex, religion, age, disability, AIDS, sexual orientation, and veteran and reserve status." Publisher's note

Perritt, Henry H., Jr.
Americans with Disabilities Act handbook; [by] Henry H. Perritt, Jr. 4th ed. Aspen Pubs. 2003 2v + 1 computer laser optical disc set $450   **344**
1. Handicapped—Law and legislation 2. Handicapped—Civil rights
ISBN 0-7355-3148-X   LC 2003-265473
First published 1992 by Excellent Bks.
"Supplemented twice a year for complete currency, these volumes . . . explore the statutory definition of disability, the concept of being 'otherwise qualified' for a job, and exactly how employers, business owners, and providers of governmental services must make 'reasonable accommodation.'" Publisher's note

Rubenstein, William B.

The rights of people who are HIV positive; the authoritative ACLU guide to the rights of people living with HIV disease and AIDS; [by] William B. Rubenstein, Ruth Eisenberg, Lawrence O. Gostin. Southern Ill. Univ. Press 1996 384p (American Civil Liberties Union handbook) hardcover o.p. paperback available $15   **344**

1. AIDS (Disease)—Law and legislation
ISBN 0-8093-1992-6 (pa)   LC 95-52122

This guide to the legal rights of HIV positive people is divided "in four parts: the disease itself and the related testing, public health, and confidentiality issues; day-to-day issues involving insurance, family law, and health care decision-making; discrimination in housing and work; and AIDS in prisons, schools, as a factor in immigration, and among IV drug users. . . . The authors do not shrink from complicated or difficult subjects and generally do a fine job of explaining and humanizing the material." Libr J

Sack, Steven Mitchell, 1954-

The employee rights handbook; the essential guide for people on the job. rev and updated. Warner Bks. 2000 459p $13.95
344

1. Employees—Civil rights 2. Labor—Law and legislation
ISBN 0-446-67326-9   LC 99-33758

First published 1990 by Facts on File

This "handbook advises employees on what to do when faced with illegal interview questions, sexual harassment, discrimination, illegal firings and layoffs, and defamatory job references. Practical advice is provided for when and how to hire an attorney, negotiating a job, writing a letter of protest regarding illegal interview questions, and writing a letter demanding a written explanation for discharge." Libr J

345   Criminal law

DeLaughter, Bobby

Never too late; the prosecutor's story of justice in the Medgar Evers case. Scribner 2001 313p il $27   **345**

1. De La Beckwith, Byron 2. Trials
ISBN 0-684-86503-3   LC 00-30106

"The author draws on his journals and the legal transcriptions to re-create the research and interviews that made indictment possible and the thrust and parry of trial examination and cross-examination. DeLaughter's . . . story begins with requests to reopen the case in 1989, and then follows a team's efforts to reconstruct the case over a period of years." Booklist

Dunne, Dominick

Justice; crimes, trials, and punishments. Crown 2001 337p hardcover o.p. paperback available $14   **345**

1. Trials
ISBN 0-609-80963-6 (pa)   LC 2001-28214

"Dunne describes the events surrounding several high-profile murders, including those of Nicole Simpson and Ron Goldman, Edmond Safra, Sunny von Bulow (attempted murder), Kitty and Jose Menendez, Pati Margello, Patricia Burton Lonergan, Martha Moxley, and,

in the work's most affecting piece, his own daughter, Dominique Dunne." Libr J

"Fascinating stuff, though less than complimentary about the American system of justice." Booklist

Geis, Gilbert

Crimes of the century; from Leopold & Loeb to O.J. Simpson; [by] Gilbert Geis and Leigh B. Bienen. Northeastern Univ. Press 1998 227p $40; pa $18.95   **345**

1. Trials 2. Crime—United States
ISBN 1-55553-360-4; 1-55553-427-9 (pa)
LC 98-23180

The authors discuss "five of the most famous crimes and trials of the 20th century. The cases of Leopold and Loeb, the Scottsboro boys, the Lindbergh kidnapping, Alger Hiss, and O.J. Simpson. . . . Though each case is covered from crime through punishment (or acquittal) in fewer than 50 pages, the depth of historical detail and legal analysis is remarkable. The authors are particularly adept at placing these crimes within both their immediate historical settings and the larger societal issues." Libr J

Includes bibliographical references

Geoghegan, Thomas

In America's court; how a civil lawyer who likes to settle stumbled into a criminal trial. New Press (NY) 2002 206p $23.95; pa $15.95   **345**

1. Administration of criminal justice
ISBN 1-56584-732-6; 1-56584-817-9 (pa)
LC 2002-20065

The author "describes participating in a criminal trial after arranging to assist in the defense of a young man accused of committing a felony murder. As the trial proceeds, he talks about his work as a civil lawyer, what it means to be a lawyer, and the issues lawyers face." Libr J

Hoffer, Peter Charles

The Salem witchcraft trials; a legal history. University Press of Kan. 1997 165p (Landmark law cases & American society) hardcover o.p. paperback available $12.95
345

1. Trials 2. Salem (Mass.)—History
ISBN 0-7006-0859-1 (pa)   LC 97-19986

"Hoffer discusses the legal nature of the charges of witchcraft, the evidential and procedural characteristics of the trials of the accused, and the roles and attitudes of the ministers and magistrates who controlled the proceedings. . . . Hoffer offers little that is new in terms of interpretation, but he presents it well and in a manner easily grasped by the general reader." Choice

Includes bibliographical references

Mack, Raneta Lawson, 1963-

A layperson's guide to criminal law. Greenwood Press 1999 201p $69.95   **345**

1. Criminal law
ISBN 0-313-30556-0   LC 98-53382

This explanation of the basics of criminal law includes numerous hypothetical situations that place some of the more difficult concepts in an "everyday" context. An overview of the criminal trial process, from the arrest to the final verdict is also provided

Includes bibliographical references

Neff, James
The wrong man; the final verdict on the Dr. Sam Sheppard murder case. Random House 2001 414p il hardcover o.p. paperback available $13.95   **345**
1. Sheppard, Sam, d. 1970 2. Trials 3. Homicide
ISBN 0-375-76105-5 (pa)   LC 2001-41917
A reexamination of the Sheppard case "from Marilyn Sheppard's brutal murder before dawn July 4, 1954, in suburban Cleveland, to her husband's trial, years in prison, release, retrial, and sad final years, as well as the son's effort to force Ohio to declare Sheppard innocent. . . . Neff brings to life family members, neighbors, defense and prosecuting attorneys, witnesses, and the critical 'other suspect,' and analyzes courtroom arguments and evidence effectively. Will appeal to legal-thriller fans and readers concerned about abuse of prosecutorial power." Booklist

Walsh, John Evangelist, 1927-
Moonlight; Abraham Lincoln and the Almanac trial. St. Martin's Press 2000 166p il $22.95   **345**
1. Lincoln, Abraham, 1809-1865 2. Trials
ISBN 0-312-22922-4   LC 99-59606
This is "the story of how Abraham Lincoln secured the acquittal of murder suspect William 'Duff' Armstrong, the son of an old New Salem friend, by making use of an almanac to discredit a witness's description of the position of the moon on the night in question." Libr J
Includes bibliographical references

346.01   Law of persons and domestic relations

The **American** Bar Association guide to family law; the complete and easy guide to all the laws of marriage, parenthood, separation and divorce. Times Bks.; Random House 1996 179p maps pa $13   **346.01**
1. Domestic relations 2. Law—United States
ISBN 0-8129-2791-5   LC 95-52854
This guide offers advice on such legal issues as divorce, child custody, adoption, premarital agreements, unmarried cohabitation, domestic violence, and child support

The **American** Bar Association legal guide for older Americans; the law every American over fifty needs to know. Times Bks.; [distributed by] American Bar Assn. 1998 251p il pa $13   **346.01**
1. Elderly—Law and legislation
ISBN 0-8129-2937-3   LC 97-22270
This guide covers such topics as age discrimination in employment, disability rights, Medicare benefits, estate planning, retirement, health insurance, and grandparents' visitation rights

Boland, Mary L.
Your right to child custody, visitation, and support. 2nd ed. Sphinx Pub. (Naperville) 2001 328p (Legal survival guides) pa $24.95   **346.01**
1. Child custody 2. Visitation rights (Domestic relations) 3. Child support
ISBN 1-57248-162-5   LC 2001-41175
First published 2000
The author "describes all the legal issues affecting the balance between the rights of parents and those of the child. Problems such as child kidnapping, financial support, and determining custody are discussed." Libr J [review of 2000 edition]

Kennedy, Randall
Interracial intimacies; sex, marriage, identity, and adoption. Pantheon Bks. 2003 676p $30   **346.01**
1. Interracial marriage—Law and legislation 2. Interracial adoption
ISBN 0-375-40255-1   LC 2002-72786
The author "surveys 400 years of interracial intimacy, from the knotty relationship between master and slave to recent adoption reforms and politicization of multiethnic people, and interweaves a compelling argument for racial egalitarianism and against race matching in adoption. Short on jargon and full of fascinating illustrative anecdotes, his book will appeal to both general readers and scholars." Libr J
Includes bibliographical references

The **Rights** of women; the basic ACLU guide to women's rights; [by] Susan Deller Ross [et al.] 3rd ed, completely rev and up-to-date. Southern Ill. Univ. Press 1993 317p (American Civil Liberties Union handbook) $27.50; pa $19.95   **346.01**
1. Women—Law and legislation 2. Women's rights
ISBN 0-8093-1898-9; 0-8093-1633-1 (pa)
                          LC 92-34244
First published 1973 by Sunrise Books/Dutton
Topics covered "include employment, education, parenting, family law, and reproductive freedom. This handbook also examines criminal proceedings, insurance, the military, credit, and the rights of homeless women." Publisher's note
Includes bibliographical references

Sitarz, Daniel, 1948-
Divorce yourself; the national no-fault divorce kit. Nova Pub. Co. (Legal self-help series) $24.95   **346.01**
1. Divorce—Law and legislation
Also available with CD-ROM for $34.95
First published 1990. (5th edition 2002) Periodically revised
"Legally valid in all 50 states and Washington D.C." Cover
This book "includes clear explanations of divorce-related legal issues and terminology, checklists that facilitate discussion of financial and custodial arrangements, and advice regarding tax consequences and name changes. Sample forms are included, along with precise instructions for preparing and filing them, and also a chapter that advises the user on court appearance and procedures. The appendix consists of a summary of the divorce laws of all 50 states with appropriate citations

Sitarz, Daniel, 1948-—*Continued*
and the advice to check the latest version for possible changes." Booklist
Includes bibliographical references

Women's legal guide; editor, Barbara R. Hauser with Julie A. Tigges. Fulcrum 1996 526p hardcover o.p. paperback available $22.95 **346.01**
1. Women—Law and legislation
ISBN 1-55591-303-2 (pa)   LC 95-46893
"This is a collection of essays written by women attorneys for women who need legal information. Family- and health- related issues such as divorce, family violence, and reproductive rights are covered, as are business topics of particular concern to women. . . . Estate planning, sexual discrimination, dealing with disabilities, and the rights of lesbian women are considered as well. The writing is consistently clear, objective, and practical." Libr J
Includes bibliographical references

Woodhouse, Violet, 1948-
Divorce and money; how to make the best financial decisions during divorce; by Violet Woodhouse and Victoria Felton-Collins, with M.C. Blakeman; edited by Robin Leonard and Stephen Elias. Nolo Press (Berkeley) pa $34.99 **346.01**
1. Divorce—Law and legislation 2. Property—Law and legislation
First published 1991. (6th edition 2002) Periodically revised
A guide to financial problems that arise as a result of divorce proceedings

346.03 Torts (delicts)

Matthews, Joseph L.
How to win your personal injury claim; edited by Kimberly Carver. 4th ed. Nolo Press (Berkeley) 2002 various paging il pa $29.99 **346.03**
1. Liability (Law) 2. Accident insurance
ISBN 0-87337-834-2   LC 2002-24275
First published 1992
This offers advice and instruction on how to make a personal injury claim without a lawyer. Gathering evidence, calculating a claim's worth, and negotiating tactics are discussed

346.04 Property law

The **American** Bar Association guide to home ownership; the complete and easy guide to all the law every home owner should know. Times Bks. 1995 193p pa $13 **346.04**
1. Real estate 2. Houses—Buying and selling
ISBN 0-8129-2535-1   LC 94-40827
This volume covers "such basics as deeds and titles, shared ownership, taxes, insurance, refinancing, neighborhood disputes, and liability issues. A chapter entitled 'Getting Older' answers questions about reverse mortgages and discusses what to look for in retirement communities. Contemporary concerns about lead, asbestos, and radon are introduced, and there are forms, phone numbers, and references to other sources." Libr J
"This easy-to-read, jargon-free book provides answers to legal questions most readers would never associate with home ownership." Booklist

Crews, Kenneth D.
Copyright essentials for librarians and educators; [by] Kenneth D. Crews with contributions from Dwayne K. Buttler [et al.] American Lib. Assn. 2001 143p pa $45 **346.04**
1. Copyright
ISBN 0-8389-0797-0   LC 00-59421
This reference is "designed to instruct today's information providers on the fundamentals of current copyright law. . . . [It answers such questions as]: What makes a work copyright-protected or not? How long do copyrights last? What are the rights of copyright owners? How can I determine what qualifies as fair use? What are the need-to-knows regarding copyright and the Internet? Publisher's note

Elias, Stephen
Patent, copyright & trademark; by Stephen Elias and Richard Stim. Nolo Press (Berkeley) il pa $39.99 **346.04**
1. Patents 2. Copyright 3. Trademarks
First published 1996. (5th edition 2002) Periodically revised
The author explains concepts, issues, and terms concerning intellectual property, discusses trade secret, copyright, patent, and trademark law, and provides sample forms

Trademark; legal care for your business & product name. Nolo Press (Berkeley) il $39.99 **346.04**
1. Trademarks
First published 1992. (6th edition 2003) Periodically revised
The authors explain "how to: choose a distinctive name or logo that others can't copy, conduct a trademark search, register the trademark, protect and maintain the trademark, handle disputes out of Court. Contains all the official forms with step-by-step instructions." Publisher's note

Fishman, Stephen
The copyright handbook. Nolo Press (Berkeley) pa $39.99 **346.04**
1. Copyright
First published 1991. (7th edition 2003) Frequently revised
"Designed as a practical handbook for writers and publishers. Includes a list of legal aid groups and sample forms." Guide to Ref Books. 11th edition

Hoffmann, Gretchen McCord

Copyright in cyberspace; questions and answers for librarians. Neal-Schuman 2001 264p (Neal-Schuman netguide series) pa $65

346.04

1. Copyright 2. Internet

ISBN 1-55570-410-7   LC 00-67869

"This book covers all aspects of copyright law of interest to public librarians, academic librarians, and school library media specialists." Book Rep

"This volume will be indispensable for school districts and public libraries." SLJ

Includes bibliographical references

Lessig, Lawrence

The future of ideas; the fate of the commons in a connected world. Random House 2001 352p hardcover o.p. paperback available $15   **346.04**

1. Copyright 2. Internet 3. Information society

ISBN 0-375-72644-6 (pa)   LC 2001-31968

The author "argues that as the Internet faces the challenges of intellectual property laws, it should not become so controlled that it discourages innovation and creativity in the digital world." Libr J

"Some of Lessig's sweeping proposals are sure to spark a lively debate, but his well-reasoned, clearly written argument is powerful." Publ Wkly

Portman, Janet

Every landlord's legal guide; by Marcia Stewart, and Ralph Warner & Janet Portman. Nolo Press (Berkeley) il $44.99   **346.04**

1. Landlord and tenant

First published 1996. (6th edition 2003) Frequently revised

Includes CD-ROM

This guide explains how to "screen and choose prospective tenants, write a legal rental agreement or lease, hire a property manager, deal with problem tenants, understand repair, maintenance and security responsibilities, avoid lawsuits, comply with laws regarding security deposits, privacy, discrimination, housing, habitability and . . . more." Publisher's note

Every tenant's legal guide; by Janet Portman & Marcia Stewart. 3rd ed. Nolo Press (Berkeley) 2002 various paging il $20.99   **346.04**

1. Landlord and tenant

ISBN 0-87337-825-3   LC 2002-19574

First published 1997

This guide explains how to find and inspect a home, negotiate clauses in a lease or rental agreement, understand rules on rent increases, late rent and rent control, get repairs and maintenance, protect privacy rights, fight discrimination, deal with environmental hazards, security deposits, evictions and legal procedures

Strauss, Steven D., 1958-

Landlord and tenant. Norton 1998 155p (Ask a lawyer) $25; pa $14   **346.04**

1. Landlord and tenant

ISBN 0-393-04585-4; 0-393-31730-7 (pa)
LC 97-33617

This book covers the legal rights and responsibilities of tenants and landlords including such topics as what to look for in an apartment or lease, how to evict tenants or avoid eviction, and how to break a lease

Talab, Rosemary Sturdevant

Commonsense copyright; a guide for educators and librarians; by R. S. Talab. 2nd ed. McFarland & Co. 1999 292p pa $45

346.04

1. Copyright

ISBN 0-7864-0675-5   LC 99-12915

First published 1986

This volume "highlights recent copyright legislation and the impact of current copyright protection on new technologies. The text includes an entire section on 'Computer-Based Systems' detailing copyright and electronic publishing, educational multimedia, distance learning, and the Internet and World Wide Web. The accurate, well-organized guide describes the legal and ethical 'fair use' of copyrighted materials and provides the librarian and the educator with an excellent resource for dealing with current copyright issues." Libr J

346.05 Law regarding inheritance, succession, trusts

The **American** Bar Association guide to wills and estates; everythng you need to know about wills, trusts, estates, and taxes. Times Bks. 1995 225p pa $13   **346.05**

1. Wills 2. Estate planning

ISBN 0-8129-2536-X   LC 95-2489

This guide includes information about crafting wills, avoiding unnecessary inheritance taxes, minimizing probate, creating living trusts, choosing an executor, transfering property without a will, and protecting property in case of incapacitation

Clifford, Denis

Make your own living trust. Nolo Press (Berkeley) $39.99   **346.05**

1. Estate planning 2. Inheritance and succession

First published 1993. (5th edition 2002) Periodically revised

Accompanied by CD-ROM

This explains how to create a living trust, how to transfer property to it, and how to manage it. Includes forms and instructions

Nolo's simple will book. 5th ed. Nolo Press (Berkeley) 2003 various paging il + 1 computer laser optical disc $36.99   **346.05**

1. Wills

ISBN 0-87337-939-X   LC 2001-42764

First published 1986

This guide offers instructions in creating a legal will, including seven sample documents, worksheets as tearouts, and a CD-ROM. A detailed discussion of estate planning is also provided for those who may want more than a will

"This is an excellent resource for those who want to go it alone and for those who are trying to get organized before working with an attorney." Libr J

Plan your estate; by Denis Clifford & Cora Jordan. Nolo Press (Berkeley) pa $44.99

346.05

1. Estate planning

First published 1989. (6th edition 2002) Periodically revised

This guide covers basic estate planning, probate avoidance, living wills, federal estate and gift taxes, trusts, durable powers of attorney, and more

Clifford, Denis—*Continued*

Quick & legal will book. 3rd ed. Nolo Press (Berkeley) 2003 various paging il pa $16.99   **346.05**

1. Wills
ISBN 0-87337-948-9

First published 1996

"Written for people under age 50 with less than $600,000 in assets, the book instructs readers in how to designate who gets their property, name someone to care for minor children, manage property left to them, and name an executor." Libr J [review of 1996 edition]

Plotnick, Charles

How to settle an estate; a manual for executors and trustees; [by] Charles K. Plotnick, Stephan R. Leimberg. 3rd rev ed. Plume Bks. 2002 354p pa $16   **346.05**

1. Executors and administrators
ISBN 0-452-28342-6   LC 2002-727766

First published 1986 by Doubleday with title: The executors manual

This guide offers estate executors and trustees advice on such topics as "How to raise cash for immediate estate expenses; Dealing with insurance claims; Knowing when to hire a lawyer, an accountant, and a stock broker; Managing real estate [and] Distributing assets." Publisher's note

Shotwell, Barbara, 1946-

Pass it on; a practical approach to the fears and facts of planning your estate; [by] Barbara Shotwell and Nancy R. Greenway. Hyperion 2000 286p il $22.95; pa $14.95
                                                    346.05

1. Estate planning
ISBN 0-7868-6580-6; 0-7868-8494-0 (pa)
                                                  LC 99-49481

The authors explain "the essential estate-planning documents, various kinds of trusts, retirement plans, business considerations, and the probate process. . . . The text is replete with cartoons, quotes, illustrative song titles, and anecdotes that add levity and accessibility without oversimplifying the treatment of the subject." Libr J

Sitarz, Daniel, 1948-

Prepare your own will; the national will kit. Nova Pub. Co. (Legal self-help series) pa $27.95   **346.05**

1. Wills
Accompanied by CD-ROM

First published 1988 with title: Prepare your own last will and testament—without a lawyer. (5th edition 2000) Periodically revised

This offers instructions and forms for preparing a will, with assessment questionnaires on property and beneficiaries, checklists, and sample wills, an appendix of state laws relating to wills, and forms on CD-ROM

Strauss, Steven D., 1958-

Wills and trusts. Norton 1998 176p (Ask a lawyer) $25; pa $14   **346.05**

1. Wills 2. Estate planning
ISBN 0-393-04583-8; 0-393-31728-5 (pa)
                                                  LC 97-33619

This guide describes "The various phases of wills, trusts, and estate planning and provides legal definitions, tips, sample scenarios, and a typical will." Publisher's note

"Strauss specializes in transforming the arcane and obtuse into everyman's lingo and comprehension." Booklist

346.07   Commercial law

How to file for chapter 7 bankruptcy; by Stephen Elias [et al.] Nolo Press (Berkeley) $34.99   **346.07**

1. Bankruptcy

First published 1989. (10th edition 2002) Periodically revised; variant title: How to file for bankruptcy

This offers advice on such topics as personal debt, property liability, asset protection, rebuilding credit, and filling out and filing forms

347   Civil procedure and courts

Bergman, Paul, 1943-

Represent yourself in court; how to prepare and try a winning case; by Paul Bergman & Sara J. Berman-Barrett; edited by Lisa Guerin. 4th ed. Nolo Press (Berkeley) 2003 various paging il $34.99   **347**

1. Litigation
ISBN 0-87337-908-X   LC 2002-43202

First published 1993

The authors describe the legal process for the layman in dealing with such cases as personal injury claims, landlord-tenant and small business disputes, divorce, child custody and child support

Includes bibliographical references

BNA's directory of state and federal courts, judges, and clerks. Bureau of Natl. Affairs pa $165   **347**

1. Courts—United States—Directories

Annual. First published 1986

A state-by-state and federal listing

This directory lists the names, addresses, and telephone numbers of over 14,000 judges and approximately 5,300 clerks and administrators, in more than 2,400 courts at the three highest levels of all US states and territories

Dwyer, Jim, 1957-

Actual innocence; five days to execution and other dispatches from the wrongly convicted; [by] Jim Dwyer, Peter Neufeld, Barry Scheck. Doubleday 2000 297p il maps $27.50   **347**

1. Administration of criminal justice
ISBN 0-385-49341-X   LC 99-45876

This book deals with "men wrongly convicted of rape and murder, some of them sentenced to die, who were able to prove they were innocent. They largely owe their exoneration to the Innocence Project, a program based at Cardozo Law School in New York. . . . The Innocence Project works to reopen old convictions, using DNA evidence." N Y Times Book Rev

Includes bibliographical references

Dwyer, William L., 1929-2002
In the hands of the people; the trial jury's origins, triumphs, troubles, and future in American democracy. Thomas Dunne Bks. 2002 237p $24.95 **347**
1. Jury
ISBN 0-312-27812-8   LC 2001-54756
This is an "examination of the history and future direction of the trial jury. Despite criticisms aimed at juries following verdicts in some high-profile, complicated trials, Dwyer firmly believes the system is worth preserving—with some fine-tuning." Booklist
"Dwyer's book is well written and accessible to non-attorneys." Libr J
Includes bibliographical references

Finkelman, Paul, 1949-
Landmark decisions of the United States Supreme Court; [by] Paul Finkelman, Melvin I. Urofsky. CQ Press 2003 687p $225 **347**
1. United States. Supreme Court 2. Constitutional law—United States
ISBN 1-56802-720-6   LC 2002-153035
"More than 1,000 of the Court's most important decisions are discussed in this title. The cases selected for inclusion fall into three categories: decisions recognized as the most important (*Dred Scott v. Sandford, Roe v. Wade*); cases that are significant but of lesser impact; and those that were narrow in influence. . . . Summaries are preceded by the type and date of the decision, the vote of each justice, and the authors of the majority and dissenting opinion. The summaries give the background, relevant legal points, and impact of each decision. Underlying principles are clearly explained." Booklist
Includes bibliographical references

Garbus, Martin, 1934-
Courting disaster; the Supreme Court and the dangerous unmaking of American law. Times Bks. 2002 322p $25; pa $15 **347**
1. United States. Supreme Court 2. Constitutional history—United States
ISBN 0-8050-6918-6; 0-8050-7287-X (pa)
                                LC 2002-20314
"Garbus sees the Rehnquist Court as undermining the ability of both the Federal judiciary and especially Congress to play a prominent role in the progressive evolution of the modern state. . . . Carefully explicating the conflicting Court perceptions of federalism, he paints a vivid picture of internal conflict among the justices." Libr J
Includes bibliographical references

Great American court cases; Mark F. Mikula and L. Mpho Mabunda, editors; Allison McClintic Marion, associate editor. Gale Group 1999 4v set $415 **347**
1. Law—United States 2. Trials
ISBN 0-7876-2947-2   LC 99-11419
Contents: v1 Individual liberties; v2 Criminal justice; v3 Equal protection and family law; v4 Business and government
This set includes approximately eight hundred cases, most of them cases before the Supreme Court, but major federal and state cases that set precedents are also dealt with
"An extensive, attractive, well-organized resource, recommended for high-school, public, and academic libraries." Booklist
Includes bibliographical references

Great American trials; Edward W. Knappman, editor; Stephen G. Christianson and Lisa Paddock, consulting legal editors. 2nd ed. Gale Group 2002 2v il set $170 **347**
1. Trials
ISBN 0-7876-4901-5
"A New England Publishing Associates book"
First published 1994
Contents: v1 1637-1949; v2 1950-2001
Featuring approximately 360 trials from the 1800s to the present, entries "cover the principals involved, the crime charged, the verdict and sentence, and the significance and impact of each trial." Publisher's note
Includes bibliographical references

Great world trials; Edward W. Knappman, editor. Gale Res. 1997 xxviii, 536p il $90 **347**
1. Trials
ISBN 0-7876-0805-X   LC 96-38793
This is a "narrative of 100 international trials of historical, political, or social significance." Libr J
"From the Alcibiades trial in 415 B.C. to the 1996 trial of Yigal Amir and covering crimes such as murder, treason, fraud, and negligence, this work paints a vivid portrait of international jurisprudence through the ages." Booklist
Includes bibliographical references

Irons, Peter H., 1940-
A people's history of the Supreme Court; by Peter Irons. Viking 1999 542p $32.95; pa $15.95 **347**
1. United States. Supreme Court
ISBN 0-670-87006-4; 0-14-029201-2 (pa)
                                LC 98-53706
In this history of the Supreme Court the author "focuses on the human aspect of decisions, from the impact of the slave trade and related issues in the formation of the nation to the contradictory values of the founding fathers and subsequent lawmakers. . . . Irons clearly and repeatedly shows how the law reflects political reality above esoteric legal mandates." Booklist
Includes bibliographical references

Lewis, Anthony, 1927-
Gideon's trumpet. Random House 1964 262p hardcover o.p. paperback available $12 **347**
1. Gideon, Clarence Earl 2. United States. Supreme Court 3. Law—United States
ISBN 0-679-72312-9 (pa)
An account of the case of a Florida man convicted of burglary which brought about a historic decision of the Supreme Court decreeing that in all states a defendant is entitled to counsel
Includes bibliographical references

O'Brien, David M.
Storm center; the Supreme Court in American politics. Norton il pa $24.85 **347**
1. United States. Supreme Court
First published 1986. (6th edition 2002) Periodically revised
The author discusses "the day-to-day workings of the Court justices and their law clerks, how cases are accept-

O'Brien, David M.—*Continued*
ed for hearing, what negotiations and compromises go on, how case opinions get written—and what happens to American society when two conservative presidents, Reagan and Bush, appoint the majority of justices." Publisher's note
Includes bibliographical references

O'Connor, Sandra Day
The majesty of the law; reflections of a Supreme Court justice; edited by Craig Joyce. Random House 2003 xx, 330p il $24.95
347
1. United States. Supreme Court 2. Judges
ISBN 0-375-50925-9   LC 2002-68210
"The first female Supreme Court justice offers a broad-ranging look at the most revered and enigmatic institution of the federal government, from the day-to-day activities of the court to portraits of individual justices of historic perspective on how the court has evolved." Booklist
Includes bibliographical references

The **Oxford** companion to the Supreme Court of the United States; editor in chief, Kermit L. Hall; editors, James W. Ely, Jr., Joel B. Grossman, William M. Wiecek. Oxford Univ. Press 1992 xx, 1032p il $70   **347**
1. United States. Supreme Court
ISBN 0-19-505835-6   LC 92-3863
"An encyclopedia of constitutional law, the Supreme Court, and the American judicial system, with more than 1,000 signed alphabetically arranged entries. Ranging in length from one paragraph to a 30-page History of the Court, articles cover major cases, terms and legal concepts, constitutional law issues, and justices and other historical figures. Illustrated with portraits of justices." Guide to Ref Books. 11th edition

The **Supreme** Court A to Z; Kenneth Jost, editor. 3rd ed. CQ Press 2003 576p $125
347
1. United States. Supreme Court
ISBN 1-56802-802-4
First published 1993
"Topics, which range from abortion to zoning, are arranged alphabetically with appropriate cross references to sections that provide further information. For most issues discussed, a historical overview essay is provided for all relevant cases, as is an explanation of how the Court's decisions have changed (or not changed) over the years as interpretations evolve." Libr J [review of 1993 edition]

The **Supreme** Court compendium; data, decisions, and developments; [by] Lee Epstein [et al.] 3rd ed. CQ Press 2003 xx, 780p $100   **347**
1. United States. Supreme Court 2. Judges
ISBN 1-56802-592-0   LC 2002-41345
First published 1994
This offers "a copious amount of data concerning the Supreme Court, its judges and judicial staff, petitions and decisions, political climate, public opinion, and much more, in a well-organized reference work. . . . There are nine chapters, each with suggested methods of using the information and the rationale for the data collection and inclusion. The date, in tabular format, present a concise,

easily accessible presentation. . . . The inclusion of current Internet/Websites in this edition is welcomed by those users pursuing online research." Am Ref Books Annu, 1997 [review of 1996 edition]
Includes bibliographical references

Warner, Ralph E.
Everybody's guide to small claims court; [by] Ralph Warner. Nolo Press (Berkeley) various paging il pa $26.99   **347**
1. Small claims court
First published 1980 by Addison-Wesley. (9th edition 2003) Periodically revised
The author "discusses filing court papers, paying fees, and using witnesses and examines typical kinds of small claims. The appendixes detail procedures, list monetary thresholds, and reference statutory citations." Libr J

348 Laws (Statutes), regulations, cases

Howard, Philip
The death of common sense; how the law is suffocating America; [by] Philip K. Howard. Random House 1995 c1994 202p o.p.; Warner Bks. paperback available $13.95
348
1. Law—United States 2. Law reform 3. Bureaucracy
ISBN 0-446-67228-9 (pa)   LC 94-34349
The author contends "that we need less law, fewer rules and more common sense. He thinks that American law is now endangering both freedom and prosperity precisely because it is so excruciatingly rule-bound." N Y Times Book Rev
This book "is absolutely wonderful to read. It is accessible to general readers, yet it should at the same time serve as a clarion call to the legal profession to clean up its house and to the legislatures to pass functional statutes." Choice

349 Law of specific jurisdictions

1001 legal words you need to know; Jay M. Feinman, editor; with topical essays by James E. Clapp. Oxford Univ. Press 2003 239p $17.95   **349**
1. Law—United States—Dictionaries
ISBN 0-19-516503-9   LC 2003-9869
This "guide to the language of the American legal system . . . defines and explains every term with a sample sentence, and many entries have supplementary notes. In addition, the book includes a number of quick miniguides to legal troubleshooting that includes information on understanding wills, trusts, and inheritance, granting someone the power of attorney, understanding contracts, what to do if you're sued, how to choose a lawyer, exploring law school, and enjoying cop and lawyer dramas." Publisher's note
Includes bibliographical references

Encyclopedia of American law; [edited by] David Schultz. Facts on File 2002 542p il $75   **349**
1. Law—United States—Encyclopedias
ISBN 0-8160-4329-9   LC 2001-40206
"This encyclopedia's entries average a page in length and include contemporary topics such as affirmative action and recent court cases as well as concepts such as entrapment, equity, and insanity. . . . This resource packs a lot of material and is easy to read and navigate." Book Rep
For a fuller review see: Booklist, July, 2002

Friedman, Lawrence Meir, 1930-
American law in the 20th century; [by] Lawrence M. Friedman. Yale Univ. Press 2002 722p $38   **349**
1. Law—United States
ISBN 0-300-09137-0   LC 2001-3332
The author "examines the American legal system as an integral part of the larger society, both reflecting and causing changes therein. By adopting such a focus, the author makes his book accessible to readers who are not legal scholars." Booklist
Includes bibliographical references

Gale encyclopedia of everyday law; Shirelle Phelps, editor. Gale Group 2003 2v set $250   **349**
1. Law—United States
ISBN 0-7876-5759-X   LC 2002-8407
This set "provides short (2000- to 5000-word) essays in 24 alphabetically arranged subject areas (e.g., automobiles, civil rights, consumer issues, estate planning, First Amendment issues, retirement, and taxes). The text starts with an overview of the American legal system, explaining the various types of laws and tribunals. The essays in the first section, on the Americans with Disabilities Act, contain a short overview of the law, using boldface for terms (e.g., discrimination) defined in the glossary. Essays in other sections cover issues ranging from buying and selling real estate to traveling with children to elder abuse. Each essay includes a list of additional resources and organizations, including numerous web sites." Libr J
For a fuller review see: Booklist, May 1, 2003

National survey of state laws; Richard A. Leiter, editor. 4th ed. Gale Group 2003 693p $105   **349**
1. Law—United States
ISSN 1078-2095
Irregular. First published 1993
Summarizes state laws on 45 subjects, divided into general legal categories: business and consumer, criminal, education, employment, family, general civil, real estate, and tax

The **Oxford** companion to American law; editor in chief, Kermit L. Hall; editors, David S. Clark [et al.] Oxford Univ. Press 2002 xxvi, 912p $75   **349**
1. Law—United States
ISBN 0-19-508878-6   LC 2002-284010
The alphabetically arranged "entries consider how law, legal institutions, and court decisions are related to social demands and legal responses. . . . The volume also includes standard legal terms and key legal concepts, such

as verdicts and venues, as well as biographical statements about leading individuals in the legal profession. . . . With a substantial breadth of information and analysis, this volume is accessible to every reader. All libraries will find it an invaluable reference source." Libr J

Van Susteren, Greta, 1954-
My turn at the bully pulpit; straight talk about the things that drive me nuts; by Greta Van Susteren and Elaine Lafferty. Crown 2003 233p $25   **349**
1. Law—United States
ISBN 1-4000-4662-9   LC 2003-7601
Contents: Anatomy of a cable news show; New patriotism and the military; The death penalty; On loyalty and disagreement; Lifting the veil: on cameras in the courtroom; Looking good; No patience with poor education and no tolerance for zero tolerance; Hot coffee, personal responsibility, and gold chains; The wonderful world of torts; Fun; Sports, fairness, and competing for the highest score; Getting rich through failure and fraud; A final word from the viewers
The former criminal defense attorney "offers her opinions on a variety of controversial issues, including the death penalty, corporate greed, the politics of patriotism, and tort reform. All couched in candor and humor." Booklist

351.076   Civil service examinations

Civil service arithmetic and vocabulary. Arco pa $14.95   **351.076**
1. Civil service—Examinations
First published 1951. (14th edition 2002) Periodically revised
Contains basic instructions for working every type of math problem found on the exams. The vocabulary section includes a review of vocabulary words, verbal analogies, and sentence completion problems

Civil service handbook; everything you need to know to get a civil service job; edited by Gabriel Heilig. 14th ed. Thomson/Arco 2000 c2002 224p il pa $12.95   **351.076**
1. Civil service—United States 2. Civil service—Examinations
ISBN 0-02-863541-8
At head of title: Arco
This handbook covers where to look and how to apply for civil service jobs as well as job requirements, salaries, and promotional opportunities. Sample exam questions are included

Federal civil service jobs. 14th ed, [by] Dawn Rosenberg McKay, Michele Lipson. Thomson/Arco 2003 194p pa $14.95
                                       351.076
1. Civil service—United States
ISBN 0-7689-0921-X
11th-13th editions by Hy Hammer
This is a guide on how to search and apply for federal jobs. Information on eligibility requirements and promotional opportunities is included as well as a glossary of civil service hiring terms, sample questions, test strategies, and techniques for various qualifying exams

Guide to America's federal jobs; a complete directory of federal career opportunities. 2nd ed. Jist Works 2001 517p pa $18.95

351.076

1. Civil service—United States

ISBN 1-56370-526-5   LC 2001-279236

Originally published 1956 by the U.S. Govt. Ptg. Office with title: Federal careers; first published 1991 by JIST Works with title: America's federal jobs

This guide provides "tips on obtaining job vacancy announcements, application information, and employment forms. Included are details on 60 agencies and departments hiring the most employees, lists of federal job titles, lists of jobs for college graduates and particulars about special employment and volunteer programs." Libr J

352 General considerations of public administration

Moynihan, Daniel Patrick, 1927-2003

Secrecy; the American experience; [by] Daniel Patrick Moynihan; introduction by Richard Gid Powers. Yale Univ. Press 1998 262p il $38; pa $16   **352**

1. National security—United States 2. Executive power

ISBN 0-300-07756-4; 0-300-08079-4 (pa)

LC 98-8144

"Using his background as chairman of the bipartisan Commission on Protecting and Reducing Government Secrecy, Moynihan provides a fascinating account of the development of secrecy as a mode of regulation for the U.S. government since World War I: how it was born, how world events shaped it, how it has adversely affected momentous political decisions—dropping the bomb on Hiroshima, the Bay of Pigs fiasco, the Iran-contra affair—and how it has eluded efforts to curtail or end it." America

Includes bibliographical references

352.13 State and provincial administration

The **Book** of the states. Council of State Govts. $99; pa $79   **352.13**

1. State governments

ISSN 0068-0125

Also available CD-ROM version

Biennial, 1935-2001, Annual from 2002 Began publication 1935

"In addition to general articles on various aspects of state government, this source provides many statistical and directory data, the principal state officials, and such information as the nickname, motto, flower, bird, song, and tree of each state." Ref Sources for Small & Medium-sized Libr. 6th edition

Counties USA; a directory of United States Counties; Darren Smith, managing editor. 2nd ed. Omnigraphics 2003 672p il maps $120   **352.13**

1. County government 2. United States—Statistics

ISBN 0-7808-0546-1

First published 1997

The reference "provides statistical descriptions and . . . contact information for more than 3100 U.S. counties, based on information from the 2000 Census. . . . The book also offers . . . data on state rankings, percentages of total population below the poverty level, unemployment rates, and median home values." Libr J

This is "an excellent choice, offering multiple uses as a country directory, demographic source, and gazetteer." Choice

352.2 Organization of administration

United States government manual; Office of the Federal Register, National Archives and Records Service, General Services Administration. Claitor's Law Bks. pa $52

352.2

1. United States—Politics and government—Handbooks, manuals, etc.

Annual. First published 1935. Variant title: United States government organization manual

"Official handbook of the Federal government describing the purposes and programs of most Government agencies and listing the top personnel." N Y Public Libr. Ref Books for Child Collect. 2d edition

352.23 Chief executives

Guide to the presidency; Michael Nelson, editor. 3rd ed. CQ Press 2002 2v set $315

352.23

1. Presidents—United States

ISBN 1-56802-714-1   LC 2002-151619

First published 1989 with title: Congressional Quarterly's guide to the presidency

Contents: v1 Origins and development of the presidency; Selection and removal of the president; Powers of the presidency; The president, the public, and the parties; v2 The White House and the executive branch; Chief executive and federal government; Biographies of the presidents and vice presidents

This "is an essential purchase for public and academic libraries." Booklist

Includes bibliographical references

The **Presidency** A to Z; Michael Nelson, advisory editor. 3rd ed. CQ Press 2003 603p (CQ's American government A to Z series) $125   **352.23**

1. Presidents—United States—Encyclopedias

ISBN 1-56802-803-2   LC 2003-9464

First published 1992

"Approximately 300 entries describe the background of the presidents, their public experiences, daily and family life, powers and life in the White House, and deaths. Extensive essays explore concepts relating to the presidency such as Constitutional powers, the budget process, diplomatic activity, the cabinet, and the relationship of the presidency to Congress and the courts." Libr J [review of 1992 edition]

Includes bibliographical references

355 Military science

Amazons to fighter pilots; a biographical dictionary of military women; Reina Pennington, editor; foreword by Gerhard Weinberg. Greenwood Press 2003 2v il set $175 **355**
1. Women soldiers—Biography—Dictionaries
ISBN 0-313-29197-7   LC 2002-44777

"Entries profile over 300 remarkable women of the military, covering such groups as the Amazons, women in the Spanish Civil War, and Native Americans. . . . Additional tidbits—quotations, statistics, information on women and war—appear in sidebars throughout the text. Lists grouping entries by geographical regions, time periods, and branch of service serve as finding aids for researchers." Publisher's note

"This peerless work, situated at the nexus of military history and women's studies, is an essential companion to more male-biased biographical resources." Choice

Includes bibliographical references

The Book of war; edited by John Keegan. Viking 1999 492p hardcover o.p. paperback available $17 **355**
1. Military history
ISBN 0-14-029655-7 (pa)   LC 99-42660

This is an "anthology of eyewitness and participant writing covering 25 centuries, from Thucydides' history of the Peloponnesian War to a small-unit engagement between British and Iraqi infantry in the Persian Gulf war." N Y Times Book Rev

Includes bibliographical references

Buckley, Gail Lumet, 1937-
American patriots; the story of Blacks in the military from the Revolution to Desert Storm; [by] Gail Buckley. Random House 2001 xxiv, 534p il $29.95; pa $15.95 **355**
1. African American soldiers 2. United States—Military history 3. United States—Race relations
ISBN 0-375-50279-3; 0-375-76009-1 (pa)
          LC 00-51825

This is an account "of blacks in the U.S. military, both at home and abroad, from the 1770s to the 1990s. . . . This readable, spirited story deserves a place in every U.S. history collection, as well as in the black or military collections." Libr J

Includes bibliographical references

Clausewitz, Carl von, 1780-1831
On war; [by] Carl von Clausewitz; edited and translated by Michael Howard and Peter Paret; introductory essays by Peter Paret, Michael Howard and Bernard Brodie; with commentary by Bernard Brodie. Princeton Univ. Press 1976 717p $95; pa $26.95 **355**
1. Military art and science 2. War
ISBN 0-691-05657-9; 0-691-01854-5 (pa)
Original German edition, 1833

"Drawing on the experiences of Frederick the Great and Napoleon, Clausewitz tried to analyze the workings of military genius by isolating the factors that decide success in war. His conclusions have remained generally applicable, and since his work contains a minimum of technical discussion, it has retained a wide appeal." Ency Britannica

Coffey, Michael, 1954-
Days of infamy; great military blunders of the 20th century; introduction by Mike Wallace. Hyperion 1999 288p il $24.95 **355**
1. Military history 2. Errors
ISBN 0-7868-6556-3   LC 99-30839

In this companion volume to a History Channel series, the incidents covered "roam among the century's well-known military-related screwups, from a driver's poor knowledge of Sarajevo's streets in 1914, giving us World War I, to Iraq's invasion of Kuwait." Booklist

"Like the best general history volumes, Coffey's book, in clean, muscular prose, expertly informs as it artfully entertains." Publ Wkly

Cohen, Eliot A.
Supreme command; soldiers, statesmen, and leadership in wartime. Free Press 2002 288p $25 **355**
1. Military art and science 2. Leadership
ISBN 0-7432-3049-3   LC 2002-73630
Also available in paperback from Anchor Bks.

What made "Abraham Lincoln, Georges Clemenceau, Winston Churchill and David Ben Gurion . . . great wartime heads of state, according to . . . [the author] is that they were able to finesse a relationship with their military leaders that kept the balance of power squarely in (their own) civilian hands." Publ Wkly

Includes bibliographical references

De Pauw, Linda Grant
Battle cries and lullabies; women in war from prehistory to the present. University of Okla. Press 1998 395p il hardcover o.p. paperback available $21.95 **355**
1. Military history 2. Women—History 3. Women soldiers
ISBN 0-8061-3288-4 (pa)   LC 98-21219

This is a history of women in the military, "from prehistory to the Persian Gulf War and Tailhook." Booklist

"Though the book never directly states its larger claims, the wealth of evidence it provides renders the controversy over women in combat almost quaint—their presence on and near the battlefield is ancient, inescapable and irreversible." Publ Wkly

Includes bibliographical references

Dictionary of military terms; a guide to the language of warfare and military institutions; compiled by Trevor N. Dupuy [et al.] 2nd ed. Wilson, H.W. 2003 271p il $85 **355**
1. Military art and science—Dictionaries 2. Naval art and science—Dictionaries
ISBN 0-8242-1025-5   LC 2002-32960
First published 1986

This book offers "guidance to the language of contemporary warfare and military institutions, from weapons systems, strategies, and tactics to ranks, decorations, and administration." Publisher's note

"This is a very readable book for the general reader and will make a great addition to public, academic, and some high-school libraries as well as being useful for military professionals." Booklist

Encyclopedia of American military history; Spencer C. Tucker, general editor; associate editors David Coffey, John C. Fredriksen, Justin D. Murphy. Facts on File 2003 3v il maps set $225 **355**
1. United States—Military history—Encyclopedias
ISBN 0-8160-4355-8   LC 2002-29658
"More than 1,200 entries cover military leaders, wars, campaigns, battles, events, famous soldiers, military branches, key technological developments, overviews of weapons systems, and more. It covers the period from the colonial wars to the present, and gives special attention to the minorities and women who have contributed significantly to American military success." Publisher's note

Facts about the American wars; edited by John S. Bowman. Wilson, H.W. 1998 750p il maps $110 **355**
1. United States—Military history
ISBN 0-8242-0929-X   LC 97-40298
"An introduction explains the text's layout and approach to each war. The reader samples every conflict from the Franco-Spanish War of the mid-1500s to the Persian Gulf War of 1991. Most wars covered have maps; illustrations, or photographs; each has a separate bibliography. The details provided for each war are most impressive." Book Rep

Hanson, Victor Davis
The soul of battle; from ancient times to the present day, how three great liberators vanquished tyranny. Free Press 1999 480p il $30 **355**
1. Epaminondas, ca. 418-362 B.C. 2. Sherman, William T. (William Tecumseh), 1820-1891 3. Patton, George S. (George Smith), 1885-1945 4. Military history
ISBN 0-684-84502-4   LC 99-23853
Also available in paperback from Anchor Bks.
"Hanson narrates the success of three military campaigns—Epaminondas defeat of the Spartans in the fourth century B.C., Sherman's march through Georgia and the Carolinas during the Civil War, and Patton's race into Germany at the head of the Third Army in 1944-45. . . . In Hanson's view, the individual traits of spontaneity and creativity that are nourished in a free society are assets, not hindrances, in warfare." Booklist
Includes bibliographical references

Hedges, Chris
War is a force that gives us meaning. PublicAffairs 2002 211p $23 **355**
1. War
ISBN 1-58648-049-9   LC 2002-68136
Also available in paperback from Anchor Bks.
"War can only be sustained, Hedges affirms, by imbuing events with meanings they do not have. These 'mythic realities' are essential to suspending the normal rules of human behavior and justifying the mayhem and personal sacrifice war entails. Each side comes to see itself as the embodiment of absolute goodness; each demonizes the other and reduces its enemies to objects. The killing is thus made easy, but communication is thus impossible." New Leader
"This should be required reading in this post-9/11 world." Libr J
Includes bibliographical references

How to prepare for the Armed Forces test—ASVAB; Armed Services Vocational Aptitude Battery; compiled by the Editorial Department of Barron's Educational Series, Inc. Barron's Educ. Ser. il pa $14.95 **355**
1. United States—Armed forces—Examinations
Also available with CD-ROM $29.95
First published 1984. (7th edition 2003) Frequently revised
Cover title: Barron's how to prepare for the ASVAB Armed Forces test
This study guide includes practice examinations and a review of pertinent subject areas

Kindsvatter, Peter S.
American soldiers; ground combat in the World Wars, Korea, and Vietnam; foreword by Russell F. Weigley. University Press of Kan. 2003 xxiii, 432p il (Modern war studies) $34.95 **355**
1. United States. Army. Infantry 2. United States. Marine Corps 3. Soldiers—United States 4. United States—Military history
ISBN 0-7006-1229-7   LC 2002-12957
"Mining twentieth-century foot soldiers' memoirs and novels, Kindsvatter integrates this literature of personal experience into a generalized assessment of what combat was like and how men reacted to it. . . . Kindsvatter's illuminating work is about coping with . . . fear at the foxhole level, and it . . . powerfully conveys the psychology and military sociology of combat in the draft-era armies." Booklist
Includes bibliographical references

Kohn, George C.
Dictionary of wars; [by] George Childs Kohn. rev ed. Facts on File 1999 614p $82.50; pa $22.95 **355**
1. Military history—Dictionaries
ISBN 0-8160-3928-3; 0-8160-4157-1 (pa)
                                  LC 98-49684
First published 1986
"Conflicts are arranged alphabetically under their most accessible or familiar names, in double columns with running heads. Each entry includes basic descriptive information, such as dates of the conflict, sides involved, and outcome. . . . Years of birth and death of leaders who are mentioned in the text are provided. Entries are current through 1998." Booklist

Magill's guide to military history; editor, John Powell; managing editor, Christina J. Moose; project editor, Rowena Wildin. Salem Press 2001 5v il set $473 **355**
1. Military history—Dictionaries 2. Generals—Dictionaries
ISBN 0-89356-014-6   LC 00-66072
This "is a worldwide, illustrated, alphabetical survey of war, weapons, battles, civilizations, people and their place in military history, ancient times to the 21st century. Its 1,518 entries and over 300 thorough essays with keywords in boldface are all indexed by category in volume 5." Choice
For a fuller review see: Booklist, Sept 1, 2001

The **Oxford** companion to American military history; editor in chief, John Whiteclay Chambers II; editors, Fred Anderson [et al.] Oxford Univ. Press 1999 xxxiv, 916p il maps $75   **355**
1. United States—Military history—Dictionaries
ISBN 0-19-507198-0   LC 99-21181
This reference work covers "battles and soldiers, ships and weapons, services and doctrines—as well as the social and cultural impact of the U.S. military at home and around the world. . . . There are entries on relevant acts of Congress and on diplomatic policies such as the Monroe Doctrine and the Marshall Plan; on peace and antiwar movements; on war in film, literature, music, and photography; and on war viewed through the disciplinary lenses of anthropology, economics, gender studies, and psychology." Publisher's note

The **Oxford** companion to military history; edited by Richard Holmes; consultant editor Hew Strachan: associate editors, Christopher Bellamy and Hugh Bicheno. Oxford Univ. Press 2001 1048p il maps $75; pa $29.95   **355**
1. Military history
ISBN 0-19-866209-2; 0-19-860696-6 (pa)
     LC 2001-273896
This reference includes "the social, political, technological, and economic background of major conflicts. Entries cover people . . . weapons and equipment; wars, campaigns and battles; strategy and tactics; logistics; fortifications; military life; institutions; literature, art, and music. . . . The primary focus is on land warfare in Europe and America from the 18th century to the present day." Publisher's note
"This is a reference tool of remarkable quality." Libr J

Reader's guide to military history; edited by Charles Messenger. Fitzroy Dearborn Pubs. 2001 xxxvi, 948p $135   **355**
1. Military history
ISBN 1-57958-241-9   LC 2002-275907
Topics covered "include land, sea, and air services; conflicts; types of warfare; military theory; prominent military leaders; and national armed services. . . . [This] is a unique, well-designed reference tool that will be useful to academic, large public, and specialized libraries." Booklist

Ruggero, Ed
Duty first; West Point and the making of American leaders. HarperCollins Pubs. 2001 342p il $27.50; pa $14.95   **355**
1. United States Military Academy 2. Leadership
ISBN 0-06-019317-4; 0-06-093133-7 (pa)
     LC 00-59775
In this report about the contemporary West Point experience, the author "tries to explain precisely what makes the United States Military Academy, better known as West Point, a breeding ground for future leaders." Publ Wkly

Wright, Kai
Soldiers of freedom; an illustrated history of African Americans in the Armed Forces. Black Dog & Leventhal 2002 294p il $19.95   **355**
1. African American soldiers 2. United States—Armed forces
ISBN 1-57912-253-1   LC 2002-8000
This is a "look at the contributions African Americans have made to military engagements from the American Revolution through the Vietnam War up to the current war on terrorism. . . . Readers interested in African American and military history will appreciate this well-documented and -illustrated resource." Booklist
Includes bibliographical references

Ziegler, Philip
Soldiers: fighting men's lives, 1901-2001. Knopf 2002 331p $26   **355**
1. Royal Hospital (London, England) 2. Soldiers—Great Britain 3. Great Britain—Military history
ISBN 0-375-41206-9   LC 2001-38427
First published 2001 in the United Kingdom
In this work the author concentrates "on the ashes of empire by talking to residents of London's Royal Hospital Chelsea, veterans of Britain's wars from Flanders to Cyprus and Aden, men who had little to lose in life and little to gain but whose fidelity never came into question." N Y Times Book Rev
"A perceptive presentation of the military culture and mentality." Booklist
Includes bibliographical references

355.3   Organization and personnel of military forces

Connelly, Owen
On war and leadership; the words of combat commanders from Frederick the Great to Norman Schwarzkopf. Princeton Univ. Press 2002 347p $29.95   **355.3**
1. Leadership 2. Military history 3. Decision making
ISBN 0-691-03186-X   LC 2002-16914
This presents the words of twenty military leaders throughout history including such figures as William Tecumseh Sherman, Stonewall Jackson, George S. Patton, Moshe Dayan, Vo Nguyen Giap, and Harold Moore
Includes bibliographical references

356   Foot forces and warfare

Clancy, Tom, 1947-
Special forces; a guided tour of U.S. Army Special Forces; written with John Gresham. Berkley Bks. 2001 366p il $16   **356**
1. United States. Special Operations Command
ISBN 0-425-17268-6   LC 00-65121
"The book covers recruitment and training of personnel . . . equipment, which includes an exotic mixture of high, low, and no tech components; and the variety of missions special forces execute." Booklist
Includes bibliographical references

Haney, Eric L.

Inside Delta Force; the story of America's elite counterterrorist unit. Delacorte Press 2002 324p il $25.95   **356**

1. United States. Army. Delta Force
ISBN 0-385-33603-9   LC 2001-58408

The author relates his "experiences during the formation and early operations of 1st Special Forces Operational Detachment-Delta. . . . He served three times in Beirut guarding the American ambassador, participated in the invasion of Grenada, served in several Central American countries and narrowly escaped death during the abortive rescue attempt of the American hostages in Iran. . . . Readers of other special forces memoirs will find this one distinctive for Haney's attention to interservice rivalries . . . that he believes compromised several missions, as well as for Haney's nuanced, often disgusted descriptions of the human cost of war." Publ Wkly

McKinney, Mike

Chariots of the damned; helicopter special operations from Vietnam to Kosovo; [by] Mike McKinney and Mike Ryan. Thomas Dunne Bks./St. Martin's Press 2002 c2001 215p il maps $24.95; pa $6.99   **356**

1. United States. Army. Special Forces 2. Helicopters 3. Military aeronautics
ISBN 0-312-29118-3; 0-312-98980-6 (pa)
                                LC 2002-21969

First published 2001 in the United Kingdom

This recounts U.S. Army helicopter missions in the Vietnam War, the Gulf War, Bosnia, and Somalia, and describes military helicopter technology

"Readers have much to admire in these renditions of the helicopter's role in American missions." Booklist

Includes bibliographical references

358   Air and other specialized forces and warfare

Miller, Judith, 1948-

Germs; America's secret war against biological weapons; Judith Miller, Stephen Engelberg, William Broad. Simon & Schuster 2001 382p $27; pa $14   **358**

1. Biological warfare
ISBN 0-684-87158-0; 0-684-87159-9 (pa)
                                LC 2001-42690

Three reporters survey the history of biological weapons and recount incidents of their use by terrorist groups. They explain why advances in biology and the spread of germ weapons poses grave risks as countries such as Iran, Iraq and North Korea continually engage in research

Includes bibliographical references

Wright, Patrick, 1951-

Tank: the progress of a monstrous war machine. Viking 2002 499p il $29.95; pa $16   **358**

1. Military tanks
ISBN 0-670-03070-8; 0-14-200191-0 (pa)

The author "traces the cultural history of a kill vehicle variously called 'behemoth,' 'landship' and even 'Mother.' Wright's exhaustive research offers a treasure trove of facts usually eclipsed in conventional military or technical histories." Publ Wkly

358.4   Air forces and warfare

Boyne, Walter J., 1929-

Beyond the wild blue; a history of the United States Air Force, 1947-1997. St. Martin's Press 1997 442p il $29.95; pa $19.95   **358.4**

1. United States. Air Force 2. Military aeronautics
ISBN 0-312-15474-7; 0-312-18705-X (pa)
                                LC 96-53507

"A Thomas Dunne book"

In this "history of the evolution of the air force, from its beginning as a separate arm of the military in 1947 through its many roles and changes since then, Boyne asserts that the air force's effort and sacrifice won us the Cold War. . . . While his slant may be seen as controversial, this is a large, thorough, and valuable history." Libr J

Includes bibliographical references

359   Sea (Naval) forces and warfare

Bruce, Anthony

An encyclopedia of naval history; {by} Anthony Bruce and William Cogar. Facts on File 1998 440p il   **359**

1. Naval history   LC 97-7243

Available from Fitzroy Dearborn Pub.

An "encyclopedia of world naval history from the 15th century to the present. Its 1,000 articles cover all manner of detail from sea battles and great commanders to warship evolution, naval technology and tactics, organizations, and naval-oriented details of specific campaigns. Although international in scope, the work clearly emphasizes the US and Britain." Choice

Love, Robert William, 1944-

History of the U.S. Navy; [by] Robert W. Love, Jr. Stackpole Bks. 1992 2v ea $39.95   **359**

1. United States. Navy 2. United States—Naval history
ISBN 0-8117-1862-X (v1); 0-8117-1863-8 (v2)
                                LC 91-27510

Contents: v1 1775-1941; v2 1942-1991

"This pragmatic chronicle pays as much attention to the government context out of which naval policy proceeded as to campaigns at sea. The Navy's main business, in Love's view, has always been to serve as a handmaid to diplomacy and at the same time as a clenched fist of foreign policy. . . . A comprehensive, thoroughly researched review." Publ Wkly

Includes bibliographical references

Naval warfare; an international encyclopedia; edited by Spencer C. Tucker; associate editors, John Fredriksen [et al.]; introduction by James C. Bradford. ABC-CLIO 2002 3v il maps set $295   **359**

1. Naval art and science—Encyclopedias 2. Naval history—Encyclopedias
ISBN 1-57607-219-3   LC 2002-4401

This set "explores the history of combat at sea, from ancient Greek galleys to the sophisticated ships of the

Naval warfare—_Continued_
U.S. Sixth Fleet. More than 1500 signed entries . . . describe the three key eras: Age of Galley Warfare, Age of Sail, and Age of Steam or Modern Era. . . . Each new development is examined in painstaking detail." Libr J

359.9   Specialized combat forces

Couch, Dick, 1943-
The warrior elite; the forging of Seal Class 228; photographs by Cliff Hollenbeck. Crown 2001 319p il hardcover o.p. paperback available $14.95   **359.9**
1. United States. Navy. Sea Air Land Team
ISBN 1-4000-4695-5 (pa)   LC 2001-28368
This is an account of the Basic Underwater Demolition course, (BUD) training for the U.S. Navy Sea Air Land Team (SEALs)
This book "is unique. Couch, a Vietnam-era SEAL and retired naval reserve captain was given the most complete access possible. . . . On view is much serious thought by serious thinkers on the making of warriors at the dawn of the twenty-first century." Booklist

Knott, Richard C.
A heritage of wings; an illustrated history of navy aviation. Naval Inst. Press 1997 339p il maps $49.95   **359.9**
1. United States. Navy 2. Military aeronautics
ISBN 0-87021-270-2   LC 97-23625
The author examines "the history of naval aviation, from Lt. Theodore 'Spuds' Ellyson, naval aviator number one, to Lt. Commander Wendy Lawrence, the first female naval aviator in space. Knott explains the troublesome development of the aircraft carrier . . . and the specialized aircraft that call the carrier home. He also details major naval battles and tells how naval airpower influenced the outcome. His book is full of interesting facts." Libr J
Includes bibliographical references

361.2   Social action

Rieff, David
A bed for the night; humanitarianism in crisis. Simon & Schuster 2002 367p $26; pa $15   **361.2**
1. International agencies
ISBN 0-684-80977-X; 0-7432-5211-X (pa)
     LC 2002-29432
The author takes a "look at the effectiveness of humanitarian organizations, which have increasingly been drawn into the politics behind some of the disasters for which they provide relief." Booklist
Readers "will come away from this passionate, eloquent argument with a distinctly clearer understanding of the complex moral issues facing humanitarian aid in a world filled with brutality and suffering." Publ Wkly
Includes bibliographical references

361.6   Governmental action

Hancock, LynNell
Hands to work; the stories of three families racing the welfare clock. Morrow 2002 308p $25.95; pa $13.95   **361.6**
1. Poor—New York (N.Y.) 2. Public welfare
ISBN 0-688-17388-8; 0-06-051216-X (pa)
     LC 2001-31730
This "study depicts welfare in America today through the stories of three women from the South Bronx—Alina, Brenda, and Christine—who were affected by the 1996 Personal Responsibility Act . . . which limits lifetime federal financial assistance to five years for families and two years for singles. . . . Attention-holding and articulate, this important book on how America treats residents who are 'down and out' is highly recommended." Libr J
Includes bibliographical references

Katz, Michael B.
The price of citizenship; redefining America's welfare state. Metropolitan Bks. 2001 469p hardcover o.p. paperback available $17   **361.6**
1. Public welfare 2. Social policy—United States
ISBN 0-8050-6929-1 (pa)   LC 00-46906
In this "historical and political study of welfare in 20th-century America [the author] . . . focuses on the destructive influence of the market economy on social welfare programs." Libr J
Katz "has written a defining history of post-Nixon transformations of America's welfare state, including its nonprofit and private sectors (private pensions, health insurance, etc.)." Publ Wkly

362.1   Physical illness

AIDS sourcebook; edited by Dawn M. Matthews. 3rd ed. Omnigraphics 2003 664p (Health reference series) $78   **362.1**
1. AIDS (Disease)
ISBN 0-7808-0631-X   LC 2003-40531
First published 1995
"Basic consumer health information about acquired immune deficiency syndrome (AIDS) and human immunodeficiency virus (HIV) infection, including facts about transmission, prevention, diagnosis, treatment, opportunistic infections, and other complications, with a section for women and children, including details about associated gynecological concerns, pregnancy, and pediatric care ; along with updated statistical informations, reports on current research initiatives, a glossary, and directories of Internet, Hotline, and other resources." Title page

Consumers' guide to hospitals; by the editors of Consumers' checkbook magazine. Center for the Study of Services il pa $19.95
     362.1
1. Hospitals—United States
ISSN 1070-2644
Irregular. First published 1988
This guide presents statistics about U.S. hospitals with comparisons on death rates, estimated rates of complications, ratings of physicians, and outcome ratings for particular conditions and diseases. It includes advice on choosing a hospital and cutting costs and lists resources

Encyclopedia of AIDS; a social, political, cultural, and scientific record of the HIV epidemic; edited by Raymond A. Smith; forewords by James W. Curran, Peter Piot; photo editor, Jane Rosett. Fitzroy Dearborn Pubs. 1998 xli, 601p il $135   **362.1**
1. AIDS (Disease)—Encyclopedias
ISBN 1-57958-007-6   LC 98-200474
Also available in paperback from Penguin Bks.
This reference covers "aspects of the global HIV/AIDS crisis, primarily for the period 1991-96. The contents are organized into eight broad domains covering basic science and epidemiology; transmission and prevention; pathology and treatment; impacted populations; government and activism; policy and law; culture and society; and the global epidemic." Choice

Encyclopedia of public health; edited by Lester Breslow. Macmillan Ref. USA 2001 4v set $475   **362.1**
1. Public health—Encyclopedias
ISBN 0-02-865354-8   LC 2001-31501
"Information on more than 900 programs, services, organizations, health behaviors, and the prevalence, epidemiology, and costs of communicable diseases. Although the work focuses on the United States, there are also references to worldwide problems." Libr J
For a fuller review see: Booklist, July, 2002

Fisher, Mary, 1948-
Sleep with the angels; a mother challenges AIDS. Moyer Bell 1994 220p il $24.95; pa $12.95   **362.1**
1. AIDS (Disease)
ISBN 1-55921-105-9; 1-55921-103-2 (pa)
     LC 93-27216
"Fisher learned she was HIV+ in July 1991 and began telling her story in public in 1992. . . . Presented in chronological order from May 4, 1992 through June 28, 1993, the transcripts of these 24 speeches . . . include her famous address to the 1992 Republican National Convention in Houston. . . . Utilizing her position as a privileged heterosexual non-drug using white woman, she forces her audiences to confront the reality of the epidemic." Libr J

Garrett, Laurie
Betrayal of trust; the collapse of global public health. Hyperion 2000 754p il $30; pa $16.95   **362.1**
1. Public health 2. Medical care
ISBN 0-7868-6522-9; 0-7868-8440-1 (pa)
     LC 00-33425
This book examines contemporary "health systems in the former Soviet Union, India, central Africa, and the United States." N Y Times Book Rev

Greenspan, Stanley I.
The child with special needs; encouraging intellectual and emotional growth; [by] Stanley I. Greenspan, Serena Wieder, with Robin Simons. Addison-Wesley 1998 496p $32   **362.1**
1. Handicapped children 2. Child psychology
ISBN 0-201-40726-4   LC 97-32101
"A Merloyd Lawrence book"

This offers advice to parents on helping children with such disabilities as cerebral palsy, autism, retardation, ADD, and language problems
This "is an important work for libraries." Libr J
Includes bibliographical references

Hallman, Tom
Sam: the boy behind the mask. Putnam 2002 240p il $22.95   **362.1**
1. Lightner, Sam, 1985- 2. Face—Surgery 3. Birth defects
ISBN 0-399-14933-3   LC 2002-69753
This is "the story of a teenaged boy who survives a 13-hour operation for a facial deformity, then pulls through a subsequent coma with the help of an against-all-the-odds woman doctor." Libr J
"Hallman's writing is crisp and affecting. . . . This is a deeply moving story, an against-all-odds tale of bravery and faith." Publ Wkly

Halpin, Brendan
It takes a worried man; a memoir. Villard Bks. 2002 239p hardcover o.p. paperback available $12.95   **362.1**
1. Breast cancer
ISBN 0-8129-6687-2 (pa)   LC 2001-41907
This is "Halpin's memoir of his wife's struggle with breast cancer." Publ Wkly
"A poignant account with no answers and probing look at how one individual copes with dire circumstances." Booklist

Havemann, Joel
A life shaken; my encounter with Parkinson's disease; foreword by Stephen G. Reich. Johns Hopkins Univ. Press 2002 181p il $26; pa $14.95   **362.1**
1. Parkinson's disease—Personal narratives
ISBN 0-8018-6928-5; 0-8018-7888-8 (pa)
     LC 2001-4650
The author "chronicles the physical and emotional effects . . . [Parkinson's] disease has had on his life since his diagnosis in 1990. While he briefly discusses PD's history, possible causes, medical and surgical treatments, and research progress, it is the account of his personal struggle that is the heart of this book." Libr J
Includes bibliographical references

Kondracke, Morton
Saving Milly; love, politics, and Parkinson's disease. PublicAffairs 2001 xxii, 288p $25   **362.1**
1. Kondracke, Milly 2. Parkinson's disease
ISBN 1-58648-037-5   LC 2001-19181
Also available Thorndike Press large print editon and in paperback from Ballantine Bks.
This is Kondracke's "account of how he and his wife, Milly, have coped with her diagnosis of Parkinson's disease." Publ Wkly
"Kondracke pleads eloquently for Parkinson's research while telling a story almost too painful to read." N Y Times Book Rev

Monette, Paul
Borrowed time; an AIDS memoir. Harcourt Brace Jovanovich 1988 342p $22; pa $13
362.1
1. AIDS (Disease)
ISBN 0-15-113598-3; 0-15-600581-6 (pa)
LC 88-7215
"In March 1985, after a period of intermittent ill-health, Roger Horwitz was diagnosed as having AIDS, he died in October 1986. [This volume] is his lover's memoir." New Statesman Soc
"The memoir transcends the particulars of the AIDS epidemic to stand as an eloquent testimonial to the power of love and the devastation of loss." Publ Wkly

Rovner, Julie
Health care policy and politics A to Z. 2nd ed. CQ Press 2004 275p $58 **362.1**
1. Medical care 2. Public health
ISBN 1-56802-852-0 LC 2003-23089
This reference explores changes made in the nation's health system by the private sector, Congress, federal and state courts, and state legislatures. Updated entries cover such topics as prescription drug benefits, key programs and agencies, committees and organizations, statistics, and the history and background shaping major health policies
Includes bibliographical references

Shilts, Randy
And the band played on; politics, people, and the AIDS epidemic. St. Martin's Press 1987 xxiii, 630p hardcover o.p. paperback available $16.95 **362.1**
1. AIDS (Disease)
ISBN 0-312-24135-6 (pa) LC 87-16528
A "chronicle of the five-year political, scientific, and social battle to force government, the medical and blood-bank establishments, the news media, and gay men to take AIDS seriously." Booklist
"Shilts successfully weaves comprehensive investigative reporting and commercial page-turner pacing, political intrigue and personal tragedy into a landmark work." Publ Wkly
Includes bibliographical references

Warner, Mark L., 1948-
The complete guide to Alzheimer's-proofing your home. rev ed. Purdue Univ. Press 2000 477p il $54.95
362.1
1. Alzheimer's disease 2. Home accidents
ISBN 1-55753-202-8 LC 99-462016
First published 1998
This is a "design guide to help caregivers and family members create a home environment that will enable them and Alzheimer's patients to handle the difficulties associated with the disease." Libr J [review of 1998 edition]
"A generous directory of relevant products and manufacturers and a helpful glossary further distinguish this superlative resource for home caregivers." Booklist [review of 1998 edition]
Includes bibliographical references

362.28 Suicide

Ackerman, Diane
A slender thread. Random House 1997 305p hardcover o.p. paperback available $14
362.28
1. Crisis centers 2. Hotlines (Telephone counseling) 3. Suicide
ISBN 0-679-77133-6 (pa) LC 96-8721
This is an account of the author's work as a volunteer counselor at a suicide-prevention and crisis center in a New York college town
"In a narrative that is lush with her signature gift for metaphor and delight in the senses and taut with the drama of her often frightening negotiations with people in the throes of every imaginable form of crisis, Ackerman illuminates the bewildering workings of the resilient human psyche." Booklist

Evans, Glen
The encyclopedia of suicide; [by] Glen Evans, Norman L. Farberow; foreword by Alan L. Berman. 2nd ed. Facts on File 2003 xxxiii, 329p $65 **362.28**
1. Suicide—Dictionaries
ISBN 0-8160-4525-9 LC 2002-27166
First published 1988
Arranged in A-Z format, over 500 entries cover such aspects as causes, history and psychology of suicide. Also covered are philosophical and religious issues as well as sociological viewpoints and research and treatment concerns
For a fuller review see: Booklist, Nov. 1, 2003

362.29 Substance abuse

Courtwright, David T., 1952-
Forces of habit; drugs and the making of the modern world. Harvard Univ. Press 2001 277p $24.95; pa $16.95 **362.29**
1. Drug abuse 2. Psychotropic drugs
ISBN 0-674-00458-2; 0-674-01003-5 (pa)
LC 00-61466
"In charting the mostly covert impact of drugs on modern civilization, Courtwright . . . contends that governmental, religious and economic institutions have a centuries-old love-hate relationship with psychoactive substances ranging from alcohol and caffeine to cocaine and peyote." Publ Wkly
"Reasoned and informative, Courtwright's book is a cogent source of dispassionate information on drugs and their role in society." Booklist
Includes bibliographical references

Drug abuse sourcebook; basic consumer health information about illicit substances of abuse and the diversion of prescription medications . . .; edited by Karen Bellenir. Omnigraphics 2000 629p (Health reference series) $78 **362.29**
1. Drug abuse
ISBN 0-7808-0242-X LC 00-55071
This handbook "presents information about specific drugs of abuse, including depressants, hallucinogens, inhalants, marijuana, narcotics, stimulants, and anabolic steroids. It explains the nature of addiction, describes re-

Drug abuse sourcebook—*Continued*
lated health risks, and provides information about various treatment strategies and drug abuse prevention issues. A glossary, a dictionary of street names for illicit drugs, and resource directories are also included." Publisher's note

Henderson, Elizabeth Connell
Understanding addiction. University Press of Miss. 2000 209p il (Understanding health and sickness series) hardcover o.p. paperback available $12 **362.29**
1. Compulsive behavior 2. Drug abuse
ISBN 1-57806-240-3 (pa)   LC 00-42856
The author writes "on how addictions develop, how the addicted brain works, and what the different effects of the major addictive drugs are, and on genetic, psycho logical, and behavioral factors involved in addiction." Booklist
Includes bibliographical references

Streatfeild, Dominic
Cocaine; an unauthorized biography. Thomas Dunne Bks./St. Martin's Press 2002 510p il $27.95; pa $15   **362.29**
1. Cocaine 2. Drug abuse 3. Drug traffic
ISBN 0-312-28624-4; 0-312-42226-1 (pa)
First published 2001 in the United Kingdom
This study covers "the rise of the Colombian cartels, government collusion with traffickers, the crack phenomenon, media hype, the U.S. war on drugs and the legalization debate." Publ Wkly
"Thorough, engrossing, balanced, and entertaining, it is important social history in palatable form." Booklist
Includes bibliographical references

362.292 Alcoholism

Dorris, Michael
The broken cord; with a foreword by Louise Erdrich. Harper & Row 1989 300p il hardcover o.p. paperback available $14
362.292
1. Alcoholism 2. Father-son relationship 3. Native Americans
ISBN 0-06-091682-6 (pa)   LC 88-45893
This is a memoir about Dorris' "adopted son, Adam, a victim of fetal alcohol syndrome (FAS). Although the book began as an anthropological investigation of FAS and its effect on native American communities, Dorris soon realized that he couldn't separate the theoretical from the personal." Booklist
"The alarming statistics and consequences of fetal alcohol syndrome are skillfully interwoven with the human story of one of its victims in 'The Broken Cord.' Mr. Dorris's prose is clear and affecting." N Y Times Book Rev
Includes bibliographical references

362.4 Problems of and services to people with physical disabilities

The **Encyclopedia** of blindness and vision impairment; [by] Jill Sardegna [et al.] 2nd ed. Facts on File 2002 333p (Facts on File library of health and living) $65   **362.4**
1. Blind—Dictionaries 2. Vision disorders—Dictionaries
ISBN 0-8160-4280-2   LC 2001-55653
First published 1991
"This volume incorporates a history of blindness and vision impairment with an A-to-Z presentation of health issues, types of surgery, medications, medical terminology, social issues, myths and misconceptions, economic issues, and current research trends." Publisher's note
For a review see: Booklist: Jan 1 & 15, 2003
Includes bibliographical references

Sacks, Oliver W.
Seeing voices; a journey into the world of the deaf; [by] Oliver Sacks. University of Calif. Press 1989 180p il o.p.; Vintage Bks. paperback available $13   **362.4**
1. Deaf 2. Sign language
ISBN 0-375-70407-8 (pa)   LC 89-4817
The author "scrutinizes the history of treatment of the deaf, investigates the expressive capabilities of sign language and gauges the linguistic and social pressures faced by deaf people. The closing section documents a 1988 student revolt at Gallaudet that led to the appointment of the school's first deaf president." Publ Wkly
"With his philosopher's penchant for profound discovery and his neurologist's knowledge of biology and the brain, Sacks offers provocative connections and acute observations about the nature of language and culture." Booklist
Includes bibliographical references

362.5 Problems of and services to the poor

Hombs, Mary Ellen
American homelessness; a reference handbook. 3rd ed. ABC-CLIO 2001 299p $45
362.5
1. Homeless persons
ISBN 1-57607-247-9   LC 2001-2779
First published 1990
This study of homelessness in the United States includes a chronology, a bibliography, biographies of individuals and a documents section focusing on legislation and court cases

Kozol, Jonathan
Rachel and her children; homeless families in America. Crown 1988 261p o.p.; Fawcett Columbine paperback available $12.95 **362.5**
1. Homeless persons
ISBN 0-449-90339-7 (pa)   LC 87-22273
The author introduces us to "the residents of a hotel for the homeless in New York. . . . Kozol faults everyone involved: governments, social agencies, landlords, the courts, and indifferent Americans in general." Libr J

Kozol, Jonathan—*Continued*
"While the individual stories that Kozol tells so affectingly point out the vivid realities of urban poverty, the book also supplies statistics that detail the more abstract—and inhuman—attitudes that contemporary society assumes when attempting to deal with its victims." Booklist

Zucchino, David
Myth of the welfare queen; a Pulitzer Prize-winning journalist's portrait of women on the line. Scribner 1997 366p hardcover o.p. paperback available $21.95   **362.5**
1. Public welfare 2. Poor—United States 3. African American women
ISBN 0-684-85006-5 (pa)   LC 97-9104
"From July to December 1995, David Zucchino . . . became a participant observer in the lives of two . . . women living on welfare. Zucchino wanted to answer two questions: 'What did welfare mothers do all day?' and '(Has) anyone among a class of women so despised by mainstream America attempted to improve their circumstances and to raise their children for lives beyond poverty?'" Women's Rev Books
This book "a harrowing description of daily subsistence living with very little chance of change, is a powerful exposé of the welfare myth." Libr J

362.6 Problems of and services to persons in late adulthood

Consumer reports complete guide to health services for seniors; what your family needs to know about finding and financing *Medicare *assisted living * nursing homes *home care *adult day care with ratings of Medicare HMOs and supplemental policies; [by] Trudy Lieberman and the editors of Consumer reports. Three Rivers Press (NY) 2000 xx, 568p pa $19.95   **362.6**
1. Elderly—Care 2. Medical care 3. Consumer education
ISBN 0-8129-3147-5   LC 00-23453
This guide to the "programs that make up the local, state, and national healthcare 'systems' for seniors aims to help them identify and finance needed services. The book offers detailed explanations of Medicare, Medicaid, supplemental insurance options, and HMOs, along with such long-term care choices as nursing home—and community-based care, assisted living, adult day programs, and hospices." Libr J

362.7 Problems of and services to young people

Bartholet, Elizabeth
Nobody's children; abuse and neglect, foster drift, and the adoption alternative. Beacon Press 1999 304p hardcover o.p. paperback available $17.50   **362.7**
1. Child welfare
ISBN 0-8070-2319-1 (pa)   LC 99-22976
This is a critique "of American child welfare policy. Examining legislation from all parts of the United States,

Bartholet questions why 'family preservation ideology still reigns supreme when children rather than adult women are involved.' . . . Clear and consistent." Libr J
Includes bibliographical references

Bernstein, Nina
The lost children of Wilder; the epic struggle to change foster care. Pantheon Bks. 2001 482p hardcover o.p. paperback available $15   **362.7**
1. Wilder, Shirley 2. Foster home care 3. Child welfare
ISBN 0-679-75834-8 (pa)   LC 00-57456
"Bernstein explores the genesis and aftermath of the landmark 1973 legal case filed by young ACLU attorney Marcia Lowry against the New York State foster-care system. Known as *Wilder* for its 14-year-old African-American plaintiff, Shirley 'Pinky' Wilder, the suit claimed Jewish and Catholic child welfare services had a lock on foster care funding and placements. . . . This viscerally powerful history of institutionalized child abuse and the criminalization of poverty, of civil rights and social change, is compelling and essential reading." Publ Wkly
Includes bibliographical references

Gilman, Lois
The adoption resource book. 4th ed. HarperPerennial 1998 576p pa $16.95   **362.7**
1. Adoption
ISBN 0-06-273361-3 (pa)   LC 98-21174
First published 1984
This offers information about adoption strategies including international adoptions, private and agency adoptions, and financing and lists more than 1,000 agencies and support groups
Includes bibliographical references

Kozol, Jonathan
Amazing grace; the lives of children and the conscience of a nation. Crown 1995 286p o.p.; HarperPerennial paperback available $14   **362.7**
1. Poor—New York (N.Y.) 2. Socially handicapped children 3. Inner cities
ISBN 0-06-097697-7 (pa)   LC 95-23163
In this "book, Mr. Kozol travels the Mott Haven section of the Bronx, one of the poorest neighborhoods in the nation, where he visits with children, their parents and ministers, talking with them about their lives and about what they perceive as their place in the world." NY Times Book Rev
Kozol's "powerfully understated report takes us inside rat-infested homes that are freezing in winter, overcrowded schools, dysfunctional clinics, soup kitchens. . . . While his narrative offers no specific solutions, it forcefully drives home his conviction: a civilized nation cannot allow this situation to continue." Publ Wkly
Includes bibliographical references

362.82 Problems of and services to families

Domestic violence & child abuse sourcebook; edited by Helene Henderson. Omnigraphics 2000 xx, 1064p il (Health reference series) $78 **362.82**
1. Domestic violence 2. Child abuse
ISBN 0-7808-0235-7   LC 00-58436

"Basic consumer health information about spousal/partner, child, sibling, parent, and elder abuse, covering physical, emotional, and sexual abuse, teen dating violence, and stalking; includes information about hotlines, safe houses, safety plans, and other resources for support and assistance, community initiatives, and reports on current directions in research and treatment; along with a glossary, sources for further reading, and governmental and non-governmental organizations contact information." Title page

"Because this book includes a lot of issues within one volume, this work is recommended for all public libraries." Am Ref Books Annu, 2001

Dutton, Donald G., 1943-
The batterer; a psychological profile; [by] Donald G. Dutton with Susan K. Golant. Basic Bks. 1995 209p hardcover o.p. paperback available $15   **362.82**
1. Wife abuse 2. Domestic violence 3. Men—Psychology
ISBN 0-465-03388-1 (pa)   LC 95-9556

The authors draw on the O. J. Simpson trial "to help elucidate their points regarding wife batterers. . . . Dutton and Golant provide an excellent introduction to the psychology of wife abusers, examining the different types of abusers: psychopathic, overcontrolled, and cyclical. They then narrow the focus to the cyclical abuser (the Dr. Jekyll/Mr. Hyde type exemplified by Simpson) and examine the different factors that go into making such an abuser." Libr J
Includes bibliographical references

Forward, Susan
Toxic parents: overcoming their hurtful legacy and reclaiming your life; [by] Susan Forward with Craig Buck. Bantam Bks. 1989 326p hardcover o.p. paperback available $13.95   **362.82**
1. Child abuse
ISBN 0-553-28434-7 (pa)   LC 89-6812

The authors identify types of hurtful parents, including alcoholics, verbal and physical abusers, and those who emotionally neglect their children. They also offer advice to adult child abuse victims on how to overcome the harm done
Includes bibliographical references

362.83 Problems of and services to women

Bass, Ellen
The courage to heal; a guide for women survivors of child sexual abuse: featuring "Honoring the truth, a response to the backlash"; [by] Ellen Bass and Laura Davis. 3rd ed rev & updated. HarperPerennial 1994 604p pa $22.50   **362.83**
1. Child sexual abuse 2. Adult child sexual abuse victims 3. Women—Psychology
ISBN 0-06-095066-8   LC 93-48353
First published 1988

The authors offer a three part recovery program: taking stock, the healing process, and changing patterns, followed by the personal experiences of survivors, and a response to critics who claim sexual abuse charges are based on "the false memory syndrome"
Includes bibliographical references

362.883 Problems of and services to victims of rape

Sebold, Alice
Lucky. Scribner 1999 254p o.p.; Back Bay Bks. paperback available $11.95   **362.883**
1. Rape
ISBN 0-316-09619-9 (pa)   LC 99-19697

When the author "was a college freshman at Syracuse University, she was attacked and raped on the last night of school. . . . Sebold launches her memoir headlong into the rape itself, laying out its visceral physical as well as mental violence, and from there spins a narrative of her life before and after the incident, weaving memories of parental alcoholism together with her post-rape addiction to heroin. In the midst of each wrenching episode, from the initial attack to the ensuing courtroom drama, Sebold's wit is as powerful as her searing candor." Publ Wkly

363.1 Public safety programs

Cummins, Ronnie
Genetically engineered food; a self-defense guide for consumers; by Ronnie Cummins and Ben Lilliston; foreword by Andrew Kimbrell. Marlowe & Co. 2000 208p pa $13.95   **363.1**
1. Food—Biotechnology 2. Farm produce
ISBN 1-56924-635-1   LC 00-21900

The authors discuss genetically engineered or modified food focusing on the scientific, political, economic, and health issues. They "include information on what consumers can do, from smart shopping to grassroots lobbying, to reduce the threat of genetically engineered food." Booklist

Genetically modified foods; debating biotechnology; edited by Michael Ruse, David Castle. Prometheus Bks. 2002 355p il (Contemporary issues series) $20 **363.1**
1. Food—Biotechnology 2. Farm produce
ISBN 1-57392-996-4 LC 2002-70510

In this collection of essays the first section focuses on "the history and the science of genetically modified foods. The next section focuses on the morality of modifying organisms for human use. . . . Succeeding sections include articles discussing religious attitudes toward genetically modified food, legal issues involving patenting and environmental damage, risk assessment, and possible environmental threats and benefits." Publisher's note

Includes bibliographical references

Gerson, Allan

The price of terror; one bomb, one plane, 270 lives: the history-making struggle for justice after Pan Am 103; [by] Allan Gerson and Jerry Adler. HarperCollins Pubs. 2001 322p il hardcover o.p. paperback available $13.95 **363.1**
1. Pan Am Flight 103 Bombing Incident, 1988 2. Terrorism
ISBN 0-06-095701-8 (pa) LC 2001-39962

This is an "overview of the multitude of ways in which the Pan Am Flight 103 families sought justice through the legal system. That flight, en route from Frankfurt to New York, was blown apart by a terrorist's bomb over Lockerbie, Scotland, on Dec 21, 1988, killing 270 people, including 189 Americans." N Y Times Book Rev

Lapierre, Dominique

Five past midnight in Bhopal; [by] Dominique Lapierre, Javier Moro; translated from the French by Kathryn Spink. Warner Bks. 2002 403p il map $25.95 **363.1**
1. Bhopal Union Carbide Plant Disaster, Bhopal, India, 1984 2. Pesticides industry—Accidents
ISBN 0-446-53088-3 LC 2002-100974
Original French edition, 2001

The authors relate "the story of Bhopal, India, where in 1984 16,000 to 30,000 people were killed and half a million maimed as the result of a deadly gas leak of methyl isocyanate from a Union Carbide pesticide manufacturing plant." America

Nestle, Marion

Safe food; bacteria, biotechnology, and bioterrorism. University of Calif. Press 2003 350p il (California studies in food and culture) $27.50 **363.1**
1. Food adulteration and inspection 2. Food—Biotechnology 3. Terrorism
ISBN 0-520-23292-5 LC 2002-27172

The author "argues that ensuring safe food involves more than washing hands or cooking food to higher temperatures. It involves politics. When it comes to food safety, billions of dollars are at stake, and industry, government, and consumers collide over issues of values, economics, and political power—and not always in the public interest." Publisher's note

Includes bibliographical references

Pringle, Peter

Food, inc; Mendel to Monsanto—the promises and perils of the biotech harvest. Simon & Schuster 2003 239p $24 **363.1**
1. Food—Biotechnology 2. Farm produce
ISBN 0-7432-2611-9 LC 2003-42823

The author "believes that there is nothing inherently unsafe about genetically modified (GM) foods and that technology has the potential to relieve hunger and pain for millions of people. However, in this discussion of the aspects of GM foods, he does not hesitate to point out the perils. . . . Especially troubling to the author is the degree to which plant biotechnology gives control to a few international conglomerates that own patents to the products and processes." Libr J

"This is a book to satisfy curiosity and engender concern, and any of its chapters would provide an excellent subject for discussion groups." SLJ

363.2 Police services

Cole, Simon A., 1967-

Suspect identities; a history of criminal identification and fingerprinting. Harvard Univ. Press 2001 369p il $35; pa $17.95 **363.2**
1. Fingerprints 2. Criminals—Identification
ISBN 0-674-00455-8; 0-674-01002-7 (pa)
LC 00-54054

The author discusses the history of fingerprinting and how it emerged as a separate discipline from anthropometry. He questions how reliable it is as a method of identification. "Cole suggests fingerprint examiners never proved two fingerprints can't be alike. Nor did the decentralized American criminal justice system ever develop a uniform standard for how similar a fragment must be to fingerprints on file." Christ Sci Monit

Includes bibliographical references

Conklin, Barbara Gardner

Encyclopedia of forensic science; a compendium of detective fact and fiction; [by] Barbara Gardner Conklin, Robert Gardner, and Dennis Shortelle. Oryx Press 2002 329p il $64.95 **363.2**
1. Forensic sciences—Encyclopedias 2. Criminal investigation
ISBN 1-57356-170-3 LC 2001-36638

This "illustrates the various ways that evidence can be extracted from a crime scene (e.g., ballistics, toxicology). . . . Though events in Great Britain and France are covered, the book's 85 entries focus on 19th-and 20th-century America. . . . Both famous and infamous people are listed, but what makes this book different and interesting is the inclusion of novelists (e.g., Patricia Cornwell, Jeffery Deaver, and Sir Arthur Conan Doyle) and their characters, who use forensics to solve crimes. . . . This is a solid resource." Libr J

The **FBI**: a comprehensive reference guide; edited by Athan G. Theoharis with Tony G. Poveda, Susan Rosenfeld, Richard Gid Powers. Oryx Press 1999 409p $89.95 **363.2**
1. United States. Federal Bureau of Investigation
ISBN 0-89774-991-X LC 98-26642
Also available in paperback from Checkmark Bks.

The FBI: a comprehensive reference guide—*Continued*

This work provides a "chronological history of and guide to the FBI that includes information about the facilities, the organizational structure, and biographies of key individuals. This reference source will not only please FBI enthusiasts, but it also serves as an excellent resource for those interested in U.S. history, criminal justice, and American culture. Also included is an extensive chronology of key events, a subject index, and an authoritative bibliography." Am Libr

From the secret files of J. Edgar Hoover; edited with commentary by Athan Theoharis. Dee, I.R. 1991 370p $24.95; pa $19.90   **363.2**

1. Hoover, J. Edgar (John Edgar), 1895-1972 2. United States. Federal Bureau of Investigation 3. Internal security—United States 4. Anticommunist movements 5. Subversive activities

ISBN 0-929587-67-7; 1-56663-017-7 (pa)

LC 91-3478

After a history of the Federal Bureau of Investigation, the first section of the book "presents selected files examining the alleged and real sexual indiscretions of JFK, Robert Kennedy, Eleanor Roosevelt, and Martin Luther King Jr. . . . Subsequent chapters examine the FBI's 'investigative' techniques, its relationship with Presidents and the McCarthy committee, and the uses of public relations and the role of the director." Libr J

Kessler, Ronald

The FBI; inside the world's most powerful law enforcement agency. Pocket Bks. 1993 492p il hardcover o.p. paperback available $6.99   **363.2**

1. United States. Federal Bureau of Investigation

ISBN 0-671-78658-X (pa)

LC 93-5207

"Kessler details how the bureau solved prominent cases such as Watergate and the World Trade Center bombing; covered up many detrimental internal cases; and introduced and employed ultra-modern forensic technologies for criminal investigations." Libr J

Includes bibliographical references

Whitcomb, Christopher, 1959-

Cold zero; inside the FBI Hostage Rescue Team. Little, Brown 2001 420p $25.95

363.2

1. United States. Federal Bureau of Investigation 2. Hostages

ISBN 0-316-60103-9

LC 2001-29395

Also available G.K. Hall large print edition and in paperback from Warner Bks.

The author "recounts his early years in the FBI, which included stops at Ruby Ridge and Waco as a sniper in the elite Hostage Rescue Team. . . . This fast-paced memoir never lags." Libr J

363.3 Other aspects of public safety

Censorship: a world encyclopedia; Derek Jones, editor. Fitzroy Dearborn Pubs. 2001 4v set $450   **363.3**

1. Censorship—Encyclopedias

ISBN 1-57958-135-8

"This work provides a wide-ranging view of censorship, spanning ancient Egypt to present times and covering art, literature, music, newspapers and broadcasting, and the visual arts, among many other topics. In addition, the work provides country surveys and discussions of major controversies for specific movies, books, and television shows. Some 1,550 entries, arranged in alphabetical order by subject, were written by about 600 contributors from 50 countries. Entries are enhanced by occasional illustrations, a name-subject index, and an alphabetical and thematic list of entries at the beginning of each volume." Booklist

Guns in American society; an encyclopedia of history, politics, culture, and the law; edited by Gregg Lee Carter. ABC-CLIO 2002 2v set $185   **363.3**

1. Gun control 2. Firearms—Law and legislation

ISBN 1-576-07268-1

LC 2002-14682

"The entries range widely, including many individuals past and present, both in and out of government. A variety of federal and state court cases are covered, as are the ordinances promoted by gun control advocates or opponents, and good background is provided on many issues. . . . [This encyclopedia] should serve as the standard reference on many aspects of guns, gun ownership, and gun control in the United States." Libr J

Henderson, Harry, 1951-

Gun control. Facts on File 2000 297p (Library in a book) $45   **363.3**

1. Gun control

ISBN 0-8160-4031-1

LC 99-49843

An examination of the history and issues of gun control that includes "summaries of the law (with the text of important cases and statutes), biographies; definitions of terms, a chronology of important Anglo-American events (from 871 C.E.), a lengthy annotated bibliography, selected tables from research studies, and a research section detailing how to find information." Libr J

Sugarmann, Josh, 1960-

Every handgun is aimed at you; the case for banning handguns. New Press (NY) 2001 238p il $24.95; pa $14.95   **363.3**

1. Gun control

ISBN 1-56584-629-X; 1-56584-705-9 (pa)

LC 00-60547

"The book begins with a brief historical survey that argues . . . that handguns did not become widespread in the U.S. until the Civil War, when the introduction of the Colt pistol and westward expansion fueled gun sales and deaths. But most of the book's focus is on present-day issues such as crime and self-defense." Publ Wkly

Utter, Glenn H.
Encyclopedia of gun control and gun rights.
Oryx Press 2000 xxiii, 376p il $62.50 **363.3**
1. Gun control 2. Firearms—Law and legislation
ISBN 1-57356-172-X   LC 99-43449
A "listing of the court cases, personalities, laws, and
groups involved in the regulation of guns. The book begins with an essay on the issues in the gun-control battle
and a short guide to the court cases and groups involved,
placing them in the opposing camps. The entries, which
are balanced and well written, include photographs and
charts." Libr J
Includes bibliographical references

363.34   Disasters

Halberstam, David, 1934-
Firehouse. Hyperion 2002 201p $22.95; pa
$14   **363.34**
1. New York (N.Y.). Fire Dept. 2. Fire fighters
3. World Trade Center terrorist attack, 2001
ISBN 1-4013-0005-7; 0-7868-8851-2 (pa)
"A journalist's homage to firefighters, their values,
their culture and their courage during the martyrdom imposed on the New York Fire Department by the catastrophe of the attack on the World Trade Center." N Y
Times Bk Rev

Hemingway, Lorian, 1951-
A world turned over; a killer tornado and
the lives it changed forever. Simon &
Schuster 2002 244p $23; pa $12   **363.34**
1. Tornadoes 2. Jackson (Miss.)
ISBN 0-684-85634-4; 0-7432-4767-1 (pa)
                                       LC 2002-73346
"On March 3, 1966, a devastating tornado struck the
Candlestick Shopping Center in South Jackson, Miss.,
flattening buildings and killing 14 people. Because her
family had just moved away from their home across the
road from the shopping center, Hemingway . . . missed
the disaster. All her life she has been obsessed with it,
however, and in 2000 she went back to learn about it
from childhood friends who were there. . . . Hemingway
skillfully draws the reader into the nightmare." Publ
Wkly

Smith, Dennis, 1940-
Report from ground zero; the story of the
rescue efforts at the World Trade Center.
Viking 2002 366p il maps $24.95; pa $14
                                       363.34
1. New York (N.Y.). Fire Dept. 2. World Trade Center terrorist attack, 2001 3. Fire fighters
ISBN 0-670-03116-X; 0-452-28395-7 (pa)
                                       LC 2002-19840
Based on his personal observations and interviews
with other rescue workers, the author describes the efforts of the New York City Fire Department to rescue
survivors of the September 11 attack on the World Trade
Center

363.4   Controversies related to public morals and customs

Behr, Edward, 1926-
Prohibition; thirteen years that changed
America. Arcade Pub. 1996 262p il hardcover
o.p. paperback available $13.95   **363.4**
1. Prohibition
ISBN 1-55970-394-6 (pa)   LC 96-24063
In this study Behr "tracks the 13 years of Prohibition
primarily through the actions of Wheeler, bootlegger
George Remus and Chicago mayor 'Big Bill' Thomson,
and in doing so stresses the corruption of politicians and
law enforcement officials that made carrying out the 18th
Amendment all but impossible." Publ Wkly
"This is an excellent and honest book that does not
flinch at unpalatable facts." N Y Times Book Rev
Includes bibliographical references

363.45   Drug traffic

Chepesiuk, Ronald
The war on drugs; an international
encyclopedia; [by] Ron Chepesiuk.
ABC-CLIO 1999 xxxiv, 317p il $75 **363.45**
1. Narcotics—Encyclopedias 2. Drug traffic—Encyclopedias 3. Drug abuse—Encyclopedias
ISBN 0-87436-985-1   LC 99-54389
A historical overview "is followed by 642 alphabetically arranged entries covering the legal, political, social,
economic, and environmental aspects of drugs. . . . Following the entries are a chronology beginning in 2737
B.C., selected Web sites, a 21-page bibliography, and an
index." Booklist

Davenport-Hines, R. P. T. (Richard Peter Treadwell), 1953-
The pursuit of oblivion; a global history of
narcotics; [by] Richard Davenport-Hines.
Norton 2002 576p il $29.95   **363.45**
1. Drug abuse 2. Narcotics 3. Drug traffic
ISBN 0-393-05189-7   LC 2002-71908
The author offers a "history of addictive drugs and
their abuse, spanning the globe and covering all eras for
which there exists documented evidence of such activity,
primarily from the 18th century forward." Libr J
This "is an extremely impressive work, not just for its
common-sense argumentation and encyclopedic breadth,
but also because of Davenport-Hines's sharp eye for a
good story." N Y Times Book Rev
Includes bibliographical references

363.46   Abortion

Abortion wars; a half century of struggle,
1950-2000; edited by Rickie Solinger.
University of Calif. Press 1998 413p
hardcover o.p. paperback available $21.95
                                       363.46
1. Abortion
ISBN 0-520-20952-4 (pa)   LC 97-12261
"A collection of 18 essays written by abortion providers, journalists, reproductive-rights activists, legal strate-
gists, and philosophers. In the introduction the editor
makes it clear that the book is 'unabashedly a pro-rights
book.' . . . The time line alone is so valuable that it's
practically worth the price of the book." SLJ

Reagan, Leslie J.

When abortion was a crime; women, medicine, and law in the United States, 1867-1973. University of Calif. Press 1997 387p il hardcover o.p. paperback available $19.95 **363.46**

1. Abortion 2. Women—United States
ISBN 0-520-21657-1 (pa)   LC 96-22568

This is a history of abortion in the United States from its criminalization between 1860 and 1880 to Roe v. Wade in 1973

"Important and original, vigorously written even down to the footnotes, [this book] manages with apparent ease to combine serious scholarship . . . and broad appeal." Atl Mon

Includes bibliographical references

Solinger, Rickie, 1947-

Beggars and choosers; how the politics of choice shapes adoption, abortion, and welfare in the United States. Hill & Wang 2001 290p hardcover o.p. paperback available $14

363.46

1. Pro-choice movement 2. Abortion 3. Women's rights
ISBN 0-8090-2860-3 (pa)   LC 2001-16652

"Solinger argues here that framing issues like abortion as a matter of choice is a mistake. . . . In Solinger's view, the word choice has transformed what ought to be considered a universal right into 'a consumer's privilege' that only affluent women enjoy." N Y Times Book Rev

"The juxtaposition of choice and class when considering women's reproductive rights makes for insightful reading." Libr J

Includes bibliographical references

Tribe, Laurence H.

Abortion: the clash of absolutes. new ed. Norton 1992 318p pa $12.95   **363.46**

1. Abortion
ISBN 0-393-30956-8   LC 93-111762

First published 1990

The author examines both pro-life and pro-choice arguments and analyzes major court and legislative decisions

Includes bibliographical references

Weddington, Sarah Ragle, 1945-

A question of choice. Putnam 1992 306p il o.p.; Penguin Bks. paperback available $13.95

363.46

1. Roe v. Wade 2. Abortion
ISBN 0-14-017798-1 (pa)   LC 92-14311

"Starting with her years at the University of Texas Law School at Austin, Weddington, the attorney who won Roe v. Wade, traces the history of her involvement with this . . . Supreme Court case and its aftermath." Libr J

"This description of the background and legal significance of the 1973 Supreme Court decision . . . provides a sense of how Roe happened that is at once more personal and more knowledgeable than most popular summaries. . . . A sound addition to legal history and current affairs collections." Booklist

Includes bibliographical references

363.6   Public utilities and related services

Amery, Colin

Vanishing histories; 100 endangered sites from the World Monuments Watch; by Colin Amery, with Brian Curran; foreword by John Berendt; preface by Bonnie Burnham and Marilyn Perry. Abrams 2001 207p il maps $60   **363.6**

1. Historic sites 2. Monuments
ISBN 0-8109-1435-2   LC 2001-22622

"The World Monuments Fund, which has been monitoring the state of precious architectural and artistic sites since 1965, established the World Monuments Watch in 1995 to heighten awareness of endangered cultural sites in the hope of garnering the support necessary for their preservation. Architectural expert Amery and conservator Curran present the histories of 100 such monuments in a volume as notable for the beauty of its photographs as for the urgency of its message." Booklist

363.7   Environmental problems

Christianson, Gale E.

Greenhouse; the 200-year story of global warming. Walker & Co. 1999 305p il $25

363.7

1. Greenhouse effect
ISBN 0-8027-1346-7   LC 98-55251

Also available in paperback from Greystone Bks.

Christianson discusses global warming, focusing on "the history of industrialization and fuel use over the past two centuries." Natl Rev

"A thorough bibliography with a helpful listing of web sites is an added resource. Offering an extensive historical perspective on global warming, this book is an excellent addition to any science collection." Libr J

Davis, Lee Allyn

Environmental disasters; a chronicle of individual, industrial, and governmental carelessness; [by] Lee Davis. Facts on File 1998 246p il $49.50   **363.7**

1. Pollution 2. Human influence on nature 3. Industrial accidents 4. Disasters
ISBN 0-8160-3265-3   LC 98-29134

"This volume chronicles nearly 100 different environmental tragedies. Although the concentration is on the twentieth century, Davis has also included some events, such as deforestation, that began earlier. . . . The strength of this work is in its coverage of events that did not have the international impact of Chernobyl or Bhopal. Davis makes a strong effort to include the underlying causes of these disasters." Booklist

Includes bibliographical references

Encyclopedia of global change; environmental change and human society; Andrew S. Goudie, editor in chief; David J. Cuff, associate editor. Oxford Univ. Press 2002 2v il maps set $275   **363.7**
1. Environmental sciences—Encyclopedias 2. Human influence on nature—Encyclopedias
ISBN 0-19-510825-6   LC 00-58918
"This encyclopedia of environmental science and its impact on human society reflects the global changes that have taken place during the past century. The selection of the various topics cuts across many disciplines in the social, political, and natural sciences. The physical, biological, and chemical changes in the atmosphere, in the water, and on land are related to health, industry, economics, and human welfare. Some of the topics discuss climate models, including cyclones and winter storms. . . . The importance of the world-wide effort to manage whole ecosystems and its impact on human society are also explained. . . . Topics that are discussed briefly include dams, deforestation, earth motions, El Niño, extinction of species, fires, fishing, the Gaia hypothesis, the greenhouse effect, and biological diversity." Sci Books Films

Environmental encyclopedia; edited by Marci Bortman [et al.] 3rd ed. Gale Res. 2002 2v set $275   **363.7**
1. Environmental sciences—Encyclopedias 2. Ecology—Encyclopedias 3. Earth sciences—Encyclopedias
ISBN 0-7876-5486-8
First published 1994
"Entries range from 100 to more than 2,000 words. Some are complemented by black-and-white photographs and diagrams. Each entry is signed, and topical coverage includes a broad range of environmental perspectives, including scientific, political, and social issues. . . . Additional sections include a brief (five page) 'Historical Chronology' of environmental events, a five-page chronology of 'Environmental Legislation in the United States,' organizations mentioned within the bibliographies accompanying encyclopedia entries, and an index to entries and terms." Booklist

Famous first facts about the environment; edited by Ronald J. Formica; contributors, Victoria S. Chase [et al.] Wilson, H.W. 2002 573p $150   **363.7**
1. Environmental sciences
ISBN 0-8242-0974-5   LC 2001-17704
"A New England Publishing Associates book"
This "volume lists 4000 entries of international environmental 'firsts'. . . . Entries are first listed under a major subject category, such as air pollution, climate and weather, hazardous waste, population growth, and storms, which are then broken down into various subdivisions. . . . This unique work should be purchased by any size library that needs an account of environmental 'firsts.'" Libr J
Includes bibliographical references

Gonzalez, Juan
Fallout; the environmental consequences of the World Trade Center collapse. New Press (NY) 2002 150p $20   **363.7**
1. World Trade Center terrorist attack, 2001 2. Environmental health 3. Pollution
ISBN 1-56584-754-7   LC 2002-72404
González discusses the pollution caused when the World Trade Center collapsed after the terrorist attacks on September 11, 2001. He believes that substances such as asbestos, lead, mercury, dioxins, furans, and diesel fuel were released into the surrounding environment
"This book is a tragic indictment of the breakdown of public trust when it was needed most." Libr J

Hosansky, David
The environment A-Z. CQ Press 2000 320p il maps $58   **363.7**
1. Environmental sciences—Encyclopedias 2. Environmental policy—Encyclopedias
ISBN 1-568-02583-1   LC 00-62163
"Covering mostly the last 30 years, with some treatment of earlier events when essential to provide perspective, the alphabetic entries include general issues and topics, federal agencies and laws, and individual persons . . . who have influenced environmental decisions. A few international bodies are included, and of course issues like global warming are of broader than national scope, but in these cases the emphasis is primarily on how U.S. policies relate to the agencies and issues. Most entries are one or two pages in length, and are clearly and concisely written." Am Ref Books Annu, 2002
Includes bibliographical references

Mongillo, John F.
Encyclopedia of environmental science; by John Mongillo and Linda Zierdt-Warshaw. Oryx Press 2000 450p il $99.95   **363.7**
1. Environmental sciences—Encyclopedias
ISBN 1-57356-147-9   LC 00-32657
This encyclopedia covers "the major topics of agriculture, atmosphere, biomes, ecology, endangered plant and wildlife species, energy, law and regulations, water, and wetlands. . . . The 1000 entries are arranged alphabetically and range from several paragraphs to two pages in a clear and straightforward style with plenty of cross references." Libr J
For a fuller review see: Booklist, Feb. 1, 2001

Woodard, Colin, 1968-
Ocean's end; travels through endangered seas. Basic Bks. 2000 300p hardcover o.p. paperback available $15   **363.7**
1. Marine pollution 2. Marine resources
ISBN 0-465-01571-9 (pa)   LC 99-51771
The author contends "that pollution, harmful fishing practices, ignorance and global warming are destroying the world's oceans. . . . He uncovers a colorful cast of scientists, officials, activists, divers and religious missionaries who attest to the human and economic costs of ecological decline." Publ Wkly
Includes bibliographical references

Wyman, Bruce C.

The Facts on File dictionary of environmental science; [by] Bruce Wyman, L. Harold Stevenson. new ed. Facts on File 2001 458p (Facts on File science library) $44; pa $17.95 **363.7**
1. Environmental sciences—Dictionaries
ISBN 0-8160-4233-0; 0-8160-4234-9 (pa)

LC 00-55554

First published 1991 with authors names in reverse order

This dictionary contains over 4,000 cross-referenced entries reflecting the diversity of subjects that are relevant to the environmental field

"Entries contain clear and mostly concise definitions, but with no sources given. Significant place-names (Love Canal, Three Mile Island), a few environmentalists (Thoreau) and organizations, with Web sites included in the entry, are all useful additions." Choice

363.8 Food supply

McGovern, George S. (George Stanley), 1922-

The third freedom; ending hunger in our time; [by] George McGovern. Simon & Schuster 2001 173p $22 **363.8**
1. Food relief 2. Hunger
ISBN 0-684-85334-5

LC 00-49231

Also available in paperback from Rowman & Littlefield

The author outlines his ideas for ending world hunger which includes "a five-point program to be spearheaded by the U.S. that includes free school lunches for children around the world; free food, nutrition counseling and health-care services to disadvantaged women and children; the establishment of international food reserves; aid to farmers in developing nations to improve their yields; and the genetic engineering of crops." Publ Wkly

363.9 Population problems

Family planning sourcebook; edited by Amy Marcaccio Keyzer. Omnigraphics 2000 520p (Health reference series) $78 **363.9**
1. Birth control
ISBN 0-7808-0379-5

LC 00-53029

"Basic consumer health information about planning for pregnancy and contraception, including traditional methods, barrier methods, hormonal methods, permanent methods, future methods, emergency contraception, and birth control choices for women at each stage of life." Publisher's note

Tone, Andrea, 1964-

Devices and desires; a history of contraceptives in America. Hill & Wang 2001 366p $30; pa $15 **363.9**
1. Birth control
ISBN 0-8090-3817-X; 0-8090-3816-1 (pa)

LC 00-50547

"Part 1 examines the 'contraceptive entrepreneurs' who practiced what was for many years an illegal trade, regulated by no one. In part 2, 'From Smut to Science,' Tone considers the development of relatively reliable contraceptive techniques, . . . part 3, 'The Medicalization of Contraceptives,' covers birth control pills, Norplant, and intrauterine devices." Booklist

364.03 Criminology— Encyclopedias and dictionaries

Encyclopedia of crime & justice; Joshua Dressler, editor in chief. 2nd ed. Macmillan Ref. USA 2001 c2002 4v set $475 **364.03**
1. Crime—Encyclopedias 2. Criminals—Encyclopedias 3. Administration of criminal justice
ISBN 0-02-865319-X

First published 1982

Contents: v1 Abortion to cruel & unusual punishment; v2 Delinquent & criminal subcultures to Juvenile justice: Institutions; v3 Juvenile justice: Juvenile court to Rural crime; v4 Schools & crime to Wiretapping & eavesdropping

"The signed essays are written by respected scholars in the fields of law, sociology, and criminal justice and range in length from 800 to 12,000 words. . . . This set will be in high demand by 'issues' researchers as well as by researchers in the fields of law and criminal justice." Booklist

Encyclopedia of crime and punishment; edited by David Levinson. Sage Publs. 2002 4v set $600 **364.03**
1. Crime—Encyclopedias 2. Administration of criminal justice
ISBN 0-7619-2258-X

LC 2002-1220

"The 439 signed entries cover 13 major themes: crimes and related behaviors, law and justice, policing, forensics, corrections, victimology, punishment, social and cultural context, international aspects, concepts and theories, research methods and information, organizations and institutions, and special populations. . . . [This is] easy to understand and useful for beginning research in the field of criminal justice." Booklist

Nash, Jay Robert

World encyclopedia of 20th century murder. Paragon House 1992 693p il **364.03**
1. Homicide—Encyclopedias

LC 91-40492

Available from Marlowe & Co.

This volume presents information condensed from the Encyclopedia of world crime (1990). It contains some 1,000 alphabetically arranged entries for murderers and murders varying in length from a few paragraphs to over 15 pages, and includes over 400 photographs

Newton, Michael, 1951-

The encyclopedia of serial killers. Facts on File 2000 391p il $82.50; pa $19.95 **364.03**
1. Criminals—Encyclopedias 2. Homicide—Dictionaries
ISBN 0-8160-3978-X; 0-8160-3979-8 (pa)

LC 99-14384

"Entries cover a broad range of countries and time periods, but the majority of cases occurred within the last 50 years. In addition, the majority of killers profiled are American. . . . Interspersed with the profiles of the killers are entries on general topics." Booklist

Includes bibliographical references

364.1 Criminal offenses

Best American crime writing; edited by Otto Penzler and Thomas H. Cook. Pantheon Bks. $29.50; pa $15 **364.1**
1. Crime 2. Criminals
Annual. First published 2002

Best American crime writing—*Continued*

The essays in this collection "illuminate the darker side of human nature. . . . The topics include small towns devastated by multiple deaths, a conman who also likes to kill, crooked cops, disgraced DEA agents, and in the case of Mark Singer's compelling 'Chicken Warriors,' the bizarre subculture of cockfighting. An excellent collection in what is sure to be a valuable series." Booklist [review of 2002 annual]

Bonanno, Bill
Bound by honor; a mafioso's story. St. Martin's Press 1999 282p il $24.95; pa $6.99
364.1
1. Mafia
ISBN 0-312-20388-8; 0-312-97147-8 (pa)
LC 99-14049
"Bonanno not only details Mob infighting and the struggles among rival East Coast Mob families; he also offers specifics concerning Mob influence on Presidents Kennedy, Johnson, and Nixon as well as on other important political figures, such as J. Edgar Hoover . . . and Morris Udall. Even the Mob's involvement in JFK's assassination is spelled out. . . . Straightforward rather than chatty, the book paints a revealing picture of Mob family politics and government intervention." Booklist

Brown, Elaine
The condemnation of Little B. Beacon Press 2002 391p hardcover o.p. paperback available $19
364.1
1. Lewis, Michael, 1983 or 4- 2. Homicide 3. Atlanta (Ga.)—Race relations
ISBN 0-8070-0975-X (pa)
LC 2001-37943
"Brown analyzes the social and political context of the high-profile trial and conviction, amidst media blather about 'super predators,' of 13-year-old Little B. (a legal alias) for killing another black youth in Atlanta just before the Olympics opened." Booklist
"Packed with detail, strong arguments and flashes of brilliance, Brown's book is extraordinarily powerful." Publ Wkly
Includes bibliographical references

Bugliosi, Vincent
Helter skelter; the true story of the Manson murders; [by] Vincent Bugliosi with Curt Gentry. 25th anniversary ed. Norton 1994 528p il $25
364.1
1. Manson, Charles, 1934- 2. Homicide
ISBN 0-393-08700-X
LC 94-20957
A reissue of the title published 1974
"This book by the prosecutor at the Tate-LaBianca murder trial tells the inside story of the Manson Family murders, the investigations, and the trial." Libr J

Butterfield, Fox
All God's children; the Bosket family and the American tradition of violence. Knopf 1995 389p il maps o.p.; Avon Bks. paperback available $15
364.1
1. Bosket family 2. Violence 3. United States—Race relations
ISBN 0-380-72862-1 (pa)
LC 95-1540
Willie Bosket is an inmate "in New York's Woodbourne Correction Center. . . . Butterfield, with Willie's encouragement, set out to trace Bosket's family tree. . . . Butterfield focuses on Edgefield Country in Central South Carolina, where Bosket's family served as slaves." Newsweek
Includes bibliographical references

Capote, Truman, 1924-1984
In cold blood; a true account of a multiple murder and its consequences. Random House 2002 343p $22; pa $13
364.1
1. Hickock, Richard, 1931-1965 2. Smith, Perry, 1928-1965 3. Homicide
ISBN 0-375-50790-6; 0-679-74558-0 (pa)
LC 2002-282920
Also available Modern Library edition $15.95 (0-679-60023-X)
A reissue of the title first published 1966
"Truman Capote called his account of the 1959 murder of a Kansas farm family a nonfiction novel. Using information he collected through interviews with townspeople and the killers, Capote created a vivid portrait of the criminals and graphically described the crime, the criminals' escape to Mexico, capture, trial, appeals, and hanging." HarperCollins Reader's Ency of Am Lit. 2nd edition

Carrère, Emmanuel, 1957-
The adversary; translated by Linda Coverdale. Metropolitan Bks. 2000 191p o.p.; Picador paperback available $13
364.1
1. Romand, Jean-Claude, 1954- 2. Homicide
ISBN 0-312-42060-9 (pa)
LC 00-40755
"In 1933, Jean-Claude Romand, a successful French doctor, seemed devastated when his family was killed in a house fire; then police found evidence of blunt trauma on his wife's skull, and dug bullets out of his children. Soon, the truth began to surface: Romand was not a doctor at all, and he had murdered his family to conceal a web of lies that extended across almost two decades." New Yorker
"In telling Romand's story, [the author] also writes of the process of creating this book. By injecting himself into the narrative, Carrère has managed to make this appalling story both fascinating and highly readable." Libr J

Cornwell, Patricia Daniels
Portrait of a killer; Jack the Ripper—case closed; [by] Patricia Cornwell. Putnam 2002 387p il $27.95
364.1
1. Jack the Ripper 2. Homicide
ISBN 0-399-14932-5
LC 2002-31802
The author investigates the case of Jack the Ripper, the serial murderer that terrorized 1880s London
"The book's narrative is complex, as Cornwell details her emotional involvement in the case; re-creates life in Victorian times, particularly in the late 1880s, and especially the cruel existence of the London poor; offers expertly observed scenarios of how, based on the evidence, the killings occurred and the subsequent investigations were conducted." Publ Wkly
Includes bibliographical references

Douglas, John E.
The cases that haunt us; from Jack the Ripper to JonBenet Ramsey, the FBI's legendary mindhunter sheds new light on the mysteries that won't go away; [by] John Douglas and Mark Olshaker. Scribner 2000 352p il o.p.; Pocket Bks. paperback available $7.99
364.1
1. Homicide 2. Criminal psychology
ISBN 0-671-01706-3 (pa)
LC 00-63524
"A Lisa Drew book"

Douglas, John E.—*Continued*
The authors discuss "eight controversial cases that include the Lindbergh baby kidnapping, the Boston Strangler, the Zodiac Killer, and the JonBenet Ramsey killing." Libr J

Dray, Philip
At the hands of persons unknown; the lynching of Black America. Random House 2002 528p il hardcover o.p. paperback available $14.95   **364.1**
1. Lynching 2. African Americans—Southern States 3. Southern States—Race relations
ISBN 0-375-75445-8 (pa)   LC 2001-40366
The author "looks at specific lynchings, the national history of race and politics, and anti-lynching campaigns of black and biracial organizations." Libr J
"Dray balances moral indignation with a sound understanding of history and politics. The result is vital, hard-hitting cultural history." Publ Wkly
Includes bibliographical references

Drew, Elizabeth
The corruption of American politics; what went wrong and why. Carol Pub. Group 1999 278p o.p.; Overlook Press paperback available $15.95   **364.1**
1. Political corruption 2. United States—Politics and government—1989-
ISBN 1-58567-049-9 (pa)   LC 99-28684
"Birch Lane Press book"
The author argues "that the prevalence of soft money has lowered the quality of leadership in Washington. The most successful politicians are no longer the best executives or the best legislators, she says, but rather the best fund-raisers. . . . One of the most skillfully written, as well as insightful, looks inside the Beltway to appear in a very long time." Publ Wkly

Flook, Maria
Invisible Eden; a story of love and murder on Cape Cod. Broadway Bks. 2003 406p $24.95   **364.1**
1. Worthington, Christa, 1955-2002 2. Homicide
ISBN 0-7679-1374-4   LC 2003-41853
"When Christa Worthington, an accomplished fashion writer and single mother, was found murdered in a remote Cape Cod town, national media became fascinated with the life and tragic end of a woman who appeared to have everything. Flook, a newer resident to the same small town, follows the investigation into the still unsolved murder. . . . Flook brings Worthington to life, detailing her vibrancy, character flaws, and obsessions." Booklist

Gourevitch, Philip
A cold case. Farrar, Straus & Giroux 2001 183p il o.p.; Picador paperback available $11   **364.1**
1. Koehler, Frank, 1929- 2. Homicide
ISBN 0-312-42002-1 (pa)   LC 00-68179
"In 1970, Frankie Koehler shot and killed two men after a barroom brawl in Hell's Kitchen and then disappeared; twenty-seven years later, Andy Rosenzweig, the chief investigator for the Manhattan D.A., set out to solve one last case before he retired. Gourevitch reconstructs not only the crime but an era of cops and criminals that's fast passing into myth." New Yorker

Jones, Ann, 1937-
Women who kill. Beacon Press 1996 448p pa $16   **364.1**
1. Homicide 2. Criminals
ISBN 0-8070-6775-X   LC 95-46961
First published 1980 by Holt, Rinehart & Winston
The author examines murders committed by women throughout American history, discussing such cases as Lizzie Borden, Alice Crimmins, and Jean Harris. The cases discussed shed light on women's status in American society
Includes bibliographical references

Kelly, Robert J.
Encyclopedia of organized crime in the United States; from Capone's Chicago to the new urban underworld. Greenwood Press 2000 xxx, 358p $64.95   **364.1**
1. Organized crime
ISBN 0-313-30653-2   LC 99-33801
This reference source "describes and analyzes issues, criminal personalities, and trends throughout the 20th century. Kelly also examines the conditions that produced criminal activities and organizations. More than 250 entries provide in-depth information on major underworld figures, from Al Capone to Lucky Luciano to John Gotti, as well as key criminal events, from rub outs to FBI stings." Libr J
For a fuller review see: Booklist, Nov. 1, 2000

King, Joyce
Hate crime: the story of a dragging in Jasper, Texas. Pantheon Bks. 2002 225p $24   **364.1**
1. Byrd, James, Jr. 2. Homicide 3. Hate crimes 4. African Americans—Southern States 5. Southern States—Race relations
ISBN 0-375-42132-7   LC 2001-58074
"On a Texas back road in 1998 . . . three young whites wrapped a chain around an African American man and dragged him to his death behind their truck. . . . King covers each of the three trials that followed the atrocity." Libr J
The author "provides both objective reporting and sensitive insight into the players on both sides of America's racial divide." Booklist

Larson, Erik
The devil in the white city; murder, magic, and madness at the fair that changed America. Crown 2003 447p il map $25.95   **364.1**
1. Mudgett, Herman W., 1861-1896 2. World's Columbian Exposition (1893: Chicago, Ill.) 3. Homicide
ISBN 0-609-60844-4   LC 2002-154046
This is an account of how "H.H. Holmes (born Herman Webster Mudgett) dispatched somewhere between 27 and 200 people, mostly single young women, in the churning new metropolis of Chicago; many of the murders occurred during (and exploited) the city's finest moment, the World's Fair of 1893. Larson's breathtaking new history is a novelistic yet wholly factual account of the fair and the mass murderer who lurked within it." Publ Wkly
Includes bibliographical references

Maas, Peter, 1929-2001

Manhunt. Random House 1986 301p o.p.; I Books paperback available $13 **364.1**

1. Wilson, Edwin P. 2. United States. Central Intelligence Agency 3. Criminals 4. Military weapons

ISBN 0-7434-5268-2 (pa)   LC 85-25762

This is the "story of Edwin P. Wilson, a CIA operative turned international arms dealer, who grew rich providing restricted explosives and aid to Libya's Qaddafi." Publ Wkly

"It's an old story, and Mr. Maas tells it well, with a fine eye for character and setting and a good reporter's tenacity in finding out things a whole lot of people don't want him to know." N Y Times Book Rev

Mallon, Thomas, 1951-

Mrs. Paine's garage and the murder of John F. Kennedy. Pantheon Bks. 2002 211p $22; pa $13   **364.1**

1. Paine, Ruth 2. Oswald, Lee Harvey 3. Oswald, Marina 4. Kennedy, John F. (John Fitzgerald), 1917-1963—Assassination

ISBN 0-375-42117-3; 0-15-602755-0 (pa)

LC 2001-36157

"A journalistic inquiry into Ruth Paine, the woman who welcomed Marina Oswald—and sometimes her husband, Lee—into her suburban Dallas home in 1963; it offers a new theory about the antecedents of the assassination." N Y Times Book Rev

McGinniss, Joe

Fatal vision. Putnam 1983 663p o.p.; New Am. Lib. paperback available $7.99   **364.1**

1. MacDonald, Jeffrey R. 2. Homicide

ISBN 0-451-16566-7 (pa)   LC 82-24127

"The complex story of Jeffrey MacDonald, a Princeton-educated doctor and Green Beret captain who was accused of brutally murdering his wife and their two young daughters on a dreary February night in 1970." Best Sellers

"This is a wisely observant, well-written, and understated book." Harpers

Includes bibliographical references

Milito, Lynda

Mafia wife; my story of love, murder, and madness; {by} Lynda Milito with Reg Potterton. HarperCollins Pubs. 2003 290p $24.95   **364.1**

1. Mafia

ISBN 0-06-621261-8   LC 2002-191273

"In 1988, the author's husband of 23 years, Louie, vanished. Several years later, two men confessed to being responsible for his murder. . . . Now, the dead man's widow tells her story, about her life with and without her husband. . . . This exposé offers an often-shocking glimpse inside the world of organized crime." Booklist

Murakami, Haruki, 1949-

Underground; translated from the Japanese by Alfred Birnbaum and Philip Gabriel. Vintage Bks. 2001 366p map pa $14   **364.1**

1. Aum Shinrikyō 2. Terrorism

ISBN 0-375-72580-6   LC 00-69310

"The Tokyo gas attack and the Japanese psyche." Subtitle on cover

"On March 20, 1995, followers of the religious cult Aum Shinrikyo unleashed lethal sarin gas into cars of the Tokyo subway system. Many died, many more were injured. This is [Murakami's] . . . account of this episode." Publ Wkly

Olsen, Jack

I: the creation of a serial killer. St. Martin's Press 2002 365p il $24.95; pa $6.99   **364.1**

1. Jesperson, Keith Hunter 2. Homicide

ISBN 0-312-24198-4; 0-312-98384-0 (pa)

LC 2001-58892

The author draws "on interviews and his subject's own diaries to . . . reveal the life and inner workings of Keith Hunter Jesperson, currently serving life in prison for the murders of eight women in the 1990s." Publ Wkly

"A truly horrifying account of a serial killer, told with shocking candor." Booklist

Posner, Gerald L.

Killing the dream; James Earl Ray and the assassination of Martin Luther King, Jr. Random House 1998 446p il o.p.; Harvest Bks. paperback available $15   **364.1**

1. King, Martin Luther, 1929-1968 2. Ray, James Earl, 1928-1998

ISBN 0-15-600651-0 (pa)   LC 97-40112

This book looks "at the 1968 murder of Martin Luther King Jr. in Memphis, focusing on the character of the convicted killer, the late James Earl Ray." Libr J

Posner "has written a superb book: a model of investigation, meticulous in its discovery and presentation of evidence, unbiased in its exploration of every claim. And it is a wonderfully readable book, as gripping as a first-class detective story." N Y Times Book Rev

Ruddick, James

Death at the priory; love, sex, and murder in Victorian England. Atlantic Monthly Press 2002 c2001 209p il $24   **364.1**

1. Bravo, Charles Delaunay Turner, 1845-1876 2. Bravo, Florence, 1845-1878 3. Homicide

ISBN 0-87113-832-8   LC 2001-22522

Also available in paperback from Grove Press

First published 2001 in the United Kingdom

The author examines the unsolved crime of "the fatal poisoning of Charles Bravo in his London home in 1876." N Y Times Book Rev

"This well-executed portrait of Victorian mores and malice will please the mystery and true-crime crowd and very possibly a wider audience." Publ Wkly

Includes bibliographical references

Rule, Ann

—and never let her go; Thomas Capano, the deadly seducer. Simon & Schuster 1999 479p il o.p.; Pocket Bks. paperback available $7.99   **364.1**

1. Capano, Thomas J., 1949- 2. Fahey, Anne Marie 3. Homicide 4. Trials (Homicide)

ISBN 0-671-86871-3 (pa)   LC 99-47339

"In June 1996, Anne Marie Fahey, a 30-year-old secretary to the governor of Delaware, disappeared and was reported missing by her family. In the weeks that followed, a charming, successful, and well-connected attorney, Tom Capano, was charged with her murder. Rule . . . tells the riveting story of the three-year secret affair between Fahey and Capano and a cruel obsession that led to murder." Booklist

Rule, Ann—*Continued*

Dead by sunset; perfect husband, perfect killer? Simon & Schuster 1995 429p il hardcover o.p. paperback available $7.99

364.1

1. Keeton, Cheryl, 1949-1986 2. Cunningham, Bradly Morris 3. Trials (Homicide)

ISBN 0-671-00113-2 (pa)   LC 95-38326

"Eight years after killing his divorced wife in Portland, Oregon, Brad Cunningham was finally convicted of her murder. . . . [Rule] tackles the case of the five-times-married Cunningham, whose loving personality and demeanor changed after each marriage." Booklist

"Rule's writing is crisp and well paced, full of details that give the reader clear insight into circumstances and surroundings, as well as motive." Libr J

Salamon, Julie

Facing the wind; a true story of tragedy and reconciliation. Random House 2001 302p hardcover o.p. paperback available $13.95

364.1

1. Homicide 2. Brooklyn (New York, N.Y.)—Social conditions

ISBN 0-375-75940-9 (pa)   LC 00-42532

"In 1978, Bob Rowe, an out-of-work Brooklyn lawyer, killed his two sons, his daughter and wife by bashing their heads in with a baseball bat. He was found not guilty by reason of insanity, and after several years in a mental institution was released. He later remarried and had another daughter. Although journalist Salamon . . . did not interview Rowe before his death in 1997, this expertly crafted account is informed by diligent research and interviews with his second wife, Colleen, as well as with a women's support group to which Rowe's first wife, Mary, had belonged." Publ Wkly

Schiller, Lawrence

Perfect murder, perfect town. HarperCollins Pubs. 1999 621p hardcover o.p. paperback available $7.99

364.1

1. Ramsey, JonBenet, d. 1996 2. Ramsey, Patricia 3. Ramsey, John Bennett 4. Boulder (Colo.). Police Dept. 5. Homicide

ISBN 0-06-109696-2 (pa)   LC 99-207248

This is an account of the investigation "of the murder of six-year-old child beauty-pageant winner JonBenét Ramsey in Boulder, Colorado, on the night of Christmas 1996." N Y Rev Books

Schiller argues that the "Boulder Police Department bungled the investigation, in large part out of ego and inexperience." N Y Times Book Rev

Sifakis, Carl

The Mafia encyclopedia. 2nd ed. Facts on File 1999 414p il $55

364.1

1. Mafia—Dictionaries 2. Organized crime—Dictionaries

ISBN 0-8160-3856-2   LC 98-42297

First published 1987

The more than 450 entries "cover the major personalities, events, and mores of the Mafia. Approximately half of the entries are biographical, including the heads of crime families, their minions at various levels in the organization, and the victims of Mafia blackmail, persecution, or violence." Booklist

Stewart, James B.

Blind eye; how the medical establishment let a doctor get away with murder. Simon & Schuster 1999 334p il hardcover o.p. paperback available $14

364.1

1. Swango, Michael 2. Homicide

ISBN 0-684-86563-7 (pa)   LC 99-37044

Stewart discusses the "case against Dr. Michael Swango, a . . . physician suspected of poisoning between 35 and 60 patients and co-workers." Time

This is "not only a fascinating look at a psychopath masquerading as a healer but also a disturbing exposé of the system that fails to protect the public." Libr J

Sullivan, Randall

Labyrinth; a detective investigates the murders of Tupac Shakur and Biggie Smalls, the implication of Death Row Records' Suge Knight, and the origins of the Los Angeles Police scandal. Atlantic Monthly Press 2002 324p il $25

364.1

1. Shakur, Tupac 2. Notorious B.I.G. (Musician) 3. Knight, Suge 4. Homicide 5. Police corruption

ISBN 0-87113-838-7   LC 2001-53709

Also available in paperback from Grove Press

The author makes a "case for thinking that the murders of Tupac Shakur and Biggie Smalls are connected, and the LAPD Ramparts Division scandal is connected to them. . . . You haven't got the goods on any of these notorious cases until you read this intricate show-biz true-crime thriller." Booklist

Thornhill, Randy

A natural history of rape; biological bases of sexual coercion; [by] Randy Thornhill and Craig T. Palmer. MIT Press 2000 251p $35; pa $16.95

364.1

1. Rape 2. Men—Sexual behavior

ISBN 0-262-20125-9; 0-262-70083-2 (pa)

     LC 99-31685

The authors aim "to show that human rape is a 'natural, biological phenomenon that is a product of the human evolutionary heritage.' . . . Rape, they argue, was favored by natural selection to give sexually dispossessed males the chance to have children, or males with mates the chance to have extra children. . . . They further claim that attempts to root out rape will not succeed until one accepts its evolutionary origin and uses this . . . knowledge as a basis for social policy." New Repub

Includes bibliographical references

The **Ultimate** Jack the Ripper companion; an illustrated encyclopedia; [compiled by] Stewart P. Evans & Keith Skinner. Carroll & Graf Pubs. 2000 692p il $35; pa $16

364.1

1. Jack the Ripper 2. Homicide

ISBN 0-7867-0768-2; 0-7867-0926-X (pa)

     LC 00-711560

Published in the United Kingdom with title: Ultimate Jack the Ripper sourcebook

This is a collection of primary and secondary source material pertaining to the Whitechapel murders

"This volume is undoubtedly the single largest resource on this case ever published." Libr J

Includes bibliographical references

Vollers, Maryanne

Ghosts of Mississippi; the murder of Medgar Evers, the trials of Byron de la Beckwith, and the haunting of the new South. Little, Brown 1995 411p hardcover o.p. paperback available $19.95   **364.1**
1. Evers, Medgar Wiley, 1925-1963 2. De La Beckwith, Byron
ISBN 0-316-91471-1 (pa)   LC 94-31108
The author maintains that "the murder of Mississippi NAACP field secretary Evers (1925-63) and the subsequent trials of Byron de la Beckwith sum up the terror of racial segregation, the battle for blacks' civil rights, and a generation of change in Southern bearing and behavior on race. With care for the human elements, Vollers reviews the background of race, culture, class, and personality in Evers's shooting. She then follows the trials—the two acquittals in 1964 and the conviction in 1994." Libr J
Includes bibliographical references

Walsh, John

Public enemies; the host of America's most wanted targets the nation's most notorious criminals; [by] John Walsh with Philip Lerman. Pocket Bks. 2001 310p il $24.95; pa $7.99   **364.1**
1. America's most wanted (Television program) 2. Criminals 3. Crime
ISBN 0-671-01995-3; 0-671-01996-1 (pa)
     LC 2001-34027
"From the media-popular 'Railroad Killer' to a remorseless member of the Symbionese Liberation Army with 25 years on the lam, to '70s iconoclast Ira Einhorn, who murdered his girlfriend and hid her body for 18 months in a steamer trunk, this title captures the television show's highlights." Publ Wkly

Wambaugh, Joseph

Fire lover; a true story. Morrow 2002 338p $25.95; pa $7.99   **364.1**
1. Orr, John 2. Arson
ISBN 0-06-009527-X; 0-06-009528-8 (pa)
     LC 2002-20139
"John Orr was a Glendale, Calif., fire investigator who specialized in arson in more ways than one. . . . Mr. Orr has been linked to four deaths and millions of dollars of property damage. . . . Mr. Wambaugh begins by describing the most lethal fire." N Y Times (Late N Y Ed)
"Wambaugh's painstaking research which included interviews with law-enforcement officers, survivors, and victims' families, is astonishing." Booklist

Worrall, Simon

The poet and the murderer; a true story of literary crime and the art of forgery. Dutton 2002 270p il $23.95; pa $14   **364.1**
1. Hofmann, Mark 2. Forgery 3. Homicide
ISBN 0-525-94596-2; 0-452-28402-3 (pa)
     LC 2001-53878
"In 1997, Sotheby's unveiled what experts believed was a newly discovered poem, 'That God Cannot Be Understood,' by Emily Dickinson. A few weeks later, the . . . discovery was revealed a forgery by a man who had already convincingly forged documents by more than 100 literary and historical figures, including Daniel Boone and Betsy Ross. This book examines the psychology of . . . forger and murderer (he killed two people who threatened his unmasking) Mark Hofmann." Booklist

364.3   Offenders

Rhodes, Richard, 1937-

Why they kill; the discoveries of a maverick criminologist. Knopf 1999 371p $26.95; pa $14   **364.3**
1. Athens, Lonnie H. 2. Criminal psychology 3. Violence 4. Criminals
ISBN 0-375-40249-7; 0-375-70248-2 (pa)
     LC 99-18920
The author discusses the history of violence and the work of social scientist Lonnie H. Athens. "Athens interviewed prisoners in maximum security prisons in Iowa, California and elsewhere, predominantly men. . . . His hope was to bypass inmates' typical narratives and get to what they actually thought and felt when they assaulted or raped or killed." N Y Times Book Rev
Includes bibliographical references

364.66   Capital punishment

Henderson, Harry, 1951-

Capital punishment. rev ed. Facts on File 2000 300p (Library in a book) $45   **364.66**
1. Capital punishment
ISBN 0-8160-4193-8   LC 00-28775
First published 1991 under the authorship of Stephen A. Flanders
A look at both sides of this controversial issue from social, political, ethical, and religious perspectives. Includes a glossary, bibliographies, Internet sources, and audiovisual materials

Solotaroff, Ivan

The last face you'll ever see; the private life of the American death penalty. HarperCollins Pubs. 2001 232p hardcover o.p. paperback available $12.95   **364.66**
1. Capital punishment
ISBN 0-06-093103-5 (pa)   LC 2001-16604
In this examination of the death penalty the author "interviews the executioners who carry out the sentences. He concentrates on Parchman State Penitentiary in Mississippi and on two men, Donald Cabana, who quit his job as warden because he could not stomach the death penalty, and Donald Hocutt, who appears to relish his work yet suffers from a list of physical and psychological ailments." Libr J
"Entertainingly written, well researched and documented, this is important reading for death-penalty activists, pro and con, and other concerned citizens." Booklist
Includes bibliographical references

365   Penal and related institutions

Abbott, Jack Henry, 1944-2002

In the belly of the beast; letters from prison; with an introduction by Norman Mailer. Random House 1981 166p hardcover o.p. paperback available $12   **365**
1. Prisoners 2. Prisons—United States
ISBN 0-679-73237-3 (pa)   LC 80-6038
The writer of these letters began them while "chained to the crossbar of his bed in the Butner, North Carolina

Abbott, Jack Henry, 1944-2002—*Continued*
Federal Correctional Institution. He addressed his letter to Norman Mailer. . . . [In these letters he] wished to convey something about the effect of [prison life on the individual]." Nation
Abbott's "letters belong with the best prison literature, not because of their accounts of atrocity, but for their disturbing picture of daily life behind bars." Time

Applebaum, Anne, 1964-
Gulag; a history. Doubleday 2003 677p il maps $35　　　**365**
1. Concentration camps 2. Convict labor 3. Soviet Union—Politics and government
ISBN 0-7679-0056-1　　　LC 2002-41344
This "describes how, largely under Stalin's watch, a regulated, centralized system of prison labor—unprecedented in scope—gradually arose out of the chaos of the Russian Revolution. . . . Applebaum details camp life, including strategies for survival; the experiences of women and children in the camps; sexual relationships and marriages between prisoners; and rebellions, strikes and escapes. . . . Applebaum's lucid prose and painstaking consideration of the competing theories about aspects of camp life and policy are always compelling." Publ Wkly
Includes bibliographical references

Encyclopedia of American prisons; editors, Marilyn D. McShane, Frank P. Williams III. Garland 1996 xxv, 532p il (Garland reference library of the humanities) $160　　　**365**
1. Prisons—United States—Encyclopedias
ISBN 0-8153-1350-0　　　LC 95-41593
This encyclopedia "traces the history and development of the major prisons in the United States and provides an overview of prison issues such as convicts with AIDS, prisoners' rights, and juveniles behind bars." Libr J

Oshinsky, David M., 1944-
"Worse than slavery"; Parchman Farm and the ordeal of Jim Crow justice. Free Press 1996 306p il hardcover o.p. paperback available $14　　　**365**
1. Mississippi State Penitentiary 2. Prisons—United States 3. United States—Race relations
ISBN 0-684-83095-7 (pa)　　　LC 95-52880
This book examines Mississippi's "Parchman prison farm in the context of sharecropping, convict leasing, lynching and the legalized segregation that replaced slavery." N Y Times Book Rev
"Oshinsky's beautifully constructed narrative brings to vivid life one of the most shameful chapters in American history." New Yorker
Includes bibliographical references

Rafter, Nicole Hahn, 1939-
Prisons in America; a reference handbook; [by] Nicole Hahn Rafter and Debra Stanley. ABC-CLIO 1999 226p il (Contemporary world issues) $45　　　**365**
1. Prisons—United States
ISBN 1-57607-102-2　　　LC 99-35719
"The first chapter, 'History of American Prisons,' is followed by . . . [a] section titled 'Issues and Controversies' that discusses pertinent issues like prisoners' rights, equality for women prisoners, prison violence, and healthcare. The remainder of the volume includes a chronology of major events in U.S. prison history, bibliographic sketches, and an extensive list of sources." Libr J

Rees, Siân, 1965-
The floating brothel; the extraordinary true story of an eighteenth-century ship and its cargo of female convicts. Hyperion 2002 236p il maps $23.95　　　**365**
1. Prisoners 2. Penal colonies 3. Women criminals
ISBN 0-7868-6787-6　　　LC 2001-46338
Also available Thorndike large print edition
"This work of nautical history recounts the 1789-90 voyage from England to Australia of a ship full of female convicts." Libr J
"Rees uses every scrap of information she can muster to produce a lively, vibrant sense of these women as they must have lived their lives." Publ Wkly
Includes bibliographical references

Solzhenitsyn, Aleksandr, 1918-
The Gulag Archipelago, 1918-1956; an experiment in literary investigation; {Pts} I-VII. Harper & Row 1974-1978 3v il maps o.p.; Westview Press paperback available 3v set $59　　　**365**
1. Political prisoners 2. Soviet Union—Politics and government
ISBN 0-8133-3294-X (pa)
Also available abridged paperback edition for HarperCollins Pubs. $18.95 (ISBN 0-06-000776-1)
"A 'literary investigation' of the network of Soviet prison camps as they existed between 1918 and 1956. . . . A mixture of autobiography, history, and analysis, the relentlessly grim picture of life inside the camps forms the basis for an attack not only on Stalinism and Leninism but also on the whole process of substituting Western rational and secular ideas for Russia's traditional mysticism." Benét's Reader's Ency. 4th edition

Wynn, Jennifer
Inside Rikers; stories from the world's largest penal colony. St. Martin's Press 2001 223p $24.95; pa $13.95　　　**365**
1. Rikers Island Prison (New York, N.Y.) 2. Prisoners
ISBN 0-312-26179-9; 0-312-29158-2 (pa)
LC 2001-19261
The author presents an "exploration of inmates' lives in New York's 'vast penal colony,' Rikers Island." Publ Wkly
"Wynn's study is ultimately a call for much-needed prison reform, with emphasis on rehabilitation rather than mere incarceration, and she makes her case well." Booklist
Includes bibliographical references

366　Association

Ridley, Jasper Godwin
The Freemasons; a history of the world's most powerful secret society; [by] Jasper Ridley. Arcade Pub. 2001 357p $25.95; pa $14.95　　　**366**
1. Freemasons
ISBN 1-55570-601-5; 1-55570-654-6 (pa)
LC 2001-45745
The author "traces the origins of freemasonry back to the craft guilds in medieval Europe, and then he chronicles their growth and evolution through the modern era. . . . This work of popular history sheds light on a frequently obscure subject." Booklist
Includes bibliographical references

368.3 Insurance against death, old age, illness, injury

Life insurance fact book. American Council of Life Insurance $37.50   **368.3**
1. Life insurance
ISSN 0075-9406

Also available print edition and diskette $55

Biennial. First published 1946

"A source useful to all U.S. legal reserve life insurance companies, with tables, charts, and interpretive text. Data are taken from annual statements and give statistics, yearly statements, ownership, payments, assets, officials, and so forth." Ref Sources for Small & Medium-sized Libr. 6th edition

368.4 Government-sponsored insurance

Social Security handbook; United States Department of Health and Human Services, Social Security Administration. U.S. Govt. Ptg. Office pa $55.50   **368.4**
1. Social security

First published 1960 by United States. Bureau of Old Age and Survivors Insurance. Subtitle varies. (14th edition 2001) Periodically revised

"Detailed explanation without commentary of the federal retirement, survivors, disability, black lung benefits, supplementary security income, and health insurance programs, who is entitled to benefits, and how such benefits may be obtained." Ref Sources for Small & Medium-sized Libr. 6th edition

370 Education

Encyclopedia of education; James W. Guthrie, editor in chief. 2nd ed. Macmillan Ref. USA 2003 8v il set $850   **370**
1. Education—Encyclopedias
ISBN 0-02-865594-X   LC 2002-8205

First published 1971

Contents: v1 AACSB-Commerce; v2 Common-Expertise; v3 Faculty-Hutchins; v4 IEA-Lowenfeld; v5 Macdonald-Putnam; v6 Race-State; v7 States-Zirbes; v8 Appendixes. Index

This set includes over 850 signed articles covering educational policy and curriculum issues, learning assessment, standards, history and culture, legislation, and profiles of schools, people, and organizations

"The writing is well edited and accessible." Booklist

Hirsch, E. D. (Eric Donald), 1928-
The schools we need and why we don't have them; [by] E.D. Hirsch, Jr. Doubleday 1996 317p hardcover o.p. paperback available $14.95   **370**
1. Education—United States
ISBN 0-385-49524-2 (pa)   LC 96-2192

The author argues that "our current educational system has failed to reduce social inequity or enhance our economic competitiveness. . . . Hirsch pleads for abandoning Progressivism's 'process' methodology in favor of a

curriculum based on challenging content, common knowledge acquisition, and rigorous standardized testing." Libr J

This "book presents a sophisticated, scholarly and often compelling argument and it deserves serious consideration, whatever one's political predilections." N Y Times Book Rev

Includes bibliographical references

Postman, Neil
The end of education; redefining the value of school. Knopf 1995 209p hardcover o.p. paperback available $12   **370**
1. Education—United States
ISBN 0-679-75031-2 (pa)   LC 94-46605

"The volume initially investigates American education in the earlier part of this century. . . . Part 2 shifts focus to contemporary education, describing the underlying conceptions of today's schools and considering economic utility, consumership, technology, and separatism. . . . Postman responds creatively to the problems of 'modernity,' holding out hope for regaining a sense of purpose and respect for learning." Choice

"Beautifully written, breathtakingly high-minded, this is Postman's best book on American education." Booklist

Includes bibliographical references

Unger, Harlow G., 1931-
Encyclopedia of American education. 2nd ed. Facts on File 2001 3v set $225   **370**
1. Education—United States—Encyclopedias
ISBN 0-8160-4344-2   LC 2001-17475

First published 1996

This work "includes about 2,500 entries in about 200 subject areas. Topics range from history to current issues, from leading figures and movements to legislation and Supreme Court cases, from administration to adolescence. . . . Entries range in length from a couple of sentences to several pages. . . . The humanities are covered more extensively than the sciences." Booklist

370.1 Education—Philosophy

Dewey, John, 1859-1952
Democracy and education; an introduction to the philosophy of education. Macmillan 1916 434p o.p.; Free Press paperback available $16.95   **370.1**
1. Education—Philosophy
ISBN 0-684-83631-9 (pa)

"The author's aim here is to detect and state the ideas implied in a democratic society and to apply those ideas to the problems of education." Boston Transcr

370.15 Educational psychology

Levine, Melvin D.
A mind at a time; [by] Mel Levine. Simon & Schuster 2002 352p $26; pa $14   **370.15**
1. Educational psychology 2. Child development 3. Learning disabilities
ISBN 0-7432-0222-8; 0-7432-0223-6 (pa)
    LC 2001-57670

The author discusses "eight areas of learning (the memory system, the language system, the spatial ordering system, the motor system, etc.). He provides chapters describing how each type of learning works and advises

Levine, Melvin D.—*Continued*

parents and teachers on how to help kids struggling in these areas. . . . This is a must-read for parents and educators who want to understand and improve the school lives of children." Publ Wkly

Includes bibliographical references

370.25   Education—Directories

The **Handbook** of private schools; an annual descriptive survey of independent education. Sargent Pubs. il maps $95

370.25

1. Private schools—Directories 2. Education—United States—Directories

ISSN 0072-9884

First published 1915 with title: Handbook of the best private schools of the United States and Canada

"Describes more than 1,700 boarding and day schools, providing information on age and grade ranges, whether co-educational or for boys or girls, enrollment, faculty size and background, academic orientation and curriculum, and where graduates attend college. 'Features classifield' section lists institutions offering military programs, elementary boarding divisions, programs for students with learning differences, international and bilingual schools, and schools with more than 500 or fewer than 100 students." Guide to Ref Books. 11th edition

Patterson's American education. Educational Directories $94   **370.25**

1. Education—United States—Directories

ISSN 0079-0230

Annual. First published 1904

"The first part lists public, private, and Catholic junior high school and high school districts, and combined elementary and secondary districts. Arranged by state, beginning with addresses of officials of state departments of education; then by community; then by district, with names of top officials; then by individual schools, giving names, addresses, and phone numbers of principals. . . . The second part consists of a directory of schools classified by specialty." Guide to Ref Books. 11th edition

Private independent schools. Bunting & Lyon $110   **370.25**

1. Private schools—Directories 2. Education—United States—Directories

ISSN 0079-5399

Annual. First published 1943 with title: Independent schools, a directory. Title varies

"Describes some 1,000 American and 100 foreign boarding and day schools, from kindergarten through high school, plus one-year post-high school programs. Roughly a quarter of the entries are descriptive; the remainder give the school's size, age range, application procedures, administrative control, cost, and special programs, plus a brief statement of its philosophy. A classification grid, arranged by state, identifies institutions with specific characteristics, such as military programs, church affiliation, and restriction to one sex. Separate section on summer programs emphasizing academics, recreation, or travel." Guide to Ref Books. 11th edition

370.5   Education—Serial publications

Education index. Wilson, H.W. service basis

370.5

1. Education—Periodicals—Indexes 2. Education—Bibliography

ISSN 0013-1385

Also available CD-ROM version and online

Published monthly, except in July and August, with quarterly cumulations and permanent bound annual cumulations

A cumulative index to more than 500 English-language periodicals, yearbooks, and monographs. The main body consists of subject and author entries arranged in one alphabet. In addition there is an author listing of citations to book reviews

"A cornerstone for information and research in the field of education." Am Ref Books Annu, 1982

371   Schools & their activities; special education

Gross, Martin L. (Martin Louis), 1925-

The conspiracy of ignorance; the failure of American public schools. HarperCollins Pubs. 2000 291p $25; pa $14   **371**

1. Public schools—United States 2. Education—United States

ISBN 0-06-019458-8; 0-06-093260-0 (pa)

LC 99-34783

Gross examines the current state of public schools in the United States and argues for the need for reform

Includes bibliographical references

371.04   Alternative schools

Rupp, Rebecca

The complete home learning sourcebook; the essential resource guide for homeschoolers, parents, and educators covering every subject from arithmetic to zoology. Three Rivers Press (NY) 1998 865p pa $29.95   **371.04**

1. Home schooling

ISBN 0-609-80109-0   LC 98-38440

Arranged by subject, this resource reviews: books, videos, magazines, catalogs, timelines, kits, hands-on activities, board games, CD-ROMs, and educational web sites. Icons denote format and intended age group of each resource

371.1   Teachers, teaching, and related activities

Barzun, Jacques, 1907-
Begin here; the forgotten conditions of teaching and learning; editor, Morris Philipson. University of Chicago Press 1991 222p $24.95; pa $21   **371.1**
1. Teaching 2. Psychology of learning
ISBN 0-226-03846-7; 0-226-03847-5 (pa)
         LC 90-25877
"Some of the topics Barzun addresses include the inadequate ways in which reading is taught; the demeaning methods of teacher training; the counterfeit 'social studies' programs which are the offshoot of combined geography and history curriculums; the benefits of reading the classics; and how television affects learning." Libr J
Includes bibliographical references

371.2   School administration

Kohn, Alfie
The schools our children deserve; moving beyond traditional classrooms and "tougher standards". Houghton Mifflin 1999 344p $24; pa $14   **371.2**
1. Education—United States 2. Education—Aims and objectives
ISBN 0-395-94039-7; 0-618-08345-6 (pa)
         LC 99-31122
The author challenges the "back-to-basics" approach to education and test-driven "tougher standards," advocating instead the teaching of creative and critical thinking skills
"Parents as well as educators should read this remarkable book." Libr J
Includes bibliographical references

371.3   Methods of instruction and study

Britton, Lesley
Montessori play & learn; a parents' guide to purposeful play from two to six; with an introduction by Joy Starrey Turner. Crown 1992 144p il pa $19.95   **371.3**
1. Montessori method of education 2. Parenting
ISBN 0-517-59182-0   LC 92-5446
This describes educational activities for two to six year olds according to the Montessori method which parents can introduce at home

Montessori, Maria, 1870-1952
The Montessori method; introduction by J. McV. Hunt. Schocken Bks. 1964 xxxix, 376p il hardcover o.p. paperback available $14
         371.3
1. Montessori method of education
ISBN 0-8052-0922-0 (pa)
Originally published in Italy; first published 1912 in the United States
This is an introduction to the author's teaching methods. The Montessori system emphasizes the development of individuality in the child and the careful training of the senses. Education is controlled by interpersonal relations between the children rather than between teacher and child

371.3025   Audiovisual materials— Directories

AV market place. Information Today il pa $195   **371.3025**
1. Audiovisual materials—Directories
ISSN 1044-0445
Annual. First published 1969 with title: Audiovisual market place. Subtitle varies
"The complete business directory of: audio, audio visual, computer systems, film, video, programming—with industry yellow pages." Title page

371.9   Special education

The **Directory** for exceptional children; a listing of educational and training facilities. Sargent Pubs. il $75   **371.9**
1. Exceptional children—Education—Directories
ISSN 0070-5012
First published 1954. (14th edition 2001) Periodically revised
"Contains 14 sections on facilities for specific handicaps (residential facilities for mentally retarded persons, speech and hearing clinics, etc.); within each section, entries are arranged geographically. Each entry includes names of directors, medical directors, and admissions officers, as well as information on which handicaps are targeted; grades served; academic orientation and curriculum; therapy offerings; enrollment; staff; fees and financial aid; summer programs; and organizational structure; plus descriptive text. List of associations, foundations, and societies for specific disabilities; directory of state agency personnel." Guide to Ref Books. 11th edition

Hayden, Torey L.
Beautiful child; [by] Torey Hayden. HarperCollins Pubs. 2002 326p $24.95; pa $7.50   **371.9**
1. Special education
ISBN 0-380-81339-4; 0-06-050887-6 (pa)
         LC 2001-39928
This is "the story of a scruffy seven-year-old, Venus, who is so unresponsive that Hayden searches for signs of deafness, brain damage or mental retardation. . . . Hayden sets Venus's bittersweet and complex story against the backdrop of other students. . . . In this first-person narrative, Hayden also shares her own thoughts, worries and strained relationship with a mismatched classroom aide, creating a rich tapestry of the dynamics of a group of special needs youngsters and the adults who try to help them." Publ Wkly

Kersjes, Mike

A smile as big as the moon; a teacher, his class, and their unforgettable journey; [by] Mike Kersjes with Joe Layden. St. Martin's Press 2002 276p $23.95 **371.9**

1. U.S. Space Camp (Huntsville, Ala.) 2. Special education 3. Handicapped children

ISBN 0-312-27314-2   LC 2001-48779

This is the story of a teacher who "takes a group of special-ed students to Space Camp, and they end up being one of the best teams there. . . . Kersjes and coauthor Layden tell the remarkable story in conversational prose that makes for fast reading. Genuinely inspirational." Booklist

Kozol, Jonathan

Savage inequalities; children in America's schools. Crown 1991 262p o.p.; HarperPerennial paperback available $14 **371.9**

1. Public schools 2. Socially handicapped children 3. Segregation in education

ISBN 0-06-097499-0 (pa)   LC 91-17574

In 1988, Kozol "visited schools in over 30 neighborhoods, including East St. Louis, Harlem, the Bronx, Chicago, Jersey City, and San Antonio. In this account, he concludes that real integration has seriously declined and education for minorities and the poor has moved backwards by at least several decades." Libr J

"Jonathan Kozol has written an impassioned book, laced with anger and indignation, about how our public education system scorns so many of our children. 'Savage Inequalities' is also an important book, and warrants widespread attention." N Y Times Book Rev

Siegel, Bryna

Helping children with autism learn; treatment approaches for parents and professionals. Oxford Univ. Press 2003 498p $30 **371.9**

1. Autism 2. Special education

ISBN 0-19-513811-2   LC 2002-151673

"Siegel explains how to take an inventory of a child's particular disabilities, breaks down the various kinds unique to autism, discusses our current knowledge about each, and reviews the existing strategies for treating them." Publisher's note

"Carefully tailoring her book to multiple audiences, with free use of commentary and introductory notes, Siegel . . . excels at showing what parents and educators need to do to reach autistic children. She includes a valuable section on having successful individualized educational programs (IEPs), the standard for children with special needs." Libr J

Includes bibliographical references

Turkington, Carol

The encyclopedia of learning disabilities; [by] Carol Turkington, Joseph R. Harris, [and] American Bookworks. Facts on File 2002 304p (Facts on File library of health and living) $65 **371.9**

1. Learning disabilities—Encyclopedias

ISBN 0-8160-4075-3   LC 2001040620

Approximately 400 "entries define the different types of learning disabilities and problems, including neurological damage, perceptual dysfunction, and language disorders; their causes and treatments; relevant psychological

and medical terms; pharmacology; and therapies. The volume also includes appendixes offering information on relevant directories and organizations, periodicals, standardized tests, and government regulations." Publisher's note

"The alphabetically arranged entries are in encyclopedic format and range from highly technical to controversial. . . . The thoroughness of information is shown by the entry for assistive technology, which includes a spreadsheet for strengths, weaknesses, and LD characteristics. Highly recommended for the learning disabled or people working with them." Choice

Includes bibliographical references

372   Elementary education

Dewey, John, 1859-1952

The school and society, and The child and the curriculum; introduction by Philip W. Jackson. University of Chicago Press 1990 xli, 209p hardcover o.p. paperback available $11 **372**

1. Elementary education

ISBN 0-226-14396-1 (pa)   LC 90-43528

A combined edition of two essays first published separately in 1899 and 1902 respectively

Both of these works stress the functional relationship between classroom learning activities and real life experiences and analyze the social and psychological nature of the learning process. They present and defend the underlying tenets of Dewey's philosophy of education

372.4   Reading

Flesch, Rudolf Franz, 1911-1986

Why Johnny can't read—and what you can do about it. Harper & Row 1955 222p hardcover o.p. paperback available $13 **372.4**

1. Reading 2. Phonetics—Study and teaching

ISBN 0-06-091340-1 (pa)

Also available in hardcover from Buccaneer Bks.

Companion volume to Why Johnny still can't read (1981)

The author advocates the alphabetic-phonetic system of teaching children to read. He includes step-by-step directions and phonetic drills for use by parents

372.6   Language arts (Communication skills)

Seeger, Pete

Pete Seeger's storytelling book; by Pete Seeger and Paul Du Bois Jacobs. Harcourt 2000 264p $24; pa $14 **372.6**

1. Storytelling

ISBN 0-15-100370-X; 0-15-601311-8 (pa)

LC 00-29599

"The tales themselves, tape-recorded by Seeger and rewritten by Jacobs . . . are grouped roughly by origin. They range from family stories to versions of Bible tales to stories inspired by songs, history, legends, and Seeger's own imagination. In an introduction to each chapter, Seeger explains the source of the tales and offers suggestions for scouting similar ones. Each story, ready to read aloud or tell, concludes with possible variations, themes, morals, and, sometimes, music." Booklist

373.1

How to prepare for the GED high school equivalency examination; {by} Murray Rockowitz {et al.}. Barron's Educ. Ser.
373.1
1. High school equivalency examination

First published 1968. (12th edition 2002) Frequently revised. Title varies

Accompanied by CD-ROM

General advice on how to study and specific suggestions on reviewing for and taking the tests are followed by sample questions in the five areas covered—English, mathematics, social studies, science, and literature

Master the GED; teacher-tested strategies and techniques for scoring high. Peterson's pa $29.95   **373.1**
1. High school equivalency examination

First published 1962 with title: High school equivalency diploma test (GED). (18th edition 2004) Periodically revised. Title varies

At head of title: Arco

Accompanied by CD-ROM

This guide to preparing for the General Educational Development (GED) battery of tests includes practice in reading, writing, mathematics, science, and social studies

373.2   Secondary schools and programs of specific kinds

Peterson's private secondary schools. Peterson's il pa $29.95   **373.2**
1. Private schools—Directories 2. Education—United States—Directories

ISSN 1066-5366

Annual. First published 1980. Title varies

"Describes more than 1,600 American and foreign boarding and day schools including schools that serve children with special needs. Outlines each institution's setting; enrollment by sex, race, grade, and geographic origin; faculty size and educational background; facilities; subjects offered; special programs; graduation requirements; tuition; admissions procedures; and where the graduates go to college." Guide to Ref Books. 11th edition

374   Adult education

The **Independent** study catalog. Peterson's pa $21.95   **374**
1. Correspondence schools and courses

ISSN 0733-6020

First published 1977 with title: Guide to independent study through correspondence instruction. (7th edition 1998) Periodically revised. Title varies

"Published by Peterson's for the University Continuing Education Association." Title page

"Lists approximately 12,000 correspondence courses in 1,000 subject areas at 71 colleges and universities in the U.S. and Canada. Includes courses for high school, college, and graduate credit, as well as noncredit courses. Arranged by institution. Entries include course title, department offering the course, course number, number of

credits, and level. Also includes some general information on each program, such as degree offered, availability of telecourses, time requirements, etc." Guide to Ref Books. 11th edition

378   Higher education

Fiske, Edward B.
The Fiske guide to getting into the right college; [by] Edward B. Fiske & Bruce G. Hammond. Sourcebooks 2002 257p pa $14.95
378
1. College choice 2. Colleges and universities—Entrance requirements

ISBN 1-57071-906-3   LC 2001-57590

First published 1997

"Information on everything from interviews to standardized tests, college essays, and financing is included, along with a handy 'road map' of institutions, organized into such categories as 'Small College Bargains,' 'Most Innovative Curriculums,' and 'Colleges for Students with Learning Disabilities.' In addition, there is a selective roundup of listings by subject specialty. . . . Further resources, including Web sites, appear in a separate chapter. In all, this is a first-rate introduction that will help students narrow the field while still allowing them to cover the territory." Booklist [review of 1997 edition]

Gale directory of learning worldwide; a guide to faculty and institutions of higher education, research and culture. Gale Group 3v set $425   **378**
ISSN 1529-9686

First published 2001. Periodically revised

This set provides "access to approximately 26,000 colleges, universities, academies, scholarly associations, research institutes, museums, archives, and libraries around the world. . . . A master Index of Institutions with subject categories, and a Faculty Name Index are included." Publisher's note

Women in higher education; an encyclopedia; Ana M. Martínez Alemán and Kristen A. Renn, editors. ABC-CLIO 2002 xxiv, 637p il $85   **378**
1. Higher education 2. Women—Education

ISBN 1-57607-614-8   LC 2002-11570

This resource "on women and higher education presents multipage essays organized in nine sections covering historical and cultural contexts, gender theory, feminism, curriculum, policy, and women as students, faculty, administrators, and employees. . . . Destined to become a classic." Choice

378.1   Generalities of higher education

How to prepare for SAT I. Barron's Educ. Ser. pa $14.95   **378.1**
1. Scholastic Aptitude Test 2. Colleges and universities—Entrance requirements

Also available with CD-ROM for $29.95

Study guides for SAT II subject tests are also available at various prices

First published 1954 (21th edition 2001) Frequently revised. Title and authors vary

How to prepare for SAT I—*Continued*

This guide includes a review of skills, test-taking strategies, and sample tests with answers

How to prepare for the ACT, American College Testing Assessment Program; [by] George Ehrenhaft [et al.] Barron's Educ. Ser. il pa $14.95 **378.1**

1. ACT assessment 2. Colleges and universities—Entrance requirements

Also available with CD-ROM for $29.95

First published 1972 with title: Barron's how to prepare for the American College Testing Program (ACT). (12th edition 2001) Frequently revised. Editors vary

A guide to achieving higher scores on the ACT which includes subject reviews and practice exams with answers

Includes bibliographical references

Master the CLEP. Arco il pa $16.95 **378.1**

1. College Level Examination Program

Annual. First published 2001 to replace Preparation for the CLEP published by Macmillan General Reference

A study guide for the testing program that allows the nontraditional student to transform what he knows into traditional college credit. It includes sample examinations in English composition, humanities, mathematics, natural sciences, and social sciences and history

Steinberg, Jacques

The gatekeepers; inside the admissions process of a premier college. Viking 2002 xxiii, 292p $25.95; pa $15 **378.1**

1. Wesleyan University (Middletown, Conn.)—Admission 2. College applications

ISBN 0-670-03135-6; 0-14-200308-5 (pa)

LC 2002-16884

The author follows "the procedures at Wesleyan University for a year . . . [to] see how the admissions process really looks, to the admitters as well as the applicants." N Y Times Book Rev

"This insightful and readable book should be purchased by all academic and large public libraries." Libr J

Includes bibliographical references

Toor, Rachel

Admissions confidential; an insiders account of the elite college selection process. St. Martin's Press 2001 256p $23.95; pa $12.95 **378.1**

1. Duke University 2. College applications

ISBN 0-312-28405-5; 0-312-30235-5 (pa)

LC 2001-34892

"Toor describes her first year as an admissions officer at Duke from the summer campus tours and interviews to the final push in May to persuade the students who were accepted to commit to her university." SLJ

"Toor tells all—and it's not necessarily a pretty picture. It's a funny, often irreverent overview of her work. . . . The students don't leap off the page, but Toor certainly does." Booklist

378.3 Student aid and related topics

College Entrance Examination Board

The college costs & financial aid handbook. College Bd. Publs. pa $22.95 **378.3**

1. College costs 2. Student loan funds

Also available with CD-ROM for $27.95

Annual. First published 1980 with title: The college cost book

This guide covers over 3000 two-and four-year institutions. Provides information on what each college really costs, describes aid packages and includes tips on application procedures

Feigenbaum, Richard A.

The 529 College Savings Plan; [by] Richard A. Feigenbaum and David J. Morton. Sphinx Pub. 2002 xxii, 224p pa $16.95 **378.3**

1. College costs 2. Saving and investment 3. Personal finance

ISBN 1-57248-238-9   LC 2002-75792

This is a guide to saving for college costs using the tax-free 529 plan created in 1996

Peterson's college money handbook. Peterson's pa $29.95 **378.3**

1. College costs 2. Student loan funds 3. Scholarships

ISSN 0894-9395

Annual. First published 1983. Variant title: Paying less for college

"Arranged alphabetically and covering more than $36 billion in institutional, state, and federal aid, this . . . book includes profiles of more than 1,600 colleges and universities and the need -and non-need-based scholarships they offer. It answers commonly asked questions about financial aid and provides a step-by-step explanation of the financial aid application process." Publisher's note

Schlachter, Gail A.

Directory of financial aids for women; [by] Gail Ann Schlachter. Reference Service Press $45 **378.3**

1. Scholarships 2. Women—Education

Biennial. First published 1978

Describes "scholarships, fellowships, loans, grants, awards, and internships designed primarily or exclusively for women. . . . Lists state sources of educational benefits and offers an annotated bibliography of directories that list general financial aid programs. Program title, sponsoring organization, geographic, subject, and filing date indexes." Ref Sources for Small & Medium-sized Libr. 5th edition

Financial aid for the disabled and their families; [by] Gail Ann Schlachter, R. David Weber. Reference Service Press $40 **378.3**

1. Scholarships 2. Physically handicapped

Biennial. First published 1988

"Provides information on a wide range of funding needs in such areas as education, career development, research, and travel. Includes multiple indexes; cross-referenced." N Y Public Libr Book of How & Where to Look It Up

Scholarships, fellowships and loans; a guide to education-related financial aid programs for students and professionals. Gale Group $199   **378.3**
1. Scholarships 2. Student loan funds 3. Student aid
ISSN 1058-5699

Annual. First published 1949. Frequency, editors, and publisher vary

This "resource provides detailed information about financial aid for formal and informal degree and nondegree programs at all levels beyond secondary school. Includes information about awards, grants, loans, and contests sponsored by corporations, foundations, religious groups, professional associations, and a few government sources. The index directs students to sources identified by vocational goals, level of study, residence requirements, and sponsoring organizations." Ref Sources for Small & Medium-sized Libr. 6th edition

378.73 Institutions of higher education—United States

American universities and colleges. De Gruyter $249.50   **378.73**
1. Colleges and universities—United States—Directories 2. Education—United States—Directories
ISSN 0066-0922

First published 1928. (16th edition 2001) Frequently revised

Sponsored by the American Council on Education

This directory "describes more than 1,900 accredited schools offering baccalaureate or higher degrees. Its main section, arranged by state, presents narrative data for each college, covering its history, institutional structure and control, admissions and degree requirements, enrollment and degrees conferred, fees and financial arrangements, numbers of teachers in specific departments and degrees they hold, library collections, and student life (dormitories, intercollegiate athletics, car regulations, surrounding communities). Another section lists institutions offering professional degrees at baccalaureate, masters, and doctoral levels, arranged alphabetically by course of study." Guide to Ref Books. 11th edition

Barron's guide to law schools. Barron's Educ. Ser. pa $16.95   **378.73**
1. Colleges and universities—United States—Directories

First published 1967. 1st-8th editions published under the authorship of Elliott M. Epstein, Jerome Shostak, and Lawrence M. Troy. (15th edition 2003) Frequently revised

Information includes profiles of American Bar Association approved law schools, guidelines for preparing for the LSAT, and prospects for employment

Barron's profiles of American colleges. Barron's Educ. Ser. pa $26.95   **378.73**
1. Colleges and universities—United States—Directories 2. Education—United States—Directories

Annual. First published 1964

Includes CD-ROM

"More than 1,650 schools are profiled with details on admission requirements, academic programs, tuitions and other fees, sources of available financial aid, library facilities, computer facilities, descriptions of campus environments, athletic facilities, extracurricular activities, e-

mail addresses, fax numbers, web sites, and more. Each school receives Barron's . . . academic rating system, which advises students on its degree of academic competitiveness." Publisher's note

The **College** blue book. Macmillan 6v maps set $325   **378.73**
1. Colleges and universities—United States—Directories 2. Education—United States—Directories
ISSN 0069-5572

Biennial. First published 1923

"A leading directory of American and Canadian colleges. In five volumes. Vol. 1, Narrative descriptions, provides information for some 3,000 institutions, with entries arranged by state or province. Vol. 2, Tabular data, outlines information such as costs, accreditation, enrollment, and faculty characteristics; it also gives the names of college presidents, registrars, and admissions officers. Vol. 3, is in two parts: Degrees offered by college, which lists for each school the majors it offers; Degrees offered by subject provides a list of all majors offered, showing which schools offer each major." Guide to Ref Books. 11th edition

College Entrance Examination Board
The college handbook. College Bd. Publs. pa $27.95   **378.73**
1. Colleges and universities—United States—Directories 2. Education—United States—Directories
Accompanied by CD-ROM

Annual. First published 1941 by Ginn with title: Annual handbook

This work offers "detailed information for college-bound students on such subjects as freshman admissions requirements and procedures, enrollment, majors, expenses, financial aid, and many other areas of interest." N Y Public Libr. Book of How & Where to Look It Up

Index of majors and graduate degrees. College Bd. Publs. pa $23.95   **378.73**
1. Colleges and universities—United States—Directories 2. Colleges and universities—Curricula

Annual. First published 1977 with title: The college handbook index of majors. Variant title: Index of majors

"Directory of colleges offering specific majors at bachelors, master, doctoral, professional, associate, and certificate levels. Lists of institutions and the degree levels offered for each major are arranged alphabetically by major, then by state. A section on specialized academic programs lists schools that offer cooperative education, dual majors, independent study, study abroad." Guide to Ref Books. 11th edition

Fiske, Edward B.
The Fiske guide to colleges. Times Bks. pa $22.95   **378.73**
1. Colleges and universities—United States—Directories 2. College choice

Annual. First published 1982 with title: The New York Times selective guide to colleges

This guide to some 300 of the best colleges and universities nationwide includes information on admissions, costs, financial aid, housing, social life, and academic strengths and weaknesses

Peterson's colleges with programs for students with learning disabilities or attention deficit disorders. Peterson's pa $29.95 **378.73**
1. Learning disabilities 2. Colleges and universities—United States—Directories

First published 1985 with title: Peterson's guide to colleges with programs for learning-disabled students. (7th edition 2003). Periodically revised

"Profiles more than 800 two-year and four-year colleges offering special services and programs and includes information on graduate-level options, financial aid, and special services at U.S. and Canadian schools. It's divided into two main sections: one with colleges that have comprehensive programs and the other with schools that make a number of services available." Publisher's note

Peterson's competitive colleges. Peterson's pa $18.95 **378.73**
1. Colleges and universities—United States—Directories 2. Education—United States—Directories
ISSN 0887-0152

Annual. First published 1981

"College sponsors of the book and Web resources designed for college-bound students are identified. The major portion of the book is devoted to one-page descriptions of the colleges, arranged in alphabetic order. Following the same format throughout, a statement pertaining to college setting and various contact information for admissions directors are provided at the top of the page followed by college descriptions subdivided by the following topics: academics, students, facilities and resources, campus life, campus safeety, and applying." Recomm Ref Books for Small & Medium-sized Libr & Media Cent, 2003

Peterson's guide to four-year colleges. Peterson's il pa $26.95 **378.73**
1. Colleges and universities—United States—Directories 2. Education—United States—Directories
ISSN 0894-9336

Accompanied by CD-ROM

Annual. First published 1966 as part of Peterson's annual guide to undergraduate study

"In two major sections: (1) half-page entries for some 2,000 institutions, with details of enrollment, admission requirements, expenses, housing, student aid, and programs offered; (2) two-page in-depth descriptions of more than 800 institutions, prepared by their officials, which emphasize campus environment, student activities, and lifestyle. Indexes: major, entrance difficulty, cost, and name of institution." Guide to Ref Books. 11th edition

Peterson's guide to two-year colleges. Peterson's il pa $26.95 **378.73**
1. Colleges and universities—United States—Directories 2. Education—United States—Directories
ISSN 0894-9328

Annual. First published 1966 as part of Peterson's annual guide to undergradute study

"Describes 1,400 accredited institutions in the U.S. and its territories awarding the associate degree as their most popular undergraduate offering, plus some non-degree-granting schools. . . . In addition to the usual information on admission and graduation requirements, programs, costs, etc., treats considerations peculiar to junior colleges, giving advice on profiting from two-year colleges and transferring to four-year schools, statistics

on students transferring from individual colleges, and a list by major of colleges offering associate degree programs." Guide to Ref Books. 11th edition

379 Public policy issues in education

DelFattore, Joan, 1946-
What Johnny shouldn't read; textbook censorship in America. Yale Univ. Press 1992 209p $40; pa $16.95 **379**
1. Censorship
ISBN 0-300-05709-1; 0-300-06050-5 (pa)
LC 92-3585

DelFattore "discusses the process of textbook censorship, the litigation of specific cases, the role of publishers, and the issues that have an impact on censorship. . . . She lists state policies on textbook selection and explores issues of gender, race, and ethnicity, as well as science and religion." Libr J

The author "thoughtfully presents six specific cases and their immediate and long-term effects in order to open the eyes and, hopefully, to raise the voices of those who treasure intellectual freedom." Booklist

Includes bibliographical references

381 Internal commerce (Domestic trade)

Bond's franchise guide. Source Bk. Publs. pa $29.95 **381**
1. Franchises (Retail trade)

Annual. First published 1985 by Dow Jones-Irwin with title: The source book of franchise opportunities

This guide to over 2,300 franchise opportunities in 54 categories gives background, capital requirements, support and training information as well as specifics on expansion in the U.S and Canada

Cassidy, John
Dot.con; the greatest story ever sold. HarperCollins Pubs. 2002 372p hardcover o.p. paperback available $13.95 **381**
1. Electronic commerce 2. Stocks
ISBN 0-06-000881-4 (pa)
LC 2001-51449

"A history of the dot-com bubble by a financial writer for The New Yorker, with insightful observations about the Federal Reserve and severe views on its chairman, Alan Greenspan." N Y Times Book Rev

Consumer sourcebook. Gale Res. $305 **381**
1. Consumer protection
ISSN 0738-0518

First published 1974. (16th edition 2003) Frequently revised

This directory describes "programs and services available to the American consumer at little or no cost. Lists federal, state, county, and local governmental agencies, nongovernmental consumer organizations and associations, and consumer affairs and customer services departments of corporations. Describes consumer publications and multimedia products and provides consumer tips and recommendations." Ref Sources for Small & Medium-sized Libr. 6th edition

383   Postal communication

Barkus, Philip
Comprehensive postal exam; test battery series 460/470 for eight top positions. 2nd ed. Barron's Educ. Ser. 2000 448p il $16.95
383

1. Postal service—Examinations
ISBN 0-7641-0774-7   LC 99-32387
First published 1995 with title: How to prepare for the comprehensive postal exam
"Six full-length model exams plus a diagnostic test are presented to prepare applicants for a variety of jobs in the U.S. Postal Service. . . . The author also provides special drills designed to improve test-taking skills in memory, speed, and following oral directions." Publisher's note

Damp, Dennis V.
Post Office jobs; how to get a job with the U.S. Postal Service. 3rd ed, completely rev. Bookhaven Press 2003 256p il pa $19.95
383

1. Postal service—Vocational guidance 2. Postal service—Examinations
ISBN 0-943641-22-5   LC 2003-8268
First published 1996
This is a guide to Postal Service careers including professional and administrative positions, mail carrier, maintenance, postal inspectors, and clerical positions. It includes information on preparing for postal exams, applications, resumes, and interviews.

National five digit zip code and post office directory. U.S. Postal Service maps pa $31
383

1. Zip code
ISSN 0731-9185
Annual. Continuation of National zip code and post office directory

"Besides ZIP codes and post offices, this directory includes information on the organization of the Postal Service, addressing, parcel weights and sizes, delivery statistics, and other matters." Recomm Ref Books in Paperback. 2d edition

384.1   Telegraphy

FaxUSA; a directory of facsimile numbers for businesses and organizations nationwide. Omnigraphics pa $165   **384.1**
1. Fax transmission—Directories
ISSN 1075-7112

Annual. First published 1994
This "directory provides fax numbers, along with other . . . contact data, for nearly 108,000 businesses and organizations in the United States and Canada. Each listing in *FaxUSA* includes the official name of a company, institution, agency, or other business-related organizations, along with its full mailing address, telephone number, and fax number. In addition, stock symbols are provided for companies whose stock is traded on the New York, NASDAQ, or American Stock Exchange." Publisher's note

Gordon, John Steele
A thread across the ocean; the heroic story of the transatlantic cable. Walker & Co. 2002 240p il $26   **384.1**
1. Submarine cables 2. Telegraph
ISBN 0-8027-1364-5   LC 2002-66385
Also available in paperback from HarperCollins Pubs
This is an account of "the laying of the first telegraph cables between Europe and North America, completed in 1866." N Y Times Book Rev
The author "has written a lively, engaging account of the extraordinary efforts that brought about this remarkable scientific, technological, and business feat." Libr J
Includes bibliographical references

National E-mail and FAX directory. Gale Res. $170   **384.1**
1. Fax transmission—Directories 2. Electronic mail systems—Directories
ISSN 1045-9499
Annual. First published 1989 with title: National FAX directory
"The *Directory* provides more than 180,000 fax numbers and e-mail addresses for U.S. companies, organizations and government agencies." Publisher's note

384.5   Wireless communication

Murray, James B., Jr.
Wireless nation; the frenzied launch of the cellular revolution in America. Perseus Bks. 2001 338p hardcover o.p. paperback available $17.95   **384.5**
1. Cellular telephones
ISBN 0-7382-0391-2 (pa)
An account of the development and growth of the communications industry with speculations about its future

384.54   Radiobroadcasting

Broadcasting & cable yearbook. Reed Business Information 2v set $199.95
384.54

1. Radio broadcasting 2. Cable television
ISSN 0000-1511
Annual. First published 1993
"The most comprehensive directory to the Fifth Estate, covering the history and continuing growth of every field in the industry. There are nine major sections: 'The Fifth Estate,' 'Radio,' 'Television,' 'Cable,' 'Satellites,' Programming,' 'Advertising and Marketing,' 'Technology,' and 'Professional Services.' Includes extensive equipment listings and a buyer's guide. The standard directory of AM and FM radio stations in the United States, Canada, Mexico, and the Caribbean and of U.S. and Canadian television stations." Ref Sources for Small & Medium-sized Libr. 6th edition

385 Railroad transportation

Ambrose, Stephen E.
Nothing like it in the world; the men who built the transcontinental railroad, 1863-1869. Simon & Schuster 2000 471p $28; pa $16

385

1. Central Pacific Railroad 2. Union Pacific Railroad Company 3. Railroads—United States
ISBN 0-684-84609-8; 0-7432-0317-8 (pa)

LC 00-41005

This is an account of the construction of the transcontinental railroad by the Central Pacific and Union Pacific companies

"Ambrose's scholarship seems impeccable. . . . He writes a brisk, colloquial, straightforward prose that not only is easy to read but also bears the reader on shoulders of wonder and excitement." N Y Times Book Rev
Includes bibliographical references

Bain, David Haward
Empire express; building the first transcontinental railroad. Viking 1999 797p il maps $34.95; pa $18

385

1. Railroads—United States 2. West (U.S.)—History
ISBN 0-670-80889-X; 0-14-008499-1 (pa)

LC 99-33375

In this account of the history of the transcontinental railroad, Bain focuses on "the visionaries who dreamed of the railroad, the building of the railroad, and, most of all, the capitalists who organized and promoted the railroads and the engineers who surveyed and planned the road." New Repub

"Bain knits together excellent storytelling and exhaustive research in a rich contextual tale of vision, ambition, and, ultimately, political and personal corruption." Libr J
Includes bibliographical references

387.7 Air transportation

Blatner, David
The flying book; everything you've ever wondered about flying on airplanes. Walker & Co. 2003 248p il $22

387.7

1. Commercial aeronautics 2. Airplanes
ISBN 0-8027-1378-5

"Concentrating on commercial aviation, [the author] offers a compendium of fascinating facts. Chapters zero in on specific aspects of flight: what keeps planes in the air, for example, or how a jet engine functions, or the workings of air-traffic control, or airplane maintenance, or the often-bewildering universe of ticket prices. In addition to technological facts, he also covers the human side of air travel: fear of flying and how to control it, what the pilots are up to in the cockpit, even the horrors of airline food." Booklist

"Engaging, upbeat, and fact-filled, *The Flying Book* features an open, airy design with lots of charts and sidebars." SLJ
Includes bibliographical references

Smith, Myron J.
The airline encyclopedia, 1909-2000. Scarecrow Press 2002 3v il set $695 **387.7**

1. Airlines—Encyclopedias
ISBN 0-8108-3790-0

LC 00-44000

Contents: v1 [without special title]; v2 Company profiles: D & D Aviation to Pyramid Airlines; v3 Company profiles: Quantas to Zuliana de Aviacion

This "reference source provides operational and statistical profiles of more than 6000 commercial air transport companies that flourished in the 20th century. Fascinating facts combine with profiles that include aircraft, routes, services, personnel, alliances, accidents and incidents, terrorism and in-flight crime, government service in war and peace, natural disasters, literary or film references, and unusual anecdotes." Libr J

391 Costume and personal appearance

Boucher, François, b. 1885
20,000 years of fashion; the history of costume and personal adornment; by François Boucher, with a new chapter by Yvonne Deslandres. expanded ed. Abrams 1987 459p il $49.50

391

1. Costume—History
ISBN 0-8109-1693-2

LC 86-72852

First published 1967; published in the United Kingdom with title: A history of costume in the West

"Begins divided into historical-regional sections but quickly moves to the history of European costume. Discusses materials, ornaments, accessories, and functions." N Y Public Libr Book of How & Where to Look It Up

Calasibetta, Charlotte Mankey
The Fairchild dictionary of fashion; [by] Charlotte Mankey Calasibetta, Phyllis Tortora; illustrated by Bina Abling. 3rd ed. Fairchild Publs. 2003 522p il $75 **391**

1. Fashion design—Dictionaries 2. Costume—Dictionaries
ISBN 1-5636-7235-9

LC 2002-103884

First published 1975

This work provides definitions of fashion terms, line drawings, and biographical sketches of designers

Cassin-Scott, Jack
The illustrated encyclopaedia of costume and fashion from 1066 to the present. Studio Vista; [distributed by] Sterling 1994 192p il $27.95

391

1. Costume—History
ISBN 0-289-80093-5

LC 94-242055

First published 1986 by Blandford Press with title: The illustrated edition of costume and fashion, 1550-1920

This volume includes "180 color illustrations, which depict in rich detail figures representing varied social classes of European (and later American) society from 1066 to 1990. A succinct glossary and a one-page introduction provide complementary text to the parade of the 'great years of fashions' and the full descriptions that follow. . . . Fashion/costume students or enthusiasts, fashion designers, and theater wardrobe designers will find this a valuable and interesting research tool." Libr J

Contemporary fashion; editor, Taryn Benbow-Pfalzgraf. 2nd ed. St. James Press 2002 xxi, 743p il $185 **391**

1. Fashion design 2. Clothing industry 3. Fashion—History
ISBN 1-55862-348-5

LC 2002-17801

First edition edited by Richard Martin published 1995

Contemporary fashion—*Continued*

This volume "includes coverage of more than 450 designers, milliners, footwear designers, fashion companies and textile houses. Entries . . . include a biographical summary; primary and secondary bibliography, including articles and exhibition catalogs; and a signed, critical essay written by an expert in the field." Publisher's note

Cosgrave, Bronwyn

The complete history of costume and fashion; from ancient Egypt to the present day. Checkmark Bks. 2001 256p il $37.95

391

1. Costume—History
ISBN 0-8160-4574-7   LC 00-64401
"This book explores the development of fashion from its simple and practical beginnings to the growth of the multibillion dollar global industry that it is today. . . . Trends in clothing style, fabric, accessories, and footwear [are examined]." Publisher's note
Includes bibliographical references

De Marly, Diana

Dress in North America. v1: The New World, 1492-1800. Holmes & Meier 1990 221p il $59.95   **391**

1. Costume—History 2. United States—Social life and customs—1600-1775, Colonial period
ISBN 0-8419-1199-1   LC 90-4905
"Volume 1 of this projected three-volume series is a historical narrative of the development of clothing styles and industries in Colonial America. Beautifully reproduced art works, mostly portrait paintings, are accompanied by excellent fashion commentary." Libr J
Includes bibliographical references

Etcoff, Nancy L., 1955-

Survival of the prettiest; the science of beauty; [by] Nancy Etcoff. Doubleday 1999 325p il hardcover o.p. paperback available $14   **391**

1. Personal appearance 2. Sexual behavior 3. Natural selection
ISBN 0-385-47942-5 (pa)   LC 98-41332
The author "presents the evolution of our conception of beauty as a biological adaptation that seeks healthy, fertile mates and makes us instinctively seek partners whose physical characteristics reflect this likelihood." Libr J
"Topics as wide-ranging as penis- or breast-enlargement surgery and the basics of haute couture are treated with wit and insight. Etcoff's arguments are certain to initiate a great deal of discussion." Publ Wkly
Includes bibliographical references

Hunnisett, Jean

Period costume for stage & screen; patterns for women's dress, 1500-1800; illustrations by Janette Haslam. Players Press 1991 176p il $55   **391**

1. Costume—History 2. Dressmaking
ISBN 0-88734-610-3   LC 90-50385
Also available volume covering years 1800-1909 $55 (ISBN 0-88734-609-X) and volume covering medieval-1500 $55 (ISBN 0-88734-653-7)
First published 1986 in the United Kingdom
Contains patterns, illustrations, and instructions for more than twenty garments
Includes bibliographical references

In an influential fashion; an encyclopedia of nineteenth- and twentieth-century fashion designers and retailers who transformed dress; [by] Ann T. Kellogg [et al.]; with illustrations by Kamila Dominik. Greenwood Press 2002 371p il $49.95

391

1. Fashion design 2. Clothing industry 3. Fashion—History
ISBN 0-313-31220-6   LC 2001-45124
"This volume chronicles the achievements of 164 renowned international designers and retailers who have most influenced American dress and culture from the late 19th century to the present. . . . The alphabetically arranged entries include biographical data, education, influences, awards, additional references, and the contribution the subject made to fashion." Libr J

Laver, James, 1899-1975

Costume and fashion; a concise history. 4th ed, concluding chapter by Amy de la Haye and Andrew Tucker. Thames & Hudson 2002 304p il (World of art) pa $16.95   **391**

1. Costume—History 2. Fashion—History
ISBN 0-500-20348-2   LC 2001-87366
First published 1969 with title: A concise history of costume
This "guide covers the landmarks of costume history, the forms and materials used through the ages, as well as the underlying motives of fashion and the ways in which clothes have been used to protect, to express identity, and to attract or to influence others." Publisher's note
Includes bibliographical references

Nunn, Joan

Fashion in costume, 1200-2000. 2nd ed. New Amsterdam Bks. 2000 280p pa $18.95

391

1. Costume—History
ISBN 1-56663-279-X   LC 99-47516
First published 1984 by Schocken Bks. with title: Fashion in costume, 1200-1980
This history of American and European costume covers men's, women's, and children's dress, accessories and jewelry, fabrics, and color. Discusses how historical, social, economic, and artistic events influence fashion
Includes bibliographical references

Paterek, Josephine

Encyclopedia of American Indian costume. ABC-CLIO 1994 516p il maps o.p.; Norton paperback available $23.95   **391**

1. Native American costume
ISBN 0-393-31382-4 (pa)   LC 93-39337
Paterek describes "the clothing used for everyday, war, rites, and ceremonies for men, women, and children in hundreds of tribes in diverse climates stretching over centuries. Well-organized text and 400 drawings and authentic photos plus the cultural essays prefacing the 10 regional groupings and each tribe put the costumes in historical, social, and geographic context. Appendixes cover terminology and the materials used in clothing. The excellent bibliographies in this classic work both document and encourage further reading." Am Libr

Peacock, John, 1943-
20th-century fashion; the complete sourcebook; with a preface by Christian Lacroix. Thames & Hudson 1993 240p il $34.95   **391**
1. Costume—History
ISBN 0-500-01564-3   LC 93-60138
This book illustrates "90 years in the development of women's fashions. Each division, representing a decade, begins with [the author's] choice of the 'ideal' work of leading couturiers, followed by sketches of leisure, day, evening, and bridal wear, as well as underwear and accessories. Principal changes for five-year periods are depicted through a fashionable silhouetted outline, with notes on various modifications. Brief biographical data are included for selected designers. . . . Recommended as a valuable source of inspiration and a visual history for the fashion enthusiast, historian, designer, and theater arts students." Libr J

The chronicle of Western fashion; from ancient times to the present day. Abrams 1991 224p il $45   **391**
1. Costume—History 2. Fashion—History
ISBN 0-8109-3953-3   LC 90-1053
A survey of "Western costume from ancient Egypt to 1980. Presented chronologically, the 8 to 10 illustrations per page are lavishly colored and use color schemes appropriate to each period. All illustrations are labeled with country of origin and wearer's societal status. Every century is followed up by concise captions corresponding to the illustrations." Booklist
Includes bibliographical references

Men's fashion; the complete sourcebook. Thames & Hudson 1996 216p il $29.95
                                                    391
1. Costume—History 2. Men's clothing 3. Fashion—History
ISBN 0-500-01725-5   LC 96-60141
This is an illustrated survey of "men's fashion and accessories from roughly the French revolutionary era to the present (1789-1995). The 1000 colored line drawings are hand-rendered, showing a variety of front, side, and rear views of day wear, sportswear, evening wear, negligee, and underwear, as well as accessories and hairstyles. Brief biographies of designers, tailors, and outfitters and a bibliography of related books conclude the work." Libr J
"A highly practical and useful volume." Choice

Peiss, Kathy Lee
Hope in a jar; the making of America's beauty culture; [by] Kathy Peiss. Metropolitan Bks. 1998 334p il hardcover o.p. paperback available $15.95   **391**
1. Personal appearance 2. Cosmetics
ISBN 0-8050-5551-7 (pa)   LC 97-42706
This is a "social history of the origin and development of the U.S. cosmetics industry. . . . An engrossing, highly readable book that should be welcomed by scholars and general readers alike." Libr J
Includes bibliographical references

392   Customs of life cycle and domestic life

Gollaher, David, 1949-
Circumcision; a history of the world's most controversial surgery; [by] David L. Gollaher. Basic Bks. 2000 253p hardcover o.p. paperback available $18   **392**
1. Circumcision
ISBN 0-465-02653-2 (pa)   LC 99-40015
This history of circumcision discusses Jewish, Muslim, and tribal rituals, medical procedures and complications, reasons for the procedure, and its social significance in various cultures and eras

393   Death customs

Brier, Bob
The encyclopedia of mummies. Facts on File 1998 248p il $38.50   **393**
1. Mummies—Encyclopedias
ISBN 0-8160-3108-8   LC 97-16588
"Brier pulls together a wide variety of facts and descriptions that provide cultural and popular perspectives about preserved human and animal life along with the scientific information. The alphabetical entries contain a definition, an explanation of how the entry fits into a historical context, and photographs for certain selected subjects." SLJ
For a fuller review see: Booklist, Mar. 15, 1998

Mitford, Jessica, 1917-1996
The American way of death revisited. Knopf 1998 296p hardcover o.p. paperback available $14   **393**
1. Undertakers and undertaking 2. Funeral rites and ceremonies
ISBN 0-679-77186-7 (pa)   LC 97-49349
First published 1963 by Simon & Schuster with title: The American way of death
The author offers a "scathing critique of the U.S. funeral industry. . . . Furthermore, she charges, the Federal Trade Commission's lax enforcement of its 1984 rule banning morticians' deceptive practices has contributed to an upward spiral of prices and profits. Other developments of the 1990s perceptively analyzed here include the refusal of many funeral directors to embalm AIDS victims and the growing popularity of low-cost funeral and memorial service organizations, which are listed in an appendix." Publ Wkly
"Very interesting, informative, and easy to read, this book is written with wit, solid information, and refreshing bluntness." Libr J

Pringle, Heather Anne, 1952-
The mummy congress; science, obsession, and the everlasting dead; [by] Heather Pringle. Hyperion 2001 368p il $23.95; pa $13.95   **393**
1. Mummies 2. Forensic anthropology
ISBN 0-7868-6551-2; 0-7868-8463-0 (pa)
                                         LC 00-54487
"Besides outstanding members of the scientific association that gathers as the Mummy Congress, Pringle limns the many varieties of mummies, from the world's oldest, preserved by the high-altitude climate of the Andes, to

Pringle, Heather Anne, 1952-—*Continued*
modern Communist dictators, self-mummifying Buddhists, and the subjects of extreme cosmetic surgery. More astounding than all the fright flicks about shambling, gauze-wrapped menaces wound together." Booklist
Includes bibliographical references

Young, Gregory W.
The high cost of dying; a guide to funeral planning. Prometheus Bks. 1994 142p il $32.50; pa $20   393
1. Death 2. Funeral rites and ceremonies
ISBN 0-87975-868-6; 0-87975-874-0 (pa)
LC 93-41859
The author "discusses working with the funeral director, working out a contract, avoiding ripoffs, and planning a prearranged funeral. . . . Young, a former director of a funeral home chain, sensitively and clearly offers practical guidelines and presents an overview of the funeral service industry." Libr J
Includes bibliographical references

394.1   Eating, drinking; using drugs

Encyclopedia of food and culture; Solomon H. Katz, editor in chief; William Woys Weaver, associate editor. Scribner 2003 3v il (Scribner library of daily life) set $395
394.1
1. Eating customs 2. Food—Encyclopedias
ISBN 0-684-80568-5   LC 2002-14607
This reference includes "600 signed articles covering topics such as individual staple foods; the preparation, distribution, and storage of various foods; the role of food in different holidays and festivals; nutrition and food science; food symbolism and its use in various arts; national cuisines; and biographies of influential individuals in food history. Entries range in length from one page to 20 or more." Libr J
For a fuller review see: Booklist, June 1 & 15, 2003

Gately, Iain
Tobacco; the story of how tobacco seduced the world. Grove Press 2002 c2001 403p il $25; pa $15   394.1
1. Tobacco
ISBN 0-8021-1705-8; 0-8021-3960-4 (pa)
LC 2001-54493
First published 2001 in the United Kingdom with title: La diva nicotina
This is a "historical survey of humanity's love/hate relationship with tobacco. . . . Gately pays particular attention to the evolving methods of ingesting tobacco, pays respect to the pleasurable ambience of the smoking experience, and even offers a final chapter on how to grow tobacco in your backyard." Libr J
"An entertaining story of humanity's Faustian bargain with tobacco." Booklist
Includes bibliographical references

Haber, Barbara
From hardtack to home fries; an uncommon history of American cooks and meals. Free Press 2002 244p il $25   394.1
1. Cooking 2. Eating customs
ISBN 0-684-84217-3   LC 2001-58482
Also available in paperback from Penguin Bks.

"Drawing on cookbooks, diaries, and memoirs, . . . Haber here presents some of the major events of American history through the lens of food history. Chapters cover such topics as the diets of POWs during World War II, why the food was so bad in the FDR White House, the role of the Harvey Girls in feeding the Western expansion, and the 'diet kitchens' run by Civil War nurses. . . . An annotated bibliography, photographs, and several illustrative recipes are also included." Libr J

Kluger, Richard
Ashes to ashes; America's hundred-year cigarette war, the public health, and the unabashed triumph of Philip Morris. Knopf 1996 807p hardcover o.p. paperback available $19   394.1
1. Philip Morris, Inc. 2. Smoking 3. Tobacco habit 4. Tobacco industry
ISBN 0-375-70036-6 (pa)   LC 95-42103
"From the Native American usage of tobacco through the law-suits of the 1990s, Kluger follows the industry's agricultural and labor practices, technical advances, and marketing campaigns; he also considers research on tobacco's deleterious health effects and the tobacco control movement. Significant personalities and events such as the invention of the cigarette-rolling machine are featured. . . . Suitable for readers of high school age on up, this book belongs in every library." Libr J
Includes bibliographical references

Mayle, Peter
French lessons; adventures with knife, fork, and corkscrew. Knopf 2001 227p il $24; pa $12.95   394.1
1. Eating customs 2. France—Social life and customs
ISBN 0-375-40590-9; 0-375-70561-9 (pa)
Also available large print edition $24 (ISBN 0-375-43119-5)
Mayle "relives some of his most precious moments reveling in the cuisine of his adopted homeland. . . . [He tells] savory, sensual, positively transporting stories about his encounters with Gallic gustatory delights and about his growing appreciation of the central place food occupies in French life." Booklist

Schlosser, Eric
Fast food nation; the dark side of the all-American meal. Houghton Mifflin 2001 356p il $25   394.1
1. Restaurants 2. Convenience foods 3. Food industry
ISBN 0-395-97789-4   LC 00-53886
Also available G.K. Hall large print edition and in paperback from HarperCollins Pubs.
"Schlosser documents the effects of fast food on America's economy, its youth culture, and allied industries. . . . Starting with a young woman who makes minimum wage working at a Colorado fast-food restaurant, Schlosser relates the oft-told story of Ray Kroc's founding of McDonald's. The author also tells about the development of the franchise method of business ownership and the health and nutrition implications of fast-food consumption." Booklist
Includes bibliographical references

394.25 Carnivals

Danticat, Edwidge, 1969-
After the dance; a walk through carnival in Jacmel, Haiti. Crown 2002 158p (Crown journeys series) $16 **394.25**
1. Carnival 2. Haiti—Social life and customs
ISBN 0-609-60908-4 LC 2002-24165
The author "journeyed back to her native Haiti to explore what had been forbidden in her childhood: the colorful, raucous, dangerous carnival. . . . She sought out some of the island's more unusual residents while exploring the history, folklore, and meaning of the many images of carnival. Her lively narrative describes a rich and complicated cultural history." Libr J

394.26 Holidays

The **American** book of days. 4th ed, compiled and edited by Stephen G. Christianson. Wilson, H.W. 2000 xxvi, 945p $130 **394.26**
1. Holidays 2. Festivals—United States
ISBN 0-8242-0954-0 LC 99-86611
First edition, by George William Douglas, published 1937
This work "consists of essays that are a day-to-day recounting of selective American historic events, including those of festivals and celebrations. . . . The topics of these essays vary, with the editor highlighting notable activities from military, scientific, ethnic, political, and cultural occurrences. Not limited strictly to events, essays are also devoted to individuals who played a significant role in American history. . . . A comprehensive index and table of contents provide excellent means for finding specific topics." Am Ref Books Annu, 2001

Chase's calendar of events. Contemporary Bks. pa $54.95 **394.26**
1. Calendars 2. Holidays 3. Almanacs
Annual. First published 1958 with title: Chase's calendar of annual events, under the editorship of William D. and Helen M. Chase. Variant title: Chase's annual events
"Day-by-day listing of national and state holidays, religious observances, special events, festivals and fairs, and historical anniversaries and birthdays. Covers U.S. events primarily, but some international occasions and anniversaries are included." N Y Public Libr Book of How & Where to Look It Up

The **Folklore** of the American holidays; Hennig Cohen and Tristram Potter Coffin, editors. 3rd ed. Gale Res. 1998 c1999 573p $140 **394.26**
1. Holidays 2. Festivals—United States 3. Folklore—United States
ISBN 0-8138-8642-2 LC 98-37035
First published 1987
"A compilation of more than 600 beliefs, legends, superstitions, proverbs, riddles, poems, songs, dances, games, plays, pageants, fairs, foods, and processions associated with over 140 American calendar customs and festivals." Title page

The **Folklore** of world holidays; Robert Griffin and Ann H. Shurgin, editors. 2nd ed. Gale Res. 1998 c1999 841p $125
394.26
1. Holidays 2. Festivals 3. Folklore
ISBN 0-8103-8901-0 LC 98-37030
First published 1992 under the editorship of Margaret Read MacDonald
"Provides descriptive information on nearly 2,000 beliefs, stories, superstitions, proverbs, recipes, games, pageants, fairs, processions and other lore related to more than 350 special dates from 150 countries." Publisher's note

Gulevich, Tanya
Encyclopedia of Christmas and New Year's celebrations; illustrated by Mary Ann Stavros-Lanning. Omnigraphics 2003 xx, 977p il $68 **394.26**
1. Christmas 2. New Year
ISBN 0-7808-0625-5 LC 2003-40580
First published 2000 with title: Encyclopedia of Christmas
"Over 240 alphabetically arranged entries covering Christmas, New Year's, and related days of observance, including folk and religious customs, history, legends, and symbols from around the world; supplemented by a bibliography and lists of Christmas Web sites and associations . . ." Title page
The author "covers a variety of secular and sacred aspects of Christmas and New Year's celebrations. The volume discusses the history and meaning of the well known, such as Saint Nicholas, and the lesser well known, such as Knecht Ruprecht who was Saint Nicholas' companion visiting the not-so-good children . . . This encyclopedic work is useful for those schools where folklore is covered, or for those interested in origins of the holidays." Lib Media Connect

Holidays and anniversaries of the world; Beth A. Baker, editor. 3rd ed. Gale Res. 1998 c1999 1184p $130 **394.26**
1. Holidays 2. Festivals 3. Historical chronology
ISBN 0-8103-5477-2 LC 98-38866
First published 1985
"A comprehensive catalogue containing detailed information on every month and day of the year, with coverage of more than 26,000 holidays, anniversaries, fasts and feasts, holy days of the saints, the blesseds, and other days of religious significance, birthdays of the famous, important dates in history, and special events and their sponsors." Title page

Holidays, festivals and celebrations of the world dictionary; detailing 2,500 observances from all 50 states and more than 100 nations; edited by Helene Henderson and Sue Ellen Thompson. 3rd ed. Omnigraphics 2001 1000p $98 **394.26**
1. Holidays 2. Festivals
ISBN 0-7808-0422-8
First edition published 1994 compiled by Sue Ellen Thompson and Barbara W. Carlson
This "describes 2,500 holidays, festivals, commemorations, holy days, feasts and fasts, and other observances from all parts of the world. The entries cover popular, secular, and religious events." Publisher's note

Marling, Karal Ann

Merry Christmas! celebrating America's greatest holiday. Harvard Univ. Press 2000 442p il $29.95; pa $16.95   **394.26**

1. Christmas 2. United States—Social life and customs

ISBN 0-674-00318-7; 0-674-00679-8 (pa)

LC 00-31935

Topics covered include The Christmas tree, Santa, wrapping paper, cards, gifts, decorating, baking cookies, movies and music

"Imaginatively researched and strewn with surprising details, this engaging cultural history traces the rise of the consumerism that has become . . . integral to the celebration of Christmas in the United States." Publ Wkly

Includes bibliographical references

Thompson, Sue Ellen, 1948-

Holiday symbols and customs. 3rd ed. Omnigraphics 2002 895p $68   **394.26**

1. Holidays 2. Festivals

ISBN 0-7808-0501-1   LC 2002-193028

First published 1998 with title: Holiday symbols

"A guide to the legend and lore behind the traditions, rituals, foods, games, animals, and other symbols and activities associated with holidays and holy days, feasts and fasts, and other celebrations, covering calendar, ethnic, religious, historic, cultural, national, promotional, sporting, and ancient events, as observed in the United States and around the world." Title page

For a review see: Booklist, Jan. 1 and 15, 2004

Includes bibliographical references

395 Etiquette (Manners)

Baldrige, Letitia

Letitia Baldrige's new complete guide to executive manners. Rawson Assocs. 1993 xxx, 590p il $40   **395**

1. Business etiquette

ISBN 0-89256-362-1   LC 93-14166

First published 1985 with title: Letitia Baldrige's complete guide to executive manners

The author provides advice on such issues in the workplace as sexual harassment; using nonsexist, ethnically correct forms of address and language; romantic involvement among co-workers; dealing with HIV-positive employees and clients; working with the physically-challenged; and international business manners

Letitia Baldrige's new manners for new times; a complete guide to etiquette; illustrations by Denise Cavalieri Fike. Scribner 2003 xxvi, 709p il $35   **395**

1. Etiquette

ISBN 0-7432-1062-X   LC 2003-65666

First published 1990 with title: Letitia Baldrige's complete guide to the new manners for the 90's

"Combining correctness, consideration, and common sense in equal measure, Baldrige advises readers on proper ways to approach intricate situations. She addresses same-sex unions, pregnant brides, blended and extended families, and sexual harassment with aplomb." Libr J

Bride's

Bride's book of etiquette; [by] the editors of Bride's magazine. Perigee Bks. il pa $16.95   **395**

1. Etiquette 2. Weddings 3. Marriage customs and rites

First published 1948. Periodically revised. Publisher and title vary

A guide to planning a wedding ceremony and reception, from announcements to honeymoon plans

Includes bibliographical references

Dresser, Norine

Multicultural manners; new rules of etiquette for a changing society. Wiley 1996 285p pa $17.95   **395**

1. Etiquette 2. Manners and customs

ISBN 0-471-11819-2   LC 96-139921

"From body language and table manners to classroom behavior and gift giving, this guide to etiquette provides fascinating information about relations in our multicultural society." Booklist

Martin, Judith, 1938-

Miss Manners' basic training: the right thing to say. Crown 1998 179p $17.95   **395**

1. Conversation 2. Etiquette

ISBN 0-609-60051-6   LC 97-28967

The author offers advice on conversational manners, including suggestions about how to respond to awkward, embarrassing, or rude comments, how to make small talk, and when to use euphemisms and polite lies

"Martin is an amusingly sardonic arbiter, and her manual should be popular." Booklist

Miss Manners' guide to domestic tranquility; the authoritative manual for every civilized household, however harried. Crown 1999 372p hardcover o.p. paperback available $18   **395**

1. Etiquette

ISBN 0-609-80539-8 (pa)   LC 99-22824

This guide to etiquette focusing on the home "considers the myriad facets of living with family, friends, guests, and society in general." Libr J

Miss Manners on weddings; illustrated by Gloria Kamen. Crown 1999 208p il $16   **395**

1. Etiquette 2. Weddings 3. Marriage customs and rites

ISBN 0-609-60431-7   LC 98-40684

First published 1995 with title: Miss Manners on painfully proper weddings

This guide to wedding etiquette outlines the responsibilities of family and friends and offers advice on engagements, bridal showers, invitations, gifts, and receptions

Post, Peggy, 1945-

Emily Post wedding etiquette; cherished traditions and contemporary ideas for a joyous celebration. 4th ed. HarperResource 2001 400p il $27.50   **395**

1. Etiquette 2. Weddings 3. Marriage customs and rites

ISBN 0-06-019883-4   LC 2001-268791

First published 1982 under the authorship of Emily Post with title: Emily Post's complete book of wedding etiquette

Post, Peggy, 1945-—*Continued*

This guide to wedding planning covers such topics as multicultural and interfaith marriages, second marriages, engagements, prewedding events, postwedding duties, financial matters, working with consultants, and responsibilities of participants, and includes flow charts and ckecklists

Emily Post's etiquette. HarperCollins Pubs. il $38 **395**

1. Etiquette

First published 1922 under the authorship of Emily Post. Periodically revised and updated. Title varies. 11th-15th editions revised by Elizabeth Post; 16th edition 1997 revised by Peggy Post

"The classic reference for which fork to use has been expanded to include such modern situations as dating, living together, second marriages, and co-ed business traveling." N Y Public Libr Book of How & Where to Look It Up

Tuckerman, Nancy, 1928-

The Amy Vanderbilt complete book of etiquette; entirely rewritten and updated by Nancy Tuckerman and Nancy Dunnan; illustrations by Jackie Aher. Doubleday 1995 786p il $32 **395**

1. Etiquette
ISBN 0-385-41342-4   LC 93-44452

First published 1952 under the authorship of Amy Vanderbilt

This guide includes "discussions of cellular phones, unmarried couples living together, either heterosexual or gay, business travel, especially for women, and many other new topics, as well as the standard information on table settings, weddings, funerals, and tipping. . . . This is a very comprehensive work that belongs in every public library." Libr J

Warner, Diane, 1937-

How to have a big wedding on a small budget; cut your wedding costs in half. 4th ed. Betterway Bks. 2003 185p il pa $12.99 **395**

1. Weddings
ISBN 1-55870-646-1   LC 2002-26191

First published 1990

The author provides consumer tips on such subjects as invitations, dresses, food, flowers, and pictures

Includes bibliographical references

398 Folklore

Bernstein, Peter L.

The power of gold; the history of an obsession. Wiley 2000 432p $27.95; pa $16.96 **398**

1. Gold
ISBN 0-471-25210-7; 0-471-00478-6 (pa)
LC 00-36647

The author "recounts the magical, religious, and artistic qualities of gold and moves through the invention of coins, the transformation of gold into money, and the history of the gold standard." Libr J

"Bernstein's prose is lucid if not vivid, and he covers a lot of time and territory in relatively few pages." N Y Times Book Rev

Includes bibliographical references

Bunson, Matthew

The vampire encyclopedia. Crown 1993 303p il **398**

1. Vampires—Encyclopedias   LC 92-42005

Available from Random House Value Pub.

This "is an A-Z arrangement of more than 2000 entries drawn from folklore, literature, and popular culture. Entries range in length from a line to over a page, with a few tables (film, literature, etc.) running to several pages. *See* and *See also* references are frequent, . . . appendixes list more novels and anthologies, major works consulted, and vampire societies." Libr J

Melton, J. Gordon

The vampire book; the encyclopedia of the undead. Visible Ink Press 1998 c1999 919p il pa $24.95 **398**

1. Vampires
ISBN 1-57859-071-X

First published 1994

This work "has 375 entries ranging in length from 100 to 5,000 words. The work is illustrated with black-and-white photographs. . . . Four appendixes list vampire organizations and fanzines; a filmography of 650 feature films; a section of vampire drama, opera, and ballet; and a bibliography of vampire books beginning with *Dracula* in 1897 up to the present." Booklist [review of 1994 edition]

398.03 Folklore—Encyclopedias and dictionaries

American folklore; an encyclopedia; edited by Jan Harold Brunvand. Garland 1996 794p il (Garland reference library of the humanities) hardcover o.p. paperback available $42 **398.03**

1. Folklore—United States 2. North America—Social life and customs
ISBN 0-8153-3350-1 (pa)   LC 95-53734

This volume contains "more than 500 articles covering American and Canadian folklore from holidays, festivals, and rituals to crafts, music, dance, and occupations. Well-chosen black-and-white photographs illustrate many aspects of our rich folklife tradition. Twenty-three ethnic groups receive lengthy articles describing their traditional and contemporary folklore—with the exception of Native Americans." Am Libr

Radford, Edwin, 1891-1973

Encyclopaedia of superstitions; by E. and M. A. Radford; with a foreword by Sir John Hammerton. Philosophical Lib. 1949 269p o.p.; Greenwood Press reprint available $72.95 **398.03**

1. Superstition—Dictionaries 2. Folklore—Dictionaries
ISBN 0-8371-2115-9

First published 1948 in the United Kingdom

This volume "contains over two thousand superstitions of Britain ranging over the past six hundred years, with many references to present day beliefs." Wilson Libr Bull

Rose, Carol, 1943-
Giants, monsters, and dragons; an encyclopedia of folklore, legend, and myth. ABC-CLIO 2000 xxix, 428p il o.p.; Norton paperback available $17.95   **398.03**
1. Monsters—Encyclopedias 2. Giants—Encyclopedias 3. Dragons—Encyclopedias
ISBN 0-393-32211-4 (pa)   LC 00-9117
For inclusion in this reference work "the creature cannot be divine, it must be a supernatural being from mythology, legend, folklore, or classic literature, and it may be a cryptozoological or symbolic being, such as a heraldic beast. . . . Entries give basic descriptions of each creature as well as its activities, region, culture, and historical period." Libr J

Sax, Boria
The mythical zoo; an encyclopedia of animals in world myth, legend, and literature. ABC-CLIO 2001 xxi, 298p il $85   **398.03**
1. Animals—Folklore—Encyclopedias 2. Mythical animals—Encyclopedias 3. Animals in literature
ISBN 1-57607-612-1   LC 2001-4422
An encyclopedia of animals as they have appeared in myth and legend throughout history
This "is a handy reference book that will be useful to just about anyone from storywriters to television producers, newspaper editors, or just plain interested readers. Anyone checking some background information or some last minute facts will find this book a must." Am Ref Books Annu, 2003
Includes bibliographical references

Seal, Graham, 1950-
Encyclopedia of folk heroes. ABC-CLIO 2001 xxiii, 347p $85   **398.03**
1. Folklore—Encyclopedias 2. Heroes and heroines
ISBN 1-57607-216-9   LC 2001-4423
"This volume describes folk heroes from all times and cultures, both individually and as groups. . . . There are indexes by heroic type, country/culture, and a chronology of folk heroes by century." SLJ
This "includes a number of figures not easily found elsewhere. Larger public and academic libraries with folklore collections may find it useful." Booklist

Storytelling encyclopedia; historical, cultural, and multiethnic approaches to oral traditions around the world; general editor, David Adams Leeming; project editor, Marion Sader. Oryx Press 1997 543p $69.95   **398.03**
1. Storytelling—Encyclopedias 2. Folklore—Encyclopedias
ISBN 1-57356-025-1   LC 97-23081
This volume "includes entries on characters from both mythology and folklore as well as authors, storytellers, scholars, tale types, terminology, cultural traditions, and more. A selected bibliography is included, and most entries are followed by references to further reading." Libr J
"A valuable source on various aspects of folklore and storytelling around the world from early times to the present. It should prove of interest to librarians, teachers, students, and others interested in the subject." Booklist

398.2   Folk literature

American Indian myths and legends; selected and edited by Richard Erdoes and Alfonso Ortiz. Pantheon Bks. 1984 527p il hardcover o.p. paperback available $18   **398.2**
1. Native Americans—Folklore 2. Native Americans—Religion
ISBN 0-394-74018-1 (pa)   LC 84-42669
"This volume comprises 160 tales of native folklore and myth ranging from one geographical end of our continent to the other. The book is organized according to type of myth. . . . Erdoes and Ortiz seek to keep Indian myth intact and pure through their retellings, using, as often as possible, primary sources." Booklist
Includes bibliographical references

Brunvand, Jan Harold
The choking Doberman and other "new" urban legends. Norton 1984 240p il hardcover o.p. paperback available $11.95   **398.2**
1. Folklore—United States 2. Legends—United States
ISBN 0-393-30321-7 (pa)   LC 83-22031
"These fictitious narratives . . . circulate widely as true incidents. Brunvand details more than 40 . . . anecdotes, ranging from grisly reports of alleged mutilations to comical tales of sexual mishaps." Libr J
"Brunvand is especially adept at tracing apparently fresh stories to ancient roots." Time
Includes bibliographical references

Encyclopedia of urban legends; artwork by Randy Hickman. ABC-CLIO 2001 xxxiv, 524p il $75   **398.2**
1. Folklore 2. Legends
ISBN 1-57607-076-X   LC 2001-883
Also available in paperback from Norton
"Among the nearly 500 entries are specific legends . . . along with common legend topics, categories, and themes. . . . Other entries deal with terms and concepts related to the study of urban legends. . . . Coverage focuses on the U.S. but also extends to Canada, England, and other English-speaking countries and to countries, such as Romania, in which published urban-legend collections are available." Booklist

Too good to be true; the colossal book of urban legends. Norton 1999 480p il $29.95; pa $17.95   **398.2**
1. Folklore—United States 2. Legends—United States
ISBN 0-393-04734-2; 0-393-32088-X (pa)
LC 99-17562
"This anthology embraces over 200 fanciful, amusing, and often exaggerated stories and beliefs that have, through repetition, become part of the American oral heritage. . . . Thoroughly researched and exhaustive, this fascinating work is characterized by impressive scholarship." Libr J

Brunvand, Jan Harold—*Continued*
The vanishing hitchhiker; American urban legends and their meaning. Norton 1981 208p hardcover o.p. paperback available $13.95
398.2
1. Folklore—United States 2. Legends—United States
ISBN 0-393-95169-3 (pa)   LC 81-4744
A collection of modern urban folktales with an ironic or supernatural twist. The author reports on how such tales are disseminated and discusses their inherent messages for contemporary society
Includes bibliographical references

Favorite folktales from around the world; edited by Jane Yolen. Pantheon Bks. 1986 498p hardcover o.p. paperback available $18   **398.2**
1. Folklore 2. Fairy tales
ISBN 0-394-75188-4 (pa)   LC 86-42644
"Selections include tales from the American Indians, the brothers Grimm, Italo Calvino's Italian folk-tales, as well as stories from Iceland, Afghanistan, Scotland, and many other countries. Yolen provides each section with a relevant introduction, often including historical and literary factors, thus alerting readers as to what to look for." SLJ

From my people; 400 years of African American folklore; edited by Daryl Cumber Dance. Norton 2002 xliii, 736p il $35
398.2
1. African Americans—Folklore
ISBN 0-393-04798-9   LC 2001-44843
"Folktales, work songs, proverbs, sermons, and speeches . . . are presented along with a color insert on folk arts and crafts. . . . The collection includes contributions from Zora Neale Hurston, Ralph Ellison, Nikki Giovanni, W. C. Handy and Bessie Smith, as well as a host of proverbs, superstitions, and riddles collected over the years from anonymous and obscure contributors. This is a rich collection." Booklist
Includes bibliographical references

Grimm, Jacob, 1785-1863
The complete fairy tales of the Brothers Grimm; translated and with an introduction by Jack Zipes; illustrations by John B. Gruelle. Bantam Bks. 1992 xxxiv, 750p il pa $19.95   **398.2**
1. Fairy tales
ISBN 0-553-37101-0   LC 94-124913
This edition first published 1987
"The inside illustrations by John B. Gruelle first appeared in Grimm's fairy tales, translated by Margaret Hunt in 1914." Verso of title page
This collection contains the classic tales plus others recently discovered in the Grimm archives. Oral and literary sources are included

Index to fairy tales; including folklore, legends, and myths in collections. Scarecrow Press 1985-1994 4v   **398.2**
1. Folklore—Indexes 2. Fairy tales—Indexes 3. Legends—Indexes 4. Mythology—Indexes
Volumes covering 1949-1972 and 1973-1977 first published by Faxon 1973 and 1979 respectively
A continuation of Index to fairy tales, myths and legends and its two supplements, compiled by Mary Huse Eastman, published 1926-1952 by Faxon (o.p.)

Volume covering 1949-1972 compiled by Norma Olin Ireland $75 (ISBN 0-8108-2011-0); volume covering 1973-1977 compiled by Norma Olin Ireland $45 (ISBN 0-8108-1855-8); volume covering 1978-1986 compiled by Norma Olin Ireland and Joseph W. Sprug $85 (ISBN 0-8108-2194-X); volume covering 1987-1992 compiled by Joseph W. Sprug $85 (ISBN 0-8108-2750-6)
"Although this is an essential reference book for the children's department, it is also a valuable source for the location of much folklore and fairy-tale material and should be available in adult book collections as well." Ref Sources for Small & Medium-sized Libr. 6th edition

MacDonald, Margaret Read
Celebrate the world; twenty tellable folktales for multicultural festivals; illustrations by Roxane Murphy Smith. Wilson, H.W. 1994 225p il $60   **398.2**
1. Folklore 2. Festivals 3. Storytelling
ISBN 0-8242-0862-5   LC 94-6682
In this collection MacDonald "has interwoven the stories with holidays and festivals from various countries and presented tips on how to present both the story and the holiday in a storytelling program." J Youth Serv Libr
Includes bibliographical references

Malory, Sir Thomas, 15th cent.
Le morte d'Arthur   **398.2**
1. Arthur, King
Hardcover and paperback editions available from various publishers
Originally published 1485
"The work is a skillful selection and blending of materials taken from the mass of Arthurian legends. The central story consists of two main elements: the reign of King Arthur ending in catastrophe and the dissolution of the Round Table; and the quest of the Holy Grail." Oxford Companion to Engl Lit

The **Oxford** companion to fairy tales; edited by Jack Zipes. Oxford Univ. Press 2000 xxxii, 601p hardcover o.p. paperback available $24.95   **398.2**
1. Fairy tales—History and criticism
ISBN 0-19-860509-9 (pa)   LC 99-14271
This is a "collection of brief essays on classic tales, both modern and ancient. In alphabetical order, the companion profiles noted authors, illustrators, filmmakers, choreographers, and composers; more broadly, it covers film, art, opera, ballet, music, and commercial use. . . . Attractive, well written, and approachable, this solid guide to the fairy-tale world is without equal." Libr J

Petro, Pamela, 1960-
Sitting up with the dead; a storied journey through the American South. Arcade Pub. 2002 414p $25.95   **398.2**
1. Folklore—Southern States 2. Southern States—Description
ISBN 1-55970-612-0   LC 2002-18310
The author "embarked on four meandering trips through the South. . . . Folktales and their tellers serve as her maps and guides; her travelogue is peppered with transcribed stories she hears on the way. The resulting chronicle is an impressive piece of cultural conservation, reportage and memoir that subtly mourns the passing of a rural way of life." Publ Wkly

Pickering, David, 1958-
A dictionary of folklore. Facts on File 1999
324p $44   **398.2**
1. Folklore—Dictionaries 2. Mythology—Dictionaries
ISBN 0-8160-4550-0
The author provides entries "on such subjects as herbal remedies, the superstitions connected with various gemstones, the folklore associated with selected trees, plants, birds, and animals. He also covers the ritual tradition of holidays and festivals and the origins of proverbs and sayings. In addition, the dictionary mentions characters and heroes from selkies to Joe Magarac, fantasy beings such as sprites and pixies, and some urban myths." Libr J
For a fuller review see: Booklist, May 15, 2000

398.8   Rhymes and rhyming games

The **Oxford** dictionary of nursery rhymes; edited by Iona and Peter Opie. 2nd ed. Oxford Univ. Press 1997 xxix, 559p il $55
       398.8
1. Nursery rhymes—Dictionaries
ISBN 0-19-860088-7   LC 98-140995
First published 1951
"A scholarly collection of nursery rhymes with notes and explanations concerning history, literary associations, social uses, and possible portrayal of real people. Both standard and earliest recorded versions (where available) are included. Indexes for 'notable figures' and first lines." Ref Sources for Small & Medium-sized Libr. 5th edition [entry for 1951 edition]

398.9   Proverbs

The **Concise** Oxford dictionary of proverbs; [compiled by John Simpson & Jennifer Speake] 3rd ed. Oxford Univ. Press 1998 333p pa $12.95   **398.9**
1. Proverbs
ISBN 0-19-280084-1   LC 99-234790
First published 1982
This volume "contains over 1000 proverbs commonly used in 20th-century Britain. . . . Arranged alphabetically by the first significant word, each one includes illustrative quotations, beginning with the earliest known use." SLJ [review of 1992 edition]

Cordry, Harold V., 1943-
The multicultural dictionary of proverbs; over 20,000 adages from more than 120 languages, nationalities and ethnic groups. McFarland & Co. 1997 406p $49   **398.9**
1. Proverbs
ISBN 0-7864-0251-2   LC 96-33264
"The proverbs are arranged under 1300 headings (e.g., accidents, divided loyalty, marriage, and shame), and each includes the nationality, group or language in which it originated." Publisher's note
"This well-organized multicultural dictionary of proverbs not only illustrates the common insights that different cultures share but also provides a rich resource of wisdom that the casual reader can glean from perusing the proverbs in an entry." Am Ref Books Annu, 1998

A **Dictionary** of American proverbs; Wolfgang Mieder, editor in chief; Stewart A. Kingsbury and Kelsie B. Harder, editors. Oxford Univ. Press 1992 710p $65; pa $19.95   **398.9**
1. Proverbs
ISBN 0-19-505399-0; 0-19-511133-8 (pa)
     LC 91-15508
"This scholarly work includes 15,000 proverbs with variants currently used in the United States and parts of Canada. Entries are arranged alphabetically under key words and are often followed by variants and cross references. . . . This collection differs from most such compilations because the proverbs were collected by field workers rather than from written sources. The work sets new standards for understanding the oral tradition in America and is an essential purchase for ready-reference collections." Libr J

Manser, Martin H.
The Facts on File dictionary of proverbs; associate editor: Rosalind Fergusson. Facts on File 2002 440p (Facts on File library of language and literature) $45   **398.9**
1. Proverbs
ISBN 0-8160-4607-7   LC 2002-67832
Original edition published 1983 compiled by Rosalind Fergusson
This reference "includes more than 1,500 English-language proverbs that are widely recognized today. Arranged alphabetically, entries provide the meaning of each proverb, the date it was first recorded, variant forms of the proverb, other proverbs that are similar and opposite to it in meaning, and examples of the proverb's use." Publisher's note
"A very readable, easy-to-use collection of proverbs, this book will be useful either at home or in most types of libraries." Am Ref Books Annu, 2003

Pickering, David, 1958-
Cassell dictionary of proverbs. Cassell 1997 297p $24.95   **398.9**
1. Proverbs
ISBN 0-304-34911-9   LC 97-152081
"Collected here are more than 3,000 entries, covering familiar and unfamiliar proverbs from the English-speaking world as well as a wide representative selection from other cultures. Entries attempt to pinpoint each proverb's precise meaning, where it originated, when it was first used, and what its subsequent history has been." Booklist

400   LANGUAGE

Crystal, David, 1941-
The Cambridge encyclopedia of language. 2nd ed. Cambridge Univ. Press 1997 480p il $85; pa $30   **400**
1. Language and languages—Encyclopedias
ISBN 0-521-55050-5; 0-521-55967-7 (pa)
     LC 96-3104
First published 1987
This encyclopedia "covers all the major themes of language study, including popular ideas about language, language and identity, the structure of language, speaking and listening, writing, reading, and signing, language acquisition, the neurological basis of language, and lan-

Crystal, David, 1941-—*Continued*
guages of the world. . . . [Also includes] advances in areas such as machine translation, speech interaction with machines, and language teaching." Univ Press Books for Public and Second Sch Libr, 1997

Language and the Internet. Cambridge Univ. Press 2001 272p $23 **400**
1. Language and languages 2. Internet
ISBN 0-521-80212-1   LC 2001-25792
The author "explores the role of language in the Internet and the effect of the Internet on language. In four central chapters, he details the significant linguistic features at work in the four major 'situations' of the Internet: e-mail, chat-groups (including listservs and discussion groups), virtual worlds, and the web. He concludes that Netspeak (his word for the language of the Internet) is a new medium." Libr J
Includes bibliographical references

Facts about the world's languages: an encyclopedia of the world's major languages, past and present; edited by Jane Garry and Carl Rubino; contributing linguistics editors Adams B. Bodomo, Alice Faber, Robert French. Wilson, H.W. 2000 896p $170 **400**
1. Language and languages—Encyclopedias
ISBN 0-8242-0970-2   LC 00-49430
"A New England Publishing Associates book"
"The encyclopedia includes descriptions of most languages with two million or more current speakers, as well as several ancient languages. Each of its 191 articles, written by a recognized authority, follows a similar format: language name, family, number of speakers, and narrative descriptions of its history, orthography, phonology, morphology, syntax, contact with other languages, and sample words and sentences. Refreshingly, the contributors do not neglect to mention social and political factors that have influenced linguistic change." Choice

Nunberg, Geoffrey, 1945-
The way we talk now; commentaries on language and culture from NPR's "Fresh air". Houghton Mifflin 2001 256p $22; pa $14 **400**
1. Language and languages
ISBN 0-618-11602-8; 0-618-11603-6 (pa)
    LC 2001-24797
Topics covered include "the long-lasting linguistic impact of movies, software that checks grammar, and word histories. . . . Politics is one of six categories in which the essays are chronologically organized." Libr J
"Nunberg never fails to reveal some bit of history embedded in language, and, despite his occasionally stuffy responses to contemporary jargon, his acuity and fixation on funny pop-phenomena keep the book fresh." Publ Wkly

Pinker, Steven, 1954-
The language instinct. Morrow 1994 494p o.p.; HarperCollins Pubs. paperback available $15 **400**
1. Language and languages
ISBN 0-06-095833-2 (pa)   LC 93-31842
The author "argues that an 'innate grammatical machinery of the brain' exists, which allows children to 'reinvent' language on their own. Basing his ideas on Noam Chomsky's Universal Grammar theory, Pinker describes language as a 'discrete combinatorial system' that might easily have evolved via natural selection. Pinker steps on a few toes . . . but his work, while controversial, is well argued, challenging, often humorous, and always fascinating." Libr J
Includes bibliographical references

Science times book of language and linguistics; edited by Nicholas Wade. Lyons Press 2000 193p il $25 **400**
1. Language and languages 2. Linguistics
ISBN 1-55821-934-X   LC 99-43156
This is a compilation of articles from the New York Times concerning such topics as the origins of language, animal communication, sex differences in language, language and the brain, language and learning, and language and society
"This book is sure to fascinate anyone who has an interest in language and culture." Booklist

The **World's** major languages; edited by Bernard Comrie. Oxford Univ. Press 1987 1025p hardcover o.p. paperback available $42 **400**
1. Language and languages
ISBN 0-19-506511-5 (pa)   LC 86-12795
"Ranging from English, French, Spanish, and Russian to Swahili, this comprehensive reference work provides [a] . . . detailed guide to the world's forty major languages. With a general introduction on languages and language families, and authoritative entries written by acknowledged specialists, this is an indispensable resource for anyone seeking a fuller appreciation of the origins of and nature of language." Univ Press Books for Public Libr

401 Language—Philosophy and theory

Golinkoff, Roberta M.
How babies talk; the magic and mystery of language in the first three years of life; [by] Roberta Michnick Golinkoff and Kathy Hirsh-Pasek. Dutton 1999 256p o.p.; Plume Bks. paperback available $14 **401**
1. Language and languages—Psychology 2. Children—Language
ISBN 0-452-28173-3 (pa)   LC 99-22282
"Beginning with the fetus and newborn, the authors take the reader through the steps and stages of language learning. The text is interspersed with activities readers can use to assess the specific development of their own children." Libr J
Includes bibliographical references

Pinker, Steven, 1954-
Words and rules; the ingredients of language. Basic Bks. 1999 348p il o.p.; HarperCollins Pubs. paperback available $15 **401**
1. Language and languages 2. Grammar
ISBN 0-06-095840-5 (pa)   LC 99-43013
Pinker "studies how the mind works by examining the nature of language. In 'Words and Rules,' he examines

Pinker, Steven, 1954-—*Continued*
irregularities, especially irregular verbs and plurals, from the points of view of biology, child development, psychology, philology, and linguistics." Christ Sci Monit

This book "with its crisp prose and neat analogies, makes required reading for anyone interested in cognition and language." Publ Wkly

Includes bibliographical references

410 Linguistics

Crystal, David, 1941-
A dictionary of language. 2nd ed. University of Chicago Press 2001 390p il pa $17.50 **410**
1. Language and languages—Dictionaries
ISBN 0-226-12203-4   LC 00-69076
First published 1992 with title: An encyclopedic dictionary of language and languages; present edition first published in the United Kingdom with title: The Penguin dictionary of language

This dictionary "offers explanations of the most frequently used linguistic terms, particularly those that can occur in texts read by beginners and by interested laypersons. . . . There are also entries concerned with graphology, shorthand writing, and similar peripheral, but interesting, topics. The impression that this dictionary has been written mainly for the general public is enhanced by the humorous jocose caricatures interspersed throughout the text, but the information is still solid. The author has succeeded in creating a handy dictionary that will serve students and laypeople equally well, for both browsing and study." Am Ref Book Annu, 2002

Dalby, Andrew
Dictionary of languages; the definitive reference to more than 400 languages. Columbia Univ. Press 1999 734p il maps $57.50 **410**
1. Language and languages—Dictionaries
ISBN 0-231-11568-7   LC 98-87178
This dictionary includes alphabetical entries that "cover all languages with official status as well as those with a written literature and 175 minor languages with significant historical and/or anthropological interest. A preface explains the author's pronunciation scheme. . . . The entries themselves are from two to four pages long. Each one discusses a specific language. . . . With coverage of languages from Abkhaz to Zulu, explanations of Egyptian hieroglyphics and Sumerian script, and a discussion of Chinese dialects and characters, [this] . . . is a welcome addition to public and academic library collections." Booklist

International encyclopedia of linguistics; William J. Frawley, editor-in chief. 2nd ed. Oxford Univ. Press 2003 4v set $495 **410**
1. Linguistics—Encyclopedias
ISBN 0-19-513977-1   LC 2003-430
First published 1992 under the editorship of William Bright

This work includes "historical, comparative, formal, mathematical, functional, and philosophical linguistics with special attention given to interrelations within branches of linguistics and to relations of linguistics with other disciplines. Areas of intersection with the social and behavioral sciences—ethnolinguistics, sociolinguistics, psycholinguistics, and behavioral linguistics

. . . [are covered] along with interdisciplinary work in language and literature, mathematical linguistics, computational linguistics, and applied linguistics." Publisher's note

This reference "remains an important scholarly source." Libr J

412 Etymology

Hayakawa, S. I.
Language in thought and action; [by] S.I. Hayakawa and Alan R. Hayakawa. 5th ed. Harcourt Brace Jovanovich 1990 287p il $49.95; pa $16 **412**
1. Semantics 2. Thought and thinking 3. English language
ISBN 0-15-550120-8; 0-15-648240-1 (pa)
        LC 89-84371
First published 1939 with title: Language in action

The author analyzes the nature of language, discusses the processes of thinking and writing, and gives advice on thinking and writing clearly

Includes bibliographical references

419 Verbal language not spoken and written

Butterworth, Rod R.
Signing made easy; a complete program for learning sign language. Includes sentence drills and exercises for increased comprehension and signing skill; [by] Rod R. Butterworth and Mickey Flodin. Putnam 1989 224p il pa $13.95 **419**
1. Sign language
ISBN 0-399-51490-2   LC 88-23878
"A Perigee book"

This volume "is organized into general subject areas such as Family and Friends, Work, Food, and Travel. Each chapter builds progressively on the vocabulary and grammar of the previous lesson." Publisher's note

Chambers, Diane P., 1959-
Communicating in sign; creative ways to learn American Sign Language (ASL); written by Diane P. Chambers, with Lee Ann Chearney; edited by D. Keith Robertson; illustrations by Paul M. Setzer; with an introduction by Bernard Bragg. Fireside 1998 165p il (Flying hands book) pa $12 **419**
1. Sign language
ISBN 0-684-83520-7   LC 97-51145
"By combining vocabulary, grammar, syntax, expression, and movement with commentary on etiquette and other cultural issues, Chambers . . . has created a general resource intended for the lay public." Libr J

Includes bibliographical references

Costello, Elaine

Random House Webster's American sign language dictionary; illustrated by Lois Lenderman, Paul M. Setzer, Linda C. Tom. Random House 1998 xxxvi, 539p pa $20 **419**

1. Sign language
ISBN 0-679-78011-4 LC 97-21538
Also available Concise American sign language dictionary pa $6.99 (ISBN 0-553-58474-X)
First published 1994 with title: Random House American sign language dictionary
This illustrated sign language dictionary includes over 4,500 signs with complete description of each sign, plus full-torso illustrations. Includes alternate signs for the same meaning and different signs for different meanings of the same word

Lane, Leonard G.

Gallaudet survival guide to signing; illustrations by Jan Skrobisz. new rev ed. Gallaudet Univ. Press 1990 203p il pa $7.95 **419**

1. Sign language
ISBN 0-930323-67-X LC 89-25686
First published 1987
Line drawings illustrate approximately five hundred signs representing words and concepts as expressed in American Sign Language. Separate charts of the basic handshapes, the American Manual Alphabet, and signed numbers are also included

Proctor, Claude O.

NTC's multilingual dictionary of American sign language. National Textbook 1995 767p il hardcover o.p. paperback available $29.95 **419**

1. Sign language
ISBN 0-8442-0732-2 (pa)
This work contains "2,446 entries arranged alphabetically by the English word, followed by an abbreviation denoting the part of speech and a small line drawing showing the American Sign Language (ASL) gesture with arrow(s) indicating direction of motion of the hand(s). There are four entries per page. Following the ASL illustration are equivalents in 12 languages, Arabic through Swedish, including 3 Asian and 8 European languages. For Russian and Asian words, a romanized spelling is given before the native script itself." Recommended Ref Books for Small & Medium-sized Libr & Media Cent, 1997

Riekehof, Lottie L.

The joy of signing; the illustrated guide for mastering sign language and the manual alphabet. 2nd ed. Gospel Pub. House 1987 352p il $23.95 **419**

1. Sign language
ISBN 0-88243-520-5 LC 86-80173
First published 1963 with title: Talk to the deaf
This manual presents over 1300 signs used for communicating with deaf adults, and provides basic vocabulary needed for entering interpreter training programs. Signs are arranged in 25 categories with an alphabetical index. For each sign there is a line drawing, description of how to make the sign, origin (concept) and notes on usage
Includes bibliographical references

Sternberg, Martin L. A.

American Sign Language; a comprehensive dictionary; illustrated by Herbert Rogoff. Unabridged. HarperCollins Pubs. 1998 xxi, 983p il $60; pa $24 **419**

1. Sign language
ISBN 0-06-271608-5; 0-06-273634-5 (pa)
LC 98-26649
First published 1981
Arranged alphabetically, this dictionary features 7,000 sign entries, with cross-references and more than 12,000 illustrations
Includes bibliographical references

Tennant, Richard A.

The American Sign Language handshape dictionary; [by] Richard A. Tennant, Marianne Gluszak Brown; illustrated by Valerie Nelson-Metlay. Gallaudet Univ. Press 1998 407p il $39.95 **419**

1. Sign language
ISBN 1-56368-043-2 LC 97-48389
This work organizes "signs by handshape rather than alphabetically by English word order. In so doing, it acts best as a recognition tool for the ASL learner, leading the user quickly to specific signs without having first to refer to an English-equivalent word." Libr J

420 English and Old English

Bryson, Bill

Made in America; an informal history of the English language in the United States. Morrow 1995 417p o.p.; Avon Bks. paperback available $14 **420**

1. English language—History 2. Americanisms
ISBN 0-380-71381-0 (pa) LC 94-46451
The author "explains the original meanings of words and phrases by establishing the contexts in which they were popularized, describing particular eras in American history as well as major events and institutions, e.g., war, politics, sports, advertising and movies, that have contributed to language usage." Publ Wkly
"For Bryson's wonderfully sane and reasoned discussion of the issues surrounding 'politically correct' language alone, this book is a worthwhile read." Libr J
Includes bibliographical references

The mother tongue: English & how it got that way. Morrow 1990 270p o.p.; Avon Bks. paperback available $14 **420**

1. English language—History
ISBN 0-380-71543-0 (pa) LC 89-77521
Topics discussed include "etymology, pronunciation, spelling, dialects, grammar, the origins of proper names, [and] wordplay." N Y Times Book Rev
Includes bibliographical references

Crystal, David, 1941-

The Cambridge encyclopedia of the English language. 2nd ed. Cambridge Univ. Press 2003 499p il $75; pa $35 **420**

1. English language
ISBN 0-521-82348-X; 0-521-53033-4 (pa)
LC 2003-272259
First published 1995

Crystal, David, 1941-—*Continued*
This "volume is divided into six broad topics that cover the English language's history, vocabulary, grammar, writing and speech systems, usage, and acquisition. Within these major topics, the book is divided into logical subtopics and finally into the basic unit of the text—the two-page spread. . . . The clear and spirited text is stunning, enhanced with over 500 illustrations, making this a particularly rich reference work and a browser's dream." Libr J [review of 1995 edition]

English as a global language. 2nd ed. Cambridge Univ. Press 2003 212p il maps $45; pa $15 **420**
1. English language—Social aspects
ISBN 0-521-82347-1; 0-521-53032-6 (pa)
LC 2003-282119
First published 1997
Crystal's "account of the rise of English as a global language explores the history, current status and potential of English as the international language of communication. [Includes] sections on the future of English as a world language, English on the Internet, and the possibility of an English 'family' of languages." Publisher's note
"This is a fascinating and useful book. . . . a fine introduction for a wide variety of potential users." Choice
Includes bibliographical references

McCrum, Robert
The story of English; [by] Robert McCrum, Willam Cran, Robert MacNeil. 3rd rev ed. Penguin Bks. 2003 xxi, 468p maps pa $16 **420**
1. English language—History
ISBN 0-14-200231-3 LC 2002-29818
First published 1986 by Viking
A "companion to the PBS television series of the same name. . . . The text covers the history of our language from its roots in Latin through its transplanting to other shores and its infusions from other cultures and languages. . . . Good for browsing, this book is a must for word and history buffs." SLJ [review of 1986 edition]
Includes bibliographical references

Metcalf, Allan A.
Predicting new words; the secrets of their success; [by] Allan Metcalf. Houghton Mifflin 2002 206p il $22 **420**
1. New words 2. English language—Terms and phrases
ISBN 0-618-13006-3 LC 2002-68593
This book traces the origins of an "array of words and phrases: *Marlboro Man, Frankenfood, blurb, skycap, quark, scofflaw*. It also introduces us to a fascinating array of would-be words, coinages that never quite caught on. . . . The book is jam-packed with treats for word lovers." Booklist

The **Oxford** companion to the English language; edited by Tom McArthur; managing editor, Feri McArthur. Oxford Univ. Press 1992 xxvii, 1184p il $65 **420**
1. English language—Dictionaries
ISBN 0-19-214183-X
"This Oxford companion—part dictionary, part usage guide, part linguistic encyclopedia—offers the broadest range of reference information to be found in any single source. Included are entries on grammar, prosody, language acquisition, and sexist language, on every nation where English is widely spoken, and on writers and lexicographers whose works have significantly affected the development of the language—about 5,000 entries all told." Am Libr

421 Written and spoken codes of standard English

Vos Savant, Marilyn Mach
The art of spelling; the madness and the method; by Marilyn vos Savant; illustrations by Joan Reilly. Norton 2000 204p il hardcover o.p. paperback available $12.95 **421**
1. English language—Spelling
ISBN 0-393-32208-4 (pa) LC 00-37228
The author "offers some suggestions for spelling improvement, supplying common roots like anim-, arch-, and spec- and a list of 500 commonly misspelled words. She also includes a few quizzes, with answers in the back of the book. This is not a how-to book, however, for more than half of it examines what spelling ability tells us about intelligence and personality. . . . The bibliography and web site list are nice additions as well." Libr J

421.03 Written and spoken codes of standard English—Dictionaries

Acronyms, initialisms, & abbreviations dictionary. Gale Res. 4v set $865 **421.03**
1. Acronyms—Dictionaries 2. Abbreviations—Dictionaries
ISSN 0270-4404
Also available: Reverse acronyms, initialisms, & abbreviations dictionary
First published 1960 in one volume with title: Acronyms dictionary. (32nd edition 2003) Frequently revised
A guide to acronyms, initialisms, abbreviations, contractions, alphabetic symbols, and similar condensed apellations

Stahl, Dean
Abbreviations dictionary; [by] Dean Stahl, Karen Kerchelich; originated by Ralph De Sola. 10th ed. CRC Press 2001 1529p $79.95 **421.03**
1. Abbreviations—Dictionaries 2. Acronyms—Dictionaries 3. Signs and symbols
ISBN 0-8493-9003-6 LC 00-58549
First published 1958 under the authorship of Ralph De Sola
"The classic status of this title endures: abbreviations are again joined by a dazzling array of acronyms, contractions, initials, nicknames, short forms, signs, and symbols. Its 15,000 new terms swell the dictionary to nearly 300,000 entries. Domestic and international terms are harvested from diverse fields, criminology to music. Computing, technology, and government draw special attention due to active abbreviating. Entries are alphabetically and numerically ordered." Choice

422 Etymology of standard English

Barnhart, David K.
America in so many words; words that have shaped America; [by] David K. Barnhart and Allan A. Metcalf. Houghton Mifflin 1997 308p il hardcover o.p. paperback available $12   **422**
1. English language—Etymology 2. English language—History 3. Americanisms
ISBN 0-618-00270-7 (pa)   LC 97-14510
A "year-by-year review highlights words that have had an indelible American origin or meaning. Barnhart and Metcalf . . . have selected one particularly significant word for each year and, through anecdotes and historical details, discuss its roots, development, and importance." Libr J
Includes bibliographical references

Buckley, William F. (William Frank), 1925-
Buckley, the right word; [by] William F. Buckley, Jr.; selected, assembled, and edited by Samuel S. Vaughan with an introduction & sundry commentaries. Random House 1996 524p o.p.; Harcourt paperback available $15   **422**
1. English language—Usage 2. Vocabulary
ISBN 0-15-600569-7 (pa)   LC 96-8928
"Vaughan has included Buckley's pieces on the uses and abuses of language, reviews, letters, and journalism, among many other things. Whether responding to letters to *National Review*, being interviewed, or skewering a reviewer, Buckley is prolific and provocative, influential and infuriating, and always intellectually stimulating." Libr J

Korach, Myron
Common phrases and where they come from; [by] Myron Korach in collaboration with John B. Mordock. Lyons Press 2001 200p hardcover o.p. paperback available $9.95   **422**
1. English language—Etymology 2. English language—Terms and phrases
ISBN 1-58574-682-7 (pa)   LC 00-69016
Korach and Mordock "show how much our culture relies on idiomatic speech to enliven discourse, a point further demonstrated by the more than 150 well-known phrases whose interesting histories they have provided. The arrangement of phrases is loosely thematic, with one to several paragraphs devoted to each." Libr J

422.03 Etymology of standard English—Dictionaries

The **Barnhart** dictionary of etymology; Robert K. Barnhart, editor; Sol Steinmetz, managing editor. Wilson, H.W. 1988 xxvii, 1284p $100   **422.03**
1. English language—Etymology—Dictionaries
ISBN 0-8242-0745-9   LC 87-27994
Also available The Barnhart concise dictionary of etymology (HarperCollins Pubs. 1995)

This dictionary "focuses on words used in contemporary American English and words of American origin and incorporates current American scholarship. Entries give spelling variations, pronunciation for difficult words, part of speech, definition, and information on word origins. Written for a wide audience, this is a very attractive, readable work suited for most library users." Ref Sources for Small & Medium-sized Libr. 6th edition

The **Concise** Oxford dictionary of English etymology; edited by T. F. Hoad. Oxford Univ. Press 1986 hardcover o.p. paperback available $16.95   **422.03**
1. English language—Etymology—Dictionaries
ISBN 0-19-283098-8 (pa)   LC 85-31970
Based on The Oxford dictionary of English etymology
"Provides concise statements on the origins of words and their development once they became part of the English language." N Y Public Libr Book of How & Where to Look It Up

Guinagh, Kevin, 1897-
Dictionary of foreign phrases and abbreviations; translated and compiled by Kevin Guinagh. 3rd ed. Wilson, H.W. 1983 261p $70   **422.03**
1. English language—Foreign words and phrases—Dictionaries 2. Quotations 3. Abbreviations—Dictionaries
ISBN 0-8242-0675-4   LC 82-8486
First published 1965
This dictionary "contains more than 5,000 foreign phrases, proverbs, and abbreviations frequently used in written and spoken English. Provides translations and pronunciations, and for some entries brief explanatory notes; includes a list of phrases by languages." Ref Sources for Small & Medium-sized Libr. 6th edition

Hendrickson, Robert, 1933-
The Facts on File encyclopedia of word and phrase origins. 3rd ed. Facts on File 2003 822p $82.50   **422.03**
1. English language—Etymology—Dictionaries 2. English language—Terms and phrases
ISBN 0-8160-4813-4   LC 2003-44948
First published 1987
This work "contains definitions and origins of more than 12,500 words and expressions. . . . Anecdotes and information on the development of a wide range of words, including slang, proverbs, animal and plant names, place names, nicknames, historical expressions, foreign language expressions, and phrases from literature, are included. . . . The emphasis throughout is on words and expressions whose origins are not adequately explained, or not addressed at all, in standard dictionaries." Publisher's note

Manser, Martin H.
The Facts on File dictionary of foreign words and phrases; associate editor, David H. Pickering. Facts on File 2002 432p $45; pa $16.95   **422.03**
1. English language—Foreign words and phrases
ISBN 0-8160-4458-9; 0-8160-4459-7 (pa)
LC 2001-42302
This dictionary includes more than 4,000 entries for terms that have entered the English lexicon from foreign languages in the fields of language and literature, religion, law, politics, economics, music, entertainment and cuisine. Examples or quotations are provided to illustrate usage

Morris, William, 1913-1994
Morris dictionary of word and phrase
origins; [by] William and Mary Morris;
foreword by Isaac Asimov. 2nd ed. Harper &
Row 1988 669p $38   **422.03**
1. English language—Etymology—Dictionaries 2. English language—Terms and phrases
ISBN 0-06-015862-X   LC 87-45651
Original three volume edition published 1962-1971;
one volume edition first published 1977
"Traces the origins of several thousand words and
phrases commonly used in the English language, including slang terms and clichés not usually found in more
formal works. Entries are listed alphabetically by the first
word in the phrase, with an index at the end." Ref
Sources for Small & Medium-sized Libr. 6th edition

The **Oxford** dictionary of foreign words and
phrases; edited by Jennifer Speake. Oxford
Univ. Press 1997 512p $37.95; pa $12.95
     422.03
1. English language—Foreign words and phrases—
Dictionaries
ISBN 0-19-863159-6; 0-19-280112-0 (pa)
     LC 96-49006
This dictionary features "a pronunciation guide for
each word based on the International Phonetic Alphabet,
and examples of usage. Some entries also feature notes
on the historical or etymological background of the word
or phrase. Approximately 8,000 words and phrases from
more than 40 languages make up the main entries. . . .
Included are words and phrases that have meaning in
more than one sense or have come into general use in
this century." Choice

The **Oxford** dictionary of word histories;
edited by Glynnis Chantrell. Oxford Univ.
Press 2002 559p $27.95   **422.03**
1. English language—Etymology—Dictionaries
ISBN 0-19-863121-9   LC 2001-44807
"This book describes the origins and sense development of over 11,000 words in the English language, with
dates of the first recorded evidence from ongoing research for the OED. Well-known idioms are included,
with dates of original use and details of how and when
they came about. . . . Colorful popular beliefs about the
origins of words like 'posh' and 'snob' are explored and
insights are given into our social history revealed by language development. . . . Throughout, boxed word-building elements show the various meanings of a shared
prefix, such as in 'hyperspace,' 'hypersonic,' and
'hyperlink.'" Publisher's note
"Written in straightforward prose and boasting an
easy-to-read font and page layout. . . . This delightful
and affordable handbook is well recommended for all libraries." Libr J

423   English language—
Dictionaries

The **American** Heritage college dictionary.
4th ed. Houghton Mifflin 2002 xxviii,
1636p il maps $26   **423**
1. English language—Dictionaries
ISBN 0-618-09848-8   LC 2001-39826
First published 1975 as an abridgment of The
American Heritage dictionary of the English language

This dictionary is derived from the fourth edition of
the American Heritage Dictionary of the English language. This edition includes over 2,000 photographs and
drawings, usage advice, notes on synonyms, regionalisms, and word histories, biographical and geographical
entries as well as a style manual

The **American** Heritage dictionary of the
English language. 4th ed. Houghton Mifflin
2000 xxxvi, 2074p il $60   **423**
1. English language—Dictionaries
ISBN 0-395-82517-2   LC 00-25369
Also available CD-ROM version; print and CD-ROM
edition $75 (ISBN 0-618-08230-1)
First published 1969
This dictionary provides some 210,000 main entries
with over 4,000 full-color illustrations. Word histories,
synonym paragraphs and regionalisms are also explored.
The work also examines the influence of social factors
such as age and ethnicity on how American English has
been shaped by speakers from every social class

Bartlett's Roget's thesaurus. Little, Brown
1996 xxxii, 1415p $21.95   **423**
1. English language—Synonyms and antonyms
2. Americanisms
ISBN 0-316-10138-9   LC 96-18343
This thesaurus "reflects the current state of American
English, including terminology from the worlds of composers and television, with such sub-categories as 'Living
Things,' 'The Arts,' 'Feelings.' But what really makes
the book a joy to use is the tremendously useful lists—
everything from phobias to styles and periods of furniture." Am Libr

The **Cassell** dictionary of English idioms;
[editor, Rosalind Fergusson] Cassell 2000
392p hardcover o.p. paperback available
$14.95   **423**
1. English language—Idioms 2. English language—
Terms and phrases
ISBN 0-304-36384-7 (pa)   LC 00-340364
"Idiomatic expressions are arranged alphabetically by
their 'core' or key terms. . . . Approximately 10,000 idioms have been selected from English as it is used today
in North America, Australia, New Zealand, and the British Isles. Usage notes identify country of origin of expressions tied closely to one culture. Notes also label
terms as colloquial or slang as appropriate." Booklist

Choose the right word; a contemporary guide
to selecting the precise word for every
situation; [edited by] S.I. Hayakawa. 2nd
ed, Eugene Ehrlich, revising editor.
HarperPerennial 1994 532p hardcover o.p.
paperback available $21.95   **423**
1. English language—Synonyms and antonyms
ISBN 0-06-273131-9 (pa)   LC 93-34206
First published 1968 with title: Funk & Wagnalls
Modern guide to synonyms & related words
This work contains over 1,000 key word entries which
define and compare 6,000 commonly used synonyms and
related words. Short explanatory essays provide illustrative sentences

Corbeil, Jean-Claude

The Firefly visual dictionary; [by] Jean-Claude Corbeil, Ariane Archambault. Firefly Bks. 2002 952p il $49.95   **423**
1. Picture dictionaries
ISBN 1-55297-585-1   LC 2002-726880
First published 1992 by Macmillan International with title: The Macmillan visual dictionary
"Created and produced by QA International." Verso of title page
This contains an "inventory of 35,000 terms and 6000 illustrations. Organized into 17 color-coded chapters and according to 94 broad themes, this wonderful resource will help the terminology-challenged, especially since today's gadgets and gizmos are included. . . . The clarity, schematic detail, and contrast of the computer-generated art are stunning." Libr J

Dictionary of confusable words; [edited by] Adrian Room. Fitzroy Dearborn Pubs. 2000 251p $35   **423**
1. English language—Synonyms and antonyms 2. English language—Usage
ISBN 1-57958-271-0
A "guide to potentially confusing words. . . . The brief entries give definitions of each of the terms. Each word is then used in at least one sample sentence, clarifying the differences between like terms. The definitions and examples are in simple language and are easy to understand." Libr J
For a fuller review see: Booklist, Nov. 19, 2000

The **Doubleday** Roget's thesaurus in dictionary form; Sidney I. Landau, editor in chief; Ronald J. Bogus, managing editor. rev ed. Doubleday 1987 804p thumb-indexed $16.95   **423**
1. English language—Synonyms and antonyms 2. Americanisms
ISBN 0-385-23997-1   LC 86-24184
First published 1977
"Despite the words 'Roget' and 'thesaurus' in the title, which may imply a classified arrangement, the entry words in this volume are listed in alphabetical order. Some 250,000 synonyms and antonyms, including slang, are provided, but with little guidance in word selection. This work's arrangement will appeal to those who find *Roget's International Thesaurus* awkward to use." Nichols. Guide to Ref Books for Sch Media Cent. 4th edition

Espy, Willard R.

Words to rhyme with; for poets and songwriters; foreword and further thoughts on rhyme by Louis Phillips. Updated ed. Facts on File 2001 676p $65; pa $21.95   **423**
1. English language—Rhyme
ISBN 0-8160-4312-4; 0-8160-4313-2 (pa)
LC 00-52803
First published 1986
"Including a Primer of prosody, a list of more than 80,000 words that rhyme, a glossary defining 9,000 of the more eccentric rhyming words, and a variety of exemplary verses, one of which does not rhyme at all." Title page

Garner, Bryan A.

Garner's modern American usage. 2nd ed. Oxford Univ. Press 2003 848p $39.95   **423**
1. English language—Usage 2. Americanisms
ISBN 0-19-516191-2
First published 1998 with title: A dictionary of modern American usage
"Containing roughly 7000 main entries and many cross references, the dictionary offers intelligent, sensible, readable advice concerning usage demons involving problems of grammar, spelling, homonyms, variants, clichés, skunked words, redundancies, phrasal adjectives and verbs, and more." Libr J [review of 1998 edition]

Holder, R. W.

How not to say what you mean; a dictionary of euphemisms. 3rd ed. Oxford Univ. Press 2002 xx, 501p $18.95   **423**
1. Euphemism—Dictionaries
ISBN 0-19-860402-5   LC 2002-74261
Replaces A dictionary of euphemisms, published 1995
This edition contains thousands of alphabetized entries for such expressions as a 'fruit salad' (mixture of illegal narcotics), 'arm candy' (a good-looking female companion), and 'birthday suit' (nakedness). Historical explanations, definitions, and examples are provided
"Delightful, quirky and exhaustive, Holder's dictionary of American and British circumlocutions is the kind of reference work that one can spend hours browsing through happily." Publ Wkly

Kipfer, Barbara Ann

Roget's 21st century thesaurus in dictionary form; the essential reference for home, school, or office; edited by the Princeton Language Institute; Barbara Ann Kipfer, head lexicographer. 2nd ed. Dell 1999 957p (21st century reference) pa $14.95   **423**
1. English language—Synonyms and antonyms
ISBN 0-385-33415-X   LC 99-462557
First published 1992
Produced by The Philip Lief Group, Inc.
This thesaurus, cross referencing each word with the same concept, provides 17,000 main entry words and 450,000 synonyms in a dictionary format
"Exceptional . . . unique words and groupings. . . . This resource is a gem!" Booklist

Lees, Gene

The modern rhyming dictionary; how to write lyrics; including a practical guide to lyric writing for songwriters and poets. Cherry Lane Bks. 1981 360p hardcover o.p. paperback available $14.95   **423**
1. English language—Rhyme
ISBN 0-89524-317-2 (pa)   LC 81-4832
"Lees' dictionary is arranged in three sections—masculine (one-syllable), feminine (two-syllable), and three-syllable rhymes—with each section subdivided by vowels and then into subgroups by the consonant beginning the final syllable of the word." Ref Sources for Small & Medium-sized Libr. 5th edition

Lutz, William, 1940-
The Cambridge thesaurus of American English; [by] William D. Lutz. Cambridge Univ. Press 1994 515p $25   **423**
1. English language—Synonyms and antonyms 2. Americanisms
ISBN 0-521-41427-X   LC 93-31878
This thesaurus lists "over 200,000 synonyms and antonyms. . . . Lutz concentrates on idioms, verb phrases, and slang. Phrases are listed under the 'main' word in the phrase. 'Play it by ear,' for example, is found under the noun *ear* instead of the verb *play*. . . . The *Cambridge* is a welcome addition to the list of modern thesauruses and highly recommended for users who need a concise work that provides quick and easy access." Libr J

Merriam-Webster's collegiate dictionary. Eleventh ed. Merriam-Webster 2003 1623p il $23.95   **423**
1. English language—Dictionaries
ISBN 0-87779-808-7   LC 2003-3674
Also available thumb-indexed print and CD-ROM edition $26.95 (ISBN 0-87779-809-5)
First published 1898
This edition includes over 165,000 entries, 10,000 new words and meanings, 38,000 etymologies, a handbook of style, an essay on the English language, a special section on signs and symbols, and a free one-year subscription to the Collegiate Web site

Merriam-Webster's collegiate thesaurus. Merriam-Webster 1993 868p $17.95   **423**
1. English language—Synonyms and antonyms
ISBN 0-87779-169-4   LC 93-3177
Also available on CD-ROM as part of Merriam-Webster's collegiate dictionary & thesaurus
First published 1976 with title: Webster's collegiate thesaurus
"Employs a conventional dictionary arrangement, and gives synonyms, related terms, idiomatic equivalents, antonyms, and contrasted words as applicable. Cross-references in small capitals." Guide to Ref Books. 11th edition

Metaphors dictionary; [edited by] Elyse Sommer, with Dorrie Weiss. Visible Ink Press 2001 xlvi, 612p $24.95   **423**
1. English language—Terms and phrases
ISBN 1-57859-137-6
First published 1995 by Gale Res.
This is a "collection of 6,500 colorful classic and contemporary comparative phrases (with full annotations and a complete bibliography of sources) . . . organized under 500 timeless and timely themes, ranging from Aloneness to Love to Zeal." Publisher's note
"Any library serving patrons involved in creative writing, composition, public speaking, or literary criticism should add this volume." Am Ref Books Annu, 1996 [entry for 1995 edition]

Microsoft Encarta college thesaurus; general editor, Susan Jellis. St. Martin's Press 2002 xxvi, 1166p $21.95   **423**
1. English language—Synonyms and antonyms
ISBN 0-312-28906-5   LC 2001-48999
Companion to Microsoft Encarta college dictionary (2001)
"A Bloomsbury reference book"

This thesaurus "has 40,000 alphabetically arranged entries with 350,000 synonyms and antonyms. . . . In addition to single words the alphabetic section contains phrases like *full of beans* and *walk a tightrope*. Interspersed between the entries are 'Compare and Contrast' boxes that explain nuances in meaning. . . . The alphabetic section serves as an index to the thematic section, and the editor has done a good job of linking the two. . . . [This] is an excellent choice for libraries or individuals that need a current thesaurus that reflects today's culture." Booklist

The **New** Oxford American dictionary; edited by Frank Abate, Elizabeth J. Jewell. Oxford Univ. Press 2001 xxxvii, 2023p il maps + 1 computer laser optical disc $55   **423**
1. English language—Dictionaries 2. Americanisms
ISBN 0-19-515060-0   LC 2001-45172
Also available CD-ROM version
First published 1980 with title: The Oxford American dictionary
In this dictionary "entries are organized around core meanings. . . . The structure of each entry . . . shows the major meaning or meanings of the word, plus any related senses, supplemented by illustrative, in-context examples of actual usage." Publisher's note
"Entries have a clean appearance; definitions are readable and understandable. Examples are drawn from modern usage rather than from oldest known or literary occurrences. Definitions for technical, scientific, and other terms strike an excellent balance by providing clear understanding for nonspecialists while not being too elementary in tone. . . . A well-designed dictionary, recommended for all libraries." Choice

The **Oxford** American dictionary and language guide. Oxford Univ. Press 1999 1306, 36p il maps $35   **423**
1. English language—Dictionaries 2. Americanisms
ISBN 0-19-513449-4   LC 00-265059
"The 'language guide' portion of this publication is reprinted (with adaptation) from The world book dictionary." Verso of title page
"Headwords in boldface are arranged letter by letter; entries provide pronunciation, part of speech, identifier, variants in spelling (British, American, Australian, New Zealand), inflected forms (plurals of nouns, forms of verbs, comparative and superlative of adjectives and adverbs), lexical meanings, syntax notes, illustrative examples, phrases and idioms, derivatives, and etymology." Choice

The **Oxford** American dictionary of current English. Oxford Univ. Press 1999 966p il $17.95; pa $9.95   **423**
1. English language—Dictionaries 2. Americanisms
ISBN 0-19-513374-9; 0-19-515082-1 (pa)
     LC 99-39972
Edited by Frank Abate
This dictionary contains approximately 180,000 definitions and entries as well as hundreds of word histories and grammar, style, and usage notes. 3,000 biographical and geographical entries are included

The **Oxford** American thesaurus of current English; edited by Christine A. Lindberg. Oxford Univ. Press 1999 863p $17.95; pa $9.95 **423**

1. English language—Synonyms and antonyms
ISBN 0-19-513375-7; 0-19-515083-X (pa)
LC 99-31092

"First British edition published in 1997 as The concise Oxford thesaurus, based on The Oxford paperback thesaurus (1995), edited by Betty Kirkpatrick." Verso of title page

This "thesaurus has 15,000 main entries and 350,000 synonyms. Headwords, printed in bold type, are listed in strict alphabetical order. For each headword, the part of speech is provided. Within entries, synonyms that convey different senses of a word appear in numbered groups. In addition to lists of synonyms, entries may include example phrases (which are sometimes complete sentences), usage labels, cross-references, and antonyms." Booklist

The **Oxford** English dictionary. 2nd ed, prepared by J.A. Simpson and E.S.C. Weiner. Oxford Univ. Press 1989 20v apply to publisher for price **423**

1. English language—Dictionaries
ISBN 0-19-861186-2
LC 88-5330

Also available CD-ROM version and online; print and CD-ROM edition also available

Compact edition reproduced micrographically from first edition and supplements available for $395

First published 1888 with title: New English dictionary on historical principles

"This is an etymological or word-source dictionary. In addition to definitions, this work gives the history of 290,500 words, both current and archaic, in the English language. Slang entries are very limited. Word histories include early forms, variant forms and roots, and first or exemplary usages in English from ancient to modern times. Short explanatory notes are provided for more common words." N Y Public Libr Book of How & Where to Look It Up

The **Oxford** reverse dictionary; compiled by David Edmonds. Oxford Univ. Press 1999 403p pa $15.95 **423**

1. English language—Synonyms and antonyms 2. English language—Dictionaries
ISBN 0-19-860176-X
LC 99-21464

"This book is a collection of words linked by concept that offers a way for readers to look up words they may already know but are unable to recall. . . . The book makes no attempt to be comprehensive, either in its choice of main entries or in the included definitions; it is limited to 31,000 entries, omitting specialist vocabularies and slang. . . . This is a quite useful resource for the curious, students, and the general public." Libr J

Pronouncing dictionary of proper names; pronunciations for more than 28,000 proper names, selected for currency, frequency, or difficulty of pronunciation; editor, John K. Bollard [et al.] 2nd ed. Omnigraphics 1998 xxxv, 1097p $110 **423**

1. English language—Pronunciation—Dictionaries
2. Names—Pronunciation
ISBN 0-7808-0098-2
LC 97-23664

First published 1994

Including place names; given names; names of famous individuals; cultural, literary, historical, and Biblical names; mythological names; names of peoples and tribes; company names and product names; with pronunciations transcribed into the international phonetic alphabet and a simplifed phonetic respelling; and including an explanatory introduction

Random House Webster's college dictionary. Random House il maps $24.95 **423**

1. English language—Dictionaries
ISBN 0-375-42560-8
LC 99-12620

First published 1991 as a successor to The Random House college dictionary. (2002 edition) Frequently revised

"Each entry in the dictionary presents spelling, along with alternatives, syllabication, pronunciation used in conversational speech (with alternatives), and part of speech. Entries also include meanings and definitions, with the most common usage listed first; historical, technical, or other usages of the term; date of first usage, including place of origin; and other related words that use the same root or stem. . . . The dictionary includes over 207,000 definitions, many of them so new they are not yet found in competing products. . . . For libraries seeking a wide variety of dictionaries, this work will prove especially useful for its inclusion of recent terms and idioms." Am Ref Books Annu, 2001 [entry for 2000 edition]

Random House Webster's unabridged dictionary. 2nd ed. Random House 2001 xxvi, 2230p il maps $49.95 **423**

1. English language—Dictionaries
ISBN 0-375-42566-7

Also available CD-ROM version; print and CD-ROM edition $64.95 (ISBN 0-375-42573-X)

This dictionary contains over 315,000 entries. A newwords section and an essay on the growth of English are included. 2,400 spot maps and illustrations complement the text

Roget's international thesaurus. 6th ed, edited by Barbara Ann Kipfer; Robert L. Chapman, consulting editor. HarperResource 2001 xxv, 1248p $20.95; pa $16.95 **423**

1. English language—Synonyms and antonyms
ISBN 0-06-273693-0; 0-06-093544-8 (pa)
LC 2002-276277

Also available thumb-indexed edition

First copyright edition published 1911 with title: The standard thesaurus of English words and phrases classified and arranged so as to facilitate the expression of ideas and assist in literary composition

This edition includes 330,000 words and phrases organized into 1,075 categories and a pinpoint reference system that directs the user from a comprehensive index to the numbered category of the right word. Crossreferences throughout lead to other categories. Also included are supplemental word lists that supply the names of things which have no synonyms (measurements, wines, state mottoes) as well as quotations that amplify the meanings of selected words

Shorter Oxford English dictionary on historical principles. 5th ed. Oxford Univ. Press 2002 2v set $150   **423**
1. English language—Dictionaries
ISBN 0-19-860457-2   LC 2002-70244
Also available print and CD-ROM edition $199.95 (ISBN 0-19-521955-4)

First published 1933

Editor-in-chief, Lesley Brown

This "set offers over 33% of the complete *Oxford English Dictionary*, with over a half million definitions, the same emphasis on etymology and the evolving usage of a word through history. Examples of usage, presented in specially tinted boxes, are taken from great works of literature, period newspapers and political oratory, with sources ranging from Gibbon to S.J. Perelman; there are 83,500 illustrative quotes from 7,000 authors." Publ Wkly

Ultimate visual dictionary. Dorling Kindersley il maps $40   **423**
1. Picture dictionaries 2. English language—Dictionaries
First published 1994 with title: Dorling Kindersley ultimate visual dictionary. Frequently revised. Variant title: DK ultimate visual dictionary

This dictionary features over 30,000 terms and more than 6,000 color illustrations detailing everything from the prehistoric earth, the physical and biological science, to the visual arts, architecture, music, sports and common, ordinary everyday things

Webster's third new international dictionary of the English language, unabridged. Merriam-Webster il   **423**
1. English language—Dictionaries
Prices vary according to binding
Also available CD-ROM version; print and CD-ROM edition also available

Original edition by Noah Webster published 1828 with title: An American dictionary of the English language. Has also appeared under various other titles. First published with present title 1961. Frequently reprinted with additions and changes to keep it up to date

"Clear, accurate definitions are given in historical order. Outstanding for its numerous illustrative quotations, impeccable authority, and etymologies, *Webster's third* is regarded as the most reliable, comprehensive general unabridged dictionary." Ref Sources for Small & Medium-sized Libr. 6th edition

Winchester, Simon
The professor and the madman; a tale of murder, insanity, and the making of the Oxford English dictionary. HarperCollins Pubs. 1998 242p il $22; pa $13   **423**
1. Murray, Sir James Augustus Henry, 1837-1915 2. Minor, William C., d. 1920 3. Oxford English dictionary
ISBN 0-06-017596-6; 0-06-099486-X (pa)
     LC 98-10204
The author relates the "story of the *Oxford English Dictionary's* first editor and the expatriate American murderer who contributed more than 10,000 quotations as examples. Best of all, among the entertaining tangents one learns a great deal about the making of that grandest of all reference works." Libr J
Includes bibliographical references

Young, Sue
The new comprehensive American rhyming dictionary. Morrow 1991 622p o.p.; Avon Bks. paperback available $14   **423**
1. English language—Rhyme 2. Americanisms
ISBN 0-380-71392-6 (pa)   LC 90-19165
This book contains over 65,000 words and phrases categorized by sound, rather than spelling. It includes many colloquialisms and slang expressions

425   English language— Grammar

Huddleston, Rodney D.
The Cambridge grammar of the English language; [by] Rodney Huddleston, Geoffrey K. Pullum in collaboration with Laurie Bauer [et al.] Cambridge Univ. Press 2002 1842p il $160   **425**
1. English language—Grammar
ISBN 0-521-43146-8   LC 2001-25630
"Each chapter comprises core definitions, detailed analyses, notes explaining alternative interpretations of difficult or controversial points, and brief notes on usage and history." Publisher's note
This "comprehensive and detailed look at the principles of the English language . . . [is] an authoritative addition to the fields of both English grammar and linguistics." Libr J
Includes bibliographical references

427   English language variations

Ammer, Christine
The American Heritage dictionary of idioms. Houghton Mifflin 1997 729p $32; pa $14.95   **427**
1. English language—Idioms 2. English language— Terms and phrases 3. Americanisms
ISBN 0-395-72774-X; 0-618-24953-2 (pa)
     LC 97-12390
"In addition to idioms, the dictionary includes common figures of speech, formula phrases such as 'take care,' emphatic redundancies whose word order cannot be reversed such as 'cease and desist,' common proverbs, colloquialisms, and slang phrases. Each expression is defined briefly and then illustrated by a short, simple sentence showing how it is used in context." SLJ
Includes bibliographical references

Dalzell, Tom, 1951-
Flappers 2 rappers; American youth slang. Merriam-Webster 1996 256p il pa $14.95
    427
1. English language—Slang 2. Americanisms
ISBN 0-87779-612-2   LC 96-50258
Dalzell "begins with a brief look at the time before the flapper, that is, back to the 1850s, and then proceeds chronologically in decades to the present. Each chapter includes numerous word lists and definitions, as well as innumerable essays on the development and occurrence of particular slang terms." Recommended Ref Books for Small & Medium-sized Libr & Media Cent, 1997
Includes bibliographical references

Dictionary of American regional English; Frederic G. Cassidy, chief editor. Belknap Press 1985-2002 4v maps   427

1. English language—Dictionaries 2. Americanisms

The first four volumes of a projected five volume work

Contents: v1 Introduction and A-C $92 (ISBN 0-674-20511-1); v2 D-H $92 (ISBN 0-674-20512-X); v3 I-0 $92 (ISBN 0-674-20519-7); v4 P-Sk $89.95 (ISBN 0-674-00884-7)

This dictionary "offers detailed information on non-standard, regional, or folk American speech. . . . Entries do not merely define, but include part of speech, pronunciation, variant forms, etymology, geographic range, usage, cross-references, editorial notes, and dated quotations defining the word. Where appropriate, a computer-generated map . . . illustrates the regional distribution of a word. When it is completed . . . this work will definitely take its place beside the OED as a classic." Am Libr

Dictionary of American slang; edited by Robert L. Chapman. 3rd ed. HarperCollins Pubs. 1995 xxii, 617p $42.95   427

1. English language—Slang 2. Americanisms

ISBN 0-06-270107-X   LC 97-2771

First published 1960 by Crowell. Variant title: New dictionary of American slang

This dictionary defines over 17,000 terms. Examples of usage are provided and derivations noted. Particular emphasis has been placed on language pertaining to technology, business and the media

Green, Jonathon

The Cassell dictionary of slang; [compiled by] Jonathon Green. Cassell 1998 1316p hardcover o.p. paperback available $19.95   427

1. English language—Slang

ISBN 0-304-35167-9 (pa)   LC 99-209227

"Green includes words from the seventeenth century to the present with slang from all English-speaking areas: U.S., U.K., Canada, the Caribbean, New Zealand, Australia, and India. Each entry includes the part of speech, date of use, and definition. In a volume of this size it would be impossible to cite each source, so instead Green includes a bibliography of more than 200 books and numerous newspapers, comics, films, television scripts, and even Internet sites." Booklist

Hendrickson, Robert, 1933-

The Facts on File dictionary of American regionalisms. Facts on File 2000 786p $82.50   427

1. English language—Dictionaries 2. Americanisms

ISBN 0-8160-4156-3   LC 00-28808

This "resource covers colorful and ordinary expressions spoken in several geographical regions, samples from the dialects spoken by Hawaiian and Pennsylvania Dutch people, and brief information about the dialects Bawlamerese, Bonac, Conch, Gullah, and Boont. A typical section includes a general discussion of the regional language or dialect (etymology, pronunciation, and grammatical variations) followed by alphabetized words and phrases briefly defined." Libr J

Herman, Lewis

American dialects; a manual for actors, directors, and writers; by Lewis Herman and Marguerite Shalett Herman. Theatre Arts Bks. 1959 328p il hardcover o.p. paperback available $23.95   427

1. English language—Dialects 2. Americanisms

ISBN 0-87830-049-X (pa)

First published 1947 with title: Manual of American dialects, for radio, stage, screen, and television

"An invaluable guide to reproducing the sounds, rhythms, lilts, and stresses of representative dialects of every major section of the continental United States." Libr J

Lutz, William, 1940-

The new doublespeak; why no one knows what anyone's saying anymore. HarperCollins Pubs. 1996 244p hardcover o.p. paperback available $13.95   427

1. English language—Jargon

ISBN 0-06-092839-5 (pa)   LC 96-165038

Companion volume to Doublespeak (1989)

"Focusing on the misuse of language by government employees, journalists, and economists, Lutz argues passionately that doublespeak . . . is dangerous to the welfare of the nation. He shows how both Democrats and Republicans engage in doublespeak and is especially good in his description and explanation of the language of law and the Supreme Court. A fair and outspoken view of American political life and the degradation of language." Libr J

Includes bibliographical references

Mencken, H. L. (Henry Louis), 1880-1956

The American language; an inquiry into the development of English in the United States. 4th ed, corrected and rewritten. Knopf 1936 769, xxixp $55   427

1. English language 2. Names 3. Americanisms

ISBN 0-394-40075-5

Supplements 1-2 ea $50 (ISBN 0-394-40076-3; 0-394-40077-1)

Analyzed in Essay and general literature index

First published 1919

An historical treatment of the development of American English covering such subjects as pronunciation and spelling, slang, proper names, and common speech

Includes bibliographical references

Metcalf, Allan A.

How we talk; American regional English today; [by] Allan Metcalf. Houghton Mifflin 2000 206p il hardcover o.p. paperback available $14   427

1. English language—Dictionaries 2. Americanisms

ISBN 0-618-04362-4 (pa)   LC 00-59777

The author "discusses the origins of American regional dialects and explains why different parts of the country use different words to mean the same thing (*carry* versus *tote*, for example) or why the same words are pronounced differently in the South as opposed to the North. For fiction writers hoping to create authentic-sounding dialogue, this book could function as an indispensable guide." Booklist

The **Oxford** dictionary of slang; a unique topic-by-topic review of English slang; [compiled by] John Ayto. Oxford Univ. Press 1998 474p hardcover o.p. paperback available $13.95   **427**
ISBN 0-19-280104-X (pa)   LC 99-201836

"The 10,000 slang terms defined here originated mainly in the United States, Britain, Australia, or New Zealand and include both old and new coinages. The dictionary's arrangement is topical in thesaurus fashion." Libr J

Partridge, Eric, 1894-1979
A dictionary of slang and unconventional English; edited by Paul Beale. Routledge pa $39.95   **427**
1. English language—Slang
First published 1937. Periodically revised
"Colloquialisms and catch phrases, fossilised jokes and puns, general nicknames, vulgarisms and such Americanisms as have been naturalised." Title page
Entries are "in one alphabet; front matter includes a helpful note, 'Arrangement Within Entries.' Entries trace, in a way that recalls the 'Oxford English Dictionary,' the development of terms and usages." Booklist
"Partridge remains essential for all reference collections, an irresistable distraction to browsers." Am Ref Books Annu, 1986

Random House historical dictionary of American slang; J. E. Lighter, editor; assistant editors, J. Ball, J. O'Connor. Random House 1994-1997 2v   **427**
1. English language—Slang 2. Americanisms
LC 94-9721
First two volumes of a projected three volume set; volume three in preparation
Contents: v1 A-G $79.95 (ISBN 0-394-54427-7); v2 H-R $75.95 (ISBN 0-679-43465-8)
In this dictionary "terms are not only defined but their etymological development is traced chronologically through dated citations. . . . Lighter's dictionary represents a major contribution to lexicographic scholarship. It belongs in every serious reference collection." Libr J

Spears, Richard A.
NTC's dictionary of American slang and colloquial expressions. 3rd ed. NTC Pub. Group 2000 560p $18.95; pa $14.95   **427**
1. English language—Slang 2. Americanisms
ISBN 0-8442-0461-7; 0-8442-0462-5 (pa)
LC 99-39117
First published 1989
This dictionary "includes street slang, popular culture terms, and the telegraphic language peculiar to the Internet. Arranged alphabetically, entries include usage information, slang type or source, and additional information about whether the term is, e.g., objectionable, derogatory, or standard English." Libr J
For a fuller review see: Booklist, July 2000

428   Standard English usage

Chalker, Sylvia
The Oxford dictionary of English grammar; [by] Sylvia Chalker, Edmund Weiner. Oxford Univ. Press 1994 448p il hardcover o.p. paperback available $15.95   **428**
1. English language—Grammar 2. English language—Dictionaries
ISBN 0-19-280087-6 (pa)   LC 94-19818
"Offering 1,000 grammatical terms and their meanings, this title is a comprehensive reference tool and an updated guide to grammatical and linguistic terms, including entries related to phonetics and semantics. Its emphasis is on the terminology of current mainstream grammar, including Chomskyan generative grammar." Choice

Fowler, H. W.
The new Fowler's modern English usage; first edition by H. W. Fowler. rev 3rd ed, [edited] by R. W. Burchfield. Oxford Univ. Press 2000 xxi, 873p $29.95   **428**
1. English language—Etymology 2. English language—Idioms 3. English language—Usage
ISBN 0-19-860263-4   LC 00-267266
First published 1926 with title: A dictionary of modern English usage
"In a simple, alphabetical arrangement, the third edition covers grammar, syntax, style, word choice, and advice on usage." Libr J [review of 1996 edition]

Lovinger, Paul W.
The Penguin dictionary of English usage and style; a readable reference book, illuminating thousands of traps that snare writers and speakers. Penguin Bks. 2000 491p hardcover o.p. paperback available $18 **428**
1. English language—Usage
ISBN 0-14-200046-9 (pa)   LC 99-53704
"This alphabetically arranged resource features specific words and general-usage topics. . . . The 75 topic entries cover subjects as varied as abbreviations, collective nouns, homophones, prepositions, punctuation, and, interestingly, Iran, often erroneously referred to as Arab. . . . Numerous cross references and 2000 richly contemporary examples replete with quotations add to this tool's usefulness." Libr J
For a fuller review see: Booklist, Nov. 15, 2000

O'Conner, Patricia T.
Woe is I; the grammarphobe's guide to better English in plain English. Riverhead Bks. 2003 240p $19.95   **428**
1. English language—Grammar 2. English language—Usage
ISBN 1-57322-252-6   LC 2003-41416
First published 1996
This guide to good English offers advice on punctuation, usage, style and grammar as well as e-mail
"The author doesn't take herself or the subject matter too seriously, offering a delightful romp through the intricacies of our language. . . . She knows her subject, can convey her message with wit and ease, and does it all in a compact, easy-to-read format. In short, this is an entertaining and useful grammar reference." Libr J
Includes bibliographical references

The **Oxford** dictionary for writers and editors; edited and compiled by R.M. Ritter. 2nd ed. Oxford Univ. Press 2000 404p $24.95 **428**
1. English language—Usage 2. English language—Dictionaries
ISBN 0-19-866239-4 LC 00-268520
First published 1981 as a successor to the eleventh edition of Collins' Authors' and printers' dictionary
This work "provides guidance on common spelling errors, abbreviations, confusable words, foreign words and phrases, differences between British and American English, allusions, and more." Booklist

Wilson, Kenneth G. (Kenneth George), 1923-
The Columbia guide to standard American English. Columbia Univ. Press 1993 482p hardcover o.p. paperback available $21 **428**
1. English language—Dictionaries 2. English language—Usage 3. Americanisms
ISBN 0-231-06989-8 (pa) LC 92-37887
Available in hardcover from Fine Communications
"The 6,500 entries in this book provide a unique approach to spoken and written English. Wilson diagrams five levels of speech, from intimate to oratorical, and three levels of writing, from informal to formal. His descriptive discussion of usage is intended to assist in making choices. . . . Cross references are numerous, and a helpful guide to pronunciation is included." Am Libr

433 German language— Dictionaries

Cassell's German dictionary; German-English, English-German; completely revised by Harold Betteridge. Wiley 2002 xx, 1580p thumb-indexed $27 **433**
1. German language—Dictionaries
ISBN 0-02-522930-3
First compiled 1888 by Elizabeth Weir and published by Heath. Previous American editions published by Funk & Wagnalls with title: The New Cassell's German dictionary
This dictionary provides the words and phrases most commonly used in normal speech and contemporary literature and includes a key to German pronunciation as well as a bibliography of technical and specialist dictionaries
"One of the most useful bilingual dictionaries." Guide to Ref Books. 11th edition

Collins German-English, English-German dictionary; unabridged; by Peter Terrell [et al.] 4th ed. HarperCollins Pubs. 1999 xxvi, 2056p il $55 **433**
1. German language—Dictionaries
ISBN 0-06-270235-1 LC 98-38494
First published 1980
This unabridged dictionary includes coverage of new vocabulary from the fields of computers, business, medicine and politics. A Language in use section features context-based examples

The **Oxford-Duden** German dictionary; German-English, English-German; edited by the Dudenredaktion and the German Section of the Oxford University Press Dictionary Department; chief editors, W. Scholze-Stubenrecht, J.B. Sykes. 2nd ed, edited by M. Clark, O. Thyen. Oxford Univ. Press 1999 1728p il thumb-indexed $49.95 **433**
1. German language—Dictionaries
ISBN 0-19-860248-0 LC 00-502733
Also available concise Oxford-Duden German dictionary $32.95 (ISBN 0-19-864230-X)
First published 1990
This dictionary includes over 260,000 words and phrases, some 450,000 translations, thousands of example sentences, in-text features covering grammar, usage, and vocabulary building, preferred spellings, and numerous full-page maps

439 Other Germanic languages. Yiddish

Rosten, Leo, 1908-1997
The new joys of Yiddish; revisions and commentary by Lawrence Bush; illustrations by R. O. Blechman. Rev ed. Crown 2001 xxxii, 458p il $35; pa $18 **439**
1. Yiddish language 2. English language—Foreign words and phrases
ISBN 0-609-60785-5; 0-609-80692-0 (pa)
LC 2001-28366
First published 1968 with title: The joys of Yiddish
This "work explores the nuances and complexities of language, clarifying the interrelationship between Yiddish and English (Yinglish, according to Rosten). The lengthy alphabetical listing not only presents multiple spellings, pronunciation guides, definitions, and cross references but also illustrates usage with background information, anecdotes, and jokes, as well as breezy erudition in the form of tidbits of cultural history, Talmudic and biblical references, tips on pronunciation, and thoughtful commentary. . . . The revision incorporates additional material on modern Yiddish literature and culture and updates on changes in American Jewish life and faith. Also included as an appendix is an English-Yiddish dictionary." Libr J
Includes bibliographical references

Weinreich, Uriel
Modern English-Yiddish, Yiddish-English dictionary. Schocken Bks. 1977 xliii, 789, 15p pa $30 **439**
1. Yiddish language—Dictionaries
ISBN 0-8052-0575-6 LC 77-76038
A reissue of the title first published 1968 by Yivo
"This dictionary is designed in the main for persons who have a firm grounding in English and at least a rudimentary command of Yiddish. . . . Accordingly, the Yiddish rather than the English material has been phonetically and grammatically analyzed, and English glosses have been used, wherever appropriate, to specify sermantic detail."—Author's pref. A scholarly and useful work." Guide to Ref Books. 11th edition

Weinstein, Miriam
Yiddish; a nation of words. Steerforth Press 2001 303p il $26   **439**
1. Yiddish language
ISBN 1-58642-027-5   LC 2001-2706
Also available in paperback from Ballantine Bks.
The author "traces the language's roots in German lands and in Poland, then sketches Yiddish-drenched shtetl life, drawing on the writing of Israel Joshua Singer and Isaac Bashevis Singer, before describing how Yiddish both influenced and was shaped by two late-19th-century movements, Bundism and Zionism." Publ Wkly
"Aspects of 20th-century history, such as the Holocaust, the revival of Hebrew, the popularity of klezmer (Yiddish) music, and the language's future, receive special attention." Libr J

439.3   Dutch, Flemish, Afrikaans languages

Dutch-English, English-Dutch dictionary; with a brief introduction to Dutch grammar. Hippocrene Bks. 1990 418p (Hippocrene concise dictionary) pa $11.95   **439.3**
1. Dutch language—Dictionaries
ISBN 0-87052-910-2
This dictionary offers a concise overview of English and Dutch grammar with over 7,000 entries each way and notation of common irregularities

Osselton, N. E.
The new Routledge Dutch dictionary; Dutch-English/English-Dutch; [by] N. Osselton and R. Hempelman. Routledge 2003 908p $90; pa $27.95   **439.3**
1. Dutch language—Dictionaries
ISBN 0-415-30040-1; 0-415-30041-X (pa)
LC 2002-153868
First published 2002 in the United Kingdom
This dictionary is "for Dutch language learners and users at all levels. Key features of the dictionary include: over 25,000 Dutch entries, the use of colloquial and idiomatic language, useful contextual information within glosses, phonetic transcription for all Dutch headwords, aiding pronunciation, gender marked for all Dutch nouns, [and an] appendix of Dutch irregular verbs." Publisher's note

443   French language— Dictionaries

Cassell's French dictionary; French-English, English-French; completely revised by Denis Girard with the assistance of Gaston Dulong, Oliver Van Oss, and Charles Guinness. Wiley 2002 thumb-indexed $24.95   **443**
1. French language—Dictionaries
ISBN 0-02-522620-7
First published 1920 with title: Cassell's French-English, English-French dictionary. Previous American editions published by Funk & Wagnalls with title: The New Cassell's French dictionary

"New words including colloquialisms, slang, American English and French-Canadian terms [are included]. . . . There are also sections on French verbs and French and English abbreviations. Reliable, standard dictionary. A first choice." N Y Public Libr. Ref Books for Child Collect. 2d edition

Larousse French-English, English-French dictionary. Nouvelle éd. Larousse (Paris); [distributed by] Houghton Mifflin 2003 xx, 1221p il maps $43.95   **443**
1. French language—Dictionaries
ISBN 2-03-542050-4   LC 2003-503788
Previous edition published with title: Grand dictionnaire français-anglais, anglais-français
Cover title: Larousse Chambers dictionnaire français-anglais, English-French
Added title page: Dictionnaire Larousse français-anglais, anglais-français
This dictionary contains over 250,000 entries and 400,000 translations, an updated vocabulary including technical, IT, and Internet terms, coverage of Canadian, Belgian, and Swiss French, models of letters, faxes, and e-mails, and informative sidebars on French life and culture

The **Oxford-Hachette** French dictionary; French-English, English-French; edited by Marie-Hélène Corréard, Valerie Grundy. 3rd ed, edited by Jean-Benoit Ormal-Grenon, Natalie Pomier. Oxford Univ. Press 2001 xxxviii, 1945p il $45   **443**
1. French language—Dictionaries
ISBN 0-19-860363-0
First published 1994
This work provides coverage of French and English vocabulary in general as well as scientific and technical areas with some 350,000 words and phrases and some 530,000 translations. Supplementary material includes information on French society and culture, including famous places, people and much practical information for those planning to reside in France

453   Italian language— Dictionaries

Cassell's Italian dictionary; Italian-English, English-Italian; compiled by Piero Rebora, with the assistance of Francis M. Guercio and Arthur L. Hayward. Wiley 2002 xxi, 1128p thumb-indexed $24.95   **453**
ISBN 0-02-522540-5
First published 1958 in the United Kingdom with title: Cassell's Italian-English, English-Italian dictionary. Previous United States editions published by Funk & Wagnalls
"A general dictionary of the Italian language as currently written and spoken." Ref Sources for Small & Medium-sized Libr. 5th edition

463 Spanish language— Dictionaries

The **American** Heritage Spanish dictionary; Spanish/English, inglés/español. 2nd ed. Houghton Mifflin 2001 xxx, 1103p $26 **463**

1. Spanish language—Dictionaries
ISBN 0-618-12770-4   LC 2001-24524
Also available The Concise American Heritage Spanish dictionary, 2nd edition published 2001

"With an emphasis on American English and Latin American Spanish, . . . this bilingual dictionary includes new technological, scientific, and business terms. Speakers of all the Americas will appreciate the different meanings of more than 120,000 words, presented in an easy-to-understand design. Notes on grammar usage are a plus." Booklist

Cassell's Spanish-English, English-Spanish dictionary; completely revised by Anthony Gooch, Angel Garcia de Paredes. Wiley 2002 xxv, 1109p $22.95 **463**
ISBN 0-02-522910-9
Also available in a concise edition for $13 (ISBN 0-02-522660-6)

Previously published in 1978 by Macmillan

This dictionary emphasizes the Spanish of Latin America, and includes both classical and literary Spanish as well as the language of the modern Spanish-speaking world

The **Concise** American Heritage Spanish dictionary. 2nd ed. Houghton Mifflin 2001 xxiv, 616p $14 **463**
1. Spanish language—Dictionaries
ISBN 0-618-11769-5   LC 00-66461
"This bilingual dictionary includes more than 70,000 words and phrases. The emphasis on American English and Latin American Spanish as well as the informative guides and tables will assist students of either language." Booklist

Gran diccionario español-inglés. English-Spanish dictionary; dirigido y realizado por Ramón García-Pelayo y Gross; con la colaboración de Micheline Durand [et al.] unabridged ed. Larousse (Paris) 1994 various paging maps $55 **463**
1. Spanish language—Dictionaries
ISBN 2-03-420201-5
New edition of Gran diccionario moderno: español/inglés, published 1984
This dictionary includes slang, acronyms, abbreviations, and geographical names. Terms reflect recent advances in such areas as information technology, telecommunications, economics, medicine and biology. A full-color bilingual atlas is included

Larousse diccionario compact: español inglés, inglés español. [New & rev ed] Larousse (Paris) 2002 various paging il maps $21.95; pa $11.95 **463**
1. Spanish language—Dictionaries
ISBN 2-03-542018-0; 2-03-542017-2 (pa)
LC 2003-275808
First published 1993 with title: Larousse diccionario manual: español-inglés, inglés-español. Variant title: Larousse concise dictionary, Spanish-English, English-Spanish

This edition includes over 90,000 words and phrases, 120,000 translations, updated vocabulary in all subject areas, idioms, abbreviations, acronyms, and proper nouns. A supplement on life and culture in Latin America is also provided

Larousse English-Spanish Spanish-English dictionary. new ed. Larousse (Paris) 1996 xxiii, 665, xxii, 717p $32.95 **463**
1. Spanish language—Dictionaries
ISBN 2-03-420281-3
General editor: Elvira D. Moragas
With over 160,000 references and 260,000 translations this dictionary covers general, professional and literary vocabulary. Abbreviations, acronyms and proper nouns are included. Contains special sections on language usage arranged alphabetically in main dictionary text

The **Oxford** Spanish dictionary; Spanish-English/English-Spanish; chief editors, Beatriz Galimberti Jarman, Roy Russell; edited by Carol Styles Carvajal, Jane Horwood. 3rd ed. Oxford Univ. Press 2003 xlviii, 1977p + 1 computer laser optical disc $49.95 **463**
1. Spanish language—Dictionaries
ISBN 0-19-860475-0   LC 2003-272816
First published 1994
Title page in English and Spanish
This dictionary contains over 300,000 words and phrases, 500,000 translations and "covers over 24 varieties of Spanish as it is written and spoken throughout the Spanish-speaking world. . . . Special entries on life and culture explain the differences between institutions, administrative systems, educational systems, and general life in the Spanish and English-speaking worlds, offering vital background to the language." Publisher's note

Random House Latin-American Spanish dictionary; [edited by] David L. Gold. 2nd ed, revised and updated by Kathleen O'Connor. Random House 1999 680p hardcover o.p. paperback available $12.95 **463**
ISBN 0-375-70736-0 (pa)   LC 96-27274
First published 1997
This dictionary has over 10,000 entries and it includes vocabulary and usage unique to Latin America, Central America, Mexico, Argentina, Chile, and Cuba

The **University** of Chicago Spanish dictionary; Spanish-English, English-Spanish; originally compiled by Carlos Castillo and Otto F. Bond. 5th ed David Pharies, editor in chief; María Irene Moyna, associate editor [et al.] University of Chicago Press 2002 586p $27.50; pa $11
463

1. Spanish language—Dictionaries
ISBN 0-226-66688-3; 0-226-66689-1 (pa)
LC 2002-17358

First published 1948

This dictionary "includes 80,000 entries, divided into two sections, each with a list of abbreviations, guide to pronunciation, and notes on grammar. The brief definitions include pronunciation (English), grammatical category, and illustrative phrases. . . . The dictionary is well organized and easy to read. . . . It aims to provide a core, up-to-date vocabulary, one that is concise yet comprehensive enough to satisfy both beginners and advanced speakers. Its scope is broad, including new terms in science, technology, medicine, business, politics, and popular culture." Am Ref Books Annu, 2003

473   Latin language—Dictionaries

Oxford Latin dictionary; edited by P. G. W. Glare. Oxford Univ. Press 1982 xxiii, 2126p $295
473
1. Latin language—Dictionaries
ISBN 0-19-864224-5
LC 82-8162

"Authorized in 1931 and begun two years later, [this dictionary] appeared in eight fascicles published between 1968 and 1982. These have been combined in a single volume." Wilson Libr Bull

This dictionary looks at the meaning and development of more than 40,000 classical Latin words and phrases

Stone, Jon R., 1959-
Latin for the illiterati; exorcizing the ghosts of a dead language. Routledge 1996 201p $80; pa $18.95
473
1. Latin language—Dictionaries
ISBN 0-415-91774-3; 0-415-91775-1 (pa)
LC 95-47985

"Here are nearly 6,000 words, phrases, and abbreviations culled from the arts, music, law, philosophy, theology, medicine, and the works of ancient writers. Stone has also included a section of handy lists: the Seven Hills of Rome, countries and regions, colors, and, of course, Roman numerals, both cardinal and ordinal. . . . A ready-reference dream come true." Am Libr

More Latin for the illiterati; exorcizing the ghosts of a dead language. Routledge 1999 201p $75; pa $17.95
473
1. Latin language—Dictionaries
ISBN 0-415-92210-0; 0-415-92211-9 (pa)
LC 98-43820

This dictionary focuses on "three areas: medicine, law, and religion. Translations are brief and literal. The dictionary concludes with some of the same information given in *Latin for the Illiterati* as well as newer miscellaneous information, including Latin selections (with English translations) from the Roman Catholic liturgy." Libr J

Includes bibliographical references

483   Classical Greek language— Dictionaries

Liddell, Henry George, 1811-1898
A Greek-English lexicon; compiled by Henry George Liddell and Robert Scott; revised and augmented throughout by Sir Henry Stuart Jones, with the assistance of Roderick McKenzie, and with the cooperation of many scholars. Clarendon Press; Oxford Univ. Press 1996 xlv, 2042, xxxi, 320p $145
483
1. Greek language—Dictionaries
ISBN 0-19-864226-1
LC 95-32369

First edition 1843; this is a reprint of the 9th edition (1925-1940) with a new supplement edited by P. G. W. Glare

Originally issued in ten parts. Frequently reprinted. Preliminary leaves include: List of authors and works; Epigraphical publications; Papyrological publications; Periodicals; General list of abbreviations. Addenda and corrigenda

"The standard Greek and English lexicon, covering the language to about 600 A.D., omitting Patristic and Byzantine Greek." Ref Sources for Small & Medium-sized Libr. 6th edition

491   East Indo-European and Celtic languages

The **Oxford** Hindi-English dictionary; edited by R.S. McGregor. Oxford Univ. Press 1993 xx, 1083p hardcover o.p. paperback available $30
491
1. Hindi language—Dictionaries
ISBN 0-19-864339-X (pa)
LC 92-42314

A dictionary of historical Hindi together with current colloquial and literary vocabulary

Includes bibliographical references

491.7   East Slavic languages. Russian

The **Concise** Oxford Russian dictionary; Russian-English, edited by Marcus Wheeler and Boris Unbegaun; English-Russian, edited by Paul Falla; thematic wordfinder prepared by David Taylor; guide to exploring the Internet prepared by Geoffrey Rolfe. Rev ed. Oxford Univ. Press 1998 1007p $35
491.7
1. Russian language—Dictionaries
ISBN 0-19-860152-2
LC 98-33740

"This dictionary provides coverage of 120,000 words and phrases, and over 190,000 translations. It includes . . . treatment of contemporary Russian and English, including *amniocentesis, global warming, information superhighway, multimedia, streetwise,* and *time-share.* There is extra in-text grammatical information; extended constructions, complementation, and difficult points of grammar. It records Russian as it is used today, with special emphasis on modern idioms and colloquial usage, highlighted by numerous illustrative examples. . . . A new guide to email and the Internet [is also included]." Publisher's note

The **Oxford** Russian dictionary; Russian-English, edited by Marcus Wheeler and Boris Unbegaun; English-Russian, edited by Paul Falla; revised and updated by Della Thompson. 3rd ed. Oxford Univ. Press 2000 xxi, 1293p $60 **491.7**
1. Russian language—Dictionaries
ISBN 0-19-860160-3 LC 00-708887
First published 1972 with title: The Oxford Russian-English dictionary

This dictionary "includes over 185,000 words and phrases and 290,000 translations. The dictionary provides . . . coverage of regional Russian, British, and American dialects as well as of modern idioms and colloquial usage, with numerous illustrative examples. It also includes all common abbreviations and acronyms, such as DTP, ROM, AIDS, and others." Publisher's note

492 Afro-Asiatic languages. Semitic languages

The **Oxford** English-Arabic dictionary of current usage; edited by N. S. Doniach. Oxford Univ. Press 1972 1392p $95 **492**
1. Arabic language—Dictionaries
ISBN 0-19-864312-8

"Intended both for the English-speaking students of Arabic and for Arabic-speaking students of English. Includes formal literary English, colloquial and slang usage, with the closest Arabic equivalent at the same level of usage." Guide to Ref Books. 11th edition

492.4 Hebrew language

Baltsan, Hayim
Webster's New World Hebrew dictionary; Hebrew/English, English/Hebrew. Prentice-Hall 1992 xxx, 827p o.p.; Macmillan paperback available $18 **492.4**
1. Hebrew language—Dictionaries
ISBN 0-671-88991-5 (pa) LC 91-32079
"The work includes two main sequences with a total of 60,000 entries: a Hebrew-English section in which headwords or proper names are Romanized, and an English-Hebrew section in which definitions are given in Roman characters. . . . Besides the guide to the dictionary, there is a 13-page introduction to Hebrew that contains basic information about the alphabet and the structure of the language." Am Ref Books Annu, 1993

The **Oxford** English-Hebrew dictionary; {published} in collaboration with the Oxford Centre for Hebrew and Jewish Studies. Oxford Univ. Press 1996 1091p hardcover o.p. paperback available $29.95 **492.4**
1. Hebrew language—Dictionaries
ISBN 0-19-860172-7 (pa) LC 95-21451
In this dictionary, containing more than 50,000 entries, the "goal of the editors was to describe the language as it is actually used, and thus they list only words currently attested to in usage, including non-Semitic loan words. The editors did not intend the work to be fully comprehensive, but rather sought to furnish the most

common words that would be most likely needed by an average user—slang, idioms and phrases, and specialized terminology." Recommended Ref Books for Small & Medium-sized Libr & Media Cent, 1997

Zilkha, Avraham
Modern English-Hebrew dictionary. Yale Univ. Press 2002 457p (Yale language series) $55; pa $30 **492.4**
1. Hebrew language—Dictionaries
ISBN 0-300-09004-8; 0-300-09005-6 (pa) LC 2001-26830
This dictionary includes 30,000 entries, with listings for translating words with multiple meanings, newly coined and slang words, common idioms, vocalization of Hebrew words, acronyms, and gender identification and plural forms of irregular nouns

493 Non-Semitic Afro-Asiatic languages

Roth, Ann Macy, 1954-
Hieroglyphs without mystery; an introduction to ancient Egyptian writing; translated and adapted for English-speaking readers by Ann Macy Roth. University of Tex. Press 1992 121p il hardcover o.p. paperback available $17.95 **493**
1. Egyptian language 2. Hieroglyphics
ISBN 0-292-79804-0 (pa) LC 91-47600
"Written for ordinary people with no special language skills, the book quickly demonstrates that hieroglyphic writing can be read, once a few simple principles are understood." Univ Press Books for Public and Second Sch Libr
Includes bibliographical references

495.1 Chinese language

The **Oxford** starter Chinese dictionary; edited by Boping Yuan and Sally K. Church. Oxford Univ. Press 2000 xxix, 450p pa $15.95 **495.1**
1. Chinese language—Dictionaries
ISBN 0-19-860258-8 LC 2001-21702
This "dictionary features color headwords and translations . . . and warning symbols show potential problem areas. It includes thousands of example phrases drawn from real-life situations and full romanization of the Chinese text with Chinese script following in simplified characters. It also offers a guide on how to write Chinese characters and provides full guidance on the pronunciation of Mandarin Chinese." Publisher's note

495.6 Japanese language

Basic Japanese-English dictionary; Kiso Nihongo gakushū jiten; [by] The Japan Foundation. Paperback ed. Oxford Univ. Press 1993 958p pa $18.95 **495.6**
1. Japanese language—Dictionaries
ISBN 0-19-864328-4 LC 92-38748
First published 1986 in Japan; 1989 by Oxford University Press

Basic Japanese-English dictionary—*Continued*

"This desk dictionary provides basic vocabulary for the daily use of those learning Japanese. The nearly 2,900 entries are written in Roman letters followed by Kanji and/or Kana. Example sentences are included." Guide to Ref Books. 11th edition

The **Oxford-Duden** pictorial English-Japanese dictionary. Oxford Univ. Press 1983 864p il hardcover o.p. paperback available $25 **495.6**

1. Japanese language—Dictionaries 2. Picture dictionaries

ISBN 0-19-860119-0 (pa) LC 83-163303

"This topically arranged picture dictionary will be of value chiefly to Japanese speakers engaged in the conversion of English into Japanese (though, with some limitations, thanks to its English and Japanese indexes, it can serve as a regular bilingual dictionary as well). . . . Needless to say, the entries are largely nouns (or nominal phrases). Within the narrow domain of its usability, a fine piece of lexicography." Libr J

495.9 Miscellaneous languages of Southeast Asia

Nguyen, Dinh Hoa, 1924-

NTC's Vietnamese-English dictionary. NTC Pub. Group 1995 728p $24.95; pa $17.95 **495.9**

1. Vietnamese language—Dictionaries

ISBN 0-8442-8356-8; 0-8442-8357-6 (pa)

LC 95-18670

First published 1955 with title: Vietnamese-English vocabulary

This work "contains approximately 50,000 Vietnamese words, morphemes, compound words, and phrases. . . . Entries are accompanied by their English equivalents and, where appropriate, synonyms, antonyms, and usage are provided. Also included are a guide to pronunciation and a 50-page supplement of new Vietnamese words." Recommended Ref Books for Small & Medium-sized Libr & Media Cent, 1997

499 Austronesian & other languages

Pukui, Mary Kawena, 1895-1986

Hawaiian dictionary; Hawaiian-English, English-Hawaiian; [by] Mary Kawena Pukui, Samuel H. Elbert. rev & enl ed. University of Hawaii Press 1986 xxvi, 572p $32.95 **499**

1. Hawaiian language—Dictionaries

ISBN 0-8248-0703-0 LC 85-24583

Originally published in two separate parts in 1957 and 1964. First combined edition published 1971

"The Hawaiian-English part now comprises 29,000 entries. It is the most comprehensive and up-to-date dictionary for the language." Guide to Ref Books. 11th edition

Includes bibliographical references

500 NATURAL SCIENCES & MATHEMATICS

The **Best** American science and nature writing. Houghton Mifflin $27.50; pa $13 **500**

1. Science 2. Nature

Annual. First published 2000

Editors vary

The "essays collected here were chosen not only for their compelling subject matter—which ranges from camels and toads to sex and evolution, AIDS, smallpox, computers, and string theory—but for their emphasis on reflection rather than mere information." Booklist [review of 2000 annual]

The **Best** American science writing. Ecco Press $27.50; pa $14 **500**

1. Science

Annual. First published 2000

Editors vary

A "collection of accessible scientific papers, science-related personal essays and journalistic prose about evolutionary biology, medicine, paleoanthropology, particle physics and more." Publ Wkly [review of 2000 annual]

Biddle, Wayne

A field guide to the invisible. Holt & Co. 1998 185p il $23 **500**

1. Science

ISBN 0-8050-5069-8 LC 97-39178

This book "explains 58 subjects that are invisible or tiny. Sixteen gases are discussed, 12 types of radiation, some chemical and allergenic air pollutants, a few lifeforms and odors, and even God, thoughts, and an abstract concept such as zeitgeist. Most of the topics relate to health and the environment." Sci Books Films

This "offers a well-researched yet enjoyably irreverent look at the 'parallel world' that 'we inhabit simultaneously with the one before our very eyes.'" N Y Times Book Rev

Includes bibliographical references

Bronowski, Jacob, 1908-1974

Science and human values; revised edition with a new dialogue, The abacus and the rose. Harper & Row 1965 119p il hardcover o.p. paperback available $12 **500**

1. Science

ISBN 0-06-097281-5 (pa)

First published 1958 by Messner

Contains the following three essays, which were first given as lectures at the Massachusetts Institute of Technology in 1953: The creative mind; The habit of truth; The sense of human dignity. The abacus and the rose was originally broadcast by the BBC Third Programme in 1962

The dialogue "discusses the theme that 'science is as integral a part of the culture of our age as the arts are.'" Sci Am

Bryson, Bill

A short history of nearly everything. Broadway Bks. 2003 544p $27.50 **500**

1. Science

ISBN 0-7679-0817-1 LC 2003-46006

Also available Random House large print edition

Bryson, Bill—*Continued*

In presenting this history of science, Bryson's "interest is not simply to discover what we know but to find out how we know it. How do we know what is in the center of the earth, thousands of miles beneath the surface? How can we know the extent and the composition of the universe, or what a black hole is? How can we know where the continents were 600 million years ago?" Publisher's note

"Neither oversimplified nor overstuffed, this exceptionally skillful tour of the physical world covers the basic principles and still has room for profiles of some of the more engaging scientists." N Y Times Book Rev

Includes bibliographical references

Clarke, Arthur C., 1917-

Greetings, carbon-based bipeds! collected essays, 1934-1998; edited by Ian T. Macauley. St. Martin's Press 1999 558p hardcover o.p. paperback available $16.95

500

1. Science 2. Technology
ISBN 0-312-26745-2 (pa)   LC 99-22074

These essays "cover a range of science topics—especially space exploration. Arranged chronologically with an introduction by Clarke for each decade, they provide a kind of eyewitness history of how the scientific community's dreams and hopes changed over the course of the 20th century." Libr J

Includes bibliographical references

Eiseley, Loren C., 1907-1977

The unexpected universe. Harcourt Brace & World 1969 239p hardcover o.p. paperback available $14   **500**

1. Natural history 2. Science
ISBN 0-15-692850-7 (pa)

This volume contains personal interpretative meditations on mankind's relationship to nature

Includes bibliographical references

Feynman, Richard Phillips

The meaning of it all; thoughts of a citizen scientist; [by] Richard P. Feynman. Addison-Wesley 1998 133p o.p.; Perseus Bks. paperback available $15   **500**

1. Science 2. Religion and science
ISBN 0-7382-0166-9 (pa)   LC 97-48250

"Originally delivered as a three-part lecture series at the University of Washington in 1963, this collection touches on such far-ranging topics as the existence or nonexistence of God; the Constitution; and UFOs. . . . These memorable lectures confirm that Feynman's gift of insight extended from the subatomic world to the cosmic, and to the very human as well." Publ Wkly

The pleasure of finding things out; the best short works of Richard P. Feynman; by Richard P. Feynman; edited by Jeffrey Robbins; foreword by Freeman Dyson. Perseus Bks. 1999 270p hardcover o.p. paperback available $15.95   **500**

1. Science
ISBN 0-7382-0349-1 (pa)   LC 99-64775

These lectures and interviews are "expositions about [Feynman's] life, about technical topics in computing and physics, and about science's general place in society." Booklist

Gardner, Martin, 1914-

Did Adam and Eve have navels? discourses on reflexology, numerology, urine therapy and other dubious subjects. Norton 2000 333p il hardcover o.p. paperback available $15.95

500

1. Science
ISBN 0-393-32238-6 (pa)   LC 00-34870

This is a collection of the author's pieces culled from the *Skeptical Inquirer.* Gardner "gives succinct and amusing critiques of a number of the fallacies that abound in alternative medicine (including the very peculiar urine-therapy treatment) and many other 'dubious subjects.'" Libr J

Includes bibliographical references

On the wild side. Prometheus Bks. 1992 257p il $32   **500**

1. Science
ISBN 0-87975-713-2   LC 91-43151

"This is a collection of 32 reviews and essays. . . . All deal with one aspect or another of pseudoscience. . . . Gardner is a witty and good-humored antidote to the occult, psychic, New Age trash we are inundated with." Sci Books Films

Includes bibliographical references

Gribbin, John R.

Almost everyone's guide to science; the universe, life and everything; [by] John Gribbin with Mary Gribbin. Yale Univ. Press 1999 232p $30; pa $11.95   **500**

1. Science
ISBN 0-300-08101-4; 0-300-08460-9 (pa)

LC 99-26755

First published 1998 in the United Kingdom

In this "general guide to science for the layperson . . . Gribbin combines biographies and history, on the one hand, with the major theories in science, on the other. . . . The text is clear, is based on solid research, and clearly reflects a lifetime love for science." Sci Books Films

Includes bibliographical references

The **Handy** science answer book; compiled by the Science and Technology Department of the Carnegie Library of Pittsburgh; edited by James E. Bobick and Naomi E. Balaban. Centennial ed. Visible Ink Press 2003 660p pa $21.95   **500**

1. Science 2. Technology
ISBN 1-57859-140-6   LC 2002-15562

First published 1994

"The text is divided into various subject areas including physics and chemistry, space, earth, climate and weather, minerals and other materials, energy, technology, and environment, gathering answers to reference questions. . . . A comprehensive index . . . makes the material accessible and easy to find. Pages are full of fascinating tidbits, complemented by illustrations, photos, charts, graphs, and maps. . . . A librarian will want a copy of this book behind the desk for ready reference, but students will want a copy for themselves to peruse time and again just for fun." Voice Youth Advocates

Hazen, Robert M., 1948-

Science matters: achieving scientific literacy; [by] Robert M. Hazen and James Trefil. Doubleday 1991 294p il hardcover o.p. paperback available $12.95 **500**

1. Science
ISBN 0-385-26108-X (pa)   LC 90-3786

"This book attempts to acquaint the educated (or mis-educated) layperson with the major concepts of modern science. . . . Although many concepts are, perforce, oversimplified, offering the reader only a superficial understanding of some of them, this book is a step in the right direction." Libr J

Includes bibliographical references

Highfield, Roger

The science of Harry Potter; how magic really works. Viking 2002 xxii, 322p $23.95 **500**

1. Rowling, J. K.—Characters—Harry Potter 2. Science 3. Magic
ISBN 0-670-03153-4   LC 2002-28878

The author "takes on J.K. Rowling's Harry Potter series 'to show how many elements of her books can be found in and explained by modern science.'" Publ Wkly

"Fans of such science popularizers as Gould and Asimov will certainly get a kick out of Highfield's utterly fascinating take on the subject." Booklist

Includes bibliographical references

Ingram, Jay

The barmaid's brain and other strange tales from science. Freeman, W.H. 2000 271p il o.p.; Holt & Co. paperback available $15 **500**

1. Science
ISBN 0-7167-4702-2 (pa)   LC 00-55158

First published 1998 in Canada

A collection of essays about such topics as "the nature of laughter; perpetual-motion machines; optical illusions . . . the phenomenon of simultaneous discovery; and a possible scientific explanation for the curious behavior that provoked the Salem witch trials. Ingram is an accomplished writer . . . and fans of science books that spotlight the offbeat, the unusual, and the colorful will flock to this title." Booklist

Includes bibliographical references

Maddox, John Royden, 1925-

What remains to be discovered; mapping the secrets of the universe, the origins of life, and the future of the human race; [by] John Maddox. Kessler Bks. 1998 434p $26 **500**

1. Science
ISBN 0-684-82292-X   LC 98-29137

Also available in paperback from Simon & Schuster

The author reflects "on the nature of science, both its successes and its challenges. . . . By focusing on some of the 'big' fields of science—cosmology, quantum mechanics, cell biology, genetics, evolution and neuroscience, for example—he has crafted a primer worthy of study. But this is not an introduction for the uninitiated." Publ Wkly

Includes bibliographical references

Marshall, I. N.

Who's afraid of Schrödinger's cat? all the new science ideas you need to keep up with the new thinking; [by] Ian Marshall & Danah Zohar, with contributions by F. David Peat. Morrow 1997 xxx, 402p map hardcover o.p. paperback available $15 **500**

1. Science
ISBN 0-688-16107-3 (pa)   LC 96-20769

This "is an alphabetically organized, heavily cross-listed compendium of brief descriptions of new areas of science, such as 'Artificial Intelligence,' 'The Edge of Chaos,' 'Mesons' and 'Transpersonal Psychology.' While the 201 entries are weighted toward new areas of physics, the book does justice to every area of natural and social science." Sci Books Films

Park, Robert L.

Voodoo science; the road from foolishness to fraud. Oxford Univ. Press 2000 230p hardcover o.p. paperback available $14.95 **500**

1. Science 2. Fraud
ISBN 0-19-860443-2 (pa)   LC 99-40911

The author "aims to expose various beliefs and schemes put forth in the popular press and other places as scientifically real and factual. . . . [He] turns a critical eye on cold fusion, magnet therapy, homeopathy, perpetual motion, and other recent examples of fringe science. . . . Park's book should be required reading for all science writers, journalists, and politicians." Libr J

Pohl, Frederik, 1919-

Chasing science; science as a spectator sport. TOR Bks. 2000 251p $23.95; pa $14.95 **500**

1. Science
ISBN 0-312-86711-5; 0-7653-0829-0 (pa)
                LC 00-57768

In order to witness science in action, Pohl traveled to a variety of sites, museums, laboratories, and observatories around the world. This is an account of his experiences and impressions

Ray, C. Claiborne

The New York Times second book of science questions and answers; 225 new, intriguing, and just plain bizarre inquiries into everyday scientific mysteries; drawings by Victoria Roberts; edited by Henry Fountain. Anchor Bks. (NY) 2003 228p il pa $13 **500**

1. Science
ISBN 0-385-72258-3   LC 2002-26192

Also available The New York Times book of science questions and answers published 1997 pa $15 (ISBN 0-385-48660-X)

These selections from the author's weekly column in the science section of The New York Times answer such questions as "What would kill you if you fell into a black hole? Once people finally get to Mars, how will they get back? What makes the holes in Swiss cheese?" Publisher's note

"This eclectic volume of 228 questions with 200-word answers entices readers' interest in science. . . . There is no index and not much structure in this volume, but its charm and interest make up for its informality." Sci Books Films

Includes bibliographical references

Sagan, Carl, 1934-1996

Billions and billions; thoughts on life and death at the brink of the millennium. Random House 1997 241p hardcover o.p. paperback available $14.95 **500**

1. Science

ISBN 0-345-37918-7 (pa)   LC 96-52730

This collection of essays covers such topics as: "the invention of chess, life on Mars, global warming, abortion, international affairs, the nature of government, and the meaning of morality. Writing with clarity and an understanding of human nature, Sagan offers hope for humanity's future." Libr J

Includes bibliographical references

Broca's brain; reflections on the romance of science. Random House 1979 347p hardcover o.p. paperback available $6.99 **500**

1. Science 2. Philosophy

ISBN 0-345-33689-5 (pa)   LC 78-21810

In this volume Sagan considers the following: "the quest for extraterrestrial life, popular science, and religious questions, as well as numerous concerns more immediate to his own specialty, astronomy." Libr J

The author "is a lucid, logical writer with a gift for explaining science to the layman and infecting the reader with his own boundless enthusiasm and curiosity." Natl Rev

Includes bibliographical references

Science and technology desk reference; 1,700 answers to frequently-asked or difficult-to-answer questions; [by] the Carnegie Library of Pittsburgh, Science and Technology Department. Gale Res. 1996 xxx, 795p il $90 **500**

1. Science 2. Technology

ISBN 0-8103-9176-7   LC 96-26601

First published 1993 with subtitle: 1,500 answers to frequently-asked or difficult-to-answer questions

This work "consists of approximately 1,500 questions and answers arranged within broad subject chapters. Entries include: an entry number; the question and answer (some with a table or illustration), and up to three source citations with full bibliographic data for follow-up research. Approximately 100 line drawings and charts help illustrate selected answers. Subjects covered include the animal world, astronomy, chemistry, the earth, the environment, health and medicine." Publisher's note

The **Scientific** American science desk reference. Wiley 1999 690p il $39.95 **500**

1. Science

ISBN 0-471-35675-1   LC 99-32007

This reference "covers the physical, biological/health, and applied sciences. Fifteen chapters each provide a definition of scope, then a topical arrangement, with headings and subheadings in boldface type. . . . Each chapter concludes with a highly effective pattern: chronology, biographies, glossary, and brief-entry bibliography." Choice

For a fuller review see: Booklist, March 1, 2000

Wynn, Charles M.

The five biggest ideas in science; [by] Charles M. Wynn and Arthur W. Wiggins; with cartoon commentary by Sidney Harris. Wiley 1997 200p il maps pa $15.95 **500**

1. Science

ISBN 0-471-13812-6   LC 96-27469

Presents five basic scientific hypotheses: the atomic model, the periodic law, the big bang theory, plate tectonics, and evolution

"Each 'Big Idea' is thoroughly described. . . . In explaining the thinking that led to each 'Big Idea,' the authors clearly outline the scientific method and demystify the process." Libr J

Includes bibliographical references

500.2   Physical sciences

Encyclopedia of earth and physical sciences. Marshall Cavendish 1998 11v set $459.95 **500.2**

1. Earth sciences—Encyclopedias 2. Physical sciences—Encyclopedias

ISBN 0-7614-0551-8   LC 96-49660

Contents: Absolute zero-Calendars; Cambrian period-Crystals and crystallography; Currents, oceanic-Extinctions; Faults-Hydrocarbons; Hydrogen-Marine exploration; Mariner probes-Novas and supernovas; Nuclear physics-Plate tectonics; Platinum metals-Silicon; Silurian period-Time; Time travel-Zinc

500.5   Space sciences

Space sciences; Pat Dasch, editor in chief. Macmillan Ref. USA 2002 4v il set $395 **500.5**

1. Space sciences

ISBN 0-02-865546-X   LC 2002-1707

"The Macmillan science library." On cover

Contents: v1 Space business; v2 Planetary science and astronomy; v3 Humans in space; v4 Our future in space

"The entries in each volume are in alphabetical order and range from a single paragraph to several pages in length, with most being one or two pages long. The front and back matter are the same in each volume and include a few pages of reference tables such as conversion charts, time lines of milestones in space history and human achievements in space, a list of contributors, a table of contents for the set, and a glossary." Booklist

"A comprehensive and usable survey of space exploration, this marvelous encyclopedia works equally well as a multivolume set and as four standalone volumes. . . . The photographs are excellent." Libr J

501   Science—Philosophy and theory

Dawkins, Richard, 1941-

Unweaving the rainbow; science, delusion, and the appetite for wonder. Houghton Mifflin 1998 336p $26; pa $14   **501**

1. Science—Philosophy

ISBN 0-395-88382-2; 0-618-05673-4 (pa)

        LC 98-40879

Dawkins "argues that scientific fact is both intellectually and esthetically more pleasing than pseudoscientific fantasy." N Y Times Book Rev

Dawkins is a "witty popularizer, whether he is offering a crash course in DNA fingerprinting, explaining the origins of 'mad cow disease' in weird proteins that spread like self-replicating viruses or discussing male birdsong as an auditory aphrodisiac for female birds." Publ Wkly

Includes bibliographical references

Morris, Richard, 1939-

The big questions; probing the promise and limits of science. Times Bks. 2002 272p $26   **501**

1. Science—Philosophy

ISBN 0-8050-7092-3   LC 2001-57362

The author discusses the following questions: "What is time? Does the future already exist? Is there a God? Surveying the latest scientific theories for the answers to those questions, Morris is quite effective in describing quantum mechanics, superstring theory, cosmology, genetics, and cognitive research." Booklist

Includes bibliographical references

502   Science—Miscellany

Ochoa, George

The Wilson chronology of science and technology; [by] George Ochoa and Melinda Corey. Wilson, H.W. 1997 440p $100   **502**

1. Science—History 2. Technology—History

ISBN 0-8242-0933-8   LC 97-22060

This chronology begins in 2,500,000 B.C. and continues into 1997. "Within each year, entries are arranged alphabetically according to one of 13 categories: archaeology; astronomy, space science, and space exploration; biology, biochemistry, agriculture, and ecology; chemistry; earth sciences (geology, oceanography, meteorology) and earth exploration; mathematics; medicine; miscellaneous; paleontology; physics; psychology, neuroscience, and artificial intelligence; social sciences (anthropology, sociology, economics, political science) and linguistics; and technology and engineering." Publisher's note

Includes bibliographical references

502.8   Science—Auxiliary techniques and procedures; apparatus, equipment, materials

Instruments of science; an historical encyclopedia; editors, Robert Bud, Deborah Jean Warner; associate editor, Stephen Johnston; managing editor, Betsy Bahr Peterson; picture editor, Simon Chaplin. Science Mus. 1998 xxv, 709p il (Garland encyclopedias in the history of science) $175   **502.8**

1. Scientific apparatus and instruments—Encyclopedias

ISBN 0-8153-1561-9   LC 97-15296

This "encyclopedia presents 325 historically significant scientific instruments from antiquity to the present. Instruments used for testing and monitoring in addition to those used for research are studied, including laboratory organisms such as *E coli*. Each of the signed entries explains how the instrument works and how it is used, as well as tracing its invention, development, and distribution. . . . Beautiful illustrations accompany many of the entries." Am Libr

503   Science—Encyclopedias and dictionaries

Academic Press dictionary of science and technology; edited by Christopher Morris. Academic Press 1992 xxxii, 2432p il $99.95   **503**

1. Science—Dictionaries 2. Technology—Dictionaries

ISBN 0-12-200400-0   LC 90-29032

"With over 133,000 entries, this title provides current, concise definitions of the specialized vocabulary used in 124 designated fields from acoustical engineering to zoology. . . . This authoritative, attractive dictionary will be useful to anyone seeking to understand the language of science and technology." Am Libr

Bunch, Bryan H.

The Penguin desk encyclopedia of science and mathematics; [by] Bryan Bunch and Jennie Tesar. Penguin Ref. 2000 696p il hardcover o.p. paperback available $25   **503**

1. Science—Encyclopedias 2. Mathematics—Encyclopedias

ISBN 0-14-051429-5 (pa)   LC 00-39970

This reference offers thousands of alphabetically arranged brief entries on scientific and mathematical topics with drawings, tables, cross-references and an exhaustive index

The **Encyclopedia** of science and technology; James S. Trefil, general editor; contributing editors, Harold Morowitz, Paul Ceruzzi. Routledge 2001 554p il maps $50   **503**

1. Science—Encyclopedias 2. Technology—Encyclopedias

ISBN 0-415-93724-8   LC 2001-19983

This reference includes "1000 entries, arranged alphabetically and color-coded to indicate whether the topic is related to life science, physical science, or technology.

The Encyclopedia of science and technology—*Continued*

Accessible to the general reader, the articles range widely. . . . The excellent cross references direct the reader to related articles that cover either more fundamental or more advanced information. . . . A true pleasure to browse and read; highly recommended." Libr J

The **Facts** on File encyclopedia of science. Facts on File 1999 2v il set $137.50 **503**

1. Science—Dictionaries
ISBN 0-8160-4008-7   LC 98-53201

"Over 10,000 terms are defined from all areas of the sciences, including medicine and the applied sciences. A series of feature essays gives more depth to certain topics, ranging from the millennium bug to miners' safety lamps, though most are items of current news interest. The work is remarkably current, with many up-to-date entries (e.g., 'FAQ' and 'browser'); photographs and diagrams enhance the text." Libr J

Gale encyclopedia of science; K. Lee Lerner & Brenda Wilmoth Lerner, editors. 3rd ed. Gale Group 2004 6v il maps set $575 **503**

1. Science—Encyclopedias
ISBN 0-7876-7554-7   LC 2003-15731

First published 1996

Including over 2000 alphabetically arranged entries, this "set covers all major areas of science, engineering, technology, as well as mathematics and the medical and health sciences. Entries typically describe scientific concepts, provide overviews of scientific areas and, in some cases, define terms. Longer entries conclude with a bibliography." Publisher's note

McGraw-Hill concise encyclopedia of science & technology; Sybil P. Parker, editor-in-chief. McGraw-Hill $150 **503**

1. Science—Encyclopedias 2. Technology—Encyclopedias

First published 1984. (5th edition 2003) Periodically revised

A condensed version of the McGraw-Hill encyclopedia of science & technology

"This excellent one-volume science encyclopedia has been created by extracting 'the essential text from each article in the parent work while retaining the same proportionality between subjects.'" Malinowsky. Best Sci & Technol Ref Books for Young People

McGraw-Hill dictionary of scientific and technical terms. 6th ed. McGraw-Hill 2003 2380p il $150 **503**

1. Science—Dictionaries 2. Technology—Dictionaries
ISBN 0-07-042313-X   LC 2002-26436

First published 1974

This dictionary provides "over 100,000 succinct definitions ranging through 102 fields of science, from acoustics to zoology. Many of the definitions contain clear-cut illustrations with labels in the margins of the pages. Phonetics for pronunciation appear at the end of the definition." Sci Books Films

"This continues to be the most comprehensive science and technology dictionary for the student, researcher, and layperson." Booklist

McGraw-Hill encyclopedia of science & technology; an international reference work in twenty volumes including an index. 9th ed. McGraw-Hill 2002 20v il set $2,495 **503**

1. Science—Encyclopedias 2. Technology—Encyclopedias
ISBN 0-07-913665-6   LC 2001-57910

First published 1960 in fifteen volumes

This encyclopedia "contains approximately 7,100 articles on major topics in all categories of science and technology, written for the non-specialist. Each entry begins with general information on the topic. Detailed information follows under headings so the reader can focus on specific areas of interest. All but general survey articles have a bibliography at the end. There is extensive cross-referencing between articles that leads to related topics. Scientists who have been major contributors to their field wrote many articles. The index volume contains a list of contributors, a guide to scientific notation, study guides, a topical index, and an analytical index." Sci Books Films

The **new** encyclopedia of science. 2nd ed. Oxford University Press 2003 9v il set $299 **503**

1. Science—Encyclopedias
ISBN 0-19-521918-X   LC 2003-41937

First published 1995

Contents: v1. Matter and energy by J.O.E. Clark; v2. Animals and plants by J. Bailey and M. Allaby; v3. Chemistry in action by N. Morgan and J.O.E. Clark; v4. Stars and atoms by S. Clark; 5. Earth and other planets by P. Cattermole and S. Clark; v6. Ecology and environment by S. Morgan and M. Allaby; v7. Computing by T. Dodd and M. Allaby; v8. Evolution and genetics by J. Bailey; v9. Reference and set index

"Each volume begins with a 'Knowledge Map' that shows how the pertinent areas of science are interrelated as well as defining the major fields. Next, there is an extensive 'Time Chart' that traces the development of the science through the key discoveries that shaped it. Each volume concludes with its own 'Factfile' offering a wealth of quick information for the casual browser, including data, tables, and statistics chosen for their relevance to the subject. ... It also contains a listing of scientific institutions worldwide, recommended Web sites, and places to visit. ... The text is written for the less well informed reader and should be accessible to most. The layout is bright and appealing. Color photographs and illustrations appear on almost every page. ...Each of these ... volumes is excellent as a stand-alone. The addition of a cumulative index enhances their value as a reference set." Booklist

Van Nostrand's concise encyclopedia of science; Christopher G. De Pree, Alan Axelrod, editors; with a foreword by Glenn D. Considine. Wiley 2003 821p il $40 **503**

1. Science—Encyclopedias 2. Engineering—Encyclopedias
ISBN 0-471-36331-6   LC 2002-34327

Based on the ninth edition of Van Nostrand's scientific encyclopedia

"Written at a level accessible to the general reader, the alphabetically arranged entries range in length from about a sentence to a page. The 5,000 entries cover physics, chemistry, earth sciences, space sciences, life

Van Nostrand's concise encyclopedia of science—*Continued*

sciences, energy, environmental sciences, materials sciences, and information sciences." Booklist

"This encyclopedia is a great resource for quick and short answers to many scientific questions. There are no references, so it is not a good conduit to further information, but if you need a book that will provide concise answers quickly, this is it." Sci Books Films

Van Nostrand's scientific encyclopedia. 9th ed, Glenn D. Considine, editor; Peter H. Kulik, associate editor. Wiley-Interscience 2002 2v il maps set $350   **503**
1. Science—Encyclopedias 2. Engineering—Encyclopedias
ISBN 0-471-33230-5
First published 1938

"Animal life; biosciences; chemistry; earth and atmospheric sciences; energy sources and power technology; mathematics and engineering sciences, medicine, anatomy, and physiology; physics; plant science; space and planetary sciences." Title page

Volti, Rudi

The Facts on File encyclopedia of science, technology, and society. Facts on File 1999 3v il set $247.50   **503**
1. Science—Encyclopedias 2. Technology—Encyclopedias
ISBN 0-8160-3123-1   LC 98-39014

"In 900 alphabetically arranged entries, this title aims to be 'a presentation of the social settings in which science and technology have emerged, been developed, and put to use.' . . . It includes articles on a wide range of topics, such as the origin and chemistry of cheese, the historical development of software, and the rise and fall of drive-in movies." Booklist

505 Science—Serial publications

General science index. Wilson, H.W. service basis   **505**
1. Science—Periodicals—Indexes
ISSN 0162-1963

Also available CD-ROM version and online

First published July 1978. Monthly, except June and December, with quarterly and bound annual cumulations

"Cumulative subject index to English-language science journals covering 150 essential periodicals. Its accessible subject headings, extremely broad coverage, and identification of articles on current topics in widely owned periodicals are helpful for high school and college students and public library patrons alike." Ref Sources for Small and Medium-sized Libr. 6th edition

507.8 Science—Use of apparatus and equipment in study and teaching

Experiment central; understanding scientific principles through projects; John T. Tanacredi & John Loret, general editors. U.X.L 2000 4v set $165   **507.8**
1. Science—Experiments
ISBN 0-7876-2892-1   LC 99-54142

Also available additional two volume set published 2003, designated volume five and six $99 (ISBN 0-7876-7615-2)

Demonstrates scientific concepts by means of experiments, including step-by-step instructions, lists of materials, troubleshooter's guide, and interpretation and explanation of the results

For a review see: Booklist, Oct. 1, 2000

Sheldrake, Rupert

Seven experiments that could change the world; a do-it-yourself guide to revolutionary science. [2nd ed] Park St. Press 2002 303p pa $16.95   **507.8**
1. Science—Experiments
ISBN 0-89281-989-8   LC 2002-728157

First published 1995 by Riverhead Bks.

"Sheldrake questions many tenets of the mechanistic-materialistic orthodoxy governing most science today and proposes certain practical experiments to raise further doubts about it. He presents experiments by which we can determine how some pets know when their owners are coming home, how homing pigeons find their way, how insect colonies operate, how people know that they are being stared at from behind and how phantom limbs sometimes seem to amputees to be still attached. . . . Finally, he offers details of experiments by which even those who are not trained scientists can measure some of these possibly paranormal phenomena. A well-reasoned, accessible and provocative book." Publ Wkly

Includes bibliographical references

508 Natural history

Ackerman, Diane

Cultivating delight; a natural history of my garden. HarperCollins Pubs. 2001 261p hardcover o.p. paperback available $13.95   **508**
1. Natural history 2. Gardens
ISBN 0-06-050536-2 (pa)   LC 2001-16607

Also available G.K. Hall large print edition

Although Ackerman's "book is presented as a gardening journal, with sections on the four seasons, her musings know no bounds and verge on stream-of-consciousness. One typical chapter ranges over topics that include landscape architecture, lawns, fences, autumn colors, childhood memories, the difference between labyrinths and mazes, the history and definition of gardens, and compost, all peppered with quotations from a dozen authors." Libr J

Asma, Stephen T.

Stuffed animals & pickled heads; the culture and evolution of natural history museums. Oxford Univ. Press 2001 302p il $30; pa $16.95   **508**
1. Natural history 2. Museums
ISBN 0-19-513050-2; 0-19-516336-2 (pa)
LC 00-40674
The author discusses the development of natural history museums, beginning with the "'cabinets of curiosities', put together in the 17th century. . . . The cabinets changed when Darwin's theory of evolution became widely accepted in the late 19th century, with less emphasis on the exceptional, more on showing how each species fitted into the supposed scheme of things." Economist
Includes bibliographical references

Darwin, Charles, 1809-1882

The voyage of the Beagle   **508**
1. Beagle Expedition (1831-1836) 2. Natural history 3. South America—Description
Available in paperback from Modern Lib and Penguin Bks.
First published 1839 with title: Journal of researches into the geology and natural history of the various countries visited by H.M.S. Beagle
This journal records the author's five year voyage around the world as a naturalist aboard H.M.S. Beagle. The trip was influential in the formulation of Darwin's theories of evolution. During the journey he collected data on wildlife, geological formations, weather, and local customs

De Villiers, Marq

Sahara: a natural history; [by] Marq de Villiers and Sheila Hirtle. Walker & Co. 2002 326p il maps $28; pa $13   **508**
1. Sahara Desert 2. Natural history—Africa
ISBN 0-8027-1372-6; 0-8027-7678-7 (pa)
LC 2002-71391
This volume includes the Sahara's "history (both natural and human), as well as a look at the complicated ethnology and present-day life of the various tribes (Tauregs, Berbers, Moors, and Tubu) that have adapted to this incredibly harsh climate." Libr J
"Insightful and intelligent, this fascinating book will appeal to anyone with a curiosity about the world's largest desert and the people who inhabit it." Booklist
Includes bibliographical references

Elias, Scott A.

Rocky Mountains. Smithsonian Institution Press 2002 164p il maps (Smithsonian natural history series) $34.95   **508**
1. Natural history—Rocky Mountains
ISBN 1-58834-042-2   LC 2001-57645
The author offers an "overview of the vast mountain system that forms the topographic backbone of North America. . . . [He] treats, in separate chapters, geophysics and geology, fossils, plant life, animals, first peoples, and written history. A brief epilogue states the case for conservation. Some 47 excellent color photos occupy the book's center, and monochromes are scattered throughout." Choice
Includes bibliographical references

Flannery, Tim F. (Tim Fridjof), 1956-

The eternal frontier; an ecological history of North America and its peoples; [by] Tim Flannery. Atlantic Monthly Press 2001 404p il maps $27.50; pa $16   **508**
1. Natural history—North America
ISBN 0-87113-789-5; 0-8021-3888-8 (pa)
LC 2001-18841
This "book explores approximately 65 million years of the ecology of the entire North American continent." Libr J
"This book weaves ecological, cultural, and social history together in a marvelous way." Sci Books Films

Gould, Stephen Jay, 1941-2002

Bully for brontosaurus; reflections in natural history. Norton 1991 540p il hardcover o.p. paperback available $15.95
508
1. Natural history 2. Evolution
ISBN 0-393-30857-X (pa)   LC 91-6916
A collection of essays from the author's monthly columns in Natural History magazine
"These pithy essays focus on evolution and the workings of science. Gould's fans . . . will find these works fascinating, literate, and often challenging—vintage Gould." Libr J

Dinosaur in a haystack; reflections in natural history. Harmony Bks. 1995 480p il hardcover o.p. paperback available $15   **508**
1. Natural history
ISBN 0-517-88824-6 (pa)   LC 95-51333
Analyzed in Essay and general literature index
In this collection the author "relates anecdotes from the history of science and demonstrates their relevance to contemporary scientific disputes and social trends." Libr J
"A discovery awaits in every essay—in every haystack—which solidifies Gould as one of the most eloquent science popularizers writing today." Booklist
Includes bibliographical references

The flamingo's smile; reflections in natural history. Norton 1985 476p il hardcover o.p. paperback available $15.95   **508**
1. Natural history
ISBN 0-393-30375-6 (pa)   LC 85-4916
In this collection "the theme is history, both natural and human. . . . The essays are marked by Gould's usual careful scholarship and erudition and clear and nontechnical language." Sci Books Films
Includes bibliographical references

Leonardo's mountain of clams and the Diet of Worms; essays on natural history. Harmony Bks. 1998 422p il hardcover o.p. paperback available $15   **508**
1. Natural history 2. Evolution
ISBN 0-609-80475-8 (pa)   LC 98-11500
In this collection of essays, Gould "peers less at nature than at scientists' attempts to understand and explain its wonders. Ranging far and wide through the history of science, Gould's sketches in 'humanistic natural history' examine the 'grand false starts in the history of natural science.'" Publ Wkly
"Gould's incomparable style, by turns colloquial, hu-

Gould, Stephen Jay, 1941-2002—*Continued*
morous, ironic and insightful, allows readers to revel in his unabashed and contagious enthusiasm." N Y Times Book Rev

Includes bibliographical references

The lying stones of Marrakesh; penultimate reflections to natural history. Harmony Bks. 2000 372p il hardcover o.p. paperback available $15 **508**
1. Natural history 2. Evolution
ISBN 0-609-80755-2 (pa)   LC 99-36148

In this collection of essays Gould "chronicles the history of paleontology through a biographical lens, then trains his scientific acumen and keen humor on such subjects as Mozart's *Requiem* and the tragic 1911 Triangle Shirt Factory fire." Booklist

Keynes, R. D.
Fossils, finches, and Fuegians; Darwin's adventures and discoveries on the Beagle; by Richard Keynes. Oxford Univ. Press 2003 428p il maps $35   **508**
1. Darwin, Charles, 1809-1882 2. Beagle Expedition (1831-1836) 3. Natural history
ISBN 0-19-516649-3   LC 2002-154176
First published 2002 in the United Kingdom

The author "tracks Darwin's storied 1831-36 voyage of science and surveying on the *Beagle,* quoting unexpurgated tracts not only from Darwin's letters and journals but also from those of the *Beagle's* captain, . . . Robert FitzRoy." Booklist

"Keynes shows readers how his great-grandfather's belief in the immutability of species slowly began to change during his travels. Handsomely illustrated with sketches and paintings made by Darwin and others associated with the *Beagle,* this is an excellent introduction to the events that led 20 years later to *On the Origin of Species.*" Publ Wkly
Includes bibliographical references

Kricher, John C.
Galapagos; [by] John Kricher. Smithsonian Institution Press 2002 221p il $34.95   **508**
1. Natural history—Galapagos Islands 2. Galapagos Islands
ISBN 1-58834-041-4   LC 2001-55134

The author examines the different wildlife of the Galapagos Islands along with the island's geology and natural history. He also discusses the special conservation issues the islands face. This volume features 27 black & white photographs and 50 color photographs
Includes bibliographical references

Lincoln, Roger J.
The Cambridge illustrated dictionary of natural history; [by] R. J. Lincoln and G. A. Boxshall; illustrations by Roberta Smith. Cambridge Univ. Press 1987 413p il hardcover o.p. paperback available $29   **508**
1. Natural history—Dictionaries
ISBN 0-521-39941-6 (pa)   LC 87-8018

This "is principally a dictionary of taxonomic groups down to the level of family, with common names cross-referenced to Latin ones, and frequent illustrations. Technical terms are few, and paleontology is given less attention than current classes of plants, animals, and microorganisms." Recomm Ref Books in Paperback. 2d edition

Matthiessen, Peter
End of the earth; voyaging to Antarctica. National Geographic Soc. 2003 242p il maps $26   **508**
1. Antarctica—Exploration 2. Animals—Antarctica
ISBN 0-7922-5059-1   LC 2003-51254

This account of the author's voyage describes the wildlife he encountered in the region

"Vivid and empathic accounts of the high drama and petty rivalries of Antarctic exploration alternate with Matthiessen's own adventures as he shares his indelible impressions of this cold, white wonderland in the hope that they will inspire readers to appreciate the beauty and bounty of the earth's 'shimmering web of biodiversity' enough to defend and preserve it." Booklist
Includes bibliographical references

Nature encyclopedia. Oxford Univ. Press 2001 472p il maps $65   **508**
1. Natural history—Encyclopedias
ISBN 0-19-521834-5

At head of title: Oxford

"Covers earth sciences, life sciences, flora and fauna, and biographies." Preface

"Besides the general entries, 30 special interest topics are covered in more detail with comprehensive illustrations. The volume also includes an extensive chronology of science, a ready reference to facts and statistics, 10,000 cross-references to the main entries and articles, and a nomenclature relating common to scientific names and classifications. The book will attract a broad band of users, young people to experienced nature lovers." Choice

Nature writing; the tradition in English; edited by Robert Finch and John Elder. Norton 2002 1152p $39.95   **508**
1. Natural history
ISBN 0-393-04966-3   LC 2001-55825
First published 1990 with title: The Norton book of nature writing

This anthology of nature writings from 1789 to 1987 includes such authors as Henry David Thoreau, John Muir, Annie Dillard, and Barry Lopez
Includes bibliographical references

Quammen, David, 1948-
The boilerplate rhino; nature in the eye of the beholder. Scribner 2000 287p hardcover o.p. paperback available $13   **508**
1. Natural history 2. Nature
ISBN 0-7432-0032-2 (pa)   LC 99-56894

In this "collection of David Quammen's columns for Outside magazine, the focus is on man's interaction with nature. Sometimes Quammen interacts with the nature he's writing about; at other times he just thinks about it, reads up and summarizes what he's read." N Y Times Book Rev
Includes bibliographical references

Thapar, Valmik
Land of the tiger; a natural history of the Indian subcontinent. University of Calif. Press 1998 c1997 288p il $34.95   **508**
1. Natural history—South Asia 2. Tigers
ISBN 0-520-21470-6   LC 98-181919

In this illustrated companion volume to a PBS series Thapar "weaves together natural history, folklore, reli-

Thapar, Valmik—*Continued*

gious tradition and personal anecdotes. His tour starts in the Nepal Himalayas, follows sacred rivers of India, touches on oceans, island, and coasts and visits harsh deserts and lush rain forests. Throughout, Thapar urges protection of endangered creatures and ecosystems." Publ Wkly

Wallace, Joseph, 1957-

A gathering of wonders; behind the scenes at the American Museum of Natural History. St. Martin's Press 2000 288p il $24.95; pa $14.95 **508**

1. American Museum of Natural History 2. Natural history

ISBN 0-312-25221-8; 0-312-28039-4 (pa)

LC 00-25481

This describes the American Museum of Natural History "through its most famous, colorful or important scientists and administrators, from the 1880s to the 1970s." Publ Wkly

509 Science—Historical and geographic treatment

Adler, Robert E., 1946-

Science firsts: from the creation of science to the science of creation; [by] Robert Adler. Wiley 2002 232p il $24.95 **509**

1. Science—History 2. Scientists

ISBN 0-471-40174-9 LC 2002-727233

Contents: Thales and natural causation; Anaximander orders the cosmos; Pythagoras numbers the cosmos; Atoms and the void; Aristotle and the birth of biology; Aristarchus, the forgotten Copernicus; Archimedes's physics; Ibn al-Haitham illuminates vision; Copernicus moves the earth; Galileo discovers the skies; Kepler solves the planetary puzzle; Van Leeuwenhoek eplores the microcosm; Newton: gravity and light; A breath of fresh air; Humphry Davy, intoxicated with discovery; Visionaries of the computer; Darwin's great truth; A genius in the garden; Mendeleev charts the elements; In the realm of radioactivity; Planck's quantum leap; Wired on wireless; Rutherford dissects the atom; Einstein: matter, energy, space, and time; Wegener sets the continents adrift; Hubble's expanding universe; Out of Africa; Fermi and the fire of the gods; McClintock's chromosomes; A bit of genius; The dynamic duo of DNA; Echoes of creation; We are not what we seem; Planetary pioneers; After Dolly, life will never be the same

The author tells the engaging and inspiring stories of thirty-five landmark scientific discoveries from the first accurate prediction of an eclipse in 585 B.C. to the cloning of Dolly the sheep

Includes bibliographical references

The **Chronology** of science; from Stonehenge to the human genome project; consulting editor, Lisa Rosner. ABC-CLIO 2002 566p $85 **509**

1. Science—History 2. Scientists

ISBN 1-57607-954-6 LC 2001-7692

The chronologies are "divided into subject areas, including astronomy, biology, chemistry, ecology, mathematics, and physics; 16 feature essays on critical scientific discoveries . . . [are included as well as] biographies of key scientists." Publisher's note

For a review see: Booklist, Sept. 15, 2002

Crump, Thomas

A brief history of science; as seen through the development of scientific instruments. Carroll & Graf Pubs. 2001 xxi, 425p il maps $28 **509**

1. Science—History 2. Scientific apparatus and instruments

ISBN 0-7867-0907-3

"Crump begins with mankind's discovery of how to create fire and ends with SQUIDs superconducting quantum interference devices. In between, there is chemistry, astronomy and 20th-century physics. The sections on advances in electricity and energy measurement make for particularly fascinating reading. . . . Crump's prose is generally reader-friendly, and mathematical and chemical notation are kept to a minimum." Publ Wkly

Includes bibliographical references

Encyclopedia of the scientific revolution; from Copernicus to Newton; editor Wilbur Applebaum. Garland 2000 xxxv, 758p il (Garland reference library of the humanities) $160 **509**

1. Science—History—Encyclopedias

ISBN 0-8153-1503-1 LC 00-25149

A "collection of articles on the progress of scientific discovery in the 16th and 17th centuries. . . . The 437 entries vary in length from just half a page to five pages, and each has a short bibliography directing the reader to recent articles and monographs as well as primary sources." Libr J

For a fuller review see: Booklist, Dec. 1, 2000

Flowers, Charles

Instability rules; the ten most amazing ideas of modern science. Wiley 2002 228p $24.95 **509**

1. Science—History

ISBN 0-471-38042-3 LC 2001-6729

Contents: Hubble and the expanding universe; Einstein and the wonder of light; Bohr and the puzzles of the quantum world; Wegener and the dance of the continents; Big bang; Fermat, Godel, and fuzzy math; Mendel, Watson, Crick, and the human genome; Hominids to humans, and continuing; Turing, the brain as computer, and vice versa; Freud, the unconscious, and other views

Great events from history II, Science and technology; edited by Frank N. Magill. Salem Press 1991 5v set $394 **509**

1. Science—History 2. Technology—History

ISBN 0-89356-637-3 LC 91-23313

Contents: v1, 1888-1910; v2, 1910-1931; v3, 1931-1952; v4, 1952-1969; v5, 1969-1991

These volumes cover the major events in the history of science and technology from 1888 through 1991 in 458 chronologically arranged articles

"The articles in the set are well written and most are accessible to the general reader. Although many of the discoveries can be found in other sources, the set provides a clear description of each event and places it in its proper historical context." Booklist

Hargittai, István
The road to Stockholm; Nobel Prizes, science, and scientists. Oxford Univ. Press 2002 342p il $29.95   **509**
1. Scientists 2. Nobel Prizes
ISBN 0-19-850912-X   LC 2002-283888
This book discusses the process by which Nobel Prize laureates are selected and the steps scientists take to be recognized for their discoveries as well as the characteristics of winners. It includes a chapter on scientists and discoveries that did not win. 80 photographs are included

History of modern science and mathematics; Brian S. Baigrie, editor. Scribner 2002 4v il set $395   **509**
1. Science—History 2. Mathematics—History
ISBN 0-684-80636-3   LC 2002-4042
This "set attempts to synthesize the history of scientific developments in anthropology, astronomy, biology, chemistry, mathematics, physics, psychology, and the earth sciences. . . . This work ranges from the 17th century to the present without trying to include the most recent developments." Libr J
For a fuller review see: Booklist, Dec. 1, 2002

The **History** of science in the United States; an encyclopedia; edited by Marc Rothenberg. Garland 2000 xx, 615p (Garland reference library of social science, Special-reference) $160   **509**
1. Science—History—Encyclopedias
ISBN 0-8153-0762-4   LC 99-43757
This "encyclopedia comprises 500 short- to medium-length articles . . . on the development of science and medicine in the United States. The typical article runs a page, though broad topics . . . receive longer treatments." Libr J
"This book will become a standard reference and belongs in every high school, college, and public library." Sci Books Films

Horvitz, Leslie Alan
Eureka!: scientific breakthroughs that changed the world. Wiley 2002 246p il $24.95   **509**
1. Science—History
ISBN 0-471-40276-1   LC 2001-46890
This examines twelve scientific discoveries and their discoverers, including Joseph Priestley and oxygen, Friedrich Kekulé and the structure of carbon compounds, Dmitri Mendeleev and the periodic table, Isaac Newton and gravity, Einstein and the theory of relativity, Philo Farnsworth and television, Alexander Fleming and penicillin, Charles Townes and the laser, Alfred Wegener and continental drift, Darwin and the origin of species, Watson and Crick and the double helix, and Benoit Mandelbrot and fractal geometry
Includes bibliographical references

Jardine, Lisa, 1944-
Ingenious pursuits; building the scientific revolution. Talese 1999 444p il hardcover o.p. paperback available $16   **509**
1. Science—History
ISBN 0-385-72001-7 (pa)   LC 99-41985
In this history of science in the 17th and early 18th centuries the author "chronicles improvements in the tools of observation (telescopes, microscopes) and mea-

surement (clocks) that were used by a pungent cast of characters who collaborated and squabbled with one another as they sorted out comets and discovered microbes." New Yorker
Includes bibliographical references

The **Oxford** companion to the history of modern science; editor in chief, J.L. Heilbron; editors, James Bartholomew [et al.] Oxford Univ. Press 2003 xxviii, 941p il $110   **509**
1. Science—History
ISBN 0-19-511229-6   LC 2002-153783
This reference on the history of science from the Renaissance through the 20th century includes some 600 articles covering "a broad spectrum of topics in all scientific disciplines (e.g., biotechnology, geology) as well as disciplines that influenced science, such as religion and politics. Also included are the biographies of 100 leading figures (e.g., Isaac Newton, Marie Curie) and coverage of scientific instruments (e.g., microscopes, Geiger counters). Organized alphabetically, the well-written articles include plenty of cross references. Over 100 black-and-white illustrations appear within their appropriate articles, but the eight pages of color illustrations in the middle of the volume are not associated with any article." Libr J
Includes bibliographical references

Piel, Gerard, 1915-
The age of science; what scientists learned in the 20th century; with illustrations by Peter Bradford. Basic Bks. 2001 xx, 460p il maps $40   **509**
1. Science—History
ISBN 0-465-05755-1   LC 2001-43178
"A Cornelia and Michael Bessie book"
This "survey explores quantum mechanics, subatomic particles, astrophysics, genetics, cell biology, planetary geology, and evolution. . . . While it generally succeeds in making science intelligible to the lay reader, this book is still challenging if rewarding." Libr J
Includes bibliographical references

Pyenson, Lewis
Servants of nature; a history of scientific institutions, enterprises, and sensibilities; [by] Lewis Pyenson and Susan Sheets-Pyenson. Norton 1999 496p il (Norton history of science) hardcover o.p. paperback available $17.95   **509**
1. Science—History
ISBN 0-393-31736-6 (pa)   LC 98-53198
"This survey ranges in time and space from Sumerian astronomy to the formulation of the theory of relativity, in New Jersey. It demonstrates how science has evolved in different societies, spawning innumerable organizations—universities, museums, observatories—for teaching, research, and popularization. The book's inclusiveness helps us recognize not only how science affects everything, from daily life to government budgets, but also the way we think about everything, from politics to poetry." New Yorker
Includes bibliographical references

Reader's guide to the history of science; edited by Arne Hessenbruch. Fitzroy Dearborn Pubs. 2000 xxix, 934p $135
509

1. Science—History—Encyclopedias
ISBN 1-884964-29-X   LC 2001-270888

"This volume contains about 600 entries on various aspects of the history of science, including individuals (e.g., Galileo), disciplines (e.g., astronomy), and broad topics (e.g., religion)." Libr J
For a fuller review see: Booklist, Aug. 2001

Science: a history of discovery in the twentieth century; [edited by] Trevor I. Williams. Oxford Univ. Press 1990 256p il $45
509

1. Science—History 2. Technology—History
ISBN 0-19-520843-9   LC 90-39705

"An Equinox book"

This survey of science and technology in the twentieth century relates advances in aeronautics, transportation, physics, medicine, and agriculture, and includes brief biographies of prominent scientists
Includes bibliographical references

Science and its times; understanding the social significance of scientific discovery; Neil Schlager, editor; Josh Lauer, associate editor. Gale Group 2000-2001 8v set $625
509

1. Science—History
ISBN 0-7876-3932-X   LC 00-37542

Contents: v1 2000 B.C.-700 A.D.; v2 700-1450; v3 1450-1699; v4 1700-1799; v5 19th century; v6 1900-1950; v7 1950-present; v8 Cumulative index

This set addresses "a wide variety of scientific developments with explanations of underlying factors and their effects on politics, economics, culture and daily life. [It includes] more than 20 topical essays, 25 full biographies and 85 sketches of notable people in each volume." Publisher's note
For a review see: Booklist Oct. 1, 2000

Science, technology, and society: the impact of science in the 20th century; Phillis Engelbert, editor. U.X.L 2002 3v il set $145
509

1. Science—History 2. Science and civilization 3. Technology—History 4. Technology and civilization
ISBN 0-7876-5649-6   LC 2002-4668

Also available 2 volume companion set covering the impact of science in the 19th century and a 3 volume companion set covering the impact of science from 2000 B.C. to the 18th century

"Each volume begins with the same table of contents, chronology, and list of words to know. Volumes cover specific fields of science: volume 1, *Life Science*; volume 2, *Mathematics and Medicine*; volume 3, *Physical Science and Technology*. The format for each of the five topics is the same: 'Chronology,' 'Overview,' 'Essays' on specific discoveries and inventions, 'Biographies' (nine or ten two-page profiles), 'Brief Biographies' (additional paragraph-length treatments), 'Research and Activity Ideas,' and a bibliography for more information." Booklist

Silver, Brian L.
The ascent of science. Oxford Univ. Press 1998 534p il hardcover o.p. paperback available $29.95
509

1. Science—History   2. Science—Philosophy 3. Thought and thinking
ISBN 0-19-513427-3 (pa)   LC 97-15430

"A Solomon Press book"

The author discusses a "variety of topics, from Pythagorean musings and lodestones to quantum mechanical puzzles and DNA structures. Yes, chaos theory and cosmology are included too. All this is sandwiched between interesting references to historical matters, philosophical positions, some controversies, and to Shakespeare, Shelley, and Shaw also. A book commendable for its breadth, depth, and vision." Choice
Includes bibliographical references

Suplee, Curt
Milestones of science. National Geographic Soc. 2000 287p il $35
509

1. Science—History
ISBN 0-7922-7906-9   LC 00-36149

In this history of science the author begins "with modern science's antecedents in classical Greece, and he narratively develops science's core dynamic, the recurring overthrow of an orthodox viewpoint by a revolutionary one. . . . An eminently browsable entrée to the vast universe of scientific knowledge." Booklist

Teresi, Dick
Lost discoveries; the ancient roots of modern science, from the Babylonians to the Maya. Simon & Schuster 2002 453p il $27; pa $15
509

1. Science—History 2. Ancient civilization
ISBN 0-684-83718-8; 0-7432-4379-X (pa)
          LC 2002-75457

"This is a compendium of premodern knowledge of the natural world. Teresi structures his exploration into the science of Sumerian, Babylonian, Mayan, Chinese, and other non-European, premodern cultures around the thesis that classical Greece is not the sole fount of Western science." Booklist
"Teresi offers a great deal of fascinating material largely ignored by many histories of science." Publ Wkly
Includes bibliographical references

Walker, Mark
Nazi science; myth, truth, and the German atomic bomb. Plenum Press 1995 325p il o.p.; Perseus Bks. paperback available $22.50
509

1. Science—Germany 2. Atomic bomb 3. National socialism
ISBN 0-7382-0585-0 (pa)   LC 95-6102

"Walker examines the effect of the Nazi years on German science. Focusing primarily on physics and such . . . individuals as Einstein, Heisenberg, Gerlach, von Weizsächer, Stark, von Laue, and Planck, the author devotes the first seven of 11 chapters to an . . . analysis of how the German physics community evolved during the growth of the Third Reich. In chapters 8-10, the German work on nuclear fission is discussed." Choice
"Although scholarly, this will be accessible to general readers." Libr J
Includes bibliographical references

Webster, Raymond B.

African American firsts in science and technology; foreword by Wesley L. Harris. Gale Group 1999 462p $80   **509**

1. Scientists 2. African American inventors

ISBN 0-7876-3876-5   LC 99-27346

Presents capsule accounts of notable first achievements by African Americans, arranged in the categories "Agriculture and Everyday Life," "Dentistry and Nursing," "Life Science," "Math and Engineering," "Medicine," "Physical Science," and "Transportation"

For a review see: Booklist, Feb. 15, 2000

Includes bibliographical references

Whitfield, Peter

Landmarks in western science; from prehistory to the atomic age. Routledge 1999 256p il $65   **509**

1. Science—History

ISBN 0-415-92533-9   LC 99-24976

This survey "highlights significant discoveries and turning points in mathematics, astronomy, physics, medicine, geology, and many other fields." Publisher's note

Includes bibliographical references

510   Mathematics

Acheson, D. J.

1089 and all that; a journey into mathematics; [by] David Acheson. Oxford Univ. Press 2002 178p il $19.95   **510**

1. Mathematics

ISBN 0-19-851623-1   LC 2002-71547

"This book aims to make mathematics accessible to non-experts and the lay reader. Providing an . . . overview of the subject, the text includes several . . . mathematical conundrums. . . . The book contains several cartoons, sketches and photos." Publisher's note

"Not a page passes without at least one intriguing insight. . . . Anyone who is baffled by mathematics should buy it." New Sci

Boyer, Carl B. (Carl Benjamin), 1906-

A history of mathematics; revised by Uta C. Merzbach. 2nd ed. Wiley 1989 762p il $101.95; pa $39.95   **510**

1. Mathematics

ISBN 0-471-09763-2; 0-471-54397-7 (pa)

LC 89-5325

First published 1969

"This good general history of mathematics is understandable to the student as well as authoritative for the mathematician." Malinowsky. Best Sci & Technol Ref Books for Young People

Includes bibliographical references

Cole, K. C.

The universe and the teacup; the mathematics of truth and beauty. Harcourt Brace & Co. 1998 214p hardcover o.p. paperback available $13   **510**

1. Mathematics 2. Truth

ISBN 0-15-600656-1 (pa)   LC 97-22338

The author "leads readers through the mathematical concepts that apply equally well to the behavior of planetary bodies and our own. . . . Cole's arguments occasionally meander, but that doesn't detract from the

book's overall clarity and balance, including a well-chosen, succinct list of suggested readings. From the symmetry of spheres to altruism, Cole shows that truth does indeed add up to beauty, and beauty to truth." Publ Wkly

CRC standard mathematical tables and formulae. CRC Press $49.95   **510**

1. Mathematics—Tables

First published 1929 with title: Math tables from the Handbook of Chemistry and Physics. (31st edition 2002) Periodically revised

"This standard mathematical handbook contains both textual and tabular material. The contents include constants and conversion factors; algebra; combinatorial analysis; geometry; trigonometry; logarithmic, exponential, and hyperbolic functions; analytical geometry; calculus; differential equations; special functions; numerical methods; probability and statistics; and financial tables." Malinowsky. Best Sci & Technol Ref Books for Young People

Devlin, Keith J.

The math gene; how mathematical thinking evolved and why numbers are like gossip; [by] Keith Devlin. Basic Bks. 2000 328p il hardcover o.p. paperback available $17   **510**

1. Number concept 2. Mathematics

ISBN 0-465-01619-7 (pa)   LC 2001-520984

"Is the human brain hardwired for mathematical thinking? Just as we have an instinct for language acquisition, Devlin argues that we also possess an innate ability for logical and algorithmic reasoning. This book is an eye-opener for all math phobics." Libr J

Includes bibliographical references

The millennium problems; the seven greatest unsolved mathematical puzzles of our time; [by] Keith Devlin. Basic Bks. 2002 237p il $26   **510**

1. Mathematics

ISBN 0-465-01729-0   LC 2003-535468

Partial contents: The Riemann hypothesis; Yang-Mills theory and the mass gap hypothesis; The P vs. NP problem; The Navier-Stokes equations; The poincare conjecture; The Birch and Swinnerton-Dyer conjecture; The Hodge conjecture

The author attempts to explain difficult mathematical problems in such a way that non-experts can easily understand them. It features diagrams, cartoons, photos, and sketches to help illustrate many mathematical concepts

Dewdney, A. K.

200% of nothing; an eye-opening tour through the twists and turns of math abuse and innumeracy. Wiley 1993 182p il $22.95; pa $15.95   **510**

1. Mathematics

ISBN 0-471-57776-6; 0-471-14574-2 (pa)

LC 92-42173

The author discusses the media abuse of numbers "as well as 'percentage pumping,' 'irrational ratios,' 'compound blindness,' 'filtering,' and 'dimensional dementia.'" Libr J

Includes bibliographical references

Dewdney, A. K.—*Continued*

A mathematical mystery tour; discovering the truth and beauty of the cosmos. Wiley 1999 218p il $22.95; pa $15.95   **510**
1. Mathematics
ISBN 0-471-23847-3; 0-471-40734-8 (pa)
LC 98-36470

Dewdney "addresses two closely related, long-pondered questions. Why is mathematics so uncannily effective in describing the physical universe? Is 'new' mathematics invented, or is it a preexisting something that is discovered?. . . He explores these fundamental questions via discussions of the mathematical work of Pythagoras, the medieval Arab mathematicians, modern theoretical physicists, and modern mathematicians." Libr J

A **Dictionary** of quotations in mathematics; compiled and edited by Robert A. Nowlan. McFarland & Co. 2002 314p pa $45   **510**
1. Mathematics—Quotations 2. Quotations
ISBN 0-7864-1284-4   LC 2002-5268

"This work contains almost 3,000 quotations in mathematics. It is divided into thirty-eight chapters and 389 sections that present quotations over a spectrum from God and religion to the nature of infinity. . . . Areas covered [include] historical origins, linguistics, the arts, mathematicians themselves, logic, real and idealized space, number theory, algebra, computers, probability theory, and statistics." Publisher's note

"For anyone writing a term paper, professional paper, or giving a presentation, whether in mathematics, science, or a related discipline, this reference will be a useful resource. For the rest of us, this book is a delightful read all by itself." Am Ref Books Annu, 2003

Dunham, William, 1947-

The mathematical universe; an alphabetical journey through the great proofs, problems, and personalities. Wiley 1994 314p il hardcover o.p. paperback available $19.95   **510**
1. Mathematics 2. Mathematicians
ISBN 0-471-17661-3 (pa)   LC 93-46702

In this history of mathematics, "Dunham sheds light not only on the personalities—eccentric, vain, brilliant—of major mathematicians, but also on contemporary social issues, such as multiculturalism and gender equity. Readers who want to understand the cultural significance of mathematics would do well to begin with this book." Booklist
Includes bibliographical references

Glazer, Evan, 1971-

Real-life math; everyday use of mathematical concepts; [by] Evan M. Glazer and John W. McConnell. Greenwood Press 2002 165p il $49.95   **510**
1. Mathematics
ISBN 0-313-31998-7   LC 2001-58635

The authors "have written this book as a reply to students' complaints that they'll never use the mathematical concepts they're being taught. They look at dozens of mathematical concepts and . . . show how these math ideas relate to the world in which students live. . . . The book is thorough and accurate." Libr Media Connect
For a fuller review see: Booklist, Dec. 15, 2002
Includes bibliographical references

Mankiewicz, Richard

The story of mathematics. Princeton Univ. Press 2000 192p il $29.95   **510**
1. Mathematics
ISBN 0-691-08808-X   LC 00-107068

A history of mathematics from prehistory to the present, including cultural influences and practical applications

"Mathematics here receives the multifaceted treatment it deserves. In a text laced with beautiful illustrations and piquant anecdotes, Mankiewicz traces the rise of this profoundly human pursuit." Booklist

Paulos, John Allen

Beyond numeracy; ruminations of a numbers man. Knopf 1991 285p il hardcover o.p. paperback available $14   **510**
1. Mathematics
ISBN 0-679-73807-X (pa)   LC 90-44999

These seventy short essays "range from summaries of whole disciplines (calculus, trigonometry, topology) to biographical and historical asides (Gödel, Pythagoras, non-Euclidean geometry) to bits of mathematical or quasi-mathematical folklore (infinite sets, Platonic solids, QED)." Introduction

"This well-written and easy-to-follow book gently guides readers through many interesting mathematical topics." SLJ
Includes bibliographical references

Innumeracy; mathematical illiteracy and its consequences. Hill & Wang 1989 135p o.p.; Random House paperback available $12 **510**
1. Mathematics
ISBN 0-679-72601-2 (pa)   LC 88-17001

The author contends that "innumeracy, an inability to deal comfortably with the fundamental notions of number and chance, plagues far too many otherwise knowledgeable citizens." Introduction

Paulos presents "his concepts entirely in words. Such hitherto abstruse topics as conditional probability, or permutations and combinations, are treated in a brief, entertaining, and comprehensible way without use of a single equation." Christ Sci Monit

A mathematician reads the newspaper. Basic Bks. 1995 212p il o.p.; Anchor Bks. paperback available $12.95   **510**
1. Mathematics
ISBN 0-385-48254-X (pa)   LC 94-48206

The author uses newspaper features "as vehicles for explaining mathematical concepts and how they figure in the business of being a well-informed citizen. For instance, he uses stories on the economy to illustrate prediction, regression analysis, statistics, and game theory and how those tools are used to both illuminate and obfuscate underlying truth." Booklist

This is "mathematically undemanding, humorous, and instructive." Libr J
Includes bibliographical references

Sperling, Abraham Paul, 1912-
Mathematics made simple; [by] Abraham Sperling and Monroe Stuart; edited and prepared for publication by the Stonesong Press, Inc. 5th ed, rev. by Christine M. Peckaitis. Doubleday 1991 272p il pa $12.95
510

1. Mathematics
ISBN 0-385-26584-0   LC 89-49249
"A Made simple book"
First published 1943 by Kenmore Pub. Co.
"This book serves as a review of arithmetic, and an introduction to algebra, geometry, and trigonometry. Combinations and permutations are covered . . . in the Probability chapter. The exercises and answers in this book provide readers with opportunities to test their mastery of each step in these common branches of mathematics." Introduction

Stewart, Ian, 1945-
The magical maze; seeing the world through mathematical eyes. Wiley 1998 268p il $24.95; pa $16.95
510

1. Mathematics 2. Mathematical recreations
ISBN 0-471-19297-X; 0-471-35065-6 (pa)
     LC 98-13185
Stewart presents various mathematical puzzles and problems through the metaphorical structure of a maze
Chapters "contain good discussions of such topics as modular arithmetic, Marilyn vos Savant's Monty-Hall problem, depth-first and other search strategies, static and dynamic symmetry, Turing machines, optimization, fractals, and chaos. This is an excellent mix of topics and the material is very much up-to-date." Choice

Szpiro, George G., 1950-
Kepler's conjecture; how some of the greatest minds in history helped solve one of the oldest math problems in the world; by George Szpiro. Wiley 2002 296p $24.95
510

1. Mathematics
ISBN 0-471-08601-0   LC 2002-14422
Contents: Cannonballs and tomatoes; The puzzle of the dozen spheres; Parasols, water hydrants, and soccer players; Thue's two attempts and Fejes-Tóth's achievement; Twelve's company, thirteen's a crowd; Nets and knots; Twisted boxes; No dancing at this congress; The race for the upper bound; Right angles for round spaces; Wobbly balls and hybrid stars; Simplex, Cplex, and symbolic mathematics; But is it really a proof?; Beehives again ...; This is not an epilogue
"Using an engaging historical context, Szpiro makes the mathematics understandable, relegating the more difficult material to appendixes. Helpful reference list." Choice
Includes bibliographical references

Tobias, Sheila
Overcoming math anxiety. rev and expanded. Norton 1993 260p il $23; pa $14.95
510

1. Mathematics
ISBN 0-393-03577-8; 0-393-31307-7 (pa)
     LC 93-3648
First published 1978
The author explains common misconceptions about mathematical concepts, analyzes what makes math seem difficult, discusses alleged sex differences in brain function in relation to math, and describes math programs aimed at women
Includes bibliographical references

511   General principles of mathematics

Berlinski, David, 1942-
The advent of the algorithm; the idea that rules the world. Harcourt 2000 345p $28; pa $14
511

1. Algorithms
ISBN 0-15-100338-6; 0-15-601391-6 (pa)
     LC 98-43755
Berlinski "chronicles the discovery of algorithms, the codes that control computers, vividly profiling the key thinkers involved. He also identifies the hidden sources of the algorithm's power as a calculating tool, and exposes its defects as a scientific metaphor for explaining the human intellect." Booklist
Includes bibliographical references

Kaplan, Robert
The nothing that is; a natural history of zero; illustrations by Ellen Kaplan. Oxford Univ. Press 2000 225p $40; pa $11.95   **511**

1. Zero (The number)
ISBN 0-19-512842-7; 0-19-514237-3 (pa)
     LC 99-29000
"Kaplan presents cultural, philosophical, historical, and mathematical developments that either encouraged or discouraged the recognition of the role of zero in counting and computation." Sci Books Films

Seife, Charles
Zero; the biography of a dangerous idea. Viking 2000 248p il hardcover o.p. paperback available $13
511

1. Zero (The number)
ISBN 0-14-029647-6 (pa)   LC 99-36693
"The zero emerges as a daunting intellectual riddle in this . . . chronicle of a once controversial concept as Seife deftly traces the gradual acceptance of the zero and its role as catalyst for the evolution of everything from business to physics to moral thought." Booklist
Includes bibliographical references

512   Algebra, number theory

Aczel, Amir D.
Fermat's last theorem; unlocking the secret of an ancient mathematical problem. Four Walls Eight Windows 1996 147p il map $18
512

1. Wiles, Andrew 2. Number theory
ISBN 1-56858-077-0   LC 96-9029
Also available in paperback from Delacorte
An "informal history of Fermat's Last Theorem (FLT), this work reaches back to antiquity and culminates in Andrew Wiles's magnificent and climactic achievement in 1994 of a proof of a major portion of the Shimura-Taniyama-Weil conjecture that was known to imply FLT. Aczel has chosen to place considerable emphasis on the personalities of the multitude of mathematicians who played a role in the story." Choice
Includes bibliographical references

Clawson, Calvin C.

Mathematical mysteries; the beauty and magic of numbers. Plenum Press 1996 313p il o.p.; Perseus Bks. paperback available $18.95   **512**

1. Number theory
ISBN 0-7382-0259-2 (pa)   LC 96-31715
Topics discussed include "numeric origins, Greek achievements, famous sequences and series, different infinities, prime numbers and secret codes, Goldbach's conjectures, [and] Ramanujan's equations. . . . Various philosophical bases of mathematics are . . . presented at the end of the book." Choice
"A writer in love with his subject, Clawson offers the perfect antidote to the phobias and misconceptions surrounding mathematics." Booklist
Includes bibliographical references

Conway, John Horton

The book of numbers; [by] John Horton Conway, Richard K. Guy. Copernicus 1996 310p il $35   **512**

1. Number theory
ISBN 0-387-97993-X   LC 95-32588
Topics examined include "Ramanujan's formula for partitions, the factors of the 13th Fermat number, 17-sided polygons, Farey sequences, Pythagorean fractions, the game of Hackenbush and surreal numbers." New Sci
"The authors take such joy in the order and patterns of numbers that you can't help being fascinated by what is actually a fairly difficult subject." Libr J
Includes bibliographical references

Mazur, Barry, 1937-

Imagining numbers; (particularly the square root of minus fifteen). Farrar, Straus & Giroux 2002 270p il $22   **512**

1. Numbers
ISBN 0-374-17469-5   LC 2002-75402
"Imaginary numbers entered into mathematics in sixteenth-century Italy, . . . [but] it took more than two hundred years for mathematicians to discover a satisfactory way of 'imagining' these numbers. With discussions about how we comprehend ideas both in poetry and in mathematics, Mazur reviews some of the writings of the earliest explorers of these elusive figures, such as Rafael Bombelli, an engineer . . . who in his spare moments composed his great treatise 'L'Algebra.' . . . [He discusses] how to begin imagining, ourselves, imaginary numbers." Publisher's note
Includes bibliographical references

Reid, Constance

From zero to infinity; what makes numbers interesting. 4th ed. Mathematical Assn. of Am. 1992 186p pa $21.95   **512**

1. Number theory
ISBN 0-88385-505-4
First published 1955 by Crowell
"This book covers selected topics in number theory. Partly expository, it nonetheless challenges the reader's mind in clever and nonthreatening ways." Sci Books Films

Singh, Simon

Fermat's enigma; the quest to solve the world's greatest mathematical problem; foreword by John Lynch. Walker & Co. 1997 315p il $23   **512**

1. Wiles, Andrew 2. Number theory
ISBN 0-8027-1331-9   LC 97-20748
Also available in paperback from Bantam Bks.
Published in the United Kingdom with title: Fermat's last theorem
"For 350 years, mathematicians staked whole careers—even lives—on solving Fermat's Last Theorem. The story of this immensely difficult problem involves failure, despair, obsession, and, ultimately triumph." Libr J
"This vivid account is fascinating reading for anyone interested in mathematics, its history, and the passionate quest for solutions to unsolved riddles." SLJ
Includes bibliographical references

513 Arithmetic

Bunch, Bryan H.

The kingdom of infinite number; a field guide; [by] Bryan Bunch. Freeman, W.H. 2000 388p il $23.95   **513**

1. Numbers 2. Number concept
ISBN 0-7167-3388-9   LC 99-53641
Also available in paperback from Holt & Co.
"Bunch limns the personalities, the species linkages, and the field marks of all kinds of numbers—from simple odds and evens to intricate logarithms and transcendentals." Booklist
"The reader will inevitably get caught up in the book's spellbinding mixture of history, language, mathematics, and science." Sci Books Films
Includes bibliographical references

Kogelman, Stanley

The only math book you'll ever need; [by] Stanley Kogelman and Barbara R. Heller. rev ed. Facts on File 1994 xx, 268p il $22.95   **513**

1. Mathematics
ISBN 0-8160-2767-6   LC 93-10539
Also available in paperback from HarperCollins Pubs.
First published 1986
Step-by-step operations are reviewed in problems encountered on a daily basis such as comparing credit cards, evaluating investments, estimating interest rates, and converting area measurements

515 Analysis

Berlinski, David, 1942-

A tour of the calculus. Pantheon Bks. 1995 331p il hardcover o.p. paperback available $14   **515**

1. Calculus
ISBN 0-679-74788-5 (pa)   LC 95-4042
This is an introduction to "the foundations of calculus. It is in part an informal history of the subject; the author interweaves the historical fragments with expository sections that [seek to] explain the concepts from a modern viewpoint." Libr J
"Berlinski tangibly grounds the abstract notions, so that attentive readers can ease into and grasp the several full-blown proofs he sets forth." Booklist

Kaplan, Robert

The art of the infinite; the pleasures of mathematics; [by] Robert Kaplan and Ellen Kaplan; illustrations by Ellen Kaplan. Oxford Univ. Press 2003 c2002 324p il $26   **515**

1. Mathematics

ISBN 0-19-514743-X

"From ancient ideas such as the development of counting to recent ideas involving different orders of infinity (Cantor), the Kaplans present the infinite as an inevitable consequence in mathematical thinking. Through their presentation, they help readers understand many mathematical basics, such as why the product of two negatives is a positive and the nature of proof by contradiction." Choice

"Most of the math discussed can be followed by anyone with a smattering of algebra and geometry, and always it is accompanied by stories of how people first discovered the mathematical principles, with illustrations of the protagonists." SLJ

Includes bibliographical references

516 Geometry

Gorini, Catherine A.

The Facts on File geometry handbook. Facts on File 2003 280p il (Facts on File science library) $35   **516**

1. Geometry

ISBN 0-8160-4875-4   LC 2002-12343

This includes a glossary of 3,000 entries with labeled diagrams, biographies of 300 scientists and mathematicians from ancient times to the present, a chronology of geometry history, charts, tables, recommended reading and websites

Includes bibliographical references

Mlodinow, Leonard

Euclid's window; the story of geometry from parallel lines to hyperspace. Free Press 2001 306p il hardcover o.p. paperback available $14   **516**

1. Geometry

ISBN 0-684-86524-6 (pa)   LC 00-54351

Mlodinow's monograph "takes the form of five biographical stories, each about a key figure in the development of geometry: Euclid, Descartes, Gauss, Einstein and Witten." New Sci

"This engaging history does an excellent job of explaining the importance of the study of geometry without making the reader learn any geometry." Libr J

Includes bibliographical references

516.2 Euclidean geometry. Trigonometry

Blatner, David

The joy of π. Walker & Co. 1997 129p il $18; pa $12   **516.2**

1. Pi

ISBN 0-8027-1332-7; 0-8027-7562-4 (pa)

LC 97-23705

The author discusses the history of the number π, as well as the process of "calculating the ratio of a circle's circumference to its diameter, which has advanced from measuring lengths of string and the 'brute force' of mea-

suring polygons to feeding supercomputers sophisticated algorithms. Sidebars . . . abound, containing a factoid, joke, or doggerel inspired by π." Booklist

Includes bibliographical references

Livio, Mario, 1945-

The golden ratio; the story of phi, the world's most astonishing number. Broadway Bks. 2002 294p $24.95   **516.2**

1. Geometry

ISBN 0-7679-0815-5   LC 2002-23084

The author examines the history and myths of phi, the "golden ratio" of 1.6180339887 that has been related to phenomena as diverse as the arrangements of petals on roses and the breeding patterns of rabbits

"Overall, an enjoyable work, amply supported by index, extensive references, and ten appendixes presenting mathematical elaborations of text material." Choice

Includes bibliographical references

519.2 Probabilities

Orkin, Michael

What are the odds? chance in everyday life; [by] Mike Orkin. Freeman, W.H. 1999 154p pa $14.95   **519.2**

1. Probabilities 2. Chance

ISBN 0-7167-3560-1   LC 99-51731

This "treatise covers the role of chance and probability, ranging from coin tosses to Heisenberg's uncertainty principle. . . . The author explains the role of chance and probability in terms that can, on the whole, be understood by those who have had neither course work nor any other type of exposure to probability and statistics." Sci Books Films

Includes bibliographical references

519.5 Statistical mathematics

Everitt, Brian

The Cambridge dictionary of statistics. 2nd ed. Cambridge Univ. Press 2002 410p il $50

519.5

1. Statistics—Dictionaries

ISBN 0-521-81099-X   LC 2002-514499

First published 1998

This dictionary contains definitions for 3500 terms, covering "medical, survey, theoretical, applied statistics, etc. In addition, short biographies of over 100 important statisticians are included." Publisher's note

"A valuable added feature is the inclusion of bibliographies and examples with nearly all the definitions. Highly recommended for most libraries." Choice

520 Astronomy and allied sciences

The **Amateur** astronomer; edited by Shawn Carlson. Wiley 2001 271p il pa $16.95

520

1. Astronomy

ISBN 0-471-38282-5   LC 00-47773

At head of title: Scientific American

The Amateur astronomer—*Continued*

A collection of articles on the subject of astronomy published in Scientific American magazine from the 1950s to the 1990s

"Carlson provides fascinating assessments of both how much and how little was known 50 years ago, and he charts the evolution of theories and the rise and resolution of controversies, thus offering invaluable insights into the history of scientific thought and methodology. Technically precise yet always clear, these popular science columns remain vital and exciting." Booklist

Includes bibliographical references

Angelo, Joseph A.

The Facts on File space and astronomy handbook; [by] Joseph A. Angelo, Jr. Facts on File 2002 278p il $35; pa $17.95   **520**
1. Astronomy 2. Space sciences
ISBN 0-8160-4542-9; 0-8160-4960-2 (pa)
LC 2001-54323

"Facts on File science library"

This handbook "is organized into four sections: a 1,200-entry glossary, 400 short (one sentence to one paragraph in length) biographies, a 45-page chronology of 8,000 years of discoveries in astronomy and space science, and 17 pages of charts and tables. The glossary provides brief descriptions or definitions for terms such as *Blastoff, Extraterrestrial catastrophe theory, Gemini Project, Galactic cannibalism, Habitable payload, Orion Nebula, Planck's radiation law,* and *Zenith.* Biographies include well-known people such as Galileo Galilei, John Glenn, and Sally Ride as well as some that one would not expect to find in an astronomy resource." Booklist

Asimov, Isaac, 1920-1992

Isaac Asimov's guide to earth & space. Random House 1991 285p il hardcover o.p. paperback available $6.99   **520**
1. Astronomy 2. Earth
ISBN 0-449-22059-1 (pa)
LC 91-11097

Written as if "Asimov were chatting with an interesting but unsophisticated companion, this guide covers a wide range: ancient history; new discoveries; specific properties of the sun, moon, stars and Earth; as well as general information about the universe." Voice Youth Advocates

Astronomy encyclopedia; foreword by Leif J. Robinson; star maps created by Wil Tirion; general editor, Patrick Moore. fully rev and expanded ed. Oxford Univ. Press 2002 456p il maps $50   **520**
1. Astronomy—Encyclopedias
ISBN 0-19-521833-7
LC 2003-535058

First published 1987 with title: International encyclopedia of astronomy

This encyclopedia ranges "from adaptive optics and cold dark matter, to Islamic astronomy and the lens defect known as vignetting. It includes . . . articles on the cornerstones of astronomical investigation, such as the Milky Way, the sun and the planets, optical and radio telescopes, stars, black holes, astrophysics, observatories, astronomical photography, space programs, the constellations, and famous astronomers. And there are concise entries on planetary features and satellites, asteroids, observational techniques, comets, satellite launchers, meteors, and subjects as diverse as life in the Universe and the structure of meteorites." Publisher's note

"This is a beautiful book, replacing many older ency-

clopedias that may be on the reference shelves. If a library has funds to purchase only one encyclopedia covering astronomy, this is the one to select." Booklist

Berman, Bob

Secrets of the night sky; the most amazing things in the universe you can see with the naked eye; illustrations by Alan McKnight. Morrow 1995 320p il o.p.; HarperCollins Pubs. paperback available $16   **520**
1. Astronomy
ISBN 0-06-097687-X (pa)
LC 94-21604

Berman discusses a "variety of interesting celestial objects and how to view some of them and reviews a number of important concepts of physical science and how they are related to the objects we are able to see through binoculars and small telescopes. . . . Fun to read, with virtually all the astronomical subject information timely and generally accurate." Sci Books Films

Includes bibliographical references

The **Cambridge** illustrated history of astronomy; edited by Michael Hoskin. Cambridge Univ. Press 1997 392p il maps $40   **520**
1. Astronomy—History
ISBN 0-521-41158-0
LC 95-40923

This is a "record of human intellectual progress embracing Mayan, Babylonian, Greek, Islamic, and medieval Latin astronomy and leading up to the arrival of Copernicus, Galileo, and Newton. Their influence provided the needed change in approach from geometry to physics and forced long-delayed acceptance of the elliptical orbits of planets, a sun-centered system, and an earth that moved within it." Libr J

"This volume is a triumph: authoritative, current, elegantly written, lavishly illustrated, thoughtfully and aesthetically designed, and handsomely executed. If there is to be only one history of astronomy on one's bookshelf, this is the one to have." Sci Books Films

Includes bibliographical references

Cosmic dispatches; the New York Times reports on astronomy and cosmology; John Noble Wilford, editor. Norton 2000 316p il hardcover o.p. paperback available $16.95   **520**
1. Astronomy 2. Cosmology
ISBN 0-393-32277-7 (pa)
LC 00-41861

A collection of some 75 articles on astronomy and cosmology from the New York Times

These articles convey "the astounding significance of recent breakthroughs in astronomy and cosmology—without entangling us in the technical complexities." Booklist

Dickinson, Terence

From the big bang to Planet X; the 50 most-asked questions about the universe—and their answers. Camden House (Camden East) 1993 151p il pa $12.95   **520**
1. Astronomy
ISBN 0-921820-71-2

This book answers 50 commonly asked astronomical questions

"The author has succeeded in writing a useful, enjoyable, and eminently readable book. The questions range over the whole domain of astronomy and include those concerned with current areas of astronomical research." Sci Books Films

Ferris, Timothy
Seeing in the dark; how backyard stargazers are probing deep space and guarding earth from interplanetary peril. Simon & Schuster 2002 379p il $26; pa $14 **520**
1. Astronomy 2. Astronomers
ISBN 0-684-86579-3; 0-684-86580-7 (pa)
LC 2002-20693
Ferris examines "the 20th-century in spectroscopic analysis of very distant light from celestial bodies through the personal experiences of . . . astronomers, mostly amateurs." Christ Sci Monit
"This book should turn many novices on to astronomy and captivate those already fascinated by the heavens." Publ Wkly

On the shoulders of giants; the great works of physics and astronomy; edited, with commentary, by Stephen Hawking. Running Press 2002 1264p il $29.95 **520**
1. Physics 2. Astronomy
ISBN 0-7624-1348-4   LC 2002-100441
Contents: Nicolaus Copernicus (1473-1543): his life and work; On the revolution of heavenly spheres—Galileo Galilei (1564-1642): his life and work; Dialogues concerning two sciences—Johannes Kepler (1571-1630): his life and work; Harmony of the world, Book 5—Sir Isaac Newton (1643-1727): his life and work; Principia—Albert Einstein (1879-1955): his life and work; Selections from The principle of relativity
"Physicist Hawking has collected in this single illuminating volume the classic works of physics and astronomy that in their day revolutionized humankind's perception of the world. . . . Despite the volume's heftiness, Hawking has given these works a setting that is elegantly simple and, in its simplicity, effectively broadening." Publ Wkly

Plait, Philip C.
Bad astronomy; misconceptions and misuses revealed, from astrology to the moon landing 'hoax'; [illustrations by Tina Cash Walch] Wiley 2002 277p il pa $15.95 **520**
1. Astronomy 2. Errors
ISBN 0-471-40976-6   LC 2002-277382
"The work describes 24 common astronomical fallacies. . . . The author . . . dismisses astrology, creationism, and UFO sightings and explains the principles behind basic general concepts (the Big Bang, why the sky is blue, etc." Libr J
"...everything's beautifully explained. [The author] . . . gives the neatest explanation of tides I've ever seen . . . for that alone, this book should be in every school library on the planet." New Scientist
Includes bibliographical references

Raymo, Chet
An intimate look at the night sky. Walker & Co. 2001 242p il $25; pa $16 **520**
1. Astronomy
ISBN 0-8027-1369-6; 0-8027-7670-1 (pa)
Raymo discusses astronomy and cosmology. "The narrative follows earth's path through the four seasons [around the sun]." Christ Sci Monit
"A delightful, inspiring introduction to astronomy." Booklist
Includes bibliographical references

Ridpath, Ian
Stars and planets; illustrated by Wil Tirion. 3rd ed. Princeton Univ. Press 2001 400p il (Princeton field guides) $60; pa $19.95 **520**
1. Astronomy 2. Stars 3. Planets
ISBN 0-691-08912-4; 0-691-08913-2 (pa)
LC 00-110474
First published 1998 by DK Pub.
This book features "full-color photos and data, including recent planetary images; monthly maps of the night sky as seen from latitudes throughout the world; charts of all 88 constellations, with data and notes on bright stars and other objects of interest; illustrated introduction to stars, nebulae, galaxies, and the Solar System; advice on choosing and using binoculars and telescopes." Publisher's note

Sagan, Carl, 1934-1996
Cosmos. Random House 2002 365p $35 **520**
1. Astronomy
ISBN 0-375-50832-5   LC 2002-69744
A reissue of the title first published 1980
Based on the author's television series of the same name, this volume covers "the 10- to 20-billion-year history of the universe, from the big bang and subsequent evolution of molecular material through the evolution of human culture." Libr J [review of 1980 edition]
Includes bibliographical references

Pale blue dot; a vision of the human future in space. Random House 1994 429p il o.p.; Ballantine Bks. paperback available $13.95 **520**
1. Outer space—Exploration
ISBN 0-345-37659-5 (pa)   LC 94-18121
"In a tour of our solar system, galaxy and beyond . . . Sagan meshes a history of astronomical discovery, a cogent brief for space exploration and an overview of life. . . . His exploration of our place in the universe is illustrated with photographs, relief maps and paintings, including high-resolution images made by *Voyager 1* and *2*, as well as photos taken by the *Galileo* spacecraft, the Hubble Space Telescope and satellites orbiting Earth." Publ Wkly
Includes bibliographical references

Schaaf, Fred
40 nights to knowing the sky; a night-by-night skywatching primer. Holt & Co. 1998 252p il maps pa $19 **520**
1. Astronomy
ISBN 0-8050-4668-2   LC 97-48507
"An Owl book"
This is a series of forty interactive activities for observing stars, planets, the moon and other visible phenomena in the sky
"An excellent, well-designed start in a subject where all one needs is desire, binoculars, and a dark and unstormy night." Booklist
Includes bibliographical references

Upgren, Arthur R.

The turtle and the stars; observations of an earthbound astronomer; [by] Arthur Upgren. Times Bks.; Holt & Co. 2002 xx, 250p $26; pa $15 **520**
1. Astronomy
ISBN 0-8050-7094-X; 0-8050-7290-X (pa)
LC 2001-52741
Upgren's "series of musings on the sky's changing appearance . . . offers interesting explanations of the sky's look resulting from the earth's spin and the slight eccentricity of its orbit. He also incorporates the major historical steps in discovering the distances to the moon, sun, and nearer stars. . . . An approachable potpourri, Upgren's essays will delight and inform astronomy buffs." Booklist
Includes bibliographical references

Voit, Mark

Hubble space telescope; new views of the universe. Abrams 2000 64p il pa $19.95
520
1. Hubble Space Telescope 2. Universe
ISBN 0-8109-2923-6 LC 00-29316
This includes over 100 photographs of space taken by the Hubble Space Telescope, with explanatory text
"Incredible color photography and refreshing understandable text re-create the wonder and magic of space. Through these fantastic reproductions, the amazing ability of the Hubble Space Telescope is defined and showcased." SLJ
Includes bibliographical references

520.3 Astronomy—Encyclopedias and dictionaries

Encyclopedia of astronomy and astrophysics; editor-in-chief Paul Murdin. Institute of Physics Nature Publishing Group 2001 4v il set $650 **520.3**
1. Astronomy—Encyclopedias 2. Astrophysics—Encyclopedias
ISBN 1-56159-268-4
Also available online
This reference "consists of more than 3,000 entries, of which 630 are primary articles discussing important theoretical and observational results of astronomical research, including entries as varied as *Climate, Galaxies, Jupiter,* and *Telescope engineering.* The work is especially strong in its coverage of topics related to the sun and solar physics. All of these lengthy articles provide both an overview and state-of-the-art review of the subject matter. Each includes at least three illustrations and a bibliography of relevant print and Web resources." Booklist
"A monumental work, this set displays impeccable credentials, including a large group of contributors, an experienced editorial board, and the careful and extensive efforts of the publishers who themselves have an excellent reputation." Choice

History of astronomy; an encyclopedia; edited by John Lankford. Garland 1997 594p il (Garland encyclopedias in the history of science) $155 **520.3**
1. Astronomy—History—Encyclopedias
ISBN 0-8153-0322-X LC 96-28558
"Focusing on developments since the Scientific Revolution, the signed articles . . . fall into five broad categories: an historical overview of astronomy, astronomy in national contexts (e.g., Chinese astronomy), the history of observatories, the social history of astronomy (e.g., Women in Astronomy), and biographies. . . . Recommendations for further reading are well chosen and current. An excellent and much-needed work." Libr J

Mitton, Jacqueline

Cambridge dictionary of astronomy. Cambridge Univ. Press 2001 443p il hardcover o.p. paperback available $19

520.3
1. Astronomy—Dictionaries
ISBN 0-521-80480-9 (pa) LC 00-64220
Published in the United Kingdom with title: The Penguin dictionary of astronomy
This "work provides definitions of over 3200 words, names, and abbreviations commonly found in astronomy. . . . The definitions vary in length from a few sentences to several paragraphs and are clearly written and very informative. Appendixes include tables providing data on the constellations, planets, natural satellites, planetary ring systems, and brightest stars." Libr J

521 Celestial mechanics

Goodstein, David L., 1939-

Feynman's lost lecture; the motion of planets around the sun; [by] David L. Goodstein and Judith R. Goodstein. Norton 1996 191p il $35; pa $19.95 **521**
1. Feynman, Richard Phillips 2. Universe 3. Astrophysics
ISBN 0-393-03918-8; 0-393-31995-4 (pa)
LC 95-38719
Includes audio CD
This "book consists of four chapters. The first and largest is a brief history of the establishment of the Copernican cosmology, which Feynman gave as a lecture to the freshman class at Caltech. Feynman then revisits the work of Isaac Newton and the watershed proof that separated the ancient world from the modern. There is also a chapter with some wonderful reminiscences of Feynman." Libr J
Includes bibliographical references

Rubin, Alan E.

Disturbing the solar system; impacts, close encounters, and coming attractions. Princeton Univ. Press 2002 361p il $29.95 **521**
1. Gravitation 2. Catastrophes (Geology) 3. Life on other planets
ISBN 0-691-07474-7 LC 2001-55197
"After relating a brief history of the solar system, Alan Rubin describes how astronomers determined our location in the Milky Way. He provides . . . accounts of the energetic interactions among planetary bodies, the generation of the Earth's magnetic field, the effects of other solar-system objects on our climate, the moon's genesis, the heating of asteroids, and the origin of the mysterious tektites. . . . He chronicles the history of the search for life on Mars and describes cutting-edge lines of astrobiological inquiry." Publisher's note
Includes bibliographical references

522 Techniques, equipment, materials of astronomy

Chaisson, Eric

The Hubble wars; astrophysics meets astropolitics in the two-billion-dollar struggle over the Hubble Space Telescope; [by] Eric J. Chaisson. HarperCollins Pubs. 1994 386p il maps o.p.; Harvard Univ. Press paperback available $17.95   **522**

1. Hubble Space Telescope
ISBN 0-06-092629-5 (pa)   LC 93-37468

The author "recounts the launching and initial experiments of the Hubble Space Telescope, the largest, most complex, and most powerful observatory ever launched into space." Booklist

"Despite its literary imperfections, this book is a good chronicle of the Hubble episode and how 'Big Science' can become counterproductive." Libr J

Includes bibliographical references

Dickinson, Terence

The backyard astronomer's guide; [by] Terence Dickinson, Alan Dyer. 2nd ed. Firefly Bks. 2002 336p il $49.95   **522**

1. Astronomy
ISBN 1-55209-507-X

First published 1991 by Camden House

"The authors survey astronomy from the hobbyist's viewpoint, acknowledging some of the most active amateurs and their accomplishments and encouraging readers to contribute to knowledge of the heavens. The book's three parts, respectively on optical equipment, observing techniques, and astrophotography, are full of specifics on their subjects. Equipment reviews are detailed; techniques covered include naked-eye, binocular, and telescope observation; and photography is suggested for a range of camera equipment and film capabilities." Booklist [review of 1991 edition]

"Its nontechnical language makes astronomy an avocation accessible to everyone." Libr J

Harrington, Philip S.

Star ware; the amateur astronomer's ultimate guide to choosing, buying, and using telescopes and accessories. 3rd ed. Wiley 2002 424p il pa $19.95   **522**

1. Telescopes
ISBN 0-471-41806-4   LC 2002-282308

First published 1994

This guidebook on choosing and caring for telescopes and related equipment also features advice on practical issues such as keeping dew off a corrector plate, warding off mosquitoes, and staying warm outside

Includes bibliographical references

Katz, Jonathan I.

The biggest bangs; the mystery of gamma-ray bursts, the most violent explosions in the universe. Oxford Univ. Press 2002 218p il $28   **522**

1. Gamma ray bursts
ISBN 0-19-514570-4   LC 2001-36545

"Discovered in the 1960s, gamma-ray bursts were not as easily measured or explained as quasars and pulsars. Besides recounting the journey to our current understanding of these bursts—which are thought to be explosions from neutron stars either hitting each other or being dragged into a black hole—physicist Katz also elucidates the scientific thinking process." Booklist

Includes bibliographical references

Panek, Richard

Seeing and believing; how the telescope opened our eyes and minds to the heavens. Viking 1998 198p hardcover o.p. paperback available $11.94   **522**

1. Telescopes 2. Astronomy
ISBN 0-14-028061-8 (pa)   LC 98-18766

"From Galileo's observations of the moon and planets to . . . the 1996 discovery, thanks to the Hubble space telescope, that the universe contains 40 billion more galaxies than we had thought, Panek describes how the technology of telescopes has changed and how our ideas of nature and science and of the universe and our place in it have slowly adjusted to that improving technology. A gracefully written and useful blending of science, biography, and analysis of philosophical consequences." Booklist

Includes bibliographical references

Schilling, Govert

Flash! the hunt for the biggest explosions in the universe; translated by Naomi Greenberg-Slovin. Cambridge Univ. Press 2002 291p il $28   **522**

1. Gamma ray bursts 2. Black holes (Astronomy)
ISBN 0-521-80053-6   LC 2002-283188

This book "describes the fast moving field of gamma ray burst research. . . . [It] provides an inside view of the scientific challenges involved in unravelling the mystery of gamma-ray bursts." Publisher's note

"Everday examples are frequently used to illustrate the more difficult concepts. Those who want more details will appreciate the glossary and references to the scientific literature. Almost without realizing it, readers will also get a good introduction to elementary astronomy as a bonus. A must-read for anyone interested in GRBs!" Choice

Includes bibliographical references

523 Specific celestial bodies and phenomena

Chartrand, Mark R.

The Audubon Society field guide to the night sky; astronomical charts by Wil Tirion. Knopf 1991 714p il maps $19.95   **523**

1. Astronomy
ISBN 0-679-40852-5   LC 91-52708

"A Chanticleer Press edition. The Audubon Society field guide series"

This guide includes monthly star charts, charts and photographs of the constellations, detailed information on stars, galaxies, and nebulae, hints on observing the sky, dates of solar and lunar eclipses, meteor showers, and comets, and the Messier catalog

Includes bibliographical references

Croswell, Ken

Planet quest; the epic discovery of alien solar systems. Free Press 1997 324p il o.p.; Harcourt paperback available $14 **523**

1. Planets 2. Outer space—Exploration
ISBN 0-15-600612-X (pa)   LC 97-9473
"After summarizing the history of the discovery of the outer planets in our solar system, science writer Croswell . . . moves on to the . . . recent discoveries of planets revolving around stars other than our Sun." Libr J
This book "is fascinating and worthwhile." N Y Times Book Rev
Includes bibliographical references

Gribbin, John R.

Stardust; supernovae and life: the cosmic connection; [by] John Gribbin with Mary Gribbin. Yale Univ. Press 2000 238p $35; pa $13.95 **523**

1. Supernovas 2. Universe 3. Life (Biology)
ISBN 0-300-08419-6; 0-300-09097-8 (pa)
LC 00-35944
"All the carbon, hydrogen, oxygen and nitrogen (CHON) in our DNA was once floating around in a planetary nebula, to which it had been expelled violently from a red giant star. So how did it get here? Most likely via comets, says Gribbin. . . . The author also argues that we shouldn't necessarily look for life on other planets, but rather on the large moons revolving around the giant planets that orbit distant stars. . . . In a short appendix . . . Gribbin discusses current theories about the evolution of multiple universes." Publ Wkly
"A fine summary of the origin of our elemental constitution." Booklist
Includes bibliographical references

Moore, Patrick

Atlas of the universe; introduction by Arnold Wolfendale. Firefly Bks. 2003 288p il $45 **523**

1. Astronomy
ISBN 1-55297-819-2
Replaces the revised Cambridge Univ. Press edition published 1988. Variant title: Philip's atlas of the universe
At head of title: Firefly
This work begins with a "general historical overview, followed by individual sections on the solar system, the sun, the stars, the structure of the universe and our galaxy's place in it, and over 20 useful star maps, all incorporating the newest scientific data." Libr J

The **Universe** revealed; general editor, Pam Spence. Cambridge Univ. Press 1999 192p il $40 **523**

1. Astronomy 2. Universe
ISBN 0-521-64239-6   LC 99-163022
"Sections on the solar system, cosmology, and observational techniques cover everything from global warming to the size of the universe. Informative facts and figures are provided in side entries, and innovative cross-indexing eases usage and leads the reader to related topics." Libr J

523.1 The universe, galaxies, quasars

Aczel, Amir D.

God's equation; Einstein, relativity, and the expanding universe. Four Walls Eight Windows 1999 236p il o.p.; Dell paperback available $11.95 **523.1**

1. Einstein, Albert, 1879-1955 2. Cosmology 3. Relativity (Physics)
ISBN 0-385-33485-0 (pa)   LC 99-36319
"Conventional wisdom has it that Einstein made an embarrassing error in introducing a 'cosmological constant' into his formula for the dynamics of the universe, but, as Aczel's . . . scientific detective story reveals, Einstein's infamous mistake was in fact a brilliant discovery." Booklist
"Though Aczel's analysis of Einstein's work requires familiarity with advanced mathematics, that analysis makes up only a minor portion of his book, and most readers will appreciate the author's inclusion of the great physicist's letters to astronomer Erwin Freundlich." Publ Wkly
Includes bibliographical references

Adams, Fred C.

The five ages of the universe; inside the physics of eternity; [by] Fred Adams, Greg Laughlin. Free Press 1999 251p il hardcover o.p. paperback available $14 **523.1**

1. Cosmology
ISBN 0-684-86576-9 (pa)   LC 99-18139
"In order to tell the story of the universe from its origin to its ultimate demise, the authors . . . have divided all of time into five eras. . . . Good illustrations help explain complex concepts, and the glossary is useful. This unusual history of the universe is accessible to the educated general reader." Libr J
Includes bibliographical references

Barrow, John D., 1952-

The origin of the universe. Basic Bks. 1994 150p il (Science masters series) hardcover o.p. paperback available $16 **523.1**

1. Cosmology 2. Astrophysics
ISBN 0-465-05314-9 (pa)   LC 94-6343
The author explains current theories in cosmology including the big bang, the inflationary universe, wormholes and the origin of physical constants
"The attentive reader will be rewarded with a gigantic feast for continued contemplation, especially if one comes to the book with fundamental concepts of astronomy and physics well in hand. . . . This is an extremely stimulating book." Sci Books Films
Includes bibliographical references

The **Book** of the cosmos; imagining the universe from Heraclitus to Hawking; edited by Dennis Richard Danielson. Perseus Bks. 2000 xxxiii, 556p il hardcover o.p. paperback available $20 **523.1**

1. Cosmology 2. Physics
ISBN 0-7382-0498-6 (pa)   LC 2001-268173
This book presents "short bits of prose . . . [from an] assortment of cosmological authors. . . . [These include] Tycho, Galileo, Kepler, and Newton. Modern commentators are represented as well, including Samuel Y. Edgerton, who realized that Galileo was able to interpret his observations of the Moon as craters because of his artistic training in Renaissance Italy." Sci Books Films

Chown, Marcus

The universe next door; the making of tomorrow's science. Oxford Univ. Press 2002 191p $26; pa $13.95   **523.1**

1. Physics 2. Cosmology 3. Life on other planets
ISBN 0-19-514382-5; 0-19-516884-4 (pa)

LC 2001-36400

The author attempts to answer such questions as "could time run backwards? Is there a fifth dimension? Does quantum theory promise immortality? . . . Was our universe created by super-intelligent beings from another universe? Is there evidence of extraterrestrial life lying right beneath our feet?" Publisher's note

"Chown frees readers from the technical rigors of theorizing but ceaselessly challenges us to enlarge our imaginative horizons. . . . For sheer intellectual exhilaration, few books offer more." Booklist

Croswell, Ken

The alchemy of the heavens; searching for meaning in the Milky Way; illustrations by Philippe Van. Anchor Bks. (NY) 1995 340p il hardcover o.p. paperback available $14.95

     523.1

1. Milky Way 2. Universe
ISBN 0-385-47214-5 (pa)   LC 94-30452

This is an "overview of our present knowledge concerning the Milky Way. . . . Examples of the numerous topics considered are stellar populations, conflicting models of galactic birth and the origin of the elements." Publ Wkly

A "well-written, crystal-clear presentation. . . . This work will snare all general reading interests." Booklist
Includes bibliographical references

The universe at midnight; observations illuminating the cosmos. Free Press 2001 338p $27   **523.1**

1. Cosmology
ISBN 0-684-85931-9   LC 2001-40232

"Astronomers and physicists, working together, have developed what is known as the standard hot Big Bang model of the universe. . . . [Croswell] chronicles the rise of the standard model in 'The Universe at Midnight.'" NY Times Book Rev

"A clearly written overview that demystifies cosmology for the general reader." Booklist
Includes bibliographical references

Dauber, Philip M.

The three big bangs; comet crashes, exploding stars, and the creation of the universe; [by] Philip M. Dauber and Richard A. Muller. Addison-Wesley 1996 207p il o.p.; Perseus Bks. paperback available $15   **523.1**

1. Cosmology 2. Catastrophes (Geology) 3. Supernovas
ISBN 0-201-15495-1 (pa)   LC 95-24451

The authors discuss the origins of the universe and of life on Earth

"Dauber and Muller have not only chosen three 'hot topics' in . . . astronomy but also have masterfully woven the underlying scientific strands together. They paint a colorful picture of the theories and techniques of modern astronomy." Choice
Includes bibliographical references

Davies, P. C. W., 1946-

The last three minutes; conjectures about the ultimate fate of the universe; [by] Paul Davies. Basic Bks. 1994 162p il (Science masters series) hardcover o.p. paperback available $14   **523.1**

1. Cosmology
ISBN 0-465-03851-4 (pa)   LC 94-6345

In this volume, Davies addresses the question of the ultimate demise of the universe. Topics covered include "the big bang theory, the expansion of the universe, the nature of black holes, and the life cycle of stars." Sci Books Films

"The reader will discover that science can sometimes be more creative than art, more stimulating than philosophy, more revelatory than any religion, and more frightening than any fiction thriller." Choice
Includes bibliographical references

Ferguson, Kitty

Measuring the universe; our historic quest to chart the horizons of space and time. Walker & Co. 1999 342p il $27; pa $16.95

     523.1

1. Cosmology 2. Measurement
ISBN 0-8027-1351-3; 0-8027-7592-6 (pa)

LC 99-19476

"Starting with Eratosthenes and his calculation of the earth's circumference using the shadows cast in a well, and moving through Stephen Hawking's work on black holes, Ferguson tells the tale of our search for our place in the universe. This book is nicely illustrated with photos, tables, and diagrams." Libr J
Includes bibliographical references

Ferris, Timothy

The whole shebang; a state-of-the-universe(s) report. Simon & Schuster 1997 393p hardcover o.p. paperback available $14   **523.1**

1. Cosmology
ISBN 0-684-83861-3 (pa)   LC 96-49768

The author "reviews the current state of scientific cosmology, including the now-considerable overlap between astronomical findings and the theories of elementary particle physicists. . . . Ferris adheres to the orthodox Big Bang theory, giving little attention to its critics, but he is candid about the many uncertainties in modern cosmology. He writes clearly, often with considerable eloquence." Libr J
Includes bibliographical references

Gleiser, Marcelo

The prophet and the astronomer; a scientific journey to the end of time. Norton 2002 256p il $26.95; pa $15.95   **523.1**

1. Cosmology 2. Religion and science 3. End of the world
ISBN 0-393-04987-6; 0-393-32431-1 (pa)

LC 2002-538

"Gleiser ponders the dark parallels between the apocalyptic visions of ancient seers and the cosmic predictions of modern scientists. . . . Gleiser's musings . . . occasionally will baffle the nonspecialist, but most readers will consider a few moments of perplexity a small price to pay for the opportunity to probe humanity's oldest nightmares and newest aspirations." Booklist
Includes bibliographical references

Gribbin, John R.

The birth of time; how astronomers measured the age of the universe; [by] John Gribbin. Yale Univ. Press 2000 237p $40; pa $11.95 **523.1**

1. Cosmology
ISBN 0-300-08346-7; 0-300-08914-7 (pa)
LC 99-52835
First published 1999 in the United Kingdom

The author "recounts the history of the problem and describes the people who have worked on it. Since the age of the universe is inextricably linked to its size, he devotes most of his work to dealing with methods that have been used, are being used, and are proposed as future means to determine cosmic distances." Libr J
Includes bibliographical references

Guth, Alan H.

The inflationary universe; the quest for a new theory of cosmic origins; with a foreword by Alan Lightman. Addison-Wesley 1997 358p il o.p.; Perseus Bks. paperback available $18.50 **523.1**

1. Cosmology
ISBN 0-201-32840-2 (pa)
LC 96-46117

"In the 1970s as scientists struggled to reconcile several discrepancies in the Big Bang theory, Guth, a young, unknown astrophysicist, put forward his model of an inflationary universe. This is his firsthand account of one of the most astonishing theories of the 20th century." Libr J

This "is a user-friendly guide to getting one's mind round the big bang and . . . the events that preceded it. . . . A significant document in the history of science." N Y Times Book Rev
Includes bibliographical references

Hawking, S. W. (Stephen W.)

Black holes and baby universes and other essays; [by] Stephen Hawking. Bantam Bks. 1993 182p hardcover o.p. paperback available $16.95 **523.1**

1. Cosmology 2. Science—Philosophy
ISBN 0-553-37411-7 (pa)
LC 93-8269
Analyzed in Essay and general literature index

A collection of essays and speeches ranging from autobiographical sketches to theoretical discussions of black holes, relativity and quantum mechanics

The author "sprinkles his explanations with a wry sense of humor and a keen awareness that the sciences today delve not only into the far reaches of the cosmos, but into the inner philosophical world as well." N Y Times Book Rev

A brief history of time; [by] Stephen Hawking. Updated and expanded tenth anniversary ed. Bantam Bks. 1998 212p il $27.95; pa $16.95 **523.1**

1. Cosmology
ISBN 0-553-10953-7; 0-553-38016-8 (pa)
LC 98-21874
Also available The illustrated brief history of time $39.95 (ISBN 0-553-10374-1)
First published 1988

The author describes concepts about space and time, black holes, the origin and nature of the universe, the uncertainty principle, and the unification of physics. This edition includes a new introduction and a new chapter about wormholes and time travel

Jastrow, Robert, 1925-

God and the astronomers. 2nd ed. Norton 1992 149p il hardcover o.p. paperback available $12.95 **523.1**

1. Cosmology 2. Astronomy 3. Religion and science
ISBN 0-393-85006-4 (pa)
LC 92-32186
First published 1978

The author considers the theological implications of the big bang theory of creation, and summarizes the evidence for the theory including the relativity theory, the life story of stars, and the discovery of the retreat of the galaxies. Includes chapters by a Catholic astronomer and a Jewish theologian with their viewpoints on the origin and destiny of the universe
Includes bibliographical references

Kolb, Rocky

Blind watchers of the sky; the people and ideas that shaped our view of the universe. Addison-Wesley 1996 338p il o.p.; Perseus Bks. paperback available $18 **523.1**

1. Cosmology 2. Solar system
ISBN 0-201-15496-X (pa)
LC 95-41438

The author "presents a popular history of astronomy and scientific cosmology from Tycho Brahe to the second half of the 20th century." Libr J
Includes bibliographical references

Krauss, Lawrence Maxwell

Atom; an odyssey from the big bang to life on earth . . . and beyond; [by] Lawrence M. Krauss. Little, Brown 2001 305p $26.95 **523.1**

1. Universe
ISBN 0-316-49946-3
LC 00-55795

"Starting with one atom of oxygen that arises as an effect of the big bang, Krauss . . . traces the atom's travels from the early moments of the universe to its participation in life on Earth and then considers what might become of it after life on Earth ends." Sci Am

Lightman, Alan P., 1948-

Ancient light; our changing view of the universe; [by] Alan Lightman. Harvard Univ. Press 1991 170p il hardcover o.p. paperback available $14.95 **523.1**

1. Cosmology 2. Astronomers
ISBN 0-674-03363-9 (pa)
LC 91-12459

"Adapted from Origins: the lives and worlds of modern cosmologists, by Alan Lightman and Roberta Brawer, published by Harvard University Press, 1990"

The author discusses the development of modern cosmology, the big bang model, and recent challenges to that model

"Lightman's book is a short and simple introduction to modern cosmology, with a strong emphasis upon observation and its interaction with theory. . . . Its merits are that it is accurate and does not go further than current observations warrant." Nat Hist
Includes bibliographical references

Rees, Martin J., 1942-

Just six numbers; the deep forces that shape the universe; [by] Martin Rees. Basic Bks. 2000 173p il hardcover o.p. paperback available $14.95 **523.1**

1. Cosmology 2. Big bang theory
ISBN 0-465-03673-2 (pa)
LC 00-268248
First published 1999 in the United Kingdom

Rees, Martin J., 1942-—*Continued*
"Rees summarizes the history of the universe, pointing out that six numbers related to basic physical constants (for example, the relative strengths of the gravitational and electromagnetic attraction) determine how the universe developed." Libr J
"A brief, readable, and profoundly instructive account of where cosmological knowledge stands at this moment." New Yorker
Includes bibliographical references

Our cosmic habitat; [by] Martin Rees. Princeton Univ. Press 2001 205p il $35; pa $14.95   **523.1**
1. Cosmology
ISBN 0-691-08926-4; 0-691-11477-3 (pa)
LC 2001-27835
"Rees explores the notion that our universe is just a part of a vast 'multiverse,' or ensemble of universes, in which most of the other universes are lifeless. . . . In this scenario, our cosmic habitat would be a special, possibly unique universe where the prevailing laws of physics allowed life to emerge." Publisher's note
"In the crowded field of popular writing about the universe, Rees is genuinely in the forefront—an accomplished scientist with the superior writing skills that enable him to connect with nonspecialists." Booklist
Includes bibliographical references

Siegfried, Tom
Strange matters; undiscovered ideas at the frontiers of space and time. Joseph Henry Press 2002 307p il $24.95   **523.1**
1. Cosmology 2. Physics
ISBN 0-309-08407-5   LC 2002-6045
Also available online
"Siegfried attempts to provide answers to the two basic questions that absorb physicists today: 'What is the universe made of?' and 'How does the universe work?'" Publ Wkly
"A light, energetic introduction to cutting-edge physics and cosmology." Booklist

Smoot, George
Wrinkles in time; [by] George Smoot and Keay Davidson. Morrow 1993 331p il o.p.; Avon Bks. paperback available $14   **523.1**
1. Cosmology
ISBN 0-380-72044-2 (pa)   LC 93-8500
"Smoot and Davidson present a historical review of cosmology that takes the reader from the work of Galileo to the recent . . . work on 'COBE' (the Cosmic Background Explorer satellite). An excellent nontechnical study of research into what makes the universe the way it is, the book provides a detailed discussion of the search for and the eventual discovery of what are called the 'wrinkles in time' from the viewpoint of the authors' own experiences in the field." Choice

Tyson, Neil De Grasse
Universe down to Earth. Columbia Univ. Press 1994 277p il $60; pa $19   **523.1**
1. Cosmology
ISBN 0-231-07560-X; 0-231-07561-8 (pa)
LC 93-32259
The author "guides readers through the methods, history, and jargon of cosmology." Booklist
"This book is a genuine joy to read. . . . It is at once witty and profound in its treatment of some of the most 'far-out' concepts of the universe." Sci Books Films
Includes bibliographical references

523.2 Solar system

Greeley, Ronald
The compact NASA atlas of the solar system; [by] Ronald Greeley, Raymond Batson. Cambridge Univ. Press 2002 408p il maps $65   **523.2**
1. Solar system
ISBN 0-521-80633-X   LC 2001-18259
"Derived from The NASA atlas of the solar system ... first published 1997." Verso of title page
"Featuring over 150 maps, 214 color illustrations and a gazetteer that lists the names of all features officially approved by the International Astronomical Union, The Compact NASA Atlas of the Solar System includes the full range of information gathered from NASA missions throughout the Solar System." Publisher's note
"An excellent collection of systematic maps, photographs, and overviews of planets and major satellites. . . . It is unique in scope and its use of uniform formats and consistent scales . . . highly recommended." Libr J

Trefil, James S., 1938-
Other worlds; images of the cosmos from earth and space; [by] James Trefil; foreword by David H. Levy. National Geographic Soc. 1999 255p il $35   **523.2**
1. Cosmology 2. Solar system
ISBN 0-7922-7491-1   LC 99-14601
In this illustrated overview of cosmology Trefil "examines the birth of the solar system and then its inner and outer planets. He closes with a discussion of the universe beyond our solar system." Booklist

523.3 Moon

Mackenzie, Dana
The big splat; or, How our moon came to be. Wiley 2003 232p il $24.95   **523.3**
1. Moon
ISBN 0-471-15057-6   LC 2003-535402
"Mackenzie's account of humanity's long relationship with Earth's only natural satellite, from a probable lunar calendar found in the Lascaux caves to the new 'giant impact' theory of the moon's origin, is magnetically readable, preternaturally clear, and amazingly concise." Booklist
Includes bibliographical references

523.4 Planets

Bakich, Michael E.
The Cambridge planetary handbook. Cambridge Univ. Press 2000 336p il $30
523.4
1. Planets
ISBN 0-521-63280-3   LC 99-10171
"The book is arranged in two parts. Part one presents planetary data, such as atmospheric pressure, composition, and future conjunctions and transits. Part two contains a summary on each planet, including its moons. . . . The handbook is well suited for amateur astronomers and students of astronomy." Booklist

Beebe, Reta F.
Jupiter; the giant planet; [by] Reta Beebe. 2nd ed. Smithsonian Institution Press 1997 261p il (Smithsonian library of the solar system) hardcover o.p. paperback available $17.95 **523.4**
1. Jupiter (Planet)
ISBN 1-56098-685-9 (pa)   LC 96-38604
First published 1994
The author describes the history of discoveries about Jupiter, its atmosphere and interior composition. Includes findings from the 1994 collision of Comet Shoemaker-Levy/9 and observations of the Galileo probe
Includes bibliographical references

Grinspoon, David Harry
Venus revealed; a new look below the clouds of our mysterious twin planet. Addison-Wesley 1997 355p il hardcover o.p. paperback available $20   **523.4**
1. Venus (Planet)
ISBN 0-201-32839-9 (pa)   LC 96-38448
The author discusses "the orbital, geological, and atmospheric processes of Venus gathered through Earth-based observations and various U.S. and Soviet probes." Libr J
The author "makes science fun, not forbidding." Booklist

Morton, Oliver
Mapping Mars; science, imagination, and the birth of a world. Picador 2002 357p il maps $30; pa $16   **523.4**
1. Mars (Planet)
ISBN 0-312-24551-3; 0-312-42261-X (pa)
The author "traces scientists' efforts to map and understand the surface of Mars. . . . Morton writes eloquently and displays a breadth of knowledge not often found in science writing." Publ Wkly
Includes bibliographical references

Peebles, Curtis
Asteroids; a history. Smithsonian Institution Press 2000 280p il $29.95; pa $17.95 **523.4**
1. Asteroids
ISBN 1-56098-389-2; 1-56098-982-3 (pa)
          LC 00-20733
Surveys the equipment, techniques, and controversies of 200 years of asteroid research. Prominent theorists are profiled. Impact threats and the mystery of the dinosaurs' extinction are discussed
"For a book aimed at general audiences, Peeble's excellent review of asteroids is unusually well documented. . . . [His] book clearly has a place on the bookshelves of specialists, students, and advanced amateurs." Choice
Includes bibliographical references

Sheehan, William, 1954-
Mars; the lure of the red planet; [by] William Sheehan & Stephen James O'Meara. Prometheus Bks. 2001 406p il $28   **523.4**
1. Mars (Planet)
ISBN 1-57392-900-X   LC 00-67358
The authors look "at the personalities of the great astronomers who gazed at Mars and, in particular, the aspects of or mysteries about Mars that captivated them. . . . An informative overview of sky watchers' enduring fascination with Mars." Booklist
Includes bibliographical references

The planet Mars; a history of observation & discovery. University of Ariz. Press 1996 270p il maps hardcover o.p. paperback available $19.95   **523.4**
1. Mars (Planet)
ISBN 0-8165-1641-3 (pa)   LC 96-4485
"Sheehan documents the discoveries made by earlier astronomers on through the Mariner and Viking spacecraft." Libr J
"This well-written book presents a fascinating chronological history of Martian discovery." Choice
Includes bibliographical references

523.5 Meteoroids, solar wind, zodiacal light

Bevan, A. W. R.
Meteorites: a journey through space and time; [by] Alex Bevan and John de Laeter. Smithsonian Institution Press 2002 215p il maps $35.95   **523.5**
ISBN 1-58834-021-X   LC 2001-49551
"The authors trace the formation and breakup of the planets, asteroids, and comets where meteorites originated, their long journey through space, their fall to Earth, their recovery, and what scientists are learning from them. The book contains a great deal of material about the '84001 Martian meteorite, which has raised provocative new questions about life on the red planet." Publisher's note
"Informative and visually appealing, this title meets any library's need for a basic source on meteorites." Booklist
Includes bibliographical references

Norton, O. Richard
The Cambridge encyclopedia of meteorites; fragments of other worlds. Cambridge Univ. Press 2002 xx, 354p il maps $50   **523.5**
1. Meteorites
ISBN 0-521-62143-7   LC 2001-35621
This reference describes the classification, structure, history, and origins of meteorites
"Anyone wishing to know what meteorites are, where they come from, and what they reveal about the history of the universe need look no further. This thorough and accessible compilation covers all facets of the field." Libr J
Includes bibliographical references

Rocks from space; meteorites and meteorite hunters; illustrated by Dorothy S. Norton. 2nd ed. Mountain Press 1998 447p il maps $55; pa $32   **523.5**
1. Meteorites 2. Asteroids 3. Comets
ISBN 0-87842-438-5; 0-87842-373-7 (pa)
          LC 97-51574
First published 1994
This illustrated introduction to meteorites and meteoritics includes "sections devoted to meteorite falls, finds, and craters in addition to descriptions of meteorites, how they are classified, their origins, and what they are. Also [included] . . . is a section on the history of meteoritics and the prominent personalities associated with the science." Choice [review of 1994 edition]
Includes bibliographical references

523.6   Comets

Levy, David H., 1948-
Comets; creators and destroyers. Simon &
Schuster 1998 256p il pa $12   **523.6**
1. Comets
ISBN 0-684-85255-1   LC 98-3113
In this study of comets, "Levy explains how astronomers developed an understanding of their real nature and locations in the solar system, their possible role in supplying the earth's life-giving water and carbon, and the evidence of their contribution to cataclysmic extinctions."
Booklist
Includes bibliographical references

Sagan, Carl, 1934-1996
Comet; [by] Carl Sagan and Ann Druyan.
Random House 1985 398p il o.p.; Ballantine
Bks. paperback available $16   **523.6**
1. Comets 2. Halley's comet
ISBN 0-345-41222-2 (pa)   LC 85-8308
"The authors explore the myth and science of comets in a lavishly illustrated, slightly oversize volume that is both fascinating and authoritative." Booklist
Includes bibliographical references

523.7   Sun

Golub, Leon
Nearest star; the surprising science of our
sun; [by] Leon Golub & Jay M. Pasachoff.
Harvard Univ. Press 2001 267p il $29.95; pa
$16.95   **523.7**
1. Sun
ISBN 0-674-00467-1; 0-674-01006-X (pa)
      LC 00-63213
The authors "describe for a nonspecialist audience what is currently known of the structure of the sun, the source of its enormous energy, its history and future, its various effects on Earth and its atmosphere." Libr J
This is "a brilliant, richly illustrated survey." Booklist
Includes bibliographical references

523.8   Stars

Bakich, Michael E.
The Cambridge guide to the constellations.
Cambridge Univ. Press 1995 320p il maps
hardcover o.p. paperback available $29
    523.8
1. Constellations
ISBN 0-521-44921-9 (pa)   LC 94-4678
"This book is the ultimate constellation reference book that brings together a variety of information about constellations, including: the size, visibility and relative brightness of all eighty-eight constellations; former location of extinct constellations; the number of visible stars in each constellation, and more." Univ Press Books for Public and Second Sch Libr
Includes bibliographical references

Ferguson, Kitty
Prisons of light; black holes. Cambridge
Univ. Press 1996 214p il $48; pa $17 **523.8**
1. Black holes (Astronomy)
ISBN 0-521-49518-0; 0-521-62571-8 (pa)
      LC 96-11729
The author discusses the origin, properties, and behavior of black holes and reviews the scientific evidence for their existence
"The typical reader will find this book an easily understood overview of an interesting subject. . . . A clear and accurate introduction to black holes for the general science reader." Sci Books Films
Includes bibliographical references

Hirshfeld, Alan
Parallax; the race to measure the cosmos;
[by] Alan W. Hirshfeld. Freeman, W.H. 2001
314p il $23.95; pa $16   **523.8**
1. Stars
ISBN 0-7167-3711-6; 0-8050-7133-4 (pa)
      LC 00-68147
This book chronicles the efforts to secure the first distance to a star through detection of stellar parallax. Scientists involved in the challenge included Tycho Brahe, Robert Hooke, James Bradley and William Herschel
This "is a lively gallery of colorful and, of course, calculating characters. . . . A delightful history of a crucial advance in knowledge." Booklist
Includes bibliographical references

Kaler, James B.
Extreme stars; at the edge of creation.
Cambridge Univ. Press 2001 236p il maps
$40   **523.8**
1. Stars
ISBN 0-521-40262-X   LC 00-58522
"Each chapter covers extreme stars of a different kind, including the faintest, the coolest, the brightest, the largest, the smallest, the youngest, the oldest, and the strangest. . . . [Kaler] piques the curiosity of the novice, while encouraging knowledgeable readers to think about stars from a different perspective. There is a wealth of information, much of it not available elsewhere at this semipopular level." Choice

Tirion, Wil
The Cambridge star atlas. 3rd ed.
Cambridge Univ. Press 2001 90p il maps $25
    523.8
1. Stars—Atlases
ISBN 0-521-80084-6   LC 2001-622030
First published 1991 with title: Cambridge star atlas
2000.0
This star atlas "includes a series of twenty-four monthly sky maps, designed to be of use for almost anywhere on Earth and a series of twenty . . . star charts, covering the whole heavens, with all stars visible to the naked eye under good circumstances." Publisher's note
"Recommended for anyone who plans to observe with the naked eye, binoculars, or small telescope... The printing is excellent, and the pages easily lie flat." Choice

526 Mathematical geography

Alder, Ken
The measure of all things; the seven-year odyssey and hidden error that transformed the world. Free Press 2002 422p $27; pa $15
526
1. Delambre, J. B. J., 1749-1822 2. Méchain, Pierre-François-André, 1744-1804 3. Metric system 4. Geography
ISBN 0-7432-1675-X; 0-7432-1676-8 (pa)
LC 2002-70267
"In 1792, two astronomers set out from Paris in opposite directions to measure the meridian and thereby define the length of the meter. Alder's marvelous account of their quest is a dramatic tale of revolution, science, and human error." Libr J
Includes bibliographical references

Carter, Bill, 1939-
Latitude; how American astronomers solved the mystery of variation; [by] Bill Carter and Merri Sue Carter. Naval Inst. Press 2002 252p il $24.95
526
1. Chandler, Seth Carlo, 1846-1913 2. Newcomb, Simon, 1835-1909 3. Latitude
ISBN 1-55750-016-9
LC 2002-9396
This is an "account of Seth Chandler's solution to the problem of the variation between observed and theoretical measurements of latitude, a problem that plagued European astronomers for decades." Libr J
"Readers who thrill to the unlikely triumphs of amateurs will greatly enjoy the compelling story of Seth Carlo Chandler Jr. . . . Throughout, the Carters allow nonspecialists to share in a rare intellectual adventure, punctuated with piquant personal episodes." Booklist
Includes bibliographical references

Keay, John
The great arc; the dramatic tale of how India was mapped and Everest was named. HarperCollins Pubs. 2000 xxi, 182p il maps hardcover o.p. paperback available $13 **526**
1. Lambton, William, 1756-1823 2. Everest, George, 1790-1866 3. India—Surveys 4. Himalaya Mountains
ISBN 0-06-093295-3 (pa)
LC 00-38292
This "history of the Great Trigonometrical Survey of India presents indelible descriptions of the vast subcontinent and resonant profiles of the visionary yet forgotten surveyor William Lambton and George Everest, who completed Lambton's project and then was immortalized in the naming of the highest peak in the Himalayas." Booklist

Sobel, Dava
Longitude; the true story of a lone genius who solved the greatest scientific problem of his time. Walker & Co. 1995 184p $19 **526**
1. Harrison, John, 1693-1776 2. Longitude
ISBN 0-8027-1312-2
LC 95-17402
Also available illustrated edition for $32.95; pa $22.95 (ISBN 0-8027-1344-0; 0-8027-7593-4)
"In 1714, Britain's Parliament offered the modern equivalent of $12 to anybody who could develop a means of determining longitude at sea. While the likes of Isaac Newton and Edmund Halley sought to calculate longitude by celestial measurement, John Harrison, an uneducated clockmaker, solved the problem with his in-vention of the chronometer. Science writer Sobel tells this story in a way that enables readers 'to see the globe anew.'" Libr J
Includes bibliographical references

528 Astronomical and nautical almanacs

The **Astronomical** almanac; issued by the Nautical Almanac Office, United States Naval Observatory. . . . U.S. Govt. Ptg. Office $54
528
1. Nautical almanacs
Annual
Formed by the union in 1981 of The American ephemeris and nautical almanac and The Astronomical ephemeris published by Her Majesty's Nautical Almanac Office
"With basic information contributed by the ephemeris offices of a number of countries, this collection of tables is the authoritative source for annual astronomical data from the movement of heavenly bodies to the calculation of calendars." Ref Sources for Small & Medium-sized Libr. 6th edition

529 Chronology

Aveni, Anthony F.
Empires of time; calendars, clocks, and cultures; [by] Anthony Aveni. rev ed. University Press of Colo. 2002 332p il pa $22.95
529
1. Time
ISBN 0-87081-672-1
LC 2002-7120
First published 1989 by Basic Bks.
The author "traces the modern calendar's roots back to Greek pastoral poetry and prehistoric African bone markings, then compares Western, Chinese, Maya, Inca and tribal time systems. He also fathoms our division of time into days, weeks, months, seasons and years for clues to our psychology and worldview." Publ Wkly
Includes bibliographical references

Barnett, Jo Ellen
Time's pendulum; the quest to capture time—from sundials to atomic clocks. Plenum Trade 1998 340p il $27.95
529
1. Time
ISBN 0-306-45787-3
LC 98-4624
Also available in paperback from Harcourt
The author "shows how our notion of time is relative on a very human level. Time has undergone a long process of standardization over the centuries, she explains. . . . Barnett's book is a triumph of interdisciplinary scholarship that could appeal to a wide variety of readers." Publ Wkly
Includes bibliographical references

Duncan, David Ewing

Calendar; humanity's epic struggle to determine a true and accurate year. Avon Bks. 1998 266p il hardcover o.p. paperback available $13.50   **529**

1. Calendars 2. Time

ISBN 0-380-79324-5 (pa)   LC 98-10434

The author "chronicles the evolution of human attempts to chart time accurately and reviews the time periods, events, and principle figures involved in this process. Introductory material includes a short 'Calendar Index' containing statistics, a comparison of major calendar systems, and a brief timeline of Gregorian calendar development." Libr J

Includes bibliographical references

Galison, Peter Louis

Einstein's clocks and Poincaré's maps; empires of time; by Peter Galison. Norton 2003 389p il $23.95   **529**

1. Einstein, Albert, 1879-1955 2. Poincaré, Henri, 1854-1912 3. Time 4. Relativity (Physics)

ISBN 0-393-02001-0   LC 2002-155114

Contents: Synchrony; Coal and chaos; The electric worldmap; Poincaré's maps; Einstein's clocks; The place of time

"Gallison shows how Einstein's work was influenced by French cartographer Henri Poincaré and by the physicist's own experience working in a Bern patent office, where the numerous patent requests for devices designed to coordinate distant clocks may have prompted further inquiry into the problem of simultaneity, which lies at the heart of relativity. Few books have ever made Einstein's theories more accessible—or more engrossing—for general readers." Booklist

Includes bibliographical references

Gleick, James

Faster; the acceleration of just about everything. Pantheon Bks. 1999 324p il hardcover o.p. paperback available $14   **529**

1. Time

ISBN 0-679-77548-X (pa)   LC 99-21640

Gleick focuses on time and argues that the pace of life has grown faster. He discusses technologies such as "the watch, the typewriter, the phone, the TV, and [the computer, and] . . . the ways these 'time-saving' devices have influenced our world." Christ Sci Monit

The author's "shrewd dissection of the 'psychology of hurriedness' leads to many provocative observations." Booklist

Richards, E. G. (Edward Graham)

Mapping time; the calendar and its history. Oxford Univ. Press 1999 xxi, 438p il hardcover o.p. paperback available $16.95   **529**

1. Calendars 2. Time

ISBN 0-19-286205-7 (pa)   LC 98-24957

"An overview of astronomy, time, clocks, writing, arithmetic, and other theoretical issues lays the groundwork for a description of calendar systems from prehistory to the present. Illustrations, charts, and diagrams, including algorithms for the conversion of calendar systems, are also provided." Libr J

Includes bibliographical references

530 Physics

Bloomfield, Louis

How things work; the physics of everyday life; [by] Louis A. Bloomfield. 2nd ed. Wiley 2001 xxiv, 512p il pa $83.95   **530**

1. Physics

ISBN 0-471-38151-9   LC 00-64917

First published 1997

"After an introduction to the principles of physics, such as those involving kinetic and potential energy, torque, and acceleration, the reader learns how a seesaw works, how a vacuum cleaner works, and even how air conditioners work. The list of 51 everyday objects is used to illustrate how the principles of physics manifest themselves around us. . . . The book is liberally sprinkled with diagrams designed to illustrate the points made. The writing is clear, and principles easily extracted from the text." Sci Books Films [review of 1997 edition]

Buchanan, Mark

Nexus: small worlds and the groundbreaking science of networks. Norton 2002 235p $25.95; pa $14.95   **530**

1. Patterns (Mathematics) 2. System analysis

ISBN 0-393-04153-0; 0-393-32442-7 (pa)

LC 2002-518

The author "introduces readers to the dynamics of networks and shows how these networks affect behaviors in both the natural and the social world. . . . [Buchanan] finds the same patterns taking shape in food chains, in the neuronal networks of insects, in the architecture of the Internet and in the cultural backgrounds of elite CEOs. . . . Buchanan's ability as an affable, easygoing storyteller makes up for myriad digressions, and the narrative is, at times, spellbinding." Publ Wkly

Includes bibliographical references

The **Cambridge** companion to Newton; edited by I. Bernard Cohen and George E. Smith. Cambridge Univ. Press 2002 500p il $65; pa $23   **530**

1. Newton, Sir Isaac, 1642-1727

ISBN 0-521-65177-8; 0-521-65696-6 (pa)

LC 2001-37836

"A team of . . . contributors examines the principal aspects of Newton's thought. They include not only his approach to space, time, mechanics, and universal gravity in Principia and his research in optics and mathematics, but also his lesser known clandestine investigations into alchemy, theology, and prophecy." Publisher's note

This is "the best available brief overview of Newton's contributions to mechanics, cosmology, optics, mathematics, alchemy, and theology. The contributors have produced 16 well-written and admirably focused chapters. Some will be challenging for nonspecialist readers, but even those that discuss mechanics in detail are so well organized and clearly written that they amply repay close attention." Choice

Includes bibliographical references

Cole, K. C.

First you build a cloud; and other reflections on physics as a way of life. Harcourt Brace & Co. 1999 231p il pa $14   **530**

1. Physics

ISBN 0-15-600646-4   LC 98-47050

"A Harvest book"

Cole, K. C.—*Continued*

Originally published 1985 by Morrow with title: Sympathetic vibrations

"Cole offers reflections on the place of physics in modern life. . . . Especially compelling are the essays on the aesthetic force behind scientific endeavors—the beauties of theory. For readers without scientific background, Cole gracefully introduces relativity, quantum theory, optics, astrophysics, and other significant disciplines, never getting bogged down in unnecessary explanation." Booklist

Includes bibliographical references

The hole in the universe; how scientists peered over the edge of emptiness and found everything. Harcourt 2001 274p il hardcover o.p. paperback available $14   **530**
1. Physics
ISBN 0-15-601317-7 (pa)   LC 00-44947

Cole discusses the history of nothing, "combining the history of zero (a mathematical nothing) with that of the vacuum (a physical nothing). . . . Until Einstein showed that light needed no tangible medium through which to travel, theorists filled the vacuum with 'ether'—the 'enfant terrible' of substances, as Einstein put it. It was subsequently banished." Atl Mon

Includes bibliographical references

Davies, P. C. W., 1946-

The matter myth; dramatic discoveries that challenge our understanding of physical reality; [by] Paul Davies and John Gribbin. Simon & Schuster 1992 320p il hardcover o.p. paperback available $14   **530**
1. Reality 2. Physics
ISBN 0-671-72841-5 (pa)   LC 91-39522

Topics discussed include "chaos, solitons, the topology of space, quantum field theory, antimatter, magnetic monopoles, special and general relativity, the big bang, inflationary cosmology, the omega point, dark matter, cosmic strings and superstrings, wormholes, and the many-universe model." Sci Books Films

Includes bibliographical references

Deutsch, David

The fabric of reality; the science of parallel universes—and its implications. Allen Lane/The Penguin Press 1997 390p il hardcover o.p. paperback available $16   **530**
1. Reality 2. Physics—Philosophy 3. Life 4. Cosmology
ISBN 0-14-027541-X (pa)   LC 97-6171

"Deutsch describes a reality where parallel universes are 'stacked like a pack of playing cards' to comprise a 'multiverse,' with computers communicating between them, where the mechanics and likelihood of time travel exist and where the universe comes to an end. . . . An intellectually stimulating read for the science-literate and motivated lay person." Publ Wkly

"A thoroughly mesmerizing scientific/philosophical view of reality." Libr J

Includes bibliographical references

Einstein, Albert, 1879-1955

The evolution of physics; the growth of ideas from early concepts to relativity and quanta; by Albert Einstein and Leopold Infeld. Simon & Schuster 1938 320p il hardcover o.p. paperback available $13   **530**
1. Physics—History 2. Relativity (Physics) 3. Quantum theory
ISBN 0-671-20156-5 (pa)

An "exposition for the layman of the growth of ideas in physical science." Publ Wkly

Feynman, Richard Phillips

Six easy pieces; essentials of physics, explained by its most brilliant teacher; [by] Richard P. Feynman; originally prepared for publication by Robert B. Leighton and Matthew Sands; new introduction by Paul Davies. Helix Bks. (Reading) 1995 xxix, 145p il o.p.; Perseus Bks. paperback available $15   **530**
1. Physics
ISBN 0-201-40825-2 (pa)   LC 94-30894

This book reprints six chapters from Feynman's Lectures on Physics, which the "scientist delivered from 1961 to 1963 at the California Institute of Technology. . . . They discuss atoms, basic physics, the relation of physics to other sciences, the conservation of energy, gravitation, and quantum behavior." Libr J

"These 'easy pieces' cover key topics with a minimum of mathematics and a wealth of excellent analogies and vivid descriptions." Booklist

Kragh, Helge, 1944-

Quantum generations; a history of physics in the twentieth century. Princeton Univ. Press 1999 494p $65; pa $22.95   **530**
1. Physics—History
ISBN 0-691-01206-7; 0-691-09552-3 (pa)
LC 99-17903

The author "details the explosive course physics has taken from the introduction of X rays in the mid-1890's to superstring theory in the present day. . . . [He] explains not only how the groundbreaking ideas of physics progressed but also how they are actively applied." Publisher's note

Includes bibliographical references

Krauss, Lawrence Maxwell

Fear of physics; a guide for the perplexed. Basic Bks. 1993 206p il hardcover o.p. paperback available $18   **530**
1. Physics
ISBN 0-465-02367-3 (pa)   LC 92-54523

The author uses "examples and analogies to introduce many of the central ideas of current physics theories without using equations. The book begins with the concept of scaling, using the 'spherical cow' as an example, and ends with contemplation of a 'Theory of Everything.' Along the way, topics such as the expanding universe, uses of numerical estimation, the creation and development of physical theories . . . and the Standard Model are clearly discussed at a level appropriate for the educated general reader." Choice

Includes bibliographical references

Macmillan encyclopedia of physics; John S. Rigden, editor in chief. Simon & Schuster Macmillan 1996 4v il set $475　　**530**
1. Physics—Encyclopedias
ISBN 0-02-897359-3　　　　　LC 96-30977
Also available supplementary volume Building blocks of matter published 2003
This set covers "all of the subdisciplines of the field of physics. In approximately 1,000 articles, it discusses concepts and important people from throughout the history of the field." Booklist
"This excellent encyclopedia is recommended for libraries seeking to serve a broad clientele." Libr J

Peat, F. David, 1938-
From certainty to uncertainty; the story of science and ideas in the twentieth century. Joseph Henry Press 2002 230p $24.95　**530**
1. Physics 2. Chaos (Science)
ISBN 0-309-07641-2　　　　　LC 2002-1482
Contents: Quantum uncertainty; On incompleteness; From object to process; Language; The end of representation; From clockwork to chaos; Re-envisioning the planet; Pausing the cosmos

Suplee, Curt
Physics in the 20th century; edited by Judith R. Franz and John S. Rigden. Abrams 1999 223p il $49.50; pa $19.95　　**530**
1. Physics
ISBN 0-8109-4364-6; 0-8109-9084-9 (pa)
　　　　　　　　　　　　　LC 98-41306
In this overview of physics Suplee "leads us through the structure and function of atoms, the astonishing intimacy of light and matter, the often amusing improbabilities of quantum mechanics, the architecture of exotic materials, the elusive lives of subatomic particles that are the stuff of all creation, and chaos and order in nature—until we arrive at a vision of the entire universe. He does it without equations or misleading analogies, and often with humor." N Y Times Book Rev

Teller, Edward, 1908-2003
Conversations on the dark secrets of physics; [by] Edward Teller, Wendy Teller, and Wilson Talley. Plenum Press 1991 247p il o.p.; Perseus Bks. paperback available $16
　　　　　　　　　　　　　　　　530
1. Physics
ISBN 0-7382-0765-9 (pa)　　　LC 91-8626
The authors discuss the work of major physicists starting with Pythagoras and the ancient Greeks and including Einstein, Galileo, Johann Kepler, Isaac Newton, Niels Bohr, and Louis de Broglie, and explain such topics as quantum theory, superconductivity, and lasers
"Each chapter starts at a low level of understanding, but often ends up at a dramatically high one. Questions at the end of each chapter have answers that are both expansive and illuminating." New Sci
Includes bibliographical references

530.1　Physics—Theories and mathematical physics

Aczel, Amir D.
Entanglement; the greatest mystery in physics. Four Walls Eight Windows 2002 284p il $25　　　　　　　　**530.1**
1. Quantum theory
ISBN 1-56858-232-3　　　　　LC 2002-69338
The author discusses "the concept of entanglement in quantum physics. He begins by explaining that 'entanglement' occurs when two subatomic particles are somehow connected or 'entangled' with one another, so that when something happens to one particle, the same thing simultaneously happens to the other particle, even if it's miles away. However, this concept violates the theory of special relativity, since communication between two places cannot occur faster than the speed of light. Einstein knew that the mathematics of quantum theory predicted that this could happen, but he didn't believe it. In the last decade, researchers have shown in laboratory experiments that entanglement does indeed happen." Publ Wkly
Includes bibliographical references

Barbour, Julian B.
The end of time; the next revolution in physics; [by] Julian Barbour. Oxford Univ. Press 2000 371p il $32.50; pa $17.95　**530.1**
1. Space and time 2. Relativity (Physics) 3. Quantum theory
ISBN 0-19-511729-8; 0-19-514592-5 (pa)
　　　　　　　　　　　　　LC 99-44319
This "book is about time and its history—how it is treated in various physical theories. . . . Barbour asks what time really is. His answer, in light of all we know of the physics involved: nothing; time does not exist." NY Times Book Rev
Includes bibliographical references

Bodanis, David
$E=mc^2$; a biography of the world's most famous equation. Walker & Co. 2000 337p il $25　　　　　　　　　　　　**530.1**
1. Einstein, Albert, 1879-1955 2. Force and energy 3. Space and time
ISBN 0-8027-1352-1　　　　　LC 00-40857
Also available in paperback from Berkley Pub. Group
The author relates the story of "Einstein's formulation of the equation in 1905 and its association ever after with relativity and nuclear energy. Parallel with the science, Bodanis populates his tale with dramatic lives." Booklist

Davies, P. C. W., 1946-
About time; Einstein's unfinished revolution; [by] Paul Davies. Simon & Schuster 1995 316p il hardcover o.p. paperback available $14　　　　**530.1**
1. Einstein, Albert, 1879-1955 2. Space and time 3. Relativity (Physics) 4. Astrophysics
ISBN 0-684-81822-1 (pa)　　　LC 94-40281
This book examines scientific "theories about the origin, direction, and end of time." Booklist
This "is intelligent, fascinating, and eminently readable." Sci Books Films
Includes bibliographical references

Einstein, Albert, 1879-1955
The meaning of relativity; including the Relativistic theory of the non-symmetric field. 5th ed. Princeton Univ. Press 1956 166p hardcover o.p. paperback available $13.95
530.1
1. Relativity (Physics)
ISBN 0-691-02352-2 (pa)
First published 1922. Translated by Edwin Plimpton Adams, Ernst G. Straus and Bruria Kaufman
The Stafford Little lectures of Princeton University, May 1921
"Though few can understand it, most readers in physics and librarians in charge of science collections know this book as one of the landmarks of modern knowledge. . . . The book is not intended for general reading. Instead it is addressed to . . . [those whose training enables] them to understand the mathematical expressions of relativity." N Y Public Libr. New Tech Books

Fritzsch, Harald, 1943-
An equation that changed the world; Newton, Einstein, and the theory of relativity; translated by Karin Heusch. University of Chicago Press 1994 279p il $32.50; pa $16
530.1
1. Einstein, Albert, 1879-1955 2. Newton, Sir Isaac, 1642-1727 3. Relativity (Physics)
ISBN 0-226-26557-9; 0-226-26558-7 (pa)
LC 94-3876
"Bridging the gap between classical and relativistic concepts, the author describes a variety of phenomena of modern physics. . . . Fritzsch accomplishes his goal by introducing three characters: Sir Isaac Newton and Albert Einstein return from the dead and meet Professor Adrian Haller [a fictitious] . . . American physicist from the present." Sci Books Films
"Many readers will applaud Fritzsch for this lively but profoundly insightful book." Booklist
Includes bibliographical references

Gell-Mann, Murray, 1929-
The quark and the jaguar; adventures in the simple and the complex. Freeman, W.H. 1994 392p il o.p.; Holt & Co. paperback available $17
530.1
1. Particles (Nuclear physics) 2. Science—Philosophy
ISBN 0-8050-7253-5 (pa)
LC 94-1642
The author "ponders the universe's mix of simplicity and complexity, regularity and randomness, as he ranges from quarks (the fundamental subatomic particles which he discovered) to complex adaptive systems like bacteria developing resistance to antibiotics, mobile robots, jaguars, and people interacting with and learning from their environment." Publ Wkly
"While the topics are technical in nature, Gell-Mann's presentation is clear and will be readily understood by scholars and informed lay readers." Libr J

Gott, J. Richard, 1947-
Time travel in Einstein's universe; the physical possibilities of travel through time; [by] J. Richard Gott, III. Houghton Mifflin 2001 291p il $24; pa $14
530.1
1. Space and time 2. Fourth dimension
ISBN 0-395-95563-7; 0-618-25735-7 (pa)
LC 00-54243
"Gott tackles the complexities of attempting to turn the fantasy of time travel into a theoretical possibility in

a lively and lucid discussion." Booklist
Includes bibliographical references

Gribbin, John R.
In search of Schrödinger's cat; quantum physics and reality. Bantam Bks. 1984 302p il pa $15.95
530.1
1. Quantum theory 2. Reality
ISBN 0-553-34253-3
LC 84-2975
This history of quantum mechanics discusses the work of Huygens, Einstein, Schrödinger, Bohr, Planck and Everett
This book "contains many vignettes from the history of science and many insights into the researchers and the work that has led to our current understanding of the quantum theory. Excellent analogies and graphic illustrations are used to present difficult ideas." Sci Books Films
Includes bibliographical references

Schrödinger's kittens and the search for reality; solving the quantum mysteries; [by] John Gribbin. Little, Brown 1995 261p il hardcover o.p. paperback available $14.95
530.1
1. Schrödinger, Erwin, 1887-1961 2. Quantum theory 3. Reality
ISBN 0-316-32819-7 (pa)
LC 95-75652
In this sequel to In search of Schrödinger's cat, Gribbin attempts to "explain recent experimental and theoretical findings about the . . . nature of the submicroscopic world of the atom. The 'Copenhagen interpretation' of quantum mechanics offered by Niels Bohr and his colleagues has prevailed for almost 70 years, but there [are] now . . . competing interpretations. Gribbin reviews this . . . [field and] indicates his personal preference for one of the new theoretical models." Libr J
Includes bibliographical references

Guillen, Michael
Five equations that changed the world; the power and poetry of mathematics. Hyperion 1995 277p $22.95; pa $14.95
530.1
1. Physics 2. Mathematics
ISBN 0-7868-6103-7; 0-7868-8187-9 (pa)
LC 95-15199
The author discusses "five significant equations in physics and the individuals who developed them. The individuals are Isaac Newton (Universal gravitation), Daniel Bernoulli (hydrodynamic pressure), Michael Faraday (thermodynamics), Rudolf Clausius (thermodynamics), and Albert Einstein (special relativity)." Libr J
"A seamless blend of dramatic biography and mathematical documentary that links the personal with the scientific." Publ Wkly

Hawking, S. W. (Stephen W.)
The nature of space and time; [by] Stephen Hawking and Roger Penrose. Princeton Univ. Press 1996 141p il (Isaac Newton Institute series of lectures) $49.50; pa $18.95 **530.1**
1. Space and time 2. Quantum theory 3. Astrophysics
ISBN 0-691-03791-4; 0-691-05084-8 (pa)
LC 95-35582
This volume "takes the form of a debate between Hawking and Penrose at Cambridge in 1994. At the center of the discussion is a pair of powerful theories: the quantum theory of fields and the general theory of rela-

Hawking, S. W. (Stephen W.)—*Continued*

tivity. The issue is how—if at all—one can merge the two into a quantum theory of gravity. . . . A substantial background in theoretical physics is needed for full comprehension." Libr J

Includes bibliographical references

The universe in a nutshell; [by] Stephen Hawking. Bantam Bks. 2001 216p il $35

530.1

1. Quantum theory
ISBN 0-553-80202-X   LC 2001-35757

Companion volume to A brief history of time

Hawking "explains the basic laws of physics that govern the universe, beginning with a brief history of the concept of relativity, and then he is off and running to explore time, space, the future, and the possibility of time travel, among other fundamental rules of the universe's road. Admirers of Hawking's previous book will continue to appreciate his ability not only to air fresh, provocative ideas but also to say what he means clearly and without watering down his material or condescending to his audience—he even injects humor into his narrative. The profuse, beautifully rendered illustrations contribute greatly to the reader's understanding of his points." Booklist

Kaku, Michio

Hyperspace; a scientific odyssey through parallel universes, time warps, and the tenth dimension; illustrations by Robert O'Keefe. Oxford Univ. Press 1994 359p il $35   **530.1**

1. Relativity (Physics) 2. Space and time
ISBN 0-19-508514-0   LC 93-7910

Also available in paperback from Anchor Bks.

This is an "overview of the major scientists, discoveries, and ideas involved in an ongoing quest for synthesizing quantum mechanics and relativity physics into a superstring theory of our entire universe." Libr J

Includes bibliographical references

Parker, Barry R.

Quantum legacy; the discovery that changed our universe; [by] Barry Parker. Prometheus Bks. 2002 282p il $29   **530.1**

1. Quantum theory
ISBN 1-57392-993-X   LC 2002-67966

The author describes the theory of quantum mechanics, its practical applications, and the work of such scientists as Max Planck, Albert Einstein, Niels Bohr, Werner Heisenberg, Erwin Schrodinger, and Richard Feynman

Includes bibliographical references

Thorne, Kip S.

Black holes and time warps; Einstein's outrageous legacy. Norton 1994 619p il hardcover o.p. paperback available $18.95

530.1

1. Physics 2. Relativity (Physics) 3. Astrophysics 4. Black holes (Astronomy)
ISBN 0-393-31276-3 (pa)   LC 93-2014

This book is "about black holes, white holes, wormholes, parallel universes, time travel, 10-dimensional space-time, the origin and fate of the universe and a lot of other subjects dear to science fiction fans." N Y Times Book Rev

Includes bibliographical references

Wolfson, Richard, 1947-

Simply Einstein; relativity demystified. Norton 2003 261p il $24.95   **530.1**

1. Relativity (Physics)
ISBN 0-393-05154-4   LC 2002-2984

Contents: The self-creating universe and other absurdities; Tennis, tea, and time travel; Moving heaven and earth; Let there be light; Ether dreams; Crisis in physics; Einstein to the rescue; Stretching time; Star trips and squeezed space; The same time?; Past, present, future, and—elsewhere; Faster than light?; Is everything relative?; A problem of gravity; Into the black hole; Einstein's universe

"Wolfson's economical and vivid tutorial should open doors for lay readers encountering Einstein's principles for the first time. His popular style, with a minimum of math, should make this a must-have book for Einstein buffs as well." Publ Wkly

Includes bibliographical references

530.8   Measurement

The **Economist** desk companion; how to measure, convert, calculate, and define practically anything. Wiley 1998 272p il map $27.95   **530.8**

1. Weights and measures
ISBN 0-471-24953-X   LC 98-17615

First published 1992 by Holt & Co.

"This reference manual provides essential information on measurements, formulas, and calculations on a wide variety of scientific, industrial, economic, and applied technological topics. The introductory section describes the three major world measurement systems, followed by sections containing conversion tables, local units of measurements around the world, and abbreviations and country codes. Subjects include agriculture, finance, health, and transport, among many other topics. . . . This ready-reference volume serves as a superb compilation of material scattered in numerous sources." Libr J

535   Light and paraphotic phenomena

Magueijo, João

Faster than the speed of light; the story of a scientific speculation. Perseus Bks. 2003 279p il $26   **535**

1. Light 2. Physics
ISBN 0-7382-0525-7   LC 2002-112394

Contents: Very silly; pt1 The story of C: Einstein's bovine dreams; Matters of gravity; His biggest error; The sphinx universe; God on amphetamine; pt2 Light years: On a damp winter morning; Goan nights; Middle age crisis; The Gutenberg battle; The morning after; Altitude sickness; Epilogue: faster than light

In this study theoretical physicist Magueijo presents the idea that light traveled faster in the early universe than it does today. He also documents the reactions other scientists are having to this theory, which contradicts Einstein's theory of relativity

"Breaking the old speed limit posted by . . . Albert Einstein in his 20s, this book deploys a racy and provocative text to convey its popularized content of a new cosmology. Jocular, ironic, witty, self-centered, even indignant, Magueijo is all too ready to castigate his adversaries." Sci Am

Park, David

The fire within the eye; a historical essay on the nature and meaning of light. Princeton Univ. Press 1997 377p il hardcover o.p. paperback available $19.95 **535**

1. Light 2. Optics

ISBN 0-691-05051-1 (pa)   LC 96-45573

A history of the concept and science of light from classical times to the present. Cultural, philosophical, intellectual and theological perspectives are explored and works by Aristotle, Grosseteste, Plotinus and Bohr are among those discussed

"Whether it is Fermat and Huygens on optics or Faraday and Maxwell on electromagnetism, the writing is lively and informed. . . . The very readable style and helpful glossary, along with an excellent bibliography and references, make this work suitable for . . . general readers." Choice

Perkowitz, S., 1939-

Empire of light; a history of discovery in science and art; [by] Sidney Perkowitz. Holt & Co. 1996 227p o.p.; Joseph Henry Press paperback available $16.95 **535**

1. Light

ISBN 0-309-06556-9 (pa)   LC 95-50778

"A John Macrae book"

The author traces "humanity's understanding of light from both scientific and artistic viewpoints. Later portions of his text deal with light in contemporary physics research and in astronomy and cosmology." Libr J

"This is a wonderful, well-written book that not only enlightens, but also entertains the reader." Sci Books Films

Includes bibliographical references

Zajonc, Arthur

Catching the light; the entwined history of light and mind. Bantam Bks. 1993 388p il o.p.; Oxford Univ. Press paperback available $17.95 **535**

1. Light

ISBN 0-19-509575-8 (pa)   LC 92-20204

The author "provides a capsule history of humans' changing understanding of the nature of light; scientific developments are interspersed with the comments of numerous philosophers, literary figures, and miscellaneous other nonscientists." Libr J

"Reading this creative, learned, anecdotal, poetic, cross-cultural, and interdisciplinary volume is a profound challenge and a deep pleasure." Booklist

Includes bibliographical references

536   Heat

Segrè, Gino

A matter of degrees; what temperature reveals about the past and future of our species, planet, and universe. Viking 2002 300p il $24.95; pa $15 **536**

1. Temperature

ISBN 0-670-03101-1; 0-14-200278-X (pa)

LC 2001-46942

The author "first gives background on the inventors of the thermometer, which prepares the way for the major discoveries in the 1800s about the nature of heat. . . . Segre recounts heat's role in the earth's formation, climate history, and thermophilic life on the ocean bottom, and . . . the temperature of stellar interiors." Booklist

Segre "brings humor and passion to his subject and excels in showing its relevance to both current policy and future research." Publ Wkly

Includes bibliographical references

Shachtman, Tom, 1942-

Absolute zero and the conquest of cold. Houghton Mifflin 1999 261p $25; pa $14 **536**

1. Low temperatures—Research

ISBN 0-395-93888-0; 0-618-08239-5 (pa)

LC 99-33305

The author "analyzes the social impact of the chill factor, explains the science of cold and tells the curious tales behind inventions like the thermometer, the fridge and the thermos flask." N Y Times Book Rev

Von Baeyer, Hans Christian

Maxwell's demon; why warmth disperses and time passes. Random House 1998 xxi, 207p hardcover o.p. paperback available $15 **536**

1. Thermodynamics 2. Time

ISBN 0-375-75372-9 (pa)   LC 97-41543

The author "traces the development of the laws of thermodynamics in a narrative spanning a period from 13th-century perpetual motion machines to contemporary thinking about laser technology, information theory, and algorithmic randomness. . . . The star of the story is James Clerk Maxwell's molecule-manipulating demon, who conceivably could challenge the Second Law of Thermodynamics." Choice

538   Magnetism

Livingston, James D., 1930-

Driving force; the natural magic of magnets. Harvard Univ. Press 1996 311p il maps hardcover o.p. paperback available $16.95 **538**

1. Magnets

ISBN 0-674-21645-8 (pa)   LC 95-39595

The author "explains the uses of magnets, the properties of magnetism, and how modern materials science uses both." Libr J

"A stimulating variety of science, history, and technology delivered enthusiastically." Booklist

Includes bibliographical references

Savage, Candace, 1949-

Aurora; the mysterious northern lights. Sierra Club Bks. 1994 144p il maps o.p.; Firefly Bks. paperback available $19.95 **538**

1. Auroras

ISBN 1-55209-583-5 (pa)   LC 94-1458

In text and photographs, this book examines the science, history, and mythology of the aurora, otherwise known as the polar or northern lights

"With the publication of this volume everyone can experience the aurora vicariously through the magnificent photographs and prose contained within." Choice

Includes bibliographical references

539.7   Atomic and nuclear physics

Asimov, Isaac, 1920-1992

Atom; journey across the subatomic cosmos; illustrated by D.F. Bach. Dutton 1991 319p il hardcover o.p. paperback available $15.95   **539.7**
1. Atoms 2. Nuclear physics
ISBN 0-452-26834-6 (pa)   LC 90-21343
"A Truman Talley book"

The author "presents the history of atomic and subatomic research from the speculation of ancient Greek philosophers to the cosmological theorizing of the late 20th century. Somewhat less than half the book is devoted to the story of how the existence of atoms was confirmed and their structure was determined. The remainder of the work deals with the internal structure of the nucleus and with the many particles . . . disclosed by modern physicists." Libr J

Building blocks of matter; a supplement to the Macmillan encyclopedia of physics; edited by John S. Rigden. Macmillan Ref. 2003 xxxi, 530p il $162.50   **539.7**
1. Particles (Nuclear physics)
ISBN 0-02-865703-9   LC 2002-13396

This supplement to the Macmillan encyclopedia of physics "covers topics in particle physics—including laboratories and facilities for study in elementary particle physics, biographies of prominent physicists, historical articles, experiments and case studies, and physical concepts, processes, and procedures. Each signed entry runs one to five pages and includes a bibliography, references, and photos and black-and-white illustrations." Libr J

Close, F. E.

The particle odyssey; a journey to the heart of the matter; [by] Frank Close, Michael Marten, Christine Sutton. New ed. Oxford Univ. Press 2002 240p il $45   **539.7**
1. Particles (Nuclear physics)
ISBN 0-19-850486-1   LC 2002-512235

First published 1987 with title: The particle explosion

"The authors describe the history of experimental particle physics: its origins in the discovery of X-rays in 1895; the dissection of the atom by Rutherford and others; the unexpected revelations of the cosmic rays; the discovery of quarks and the rise of the 'standard model' in the last part of the 20th century." Publisher's note

This "well-written text succeeds in explaining complex scientific concepts for lay readers without oversimplifying them or patronizing the audience. The color illustrations are dazzlingly attractive and complement the text. Captions on the bubble chamber photos are a great help in unraveling the particle interactions shown. This superb explication of fundamental physical science is highly recommended for academic and public libraries." Libr J

Includes bibliographical references

The **Facts** on File dictionary of atomic and nuclear physics; edited by Richard Rennie. Facts on File 2002 250p il $49.50; pa $19.95   **539.7**
1. Nuclear physics—Dictionaries 2. Atoms—Dictionaries
ISBN 0-8160-4916-5; 0-8160-4917-3 (pa)
LC 2002-32545

This dictionary "covers areas such as atomic theory, the structure of matter, spectroscopy, quantum theory, nuclear physics, particle physics, and cosmology. Examples of specific entries are *Bohr model; Carbon dating; Grand unified theories* (GUTs); *Hadron; Hawking, Stephen William; Rydberg constant*; and *Self-organization*. Appendixes provide tables of fundamental constants, elementary particles, chemical elements, and a selected list of organizational Web pages." Booklist

Feynman, Richard Phillips

QED; the strange theory of light and matter; [by] Richard Feynman. Princeton Univ. Press 1985 158p (Alix G. Mautner memorial lectures) $55; pa $15.95   **539.7**
1. Electrons 2. Light 3. Quantum theory
ISBN 0-691-08388-6; 0-691-02417-0 (pa)
LC 85-42685

The author attempts to describe the interaction between light and electrons

"Feynman describes with accuracy, insight, self-deprecating humor, and clarity the centerpiece of modern elementary particle theory—quantum electrodynamics. . . . 'QED' will challenge the mind." Christ Sci Monit

Greene, Brian R., 1963-

The elegant universe; superstrings, hidden dimensions, and the quest for the ultimate theory; [by] Brian Greene. Norton 1999 448p il o.p.; Vintage Bks. paperback available $15.95   **539.7**
1. Nuclear physics
ISBN 0-375-70811-1 (pa)   LC 98-25695

"Greene aims to acquaint lay readers with string theory, a hypothesis concerning strings of subatomic particles that could help scientists explain all of nature's forces in one Unified Field Theory." Libr J

The author "makes the terribly complex theory of strings accessible to all. He possesses a remarkable gift for using the everyday to illustrate what may be going on in dimensions beyond our feeble human perception." Publ Wkly

Includes bibliographical references

Gribbin, John R.

Q is for quantum; an encyclopedia of particle physics; [by] John Gribbin; edited by Mary Gribbin; illustrations by Jonathan Gribbin; timelines by Benjamin Gribbin. Free Press 1998 545p il $35; pa $20   **539.7**
1. Particles (Nuclear physics)—Dictionaries
ISBN 0-684-85578-X; 0-684-86315-4 (pa)
LC 98-9918

"There are entries for people (Feynman, Richard Phillips; Huygens, Christiaan; Oppenheimer, Robert), places (Brookhaven National Laboratory, Fermilab), and historical highlights (Manhattan Project). . . . Following the entries is a bibliography that lists the books referred to in the text, together with others; the more technical titles are indicated with an asterisk. The volume concludes

Gribbin, John R.—*Continued*
with time lines of birth dates of famous scientists, key dates in physical sciences, and key dates in history." Booklist

The search for superstrings, symmetry, and the theory of everything; [by] John Gribbin. Little, Brown 1999 c1998 212p $23; pa $14.95 **539.7**
1. Nuclear physics
ISBN 0-316-32975-4; 0-316-32614-3 (pa)
LC 98-34711
First published 1998 in the United Kingdom with title: In search of Susy

This introduction to the world of high-energy physics traces "research from the foundation work done in the 19th century to the latest concepts of superstrings." Libr J

"Diligent readers without any specialized knowledge of physics or mathematics will come away with a flavor of the latest ideas theorists are grappling with." Publ Wkly

Includes bibliographical references

Kane, Gordon, 1937-
The particle garden; our universe as understood by particle physicists. Addison-Wesley 1995 224p il hardcover o.p. paperback available $15 **539.7**
1. Particles (Nuclear physics) 2. Nuclear physics
ISBN 0-201-40826-0 (pa)
LC 94-25804
The author explains "the physics of subatomic particles: electrons, quarks, photons, bosons and company. . . . Topics covered include a history of particle physics, the Standard Theory, 'grand unification' and beyond and the relation of particle physics to cosmology and astrophysics." Publ Wkly

"This is an accurate, well-written, up-to-date account of particle physics by an expert in the field." Sci Books Films

Lederman, Leon M.
The God particle; if the universe is the answer, what is the question? [by] Leon Lederman with Dick Teresi. Houghton Mifflin 1993 434p o.p.; Dell paperback available $15.95 **539.7**
1. Particles (Nuclear physics) 2. Science—Philosophy 3. Universe
ISBN 0-385-31211-3 (pa)
LC 92-43583
Lederman examines "the course of experimental physics from 430 B.C. to the planned opening of the Superconducting Supercollider (SSC), of which he is one of the principal architects." Libr J

The author "pokes fun at the theorists and dazzles us with descriptions of the seemingly impossible experiments he and his fellow genius tinkerers executed to prove the existence of those massless, charmed, and strange entities, quarks and leptons." Booklist

Includes bibliographical references

Lindley, David
The end of physics; the myth of a unified theory. Basic Bks. 1993 275p hardcover o.p. paperback available $18 **539.7**
1. Nuclear physics 2. Physics
ISBN 0-465-01976-5 (pa)
LC 92-54524
The author has written an "account of the transition made by physicists from the physical world to a theoretical one. . . . As a primer for a history of physical science and experimentation, this book is an invaluable tonic, written in a gentle and pleasing way and with a critical eye. The early chapters on pre-20th century theory and experimentation are especially fine: clear, precise, and highly accessible." Libr J

Includes bibliographical references

540 Chemistry & allied sciences

Cobb, Cathy
Creations of fire; chemistry's lively history from alchemy to the atomic age; [by] Cathy Cobb and Harold Goldwhite. Plenum Press 1995 475p il o.p.; Perseus Bks. paperback available $18 **540**
1. Chemistry—History
ISBN 0-7382-0594-X (pa)
LC 95-24804
This history "begins with chemistry in the Stone Age and ends with current areas of interest such as superheavy elements and the polymerase chain reaction. Along the way, the coverage includes alchemy, cold fusion, and . . . topics like the contributions of Lise Meitner and Marie Lavoisier. . . . This book's light and often humorous style makes it especially appealing to the general reader." Libr J

Includes bibliographical references

CRC handbook of chemistry and physics; a ready-reference book of chemical and physical data. CRC Press $139.95 **540**
1. Chemistry—Tables 2. Physics—Tables
Also available CD-ROM version and online
First published 1913. (84th edition 2003) Periodically revised

A "reference book containing much-used information on mathematics, chemistry, and physics, including tables, physical constants of chemical elements and compounds, definitions, formulae, etc." AAAS Sci Book List for Young Adults

Includes bibliographical references

Greenberg, Arthur
The art of chemistry; myths, medicines, and materials. Wiley 2003 357p $59.95 **540**
1. Chemistry—History 2. Alchemy 3. Medicine—History
ISBN 0-471-07180-3
LC 2002-9950
Contents: Spiritual and myphological roots; Stills, cupels and weapons; Medicines, purges and ointments; Emerging science; Two revolutions in France; Young country and a young theory; Specialization and systemization; Some fun

This book "tracks chemistry's incremental progress from myth to modern science, featuring the figures and diagrams that early chemists used to explain their craft." Publisher's note

"A very interesting mix of information. Although it is not something that a reader would sit down and read through in one sitting, each of the eight sections was interesting by itself." Sci Books Films

Includes bibliographical references

Lange's handbook of chemistry. McGraw-Hill $125 **540**
1. Chemistry—Tables
First published 1934. (15th edition 1998) Periodically revised

Lange's handbook of chemistry—*Continued*

Editors vary

"A standard reference source for both students and professional chemists. Sections for: organic compounds; general information, conversion tables, and mathematics; inorganic chemistry; properties of atoms, radicals, and bonds; physical properties; thermodynamic properties; spectroscopy; electrolytes, electromotive force, and chemical equilibrium; physiochemical relationships; polymers, rubbers, fats, oils, and waxes; and practical laboratory information." Guide to Ref Books. 11th edition

Salzberg, Hugh W.

From caveman to chemist; circumstances and achievements. American Chemical Soc. 1991 294p il maps $24.95; pa $19.95   **540**
1. Chemistry—History
ISBN 0-8412-1786-6; 0-8412-1787-4 (pa)
         LC 90-44612
"A world history of chemistry from ancient times to the dawn of the 20th century. Like astronomy, chemistry developed from a discipline shrouded in myth and magic into a legitimate science, and Salzberg, a retired chemist, describes this evolution in a sweeping historical sketch. Further, the author shows that advancements in the understanding of chemistry invariably led to improvements in medicine and technology." Libr J
Includes bibliographical references

540.3   Chemistry—Encyclopedias and dictionaries

Hawley's condensed chemical dictionary. Van Nostrand Reinhold $155   **540.3**
1. Chemistry—Dictionaries
Also available CD-ROM version
First published 1919. (14th edition 2001) Periodically revised
Editors vary
"Describes industrial and scientific chemicals, terms, processes, reactions, and related terminology and phenomena. Charts chemical structures; gives uses and trademarked products that employ these chemicals. Some emphasis is on environment and energy sources. Includes appendices." N Y Public Libr Book of How & Where to Look It Up

540.9   Chemistry—Historical and geographic treatment

Strathern, Paul, 1940-

Mendeleyev's dream; the quest for the elements. Thomas Dunne Bks. 2001 c2000 308p il $23.95   **540.9**
1. Mendeleev, Dmitri I. 2. Chemical elements 3. Chemistry—History
ISBN 0-312-26204-3
Also available in paperback from Berkley Pub. Group
First published 2000 in the United Kingdom
The author "uses the creation of the periodic table by the great Russian scientist Dmitri Mendeleyev, who literally dreamed it up, to bookend a journey through the history of chemistry." Publ Wkly
"A book that brings lucidity to science while restoring human complexity to the scientists who do it." Booklist
Includes bibliographical references

541.2   Theoretical chemistry

Atkins, P. W. (Peter William), 1940-

The periodic kingdom; a journey into the land of the chemical elements. Basic Bks. 1995 161p il (Science masters series) hardcover o.p. paperback available $14
         541.2
1. Chemical elements 2. Periodic law
ISBN 0-465-07266-6 (pa)   LC 95-7362
"Depicting the periodic table of elements as a map, Atkins explores the territories that it represents, from metallic 'deserts' to the hydrogen 'island.' Basic chemistry has never been presented in a more creative and readily comprehensible manner." Libr J
Includes bibliographical references

Ball, Philip, 1962-

Stories of the invisible; a guided tour of molecules. Oxford Univ. Press 2001 204p il $22.50; pa $14.95   **541.2**
1. Molecules 2. Chemistry
ISBN 0-19-280214-3; 0-19-280317-4 (pa)
         LC 2001-36601
This "outlines the advances in the molecular sciences from the discovery of molecules to the present-day widespread use of chemical compounds and chemical processes. . . . This volume presents topics that are exact, instructive, and interesting while providing a unique insight into the molecular nature of living systems." Sci Books Films
Includes bibliographical references

546   Inorganic chemistry

Rigden, John S.

Hydrogen; the essential element. Harvard Univ. Press 2002 280p il $28; pa $15.95
         546
1. Hydrogen 2. Science—History
ISBN 0-674-00738-7; 0-674-01252-6 (pa)
         LC 2001-51708
The author chronicles "how one enduring conundrum—that of explaining the element hydrogen—has challenged two centuries of brilliant scientists. . . . In the process, he clarifies for general readers the nature of the scientific enterprise, in which elegant theories must meet the test of empirical verification." Booklist
Includes bibliographical references

548   Crystallography

Holden, Alan

Crystals and crystal growing; [by] Alan Holden and Phylis Morrison; introduction by Philip Morrison. MIT Press 1982 318p il pa $19.95   **548**
1. Crystals
ISBN 0-262-58050-0   LC 81-23639
First published 1960 by Anchor Bks.
This book "sets for itself three major goals: 1. Describing the atomistic character of crystallinity; 2. Describing some techniques for preparing large single crystals; and 3. Describing some experiments that display the unexpected properties which flow from crystallinity." Preface
"An excellent introduction to crystallography (and, incidentally, to much basic physics) written in plain language." Libr J

549 Mineralogy

Chesterman, Charles W.

The Audubon Society field guide to North American rocks and minerals; scientific consultant, Kurt E. Lowe. Knopf 1979 c1978 850p il $19.95   **549**
1. Minerals 2. Rocks
ISBN 0-394-50269-8   LC 78-54893
"Pocket guide providing color photos and descriptions of some 232 mineral species and forty types of rocks. Includes guide to mineral environments, glossary, bibliography, and indexes by name and locality." Ref Sources for Small & Medium-sized Libr. 5th edition

Johnsen, Ole

Minerals of the world. Princeton Univ. Press 2002 439p il (Princeton field guides) pa $24.95   **549**
1. Minerals 2. Crystals
ISBN 0-691-09537-X   LC 2001-97695
Originally published in hardcover with title: Photographic guide to minerals of the world
The author "provides descriptive information for the identification of more than 500 minerals. . . . This book follows the standard mineralogy textbook approach in which the mineral sections are arranged according to mineral composition and structure. . . . The book's suitability as a field guide is completed by the addition of hundreds of excellent color photographs and drawings. . . . The content material is solid, and superb illustrations on high-quality paper make for an attractive volume." Choice

Manual of mineral science. Wiley il $115.95
549
1. Minerals
Also available CD-ROM version
First published 1848 under the authorship of James D. Dana. (22nd edition 2001) Periodically revised. Variant title Manual of mineralogy
Current edition by Cornelis Klein
This is a standard introductory reference book for the use of students and collectors. It covers physical, chemical, determinative, and descriptive mineralogy, discusses mineral occurrence, association, and use, and includes both a subject and mineral index

Pellant, Chris

Rocks and minerals; Helen Pellant, editorial consultant; photography by Harry Taylor. Dorling Kindersley 1992 256p il (Eyewitness handbooks)   **549**
1. Minerals 2. Rocks   LC 91-58222
Available in paperback in the Smithsonian handbook series $20 (ISBN 0-7894-9106-0)
This field guide to identification of rocks and minerals includes techniques for collection and classification, and facts about physical and chemical composition and formation
"Visually attractive, with many color photographs [this provides] detail and information that would benefit either new or experienced naturalists." SLJ

Pough, Frederick H. (Frederick Harvey), 1906-

A field guide to rocks and minerals; photographs by Jeffrey Scovil. Houghton Mifflin pa $20   **549**
1. Minerals 2. Rocks   LC 94-49005
"The Peterson field guide series"
First published 1953. (5th edition 1996) Periodically revised
"Sponsored by the National Audubon Society, the National Wildlife Federation, and the Roger Tory Peterson Institute"
This illustrated guide utilizes traditional identification methods and includes discussions of crystallography, mineralogy and home laboratory techniques
Includes bibliographical references

Simon and Schuster's guide to rocks and minerals; edited by Martin Prinz, George Harlow, and Joseph Peters. Simon & Schuster 1978 607p il hardcover o.p. paperback available $17   **549**
1. Minerals 2. Rocks
ISBN 0-671-24417-5 (pa)   LC 78-8610
Original Italian edition, 1977
"Half of this book consists of color plates; the other half is an authoritative text which describes the elements of mineralogy and petrology. Crystal system or family, physical and chemical properties, occurrence, uses, and rarity are included for each species." Libr J

Sofianides, Anna S.

Gems & crystals from the American Museum of Natural History; [by] Anna S. Sofianides and George E. Harlow; photographs by Erica and Harold Van Pelt. Simon & Schuster 1990 208p il $40   **549**
1. Minerals 2. Precious stones
ISBN 0-671-68704-2   LC 89-11574
Color photographs "picture familiar gems, which are briefly described in terms of their particular properties and the legends associated with them." Booklist
Includes bibliographical references

550 Earth sciences

Earth almanac; an annual geophysical review of the state of the planet. Oryx Press 2002 il maps pa $69.95   **550**
1. Earth sciences 2. Earth
ISSN 1533-0605
Annual. First published 2000
Vols. for 2000- by: N. Goldstein
This "almanac reviews geophysical processes in four major areas: the Earth's atmosphere, oceans, land, and fresh water. For each area, Goldstein . . . summarizes research, covers major events . . . and describes processes, cycles, and pertinent data. Appendixes outline selected treaties and law as well as selected national and international scientific programs. . . . Highly recommended for public and academic libraries for its solid presentation of basic scientific background information and socially and scientifically relevant data." Libr J

Erickson, Jon, 1948-
Quakes, eruptions, and other geologic cataclysms; revealing the earth's hazards. rev ed, foreword [by] Alexander E. Gates. Facts on File 2001 310p il (Facts on File science library) $55; pa $19.95   **550**
1. Natural disasters
ISBN 0-8160-4516-X; 0-8160-4904-1 (pa)
LC 01-23055
First published 1994
At head of title: The living earth
"An introductory chapter details the dynamic forces at work beneath the Earth's crust, while the subsequent chapters—each dedicated to a single type of disaster—explain causes and myriad effects of these disturbances, enhanced with numerous examples." Publisher's note
Includes bibliographical references

Morton, R. L. (Ronald Lee)
Music of the earth; volcanoes, earthquakes, and other geological wonders. Plenum Press 1996 312p il o.p.; Perseus Bks. paperback available $25   **550**
1. Earth sciences
ISBN 0-7382-0870-1 (pa)   LC 96-1764
"Using music as an overall metaphor for the various geologic processes described, Morton . . . [discusses] tectonics, volcanoes, earthquakes, mass wasting, thermal waters, ore deposits, glaciers, coastal processes, deserts, and mass extinctions." Choice
"An entertaining and readable account of the earth that is full of humor and anecdotes." Sci Books Films
Includes bibliographical references

550.3 Earth sciences—Encyclopedias and dictionaries

Encyclopedia of earth sciences; E. Julius Dasch, editor in chief. Macmillan Lib. Ref. USA 1996 2v il maps set $295   **550.3**
1. Earth sciences—Encyclopedias
ISBN 0-02-883000-8   LC 96-11302
Spine title: Macmillan encyclopedia of earth sciences
"This two-volume set covers not only the sciences of the solid earth, the oceanographic and atmospheric sciences, and the biological sciences, but also the study of the solar system and its place in the galaxy and the universe. Well written and indexed, this encyclopedia will find an audience with both high school and college students as well as with decision makers and the interested layperson." Am Libr

The **Facts** on File dictionary of earth science; edited by John O.E. Clark and Stella Stiegeler. Facts on File 2000 362p il maps $49.50; pa $17.95   **550.3**
1. Earth sciences—Dictionaries
ISBN 0-8160-4287-X; 0-8160-4288-8 (pa)
LC 00-61772
In this reference work some 3,000 entries cover "geomorphology, stratigraphy, mineralogy, petrology, climatology, oceanography, paleontology, hydrology, geophysics, cartography, surveying, and soil science. Key concepts in physics, chemistry, biology, and mathematics are also defined." Publisher's note

The **Oxford** companion to the earth; editors Paul L. Hancock and Brian J. Skinner; associate editor David L. Dineley: subject editor, Alistair G. Dawson. Oxford Univ. Press 2000 1174p il $75   **550.3**
1. Earth sciences—Dictionaries
ISBN 0-19-854039-6   LC 2001-16311
This "resource offers concise explanations of earth phenomena and processes, with over 800 entries written by 200 experts. . . . Each entry is well written, with information suitable for undergraduates as well as researchers needing an overview." Libr J

551 Geology, hydrology, meteorology

Interdisciplinary encyclopedia of marine sciences; edited by James W. Nybakken, William W. Broenkow, Tracy L. Vallier. Grolier 2002 3v set $349   **551**
1. Marine sciences—Encyclopedias 2. Oceanography
ISBN 0-7172-5946-3   LC 2002-192707
"More than 800 alphabetical enries vary in length from 250 to 2500 words and discuss topics ranging from 'Abyssal Gigantism' to 'Zooxanthellae'. The . . . articles cover the subdiscipline of oceanography (biological, chemical, geological, and physical) in addition to economics, marine life, and ecology of the oceans. Technologies used to explore this environment and biographies of important individuals are also included. Each accessible, signed entry concludes with a list of related articles and suggestions for further reading that will be useful for students." SLJ
Includes bibliographical references

Lambert, David, 1932-
The field guide to geology; [by] David Lambert and the Diagram Group. updated ed. Facts on File 1998 256p il $30.75; pa $14.95   **551**
1. Geology
ISBN 0-8160-3840-6; 0-8160-3823-6 (pa)
LC 98-168173
First published 1988
This "introductory field guide to geology for students and the general public is well-illustrated, depicting all aspects of geology." Malinowsky. Best Sci & Technol Ref Books for Young People [entry for 1998 edition]
Includes bibliographical references

Oldroyd, D. R. (David Roger)
Thinking about the earth; a history of ideas in geology. Harvard Univ. Press 1996 xxx, 410p il maps (Studies in the history and philosophy of the earth sciences) $55.50   **551**
1. Geology
ISBN 0-674-88382-9   LC 95-48234
"Oldroyd surveys Greek and Islamic philosophers on stones, seventeenth-century theologians on the origins of the world, Enlightenment philosophers on the workings of the earth machine, . . . [and modern] ideas about plate tectonics and the chemical formation of life." Times Lit Suppl
"The sections on mountain-building, seismology, and, especially, the Gaia hypothesis . . . are new to the his-

Oldroyd, D. R. (David Roger)—*Continued*
tory of geology. Because of this book, these subjects will now be added to the standard lists of topics that are required reading for the 'complete' geologist." Choice
Includes bibliographical references

551.2 Volcanoes, earthquakes, thermal waters and gases

Carson, Rob, 1950-
Mount St. Helens: the eruption and recovery of a volcano; with selected photographs by Geff Hinds, Cheryl Haselhorst and Gary Braasch. Sasquatch Bks. 1990 160p il hardcover o.p. paperback available $19.95 **551.2**
1. Mount Saint Helens (Wash.)
ISBN 1-5706-1248-X (pa) LC 90-31009
The author "describes the eruption of Mount St. Helens in 1980, and goes on to report what has happened in the devastated area since then. . . . Mr. Carson has a lively story to tell and does it well. The photographs . . . provide beauty as well as information." Atl Mon

Ritchie, David, 1952-
Encyclopedia of earthquakes and volcanoes; [by] David Ritchie and Alexander E. Gates. New ed. Facts on File 2001 306p il maps (Facts on File science library) $55; pa $18.95 **551.2**
1. Earthquakes—Encyclopedias 2. Volcanoes—Encyclopedias
ISBN 0-8160-4372-8; 0-8160-4583-6 (pa) LC 00-49492
First published 1994
This "explains the science of seismology and volcanology through facts about the disasters themselves, historical and eyewitness accounts, and how they affect the political landscape." Publisher's note
Includes bibliographical references

Thompson, Dick
Volcano cowboys; the rocky evolution of a dangerous science. St. Martin's Press 2000 326p il map $26.95; pa $14.95 **551.2**
1. Volcanoes
ISBN 0-312-20881-2; 0-312-28668-6 (pa) LC 00-26158
This describes the work of U.S. Geological Survey scientists in predicting volcanic eruptions, focusing on the eruptions of Mount St. Helens in 1980 and Mount Pinatubo in 1991
"An informative book about science's communication with the lay public." Booklist
Includes bibliographical references

Winchester, Simon
Krakatoa: the day the world exploded, August 27, 1883. HarperCollins Pubs. 2003 416p il maps $25.95 **551.2**
1. Volcanoes
ISBN 0-06-621285-5
Also available Thorndike Press large print edition
"This book chronicles the underlying causes, utter devastation and lasting effects of the cataclysmic 1883 eruption of the volcano island Krakatoa in what is now

Indonesia. . . . [The author] demonstrates a keen knack for balancing rich and often rigorous historical detail with dramatic tension and storytelling." Publ Wkly
"As a rich blend of science and history, this book is highly recommended for most public and academic libraries." Libr J

551.46 Hydrosphere. Oceanography

Ballard, Robert D.
The eternal darkness; a personal history of deep-sea exploration; [by] Robert D. Ballard with Will Hively. Princeton Univ. Press 2000 388p il maps $55; pa $18.95 **551.46**
1. Underwater exploration
ISBN 0-691-02740-4; 0-691-09554-X (pa) LC 99-43072
Ballard "blends his personal experiences exploring hydrothermal vents and shipwrecks with stories of earlier deep-sea pioneers, focusing especially on the technology. . . . Ballard's volume is easy to read and will be an excellent addition to collections at all levels on oceanography, history of science, and exploration." Libr J
Includes bibliographical references

Broad, William, 1951-
The universe below; discovering the secrets of the deep sea; [by] William J. Broad; illustrations by Dimitry Schidlovsky. Simon & Schuster 1997 432p il maps hardcover o.p. paperback available $15 **551.46**
1. Oceanography 2. Underwater exploration
ISBN 0-684-83852-4 (pa) LC 96-50337
This work focuses "on the ships, subs, divers, underwater vehicles both manned and robotic, and satellites used in a variety of applications, from discovering the *Titanic* to observing unusual or new marine species." Libr J
"Intensively researched and crisply told, this is an illuminating, stimulating portrait of one of Earth's last frontiers." Publ Wkly
Includes bibliographical references

Carson, Rachel, 1907-1964
The sea around us. Oxford Univ. Press 2003 274p il maps $45 **551.46**
1. Ocean
ISBN 0-19-514701-4 LC 2002-29299
This is a reissue of the title first published 1951
Beginning with a description of how the earth acquired its oceans, the book covers such topics as how life began in the primeval sea, the hidden lands, the life discovered in the abyss by highly delicate sounding apparatus, currents and tides, the formation of volcanic islands, and mineral resources

Day, Trevor, 1955-
Oceans. Facts on File 1999 216p il maps (Ecosystem) $65 **551.46**
1. Oceanography
ISBN 0-8160-3647-0 LC 98-18110
This volume describes the oceans of the world with regard to their geography, geology, history, chemistry, exploration, relationship to the atmosphere, economic resources, and management
Includes bibliographical references

Ellis, Richard, 1938-

Encyclopedia of the sea; written and illustrated by Richard Ellis. Knopf 2000 380p il $35   **551.46**

1. Oceanography—Encyclopedias 2. Marine ecology—Encyclopedias

ISBN 0-375-40374-4   LC 99-42401

"The alphabetically arranged text consists of short paragraphs on topics in marine biology, oceanography, fisheries, geography, and maritime and naval history. . . . Eight pages of Ellis's color paintings . . . and hundreds of his own illustrations enhance the text. . . . The handy format makes the book useful as a ready-reference source for public and college libraries." Libr J

For a fuller review see: Booklist, Feb. 1, 2001

Kunzig, Robert

The restless sea; exploring the world beneath the waves. Norton 1999 336p il maps $24.95   **551.46**

1. Ocean

ISBN 0-393-04562-5   LC 98-38704

The author "chronicles the history of oceans from the Big Bang to the present. Although some of the material Kunzig sets down as fact is still hotly debated, his writing is clear and easy to understand. His descriptions of the ocean are visual, almost poetic." Libr J

551.48   Hydrology

Outwater, Alice B.

Water; a natural history; [by] Alice Outwater; illustrations by Billy Brauer. Basic Bks. 1996 212p hardcover o.p. paperback available $16   **551.48**

1. Water 2. Hydraulic engineering 3. Water supply 4. Water pollution

ISBN 0-465-03780-1 (pa)   LC 96-24182

The author "tells why our water is not all it should be, even though very little new industrial waste is being added. She describes how once plentiful species—beavers, prairie dogs, bison, alligators—indirectly contributed to cleaning water, and how the loss of forest and the decline of forest fires have affected water quality. Her tone is attractively specific: stylish in its directness, and realistic in its proposals." New Yorker

Includes bibliographical references

551.5   Meteorology

Encyclopedia of atmospheric sciences; editor-in-chief, James R. Holton; editors, Judith A. Curry, John A. Pyle. Academic Press 2003 6v il set $1,400   **551.5**

1. Atmosphere—Encyclopedias 2. Meteorology—Encyclopedias

ISBN 0-12-227090-8   LC 2002-114120

This reference set "includes the work of 400 scientists worldwide. The 330 authoritative and concise articles review such complex subjects as weather prediction, climate change and variability, and atmospheric chemistry. Beautifully illustrated with maps, charts, photos and illustrations." Libr J

Includes bibliographical references

Reynolds, Ross

Cambridge guide to the weather. Cambridge Univ. Press 2000 192p il pa $17   **551.5**

1. Weather 2. Meteorology 3. Weather forecasting

ISBN 0-521-77489-6   LC 00-266555

This offers "country-by-country climate data and statistics, along with in-depth explanations of global weather patterns. . . . In addition, Ross Reynolds gives . . . [an] account of the implications of environmental issues currently in the headlines, such as global warming and the depletion of the ozone layer, as well as the effects of El Niño and other phenomena on world weather patterns." Publisher's note

This book's "rather complete coverage of all major topics is enhanced by excellent illustrations, including clear photographs, drawn figures, and maps." Sci Books Films

Includes bibliographical references

Stevens, William K., 1935-

The change in the weather; people, weather, and the science of climate. Delacorte Press 1999 xxiii, 357p hardcover o.p. paperback available $13.95   **551.5**

1. Climate 2. Weather

ISBN 0-385-32007-8 (pa)   LC 99-38592

This account of the ever-changing climate examines the problem of global warming

"Stevens approaches climate change from a historical point of view. Starting with evidence from the geological record, he outlines current knowledge of paleoclimatology and what it may predict about current and future weather trends. He also examines weather's role in the world's religious and literary traditions. . . . The author's evenhandedness in presenting all viewpoints in the politically charged global warming debate adds to his work's credibility." Booklist

Includes bibliographical references

Weather. Reader's Digest Assn. 1997 159p il maps (Reader's digest explores) $24.95   **551.5**

1. Weather 2. Climate

ISBN 0-89577-975-7   LC 97-3324

This volume covers such topics as rainbows, hurricanes, global warming, acid rain and ozone depletion. The difference between weather and climate, what causes seasons, and the limitations of forecasting are also discussed

551.51   Composition, regions, dynamics of atmosphere

DeBlieu, Jan

Wind; how the flow of air has shaped life, myth, and the land. Houghton Mifflin 1998 294p $24; pa $14   **551.51**

1. Winds

ISBN 0-395-78033-0; 0-395-95794-X (pa)

     LC 98-16851

The author discusses "ancient myths that attest to the enormous influence wind has had on our cosmologies, and lucidly explains the physics of wind. One facet of this wide-ranging discussion involves how wind determines the distribution of moisture on the planet, thus playing an integral role in the rise and fall of civilizations. . . . This is nature writing at its most expansive and rewarding." Booklist

Includes bibliographical references

Holmes, Hannah, 1963-
The secret life of dust; from the cosmos to the kitchen counter, the big consequences of little things. Wiley 2001 240p $22.95; pa $14.95 **551.51**
1. Dust 2. Science—Philosophy
ISBN 0-471-37743-0; 0-471-42635-0 (pa)
LC 2001-22368
"Holmes explores how dust has been crucial in the birth of planets, how it affects the earth's environment and weather, and how humans create it as well. Out to communicate straight facts and science, she considers technical points in language that is clear and comprehensible even for those lacking a science background. In addition to the bibliography, Holmes provides a listing of web sites for each chapter so that readers may easily obtain current information and graphics." Libr J

551.55 Atmospheric disturbances and formations

Davies, Pete, 1959-
Inside the hurricane; face to face with nature's deadliest storms. Holt & Co. 2000 264p hardcover o.p. paperback available $14 **551.55**
1. Hurricanes
ISBN 0-8050-6611-X (pa)
LC 00-29562
The author "surveys the 1999 Atlantic hurricane season, focusing on the experiences of a small group of hurricane researchers and forecasters. . . . Vivid and engrossing; recommended for both public and academic libraries." Libr J
Includes bibliographical references

Longshore, David
Encyclopedia of hurricanes, typhoons and cyclones. Facts on File 1998 372p il maps $55; pa $19.95 **551.55**
1. Hurricanes 2. Typhoons 3. Cyclones
ISBN 0-8160-3398-6; 0-8160-4291-8 (pa)
LC 97-20860
This encyclopedia describes named hurricanes, typhoons and cyclones, explains meteorological terms and instruments, and includes biographical data, a chronology, and a list of hurricane safety procedures

551.57 Hydrometeorology

Hamblyn, Richard, 1965-
The invention of clouds; how an amateur meteorologist forged the language of the skies. Farrar, Straus & Giroux 2001 403p il o.p.; Picador paperback available $14 **551.57**
1. Howard, Luke, 1772-1864 2. Clouds 3. Meteorology
ISBN 0-312-42001-3 (pa)
LC 00-68189
This is a study of Luke Howard, an unknown amateur scientist who in 1802 "gave a lecture in which he named and defined the different types of clouds—cirrus, cumulus, stratus and their various hybrid forms. . . . [His taxonomy] gave scientists a standardised way to record and compare observations and begin to form theories." Economist
"A remarkable, remarkably pleasing story." Booklist

Mergen, Bernard
Snow in America. Smithsonian Institution Press 1997 xxi, 321p il $24.95; pa $16.95 **551.57**
1. Snow
ISBN 1-56098-780-4; 1-56098-381-7 (pa)
LC 97-12247
This study traces the development of snow technology, explains the importance of snow surveys for climate regulation, and looks at the ski industry, water usage, winter fashions and street cleaning. The author also explores snow in popular culture and its role in the emotional development of the American character
Includes bibliographical references

551.6 Climatology and weather

Allaby, Michael, 1933-
The Facts on File weather and climate handbook. Facts on File 2002 290p il (Facts on File science library) $35; pa $17.95
551.6
1. Climate 2. Weather
ISBN 0-8160-4517-8; 0-8160-4961-0 (pa)
LC 2001-50114
This book covers weather-related issues such as "Area forecast; Bioclimatology; Dust bowl; Greenhouse gas; La Niña; Severe-storm observation [and] Veil of cloud." Publisher's note
"This work is a comprehensive, handy reference tool for weather and climate. The glossary is especially comprehensive . . . [and] is recommended for all reference collections." Am Ref Books Annu, 2003
Includes bibliographical references

Encyclopedia of climate and weather; Stephen H. Schneider, editor in chief. Oxford Univ. Press 1996 2v il maps set $275 **551.6**
1. Climate 2. Weather
ISBN 0-19-509485-9
LC 95-31019
This "is an alphabetical arrangement of over 300 short articles . . . on everything from clouds and tornadoes to human influences on weather and climate (e.g., acid rain, deforestation, and effects of aerosols on the ozone layer). . . . The set contains over 400 black-and-white line drawings, photographs, charts, and maps, as well as a glossary." Libr J

Laskin, David, 1953-
Braving the elements; the stormy history of American weather. Doubleday 1995 241p il hardcover o.p. paperback available $12.95
551.6
1. United States—Climate
ISBN 0-385-46956-X (pa)
LC 95-19851
The author presents a "history of our weather and our interpretations of it, covering everything from spiritual perspectives—weather as signs from God—to our obsession with televised forecasts. Laskin articulates the myriad ways weather affects us, from the obvious, such as the destructiveness of hurricanes, to more subtle manifestations, such as how it influences our moods." Booklist
Includes bibliographical references

Ludlum, David M., 1910-1997
The Audubon Society field guide to North American weather. Knopf 1991 656p il maps $19.95 **551.6**
1. Weather forecasting
ISBN 0-679-40851-7 LC 91-52707
"A Chanticleer Press edition"
"The opening essays provide in-depth information on topics such as clouds, snowstorms, floods, etc. About half of the book is comprised of labelled, high-quality photographs. The third section gives description, environment, season, range, and significance of each type of weather. Clear diagrams, simple definitions, and a readable text make this an excellent selection." SLJ

Lyons, Walter A. (Walter Andrew), 1943-
The handy weather answer book. Visible Ink Press 1997 397p il pa $19.95 **551.6**
1. Weather
ISBN 0-7876-1034-8 LC 96-30555
This book provides "answers to more than 1,000 frequently asked questions about the weather. It also provides information on such . . . topics as hurricanes, droughts, flash floods, volcanoes . . . the greenhouse effect, Aurora Borealis and St. Elmo's fire." Publisher's note
Includes bibliographical references

Monmonier, Mark S. (Mark Stephen), 1943-
Air apparent; how meteorologists learned to map, predict, and dramatize weather; [by] Mark Monmonier. University of Chicago Press 1999 309p il $27.50; pa $17 **551.6**
1. Meteorology 2. Weather forecasting
ISBN 0-226-53422-7; 0-226-53423-5 (pa)
LC 98-25797
The author presents a "history of more than 200 years of weather maps, an account that embraces technological advances from the telegraph and mercury barometer to the satellite and Doppler radar." Booklist
Includes bibliographical references

Weather almanac. Gale Res. il maps $165 **551.6**
1. United States—Climate 2. Weather
First published 1974. (11th edition 2003) Periodically revised
Editors vary
"Definitions and articles on major weather events and meteorological issues. Includes layperson's guide to 'weather fundamentals' and a glossary. Provides meteorological and climatological information and statistics for major U.S. and world cities." N Y Public Libr Book of How & Where to Look It Up

Williams, Jack, 1936-
The weather book. 2nd ed, rev and updated. Vintage Bks. 1997 227p il maps pa $20 **551.6**
1. Weather 2. United States—Climate
ISBN 0-679-77665-6 LC 97-197544
First published 1992
At head of title: USA today
This guide to America's weather features full-color graphics from USA Today and discussions of hurricanes, blizzards, heat waves, cold fronts, tornadoes, and droughts, as well as the latest information on computer forecasting, explanations on how events in space affect Earth's weather, reasons for our increasingly wild weather, coverage of recent hurricanes, etc.
Includes bibliographical references

551.7 Historical geology

Alvarez, Walter, 1940-
T. rex and the Crater of Doom. Princeton Univ. Press 1997 185p il $35 **551.7**
1. Catastrophes (Geology) 2. Dinosaurs
ISBN 0-691-01630-5 LC 96-49208
Also available in paperback from Vintage Bks.
The author relates the story of how he "along with four other Berkeley scientists, found the geologic evidence that implicated a cosmic collision in the extinction of the dinosaurs. . . . [Their research involved] the evaluation of a thin iridium-rich layer of clay found in Italy and the search for an impact crater." Booklist
This book "gets the facts across in a lighthearted, almost playful manner. But it's also solid science, a clear and efficient exposition." N Y Times Book Rev
Includes bibliographical references

Hancock, Graham
Underworld: the mysterious origins of civilization; photographs by Santha Faiia. Crown 2002 769p il maps $27.50; pa $16.95 **551.7**
1. Stratigraphic geology 2. Ancient civilization 3. Prehistoric peoples
ISBN 1-4000-4612-2; 1-4000-4951-2 (pa)
The author presents theories on how "civilization rose about 17,000 years ago (rather than about 6,000) and vanished beneath a rising sea level, leaving its traces in flood myths in Sumerian and Vedic texts, in early maps of the Age of Discovery, and more plausibly, in submerged ruins. Hancock throws up a fantastic amount of data on these points in this work, ranging from his personal textual interpretations to his dives at coastal sites in Malta, India, Japan, and the Bahamas." Booklist
Includes bibliographical references

Macdougall, J. D., 1944-
A short history of planet earth; mountains, mammals, fire, and ice. Wiley 1996 266p il maps (Wiley popular science) hardcover o.p. paperback available $16.95 **551.7**
1. Stratigraphic geology 2. Life—Origin
ISBN 0-471-19703-3 (pa) LC 95-46399
In "this survey of four-and-a-half billion years of Earth's past . . . MacDougall traces the rise of continents and the origins of life in each era. He discusses tectonic plates, the major extinctions and their probable causes, climate and the Ice Ages, and he speculates on the future of our planet. To compress Earth's history into a single, lucidly written volume is a major achievement." Publ Wkly
Includes bibliographical references

553.2 Carbonaceous materials

Freese, Barbara
Coal: a human history. Perseus Bks. 2003 308p il $37.95 **553.2**
1. Coal
ISBN 0-7382-0400-5 LC 2002-114066
Also available in paperback from Penguin Bks.

Freese, Barbara—*Continued*

This is "an engrossing account of the comparatively cheap, usually dirty fuel that supported the Industrial Revolution, inspired the building of canals and railroads to move it, and once made London and Pittsburgh famous for their air." N Y Times Book Rev

The author's "balancing of ecological concerns with realistic analyses of resource use is impressive. Although the ecological implications of coal use are great, Freese effectively demonstrates the dependence on coal of countries around the world for sustaining economic growth. Most important, she offers clearheaded opinions on what we need to do to make our use of coal as clean as possible and what we must eventually do to replace it. Highly recommended for all libraries." Libr J

Includes bibliographical references

553.6 Other economic materials

Kurlansky, Mark

Salt: a world history. Walker & Co. 2002 484p il maps $28   **553.6**

1. Salt

ISBN 0-8027-1373-4

Also available Thorndike Press large print edition and in paperback from Penguin Bks.

The author shows how salt "has influenced and affected wars, cultures, governments, religions, societies, economies, cooking (there are a few recipes), and foods. In addition, he provides information on the chemistry, geology, mining, refining, and production of salt." Libr J

"Throughout his engaging, well-researched history, Kurlansky sprinkles witty asides and amusing anecdotes. A piquant blend of the historic, political, commercial, scientific and culinary, the book is sure to entertain as well as educate." Publ Wkly

Includes bibliographical references

553.7 Water

Ball, Philip, 1962-

Life's matrix; a biography of water. Farrar, Straus & Giroux 2000 417p il o.p.; University of Calif. Press paperback available $18.95   **553.7**

1. Water

ISBN 0-520-23008-6 (pa)   LC 99-59110

First published 1999 in the United Kingdom with title: H20: a biography of water

Ball aims to "explain water's physical and chemical properties, examine its role in the development of civilization and explore its presence in space." N Y Times Book Rev

Includes bibliographical references

Kandel, Robert S.

Water from heaven; the story of water from the big bang to the rise of civilization, and beyond; [by] Robert Kandel. Columbia Univ. Press 2003 311p il maps $29.95   **553.7**

1. Water

ISBN 0-231-12244-6   LC 2002-31229

The author "explains the earth's elaborate and essential-to-life water cycle . . . beginning cosmologically with the birth of the solar system and an analysis of various theories as to where the earth's water . . . originated." Booklist

"While dense with facts and figures, Kandel's aquatic history is riveting, an exhaustive and complex examination of our most precious chemical compound." Publ Wkly

Includes bibliographical references

Pielou, E. C., 1924-

Fresh water. University of Chicago Press 1998 275p il maps $24; pa $14   **553.7**

1. Water

ISBN 0-226-66815-0; 0-226-66816-9 (pa)

LC 97-51562

Pielou provides an "introduction to hydrology as she conducts a guided tour to freshwater's gathering places underground and in streams, rivers, wetlands, lakes, and clouds, then turns to a discussion of how civilization has used this limited resource, and why water conservation must be established as a permanent aspect of life on earth." Booklist

This "is a wonderful natural history of one of life's necessities, a refreshing break from grand theory and special pleading of many a science book. . . . Sometimes Pielou gets political. . . . But the mind-boggling details always hold the attention best." New Scientist

Includes bibliographical references

Water: science and issues; E. Julius Dasch, editor in chief. Macmillan Ref. USA 2003 4v il maps set $395   **553.7**

1. Water—Encyclopedias

ISBN 0-02-865611-3

Contents: v1 Acid-Drought; v2 Earle-Lakes; v3 Land-Pricing; v4 Prior-Women

"This reference contains more than 300 topical entries . . . about a wide array of topics surrounding the nature, sources, use, desecration, and protection of this most valuable resource. *Acid rain, Bottled water, Careers in oceanography, Hoover Dam, Leonardo da Vinci, Plankton, Salmon decline and recovery* and *Wetlands* are examples of entries and help illustrate the set's range. . . . At the beginnig of each volume are several tables: metric conversions; symbols, abbreviations, and acronyms; and geologic eras, periods and epochs. Entries range in length from 500 to 2,500 words and include short bibliographies of print and electronic sources. Pages have wide margins, which contain picture captions, definitions of key terms, and boxes of important facts and explanations. . . . Photographs, illustrations, and tables are attractive and add meaning to the text. Each volume concludes with the 36-page, detailed cumulative index and the 60-page glossary. . . . The scientific and social aspects of water are well introduced in this set, which is recommended for high-school, public, and undergraduate libraries." Booklist

553.8 Gems

Hart, Matthew, 1945-

Diamond: a journey to the heart of an obsession. Walker & Co. 2001 276p il maps $26   **553.8**

1. Diamonds

ISBN 0-8027-1368-8   LC 2001-26348

Also available in paperback from Plume Bks.

Hart's "account of the glittering business of mining and marketing diamonds is also a story of avarice, theft, aesthetics, monopoly, and war. A thoroughly entrancing book." Booklist

Includes bibliographical references

Levy, Adrian, 1965-
The stone of heaven; unearthing the secret history of imperial green jade; [by] Adrian Levy and Cathy Scott-Clark. Little, Brown 2002 xxii, 408p il map $24.95; pa $15.96
553.8
1. Jadeite 2. Myanmar—Description
ISBN 0-316-52596-0; 0-316-09558-3 (pa)
LC 2001-37742
This "chronicle interweaves legend, mythology, and history with a shocking contemporary exposé of the Burmese jadeite mines. . . . An engrossing combination of narrative history and undercover journalism." Booklist
Includes bibliographical references

The **Nature** of diamonds; edited by George E. Harlow. Cambridge Univ. Press 1997 278p maps $95; pa $35
553.8
1. Diamonds
ISBN 0-521-62083-X; 0-521-62935-7 (pa)
LC 97-29176
This volume covers "every facet of the stone, from its formation in the depths of the Earth, its ascent to the surface, and its economic, regal, social, and technological roles. . . . Wide-ranging illustrations explain the geology of diamonds, chart the history of mining from its origins in India and Brazil through the diamond rush in South Africa and today's high-tech enterprises, and capture the brilliance and beauty of this extraordinary gem." Univ Press Books for Public and Second Sch Libr
Includes bibliographical references

Webster, Robert
Gems; their sources, descriptions, and identification. 5th ed, revised by Peter G. Read. Butterworth-Heinemann 1994 xxviii, 1026p il maps $150
553.8
1. Precious stones
ISBN 0-7506-1674-1
LC 93-44841
First published 1962
This guide to gemstones also includes descriptions of the newer synthetic stones and of the methods used to change the colors of gemstones
"A useful, comprehensive work." Guide to Ref Books. 11th edition
Includes bibliographical references

557 Earth sciences—North America

McPhee, John A.
Annals of the former world; [by] John McPhee. Farrar, Straus & Giroux 1998 695p maps $35; pa $20
557
1. Geology—United States
ISBN 0-374-10520-0; 0-374-51873-4 (pa)
LC 97-39660
This volume combines edited and revised sections from Basin and range (1981), In suspect terrain (1983), Rising from the plains (1986), and Assembling California (1993), with two new essays
McPhee provides a "portrait of the continent—a. . . narrative that not only tracks the drama of North American geological history but also chronicles the rapid evolution of the theories and practice of geology itself and tells the intriguing stories of people for whom love of rocks has meant love of life." Booklist

"As in any McPhee work, there are gemlike sentences, richly rhythmic paragraphs, nicely burnished synecdoches, metaphors as pungent as wasabi and, behind those felicities, vast amounts of painstaking research." N Y Times Book Rev

560 Paleontology. Paleozoology

Arduini, Paolo
Simon & Schuster's guide to fossils; [by] Paolo Arduini and Giorgio Teruzzi. Simon & Schuster 1986 317p il hardcover o.p. paperback available $16
560
1. Fossils
ISBN 0-671-63132-2 (pa)
LC 86-22043
Original Italian edition, 1986
"This is an excellent field guide to identifying collecting fossils. Each fossil is described and locations of where they can be found are indicated. Notes are given on the preservation of fossil sites so that areas are not destroyed." Malinowsky. Best Sci & Technol Ref Books for Young People

Eldredge, Niles
Fossils; the evolution and extinction of species; photography by Murray Alcosser; introduction by Stephen Jay Gould. Princeton Univ. Press 1997 xx, 220p pa $45
560
1. Fossils 2. Evolution
ISBN 0-691-02695-5
LC 96-26969
A reissue of the title first published 1991 by Abrams
The author "examines what the fossilized remains of earth's ancient flora and fauna reveal about mass extinction and the origin of species." Publisher's note
"Full-page photographs adorn about half the pages of this beautiful book. . . . These essays are not intended as detailed academic treatments; rather, they provide a touch of the history of discovery, and the excitement of delving into the unknown—doing paleontology. The anatomical descriptions are easy to understand. This is a 'coffee table book' of the highest quality." Sci Book Films
Includes bibliographical references

The **miner's** canary; unravelling the mysteries of extinction. Prentice Hall Press 1991 246p il o.p.; Princeton Univ. Press paperback available $29.95
560
1. Extinct animals 2. Fossils
ISBN 0-691-03655-1 (pa)
LC 91-9140
The author "reviews the evidence for extinction and its causes, primarily using fossil evidence and focusing on climatic change and loss of habitat." Libr J
The book "rings with integrity. The author seems almost apologetic about offering views of his own that stray somewhat from his self-imposed syllabus, and he takes care to present opposing views." N Y Times Book Rev
Includes bibliographical references

Encyclopedia of paleontology; editor, Ronald Singer. Fitzroy Dearborn Pubs. 1999 2v il set $295
560
1. Fossils—Encyclopedias
ISBN 1-88496-496-6
LC 00-271769
This work has "328 articles that cover all areas of paleontology, including 79 biographies for individuals such

Encyclopedia of paleontology—*Continued*

as Jean Agassiz, Charles Darwin, and Louis Leakey. The articles are extremely well written, with line drawings, photographs, charts, and other illustrative matter, plus a list of works cited and a further reading list." Booklist

Erickson, Jon, 1948-

An introduction to fossils and minerals; seeking clues to the earth's past; foreword by Donald R. Coates. rev ed. Facts on File 2000 272p il maps (Facts on File science library) $55; pa $19.95 **560**

1. Fossils 2. Minerals 3. Geology
ISBN 0-8160-4236-5; 0-8160-4237-3 (pa)
LC 00-37203

First published 1992

At head of title: Living Earth

"The focus of this book is primarily the geological occurrence of fossils and minerals. . . . The kinds of enclosing rock formations and the geologic processes that produced them are explained. Types of fossils, mostly of animals, but some of plants, and their geographic distributions are . . . described. The occurrence of minerals, gems, and natural metal in the earth are explained." Sci Bks

Includes bibliographical references

Fortey, Richard A.

Fossils; the key to the past; [by] Richard Fortey. 3rd ed. Smithsonian Institution Press 2002 232p il maps $55; pa $27.50 **560**

1. Fossils
ISBN 1-58834-023-6; 1-58834-048-1 (pa)
LC 2001-49439

First published 1982 by Van Nostrand Reinhold

In this volume, fossils "from earliest Precambrian forms onward are discussed, emphasizing evolutionary trends and extinctions, and relationships with habitat environments and geologic processes, such as volcanism and meteorite impacts, are evaluated. . . . Aspects of preservation, discovery, collection, and identification are discussed." Choice [review of 1991 edition]

Includes bibliographical references

Trilobite! eyewitness to evolution; by Richard Fortey. Knopf 2000 284p il $26; pa $14 **560**

1. Fossils 2. Evolution
ISBN 0-375-40625-5; 0-375-70621-6 (pa)
LC 00-34908

This is an introduction to the study of extinct marine arthropods called trilobites

The author's "unabashed trilobite-centric view of the evolution of life on Earth is full of personal anecdotes and asides, but it's also full of excellent science." Libr J

Gould, Stephen Jay, 1941-2002

Wonderful life: the Burgess Shale and the nature of history. Norton 1989 347p il hardcover o.p. paperback available $15.95 **560**

1. Fossils 2. Evolution
ISBN 0-393-30700-X (pa)
LC 88-37469

"The Burgess Shale is a rock formation containing the fossilized remains of a large number of marine creatures that no longer exist, and also the remains of some that do. The nonsurvivors appear to have been as well equipped to flourish as their contemporaries. Why did they not? . . . [This is an] account of the studies, the misinterpretations, and the revisions of opinion arising from the Burgess Shale material." Atlantic

"With his usual grace and wit Gould guides readers through the technical terminology and explains the significance of these fossils that exploded past assumptions about the history of life." Libr J

Includes bibliographical references

Poinar, George O.

The quest for life in amber; [by] George and Roberta Poinar. Addison-Wesley 1994 219p il hardcover o.p. paperback available $18 **560**

1. Fossils 2. Amber
ISBN 0-201-48928-7 (pa)
LC 94-3043

This is an account of the authors' search for and work with amber, a fossilized resin. The Poinars also include details of the scientific analyses of the insects trapped within this host material

This is "one of those books that educates the general reader about a scientific topic without requiring very much scientific background. Although educational, it is also highly entertaining and should be read for pleasure as much as for knowledge." Choice

Includes bibliographical references

Raup, David M.

Extinction; bad genes or bad luck? Norton 1991 210p hardcover o.p. paperback available $12.95 **560**

1. Mass extinction of species
ISBN 0-393-30927-4 (pa)
LC 90-27192

In this study of extinction, the author challenges the view that internal factors are critical in explaining the death of a species. Surveying past extinctions, Raup seeks to locate their cause in external factors, specifically the impact of meteorites

"Neither [Raup's] readers nor his scientific colleagues are likely to endorse everything he says, but his book is an eminently entertaining and informative read." N Y Times Book Rev

Includes bibliographical references

Rea, Tom, 1950-

Bone wars; the excavation and celebrity of Andrew Carnegie's dinosaur. University of Pittsburgh Press 2001 276p il $25 **560**

1. Carnegie, Andrew, 1835-1919 2. Fossils 3. Dinosaurs
ISBN 0-8229-4173-2
LC 2001-3336

This describes the history of the excavation of the dinosaur fossil Diplodocus carnegii in 1899 which was financed by Andrew Carnegie

"Rea pieces together countless bits of information to construct an overall picture of this period of scientific discovery." Booklist

Includes bibliographical references

Thompson, Ida

The Audubon Society field guide to North American fossils; with photographs by Townsend P. Dickinson; visual key by Carol Nehring. Knopf 1982 846p il maps flexible bdg $19.95 **560**

1. Fossils
ISBN 0-394-52412-8
LC 81-84772

"A Chanticleer Press edition. The Audubon Society field guide series"

Thompson, Ida—*Continued*

"This softbound field guide to fossils is divided into a section of color photographs followed by a section of detailed descriptions. It covers 420 fossils of marine and freshwater invertebrates, insects, plants, and vertebrates that are likely to be found by the amateur." Malinowsky. Best Sci & Technol Ref Books for Young People

Travels with the fossil hunters; edited by Peter Whybrow. Cambridge Univ. Press 2000 211p il $40   **560**

1. Fossils 2. Scientists

ISBN 0-521-66301-6   LC 99-30134

A collection of essays by paleontologists from London's Natural History Museum describing their work in such places as China, India, the Sahara, Latvia, and Antarctica

"The essayists give enough details of their quests to explain their presence in these places and keep science buffs entertained. . . . Heightening the impact of the stories is an abundance of beautiful, colorful photos of the places, the people, and the fossils." SLJ

Wallace, David Rains, 1945-

The bonehunters' revenge; dinosaurs, greed, and the greatest scientific feud of the gilded age. Houghton Mifflin 1999 366p il $25; pa $14   **560**

1. Cope, E. D. (Edward Drinker), 1840-1897 2. Marsh, Othniel Charles, 1831-1899 3. Fossils

ISBN 0-395-85089-4; 0-618-08240-9 (pa)

LC 99-31904

This is an account of the rivalry between 19th century paleontologists Edward Drinker Cope and Othniel Charles Marsh

"This curious century-old feud comes alive with momentum and understanding in Wallace's skillful hands." Booklist

Includes bibliographical references

567.9   Fossil reptiles. Dinosaurs

Chiappe, Luis M.

Walking on eggs; the astonishing discovery of thousands of dinosaur eggs in the badlands of Patagonia; [by] Luis M. Chiappe and Lowell Dingus. Scribner 2001 219p il maps $25   **567.9**

1. Dinosaurs 2. Fossils

ISBN 0-7432-1211-8   LC 2001-20280

"The authors, both paleontologists, describe the biologic and geologic aspects of three trips (in 1997, 1999, and 2000) to the badlands of northern Patagonia. While the expeditions focused on the discovery of large numbers of sauropod dinosaur eggs, dinosaur skeletal fossils were also discovered and collected, and a new carnivorous dinosaur that was found is described and named. . . . The authors successfully convey the ecstatic thrill of discovery." Sci Books Films

Includes bibliographical references

Encyclopedia of dinosaurs; edited by Philip J. Currie, Kevin Padian. Academic Press 1997 xxx, 869p il $110.95   **567.9**

1. Dinosaurs—Encyclopedias

ISBN 0-12-226810-5   LC 97-23430

"Organized alphabetically by subject, the signed articles cover kinds of dinosaurs, biology, geology, research, and museums where dinosaurs are on display, including a worldwide list of museums and sites." Libr J

Fiffer, Steve

Tyrannosaurus Sue; the extraordinary saga of the largest, most fought over T. rex ever found; foreword by Robert T. Bakker. Freeman, W.H. 2000 248p hardcover o.p. paperback available $14.95   **567.9**

1. Larson, Peter 2. Dinosaurs

ISBN 0-7167-9462-4 (pa)   LC 00-21596

In 1990 "South Dakota fossil-hunters Sue Hendrickson and Peter Larson dug up an exceptional T. rex—only the 12th tyrannosaur ever found, and the biggest and best-preserved to date. . . . The ensuing legal, political and scientific imbroglio set Native Americans against the federal government, the government against itself, the feds against established scientists and the world's great research universities against independent operators like Larson. Fiffer's thorough account should prove irresistible to readers with even a marginal interest in the legendary lizards." Publ Wkly

Gillette, David D.

Seismosaurus; the earth shaker; with illustrations by Mark Hallett. Columbia Univ. Press 1994 205p il maps $60; pa $21.95

     567.9

1. Dinosaurs

ISBN 0-231-07874-9; 0-231-07875-7 (pa)

LC 93-40318

"Seismosaurus (Sam, for short) is a new dinosaur discovered by hikers in New Mexico and excavated by the author. . . . Gillette's step-by-step story of the discovery of the first bones of the Seismosaurus details how it was named, unearthed, funded, and shared with the scientific community. He discusses how Sam fits in among the better-known Jurassic specimens as well as the potential uses for some exciting new field sensing techniques." Booklist

Includes bibliographical references

Glut, Donald F.

Dinosaurs, the encyclopedia; foreword by Michael K. Brett-Surman. McFarland & Co. 1997 1076p il $195   **567.9**

1. Dinosaurs—Encyclopedias

ISBN 0-89950-917-7   LC 95-47668

Also available supplementary volumes 1-3 published 1999-2003, v1 $60 v2-3 $95

"Opening with an overview and historical background on dinosaurians, the encyclopedia is devoted to an alphabetical list of dinosaur genera. Each article provides genus name; derivations of that name; the genus's extended classification of order, suborder, and family; a list of the locations specimens have been found; and drawings or black-and-white photographs of bones or the whole creature's skeleton. Each entry describes the physical characteristics of the animal and how its genus was established as well as how research and analysis have extended our understanding of it." Am Libr

Haines, Tim

Walking with dinosaurs; a natural history. DK Pub. 2000 288p il maps $25   **567.9**

1. Dinosaurs

ISBN 0-7894-5187-5   LC 99-37311

First published 1999 in the United Kingdom

Describes the earth's environment when dinosaurs flourished, the characteristics and habits of various species, and how changes in climate, landmasses, and vegetation led to the extinction of these massive reptiles

Haines, Tim—*Continued*

"Although published to accompany the BBC television series of the same name, this book by zoologist Haines can stand alone. . . . The you-are-there text is lavishly supplemented with graphics and with brief essays filled with scientific background information." Nat Hist

Lambert, David, 1932-

Dinosaur encyclopedia; from dinosaurs to the dawn of man; [by David Lambert, Darren Naish, Elizabeth Wyse] Dorling Kindersley 2001 376p il maps $29.95   **567.9**

1. Dinosaurs—Encyclopedias
ISBN 0-7894-7935-4   LC 2001-28433

In association with the American Museum of Natural History

"After a brief discussion of how paleontologists reconstruct the details of prehistory, this comprehensive volume breaks the animal kingdom into four major sections, 'Fish and Invertebrates,' 'Amphibians and Reptiles,' 'Dinosaurs and Birds' and 'Mammals and Their Ancestors.'" Publ Wkly

"This book is an excellent volume for both the uninitiated and the person who wishes to expand his or her knowledge from the basics. The book is logically laid out by groups of animals, and evolutionary connections between the animals are explained clearly. . . . As an encyclopedia, this one accomplishes its mission of providing a good basic foundation for each animal group it presents." Sci Books Films

The ultimate dinosaur book; foreword by John H. Ostrom. Dorling Kindersley 1993 192p il maps $29.95   **567.9**

1. Dinosaurs
ISBN 1-56458-304-X   LC 93-21885

Published in association with The Natural History Museum, London

"The opening section defines dinosaurs, describes the world they lived in, how they lived, and possible reasons for their extinction. . . . Profiles of 55 representative genera are illustrated with skeletons and museum models, plus a Fact File for each showing location, diet, classification, size and geologic era in which they lived. An A to Z of Dinosaurs (with pronunciation of names) includes 638 genera. Every page of this book includes color photos and detailed drawings." Book Rep

This "is a remarkable book, filled with information and high-quality illustrations." Sci Books Films

Larson, Peter L.

Rex appeal; the amazing story of Sue, the dinosaur that changed science, the law, and my life; [by] Peter Larson, Kristin Donnan. Invisible Cities Press 2002 404p il $26.95   **567.9**

1. Dinosaurs 2. Fossils
ISBN 1-931229-07-4   LC 2002-24207

Larson's "team discovered the largest and most complete Tyrannosaurus rex skeleton that the world had seen. Almost immediately, however, the team . . . became embroiled in a dispute with the U.S. government about who owns the fossil, during which the skeleton was seized by the National Guard. . . . The book recounts the heated legal battles but focuses primarily on Larson's adventures in South Dakota, where his group eventually found six more T. rex fossils." Publ Wkly

Includes bibliographical references

Nothdurft, William E.

The lost dinosaurs of Egypt; [by] William Nothdurft with Josh Smith [et al.] Random House 2002 242p il maps $24.95; pa $13.95   **567.9**

1. Stromer, Ernst 2. Dinosaurs 3. Fossils
ISBN 0-375-50795-7; 0-375-75979-4 (pa)
        LC 2002-75172

"Between 1910 and 1914, Ernst Stromer . . . unearthed a wealth of dinosaur fossils in Egypt's Bahariya Oasis. Thirty years later, Stromer's discoveries were destroyed in a WWII Allied bombing raid, and the oasis lay neglected for decades until Josh Smith, a Penn State doctoral candidate in paleontology, decided to retrace Stromer's footsteps in 1999. . . . [This] account highlights Stromer's discoveries . . . and chronicles recent findings by Smith and his colleagues. . . . An engaging mix of history and desert drama, this . . . is first-rate popular science." Publ Wkly

The **Scientific** American book of dinosaurs; Gregory S. Paul, editor. St. Martin's Press 2000 424p il maps $32.95; pa $19.95   **567.9**

1. Dinosaurs
ISBN 0-312-26226-4; 0-312-31008-0 (pa)
        LC 2001-269051

"A Byron Preiss book"

This book features information on "how dinosaurs evolved, how they looked, where they lived, how they behaved, and why they died . . . [as well as] stories about the first discoveries of dinosaur fossils, the beginnings of dinosaur paleontology, how the field has changed with modern technology, the most sensational finds, and the latest theories." Publisher's note

Includes bibliographical references

568 Fossil birds

Shipman, Pat

Taking wing; Archaeopteryx and the evolution of bird flight. Simon & Schuster 1998 336p il hardcover o.p. paperback available $22.95   **568**

1. Archaeopteryx 2. Birds—Flight
ISBN 0-684-84965-8 (pa)   LC 97-27527

The author focuses on "how adaptations needed for animal flight came about. Using the well-known *Archaeopteryx* fossils as a keystone, she discusses historical and current hypotheses about bird evolution, along with the provocative debates they spurred." Libr J

"Shipman brings to her excellent book the authority of a paleontologist and the talent of an accomplished writer on science for popular audiences." N Y Times Book Rev

Includes bibliographical references

570 Life sciences. Biology

Carson, Rachel, 1907-1964
Lost woods; the discovered writing of Rachel Carson; edited and with an introduction by Linda Lear. Beacon Press 1998 267p hardcover o.p. paperback available $16 **570**
1. Nature 2. Wildlife conservation
ISBN 0-8070-8547-2 (pa) LC 98-20058
This is a collection of previously unpublished essays, speeches, field notes, letters, and other writings by the pioneering environmentalist
These excerpts provide readers "with samples of some of the most lyrical, clear scientific writing available in the fields of biology, ecology, and wildlife and wilderness conservation." SLJ
Includes bibliographical references

Gould, Stephen Jay, 1941-2002
An urchin in the storm; essays about books and ideas. Norton 1987 255p il hardcover o.p. paperback available $11.95 **570**
1. Biology
ISBN 0-393-30537-6 (pa) LC 87-21718
Analyzed in Essay and general literature index
This collection of Gould's book reviews is arranged in broad subject areas: evolutionary theory, biological determinism, time and geology

Hoagland, Mahlon B., 1921-
The way life works; [by] Mahlon Hoagland, Bert Dodson. Times Bks. 1995 xxi, 233p il hardcover o.p. paperback available $27 **570**
1. Life (Biology)
ISBN 0-8129-2888-1 (pa) LC 94-48780
Hoagland's text and Dodson's illustrations "present the mechanics of everything from DNA to neural circuits and evolution. As they move from discussion of 16 key patterns in life to chapters titled 'Energy,' 'Information,' 'Feedback,' 'Community,' and 'Evolution,' Hoagland and Dodson link the mechanics of the invisible world of molecules to the observable working world of plants and animals, water and light, and human beings and even machines. There is a lively sense of discovery here." Booklist
Includes bibliographical references

Margulis, Lynn, 1938-
Five kingdoms; an illustrated guide to the phyla of life on earth; [by] Lynn Margulis, Karlene V. Schwartz. 3rd ed. Freeman, W.H. 1998 xx, 520p il hardcover o.p. paperback available $29.95 **570**
1. Biology
ISBN 0-7167-3027-8 (pa) LC 97-21338
First published 1982
This classifies life on Earth into nearly 100 phyla, and discusses techniques such as molecular biology and gene sequencing that illuminate the relationship between microorganisms and larger life forms. Introductory sections define the general features of each of the five kingdoms (Bacteria, Protoctists, Animals, Fungi, and Plants). Brief essays and illustrations describe representative members of each phylum
Includes bibliographical references

Mayr, Ernst, 1904-
This is biology; the science of the living world. Harvard Univ. Press 1997 327p il hardcover o.p. paperback available $17.95 **570**
1. Biology
ISBN 0-674-88469-8 (pa) LC 96-42192
This is an overview of the major concepts and issues surrounding biology from Aristotle to the present. Topics discussed include genetics, cytology, evolution, development, and biodiversity
"This is an extremely well-thought-out and eminently scholarly work. . . . Mayr is definitely a grand old man of biology, and this book demonstrates his grasp of the development of the field." Sci Books Films
Includes bibliographical references

Serafini, Anthony
The epic history of biology. Plenum 1993 395p il hardcover o.p. paperback available $25 **570**
1. Biology
ISBN 0-7382-0577-X (pa) LC 93-27895
This volume traces the origins and evolution of the discipline "of biology from prehistoric times through the modern revolution in molecular biology." Sci Books Films
Includes bibliographical references

570.1 Life sciences—Philosophy and theory

Bentley, P. J.
Digital biology; how nature is transforming our technology and our lives; [by] Peter J. Bentley. Simon & Schuster 2002 c2001 272p il $25 **570.1**
1. Biology—Computer simulation 2. System analysis
ISBN 0-7432-0447-6 LC 2001-54987
The author "reveals the unexpected ways in which cybertechnicians are taking their research cues from evolutionists and geneticists. . . . Bentley adduces strong evidence that the digital plants now sprouting in computer systems must count as part of nature, not merely as copies. . . . A thrilling vision of the future for some; *Brave New World* revisited for others." Booklist
Includes bibliographical references

Capra, Fritjof
The web of life; a new scientific understanding of living systems. Anchor Bks. (NY) 1996 347p il hardcover o.p. paperback available $14.95 **570.1**
1. Life (Biology) 2. System theory
ISBN 0-385-47676-0 (pa) LC 96-12576
This discourse on the life sciences incorporates "elements from such contemporary schools of thought as the Gaia hypothesis, deep ecology, complexity theory, systems theory, and . . . eco-feminism." Libr J
This is "a rewarding synthesis that will challenge serious readers." Publ Wkly
Includes bibliographical references

Duve, Christian de, 1917-
Vital dust; life as a cosmic imperative. Basic Bks. 1994 362p il hardcover o.p. paperback available $24 **570.1**
1. Life—Origin 2. Life (Biology) 3. Evolution
ISBN 0-465-09045-1 (pa)   LC 94-12964
"De Duve begins with hypotheses about the origin of life and ends with speculations about the future and meaning of life and the abundance of life in the universe. He argues . . . for the view that life—including intelligent life—is probably found liberally scattered throughout the universe. In the intervening pages, he reviews the major stages, or innovations, in the history of life on planet Earth. . . . Not always easy reading at times, this book is guaranteed to make the patient reader think and question." Sci Books Films
Includes bibliographical references

Keller, Evelyn Fox, 1936-
Making sense of life; explaining biological development with models, metaphors, and machines. Harvard Univ. Press 2002 388p il $29.95 **570.1**
1. Biology—Philosophy 2. Life (Biology)
ISBN 0-674-00746-8   LC 2001-51559
The author "analyzes the history of developmental biology. She explains the type of information scientists have accepted, why changes in acceptance may occur and, on a broader scale, what it means to understand the natural world. . . . While Keller's prose is graceful and informed, her thesis is complex and unlikely to be fully appreciated by those without significant grounding in philosophy and biology." Publ Wkly
Includes bibliographical references

Lovelock, James
The ages of Gaia; a biography of our living earth. Norton 1988 xx, 252p il hardcover o.p. paperback available $13.95 **570.1**
1. Biology—Philosophy 2. Gaia hypothesis 3. Biosphere 4. Life (Biology)
ISBN 0-393-31239-9 (pa)   LC 87-36567
"A volume of the Commonwealth Fund Book Program, under the editorship of Lewis Thomas"
"Gaia is the Greek goddess of the earth. For James Lovelock she is the embodiment of a hypothesis: the earth is not merely the abode of life but is a single living organism. He proposes that all living species are components of that organism, as cells are components of the human body." N Y Times Book Rev
Includes bibliographical references

Margulis, Lynn, 1938-
What is life? [by] Lynn Margulis and Dorion Sagan; foreword by Niles Eldredge. Simon & Schuster 1995 207p il o.p.; University of Calif. Press paperback available $24.95 **570.1**
1. Life (Biology) 2. Biology—Philosophy 3. Biological diversity 4. Life—Origin
ISBN 0-520-22021-8 (pa)   LC 94-44213
"A Peter N. Nevraumont book"
"Continuing Margulis's contention that organelles within cells, such as mitochondria, were originally free-living organisms that fused with others to form complex cells and bodies, the authors extend this concept to the Earth as a superorganism. Although following traditional evolutionary pathways, the authors argue that life has played a role in its own evolution." Choice
Includes bibliographical references

Sagan, Carl, 1934-1996
Shadows of forgotten ancestors; a search for who we are; [by] Carl Sagan, Ann Druyan. Random House 1992 505p hardcover o.p. paperback available $15.95 **570.1**
1. Life—Origin 2. Evolution
ISBN 0-345-38472-5 (pa)   LC 92-50155
The authors "trace the roots of the *Homo sapiens* family tree down to life at its tiniest. . . . As Sagan and Druyan move up the evolutionary ladder from microorganisms to more complex creatures including insects, snakes, fish, birds, and primates, they track the emergence of sexuality, survival tactics, instinct, and thinking, all sparked by the basic interplay between heredity and environment." Booklist
"Despite a preference for the overly dramatic phrase at the expense of scientific clarity, the argument is coherent throughout." Libr J
Includes bibliographical references

Thomas, Lewis, 1913-1993
The lives of a cell; notes of a biology watcher. Viking 1974 153p hardcover o.p. paperback available $13 **570.1**
1. Biology—Philosophy
ISBN 0-14-004743-3 (pa)
Also available in paperback from Bantam Bks.
In this collection of twenty-nine short essays "the author does not confine his scientist's eye to a microscope. He takes a much wider view of the world, looking at insect behavior and the possibility of intelligent life in outer space or bird songs and the evolution of language. He also offers a modest proposal for saving ourselves from nuclear self-destruction." Time
Includes bibliographical references

570.3 Life sciences— Encyclopedias and dictionaries

McGraw-Hill dictionary of bioscience. 2nd ed. McGraw-Hill 2002 662p pa $19.95 **570.3**
1. Biology—Dictionaries 2. Life sciences—Dictionaries
ISBN 0-07-141043-0   LC 2002-33193
First published 1997
This dictionary includes 18,000 entries in more than 20 areas of life science and includes synonyms, acronyms, abbreviations, pronunciations, and an appendix of data tables
"Given its reasonable price, the dictionary . . . would be useful for offices, laboratories, or classrooms. The source of the definitions is a guarantee of quality." Am Ref Books Annu, 1998

571 Physiology and related subjects

Widmaier, Eric P.
Why geese don't get obese (and we do); how evolution's strategies for survival affect our everyday lives. Freeman, W.H. 1998 213p il hardcover o.p. paperback available $14.95   **571**
1. Comparative physiology
ISBN 0-7167-3649-7 (pa)   LC 98-2698
This book examines "the evolution of normal human and animal physiology, why we work the way we do, and a few conditions where adaptations from our ancestors are not so useful in modern life, for example, diabetes, stress, and the obesity mentioned in the title. What really makes this book stand out are the lucid explanations of how scientific method . . . is used to learn about human and animal physiology." Libr J

571.4 Biophysics

Vogel, Steven, 1940-
Cats' paws and catapults; mechanical worlds of nature and people; illustrated by Kathryn K. Davis with the author. Norton 1998 382p il $27.50; pa $15.95   **571.4**
1. Human engineering 2. Mechanics
ISBN 0-393-04641-9; 0-393-31990-3 (pa)
                  LC 97-44807
"This work is a comparison of natural mechanical devices, the cats' paws of the title, and human inventions, the catapults and dozens more of the components of modern life." N Y Times Book Rev
"Composed of curiosity and counter-intuition, this amply illustrated work should attract anyone interested in biology." Booklist
Includes bibliographical references

571.6 Cell biology

The **Facts** on File dictionary of cell and molecular biology; edited by Robert Hine. Facts on File 2002 248p il $49.50; pa $19.95   **571.6**
1. Cells—Dictionaries 2. Molecular biology—Dictionaries
ISBN 0-8160-4912-2; 0-8160-4913-0 (pa)
                  LC 2002-32540
"There are 2,000 entries for terms in all major areas of biochemistry, molecular biology, molecular genetics, and cell biology. . . . Brief biographies of significant scientists are included. The appendixes include a chronology of the major discoveries in biochemistry and molecular biology. Also provided are molecular diagrams of 20 amino acids, a chart of the genetic code, a brief list of Web pages, and a bibliography. . . . Each entry is well written and clear. The illustrations are good, and there appear to be all the major terms needed for the purpose of this dictionary." Am Ref Books Annu, 2003

Harold, Franklin M.
The way of the cell; molecules, organisms, and the order of life. Oxford Univ. Press 2001 305p il $37.50; pa $17.95   **571.6**
1. Cells 2. Life (Biology)
ISBN 0-19-513512-1; 0-19-516338-9 (pa)
                  LC 00-56670
"Harold tackles the largest of questions (What is life?) within the smallest of settings (the cell) in order to consider where and why a strictly genetic approach to life leads us astray." Booklist
Includes bibliographical references

Loewenstein, Werner R.
The touchstone of life; molecular information, cell communication, and the foundations of life. Oxford Univ. Press 1999 366p il $45; pa $17.95   **571.6**
1. Cells 2. Evolution
ISBN 0-19-511828-6; 0-19-514057-5 (pa)
                  LC 97-43408
This work "focuses on the role information transfer has played in the evolution of life over the past four million years. By merging principles of biology and physics, Loewenstein explains the workings of cell biology and biochemistry." Publ Wkly
"Loewenstein writes engagingly, and he provides the background material a nonspecialist needs to follow the intricate story." N Y Times Book Rev
Includes bibliographical references

Rensberger, Boyce
Life itself; exploring the realm of the living cell; illustrations by Nigel Orme. Oxford Univ. Press 1996 290p il hardcover o.p. paperback available $16.95   **571.6**
1. Cells 2. Molecular biology
ISBN 0-19-512500-2 (pa)   LC 96-33679
This is an overview of what is "currently known about the mechanisms by which living cells perform their myriad tasks." N Y Times Book Rev
This is "an elegant, authoritative, yet felicitously written book that will appeal to anyone who is interested in how cells work." New Sci
Includes bibliographical references

572 Biochemistry

The **Facts** on File dictionary of biochemistry; edited by John Daintith. Facts on File 2002 247p il $49.50; pa $19.95   **572**
1. Biochemistry—Dictionaries
ISBN 0-8160-4914-9; 0-8160-4915-7 (pa)
                  LC 2002-35203
"Facts on File science library"
"General areas included in the *Dictionary of Biochemistry* are basic organic and physical chemistry, classes of compounds, cytology and histology, nutrition and metabolism, and natural-product chemistry. Examples of specific entries are *Beta-pleated sheet; cyano-bacteria; Enzyme; G protein; Guanine; Isomerase; McClintock, Barbara; Pollution; Sex determination; Sugar; Vector*; and *Zeolite*. Appendixes provide a chronology of major events in the development of biochemistry and molecular biology, a table of the genetic code, amino acid structures, the periodic table, chemical elements, the Greek alphabet, and suggested Web pages." Booklist

572.8 Biochemical genetics

Bodmer, W. F. (Walter Fred), 1936-
The book of man; the Human Genome Project and the quest to discover our genetic heritage; [by] Walter Bodmer and Robin McKie. Scribner 1995 c1994 259p il maps o.p.; Oxford Univ. Press paperback available $21.50   **572.8**
1. Human Genome Project 2. Gene. mapping
ISBN 0-19-511487-6 (pa)   LC 94-38081
First published 1994 in the United Kingdom with subtitle: The quest to discover our genetic heritage
This book discusses the Human Genome Project and contains "information on how human genes are mapped and why this mapping is important in medical, evolutionary, and sociological terms." Libr J
This "is highly readable, clear and accurate." New Sci

Cook-Deegan, Robert M.
The gene wars; science, politics, and the human genome. Norton 1994 416p il $25; pa $14.95   **572.8**
1. Human Genome Project 2. Gene mapping
ISBN 0-393-03572-7; 0-393-31399-9 (pa)
LC 93-10762
This "account of the Human Genome Project is as much about the politics, economics, and personalities as it is about the science of this . . . project to map the 100,000 chromosome sequences of the human genome." Libr J
Includes bibliographical references

Danchin, Antoine
The Delphic boat; what genomes tell us; translated by Alison Quayle. Harvard Univ. Press 2002 368p $35   **572.8**
1. Genomes
ISBN 0-674-00930-4   LC 2002-27273
Original French edition, 1998
"The book explores how researchers identify the roles of genes and the proteins they produce, and how understanding genomes leads us to a reconsideration of the very idea of life." Publ Wkly
"Danchin conducts intelligent amateurs surprisingly far into the [book's] central issues. This timely book offers hope that the rhetoric and hype of the antagonists fighting over the genome agenda will not drown out rational dialogue." Booklist
Includes bibliographical references

Lewontin, Richard C., 1929-
The triple helix; gene, organism, and environment; [by] Richard Lewontin. Harvard Univ. Press 2000 136p il $25; pa $15 **572.8**
1. Molecular biology 2. Genetic code
ISBN 0-674-00159-1; 0-674-00677-1 (pa)
LC 99-53879
In this book the author "demonstrates how all organisms, including humans, are the product of intricate interactions between their genes and the environment in which they live. . . . Although the issues Lewontin addresses are huge, he writes about them in a manner fully accessible to the nonspecialist." Publ Wkly
Includes bibliographical references

Morange, Michel
A history of molecular biology; translated by Matthew Cobb. Harvard Univ. Press 1998 336p $39.95; pa $22.50   **572.8**
1. Molecular biology
ISBN 0-674-39855-6; 0-674-00169-9 (pa)
LC 97-47158
"Molecular biology is responsible for the recent high-profile developments in cloning, genetic engineering, DNA fingerprinting, etc. Morange . . . covers the birth of the field at the beginning of this century, the discovery of DNA and the deciphering of the genetic code, and the practical applications resulting from the revelations of the last 50 years." Libr J
Includes bibliographical references

Rabinow, Paul
Making PCR; a story of biotechnology. University of Chicago Press 1996 190p il $22.50; pa $14   **572.8**
1. Polymers 2. Chemical reactions
ISBN 0-226-70146-8; 0-226-70147-6 (pa)
LC 95-49103
The author provides "an 'ethnographic account' of the Cetus Corporation during the invention of PCR, the polymerase chain reaction, a method for increasing the DNA in samples to usable levels and one of the most important techniques in biotechnology." Publ Wkly
"An intriguing read that raises many questions about our understanding of the twisting process of discovery itself." New Sci
Includes bibliographical references

Sulston, John, 1942-
The common thread; a story of science, politics, ethics, and the human genome; [by] John Sulston, Georgina Ferry. Joseph Henry Press 2002 310p il $24.95   **572.8**
1. Human Genome Project
ISBN 0-309-08409-1   LC 2002-14007
The author gives an "account of the excitement, hard work, vision, and daring needed to move from worm biology to recommending sequencing of the human genome, while senior and influential colleagues argued vigorously against it. He speaks forcefully of the necessity of keeping the sequence public and freely available. . . . [This title is] recommended for almost any library, particularly those with readers willing to go beyond sound bites and media hype." Libr J
Includes bibliographical references

Watson, James D., 1928-
The double helix; a personal account of the discovery of the structure of DNA. Scribner 1998 226p il $25; pa $14   **572.8**
1. DNA 2. Biochemistry—Research
ISBN 0-684-85279-9; 0-7432-1630-X (pa)
LC 98-136787
Also available in paperback from Norton
A reissue of the title first published 1968 by Atheneum Pubs.
This book is a "personal, day-by-day account of how Watson, [Francis] Crick and their collaborators in the years between 1951 and 1963 hit upon the famous 'double helix' model of the 'DNA' [deoxyribonucleic acid] molecule, the fundamental genetical material." America

573.6 Reproductive system

Friedman, David M., 1949-
A mind of its own; a cultural history of the penis. Free Press 2001 358p il o.p.; Penguin Bks. paperback available $15 **573.6**
1. Penis
ISBN 0-14-200259-3 (pa) LC 2001-45208
This is a social and medical history of the male organ. Topics discussed include religious teachings about sex, efforts to overcome male impotence throughout history, attitudes toward masturbation, and racial stereotypes relating to phallus size
"This valuable analysis of the origins of male sexuality and how the conception of maleness has shaped understanding of female sexuality isn't just educational . . . it's entertaining." Booklist
Includes bibliographical references

573.8 Nervous and sensory systems

Hughes, Howard C.
Sensory exotica; a world beyond human experience. MIT Press 1999 345p $40; pa $18.95 **573.8**
1. Senses and sensation 2. Comparative physiology
ISBN 0-262-08279-9; 0-262-58204-X (pa)
LC 98-51875
This is a compendium of stories and information regarding the vast array of sensory systems that are utilized by different species, ranging from insects to aquatic mammals to humans. . . . Hughes does an excellent job of presenting the facts and the science behind the vast array of sensory systems." Sci Books Films
Includes bibliographical references

576 Genetics and evolution

Dawkins, Richard, 1941-
Climbing Mount Improbable; original drawings by Lalla Ward. Norton 1996 340p il hardcover o.p. paperback available $15.95 **576**
1. Natural selection 2. Evolution 3. Genetics
ISBN 0-393-31682-3 (pa) LC 96-19138
"Dawkins discusses genetics, natural selection, and embryology for hundreds of species spanning millions of years. . . . An invigorating trip through the history of life led by one of Darwin's most articulate disciples." Libr J
Includes bibliographical references

River out of Eden; a Darwinian view of life; illustrations by Lalla Ward. Basic Bks. 1995 172p il (Science masters series) hardcover o.p. paperback available $14 **576**
1. Genetics 2. Evolution
ISBN 0-465-06990-8 (pa) LC 94-37146
The author "explores the evolution of humans from a single ancestor; evolutions of specific organs (e.g., eyes) and coadaptation of species (e.g., wasps and orchids); nature's physical and behavioral mechanisms to maximize survival of DNA; and, finally, the ultimate results when our DNA reaches out in space. His arguments and examples are clear, compelling, and often amusing." Libr J
Includes bibliographical references

The selfish gene. new ed. Oxford Univ. Press 1989 352p il hardcover o.p. paperback available $14.95 **576**
1. Genetics 2. Evolution
ISBN 0-19-286092-5 (pa) LC 89-16077
First published 1976
The author examines evolution and contends that genes that benefit individual members of a species will be passed on to future generations, rather than those which may benefit the entire group
Includes bibliographical references

Genetics; Richard Robinson [editor in chief] Macmillan Ref. USA 2003 4v set $395 **576**
1. Genetics—Encyclopedias
ISBN 0-02-865606-7 LC 2002-3560
This set contains "approximately 250 signed entries from *Accelerated aging: Progeria* to *Zebrafish*. Articles range from a few paragraphs to a few pages in length and focus on a variety of topics, including inheritance, genes and chromosomes, genetic diseases, biotechnology, history, careers, and the ethical, legal, and social issues associated with genetically modified foods and cloning. The entries appear in alphabetical order and include cross-references to related entries. Most have a list of suggested readings and Internet resources. . . . The clear and well-written articles are informative and should meet the needs of most students." Booklist

Goodwin, Brian C.
How the leopard changed its spots; the evolution of complexity; [by] Brian Goodwin. Scribner 1994 252p il o.p.; Princeton Univ. Press paperback available $19.95 **576**
1. Evolution 2. Biology
ISBN 0-691-08809-8 (pa) LC 94-16891
"Arguing that Darwin's theory of natural selection cannot explain the emergence of distinctive species, British biologist Goodwin proposes an alternative theory of evolution. He views organisms as dynamic systems, themselves the primary agents of creative evolutionary adaptation and change that occurs in a matrix of relationships with other members of the same species." Publ Wkly
"Although light on data, this is a serious presentation for the informed lay reader of the philosophical direction some avant-garde biological thought is taking." Libr J
Includes bibliographical references

576.5 Genetics

Berg, Paul, 1926-
Dealing with genes; the language of heredity; [by] Paul Berg, Maxine Singer. University Science Bks. 1992 269p il $38 **576.5**
1. Genetics
ISBN 0-935702-69-5 LC 91-75179
"This book about molecular genetics covers basic chemistry and cell biology, as well as the structure and fundamental role of DNA and the information it contains." Sci Books Films
Includes bibliographical references

Keller, Evelyn Fox, 1936-

The century of the gene. Harvard Univ. Press 2000 186p il $25; pa $15.95   **576.5**

1. Genetics
ISBN 0-674-00372-1; 0-674-99825-1 (pa)

LC 00-38319

The author "traces the evolution of genetic science over the course of the twentieth century, during which Gregor Mendel's theories of inheritance were rediscovered, the structure of DNA revealed, and the human genome mapped." Booklist

"In this tight, clearly written survey, Keller does a wonderful job of explaining and demonstrating how our knowledge of genetics has accumulated to the extent that we can fathom what we don't understand." Publ Wkly

Includes bibliographical references

Tudge, Colin

The impact of the gene; from Mendel's peas to designer babies. Hill & Wang 2001 375p $27; pa $15   **576.5**

1. Genetics
ISBN 0-374-17523-3; 0-8090-5743-3 (pa)

LC 00-67306

This is a "narrative on the development of genetics from Gregor Mendel's 19th-century pea experiments to the present. . . . Tudge manages to weave the contributions of hundreds of scientists into a story that is coherent, logical, and readable. He also tackles the social implications of genetics . . . and offers thoughtful and persuasive discussions of difficult topics such as evolutionary psychology." Libr J

Includes bibliographical references

Watson, James D., 1928-

DNA: the secret of life; [by] James D. Watson, with Andrew Berry. Knopf 2003 446p il $39.95   **576.5**

1. Genetics 2. DNA
ISBN 0-375-41546-7   LC 2002-190725

"Watson begins by describing the history of molecular genetics, pausing at times to introduce the scientific players and to describe the . . . experiments showing how DNA is replicated, how its code is translated into the proteins that compose our bodies and how genes are turned on and off as needed. The remaining two-thirds of the book treats the implications of the new genetics: biotechnology, genetically modified food, the forensic use of DNA, the sequencing of the human genome, the development of genetically based medicine and the search for genes affecting human behavior. . . . [There is] a chapter on DNA-based approaches to understanding the human past." N Y Times Book Rev

"Watson sensitively and sensibly treats the controversies aroused by genetically modified foods and organisms, patenting genes, and playing with the 'stuff of life.' Written for the educated and biologically aware reader, this is recommended for most public and academic libraries." Libr J

Includes bibliographical references

576.8   Evolution

Adams, Fred C.

Origins of existence; how life emerged in the universe; [by] Fred Adams. Free Press 2002 266p il $25   **576.8**

1. Life—Origin
ISBN 0-7432-1262-2   LC 2002-73877

The author "argues that life followed naturally from the laws of physics—which were established as the universe burst into existence at the big bang. Those elegant laws drove the formation of galaxies, stars, and planets—including some like our Earth." Publisher's note

Includes bibliographical references

Behe, Michael J., 1952-

Darwin's black box; the biochemical challenge to evolution. Free Press 1996 307p il hardcover o.p. paperback available $14.99   **576.8**

1. Evolution
ISBN 0-684-83493-6 (pa)   LC 96-695

The author "argues that the biochemical basis of complex life could not have developed through gradual evolutionary change because too many dependent variables would have had to have been altered simultaneously. Through explanations of the functions of the eye, blood clotting, and the immune system, he sets out to argue against evolution as a sole explanation for their existence." Libr J

Includes bibliographical references

Boulter, Michael Charles

Extinction: evolution and the end of man; [by] Michael Boulter. Columbia Univ. Press 2002 210p il maps $26   **576.8**

1. Mass extinction of species 2. Evolution 3. Human influence on nature
ISBN 0-231-12836-3   LC 2002-34783

"This book is . . . [an] introduction to the new developments in the science of life and [an] . . . account of the effects that humans have had on the planet." Publisher's note

Darwin, Charles, 1809-1882

The Darwin reader; edited by Mark Ridley. 2nd ed. Norton 1996 315p il pa $21.30   **576.8**

1. Evolution 2. Natural selection
ISBN 0-393-96967-3   LC 95-50297

First published in the United Kingdom with title: The essential Darwin; first Norton edition published 1987

This collection presents excerpts from Darwin's most important works including Origin of the species, The descent of man and Coral reef. Illustrations are taken from the original editions

Includes bibliographical references

The origin of species   **576.8**

1. Evolution 2. Natural selection 3. Human origins 4. Heredity

Available in hardcover and paperback from various publishers

First published 1859. Variant title: The origin of species by means of natural selection

The classic exposition of the "theory of evolution by natural selection. Darwin argues that every species devel-

Darwin, Charles, 1809-1882—*Continued*

ops or evolves from a previous one and that all life is
a continuing pattern. His objects of study were the variations from generation to generation in domestic plants
and animals. . . . While subsequent investigation has superseded some of Darwin's arguments, *Origin of Species*
remains one of the most influential books ever published." Reader's Ency. 4th edition

Davies, P. C. W., 1946-

The fifth miracle; the search for the origin
and meaning of life; [by] Paul Davies. Simon
& Schuster 1999 304p il hardcover o.p.
paperback available $14   **576.8**
  1. Life—Origin
  ISBN 0-684-86309-X (pa)   LC 98-33421
  "Life on earth—God's fifth miracle according to Genesis—may have begun with rock-eating microbes far below the surface of Mars. So suggests Davies in this provocative investigation into the origins of life. . . . In his
remarkably lucid style, Davies lays out the evidence for
a universe inherently friendly to life. A ground-breaking
book." Booklist
  Includes bibliographical references

Duve, Christian de, 1917-

Life evolving; molecules, mind, and
meaning. Oxford Univ. Press 2002 341p il
$30   **576.8**
  1. Life—Origin 2. Evolution 3. Life (Biology)
  ISBN 0-19-515605-6   LC 2002-75407
  The author "surveys the scientific approach to understanding how life began, crucial bottlenecks in its increasing complexity, and the question of the contingency
versus the inevitability of the entire process. . . . Beneath the philosophizing, de Duve delineates biology excellently and authoritatively, introducing it with wonder
and curiosity that are bound to excite the next generation." Booklist
  "A masterful work of synthesis recommended for all
collections." Choice
  Includes bibliographical references

Eiseley, Loren C., 1907-1977

The immense journey; [by] Loren Eisley.
Random House 1957 210p hardcover o.p.
paperback available $10   **576.8**
  1. Evolution 2. Human origins
  ISBN 0-394-70157-7 (pa)
  "Essays on biology and paleontology by an anthropologist speculating on the origin of man and the theory of
evolution." Publ Wkly
  Dr Eiseley's "style is beautiful, compelling in impact
and poetic in its imagery. His subject is one of the epics
of natural science—the 'immense journey' of life as
known on this planet." Christ Sci Monit

Encyclopedia of evolution; Mark Pagel,
editor in chief. Oxford Univ. Press 2002 2v
il set $325   **576.8**
  1. Evolution—Encyclopedias
  ISBN 0-19-512200-3   LC 2001-21588
  This reference covers topics in evolutionary theory
"including developmental biology, social behavior, consciousness, evolution of disease, systematics, population
biology, complexity theory, and even art in prehistory.
Some biographical articles are also included. . . .
[Contributors include] Stephen Jay Gould, Jane Goodall,
Sarah Blaffer Hrdy, and John Maynard Smith." Libr J

Fortey, Richard A.

Life; a natural history of the first four
billion years of life on earth; {by} Richard
Fortey. Knopf 1998 346p il $32.59; pa $15
                                           576.8
  1. Evolution 2. Life—Origin
  ISBN 0-375-40119-9; 0-375-70261-X (pa)
                                        LC 97-49466
  First published 1997 in the United Kingdom with subtitle: an unauthorized biography
  In this survey Fortey summarizes "what we know
about the history of life on the planet. Because not all
life forms left fossil evidence and because interpretations
are subject to change, he offers a provisional, personal,
and sometimes speculative picture. Fortey points out how
discoveries in such areas as historical geology, molecular
biology, and genetics have changed past assumptions
about the evolution of life forms." Libr J
  This work is "written for readers with no science. It
will help them understand the specialized and often technical books on evolution that make headlines but leave
most people wondering why." N Y Times Book Rev
  Includes bibliographical references

Gould, Stephen Jay, 1941-2002

Eight little piggies; reflections in natural
history. Norton 1993 479p il hardcover o.p.
paperback available $15.95   **576.8**
  1. Natural history 2. Evolution
  ISBN 0-393-31139-2 (pa)   LC 92-18737
  In this collection of essays originally published in Natural History magazine "Gould critically explores a cas-
cade of ideas that shed new light on ecology, human nature, vertebrate anatomy, neo-Darwinism, and mass extinctions; he even includes personal musings." Libr J
  Includes bibliographical references

Ever since Darwin; reflections in natural
history. Norton 1977 285p il hardcover o.p.
paperback available $14.95   **576.8**
  1. Darwin, Charles, 1809-1882 2. Evolution 3. Natural selection
  ISBN 0-393-30818-9 (pa)   LC 77-22504
  "In a series of essays written originally for Natural
History magazine Gould explores the impact of Darwin's
evolutionary theory on the study of man and other organisms." Libr J
  Gould "not only explains scientific theory but comments on science itself, with clarity and wit, simultaneously entertaining and teaching." N Y Times Book
Rev
  Includes bibliographical references

Hen's teeth and horse's toes. Norton 1983
413p il hardcover o.p. paperback available
$15.95   **576.8**
  1. Evolution
  ISBN 0-393-31103-1 (pa)   LC 82-22259
  The theme of this collection is "biological evolution.
[The author] has grouped the 30 essays into seven cate-
gories: Sensible Oddities, Personalities, Adaptation and
Development, Teilhard and Piltdown, Science and Poli-
tics, Extinction and a Zebra Trilogy." America
  Includes bibliographical references

Gould, Stephen Jay, 1941-2002—*Continued*

The panda's thumb; more reflections in natural history; Stephen Jay Gould. Norton 1980 343p il hardcover o.p. paperback available $15.95 **576.8**
1. Evolution 2. Natural selection
ISBN 0-393-30819-7 (pa)   LC 80-15952
In these essays "a variety of creatures, including humans, dinosaurs, pandas, turtles, and microscopic organisms, are considered in light of their reflection of Darwin's theory. One intriguing theme which runs throughout the selections is how imperfectly designed anatomy or haphazardly applied anatomical evolution best supports Darwinism." Booklist
Includes bibliographical references

The structure of evolutionary theory. Belknap Press 2002 xxii, 1433p il $39.95 **576.8**
1. Evolution
ISBN 0-674-00613-5   LC 2001-43556
This is a "history and analysis of classical and twentieth-century evolutionary theory." Booklist
Includes bibliographical references

Hooper, Judith

Of moths and men; an evolutionary tale: the untold story of science and the peppered moth. Norton 2002 xx, 377p il $26.95; pa $15.95 **576.8**
1. Kettlewell, Henry Bernard David, 1907-1979 2. Majerus, M. E. N., 1954- 3. Natural selection 4. Evolution 5. Moths 6. Fraud
ISBN 0-393-05121-8; 0-393-32525-3 (pa)
LC 2002-26315
This is an "account of H.B.D. Kettlewell's famous field experiments on the peppered moth, which were widely known as 'Darwin's missing evidence,' proof of natural selection in action—until 1998, that is, when biologist Michael Majerus showed Kettlewell's findings to be falsified and wrong." Publ Wkly
"A fascinating look at the people behind scientific theories." Booklist
Includes bibliographical references

Jakosky, Bruce M.

The search for life on other planets; by Bruce Jakosky. Cambridge Univ. Press 1998 326p il hardcover o.p. paperback available $19.95 **576.8**
1. Life on other planets
ISBN 0-521-59837-0 (pa)   LC 97-51549
"After opening with a look at the development of and requirements for terrestrial life, Jakosky conducts a tour of the universe, steadily progressing toward more speculative venues. The first stop is Mars and the controversial evidence of bacterial life there in ancient epochs. Then it's onward to Venus, the satellites of Jupiter and Saturn and then to possible terrestrial planets in orbit around other stars." Publ Wkly
Includes bibliographical references

Jones, Steve, 1944-

Darwin's ghost; the origin of species updated. Random House 2000 xxix, 377p il hardcover o.p. paperback available $15 **576.8**
1. Natural selection 2. Evolution
ISBN 0-345-42277-5 (pa)   LC 99-53246
First published 1999 in the United Kingdom with title: Almost like a whale
Jones "has updated Charles Darwin's *On the origin of species* (1859) so that the fact of organic evolution is both understandable and relevant to today's general reader. . . . Very informative and cogently argued, this book is an important addition to the natural history literature." Libr J
Includes bibliographical references

Koerner, David

Here be dragons; the scientific quest for extraterrestrial life; [by] David Koerner, Simon LeVay. Oxford Univ. Press 2000 264p il hardcover o.p. paperback available $15.95 **576.8**
1. Life on other planets 2. Life—Origin
ISBN 0-19-514600-X (pa)   LC 99-38170
In this book the authors explore "the origin of life and its occurrence outside Earth. . . . They offer a broad overview of up-to-date research and thought on topics ranging from the chemistry of life's origins to the search for extra-solar planets, the process of evolution, and the nature of life and the cosmos." Booklist
Includes bibliographical references

Lemonick, Michael D.

Other worlds; the search for life in the universe. Simon & Schuster 1998 272p il hardcover o.p. paperback available $14 **576.8**
1. Life on other planets
ISBN 0-684-85313-2 (pa)   LC 97-49006
"Lemonick surveys the scientists and the science involved in . . . [the study of] the possibility of life beyond Earth." Booklist
"*Other Worlds* is a very informative, readable, captivating, well-written account of a fascinating topic." Sci Books Films
Includes bibliographical references

Margulis, Lynn, 1938-

Symbiotic planet; a new look at evolution. Basic Bks. 1998 147p il (Science masters series) hardcover o.p. paperback available $14 **576.8**
1. Symbiosis 2. Evolution 3. Gaia hypothesis
ISBN 0-465-07272-0 (pa)   LC 98-38921
"From the origin of life to the classification and phylogeny of living organisms, from a discussion of Gaia—the belief that Earth operates like a living being—to a discussion of the underlying reasons for sex, iconoclastic biologist Margulis . . . takes on many of the big questions in biology. . . . In a book that is part autobiography and part biological primer, Margulis . . . advances the idea that a large part of organic evolution can be explained by symbiosis." Publ Wkly
Includes bibliographical references

Mayr, Ernst, 1904-
What evolution is. Basic Bks. 2001 318p il
maps hardcover o.p. paperback available $16
576.8

1. Evolution
ISBN 0-465-04426-3 (pa)   LC 2001-36562
This introduction to the theory of evolution offers "insights into taxonomy, adaptation, common descent, biodiversity, and those mechanisms of organic evolution that result in the process of speciation." Libr J
"A wise and illuminating examination, by an illustrious evolutionary biologist, that sorts out the complexities of evolution." N Y Times Book Rev
Includes bibliographical references

Palumbi, Stephen R.
The evolution explosion; how humans
cause rapid evolutionary change. Norton 2001
277p il $24.95; pa $14.95   **576.8**
1. Evolution 2. Human influence on nature
ISBN 0-393-02011-8; 0-393-32338-2 (pa)
LC 00-67004
This describes human causes of rapid evolutionary change, focusing on bacteria which have evolved strains resistant to antibiotics and insects resistant to pesticides
"Palumbi's writing is lively and lucid, and his analogies are felicitous." Booklist
Includes bibliographical references

Pennock, Robert T.
Tower of Babel; the evidence against the
new creationism. MIT Press 1999 429p $55;
pa $21.95   **576.8**
1. Evolution 2. Creationism 3. Religion and science
ISBN 0-262-16180-X; 0-262-66165-9 (pa)
LC 98-27286
"A Bradford book"
The author "catalogues the wide range of creationist beliefs, dissects their main arguments and highlights what he sees as their internal inconsistencies." Publ Wkly
By "disentangling the scientific issues from the religious and philosophic ones, Pennock has made a valuable contribution to a too-often-overheated debate."
Booklist
Includes bibliographical references

Powell, James Lawrence, 1936-
Night comes to the Cretaceous; dinosaur
extinction and the transformation of modern
geology; [by] James L. Powell. Freeman,
W.H. 1998 250p il map $22.95   **576.8**
1. Catastrophes (Geology) 2. Mass extinction of species 3. Dinosaurs
ISBN 0-7167-3117-7   LC 98-13192
Also available in paperback from Harcourt
The author "summarizes arguments for and against the controversial 'impact theory' of the extinction of the dinosaurs first proposed by Nobel physicist Luis Alvarez and his geologist son Walter and others in 1980. . . . Powell's book is written for a broad audience. It is slow reading in places, but explanations added in parentheses clarify technical materials." Sci Books Films
Includes bibliographical references

Rose, Michael R. (Michael Robertson), 1955-
Darwin's spectre; evolutionary biology in
the modern world. Princeton Univ. Press
1998 233p hardcover o.p. paperback available
$20.95   **576.8**
1. Evolution 2. Natural selection
ISBN 0-691-05008-2 (pa)   LC 98-11494
Rose "outlines the elements of evolutionary theory and then examines its contemporary applications in agriculture, where it is manifested in genetically engineered crops and animals, and in the new and developed field of 'Darwinian medicine', which is transforming our understanding of pathogens and how to treat certain diseases." Libr J
Includes bibliographical references

Schopf, J. William, 1941-
Cradle of life; the discovery of earth's
earliest fossils. Princeton Univ. Press 1999
367p il $55; pa $20.95   **576.8**
1. Life—Origin 2. Fossils
ISBN 0-691-00230-4; 0-691-08864-0 (pa)
LC 98-42443
An "exploration of how Precambrian fossils came to light and what they've taught us. The author covers the history of evolutionary thought and the exploits of field paleontologists, as well as the trajectory of his own career." Publ Wkly
"Schopf's chapter on the evolution of biochemical pathways is a fascinating and wonderfully clear exposition of a difficult topic." Libr J
Includes bibliographical references

Small, Meredith F.
What's love got to do with it? the
evolution of human mating. Anchor Bks.
(NY) 1995 xx, 249p hardcover o.p. paperback
available $14.95   **576.8**
1. Evolution 2. Sex (Biology) 3. Sexual behavior
ISBN 0-385-47702-3 (pa)   LC 95-1359
The author reviews various "experimental and observational studies on male and female sexuality, choosing a mate, homosexuality, and the impact of technology on sexual behavior, among other topics." Sci Books Films
"Extensively documented and indexed, Small's text is . . . highly readable." Libr J
Includes bibliographical references

Ward, Peter Douglas, 1949-
Rare earth; why complex life is uncommon
in the universe; [by] Peter Ward, Don
Brownlee. Copernicus 1999 xxviii, 333p il
$27.50; pa $16.95   **576.8**
1. Life on other planets
ISBN 0-387-98701-0; 0-387-95289-6 (pa)
LC 99-20532
Partial contents: Why life might be widespread in the universe; Habitable zones of the universe; Life's first appearance on Earth; The enigma of the Cambrian explosion; Mass extinctions and the Rare Earth Hypothesis; The surprising importance of plate tectonics; Assessing the odds
"Arguing that complex life is a rare event in the universe, this compelling book magnifies the significance—and tragedy—of species extinction." Libr J
Includes bibliographical references

577 Ecology

Baskin, Yvonne
A plague of rats and rubbervines; the growing threat of species invasions. Island Press (Washington, D.C.) 2002 377p il $35; pa $16 **577**
1. Biological invasions 2. Nature conservation
ISBN 1-55963-876-1; 1-55963-051-5 (pa)
LC 2002-4029
"Shearwater books"
"A project of SCOPE, the Scientific Committee on Problems of the Environment, in collaboration with the World Conservation Union—IUCN and CAB International"
The author goes "on a worldwide tour of grasslands, gardens, waterways, and forests, describing the troubles caused by exotic organisms that run amok in new settings and examining how commerce and travel on an increasingly connected planet are exacerbating this oldest of human-created problems. She offers examples of potential solutions and profiles dedicated individuals worldwide who are working tirelessly to protect the places and creatures they love." Publisher's note
The author "describes her visits to several environments where alien species have run amok, such as Hawaii, the Galapagos Islands, South Africa, and New Zealand, skillfully revealing her zoological and botanical knowledge. . . . Her survey—with historical perspective on biological interchange since the time of Columbus—of an extinction threat second only to habitat destruction will appeal to ecologically minded readers." Booklist
Includes bibliographical references

Bright, Chris
Life out of bounds; bioinvasion in a borderless world. Norton 1998 287p il (Worldwatch environmental alert series) pa $13.95 **577**
1. Biological invasions 2. Ecology
ISBN 0-393-31814-1
LC 99-163011
"Bright discusses the increasingly urgent issue of invasive exotic plants and animals and their ecological impact worldwide on native species. An excellent introduction to the field, loaded with historical examples and heavily referenced." Libr J

Buchmann, Stephen
The forgotten pollinators; [by] Stephen L. Buchmann and Gary Paul Nabhan; with a foreword by Edward O. Wilson; illustrations by Paul Mirocha. Island Press (Covelo) 1996 xx, 292p il $30; pa $18 **577**
1. Fertilization of plants 2. Biological diversity 3. Ecology
ISBN 1-55963-352-2; 1-55963-353-0 (pa)
LC 96-802
The authors explore the "link between plants and their pollinators. It is a disturbing story of disappearing insects and diminishing plant reproduction, owing to overuse of pesticide and fragmented habitat. The authors combine anecdotes from the field with discussions of ecology, entomology, botany, crop science and the economics of pollination." Publ Wkly
Includes bibliographical references

Smil, Vaclav
The earth's biosphere; evolution, dynamics, and change. MIT Press 2002 346p il maps $32.95; pa $19.95 **577**
1. Biosphere
ISBN 0-262-19472-4; 0-262-69298-8 (pa)
LC 2001-58705
This study of the Earth's biosphere "examines the biosphere's physics, chemistry, biology, geology, oceanography, energy, climatology, and ecology, as well as the changes caused by human activity." Publisher's note
"A presentation marked by balance and clarity. . . . A superior, comprehensive survey." Booklist
Includes bibliographical references

Wilson, Edward O., 1929-
The diversity of life. Harvard Univ. Press 1992 424p il maps (Questions of science) $31.50 **577**
1. Ecology 2. Nature conservation
ISBN 0-674-21298-3
LC 92-9018
Also available in paperback from Norton
"Identifying five natural events that have disrupted evolution and global diversity (climatic changes, meteorite strikes), Wilson maintains that the present sixth great extinction is being caused by human neglect and ignorance. This important book is highly recommended." Libr J
Includes bibliographical references

577.2 Specific factors affecting ecology

Winston, Mark L.
Nature wars; people vs. pests. Harvard Univ. Press 1997 210p $27.50; pa $15.95 **577.2**
1. Pesticides—Environmental aspects 2. Pest control 3. Human influence on nature
ISBN 0-674-60541-1; 0-674-60542-X (pa)
LC 97-17302
"Winston provides case studies demonstrating alternative methods of pest control, explaining how political, social, economic, and biologic interactions behind pest-management decisions have contributed to our failure to replace toxic chemicals as our first method of choice. . . . Winston has written a convincing and necessary book." Libr J
Includes bibliographical references

577.3 Forest ecology

Heinrich, Bernd, 1940-
The trees in my forest. Cliff St. Bks. 1997 239p il hardcover o.p. paperback available $13 **577.3**
1. Forest ecology 2. Trees
ISBN 0-06-092942-1 (pa)
LC 97-16885
"Heinrich's 20-year relationship with his plot of land in the Maine wilderness provides the inspiration for this collection of observations, reflections and ecology lessons. . . . This is a deeply satisfying look into the ways and pleasures of the woods." Publ Wkly
Includes bibliographical references

Royte, Elizabeth
The Tapir's morning bath; mysteries of the tropical rain forest and the scientists who are trying to solve them. Houghton Mifflin 2001 328p maps $25; pa $14   **577.3**
1. Rain forest ecology 2. Panama—Description
ISBN 0-395-97997-8; 0-618-25758-6 (pa)
LC 2001-24989
Royte discusses time spent with scientists studying the ecology of Barro Colorado, an island in the Panama Canal
This is "a superb introduction to tropical ecology and theoretical biology, as well as original and thoroughly engaging travel writing." Publ Wkly
Includes bibliographical references

577.4   Grassland ecology

Manning, Richard, 1951-
Grassland; the history, biology, politics, and promise of the American prairie. Viking 1995 306p hardcover o.p. paperback available $15   **577.4**
1. Grassland ecology 2. Human influence on nature
ISBN 0-14-023388-1 (pa)   LC 95-10073
"Our culture's disrespect for grasslands has produced an environmental catastrophe, charges the author. By allowing overgrazing on public lands, our government is wiping out an ecosystem as vital as the Brazilian rain forests. In this sweeping exploration of the prairie, Manning . . . makes an eloquent plea to restore it." Publ Wkly
Includes bibliographical references

577.6   Aquatic ecology. Freshwater ecology

Douglas, Marjory Stoneman
The Everglades: river of grass; illustrated by Robert Fink. 50th anniversary ed. Pineapple Press (Sarasota) 1997 478p il map $18.95   **577.6**
1. Everglades (Fla.)
ISBN 1-56164-135-9   LC 97-1594
A reissue of the title first published 1947
A natural history of South Florida focusing on the unique ecosystem of the Everglades. Discusses environmental changes, scientific research, and political responses to conservation efforts
Includes bibliographical references

577.7   Marine ecology

Carson, Rachel, 1907-1964
The edge of the sea; with illustrations by Bob Hines. Houghton Mifflin 1955 276p il hardcover o.p. paperback available $14
577.7
1. Marine biology 2. Seashore
ISBN 0-395-28519-4 (pa)
Also available in hardcover from P. Smith
"The seashores of the world may be divided into three basic types: the rugged shores of rock, the sand beaches,

and the coral reefs and all their associated features. Each has its typical community of plants and animals. The Atlantic coast of the United States [provides] clear examples of each of these types. I have chosen it as the setting for my pictures of shore life." Preface

Under the sea wind; [by] Rachel L. Carson; illustrations by Bob Hines. 50th anniversary ed. Dutton 1991 304p il o.p.; Penguin Bks. paperback available $14   **577.7**
1. Marine biology
ISBN 0-14-025380-7 (pa)   LC 90-47451
"A Truman Talley book"
A newly illustrated edition of the title first published 1941 by Simon & Schuster
A series of narratives describe the birds and sea creatures that inhabit the Eastern coasts of North America

578   Natural history of organisms and related subjects

Gould, Stephen Jay, 1941-2002
I have landed; the end of a beginning in natural history. Harmony Bks. 2002 418p il $25.95; pa $16   **578**
1. Natural history 2. Evolution
ISBN 0-609-60143-1; 1-4000-4804-4 (pa)
LC 2002-24145
In this anthology of "essays from Natural History magazine . . . Gould writes on Darwinism, evolutionary theory, the history of science, and the joys of doing scientific research." Libr J
"Gould is at the peak of his abilities in this latest menagerie of wonders." Publ Wkly

Tudge, Colin
The variety of life; a survey and a celebration of all the creatures that have ever lived. Oxford Univ. Press 2000 684p il $60
578
1. Biology—Classification 2. Biological diversity
ISBN 0-19-850311-3   LC 99-50043
"Tudge writes with a lively style that renders the most opaque terms lucid and meaningful." Booklist
Includes bibliographical references

Wolfe, David W.
Tales from the underground; a natural history of subterranean life. Perseus Bks. 2001 221p il hardcover o.p. paperback available $18   **578**
1. Soil microbiology
ISBN 0-7382-0679-2 (pa)
The author discusses the ecology of life in the soil and the earth's rocky crust, including Darwin's experiments with earthworms, Lewis and Clark's first encounter with prairie dogs, the use of genetic tools, and the possible role of primitive underground microbes in evolution
Wolfe "explains in a straightforward, readable style that there is probably as much biodiversity and even as much biomass below ground as above." New Sci
Includes bibliographical references

578.68 Rare and endangered species

Ackerman, Diane
The rarest of the rare; vanishing animals, timeless worlds. Random House 1995 xxi, 184p hardcover o.p. paperback available $12
578.68
1. Endangered species 2. Rare animals
ISBN 0-679-77623-0 (pa)   LC 95-8499
In these essays the author "tells of her adventures in several relatively isolated habitats of several endangered animal species: monk seals in Hawaii, golden lion tamarins in the Brazilian rain forest, short-tailed albatrosses on a Japanese volcanic island, and monarch butterflies in southern California. For each of the habitats Ackerman has recruited the company of one or more biologically sophisticated guides." Choice
"Every species that is endangered or becomes extinct deserves so poetic a chronicler as Ackerman." Libr J

Beacham's guide to the endangered species of North America; edited by Walton Beacham, Frank V. Castronova, Suzanne Sessine. Gale Group 2001 6v set $650
578.68
1. Endangered species 2. Nature conservation
ISBN 0-7876-5028-5   LC 00-62297
Replaces The Official World Wilflife Fund guide to the endangered species of North America, published 1990-1994 by Beacham
Contents: v1 Mammals, birds, reptiles; v2 Amphibians, fishes, snails, mussels, and clams; v3 Arachnids and crustaceans, insects, lichens, fern allies, true ferns, conifers, dicots; v4-5 Dicots; v6 dicots, monocots, glossary, organizations, indexes
"More than 1200 plants and animals identified as threatened or endangered by the U.S. Fish and Wildlife Service are described in this remarkable encyclopedia. . . . The articles for each species include a shaded box of bulleted summary information with one or more full-color images, followed by information on species, behavior, habitat, distribution (past and present), threats, conservation and recovery efforts, organizational contacts, and references. The writing is clear and information is thorough and current." SLJ
For a fuller review see: Booklist May 15, 2001

Crawford, Mark
Habitats and ecosystems; an encyclopedia of endangered America. ABC-CLIO 1999 398p $75   **578.68**
1. Endangered species 2. Environmental protection
ISBN 0-87436-997-5   LC 00-698072
Companion volume to Toxic waste sites (1997)
This "is a state-by-state listing of sites having special or unique natural resource value. Included also are sites that have natural communities of high biodiversity or habitats for rare, unique, threatened, or endangered species." Libr J
For a fuller review see: Booklist, April 1, 2000

Encyclopedia of endangered species; edited by Mary Emanoil; in association with IUCN-the World Conservation Union, Species Survival Commission. Gale Res. 1994-1998 2v il maps ea $130   **578.68**
1. Endangered species
ISBN 0-8103-8857-X (v1); 0-8103-9315-8 (v2)
"This book contains synopses of 700 endangered species. . . . There are eight broad taxonomic sections arranged by family and genus. . . . The accounts are clearly written, with sections on description and biology, habitat and current distribution, and conservation measures." Am Ref Books Annu, 1995

Endangered wildlife and plants of the world. Marshall Cavendish 2001 13v set $657.07
578.68
1. Endangered species
ISBN 0-7614-7194-4   LC 99-86194
First published 1993 with title: Endangered wildlife of the world
For this reference "more than 1,400 species threatened with extinction were selected from data provided by the U.S. Fish and Wildlife Services and IUCN (International Union for Conservation of Nature). . . . Each entry is signed and presented in a clear, user-friendly format combining succinct scientific information and statistics." Booklist

578.7 Organisms characteristic of specific kinds of environments

Jukofsky, Diane
Encyclopedia of rainforests; by Diane Jukofsky for the Rainforest Alliance. Oryx Press 2001 xxxi, 328p il $84.95   **578.7**
1. Rain forests—Encyclopedias
ISBN 1-57356-259-9   LC 2001-32154
This "encyclopedia surveys the flora, fauna, and native peoples of the tropical rainforest, including 261 families of plants and 818 taxonomic groups of animals. The work has five parts: tropical forest wildlife, tropical forest plants, people and tropical forests, saving tropical forests, and rainforests resources. Topics are arranged alphabetically; within the plant and animal sections, related articles are arranged taxonomically." Choice
"The text as a whole, which . . . includes sections on peoples, noted naturalists, and conservation efforts, . . . provides a fine introduction to the world of the rainforest and would be appreciated by any high school/undergraduate library." Libr J
For a fuller review see: Booklist, August 2002

579 Microorganisms, fungi, algae

Sankaran, Neeraja
Microbes and people: an A-Z of microorganisms in our lives. Oryx Press 2000 297p il $62.95   **579**
1. Microbiology—Dictionaries
ISBN 1-57356-217-3   LC 00-10117
"Entries cover environmental, industrial, and food microbiology, in addition to the microbiology of health and disease. Scientific techniques used for studying microor-

Sankaran, Neeraja—*Continued*
ganisms are discussed, and biographies of key individuals
are provided. A chronology of infections and disease epidemics from 430 BC to the present is included as an appendix." Publisher's note
"Because it provides very readable coverage of topics
so much in the news lately, this dictionary will be much
used in high school, undergraduate, and public libraries."
Booklist
Includes bibliographical references

579.3   Prokaryotes (Bacteria)

Karlen, Arno
Biography of a germ. Pantheon Bks. 2000
178p hardcover o.p. paperback available $12
579.3
1. Microorganisms 2. Lyme disease
ISBN 0-385-72066-1 (pa)   LC 99-57304
This "book examines *Borrelia burgdorferi*, the elusive
spirochete that causes Lyme disease." New Yorker
"Karlen has created a vigorous, compact account of
Bb's life and times." Publ Wkly

579.5   Fungi

Hudler, George W.
Magical mushrooms, mischievous molds.
Princeton Univ. Press 1998 248p il hardcover
o.p. paperback available $18.95   **579.5**
1. Fungi
ISBN 0-691-07016-4 (pa)   LC 98-10163
The author shows how fungi "have dramatically influenced the course of human history. With chapters on
yeasts used to make bread and to brew alcoholic beverages, on the medicinal uses of fungi from penicillin to
possible treatments for AIDS, on edible mushrooms like
the common button mushroom and the more exotic truf-
fle, and on hallucinogenic mushrooms, Hudler takes
readers on an enthralling and informative tour of this
much maligned kingdom." Publ Wkly

Money, Nicholas P.
Mr. Bloomfield's orchard; the mysterious
world of mushrooms, molds, and mycologists.
Oxford Univ. Press 2002 208p il $26 **579.5**
1. Fungi
ISBN 0-19-515457-6   LC 2002-72654
The author "introduces readers to . . . [an] array of
fungi, from brewer's yeast and *Penicillium* to the highly
lethal death cap." Publisher's note
"Assuredly fascinating and highly entertaining, Money's chronicle boasts an inimitable style that mixes up
fact-based information and creative analogies. . . . Not
for the faint of heart, but definitely for science devotees
who appreciate rollicking good humor." Booklist
Includes bibliographical references

579.6   Mushrooms

Lincoff, Gary
The Audubon Society field guide to North
American mushrooms; [by] Gary H. Lincoff;
visual key by Carol Nehring. Knopf 1981
926p il flexible bdg $19.95   **579.6**
1. Mushrooms
ISBN 0-394-51992-2   LC 81-80827
"A Chanticleer Press edition. The Audubon Society
field guide series"
This guide to 703 species of common mushrooms provides 762 color photographs and descriptions as keys to
identifying these plants
"The author is an expert on mushroom toxins and in-
stills responsible cautions. The photos are uncommonly
beautiful." SLJ

McKnight, Kent H.
A field guide to mushrooms, North
America; [by] Kent H. McKnight and Vera
B. McKnight; illustrations by Vera B.
McKnight. Houghton Mifflin 1987 429p il
hardcover o.p. paperback available $19
579.6
1. Mushrooms
ISBN 0-395-91090-0 (pa)   LC 86-27799
"The Peterson field guide series"
"Sponsored by the National Audubon Society and the
National Wildlife Federation"
"More than 500 species [of mushrooms] are described
and depicted. . . . Edibility of each species is noted and
signified by marginal pictograms both in the text and on
the colorplates. . . . Appended: a genial chapter of recipes by Anne Dow, glossary, selected references, and index." Booklist

Smith, Alexander Hanchett, 1904-1988
The mushroom hunter's field guide; [by]
Alexander H. Smith and Nancy Smith Weber.
all color & enlarged. University of Mich.
Press 1980 316p il $24.95   **579.6**
1. Mushrooms
ISBN 0-472-85610-3   LC 80-10514
First published 1958
This is a "field guide for both novices and experts
alike. The introductory chapter explains basic terminolo-
gy and what to look for when identifying fungi. More
than 280 mushrooms are described, including identifying
marks, edibility, habitat, native range, and type of spore.
A color photograph . . . of each mushroom is most valuable for accurate information." Booklist
Includes bibliographical references

580   Plants

The **Facts** on File dictionary of botany;
edited by Jill Bailey. Facts on File 2002
250p il $49.50; pa $19.95   **580**
1. Botany—Dictionaries
ISBN 0-8160-4910-6; 0-8160-4911-4 (pa)
LC 2002-35202
"Facts on File science library"
This dictionary covers "pure and applied plant science,
including the taxonomy and classification of plants, with
entries for the higher-ranking taxa. Techniques of nucleic
acid technology are included, with references made to
applications in horticulture and agriculture." Publisher's
note

Sabbagh, Karl

A Rum affair; true story of botanical fraud. Farrar, Straus & Giroux 2000 276p il o.p.; Perseus Bks. paperback available $15   **580**

1. Heslop-Harrison, J. W. 2. Fraud 3. Botany
ISBN 0-306-81060-3 (pa)   LC 99-87543
First published 1999 in the United Kingdom
"In the late 1940's, John Raven, a British classics scholar, . . . [investigated] Prof. John Heslop Harrison of the Royal Society, for fraudulently introducing alien sedges on the Hebridean island of Rum in order to advance a pet theory." N Y Times Book Rev
Includes bibliographical references

581.6 Miscellaneous nontaxonomic kinds of plants

Angier, Bradford

Field guide to edible wild plants; jacket and book illustrated by Arthur J. Anderson. Stackpole Bks. 1974 256p il hardcover o.p. paperback available $16.95   **581.6**

1. Edible plants
ISBN 0-8117-2018-7 (pa)
"Plants are arranged alphabetically by one of their common names. Each entry includes genus, family affiliation, other common names, a lengthy plant description (including many interesting facts about the plant), notes on distribution, and a statement concerning edibility and preparation of the plant parts." Libr J

Bown, Deni

New encyclopedia of herbs & their uses. Dorling Kindersley 2001 448p il $40   **581.6**

1. Herbs 2. Herb gardening
ISBN 0-7894-8031-X   LC 2001-28790
First published 1995 with title: Encyclopedia of herbs and their uses
At head of title: The Herb Society of America
This reference in A-Z format lists the culinary and medicinal properties of herbs alongside information about cultivation, and includes a quick identification guide with color photographs. Also includes a history of herbs and their roles in various cultures

Davis, Wade

One river; explorations and discoveries in the Amazon rain forest. Simon & Schuster 1996 537p il hardcover o.p. paperback available $16   **581.6**

1. Schultes, Richard Evans, 1915-2001 2. Plowman, Timothy Charles, 1944-1989 3. Ethnobotany 4. Hallucinogens 5. Medical botany
ISBN 0-684-83496-0 (pa)   LC 96-21516
"This is the story of Timothy Plowman, a young ethnobotanist who died while looking for medicinal plants in the South American rain forests. . . . Plowman was the brilliant protégé of Richard Evans Schultes, one of the world's leading authorities on hallucinogenic plants and the Amazon rain forest. The author mixes the backgrounds and travels of the two men with sociology of South American tribes and their sacred plants." Libr J

Davis "writes magnificently, with verve when describing his many adventurous field trips, accurately and efficiently when telling science or history, and with vivid fantasy when portraying hallucinogenic trances." N Y Times Book Rev
Includes bibliographical references

Gibbons, Euell

Stalking the wild asparagus; with illustrations by Margaret F. Schroeder; including a remembrance of the author by John McPhee. 25th anniversary ed. Hood, A.C. 1987 c1962 303p il hardcover o.p. paperback available $17.50   **581.6**

1. Edible plants 2. Cooking
ISBN 0-911469-03-6 (pa)   LC 87-16933
A reprint of the title first published 1962 by McKay
In this series of brief anecdotal essays the naturalist discourses on the identification and preparation of roots, flowers and plants, old Indian legends, and wilderness survival

Pollan, Michael

The botany of desire; a plant's eye view of the world. Random House 2001 xxv, 271p $24.95; pa $13.95   **581.6**

1. Economic botany
ISBN 0-375-50129-0; 0-375-76039-3 (pa)
      LC 00-66479
Also available G.K. Hall large print edition
"Pollan intertwines history, anecdote, and revelation as he investigates the connection between four plants that have thrived under human care—apples, tulips, marijuana, and potatoes—and the four human desires they satisfy in return: sweetness, beauty, intoxication, and control. . . . Pollan's dynamic, intelligent, and intrepid parsing of the wondrous dialogue between plants and humans is positively paradigm-altering." Booklist
Includes bibliographical references

Sumner, Judith

The natural history of medicinal plants; foreword by Mark Plotkin. Timber Press 2000 235p il $24.95   **581.6**

1. Medical botany
ISBN 0-88192-483-0   LC 99-76555
In this "introduction to the botanical compounds used medicinally, Dr. Sumner describes their biological and ecological importance as toxins and deterrents in protecting plants." Publisher's note
Sumner presents an "accessible introduction to the world of medicinal plants. . . . Some of her most interesting revelations are about the relationships that animals have with plants." Booklist
Includes bibliographical references

Thoreau, Henry David, 1817-1862

Wild fruits; Thoreau's rediscovered last manuscript; edited and introduced by Bradley P. Dean; illustrations by Abigail Rorer. Norton 1999 409p il hardcover o.p. paperback available $17.95   **581.6**

1. Edible plants 2. Fruit
ISBN 0-393-32115-0 (pa)   LC 99-31377
Thoreau "offers a series of paragraphs or brief essays describing the condition of each of the wild fruits he finds around Concord and supplementing these accounts with notes on the relevant lore. . . . Dean includes textual notes, a glossary, and a chronology as well as a succinct but substantive introduction." Libr J

Turner, Nancy J.

Common poisonous plants and mushrooms of North America; [by] Nancy J. Turner and Adam F. Szczawinski. Timber Press 1991 311p il $55; pa $24.95   **581.6**
1. Poisonous plants 2. Mushrooms
ISBN 0-88192-179-3; 0-88192-312-5 (pa)

           LC 90-37574

This "presents over 150 of the most common and dangerous poisonous plants, describing not only those of wild areas of temperate North America but also garden and crop plants, house plants, and plant products. Information about each plant includes a description, occurrence, toxicity, symptoms, and treatment for poisoning." Am Libr
Includes bibliographical references

582.1   Herbaceous and woody plants, plants noted for their flowers

Symonds, George W. D.

The shrub identification book; photographs by A. W. Merwin. Barrows 1963 379p il o.p.; Morrow paperback available $22   **582.1**
1. Shrubs
ISBN 0-688-05040-9 (pa)
"The visual method for the practical identification of shrubs, including woody vines and ground covers." Subtitle
"Part I gives pictorial keys for thorns, leaves, flowers, fruit, twigs and bark of broad-leaved upright shrubs. Part II contains 200 master pages arranged under four categories, with data on habitat, blooming period, etc., accompanying the photographs." Wilson Libr Bull
Includes bibliographical references

582.13   Plants noted for their flowers

Coffey, Timothy

The history and folklore of North American wildflowers; foreword by Stephen Foster. Facts on File 1993 xxiv, 356p il o.p.; Houghton Mifflin paperback available $17
           582.13
1. Wild flowers 2. Economic botany 3. Medical botany
ISBN 0-395-51593-9 (pa)   LC 92-18392
"Entries discuss about 700 plants from over 90 families. Plants featured were those used by the Indians and/or colonists. Arrangement is by family according to evolutionary development. . . . For each of the entries, basic information includes the common name, the Latin name and its translation, and any vernacular names. One or more paragraphs quote what various writers have observed about the plant." Booklist
"This book brings together a wealth of information that is otherwise scattered throughout many obscure sources." Libr J

Johnson, Lady Bird, 1912-

Wildflowers across America; [by] Lady Bird Johnson and Carlton B. Lees; photographs selected by Les Line. Abbeville Press 1988 309p il $39.95   **582.13**
1. Wild flowers
ISBN 0-89659-770-9   LC 88-1275
"The former first lady . . . shares recollections of wildflowers she has loved, especially in the Southwest; the founding of the National Wildflower Research Center; and her work with highway beautification. Lees writes of native plants, their distribution, introductions now at home in America, and wildflowers in the new trend toward natural landscaping. This handsome book abounds with color photographs." Libr J
Includes bibliographical references

Spellenberg, Richard

National Audubon Society field guide to North American wildflowers, western region. 2nd ed rev. Knopf 2001 862p il map $19.95
           582.13
1. Wild flowers
ISBN 0-375-40233-0   LC 2001-269242
"A Chanticleer Press edition"
First published 1979
"More than 940 . . . full-color images show the wildflowers of western North America close-up and in their natural habitats. . . . Images are grouped by flower color and shape and keyed to . . . descriptions that reflect current taxonomy." Publisher's note

Thieret, John W.

National Audubon Society field guide to North American wildflowers: eastern region; revising author, John W. Thieret; original authors, William A. Niering and Nancy C. Olmstead. Knopf 2001 879p il map (National Audubon Society field guide series) $19.95
           582.13
1. Wild flowers
ISBN 0-375-40232-2   LC 2001-269241
"A Chanticleer Press edition"
First published 1979 under the authorship of William A. Niering and Nancy C. Olmstead
    Spine title: Field guide to wildflowers, eastern region
"Covers the area east of the Rockies and east of the Big Bend area of Texas to the Atlantic. Color photographs together with family and species descriptions make this a most useful field guide." Sci News [review of 1979 edition]

Wells, Diana

100 flowers and how they got their names; illustrated by Ippy Patterson. Algonquin Bks. 1997 257p il $17.95   **582.13**
1. Flowers 2. Popular plant names
ISBN 1-56512-138-4   LC 96-22296
The author "describes the mythology and history behind 100 favorite garden plants, emphasizing the exploits of botanists and plant explorers who brought them out of their native habitats." Libr J
"This is a delightful book for browsing." Booklist
Includes bibliographical references

582.16 Trees

Benvie, Sam
The encyclopedia of North American trees.
Firefly Bks. (Buffalo) 2000 304p il maps
hardcover o.p. paperback available $24.95
582.16

1. Trees—North America
ISBN 1-55297-641-6 (pa)   LC 2001-521107
In this tree encyclopedia the species "are listed alphabetically by Latin name with the common name given in
dark print at the top of the entry as well as on the top
of the right-hand page. Each species is described in a
page or less. . . . For the most common trees, a box lists
key features. . . . Additional larger boxes provide a detailed history of the species and line drawings of the
leaves, buds, and flowers." Booklist
Includes bibliographical references

Little, Elbert Luther, 1907-
The Audubon Society field guide to North
American trees; [by] Elbert L. Little;
photographs by Sonja Bullaty and Angelo
Lomeo [et. al.]; visual key by Susan Rayfield
and Olivia Buehl. Knopf 1980 2v il ea
$19.95   **582.16**

1. Trees—North America   LC 79-3474
"A Chanticleer Press edition. The Audubon Society
field guide series"
Contents: [v1] Eastern region (ISBN 0-394-50760-6);
[v2] Western region (0-394-50761-4)
These "guides are unusual in that they contain many
color photographs of parts of a living tree. The identification keys are easy to use, being based on an arrangement by leaf shapes, flowers, fruit, and fall leaves, and
giving drawings of winter silhouettes. The eastern guide
covers 364 species, the western guide describes 314 species; they divide the country at central Texas and the
Rockies." Libr J

Pakenham, Thomas, 1933-
Remarkable trees of the world; text and
photographs by Thomas Pakenham. Norton
2002 191p il $49.95; pa $27.95   **582.16**

1. Trees
ISBN 0-393-04911-6; 0-393-32529-6 (pa)
LC 2002-21934
The author presents descriptions and photographs of
sixty exceptional trees from around the world
"This beautiful and unique book is sure to be appreciated by nature lovers. And though it is a highly personal
work and not a scientific text, it demonstrates keen and
accurate observation; it could also serve as an excellent
supplement to studies in science, history, and geography." SLJ
Includes bibliographical references

Simon and Schuster's guide to trees; English
translation by Hugh Young. Simon &
Schuster 1978 c1977 various paging il
hardcover o.p. paperback available $16
582.16

1. Trees
ISBN 0-671-24125-7 (pa)   LC 77-17896
"A Fireside book"
Original Italian edition by P. Lanzara and M. Pizzetti

This is "a field guide to 300 species of trees from
around the world. A 50-page introduction ranges over the
history of the trees, their ecosystems and names, wood,
and its uses, leaves, flowers, seeds, and ecological concerns. The descriptions cover habitat, physical characteristics, propagation, and conditions of growth. Each is accompanied by a drawing showing the tree's shape and a
handsome color photograph." Wilson Libr Bull

583 Dicotyledons

Anderson, Edward F., 1932-2001
The cactus family; with a foreword by
Wilhelm Barthlott; and a chapter on cactus
cultivation by Roger Brown. Timber Press
2001 776p il maps $99.95   **583**

1. Cactus
ISBN 0-88192-498-9   LC 00-60700
This reference work on cactaceae covers 125 genera
and 1810 species
"While more than 1,000 photographs overall illustrate
the extraordinary diversity and beautiful flowers of cacti,
the main section—an alphabetically arranged reference—
will arguably rank as the definitive work readers will use
to examine and identify cactus genera, species, and subspecies." Booklist
Includes bibliographical references

587 Vascular seedless plants

Sacks, Oliver W.
Oaxaca journal; [by] Oliver Sacks. National
Geographic Soc. 2002 159p il (National
Geographic directions) $20   **587**

1. Ferns 2. Mexico—Description
ISBN 0-7922-6521-1   LC 2001-57920
Sacks "joined fellow members of the American Fern
Society on a 10-day foray to Oaxaca. . . . [This book]
is the story of his search for the fern—and his discovery
of Mexico." N Y Times Book Rev

590 Animals

Grzimek's animal life encyclopedia. 2nd ed.
Gale Group 2003 17v il maps set $1,750
590

1. Zoology
ISBN 0-7876-5362-4   LC 2002-3351
Original German edition, 1968; first English language
edition published 1972-1975 by Van Nostrand Reinhold
Contents: v1 Lower metazoans and lesser
deuterosomes; v2 Protostomes; v3 Insects; v4-5 Fishes I-
II; v6 Amphibians; v7 Reptiles; v8-11 Birds I-IV; v12-16
Mammals I-V; v17 Cumulative index
"Even after 30 years, the original Grzimek's is still
considered a core title for reference collections. Biologists and nonbiologists alike will appreciate the excellent
organization, well-written text, and beautiful illustrations.
. . . Highly recommended for all types of libraries." Libr
J
Includes bibliographical references

Lavers, Chris
Why elephants have big ears; understanding patterns of life on Earth. St. Martin's Press 2001 269p il $24.95; pa $13.95   **590**
1. Animals 2. Evolution
ISBN 0-312-26902-1; 0-312-30333-5 (pa)
              LC 00-45997
"Lavers analyzes why animals look the way they do, why they live where they live, and why their physiology is either warm or cold-blooded. . . . He then examines the evolution of animal life and the corollary evolution of warmbloodedness." Booklist
Includes bibliographical references

590.73   Collections and exhibits of living animals

Baratay, Eric, 1960-
Zoo: a history of zoological gardens in the West; [by] Eric Baratay, Elisabeth Hardouin-Fugier. Reaktion Bks.; [distributed by] Consortium Bk. Sales & Distr. 2002 400p il $40   **590.73**
1. Zoos
ISBN 1-86189-111-3
In this history of zoos the authors "take a social history focus, examining how people view wild animals and how that has changed over time. . . . One can read the text or spend hours simply enjoying the images. Libraries that have other titles on zoos will still want to purchase this." Libr J

Encyclopedia of the world's zoos; editor, Catharine E. Bell; senior advisor, Lester E. Fisher; photo editor, Catharine E. Bell; associate photo editor, Laura Mizicko. Fitzroy Dearborn Pubs. 2001 3v il set $325   **590.73**
1. Zoos
ISBN 1-57958-174-9   LC 2002-665421
This "encyclopedia includes individual profiles of animals found in most zoos, associations affiliated with zoos, and individuals who have made major contributions to the development of zoos. Only 146 of the more than 400 entries are actual descriptions of zoos." Choice
For a fuller review see: Booklist, Sept. 15, 2001

Hanson, Elizabeth, 1962-
Animal attractions; nature on display in American zoos. Princeton Univ. Press 2002 243p il $29.95   **590.73**
1. Zoos
ISBN 0-691-05992-6   LC 2001-55198
This book "examines the meaning of nature in the city by looking at the ways zoos have assembled and displayed their animal collections." Publisher's note
"If ever a book lived up to its title and subtitle, this one, an interesting and readable history of zoos and influences on their development in the US, certainly does." Choice
Includes bibliographical references

591.3   Genetics, evolution, young of animals

Avise, John C.
Genetics in the wild; illustration by Trudy Nicholson. Smithsonian Institution Press 2002 248p il $27.95   **591.3**
1. Genetics 2. Animal behavior 3. Evolution
ISBN 1-58834-069-4   LC 2002-17576
Partial contents: Some evolutionary oddities, Clones and chimeras, Hermaphroditism, Unusual mating practices, Dispersal and migration, Some genetic world records, Fossil DNA
The author "demonstrates how scientists directly examine DNA to address long-standing questions about wild animals, plants, and microbes." Publisher's note
Includes bibliographical references

591.5   Behavior

Bekoff, Marc
Minding animals; awareness, emotions, and heart; [by] Marc Bekoff; with a foreword by Jane Goodall. Oxford Univ. Press 2002 xxiv, 230p il $27.50; pa $15.95   **591.5**
1. Animal behavior
ISBN 0-19-515077-5; 0-19-516337-0 (pa)
              LC 2001-51341
"Chapters cover such broad topics as the richness of behavioral diversity, animal emotions, play and cooperation, and human intrusion into animals' lives. . . . The conversational writing style makes for a highly accessible book." Booklist
Includes bibliographical references

Griffin, Donald Redfield, 1915-
Animal minds; beyond cognition to consciousness; [by] Donald R. Griffin. [Rev and expanded] University of Chicago Press 2001 355p $27.50   **591.5**
1. Animal behavior
ISBN 0-226-30865-0   LC 00-10006
First published 1992
The author "moves beyond considerations of animal cognition to argue that scientists can and should investigate questions of animal consciousness. Using examples from studies of species ranging from chimpanzees and dolphins to birds and honeybees, he demonstrates how communication among animals can serve as a 'window' into what animals think and feel, just as human speech and nonverbal communication tell us most of what we know about the thoughts and feelings of other people." Publisher's note
"Griffin's book will enlighten, delight and even ruffle some feathers." Publ Wkly
Includes bibliographical references

Hauser, Marc D.
Wild minds; what animals really think; illustrations by Ted Dewen. Holt & Co. 2000 xx, 315p il hardcover o.p. paperback available $15   **591.5**
1. Animal intelligence 2. Animal behavior
ISBN 0-8050-5670-X (pa)   LC 99-36204
"The first section explores how animals view material objects, their ability to count, and their navigational

Hauser, Marc D.—*Continued*
skills. . . . The second section covers mental abilities, such as self-knowledge, how animals learn, and deception. The final section discusses skills necessary for living in groups—communication and a sense of morals. This entertaining yet highly scientific work is a terrific antidote to all the badly researched popular writing on animal emotions and intelligence." Booklist
Includes bibliographical references

Linden, Eugene
The octopus and the orangutan; more true tales of animal intrigue, intelligence, and ingenuity. Dutton 2002 242p $23.95; pa $14
        591.5
  1. Animal intelligence 2. Animal behavior
  ISBN 0-525-94661-6; 0-452-28411-2 (pa)
        LC 2002-67434
The author "presents anecdotes that illustrate the workings of the minds of both domestic and wild creatures—how they use tools, play games and adapt to change." Publ Wkly
"Linden's chatty writing style, along with the science behind the stories that he occasionally slips in, makes for entertaining and enlightening reading." Booklist
Includes bibliographical references

Masson, J. Moussaieff (Jeffrey Moussaieff), 1941-
When elephants weep; the emotional lives of animals; [by] Jeffrey Moussaieff Masson and Susan McCarthy. Delacorte Press 1995 xxiii, 291p il hardcover o.p. paperback available $15.95
        591.5
  1. Animal intelligence 2. Animal behavior
  ISBN 0-385-31428-0 (pa)   LC 94-23819
The authors gather "the evidence to date for the existence of emotions and, hence, something approaching human consciousness in animals. . . . Masson and McCarthy do a commendable job of synthesizing the material they tackle . . . making it efficiently readable." Booklist
Includes bibliographical references

Page, George
Inside the animal mind; a groundbreaking exploration of animal intelligence. Doubleday 1999 285p il hardcover o.p. paperback available $14.95
        591.5
  1. Animal intelligence
  ISBN 0-7679-0559-8 (pa)   LC 99-32431
"In discussing whether animals think and feel the way we do, George Page explores the work of scientists like Charles Darwin, Jane Goodall and Donald Griffin, as well as books on the subject, including Jeffrey Moussaieff Masson's 'When elephants weep;' and Elizabeth Marshall Thomas's 'Hidden life of dogs.'" N Y Times Book Rev
"An accessible book replete with illustrative stories and anecdotal evidence." Libr J
Includes bibliographical references

Weiner, Jonathan
Time, love, memory; a great biologist and his quest for the origins of behavior. Knopf 1999 300p il $27.50; pa $14
        591.5
  1. Benzer, Seymour, 1921- 2. Behavior genetics
  ISBN 0-679-44435-1; 0-679-76390-2 (pa)
        LC 98-43128
An exploration of the work of "one of the unsung pioneers of molecular biology: brash, eccentric physicist-turned-biologist Seymour Benzer. By studying tiny genetic mutations in the fruit fly, Benzer seeks to shed light on the question of whether genes determine behavior. Weiner . . . presents an elegant scientific detective story." Publ Wkly
Includes bibliographical references

Yoerg, Sonja, 1959-
Clever as a fox; what animal intelligence can teach us about ourselves; [by] Sonja I. Yoerg. Bloomsbury Pub. 2001 228p $24.95
        591.5
  1. Animal intelligence
  ISBN 1-58234-115-X   LC 00-46801
Also available in paperback from Harvard Univ. Press
"The author quotes studies of animals as disparate as crabs, primates, parrots, and humans to make her main point: there are different kinds of intelligence, evolved in the face of different environmental pressures. Leavened with humor, Yoerg's clear, logical, and well-written discussion of a complex subject will lead even the casual reader into a much better understanding of the many answers to the question 'what is intelligence?'" Booklist
Includes bibliographical references

591.56 Behavior relating to life cycle

Bagemihl, Bruce
Biological exuberance; animal homosexuality and natural diversity; illustrated by John Megahan. St. Martin's Press 1999 751p il map $40; pa $21.95
        591.56
  1. Animal behavior 2. Homosexuality
  ISBN 0-312-19239-8; 0-312-25377-X (pa)
        LC 98-28528
The author "challenges the belief that homosexuality is an aberration in nature by revealing the documented homosexual or transgendered behavior of 450 animal species. Contesting the idea that scarcity and functionality are the primary agents of biological change, biologist Bagemihl persuasively argues that abundance and extravagance are just as crucial to the mosaic of life." Publ Wkly
Includes bibliographical references

Dugatkin, Lee Alan, 1962-
Cheating monkeys and citizen bees; the nature of cooperation in animals and humans; [by] Lee Dugatkin. Free Press 1999 208p il $25
        591.56
  1. Animal behavior
  ISBN 0-684-84341-2   LC 98-27768
Also available in paperback from Harvard Univ. Press
The author contends "that animal cooperation could provide a new perspective on human cooperation, as we

Dugatkin, Lee Alan, 1962-—*Continued*
look at the animal world without the human strictures of morality and free will. He also acknowledges the potential weaknesses of this research. . . . He supports his arguments with many examples from animal behavior studies." Libr J

Includes bibliographical references

Zuk, M. (Marlene), 1956-
Sexual selections; what we can and can't learn about sex from animals; [by] Marlene Zuk. University of Calif. Press 2002 239p il $40; pa $16.95   **591.56**
1. Sexual behavior in animals
ISBN 0-520-21974-0; 0-520-24075-8 (pa)
LC 2001-5771
This book "exposes the anthropomorphism and gender politics that have colored our understanding of the natural world and shows how feminism can help move us away from our ideological biases." Publisher's note

"Fascinating and persuasive. Zuk is not an idealogue, just an unusually clear-eyed scholar." N Y Times Book Rev

Includes bibliographical references

591.6 Miscellaneous nontaxonomic kinds of animals

Quammen, David, 1948-
Monster of God; the man-eating predator in the jungles of history and the mind. Norton 2003 513p maps $26.95   **591.6**
1. Dangerous animals 2. Predatory animals 3. Endangered species
ISBN 0-393-05140-4   LC 2003-7812
This is an "account of efforts to preserve large top-of-the-food-chain carnivores like tigers and crocodiles, and a meditation on what life would be like without them." N Y Times Book Rev

"Rich with personal stories that clarify humanity's true place in the universe, this book will leave the reader eager for more. . . . This has all the makings of a science book of the year. Highly recommended." Libr J

Includes bibliographical references

Todd, Kim, 1970-
Tinkering with Eden; a natural history of exotics in America; illustrations by Claire Emery. Norton 2001 302p il hardcover o.p. paperback available $15.95   **591.6**
1. Animal introduction
ISBN 0-393-32324-2 (pa)   LC 00-58740
"Exotics include such now prosaic, nonnative bird species as starlings, pigeons, and house sparrows. Todd's intriguing history of their introduction in the U.S., some deliberate . . . others accidental, develops into an essential look at the unexpected and, all too often, unwelcome impact exotics have on the ecosystem in which they thrive." Booklist

Includes bibliographical references

591.68 Rare and endangered animals

Chadwick, Douglas H.
The company we keep; America's endangered species; [by] Douglas H. Chadwick and Joel Sartore. National Geographic Soc. 1996 157p il hardcover o.p. paperback available $16   **591.68**
1. Endangered species 2. Wildlife conservation 3. Environmental policy—United States
ISBN 0-7922-7132-7 (pa)   LC 96-18874
Topics covered "include a history of the conservation effort (including a description of the Endangered Species Act), accounts of representative species, . . . and the human activities that threaten the Pacific Northwest, desert Southwest, and southern Florida ecosystems." Choice

"The book is not built solely around the photographs. But the pictures are collectively a good storyteller. They're well-edited, and accompanied by maps and charts that help explain how man is threatening many species." Christ Sci Monit

Includes bibliographical references

Weidensaul, Scott
The ghost with trembling wings; science, wishful thinking, and the search for lost species. North Point Press 2002 341p il maps $26; pa $15   **591.68**
1. Rare animals 2. Extinct animals
ISBN 0-374-24664-5; 0-86547-668-3 (pa)
LC 2001-54605
"Weidensaul's narrative concerns those rare occurrences when a supposedly extinct animal makes a surprise reappearance, and the much more frequent occasions when scientists or civilians only think they've sighted a vanished creature." Publ Wkly

"Weidensaul is a graceful writer who works an amazing amount of scientific theory into his narrative." Booklist

Includes bibliographical references

591.7 Animals characteristic of specific environments, animal ecology

Zimmer, Carl
Parasite rex; inside the bizarre world of nature's most dangerous creatures. Free Press 2000 xxii, 298p il hardcover o.p. paperback available $14   **591.7**
1. Parasites
ISBN 0-7432-0011-X (pa)   LC 00-37593
This is a chronicle of the effects of parasites on plants and animals

"The importance of Zimmer's book lies not only in its accessible presentation of the new science of evolutionary parasitology but in its thoughtful treatment of the global strategies and policies that scientists, health workers and governments will have to consider in order to manage parasites in the future." N Y Times Book Rev

Includes bibliographical references

591.9 Treatment of animals by continents, countries, localities

Stuart, Chris

Africa's vanishing wildlife; [by] Chris & Tilde Stuart. Smithsonian Institution Press 1996 198p il maps $45   **591.9**

1. Animals—Africa 2. Rare animals 3. Endangered species

ISBN 1-56098-678-6   LC 97-147179

The authors provide an "account of the many species endangered by habitat destruction, poaching, and desertification in Africa. Encyclopedia-style entries are arranged in chapters on elephants, rhinos, carnivores, primates, antelopes, other mammals, birds, and reptiles, amphibians, and fish." Libr J

Includes bibliographical references

592 Invertebrates

Barnes, Robert D.

Invertebrate zoology. Saunders College Pub. il $104.95   **592**

1. Invertebrates   LC 86-10023

First published 1963. (7th edition 2003) Periodically revised

A comprehensive text which discusses all aspects of the biology of the invertebrates

Includes bibliographical references

Hubbell, Sue

Waiting for Aphrodite; journeys into the time before bones; with illustrations by Liddy Hubbell. Houghton Mifflin 1999 242p il $24; pa $13   **592**

1. Invertebrates

ISBN 0-395-83703-0; 0-618-05684-X (pa)   LC 98-49811

"These essays on natural history discuss everything from the orange-humped crickets that are unique to Missouri and the iridescent butterflies of Costa Rica to the furry sea mice that live in the coastal waters near the writer's new house, in Maine. Hubbell is both a delighted home scientist and a glinting memoirist, and her observations are interspersed with accounts of her fresh life in the East." New Yorker

Includes bibliographical references

594 Mollusks and mollusk-like animals

Ellis, Richard, 1938-

The search for the giant squid. Lyons Press 1998 322p il o.p.; Penguin Bks. paperback available $14.95   **594**

1. Squids

ISBN 0-14-028676-4 (pa)   LC 98-10436

The giant squid (Architeuthis) "has never positively been seen by human eyes in its living, active form. . . . With everything about the giant squid's life, behavior, and geographical range as a mysterious background, Ellis roams through speculative tracts, dating back to Pliny the Elder, about *Architeuthis*." Booklist

"Some of the appeal of this book is visual, as it presents 30 b&w photographs and 35 line drawings, many historical, several of the drawings by Ellis himself." Publ Wkly

Includes bibliographical references

595.7 Insects

Alcock, John, 1942-

In a desert garden; love and death among the insects; with illustrations by Turid Forsyth. Norton 1997 186p il $27.50   **595.7**

1. Insects 2. Desert ecology

ISBN 0-393-04118-2   LC 97-589

Also available in paperback from University of Ariz. Press

The focus of this "work is the author's own front yard in Tempe, Arizona, and its insect inhabitants. . . . Readers will gain insights into how science is practiced as the author's lively, often humorous observations of assorted beetles, bugs, wasps, bees, caterpillars, and butterflies are related to broad concepts of animal behavior, ecology, and survival." Libr J

Includes bibliographical references

Evans, Arthur V.

An inordinate fondness for beetles; [by] Arthur V. Evans, Charles L. Bellamy; photography by Lisa Charles Watson; illustrations, Patricia Wynne. Holt & Co. 1996 208p il (Henry Holt reference book) o.p.; University of Calif. Press paperback available $29.95   **595.7**

1. Beetles

ISBN 0-520-22323-3 (pa)   LC 96-5245

"A Peter N. Nevraumont book"

"The six chapters cover beetle numbers and diversity, their body plan and functions, their life histories, habits, and defenses, their evolution, their interactions with humans, and their aesthetic importance and conservation." Libr J

"The incredible full-color photographs bring readers up close without a magnifying lens at hand, and the seemingly infinite variations within the species due to size, structure, and color are easily seen. . . . While the text is scientific, it is very readable." SLJ

Includes bibliographical references

The **Firefly** encyclopedia of insects and spiders; edited by Christopher O'Toole. Firefly Bks. 2002 240p il $40   **595.7**

1. Insects 2. Spiders

ISBN 1-55297-612-2

First published 1986 by Facts on File with title: The Encyclopedia of insects

This work "treats all the major taxonomic groups of arthropods except for the marine groups. The 28 orders of insects are all given separate treatment, as well as millipedes, centipedes, and arachnids. The work focuses in fascinating detail on behavior, morphology, ecology, life cycles, and economic or medical importance. Strikingly beautiful photographs of arthropods around the world supplement drawings that illustrate specific features. Separate essays discuss topics such as flight, pheromones and mating, mimicry, and social life. . . . There is no rival encyclopedia." Choice

Halpern, Sue M.

Four wings and a prayer; caught in the mystery of the monarch butterflies; [by] Sue Halpern. Pantheon Bks. 2001 212p il maps hardcover o.p. paperback available $12

595.7

1. Monarch butterflies

ISBN 0-375-70194-X (pa)   LC 00-51055

Halpern discusses her experiences studying the migration of monarch butterflies. "She spends much of her time assisting Bill Calvert, a . . . field biologist, as they drive through rural Mexico tagging, weighing, and counting butterflies." Christ Sci Monit

Hölldobler, Bert, 1936-

The ants; [by] Bert Hölldobler and Edward O. Wilson. Belknap Press 1990 732p il $95

595.7

1. Ants

ISBN 0-674-04075-9   LC 89-30653

This volume includes coverage of ant "evolution, taxonomy, life history, chemical ecology, kin recognition, community organization, [and] symbiosis. . . . Army ants, fungus growers, harvesting ants and weaver ants . . . are each given a chapter of their own. . . . The book's last chapter tells the reader how to collect, culture and observe live ants." Sci Am

"Science is rarely good literature. 'The Ants' is an exalting exception." N Y Times Book Rev

Includes bibliographical references

Journey to the ants; a story of scientific exploration; [by] Bert Hölldobler and Edward O. Wilson. Belknap Press 1994 228p il $27.50; pa $16.95   **595.7**

1. Ants

ISBN 0-674-48525-4; 0-674-48526-2 (pa)

LC 94-13386

"Based on their field studies ranging from the Arctic Circle and Finland to rain forests in Brazil, the authors relate various aspects of ant natural history including foraging behavior, colony structure and organization, and chemical communication." Choice

"A skillful blend of natural lore, autobiography, and history." Libr J

Insect lives; stories of mystery and romance from a hidden world; edited by Erich Hoyt and Ted Schultz. Wiley 1999 360p il o.p.; Harvard Univ. Press paperback available $18.95   **595.7**

1. Insects

ISBN 0-674-00952-5 (pa)   LC 99-24788

"The selections for this volume come from Aristotle, Charles Darwin, William Wordsworth, the Bible, contemporary entomologists such as Edward O. Wilson, and dozens of other sources. The editors have arranged the material into ten chapters on themes dealing with insects both praised and reviled, insect societies, mating, metamorphosis, behavior, and more. The book is well suited for browsing, with many illustrations, relatively short entries, and a wide variety of topics and writing styles." Libr J

Milne, Lorus Johnson, 1912-

The Audubon Society field guide to North American insects and spiders; [by] Lorus and Margery Milne; visual key by Susan Rayfield. Knopf 1980 989p il $19.95   **595.7**

1. Insects 2. Spiders

ISBN 0-394-50763-0   LC 80-7620

"A Chanticleer Press edition. The Audubon Society field guide series"

The authors "have based their field guide on 702 excellent color photographs (75 of which are of spiders and other arachnids). In addition to some general information, the text (two thirds of the book) is made up of brief comments on each kind of arthropod pictured." Choice

Pyle, Robert Michael

The Audubon Society field guide to North American butterflies; visual key by Carol Nehring and Jane Opper. Knopf 1981 916p il $19.95   **595.7**

1. Butterflies

ISBN 0-394-51914-0   LC 80-84240

"A Chanticleer Press edition. The Audubon Society field guide series"

This guide "introduces more than 600 species of North American butterfly, including those native to the Hawaiian Islands. A section of brilliant color plates (more than 1,000 of them) featuring butterflies in their natural habitats, follows a general introduction and notes on text organization and use." Booklist

Schappert, Phil, 1956-

A world for butterflies; their lives, behavior and future. Firefly Bks. 2000 320p il $35

595.7

1. Butterflies

ISBN 1-55209-550-9

"The first chapter explains what a butterfly is, the difference between butterflies and their more numerous cousins the moths, and their anatomy. Taxonomy and the butterfly families of the world are covered in the second chapter, with diversity and where they live comprising the third . . . the fourth chapter, on the natural history and behavior of butterflies, is the most fascinating portion of the book and illustrates the complex relationships between butterflies and their environment. The final chapter, on conservation, is an eloquent plea for the continued existence of these most intriguing insects." Booklist

Spielman, A. (Andrew), 1930-

Mosquito; a natural history of man's most persistent and deadly foe; [by] Andrew Spielman and Michael D'Antonio. Hyperion 2001 247p il maps hardcover o.p. paperback available $12   **595.7**

1. Mosquitoes

ISBN 0-7868-8667-6 (pa)   LC 2001-16815

The authors tell us about the mosquito's "life cycle, its natural enemies and predators, and, of course, its monumental impact on human history. . . . This is truly an unexpected delight, an informative, entertaining, and sometimes skin-crawly book that should appeal to anyone with a taste for popular science." Booklist

Stokes, Donald W.

The butterfly book; an easy guide to butterfly gardening, identification, and behavior; [by] Donald and Lillian Stokes and Ernest Williams. Little, Brown 1991 95p il maps pa $12.95   **595.7**

1. Butterflies

ISBN 0-316-81780-5   LC 91-15323

This book discusses plants which will attract butterflies, explains butterfly life cycles and behavior, and provides information for identification of over 140 species

Waldbauer, Gilbert

Insects through the seasons. Harvard Univ. Press 1996 289p il $27.50; pa $14.95 **595.7**

1. Moths

ISBN 0-674-45488-X; 0-674-45489-8 (pa)

LC 95-35171

"Waldbauer uses the yearly cycle of the cecropia moth as a base to which he periodically returns while presenting an impressive array of the tactics the moth's fellow insects and arthropod relatives use to live and thrive." Booklist

"The scientific information is excellent and the writing is fascinating." Sci Books Films

Includes bibliographical references

Millions of monarchs, bunches of beetles; how bugs find strength in numbers. Harvard Univ. Press 2000 264p il $27.50; pa $16.95
595.7

1. Insects

ISBN 0-674-00090-0; 0-674-00686-0 (pa)

LC 99-42453

The author "examines many of the reasons that insects form groups. . . . Insects come together for a host of reasons, Waldbauer explains: to find mates, to avoid predators, to enhance their food-gathering abilities, to manipulate their environment and to subdue prey. In each case, Waldbauer provides evocative descriptions of particular species' behaviors while discussing the underlying evolutionary reasons for that behavior." Publ Wkly

Includes bibliographical references

Wilson, Edward O., 1929-

Insect societies. Belknap Press 1971 548p il hardcover o.p. paperback available $33.95
595.7

1. Insects

ISBN 0-674-45495-2 (pa)

In addition to "descriptions of specific groups of organisms, Wilson attempts to bring much diverse information, including fundamental concepts of evolution and ecology, into a conceptual format he terms unified sociobiology. He devotes several chapters to detailed descriptions of various activities necessary to maintenance of the societies, including a chapter on genetic theories relating to social behavior." Libr J

Includes bibliographical references

597   Cold-blooded vertebrates. Fishes

Allen, Thomas B., 1929-

The shark almanac. Lyons Press 1999 274p il hardcover o.p. paperback available $19.95
597

1. Sharks

ISBN 1-58474-808-0 (pa)   LC 98-38524

The author "discusses the evolution, anatomy, and physiology of more than 100 shark species. A description and illustration of each family is presented, giving its common name, size, distribution, and degree of danger to humans. The same information is given for the related skates and rays. Detailed historical information on shark attacks, a list of shark avoidance rules, and an extensive bibliography are included." Libr J

The **Audubon** Society field guide to North American fishes, whales, and dolphins; [by] Herbert T. Boschung, Jr. [et al.]; visual key by Carol Nehring and Jordan Verner. Knopf 1983 848p il $19   **597**

1. Fishes—North America 2. Whales 3. Dolphins

ISBN 0-394-53405-0   LC 83-47962

"A Chanticleer Press edition. The Audubon Society field guide series"

This guide has "a first section containing excellent photographs of 529 marine and freshwater fishes and 45 cetacean species found in or near North America north of Mexico, and a second section giving brief descriptions of each species. . . . The well-organized and well-written text includes descriptions of physical features, habitat, range (generally with a small map), and related or similar species." Choice

Behnke, Robert J.

Trout and salmon of North America; illustrated by Joseph R. Tomelleri; foreword by Thomas McGuane; introduction by Donald S. Proebstel; edited by George Scott. Free Press 2002 359p il maps $40   **597**

1. Trout 2. Salmon

ISBN 0-7432-2220-2   LC 2002-69256

This is a "guide to the more than 70 types of trout and salmon of North America." Libr J

"Along with full and clearly written scientific explanations, statistics and analysis, the author provides anecdotal and historical details that make this not just a field guide, but a fascinating read for those interested in the natural world." Publ Wkly

Includes bibliographical references

Benchley, Peter

Shark trouble; true stories about sharks and the sea. Random House 2002 186p il $21.95; pa $12.95   **597**

1. Sharks 2. Marine animals

ISBN 0-375-50824-4; 0-8129-6633-3 (pa)

LC 2002-283533

Also available Thorndike Prss large print edition

"Benchley describes the many types of sharks (including the ones that pose a genuine threat to man), what is and isn't known about shark behavior, the odds against an attack and how to reduce them even further—all reinforced with the lessons he has learned, the mistakes he has made, and the personal perils he has encountered."

Benchley, Peter—*Continued*
Publisher's note
"Handy with statistics and quick to crack a joke with himself as the target, Benchley offers riveting accounts of his and his family's up close and personal encounters with sharks, a gigantic manta ray, a friendly killer whale, barracuda, and sundry other wild creatures." Booklist

Capuzzo, Mike
Close to shore; a true story of terror in an age of innocence. Broadway Bks. 2001 317p map hardcover o.p. paperback available $14.95   **597**
1. Sharks 2. Animal attacks
ISBN 0-7679-0414-1 (pa)   LC 2001-25750
Also available G.K. Hall large print edition
This describes a series of shark attacks in 1916 off the coast of New Jersey
"A book full of adventure, mounting tension, some gore and excitement, and lots of history." SLJ
Includes bibliographical references

Ellis, Richard, 1938-
Great white shark; [by] Richard Ellis and John E. McCosker; with photographs by Al Giddings and others, and paintings by Richard Ellis. HarperCollins Pubs. 1991 270p il maps o.p.; Stanford Univ. Press paperback available $35.95   **597**
1. Sharks
ISBN 0-8047-2529-2 (pa)   LC 89-46528
"In collaboration with Stanford University Press"
The authors discuss the great white shark's "unique biology (it's warm blooded), size, distribution, and evolution. They also describe the sport of shark fishing and the efforts . . . [to save] the white from threats of extinction. Handsomely illustrated with Ellis's paintings and many simply awesome photographs, . . . the text has enough scientific fact for armchair icthyologists but not enough to confuse the casual reader." Libr J
Includes bibliographical references

Ferrari, Andrea
Sharks; [by] Andrea and Antonella Ferrari; foreword by Doug Perrine. Firefly Bks. 2002 256p il pa $24.95   **597**
1. Sharks
ISBN 1-55209-629-7   LC 2002-511486
Original Italian edition, 2000
"A guide to the appearance and behavior of 120 species of sharks and rays. . . . Illustrated with photographs of sharks and rays in their natural environment. Essays on history, biology, and ecology accompany the text." Publisher's note
"Perrine offers a spellbinding shark gallery." Booklist
Includes bibliographical references

McPhee, John A.
The founding fish; [by] John McPhee. Farrar, Straus & Giroux 2002 358p $25; pa $14   **597**
1. Shad
ISBN 0-374-10444-1; 0-374-52883-7 (pa)
                                    LC 2002-25012
The author considers the shad's "role in nature and American history." Libr J
"McPhee is in great form here, as informative as always but also funny, unusually self-revealing, and quite passionate." Booklist

Page, Lawrence M.
A field guide to freshwater fishes: North America north of Mexico; [by] Lawrence M. Page, Brooks M. Burr; illustrations by Eugene C. Beckham III, John Parker Sherrod, Craig W. Ronto. Houghton Mifflin 1991 432p il maps hardcover o.p. paperback available $19   **597**
1. Fishes—North America
ISBN 0-395-91091-9 (pa)   LC 90-42049
"The Peterson field guide series"
"Sponsored by the National Audubon Society, the National Wildlife Federation, and the Roger Tory Peterson Institute"
This guide "covers all 790 species known in North America north of Mexico. Over 700 illustrations, most in color, show identifying marks. Also includes 377 distribution maps and additional line drawings of key details." Publisher's note
Includes bibliographical references

Smith, C. Lavett, 1927-
National Audubon Society field guide to tropical marine fishes of the Caribbean, the Gulf of Mexico, Florida, the Bahamas, and Bermuda. Knopf 1997 720p il maps $19.95   **597**
1. Tropical fish
ISBN 0-679-44601-X   LC 97-7690
"A Chanticleer Press edition"
This illustrated guide to tropical fishes describes nearly 1,200 species and includes color photographs, classification and identification information

Springer, Victor Gruschka, 1928-
Sharks in question; the Smithsonian answer book; [by] Victor G. Springer and Joy P. Gold. Smithsonian Institution Press 1989 187p il hardcover o.p. paperback available $24.95   **597**
1. Sharks
ISBN 0-87474-877-1 (pa)   LC 88-18185
"At first, the book deals with the general life history of these fish and presents detailed answers to the most commonly asked questions. The remainder of the book discusses the biology of some spectacular shark species and presents a balanced picture of the question of shark attack on humans. Several appendices with information on shark classification, taxonomy, and sizes of selected sharks are also included." Sci Books Films
Includes bibliographical references

Steel, Rodney
Sharks of the world. Facts on File 2003 192p il $35   **597**
1. Sharks
ISBN 0-8160-5212-3   LC 2002-35228
First published 1985
This volume covers shark classification, anatomy, evolution, behavior, and reproduction
Includes bibliographical references

Thomson, Keith Stewart
Living fossil; the story of the coelacanth. Norton 1991 252p il maps hardcover o.p. paperback available $9.95 **597**
1. Coelacanth
ISBN 0-393-30868-5 (pa)   LC 90-43053
This study of the coelacanth discusses "the 1938 discovery of a fish thought to be extinct for 70 million years and the subsequent collection and examination of this [species]." Libr J
"Brisk and engrossing, this is a winning mix of science and adventure." Booklist

Weinberg, Samantha, 1966-
A fish caught in time; the search for the coelacanth. HarperCollins Pubs. 2000 xx, 220p il map hardcover o.p. paperback available $13   **597**
1. Coelacanth
ISBN 0-06-093285-6 (pa)   LC 99-44800
First published 1999 in the United Kingdom
"In 1938, a fish believed to be extinct for 70 million years was caught off the South African coast, triggering the 'greatest scientific find of the century.' The search for the coelacanth . . . is a fascinating story, and Weinberg . . . tells it well." Libr J
Includes bibliographical references

597.8 Amphibians

Amphibians: the world of frogs, toads, salamanders and newts; Robert Hofrichter, editor. Firefly Bks. 2000 264p il maps $49.95   **597.8**
1. Amphibians
ISBN 1-55209-541-X   LC 2001-368012
Original German edition, 1998
Contents: Evolution, systematics, and biogeography; Biology and physiology; Ecology and ethology; The meaning of amphibians for mankind; Amphibians: endangerment and species
"This book is an interesting hybrid: on the one hand, it is an introductory textbook to the biology of the amphibians, and on the other, it is a coffee-table book of beautiful photographs of amphibians." Booklist
Includes bibliographical references

Souder, William, 1949-
A plague of frogs; the horrifying true story. Hyperion 2000 299p il $23.95   **597.8**
1. Frogs
ISBN 0-7868-6360-9   LC 99-49564
The author examines "the disturbing increase in deformed frogs found in Minnesota in 1995. . . . So far, the biologists have not reached a consensus, but Souder's deep-drilling reportage of their work informs readers how these sentinels of science track 'indicator' species such as frogs." Booklist
Includes bibliographical references

597.9 Reptiles

Badger, David
Snakes; text by David Badger; photography by John Netherton. Voyageur Press 1999 144p $35   **597.9**
1. Snakes
ISBN 0-89658-408-9   LC 98-52379
"The first chapter is a general overview of humans and snakes. . . . The second chapter presents a primer on snake biology and behavior, and the very long third chapter is an overview of various families and species of snakes (mostly native to North America). The photographs are breathtaking in their composition, clarity, and sheer beauty." Booklist
Includes bibliographical references

Conant, Roger, 1909-
A field guide to reptiles & amphibians; eastern and central North America; [by] Roger Conant and Joseph T. Collins; illustrated by Isabelle Hunt Conant and Tom R. Johnson. 3rd ed, expanded. Houghton Mifflin 1998 616p il maps (Peterson field guide series) $21   **597.9**
1. Reptiles 2. Amphibians
ISBN 0-395-90452-8   LC 98-13622
First published 1958 with title: A field guide to reptiles and amphibians of the United States and Canada east of the 100th meridian
"Sponsored by the National Audubon Society, the National Wildlife Federation, and the Roger Tory Peterson Institute"
This guide describes 595 species and subspecies, featuring color photos, black and white drawings, and color distribution maps of reptiles and amphibians of the region. Also includes information on transporting live reptiles and amphibians
Includes bibliographical references

Ernst, Carl H.
Snakes in question; the Smithsonian answer book; [by] Carl H. Ernst and George R. Zug; illustrations by Molly Dwyer Griffin. Smithsonian Institution Press 1996 203p il hardcover o.p. paperback available $24.95
597.9
1. Snakes
ISBN 1-56098-649-2 (pa)   LC 96-9367
"The book is organized into five sections: 'Snake Facts,' 'Folk Tales,' 'Giant Snakes: Big and Biggest,' 'Snakebite,' and 'Snakes and Us.' Appendices, a glossary, and general and subject bibliographies are included." Sci Books Films
"The questions and answer format is effective, and readers with no background and others more familiar with snake biology but seeking some biological information or specific data will find the text and tables useful. The careful answers are based on long-term observations as well as current research." Choice

Ferri, Vincenzo
Tortoises and turtles. Firefly Bks. 2002 c1999 255p il pa $24.95   **597.9**
1. Turtles
ISBN 1-55209-631-9
Original Italian edition, 1999
Cover title: Turtles & tortoises

Ferri, Vincenzo—*Continued*

An "illustrated guide to 190 land, marine and freshwater turtles and tortoises . . . describing the physical and biological characteristics of the majority of species." Publisher's note

"Turtle enthusiasts and students writing papers will find this guide and the additional resources it cites invaluable." Voice Youth Advocates

Includes bibliographical references

Firefly encyclopedia of reptiles and amphibians; edited by Tim Halliday and Kraig Adler. Firefly Bks. 2002 240p il maps $40   **597.9**
1. Reptiles 2. Amphibians
ISBN 1-55297-613-0

First published 1986 by Facts on File with title: The Encyclopedia of reptiles and amphibians

This volume "presents information about evolution, form, function, distribution, diet, reproduction, development, locomotion, social behavior, and conservation of the various families of amphibians and reptiles. Special feature articles cover other important aspects of their lives, from vocal communication to play. . . . The book includes a glossary, a bibliography with Web sites, and an extensive index." Choice

Greene, Harry W.

Snakes; the evolution of mystery in nature; with photographs by Michael and Patricia Fodgen. University of Calif. Press 1997 351p il $55; pa $29.95   **597.9**
1. Snakes
ISBN 0-520-20014-4; 0-520-22487-6 (pa)
LC 96-21928

The author examines the "biology and ecology of snakes. Throughout, facts on the form, function, habitat, and evolution of these reptiles are mixed with the author's experiences, and the over 200 natural-setting color photographs that complement the text are commendable in their own right." Libr J

Includes bibliographical references

Mattison, Christopher

The encyclopedia of snakes; [by] Chris Mattison. Facts on File 1995 256p il maps $35   **597.9**
1. Snakes
ISBN 0-8160-3072-3   LC 95-2501

This study of snakes covers "their taxonomy, morphology, habitats, diet, reproduction, and protective mechanisms. Especially interesting are the discussions of the snake's relationship with humans in myth and reality. Color photographs illustrate the discussion throughout." Booklist

Includes bibliographical references

Snakes of the world; [by] Chris Mattison. Facts on File 2003 190p il maps $35 **597.9**
1. Snakes
ISBN 0-8160-5213-1   LC 2002-34737

A reissue of the title first published 1986

Snake morphology, reproduction, diet, self-defense, ecology and behavior are discussed

"Mattison provides an enjoyable introduction to snake biology and snake diversity for the interested general reader. . . . Many of the numerous color photographs are spectacular." Choice [review of 1986 edition]

Includes bibliographical references

Murphy, John C., 1947-

Tales of giant snakes; a historical natural history of anacondas and pythons; [by] John C. Murphy and Robert W. Henderson. Krieger 1997 221p il maps $32.50   **597.9**
1. Anacondas 2. Pythons
ISBN 0-89464-995-7   LC 96-54033

Accounts of encounters between large snakes and humans include newspaper articles, adventure writings, and reports of explorers

Includes bibliographical references

Orenstein, Ronald I. (Ronald Isaac), 1946-

Turtles, tortoises and terrapins; survivors in armor; [by] Ronald Orenstein. Firefly Bks. 2001 308p il maps $45   **597.9**
1. Turtles
ISBN 1-55209-605-X   LC 2003-389052

This book "surveys the myriad of turtle anatomy, habitat, and life cycles throughout the ages." Publisher's note

"Orenstein has produced a superbly illustrated, highly informative, and exceptionally readable volume on world turtles. . . . Easily one of the best books ever published on turtles. Highly recommended." Choice

Includes bibliographical references

Rubio, Manny

Rattlesnake; portrait of a predator. Smithsonian Institution Press 1998 xxvii, 239p il $49.95   **597.9**
1. Rattlesnakes
ISBN 1-56098-808-8   LC 98-22935

This book contains "more than 120 color photographs of various North American rattlesnakes. . . . The text discusses many aspects of rattlesnake evolution, anatomy and physiology, and ecology, including several chapters on interactions between snakes and people." Sci Books Films

Includes bibliographical references

Stebbins, Robert C. (Robert Cyril), 1915-

A field guide to Western reptiles and amphibians; text and illustrations by Robert C. Stebbins. 3rd ed newly rev. Houghton Mifflin 2003 533p il maps $22   **597.9**
1. Reptiles 2. Amphibians
ISBN 0-395-98272-3   LC 2002-27561

"The Peterson field guide series"

First published 1966

"Sponsored by The National Wildlife Federation and the Roger Tory Peterson Institute"

This "covers all the species of reptiles and amphibians found in western North America. More than 650 full-color paintings and photographs show key details for making accurate identifications. . . . Color range maps give species' distributions. . . . [Includes] information on conservation efforts and survival status." Publisher's note

Includes bibliographical references

Tyning, Thomas F.

A guide to amphibians and reptiles; edited by Donald W. Stokes and Lillian Q. Stokes; illustrations by Andrew Finch Magee; range maps by Thomas F. Tyning and Timothy J. Flanagan. Little, Brown 1990 400p il hardcover o.p. paperback available $14.95

597.9

1. Amphibians 2. Reptiles
ISBN 0-316-81713-9 (pa)   LC 89-28444
This guide covers common frogs, salamanders, alligators, snakes, turtles, and lizards
Includes bibliographical references

598 Birds

Adams, George Martin

Birdscaping your garden; a practical guide to backyard birds and the plants that attract them; [by] George Adams. Rodale Press 1994 208p il maps hardcover o.p. paperback available $18.95   **598**

1. Bird watching
ISBN 0-87596-956-9 (pa)   LC 93-43391
In this guide to 64 species each entry includes a photograph and description of the bird's habitats, song, preferred habitat, breeding behavior, nesting style, and diet. A list of plants that provide food and shelter for the bird is included
Includes bibliographical references

Attenborough, David, 1926-

The life of birds. Princeton Univ. Press 1998 320p il $29.95   **598**

1. Birds
ISBN 0-691-01633-X   LC 98-30705
This survey of bird behavior describes "eating habits, flight, communication, mating, parenthood and environmental adaptability." Publ Wkly
"Well illustrated with color photographs, Attenborough's latest goes a long way to converting all readers into bird lovers." Booklist
Includes bibliographical references

Beans, Bruce E.

Eagle's plume; the struggle to preserve the life and haunts of America's bald eagle. Scribner 1996 318p il o.p.; University of Neb. Press paperback available $17.95   **598**

1. Bald eagle 2. Birds—Protection
ISBN 0-8032-6142-X (pa)   LC 96-31485
This book "deals with the conservation of eagles and their habitat. [It] also contains details on the biology, behavior, and ecology of eagles." Sci Books Films
Includes bibliographical references

Book of North American birds. Reader's Digest Assn. 1990 576p il maps $32.95

598

1. Birds—North America
ISBN 0-89577-351-1   LC 89-70261
This book "consists of over 450 page-length species accounts which feature a . . . color painting, a half-page anecdotal narrative essay, a range map, a drawing, plus small sections detailing the bird's identification, habitat,

and food. Smaller accounts (three per page) for 117 scarcer birds follow the full-page ones. Appended is a 40-page section with thumbnail sketches of the best birding areas in the United States and Canada." Libr J
Includes bibliographical references

Bull, John L.

The National Audubon Society field guide to North American birds, Eastern region; [by] John Bull and John Farrand, Jr.; revised by John Farrand, Jr.; visual key by Amanda Wilson and Lori Hogan. rev ed. Knopf 1994 797p il maps pa $19.95   **598**

1. Birds—North America
ISBN 0-679-42852-6   LC 94-7768
Companion volume to National Audubon Society field guide to North American birds, Western region, by Miklos D. F. Udvardy
"A Chanticleer Press edition"
First published 1977
This pictorial guide to 508 eastern species arranges birds by color and shape to simplify identification. It also includes information on bird-watching and conservation status
Includes bibliographical references

Clark, William S., 1937-

A field guide to hawks of North America; [by] William S. Clark and Brian K. Wheeler; illustrations by Brian K. Wheeler. 2nd ed. Houghton Mifflin 2001 316p il maps $30; pa $22   **598**

1. Hawks
ISBN 0-395-67068-3; 0-395-67067-5 (pa)
                                           LC 2001-2477
"The Peterson field guide series"
First published 1987
"Accounts are presented for all 39 of North America's diurnal raptors, including eagles, falcons, and vultures. Each species account reviews details of plumages and molts, useful identification features, patterns of flight, and general behavior. . . . The guide also provides size data (weight, length, and wingspread) for all species, as well as the etymology of common and scientific names. Basically, the reference is essential for any student of raptors and useful for serious birders in general." Am Ref Books Annu, 2002
Includes bibliographical references

Cocker, Mark

Birders; tales of a tribe. Atlantic Monthly Press 2002 c2001 229p $24; pa $13   **598**

1. Bird watching
ISBN 0-87113-844-1; 0-8021-3996-5 (pa)
                                           LC 2001-56490
First published 2001 in the United Kingdom
In a "memoir cum essay collection, the author brings the reader into the sometimes obsessive world of bird-watching. . . . Stories of the author and friends going to great lengths and distances to see rare birds, of birding in exotic locales, or of unmasking a fellow birder's claims to finding a rare species are both thought-provoking and amusing." Booklist
Includes bibliographical references

Cokinos, Christopher

Hope is the thing with feathers; a personal chronicle of vanished birds. Tarcher/Putnam 2000 359p il o.p.; Warner Bks. paperback available $13.95   **598**

1. Birds—North America 2. Extinct animals
ISBN 0-446-67749-3 (pa)   LC 99-52846

This is an "account of the context and circumstances of the extinctions of six North American birds: the passenger pigeon, Carolina parakeet, ivory-billed woodpecker, heath hen, Labrador duck, and great auk. . . . [This] well-researched book takes an engaging, lively look at American history and science as well as the possibility of re-creating vanished creatures through DNA cloning." Libr J

Includes bibliographical references

Dunn, Erica H.

Birds at your feeder; a guide to the feeding habits, behavior, distribution, and abundance; [by] Erica H. Dunn and Diane L. Tessaglia-Hymes; illustrations by Peter Burke; abundance maps by Jeffrey Price; sponsored by Cornell Laboratory of Ornithology [et al.] Norton 1999 418p il maps hardcover o.p. paperback available $15.95   **598**

1. Birds—North America
ISBN 0-393-32231-9 (pa)   LC 98-35661

"For the 93 most widespread feeder species, the authors present several pages of excellent commentary plus two range maps and four bar graphs. For each bird, there is textual and graphic information on its abundance . . . food preferences, behavior, habits, a drawing of the bird, and more." Libr J

Includes bibliographical references

Ehrlich, Paul R.

The birder's handbook; a field guide to the natural history of North American birds: including all species that regularly breed north of Mexico; [by] Paul R. Ehrlich, David S. Dobkin, Daryl Wheye. Simon & Schuster 1988 xxx, 785p il hardcover o.p. paperback available $20   **598**

1. Birds—North America
ISBN 0-671-65989-8 (pa)   LC 87-32404

This volume contains "basic information on each of the 646 species of birds in North America, enriched by 250 short essays on all aspects of avian behavior and biology. This book is a companion volume to any illustrated field guide." Am Libr

Includes bibliographical references

Field guide to the birds of North America.

4th ed, Fully rev & updated. National Geographic Soc. 2002 480p il maps $21.95   **598**

1. Birds—North America
ISBN 0-7922-6877-6   LC 2003-269768

First published 1983

An identification guide to more than 800 species of North American birds. Arranged in family groups, the information for each species includes a full-color illustration, a range map, common and scientific names, measurement, and a description of plumage, distinctive songs and calls, behavior, abundance, and habitat

Firefly encyclopedia of birds; edited by

Christopher Perrins. Firefly Bks. 2003 655p il maps $59.95   **598**

1. Birds
ISBN 1-55297-777-3

"An Andromeda book"

Replaces The encyclopedia of birds, published 1985 by Facts on File

"Organized in phylogenetic order, the volume covers almost 10,000 bird species; for each bird family (owls, woodpeckers, thrushes, et al.) there is a map, a general text, and sidebars with paragraphs on nesting, voice, size, diet, plumage, habitat, etc. There are also random essays on appropriate related subjects, such as conservation, courtship, and many family-specific topics of interest as well as a helpful glossary. The volume is highly illustrated in color, both by quality paintings and the approximately 1000 lively, engaging photographs. This excellent reference title in an attractive format is highly recommended for most public and academic libraries." Libr J

Gessner, David, 1961-

Return of the osprey; a season of flight and wonder. Algonquin Bks. 2001 286p map $23.95   **598**

1. Ospreys
ISBN 1-56512-254-2   LC 00-68230

Also available in paperback from Ballantine Bks.

"Over 90 percent of the osprey population in New England was wiped out between 1950 and 1975, and then DDT was banned. Gessner writes of the return of nesting ospreys to Cape Cod. . . . This beautifully written story of a season with birds of prey makes for engrossing reading as we learn about osprey life from a master essayist." Booklist

Includes bibliographical references

Harrison, Kit

America's favorite backyard birds; [by] Kit and George Harrison. Simon & Schuster 1983 288p il hardcover o.p. paperback available $12   **598**

1. Birds—United States
ISBN 0-671-67341-6 (pa)   LC 83-11341

This book presents "life histories and behavior of ten of the most popular American birds. One chapter each is devoted to the robin, black-capped chicadee, mockingbird, cardinal, mourning dove, American goldfinch, downy woodpecker, house wren, blue jay, and white-breasted nut-hatch, describing their habits, and how to attract them." Libr J

Includes bibliographical references

Heinrich, Bernd, 1940-

Mind of the raven; investigations and adventures with wolf-birds. Cliff St. Bks. 1999 380p il $25; pa $13   **598**

1. Ravens
ISBN 0-06-017447-1; 0-06-093063-2 (pa)
    LC 99-18129

Heinrich "describes his field experiments in the feeding habits, play, intelligence, social structure, territoriality, and hunting methods of ravens as well as an array of topics from their skill as mimics to their suspected emotional natures. He brings alive the romance of field research, where the discipline of science is often harder to achieve than in the lab but is at least as rewarding. A splendid book." Libr J

Includes bibliographical references

Kaufman, Kenn

Birds of North America; [by] Kenn Kaufmann with the collaboration of Rick and Nora Bowers and Lynn Hassler Kaufman. Houghton Mifflin 2000 383p (Kaufman focus guides) $30; pa $22 **598**
1. Birds—North America
ISBN 0-618-07324-8; 0-618-13219-8 (pa)
LC 00-56717
For this identification guide "Kaufman selected over 2000 digitally edited photographs, enhanced to improve contrast, color, and the like. The excellent result will appeal to beginning birders perhaps intimidated by illustrations. . . . Kaufman's text is simple and uncluttered, a plus for novices." Libr J
Includes bibliographical references

Kress, Stephen W.

The bird garden; foreword by Roger Tory Peterson. Dorling Kindersley 1995 176p il $25 **598**
1. Birds—North America 2. Gardening
ISBN 0-7894-0139-8
LC 95-6748
At head of title: National Audubon Society
A guide to selecting and planting vegetation to attract birds, building nesting structures and feeders, and ways to provide water throughout the year
"A comprehensive, first-rate guide." Booklist

Matthiessen, Peter

The birds of heaven; travels with cranes; paintings and drawings by Robert Bateman. North Point Press 2001 349p il $27.50; pa $16 **598**
1. Cranes (Birds) 2. Endangered species
ISBN 0-374-19944-2; 0-86547-657-8 (pa)
LC 2001-32986
The author writes "of his journeys in search of all the crane species and of his conversations with the scientists working to understand and preserve them." Booklist
"Eloquent and graceful, this lovely, moving narrative will inspire and delight readers with or without ornithological background or interests." Publ Wkly

Peterson, Roger Tory, 1908-1996

A field guide to the birds of Britain and Europe; [by] Roger Tory Peterson, Guy Mountfort, P.A.D. Hollom. 5th ed, in collaboration with D.I.M. Wallace. Houghton Mifflin 1993 261p il hardcover o.p. paperback available $22 **598**
1. Birds—Great Britain 2. Birds—Europe
ISBN 0-618-16675-0 (pa)
LC 93-22426
"The Peterson field guide series"
First published 1954
"Sponsored by the National Audubon Society, the National Wildlife Federation, and the Roger Tory Peterson Institute"
Covers the British Isles, Iceland, continental Europe and the islands of the Mediterranean. Includes identification, voice and habitat, and names in the foreign language pertinent to location

A field guide to the birds of eastern and central North America; by Roger Tory Peterson and Virginia Marie Peterson. 5th ed. Houghton Mifflin 2002 xxii, 427p il maps $30 **598**
1. Birds—North America
ISBN 0-395-74047-9
LC 2001-51879
Also available large print edition $24 (ISBN 0-395-96371-0)
"The Peterson field guide series"
First published 1934 with title: A field guide to the birds
"Sponsored by the National Audubon Society, the National Wildlife Federation, and the Roger Tory Peterson Institute"
This guide to birds found east of the Rocky Mountains contains colored illustrations painted by the author, with a description of each species on the facing page. Views of young birds and seasonal variations in plumage are included. Birds are arranged in eight major groups of body shape

A field guide to western birds; text and illustrations by Roger Tory Peterson; maps by Virginia Marie Peterson. 3rd ed, completely rev and enl. Houghton Mifflin 1998 432p il maps $27; pa $18 **598**
1. Birds—West (U.S.)
ISBN 0-395-91174-5; 0-395-91173-7 (pa)
LC 89-31517
"The Peterson field guide series"
First published 1941
"A completely new guide to field marks of all species found in North America west of the 100th meridian and north of Mexico." Title page
Sponsored by the National Audubon Society, the National Wildlife Federation, and the Roger Tory Peterson Institute
This guide illustrates over 1,000 birds (700 species) on 165 color plates. In addition, over 400 distribution maps are included

Robbins, Chandler S., 1918-

Birds of North America; a guide to field identification; by Chandler S. Robbins, Bertel Bruun, and Herbert S. Zim; revised by Jonathan P. Latimer and Karen Stray Nolting and James Coe; illustrated by Arthur Singer. rev and updated. St. Martin's Press 2001 359p il maps $19.95; pa $15.95 **598**
1. Birds—North America
ISBN 1-58238-091-0; 1-58238-090-2 (pa)
LC 2001-271739
"A Golden field guide"
First published 1966
This resource includes over 800 species and 600 range maps; illustrations featuring male, female, and juvenile plumage; and sonograms picturing sound for song recognition. Feeding habits, migration routes, and characteristic flight patterns as well as American Ornithologists' classifications are also provided

Roth, Sally

The backyard bird feeder's bible; the A-to-Z guide to feeders, seed mixes, projects, and treats. Rodale 2000 268p il $29.95; pa $18.95 **598**

1. Birds

ISBN 0-87596-834-1; 0-87596-918-6 (pa)

LC 00-9063

Conveying "information on attracting, feeding, and observing birds, the entries vary in length from half a page to multiple pages for broad or complex topics such as the benefits of fruiting plants . . . as a source of both food and shelter." Libr J

This "truly is a comprehensive guide for bird enthusiasts." Booklist

Includes bibliographical references

Safina, Carl

Eye of the albatross; visions of hope and survival. Holt & Co. 2002 377p il maps hardcover o.p. paperback available $16 **598**

1. Albatrosses

ISBN 0-8050-6229-7 (pa)

LC 2001-51644

"A John Macrae book"

The author "recounts his travels to remote portions of the northwest Hawaiian Islands to witness albatross breeding season, during which parent birds fly across entire oceans—as much as 25,000 miles—to hunt sufficient food to nourish their single chicks. . . . Safina's encyclopedic knowledge and spirited prose provide a stunningly intimate portrait of an environment." Publ Wkly

Includes bibliographical references

Sibley, David

The Sibley field guide to birds of eastern North America; written and illustrated by David Allen Sibley. Knopf 2003 431p il pa $19.95 **598**

1. Birds—North America

ISBN 0-679-45120-X

LC 2002-114931

Companion volume to The Sibley field guide to birds of western North America

This portable "guide features 650 bird species, plus regional populations found east of the Rocky Mountains. Accounts include . . . illustrations . . . with descriptive caption text pointing out the most important field marks. Each entry contains . . . text concerning frequency, nesting, behavior, food and feeding, voice description, and key identification features." Publisher's note

"All the qualities to be expected in a field guide are here. . . . Image reproduction is crisp, colors are distinct, shading shows well, and despite the very small size, range map colors are clear. . . . Sibley has accomplished the difficult task of condensing . . . [The Sibley guide to birds] to practical field size." Libr J

The Sibley field guide to birds of western North America. Knopf 2003 471p il pa $19.95 **598**

1. Birds—North America

ISBN 0-679-45121-8

LC 2002-114930

Companion volume to The Sibley field guide to birds of eastern North America

This portable "guide features 703 bird species, plus regional populations found west of the Rocky Mountains. Accounts include . . . illustrations . . . with descriptive caption text pointing out the most important field marks. Each entry contains . . . text concerning frequency, nesting, behavior, food and feeding, voice description, and

key identification features." Publisher's note

"All the qualities to be expected in a field guide are here. . . . Image reproduction is crisp, colors are distinct, shading shows well, and despite the very small size, range map colors are clear. . . . Sibley has accomplished the difficult task of condensing . . . [The Sibley guide to birds] to practical field size." Libr J

The Sibley guide to bird life & behavior; illustrated by David Allen Sibley; edited by Chris Elphick, John B. Dunning, Jr., David Allen Sibley. Knopf 2001 588p il maps $45 **598**

1. Birds—North America

ISBN 0-679-45123-4

LC 2001-33903

At head of title: National Audubon Society

This companion volume to The Sibley guide to birds provides "information about birds' lives and behavior. . . . Part 1 ('The World of Birds') discusses basic avian biology, including form, distribution, population, and conservation, in about 100 pages. Part 2 ('Bird Families of North America'), to which over 40 ornithologists contributed, uses a standard format to describe taxonomy, foraging, breeding, range, nests, eggs, longevity, conservation, and more." Libr J

The Sibley guide to birds; written and illustrated by David Sibley. Knopf 2000 544p il maps pa $35 **598**

1. Birds—North America

ISBN 0-679-45122-6

LC 00-41239

"A Chanticleer Press edition"

At head of title: National Audubon Society

"The treatments of each of the 810 species have detailed paintings to show the natural variations in plumage (e.g., juveniles, male/female adults, seasonal and geographic changes). In all, there are more than 6,600 full-color illustrations. . . . The text for each species has a short summary of identification key points, description of vocalizations, and an up-to-date range map." Choice

"This stunning volume stands out as a must have for even casual birders." SLJ

Sibley's birding basics; written and illustrated by David Allen Sibley. Knopf 2002 154p il pa $15.95 **598**

1. Bird watching 2. Birds

ISBN 0-375-70966-5

LC 2002-20768

Sibley "explores general aspects of birding such as getting started, misidentification, voice, understanding feathers, age variation, ethics and conservation, taxonomy, and finding birds. If being a field naturalist is a craft, then this book is essential in helping to develop and understand the required skills." Libr J

Stokes, Donald W.

The bird feeder book; an easy guide to attracting, identifying, and understanding your feeder birds; [by] Donald and Lillian Stokes; illustrations of feeders by Gordon Morrison; range maps by Leslie Cowperthwaite. Little, Brown 1987 90p il maps pa $12.95 **598**

1. Bird watching

ISBN 0-316-81733-3

LC 87-3016

"This guide for beginners features 72 dramatic color photographs of the most common backyard birds. The text offers chapters on attracting and identifying birds (which types of feeders to use, etc.), dealing with squir-

Stokes, Donald W.—*Continued*

rels and other yard pests, and planting shrubbery layouts that offer food and nest sites. A nicely illustrated, logically organized handbook." Booklist
Includes bibliographical references

Stokes field guide to birds: Eastern region; [by] Donald and Lillian Stokes. Little, Brown 1996 xxiv, 471p il pa $17.95   **598**
  1. Birds—North America
  ISBN 0-316-81809-7   LC 95-6611
In this field guide to birds "a page is devoted to each species with identification remarks, feeding habits, nesting information, other behavior notes, range map, voice explanation, and conservation notes. . . .[There is information on] whether the species is increasing, decreasing, or remaining stable. The book [is] arranged phylogenetically, beginning with seabirds and ending with finches." Booklist
"The text is clearly written, accurate, and up-to-date. . . . The inclusion of population data is unique and valuable." Libr J

Stokes field guide to birds: Western region; {by} Donald and Lillian Q. Stokes. Little, Brown 1995 xxiv, 519p il pa $17.95   **598**
  1. Birds—North America
  ISBN 0-316-81810-0   LC 95-6610
This field guide is "arranged phylogenetically, beginning with seabirds and ending with finches. . . . {An} alphabetical index of the more common bird names is at the front of . . . {the} volume, with a more detailed index at the end." Booklist

Udvardy, Miklos D. F., 1919-1998

National Audubon Society field guide to North American birds, Western region; revised by John Farrand, Jr.; visual key by Amanda Wilson and Lori Hogan. rev ed. Knopf 1994 822p il maps pa $19.95   **598**
  1. Birds—North America
  ISBN 0-679-42851-8   LC 94-7415
Companion volume to National Audubon Society field guide to North American birds, Eastern region by John L. Bull
"A Chanticleer Press edition"
First published 1977
This pictorial guide to 544 western species arranges birds by color and shape to simplify identification. It also includes information on bird-watching and conservation status
Includes bibliographical references

Weidensaul, Scott

Living on the wind; across the hemisphere with migratory birds. North Point Press 1999 420p il hardcover o.p. paperback available $15   **598**
  1. Birds—Migration
  ISBN 0-86547-591-1 (pa)   LC 99-11693
"Starting at a wildlife refuge in Alaska, the author follows birds on their southward migration; watches them on their wintering grounds in Central America, Jamaica, Argentina, and the U.S. . . . and then follows them north again. Along the way he discovers how birds navigate on their journeys, using the sun during the day, the stars to orient by night, or even the Earth's magnetic field as a compass." Booklist

"The book will be of interest to biologists and amateur naturalists; birders will particularly appreciate the discussion of key 'fallout' areas." Libr J
Includes bibliographical references

Weiner, Jonathan

The beak of the finch; a story of evolution in our time. Knopf 1994 332p il hardcover o.p. paperback available $14   **598**
  1. Grant, Peter R., 1936- 2. Grant, B. Rosemary 3. Finches 4. Evolution
  ISBN 0-698-73337-X (pa)   LC 93-36755
"This is an account of Peter and Rosemary Grant's research on the microevolutionary modifications that occur in finch beaks as they adapt to environmental changes. Analysis of data collected from 18,000 birds on a Galápagos island over 21 years conclusively demonstrates that the pressures of natural selection are currently altering wild populations." Libr J
Includes bibliographical references

Williamson, Sheri L.

A field guide to hummingbirds of North America; [by] Sheri L. Williamson. Houghton Mifflin 2001 263p il maps $30; pa $22 **598**
  1. Hummingbirds
  ISBN 0-618-02495-6; 0-618-02496-4 (pa)
             LC 2001-24473
"The Peterson field guide series"
"The habits, habitats, migratory patterns, physical traits, diet, mating practices, where to find them in short, all the information that a good wildlife guide offers are the stuff of Williamson's book. Clear, engaging prose and 180 full color photographs make this a natural for birdwatchers everywhere." Publ Wkly

599   Mammals

Burt, William Henry, 1903-1987

A field guide to the mammals; text and maps by William Henry Burt; illustrated by Richard Philip Grossenheider. 3d ed. Houghton Mifflin 1976 xxv, 289p il maps hardcover o.p. paperback available $19 **599**
  1. Mammals
  ISBN 0-395-91098-6 (pa)
Also available in abridged form in paperback with title: Peterson first guide to mammals of North America
"The Peterson field guide series"
First published 1952
"Sponsored by the National Audubon Society and National Wildlife Federation"
"Field marks of all North American species found north of Mexico." Title page
"This field guide covers 380 species of mammals, including whales, dolphins, and porpoises. Each one is described in detail and most are depicted in color photographs and additional black-and-white sketches. Range maps are included. The description includes information on distinguishing marks, habitat, litter size, appearance of young, specimen tracks, and representations of nests." Malinowsky. Best Sci & Technol Ref Books for Young People

Elbroch, Mark

Mammal tracks & sign; a guide to North American species. Stackpole Bks. 2003 779p il maps $44.95   **599**

1. Animal tracks

ISBN 0-8117-2626-6   LC 2002-10549

This guide provides "track and trail illustrations, range maps, and full-color photographs showing feeding signs, scat, tunnels, burrows, bedding areas, remains, and more. . . . [It explains] how to find, identify, measure, and interpret the clues mammals leave behind. . . . Includes essays that contextualize tracking as a developing science." Publisher's note

The author "brings an ideal combination of practical experience and careful research to this work. . . . A definitive treatment, Elbroch's book will set the standard for years to come and is essential to anyone interested in tracking this continent's mammals." Libr J

Includes bibliographical references

Mares, Michael A.

A desert calling; life in a forbidding landscape. Harvard Univ. Press 2002 318p il maps $29.95   **599**

1. Mammals 2. Desert animals

ISBN 0-674-00747-6   LC 2001-51786

The author describes his studies of "small mammals in the deserts of North America, South America, Egypt, and Iran. . . . The wonder of field research and of the discoveries that result shines through his matter-of-fact tone." Booklist

Includes bibliographical references

Murie, Olaus Johan, 1889-1963

A field guide to animal tracks; text and illustrations by Olaus J. Murie. 2nd ed. Houghton Mifflin 1975 c1974 xxi, 375p il hardcover o.p. paperback available $18   **599**

1. Animal tracks

ISBN 0-395-18323-5 (pa)

"The Peterson field guide series"

First published 1954

"Murie's handbook is recognized as the classic work on the subject. . . . The illustrated guide describes the tracks, droppings, and marks left on bones and leaves by an army of wild animals—bats, bears, rabbits, reptiles, moles, weasels, and others. A fascinating collection of miscellaneous information about the habits of these creatures is part of the descriptive text." Wynar. Ref Books in Paperback. 2d edition

Nowak, Ronald M.

Walker's mammals of the world. 6th ed. Johns Hopkins Univ. Press 1999 2v il set $135   **599**

1. Mammals

ISBN 0-8018-5789-9   LC 98-23686

Also available online

First published 1964

"A goal of the work . . . [is] to provide a quality photograph of a living representative of every genus of mammal. . . . Each genus entry contains information on the number of species known, key literature references, physical description, comparison of characteristics of representative species, description of habitat, general behavior, breeding and care of young, and information on the species' endangered status." Am Ref Books Annu, 2000

Includes bibliographical references

The **Smithsonian** book of North American mammals; edited by Don E. Wilson and Sue Ruff. Smithsonian Institution Press 1999 xxv, 750p il maps $75   **599**

1. Mammals

ISBN 1-56098-845-2   LC 98-43735

"In association with the American Society of Mammalogists."

This volume "covers every species known in the United States, Canada, and the surrounding islands and waters. The book is arranged by evolutionary relationships, with each species account including information on identification guidelines, scientific and common names, geographic distribution, behavior, diet, habitat, reproduction, growth and development, longevity, predation, population status, and impact of human activity. Each entry also includes a distribution map and photograph, usually in color, and a brief list of references providing additional information." Libr J

This is "an indispensable reference to the scientific literature, making it a primary source for reference librarians for years to come." Booklist

Whitaker, John O., Jr.

National Audubon Society field guide to North American mammals. rev ed. Knopf 1996 937p il maps pa $19.95   **599**

1. Mammals

ISBN 0-679-44631-1   LC 95-81456

First published 1980

This field guide describes 390 species of mammals of North America and includes keys for identification, range maps, information on tracks and anatomy, and 375 color photos

599.5   Cetaceans and sea cows

Montgomery, Sy

Journey of the pink dolphins; an Amazon quest. Simon & Schuster 2000 317p il maps hardcover o.p. paperback available $16

599.5

1. Dolphins 2. Amazon River valley

ISBN 0-7432-0026-8 (pa)   LC 99-45840

The author "recounts her Amazonian adventures in search of the *botos,* the famously elusive freshwater pink dolphins, a quest that yields not only invaluable scientific observations but profound insights into the significance of myth." Booklist

Includes bibliographical references

Morton, Alexandra, 1957-

Listening to whales; what the orcas have taught us. Ballantine Bks. 2002 309p il maps $26.95   **599.5**

1. Whales

ISBN 0-345-43794-2   LC 2002-283315

"Morton describes her more than 20 years studying the movements and sounds of orcas, the mammals, actually dolphins, commonly known as killer whales." Publ Wkly

The author "weaves a tremendous amount of whale science into her narrative. . . . This is biographical natural history at its best." Booklist

National Audubon Society guide to marine mammals of the world; illustrated by Pieter A. Folkens; written by Randall R. Reeves [et al.] Knopf 2002 527p il maps $26.95
599.5

1. Marine mammals
ISBN 0-375-41141-0   LC 2001-38103
"A Chanticleer Press edition"
This describes "120 species of the world's whales, dolphins, porpoises, seals and sea lions, manatees, Marine and Sea Otters, and [Polar Bears]." Publisher's note
"Just about everything one could hope for in a guide can be found in this info-packed yet extremely user-friendly tome. . . . A liberal dose of superb, high-quality action color photographs shows the creatures in their natural surroundings." SLJ
Includes bibliographical references

Russell, Dick
Eye of the whale; epic passage from Baja to Siberia; maps by Eben Given. Simon & Schuster 2001 689p il maps $35   **599.5**
1. Whales
ISBN 0-684-86608-0   LC 2001-20572
The author follows gray whales' "migrations from Baja California to the top of the map and around to Siberia, talking along the way to scientists, sailors, and fishermen." New Yorker
"Better than anyone else to date, Russell has documented the historical and cultural importance of the gray whale to the peoples, past and present, of the Pacific Coast." N Y Times Book Rev
Includes bibliographical references

Whales, dolphins, and porpoises; consultant editor, Mark Carwardine. 2nd ed. Checkmark Bks. 1999 240p il maps $39.95
599.5

1. Whales 2. Dolphins 3. Porpoises
ISBN 0-8160-3991-7   LC 99-461832
First published 1988 by Facts on File
"A Weldon Owen production." Verso of title page
This book's subjects range "from evolution, biology, and behavior to an examination of the history of commercial whaling. The place of whales in ecology is considered, together with an overview of their intelligence, social sophistication, and the potential for communication between humans and whales." Publisher's note
Includes bibliographical references

599.64   Bovids

Lott, Dale F.
American bison; a natural history; with a foreword by Harry W. Greene. University of Calif. Press 2002 229p il (Organisms and environments) $29.95   **599.64**
1. Bison
ISBN 0-520-23338-7   LC 2002-243
The author "spent his early years on a national bison range and has been watching these magnificent beasts ever since. . . . Lott's seasonal observations add up to a life's work of unique natural history, as readable as it is assured." Libr J
Includes bibliographical references

599.67   Elephants

Alexander, Shana
The astonishing elephant. Random House 2000 300p il $25.95   **599.67**
1. Elephants
ISBN 0-679-45660-0   LC 99-50038
Writing about elephants, the author presents "a combination of historical facts, personal anecdotes and scientific studies. . . . Alexander devotes several chapters to scientists and veterinarians who have dedicated their lives to saving elephants from extinction. She also discusses the important role elephants play in Hinduism and Buddhism." N Y Times Book Rev
Includes bibliographical references

Ellis, Gerry
Wild orphans; photographs and text by Gerry Ellis. Welcome Enterprises 2002 135p $24.95   **599.67**
1. Elephants 2. Wildlife refuges
ISBN 0-941807-58-4   LC 2001-56779
"In this book, Ellis documents the story of eight baby elephants brought to the David Sheldrick Wildlife Trust in Kenya during the drought-plagued summer of 1999." Sci Am
"The care and concern pictured in Ellis' heartwarming photos must be seen to be believed. The intimate text explains the reasons for many of the techniques used when rearing baby elephants and is often as evocative as the photos." Booklist

Payne, Katharine, 1937-
Silent thunder; in the presence of elephants; [by] Katy Payne. Simon & Schuster 1998 288p il o.p.; Penguin Bks. paperback available $13.95   **599.67**
1. Elephants
ISBN 0-14-028596-2 (pa)   LC 98-4255
The author "describes her role in the discovery of infrasonic communication between elephants. As she does so, she recounts her 13 years' study of African elephants—observing their social and family structures and behaviors. . . . This book will make a wonderful addition to the library of any animal lover or of anyone fascinated by intra- and interspecies communication." Publ Wkly

Scigliano, Eric, 1953-
Love, war, and circuses; the age-old relationship between elephants and humans. Houghton Mifflin 2002 358p il $25   **599.67**
1. Elephants
ISBN 0-618-01583-3   LC 2002-22591
The author discusses human interaction with elephants and his travels in "Sri Lanka, Malaysia, Thailand, Burma (Myanmar), and India." Christ Sci Monit
This is an "eminently readable book." Booklist
Includes bibliographical references

599.75   Cat family

Adamson, Joy, 1910-1980
Born free; a lioness of two worlds. Pantheon Bks. 1987 220p il o.p.; Schocken Bks. paperback available $14.95   **599.75**
1. Lions 2. Kenya—Description
ISBN 0-375-71438-3 (pa)   LC 86-42972
A reissue of the title first published 1960

Adamson, Joy, 1910-1980—*Continued*

This is the "story of a lioness who bridged the gulf between two worlds, that of the jungle and of man. The author and her husband, a Kenya game warden, reared a cub to kill and fend for herself when she was returned to the jungle. At the same time they were able to preserve the bond of confidence and affection established with her as a pet." Cincinnati Public Libr

Caputo, Philip

Ghosts of Tsavo; stalking the mystery lions of East Africa. National Geographic Soc. 2002 275p il $27; pa $15   **599.75**

1. Lions 2. Tsavo National Park (Kenya)

ISBN 0-7922-6362-6; 0-7922-4100-2 (pa)

LC 2002-22642

This is a study of the Tsavo lions of Kenya. Philip Caputo discusses "why they are bigger than their counterparts of the Serengeti plains, why the males do not normally grow manes, and why Tsavo lions are more prone than Serengeti lions to make humans a part of their diet. The observable differences between Tsavo lions and Serengeti lions have led some behavioral scientists whom Mr. Caputo interviews to believe that the Tsavo lions are actually a different species." N Y Times (Late N Y Ed)

Kitchener, Andrew

The natural history of the wild cats. Comstock 1991 xxi, 280p il maps (Natural history of mammals series) hardcover o.p. paperback available $23.95   **599.75**

1. Wild cats

ISBN 0-8014-8498-7 (pa)   LC 90-45833

The author provides a "synthesis of what we know about cats, his account always strengthened by the comparative point of view. There are eight vivid chapters packed with graphs, maps and feline parameters. He includes a cat Who's Who in fine color photographs; it shows us most of the small cat species, plus three big cats that, unlike lions and tigers and leopards, are not in the public eye." Sci Am

Includes bibliographical references

Matthiessen, Peter

Tigers in the snow; introduction and photographs by Maurice Hornocker. Farrar, Straus & Giroux 1999 169p il o.p. paperback available $15   **599.75**

1. Tigers 2. Endangered species

ISBN 0-86547-596-2 (pa)   LC 99-44866

Matthiessen's book focuses on "the Siberian tiger. His account also touches on the fate of other tiger populations that once ranged from Eastern Turkey to the Sea of Japan." Nat Hist

"Mixing information about the lives of all the races of wild tigers with firsthand tales of his visits to Russia, the author brings an immediacy to his narrative that stirs the reader to awe of these great cats. . . . [An] evocative look at one of our rarest animals." Booklist

Includes bibliographical references

Thomas, Elizabeth Marshall, 1931-

The tribe of tiger; cats and their culture; illustrated by Jared Taylor Williams. Simon & Schuster 1994 240p il hardcover o.p. paperback available $13.95   **599.75**

1. Cats 2. Tigers 3. Lions

ISBN 0-7434-2689-4 (pa)   LC 94-20195

The author offers a "look into the lives of various members of the cat family—small and large, domestic and wild, Old World and New. She begins with the evolution and spread of different feline species, explaining the physiology and behavior of cats, including house cats, as meat eaters, that is, in the light of their hunting instincts. She then examines the changes over a period of more than 30 years in the culture . . . of different lion communities in several parts of Africa. In conclusion, she discusses the need for tiger conservation." Booklist

Includes bibliographical references

599.77   Dog family

Busch, Robert

The wolf almanac; [by] Robert H. Busch. Fully rev and updated. Lyons Press 1998 226p il maps pa $18.95   **599.77**

1. Wolves

ISBN 1-55821-557-3   LC 98-141297

First published 1995

This offers information about "the evolution and history of wolves; their biology and physiology; their behavior and sociology; and their influence in ancient cultures and mythology. . . . [The author also discusses] the conservation politics of all wolf species." Publisher's note

Includes bibliographical references

Lopez, Barry Holstun, 1945-

Of wolves and men. Scribner 1978 309p il hardcover o.p. paperback available $18

     599.77

1. Wolves

ISBN 0-684-16322-5 (pa)   LC 78-6070

"In succeeding chapters we see the wolf as an expert if cruel killer and as part of a highly organized, loving family and social group. Some myths about the animal are disproved, others are confirmed." Publ Wkly

"This is a history of ideas, written without prejudice, a successful contribution to the difficult study of the relationship between man and the world around him." Booklist

McNamee, Thomas, 1947-

The return of the wolf to Yellowstone. Holt & Co. 1997 354p il maps hardcover o.p. paperback available $15   **599.77**

1. Wolves 2. Endangered species 3. Yellowstone National Park

ISBN 0-8050-5792-7 (pa)   LC 96-39702

"An advocate for the reintroduction of the gray wolf to Yellowstone National Park, McNamee kept careful watch over the legal wrangling that accompanied this controversial endeavor, the challenges of its execution, and the complex questions it has raised, then recorded the entire story in this vivid day-by-day chronicle." Booklist

Includes bibliographical references

Mech, L. David

The way of the wolf; foreword by Robert Bateman; photography by Tom Brakefield [et al.] Voyageur Press 1991 120p il maps hardcover o.p. paperback available $19.95

599.77

1. Wolves
ISBN 0-89658-179-9 (pa)   LC 91-14415
This covers wolf behavior, biology, reproduction, communication and feeding habits and pleads for wolf conservation. Illustrated with color photographs
Includes bibliographical references

Mowat, Farley

Never cry wolf. Little, Brown 1963 247p o.p.; Back Bay Bks. paperback available $12.95   **599.77**

1. Wolves
ISBN 0-316-88179-1 (pa)
"An Atlantic Monthly Press book"
"A biologist for the Canadian government describes his experiences in the Arctic watching and tracking the activities of a wolf family." Publ Wkly

599.78 Bears

Busch, Robert

The grizzly almanac; [by] Robert H. Busch. Lyons Press 2000 229p il maps $29.95

599.78

1. Grizzly bear
ISBN 1-58574-143-4   LC 00-58587
The author "traces the evolution of the 'big bear' from its earliest days, describes its habitat and behavior, and recounts grizzly folklore and tales of grizzly attacks. Maintaining that the grizzly's reputation as a vicious killer is undeserved, he makes recommendations for a more peaceful coexistence with humans." Libr J
Includes bibliographical references

Craighead, Lance

Bears of the world. Voyageur Press 2000 132p il maps $29.95; pa $19.95   **599.78**

1. Bears
ISBN 0-89658-503-4; 0-89658-008-3 (pa)
          LC 00-31983
"Overview chapters look at the bears of the world in general, covering evolution, behavior, and conservation. . . . Good basic information is given on general biology, behavior, reproduction, and diet for each species, along with their relationships with humans. Clearly delineated range maps and capsule facts complete this nicely illustrated introduction to the world's bears." Booklist
Includes bibliographical references

Mangelsen, Thomas D.

Polar dance; born of the north wind; photographs by Thomas D. Mangelsen; story by Fred Bruemmer; design by Lee Carlman Riddell; text edited by Cara Blessley. Images of Nature 1997 264p il $65   **599.78**

1. Polar bear 2. Arctic regions
ISBN 1-890310-03-4   LC 97-71666
A pictorial documentary of the lives of polar bears focusing on a female bear and her two cubs through four seasons

The "evocative photos of white bears covered in snow, lying spread-eagled on pack ice, or swimming among ice floes give the reader a sense of this harsh habitat. Bruemmer's text is a factual account of arctic ecology and the niche the polar bear fills in this surprisingly rich ecosystem." Booklist

Montgomery, Sy

Search for the golden moon bear; science and adventure in Southeast Asia. Simon & Schuster 2002 324p il maps $26   **599.78**

1. Bears
ISBN 0-7432-0584-7
Subtitle on jacket: Science and adventure in pursuit of a new species
The author describes her travels "in Southeast Asia along with evolutionary biologist Gary Galbreath, as they search for the mysterious golden moon bear and confront the horrors of the illegal wildlife trade." Booklist
"Montgomery vividly recounts her sometimes humorous, sometimes horrifying experiences with a reporter's keen eye, a conservationist's outrage and a poet's lyricism." Publ Wkly

Schooler, Lynn

The blue bear; a true story of friendship, tragedy, and survival in the Alaskan wilderness. Ecco Press 2002 272p il $25.95; pa $13.95   **599.78**

1. Bears 2. Alaska—Description
ISBN 0-06-621085-2; 0-06-093573-1 (pa)
          LC 2001-51079
The author describes his experiences as a wilderness guide in Alaska. "The story centers on the renowned nature photographer Michio Hoshino, a client who became a friend, and the two men's ongoing search for the elusive glacier bear, a blue variant of the North American black bear. . . . [Schooler's] writing reveals an abundance of wilderness savvy, and a mind scrupulous about getting the world down as accurately as possible." New Yorker

Treadwell, Timothy

Among grizzlies; living with wild bears in Alaska; [by] Timothy Treadwell and Jewel Palovak. HarperCollins Pubs. 1997 199p il o.p.; Ballantine Bks. paperback available $14

599.78

1. Grizzly bear
ISBN 0-345-42605-3 (pa)   LC 96-53501
"This firsthand account of living among grizzly bears in a place Treadwell calls the Grizzly Sanctuary, just south of the Arctic Circle, reveals intimate details of the summer lives of these great bears. Fleeing a life of drug and alcohol addiction, Treadwell made an initial foray to Alaska. . . . He returned to Alaska in subsequent summers to live among the bears and observe them close at hand. . . . Full of anecdotal stories about the details of the daily routine of grizzly life, this story of salvation through grizzly bears will help engender concern for their future in the wild." Booklist
Includes bibliographical references

599.8   Primates

Fossey, Dian

Gorillas in the mist. Houghton Mifflin 1983
326p il hardcover o.p. paperback available
$14   **599.8**
1. Gorillas
ISBN 0-618-08360-X (pa)   LC 82-23332
This book "recounts some of the events of the thirteen
years that I have spent with the mountain gorillas in their
natural habitat and includes data from the fifteen years
of continuing field study." Preface
Includes bibliographical references

Galdikas, Biruté

Orangutan odyssey; [by] Biruté M.F.
Galdikas and Nancy Briggs; photographs by
Karl Ammann; introduction by Jane Goodall.
Abrams 1999 144p il map $39.95   **599.8**
1. Orangutan
ISBN 0-8109-3694-1   LC 99-25446
This is "a photographic essay on the current plight of
orangutans, with a particular emphasis on environmental
degradation in Borneo, especially in recent years when
logging, forest fires, and gold mining have destroyed
much of the habitat these animals need for survival."
Libr J
"Memorable, informal and attractive." Publ Wkly

Reflections of Eden; my years with the
orangutans of Borneo; [by] Biruté M.F.
Galdikas. Little, Brown 1995 408p il maps
hardcover o.p. paperback available $19.99
      599.8
1. Orangutan 2. Borneo—Description
ISBN 0-316-30186-8 (pa)   LC 94-22948
The author discusses her life in Borneo and her research into the lives of the orangutans of Borneo's rain
forest
"Highly recommended for all libraries, this book will
inspire young scientists and enthrall anyone interested in
orangutans and the rigors of modern field research." Libr
J

Goodall, Jane, 1934-

In the shadow of man; photographs by
Hugo van Lawick. rev ed. Houghton Mifflin
1988 297p il map pa $15   **599.8**
1. Chimpanzees
ISBN 0-618-05679-9   LC 87-36965
First published 1971
The author describes the chimpanzee group she stud-
ied during ten years of field observation in the Gombe
Stream Chimpanzee Reserve in Tanzania
Includes bibliographical references

Through a window; my thirty years with
the chimpanzees of Gombe. Houghton Mifflin
1990 268p il map hardcover o.p. paperback
available $14   **599.8**
1. Chimpanzees
ISBN 0-618-05677-7 (pa)   LC 90-36974
This continuation of In the shadow of man "tells two
stories: first of how the chimps of Gombe in Tanzania
have grown, changed and died, and second, how Goodall
and her dedicated group of Tanzanian observers have
survived the rigours of the past thirty years. It is beautifully written, and evokes both sympathy and understanding of these animals." Times Lit Suppl

Sapolsky, Robert M.

A primate's memoir. Scribner 2001 304p
$25; pa $14   **599.8**
1. Baboons
ISBN 0-7432-0247-3; 0-7432-0241-4 (pa)
      LC 00-63522
This is an account of the author's experiences observing baboons in Kenya
"One closes Sapolsky's book a lot more knowledgeable about plenty of baboon-related matters. But mostly
one has already begun to miss the company of this
sometimes cranky but always impassioned, learned and
winningly irreverent man." N Y Times Book Rev

Waal, Frans de, 1948-

Bonobo; the forgotten ape; photographs,
Frans Lanting. University of Calif. Press 1997
210p il maps $50; pa $29.95   **599.8**
1. Apes
ISBN 0-520-20535-9; 0-520-21651-2 (pa)
      LC 96-41095
The subject of this monograph is the bonobo, a species of ape. "In six chapters, de Waal describes the history of the discovery of bonobos as a separate species;
he compares them with common chimps; he describes
their natural habitat and their . . . use of sex as social
currency, particularly in moderating aggression; he examines bonobo social structure in relation to that of common chimps and humans; and he finishes with an exploration of bonobos' highly developed sense of empathy."
New Sci
Includes bibliographical references

599.9   Hominids. Humans

Olson, Steve, 1956-

Mapping human history; discovering the
past through our genes. Houghton Mifflin
2002 292p il $25; pa $14   **599.9**
1. Human beings 2. Physical anthropology
ISBN 0-618-09157-2; 0-618-35210-4 (pa)
      LC 2001-51880
The author "traces the history of human civilization in
five regions of the world—Africa, the Middle East, Asia,
Australia, and Europe and the Americas, plus a final
chapter on Hawaii—to explain how physical differences
originated and to provide evidence of our essential same-
ness." Publ Wkly
Includes bibliographical references

Richardson, John H., 1954-

In the little world; a true story of dwarfs,
love, and trouble. HarperCollins Pubs. 2001
257p il hardcover o.p. paperback available
$13.95   **599.9**
1. Dwarfism
ISBN 0-06-093131-0 (pa)   LC 2001-16838
"What began as a feature article for *Esquire* in February 1998, in which contributing editor Richardson introduces several people, tall and small, looking for love and
miracles at the annual Little People of America convention, has culminated in this full-blown narrative. Here
Richardson explores the intimate stories and relationships
he cultivated with the individuals initially profiled." Libr
J
"Because of its naked honesty, *In the Little World* is
both phenomenal and unique." Booklist

599.93 Genetics, sex and age characteristics, evolution

The **Cambridge** encyclopedia of human evolution; edited by Steve Jones, Robert Martin and David Pilbeam; executive editor, Sarah Bunney; foreword by Richard Dawkins. Cambridge Univ. Press 1993 506p il maps $120; pa $42   **599.93**
1. Human origins 2. Evolution
ISBN 0-521-32370-3; 0-521-46786-1 (pa)
LC 92-18037
"This encyclopedia of the human species places modern man in evolutionary perspective, showing the descent of humankind from Mitochondrial Eve and its relationship to other living primates. Genetics, fossils, biology, brain function, disease, the biology, evolution, and ecology of humans and other modern primates are the major themes arranged topically in this encyclopedia. Excellent black-and-white photos, drawings, tables, and maps complement a work with over 70 contributors." Am Libr

Davies, Kevin, 1960-
Cracking the genome; inside the race to unlock human DNA. Free Press 2001 310p $25   **599.93**
1. Human Genome Project 2. Genomes
ISBN 0-7432-0479-4   LC 00-48430
Also available in paperback from Johns Hopkins Univ. Press
This describes the Human Genome Project, highlighting the competition between J. Craig Venter and federal scientist Francis Collins
Davies "does an impressive job of contextualizing the science within a political, economic and social framework, creating a lively tale as accessible to nonspecialists as it is to scientists." Publ Wkly
Includes bibliographical references

Dennis, Carina
The human genome; edited by Carina Dennis and Richard Gallagher; foreword by James D. Watson. Nature/Palgrave 2001 140p il $32   **599.93**
1. Human Genome Project 2. Genomes 3. Gene mapping
ISBN 0-333-97143-4   LC 2001-133051
This "volume [covering] the history of the Human Genome Project . . . contains [an] . . . introduction; a timeline of significant events, including a few political cartoons; . . . color photographs and graphics [and] a depiction of the actual human genetic map." Sci Books Films
Includes glossary and bibliographical references

Diamond, Jared M.
The third chimpanzee; the evolution and future of the human animal; [by] Jared Diamond. HarperCollins Pubs. 1992 407p il maps hardcover o.p. paperback available $15   **599.93**
1. Human origins 2. Evolution
ISBN 0-06-098403-1 (pa)   LC 91-50455
First published 1991 in the United Kingdom with title: The rise and fall of the third chimpanzee
The author "argues that the human being is just a third species of chimpanzee but nevertheless a unique animal essentially due to its capacity for innovation, which caused a great leap forward in hominoid evolution. After stressing the significance of spoken language, along with art and technology, Diamond focuses on the self-destructive propensities of our species." Libr J
Includes bibliographical references

The **Double-edged** helix; social implications of genetics in a diverse society; edited by Joseph S. Alper [et al.] Johns Hopkins Univ. Press 2002 293p $49.95; pa $26.95   **599.93**
1. Genetic engineering 2. Bioethics 3. Genetics 4. Medical genetics
ISBN 0-8018-6964-1; 0-8018-7926-4 (pa)
LC 2001-6618
This "explores the impact of recent genetic discoveries on both different population segments and society as a whole. The authors address the medical and ethical implications of the new technologies, outlining potential positive and negative effects of genetic research on minorities, individuals with disabilities, and those of diverse sexual orientations. . . . This book emphasizes the need to ensure that research into genetics research does not result in discrimination against people on the basis of their DNA." Publisher's note
"Bringing the concerns of different communities together in a single volume makes it possible to appreciate the mosaic of human issues fully and forces us to anticipate the challenges that may arise—and that will require our attention—as the genetic revolution proceeds. . . . A much needed antidote to the current genetic hoopla." JAMA
Includes bibliographical references

Dunbar, R. I. M. (Robin Ian MacDonald), 1947-
Grooming, gossip, and the evolution of language; [by] Robin Dunbar. Harvard Univ. Press 1996 230p $25; pa $17.95   **599.93**
1. Human origins 2. Language and languages 3. Gossip 4. Human behavior
ISBN 0-674-36334-5; 0-674-36336-1 (pa)
LC 96-15934
"Dunbar, a psychologist, thinks that gossip has the same social function in humans as does grooming in other primates and that language evolved to enable humans to chat about their friends and families." Libr J
"Concisely and clearly written for lay readers, Dunbar exhibits a gift for argument and explanation." Publ Wkly
Includes bibliographical references

The **Genomic** revolution; unveiling the unity of life; Michael Yudell and Robert DeSalle, editors. Joseph Henry Press 2002 $27.95   **599.93**
1. Human Genome Project 2. Genomes
ISBN 0-309-07436-3   LC 2002-4016
Published with the American Museum of Natural History
This book looks at genomics "from the basic presentation of ideas about heredity through the essential principles of molecular biology, including an exploration of the ethical implications of the genome project for individuals and society." Publisher's note
"...some of the best and most current thought in genomics. . . . The essays are well written and accessible to almost anyone interested in the areas represented. . . . All in all, a unique snapshot of a pivotal period in sci-

The Genomic revolution—*Continued*
ence and a valuable addition to most libraries. Summing up: Highly recommended." Choice
Includes bibliographical references

Johanson, Donald C.
From Lucy to language; [by] Donald Johanson & Blake Edgar; principal photography, David Brill. Simon & Schuster 1996 272p il map $60   **599.93**
1. Human origins 2. Fossil hominids
ISBN 0-684-81023-9   LC 96-31576
"A Peter N. Nevraumont book"
"The focus of this album is the hundreds of photographs of the small inventory of hominid fossils from which evolutionary history is inferred. . . . After he has stated the principal issues being pursued in paleoanthropology, Johanson, [who discovered the 'Lucy' fossil], displays in sidebar style features about individual fossils: who found them, where, and how they fit into the evolutionary scheme." Booklist
"No serious student of paleoanthropology can afford to miss this magnificent, encyclopedic survey of human origins." Publ Wkly
Includes bibliographical references

Lucy: the beginnings of humankind; [by] Donald C. Johanson and Maitland A. Edey. Simon & Schuster 1981 409p il hardcover o.p. paperback available $15   **599.93**
1. Human origins 2. Fossil mammals
ISBN 0-671-72499-1 (pa)   LC 80-21759
In November 1974 at a place called Hadar in Ethiopia Donald Johanson "discovered the partial skeleton of an extremely primitive female, erect-walking primate or hominid. . . . The skeleton received the name 'Lucy.' Much later, Lucy received the scientific name, Australopithecus afarensis, and it was determined she was some 3.5 million years old. . . . This book is Johanson's own story of the events leading up to and subsequent to Lucy's discovery." Best Sellers
Includes bibliographical references

Jolly, Alison
Lucy's legacy; sex and intelligence in human evolution. Harvard Univ. Press 1999 518p il $31.50; pa $18.95   **599.93**
1. Evolution 2. Intellect
ISBN 0-674-00069-2; 0-674-00540-6 (pa)
    LC 99-32252
"Lucy is the name given to the fossil skeleton of an Australopithecine, a human ancestor, discovered in Ethiopia. The name may be a misnomer, since there's no way yet of telling whether Lucy was female. No matter. Primatologist Jolly's interest is not so much in Lucy as in the crucial role that females in general have played in human evolution. . . . In clear and clever prose, Jolly shows us how we got so smart, what sex had to do with it, and how our brains have become the central force in evolution." Booklist
Includes bibliographical references

Klein, Richard G.
The dawn of human culture; [by] Richard G. Klein with Blake Edgar. Wiley 2002 288p il maps $27.95   **599.93**
1. Human origins 2. Culture
ISBN 0-471-25252-2   LC 2002-277680
"A Peter N. Nevraumont book"

This book "traces the origin of modern humans from their five-million-year-old roots in East Africa up through the replacement of Neanderthals in Europe some 40,000 years ago. . . . The clarity and information conveyed by the illustrations are superb, adding substantially to the book's value as a reference guide. The index is excellent. The book will appeal to all readers interested in human evolution, regardless of how much paleoanthropological background they have, and will serve admirably for courses on human evolution at any level." Choice
Includes bibliographical references

Leakey, Richard E., 1944-
The origin of humankind; [by] Richard Leakey. Basic Bks. 1994 171p il maps (Science masters series) hardcover o.p. paperback available $14.95   **599.93**
1. Human origins
ISBN 0-465-05313-0 (pa)   LC 94-3617
"Leakey summarizes the evolution of theories, from Darwin's to his own, in the process demonstrating the scientific method in action. . . . Covering the taxonomy of skeletons and craniums, shapes of tools, and the first sprouts of art and culture, Leakey knowledgeably points the enthralled neophyte to the wide avenues of future discoveries." Booklist
This "is a worthwhile addition to many kinds of libraries—public, general, science, biological, and psychological." Sci Books Films
Includes bibliographical references

Origins reconsidered; in search of what makes us human; [by] Richard Leakey and Roger Lewin. Doubleday 1992 375p il hardcover o.p. paperback available $16.95
    599.93
1. Human origins
ISBN 0-385-46792-3 (pa)   LC 92-6661
"Leakey and Lewin discuss how conceptions of human anatomical and behavioral development have been radically altered within the last 12 years by new discoveries and research in other fields. They review the developments and assert Leakey's own hypotheses based on these discoveries. . . . This is an engrossing book written for the layperson, fully explaining anthropological terms and theories when necessary. It's a solid introduction to current theory concerning human development." SLJ

Marks, Jonathan
What it means to be 98% chimpanzee; apes, people, and their genes. University of Calif. Press 2002 312p $27.50   **599.93**
1. Human beings 2. Genetics 3. Evolution
ISBN 0-520-22615-1   LC 2001-7085
Contents: Introduction; Molecular anthropology; The ape in you; How people differ from one another; The meaning of human variation; Behavioral genetics; Folk heredity; Human nature; Human rights ... for apes?; A human gene museum; Identity and descent; Is blood really so damn thick?
"With plenty of entertaining sarcasm as well as scientific argument and moral indignation, Marks blasts the pretensions of grandiose geneticists pretty thoroughly out of the water. This may be *the* science book to read this year." Booklist
Includes bibliographical references

Ridley, Matt

Genome; the autobiography of a species in 23 chapters. HarperCollins Pubs. 2000 344p hardcover o.p. paperback available $14

599.93

1. Genomes 2. Genetics
ISBN 0-06-093290-2 (pa)   LC 99-40933

Ridley presents a "summation of our ever increasing understanding of the roles that genes play in disease, behavior, sexual differences, and even intelligence. More important, though, he addresses not only the ethical quandaries faced by contemporary scientists but the reductionist danger in equating inheritability with inevitability." New Yorker

Includes bibliographical references

Rothman, Barbara Katz

Genetic maps and human imaginations; the limits of science in understanding who we are. Norton 1998 272p $24.95   **599.93**

1. Genetics 2. Genomes 3. Human beings
ISBN 0-393-04703-2   LC 98-18800

A discussion of "the bioethics and consequences of mapping the human genome. . . . Rothman has concentrated on how 'genetic thinking' affects the way we see race, illness and cancer, and reproduction. Scientists may not like a couple of phrases Rothman has coined . . . but most other readers will probably find that the terms make sense as they read." Libr J

Includes bibliographical references

Schwartz, Jeffrey H.

What the bones tell us. Holt & Co. 1993 292p o.p.; University of Ariz. Press paperback available $18.95   **599.93**

1. Physical anthropology
ISBN 0-8165-1855-6 (pa)   LC 92-12473

"A John Macrae book"

This volume discusses "the nature and limits of osteology and paleontology and the scientific knowledge the two sciences provide. Part one describes the kinds of fossils and artifacts archaeologists find. [Part two addresses] . . . the places of Darwin, Huxley, and Raymond Dart in human evolutionary theory." Booklist

Stringer, Christopher B.

African exodus; the origins of modern humanity; [by] Christopher Stringer and Robin McKie. Holt & Co. 1997 xx, 282p il maps hardcover o.p. paperback available $17

599.93

1. Human origins
ISBN 0-8050-5814-1 (pa)   LC 96-37718

First published 1996 in the United Kingdom

The authors "argue for a single-origin theory for the recent emergence and essential unity of our species. The authors maintain that the *erectus-sapiens* transition happened only once, with *Homo sapiens sapiens* migrating out of Africa about 100,000 years ago and subsequently spreading worldwide." Libr J

"This intellectually potent yet eminently accessible volume . . . stands tall. It provides broad insight into a complex field." Publ Wkly

Includes bibliographical references

Swisher, Carl C.

Java man; how two geologists' dramatic discoveries changed our understanding of the evolutionary path to modern humans; [by] Carl Swisher, Garniss H. Curtis, Roger Lewin. Scribner 2000 256p il map $27.50

599.93

1. Fossil hominids 2. Human origins
ISBN 0-684-80000-4   LC 00-61187

Also available in paperback from University of Chicago Press

"In the early 1990s, geologists Garniss H. Curtis and Carl C. Swisher III . . . used radiometric rock dating to pin more accurate dates on some Asian 'missing-link' fossils and prove that our close evolutionary relative *Homo erectus* coexisted with *Homo sapiens* and was probably not a precursor after all." Libr J

The authors "offer a lively write-up of the technicalities of geochronology, bio-sketches of the discoverers of the *erectus* fossils, travelogues of their travel in Java, and their side of a spat with paleoanthropology celebrity Don Johansen. An engrossing contribution to the general-interest literature about human origins." Booklist

Includes bibliographical references

Sykes, Bryan

The seven daughters of Eve. Norton 2001 306p il map hardcover o.p. paperback available $15.95   **599.93**

1. Genetics 2. Human origins
ISBN 0-393-32314-5 (pa)

The author "contends that most Europeans can trace their roots back to seven women—seven daughters of Eve. One of them lived about 10,000 years ago, around the time farmers first cultivated European soil; the six others go back much farther, to Europe's early hunter-gatherers." N Y Times Book Rev

Tattersall, Ian

Extinct humans; by Ian Tattersall and Jeffrey H. Schwartz. Westview Press 2000 256p il hardcover o.p. paperback available $35   **599.93**

1. Human origins 2. Fossil hominids 3. Evolution
ISBN 0-8133-3918-9 (pa)   LC 00-22088

The authors explain "why the idea of the one-track, lineal descent of human beings is obsolete and the notion of a 'bushy' evolutionary history, like that of other genera, fits the fossil evidence better." Booklist

Includes bibliographical references

The fossil trail; how we know what we think we know about human evolution. Oxford Univ. Press 1995 276p il maps $35; pa $17.95   **599.93**

1. Evolution 2. Human origins 3. Fossils
ISBN 0-19-506101-2; 0-19-510981-3 (pa)

LC 94-31633

"As much concerned with the dialectic of scientific advancement as with the specific, though fragmentary, fossil evidence, Tattersall courses through the interpretations of excavated discoveries since the days of Darwin." Booklist

"The task of organising such complex material into a narrative account would have defeated most writers, but Tattersall has mastered it with remarkable skill." New Sci

Includes bibliographical references

Tattersall, Ian—*Continued*

The monkey in the mirror; essays on science and what makes us human. Harcourt 2002 203p hardcover o.p. paperback available $13   **599.93**

1. Evolution 2. Human origins
ISBN 0-15-602706-2 (pa)   LC 2001-24122

The author "explores the current understanding of organic evolution in terms of science and reason." Libr J

"A perceptive and persuasive introduction to human origins." Booklist

Tudge, Colin

The time before history; 5 million years of human impact. Scribner 1996 366p il maps hardcover o.p. paperback available $16

599.93

1. Human origins 2. Evolution 3. Mammals
ISBN 0-684-83052-3 (pa)   LC 95-42026

Tudge "begins by putting time into perspective so that we can understand how vast is our past; he helps us see that all evolution is part of a bigger whole—an unfolding process affected by shifting continents, climatic changes, and our own impact on the planet and its ecosystems. . . . He defines our origins in a biological, as well as historical context and applies the lessons that we should learn from our mistakes as well as our achievements to provide a blueprint for the future." Libr J

"With majestic sweep and subtle wit, . . . Tudge brings an astonishing perspective to the story of humanity." Publ Wkly

Includes bibliographical references

Walker, Alan

The wisdom of the bones; in search of human origins; [by] Alan Walker and Pat Shipman. Knopf 1996 338p il maps hardcover o.p. paperback available $14

599.93

1. Human origins 2. Evolution 3. Fossil hominids
ISBN 0-679-74783-4 (pa)   LC 95-37525

"In 1984 Walker, along with colleague Richard Leakey and their 'hominidgang' of experienced Kenyan excavators, discovered a near-intact fossil of *Homo erectus*. The find was a veritable trove of theory-busting information, which the authors take up after recounting the scientists who preceded Walker in investigating the species. . . . A fluidly presented portrait of the people and process of paleoanthropology." Booklist

Includes bibliographical references

Wickelgren, Ingrid

The gene masters; how a new breed of scientific entrepreneurs raced for the biggest prize in biology. Holt & Co. 2002 291p il $26   **599.93**

1. Human Genome Project 2. Gene mapping 3. Genomes 4. Genetic engineering
ISBN 0-8050-7174-1   LC 2002-67321

A look at the Human Genome Project and the scientists who competed with each other in a race to map the human genome, including Craig Venter, Francis Collins, and Kari Stefannson

This book "sharply highlight[s] the fundamental tensions and interdependencies between both academic and industrial research and international competition and collaboration, and . . . [it] also show[s] the extent to which the biopharmaceutical industry is both science-and profit-

driven. . . . Recommended for almost any library, particularly those with readers willing to go beyond sound bites and media hype." Libr J

Includes bibliographical references

599.97   Human races

Wolpoff, Milford H., 1942-

Race and human evolution; [by] Milford Wolpoff and Rachel Caspari. Simon & Schuster 1997 462p il maps $26   **599.97**

1. Human origins 2. Fossil hominids 3. Race
ISBN 0-684-81013-1   LC 96-33466

Also available in paperback from Westview Press

The authors present an "intellectual history behind two primary, diametrically opposed hypotheses: the Eve theory, which states that all races have a single origin, and the multiregional hypothesis, which posits 'multiple origins, different and separate developments, and fundamental and essential racial differences.' The authors support the second theory but present both viewpoints with equal attention in their invaluable, even dramatic chronicle of more than two centuries of evolutionary science." Booklist

Includes bibliographical references

600   TECHNOLOGY (APPLIED SCIENCES)

Brain, Marshall

Marshall Brain's more how stuff works; [by] Marshall Brain and the staff at HowStuffWorks.com. Wiley 2003 309p il $24.99   **600**

1. Technology 2. Inventions
ISBN 0-7645-6711-X   LC 2003-268792

Also available Marshall Brain's how stuff works (2001)

The author "travels inside your computer, to the depths of diamond mines, across the African plains, and on board an Apache helicopter to explain the magic behind how stuff works." Publisher's note

Macaulay, David, 1946-

The new way things work; [by] David Macaulay with Neil Ardley. Houghton Mifflin 1998 400p il $35   **600**

1. Technology 2. Machinery 3. Inventions
ISBN 0-395-93847-3   LC 98-14224

First published 1988 with title: The way things work

Arranged in five sections this volume provides information on "the workings of hundreds of machines and devices—holograms, helicopters, airplanes, mobile phones, compact disks, hard disks, bits and bytes, cash machines. . . . Explanations [are also given] of the scientific principles behind each machine—how gears make work easier, why jumbo jets are able to fly, how computers actually compute." Publisher's note

609 Technology—Historical and geographic treatment

Brown, David E.

Inventing modern America; from the microwave to the mouse; text by David E. Brown; foreword by Lester C. Thurow; introductions by James Burke. MIT Press 2001 c2002 209p il $32.95; pa $19.95 **609**

1. Inventions 2. Inventors

ISBN 0-262-02508-6; 0-262-52349-3 (pa)

LC 2001-44768

"A publication of the Lemelson-MIT program for invention and innovation"

This "profiles thirty-five inventors . . . [including] such well-known figures as George Washington Carver, Henry Ford, and Steve Wozniak, as well as . . . Stephanie Kwolek, inventor of Kevlar, and Wilson Greatbatch, inventor of the first implantable cardiac pacemaker." Publisher's note

"Brown simplifies technical data and uses an enthusiastic, almost proselytizing tone. . . . Full color photographs, diagrams and intriguing tidbits . . . make this a good book for most to browse." Publ Wkly

Includes bibliographical references

Bruno, Leonard C.

Science & technology firsts; Daniel J. Boorstin, guest foreword; Donna Olendorf, editor. Gale Res. 1997 636p il $90 **609**

1. Technology—History 2. Science—History

ISBN 0-7876-0256-6 LC 96-43595

"Chapters on agriculture, astronomy, biology, chemistry, communications, computers, Earth science, energy, mathematics, medicine, physics, and transportation give quick snapshots of verifiable first occurrences. The more than 4000 entries range from ancient times to 1996 and contain 20 to 80 words." SLJ

Includes bibliographical references

Burke, James, 1936-

Circles: 50 round trips through history, technology, science, culture. Simon & Schuster 2000 286p $24; pa $13 **609**

1. Technology—History 2. Science—History

ISBN 0-7432-0008-X; 0-7432-4976-3 (pa)

LC 00-57335

"The 50 essays collected here, which concern the history of technology, first appeared in Burke's *Scientific American* column between 1995 and 1999." Libr J

"Readers will be fascinated by Burke's route through the labyrinthine corridors of history. This book is ideal for dipping into, a few essays at a time." Publ Wkly

Includes bibliographical references

The knowledge web; from electronic agents to Stonehenge and back—and other journeys through knowledge. Simon & Schuster 1999 285p il $25; pa $14 **609**

1. Technology—History

ISBN 0-684-85934-3; 0-684-85935-1 (pa)

LC 99-24539

This work "is Burke's effort to replicate, in linear form, the sort of 'webbed' knowledge available to Internet surfers. Its 20 chapters trace often serendipitous developments of particular products or scientific discoveries." Booklist

Burke's "style matches his subject as he skips from one topic to another, moving at the speed of hypertext. . . . This manic, associative tour of the cultural underpinnings of technological advancement is fast, sexy and packed with information." Publ Wkly

Includes bibliographical references

Flatow, Ira

They all laughed; from lightbulbs to lasers, the fascinating stories behind the great inventions that have changed our lives. HarperCollins Pubs. 1992 238p il hardcover o.p. paperback available $13 **609**

1. Inventions

ISBN 0-06-092415-2 (pa) LC 91-58336

The author has put together an "overview of how some of our more interesting scientific discoveries and inventions have come to be. From teflon to lasers, from xerography to velcro, the author humorously describes the often serendipitous events leading to the particular breakthrough. The treatment is enthusiastic and lighthearted and not organized in any thematic or chronological fashion. It's a quick read and informative." Libr J

Includes bibliographical references

Karwatka, Dennis

Technology's past. Prakken Publs. 1996-1999 2v il pa ea $29.95 **609**

1. Inventions—History 2. Inventors 3. Technology—History LC 95-72938

Contents: [v1] America's industrial revolution and the people who delivered the goods (ISBN 0-911168-91-5); v2 More heroes of invention and innovation (ISBN 0-911168-96-6)

"This volume profiles 76 Americans who influenced technology in the United States from the Industrial Revolution through the beginning years of World War II. . . . Biographies are three pages long and are arranged chronologically by the birth date of the inventor. . . . The final section of the book covers four areas of technology: computers, television, manned space flight, robotics." Book Rep [review of 1996 volume]

"This is a readable, well-documented selection." SLJ [review of 1996 volume]

Includes bibliographical references

Lindsay, David, 1957-

House of invention; the secret life of everyday products. Lyons Press 1999 179p il hardcover o.p. paperback available $9.95 **609**

1. Inventions

ISBN 1-58574-625-8 (pa) LC 99-53253

"Lindsay not only recounts the improbable origins of many most-used gadgets but also expounds on the occasionally wacky, always interesting individuals who came up with inventions so marvelous that they became ubiquitous." Booklist

Macdonald, Anne L., 1920-

Feminine ingenuity; women and invention in America; [by] Anne Macdonald. Ballantine Bks. 1992 xxiv, 514p il hardcover o.p. paperback available $25 **609**

1. Women inventors 2. Inventions

ISBN 0-345-38314-1 (pa) LC 91-55502

This is a "study of American women's contribution to science, engineering, and technology as represented in

Macdonald, Anne L., 1920-—*Continued*

the issuance of U.S. patents. From the first patent issued to a woman in 1809, Macdonald traces the uphill struggle women have faced in their efforts to obtain equal rights—in the area of patent awards as well as in the broader educational, economic, and social arenas." Libr J

Includes bibliographical references

Petroski, Henry

The evolution of useful things. Knopf 1992 288p il hardcover o.p. paperback available $13.95   **609**

1. Inventions 2. Patents

ISBN 0-679-74039-2 (pa)   LC 91-39524

The author "provides an intricate look, in lay reader's terms, at the technology and basic rationale behind a number of items we often take for granted. The list is comprehensive: kitchen utensils, zippers, tools, paper clips, fast-food packaging, and more. The text is far from a recital of mere facts. Petroski's anecdotes and stories about individual designers and inventors are told with warm regard. He also provides illuminating thoughts on the theoretical, historical, and cultural frameworks that influenced these creations." Libr J

Includes bibliographical references

Technology & American history; a historical anthology from Technology & culture; edited by Stephen H. Cutcliffe and Terry S. Reynolds. University of Chicago Press 1997 448p il maps $37.50; pa $18.95 **609**

1. Technology—History

ISBN 0-226-71027-0; 0-226-71028-9 (pa)

     LC 97-5925

This is a collection of 15 articles reprinted from Technology and Culture magazine from 1963 to 1996, which trace the impact of technology throughout the history of the United States

Includes bibliographical references

Van Dulken, Stephen, 1952-

Inventing the 19th century; 100 inventions that shaped the Victorian Age from aspirin to the Zeppelin. New York Univ. Press 2001 218p il $30   **609**

1. Inventions

ISBN 0-8147-8810-6   LC 2001-30831

This briefly describes the inventions of the 19th century with text and diagrams from the patent applications

Includes bibliographical references

Inventing the 20th century; 100 inventions that shaped the world: from the airplane to the zipper; [by] Stephen Van Dulken; with an introduction by Andrew Phillips. New York Univ. Press 2000 246p il $30; pa $17.95

    609

1. Inventions

ISBN 0-8147-8808-4; 0-8147-8812-2 (pa)

     LC 00-41141

This briefly describes inventions of the 20th century, arranged by decade, with text and diagrams from the patent applications

"A fascinating compendium for trivia seekers." Publ Wkly

Includes bibliographical references

Williams, Trevor Illtyd

A history of invention; from stone axes to silicon chips; [by] Trevor I. Williams. updated & rev ed, by William E. Schaaf, Jr. with Adrianne E. Burnette. Checkmark Bks. 2000 367p il $45   **609**

1. Technology—History 2. Inventions—History

ISBN 0-8160-4072-9   LC 99-57476

First published 1987

"The authors organize the material in broad themes, including agriculture; buildings and architecture; transportation and communication; machinery, power, and mechanization; the technologies of war; and several others. . . . The material is presented in an objective and evenhanded style, properly in the context of the political, social, and economic conditions of each age." Sci Books Films

610   Medical sciences. Medicine

Groopman, Jerome E.

Second opinions; stories of intuition and choice in a changing world of medicine; [by] Jerome Groopman. Viking 2000 243p hardcover o.p. paperback available $14 **610**

1. Medicine 2. Diagnosis

ISBN 0-14-029862-2 (pa)   LC 99-36692

Groopman "focuses on medical decision-making; in eight dramatic case studies, he reveals the importance of honoring intuition in the evaluation and treatment of illness." Libr J

"Through vivid accounts of the dilemmas he has faced—not only as a doctor but as a patient, a parent, a grandson and a friend—the author illuminates the art, and the perils, of interpreting other people's symptoms." Newsweek

The **Harvard** Medical School family health guide; edited by Anthony L. Komaroff. Simon & Schuster 1999 1288p il $40 **610**

1. Medicine 2. Health

ISBN 0-684-84703-5   LC 99-27223

"Divided into ten parts, the text begins with a discussion on how to navigate current healthcare systems; the major areas then covered include health maintenance, how diseases are diagnosed, symptom management illustrated by numerous decision trees, and diseases and disorders." Libr J

Lown, Bernard

The lost art of healing. Houghton Mifflin 1996 332p o.p.; Ballantine Bks. paperback available $14.95   **610**

1. Holistic medicine 2. Physicians 3. Sick

ISBN 0-345-42597-9 (pa)   LC 96-18184

"Cardiologist Lown combines autobiography with a plea for thoughtful and individual medical care of each patient. . . . Healing, he asserts, has been replaced in his time by treating, caring by managing, and the art of listening by technological procedures." Booklist

The author's "stimulating inquiry is sound medicine for doctors and patients alike." Publ Wkly

Includes bibliographical references

Pollack, Robert, 1940-

The missing moment; how the unconscious shapes modern science. Houghton Mifflin 1999 240p $25 **610**

1. Medicine—Philosophy 2. Psychology
ISBN 0-395-70985-7   LC 99-26241

"The collective myth of science and of biomedicine, in Pollack's diagnosis, involves misplaced beliefs in the omnipotence of rational thought, absolute control over nature and triumph over death. With eloquence and wit, he contends that biomedicine's heroic goals of beating infectious microbes into total submission, of eradicating cancer and of dramatically extended life expectancy should give way to emphasis on disease prevention and methods to slow the aging process." Publ Wkly

610.3 Medical sciences— Encyclopedias and dictionaries

American Medical Association complete medical encyclopedia; medical editors, Jerrold B. Leikin, Martin S. Lipsky. Crown 2003 1408p il $45 **610.3**

1. Medicine—Encyclopedias
ISBN 0-8129-9100-1   LC 2002-67340

This "medical compendium contains over 5000 alphabetically arranged entries (with 2000 on illnesses) and 1750 illustrations (mostly line drawings, as well as photographs). . . . Definitions include parts of the body (e.g., the spinal cord, with a line drawing of the 'Communication Highway,' as the book calls it), procedures (e.g., in vitro fertilization, with four detailed line drawings of the steps involved), disorders (e.g., ectropion, with a line drawing of a sagging lower eyelid), and specialties (e.g., oncologist). . . . Owing to its relatively modest price, reliability of source, and coverage of popular areas in medicine, it is recommended not only for public libraries and consumer health collections but also for high school libraries." Libr J

Current medical diagnosis and treatment. Lange Medical Bks. pa $59.95 **610.3**

1. Medicine—Handbooks, manuals, etc.
ISSN 0092-8682

Also available CD-ROM version

Annual. First published 1974 as a successor to Current diagnosis & treatment

Editors vary

"Provides concise information on the diagnosis and treatment of diseases and disorders for medical practitioners. Uses common medical terminology, but is generally understandable to the layperson." N Y Public Libr Book of How & Where to Look It Up

Dorland's illustrated medical dictionary. Saunders il $49.95 **610.3**

1. Medicine—Dictionaries

Also available CD-ROM version

First published 1900. (30th edition 2003) Periodically revised

This standard reference includes terms used in medicine, surgery, dentistry, pharmacy, chemistry, nursing, veterinary science, biology, and medical biology. Pronunciation, derivation, and definitions are given

"This is considered one of the most comprehensive medical dictionaries in print." N Y Public Libr Book of How & Where to Look It Up

Gale encyclopedia of medicine; Jacqueline L. Longe, editor; Deirdre S. Blanchfield, associate editor. 2nd ed. Gale Group 2001 5v set $550 **610.3**

1. Medicine—Encyclopedias
ISBN 0-7876-5489-2   LC 2001-51245

First published 1999

This encyclopedia includes approximately 1,700 alphabetical entries covering over 900 disorders and conditions, describing their causes, symptoms, diagnoses, treatments, and prevention

Merck manual of diagnosis and therapy. Merck & Co. $35 **610.3**

1. Medicine—Handbooks, manuals, etc.

Also available online

First published 1899. (17th edition 1999) Periodically revised

"A one-volume reference that attempts to cover all but the most obscure diseases. Sections are organized by type of disease or medical specialty." N Y Public Libr Book of How & Where to Look It Up

Mosby's medical, nursing, & allied health dictionary. Mosby $36.95 **610.3**

1. Medicine—Dictionaries 2. Nursing—Dictionaries

Also available in abridged form with title: Mosby's pocket dictionary of medicine, nursing & allied health

First published 1983 with title: Mosby's medical & nursing dictionary. (6th edition 2002) Periodically revised

"Many definitions are discursive. Emphasizes allied health professions, with . . . categories of entries in physical therapy, occupational therapy, and respiratory care." Guide to Ref Books. 11th edition

The **Oxford** illustrated companion to medicine; edited by Stephen Lock, John M. Last, and George Dunea; emeritus editors, John Walton, Paul B. Beeson, Jeremiah A. Barondess. Oxford Univ. Press 2001 891p il $75 **610.3**

1. Medicine—Dictionaries
ISBN 0-19-262950-6   LC 2001-21799

First published 1986 with title: The Oxford companion to medicine; variant title: The Oxford medical companion

"More than 500 articles cover the major diseases and medical specialities, national medical systems, history of medicine, and how medicine intersects with such topics as art." Booklist

"An essential reference work that is also a pleasure to browse. . . . The alphabetically arranged entries . . . are well written and highly informative." Libr J

Includes bibliographical references

Sloane, Sheila B.

Medical abbreviations & eponyms. 2nd ed. Saunders 1997 905p pa $41 **610.3**

1. Medicine—Dictionaries
ISBN 0-7216-7088-1   LC 96-28595
First published 1985

This dictionary provides a list of medical abbreviations, acronyms, symbols, and eponyms. Also included are definitions for common diseases, syndromes, and operations. An appendix which lists over 400 anticancer drug combinations is provided

Stedman's medical dictionary. Williams & Wilkins $49.95   **610.3**
1. Medicine—Dictionaries
First published 1911. (27th edition 2000) Periodically revised

Provides definitions, pronunciation and derivations for terms used in general medicine, veterinary medicine, biochemistry and other related fields

Taber's cyclopedic medical dictionary. Davis, F.A. $33.95   **610.3**
1. Medicine—Dictionaries
Also available CD-ROM version and thumb-indexed version

First published 1940. (19th edition 2001) Periodically revised

This work gives "definitions of medical terms and words. Pronunciation is given for all but very common terms and the etymology of most words is included. Appendixes include such information as emergency treatment, dietetic charts, Latin and Greek nomenclature, and normal reference laboratory values." Guide to Ref Books. 11th edition

610.69   Medical personnel

America's top doctors. Castle Connolly Medical $79.95; pa $29.95   **610.69**
1. Physicians—Directories
ISBN 1-883769-38-8; 1-883769-36-1 (pa)
LC 2003-100260

"A Castle Connolly guide"
First published 2001

This guide identifies and provides information about more than 4,000 top specialists for care and treatment of more than 2,000 diseases and medical conditions, provides information about accessing and using clinical trials, and explains services provided at the National Institutes of Health and how to get the most from your specialist's appointment

Directory of physicians in the United States. American Medical Assn. 4v set $750
610.69
1. Physicians—Directories
Also available CD-ROM version
First published 1906 with title: American medical directory. (38th edition 2003) Periodically revised

At head of title: American Medical Association

This directory lists names, addresses, and zip codes; includes information on medical school of graduation; year first licensed in state; primary and secondary practice specialties; type of practice; American Board of Medical Specialties Certification; and Physician's Recognition Award status

The **Official** ABMS directory of board certified medical specialists. Marquis Who's Who 4v set $599   **610.69**
1. Physicians—Directories
Also available CD-ROM version
Formed by the merger of Directory of medical specialists and ABMS compendium of certified medical specialists. Started publication 1994 retaining volume numbering of the Directory. (35th edition 2002) Periodically revised

"For each physician, lists name, certification(s), type of practice, birth date and place, education, career history, teaching positions, military record, professional memberships, office address and phone number. Includes an outline of certification requirements for each specialty." Guide to Ref Books. 11th edition

Wischnitzer, Saul
Barron's guide to medical & dental schools. Barron's Educ. Ser. il maps pa $18.95   **610.69**
1. Medicine—Vocational guidance 2. Dentistry—Vocational guidance 3. Osteopathic medicine—Vocational guidance
First published 1982. (10th edition 2003) Periodically revised

This guide profiles "AMA-accredited American and Canadian schools, ADA-accredited dental schools, as well as osteopathic schools, accredited by the American Osteopathic Association. Advice is also given on applying to schools, with specific recommended courses and procedures for maximizing chances of acceptance." Publisher's note

610.9   Medical sciences—Historical and geographic treatment

The **Cambridge** illustrated history of medicine; edited by Roy Porter. Cambridge Univ. Press 1996 400p il maps $55; pa $35
610.9
1. Medicine—History
ISBN 0-521-44211-7; 0-521-00252-4 (pa)
LC 95-38000
This is a history of medicine from antiquity to the present. In ten "chapters, Roy Porter and his collaborators examine the changing form of medicine and . . . [the] technical successes that it has achieved." Sci Am
Includes bibliographical references

Cassedy, James H.
Medicine in America: a short history. Johns Hopkins Univ. Press 1991 187p (American moment) hardcover o.p. paperback available $18.95   **610.9**
1. Medicine—United States—History
ISBN 0-8018-4208-5 (pa)
LC 91-7058
This history of American medicine traces medical and health-related matters from colonial times to the present
This book "is scholarly, well written, very useful, and fills a void." Choice
Includes bibliographical references

Friedman, Meyer, 1910-2001
Medicine's 10 greatest discoveries; [by] Meyer Friedman, Gerald W. Friedland. Yale Univ. Press 1998 363p il $35; pa $14.95
610.9
1. Medicine—History 2. Scientists
ISBN 0-300-07598-7; 0-300-08278-9 (pa)
LC 98-19921
This describes such medical discoveries as the circulation of blood by William Harvey, the X-ray by Roentgen, Penicillin by Alexander Fleming, and DNA by Watson, Crick and Maurice Hugh Frederick Wilkins
Includes bibliographical references

Porter, Roy, 1946-2002

Blood and guts; a short history of medicine. Norton 2003 199p il $21.95 **610.9**
1. Medicine—History
ISBN 0-393-03762-2   LC 2003-42078
The author "examines the war fought between disease and doctors on the battleground of the flesh from ancient times to the present. He explores the many ingenious ways in which we have attempted to overcome disease through the ages." Publisher's note
"A delightful and informative introduction to an important subject by one of the outstanding scholars of his generation." New Engl J Med
Includes bibliographical references

The greatest benefit to mankind; a medical history of humanity. Norton 1998 831p il $35; pa $18.95   **610.9**
1. Medicine—History 2. Social medicine—History
ISBN 0-393-04634-6; 0-393-31980-6 (pa)
LC 98-10219
First published 1997 in the United Kingdom
Porter's "study traces Western medical thought and practices from their origins in classical Greece to today's biomedical developments. Although scholarly, the text is elegantly written, accessible to the general reader, and filled with fascinating details." Libr J
Includes bibliographical references

Western medicine: an illustrated history; edited by Irvine Loudon. Oxford Univ. Press 1997 347p il $65; pa $27.50 **610.9**
1. Medicine—History
ISBN 0-19-820509-0; 0-19-924813-3 (pa)
LC 97-218848
Spine title: The Oxford illustrated history of Western medicine
This history "extends from ancient Greece to the present. . . . The book consists of chapters by 20 historians from England, Germany, and the United States. An introductory chapter describes the long historical relationship between medicine and the visual arts. Seven subsequent chapters offer a chronological history of medicine, including a discussion of the influence of Islamic medicine on medieval and Renaissance physicians. The 11 final chapters deal with medicine in its social context, such as histories of childbirth, nursing, and mental illness." Libr J
Includes bibliographical references

611 Human anatomy, cytology, histology

Anatomica's body atlas; text editors, Denise Imwold, Janet Parker. Laurel Glen Pub. 2003 560p il $24.95   **611**
1. Human anatomy 2. Physiology
ISBN 1-57145-923-5   LC 2002-35361
This "human anatomy reference, arranged by physiological system, includes body parts, functions, conditions, disorders, and symptoms." Publisher's note

Netter, Frank H., 1906-1991

Atlas of human anatomy; John T. Hansen, consulting editor. 3d ed. Icon Learning Systems; [distributed by] Lippincott Williams & Wilkins 2003 various paging il $69.95
611
1. Human anatomy
Also available CD-ROM version
First published 1989 by CIBA-GEIGY Corp.
This human anatomy atlas features 542 illustrations of the human body and its systems and organs
"Organized by anatomical regions, the illustrations are colorful, easily defined, and clearly labeled. . . . Highly recommended for public and academic libraries." Libr J [review of 1997 edition]
Includes bibliographical references

Roach, Mary

Stiff; the curious lives of human cadavers. Norton 2003 303p il $23.95   **611**
1. Human experimentation in medicine 2. Dead 3. Dissection
ISBN 0-393-05093-9   LC 2002-152908
Also available Thorndike Press large print edition
Contents: A head is a terrible thing to waste; Practicing surgery on the dead; Crimes of anatomy; Body-snatching and other sordid tales from the dawn of human dissection; Life after death; On human decay and what can be done about it; Dead man driving; Human crash test dummies and the ghastly, necessary science of impact tolerance; The cadaver that joined the army; The sticky ethics of bullets and bombs; Holy cadaver; The crucifixion experiments; How to know if you're dead; Beating-heart cadavers, live burial, and the scientific search for the soul; Just a head; Decapitation, reanimation, and the human head transplant; Eat me; Medicinal cannibalism and the case of the human dumplings; Out of the fire, into the tissue digestor; And other new ways to end up; Remains of the author; Will she or wont she?
The author "explains how surgeons and doctors use cadavers donated for research purposes to help the living, and also examines potential new variations on how we bury the dead." Libr J
"For those who are interested in the fields of medicine or forensics and are aware of some of the procedures, this book makes excellent reading." SLJ
Includes bibliographical references

612 Human physiology

The **Human** body; an illustrated guide to its structure, function, and disorders; editor-in-chief, Charles Clayman. Dorling Kindersley 1995 240p il $30   **612**
1. Physiology 2. Human anatomy
ISBN 1-56458-992-7   LC 94-37165
"This body atlas uses current medical illustration techniques to provide unique views of human anatomical features. Color-enhanced microscope photographs and computer-generated images accompany detailed drawings to illustrate various organs, demonstrate body functions, and depict problems or complications. The introduction explains various types of medical illustration such as computerized tomography, ultrasound, and magnetic resonance imaging." Booklist
"This absolutely stunning book succeeds immeasurably as a guide to the human body." Sci Books Films

Wilson, Frank R.

The hand; how its use shapes the brain, language, and human culture. Pantheon Bks. 1998 397p il $30; pa $16 **612**

1. Hand

ISBN 0-679-41249-2; 0-679-74047-3 (pa)

LC 97-46427

The author "explores anatomy, anthropology, and evolution to show how the hand shapes human language and thought. He aruges convincingly that a less rigid, more individualized approach to education will yield a student with a unified body and mind. His most inspiring evidence is blessedly anecdotal: interviews with people whose vocations involve the skilled use of their hands." New Yorker

Includes bibliographical references

World of anatomy and physiology; K. Lee Lerner and Brenda Wilmoth Lerner, editors. Gale Group 2002 2v set $160 **612**

1. Physiology—Encyclopedias 2. Anatomy—Encyclopedias

ISBN 0-7876-5684-4 LC 2002-5517

"This reference provides basic information on human anatomy and physiology. The 650 alphabetically arranged entries, ranging in length from several paragraphs to several pages, are written at a level accessible to high school students and the general reader. Topics covered range from classical human anatomy and physiology to developmental and reproductive biology. . . . Lengthy biographies of about 200 famous as well as lesser-known scientists, among them Francis Crick, Herophilus, Rita Levi-Montalcini, Susumu Tonegawa, and Otto Heinrich Warburg, are also included. . . . Although primarily aimed at high-school students and general readers, this reference source could also be of use to undergraduate students in introductory courses." Booklist

Includes bibliographical references

612.6 Reproduction, development, maturation

Angier, Natalie

Woman; an intimate geography. Houghton Mifflin 1999 398p $25 **612.6**

1. Physiology 2. Women—Psychology 3. Sex role

ISBN 0-395-69130-3 LC 98-47634

Also available in paperback from Anchor Bks.

"A Peter Davison book"

The author "presents new theories on the evolution of women's anatomy, physiology and social behaviors. . . . Angier discusses such topics as ovulation, conception and birth; the social and physiological functions of breasts; orgasm, mate selection and child-rearing behavior; the complex workings of estrogen; hysterectomy; muscle strength; and female aggression and bonding." Publ Wkly

"Angier proves a knowledgeable, witty guide on our illustrative journey through hordes of cultures and species." Ms

Includes bibliographical references

Benecke, Mark

The dream of eternal life; biomedicine, aging, and immortality; translated by Rachel Rubenstein. Columbia Univ. Press 2002 196p il $29.95 **612.6**

1. Longevity 2. Death 3. Life 4. Immortality

ISBN 0-231-11672-1 LC 2001-47366

"The first section of the book discusses the biological fundamentals of why death exists and what modern biology, especially the biology of genetics, tells us about aging and death. . . . In the second part Benecke assesses the various ways that we humans cope with a finite life span and the looming certainty of death. . . . The third part looks at the possibility for extending our lives through cloning, organ and brain transplants, live cell therapy . . . and deep freezing of humans for reawakening in a future age." Publisher's note

An "informative and engaging examination of aging and the meaning of death." Booklist

Includes bibliographical references

Blum, Deborah

Sex on the brain; the biological differences between men and women. Viking 1997 xxii, 329p hardcover o.p. paperback available $13.95 **612.6**

1. Sex differences (Psychology) 2. Sex (Biology)

ISBN 0-14-026348-9 (pa) LC 96-52034

The author examines "the origins of sex, differences in male and female brains, hormones and emotions, monogamy, sexual orientation, love, rape, and power." Libr J

Blum "has a skilled journalist's ability to take abstract and confusing genetic, hormonal, endocrinological and neuroscientific findings and make them intelligible." Publ Wkly

Includes bibliographical references

Chopra, Deepak

Ageless body, timeless mind; the quantum alternative to growing old. Harmony Bks. 1993 342p hardcover o.p. paperback available $14 **612.6**

1. Longevity 2. Mind and body 3. Aging 4. Holistic medicine

ISBN 0-517-88212-4 (pa) LC 93-16766

Chopra argues that "the mind-body connection is a major player in all facets of health. . . . [He advises] readers to realize that the body is a product of awareness, that beliefs, thoughts, and emotions cause chemical reactions in cells, and that if you change your perception, you can change the experience of your body and the world." Booklist

Kirkwood, Tom

Time of our lives; the science of human aging. Oxford Univ. Press 1999 277p $37.50 **612.6**

1. Aging

ISBN 0-19-512824-9 LC 98-46932

Among the topics Kirkwood "addresses are the evolutionary advantage of aging, the relationship of aging and cancer, why women live longer then men, Alzheimer's, and the future of gene therapy. He also addresses how to prolong life or at least improve the quality of it in later years." Libr J

Kirkwood "conveys scientific matters lucidly and thought provokingly, posing good questions to show what is definitely known, disposing of myths, and point-

Kirkwood, Tom—_Continued_
ing out where more information needs to be ascertained."
Booklist
Includes bibliographical references

Medina, John, 1956-
The clock of ages; why we age—how we age—winding back the clock; [by] John J. Medina. Cambridge Univ. Press 1996 332p il hardcover o.p. paperback available $25

612.6
1. Aging
ISBN 0-521-59456-1 (pa)   LC 95-40712
This "biological explanation of the aging process explores the changes that occur in the human body as it approaches death." Book Rep
"This is the best biology book written for the lay public to appear in many years." Libr J
Includes bibliographical references

Nilsson, Lennart, 1922-
A child is born; [photography], Lennart Nilsson; text, Lars Hamberger; translated from the Swedish by Linda Schenck. 4th ed, completely rev and updated. Delacorte Press 2003 239p il $35   **612.6**
1. Pregnancy 2. Embryology 3. Childbirth
ISBN 0-385-33754-X   LC 2003-43854
"A Merloyd Lawrence book"
Original Swedish edition, 1965; first United States edition, 1966
An illustrated look at male and female reproductive anatomy and physiology, the processes of ovulation and fertilization, fetal development, and labor and delivery

Rowe, John W. (John Wallis), 1944-
Successful aging; [by] John W. Rowe and Robert L. Kahn. Pantheon Bks. 1998 265p hardcover o.p. paperback available $13.95

612.6
1. Longevity 2. Aging
ISBN 0-440-50863-0 (pa)   LC 97-36900
The authors "report on a 10-year, MacArthur Foundation-funded inquiry into 'successful aging'—that is, remaining healthy, vigorous, mentally acute, and independent well into the ninth and tenth decades of life. . . . Separate chapters illustrate, with the experience of the study's elderly subjects, that good diet and exercise, maintaining and enhancing mental functions, positive social connections, and productive work are essential to living well while living longer." Booklist
Includes bibliographical references

Schneider, Edward L.
Ageless: take control of your age and stay youthful for life; [by] Edward L. Schneider and Elizabeth Miles. Rodale 2003 310p il $24.95   **612.6**
1. Longevity 2. Health
ISBN 1-57954-621-8   LC 2003-252
Schneider offers "tips on the areas essential to controlling the aging process: diet, exercise, sleep, weight control, stress, and sex. His moderate approach promotes the benefits of life-extending foods, sensible exercise, and lifestyle changes rather than exotic supplements and more extreme measures promoted by other antiaging writers." Libr J
Includes bibliographical references

612.8　Nervous functions. Sensory functions

Dement, William C., 1928-
The promise of sleep; a pioneer in sleep medicine explores the vital connection between health, happiness, and a good night's sleep; by William C. Dement with Christopher Vaughan. Delacorte Press 1999 524p il hardcover o.p. paperback available $15.95   **612.8**
1. Sleep
ISBN 0-440-50901-7 (pa)   LC 98-23527
This work "offers scientific data on sleep, advice on sleep hygiene and a scenario for a restorative 'sleep camp'. Dement's outstanding book also includes helpful appendixes listing sleep-disorder clinics and Web sites." Libr J

Dowling, John E.
Creating mind; how the brain works. Norton 1998 212p il hardcover o.p. paperback available $17.50   **612.8**
1. Brain
ISBN 0-393-97446-4 (pa)   LC 98-9365
"In this guide to the 'nuts and bolts' of the human brain, neurobiologist Dowling explains how basic brain functions work and are interconnected. He then explores in clear, concise prose the brain's major functions: vision, language, memory, emotion, perception, and consciousness. A good jumping off point for learning about neuroscience and its fascinating discoveries." Libr J
Includes bibliographical references

Eliot, Lise
What's going on in there? how the brain and mind develop in the first five years of life. Bantam Bks. 1999 533p hardcover o.p. paperback available $18   **612.8**
1. Brain 2. Developmental psychology
ISBN 0-553-37825-2 (pa)   LC 99-35423
"This book is both theoretical and practical, combining scientific reportage with 'how-to' advice for new parents. . . . With clear, mostly simple language, [Eliot] guides readers through a fascinating array of new research—on infant balance, the development of language and memory, and the relationship between the birthing process and the brain." Libr J

Glynn, Ian, 1928-
An anatomy of thought; the origin and machinery of mind. Oxford Univ. Press 2000 456p $35; pa $17.95   **612.8**
1. Brain 2. Consciousness
ISBN 0-19-513696-9; 0-19-515803-2 (pa)
LC 99-41218
Glynn offers a "summary of what we know about the brain—both its evolution and its mechanisms. Among the topics he covers are natural selection, molecular evolution, nerves and the nervous system, sensory perception, and the specific structures responsible for our intellect." Libr J
Includes bibliographical references

Greenfield, Susan
The private life of the brain; emotions, consciousness, and the secret of the self. Wiley 2000 258p $27.95; pa $16.95   **612.8**
1. Brain
ISBN 0-471-18343-1; 0-471-39975-2 (pa)
LC 99-46191
The author "explores how consciousness and various brain functions differ in a child, a drug user, someone experiencing a nightmare, and a depressive. Examining how emotions affect all states of consciousness, she attempts to make sense of how brain activities constituting the mind and consciousness are interrelated." Libr J
"Greenfield presents a subtle model in everyday language, introducing her readers skillfully to her precedents and rivals in neurobiology and cognitive science." Publ Wkly

Lavie, P. (Peretz), 1949-
The enchanted world of sleep; [by] Peretz Lavie; translated by Anthony Berris. Yale Univ. Press 1996 270p il $47.50; pa $14.35   **612.8**
1. Sleep
ISBN 0-300-06602-3; 0-300-07436-0 (pa)
LC 95-41304
The author "describes our historical fascination with sleep and reviews notable research in the field. Among the topics he covers are the physiological changes that occur during a normal period of sleep, sleep disorders, the purpose of dreams, and the 'evolution' of the sleep cycle from birth to old age." Libr J
Includes bibliographical references

LeDoux, Joseph E.
Synaptic self; how our brains become who we are; [by] Joseph LeDoux. Viking 2002 406p il $29.95; pa $16   **612.8**
1. Personality 2. Self
ISBN 0-670-03028-7; 0-14-200178-3 (pa)
LC 2001-45356
The author puts forth the theory that "it's the neural pathways—the synaptic relationships—in our brains that make us who we are. . . . Writing for a general audience, he succeeds in making his subject accessible to the dedicated nonspecialist. He offers absorbing descriptions of some of the most fascinating case studies in his field, provides insight into the shortcomings of psychopharmacology and suggests new directions for research on the biology of mental illness." Publ Wkly

Pert, Candace, 1946-
Molecules of emotion; why you feel the way you feel; [by] Candace B. Pert; with a foreword by Deepak Chopra. Scribner 1997 368p $25; pa $14   **612.8**
1. Emotions 2. Psychosomatic medicine 3. Mind and body
ISBN 0-684-83187-2; 0-684-84634-9 (pa)
LC 97-17463
The author "has been at the forefront of key discoveries in the fields of neuroscience and AIDS therapy, and was intimately involved in the discovery of the brain's opiate receptors in 1972. Her memoir describes some of her breakthroughs while providing very real insight into the processes and politics at the core of modern science. . . . This is an important look at what really goes on inside the human body—and inside the scientific elite." Publ Wkly
Includes bibliographical references

Ratey, John J., 1948-
A user's guide to the brain; perception, attention, and the four theaters of the brain. Pantheon Bks. 2001 404p il hardcover o.p. paperback available $14.95   **612.8**
1. Brain
ISBN 0-375-70107-9 (pa)
LC 98-27796
The author explains the intricacies of the brain and its functions, he "organizes his material by functional category—development, perception, attention, memory, emotion, language, and socialization." Libr J
"Far more than a map of the brain's exotic jungles, this study can serve as a life-enriching guide for keeping the richest mental fields in cultivation." Booklist
Includes bibliographical references

Restak, Richard M., 1942-
Mozart's brain and the fighter pilot; unleashing your brain's potential; by Richard Restak. Harmony Bks. 2001 220p il hardcover o.p. paperback available $12   **612.8**
1. Brain 2. Mental health
ISBN 0-609-81005-7 (pa)
LC 2001-24779
The author "offers 28 ways to improve mental fitness, including exercises to enhance memory, concentration, creativity, and analytical ability. . . . Restak's upbeat and enlightening guide will certainly be a popular addition to public libraries." Libr J

Mysteries of the mind; [by] Richard Restak. National Geographic Soc. 2000 256p il $35   **612.8**
1. Brain
ISBN 0-7922-7941-7
LC 00-27668
This overview of modern neuroscience includes several real-life case studies. Illustrations and photographs accompany the text

The **Scientific** American book of the brain; from the editors of Scientific American; introduction by Antonio Damasio. Lyons Press 1999 340p il hardcover o.p. paperback available $19.95   **612.8**
1. Brain
ISBN 1-58574-285-6 (pa)
LC 99-39387
The articles in this anthology "include overviews of research and clinical medicine and focused discussions of such specific diseases as Parkinson's, Alzheimer's, and depression. They not only present recent accomplishments and research but also show, most intriguingly, how brain scientists think about a problem and develop its solution." Booklist

Thorpy, Michael J., 1948-
The encyclopedia of sleep and sleep disorders; [by] Michael J. Thorpy and Jan Yager. 2nd ed, updated and rev. Facts on File 2001 xxxvii, 314p $65   **612.8**
1. Sleep—Encyclopedias
ISBN 0-8160-4089-3
LC 00-64028
First published 1990 with authors' names in reverse order
"Terms covered include those for syndromes, medications, disorders, individuals, organizations, treatments, symptoms, and conditions. The readable and informative material is useful to the layperson as well as the profes-

Thorpy, Michael J., 1948-—_Continued_
sional. Extensive appendixes include a state-by-state listing of sleep centers and laboratory members of the AASM, Websites, and international and diagnostic classifications of sleep disorders." Am Ref Books Annu, 2002
Includes bibliographical references

Turkington, Carol
The encyclopedia of the brain and brain disorders; foreword by Joseph R. Harris. 2nd ed. Facts on File 2002 369p $65   **612.8**
1. Brain—Encyclopedias
ISBN 0-8160-4774-X   LC 2002-66512
"Library of health and living series"
First published 1996 with title: The brain encyclopedia
This volume "includes more than 600 clear, concise entries about the brain and treatments for neurological disorders. Articles, alphabetically arranged, are followed by directories of self-help organizations and of professional and government organizations in the fields of neurology, chronic pain, and mental illness. The list of references is extensive, the subject index is well organized." Choice

Victoroff, Jeffrey Ivan
Saving your brain; the revolutionary plan to boost brain power, improve memory, and protect yourself against aging and Alzheimer's; [by] Jeff Victoroff. Bantam Bks. 2002 450p il $25.95; pa $14.95   **612.8**
1. Brain 2. Aging 3. Memory 4. Alzheimer's disease
ISBN 0-553-10944-8; 0-553-37980-1 (pa)
    LC 2001-56732
"Contradicting popular scientific opinion, the author argues memory loss may be a natural part of the aging process. Using his own clinical experiences and reviews of 14,000 research studies, [he] explores the many ways the human brain can be damaged and offers tips for improving brain function and preventing memory loss, from avoiding exposure to chemicals to not watching television." Libr J
Includes bibliographical references

Watson, Lyall
Jacobson's organ and the remarkable nature of smell. Norton 2000 255p il o.p.; Plume Bks. paperback available $14   **612.8**
1. Nose 2. Smell
ISBN 0-452-28258-6 (pa)   LC 99-56864
First published 1999 in the United Kingdom
"Drawing on both biology and cultural history, Watson employs intriguing and instructive examples as he describes how humans, animals, and plants secrete and decode odors; and explains how smell is essential to sexuality, and underlies emotions and many other forms of subconscious knowledge." Booklist
Includes bibliographical references

613   Promotion of health

Allison, Kathleen Cahill
American Medical Association complete guide to women's health; Ramona I. Slupik, medical editor; produced by Alison Brown Cerier Book Development, Inc. Random House 1996 759p il $39.95   **613**
1. Women—Health and hygiene
ISBN 0-679-43122-5   LC 96-33738
This guide covers fitness, nutrition, preventive care, sex and reproduction, cosmetic surgery, domestic violence and mental health

Atkins, Robert C.
Dr. Atkins' age-defying diet revolution. St. Martin's Press 2000 335p hardcover o.p. paperback available $7.99   **613**
1. Nutrition 2. Aging 3. Health
ISBN 0-312-97701-8 (pa)   LC 99-55690
The author "argues here that the use of supplements and a change in diet can eliminate many health problems, including cardiovascular disease, diabetes and stroke." Publ Wkly

The **Black** women's health book; speaking for ourselves; edited by Evelyn C. White. new expanded ed. Seal Press 1994 375p pa $16.95   **613**
1. African American women—Health and hygiene
ISBN 1-878067-40-0   LC 93-28901
First published 1990
Contributors to this collection include Zora Neale Hurston, Lucille Clifton, Marian Wright Edelman, bell hooks, and Toni Morrison. Topics covered include: suicide, midwives, the politics of black women's health, sexual abuse, domestic violence, skin color, HIV infection, menopause, etc.
Includes bibliographical references

Buhner, Stephen Harrod
Vital man; natural health care for men at midlife. Avery 2003 399p pa $16.95   **613**
1. Men—Health and hygiene 2. Alternative medicine 3. Health
ISBN 1-58333-136-0   LC 2002-74603
This book provides "a comprehensive overview of natural health care for men entering middle ages. . . . [The author] offers practical knowledge to help men navigate the forty-five most common disorders that occur at age forty and above." Publisher's note
"If readers want to know how juniper berries can aid urinary tract infections, or how ginkgo can be used in treating the heart and the mind, Buhner is a knowledgeable guide." Publ Wkly
Includes bibliographical references

Dollemore, Doug
The doctors book of home remedies for seniors; an A-to-Z guide to staying physically active, mentally sharp, and disease-free; by Doug Dollemore and the Editors of Prevention Health Books for Seniors. Rodale Press 1999 578p il $29.95   **613**
1. Aging 2. Health self-care 3. Medicine
ISBN 1-57954-011-2   LC 99-11451
Also available in paperback from Bantam Bks.

Dollemore, Doug—*Continued*

This guide addresses exercise, diet, accident prevention, medical care, and mental health. Medical problems discussed range from varicose veins to angina. Drug interactions and alternative therapies are covered

Fitness over fifty; an exercise guide from the National Institute on Aging; with a foreword by John Glenn. Special illustrated ed. Healthy Living Bks. 2003 134p il pa $15.95   **613**

1. Exercise 2. Physical fitness 3. Aging

ISBN 1-57826-136-8

First published 2001 with title: Exercise: a guide from the National Institute on Aging

"Strenght flexibility, vitality, balance. 25 easy exercises for better health." Cover

"A panel of experts in exercise for older adults explain the benefits of physical activity and present basic fitness routines (with illustrated step-by-step instructions) to improve endurance, strength, balance, and flexibility. There are also useful tips for finding a fitness professional, incorporating exercise into daily routines, computing target heart rates, and creating exercise plans and progress charts. Excellent for beginners." Libr J

Gay, Kathlyn, 1930-

Encyclopedia of women's health issues. Oryx Press 2001 300p $74.95   **613**

1. Women—Health and hygiene 2. Women—Diseases

ISBN 1-57356-303-X   LC 2001-37342

This encyclopedia covers "the issues and history surrounding diseases and medical procedures faced by women; health concerns of different ethnic groups of women; information on organizations and programs that deal with women's health; profiles on the people who have pioneered women's health services and information; and legal decisions related to women's health." Publisher's note

For a review see: Booklist, August, 2002

The **"Go** ask Alice" book of answers; a guide to good physical, sexual, and emotional health; [by] Columbia University's Health Education Program. Holt & Co. 1998 345p pa $15.95   **613**

1. Youth—Health and hygiene 2. Adolescence 3. Sex education

ISBN 0-8050-5570-3   LC 98-3318

"An Owl book"

"The title within the title refers to a Web site maintained by Columbia University Health Services. Set up to answer questions about relationships, sex, physical and mental health, nutrition, and related matters, the site eventually was opened to the general public as a quick-reference forum. The book's seven chapters round up queries the site has received and responses to them from Columbia-associated health educators." Booklist

Includes bibliographical references

Health matters! general editor William M. Kane . Grolier Educ. 2002 8v il set $419   **613**

1. Health

ISBN 0-7172-5575-1   LC 2001-40248

Contents: v1 Addiction: tobacco, alcohol, and other drugs; v2 Mental health: depression, suicide, and other

issues; v3 Sexuality and pregnancy; v4 Physical activity, weight, and eating disorders; v5 Injuries and violence; v6 Environmental poisoning; v7 HIV infections, AIDS, and STDs; v8 Diseases and disabling conditions

"This set serves two purposes: it is a means of answering young adults' questions about their health and empowering them to make sound decisions and also a reference source for school reports pertaining to health topics. . . . A useful addition to high-school or public libraries." Booklist

Healthy women, healthy lives; a guide to preventing disease from the landmark Nurses' Health Study; senior editors, Susan E. Hankinson [et al.] Simon & Schuster 2001 xxviii, 546p il $26; pa $16   **613**

1. Women—Health and hygiene

ISBN 0-684-85519-4; 0-7432-1774-8 (pa)

   LC 2001-34154

"A Harvard Medical School book"

"In 'Lowering the Risk of Disease', the risks of coronary heart disease, breast cancer, lung cancer, stroke, diabetes, colon cancer, osteoporosis, endometrial cancer, ovarian cancer, and skin cancer are discussed. Another chapter covers asthma, arthritis, age-related eye disease, and Alzheimer's disease. . . . The final chapters look at changing behaviors and making decisions that can affect women's health." Libr J

Includes bibliographical references

The **Johns** Hopkins medical guide to health after 50; the latest recommendations from the Hopkins specialists; medical editor, Simeon Margolis; prepared by the editors of The John Hopkins medical letter health after 50. Rebus 2002 704p il $39.95 **613**

1. Elderly—Health and hygiene 2. Elderly—Diseases

ISBN 0-929661-73-7   LC 2002-69670

Partial contents: Guide to disease prevention; Body atlas; Guide to medical disorders; Organizations and support groups

This handbook "explains which measures you can take to increase longevity and protect yourself from the avoidable ailments of aging—and how to deal effectively with those ailments you can't avoid." Publisher's note

Looking after your body; an owner's guide to successful aging. Reader's Digest Assn. 2001 416p il $30   **613**

1. Aging 2. Health

ISBN 0-7621-0302-7   LC 00-47071

This "guide covers the basics of good health: diet, weight control, fitness, essential medical tests, 'health traps' (smoking, alcohol use), medication management, stress reduction and emotional health, sexuality, memory, sleep, and personal appearance. Part 2 is an alphabetical encyclopedia of common late-life diseases, with details on diagnosis, treatments (including herbs and supplements), prevention plans, and lifestyle modifications. Clear, interesting explanations of complex concepts are fortified with numerous illustrations, charts, lists, and current medical research findings." Libr J

Mayo Clinic family health book; Scott C. Litin, editor-in-chief. 3rd ed. HarperResource 2003 1448p il $49.95 **613**

1. Medicine

ISBN 0-06-000250-6   LC 2002-27349

First published 1990 by Morrow

Mayo Clinic family health book—*Continued*

This edition covers over 1,000 illnesses and includes information on immunizations, breast health, genetics, sleep disorders, complementary and alternative medicine, pain management, and end-of-life issues. A medications guide covering more than 500 prescription and over-the-counter drugs is also included

Men's health concerns sourcebook; basic information about health issues that affect men . . .; edited by Allan R. Cook. Omnigraphics 1998 738p il maps (Health reference series) $78   **613**
1. Men—Health and hygiene
ISBN 0-7808-0212-8   LC 98-33612
Among the topics discussed are: prostate enlargement, impotence, vasectomies, snoring, sleep apnea, urological disorders, hair loss and pulmonary diseases

Null, Gary

For women only! your guide to health empowerment; [by] Gary Null and Barbara Seaman. Seven Stories Press 1999 xxiv, 1571p il $49.95; pa $29.95   **613**
1. Women—Health and hygiene 2. Alternative medicine
ISBN 1-58322-015-1; 1-58322-278-2 (pa)
                                       LC 99-39822
"The first 600 pages of this . . . [book] offer alternative practitioner Null's thoughts on the causes, symptoms, prevention, and treatment of conditions and illnesses, from addiction and arthritis to violence and varicose veins. The remainder is Seaman's history of the women's health movement, featuring selections from . . . feminist writers." Booklist
Includes bibliographical references

Our bodies, ourselves for the new century; a book by and for women; [by] The Boston Women's Health Book Collective. Simon & Schuster 1998 780p il pa $24   **613**
1. Women—Health and hygiene 2. Women—Psychology
ISBN 0-684-84231-9   LC 98-12725
"A Touchstone book"
First published 1971 with title: Our bodies, ourselves
This encyclopedia of women's health covers such topics as body image, food, alcohol and drugs, holistic healing, psychotherapy, occupational health, violence, relationships and sexuality, sexual health and controlling fertility, child-bearing, aging and politics of women and health
Includes bibliographical references

Peck, Brian

The baby boomer body book; the complete health reference for our generation. Sourcebooks 2001 447p il pa $21.94   **613**
1. Middle age 2. Health 3. Aging
ISBN 1-57071-715-X   LC 00-66169
The author "draws on case histories from his practice to discuss age-related physical changes, memory problems, depression, dietary supplements, medical tests, and weight loss. Separate sections on men's and women's health issues cover sexual dysfunction and osteoporosis in men—an often unrecognized condition. Peck also addresses recreational drug use and midlife self-image. His

breezy, approachable style will appeal to midlifers (especially men not attracted by conventional resources)." Libr J
Includes bibliographical references

Prevention's ultimate guide to women's health and wellness; action plans for more than 100 women's health problems; by the editors of Prevention Health Books for Women. Rodale 2002 532p il $31.95   **613**
1. Women—Health and hygiene 2. Women—Diseases
ISBN 1-579-54491-6   LC 2002-6637
This book features "remedies for more than 100 health problems—colds, back pain, fatigue, allergies, headaches, depression, and dozens more. . . . The advice is tailored to women's unique biological needs." Publisher's note

Reed, James, 1944-
The black man's guide to good health. Hilton Pub. 2000 304p il pa $16.95   **613**
1. African Americans—Health and hygiene 2. Men—Health and hygiene
ISBN 0-9675258-1-0
First published 1994 by The Berkley Publishing Group
Health problems covered include "high blood pressure, diabetes, heart disease and stroke, cancer, sickle cell anemia, AIDS, sexually transmitted diseases, and substance abuse. Definitions, conditions, and symptoms are included, along with the names, addresses, and telephone numbers of resource organizations to contact. There is a great deal of solid information on prevention and treatment here. Proper diet, cholesterol levels, and ways to control fat and salt intake are discussed. The importance of exercise is stressed and various types are recommended." SLJ [review of 1994 edition]

Roan, Sharon

Our daughters' health; practical and invaluable advice for raising confident girls ages 6 to 16; [by] Sharon L. Roan. Hyperion 2000 399p il pa $14.95   **613**
1. Girls—Health and hygiene 2. Parenting
ISBN 0-7868-8500-9   LC 00-38837
The author "explains the importance of regular healthcare, stressing disease prevention, nutrition, calcium to insure strong bones, skin care, and mental health. She also stresses participation in sports and the importance of exercise and examines eating disorders, education, sexuality, violence and personal safety, and substance abuse. . . . Her nonjudgmental tone and reassuring advice make this an excellent addition to all parenting collections." Libr J

Simon, Harvey B. (Harvey Bruce), 1942-
The Harvard Medical School guide to men's health. Free Press 2002 485p il $27
                                       613
1. Men—Health and hygiene 2. Health self-care
ISBN 0-684-87181-5   LC 2002-21723
"Major areas covered include the prostate, vitamins and supplements, depression, and the very fine line between healthful and hazardous drinking. The contents are disposed in three parts on basic information, what keeps men healthy, and what can go wrong." Booklist
"This comprehensive, informative, engagingly written guide is a standout among a slew of similar titles." Libr J

Weil, Andrew

Eight weeks to optimum health; a proven program for taking full advantage of your body's natural healing power. Knopf 1997 276p $25; pa $13.95   **613**

1. Health self-care 2. Alternative medicine
ISBN 0-679-44715-6; 0-449-00026-5 (pa)
                                        LC 96-51918

The program consists of "a schedule of incremental changes in diet (recipes are included), dietary supplements, exercise, and such mental-spiritual practices as breath work, art and music appreciation, and spending some time in a sauna." Booklist

The book's "strength lies in its design, which uses small easy steps to achieve big changes. . . . As a physician, Weil is careful to substantiate every claim, and he debunks some of today's more extreme alternative health theories." Libr J

Includes bibliographical references

613.2   Dietetics

Atkins, Robert C.

Dr. Atkins' new diet revolution. Avon Bks. 2002 540p il pa $7.99   **613.2**

1. Weight loss 2. Low-carbohydrate diet
ISBN 0-06-001203-X   LC 2002-278407
Also available G.K. Hall large print edition
First published 1972 by D. McKay with title: Dr. Atkins' diet revolution: the high calorie way to stay thin forever

Completely updated

In this "holistic approach to health and well-being . . . Atkins promotes a diet of protein and fat in four stages: induction, ongoing weight loss, premaintenance, and maintenance. Case histories document his achievements. . . . Useful appendixes include menus, recipes, and a carbohydrate gram counter." Libr J

Includes bibliographical references

Beling, Stephanie

Powerfoods; good food, good health with phytochemicals, nature's own energy boosters; featuring 140 delicious recipes by executive chefs, Barry Correia and Carl Deluce. HarperCollins Pubs. 1997 372p il hardcover o.p. paperback available $15

                                        613.2

1. Nutrition 2. Botanical chemistry 3. Vegetables
ISBN 0-06-092954-5 (pa)   LC 97-1046

The author "presents eating 'guidelines and strategies' to enhance good health and, especially, to strengthen the immune system. She focuses on foods—certain fruits and vegetables, garlic, grains and legumes—that contain phytochemicals. . . . Beling offers 140 easy and appealing recipes." Publ Wkly

Includes bibliographical references

Cox, Peter, 1955-

You don't need meat. Thomas Dunne Bks. 2002 xxii, 378p il $24.95; pa $14.95   **613.2**

1. Vegetarianism 2. Vegetarian cooking
ISBN 0-312-27761-X; 0-312-30338-6 (pa)
                                        LC 2001-54814

"Cox's defense of vegetarianism rests largely on health and nutritional issues, but he uses plenty of anthropomorphic imagery to discourage eating animals. He

cites low rates of heart disease among Seventh-Day Adventists as empirical evidence for the better health of those who refuse to eat meat. . . . A few recipes illustrate general principles of vegetarian cooking." Booklist

Includes bibliographical references

Critser, Greg

Fat land; how Americans became the fattest people in the world. Houghton Mifflin 2003 232p il $24; pa $13   **613.2**

1. Obesity
ISBN 0-618-16472-3; 0-618-38060-4 (pa)
                                        LC 2002-32282

The author "presents a critical analysis of the many social and economic factors that make Americans, contrary to the book's subtitle, the second-fattest people in the world. . . . He blames parents' reluctance to monitor their children's eating habits; the marketing tactics of fast-food companies, which influence us to overeat; the preponderance of fad diets; the phasing out of physical education programs in schools; and the sale of fast foods at schools to save money on dining facilities." Libr J

The author "succeeds in letting laypersons grasp agricultural policy, astute marketing ploys, lipid chemistry, human physioloy, and the follies of institutional feeding schemes and weight-loss quackery." Choice

Diet and nutrition sourcebook . . .; edited by Karen Bellenir. 2nd ed. Omnigraphics 1999 650p il (Health reference series) $78

                                        613.2

1. Nutrition
ISBN 0-7808-0228-4   LC 99-17687
First published 1996

"Basic consumer health information about dietary guidelines, recommended daily intake values, vitamins, minerals, fiber, fat, weight control, dietary supplements, and food additives: along with special sections on nutrition needs throughout life and nutrition for people with such specific medical concerns as allergies, high blood cholesterol, hypertension, diabetes, celiac disease, seizure disorders, phenylketonuria (PKU), cancer, and eating disorders, and including reports on current nutrition research and source listings for additional help and information." Title page

Duyff, Roberta Larson

American Dietetic Association complete food and nutrition guide. 2nd ed. Wiley 2002 658p il $45; pa $24.95   **613.2**

1. Nutrition
ISBN 0-471-22924-5; 0-471-44144-9 (pa)
First published 1996 by Chronimed Pub.

This book "covers safe weight control; nutritional needs of women, children, teens, and seniors; shopping, eating out, reading labels, and food safety." Booklist [review of 1996 edition]

"Duyff gives sound advice." Libr J [review of 1996 edition]

Foods that harm, foods that heal; an A-Z guide to safe and healthy eating. Reader's Digest Assn. 1997 400p il $30   **613.2**

1. Nutrition
ISBN 0-89577-912-9   LC 96-24477
At head of title: Reader's Digest

"Alphabetical listings in this . . . resource span general categories of illnesses, food groups, additives, and nor-

Foods that harm, foods that heal—*Continued*

mal life passages, such as aging. Other entries refer to specific medical conditions or individual dietary elements. . . . Each medical entry recommends helpful foods, followed by those that should be avoided." Booklist

"Over 300 medical and nutrition experts collaborated to ensure that the information presented in this book is not only up-to-date but also supported by scientific evidence." Libr J

Kraus, Barbara

Calories and carbohydrates. Signet Bks. pa $6.99   **613.2**

1. Food—Composition
First published 1971 by Grosset & Dunlap. (15th edition 2003) Title varies
This lists the calorie and carbohydrate count of more than 8,500 brand-name and natural foods, according to portion size, with cross references

Mindell, Earl, 1940-

Dr. Earl Mindell's unsafe at any meal; how to avoid hidden toxins in your food; [by] Earl Mindell with Hester Mundis. rev and updated. Contemporary Bks. 2002 274p pa $14.95
     613.2

1. Nutrition 2. Food—Composition 3. Natural foods
ISBN 0-658-02115-X   LC 2001-58223
First published 1987
The author discusses the food industry's chemical cover-ups and looks at "labelese", pros and cons of new products, genetically modified foods and natural foods fortified with vitamins, minerals, and antioxidants
Includes bibliographical references

Murray, Michael T.

Encyclopedia of nutritional supplements; the essential guide for improving your health naturally. Prima Pub. 1996 564p pa $22.95
     613.2

1. Vitamins 2. Nutrition
ISBN 0-7615-0410-9   LC 96-3804
"Written to help users make sense of the voluminous information available on nutritional supplements, this book includes detailed profiles of all the major ones—vitamins, minerals, essential fatty acids, accessory nutrients, and glandular extracts—and tells how they can help one live longer, feel better, and fight the effects of aging. A concluding section counsels which nutritional supplements to take for a host of conditions, including high cholesterol, depression, and fatigue." Am Ref Books Annu, 1997
Includes bibliographical references

Nelson, Miriam E.

Strong women eat well; nutritional strategies for a healthy body and mind; [by] Miriam E. Nelson with Judy Knipe. Putnam 2001 268p il $24.95; pa $13.95   **613.2**

1. Nutrition 2. Women—Health and hygiene
ISBN 0-399-14740-3; 0-399-52782-6 (pa)
     LC 00-69677
"The main body of the work discusses each level of the Food Guide Pyramid—grains; fruits and vegetables; milk and meat products; and fats, oils, and sugars—as well as the importance of water. . . . A large number of

recipes . . . provide ways to increase the use and intake of some foods that most of us may be hesitant to try." Libr J
Includes bibliographical references

Nichter, Mimi

Fat talk; what girls and their parents say about dieting. Harvard Univ. Press 2000 263p $25; pa $16.95   **613.2**

1. Obesity 2. Weight loss 3. Girls—Health and hygiene
ISBN 0-674-00229-6; 0-674-00681-X (pa)
     LC 99-59521
The author "spent three years studying and interviewing teenage girls about their attitudes toward appearance, eating habits, and dieting. . . . Over two hundred girls were followed over a three-year period so that changing attitudes could be measured. The reader gains a better understanding of teenage girls through the readable narrative that describes the results of the study." Voice Youth Advocates
Includes bibliographical references

Ronzio, Robert A.

The encyclopedia of nutrition and good health; [by] Robert Ronzio. 2nd ed. Facts on File 2003 726p $71.50   **613.2**

1. Nutrition—Encyclopedias
ISBN 0-8160-4966-1   LC 2002-35221
First published 1997
"The alphabetical entries cover a broad range of topics. Foods, their ingredients, and nutritional values are described. Specific diets (Atkins, Mediterranean) are discussed objectively, with the basic premise of the diet explained along with its pros and cons. Entries on foods and the components implicated in diseases and disorders explain how and why the problem occurs and offer dietary recommendations. Some articles reflect new health concerns. For example, the *Transfatty acids* entry gives a clear explanation of the health risks and offers alternative food options. There is useful information on the food pyramid and food labels. Medical terms, tests, and current research are also covered." Booklist
Includes bibliographical references

Sears, William

The family nutrition book; everything you need to know about feeding your children from birth through adolescence. Little, Brown 1999 416p il hardcover o.p. paperback available $19   **613.2**

1. Children—Nutrition 2. Infants—Nutrition
ISBN 0-316-77715-3 (pa)   LC 98-51879
"The book progresses from an overview of nutrients (water and fiber among them) to an extensive evaluation of food groups, including discussions of vegetarianism, organic foods and decoding packaging labels. Additional sections address weight control and the specific roles various foods play in disease prevention, stamina building, etc. Reference tables and an updated food pyramid will prove indispensable to the reader." Publ Wkly
Includes bibliographical references

Shintani, Terry
The good carbohydrate revolution. Pocket
Bks. 2002 432p il $23; pa $14   **613.2**
1. High-carbohydrate diet 2. Diet
ISBN 0-7434-0598-6; 0-7434-0599-4 (pa)
                              LC 2001-55416
The author introduces a "way to control weight and
blood sugar levels by eating more of the right kinds of
carbohydrates. . . . Designed to maximize your health
and keep you lean for life, Dr. Shintani's . . . program
centers on 'good' carbohydrates such as whole-grain pasta, pita bread, corn, sweet potatoes, and brown rice, as
well as an array of vitamin-rich fruits and vegetables."
Publisher's note
Includes bibliographical references

Spencer, Colin
Vegetarianism; a history. Four Walls Eight
Windows 2002 384p $28   **613.2**
1. Vegetarianism
ISBN 1-56858-238-2   LC 2002-69298
First published 1996 by University Press of New Eng-
land with title: The heretic's feast (available pa $24.95
ISBN 0-87451-760-5)
The author "chronicles meat abstinence throughout
history, describing its ancient origins and the myriad
struggles of this growing movement." Publisher's note
Includes bibliographical references

Vegetarian Times vegetarian beginner's
guide; by the editors of Vegetarian Times.
Macmillan 1996 181p il pa $13.95   **613.2**
1. Vegetarianism
ISBN 0-02-860386-9   LC 96-4120
The authors "describe the various types of vegetarianism. Stressing the health value of the vegetarian lifestyle,
especially in the treatment of various diseases, they point
out the possible dangers of dairy foods, discuss whether
to use vitamin supplements, and encourage the use of
low-fat ingredients. Tips on the basic vegetarian pantry,
along with two-weeks' worth of easy recipes and menus,
are given for the beginner." Libr J

Weil, Andrew
Eating well for optimum health; the
essential guide to food, diet, and nutrition.
Knopf 2000 307p $25   **613.2**
1. Nutrition 2. Food 3. Health
ISBN 0-375-40754-5   LC 99-52730
Also available in paperback from Guill
"Weil illuminates the often confusing and conflicting
ideas circulating about good nutrition, addressing specific
health issues and offering nutritional guidance to help
heal and prevent major illnesses. Of particular value is
his examination of recent fads, such as low-carbohydrate,
vegan and 'Asian' diets, with an eye toward debunking
the myths about them while highlighting their valuable
aspects." Publ Wkly
Includes bibliographical references

Wenner, Paul F.
Garden cuisine; heal yourself and the
planet through low-fat meatless eating; [by]
Paul Wenner. Simon & Schuster 1997 367p
il hardcover o.p. paperback available $21.95
                                    613.2
1. Low-fat diet 2. Vegetarian cooking
ISBN 0-684-83882-6 (pa)   LC 96-53990
The author "begins by outlining the ethical, health,
and environmental benefits of reducing the amount of
meat in our diets. He then proposes what is called the
Garden Plan for a healthier lifestyle, including three
weeks worth of menu plans, a shopping list, and an
eight-page list of educational and organizational resources. Wenner's recommendations are easy to follow
and commonsensical. . . . The recipes are, for the most
part, light and easy to prepare." Libr J
Includes bibliographical references

Willett, Walter
Eat, drink and be healthy; the Harvard
Medical School guide to healthy eating; [by]
Walter C. Willett with P. J. Skerrett;
contributions by Edward L. Giovannucci;
recipes by Maureen Callahan. Simon &
Schuster 2001 299p il $25; pa $13   **613.2**
1. Nutrition
ISBN 0-684-86337-5; 0-7432-2322-5 (pa)
                              LC 2001-20565
The author contends that the USDA Food Pyramid,
which recommends 6 to 11 servings of carbohydrate-rich
foods per day, is wrong and dangerous, and he offers an
alternate nutritional plan emphasizing fruits, vegetables,
fish, chicken, legumes, and whole grains
Includes bibliographical references

The **Yale** guide to children's nutrition;
William V. Tamborlane, editor-in-chief;
Janet Z. Weiswasser, managing editor;
editors, Teresa Fung, Nancy A. Held, Tara
Prather Liskov; foreword by Jane E. Brody;
recipes compiled with cooperation from the
James Beard Foundation. Yale Univ. Press
1997 415p il $52; pa $19.95   **613.2**
1. Children—Nutrition
ISBN 0-300-06965-0; 0-300-07169-8 (pa)
                              LC 96-44774
Divided as follows: "From Infancy to Adolescence,
which treats developmental nutrition; Common Concerns,
which tackles such issues as proper weight gain and
dealing with picky eaters; Beyond the Basics, which addresses special problems, such as feeding children with
diabetes, cystic fibrosis or food allergies; Building
Blocks for Good Nutrition; Eating in, Eating Out, which
proffers practical advice on school lunches and fast
foods; and Recipes." Publ Wkly
"Comprehensive in its coverage, well organized, and
easily understood, this book is highly recommended for
any consumer health collection." Libr J
Includes bibliographical references

613.6 Special topics of health and safety

Frist, William H.
When every moment counts; what you need to know about bioterrorism from the Senate's only doctor; [by] Bill Frist. Rowman & Littlefield 2002 181p il pa $14.95   **613.6**
1. Biological warfare 2. Terrorism
ISBN 0-7425-2245-8   LC 2001-8752
Contents: Anthrax in the capitol; Safe at home; Anthrax; Plague; Small pox; Botulism; Tularemia; Ebola and viral hemorrhagic fevers; Chemical weapons; The threat to our food and water supply; A nation prepared

613.7 Physical fitness

Active living every day; [by] Steven N. Blair [et al.] Human Kinetics 2001 194p il pa $22.95   **613.7**
1. Exercise 2. Physical fitness 3. Health
ISBN 0-7360-3701-2   LC 00-47238
The authors "present a week-by-week, self-paced plan for couch potatoes to incorporate physical activity gradually into their daily lives. . . . There is also sensible advice on proper nutrition and additional interactive exercises on the net." Libr J
Includes bibliographical references

Bailey, Covert
Smart exercise; burning fat, getting fit. Houghton Mifflin 1994 292p hardcover o.p. paperback available $12   **613.7**
1. Exercise 2. Physical fitness
ISBN 0-395-66114-5 (pa)   LC 94-1667
This fitness guide discusses metabolism, dieting, muscle tone, aerobics, exercise machines, swimming, walking and the benefits and drawbacks of various sports

Callahan, Lisa
The fitness factor; every woman's key to a lifetime of health and wellbeing. Lyons Press 2002 xxi, 314p il $24.95   **613.7**
1. Exercise 2. Physical fitness 3. Women—Health and hygiene
ISBN 1-58574-501-4   LC 2001-50729
In this guide the author stresses the importance of exercise in "preventing heart disease; beating osteoporosis; lowering cholesterol; decreasing cancer risk; losing weight; increasing energy; reducing stress; having better sex and much more." Publisher's note

Fitness and exercise sourcebook; edited by Kristen M. Gledhill. 2nd ed. Omnigraphics 2001 646p il (Health reference series) lib bdg $78   **613.7**
1. Physical fitness 2. Exercise
ISBN 0-7808-0334-5   LC 2001-21453
First published 1996
"Basic consumer health information about the fundamentals of fitness and exercise, including how to begin and maintain a fitness program, fitness as a lifestyle, the link between fitness and diet, advice for specific groups of people, exercise as it relates to specific medical conditions, and recent research in fitness and exercise; along with a glossary of important terms and resources for additional help and information." Title page

"An essential reference for most collections." Libr J

Iyengar, B. K. S., 1918-
Yoga; the path to holistic health. DK Pub. 2001 416p il $40   **613.7**
1. Yoga
ISBN 0-7894-7165-5   LC 00-45198
This introduction to yoga offers "sharply detailed, step-by-step color photographs; generous page layouts; clear explanations of how to do the various poses and the benefits of each; and in-depth section on yoga therapy for specific ailments." Booklist

McFarlane, Stewart
The complete book of t'ai chi. DK Pub. 1997 120p il hardcover o.p. paperback available $15   **613.7**
1. T'ai chi ch'üan
ISBN 0-7894-4259-0 (pa)   LC 96-33596
This is an illustrated guide to the Chinese art of t'ai chi, which is aimed at promoting physical and mental well-being
"The gentle movements are diagrammed in detail with full-color step-by-step photographs and precise explanations. A good how-to book for beginners." BAYA Book Rev

Reichmann, Rosie, 1917-
Ageless yoga; yoga exercises for improving your life at any age! Astrolog; [distributed by] Independent Pubs. Group 2001 192p il pa $18.95   **613.7**
1. Yoga
ISBN 9-6549-4124-4
The author discusses how her "program of gentle stretching and breathing techniques can be used to create specific workouts to relieve tension, increase flexibility, and reduce age-related functional losses in various parts of the body. Her readable text is illustrated with photos of the author demonstrating the poses, with modifications for those who must use a chair or mattress." Libr J

Spilner, Maggie
Prevention's complete book of walking; everything you need to know to walk your way to better health. Rodale 2000 292p il hardcover o.p. paperback available $14.95   **613.7**
1. Walking 2. Physical fitness
ISBN 1-57954-236-0 (pa)   LC 00-25877
This guide to the tools and techniques of fitness walking features workout plans, training programs, and tips on buying shoes and treadmills. Yoga positions to facilitate a fluid stride are discussed. Includes cassette tape

613.9 Birth control, reproductive technology, sex hygiene

Block, Joel D.
Sex over 50; [by] Joel D. Block with Susan Crain Bakos. Parker Pub. 1999 302p $34; pa $15   **613.9**
1. Sexual behavior
ISBN 0-13-080968-3; 0-7352-0058-0 (pa)
LC 98-42503
"Highlighting the 'potent sexual benefits' that come with midlife, this light-hearted but informative guide by

Block, Joel D.—*Continued*

a psychotherapist and journalist presents exercises to reenergize a routine sex life, suggests how to create moods and fantasies, describes alternative forms of love-making (bondage, etc.), and covers the more mundane aspects of midlife sexuality (health issues, impotence, hormonal changes)." Libr J

Comfort, Alex, 1920-2000

The joy of sex; foreword by Claire Rayner. Crown 2002 240p il $29.95; pa $10   **613.9**

1. Sexual behavior

ISBN 1-400-04614-9; 0-7434-7774-X (pa)

LC 2002-67455

"30th anniversary edition of original 1972 publication." Verso of title page

Variant title: The new joy of sex

Describes with illustrations a variety of sexual behaviors, addresses causes and risks of sexually transmitted diseases, and emphasizes the importance of love

Djerassi, Carl

This man's pill; reflections on the 50th birthday of the pill. Oxford Univ. Press 2001 308p il $22.50   **613.9**

1. Oral contraceptives

ISBN 0-19-850872-7   LC 2001-21982

"The first five essays of this . . . book deal with the development and distribution of the Pill. . . . The most interesting essays here are those in which [Djerassi] expounds upon his forays into literature and the arts—a later life passion that he credits to perspective gained as a result of what he had experienced because of the Pill." Libr J

614 Forensic medicine, incidence & prevention of disease

Evans, Colin

The casebook of forensic detection; how science solved 100 of history's most baffling crimes. Wiley 1996 310p il hardcover o.p. paperback available $17.95   **614**

1. Forensic sciences 2. Medical jurisprudence 3. Criminal investigation

ISBN 0-471-28369-X (pa)   LC 95-26002

"Covers cases from 1751 to 1991, arranged according to the methodology by which they were solved. Fifteen areas are listed alphabetically, ranging from ballistics through DNA typing, fingerprinting, odontology, serology and toxicology to the still-disputed voiceprint analysis." Publ Wkly

"Written in a popular style as clear as it is brief, this book is suitable for general true-crime collections." Libr J

Kirwin, Barbara

The mad, the bad, and the innocent; the criminal mind on trial. Little, Brown 1997 306p $23.95   **614**

1. Insanity defense 2. Criminal psychology

ISBN 0-316-49499-2   LC 97-7833

Also available in paperback from HarperCollins Pubs.

"Arguing that the insanity defense is alternately abused and neglected in our legal system, criminal psychologist Kirwin analyzes what true insanity is through the many criminals she has diagnosed. . . . Balanced and penetrating, this is a solid addition to true-crime holdings." Booklist

Lee, Henry C.

Blood evidence; how DNA is revolutionizing the way we solve crimes; [by] Henry C. Lee, Frank Tirnady. Perseus Bks. 2003 xxx, 418p $26   **614**

1. DNA fingerprinting 2. Forensic sciences

ISBN 0-7382-0602-4   LC 2002-105970

This book "explains the principles and science behind DNA testing and shows how it has both helped solve some of the most puzzling criminal cases in recent history and been used to discredit eyewitness accounts and physical evidence found at the crime scene." Publisher's note

"This volume is an excellent introduction to the science and use of DNA analysis." Publ Wkly

Includes bibliographical references

Maples, William R., 1937-1997

Dead men do tell tales; [by] William R. Maples and Michael Browning. Doubleday 1994 292p il hardcover o.p. paperback available $15.95   **614**

1. Forensic anthropology

ISBN 0-385-47968-9 (pa)   LC 94-12290

Maples, a forensic anthropologist, "describes the remains (or, when burnt, cremains) presented to him, describes what he looks for, and guides us through his thinking and the search for additional clues and information. His most difficult, fascinating, and perplexing case dealt with a 1985 apparent double murder and burning, while among historic bodies, Maples dealt with those of Francisco Pizarro, Zachary Taylor, Czar Nicholas II, and Joseph Merrick, 'the Elephant Man.'" Booklist

614.4 Incidence of and public measures to prevent disease

Drexler, Madeline, 1954-

Secret agents; the menace of emerging infections. Joseph Henry Press 2002 316p il $24.95   **614.4**

1. Epidemiology 2. Communicable diseases

ISBN 0-309-07638-2   LC 2001-7832

Also available in paperback from Penguin Bks.

This discusses such topics as food-borne pathogens, antibiotic resistance, animals and insect-borne pathogens, pandemic influenza, infectious causes of chronic disease, and bioterrorism, including the threats of anthrax and smallpox

This is a "fascinating thought-provoking book. . . . A substantial contribution to public information about infectious diseases." Booklist

Includes bibliographical references

Epidemic! the world of infectious diseases; Rob DeSalle, editor. New Press (NY) 1999 246p pa $19.95   **614.4**

1. Epidemics 2. Communicable diseases

ISBN 1-56584-546-3   LC 99-14127

"Published in conjunction with the American Museum of Natural History"

The editor has collected "information about pathogens, methods of infection, the cultural implications of disease, and prevention and presented it in three ways: in brief essays written by scientific experts, profiles of renowned scientists, and case studies. Throughout, major emphasis is placed on the correlation between ecological changes

Epidemic! the world of infectious diseases—*Continued*

and the spread of disease as well as on pathogens' ability to adapt rapidly to prevention and treatment methods." Libr J

Includes bibliographical references

Garrett, Laurie

The coming plague; newly emerging diseases in a world out of balance. Farrar, Straus & Giroux 1994 750p il maps o.p.; Penguin Bks. paperback available $15.95

614.4

1. Epidemics 2. Communicable diseases
ISBN 0-14-025091-3 (pa)   LC 94-26285
"The author demonstrates that the emerging global village means not only superior communication and trade among nations but also the deadly swap of microbes. Analyzing the spread of both familiar diseases like cholera and new viruses like Ebola, this is 'a meticulously researched, genuinely disturbing' account." N Y Times Book Rev

Includes bibliographical references

Karlen, Arno

Man and microbes; disease and plagues in history and modern times. Putnam 1995 266p o.p.; Touchstone paperback available $14

614.4

1. Epidemics 2. Communicable diseases
ISBN 0-684-82270-9 (pa)   LC 94-36164
"A Jeremy P. Tarcher/Putnam book"
Karlen presents a "report on the current global crisis of new and resurgent diseases. Covering cholera, leprosy, cancer, AIDS, viral encephalitis, lethal Ebola fever, streptococcal 'flesh-eating' infections and a host of other killers, he shows how the present wave of diseases arose with drastic environmental change, wars, acceleration of travel, the breakdown of public health measures, and microbial adaptation." Publ Wkly
"The educated adult should read the work as a well-crafted entrepôt on the subject and its literature." Sci Books Films

Includes bibliographical references

Oldstone, Michael B. A.

Viruses, plagues, and history. Oxford Univ. Press 1998 211p il maps $27.50; pa $15.95

614.4

1. Communicable diseases 2. Viruses 3. Epidemics
ISBN 0-19-511723-9; 0-19-513422-2 (pa)
LC 97-9545
The author "starts with accounts of smallpox, yellow fever, measles, and polio, providing lively, well-documented stories about those diseases and their investigators. He well understands historical contexts and developments, and he has interviewed scientists involved in pertinent clinical and research work when that was possible. . . . He moves on to Ebola and other terrifying fevers, mad cow disease, and influenza, thoughtfully exploring the problems mutation poses for prevention and treatment." Booklist

Includes bibliographical references

Ryan, Frank, 1944-

Virus-X; tracking the new killer plagues: out of the present and into the future. Little, Brown 1997 430p il maps hardcover o.p. paperback available $15   **614.4**

1. Communicable diseases 2. Epidemics 3. Viruses
ISBN 0-316-76306-3 (pa)   LC 96-30495
Ryan discusses "emerging viruses and potential global crises. He defines the issue by reviewing the political, medical, and social history of past and recent epidemics . . . [and presents] his hypothesis for the rise of an emerging virus and the potential global risks." Choice
"Of the many recent books about emerging diseases, this is one of the most interesting and disquieting, not only because of its gripping accounts of recent disease outbreaks such as hantavirus and AIDS but because of what it says about the nature of viruses." Libr J

Includes bibliographical references

Wills, Christopher

Yellow fever, black goddess; the coevolution of people and plagues. Addison-Wesley 1996 324p il hardcover o.p. paperback available $16.50   **614.4**

1. Epidemics 2. Communicable diseases
ISBN 0-201-32818-6 (pa)   LC 96-23934
Published in the United Kingdom with title: Plagues: their origins, history, and future
The book's contents range "from the history of particular diseases such as cholera and AIDS (but not yellow fever) to accounts of the author's travels in disease-ridden places to explanations of the genetic mechanisms of evolutionary change." Libr J
The author manages "to provide a good read while weaving seamlessly between historical accounts, scientific detective stories, and personal (or family) anecdotes." New Sci

Includes bibliographical references

614.5 Incidence & prevention of specific diseases

Cantor, Norman F.

In the wake of the plague; the Black Death and the world it made. Free Press 2001 245p il maps $25   **614.5**

1. Plague
ISBN 0-684-85735-9   LC 00-53555
Also available in paperback from Perennial
The author "looks at the effects of the Black Death on 14th-century Europe." Libr J
"By animating history and demonstrating our times' connections to even as remote an event as the Black Death, Cantor's erudite excursion proves most engrossing." Booklist

Includes bibliographical references

Davies, Pete, 1959-

The devil's flu; the world's deadliest influenza epidemic and the scientific hunt for the virus that caused it. Holt & Co. 2000 306p pa $14   **614.5**

1. Influenza 2. Epidemiology
ISBN 0-8050-6622-5   LC 00-36963
First published 1999 in the United Kingdom with title: Catching cold

Davies, Pete, 1959- *—Continued*

"In 1918, in the shadow of the First World War, influenza killed some 40 million people, in the world's worst ever pandemic. . . . Scientists working with influenza . . . know that, in the nature of things, there will be another flu pandemic, that the virus is unstable and unpredictable, that the next outbreak could be a repeat of 1918. In 1997, they thought that repeat had arrived. The story of these influenza scientists, and of their attempts to elucidate the mystery of why the 1918 virus was so lethal, is told in [Davies's book]." Times Lit Suppl

This is "a lively read and a wake-up call about current threats from an old disease." Publ Wkly

Fenn, Elizabeth A. (Elizabeth Anne), 1959-

Pox Americana; the great smallpox epidemic of 1775-82. Hill & Wang 2001 370p $25; pa $15   **614.5**

1. Smallpox 2. United States—History—1775-1783, Revolution

ISBN 0-8090-7820-1; 0-8090-7821-X (pa)

LC 2001-16886

The author describes the effects of smallpox during the American Revolution, including the disease's toll on Native Americans, the greater vulnerability of Americans as compared to the British, and the conditions which transmitted the disease

"Noteworthy as scholarship, Fenn's insightful, readable narrative is a welcome addition to literature about the revolutionary period." Booklist

Includes bibliographical references

Kolata, Gina

Flu; the story of the great influenza pandemic of 1918 and the search for the virus that caused it. Farrar, Straus & Giroux 1999 329p o.p.; Touchstone paperback available $14   **614.5**

1. Influenza 2. Epidemiology

ISBN 0-7432-0398-4 (pa)   LC 99-39665

Also available G.K. Hall large print edition in paperback from Touchstone Bks.

Kolata focuses on the influenza epidemic of 1918, during which "at least 20 million people and possibly more than 40 million people throughout the world took sick and died." Time

"Clearly explaining both the science and the social toll of the pandemic, Kolata writes an admirable history and soberly spells out how the U.S. government is prepared—or unprepared—for a similar public health threat today." Publ Wkly

Marriott, Edward, 1966-

Plague: a story of science, rivalry, and the scourge that won't go away. Metropolitan Bks. 2003 302p il $25   **614.5**

1. Plague

ISBN 0-8050-6680-2   LC 2002-26325

First published 2002 in the United Kingdom with title: The plague race

This is "a contemporary history of the plague, from 1894, when top scientists Alexandre Yersin and Shibasaburo Kitasato vied to discover the source of a Hong Kong outbreak, to contemporary New York, which has as many rats as people." Libr J

"The scientists' competition is the stuff of movies, gripping even though Marriott reveals the ending early." Booklist

Includes bibliographical references

Peters, C. J., 1940-

Virus hunter; thirty years of battling hot viruses around the world; [by] C.J. Peters, with Mark Olshaker. Anchor Bks. (NY) 1997 323p il hardcover o.p. paperback available $14.95   **614.5**

1. Medicine—Research

ISBN 0-385-48558-1 (pa)   LC 97-977

Peters describes his career battling deadly diseases in the lab and in the field. He presents "details about generally ignored medical struggles in less-industrialized nations and warnings about the myriad human factors—from crowded slums, agricultural monocultures, and bureaucratic infighting to reduced science funding and managed health care—that make a future viral disaster possible, perhaps probable." Booklist

This book is "smoothly written and provides an interesting overview of its author's career and education in the workings of medical bureaucracies." Libr J

Preston, Richard

The hot zone. Random House 1994 300p o.p.; Anchor Bks. paperback available $7.99   **614.5**

1. Ebola virus 2. Animal experimentation

ISBN 0-385-47956-5 (pa)   LC 94-13415

"Ebola, a lethal virus that slumbers in an unknown host somewhere in the rain forest, sneaked into the United States in 1989 in a shipment of primates that ended up in a monkey house in Reston, Virginia. This virus jumps between species easily, and takes only weeks to kill its victim, with gory hemorrhaging from various orifices. Preston tells the suspenseful tale of its detection, and gives vivid life to the members of the SWAT team that, for eighteen bio-hazardous days, combatted the strain now known as Ebola Reston." New Yorker

Rhodes, Richard, 1937-

Deadly feasts; tracking the secrets of a terrifying new plague. Simon & Schuster 1997 259p il hardcover o.p. paperback available $13   **614.5**

1. Prion diseases

ISBN 0-684-84425-7 (pa)   LC 97-320

This is an "account of how scientists have tracked the emergence of a new group of fatal brain diseases—transmissible spongiform encephalopathies (TSEs)—that affect humans (Creutzfeldt-Jakob disease) and animals (mad cow disease). . . . These diseases are spread via 'industrial cannibalism' (e.g., infected animal remains fed to animals, humans eating contaminated meat)." Libr J

"Rhodes offers the first popular documentation of a disaster with profound implications." Booklist

615 Pharmacology and therapeutics

Booth, Martin, 1944-

Opium; a history. St. Martin's Press 1998 381p hardcover o.p. paperback available $14.95   **615**

1. Opium

ISBN 0-312-20667-4 (pa)   LC 98-14951

First published 1997 in the United Kingdom

"The first six chapters set the historical scene over time, explore the scientific dimensions and consider the uses and preparations of opium in different cultures,

Booth, Martin, 1944-—*Continued*
from the medicinal to the escapist and the allegedly creative. The next three chapters focus largely on China. . . . The last seven chapters explore the international criminal distribution of opium in the recent era." N Y Times Book Rev
"An excellent historical treatment of the development, use, and misuse of the drug, as well as of society's efforts to control it." Libr J
Includes bibliographical references

Chevallier, Andrew
Encyclopedia of herbal medicine. 2nd ed.
DK Pub. 2000 336p il $40 **615**
1. Materia medica 2. Medical botany
ISBN 0-7894-6783-6 LC 2001-268250
First published 1996 with title: The encyclopedia of medicinal plants
This provides information about the current uses, cultivation, habitat, and folklore of over 550 herbs
This "volume remains a top choice for a library reference on the medicinal use of herbs for the public." Libr J

Consumer drug reference. Consumer Repts.
Bks. il $44.95 **615**
1. Drugs
Annual. First published 1980 with title: United States Pharmacopeia drug information for the consumer. Variant title: Complete drug reference
At head of title on cover: Consumer reports
Published simultaneously with: USP DI. Volume II (Advice for the patient), 22nd edition, 2002
"Including more than 5,500 drugs, this work presents drug information to the patient in clear and easy-to-read language. The drugs are listed by their generic names. The drug monographs make up the greatest portion of the source. Information provided for each drug includes brand names, general description, risks to be considered before taking the medicine (e.g., allergies, pregnancy, breast-feeding), proper use, precautions to be taken while using the medicine, and side effects." Am Ref Books Annu, 1993

Graedon, Joe
The people's pharmacy guide to home and herbal remedies; [by] Joe Graedon and Teresa Graedon. St. Martin's Press 1999 428p $27.95; pa $17.95 **615**
1. Herbs—Therapeutic use 2. Vitamins
ISBN 0-312-20779-4; 0-312-26764-9 (pa)
LC 99-26613
"The first section combines tested scientific research and accumulated folk wisdom to provide the health consumer with treatment suggestions for common ailments. Also included are possible causes and symptoms for selected conditions, as well as contact information for product manufacturers. The second section lists the 50 most commonly used herbs, including their ingredients and information on usage, dose, adverse effects, and drug interactions." Libr J

Karch, Steven B.
The consumer's guide to herbal medicine.
Advanced Res. Press 1999 240p il $29.95
615
1. Herbs—Therapeutic use 2. Materia medica
ISBN 1-889462-06-3
This "guide reviews 67 of the most popular medicinal herbs, including chamomile, echinacea, garlic, ginseng,

and St. John's wort. . . . Each two- to three-page entry contains an illustration of the plant. Full botanical and common names are given as well as the plant's geographic origin and the documented and legendary history of its use. Proven effects (based on recent research data), potential problems, warnings, and safe dosage amounts are included." Booklist

Kuhn, Cynthia
Buzzed; the straight facts about the most used and abused drugs from alcohol to ecstasy; [by] Cynthia Kuhn, Scott Swartzwelder, Wilkie Wilson; with Leigh Heather Wilson and Jeremy Foster. 2nd ed.
Norton 2003 345p il pa $16.95 **615**
1. Drugs 2. Drug abuse
ISBN 0-393-32493-1 LC 2003-11411
First published 1998
This guide discusses "drugs, from alcohol, caffeine, and nicotine to heroin, ecstasy, and Special K. In both quick-reference summaries and in-depth analysis, it reports on how these drugs enter the body, how they manipulate the brain, their short-term and long-term effects, the kinds of 'high' they produce, and the circumstances in which they can be deadly." Publisher's note
"The book adopts a straight, neutral tone that reflects its commitment to providing unbiased, scientific fact. . . . Best of all, the descriptions are jargon-free, making this book a great choice for anyone looking for clear, reliable information about any kind of drug." Publ Wkly
Includes bibliographical references

Long, James W.
The essential guide to prescription drugs.
HarperCollins Pubs. pa $20.95 **615**
1. Drugs
Annual. First published 1977
This reference work gives "drug profiles, including major prescription drugs, arranged by generic name. Each profile provides brand names, dosage, actions, and precautions for use. Supplementary tables present drug interactions with food, diseases, light, and other drugs. Access is available through the index by brand or generic name. Considered the standard of directories compiled for the layperson." Ref Sources for Small & Medium-sized Libr. 5th edition

The **Merck** index; an encyclopedia of chemicals, drugs and biologicals. Merck & Co. il $45 **615**
1. Materia medica 2. Drugs
Also available CD-ROM version
First published 1889. (13th edition 2001) Periodically revised
"Technical descriptions of the preparation, properties, uses, commercial names, and toxicity of drugs and medicines." N Y Public Libr Book of How & Where to Look It Up

Miller, Richard Lawrence
The encyclopedia of addictive drugs.
Greenwood Press 2002 491p $75 **615**
1. Drugs—Encyclopedias 2. Drug abuse—Encyclopedias
ISBN 0-313-31807-7 LC 2002-75332
"The more than 130 substances included are both natural and pharmaceutical products, all associated with misuse and addiction. Listed by common name, the initial citation includes pronunciation, Chemical Abstracts

Miller, Richard Lawrence—*Continued*

Service Registry Number, formal and informal names, drug type, U.S. availability, and more. The accompanying article discusses uses, drawbacks, abuse factors, drug interactions, cancer risks, and effects on pregnancy, and concludes with a bibliography." SLJ

Physician's desk reference. Medical Economics $92.95   **615**

1. Materia medica
ISSN 0093-4461

Annual. First published 1947. Title varies

2004 edition includes CD-ROM offer

"Latest available information intended for physicians on over 2,000 products. Covers dosage, contraindications, precautions, side effects, and undesirable interactions. The information is furnished by the manufacturers of the various products. Product identification in color." N Y Public Libr Book of How & Where to Look It Up

Physicians desk reference for nonprescription drugs. Medical Economics $58.95   **615**

1. Nonprescription drugs
ISSN 1044-1395

Annual. First published 1980

"A companion to the *Physician's Desk Reference*. Provides essential information on nonprescription drugs. Indexed by manufacturer, product name, product category, and active ingredients." N Y Public Libr Book of How & Where to Look It Up

Plotkin, Mark

Medicine quest; in search of nature's healing secrets; [by] Mark J. Plotkin. Viking 2000 224p il hardcover o.p. paperback available $14   **615**

1. Materia medica
ISBN 0-14-026210-5 (pa)   LC 99-42822

The author "takes the reader on many 'voyages,' from high mountains, deep jungles, and archeological excavations, on into the deepest depths of the oceans—all in quest of the biological materials that may be analyzed and then utilized in the prevention and overcoming of human, animal, and plant diseases." Sci Books Films

Includes bibliographical references

Seaman, Barbara

The greatest experiment ever performed on women; exploding the estrogen myth. Hyperion 2003 332p $24.95   **615**

1. Estrogen 2. Menopause
ISBN 0-7868-6853-8

The author "demonstrates that the pandemic abuse of the trust women place in their doctors begins with medical practitioners, abetted by drug manufacturers and the Food and Drug Administration, from synthetic estrogen's 1938 debut onward." Booklist

"Seaman passionately and convincingly argues that women have been unneccessarily put at risk by doctors treating menopause as a disease." Publ Wkly

Talbott, Shawn

A guide to understanding dietary supplements; magic bullets or modern snake oil? [by] Shawn M. Talbott. Haworth Press 2003 xxv, 713p il $119.95; pa $59.95   **615**

1. Dietary supplements 2. Drug industry
ISBN 0-7890-1455-6; 0-7890-1456-4 (pa)
LC 2002-68770

This overview of the dietary supplement industry and its products "examines more than 140 supplements arranged under broad categories such as weight loss and joint health." Booklist

Includes bibliographical references

615.5 Therapeutics

Blackwell complementary and alternative medicine; fast facts for medical practice; edited by Mary A. Herring, Molly M. Roberts. Blackwell Science 2002 142p pa $22.95   **615.5**

1. Alternative medicine 2. Medical practice
ISBN 0-632-04583-3   LC 2001-7573

Partial contents: Foundational concepts of complementary & alternative medicine; Significance of CAM in healthcare, by S. Roe; Guidelines for advising patients on CAM, by M. Herring; Politics of CAM, by K. Lawson; Psychoneuroimmunology, by K. Lawson; Common modalities; Acupuncture, by S. Shannon; Aroma therapy, by L. Halcon & A. Levitan; Biofields and energy therapies, by E. Baruch; Feldenkrais method & Alexander technique, by J. Ziff & J. D. Grotte; Guided imagery, by M. Rossman; Homeopathy, by E. Anderson; Hypnosis, by D. Handel; Massage therapies, by A. Reinking-Hanf; Music therapy, by J. Graham-Pole; Naturopathy, by S. Ehrlich; Reiki, by L. Thrapp; Tai Chi & Qigong, by A. Kuramoto; Therapeutic touch-healing touch therapy, by A. Quinlan-Colwell; CAM's impact on medical practice; Issues of blended practice, by S. Roe; A glimpse of U.S. CAM resources, by T. Throckmorton

This guide features summaries of 15 common complementary and alternative medicine therapies, each written by practitioners of alternative medicine. It covers information such as uses for these therapies, how they work, histories, facts, and guidelines

Includes bibliographical references

Cassileth, Barrie R.

The alternative medicine handbook; the complete reference guide to alternative and complementary therapies. Norton 1998 340p il hardcover o.p. paperback available $19.95   **615.5**

1. Alternative medicine
ISBN 0-393-31816-8 (pa)   LC 97-16268

"Describes over 50 techniques, from acupuncture and apitherapy to yoga and shamanism. Grouping them alphabetically within seven broad approaches, she describes the claims of each one's practitioners and the theories or beliefs on which it is based, discusses available scientific research on the subject, and notes what the therapy can actually accomplish, any relevant licensing regulations and sources of further information. Explanations are concise and warnings are clear." Publ Wkly

The **Illustrated** encyclopedia of body-mind disciplines; Nancy Allison, editor. Rosen Pub. Group 1999 xxxii, 448p il $105.95
615.5

1. Alternative medicine
ISBN 0-8239-2546-3   LC 98-24969
This "text is divided into 16 sections, each of which begins with an introductory essay discussing the disciplines included in that section. Each discipline is described by a certified practitioner in terms of history, basic principles, and potential benefits and risks. Short resources/reading lists follow each discipline description." Libr J

Maleskey, Gale
Nature's medicines; from asthma to weight gain, from colds to high cholesterol: the most powerful all-natural cures; by Gale Maleskey, and the editors of Prevention Health Books. Rodale Press 1999 688p $31.95   **615.5**
1. Naturopathy 2. Alternative medicine
ISBN 1-57954-028-7   LC 99-15694
The first three sections of this health guide cover "vitamins, minerals, herbs, and emerging supplements. The major portion of [the book] follows, with an . . . A-Z listing of 61 substances, from Acidophilus to Zinc. Sidebars provide botanical names and highlight special instructions and cautions. Following this section is an A-Z listing of more than 75 health concerns." Booklist

Marti, James
The alternative health & medicine encyclopedia; [by] James Marti with Andrea Hine; foreword by Michael T. Murray. 2nd ed. Gale Res. 1998 xxiii, 462p $75   **615.5**
1. Alternative medicine 2. Health
ISBN 0-7876-0073-3   LC 97-31144
First published 1995
This guide offers information on such therapies as biofeedback, acupuncture, acupressure, hypnosis, nutrition, reflexology, botanical medicine, homeopathy, chiropractics, detoxification, and massage
Includes bibliographical references

McTaggart, Lynne
The field: the quest for the secret force of the universe. HarperCollins Pubs. 2002 288p hardcover o.p. paperback available $12.95
615.5
1. Alternative medicine 2. Mind and body
ISBN 0-06-093117-5 (pa)   LC 2002-17348
The author "describes scientific discoveries that she believes point to a unifying concept of the universe, one that reconciles mind with matter, classic Newtonian science with quantum physics and, most importantly, science with religion." Publ Wkly
Includes bibliographical references

Murray, Michael T.
Encyclopedia of natural medicine; [by] Michael T. Murray, Joseph Pizzorno. rev 2nd ed. Prima Pub. 1998 946p il pa $24.95
615.5
1. Naturopathy—Encyclopedias
ISBN 0-7615-1157-1   LC 97-50569
First published 1991

This volume is divided into three parts. Part I explains the philosophy and principles of natural medicine; Part II covers body systems, and specific health problems are dealt with in Part III

The **New** York Times guide to alternative health; a consumer reference; by Jane E. Brody, Denise Grady, and the reporters of the New York Times. Times Bks. 2001 394p il pa $16   **615.5**
1. Alternative medicine 2. Consumer education
ISBN 0-8050-6743-4   LC 2001-17160
This guide "offers facts, theories, and anecdotal evidence related to several of the most popular alternative therapies, including acupuncture, massage therapy, herbal medicine, and chiropractic. . . . This is a useful resource for libraries that receive frequent questions about alternative therapies. It will also be a good resource for students who are writing papers on alternative therapies, as it includes both historical and current information about the therapies." Libr J

Pelletier, Kenneth R.
The best alternative medicine; What works? What does not? introduction by Andrew Weil. Simon & Schuster 2000 448p $26; pa $15   **615.5**
1. Alternative medicine
ISBN 0-684-84207-6; 0-7432-00027-6 (pa)
          LC 99-26629
Pelletier "explains alternative and complementary medicine including commonly used treatment modalities and 75 medical conditions and correlating therapies. What sets Pelletier's work apart in this genre are cited studies and references. The selected bibliography alone is more than 50 pages long." Libr J

Whorton, James C., 1942-
Nature cures; the history of alternative medicine in America. Oxford Univ. Press 2002 368p il $30   **615.5**
1. Alternative medicine
ISBN 0-19-514071-0   LC 2002-22023
"This study documents the major 'unconventional' healing movements of 19th- and 20th century America. Whorton . . . traces the origins and influences of Thomsonianism, homeopathy, mesmerism, Christian Science, osteopathy, chiropractic, naturopathy, and acupuncture, briefly discussing therapeutic touch, visualization, and prayer as well." Libr J
Includes bibliographical references

615.8 Specific therapies and kinds of therapies

Campbell, Don G.
The Mozart effect; tapping the power of music to heal the body, strengthen the mind, and unlock the creative spirit; [by] Don Campbell. Avon Bks. 1997 332p il hardcover o.p. paperback available $14   **615.8**
1. Music therapy 2. Music—Psychological aspects
ISBN 0-06-093720-3 (pa)   LC 97-27570
The author "uses case histories to show how music can enhance memory, learning, and creativity. Properly chosen and presented, music can also alleviate and in some cases apparently cure medical problems, he says." Booklist
Includes bibliographical references

Mitchell, Deborah R.

The Botox miracle; [by] Deborah Mitchell; consulting medical editor, Roberta D. Sengelmann. Pocket Bks. 2002 212p il pa $11 **615.8**

1. Botulinum toxin 2. Skin—Care
ISBN 0-7434-6463-X   LC 2003-544572
"A Lynn Sonberg book"

The author "describes how wrinkles develop and how Botox works to reduce or eliminate them. Covered are how to find a doctor, what to expect during treatment, the frequency of treatments, side effects, and possible complications. Also describes other wrinkle remedies for Botox-resistant areas. Simply written, this is a good introduction to the subject." Libr J

Wise, Anna

Awakening the mind; a guide to mastering the power of your brain waves. Tarcher/Putnam 2002 255p il pa $16.95

615.8

1. Mental healing 2. Spiritual healing 3. Brain
ISBN 1-58542-145-6   LC 2001-53501

"This work aims to help readers improve their mental powers by optimizing brain-wave patterns. . . . [Wise discusses] the four types of brain-wave patterns, or EEGs, giving readers 'subjective landmarks' to help them gauge their own patterns without an EEG biofeedback machine." Libr J

615.9   Toxicology

Barker, Rodney, 1946-

And the waters turned to blood; the ultimate biological threat. Simon & Schuster 1997 346p il hardcover o.p. paperback available $14   **615.9**

1. Burkholder, JoAnn M., 1953- 2. Algae 3. Poisons and poisoning
ISBN 0-684-83845-1 (pa)   LC 97-86

"Barker follows the work of Dr. JoAnn Burkholder, a scientist from North Carolina State University, as she attempts to obtain academic respect and funding for her research on a new species of dinoflagellate that is responsible for a number of major fish kills. . . . He presents a detailed discussion of Burkholder's struggles with state officials as she becomes convinced that the organism is toxic, not only to fish but also to humans. Written in a clear, non-technical style." Libr J

Callahan, Joan R.

Biological hazards; an Oryx sourcebook. Oryx Press 2002 385p il (Oryx sourcebooks on hazards and disasters) $64.95   **615.9**

1. Communicable diseases 2. Poisons and poisoning 3. Environmental health
ISBN 1-57356-385-4   LC 2001-55184

This sourcebook provides "introductory information on a wide range of biological hazards. . . . Chapters divide hazards into categories: human pathogens in water, food, and air; those transmitted by contact; plant and animal pathogens and pests; venoms, toxins, and allergens; and animals that are a threat for predatory or other behavior. Another chapter provides information on controversial topics such as immunization and biological warfare. . . . The chapters that deal with different kinds of hazards offer extensive references and recommended readings. Lists of additional resources, including statistics and documents, print resources, nonprint resources, and organizations, comprise the final chapters." Booklist

Davis, Devra Lee

When smoke ran like water; tales of environmental deception and the battle against pollution; [by] Devra Davis. Basic Bks. 2002 336p $26   **615.9**

1. Environmental health 2. Pollution
ISBN 0-465-01521-2   LC 2002-10562

Contents: Where I come from; The phantom epidemic; How to become a statistic; How the game is played; Zones of incomprehension; The new sisterhood of breast cancer; Save the males; Earthquakes and spouting bowls; A grand experiment; Defiant figures

"This is an exposé on how industrial polluters deceived the public, belittled scientists and academics, and pressured government agencies to stifle regulations." Libr J

Includes bibliographical references

Fagin, Dan

Toxic deception; how the chemical industry manipulates science, bends the law, and endangers your health; [by] Dan Fagin, Marianne Lavelle, and the Center for Public Integrity. Carol Pub. Group 1996 xxv, 294p o.p.; Common Courage Press paperback available $17.95   **615.9**

1. Chemicals 2. Chemical industry
ISBN 1-56751-162-7 (pa)   LC 96-41045
"A Birch Lane Press book"

This work examines "the regulatory foundations of four suspect chemicals—atrazine, alachor, formaldehyde, and perchloroethylene—and the chemical industry's role in the design and calculation of risk assessments. . . . This well-researched exposé is recommended." Libr J

Includes bibliographical references

Markowitz, Gerald E.

Deceit and denial; the deadly politics of industrial pollution; [by] Gerald Markowitz and David Rosner. University of Calif. Press 2002 xx, 408p il $45; pa $19.95   **615.9**

1. Environmental health 2. Industrial waste 3. Pollution
ISBN 0-520-21749-7; 0-520-24063-4 (pa)
LC 2001-58515

"This is a historical acccount of corporate control of the lead, plastics, and petroleum industries and the campaign of denial regarding the toxic effects on workers, consumers, and the general public of chemicals used in the manufacture of paint, toys, furniture, plastics, and other products. . . . This is not another diatribe about industrial pollution. Instead, it is a well-researched work that analyzes the conflict between industry's need to provide products that make life easier for consumers and the public's demand for legislation and standards to protect them from toxic pollution caused by the manufacture of these products. Recommended for health, environment, and law collections." Libr J

Includes bibliographical references

Turkington, Carol

The poisons and antidotes sourcebook; foreword by Shirley K. Osterhout. 2nd ed. Facts on File 1999 408p $38.50; pa $16.95

615.9

1. Poisons and poisoning
ISBN 0-8160-3959-3; 0-8160-3960-7 (pa)
LC 98-55190

First published 1994 with title: Poisons and antidotes

Turkington, Carol—*Continued*

This book "describes more than 600 toxins and their sources, including: common household poisons; insecticides and fertilizers; poisonous spiders, snakes, and other venomous creatures; addictive drugs, such as nicotine and cocaine; poison ivy, sumac, and other toxic shrubs." Publisher's note

Includes bibliographical references

616 Diseases

Bakalar, Nick

Where the germs are; a scientific safari; [by] Nicholas Bakalar. Wiley 2003 262p il $24.95   **616**

1. Microbiology 2. Germ theory of disease 3. Bacteria

ISBN 0-471-15589-6   LC 2003-271569

This book is "about our everyday interactions with microbes. . . . It reveals some of the extraordinary things scientists now know about these most ordinary companions. . . . You'll learn, for example, that your nice clean kitchen is a more likely source of illness than your bathroom; that fast-food restaurants are less contaminated with E. coli than fancier table-service establishments; that your luxurious daily bath or shower is doing almost nothing for your hygiene; that a certain bacterium can make you sick even after it's been boiled to death; and that one California scientist found the cure for smelly socks by creating cloth that kills germs." Publisher's note

The author's "excellent chapter on childhood diseases and vaccines should be required reading for parents, and teenagers should be plunked down in a chair with the chapter on sexually transmitted diseases. . . . His writing is witty, and he gives all the details of germs and illnesses without medical school jargon." Publ Wkly

Biddle, Wayne

A field guide to germs. 2nd Anchor Books ed. Anchor Bks. (NY) 2002 209p il pa $13.95   **616**

1. Microbiology 2. Germ theory of disease

ISBN 1-400-03051-X   LC 2002-511927

First published 1995 by Holt & Co.

"Relaying essential information about the 100 most prevalent, powerful, or literarily famous microbiological malefactors in dictionary-encyclopedia style, Biddle injects social and political history into the exposition to provide fuller understanding of germs, their roles in society, their histories, and their current statuses. . . . Eminently entertaining, the book yet has the serious purpose of showing how concerns other than science and the relief of human suffering have affected the course of medical history." Booklist [review of 1995 edition]

Crawford, Dorothy H.

The invisible enemy; a natural history of viruses. Oxford Univ. Press 2000 275p il $27.50; pa $14.95   **616**

1. Viruses

ISBN 0-19-850332-6; 0-19-856481-3 (pa)

LC 00-36756

The author begins by explaining how viruses "subvert the internal machinery of living cells to reproduce and spread. . . . Ms. Crawford examines the threats posed by the Lassa and Hanta viruses—as well as Ebola, . . . and assesses the prospects for a flu pandemic like that of 1918, which infected half the world's population." Economist

"Crawford offers new knowledge and insights for any reader, regardless of the depth of their science education." New Sci

Dillard, James

The chronic pain solution; your personal path to pain relief; [by] James N. Dillard with Leigh Ann Hirschman. Bantam Bks. 2002 xxiii, 439p il $24.95; pa $13.95   **616**

1. Pain

ISBN 0-553-80183-X; 0-553-38111-3 (pa)

LC 2002-23225

The author discusses how pain affects your body and mind. He outlines treatment methods, from state-of-the-art microsurgery and pharmaceuticals to acupuncture, yoga and feedback. He provides chapters on various forms of pain, from arthritis and back pain to migraines and fibromyalgia and includes a pain-control diet

Includes bibliographical references

Grob, Gerald N., 1931-

The deadly truth; a history of disease in America. Harvard Univ. Press 2002 349p il $35   **616**

1. Diseases 2. Medicine—United States—History

ISBN 0-674-00881-2   LC 2002-17267

"Is it possible to eradicate disease? Grob . . . addresses this question while offering a history of disease in America to illustrate the ongoing relationships among society, environment, and human health." Libr J

Includes bibliographical references

Human diseases and conditions; Neil Izenberg, editor in chief. Scribner 2000 3v il set $295   **616**

1. Medicine

ISBN 0-684-80543-X   LC 99-51442

Also available: Supplement 1, Behavioral health $100 (ISBN 0-684-80643-6); Supplement II, Infectious diseases and the immune system $100 (ISBN 0-684-31260-3)

Published in association with the Center for Children's Health Media, the Nemours Foundation

"Almost 300 diseases and conditions are included (with an equal number of color photographs, charts, and illustrations), covering such topics as cleft palate, kuru, obsessive-compulsive disorder, slipped disk, and typhoid fever. . . . Each entry, ranging in length from one to eight pages, contains information on natural history, causes, cures, and prevention, when appropriate. . . . Children and teenagers are obviously the intended audience, though any adult would find this book valuable." Libr J

For a fuller review see: Booklist, July, 2000

Koestler, Angela J.

Understanding chronic pain; [by] Angela J. Koestler, Ann Myers. University Press of Miss. 2002 162p il (Understanding health and sickness series) $28; pa $12   **616**

1. Pain

ISBN 1-57806-439-2; 1-57806-440-6 (pa)

LC 2002-1017

Contents: What is chronic pain?; What causes chronic pain?; Seeking relief; Taking care of yourself; Low back pain; Nerve pain; Rheumatic pain; Cancer pain; Other chronic pain conditions; The search for cures

Koestler, Angela J.—*Continued*

The authors "provide basic information about cultural history, definitions, theories, and causes of pain. They describe treatment specialists and the usual and varied approaches to pain relief and the responsibility of self-care. . . . This is a compact and readable self-help handbook for patients and their families." Choice

Moyers, Bill

Healing and the mind; [by] Bill Moyers; Betty Sue Flowers, editor; David Grubin, executive editor; Elizabeth Meryman-Brunner, art research. Doubleday 1993 369p il hardcover o.p. paperback available $21.95
     616

1. Medicine 2. Mind and body 3. Psychophysiology
ISBN 0-385-47687-6 (pa)   LC 92-31074
In this "companion volume to a PBS TV series, Moyers explores the roles of thoughts and emotions in illness and health through interviews with 16 doctors and scientists." Publ Wkly

Stoffman, Phyllis, 1948-

The family guide to preventing and treating 100 infectious illnesses; foreword by Ronald Gold. Wiley 1995 406p pa $18.95   **616**

1. Communicable diseases
ISBN 0-471-00014-0   LC 94-23832
"Parts 1 and 2 provide an overview of infectious disease and how to prevent it, including lists of recommended vaccinations and a guide for travelers. Part 3 covers 100 diseases such as hantavirus, croup, and AIDS. . . . Unlike many such guides, this one tells you not only how to care for a sick child but which antibiotics are used to treat the disease, the length of its infectious period, possible complications, and how to avoid or minimize chances of getting it." Libr J

Teichler-Zallen, Doris

Does it run in the family? a consumer's guide to DNA testing for genetic disorders. Rutgers Univ. Press 1997 201p il $24.95
     616

1. Medical genetics
ISBN 0-8135-2446-6   LC 96-49677
The author explains "the basics of genetics, outlining likely scenarios for individuals and families who suddenly (often through prenatal testing or with the birth of a child with a genetic disorder) or eventually (as a possible carrier or family member) need more information on the potential uses of genetic tests. Zallen is clear, concise, and sensitive to the difficult decisions that families will have to make." Libr J
Includes bibliographical references

Vertosick, Frank T.

Why we hurt; the natural history of pain; [by] Frank T. Vertosick, Jr. Harcourt 2000 292p hardcover o.p. paperback available $14
     616

1. Pain
ISBN 0-15-601403-3 (pa)   LC 99-45848
"The types of pain profiled range from the common, like migraine, angina pectoris and ruptured disc, to the arcane, like tic douloureux and phantom limb pain. Each chapter is a triptych, presenting a clinical case, the relevant biology and the way different cultures have viewed the disorder." N Y Times Book Rev

Wade, Nicholas

Life script; how the human genome discoveries will transform medicine and enhance your health. Simon & Schuster 2001 204p $24; pa $12   **616**

1. Human Genome Project 2. Medical genetics
ISBN 0-7432-1605-9; 0-7432-2318-7 (pa)
     LC 2001-42627
This is an "account of how the human genome was decoded and its effect on health, medicine, and society." Libr J
"Without dumbing down the issues or clogging them with data, Wade allows readers to ponder . . . questions for themselves." Publ Wkly
Includes bibliographical references

616.02   Domestic medicine and medical emergencies

American College of Physicians complete home medical guide; editor-in-chief David R. Goldmann; associate editor David A. Horowitz. 2nd American ed. DK Pub. 2003 1104p il $50   **616.02**

1. Medicine 2. Health self-care
ISBN 0-7894-9673-9
First published 1999
"Completely revised and updated." Cover
This guide discusses genetics, health, and health care; lifestyle issues such as diet, exercise, and substance abuse, medical examinations, lab tests and imaging techniques; drug treatment, surgery, and therapies. Illustrated with diagrams, anatomical artworks, and over 2000 photographs. A select listing of online medical sites is also included

American Medical Association family medical guide; medical editor, Charles B. Clayman. rev & updated 3rd ed. Random House 1994 880p il $39.95   **616.02**

1. Medicine 2. Health self-care
ISBN 0-679-41290-5   LC 94-2116
First published 1982
"Aimed at general readers, this guide is in four main sections: general discussion of the healthy body, self-diagnosis symptom charts with visual aids to diagnosis, diseases and other disorders and problems, and caring for the sick, including a section on accidents and emergencies. Glossary and subject index." Guide to Ref Books. 11th edition

The **Doctors** book of home remedies; simple, doctor-approved self-care solutions for 146 common health conditions; by the editors of Prevention Health Books. Rodale 2002 672p $29.95   **616.02**

1. Medicine 2. Health self-care
ISBN 1-57954-611-0   LC 2002-9240
First published 1990
"Employing advice culled from hundreds of doctors, the editors present an A-to-Z of common ailments from asthma to menopause to warts, and multiple suggestions about what to do about them. Included within are '8 Tips to Stop the Cough,' '14 Soothing Ideas' for lactose intolerance '12 Comforting Steps' for vaginal infections and '35 Hints for a High-Energy Life.'" Publ Wkly

Johns Hopkins symptoms and remedies; the complete home medical reference; medical editor, Simeon Margolis; prepared by the editors of The Johns Hopkins medical letter health after 50. Rebus; [distributed by] Random House 2003 736p il $39.95

616.02

1. Medicine 2. Health self-care
ISBN 0-929661-79-6   LC 2002-37036

This work attempts to guide the reader from symptom to possible diagnosis with the use of checklists and charts. Prevention, treatments, medications and when to consult a doctor are also discussed

The **Merck** manual of medical information; Mark H. Beers, editor-in-chief; Andrew J. Fletcher, Thomas V. Jones, and Robert Porter, senior assistant editors; Michael Berkwitz, and Justin L. Kaplan, assistant editors. 2nd home ed. Merck Res. Labs. 2003 xxxviii, 1907p il $37.50   **616.02**

1. Medicine
ISBN 0-9119-1035-2   LC 2002-115250

Also available online

First published 1997

"A detailed table of contents lists 25 sections divided into chapters. The first, 'Fundamentals,' explains basic anatomy and physiology, the aging process, fitness, communicating with health professionals, and legal and ethical issues. The others cover specific organs, systems, diseases and disorders, drugs, and first aid. The sections dealing with organs and systems begin with the biology of the system and then explain the symptoms, diagnosis, prognosis, and treatment of diseases that may affect it. There are color diagrams of relevant anatomy as well as an eight-page insert of anatomical charts." Booklist

"Written for the layperson, articles are clear, comprehensive and detailed. There are excellent charts and illustrations to further make the material more understandable. Almost every conceivable medical condition is covered." Publ Wkly

616.07   Pathology

Boaz, Noel Thomas

Evolving health; the origins of illness and how the modern world is making us sick; [by] Noel T. Boaz. Wiley 2002 250p $27.95

616.07

1. Diseases 2. Evolution 3. Adaptation (Biology)
ISBN 0-471-35261-6   LC 2001-6727

The author posits that "human illnesses can be understood as damage to those adaptations that we took on at various stages in our evolution from pre-life molecules to modern Homo sapiens. Preventing these illnesses entails avoiding what causes the damage—which too frequently are the everyday hazards of twenty-first-century life." Publisher's note

Includes bibliographical references

Hall, Stephen S.

A commotion in the blood; life, death, and the immune system. Holt & Co. 1997 544p il (Sloan technology series) hardcover o.p. paperback available $16.95   **616.07**

1. Immune system 2. Cancer
ISBN 0-8050-5841-9 (pa)   LC 97-404

"This history of immunology focuses on efforts to fight off cancer using T cells, antibodies, and mysterious substances like TNF (tumor necrosis factor), all of which can act in concert to kill malignant tissue." New Yorker

"This is an impressive, if not entirely successful, look at scientists' understanding of the immune system, and at the marketing culture that now surrounds it." Publ Wkly

Includes bibliographical references

The **Johns** Hopkins consumer guide to medical tests; what you can expect, how you should prepare, what your results mean; Simeon Margolis, medical editor. Rebus 2001 400p il $39.95   **616.07**

1. Diagnosis
ISBN 0-929661-63-X   LC 2001-19980

"A John Hopkins health after 50 book"

This is a "guide to over 170 medical tests. . . . The entries, generally about two pages long, list the test's purpose and special concerns, what the results may mean, pretest preparations, risks and complications, and estimated cost." Libr J

Nuland, Sherwin B.

How we die; reflections on life's final chapter. Knopf 1994 278p hardcover o.p. paperback available $14   **616.07**

1. Death
ISBN 0-679-74244-1 (pa)   LC 93-24590

The author provides "information on the clinical, biological and emotional details of deaths resulting from heart disease, stroke, cancer, AIDS, Alzheimer's disease, old age, accidents, suicide, euthanasia and murder or violent physical assault." Publ Wkly

"Nuland is one of those rare physicians who know a great deal about a great deal, not only medicine but also its history and, beyond that, literature and the humanities." Commentary

Pagana, Kathleen Deska, 1952-

Mosby's diagnostic and laboratory test reference; [by] Kathleen Deska Pagana, Timothy James Pagana. Mosby $36.95

616.07

1. Diagnosis 2. Nursing
First published 1992. (6th edition 2003) Frequently revised

This handbook features alphabetically organized laboratory and diagnostic tests which "are presented in a consistent format. . . . Each test entry includes, where relevant, alternate or abbreviated test names; type of test; normal findings; possible critical values; test explanation and related physiology; contraindications; potential complications; interfering factors; procedure and patient care (before, during, and after); and abnormal findings." Publisher's note

Segen, J. C.
The patient's guide to medical tests; everything you need to know about the tests your doctor orders; {by} Joseph C. Segen and Josie Wade. 2nd ed. Facts on File 2002 418p (Facts on File library of health and living) $44; pa $17.95 **616.07**
1. Diagnosis
ISBN 0-8160-4651-4; 0-8160-4652-2 (pa)
LC 2002-18824
First published 1997 with Joseph Stauffer as joint author
This "guide presents information on more than 1,000 commonly prescribed tests and procedures. Each entry includes a description of the test, patient preparation required, a description of the procedure itself, the reference range, what abnormal values may signify, and the approximate cost of each test." Publisher's note

616.1 Diseases of the cardiovascular system

Bloom, Miriam, 1934-
Understanding sickle cell disease. University Press of Miss. 1995 126p il map (Understanding health and sickness series) hardcover o.p. paperback available $11.95
616.1
1. Sickle cell anemia
ISBN 0-87805-745-5 (pa) LC 94-44275
Topics covered "include a discussion of who gets the disease (which includes not only people of African descent but of Mediterranean ancestry as well), the red blood cell, effects of the disease, care of sickle cell patients, family planning, and the search for a cure. An extensive list of organizations and support groups is included." Libr J
"Although it imparts much technical information, the book is very much for the lay reader." Booklist
Includes bibliographical references

Cooke, John P.
The cardiovascular cure; how to strengthen your self-defense against heart attack and stroke; [by] John P. Cooke and Judith Zimmer. Broadway Bks. 2002 xxvi, 310p $25; pa $14.95 **616.1**
1. Cardiovascular system—Diseases
ISBN 0-7679-0881-3; 0-7679-0882-1 (pa)
LC 2001-55369
The author outlines a program for fighting cardiovascular disease by enhancing your body's natural defenses with a diet, supplements, and an exercise program

DeBakey, Michael E., 1908-
The new living heart; [by] Michael E. DeBakey, Antonio M. Gotto. Adams Media Corp. 1997 495p il pa $18.95 **616.1**
1. Heart diseases 2. Cardiovascular system—Diseases
ISBN 1-55850-722-1 LC 97-365
First published 1977 with title: The living heart
This book covers "diagnostic procedures; conditions such as atherosclerosis, aneurysms, hypertension, stroke, and congenital and acquired heart diseases; risk factors and healthy-heart lifestyles; surgical and drug therapies; and the vascular system." Libr J

Gould, K. Lance
Heal your heart; how you can prevent or reverse heart disease. Rutgers Univ. Press 1998 xxxi, 274p il hardcover o.p. paperback available $20 **616.1**
1. Heart diseases
ISBN 0-8135-2896-8 (pa) LC 97-39172
The author "advocates early diagnosis to minimize risk [of heart disease], a very low-fat diet, moderate exercise, and the use of cholesterol-lowering drugs." Libr J
"Although Gould's lucid style . . . makes things easy for the reader, the uncluttered, well-labeled illustrations help substantially, too." Booklist
Includes bibliographical references

Heart attack! advice for patients by patients; [by] Kathleen Berra [et al.] Yale Univ. Press 2002 232p $32.50; pa $14.95 **616.1**
1. Heart diseases
ISBN 0-300-08980-5; 0-300-09190-7 (pa)
LC 2001-33256
This "book on the current state of the diagnosis and treatment of heart attacks includes 11 personal accounts by patients and 5 chapters by health professionals. . . . Succinct yet detailed, this collection should prove valuable to both health professionals and the general public." Booklist
Includes bibliographical references

Klaidman, Stephen
Saving the heart; the battle to conquer coronary disease. Oxford Univ. Press 1999 272p il $27.50 **616.1**
1. Heart diseases
ISBN 0-19-511279-2 LC 99-28930
Klaidman examines "the people, the business aspects, and the ethical issues relating to cardiology. Using clear lay language, he humanizes the history of cardiology and explains the evolution of many of the procedures commonly used today—including angioplasty, bypass surgery, and stenting. He also carefully weighs the advantages and disadvantages of commercialism in medical device technology." Libr J
Includes bibliographical references

Kra, Siegfried J.
What every woman must know about heart disease; a no-nonsense approach to diagnosing, treating, and preventing the #1 killer of women. Warner Bks. 1996 226p hardcover o.p. paperback available $14.99
616.1
1. Heart diseases 2. Women—Diseases
ISBN 0-446-39532-3 (pa) LC 94-24691
The author discusses the rapid growth of heart disease and "its symptoms in women, which often differ from those in men. Particular chapters treat such topics as the diagnosis and treatment of heart attacks, mitral valve prolapse, palpitations, vascular disease, and varicose veins; and, in the book's second part, topics in prevention and treatment." Booklist

McGowan, Mary P., 1959-
Heart fitness for life; the essential guide to preventing and reversing heart disease; by Mary P. McGowan, with Jo McGowan Chopra. Oxford Univ. Press 1997 322p il hardcover o.p. paperback available $16.95

616.1

1. Heart diseases—Prevention
ISBN 0-19-512909-1 (pa)   LC 97-29834
The author "seeks to cover all the bases of a heart-healthy lifestyle, particularly for those recovering from heart disease, by discussing diet, exercise, stress relief, smoking, and medications. The information is current, and much is drawn from the work of other experts in the field." Libr J
Includes bibliographical references

The **New** living heart diet; [by] Michael E. DeBakey [et al.] [Completely rev and updated] Simon & Schuster 1996 414p pa $16   **616.1**
1. Heart diseases—Diet therapy
ISBN 0-684-81188-X   LC 95-40787
"A Fireside book"
First published 1984 with title: The living heart diet
This book includes "information about risk factors for coronary heart disease and . . . dietary recommendations for preventing it. The first half relates such health considerations as cholesterol, diabetes and blood pressure to diet; menus and 300-plus recipes with complete nutritional analyses constitute the second half." Publ Wkly

Ornish, Dean
Love & survival; the scientific basis for the healing power of intimacy. HarperCollins Pubs. 1998 284p il hardcover o.p. paperback available $14   **616.1**
1. Heart diseases 2. Health
ISBN 0-06-093020-9 (pa)   LC 98-141279
"Ornish argues that affection is crucial to health with research findings as well as clinical-anecdotal evidence. The second of six . . . chapters presents studies demonstrating that those who give and receive love are healthier than those who don't; this is intriguing and persuasive testimony that many may find squares with common sense. Succeeding chapters present the anecdotal evidence." Booklist

Pashkow, Fredric J., 1945-
The women's heart book; the complete guide to keeping your heart healthy; [by] Fredric J. Pashkow and Charlotte Libov. Hyperion 2001 364p il pa $14.95   **616.1**
1. Heart diseases 2. Women—Diseases
ISBN 0-7868-8428-2   LC 00-58056
First published 1993 by Dutton with title: The woman's heart book
This book discusses "risk factors, the diagnosis and treatment of heart attacks, other cardiac conditions, and the specific concerns of women. The advice on when to see a doctor, which questions to ask, and how to evaluate the hospital's and physician's credentials are outstanding. . . . Pregnancy, hormone replacement therapies, gender bias, and even the 'zipper' scar resulting from open-heart surgery are discussed, as are the financial aspects of insurance and healthcare. . . . Empathetic in tone and realistic in advice, this should be essential for all consumer health collections." Libr J
Includes bibliographical references

Reaven, Gerald M.
Syndrome X; overcoming the silent killer that can give you a heart attack; [by] Gerald Reaven, Terry Kristen Strom, Barry Fox. Simon & Schuster 2000 284p il hardcover o.p. paperback available $13   **616.1**
1. Heart diseases
ISBN 0-684-86863-6 (pa)
"Syndrome X is a metabolic disorder that interferes with the body's ability to use insulin to move glucose into cells. It causes insulin resistance or diabetes, hyperlipidemia, and hypertension and results in obesity and heart disease. . . . Reaven and his coauthors clearly explain what the syndrome is; its impact on the body, especially the heart and circulatory system, is well described." Libr J

616.2 Diseases of the respiratory system

Adams, Francis V.
The breathing disorders sourcebook. Lowell House 1998 235p il pa $17   **616.2**
1. Respiratory system—Diseases 2. Lungs—Diseases
ISBN 0-7373-0006-X   LC 98-27806
The author "enumerates the steps taken in diagnosing a breathing disorder and discusses many disorders in detail, covering causes, symptoms, and treatments. . . . An appendix of relevant sources, including publications, organizations, and Internet sites, completes this valuable book." Libr J

Brody, Jane E.
Jane Brody's allergy fighter. Norton 1997 127p il hardcover o.p. paperback available $10   **616.2**
1. Allergy
ISBN 0-393-31635-1 (pa)   LC 96-34499
"Discussing the elements that cause allergies, the various OTC and prescription medications that may relieve symptoms, and special strategies for dealing with allergies in children, Brody also supplies a glossary and an information and product guide." Publ Wkly

Freedman, Michael R.
Living well with asthma; [by] Michael R. Freedman, Samuel J. Rosenberg, Cynthia L. Divino. Guilford Press 1998 213p pa $15.95   **616.2**
1. Asthma
ISBN 1-57230-051-5   LC 97-48747
The authors consider the "potentially serious psychological aspects of having a chronic disease. Aimed directly at the asthma sufferer, it includes case studies of commonly encountered problems and discusses family and broader issues that can constrain one's life." Libr J
Includes bibliographical references

Lung disorders sourcebook; edited by Dawn D. Matthews. Omnigraphics 2002 678p il (Health reference series) $78   **616.2**
1. Lungs—Diseases
ISBN 0-7808-0339-6   LC 2002-16976
"Basic consumer health information about emphysema, pneumonia, tuberculosis, asthma, cystic fibrosis, and other lung disorders. Including facts about diagnostic proce-

Lung disorders sourcebook—*Continued*
dures, treatment strategies, disease prevention efforts, and
such risk factors as smoking, air pollution, and exposure
to asbestos, radon, and other agents: along with a glossary and resources for additional help and information." Title page

"This title is a great addition for public and school libraries because it provides concise health information on
the lungs. Readers can start with this reference source
and get satisfactory answers before proceeding to other
medical reference tools for more in-depth information."
Am Ref Books Annu, 2003

Wray, Betty B.
Taking charge of asthma; a lifetime
strategy. Wiley 1998 231p pa $14.95   **616.2**
1. Asthma
ISBN 0-471-24704-9   LC 97-48749
The author "offers asthma sufferers practical steps for
living with their disease. She includes many lists and
quizzes, and at the end of every chapter an 'Ask your
Doctor. . .' section with suggested questions." Libr J
Includes bibliographical references

616.3   Diseases of the digestive system

Achord, James L.
Understanding hepatitis. University Press of
Miss. 2002 132p il (Understanding health and
sickness series) $28; pa $12   **616.3**
1. Liver—Diseases
ISBN 1-57806-435-X; 1-57806-436-8 (pa)
      LC 2001-49243
"The book is divided into seven sections: the liver and
hepatitis; symptoms and complications of acute and
chronic viral hepatitis; hepatitis A; hepatitis B; hepatitis
C; other viruses and nonviral causes of hepatitis; and
current research. . . . The book's all-encompassing and
easy-to-read format helps readers better understand the
scope of the disease." Choice
Includes bibliographical references

Janowitz, Henry D.
Good food for bad stomachs. Oxford Univ.
Press 1997 224p il $28; pa $15.95   **616.3**
1. Indigestion 2. Diet therapy
ISBN 0-19-508792-5; 0-19-512655-6 (pa)
      LC 96-9409
The author outlines a "low-fat, high-fiber diet and describes its role in maintaining digestive health. He also
explains the mechanisms of digestion and the effect of
diet on specific digestive disorders. Janowitz uses easy-
to-understand language." Libr J

Palmer, Melissa
Dr. Melissa Palmer's guide to hepatitis &
liver disease; what you need to know. Avery
Pub. Group 1999 457p pa $14.95   **616.3**
1. Liver—Diseases
ISBN 0-89529-922-4   LC 99-44886
Palmer explains the liver's "function and the diagnosis
and treatment of hepatitis, cancers, and other liver diseases. She also discusses choosing a doctor and finding
information in print and online sources. The
comprehensive information includes nutrition, alternative
therapies, surgery, the liver during pregnancy, and living
with liver dysfunction. Simply the most complete resource on liver disease for lay readers." Libr J
Includes bibliographical references

Pool, Robert, 1955-
Fat; fighting the obesity epidemic. Oxford
Univ. Press 2000 292p $27.50   **616.3**
1. Obesity
ISBN 0-19-511853-7   LC 00-36731
The author "traces the history of obesity in Western
society and the ups and downs of medical science's ability to determine what causes some people to gain a considerable amount of weight." Publ Wkly
"This fascinating investigative journey into the history
of obesity will go a long way toward removing the stigma attached to being overweight and will increase our
understanding of the complex issues that contribute to
the obesity epidemic." Libr J

Zonderman, Jon
Understanding Crohn disease and ulcerative
colitis; [by] Jon Zonderman and Ronald
Vender. University Press of Miss. 2000 116p
il (Understanding health and sickness series)
$28; pa $12   **616.3**
1. Inflammatory bowel diseases
ISBN 1-57806-202-0; 1-57806-203-9 (pa)
      LC 99-52483
"After describing how the digestive system functions,
[the authors] show how it can go wrong. They deal with
related medical conditions and how Crohn disease and
ulcerative colitis can affect persons of different ages differently. Treatment can involve careful dieting . . . and
medical and surgical procedures." Booklist
Includes bibliographical references

616.4   Diabetes

American Diabetes Association complete
guide to diabetes; the ultimate home
reference from the diabetes experts. 3rd ed,
completely rev. American Diabetes Assn.
2002 517p il pa $29.95   **616.4**
1. Diabetes
ISBN 1-580-40161-9   LC 2002-27941
First published 1996
This edition features new types of insulin and the best
ways to use them, insulin pumps and injection-free insulin techniques in research, new oral diabetes medications
and therapies, the use of carbohydrate counting techniques as a meal planning tool as well as information on
diabetes in the workplace, school, and day care. Links to
web sites are also included

Beaser, Richard S.
The Joslin guide to diabetes; a program for
managing your treatment; [by] Richard S.
Beaser, with Joan C.V. Hill and the Joslin
Education Committee. Simon & Schuster
1995 351p il pa $15   **616.4**
1. Diabetes
ISBN 0-684-80208-2   LC 95-12169
"A Fireside book"
In this "introduction to self-care for both insulin-
dependent and noninsulin-dependent diabetics, Beaser
emphasizes the need for proper diet, weight control and
exercise, and for frequent monitoring of blood sugar and
ongoing medical supervision. Suggesting guidelines for
office visits, medical tests that should be done regularly
and questions to ask one's healthcare team, Beaser discusses insulin pumps, diabetes pills and what lies on the

Beaser, Richard S.—*Continued*
horizon of current diabetes research." Publ Wkly
"Essential for all health collections." Libr J
Includes bibliographical references

Diabetes sourcebook; edited by Dawn D. Matthews. 3rd ed. Omnigraphics 2003 621p il (Health reference series) $78 **616.4**
1. Diabetes
ISBN 0-7808-0629-8   LC 2003-40577
First published 1994

"Basic consumer health information about Type 1 diabetes (insulin-dependent or juvenile-onset diabetes), Type 2 diabetes (noninsulin-dependent or adult-onset diabetes), gestational diabetes, impaired glucose tolerance (IGT), and related complications, such as amputation, eye disease, gum disease, nerve damage, and end-stage renal disease: including facts about insulin, oral diabetes medications, blood sugar testing, and the role of exercise and nutrition in the control of diabetes: along with a glossary and resources for further help and information." Title page

Includes bibliographical references

Ditkoff, Beth Ann
The thyroid guide; [by] Beth Ann Ditkoff, and Paul LoGerfo. HarperPerennial 2000 xx, 171p il pa $13.95   **616.4**
1. Thyroid gland—Diseases
ISBN 0-06-095260-1   LC 99-34742
A guide to the detection, diagnosis and treatment of thyroid diseases

Mayo Clinic on managing diabetes; Maria Collazo-Clavell, editor in chief. Mayo Clinic; [distributed by] Mason Crest 2002 c2001 194p il Mayo Clinic $29.95; Mason Crest pa $14.95   **616.4**
1. Diabetes
ISBN 1-893005-06-2; 1-59084-227-8 (pa)
LC 00-134265

"The facts section discusses diabetes and its long-term health problems. The second section, Taking Control, covers healthy eating, monitoring blood sugar, and physical activity. Next, Medical Therapies deals with Type 1 and Type 2 medications and transplantation. Living Well, the fourth section, provides information on medical tests, self-care, and sexual issues, including graphic drawings of methods used to treat impotence." Voice Youth Advocates

Poirier, Laurinda M., 1960-
Women & diabetes; staying healthy in body, mind, and spirit; by Laurinda M. Poirier, Katharine M. Coburn. 2nd ed. American Diabetes Assn. 2000 230p il pa $14.95   **616.4**
1. Diabetes 2. Women—Diseases 3. Women—Health and hygiene
ISBN 1-580-40058-2   LC 00-38104
First published 1997 with subtitle: Life planning for health and wellness

"Quality-of-life issues are emphasized, and short activities are included to assist the reader in determining her own areas of need and support. Special concerns for women with diabetes, such as monthly hormonal changes, pregnancy, and estrogen replacement therapy, are addressed." Libr J [review of 1997 edition]

Includes bibliographical references

Saudek, Christopher D.
The Johns Hopkins guide to diabetes; for today and tomorrow; [by] Christopher D. Saudek, Richard R. Rubin, Cynthia S. Shump. Johns Hopkins Univ. Press 1997 422p (Johns Hopkins health book) $54; pa $17.95   **616.4**
1. Diabetes
ISBN 0-8018-5580-2; 0-8018-5581-0 (pa)
LC 96-49161
Also available large print paperback edition $23.95 (ISBN 0-8018-6657-X)

This guide presents "information about the physical, emotional, and psychological effects of diabetes. The nature of the disease, diet and exercise, treatments, complications, sexuality, pregnancy, and research are covered. . . . The language used, while sometimes complex in concept, is clear, enlightening, and reassuring to the reader. Positive examples stress the importance of individual knowledge and flexibility in daily life. An excellent beginner's guide." Libr J

616.5 Diseases of integument, hair, nails

Cram, David L. (David Lee), 1934-
Coping with psoriasis; a patient's guide to treatment. Addicus Bks. 2000 132p pa $14.95   **616.5**
1. Psoriasis
ISBN 1-886039-47-X   LC 0000-8220
This book "covers how the disease starts, choosing the right doctor, treatment options, the importance of treating the emotional symptoms, the role of special diets, alternative therapies, and advances in treatment." Publisher's note

Includes bibliographical references

Greenwood-Robinson, Maggie
Hair savers for women; a complete guide to preventing and treating hair loss. Three Rivers Press (NY) 2000 261p pa $14 **616.5**
1. Hair—Diseases 2. Women—Health and hygiene
ISBN 0-609-80445-6   LC 99-39185
The author discusses "solutions and advances in treating female hair loss, from medicine to natural remedies, and introduces women to . . . safe, clinically proven baldness remedies. For women whose hair loss persists, the book discusses surgical alternatives such as hair transplants and scalp reductions, as well as the pros and cons of hair weaves and wigs." Publisher's note

Includes bibliographical references

Leffell, David J.
Total skin; the definitive guide to skin health for life. Hyperion 2000 401p il $27.95
616.5
1. Skin—Care
ISBN 0-7868-6504-0   LC 99-47396
"How does the skin grow and perform its varied tasks? What roles does the skin play in health, disease, and appearance? What really protects the skin from the effects of sun, aging, and other potential enemies? Leffell answers such questions practically, complete with counsel on when to see a physician and when to handle a skin condition on one's own." Booklist

Mayes, Maureen D.

The scleroderma book; a guide for patients and families. Oxford Univ. Press 1999 182p il $30 **616.5**

1. Scleroderma (Disease)

ISBN 0-19-511507-4   LC 98-54669

"Neither the cause nor the cure of the autoimmune connective tissue disease is known. Mayes describes the two main types of scleroderma; discusses who is likely to get the malady, which affects the whole body, as well as sexuality and pregnancy; and zeroes in on such organs as the kidneys, GI tract, lungs, heart, joints, tendons, muscles, and nerves." Booklist

Skin disorders sourcebook; edited by Allan R. Cook. Omnigraphics 1997 647p il (Health reference series) $78 **616.5**

1. Skin—Diseases

ISBN 0-7808-0080-X   LC 97-6570

"Basic information about common skin and scalp conditions caused by aging, allergies, immune reactions, sun exposure, infectious organisms, parasites, cosmetics, and skin traumas including abrasions, cuts, and pressure sores along with information on prevention and treatment." Title page

Includes bibliographical references

Thompson, Wendy J. A.

Alopecia areata; understanding and coping with hair loss; [by] Wendy Thompson, Jerry Shapiro; foreword by Vera H. Price. Johns Hopkins Univ. Press 1996 180p hardcover o.p. paperback available $17.95 **616.5**

1. Hair—Diseases

ISBN 0-8018-6472-0 (pa)   LC 96-33971

This book discusses "a disorder that causes hair loss ranging from bald patches to total loss of head and body hair. . . . This easy-to-read, helpful, and straightforward guide provides in-depth information on the diagnosis, treatment, and cosmetic concerns of [this disorder]." Libr J

Includes bibliographical references

Turkington, Carol

The encyclopedia of skin and skin disorders; [by] Carol Turkington, Jeffrey S. Dover; medical illustrations, Birck Cox. 2nd ed. Facts on File 2002 436p (Facts on File library of health and living) $71.50 **616.5**

1. Skin—Diseases

ISBN 0-8160-4776-6   LC 2001-53232

First published 1996 with title: Skin deep

Entries in this resource range "from elements of the skin and their roles in the human anatomy to cosmetics, medications, and preventive care. This reference also examines the histories of skin disorders, skin traumas, their symptoms, and treatments." Publisher's note

For a review see: Booklist, Oct. 15, 2002

616.6 Diseases of the urogenital system. Diseases of the urinary system

Dierich, Mary

Overcoming incontinence; a straightforward guide to your options for treating this common problem; [by] Mary Dierich, Felicia Froe. Wiley 2000 120p il pa $14.95 **616.6**

1. Urinary incontinence

ISBN 0-471-34795-7   LC 99-36372

The authors "explain the different types of urinary incontinence: stress, urge, overflow, functional, iatrogenic, and mixed. . . . They explain in detail the different types of treatment (drugs, Kegel exercises, biofeedback, muscle therapy, pessaries, and surgery) and delineate the advantages and disadvantages of each." Libr J

Marrs, Richard P.

Dr. Richard Marr's fertility book; America's leading fertility expert tells you everything you need to know about getting pregnant; [by] Richard Marrs, and Lisa Friedman Bloch, and Kathy Kirtland Silverman. Delacorte Press 1997 506p il o.p.; Dell paperback available $16.95 **616.6**

1. Infertility

ISBN 0-440-50803-7 (pa)   LC 96-11350

This guide to infertility discusses causes and treatments, outlines assisted reproductive technologies, considers immunological problems as well as emotional and financial issues

"A necessary primer for any couple faced with infertility, this is essential for public libraries." Libr J

Turkington, Carol

The encyclopedia of fertility and infertility; [by] Carol Turkington and Michael M. Alper. Facts on File 2001 308p (Facts on File library of health and living) $71.50 **616.6**

1. Infertility

ISBN 0-8160-4154-7   LC 00-67749

This A-Z reference volume "is designed to give basic definitions of the many terms associated with fertility and infertility. Intended for the layperson, the 600 entries range in length from a sentence to several paragraphs." Booklist

Walsh, Patrick C., 1938-

The prostate; a guide for men and the women who love them; [by] Patrick C. Walsh and Janet Farrar Worthington; illustrations by Leon Schlossberg. Johns Hopkins Univ. Press 1995 322p il hardcover o.p. paperback available $18.95 **616.6**

1. Prostate—Diseases

ISBN 0-8018-4989-6 (pa)   LC 94-33397

The authors survey current medical knowledge of the prostate and its disorders. Prevention is emphasized

616.7 Diseases of the musculoskeletal system

Arthritis sourcebook . . .; edited by Allan R. Cook. Omnigraphics 1999 550p $78 **616.7**

1. Arthritis
ISBN 0-7808-0201-2   LC 98-42073

"Basic consumer health information about specific forms of arthritis and related disorders, including rheumatoid arthritis, osteoarthritis, gout, polymyalgia rheumatica, psoriatic arthritis, spondyloarthropathies, juvenile rheumatoid arthritis, and juvenile ankylosing spondylitis; along with information about medical, surgical, and alternative treatment options, and including strategies for coping with pain, fatigue, and stress." Title page

Lahita, Robert G. (Robert George), 1945-

Lupus; everything you need to know; [by] Robert G. Lahita, Robert H. Phillips. Avery Pub. Group 1998 224p pa $13.95   **616.7**

1. Systemic lupus erythematosus
ISBN 0-89529-833-3   LC 97-34718

This book "discusses the different types of the disease. Because lupus can be so confusing, Lahita and Phillips also discuss medical disorders similar to it. They subsequently turn to the immune system, which is the body system most likely to be involved in lupus, to tests and diagnosis, and to descriptions of symptoms and complications, usefully conveyed in question-and-answer format." Booklist

Lane, Nancy E.

The osteoporosis book. Oxford Univ. Press 1998 206p il hardcover o.p. paperback available $13.95   **616.7**

1. Osteoporosis
ISBN 0-19-514238-1 (pa)   LC 98-19650

This work is "organized in two parts, with early chapters devoted to educating the lay reader on the life cycle of bone and reasons for its loss. Risk factors and different types of fractures are identified, and diagnostic tests are explained. Later chapters discuss the many types of estrogen replacement therapy and medications other than hormones to prevent and treat osteoporosis." Libr J

Includes bibliographical references

Lawrence, Ronald Melvin, 1926-

Preventing arthritis; a holistic approach to life without pain; by Ronald M. Lawrence and Martin Zucker. Putnam 2001 286p il hardcover o.p. paperback available $14

616.7

1. Arthritis
ISBN 0-425-18468-4 (pa)   LC 00-68857

This "discusses the osteoarthritis disease process and how it can be prevented or minimized by exercise, appropriate body mechanics, diet, supplements, and complementary alternative therapies." Libr J

Includes bibliographical references

Nelson, Miriam E.

Strong women, strong bones; everything you need to know to prevent, treat, and beat osteoporosis; [by] Miriam E. Nelson with Sarah Wernick. Putnam 2000 318p il hardcover o.p. paperback available $13.95

616.7

1. Osteoporosis
ISBN 0-399-52656-0 (pa)   LC 99-57570

The authors explain "how bones grow; osteoporosis risk factors; how to adjust the diet to include calcium, vitamin D, and other bone-essential nutrients; the types of weight-bearing exercises that should be performed to promote maximum bone health; and the latest osteoporosis treatment options." Libr J

Includes bibliographical references

Patarca, Roberto

The concise encyclopedia of fibromyalgia and myofascial pain. Haworth Medical Press 2002 201p $49.95; pa $24.95   **616.7**

1. Fibromyalgia—Encyclopedias
ISBN 0-7890-1527-7; 0-7890-1528-5 (pa)
LC 2001-51687

This source of information on fibromyalgia and myofascial pain is in dictionary form and includes entries on symptoms, medication, condition, and findings on related disorders. Also covered are "advances in rheumatology, cardiovascular medicine, endocrinology, epidemiology, immunology, infectious diseases, neurology, psychiatry, and psychology that form the basis for new lines of research and therapeutic intervention." Publisher's note

Includes bibliographical references

Selfridge, Nancy

Freedom from fibromyalgia; the 5-week program proven to conquer pain; [by] Nancy Selfridge and Franklynn Peterson. Three Rivers Press (NY) 2001 156p il pa $14

616.7

1. Fibromyalgia
ISBN 0-8129-3375-3   LC 00-46668

"The authors believe 'rogue' brain chemicals are the culprits behind the all-over body pain of FMS. Since there are no pills to combat these chemicals, the authors have developed a five-week, self-directed recovery program based upon mind-body principles. . . . The structured program the authors have developed focuses on meditation, journal writing, and self-talk aimed at creating a psychological awareness of the emotions, thoughts, and feelings that produce pain in the body." Libr J

Includes bibliographical references

Starlanyl, Devin

Fibromyalgia & chronic myofascial pain syndrome; a survival manual; [by] Devin Starlanyl, Mary Ellen Copeland; foreword by Christopher R. Brown. 2nd ed. New Harbinger Publs. 2001 398p il $19.95 **616.7**

1. Fibromyalgia
ISBN 1-57224-238-8   LC 2001-132299

First published 1996

In this overview of fibromyalgia syndrome (FMS) and myofascial pain syndrome (MPS) the authors "offer information on the latest medications, tips for bodywork, and suggestions for coping with family and work, getting support, and dealing with the healthcare system." Libr J [review of 1996 edition]

Includes bibliographical references

Wallace, Daniel J. (Daniel Jeffrey), 1949-

Fibromyalgia: an essential guide for patients and their families; [by] Daniel J. Wallace, Janice Brock Wallace. Oxford Univ. Press 2003 196p il pa $12.95   **616.7**

1. Fibromyalgia
ISBN 0-19-514931-9   LC 2002-17096

This guide to fibromyalgia, a form of chronic neuro-muscular pain, provides an explanation of the syndrome and its symptoms and also outlines recent advances in treatment and new drugs available

Includes bibliographical references

616.8   Diseases of the nervous system and mental disorders

Bruno, Richard L.

The polio paradox; uncovering the hidden history of polio to understand and treat "post-polio syndrome" and chronic fatigue. Warner Bks. 2002 350p il $25.95; pa $15.95   **616.8**

1. Poliomyelitis
ISBN 0-446-52907-9; 0-446-69069-4 (pa)

The author "discusses the history and care of polio patients, the identification of and research into PPS [post-polio syndrome], and the approach to treating the symptoms. . . . [He] also addresses chronic fatigue (CF), multiple sclerosis, fibromyalgia, Gulf War syndrome, and spina bifida disorders that share symptoms, brain changes, and stress links similar to PPS." Libr J

Includes bibliographical references

Cram, David L. (David Lee), 1934-

Answers to frequently asked questions in Parkinson's disease; a resource book for patients and families; [by] David L. Cram, M.D. Acorn Pub. 2002 170p pa $19.95

     616.8

1. Parkinson's disease
ISBN 0-9710988-8-3   LC 2002-1074

Contents: Financial Considerations. Where to turn for help. Staying in the workforce—Diagnosing early disease and tremor. Early stages of Parkinson's disease. Young-onset Parkinson's disease. Essential tremor—Parkinson's disease and heredity. What have we learned so far? Twin study. Families with Parkinson's disease. Genetics and the environment—Medications in Parkinson's disease. Tips on taking medications. Drug-related parkinsonism drugs that may interfere with Parkinson's disease. Drugs that can interact with Parkinson's disease medications. Drugs that can produce Parkinson's disease-like symptoms—Stress and exercise. The role of stress in Parkinson's disease. Good and bad stress. The effects of stress. Does stress cause Parkinson's disease? Stress and your partner. Coping with fear. Managing stress. The importance of exercise. Use it or lose it. Facts about exercise in Parkinson's disease. The benefits of exercise. A word about

Includes bibliographical references

Cutler, Neal R.

Understanding Alzheimer's disease; [by] Neal R. Cutler and John J. Sramek. University Press of Miss. 1996 151p (Understanding health and sickness series) $28; pa $12   **616.8**

1. Alzheimer's disease
ISBN 0-87805-910-5; 0-87805-911-3 (pa)

     LC 96-20284

The authors describe the incidence, risk factors and possible causes of Alzheimer's disease. Treatment and research programs are discussed

This "comprehensive guide . . . is a must read for the early Alzheimer's patient and his or her immediate care-givers and family, as well as all professionals involved in long-term planning for the medical, social, economic, and legal affairs of the patient." Sci Books Films

Includes bibliographical referneces

Duvoisin, Roger C., 1927-

Parkinson's disease; a guide for patient and family; [by] Roger C. Duvoisin, Jacob Sage. 5th ed. Lippincott Williams & Wilkins 2001 195p il pa $32.95   **616.8**

1. Parkinson's disease
ISBN 0-7817-2977-7   LC 2001-29689

First published 1978 by Raven Press

The authors "explain the pathology, symptoms, and course of Parkinson's Disease, discuss current drug therapies and surgical procedures, and examine the latest research on the genetics of parkinsonism." Publisher's note

"The complications of advancing disease are particularly well described. While the reading level is high, the determined reader can find a great deal of detailed information not found in other guides." Libr J

Freed, Curt

Healing the brain; [by] Curt Freed and Simon LeVay. Times Bks. 2002 269p $26

     616.8

1. Parkinson's disease 2. Transplantation of organs, tissues, etc.
ISBN 0-8050-7091-5   LC 2002-19671

"Freed gives a brief background on the biology of the disease and the history of Parkinson's treatments, but most of the book is devoted to his own surgical experiment, which involved 40 volunteer Parkinson's patients, half of whom received transplanted cells while the other group underwent sham surgeries." Publ Wkly

"Parkinson's patients and others interested in the issue will find this an absorbing account." Libr J

Hauser, Robert A.

Parkinson's disease: questions and answers. 4th ed. Merit Pub. Int. 2003 204p $34.95

     616.8

1. Parkinson's disease
ISBN 1-873413-68-8

First published 1996

"Although primarily aimed at general clinicians, this manual may be useful for patients wishing more in-depth knowledge than what the consumer guides offer. Hauser . . . covers test, clinical characteristics, staging and classifications, medical management, and issues frequently missed in the lay literature." Libr J [review of 2000 edition]

Kuhn, Daniel

Alzheimer's early stages; first steps for families, friends and caregivers. 2nd ed. Hunter House 2003 306p $27.95; pa $15.95

616.8

1. Alzheimer's disease
ISBN 0-89793-398-2; 0-89793-397-4 (pa)
LC 2002-151932
First published 1999

This book covers "the importance of getting a diagnosis, risk factors (including the role of depression), early symptoms, treatment and prevention, and information on physical health, safety concerns, caring for the caregiver, and financial and end-of-life planning—all illustrated with brief, first-person narratives. Of special interest are chapters on relationships, including telling others about the diagnosis, and the . . . section on current available treatments. . . . Intelligently written with numerous references to professional and consumer literature, this book is an excellent choice for Alzheimer's and consumer health collections." Libr J

Includes bibliographical references

Kushner, Howard I.

A cursing brain? the histories of Tourette syndrome. Harvard Univ. Press 1999 303p il $32.50; pa $16,95

616.8

1. Tourette syndrome
ISBN 0-674-18022-4; 0-674-00386-1 (pa)
LC 98-38733

The author presents a "narrative of the development of knowledge about, treatments of, and medical and lay attitudes toward Tourette's syndrome (TS) patients." Booklist

"A compassionate and absorbing work of medical history." Libr J

Includes bibliographical references

Lieberman, A. (Abraham), 1938-

100 questions & answers about Parkinson [sic] disease; [by] Abraham Lieberman, with Marcia McCall. Jones & Bartlett 2003 238p il pa $16.95

616.8

1. Parkinson's disease
ISBN 0-7637-0433-4
LC 2002-152130

A patient-oriented guide to the symptoms, diagnosis, and treatment of Parkinson's disease

"Lieberman is particularly good at telling patients what they should expect from their physicians, how they can select a competent movement disorders specialist, how they can make the most of living with PD, and what they should know about the new advances in medical, alternative, and surgical therapies. An optimistic resource that should be much in demand." Libr J

Shaking-up Parkinson disease; fighting like a tiger, thinking like a fox: a book for the puzzled, the hopeful, the willing and the prepared; by Abraham Lieberman. Jones & Bartlett 2002 250p il pa $18.95

616.8

1. Parkinson's disease
ISBN 0-7637-1866-1
LC 2001-25721

This book "explains PD and its symptoms (with steps to alleviate them) and extensively covers treatment options such as drugs and surgery. A plus is the author's discussion of anxiety and depression as a biological rather than a psychological symptom of the disease. . . . Although nonreligious readers may be put off by the biblical quotes, this is still an outstanding text." Libr J

Lukeman, Alex, 1941-

Sleep well, sleep deep. Evans & Co. 1999 209p hardcover o.p. paperback available $14.95

616.8

1. Sleep
ISBN 0-87131-941-1 (pa)
LC 99-47495

This volume "covers: How sleeping well can change your life; What to do when you can't sleep; Sleeping disorders—from sleepwalking to insomnia; Dreams and how they affect your health; Medications—over the counter prescription, and holistic; What to do when your child can't sleep; Myths, folklore, and history of sleep; School of thought on sleep." Publisher's note

Includes bibliographical references

Managing stroke; a guide to living well after stroke; edited by Paul R. Rao, Mark N. Ozer, John E. Toerge; foreword by Don A. Olson. ABI Professional Publs. 2000 299p il $27

616.8

1. Stroke
ISBN 1-886236-24-0

"With information on physical therapy, occupational therapy, and daily living skills, this is primarily a guide to rehabilitation for stroke patients or their families rather than a quick reference book or a guide to prevention." Libr J

Marks, David R.

The headache prevention cookbook; eating right to prevent migraines and other headaches; [by] David R. Marks, with Laura Marks. Houghton Mifflin 2000 208p pa $16

616.8

1. Headache 2. Diet therapy
ISBN 0-395-96716-3
LC 00-33435

The authors explain how ordinary foods may serve as triggers for headache pain. To help readers with undiagnosed food sensitivities they include more than 100 easy-to-prepare recipes

Mayo Clinic on Alzheimer's disease; Ronald Petersen, editor in chief. Mayo Clinic 2002 210p il $16.95

616.8

1. Alzheimer's disease
ISBN 1-89300-522-4
LC 2002-104996

This book "covers the basics of brain function; the causes, signs, and symptoms of late-life memory loss; how it is diagnosed; the latest in available treatments; and current research on promising new remedies, as well as details about the effects of memory disorders on the ill person, families, and caregivers . . . [It features a] 'Quick Guide for Caregivers,' offering an overview of medical complications, home safety, managing medications, and problem behaviors caused by failing memory, among other essential topics. . . . Those unfamiliar with memory disorders are well served by this concise guide." Libr J

Moore, Elaine A., 1948-
Encyclopedia of Alzheimer's disease; with directories of research, treatment, and care facilities; [by] Elaine A. Moore; with Lisa Moore; illustrations by Marvin G. Miller. McFarland & Co. 2003 401p il $75 **616.8**
1. Alzheimer's disease—Encyclopedias
ISBN 0-7864-1438-3   LC 2002-12202
"The first section of this encyclopedia explains terms (e.g., scientific, health plans, organizations) relating directly or indirectly to the disease. . . . The next section has three directories (treatment centers listed by state and city, research facilities by state, and resources) followed by an index. . . . For a comprehensive reference on Alzheimer's, the Moores' resource would be an excellent choice." Choice
> For a fuller review see: Booklist, Sept. 15, 2003
> Includes bibliographical references

Parkinson's disease; a self-help guide; [by] Marjan Jahanshahi, C. David Marsdan; with contributions from Richard G. Brown [et al.] Demos 2000 392p il pa $24.95 **616.8**
1. Parkinson's disease 2. Health self-care
ISBN 1-88879-938-2   LC 00-35859
This "handbook gives . . . information to PD patients and their families on how best to cope with the life changes brought about by the disease. The authors emphasize patient empowerment through information, resources, and assistive devices." Libr J

Parkinson's disease and quality of life; Lucien Côté [et al.] editors. Haworth Press 2000 199p $49.95; pa $19.95 **616.8**
1. Parkinson's disease 2. Quality of life
ISBN 0-7890-0763-0; 0-7890-0810-6 (pa)
                                 LC 00-28034
"Parkinson's disease and quality of life has been co-published simultaneously as Loss, grief & care, Volume 8, Numbers 3/4, 2000"
"This volume features 31 contributors (nurses, doctors, patients, speech therapists, etc.) who cover a wide array of topics avout PD not found in other guides: dental health, shortness of breath, sexuality, incontinence, medical expenses and health insurance benefits, tax planning, and occupational therapy, among others. Some essays are more technical, but this is still a valuable resource." Libr J

Includes bibliographical references

Rosenstein, Ann, 1958-
Water exercises for Parkinson's; maintaining balance, strength, endurance, and flexibility; [by] Ann A. Rosenstein; foreword by Len Kalakian. Idyll Arbor 2002 242p il pa $18 **616.8**
1. Parkinson's disease 2. Exercise
ISBN 1-88288-349-7   LC 2001-51720
The author argues "that water exercises can significantly enhance mobility and ease the physical impact of PD, as well as ward off depression and improve self-esteem. She addresses pool safety, drugs, proper attire, equipment, and methods of entering the pool; her exercises are well illustrated." Libr J
Includes bibliographical references

Sacks, Oliver W.
An anthropologist on Mars; seven paradoxical tales; [by] Oliver Sacks. Knopf 1995 327p il hardcover o.p. paperback available $14 **616.8**
1. Nervous system—Diseases
ISBN 0-679-75697-3 (pa)   LC 94-26733
In this "collection of previously published essays, the noted neurologist describes his meetings with seven people whose 'abnormalities' in brain function generate new perspectives on the workings of that organ, the nature of experience and concepts of personality and consciousness. . . . Writing with eloquent particularity and compassionate respect, Sacks enlarges our view of the nature of human experience." Publ Wkly
Includes bibliographical references

The man who mistook his wife for a hat and other clinical tales; [by] Oliver Sacks. Simon & Schuster 1998 243p il pa $14
616.8
1. Nervous system—Diseases
ISBN 0-684-85394-9   LC 98-4723
"A Touchstone book"
First published 1985 by Summit Bks.
"Sacks introduces the reader to real people who suffer from a variety of neurological syndromes which includes symptoms such as amnesia, uncontrolled movements, and musical hallucinations. Sacks recounts their stories in a riveting, compassionate, and thoughtful manner." Libr J
Includes bibliographical references

Schwarz, Shelley Peterman, 1946-
Parkinson's disease: 300 tips for making life easier. Demos Medical Pub. 2002 124p pa $18.95 **616.8**
1. Parkinson's disease
ISBN 1-88879-965-X   LC 2002-363
The author "offers tips, techniques, shortcuts, and resources that can assist Parkinsonians adapt to their environment and maintain their daily personal living skills. She also gives advice to caregivers." Libr J

Shenk, David, 1966-
The forgetting: Alzheimer's, portrait of an epidemic. Doubleday 2001 290p $24.95; pa $13.95 **616.8**
1. Alzheimer's disease
ISBN 0-385-49837-3; 0-385-49838-1 (pa)
                                 LC 2001-28012
The author "traces the development of knowledge about Alzheimer's in the work of individuals and such groups as the National Institute of Aging; describes various tests that help in identifying possible sufferers; and discusses the early, middle, and end stages of the malady. . . . Lucid and well organized, this is one of the best books on this increasingly prevalent illness." Booklist
Includes bibliographical references

Sleep disorders sourcebook . . .; edited by Jenifer Swanson. Omnigraphics 1999 439p (Health reference series) $78 **616.8**
1. Sleep 2. Consumer education
ISBN 0-7808-0234-9   LC 98-37257
"Basic consumer health information about sleep and its disorders including insomnia, sleepwalking, sleep apnea, restless leg syndrome, and narcolepsy; along with

Sleep disorders sourcebook . . .—*Continued*

data about shiftwork and its effects, information on the societal costs of sleep deprivation, descriptions of treatment options, a glossary of terms, and resource listings for additional help." Title page

Tanzi, Rudolph E.

Decoding darkness; the search for the genetic causes of Alzheimer's disease; [by] Rudolph E. Tanzi & Ann B. Parson. Perseus Bks. 2000 281p il hardcover o.p. paperback available $16   **616.8**

1. Alzheimer's disease
ISBN 0-7382-0526-5 (pa)
This is an "account of the race to uncover the genetics behind Alzheimer's disease. . . . [The author discusses] his research and the work of others that led to recent genetic discoveries associated with early-onset and late-onset Alzheimer's disease." Libr J
"This is a gripping book with a vast amount of fascinating information." Booklist

Turkington, Carol

The encyclopedia of Alzheimer's disease; foreword by James E. Galvin. Facts on File 2003 286p $71.50   **616.8**

1. Alzheimer's disease—Encyclopedias
ISBN 0-8160-4818-5   LC 2002-11981
This encyclopedia provides "coverage of the disease and its causes and symptoms, as well as related health conditions and terms . . . advances in treatment, drugs and research; social issues related to Alzheimer's; and . . . organizations." Publisher's note
This is "a useful addition to most consumer health collections." Libr J
Includes bibliographical references

Weiner, William J.

Parkinson's disease; a complete guide for patients and families; [by] William J. Weiner, Lisa M. Shulman, and Anthony E. Lang. Johns Hopkins Univ. Press 2001 256p il $62; pa $16.95   **616.8**

1. Parkinson's disease
ISBN 0-8018-6555-7; 0-8018-6556-5 (pa)
     LC 00-9630
Also available large print edition $20.95 (ISBN 0-8018-6880-7)
"A Johns Hopkins Press health book"
The author "presents known facts and clarification about this degenerative neurological disease. Physical, behavioral, and psychiatric signs and symptoms exhibited during mild, moderate, and advanced stages of the disease are examined, as are diseases that can mimic Parkinson's. . . . He outlines drug and surgical treatments, including alternative and complementary therapies." Libr J

When Parkinson's strikes early; voices, choices, resources, and treatment; [edited by] Blake-Krebs & Linda Herman. Hunter House 2001 270p il pa $15.95   **616.8**

1. Parkinson's disease
ISBN 0-89793-340-0   LC 2001-16619
This "guide incorporates e-mailings from the members of the Parkinson's Information Exchange Network

(PIEN), with detailed advice on diagnosis, treatment, and self-help options. The vivid essays, poetry, and stories personalize the disease's impact; the resources section is outstanding." Libr J
Includes bibliographical references

616.85 Neuroses; speech and language disorders; disorders of personality, intellect, impulse control

Ainsworth, Patricia, 1932-

Understanding depression. University Press of Miss. 2000 174p il (Understanding health and sickness series) $28; pa $12   **616.85**

1. Depression (Psychology)
ISBN 1-57806-168-7; 1-57806-169-5 (pa)
     LC 99-35416
"The author discusses the different types of depression, the kinds of people at risk, and the risk factors of suicide. . . . The book looks at the way the brain works and how the body communicates with it, including recent discoveries about how the process fails in depression." Publisher's note
"Ainsworth's levelheaded approach should help many depressed persons decide to seek professional help, not least because she disposes of widely accepted myths, offers practical tips for self-care and helping someone else, and appends helpful material on the many drugs involved in treatment." Booklist
Includes bibliographical references

Beardslee, William R.

Out of the darkened room; when a parent is depressed: protecting the children and strengthening the family. Little, Brown 2002 304p $25.95   **616.85**

1. Depression (Psychology)
ISBN 0-316-08549-9   LC 2001-38400
"Beardslee outlines the symptoms of depression as well as the biological bases and causes of the disease. . . . [He] takes a preventive approach to help families recognize depression, develop resiliency, and reduce the risks. Profiles of families who have coped well with a range of challenges, from divorce, death, job loss, and other life woes, show the characteristics associated with triumphing over adversity and avoiding depression." Booklist

Bremner, J. Douglas, 1961-

Does stress damage the brain? understanding trauma-related disorders from a mind-body perspective. Norton 2002 311p il $30   **616.85**

1. Post-traumatic stress disorder 2. Stress (Psychology) 3. Stress (Physiology) 4. Psychiatry
ISBN 0-393-70345-2   LC 2002-70265
The author offers an "argument for revising the current diagnostic schema of the *Diagnostic and Statistical Manual IV* (which currently classifies numerous trauma as distinct conditions) to provide for one single spectrum of disorders, including both acute and chronic posttraumatic stress disorder and related conditions. . . . Bremner offers an interesting and valuable perspective on the subject of traumatic stress. His book will particularly interest professionals." Libr J
Includes bibliographical references

Claude-Pierre, Peggy

The secret language of eating disorders; the revolutionary new approach to understanding and curing anorexia and bulimia. Times Bks. 1997 288p il o.p.; Vintage Bks. paperback available $14.95 **616.85**

1. Eating disorders
ISBN 0-375-75018-5 (pa)   LC 97-11899

According to the author, "the primary cause of an eating disorder is rooted in confirmed negativity condition, or CNC. . . . She discusses how CNC manifests itself and the stages of recovery from it, with appropriate intervention strategies. . . . Her message and tone are supportive and should comfort those, including desperate parents, dealing with these complex, puzzling afflictions." Booklist

Includes bibliographical references

Dalton, Katharina, 1916-

Depression after childbirth; how to recognize, treat, and prevent postnatal depression; [by] Katharina Dalton, with Wendy Holton. 4th ed. Oxford Univ. Press 2001 240p il $19.95 **616.85**

1. Postpartum depression
ISBN 0-19-263277-9   LC 00-53754

First published 1980

This guide for women and their partners for recognizing, treating and preventing postpartum depression discusses such topics as the role of hormones, symptoms such as exhaustion and irritability, and careers and motherhood

Includes bibliographical references

DePaulo, J. Raymond

Understanding depression; what we know and what you can do about it; [by] J. Raymond DePaulo, Leslie Alan Horvitz. Wiley 2002 296p il $24.95; pa $14.95 **616.85**

1. Depression (Psychology)
ISBN 0-471-39552-8; 0-471-43030-7 (pa)
    LC 2001-45449

This describes the nature, causes, effects, and treatment of depression and manic-depressive illness

"The chapters on finding the right treatment and how doctors make diagnoses will be extremely useful for those suffering from the disease. . . . Readers will find this an invaluable resource." Publ Wkly

Includes bibliographical references

Doctor, Ronald M.

The encyclopedia of phobias, fears, and anxieties; [by] Ronald M. Doctor and Ada P. Kahn. 2nd ed. Facts on File 2000 568p il (Facts on File library of health and living) $71.50 **616.85**

1. Phobias 2. Fear
ISBN 0-8160-3989-5   LC 99-56020

First published 1989

This reference includes "over 2,000 entries . . . that describe things, feelings, and situations that impact people's lives in a negative way. There are a few biographical entries for professionals (Abraham Maslow, Rollo May) whose theories and research have influenced treatment of these conditions or have explained their origins. Some entries are single-sentence definitions. Others run

for several pages and include examples of how the phobia is manifested, historical background, causation theories, and treatment approaches." Booklist

Includes bibliographical references

Glenmullen, Joseph, 1950-

Prozac backlash; overcoming the dangers of prozac, zoloft, paxil, and other antidepressants with safe, effective alternatives. Simon & Schuster 2000 383p hardcover o.p. paperback available $14 **616.85**

1. Antidepressants 2. Depression (Psychology)
ISBN 0-7432-0062-4 (pa)   LC 99-59911

The author presents a "survey of recent studies on the negative effects of antidepressants and their less-publicized alternatives. His title refers not to the growing skepticism toward psychiatric medications but to the brain's compensatory reactions to the artificial elevation of serotonin, including potentially permanent tics, dependence, sexual dysfunction, memory problems, sudden suicidal feelings and violence." Publ Wkly

Includes bibliographical references

Hallowell, Edward M.

Driven to distraction; [by] Edward M. Hallowell and John Ratey. Pantheon Bks. 1994 319p o.p.; Touchstone paperback available $14 **616.85**

1. Attention deficit disorder
ISBN 0-684-80128-0 (pa)   LC 93-29536

This study of Attention Deficit Disorder in children as well as in adults covers biology, neurology, pharmacology, clinical findings and personal and professional experiences

"This is an absorbing look at efforts to understand troubling and exasperating behaviors." Booklist

Worry; controlling it and using it wisely. Pantheon Bks. 1997 331p hardcover o.p. paperback available $16.95 **616.85**

1. Anxiety 2. Worry
ISBN 0-345-42458-1 (pa)   LC 97-8609

The author explains "the difference between worry rooted in in-born predispositions and worry that signals other, deeper problems." Libr J

"The book offers useful advice and entertaining stories, and readers can find something here to help them worry less." Booklist

Includes bibliographical references

Hornbacher, Marya, 1974-

Wasted: a memoir of anorexia and bulimia. HarperCollins Pubs. 1998 268p hardcover o.p. paperback available $13 **616.85**

1. Anorexia nervosa 2. Bulimia
ISBN 0-06-093093-4 (pa)   LC 97-21375

This is the author's "account of her bout with anorexia and bulimia, a decade-long struggle that brought her to the brink of death at age 18 and left her with chronic physical ailments." Publ Wkly

This "is a gritty, unflinching look at eating disorders. . . . Hornbacher is at her best when she zeroes in on the specifics of eating disorders and their origins." N Y Times Book Rev

Includes bibliographical references

Kramer, Peter D.

Listening to Prozac; a psychiatrist explores mood-altering drugs and the new meaning of the self. Viking 1993 409p hardcover o.p. paperback available $15 **616.85**

1. Psychotropic drugs 2. Psychiatry 3. Personality disorders 4. Psychotherapy
ISBN 0-14-026671-2 (pa)   LC 92-50733

"Kramer's thesis is that Prozac, in addition to its antidepressant effects, can also act upon aspects of the personality that were previously conceptualized as enduring individual traits (i.e., sensitivity to rejection, social inhibition, and reactivity to stressors). Medication with Prozac appears to have beneficial effects on self-esteem, the ability to experience pleasure, and mental acuity. Kramer is favorable to Prozac, although he documents its side effects, unknown long-term affects, and controversial publicity." Choice

Maté, Gabor

Scattered; how attention deficit disorder originates and what you can do about it. Dutton 1999 348p $24.95; pa $14.95 **616.85**

1. Attention deficit disorder
ISBN 0-525-94412-5; 0-452-27963-1 (pa)
    LC 99-12999

"A victim of ADD since childhood and now a practicing physician, Maté writes about living with the disorder as both a child and an adult. . . . He does not support the disease model of ADD. He recognizes the physiological correlates of sensitive children who develop ADD, but he argues for an exclusively socioenvironmental model. Maté focuses on parent-child attachment failures, which create disconnected children who develop ADD." Choice
Includes bibliographical references

Matsakis, Aphrodite

Vietnam wives; facing the challenges of life with veterans suffering post-traumatic stress. 2nd ed. Sidran Press 1996 440p pa $24.95 **616.85**

1. Post-traumatic stress disorder 2. Veterans 3. Vietnam War, 1961-1975
ISBN 1-88696-800-4   LC 96-15876
First published 1988 by Woodbine House

The author describes post-traumatic stress disorder (PTSD) as it effects Vietnam War veterans and their wives, often resulting in psychic numbness, sexual impotence, alcohol and drug addiction, family violence and depression. The book outlines therapy and coping techniques and includes a resource guide
Includes bibliographical references

Mondimore, Francis Mark, 1953-

Adolescent depression; a guide for parents. Johns Hopkins Univ. Press 2002 287p il (A Johns Hopkins Press health book) $45; pa $17.95 **616.85**

1. Depression (Psychology) 2. Adolescent psychology
ISBN 0-8018-7058-5; 0-8018-7065-9 (pa)
    LC 2001-7992

Mondimore contends "that serious depression in adolescents is an illness. . . . He describes the many forms of depression and the many way it can appear in young people—from intensely sad feelings to irritability, anger, and destructive rages." Publisher's note

"The author provides a solid reference tool for anyone who works with adolescents. It is highly recommended for education professionals as well as public libraries." Voice Youth Advocates
Includes bibliographical references

Morrison, Andrew L.

The antidepressant sourcebook; a user's guide for patients and families. Doubleday 1999 286p pa $12.95 **616.85**

1. Antidepressants
ISBN 0-385-49665-6   LC 99-29949
"A Main Street book"

"After a brief explanation of the major types of antidepressants and the difference between clinical depression and an ordinary 'blue' mood, [the author] tells how antidepressants, combined with talk therapy, can be used to treat not only depression but other conditions such as obsessive-compulsive disorders, panic attacks, general anxiety, social phobia and eating disorders." Publ Wkly
Includes bibliographical references

Normandi, Carol Emery

It's not about food; [by] Carol Emery Normandi and Laurelee Roark. Grosset/Putnam 1998 xxi, 216p il hardcover o.p. paperback available $13.95 **616.85**

1. Eating disorders 2. Obsessive-compulsive neurosis
ISBN 0-399-52502-5 (pa)   LC 97-36328

"The authors' philosophy is that extra weight is an emotional as well as a physical issue, and that it can be handled, in part, by learning to distinguish between emotional and physical hunger." SLJ
Includes bibliographical references

Osborn, Ian

Tormenting thoughts and secret rituals; the hidden epidemic of obsessive-compulsive disorder. Pantheon Bks. 1998 325p hardcover o.p. paperback available $14.95 **616.85**

1. Obsessive-compulsive neurosis
ISBN 0-440-50847-9 (pa)   LC 97-31226

"Osborn shows that OCD is caused by a chemical imbalance in the brain and that behavior therapy and drugs, preferably together, can take care of it for most patients; Osborn personalizes this part of the discussion with case histories of individuals. . . . He concludes with a long list of OCD support groups and other helpful information." Booklist
Includes bibliographical references

Penzel, Fred

Obsessive-compulsive disorders; a complete guide to getting well and staying well. Oxford Univ. Press 2000 428p il $35

616.85

1. Obsessive-compulsive neurosis
ISBN 0-19-514092-3   LC 00-32419

This study of OCD (obsssive-compulsive disorder) outlines behavior patterns, discusses new antidepressants and behavior therapy techniques, and includes a do-it-yourself guide for a self-administered program of behavior therapy

"New antidepressants and behavioral therapy techniques have led to great improvements in the condition of sufferers of this biologically based illness. Psychologist Penzel has written a do-it-yourself guide that outlines in great detail procedures for a self-administered program of behavioral therapy. . . . This title is the most useful of the recent books on OCD and is highly recommended to all public libraries." Libr J

Roesch, Roberta
The encyclopedia of depression. 2nd ed.
Facts on File 2001 278p il $65   **616.85**
1. Depression (Psychology)—Encyclopedias
ISBN 0-8160-4047-8   LC 00-39353
First published 1991
"More than 570 A-to-Z entries include . . . information on the history of the disease, current research, treatment options, and the role of various mental health professional and government programs in addressing depression." Publisher's note

Root, Benjamin A., Jr.
Understanding panic and other anxiety disorders; [by] Benjamin A. Root, Jr. University Press of Miss. 2000 109p il (Understanding health and sickness series) hardcover o.p. paperback available $12

616.85
1. Panic disorders 2. Anxiety
ISBN 1-57806-245-4 (pa)   LC 00-21977
"Root explains physical and mental problems that can mimic panic disorders and that the differentiating diagnosis in emergency room or clinic is often a major hurdle. The unpredictable nature of attacks in panic disorders and their frequent accompaniment, agoraphobia . . . add to the anxiety involved. Root describes those likely to suffer from panic attacks, discusses drug and psychotherapy treatments, and includes a chapter on pertinent research projects." Booklist

Schreiber, Flora Rheta
Sybil. Regnery Pub. 1973 350p o.p.; Warner Bks. paperback available $7.99

616.85
1. Multiple personality
ISBN 0-446-35940-8 (pa)
This is the "true story of Sybil I. Dorsett, a battered child possessed by 16 different personalities. . . . The author skillfully evokes Sybil's patient work during 11 years of psychoanalysis and her eventual success in integrating these selves into a unified personality." Libr J

Solden, Sari
Journeys through ADDulthood; discover a new sense of identity and meaning while living with attention deficit disorder. Walker & Co. 2002 300p il $24; pa $13   **616.85**
1. Attention deficit disorder
ISBN 0-8027-1376-9; 0-8027-7679-5 (pa)
                                 LC 2003-268751
"The material is organized into three stages: understanding the brain and primary symptoms of ADD, discovering one's true identity and accepting one's uniqueness, and learning to share one's self with others. . . . This important work stands out among the growing number of books on ADD for its focus on adults and the author's emphasis on learning how to come to terms with and live comfortably with the disease. Highly recommended for all public libraries." Libr J
Includes bibliographical references

Solomon, Andrew, 1963-
The noonday demon; an atlas of depression. Scribner 2001 569p $28; pa $16
                                          616.85
1. Depression (Psychology)
ISBN 0-684-85466-X; 0-684-85467-8 (pa)
                                 LC 2001-18884
"The author draws on his own life story and other sources for a deeply moving and provocative exploration of depression." Booklist
Includes bibliographical references

Styron, William, 1925-
Darkness visible; a memoir of madness. Random House 1990 84p hardcover o.p. paperback available $11   **616.85**
1. Depression (Psychology)
ISBN 0-679-73639-5 (pa)   LC 90-53141
This is an account of the author's experience of suicidal depression and his recovery
"The book's virtues—considerable—are twofold. First, it is a pitiless and chastened record of a nearly fatal human trial far commoner than assumed—and then a literary discourse on the ways and means of our cultural discontents." Publ Wkly

616.86   Substance abuse (Drug abuse)

Beattie, Melody
Beyond codependency; and getting better all the time. Harper & Row 1989 252p o.p.; Hazelden Foundation paperback available $15.95   **616.86**
1. Applied psychology 2. Drug abuse
ISBN 0-89486-583-8 (pa)   LC 88-45986
"A Harper/Hazelden book"
The author discusses "the process of recovering from the self-defeating behaviors adopted as survival tactics by adult children of families rendered dysfunctional by parental alcoholism or similar traumas." Publ Wkly
Includes bibliographical references

Codependents' guide to the twelve steps. Prentice Hall Press 1990 273p o.p.; Simon & Schuster paperback available $12   **616.86**
1. Drug abuse
ISBN 0-671-76227-3 (pa)   LC 90-52819
"A Prentice Hall/Parkside book"
"Beattie offers an interpretation of the 12 steps based on her own experience as a recovering addict, codependent, and practicing therapist. This includes an excellent annotated bibliography of recovery titles." Libr J

Chopra, Deepak
Overcoming addictions; the spiritual solution. Harmony Bks. 1997 136p il hardcover o.p. paperback available $12

616.86
1. Drug abuse 2. Mind and body
ISBN 0-609-80195-3 (pa)
The author "addresses the topic of dependencies on psychoactive and mood-altering substances and guides the reader to replace addictive behavior with deeper sources of joy and spiritual fulfillment." Publisher's note

Drugs and controlled substances; information for students; Stacey Blachford, Kristine Krapp, editors. Gale Group 2002 c2003 xxvi, 495p il $115   **616.86**
1. Drugs 2. Drug abuse
ISBN 0-7876-6264-X   LC 2002-10925
Provides detailed information about the composition, history, effects, uses and abuses of common drugs, including illegal drugs and addictive substances, as well as commonly abused classes of prescription drugs
"In addition to the well-written essays, sidebars discussing legal issues, misconceptions, history, and news stories add depth to each topic. . . . Currency, scope, and authority are the hallmarks of this highly recommended reference work." Booklist
Includes bibliographical references

Fisher, Edwin B., 1946-
American Lung Association 7 steps to a smoke-free life; [by] Edwin B. Fisher, Jr. with Toni L. Goldfarb. Wiley 1998 226p pa $14.95   **616.86**
1. Smoking cessation programs 2. Tobacco habit
ISBN 0-471-24700-6   LC 97-38826
"Based on the American Lung Association's smoking cessation program, this book coaches smokers through discovering their own motivations and obstacles to quitting, planning effective strategies to meet and conquer the temptation to pick up a cigarette, and tailoring a cessation program to individual lifestyles." Libr J

Substance abuse sourcebook; edited by Karen Bellenir. Omnigraphics 1996 573p (Health reference series) $78   **616.86**
1. Drug abuse
ISBN 0-7808-0038-9   LC 96-9511
"Basic health-related information about the abuse of legal and illegal substances such as alcohol, tobacco, prescription drugs, marijuana, cocaine, and heroin; and including facts about substance abuse prevention strategies, intervention methods, treatment and recovery programs, and a section addressing the special problems related to substance abuse during pregnancy." Title page
"A valuable addition to any health reference section." Book Rep
Includes bibliographical references

Weil, Andrew
From chocolate to morphine; everything you need to know about mind-altering drugs; [by] Andrew Weil and Winifred Rosen. rev & updated. Houghton Mifflin 1993 240p il pa $16   **616.86**
1. Psychotropic drugs
ISBN 0-395-91152-4   LC 92-31727
First published 1983 with title: Chocolate to morphine
"Neither condoning nor condemning drug use, the authors cover a wide range of available substances, from coffee to marijuana, from antihistamines to psychedelics, from steroids to the new 'smart drugs.' Besides describing the likely effects of each substance, the authors discuss precautions and alternatives." Publisher's note
"Because drug use (legal or illegal) is not condemned, this volume may be considered unorthodox by some. . . . Aimed at young people, their parents and teachers, this book offers an alternative way of looking at drug use." Libr J
Includes bibliographical references

West, James W.
The Betty Ford Center book of answers; help for those struggling with substance abuse and for the people who love them; foreword by Betty Ford. Pocket Bks. 1997 206p pa $16.95   **616.86**
1. Drug abuse 2. Alcoholism
ISBN 0-671-00182-5   LC 96-41485
"Chapters include straighforward information on how to identify an alcoholic, intervention, effects of substance abuse on the brain and other parts of the body, treatment, prevention, and relapse." Libr J

616.89   Mental disorders

Amen, Daniel
Change your brain, change your life; the breakthrough program for conquering anxiety, depression, obsessiveness, anger, and impulsiveness. Times Bks. 1998 337p il hardcover o.p. paperback available $15   **616.89**
1. Mental illness 2. Brain
ISBN 0-8129-2998-5 (pa)   LC 98-15043
Using brain imaging technology the author identifies which brain systems are associated with specific problems. In addition to changes in diet the author advocates the use of fragrances, music, lighting, and cognitive exercises in combating certain negative behaviors

Andreasen, Nancy C.
Brave new brain; conquering mental illness in the era of the genome. Oxford Univ. Press 2001 368p il $35   **616.89**
1. Mental illness 2. Gene mapping
ISBN 0-19-514509-7   LC 00-50141
The author "argues that by combining our knowledge of the human genome with that of the human brain we can effectively 'wage war' on mental illness. She summarizes what we know about the etiology, diagnosis, and treatment of schizophrenia, dementia, and various mood and anxiety disorders. . . . Written with clarity and sensitivity, this study offers a refreshing, optimistic vision of the future." Libr J
Includes bibliographical references

Attwood, Tony, 1952-
Asperger's syndrome; a guide for parents and professionals. Kingsley, J. 1998 224p il pa $18.95   **616.89**
1. Asperger's syndrome 2. Autism
ISBN 1-85302-577-1   LC 98-130894
This is a guide to the "identification, treatment and care of both children and adults with Asperger's Syndrome. The book provides a description and analysis of the unusual characteristics of the syndrome and practical strategies to reduce those that are most conspicuous or debilitating. Beginning with a chapter on diagnosis, including an assessment test, the book covers . . . aspects of the syndrome from language to social behaviour and motor clumsiness, concluding with a chapter based on the questions most frequently asked by those who come into contact with individuals with this syndrome." Publisher's note
This book "offers tremendous insight into the identification and treatment of children on the higher functioning end of ASD." Libr J
Includes bibliographical references

Carter, Rosalynn

Helping someone with mental illness; a compassionate guide for families, friends, and caregivers; [by] Rosalynn Carter, with Susan K. Golant. Times Bks. 1998 348p hardcover o.p. paperback available $15   **616.89**

1. Mental illness
ISBN 0-8129-2898-9 (pa)   LC 97-39218

"The chapters of part 1 relate what spurred Carter's involvement with mental-health issues and profile families dealing with mental illness. . . . Part 2 sketches scientific and technological advances that are empowering treatment and homes in on understanding schizophrenia, depression, manic-depression, and anxiety disorders—the four basic kinds of mental illness. The third part discusses intervention, prevention, caregiving, and advocating in respect to mental illness." Booklist

Includes bibliographical references

Duke, Patty

A brilliant madness; living with manic-depressive illness; [by] Patty Duke and Gloria Hochman. Bantam Bks. 1992 285p hardcover o.p. paperback available $7.99   **616.89**

1. Manic-depressive illness
ISBN 0-553-56072-7 (pa)   LC 92-5878

This work "alternates between the actress's first-person description of her experiences as a manic-depressive and Ms. Hochman's informative narrative about this sickness. . . . Ms. Duke is a comforting guide through the terror of mental illness, and Ms. Hochman lightens a weighty topic with interesting, animated writing." N Y Times Book Rev

Includes bibliographical references

Encyclopedia of mental health; editor-in-chief, Howard S. Friedman. Academic Press 1998 3v il set $600

616.89

1. Mental health—Dictionaries 2. Psychiatry—Encyclopedias 3. Mental illness—Dictionaries
ISBN 0-12-226675-7   LC 98-84208

"In addition to discussing mental disorders, treatments, and personality attributes, articles focus on such subjects as burnout, caffeine, and commuting and mental health. Each article is formatted clearly with an outline describing its content and a short glossary to explain terminology. . . . Bibliographies for further reading at the end of every article, and an extensive index aid use." Am Libr

The Gale encyclopedia of mental disorders; Ellen Thackery and Madeline Harris, editors. Gale Group 2003 2v il set $295

616.89

1. Psychiatry—Encyclopedias 2. Mental illness—Encyclopedias
ISBN 0-7876-5768-9   LC 2002-23257

"Entries for mental disorders use the following pattern: definitions, descriptions, causes and symptoms, demographics, diagnosis, treatments, prognosis, prevention, and resources. . . . Entries for prescription medications, herbal medications, and dietary supplements include definition, purpose, description, recommended dosage, precautions, side effects, interactions, and resources. Entries are arranged in alphabetical order." Choice

For a fuller review see: Booklist, March 15, 2003

Includes bibliographical references

Hewetson, Ann

The stolen child; aspects of autism and Asperger syndrome; foreword by Susan J. Moreno. Bergin & Garvey Pubs. 2002 240p $26.95   **616.89**

1. Autism 2. Asperger's syndrome
ISBN 0-89789-844-3   LC 2001-43015

"A compendium of historical facts along with the latest thinking about the puzzling field of autism-spectrum disorders, this volume covers theories about what might cause autism and current treatments. Hewetson uses many levels of evidence—including case history, anecdotal observations, correlational studies, controlled research findings—and critiques." Choice

"A strong introductory text. . . . Hewetson, the mother of a son with high-ability autism, carefully balances the different approaches and does not promote one treatment over another as the cure for all people with ASD." Libr J

Hobson, J. Allan

Out of its mind; psychiatry in crisis; a call for reform; [by] J. Allan Hobson, Jonathan A. Leonard. Perseus Bks. 2001 292p il hardcover o.p. paperback available $17   **616.89**

1. Psychiatry
ISBN 0-7382-0685-7 (pa)

The authors contend that psychiatry "has lost its way, and without a new integration of its medical, psychological, and social components, it may well die, giving up its functions and ill-served patients to neurology and psychology. . . . The authors' proposed reforms are exciting and important." Libr J

Kramer, Peter D.

Should you leave? Scribner 1997 320p o.p.; Penguin Bks. paperback available $16

616.89

1. Psychotherapy 2. Marriage counseling
ISBN 0-14-027279-8 (pa)   LC 97-19060

This book "examines how people seek an answer to this crucial question of the heart. . . . It also delves into the intricate and complicated issue of psychotherapy and advice itself. Kramer contemplates the role of the therapist as well as the unspoken law against offering advice to his clients. Written with a keen ear for narrative, this nonfiction title reads more like well-written fiction." Libr J

Includes bibliographical references

Neugeboren, Jay, 1938-

Transforming madness; new lives for people living with mental illness. Morrow 1999 390p o.p.; University of Calif. Press paperback available $16.95   **616.89**

1. Mentally ill 2. Mental illness
ISBN 0-520-22875-8 (pa)   LC 98-50056

"A quiet revolution is taking place in the care and treatment of the mentally ill, observes Neugeboren in this . . . report. Within the last five to 10 years, antipsychotic medications have become much more effective and their side effects less debilitating. Just as important, he notes, is the emergence of recovery programs, peer support centers and community treatment facilities that make it possible for the severely mentally ill to go to college, hold down jobs, marry and raise children—even without being fully cured." Publ Wkly

The author "provides a literate, lively guide, rich in history, biography, and economics as well as psychology and neurochemistry." Libr J

Noll, Richard

The encyclopedia of schizophrenia and other psychotic disorders; foreword by Susan Naylor. 2nd ed. Facts on File 2000 xxi, 344p $65 **616.89**

1. Schizophrenia—Encyclopedias
ISBN 0-8160-4070-2   LC 99-44166
First published 1992
"This dictionary contains an alphabetical listing of entries that include therapy, treatments, theories, organizations, terms, related diseases, and more. One of four appendixes includes contact information for organizations. The extensive historical, biographical, and clinical information includes facts about the history of mental illness, current genetic research, and possibly related diseases." Book Rep
For a fuller review see: Booklist, Feb. 1, 2001

Osborne, Lawrence

American normal; the hidden world of Asperger syndrome. Copernicus 2002 224p $27.50   **616.89**

1. Asperger's syndrome
ISBN 0-387-95307-8   LC 2002-73782
"Basing his report on memoirs, clinical histories, poems and stories, and visits with dozens of individuals afflicted with the disorder, journalist and essayist Lawrence Osborne shows us what life with Asperger's is really like." Publisher's note
"Osborne uses his considerable journalistic talents to interview a number of well-known and not so well-known people diagnosed with an enigmatic disorder known as Asperger's Syndrome. . . . Recommended for readers at all levels." Choice
Includes bibliographical references

Park, Clara Claiborne

Exiting nirvana; a daughter's life with autism; foreword by Oliver Sacks. Little, Brown 2001 225p il $23.95; pa $14.95
616.89

1. Park, Jessy, 1958- 2. Autism
ISBN 0-316-69117-8; 0-316-69124-0 (pa)
LC 00-33554
The author "covers the past 40 years of her daughter Jessy's life and . . . describes what Jessy has been able to accomplish, as well as setbacks along the way. Also included are color illustrations of Jessy's . . . artwork." Libr J
"A perceptive, detailed, and empathetic account not of autism but of the experience of autism. . . . A warm, levelheaded, neither overly optimistic nor overly glorified book that proves very rewarding." Booklist
Includes bibliographical references

Porter, Roy, 1946-2002

Madness; a brief history. Oxford Univ. Press 2002 241p il hardcover o.p. paperback available $12.95   **616.89**

1. Mental illness 2. Psychiatry
ISBN 0-19-280267-4 (pa)   LC 2001-52329
This is a study on the many ways madness has been perceived and misperceived from antiquity to modern times. The author "also discusses topical issues, including the relationship between lunacy and creativity, the drive to institutionalize, which peaked in the mid-20th century; the rise and demise of psychoanalysis; and the development of the antipsychiatry movement. This book combines the appeal of history as narrative with the in-

tellectual stimulation derived from cogent analysis." Libr J
Includes bibliographical references

Rogers, Carl R. (Carl Ransom), 1902-1987

On becoming a person; a therapist's view of psychotherapy. Houghton Mifflin 1961 420p hardcover o.p. paperback available $16
616.89

1. Psychotherapy
ISBN 0-395-75531-X (pa)
This collection begins with "two talks in which Dr. Rogers gives some biographical data and outlines his progress toward his concept of client-centered therapy; succeeding chapters express his views on helping others toward personal growth, the therapeutic process, his philosophy of the fully functioning person, the place of research in psychotherapy, its implications for living and the new discipline of behavioral sciences." Booklist
Includes bibliographical references

Shorter, Edward

A history of psychiatry; from the era of the asylum to the age of Prozac. Wiley 1997 436p il hardcover o.p. paperback available $30   **616.89**

1. Psychiatry
ISBN 0-471-24531-3 (pa)   LC 96-15292
Shorter traces "the development of modern psychiatry from the asylum era of the late 18th and 19th centuries . . . to the recent advent of mind-altering pharmaceuticals (i.e., Thorazine, Valium, Prozac, etc.)." Choice
This "social history of 200 years of psychiatry in the U.S., Great Britain, France, and Germany is informative and at times lively. . . . Dealing ably with the major trends, Shorter does not fail to also illuminate such engaging and horrifying byways as the 'fever cure' and ice pick lobotomy." Booklist
Includes bibliographical references

Sichel, Deborah

Women's moods; what every woman must know about hormones, the brain, and emotional health; [by] Deborah Sichel and Jeanne Watson Driscoll. Morrow 1999 352p hardcover o.p. paperback available $14
616.89

1. Women—Health and hygiene 2. Women—Psychology
ISBN 0-380-72852-4 (pa)   LC 99-25412
"Drawing on their own personal experiences, the experiences of their patients, and their own research as well as that of others, the authors discuss why the unique brain chemistry of women and the sensitivity of the brain to female hormones make women more susceptible to mood disorders and anxiety problems. They outline the program they use with their patients, which includes some medications and a great deal of self-care." Libr J
Includes bibliographical references

Slater, Lauren

Prozac diary. Random House 1998 203p o.p.; Penguin Bks. paperback available $13
616.89

1. Psychotropic drugs 2. Mental illness
ISBN 0-14-026394-2 (pa)   LC 97-35727
The author "was among the first patients to be given Prozac, and she has now been on it, almost without in-

Slater, Lauren—*Continued*

terruption, for ten years. She credits the drug with enabling her, after an incapacitating adolescence, not only to taste and see but to complete a doctorate; marry; and, as director of a clinic, be useful. But she also ponders what it means to one's sense of self to be more or less permanently under the influence of a personality- (and libido-) altering drug." New Yorker

Stone, Michael H., 1933-

Healing the mind; a history of psychiatry from antiquity to the present. Norton 1997 516p il $49   **616.89**

1. Psychiatry

ISBN 0-393-70222-7   LC 96-28209

The author "chronicles the persons, movements, and events that have contributed to modern psychiatry. Starting with accounts of aberrant behavior in religious texts, he traces the diagnosis and treatment of mental illness from ancient Greece to present times." Libr J

Includes bibliographical references

Whitaker, Robert

Mad in America; bad science, bad medicine, and the enduring mistreatment of the mentally ill. Perseus Bks. 2002 334p $27; pa $17.50   **616.89**

1. Mental illness 2. Schizophrenia 3. Psychiatric hospitals

ISBN 0-7382-0385-8; 0-7382-0799-3 (pa)

LC 2001-98251

The author "argues that mental asylums in the U.S. have been run largely as 'places of confinement—facilities that served to segregate the misfits from society— rather than as hospitals that provided medical care.' . . . Whitaker's . . . book will appeal to those interested in medical history, as well as anyone fascinated by Western culture's obsessive need to define and subdue the mentally ill." Publ Wkly

Includes bibliographical references

Whybrow, Peter C.

A mood apart; depression, mania, and other afflictions of the self. Basic Bks. 1997 xx, 363p il map o.p. Perennial Bks. paperback available $15   **616.89**

1. Personality disorders 2. Self 3. Personality

ISBN 0-06-097740-X (pa)   LC 96-47974

"Whybrow examines mania and depression, . . . describing several individual cases. . . . The author guides us through the evolutionary growth of both the so-called lizard, ancient mammal and the new mammal brains within the human brain, then examines areas of behavior, types of diseases, precipitating causes of disease, and treatments." Booklist

"Seldom has the inner emotional landscape of melancholic depression, mania and manic-depressive illness been mapped with so much clarity, empathy and sensitivity." Publ Wkly

Yalom, Irvin D., 1931-

The gift of therapy; an open letter to a new generation of therapists and their patients. HarperCollins Pubs. 2002 xxi, 263p $23.95; pa $12.95   **616.89**

1. Psychotherapy

ISBN 0-06-621440-8; 0-06-093811-0 (pa)

LC 2001-39319

"Yalom offers what he calls a series of tips for therapists, emphasizing process rather than content. . . . His 85 brief advices, while certainly helpful to therapists and patients, may also help any thoughtful person seeking to improve relationships with others and self-understanding." Booklist

Includes bibliographical references

616.9 Other diseases

Honigsbaum, Mark

The fever trail; in search of the cure for malaria. Farrar, Straus & Giroux 2002 397p maps $25   **616.9**

1. Malaria

ISBN 0-374-15469-4   LC 2001-40871

Also available in paperback from Picador USA

First published 2001 in the United Kingdom

This is a history of attempts to find medical treatments for malaria, beginning with quinine "from the bark of the cinchona tree, [found] . . . on slopes of the Andes Mountains. . . . The bulk of the [book] is an account of three British adventurers who [searched] . . . for the tree: Richard Spruce, a hypochondriac Yorkshire moss collector; Charles Ledger, a cockney trader who hoped to make a fortune; and Clements Markham, a historian, linguist and patron of Robert Scott's expeditions to the Arctic. . . . Entering the present, Honigsbaum reports on recent efforts to eradicate or control malaria and attempts to discover better drugs, or a vaccine." N Y Times Book Rev

"This tale is impeccably researched; moreover, Honigsbaum's aptitude for clarifying epidemiology and disease organisms is rivaled only by his knack for telling tales of reeling adventure and colonialist history." Publ Wkly

Includes bibliographical references

Kahn, Ada P.

Stress A-Z; a sourcebook for facing everyday challenges. Facts on File 1998 390p $44   **616.9**

1. Stress (Physiology) 2. Stress (Psychology)

ISBN 0-8160-3295-5   LC 97-51580

In addition to describing how to identify and manage stress this work explores causes and a variety of traditional and alternative methods of treatment

"The scope of the book is wide and current—most of the references are from the 1990s, with a few from the late 1980s. Almost all of the entries include cross references, sources for further information, and bibliographies." Libr J

Koplow, David A., 1951-

Smallpox: the fight to eradicate a global scourge. University of Calif. Press 2003 265p $30; pa $14.95 **616.9**

1. Smallpox
ISBN 0-520-23732-3; 0-520-24220-3 (pa)

LC 2002-5539

The author "provides a brief overview of the disease's history, its basic biology, biodiversity concerns, and the role of the World Health Organization in the virus's eradication. He concludes his timely book with a lengthy consideration of the pros and cons of eliminating the smallpox stockpiles." Libr J

Includes bibliographical references

Preston, Richard

The demon in the freezer; a true story. Random House 2002 240p $24.95 **616.9**

1. Smallpox 2. Biological warfare
ISBN 0-375-50856-2

Also available large print edition $26.95 (ISBN 0-375-43186-1) and in paperback from Fawcett Bks.

Contents: Something in the air; The dreaming demon; To Bhola Island; The other side of the moon; A woman with a peaceful life; The demon's eyes; The anthrax skulls; Superpox

The author explains "the chemical properties of the smallpox virus; how a single infected person . . . can set off an epidemic; and what this horrendous disease can be like. . . . We learn how the disease was eliminated by an international vaccination campaign in the 1970's; why there are reasons to believe that the Soviet Union grew staggering quantities of the virus, allegedly in part to arm intercontinental missiles; and how the virus might now be used by others as a 'strategic weapon.'" N Y Times Book Rev

Rocco, Fiammetta

The miraculous fever tree; malaria and the quest for a cure that changed the world. HarperCollins Pubs. 2003 348p il maps $24.95 **616.9**

1. Malaria 2. Quinine
ISBN 0-06-019951-2

LC 2003-51128

Rocco's "clear prose and personal investment—having grown up in Africa, she knows malaria and quinine all too personally—ensure that every episode of her narrative enthralls." Booklist

Includes bibliographical references

Turkington, Carol

The encyclopedia of infectious diseases; {by} Carol Turkington, Bonnie Lee Ashby. 2nd ed. Facts on File 2003 397p $71.50

616.9

1. Communicable diseases—Encyclopedias
ISBN 0-8160-4775-8

LC 2002-29418

First published 1998

"The alphabetically arranged volume covers diseases, treatment options, and relevant organizations. . . . Information is provided for each disease and includes its cause, symptoms, treatment, and prevention. Major diseases that have had an impact on the world's population (tuberculosis, AIDS) are covered . . . and include a history. This feature makes the volume useful to researchers and students." Booklist

Includes bibliographical references

Vanderhoof-Forschner, Karen

Everything you need to know about Lyme disease and other tick-borne disorders; foreword by Willy Burgdorfer. 2nd ed. Wiley 2003 270p il pa $15.95 **616.9**

1. Lyme disease 2. Ticks
ISBN 0-471-40793-3

LC 2003-45066

First published 1997

The author "discusses the status of Lyme disease as a public health threat; the nature and characteristics of ticks; the history of Lyme disease; its symptoms, diagnosis, and treatment; and the search for vaccines. . . . The author's writing is conversational and clear even when discussing complex topics, and her appendixes are outstanding." Libr J

Includes bibliographical references

616.95 Sexually transmitted diseases

Hayden, Deborah

Pox: genius, madness, and the mysteries of syphilis. Basic Bks. 2003 xx, 379p il $27.50

616.95

1. Syphilis
ISBN 0-465-02881-0

LC 2002-15847

The author "presents case studies of various nineteenth- and twentieth-century luminaries rumored to have been syphilitic. The . . . accounts allow readers to draw their own conclusions about men as diverse as Beethoven, Flaubert, Lincoln, and Hitler." Booklist

"A fascinating account . . . any book that combines genius, madness, sex, and disease is bound to find an audience." Libr J

Includes bibliographical references

Marr, Lisa

Sexually transmitted diseases; a physician tells you what you need to know. Johns Hopkins Univ. Press 1998 341p il (Johns Hopkins Press health book) $55; pa $17.95

616.95

1. Sexually transmitted diseases
ISBN 0-8018-6042-3; 0-8018-6043-1 (pa)

LC 98-25952

The author "begins with basic anatomy, symptoms, and the components of a medical examination for men and women. She then offers important advice about communications with sex partners and safe sex. The second part of her book discusses specific diseases and their symptoms, diagnosis, and treatment." Libr J

Includes bibliographical references

616.97 Diseases of the immune system

Gallo, Robert C.

Virus hunting; AIDS, cancer, and the human retrovirus: a story of scientific discovery. Basic Bks. 1991 352p hardcover o.p. paperback available $17.50 **616.97**

1. AIDS (Disease) 2. Medicine—Research
ISBN 0-465-09815-0 (pa)

LC 90-55600

"A New Republic book"

The author describes his biomedical research of the cancer-causing retrovirus, how it led to the discovery of the AIDS virus, and the political and ethical controversies surrounding AIDS research

Grmek, Mirko D., 1924-2000

History of AIDS; emergence and origin of a modern pandemic; translated by Russell C. Maulitz and Jacalyn Duffin. Princeton Univ. Press 1990 279p hardcover o.p. paperback available $30   **616.97**

1. AIDS (Disease)
ISBN 0-691-02477-4 (pa)   LC 90-32514
Original French edition, 1989

In this "medical and social history of the disease, Dr. Grmek . . . speculates about the prehistory of AIDS, before its seemingly sudden appearance from nowhere in 1981. He argues that while today's runaway epidemic is a new phenomenon, the viruses that cause AIDS have infected people for many decades, if not for centuries." NY Times Book Rev

Includes bibliographical references

Lipkowitz, Myron

Encyclopedia of allergies; [by] Myron A. Lipkowitz, Tova Navarra. 2nd ed. Facts on File 2001 340p (Library of health and living) $65; pa $19.95   **616.97**

1. Allergy—Encyclopedias
ISBN 0-8160-4404-X; 0-8160-4405-8 (pa)
                                 LC 00-49490
First published 1994 with title: Allergies A-Z

This guide to the symptoms and treatments of a variety of allergies includes over 1,000 entries that provide information on medications, occupational and environmental allergies, inherited allergies, and antihistamines, etc.

Includes bibliographical references

Null, Gary

AIDS: a second opinion. Seven Stories Press 2001 750p $34.95   **616.97**

1. AIDS (Disease)
ISBN 1-58322-062-3   LC 00-51013

The author "argues that the AIDS drama has exposed problematic issues having to do with the functioning of U.S. medical institutions. . . . The book dissects the claims of the AZT and drug-cocktail approach to treating AIDS and offers a trilogy of treatment strategies based on wide views of how to enhance the immune system and improve overall functioning." Publisher's note

Includes bibliographical references

Pescatore, Fred, 1961-

The allergy and asthma cure; a complete 8-step nutritional program. Wiley 2003 251p $24.95   **616.97**

1. Allergy 2. Asthma 3. Food allergy 4. Diet therapy
ISBN 0-471-21468-X   LC 2002-14024

Contents: Understanding and diagnosing allergies; Understanding and diagnosing asthma; Conventional therapies for the treatment of allergies; Conventional therapies for the treatment of asthma; Understanding food sensitivities: the allergy and asthma step one; Understanding candida and yeast: the allergy and asthma cure step two; Setting the stage: the allergy and asthma cure step three; The healing phase diet: the allergy and asthma cure step four; The healing phase diet—weight loss: the allergy and asthma cure step five; Breathing better: the allergy and asthma cure step six; Nutritional supplements to treat allergies: the allergy and asthma cure step seven; Nutritional supplements to treat asthma: the allergy and asthma cure step eight; Meal plans; Recipes; A resource guide

Rumpf, Teri P.

The Sjogren's syndrome survival guide; [by] Teri P. Rumpf, Katherine Morland Hammitt. New Harbinger Publs. 2003 234p pa $15.95   **616.97**

1. Immune system—Diseases
ISBN 1-57224-356-2

This discusses Sjogren's syndrome, the most prevalent autoimmune disorder in the U.S. and includes medical information, methods of treatment, and advice on how to cope with the disorder

Walsh, William E.

Food allergies; the complete guide to understanding and relieving your food allergies. Wiley 2000 286p pa $16.95
                                 616.97

1. Allergy
ISBN 0-471-38268-X   LC 00-24608

"While providing an overview of the physiology and types of food allergies, Walsh concentrates on what he terms 'MALS' (monosodium glutamate, acidic foods, low-calorie sweeteners, and refined sugar), the most common allergens identified in his patients. He lists MALS foods, provides a sample elimination diet, and includes information on common fast-food restaurant choices." Libr J

Includes bibliographical references

Watstein, Sarah B.

The encyclopedia of HIV and AIDS; {by} Sarah Barbara Watstein, Stephen E. Stratton; foreword by Evelyn J. Fisher. 2nd ed. Facts on File 2003 660p $71.50   **616.97**

1. AIDS (Disease)—Dictionaries
ISBN 0-8160-4808-8   LC 2002-35220
"Facts on File library of health and living"
First published 1998 with title: The AIDS dictionary

This volume includes "entries covering the basic biological, medical, financial, legal, political, and social issues and terms associated with HIV and AIDS. Entries explain symptoms and treatments, opportunistic infections, prevention strategies, and much more. Appendixes include HIV/AIDS associations, education centers, clinical trials, hotlines, publications, and additional material." Publisher's note

"The coverage is . . . broad and the language is pitched for the intended audience of nonspecialists . . . vastly expanded and brought up to date . . . Recommended." Choice

Young, Stuart, 1938-

Allergies; the complete guide to diagnosis, treatment, and daily management; [by] Stuart H. Young, Bruce S. Dobozin, Margaret Miner. rev ed. Plume Bks. 1999 337p pa $13.95   **616.97**

1. Allergy
ISBN 0-452-27966-6   LC 98-50350
First published 1991

"Covering all kinds of allergies from hay fever and sinus problems to food and drug allergies, [the authors] address aspects of allergy management such as visiting the doctor and psychological issues." Libr J

Includes bibliographical references

616.99 Tumors

Adrouny, A. Richard, 1952-
Understanding colon cancer. University Press of Miss. 2002 146p il (Understanding health and sickness series) hardcover o.p. paperback available $12   **616.99**
1. Colon (Anatomy) 2. Cancer
ISBN 1-57806-473-2 (pa)   LC 2002-788
Contents: Who gets colon cancer and why; The colon; How colon cancer develops; The "look" of colon cancer; The "feel" of colon cancer; Stages and prognosis of colon cancer; Surgical treatment of colon cancer; Treatment of later stages of colon cancer; Prevention; The future
The author "describes the anatomy and physiology of the colon. A detailed chapter makes clear the stages of the disease and how they affect the prognosis. Adrouny describes various surgical procedures, their results, and possible complications. . . . The understandable, thorough book concludes with a resources list and a glossary." Booklist
Includes bibliographical references

American Cancer Society's Guide to complementary and alternative cancer methods. American Cancer Soc. 2000 438p $32.95; pa $24.95   **616.99**
1. Cancer 2. Alternative medicine
ISBN 0-944235-29-8; 0-944235-24-7 (pa)
LC 00-40596
"The first part of the book defines complementary and alternative methods and commonly used terms; it also explains how to evaluate treatment and discusses types of research, safety, and usage guidelines. The second section covers a wide range of treatment methodologies, arranged into five categories: Mind, Body, and Spirit; Manual Healing and Physical Touch; Herb, Vitamin, and Mineral; Diet and Nutrition; and Pharmacological and Biological Treatment." Libr J
Includes bibliographical references

Arnot, Bob
The breast cancer prevention diet; the powerful foods, supplements, and drugs that can save your life. Little, Brown 1998 258p $28; pa $14.95   **616.99**
1. Breast cancer 2. Cancer—Diet therapy
ISBN 0-316-05114-4; 0-316-05109-8 (pa)
LC 98-20432
The author "discusses a 12-step plan with a main focus on good nutrition—less fat, less glucose, more fiber, a lower oxidative load, and no chemical estrogens or alcohol. Menus and recipes are supplied." Libr J
Includes bibliographical references

The breast health cookbook; fast and simple recipes to reduce the risk of cancer; recipes and menus by Barbara Sutherland and Rita Mitchell. Little, Brown 2001 262p $25.95; pa $14.95   **616.99**
1. Breast cancer 2. Cancer—Diet therapy
ISBN 0-316-05133-0; 0-316-09528-1 (pa)
LC 00-046942
"In this companion volume to . . . The Breast Cancer Prevention Diet, Arnot offers an array of recipes featuring the foods most likely to help people avoid breast cancer (and prostate cancer as well). With more than 150 recipes from nutritionists Rita Mitchell and Barbara Sutherland, the book is structured around ethnic categories of diet Asian, New American, Mediterranean along with suggested meals. Recipes are provided for main courses, sandwiches, soups, desserts and more. The recipes frequently involve soy products, which Arnot believes are key for preventing cancer." Publ Wkly

Bernard, Jami
Breast cancer, there and back; a woman-to-woman guide. Warner Bks. 2001 xxi, 246p pa $13.95   **616.99**
1. Breast cancer
ISBN 0-446-67753-1   LC 2001-17943
"Breast cancer survivor Bernard describes what it is really like to undergo chemotherapy and radiation treatments. Besides advising on coping with such side effects as hair loss, she also discusses how the disease affects relationships, finding support groups, and alternative therapies." Libr J
Includes bibliographical references

Breast cancer; beyond convention: the world's foremost authorities on complementary and alternative medicine offer advice on healing; edited by Mary Tagliaferri, Isaac Cohen, and Debu Tripathy. Atria Bks. 2002 478p il $27; pa $16   **616.99**
1. Breast cancer 2. Alternative medicine
ISBN 0-7434-1011-4; 0-7434-1012-2 (pa)
LC 2002-16930
This collection of essays "is intended to serve as a guide to the alternative therapies most often used by women with breast cancer. The book includes . . . chapters on approaches such as Chinese Medicine, vitamin and mineral supplementation, meditation and prayer. . . . Women with breast cancer looking for alternative therapies might find this book to be a good start in their own research." Publ Wkly
Includes bibliographical references

Breast cancer sourcebook; edited by Edward J. Prucha and Karen Bellenir. Omnigraphics 2001 580p (Health reference series) $78
616.99
1. Breast cancer
ISBN 0-7808-0244-6   LC 2001-36253
"Basic consumer health information about breast cancer, including diagnostic methods, treatment options, alternative therapies, help and self-help information, related health concerns, statistical and demographic data, and facts for men with breast cancer, along with reports on current research initiatives, a glossary of related medical terms, and a directory of sources for further help and information." Title page
This is a "thoroughgoing, very readable reference." Libr J

The **Cancer** pain sourcebook; Roger S. Cicala [editor] Contemporary 2001 301p il pa $17.95   **616.99**
1. Cancer 2. Pain
ISBN 0-7373-0423-5   LC 00-53478
This offers information "on treating and handling cancer pain. The causes of pain and the factors that worsen it are covered in the first part of the book. . . . The second section of the book . . . details standard cancer pain

The Cancer pain sourcebook—*Continued*
treatments. Several helpful appendixes follow the third section, which delves into advanced pain treatment." Libr J

Includes bibliographical references

Cancer sourcebook; basic consumer health information about major forms and stages of cancer, featuring facts about head and neck cancers, lung cancers . . .; edited by Karen Bellenir. 4th ed. Omnigraphics 2003 1119p il (Health reference series) $78

616.99

1. Cancer
ISBN 0-7808-0633-6   LC 2003-46975
First published 1991

This book "offers descriptions of the major forms and stages of cancers affecting specific organs and systems. It provides facts about treatments, side effects, alternative therapies, clinical trials, and coping strategies. The book's 138 articles are organized in six parts: Cancer Overview . . . Identifying and Reducing Cancer Risks . . . Types of Cancer . . . Cancer Treatments and Therapies . . . Coping with Cancer and the Side Effects of Treatments . . . [and] Additional Help and Information." Publisher's note

"An excellent fourth edition of this useful source. Recommended." Choice

Coleman, C. Norman
Understanding cancer; a patient's guide to diagnosis, prognosis, and treatment; foreword by Ellen L. Stovall. Johns Hopkins Univ. Press 1998 176p il hardcover o.p. paperback available $16.95   **616.99**
1. Cancer
ISBN 0-8018-6020-2 (pa)   LC 98-18732
The author "explains such concepts as cancer etiology, diagnostic tests, treatment options, and clinical trials. . . . Using patient checklists and case studies, Coleman describes the steps involved in the initial diagnosis, staging (the growth pattern of a tumor), and the risks and benefits of different treatments." Libr J
Includes bibliographical references

Everyone's guide to cancer therapy; how cancer is diagnosed, treated, and managed day to day; [by] Malin Dollinger [et al.] 4th ed. Andrews McMeel Pub. 2003 xxxiv, 925p il $29.95   **616.99**
1. Cancer
ISBN 0-7407-1856-8   LC 2002-28289
First published 1991

This offers information on cancer diagnosis and treatment options and includes chapters on cryotherapy, radio frequency treatment, genetic risk assessment, and managed care

Gordon, James Samuel, 1941-
Comprehensive cancer care; integrating alternative, complementary and conventional therapies; the complete guide; [by] James Gordon and Sharon Curtin. Perseus Bks. 2000 hardcover o.p. paperback available $18.50

616.99

1. Cancer
ISBN 0-7382-0486-2 (pa)
"Based on a series of medical conferences exploring new approaches to cancer, this guide discusses a wide variety of cancer-fighting modalities. Throughout . . . [the authors] encourage readers to consider unfamiliar ideas, form effective patient/doctor partnerships and adopt empowered, informed patient attitudes." Publ Wkly

Harpham, Wendy Schlessel
Diagnosis, cancer; your guide through the first few months; illustrations by Ann Bliss Pilcher. [rev and updated] Norton 1998 xxvi, 230p pa $13.95   **616.99**
1. Cancer
ISBN 0-393-31691-2   LC 97-9291
First published 1992
The author discusses current developments in cancer diagnosis and treatments for the newly diagnosed patient, with advice on decision making and emotional and practical problems
Includes bibliographical references

Henschke, Claudia I.
Lung cancer; myths, facts, choices—and hope; [by] Claudia I. Henschke, and Peggy McCarthy, with Sarah Wernick. Norton 2002 389p il $27.95; pa $16.95   **616.99**
1. Lung cancer
ISBN 0-393-04154-9; 0-393-32498-2 (pa)
LC 2002-513
The authors present a "guide to the basics of how lung cancer develops, risk factors, diagnosis, treatment options, and living well with lung cancer. . . . Treatment modalities detailed here include surgery, chemotherapy, and radiation, with additional chapters on alternative therapies such as acupuncture for pain and getting access to the latest treatment through clinical trials." Libr J

Informed decisions; the complete book of cancer diagnosis, treatment, and recovery; [edited by] Harmon Eyre, Dianne Partie Lange; Lois B. Morris, consulting editor. 2nd ed. American Cancer Soc. 2001 768p il pa $29.95   **616.99**
1. Cancer
ISBN 0-944235-27-1   LC 2001-1880
First published 1997 by Viking
"Covering all types of cancer in general terms, this tome from the American Cancer Society discusses detection, diagnosis, and treatment in five parts, subdivided into 31 chapters. Throughout, the information is presented logically, clearly, and in a visually accessible manner, with copious subheads, sidebars (case histories, checklists, dos and don'ts, etc.), headnotes (Tips and Advice, Cancer Basics), and questions to ask the doctor." Libr J

Leopold, Ellen, 1944-

A darker ribbon; breast cancer, women, and their doctors in the twentieth century. Beacon Press 1999 334p hardcover o.p. paperback available $18   **616.99**

1. Breast cancer

ISBN 0-8070-6513-7 (pa)   LC 99-27201

The author "offers a social history of the disease and how it has affected individuals and attitudes. . . . She has brought in a personal flavor by drawing on two groups of letters, one between a pseudonymous patient and surgeon William Stewart Halsted, inventor of radical mastectomy, and the other between Rachel Carson and surgeon George Crile Jr., who preferred lumpectomy whenever possible. This is a considerable contribution to social and medical history as well as women's studies." Booklist

Includes bibliographical references

Lerner, Barron H.

The breast cancer wars; hope, fear, and the pursuit of a cure in twentieth century America. Oxford Univ. Press 2001 383p il $30; pa $16.95   **616.99**

1. Breast cancer

ISBN 0-19-514261-6; 0-19-516106-8 (pa)

LC 00-63691

This is an account of the development of breast cancer treatments in the United States from the nineteenth-century to the present

"Lerner's book is essential for women's studies and history of medicine collections, but no public or academic library could go wrong in adding it to its collection." Libr J

Includes bibliographical references

Link, John

The breast cancer survival manual; a step-by-step guide for the woman with newly diagnosed breast cancer; [by] John Link, Cynthia Forsthoff, James Waisman. Holt & Co. 2003 222p il pa $15   **616.99**

1. Breast cancer

ISBN 0-8050-7059-1   LC 2003-41742

"An Owl book"

First published 1998

The author "explains how to get a second opinion, read a pathology report and work the medical system in order to become the leader of one's own treatment team. This is a good start to assist newly diagnosed patients, accelerate recovery and reduce the side effects of treatment." Publ Wkly [review of 1998 edition]

Includes bibliographical references

Take charge of your breast cancer; a guide to getting the best possible treatment. Holt & Co. 2002 189p pa $15   **616.99**

1. Breast cancer

ISBN 0-8050-7056-7   LC 2002-68541

Companion volume to The breast cancer survival manual

"Link believes that women are generally overtreated or undertreated for this disease, and he hopes that they each will eventually receive the 'correct' treatment. He emphasizes self-advocacy and establishing strong, healing relationships with a team of physicians who consider treating the woman as a combination of mind and body." Libr J

The author's "warm and encouraging tone, as well as the nuanced information he offers, should, as the book's title suggests, help readers obtain individualized treatment in a health care system that is often dehumanizing." Publ Wkly

Olson, James Stuart, 1946-

Bathsheba's breast; women, cancer, and history; by James S. Olson. Johns Hopkins Univ. Press 2002 302p $24.95   **616.99**

1. Breast cancer

ISBN 0-8018-6936-6   LC 2001-6265

"Olson examines the evolution of cancer research, the politics and economics of the disease, the gender dynamics of female patients and male physicians, and the rise of patient activism. The book chronicles advances in breast-cancer diagnosis and treatment and the uncertainty that women must face while making difficult choices." Libr J

Includes bibliographical references

Scott, Walter J., 1954-

Lung cancer; a guide to diagnosis and treatment. Addicus Bks. 2000 156p il pa $14.95   **616.99**

1. Lung cancer

ISBN 1-886039-43-7   LC 00-8028

Scott "explains how the lungs work, the different types of lung cancer, diagnosis, treatment, and end-of-life care. An appendix contains a list of chemotherapy agents, a resource list, and a glossary." Libr J

Teeley, Peter

The complete cancer survival guide; the most comprehensive, up-to-date guide for patients and their families: with advice from dozens of leading cancer specialists at more than 30 major cancer centers; [by] Peter Teeley and Philip Bashe. Doubleday 2000 xx, 972p il $21.95   **616.99**

1. Cancer

ISBN 0-385-48605-7   LC 98-28588

A "manual on the 25 most common cancer types. Exceptional in its fusing of facts with practical advice and straightforward strategies, the text covers disease basics, navigating the healthcare system, standard and experimental treatments (i.e., clinical trials), insurance options, and the psychosocial aspects of cancer." Libr J

617 Miscellaneous branches of medicine. Surgery

Arem, Arnold

In our hands; a hand surgeon's tales of the body's most exquisite instrument. Times Bks. 2002 271p $24; pa $14   **617**

1. Hand—Surgery

ISBN 0-8050-7179-2; 0-8050-7435-X (pa)

LC 2002-22191

A look at "the world of hand surgery from the perspectives of both the patient and the surgeon. . . . [In Part 1 the author presents] 11 case studies of his patients, from infants to the middle aged, whose lives were scrambled from hand injuries. . . . Part 2 covers specific hand problems, such as replantation, carpal tunnel syndrome, and rheumatoid disease." Libr J

Current surgical diagnosis & treatment. Appleton & Lange pa $59.95   **617**
1. Surgery
ISSN 0894-2277

Also available CD-ROM version

First published 1977. (11th edition 2003) Periodically revised

This book "covers over 1,000 diseases and disorders managed by surgeons . . . [and] emphasizes quick recall of major diagnostic features and succinct descriptions of disease processes, followed by procedures for definitive diagnosis and treatment, epidemiology, pathophysiology, and pathology." Publisher's note

Gawande, Atul
Complications: a young surgeon's notes on an imperfect science. Metropolitan Bks. 2002 269p $24   **617**
1. Surgery
ISBN 0-8050-6319-6   LC 2001-55884

Also available in paperback from Picador USA

The author describes the work of a trainee surgeon. The pieces "range from edgy accounts of medical traumas to sobering analyses of doctors' anxieties and burnout. . . . These exquisitely crafted essays, in which medical subjects segue into explorations of much larger themes, place Gawande among the best in the field." Publ Wkly

Includes bibliographical references

Mailhot, Claire B.
Surgery: a patient's guide from diagnosis to recovery; [by] Claire Mailhot, Melinda Brubaker, Linda Garratt Slezak. University of Calif. Press 1999 253p il $20   **617**
1. Surgery
ISBN 0-943671-19-1

"Starting from the moment of diagnosis, the authors walk readers through general topics common to all inpatient treatment, including getting a second opinion; decoding insurance policies; understanding surgical procedures, anesthesia, and medications; preadmission testing (e.g., blood work, chest X-rays); discharge; and home care." Libr J

Includes bibliographical references

McLanahan, Sandra A.
Surgery and its alternatives; how to make the right choices for your health; by Sandra A. McLanahan, David J. McLanahan; preface by Bernie S. Siegel. Twin Streams 2002 814p $35; pa $22   **617**
1. Surgery
ISBN 0-7582-0201-6; 1-57566-739-8 (pa)
LC 2001-92972

The authors discuss "the surgical perspective for conditions that include many types of cancer, coronary artery disease, varicose veins, gallstones and hernias . . . [describing] the surgical techniques available, various anesthetics and preoperative tests. [Also outlined are] alternative methods to surgery as well as ways to utilize complementary medical strategies that improve both body and mind when an operation is necessary." Publ Wkly

Includes bibliographical references

Palmer, Sara
Spinal cord injury; a guide for living; [by] Sara Palmer, Kay Harris Kriegsman, and Jeffrey B. Palmer. Johns Hopkins Univ. Press 2000 290p il (Johns Hopkins Press health book) $55; pa $16.95   **617**
1. Spinal cord
ISBN 0-8018-6352-X; 0-8018-6353-8 (pa)
LC 99-52572

This volume "covers what will happen during initial hospitalization, rehabilitation therapy, readjusting to home, the effects of spinal cord injury on other family members, dating and sexuality, independent living choices, and current research." Libr J

Includes bibliographical references

Rutkow, Ira M.
American surgery; an illustrated history; Stanley B. Burns, photohistorian. Lippincott-Raven Pubs. 1997 c1998 638p il map $99   **617**
1. Surgery
ISBN 0-316-76352-7   LC 97-17654

This history of American surgery focuses "on the dramatic leaps forward in surgical technology in the United States. Rutkow has included time lines, linking historic events to developments in surgery, and an excellent bibliography to make this work a useful reference source." Libr J

617.1 Injuries and wounds. Sports medicine

Burns sourcebook . . .; edited by Allan R. Cook. Omnigraphics 1999 604p il (Health reference series) $78   **617.1**
1. Burns and scalds
ISBN 0-7808-0204-7   LC 99-24510

"Basic consumer health information about various types of burns and scalds, including flame, heat, cold, electrical, chemical, and sun burns; along with information on short-term and long-term treatments, tissue reconstruction, plastic surgery, prevention suggestions, and first aid." Title page

Garrick, James G.
Anybody's sports medicine book; the complete guide to quick recovery from injuries; [by] James G. Garrick, Peter Radetsky. Ten Speed Press 2000 329p il pa $16.95   **617.1**
1. Sports medicine
ISBN 1-58008-144-4

The authors "start at the bottom, with feet and ankles, and work their way up the body, describing injuries (both common and rare) that can occur and how to treat them. Sidebars touch on age and gender factors, and they offer sound advice on prevention as well." Libr J

Kuhn, Cynthia

Pumped; straight facts for athletes about drugs, supplements, and training; by Cynthia Kuhn, Scott Swartzwelder, and Wilkie Wilson. Norton 2000 190p il pa $14.95

617.1

1. Athletes—Drug use 2. Dietary supplements
ISBN 0-393-32129-0 LC 00-30455

The authors offer "advice regarding drugs and supplements. Some of them work but are dangerous; some are dangerous and don't work; many are harmless and have little effect other than to fill the coffers of the sellers. . . . This is an excellent book that provides a realistic overview on the topic of drugs, dietary supplements, and athletics." Booklist

Includes bibliographical references

Micheli, Lyle J., 1940-

The sports medicine bible for young athletes; [by] Lyle J. Micheli, with Mark Jenkins; foreword by T. Barry Brazelton. Sourcebooks 2001 252p il hardcover o.p. paperback available $19.95 **617.1**

1. Sports medicine 2. Children—Health and hygiene
ISBN 1-57071-710-9 (pa) LC 2001-31322

The author provides "advice for parents about choosing a good coach, proper nutrition, stress, and the concerns of young athletes. He then discusses each body system, specific injuries that can occur, and their treatment." Libr J

617.6 Dentistry

Dental care and oral health sourcebook; edited by Amy L. Sutton. 2nd ed. Omnigraphics 2003 609p (Health reference series) $78 **617.6**

1. Dentistry 2. Mouth—Diseases
ISBN 0-7808-0634-4 LC 2003-58485

First published 1997 with title: Oral health sourcebook

"Basic consumer health information about dental care, including oral hygiene, dental visits, pain management, cavities, crowns, bridges, dental implants, and fillings, and other oral health concerns, such as gum disease, bad breath, dry mouth, genetic and developmental abnormalities, oral cancers, orthodontics, and temporomandibular disorders; along with updates on current research in oral health, a glossary, a directory of dental and oral health organizations, and resources for people with dental and oral health disorders." Title page

Includes bibliographical references

Wynbrandt, James

The excruciating history of dentistry; toothsome tales & oral oddities from Babylon to braces. St. Martin's Press 1998 248p il hardcover o.p. paperback available $14.95

617.6

1. Dentistry—History
ISBN 0-312-26319-8 (pa) LC 98-9794

The author "discusses the development of dentistry as a profession, the use of different anesthetics, and the evolution of dentures and dental prosthetics, among other topics. Much of the book is devoted to anecdotes illustrating discontinued dental practices." Libr J

Includes bibliographical references

617.7 Ophthalmology

Cassel, Gary H., 1953-

The eye book; a complete guide to eye disorders and health; [by] Gary H. Cassel, Michael D. Billig, Harry G. Randall. Johns Hopkins Univ. Press 1998 367p il (Johns Hopkins Press health book) $53; pa $19.95

617.7

1. Eye—Diseases
ISBN 0-8018-5835-6; 0-8018-5847-X (pa)
LC 97-35348

Also available large print edition $22.95 (ISBN 0-8018-6520-4)

This "guide covers routine eye care and the more common eye diseases, providing up-to-date facts on refractive surgery, treatment for optical neuritis, and possible nutritional therapies for cataracts and macular degeneration." Libr J

Includes bibliographical references

Sacks, Oliver W.

The island of the colorblind; and, Cycad island; [by] Oliver Sacks. Knopf 1997 c1996 298p il maps hardcover o.p. paperback available $13 **617.7**

1. Color blindness 2. Parkinson's disease 3. Islands of the Pacific
ISBN 0-375-70073-0 (pa) LC 96-34252

First published 1996 in the United Kingdom

Contents: Book 1 The island of the colorblind; Book 2 Cycad island

In this "travelogue, the neurologist Oliver Sacks investigates Pingelap, a Pacific atoll where the incidence of total congenital color blindness is an astonishing one in twelve; he also visits Guam, where a mysterious neurodegenerative disorder has had tragic consequences for the native population. Sacks's empathy has always been uncanny, but equally remarkable is his contagious fascination with just about everything." New Yorker

"As a travel writer, Sacks ranks with Paul Theroux and Bruce Chatwin. As an investigator of the mind's mysteries, he is in a class by himself." Publ Wkly

Includes bibliographical references

617.8 Otology and audiology

Myers, David G.

A quiet world; living with hearing loss. Yale Univ. Press 2000 211p $23 **617.8**

1. Deafness 2. Hearing aids
ISBN 0-300-08439-0 LC 00-38153

Also available Thorndike Press large print edition

The author "explores the problems faced by the hard of hearing at home and at work and provides information on the new technology and groundbreaking surgical procedures that are available." Publisher's note

Turkington, Carol

The encyclopedia of deafness and hearing disorders; [by] Carol Turkington and Allen E. Sussman. 2nd ed, [updated] Facts on File 2003 304p (Facts on File library of health and living) $65 **617.8**

1. Deafness—Encyclopedias 2. Ear—Diseases
ISBN 0-8160-5615-3 LC 2003-49358

First published 1992

Turkington, Carol—*Continued*
This encyclopedia features "information to help readers understand hearing impairment and how it can be successfully treated. More than 800 entries cover parts of the ear, clinical terms, specialists, devices and equipment, organizations, diseases, and more." Publisher's note
Includes bibliographical references

617.9 Transplantation of tissue and organs

Copeland, Michelle
Change your looks, change your life; quick fixes and cosmetic surgery solutions for looking younger, feeling healthier, and living better; [by] Michelle Copeland with Alexandra S. Postman. HarperResource 2003 267p il $27; pa $15.95 **617.9**
1. Plastic surgery
ISBN 0-06-621373-8; 0-06-051897-9 (pa)
LC 2002-24093
"The book takes readers from making the cosmetic surgery decision through finding a doctor, to 'Skin Savers and Quick Fixes' that don't involve surgery, and separate chapters on the face, breasts . . . body contouring, and healing that do. . . . The book's upbeat, go-go encouragement is infectious." Publ Wkly

Finn, Robert
Organ transplants; making the most of your gift of life. O'Reilly & Assocs. 2000 311p (Patient-centered guides) pa $19.95 **617.9**
1. Transplantation of organs, tissues, etc.
ISBN 1-56592-634-X LC 00-29837
This guide is "sprinkled with comments from actual recipients, their families, and members of the transplant teams. . . . Appendixes include Internet discussion groups, mailing lists and other web sites, pharmaceutical and financial assistance programs, and contact information for scores of transplant-related organizations." Libr J
Includes bibliographical references

Gilman, Sander L.
Making the body beautiful; a cultural history of aesthetic surgery. Princeton Univ. Press 1999 396p il hardcover o.p. paperback available $20.95 **617.9**
1. Plastic surgery
ISBN 0-691-07053-9 (pa) LC 98-48423
An "inquiry into how aesthetic surgery has evolved into a major area of modern medicine, this book combines cultural perspectives on the body beautiful with a medical chronology." Publ Wkly
Gilman's "book shows a dazzling European erudition. . . . He tells a strange, macabre, and often richly comic story of shifting desires." N Y Rev Books
Includes bibliographical references

Reconstructive and cosmetic surgery sourcebook; edited by M. Lisa Weatherford. Omnigraphics 2001 374p il (Health reference series) $78 **617.9**
1. Plastic surgery 2. Consumer education
ISBN 0-7808-0214-4 LC 00-66880
"Basic consumer health information on cosmetic and reconstructive plastic surgery, including statistical information about different surgical procedures, things to consider prior to surgery, plastic surgery techniques and tools, emotional and psychological considerations, and procedure-specific information." Title page

Transplantation sourcebook; edited by Joyce Brennfleck Shannon. Omnigraphics 2002 628p il (Health reference series) $78
617.9
1. Transplantation of organs, tissues, etc.
ISBN 0-7808-0322-1 LC 2002-16975
"Basic consumer health information about organ and tissue transplantation, including physical and financial preparations, procedures and issues relating to specific solid organ and tissue transplants, rehabilitation, pediatric transplant information, the future of transplantation, and organ and tissue donation." Publisher's note

618.1 Gynecology

Greer, Germaine, 1939-
The change; women, aging, and the menopause. Knopf 1992 422p o.p.; Fawcett Columbine paperback available $14 **618.1**
1. Menopause 2. Women—Psychology 3. Self-realization 4. Aging
ISBN 0-449-90853-4 (pa) LC 92-52949
This is a discussion of menopause in Western society. Greer looks at medical, psychological and social aspects of the cessation of menstruation and the aging process. She views the climateric as an important turning-point in a woman's life
"In a wise, witty and inspiring book, Greer rebukes doctors, psychiatrists—and women themselves—who blame the aging female for her menopausal distress. . . . Greer dispels all manner of myths and misconceptions about menopause." Publ Wkly
Includes bibliographical references

Huston, James E.
Menopause; a guide to health and happiness. Facts on File 1998 244p il $28.55; pa $15.95 **618.1**
1. Menopause
ISBN 0-8160-3675-6; 0-8160-3693-4 (pa)
LC 97-36897
This guide discusses various therapy treatments, nutrition, fitness, stress management as well as alternative therapies
Includes bibliographical references

Love, Susan M.
Dr Susan Love's breast book; [by] Susan M. Love with Karen Lindsey; illustrations by Marcia Williams. 3rd ed fully rev. Perseus Pub. 2000 xx, 700p il $22.50 **618.1**
1. Breast
ISBN 0-7382-0235-5
"A Merloyd Lawrence book"
First published 1990 by Addison-Wesley
This offers "information on breast health and care, with advice on self-examination, anatomy, cancer, cosmetic surgery, benign tisssue changes, and breast feeding." Booklist [review of 1995 edition]
"A highly readable book that educates, supports and encourages women to become their own advocates of breast health." Publ Wkly [review of 1995 edition]
Includes bibliographical references

Love, Susan M.—*Continued*

Dr. Susan Love's menopause and hormone book; making informed choices; {by} Susan M. Love with Karen Lindsey. Rev. pbk. ed. Three Rivers Press (NY) 2003 420p il pa $15.95   **618.1**
1. Menopause 2. Hormones 3. Women—Health and hygiene
ISBN 0-609-80996-2   LC 2002-15811
First published 1997 with title: Dr. Susan Love's hormone book

Contents: What is menopause?; The medicalization of menopause; What does it feel like?; Prevention and risk: understanding research; Osteoporosis: are we all going to crumble?; Heart disease: what's your real risk?; Breast cancer: every women's fear?; Endometrial cancer: the first problem with estrogen; For better or worse: hormone therapy and other diseases; Approaches to symptom relief; From flashes to fuzzy thinking: what you can do right now?; For prevention: first, look to your lifestyle!; Alternatives: from acupuncture to herbs; Drugs: other means of prevention; Hormones: the menu of options; Decisions: what should I do?
Includes bibliographical references

Minkin, Mary Jane
The Yale guide to women's reproductive health; [by] Mary Jane Minkin, Carol V. Wright. Yale Univ. Press 2003 448p il $29.95
                                              618.1
1. Women—Health and hygiene
ISBN 0-300-09820-0   LC 2002-35738
"Aiming to provide readers with information needed to make choices that may be presented in a gynecologist's office, the text covers menstruation, contraceptives, infections and sexually transmitted diseases, breast and genital tract cancer, pregnancy and infertility, and abortion and miscarriage." Libr J
Includes bibliographical references

Moore, Michele
The only menopause guide you'll need. Johns Hopkins Univ. Press 2000 166p il $52; pa $14.95   **618.1**
1. Menopause
ISBN 0-8018-6407-0; 0-8018-6408-9 (pa)
This guide tells "women how to remain healthy and treat the annoying symptoms that may accompany the change. . . . [The author recommends] vitamins, herbs, and homeopathic remedies as well as hormone replacement therapy." Libr J
Includes bibliographical references

Seibel, Machelle M.
The soy solution for menopause; the estrogen alternative. Simon & Schuster 2003 xxii, 340p pa $14   **618.1**
1. Menopause 2. Soybean 3. Women—Health and hygiene
ISBN 0-7434-2152-3   LC 2002-106981
"A Fireside book"
The author "reveals how the soybean and its by-products afford new hope to menopausal women. . . . Seibel explains how the female body processes soy, how soy products naturally restore hormonal balance by behaving like estrogen, and how to add soy to [one's] diet for maximum effect." Publisher's note
Includes bibliographical references

Sheehy, Gail
The silent passage: menopause. Rev and updated with four brand-new chapters. Pocket Bks. 1998 xxvi, 293p pa $7.50   **618.1**
1. Menopause
ISBN 0-671-56777-2   LC 98-65873
First published 1992
The author examines the medical, psychological, and social aspects of menopause and includes interviews with women in various stages of menopause and with experts. Discussions of herbal remedies, exercise and diet, menopause in the workplace, estrogen and brainpower, and new frontiers in treatment are included

Warga, Claire L.
Menopause and the mind; the complete guide to coping with memory loss, foggy thinking, verbal slips, and other cognitive effects of perimenopause and menopause. Free Press 1999 xxiii, 388p il $24; pa $14
                                              618.1
1. Menopause 2. Estrogen
ISBN 0-684-85456-2; 0-684-85479-1 (pa)
                                      LC 99-11244
The author explores the "link between hormonal change and lapses in the cognitive faculties of women in the years leading up to and during menopause. Citing studies that relate declining estrogen levels to a range of 'slips' in memory, speech, thinking, attention span and sense of time and space, Warga makes a fascinating argument for the biological, even evolutionary basis of such behaviors." Publ Wkly
Includes bibliographical references

West, Stanley
The hysterectomy hoax; the truth about why many hysterectomies are unnecessary and how to avoid them; by Stanley West with Paula Dranov. 3rd ed. Next Decade 2002 243p il pa $19.95   **618.1**
1. Hysterectomy 2. Consumer education
ISBN 0-9700908-1-1   LC 2001-55868
First published 1994 by Doubleday
"West, an infertility specialist, makes a strong case against hysterectomy unless a woman has cancer. Providing clear, illustrated explanations of female anatomy and physiology, he also thoroughly discusses fibroids, endometriosis, uterine prolapse, ovarian cysts, and precancerous conditions. West offers effective treatments that enable women to preserve their ovaries and uterus as these organs are important for sexuality and hormone production, even after menopause." Libr J [review of 1994 edition]

618.2   Obstetrics

Bruce, Debra Fulghum, 1951-
Making a baby; everything you need to know to get pregnant; [by] Debra Fulghum Bruce and Samuel Thatcher. Ballantine Bks. 2000 379p pa $14.95   **618.2**
1. Pregnancy 2. Infertility
ISBN 0-345-43543-5
The authors offer a guide to "babyboosting medicines, IVF, sperm injection, and egg donation. They explain how the male and female reproductive systems work and detail the many common, and sometimes hidden, threats

Bruce, Debra Fulghum, 1951— *Continued*
to fertility. They offer practical, low-tech-solutions, such as lifestyle changes, as well as the more advanced therapies." Libr J

Kitzinger, Sheila, 1929-
The complete book of pregnancy and childbirth; black-and-white photography by Marcia May. rev ed. Knopf 2003 448p $35; pa $19.95   **618.2**
1. Pregnancy 2. Childbirth 3. Infants—Care
ISBN 1-400-04108-2; 0-375-71047-7 (pa)
                                      LC 2002-43433
First published 1980
After an overview of basic embryology the author covers health, nutrition and emotional well-being during pregnancy. Hospital facilities, home birthing rooms, drugs and exercise are discussed
Includes bibliographical references

Lees, Christoph C.
Pregnancy and birth; your questions answered; [by] Christoph Lees, Karina Reynolds, Grainne McCartan. rev ed, [expanded & updated] DK Pub. 2002 264p il pa $19.95   **618.2**
1. Pregnancy 2. Childbirth 3. Infants—Care
ISBN 0-7894-8789-6   LC 2002-281852
First published 1997
This title provides answers on common questions related to human reproduction and newborn care
"Particular highlights include its very clear, conversational style; profuse, interesting, and colorful illustrations; and a nice section on sex during pregnancy. The only potential shortcomings are a fair amount of what some might consider graphic nudity." Booklist [review of 1997 edition]

Mayo Clinic complete book of pregnancy & baby's first year; Robert V. Johnson, editor-in-chief. Morrow 1994 750p il $33
                                      618.2
1. Pregnancy 2. Infants—Care 3. Childbirth
ISBN 0-688-11761-9   LC 94-7264
This volume contains "reviews of prenatal tests and their purposes and of fetal development during the stages of pregnancy, a frank account of labor, advice on coping with the health problems associated with premature birth, and detailed guidance to developmental milestones, health care needs, daily care, and parental fears during the first few months of life. This guide's illustrations . . . are equally practical and more useful than those in most parenting guides." Booklist

Murkoff, Heidi Eisenberg
What to expect when you're expecting; [by] Heidi Murkoff, Arlene Eisenberg & Sandee Hathaway; medical consultant, Richard Aubry; research consultant, Sharon Mazel. 3rd ed. Workman 2002 xxv, 597p il $23.95; pa $13.95   **618.2**
1. Pregnancy 2. Childbirth
ISBN 0-7611-2549-3; 0-7611-2132-3 (pa)
                                      LC 2001-43523
First published 1984 with authors' names in reverse order

"The book is arranged by month, from pregnancy test through labor and delivery. Each section offers answers to frequently asked questions, along with features such as 'What You May Be Feeling' and 'What You May Be Concerned About.'. . . This book remains an indispensable guide for pregnant women and their partners." Publ Wkly

Sears, William
The pregnancy book; a month-by-month guide; [by] William Sears and Martha Sears, with Linda Hughey Holt. Little, Brown 1997 430p il hardcover o.p. paperback available $13.95   **618.2**
1. Pregnancy 2. Childbirth
ISBN 0-316-77914-8 (pa)   LC 96-48905
"Using a month-by-month format with nice illustrations that show normal fetal development [the authors] discuss a wide range of pregnancy options without judgmental bias. Scattered throughout are helpful hints and stories from other pregnant mothers that give the book a comfortable feel." Libr J

Steingraber, Sandra
Having faith; an ecologist's journey to motherhood. Perseus Bks. 2001 341p $27
                                      618.2
1. Pregnancy 2. Breast feeding 3. Mothers
ISBN 0-7382-0467-6   LC 2001-277000
Also available in paperback from Berkley Books
"This ecologist, who became pregnant at age 38, describes her experience as becoming a habitat. Based on her dogged personal investigations, she reveals new information on pregnancy and childbirth, including environmental hazards to mothers and babies. A fabulous book." Booklist

Vincent, Peggy, 1942-
Baby catcher; chronicles of a modern midwife. Scribner 2002 336p $26; pa $13
                                      618.2
1. Midwives
ISBN 0-7432-1933-3; 0-7432-1934-1 (pa)
                                      LC 2001-54988
This is an account of a midwife specializing in home births who "over the course of 40 years, brought some 2,000 babies into the world. . . . A solid writer, Vincent doesn't preach the virtues of unmedicated birthing; she just lays consistent stories of women doing it—Christian Science moms, Muslim moms, spiritualist moms, lesbian moms, teen moms and just plain ordinary moms." Publ Wkly

Wolf, Naomi
Misconceptions; truth, lies, and the unexpected on the journey to motherhood. Doubleday 2001 326p $24.95   **618.2**
1. Pregnancy 2. Childbirth 3. Mothers
ISBN 0-385-49302-9   LC 2001-28831
Wolf discusses her experiences with pregnancy and childbirth and what she sees as "the problems that can surround childbirth in America. . . . [Wolf] calls for changes in obstetrical practices that would give parents more control. And she pleads for more support for mothers." Christ Sci Monit
Includes bibliographical references

618.3 Diseases and complications of pregnancy

Kohn, Ingrid

A silent sorrow; pregnancy loss: guidance and support for you and your family; [by] Ingrid Kohn and Perry-Lynn Moffitt, with Isabelle A. Wilkins. 2nd ed. Routledge 2000 xx, 299p pa $16.95   **618.3**
1. Miscarriage 2. Bereavement
ISBN 0-415-92481-2   LC 99-25720
First published 1993 by Delacorte Press
The authors provide "suggestions to validate parents' grief; cope with the unique concerns of early loss, crisis pregnancies, stillbirth, and newborn death; find medical, religious, and family support; and manage their lives afterwards. The writing is insightful and the tone respectful and supportive." Libr J [review of 1993 edition]
Includes bibliographical references

Lerner, Henry M.

Miscarriage: a doctor's guide to the facts; why it happens and how best to reduce your risks; with contributions by Alice Domar; introduction by Robert Barbieri. Perseus Bks. 2003 291p pa $16.95   **618.3**
1. Miscarriage
ISBN 0-7382-0634-2   LC 2002-114586
This book provides "explanations to questions concerning the etiology, diagnosis, prevention, and treatment of miscarriage. His medical and scientific discussion, while exceedingly thorough, is easy to understand. . . . Especially helpful are the concluding chapters, which focus on dealing with the emotional trauma of miscarriage." Libr J

618.4 Childbirth. Labor

Leboyer, Frédérick

Birth without violence; new translation by Yvonne Fitzgerald. rev ed. Healing Arts Press 2002 131p il pa $16.95   **618.4**
1. Natural childbirth
ISBN 0-89281-983-9   LC 2002-3503
Original French edition, 1974; first English translation published 1975 by Knopf
"The work's stylistic qualities, in addition to the beautiful photographs, jar the reader into thinking about childbirth in a unique and revolutionary way." Choice [review of 1975 edition]

618.92 Pediatrics

American Academy of Pediatrics guide to your child's sleep; birth through adolescence; editor, George J. Cohen. Villard Bks. 1999 209p pa $12.95 **618.92**
1. Sleep 2. Infants—Care 3. Children—Health and hygiene
ISBN 0-679-76981-1   LC 99-27284
This work provides "explanations of normal sleep patterns and common problems such as night waking and monsters under the bed. The guide emphasizes the importance of bedtime rituals and good sleep hygiene, physical problems that may affect sleep quality, and differences in temperament and developmental stages. Controversies such as the family bed vs. cribs for newborns and whether—or for how long—to allow a baby to cry at bedtime are also addressed." Libr J

American Medical Association complete guide to children's health; written by Donna Kotulak, Dennis Connaughton; Edward S. Traisman, medical editor [et al.] Random House 1999 710p il $39.95
    618.92
1. Children—Diseases 2. Children—Health and hygiene 3. Child rearing
ISBN 0-679-45776-3   LC 98-6970
"This multipurpose reference book combines a medical encyclopedia covering childhood ailments, a full-color atlas of the human body, symptoms charts, and a first-aid and emergency-care primer." Libr J

Barkley, Russell A., 1949-

Taking charge of ADHD; the complete, authoritative guide for parents. rev ed. Guilford Press 2000 321p $42; pa $19.95
    618.92
1. Attention deficit disorder 2. Child rearing
ISBN 1-57230-600-9; 1-57230-560-6 (pa)
    LC 00-34130
First published 1995
The author "reports on his own theory, recent research, and strategies for parents in the challenge of raising children with attention problems. His view is that attention-deficit hyperactivity disorder (ADHD) is a 'disorder of self-regulation' and that the problems of inattention, overactivity, and lack of inhibition become a developmental disability when extreme. ADHD is described as a neurologically based disorder with a probable genetic base." Sci Books Films
Includes bibliographical references

Bashe, Patricia Romanowski

The oasis guide to asperger syndrome; advice, support, insights, and inspiration; [by] Patricia Romanowski Bashe and Barbara L. Kirby; foreword by Tony Attwood. Crown 2001 467p $27.50   **618.92**
1. Asperger's syndrome 2. Autism
ISBN 0-609-60811-8   LC 2001-28369
The authors discuss "what AS looks like and how it is diagnosed; how parents can accept and work with the diagnosis; what interventions, therapies, and medications are available; how to navigate through the school system, including the ins and outs of special ed; how parents can raise their unique child, guiding him or her through the social, emotional, and intellectual challenges on the way to adulthood." Publisher's note
"These authors have certainly done their homework. Besides invaluable practical information, parents and other interested persons will find comfort in the book's welcoming tone and the knowledge that they are not alone." Publ Wkly
Includes bibliographical references

Childhood cancer; a handbook from St. Jude Children's Research Hospital with contributions from St. Jude clinicians and scientists; [edited] by R. Grant Steen & Joseph Mirro Jr. Perseus Bks. 2000 606p il $30   **618.92**
1. Cancer 2. Children—Diseases
ISBN 0-7382-0277-0
"Organized around seven broad sections for the comprehensive coverage of key issues (basics, diagnosis, treatment, patient care, cancer types, and recovery), the 56 chapters are each authored by a specialist in the field. The writing is intelligent and clear but never patronizing." Libr J

Children with autism; a parent's guide; edited by Michael D. Powers; foreword by Temple Grandin. 2nd ed. Woodbine House 2000 xxvii, 427p il pa $17.95   **618.92**
1. Autism
ISBN 1-89062-704-6   LC 00-35165
First published 1989
Coverage includes "daily and family life, early intervention, educational programs, legal rights, advocacy, and a look at the years ahead with a chapter on adults with autism. . . . [Information is also provided] on current diagnostic criteria, Applied Behavior Analysis, the Individuals with Disabilities Education Act (IDEA), autism advocacy via the Internet, and much more." Publisher's note
Includes bibliographical references

Children with spina bifida; a parent's guide; edited by Marlene Lutkenhoff. Woodbine House 1999 405p il pa $16.95   **618.92**
1. Spina bifida
ISBN 0-933149-60-3   LC 99-35403
"The chapters deal with issues parents will face, from prenatal diagnosis to adulthood—legal issues, education, health concerns, treatments, therapies, and causes. The extensive Resource Guide at the back of the book is remarkable." Libr J

The **Children's** Hospital guide to your child's health and development; with a foreword by T. Berry Brazelton. Perseus Bks. 2001 xx, 796p il hardcover o.p. paperback available $20   **618.92**
1. Children—Health and hygiene 2. Children—Diseases 3. Child development
ISBN 0-7382-0743-8 (pa)
"A Merloyd Lawrence book"
This is a "parental guide to a child's physical, behavioral, and psychological health and development. The book is divided into five sections: prenatal preparation and birth of the newborn; norms at one month, one year, toddler, preschooler, and school age; choosing a doctor and childcare; sickness and emergencies and . . . an alphabetical list of common childhood illnesses and injuries." Libr J
"Presented in a friendly, matter-of-fact style with simple but helpful illustrations, it is a veritable encyclopedia on current developmental theory, medical recommendations, and diverse parenting ideas." Publ Wkly

Cohen, Shirley
Targeting autism; what we know, don't know, and can do to help young children with autism and related disorders. Updated ed. University of Calif. Press 2002 xxiii, 215p pa $16.95   **618.92**
1. Autism
ISBN 0-520-23480-4   LC 2002-22505
First published 1998
This book presents "overviews of current work being done with autism and addresses the different life cycles of children with the condition through preschool, elementary school, and adolescence. She effectively uses narratives to help illustrate her points and the treatment methods that parents and educators should consider." Libr J
Includes bibliographical references

DeGrandpre, Richard J.
Ritalin nation; rapid-fire culture and the transformation of human consciousness. Norton 1999 284p hardcover o.p. paperback available $13.95   **618.92**
1. Attention deficit disorder 2. Ritalin
ISBN 0-393-32025-1 (pa)   LC 98-20687
The author questions "psychiatry's identification of ADHD as a biologically based brain disease. He argues that societal adjustments and a change in human consciousness are the real antidotes for this development disorder. Viewing hyperactivity in a multidisciplinary context, *Ritalin Nation* is richly referenced and offers a critical perspective suited to academic and specialized collections." Libr J
Includes bibliographical references

Diller, Lawrence H.
Running on Ritalin; a physician reflects on children, society, and performance in a pill. Bantam Bks. 1998 386p hardcover o.p. paperback available $12.95   **618.92**
1. Attention deficit disorder 2. Ritalin 3. Children—Health and hygiene
ISBN 0-553-37906-2 (pa)   LC 98-232695
The author discusses Attention deficit disorder (ADD), "the effects of Ritalin and behavior therapy, societal and parental expectations, ADD in adults, and treatment options." Libr J
Includes bibliographical references

First aid for children fast. rev ed. DK Pub. 2002 128p il pa $13   **618.92**
1. First aid 2. Children—Health and hygiene
ISBN 0-7894-8960-0   LC 2002-19493
First published 1995
At head of title: Johns Hopkins Children's Center
An illustrated step-by-step guide to pediatric emergency care. Includes sections on assembling a first-aid kit, basic dressings, and home safety

Frith, Uta, 1941-
Autism: explaining the enigma. 2nd ed. Blackwell 2003 249p il $59.95; pa $26.95   **618.92**
1. Autism
ISBN 0-631-22900-0; 0-631-22901-9 (pa)
     LC 2002-12932
First published 1989

Frith, Uta, 1941——*Continued*
Contents: What is autism?; The enchantment of autism; Lessons from history; Is there an autism epidemic?; Mind-reading and mind-blindness; Autism aloneness; The difficulty of talking to others; Intelligence and special talent; A fragmented world; Sensations and repetitions; Seeing the brain through a scanner
This "book is valuable for educated parents interested in learning about autism in a larger historical context. Frith writes a great deal on the problem that autistic people have with 'mind blindness,' the inability to look at and see other people." Libr J
Includes bibliographical references

Ives, Martine, 1975-
Caring for a child with autism; a practical guide for parents; [by] Martine Ives and Nell Munro; illustrations by Fiona Bleach. Kingsley, J. 2002 304p il pa $18.95 **618.92**
1. Autism
ISBN 1-85302-996-3   LC 2001-38436
Published with the National Autistic Society
This "guide answers the questions commonly asked by parents and carers following a diagnosis of autism, and discusses the challenges that can arise in home life, education and socializing." Publisher's note
Includes bibliographical references

Jackson, Luke
Freaks, geeks and asperger syndrome; a user guide to adolescence; foreword by Tony Attwood. Kingsley, J. 2002 217p il pa $17.95
618.92
1. Asperger's syndrome 2. Autism 3. Adolescent psychology
ISBN 1-8431-0098-3   LC 2002-70930
"In this terrific book that is sure to inspire other adolescents with the same condition, 13-year-old Jackson offers a teenager's perspective on what it's like to live with Asperger's. He also writes about his younger brother, who has a more severe condition on the ASD spectrum." Libr J

Janes-Hodder, Honna, 1966-
Childhood cancer; a parent's guide to solid tumor cancers; [by] Honna Janes-Hodder, Nancy Keene. 2nd ed. O'Reilly & Assocs. 2002 xx, 537p il (Patient-centered guides) pa $29.95 **618.92**
1. Cancer 2. Children—Diseases
ISBN 0-59650-014-9   LC 2002-72284
First published 1999
This guide provides information on solid tumor childhood cancers, including neuroblastoma, Wilms tumor, liver tumors, soft tissue sarcomas, bone sarcomas and retinoblastoma. Medical terminology, diagnosis, treatment and hospitalization are discussed

Karasik, Judy
The ride together; a brother and sister's memoir of autism in the family; text chapters by Judy Karasik; comic chapters by Paul Karasik. Washington Sq. Press 2003 199p il $20 **618.92**
1. Autism 2. Siblings
ISBN 0-7434-2336-4   LC 2002-104625
"This exceptional account of a family's experience with autism fills a gap in the literature by featuring the siblings' point of view. In chapters that alternate between Judy's prose and Paul's graphic illustrations, the Karasiks chronicle the life of their autistic brother from the 1950s, to the present." Libr J

Linden, Dana Wechsler
Preemies; the essential guide for parents of premature babies; [by] Dana Wechsler Linden, Emma Trenti Paroli, and Mia Wechsler Doron. Pocket Bks. 2000 578p il pa $24.95 **618.92**
1. Premature infants
ISBN 0-671-03491-X   LC 00-28554
This guide "covers risk factors, the first day, the first week, surgery, taking the baby home and many other topics. Each section contains personal observations from parents of preemies, insightful comments from 'the doctor's perspective' and information on procedures, equipment, common problems and other issues." Publ Wkly

Martin, Katherine L., 1960-
Does my child have a speech problem? Chicago Review Press 1997 160p il pa $16.95 **618.92**
1. Speech disorders 2. Children—Health and hygiene
ISBN 1-55652-315-7   LC 96-35302
The author addresses stuttering, fluency and articulation issues. Listening and auditory processing skills are discussed
"Martin's writing style is clear and engaging, making this slim volume a quick, easy read." Libr J
Includes bibliographical references

Ozonoff, Sally
A parent's guide to asperger syndrome and high-functioning autism; how to meet the challenges and help your child thrive; [by] Sally Ozonoff, Geraldine Dawson, James McPartland. Guilford Press 2002 278p il $38; pa $17.95 **618.92**
1. Autism 2. Parenting
ISBN 1-57230-767-6; 1-57230-531-2 (pa)
LC 2002-5507
Partial contents: Part I: Understanding asperger syndrome and high-functioning autism; What are asperger syndrome and high-functioning autism?; The diagnostic process; Causes of autism spectrum disorders; Treatments for asperger syndrome and high-functioning autism?; Part II: Living with asperger syndrome and high-functioning autism; Channeling your child's strengths: a guiding principle; Asperger syndrome and high-functioning autism at home; Asperger syndrome and high-functioning autism at school; The social world of children and adolescents with asperger syndrome and high-functioning autism; Looking ahead: asperger syndrome and high-functioning autism in late adolescence and adulthood
"This is an excellent resource for parents of children of the higher end of the autistic spectrum. All educators, the authors provide the basics on diagnosis, causes, and treatment. What makes their title essential is their positive emphasis on finding and channeling a child's strengths, as well as a sensitive discussion of home life, school, and the social world and life as an adult." Libr J
Includes bibliographical references

Papolos, Demitri F.

The bipolar child; the definitive and reassuring guide to childhood's most misunderstood disorder; [by] Demitri F. Papolos and Janice Papolos. rev and expanded ed. Broadway Bks. 2002 xx, 452p il $26 **618.92**

1. Manic-depressive illness 2. Depression (Psychology) 3. Child psychology
ISBN 0-7679-1285-3   LC 2003-269309
First published 2000

Demitri and Janice Papolos discuss "early-onset bipolar disorder, focusing on how this complicated illness evolves in children. The authors warn that nearly one-third of children diagnosed with attention deficit hyperactivity disorder (ADHD) may actually be bipolar (previously called manic depression), and they stress the importance of getting early diagnosis and treatment. . . . In addition to diagnosis and treatment, the authors discuss practical ways to deal with the condition itself, as well as the impact it has on the entire family. An important guide for parents seeking ways to cope with this potentially devastating disorder." Publ Wkly

Includes bibliographical references

Pediatric cancer sourcebook; edited by Edward J. Prucha. Omnigraphics 1999 587p (Health reference series) $78 **618.92**

1. Cancer 2. Children—Diseases
ISBN 0-7808-0245-4   LC 99-41613

"Basic consumer health information about leukemias, brain tumors, sarcomas, lymphomas, and other cancers in infants, children, and adolescents, including descriptions of cancers, treatments, and coping strategies; along with suggestions for parents, caregivers, and concerned relatives, a glossary of cancer terms, and resource listings." Title page

Richman, Shira, 1972-

Raising a child with autism; a guide to applied behavior analysis for parents. Kingsley, J. 2000 173p pa $19.95 **618.92**

1. Autism 2. Parent-child relationship
ISBN 1-85302-910-6   LC 00-47818

"Behavior therapy consultant Richman clearly outlines the applied behavior analysis (ABA) activities that parents can use with ASD children. Included is helpful guidance for toilet training, daily living, and increasing communication and sibling interaction. Since ABA consultants may be out of the financial or geographic reach of many parents, having a strong resource like this is invaluable." Libr J

Includes bibliographical references

Sandler, Adrian

Living with spina bifida; a guide for families and professionals; illustrations by Peter Bedick. University of N.C. Press 1997 xxvii, 262p il hardcover o.p. paperback available $19.95 **618.92**

1. Spina bifida
ISBN 0-8078-4657-0 (pa)   LC 96-47697

This guide covers "issues of clinical management, habilitation, and early intervention from an interdisciplinary, holistic, and family-based perspective. In a series of chapters arranged according to the developmental stages of childhood—from birth through infancy, school age, adolescence, and young adulthood—Sandler discusses relevant medical, health, and psychosocial aspects of spina bifida. He addresses such concerns as education, daily living, and family relationships." Publisher's note

Selikowitz, Mark

Down syndrome; the facts. 2nd ed. Oxford Univ. Press 1997 192p il pa $19.95 **618.92**

1. Down syndrome 2. Children—Diseases
ISBN 0-19-262662-0   LC 96-29562
"Oxford medical publications"
First published 1990

Discusses possible causes of Down's syndrome, development of the child with the disease, medical problems and educational strategies, and includes advice for parents about future pregnancies

Seroussi, Karyn

Unraveling the mystery of autism and pervasive developmental disorder; a mother's story of research and recovery. Simon & Schuster 2000 288p $24 **618.92**

1. Autism
ISBN 0-684-83164-3   LC 99-53954
Also available in paperback from Broadway Bks.

This is an account of the author's experiences with her son, who was diagnosed with autism at 19 months. She discusses various therapies and the possible connections between autism and diet

Includes bibliographical references

Stein, David B.

Ritalin is not the answer; a drug-free, practical program for children diagnosed with ADD or ADHD; foreword by Peter R. Breggin. Jossey-Bass 1999 203p il pa $15 **618.92**

1. Attention deficit disorder 2. Ritalin 3. Children—Health and hygiene
ISBN 0-7879-4514-5   LC 98-25535
Also available Ritalin is not the answer action guide pa $19.95 (ISBN 0-7879-6044-6)

The author offers parents and educators a program designed to work as an alternative to the use of medication in treating children with attention deficit disorder or attention deficit with hyperactivity disorder

Includes bibliographical references

Thompson, Charlotte E.

Raising a child with a neuromuscular disorder; a guide for parents, grandparents, friends, and professionals. Oxford Univ. Press 1999 275p $25 **618.92**

1. Musculoskeletal system—Diseases 2. Children—Diseases
ISBN 0-19-512843-5   LC 99-30834

Thompson "suggests ways parents can be strong advocates for their children. . . . In addition to a chapter with descriptions and treatments of various neuromuscular disorders, there is a brief overview on genetics, a table summarizing the characteristics of various neuromuscular diseases, and a glossary of medical terms." Libr J

Includes bibliographical references

Waltz, Mitzi

Autistic spectrum disorders; understanding the diagnosis and getting help. 2nd ed. O'Reilly & Assocs. 2002 511p il (Patient-centered guides) pa $29.95 **618.92**

1. Autism
ISBN 0-596-50013-0   LC 2002-66219
First published 1999 with title: Pervasive developmental disorders

Waltz, Mitzi—*Continued*

Waltz covers autism-related "developments in medical and therapeutic interventions and environmental links, insurance, education, family issues, support, and resources for the English-speaking world. Throughout, she intersperses numerous personal accounts from interviews held with families, caretakers, and ASD patients. . . . Strongly recommended for public libraries and for academic libraries with education or autism collections." Libr J

Includes bibliographical references

Wing, Lorna

The autistic spectrum; a parents' guide to understanding and helping your child. Ulysses Press 2001 240p pa $14.95   **618.92**

1. Autism

ISBN 1-56975-257-5

This guide "shows parents how to understand their child and teach basic skills, improve communication, develop potential abilities, and expand social interaction skills." Publisher's note

"While the depth of information here may be overwhelming to the parents of a newly diagnosed child . . . it is an excellent choice for those who require a text with more substance." Libr J

Includes bibliographical references

618.97   Geriatrics

Hutton, J. Thomas

Preventing falls; a defensive approach. Prometheus Bks. 2000 115p il pa $19

618.97

1. Accidents—Prevention 2. Parkinson's disease

ISBN 1-57392-761-9   LC 99-40082

The author "explains major causes of falls and what the caregiver or patient can do to anticipate and minimize risks. He includes some assessment tools and a . . . chapter on how to recover from a fall." Libr J

Includes bibliographical references

Mace, Nancy L.

The 36-hour day; a family guide to caring for persons with Alzheimer disease, related dementing illnesses, and memory loss in later life; [by] Nancy L. Mace, Peter V. Rabins. 3rd ed. Johns Hopkins Univ. Press 1999 xx, 339p (Johns Hopkins Press health book) $54; pa $14.95   **618.97**

1. Alzheimer's disease

ISBN 0-8018-6148-9; 0-8018-6149-7 (pa)

LC 98-43608

Also available large print edition (ISBN 0-8018-6521-2 $19.95) and in paperback from Warner Bks.

First published 1981

A guide designed for families of Alzheimer's sufferers. Current research on the brain, behavior and personality is included

Includes bibliographical references

620   Engineering and allied operations

Berlow, Lawrence H., 1945-

The reference guide to famous engineering landmarks of the world; bridges, tunnels, dams, roads, and other structures. Oryx Press 1997 c1998 250p il $73.95   **620**

1. Engineering—History

ISBN 0-89774-966-9   LC 97-36051

"The main section is an alphabetically arranged, double-column compendium of facts and histories of 600 structures. The format of each entry begins with the structure's location and date of construction. Size is often given, including metric, and the basic facts of the construction are provided. . . . A biography section provides background on 52 significant engineers or designers. A chronology section begins with the oldest surviving dam in the world (in Egypt) and continues to 2010, when a monster skyscraper, Millennium Tower, will be completed in Tokyo." Booklist

Esser, Teresa

The venture cafe; secrets, strategies, and stories from America's high-tech entrepreneurs. Warner Bks. 2002 292p $24.95

620

1. High technology industry 2. Entrepreneurship

ISBN 0-446-52783-1   LC 2001-46533

The author "has gathered case studies of small business successes and failures in order to explore the nature of the entrepreneurial spirit. Along the way and using real-life stories, she teaches readers how to find funding, attract good employees, use the press, and set up a vesting schedule." Booklist

Includes bibliographical references

Molotch, Harvey Luskin

Where stuff comes from; how toasters, toilets, cars, computers, and many other things come to be as they are; [by] Harvey Molotch. Routledge 2003 324p il $24.95

620

1. Engineering

ISBN 0-415-94400-7   LC 2003-1191

The author examines "the complicated, dynamic relationships between inventor, society, corporation, regulator, shopkeeper, community, family and customer. . . . Myriad links, he argues, ultimately produce and constantly change what we want, buy, keep and throw away; thus, neither consumers nor producers are to be blamed for our numerous possessions. . . . Molotch's description of systemic person-product complexes could work to end blame-the-consumer guilt-mongering in the popular discourse." Publ Wkly

Includes bibliographical references

Petroski, Henry

Invention by design; how engineers get from thought to thing. Harvard Univ. Press 1996 242p il map hardcover o.p. paperback available $14.95   **620**

1. Engineering 2. Inventions

ISBN 0-674-46368-4 (pa)   LC 96-19227

"By examining the relationship between the invention of devices and their refinement over time by others, Petroski identifies design principles that engineers use to

Petroski, Henry—*Continued*
make things work. Written as a series of case studies ranging from the paper clip to the zipper to the FAX machine to the Boeing 777." Libr J

"Every case study includes well-chosen pictures and schematic drawings to clarify how inventors resolve technical difficulties, and the carefully research text explains how they make their new creations economically feasible and socially acceptable." Booklist

Includes bibliographical references

Remaking the world; adventures in engineering. Knopf 1997 239p il hardcover o.p. paperback available $13   **620**
1. Engineering
ISBN 0-375-70024-2 (pa)   LC 97-29328
A collection of the author's essays originally written for American Scientist. "Several pieces are about particular engineers . . . or engineering projects (the Channel Tunnel, the Ferris Wheel); others are provocative (the flaws of engineering software, the creep of technology)." Libr J

Includes bibliographical references

Tobin, James, 1956-
Great projects; the epic story of the building of America: from the taming of the Mississippi to the invention of the Internet. Free Press 2001 322p il maps $40   **620**
1. Engineering—History
ISBN 0-7432-1064-6   LC 2001-33016
This describes eight construction projects and innovations including "the flood-control works of the lower Mississippi, Hoover Dam, Edison's lighting system, the spread of electricity across the nation, the great Croton Aqueduct, the bridges of New York City, Boston's revamped street system, known as the Big Dig, and the [Internet]." Publisher's note

"The clearly written, nontechnical narratives are lively and comprehensive." Libr J

Includes bibliographical references

620.1   Engineering mechanics and materials

Brady, George S. (George Stuart)
Materials handbook; an encyclopedia for managers, technical professionals, purchasing and production managers, technicians, supervisors, and foremen; [by] George S. Brady, Henry R. Clauser. McGraw-Hill $99.95   **620.1**
1. Materials—Encyclopedias 2. Building materials—Encyclopedias 3. Commercial products—Encyclopedias
First published 1929. (15th edition 2002) Periodically revised. Subtitle varies

"Covers more than 15,000 minerals, animal and plant substances, and commercial and engineering materials. Uses, production methods, and trade names are included for common items. Most entries are shorter than half a page. The special chapter on structure and properties of materials includes charts, tables, and a glossary of terms. Uses both SI and U.S. customary units. Subject index is very important because the main text has no cross-references." Guide to Ref Books. 11th edition

620.8   Human factors and safety engineering

Evan, William M.
Minding the machines; preventing technological disasters; [by] William M. Evan, Mark Manion. Prentice-Hall 2002 xxiv, 485p il $29.99   **620.8**
1. Engineering 2. Disasters
ISBN 0-13-065646-1   LC 2001-54867
The authors "analyze more than 30 disasters—from the Titanic sinking to Exxon Valdez oil spill, the Challenger shuttle disaster to Chernobyl nuclear catastrophe, the Love Canal toxic waste contamination to Bhopal poison gas release. They present lessons learned and preventive strategies for all four leading causes of technological disasters: technical design factors, human factors, organizational systems factors, and socio-cultural factors. They also identify appropriate roles for every participant in technological systems—from corporations to regulators, engineering schools to individual citizens." Publisher's note

Includes bibliographical references

621   Applied physics

Landmarks in mechanical engineering; [by] ASME International History and Heritage. Purdue Univ. Press 1997 364p il $62.95; pa $24.95   **621**
1. Mechanical engineering
ISBN 1-55753-093-9; 1-55753-094-7 (pa)
     LC 96-31573
This collection of essays on "American 'industrial archaeology' discusses still-existing artifacts ranging from the Saugus Ironworks (1640s) to the Saturn V rocket. . . . [Areas considered] include pumping, mechanical and electrical power, power tranmission, minerals extraction and refining, manufacturing, food processing, materials handling, environmental control, water transportation through space transportation, research, communications and processing, and biomedical engineering." Choice

Includes bibliographical references

Marks' standard handbook for mechanical engineers. McGraw-Hill il $150   **621**
1. Mechanical engineering—Handbooks, manuals, etc.

Also available from American Soc. of Mechanical Engs.; CD-ROM version also available

First published 1916 under the editorship of Lionel S. Marks with title: Mechanical engineers' handbook. (10th edition 1996) Periodically revised. Editors vary

Known as Standard handbook for mechanical engineers

This volume presents concisely the basic scientific and technical data of mechanical engineering, covering theory, basic mechanism, standard practice, often-needed mathematical formulae and technical data

Includes bibliographical references

621.3 Electrical engineering; superconductivity; electronics; communication engineering; computers

American electricians' handbook. McGraw-Hill il $89.95 **621.3**

1. Electrical engineering—Handbooks, manuals, etc.

First published 1913. (14th edition 2002) Periodically revised

"A Standard handbook, written to be in accordance with the latest ed. of the National Electrical code." Guide to Ref Books. 11th edition

Gibilisco, Stan

Teach yourself electricity and electronics. 3rd ed. McGraw-Hill 2002 xx, 727p il $34.95 **621.3**

1. Electronics 2. Electricity
ISBN 0-07-137730-1   LC 2001-45265
First published 1993

This is a self-instructional guide for hobbyists, professionals, and techicians who wish to learn more about AC and DC currents, batteries, resistors, semiconductors, and computers. It features multiple-choice quizzes at the ends of each section

Includes bibliographical references

McGraw-Hill's National Electrical Code handbook. McGraw-Hill $75   **621.3**

1. Electrical engineering—Handbooks, manuals, etc.

First published 1932 with title: National Electrical Code handbook. (24th edition 2002) Periodically revised to reflect changes in the code. Title varies

This handbook presents analysis and commentary on the National Electrical Code, as it pertains to wiring of appliances, buildings, emergency systems, and other types of electrical construction

National Electrical Code handbook. National Fire Protection Assn. $109.95   **621.3**

1. Electrical engineering—Handbooks, manuals, etc.

Also available CD-ROM version

First published 1978. (9th edition 2002) Periodically revised

This "is a nationally accepted guide to the safe installation of electrical conductors and equipment, and is, in fact, the basis for all electrical codes used in the United States." Ref Sources for Small & Medium-sized Libr. 5th edition

Standard handbook for electrical engineers. McGraw-Hill $150   **621.3**

1. Electrical engineering—Handbooks, manuals, etc.

First published 1908. (14th edition 2000) Periodically revised

Contains data on all branches of electrical engineering including material in the field of nuclear physics, plastics and resins, transistors and television

621.319 Transmission of electric power

Cauldwell, Rex

Safe home wiring projects. Taunton Press 1997 151p il pa $19.95   **621.319**

1. Electric wiring
ISBN 1-56158-164-X   LC 97-5789

"A Fine woodworking book"

The author "starts by explaining basic electrical principles and shows which tools to use. A section on inspecting your home's electrical system is particularly helpful, describing various hazards and pitfalls. Other sections cover repairing wiring switches and receptacles and installing light fixtures, ceiling and bathroom fans and home entertainment systems. . . . This is an excellent title for beginners." Libr J

621.381 Electronics

Electronics engineers' handbook. McGraw-Hill $150   **621.381**

1. Electronics—Handbooks, manuals, etc.

First published 1975. (4th edition 1997) Periodically revised

Current editor: Donald Christiansen

Covers essential principles, data, and design information on the components, circuits, equipment, and systems of electronics engineering. Emphasizes practical use of basic principles. Includes computer-aided design and electronic data processing

Goodman, Robert L.

How electronic things work—and what to do when they don't. 2nd ed. TAB Electronics 2003 xx, 426p il $24.95   **621.381**

1. Electronic apparatus and appliances—Maintenance and repair
ISBN 0-07-138745-5   LC 2003-265249
First published 1999

"Explains the practical side of electronics—troubleshooting problems, testing, repair, and servicing. Although the reader may not learn all the basics of electronics here, there is certainly a lot to be learned about resolving typical problems with common household items." Libr J

Grob, Bernard

Basic electronics. McGraw-Hill   **621.381**

1. Electricity 2. Electronics

First published 1959. (9th edition 2003) Periodically revised

Accompanied by computer laser optical disc

An introductory text on the fundamentals of electricity and electronics for technicians in radio, television, and industrial electronics

Includes bibliographical references

The **Illustrated** dictionary of electronics; edited by Stan Gibilisco. McGraw-Hill il $44.95   **621.381**

1. Electronics—Dictionaries

First published 1980 under the authorship of Rufus P. Turner. (8th edition 2001) Periodically revised

This illustrated dictionary contains nearly 28,000 entries—definitions, abbreviations, and acronyms—includ-

The Illustrated dictionary of electronics—
Continued
ing terms in the fields of robotics, artificial intelligence, and personal computing as they relate to electronics. Also included is terminology in: lasers; television; radio; IC technology; digital and analog electronics; audio and video; power supplies; fiber optic communications, etc.

621.382 Communications engineering

Bourne, Jennie, 1951-
DSL: a Wiley tech brief; [by] Jennie Bourne, Dave Burstein. Wiley 2001 210p il (Wiley tech brief series) pa $34.99 **621.382**
1. Digital subscriber lines 2. Computer networks
ISBN 0-471-08390-9 LC 2001-46621
"The book moves . . . from the basics of the equipment through security, applications, and network management. . . . [The authors provide] evaluations of the providers and manufacturers and offer technical managers a . . . guide to make . . . strategic decisions on DSL, reduce costs, and ensure a system that will run reliably and smoothly." Publisher's note

Clayton, Jade
McGraw-Hill illustrated telecom dictionary. McGraw-Hill il $34.95 **621.382**
1. Telecommunication—Dictionaries
ISBN 0-07-139508-3 LC 2002-25519
Accompanied by computer laser optical disc
Annual. First published 1998
"Package includes more than 4,000 definitions, 600 illustrations, seven appendixes, and the complete text on a searchable CD-ROM. The CD-ROM offers an additional 1,000 pages of cross-referenced material. . . . The additional articles give a look in greater depth at certain definitions in the text. . . . A good reference source for professionals and students." Choice

Naughton, John, 1946-
A brief history of the future; from radio days to Internet years in a lifetime. Overlook Press 2000 327p $29.95 **621.382**
1. Telecommunication 2. Internet
ISBN 1-58567-032-4 LC 00-26265
This "volume offers a selective history of computing as it traces the dawn of the World Wide Web and honors the engineers who created it." Publ Wkly
"Naughton's history reads like a drama, detailing the major players in the battles of the 1990s involving Bill Gates, Netscape, and Linus Torvalds, among others. This is a book for anyone who wants a clear picture of the growth of the net and an understanding of what led to its ubiquity." Libr J
Includes bibliographical references

Weems, David B.
Designing, building, and testing your own speaker system with projects. McGraw-Hill pa $19.95 **621.382**
1. Intercommunication systems
Also available the author's Great sound stereo speaker manual pa $34.95 (ISBN 0-07-134874-3)
First published 1981. (4th edition 1996) Periodically revised
This manual offers instructions on building low cost high quality loudspeaker systems using the latest audio technology

621.384 Radio and radar

Carr, Joseph J.
Old time radios! restoration and repair. TAB Bks. 1991 256p il hardcover o.p. paperback available $19.95 **621.384**
1. Radio—Repairing
ISBN 0-8306-3342-1 (pa) LC 90-44411
This guide includes the history, theory and practical operation of old-time radio sets and detailed instructions and schematics for repairing and rebuilding them

621.3841 Amateur (Ham) radio

The **ARRL** handbook for radio amateurs. American Radio Relay League il $32
621.3841
1. Radio—Handbooks, manuals, etc. 2. Amateur radio stations—Handbooks, manuals, etc.
ISSN 0890-3565
Also available CD-ROM version
Annual. Began publication 1926. Editions 1 through 61 published with title: The Radio amateur's handbook
"Chapters cover fundamentals and changing technology in the field and include many tables, circuit diagrams, photographs, and occasional references" Guide to Ref Books. 11th edition

621.3848 Radar

Buderi, Robert
The invention that changed the world; how a small group of radar pioneers won the Second World War and launched a technological revolution. Simon & Schuster 1996 575p il (Sloan technology series) hardcover o.p. paperback available $16
621.3848
1. Radar 2. World War, 1939-1945
ISBN 0-684-83529-0 (pa) LC 96-9404
Buderi presents a narrative account of the development of radar during the Second World War. In addition, he chronicles the subsequent applications of radar technology in the postwar era
"Buderi provides an impressive overview of his subject." N Y Times Book Rev
Includes bibliographical references

621.385 Telephony

Steuernagel, Robert
The cellular connection; a guide to cellular telephones. 4th ed. Wiley 2000 132p il pa $32.95 **621.385**
1. Cellular telephones
ISBN 0-471-31652-0 LC 99-21916
First published 1987 by Quantum Pub.
This book features information on cell phones, including "How the cellular system works; The purposes and advantages of various features; How to choose, install, and operate your phone; How to make sense of your phone bill; What to do when traveling outside your home area; How to tell when you're roaming [and] What's in the future, including digital cellular and PCS." Publisher's note

621.388 Television

Abramson, Albert
The history of television, 1942 to 2000; foreword by Christopher H. Sterling. McFarland & Co. 2003 309p il $75 **621.388**
1. Television—History
ISBN 0-7864-1220-8   LC 2002-326
Also available The history of television, 1880 to 1941, published 1987
"Chapters are devoted to television and World War II and the postwar era, the development of color television, Ampex Corporation's contributions, television in Europe, the change from helical to high band technology, solid state cameras, the television coverage of Apollo II, the rise of electronic journalism, television entering the studios, the introduction of the camcorder, the demise of RCA at the hands of GE, the domination of Sony and Matsushita, and the future of television in e-cinema and the 1080 P24 format." Publisher's note
"No reference work available in print right now matches the attention to detail that is obvious here. A significant work on how the machinery of television has evolved, this . . . should stand as the authority for years to come." Libr J
Includes bibliographical references

Capelo, Gregory R.
VCR troubleshooting & repair; [by] Gregory R. Capelo, Robert C. Brenner. 3rd ed. Newnes 1998 434p il $34.95   **621.388**
1. Home video systems—Maintenance and repair
ISBN 0-7506-9940-X   LC 97-27610
First published 1987 by Sams with authors in reverse order
This is a guide to caring for VCRs including preventative maintenance, diagnosing problems and making repairs

Davidson, Homer L.
TV repair for beginners. McGraw-Hill $44.95; pa $29.95   **621.388**
1. Television—Repairing
First published under the authorship of George Zwick with title: Beginner's guide to TV repair. (5th edition 1997) Periodically revised
This is a guide to the operation and repair of standard TV components as well as universal remote transmitters, stereo TV, digital controls, new color circuits and picture tube sizes, and digital satellite receivers

Wilkins, Richard C.
Home VCR repair illustrated; [by] Richard C. Wilkins, Vicki Wilkins. 2nd ed. McGraw-Hill 1999 xxiii, 615p il $29.95
          621.388
1. Home video systems—Maintenance and repair
ISBN 0-07-070769-3   LC 99-35899
First published 1991
This VCR repair guide features instructions on how to "Clean the video heads plus pinpoint and correct head problems; Remove and service cassette carriages; Align the video tape path, audio heads, and gears; Replace fuses, audio heads, and video heads; Solve problems with take-up spindles, capstan shafts, and jammed cassettes; Check and replace DC motors; Diagnose common malfunctions—from video jitter to distorted audio to freeze ups; Repair damage from water or spilled beverages [and] Bring a dropped VCR back to life." Publisher's note

621.39 Computer engineering

Mueller, Scott
Upgrading and repairing PCs. Que il $59.99   **621.39**
1. Microcomputers—Maintenance and repair
2. Microcomputers—Upgrading
First published 1988. (15th edition 2003) Periodically revised
This guide to maintaining, upgrading, and repairing personal computers explains physical disassembly and reassembly, primary system components, input/output hardware, mass storage systems, maintenance, troubleshooting and diagnostics. It includes a technical reference, a glossary, and lists vendors of replacement parts. CD-ROM containing electronic books and information included in 8th edition

621.43 Internal-combustion engines

Weil, Elizabeth
They all laughed at Christopher Columbus; an incurable dreamer builds the first civilian spaceship. Bantam Bks. 2002 230p il hardcover o.p. paperback available $13.95
          621.43
1. Hudson, Gary 2. Rotary Rocket Company 3. Rocketry 4. Space flight 5. Outer space
ISBN 0-553-38236-5 (pa)   LC 2002-18665
"Gary Hudson, the subject of the book, was a space enthusiast of the 1950s. He believed that NASA engineers were wrong in their approach to space travel. He was convinced that private industry could build a vehicle to deliver humans into space more cheaply and more effectively than the government. . . . He sketched a rough drawing of his idea for a space vehicle he called the Roton. It looked like a 60-foot nose cone with a helicopter blade." Sci Books Films

621.9 Tools

Hack, Garrett
Classic hand tools; photographs by John S. Sheldon. Taunton Press 1999 218p il $34.95; pa $24.95   **621.9**
1. Tools
ISBN 1-56158-273-5; 1-56158-507-6 (pa)
          LC 99-23719
In this look at old, muscle-powered tools Hack discusses "how to maintain them; and, for some of the obscurer ones, what exactly their purposes are. The resulting book is surprisingly comprehensive, covering just about everything from scrapers to saws and including a most interesting chapter on antique-tool collecting." Booklist
Includes bibliographical references

Nagyszalanczy, Sandor

Power tools; an electrifying celebration and grounded guide; written and photographed by Sandor Nagyszalanczy. Taunton Press 2001 266p il $40; pa $24.95　　　**621.9**

1. Power tools
ISBN 1-56158-427-4; 1-56158-576-9 (pa)
LC 2001-33097

This work covers the history, design, accessories and recent developments of portable and stationary power tools

"Tool collectors and those considering tool purchases will find this title invaluable." Libr J

623　Military and nautical engineering

Volkman, Ernest

Science goes to war; the search for the ultimate weapon, from Greek fire to Star Wars. Wiley 2002 278p $24.95　　　**623**

1. Military art and science 2. Weapons
ISBN 0-4714-1007-1

The author "traces the long, often contentious relationship between science and warfare. Beginning with the Assyrians, who established the first military R&D program more than 3,000 years ago, Volkman details the never-ending search for the ultimate weapon. He examines the military research of history's most renowned scientists and explains the military significance of many nonmilitary inventions, such as the printing press, the compass, and canned food." Publisher's note

623.4　Ordnance

Gun digest. DBI Bks. pa $27.99　　　**623.4**

1. Firearms 2. Shooting

Annual. First published 1944. Editors vary

This reference work covers information relating to shotguns, rifles, cartridges, sights and scopes, availability of arms and accessories, technical articles on hunting, gun control, foreign arms, etc.

Light, Michael

100 suns, 1945-1962. Knopf 2003 unp il $45　　　**623.4**

1. Nuclear weapons—Pictorial works
ISBN 1-4000-4113-9　　　LC 2003-106275

"The 'suns' Light presents to readers in this . . . photography collection are manmade: aboveground atomic detonations captured on film both in the Nevada desert and at sea, terrifyingly beautiful images that remind readers of the apocalyptic might of nuclear weapons." Booklist

Includes bibliographical references

O'Connell, Robert L.

Soul of the sword; an illustrated history of weaponry and warfare from prehistory to the present; illustrations by John Batchelor. Free Press 2002 390p il $35　　　**623.4**

1. Weapons 2. Military art and science
ISBN 0-684-84407-9　　　LC 2002-726645

"From the use of a sharpened stick by prehistoric humans to today's warfare by virus, O'Connell . . . traces the vast history of weapons and in the process explains how major conflicts and strategies have been affected by weaponry. . . . Throughout, O'Connell's captivating writing is surprisingly witty, given the serious nature of the subject. . . . Highly recommended for all academic military history collections and larger public libraries." Libr J

Includes bibliographical references

Rhodes, Richard, 1937-

Dark sun; the making of the hydrogen bomb. Simon & Schuster 1995 731p il hardcover o.p. paperback available $18

623.4

1. Hydrogen bomb
ISBN 0-684-82414-0 (pa)　　　LC 95-11070

This is a "chronicle of the rivalry between the U.S. and the U.S.S.R. to invent, build, test and stockpile hydrogen bombs. . . . Rhodes places the story of the bomb's development in the context of politics, science, technical hurdles and espionage. . . . He also brings in the case of convicted atomic spies Julius and Ethel Rosenberg." Publ Wkly

"This meticulously documented treatise presents a gripping story." Libr J

The making of the atomic bomb. Simon & Schuster 1986 886p il hardcover o.p. paperback available $20　　　**623.4**

1. Atomic bomb
ISBN 0-684-81378-5 (pa)　　　LC 86-15445

This book chronicles the development of the bomb "from the birth of modern physics in the late 19th century to the first tests of hydrogen bombs, by the United States in 1954 and the Soviet Union in 1955." Science

"The book provides portraits of the many players from Szilard and Einstein to Oppenheimer. . . . The book is heavily documented and includes a 13-page bibliography. This is a definitive work, well written, with a gripping story. It is not an easy book to read, but is well worth the effort." Libr J

Shooter's bible. Stoeger il pa $23.95　　**623.4**

1. Firearms—Catalogs

Annual. First published 1925 by Follett

Contains specifications and manufacturers' current prices for a variety of firearms and accessories. Also includes articles on related subjects, gun finder index, and caliber finder index

Weapons & warfare; editor, John Powell; managing editor, Christina J. Moose. Salem Press 2001 2v il maps $194　　　**623.4**

1. Military weapons 2. Military art and science
ISBN 1-58765-000-2　　　LC 2001-34150

Contents: v1 Ancient and medieval weapons and warfare (to 1500); v2 Modern weapons and warfare (since 1500)

"Each of the volumes is arranged with the same scheme. Discussions of major weapon groups are followed by sections that survey historical periods and are further divided by geographic region. The total number of topics covered in the two volumes exceeds 100, ranging from 2,000 to 7,000 words." Booklist

Includes bibliographical references

623.7 Military vehicles

Fredriksen, John C.
Warbirds; an illustrated guide to U.S. military aircraft, 1915-2000. ABC-CLIO 1999 363p il $75 **623.7**
1. Military airplanes
ISBN 1-57607-131-6   LC 99-16624
This guide "covers all fighters, bombers, trainers, patrol craft, transports, and helicopters manufactured and deployed by military or naval units. . . . There are 325 entries, each with a black-and-white photograph of the aircraft and a listing of performance, power plant, armament, and service dates and a brief narrative detailing the development, deployment, and eventual retirement of the machines." Booklist

623.8 Nautical engineering and seamanship

Jane's fighting ships. Jane's Information Group $630 **623.8**
1. Warships 2. Navies
Also available CD-ROM version and online
Annual. First published 1898. Title and publisher vary
"Arranged alphabetically by country, subdivided by class of ship. Gives numbers and names of ships in each class; builders; dates of laying down, launching, and completion; a photograph of a ship in the class; and specifications for the class." Guide to Ref Books. 11th edition

Tall, J. J.
Submarines & deep-sea vehicles; [by] Jeffrey Tall. Thunder Bay Press (San Diego) 2002 256p il $24.98 **623.8**
1. Submarines 2. Submersibles
ISBN 1-57145-778-X   LC 2002-71951
This book traces the history of deep sea vehicles "starting with the earliest submersible craft, right up to the stealthy nuclear giants of the modern age." Publisher's note
Includes bibliographical references

623.88 Seamanship

Day, Cyrus Lawrence, 1900-1968
The art of knotting & splicing; edited by Ray O. Beard, Jr. and M. Lee Hoffman, Jr. 4th ed. Naval Inst. Press 1986 235p il $32.95 **623.88**
1. Knots and splices
ISBN 0-87021-062-9   LC 86-16299
First published 1947 by Dodd, Mead
A series of photographs in sequence demonstrates splicing and the tying of knots in actual use today, giving their origins, backgrounds, comparative strengths and uses
Includes bibliographical references

Pawson, Des
The handbook of knots. DK Pub. 1998 160p il pa $17 **623.88**
1. Knots and splices
ISBN 0-7894-2395-2   LC 97-38707
"This is a step-by-step guide to tying and using more than 100 knots. . . . There's a chapter on rope construction, rope materials, and properties of ropes and their main uses. It's very informative and put together concisely." BAYA Book Rev

623.89 Navigation

Bathurst, Bella
The lighthouse Stevensons; the extraordinary story of the building of the Scottish lighthouses by the ancestors of Robert Louis Stevenson. HarperCollins Pubs. 1999 xxiv, 278p il map hardcover o.p. paperback available $14 **623.89**
1. Stevenson family 2. Lighthouses
ISBN 0-06-093226-0 (pa)   LC 99-26174
Also available G.K. Hall large print edition
The author "tells how four generations of Robert Louis Stevenson's family designed and built the 97 manned lighthouses that speckle the Scottish coast." Publ Wkly
"Writing with an enchanting eloquence . . . Bathurst delivers a family saga that shows how the ingenuity and perseverance of a few could be 'for the benefit of the nation as a whole.'" N Y Times Book Rev
Includes bibliographical references

Dutton's nautical navigation. Naval Inst. Press il $49.95 **623.89**
1. Navigation
First published 1926 under the authorship of Benjamin Dutton with title: Navigation and nautical astronomy. (15th edition 2003 by Thomas J. Cutler. Variant title: Dutton's navigation & piloting)
This guide for the coastal and seagoing mariner focuses on piloting, celestial navigation, radio navigation and dead reckoning

624 Civil engineering

Brown, David J., 1946-
Bridges. Macmillan 1993 176p il maps o.p.; MBI Pub. paperback available $19.95 **624**
1. Bridges
ISBN 0-7603-1234-6 (pa)   LC 93-9747
Illustrated with photographs, construction diagrams, and historical drawings and engravings, this book presents profiles of more than one hundred bridges, organized chronologically from ancient times to the twenty-first century. Each account includes the bridge's location, date of construction, designer, materials, dimensions, and the story behind its creation
Includes bibliographical references

Graf, Bernhard
Bridges that changed the world. Prestel 2002 127p il $29.95   **624**
1. Bridges
ISBN 3-7913-2701-1   LC 2002-109555
This book examines fifty of the world's most important bridges and the history, legends, and people behind them. . . . Bridges examined include Florence's Ponte Vecchio, Bosnia's Stari Most, the An Ji Bridge in China, and the Iron Bridge in Britain
"An appealing diversion for browsers." Booklist
Includes bibliographical references

Petroski, Henry
Engineers of dreams; great bridge builders and the spanning of America. Knopf 1995 479p il hardcover o.p. paperback available $16   **624**
1. Bridges 2. Civil engineering
ISBN 0-679-76021-0 (pa)   LC 94-48893
Focusing on the men who designed them, "Petroski depicts the building of several famous American bridges—New York's George Washington, St. Louis's Eads, and Michigan's Mackinaw, among others." Libr J
"An exhilarating saga of ingenuity and sheer determination." Publ Wkly
Includes bibliographical references

627   Hydraulic engineering

Matson, Tim, 1943-
Earth ponds A to Z; an illustrated encyclopedia; illustrated by Frank Fretz. Countryman Press 2003 225p il pa $18.95   **627**
1. Water supply engineering 2. Ponds
ISBN 0-88150-494-7   LC 2002-67672
"From Acid Rain to Zooplankton . . . Tim Matson defines and explains . . . {over} two hundred terms associated with pond building and maintenance. . . . The reader will find descriptions and definitions of . . . pond elements, including: structural features; construction materials; water conditions and treatments; aquacultural topics and crops; environmental concerns; government support and regulatory agencies {and} landscaping." Publisher's note
Includes bibliographical references

628.9   Fire-fighting technology

Golway, Terry, 1955-
So others might live; a history of New York's bravest; the FDNY from 1700 to the present. Basic Bks. 2002 368p $27.50; pa $17   **628.9**
1. New York (N.Y.). Fire Dept. 2. Fire fighting
ISBN 0-465-02740-7; 0-465-02741-5 (pa)
The author describes the New York City Fire Department's "emergence from amateur bucket brigades into the beginnings of a specialized force and up to the present, never letting a memorable figure or vivid moment escape his narrative." Libr J
Includes bibliographical references

Gottschalk, Jack
Firefighting. DK Pub. 2002 160p il $30   **628.9**
1. Fire fighting 2. Fires
ISBN 0-7894-8909-0   LC 2002-67201
This book "examines history's most formidable fires, showing how each influenced the evolution of firefighting technology, equipment, and tactics." Publisher's note

National Fire Protection Association
Fire protection handbook. National Fire Protection Assn. il $149.95   **628.9**
1. Fire prevention
First published 1896. (19th edition 2003) Periodically revised. Title varies
"A handbook of approved practice in the fields of fire prevention and fire protection. Will be useful to owners and superintendents of buildings, and to architects and engineers interested in designing safe buildings and planning for their protection against fire." Carnegie Libr of Pittsburgh

629   Other branches of engineering

Space exploration; edited by Christopher Mari. Wilson, H.W. 1999 157p (Reference shelf) pa $50   **629**
1. United States. National Aeronautics and Space Administration 2. Astronautics—United States 3. Outer space—Exploration
ISBN 0-8242-0963-X   LC 99-25424
Contents: John Glenn's return to space; Exploration of Mars; The international space station; Private enterprise and space exploration; New technologies and discoveries
Includes bibliographical references

629.13   Aeronautics

Chaikin, Andrew, 1956-
Air and space; the National Air and Space Museum's story of flight. Little, Brown 1997 317p il $50; pa $29.95   **629.13**
1. National Air and Space Museum (U.S.)
ISBN 0-8212-2082-9; 0-8212-2670-3 (pa)
     LC 96-31929
This illustrated work connects artifacts on display at the Smithsonian's aeronautics museum with a brief history of air and space flight
"A few photos, as of the DC-3, show the vehicle in its exhibit hall, but most pictures depict planes or rockets in action, right up through the latest images of the space age—Mars as viewed from Pathfinder. An enthusiast's delight." Booklist

Chant, Christopher
A century of triumph; the history of aviation; illustrations by John Batchelor. Free Press 2002 388p il $50   **629.13**
1. Aeronautics—History
ISBN 0-7432-3479-0   LC 2002-73944
The author "covers every aspect of aviation history: early biplanes, the age of the Zeppelins, the birth of civil aviation, and the beginning of airmail service. He also

Chant, Christopher—*Continued*

chronicles the race for speed and distance, World War I and World War II fighters and bombers, commercial air travel, the invention and uses of helicopters, the jet age, and what Chant describes as the modern age of flight with its huge airliners and stealth warplanes." Booklist
This is "the best overview to date of aviation's first century." Publ Wkly

Demetz, Peter, 1922-

The air show at Brescia, 1909. Farrar, Straus & Giroux 2002 254p $24   **629.13**
1. Aeronautics—History 2. Brescia (Italy)—History
ISBN 0-374-10259-7   LC 2002-23259
This is an "account of a flying competition that took place in northern Italy during the early days of aviation. Attending the event, among other notables, were Franz Kafka and Italian poet Gabriele d'Annunzio. Kafka, who traveled to Brescia with several friends, including novelist and editor Max Brod, published a journalistic article about the show. . . . Those interested in aviation history as well as a glimpse of the young Kafka will greatly enjoy this serendipitous account." Publ Wkly
Includes bibliographical references

Gorn, Michael H.

Expanding the envelope; flight research at NACA and NASA. University Press of Ky. 2001 472p il $35   **629.13**
1. United States. National Aeronautics and Space Administration 2. United States. National Advisory Committee for Aeronautics 3. Aeronautics
ISBN 0-8131-2205-8   LC 00-12287
"A history of government-sponsored flight research, from the testing of kites and gliders in the 19th century through the Wright brothers, the creation of the National Advisory Committee on Aeronautics, and NASA in the 20th century." Choice
Includes bibliographical references

Grant, R. G. (Reg G.)

Flight: 100 years of aviation. DK Pub. 2002 440p il $50   **629.13**
1. Aeronautics—History
ISBN 0-7894-8910-4   LC 2002-73935
Grant "divides this book into sections that include a prehistory of flight and the Wright brothers; accounts of air combat in World War I, and a focus on the 'golden age' that recounts the flights of Charles Lindbergh, Amelia Earhart, Jimmy Doolittle, and the great airships and flying boats. He also presents a history of aircraft's role in World War II (the Battle of Britain, the air war at sea, and the Allied bombing raids on Axis cities); the cold war and Vietnam; space travel; and jet passenger travel." Booklist
"The impressive illustrations include over 300 gorgeous, full-color profiles of the world's major military and civilian aircraft and space vehicles. Libr J

Haynsworth, Leslie

Amelia Earhart's daughters; the wild and glorious story of American women aviators from World War II to the dawn of the space age; [by] Leslie Haynsworth and David Toomey. Morrow 1998 322p il hardcover o.p. paperback available $14   **629.13**
1. Women air pilots 2. Women astronauts
ISBN 0-380-72954-9 (pa)   LC 98-8727
This "study of American women aviators concentrates almost exclusively on the WASPs of World War II and the would-be female astronauts of the early 1960s." Booklist
Includes bibliographical references

Heppenheimer, T. A., 1947-

First flight; the Wright brothers and the invention of the airplane. Wiley 2003 394p il $30   **629.13**
1. Wright, Orville, 1871-1948 2. Wright, Wilbur, 1867-1912 3. Aeronautics—History
ISBN 0-471-40124-2   LC 2003-268729
"Debunking the standard view that the brothers more or less invented their flying machine by luck and persistence, Heppenheimer . . . establishes a number of . . . facts about Orville and Wilbur that challenge current assumptions." Publ Wkly
This book "will appeal to aviation scholars and enthusiasts. Recommended for all aeronautical collections and large libraries." Libr J
Includes bibliographical references

Lindbergh, Charles, 1902-1974

The spirit of St. Louis; {by} Charles A. Lindbergh. Scribner 1998 562p il $35   **629.13**
1. Aeronautics—Flights 2. Spirit of St. Louis (Airplane)
ISBN 0-684-85277-2   LC 98-33556
Also available in paperback from Minnesota Historical Society
A reissue of the title first published 1953
This is an account of the first solo transatlantic flight from New York to Paris, as well as a detailed description of the preparation for the flight which in turn mirrors aviation of the 1920's

Tobin, James, 1956-

To conquer the air; the Wright Brothers and the great race for flight. Free Press 2003 433p il $28   **629.13**
1. Wright, Orville, 1871-1948 2. Wright, Wilbur, 1867-1912 3. Aeronautics—History 4. Flight—History
ISBN 0-684-85688-3   LC 2002-44778
Also available Thorndike Press large print edition
"In this centenary of the airplane, Tobin recreates the course, in its technological and biographical dimensions, of the Wright brothers' claim to its invention." Booklist
"This book represents the most forceful argument to date for the brothers' monumental legacy to the history of flight. . . . This lucidly written and exhaustively researched study is recommended for all aviation collections and all libraries." Libr J
Includes bibliographical references

Wright, Orville, 1871-1948

How we invented the airplane; an illustrated history; edited with an introduction and commentary by Fred C. Kelly; additional text by Alan Weissman. Dover Publs. 1988 c1953 87p il pa $9.95   **629.13**
1. Wright, Wilbur, 1867-1912 2. Airplanes
ISBN 0-486-25662-6   LC 87-33037
First published 1953 by D. McKay
This "account by the two inventors . . . covers experiments, discovery of aeronautical principles, construction of planes and motors, first flights, and much more. Also included is a later account written by both brothers." Publisher's note
Includes bibliographical references

629.133   Aircraft types

Botting, Douglas
Dr. Eckener's dream machine; the great Zeppelin and the dawn of air travel. Holt & Co. 2001 331p il maps $27.50; pa $16

629.133

1. Eckener, Hugo, 1868-1954 2. Graf Zeppelin (Airship) 3. Airships 4. Aeronautics—Flights
ISBN 0-8050-6458-3; 0-8050-6459-1 (pa)
LC 2001-24770
Botting discusses the history of the Zeppelin, a rigid airship designed by a Prussian army officer, Ferdinand Count von Zeppelin, and the career of Hugo Eckener, who promoted and flew the dirigible
"A truly exciting book, filled with colorful characters and plenty of derring-do and laced with just the right amount of sadness and tragedy." Booklist
Includes bibliographical references

Jane's all the world's aircraft. Jane's Information Group il $630   **629.133**
1. Aeronautics
ISSN 0075-3017

Also available CD-ROM version and online
Annual. First published 1909
"Offers illustrations, descriptions, and specifications of aircraft of various countries of the world including: airplanes, drones, sailplanes, airships, military missiles, research rockets, space vehicles, aero-engines. Arranged in sections by: Aircraft; Lighter than air; Aero engines, then alphabetically by country of manufacture." Guide to Ref Books. 11th edition

629.2   Motor land vehicles, and cycles

Bradsher, Keith
High and mighty; SUVs—the world's most dangerous vehicles and how they got that way. PublicAffairs 2002 468p il $28; pa $14

629.2

1. Sport utility vehicles 2. Consumer protection 3. Automobile industry
ISBN 1-58648-123-1; 1-58648-203-3 (pa)
LC 2002-28722
The author discusses sport utility vehicles (S.U.V.'s), which are classified as light trucks and therefore exempt from the environmental and safety rules that apply to cars. Bradsher examines their marketing, environmental impact, safety record, and user psychology
"This fascinating history and troubling analysis of both the politics and the design of the SUV should appeal to readers on both sides of the debate." Booklist
Includes bibliographical references

629.222   Passenger automobiles

Adler, Dennis, 1948-
The art of the sports car; the greatest designs of the 20th century; written and with photographs by Dennis Adler. HarperCollins Pubs. 2002 236p il $44.95   **629.222**
1. Sports cars
ISBN 0-06-018885-5   LC 2001-51810
In this illustrated history of the sports car the author provides an "account of the evolution of small cars with big engines, recounting the travails of famous auto designers, the engineering and styling innovations they pioneered and the races and road rallies at which cars proved (and advertised) themselves. His narrative dwells mostly on European makes such as Jaguar, Porsche and Ferrari, but also discusses the American Corvette and muscle cars like the Ford Thunderbird and the Dodge Challenger. . . . Hard-core aficionados will derive much gratification from the detailed descriptions of mechanical design and performance. . . . But just about anyone will be entranced at the pictures of classic cars meticulously restored, polished to a sheen and photographed on opulent country estates." Publ Wkly

The **Beaulieu** encyclopedia of the automobile; editor in chief, Nick Georgano; foreword by Lord Montagu of Beaulieu. Fitzroy Dearborn Pubs. 2000 2v il set $325

629.222

1. Automobiles—Encyclopedias
ISBN 1-57958-293-1   LC 2001-316285
This encyclopedia "provides A-Z coverage of almost every make of car that was intended to be manufactured and sold. . . . Most entries are brief descriptions of individual makes, although major names (Chrysler, Citroën, Toyota, etc.) are accorded long entries within which their models are discussed." Booklist
"The most comprehensive automobile encyclopedia available today." Am Libr

Kimes, Beverly Rae
Standard catalog of American cars, 1805-1942; Henry Austin Clark, Jr., chief of research; Ralph Dunwoodie, Keith Marvin, consultants to the author; Marque researchers, Robert C. Ackerson [et al.] 3rd ed. Krause Publs. 1996 1612p il pa $55   **629.222**
1. Automobiles—History
ISBN 0-87341-428-4   LC 96-199824
Also available Standard catalog of American cars, 1946-1975 and Standard catalog of American cars, 1976-1999
First published 1985
This catalog describes American automobiles manufactured between 1805 and 1942, including current pricing according to condition, more than 5,000 photos, and histories of the cars and their manufacturers
Includes bibliographical references

Standard guide to American muscle cars; a supercar source book, 1960-2000; edited by John Gunnell. 3rd ed. Krause Publs. 2002 304p il pa $24.95   **629.222**
1. Automobiles
ISBN 0-87349-262-5   LC 2002-282579
First edition published 1993 covered 1949-1992

Standard guide to American muscle cars—
Continued

"Featuring more than 300 American muscle cars produced during the last 40 years. . . . This full-color reference features more than four decades of muscle cars from American manufacturers including, AMC, GM, Chrysler, Ford, and Studebaker." Publisher's note

629.227 Cycles

Sloane, Eugene A.

Sloane's complete book of bicycling. 25th anniversary ed. Simon & Schuster 1995 429p il pa $21.95   **629.227**

1. Cycling 2. Bicycles
ISBN 0-671-87075-0   LC 94-46788
"A Fireside book"

First published 1970 by Trident Press with title: The complete book of bicycling. Variant titles: The new Complete book of bicycling; The all new Complete book of bicycling

Covers choosing a bicycle, repair and tools, preventive maintenance, safety tips for commuters, new technologies, bike touring, all-terrain and mountain bikes, and facts on health

Includes bibliographical references

629.28 Motor land vehicles and cycles—Tests, driving, maintenance, repairs

Bennett, James S.

The complete motorcycle book; a consumer's guide. 2nd ed. Facts on File 1999 258p il $30.75; pa $14.95   **629.28**

1. Motorcycles
ISBN 0-8160-3853-8; 0-8160-3854-6 (pa)
    LC 98-30311
First published 1995

This book covers "motorcycle mechanics, road skills, buying, riding, and caring for motorcycles. Information about factors to consider in buying a motorcycle are covered as well as advice about how to find a new or used bike to meet the rider's needs. Thorough evaluations of many top brands such as BMW, Harley-Davidson, Honda, Suzuki, Yamaha, and others are included. This book offers the most information for the widest variety of motorcyle enthusiasts." Libr J

Bicycling magazine's basic maintenance and repair; simple techniques to make your bike ride better and last longer; edited by Ed Pavelka. Rodale Press 1999 135p il pa $9.99   **629.28**

1. Bicycles—Maintenance and repair
ISBN 1-57954-170-4   LC 99-35338

An illustrated guide to do-it-yourself repairs and maintenance procedures designed to prevent on-road breakdowns

Chilton's auto repair manual. Chilton il
    629.28

1. Automobiles—Maintenance and repair
ISSN 0069-3634

For information on availability and price contact publisher

First published 1953 with title: Chilton's automobile repair manual

"Covers all mass-produced American cars of the past six or seven years plus the current year. Illustrated; includes charts to help diagnose problems. Useful for both novices and experts." N Y Public Libr Book of How & Where to Look It Up

Chilton's import car repair manual. Chilton il
    629.28

1. Foreign automobiles—Maintenance and repair
ISSN 0271-3608

For information on availability and price contact publisher

First published 1971-1972 in two volumes with title: Chilton's foreign car repair manual. Title varies

This manual covers maintenance, specifications and repair of European and Japanese cars and pick-up trucks. Many photographs and diagrams are included

Kachur, Bridget

Every woman's quick & easy car care; a worry-free guide to car troubles, trials & travels. Storey Bks. 2002 262p il pa $14.95
    629.28

1. Automobiles—Maintenance and repair
ISBN 1-58017-451-5   LC 2002-1117

This "guide presents a complete lesson in Auto Mechanics 101, from identifying the different parts of the engine to improving gas mileage to checking the air pressure in tires. . . . [It features] illustrated tutorials on changing a tire, jumpstarting a car, installing a car seat, replacing belts and hoses, changing the oil, detailing, winterizing, performing seasonal maintenance, and much more." Publisher's note

Langley, Jim

Bicycling magazine's complete guide to bicycle maintenance and repair for road and mountain bikes; over 1,000 tips, tricks, and techniques to maximize performance, minimize repairs, and save money. Expanded & rev 4th ed. Rodale Press 1999 351p il pa $19.95   **629.28**

1. Bicycles—Maintenance and repair
ISBN 1-57954-009-0   LC 99-17760

First edition by the editors of Bicycle magazine published 1986

This illustrated guide includes step-by-step instructions for major and minor repairs and maintenance for many types of bicycles. Web sites and phone numbers of bicyles and parts manufacturers is provided

Plas, Rob van der, 1938-

Bicycle repair step by step; how to maintain and repair your bicycle. Van der Plas Publs. 2002 144p il pa $18.95   **629.28**

1. Bicycles—Maintenance and repair
ISBN 1-89249-539-2   LC 2002-104475

First published 1994

This illustrated volume covers the proper maintenance and repair of a bicycle's mechanical systems from changing tires to complex overhauls

Includes bibliographical references

Volpe, Ren
The lady mechanic's total car care for the clueless. St. Martin's Griffin 1998 197p il pa $13.95   **629.28**
1. Automobiles—Maintenance and repair
ISBN 0-312-18733-5   LC 98-9435
A "guide to basic car care with a focus on preventive maintenance. . . . {The author} covers everything from @checking fluids' . . . to changing a tire to jump-starting a battery. . . . She discusses buying and selling vehicles. . . . The directions are clear, precise, and easy to follow; the style is engaging; and the author's sense of humor helps to make the topic less intimidating. This is an upbeat, comprehensive guide." SLJ

Wilson, Hugo
Motorcycle owner's manual. DK Pub. 1997 112p il pa $10   **629.28**
1. Motorcycles—Maintenance and repair
ISBN 0-7894-1615-8   LC 96-35925
This guide to motorcycle maintenance starts with simple procedures and routines then goes on to basic servicing and complex jobs
"Handy, attractive, and easy to follow." Booklist

629.4   Astronautics

Angelo, Joseph A.
Encyclopedia of space exploration; [by] Joseph A. Angelo, Jr. Facts on File 2000 305p il (Facts on File science library) $55; pa $21.95   **629.4**
1. Outer space—Exploration—Encyclopedias
ISBN 0-8160-3942-9; 0-8160-4902-5 (pa)
    LC 99-59659
In an A to Z format, this reference "presents the most recent lunar missions, the exploration of Mars, the latest images and discoveries via the *Hubble Space Telescope*, a special focus on Mission to planet Earth and the use of space to monitor and protect the biosphere, an update on the *International Space Station*, a focus on asteroid detection and negation systems, and the role of robotics and virtual reality in exploring the solar system." Publisher's note
Includes bibliographical references

The Facts on File dictionary of space technology; [by] Joseph A. Angelo, Jr. rev ed. Facts on File 2004 474p $49.95   **629.4**
1. Astronautics—Dictionaries
ISBN 0-8160-5222-0   LC 2003-49148
"Facts on File science library"
First published 1982 with title: The dictionary of space technology
This dictionary contains approximately 1,500 cross-referenced entries that present the basic concepts and phrases in the science of space, spaceflight, and space technology. Among the topics covered are: abort modes; ballistic missile defense; launch vehicles; Milstar; ocean remote sensing; robotics and space stations

Burrows, William E.
This new ocean; the story of the first space age. Random House 1998 723p il hardcover o.p. paperback available $16.95   **629.4**
1. Astronautics 2. Outer space—Exploration
ISBN 0-375-75485-7 (pa)   LC 98-3252
This is a "history of space exploration, from its ancient roots in mythology and literature to the theoreticians and pioneering engineers who made it a reality in this century." Libr J
"'This New Ocean' is most distinguished by the successful integration of three different story lines: manned space flight, the militarization of space and space science." N Y Times Book Rev
Includes bibliographical references

Heppenheimer, T. A., 1947-
Countdown; a history of space flight. Wiley 1997 398p il hardcover o.p. paperback available $17.95   **629.4**
1. Space flight 2. Astronautics 3. Cold war
ISBN 0-471-29105-6 (pa)   LC 96-28245
This is a "historical overview of the early visionaries, the engineers, and the geopolitical forces that placed men on the moon and created today's aerospace industry. Drawing on newly available Russian sources, the author places both Russian and American programs in their historical contexts." Libr J
Includes bibliographical references

Walsh, Patrick J.
Echoes among the stars; a short history of the U.S. space program. Sharpe, M.E. 2000 204p $35.95   **629.4**
1. Astronautics—United States
ISBN 0-7656-0537-6   LC 99-38899
Walsh "recounts the early successes of the Mercury and Gemini missions that paved the way for the Apollo moon landings as well as the Skylab and Apollo-Soyuz mission that marked the end of the first era of U.S. manned space flight." Libr J
Includes bibliographical references

Williamson, Mark
The Cambridge dictionary of space technology. Cambridge Univ. Press 2001 464p il maps $50   **629.4**
1. Astronautics—Dictionaries 2. Astronomy—Dictionaries
ISBN 0-521-66077-7   LC 00-59884
First published 1990 by Hilger with title: Dictionary of space technology
"This dictionary is a comprehensive reference on the words and phrases related to many aspects of the evolving field of space technology. The work contains material ranging from basic concepts to advanced applications and includes over 2,000 entries. The extraordinary breadth of coverage ensures that there are entries on all major space technology subject areas. While the emphasis on each entry is on defining the meaning of the word or phrase, entries have been written with the intention of enhancing the understanding of the subject for a variety of users, ranging from the practicing specialist to the layperson to the student." Sci Books & Films

Zimmerman, Robert
The chronological encyclopedia of discoveries in space. Oryx Press 2000 410p il maps $95 **629.4**
1. Outer space—Exploration 2. Astronautics
ISBN 1-57356-196-7
"Over 1,000 entries record the date of launch, name of the spacecraft(s), summary of the mission, names of the crew members, experiments, problems, and discoveries in a clear and concise fashion. Seemingly every single space mission is included, encompassing spaceflight with and without human crews, military and civilian ventures, public and commercial ventures, planetary probes, and communications satellites. . . . An excellent, cross-referencing system within the text, as well as extensive subject indices by satellite, mission, and nation or consortia, helps the reader follow particular interests in detail. . . . There is no comparable source to this volume for its comprehensiveness and conciseness." Sci Books Films

629.45 Manned space flight

Chaikin, Andrew, 1956-
A man on the moon; the voyages of the Apollo astronauts. Viking 1994 670p il hardcover o.p. paperback available $15.95 **629.45**
1. Apollo project 2. Space flight to the moon
ISBN 0-14-027201-1 (pa) LC 93-48680
In this chronicle of NASA's Apollo program "diary-like reports mix with first- and third-person accounts as Chaikin . . . delivers a chronological view of the missions and those who planned and flew them. Focusing closely on the Apollo astronauts, including Buzz Aldrin, Pete Conrad and Neil Armstrong, Chaikin gives his topic a sense of immediacy." Publ Wkly
Includes bibliographical references

Kranz, Eugene F., 1933-
Failure is not an option; mission control from Mercury to Apollo 13 and beyond; [by] Gene Kranz. Simon & Schuster 2000 415p il $26 **629.45**
1. United States. National Aeronautics and Space Administration 2. Space flight 3. Astronautics—United States
ISBN 0-7432-0079-9 LC 00-27720
Also available G.K. Hall large print edition and in paperback from Berkley Pub. Group
This memoir by the NASA flight director "follows his and NASA's careers from the start of the space race through 'the last lunar strike,' Apollo 17 (1972-1973)." Publ Wkly
"A welcome contribution to the history of space flight. More than any previous book, it gives the view of that history as lived by the brotherhood of Mission Control. The writing, like Kranz himself, is brisk, unadorned and informative, but warmed from time to time by characteristic expressions of irony and humor." N Y Times Book Rev

Launius, Roger D.
Frontiers of space exploration. Greenwood Press 1998 xxxi, 204p il (Greenwood Press guides to historic events of the twentieth century) $46.95 **629.45**
1. Astronautics 2. Outer space—Exploration
ISBN 0-313-29968-4 LC 97-34788
New edition in preparation

Launius presents "a historical overview of space exploration, the race to the moon, the scientific explorations in the space age, and the pursuit of a permanent, manned presence in space." Choice
The author "does an excellent job summarizing the early history of spaceflight with his essays—the real meat of the book—and the inclusion of the primary documents provides interesting insights into how major policy decisions were reached." Libr J
Includes bibliographical references

Reynolds, David West
Apollo: the epic journey to the moon. Harcourt 2002 272p $35 **629.45**
1. Apollo project 2. Space flight to the moon
ISBN 0-15-100964-3 LC 2001-51930
"A Tehabi book"
This is an illustrated history of the U.S. project of manned flight to the moon
"This title is definitely one of the best books written about Apollo in recent years. . . . Almost every major component of the Apollo complex is displayed, from the ground installations, to the titanic first stage, up to the moonwalker's spacesuit." Booklist
Includes bibliographical references

Schefter, James L.
The race; the uncensored story of how America beat Russia to the moon; by James Schefter. Doubleday 1999 303p il hardcover o.p. paperback available $14 **629.45**
1. Astronautics 2. Space flight to the moon 3. Apollo project
ISBN 0-385-49254-5 (pa) LC 98-54430
Schefter chronicles the early days of space flight competition describing "the subtle infighting among the astronauts, the complex nature of lesser-known people like manned-flight champion Bob Gilruth, and the American leaders struggling with military, scientific and public relations concerns." Publ Wkly

Space shuttle; the first 20 years; edited by Tony Reichhardt for Air & Space/Smithsonian magazine. DK Ink 2002 320p il $40 **629.45**
1. Space shuttles 2. Space flight
ISBN 0-7894-8425-0
"The astronauts' experiences in their own words." On cover
This "book documents the history of the space shuttle program by collecting anecdotes and reminiscences from the astronauts and some remarkable pictures of the shuttle and Earth from space." Libr J
"Some stories concern the oddities of zero-gravity housekeeping; others, the exhilaration of a space walk. Taken together with the spectacular pictures, the accounts create an intimacy with the reader and guarantee the high popularity of this work with spaceflight fans." Booklist
Includes bibliographical references

Wolfe, Tom
The right stuff. new ed. Farrar, Straus & Giroux 1983 436p $30 **629.45**
1. Astronauts 2. Astronautics—United States
ISBN 0-374-25033-2 LC 84-162805
Also available in paperback from Bantam Bks.
A reissue of the title first published 1979
This is a "history of the early years of the space program. Starting with an account of the lives of military pi-

Wolfe, Tom—*Continued*
lots [the book progresses] through the selection of the first seven astronauts, their training, and the Mercury flights." Libr J

Zimmerman, Robert
Genesis; the story of Apollo 8: the first manned flight to another world. Four Walls Eight Windows 1998 299p il $25.95 **629.45**
1. Apollo project 2. Space flight to the moon
ISBN 1-56858-118-1   LC 98-29963
Also available in paperback from Dell
The author tells the story of "*Apollo 8* from the time it blasted into space on December 21, 1968, until it splashed down in the Pacific nearly a week later. He focuses on three brave men—Frank Borman, Jim Lovell, and Bill Anders—who volunteered to ride an inadequately tested space vehicle equipped with a primitive computer on a journey of some quarter-million miles to orbit the Moon and return. He also focuses on the astronauts' wives." Choice
Includes bibliographical references

629.46 Engineering of unmanned spacecraft

Dickson, Paul
Sputnik: the shock of the century. Walker & Co. 2001 310p il $28   **629.46**
1. Artificial satellites 2. Astronautics 3. United States—Politics and government—20th century
ISBN 0-8027-1365-3   LC 2001-26156
Also available G.K. Hall large print edition and in paperback from Berkley Pub. Group
This is an "analysis of the impact of the Soviet space program on American politics, as well as on the military, public opinion, education, science, and research." Sci Books Films
"Paul Dickson skillfully puts the story of Sputnik and its aftermath into . . . perspective in his informative and readable book." Christ Sci Monit
Includes bibliographical references

629.47 Astronautical engineering

Dyson, George, 1953-
Project Orion; the true story of the atomic spaceship. Holt & Co. 2002 345p il $26; pa $16   **629.47**
1. Nuclear rockets 2. Astronautics
ISBN 0-8050-5985-7; 0-8050-7284-5 (pa)
LC 2001-46500
The author "charts the history of the failed Project Orion, which called for a massive rocket to be built atop a nuclear-powered piston. . . . Dyson's explanations of the nuclear science behind the system are lucid. A great strength of Dyson's project is the interviews he conducted with surviving Orion team members." Publ Wkly
Includes bibliographical references

Stine, G. Harry (George Harry), 1928-1997
Handbook of model rocketry. Wiley il pa $24.95   **629.47**
1. Rockets (Aeronautics)—Models
First published 1965 by Follett. (6th edition 1994) Periodically revised. Publisher varies
"NAR official handbook"

"Stine, an authority on model rocketry, describes all aspects of the subject from basics to international competition." Ref Sources for Small & Medium-sized Libr. 4th edition

629.8 Automatic control engineering

Brooks, Rodney Allen
Flesh and machines; how robots will change us. Pantheon Bks. 2002 260p il $26; pa $14   **629.8**
1. Robots 2. Artificial intelligence
ISBN 0-375-42079-7; 0-375-72527-X (pa)
LC 2001-36636
"A scientist at MIT's famous artificial intelligence lab, Brooks here splits his book in two: the first part describes various robots he and his group have built; the second part philosophizes on the nature of artificial intelligence." Booklist
A "stimulating book written by one of the major players in the field . . . about the state of robotics and its short-term future. It also offers surprisingly deep glimpses into what it is to be human. Brooks appears to have gained a boundless appreciation for human beings by attempting to copy them." N Y Times Book Rev

Cook, David
Robot building for beginners. APress 2002 568p il (Technology in action) pa $29.95
629.8
1. Robots—Design and construction
ISBN 1-893115-44-5
This book contains instructions on how to build a robot. "General sources for tools and parts are provided in a consolidated list, and specific parts are recommended throughout the book. . . . {The book also features information on} basic safety precautions and essential numbering and measuring systems." Publisher's note

McComb, Gordon
Robot builder's sourcebook. McGraw-Hill 2002 711p il pa $24.95   **629.8**
1. Robots
ISBN 0-07-140685-9   LC 2002-31999
A "listing (with address, phone numbers, web sites) of over 2500 suppliers and manufacturers of robot components, materials, tools, and much more. There are even sources for tracking down older and hard-to-find parts. Also listed are books, journals, magazines, professional societies, and Internet resources, including education sites, competition information, and web sites where hobbyists can find examples of program code. Dozens of sidebars and articles on various robotics topics break up the directory feel. The author also indicates recommended sources based on his own experiences and identifies 'premium' sources that are dedicated to robot hobbyists." Libr J

Menzel, Peter
Robo sapiens: evolution of a new species; [by] Peter Menzel and Faith D'Aluisio. MIT Press 2000 239p il $29.95; pa $19.95 **629.8**
1. Robots 2. Artificial intelligence
ISBN 0-262-13382-2; 0-262-63245-4 (pa)
LC 00-33946
"A Material world book"

Menzel, Peter—*Continued*

This book is a collection of "interviews, essays, illustrations, and numerous photographs of all aspects of current research and actual production locations using robots, some of which approach the 'intelligent' level. The coverage includes more than 100 different researchers and developers with their robots. . . . The interviews are interesting, and the range of applications areas is fascinating; from medicine to housecleaning, from game playing to dancing robots, there is something for everyone in this collection." Libr J

Includes bibliographical references

Moravec, Hans P.

Robot; mere machine to transcendent mind; by Hans Moravec. Oxford Univ. Press 1999 227p il hardcover o.p. paperback available $17.95   **629.8**

1. Robots 2. Artificial intelligence
ISBN 0-19-513630-6 (pa)   LC 97-47328

The author "predicts that artificial intelligence will exceed human intelligence by 2050. He argues further that it is only a matter of time before we have computer simulations that will substitute for human functionality." Libr J

"Moravec's vision, a bewildering but amazingly interconnected set of ideas, is enthusiastically presented and reasonably argued, and will captivate futurists." Booklist

Rosheim, Mark E.

Robot evolution; the development of anthrobotics. Wiley 1994 423p il $140
    629.8

1. Robots
ISBN 0-471-02622-0   LC 94-13687

This book "offers a blend of robotic history, technology, ideas, and trends. It surveys robotics history from the days of Greeks up to Joseph Engelberger, the father of modern robotics." Choice

This "book is highly recommended because of its content, organization, completeness, quality of illustrations, and value." Sci Books Films

Wood, Gaby

Edison's Eve; a magical history of the quest for mechanical life. Knopf 2002 xxviii, 304p il $24; pa $14   **629.8**

1. Robots 2. Artificial intelligence
ISBN 0-679-45112-9; 1-4000-3158-3 (pa)
    LC 2002-25467

The author discusses "the thinking, hoaxes, and inventions that presage contemporary robotics and the current experiments with artificial intelligence." Publisher's note

This is "a lively, elegant and surprising book, packed with curious details and enticing anecdotes." N Y Times Book Rev

630   Agriculture & related technologies

Fatal harvest; the tragedy of industrial agriculture; edited by Andrew Kimbrell. Island Press (Washington, D.C.) 2002 384p il $75; pa $45   **630**

1. Agriculture—Environmental aspects
ISBN 1-55963-940-7; 1-55963-941-5 (pa)
    LC 2001-5800

The contributors to this "volume trace the shift from agrarian to industrial agriculture, assess how and why the latter is now wreaking environmental havoc, and analyze alternative practices." Booklist

Includes bibliographical references

Hurt, R. Douglas

Problems of plenty; the American farmer in the twentieth century. Dee, I.R. 2002 192p (American ways series) $24.95; pa $13.95
    630

1. Agriculture—United States 2. Agriculture—Government policy 3. Agriculture—Economic aspects
ISBN 1-56663-463-6; 1-56663-462-8 (pa)
    LC 2002-67431

The author argues "that farmers face the same fundamental issues they did a century ago: overproduction, low commodity prices coupled with high production costs, and ineffective government intervention that often encourages rather than discourages overproduction. . . . He focuses chiefly on macroeconomic threads into which he incorporates the influence of farm organizations, technological developments (especially the gasoline tractor and later biotechnology), and federal farm programs. . . . Hurt has produced a very solid, readable history which should be useful for collections in general agriculture, agricultural economics and history, or rural sociology." Choice

Includes bibliographical references

631.4   Soil science

Stoll, Steven

Larding the lean Earth; soil and society in nineteenth-century America. Hill & Wang 2002 287p il maps $30; pa $15   **631.4**

1. Soil conservation 2. Agriculture—Environmental aspects 3. Land settlement—United States
ISBN 0-8090-6431-6; 0-8090-6430-8 (pa)
    LC 2002-23279

"Stoll blends biology and history in this . . . study of soil, which performs more ecological functions than most people realize and which is being lost at an alarming rate." Booklist

Includes bibliographical references

631.5   Cultivation and harvesting

Lurquin, Paul F.

High tech harvest; understanding genetically modified food plants. Westview Press 2002 218p il $25   **631.5**

1. Food—Biotechnology 2. Genetic engineering
ISBN 0-8133-3946-4   LC 2002-4938

The author attempts to explain "the scientific foundations of the current controversy over enhancing the quali-

Lurquin, Paul F.—*Continued*

ty and quantity of the world's food supply through genetic engineering. . . . This book's focus on scientific issues as opposed to political posturing gives it a substantive voice in the current noisy debate over genetic manipulation of the foods we all eat." Booklist

Includes bibliographical references

633   Field and plantation crops

Vaughan, J. G. (John Griffith)

The new Oxford book of food plants; [by] J.G. Vaughan and C. Geissler; illustrated by B.E. Nicholson; with additional illustrations by Elisabeth Dowle and Elizabeth Rice. Oxford Univ. Press 1998 xx, 239p il $45; pa $25   **633**

1. Edible plants
ISBN 0-19-854825-7; 0-19-850567-1 (pa)
LC 97-6803
First published 1969 with title: The Oxford book of food plants

This work "describes the origin, distribution, structure, cultivation, utilization, and nutritive value of the world's common food plants, as well as some lesser-known species. . . . All the plants are illustrated in color and each entry gives information on the plant's historical and current uses and in its nutritional value. Cooks, gardeners, naturalists, nutritionists, and dietitians will find the book both absorbing and helpful." Booklist

634.9   Forestry

Taylor, Murry A.

Jumping fire; a smokejumper's memoir of fighting wildfire. Harcourt 2000 445p il hardcover o.p. paperback available $14

    634.9

1. Forest fires 2. Fire fighting
ISBN 0-15-601397-5 (pa)   LC 99-87608

"The oldest smoke jumper in the 60-year history of Alaskan firefighting, Taylor gives a detailed and exciting account of his adventures parachuting into the wilderness to combat wildfires during the summer of 1991." Publ Wkly

635   Garden crops (Horticulture)

1,001 ingenious gardening ideas; new, fun, and fabulous tips that will change the way you garden-forever! Deborah L. Martin, editor; contributing writers, Sally Jean Cunningham [et al.] Rodale Press 1999 342p il map $27.95   **635**

1. Gardening 2. Organic gardening
ISBN 0-87596-809-0   LC 99-6038

This volume "begins with a chapter on making, recycling, and reusing gardening tools, and continues with one on compost tips. Other subjects covered include making mulch (from shredded junk mail); ways to support plants, watering, creating garden paths; extending the growing season by using containers, hanging baskets, cold frames, and pit greenhouses; and starting seeds." Booklist

Includes bibliographical references

Adam, Judith

Landscape planning; practical techniques for the home gardener. Firefly Bks. 2002 224p il $39.95; pa $27.95   **635**

1. Landscape gardening
ISBN 1-55209-620-3; 1-55209-618-1 (pa)

"Addressing the basics like tool selection, planning, design features, hiring a landscaper versus doing it yourself, designer Adam dispenses fundamental advice for a beginning gardener but also incorporates interesting details and ideas relevant to those who are no longer novices. . . . Adam's language is both practical and reflective of a love of gardening. A sound resource for any size collection." Libr J

American Horticultural Society encyclopedia of gardening; editor-in-chief, Christopher Brickell. Rev. US ed., Rev. & expanded ed. DK Pub. 2003 752p il map $60   **635**

1. Gardening—Encyclopedias
ISBN 0-7894-9653-4   LC 2003-279089
First published 1993

"Originally a British publication, this beautifully illustrated encyclopedia . . . has been thoroughly revised for the American gardener. The book covers all aspects of gardening including techniques, plants, and maintenance for indoor and outdoor plants. It also discusses equipping the garden, the garden environment, and plant problems. An outstanding feature of the book is the 3,000-plus color photos that illustrate clearly written instructions and make gardening procedures easy to follow. While extremely valuable as a reference, some patrons will want more time to explore the book so a circulating copy is also recommended." Am Libr {review of 1993 edition}

An "essential purchase for all public libraries." Libr J {review of 1993 edition}

For a fuller review see: Booklist Jan. 1 & 15, 2004

The **American** Horticultural Society gardening manual. Dorling Kindersley 2000 420p il map $40   **635**

1. Gardening
ISBN 0-7894-5952-3   LC 00-22644
Published simultaneously under title: The Royal Horticultural Society gardening manual

"The book is divided into four parts, the first of which covers garden planning, illustrating various garden styles, hardscape choices, and advice on designing the space. . . . Part 2, which is arranged by plant type . . . covers the care and maintenance of the plants. . . . Part 3 offers thumbnail descriptions, including hardiness zones and the mature size of reliable, recommended plants arranged by the season they are at their best. The final part summarizes the routine but essential tasks the gardener should do each month." Libr J

Burpee complete gardener; a comprehensive, up-to-date, fully illustrated reference for gardeners at all levels; [by] Maureen Heffernan [et al.]; edited by Barbara W. Ellis. Macmillan 1995 422p il $29.95   **635**

1. Gardening
ISBN 0-02-860378-8   LC 95-13141

This volume presents "information on 420 annuals, biennials, perennials, bulbs, roses, vegetables, herbs, ground covers, and vines. There's a description of each plant, along with growing instructions and its uses. Other chapters cover designing, starting, planting, and caring

Burpee complete gardener—*Continued*
for a garden; tools and equipment; and pests and diseases." Booklist

Includes bibliographical references

Cuthbertson, Yvonne, 1944-
Beginners' guide to herb gardening. Guild of Master Craftsman Publs.; [distributed by] Sterling 2001 168p il pa $17.95   **635**
1. Herb gardening
ISBN 1-86108-198-7
This covers such topics as designing and planning an herb garden, choosing and planting herbs, propagation and pruning, culinary herbs and herbs for fragrance and color, growing herbs in containers or indoors, and harvesting and drying
This "guide provides a thorough overview of the subject. . . . All the basics are presented in an informative, attractively illustrated format." Booklist

Denckla, Tanya
The organic gardener's home reference; a plant-by-plant guide to growing fresh, healthy food. Storey Communications 1994 273p il hardcover o.p. paperback available $21.95
          635
1. Organic gardening
ISBN 0-88266-839-0 (pa)   LC 93-22835
"A Garden Way Publishing book"
First published 1991 with title: Gardening at a glance
This work "covers vegetables, herbs, fruits and nuts, and pest and disease control. The book has a good introduction on garden stewardship, followed by chapters on vegetables, fruits and nuts, herbs, macro- and microdestructive agents with organic remedies, and allies and companions. For those who want to know about an edible plant, the book describes growth conditions, harvesting, storage requirements, growing tips, and selected varieties." Recomm Ref Books for Small & Medium-sized Libr & Media Cent, 1996
Includes bibliographical references

Encyclopedia of gardens; history and design; editor, by Candice A. Shoemaker. Fitzroy Dearborn Pubs. 2001 3v set $385   **635**
ISBN 1-57958-173-0
At head of title: Chicago Botanic Garden
"Produced under the auspices of the Chicago Botanic Garden . . . this comprehensive resource provides information on garden history and design. The contributors . . . describe and provide analysis of garden-related individuals, places, and topics. The entries are alphabetically arranged and vary in length from a page to more than 10 pages for the entry *United States*. Depending on whether the entry deals with an individual, a place, or a topic, it includes an essay, a biography, a list of works, a chronology, and a bibliography." Booklist

Gardening basics; a complete guide to designing, planting, and maintaining gardens; [by Ken Beckett et al.; consulting editor, John E. Elsley] Sterling 1999 276p hardcover o.p. paperback available $19.95
          635
1. Gardening
ISBN 0-8069-2429-2 (pa)   LC 99-20247
This is "a comprehensive introduction to gardening, with basic information on designing and creating family

gardens, patio gardens, large gardens, and low-maintenance gardens. From fences to hedges to soil types to fundamental plants for most gardens, the contributors bring great expertise and detail." Booklist

Great garden formulas; the ultimate book of mix-it-yourself concoctions for your garden; Joan Benjamin and Deborah L. Martin, editors; contributing writers, Erin Hynes [et al.] Rodale Press 1998 342p il map hardcover o.p. paperback available $17.95   **635**
1. Organic gardening
ISBN 0-87596-848-1 (pa)   LC 98-8915
Organic recipes and techniques for gardeners to "improve their soil, fertilize their plants, reduce weeds and pests, and even concoct a soothing hand cream to use when the work is done. Grouped thematically by chapter, these formulas employ either natural ingredients or simple chemicals such as Epsom salts, and most are easy to make and use." Libr J
Includes bibliographical references

Greenwood, Pippa
AHS garden problem solver. DK Pub. 2002 192p il pa $25   **635**
1. Gardening
ISBN 0-7894-8380-7   LC 2001-47634
First published 2001 in the United Kingdom with title: Garden problem solver
"Greenwood offers practical solutions to such major horticultural problems as when to prune or how to prevent winter weather damage to plants. She also discusses the allergic or aching gardener, lawn discoloration, planting depths for perennials, how to correct design mistakes, and more. Even experienced gardeners will find her volume useful." Libr J

Hortus third; a concise dictionary of plants cultivated in the United States and Canada; initially compiled by Liberty Hyde Bailey and Ethel Zoe Bailey; revised and expanded by the staff of the Liberty Hyde Bailey Hortorium. Macmillan 1976 1290p il $150   **635**
1. Gardening—Dictionaries 2. Botany—Dictionaries 3. Agriculture—Dictionaries
ISBN 0-02-505470-8
First published 1930 with title: Hortus
"More than 34,000 A-to-Z listings cover all plants cultivated in North America, from a botanical point of view. Almost 200 general entries treat such subjects as bulbs, evergreens, and propagation. Illustrated, and has glossary of terms." N Y Public Libr Book of How & Where to Look It Up

Long, Cheryl
Rodale organic gardening solutions; over 500 answers to real-life questions from backyard gardeners; [by] Cheryl Long and the editors of Organic gardening magazine. Rodale 2000 246p il map pa $23.95   **635**
1. Organic gardening
ISBN 0-87596-852-X   LC 00-8144
Contains "advice and answers to more than 500 questions asked by new and veteran backyard gardeners. The easy-to-read chapters are divided into subject categories,

Long, Cheryl—_Continued_
ranging from vegetables, fruits, and herbs to essentials of starting and saving seeds, composting, and maintaining carefree lawns." Booklist
Includes bibliographical references

Pollock, Michael, 1938-
The Royal Horticultural Society shorter dictionary of gardening; [by] Michael Pollock and Mark Griffiths. Macmillan; [distributed by] Trafalgar Sq. 1998 836p il $65 **635**
1. Gardening—Dictionaries
ISBN 0-333-65440-4
Illustrated with photographs, this dictionary provides definitions of gardening terms and describes a variety of plants. Plant nutrition and geographical considerations are addressed

Rodale's all-new encyclopedia of organic gardening; the indispensable resource for every gardener; edited by Fern Marshall Bradley and Barbara W. Ellis. Rodale Press 1992 690p il $29.95; pa $19.95 **635**
1. Organic gardening
ISBN 0-87857-999-0; 0-87596-599-7 (pa)
LC 91-32088
First published 1959 with title: Rodale's encyclopedia of organic gardening
"Entries are cross referenced and include further reading lists, related organizations, and key words. Common and botanical names are listed, and while food plants are entered under their common names, ornamentals and herbs are entered under their botanical names. This is an important, complete, well-arranged, and attractive reference tool." Libr J

Rodale's illustrated encyclopedia of herbs; Claire Kowalchik & William H. Hylton, editors; writers: Anna Carr [et al.] Rodale Press 1987 545p il hardcover o.p. paperback available $17.95 **635**
1. Herbs 2. Medical botany
ISBN 0-87696-964-X (pa)
LC 87-16019
Provides "the history, uses, and cultivation of over 100 herbs, plus information on making teas, lotions, scents, and dyes. Other sections include herbs as houseplants, the history and botany of herbs, and a particularly valuable chapter on the dangers of herbs. The book is attractive and well illustrated." Libr J
Includes bibliographical references

Seymour, Miranda
A brief history of thyme and other herbs; illustrations by Jane Macfarlane. Grove Press 2002 129p il pa $14.95 **635**
1. Herbs
ISBN 0-8021-4008-4
LC 2002-44684
"A compendium of herbs from A to Z. . . . Each piece covers a single herb—from comfrey, angelica, and woad . . . to the more familiar parsley, sage, rosemary, and thyme—and describes its characteristics, the history of its use, and the myth and beliefs attached to it." Publisher's note
Includes bibliographical references

Silber, Mark
Growing herbs and vegetables; from seeds to harvest; [by] Mark and Terry Silber. Knopf 1999 274p il $35 **635**
1. Herb gardening 2. Vegetable gardening
ISBN 0-394-57346-3
LC 98-38189
The authors offer "advice on how to start vegetables and herbs from seed—both indoors and planting seeds directly into garden beds. They discuss the entire process from choosing varieties of seed to starting the seed to planting the beds. Next the authors discuss individual species of vegetables and herbs. . . . A final chapter covers preparing and storing seeds. Useful, easy-to-read charts summarize seeding specifics." Libr J
Includes bibliographical references

Smith, Charles W. G.
The big book of gardening secrets. Storey Communications 1998 341p il hardcover o.p. paperback available $22.95 **635**
1. Gardening 2. Organic gardening
ISBN 1-58017-000-5 (pa)
LC 97-43037
This work covers "ways to improve soil by using organic matter and nutrients; how to make and use compost; ways to propagate plants by cuttings, layering, and dividing; how to grow better cool-season and warm-season vegetables; and how to achieve longer growing seasons and higher yields of vegetables." Booklist
Includes bibliographical references

Smith, Edward C., 1941-
The vegetable gardener's bible; discover Ed's high-yield W-O-R-D system for growing your best garden ever! for all North American gardening regions; foreword by John Storey. Storey Bks. 2000 309p il maps $35; pa $24.95 **635**
1. Vegetable gardening 2. Organic gardening
ISBN 1-58017-213-X; 1-58017-212-1 (pa)
LC 99-52610
Smith "recommends a method of gardening that calls for wide, raised, deep beds, resulting in more vegetables with less work. In part 1 Smith explains how this is achieved. . . . Part 2 deals with soil requirements, making and using compost, and pest and disease control. Part 3 is an A-to-Z listing of vegetables and herbs, with details on growing, harvesting, and storing." Booklist

Springer, Lauren
Passionate gardening; good advice for challenging climates; essays and photography by Lauren Springer & Rob Proctor. Fulcrum 2000 336p il $34.95 **635**
1. Gardening
ISBN 1-55591-348-2
LC 99-49511
The "authors dispense practical advice to gardeners facing difficult growing conditions, such as poor soil, dry shade, etc. . . . [They also] discuss what plants to select—whether working with bulbs or ornamental grasses—and how to use them in conjunction with other plants." Libr J
Includes bibliographical references

Step-by-step yard & garden basics. Better Homes & Gardens Bks. 2000 323p il pa $24.95 **635**
1. Gardening 2. Lawns 3. Landscape architecture
ISBN 0-6962-1288-9
LC 0013-4297
At head of title: Better homes and gardens
"Writer, Liz Ball." Verso of title page

Step-by-step yard & garden basics—_Continued_

This guidebook covers "starting a lawn and growing roses . . . pruning trees and creating a front yard garden. It provides 200 . . . weather-related tips for lawns and lawn alternatives—flowers, vines, edibles, trees, shrubs and ornaments. [It features] more than 750 photos . . . plus a . . . list of tools and supplies needed for each project. Each chapter closes with a seasonal checklist of related chores for yards and gardens in both northern and southern climates." Publisher's note

Wyman, Donald, 1903-1993

Wyman's gardening encyclopedia. new expanded 2nd ed. Macmillan 1986 xxvi, 1221p il $65   **635**

1. Gardening—Encyclopedias 2. Ornamental plants—Encyclopedias

ISBN 0-02-632070-3   LC 86-12509

First published 1961

Contains information on major horticultural practices, including use of pesticides and herbicides, and on ornamental and agricultural plant species. Includes scientific names according to Hortus third, with cross-references for common names

635.9   Flowers and ornamental plants

The **American** Horticultural Society A-Z encyclopedia of garden plants; Christopher Brickell, Judith D. Zuk, editors-in-chief. DK Pub. 1997 1092p il $80   **635.9**

1. Ornamental plants—Encyclopedias

ISBN 0-7894-1943-2   LC 97-10941

First published 1989 in the United Kingdom with title: The Royal Horticultural Society encyclopedia of gardening

This volume is "arranged in four major sections: an introduction to gardening, alphabetical plant directory, extensive glossary, and common name index. Plants are arranged by their botanical names with ample cross references." Libr J

American Horticultural Society encyclopedia of plants and flowers; editors in chief, Christopher Brickell & Trevor Cole. Rev and updated ed. DK Pub. 2002 720p il $60   **635.9**

1. Ornamental plants

ISBN 0-7894-8993-7   LC 2002-73553

First published 1989 in the United Kingdom with title: The Royal Horticultural Society gardeners' encyclopedia of plants and flowers

This "volume features design information, an illustrated catalog of plants arranged by color as well as kind, and a plant dictionary. With over 8000 trees, shrubs, water plants, cacti, succulents, and more profiled here, there is something for nearly every kind of garden." Libr J

Anderton, Stephen

Urban sanctuaries; peaceful havens for the city gardener. Timber Press 2001 144p il $29.95   **635.9**

1. Landscape gardening 2. Garden design

ISBN 0-88192-502-0   LC 2001-27684

This "guide covers basic gardening concerns like soil, light, and water before explaining how to use different design styles to evoke moods." Libr J

"A treasury of photographs wraps around the descriptive, instructional text. . . . Anderton looks at special problems and overall schemes in a manner that should appeal to gardeners of all levels." Booklist

Armitage, Allan M.

Armitage's manual of annuals, biennials, and half-hardy perennials; illustrations by Asha Kays and Chris Johnson. Timber Press 2001 539p il $39.95   **635.9**

1. Annuals (Plants) 2. Perennials

ISBN 0-88192-505-5   LC 00-66789

"Armitage has compiled descriptions and assessments of 245 genera of true annuals as well as plants that behave like annuals in USDA zones 1-7. Focusing on plant identification, successful culture, and garden uses, he discusses 279 species." Publisher's note

"A wonderfully written resource chockablock with gardening information." Booklist

Includes bibliographical references

Brookes, John, 1933-

John Brookes' natural landscapes; how to design and plant a garden in tune with the landscape. DK Pub. 2002 192p il maps pa $19.95   **635.9**

1. Landscape gardening

ISBN 0-7894-8383-1   LC 2002-282568

First published 1998 with title: The new garden

"Brookes explains the concept and design elements of a natural garden. He then presents examples of gardens from around the world representing different climatic conditions. . . . For each, Brookes explores the nature of the particular environment and its gardening challenges; provides details about climate, soil, and terrain; and demonstrates the model garden with plans, plant selections, and photographs to indicate particular landscape and design effects." Libr J

Includes bibliographical references

The **Brooklyn** Botanic Garden gardener's desk reference; Janet Marinelli, general editor; principal illustrations by Stephen K-M. Tim. Holt & Co. 1998 816p il $40   **635.9**

1. Gardening 2. Botany

ISBN 0-8050-5095-7   LC 98-6314

This book "presents 17 horticultural topics plus a glossary, a list of 'essential resources,' and a list of weights, measures, and conversions." Libr J

Bulbs of North America; Jane McGary, editor. Timber Press 2001 251p il maps $34.95   **635.9**

1. Bulbs

ISBN 0-88192-511-X   LC 2001-25348

This volume discusses "bulbous plants (with the exception of orchids) and their growing conditions in the

Bulbs of North America—*Continued*
Northwest, Southwest, and Eastern United States. . . .
Plant details include propagation techniques and
sources." Libr J
Includes bibliographical references

Cave, Yvonne
Succulents for the contemporary garden.
Timber Press 2003 176p il $29.95   635.9
1. Succulent plants
ISBN 0-88192-573-X   LC 2003-271441
"After defining succulents or xerophytes, Cave
presents short discussions of succulent's cultivation, pests
and diseases, and propagation. The real core of this work
is the A-Z of genera, which lists 60 genera and hundreds
of their species. Each entry contains a detailed description, with shape, size, color, and country of origin for
each plant, often with a beautiful close-up photograph
and cultivation and propagation information. . . . This
first-rate reference belongs in . . . libraries everywhere."
Am Ref Books Annu, 2003

The **Complete** encyclopedia of trees and
shrubs; chief consultant, Ernie Wasson.
Thunder Bay Press (San Diego) 2003 816p
il $24.98   635.9
1. Trees 2. Shrubs
ISBN 1-59223-055-5
This encyclopedia describes "some 8,500 plants
around the world, illustrating most with photographs.
Plant descriptions tell whether a tree or shrub can survive
in a particular region of the country, whether it bears
fruit or flowers, how large it can get when it matures,
and how it should be planted and pruned. Entries are arranged in alphabetical order by genus then species, and
the index makes it easy to find a plant by either its scientific or common name. An excellent introductory chapter discusses the geography and habitats of plants, their
structure and function, and the industrial products derived
from them. A chapter covers selecting, planting, pruning,
and propagating plants, and another basic plant classification. One- and two page illustrated guides to leaf, flower,
and fruit types are very helpful. This excellent book for
gardeners will probably become the standard reference
work on trees and shrubs." Choice

Courtier, Jane
Indoor plants; the essential guide to
choosing and caring for houseplants; [by]
Jane Courtier & Graham Clarke; consultant,
Anne Halpin. Reader's Digest Assn. 1997
240p il $30   635.9
1. House plants 2. Indoor gardening
ISBN 0-89577-921-8   LC 96-42046
At head of title: Reader's Digest
This discussion of houseplants includes information on
care, feeding, temperature control, propagation, and pests
and diseases. Display ideas are also provided

Cox, Jeff, 1940-
Landscape with roses; photographs by Jerry
Pavia. Taunton Press 2002 234p il pa $27.95
635.9
1. Roses 2. Landscape gardening
ISBN 1-56158-382-0   LC 2001-43371
The author "incorporates roses into a variety of landscape designs, including the natural garden. His plant
lists suggest optimal rose choices for different effects,
and the author gives full treatment to plant selection,
care, and growth." Libr J

Perennial all-stars; the 150 best perennials
for great-looking, trouble-free gardens.
Rodale Press 1998 344p il map $29.95; pa
$16.95   635.9
1. Perennials
ISBN 0-87596-780-9; 0-87596-889-9 (pa)
LC 97-33811
Each perennial "is highlighted in a two-page spread
that includes information on how to grow, propagation,
picking the right site, and the best companion plants. In
addition to the individual entries, there is a chapter on
'ten steps to starting a perennial garden' and lists of the
perennials categorized by color, size, bloom time, specific conditions, and those that will attract butterflies and
hummingbirds." Libr J
Includes bibliographical references

Darke, Rick
The American woodland garden; capturing
the spirit of the deciduous forest; text and
photography by Rick Darke. Timber Press
2002 377p il $49.95   635.9
1. Gardening 2. Forest plants
ISBN 0-88192-545-4   LC 2002-20474
This "is both a pictorial and narrative account of a
wooded locale in Pennsylvania that the author spent
years studying, as well as a design and planting guide.
. . . He explains the different elements of a woodland
garden and thoroughly describes the plants (features,
zones, and growth ranges) that will perform well. The
author's photographs illustrate both the overall effect and
the beauty of individual plants." Libr J
Includes bibliographical references

The color encyclopedia of ornamental
grasses; sedges, rushes, restios, cat-tails, and
selected bamboos. Timber Press 1999 325p il
maps $49.95   635.9
1. Grasses—Encyclopedias 2. Ornamental plants
ISBN 0-88192-464-4   LC 98-23440
Also available CD-ROM version
This volume "provides details on the biology of grasses as well as their use in garden design. The plant profiles section includes data on native habitat, physical features, culture, and cultivars." Libr J
Includes bibliographical references

Dash, Mike
Tulipomania; the story of the world's most
coveted flower and the extraordinary passions
it aroused. Crown 2000 273p hardcover o.p.
paperback available $13   635.9
1. Tulips 2. Netherlands—History
ISBN 0-609-80765-X (pa)   LC 99-39186
Also available G.K. Hall large print edition
"The centerpiece of this story is a stunning two
months, December 1636 and January 1637, when fortunes were made and lost in the Netherlands—in tulip
bulb futures trading. Stripped to its basics, this would be
a dry case study in an economics textbook. But Dash
adds depth to the tale by including relevant bits of botany, sociology and history, as well as glimpses of the personalities involved in the creation of the tulip market."
Publ Wkly
Includes bibliographical references

Dirr, Michael

Dirr's Hardy trees and shrubs; an illustrated encyclopedia; by Michael A. Dirr. Timber Press 1997 493p il $69.95   **635.9**

1. Trees 2. Shrubs 3. Landscape gardening
ISBN 0-88192-404-0   LC 96-54032

"Depicting both character and traits (fruit, flower, bark, or autumn color), the volume covers over 500 species and some additional varieties and cultivars. Each entry enumerates scientific name, common name, detailed plant description, environmental conditions, place in the landscape, i.e., woodlawn tree or lawn tree, and hardiness zones." Libr J

Dirr's trees and shrubs for warm climates; an illustrated encyclopedia; by Michael A. Dirr. Timber Press 2002 446p il map $69.95   **635.9**

1. Ornamental plants 2. Trees 3. Shrubs 4. Landscape gardening
ISBN 0-88192-525-X   LC 2001-35810

"This volume, in conjunction with *Dirr's Hardy Trees and Shrubs*, completes [the author's] coverage of the woody ornamentals cultivated in North America. In a witty and informative style, Dirr presents botanic, cultural, and landscaping details on over 400 species. Entries are accompanied by magnificent color photos." Libr J

DiSabato-Aust, Tracy

The well-tended perennial garden; planting & pruning techniques. Timber Press 1998 269p il maps $29.95   **635.9**

1. Perennials
ISBN 0-88192-414-8   LC 97-29768

In addition to details on pruning and maintenance this work contains an A-Z encyclopedia of perennials
Includes bibliographical references

Duffield, Mary Rose

Plants for dry climates; how to select, grow, and enjoy; [by] Mary Rose Duffield and Warren D. Jones. rev ed. Perseus Pub. 2001 216p il pa $27.50   **635.9**

1. Desert plants 2. Gardening
ISBN 1-55561-251-2   LC 2001-280011
First published 1981

The authors "explore strategies for gardening in dry or arid climates. . . . They cover climate conditions and predesign concerns such as possible planting restrictions by neighborhood covenants, the use of professional landscaping services, costs, and maintenance. A detailed plant guide identifies more than 300 species best suited to arid gardens, explaining conditions in which they thrive or are compromised." Libr J
Includes bibliographical references

Ellis, Barbara W.

Taylor's guide to annuals; how to select and grow more than 400 annuals, biennials, and tender perennials. Houghton Mifflin 1999 441p il (Taylor's guides to gardening) pa $23   **635.9**

1. Annuals (Plants) 2. Flower gardening
ISBN 0-395-94352-3   LC 99-33188
First published 1986

This guide features information on over five hundred popular plants and cultivars for landscaping and gardening

Taylor's guide to bulbs; how to select and grow 480 species of spring and summer bulbs. Houghton Mifflin 2001 439p il map (Taylor's guides to gardening) pa $23   **635.9**

1. Bulbs 2. Flower gardening
ISBN 0-618-06890-2   LC 00-53884
First published 1986

This guide covers popular bulbs such as daffodils and tulips and provides information on sun and soil requirements

Taylor's guide to perennials; more than 600 flowering and foliage plants, including ferns and ornamental grasses. Houghton Mifflin 2001 490p il map (Taylor's guide to gardening) pa $23   **635.9**

1. Perennials 2. Flower gardening
ISBN 0-395-98363-0   LC 00-33436
First published 1986

Text and numerous illustrations cover popular perennials, their cultivars, ornamental grasses, and ferns

Fenton, James, 1949-

A Garden from a hundred packets of seed. Farrar, Straus & Giroux 2002 125p il $18   **635.9**

1. Gardening
ISBN 0-374-16029-5   LC 2001-54452

The author "selects one hundred plants he would choose to grow from seed. Flowers for color, size, and exotic interest; herbs and meadow flowers; climbing vines, tropical species—Fenton describes one hundred readily available varieties, and tells how to acquire and grow them." Publisher's note

Fenton "has created a wee gem of a book, hardly bigger than the packet of seeds he rhapsodizes about, based on a fascinating premise: given an empty garden and starting solely by seed, what plants would you choose to grow?" Booklist

Fisher, Kathleen

Taylor's guide to shrubs; how to select and grow more than 500 ornamental and useful shrubs for privacy, ground covers, and specimen plantings. Houghton Mifflin 2001 441p il map (Taylor's guides to gardening) pa $23   **635.9**

1. Shrubs
ISBN 0-618-00437-8   LC 00-36941
First published 1987

This guide covers information on popular shrubs and their cultivars and includes growing instructions

Freeman, Mark, 1927-

Gardening in your greenhouse; illustrations by Heather Bellanca. Stackpole Bks. 1998 200p il pa $19.95   **635.9**

1. Greenhouses 2. Gardening
ISBN 0-8117-2776-9   LC 98-4842

Companion volume to Building your own greenhouse (1997)

This work "begins with chapters on types of greenhouses, equipment, soil, air, water, heat, light, pests, and diseases. The rest of the book covers growing seedlings for transplanting into the outdoor garden and raising vegetables and herbs in the greenhouse. Freeman lists vegetable, flower, and herb species suitable for growing to maturity in a greenhouse." Libr J

Hansen, Eric
Orchid fever; a horticultural tale of love, lust, and lunacy. Pantheon Bks. 2000 288p hardcover o.p. paperback available $13

635.9

1. Orchids
ISBN 0-679-77183-2 (pa)   LC 99-44582
This book focuses on "the failure of the 1973 Convention on International Trade in Endangered Species of Wild Fauna and Flora (CITES) to protect orchids." Nat Hist
"Most of Hansen's sketches are fundamentally vehicles for illustrating his serious and provocative argument against CITES (the Convention on International Trade in Endangered Species of Wild Fauna and Flora). According to the author, CITES thwarts orchid conservation and perversely legitimizes plant smuggling by botanical institutions." Libr J

Heffernan, Cecelia
Flowers A to Z; buying, growing, cutting, arranging; photography T.K. Hill. Abrams 2001 160p $49.50; pa $17.95   **635.9**
1. Flowers 2. Flower gardening 3. Flower arrangement
ISBN 0-8109-3348-9; 0-8109-2122-7 (pa)
LC 00-64282
"Recommendations for the best tools and containers are followed by in-depth profiles of 55 of the most popular garden and hothouse flowers, in which Heffernan shares such trade secrets as the flower's vase life and its cost at different seasons. . . .Straightforward directions are supported by close-up photographs." Booklist

Hewitt, Terry
The complete book of cacti & succulents. Dorling Kindersley 1993 176p il hardcover o.p. paperback available $20   **635.9**
1. Cactus 2. Succulent plants
ISBN 0-7894-1657-3 (pa)   LC 93-22107
An illustrated look at the history and cultivation of more than 300 plants. Ideas for containers and display are included

Hill, Lewis, 1924-
Bulbs; four seasons of beautiful blooms; [by] Lewis & Nancy Hill. Storey Communications 1994 218p il hardcover o.p. paperback available $19.95   **635.9**
1. Bulbs
ISBN 0-88266-877-3 (pa)   LC 94-14240
"A Garden Way Publishing book"
The authors "examine bulbs that will bloom in each of four seasons, as well as give guidance on such subjects as forcing bulbs successfully, pests and disease, and naturalizing bulbs. They go into the 'big four' (crocuses, hyacinths, narcissus and tulips) in wonderful detail and pique our interest in lesser-known bulbs." Publ Wkly
Includes bibliographical references

Hillier, Malcolm
Container gardening through the year; photography by Matthew Ward. Dorling Kindersley 1995 160p il hardcover o.p. paperback available $13.95   **635.9**
1. Container gardening
ISBN 0-7894-3296-X (pa)   LC 94-26717
"Hillier advises on how to match surprising plant combinations with an array of containers. Various themes (shape and proportion, texture, and harmonizing or contrasting colors) are represented in lovely color plates that provide a pleasing supplement to Hillier's reassuring guidance." Booklist

The **Hillier** gardener's guide to trees & shrubs; editor, John Kelly; consultant editor, John Hillier. Reader's Digest Assn. 1997 640p il maps $50   **635.9**
1. Trees 2. Shrubs
ISBN 0-89577-973-0   LC 97-4282
First published 1995 in the United Kingdom
"Alphabetically arranged plant directory covering more than 4000 plants with over 400 genres represented. . . . [It discusses] basic biology, theory and practice, selection and purchase, care and maintenance, pest and diseases, plant propagation, plant names, and plant selection." Libr J

Hodgson, Larry
Perennials for every purpose; choose the plants you need for your conditions, your garden, and your taste. Rodale 2000 502p il $29.95; pa $19.95   **635.9**
1. Perennials
ISBN 0-87596-823-6; 0-87596-893-7 (pa)
LC 99-6968
"Preliminary chapters cover the basics such as getting started, creating a design, and keeping plants healthy. The highlight, however, is the 14 chapters that profile perennials that can be used in unique situations (e.g., dry, wet, sunny, shade, easy-care). Each plant profile includes a photograph, a sidebar listing plant characteristics, and informative paragraphs detailing good companion plants, problems and solutions, and the top performers and recommended varieties for each plant." Libr J
Includes bibliographical references

Joyce, David
Topiary and the art of training plants; illustrated by Laura Stoddart. Firefly Bks. 2000 160p il $40; pa $24.95   **635.9**
1. Ornamental plants 2. Landscape gardening
ISBN 1-55209-420-0; 1-55209-442-7 (pa)
The author "explains the technical steps necessary to achieve an array of plant forms that will function in the garden as living sculptures. . . . Joyce's handbook offers an instructive tour that will surely fire up the imagination of keen gardeners. A directory of recommended plants and suppliers is included." Booklist

King, Michael, 1952-
Gardening with grasses; [by] Michael King and Piet Oudolf; foreword by Beth Chatto. Timber Press 1998 152p il $34.95   **635.9**
1. Grasses 2. Landscape gardening
ISBN 0-88192-411-3   LC 97-24467
The authors discuss the application of grasses "in comtemporary settings from lawns to urban landscaping

King, Michael, 1952-—*Continued*
projects. . . . Plant lists for particular situations augment the text, and the many color photographs illustrate the roles grasses can play in a natural garden design." Libr J
Includes bibliographical references

Lloyd, Christopher, 1921-
Color for adventurous gardeners; edited by Erica Hunninger; photographs by Jonathan Buckley. Firefly Bks. 2001 92p il $35; pa $19.95   **635.9**
    1. Gardening
    ISBN 1-55297-532-0; 1-55297-530-4 (pa)
    The author "shows gardeners how to incorporate a range of colors in their plantings. . . . Organizing his chapters by color, Lloyd pays attention not just to flowers but to foliage. Buckley's photographs depict the effectiveness of many unusual, subtle, and beautiful plant combinations." Libr J

Lord, Tony
The encyclopedia of planting combinations; photography by Andrew Lawson. Firefly Bks. 2002 416p il maps $59.95   **635.9**
    1. Gardening—Encyclopedias
    ISBN 1-55209-623-8
    This is a "visual resource of suggested companion plants, botanical names, flowering season, awards, horticultural characteristics, and growing information. A short introduction on general design considerations precedes sections on shrubs and small trees, climbing plants such as clematis, roses, perennials, bulbs, and annuals." Libr J
    "Few guides could rival [this] treatise for the practicality of its structure or for the quality of its information. Each entry contains at-a-glance information on plant companions and cultural requirements, and helpfully lists photographic cross-references. For professionals and amateurs alike, this guide is a godsend." Booklist

Michener, David
Taylor's guide to ground covers; more than 400 flowering and foliage ground covers for every garden situation; [by] David Michener and Nan Sinton. completely rev and updated. Houghton Mifflin 2001 375p il maps (Taylor's guides to gardening) pa $23 **635.9**
    1. Ornamental plants 2. Climbing plants 3. Grasses
    ISBN 0-618-03010-7   LC 2001-39566
    First published 1987 with title: Taylor's guide to ground covers, vines & grasses
    This guide features instructions on how "to stabilize banks and control erosion; to substitute for turf where grass won't grow or is hard to mow; to line curbs and driveways, where salt will damage ordinary plants [and] to enhance a landscape with broad, dramatic sweeps." Publisher's note
    "In this guide luscious photographs of 400 ground covers are paired with information about gardening zones and sun tolerance. . . . The splendor of the photography aside, the no-nonsense approaches are recommended." Am Ref Books Annu, 2003

Ondra, Nancy J.
Taylor's guide to roses; how to select, grow, and enjoy more than 380 roses. Houghton Mifflin 2001 474p il maps (Taylor's guides to gardening) pa $23 **635.9**
    1. Roses
    ISBN 0-618-06888-0   LC 00-68248
    First published 1986
    Text and numerous full color illustrations describe classes of roses including floribundas, grandifloras, miniatures, and climbers. Suggestions are provided for carefree border and ground cover roses. Entries are given for each plant, noting its uses and limitations

Phillips, Ellen
Rodale's illustrated encyclopedia of perennials; [by] Ellen Phillips & C. Colston Burrell. Rodale Press 1993 533p il hardcover o.p. paperback available $19.95   **635.9**
    1. Perennials
    ISBN 0-87596-999-2 (pa)   LC 92-30109
    "The book is divided into three major sections, focusing on designing gardens, growing perennials, and an A-Z dictionary of plant types. . . . The last half of the book is devoted to the individual perennials. One hundred sixty-one flowers, foliage plants, and ground covers are described. Besides descriptions, pointers are given on how to grow them and on their landscape uses. . . . The volume closes with a glossary, lists of sources and organizations, and suggested reading." Booklist

Phillips, Roger, 1932-
Annuals and biennials; the definitive reference with over 1,000 photographs; [by] Roger Phillips & Martyn Rix; assisted by James Compton & Alison Rix; layout by Jill Bryan. Firefly Bks. 2002 288p il pa $24.95   **635.9**
    1. Annuals (Plants)
    ISBN 1-55297-566-5   LC 2002-511785
    "The introduction includes brief information on the book's general organization. Within the work are descriptions of the photographs and explanations of plant names and hardiness as used in the text. Longer sections on the main wild localities of annuals and biennials, the uses of annuals in the garden, and seed raising and cultivation follow. . . . The strengths of *Annuals & Biennials* include the large number of plants it covers, the outstanding photographs, and country of origin information." Am Ref Books Annu, 2003

Pruning & training; Christopher Brickell, editor in chief. DK Pub. 1996 336p il $35   **635.9**
    1. Pruning 2. Plants—Training
    ISBN 1-56458-331-7   LC 96-10836
    At head of title: American Horticultural Society
    "The authors begin by explaining how plants grow and offer general information on the principles of pruning and training and on tools and equipment. They follow this with chapters on ornamental trees, fruit trees, ornamental shrubs, soft fruits . . . climbing plants, and roses. In each category are instructions on basic techniques, initial training, and renovation. Also included is a dictionary of ornamental trees and shrubs. This comprehensive and practical guide lists more than 800 plants and contains more than 1,500 color photographs and illustrations." Booklist

Regel, Pat, 1947-
The houseplant survival guide. Taunton
Press 1997 153p il pa $19.95   **635.9**
1. House plants
ISBN 1-56158-186-0   LC 96-29564
The author offers "advice on houseplant care and plant
selection. Special sections include summering plants outdoors and how to take care of plants when you're on vacation. Regel profiles a few plants but emphasizes general houseplant culture. Especially helpful for beginners."
Libr J

Rice, Graham
Discovering annuals. Timber Press 1999
192p il $34.95   **635.9**
1. Annuals (Plants)
ISBN 0-88192-465-2   LC 99-11612
In addition to presenting his choice of various annuals
the author suggests color combinations and planting
schemes
Includes bibliographical references

Robinson, Peter, 1938-
The American Horticultural Society
complete guide to water gardening. DK Pub.
1997 216p il $35   **635.9**
1. Landscape gardening 2. Ornamental plants
ISBN 0-7894-1478-3   LC 96-30989
This is an "introduction to water gardening, with an
emphasis on the mechanics of design, construction, and
maintenance. A brief catalog of water plants is also included. The text is terse, but supplemented by numerous
color photographs showing the principles under discussion." Sci Books Films

Rodale's illustrated encyclopedia of organic
gardening; Henry Doubleday Research
Association; editor-in-chief, Pauline Pears.
DK Pub. 2002 416p il $39.95   **635.9**
1. Organic gardening
ISBN 0-7894-8908-2   LC 2002-73477
First published 2001 in the United Kingdom with title:
HDRA encyclopedia of organic gardening
This "encyclopedia offers guidance on growing flow-
ers, herbs, and fruits and vegetables the organic, chemi-
cal-free way." Booklist
Includes bibliographical references

Seale, Allan
New life for old gardens; designs for
reviving your garden; illustrations by Lorrie
Lawrence. New Holland; [distributed by]
Sterling 2002 128p il pa $19.95   **635.9**
1. Garden design 2. Landscape gardening
ISBN 1-84330-312-4
First published 1999 in Australia
"This guide gives plans and illustrated instructions for
rejuvenating a mature garden. Also covered: plant sug-
gestions to achieve particular design effects and ideas on
how to work with older plants and existing hardscape."
Libr J

Swindells, Philip
The water garden encyclopedia. Firefly
Bks. 2003 256p il $45; pa $29.95   **635.9**
1. Hydroponics
ISBN 1-55297-715-3; 1-55297-717-X (pa)
    LC 2003-271624
This book "offers a host of ideas for creating and
maintaining many types of water gardens, from small
containers with fountains to re-creations of natural landscape settings. . . . Instructions for making each type of
garden are given through a combination of text and photographs that . . . illustrate each step in the process,
from choosing and marking out the site to finishing the
project with suitable aquatic plants. Accompanying each
design idea are lists of water-loving plants suitable for
that type of garden—including water lilies, reeds and
rushes, bog plants, and floating and submerged aquat-
ics—and there are chapters on how to buy, plant, fertilize, divide, propagate and care for these plants." Publ
Wkly

Taylor's guide to vegetables & herbs.
Houghton Mifflin 1987 479p il (Taylor's
guides to gardening) pa $19.95   **635.9**
1. Vegetable gardening 2. Herb gardening
ISBN 0-395-43092-5   LC 86-20018
"A Chanticleer Press edition"
These volumes are "drawn from 'Taylor's Encyclopedia of gardening'. . . . Each volume begins with general
horticultural information and points of basic botany. Following this is a section of color photographs of individual species arranged as an identification guide. Particular
information on each species is supplied in a third section,
which is also keyed to the color illustrations. This
comprehensive and authoritative set features a lucid text
and easy-to-follow instructions." Booklist

Taylor's master guide to gardening;
editor-in-chief: Frances Tenenbaum;
editors: Rita Buchanan, Roger Holmes;
designer: Deborah Fillion; illustrator: Steve
Buchanan; copy editor: Nancy J. Stabile.
Houghton Mifflin 1994 612p il $60   **635.9**
1. Landscape gardening 2. Gardening
ISBN 0-618-15907-X   LC 93-48865
The first part of this book consists of a discussion of
"30 topics (annuals, perennials, trees, design, color, containers, shade, water, etc.) . . . Next, a 200-page 'Gallery' of recommended plants is arranged alphabetically
by Latin name, with photographs and climate zone numbers. The third section, a 300-page encyclopedia, list
3000 unillustrated species and cultivars with a short paragraph about each." Libr J
Includes bibliographical references

636.089   Veterinary sciences. Veterinary medicine

Black's veterinary dictionary. Rowman &
Littlefield il $129   **636.089**
1. Veterinary medicine—Dictionaries
First published 1928 by Macmillan with title: Black's
veterinary cyclopedia. (20th edition 2002) Title and publisher vary
"Gives comprehensive coverage of terms in veterinary
medicine and animal husbandry, as well as the anatomy
and physiology of domesticated animals. Includes 'infor-

Black's veterinary dictionary—*Continued*
mation on accidents, worldwide disease eradication campaigns, health promotion, the housing of animals, and pest control.'—*Pref.* Includes references and cross-references." Guide to Ref Books. 11th edition

Goldstein, Martin, 1947-
The nature of animal healing; the path to your pet's health, happiness, and longevity. Knopf 1999 357p hardcover o.p. paperback available $16   **636.089**
1. Pets 2. Veterinary medicine
ISBN 0-345-43919-8 (pa)   LC 98-38193
"Goldstein outlines an approach to healing that revolves around strengthening the immune system through diet and such holistic healing techniques as acupuncture and homeopathy, so that an animal can heal itself. . . . This is a life-affirming book that should interest any pet owner." Publ Wkly

Herriot, James
James Herriot's animal stories; with an introduction by Jim Wright; illustrations by Lesley Holmes. St. Martin's Press 1997 142p il   **636.089**
1. Veterinary medicine 2. Domestic animals
LC 97-13863
Available Thorndike Press large print edition
This is a compilation of ten previously published stories from the author's autobiographical accounts of the practice of veterinary medicine in 1930's Yorkshire England

The Merck veterinary manual; a handbook of diagnosis and therapy for the veterinarian. Merck & Co. $32   **636.089**
1. Veterinary medicine—Handbooks, manuals, etc.
Also available online
First published 1955. (8th edition 1998) Periodically revised
"Technical manual for use by veterinarians in the diagnosis and treatment of animal diseases. Authoritative, up-to-date information presented in a brief, convenient format; includes recommended prescriptions." Ref Sources for Small & Medium-sized Libr. 6th edition

Petspeak; you're closer than you think to a great relationship with your dog or cat! by the editors of Pets, part of the family books. Rodale 2000 485p il $29.95; pa $16.95   **636.089**
1. Dogs 2. Cats
ISBN 1-57954-077-5; 1-57954-337-5 (pa)
LC 00-9290
This volume "attempts to explain pet behavior to improve pet-owner relationships. Addressing the habits of both cats and dogs, this book helps make sense out of pet peculiarities and offers practical solutions and advice." Booklist

Pinney, Chris C.
The complete home veterinary guide. McGraw-Hill 2004 736p il $29.95   **636.089**
1. Pets—Diseases 2. Veterinary medicine
ISBN 0-07-141272-7   LC 2003-52668
First published 1992 by Tab Bks. with title: The illustrated veterinary guide for dogs, cats, birds & exotic pets

This guide covers "preventive health care, diet, grooming, training, diseases, traveling with pets, selection, first aid, anatomy, [and] holistic pet care." Publisher's note

Schoen, Allen M.
Kindred spirits; how the remarkable bond between humans and animals can change the way we live. Broadway Bks. 2001 280p hardcover o.p. paperback available $14
636.089
1. Veterinary medicine 2. Pets
ISBN 0-7679-0431-1 (pa)   LC 00-57891
This book "covers the benefits of the human-animal bond; seven ways to foster a spiritual bond with your animal; wellness approaches, such as diet therapy and preventing and treating cancer the natural way; finding veterinary support; and how to let go when there is nothing further that can be done." Libr J
Includes bibliographical references

Tufts University. School of Veterinary Medicine
Animal ER; extraordinary stories of hope and healing from one of the world's leading veterinary hospitals; [by] the Tufts University School of Veterinary Medicine with Vicki Croke. Dutton 1999 194p hardcover o.p. paperback available $12   **636.089**
1. Foster Hospital for Small Animals (Medford, Mass.) 2. Veterinary medicine
ISBN 0-452-28101-6 (pa)   LC 99-32017
Also available G.K. Hall large print edition
An account of medical emergencies at the Foster Hospital for Small Animals
"Good background information and definitions of medical terms help in understanding the complex conditions and courses of treatment described in Croke's taut text." Booklist

636.1 Equines. Horses

Edwards, Elwyn Hartley
The new encyclopedia of the horse; photography by Bob Langrish, Kit Houghton; foreword by Sharon Ralls Lemon. [rev ed] DK Pub. 2000 464p il maps $40   **636.1**
1. Horses
ISBN 0-7894-7181-7   LC 2001-271665
"A Dorling Kindersley book"
First published 1994 with title: The encyclopedia of the horse
The author "traces the evolution of the horse, covering every major breed of horse and pony as well as the contribution the horse has made to civilization—in the wild, at work, at war, and in sport and recreation. . . . The origin, history, and uses of each breed are explained. . . . Specimens of familiar as well as obscure breeds are featured, including Dutch Warmbloods and Camargues, Icelandic and Timor Ponies, Morgans and Shetlands, Andalucian and Lusitano, and the Cutting Horse. . . . Sections on horse management, training, and equipment explain the basics of the proper care of the horse. Information is also included on farriers, feeding, grooming, horse behavior, training techniques, and which equipment to use, including saddles, bridles, and bits." Publisher's note
"A beautiful reference work for the true horse enthusiast." Libr J

Edwards, Elwyn Hartley—*Continued*

Ultimate horse. Rev ed. DK Pub. 2002 272p il $35   **636.1**
1. Horses
ISBN 0-7894-8928-7   LC 2002-71493
First published 1991 with title: The ultimate horse book

The author "delves into the origins of the equine species, the 6,000-year relationship between horse and human, and equine anatomy and behavior. More than 80 breeds of horse and pony are described in . . . two-page spreads highlighting each breed's history and distinctive physical traits and temperaments. Owning and caring for a horse are covered in . . . illustrated discussions of equipment, health, and stable management." Booklist [review of 1991 edition]

"A brilliantly conceived and executed work, this book has captured in color photos what other horse books have previously illustrated in drawings or descriptive text. . . . Recommended for all equine collections. This will be a classic." Libr J

Faurie, Bernadette
The horse riding & care handbook. Lyons Press 2000 160p il $29.95; pa $19.95 **636.1**
1. Horses 2. Horsemanship
ISBN 1-58574-058-6; 1-58574-517-0 (pa)
"Each section contains pictures or diagrams to clarify the explanations, from horse evolution and history with humans to markings, colors, and breeds. Topics such as tack, how to mount, a first riding lesson, and techniques of western riding are all simply described with wonderful graphics." Libr J

Hermsen, Josèe
The horse encyclopedia. Firefly Bks. 1998 c1997 312p il $19.95   **636.1**
1. Horses
ISBN 1-55209-305-0
Translated from the Dutch by Stephen Challacombe
"There are two main sections: one covering breeds of horses and the other dealing with the care of the horse and equestrian activities. Fifty breeds of horses and ponies are described in terms of their origins and physical characteristics. A color photograph accompanies the description of each breed." Booklist

Morris, Desmond
Horsewatching. Crown 1989 c1988 150p il $16   **636.1**
1. Horses
ISBN 0-517-57267-2   LC 88-34019
First published 1988 in the United Kingdom
"Morris answers many questions about the anatomy, history, traditions, physiology, and interrelationships of horses. The inquiries on how a horse sleeps, eats, sees, hears, and mates give way to more complex questions that are just as succinctly answered in a page or two. . . . An intriguing browsing item and reference that will have wide appeal." Booklist

Storey's horse-lover's encyclopedia; an English and Western A-to-Z guide; edited by Deborah Burns. Storey Bks. 2001 471p il $37.50; pa $24.95   **636.1**
1. Horses
ISBN 1-58017-336-5; 1-58017-317-9 (pa)
     LC 00-46329
"The alphabetically arranged entries vary in length from a few sentences to a few pages, with the most thorough coverage going to extensive topics like breeding, foot care, and feeding. Most entries consist of one or two paragraphs and provide a good definition of the term at hand." Libr J
For a fuller review see: Booklist, Sept. 15, 2001

636.2   Ruminants. Bovines. Cattle

Lovenheim, Peter
Portrait of a burger as a young calf; the true story of one man, two cows, and the feeding of a nation. Harmony Bks. 2002 272p il $23; pa $14   **636.2**
1. Cattle 2. Livestock industry
ISBN 0-609-60591-7; 0-609-80544-4 (pa)
     LC 2001-46509
"Purchasing several calves from a herd of cattle on an upstate New York dairy farm, Lovenheim follows their progress from birth to death. . . . By focusing on the people involved at each step of this process, and by neither sentimentalizing nor anthropomorphizing the cattle, Lovenheim offers a graphic portrait of those whose labor and lives feed a nation and a world." Booklist
Includes bibliographical references

636.4   Swine

Rath, Sara
The complete pig. Voyageur Press 2000 144p $29.95   **636.4**
1. Pigs
ISBN 0-89658-435-6   LC 99-45618
"A Town Square book"
This book contains "accounts of pigs in history, art and literature." N Y Times Book Rev
This book is "liberally illustrated with color photographs, lithographs, advertisements, and vintage photographs. A good bibliography rounds out a book that is not only fun but informative." Booklist

636.5   Poultry. Chickens

Grimes, William
My fine feathered friend. North Point Press 2002 84p il $15   **636.5**
1. Chickens
ISBN 0-86547-632-2   LC 2001-59096
This is an account of the author's experiences with a chicken that appeared in his Astoria, Queens backyard
"Grimes deftly sprinkles historical background and anecdotes about chickens into his chronicle of the bird's behavior and the reaction of neighbors and colleagues." Publ Wkly

636.6 Birds other than poultry

Lantermann, Werner, 1956-
The new parrot handbook; everything about purchase, acclimation, care, diet, disease, and behavior of parrots, with a special chapter on raising parrots; 50 color photographs by outstanding animal photographers, 30 drawings by Fritz W. Köhler, and 35 maps indicating distribution; translated from the German by Rita and Robert Kimber; American advisory editor, Matthew M. Vriends. Barron's Educ. Ser. 1986 144p il maps pa $11.95   **636.6**
1. Parrots
ISBN 0-8120-3729-4   LC 86-17289
This book "is divided into two parts, the first about selecting, housing, and caring for a bird; the other devoted to breeding and behavior and including a large section of descriptions of individual species." Booklist
Includes bibliographical references

636.7 Dogs

American Kennel Club
The complete dog book. Howell Bk. House il $32.95   **636.7**
1. Dogs
First published 1935. (19th edition 1997) Periodically revised
"The official guide to 124 AKC registered breeds and their history, appearance, selection, training, care and feeding, and first aid. Some color plates." N Y Public Libr. Ref Books for Child Collect. 2d edition

Budiansky, Stephen
The truth about dogs; an inquiry into the ancestry, social conventions, mental habits, and moral fiber of Canis familiaris. Viking 2000 263p il hardcover o.p. paperback available $13   **636.7**
1. Dogs
ISBN 0-14-100228-X (pa)   LC 00-34966
The author "uses scientific and genetic research to explain why dogs do what they do and are the way they are. In a conversational and entertaining way, the author shows how dog behavior is much more complex and interesting than we have previously thought, and how that behavior is firmly grounded in the breed's successful evolution." Booklist
Includes bibliographical references

Coile, D. Caroline
Encyclopedia of dog breeds; illustrations by Michele Earle-Bridges. Barron's Educ. Ser. 1998 328p il $26.95   **636.7**
1. Dogs—Encyclopedias
ISBN 0-7641-5097-9   LC 98-20368
This source provides profiles and histories of 150 American Kennel Club breeds. Each is covered in two pages with two color photographs. A glossary of terms is included

Coppinger, Raymond
Dogs; a startling new understanding of canine origin, behavior, and evolution; [by] Raymond Coppinger and Lorna Coppinger. Scribner 2001 352p il $26   **636.7**
1. Dogs
ISBN 0-684-85530-5   LC 00-54137
"Taking a biological approach to the study of canine behavior and intelligence, the authors promulgate a theory of how the dog evolved. They explain in depth how the interplay of nature and nurture and critical periods of development produced an animal that has more shapes and sizes and uses than any other. . . . They define what constitutes a breed and criticize today's purebred breeding programs." Libr J
"This important book belongs in all libraries." Booklist
Includes bibliographical references

Coren, Stanley
Why we love the dogs we do; how to find the dog that matches your personality. Free Press 1998 308p il hardcover o.p. paperback available $13   **636.7**
1. Dogs
ISBN 0-684-85502-X (pa)   LC 97-50333
"Coren offers insight into dog-and-owner personality conflicts and shows prospective owners how to choose the dog that is right for them. His book shows why some breeds of dogs turn out to be disasters for certain people, provides personality tests for readers to determine their own distinctive personality types, and includes amusing 'famous pet' anecdotes. Humanitarian, witty, and full of common sense, this is a perfect primer for novice dog owners." Booklist
Includes bibliographical references

Dibra, Bashkim
Dogspeak; how to learn it, speak it, and use it to have a happy, healthy, well-behaved dog; [by] Bash Dibra; with Mary Ann Crenshaw; illustrations by José Dennis. Simon & Schuster 1999 270p il hardcover o.p. paperback available $13   **636.7**
1. Dogs
ISBN 0-684-86548-3 (pa)   LC 99-30194
"Discusses the social, or pack, nature of dogs and explains eight factors important to pack dynamics: the dominance hierarchy aggression, territorial behavior, food guarding, flight behavior, chase behavior, socialization, and vocalization. Throughout, Dibra provides examples of how these factors come into play when training the family dog." Libr J

The **Doctor's** book of home remedies for dogs and cats; over 1,000 solutions to your pet's problems—from top vets, trainers, breeders, and other animal experts; by the editors of Prevention Magazine Health Books; edited by Matthew Hoffman. Rodale Press 1996 403p il hardcover o.p. paperback available $16.95   **636.7**
1. Dogs 2. Cats
ISBN 0-87596-010-4 (pa)   LC 95-46481
This volume "provides hints for everyday pet healthcare. Each section includes descriptions and suggestions for coping with or curing ailments ranging from arthritis to shedding. Almost 100 different symptoms and problems are covered." Libr J

Dodman, Nicholas H.

Dogs behaving badly; an A to Z guide to understanding and curing behavioral problems in dogs. Bantam Bks. 1999 284p hardcover o.p. paperback available $13.95   **636.7**

1. Dogs

ISBN 0-553-37968-2 (pa)   LC 98-46042

The author covers "behavorial traits and problems from A (aggression) to Z (zoonosis) . . . he describes canine foibles such as chewing, barking, and eating everything they can find, he shows how these little problems can mutate into major behavioral abnormalities. Many of the definitions are illustrated with tales from the author's practice treating behavioral problems, making the book extremely user-friendly." Booklist

Dogs: the ultimate care guide; good health, loving care, maximum longevity; edited by Matthew Hoffman; medical advisor, Lowell Ackerman. Rodale Press 1998 450p il hardcover o.p. paperback available $19.95   **636.7**

1. Dogs

ISBN 1-57954-244-1 (pa)   LC 97-46600

Subjects covered range "from bringing up puppy, basic training, and emergency first aid, to easing common complaints." Booklist

Fogle, Bruce

ASPCA complete dog care manual; foreword by Roger Caras. Dorling Kindersley 1993 192p il $24.95   **636.7**

1. Dogs

ISBN 1-56458-168-3   LC 92-53474

This book "presents the history, grooming, training, and showing of canines while emphasizing basic nursing, first aid, and breeding. The author gives commonsense tips, answers myriad questions, promotes owners' responsibility for pets, and discourages buying puppies from pet shops and the cruel practice of docking tails. The . . . text is supplemented by detailed diagrams and clear instructions." SLJ

Dog owner's manual. DK Pub. 2003 288p il pa $25   **636.7**

1. Dogs

ISBN 0-7894-9321-7   LC 2002-41146

This is a "guide to dog care, including first aid, training, and behavior." Publisher's note

"Fogle's succinct writing style packs a tremendous amount of information into each sentence. Heavily illustrated with beautiful photographs." Booklist

New complete dog training manual; [by] Bruce Fogle and Patricia Holden White. Dorling Kindersley 2002 176p il $25   **636.7**

1. Dogs—Training

ISBN 0-7894-8398-X   LC 2001-47931

First published 1994 with title: ASPCA complete dog training manual

This book "shows you how to establish routines, implement commands, break bad habits, and learn how to train various breeds." Publisher's note

The new encyclopedia of the dog; photography by Tracy Morgan. 2nd American ed. Dorling Kindersley 2000 416p il $40   **636.7**

1. Dogs—Encyclopedias

ISBN 0-7894-6130-7   LC 00-22642

First published 1995 with title: The encyclopedia of the dog

This describes over 420 breeds and varieties of dogs, including their histories, temperaments, and physical features

Giffin, James M.

Dog owner's home veterinary handbook; [by] James M. Giffin and Liisa Carlson. 3rd ed. Howell Bk. House 2000 xxvi, 558p il $29.95   **636.7**

1. Dogs—Diseases

ISBN 0-87605-201-4   LC 99-62755

First published 1980

"The authors discuss all of the major organ systems with descriptions of normal functions and infectious and parasitic diseases. Writing in easy-to-understand terms, they identify emergency situations and explain first-aid care. . . . It contains information on Lyme disease and other recently recognized problems." Libr J [review of 1992 edition]

Includes bibliographical references

Herriot, James

James Herriot's dog stories. St. Martin's Press 1986 xxxiii, 426p il $23.95; pa $7.99   **636.7**

1. Dogs

ISBN 0-312-43968-7; 0-312-92558-1 (pa)

LC 86-6637

Herriot "has gathered 50 recollections of canines, some of them sentimental, a few tragic and at least one—the story of a terrier male who abruptly becomes attractive to other males—as odd as anything in the Decameron. Herriot recalls that in his student days domestic animals were customarily listed in descending order of importance: horse, ox, sheep, pig, dog. In the latest work, he has brought his favorites to the front and given them a new leash on life." Time

Lane, Marion

The Humane Society of the United States complete guide to dog care; [by] Marion S. Lane and the staff of the Humane Society of the United States. Little, Brown 1998 390p il $24.95; pa $16.95   **636.7**

1. Dogs

ISBN 0-316-51305-9; 0-316-59547-0 (pa)

LC 97-44392

"Emphasizing the importance of companionship between dogs and owners, this guide offers activities and ideas for including your dog in your lifestyle as much as possible." Booklist

McGinnis, Terri

The well dog book; the classic, comprehensive handbook of dog care; illustrated by Pat Stewart. rev ed. Random House 1991 287p il pa $19   **636.7**

1. Dogs 2. Dogs—Diseases

ISBN 0-679-77001-1 (pa)   LC 91-52680

First published 1974

McGinnis, Terri—*Continued*

This illustrated manual introduces canine anatomy and offers training, grooming and nutrition guidelines. Diagnostic and preventive information is included

Monks of New Skete

How to be your dog's best friend; the classic training manual for dog owners; [by] the Monks of New Skete. completely rev and updated, 2nd ed. Little, Brown 2002 336p il $25.95 **636.7**

1. Dogs—Training
ISBN 0-316-61000-3   LC 2002-102894
First published 1978

This guide to dog training focuses on important aspects of the canine-human relationship, including discipline and choosing a breed that fits the owner's personality and lifestyle

This book's "unique value lies in the monks' insights and thoughts about the human-canine bond. . . . Without devolving into New Age psychobabble, the monks make philosophical and spiritual observations that no dog lover could resist." Publ Wkly

Includes bibliographical references

Morris, Desmond

Dogs: the ultimate dictionary of over 1,000 dog breeds. Trafalgar Sq. 2002 752p il $24.95 **636.7**

1. Dogs
ISBN 1-57076-219-8

This reference on dog breeds from around the world discusses over 1000 breeds accompanied by 600 illustrations

"Although the sheer number of dog breeds cited would be sufficient to make this volume a highly recommended purchase for all public libraries, Morris's painstaking scholarship and research truly set the book apart from standard breed dictionaries." Libr J

Palika, Liz, 1954-

K.I.S.S. guide to raising a puppy; foreword by Alan Gomberg. DK Pub. 2002 288p il (Keep it simple series) pa $20 **636.7**

1. Dogs
ISBN 0-7894-8947-3   LC 2001-58418

This guide provides instructions on feeding, grooming, exercising, trips to the vet, and other important aspects of caring for a puppy

Includes bibliographical references

Ross, John

Adoptable dog; teaching your adopted pet to obey, trust, and love you; [by] John Ross and Barbara McKinney. Norton 2003 353p il $24.95 **636.7**

1. Dogs
ISBN 0-393-05079-3   LC 2002-13395

This is a "guide for the lay reader who wants to turn the adopted shelter dog into a well-behaved family pet. The authors cover such topics as evaluating a shelter dog as a prospective pet, equipment, grooming, housebreaking, loose leash walking, and basics obedience commands: sit, down, come, and stay." Libr J

"This is a useful book that should be read by people before they start looking at dogs and 'falling in love' with a particular one." Publ Wkly

Includes bibliographical references

Taylor, David, 1934-

The ultimate dog book; consulting editor, Connie Vanacore; commissioned photography by Dave King, Jane Burton. Simon & Schuster 1990 240p il $29.95 **636.7**

1. Dogs
ISBN 0-671-70988-7   LC 90-32242
"A Dorling Kindersley book"

"Each representative breed . . . is reproduced in a large, vibrantly colored photograph, while smaller illustrations embellish the information on the canine's history, temperament, and physical characteristics. The concluding chapters address dog care, maintenance, and breeding. Highly recommended for browsing and reference." Booklist

Thomas, Elizabeth Marshall, 1931-

The social lives of dogs; the grace of canine company; illustrated by Jared Taylor Williams. Simon & Schuster 2000 253p hardcover o.p. paperback available $13.95 **636.7**

1. Dogs
ISBN 0-7434-2236-8 (pa)   LC 99-87357
Also available G.K. Hall large print edition

Thomas discusses how dogs interact with various members of the household, including other dogs and pets of other species

The author "draws upon her extensive knowledge of the behavior and treatment of feral dogs in East Africa to explain the domestication of the dog. Appendixes containing advice on controlling dogs' behavior and on keeping parrots as pets conclude this entertaining and informative book." Libr J

Wilcox, Bonnie

Atlas of dog breeds of the world; [by] Bonnie Wilcox and Chris Walkowicz. T.F.H. Publs. $89.95 **636.7**

1. Dogs
First published 1989. (5th edition 1995) Periodically revised

"Contains chapters on eight groups of dogs . . . describing general characteristics and historical evolution and including a complete listing of breeds in the group. The main section (Dogs of the world) is arranged alphabetically by breed name. Includes complete list of sources, contributors, and owners of the dogs portrayed as well as breed name." Guide to Ref Books. 11th edition

636.8 Cats

The **Cornell** book of cats; a comprehensive and authoritative medical reference for every cat and kitten; by the faculty, staff, and associates, Cornell Feline Health Center, College of Veterinary Medicine, Cornell University; edited by Mordecai Siegal; consulting editor, James R. Richards. 2nd ed completely updated & rev. Villard Bks. 1997 xxx, 465p il $35 **636.8**

1. Cats—Diseases
ISBN 0-679-44953-1   LC 96-41131
First published 1989

The Cornell book of cats—*Continued*
This medical reference for the care of cats includes information on nutrition, reproduction, genetics, first aid, breeds, anatomy, medical advances, preventive care, etc.

Edney, A. T. B.
ASPCA complete cat care manual; [by] Andrew Edney; foreword by Roger Caras. Dorling Kindersley 1992 192p il $25 **636.8**
1. Cats
ISBN 1-56458-064-4   LC 92-52783
"Cat care is made easy through step-by-step photographs that illustrate grooming, handling, detecting illness, first aid, and other concerns. Difficult-to-explain procedures, such as how to administer medication or transport an injured cat, are clearly understandable." Libr J

Includes bibliographical references

Fogle, Bruce
The new encyclopedia of the cat. DK Pub. 2001 288p il maps $35 **636.8**
1. Cats
ISBN 0-7894-8021-2   LC 2001-275714
First published 1997 with title: The encyclopedia of the cat
"Opening sections cover the cat family, cats and people, and feline design and behavior. Entries on more than 60 longhair and shorthair breeds include discussions on the ancestry of each breed, shape and form, colors and patterns, and standards and temperament. Over 1300 beautiful color illustrations make this an essential purchase for both circulating and reference collections." Libr J [review of 1997 edition]
Includes bibliographical references

Herriot, James
James Herriot's cat stories; with illustrations by Lesley Holmes. St. Martin's Press 1994 161p $17.95 **636.8**
1. Cats
ISBN 0-312-11342-0   LC 94-20131
A "collection of favorite cat tales from Herriot's veterinary practice. Retired after over 50 years in practice, Herriot continues to entertain young and old alike with his storytelling ability. His current collection includes 'Alfred, the Sweet-Shop Cat,' 'Boris and Mrs. Bond's Cat Establishment,' 'Moses Found Among the Rushes,' and others." Libr J

Masson, J. Moussaieff (Jeffrey Moussaieff), 1941-
The nine emotional lives of cats; a journey into the feline heart. Ballantine Bks. 2002 xxv, 259p il $24.95 **636.8**
1. Cats
ISBN 0-345-44882-0   LC 2003-266414
Also available Thorndike Press large print edition
In this book the author explores "the range of feline emotions and relationships that take place between cats and humans. . . . He addresses in each chapter a particular feline emotion (narcissism, love, contentment, attachment, jealousy, fear, anger, curiosity, and playfulness), using the comings and goings of his five cats as examples. . . . This should be very popular with cat lovers everywhere, especially those who want something more than a personal account but less than a behavioral treatise. Highly recommended." Libr J
Includes bibliographical references

McGinnis, Terri
The well cat book; the classic comprehensive handbook of cat care; illustrated by Pat Stewart. 2nd ed. Random House 1993 325p il hardcover o.p. paperback available $19 **636.8**
1. Cats 2. Cats—Diseases
ISBN 0-679-77000-3 (pa)   LC 92-56834
First published 1975
The author provides "professional advice on nutrition, diagnosing illnesses, treating injuries, and preventing health problems. . . . [She also includes] information on new illnesses such as feline infectious peritonitis and feline immunodeficiency virus, and she clearly explains their symptoms. Among her work's other useful features is the chapter on emergency first aid. . . . Highly recommended for all pet care collections." Libr J

Morris, Desmond
Cat watching. Crown 1987 c1986 136p hardcover o.p. paperback available $8.95 **636.8**
1. Cats
ISBN 0-517-88053-9 (pa)   LC 86-23938
First published 1986 in the United Kingdom
Spine title: Catwatching
In question-and-answer format, the author examines mating, hunting behavior and physical characteristics of cats

Richards, James R., 1960-
ASPCA complete guide to cats. Chronicle Bks. 1999 368p il pa $24.95 **636.8**
1. Cats
ISBN 0-8118-1929-9   LC 99-12354
This guide offers advice on feeding, grooming, veterinary care, litterbox training, and the special needs of kittens, old cats, and cats from shelters. The text is accompanied by over 450 illustrations and photos

Wilbourn, Carole, 1940-
The total cat; understanding your cat's physical and emotional behavior from kitten to old age. HarperCollins Pubs. 2000 xxxvii, 233p il pa $14 **636.8**
1. Cats
ISBN 0-380-79051-3   LC 00-40846
Wilbourn presents "general information about the care, feeding, and medical needs of cats. . . . From the selection of a cat by its age and personality type, along with suggestions for finding a good match for the character and lifestyle of the potential owner, to fitting a cat into a household that may include other pets to causes and cures of less desirable feline behavioral traits, the author covers all aspects of cat behavior." Booklist

638 Insect culture

Hubbell, Sue
A book of bees—and how to keep them; drawings by Sam Potthoff. Random House 1988 193p il o.p.; Houghton Mifflin paperback available $13 **638**
1. Bees
ISBN 0-395-88324-5 (pa)   LC 88-42655
"Following the seasons of the beekeeper's year [the author] imparts practical hints along with literary, mythological, entomological, and anecdotal commentary." Booklist

639 Hunting, fishing, conservation, related technologies

Greenlaw, Linda, 1960-
The lobster chronicles; life on a very small island. Hyperion 2002 238p $22.95; pa $13.95   **639**
1. Lobster fisheries 2. Isle au Haut (Maine)
ISBN 0-7868-6677-2; 0-7868-8591-2 (pa)
In this companion to The hungry ocean, the author gives "up swordfishing to return to her parents' home on Isle Au Haut off the coast of Maine and fish for lobster. . . . She intersperses her narrative with plenty of eccentrics who live on her tiny island. . . . Self-speculation and uncertainties . . . nicely balance her delightfully cocky essays of island life." Publ Wkly

639.2 Commercial fishing, whaling, sealing

Greenlaw, Linda, 1960-
The hungry ocean; a swordboat captain's journey. Hyperion 1999 265p map $22.95; pa $14   **639.2**
1. Fishing
ISBN 0-7868-6451-6; 0-7868-8541-6 (pa)
    LC 98-51985
The author "details a 30-day swordfishing trip from Gloucester to the Grand Banks. Greenlaw describes her boat, equipment, and various electronic gear, including the 'temperature bird' that is lowered to measure the temperature at the fishing depth, as well as her technique for finding just the right area to fish. . . . An exciting and detailed look inside the commercial fishing industry." Libr J

Kurlansky, Mark
Cod; a biography of the fish that changed the world. Walker & Co. 1997 294p il maps $21   **639.2**
1. Codfish 2. Commercial fishing 3. Cooking—Fish
ISBN 0-8027-1326-2   LC 97-12165
Also available in paperback from Penguin Bks.
Kurlansky discusses the history of commercial cod fishing and the plight of the Atlantic fish and fisheries today as the cod faces extinction
This book offers "maximum readability, plenty of handsome illustrations, and a 40-page appendix of superlatively annotated recipes." Booklist
Includes bibliographical references

639.34 Aquariums

Mills, Dick
Aquarium fish; photography by Jerry Young. Dorling Kindersley 1993 304p il (Eyewitness handbooks) hardcover o.p. paperback available $20   **639.34**
1. Fishes 2. Aquariums
ISBN 1-56458-293-0 (pa)   LC 93-3155
This illustrated "guide provides general information on the choice and care of fish, natural habitats, required aquarium conditions, and specific details on freshwater and marine tropical and coldwater fishes. Data for each species include family, common name, maximum adult size, physical characteristics of species, habitat, range, geographical distribution, peculiarites of species, alternative names, and a small, attractive photograph showing the male of the species." Libr J

Sandford, Gina
Aquarium: owner's manual. DK Pub. 1999 256p il pa $17   **639.34**
1. Aquariums
ISBN 0-7894-4614-6   LC 99-27002
New edition in preparation
Published simultaneously under title: The complete aquarium handbook
Full color pictures accompany information on creating, stocking, and maintaining a home aquarium. Types of fish, water, and aquarium environments are discussed
Includes bibliographical references

640 Home economics and family living

Heloise
All-new hints from Heloise; a household guide for the '90s. Putnam 1989 416p il pa $13.95   **640**
1. Home economics
ISBN 0-399-51510-0   LC 88-33651
Also available Hints from Heloise (1980) from Avon Bks. $12 (ISBN 0-380-53066-X)
"A Perigee book"
The author "offers a mother lode of salient tips on cleaning, child-care, pet care, traveling and much more. . . . She is at her most ingenious and credible in the kitchen and on household maintenance." Publ Wkly

Huff, Darrell
The complete how to figure it; [by] Darrell Huff with Kristy Maria Huff; illustrated by Carolyn R. Kinsey; designed by Kristy Maria Huff. Norton 1996 470p il hardcover o.p. paperback available $17.95   **640**
1. Mathematics 2. Personal finance
ISBN 0-393-31924-5 (pa)   LC 95-46480
The author presents "solutions (with and without a pocket calculator) to the . . . calculations we need to make day by day, from budgeting current expenses to planning for retirement, from purchasing a home to travel, sports, and entertainment." Publisher's note
"This makes an ideal browser on a rainy afternoon, and it is especially friendly to those who can't quite cope with calculators." Booklist

Marken, Bill
How to fix (just about) everything. Free Press 2002 551p il $27   **640**
1. Repairing 2. Houses—Maintenance and repair
ISBN 0-7432-3468-5   LC 2002-21451
Pagination applies to instruction titles
"More than 550 step-by-step instructions for everything from fixing a faucet to removing mystery stains to curing a hangover." Title page
"Marken's manual is aimed at the amateur needing brief, step-by-step instructions. Entries on repairing objects, improving skills, and even mending relationships are included in 13 broad categories." Libr J

Mendelson, Cheryl
Home comforts; the art and science of
keeping house; illustrations by Harry Bates.
Scribner 1999 884p il $35   **640**
1. Home economics
ISBN 0-684-81465-X   LC 99-37555
Mendelson includes "sections on food, clothing, clean-
liness, daily life, and safety, with information on negligence, domestic employment laws, insurance, and even
the impact of clothing label laws on our laundry. Preferred methods are explained in detail, and some alternatives are offered for those who need to compromise. This
is a valuable tool." Libr J
Includes bibliographical references

641   Food and drink

Allen, Stewart Lee
In the devil's garden; a sinful history of
forbidden food. Ballantine Bks. 2002 315p
$24; pa $13.95   **641**
1. Food 2. Eating customs 3. Cooking 4. Menus
ISBN 0-345-44015-3; 0-345-44016-1 (pa)
     LC 2001-43882
"Different cultures and religions have defined certain
foods as taboo over the centuries. Allen examines these
taboos and looks for possible explanations for forbidding
some otherwise edible foodstuffs from human consumption." Booklist
"The historical and cultural links between food, sex
and religion make for fascinating reading." Publ Wkly
Includes bibliographical references

Bourdain, Anthony
A cook's tour; in search of a perfect meal.
Bloomsbury Press 2001 274p $25.95   **641**
1. Cooking 2. Food
ISBN 1-58234-140-0   LC 0001-52428
Also available in paperback from Ecco Press
This is an "account of the author's global search for
the 'perfect mix of food and context' that takes the read-
er to the culinary corners of the earth: from Vietnam (a
live cobra heart) and Japan (poisonous blowfish) to Eng-
land (roasted bone marrow) and Scotland (deep-fried
Mars bar)." N Y Times Book Rev

Wright, Clifford A., 1951-
A Mediterranean feast; the story of the
birth of the celebrated cuisines of the
Mediterranean, from the Merchants of Venice
to the Barbary Corsairs: with more than 500
recipes. Morrow 1999 xxiv, 815p il $35
     641
1. Food 2. Eating customs 3. Mediterranean region—
Social life and customs
ISBN 0-688-15305-4   LC 98-49155
Wright "traces the influences and interconnections
among the food and cooking of the diverse cultures that
ring the Mediterranean Sea. . . . A unique work, this is
recommended for history as well as cookery collections."
Libr J
Includes bibliographical references

641.03   Food and drink— Encyclopedias and dictionaries

Ayto, John
An A-Z of food and drink; with a preface
by Alan Davidson. Oxford Univ. Press 2002
375p $30   **641.03**
1. Food 2. Beverages 3. Cooking
ISBN 0-19-280352-2   LC 2002-510043
First published 1993 with title: The diner's dictionary
This "collection of about 1,200 terms from all countries describes the origin, meaning, and development of
words about food and traces changes in ingredients,
cooking, and diet." Choice

International dictionary of food & cooking;
compiled by Charles G. Sinclair. Fitzroy
Dearborn Pubs. 1998 594p $60   **641.03**
1. Food—Dictionaries 2. Cooking—Dictionaries
ISBN 1-57958-057-2
This work contains over "24,000 words and terms that
professional chefs and amateur cooks encounter in their
kitchens. The entries, varying in length from a few words
to a paragraph at most, are arranged alphabetically, with
the country of origin for foreign words and phrases indicated within those entries." Libr J

Larousse gastronomique; with the assistance
of the Gastronomic Committee, president
Joël Robuchon. [rev ed] Potter 2001 1350p
il $75   **641.03**
1. Cooking 2. Food—Encyclopedias 3. French cooking
ISBN 0-609-60971-8   LC 2001-32863
Original French edition published 1938 under the authorship of Prosper Montagné; first United States edition
1961
This book "presents the history of foods, eating, and
restaurants; cooking terms; techniques from elementary to
advanced; a review of basic ingredients with advice on
recognizing, buying, storing, and using them; biographies
of important culinary figures; and recommendations for
cooking nearly everything." Publisher's note
This "will probably be the first choice of cooks who
need information on culinary terms and cooking techniques, and . . . it contains more than 3500 recipes and
an array of gorgeous color photographs. An indispensable
part of any culinary reference collection, this is highly
recommended for all libraries." Libr J

The Oxford companion to food. Oxford
Univ. Press 1999 829p il $65   **641.03**
1. Food—Dictionaries
ISBN 0-19-211579-0
Also available in paperback from Penguin with title:
The Penguin companion to food
This work contains "2650 alphabetically arranged entries as well as 39 longer articles on staples such as rice.
. . . Everything from individual ingredients, cooking
terms, and prepared dishes to national cuisines and cookbooks and their authors is covered. Each entry is written
in a clear, engaging style often seasoned with a dash of
wit." Libr J

641.2 Beverages (Drinks)

Gaiter, Dorothy J.
The Wall Street journal guide to wine; new and improved; [by] Dorothy J. Gaiter & John Brecher. 2nd ed. Broadway Bks. 2002 345p $26 **641.2**
1. Wine and wine making
ISBN 0-7679-0814-7   LC 2002-74450
First published 1999
The authors "help readers develop their own insight and taste by giving information and advice regarding wines they might enjoy. The white wine section includes some unusual varietals, while a little background about Merlot's recent popularity, a decent explanation of 'first growth,' a discussion of Dolcetto, and some worthy predictions about Shiraz are given in the red wine chapters. Three short sections cover rosés, sparkling wines, and dessert wines. Each chapter concludes with a list of recommended wines/vintners and approximate prices." Libr J [review of 1999 edition]

Kolpan, Steven
Exploring wine; the Culinary Institute of America's complete guide to wines of the world; [by] Steven Kolpan, Brian H. Smith, Michael A. Weiss. 2nd ed. Wiley 2001 820p il maps $65 **641.2**
1. Wine and wine making
ISBN 0-471-35295-0   LC 2001-24345
First published 1996 by Van Nostrand Reinhold
The authors "cover wine tasting, wine making, and the wines of the world. They provide information about health and pairing wine with food and offer detailed coverage of service, storage, and purchasing, including buying wine at auctions." Booklist
Includes bibliographical references

Larousse encyclopedia of wine; general editor, Christopher Foulkes. Ed fully updated in 2001 by Larousse. Larousse 2001 624p il maps $45 **641.2**
1. Wine and wine making
ISBN 2-03-585013-4   LC 2003-269288
First published 1994
This book is a "reference to the world's vineyards and to the enjoyment of wine. . . . Full-color photographs, maps and drawings illustrate the country-by-country, vineyard-by-vineyard descriptions of all the world's wine regions from the United States and Europe to New Zealand and the Orient. . . . The book also details the intricacies of pairing wine with food, wine selection and etiquette, as well as historical and technical information about how wine is made." Publisher's note

Peynaud, Emile
The taste of wine; the art and science of wine appreciation; [by] Emile Peynaud; with the assistance of Jacques Blouin; translated from the French by Michael Schuster; with a foreword by Michael Broadbent. 2nd ed. Wiley 1996 xxi, 346p il $95 **641.2**
1. Wine and wine making
ISBN 0-471-11376-X   LC 96-24181
Original French edition 1980; first English translation published 1987 in the United Kingdom

This volume "covers the visual aspects of wine, sense of smell, taste and tasters, and errors in perception. It includes a wine tasting vocabulary and other elements essential to evaluating a wine's quality." Publisher's note
"Long considered the definitive tome on winetasting." Libr J
Includes bibliographical references

641.3 Food

The **Cambridge** world history of food; editors, Kenneth F. Kiple, Kriemhild Coneè Ornelas. Cambridge Univ. Press 2000 2v set $190 **641.3**
1. Food—History
ISBN 0-521-40216-6   LC 00-57181
"The two volumes are arranged in eight parts covering the diet of early man, staple foods, dietary liquids, nutrients and food-related disorders, food and drink around the world, nutrition and health, current food-related issues and concluding with a dictionary of plant foods. . . . The Cambridge World History of Food is a thorough study of a topic that is eternally popular. It should become a standard source in reference collections." Booklist
Includes bibliographical references

Chilies to chocolate; food the Americas gave the world; edited by Nelson Foster & Linda S. Cordell. University of Ariz. Press 1992 191p hardcover o.p. paperback available $15.95 **641.3**
1. Edible plants
ISBN 0-8165-1324-4 (pa)   LC 92-5243
Essays explore the biological and cultural history of crops cultivated by indigenous peoples of the Americas and trace their dispersion into the fields and kitchens of the Old World
Includes bibliographical references

Fernández-Armesto, Felipe
Near a thousand tables; a history of food. Free Press 2002 258p $25; pa $14 **641.3**
1. Food—History
ISBN 0-7432-2644-5; 0-7432-2740-9 (pa)
LC 2002-23318
The author "charts how the evolution of human culture is directly connected to the way food is obtained. The logistics of agriculture and hunting have shaped notions of gender and community; food is often integral to concepts of the sacred in a society; and the 'loneliness of the fast food eater'—aided by such inventions as the microwave—has become emblematic of contemporary society's fragmentation." Publ Wkly
This is a "well-written, thought-provoking overview of food history." Libr J
Includes bibliographical references

Goldstein, Myrna Chandler, 1948-
Controversies in food and nutrition; {by} Myrna Chandler Goldstein and Mark A. Goldstein. Greenwood Press 2002 260p il (Contemporary controversies) $45 **641.3**
1. Food 2. Nutrition
ISBN 0-313-31787-9   LC 2002-69605
This book explains varying opinions and underlying issues that surround such topics as popular diets, vegetar-

Goldstein, Myrna Chandler, 1948-—*Continued*

ianism, food irradiation, organic and imported food, vitamin supplementation, food allergies, and genetic modifications

"For anyone confused about the barrage of messages we get every day about nutrition, this is an excellent book. . . . Thoroughly enjoyable to read, the book is designed as a high school or college reference text, but it would also interest the general public." Choice

Includes bibliographical references

Harrison, Jim, 1937-

The raw and the cooked; adventures of a roving gourmand. Grove Press 2001 271p $25; pa $13   **641.3**

1. Food

ISBN 0-8021-1698-1; 0-8021-3937-X (pa)

LC 2001-33464

"The essays—filled with sightings of big names (Jack Nicholson, Peter Mattiessen)—take readers from meals in Harrison's homes in northern Michigan and New Mexico, to delicacies in New York, Los Angeles and Paris. . . . He is a lover of duck thighs, pigs' feet, calves' brains, foie gras, confit, sweetbreads, game birds and mussels, served with exquisite wines and 'shovels of garlic.' Perhaps not surprisingly, Harrison also ruminates on gout, weight and indigestion." Publ Wkly

Hemphill, Ian

The spice and herb bible; a cook's guide. Robert Rose 2002 498p il $35; pa $22.95   **641.3**

1. Herbs 2. Spices

ISBN 0-7788-0047-4; 0-7788-0042-3 (pa)

This "reference work covers more than 95 herbs and spices, ranging from ajowan to zedoary and including both the familiar and the exotic. The detailed entries . . . provide common and botanical names, origin and history, 'flavor group,' and tips on buying, storage, and use, along with a wealth of other information; most also include a recipe, and there are color photographs of the herbs and spices as well. . . . This invaluable reference is essential for most collections." Libr J

Includes bibliographical references

McHughen, Alan, 1954-

Pandora's picnic basket; the potential and hazards of genetically modified foods. Oxford Univ. Press 2000 277p il $36   **641.3**

1. Food

ISBN 0-19-850674-0   LC 00-25169

The author explains the technologies involved in the production of genetically modified foods and compares them with other methods of plant breeding and production. He also examines the regulatory processes established to protect consumers. The views of scientists, entrepreneurs, consumer advocates, and environmentalists are discussed

Includes bibliographical references

Rinzler, Carol Ann

The new complete book of food; a nutritional, medical, and culinary guide; with an introduction by Jane E. Brody; foreword by Michael D. Jensen. Facts on File 1999 440p $49.50; pa $19.95   **641.3**

1. Food 2. Nutrition

ISBN 0-8160-3987-9; 0-8160-3988-7 (pa)

LC 99-21200

First published 1987 by World Almanac with title: The complete book of food

This resource contains entries on more than 200 separate foods. Each entry contains: a nutritional profile of basic components, vitamins, and minerals; tips on how to buy, store, handle and prepare foods while maximizing their nutritional value; medical uses of foods; dietary restrictions; food and drug interactions

Includes bibliographical references

The new complete book of herbs, spices, and condiments; foreword by Wendell L. Combest. Facts on File 2001 422p $49.50; pa $19.95   **641.3**

1. Herbs 2. Spices 3. Condiments

ISBN 0-8160-4152-0; 0-8160-4153-9 (pa)

LC 00-32164

First published 1990 with title: The complete book of herbs, spices, and condiments

This volume pulls together a "group of ingestible substances to explain how they affect the human body. Along with popular healing herbs and food supplements such as *echinacea* and *St. John's wort*, entries summarize the good and bad effects of such substances as *allspice, coffee, lemon, salsa,* and *soy sauce*. The text concludes with an appendix of herbs, like foxglove, that are used in commercial drugs and a listing of such toxic plants as blue flag and wormwood." Booklist

Includes bibliographical references

Shulman, Martha Rose

Foodlover's atlas of the world. Firefly Bks. 2002 288p il $35   **641.3**

ISBN 1-55297-571-1   LC 2003-535048

"This overview of food around the world is divided into 'Europe,' 'Africa and the Middle East,' 'Asia and Australia' and 'the Americas,' and is subdivided by country and region. In each section Shulman discusses the staple foods, culinary history, specialties and mealtime customs of each area. Sidebars spotlight signature dishes and special ingredients, beverages and . . . concoctions. . . . The book concludes with a sampling of 80-plus recipes from every continent." Publ Wkly

"An excellent resource for geography, foreign language, and home-economics students." SLJ

Includes bibliographical references

641.4   Food preservation and storage

Costenbader, Carol W.

The big book of preserving the harvest; [foreword by Joanne Lamb Hayes] [rev ed] Storey Bks. 2002 347p il pa $18.95   **641.4**

1. Canning and preserving

ISBN 1-58017-458-2   LC 2002-21172

First published 1997

Costenbader, Carol W.—*Continued*

In addition to recipes this book provides instructions for food preservation techniques, including canning, drying, freezing, the preparation of jams and jellies, pickles, relishes and chutneys, vinegars and seasonings, and cold storage. Includes a section on gift giving, directions on building a food dehydrator, a table of equivalents, and a conversion chart to metric measures

Includes bibliographical references

Shephard, Sue

Pickled, potted, and canned; how the art and science of food preserving changed the world. Simon & Schuster 2001 366p $26

641.4

1. Canning and preserving 2. Food—Preservation

ISBN 0-7432-1633-4   LC 2001-32065

First published 2000 in the United Kingdom

"This book recounts the development of food preserving from the time of the ancients to the era of the space program, from East to West and all points in between." Libr J

"Nearly every page contains something either practical or historically fascinating or both. . . . The book is so lively and informative that even those readers who think they have no interest whatsoever in the subject will find themselves changing their minds in a hurry." Booklist

Includes bibliographical references

Ziedrich, Linda

The joy of pickling; 200 flavor-packed recipes for all kinds of produce from garden or market. Harvard Common Press 1998 382p il hardcover o.p. paperback available $19.95

641.4

1. Canning and preserving

ISBN 1-55832-133-0 (pa)   LC 98-22880

This is a "guide to pickles of all sorts, including kimchi and others from Asia, chutneys and salsas, and 'freezer pickles,' along with traditional favorites like Half-Sours by the Quart." Libr J

Includes bibliographical references

641.5   Cooking

Abadi, Jennifer Felicia

A fistful of lentils; Syrian-Jewish recipes from grandma Fritzie's kitchen. Harvard Common Press 2002 372p il $24.95   **641.5**

1. Syrian cooking 2. Jewish cooking

ISBN 1-55832-218-3   LC 2001-47060

"Abadi's recipes, collected with the help of her feisty grandmother Fritzie, feature lots of spices, sweet-and-tart sauces, flatbreads and flaky pastry doughs, and ingredients such as dates and pomegranates, pine nuts and pistachios. Her well-written, readable text provides historical context as well as family reminiscences and anecdotes." Libr J

Adams, Jody

In the hands of a chef; cooking with Jody Adams; [by] Jody Adams and Ken Rivard. Morrow 2002 374p il $34.95   **641.5**

1. Cooking

ISBN 0-688-16837-X   LC 2001-32946

The author offers over 200 recipes for such dishes as "Soupe de Poisson and Roasted Marinated Long Island Duck with Green Olive and Balsamic Vinegar Sauce. . . . The recipes are clearly written and certainly delectable." Publ Wkly

Adams, Marcia

New recipes from quilt country; more food & folkways from the Amish & Mennonites. Potter 1997 294p il $32.50   **641.5**

1. Cooking 2. Amish

ISBN 0-517-70562-1   LC 97-22620

Also available Cooking from quilt country (1989)

This book offers "stories and simple recipes from Amish and conservative Mennonite communities across the country, providing a sometimes surprisingly intimate look into the lives of these private people. . . . Some of the readable instructions focus on a particular family or activity, others on customs or topics like 'Growing Up Amish.' Most of the recipes are for hearty, homey fare, from frugal cooks used to feeding lots of people. . . . There are lots of delicious cookies, pies, and breads here." Libr J

Includes bibliographical references

Algar, Ayla Esen

Classical Turkish cooking; traditional Turkish food for the American kitchen; [by] Ayla Algar. HarperCollins Pubs. 1991 306p $35; pa $17   **641.5**

1. Turkish cooking

ISBN 0-06-016317-8; 0-06-093163-9 (pa)

LC 91-55096

"A cuisine that melds the fragrances and flavors of the Far East, Central Asia, Iran, Anatolia, and the Mediterranean is enriched by Algar as she goes well beyond the standard recipes (160 of them) to explain Turkey's historical, cultural, and culinary traditions—and, along the way, to include a glimpse of her personal family heritage." Booklist

Includes bibliographical references

American Heart Association cookbook. Times Bks. $30; pa $19.95   **641.5**

1. Cooking 2. Low-cholesterol diet

Also available in paperback from Ballantine Bks.

First published 1973. (6th edition 1998) Periodically revised

Sixth edition 1998 has title: The new American Heart Association cookbook

"Prepared under the guidance of heart specialists, this cookbook provides, aside from 600 healthy recipes, important information on the proper selecting, cooking, and storing of foods. There is a good introduction to low-fat and low-cholesterol cooking and extensive information on the physical effects that various foods have on the body and the heart in particular. Includes advice on changing to a more healthy diet, substituting ingredients, dining out, and analyzing nutrients. It is an established classic." Ref Sources for Small & Medium-sized Libr. 6th edition

American Heart Association low-fat, low-cholesterol cookbook; heart-healthy, easy-to-make recipes that taste great. 2nd ed. Times Bks. 1997 372p il spiral bdg $25.95; pa $15.95   **641.5**

1. Cooking 2. Low-fat diet 3. Low-cholesterol diet

ISBN 0-8129-2684-6; 0-609-80861-3 (pa)

LC 97-17099

New edition in preparation

First published 1989

"The dishes are, indeed, low in fat and cholesterol; as a bonus, they are also low in sodium. The recipes are

American Heart Association low-fat, low-cholesterol cookbook—_Continued_
not, by and large, for adventurous cooks—golden rice, chili, broiled fish, melon with sherbert. There are, however, a few surprises . . . and the preparation is easy enough for cooks who need to watch the time as well as the calories and nutritional content." Booklist

The **American** Heart Association low-salt cookbook; a complete guide to reducing sodium and fat in your diet. 2nd ed. Potter 2001 353p $22.95; pa $15.95   **641.5**
1. Salt-free diet 2. Cooking
ISBN 0-8129-9107-9; 0-609-80968-7 (pa)
LC 00-61184

First published 1990
This low-salt cookbook is aimed at those seeking to change their eating and cooking habits to avoid cardiovascular disease. In addition to the recipes, the book includes nutritional information and two diet plans

American Heart Association meals in minutes; over 200 all-new quick and easy low-fat recipes; [by] American Heart Association. Random House 2000 348p il $26.95; pa $15.95   **641.5**
1. Cooking 2. Low-cholesterol diet
ISBN 0-8129-3332-X; 0-609-80977-6 (pa)
LC 99-52989

An illustrated step-by-step compendium of easy-to-make low-fat recipes

American Heart Association quick-and-easy cookbook; by the American Heart Association. Times Bks. 1995 274p il $25.95; pa $15.95   **641.5**
1. Cooking 2. Low-cholesterol diet 3. Low-fat diet
ISBN 0-8129-2251-4; 0-609-80862-1 (pa)
LC 94-19973

Includes illustrated step-by-step instructions for over 200 easy-to-prepare low-fat low-cholesterol recipes

Anderson, Jean, 1929-
The food of Portugal; color photography by the author. Morrow 1986 304p il map hardcover o.p. paperback available $19.95
    641.5
1. Portuguese cooking
ISBN 0-688-13415-7 (pa)   LC 86-2510
The author "first covers Portugal's geography and touches on distinctive regional cooking styles. The following glossary delineates Portuguese food, drink, and dining terminology. . . . Part 2, . . . is a guide to the country's best food." Booklist
Includes bibliographical references

The new German cookbook; more than 230 contemporary and traditional recipes; [by] Jean Anderson and Hedy Würz. HarperCollins Pubs. 1993 416p $30   **641.5**
1. German cooking
ISBN 0-06-016202-3   LC 92-56211
"This book should give many cooks a new perspective on German cooking. All of the ingredients traditionally associated with this cuisine appear, but veal, for example, shows up in a Riesling wine sauce as well as in Wiener schnitzel, and dumplings are scented with tarragon and tossed into a clear asparagus soup." Libr J
Includes bibliographical references

Anderson, Pam
How to cook without a book; recipes and techniques every cook should know by heart. Broadway Bks. 2000 290p $25   **641.5**
1. Cooking
ISBN 0-7679-0279-3   LC 99-43776
"In chapters organized mostly by course or by technique, Anderson provides basic templates for tossed salads, pasta dishes with vegetables, simple stir-fries, and so forth, with easy suggestions for variations on the theme." Libr J

Barrenechea, Teresa, 1956-
The Basque table; passionate home cooking from one of Europe's great regional cuisines; [by] Teresa Barrenechea, with Mary Goodbody. Harvard Common Press 1998 232p il $27.95   **641.5**
1. Basque cooking
ISBN 1-55832-140-3   LC 98-29295
The author's "Basque dishes are characterized by fresh, lively flavors; garlic, hot chilis, and roasted sweet peppers, fish of all types, and beef and lamb are favorite ingredients. While home-style dishes are her emphasis here, there are some entries from _nueva cocina_ as well. A chapter on pinchos, the Basque version of tapas, is a highlight, and there are sidebars on Basque ingredients and traditions throughout." Libr J

Bastianich, Lidia
Lidia's Italian-American kitchen; by Lidia Matticchio Bastianich; photographs by Christopher Hirsheimer. Knopf 2001 xxvi, 432p il $35   **641.5**
1. Italian cooking
ISBN 0-375-41150-X   LC 2001-45009
In this cookbook "recipes are divided into antipasto, soups, pasta and risotto, pizza, entrees, side dishes and desserts." Publ Wkly
"Bastianich has a warm, engaging style, and she's a teacher as well as a chef: throughout, she provides thoughtful head-notes and sidebars along with useful boxes on cooking with wine, 'resting' soup, and other such practicalities." Libr J

Lidia's Italian table; edited by Christopher Styler; photography by Christopher Hirscheimer. Morrow 1998 390p il $30
    641.5
1. Italian cooking
ISBN 0-688-15410-7   LC 98-2949
This companion to the PBS series centers on Istrian cuisine which "represents a transition zone, Italian cooking gradually merging with Slavic traditions to create some unique flavor pairings." Booklist
This book contains recipes that "are unusual, not to be found in the average Italian cookbook, and Bastianich's considerable knowledge and experience, as well as her enthusiasm, are evident throughout." Libr J

Bayless, Rick

Rick Bayless's Mexican kitchen; capturing the vibrant flavors of a world-class cuisine; [by] Rick Bayless with Deann Groen Bayless and JeanMarie Brownson; photographs by Maria Robledo; illustrations by John Sandford. Scribner 1996 448p il $35 **641.5**

1. Mexican cooking
ISBN 0-684-80006-3 LC 96-218444

This cookbook "includes more than 200 tantalizing recipes and is packed with information on Mexican ingredients and cooking techniques, regional cuisine, and history. . . . A serious guide to an often underestimated cuisine, this is important as both a reference and a cookbook." Libr J

Includes bibliographical references

Beard, James, 1903-1985

The armchair James Beard; edited by John Ferrone; foreword by Barbara Kafka. Lyons Press 1999 346p $24.95 **641.5**

1. Cooking
ISBN 1-55821-737-1 LC 98-29728

This collection assembles "essays on everything from main courses to condiments; dining in restaurants, hospitals, and al fresco; libations and desserts; and broader philosophical concerns on gastronomy. Each chapter has captured Beard's feeling for food, his wicked sense of humor, his consummate excellence as a writer, and even his love of controversy. . . . The 150 recipes cover the globe and honor the palate." Libr J

James Beard's American cookery; with illustrations by Earl Thollander. Little, Brown 1972 877p il hardcover o.p. paperback available $24.95 **641.5**

1. Cooking
ISBN 0-316-08566-9 (pa)

"Comprehensive in scope the cookbook gives eighteenth-and nineteenth-century recipes as well as modern directions for preparation of a full range of U.S. cookery. . . . The format is attractive and the historical data add to the value of an authoritative guide." Booklist

Includes bibliographical references

Berley, Peter

The modern vegetarian kitchen; [by] Peter Berley with Melissa Clark. ReganBooks 2000 450p il $35 **641.5**

1. Vegetarian cooking
ISBN 0-06-039295-9 LC 00-42524

The author "organizes his recipes first by type (e.g., soups, salads, pasta, and beans) and then by season. . . . He also provides lots of background information and recommendations on ingredients, necessary utensils and appliances, and techniques." Libr J

Includes bibliographical references

The **Best** American recipes. Houghton Mifflin il $26 **641.5**

1. Cooking
ISSN 1525-1101

Annual. First published 1999

Editors vary

This is a compilation of popular recipes taken from cookbooks, newspapers, magazines, and other sources

Better Homes and Gardens new cook book. Meredith Corp. $29.95; pa $16.95 **641.5**

1. Cooking

Also available in ringbound edition

First published 1930 with title: My Better Homes and Gardens cookbook. (12th edition 2002) Periodically revised

"The lead chapter, Cooking Basics, covers ingredients, techniques and menu plans. The following 20 chapters are arranged alphabetically by main ingredients (Beans, Rice & Grains; Meat) or course (Appetizers & Snacks; Desserts)." Publ Wkly [review of 1996 edition]

Betty Crocker's best loved recipes. Macmillan 1998 384p il $24.95 **641.5**

1. Cooking
ISBN 0-02-862450-5 LC 98-38261

In addition to the over 200 illustrated step-by-step recipes this work also discusses cooking techniques and equipment

Betty Crocker's cooking basics; learning to cook with confidence. Macmillan 1998 280p il $19.95 **641.5**

1. Cooking
ISBN 0-02-862451-3 LC 98-20522

In addition to recipes, this illustrated volume contains tips on food selection, grocery shopping, thawing, and nutrition. Cooking equipment is discussed

Bishop, Jack

The complete Italian vegetarian cookbook; 350 essential recipes for inspired, everyday eating; photography by Ann Stratton. Houghton Mifflin 1997 568p il $35 **641.5**

1. Vegetarian cooking 2. Italian cooking
ISBN 1-57630-044-7 LC 97-16879

"A Chapters book"

This includes "vegetarian recipes for all courses of a meal, from cold and hot antipasti to dessert." Libr J

Bittman, Mark

How to cook everything; simple recipes for great food; illustrations by Alan Witschonke. Macmillan 1998 944p il $29.95 **641.5**

1. Cooking
ISBN 0-02-861010-5 LC 98-22959

The author presents "more than 1000 basic recipes and simple and inventive variations. The enormous breadth of recipes along with Bittman's engaging, straightforward prose will appeal to cooks looking for reliable help with kitchen fundamentals." Publ Wkly

Brill, Steve

The wild vegetarian cookbook; a forager's culinary guide (in the field or in the supermarket) to preparing and savoring wild (and not so wild) natural foods, with more than 500 recipes; by "Wildman" Steve Brill; foreword by Arthur Schwartz. Harvard Common Press 2002 xxvi, 500p il $29.95 **641.5**

1. Vegetarian cooking 2. Forage plants
ISBN 1-55832-214-0 LC 2001-51929

This "book includes dozens of recipes using wild foods, from sassafras and daylily shoots to blue violets

Brill, Steve—*Continued*

and cow parsnips; each entry includes a brief description of the plant as well." Libr J

"Filled with humorous ancedotes and small descriptions. . . . The book will appeal to those who enjoy foraging in the wild as well as the vegetarian who is not only health- but also environmentally conscious." Publ Wkly

Brody, Lora, 1945-

The kitchen survival guide; a hand-holding kitchen primer with 130 recipes to get you started. Morrow 1992 308p $21.95   **641.5**

1. Cooking

ISBN 0-688-10587-4   LC 91-40663

"Written in a casual style, this primer is an excellent introduction for the person who has never set foot in a kitchen. In addition to 130 recipes for the basics (fried eggs and mashed potatoes), Brody discusses setting up a kitchen and how to shop for food." Booklist

Includes bibliographical references

Brown, Sarah

The vegetarian bible. Reader's Digest Assn. 2002 384p il $35   **641.5**

1. Vegetarian cooking

ISBN 0-7621-0359-0   LC 2001-34927

"The complete illustrated guide to vegetarian food & cooking." Cover

This vegetarian cookbook features over 250 recipes and a reference section with profiles of over 350 ingredients

Bugialli, Giuliano

Bugialli's Italy; traditional recipes from the regions of Italy; photography by John Dominis. Morrow 1998 312p il $28   **641.5**

1. Italian cooking

ISBN 0-688-15864-1   LC 98-5670

This companion volume to the PBS series contains more than 150 recipes. "Headnotes discuss provenance and point out the similarities or differences among related recipes from the various regions. . . . Recipes are organized generally by course, rather than region, with a particularly outstanding selection of pastas and a separate section of Roman vegetable dishes." Libr J

Burros, Marian Fox

The new elegant but easy cookbook; [by] Marian Burros and Lois Levine. Simon & Schuster 1998 343p hardcover o.p. paperback available $14   **641.5**

1. Entertaining 2. Cooking

ISBN 0-684-85309-4 (pa)   LC 97-46884

First published 1960 with title: Elegant but easy cookbook

Many of this book's recipes "can be assembled ahead of time, then refrigerated or frozen for later cooking. . . . Helpfully, the authors include a set of 10 different menus, complete with shopping lists and detailed game plans, along with suggestions for dishes that can be whipped up for, say, 'unexpected guests.' Here's just the push a reluctant cook might need to turn on the stove and do some entertaining." N Y Times Book Rev

Child, Julia

From Julia Child's kitchen; photographs and drawings by Paul Child; additional technical photographs by Albie Walton. Knopf 1975 687, xxvip il $13.99   **641.5**

1. French cooking

ISBN 0-517-20712-5

The author "has taken many of the recipes she demonstrated in her 72 'French Chef' TV shows; grouped them by subject [soups, appetizers, egg dishes, fish, poultry, meat, vegetables, salads, bread] added variations and additional recipes; and introduced each section and most recipes with commentaries." Libr J

Includes bibliographical references

Julia and Jacques cooking at home; by Julia Child and Jacques Pepin, with David Nussbaum. Knopf 1999 430p il $40   **641.5**

1. French cooking

ISBN 0-375-40431-7   LC 98-32418

A companion volume to the PBS series. "For each show, the two chefs started out with ideas and ingredients but no set recipes, so they improvised as they went along, cooking a lot of their favorite traditional dishes and coming up with new ones as well. . . . Dozens of boxes throughout the text provide information on a wide variety of topics." Libr J

Julia's kitchen wisdom; lessons from a lifetime of cooking; by Julia Child with David Nussbaum. Knopf 2000 127p il $19.95   **641.5**

1. Cooking

ISBN 0-375-41151-8   LC 00-62928

Also available large print edition $19.95 (ISBN 0-375-43093-8)

The focus of this cookbook "is on technique, but there are dozens of recipes as well, both 'master recipes' and their spin-offs, and others that stand alone." Libr J

"This slender book from the doyenne of gourmet cooking is a boon for those who need a refresher course in, or a handy source for, basics." Publ Wkly

Mastering the art of French cooking; by Julia Child, Louisette Bertholle, Simone Beck. updated ed. Knopf 1983 2v il v1 $40; pa $30; v2 $60; pa $30   **641.5**

1. French cooking

ISBN 0-375-41340-5; 0-394-72178-0 (v1 pa); 0-394-40152-2; 0-394-72177-2 (v2 pa)

LC 83-48113

Volume 1 first published 1961 with Beck's name first; volume 2 by Julia Child and Simone Beck

Volume one includes, in addition to usual categories, a chapter dealing with entrees and luncheon dishes, including quiches, pâtés, and crepes, and other cold buffet items. Volume two emphasizes French bread and pastries, with chapters also devoted to soups, meats, chickens, vegetables, and desserts. Appendices discuss stuffings and kitchen equipment

Child, Julia—*Continued*

The way to cook; photographs by Brian Leatart and Jim Scherer; food designer, Rosemary Manell. Knopf 1989 511p il $65; pa $39.95   **641.5**
1. Cooking
ISBN 0-394-53264-3; 0-679-74765-6 (pa)
                                    LC 88-45838
"With her sensible-as-always approach to food, Child has produced a comprehensive cooking bible, filled with stunning photographs and practical illustrations, that will aid the novice [and] inspire the gourmet. . . . A masterwork from a master chef." Libr J

Claiborne, Craig
The New York Times cook book. rev ed. Harper & Row 1990 799p $34   **641.5**
1. Cooking
ISBN 0-06-016010-1   LC 89-45640
First published 1961
A basic collection of recipes covering both traditional American food preparation and more recent culinary trends. Cooking procedures are outlined in a step-by-step approach

David, Elizabeth, 1913-1992
Is there a nutmeg in the house? compiled by Jill Norman. Viking 2001 318p il hardcover o.p. paperback available $15
                                    641.5
1. Cooking 2. Food
ISBN 0-14-200166-X (pa)   LC 2001-26185
Companion volume to An omelette and a glass of wine (1985)
This "collection of essays and more than 150 recipes, compiled by David's long-time associate Jill Norman, brings some new work to light. There are 12 sections, from 'Stocks and Soups' to 'Ice Creams and Sorbets.'" Libr J
An "evocative and entertaining exploration of cooking and the time, place and personalities that shaped it.'" Publ Wkly
Includes bibliographical references

Dojny, Brooke
The New England cookbook; 350 recipes from town and country, land and sea, hearth and home; illustrations by John MacDonald. Harvard Common Press 1999 652p il $29.95; pa $21.95   **641.5**
1. Cooking
ISBN 1-55832-138-1; 1-55832-139-X (pa)
                                    LC 99-14393
This volume includes traditional dishes as well as "dozens of ethnic specialties from the various immigrant groups who have helped populate New England: Oregano-Scented Greek Lamb Shanks, Portuguese Tuna Escabeche, and Garlicky Mussels, Italian-style, to name a few." Libr J
Includes bibliographical references

Downie, David
Cooking the Roman way; authentic recipes from the home cooks and trattorias of Rome; photographs by Alison Harris. HarperCollins Pubs. 2002 xxii, 314p il $34.95   **641.5**
1. Italian cooking 2. Rome (Italy)—Social life and customs
ISBN 0-06-018892-8   LC 2002-27279
This is a "collection of more than 125 Roman recipes, exploring the . . . food traditionally served in Roman homes and trattorie. . . . [It comes] with four-color photographs of landmarks, markets and food, stories about and profiles of food vendors . . . anecdotes, and a food lovers guide to the streets of the city." Publisher's note
"Downie has beautifully and evocatively captured the cuisine of one of the world's best-known cities." Publ Wkly
Includes bibliographical references

Edge, John T.
A gracious plenty; recipes and recollections from the American South; John T. Edge for the Center for the Study of Southern Culture at the University of Mississippi. Putnam 1999 365p il hardcover o.p. paperback available $19.95   **641.5**
1. Southern cooking 2. Southern States—Social life and customs
ISBN 1-55788-388-2 (pa)   LC 99-24119
"An Ellen Rolfes book"
Edge "has gathered more than 400 recipes for Southern home cooking, most of them from community cookbooks, which he sees as historical documents as much as recipe books. In addition to the recipes, . . . there are nostalgic reminiscences from Southern authors ranging from Eudora Welty (whose fruit-cake recipe also appears here) to Roy Blount." Libr J

Farmer, Fannie Merritt, 1857-1915
The Fannie Farmer cookbook. Knopf il $30; pa $7.99   **641.5**
1. Cooking
First published 1896. (1996 edition) Periodically revised
Recent editions by Marion Cunningham
This standard cookbook focuses on the selection, preparation, and serving of a wide variety of foods

Fowler, Damon Lee
Damon Lee Fowler's new southern kitchen; traditional flavors for contemporary cooks; photographs by Ann Stratton. Simon & Schuster 2002 431p il $26   **641.5**
1. Southern cooking
ISBN 0-684-87169-6   LC 2001-57565
This cookbook covers every course from appetizers to desserts, recipes include "Pork Tenderloin Biscuits with Chutney Butter, Shrimp and Green Tomato Gumbo, Bourbon Grilled Steak, and Lillie's Little Lemon Puddings. Thoughtful menu suggestions accompany most recipes. Highly recommended." Libr J
Includes bibliographical references

Friedland, Susan R.

Shabbat shalom; recipes and menus for the sabbath. Little, Brown 1999 304p $24.95

641.5

1. Jewish cooking 2. Sabbath
ISBN 0-316-29065-3　　　　　　　LC 99-35684

The author "draws on the very best of traditional Ashkenazic and Sephardic cuisine to find dishes that especially honor the Sabbath, that unique day of the week on which work is forbidden. . . . Friedland's clear directions make her recipes easy to follow. Highly recommended as an illuminative, celebratory guide to kosher cooking." Booklist

Includes bibliographical references

Fussell, Betty Harper

Home bistro; simple, sensual fare in the comfort of your kitchen; by Betty Fussell; wine selections by David Rosengarten and Joshua Wesson. Ecco Press 1997 249p $24

641.5

1. Cooking
ISBN 0-88001-526-8　　　　　　　LC 96-43197

Recipes from "*Eating In*" (1986) and *Home Plates* (NAL: Dutton, 1990) have been revised and collected here, along with 45 new ones. Most are one-dish meals for two people; all are for simple, vibrantly flavored dishes, presented in an unintimidating, companionable style." Libr J

Garten, Ina

Barefoot Contessa family style; easy ideas and recipes that make everyone feel like family; photographs by Maura McEvoy; food styling by Rori Trovato. Potter 2002 240p il $35

641.5

1. Cooking
ISBN 0-609-61066-X　　　　　　　LC 2002-74979

"Garten's 'family style' cooking includes dishes like Chicken Noodle Soup and Parker's Fish & Chips (separate chapters are devoted to breakfast and kids' foods), but there are also elegant dishes like Tuna Tartare, Saffron Risotto, and Lobster Cobb Salad." Libr J

This is "simple, elegant home cooking with good ingredients and a minimum of fuss. It takes a certain amount of chutzpah to include ordinary chicken noodle soup and mashed potatoes and gravy in a cookbook, but Garten pulls it off with heart and style." Publ Wkly

Giedt, Frances Towner

The Joslin Diabetes great chefs cook healthy cookbook; [by] Frances Towner Giedt and Bonnie Sanders Polin, with the nutrition services staff at Joslin Diabetes Center; foreword by Alan C. Moses. Simon & Schuster 2002 308p il $30; pa $15　**641.5**

1. Diabetes—Diet therapy 2. Cooking
ISBN 0-7432-1586-9; 0-7432-1588-5 (pa)
　　　　　　　　　　　　　　LC 2002-70745

This book features "recipes from well-known chefs, each designed to fit the special dietary requirements of diabetics." Publ Wkly

"The recipes are sophisticated and elegant—perfect dinner-party fare—but many of them are quite easy to prepare. The authors have grouped main course recipes under 'Small Plates' and 'Large Plates,' along with starters, soups, salads, vegetables and other sides, and desserts. Each recipe, of course, includes nutrition information, and there are many suggested menus scattered throughout." Libr J

The **Good** Housekeeping step-by-step cookbook; edited by Susan Westmoreland, with the assistance of Susan Deborah Goldsmith and Elizabeth Brainerd Burge. Hearst Bks. 1997 576p il $29.95　**641.5**

1. Cooking
ISBN 0-688-14716-X　　　　　　　LC 97-11375

"A Carroll & Brown book"

This offers over 1,000 basic recipes illustrated by 1,800 color photographs divided into sections such as appetizers, soups, eggs and cheese, shellfish, poultry, meat, vegetables, pasta, grains and beans, breads, and desserts

Greene, Gloria Kaufer, 1950-

The new Jewish holiday cookbook; an international collection of recipes and customs. Completely rev and updated with more than 80 new recipes! Times Bks. 1999 539p $29.95　**641.5**

1. Jewish cooking 2. Jewish holidays
ISBN 0-8129-2977-2　　　　　　　LC 98-55721

First published 1985 with title: The Jewish holiday cookbook

"Starting with the chief and weekly holiday, Sabbath, Greene offers tasty recipes that occasionally draw on ingredients outside traditional ones. . . . Greene labels each recipe as 'meat,' 'dairy,' or 'pareve' so that readers may determine instantly how the recipe correlates with dietary laws." Booklist

Hagman, Bette

The gluten-free gourmet; living well without wheat. rev ed. Holt & Co. 2000 xx, 330p pa $18　**641.5**

1. Gluten-free diet 2. Diet in disease
ISBN 0-8050-6484-2　　　　　　　LC 00-22448

First published 1990

This book features over 200 "recipes using special flours for pizza, pasta, breads, pies, cakes, and cookies. . . . A complete sourcebook on how to live healthily with celiac disease or wheat intolerance, it features . . . information on developing a celiac diet, raising a celiac child, avoiding hidden glutens, eating well while traveling or in the hospital, and locating and ordering from suppliers of gluten-free food and flour." Publisher's note

The recipes "are easy to prepare. Mail-order sources for gluten-free flours will be especially helpful. The . . . accurate information in this makes it a useful purchase for large cookbook collections." Booklist [review of 1990 edition]

Includes bibliographical references

Harris, Jessica B.

The Africa cookbook; tastes of a continent. Simon & Schuster 1998 382p il $27　**641.5**

1. African cooking
ISBN 0-684-80275-9　　　　　　　LC 98-38882

The author begins with an "introductory section that provides history, . . . background on the four general divisions of the continent, and a very good glossary of ingredients and equipment. Recipes are organized by course, with country of origin listed for each, and headnotes offer context as well as useful tips. Harris writes well, and her accounts of various visits and encounters are particularly readable. With few other cookbooks available even on specific African cuisines, her ambitious new book is unique." Libr J

Includes bibliographical references

Harris, Jessica B.—*Continued*

The welcome table; African-American heritage cooking; drawings by Patricia Eck. Simon & Schuster 1995 285p il hardcover o.p. paperback available $16   **641.5**

1. African American cooking
ISBN 0-684-81837-X (pa)   LC 94-32487

The author "presents African American recipes of all sorts, from slave cooking, the source of many classic Southern dishes, to the family favorites she grew up with to her own sophisticated reinterpretations or inventions. Headnotes are readable and informative, providing culinary and cultural background. . . . Harris's thoroughly researched book is the essential purchase." Libr J

Hazan, Marcella

Essentials of classic Italian cooking; illustrated by Karin Kretschmann. Knopf 1992 688p il $30   **641.5**

1. Italian cooking
ISBN 0-394-58404-X   LC 92-52954

Revised and updated edition of the author's The classic Italian cookbook (1973) and More classic Italian cooking (1978)

A guide to the products, techniques and dishes of classic Italian cooking. Regional specialities are dealt with at length

This "could readily assume the mantle of *the* definitive resource for Italian cuisine." Booklist

Marcella cucina; photography by Alison Harris, design by Joel Avirom. HarperCollins Pubs. 1997 471p il $35   **641.5**

1. Italian cooking
ISBN 0-06-017103-0   LC 97-1253

This book includes both the author's "old favorites and recent creations, along with her versions of regional dishes from chefs and home cooks throughout Italy. . . . She offers an intimate, at times nostalgic glimpse at her life with cooking." Libr J

Jaffrey, Madhur

Madhur Jaffrey's world vegetarian. Potter 1999 760p $40; pa $24.95   **641.5**

1. Vegetarian cooking
ISBN 0-517-59632-6; 0-609-80923-7 (pa)
LC 98-30318

A compendium of vegetarian "recipes from all over the world. Grouped mostly into broad categories by main ingredient (beans, grain, vegetables, etc.), they are as likely to come from a Palestinian restaurant in Toronto, the nuns at the Ormylia Monastery in Macedonia, or a home cook in Mexico as from Jaffrey's own Indian background or her experience as a cooking teacher." Libr J

Jamison, Cheryl Alters

American home cooking; 400 spirited recipes celebrating our rich tradition of home cooking; [by] Cheryl Alters Jamison and Bill Jamison. Broadway Bks. 1999 470p $30
641.5

1. Cooking
ISBN 0-7679-0201-7   LC 99-10814

In addition to the recipes this book contains ingredient and technique tips, culinary history, and quotes from the likes of M. F. K. Fisher and James Beard

"The Jamisons authoritatively articulate the pastiche of multicultural influences that characterize American regional cuisine, enabling readers to rediscover national (and regional) culinary treasures." Publ Wkly

Includes bibliographical references

A real American breakfast; the best meal of the day anytime of the day; [by] Cheryl Alters Jamison and Bill Jamison. Morrow 2002 454p il $34.95   **641.5**

1. Breakfasts 2. Cooking
ISBN 0-06-018824-3   LC 2001-42715

This volume includes "14 chapters featuring eggs, pancakes, cereals and breads, as well as casseroles, sandwiches and cobblers. . . . With every recipe there are helpful tips on techniques and ingredients, as well as sidebars featuring American breakfast history and trivia, all in elegantly written, snappy text." Publ Wkly

Kafka, Barbara

Party food; small & savory; photography by Tom Eckerle. Morrow 1992 xxvii, 323p il $27   **641.5**

1. Cooking 2. Entertaining
ISBN 0-688-11184-X   LC 91-45725

This book includes "more than 300 recipes—of foods meant for entertaining. . . . In raising a party giver's comfort level with feeding 4 to 40, Kafka also manages to expand even a well-practiced cook's horizons, through a variety of sidebars and a homey, personalized narrative." Booklist

Kamman, Madeleine

The new making of a cook; the art, techniques, and science of good cooking. Morrow 1997 1228p il $40   **641.5**

1. Cooking
ISBN 0-688-15254-6   LC 96-37452

First published 1971 with title: The making of a cook

This instructional cookbook combines classic French cuisine with American, Asian and South American dishes. Concerns about fat consumption are addressed and time-saving suggestions are included

"Kamman's masterwork contains an incredible amount of information not only on techniques and ingredients but also on food science, cultural and culinary history, and myriad other topics." Libr J

Includes bibliographical references

Kennedy, Diana

The essential cuisines of Mexico. Potter 2000 526p $35   **641.5**

1. Mexican cooking
ISBN 0-609-60355-8   LC 00-23156

The author has gathered "the recipes from her first cookbook, the groundbreaking *Cuisines of Mexico* (1972), as well its two successors, *The Tortilla Book* (1975) and *Mexican Regional Cooking* (1978) . . . in this new collection. She's revised the recipes and simplified some, and there are also 30 or so new recipes. Kennedy's books became classics long ago; this compilation of her early works is an essential purchase." Libr J

Includes bibliographical references

Kennedy, Diana—*Continued*

My Mexico; a culinary odyssey with more than 300 recipes; with photographs by the author. Potter 1998 550p il $35   **641.5**

1. Mexican cooking 2. Mexico—Social life and customs

ISBN 0-609-60247-0   LC 98-9181

This volume incorporates family recipes "with traditional signature dishes of various locales, as well as adaptations of restaurant favorites and classics. . . . Kennedy divides chapters by geographical region and takes readers on a meandering culinary journey, replete with detailed accounts of local topography, seasons, sights, sounds and scents." Publ Wkly

Kochilas, Diane

The glorious foods of Greece. Morrow 2000 496p map $40   **641.5**

1. Greek cooking

ISBN 0-688-15457-3   LC 00-28158

This cookbook includes over 400 recipes from various "regions, starting with the Peloponnesus and the Ionian Islands, moving on to Macedonia, the islands of the Aegean, and Crete, and finishing up in the city of Athens. . . . Kochilas also provides extensive historical background, cultural as well as culinary, along with detailed descriptions and explanations of ingredients." Libr J

Includes bibliographical references

Lacalamita, Tom

The ultimate pressure cooker cookbook; recipes from the Mediterranean tradition; photographs by Ilisa Katz; food stylist, Roscoe Betsill; prop stylist, Edward Kemper Design; illustrations by Laurie Davis. Simon & Schuster 1997 205p $25   **641.5**

1. Mediterranean cooking

ISBN 0-684-82496-5   LC 96-40229

"Tips, advice, and counsel are featured upfront, with notes on proper use, care, and accident avoidance. . . . Most of the more than 90 recipes are Mediterranean or, at least, inspired by the cuisines of the region; there is a strong emphasis on dried beans, legumes, grains, and vegetables. But the real draw of this book is the incredible time savings." Booklist

Lanza, Louis

Totally dairy-free cooking; [by] Louis Lanza and Laura Morton. Morrow 1999 c2000 246p il $25   **641.5**

1. Milk-free diet 2. Cooking

ISBN 0-688-16909-0   LC 99-30472

"The author's recipes eliminate dairy products and use soy milk and soy cheeses as alternatives to the common products of the dairy farm." Booklist

Lanza's "practical approach—using readily available, brand-name products—balances nicely his creative culinary flourishes. . . . Nutritional information accompanies each recipe." Publ Wkly

Lemlin, Jeanne

Main-course vegetarian pleasures. HarperPerennial 1995 xxiii, 216p il pa $18.95   **641.5**

1. Vegetarian cooking

ISBN 0-06-095022-6   LC 94-23966

This volume includes "125 meatless main-course recipes to which speed of preparation is the key. Most of the recipes require only 30 minutes of prep time, and many can be prepared ahead in stages." Publ Wkly

"The word *pleasures* in the title is not misplaced. . . . Even those unwilling to commit fully to meatless meals will have plenty of choices." Booklist

Lo, Eileen Yin-fei

The Chinese kitchen; recipes, techniques, ingredients, history, and memories from America's leading authority on Chinese cooking; calligraphy by San Yan Wong; photographs by Alexandra Grablewski. Morrow 1999 452p il $37.50   **641.5**

1. Chinese cooking

ISBN 0-688-15826-9   LC 99-30746

"Seventeen chapters explore the Chinese larder, teas, wines, cooking equipment and techniques, classic Chinese dishes, rice and noodles, food-as-medicine, meats and vegetables, dim sum and the evolution of Chinese-American restaurant dishes." Publ Wkly

Madison, Deborah

The Greens cook book; extraordinary vegetarian cuisine from the celebrated restaurant; by Deborah Madison with Edward Espe Brown. Bantam Bks. 1987 xx, 396p $29.95   **641.5**

1. Vegetarian cooking

ISBN 0-7679-0823-6   LC 86-47884

"There are hundreds of delicious recipes for hearty or elegant soups, pastas, salads, casseroles and tarts in which meat products are not missed." N Y Times Book Rev

Includes bibliographical references

Local flavors; cooking and eating from America's farmers' markets. Broadway Bks. 2002 xxiii, 408p il $39.95   **641.5**

1. Cooking 2. Farm produce—Marketing

ISBN 0-7679-0349-8   LC 2001-49940

The author presents such "recipes as Cabbage and Potato Gratin with sage, or Corn and Squash Simmered in Coconut Milk with Thai Basil, alongside tributes to highlighted markets. Vegetarians will welcome main courses such as Braised Root Vegetables with Black Lentils and Red Wine Sauce or Asparagus and Wild Mushroom Bread Pudding." Publ Wkly

Includes bibliographical references

Vegetarian cooking for everyone. Broadway Bks. 1997 742p il $40   **641.5**

1. Vegetarian cooking

ISBN 0-7679-0014-6   LC 97-11138

Following information on ingredients and techniques, the recipes focus "mainly on vegetables and grains, aiming at flavor and variety, both often arrived at via assorted ethnic approaches." Publ Wkly

Marks, Gil

The world of Jewish cooking; more than 500 traditional recipes from Alsace to Yemen. Simon & Schuster 1996 406p il hardcover o.p. paperback available $17

641.5

1. Jewish cooking
ISBN 0-684-83559-2 (pa)   LC 96-2848

This cookbook is "loosely arranged by food category, with chapters on appetizers, soups, and main dishes, as well as side items, breads, and desserts. . . . You'll find recipes from India, Africa, even China, here, alongside many dishes that originated in one of the two major Jewish cultural communities, Ashkenazic and Sephardic." Booklist

The **Martha** Stewart Living cookbook; [by] the editors of Martha Stewart Living. Martha Stewart Living Omnimedia LLC 2000 xlviii, 592p il   **641.5**

1. Cooking   LC 2002-277834

Available from Clarkson Potter $35 (ISBN 0-609-60750-2) and Oxmoor House $29.95 (ISBN 0-8487-2373-2)

"Published simultaneously by Clarkson N. Potter, Inc., Oxmoor House, Inc. and Leisure Arts." Verso of title page

"All of the recipes in this book have been previously published in slightly different form in Martha Stewart living magazines, 1990-2000." Verso of title page

This companion volume to the Martha Stewart cookbook "presents more than 1500 recipes from the magazine. . . . In addition to the recipes, Martha's . . . 'Good Things' and other tips are scattered throughout; there is one 32-page color insert. . . . Essential, of course." Libr J

Mercuri, Becky

Food festival, U.S.A.; red, white, & blue ribbon recipes from all 50 states; illustrated by Tom Klare. Laurel Glen Pub. 2002 430p il pa $24.95   **641.5**

1. Cooking 2. Festivals—United States
ISBN 1-57145-775-5

The author presents some 250 blue-ribbon winning recipes from all 50 states region by region, and includes a directory of festivals by month and also one by state

Molokhovets, Elena

Classic Russian cooking; Elena Molokhovets' A gift to young housewives; translated, introduced, and annotated by Joyce Toomre. Indiana Univ. Press 1992 680p il (Indiana-Michigan series in Russian and East European studies) hardcover o.p. paperback available $35   **641.5**

1. Russian cooking
ISBN 0-253-21210-3 (pa)   LC 91-46254

"Molokhovets' book was first published in 1861 but revised by the author up through 1917, thus spanning an important era in Russian history. Her compendium was a sort of a *Fannie Farmer* or *Mrs. Beeton's* that became essential for young Russian housewives. . . . Toomre, a well-known culinary historian, has done an impressive job of presenting Molokhovet's work, providing a lengthy introduction to set the stage and annotations to put the recipes in context. A glimpse into another world

that should interest cultural and culinary historians alike." Libr J

Includes bibliographical references

Nathan, Joan

The foods of Israel today. Knopf 2001 433p il $40   **641.5**

1. Israeli cooking
ISBN 0-679-45107-2   LC 00-44354

The author "explores the food and culinary traditions of modern Israel. . . . Most of the more than 300 recipes she collected come from home cooks, and their stories make this title almost as much a cultural history as cookbook." Libr J

"Modern Israel is one of the world's great culinary melting pots, and Nathan . . . does it justice in this exceptional and comprehensive examination of its diverse cultural lineage." Publ Wkly

Includes bibliographical references

Jewish cooking in America. expanded ed. Knopf 1998 518p il $35   **641.5**

1. Jewish cooking
ISBN 0-375-40276-4   LC 98-27952

First published 1994

This companion volume to the PBS television series contains nearly 300 recipes. It "is also a history of the Jewish people through their food. Nathan introduces both people and food in a preface that discusses dietary laws, Jewish holidays, Jewish immigration to the U.S., and the impact of Jews—and their food—on American culture. With every recipe comes an original story or a reprint of an article or a personal vignette that intrigues and/or edifies." Booklist

Includes bibliographical references

Negrin, Micol

Rustico: regional Italian country cooking. Potter 2002 384p il $35   **641.5**

1. Italian cooking
ISBN 0-609-60944-0   LC 2001-57793

This "cookbook/guidebook offers a tour of Italy's 20 regions, with ten . . . recipes for each. Some are 'signature' dishes intimately associated with a particular region, but more are what she describes as lesser-known 'regional gems.' Each chapter opens with a brief, scene-setting introduction and a list of favorite restaurants and shops." Libr J

"Recipes are lucid and easy to follow, and chapter introductions stylishly and accurately convey a sense of place, while sidebars offer bits of folklore." Publ Wkly

Includes bibliographical references

The **New** York Times Passover cookbook; more than 200 holiday recipes from top chefs and writers; edited by Linda Amster. Morrow 1999 xxii, 328p il $25   **641.5**

1. Jewish cooking 2. Passover
ISBN 0-688-15590-1   LC 98-41282

This book's recipes "range from the traditional to the innovative and are drawn from European, Mediterranean and Middle Eastern traditions. . . . Amster has produced what may be the definitive word in Passover cookbooks, from recipes to the feelings evoked by sitting at a beautifully set, bountifully laden table." Publ Wkly

Includes bibliographical references

Parsons, Russ
How to read a french fry; and other stories of intriguing kitchen science. Houghton Mifflin 2001 334p $25; pa $14   **641.5**
1. Cooking
ISBN 0-395-96783-X; 0-618-37943-6 (pa)
LC 00-54685
In this book "Parsons combines complex science . . . workable cooking techniques, and . . . recipes. Each chapter addresses a specific culinary-scientific process (e.g., deep-frying, the secret post-harvest life of fruits and vegetables), provides a list of rules to follow therein, then offers a range of recipes that use the technique in question." Publ Wkly

Pépin, Jacques
Jacques Pépin celebrates; by Jacques Pépin with Claudine Pépin; photographs by Christopher Hirsheimer; illustrations by Jacques Pépin. Knopf 2001 458p il $40
641.5
1. Cooking 2. Entertaining
ISBN 0-375-41209-3   LC 2001-29929
"In this companion to a new PBS series, Pépin builds on a broad definition of celebrations—encompassing holidays, special occasions, and simply nice weather—to present a collection of typically solid French recipes and numerous useful tips and techniques. . . . More valuable than the recipes . . . are the many notes on chopping, garnishing, carving and so forth." Publ Wkly

Jacques Pépin's simple and healthy cooking; written and illustrated by Jacques Pépin. Rodale Press 1994 354p il hardcover o.p. paperback available $18.95   **641.5**
1. Cooking 2. Low-cholesterol diet 3. Nutrition
ISBN 0-87596-362-5 (pa)   LC 94-29177
"The 200 recipes provided are drawn from classic French cuisine. Pepin hasn't totally eliminated high-fat items (e.g., cream), but they appear in smaller proportions than classic cuisine calls for. . . . Each recipe contains a caloric breakdown so readers can pick and choose freely. Recipes are well-written, and many have useful notes. Most recipes can be tackled by anyone, but some are time-consuming." Publ Wkly

Peterson, James
Glorious French food; a fresh approach to the classics. Wiley 2002 xxv, 742p il map $45   **641.5**
1. French cooking
ISBN 0-471-44276-3   LC 2001-46972
The author presents "50 classic recipes as the starting point for his wide-ranging exploration of French food and techniques; each recipe serves both to demonstrate a variety of techniques and as the inspiration for a diverse collection of other recipes related to it in one way or another. . . . Each chapter includes boxes and charts on improvising with different ingredients and flavors. The suggested variations for individual recipes, often mini-essays in themselves, open up dozens of other possibilities. Peterson is both passionate and knowledgeable about his subject, and his . . . book is an essential purchase." Libr J
Includes bibliographical references

Polin, Bonnie Sanders, 1941-
The Joslin Diabetes gourmet cookbook; heart-healthy, everyday recipes for family and friends; [by] Bonnie Sanders Polin and Frances Towner Giedt, with the nutrition services staff at Joslin Diabetes Center; foreword by Edward Horton. Bantam Bks. 1993 xxx, 509p il $29.95   **641.5**
1. Diabetes—Diet therapy
ISBN 0-553-08760-6   LC 93-25887
"Along with more than 300 recipes, ranging from Spicy Seafood Gazpacho to Thai Basil Chicken to Herb-Stuffed Fillet of Beef, there are lots of menu suggestions, ideas for quick meals and snacks, and background information on diabetes and health. Essential." Libr J

Prudhomme, Paul
Chef Paul Prudhomme's Louisiana kitchen; photography by Tom Jimison. Morrow 1984 351p il $28   **641.5**
1. Cooking—Louisiana
ISBN 0-688-02847-0   LC 83-63236
"These 200-plus recipes comprise authentic Cajun, Creole, and southern Louisiana cuisine. That means gumbos (seven kinds here), spicy chicken and seafood dishes, sauces and gravies, pecan-based desserts, and Prudhomme's own specialty—rabbit—along with many other dishes." Booklist

Chef Paul Prudhomme's Louisiana tastes; exciting flavors from the state that cooks. Morrow 2000 347p il $25   **641.5**
1. Cooking—Louisiana
ISBN 0-688-12224-8   LC 99-35611
"Chronicling dishes from his native state, Prudhomme acknowledges that Louisiana home cooks don't normally serve anything so fancy as appetizers, so he offers dozens of ideas for starters that may readily serve as entrees by simply increasing portion size. . . . Each recipe now has its own unique seasoning mix varying from a few to a dozen spices and herbs." Booklist

Randall, Joe
A taste of heritage; the new African-American cuisine; [by] Joe Randall & Toni Tipton-Martin. Macmillan 1998 334p hardcover o.p. paperback available $19.95
641.5
1. African American cooking
ISBN 0-7645-6701-1 (pa)   LC 97-43736
"The authors offer seasonal menus, and chefs contemplate the effects of today's African American cooking and assess its future in an increasingly homogeneous food world." Booklist

Roberts, Michael, 1949-
Parisian home cooking; conversations, recipes, and tips from the cooks and food merchants of Paris; photographs by Perre-Gilles Vidoli. Morrow 1999 335p il $28
641.5
1. French cooking
ISBN 0-688-13868-3   LC 98-41750
Roberts re-examines "a cuisine that can intimidate with its sometimes exacting procedures. He shows that Parisian home cooks are as hampered by small kitchens

Roberts, Michael, 1949——*Continued*
and time shortages as the rest of us, and that, as a result, their daily recipes are far less complicated than traditional French cookbooks suggest. Roberts proves that techniques are within the reach of anyone." Publ Wkly

Roden, Claudia
The new book of Middle Eastern food. rev ed. Knopf 2000 513p il $35   **641.5**
1. Middle Eastern cooking
ISBN 0-375-40506-2   LC 00-708864
Originally published 1968 in the United Kingdom; first United States edition published 1972 with title: A book of Middle Eastern food
This volume "includes 800 recipes and variations, as well as historical background, an introduction to essential ingredients and regional dietary practices, folktales, and a vast amount of other information." Libr J
Includes bibliographical references

Rombauer, Irma von Starkloff, 1877-1962
Joy of cooking; [by] Irma S. Rombauer, Marion Rombauer Becker; illustrated by Ginnie Hofmann and Ikki Matsumoto. Scribner il $35   **641.5**
1. Cooking
Also available two volume paperback edition from New Am Lib.
First published 1931. (1997 edition) Periodically revised
"All-purpose cookbook for informal and formal use with American and foreign recipes. Includes menu planning suggestions, nutrition, basic information on foods, basic cooking terminology, and methods of preparation." N Y Public Libr Book of How & Where to Look It Up

Sass, Lorna J.
Great vegetarian cooking under pressure; two-hour taste in ten minutes. Morrow 1994 272p il $27   **641.5**
1. Vegetarian cooking
ISBN 0-688-12326-0   LC 94-10054
This is a collection of "soup, vegetable, grain, and bean recipes that can be made in the pressure cooker, most in a fraction of the time they would ordinarily take. . . . Most of the recipes will appeal to vegetarians and nonvegetarians alike." Libr J
Includes bibliographical references

Shaw, Diana, 1958-
The essential vegetarian cookbook; your guide to the best foods on earth. Potter 1997 611p il hardcover o.p. paperback available $24.95   **641.5**
1. Vegetarian cooking
ISBN 0-517-88268-X (pa)   LC 96-22290
"Shaw's recipes appeal to any educated palate, with dishes, such as fresh corn custard with polenta crust, that could be offered in any mainstream contemporary cookbook. Soups and breads abound here, and she encourages cooks to use her recipes as starting points to show off their own creative urges. Each recipe has a nutritional analysis appended, including a protein index." Booklist

Shimbo, Hiroko
The Japanese kitchen; 250 recipes in a traditional spirit; illustrations by Rodica Prato. Harvard Common Press; [distributed by] National Bk. Network 2000 512p il hardcover o.p. paperback available $21.95   **641.5**
1. Japanese cooking
ISBN 1-55832-177-2 (pa)   LC 00-33505
The author provides a "guide to equipment, techniques, and ingredients, followed by a wide-ranging selection of recipes of all sorts. There are both the homestyle dishes she grew up on and more elaborate ones for special occasions, as well as the traditional Japanese classics, with her own touches, of course, and innovative new recipes. . . . An essential purchase." Libr J

Smith, Chris, 1966-
Cooking with the diabetic chef. American Diabetes Assn. 2000 xxi, 169p il pa $19.95   **641.5**
1. Diabetes—Diet therapy 2. Cooking
ISBN 1-58040-043-4   LC 00-36208
"Recipes are divided by season to reflect the abundance of fresh foods available at different times of year. Emphasis is placed on the use of the freshest meats and vegetables for optimum flavor. . . . Complete dietary data, including exchanges, are included with each recipe. The bulk of the recipes are for meats, main dishes, and vegetables, with a smattering for salads and desserts." Libr J
"Collections lacking good contemporary recipes for diabetics would do well to add this volume." Booklist

Somerville, Annie
Fields of Greens; new vegetarian recipes from the celebrated Greens Restaurant. Bantam Bks. 1993 xxiv, 437p il $32.95   **641.5**
1. Vegetarian cooking
ISBN 0-553-09139-5   LC 92-42931
"Greens is known for its unique and sophisticated vegetarian fare, with an emphasis on fresh ingredients and flavor. Somerville, the executive chef, presents more than 300 inventive recipes, including appetizing creations like Grilled New Potato Salad, Mushroom Risotto with Leeks and Fennel, and Lemon Pots de Creme, along with lots of beautiful soups, pastas and pizzas, delicious sandwiches, and a variety of sauces and condiments." Libr J

Sorosky, Marlene
Fast & festive meals for the Jewish holidays; complete menus, rituals, and party-planning ideas for every holiday of the year; [by] Marlene Sorosky, in collaboration with Joanne Neuman and Debbie Shahvar. Morrow 1997 223p il $29.95   **641.5**
1. Jewish cooking 2. Jewish holidays 3. Entertaining 4. Menus
ISBN 0-688-14570-1   LC 97-11188
"Sorosky provides menus for all the major holidays or holy days and some minor ones, as well as for a bar/bat mitzvah, Israel Independence Day, and other events. . . . She also offers decorating tips, ideas for kids' activities, and 'game plans' and provides brief descriptions of the rituals involved, with appropriate blessings." Libr J
"Jewish cuisine will achieve new and tasty accolades under Sorosky's wise tutelage. . . . Cholesterol-packed ingredients have been reduced if not completely eliminated." Booklist

Stewart, Martha

The Martha Stewart cookbook; collected recipes for every day; edited by Roy Finamore; design by the Valentine Group; illustrations by Rodica Prato. Potter 1995 620p il $30   **641.5**

1. Cooking 2. Entertaining

ISBN 0-517-70335-1   LC 95-34600

This volume contains some 1,600 recipes and variations from Stewart's previously published collections. It includes "new step-by-step illustrations, new menus, and sidebars and tips on [such] subjects as . . . freezing pastry, selecting the best fruit, and setting the table." Publisher's note

Martha Stewart's healthy quick cook; four seasons of great menus to make every day; photographs by James Merrell. Potter 1997 224p il $32.50   **641.5**

1. Cooking 2. Low-fat diet

ISBN 0-517-57702-X   LC 96-31766

"Stewart's low-fat cooking depends heavily for its success on the use of seasonally fresh produce, so she organizes recipes by the year's cycles to take advantage of markets. . . . Citrus abounds: lemon scents risotto, orange enlivens spaghetti squash, tangerine spruces arugula and endive. Stewart's most inventive ideas, such as her portobello mushroom 'pizzas,' showcase her real talents." Booklist

Special occasions; the best of Martha Stewart living. Potter 1995 144p il pa $20

641.5

1. Cooking 2. Entertaining

ISBN 0-517-88402-X   LC 94-40128

This volume includes "recipes, decorating ideas, and gardening tips culled from previously published holiday features in Stewart's *Living* magazine. From a New Year's meal bedecked with cut branches that have been forced into bloom, the reader proceeds to spectacular cakes designed for a lavish Mother's Day get-together, onward to a Labor Day bash with crayfish and French Provençal dishes." Booklist

Stow, Josie

The African kitchen; a day in the life of a safari chef; [by] Josie Stow and Jan Baldwin. Interlink Bks. 1999 144p il $25   **641.5**

1. African cooking

ISBN 1-56656-354-2   LC 99-52120

"When Stow first took over the kitchen at a game preserve in South Africa, she found that most such establishments were serving European-style food. Drawing on the knowledge and experience of the cooks working with her, she developed a repertoire of traditional and modern African dishes. . . . Beautiful photographs of African nightcapes, people, and Stow's food illustrate the text." Libr J

Tausend, Marilyn

Cocina de la familia; more than 200 authentic recipes from Mexican-American home kitchens; [by] Marilyn Tausend with Miguel Ravago. Simon & Schuster 1997 415p hardcover o.p. paperback available $20

641.5

1. Mexican American cooking

ISBN 0-684-85259-4 (pa)   LC 97-26979

This cookbook includes recipes for "Green Enchiladas with Spinach and Tofu, Chicken with Spicy Prune Sauce made with Coca-Cola, and Mexican Beef Chow Mein, [as well as] more traditional Mexican fare like Guacamole and Braised Chicken with Rice and Vegetables." Publ Wkly

Includes bibliographical references

Tsai, Ming, 1964-

Blue Ginger; East-meets-West cooking with Ming Tsai; by Ming Tsai and Arthur Boehm. Potter 1999 275p $32.50   **641.5**

1. Cooking

ISBN 0-609-60530-5   LC 99-36393

"Chapters divide the 125-plus recipes into soups, dim sum, rice and noodles, poultry, meat, seafood, elaborate side dishes and desserts, with mail-order sources. . . . Instructions are clearly written and often include tips for wine and food pairings and advice on ingredient substitutions and techniques." Publ Wkly

Weil, Andrew

The healthy kitchen; recipes for a better body, life, and spirit; [by] Andrew Weil and Rosie Daley; photographs by Sang An, Amy Haskell, and Eric Studer. Knopf 2002 xxxvii, 325p il $24.95; pa $16.95   **641.5**

1. Cooking 2. Natural foods

ISBN 0-375-41306-5; 0-375-71031-0 (pa)

LC 2001-50391

Also available large print edition $24.95 (ISBN 0-375-43161-6)

This volume features "healthful recipes and information on topics ranging from growing herbs to wine to the Mediterranean diet. Recipes contain nutrition information, but this is not 'diet food': recipes include Smoked Fish with Horseradish Sauce, Roasted Cornish Hens with Roasted Garlic, and Thai Shrimp and Papaya Salad." Libr J

This is "a stimulating invitation to healthy, pleasurable eating." Publ Wkly

White, Joyce, 1942-

Soul food; recipes and reflections from African-American churches. HarperCollins Pubs. 1998 355p il $25   **641.5**

1. African American cooking

ISBN 0-06-018716-6   LC 97-22454

The author "brings together reminiscences and stories of African American women with 150 of their best recipes, including crab cakes, West African chicken, and lemon chess pie." Libr J

Zanger, Mark H.

The American history cookbook. Greenwood Press 2003 xxiii, 459p il (Cookbooks for students) $29.95   **641.5**

1. Cooking

ISBN 1-573-56376-5   LC 2002-69608

"An Oryx book"

Zanger, Mark H.—*Continued*

"This book uses historical commentary and recipes to trace the history of American cooking from the first European contact with Native Americans to the 1970s. Each of 50 chronologically arranged topical chapters contain 500-1,000 words of general commentary followed by descriptions and . . . step-by-step instructions for 3-4 recipes. The recipes are drawn from a wide variety of historical cookbooks and other historical sources." Publisher's note

For a review see: Booklist, Nov. 1, 2003
Includes bibliographical references

641.6 Cooking specific materials

Aidells, Bruce

The complete meat cookbook; a juicy and authorative guide to selecting, seasoning, and cooking today's beef, pork, lamb, and veal; [by] Bruce Aidelle and Denis Kelly; photographs by Beatriz Da Costa; illustrations by Mary De Palma. Houghton Mifflin 1998 604p il $35   **641.6**
1. Cooking—Meat
ISBN 0-618-13512-X   LC 98-28216
"More than 230 recipes, many with several variations, are presented along with charts and illustrations to help the reader understand different types of meat." Libr J

Brody, Jane E.

Jane Brody's good seafood book; by Jane E. Brody with Richard Flaste; illustrations by Pat Stewart. Norton 1994 577p il $27.50
                                      641.6
1. Cooking—Seafood 2. Seafood
ISBN 0-393-03687-1   LC 94-16482
Also available in paperback from Fawcett Bk. Group
Part One of this book is an "overview of seafood lore that includes chapters on how to select fish; how to clean, fillet, and store it. . . . Part Two is a collection of some 250 recipes for hors d'oeuvres and appetizers, soups, salads, and main courses, including special sections on grilling and microwaving." Publisher's note
"This is a more than usually comprehensive, conscientious and trustworthy cookbook." Publ Wkly

Cameron, Angus

The L.L. Bean game and fish cookbook; by Angus Cameron and Judith Jones; illustrations by Bill Elliott. Random House 1983 475p il $25.95   **641.6**
1. Cooking—Game 2. Cooking—Fish
ISBN 0-394-51191-3   LC 82-15089
This book "explains how to dress, hang, smoke, age and clean fish and game. It . . . covers field dressing of deer, moose, elk and bear. There are also directions for smoking, grilling, barbecuing, poaching, marinating and larding." N Y Times Book Rev
"With handsome wildlife and botanical drawings by Bill Elliott, the book was written by two experts and is complete and comprehensive." Christ Sci Monit

Czarnecki, Jack

A cook's book of mushrooms; with 100 recipes for common and uncommon varieties; photographs by Louis B. Wallach. Artisan 1995 208p il $30   **641.6**
1. Cooking—Mushrooms 2. Mushrooms
ISBN 1-885183-07-0   LC 94-48906
The author "writes about mushroom hunting in almost mystical terms while providing reliable information on a great variety of common and exotic mushrooms, both cultivated and wild. He also includes 100 mushroom recipes, many of them quite unusual; all are accompanied by wine suggestions." Libr J
Includes bibliographical references

Desaulniers, Marcel

Celebrate with chocolate; totally over-the-top recipes; recipes with Ganache Hill test kitchen chef Brett Bailey; photographs by Ron Manville. Morrow 2002 175p il $24.95   **641.6**
1. Cooking—Chocolate 2. Desserts
ISBN 0-688-16298-3   LC 2002-71777
This cookbook features "recipes ranging from Dancing Gingerbread Men Peppermint Fudge Cake to Chocolate-Peanut Butter Fusion Brownies. Many of the recipes are complicated, but the instructions are detailed and clear, and there are mouth-watering color photographs of selected showstoppers. For all baking collections." Libr J
Includes bibliographical references

Fowler, Damon Lee

Fried chicken; the world's best recipes from Memphis to Milan, from Buffalo to Bangkok. Broadway Bks. 1999 196p maps pa $15   **641.6**
1. Cooking—Poultry
ISBN 0-7679-0183-5   LC 98-19140
Fowler describes the different methods for preparing fried chicken from around the world. Suggestions for making gravies and side dishes are included
Includes bibliographical references

Griffith, Linda

Garlic, garlic, garlic; exceptional recipes from the world's most indispensable ingredient; [by] Linda & Fred Griffith; illustrations by Michael Halbert. Houghton Mifflin 1998 432p il pa $16   **641.6**
1. Cooking 2. Garlic
ISBN 0-395-89254-6   LC 98-28213
The Griffiths "cover 'designer' garlic, garlic festivals, growing your own, and more, with lots of esoteric information and trivia along the way. . . . Entertaining and filled with delicious recipes, this is recommended for most collections." Libr J
Includes bibliographical references

Marshall, Lydie

A passion for potatoes. HarperCollins Pubs. 1992 xxiii, 248p il hardcover o.p. paperback available $16.95   **641.6**
1. Cooking—Potatoes
ISBN 0-06-096910-5 (pa)   LC 91-50516
This book contains "recipes for all courses of a meal, including dessert, along with separate chapters on favorite potato preparations, from mashing through frying. . . . Headnotes include potato and other culinary lore, and the recipes are clear and well written. A charming and knowledgeable work." Libr J

Morash, Marian

The victory garden cookbook. Knopf 1982 374p il hardcover o.p. paperback available $29.95   **641.6**

1. Cooking—Vegetables 2. Vegetable gardening
ISBN 0-394-70780-X (pa)   LC 81-48132

"Basic gardening methods and preparation and storage techniques are reviewed, as are special characteristics of a particular vegetable. Numerous recipes are included for each vegetable and range from unadorned braising, baking, grilling, and broiling methods to special dishes." Booklist

Peterson, James

Fish & shellfish; the cook's indispensable companion; photographs by James Peterson. Morrow 1996 413p il $40   **641.6**

1. Cooking—Seafood
ISBN 0-688-12737-1   LC 95-38375

This cookbook includes "more than 160 step-by-step technique photographs—in color. The section on finfish is organized by method of preparation, including curing, smoking, and serving raw, while the different types of shellfish, which require more individualized treatment, are allowed a chapter each. Then there are recipes for 'seafood in other guises'—soups, stews, etc.—and accompaniments, followed by a detailed glossary of fresh and saltwater finfish." Libr J

Vegetables. Morrow 1998 429p il $35   **641.6**

1. Cooking—Vegetables
ISBN 0-688-14658-9   LC 97-42104

The author "suggests cooking techniques for some 60 vegetables. His unpretentious tone and deft way of making vegetables alluring to all render this book uncommonly captivating." Publ Wkly

Ross, Rosa Lo San

Beyond bok choy; a cook's guide to Asian vegetables; photographs by Martin Jacobs. Artisan 1996 191p il $25   **641.6**

1. Cooking—Vegetables 2. Oriental cooking
ISBN 1-885183-23-2   LC 95-47566

In this guide to Asian vegetables the author "describes each vegetable, tells how to store it and use it, offers brief gardening tips for those inclined to grow their own, and includes a recipe or two. Beautiful full-page color photographs make identification of these exotic marketplace items easy." Libr J

Includes bibliographical references

Schlesinger, Chris

How to cook meat; [by] Chris Schlesinger and John Willoughby. Morrow 2000 466p il hardcover o.p. paperback available $24.95   **641.6**

1. Cooking—Meat
ISBN 0-06-050771-3 (pa)   LC 00-62482

This cookbook includes 200 recipes for beef, veal, lamb and pork dishes. "Most every recipe is accompanied by useful sidebars that detail the cut of meat to use, offer alternative cuts and even tell you how the dish holds up as a leftover. With humor, clarity and expertise, these two renowned food writers have created a requisite text for any serious meat lover." Publ Wkly

Schneider, Elizabeth, 1943-

Vegetables from amaranth to zucchini; the essential reference: 500 recipes and 275 photographs; photographs by Amos Chan. Morrow 2001 xxiv, 777p il $60   **641.6**

1. Cooking—Vegetables 2. Vegetables
ISBN 0-688-15260-0   LC 2001-30423

This is a reference to more than 350 vegetables with information on availability, selection, storage, preparation, use, and recipes

"Schneider treats each vegetable with poetic directness, consulting authorities from around the world. . . . [This is a] landmark volume, a tribute to one writer's passion and patience." N Y Times Book Rev

Includes bibliographical references

Shurtleff, William, 1941-

The book of tofu; protein source of the future—now! [by] William Shurtleff & Akiko Aoyagi; illustrated by Akiko Aoyagi. rev & updated ed. Ten Speed Press 1983 v1 335p il hardcover o.p. paperback available $24.95   **641.6**

1. Cooking—Tofu
ISBN 1-58008-013-8 (pa)   LC 83-70113

Also available in paperback from Ballantine Bks.

"A Soyfoods Center book"

First publsihed 1975

This book contains over 500 recipes from East and West, with step-by-step instructions for making tofu at home, or in a commercial tofu shop. It also features an analysis of tofu's nutritional value

Includes bibliographical references

Waters, Alice

Chez Panisse vegetables; [by] Alice Waters and the cooks of Chez Panisse; illustrations by Patricia Curtan. HarperCollins Pubs. 1996 344p il $35   **641.6**

1. Chez Panisse (Berkeley, Calif.: Restaurant) 2. Cooking—Vegetables
ISBN 0-06-017147-2   LC 96-11305

The author "includes more than 40 vegetables in this beautifully illustrated book, describing them and how to prepare them in detail and offering more than 250 recipes. . . . An invaluable resource." Libr J

Includes bibliographical references

Willinger, Faith Heller

Red, white, and greens; the Italian way with vegetables; [by] Faith Willinger. HarperCollins Pubs. 1996 339p $25; pa $15   **641.6**

1. Cooking—Vegetables 2. Italian cooking
ISBN 0-06-018366-7; 0-06-093050-0 (pa)
     LC 96-1664

Willinger "presents 150 recipes that show Italian vegetable cookery at its best, from Florentine Artichoke Tortino to Pantelleria Potato Salad. . . . [A] wonderful collection of vegetable dishes from a spirited and knowledgeable writer." Libr J

641.7 Specific cooking processes and techniques

Kafka, Barbara
Roasting; a simple art; photographs by Maria Robledo. Morrow 1995 452p il $28

641.7

1. Cooking
ISBN 0-688-13135-2   LC 95-18259
The author "offers a detailed guide, with recipes, to roasting poultry, meats, and game, including a section on vegetables that is almost a book in itself." Libr J

Schlesinger, Chris
The thrill of the grill; techniques, recipes & down-home barbecue; [by] Chris Schlesinger & John Willoughby, line drawings by Laura Hartman Maestro; photography by Vincent Lee. Morrow 1990 395p il $30; pa $17.95

641.7

1. Barbecue cooking
ISBN 0-688-08832-5; 0-06-008449-9 (pa)
LC 89-77522
The authors present a collection of recipes as well as advice about grilling and barbecuing food
Schlesinger "favors what he calls 'equatorial cuisine,' and Caribbean, Mexican, and Southeast Asian influences are evident in his recipes. His grilled dishes are full-flavored and often hot and spicy." Libr J

641.8 Cooking specific kinds of composite dishes

American Heart Association low-fat & luscious desserts. Potter 2000 187p il $24.50

641.8

1. Low-fat diet 2. Desserts
ISBN 0-8129-3336-2   LC 00-35698
"At the bottom of each recipe is a nutritional chart detailing the calories, fat grams, cholesterol, and fiber count per serving. The introduction and appendixes cover a wide range of topics, including basic equipment, a well-stocked pantry, a heart health and body mass index, and tips on how to read labels. This slim volume is essential for public libraries." Libr J

Beard, James, 1903-1985
Beard on bread; drawings by Karl Stuecklen. Knopf 1973 230p il hardcover o.p. paperback available $15

641.8

1. Bread
ISBN 0-679-75504-7 (pa)
"An inclusive guide to the preparation of a variety of breads with recipes for coffee cakes, rolls, flat breads, fried cakes. . . . The recipes included are those Beard considers the best from around the world which can be made in a U.S. kitchen." Booklist

Beranbaum, Rose Levy
The cake bible; edited by Maria D. Guarnaschelli; photographs by Vincent Lee; foreword by Maida Heatter. Morrow 1988 555p il $35

641.8

1. Cake
ISBN 0-688-04402-6   LC 88-1369
A collection of recipes for classic cakes, buttercreams, icings, fillings and toppings. Ingredients are listed in tabular form with weights given in both ounces and grams. Assembly and storage instructions are included
Includes bibliographical references

The pie and pastry bible; illustrations by Laura Hartman Maestro; photographs by Gentl & Hyers. Scribner 1998 692p il $45

641.8

1. Baking
ISBN 0-684-81348-3   LC 98-42869
This is a "collection of more than 200 recipes for sweet and savory treats, including pies, puff pastry, biscuits, and fillings. Both culinary novices and experienced bakers will appreciate the precise preparation instructions provided for every recipe." Libr J

Collister, Linda
The bread book; by Linda Collister and Anthony Blake. [rev and updated ed] Lyons Press 2000 192p il $35; pa $19.95   **641.8**

1. Bread
ISBN 1-58574-057-8; 1-58574-447-6 (pa)
First published 1993 in the United Kingdom
"Detailed photographs accompanying each recipe usefully assist the beginner, showing doughs at various stages of kneading, rising, and forming. An attractive, worthwhile addition to the field of bread books." Booklist

The **Complete** book of pasta and noodles; by the editors of Cook's illustrated; preface by Christopher Kimball; illustrations by Judy Love; photographs by Daniel J. van Ackere. Potter 2000 483p il hardcover o.p. paperback available $19.95   **641.8**

1. Cooking—Pasta products
ISBN 0-609-80930-X (pa)   LC 99-40076
This work brings "together information and recipes covering pasta's worldwide range from North America's beloved macaroni and cheese through Italy's sophisticated sauces, across China's exotic rice noodles, and up to Japan's modest Zen noodles in broth. . . . Content and organization combine to make this a superior cooking reference book for libraries." Booklist

Crocker, Betty
Betty Crocker cookie book. rev ed. Wiley 2003 xxix, 322p il $22.95   **641.8**
ISBN 0-7645-3940-X   LC 2003-270127
First published 1963 by Golden Press with title: Cooky book
This book features "over 240 cookie favorites, from heirloom showstoppers to contemporary treats . . . [including] everything from chocolate chip cookies to brownies, oatmeal cookies to date bars and more." Publisher's note

Cunningham, Marion

The Fannie Farmer baking book; illustrated by Lauren Jarrett. Knopf 1984 624p il o.p.; Wings Bks. paperback available $9.99   **641.8**
1. Baking
ISBN 0-517-14829-3 (pa)   LC 84-47862
"Separate chapters cover pies and tarts, cookies, cakes, yeast breads, quick breads, and crackers in encyclopedic detail with brisk but reassuring professionalism. Many of the 800 recipes are standard favorites." Libr J

Dalsass, Diana

The new good cake book; over 125 delicious recipes that can be prepared in 30 minutes or less. Norton 1996 203p hardcover o.p. paperback available $14.95   **641.8**
1. Cake 2. Quick and easy cooking
ISBN 0-393-31882-6 (pa)   LC 96-13352
First published 1982 with title: The good cake book
"In addition to Orange Syrup Cake and Sour Cream-Fig Cake, Dalsass . . . includes recipes for 'bar cakes' such as Fudge-Filled Blondies and for biscotti. She likes plain, easy cakes, but many of these are rich and indulgent as well. . . . With its simple but mouth-watering recipes, this book is recommended for most collections." Libr J

Desaulniers, Marcel

Death by chocolate cakes; an astonishing array of chocolate enchantment; recipes with Brett Bailey and Kelly Bailey; photography by Duane Winfield. Morrow 2000 216p il $35   **641.8**
1. Cake 2. Cooking—Chocolate
ISBN 0-688-16297-5   LC 00-56247
This "cookbook features indulgent showstoppers, from Happy All the Time Cakes to Excessively Expressive Espresso Ecstasy, each one shown in a full-page color photograph. Although many of the recipes are complicated, instructions are detailed and clear; there are no headnotes per se to introduce these creations, but 'The Chef's Touch' section at the end of each recipe provides tips and some background." Libr J
Includes bibliographical references

Greenspan, Dorie

Baking with Julia; based on the PBS series hosted by Julia Child; written by Dorie Greenspan; photographs by Gentl & Hyers. Morrow 1996 480p il $40   **641.8**
1. Baking
ISBN 0-688-14657-0   LC 96-23061
"The 200 recipes are organized as a course in baking, with an early, energetic section on the basic batters and doughs for cakes and pastries. The book moves on to recipes of varying degrees of complexity. . . . But the book's success is due to more than organization: the text never misses a chance to explain, expand and entertain." N Y Times Book Rev
Includes bibliographical references

Heatter, Maida

Maida Heatter's book of great desserts; drawings by Toni Evins. Andrew McMeel 1999 xxxii, 528p il $26.95   **641.8**
1. Desserts
ISBN 0-8362-7861-5   LC 98-45993
First published 1974 by Knopf

This cookbook features nearly 300 dessert recipes for both light and rich desserts including Queen Mother's Cake, Mushroom Meringues, and East 62nd Street Lemon Cake

Maida Heatter's brand-new book of great cookies; illustrations by the author. Random House 1995 244p il hardcover o.p. paperback available $19   **641.8**
1. Cookies
ISBN 0-8129-9175-3 (pa)   LC 95-5250
First published 1977 with title: Book of great cookies
This volume contains "recipes for biscotti, drop cookies, icebox cookies, bar cookies, zweiback, . . . crackers, and some desserts." Libr J
"The instructions here are true to a long line of Heatter recipes: foolproof. Ms. Heatter's instructions are famously meticulous. They are also lengthy and chatty, full of learned asides." N Y Times Book Rev

Hensperger, Beth

The best quick breads; 150 recipes for muffins, scones, shortcakes, gingerbreads, cornbreads, coffeecakes, and more; Beth Hensperger. Harvard Common Press; [distributed by] National Bk. Network 2000 256p pa $22.95   **641.8**
1. Bread
ISBN 1-55832-171-3   LC 00-36962
First published 1994 by Chronicle Books with title: The art of quick breads
This book includes about 150 recipes. "In addition to quick loaves, both sweet and savory, there are waffles, dumplings, biscuits, popovers, and a variety of other easy baked goods, along with some tasty accompaniments, such as the Fruit Salsa for her Hopi Blue Corn Hotcakes." Libr J

The bread lover's bread machine cookbook; a master baker's 300 favorite recipes for perfect-every-time bread, from every kind of machine; illustrations by Kristin Hurlin. Harvard Common Press; [distributed by] National Bk. Network 2000 643p hardcover o.p. paperback available $21.95   **641.8**
1. Bread
ISBN 1-55832-156-X (pa)   LC 99-87358
Hensperger discusses the automatic bread maker and provides instructions for producing loaves of bread that differ in shape and taste
The author's "impressive bread machine book should tempt many bakers, experienced and novice alike, to try what she refers to as 'the new generation' of these appliances." Libr J
Includes bibliographical references

Malgieri, Nick

How to bake. HarperCollins Pubs. 1995 457p il $37.50   **641.8**
1. Baking
ISBN 0-06-016819-6   LC 95-32231
This introduction to baking covers "breads, savory pastries, and sweet baked goods of all kinds. Chapters are organized as an extended cooking course, with fundamental techniques included in earlier recipes, more complicated skills in the later ones." Libr J
Includes bibliographical references

Malgieri, Nick—*Continued*

Perfect cakes; photographs by Tom Eckerle. HarperCollins Pubs. 2002 xxvi, 326p il $37.50   **641.8**

1. Cake
ISBN 0-06-019879-6   LC 2002-17338

The author "dedicates individual chapters to various types of cakes, including coffee cakes, chocolate cakes, and layer cakes, before concluding with a look at frostings, fillings, and cake decorating. Among the 200 recipes included are such tempting treats as classic pound cake, Swiss apricot cake, and milk chocolate mousse cake, and the author offers a nice balance between basic, simple recipes for the beginner and more challenging recipes for the experienced baker." Libr J

"Where many compendiums tend to be overwhelming or scattershot, this book stylishly covers just what home cooks need." Publ Wkly

Includes bibliographical references

Moosewood Restaurant book of desserts; [by] the Moosewood Collective. Potter 1997 398p il hardcover o.p. paperback available $22   **641.8**

1. Desserts
ISBN 0-517-88493-3 (pa)   LC 97-1234

This volume offers a variety of recipes for cakes, cookies, pies, candies, and frozen and fruit desserts

"Recipes are clear and generally easily re-created in the home kitchen." Booklist

Nathan, Joan

The Jewish holiday baker; illustrated by Emma Celia Gardner. Schocken Bks. 1997 211p il $23; pa $16.95   **641.8**

1. Baking 2. Jewish cooking 3. Jewish holidays
ISBN 0-8052-4142-6; 0-8052-1117-9 (pa)
                    LC 97-9775

This provides fifty recipes for baked goods associated with Jewish holidays, such as hamantashen, macaroons, honey cake and challah, from various countries including Turkey, Hungary, Germany, and Russia. Reminiscences of Jewish bakers are also included

Patent, Greg, 1939-

Baking in America; traditional and contemporary favorites from the past 200 years. Houghton Mifflin 2002 552p il $35
                    641.8

1. Baking
ISBN 0-618-04831-6

In this "collection of baking recipes, Patent . . . takes classics from old American cookbooks and makes them work with modern-day ingredients, encompassing all aspects of baking from Savory Yeast Breads through Pound Cakes to Pies and Tarts. After explaining the ingredients and equipment, he moves on to the recipes, which include timeless treasures of America's baking tradition such as Parker House Rolls, Lindy's Cheesecake and Lady Baltimore Cake." Publ Wkly

"Patent's cookbook will be irresistible to anyone interested in the rich traditions and history of American baking." Libr J

Peters, Colette

Colette's cakes; the art of cake decorating. Little, Brown 1991 163p il $35   **641.8**

1. Cake decorating
ISBN 0-316-70205-6   LC 90-24676

"This is not intended as a cookbook, although recipes for a white as well as a chocolate cake precede instructions for basic cake decorating. The bulk of the guide contains step-by-step directions for assembling four fabulous cake designs that range from an impressive seashell cake to multitiered wedding cakes." Booklist

Includes bibliographical references

Pillsbury best cookies cookbook; favorite recipes from America's most-trusted kitchens; [by] the Pillsbury Company. Potter 1997 255p il $21.95   **641.8**

1. Cookies
ISBN 0-609-60084-2   LC 97-1773

This "cookbook includes more than 175 recipes for cookies, brownies, and other bars, from old favorites like Chocolate Chips to new ones like Cherry Poppy Seed Twinks. . . . There are also lots of tips and hints, suggestions to 'Make It Special,' and variations, as well as 'real-time' prep times and nutrition analyses for each recipe." Libr J

"An unpretentious, well-presented and -illustrated cookie compendium sure to please bakers of every stripe." Booklist

Puck, Wolfgang

Wolfgang Puck's pizza, pasta and more! photographs by Steven Rothfeld. Random House 2000 205p il $35   **641.8**

1. Pizza 2. Cooking—Pasta products
ISBN 0-679-43887-4   LC 00-38715

This volume includes recipes for Puck's "signature Smoked Salmon Pizza and others, along with a dozen or so salads and soups, and a wide variety of pastas, from Angel Hair with Goat Cheese, Broccoli, and Pine Nuts to Spicy Thai Cold Noodles with Cilantro." Libr J

"A lively and inspired collection of popular recipes." Publ Wkly

Stewart, Martha

Martha Stewart's hors d'oeuvres handbook; by Martha Stewart with Susan Spungen; photographs by Dana Gallagher. Potter 1999 495p il $35   **641.8**

1. Appetizers
ISBN 0-609-60310-8   LC 98-39161

"This handbook is divided into two main sections: first, the photographs, of which there are more than 300, with every recipe shown in full color, and then over 350 recipes. . . . These are followed by a smaller section called 'The Guide,' with menus, party-planning ideas, and glossaries of ingredients and equipment." Libr J

Vollstedt, Maryana

The big book of soups & stews; 262 recipes for serious comfort food. Chronicle Bks. 2001 334p pa $19.95   **641.8**

1. Soups 2. Stews
ISBN 0-8118-3056-X   LC 2001-28034

These recipes range "from a hearty Beef and Chile Stew with Cornmeal Dumplings to a more sophisticated Shrimp and Scallop Chowder; there are many kid-friendly recipes as well, including several hamburger soups. Some of the recipes are staples (such as a classic Irish Stew), but many busy cooks will find it handy to have such favorites gathered in one place." Libr J

Walter, Carole

Great pies & tarts; foreword by Arthur Schwartz; photographs by Gentl & Hyers; illustrations by Rodica Prato. Potter 1998 488p il $35   **641.8**

1. Baking

ISBN 0-517-70398-X   LC 97-29148

"Walter begins with an extensive inventorying and analysis of the ingredients that make up today's pies, from crusts' shortening and flour to the various fruits (and vegetables) that fill them. Detailed instructions for preparing piecrust, that touchstone of home kitchen expertise, follow. . . . A glossary, a listing of mail-order sources, and a comprehensive bibliography ensure that no pie-related topic goes unaddressed." Booklist

642   Meals and table service

Lagasse, Emeril

Every day's a party; Louisiana recipes for celebrating with family and friends; [by] Emeril Lagasse, with Marcelle Bienvenu and Felicia Willett; photography by Philip Gould. Morrow 1999 338p il $26   **642**

1. Entertaining 2. Cooking 3. Menus

ISBN 0-688-16430-7   LC 99-29341

This cookbook collects Louisiana-style recipes for holidays and for regional and personal celebrations

"Recipes vary from simple to complex, but precise instructions enable an experienced cook in a home kitchen to produce delicious results; dishes are well seasoned but not incendiary." Libr J

Mills, Beverly

Desperation entertaining; by Beverly Mills and Alicia Ross; illustrated by Robin Zingone. Workman 2002 351p $25.95; pa $14.95   **642**

1. Entertaining

ISBN 0-7611-2796-8; 0-7611-1815-2 (pa)

LC 2002-16826

Companion volume Desperation dinners (1997)

"The recipes are organized into such chapters as 'Welcoming Light Bites,' 'The Good Ol' Crock-Pot,' and 'The Casual Cookout' and then into two categories within them: 'Fast and Fabulous,' dishes that take only minutes from start to finish; and 'Phased and Flexible,' which take a bit more time but can be prepared in stages, often almost entirely in advance." Libr J

Ohrbach, Barbara Milo

Tabletops; easy, practical, beautiful ways to decorate the table; photographs by John Hall. Potter 1997 136p il $24   **642**

1. Table setting and decoration 2. Entertaining

ISBN 0-517-70332-7   LC 97-219769

The author offers advice on table decoration with flowers, fruits, leaves, candles, table linens, silver, and china and includes recipes and entertainment ideas

Stewart, Martha

Great parties; recipes, menus, and ideas for perfect gatherings: the best of Martha Stewart living. Potter 1997 144p il pa $20   **642**

1. Entertaining 2. Cooking 3. Menus

ISBN 0-609-80099-X   LC 97-30271

This describes such parties as a Louisiana lunch, a Polynesian fantasy picnic, an East Hampton garden harvest party, a Vietnamese-Thai feast, and a Harlem soul food brunch, including menus, recipes, and table decorations

Martha Stewart's menus for entertaining; photographs by Dana Gallagher; design by Robert Valentine Incorporated. Potter 1994 224p il $30; pa $20   **642**

1. Cooking 2. Entertaining 3. Menus

ISBN 0-517-59099-9; 1-4000-4660-2 (pa)

LC 94-12930

Full-color photographs accompany step-by-step instructions for preparing 20 complete menus for a variety of gatherings. Over 150 recipes are included as well as tips on table settings and flower arrangements

643   Housing and household equipment

Becker, Norman

The complete book of home inspection. 3rd ed. McGraw-Hill 2002 289p il pa $19.95   **643**

1. Houses—Inspection

ISBN 0-07-139125-8   LC 2002-27892

First published 1980

The author "provides the novice homebuilder and buyer with inspection information for roofs, exterior landscaping, plumbing, and electrical, as well as tips on searching for insects and rotting materials. Helpful checklists guide readers in inspecting all parts of a home from the exterior walkway to the interior basement." Libr J

Beckstrom, Robert J.

Ortho's home repair problem solver; created and designed by the editorial staff of Ortho Books; writers Robert J. Beckstrom [et al.]; project editor, Sally W. Smith; illustration manager, Cyndie C. H. Wooley; designers, Barbara Ziller and John Williams, Barbara Ziller Design. Ortho Bks. 1995 320p il pa $24.95   **643**

1. Houses—Maintenance and repair

ISBN 0-89721-260-6   LC 94-69604

This volume offers step-by-step instructions on how to cope with over 1,000 problems around the home, ranging from chimney caps to basement drains. Includes over 400 color photographs and illustrations

Better Homes and Gardens new complete guide to home repair & improvement. 2nd ed. Meredith Corp. 1997 600p il hardcover o.p. paperback available $24.95   **643**

1. Houses—Maintenance and repair

ISBN 0-696-21189-0 (pa)   LC 97-71323

First published 1980 with title: Better homes and gardens complete guide to home repair, maintenance and improvement

Better Homes and Gardens new complete guide to home repair & improvement— *Continued*

This manual "includes 500 projects and more than 3,000 full-color illustrations. Organized in four large sections that cover basics as well as a homes' inside, outside, and systems. Projects list skills, time, and tools necessary for completion." Publisher's note

"This all-in-one, do-it-yourself guide offers exceptionally good tool coverage—an entire 60-pages are devoted to tools and their use, including uncommon information such as threading with taps and dies." Libr J

Bouknight, Joanne Kellar

The kitchen idea book. Taunton Press 1999 201p il $29.95; pa $24.95 **643**
1. Kitchens
ISBN 1-56158-161-5; 1-56158-393-6 (pa)
LC 98-41873
The author covers "cabinets, shelves, countertops, appliances, flooring, and light. Information on the choices with the advantages and disadvantages of each is provided. What makes this book especially useful are the numerous photographs that illustrate how all these materials have been used in actual kitchens." Libr J

Bower, Lynn Marie

Creating a healthy household; the ultimate guide for healthier, safer, less-toxic living. Healthy House Inst. 2000 700p pa $23.95
643
1. Housing—Environmental aspects 2. Home economics 3. Commercial products
ISBN 0-9637156-7-4
LC 99-96306
The first part of this "book briefly discusses some of the medical conditions associated with unhealthy indoor environments and generally addresses purchasing alternative items. Six subsequent, detailed sections cover a wide range of home and personal issues, including cleaning, laundry, cosmetics, textiles, remodeling, automobiles, home safety, pests, hobbies, appliances, and water and air quality. Throughout, suppliers are listed in boldfaced type." Libr J

Complete basements, attics & bonus rooms; plan & build your dream space. Better Homes & Gardens Bks. 2002 192p il pa $19.95 **643**
1. Houses—Remodeling
ISBN 0-696-21350-8
LC 2002-109235
This guide to remodeling attic, basement, and garage includes advice on ventilation, temperature control, and toxic materials involved

Fields, Alan

Your new house; the alert consumer's guide to buying and building a quality home. Windsor Peak Press pa $15.95 **643**
1. Houses—Buying and selling 2. Mortgages
First published 1993. (4th edition 2002) Periodically revised
This "volume addresses working with real estate agents, planning a budget, designing a home, assembling a building team, and understanding home inspections." Libr J
Includes bibliographical references

Home improvement 1-2-3. 2nd ed [New ed. completely rev. and expanded] Meredith Bks. 2003 560p il $34.95 **643**
1. Houses—Maintenance and repair 2. Houses—Remodeling 3. Interior design
ISBN 0-696-21327-3
LC 2002-109107
First published 1995
"Easy step-by-step instructions; expert advice from the Home Depot." Cover
This offers illustrated instructions for home remodeling, decorating, and repair
"This well-illustrated all-in-one guide . . . is great for novices: it tells the skill level for each task and how long it should take. Boxes in the text indicate helpful hints, required tools, and how to avoid common problems." Libr J [review of 1995 edition]

Kitchens: plan, remodel, build. Creative Homeowner 2002 255p il pa $19.95 **643**
1. Kitchens
ISBN 1-58011-049-5
LC 2001-90755
At head of title: Creative homeowner
This "guide offers ideas and illustrations for the layout and design of various kitchen spaces, along with information on lighting, countertops, storage options, windows, and doors. A significant portion of the book is devoted to the kitchen do-it-your-selfer and includes projects from drywalling to installing appliances." Libr J

Lee, Vinny

Kitchens: a design sourcebook; with photographs by James Merrell. Updated ed. Ryland Peters & Small 2001 192p il $29.95
643
1. Kitchens
ISBN 1-8417-2227-8
LC 2003-267094
Also available in paperback from Pavilion Bks.
First published 1998 by Stewart, Tabori & Chang
Over 400 color photos illustrate this guide to remodeling, renovating or building an entirely new kitchen. A resources list is included

Litchfield, Michael W.

Renovation; a complete guide. 2nd ed. Sterling 1997 xx, 566p il pa $24.95 **643**
1. Houses—Remodeling
ISBN 0-8069-9775-3
LC 96-49513
First published 1982 by Wiley
This "guide covers all aspects of home renovation, including how to assess a house's structure, tools, materials, wiring, plumbing, painting, flooring, etc. Instructions are to the point—there is less hand-holding here than in other titles because some remodeling experience is assumed. A classic." Libr J
Includes bibliographical references

New complete do-it-yourself manual. Reader's Digest Assn. 1991 528p il $35
643
1. Houses—Maintenance and repair
ISBN 0-89577-378-3
LC 90-46830
First published 1973 with title: Reader's Digest complete do-it-yourself manual
At head of title: Reader's Digest
"For homeowner and apartment dweller alike, [this] provides details, photographs, and diagrams for projects within the capability of the do-it-yourselfer. It also offers guidance as to when a contractor or specialist is needed." N Y Public Libr Book of How & Where to Look It Up

New fix-it-yourself manual. Reader's Digest Assn. 1996 448p il $35   **643**

1. Repairing 2. Household equipment and supplies—Maintenance and repair
ISBN 0-89577-871-8   LC 96-15189
First published 1977 with title: Reader's Digest fix-it-yourself manual

This illustrated book offers instructions for repairing, buying, cleaning and maintaining a wide variety of household items including appliances, furniture, plumbing fixtures, air conditioners, electronic and sports equipment

Papolos, Janice

The virgin homeowner; the essential guide to owning, maintaining, and surviving your first home. Norton 1997 444p il $27.50 **643**

1. Houses
ISBN 0-393-04035-6   LC 96-31304
Also available in paperback from Penguin Bks.

"Beginning with how to get the most out of the initial home inspection, Papolos takes the reader through a house, describing each system, its quirks, and its potential problems. Later, she covers pest control, security, and safety. This highly readable book will prove useful to both new homeowners and those just thinking of making a purchase, and veteran homeowners will undoubtedly learn something, too." Libr J

Includes bibliographical references

Riha, John

Deck & patio planner. Better Homes & Gardens Bks. 2000 128p il pa $14.95   **643**

1. Patios
ISBN 0-696-21194-7   LC 00-134291
At head of title: Better homes and gardens

This book features advice on building and remodeling decks and patios and includes photos of examples, planning information and evaluations of building materials

Roofing: the best of Fine homebuilding. Taunton Press 1996 111p il pa $14.95

643

1. Roofs—Maintenance and repair
ISBN 1-56158-141-0   LC 96-5432
"A Fine homebuilding book"

An illustrated guide to the installation, maintenance and repair of shingle, slate, tile, thatch and metal roofs

Sussman, Julie

Dare to repair; a do-it-herself guide to fixing (almost) anything in the home; [by] Julie Sussman and Stephanie Glakas-Tenet; illustrations by Yeorgos Lampathakis. HarperCollins Pubs. 2002 253p il pa $14.95

643

1. Houses—Maintenance and repair
ISBN 0-06-095984-3   LC 2002-27625
The authors "show women how to perform a number of the most common repairs, including unclogging drains and toilets, replacing electrical switches and outlets, leveling appliances, lighting pilot lights, unsticking windows, and installing a door peephole. . . . This is a wonderful book that should be purchased by every public library." Libr J

Thomas, Steve, 1942-

This Old House kitchens; a guide to design and renovation; [by] Steve Thomas and Philip Langdon. Little, Brown 1992 273p il hardcover o.p. paperback available $27 **643**

1. Kitchens
ISBN 0-316-84107-2 (pa)   LC 91-20413
"Arguing that there is no single best way to design a kitchen, the host of the popular PBS program leads the reader through the process of selecting countertops, ventilation, heating, lighting, flooring, and equipment." Libr J

Vila, Bob

Bob Vila's complete guide to remodeling your home; everything you need to know about home renovation from the #1 home improvement expert; by Bob Vila and Hugh Howard; principal photography by Michael Fredericks, line drawings by Nancy Hull. Avon Bks. 1999 335p il hardcover o.p. paperback available $23.95   **643**

1. Houses—Remodeling
ISBN 0-380-79955-3 (pa)   LC 99-25410
In this book, Vila "details the remodeling of his own family dwelling, explaining his choices along the way. In nine chapters, he details house examination, planning, and implementation. His prose is lively, encouraging, and well written." Libr J

Wing, Charlie, 1939-

The big book of small household repairs; your goof-proof guide to fixing over 200 annoying breakdowns. Rodale Press 1995 308p il hardcover o.p. paperback available $15.95

643

1. Houses—Maintenance and repair 2. Household equipment and supplies—Maintenance and repair
ISBN 0-7621-0162-8 (pa)   LC 95-7408
Illustrations accompany step-by-step instructions for 243 home repair projects that are considered 'too small' to involve professionals. Lists of recommended tools and materials are provided for each job

645   Household furnishings

Engelbreit, Mary

Mary Engelbreit's children's companion; the Mary Engelbreit look and how to get it; illustrations by Mary Engelbreit; written by Charlotte Lyons; photographs by Barbara Elliott Martin. Andrews & McMeel 1997 144p il $24.95   **645**

1. Interior design 2. Handicraft
ISBN 0-8362-3675-0   LC 97-7261
This book offers ideas for designing and decorating children's rooms, parties, and backyard and garden play areas

646.2 Sewing and related operations

Bednar, Nancy
The encyclopedia of sewing machine techniques; [by] Nancy Bednar, JoAnn Pugh-Gannon. Sterling 1999 336p il hardcover o.p. paperback available $24.95
646.2
1. Sewing
ISBN 0-8069-6365-4 (pa)   LC 99-53581
Among the techniques covered in this illustrated step-by-step guide are beading, fringing, pintucks, and puffing

Betzina, Sandra
Fabric savvy; essential advice for every sewer. Taunton Press 1999 203p il $24.95; pa $17.95
646.2
1. Fabrics 2. Dressmaking
ISBN 1-56158-267-0; 1-56158-573-4 (pa)
LC 98-44107
"A guidebook to 85 different fabrics available to the home sewer, from African mudcloth to wool melton. Each fabric is given a two-page spread that includes information on recommended thread and needles, stitch length, presser foot, finishing, seams, marking, interfacing, cutting, types of hems, topstitching, and closures as well as basic information about the fabric and the types of garments for which it is suitable." Libr J

Sandra Betzina sews for your home; [by] Sandra Betzina and Debbie Valentine. Taunton Press 2002 202p il $29.95   **646.2**
1. Sewing
ISBN 1-56158-446-0   LC 2002-3395
The authors offer ideas and instructions for "sewing accessories for the home. In addition to complete, richly illustrated instructions for dozens of pillows, window treatments, table coverings, bed linens, and gifts for children and pets, there are solid sewing instructions that the reader can use in myriad future sewing projects." Libr J

Giordano, John
The sewing machine guide; tips on choosing, buying, and refurbishing. Taunton Press 1997 105p il pa $15.95   **646.2**
1. Sewing 2. Sewing machines
ISBN 1-56158-220-4   LC 97-13895
"A Threads book"
The author "discusses strategies for choosing the right machine. He explains how to test a machine, how to bargain for a good deal, and how to set up your sewing space once you get your purchase home. With its mixture of practical advice and money-saving tips, this book is engaging reading." Libr J

James, Chris
The complete serger handbook. Sterling 1997 159p il hardcover o.p. paperback available $17.95
646.2
1. Sewing 2. Sewing machines
ISBN 0-8069-9807-5 (pa)   LC 96-39316
"A Sterling/Sewing Information Resources book"
This "is a concise guide to the serger and serger techniques. Major sections of the book include identifying the parts of a serger (with photos of each part), serger accessories, types of threads, threading and testing the threading, learning to regulate tension, and techniques." Libr J

Lee, Linda, 1948-
Sewing edges and corners. Taunton Press 2000 134p il pa $19.95   **646.2**
1. Sewing
ISBN 1-56158-418-5   LC 00-29919
"An embellishment idea book"
The author offers about 40 corner and edge techniques for garments and home decorating projects
"Readers appreciate the clarity of Lee's instructions, since each step is numbered, photographs and other illustrations ease difficult tasks, and sidebars ensure the comfortableness of the sewing." Booklist

New complete guide to sewing; step-by-step techniques for making clothes and home accessories; from the editors at Reader's digest. Reader's Digest Assn. 2002 384p il $35   **646.2**
1. Sewing
ISBN 0-7621-0420-1   LC 2002-69944
First published 1976 with title: Complete guide to sewing
This illustrated guide begins with an overview of basic equipment and techniques. A discussion of patterns and fabrics is included. The bulk of the book provides step-by-step instructions for making clothes and home furnishings

646.4 Clothing and accessories construction

Armstrong, Helen Joseph
Patternmaking for fashion design; technical illustrator, Vincent James Maruzzi; fashion illustrator, Mia Carpenter. 3rd ed. Prentice-Hall 2000 821p il $89   **646.4**
1. Dressmaking—Patterns
ISBN 0-321-03423-6   LC 99-43802
First published 1987 by Harper & Row
"Covers the three steps in the development of design patterns—dart manipulation, added fullness, and contouring—with a central theme that all designs are based on one, or more of these three major patternmaking and design principles." Publisher's note

Betzina, Sandra
Power sewing step-by-step. Taunton Press 2000 231p il $34.95; pa $24.95   **646.4**
1. Sewing 2. Dressmaking
ISBN 1-56158-363-4; 1-56158-572-6 (pa)
LC 00-23431
"Vests, pants, shirts, dresses, and jackets for women are the focus of this book, with Betzina guiding the reader step by step through her thinking process in planning, constructing, fitting, customizing, and finishing each type of garments. More than 500 color photos illustrate many tricks of the trade, shortcuts, and tips. This will be a core title in any sewing collection." Libr J

The **Complete** book of sewing; a practical step-by-step guide to every technique. rev ed. DK Pub. 2003 320p il $40   **646.4**
1. Sewing 2. Dressmaking
ISBN 0-7894-9658-5   LC 2002-41761
First published 1996

The Complete book of sewing—*Continued*

This "sewing guide provides a detailed reference for both novices and experts. . . . Chapters explain how to pick and use patterns; select fabrics and notions; sew basic stitches and seams; attach interfacings and interlinings; form darts, tucks, pleats, and gathers; sew necklines, collars, waistlines, sleeves, and cuffs; hem; and add edges, fastenings, and pockets." SLJ [review of 1996 edition]

Morris, Mary, 1940-

Every sewer's guide to the perfect fit; customizing your patterns for a sensational look; [by] Mary Morris & Sally McCann. Lark Bks. 1997 144p il $27.95   **646.4**

1. Sewing 2. Clothing and dress
ISBN 1-88737-443-4   LC 97-6496
"G Street fabrics"

This offers instruction in adapting commercial sewing patterns for accurate custom fitting

646.5   Construction of headgear

Albrizio, Ann

Classic millinery techniques; a complete guide to making & designing today's hats; coauthored & illustrated by Osnat Lustig; photographs by Ted Morrison. Lark Bks.; [distributed by] Random House 1998 143p il hardcover o.p. paperback available $19.95

      646.5

1. Hats
ISBN 1-57990-274-X (pa)   LC 97-45828
The authors "offer step-by-step projects for making berets, pillboxes, or turbans from scratch." Libr J

646.7   Management of personal and family living. Grooming

Begoun, Paula, 1953-

Don't go to the cosmetics counter without me; a unique guide to over 35,000 products, plus the latest skin-care research. 6th ed [completely rev. and updated] Beginning Press 2003 1362p pa $27.95   **646.7**

1. Cosmetics 2. Consumer education 3. Skin—Care
ISBN 1-877988-30-8
First published 1992

The author "reviews thousands of products from cleansers and moisturizers through foundations, lip and eye colors, blushers, and mascaras while inspecting their ingredients. Arranging the book by product type, she notes possible irritants, carcinogens, companies against animal testing, and products that make unsubstantiated claims. Separates the hype from the reality." Libr J

Berg, Rona

Beauty: the new basics; illustrations by Anja Kroencke; photography by Deborah Jaffe. Workman 2001 404p il pa $19.95

      646.7

1. Personal appearance
ISBN 0-7611-0186-1   LC 00-43631

The author discusses "hair and skin care, bath and body, aging, skin cancer, makeup, home spa treatments, aromatherapy, and cosmetic surgery. She includes a directory of day and destination spas and recommended salons. Amusing time lines give thumbnail histories of style and popular products. Essential for small collections in particular." Libr J

Bonner, Lonnice Brittenum

Good hair; for colored girls who've considered weaves when the chemicals became too ruff. Crown Trade Paperbacks 1994 98p il pa $9.95   **646.7**

1. Hair
ISBN 0-517-88151-9   LC 93-42027
Reprint. First published 1991 by Sapphire Bks.

The author explains hair "structure and texture while exploring the damaging effects of hot combs and chemical relaxants, in addition to hair care essentials and how to style crimps and corkscrews. Although she doesn't cover a wide range of natural 'dos, her overarching message—that black women should embrace rather than tame their hair—makes this essential." Libr J

Includes bibliographical references

Plaited glory; for colored girls who've considered braids, locks, and twists. Crown Trade Paperbacks 1996 122p il pa $12

      646.7

1. Hair
ISBN 0-517-88498-4   LC 96-4108

The author examines "locks and braids (both with and without extensions), twists, Nubian knots, and other natural styles. Bonner also discusses the maintenance of such styles and what to do when they have grown out." Libr J

Includes bibliographical references

Brown, Bobbi

Bobbi Brown beauty evolution; a guide to a lifetime of beauty; [by] Bobbi Brown, with Sally Wadyka. HarperCollins Pubs. 2002 211p il $29.95   **646.7**

1. Personal appearance 2. Women—Health and hygiene
ISBN 0-06-008881-8   LC 2002-22988

The author suggests "that readers look beyond the retouched images in magazines to see the possibilities of individual features. Addressing all ages and races, she recommends products that enhance your assets, even during pregnancy and illness. With a chapter on men." Libr J

DuPriest, Laura

Natural beauty; pamper yourself with salon secrets at home. Prima Pub. 2002 230p il pa $10.95   **646.7**

1. Personal appearance 2. Cosmetics 3. Skin—Care
ISBN 0-7615-2099-6   LC 2002-72554

"This provides recipes for at-home beauty treatments, including facials, manicures, and waxing. Warns against

DuPriest, Laura—*Continued*
the hyped claims of cosmetic-counter products and emphasizes useful kitchen ingredients that produce the same results at a fraction of the cost." Libr J
The author's "obvious knowledge about everything from waxing to massaging to not being taken in at the cosmetics counter, as well as her inventive concoctions . . . make this a solid beauty resource." Publ Wkly

Essence total makeover; body, beauty, spirit; [by the editors of Essence]; Patricia Mignon Hinds, editor; introduction by Susan L. Taylor. Crown 2000 216p il hardcover o.p. paperback available $18
646.7
1. Personal appearance 2. African American women—Health and hygiene
ISBN 0-609-80527-4 (pa)   LC 99-14442
"Hinds provides practical tips on caring for skin, hair, body, and spirit. Glossy and attractive, this comprehensive volume is aimed at African American women." Libr J
Includes bibliographical references

Ferrell, Pamela
Let's talk hair; every black woman's personal consultation for healthy growing hair; foreword by A'Lelia Perry Bundles. Cornrows 1996 239p il pa $24.95   **646.7**
1. Hair 2. African American women—Health and hygiene
ISBN 0-939183-02-1   LC 96-85919
The author "emphasizes gentle cleansing, moisturizing, and overall protection from breakage and splitting and discusses hairstyles besides locks and braids. A good list of products to avoid is included." Libr J
Includes bibliographical references

Fornay, Alfred
The African American woman's guide to successful makeup and skincare. rev ed. Wiley 2002 184p il pa $16.95   **646.7**
1. Skin—Care 2. Personal appearance 3. African American women—Health and hygiene
ISBN 0-471-40278-8   LC 2001-56781
"An Amber book"
First published 1998 by Amber Bks.
The author "covers basic skin care and types, aging, and special problems such as acne and facial hair. He also provides guidance in selecting colors to complement skin tone and applying makeup to downplay flaws and accentuate good points. With a chapter on skin care for men." Libr J

Gross, Kim Johnson
Woman's face; skin care and makeup; [by Kim Johnson Gross, Jeff Stone; written by Rachel Urquhart] Knopf 1997 190p il (Chic simple) $30   **646.7**
1. Personal grooming 2. Face—Care 3. Cosmetics
ISBN 0-679-44578-1   LC 97-5164
This answers nearly 100 frequently asked questions about make-up and skin care, including advice on the best products, and describing how to accentuate a woman's best features

Hadadi, Letha
Healthy beauty; using nature's secrets to look great and feel terrific; [by] Letha Hadady; illustrated by Letha Elizabeth Hadady. Wiley 2003 260p il $24.95   **646.7**
1. Personal appearance 2. Women—Health and hygiene
ISBN 0-471-07534-5   LC 2002-14025
Contents: Your mirror image; Lola's way; Stress fighters; Your seasons of beauty; Your new body; Your walk; Spot slimming; Your body beautiful; Fragrance from the inside out; Pretty hands and feet; Beautiful you; Sexy hair shines from within; Alluring eyes; Your flawless complexion; Out, out damned spots; Your best face forward ; Style genius; Your voice tells a story; Beauty karma; Beauty survival skills; Look young, feel young; Annotated resource guide
The author "incorporates Asian and Western therapies and tips from celebrities to develop a physical and spiritual beauty regimen that relies on herbs, homeopathic remedies, and stress reduction." Libr J
Includes bibliographical references

Handel, Gloria
Cutting your family's hair. Sterling 2002 128p il pa $14.95   **646.7**
1. Hair
ISBN 0-8069-5851-0   LC 2002-280566
Featuring recipes for homemade shampoos, conditioners, and rinses, this is a "guide to long, medium, and short cuts for men, women, and children of all ages. Generously illustrated with a concentration on straight or only slightly wavy Caucasian hair." Libr J

Kashuk, Sonia
Real beauty; concept by Sonia Kashuk; written with Amie Valentine. Potter 2003 137p il + 1 DVD ROM $27.50   **646.7**
1. Personal appearance 2. Women—Health and hygiene
ISBN 1-4000-4774-2   LC 2003-535298
The author "showcases women of all ages and ethnic types, covering nutrition and fitness in addition to the usual hair and skin care. The accompanying DVD shows the suggested makeup techniques being performed." Libr J

Massey, Lorraine
Curly girl; more than just hair—it's an attitude: a celebration of curls: how to cut them, care for them, love them & set them free. Workman 2001 148p il pa $9.95 **646.7**
1. Hair
ISBN 0-7611-2300-8   LC 2001-26842
This book features "tips on shampoo . . . conditioners . . . drying, combing . . . styling, getting the right cut, and how to Heal Thy Hair after years of strong detergents and damaging blow-dryers. There are before-and-after photographs . . . self-help tests, confessions from curly girls [and] advice." Publisher's note

Pedersen, Stephanie
K-I-S-S beauty; foreword by Victoria Moran. DK Pub. 2001 352p il (Keep it simple series) pa $19.95   **646.7**
1. Personal appearance
ISBN 0-7894-8146-4   LC 2001-2551
"A Dorling Kindersley book"
Spine title: KISS guide to beauty

Pedersen, Stephanie—*Continued*

This guide features advice on hair, nail, and skin care and discusses issues such as cosmetic surgery, the effects of sleep, nutrition, stress, and UV rays on your appearance

"Clearly written, it will appeal to people who are intimidated by the higher-end guides." Libr J

Worthington, Charles

The complete book of hairstyling. Firefly Bks. 2002 304p il pa $19.95   **646.7**

1. Hair

ISBN 1-55297-576-2   LC 2002-277803

This describes over 100 hairstyles and offers advice on coloring and cutting hair, maintenance of hair style and health, and hair products

647.9   Multiple dwellings for transients, eating and drinking places

Hostelling North America. American Youth Hostels maps pa $13   **647.9**

1. Youth hostels—Directories

ISSN 1540-8124

First published 1934. Title varies

An annual directory of the youth hostels in the United States and Canada, published by American Youth Hostels and Canadian Hostelling Association

Sakach, Deborah

Bed & breakfast encyclopedia; [by] Deborah Edwards Sakach, Tiffany Crosswy. 3rd ed. American Hist. Inns 2001 1044p il maps pa $18.95   **647.9**

1. Hotels and motels

ISBN 1-888050-06-3

First published 1997

This volume describes 15,000 bed-and-breakfast accommodations in the U.S. and Canada, and includes contact information, setting and history

Includes bibliographical references

Bed & breakfasts, country inns. American Hist. Inns il maps pa $21.95   **647.9**

1. Hotels and motels

ISSN 1532-3587   LC 00-208629

First published 1991. (15th edition 2003) Periodically revised

This describes approximately 2000 selected accommodations in the U.S. and Canada

648   Housekeeping

Friedman, Virginia M.

Field guide to stains; how to identify and remove virtually every stain known to man; by Virginia M. Friedman, Melissa Wagner, and Nancy Armstrong. Quirk Bks. 2003 280p il pa $14.95   **648**

1. Cleaning

ISBN 1-931686-07-6   LC 2002-104065

This guide to identifying and removing over 100 stains features sections on sauces, fruits and vegetables, office products, and yard and garage stains. It also includes information on when and where certain stains are most likely to occur

How to clean practically anything; [by] the editors of Consumer Reports Books with Edward Kippel. Consumer Repts. Bks. pa $16.95   **648**

1. House cleaning 2. Cleaning

First published 1986. (2002 edition) Periodically revised. Variant title How to clean and care for practically anything

This volume offers advice on buying and using cleaning products and appliances and includes a stain removal chart for fabrics

649   Child rearing & home care of persons

Agnew, Connie L., 1957-

Twins! expert advice from two practicing physicians on pregnancy, birth, and the first year of life with twins; [by] Connie L. Agnew, Alan H. Klein, Jill Alison Ganon. HarperCollins Pubs. 1997 304p pa $18   **649**

1. Twins

ISBN 0-06-273460-1   LC 97-14657

An overview of the physical, medical, emotional, and psychological issues involved in having twins. Fetal and embryonic development, nutrition, and exercise are among the topics covered. Includes interviews with parents of twins

Ames, Louise Bates

Your eight-year-old; lively and outgoing; by Louise Bates Ames and Carol Chase Haber; illustrated with photographs by Betty David. Delacorte Press 1989 147p il hardcover o.p. paperback available $12.95   **649**

1. Child rearing

ISBN 0-440-50681-6 (pa)   LC 88-31150

A discussion of the basic personality and typical physical and mental development of the eight-year-old

Includes bibliographical references

Your five-year-old; sunny and serene; by Louise Bates Ames and Frances L. Ilg, Gesell Institute of Child Development; illustrated with photographs by Betty David. Delacorte Press 1979 123p il hardcover o.p. paperback available $12.95   **649**

1. Child rearing

ISBN 0-440-50673-5 (pa)   LC 78-11622

Beginning with a description of the general characteristics of the five-year-old, the authors go on to discuss how the child relates to parents and others

Includes bibliographical references

Your four-year-old; wild and wonderful; by Louise Bates Ames and Frances L. Ilg, Gesell Institute of Child Development. Delacorte Press 1976 152p il hardcover o.p. paperback available $12.95   **649**

1. Child rearing

ISBN 0-440-50675-1 (pa)

A discussion of the basic personality and typical physical and mental development of the four-year-old

Includes bibliographical references

Ames, Louise Bates—*Continued*

Your one-year-old; the fun-loving, fussy 12-to-24-month-old; by Louise Bates Ames, Frances L. Ilg, and Carol Chase Haber (Gesell Institute of Child Development); illustrated with photographs by Betty David. Delacorte Press 1982 178p il hardcover o.p. paperback available $12.95 **649**
1. Child rearing
ISBN 0-440-50672-7 (pa)   LC 81-17275
A discussion of the basic personality and typical physical and mental development of the one-year-old
Includes bibliographical references

Your seven-year-old; life in a minor key; by Louise Bates Ames and Carol Chase Haber; illustrated with photographs by Betty David. Delacorte Press 1985 165p il hardcover o.p. paperback available $12.95 **649**
1. Child rearing
ISBN 0-440-50650-6 (pa)   LC 84-15627
A discussion of the basic personality and typical physical and mental development of the seven-year-old
Includes bibliographical references

Your six-year-old; defiant but loving; by Louise Bates Ames and Frances L. Ilg, Gesell Institute of Child Development. Delacorte Press 1976 132p il hardcover o.p. paperback available $12.95 **649**
1. Child rearing
ISBN 0-440-50674-3 (pa)
A discussion of the basic personality and typical physical and mental development of the six-year-old
Includes bibliographical references

Your three-year-old; friend or enemy; by Louise Bates Ames, and Frances L. Ilg, Gesell Institute of Child Development. Delacorte Press 1976 168p il hardcover o.p. paperback available $12.95 **649**
1. Child rearing
ISBN 0-440-50649-2 (pa)
A discussion of the basic personality and typical physical and mental development of the three-year-old
Includes bibliographical references

Your two-year-old; terrible or tender; by Louise Bates Ames, and Frances L. Ilg, Gesell Institute of Child Development. Delacorte Press 1976 149p il hardcover o.p. paperback available $12.95 **649**
1. Child rearing
ISBN 0-440-50638-7 (pa)
A discussion of the basic personality and typical physical and mental development of the two-year-old
Includes bibliographical references

The **Baby** book; everything you need to know about your baby—from birth to age two; [by] William Sears [et al.] 2nd ed. [rev. and updated] Little, Brown 2003 769p il pa $21.95 **649**
1. Infants—Care 2. Infants—Development
ISBN 0-316-77800-1   LC 2002-016142
First published 1993
"The authors teach new parents how to bond with their babies through seven fundamental behaviors, including breastfeeding, 'babywearing' and setting proper boundaries. . . . From tips for a healthy birth, getting your baby to sleep and feeding him the 'right fats,' to information about early health concerns, the major steps in infant development and troublesome but typical toddler behavior, the authors of this comprehensive volume . . . are assured and reassuring experts." Publ Wkly

Bailey, Rebecca Anne, 1952-
Easy to love, difficult to discipline; the 7 basic skills for turning conflict into cooperation; [by] Becky A. Bailey. Morrow 2000 285p hardcover o.p. paperback available $12.95 **649**
1. Child rearing 2. Parenting
ISBN 0-06-000775-3 (pa)   LC 99-44313
"Bailey contends that the difficult but rewarding task of guiding children's behavior starts only when parents are able to discipline themselves and become models of self-control. . . . Bailey's underlying message is positive and hopeful, supported with humorous anecdotes and helpful solutions." Publ Wkly
Includes bibliographical references

Baldrige, Letitia
Letitia Baldrige's more than manners! raising today's kids to have kind manners & good hearts. Rawson Assocs. 1997 283p $23 **649**
1. Child rearing 2. Etiquette
ISBN 0-684-81875-2   LC 96-50980
This guide covers "proper conduct at school, restaurants, churches, and parties; how to communicate by telephone, letters, and e-mail; and how to act at weddings, holiday gatherings, and even funerals. A final section shows how to contend with the intricacies of New Age family life, including divorce, remarriage, and stepfamilies." Booklist

Beal, Anne C.
The black parenting book; [by] Anne C. Beal, Linda Villaros, and Allison Abner. Broadway Bks. 1998 412p il pa $20 **649**
1. African American children 2. Child rearing 3. Parent-child relationship
ISBN 0-7679-0196-7   LC 98-28120
In this guide for African American parents the authors offer some of the usual "advice: be a good listener, set a good example, respect the child, have a sense of humor. But they also examine issues that are very specific for black parents: the fear of vaccinating infants because of a mistrust of the health care system, the higher likelihood of lower birth weight babies, nurturing budding awareness of race differences, caring for black children's hair." Booklist

Brazelton, T. Berry, 1918-

Touchpoints; your child's emotional and behavioral development. Addison-Wesley 1992 xxiv, 479p il o.p.; Perseus Bks. paperback available $18.95 **649**
1. Child development 2. Child rearing
ISBN 0-201-62690-X (pa)   LC 92-23004
"A Merloyd Lawrence book"

The author "defines 'touchpoints' as the periods of development and regression which every child experiences while growing up. He describes the first six years of life and the touchpoints of that period. . . . Worried new parents will be put at ease after reading this book. Brazelton is knowledgeable, warm, and kind, and his book is a pleasure to read." Libr J
Includes bibliographical references

Touchpoints three to six; your child's emotional and behavioral development; [by] T. Berry Brazelton, Joshua D. Sparrow. Perseus Bks. 2001 xxiii, 502p il $27; pa $18 **649**
1. Child development 2. Child rearing
ISBN 0-7382-0199-5; 0-7382-0678-4 (pa)
                                         LC 2001-92010

Companion volume to Touchpoints
"A Merloyd Lawrence book"
"This book follows children from early language development to entry into first grade, charting temperament, learning, moral development, relationships, independence, and separation at each stage. The second part is arranged alphabetically by topics from adoption to parents working and caring for children in a range of family situations and backgrounds." Booklist
"Destined to become required reading for parents and early childhood educators, this is a valuable addition to any public library." Libr J
Includes bibliographical references

Brooks, Robert B.

Raising resilient children; fostering strength, hope, and optimism in your child; [by] Robert Brooks, Sam Goldstein. Contemporary Bks. 2001 317p hardcover o.p. paperback available $14.95 **649**
1. Child rearing 2. Parent-child relationship
ISBN 0-8092-9765-5 (pa)   LC 00-60316
The authors "synthesize research on children's coping skills; define and describe resilience (the capacity to cope and feel competent); and offer specific strategies for nurturing resilience in children." Booklist
Includes bibliographical references

Bullard, Sara

Teaching tolerance; raising open-minded empathetic children. Doubleday 1996 235p hardcover o.p. paperback available $19 **649**
1. Prejudices 2. Children 3. Toleration 4. Parenting
ISBN 0-385-47265-X (pa)   LC 95-36045
Bullard "states the principles of tolerance adults need to impart to children and provides guidelines for modeling the behavior we want to encourage." Libr J
"Also included is an extensive list of books, toys, games and music that explore ethnicity and promote tolerance. More thought-provoking than prescriptive, Bullard's reasoned and persuasive essay offers convincing inspiration for parents to serve as open-minded models for their children." Publ Wkly

Caring for your school-age child; ages 5 to 12; editor-in-chief, Edward L. Schor. rev trade pa. ed. Bantam Bks. 1999 xxviii, 624p il pa $19.95 **649**
1. Child care 2. Child rearing
ISBN 0-553-37992-5   LC 99-12639
Also available Caring for your baby and young child (1998)

First published 1995
On cover: The American Academy of Pediatrics
This book "offers comprehensive information about the growth, development, and behavior of children from five to 12 years of age. . . . Bicycle safety, latchkey children, dealing with violence and crime, guns in the home, prejudice, gender identity and sexual orientation, and physical and sexual abuse appear along with the usual information about immunization, diet, school problems, illness, and first aid. The text also offers sound, practical advice about how parents in traditional and nontraditional families can handle a wide variety of situations, stating clearly when they should seek professional help. . . . This book belongs in all parenting and consumer health collections." Libr J [review of 1995 edition]

Cohen, Lawrence J.

Playful parenting; a bold new way to use play in raising your children. Ballantine Bks. 2001 307p $23.95; pa $14 **649**
1. Parenting 2. Play 3. Games
ISBN 0-345-43897-3; 0-345-44286-5 (pa)
                                         LC 00-66809
"A Living Planet book"
"According to Cohen, children of all ages have an ongoing need for connectedness, security and attachment; playful interaction with parents is an important way to develop such bonds. Through play, parents can help their kids develop greater confidence, express bottled up or difficult feelings, recover from daily emotional upheavals, negotiate agreements, express love and—not least— have fun." Publ Wkly

Deak, JoAnn

Girls will be girls; a parent's guide to cultivating confident, competent and connected daughters; by JoAnn Deak with Teresa Barker. Hyperion 2002 287p $23.95; pa $14.95 **649**
1. Girls 2. Child rearing 3. Teenagers
ISBN 0-7868-6768-X; 0-7868-8657-9 (pa)
                                         LC 2001-39247
"Deak discusses the differences between fathers and daughters and mothers and daughters and also some of the more common problems faced by teens, such as body image and peer pressure." Publ Wkly
"This no-nonsense book offers a wealth of practical advice for parents and teachers." Booklist

Deutsch, Francine, 1948-

Halving it all; how equally shared parenting works. Harvard Univ. Press 1999 327p $27.50; pa $14.95 **649**
1. Parenting 2. Sex role 3. Dual-career families 4. Child rearing
ISBN 0-674-36800-2; 0-674-00209-1 (pa)
                                         LC 98-30738
Based on interviews, Deutsch "describes four groups of working parents: those who share responsibilities and duties equally; those in which one parent, usually the

Deutsch, Francine, 1948-—_Continued_
mother, does somewhat more; those in which the mother
provides most of the childcare; and parents, primarily
blue collar workers, who choose alternate work shifts to
share duties." Libr J
Includes bibliographical references

Donovan, Denis M.
What did I just say!?! how new insights
into childhood thinking can help you
communicate more effectively with your
child; [by Denis M. Donovan, Deborah
McIntyre] Holt & Co. 1999 230p il hardcover
o.p. paperback available $14   **649**
1. Parent-child relationship 2. Communication
ISBN 0-8050-6502-4 (pa)   LC 99-11987
"Unless parents state what they want of a child explicitly, literally, logically, and in simple, commonsense
terms, what they say and what the child hears and does
will rarely be in sync. Donovan and McIntyre scrutinize
many phrases . . . through the lens of logic to demonstrate embarrassingly ineffective ways for parents to
communicate." Booklist
Includes bibliographical references

Dosick, Wayne D., 1947-
Golden rules; the ten ethical values parents
need to teach their children; [by] Wayne
Dosick. HarperSanFrancisco 1995 221p
hardcover o.p. paperback available $13   **649**
1. Child rearing 2. Moral education
ISBN 0-06-251249-8 (pa)   LC 94-37098
The author "has chosen 10 values that he feels parents
must teach their children if they are to have any hope of
becoming 'good, decent, honorable human beings, with
strength of character and depth of moral commitment.'
Each chapter of 'Golden Rules' embodies one of these
ethical values—respect, honesty, fairness, responsibility,
compassion, gratitude, friendship, peace, maturity and
faith. The value is amplified by admonitions to parents,
and by stories, poems, prayers, activities to share and
discussion questions for various age levels." N Y Times
Book Rev
Includes bibliographical references

Douglas, Ann, 1963-
The mother of all baby books. Hungry
Minds 2002 c2001 604p pa $15.99   **649**
1. Infants—Care 2. Childbirth 3. Parenting
ISBN 0-7645-6616-4
First published 2001 in Canada
Baby care basics covered in this guide include "basic
childcare, nutrition, health, and physical, emotional, and
social development. [Also discussed are] facts about
sleeping patterns, breastfeeding, circumcision, and immu-
nization issues." Publisher's note
Includes bibliographical references

Eisenberg, Arlene
What to expect the toddler years; [by]
Arlene Eisenberg, Heidi E. Murkoff, and
Sandee E. Hathaway. Workman 1994 xx,
904p il pa $16.95   **649**
1. Child rearing
ISBN 0-89480-994-6   LC 93-8932
This guide for parents of two- and three-year-olds
covers such topics as pediatric checkups, toilet training,
sibling rivalry, and working parents
"This is an outstanding source written by and for parents. Easy to use, affordable and reassuring, it encourages parents to enjoy their children." Libr J

Elias, Maurice J.
Emotionally intelligent parenting; how to
raise a self-disciplined, responsible, socially
skilled child; [by] Maurice J. Elias, Steven E.
Tobias, and Brian S. Friedlander; foreword by
Daniel Goleman. Harmony Bks. 1999 246p
hardcover o.p. paperback available $13   **649**
1. Child rearing 2. Parenting
ISBN 0-609-80483-9 (pa)   LC 98-20835
The authors encourage parents to "try to see things
from the child's perspective; stop nagging, threatening
and yelling to get your point across; foster positive, and
discourage negative, behaviors." Publ Wkly

Füredi, Frank
Paranoid parenting; why ignoring the
experts may be best for your child. Chicago
Review Press 2002 233p pa $14.95   **649**
1. Parenting 2. Child rearing 3. Parent-child relationship
ISBN 1-55652-464-1   LC 2002-4121
"Previously published in a substantially different form
in the U.K. in 2001." Verso of title page
The author contends "that parents are not just worried
but downright paranoid, due, in part, to a glut of much-
publicized expert advice. . . . Claiming that society had
become 'child-obsessed rather than child-centered' Furedi
calls for a return to reliance on parents' own instincts,
and for the re-establishment of adult trust and collaboration in caring for children." Publ Wkly
"This book is provocative, well argued, and clearly
written, though the rhetoric can be stinging." Libr J
Includes bibliographical references

Garbarino, James
Parents under siege; why you are the
solution, not the problem in your child's life;
[by] James Garbarino, Claire Bedard. Free
Press 2001 246p $24; pa $13   **649**
1. Parent-child relationship 2. Child rearing
ISBN 0-7432-0134-5; 0-7432-2383-7 (pa)
          LC 2001-23692
"In Part 1, the toxic cultural environment of the last
decade is described; in Part 2, parents are offered some
usable tools to help them become more in control." Libr
J
"This book offers a sound theoretical starting point for
parents grappling with a difficult child. It also lists many
helpful resources, Web sites and groups, along with suggested further reading." Publ Wkly

Garber, Stephen W., 1946-
Monsters under the bed and other
childhood fears; helping your child overcome
anxieties, fears, and phobias; [by] Stephen W.
Garber, Marianne Daniels Garber, and Robyn
Freedman Spizman. Villard Bks. 1993 378p
hardcover o.p. paperback available $23   **649**
1. Child rearing 2. Fear
ISBN 0-8129-9222-9 (pa)   LC 92-56812
"Following opening chapters on understanding and
identifying a child's fear and some overall guidelines on
teaching basic relaxation techniques, the authors introduce their basic plan for overcoming fear through imagination, information, observation, and exposure. Subsequent chapters apply these four techniques to specific
fears." Libr J
Includes bibliographical references

Ginsberg, Barry G., 1936-
50 wonderful ways to be a single-parent
family. New Harbinger Publs. 2002 123p pa
$12.95 **649**
1. Single parent family 2. Parenting
ISBN 1-57224-308-2 LC 2003-273432
This is a "guide for the single-parent family on how
to have fun together, learn to share decisions, develop
family traditions and rituals, find common ground, relax
with each other, and feel like a team." Publisher's note

Harris, Sandra L.
Siblings of children with autism; a guide
for families; [by] Sandra L. Harris and Beth
A. Glasberg. 2nd ed. Woodbine House 2003
180p il pa $16.95 **649**
1. Autism 2. Siblings
ISBN 1-89062-729-1 LC 2003-1239
First published 1994
Contents: Brothers and sisters; He doesn't know what
angels are; Why does he do that?; Let's talk; The balancing act; Children at play; An adult perspective
This "resource for families with autistic children and
nonautistic siblings examines the perceptions, needs,
compromises, and inevitable stresses that brothers and
sisters face." Libr J
Includes bibliographical references

Hewlett, Sylvia Ann, 1946-
The war against parents; what we can do
for America's beleaguered moms and dads;
[by] Sylvia Ann Hewlett and Cornel West.
Houghton Mifflin 1998 302p il hardcover o.p.
paperback available $14 **649**
1. Parenting 2. Family
ISBN 0-395-95797-4 (pa) LC 98-5779
The authors contend that "current American political
and economic policy, as well as the popular media, dis-
criminate severely against people trying to bring up children. . . . This salutary jeremiad should be required
reading in Washington and Hollywood." Publ Wkly

Huggins, Kathleen
The nursing mother's companion; foreword
by Ruth A. Lawrence; photographs by
Harriette Hartigan. 4th ed. Harvard Common
Press 1999 284p il $24.95; pa $13.95 **649**
1. Breast feeding
ISBN 1-55832-151-9; 1-55832-152-7 (pa)
LC 98-51793
First published 1986
This offers advice on preventing and solving breast
feeding problems and includes sections on premature ba-
bies, babies at risk for underfeeding, and breast pumps,
as well as an appendix on drug safety
Includes bibliographical references

Karp, Harvey
The happiest baby on the block; the new
way to calm crying and help your baby sleep
longer. Bantam Bks. 2002 267p il $21.95; pa
$13.95 **649**
1. Infants—Care 2. Parent-child relationship 3. Child
rearing
ISBN 0-553-80255-0; 0-553-38146-6 (pa)
LC 2001-56734
To calm a crying baby the author "recommends a series of five steps designed to imitate the uterus. These

steps include swaddling, side/stomach position, shhh
sounds, swinging and sucking. The book includes detailed advice on the proper way to swaddle a child, the
difference between a gentle rocking versus shaking and
more." Publ Wkly

Leach, Penelope
Your baby & child; from birth to age five;
photographs by Jenny Matthews. 3rd ed
completely rev. Knopf 1997 559p il $35; pa
$20 **649**
1. Infants—Care 2. Child care 3. Child development
ISBN 0-375-40007-9; 0-375-70000-5 (pa)
LC 97-29325
First published 1977 in the United Kingdom with title:
Baby and child; first United States edition 1978
The author explores the psychosocial needs of children
along with their physical growth and progress. Parental
concerns are addressed
"Public and academic libraries would do well to stock
. . . this primer on children and their development for
circulation as well as for the reference shelf." Libr J

Marzollo, Jean
Fathers & babies; how babies grow and
what they need from you from birth to 18
months; illustrated by Irene Trivas.
HarperPerennial 1993 235p il pa $13.95
649
1. Infants—Care 2. Father-child relationship
ISBN 0-06-096908-3 LC 92-53386
Marzollo covers "infant development from the physical and social to the intellectual, psychological and creative. . . . Her book provides step-by-step instructions
on fixing bottles, bathing and feeding, changing a diaper,
toilet training, helping a child develop langauge skills,
and disciplining the older baby." Libr J

Mayes, Linda C.
The Yale Child Study Center guide to
understanding your child; healthy
development from birth to adolescence; [by]
Linda C. Mayes and Donald J. Cohen with
John E. Schowalter and Richard H. Granger;
J. L. Bell, editorial consultant; W. Rodney
Torbert, illustrator. Little, Brown 2002 548p
$40; pa $21.95 **649**
1. Child rearing 2. Child development 3. Parent-child
relationship
ISBN 0-316-95432-2; 0-316-79432-5 (pa)
LC 00-39116
"The book offers three perspectives: the scientific,
with basic information about meeting a growing child's
needs; the emotional, with attention to understanding a
child's feelings; and the parental, with emphasis on the
feelings and expectations the parent brings to the relationship. . . . The objective is to help parents balance
the three perspectives. . . . This approach lends the
guide a broad and deep perspective on parenting even as
it covers typical issues such as imaginary friends and sibling rivalry." Booklist

Murkoff, Heidi Eisenberg

What to expect the first year; [by] Heidi Murkoff, Arlene Eisenberg & Sandee Hathaway. 2nd ed, rev and updated. Workman 2003 704p $25.95; pa $15.95 **649**
1. Infants—Care 2. Child rearing
ISBN 0-7611-3184-1; 0-7611-2958-8 (pa)
LC 2003-57578
First published 1996 with Eisenberg's name appearing first
This guide to "taking care of a newborn through the milestone of his or her first birthday . . . [covers] issues such as newborn screening, home births and the resulting at-home newborn care, vitamins and vaccines, milk allergies, causes of colic, sleep problems, SIDS, returning to work, dealing with siblings, weaning, sippy cups, . . . [and] the expanded role of the father." Publisher's note

Nachman, Patricia Ann

You and your only child; the joys, myths, and challenges of raising an only child; [by] Patricia Nachman with Andrea Thompson. HarperCollins Pubs. 1997 244p hardcover o.p. paperback available $12 **649**
1. Only child 2. Parenting
ISBN 0-06-092896-4 (pa) LC 96-32531
"A Skylight Press book"
The authors discuss social attitudes about only children and offer advice on issues ranging from friendships and stereotyping to the only child and divorce
Includes bibliographical references

The **Nursing** mother's problem solver; Claire Martin [with Nancy Funnemark Krebs, editor; foreword by William Sears and Martha Sears] Fireside 2000 336p il pa $13 **649**
1. Breast feeding
ISBN 0-684-85784-7 LC 00-37198
"Based on questions that were asked on the lactation consultant hot-line at the Children's Hospital of Denver, this book addresses common issues of new mothers (e.g., 'latching on', sore nipples, night feedings) as well as less common situations, such as breastfeeding babies with special needs. The scope of the Q&A is wide, providing a wealth of detailed information from a modern-day perspective." Libr J

Overcoming the odds; raising academically successful African American young women; [by] Freeman A. Hrabowski III [et al.] Oxford Univ. Press 2002 272p $25 **649**
1. African American women 2. African Americans—Education
ISBN 0-19-512642-4 LC 2001-32152
Companion volume to Beating the odds; raising academically successful African American males (1998)
This volume "focuses on young black women overcoming the stereotypical image: high-school dropout, unwed mother, welfare recipient. Based on interviews with students and parents, the book answers the question, What does it take to succeed academically?" Booklist
Includes bibliographical references

Pryor, Gale

Nursing mother, working mother; the essential guide for breastfeeding and staying close to your baby after you return to work. Harvard Common Press 1997 184p il $19.95; pa $11.95 **649**
1. Breast feeding 2. Mothers
ISBN 1-55832-116-0; 1-55832-117-9 (pa)
LC 96-46491
Among the topics discussed in this guide for working mothers are: bonding, maternity leave, routine, selecting a breast pump, maintaining a milk supply, and integrating pumping sessions into work schedules

Rosenfeld, Alvin A.

Hyper-parenting; are you hurting your child by trying too hard? [by] Alvin Rosenfeld and Nicole Wise; foreword by Robert Coles. St. Martin's Press 2000 xxix, 257p hardcover o.p. paperback available $13.95 **649**
1. Parenting 2. Child rearing
ISBN 0-312-26339-2 (pa) LC 99-56670
The author "advocates 'just playing' and just spending time with one's children rather than living the overbooked family life of a stereotypical soccer mom. He notes that family schedules are at a breaking point and that parents face a great deal of guilt and anxiety because they cannot give their children everything. He promotes the need for more balance and suggests that parents take to heart Dr. Spock's advice for parents to trust themselves." Libr J
Includes bibliographical references

Sears, William

Parenting the fussy baby and high-need child; everything you need to know—from birth to age five; [by] William Sears and Martha Sears. Little, Brown 1996 237p il hardcover o.p. paperback available $12.95 **649**
1. Parenting 2. Child psychology
ISBN 0-316-77916-4 (pa) LC 95-48381
To cope with a high-need child the authors "recommend the approach they label *attachment parenting*; it includes techniques such as on-demand feeding and weaning; nighttime parenting; sharing sleep; soothing through motion, sound, visual distraction, and physical contact; and learning via close study how to anticipate the baby's needs." Booklist
Includes bibliographical references

Shapiro, Lawrence E.

How to raise a child with a high EQ; a parent's guide to emotional intelligence. HarperCollins Pubs. 1997 256p hardcover o.p. paperback available $13 **649**
1. Parenting 2. Emotions 3. Child psychology
ISBN 0-06-092891-3 (pa) LC 97-5533
"Through games, activities, tricks, skills, and habits, [this book] guides parents in developing the moral emotions of empathy, honesty, shame, and guilt; thinking skills such as realism and optimism; resourcefulness; social skills including conversation, humor, manners, and friendliness; persistence and motivation; and emotional control." Booklist
Includes bibliographical references

Shore, Kenneth

Keeping kids safe; a guide for parents of toddlers and teens, and all the years in between. Prentice Hall Press 2001 248p pa $12 **649**

1. Parenting 2. Accidents—Prevention

ISBN 0-7352-0214-1 LC 2001-35298

"Compilation of information, facts, tips, and checklists for keeping children safe in and around home and school. In 11 chapters, Shore covers everything from child care and sexual predators to school violence and Internet safety." Libr J

Includes bibliographical references

Small, Meredith F.

Our babies, ourselves; how biology and culture shape the way we parent. Anchor Bks. (NY) 1998 xxii, 292p il hardcover o.p. paperback available $14.95 **649**

1. Infants—Care 2. Infants—Development 3. Parent-child relationship

ISBN 0-385-48362-7 (pa) LC 97-44348

The author "explores ethnopediatrics, an interdisciplinary science that combines anthropology, pediatrics, and child development research in order to examine how child-rearing styles across cultures affect the health and survival of infants. Small describes the different parenting styles of several cultures, including . . . the nomadic Ache tribe of Paraguay, the agrarian !Kung San society of the Kalahari Desert in Africa, and the American industrialized society." Libr J

Includes bibliographical references

Spock, Benjamin, 1903-1998

Dr. Spock on parenting; sensible advice from America's most trusted child care expert. Simon & Schuster 1988 318p hardcover o.p. paperback available $16.95 **649**

1. Parenting

ISBN 0-7434-2683-5 (pa) LC 88-15792

"The author presents a personal critique on parenting, often bordering on the autobiographical. . . . He discusses in depth and with great conviction contemporary and traditional parent concerns, such as divorce, discipline, sex education, and the father's role." Libr J

Dr. Spock's the first two years; the emotional and physical needs of children from birth to age two; edited by Martin T. Stein. Pocket Bks. 2001 153p pa $13.95 **649**

1. Child development 2. Child care 3. Child rearing

ISBN 0-7434-1122-6

In these articles culled from *Redbook* and *Parenting* Spock's advice to parents is that they should "trust themselves" and "expands on this idea in his reply to the question, 'What has eroded so many parents' self-asssurance in asking for reasonably good behavior?'" Libr J

Dr. Spock's the school years; the emotional and social development of children; edited by Martin T. Stein. Pocket Bks. 2001 283p pa $15.95 **649**

1. Child development 2. Child care 3. Child rearing

ISBN 0-7434-1123-4

This volume collects Spock's essays published in *Redbook* and *Parenting*. They address "our contemporary culture's tendency to overschedule children." Libr J

Stoppard, Miriam

Complete baby and child care. Rev American ed. Dorling Kindersley 2001 351p il $15 **649**

1. Child care 2. Infants—Care 3. Child development 4. Child rearing

ISBN 0-7894-7151-5 LC 2001-268266

First published 1995 in the United Kingdom

The author offers advice on behavior, clothing, choosing nursery equipment and supplies, and traveling with children

"The illustrations showing how to bathe an infant, positions for breastfeeding, methods of expressing breast milk, and first aid are outstanding. . . . A fine addition to parenting collections." Libr J [review of 1995 edition]

White, Burton L., 1929-

Raising a happy, unspoiled child. Simon & Schuster 1994 253p il hardcover o.p. paperback available $13 **649**

1. Child rearing 2. Parenting

ISBN 0-684-80134-5 (pa) LC 94-7838

The author argues "that many difficulties—testing parental authority, refusal to share toys with playmates, etc.—can virtually be eliminated if parents are not overly permissive with children of more than five months old." Publ Wkly

Includes bibliographical references

The **Womanly** art of breastfeeding. La Leche League Int. pa $15.95 **649**

1. Breast feeding

First published 1956. (6th edition 1997) Periodically revised

This guide explains the benefits of breastfeeding and offers advice on avoiding problems, breastfeeding and working mothers, family life, and weaning

Includes bibliographical references

649.8 Home care of sick and infirm

Caregiving: a step-by-step resource for caring for the person with cancer at home; editors, Peter S. Houts, Julia A. Bucher. rev ed. American Cancer Soc. 2003 288p il pa $18.95 **649.8**

1. Cancer 2. Caregivers

ISBN 0-944235-45-X LC 2003-1115

First published 1994 by The American College of Physicians with title: American College of Physicians home care guide for cancer

Contents: How to use this book; Cancer treatments; Surgery; Chemotherapy; Radiation therapy; Biological therapies; Hormone therapy; Bone marrow and peripheral

Caregiving: a step-by-step resource for caring for the person with cancer at home—*Continued*

blood stem cell transplants; Clinical trials; Paying for treatments; Managing care; Understanding caregiving; Helping children understand; Coordinating care from one treatment setting to another; Getting help from community agencies and volunteer groups; Getting information from medical staff; Emotional conditions; Anxiety; Depression; Physical conditions; Appetite; Bleeding; Confusion and seizures; Constipation; Diarrhea; Fever and infections; Mouth conditions; Nausea and vomiting; Pain; Skin conditions; Vein conditions; Living with cancer and cancer treatments; Hair loss; Lymphedema; Mobility (moving around the house); Ostomies and prostheses; Tiredness and fatigue; Sexual conditions

This book "explains each major kind of cancer treatment, obstacles to recovery, when it is time to call in professional help, plentiful examples of how individuals can help their loved ones, and how to adjust your plan of action as needed. Also addressed are topics such as managing care by involving other family members and using available community resources, emotional conditions such as anxiety or depression, and the most common physical side effects of cancer treatments such as nausea, pain, and fatigue and how to cope with them. A six-step plan successfully solving problems forms the backbone of each chapter. Chockfull of sensible and reassuring information, this guide is easily accessible to the average reader." Libr J [review of 2000 edition]

Carter, Rosalynn

Helping yourself help others; a book for caregivers; [by] Rosalynn Carter with Susan K. Golant. Times Bks. 1994 278p hardcover o.p. paperback available $14   **649.8**

1. Home care services 2. Caregivers
ISBN 0-8129-2591-2 (pa)   LC 94-11924

The authors "describe the stages the caregiver progresses through, from first facing the illness or declining health of a loved one to the 'long-term, hard-work phase of caregiving.' Questions regarding in-home professional care and nursing homes are addressed, and the authors provide information on strategies, support groups, program recommendations, helpful organizations, and books." Booklist

McFarlane, Rodger

The complete bedside companion; no-nonsense advice on caring for the seriously ill; [by] Rodger McFarlane, Philip Bashe. Simon & Schuster 1998 544p hardcover o.p. paperback available $25.95   **649.8**

1. Home nursing 2. Caregivers 3. Terminal care
ISBN 0-684-84319-6 (pa)   LC 97-43746

"This primer provides information on general illness and specific diseases, questions to ask the physician, basic nursing skills, making hospital visits, dealing with insurance companies, sources of additional information, and support groups. The authors . . . supplement this material with case studies and personal experiences." Libr J

Includes bibliographical references

650   Management and auxiliary services

Business periodicals index. Wilson, H.W. service basis   **650**

1. Business—Periodicals—Indexes 2. Industries—Periodicals—Indexes 3. Economics—Periodicals—Indexes
ISSN 0007-6961
Also available CD-ROM version and online
Started publication in 1958 as a result of the division of the Industrial arts index to form the Business periodicals index and the Applied Science & technology index
Monthly (except August) with quarterly cumulations and a bound annual volume
A subject guide to periodicals in accounting, advertising, banking, communications, economics, finance and investments, insurance, management, marketing, taxation, and related fields

Encyclopedia of busine$$ and finance; Burton S. Kaliski, editor-in-chief. Macmillan Ref. USA 2001 2v il set $275   **650**

1. Business—Encyclopedias 2. Finance—Encyclopedias
ISBN 0-02-865065-4   LC 00-107932
Replaces The Encyclopedia of business, edited by Jane A. Malonis, published 2000
This set covers "accounting, management, marketing, law, finance, and economics. . . . Special emphasis is placed on careers and ethics in various areas of business. . . . The 300-plus alphabetically arranged entries do more than simply define a term; for example, the entry for accounting also describes its history, principles, and agencies, shows how students can enter the profession, and provides cross references to related topics. . . . This work is highly recommended for school, academic, and public libraries." Libr J

Encyclopedia of business information sources. Gale Res. $390   **650**

1. Business—Information services
ISSN 0071-0210
First published 1970. (18th edition 2003) Frequently revised
This is a comprehensive listing of business related finding aids including abstracting and indexing services, almanacs and yearbooks, bibliographies, biographical sources, directories, encyclopedias and dictionaries, financial ratios, handbooks and manuals, online databases, periodicals and newsletters, price sources, research centers and institutes, statistical sources, trade associations and professional societies, and other related sources of information on each topic

Folsom, W. Davis

Understanding American business jargon; a dictionary. Greenwood Press 1997 235p $73.95   **650**

1. Business—Dictionaries
ISBN 0-313-29991-9   LC 96-50211

"This compilation of approximately 2,500 business terms and expressions focuses on American English phrases that are frequently used in the business environment. . . . The dictionary concludes with approximately 400 acronyms and a bibliography of 11 dictionaries that

Folsom, W. Davis—*Continued*
were used in preparing the manuscript. . . . *Understanding American Business Jargon* fills an important gap in most business dictionary collections." Booklist
Includes bibliographical references

Pagell, Ruth A.
International business information; how to find it, how to use it; by Ruth A. Pagell and Michael Halperin. 2nd ed. Oryx Press 1998 445p il $95   **650**
1. Business—Information services 2. Business—Bibliography
ISBN 1-57356-050-2   LC 97-31548
Also available in paperback from AMACOM
First published 1994
This volume describes international business databases and publications
"Clear and simple instructions for using sources are accompanied by discussion of the concepts that enable researchers to make sense of the business information they find. The editors include examples of data, called exhibits, from a variety of sources and methodically explain how to interpret them." Booklist

650.1   Personal success in business

Adams, Scott
The Dilbert principle; a cubicle's-eye view of bosses, meetings, management fads & other workplace afflictions. HarperBusiness 1996 336p il hardcover o.p. paperback available $14.95   **650.1**
1. Dilbert (Comic strip) 2. Business
ISBN 0-88730-858-9 (pa)   LC 96-388
"Dilbert, Scott Adams' cartoon character, has become the workplace hero for the 1990s. . . . More than a compilation of past strips—though over 100 do appear—this book includes new essays on all aspects of corporate life and culture, and each one is on target and deliciously sardonic!" Booklist

Bing, Stanley
Throwing the elephant; Zen and the art of managing up. HarperBusiness 2002 xxxiv, 201p il hardcover o.p. paperback available $14.95   **650.1**
1. Business 2. Interpersonal relations 3. Zen Buddhism
ISBN 0-06-093422-0 (pa)   LC 2001-39801
"Taking the side of workers everywhere and applying the art of Zen Buddhism to the daily grind, the author provides an essential read for anyone who hates his or her boss and the whole corporate structure." Booklist

Graham, Stedman
You can make it happen; a nine-step plan for success. Simon & Schuster 1997 270p il hardcover o.p. paperback available $13
    650.1
1. Success
ISBN 0-684-83866-4 (pa)   LC 96-45457
Graham's "nine-step plan involves increasing self-awareness, creating a vision, developing a plan, under-

standing and following personal values, taking risks, managing responses to those risks, building a support team, making wise decisions, and forming a total commitment. Although his plan may be most applicable to people focusing on business and career goals, Graham notes that this plan can also be applied to other aspects of life." Libr J

McCormack, Mark H.
What they don't teach you at Harvard Business School. Bantam Bks. 1984 256p hardcover o.p. paperback available $16.95
    650.1
1. Success 2. Management
ISBN 0-553-34583-4 (pa)   LC 84-45172
"A John Boswell Associates book"
McCormack's firm, the International Management Group, merchandises professional sports figures and markets the international television rights to sporting events. In this book, McCormack offers advice on business management

Popcorn, Faith
Clicking; 16 trends to future fit your life, your work, and your business; [by] Faith Popcorn and Lys Marigold; illustrated by Gerti Bierenbroodsot. HarperCollins Pubs. 1996 498p il hardcover o.p. paperback available $14   **650.1**
1. Success
ISBN 0-88730-857-0 (pa)   LC 96-379
The authors provide tips on how to find one's proper slot in a rapidly changing world. Recognizing and adapting to new trends is discussed. Includes tips on finding a new career
Includes bibliographical references

Reinhold, Barbara Bailey
Toxic work; how to overcome stress, overload, and burnout and revitalize your career. Dutton 1996 245p il hardcover o.p. paperback available $12.95   **650.1**
1. Job stress 2. Vocational guidance 3. Work—Psychological aspects
ISBN 0-452-27275-0 (pa)   LC 95-26490
"Reinhold examines work-induced stress and its influence on psychological and physical well-being." Libr J
The author "offers a variety of probing self-tests, illuminating case histories and sequenced, focused suggestions for transforming workplace problems into opportunities for growth." Publ Wkly
Includes bibliographical references

650.14   Success in obtaining jobs and promotions

The **Adams** cover letter almanac & disk. Adams Media Corp. 1996 16,735p pa $19.95   **650.14**
1. Applications for positions 2. Job hunting
ISBN 1-55850-619-5   LC 96-7853
600 individualized samples provide detailed how-to information including strategies for career changers
Includes bibliographical references

The **Adams** resume almanac. Adams Media Corp. 1996 768p pa $19.95   **650.14**
1. Résumés (Employment) 2. Applications for positions
ISBN 1-55850-618-7   LC 96-15500
This "guide reviews résumé layouts and various formats and strategies, along with 600 samples and 25 cover letters. With the disk, the job seeker can actually generate a résumé." Libr J

Asher, Donald
The overnight résumé. 2nd ed. Ten Speed Press 1999 157p il pa $14.95   **650.14**
1. Résumés (Employment)
ISBN 1-58008-041-3   LC 98-54145
First published 1991
This book provides instructions on how to write a good résumé quickly as well as job-hunting advice and information on internet résumés, HTML résumés, scannable résumés and keyword clusters
"Asher's methods encourage clear and concise writing quickly . . . and his good humor and the 15 delightful cartoons that punctuate the book make resume writing a less agonizing experience. . . . Highly recommended for all resume collections." Libr J [review of 1991 edition]

Beatty, Richard H., 1939-
175 high-impact cover letters. 3rd ed. Wiley 2002 244p pa $14.95   **650.14**
1. Applications for positions 2. Job hunting
ISBN 0-471-21084-6   LC 2001-46963
First published 1992
Contents: Importance of cover letters; Letters to employers; Letters to search firms; Advertising response cover letters; Networking cover letters; The resume letter; Thank-you letters; Cover letters "Do's" and "Don'ts"

The interview kit. 3rd ed. Wiley 2003 248p pa $14.95   **650.14**
1. Interviewing 2. Applications for positions
ISBN 0-471-44925-3   LC 2003-45071
First published 1995
This offers advice for success in job interviews, with answers to 500 questions, strategies for making a good impression, and negotiating salaries and benefits

Enelow, Wendy S.
Cover letter magic; [by] Wendy S. Enelow [and] Louise Kursmark. 2nd ed. JIST Works 2004 412p pa $16.95   **650.14**
1. Applications for positions 2. Résumés (Employment)
ISBN 1-563-70986-4   LC 2003-23186
First published 2000
This guide to writing cover letters includes "more than 150 . . . cover letters for every profession and situation. Before-and-after transformations . . . tips on resumes, e-mail and scannable cover letters, thank-you letters [and] . . . dozens of sample opening paragraphs [are included.]DD Publisher's note

Fisher, Anne B.
If my career's on the fast track, where do I get a road map? surviving and thriving in the real world of work; [by] Anne Fisher. Morrow 2001 272p hardcover o.p. paperback available $12.95   **650.14**
1. Vocational guidance 2. Work 3. Interpersonal relations 4. Life skills
ISBN 0-06-000796-6 (pa)   LC 2001-269726
"*Fortune* magazine's career columnist offers savvy advice from results of interviews and conversations with recruiters, executives, lawyers, consultants, and other experts on a wide range of topics (e.g., salaries, benefits, interviewing)." Libr J
Includes bibliographical references

Fry, Ronald W.
Your first resume; for students and anyone preparing to enter today's job market; by Ron Fry. 5th ed. Career Press 2001 188p pa $11.99   **650.14**
1. Résumés (Employment)
ISBN 1-56414-583-2   LC 2001-35875
First published 1988
A step-by-step guide for preparing a successful résumé. Numerous examples accompany the text

Gardella, Robert
The Harvard Business School guide to finding your next job; [by] Robert S. Gardella. Harvard Business School Press 2000 143p pa $16.95   **650.14**
1. Job hunting
ISBN 1-57851-223-9   LC 99-58454
"Gardella covers references, résumés, letters, interviews, and negotiation. He also details a strategy for planning and executing a job search campaign, and discusses the emotional aspects of looking for work. Special topics include the 'long-distance' job search, job fairs, and overcoming age discrimination." Booklist
Includes bibliographical references

Jackson, Tom
The new perfect resume; {by} Tom Jackson and Ellen Jackson. Doubleday 1996 226p il pa $12.95   **650.14**
1. Résumés (Employment) 2. Applications for positions
ISBN 0-385-48190-X   LC 96-12401
"A Main Street book"
First published 1980 with title: The perfect resume
New edition in preparation
This guide to resumes and job applications emphasizes temporary, freelance, and consulting positions, and offers advice on preparing a capabilities portfolio, on using e-mail, talents banks on the Internet, and electronic job searches
Includes bibliographical references

McGraw-Hill's big red book of resumes; [compiled by Luisa Gerasimo] McGraw-Hill 2002 473p pa $16.95 **650.14**
1. Résumés (Employment)
ISBN 0-07-140195-4   LC 2002-25523
"Some 300 résumés target a wide variety of jobs, experience, and styles that will prove useful as models." Libr J

Moreira, Paula

Ace the IT job interview! Osborne/McGraw-Hill 2002 371p pa $24.99 **650.14**

1. Interviewing 2. Information technology—Vocational guidance

ISBN 0-07-222581-5   LC 2003-266138

This offers advice for preparing for interviews for applications for employment opportunities in information technology

Mornell, Pierre

Games companies play; the job hunter's guide to playing smart & winning big in the high-stakes hiring game; designed by Kit Hinrichs; illustrations by Regan Dunnick. Ten Speed Press 2000 208p il hardcover o.p. paperback available $17.95 **650.14**

1. Job hunting

ISBN 1-58008-408-7 (pa)   LC 00-26736

The author "offers advice on how to ready résumés and recommendations, write eye-catching cover letters, shine in the most difficult interview situation, and finalize job offers. He includes more than 40 sample interview questions and answers, legal considerations, and a list of important web and print resources." Libr J

Includes bibliographical references

Parker, Yana

The damn good resume guide; a crash course in resume writing. 4th ed. Ten Speed Press 2002 73p il pa $9.95 **650.14**

1. Résumés (Employment)

ISBN 1-58008-444-3   LC 2002-9177

First published 1983

This guide offers a ten-step approach to resume writing, providing creative solutions and strategies to various resume problems. Also included are sections on formatting resumes and submitting resumes over the Internet

Resumes and cover letters that have worked; [edited by Anne McKinney] PREP Pub. 1996 270p pa $25 **650.14**

1. Résumés (Employment) 2. Applications for positions

ISBN 1-88528-804-2   LC 95-19458

"The superior, readable samples, customized to professionals, college graduates, and career changers, distinguish this work from others." Libr J

Richardson, Bradley G.

Career comeback; 8 steps to getting back on your feet when you're fired, laid off, or your business venture has failed—and finding more job satisfaction than ever. Broadway Bks. 2004 319p pa $14.95 **650.14**

1. Job hunting 2. Employees—Dismissal 3. Vocational guidance

ISBN 0-767-91557-7   LC 2003-56271

"In addition to providing detailed suggestions for sharpening skills—such as resume writing, interviewing, working with recruiters and networking—[the author] addresses the psychological and emotional problems that often accompany the loss of a job. . . . Upbeat and clearly written, Richardson's comeback program will be welcomed by many." Publ Wkly

Includes bibliographical references

Rosenberg, Arthur D.

The resume handbook; how to write outstanding resumes & cover letters for every situation; [by] Arthur D. Rosenberg & David Hizer. 4th ed. Adams Media Corp. 2003 144p pa $9.95 **650.14**

1. Résumés (Employment) 2. Applications for positions

ISBN 1-580-62854-0   LC 2003-4613

First published 1985

This offers advice on writing resumes and cover letters and includes 32 examples.

Wendleton, Kate

Building a great résumé; for job hunters, career changers, consultants, and freelancers; with hints for new grads by Mark Gonska. 2nd ed. Career Press 1999 195p il pa $13.99 **650.14**

1. Résumés (Employment) 2. Job hunting 3. Career changes

ISBN 1-56414-433-X   LC 99-38052

First published 1997 by Five O'Clock Books

"Creator of the career-counseling network The Five O'Clock Club, Wendleton uses the club's case study approach with before-and-after examples (over 80 industries are featured) to address the entire process of résumé writing for career changers, consultants, freelancers, and job-hunters." Libr J

Yate, Martin John

Cover letters that knock 'em dead; [by] Martin Yate. 4th ed., completely rev. and expanded. Adams Media Corp. 2001 xx, 278p il pa $12.95 **650.14**

1. Résumés (Employment) 2. Applications for positions

ISBN 1-580-62423-5

First published 1992

This guide to writing cover letters includes "cover letters for new occupations... information on electronic cover letters and online job searching...[and] how to customize letters to make employers want to know more about you." Publisher's note

Knock 'em dead; [by] Martin Yate. Adams Media Corp. pa $14.95 **650.14**

1. Interviewing 2. Applications for positions 3. Job hunting

Annual. First published 1985

"Great answers to over 200 tough interview questions—plus the latest electronic job search strategies." Cover

"Updated regularly since 1987, Yate's comprehensive how-to covers the entire job search process from résumé writing and interviewing to salary negotiation and psychological and drug testing, with information on recent developments in the job market. Three appendixes address online searching with valuable listings of web sites and resources arranged by subject." Libr J

Resumes that knock 'em dead; by Martin Yate. 4th ed., completely rev. and expanded. Adams Media Corp. 2001 293p pa $12.95 **650.14**

1. Résumés (Employment) 2. Applications for positions

ISBN 1-580-62422-7

First published 1988

Yate, Martin John—*Continued*

This guide to resume writing includes "resumes used in successful job searches · Information on new occupations ...[and] information on electronic cover letters and online job searching" Publisher's note

651   Office services

The **New** York Public Library business desk reference. Wiley 1998 494p il map $29.95; pa $24.95   **651**
1. Office practice—Handbooks, manuals, etc.
ISBN 0-471-14442-8; 0-471-32835-9 (pa)

LC 97-7408

"A Stonesong Press book"

This work "has sections focusing on information delivery, communications, the office environment, equipment, supplies and systems, human resources, finances, law, public relations, marketing, travel, and information resources. The lists of further information that end each section include organizations, service providers, books, and online resources." Booklist

651.3   Office management

Burton, Sharon

Procedures for the automated office; {by} Sharon Burton, Nelda Shelton, Lucy Mae Jennings. Prentice-Hall pa $66   **651.3**
1. Office practice—Handbooks, manuals, etc. 2. Secretaries—Handbooks, manuals, etc.
First published 1981 under the authorship of Lucy Mae Jennings with title: Secretarial and general office procedures (5th edition 2001) Periodically revised

This covers business math and language arts skills, the role of office support staff, interpersonal communication, records management, telecommunications, computers and job search skills. Includes application exercises, projects, sample forms and documents

Includes bibliographical references

De Vries, Mary Ann

The professional secretary's book of lists & tips; [by] Mary A. De Vries. Prentice-Hall 1996 433p il $36.95   **651.3**
1. Office practice—Handbooks, manuals, etc. 2. Secretaries—Handbooks, manuals, etc.
ISBN 0-13-149345-0

LC 95-24338

This offers information to secretaries and office professionals in the form of lists and tables covering over 100 topics that impact the proper office management

Stroman, James

Administrative assistant's & secretary's handbook; [by] James Stroman, Kevin Wilson, Jennifer Wauson. 2nd ed. AMACOM 2004 556p il $34.95   **651.3**
1. Secretaries—Handbooks, manuals, etc. 2. Office practice—Handbooks, manuals, etc.
ISBN 0-8144-0784-6

LC 2003-10063

First published 1995

This handbook provides information on general procedures and techniques covering such topics as telephone usage and mailing, office equipment and computers, language usage, financial activities, banking, etc.

Includes bibliographical references

651.7   Business communication. Creation and transmission of records

Phillips, Ellen Haygood, 1947-

Shocked, appalled, and dismayed! How to write letters of complaint that get results. Vintage Bks. 1999 333p pa $12   **651.7**
1. Business letters 2. Customer relations
ISBN 0-375-70120-6

LC 98-13819

A guide to writing effective letters of complaint. Legal advice, illustrative anecdotes, and sample letters are provided. An appendix lists the names and addresses of over 600 major companies, government agencies, and consumer organizations

Seglin, Jeffrey L., 1956-

The AMA handbook of business letters; [by] Jeffrey L. Seglin with Edward Coleman. 3rd ed. AMACOM 2002 519p $69.95   **651.7**
1. Business letters
ISBN 0-8144-0665-3

LC 2001-53995

First published 1989

Accompanied by computer disk

"This volume offers 365 sample letters of different business scenarios in which a formal letter is appropriate. The letters vary in topic, from sales, marketing, and public relations to credit and collection letters. . . . This is a practical guide for those already established in the business world as well as those just out of college looking for an office support position. Public and business libraries will want to keep a copy on hand as it will answer a number of business-related questions related to writing business letters." Am Ref Books Annu, 2003

Includes bibliographical references

651.8   Data processing. Computer applications

Jaderstrom, Susan

Complete office handbook; the definitive reference for today's electronic office; {by} Susan Jaderstrom, Leonard Kruk, and Joanne Miller; general editor, Susan W. Fenner. 3rd ed. Random House Ref. 2002 596p il maps pa $21.95   **651.8**
1. Office practice—Handbooks, manuals, etc.
ISBN 0-375-70929-0

LC 2002-727980

First published 1992 with title: Professional Secretaries International complete office handbook

This book "is designed to assist the individual who serves as an administrative assistant, executive assistant, or project manager. . . . It covers, in detail, every facet of office operations, from office supplies and financial record keeping to complex operations, including computers, dictation equipment, and telecommunications equipment. . . . This handbook is just as useful for the entry-level office worker as it is for the professional advancing to the level of executive assistant." Recomm Ref Books for Small & Medium-sized Libr & Media Cent, 2003

652   Processes of written communication

Singh, Simon
The code book; the evolution of secrecy from Mary, Queen of Scots, to quantum cryptography. Doubleday 1999 402p il map $24.95; pa $15   **652**
1. Cryptography
ISBN 0-385-49531-5; 0-385-49532-3 (pa)
         LC 99-35261
This survey explores the evolution of cryptography. "Along the way, we encounter Charles Babbage, the nineteenth-century British polymath who conceived of a steam-powered computer; archeologists who used cryptographic methods to translate Egyptian hieroglyphics; and Navajo code-talkers employed by the U.S. military in the Second World War." New Yorker
Includes bibliographical references

652.3   Typing

Century 21 keyboarding & information processing. South-Western il   **652.3**
1. Keyboarding (Electronics) 2. Word processing
Replaces Century 21 keyboarding, formatting, and document processing. Periodically revised. Title varies
Various courses are available as well as accompanying workbooks and manuals for building skills in keyboarding and automated information processing. Apply to publisher for complete listing and price

657   Accounting

Century 21 accounting: advanced course. South-Western il $60.95   **657**
1. Accounting 2. Bookkeeping
First published with title: 20th century bookkeeping and accounting: advanced course. (7th edition 2002) Periodically revised
The second volume in a two-volume textbook teaching accounting principles, procedures and applications. The advanced course is preceded by the first course

Century 21 accounting: first-year course. South-Western il $60.95   **657**
1. Accounting 2. Bookkeeping
Also available various workbooks, manuals and disks to accompany the first-year course and the advanced course. Apply to publisher for complete listing
First published with title: 20th century bookkeeping and accounting: first year course. (7th edition 2003) Periodically revised
The first volume in a two-volume textbook teaching accounting principles, procedures and applications

Siegel, Joel G.
Accounting handbook; [by] Joel G. Siegel, Jae K. Shim. 3rd ed. Barron's Educ. Ser. 2000 986p il $35   **657**
1. Accounting
ISBN 0-7641-5282-3   LC 00-106978
First published 1990
This reference includes sections on financial accounting, tax preparation, auditing, personal financial planning, and governmental and nonprofit accounting and includes a dictionary of accounting terms

658   General management

Bredin, Alice, 1962-
The virtual office survival handbook; what telecommuters and entrepreneurs need to succeed in today's nontraditional workplace. Wiley 1996 259p hardcover o.p. paperback available $16.95   **658**
1. Home-based business 2. Telecommuting
ISBN 0-471-12059-6 (pa)   LC 96-1327
The author "starts by describing the professions and industries most suited to virtual or home offices and the employee personality and temperament that will thrive in the situation. Then she offers first-rate nitty-gritty advice on setting up an office, from choosing computer systems, legal and tax requirements for home business, time management and more." Publ Wkly
Includes bibliographical references

Business: the ultimate resource. Perseus Bks. 2002 xxxv, 2172p il maps $59.95   **658**
1. Management 2. Entrepreneurship
ISBN 0-7382-9242-8
This volume covers "intellectual, practical, and factual areas in the field of management. A major feature of Business is . . . a world almanac featuring 26 industry sector surveys and profiles of 150 countries and all U.S states. . . . Biographies of the management thinkers who have shaped the world as we know it—from Adam Smith to Peter Drucker, from Henry Ford to Estée Lauder [are included]." Publisher's note
"Any library or personal business collection will want a copy of this unique . . . reference." Libr J
Includes bibliographical references

Collins, James C.
Good to great; why some companies make the leap, and others don't; [by] Jim Collins. HarperBusiness 2001 300p il $27.50   **658**
1. Leadership 2. Management
ISBN 0-06-662099-6   LC 2001-24818
"Starting with every company that ever appeared in the Fortune 500, Collins identifies 11 great ones and looks for similarities among them, and what he finds will both surprise and fascinate anyone involved in management." Booklist
Includes bibliographical references

Drucker, Peter Ferdinand, 1909-
Management challenges for the 21st century; [by] Peter F. Drucker. HarperBusiness 1999 207p $27.50; pa $18   **658**
1. Management
ISBN 0-88730-998-4; 0-88730-999-2 (pa)
         LC 99-17087
"Drucker outlines the changing role of management, the new realities of strategy, how to lead in times of great change, how to develop new information sources for effective decision-making, and how individual workers must assume responsibility for managing their own careers." Libr J

Drucker, Peter Ferdinand, 1909-—*Continued*

Managing in a time of great change; [by] Peter F. Drucker. Truman Talley Bks. 1995 371p hardcover o.p. paperback available $14.95 **658**
1. Management
ISBN 0-452-27837-6 (pa)   LC 95-13316
This collection of previously published essays and articles is "arranged by four topics: management, information-based organization, the economy, and society." Libr J

Managing the non-profit organization; practices and principles; [by] Peter F. Drucker. HarperCollins Pubs. 1990 235p hardcover o.p. paperback available $16.95 **658**
1. Management 2. Corporations
ISBN 0-88730-601-2 (pa)   LC 89-46525
The author discusses "his ideas on tasks, responsibilities, and practices necessary to manage nonprofit organizations." Libr J

Encyclopedia of small business; [edited by] Kevin Hillstrom, Laurie Collier Hillstrom. 2nd ed. Gale Group 2001 c2002 2v set $450 **658**
1. Small business
ISBN 0-7876-4906-6   LC 2001-33781
First published 1998
This reference arranged in A-Z format contains some 600 articles and overviews on areas "including financing; financial planning; business plan creation; market analysis; sales strategy; tax planning, human resource issues and more. Also covered are narrower topics such as 'keough Plan,' 'working capital,' 'Self-Employment Contributions Act' and 'equity.'" Publisher's note
Includes bibliographical references

Giuliani, Rudolph W.
Leadership; by Rudolph W. Giuliani with Ken Kurson. Miramax Bks. 2002 407p $25.95 **658**
1. Management
ISBN 0-7868-6841-4
This is a "book of guidelines about exemplary management skills {by} New York City's former mayor. . . . {He includes} opening and closing segments about the destruction of the World Trade Center." N Y Times (Late N Y Ed)

Kelley, Robert Earl
How to be a star at work; nine breakthrough strategies you need to succeed. Times Business 1998 xxi, 312p il hardcover o.p. paperback available $13 **658**
1. Office workers 2. Success
ISBN 0-8129-3169-6 (pa)   LC 97-28117
Kelley's "program is commonsense advice to workers: take initiatives, network for useful information, self-manage, know whom you're trying to please, be a biddable follower when necessary, be a reliable leader when that's called for, work effectively in teams, know your organization and how to present your ideas." Publ Wkly

Lonier, Terri
Working solo; the real guide to freedom & financial success with your own business. 2nd ed. Wiley 1998 xxiv, 354p il pa $14.95 **658**
1. Self-employed 2. Small business
ISBN 0-471-24713-8   LC 98-10660
Also available companion volume The working solo sourcebook (1998)
First published 1994 by Portico Press
This offers advice on starting a small business covering such topics as time management, buying a computer, setting up an office, business planning, low-cost marketing techniques, using technology and the Internet. Includes a resource section on books, on-line services, and software

O'Reilly, Charles A., III
Hidden value; how great companies achieve extraordinary results with ordinary people; [by] Charles A. O'Reilly III, Jeffrey Pfeffer. Harvard Business School Press 2000 286p il $29.95 **658**
1. Management 2. Human capital
ISBN 0-87584-898-2   LC 00-25016
"Through eight case studies, *Hidden Value* shows how a firm can use existing talent rather than how firms can attract talent. Smart organizations make it possible for ordinary people to perform as stars by engaging their emotional and intellectual resources." Libr J

Webb, Philip, 1964-
The small business handbook; the entrepreneur's definitive guide to starting and growing a business; [by] Philip Webb and Sandra Webb. 2nd ed. Prentice-Hall 2001 318p il pa $54.50 **658**
1. Small business 2. Entrepreneurship
ISBN 0-273-65432-2
First published 1999 by Financial Times
Includes CD-ROM
This is a guide to starting a new business covering such topics as sales and marketing strategies, employment and management of staff, accounting and stress management. A list of addresses and web sites is provided
Includes bibliographical references

658.1 Business organization and finance

Burstiner, Irving
The small business handbook; a comprehensive guide to starting and running your own business. 3rd ed. Simon & Schuster 1997 395p il pa $20 **658.1**
1. Small business
ISBN 0-684-83022-1   LC 97-20330
"A Fireside book"
First published 1979 by Prentice Hall Press
Topics discussed include writing a business plan, finding capital, reaching high-potential markets, pricing, safeguarding assets, distribution, advertising, sales promotion, and computerized operations
Includes bibliographical references

How to run a small business; [by] J.K. Lasser
Tax Institute. McGraw-Hill $27.95   **658.1**
1. Small business

First edition by J. K. Lasser published 1950. (7th edition 1993) Periodically revised

"Practical advice for small businesses and for people considering opening them. Details everything from choosing a location to financing to tax management, bookkeeping, accounting, personal management, and computer technology. Concisely written and well-organized." N Y Public Libr Book of How & Where to Look It Up

Small business sourcebook. Gale Res. 2v set
$405   **658.1**
1. Small business

ISSN 0883-3397

Annual. First published 1983

This "is a standard reference work for identifying information resources for starting, developing, and growing 341 specific small businesses as well as for finding information on general small business topics and sources of assistance at the state and federal levels and by Canadian province. . . . The strength of the reference work lies in its catalog of resources for specific kinds of small businesses as well as the variety of sources covered and the copious annotations. It will aid entrepreneurs who need both general and specific information to help them solve problems." Am Ref Books Annu, 2003

Sullivan, Robert, 1940-
The small business start-up guide. Rev 3rd
ed. Information Int. 2000 xx, 339p il pa
$17.95   **658.1**
1. Small business

ISBN 1-882480-19-8   LC 99-73135

Also available online

First published 1996

"Sullivan suggests how one can evaluate his or her 'entrepreneurial aptitude' and advises how to get started, obtain financing, select partners, prepare a business plan, establish banking relationships, set up home-based operations, and market effectively. He also considers legal, tax, and personnel issues. Each chapter includes useful checklists and recommends additional sources of information." Booklist [review of 1998 edition]

658.3   Personnel management

Lancaster, Lynne C.
When generations collide; who they are, why they clash, how to solve the generational puzzle at work; by Lynne C. Lancaster and David Stillman. HarperCollins Pubs. 2002
xxv, 352p $25.95; pa $15.95   **658.3**
1. Personnel management 2. Conflict of generations

ISBN 0-06-662106-2; 0-06-662107-0 (pa)
     LC 2001-39221

At head of title: Traditionalists, baby boomers, generation Xers, millennials

The authors address the "ways of attracting and retaining individuals from the four generations that make up the American workforce. . . . Their book is a guide for employers and employees on how to take advantage of generational differences rather than allowing those differences to drain productivity. As with all outstanding business books, this wise and personable one will appeal to a wide range of readers." Booklist

Includes bibliographical references

658.4   Executive management

Batstone, David B., 1958-
Saving the corporate soul & (who knows?) maybe your own; eight principles for creating and preserving integrity and profitability without selling out; [by] David Batstone.
Jossey-Bass 2003 270p $26.95   **658.4**
1. Leadership 2. Business ethics

ISBN 0-7879-6480-8   LC 2002-154858

Contents: Leadership and governance; Transparency and integrity; Community; Customer care; Valuing the worker; Respect for the environment; Equality and diversity; Globalization

The author sends a "message to business leaders that conscience and profit go hand in hand. He believes principled companies excel financially over the long haul, are respected more by the public, and are rated as better places to work." Booklist

Includes bibliographical references

Bossidy, Lawrence A.
Execution: the discipline of getting things done; [by] Larry Bossidy & Ram Charan; with Charles Burck. Crown Business 2002
278p $27.50   **658.4**
1. Executive ability 2. Management

ISBN 0-609-61057-0   LC 2002-18743

The authors "present the viewpoint that execution (that is, linking a company's people, strategy, and operations) is what will determine success in today's business world. . . . Details of both successful and unsuccessful executions at corporations such as Dell, Johnson & Johnson, and Xerox, to name a few, support not only their how-to method for bringing execution to the forefront but also the need for it." Libr J

"This is a terrific book that will make smart managers rethink how business gets done within every level of their organization or department." Publ Wkly

Camp, Jim
Start with no; the negotiating tools that the pros don't want you to know. Crown Business 2002 271p $22.95   **658.4**
1. Negotiation 2. Business 3. Management

ISBN 0-609-60800-2   LC 2001-47742

"Camp has developed a system of negotiating that reflects the common concept of 'win-win,' and the result is an excellent book with valuable insights." Booklist

Goleman, Daniel
Primal leadership; realizing the power of emotional intelligence; [by] Daniel Goleman, Richard Boyatzis, Annie McKee. Harvard Business School Press 2002 306p $26.95
   658.4
1. Leadership 2. Management 3. Executive ability

ISBN 1-57851-486-X   LC 2001-41207

This title focuses "on the relationship between Emotional Intelligence (EI) and successful leadership. . . . The book is arranged in three sections, with the first section describing the characteristics of resonant and dissonant leadership as well as the four dimensions of EI, which are self-awareness, self-management, social awareness, and relationship management. This section also describes the different types of leadership styles, such as visionary, coaching, and commanding. The second section outlines the steps one needs to take to become a

Goleman, Daniel—*Continued*
more positive leader, and the third section discusses how to use these newfound skills to build a better organization." Libr J
This "book is well written, intelligent, approachable, and stimulating." Booklist
Includes bibliographical references

Heller, Robert, 1932-
Essential manager's manual; [by] Robert Heller & Tim Hindle. DK Pub. 1998 864p il $40 **658.4**
1. Management 2. Time management 3. Decision making
ISBN 0-7894-3519-5 LC 98-6507
The authors "focus on time management, decision making, and communication, but subjects also include successful delegation, interviewing, stress reduction, and managing change. This sturdy manual is well organized and well written, and it has an excellent index." Booklist

Krames, Jeffrey A.
The Rumsfeld way; leadership wisdom of a battle-hardened maverick. McGraw-Hill 2002 244p il $18.95; pa $12.95 **658.4**
1. Rumsfeld, Donald H. 2. Leadership
ISBN 0-07-140641-7; 0-07-141516-5 (pa)
LC 2002-523119
This book looks "at the leadership skills, methods, and strategies that have made Secretary of Defense Donald Rumsfeld an accomplished public figure." Libr J
Includes bibliographical references

Peters, Thomas J.
The circle of innovation; you can't shrink your way to greatness; by Tom Peters. Knopf 1997 xxi, 518p il $35; pa $16 **658.4**
1. Success 2. Executive ability 3. Management
ISBN 0-375-40157-1; 0-679-75765-1 (pa)
LC 97-74755
The author argues for constant innovation as a survival strategy for both the individual and the organization. Topics discussed include company decentralization, product design, empowering customers, system building, and corporate willingness to experiment

658.8 Management of distribution (Marketing)

Gerhards, Paul
How to sell what you make; the business of marketing crafts. rev & updated ed. Stackpole Bks. 1996 151p il pa $12.95
658.8
1. Selling 2. Handicraft
ISBN 0-8117-2436-0 LC 95-37330
First published 1990
This offers advice on how to market crafts through fairs, trade shows, and galleries, and includes information on small business management
Includes bibliographical references

Underhill, Paco
Why we buy; the science of shopping. Simon & Schuster 1999 255p $25; pa $15
658.8
1. Marketing 2. Consumers
ISBN 0-684-84913-5; 0-684-84914-3 (pa)
LC 99-12125
"Each chapter delves into a particular aspect of a store environment and its interface with customers: the importance of signage and why less is more, how men shop, . . . the need to cater to boomers, and clues about waiting time. Throughout, insights are peppered with one or several examples." Booklist

659.1 Advertising

The **Advertising** age encyclopedia of advertising; editors, John McDonough and the Museum of Broadcast Communications, Karen Egolf; illustration editor, Jacqueline V. Reid. Fitzroy Dearborn Pubs. 2003 3v il set $385 **659.1**
1. Advertising—Encyclopedias
ISBN 1-57958-172-2 LC 2003-270744
This encyclopedia provides "historic surveys of the world's leading agencies and major advertisers, as well as brand and market histories; it also profiles the influential men and women in advertising, overviews advertising in the major countries of the world, covers important issues affecting the field, and discusses the key aspects of methodology, practice, strategy, and theory." Publisher's note
"Well-researched, thorough, and fascinating, it belongs in all business collections and most academic and large public libraries." Booklist

Standard directory of advertisers. LEXIS-NEXIS il $799 **659.1**
1. Advertising—Directories
ISSN 0081-4229
Also available CD-ROM version and online
Also available with supplements for $999
Annual. First published 1916 by National Register Pub. Title varies
Covers "U.S. corporations, listing advertising budgets, key managment and marketing directors, and company subsidiaries and divisions, and giving addresses and lists of products. Indexed by type of business, personnel, and product trade name." Guide to Ref Books. 11th edition

Standard directory of advertising agencies. LEXIS-NEXIS For subscription options contact publisher **659.1**
1. Advertising—Directories
ISSN 0085-6614
Also available CD-ROM version and online
Semi-annual. First published 1917 by National Register Pub.
Known as The agency red book
"Lists approximately 9,700 advertising agencies in the U.S. and other countries. Arranged by type of agency: advertising agencies, house agencies, media buying services, sales promotion firms, and public relations firms. Lists major clients of each agency. Geographic and name indexes." Guide to Ref Books. 11th edition

660   Chemical engineering

The **Chemical** formulary. Chemical Pub. Co. Apply to publisher for price and availability   **660**
1. Chemical engineering
Cumulative index available for volumes 1-35
First published 1933. New volumes issued periodically
"Useful both to general readers and to chemists requiring information on chemical compounding and treatment in areas foreign to him. Formulas have been provided and reviewed by chemists and engineers engaged in many industries. Each volume presents a collection of new, up-to-date formulas not appearing in previous volumes. Grouping is under broad headings such as: Adhesives, Cosmetics and drugs, Foods and beverages, Paints and lacquers, Soaps and cleaners. Includes lists of chemicals and suppliers." Guide to Ref Books. 11th edition

660.6   Biotechnology

Hubbell, Sue
Shrinking the cat; genetic engineering before we knew about genes; with illustrations by Liddy Hubbell. Houghton Mifflin 2001 175p il $25; pa $13   **660.6**
1. Breeding 2. Genetic engineering
ISBN 0-618-04027-7; 0-618-25748-9 (pa)
                 LC 2001-24547
This is a "history of how genetic engineering began, how it has been used, and how humankind has benefited from a combination of natural selection and scientific manipulation of genes. Hubbell . . . shows that genetic engineering has always been with us, illustrating by way of silkworm breeding from its origins in China to the New World, where it spawned an industry that depends on genetics to thrive; the domestication of corn from its wild state to the product we eat today; [and] how we turned wildcats into house cats by selective breeding that changed size, color, and demeanor." Libr J
"An engaging synthesis of material that will appeal to Hubbell's well-established audience." Booklist
Includes bibliographical references

Steinberg, Mark L.
The Facts on File dictionary of biotechnology and genetic engineering; [by] Mark L. Steinberg and Sharon D. Cosloy. new ed. Facts on File 2000 228p il (Facts on File science library) $44; pa $17.95   **660.6**
1. Biotechnology—Dictionaries 2. Genetic engineering—Dictionaries
ISBN 0-8160-4274-8; 0-8160-4275-6 (pa)
                 LC 00-35463
First published 1994
This dictionary includes over 2,000 entries that "define terms and phrases from A-DNA to Zoo Blot. Among the topics covered are: Medicine, agriculture, and biochemistry, including fields related to biochemical research; cancer treatments and genetically engineered growth hormones; vaccines; the scientists responsible for major research breakthroughs and the products they've helped to create." Publisher's note

664   Food technology

Charles, Daniel
Lords of the harvest; biotech, big money, and the future of food. Perseus Bks. 2001 348p il hardcover o.p. paperback available $17.50   **664**
1. Food—Biotechnology 2. Genetic engineering 3. Agricultural industry 4. Farm produce
ISBN 0-7382-0773-X (pa)
The author "covers the history of genetic engineering in plant crops from the early 1980s to the present. . . . What makes this book particularly interesting are the author's tales of the key individuals and groups involved in the biotechnology controversy. . . . This carefully researched and balanced account is intended to help the reader understand the how and the why of genetic engineering rather than make an argument for or against it." Libr J
Includes bibliographical references

Winston, Mark L.
Travels in the genetically modified zone. Harvard Univ. Press 2002 280p $27.95   **664**
1. Food—Biotechnology 2. Farm produce
ISBN 0-674-00867-7   LC 2002-17192
The author "first describes the development of hybrid corn, then delves into the use of genetic modifications to combat weeds and diseases. The facets of genetic modification he takes into account include research, industrial processes, growing modified crops, protecting nearby crops, the safety of consumers, and the profits of agribusiness. . . . Winston also fields practical ideas for solving the major problems involved in the rapidly growing field of genetically modified crops. Throughout, however, he maintains a moderate stance on his controversial subject." Booklist
Includes bibliographical references

Winter, Ruth, 1930-
A consumer's dictionary of food additives. Three Rivers Press (NY) pa $16   **664**
1. Food additives—Dictionaries
First published 1972 (5th edition 1999) Periodically revised
This volume gives you "the facts about the relative safety and side effects of more than 8,000 ingredients that end up indirectly in your food as a result of processing and curing, such as preservatives, food-tainting pesticides, and animal drugs." Publisher's note

666   Ceramic and allied technologies

Ellis, William S.
Glass; from the first mirror to fiber optics, the story of the substance that changed the world. Avon Bks. 1998 306p hardcover o.p. paperback available $14   **666**
1. Glass
ISBN 0-380-79139-0 (pa)   LC 98-21943
This "survey of glass, from the artifacts of ancient Mesopotamia and Egypt to modern lasers and telescopes, . . . [offers an] excursion into science, history, culture and invention. . . . Ellis's amazing exploration of glass's resurgence in technology and art proves that glass, despite appearances, has muscle as well as soul." Publ Wkly
Includes bibliographical references

Macfarlane, Alan

Glass: a world history; [by] Alan Macfarlane and Gerry Martin. University of Chicago Press 2002 255p il $27.50 **666**

1. Glass

ISBN 0-226-50028-4 LC 2002-20493

The authors "make the case for the centrality of glass in the artistic renaissance and scientific revolution that took place in Western Europe from the 14th to 17th centuries. They discuss the origins of glass making and trace its development and usage across centuries and multiple cultures (Europe, the Middle East, China, India, and Japan). Their discussion combines cultural, artistic, and aesthetic viewpoints of glass within these cultures with history and developments in science. The result is a thoroughly readable, carefully argued work, filled with delightful surprises. . . . An excellent example of microhistory . . . this is required for history of science collections and recommended for large public and academic collections." Libr J

Includes bibliographical references

667 Cleaning, color, coating, related technologies

Garfield, Simon

Mauve; how one man invented a color that changed the world. Norton 2001 222p il hardcover o.p. paperback available $13.95 **667**

1. Perkin, William Henry, 1838-1907 2. Dyes and dyeing

ISBN 0-393-32313-7 (pa) LC 00-69533

This volume discusses how a British student, William Henry Perkin, while trying to synthesize quinine from coal tar, developed mauve, "the first mass-produced artificial dye. . . . By the turn of the 20th century, because of Perkin's novel idea, dye makers had 2,000 synthesized colors at their disposal." N Y Times Book Rev

"The text is understandable by the average layman and is enjoyable reading for the scientist and non-scientist alike." Sci Books Films

Includes bibliographical references

668 Technology of other organic products

Winter, Ruth, 1930-

A consumer's dictionary of cosmetic ingredients. Three Rivers Press (NY) pa $16 **668**

1. Cosmetics—Dictionaries

First published 1974. (5th edition 1999) Periodically revised

This volume describes over 6,000 ingredients used in cosmetics including preservatives, coloring agents, flavorings, fragrances, and preserving agents, their effectiveness and possible toxic and allergic effects

Includes bibliographical references

670 Manufacturing

How products are made; an illustrated guide to product manufacturing; Neil Schlager, editor. Gale Res. il ea $125 **670**

1. Commercial products

ISSN 1072-5091 LC 94-648208

Irregular. First published 1994

Each of these volumes in this on going series describes the manufacture of approximately 100 products, and includes historical information, raw materials, byproducts, quality control, future applications and sources of additional information

671.5 Joining and cutting of metals

Geary, Don

Welding. McGraw-Hill 2000 264p il pa $34.95 **671.5**

1. Welding

ISBN 0-07-134245-1 LC 99-35501

"Starting with the basics of setting up a welding outfit and with a focus on oxyacetylene welding, this book discusses . . . processes, fuels, equipment, supplies and welding techniques. . . . It even covers safety issues and how to set up your own welding workshop. It also provides welding projects for beginners to try out what they've learned." Publisher's note

674 Lumber processing, wood products, cork

The **Encyclopedia** of wood; a tree-by-tree guide to the world's most versatile resource; foreword by John Makepeace; general editor, Aidan Walker. Facts on File 1989 192p il maps $29.95 **674**

1. Wood

ISBN 0-8160-2159-7 LC 89-33439

This book describes the properties, appearance, geographic distribution, and uses of seventy-five types of wood, and discusses trees, forest types, and logging procedures

Petroski, Henry

The pencil; a history of design and circumstance. Knopf 1990 434p il hardcover o.p. paperback available $20 **674**

1. Pencils

ISBN 0-679-73415-5 (pa) LC 89-45362

The author discusses the manufacture, design, history, and sociological significance of the pencil

"An incredibly rich and complex history of this entirely unremarkable instrument of communication." SLJ

Includes bibliographical references

676 Pulp and paper technology

Dawson, Sophie

The art and craft of papermaking. Lark Bks. 1996 144p pa $19.95 **676**

1. Papermaking

ISBN 1-88737-424-8 LC 96-42365

A reprint of the edition published 1992 by Running Press

Dawson, Sophie—*Continued*

This guide "features step-by-step instructions, from selecting the pulp fiber to sculpting and molding the final product. It emphasizes making paper to be used as an artistic medium, rather than for printing. There are good instructions for constructing papermaking equipment such as molds and deckles. . . . Recommended for public libraries and schools." Libr J

677 Textiles

Fairchild's dictionary of textiles. Fairchild Publs. il $75   **677**

1. Textile industry—Dictionaries 2. Fabrics—Dictionaries

First published 1959. (7th edition 1996) Periodically revised

Editor: 1959 Stephen S. Marks; 1967- Isabel B. Wingate

"Reference source for all branches of the industry. Includes entries on fibers, yarns, fabric construction, finishing and sale, inventors and developers, and government standards and regulations. Includes appendix of organizations involved with the textile industry." N Y Public Libr Book of How & Where to Look It Up

682 Small forge work (Blacksmithing)

Parkinson, Peter, 1942-

The artist blacksmith; design and techniques. Crowood Press; [distributed by] Trafalgar Sq. Pub. 2002 160p il $40   **682**

1. Blacksmithing

ISBN 1-86126-428-3

"Parkinson explains the tools, materials, and equipment needed by blacksmiths as well as the most commonly used techniques. Numerous illustrations of beautiful creations (such as gates, sculptures, household items, and furniture) appear throughout this fascinating title." Libr J

683 Hardware and household appliances

The **New** cooks' catalogue; edited by Burt Wolf, Emily Aronson and Florence Fabricant. Knopf 2000 508p il $35   **683**

1. Kitchen utensils—Catalogs

ISBN 0-375-40673-5   LC 00-34914

First published 1975 by Harper with title: Cooks' catalogue

This book offers evaluations of "kitchen equipment—from paring knives to grill pans to espresso machines—providing you with . . . information about brands, models, size, function, and performance. Each entry is accompanied by a color photograph and includes features and tips on care and usage. Also included are sections on what to look for when purchasing, as well as recipes and sidebars by more than a hundred culinary celebrities." Publisher's note

Includes bibliographical references

684 Furnishings and home workshops

Abram, Norm

Measure twice, cut once; lessons from a master carpenter. Little, Brown 1996 196p il $18.95   **684**

1. Woodwork 2. Carpentry

ISBN 0-316-00494-4   LC 96-7584

In this book about woodwork and carpentry the author "deals mainly with hand tools. Abram covers items such as levels, chalk lines, and plumb-bobs, detailing his experiences with them and his preferences. . . . Even experienced woodworkers will pick up a tip or two from this book." Libr J

Bird, Lonnie

The complete illustrated guide to shaping wood. Taunton Press 2001 294p il $39.95   **684**

1. Woodwork

ISBN 1-56158-400-2   LC 2001-27430

This guide shows "the many ways of shaping wood (cutting, edge treatments, decorative techniques, turning, and carving). Techniques of all types and complexity are covered, usually including several means to accomplish each task, such as using hand or power tools. Profusely illustrated with drawings and photos, this book offers something for every woodworker." Libr J

Includes bibliographical references

The **Complete** book of woodworking. Landauer 2002 480p il $34.95   **684**

1. Woodwork

ISBN 1-890621-35-8

"Step-by-step guide to essential woodworking skills, techniques, tools and tips." On cover

"The first half shows how to set up a workshop, describes the species and types of wood, and covers nearly every commonly used woodworking tool and technique. The latter half offers a variety of plans that include household accessories, furniture, outdoor projects, and workshop furnishings. . . . If you are going to buy only one woodworking book, this should be it." Libr J

Guidice, Anthony

The seven essentials of woodworking. Sterling 2001 128p il pa $17.95   **684**

1. Woodwork

ISBN 0-8069-2527-2   LC 2001-20643

The author "contends that woodworkers need to be proficient in seven essential skills: joint making, measuring and marking, sawing to a line, sharpening, using hand planes, making mortise-and-tenon joints, and wood finishing. . . . Required reading for every woodworker, this is an essential purchase." Libr J

Hoadley, R. Bruce, 1933-

Understanding wood; a craftsman's guide to wood technology. 2nd ed. Taunton Press 2000 280p il $39.95   **684**

1. Woodwork 2. Wood

ISBN 1-56158-358-8   LC 00-44322

First published 1980

This guide "covers the nature of wood and its properties, the basics of wood technology, and the woodworker's raw materials." Publisher's note

Includes bibliographical references

Peters, Rick
Woodworker's guide to wood; softwoods, hardwoods, plywoods, composites, veneers. Sterling 2000 192p il pa $24.95   **684**
1. Wood 2. Lumber and lumbering
ISBN 0-8069-3687-8   LC 99-86641
Peters' book is "geared toward hobbyist woodworkers. He covers the process of making lumber from start to finish, including how trees grow, their structure, common ways of milling and drying lumber, grading, and possible defects found in wood. One section shows wood samples (both finished and plain) and describes their basic working characteristics." Libr J

Reed, Carol
Router joinery workshop; common joints, simple setups & clever jigs. Lark Bks. 2003 160p il pa $19.95   **684**
1. Woodworking machinery 2. Woodwork
ISBN 1-57990-328-2   LC 2002-30169
"Part 1 covers router features and tool selection, bits, maintenance, the creation of a number of utilitarian (but effective) jigs from common materials, and basic tool use. Part 2 shows how to make several popular joints: rabbets, dadoes, dovetails, box joints, and mortise and tenons. . . . Reed does a thorough job of explaining a somewhat complicated tool and its numerous accessories. Routers are very popular because they are so versatile; this title is among the best on the subject and should be considered by all public libraries." Libr J

Underhill, Roy
The woodwright's apprentice; twenty favorite projects from the Woodwright's shop; with drawings & photographs by the author. University of N.C. Press 1996 196p il $34.95; pa $22.50   **684**
1. Woodwork
ISBN 0-8078-2304-X; 0-8078-4612-0 (pa)
LC 96-14911
Photographs and measured drawings accompany step-by-step directions for 20 projects, among them: a workbench, a music stand, a fireplace bellows and a revolving Windsor chair. Skills covered include dovetailing, turning, steam-bending, and carving. An illustrated glossary of tools and terms is included

Warner, Pat
The router book. Taunton Press 2001 185p pa $19.95   **684**
1. Power tools 2. Woodwork
ISBN 1-56158-423-1   LC 2001-27149
"Warner shows readers how to get the most from their router, covering tools, accessories, and its use. Fixed-base, plunge routers, and laminate trimmers are introduced with excellent evaluations of specific models of each type." Libr J

684.1   Furniture

Grotz, George
The furniture doctor. rev & expanded ed. Doubleday 1989 c1983 366p il pa $15.95
   684.1
1. Furniture—Repairing 2. Furniture finishing
ISBN 0-385-26670-7   LC 89-31315
First published 1962; this is a reissue of the 1983 edition

The author presents practical information on the care, repair and finishing of furniture, using commonly available materials

686.3   Bookbinding

Fox, Gabrielle, 1955-
The essential guide to making handmade books. North Light Bks. 2000 128p il pa $24.99   **686.3**
1. Bookbinding 2. Books—Handbooks, manuals, etc.
ISBN 1-58180-019-3   LC 00-24563
"The book begins by describing the various tools involved, from bodkins and bone folders to adhesives. . . . The section on tools is followed by a chapter on terminology and techniques. Projects range from a simple folded tunnel book and nonadhesive accordion book to several sewn bindings to a slipcase and a portfolio. For each project Fox includes examples of more complex variations, and she also provides a list of suppliers." Booklist

690   Buildings

The **Art** of natural building; design, construction, resources; editors: Joseph F. Kennedy, Michael Smith, Catherine Wanek; illustrated by Joseph F. Kennedy. New Soc. Pubs. 2002 291p il pa $26.95   **690**
1. Building 2. Building materials 3. House construction
ISBN 0-86571-433-9
"The authors, who are practitioners in the natural building movement, introduce a variety of nontraditional construction options, including underground building and building with alternative materials such as adobe, recycled agricultural materials, rammed earth, and straw bale. They also address energy efficiency, design, and the desire to create a healthy environment. The final chapters include case studies." Libr J
Includes bibliographical references

Buchholz, Barbara Ballinger
Successful homebuilding and remodeling; real-life advice for getting the house you want without the roof (or sky) falling in; [by] Barbara B. Buchholz and Margaret Crane. Real Estate Educ. Co. 1999 336p il $22.95
   690
1. House construction 2. Houses—Remodeling
ISBN 0-7931-2883-8   LC 98-34007
This volume discusses "consumer issues of home building and remodeling. Part of the interest here is the comparatively unique perspective of women in a male-dominated field. . . . The forethought and process required for successful completion of a project is lucidly detailed." Libr J
Includes bibliographical references

Bukowski, Steven J.
Flooring instant answers. McGraw-Hill 2003 xxv, 285p il pa $49.95   **690**
1. Floors
ISBN 0-07-140204-7   LC 2003-266285
"This ready-reference covers flooring materials (marble, hardwood, carpet, and vinyl), installing procedures, layout, and more. For each material there is a discussion of the varying qualities of products as well as information on installation, maintenance, and repair." Libr J

Gonzalez, Steve, 1959-
Before you hire a contractor; a construction guidebook for consumers. Consumer's Press 1994 180p il pa $12.95   **690**
1. House construction 2. Consumer education
ISBN 1-8912-6465-6   LC 94-37497
The author "discusses the essentials of selecting a contractor, negotiating contracts, and avoiding scams and provides rudimentary information about liens, insurance, bonding, and consumer rights. . . . The numbers and addresses of consumer protection agencies are listed state by state, as are construction regulatory offices." Libr J

Inwood, Robert
Creative country construction; building & living in harmony with nature; [by] Robert Inwood & Christian Bruyere. Sterling 2000 288p il pa $19.95   **690**
1. House construction
ISBN 0-8069-7115-0   LC 99-86650
A combined and revised edition of In harmony with nature and Country comforts, first published 1975 and 1976 respectively by Drake Pub.
This is "a general resource with illustrations depicting various construction practices derived from the building techniques of early American homesteaders. Chapters focus on stone masonry, wood-frame construction, log homes, and post-and-beam construction." Libr J

Kidder, Tracy
House. Houghton Mifflin 1985 341p il hardcover o.p. paperback available $14   **690**
1. House construction
ISBN 0-618-00191-3 (pa)   LC 85-7630
"A Richard Todd book"
"The saga of a couple who supervised the building of their house in Massachusetts, this report interweaves the personal lives of those involved in the project with New England history, the sociology of building, popular lore and practical tips for would-be homebuilders." Publ Wkly
Includes bibliographical references

Levy, Matthys
Why buildings fall down; how structures fail; [by] Matthys Levy and Mario Salvadori; illustrations by Kevin Woest. Norton 1992 334p il hardcover o.p. paperback available $14.95   **690**
1. Building failures 2. Structural failures
ISBN 0-393-31152-X (pa)   LC 91-34954
"Two structural engineers examine puzzling structural failures and collapses and the destruction of ancient and modern buildings, bridges, dams, and other constructions. Plenty of illustrations accent the lively text." Booklist

Means illustrated construction dictionary. 3rd ed, unabridged. Means 2000 790p il + 1 computer optical disc $99.95   **690**
1. Building—Dictionaries
ISBN 0-87629-538-3   LC 2001-266365
Also available paperback condensed edition $59.95 (ISBN 0-87629-697-5)
First published 1985
Over 19,000 definitions of words, terms, and concepts related to the construction industry. Tables of weights, measures, conversions, size determinations, and symbols

are included
"This is an indispensable resource for large do-it-yourself, homeowner, or construction collections. Highly recommended." Libr J

Nash, George, 1949-
Do-it-yourself housebuilding; the complete handbook; illustrations by Roland Dahlquist. Sterling 1995 704p il pa $24.95   **690**
1. House construction
ISBN 0-8069-0424-0   LC 94-2371
This "book covers every step of house construction from site selection to finishing touches. The authors discuss both rough and finish carpentry and show how to install plumbing, and electrical, heating, and air-conditioning systems. The text is supplemented by numerous excellent photographs and illustrations." Libr J
Includes bibliographical references

Preves, Richard
New house/more house; solving the residential construction project puzzle. Portico Publs. 2001 237p il pa $26.95   **690**
1. House construction
ISBN 0-9711044-0-9   LC 2001-132443
"An architect who has worked with clients building custom homes, Preves here explains common problems most novices encounter. He familiarizes the reader with the process of building, from design through construction, and outlines the advantages and disadvantages of making specific choices during the process. The appendix includes sample contracts and agreements that will be invaluable for homebuilders." Libr J

Schuttner, Scott
Building and designing decks. Taunton Press 1993 153p il $19.95   **690**
1. Patios
ISBN 1-56158-320-0   LC 92-30687
"A Fine Homebuilding book"
"With step-by-step instructions, this book shows how to build a deck from design to completion, including finishing touches such as seats and planters. A 'gallery of deck designs' portrays a number of beautiful decks." Libr J

Scutella, Richard M.
How to plan, contract, and build your own home; [by] Richard M. Scutella & Dave Heberle; illustrations by Jay Marcinowski. 3rd ed. McGraw-Hill 1999 xxiii, 801p il pa $34.95   **690**
1. House construction 2. Building
ISBN 0-07-134609-0   LC 99-35570
First published 1987 by Tab Bks.
"Full of basic technical information for the owner who wants to gain building knowledge for a home project, this book goes beyond floor plans and appearances to focus on construction details and considerations, from building a foundation to planning a bathroom or kitchen. Every chapter ends with a 'Points to Ponder' section that summarizes what to consider when choosing building methods and addresses details that should be discussed with builders and contractors." Libr J

Spence, William P. (William Perkins), 1925-
Encyclopedia of construction methods & materials. Sterling 2000 608p il pa $24.95
690
1. Building
ISBN 0-8069-6851-6 LC 00-37289
"This technical reference book provides sketches and photographs to illustrate construction methods. Spence . . . covers such topics as insulation and refrigeration, as well as analyses of building sites. This is not a DIY manual but rather a guide to assist homebuilders in understanding the components of construction and the varying qualities of materials." Libr J
Includes bibliographical references

Thomas, Lawrence
Homebuilding pitfalls; [by] Lawrence Thomas with Robert Batcheller. New Community Press 2003 199p pa $24.95 **690**
1. House construction
ISBN 0-971955-09-3 LC 2002-110221
"Aimed primarily at readers having homes built by big builders in planned communities, this volume offers specific advice on researching builders and neighborhoods, understanding the visual traps found in model homes and enticing 'upgrades,' negotiating the sale of the home and lot, understanding contracts and warranties, hiring a home inspector, and communicating with the job supervisor. A series of good appendixes discuss common problems with moisture, concrete, plumbing, and wood construction." Libr J

Wenz, Philip S.
Adding to a house; planning, design & construction. Taunton Press 1995 263p il $34.95 **690**
1. Houses—Remodeling
ISBN 1-56158-072-4 LC 95-22406
"This guide helps homeowners decide if they should add on to an existing structure or move into a new house. Wenz ranges over different types of designs and how best to combine them with the original structure. Although some building techniques are covered, the author assumes that the reader already has a firm grasp of these topics." Libr J
Includes bibliographical references

Woodson, R. Dodge (Roger Dodge), 1955-
Build your dream home for less. Betterway Bks. 1995 185p pa $18.99 **690**
1. House construction 2. Building
ISBN 1-55870-383-7 LC 95-9087
This "explains the unknown elements of general contracting to the novice homebuilder. The author organizes the building process, proposes ways to save money, and suggests valuable DIY projects for the homeowner." Libr J

692 Auxiliary construction practices

American Institute of Architects
Architectural graphic standards. Wiley il $250 **692**
1. Architecture—Details
Also available CD-ROM version and edition with CD-ROM $675 (ISBN 0-471-39186-7)

"A Wiley-Interscience publication"
First published 1932 under the authorship of Charles G. Ramsey and Harold R. Sleeper. (10th edition 2000) Periodically revised
A guide to structural elements and details, types and dimensions of modern building materials, hardware and furniture

693 Construction in specific types of materials and for specific purposes

Thorson, Robert M., 1951-
Stone by stone; the magnificent history in New England's stone walls. Walker & Co. 2002 287p il maps $26 **693**
1. Walls 2. New England—History
ISBN 0-8027-1394-7 LC 2002-71356
"The author describes how the size, shape, and color of stones indicate how and where they were formed. These stones, as a natural resource of New England, shaped the culture of the region, beginning with the soil movement that yielded the stones from the ground. The resulting walls created microclimates and supported plant life while delineating property boundaries of the small family farms. Thorson traces the growth and decline of the farms and discusses the technological changes that resulted in the transition from an agricultural to an industrial nation." Libr J
"Yielding plentiful insights about New England's signature stone walls, geologist Thorson's scientific treatment deepens appreciation of them as more than quaint artifacts. . . . An enlightening excursion that goes well beyond the romantic notions surrounding the walls." Booklist
Includes bibliographical references

Watkins, A. M. (Arthur Martin), 1924-
Manufactured houses; finding and buying your dream home for less. 5th ed. Real Estate Educ. Co. 1994 189p il pa $14.95 **693**
1. Houses—Buying and selling 2. Prefabricated houses
ISBN 0-7931-1149-8 LC 94-13201
First published 1980 by Dutton with title: The complete guide to factory-made houses
"This volume discusses types of manufactured houses available from mobile homes to precut 'kit' homes such as log homes and dome homes. The author covers floor plan designs and ways to reduce energy costs and briefly looks at choosing land and a suitable builder. He also includes a list of home manufacturers in the United States and Canada." Libr J

694 Wood construction. Carpentry

Bollinger, Don
Hardwood floors; laying, sanding and finishing. Taunton Press 1990 137p il pa $19.95 **694**
1. Floors
ISBN 0-942391-62-4 LC 90-11065
The author "addresses the three types of flooring: strip, plank, and parquet—covering such topics as estimating costs; selecting wood types and grades; preparing the underlayment; planning the layout; sanding; and applying various finishes." Libr J
Includes bibliographical references

Burch, Monte, 1943-
Complete guide to building log homes; drawings by Richard J. Meyer and Lloyd P. Birmingham. Sterling 1990 406p il pa $19.95
694

1. Log cabins and houses
ISBN 0-8069-7486-9   LC 90-39505
This offers instruction in building log cabins including purchasing the land, making floor plans, shaping the logs, and construction techniques

695 Roof covering

Kennedy, Terry
Roofing instant answers. McGraw-Hill 2002 500p il pa $49.95   **695**
1. Roofs
ISBN 0-07-138712-9   LC 2002-284416
Contents: Before the job starts; Job mobilization; Safety means success; Maintenance, callbacks amd ancillary business; Built-up roofing; Single-ply roofs; Asphalt roofs; Wood shingles; Slate roofs; Clay and concrete tiles; Metal roofs; Reroofing; Resources
This companion volume to Steven Bukowski's Flooring instant answers provides answers to questions about roofing, including more than 300 photos, drawings, tables and checklists
Includes bibliographical references

697 Heating, ventilating, air-conditioning engineering

Kittle, James L., 1913-
Home heating and air conditioning systems; line drawings by Gary McKinney. TAB Bks. 1990 230p il hardcover o.p. paperback available $19.95   **697**
1. Houses—Heating and ventilation 2. Air conditioning
ISBN 0-8306-3257-3 (pa)   LC 89-29159
A guide to the examination and repair of gas- and oil-fired furnaces, boilers, air-conditioning systems, and heat pumps. A troubleshooting chart is appended

698 Detail finishing

Donegan, Francis
Paint your home; skills, techniques, and tricks of the trade for professional looking interior painting. Reader's Digest Assn. 1997 135p il $18.95   **698**
1. House painting
ISBN 0-89577-838-6   LC 96-46950
"Preparation, application, and clean-up are detailed, with drawings to illustrate the directions given; photographs show how color can make various elements in a room look different. Donegan intersperses professional tips throughout the text and offers safety advice, information on different paint products, and solutions to commonplace problems. This is the best book currently available to the do-it-yourselfer on home painting." Libr J

Travis, Debbie
Debbie Travis' painted house; quick and easy painted finishes for walls, floors, and furniture using water-based paints; [by] Debbie Travis with Barbara Dingle. Potter 1997 184p il hardcover o.p. paperback available $19.95   **698**
1. House painting 2. Furniture finishing 3. Interior design
ISBN 0-609-80816-8 (pa)   LC 96-37440
This offers instructions for water-based paint finishes for walls and floors, including textured, patterned, and stone types, and for furniture, including antique, metallic, and stencilling methods, and techniques such as colorwashing, ragging, sponging, and dragging

700 THE ARTS. FINE & DECORATIVE ARTS

Impelluso, Lucia
Gods and heroes in art; edited by Stefano Zuffi; translated by Thomas Michael Hartmann. Getty Mus. 2003 383p il pa $19.95   **700**
1. Art and mythology—Dictionaries 2. Classical mythology—Dictionaries
ISBN 0-89236-702-4   LC 2002-13422
The characters of ancient Greek and Roman mythology "are each described in entries summarizing their distinctive stories, their special attributes, and the ways in which artists have depicted them. Each entry is . . . illustrated with reproductions of works of art in which the god or hero is pictured. . . . The book concludes with . . . indexes, including a list of iconographic symbols associated with the subjects, and a bibliography." Publisher's note

Murray, Albert
The blue devils of Nada; a contemporary American approach to aesthetic statement. Pantheon Bks. 1996 238p hardcover o.p. paperback available $19   **700**
1. African American arts 2. Blues music
ISBN 0-679-75859-3 (pa)   LC 95-23331
Analyzed in Essay and general literature index
In these essays Murray "presents Louis Armstrong, Count Basie, Duke Ellington, painter Romare Bearden and Ernest Hemingway as embodying, in their work and their lives, a peculiarly American strain of existential improvisation and epic storytelling. His theme, variously elaborated, is the effort of the engaged artist to document and give shape to the rootlessness and chaos underlying contemporary life in general—and African American life, in particular—in a way that transcends 'agitprop journalism.'" Publ Wkly

Ochoa, George
The Wilson chronology of the arts; [by] George Ochoa and Melinda Corey. Wilson, H.W. 1998 476p $100   **700**
1. Arts—History
ISBN 0-8242-0934-6   LC 97-23541
First published 1995 by Ballantine Books with title: The timeline book of the arts
"The authors provide a timeline detailing human creativity that progresses from ca. 43,000 B.C.E. to 1997,

Ochoa, George—*Continued*
with 4,000 entries spread over 13 categories of artistic endeavor. . . . The chronology is global in scope and comprehensive in coverage, emphasizing well-established art forms without neglecting the oral traditions and decorative art forms of nonliterate societies and currently emerging art forms. . . . The straightforward organization of this work makes it suitable for many different uses." Recomm Ref Books for Small & Medium-sized Libr & Media Cent, 1999

Reid, Jane Davidson, 1918-
The Oxford guide to classical mythology in the arts, 1300-1990s; {by} Jane Davidson Reid; with the assistance of Chris Rohmann. Oxford Univ. Press 1993 2v set $195　**700**
1. Classical mythology—Catalogs 2. Arts
ISBN 0-19-504998-5　　　　LC 92-35374
Contents: v1 Auchelous-Leander; v2 Leda-Zeus
This work catalogs "more than 205 mythological characters and themes as they are represented in the arts from the early Renaissance to the present. More than 30,000 representations, including those from literature, music, dance, and art, are listed. Arranged alphabetically by character or theme, each entry briefly describes the subject and its place in classical mythology, and concludes with a comprehensive bibliography. . . . This is an impressive piece of scholarship that will quickly become a standard reference source." Am Libr

Steiner, Wendy, 1949-
Venus in exile; the rejection of beauty in twentieth-century art. Free Press 2001 xxv, 280p il $26　**700**
1. Women in art 2. Modernism (Aesthetics) 3. Arts—Philosophy
ISBN 0-684-85781-2　　　　LC 2001-23146
Also available in paperback from University of Chicago Press
In this book the author "shows how traditional forms of beauty disappeared from art in the 20th century, when artists rejected this ideal as placing undue importance on ornament while often objectifying the female body. She shows how . . . citing examples from literature, popular culture, visual arts, and even pornography. . . . Steiner is both a respected scholar and a talented and accessible writer, and her book is strongly recommended." Libr J
Includes bibliographical references

701　Art—Philosophy and theory

Ball, Philip, 1962-
Bright earth; art and the invention of color. Farrar, Straus & Giroux 2002 c2001 382p il $35　**701**
1. Color in art 2. Dyes and dyeing
ISBN 0-374-11679-2　　　　LC 2001-41820
First published 2001 in the United Kingdom
The author describes "how color developed in art and science from ancient history to the present." Publ Wkly
"Ball adeptly explains how the materials at hand in any given era influenced its aesthetics. . . . By concentrating on what paintings are made of and how they're made, Ball celebrates the way 'technology opens new doors for artists' and the breathtaking results." Booklist
Includes bibliographical references

Barzun, Jacques, 1907-
The use and abuse of art. Princeton Univ. Press 1974 hardcover o.p. paperback available $14.95　**701**
1. Arts
ISBN 0-691-01804-9 (pa)
"Bollingen series"
This volume presents the "author's less-than-sanguine view of the state of modern art—chiefly the visual arts, but literature and music as well." Publ Wkly

Berger, John, 1926-
The shape of a pocket. Pantheon Bks. 2002 264p $24; pa $13　**701**
1. Art criticism
ISBN 0-375-42147-5; 0-375-71888-5 (pa)
　　　　　　　　　LC 2001-36513
First published 2001 in the United Kingdom
"This collection of essays includes a moving tribute to Frida Kahlo and a brilliant meditation on the achievement of the Italian painter Giorgio Morandi. . . . Everything Berger has written—essays, novels, criticism, screenplays—has been filled with his passionate concern for what used to be called the state of man. That preoccupation is on every page here." New Yorker
Includes bibliographical references

Kimmelman, Michael
Portraits; talking with artists at the Met, the Modern, the Louvre, and elsewhere. Random House 1998 265p il hardcover o.p. paperback available $14.95　**701**
1. Artists 2. Art appreciation 3. Art museums
ISBN 0-375-75483-0 (pa)　　　LC 98-9589
A collection of interviews originally published in The New York Times. Kimmelman invited various artists "to meet him in museums and talk about works of art that inspire or intrigue them." Booklist
This is an "incisive, at times iconoclastic, book, well illustrated in b&w--a work of art criticism that is as bold as it is engaging." Publ Wkly

702.5　Art—Directories

American art directory. National Register Pub. il $299　**702.5**
1. Art—Directories 2. American art—Directories 3. Canadian art—Directories
ISSN 0065-6968
Biennial. First published 1898 by Bowker with title: American art annual
"Now in three main sections: (1) Art organizations (national and regional associations, museums, and libraries of the U.S. and Canada); (2) Art schools and college and university departments of art and architecture (U.S. and Canada); (3) Art information (major museums and art schools abroad, state arts councils, art magazines, newspapers carrying art notes and their critics, scholarships and fellowships, open exhibitions and traveling exhibitions, etc.) Indexes of organizations, personnel, and subjects." Guide to Ref Books. 11th edition

Artist's & graphic designer's market. Writer's Digest Bks. il $24.99　**702.5**
1. Art—Marketing—Directories
ISSN 1075-0894
Annual. First published 1974 with title: Artist's market

Artist's & graphic designer's market—
Continued

"Listings of places where art can be sold and exhibited include brokers, studios, agencies, magazines, galleries, and art fairs. Each listing covers who to contact and where, how much they pay, and additional information such as shipping requirements, preparing a portfolio, etc." Ref Sources for Small & Medium-sized Libr. 5th edition

702.8 Art—Technique, procedures, apparatus, equipment, materials

Hoving, Thomas, 1931-

False impressions; the hunt for big-time art fakes. Simon & Schuster 1996 366p il hardcover o.p. paperback available $22

702.8

1. Art—Forgeries
ISBN 0-684-83148-1 (pa)   LC 95-53800
In this book the author discloses "details of major art forgeries and the intricate chicanery of con artists who have duped the world's most prestigious art institutions, art experts, and collectors." Libr J

Hoving "is a magnetic storyteller, achieving just the right blend of humor and mettle." Booklist

Includes bibliographical references

703 Art—Encyclopedias and dictionaries

The **Concise** Oxford dictionary of art and artists; edited by Ian Chilvers. 3rd ed. Oxford University Press 2003 653p pa $14.95   **703**

1. Art—Dictionaries 2. Artists—Dictionaries
ISBN 0-19-860477-7   LC 2003-278290
First published 1990

This "is an abbreviated lexicon based on 'The Oxford Dictionary of Art'.... It includes western art from the fifth century B.C.E., but has been expanded to include more recent artists born prior to 1965 instead of 1945. Entries include biographies of artists, sculptors, writers, leading collectors and dealers, materials and techniques, and galleries and museums." Am Ref Books Annu, 2004

Frazier, Nancy

The Penguin concise dictionary of art history. Penguin Ref. 1999 774p hardcover o.p. paperback available $20   **703**

1. Art—Dictionaries
ISBN 0-670-10015-3; 0-14-051420-1 (pa)
     LC 98-56089
"This volume seeks to present an interdisciplinary approach to art history. It uses information from a number of fields, such as literature, psychology, history, geography, and economics, to give a cultural context to the changes in art. There are more than 1,500 alphabetically arranged entries. . . . Each biographical entry includes birth and death dates when known, nationality, medium used, and style of work or school of art." Booklist

"An easy-to-read, scholarly yet not lofty, fascinating, and very well-organized book." Libr J

Langmuir, Erika

Yale dictionary of art and artists; [by] Erika Langmuir and Norbert Lynton. Yale Univ. Press 2000 753p $30; pa $12.95 **703**

1. Art—Dictionaries 2. Artists—Dictionaries
ISBN 0-300-08702-0; 0-300-06458-6 (pa)
     LC 00-25800
"Varying in length from a few lines to several pages for artists such as Leonardo da Vinci, Pablo Picasso, or John Constable, the 3000 entries cover Western art from 1300 until the present. The work covers painters, sculptors, graphic artists, patrons, technical processes, movements, and terminology." Libr J

Metzger, Philip W., 1931-

The artist's illustrated encyclopedia; techniques, materials, and terms; [by] Phil Metzger. North Light Bks. 2001 486p il pa $29.99 **703**

1. Art—Technique 2. Artists' materials 3. Art—Encyclopedias
ISBN 1-581-80023-1   LC 00-135978
"Metzger explains in his introduction that this book is intended to define terms, techniques, and materials but not explain how to use them. His goal is achieved with a dictionary arrangement of definitions supplemented with many illustrations and cross-references." Publisher's note

The **Oxford** companion to western art; edited by Hugh Brigstocke. Oxford Univ. Press 2001 820p il $75 **703**

1. Art—Dictionaries
ISBN 0-19-866203-3

"A partial successor to the 1970 *Oxford Companion to Art*, this title limits itself to European-language cultures, dropping architecture and non-Western subjects. The 2600 signed entries generally range in length from 100 to 1000-plus words . . . and they include artist, historian, theorist, and patron biographies as well as entries on institutions, cities and museums, styles, movements, and art historical theory and methodology." Libr J

The **Oxford** dictionary of art. 3rd ed, edited by Ian Chilvers. Oxford Univ. Press 2004 xlvi, 816p $45 **703**

1. Art—Dictionaries
ISBN 0-19-860476-9   LC 2004-41540
First published 1988

This "reference contains 3000 entries that discuss Western and Western-inspired art from antiquity on. It considers paintings, graphics, sculpture, and architecture in terms of artistic figures, periods, schools, techniques, critical terms, and museums; lesser artists are treated more concisely than major ones." Libr J

704 Art—Special topics

Borzello, Frances

A world of our own; women as artists since the Renaissance. Watson-Guptill 2000 224p il $50 **704**

1. Women artists 2. Art—History
ISBN 0-8230-5874-3   LC 00-103117
"The six mostly chronological chapters range from 'Out of the Shadows, 1500-1600' to 'The Feminist Revo-

Borzello, Frances—_Continued_
lution, 1970 and After.' Portraits of the artists, capsule
biographies, and rich, large, and fine illustrations (100 in
color and 100 in black-and white) support the essays.
Whatever point of view the reader brings to this book,
it will capture the attention." Libr J
Includes bibliographical references

Henkes, Robert
Latin American women artists of the
United States; the works of 33
twentieth-century women. McFarland & Co.
1999 245p il $49.95 **704**
1. Hispanic American art 2. Women artists
ISBN 0-7864-0519-8 LC 98-43600
"This work examines the art of 33 Latin American
artists who have lived in the United States and the manner in which these artists have merged Latino and Norte
Americano cultures in their work. Juana Alicia, Leonora
Arye, Santa Barraza, Joyce de Guatemala, and 29 other
Latin American artists are included. A critical discussion
of the work of each artist is supplemented by photographs (some in color) of many works and a compilation
of exhibitions in which they have participated." Publisher's note
Includes bibliographical references

Hessel, Ingo
Inuit art; an introduction; photography by
Dieter Hessel; with a foreword by George
Swinton. Abrams 1998 198p il o.p.; Douglas
& McIntyre paperback available $29.95 **704**
1. Inuit—Art
ISBN 1-55054-829-8 (pa) LC 98-3410
The author traces "the transformation of basic native
craft to the varied, imaginative, and lively art available
today. . . . The ethnohistory of the tribe is reviewed and
the evolution of mythic representations traced. Given few
raw materials--stone, bone, fur, and some ivory in older
times and now paper with watercolors, pencils, and pens-
-these isolated people produce art full of life and motion
and permeated with their rich mythology." Libr J
Includes bibliographical references

Patton, Sharon F.
African-American art. Oxford Univ. Press
1998 319p il maps (Oxford history of art)
hardcover o.p. paperback available $18.95
704
1. African American art
ISBN 0-19-284213-7 (pa) LC 98-190459
This "book provides a chronological examination of
the development of African American art from its earliest
manifestations to the present day." Libr J
"Comprehensively and with sharp, scholarly accuracy,
Patton has closed gaps between the chronological and
thematic directions of Black American art and complexities of Euro-American art history." Choice

704.9 Iconography

Carr-Gomm, Sarah
Hidden symbols in art. Rizzoli Int. Publs.
2001 256p il $40 **704.9**
1. Symbolism in art
ISBN 0-8478-2402-0 LC 2001-89084
"All pictures supplied by the Bridgeman Art Library"
Contents: Classical myth and legend; The Bible and
the life of Christ; Saints and their miracles; History, literature, and the arts; Symbols and allegories

The author "identifies an amalgamation of symbols
and attributes in 75 'key paintings'. These well-known
paintings date from the Renaissance to the early 20th
century and are organized into five thematic chapters.
Each receives a standard two-page treatment a large reproduction . . . a large-type introductory paragraph on
the subject and artist, a cursory explanation of the 'key
element' (saint, animal, object), and See Also references
to other paintings. . . . Suitable as a browsing reference
in public settings." Libr J

705 Art—Serial publications

Art index. Wilson, H.W. service basis **705**
1. Art—Periodicals—Indexes 2. Art—Bibliography
ISSN 0004-3222
Also available CD-ROM version and online
First published 1930
Quarterly with bound annual cumulations
An author and subject index to more than 200 periodi-
cals. Subjects covered include advertising art, architec-
ture, art history, crafts, graphic arts, and interior design.
Current book reviews are indexed in a separate section
"The easiest to use of the major indexes to visual arts
and a basic tool for arts research." Walford. Guide to
Ref Mater. 3d edition

708 Art—Galleries, museums private collections

Biddle, Flora Miller
The Whitney women and the museum they
made; a family chronicle. Arcade Pub. 1999
408p il $28.95; pa $14.95 **708**
1. Whitney, Gertrude Vanderbilt 2. Miller, Flora
Whitney 3. Whitney Museum of American Art
ISBN 1-55970-509-4; 1-55970-594-9 (pa)
LC 99-35730
"This very personal book by a granddaughter of Gertrude Vanderbilt Whitney, the founder of the Whitney
Museum of American Art, chronicles the complex relationship her family has had to that institution, and provides an account of three generations of lively, intelligent
women as they grapple with the responsibilities of wealth
and patronage." New Yorker

Feigen, Richard, 1930-
Tales from the art crypt; the painters, the
museums, the curators, the collections, the
auctions, the art. Knopf 2000 296p il $30
708
1. Art—Collectors and collecting
ISBN 0-394-57169-X LC 00-131136
"Art collector and dealer Feigen, born in Chicago in
1930, began buying paintings at age 12, established a
Chicago gallery in 1957, and then moved to New York
and opened the first gallery in what became Soho. He
has been an important force in the art world ever since,
and he now shares his remarkable adventures in this collection of engagingly urbane reminiscences, frank revelations, and peppery commentary." Booklist
Includes bibliographical references

A **Grand** design; the art of the Victoria and Albert Museum; Malcolm Baker and Brenda Richardson, general editors; with research and essays by Anthony Burton {et al.}. Abrams 1997 431p il $60   **708**
1. Victoria and Albert Museum—Exhibitions 2. Decorative arts
ISBN 0-8109-3399-3   LC 97-3644
Catalog of a traveling exhibition shown at the Baltimore Museum of Art, and other museums Oct. 1997-Jan. 2000

"The opening essays focus on the museum's history, its educational programs, and the development of its collection. The remaining thematic essays are intricately arranged and divided so that the catalog entries flow naturally with the text, highlighting British imperial rule, national heritage, and a fascination with 20th century cultural icons, among other issues. The 200 illustrated items—from majolica porcelain, stained glass, and silverware to mosaics, bronzes, sculpture, paintings, and furniture—represent a host of world-renowned artists." Libr J
Includes bibliographical references

The **Israel** Museum, Jerusalem. Vendome Press 1995 240p il $65   **708**
1. Israel Museum
ISBN 0-86565-960-5   LC 95-15860
Editor/project coordinator, Irene Lewitt
This volume "contains introductory essays on the Museum's history, which precede a chronologically and culturally organized sampling of archaeological objects. Modern painting, sculpture, graphics, and decorative arts (most donated by emigrés) follow." Choice

The **J.** Paul Getty Museum and its collections; a museum for the new century; {by} John Walsh, Deborah Gribbon. Getty Mus. 1997 288p hardcover o.p. paperback available $40   **708**
1. Getty, J. Paul, 1892-1976 2. J. Paul Getty Museum
ISBN 0-89236-476-9 (pa)   LC 97-12170
This volume is a history of the J. Paul Getty Museum and a guide to its collections
This is "a lavish visual compendium of J. Paul Getty's amazing art collection; in addition, the text reveals important background details surrounding Getty's life and his passion for art. Walsh and Gribbon communicate just how the magnate's fortunes were put to the test as planned acquisitions of artwork flourished." Booklist

Loebl, Suzanne
America's art museums; a traveler's guide to great collections large and small. Norton 2002 426p il pa $18.95   **708**
1. Art museums
ISBN 0-393-32006-5   LC 2001-44208
This is a "guide to some of America's finest art museums. Not only does it focus on the major and more familiar art museums, it also supplies some much-needed information and marketing for some of the small and little-known, yet important, art galleries in the United States. The book is alphabetically arranged by state and then by city, and provides information on times open, strengths of the museum's collection, activities for children, the museum's history, and Websites." Am Ref Books Annu, 2003
Includes bibliographical references

Meier, Richard, 1934-
Building the Getty. Knopf 1997 204p il o.p.; University of Calif. Press paperback available $24.95   **708**
1. Getty Center (Los Angeles, Calif.)
ISBN 0-520-21730-6 (pa)   LC 97-29326
"Charting his involvement in the Getty's construction, Meier recounts in an intriguingly candid, eminently personal style the formidable bureaucratic process entailed upon undertaking to realize this grandiose endeavor. Beginning with the competition itself, Meier's detailed reminiscences offer fascinating insights into the design process and the extraordinarily intricate procedures and systems, as well as endless setbacks, associated with executing a modern-day megalithic structure." Booklist

Rosenblum, Robert
Paintings in the Musée d'Orsay; foreword by Françoise Cachin. Stewart, Tabori & Chang 1989 686p il $75   **708**
1. Musée d'Orsay (Paris, France) 2. French painting 3. Painting—19th century
ISBN 1-55670-099-7   LC 89-11338
The author describes the paintings at the Paris museum of nineteenth-century French art. Some eight hundred color illustrations are included
"Rosenblum's knowledgeable commentaries place the works and their creators in their social and artistic milieu, helping us to see why certain works were praised or criticized when first exhibited and pointing out common themes or trends." Libr J

Treasures from the Art Institute of Chicago; selected by James N. Wood, with commentaries by Debra N. Mancoff; [edited by Laura J. Kozitka and Catherine A. Steinmann] Art Inst. of Chicago 2000 344p il $75   **708**
1. Art Institute of Chicago
ISBN 0-86559-182-2   LC 99-69501
"This compendium is not only a catalog of pieces owned by the museum, but it is virtually an introduction to the history of art throughout the world. . . . Superb examples from Asian, African; classical Greek and Roman; and other regional art, crafts, ceramics, and media add a wonderfully broad scope." SLJ

709 Art—Historical and geographic treatment

Art: a world history. DK Pub. 1998 720p il hardcover o.p. paperback available $40   **709**
1. Art—History
ISBN 0-7894-8904-X (pa)   LC 97-20234
Original Italian edition, 1997
This survey consists of "brief 50- to 500-word discussions of artists, topics, styles, and historic moments, presented via multiple columns, text boxes, time lines, and the like." Libr J
Includes bibliographical references

Barnitz, Jacqueline

Twentieth-century art of Latin America. University of Tex. Press 2001 400p il $70; pa $34.95 **709**

1. Latin American art 2. Art—20th century
ISBN 0-292-70857-2; 0-292-70858-0 (pa)

LC 99-50871

A survey of 20th century Latin American art which includes coverage of regional movements, and discussion of historical, political, and cultural influences

"Latin American art, the fruit of violent collisions among diverse indigenous, European, and African cultures, is revealed as provocative and vibrant in Barnitz's well-illustrated and groundbreaking overview of its dazzling twentieth-century flowering." Booklist

Includes bibliographical references

Beckett, Wendy

Sister Wendy's American collection; {by} Sister Wendy Beckett. HarperCollins Pubs. 2000 288p il $40 **709**

1. Art appreciation 2. Art—History
ISBN 0-06-019556-8   LC 00-40953

The author provides a "discussion of works in six of America's renowned art museums. . . . {She} includes a variety of media-- paintings, sculpture, decorative arts, armor, and other art objects-- and the individual works originate from a dizzying array of time periods and several countries." Libr J

Careri, Giovanni, 1958-

Baroques; with photographs by Ferrante Ferranti; {translated from the French by Alexandra Bonfante-Warren}. Princeton Univ. Press 2003 248p il $75 **709**

1. Baroque art
ISBN 0-691-11690-3   LC 2003-50431

Original French edition, 2002

This book examines different variations on the Baroque theme, including "Bernini's . . . sculptures and his . . . colonnade on St. Peter's Square, . . . palace facades, painted ceilings, crucifixes, angels, demons, piazzas, villas, gardens, and more." Publisher's note

Includes bibliographical references

Fenton, James, 1949-

Leonardo's nephew; essays on art and artists. Farrar, Straus & Giroux 1998 283p il o.p.; University of Chicago Press paperback available $15 **709**

1. Art—History
ISBN 0-226-24147-5 (pa)   LC 98-34079

Analyzed in Essay and general literature index

Fenton presents a collection of fifteen essays on various aspects of art history. Subjects "include Freud's collection of antique statuettes, Egyptian funerary portraits and Joseph Cornell. These essays educate, enlighten, surprise and thrill, unfailingly." N Y Times Book Rev

Includes bibliographical references

Gardner's art through the ages. Harcourt College Publishers 2v il map ea $84.95

709

1. Art—History

First published 1926 under the authorship of Helen Gardner. (11th edition 2001 revised by Richard G. Tansey, Fred S. Kleiner, and Christin J. Mamiya). Periodically revised

This book surveys world art from prehistoric times to the present day. Painting, sculpture, architecture and some decorative arts are considered. Although the focus is on European art, there are also chapters on ancient Near Eastern, Asian, pre-Columbian, American Indian, African and Oceanic art

Gombrich, E. H. (Ernst Hans), 1909-2001

The preference for the primitive; episodes in the history of Western taste and art. Phaidon Press 2002 324p il $59.95 **709**

1. Art criticism
ISBN 0-7148-4154-4   LC 2003-274005

Contents: Plato's preferences; Interlude: progress or decline?; The ascendancy of the sublime; The pre-Raphaelite ideal; The quest for spirituality; The emancipation of formal values; Interlude: new worlds and myths; The twentieth century: The lure of regression (1); The lure of regression (2); Primitive, in what sense?; The study of antiquities

"This book is a study of a recurring phenomenon in the history of changing taste in the visual arts, namely the feeling that older and less sophisticated (i.e. 'primitive') works are somehow morally and aesthetically superior to later works that have become soft and decadent. Gombrich traces this idea back to classical antiquity and links it both with Cicero's observation that overindulgence of the senses leads to a feeling of disgust, and with the . . . metaphor comparing the development of art to that of a living organism." Publisher's note

"Gombrich is always worth reading. . . . His text reminds us that many of the principles of Western art were, in fact, counterintuitive." N Y Times Book Rev

Includes bibliographical references

The story of art. Prentice-Hall il pa $82

709

1. Art—History

Also available in hardcover and in paperback from Phaidon Press

First published 1950 by Phaidon Press. (16th edition 1995) Periodically revised

This survey of art examines artistic achievements in historical context to consider how prevailing social, political, and economic factors may have influenced the succession and popularity of certain artistic styles

Includes bibliographical references

Harclerode, Peter, 1947-

The lost masters; World War II and the looting of Europe's treasurehouses; {by} Peter Harclerode & Brendan Pittaway. Welcome Rain 2000 402p il $27.95; pa $18.95 **709**

1. Art thefts 2. World War, 1939-1945—Destruction and pillage
ISBN 1-56649-165-7; 1-56649-253-X (pa)

LC 00-42867

The authors "trace the elusive web of collaborators, opportunists and dealers who exploited the Third Reich's lust for prestigious trophies. Gripping vignettes and revelatory anecdotes illuminate the fates of specific works of art, including the outstanding story of four paratroopers who contrived to rescue the largest cache of stolen art sequestered by the Nazis." Publ Wkly

Includes bibliographical references

Janson, H. W. (Horst Woldemar), 1913-1982
History of art. Abrams   **709**
1. Art—History
Also available in a two-volume paperback edition from Prentice-Hall
First published 1962. (6th edition 2001 revised and expanded by Anthony F. Janson) Periodically revised
A history of art from pre-historic cave paintings to video art. While the focus is primarily on Western art, brief discussions of Oriental, Near Eastern, Islamic, African and Latin American arts are included
Includes bibliographical references

Kampen O'Riley, Michael
Art beyond the west; the arts of Africa, India and Southeast Asia, China, Japan and Korea, the Pacific, and the Americas; afterword by Anne D'Alleva. Abrams 2002 c2001 344p il maps $75   **709**
1. Art
ISBN 0-8109-1433-6   LC 2001-27923
Also available from Prentice-Hall
First published 2001 in the United Kingdom
The author "has attempted to encapsulate the entirety of non-Western art in one volume. . . . [Chapters] range over Africa, India, Southeast Asia, China, Japan and Korea, the Americas, and the Pacific and consider such issues as post- and intercolonialism and postmodernism." Libr J
The author "succeeds in defining the essence of each distinct artistic tradition. Add to that impressive feat a clear, relaxed, and engaging prose style and superb illustrations, and the sum is a prime introductory guide to much of the world's art." Booklist
Includes bibliographical references

Lippard, Lucy R.
Overlay; contemporary art and the art of prehistory. Pantheon Bks. 1983 266p il o.p.; New Press (NY) paperback available $20
          709
1. Art—20th century 2. Prehistoric art 3. Symbolism
ISBN 1-56584-238-3 (pa)   LC 82-22331
This book "is a juxtaposition of the rock and earth forms of prehistoric Europe and North America and the work of contemporary Western artists who are motivated by a need to create art which is integrated into the fabric of contemporary society at a . . . fundamental and primal level." Choice
This "is an idiosyncratic piece of scholarship, speculative and rich in suggestion." Libr J
Includes bibliographical references

The **Oxford** history of western art; edited by Martin Kemp. Oxford Univ. Press 2000 564p il $65   **709**
1. Art—History
ISBN 0-19-860012-7
"About 50 essays with perhaps 150 extended-caption subject groupings (e.g., Roman sculpture, the interior, pictures and publics, design and industry, etc., which repeat as appropriate within the larger divisions), make up the body of the text. Threads running throughout include the roles of religion and the state in the creation and meaning of art and, later, the self-consciousness of art in a world conscious of art history. Kemp has done a good job of keeping an overall vision on the page and placing objects in meaningful contexts. A number of the illustra-

tions and comparisons are unusual and thoughtful." Libr J
Includes bibliographical references

Petropoulos, Jonathan
The Faustian bargain; the art world in Nazi Germany. Oxford Univ. Press 2000 395p il $42.50   **709**
1. Art thefts 2. World War, 1939-1945—Destruction and pillage 3. National socialism
ISBN 0-19-512964-4   LC 99-33372
"Spotlighting five groups--art museum directors, art dealers, art journalists, art historians, and artists--Petropoulos . . . details how each of these groups either directly or indirectly facilitated the theft of countless works of art and legitimized the Nazi regime." Libr J
Includes bibliographical references

The **Spoils** of war; World War II and its aftermath: the loss, reappearance, and recovery of cultural property; edited by Elizabeth Simpson. Abrams 1997 336p il $49.50   **709**
1. Art thefts 2. World War, 1939-1945—Destruction and pillage
ISBN 0-8109-4469-3   LC 96-33258
Papers of a symposium sponsored by the Bard Graduate Center for the Decorative Arts, Jan. 1995, in New York
"More than 50 art experts from the U.S. and Europe . . . came together to discuss the extraordinary looting of cultural treasures during and after World War II. The papers they presented—riveting accounts of the Nazis' systematic pillaging of entire library and museum collections, fine and decorative arts, religious objects, musical instruments, and archaeological artifacts—form the core of this unique and invaluable volume, which also includes photographs of lost, disputed, or reclaimed artworks and a number of key legal texts relating to the repatriation of cultural property." Booklist
Includes bibliographical references

Stokstad, Marilyn, 1929-
Art history; [by] Marilyn Stokstad in collaboration with David Cateforis with chapters by Stephen Addiss [et al.] 2nd ed. Abrams 2002 2v il maps set $95   **709**
1. Art—History
ISBN 0-8109-0610-4   LC 2001-955
Also available from Prentice-Hall
First published 1995
This presents a global view of art from prehistoric times to the present. "Arranged topically, each section opens with a color illustration and a vignette on a work representing the period covered. The numerous color illustrations, text boxes, and varying page designs are aimed at making this [an] . . . interesting and user-friendly research tool." Libr J
Includes bibliographical references

709.01 Arts of nonliterate peoples, and earliest times to 499

Bahn, Paul G.
The Cambridge illustrated history of prehistoric art. Cambridge Univ. Press 1998 xxxii, 302p il $45 **709.01**
1. Prehistoric art
ISBN 0-521-45473-5   LC 96-51099
The author "discovers the initial 'discoveries' of this art form, then weaves an excellent accounting of research, from the earliest to the recent. This discourse encompasses mobiliary art, art on rocks and walls, the application of scientific scrutiny, literal and symbolic interpretations, and the press of time. Bahn also describes current threats and future prospects. The writing is lucid and descriptive, satisfying to the advanced anthropologist or artist while quite comprehensible to uninitiated readers." Choice

Berlo, Janet Catherine
Native North American art; by Janet Catherine Berlo and Ruth B. Phillips. Oxford Univ. Press 1999 c1998 291p il map (Oxford history of art) hardcover o.p. paperback available $21.50 **709.01**
1. Native Americans—Art
ISBN 0-19-284218-8 (pa)   LC 99-177938
This survey covers the "artistic output of most Native American tribes across the northern hemisphere over a period of more than eight centuries. . . . In an introduction that stresses the commonality of themes—cosmology, vision quests, love of ornament, reverence of materials—[the authors] emphasize the importance of today's Native art as a natural extension. Five regional chapters then incorporate history, outstanding crafts and arts, some prominent figures, and social, religious, and cultural aspects." Libr J

709.02 Art—500-1499

Graham-Dixon, Andrew
Renaissance. University of Calif. Press 1999 336p il $29.95 **709.02**
1. Art—15th and 16th centuries 2. Renaissance
ISBN 0-520-22375-6   LC 00-698469
This companion to a BBC television series is an "introduction to Renaissance art and the cultural milieu that spawned it. . . . The bulk of the text is given over to canonic figures ranging from Giotto to Michelangelo. . . . In addition, the author discusses religion, humanistic thought, the changing social status of the artist, and the larger historic ebb and flow." Libr J

Lowden, John
Early Christian & Byzantine art. Chronicle Bks. 1997 447p il (Art & ideas) pa $24.95 **709.02**
1. Byzantine art 2. Medieval art 3. Christian art
ISBN 0-7148-3168-9
In this illustrated history of the origins and growth of Christian art Lowden works "deftly through fascinatingly complex and epoch-defining artistic and theological debates, including the so-called Iconoclast Controversy." Booklist
Includes bibliographical references

Snyder, James
Medieval art; painting - sculpture - architecture, 4th-14th century. Abrams 1989 511p il map **709.02**
1. Medieval art 2. Christian art 3. Medieval architecture   LC 88-10394
Available from Prentice-Hall $82.67 (ISBN 0-13-573494-0)
"Church architecture and decoration receive the bulk of Snyder's attention, with manuscript illumination and sumptuary and secular arts presented rather briefly. The volume is well illustrated, though chiefly in black-and-white photographs." Libr J
Includes bibliographical references

709.03 Art—1500-

Art nouveau; 1890-1914; edited by Paul Greenhalgh. Abrams 2000 496p il $75 **709.03**
1. Victoria and Albert Museum 2. Decorative arts
ISBN 0-8109-4219-4   LC 00-28027
Catalog of an exhibition organized by the Victoria and Albert Museum
"Twenty scholars explore this international phenomenon in all media of the decorative and fine arts, including wood furniture, metal, textiles, glass, ceramics, jewelry, posters, prints, and architecture. . . . Lavishly illustrated with color reproductions, this book is highly recommended." Libr J
Includes bibliographical references

Craske, Matthew
Art in Europe, 1700-1830; a history of the visual arts in an era of unprecedented urban economic growth. Oxford Univ. Press 1997 320p il (Oxford history of art) hardcover o.p. paperback available $21.50 **709.03**
1. Art—19th century 2. World history—18th century
ISBN 0-19-284206-4 (pa)   LC 96-37917
This study analyzes "the fundamental historical causes of change that took place from the early 1700s to 1839. . . . Craske . . . provides a series of four stimulating chapters devoted respectively to the function of the artist, art worlds, the appreciation of the visual arts, and evolving ideas of history and civilization. The text is enhanced by 129 high-quality illustrations." Choice

709.04 Art—1900-1999

Art deco 1910-1939; edited by Charlotte Benton, Tim Benton, and Ghislaine Wood. Bulfinch Press 2003 464p il $65 **709.04**
1. Art deco
ISBN 0-8212-2834-X   LC 2002-113762
Catalog of an exhibition held at the Victorian and Albert Museum, London, March 27-July 20, 2003
This exhibition catalog includes 40 essays about the Art Deco movement and its sources and expression throughout the world in such fields as architecture, ceramics, fashion, jewelry, graphic design, metalwork, glasswork, and film
Includes bibliographical references

Blistène, Bernard

A history of 20th-century art. Flammarion & Cie 2001 201p il pa $18.95 **709.04**

1. Art—20th century

ISBN 2-0801-0564-7

This thematically-organized history features over 500 illustrations and covers painting, architecture, sculpture, photography, video and industrial design

Includes bibliographical references

Brandon, Ruth

Surreal lives; the surrealists, 1917-1945. Grove Press 1999 527p il hardcover o.p. paperback available $16 **709.04**

1. Surrealism

ISBN 0-8021-1653-1; 0-8021-3727-X (pa)

LC 99-25492

This study of surrealism "gives an account of the school's major practitioners, from Apollinaire to Dali; their flamboyant eccentricities and unconventional sexual entanglements prove a lively and absorbing complement to their work." New Yorker

Includes bibliographical references

Chilvers, Ian

A dictionary of twentieth-century art. Oxford Univ. Press 1998 670p $50; pa $18.95 **709.04**

1. Modern art—1900-1999 (20th century)—Dictionaries

ISBN 0-19-211645-2; 0-19-280092-2 (pa)

LC 98-186633

Based on The Oxford companion to twentieth-century art, and The Oxford dictionary of art

This work "deals with painting, sculpture, and graphics, but also includes conceptual, video and performance art. Major movements and styles such as Cubism, Dada, and Fluxus are concisely explained." Libr J

Dempsey, Amy

Art in the modern era; a guide to styles, schools & movements 1860 to the present. Abrams 2002 304p il $55 **709.04**

1. Modern art—Encyclopedias 2. Art—20th century—Encyclopedias

ISBN 0-8109-4172-4

LC 2001-46261

This guide to art from 1860 to the present describes 300 schools and movements and includes a fold-out timeline

"All major and minor movements are mentioned in this very comprehensive guide, which could easily become a standard for modern art survey courses, making it a sensible purchase for most libraries." Libr J

Includes bibliographical references

Fineberg, Jonathan David

Art since 1940; strategies of being; [by] Jonathan Fineberg. 2nd ed. Abrams 2000 528p il $65 **709.04**

1. Art—20th century 2. Modern art

ISBN 0-18-094209-7

LC 99-51584

Also available from Prentice-Hall

First published 1995

This surveys American and European art from 1940 to 2000 through a series of biographical profiles of individual artists linked by discussions of the cultural influences on their work

"Fineberg surveys the visual arts in Europe, England, and North America from 1940 to the present, focusing on the avant-garde artist in the major Western capitals. . . . The text is arranged in 15 chapters in chronological order. Within each chapter the individual artist is discussed, as are the ideas and events relevant to understanding how cultural and social situations influenced the artist." Choice [review of 1995 edition]

Includes bibliographical references

Hughes, Robert

The shock of the new. rev ed. Knopf 1991 444p il pa $49.95 **709.04**

1. Modern art

ISBN 0-679-72876-7

LC 89-43355

First published 1980 in the United Kingdom

Originally based on a BBC television series, this survey of vanguard art covers the last one hundred years and concludes with a chapter on the 1980s

Includes bibliographical references

Lucie-Smith, Edward, 1933-

Art today. Phaidon Press 1995 511p il hardcover o.p. paperback available $45 **709.04**

1. Art—20th century

ISBN 0-7148-3888-8 (pa)

This "survey attempts to essay the scope and aims of the art of the world over the past 30 years. . . . As well as such . . . ground as Pop Art, Lucie-Smith covers Conceptual Art, Installation Art, and Neo-Expressionism. He also covers . . . artists and works from the former Soviet Union, Africa, the Far East, and Latin America. Chapters are also included on 'Racial Minorities' and 'Feminist and Gay' art. . . . The book offers brief biographies of all artists mentioned, a chronology, and bibliography." Libr J

Visual arts in the twentieth century. Abrams 1997 400p il $65 **709.04**

1. Art—20th century

ISBN 0-8109-3934-7

LC 96-18460

Also available from Prentice-Hall

This survey of twentieth century art has "an historical rather than a stylistic approach; chapters are divided by decades, which are then subdivided by media; and each has time lines with year-by-year highlights delineating and linking the political, intellectual, and cultural landscape. . . . [This] work adds the field of photography to the discussion of painting, sculpture, graphic arts, and architecture." Libr J

Includes bibliographical references

709.1 Art—Treatment by areas, regions, places in general

Stierlin, Henri

Islamic art and architecture; photographs by Anne and Henri Stierlin. Thames & Hudson 2002 319p il maps $50 **709.1**

1. Islamic art

ISBN 0-500-51100-4

LC 2002-102346

"From Isfahan to the Taj Mahal." Jacket

This study of Islamic art and architecture features locations such as Isfahan, Bukhara and Samarkand, Lahore and the Taj Mahal of Agra

This book covers "a massive span of Islamic art and history with a consistently well written text and stunning photographs, reproductions, and floor plans. . . . Fasci-

Stierlin, Henri—*Continued*
nating explications, including a myth-debunking history of the Taj Mahal's construction, accompany the artwork." Booklist
Includes bibliographical references

709.32 Ancient Egyptian art

Egyptian art in the age of the pyramids. Metropolitan Mus. of Art 1999 xxiii, 536p il **709.32**
1. Egyptian art 2. Egypt—Antiquities
LC 99-22246
Available from Yale Univ. Press $34.95 (ISBN 0-300-08595-8)
Catalogue of an exhibition to be held at the Metropolitan Museum of Art, Sept. 16, 1999-Jan. 9, 2000
This book "focuses on the Old Kingdom—a 500-year period beginning some 4,500 years ago when necropolises like the Giza pyramids were constructed and sculptural renderings of the human figure were characterized by their 'spare, tender gestures.' The book's 15 essays cover topics like the pyramids, royal reliefs, statuary and the history of the Old Kingdom." N Y Times Book Rev
Includes bibliographical references

Egyptian treasures from the Egyptian Museum in Cairo; edited by Francesco Tiradritti; photographs by Araldo De Luca. Abrams 1999 416p il $75 **709.32**
1. Egyptian Museum 2. Egyptian art 3. Egypt—Antiquities
ISBN 0-8109-3276-8
LC 99-72419
Also published in the United Kingdom with title: The Cairo Museum
This is a "descriptive guide to the ancient history exhibit at the Egyptian Museum in Cairo. . . . Following the introduction are educational essays by Egyptologists from around the world, on topics ranging from the early dynastic eras through to the later periods of invasion by the Greeks. Throughout the book, there are vivid photographs of artifacts with a narration explaining the historical and artistic significance of each piece." Booklist
Includes bibliographical references

Germond, Philippe
An Egyptian bestiary; animals in life and religion in the land of the pharaohs; [by] Philippe Germond, Jacques Livet. Thames & Hudson 2001 224p il $65 **709.32**
1. Animals in art 2. Egyptian art
ISBN 0-500-51059-8
LC 2001-88627
The author "divides the book into the secular and sacred sections. Within those sections, he groups animals by species, discussing waterfowl in one section and ibis-headed gods in another. It is Livet's photographs, though, that grab the reader. Most are life-sized, with meticulous and stunning detail. For the quality of the illustrations alone, the book is a worthy addition to most collections; Germond's text raises it to the level of a critical addition to any but the most limited of Egyptian collections." Libr J

The **Quest** for immortality; treasures of ancient Egypt; Erik Hornung and Betsy M. Bryan, editors; contributions by Betsy M. Bryan [et al.] National Gallery of Art 2002 239p il maps $65 **709.32**
1. Egyptian art 2. Egypt—Antiquities
ISBN 0-89468-303-9
LC 2002-18847
This is a catalogue of an exhibition of Egyptian funerary art presented at the National Gallery of Art in Washington D.C. in 2002, drawn from the collection of Cairo's Egyptian Museum. It includes essays exploring "Egyptian art history, customs, and worship, with specific focus on the Amduat, a book devoted to the pharaoh's twelve-hour journey to the afterlife. Additional writings detail the background of the collection and focus upon the role of art in ancient Egypt." Publisher's note
Includes bibliographical references

Robins, Gay
The art of ancient Egypt. Harvard Univ. Press 1997 271p il $42; pa $24.95 **709.32**
1. Egyptian art 2. Egypt—Antiquities
ISBN 0-674-04660-9; 0-674-00376-4 (pa)
LC 97-19458
"The first chapter orients the reader in the cultural, technical, and iconographic contexts needed to explore the evolution of the Egyptian artistic tradition in subsequent chapters. Beginning with the predynastic origins (5000 BCE) and concluding in the Ptolemaic Period (304-30 BCE), Robins traces the development of sculpture, painting, funerary and religious art, and architecture with over 300 illustrations, many in color." Libr J
Includes bibliographical references

Smith, William Stevenson, 1907-1969
The art and architecture of ancient Egypt; {by} W. Stevenson Smith. rev with additions, by William Kelly Simpson. Yale Univ. Press 1998 296p il map (Pelican history of art) $75; pa $35 **709.32**
1. Egyptian art 2. Egypt—Antiquities
ISBN 0-300-07715-7; 0-300-07747-5 (pa)
LC 98-24893
First published 1958 by Penguin Bks.
"This book shows the tombs at Thebes, including the treasure-filled burial place of Tutankhamen, the temples of Luxor and Karnak, and the palaces of Akhenaten at Tell el Amarna and of Amenhotep III at Thebes. It also presents many revealing portraits depicting a range of subjects from the kings and queens who built the pyramids at Giza and Saqqara to their own civil servants." Publisher's note
Includes bibliographical references

709.38 Ancient Greek art

Boardman, John, 1927-
Greek art. 4th ed, rev and expanded. Thames & Hudson 1996 304p il map (World of art) pa $16.95 **709.38**
1. Greek art
ISBN 0-500-20292-3
LC 96-60184
First published 1964 by Praeger Pubs.
Partial contents: The beginnings and geometric Greece; Greece and the arts of the East and Egypt; Archaic Greek art; Classical sculpture and architecture; Hellenistic art; Selected bibliography
"This is a classic in the field made even more readable and useful than before. Highly recommended for all collections." Libr J

Houses and monuments of Pompeii; the works of Fausto and Felice Niccolini; by Roberto Cassanelli [et al]; introduction by Stefano de Caro; translation by Thomas M. Hartmann. Getty Mus. 2002 223p il $75
     709.38
1. Pompeii (Extinct city)
ISBN 0-89236-684-2   LC 2002-106116
Original Italian edition, 1997
"This book reproduces, along with commentary, Le case i monumenti di Pompeii (1854) of Fausto and Felice Niccolini, the first work to present completely and systematically all the public and private buildings so far excavated in Pompeii. It features the . . . watercolors the Niccolinis created to document Pompeii. . . . [Texts] explain the documents by the Niccolinis, as well as the evolution of the Pompeian style in Europe, the pictorial representation of Pompeii in the nineteenth century from engravings to photographs, and the evolving styles of archaeological documentation." Publisher's note

709.39   Art of other parts of ancient world

Frankfort, Henri, 1897-1954
The art and architecture of the ancient Orient. 5th ed, with supplementary notes and additional bibliography and abbreviations by Michael Roaf and Donald Matthews. Yale Univ. Press 1996 483p il maps (Pelican history of art) pa $35   **709.39**
1. Ancient art 2. Middle East—Antiquities
ISBN 0-300-06470-5   LC 97-224901
First published 1954 in the United Kingdom, 1955 in the United States
This traces the development of art in the Near East from 3500 B.C. to 539 B.C., covering the Sumerians, Assyrians, Babylonians, Hittites, Aramaeans, Levants, and Phoenicians
Includes bibliographical references

709.44   French art

Kostenevich, A. G. (Al'bert Grigor'evich)
French art treasures at the Hermitage; splendid masterpieces, new discoveries; by Albert Kostenevich. Abrams 1999 469p il $75   **709.44**
1. Hermitage (Saint Petersburg, Russia) 2. French art 3. Art—19th century 4. Art—20th century
ISBN 0-8109-3889-8   LC 99-14103
This "study looks at 416 paintings, drawings, and sculptures-- most nationalized from Russian collections after the 1917 Revolution. . . . A substantial chronological narrative has been added to focus on the French art scene from 1860 to 1950. This stunning book is highly recommended." Libr J
Includes bibliographical references

Schapiro, Meyer, 1904-1996
Impressionism; reflections and perceptions. Braziller 1997 359p il $50   **709.44**
1. Impressionism (Art) 2. French art 3. Art—19th century
ISBN 0-8076-1420-3   LC 97-10632
This text is based on tapes made at Indiana University in 1961. The author explores impressionism through the disciplines of history, science, economics, politics, linguistics, philosophy and literature
"A wonderful text, nobly illustrated." N Y Times Book Rev

709.45   Italian art

The **Medici,** Michelangelo, & the art of late Renaissance Florence; essays by Christina Acidini [et al.] Yale Univ. Press 2002 381p il $60   **709.45**
1. House of Medici 2. Michelangelo Buonarroti, 1475-1564 3. Italian art 4. Art—15th and 16th centuries
ISBN 0-89558-158-2   LC 2002-66183
Published in conjunction with the exhibition "Magnificenza! The Medici, Michelangelo, and the art of late Renaissance Florence" held at Palazzo Strozzi, Florence, June 6, 2002-Sept. 2002, Art Institute of Chicago, Nov. 9, 2002-Feb. 2, 2003, and Detroit Institute of Arts, Mar. 16, 2003-June 8, 2003
"Florence, Michelangelo's beloved native city, became the capital of the Italian Renaissance thanks to the lavish arts and science patronage of the Medici dynasty. . . . [This volume] focuses on an especially fertile period, 1537-1631. . . . Richly descriptive essays offer brisk but vivid portraits of the Medici and the artists they commissioned, consider the city's illustrious if politically volatile tradition of highly skilled craftsmanship, and assess the glory of Renaissance drawing, painting, sculpture, and decorative arts." Booklist
Includes bibliographical references

Wittkower, Rudolf, 1901-1971
Art and architecture in Italy, 1600-1750; revised by Joseph Connors and Jennifer Montagu. 6th ed. Yale Univ. Press 1999 3v il maps (Pelican history of art) set $150; pa $75   **709.45**
1. Italian art 2. Baroque art   LC 98-49066
Also available as separate volumes ea $60; pa $25
First published 1958 by Penguin Bks.
Contents: v1 The early Baroque, 1600-1625; v2 The high Baroque, 1625-1675; v3 Late Baroque and Rococo, 1675-1750
The author examines works produced during the Early, High, and Late Baroque periods of Italian art, covering such artists as Caravaggio, Bernini, Borromini and Cortona
Includes bibliographical references

709.47   Russian art

Hamilton, George Heard
The art and architecture of Russia. 3rd ed. Penguin Bks. 1983 482p il (Pelican history of art) o.p.; Yale Univ. Press paperback available $30   **709.47**
1. Russian art
ISBN 0-300-0532704 (pa)   LC 81-10583
First published 1954

Hamilton, George Heard—*Continued*

Hamilton traces the development of Russian art from the height of the Byzantine Empire, through its flowering under Peter the Great, to contemporary work and the influence of Western European culture

Includes bibliographical references

McPhee, John A.

The ransom of Russian art; {by} John McPhee. Farrar, Straus & Giroux 1994 181p il $20; pa $12   **709.47**

1. Dodge, Norton T., 1927- 2. Russian art

ISBN 0-374-24682-3; 0-374-52450-5 (pa)

LC 94-14723

The author "recounts the surreptitious activities of U.S. economist Norton Dodge, who during the 1960s and 1970s, slipped by the KGB and smuggled out of the Soviet Union 8000 artworks by 600 dissident artists." Libr J

"McPhee's engaging narrative sheds light on this suppressed creative milieu." Publ Wkly

709.5   Asian art

Lee, Sherman E.

A history of Far Eastern art. 5th ed, edited by Naomi Noble Richard. Prentice Hall; Abrams 1994 576p il $80   **709.5**

1. Asian art

ISBN 0-13-393398-9   LC 93-7267

First published 1964

"The author's text covers in chronological order the art traditions of China, Japan, and India from 5000 B.C. to A.D. 1850 and also links these major national developments to neighboring cultures. Numerous black-and-white photographs, drawings, maps, and color plates serve as the excellent illustrations." Booklist {review of 1982 edition}

Includes bibliographical references

709.51   Chinese art

Hearn, Maxwell K.

Splendors of Imperial China; treasures from the National Palace Museum, Taipei. Metropolitan Mus. of Art; Rizzoli Int. Publs. 1996 144p il hardcover o.p. paperback available $29.95   **709.51**

1. National Palace Museum (Taipei, Taiwan) 2. Chinese art

ISBN 0-87099-766-1 (pa)   LC 95-46590

Hearn "selected more than 100 works to present here, drawn from an extensive traveling exhibition featuring Neolithic and Bronze Age works, as well as Sung, Ming, and other dynasty masterpieces. This beautifully produced book contains fine quality reproductions that illuminate a splendid collection of rare artwork. . . . The text describes in accessible terms important background information, including cultural climate, historical events, and artistic elements." Booklist

Sickman, Laurence, 1906-1988

The art and architecture of China; {by} Laurence Sickman, Alexander Soper. 3rd ed. Penguin Bks. 1968 xxix, 350p il map (Pelican history of art) ; Yale Univ. Press paperback available $30   **709.51**

1. Chinese art

ISBN 0-300-05334-7 (pa)

First published 1956

The authors trace the development of painting, sculpture, and architecture from the Shang dynasty to the early twentieth century

Includes bibliographical references

Tregear, Mary

Chinese art. rev ed. Thames & Hudson 1997 216p il maps (World of art) pa $14.95   **709.51**

1. Chinese art

ISBN 0-500-20299-0

First published 1980 by Oxford Univ. Press

An introduction to major decorative, ceremonial, figurative and narrative aspects of Chinese art. Coverage ranges from works of Neolithic groups and the bronzes of the Shang dynasty to Buddhist sculpture, ceramics, garden design and architecture. Emphasis is also placed on the interaction of poetry, painting and calligraphy

Includes bibliographical references

709.6   African art

An **Anthology** of African art: the twentieth century; edited by N'Goné Fall and Jean Loup Pivin. Distributed Art Pubs. 2002 407p il $80   **709.6**

1. African art

ISBN 1-89102-438-8   LC 2002-1449

This anthology presents a theoretical, historical, geographical, and critical map of 20th century art in Sub-Saharan Africa, covering such topics as art schools in the 1930s, urban design and public art, and socially-concerned art during African independence movements

"Including 500 color and 51 black-and-white images, this book provides a depth and breadth no other volume can boast of on the subject of contemporary African art. Breathtakingly thorough and overwhelming in its comprehensiveness, this volume contains a representative selection that covers all genres and reaches into every region of sub-Saharan Africa." Libr J

Includes bibliographical references

A **History** of art in Africa; [by] Monica Blackmun Visonà [et al.]; introduction by Suzanne Preston Blier; preface by Rowland Abiodun. Prentice-Hall 2000 544p il map $71   **709.6**

1. African art

ISBN 0-13-442187-6   LC 00-22796

"Treating the subject from an art historical rather than an anthropological perspective, this groundbreaking book is organized geographically to cover the entire continent. Each of the five regional sections focuses on selected major art traditions. . . . Accompanying the text are over 700 photos and scores of maps, plans, drawings, etc." Libr J

Includes bibliographical references

709.73　American art

Harlem Renaissance: art of black America; introduction by Mary Schmidt Campbell; essays by David Driskell, David Levering Lewis, and Deborah Willis Ryan. Studio Mus. in Harlem; Abrams 1987 200p il
709.73
1. African American artists 2. American art
LC 86-17229
Available from Abradale Press
This book "features four black artists: the sculptor Meta Warrick Fuller and the painters Aaron Douglas, Palmer Hayden and William H. Johnson. Also included are photographs . . . by James Van Der Zee." N Y Times Book Rev
"An eye-catching and eye-opening introduction to the black intelligensia who created the Harlem Renaissance of 1919-1930. . . . Black-and-white figures and color plates are plentiful and of fine quality." Choice
Includes bibliographical references

Haskell, Barbara, 1946-
The American century; art and culture. Norton 1999 2v v1 $60; v2 o.p.　**709.73**
1. American art 2. Arts—United States
ISBN 0-393-04723-7 (v1)　　　　LC 98-32116
Contents: v1 1900-1950; v2 1950-2000 by Lisa Phillips
Based on exhibitions at the Whitney Museum, these illustrated volumes cover 20th century American painting, sculpture, printmaking, and photography through political, historical, social, economic, and culture contexts
Includes bibliographical references

Henkes, Robert
The art of black American women; works of twenty-four artists of the twentieth century. McFarland & Co. 1993 274p il $49.95
709.73
1. African American artists 2. Women artists 3. American art 4. Artists—United States
ISBN 0-89950-818-9　　　　LC 92-50955
Artists represented include "Lois Mailou Jones, Vivian Browne, Jewel Simon, Faith Ringgold, Clementine Hunter, and Adell Westbrook. Typically, entries are 810 pages in length, accompanied by 68 black-and-white illustrations of artwork. Rather than biographical notes, the text is a discussion of the nature and vision of the artist, followed by listings of career highlights, education, awards, selected and solo exhibitions, and a bibliography. . . . This is a worthy contribution to the literature of a group of largely overlooked artists." Booklist
Includes bibliographical references

Hughes, Robert
American visions; the epic history of art in America. Knopf 1997 635p il $65; pa $39.95
709.73
1. American art
ISBN 0-679-42627-2; 0-375-70365-9 (pa)
LC 96-45111
The author examines "art and architecture in America from the earliest Spanish works in New Mexico to contemporary art done in the late 1990s." Libr J
"Hughes has orchestrated a spectacular integration of facts, observations, and insights in this ambitious, lively, and gloriously illustrated volume." Booklist
Includes bibliographical references

Marin, Cheech, 1946-
Chicano visions; American painters on the verge; essays by Max Benavidez, Constance Cortez, Tere Tomo. Little, Brown 2002 160p il $35; pa $19.95　**709.73**
1. American painting 2. Mexican Americans
ISBN 0-8212-2805-6; 0-8212-2806-4 (pa)
LC 2002-104645
This "presents the work of 30 Chicano artists whose paintings will be exhibited at the Smithsonian and tour the country." Publ Wkly
"Marin's extraordinary collection forms the foundation for this exciting and invaluable showcase . . . [which includes works by] John Valadez, Gronk, Diane Gamboa, Patssi Valdez, Adan Hernandez, and Carlos Almaraz." Booklist

709.8　Latin American art

Brazil body & soul; edited by Edward J. Sullivan; curated by Edward J. Sullivan [et al.] Abrams 2002 600p il $85　**709.8**
1. Latin American art
ISBN 0-8109-6933-5　　　　LC 2002-283106
Catalog of an exhibition held at the Solomon R. Guggenheim Museum, New York, and at the Guggenheim Museum Bilbao
This survey "concentrates on two principal areas of Brazil's art history: the 16th-18th centuries' heavily Portuguese-influenced Baroque period and the 20th-century period of self-reflection and hybrid reinvention. . . . Within these categories, the book also includes a look at 20th-century Afro-Brazilian art, the contemporary environmental sculpture of Ernesto Neto, cinema, and architecture." Libr J
"The stars of the show of this massive catalogue are the more than 350 full-page illustrations, brilliantly reproduced." Publ Wkly
Includes bibliographical references

Encyclopedia of Latin American & Caribbean art; edited by Jane Turner. Grove's Dictionaries 1999 xx, 782p il maps (Grove encyclopedias of the arts of the Americas) $250　**709.8**
1. Latin American art
ISBN 1-88444-604-3　　　　LC 99-41595
"This work covers the art of every country in Central and South America and the Caribbean, from the colonial period to the present. The entries, expanded and updated from the publisher's mammoth Dictionary of Art, cover countries, artists, and artistic styles, with cross-referencing where appropriate." Libr J
For a fuller review see Booklist April 1, 2000
Includes bibliographical references

Scott, John F., 1936-
Latin American art; ancient to modern. University Press of Fla. 1999 xxiv, 240p il $49.95　**709.8**
1. Latin American art
ISBN 0-8130-1645-2　　　　LC 98-46535
A study "of Latin American art from pre-Columbian times to the present, encompassing media ranging from sculpture, pottery, and painting to architecture. Scott . . . addresses the major styles and artists that define each period." Libr J
Includes bibliographical references

712 Landscape architecture

Brookes, John, 1933-
Garden masterclass. DK Pub. 2002 352p il $40 **712**
1. Landscape gardening 2. Garden design
ISBN 0-7894-8382-3
"A Dorling Kindersley book"
"Brookes outlines the fundamental elements of landscape design, showing with clear text, photos, and sketches how to achieve visually pleasing effects. He explains setting, shape, direction, and level, as well as other hardscape features, demonstrating different styles and approaches. He also covers design through plant combinations and encourages readers to develop gardens suited to their local environments through the use of native plants." Libr J

Buchanan, Rita
Taylor's master guide to landscaping. Houghton Mifflin 2000 384p il $40 **712**
1. Landscape gardening
ISBN 0-618-05590-8   LC 99-54110
Companion volume to Taylor's master guide to gardening
"A Frances Tenenbaum book"
"Buchanan offers a comprehensive treatment of landscape design, emphasizing designing with plants and including extensive information about choosing and caring for plants, trees, shrubs, vines, and ground covers. . . . A landmark work destined to become a classic." Libr J

Clausen, Ruth Rogers, 1938-
Dreamscaping; 25 easy designs for home gardens. Hearst Bks. 2002 127p il $30 **712**
1. Garden design
ISBN 1-58816-067-X   LC 2001-16928
The author provides "plans, plant lists, and well-illustrated planting directions for all sorts of situations in sun or shade, outdoors and in the home. Tips and reminders are used to address design issues and maintenance, and to point out poisonous species. . . . The book's pretty layout and colorful photographs should entice novices to try something new in the garden." Booklist

The **Complete** book of garden projects; a step-by-step guide to creating and maintaining your outdoor space. Betterway Bks. 2002 c2001 224p il pa $24.99 **712**
1. Garden ornaments and furniture 2. Gardening
ISBN 1-55870-627-5
This guide offers instructions for design and construction of garden structures, planting beds, laying paths, and installing special features such as lighting or fountains

Gertley, Jan
The art of the kitchen garden; {by} Jan and Michael Gertley. Taunton Press 1999 151p il $29.95 **712**
1. Gardens 2. Vegetable gardening
ISBN 1-56158-180-1   LC 97-23710
The authors "accentuate a formal approach to line, shape, color, and texture, arriving at patterned garden plans distinguished by detailed combinations of flowers, herbs, and vegetables." Booklist
"If the prose is somewhat utilitarian, the book is commendably complete, enlivened by vivid photographs that effectively illustrate the title." Publ Wkly

Griswold, Mac K.
The golden age of American gardens; proud owners, private estates, 1890-1940; {by} Mac Griswold, Eleanor Weller; with research assistance by Helen E. Rollins. Abrams 1991 408p il $75; pa $34.95 **712**
1. Gardens
ISBN 0-8109-3358-6; 0-8109-2737-3 (pa)
LC 91-8283
Published in association with the Garden Club of America
A "history of owners, designers, and the ultimate country retreats resulting from their collaborations. . . . Weller's compilation of rare, hand-colored lantern slides and hundreds of black-and-white historical photographs of the era are particularly noteworthy." Booklist
Includes bibliographical references

Harper, Pamela
Designing with perennials; [by] Pamela J. Harper. Sterling 2001 326p il pa $19.95
712
1. Perennials 2. Landscape gardening 3. Garden design
ISBN 0-8069-7478-8
First published 1991 by Macmillan
The author "addresses plant selection, use and placement, color and foliage effects, and ground cover options. Her final chapter on ornament explains the concept of the focal point and the ways ornament can embellish or be used as part of a strategic design. Harper's captioned photographs are truly instructive, clearly demonstrating the concepts and effects she describes." Libr J

Hayward, Gordon
Stone in the garden; inspiring designs and practical projects. Norton 2001 224p il $39.95
712
1. Landscape gardening
ISBN 0-393-04779-2   LC 00-69945
"The book's first half focuses on the philosophical and design considerations of stone forms as varied as walls, paths, terraces, and even benches. The second half is more practical, covering topics such as estimating the amount of stone needed for a wall, the methods of cutting and laying stone, and building pools and fountains." Libr J
Includes bibliographical references

Hudak, Joseph
Design for gardens. Timber Press 2000 217p il $29.95 **712**
1. Garden design 2. Ornamental plants
ISBN 0-88192-441-5   LC 99-39196
Starting with "a historical overview of the art of gardening . . . Hudak proceeds through essential design practices: evaluating the site, deciding on a style, and identifying those unique features that will transform the space into a distinctive sanctuary. Subsequent chapters encompass how to map a plan, create aesthetic unity, and select plant material." Booklist

Newbury, Tim
20 best garden designs. Ward Lock 1997 96p il o.p.; Cassell paperback available $16.95 **712**
1. Garden design
ISBN 1-84188-208-9 (pa)   LC 97-189037
First published 1995 with title: The ultimate garden designer

Newbury, Tim—*Continued*

This book "offers a range of designs for varied settings, from rooftop and urban gardens to family gardens and natural gardens. Plans include plant keys, photographs, and a discussion of aims and effects. Variations for yards of different sizes or shapes complete each plan. A useful, affordable resource." Libr J

Van Sweden, James A.

Architecture in the garden; [by] James van Sweden with Thomas Christopher; foreword by Penelope Hobhouse. Random House 2002 264p il $39.95   **712**

1. Landscape architecture 2. Garden design
ISBN 0-375-50154-1   LC 2002-69702

The author attempts "to show that architectural elements are essential in developing a successful garden design. Van Sweden focuses on such components as paths, edgings, fences, walls, water, and artwork, explaining that a garden is not a garden without a sound structural organization that uses these elements. . . . A well-illustrated glossary is included. Recommended for most gardening and landscape architecture collections." Libr J

Includes bibliographical references

720   Architecture

O'Gorman, James F.

ABC of architecture; drawings by Dennis E. McGrath. University of Pa. Press 1997 127p il $35; pa $13.45   **720**

1. Architecture
ISBN 0-8122-3423-5; 0-8122-1631-8 (pa)
LC 97-22616

The author discusses the history of architecture, types of buildings, advances in technology, and architectural analysis

This book, "a model of brevity and clarity, may be the best-written work on the subject in English for lay people." N Y Times Book Rev

Includes bibliographical references

Palladio, Andrea, 1508-1580

The four books on architecture; translated by Robert Tavernor and Richard Schofield. MIT Press 1997 xxxv, 436p il $69.95; pa $24.95   **720**

1. Architecture
ISBN 0-262-16162-1; 0-262-66133-0 (pa)
LC 96-36406

This is a translation of a Renaissance architectural treatise that was first published in Venice in 1570. "The new translation includes thirty-one pages of notes and forty pages of glossary." Times Lit Suppl

"Drawing on the monuments of ancient Rome as well as the author's own villas and public works, this philosophical treatise and practical guide served as the pattern book for countless Palladian buildings by other architects around the world. Elegantly translated (in the first new English translation since 1738) and illustrated with the lyrical, rarely seen woodcuts of Palladio's original." N Y Times Book Rev

Includes bibliographical references

Wright, Frank Lloyd, 1867-1959

Frank Lloyd Wright collected writings; edited by Bruce Brooks Pfeiffer; introduction by Kenneth Frampton. Rizzoli Int. Publs. 1992-1995 5v il   **720**
LC 91-40987

Apply to publisher for price and availability

Contents: v1 1894-1931 (ISBN 0-8478-1547-1); v2 1930-1932 (ISBN 0-8478-1548-X; 0-8478-1549-8); v3 1931-1939 (ISBN 0-8478-1699-0; 0-8478-1700-8); v4 1939-1949 (ISBN 0-8478-1803-9; 0-8478-1804-7); v5 1949-1959 (ISBN 0-8478-1854-3; 0-8478-1855-1)

These volumes are comprised of published and unpublished articles, lectures, reminiscences, and essays. Volume 2 includes a reprint of books 1-3 of Wright's autobiography

"Essential for both lay readers and professionals interested in art, art history, and architecture; recommended for both public and academic libraries." Libr J {review of v1}

720.3   Architecture— Encyclopedias and dictionaries

Ching, Frank, 1943-

A visual dictionary of architecture; [by] Francis D. K. Ching. Van Nostrand Reinhold 1995 319p il $44.95; pa $39.95   **720.3**

1. Architecture—Dictionaries
ISBN 0-471-28451-3; 0-471-28821-7 (pa)
LC 95-1476

This volume arranges some "5,000 entries thematically under 68 concepts covering architectural design, history, and technology. The topics, which are treated alphabetically, include building types (church, house, theater), sections (door, roof, stair), features (arch, column, vault), and materials (brick, paint, wood). Terms are logically clustered on oversize pages and defined with both line drawings and text, usually 20 to 100 words." Booklist

Curl, James Stevens, 1937-

Oxford dictionary of architecture; with line-drawings by the author and John Sambrook. Oxford Univ. Press 1999 833p il $55; pa $16.95   **720.3**

1. Architecture—Dictionaries
ISBN 0-19-210006-8; 0-19-280017-5 (pa)
LC 98-20544

This work "merges entries on individual architects with a carefully illustrated and impressively comprehensive set of building terms. In a helpful but judiciously employed device, asterisks indicate separate entries for terms with an essay; there are also bibliographic references for most of the topics. The dictionary's terse prose is more than balanced by its breadth and excellent illustrations." Libr J

Dictionary of architecture & construction; edited by Cyril M. Harris. 3rd ed. McGraw-Hill 2000 1028p il $69.95 **720.3**

1. Architecture—Dictionaries 2. Building—Dictionaries
ISBN 0-07-135178-7   LC 99-56285

First published 1975

This dictionary of architecture and contruction provides "24,500 terms and abbreviations and 2,200 drawings and diagrams. The entries are brief and clearly written, averaging approximately 20 words in length. . . . It is an exceptionally practical and comprehensive tool." Am Ref Books Annu, 2001

The **Penguin** dictionary of architecture and landscape architecture; edited by John Fleming, Hugh Honour and Nikolaus Pevsner. 5th ed. Penguin Bks. 1998 643p il hardcover o.p. paperback available $16.95

720.3

1. Architecture—Dictionaries 2. Landscape architecture—Dictionaries
ISBN 0-14-051323-X (pa)
First published 1966 with title: The Penguin dictionary of architecture

This reference covers "architecture from ancient times to the present. Major entries on key individuals, styles, movements, materials, and terms range up to several pages in length and include cross references and bibliographies for further reading." Publisher's note

"A magnificent panorama of world architecture, scholarly conciseness at its best." Art Review

720.9 Architecture—Historical and geographic treatment

Fletcher, Sir Banister Flight, 1866-1953
Sir Banister Fletcher's A history of architecture. 20th ed, edited by Dan Cruickshank; consultant eds., Andrew Saint, Peter Blundell Jones, Kenneth Frampton; asst. ed., Fleur Richards. Architectural Press 1996 xxxviii, 1794p il $145   **720.9**
1. Architecture—History
ISBN 0-7506-2267-9   LC 96-35511
First published 1896 with title: A history of architecture on the comparative method

"Overarching view of architectural history, newly rewritten and expanded to include worldwide coverage. Extensively illustrated, with glossary, index, and bibliographies appended to each chapter. Includes general introductions and background for each chapter." N Y Public Libr Book of How & Where to Look It Up [1987 edition]

Includes bibliographical references

Glancey, Jonathan
The story of architecture. Dorling Kindersley 2000 240p il $30; pa $25   **720.9**
1. Architecture—History
ISBN 0-7894-5965-5; 0-7894-9334-9 (pa)
LC 00-30434
"Devoting nearly half the text to the modern period, Glancey condenses history's panorama into a series of colorful vignettes, each described as having some contemporary relevance. Driven by a contagious enthusiasm, the narrative is enlivened by chatty, sometimes offbeat commentary." Libr J

The **Seventy** wonders of the modern world; 1500 years of extraordinary feats of engineering and construction; edited by Neil Parkyn. Thames & Hudson 2002 304p il $40   **720.9**
1. Architecture 2. Curiosities and wonders
ISBN 0-500-51047-4   LC 2002-100549
Published in the United Kingdom with title: The seventy architectural wonders of our world

"Most of the featured 'wonders' date from the second half of the 20th century. The selections are divided into seven categories: churches, palaces, public buildings, towers and skyscrapers, bridges and railways, canals and dams, and statues. Each entry includes basic information on history, structural and engineering details, innovations, aesthetics, and a sidebar 'fact-file.'" Libr J

Trachtenberg, Marvin
Architecture, from prehistory to postmodernity; [by] Marvin Trachtenberg, Isabelle Hyman. 2nd ed. Abrams 2001 624p il $95   **720.9**
1. Architecture—History
ISBN 0-8109-0607-4   LC 2001-22388
Also available from Prentice-Hall
First published 1986 with title: Architecture, from prehistory to post-modernism

This is a "historical survey of Western architecture. . . . [The authors] proceed chronologically, discussing significant styles, works, and architects. . . . Included are very recent masterworks such as Daniel Libeskind's Jewish Museum in Berlin. The high-quality graphics include 91 color plates, and an illustrated glossary is provided." Libr J

Includes bibliographical references

720.973 Architecture—United States

LeBlanc, Sydney
The architecture traveler; a guide to 250 key 20th century American buildings. Norton 2000 276p il map pa $21.95   **720.973**
1. Architecture—United States
ISBN 0-393-73050-6   LC 99-88789
First published 1993 by Whitney Library of Design with title: 20th century American architecture

This guide "'examines 250 important American buildings' and provides the information needed to visit them. . . . This book should be of use to travelers and architecture buffs alike." Libr J

Storrer, William Allin
The Frank Lloyd Wright companion. University of Chicago Press 1993 492p il $90   **720.973**
1. Wright, Frank Lloyd, 1867-1959
ISBN 0-226-77624-7   LC 93-30127
This "volume covers more than 450 buildings designed by master architect Wright between 1886 and 1959. Storrer documents each structure with plans, drawings, photographs, and commentary. Each presentation is both complete and concise, following each stage of Wright's aesthetic development, each leap of his imagination, and each instance of technical innovation." Booklist

Whiffen, Marcus
American architecture since 1780; a guide to the styles. rev ed. MIT Press 1992 326p il hardcover o.p. paperback available $21.95   **720.973**
1. Architecture—United States
ISBN 0-262-73097-9 (pa)   LC 91-32315
First published 1969
This guide contains descriptions, illustrations, and histories of more than forty architectural styles, arranged chronologically from the Adam style to various postmodern styles

Wiseman, Carter

Shaping a nation; twentieth-century American architecture and its makers. Norton 1998 412p il $45   **720.973**

1. Architecture—20th century 2. Architecture—United States 3. Architects

ISBN 0-393-04564-1   LC 97-9896

In this survey the author is "concerned to trace the ways in which buildings express an American identity. Though his subject is twentieth-century architecture, his search for roots extends back to the colonial vernacular and Thomas Jefferson. . . . Wiseman has written a solid mainstream history in which the look of buildings is seen as important. More significantly, he argues the case for social relevance alongside beauty." Archit J

Includes bibliographical references

721   Architectural structure

The **Elements** of style; an {sic} practical encyclopedia of interior architectural details, from 1485 to the present; Stephen Calloway, general editor; Elizabeth Cromley, consultant editor; foreword by J. Jackson Walter. Rev ed. Simon & Schuster 1996 568p il $70   **721**

1. Domestic architecture 2. Architecture—Details

ISBN 0-684-83521-5   LC 98-183652

First published 1991

"This pictorial dictionary surveys architectural details of British and American domestic interiors from 1475 to 1996. It is a book of illustrations supported by concise, well-written text and captions. . . . Supporting appendixes provide one-or two-paragraph biographies of major architects and designers, a glossary of more than 300 clearly defined terms, directories of British and American suppliers of architectural details, a bibliography of English-language reference sources, and an index of subjects and illustrations." Booklist

Langmead, Donald

Encyclopedia of architectural and engineering feats; [by] Donald Langmead and Christine Garnaut. ABC-CLIO 2001 388p il $99   **721**

1. Architecture 2. Engineering—History

ISBN 1-57607-112-X   LC 2001-4229

"This encyclopedia presents more than 200 judiciously selected structures and engineering innovations. . . . More than half the entries highlight buildings and achievements from the mid-19th through the 20th centuries. The one- to two-page summaries are packed with building history, architectural details, criticism, and analysis of social conditions that pushed technology and occasionally aesthetics to new limits. . . . The final entry, the World Trade Center Towers in New York City, poignantly notes their wanton destruction on September 11, 2001." Choice

For a fuller review see: Booklist, May 15, 2002

Maliszewski-Pickart, Margaret, 1963-

Architecture and ornament; an illustrated dictionary. McFarland & Co. 1998 198p il $35   **721**

1. Architecture—Details

ISBN 0-7864-0383-7   LC 97-33112

This source pairs a traditional dictionary of architectural elements with a series of illustrations of the same elements. The names located in the numbered illustrations may be found alphabetically in the dictionary; and cross-references in the dictionary refer to specific illustrations. The illustrations are grouped by category: windows and doors; walls; roofs; columns; stairs; ornament and moldings; arches, vaults, and domes

Rybczynski, Witold

The look of architecture. Oxford Univ. Press 2001 130p il $25; pa $9.95   **721**

1. Architecture 2. Design

ISBN 0-19-513443-5; 0-19-515633-1 (pa)

LC 00-53077

This book provides "commentary on the significance of style and fashion in architecture. Using anecdote, historical data, and descriptive prose to comment on Western architecture during the modern era, Rybczynski shows how the often dismissed discipline of apparel design finds its correlative in architectural fashion." Libr J

"The author's deeply informed enthusiasm is infectious, and his removal of architectural writing from an airily theoretical discourse to the realm of practical experience is empowering for the lay reader." Publ Wkly

Includes bibliographical references

724   Architecture from 1400

Gropius, Walter, 1883-1969

The new architecture and the Bauhaus; translated from the German by P. Morton Shand; with an introduction by Frank Pick. MIT Press 1965 112p il pa $14.95   **724**

1. Bauhaus 2. Architecture—20th century

ISBN 0-262-57006-8   LC 65-10279

"The MIT paperback series"

Original German edition, 1925; this is a reissue of the translation first published 1935 in the United Kingdom

The founder of the Dessau Bauhaus describes the work of that institution, and his own architectural theories

Rybczynski, Witold

The perfect house: a journey with the Renaissance architect Andrea Palladio. Scribner 2002 266p il $25; pa $15   **724**

1. Palladio, Andrea, 1508-1580 2. Architecture—15th and 16th centuries

ISBN 0-7432-0586-3; 0-7432-0587-1 (pa)

LC 2002-66838

The author offers a historical and architectural analysis of ten villas attributed to 16th century Italian architect Andrea Palladio

"With its intriguing biographical detail, precise descriptions of design elements, and engaging insights into daily life in the 16th century, Rybczynski's book is a small but lasting gift to the reader." Libr J

Includes bibliographical references

726 Buildings for religious and related purposes

Adams, Henry, 1838-1918
Mont-Saint-Michel and Chartres; with an introduction by Ralph Adams Cram. Princeton Univ. Press 1981 401p il hardcover o.p. paperback available $40   **726**
1. Mont-Saint-Michel (France). Abbey 2. Notre-Dame (Cathedral: Chartres, France) 3. Middle Ages
ISBN 0-691-00335-1 (pa)   LC 81-47279
Also available in paperback from Penguin Bks.
"This classic study of medieval civilization is written as the commentary of Henry Adams to an imaginary niece as they tour the Abbey Church at Mont-Saint-Michel and the Chartres Cathedral." Benet's Reader's Ency of Am Lit

King, Ross, 1962-
Brunelleschi's dome; how a Renaissance genius reinvented architecture. Walker & Co. 2000 194p $24   **726**
1. Brunelleschi, Filippo, 1377-1446 2. Santa Maria del Fiore (Cathedral: Florence, Italy) 3. Church buildings
ISBN 0-8027-1366-1   LC 00-43524
Also available in paperback from Penguin Bks.
"King illuminates the mysterious sources of inspiration and the secretive methods of architectural genius Filippo Brunelleschi in a fascinating chronicle of the building of his masterwork, the dome of Santa Maria del Fiore in Florence. A remarkable saga of how one incandescent mind performed the one matchless feat that would forever transform architecture from a mechanical craft into a creative art." Booklist
Includes bibliographical references

Prache, Anne
Cathedrals of Europe. Cornell Univ. Press 2000 279p il $99.95   **726**
1. Cathedrals 2. Medieval architecture
ISBN 0-8014-3781-4   LC 00-29507
Original French edition, 1999
This historical survey covers "buildings, decorations, windows, furnishings, art, illuminated liturgical manuscripts, relics, and treasures. . . . The scope is pan-European, with smaller, less-visited cathedrals also receiving attention." Libr J
Includes bibliographical references

728 Residential and related buildings

Altman, Adelaide, 1925-
Elderhouse: planning your best home ever. Chelsea Green 2002 232p il pa $19.95   **728**
1. Elderly—Housing 2. Domestic architecture—Designs and plans
ISBN 1-931498-11-3   LC 2002-31481
"The first section is full of ideas for creating a safe and comfortable home for wheelchair access or for a time in our lives when we are less nimble. The second section addresses the psychology of moving to a new smaller space in the later years of life." Libr J
Includes bibliographical references

Bakker, Rosemary
Elderdesign; designing and furnishing a home for your later years; illustrations by Thomas Kenny. Penguin Bks. 1997 228p il pa $14.95   **728**
1. Elderly—Housing 2. Domestic architecture—Designs and plans 3. Interior design
ISBN 0-14-025809-4   LC 96-48615
This guide to safe housing for the elderly covers lighting and locking systems, stairways and doorways, furniture, flooring and room arrangement, installing communication systems as well as finding professional help
Includes bibliographical references

Eck, Jeremiah
The distinctive home; a vision of timeless design. Taunton Press 2003 234p il $40   **728**
1. Domestic architecture—Designs and plans 2. Building
ISBN 1-561-58528-9   LC 2002-151820
"Eck firmly believes it is possible to build creative houses without a large budget. He discusses a home's site placement, examines the flow of activity within a modern home, and encourages the reader to think of rooms beyond their traditional uses. Eck's book encourages creativity and provides a series of color photographs for developing sound ideas." Libr J

Friedman, Avi
The adaptable house; designing homes for change. McGraw-Hill 2002 271p il $45   **728**
1. Domestic architecture—Designs and plans 2. Prefabricated houses
ISBN 0-07-137746-8   LC 2002-141433
"Friedman urges the reader to reimagine the traditional static home as dynamic space that changes as the needs of the occupants change. A single house, according to the author, should be able to accommodate an individual and/or family throughout their lives. Friedman examines how space functions within a house and the ways a house can be expanded and contracted based on the needs of its owners." Libr J
Includes bibliographical references

Jacobson, Max, 1941-
Patterns of home; the ten essentials of enduring design; [by] Max Jacobson, Murray Silverstein, Barbara Winslow. Taunton Press 2002 282p il $34.95   **728**
1. Domestic architecture—Designs and plans
ISBN 1-56158-533-5   LC 2002-7103
"Three architects argue that there are ten essential elements that comprise a well-designed home. These include the placement of the house on the site, creating rooms both inside and outside, the balance of quiet space and communal areas, the use of lighting, and the proportion of interior spaces. Each pattern's philosophy is explained and further illustrated with beautiful photographs." Libr J

Lind, Carla
The Wright style. Simon & Schuster 1992 224p il $50   **728**
1. Wright, Frank Lloyd, 1867-1959 2. Domestic architecture
ISBN 0-671-74959-5   LC 91-44553
"An Archetype Press book."

Lind, Carla—*Continued*

This book "takes us inside dozens of Frank Lloyd Wright's 'organic' houses, including his home and studio in Oak Park, Illinois, and the two Taliesins. . . . Carla Lind's text traces the development and components of Wright's unique, revolutionary aesthetic while 250 color photographs allow readers to appreciate the harmony of Wright's light-filled, graciously rectilinear rooms." Booklist

Includes bibliographical references

McAlester, Virginia, 1943-

A field guide to American houses; by Virginia and Lee McAlester; with drawings by Lauren Jarrett, and model house drawings by John Rodriquez-Arnaiz. Knopf 1984 525p il $40; pa $24.95   **728**

1. Domestic architecture 2. Architecture—United States

ISBN 0-394-51032-1; 0-394-73969-8 (pa)

                   LC 82-48740

A guide to the "numerous architectural styles of American single-family houses. Houses featured range from 17th-century Georgians to Neoeclectics of the late 1970s, with more than 1200 drawings and photographs and brief histories and notable architects of each style." Libr J

Includes bibliographical references

Nabokov, Peter

Native American architecture; {by} Peter Nabokov, Robert Easton. Oxford Univ. Press 1989 431p il hardcover o.p. paperback available $37.50   **728**

1. Native Americans—Dwellings

ISBN 0-19-506665-0 (pa)   LC 88-9944

This volume examines "the buildings and settlements created by American Indians from prehistoric times to the present." N Y Times Book Rev

"A rich, wide-ranging depiction of American Indian culture, belief, and history. . . . {The} scholarly, well-written text is complemented by a remarkable selection of photographs, drawings, and paintings." Nat Hist

Includes bibliographical references

Small house designs; edited by Kenneth R. Tremblay, Jr. & Lawrence von Bamford. Storey Communications 1997 201p il hardcover o.p. paperback available $19.95   **728**

1. Domestic architecture—Designs and plans

ISBN 0-88266-966-4 (pa)   LC 96-47252

"A Storey Publishing book"

"This compilation of small house designs by architects participating in the American Institute of Architects design competition features 34 floor plans and exterior sketches or photographs for each design. Also included are the square footage, estimated cost to build, and a short description of special or hidden elements. While not a book of ready-to-use designs, it is a good idea book for individuals looking for creative suggestions for small city lots." Libr J

Stewart, Martha

Martha Stewart's new old house; restoration, renovation, decoration, landscaping; photographs by Mathieu Roberts; illustrations by Rodica Prato. Potter 1992 288p il $45   **728**

1. Architecture—Conservation and restoration 2. Interior design

ISBN 0-517-57701-1   LC 92-15900

This work follows the step-by-step renovation, restoration, decoration and landscaping of a 19th-century Federal farmhouse in Connecticut

"Lots of atmospheric photography show workers at their labors." Publ Wkly

Susanka, Sarah

Creating the not so big house; insights and ideas for the new American home; photographs by Grey Crawford. Taunton Press 2000 258p il $34.95; pa $24.95   **728**

1. Domestic architecture 2. Interior design

ISBN 1-56158-377-4; 1-56158-605-6 (pa)

                   LC 00-44323

Susanka provides photographs and plans of houses that are designed to look bigger than their actual size

"Architect Susanka has big ideas about small design. . . . {This book promotes} well-designed, efficient, interesting modest-size homes. . . . {She} includes 25 delightful examples of houses designed by architects from around the country." Booklist

Not so big solutions for your home. Taunton Press 2002 155p il pa $22.95   **728**

1. Domestic architecture—Designs and plans 2. Interior design

ISBN 1-56158-613-7   LC 2002-7101

The author presents a compilation of 31 essays from her "Drawing Board" column in Fine Homebuilding magazine "that offer a number of solutions to household design problems both big and small. . . . Susanka offers an eclectic mix: tips on site selection, mud room design, planning to fit specific furniture, creating a family room that works, personalizing with tile, and planning window seats, pantries, TV placement, and floor plan changes." Libr J

Zega, Andrew

Palaces of the Sun King; Versailles, Trianon, Marly: the châteaux of Louis XIV; [by] Andrew Zega and Bernd H. Dams. Rizzoli Int. Publs. 2002 208p il $125   **728**

1. Louis XIV, King of France, 1638-1715 2. Palaces

ISBN 0-8478-2473-X   LC 2002-102948

This volume documents "twenty-one chateaux and pavilions commissioned by Louis XIV, France's great builder-king. These royal buildings, and over forty architectural ornaments enriching their gardens, are illustrated in . . . watercolors by authors Andrew Zega and Bernd H. Dams. . . . The authors give full attention to unrealized projects and depict completed structures not as they stand today, if indeed they stand at all, they were originally designed by the leading architects of the day." Publisher's note

Includes bibliographical references

728.8 Large and elaborate private dwellings

Wiencek, Henry
National Geographic guide to America's great houses; more than 150 outstanding mansions open to the public; by Henry Wiencek and Donna M. Lucey. National Geographic Soc. 1999 320p il pa $25 **728.8**
1. Domestic architecture 2. Architecture—United States
ISBN 0-7922-7424-5 LC 98-53013
Arranged by state, this guide includes information on past owners, furnishings, renovations, room descriptions, and excursion plans for other nearby houses of note. The text is accompanied by 170 full-color photos

729 Design and decoration of structures and accessories

Harwood, Buie
Architecture and interior design through the 18th century; an integrated history; [by] Buie Harwood, Bridget May, Curt Sherman. Prentice-Hall 2002 558p il maps $94 **729**
1. Interior design 2. Architecture 3. Decorative arts
ISBN 0-13-758590-X LC 2001-54869
This is a study of "architecture, interior design, interior architectural features, design details, motifs, furniture, space planning, color, lighting, textiles, interior surface treatments, and decorative accessories . . . from antiquity to the 18th century—from the many regions of the world." Publisher's note
Includes bibliographical references

731.4 Sculpture—Techniques and procedures

Bütz, Richard
How to carve wood; a book of projects and techniques. Taunton Press 1984 215p il pa $19.95 **731.4**
1. Wood carving
ISBN 0-918804-20-5 LC 83-50680
"A Fine Woodworking Bk."
The author introduces "the most common types of carving, whittling, chip carving, relief carving, lettering, and architectural carving. The information on tools and their care is very helpful. This is the best book available on the subject." Libr J
Includes bibliographical references

736 Carving and carvings. Paper cutting and folding

Burton, Mike, 1944-
Architectural carving; techniques for power & hand tools. Sterling 2002 224p il pa $24.95 **736**
1. Wood carving
ISBN 0-8069-6915-6 LC 2001-44678
This is a guide to techniques for architectural wood carving "explaining tool use, wood choices, and different styles of carving. This title stands out because of its great section on tool use. Burton offers a wealth of both traditional and innovative information." Libr J

737.4 Coins

A **Guide** book of United States coins; fully illustrated catalog and price list—1616 to date; by R. S. Yeoman; edited by Kenneth Bressett. Western il $15.95 **737.4**
1. Coins
ISSN 0072-8829
Annual. First published 1946 by Whitman
At head of title: The official red book of United States coins
This guide "known as the 'Red Book' is an outstanding reference on U.S. coins designed for use in identifying and grading coins. All issues from 1616 to the present are covered. The guide provides historical data, statistics, values, and detailed photographs for each coin. Additional sections deal with specialties such as Civil War and Hard Times tokens, misstruck coins, and uncirculated and proof sets." Nichols. Guide to Ref Books for Sch Media Cent. 4th edition

Handbook of United States coins; by R. S. Yeoman; edited by Kenneth Bressett. Western il pa $9.95 **737.4**
1. Coins
ISSN 0072-9949
Annual. First published 1941 by Whitman
At head of title: Official blue book of United States coins
This companion volume to A Guide book of United States coins gives the wholesale values of U.S. coins from colonial times to the present

Krause, Chester L.
Standard catalog of world coins; by Chester L. Krause and Clifford Mishler. Krause Publs. il pa $54.99 **737.4**
1. Coins
Also available volumes covering the 17th, 18th, and 19th centuries
First published 1972. (31st edition 2004) Periodically revised
This illustrated volume currently covers coins from throughout the world minted 1901-present. Prices are provided for each coin in up to four grades of preservation. Includes commemorative issues

Official know-it-all guide: coins. Frederick Fell Publishers pa $18.95 **737.4**
1. Coins
Annual. Replaced Fell's United States coin book in 2000

Official know-it-all guide: coins—*Continued*

This guide contains complete tables showing today's value of every coin minted in the United States. Along with illustrations are information on the history of coins, speculation and investment, how to start a collection, how to sell coins and recognize worthless coins

738　Ceramic arts

Coakes, Michelle

Creative pottery; a step-by-step guide and showcase. Quarry Bks. 1998 143p il $24.99
738

1. Pottery
ISBN 1-56496-315-2
"Coakes presents a diverse collection of projects with glaze recipes and tips on technique from 19 potters. Many excellent photographs of additional pieces showcase the artists' work." Libr J

Godden, Geoffrey A.

Encyclopaedia of British pottery and porcelain marks. Crown 1964 765p il map
738

1. British pottery 2. Pottery—Marks 3. Porcelain—Marks
Available in hardcover from Barrie and Jenkins
"Includes, in alphabetical arrangement, more than 4,000 British china marks ranging in date from 1050 to the present." Sheehy. Guide to Ref Books. 10th edition

Jones, Mike

Handcrafted ceramic tiles; [by] Mike Jones and Janis Fanning. Sterling 1998 144p il hardcover o.p. paperback available $17.95
738

1. Tiles 2. Interior design
ISBN 0-8069-9678-1 (pa)　　　LC 98-3591
"A Quarto book"
The authors "show how to add color designs to existing tiles without an expensive replacement job. Tiles can be painted, decoupaged, and stenciled right on the wall, changing an unimaginative tiled surface to a work of art. For the ceramic artist with a kiln, there are general instructions and step-by step projects for making, decorating, and mounting one's own clay tiles. This is a very practical book." Libr J

Karmason, Marilyn G.

Majolica: a complete and illustrated survey; [by] Marilyn G. Karmason with Joan B. Stacke. updated and enl ed. Abrams 2002 261p il $75
738

1. Ceramics
ISBN 0-8109-3595-3　　　LC 2002-105463
First published 1989
This is an "introduction to the colorful, lustrously glazed, exuberantly decorated 19th-century ceramic art called majolica. . . . [It includes a] bibliography and list of museums with majolica collections." Publisher's note

King, Joan Bolton

Enamelling. Crowood Press; [distributed by] Trafalgar Sq. 2002 111p il (Art of crafts) $35
738

1. Enamel and enameling
ISBN 1-86126-437-2
This guide to enameling "offers advice for beginners on selecting materials, firing test pieces in the kiln, and practicing basic techniques. For advanced crafters, there are chapters on painting, sgraffito, and repoussé. Mini-projects of small pieces, mainly jewelry, occur throughout the text as practice exercises." Libr J
Includes bibliographical references

Kovel, Ralph M.

Kovel's dictionary of marks: pottery and porcelain; by Ralph M. and Terry H. Kovel. 2nd ed. Crown 1995 278p il $17
738

1. Pottery—Marks 2. Porcelain—Marks
ISBN 0-517-70137-5　　　LC 95-3361
First published 1953 with title: Dictionary of marks—pottery and porcelain
On cover: Pottery and porcelain,1650-1850
This is a guide to identification of American, English, and European pottery and porcelain including an "index of 5,000 marks, listed by prominent features and with a complete cross-reference {showing} at a glance (a) geographical location of mark, (b) factory or family name of manufacturer, (c) type of ware, (d) method of producing the mark on the object, (e) color of the mark, and (f) date when the mark was used. The authors have included a foreword, bibliography, index of manufacturers and a . . . guide to the often misunderstood marks of Delft, Sevres, and England 1842-1883." Publisher's note

Kovels' new dictionary of marks; {by} Ralph and Terry Kovel. Crown 1986 290p il $19
738

1. Pottery—Marks 2. Porcelain—Marks
ISBN 0-517-55914-5　　　LC 85-15146
Covering pottery and porcelain from 1850 to the present this volume is regarded as a complimentary volume to the one covering 1650 to 1850

738.1　Ceramic arts—Techniques, equipment, materials

Burleson, Mark

The ceramic glaze handbook; materials, techniques, formulas. Lark Bks. 2001 144p il hardcover o.p. paperback available $24.95
738.1

1. Pottery 2. Glazes
ISBN 1-57990-439-4 (pa)　　　LC 00-63486
"Burleson covers glaze chemistry, application techniques, firing, and problem solving. Color photographs comparing fired samples are particularly good. A collection of formulas by other artists is categorized by type of clay body and firing temperature. Useful for studio potters and hobbyists." Libr J

Hamer, Frank, 1929-

The potter's dictionary of materials and techniques; {by} Frank and Janet Hamer. 5th ed. University of Pa. Press 2004 544p il $59.95
738.1

1. Pottery—Dictionaries 2. Ceramics—Dictionaries
ISBN 0-8122-3810-9
First published 1975 by Watson-Guptill

Hamer, Frank, 1929-—*Continued*

Articles in this "potter's reference include soda firing, paper clay, computer glaze calculations, and fuming. . . . Alphabetically arranged entries range in length from a brief paragraph or half-page . . . to longer essays on subjects such as formulas, health hazards, and cones. Subject matter ranges widely, covering all the processes and materials involved in pottery formation, decoration, and firing." Am Ref Books Annu, 1998 {entry for 4th edition}

Kenny, John B., d. 1988

The complete book of pottery making; drawings by Carla Kenny. 2nd ed. Chilton 1976 310p il (Chilton's creative crafts series) hardcover o.p. paperback available $29.95 **738.1**

1. Pottery
ISBN 0-8019-5933-0 (pa)   LC 76-302
First published 1949 by Greenberg
The whole process of pottery making is covered in a series of step-by-step photographs which explain the wheel, modeling, mold work, glaze, coil-building a teapot, etc.
Includes bibliographical references

Nelson, Glenn C.

Ceramics; a potter's handbook. Wadsworth il pa $70.95   **738.1**

1. Pottery
First published 1960. (6th edition 2002) Periodically revised
This manual for beginner to advanced potters presents forming and decorating techniques, body and glaze recipes, and sources for raw materials and equipment
Includes bibliographical references

738.5 Mosaics

Biggs, Emma, 1956-

The encyclopedia of mosaic techniques. Running Press 1999 160p il $24.95   **738.5**

1. Mosaics
ISBN 0-7624-0444-2
This is a "guide to the materials and techniques of designing and laying mosaic tiles in both indoor and outdoor settings. Well illustrated with color photographs throughout, the 'A to Z of Techniques' section has step-by-step instructions. Finished mosaics are pictured in the 'Gallery' section. Workshop set-up and safety tips are included." Libr J

739.2 Work in precious metals

Wyler, Seymour B., d. 1990

The book of old silver: English, American, foreign; with all available hallmarks including Sheffield plate marks. Profusely illustrated. Crown 1937 447p il $35   **739.2**

1. Silverwork 2. Plate 3. Hallmarks
ISBN 0-517-00089-X
Cover title: Old silver
"A short history of old English silver and a description of the varieties of silverware are followed by brief chapters on silversmithing in England, Scotland, the Continental countries, and America. The second half of the book is an unusually comprehensive collection of reproductions of hallmarks, arranged by country and indexed. Illustrated with photographs of old silver." Booklist

739.27 Jewelry

Codina, Carles

The complete book of jewelry making. Lark Bks. 2000 160p il $29.95   **739.27**

1. Jewelry
ISBN 1-57990-188-3   LC 00-42809
This book covers "the basics, from the ABCs of metallurgy to such complicated techniques as enameling and lacquering. . . . Most of the examples are contemporary, taken from European designers, and all blessed with great color photographs." Booklist

McSwiney, Sharon

The creative jeweler; inspirational projects using semi-precious and everyday materials. Krause Publs. 2000 160p il $21.95   **739.27**

1. Jewelry
ISBN 0-87341-556-6   LC 99-67513
This book presents ideas "about creating jewelry with wire and other materials. The authors give a detailed list of the tools and equipment necessary for each project, and each step is illustrated with instructive photographs that offer clear, how-to examples. . . . Novices and seasoned craftspeople alike will find projects that interest them." SLJ

741 Drawing and drawings

De Kooning, Willem, 1904-1997

Willem de Kooning: tracing the figure; organized by Cornelia H. Butler and Paul Schimmel; essays by Cornelia H. Butler [et al.] Museum of Contemporary Art (Los Angeles) 2002 199p il $55   **741**

1. Women in art
ISBN 0-691-09618-X   LC 2001-59081
Published to accompany an exhibition held at the Museum of Contemporary Art, Los Angeles, Feb. 10-Apr. 28, 2002, the San Francisco Museum of Modern Art, San Francisco, June 15-Sept. 8, 2002, and the National Gallery of Art, Washington, D.C., Sept. 29, 2002-Jan. 5, 2003
This is a collection of de Kooning's drawings and studies which led up to his controversial "Woman" series, accompanied by four essays discussing the works and their social ramifications
"Highly recommended for anyone interested in the phenomenon that was abstract expressionism. . . . Clearly written and carefully researched." Choice
Includes bibliographical references

Leonardo, da Vinci, 1452-1519

Leonardo da Vinci, master draftsman; edited by Carmen C. Bambach; with contributions by Carmen C. Bambach [et al.]; with the assistance of Rachel Stern and Alison Manges. Metropolitan Mus. of Art 2003 786p il $75; pa $50   **741**

ISBN 1-58839-033-0; 1-58839-034-9 (pa)
LC 2002-191234
Also available from Yale University Press
Catalog of an exhibition held at the Metropolitan Museum of Art, New York, Jan. 22-Mar. 30, 2003
This offers a "portrait of Leonardo as a draftsman, integrating his diverse roles as an artist, scientist, inventor,

Leonardo, da Vinci, 1452-1519—*Continued*
theorist, and teacher. Essays written by . . . Leonardo scholars investigate the significant implications of Leonardo's left-handedness . . . the relationship between word and image in Leonardo's drawings and manuscripts; problems of attribution and authenticity . . . Leonardo's early drapery studies; the role of the artist's father; and the special role of drawn frames or boundaries in Leonardo's design process. Detailed descriptions of 138 individual works survey the wide variety of drawing types that Leonardo used." Publisher's note

"This volume is unique in its in-depth inquiry into the creation, content, and significance of [Leonardo's] drawings, and in its glorious array of more than 500 superb reproductions." Booklist
Includes bibliographical references

741.2 Drawing—Techniques, equipment, materials

Blake, Marie, d. 1993
You can paint pastels; a step-by-step guide for absolute beginners. Watson-Guptill 2000 96p il pa $9.95   **741.2**
1. Pastel drawing
ISBN 0-8230-5990-1
In this introduction to paint pastels, the author "takes the student from simple marks on a page through tone, perspective, and so forth to simple still lifes, landscapes, and figures." Libr J

Harrison, Hazel
Master strokes, Pastels; a step-by-step guide to using the techniques of the masters. Sterling 1999 96p il $24.95   **741.2**
1. Drawing
ISBN 0-8069-2425-X   LC 98-46792
This work uses a series of paintings by acknowledged masters to illustrate various techniques required in contemporary pastel drawing

741.5 Cartoons, caricatures, comics

Bell, Clare
Hirschfeld's New York; text by Clare Bell; introduction by Frank Rich. Abrams 2001 95p il pa $15.95   **741.5**
1. Hirschfeld, Al, 1903-2003 2. New York (N.Y.) in art
ISBN 0-8109-2974-0   LC 2001-634
Published in association with the Museum of the City of New York
This catalog "by Clare Bell accompanies an exhibit at the Museum of the City of New York and showcases more than 100 drawings spanning [Hirschfeld's] career so far, from the 1920s through the '90s. No one and no place is safe from his gaze: Greenwich Village denizens in 1941 imitating 'movie folks in dress and manner'; wartime Broadway on a Saturday night; Upper West Side intelligentsia (including Irving Howe and Jason Epstein) thronging Zabar's in the '70s." Publ Wkly
Includes bibliographical references

Daniels, Les, 1943-
Marvel; five fabulous decades of the world's greatest comics; introduction by Stan Lee. Abrams 1991 287p il hardcover o.p. paperback available $26.95   **741.5**
1. Marvel comics (New York, N.Y.) 2. Comic books, strips, etc.
ISBN 0-8109-2566-4 (pa)   LC 91-8783
"Daniels' behind-the-scenes look at the development of Marvel, his profiles of the line's foremost heroes and villains, and biographies of leading writers and artists will entice . . . young fans. . . . But the book's strongest appeal lies in the generous samplings of artwork spread throughout." Booklist

Hart, Christopher
Cartooning for the beginner. Watson-Guptill 2000 144p il pa $19.95
                    741.5
1. Cartoons and caricatures
ISBN 0-8230-0586-0   LC 00-101905
This guide to cartooning techniques "covers the world of cartoon animals, animation, and 'edgy 'toons.'" Libr J

Hirschfeld, Al, 1903-2003
Hirschfeld on line. Applause Theatre Bk. Pubs. 1998 343p $59.95   **741.5**
1. Cartoons and caricatures 2. Entertainers
ISBN 1-55783-356-7
Hirschfeld "is the irreplaceable M.V.P. of the New York theatre world, and this compendium of his drawings amounts to a historic work of droll, generous-minded theatre criticism. The artist himself has annotated the drawings, which cover a range of the performing arts . . . and his comments are as swooping and witty as his lines." New Yorker

Kanfer, Stefan
Serious business; the art and commerce of animation in America from Betty Boop to Toy Story. Scribner 1997 256p il o.p.; Da Capo Press paperback available $17   **741.5**
1. Animated films
ISBN 0-306-80918-4 (pa)   LC 96-37819
"As an art form, animation is magically irresistible; as a reflection of broader American popular culture, it is amazingly on target. . . . Kanfer here shows how the people, politics, prejudices, trends, and technologies of various eras have been so aptly reflected in each set of frames. . . . While Kanfer's humbly stated intention is to augment previous writings on the subject, his work should certainly join the ranks of important literature in the field." Libr J
Includes bibliographical references

Leopold, David
Hirschfeld's Hollywood; the film art of Al Hirschfeld; text by David Leopold; foreword by Larry Gelbart. Abrams 2001 95p il pa $15.95   **741.5**
1. Hirschfeld, Al, 1903-2003 2. Motion pictures—Cartoons and caricatures
ISBN 0-8109-9052-0   LC 2001-2312
"Published in association with the Academy of Motion Picture Arts and Sciences"
This volume showcases Al Hirschfeld's "artwork for movie posters, billboards, murals, and theater displays

Leopold, David—*Continued*

with images of film stars from Laurel and Hardy to the Marx Brothers, Fred Astaire, and Julia Roberts; and for classic movies such as The Wizard of Oz, Singin' in the Rain, and The Manchurian Candidate." Publisher's note

McCloud, Scott

Reinventing comics; how imagination and technology are revolutionizing an art form. Paradox Press 2000 237p il pa $22.95 **741.5**

1. Comic books, strips, etc. 2. Cartoons and caricatures

ISBN 0-06-095350-0   LC 00-710457

The author maps out "'12 revolutions', which, he believes, need to take place for comics to survive and finally be recognized as a legitimate art form. The topics progress from the oldest of comic-related arguments (seeking respect) to the use of computer technology to renew and expand its audience. These brilliantly presented discussions concern comics as literature, comics as art, creators' rights, industry innovation, and public perception, among other topics." Libr J

The **World** encyclopedia of comics; edited by Maurice Horn. rev & updated. Chelsea House 1999 7v il set $87.50   **741.5**

1. Comic books, strips, etc.

ISBN 0-7910-4854-3   LC 97-50448

Also available single volume version $59.95 (ISBN 0-7910-4856-X)

First published 1976

Containing some 1400 signed entries, this reference work opens with historical and analytical essays and a chronology. "Then the listings begin, reporting on writers, artists, publishers, and characters galore, all mixed together alphabetically and covering information up to December 1997." Libr J

Wright, Bradford W., 1968-

Comic book nation; the transformation of youth culture in America. Johns Hopkins Univ. Press 2001 336p il $39.95; pa $19.95   **741.5**

1. Comic books, strips, etc.

ISBN 0-8018-6514-X; 0-8018-7450-5 (pa)   LC 00-10277

This book "traces the genre's birth, expansions, and retractions from the 1930s to the present. The fascinating result highlights an increasingly intriguing interaction between pressing events in American society and what was written and published on colorfully paneled pages." Libr J

Includes bibliographical references

741.6   Graphic design, illustration and commercial art

Carter, Alice A.

The art of National Geographic; a century of illustration; foreword by Stephen Jay Gould; afterword by Christopher P. Sloan. National Geographic Soc. 1999 239p il $50   **741.6**

ISBN 0-7922-7920-4   LC 99-13167

The images in this volume "are taken from 'National Geographic' and range from early oil paintings to ad-

vanced computer graphics—with text and biographies of illustrators such as Andrew Wyeth, James Audubon, James Gurney, and many others. Discover how, for example, N.C. Wyeth succeeded in portraying the physical as well the emotional experience of Byrd's flight over the North Pole." Publisher's note

Marcus, Leonard S., 1950-

Ways of telling; conversations on the art of the picture book. Dutton Children's Bks. 2002 247p il $29.99   **741.6**

1. Picture books for children 2. Illustrators 3. Authors

ISBN 0-525-46490-5   LC 2002-67499

Contents: Mitsumasa Anno; Ashley Brian; Eric Carle; Tana Hoban; Karla Kuskin; James Marshall; Robert McCloskey; Iona Opie; Helen Oxenbury; Jerry Pinkney; Maurice Sendak; William Steig; Rosemary Wells; Charlotte Zolotow

"This engaging volume offers insight into the creative process of each author and illustrator as well as the social and political contexts from which their work emerged." Publ Wkly

743   Drawing and drawings by subject

Hart, Christopher

Human anatomy made amazingly easy. Watson-Guptill 2000 114p il pa $19.95   **743**

1. Artistic anatomy 2. Figure drawing

ISBN 0-8230-2497-0   LC 00-43514

In this work for the beginning artist "Hart simplifies the process in an accessible manual that concentrates on line and forgoes the complexity of color." Libr J

745   Decorative arts

Designed for delight; alternative aspects of twentieth-century decorative arts; edited by Martin Eidelberg. Flammarion & Cie 1997 320p il $65   **745**

1. Decorative arts 2. Art—20th century

ISBN 2-08-013595-3   LC 96-52180

"This exhibition catalog provides color photographs of 200 objects from the permanent collection of the Montreal Museum of Decorative Arts. . . . Segments on body language, inversion and transformation, and fantasy are straightforward. The 'Is Ornament a Crime?' section traces the debate over the rightness of adorning utilitarian objects, and the opposing philosophies of the organic and geometric." Choice

Includes bibliographical references

Gifts to the tsars, 1500-1700; treasures of the Kremlin; Barry Shifman and Guy Walton, general editors. Abrams 2001 336p il $65   **745**

1. House of Romanov—Art collections 2. Decorative arts

ISBN 0-8109-0600-7   LC 2001-22185

Published in connection with an exhibition at the Indianapolis Museum of Art

This volume focuses "on the diplomatic gifts presented to Russian tsars from Ivan the Terrible to Peter the Great. . . . The photos reveal the splendor of Russian

Gifts to the tsars, 1500-1700—*Continued*
court life, while the essays focus on different aspects of diplomacy and Russian foreign relations, as well as on treasures ranging from gold and silver to furs and textiles to jewelry and decorative arts. The catalog is arranged by the gifts' country or empire of origin. . . . This dazzling and fascinating book is essential for any collection on Russian culture and history." Libr J
Includes bibliographical references

Kilby, Janice Eaton, 1955-
By hand; 25 beautiful objects to make in the American folk art tradition; {by} Janice Eaton Kilby with the assistance of Veronika Alice Gunter. Lark Bks. 2001 144p il hardcover o.p. paperback available $17.95
745
1. Handicraft
ISBN 1-57990-376-2 (pa)   LC 00-54974
This is a "survey collection of two dozen projects for familiar items, such as samplers, decoys, and copper weathervanes, that have been designed by professional artists. Each type of craft has a historic introduction and is illustrated by photographs of museum and gallery pieces. . . . A handy all-in-one source for public libraries." Libr J
Includes bibliographical references

Loring, John, 1939-
Tiffany's 20th century; a portrait of American style. Abrams 1997 240p il $60
745
1. Tiffany & Co. 2. Decorative arts
ISBN 0-8109-3887-1   LC 97-8128
In this volume "hundreds of brooches, bracelets, rings, earrings, necklaces, and accessories are shown in color against vintage photographs and drawings, including rare images from the Tiffany archives." Libr J

745.1   Antiques

Kovel, Ralph M.
Kovels' antiques and collectibles price list; [by] Ralph M. Kovel and Terry H. Kovel. Crown il pa $16.95   **745.1**
1. Antiques 2. Collectors and collecting
First published 1968 with title: The complete antiques price list. Revised annually to reflect current prices. Title varies
Current American market prices for 50,000 antiquities and collectibles. Included are photographs, factory marks and logos, catalogs, reports of sales, auctions, and tips on buying, collecting, restoring, and preserving

Kovels' know your antiques; {by} Ralph & Terry Kovel. rev & updated ed. Crown 1990 349p il pa $17   **745.1**
1. Antiques
ISBN 0-05-175786-9   LC 90-2509
First published 1967
"How to recognize and evaluate any antique, large or small, like an expert. Covers pottery, porcelain, silver, pewter, country and formal furniture, pressed and cut glass, prints, bottles, ironware, tinware, letters, sheet music, autographs, books, magazines, and more. Provides advice about caring for antiques and recognizing frauds. Has bibliographies for each specialty." N Y Public Libr Book of How & Where to Look It Up

Kovel's know your collectibles; {by} Ralph and Terry Kovel. Crown 1992 c1981 404p il hardcover o.p. paperback available $17
745.1
1. Antiques 2. Collectors and collecting
ISBN 0-517-58840-4 (pa)   LC 81-5515
"Advises on what collectible objects are likely to increase in value and how to preserve, protect, and sell them. Covers ceramics, pottery, furniture, glass, toys, print advertisements, and many other items. Has bibliographies for each major specialty." N Y Public Libr Book of How & Where to Look It Up

Maloney, David J.
Maloney's antiques & collectibles resource directory. Antique Trader Bks. pa $32.99
745.1
1. Antiques 2. Collectors and collecting
ISSN 1083-8449
First published 1992 by Wallace-Homestead with title: Collector's information clearinghouse antiques & collectibles resource directory. (7th edition 2004) Periodically revised
This includes listings of collectors, buyers, dealers, experts, clubs, periodicals, auctions, repairers, and suppliers for various categories of antiques and collectibles. Includes e-mail addresses and websites

Miller, Judith, 1951-
Care and repair of everyday treasures; a step-by-step guide to cleaning and restoring your antiques and collectibles. Reader's Digest Assn. 1997 256p il $29.95   **745.1**
1. Antiques—Conservation and restoration
ISBN 0-89577-924-2   LC 97-5506
This illustrated guide offers instructions for maintaining and restoring old furniture, leather, textiles, rugs and carpets, ceramics, glass, stone, metalware, and jewelry
"This well-illustrated guide emphasizes cleaning processes and damage repair rather than refinishing and restoration. . . . This is an excellent selection for public libraries." Libr J

Prisant, Carol
Antiques roadshow primer; the introductory guide to antiques and collectibles from the most-watched show on PBS. Workman 1999 366p il hardcover o.p. paperback available $19.95   **745.1**
1. Antiques roadshow (Television program) 2. Antiques
ISBN 0-7611-1624-9 (pa)   LC 99-29960
"The goal of this volume is to educate collectors about antiques and to help them evaluate pieces they find. . . . It highlights American antiques, focusing primarily on the types of antiques frequently seen on *Roadshow*." Libr J
Includes bibliographical references

745.2 Industrial art and design

Heskett, John
Toothpicks and logos; design in everyday life. Oxford Univ. Press 2002 214p il $24; pa $14.95 **745.2**
1. Industrial design 2. Creative ability
ISBN 0-19-280321-2; 0-19-280444-8 (pa)
LC 2001-55716
This overview of the concept of design "tackles a diverse range of subjects, from tableware to advertising campaigns. . . . [The author] takes the perspective of the end users (or receivers) and considers how they encounter design in their day-to-day lives—as objects, environments, communications materials, identities, wayfinding systems, etc." Libr J
"A notably lucid narrative rich in provocative examples." Booklist
Includes bibliographical references

745.4 Pure and applied design and decoration

The **Work** of Charles and Ray Eames; a legacy of invention; essays by Donald Albrecht ... {et al.}. Abrams 1997 205p il $49.50 **745.4**
1. Eames, Charles 2. Eames, Ray 3. Design
ISBN 0-8109-1799-8 LC 97-4086
Published "in association with the Library of Congress and the Vitra Design Museum"
This overview of the work of two prominent American postwar designers features "pictures of famous furniture, toys, exhibitions, promotional material, informal snapshots, stills from films, comics, advertisements, exhibitions for the federal government, and much more. The work features six major essays, each with extensive notes, by scholars, designers, academics, and architecture/design writers." Choice
Includes bibliographical references

745.5 Handicrafts

Lyons, Charlotte
Between friends; craft projects to share; photographs by Steven Randazzo. Simon & Schuster 2002 160p il $25 **745.5**
1. Handicraft
ISBN 0-7432-1409-9 LC 2002-17559
This book "presents ideas for 40 handmade craft projects . . . [including] papier-mâché, collage, découpage, knitting, needlework, painting, sewing, rug hooking, quilting, scrapbooking, and doll-making." Publisher's note
"Simple and to the point, each [project] is embellished with variations and scattered sidebars on forming different clubs (book, knitting, garden) and on different personal friendships." Booklist

745.54 Paper handicrafts

Ragsdale, Linda
Creative cardboard; making fabulous furniture, amazing accessories and other spectacular stuff. Lark Bks. 2002 144p il pa $18.95 **745.54**
1. Paper crafts
ISBN 1-57990-219-7 LC 2001-38516
This includes instructions for craft projects using cardboard, including frames, jewelry, a vase, room divider, display masks, wall sconces, a roll-top desk, and a "fainting couch"
"Ragsdale offers one of the most imaginative takes on paper crafts yet. Filled with groan-worthy puns, sharp color photographs, and detailed directions, this how-to tome also provides 20 patterns with upscale designs few could resist." Booklist

745.55 Shell handicrafts

Marshall, Marlene Hurley
Shell chic; the ultimate guide to decorating your home with seashells; photographs by Sabine Vollmer von Falken. Storey Bks. 2002 152p il $35 **745.55**
1. Handicraft 2. Shells
ISBN 1-58017-440-X LC 2002-1140
This "contains step-by-step projects for traditional items of shell art such as flower arrangements and shell-encrusted boxes, all interspersed with a colorful running narrative describing decorative uses of shells by contemporary designers." Libr J

745.58 Handicrafts from beads, found and other objects

Benson, Ann
Beading for the first time. Sterling 2000 112p il $19.95 **745.58**
1. Beadwork
ISBN 0-8069-6098-1 LC 00-48265
"Step-by-step instructions for jewelry and accessories are accompanied by large color photographs and line drawings. There are sections on materials and equipment with a gallery of the work of several bead artists." Libr J

Coles, Janet
Beads; an exploration of bead traditions around the world; {by} Janet Coles and Robert Budwig; photography by Jonathan Lovekin. Simon & Schuster 1997 159p il $27 **745.58**
1. Beadwork
ISBN 0-684-83462-6 LC 97-34005
The authors combine bead craft "projects with succinct explanations of history, manufacture, and artisanship. . . . They broadly separate the globe into five regions and, from that point, choose to focus on the best examples of bead making, contemporary and antique. . . . {Included} are 30 projects {mainly necklaces} that copy both old and new design styles, from a Victorian-era tasseled jet necklace to 1970s Philippine wooden jewelry." Booklist
Includes bibliographical references

Wells, Carol Wilcox

The art & elegance of beadweaving; new jewelry designs with classic stitches. Lark Bks. 2002 160p il $27.95; pa $14.95 **745.58**

1. Beadwork 2. Jewelry
ISBN 1-57990-200-6; 1-57990-533-1 (pa)
LC 2001-38958

Includes instructions for craft projects using beads and five types of weaving stitches

What the author "conjures up in more than 30 bracelets, earrings, and necklaces is nothing short of breathtaking." Booklist

745.59 Making specific objects

Banes, Helen

Fiber & bead jewelry; beautiful designs to make & wear; {by} Helen Banes with Sally Banes. Sterling 2000 128p il $27.95; pa $14.95 **745.59**

1. Beadwork 2. Jewelry
ISBN 0-8069-6082-9; 1-4027-0073-3 (pa)
LC 00-58316

"A Sterling\Chapelle book."

This "book has photos of many of {the author's} bead and fiber necklaces, with diagrammed patterns for the woven fiber parts. This off-loom needle weaving is worked over pins on a foam board in a technique similar to pillow lacemaking. . . . This unique approach to jewelry design belongs in art as well as advanced crafts collections." Libr J

Oppenheimer, Betty, 1957-

Candlemaker's companion; a complete guide to rolling, pouring, dipping, and decorating your own candles. Completely rev and updated. Storey Bks. 2001 199p il pa $18.95 **745.59**

1. Candles
ISBN 1-58017-366-7
LC 00-53802

First published 1997

This offers a brief history of candles followed by information about wicks, waxes and additives, color and scent, and equipment. Step-by-step instructions on candlemaking techniques and decoration, and a list of suppliers

Includes bibliographical references

Stewart, Martha

Handmade Christmas; the best of Martha Stewart living. Potter 1995 134p il pa $22 **745.59**

1. Christmas decorations 2. Handicraft
ISBN 0-517-88476-3
LC 95-21291

This is a "collection of recipes and projects for assembling . . . mostly easy gifts and decorations culled from the last four years worth of *Martha Stewart Living* magazine." Publ Wkly

745.6 Calligraphy, illumination, heraldic design

Child, Heather

Calligraphy today; twentieth century tradition & practice. [rev ed] Taplinger 1988 128p il $22.95 **745.6**

1. Calligraphy
ISBN 0-8008-1206-9

Original edition first published 1963 in the United Kingdom; first United States edition published 1964 by Watson-Guptill

"This largely pictorial survey embraces the development and practice of Western calligraphy. . . . Illustrations include examples of historical scripts and the work of some 100 calligraphers." Publisher's note

Includes bibliographical references

Harris, David, 1929-

The art of calligraphy. Dorling Kindersley 1995 128p il $25 **745.6**

1. Calligraphy
ISBN 1-56458-849-1
LC 94-26722

An "introduction to a wide variety of written scripts used from Roman times to modern days. The detailed, practical instructions for 26 styles focus on step-by-step, clear visuals, as well as on the proper equipment-- brushes, pens, pencils, paper, and ink. A brief history with examples from calligraphic masters introduces each style." SLJ

Lovett, Patricia

Calligraphy and illumination; a history and practical guide. Abrams 2000 320p il $39.95 **745.6**

1. Calligraphy 2. Illumination of books and manuscripts
ISBN 0-8109-4119-8
LC 00-31318

This book provides "instructions on everything from lettering techniques to a range of projects from basic page layouts to advanced design. Lovett explores the history of illuminated manuscripts as a fine art and as a design influence for today's artists. . . . The 225 illustrations, 175 in color, amply complement the text and include reproductions of some of the world's most exquisite illuminated manuscripts." Booklist

Includes bibliographical references

Shepherd, Margaret

Learn calligraphy; the complete book of lettering and design. Broadway Bks. 2001 167p il pa $16.95 **745.6**

1. Calligraphy
ISBN 0-7679-0732-9
LC 00-53016

This guide presents historical background, and advice on materials, technique, and workspace organization. Also included are recommended usages for the various alphabets. Step-by-step illustrations are provided

745.7 Decorative coloring

Fresh & fabulous painted furniture. Sterling 2000 128p il hardcover o.p. paperback available $14.95 **745.7**

1. Furniture 2. Stencil work
ISBN 0-8069-7797-3 (pa)
LC 99-55370

"A Sterling\Chapelle book."

Fresh & fabulous painted furniture—*Continued*

This describes 25 projects for painting furniture employing techniques such as stenciling, stamping, block-printing, and découpaging

Leigh, Tera, 1964-

The complete book of decorative painting. North Light Bks. 2001 256p il pa $29.99
745.7

1. Painting—Technique 2. Decoration and ornament
ISBN 1-58180-062-2   LC 2001-30364
This volume covers "materials and supplies, color, surfaces, techniques, brush strokes, lettering and borders, finishes, even five try-your-hand projects. What's unusual is the depth and breadth of the detail; Leigh features, for example, a full chapter on specialty brushes and their usage, as well as a separate one on classes, conventions, teachers, magazines, and other resources. A bible for novices *and* experienced painters." Booklist

Sloan, Annie

Modern paint effects; a guide to contemporary paint finishes from inspiration to technique. Firefly Bks. (Buffalo) 2000 128p il hardcover o.p. paperback available $19.95
745.7

1. Painting—Technique 2. Decoration and ornament
ISBN 1-55209-488-X (pa)
This book provides information on new paint products and how to use them. Advice on decorative techniques and color combinations is included

745.92   Floral arts

Hillier, Malcolm

Flowers. Dorling Kindersley 2000 516p il $40
745.92

1. Flower arrangement
ISBN 0-7894-5954-X   LC 00-29485
This book "features 150 floral display ideas using fresh and dried flowers. . . . {The author explains} elements of design (color, shape, and texture) and how to create displays for use in the home, for Thanksgiving and Christmas, at weddings, and in churches." Booklist

Jong-Stout, Alisa A. de

A master guide to the art of floral design; [by] Alisa A. de Jong-Stout with Hannah Sigur; photography by Douglas Sandberg; illustrations by Boris Jeanrenaud. Timber Press 2002 230p il $39.95
745.92

1. Flower arrangement
ISBN 0-88192-539-X   LC 2001-52465
This book "describes how shapes, forms, patterns, and textures found in the plant world reveal the key elements one calls upon when designing floral art. . . . Compelling photographs and appealing drawings accompany instructive text that expands on an aesthetic approach to the finer points of composition." Booklist
Includes bibliographical references

Miller, Cathy

Harvesting, preserving, and arranging dried flowers; photographs by Rob Gray. Artisan 1997 208p il $32.50
745.92

1. Flower arrangement 2. Flowers—Drying
ISBN 1-88518-351-8   LC 97-15287
The author "harvests the flowers from her upstate New York farm for lavish sprays and pots brimming with mixed blossoms and leaves. About half of her book is devoted to up-to-date methods for drying flowers such as microwaving and glycerinization. She provides an extensive drying chart that includes trees as well as the northern garden flowers grown in New York." Libr J
Includes bibliographical references

Pryke, Paula

Flowers, flowers! inspired arrangements for all occasions; photography by Kevin Summers. Rizzoli Int. Publs. 1993 191p il $39.95
745.92

1. Flower arrangement
ISBN 0-8478-1679-6   LC 93-862
This volume contains "sequences of photographs providing step-by-step instructions for creating arrangements. Separate sections deal with containers, the use of a single color range, and themes and period styles, while a 'Gazetteer' supplies the plant names, common and Latin, brief descriptions and necessary care instructions." Libr J

Stewart, Martha

Great American wreaths; created by Martha Stewart and Hannah Milman; directed by Gael Towey; photographs by William Abranowicz. Potter 1996 144p il maps pa $20
745.92

1. Handicraft
ISBN 0-517-88776-2   LC 96-70330
This offers instructions in creating 51 wreaths honoring the 50 states and the District of Columbia made from natural materials inspired by their locations, such as cranberries for Massachusetts and golden wheat for Oklahoma

746   Textile arts

Campbell, Thomas

Tapestry in the Renaissance; art and magnificence; [by] Thomas P. Campbell; with contributions by Maryan W. Ainsworth [et al.]; photography by Bruce White. Metropolitan Mus. of Art 2002 594p il $95
746

1. Tapestry 2. Art—15th and 16th centuries
ISBN 1-58839-021-7   LC 2001-55821
Also available from Yale University Press
Exhibition held at the Metropolitan Museum of Art from March 14 through June 19, 2002
"Contributing scholars examine the stylistic and technical development of tapestry production in the Low Countries, France, and Italy during the Renaissance, and discuss the contribution that the medium made to art, liturgy, and propaganda of the day." Publisher's note
Includes bibliographical references

746.1   Yarn preparation and weaving

Blumenthal, Betsy, 1943-
Hands on dyeing; {by} Betsy Blumenthal & Kathryn Kreider; illustrations by Ann Sabin. Interweave Press 1988 111p il pa $16.95   **746.1**
1. Dyes and dyeing
ISBN 0-934026-36-X   LC 88-12260
The authors provide techniques and tips on a variety of hand-dyeing projects. Equipment, yarns, dyes, pots, and finishing are covered
Includes bibliographical references

Brown, Rachel
The weaving, spinning, and dyeing book; illustrated by Rachel Brown and Cheryl McGowen. 2nd ed, rev and expanded. Knopf 1983 430p il pa $40   **746.1**
1. Weaving 2. Spinning 3. Dyes and dyeing
ISBN 0-394-71595-0   LC 83-176576
First published 1978
Following a chapter of general information about weaving the author discusses Navajo weaving, Hopi sash weaving, counterbalanced looms, inkle looms, card weaving, spinning and natural dyeing. Directions are provided for 50 projects. Over 400 line drawings and color illustrations accompany the text

Irwin, Bobbie
Spin off magazine presents the Spinner's companion. Interweave Press 2001 112p il pa $19.95   **746.1**
1. Spinning
ISBN 1-88301-079-9   LC 2001-39266
This handbook includes "information on spinning, drafting, plying, fiber storage, and much more. This richly illustrated manual includes an excellent bibliography and a resource list. Public libraries with any interest in this subject will want this one." Libr J

746.4   Needlework and handwork

Reader's Digest complete guide to needlework. Reader's Digest Assn. 1979 504p il $30   **746.4**
1. Needlework
ISBN 0-89577-059-8
Editor: Virginia Colton
A guide to ten different needle crafts, "containing the ABCs, stitches, and techniques anyone would need to start—and finish—a particular crafts project. All aspects of the major forms of needlecraft are covered, from appliqué to rugmaking." Booklist

746.41   Weaving, braiding, matting unaltered vegetable fibers

Sentance, Bryan
Art of the basket; traditional basketry from around the world. Thames & Hudson 2001 216p il $45   **746.41**
1. Basketwork
ISBN 0-500-51048-2   LC 2001-86840
This is a survey of basketry worldwide divided into five sections: materials, techniques, decoration, everyday basketry, and wider applications
Includes bibliographical references

746.43   Knitting, crocheting, tatting

Breiter, Barbara
The complete idiot's guide to knitting and crocheting; illustrated; by Barbara Breiter and Gail Diven. 2nd ed. Alpha Bks. (NY) 2003 xx, 231p il pa $16.95   **746.43**
1. Knitting 2. Crocheting
ISBN 1-59257-089-5   LC 2003-108338
First published 1999 under the authorship of Gail Diven and Cindy Kitchel
This offers instruction for beginners in knitting and crocheting and includes projects and illustrations

Budd, Ann, 1956-
The knitter's handy book of patterns; basic designs in multiple sizes and gauges. Interweave Press 2002 112p pa $24.95   **746.43**
1. Knitting
ISBN 1-931499-04-7   LC 2001-59208
The patterns in this book "allow the knitter to create garments in any size from toddler to extra-large adult in any weight of yarn, from fingering to bulky. The knitter has only to knit a generous swatch with yarn and needles of her/his choice and plug the resulting gauge information into the charted instructions and schematics provided. Highly recommended for all knitting collections." Libr J

Buss, Katharina
Big book of knitting. Sterling 1999 239p il hardcover o.p. paperback available $19.95   **746.43**
1. Knitting
ISBN 0-8069-6317-4 (pa)   LC 99-20386
Original German edition, 1996
This is an "illustrated knitting reference particularly strong in its coverage of both basic techniques like increasing and decreasing and more advanced techniques like knitting cables without a cable needle, working with charts, and placing sleeve increases in openwork patterns." Libr J

Ham, Catherine
25 gorgeous sweaters for the brand new knitter. Lark Bks. 2000 127p il $24.95; pa $17.95 **746.43**
1. Knitting
ISBN 1-57990-172-7; 1-57990-437-8 (pa)
LC 00-30953
This volume features "cardigans, jackets, vests, tunics, cropped tops, kid wear, and more. {Included are} tips and ideas for embellishments that transform a plain-knit sweater into a statement—specialty buttons and closures, easy embroidery, and more." Publisher's note
Includes bibliographical references

Kagan, Sasha
Sasha Kagan's country inspiration; knitwear for all seasons; photographs by Jack Deutsch. Taunton Press 2000 170p il $27.95 **746.43**
1. Knitting
ISBN 1-56158-338-3 LC 99-52956
This book features 45 knitting patterns. "Most of the patterns are for sweaters, but there are also throws, caps, and coats. Kagan takes her inspiration from the Welsh countryside where she lives. The knitwear is grouped by topics such as roses, autumn leaves, meadow flowers, and forest fruits." Booklist

KnitLit: sweaters and their stories and other writing about knitting; Linda Roghaar & Molly Wolf, editors. Three Rivers Press (NY) 2002 270p pa $13 **746.43**
1. Knitting
ISBN 0-609-80824-9 LC 2002-5962
This book "is really about what it means to create something. Sometimes, as many knitters know, there is only the dream of what could be, as unused yarn gathers dust. But that's what's so nice about this book of knitters' personal remembrances. . . . People who love to knit will love this book." Booklist
Includes bibliographical references

Newton, Deborah
Designing knitwear. Taunton Press 1992 263p il hardcover o.p. paperback available $24.95 **746.43**
1. Knitting
ISBN 1-56158-265-4 (pa) LC 91-36451
"A Threads book"
In this book for experienced knitters the author "lets out all the stops, revealing working methods, knitwear design tips, and techniques that have taken her years to perfect." Libr J
Includes bibliographical references

Tracy, Gloria
Crochet your way; a learn to crochet afghan, over 40 projects for home and family, easy-to-understand text and symbols, special instructions for left-handers; {by} Gloria Tracy and Susan Levin. Taunton Press 2000 218p il pa $22.95 **746.43**
1. Crocheting
ISBN 1-56158-310-3 LC 99-58398
An explanation of basics "including simple and complex stitches, alternative chain techniques, color tips, and felting instructions." Booklist

Turner, Pauline
How to crochet; the definitive crochet course, complete with step-by-step techniques, stitch libraries, and projects for your home and family. Collins & Brown; [distributed by] Sterling 2001 160p il $29.95 **746.43**
1. Crocheting
ISBN 1-85585-827-4
"This is a complete crochet course presented as a series of workshops that cover not only standard crochet but also those varieties of crochet that do not employ a standard crochet hook, such as Tunisian, broomstick, and hairpin crochet. Each workshop features an illustrative project, full-color illustrations of techniques, and step-by-step instructions. . . . Public libraries will want to add this title to their short list of essential crochet books." Libr J

Vogue knitting; the ultimate knitting book; by the editors of Vogue Knitting Magazine. Sixth & Spring 2003 280p il $38.95 **746.43**
1. Knitting
ISBN 1-931543-16-X LC 2002-17571
Reissue of the title first published 1989 by Pantheon Bks.
"Following an introductory chapter on the history of knitting, the editors offer tips on how to understand knitting instructions and advice on the whole range of basic and advanced techniques. A stitch dictionary containing instructions and a photo for over 120 stitches is a real bonus. The book also contains patterns for what are referred to as 'classic sweaters.'" Booklist [review of 1989 edition]

Vogue knitting American collection; edited by Trisha Malcolm. Butterick Pub. Co 2000 160p il $29.95; pa $19.95 **746.43**
1. Knitting
ISBN 1-573-89020-0; 1-931543-10-0 (pa)
LC 00-40365
This book features patterns from the top 10 American designers featured in the magazine. . . . Except for 2 patterns, all of the more than 50 of them are targeted to the intermediate or experienced knitter. Booklist

746.44 Embroidery

Greenoff, Jane
The cross stitcher's bible. David & Charles 2000 176p il hardcover o.p. paperback available $18.99 **746.44**
1. Cross-stitch
ISBN 0-7153-1470-X (pa)
The author explains the needlecraft and its techniques. He provides instructions on working with charts, tips on threads and wools as well as creative options from charms to blackwork. "A 39-stitch and 59-motif library will give sewers a wide spread of available projects, whether a single-object Victorian posy or complex winter sampler." Booklist
Includes bibliographical references

746.46   Patchwork and quilting

Barnes, Christine
Color; the quilter's guide. That Patchwork Place 1997 127p il pa $29.95   **746.46**
1. Quilting
ISBN 1-56477-164-4   LC 96-37060
The author emphasizes the importance of color value to quilters and provides exercises and examples geared to individuals and classes
"An excellent book that should be a popular addition to all public library quilting collections." Libr J
Includes bibliographical references

Fassett, Kaffe
Glorious patchwork; more than 25 glorious quilt designs; {by} Kaffe Fassett with Liza Prior Lucy; special photography by Debbie Patterson. Potter 1997 160p il $35   **746.46**
1. Quilting
ISBN 0-517-70853-1   LC 97-24317
The author offers instructions and diagrams for patchwork projects for curtains, cushions, and table covers as well as quilts. The projects are divided into five color themes: soft pastels, circus, leafy gardens, antique stone, and Renaissance

Kavaya, Karol
Community quilts; how to organize, design, and make a group quilt; by Karol Kavaya and Vicki Skemp. Lark Bks. 2001 136p il $27.95; pa $17.95   **746.46**
1. Quilts 2. Quilting
ISBN 1-57990-181-6; 1-57990-377-0 (pa)
     LC 00-46378
This work presents three beginners projects and "a gallery of community quilts that includes background information, full-color photos, and working notes as well as a practical, step by-step method for planning, organizing, and making a group quilt." Libr J
Includes bibliographical references

Michler, J. Marsha
The magic of crazy quilting; a complete resource for embellished quilting. 2nd ed. Krause Publs. 2004 160p il pa $24.99
   746.46
1. Quilting 2. Needlework
ISBN 0-87349-724-4
First published 1998
"Michler takes the reader step by step through the creation of a crazy quilt and in the process teaches four different piecing methods, 15 embellishments, and more than 1000 embroidery stitch variations. Stitches are divided into broad groups and include stitch diagrams, color photos, and suggestions for use." Libr J
Includes bibliographical references

746.6   Textile printing, painting, dyeing

Wells, Kate, 1959-
Fabric dyeing & printing. Interweave Press 1997 192p il $39.95   **746.6**
1. Dyes and dyeing 2. Textile printing
ISBN 1-88301-035-7   LC 97-16366
This describes more than 30 fabric dyeing and printing techniques including block, screen, and resist dyeing, devore, and others
The techniques espoused by "Wells, and the resulting fabrics, are brilliant enough to inspire any and all attempts at dyeing and printing textiles." Booklist
Includes bibliographical references

747   Interior decoration

Decorating basics; styles, colors, furnishings. Meredith Press (NY) 2001 160p il pa $19.95   **747**
1. Interior design
ISBN 0-696-21197-1   LC 2001-130197
Cover title: Better Homes and Gardens decorating basics
"This book provides a look at homeowners' decorating schemes in a variety of styles, such as traditional, mid-century modern, and southwestern, through numerous color photographs captioned with budget-stretching tips and the homeowners' decorating tips. Chapters that illustrate the use of color, pattern, furniture, and wall and window treatments . . . follow these real-life decorating examples." Libr J

Gilliatt, Mary
The complete book of home design. rev ed. Little, Brown 1989 384p il $50   **747**
1. Interior design
ISBN 0-316-31406-4   LC 88-83396
First published 1984
"Emphasis is on use of space; choice of fabrics, prints, furniture, and accessories and their arrangement; and technical considerations, such as lighting. The beautifully designed format makes effective use of many high-quality color photographs and line drawings." Libr J

Jordan, Wendy Adler, 1946-
The kidspace idea book; [by] Wendy A. Jordan. Taunton Press 2001 168p il $29.95; pa $24.95   **747**
1. Interior design
ISBN 1-56158-352-9; 1-56158-617-X (pa)
     LC 00-51026
"Jordan believes that functional space should be designed for children and adults throughout the house. Large and colorful photographs illustrate details described in the text. Ideas include creating fun yet safe bathrooms, dynamic and playful bedrooms, and built-in storage space." Libr J
Includes bibliographical references

Michael, Michele

The new apartment book; {by} Michele Michael; text with Wendy S. Israel; photographs by Jeff McNamara. Potter 1996 207p il pa $30 **747**
1. Interior design
ISBN 0-517-88759-2   LC 96-296
First published 1979 with title: The apartment book
This offers ideas for apartment decoration discussing principals of function, style, and color in terms of time, space, and budget constraints
"More than 250 color photos and some valuable tips, such as buying the best sofa that one can afford, make this a handsome guide." Publ Wkly

The **New** decorating book. Better Homes & Gardens Bks. $34.95; pa $24.95 **747**
1. Interior design
First published 1956 with title: Better Homes and Gardens decorating book. (8th edition 2003) Periodically revised
This guide to home decorating discusses style, budgeting, color schemes, furniture, fabrics and patterns, window treatments, and accessories and includes floor plans, and furniture templates

Saunders, Gill

Wallpaper in interior decoration. Watson-Guptill 2002 160p il $40 **747**
1. Wallpaper 2. Interior design
ISBN 0-8230-5622-8   LC 2001-96618
"Beginning in the 17th century and continuing to the present [the author] details the use of wallpaper in domestic interiors, primarily in Great Britain but also including some examples from the United States. The book is illustrated with historic photos, paintings, sample books, and in-situ examples and employs text from literature and contemporary social commentary. Also discussed is the evolution of the decorative designs." Libr J

Includes bibliographical references

747.2 Interior decoration— Historical and geographic treatment

Slesin, Suzanne, 1944-

Japanese style; {by} Suzanne Slesin, Stafford Cliff & Daniel Rosensztroch; photographs by Gilles De Chabaneix. Potter 1987 287p il $45 **747.2**
1. Japanese decoration and ornament 2. Interior design
ISBN 0-517-56080-1   LC 87-2269
Photographs and a brief text illustrate traditional and modern extremes in Japanese homes, ranging from centuries-old country houses to contemporary apartments

748.5 Stained, painted, leaded, mosaic glass

Zaccaria, Donatella

Stained glass crafting. Sterling 1998 159p il hardcover o.p. paperback available $19.95 **748.5**
1. Glass painting and staining
ISBN 0-8069-4329-7 (pa)   LC 98-3575
The author "gears her explanations to both beginners and experienced crafters through step-by-step projects illustrated with photographs. Five patterns . . . become the basis for learning two stained-glass techniques: copper foil with lead and 'straight' lead soldering. Each technique includes excellent closeup photographs of the cutting, trimming, welding, and sealing processes, with enough text to guide unsteady hands." Booklist

749 Furniture and accessories

Lloyd, John, 1956-

Furniture restoration; a professional at work. Guild of Master Craftsman Publs.; [distributed by] Sterling 2001 121p il pa $17.95 **749**
1. Furniture—Repairing 2. Furniture finishing
ISBN 1-86108-220-7   LC 2002-391624
"In a collection of articles originally published in *Furniture & Cabinetmaking* magazine, British furniture restorer Lloyd shows how to fix a variety of furnishings properly. . . . More a survey than a step-by-step guide, this work assumes that the reader has some woodworking knowledge and should be of value to anyone with an in-depth interest in furniture restoration." Libr J

Logan, M. David

Mat, mount and frame it yourself. Watson-Guptill 2002 160p il pa $24.95 **749**
1. Picture frames and framing 2. Decoration and ornament
ISBN 0-8230-3038-5   LC 2001-93246
This describes how to mat, mount, and frame art on paper or cloth, how to determine measurements and proportions, select colors, and glaze, install, and hang framed art
"Logan does a great job of explaining everything and supplements the text with attractive photos. . . . There is something here for framers of all skill levels." Libr J

749.2 Furniture—Historical and geographic treatment

Keno, Leigh

Hidden treasures; searching for masterpieces of American furniture; {by} Leigh Keno and Leslie Keno with Joan Barzilay Freund. Warner Bks. 2000 304p il hardcover o.p. paperback available $15.95 **749.2**
1. Antiques 2. Furniture
ISBN 0-446-67816-3 (pa)   LC 00-39891
The authors, who appear on the television program Antiques Roadshow, discuss collecting antiques
"Part autobiography, part antiques history and auction

Keno, Leigh—*Continued*
lore, {this book} captures the same irrepressible enthusiam for American furniture that the two men exhibit on television." Christ Sci Monit
Includes bibliographical references

Kirk, John T.
American furniture; understanding styles, construction, and quality. Abrams 2000 234p il $39.95   **749.2**
1. American furniture
ISBN 0-8109-4220-8   LC 00-27157
"Organized by period and style, the text covers . . . the evolutionary development of furniture from the 17th century to the present, forcusing on the regional movements and variations found in certain pieces." Libr J
Includes bibliographical references

Morley, John, 1933-2001
The history of furniture; twenty-five centuries of style and design in the Western tradition. Little, Brown 1999 352p il $75
     749.2
1. Furniture
ISBN 0-8212-2624-X   LC 99-65084
Published in the United Kingdom with title: Furniture: the western tradition
This volume "explicates the use of various design features, motifs, and ornaments throughout history. The 12 broad sections, which focus on such categories as antiquity, classicism, neoclassicism, eclectic revivalism, functionalism, and non-Western styles, are subdivided into individual chapters. . . . This book is invaluable to most reference collections focusing on the decorative arts." Libr J
Includes bibliographical references

750 Painting and paintings

Manguel, Alberto
Reading pictures; a history of love and hate. Random House 2001 337p il hardcover o.p. paperback available $16.95   **750**
1. Art criticism 2. Art appreciation
ISBN 0-375-75922-0 (pa)   LC 2001-19428
Manguel "explores works from a diverse collection of artists, ranging across Western art history, from the ancient Greek painter Philoxenus, to Lavinia Fontana and Caravaggio, to artists of our own century, including Picasso, Joan Mitchell, and Tina Modotti." Libr J
This is an "intellectual joyride through various 'readings' of images." Booklist
Includes bibliographical references

750.1 Painting—Philosophy and theory

Livingstone, Margaret S.
Vision and art; the biology of seeing; by Margaret Livingstone; foreword by David Hubel. Abrams 2002 208p il $45   **750.1**
1. Perception 2. Vision 3. Painting
ISBN 0-8109-0406-3   LC 2001-46508
The author "explains how great artists exploit the functions of the human eye and brain. . . . [She] offers

a detailed explanation of how elements like perspective, luminance, color mixing, shading and chiaroscuro produce certain effects in art works." Publ Wkly
Livingstone's "enthusiasm for her subject electrifies even the most technical of her excursions. . . . [She combines] lively prose, outstanding illustrations, including works by Renoir, Degas, Seurat, and Chuck Close, and easily performed visual experiments." Booklist
Includes bibliographical references

751 Techniques, procedures, apparatus, equipment, materials, forms

Hockney, David
Secret knowledge; rediscovering the lost techniques of the old masters. Viking 2001 296p il $60   **751**
1. Painting—Technique 2. Drawing
ISBN 0-670-03026-0   LC 2001-26022
This book argues that "Western art took its decisive turn, into the age of photographic realism, 400 years before chemical photography. From the 1430's onward, many major artists . . . secretly used optical devices to make their masterpieces." N Y Times Book Rev
"David Hockney is blessed with an ability to write in a way that illuminates the work of others and to encourage a new intensity of seeing." New Statesman (Engl)
Includes bibliographical references

The **Tale** of Genji; legends and paintings; introduction by Miyeko Murase. Braziller 2001 136p il $45   **751**
1. Murasaki Shikibu, b. 978? Tale of Genji
ISBN 0-8076-1500-5   LC 2001-35321
54 paintings from the Burke albums "attributed to Tosa Mitsuoki (1617-1691) . . . however, they were more likely done by an anonymous artist of the Tosa school." Cf. Introduction, p. 2
This volume presents "a cycle of small, square-format seventeenth-century images that follow the chapters of Lady Murasaki's classic novel of courtly intrigue and love." New Repub
"Exquisitely made, this volume is a delight to hold and to read." Libr J
Includes bibliographical references

751.2 Painting—Materials

Mayer, Ralph, 1895-1979
The artist's handbook of materials and techniques. 5th ed, revised and updated by Steven Sheehan. Viking 1991 761p il $45
     751.2
1. Artists' materials 2. Pigments 3. Painting—Technique
ISBN 0-670-83701-6   LC 90-50357
First published 1940
Partial contents: Pigments; Oil painting; Acrylics; Tempera painting; Watercolor and gouache; Pastel; Solvents and thinners; Conservation of pictures
Includes bibliographical references

751.4 Painting—Techniques and procedures

Weber, Mark Christopher, 1949-
Brushwork essentials; how to render expressive form and texture with every stroke. North Light Bks. 2002 143p il $28.99
751.4
1. Painting—Technique
ISBN 1-58180-168-8   LC 2001-52162
This "book deals exclusively with oil brushwork. Painters learn how to render expressive form and texture using the myriad shapes and types of brushes available. Mixing and loading paint, cleaning and shaping brushes for maximum control, and picking the right paint for specific types of strokes are all covered." Libr J
"Weber writes with humor and confidence, keeping things lighthearted whether he is teaching the mechanics of holding a brush or a wet-into-wet application of paint on canvas." Booklist

751.42 Watercolor painting

Crawshaw, Alwyn
You can paint watercolors; a step-by-step guide for absolute beginners. Watson-Guptill 2000 96p il pa $9.95   **751.42**
1. Watercolor painting—Technique
ISBN 0-8230-5989-8   LC 00-104483
This introduction to watercolors covers basic washes, color mixing, light and shadow, a variety of still life subjects, and composition

Kunz, Jan, 1942-
Painting beautiful watercolors from photographs. North Light Bks. 1998 128p il hardcover o.p. paperback available $22.99
751.42
1. Watercolor painting—Technique
ISBN 1-581-80431-8 (pa)   LC 97-27742
The author makes a "case for painting from photographs. While this method is often maligned, Kunz points out that it allows one to paint in a situation where weather doesn't change, children don't wiggle, flowers don't wilt, and reflections stay in place. To keep such paintings from seeming static, she suggests doing outdoor sketches and keeping notes at the time of each photo session. Kunz includes instruction on shooting photographs and transferring them to sketches, along with nine nicely done demonstrations." Libr J

Lindsay, Ann K., 1948-
Watercolor; a new beginning: a Holistic approach to painting. Watson-Guptill 1997 144p il pa $24.95   **751.42**
1. Watercolor painting—Technique
ISBN 0-8230-5638-4   LC 97-30967
The author's "approach to teaching watercolor emerges from somewhere between the traditional art world and the deep, mystic spaces of the self. . . . Lindsay's unique work will strike a chord with many beginning artists who respond to a more personal, even spiritual tone. So handsomely designed that it's hard to resist leafing through it." Libr J

MacKenzie, Gordon
The watercolorist's essential notebook. North Light Bks. 1999 144p il $24.99
751.42
1. Watercolor painting—Technique
ISBN 0-89134-919-7   LC 99-40862
This "guide to watercolor materials and processes . . . {includes} observations, tips, and methods for designing strong compositions, achieving different textures, utilizing masking materials, setting up a palette, and working with transparent as well as deeply hued colors." Booklist

751.7 Paintings—Specific forms

Seligman, Patricia, 1950-
Painting murals; images, ideas, and techniques. North Light Bks. 1988 c1987 168p il pa $22.99   **751.7**
1. Mural painting and decoration
ISBN 1-5818-0470-9   LC 88-9963
"A Macdonald Orbis book"
First published 1987 in the United Kingdom
A "do-it-yourself course in mural painting. . . . Seligman covers all the procedures and processes involved, providing clear and thorough instructions. Materials, equipment, techniques, designs, and procedures are all examined as the author shows how to create trompe l'oeil effects ranging from small designs to huge wall-sized murals." Booklist
Includes bibliographical references

752 Color in painting

Pyle, David
What every artist needs to know about paints & colors. Krause Publs. 2000 144p il $29.95   **752**
1. Color 2. Painting
ISBN 0-87341-831-X   LC 99-69484
"Covers the history of how color is used, how paints and colors are made, pigment characteristics, and how to choose and use modern artists' colors." Libr J
Includes bibliographical references

757 Human figures

Virtue & beauty; Leonardo's Ginevra de' Benci and Renaissance portraits of women; [by] David Alan Brown [et al.] National Gallery of Art 2001 236p il $60   **757**
1. Leonardo, da Vinci, 1452-1519. Ginevra de' Benci 2. Women—Portraits 3. Women in art
ISBN 0-691-09057-2   LC 2001-30333
Also available in paperback from Princeton Univ. Press
Catalog of an exhibition held at the National Gallery of Art
This "volume of paintings, sculpture, medals, and drawings celebrates the flowering of female portraiture in Florence beginning in the latter half of the fifteenth century. Included are many of the finest portraits of women (and a few of men) by Sandro Botticelli, Domenico Ghirlandaio, Filippo Lippi, Antonio del Pollaiuolo, Andrea del Verrocchio, and Leonardo da Vin-

Virtue & beauty—*Continued*

ci." Publisher's note

"Illustrated with beautiful color reproductions, this highly readable volume is recommended for all libraries with art collections." Libr J

Includes bibliographic references

758 Other subjects in painting

Rowell, Margit

Objects of desire; the modern still life. Museum of Modern Art 1997 231p il $50

    758

1. Still-life painting 2. Art—20th century

ISBN 0-87070-110-X   LC 96-80496

This is the catalog of an exhibition at the Museum of Modern Art on 20th-century still lifes. There are "more than 130 pieces in the survey—opening with Picasso's proto-Cubist 'Pitcher, Bowl, and Lemon' (1907); proceeding through Dada objects, Surrealist allegories, and Pop icons; and concluding with mostly sculptural works from the 1990s. . . . The book provides access to works from many of the world's greatest collections and a very readable text." Libr J

759 Painting—Historical and geographic treatment

Beckett, Wendy

Sister Wendy's 1000 masterpieces; [by] Sister Wendy Beckett; contributing consultant, Patricia Wright. DK Pub. 1999 512p il $40   **759**

1. Painting 2. Art appreciation

ISBN 0-7894-4603-0   LC 99-20355

This work reproduces 1000 works of art from over 500 artists. Arranged alphabetically, each artist is represented by two paintings. Use of symbolism, technique and artistic inspiration are discussed. Includes a directory of museums and galleries where the original works are displayed

The story of painting; contributing consultant, Patricia Wright. 2nd American ed, enhanced & expanded ed. Dorling Kindersley 2000 736p il $40   **759**

1. Painting

ISBN 0-7894-6805-0   LC 2001-266885

First published 1994

"In association with the National Gallery of Art, Washington, D.C."

This history of painting over the past 800 years chronicles movements such as Romanticism, Impressionism, Post-Impressionism and Modernism, focusing on 450 masterpieces and including timelines

Understanding paintings; themes in art explored and explained; general editor, Alexander Sturgis; consultant editor, Hollis Clayton. Watson-Guptill 2000 272p il $45

    759

1. Painting

ISBN 0-8230-5579-5

This volume covers "the history of painting on a thematic and topical basis. Rather than focusing on impor-

tant epochs or 'big' names, the authors slice the time line into nine categories: religious painting, mythology, the nude, history painting, portraiture, landscape painting, genre, still life, and abstraction. Within each category, numerous variations of each are summarized in brief essays and illustrated by well-selected high points of the form." Libr J

Includes bibliographic references

759.13 American painting

Avery, Kevin J.

American drawings and watercolors in the Metropolitan Museum of Art; [by] Kevin J. Avery with essay by Marjorie Shelley and contributions by Claire A. Conway; catalogue entries by Kevin J. Avery [et al.] v1: A catalogue of works by artists born before 1835. Metropolitan Mus. of Art 2002 424p il $90   **759.13**

1. Metropolitan Museum of Art (New York, N.Y.) 2. American art 3. Watercolor painting

ISBN 1-58839-060-8   LC 2002-67772

Catalog of an exhibition at the Metropolitan Museum of Art held Sept. 3, 2002 to Jan. 5, 2003

"This volume documents the draftsmanship of more than 150 known artists before 1835 and that of about 60 unidentified artists of the period. It includes drawings and watercolors by such American masters as John Singleton Copley, John Trumbull, John Vanderlyn, Thomas Cole, Asher Brown Durand, George Inness, and James Abbott McNeill Whistler." Publisher's note

"A collection catalog as well made and as important as this one deserves to be on the shelves of all larger libraries, and academic and museum libraries in particular would be embarrassed not to have it in their collections." Libr J

Includes bibliographic references

Carter, Alice A.

The Red Rose girls; an uncommon story of art and love. Abrams 2000 216p il hardcover o.p. paperback available $19.95   **759.13**

1. Smith, Jessie Willcox, 1863-1935 2. Green, Elizabeth Shippen, 1871-1954 3. Oakley, Violet, 1874-1961

ISBN 0-8109-9068-7 (pa)   LC 99-39866

"Three of the first American women artists to achieve fame and fortune in the Victorian era—Jessie Willcox Smith, Elizabeth Shippen Green and Violet Oakley—lived unconventional lives marked by a remarkable degree of collaboration. In this . . . study, Carter explores the trio's internecine artistic and romantic relations." Publ Wkly

Includes bibliographic references

Cassatt, Mary, 1844-1926

Mary Cassatt, modern woman; organized by Judith A. Barter; with contributions by Erica E. Hirshler {et al.}. Abrams 1998 376p il $65   **759.13**

ISBN 0-8109-4089-2   LC 98-7306

Published to accompany a traveling exhibition opening at the Art Institute of Chicago

The contributors to this volume provide data on the life and work of Cassatt and to Impressionist art history in general. Six independent essays reveal new aspects of

Cassatt, Mary, 1844-1926—*Continued*

the artist's work and personality. . . . In addition, there are 300 illustrations, including 124 excellent color plates, and a 25-page illustrated chronology with maps. Libr J
Includes bibliographical references

Cikovsky, Nicolai, Jr.

Winslow Homer; {by} Nicolai Cikovsky, Jr., Franklin Kelly; with contributions by Judith Walsh and Charles Brock. National Gallery of Art; Yale Univ. Press 1995 420p il $80   **759.13**
1. Homer, Winslow, 1836-1910
ISBN 0-300-06555-8 (Yale Univ. Press)
LC 95-19025
In this catalog of the American artist's retrospective exhibition, the contributors "present a contextually rich and vibrant analysis of Homer's life and groundbreaking work." Booklist
Includes bibliographical references

Cohen-Solal, Annie

Painting American; the rise of American artists, Paris 1867-New York 1948; translated from the French with Laurie Hurwitz-Attias. Knopf 2001 436p il $30   **759.13**
1. American painting
ISBN 0-679-45093-9   LC 2001-32669
Original French edition, 2000
The author "offers a broad overview of the shift of artistic center from Paris to New York throughout the late 19th and early 20th centuries." Libr J
"When writing about the founders, trustees, directors and staffs of museums, [the author] is consistently rewarding. . . . Ms Cohen-Solal is at her best when mining the private history of the art trade." Economist
Includes bibliographical references

Discovered lands, invented pasts; transforming visions of the American West; {by} Jules David Prown {et al.}. Yale Univ. Press 1992 217p il pa $37.50

759.13
1. West (U.S.) in art 2. Native Americans—Pictorial works 3. American art
ISBN 0-300-05731-8   LC 92-53537
This "reinterpretation of western American art of the past three centuries reevaluates works by such artists as Bierstadt, Moran, and O'Keeffe from the perspectives of history, art history, and American studies." Univ Press Books for Public and Second Sch Libr
Includes bibliographical references

Edward Hopper and the American imagination; [by] Deborah Lyons and Adam D. Weinberg; Julie Grau, editor; with contributions by Paul Auster [et al.] Norton 1995 252p il $25   **759.13**

1. Hopper, Edward, 1882-1967
ISBN 0-393-31329-8   LC 95-4133
Catalog of an exhibition held at the Whitney Museum, 1995
This volume "reproduces 59 Hopper paintings interspersed with short pieces by major American writers. Entries include selections from William Kennedy's *Ironweed* and Paul Auster's *Moon Palace*; there are stories from Ann Beattie, James Salter and Grace Paley and

poems from Galway Kinnell, Thom Gunn, John Hollander, Tess Gallagher and others." Publ Wkly
Includes bibliographical references

Ferber, Linda S.

Masters of color and light; Homer, Sargent, and the American watercolor movement; {by} Linda S. Ferber and Barbara Dayer Gallati. Smithsonian Institution Press 1998 223p il $55   **759.13**
1. Homer, Winslow, 1836-1910 2. Sargent, John Singer, 1856-1925 3. Brooklyn Museum 4. Watercolor painting
ISBN 1-56098-572-0   LC 98-10924
In this catalog the authors trace the Brooklyn Museum's "role in the early purchase of works by such artists as Sargent, Homer, and major figures of the 20th century. A chronology distills events and provides a framework from which Brooklyn's contributions to art in America can be told. Some 46 black-and-white illustrations augment the 150 color plates; works range from landscapes and seascapes to figurative portraits and abstractions." Libr J
Includes bibliographical references

Gerdts, William H.

California impressionism; [by] William H. Gerdts, Will South. Abbeville Press 1998 284p il $65   **759.13**
1. Impressionism (Art) 2. American painting
ISBN 0-7892-0176-3   LC 97-32267
The introductory essay explores California Impressionism, examining its sources from abroad, describing exhibitions in America and the critical responses to the artists. Works by Franz Bischoff, Alson Clark, Joseph Raphael, Guy Rose, William Wendt, John Frost, Evelyn McCormack, Bruce Nelson, and others
Includes bibliographical references

Hennessey, Maureen Hart

Norman Rockwell; pictures for the American people; [by] Maureen Hart Hennessey and Ann Knutson. Abrams 1999 199p il $35   **759.13**
1. Rockwell, Norman, 1894-1978
ISBN 0-8109-6392-2   LC 99-73071
A catalogue of a traveling exhibition of Rockwell's work. "Colorplates reproduce Rockwell's paintings in . . . detail, and the essays set them in fresh contexts, discussing such themes as Rockwell's urban scenes; the reaction by both black and white Southerners to Rockwell's historic civil rights painting *The Problem We All Live With*; and Rockwell's role in the development of American illustration." Publisher's note
Includes bibliographical references

Hopper, Edward, 1882-1967

Edward Hopper: the art and the artist; {by} Gail Levin. Norton 1982 299p il $50; pa $39.95   **759.13**
ISBN 0-393-01374-X; 0-393-31577-0 (pa)
Published in association with the Whitney Museum of American Art
This "introduction to the paintings and drawings of the American realist stems from a {1981} exhibition at New York City's Whitney Museum. Curator Levin traces Hopper's development as an artist and illustrates the painter's characteristic themes in a lengthy introductory essay. Following this text is a large section of plates, in color and black and white." Booklist
Includes bibliographical references

Livingston, Jane, 1944-
The paintings of Joan Mitchell; with essays by Linda Nochlin, Yvette Lee. University of Calif. Press 2002 237p il $65; pa $35

759.13

1. Mitchell, Joan
ISBN 0-520-23568-1; 0-520-23570-3 (pa)
LC 2001-58514
Catalog of an exhibition held at the Whitney Museum of American Art, New York, June-Oct. 2002
"Using Mitchell's journals and correspondence, Livingston . . . follows the evolution of Mitchell's painting and discusses her technique. . . . Linda Nochlin demonstrates that Mitchell's rage at being viewed as a 'feminine other' was transformed into a positive energy that brought emotional intensity to her paintings. . . . Yvette Lee discusses the 'Grand Vall,e' series of 16 paintings (1983-84) as some of Mitchell's most luminous and lyrical." Libr J
This is a "vivid portrait of the artist. . . . Mitchell's compositions [are] gorgeously reproduced here in vibrant color." Booklist
Includes bibliographical references

Marling, Karal Ann
Norman Rockwell. Abrams 1997 159p il (Library of American art) $45   **759.13**
1. Rockwell, Norman, 1894-1978
ISBN 0-8109-3794-8   LC 97-7635
Published in association with the National Museum of American Art, Smithsonian Institution
This is a survey of the work of the popular American artist
The author's "exuberant, incisive readings continually reveal how much depth--personal, political, artistic, social--lay beneath Rockwell's deceptively simple surfaces." Publ Wkly
Includes bibliographical references

Mecklenburg, Virginia M. (Virginia McCord), 1946-
Edward Hopper: the watercolors; [by] Virginia M. Mecklenburg; with contributions by Margaret Lynne Ausfeld; National Museum of American Art, Smithsonian Institution. Norton 1999 181p il $39.95

759.13

1. Hopper, Edward, 1882-1967
ISBN 0-393-04849-7   LC 99-6287
Catalog of an exhibition held at the National Museum of American Art, Smithsonian Institution, Washington, D.C., Oct. 22, 1999-Jan. 3, 2000, and at the Montgomery Museum of Fine Arts, Montgomery, Ala., Jan. 30 - Mar. 26, 2000
This "book reproduces and examines over one hundred of Hopper's greatest watercolors in the context of his life and travels." Publisher's note
Includes bibliographical references

Neel, Alice, 1900-1984
Alice Neel; edited by Ann Temkin; with essays by Ann Temkin, Susan Rosenberg, and Richard Flood. Philadelphia Mus. of Art 2000 198p il $45   **759.13**
ISBN 0-8109-4215-1   LC 00-37451
Published on the occasion of an exhibition held at the Whitney Museum of American Art, New York, N.Y., and four other institutions between June 29, 2000 and Dec. 30, 2001

"This exhibit catalog of the proud feminist's work . . . with 224 illustrations, 86 in color, and essays by curators from various museum venues . . . is the most comprehensive and up-to date view of her work." Libr J
Includes bibliographical references

Thomas Eakins; organized by Darrel Sewell with essays by Kathleen A. Foster [et al.]; chronology by Kathleen Brown. Yale Univ. Press 2001 xli, 446p il $75   **759.13**
1. Eakins, Thomas, 1844-1916
ISBN 0-300-09111-7   LC 2001-53142
This is a catalog of an exhibition held at the Philadelphia Museum of Art, Musée d'Orsay, Paris, and the Metropolitan Museum of Art, New York
"This enormous volume accompanies the largest retrospective of [Eakins' work]. . . . [It] includes some 120 photographs as well as examples of his work in watercolor, drawing, and sculpture. . . . Several lengthy and interesting biocritical essays, themselves making up 175 pages of text, separate four sections of color plates. This is clearly the definitive monograph on one of the most significant artists America has produced." Libr J
Includes bibliographical references

Wilton, Andrew
American sublime; landscape painting in the United States, 1820-1880; [by] Andrew Wilton & Tim Barringer. Princeton Univ. Press 2002 284p il $49.95; pa $35   **759.13**
1. American painting 2. Landscape painting
ISBN 0-691-09670-8; 0-691-11556-7 (pa)
Published to accompany an exhibition at Tate Britain, London 21 February- 19 May 2002
"Wilton, of the Tate Gallery, considers the influence of Edmund Burke's theory of sublimity and the surge in scientific development on American painters, while Barringer . . . discusses the profound effect on the painters' imaginations of a pristine land free of Western religious, literary, and historical associations. . . . Wilton and Barringer's commentary is stimulating and important, and the exceptional plates are bliss unadulterated." Booklist
Includes bibliographical references

759.2   British painting

Asleson, Robyn, 1961-
Albert Moore. Phaidon Press 2000 240p il $59.95   **759.2**
1. Moore, Albert Joseph, 1841-1893
ISBN 0-7148-3846-2   LC 00-421386
"This book focuses on the artist's interaction with the Victorian art world as well as his formal pictorial concerns. . . . In addition, the author looks at the politics of Victorian art institutions. This is an excellent book filled with gorgeous color reproductions. Recommended for general collections as well as libraries that support art programs." Libr J
Includes bibliographical references

Wendorf, Richard

Sir Joshua Reynolds; the painter in society. Harvard Univ. Press 1996 265p il $59.95

759.2

1. Reynolds, Sir Joshua, 1723-1792
ISBN 0-674-80966-1   LC 95-51750
This work of cultural criticism explores how Sir Joshua Reynolds became the most fashionable painter of his time. Incorporating art history and literary studies, the author examines the place of portrait-painting in the social fabric of a given culture
Includes bibliographical references

759.3 German painting

Storr, Robert

Gerhard Richter: forty years of painting. Museum of Modern Art 2003 340p il $69; pa $39   **759.3**

1. Richter, Gerhard
ISBN 0-87070-357-9; 0-87070-358-7 (pa)
LC 2001-99460
Also available in hardcover from Distributed Art Pubs.
Tour of the exhibition held at the Museum of Modern Art, New York, Feb. 14-May 21, 2002 and others
Storr's "introductory and biographical essay frames the historical, art, and personal movements that have provoked Richter's exploration of painting's place in a world rent by World War II, photography, and abstraction. Among other insights, Storr hits on the distancing discomfort of studying Richter's photo-based paintings when he cites the painter's 'calculated discretion' in dealing with catastrophic subject matter, such as aspects of the Holocaust. Over 200 color and duotone images, gorgeously reproduced, firmly document the full range of this vital artist, encompassing everything from his intense, colorful abstractions to his gray-scale photo-reproductions to his highly realistic portraits and still lifes, and more. An interview with Richter fills out the book. This will be the standard on Richter for some time to come, and it is essential for all serious art collections." Libr J
Includes bibliographical references

759.36 Austrian painting

Klimt, Gustav, 1862-1918

Gustav Klimt: landscapes; edited by Stephan Koja; with contributions by Christian Huemer [et al.]; translated from the German by John Gabriel. Prestel 2002 223p il $65

759.36

1. Landscape painting
ISBN 3-7913-2677-5   LC 2002-103179
This "volume reproduces all of Klimt's landscape paintings, many of them painted during his holidays in Austria and Italy. The seductive views are utopian in spirit. . . . At the same time, as Carl Schorske . . . notes in one of seven essays by various hands included here, the landscapes are 'mildly melancholic.'" N Y Times Book Rev
Includes bibliographical references

Nebehay, Christian Michael, 1909-

Gustav Klimt; from drawing to painting; {by} Christian M. Nebehay. Abrams 1994 288p il $85   **759.36**

1. Klimt, Gustav, 1862-1918
ISBN 0-8109-3510-4   LC 94-1415
The author offers a "behind-the-finished-canvas analysis of Klimt's most famous work. Nebehay . . . traces Klimt's artistic and personal evolution, but the most exciting aspect of this handsome volume is the juxtaposition of Klimt's rarely reproduced drawings and paintings." Booklist
Includes bibliographical references

759.4 French painting

Bailey, Colin B., 1955-

Renoir's portraits; impressions of an age; {by} Colin B. Bailey with the assistance of John B. Collins; essays by Colin B. Bailey, Linda Nochlin, and Anne Distel. Yale Univ. Press 1997 384p il pa $45   **759.4**

1. Renoir, Auguste, 1841-1919
ISBN 0-300-07134-5   LC 97-60428
Published in conjunction with the exhibition Renoir's Portraits: Impressions of an Age, organized and circulated by the National Gallery of Canada
This exhibition catalog focuses on "Renoir's work that depicts his family, colleagues, friends, children, and the Parisian 'beau monde' in idealized settings. Bailey . . . provides richly detailed descriptions for the 69 vibrant color plates presented here. . . . A definitive source for scholars and a delight for lay readers." Libr J

Cézanne, Paul, 1839-1906

Cézanne; [by] Françoise Cachin, [et al.] Abrams 1996 600p il $70; pa $45   **759.4**

1. Cézanne, Paul, 1839-1906
ISBN 0-8109-4039-6; 0-876-33100-2 (pa)
LC 95-51493
This "exhibition catalogue, published in conjunction with a major international Cézanne retrospective, is a handsome tribute to the artist who revolutionized modern painting. The 258 color and 350 black-and-white reproductions of Cézanne's (1839-1906) oil paintings, watercolors, drawings and sketchbook pages are splendid, and they are accompanied by lucid, insightful commentaries." Publ Wkly
Includes bibliographical references

Courthion, Pierre

Georges Seurat. Abrams 1988 129p il $24.95   **759.4**

1. Seurat, Georges Pierre, 1859-1891
ISBN 0-8109-1519-7
Concise edition of the author's Georges Seurat, originally published 1968
This volume features a biographical essay, followed by an annotated portfolio of 40 full-page color plates. A selected bibliography is also included

Cowling, Elizabeth

Picasso: style and meaning. Phaidon Press 2002 703p il $125   **759.4**

1. Picasso, Pablo, 1881-1973
ISBN 0-7148-2950-1
The authors "focus on 'style' in Picasso's work moves beyond the limitations of formal analysis to look anew

Cowling, Elizabeth—*Continued*
at the plurality that converges as his personal style.
Cowling's scholarly and well-written prose assesses Picasso's career chronologically, illustrating familiar and unfamiliar works (626 useful illustrations). Although biographical elements enter this account, its focus on the art anchors readers in the works themselves, not in speculation." Choice
Includes bibliographical references

De Vonyar, Jill
Degas and the dance; [by] Jill De Vonyar and Richard Kendall. Abrams 2002 303p il $49.95   **759.4**
1. Degas, Edgar, 1834-1917 2. Ballet
ISBN 0-8109-3282-2   LC 2002-18230
Published in association with the American Federation of Arts
Published in conjunction with an exhibition held at the Detroit Institute of Arts, Oct. 18, 2002-Jan. 12, 2003 and the Philadelphia Museum of Art, Feb. 16-May 11, 2003
This explores Degas' fascination with ballet and his intimate relationship with the Paris Opera ballet company
"Beyond the gorgeous reproductions of 144 paintings, drawings, and sculptures, eight original and probing essays delve into the artist's working methods backstage . . . and the evolution of his prolific dance oeuvre." Libr J
Includes bibliographical references

Edouard Vuillard; {by} Guy Cogeval with Kimberly Jones {et al.}. National Gallery of Art 2003 501p il   **759.4**
1. Vuillard, Édouard, 1868-1940
     LC 2002-151120
Available from Yale Univ. Press $65 (ISBN 0-330-09737-9) and in paperback from National Gallery of Art
"National Gallery of Art, Washington, 19 January-20 April 2003, Montreal Museum of Fine Arts, 15 May-24 August 2003, Galeries nationales du Grand Palais, Paris, 23 September 2003-4 January 2004, Royal Academy of Arts, London, 27 January-27 April 2004"
"In a series of illustrated essays, the authors explore Vuillard's . . . career, which began with his academic training in Paris in the late 1880s. . . . The book concludes with an examination of Vuillard's sumptuous large-scale decorations, luminous landscapes, and elegant portraits from the last decades of his career as well as a substantial selection of his pastels and prints, in addition to his photographs." Publisher's note
"A superb display of the surprising colors, forceful textures, and mysterious atmosphere of Vuillard's paintings, accompanied by commentaries in which aesthetics, art history, and biography are perfectly balanced." Booklist
Includes bibliographical references

Flam, Jack D.
Matisse and Picasso; the story of their rivalry and friendship; [by] Jack Flam. Westview Press 2003 276p il $27.50   **759.4**
1. Matisse, Henri 2. Picasso, Pablo, 1881-1973
ISBN 0-8133-6581-3   LC 2002-154120
"This volume examines the enmity and amity between the 20th century's two greatest painters, mostly as evidenced by their art. . . . [This is a] direct, jargon-free study." Publ Wkly

Krauss, Rosalind E., 1940-
The Picasso papers. Farrar, Straus & Giroux 1998 272p il o.p.; MIT Press paperback available $18.95   **759.4**
1. Picasso, Pablo, 1881-1973 2. Cubism
ISBN 0-262-61142-2 (pa)   LC 97-16471
Krauss presents an "inquiry into the meaning, if any, behind Picasso's radical changes in style. As she analyzes specific works and his abrupt shift from cubism to neoclassicism, she evaluates Picasso's eroticism, passion for subterfuge, and the tremendous influence writers, composers, and other artists had on his art. Ultimately, Krauss cites a hollowness in the protean artist's work, even a laxness, a conclusion readers will either embrace or reject, but either way, they will relish the intricate choreography and fearlessness of her performance." Booklist

Matisse, Picasso; [by] Elizabeth Cowling [et al.] Museum of Modern Art 2002 400p il $60   **759.4**
1. Matisse, Henri 2. Picasso, Pablo, 1881-1973
ISBN 0-87070-008-1   LC 2003-266103
"Published to accompany the exhibition at the Museum of Modern Art, New York, 13 February-19 May 2003; Tate Modern, London, 11 May-18 August 2002; Les Galeries Nationales du Grand Palais, Paris, 25 September 2002-6 January 2003." Verso of title page
This examines "the visual dialog between the great 20th-century artists Pablo Picasso and Henri Matisse. Chronologically divided by period and style into sections comparing and contrasting artworks by each master, the catalog offers 34 thought-provoking essays by the exhibition's curators." Libr J

Messer, Thomas M., 1920-
Vasily Kandinsky. Abrams 1997 128p il (Masters of art) $26.95   **759.4**
1. Kandinsky, Wassily, 1866-1944
ISBN 0-8109-1228-7   LC 96-37573
"The book begins with a 38-page survey of the artist's life . . . {it} is followed by superb reproductions of 39 paintings and one group of four related works, each of which is accompanied by well-informed commentary." Choice
Includes bibliographical references

Néret, Gilles
Renoir: painter of happiness 1841-1919; English translation by Josephine Bacon. Taschen, B. 2001 438p il $39.99   **759.4**
1. Renoir, Auguste, 1841-1919
ISBN 3-8228-5876-5
The author "details the artist's entire career and traces his stylistic evolution. . . . [He contends] that Renoir reinvented the woman in painting through his everyday goddesses with overly plump, round hips and breasts; this last phase in Renoir's work, in which he returned to the simple pleasure of painting the female nude in his baigneuses series, was his most innovative and stylistically influential." Publisher's note
Includes bibliographical references

Silverman, Debora, 1954-
Van Gogh and Gauguin; the search for sacred art. Farrar, Straus & Giroux 2000 494p il $60; pa $25 **759.4**
1. Gogh, Vincent van, 1853-1890 2. Gauguin, Paul, 1848-1903 3. Art and religion
ISBN 0-374-28243-9; 0-374-52932-9 (pa)
LC 00-37146
By delving "into the religious legacies of Van Gogh and Gauguin, and forging new connections between their disparate spirituality and revolutionary artistic techniques, subject matter, and styles, Silverman casts new light on these two seminal figures and their timeless masterpieces." Booklist
"Silverman's scholarship and lucid writing makes this one of the most refreshing and insightful texts on these two artists in years." Libr J
Includes bibliographical references

Staller, Natasha
A sum of destructions; Picasso's cultures & the creation of Cubism. Yale Univ. Press 2001 438p il $50 **759.4**
1. Picasso, Pablo, 1881-1973 2. Cubism
ISBN 0-300-07242-2 LC 00-43968
"Staller views 'Les Demoiselles d'Avignon' and the creation of Cubism as a defiant summation of Picasso's reactions to and interactions with his environment, beginning with Malaga, where he was born, then La Corusa, Barcelona, and eventually Paris. Drawing on 20 years of research, she investigates the backgrounds of each of these places from a social and anthropological point of view. . . . [This is] a unique, provocative, and enjoyable portrait of one of the most controversial painters in the history of 20th-century art." Libr J
Includes bibliographical references

Tucker, Paul Hayes, 1950-
Monet in the 20th century; {by} Paul Hayes Tucker with George T.M. Shackelford and MaryAnne Stevens; essays by Romi Golan, John House, and Michael Leja. Yale Univ. Press 1998 300p il $70; pa $35 **759.4**
1. Monet, Claude, 1840-1926
ISBN 0-300-07749-1; 0-300-07944-3 (pa)
LC 98-86163
"This catalog for a show at Boston's Museum of Fine Arts, . . . is the first to consider Monet as a 20th-century artist. In four focused, critical essays by specialists, it chronicles the still-powerful older painter, who was not involved with formulae but with seeing and redefining 19th-century art with experience, color, feeling, refraction, and multiplicity while freeing painting from perspective and spatial observation. His work later influenced American abstract expressionists and color field artists of the mid-20th century. The second part of the book contains resplendent full-color reproductions." Libr J

759.5 Italian painting

Brown, David Alan, 1942-
Leonardo da Vinci; origins of a genius. Yale Univ. Press 1998 240p il $65 **759.5**
1. Leonardo, da Vinci, 1452-1519
ISBN 0-300-07246-5 LC 98-15164
The author traces the "early influences and the emergence of da Vinci's intense curiosity about nature and ability to re-create it in drawing and painting. The chapter on 'Ginevra de'Benci' is a splendid example of how art history and contemporary scientific techniques can be combined in the examination and attribution of a painting. The excellent full page reproductions and small detail examples are carefully placed within the text for ease of reference." Libr J
Includes bibliographical references

De Vecchi, Pierluigi
Raphael. Abbeville Press 2002 380p il $125 **759.5**
1. Raphael, 1483-1520
ISBN 0-7892-0770-2 LC 2002-23206
This is a survey of the life and work of the Italian Renaissance painter including some 300 illustrations
Includes bibliographical references

King, Ross, 1962-
Michelangelo & the Pope's ceiling. Walker & Co. 2002 373p il $28; pa $15 **759.5**
1. Michelangelo Buonarroti, 1475-1564 2. Vatican. Cappella Sistina 3. Mural painting and decoration 4. Italy—History—0-1559
ISBN 0-8027-1395-5; 0-14-200369-7 (pa)
LC 2002-38074
The author "recounts the creation, despite the demanding patronage of irascible Pope Julius II and myriad other adversities, of the most famous painted ceiling in the world." Booklist
"This engaging narrative sets the record straight on a few points and is highly recommended for most public library collections." Libr J
Includes bibliographical references

Marani, Pietro C.
Leonardo da Vinci—the complete paintings; appendices edited by Pietro C. Marani and Edoardo Villata. Abrams 2000 384p il $85 **759.5**
1. Leonardo, da Vinci, 1452-1519
ISBN 0-8109-3581-3 LC 00-27556
Original Italian edition, 1999
This guide covers Leonardo's 31 paintings intensively, recording possible precedents for design and technique in the work of other artists, calling attention to significant details, offering preparatory drawings and cartoons for comparison with the finished, which is not to say completed, works, and presenting X rays to elucidate the gestation of the Mona Lisa and other paintings Leonardo spent years striving to perfect. Such scrupulous attention to Leonardo's total creative process boosts the number of illustrations, mostly colorplates, to 295." Booklist
Includes bibliographical references

Sassoon, Donald
Becoming Mona Lisa; the making of a global icon. Harcourt 2001 337p il $30; pa $16 **759.5**
1. Leonardo, da Vinci, 1452-1519. Mona Lisa
ISBN 0-15-100828-0; 0-15-602711-9 (pa)
LC 2001-24956
This is a history of Leonardo's most famous portrait and its meanings and popularization in the centuries since it was painted
"Sassoon's knowledge of the minutiae of history and his respect for the image drive the narrative. . . . [This work is] thoroughly researched and highly readable." Libr J
Includes bibliographical references

Steinberg, Leo, 1920-
Leonardo's incessant Last Supper. Zone
Bks. 2001 317p il $46   **759.5**
1. Leonardo, da Vinci, 1452-1519. Last Supper
ISBN 1-89095-118-8   LC 00-28315
This is a study of Leonardo da Vinci's mural of the
Last Supper, painted on the north wall of the monastery
refectory of Santa Maria delle Grazie in Milan. Steinberg
aims to "reconsider the geometry, narrative, and composition of the original while examining the thousands of
copies made during the last five centuries." Libr J
"Steinberg's close reading of . . . [the painting's] individual elements, formal aspects, and setting is an exemplary piece of criticism." New Yorker
Includes bibliographical references

759.6   Spanish painting

Hofmann, Werner, 1928-
Goya: to every story there belongs another.
Thames & Hudson 2003 336p il $75   **759.6**
1. Goya, Francisco, 1746-1828
ISBN 0-5000-9317-2   LC 2003-103605
The author "places Goya's paintings, drawings, and
prints in a biographical context, revealing the specific
character of each phase of the artist's life and work. He
discusses 'the glory and the pain of faith' evinced by
Goya's early work, the artist's parabolic representation of
the threat posed by the French Revolution, his dramatic
documentation of the French occupation of Spain, his
variations on cruelty in the *Disasters of War* etchings,
and the religious faith apparent in his late work. Hofmann also relates the artist and his work to contemporary
intellectual developments, drawing comparisons with
writers, critics, and philosophers from Goethe to William
Blake to the Marquis de Sade." Publisher's note
Includes bibliographical references

Lubar, Robert S.
Dali: the Salvador Dali Museum collection;
text by Robert S. Lubar. Bulfinch Press 2000
186p il $60   **759.6**
1. Dalí, Salvador, 1904-1989 2. Salvador Dali Museum (Saint Petersburg, Fla.)
ISBN 0-8212-2480-8   LC 99-87333
The painting collection of the Salvador Dali Museum
in St. Petersburg, FL, is reproduced here and accompanied by a text. . . . The book is most notable for the 94
full-color illustrations encompassing new acquisitions and
other notable holdings. Included are several of Dali's
best-known works and a large number of early canvases
from the 1920s."Libr J
Includes bibliographical references

759.9492   Dutch painting

Bosch, Hieronymus, d. 1516
Hieronymus Bosch; the complete paintings
and drawings; {by} Jos Koldeweij, Paul
Vandenbroeck, Bernard Vermet. Nai Pubs.
2001 207p il $60   **759.9492**
ISBN 0-8109-6735-9   LC 2001-092544
Published on the occasion of an exhibition held at the
Museum Boijmans Van Beuningen, Rotterdam, Sept. 1-
Nov 11, 2001
This volume includes all of the paintings attributed to
Bosch by current scholarly consensus, as well as all sur-

viving drawings linked to Bosch and his workshop. An
overview and one or two details from each painting are
reproduced, along with a generous selection of related
artwork by contemporaries and artists who have been influenced by Bosch including Salvador Dali, Robert
Gober, Bill Viola, and others. The essays by European
art scholars discuss what is known about Bosch and his
cultural milieu, along with the likely meanings of his
paintings and the residual interpretive mystery that has
intrigued scholars and the public for centuries."Libr J
"As keen as the book's historical and technical sections are, its most enthralling passages contain the authors' insights into Bosch's original and satiric worldview and cosmic iconography." Booklist
Includes bibliographical references

Liedtke, Walter A.
Vermeer and the Delft school; by Walter
Liedtke in collaboration with Michiel C.
Plomp and Axel Rüger; with contributions by
Reinier Baarsen {et al.}. Metropolitan Mus.
of Art; [distributed by] Yale Univ. Press 2001
626p il $85   **759.9492**
1. Vermeer, Johannes, 1632-1675 2. Dutch painting
ISBN 0-300-08848-5   LC 00-49550
"This is the catalog of an exhibition held at the Met-
ropolitan Museum of Art, New York, N.Y., Mar. 8-May
27, 2001 and at the National Gallery, London, June 20-
Sept. 16, 2001. It includes fifteen works by Vermeer and
paintings, tapestries and drawings by other Delft artists,
including Gerard Houckgeest, Emanuel de Witte, Carel
Fabritius, Paulus Potter, Leonaert Bramer, Jan de
Bisschop and Pieter de Hooch. . . . Liedtke believes that
Vermeer was nurtured and goaded exclusively by Dutch
art of his time and by the traditions of his hometown."
N Y Rev Books
Includes bibliographical references

Saltzman, Cynthia
Portrait of Dr. Gachet; the story of a van
Gogh masterpiece, modernism, money,
politics, collectors, dealers, taste, greed, and
loss. Viking 1998 xxii, 406p il hardcover o.p.
paperback available $14.95   **759.9492**
1. Gogh, Vincent van, 1853-1890. Dr. Gachet
2. Gachet, Paul, 1828-1909
ISBN 0-14-025487-0 (pa)   LC 97-37006
"In van Gogh's portrait of his physician, the painter
sought to convey the 'heartbroken expression' of his
time; Saltzman has taken up where he left off, charting
the portrait's progress through our century. From the Nazis who confiscated it as an example of 'degenerate art,'
to the Japanese tycoon who bought it for over eighty
million dollars, only to keep it hidden in a Tokyo warehouse, the list of the painting's owners is a who's who
of modernity, and touches upon the rise and fall of empires and individuals alike." New Yorker
Includes bibliographical references

759.9493 Belgian painting

From Van Eyck to Bruegel; early Netherlandish painting in the Metropolitan Museum of Art; edited by Maryan W. Ainsworth and Keith Christiansen; with contributions by Maryan W. Ainsworth {et al.}. Abrams 1998 452p il **759.9493**
1. Metropolitan Museum of Art (New York, N.Y.)
2. Flemish painting LC 98-22196
Available from Yale Univ. Press $65 (ISBN 0-300-08609-1)
Catalog of an exhibition held at the Metropolitan Museum of Art, Sept. 1998-Jan. 1999

"Introductory essays by museum staff members cover the social organization of the production and sale of this art, the interaction of Italian and Netherlandish art, the acquisition of the Metropolitan's Netherlandish collection, and the development of 20th-century European and American scholarship on Netherlandish art. The catalog is organized thematically, with additional essays covering each theme (religious art, portraiture, workshop practice) and substantial entries describing each painting." Libr J
Includes bibliographical references

Magritte, René, 1898-1967
Magritte; edited by Daniel Abadie. D.A.P. 2003 304p il $45 **759.9493**
ISBN 1-8910-2466-3 LC 2002-115229
This volume features "more than 150 paintings, sculptures, objects, and works on paper. The organization of this catalogue paints Magritte as an innovator, and an artist who has had significant influence on contemporary creators. Accompanying essays, including an introduction by Alain Robbe-Grillet . . . consider Magritte's influence on modern and contemporary art. Magritte's relationships with his surrealist contemporaries Louis Scutenaire and André Breton, and the art dealers Edward James and Alexandre Iolas, are each revealed through individual art historical texts and a selection of unpublished letters. An illustrated chronology is included as well." Publisher's note
Includes bibliographical references

759.972 Mexican painting

Frida Kahlo. Bulfinch Press 2001 c2000 245p il $85 **759.972**
1. Kahlo, Frida, 1907-1954
ISBN 0-8212-2766-1 LC 2001-89093
Original Mexican edition, 2000
Jacket title: Frida
Contributions by Luis-Martin Lozano and others
In this "illustrated survey of Frida Kahlo's work Lozano . . . explores her life and paintings in a series of essays that range from a poetic study by noted Mexican cultural critic Carlos Monsiváis to a short, prosaic piece written in 1943 by her husband, Diego Rivera, to an academic essay by Lozano himself. . . . Lozano uses Kahlo's own stunning images, offering high-quality reproductions of some of Kahlo's most famous works as well as some of her lesser-known pieces. Previously unseen photos of Kahlo at work in her studio are also included. The detail and clarity of the images is incredible." Libr J

760 Graphic arts. Printmaking and prints

Munch, Edvard, 1863-1944
Edvard Munch: theme and variation; edited by Klaus Albrecht Schröder, Antonia Hoerschelmann; contributions by Christoph Asendorf [et al.] Hatje Cantz 2003 366p il $65 **760**
ISBN 3-7757-1270-4
Catalog published on the occasion of the exhibition "Edvard Munch: thema und variation" held at the Albertina, Vienna, Mar. 15-June 22, 2003; articles translated from Norwegian and German
This survey of the work of the Norwegian painter and graphic artist includes essays on such topics as the relationship between the artist's graphic and painterly works, and various versions of paintings such as The Scream, Melancholy, and Jealousy
Includes bibliographical references

Riley, Charles A.
The art of Peter Max; by Charles Riley II. Abrams 2002 240p il $49.95 **760**
1. Max, Peter, 1937-
ISBN 0-8109-3270-9 LC 2002-18229
"Peter Max's gorgeous, technically innovative 1960s rock-music posters and album covers made him an instant success and celebrity. Amid a gallery of brilliant reproductions, Riley charts his life before and after as well as during his star turn." Booklist

769 Prints

Beckmann, Max, 1884-1950
Max Beckmann; edited by Sean Rainbird. Museum of Modern Art; [distributed by] D.A.P. 2003 293p il $64 **769**
ISBN 0-8707-0241-6 LC 2003-536801
Catalog of an exhibition held at Centre Georges Pompidiou, Paris, Sept. 10, 2002-Jan 6, 2003, Tate Modern, London, Feb. 12-May 5, 2003, MoMA QNS, New York, June 25-Sept 30, 2003
This book surveys "Beckmann's work and his influence on and interactions with the artists of his day. Essays include discussions of Beckmann's Frankfurt cityscapes, his pictures from Italy, his triptychs, his group portraits, and his relationship with cultural politics in the 1920s and 1930s; texts and interviews by artists Leon Golub and Ellsworth Kelly; curator Robert Storr on 'The Beckmann Effect'; and artist William Kentridge on Beckmann's *Death*." Publisher's note
Includes bibliographical references

770 Photography and photographs

Goldberg, Vicki
American photography; a century of images; by Vicki Goldberg and Robert Silberman. Chronicle Bks. 1999 232p il $40
770
1. Photography—History
ISBN 0-8118-2622-8   LC 99-31713
In this companion to the PBS series the authors have "divided the century into three chronological parts and written 30 brief essays, each focusing on notable aspects, from a photographic point of view, of a particular period. . . . There is a photograph for each year of the century, plus others to illustrate chosen themes like war photography or the rise of the news agencies." N Y Times Book Rev
Includes bibliographical references

Jacobs, Lou
The big picture; the professional photographer's guide to rights, rates, and negotiation; {by} Lou Jacobs Jr. Writer's Digest Bks. 2000 218p il pa $17.99   **770**
1. Commercial photography
ISBN 0-89879-969-4   LC 00-25799
The author offers "advice on the business of photography, notably on negotiating fees and permissions. . . . He also addresses the pricing of photographs, the art of negotiation (offering sample agreements and contracts), book proposals, and special-interest topics. . . . The book concludes with a listing of sources of information, including books for further reading and professional organizations." Libr J

Mizdal, Richard
Black & white photography for 35mm; a guide to photography and darkroom techniques. Amherst Media 2000 125p il $29.95
770
1. Photography
ISBN 0-936262-99-0   LC 99-72183
This volume "explores types of landscape photography, explains what equipment works best, and describes how to find a balance between creativity and technique. . . . Darkroom techniques for creating a dramatic and beautiful final print and suggestions for framing, displaying, and selling images are also covered." Publisher's note

Willis, Deborah, 1952-
Reflections in Black; a history of Black photographers, 1840-1999. Norton 2000 348p il $50; pa $35   **770**
1. Photography—History 2. African American photographers 3. African Americans in art
ISBN 0-393-04880-2; 0-393-32280-7 (pa)
LC 99-55185
Companion volume to A Smithsonian traveling exhibition
"Willis sketches important figures and traces both developments in photographic techniques and the practice of photography by African Americans. . . . A beautiful and informative album." Booklist
Includes bibliographical references

770.2 Photography—Miscellany

Drager, Kerry
Scenic photography 101; a crash course in shooting better pictures outdoors. AMPHOTO 1999 144p il $24.95   **770.2**
1. Outdoor photography
ISBN 0-8174-5819-0   LC 99-29592
This guide discusses equipment, light and color, composition, and how to capture specific details

Grimm, Tom
The basic book of photography; {by} Tom Grimm and Michele Grimm; photographs by Michele Grimm and Tom Grimm; drawings by Ezelda Garcia and Cindy King. 2004 ed. Plume Books 2003 xxi, 650p il pa $22
770.2
1. Photography—Handbooks, manuals, etc.
ISBN 0-452-28425-2   LC 2003-49789
First published 1974
"In addition to equipment and materials, the two most important elements of good photography-lighting and composition are considered. Although the emphasis is upon 35mm photography, other types of cameras, including point and shoot, Polaroid, and digital cameras, are also discussed in detail. The final chapter and appendixes offer an abundance of useful information, including recommended books, photography schools, workshops, competitions, and an extensive glossary of photographic terms." Libr J [review of 1997 edition]

McDarrah, Gloria S.
The photography encyclopedia; {by} Gloria S. McDarrah, Fred W. McDarrah, and Timothy S. McDarrah. Schirmer Bks. 1999 689p il $125   **770.2**
1. Photography—Encyclopedias
ISBN 0-02-865025-5   LC 98-46084
This work "covers all angles of photographers and the tools of their craft. . . . It is filled with carefully selected photographs portraying the irony and beauty of life seen through the camera lens. As a reference work, the photographs are the glue between biographies and terminology. Additional sections list book reviews, films about photographers, and a time line of photography. Additional appendixes include lists of US museums, galleries, manufacturers, booksellers, etc." Choice

770.9 Photography—Historical and geographic treatment

Marien, Mary Warner
Photography: a cultural history. Abrams 2002 528p il $85   **770.9**
1. Photography—History
ISBN 0-8109-0559-0   LC 2001-56749
The author "winnows the abundant photographic production of the mid-19th to the late 20th centuries to harvest a concise and essential chronology of the medium's technologies and aesthetics. . . . With 600 illustrations, 166 in color, this volume is highly recommended for public and academic libraries." Libr J
Includes bibliographical references

Newman, Cathy

Women photographers at National Geographic. National Geographic Soc. 2000 271p il $40; pa $25 **770.9**
1. National Geographic Society (U.S.) 2. Women photographers
ISBN 0-7922-7689-2; 0-7922-6934-9 (pa)
LC 00-41575
This look at the life and careers of the photographers "describes their conflicted lives as they balance assignments that took them away from families, homes, and communities for long periods of time. . . . But it is the 144 photographs that attest to the place these women deserve in the history of photography." Libr J
Includes bibliographical references

Photography past forward: Aperture at 50; with a history by R. H. Cravens; and excerpts from Aperture issues 1952-2002; [Melissa Harris, editor] Farrar, Straus & Giroux 2002 239p il $50 **770.9**
1. Aperture (Periodical) 2. Photography—History 3. Artistic photography
ISBN 0-89381-996-4
LC 2002-107716
"Aperture celebrates 50 years as the premier venue for art photography in the United States with a book worthy of its founders' ideals. An anecdotal history lovingly details its transformation from a bright idea for a magazine—conceived by the likes of Minor White and Ansel Adams—to the publisher of hundreds of books, sampled in the accompanying photos, themselves a dizzying display of artistic variety." Libr J

771 Photography—Techniques, equipment, materials

Garrett, John

John Garrett's black-and-white photography masterclass. AMPHOTO 1999 159p il pa $27.50 **771**
1. Photography
ISBN 0-8174-4044-5
LC 99-44599
This is a guide to the "photographic process, from basic visualization and composition techniques to sophisticated darkroom procedures." Publisher's note

775 Digital photography

Ang, Tom

Advanced digital photography. AMPHOTO 2003 144p il pa $29.95 **775**
1. Photography—Digital techniques 2. Photography—Processing
ISBN 0-8174-3273-6
"Ang first discusses digital imaging principles and offers tips on mastering hardware (cameras and scanners). However, he devotes most of the book to advanced image manipulation—mastering tone control, dodging and burning, retouching, 'painting', controlling color, compositing, sharpening images, and many other creative possibilities. He also addresses the digital 'darkroom,' image organization, and the output of images. . . . The illustrations are exquisite. Highly recommended for all photography collections." Libr J
Includes bibliographical references

Digital photographer's handbook. DK Pub. 2002 407p il $40 **775**
1. Photography—Digital techniques
ISBN 0-7894-8907-4
LC 2002-73312
The author "discusses digital technology, including cameras, lenses, scanners, and printers, along with computers, accessories, and software. He then goes on to explore the unique challenges and advantages of composition and exposure with digital cameras. . . . This is certainly one of the best and most comprehensive books available about digital photography." Libr J
Includes bibliographical references

778.3 Special kinds of photography

Ang, Tom

Silver pixels; an introduction to the digital darkroom. AMPHOTO 2000 c1999 127p il pa $27.50 **778.3**
1. Photography—Digital techniques
ISBN 0-8174-5889-1
"This book compares conventional and digital photography, showing the new world of effects that can be as subtle or extreme as desired, produced in black-and-white or in color. Technical sections cover equipment, the central component of resolution, color reproduction, output to print, and scanners. An extensive glossary and relevant tips on the World Wide Web are also included." Publisher's note
Includes bibliographical references

Johnson, Dave, 1964-

How to do everything with your digital camera. 3rd ed. McGraw-Hill/Osborne 2003 453p il pa $24.99 **778.3**
1. Digital cameras 2. Photography—Digital techniques
ISBN 0-07-223081-9
First published 2001
"Johnson opens by discussing virtually all of the technical essentials of working with one's camera to make correct exposures and then proceeds to address questions about working with digital film and formats and transferring files. He further explains how to compose and edit photographs on one's computer. . . . The book concludes with helpful chapters on printing one's photographs and sharing images through e-mail, web pages, and disks. Anyone who works with digital photographs will find this book quite thorough and useful." Libr J {review of 2001 edition}

May, Alex

Multimedia: digital photography. Dorling Kindersley 2000 72p il (Essential computers) pa $6.95 **778.3**
1. Photography—Digital techniques
ISBN 0-7894-5531-5
LC 99-54350
A guide to compact, rotating and SLR cameras. Topics include image editing, shot composition, file formats, special effects, and storing images

778.5 Cinematography, video production, related activities

Netzley, Patricia D.
The encyclopedia of movie special effects. Oryx Press 2000 291p il $73.95   **778.5**
1. Cinematography
ISBN 1-57356-167-3   LC 99-47733
"This volume provides 366 entries on visual, mechanical, and makeup effects and techniques used in film and includes discussions of every movie to win an Oscar for special effects." Libr J
For a fuller review see: Booklist June 1 & 15, 2000

Solnit, Rebecca
River of shadows; Eadweard Muybridge and the technological wild west. Viking 2003 305p il $25.95   **778.5**
1. Muybridge, Eadweard, 1830-1904 2. Cinematography 3. Photography—History
ISBN 0-670-03176-3   LC 2002-66384
Published in the United Kingdom with title: Motion studies
"The pioneering stop-action motion studies of colorful Englishman-turned-Californian Muybridge led ultimately, Solnit argues, to the modern estrangement from nature and immersion in the 'river of shadows' made up of film, video, and computer images." Booklist
"'River of Shadows' is never less than deeply intelligent, and often very close to inspired." N Y Times Book Rev
Includes bibliographical references

Weishar, Peter
Blue Sky; the art of computer animation: featuring Ice Age and Bunny. Abrams 2002 86p il pa $24.95   **778.5**
1. Computer animation
ISBN 0-8109-9069-5   LC 2001-58988
This goes behind the scenes at "Blue Sky Studios and uses their . . . film Ice Age to illustrate computer modeling, rigging, texture mapping, and special effects. Weishar entertainingly details the technological wizardry used to create 3-D animation of everything from storms and smoke to fully realized film sets and woolly mammoths." Libr J

779 Photographs

Bustard, Bruce I., 1954-
Picturing the century; one hundred years of photography from the National Archives. National Archives & Records Adm.; University of Wash. Press 1999 136p il pa $24.95   **779**
1. Photography—Exhibitions 2. Photojournalism
ISBN 0-295-97772-8   LC 98-44102
Catalog of exhibition held at National Archives and Records Administration in Washington, D.C., Mar. 1999-Jan. 2001
"Bustard presents 163 images, dating from 1900 to 1994, in chapters covering the early century, World War I and the 1920s, the Depression, World War II, the postwar period to the Vietnam War, and from Vietnam to the 1990s. Original caption, photographer's credit, date, and federal agency credit are given for each photo. Many

first-rate photographers have done government work, and brief portfolios draw attention to six, among them the famous Lewis Hine, Ansel Adams, and Dorothea Lange." Booklist
Includes bibliographical references

Coles, Robert
When they were young; a photographic retrospective of childhood from the Library of Congress; preface by James H. Billington. Kales Press 2002 160p il $39.95   **779**
1. Library of Congress 2. Artistic photography 3. Children—Pictorial works
ISBN 0-9670076-5-8   LC 2002-7177
"Published in conjunction with the Library of Congress exhibition." Verso of title page
This is an "illustrated portrayal of early life and the legacies that live on from coming of age. . . . Spanning the history of photography from the daguerreotype to the documentary, each tritone image in this volume is illustrated on a full page. Works by internationally renowned photographers such as Edward Curtis and Dorothea Lange are included." Publisher's note

Homer, William Innes
Stieglitz and the Photo-Secession, 1902; text by William Innes Homer; edited by Catherine Johnson. Viking Studio Bks. 2002 133p il $29.95   **779**
1. Stieglitz, Alfred, 1864-1946 2. Photo-Secession (Group) 3. Artistic photography
ISBN 0-670-03038-4   LC 2003-268369
A reconstruction of the Photo-Secession exhibition held March 5-22, 1902 at the National Arts Club, New York with a reprint of its catalog originally published under the title: American pictorial photography
This "avant-garde band of photographers, led by Arthur Stieglitz, began to champion their work as art, rather than as a mere form of documentation, in an exhibit at the National Arts Club in New York. They called themselves the Photo-Secession and were considered to be the best and most original photographers of their day. This group included luminaries such as Edward Steichen, F. Holland Day, Frank Eugene, Gertrude Käsebier, Clarence H. White, and Stieglitz himself." Publisher's note

Icons of photography; the 20th century; edited by Peter Stepan. Prestel-Verlag 1999 199p il $35   **779**
1. Artistic photography
ISBN 3-7913-2001-7   LC 99-15014
A "chronological assembly of 90 photographers, from Berenice Abbott to Heinrich Zille. . . . Each artist is given a two-page spread, including a portrait shot and an example of a key image; there are 165 images in all, representing the artists' best and most challenging work." Libr J
Includes bibliographical references

Leibovitz, Annie
Women; {photographs by} Annie Leibovitz; {essay by} Susan Sontag. Random House 1999 239p il $75; pa $49.95   **779**
1. Women—Portraits
ISBN 0-375-50020-0; 0-375-75646-9 (pa)
      LC 99-24968
Leibovitz presents a collection of photographs of women
"Leibovitz greatly increases our lexicon of woman-

Leibovitz, Annie—*Continued*

hood with her brilliant photographs of musicians, doctors, teachers, trapeze artists, gangbangers, nude women, a woman in chador, women soldiers, and girls with their Barbies, all commanding attention and respect." Booklist

Life: century of change; America in pictures, 1900-2000; edited by Richard B. Stolley; Tony Chiu, deputy editor. Little, Brown, and Co 2000 391p il $60   **779**
1. United States—History—20th century—Pictorial works 2. Photojournalism
ISBN 0-8212-2697-5   LC 00-105956

Chronologically arranged by decade, this compilation of photographs covers a variety of subjects including landscape, celebrities, and popular culture

Mitchell, John G.

National Geographic, the wildlife photographs. National Geographic Soc. 2001 304p il maps $50   **779**
1. National Geographic Society (U.S.) 2. Animals—Pictorial works
ISBN 0-7922-6356-1   LC 2001-37021

This is a collection of over 170 wildlife images from National Geographic organized by habitat. "A sidebar portfolio in each section features the work of one photographer well known for his or her images of animals from the featured habitat. Mitchell's text gives information on each region, discussing the environment, the politics of conservation, and a profile of the featured photographer. This beautiful book will be welcome in large photography collections." Booklist

National Geographic photographs; the milestones: a visual legacy of the world. National Geographic Soc. 1999 335p il $50
                    779
1. National Geographic Society (U.S.) 2. Photojournalism 3. Documentary photography
ISBN 0-7922-7520-9   LC 99-29397

Essays discuss the Society's special collections, the advent and uses of color film, underwater photography, and new technologies

"Granted their escapist agenda and the distancing, reductive effect of the explanatory captions tacked onto them, these are wonderfully gaze-worthy images, and some are artful and individual, too, such as the painting-influenced frames from early in the century and a 1996 shot of a lion in a windstorm." Booklist

Photographs then and now. National Geographic Soc. 1998 304p il $50   **779**
1. Photojournalism 2. Documentary photography
ISBN 0-7922-7202-1   LC 98-23421

At head of title: National Geographic

This volume juxtaposes "historic photographs, some in black and white or sepia, with contemporary portraits of similar places and people. . . . The book is usefully divided by region: North America, Central and South America, Europe, Asia, the Middle East and North Africa, Oceania, and the Poles. Its strengths are the technical standard and quality of composition found in virtually every photograph." Libr J

Photos that changed the world; the 20th century; edited by Peter Stepan; with contributions by Claus Biegerd [et al.] Prestel-Verlag 2000 183p il $35   **779**
1. Photojournalism
ISBN 3-7913-2395-4

Stepan provides "105 images that had the lasting visual power to capture a moment that could be the image of an era held in the instant of a shutter's click for distribution to a generation. . . . The photos are well reproduced and gain from the explanations of time, place, and context included in the excellent short essays that accompany each." Libr J

Scavullo, Francesco, 1929-

Scavullo: photographs, 50 years. Abradale Press 2000 224p il $24.98   **779**
1. Portrait photography
ISBN 0-8109-8182-3

A reissue of the title published 1997 by Abrams

This is a "collection of 225 of Francesco Scavullo's photographs (100 in color). It surveys his work from his first years at Vogue and Seventeen magazines through his years [in Hollywood]." Christ Sci Monit

"This retrospective seems to extend the impact and visual power of [Scavullo's] . . . photographs by capturing so many familiar stars, models, and actors in a large and beautiful book." Libr J

Smith, Joel

Edward Steichen: the early years. Princeton Univ. Press 1999 167p il $65   **779**
1. Steichen, Edward, 1879-1973 2. Artistic photography
ISBN 0-691-04873-8   LC 99-26617

Smith examines the photography of Edward Steichen. Alfred Stieglitz was a patron of Steichen's, and Smith discusses "the interrelationship between Steichen's work and Stieglitz's shifting aesthetic interests, as well as the influence of Paris on Steichen's development." N Y Times Book Rev
Includes bibliographical references

Spirit capture; photographs from the National Museum of the American Indian; edited by Tim Johnson. Smithsonian Institution Press 1998 205p il $60; pa $34.95   **779**
1. National Museum of the American Indian (U.S.) 2. Native Americans—Pictorial works
ISBN 1-56098-924-6; 1-56098-765-0 (pa)
                    LC 98-4173

The more than 200 reproductions included in this volume range from daguerrotypes to color slides. Essays by Native American authors explore how Indians of the Western hemisphere were documented and depicted
Includes bibliographical references

Steichen, Edward, 1879-1973

Steichen's legacy; photographs, 1895-1973; edited and with text by Joanna Steichen. Knopf 2000 xxxii, 372p il $100   **779**
1. Artistic photography
ISBN 0-679-45076-9   LC 00-20095

Joanna Steichen, the photographer's widow, presents an account "of her husband's life's work. . . . In this book she has organized more than 300 of his photographs into 19 sections, each with commentary." N Y Times Book Rev

"A labor of love, this volume grants precious insights into Steichen's abiding romance with the camera and the universal language of images." Booklist

Stieglitz, Alfred, 1864-1946

Alfred Stieglitz: the key set; the Alfred Stieglitz collection of photographs; [text by] Sarah Greenough. Abrams 2002 2v il set $150   **779**

ISBN 0-8109-3533-3   LC 2002-5066

Contents: v1 1886-1922; v2 1923-1937

This is a "captioned catalog of 1,642 Stieglitz photographs. . . . It contains 'the finest print of every mounted photograph in Stieglitz's possession at the time of his death.' . . . Greenough's essay examines 'what is and is not in the key set in order to clarify the evolution of Stieglitz's understanding of modernist photography....' The set contains very useful, dense chronologies of Stieglitz's process and techniques (1882-1944) and of exhibitions (1888-1944), a bibliography (1875-2001), and an essay on Stieglitz's concern with reproduction printing and publishing." Choice

Includes bibliographical references

Struth, Thomas, 1954-

Thomas Struth, 1977-2002; essays by Douglas Eklund [et al.] Dallas Mus. of Art 2002 189p il $60   **779**

1. Artistic photography

ISBN 0-300-09360-8   LC 2001-99024

This is a catalog of a traveling exhibition of 100 photographs by the German photographer

"As the most complete survey of Struth's work now available, this can be highly recommended for all larger collections." Libr J

Includes bibliographical references

Through the lens; National Geographic greatest photographs. National Geographic Soc. 2003 504p il $30   **779**

1. Documentary photography

ISBN 0-7922-6164-X   LC 2003-52757

This is a "collection of 250 photos, mostly in color and drawn from the National Geographic Society's archive. . . . The society's signature blend of dramatic, rigorously composed natural shots and 'family of nations'-style culture peeps are backed by broad captions and text. . . . The six sections ('Europe'; 'Asia'; 'Africa & the Middle East'; 'The Americas'; 'Oceans and Isles'; 'The Universe') include the first color underwater photographs, as well as collaborative work with NASA, and prominently credit the 84 photographers whose work is featured." Publ Wkly

780 Music

Brabec, Jeffrey

Music, money, and success; the insider's guide to making money in the music industry; [by] Jeffrey Brabec, Todd Brabec. 3rd ed. Schirmer Bks. 2002 xx, 435p pa $24.95   **780**

1. Music industry 2. Music—Economic aspects

ISBN 0-8256-7282-1   LC 2003-267423

First published 1994

This guide discusses how money can be made from music in such areas as songwriting, performance, movies, television, advertising, recordings, and theater and explains copyright, negotiating contracts, and dealing with managers, lawyers, and agents

Day, Timothy

A century of recorded music; listening to musical history. Yale Univ. Press 2000 306p il $40; pa $19   **780**

1. Sound recordings—History 2. Music—History and criticism 3. Sound—Recording and Reproducing—History

ISBN 0-300-08442-0; 0-300-09401-9 (pa)

LC 00-43490

This work provides a "narrative of the evolution of recording from cylinders (1887), shellac discs, and acoustic rerecording through the reproducing piano, electrical amplifications (1925), and magnetic tape to the long-playing record (1948) and compact disc of the 1980s. Day also discusses studio practices and the emergence of influential record producers, the role of radio and recordings in creating a mass audience, the expansion of recorded repertoire, and new ways to experience music. Recommended for all music collections." Choice

Includes bibliographical references

Krasilovsky, M. William

This business of music; by M. William Krasilovsky and Sidney Shemel. Billboard Bks. il $29.95   **780**

1. Music industry 2. Music—Economic aspects 3. Copyright—Music 4. Popular music—Writing and publishing

First published 1964. (9th edition 2003) Periodically revised

"The definitive guide to the music industry." Title page

"A compendium of useful information on contracts, copyrights, record production, music videos, agents and managers, performing-rights organizations, and other business practices specific to music." Guide to Ref Books. 11th edition

780.3 Music—Encyclopedias and dictionaries

The **Harvard** concise dictionary of music and musicians; edited by Don Michael Randel. Belknap Press 1999 757p il $35; pa $18.95   **780.3**

1. Music—Dictionaries 2. Music—Bio-bibliography

ISBN 0-674-00084-6; 0-674-00978-9 (pa)

LC 99-40644

Based on the New Harvard dictionary of music and The Harvard biographical dictionary of music (1996)

"Entries are arranged alphabetically and encompass terms, musical forms and styles, individual works, and instruments, as well as composers, performers, and theorists." Booklist

The **Harvard** dictionary of music; edited by Don Michael Randel. 4th ed. Belknap Press 2003 xxvii, 978p il $39.95   **780.3**

1. Music—Dictionaries

ISBN 0-674-01163-5   LC 2003-58262

First published 1944 under the authorship of Willi Apel

This reference "includes entries on all the styles and forms in Western music; . . . articles on the music of Africa, Asia, Latin America, and the Near East; descriptions of instruments . . . [with] historical background, and articles that reflect today's best, including popular music, jazz, and rock." Publisher's note

Hoffman, Miles

The NPR classical music companion; terms and concepts from A to Z. Houghton Mifflin 1997 306p music pa $15 **780.3**

1. Music—Dictionaries
ISBN 0-395-70742-0   LC 97-10479

This musical guide includes "entries that are at least a good-size paragraph in length and liable to include, besides technical information, historical and listener's advisory material." Booklist

Kennedy, Michael, 1926-

The Oxford dictionary of music; associate editor, Joyce Bourne. 2nd ed. Oxford Univ. Press 1994 985p il $49.95 **780.3**

1. Music—Dictionaries 2. Musicians—Dictionaries
ISBN 0-19-869162-9   LC 94-4539

First published 1985

This "dictionary encompasses musical subjects of all kinds: composers . . . musical performers in all fields; orchestras; titles and descriptions of individual works, operas, and ballets; musical forms and terms; instruments; institutions; and writers and scholars." Publisher's note

"A comprehensive and useful resource for accurate and concise definitions and biographical sketches." Choice

The **New** Grove dictionary of music and musicians; edited by Stanley Sadie; executive editor, John Tyrrell. 2nd ed. Grove's Dictionaries Inc. 2000 29v set $2,200 **780.3**

1. Music—Dictionaries
ISBN 1-56159-239-0   LC 00-55156

Also available online

First published 1980 in twenty volumes to supersede Grove's dictionary of music and musicians

This dictionary includes "29,000 signed articles written by 5,700 contributors from 98 countries. The articles include 20,000 biographies; 2,200 entries for instruments and their makers; 1,400 entries on styles, terms, and genres; 1,300 entries on world music; 1,200 entries on popular music; plus entries on other topics, such as acoustics (89 articles)." Booklist

"Grove is not fat, it is limitless. Whether Grove is on the reference shelf or online, teachers, students, researchers, and the common reader will find it an abiding source of satisfaction." Commonweal

Includes bibliographical references

The **Oxford** companion to music; edited by Alison Latham. Oxford Univ. Press 2002 1434p il $65 **780.3**

1. Music—Dictionaries 2. Musicians—Dictionaries
ISBN 0-19-866212-2   LC 2002-537302

"New edition of two quite different earlier companions ... Oxford companion to music ... The new Oxford companion to music." Preface

"Among the 8000 entries are articles on composers, theorists, and some performers; instruments, forms, and terms; subjects like electronic music, individual countries, and politics and music; and some pieces (and even some famous arias). Each entry is presented in a dictionary format, with a select index of names appended and sometimes with bibliographic references. . . . The bias is still English, but the book provides cross references to American terms and includes plenty of American com-

posers and musical subjects. A solid reference with a grand pedigree, usefully improved for home and general library use, this is highly recommended for all public libraries." Libr J

For a fuller review see: Booklist, Nov. 15, 2002

Slonimsky, Nicolas, 1894-1995

Baker's dictionary of music; edited by Richard Kassell. Schirmer Bks. 1997 xxvi, 1171p il $175 **780.3**

1. Music—Dictionaries
ISBN 0-02-864791-2   LC 97-21923

"More than 10,000 entries cover musical instruments, terms, composers, conductors, performers, and works, both popular and classical." Booklist

780.89 Music of racial, ethnic, national groups

Floyd, Samuel A.

The power of black music; interpreting its history from Africa to the United States; [by] Samuel A. Floyd, Jr. Oxford Univ. Press 1995 316p il hardcover o.p. paperback available $18.95 **780.89**

1. African American music
ISBN 0-19-510975-7 (pa)   LC 94-21

The range of genres the author discusses includes "slaves' ring shouts, turn-of-the-century cotillion dances, jazz, R & B, etc. . . . Complementing the discourse are plenty of musical examples. Academics, critics, scholars, and fans alike stand to gain much from carefully reading this impressive work." Booklist

Includes discography, filmography, and bibliographical references

780.9 Music—Historical and geographical treatment

The **Garland** encyclopedia of world music; advisory editors, Bruno Nettl and Ruth M. Stone; founding editors, James Porter and Timothy Rice. Garland; [distributed by] Routledge 1998-2002 10v il maps (Garland reference library of the humanities) set $2,500 **780.9**

1. Folk music—Encyclopedias
ISBN 0-8153-1865-0   LC 97-9671

Volumes also available separately $250 each

Volumes 6-7, 10 published by Routledge

Contents: v1 Africa, by R. M. Stone, editor; v2 South America, Mexico, Central America, and the Caribbean, by D. A. Olsen and D. E. Sheehy, editors; v3 The United States and Canada, by E. Koskoff, editor; v4 Southeast Asia, by T. E. Miller and S. Williams, editors; v5 South Asia: the Indian subcontinent, by A. Arnold, editor; v6 The Middle East, by V. Danielson, S. Marcus, and D. Reynolds, editors; v7 East Asia: China, Japan, and Korea, by R. C. Provine, Y. Tokumaru, and J. L. Witzleben, editors; v8 Europe, by T. Rice, J. Porter, and C. Goertzen, editors; v9 Australia and the Pacific Islands, by A. L. Kaeppler and J. W. Love, editors; v10 The world's music: general perspectives and reference tools, by R. M. Stone, editor

The Garland encyclopedia of world music—*Continued*

This is an "encyclopedia dedicated to exploring the social and cultural context of music around the world. Individual volumes are devoted to specific regions of the world . . . and each has an accompanying audio compact disc of representative examples keyed to the text. Articles are authoritative, well illustrated, and provide cultural and historical perspectives on the musical styles, genres, and performances of each of the nine regions covered." Ref Sources for Small & Medium-sized Libr. 6th edition

Grout, Donald Jay, 1902-1987

A history of Western music; [by] Donald Jay Grout, Claude V. Palisca. Norton il $69.60   **780.9**

1. Music—History and criticism

First published 1960. (6th edition 2001) Periodically revised

The authors survey the course of Western music from the ancient world to modern atonalism and dodecaphony. They cover vocal and instrumental forms, notation, performance, music-printing, the development of instruments, and biographical information on composers

Includes bibliographical references

Hall, Charles J.

Chronology of Western classical music. Routledge 2002 2v set $225   **780.9**

1. Music—Chronology 2. Music—History and criticism 3. Composers

ISBN 0-415-93878-3

Contents: v1 1751-1900; v2 1901-2000

This "directory provides abstracted information on music for the years 1751 through 2000, with each year having nine subject areas: births, deaths, debuts, new positions, prizes and honors, biographical highlights, cultural beginnings, musical literature, and musical compositions (each of these subdivided as appropriate). . . . This resource will certainly be of value to those seeking a cultural or historical identity for a given year." Am Ref Books Annu, 2003

Kuhn, Laura Diane

Music since 1900; [by] Laura Kuhn. 6th ed. Schirmer Bks. 2001 1174p $175   **780.9**

1. Music—History and criticism

ISBN 0-02-864787-4   LC 2001-20636

First edition 1937 thru fifth edition 1994 published under the authorship of Nicholas Slonimsky

"A chronology of musical events (with commentary on the events listed) makes up the bulk of the volume." Guide to Ref Books. 11th edition

For review of 6th ed. see Booklist, Feb. 15, 2002

Lang, Paul Henry, 1901-1991

Music in Western civilization; with a new foreword by Leon Botstein. Norton 1997 xxii, 1107p il maps $45   **780.9**

1. Music—History and criticism

ISBN 0-393-04074-7   LC 97-5883

First published 1941

This is a history of Western music from Ancient Greece to the 1920s

"Lang's volume has long been hailed as a benchmark in the field." Libr J

Includes bibliographical references

New Oxford history of music. Oxford Univ. Press 1954-1990 10v il music apply to publisher for price and availability   **780.9**

1. Music—History and criticism

Supersedes The Oxford history of music, first published 1901-1905

Contents: v1 Ancient and Oriental music, edited by Egon Wellesz; v2 2nd ed. The Early Middle Ages to 1300, edited by Richard Crocker and David Hiley; v3 Ars nova and the Renaissance, 1300-1540, edited by Dom Anselm Hughes and Gerald Abraham; v4 The Age of humanism, 1540-1630, edited by Gerald Abraham; v5 Opera and church music, 1630-1750, edited by Nigel Fortune and Anthony Lewis; v6 Concert music, 1630-1750, edited by Gerald Abraham; v7 The age of enlightenment, 1745-1790, edited by Egon Wellesz and Frederick Sternfeld; v8 The age of Beethoven, 1790-1830, edited by Gerald Abraham; v9 Romanticism, 1830-1890, edited by Gerald Abraham; v10 The modern age, 1890-1960, edited by Martin Cooper

"It would be difficult to find a scholarly multi-volume history of music of comparable stature. . . . [This work is marked by] comprehensiveness, consistency, evenness, and sheer readability." Choice

Norton anthology of western music; edited by Claude V. Palisca. 4th ed. Norton 2001 2v music pa ea $42.50   **780.9**

1. Music—History and criticism

LC 2001-545308

Also available The Norton recorded anthology of western music, consisting of 2 sets of 6 CDs each, and a concise edition consisting of 4 CDs

First published 1980

Contents: v1 Ancient to Baroque (ISBN 0-393-97690-4); v2 Classic to Modern (ISBN 0-393-97691-2)

This is a collection of musical scores designed to accompany the sixth editon of A history of western music by Donald J. Grout and Claude V. Palisca

Rosen, Charles, 1927-

The classical style; Haydn, Mozart, Beethoven. expanded ed. Norton 1997 xxx, 533p il $35; pa $19.95   **780.9**

1. Haydn, Joseph, 1732-1809 2. Mozart, Wolfgang Amadeus, 1756-1791 3. Beethoven, Ludwig van, 1770-1827 4. Music—History and criticism

ISBN 0-393-04020-8; 0-393-31712-9 (pa)

LC 96-27335

First published 1971 by Viking

This focuses on the works of Hayden, Mozart, and Beethoven and their styles. The hardcover edition includes an audio CD of the author playing two Beethoven piano sonatas

"This remains simply the most important book on the classical style in music." Choice

Includes bibliographical references

The romantic generation. Harvard Univ. Press 1995 723p il hardcover o.p. paperback available $18.95   **780.9**

1. Music—History and criticism

ISBN 0-674-77934-7 (pa)   LC 94-46239

"Based on the Charles Eliot Norton lectures"

The author "explains and describes the first half of the 19th century in conjunction with literature, art, and social changes. . . . Rosen also examines the lives of the composers and pursues some detailed analysis of numerous

Rosen, Charles, 1927-—_Continued_
compositions to make his points. The result is a fresh, challenging, and stimulating view of the society in which Chopin, Liszt, Berlioz, and Schumann flourished." Libr J

Slonimsky, Nicolas, 1894-1995
The great composers and their works; edited by Electra Yourke. Schirmer Bks. 2000 2v il set $200   **780.9**
1. Music—History and criticism 2. Music appreciation 3. Composers
ISBN 0-02-864955-9   LC 99-42808
"This alphabetically arranged work made up of . . . writings by the late Nicolas Slonimsky . . . is edited by his daughter, Electra Yourke, and treats 19 composers, from Bach to Shostakovich. Arrangement is chronological." Booklist
"These volumes will attract individuals with a serious interest in classical music, and supplement standard resources." SLJ

Women and music in America since 1900; an encyclopedia; edited by Kristine H. Burns. Oryx Press 2002 2v il set $150   **780.9**
1. Women musicians 2. American music—Encyclopedias
ISBN 1-57356-267-X   LC 2001-54570
This is an "alphabetically arranged reference set on women composers, performers, teachers, and scholars from all genres of music since 1900, as well as issues, organizations, and broad topics." Libr J
"This set will become an essential reference tool." Choice
For a fuller review see: Booklist, March 1, 2003

780.973   Music—United States

Crawford, Richard, 1935-
America's musical life; a history. Norton 2000 976p il $45   **780.973**
1. American music—History and criticism
ISBN 0-393-04810-1   LC 99-47565
This survey of music in America covers "blues, jazz, swing, pop, rock, hip hop . . . with economics and history as cultural backdrops. Well researched and sensitively constructed, this is highly recommended." Libr J
Includes bibliographical references

Hall, Charles J.
A chronicle of American music, 1700-1995. Schirmer Bks. 1996 825p $125   **780.973**
1. American music—History and criticism
ISBN 0-02-860296-X   LC 96-16458
This "reference guide covers nearly 300 years of American music in a year-by-year time line that encompasses 'Historical Highlights,' 'World Cultural Highlights,' and 'American Art and Literature Highlights,' as well as music, itself divided between 'The Vernacular/Commercial Scene' and 'The Cultivated/Art Music Scene.'" Choice
Includes bibliographical references

The **New** Grove dictionary of American music; edited by H. Wiley Hitchcock and Stanley Sadie; editorial coordinator Susan Feder. Grove's Dictionaries of Music 1986 4v il set $725   **780.973**
1. American music—Dictionaries
ISBN 0-943818-36-2   LC 86-404
"Includes names and terms germane to the musical tradition of the U.S. Expands articles from _The new Grove dictionary of music and musicians_ where appropriate, but adds many more on art music, varieties of popular music, the political and patriotic repertories, specifically American genres, music of the present day, etc. Standard music topics are treated in the American context. Signed articles, many with bibliographies, lists of works, and discographies." Guide to Ref Books. 11th edition

781.1   Music—Aesthetics, appreciation, taste

Copland, Aaron, 1900-1990
Music and imagination. Harvard Univ. Press 1952 116p hardcover o.p. paperback available $12.95   **781.1**
1. Music appreciation 2. Music—History and criticism
ISBN 0-674-58915-7 (pa)
Analyzed in Essay and general literature index
Charles Eliot Norton lectures, 1951-1952
The author "considers many of the problems of the contemporary composer . . . the qualities of the sensitive listener, the meaning of music, 'the sonorous image,' the creative mind and the interpretive mind, the pull of tradition and the attraction of innovation upon European composers of our day, the twelve-tone procedure, and distinctive contributions of American composers." Libr J

Machlis, Joseph, 1906-1998
The enjoyment of music; an introduction to perceptive listening. Norton il $73.50   **781.1**
1. Music appreciation 2. Music—History and criticism
First published 1955. (9th edition 2003) Periodically revised
This guide to music appreciation brings together biographical, historical, and analytical material, from the music of the Middle Ages to contemporary music
Includes bibliographical references

781.2   Elements of music

Piston, Walter, 1894-1976
Harmony. 5th ed, revised and expanded by Mark DeVoto. Norton 1987 575p $59.95   **781.2**
1. Harmony
ISBN 0-393-95480-3   LC 86-23901
First published 1941
A presentation of the harmonic structures utilized by composers of the 18th and 19th centuries. Includes examples and exercises

781.6 Traditions of music. Classical music

Classical music: the listener's companion; edited by Alexander Morin; foreword by Harold C. Schonberg. Backbeat Bks. 2002 1201p pa $29.95   **781.6**
1. Sound recordings—Reviews 2. Music—Discography 3. Music
ISBN 0-87930-638-6   LC 2001-52702
This "guide to classical music examines historical and contemporary works by American, British, German and other composers, some dating back to the 1500s. It focuses on the very finest recordings of symphonies, operas, choral pieces, chamber music, and more. . . Historical essays explore the classical repertory from medieval to electronic, Broadway to Hollywood, and more. . . . [This] guide also profiles conductors, artists, and instruments." Publisher's note
Includes discographies and bibliographical references

Classical music: the rough guide. 3rd ed, written by Duncan Clark. Rough Guides; [distributed by] Penguin Group 2001 610p il $23.95   **781.6**
1. Music 2. Composers 3. Music appreciation 4. Sound recordings—Reviews
ISBN 1-85828-721-9
First published 1998
This is an A-Z guide to composers, key works and top recordings. "Articles on such topics as sonata form, the concerto, atonality, and film music are also included." Publisher's note
Includes bibliographical references

Jacobson, Julius
The classical music experience; discover the music of the world's greatest composers; by Julius Jacobson II. Sourcebooks 2002 318p il $39.95   **781.6**
1. Music appreciation
ISBN 1-57071-950-0   LC 2002-3403
The author "attempts a short layperson's introduction to [classical] music, describing the lives and oeuvres of 42 composers, from Mozart and Wagner to Leonard Bernstein and Charles Ives. Arranged in roughly chronological order, the chapters range from two pages (Max Bruch) to more than 15 (Beethoven), each highlighting at least one musical work. . . . The novelty of Jacobson's book is the accompanying set of two audio CDs. Actor Kevin Kline summarizes the text in a few words, then musical examples follow." Libr J
Includes bibliographical references

Plotkin, Fred
Classical music 101; a complete guide to learning and loving classical music. Hyperion 2002 673p pa $18.95   **781.6**
1. Music appreciation
ISBN 0-7868-8627-7   LC 2002-69075
This introduction to classical music "revolves almost entirely around the orchestra's instruments and the listening experience. [The author] presents material as coursework, and his strictures about really listening (as opposed to mere 'hearing') are well taken and certainly apply to all kinds of music. A valuable feature are the interviews with classical musicians interspersed throughout. . . .

Recommended for libraries desiring an up-to-date and informative general introduction to classical music." Libr J
Includes discography and bibliographical references

Pogue, David
Classical music for dummies; by David Pogue and Scott Speck; preface by Zarin Mehta; foreword by Glenn Dicterow. IDG Bks. Worldwide 1997 xxvi, 356p il (—For dummies) pa $24.99   **781.6**
1. Music appreciation
ISBN 0-7645-5009-8   LC 97-80115
This book provides information on "the important composers, the main periods of music, the instruments, the conductors, the artists, when to applaud at a concert . . . and even what to wear to a performance. Icons throughout pinpoint tips, advanced information, listening guides, when to use the accompanying CD . . . and stories to use in conversations." Libr J

781.62 Folk music

American musical traditions; [edited by] Jeff Todd Titon, Bob Carlin. Schirmer Bks. 2002 5v il maps set $460   **781.62**
1. Folk music—United States
ISBN 0-02-864624-X   LC 01-42050
"Published in collaboration with The Smithsonian Folkways Recordings"
Contents: v1 Native American music; v2 African American music; v3 British Isles music; v4 European American music; v5 Latino and Asian American music
"This collection of 100 essays explores how American traditional music has arisen from ethnic or regional identity and culture to connect to regions abroad. . . . The essays examine the music of a representative sampling of the most important musical traditions and are complemented by interviews or artist profiles." Libr J
Includes bibliographical references, discographies, and videographies

American roots music; edited by Robert Santelli, Holly George-Warren, and Jim Brown; foreword by Bonnie Raitt. Abrams 2001 232p il $49.50   **781.62**
1. Folk music—United States 2. Popular music
ISBN 0-8109-1432-8   LC 2001-2511
"A Ginger Group/Rolling Stone Press Book"
Companion to a public television series this volume "explains and explores such strains as early blues, gospel, *musica tejana*, and Cajun/zydeco using vivid historical summaries, first-person interviews, and hundreds of rare archival photographs." Libr J
"Aside from the excellent essays, the book stands out for its selection of rare and fascinating photographs. A rich and thoughtful investigation of 'vernacular' music, this is essential reading for neophytes and connoisseurs alike." Publ Wkly

Strom, Yale
The book of Klezmer; the history, the music, the folklore. A Cappella Bks. 2002 381p il music $28   **781.62**
1. Klezmer music 2. Jews—Music
ISBN 1-55652-445-5   LC 2002-2701
This history of Klezmer music is divided into "four chapters: 'From King David to Duvid the Klezmer,'

Strom, Yale—*Continued*

'From the Enlightenment to the Holocaust,' 'Klezmer in the New World, 1880-1960,' and 'From Zev to Zorn: The Masters of the Culture.' The first appendix, 'Klezmer Memories in the Memorial Books,' is one of the most moving sections, featuring a collection of commentaries on klezmer music and musicians from hundreds of memorial books written by Holocaust survivors." Libr J

Includes discography and bibliographical references

781.64   Western popular music

All music guide; the definitive guide to popular music; edited by Vladimir Bogdanov, Chris Woodstra, Stephen Thomas Erlewine. 4th ed. Backbeat Bks. 2001 1491p $34.95   **781.64**
1. Sound recordings—Reviews 2. Popular music—Discography
ISBN 0-87930-627-0   LC 2001-52673
Also available online
First published 1992. Subtitle varies

In this guide "over 20,000 albums and 4000 artists are represented from the worlds of rock, blues, country, jazz, rap, folk, gospel, reggae, avant-garde, and more. The book is arranged into 16 genre chapters, each beginning with an overview of the genre and its various subgenres or 'styles.' . . . Artists are listed alphabetically within each chapter. . . . All albums are rated from one to five stars, with additional symbols denoting recommended first purchases and albums that are essential representations of a genre. Signed reviews from scores of contributors accompany the most significant titles." Libr J

Bronson, Fred

The Billboard book of number 1 hits. updated and expanded 5th ed. Billboard Bks. 2003 980p il pa $27.95   **781.64**
1. Popular music—Discography
ISBN 0-8230-7677-6   LC 2003-16910
First published 1985
This book covers hit songs since 1955 with a brief history of each song and its performer, listing songwriter, producer, record label and catalog number

George, Nelson

Hip hop America. Viking 1998 226p hardcover o.p. paperback available $13.95   **781.64**
1. Rap music 2. Popular culture—United States
ISBN 0-14-028022-7 (pa)   LC 98-23414
A social and economic history of the rap music industry and hip-hop culture
"This is an invaluable, entertaining and well written account from one who has not only witnessed the evolution of hip-hop but who, through his own passion and devotion to it as a critic, has had a hand in shaping it as well." N Y Times Book Rev
Includes bibliographical references

Rose, Tricia

Black noise; rap music and black culture in contemporary America. Wesleyan Univ. Press 1994 237p il (Music culture) hardcover o.p. paperback available $19.95   **781.64**
1. Rap music
ISBN 0-8195-6275-0 (pa)   LC 93-41386
The author "traces rap's sonic history . . . and gives substantial information about the innovative rhythmic manipulations made possible by the techniques of sampling. She also makes clear the connections between rap's beginnings and the political turmoils that afflicted black and Latino urban neighborhoods throughout the 1970s and 1980s. . . . Fans, scholars, and detractors alike stand to learn a great deal by studying Rose's commendable treatise." Booklist
Includes bibliographical references

Veloso, Caetano, 1942-

Tropical truth; a story of music and revolution in Brazil; translated by Isabel de Sena; edited by Barbara Einzig. Knopf 2002 354p il $26   **781.64**
1. Popular music 2. Brazil—Social life and customs
ISBN 0-375-40788-X   LC 2002-66147
Also available in paperback from Da Capo Press
Veloso traces "how in the 1960s he and his friends developed a post-bossa nova music and movement called tropicalismo (Tropiclia in English)." Libr J
"This is a must for Brazilian music fans, as well as anyone interested in how the modernist age played out in South America." Publ Wkly
Includes discography

Whitburn, Joel

The Billboard book of top 40 hits; [compiled by] Joel Whitburn. Billboard Bks. pa $24.95   **781.64**
1. Popular music—Discography
First published 1983. (7th edition 2000) Periodically revised
A guide to all single recordings that have made Billboard's Top 40 lists since 1955. Entries are alphabetical by artist and give such information as date the record made the charts, number of weeks on the charts, highest position, etc. Biographical data and trivia on most of the artists are also included

781.642   Country music

All music guide to country; the definitive guide to country music; edited by Vladimir Bogdanov, Chris Woodstra, and Stephen Thomas Erlewine. 2nd ed. Backbeat Bks. 2003 700p pa $27.95   **781.642**
ISBN 0-8793-0760-0   LC 2003-62827
Also available online
First published 1997 by Miller Freeman
"Featuring concise career biographies of more than 1,000 performers, both individuals and groups, the guide covers the entire range of country music from the early trailblazers like Jimmie Rodgers and the Sons of the Pioneers to the newest stars like LeAnn Rimes. It also covers a broad array of subgenres, ranging from traditional country to contemporary alternative country. . . . Albums considered to be essential recordings for any good country collection and those recommended as a first pur-

All music guide to country—*Continued*
chase for the particular performer are separately labeled.
More than 5,500 recordings are included, making this an
excellent resource for collectors." Am Ref Books Annu,
1998 {entry for 1997 edition}

Dawidoff, Nicholas
In the country of country; people and
places in American music. Pantheon Bks.
1997 371p il hardcover o.p. paperback
available $15   **781.642**
1. Country music
ISBN 0-375-70082-X (pa)   LC 96-34682
Among those discussed in this survey are: "Kitty
Wells, Harlan Howard, Doc Watson, Merle Haggard,
George Jones, Emmylou Harris, Johnny Cash . . . Jimmy Rodgers, the Carter Family and Ira Louvin." Publ
Wkly
The author "concludes with a rich bibliography but a
slightly disappointing discography; nevertheless, this is
excellent, no-nonsense country-music history." Booklist

The **Encyclopedia** of country music; the
ultimate guide to the music; compiled by
the staff of the Country Music Hall of
Fame and Museum; edited by Paul
Kingsbury with the assistance of Laura
Garrard, Daniel Cooper, and John Rumble.
Oxford Univ. Press 1998 634p il $55
    781.642
1. Country music—Encyclopedias
ISBN 0-19-511671-2   LC 97-51362
"Interspersed with the biographical entries are historical and sociological essays on the literature of country
music, country songwriting, gospel, folk and popular music connections, and even touring and costuming. Thirteen appendixes cover the Country Music Hall of Fame,
radio stations, and best-selling country albums." Libr J

Stambler, Irwin
Country music: the encyclopedia; {by}
Irwin Stambler & Grelun Landon. St.
Martin's Press 1997 708p il hardcover o.p.
paperback available $29.95   **781.642**
1. Country music—Encyclopedias
ISBN 0-312-26487-9 (pa)   LC 96-43043
First published 1969 with title: Encyclopedia of folk,
country & western music
This reference offers biographical sketches of country
music artists and includes notable recordings, photos,
award information, and interviews
The entries "tend to have more depth than usually
found in other encyclopedias on country music." Libr J
Includes discography, videography, and bibliography

Wolff, Kurt
Country music: the rough guide; written by
Kurt Wolff; edited by Orla Duane. Rough
Guides 2000 596p il $24.95   **781.642**
1. Country music
ISBN 1-85828-534-8
This encompasses "the genre's important niches
(Western, bluegrass, honky-tonk, rockabilly, etc.). Solid,
informative essays on each area lead into bios of varying
lengths on its key personalities as well as many of the
more colorful albeit minor artists who usually get passed
by in this type of work. Selected CD/album critiques also
appear at the end of many entries, and the text is dotted
with numerous album covers and black-and-white pictures of artists." Libr J

781.643   Blues music

Lomax, Alan, 1915-2002
The land where the blues began. Pantheon
Bks. 1993 539p il o.p.; New Press paperback
available with CD $21.95   **781.643**
1. Blues music 2. African American music 3. African
Americans—Mississippi
ISBN 1-56584-739-3 (pa)   LC 91-52627
This is an account of the folklorist and musicologist's
travels in the Mississippi Delta in the 1940s as he
recorded the work of African American blues musicians
"If it were a novel, Alan Lomax's long-awaited ac-
count of his adventures in the Mississippi Delta would be
called 'sprawling' and a 'must read.' . . . It is as delightful and hard to put down as any fictional epic."
Booklist
Includes bibliographical references

Nothing but the blues; the music and the
musicians; [edited by] Lawrence Cohn.
Abbeville Press 1993 432p il hardcover
o.p. paperback available $39.95   **781.643**
1. Blues music
ISBN 0-7892-0607-2 (pa)   LC 93-2791
This "illustrated compilation of articles by 10 notable
writers examines the origins of blues and the music's
various styles and artists, including women." Booklist
Includes discography and bibliographical references

781.646   Reggae

Bradley, Lloyd
This is reggae music; the story of
Jamaica's music. Grove Press 2001 c2000
572p il pa $17   **781.646**
1. Reggae music
ISBN 0-8021-3828-4   LC 2001-33462
First published 2000 in the United Kingdom with title:
Brass culture: when reggae was king
This "account identifies and traces the genealogy of
reggae. . . . Focusing on reggae as a commerical entity
rather than as a means of proselytizing Rastafarianism,
Bradley nevertheless describes Rasta influences on it and
how it affected Jamaican culture." Booklist
Presented "in a witty and engaging manner. . . . For
enthusiasts, this book is fabulous." Libr J
Includes bibliographical references

781.65   Jazz music

All music guide to jazz; the definitive guide
to jazz music; edited by Vladimir
Bogdanov, Chris Woodstra, and Stephen
Thomas Erlewine. Backbeat Bks. pa $32.95
    781.65
1. Jazz music—Discography 2. Sound recordings—
Reviews
Also available online
First published 1994 by Miller Freeman. (4th edition
2002) Periodically revised
This "reference reviews and rates more than 20,000
top recordings by over 1,700 musicians in all jazz styles
and eras—from New Orleans jazz to swing, bebop, cool,
hard bop, Latin jazz, fusion, and beyond." Publisher's
note

Appel, Alfred

Jazz modernism; from Ellington and Armstrong to Matisse and Joyce; [by] Alfred Appel, Jr. Knopf 2002 283p il $35 **781.65**
1. Jazz music 2. Music and literature 3. Art and music
ISBN 0-394-53393-3　　　　　LC 2002-66132
Appel aims "to 'establish the place of classic jazz (1920-50)—especially Louis Armstrong, Duke Ellington, Fats Waller, Billie Holiday, Jack Teagarden, and Charlie Parker—in the great Modernist tradition in the arts.'" Nation
"Playful, punning, and brimming with admiration, Appel nimbly makes fresh, resonant connections across artistic disciplines and racial divides." Booklist

DeVeaux, Scott Knowles

The birth of bebop; a social and musical history; [by] Scott DeVeaux. University of Calif. Press 1997 572p il hardcover o.p. paperback available $21.95 **781.65**
1. Jazz music
ISBN 0-520-21665-2 (pa)　　　　LC 96-46887
"During the 1940s, bebop shook the foundations of jazz. . . . DeVeaux makes a vital contribution to the field of jazz studies by providing not just insightful explanation of the music but also perceptive commentary on the social and political shifts that helped shape it. He knowledgeably uses musical notation and testimony from the musicians to build his narrative." Booklist
Includes bibliographical references

Friedwald, Will, 1961-

Jazz singing; America's great voices from Bessie Smith to bebop and beyond. Da Capo Press 1996 505p il pa $18.50 **781.65**
1. Jazz music 2. Singers
ISBN 0-306-80712-2　　　　　LC 96-23837
First published 1990 by Scribner, this edition has a new discography
"Starting with blues singers who laid the foundations for jazz-oriented popular singing, the author follows the development of this vocal style from Bing Crosby and Louis Armstrong through a host of performers to the present day." Publ Wkly
"This is an absolutely essential book for anybody who cares in the slightest about adult popular music." Booklist

Giddins, Gary

Visions of jazz; the first century. Oxford Univ. Press 1998 690p hardcover o.p. paperback available $18.95 **781.65**
1. Jazz musicians 2. Jazz music
ISBN 0-19-513241-6 (pa)　　　　LC 98-12199
"Alongside his virtuoso considerations of Ellington, Monk, Mingus, and the predictable greats, Giddins illuminates the contributions to be found in the likes of Al Jolson's minstrel posing and Stan Kenton's florid kitsch. His writing, like the music he loves, is joyously polyphonic, with history, legend, musicology, biography, and performance all rising out of the mix." New Yorker

Gioia, Ted

The history of jazz. Oxford Univ. Press 1997 471p il $37.50; pa $16.95 **781.65**
ISBN 0-19-509081-0; 0-19-512653-X (pa)
LC 97-102
The author "relates the story of African American music from its roots in Africa to the international respect it enjoys today. . . . This well-researched, extensively annotated volume covers the major trends and personalities that have shaped jazz. The excellent bibliography and list of recommended listening make this a valuable purchase for libraries building a jazz collection." Libr J

Hentoff, Nat

Listen to the stories; Nat Hentoff on jazz and country music. HarperCollins Pubs. 1995 220p o.p.; Da Capo Press paperback available $16 **781.65**
1. Jazz music 2. Country music
ISBN 0-306-80982-6 (pa)　　　　LC 95-1395
This collection of pieces from Hentoff's column in the Wall Street Journal "presents a combination of recollections and personal profiles introducing legendary artists such as Billie Holiday and Duke Ellington as well as contemporary musicians such as 'jazz player' Wynton Marsalis." Booklist
"The pieces are short, mostly between three and five pages, but Hentoff always manages to make his point and to pique our interest in the music." Libr J
Includes bibliographical references

Jazz: the first century; edited by John Edward Hasse; forewords by Quincy Jones and Tony Bennett; with contributions by Larry Appelbaum [et al.] Morrow 2000 246p il $42.95 **781.65**
1. Jazz music
ISBN 0-688-17074-9　　　　　LC 99-46071
"Comprising eight chapters (two authored by Hasse, the others by prominent scholars like Bob Blumenthal) that follow a chronological progression from jazz's earliest inclinations through its more recent developments, this also features numerous sidebars." Libr J
"This photo-rich, snappily laid-out survey covers its subject with genuine thoroughness." Booklist
Includes discographies and bibliographical references

Kahn, Ashley

A love supreme; the story of John Coltrane's signature album. Viking 2002 xxii, 260p il $27.95 **781.65**
1. Coltrane, John, 1926-1967. Love supreme
ISBN 0-670-03136-4　　　　　LC 2002-29623
"Foreword by Elvin Jones." Jacket
"Kahn covers the lead-up to and the follow-through from the great tenor saxophonist's most characteristic and popular album by efficiently telling Coltrane's life story and illuminating many aspects of his great record's creation, not to mention its impact." Booklist
Includes discography and bibliographical references

Milkowski, Bill, 1954-

Swing it! an annotated history of jive. Billboard Bks. 2001 288p il pa $18.95

781.65

1. Jazz music

ISBN 0-8230-7671-7   LC 00-64233

The author sorts "his biographical-discographical sketches into thematic chapters titled 'Godfathers of jive' (Louis Armstrong, Cab Calloway, etc.), 'Golden Era of jive' (Louis Jordan, Stuff Smith, etc.), 'The White Connection' (Gibson, Louis Prima, etc.), and 'Retro Jivesters' (Big Bad Voodoo Daddy, Squirrel Nut Zippers, Brian Setzer, etc.)." Booklist

Includes bibliographical references

The **New** Grove dictionary of jazz; edited by Barry Kernfeld. 2nd ed. Grove's Dictionaries Inc. 2002 3v set $250 **781.65**

1. Jazz music

ISBN 1-56159-284-6   LC 2001-40794

First published 1988 in two volumes

This reference to jazz and jazz musicians includes "more than 7750 entries. . . . {It covers} jazz styles, instruments, record labels, nicknames, guilds and associations, jazz language, libraries and archives, false fingering techniques for horns, festivals, titles of films containing jazz scenes, a list of contrafacts . . . and even biographies of a few jazz writers and critics." Libr J

For a fuller review see: Booklist, Mar. 15, 2002

The **Oxford** companion to jazz; edited by Bill Kirchner. Oxford Univ. Press 2000 852p il $49.95 **781.65**

1. Jazz music

ISBN 0-19-512510-X   LC 99-88598

For this work, Kirchner "commissioned essays from 59 jazz critics, including Dan Morgenstern, John McDonough, Gene Lees, Gene Santoro and Gunther Schuller. . . . Essays cover major historical trends and figures, discuss jazz in different countries, review the role of most instruments and consider the place of jazz in other arts, like dance, literature and film." N Y Times Book Rev

"This work is an effective single-volume device, leading current listeners to the music while including enough newer scholarship to retain the interest of connoisseurs." Libr J

Includes bibliographical references

Ratliff, Ben

Jazz: a critic's guide to the 100 most important recordings. Times Bks. 2002 xx, 250p il (New York Times essential library) pa $16 **781.65**

1. Jazz music—Discography 2. Sound recordings—Reviews

ISBN 0-8050-7068-0   LC 2002-69551

The author "presents essays on what he considers the 100 most important jazz recordings. In each, he discusses a recording's merits and shortcomings and includes a list of its performers. . . . As a guide for the uninitiated it is essential for academic music libraries and public libraries large and small. It would also be most useful for collection development librarians building a well-rounded jazz CD collection." Libr J

Shipton, Alyn

A new history of jazz. Continuum 2001 965p il $24.95 **781.65**

1. Jazz music

ISBN 0-8264-4754-6   LC 2001-17177

This volume "spans the entire history of jazz, from its mid-nineteenth-century origins to the present day. Shipton's . . . treatment seeks to rebut some of the more popular myths about the origins of jazz." Booklist

"Throughout, Shipton stresses the importance of the recording industry, which early on helped spread the form to young musicians beyond the big centers of New Orleans, Chicago and New York, and has facilitated communication between jazz musicians. This comprehensive book, with its wealth of information presented in nontechnical style accessible to the general reader, is a major contribution to the literature of jazz." Publ Wkly

Includes bibliographical references

Ward, Geoffrey C.

Jazz; a history of America's music; based on a documentary film by Ken Burns written by Geoffrey C. Ward; with a preface by Ken Burns. Knopf 2000 489p il $65; pa $29.95

781.65

1. Jazz music

ISBN 0-679-44551-X; 0-679-76539-5 (pa)

LC 00-22604

Companion volume to PBS series of the same title

The authors "have assembled a comprehensive history with a focus on the musicians and the sociology of jazz. . . . The short articles by Wynton Marsalis, Dan Morgenstern, Gerald Early, Stanley Crouch, and Gary Giddins, which are woven into the text, provide a . . . specific focus on a number of jazz's aspects." Libr J

"The illustrations are copious, including about 500 pieces and running from cover to cover; the text, picture captions, and sidebars reflect the research that went into the six-year project. A very competent and lovingly rendered history." Booklist

Includes bibliographical references

781.66   Rock (Rock 'n' roll)

The **Beatles** anthology. Chronicle Bks. 2000 367p il $60; pa $35 **781.66**

1. Beatles

ISBN 0-8118-2684-8; 0-8118-3636-3 (pa)

LC 00-23685

The story of the Beatles as "told through quotes from John, Paul, George, and Ringo, as well as the group's closest aides: George Martin, Neil Aspinall, and Derek Taylor. . . . The density of the text is daunting, but the book's browsability makes it as appealing to casual readers as it is indispensable to Beatlemaniacs." Libr J

Includes bibliographical references

Miller, Jim, 1947-

Flowers in the dustbin; the rise of rock and roll, 1947-1977. Simon & Schuster 1999 415p il hardcover o.p. paperback available $15 **781.66**

1. Rock music

ISBN 0-684-86560-2 (pa)   LC 99-21077

Miller "explores the cultural underpinnings of Fifties and Sixties rock'n'roll. In dozens of brief chapters, he identifies turning points in rock history: the rise of jump

Miller, Jim, 1947-—*Continued*
blues, the introduction of Top 40 radio, Alan Freed's rock'n'roll dances, Dick Clark's *American Bandstand*, and the payola scandal. Miller pays special attention to Elvis Presley and the Beatles." Libr J
Includes discography

The **Rolling** Stone illustrated history of rock & roll; the definitive history of the most important artists and their music; edited by Anthony DeCurtis and James Henke with Holly George-Warren; original editor: Jim Miller. [new ed] Random House 1992 710p il pa $34.95   **781.66**
1. Rock music
ISBN 0-679-73728-6   LC 92-6339
First published 1976
This history of four decades of rock music includes essays and photographs covering individual artists, groups, trends and styles

Strong, M. C. (Martin Charles), 1960-
The great rock discography. 6th ed. Canongate 2002 1185p $50; pa $30   **781.66**
1. Rock music—Discography
ISBN 1-8419-5311-3; 1-8419-5312-1 (pa)
First published 1994
This work contains: discographies listing every track by more than 1,000 groups; band histories, lineup changes, career milestones; catalog numbers for ordering recordings and evaluating collections; top U.S. and U.K. chart positions; name changes, breakups, solo albums

782   Vocal music

The **Cambridge** companion to singing; edited by John Potter. Cambridge Univ. Press 2000 286p il (Cambridge companions to music) $60; pa $24   **782**
1. Singing 2. Vocal music
ISBN 0-521-62225-5; 0-521-62709-5 (pa)
                                            LC 99-32948
"Articles on popular traditions, including world music, rock, rap, and jazz, describe the major singers and songwriters in each. Then come histories of theatrical singing encompassing twentieth-century stage and screen artists, the beginnings of opera, and grand opera. The growth of choral music and art songs is traced next. . . . The last and largest section concerns performance practices in choral and ensemble singing, medieval singing techniques, singing in the pre-romantic and contemporary periods, teaching singing, children's singing, and vocal production. . . . The guide covers its wide range of topics accessibly as well as thoroughly for a one-volume work." Booklist

782.27   Hymns

American hymns old and new; [compiled by] Albert Christ-Janer, Charles W. Hughes, Charles Sprague Smith. Columbia Univ. Press 1980 838p music $104   **782.27**
1. Hymns
ISBN 0-231-03458-X
Also published as a two-volume set, with v2 consisting of notes on the hymns and biographies, compiled by Charles W. Hughes (o.p.)

This is an interdenominational compilation of 625 hymns sung in America since 1615

782.28   Carols

The **New** Oxford book of carols; edited by Hugh Keyte and Andrew Parrott; associate editor, Clifford Bartlett. Oxford Univ. Press 1992 xxxiv, 702p music hardcover o.p. paperback available $34.95   **782.28**
1. Carols
ISBN 0-19-353322-7 (pa)   LC 92-756468
First published 1928 with title: The Oxford book of carols
This book contains over 300 settings of sacred and secular carols spanning the Catholic and Protestant traditions. The selections are drawn from: folk carols, medieval Latin songs, English medieval carols, Lutheran hymnody, and English "gallery" and American "primitive" carols

782.42   Songs

The **Books** of the American Negro spirituals; edited by James Weldon Johnson and J. Rosamond Johnson. Da Capo Press 2002 pa $25   **782.42**
1. Spirituals (Songs)
ISBN 0-306-81202-9
A reprint of the volumes first published separately in 1925 and 1926 by Viking and reissued in the present format 1940
Includes "The book of American Negro spirituals" (1925) and "The second book of Negro spirituals" (1926). Contains words and music of 120 spirituals
Musical arrangements by J. Rosamond Johnson, additional numbers by Lawrence Brown

The **Children's** song index, 1978-1993; compiled by Kay Laughlin, Pollyanne Frantz, Ann Branton. Libraries Unlimited 1996 153p $40   **782.42**
1. Songs—Indexes
ISBN 1-56308-332-9   LC 95-40236
"This book indexes more than 2,500 songs from 77 song books listed in *Cumulative Book Index*, 1977-1994. . . . [Songs are indexed] by song title, first line, or subject. . . . A quick-reference tool for those who need to locate in which songbook a particular song can be found, this index encompasses songs appealing to children prekindergarten through middle school." Booklist
Includes bibliographical references

Ferguson, Gary Lynn
Song finder; a title index to 32,000 popular songs in collections, 1854-1992; compiled by Gary Lynn Ferguson under the auspices of the State Library of Louisiana. Greenwood Press 1995 344p (Music reference collection) $88.95   **782.42**
1. Songs—Indexes
ISBN 0-313-29470-4   LC 95-9936
In this index "the song collections include theater, folk, children's, African American, military, patriotic,

Ferguson, Gary Lynn—*Continued*

pop, rock, and country music. Movie and TV themes ('M*A*S*H Theme Song') and advertising jingles ('Chiquita Banana') are also covered. . . . It provides indexing to so many songs and books not covered elsewhere that it is a useful and necessary addition to the reference collection." Booklist

Includes bibliographical references

Friedwald, Will, 1961-

Stardust melodies; the biography of twelve of America's most popular songs. Pantheon Bks. 2002 397p il $27.50   **782.42**

1. Popular music 2. Songs

ISBN 0-375-42089-4   LC 2001-36514

Contents: Star dust; St. Louis blues; Ol' man river; Mack the Knife; Body and soul; I got rhythm; As time goes by; Night and day; Stormy weather; Summertime; My funny valentine; Lush life

"The joy of these short essays—ruminative, but also filled with fascinating historical and social details—is in their intelligence and their always evident love of the music itself." Publ Wkly

Havlice, Patricia Pate

Popular song index. Scarecrow Press 1975 933p o.p. supplements available   **782.42**

1. Songs—Indexes 2. Popular music—Indexes

First supplement (1978) $60 (ISBN 0-8108-1099-9); Second supplement (1984) $65 (ISBN 0-8108-1642-3); Third supplement (1989) $72 (ISBN 0-8108-2202-4)

"Indexes 301 song collections published between 1940 and 1972 in the original volume and adds 253 collections in the supplements, mainly from the 1970-87 period, but with some published earlier. 'Popular' includes folk songs, hymns, children's songs, etc. The index is by title, first line of verse, and first line of chorus, all coded to the numbered anthologies." Ref Sources for Small & Medium-sized Libr. 5th edition

Hischak, Thomas

The American musical film song encyclopedia; [by] Thomas S. Hischak. Greenwood Press 1999 521p $83.95   **782.42**

1. Motion picture music—Encyclopedias 2. Songs—Encyclopedias

ISBN 0-313-30737-7   LC 98-34723

"Coverage is restricted to songs actually written for film. . . . Entries, arranged by song title, include vocalist, composer, lyricist, and information on the place of the song in the film, as well as recordings by artists other than those in the film. The concise entries combine a wealth of information not found in other sources." Libr J

The Tin Pan Alley song encyclopedia; [by] Thomas S. Hischak. Greenwood Press 2002 530p $74.95   **782.42**

1. Popular music—Encyclopedias

ISBN 0-313-31992-8   LC 2002-23250

Companion volume to The American musical film song encyclopedia and The American musical theatre song encyclopedia (1995)

"*Tin Pan Alley* refers to the American popular music business from the mid-nineteenth through the mid-twentieth centuries, and the songs written for parlor pianos, sing-alongs, dance orchestras, radio broadcasts, etc. This book is an A-Z listing of more than 1,200 popular songs. . . . Each entry includes the year the song was published and highly readable information about its composition and performance history." Booklist

Includes bibliographical references

National anthems of the world; edited by W.L. Reed and M.J. Bristow. Cassell; [distributed by] Sterling music $90 **782.42**

1. National songs

First published 1943 in the United Kingdom with title: National anthems of the United Nations and France. (10th edition 2002) Periodically revised. Publisher varies

This volume contains national anthems of about 195 nations, including melody and accompaniment. Words are presented in the native language with transliteration provided where necessary. English translations follow. Brief historical notes on the adoption of each anthem are included and the book concludes with a list of national holidays

Peterson, Carolyn Sue, 1938-

Index to children's songs; a title, first line, and subject index; compiled by Carolyn Sue Peterson and Ann D. Fenton. Wilson, H.W. 1979 318p $65   **782.42**

1. Songs—Indexes

ISBN 0-8242-0638-X   LC 79-14265

"A numbered indexed list of 298 children's song books published between 1909 and 1977, identifying more than 5000 songs (both American and foreign) and variations, arranged alphabetically by author. There are also a title and first line index and a subject index using more than 1000 subject headings. The titles are likely to be held in schools and public libraries." Ref Sources for Small & Medium-sized Libr. 5th edition

Porter, Cole, 1891-1964

The complete lyrics of Cole Porter; edited by Robert Kimball; with a foreword by John Updike. Knopf 1983 xxv, 354p il o.p.; Da Capo Press paperback available $30 **782.42**

1. American songs

ISBN 0-306-80483-2 (pa)   LC 83-48101

The author "has gathered 800 of Porter's lyrics, 400 of which have not been published before. Each section begins with a full-page photo of Porter or one of the many celebrated performers of his work. The shows and films for which he wrote are arranged chronologically, and each lyric comes with publishing information and the name of the performer who introduced the song." Libr J

Sandburg, Carl, 1878-1967

The American songbag; [compiled by] Carl Sandburg. Harcourt Brace & Co. 1927 xxiii, 495p il music hardcover o.p. paperback available $24   **782.42**

1. Folk songs—United States 2. American ballads

ISBN 0-15-605650-X (pa)

The song history of America is traced through this "collection of 280 songs. . . . The music includes not merely airs and melodies, but complete harmonizations or piano accompaniments." Introduction

"Each song is introduced by Mr. Sandburg, who in a few words gives the story of his discovery or of its origin. Those notes make fascinating reading, and they can be enjoyed by those who cannot read notes." Springfield Repub

Songwriter's market. Writer's Digest Bks. $24.99 **782.42**
1. Popular music—Writing and publishing
ISSN 0161-5971
Annual. First published 1978
The main section of this guide consists of listings of music publishers, record companies, producers, managers, booking agents, and firms interested in original music. Also included are articles which present an overview of the songwriting field, and listings of resources such as organizations, workshops, and contests

The **Vibe** history of hip hop; edited by Alan Light. Three Rivers Press (NY) 1999 418p il pa $27.50 **782.42**
1. Rap music
ISBN 0-609-80503-7   LC 99-36003
This history of rap music answers "questions about hip-hop culture, such as how rap got started, who the earliest performers were, etc. Even larger issues such as the role of women as rap artists, regional rivalries, money, power, and the merge of rock and roll are examined in great detail. . . . This gargantuan masterpiece is profusely illustrated." SLJ
Includes discographies

784.19   Musical instruments

The **Illustrated** encyclopedia of musical instruments; general editor Robert Dearling. Schirmer Bks. 1996 240p il $125   **784.19**
1. Musical instruments
ISBN 0-02-864667-3
"Designed to describe in words and pictures the nature and capabilities of all the families of musical instruments, this . . . volume ranges from very early drums and horns to modern electronic instruments." Booklist
"This is a serious work that discusses its complicated subject thoroughly and accurately, but the joy of the book is that it does this with flair, wit, and style. It is also a book of uncommon beauty." Recomm Ref Books for Small & Medium-sized Libr & Media Cent, 1997

784.2   Symphony orchestra

Steinberg, Michael
The symphony; a listener's guide. Oxford Univ. Press 1995 678p music $42.50; pa $25 **784.2**
1. Symphony 2. Music appreciation 3. Composers
ISBN 0-19-506177-2; 0-19-512665-3 (pa)
                                          LC 95-5568
"Steinberg describes 36 composers and, movement by movement, 118 symphonies, including all the standard repertory . . . as well as a few by less well known composers such as Gorecki, Harbison, Martinu, and Sessions. The writing varies from formal and factual to chatty, with candid asides and stories relevant to the composer, the composition, or an important performance." Libr J
Includes bibliographical references

786.2   Pianos

Rosen, Charles, 1927-
Piano notes; the world of the pianist. Free Press 2002 246p il $25   **786.2**
1. Pianists 2. Piano music
ISBN 0-7432-0382-8   LC 2002-69634
Contents: Body and mind; Listening to the sound of the piano; The instrument and its discontents; Conservatories and contests; Concerts; Recording; Styles and manners
Rosen "truly sheds light on all aspects of piano performance, and piano-music lovers and players alike will benefit from his thought-provoking and appreciation-enhancing comments." Booklist

Siepmann, Jeremy
The piano. Knopf 1997 184p il (Everyman's music companions) $47.50
                                          786.2
1. Pianos
ISBN 0-375-40022-2   LC 97-217293
Also available in paperback from Hal Leonard
Accompanied by 3 CDs
This book covers the piano's history from its modest 18th century beginnings, to society drawing rooms and Harlem honky-tonks. Special sections are devoted to technical developments, composers, performers and pieces of music

787.87   Guitars

Bacon, Tony
The ultimate guitar book; [by] Tony Bacon & Paul Day. Knopf 1991 192p il hardcover o.p. paperback available $27.50   **787.87**
1. Guitars
ISBN 0-375-70090-0 (pa)   LC 91-52714
This is a "chronological history of the guitar, beginning with an example from 1552 and continuing through current times. Covering acoustic, electrical, and bass guitars, including all the big-name manufacturers such as Fender, Gibson, Martin, and Stratocaster, this informative and beautifully illustrated work will have wide appeal." SLJ

Chapman, Richard
The complete guitarist. Dorling Kindersley 1993 192p il hardcover o.p. paperback available $20   **787.87**
1. Guitars
ISBN 1-56458-711-8 (pa)   LC 92-56493
This work ranges "from fundamentals such as tuning, scales, chords, picking, and strumming, to advanced techniques of various styles such as rock, blues, and jazz. . . . [It also] includes discussions on such topics as sound and amplification, choosing a guitar, studio and home recording, plus care and maintenance of the instrument. An appealing book in the style of the 'Eyewitness' series." SLJ

791 Public performances

Jay, Ricky

Jay's journal of anomalies; conjurers, cheats, hustlers, hoaxsters, pranksters, jokesters, impostors, pretenders, sideshow showmen, armless calligraphers, mechanical marvels, popular entertainments. Farrar, Straus & Giroux 2001 202p il $40 **791**

1. Entertainers 2. Curiosities and wonders 3. Impostors and imposture

ISBN 0-374-17867-4 LC 2001-16200

Also available in paperback from Norton

The author "gathers four years of his quarterly *Jay's Journal of Anomalies* in one volume of the same name. An expert on the improbable, Jay trains his curiosity on unusual forms of entertainment and recorded history. . . . He has unearthed gems like an advertisement for 'Miss Silvia, Skandenavian Ceiling Walker' and a centuries-long fascination with the public spectacle of nose amputation. . . . [A] witty and bizarre collection." Publ Wkly

Includes bibliographical references

Terkel, Studs, 1912-

The spectator. New Press 1999 364p $26.95; pa $16.95 **791**

1. Entertainers 2. Dramatists

ISBN 1-56584-553-6; 1-56584-633-8 (pa)

LC 99-17129

This is "a compendium of forty-five years of [Terkel's] conversations with film and theater people." Nation

"Telling portraits of a wide range of artists in conversation with a passionately involved, prodigiously well prepared interlocutor." Booklist

791.3 Circuses

McVicar, Wes

Clown act omnibus; everything you need to know about clowning plus over 200 clown stunts. 2nd ed. Meriwether 1987 184p il pa $14.95 **791.3**

1. Clowns

ISBN 0-916260-41-0 LC 87-42958

First published 1960

This volume covers "the basics of being a clown; clown equipment; walk-ons and walk-arounds; clown acts with special equipment [and includes] over 200 skit ideas, classified." Publisher's note

Includes bibliographical references

Wilkins, Charles (Charles Everett)

The circus at the edge of the earth; travels with the Great Wallenda Circus. McClelland & Stewart 1998 270p il $22.95; pa $15.95 **791.3**

1. Great Wallenda Circus

ISBN 0-7710-8847-7; 0-7710-8842-6 (pa)

LC 99-161790

"Wilkins chronicles a month on the road in his native Canada with the Great Wallenda Circus in the spring of 1997 and, in the process, offers remarkable insight into a subculture—the diverse assortment of gymnasts, animal trainers, daredevils and wanderers who identify themselves as circus folk—that is slowly disappearing from public consciousness." Publ Wkly

791.43 Motion pictures

The **Actor's** book of movie monologues; edited by Marisa Smith and Amy Schewel. Penguin Bks. 1986 xxx, 240p pa $14

791.43

1. Motion pictures 2. Monologues

ISBN 0-14-009475-X LC 86-8093

"Although designed as a sourcebook for aspiring thespians who need material for auditions, this collection of famous movie monologues makes great browsing for all film buffs. . . . Featuring memorable speeches from more than 80 films, the text is arranged chronologically." Booklist

Allen, Woody

Woody Allen on Woody Allen; in conversation with Stig Björkman. Grove Press 1995 288p il hardcover o.p. paperback available $14 **791.43**

ISBN 0-8021-3425-4 (pa) LC 94-26866

"Swedish filmmaker Björkman compiled this volume from several weeks of interviews, conducted over a six-month period, in which he led Allen through a film-by-film discussion of his quarter century as director, actor, and writer." Booklist

"This is the most comprehensive discussion so far by Allen of his films. . . . The Woody Allen that emerges is a craftsman whose real obsession is his work." Sight Sound

Includes filmography

Auiler, Dan

Vertigo; the making of a Hitchcock classic; foreword by Martin Scorsese. St. Martin's Press 1998 220p il hardcover o.p. paperback available $17.95 **791.43**

1. Hitchcock, Alfred, 1899-1980 2. Vertigo (Motion picture)

ISBN 0-312-26409-7 (pa) LC 97-31654

In this account of the film's production Auiler "reconstructs the sometimes uneasy give-and-take between Hitchcock and his players—actors Jimmy Stewart, Kim Novak and Barbara Bel Geddes; screenwriters Samuel Taylor and Alec Coppel; Robert Burks and his second-unit cameraman who created the now-famous Vertigo effect . . . and Bernard Hermann, who composed the mesmerizing score. Interesting factoids abound." Publ Wkly

Barrier, J. Michael

Hollywood cartoons; American animation in its golden age; [by] Michael Barrier. Oxford Univ. Press 1999 648p il hardcover o.p. paperback available $19.95 **791.43**

1. Animated films

ISBN 0-19-516729-5 (pa) LC 98-7471

"Based on archival research and hundreds of interviews, this volume provides a comprehensive survey of American animation up to the late 1960s. . . . Barrier traces the development of such studios as Disney, Warner Brothers, and MGM. His cast of characters includes animators like Max Fleischer, Tex Avery, Chuck Jones, and Bill Hanna and Joe Barbera." Libr J

"A genuinely thoughtful attempt to explain what makes golden-age cartoons work, and why some work better than others." N Y Times Book Rev

Includes bibliographical references

Biskind, Peter

Easy riders, raging bulls; how the sex-drugs-and-rock-'n'-roll generation saved Hollywood. Simon & Schuster 1998 506p il hardcover o.p. paperback available $15

791.43

1. Motion picture producers and directors 2. Motion pictures
ISBN 0-684-85708-1 (pa)   LC 98-2919
This is an account "of 'New Hollywood' filmmakers like Francis Ford Coppola, Martin Scorsese, Steven Spielberg, George Lucas, William Friedkin, Peter Bogdanovich, Hal Ashby, Robert Towne, Paul Schrader, Dennis Hopper and the producer Bert Schneider." N Y Times Book Rev
"Biskind does relish the tales of outlandish behaviour. . . . But in kicking over the traces of survivors' more or less reliable memories, he shows that libidinal and pharmaceutical urges were intrinsic to the film-makers' ferocious need to outdo each other as auteurs along the lines of the European greats they studied and worshipped." Sight Sound
Includes filmography and bibliographical references

Brownlow, Kevin

Mary Pickford rediscovered; rare pictures of a Hollywood legend; Robert Cushman, general editor. Abrams 1999 256p il $39.95

791.43

1. Pickford, Mary, 1893-1979
ISBN 0-8109-4374-3   LC 98-41302
This re-evaluation of Pickford's cinematic career is copiously illustrated with "photographs and movie stills, which range from Pickford at her most winsomely beautiful to her most unrecognizably, even grotesquely, plain. Brownlow, one of our most eloquent guides to silent cinema, provides fascinating background stories and appreciations of the films themselves and of Pickford's amazingly varied incarnations." N Y Times Book Rev
Includes bibliographical references

Canby, Vincent

The New York times guide to the best 1,000 movies ever made; [by] Vincent Canby, Janet Maslin, and the film critics of the New York Times; edited by Peter M. Nichols. Times Bks. 1999 xxii, 1002p pa $25 **791.43**

1. Motion pictures—Reviews
ISBN 0-8129-3001-0   LC 98-45289
"This volume compiles alphabetically the original reviews of the 1000 'best' films as selected by *New York Times* critics from 1927 to 1998. . . . The result is fascinating in two respects. First, the book provides easy access to historical criticism. . . . Second, it encourages reflection on the politics of taste." Libr J

Chadwick, Bruce

The reel Civil War; mythmaking in American film. Knopf 2001 366p il hardcover o.p. paperback available $15   **791.43**

1. Motion pictures 2. United States—History—1861-1865, Civil War—Motion pictures and the war
ISBN 0-375-70832-4 (pa)   LC 2001-91008
The author "charts the resiliency of myths about the Civil War in films dating from the silent era to the post-Civil Rights 1970s." Libr J
"One-third of 'The Reel Civil War' concentrates on {'The Birth of a Nation' and 'Gone With the Wind'}.

Given their prominence, that seems a reasonable balance, and Chadwick's dissection of the myths they helped to foster is superb." N Y Times Book Rev
Includes bibliographical references

Ciment, Michel, 1938-

Kubrick; the definitive edition; translated from the French by Gilbert Adair. additional material translated by Robert Bononno. Faber & Faber 2001 329p il $50   **791.43**

1. Kubrick, Stanley
ISBN 0-571-19986-0   LC 2001-23276
Original French edition, 1980
This is a study of Kubrick's films including Lolita, A clockwork orange and Full metal jacket. A short biography of Kubrick is included as well as interviews with the director and colleagues, actors and production crew members
Includes bibliographical references

Cook, David A.

A history of narrative film. 3rd ed. Norton 1996 xxvi, 1087p il pa $68.20   **791.43**

1. Motion pictures—History and criticism
ISBN 0-393-96819-7   LC 95-31987
First published 1981
This volume provides discussion and analysis of major films, directors, and national cinemas. In addition to historical and aesthetic concerns, the author explores the technological, social, and economic context of world cinema. Includes in-depth coverage of contemporary filmmaking in Hollywood, the Third World, and the former Soviet Union
Includes bibliographical references

Dunne, John Gregory, 1932-

Monster; living off the big screen. Random House 1997 203p hardcover o.p. paperback available $12   **791.43**

1. Up close and personal (Motion picture) 2. Motion pictures—Production and direction
ISBN 0-375-75024-X (pa)   LC 96-26212
The author "traces the life of a screenplay from the first draft to the final wrap. The work in question . . . *Up Close & Personal*, is the story of two newscasters and was originally intended to follow the life of Jessica Savitch. By the end of the eight years that Dunne and his wife, author Joan Didion, worked on it, however, very little of that germinal plan remained. . . . The account is forthright and written with the wry detachment of true experience." Libr J

Ebert, Roger

Roger Ebert's movie yearbook. Andrews & McMeel pa $19.95   **791.43**

1. Motion pictures 2. Videotapes
ISSN 1532-8147
Annual. First published 1985 with title: Roger Ebert's movie home companion. Later title: Roger Ebert's video companion
In addition to reviews this volume contains interviews and essays, questions and answers, film festival information, and a rated list of previously reviewed films

Gallagher, Tag

John Ford; the man and his films. University of Calif. Press 1986 572p il hardcover o.p. paperback available $24.95

791.43

1. Ford, John, 1894-1973
ISBN 0-520-06334-1 (pa)   LC 83-18047
"Gallagher's reassessment of John Ford's life and career revels in the complexity of the film director's personality while reconsidering his cinematic achievement. . . . Ford's philosophical and intellectual character is also sketched in this honest yet sympathetic account." Booklist
Includes bibliographical references

George, Nelson

Blackface: reflections   on African-Americans and the movies. Expanded ed. Cooper Sq. Pubs. 2002 238p il pa $16.95

791.43

1. African Americans in motion pictures
ISBN 0-8154-1194-4
First published 1994 by HarperCollins Pubs.
This "book is a reflection on the African American film scene written from the perspective of a 'cheerleader, consumer, and professional participant.' The book contains a series of ruminations on Sidney Poitier, Richard Pryor, Seventies 'blaxploitation' films, Spike Lee and the current crop of black filmmakers." Libr J [review of 1994 edition]

Halliwell's film guide. HarperPerennial pa $24.95   **791.43**

1. Motion pictures
Annual. First published 1977 by Scribner. Variant title: Halliwell's film and video guide
"Arranged alphabetically by film title, entries include a critical rating of one to four stars; country of origin; year of release; running time; color or black and white; special film techniques . . . availability of videotape, laser disc, and sound-track on CD; producer and distributor; alternative titles; synopsis of plot; short critical assessment; writing, directing, photography, music, and other credits; principal actors; comments from professional critics; and Academy Award nominations and wins." Ref Sources for Small & Medium-sized Libr. 6th edition

Harvey, James

Movie love in the 50's. Knopf 2001 448p il o.p.; Da Capo Press paperback available $18   **791.43**

1. Motion pictures
ISBN 0-306-81177-4 (pa)   LC 2001-33821
"For every 'sanitized' movie that came out of the Fifties, there were others that shook up old formulas. Critic and essayist Harvey explores—and ultimately eulogizes—Hollywood films of this era, a time of transition when the Production Code was being scrapped and the studio system abandoned. . . . His movie love is inspired and infectious." Libr J
Includes bibliographical references

Howard, Jean

Jean Howard's Hollywood; a photo memoir; photographs by Jean Howard; text by Jim Watters. Abrams 1989 248p il

791.43

1. Motion picture industry—Pictorial works
LC 89-264
Available from Abradale $19.98 (ISBN 0-8109-8218-8)
"Miss Howard has recorded the rarefied behind-the-gates lives of some of the most famous personalities in the history of the motion picture business. No outsider was she, hired for the occasion to 'snap' the swells. Miss Howard is very much one of the swells herself; her pictures are shot from the intimate perspective of the insider, either as a guest at the party or, frequently, as the hostess." N Y Times Book Rev

International motion picture almanac. Quigley $130   **791.43**

1. Motion pictures
ISSN 1043-8122
Annual. First published 1929 with title: Motion picture almanac. Variant title: Motion picture and television almanac
"Includes biographical sketches of movie personalities, lists of services, distributors, film corporations, companies, theaters, suppliers, organizations, markets, and government agencies, primarily in the United States. Lists of films of the previous decade and a review of the previous year in film: awards, polls, and festivals." Ref Sources for Small & Medium-sized Libr. 6th edition

Jones, G. William

Black cinema treasures; lost and found; foreword by Ossie Davis. University of N. Tex. Press 1991 242p il hardcover o.p. paperback available $17.95   **791.43**

1. Motion pictures 2. African Americans in motion pictures
ISBN 1-57441-028-8 (pa)   LC 91-10882
This book "documents black independent filmmaking from the 1920s to the 1950s, spotlighting sixteen films salvaged from a warehouse in Tyler, Texas, by the author. . . . There are also brief biographies of pioneers such as Oscar Micheaux and Spencer Williams. . . . For anyone with an interest in the social history of the movie industry, this book helps bring to light a much-neglected body of work." San Francisco Rev Books
Includes filmography

Kael, Pauline, 1919-2001

For keeps. Dutton 1994 1291p hardcover o.p. paperback available $22   **791.43**

1. Motion pictures—Reviews
ISBN 0-452-27308-0 (pa)   LC 94-6752
"A William Abrahams book"
An anthology of over 275 reviews, essays, profiles, and radio transcripts spanning the years 1962-1992
"The work is important not so much for its scope as for the individuality and candor of its author. Kael is arguably the most pernicious, influential, and literary of film critics to have written in the postwar era. In addition to ennobling criticism itself with her masterly reviews, she has been bold enough to publish insightful, if biting, critiques of the reviews of other prominent critics." Libr J

Kashner, Sam
The bad & the beautiful; Hollywood in the fifties; {by} Sam Kashner and Jennifer MacNair. Norton 2002 380p il $26.95; pa $15.95 **791.43**
1. Motion pictures
ISBN 0-393-04321-5; 0-393-32436-2 (pa)
LC 2002-317
This "is a series of vignettes capturing a Hollywood in transition, pressured by television, the studio system's decline, and the postwar emerging permissiveness. Topics include the influence of the short-lived but much-feared Confidential; the clout of aging gossip queens Louella Parsons, Hedda Hopper, and Sheila Graham; and the uproar over an interracial romance between Sammy Davis and Kim Novak." Libr J
"These accounts, often dipped in acid, will keep readers flipping pages." Publ Wkly
Includes bibliographical references

Keaton, Eleanor, 1918-1998
Buster Keaton remembered; [by] Eleanor Keaton and Jeffrey Vance; afterword by Kevin Brownlow; Manoah Bowman, photographic editor; photographs from the collection of the Academy of Motion Picture Arts and Sciences. Abrams 2001 238p il $45 **791.43**
1. Keaton, Buster, 1895-1966
ISBN 0-8109-4227-5
LC 00-61853
This is an account of "Keaton's career, from the shorts he made with Fatty Arbuckle during the years 1917-20 to his final cameo appearances in feature films." Booklist
A "photographic tribute . . . comprising formal and behind-the-scenes stills, staged publicity shots, and previously unpublished personal photos, this book is the most comprehensive pictorial retrospective on Keaton to date." Libr J
Includes filmography and bibliographical references

Knowles, Harry
Ain't it cool? Hollywood's redheaded stepchild speaks out; [by] Harry Knowles with Paul Cullum and Mark Ebner. Warner Bks. 2002 318p hardcover o.p. paperback available $13.95 **791.43**
1. Motion pictures
ISBN 0-446-67991-7 (pa)
LC 2001-46532
Knowles's "Web site, 'Ain't It Cool,' is dedicated to movie news, from the sale of a script to a film's release. Knowles's opinions are pervasive and have frequently brought him into conflict with the Hollywood powers that be. . . . The narrative is filled with history, trivia, commentary about the ethics of today's journalists, and stories behind the stories. . . . Movie buffs will enjoy this inside look at an outsider who has made a big impact on the film industry." SLJ

Lane, Anthony
Nobody's perfect; writings from the New Yorker. Knopf 2002 xx, 752p $30; pa $16.95 **791.43**
1. Motion pictures—Reviews
ISBN 0-375-41448-7; 0-375-71434-0 (pa)
LC 2002-20809
This is a "compilation of movie reviews, which also includes several book reviews and other critical pieces

about art and other aspects of culture." Booklist
"One of the best aspects of Lane's column, and of this anthology, is that it wanders across cultural and intellectual borders." Libr J

Levy, Edmond, 1929-1998
Making a winning short; how to write, direct, edit, and produce a short film. Holt & Co. 1994 290p pa $17 **791.43**
1. Motion pictures—Production and direction
ISBN 0-8050-2680-0
LC 94-6621
"An Owl book"
"Using examples from his own career, Levy . . . explains all aspects of creating a short film, from the development of the idea to what food and drink to provide for actors and crew. After Levy's easy-to-follow lessons are finished, he offers a list of film festivals that accept short films, titles of short films that he believes to be some of the finest examples of the genre, and a reading list. . . . A worthy addition to all performing arts collections." Libr J

Lumet, Sidney
Making movies. Knopf 1995 220p hardcover o.p. paperback available $12 **791.43**
1. Motion pictures—Production and direction
ISBN 0-679-75660-4 (pa)
LC 94-34449
This is a "book about the job of being a movie director. From the creation of the screenplay to the final previews, Mr. Lumet explains every step in the process, drawing examples from his own career." N Y Times Book Rev
"A fascinating look at the artist at work." Libr J

Magill's cinema annual. Gale Group $135 **791.43**
1. Motion pictures
ISSN 0739-2141
Annual. First published 1982 by Salem Press
"Each entry includes the movie's tagline (promotional catch phrases), year-end domestic box office gross, a signed review and comments on the film's reception, cast/production credits, a bibliography of reviews from major newspapers and industry trade papers, memorable dialogue quotes, a trivia section, and awards and nominations. Reviews average about two pages in length and strive to be both entertaining and analytical. In addition to numerous specialized indexes (directors, screenwriters, editors, cinematographers, performers, and subject), the annual also features an obituaries section and a selected list of film books." Am Ref Books Annu, 2003

Maltin, Leonard
Leonard Maltin's movie and video guide. Signet Bks. pa $8.99 **791.43**
1. Motion pictures 2. Videotapes
Annual. First published 1969 with title: TV movies. Title varies
This contains summaries and capsule reviews of thousands of films, videos, DVDs, and laserdisc releases, a list of recommended family films, filmographies of famous actors, and a list of specialty video mail-order companies

Mamet, David
On directing film. Viking 1991 107p
hardcover o.p. paperback available $14
791.43
1. Motion pictures—Production and direction
ISBN 0-14-012722-4 (pa)   LC 90-50428
"Noted playwright, screenwriter, and director Mamet
offers his views on film directing taken, some in transcript form, from lectures and classes at Columbia. . . .
Refreshingly untheoretical, particularly regarding acting
technique, this is fitfully interesting stuff." Libr J

Mann, William J.
Behind the screen; how gays and lesbians
shaped Hollywood, 1910-1969. Viking 2001
xxiv, 422p il $29.95; pa $16   **791.43**
1. Homosexuality in motion pictures 2. Motion picture industry
ISBN 0-670-03017-1; 0-14-200114-7 (pa)
LC 2001-17984
In this study "Mann examines how the movie capital
of the world was transformed by a host of writers, directors, designers, actors, and producers often at odds with
the official codes, and mores of the times. . . . Mann's
book is important reading for anyone interested in the
history of American film. Essential for all film and gay
studies collections." Libr J

Mast, Gerald, 1940-1988
A short history of the movies; [by] Gerald
Mast, Bruce F. Kawin. Allyn & Bacon pa
$78   **791.43**
1. Motion pictures—History and criticism
First published 1971 by Pegasus Press. (8th edition
2002) Periodically revised
The author traces the history of motion pictures from
their birth to the present day. Among the topics discussed are the coming of sound, the studio system and
the cinemas of France, Germany and Russia. D. W. Griffith, Mack Sennet and Charlie Chaplin are among the
personalities covered
Includes bibliographical references

Mayo, Mike, 1948-
VideoHound's DVD guide; {by} Mike
Mayo {with Jim Olenski}. Visible Ink Press
2001 xxv, 728p pa $19.95   **791.43**
1. Motion pictures 2. Digital videodiscs
ISBN 1-57859-115-5   LC 00-43481
This guide's 3,000 entries each includes a movie re-
view, and a review of that movie in DVD format. Infor-
mation includes added features, price, and distributor.
Eight indexes provide the user with a variety of access
options
Includes bibliographical references

Muir, John Kenneth, 1969-
Horror films of the 1970s. McFarland &
Co. 2002 662p il $59.95   **791.43**
1. Horror films
ISBN 0-7864-1249-6   LC 2002-6759
Muir opens with a "'Brief History,' which discusses
actors Christopher Lee and Peter Cushing, the influence
of productions by Hammer Films . . . and some of the
best, worst, and most controversial flicks of the period.
Part 2, which makes up the bulk of the book, consists of
some 228 chronological entries on standout movies,
including Carrie and The Exorcist. Each entry covers

cast and crew, critical reception . . . synopsis, direct
quotes from cast when available, and commentary providing further information on the film's merits or bad
points. Muir's commentaries are well worth reading. . . .
An impressive resource for all film collections." Libr J
Includes bibliographical references

Muller, Eddie
Dark city; the lost world of film noir. St.
Martin's Griffin 1998 206p il pa $22.95
791.43
1. Motion pictures
ISBN 0-312-18076-4   LC 98-5677
"The book is organized around the city motif, with
chapters devoted to various thematic neighborhoods, for
example, 'The Precinct' (cop flicks) and 'Vixenville'
(femme fatales)." Booklist
"There are few fresh insights because the book is essentially a retro trip--and it does succeed in conveying
the patina of 40s and 50s crime films pretty magnificently." Sight Sound
Includes bibliographical references

Nowlan, Robert A.
Film quotations; 11,000 lines spoken on
screen, arranged by subject, and indexed; [by]
Robert A. Nowlan and Gwendolyn W. Nolan.
McFarland & Co. 1994 745p $75   **791.43**
1. Motion pictures—Quotations
ISBN 0-89950-786-7   LC 92-56673
This volume includes "11,000 quotations under more
than 900 headings. . . . Each entry notes the name of
the performer who spoke the lines, the film and its studio
and release date, and a sentence or two explaining the
context. . . . The chronological coverage is broad, from
the 1930s to the 1990s. As a source for some of the
most common quotations we encounter every day, this
book is a solid reference." Booklist

Osborne, Robert A.
75 years of the Oscar; the official history
of the Academy Awards; [by] Robert
Osborne. Abbeville Press 2003 416p il $75
791.43
1. Academy Awards (Motion pictures)
ISBN 0-7892-0787-7   LC 2003-45311
First published 1989 with title: 60 years of the Oscar
This includes a history of the Academy of Motion
Picture Arts and Sciences, overviews of Academy Award
nominees and winners, award ceremonies, and a complete listing of nominees and winners in every category
Includes bibliographical references

The **Oxford** history of world cinema; edited
by Geoffrey Nowell-Smith. Oxford Univ.
Press 1996 xxii, 824p il hardcover o.p.
paperback available $29.95   **791.43**
1. Motion pictures—History and criticism
ISBN 0-19-874242-8 (pa)   LC 94-36359
This volume "begins with the 'pre-cinema' era and
moves forward through silent films to sound and on to
modern and current work, tracing development by genre
and by nation. Special features on pioneers, outstanding
actors and major industry figures appear throughout the
book." Publ Wkly
This "volume should be a top purchase for all film
collections." Libr J
Includes bibliographical references

Roger Ebert's book of film; edited by Roger Ebert. Norton 1997 793p $30   **791.43**
1. Motion pictures
ISBN 0-393-04000-3   LC 96-14271

"Ebert arranges over 100 pieces—many of them book excerpts—into categories (Movie Stars, The Business, Early Days, Genres, etc.) and provides a brief introduction to each. . . . It's a first-rate collection that will stimulate interest in both the movies mentioned and the authors anthologized." Libr J

Sklar, Robert
A world history of film. rev & expanded ed. Abrams 2002 600p il $75   **791.43**
1. Motion pictures
ISBN 0-8109-0606-6   LC 2001-22853
First published 1993 with title: Film: an international history of the medium

"Beginning with such precursors of cinema as the magic lantern and such pioneer filmmakers as the Lumières and Griffith, Sklar thereafter chronicles the rise of Hollywood, the development of genres, the advent of sound, and modern developments, right up to Pixar and the Farrelly brothers. . . . Well-selected photos profusely enhance the incisive text." Booklist

Includes filmography and bibliographical references

Taub, Eric
Gaffers, grips, and best boys. rev ed. St. Martin's Press 1994 276p il pa $14.95
   791.43
1. Motion pictures—Production and direction
ISBN 0-312-11276-9   LC 94-28113
First published 1987

The author "draws on interviews with contemporary filmmakers—from director to camera operator and sound mixer—to give an insider's look at who does what in the making of a motion picture." Booklist

Thomas, Tony, 1927-1997
A wonderful life: the films and career of James Stewart. Citadel Press 1988 255p il pa $19.95   **791.43**
1. Stewart, James
ISBN 0-8065-1953-3   LC 87-37493
Black-and-white photographs of Stewart's professional and private life illustrate this look at his 77 films

Tibbetts, John C., 1946-
The encyclopedia of novels into film; [by] John C. Tibbetts, James M. Welsh; additional research by Heather Addison [et al.] Facts on File 1998 522p il $75   **791.43**
1. Film adaptations—Encyclopedias
ISBN 0-8160-3317-X   LC 97-11390

"Included are more than 300 entries, arranged alphabetically by book titles. Where the film title differs from the novel, it is cross-referenced. . . . First the novel is discussed, then the film. Where more than one film has been made from the book, all are discussed. Comparisons are made between the movie and the novel." Book Rep

Includes bibliographical references

Vanity Fair's Hollywood; edited by Graydon Carter and David Friend; with text by Christopher Hitchens. Viking Studio Bks. 2000 318p il $30   **791.43**
1. Motion pictures 2. Actors
ISBN 0-670-89141-X   LC 00-33397

This volume includes pieces from Vanity Fair magazine and photographs of such actors as Claudette Colbert, Greta Garbo, Peter Lorre, Elizabeth Taylor, Jack Nicholson, Meryl Streep, Robert De Niro, Tom Hanks, and Sophia Loren

Wiener, Thomas
The off-Hollywood film guide; the definitive guide to independent and foreign films on video and DVD; [by] Tom Wiener. Random House 2002 xxiv, 535p pa $16.95
   791.43
1. Motion pictures 2. Videotapes 3. Digital videodiscs
ISBN 0-8129-9207-5   LC 2002-69918

Wiener "annotates over 650 of the best foreign and independently produced films from the silent era through 2001, noting year and country of release, principal cast, director, MPAA rating, type of film (e.g., documentary, fantasy), and DVD features. . . . An appendix breaks out films by subgenres, and director, actor, and country indexes also facilitate access. Wiener's suggestions are excellent. . . . As a core title list for libraries and individuals, Wiener's new work ranks near the top." Libr J

791.4303 Motion pictures— Encyclopedias and dictionaries

Konigsberg, Ira
The complete film dictionary. 2nd ed. Penguin Ref. 1997 469p il hardcover o.p. paperback available $18.95   **791.4303**
1. Motion pictures—Dictionaries
ISBN 0-14-051393-0 (pa)   LC 96-52953
First published 1987 by New Am. Lib.

This dictionary's nearly 4,000 entries cover film history, techniques and theory. Artistic, technological, and financial aspects are also explored. Illustrated with more than 250 line drawings and photographs

Slide, Anthony
The new historical dictionary of the American film industry. Scarecrow Press 1998 266p hardcover o.p. paperback available $19.95   **791.4303**
1. Motion pictures—Dictionaries
ISBN 1-57886-015-6 (pa)   LC 97-35737
First published 1986 with title: The American film industry

This reference "covers studios, companies, clubs and associations, and related concepts. Lots here that is not found elsewhere." Booklist

Includes bibliographical references

791.44   Radio

Dunning, John, 1942-

On the air; the encyclopedia of old-time radio. Oxford Univ. Press 1998 822p $60
        791.44

1. Radio programs
ISBN 0-19-507678-8   LC 96-41959
First published 1976 with title: Tune in yesterday
Dunning has "compiled and organized a massive amount of research data on hundreds of radio shows aired from the 1920s through the 1960s. The entries, listed alphabetically by show title, each contain a treasure trove of information—broadcast dates, casts and personnel, anecdotes, special analyses, and a detailed overview of each show's background, format, and content." Libr J

Ely, Melvin Patrick

The adventures of Amos 'n' Andy; a social history of an American phenomenon. University Press of Va. 2001 xxi, 322p il pa $18.50   **791.44**
1. Amos 'n' Andy (Radio program) 2. Amos 'n' Andy (Television program) 3. African Americans on television
ISBN 0-8139-2092-2   LC 2001-45538
A reissue of the title first published 1991 by Free Press
A "historian examines one of America's greatest cultural enigmas—the amazing popularity, among blacks as well as whites, of 'Amos 'n' Andy' on radio for more than 30 years." N Y Times Book Rev
Includes bibliographical references

Neer, Richard

FM: the rise and fall of free-form rock radio. Villard Bks. 2001 367p hardcover o.p. paperback available $19   **791.44**
1. WNEW (Radio station: New York, N.Y.) 2. Radio broadcasting
ISBN 0-8129-9265-2 (pa)   LC 2001-33251
Neer "recalls the brief moment when FM radio, in its infancy, coincided with the extraordinary vitality of sixties rock, and FM stations became important countercultural institutions. Free to play (and say) what they wanted, disk jockeys concocted a heady, often unpredictable brew of extended album tracks, shaggy-dog stories, and political commentary." New Yorker
This is "a nice little snapshot of cultural history." Booklist

Sies, Luther F.

Encyclopedia of American radio, 1920-1960. McFarland & Co. 2000 904p $135   **791.44**
1. Radio broadcasting 2. Radio programs
ISBN 0-7864-0452-3   LC 99-24129
"In 28,848 alphabetically arranged entries, Sies attempts to identify as many broadcasters and their programs as possible. Programs from the early days of radio reflect the work mainly of individual performers and are entered that way in the encyclopedia. After 1929, entries are primarily for programs, with individual entries only for performers whose programs bear their names or for newscasters, commentators, home economists, DJs, singers, and vocal and instrumental groups. There are . . . entries on special topics such as Black radio, Networks, Sports, and Wartime radio." Booklist

791.45   Television

Bogle, Donald

Primetime blues; African Americans on network television. Farrar, Straus & Giroux 2001 520p il hardcover o.p. paperback available $18   **791.45**
1. African Americans on television
ISBN 0-374-52718-0 (pa)   LC 00-41700
Bogle examines the history of African Americans on American television programs "decade by decade, show by show, sometimes episode by episode. . . . [He] measures the shows aesthetically and sociologically . . . [and] aims to explain the influence of ratings and Hollywood politics on how blacks have been represented. He also provides brief biographies of [some] . . . of the actors whose work he describes." N Y Times Book Rev
Includes bibliographical references

Brooks, Tim

The complete directory to prime time network and cable TV shows, 1946-present; [by] Tim Brooks and Earle Marsh. Ballantine Bks. $27.95   **791.45**
1. Television programs
First published 1979. (8th edition 2003) Periodically revised
"Provides coverage of more than 5,000 nighttime series on commerical networks, with information on the type of show, broadcast history, cast, spin-offs, and plot or format. Index to actors and actresses. Appendixes list each season's prime time schedules, Emmy award winners, long-running and highly rated programs, and spin-offs. Coverage of original cable series began with the sixth edition" Ref Sources for Small & Medium-sized Libr. 6th edition

Encyclopedia of television; editor, Horace Newcomb; photo editor, Cary O'Dell; commissioning editor, Noelle Watson. Fitzroy Dearborn Pubs. 1997 3v il set $350   **791.45**

1. Television broadcasting
ISBN 1-884964-26-5   LC 97-214692
At head of title: Museum of Broadcast Communications
This "work examines the full spectrum of the television industry—its topics, programs, and personalities from its inception to the present. It reflects U.S. dominance, although the book does survey the medium in other countries such as France, Germany, Italy, and Russia. Most of the 1000 lengthy articles include excellent black-and-white photographs and bibliographies for further reading. Essential for public libraries and for most academic collections." Libr J

Lackmann, Ronald W.

The encyclopedia of American television, broadcast programming Post World War II to 2000; {by} Ron Lackmann. Facts on File 2002 466p il $75; pa $21.95   **791.45**
1. Television broadcasting—Encyclopedias
ISBN 0-8160-4554-2; 0-8160-4555-0 (pa)
            LC 2001-56856
Also available Lackmann's The encyclopedia of America radio: an A-Z guide to radio from Jack Benny to Howard Stern pa $18.95 (ISBN 0-8160-4077-X)

Lackmann, Ronald W.—*Continued*

The majority of entries are for programs and actors. Each program entry includes a description of the show, times the show aired, complete cast listings and notable guest stars, and the occasional interesting fact. Biographical entries include dates of birth and death, along with the actor's television credits. Any significant acting work done outside of television is also mentioned. All entries are enhanced with excellent cross-references to related shows and actors. Coverage of special television events and programs is also included." Am Ref Books Annu, 2003

Includes bibliographical references

McNeil, Alex, 1948-

Total television; the comprehensive guide to programming from 1948 to the present. 4th ed. Penguin Bks. 1996 1251p pa $25

791.45

1. Television programs
ISBN 0-14-024916-8   LC 95-48224
First published 1980
"Provides information on more than 6,000 daytime and prime-time series and specials, as well as prime-time network schedules, Emmy and Peabody Award winners, and lists of top-rated shows. Coverage extends to late 1995." Booklist

Morris, Bruce B.

Prime time network serials; episode guides, casts, and credits for 37 continuing television dramas, 1964-1993; with a foreword by Michele Lee. McFarland & Co. 1997 841p il $95

791.45

1. Television programs
ISBN 0-7864-0164-8   LC 96-31166
This volume provides information of thirty-seven serials that aired on the major networks from the 1964 season through 1992-93
This "work belongs in any library collection that serves a devoted television viewing public." Booklist

Richards, Thomas, 1956-

The meaning of Star Trek. Doubleday 1997 194p hardcover o.p. paperback available $15

791.45

1. Star trek: the next generation (Television program)
ISBN 0-385-48439-9 (pa)   LC 97-6845
The author "presents his own literary examination of Gene Roddenberry's creation . . . in four sections: conflict, character, story, and sense of wonder. While he draws on themes that span the canon of celluloid Trek, the examples he cites are mainly from *Star Trek: The Next Generation* televison series." Publ Wkly
"One of the best recent *Star Trek* books and also one of the most cogent, exciting recent literary analyses." Booklist

Stashower, Daniel

The boy genius and the mogul; the untold story of television. Broadway Bks. 2002 xx, 277p il $24.95

791.45

1. Farnsworth, Philo T., 1906-1971 2. Sarnoff, David, 1891-1971 3. Television—History
ISBN 0-7679-0759-0   LC 2002-283169
Stashower chronicles the life of the "farm boy who came up with the revolutionary idea that would ultimately make television possible as we know it today. Yet

young Philo Farnsworth, with limited funding and a handful of friends to help build the apparatus, could not compete with the powerful David Sarnoff, president of RCA, who was determined to become the leader in the television effort. This book intermingles biographies of both men with the broader story of television's early years. . . . The amount of technical detail [Stashower] provides . . . is enough to give the reader an idea of what the inventors had to work with, yet simplified enough to be accessible to a general audience." Booklist

Includes bibliographical references

Terrace, Vincent, 1948-

Television sitcom factbook; over 8700 details from 130 shows, 1985-2000. McFarland & Co. 2000 164p pa $25 **791.45**

1. Television programs
ISBN 0-7864-0900-2   LC 00-57865
This volume includes "over 8,700 facts concerning 130 television sitcoms broadcast from 1985 to those still current in 2000 by ABC, CBS, NBC, Fox, UPN, WB and in syndication." Publisher's note

791.8   Animal performances

Hemingway, Ernest, 1899-1961

The dangerous summer; introduction by James A. Michener. Scribner 1985 228p il hardcover o.p. paperback available $13

791.8

1. Bullfights 2. Spain—Description
ISBN 0-684-83789-7 (pa)   LC 84-27578
Originally written as a series of articles for Life magazine
A look at the "personal and professional rivalry of the two greatest bullfighters since the death of Manolete in 1947: Luis Miguel Domínguín and Antonio Ordóñez. The Dangerous Summer provides an insider's view based on extensive experience, mingles memory and desire, and is essential reading for anyone interested in the subject or the author." Natl Rev

Death in the afternoon. Scribner 1999 397p il $35 **791.8**

1. Bullfights
ISBN 0-684-85922-X   LC 99-231717
First published 1932
"A loosely organized book on bullfighting in Spain. . . . Hemingway depicts the bullfight as an emblematic tragedy, a test of courage, with a bloody and not entirely predictable end. Throughout, he digresses to philosophize on life and death in exchanges with a character he calls the Old Lady." HarperCollins Reader's Ency of Am Lit. 2nd edition

Kasson, Joy S.

Buffalo Bill's Wild West; celebrity, memory, and popular history. Hill & Wang 2000 319p il $27; pa $15 **791.8**

1. Buffalo Bill, 1846-1917
ISBN 0-8090-3243-0; 0-8090-3244-9 (pa)
LC 99-56101
"Best known for his 'Wild West' spectacles depicting scenes of the American West, highlighting conflicts between white and Native Americans, William Cody, a.k.a. 'Buffalo Bill,' was a consummate showman. . . . Kasson shows how deeply Cody was attuned to the public's impressions of the American West as he balanced fiction with authenticity." Libr J

792 Stage presentations

Adler, Stella, 1901-1992
Stella Adler: the art of acting; compiled and edited by Howard Kissel. Applause Theatre Bk. Pubs. 2000 271p il $25.95 **792**
1. Acting
ISBN 1-55783-373-7
In this collection of Adler's papers Kissel "has taken tapes, transcriptions, notebooks, and other sources to reconstruct an acting course in 22 lessons. . . . The lessons are graduated from very basic matters to quite complex issues of textual analysis and decorum. Though mostly monologs, they include enough exercises and student responses to get the flavor of Adler's work. . . . This is required reading for anyone interested in theater practice." Libr J

Bordman, Gerald Martin
American theatre: a chronicle of comedy and drama, 1869-1914; [by] Gerald Bordman. Oxford Univ. Press 1994 793p $95 **792**
1. Theater—United States 2. American drama—History and criticism
ISBN 0-19-503764-2 LC 92-16066
"For each theater season, in chronological order, [this volume] provides an overview and traces nonmusical productions, highlighting successes and failures. Each of the plays (including many of foreign origin) is described in some detail, often incorporating contemporary commentary on the production and individual performances. Indexes of plays, play sources, and people." Guide to Ref Books. 11th edition

American theatre: a chronicle of comedy and drama, 1914-1930; [by] Gerald Bordman. Oxford Univ. Press 1995 446p $72 **792**
1. Theater—United States 2. American drama—History and criticism
ISBN 0-19-509078-0 LC 94-13842
A season-by-season history of Broadway productions from World War I through the Depression

American theatre: a chronicle of comedy and drama, 1930-1969; [by] Gerald Bordman. Oxford Univ. Press 1996 472p $72 **792**
1. Theater—United States 2. American drama—History and criticism
ISBN 0-19-509079-9 LC 96-17572
This volume deals with the seasons 1930-31 through 1968-69
Continued by Thomas Hischak's volume covering 1969-2000

Briggs, Jody, 1945-
Encyclopedia of stage lighting; foreword by Scott Nolte. McFarland & Co. 2003 334p il $75 **792**
1. Stage lighting—Encyclopedias
ISBN 0-7864-1512-6 LC 2003-7619
"Peppered with some 300 simple line drawings and diagrams to illustrate basic concepts, this work emphasizes the principles and practices of the founding fathers of theatrical lighting, among whom are Stanley McCandless, Ariel Davis, Adolphe Appia, and Gordan Craig. . . . This book often goes beyond most encyclopedias, addressing standard lighting procedures and practices, brief-ly outlining the historical development of theatrical lighting, and providing strategies for dealing with theater directors and other theatrical personalities." Choice
Includes bibliographical references

Brook, Peter, 1925-
The empty space. Atheneum 1968 141p hardcover o.p. paperback available $11 **792**
1. Theater 2. Drama
ISBN 0-684-82957-6 (pa) LC 68-12531
The author "distinguishes four types of theater: the Deadly Theatre (conventional), the Holy Theatre (ritualistic), the Rough Theatre (combative), and the Immediate Theatre (mutative and organic). An impassioned treatise that is also very accessible and direct." Libr J

Chekhov, Michael, 1891-1955
To the actor. [rev and expanded ed. by Mala Powers] Routledge 2002 lii, 222p il $75; pa $19.95 **792**
1. Acting
ISBN 0-415-25875-8; 0-415-25876-6 (pa)
First published 1953 by Harper & Row
"Chekhov is among a handful of master acting teachers who have profoundly influenced not only a constellation of famous stars but also shaped an acting style and sensibility. . . . This new edition contains all of Chekhov's brilliant insights, techniques, and exercises, as well as a previously unpublished chapter on the 'Psychological Gesture,' a central precept of his system." Libr J
Includes bibliographical references

Corson, Richard
Stage makeup; [by] Richard Corson, James Glavan. Allyn & Bacon il $111.40 **792**
1. Theatrical makeup
First published 1942 by Appleton. (9th edition 2000) Periodically revised
The authors discuss the art and technique of theatrical makeup, covering such topics as facial anatomy, various methods for applying greasepaint and other makeup, and the use of beards, wigs, and prosthetic pieces

Gillette, J. Michael
Designing with light; an introduction to stage lighting. 4th ed. McGraw-Hill 2003 various paging il pa $55.45 **792**
1. Stage lighting
ISBN 0-7674-2733-5 LC 2002-19777
First published 1978 by Mayfield Pub.
The author "divides his standard text for undergraduate lighting design students into the two constituent elements of his craft—technology and design. He clearly and completely presents both technical and aesthetic design aspects." Libr J

Theatrical design and production; an introduction to scene design and construction, lighting, sound, costume, and makeup. 4th ed. Mayfield 1999 587p il $76.70 **792**
1. Theaters—Stage setting and scenery
ISBN 0-7674-1191-9 LC 99-28595
First published 1987
This is a "survey of the technical and design aspects of play production, including scene design and construction, lighting, sound, costume, and makeup. Health and safety precautions for the backstage crew appear throughout in boxes labeled 'Safety Tips,' and 'Design Inspiration' boxes show how professional designers create the desired look." Publisher's note
Includes bibliographical references

Hagen, Uta, 1919-

Respect for acting; by Uta Hagen with Haskel Frankel. Macmillan 1973 227p $19.95
792

1. Acting
ISBN 0-02-547390-5
This "classic treatise on the process and craft of acting has significantly benefited actors for three decades. Juxtaposed with Hagen's aesthetic is a wealth of practical information, creative ideas, and her uniquely useful object exercises." Libr J

Harold, Madd, 1973-

An actor's guide to performing Shakespeare; for film, television, and theatre. Lone Eagle 2002 288p pa $18.95 **792**
1. Shakespeare, William, 1564-1616—Dramatic production 2. Acting
ISBN 1-58065-046-5   LC 2002-34213
"Harold is the anti-academic incarnate, who, through his own considerable Shakespearean experience as both an actor and a director, has accrued some useful ideas, collected in this breezy vernacular guide." Libr J

Hischak, Thomas

American theatre: a chronicle of comedy and drama, 1969-2000; [by] Thomas S. Hischak. Oxford Univ. Press 2000 505p $72
792
1. Theater—United States 2. American drama—History and criticism
ISBN 0-19-512347-6   LC 00-28287
Continues Gerald Bordman's three volumes on the American theater published 1994, 1995 and 1996
"In this chronicle of New York nonmusical theater, every play produced in the years 1969 to 2000, from Broadway to Off Off Broadway, is discussed in four chapters, with seasons grouped by topical issues. . . . Each year gets an overview comment, while each play gets a summary, an actor comment, and a statement about its critical reception." Libr J

Hodge, Francis

Play directing; analysis, communication, and style. 5th ed. Allyn & Bacon 1999 c2000 396p il $86.40 **792**
1. Theater—Production and direction
ISBN 0-205-29561-4   LC 99-29772
First published 1971 by Prentice-Hall
This presents a "methodology for textual analysis, communicative relationships with actors, and understanding and cultivating a sense of interpretive style. All production areas are considered and illustrated with diagrams and photographs. Numerous exercises assist in the explanation of each area." Libr J
Includes bibliographical references

Mamet, David

True and false; heresy and common sense for the actor. Pantheon Bks. 1997 127p hardcover o.p. paperback available $11 **792**
1. Acting
ISBN 0-679-77264-2 (pa)   LC 97-19336
"Mamet exhorts actors to show up early, have their lines down cold, and have a single objective for each scene. He contends that overthinking and too much emotional interpretation is not the actor's role. Essential reading for theater collections." Libr J

Moore, Sonia, d. 1995

The Stanislavski system; the professional training of an actor; digested from the teachings of Konstantin S. Stanislavski. 2nd rev ed. Penguin Bks. 1984 96p pa $12.95
792
1. Stanislavsky, Konstantin, 1863-1938 2. Acting
ISBN 0-14-046660-6   LC 84-2855
First published 1960 with title: The Stanislavski method
This is a concise, simplified guide to the teachings of the great master of the Moscow Art Theater

The **New** York Times book of Broadway; on the aisle for the unforgettable plays of the last century; edited and with an introduction by Ben Brantley. St. Martin's Press 2001 268p il $35 **792**
1. Theater—New York (N.Y.)
ISBN 0-312-28411-X   LC 2001-41968
This is a compilation of reviews, some selected "for the quality of the writing, some for the play as seen at the time, and some because the play is likely to have a long-term effect on the world of theater. . . . Each entry has the critic's name, play or musical title, date of the performance reviewed, theater, and total number of performances, along with many vintage production photographs and credits. . . . This is an engaging collective look at the past century of drama as seen through the eyes of the *New York Times* theater critics." Libr J

Rodenburg, Patsy

Speaking Shakespeare. Palgrave 2002 355p $26.95 **792**
1. Shakespeare, William, 1564-1616—Dramatic production 2. Acting
ISBN 0-312-29420-4
The author presents a "text based on her elementary principle that 'you can't act Shakespeare until you speak him.' Her approach focuses on the mechanics of body and voice, explication of verse structure and language, imaginative textual exploration, and, finally, the application of the aforementioned to an assortment of speeches from 17 plays." Libr J

Stanislavsky, Konstantin, 1863-1938

An actor prepares; [by] Constantin Stanislavski; translated by Elizabeth Reynolds Hapgood. Routledge 1989 313p pa $18.95
792

1. Acting
ISBN 0-87830-983-7   LC 89-146170
"A Theatre Arts book"
First published 1936
"Working examples of good and bad acting described in the form of semi-fiction. The names of the actors are fictitious; the acting principles are based on the experience of the author in the Moscow art theatre." Booklist

Building a character; [by] Constantin Stanislavski; translated by Elizabeth Reynolds Hapgood. Routledge c1977 299p pa $19.95
792

1. Acting
ISBN 0-87830-982-9   LC 89-145827
"A Theater Arts book"
This "addresses the actor's external mechanics of body and movement, voice and diction, and control." Libr J

Stanislavsky, Konstantin, 1863-1938—*Continued*

Creating a role; [by] Constantin Stanislavski; translated by Elizabeth Reynolds Hapgood; edited by Hermine I. Popper; foreword by Robert Lewis. Routledge c1989 271p pa $19.95   **792**
1. Acting
ISBN 0-87830-981-0   LC 91-228412
"A Theatre Arts book"
"Stanislavski unifies his conceptual canon and applies it to detailed preparatory work for the roles of Othello and Gogol's Inspector General." Libr J

Troubridge, Emma
Scenic art and construction; [by] Emma Troubridge and Tim Blaikie. Crowood Press; [distributed by] Trafalgar Sq. 2002 192p il pa $29.95   **792**
1. Theaters—Stage setting and scenery
ISBN 1-86126-499-2
A "guide for upper-level theater students, scenic artists, and technical directors, this details the nuts and bolts of the production process, beginning with a design and culminating in a full-blown set." Libr J
Includes bibliographical references

792.03   Theater—Encyclopedias and dictionaries

Bordman, Gerald Martin
The Oxford companion to American theatre; [by] Gerald Bordman. 2nd ed. Oxford Univ. Press 1992 735p $75   **792.03**
1. Theater—United States—Dictionaries 2. American drama—Dictionaries
ISBN 0-19-507246-4   LC 91-16720
First published 1984
This reference work includes entries on playwrights, plays, actors, directors, producers, songwriters, famous playhouses, dramatic movements, and biographical sketches of prominent theatre personalities and groups

Cambridge guide to American theatre; [edited by] Don B. Wilmeth with Tice L. Miller. Cambridge Univ. Press 1996 463p pa $26   **792.03**
1. Theater—United States—Dictionaries
ISBN 0-521-56444-1   LC 95-51681
First published 1993
"Essentially a reworking of material on the American stage from *The Cambridge guide to world theatre* . . . with considerable expansion and additional information. Consists of signed articles (many by contributors to the parent work) on performers, dramatists, directors, set designers, plays, companies, theatrical forms and movements, etc." Guide to Ref Books. 11th edition [1993 edition]

The **Cambridge** guide to theatre; [edited by] Martin Banham; editorial advisory board, James Brandon [et al.] new ed. Cambridge Univ. Press 1995 1233p il $50   **792.03**
1. Theater—Dictionaries
ISBN 0-521-43437-8   LC 95-1011
First published 1988 with title: The Cambridge guide to world theatre
"A broad-ranging source of information on individuals, organizations, theatrical forms and movements, individual countries, and a variety of specific topics. Articles are signed; some longer articles have bibliographies. Covers popular theater and entertainments, as well as the legitimate stage. Because of global perspective, especially useful for country surveys of cultures outside the U.S. and Western Europe and entries for forms and individuals associated with those cultures." Guide to Ref Books. 11th edition [1988 edition]
Includes bibliographical references

The **Oxford** encyclopedia of theatre & performance; edited by Dennis Kennedy. Oxford Univ. Press 2003 2v il set $275   **792.03**
1. Theater—Encyclopedias 2. Performing arts—Encyclopedias
ISBN 0-19-860174-3   LC 2003-266308
This encyclopedia "encompasses opera and film, dance and radio, and para-theatrical, non-dramatic performances including circuses and carnivals, and parades and public executions—providing . . . coverage from ancient Greek theatre to developments in London, Paris, New York, and around the globe. The Encyclopedia pays special attention to non-Western styles." Publisher's note
This "work on theater and performance will set the standard for decades and become the reference of choice in these areas. . . . It is thorough, carefully thought out, and easy to use." Libr J

792.09   Theater—Historical and geographic treatment

Brockett, Oscar Gross, 1923-
History of the theatre. Allyn & Bacon il $95.80   **792.09**
1. Theater—History 2. Drama—History and criticism
First published 1968. (9th edition 2002) Periodically revised
This work traces the development of the theater from primitive times to the present, with an emphasis on European theater

The **Oxford** illustrated history of theatre; edited by John Russell Brown. Oxford Univ. Press 1995 582p il hardcover o.p. paperback available $27.50   **792.09**
1. Theater—History
ISBN 0-19-285442-9 (pa)   LC 95-231683
Covering theatre history from the ancient Greeks to the 1990s, this "resource provides a wide variety of information from basic theatre chronology to detailed analyses of several well-known and important plays and playwrights. . . . The emphasis is on European and Western theatre, but a chapter provides a concise summary on Southern and Eastern Asian theatre." SLJ
Includes bibliographical references

792.5 Opera

Baker's dictionary of opera; [edited] by Laura Kuhn. Schirmer Bks. 2000 1047p il $130   **792.5**

1. Opera—Dictionaries
ISBN 0-02-865349-1   LC 99-16852

This "offers 1000 alphabetical entries on opera singers, composers, and selected related artists (e.g., conductors, impresarios, and musicologists). . . . Appendixes include opera character names, terms, chronology, synopses, and descriptions of selected world opera houses." Libr J

For a fuller review see: Booklist June 1 & 15, 2000

Boyden, Matthew

The Rough Guide to opera; written by Matthew Boyden with contributions from Nick Kimberley {et al.}; edited by Joe Staines. 3rd ed, expanded and completely revised. Rough Guides 2002 735p il pa $25.95   **792.5**

1. Opera
ISBN 1-85828-749-9

First published 1997 with title: Opera: the Rough Guide

This guide provides "information on history's most renowned operas. Biographical sketches of over 150 composers . . . CD reviews of hundreds of operas . . . {and a} who's who of the finest singers on record." Publisher's note

Fiedler, Johanna

Molto agitato; the mayhem behind the music at the Metropolitan Opera. Doubleday 2001 393p il $30; pa $15.95   **792.5**

1. Metropolitan Opera (New York, N.Y.)
ISBN 0-385-48187-X; 1-4000-3231-8 (pa)
                       LC 2001-27158

This book is about "the business of New York City's Metropolitan Opera and the personalities who have shaped it from its beginnings in the late 19th century to the present day. . . . [The author] spins a fascinating account of strong egos, clashing personalities, power plays, and frequent major disasters. There are enough heroes, villains, and side plots to fill a dozen adventure novels. . . . For those interested in the dirt behind the golden curtain, this will be a feast." Libr J

Freeman, John W.

The Metropolitan Opera stories of the great operas. Metropolitan Opera Guild 1984-1996 2v v1 $29.95; v2 $35   **792.5**

1. Opera—Stories, plots, etc.
ISBN 0-393-01888-1 (v1); 0-393-04051-8 (v2)

Also available as a boxed set $75 (ISBN 0-393-04548-8)

Volume one contains the plots of 150 of the world's most popular operas including biographies of each of the 72 composers represented together with historical background information relevant to each work. Volume two includes 125 additional plot summaries covering less known works from the early operas of Monteverdi to that of contemporary composers, such as John Adams

The **New** Grove dictionary of opera; edited by Stanley Sadie. Grove's Dictionaries of Music 1992 4v il hardcover o.p. paperback available set $275   **792.5**

1. Opera—Dictionaries
ISBN 1-56159-228-5 (pa)   LC 92-36276

This set "developed from The New Grove Dictionary of Music and Musicians, covers all aspects of the modern Western opera tradition, including composers, performers, directors, companies, stagecraft, theaters, cities, terms, and individual works." Libr J

Includes bibliographical references

The **New** Kobbé's opera book; edited by the Earl of Harewood and Antony Peattie. Putnam 1997 1,012p il $60   **792.5**

1. Opera—Stories, plots, etc.
ISBN 0-399-14332-7   LC 97-10981

First published 1919 under the authorship of Gustav Kobbé with title: The complete opera book

This opera guide covers about five hundred works and provides full descriptions of the operas, plot synopses, cast lists and performance histories

The **New** Penguin opera guide; edited by Amanda Holden. Penguin Bks. 2001 xxii, 1142p il pa $30   **792.5**

1. Opera—Dictionaries
ISBN 0-14-051475-9   LC 2002-318562

First published 1993 with title: The Viking opera guide

This guide covers "nearly 2,000 operatic works by some 850 composers. From perennial favorites like Mozart and Wagner to contemporary composers like Adès and Reich, each article . . . outlines the composer's operatic career and assesses his contribution to the genre. Every significant work has its own entry, with information about the libretto, duration, cast and orchestra, background, plot, and musical highlights. . . . Selected recordings are featured." Publisher's note

Includes discographies and bibliographical references

Osborne, Charles, 1927-

The complete operas of Mozart; a critical guide. Atheneum Pubs. 1978 349p il music o.p.; Da Capo Press paperback available $17.50   **792.5**

1. Mozart, Wolfgang Amadeus, 1756-1791 2. Opera—Stories, plots, etc.
ISBN 0-306-80190-6 (pa)   LC 78-55623

In this introduction to Mozart's operas, "each opera is treated as a separate chapter. . . . Each chapter begins with a separate page containing the dramatis personae and their voice range . . . the date, place, and cast for the first performance . . . the name of the librettist, and the Köchel number." Choice

Includes bibliographical references

The complete operas of Puccini; a critical guide. Atheneum Pubs. 1982 279p il music o.p.; Da Capo Press paperback available $18   **792.5**

1. Puccini, Giacomo, 1858-1924 2. Opera—Stories, plots, etc.
ISBN 0-306-80200-7 (pa)   LC 81-69141

The author "provides general background information on all 13 Puccini operas. . . . Unencumbered by techni-

Osborne, Charles, 1927- —*Continued*
cal language, this enjoyably written book is accessible to
all admirers of one of the most popular opera composers
of all time." Choice
Includes bibliographical references

The complete operas of Richard Wagner.
Trafalgar Sq. 1991 c1990 288p il o.p.; Da
Capo Press paperback available $16   **792.5**
1. Wagner, Richard, 1813-1883 2. Opera—Stories,
plots, etc.
ISBN 0-306-80522-7 (pa)   LC 90-70513
First published 1990 in the United Kingdom
In this book, "biography—often in Wagner's own
words—combined with criticism by Wagner's contemporaries, literary background, Wagner's librettos, plot
summaries, descriptions of musical elements illustrated
with musical examples, and Osborne's own insights form
a clear picture of Wagner, his world, and the operas."
Libr J
Includes bibliographical references

Plotkin, Fred
Opera 101; a complete guide to learning
and loving opera. Hyperion 1994 494p pa
$16.95   **792.5**
1. Opera
ISBN 0-7868-8025-2   LC 94-9477
The author introduces the reader to the "basic components of an opera, including how to understand the partnership of words and music, to make oneself aware of
opera plots, to be sensitive to vocal techniques and types,
and to know something about staging. Plotkin even instructs the reader on purchasing a ticket and on behavioral rules at a performance (including the issue of applause). But all this is preliminary to the real meat of the
book: excellent, even exciting, studies of 11 operas."
Booklist
Includes discographies, videography and bibliographical references

Pogue, David
Opera for dummies; by David Pogue and
Scott Speck; foreword by Roger Pines. IDG
Bks. Worldwide 1997 xxiv, 356p il (—For
dummies) pa $24.99   **792.5**
1. Opera
ISBN 0-7645-5010-1   LC 97-80116
A guide to appreciation of opera for beginners, accompanied by a CD
"Icons throughout pinpoint tips, advanced information,
listening guides, when to use the accompanying CD, and
stories to use in conversation. . . . Recommended for
public libraries." Libr J

792.6   Musical plays

Boland, Robert, 1925-
Musicals! directing school and community
theatre; {by} Robert Boland and Paul
Argentini. Scarecrow Press 1997 xxv, 202p il
pa $35   **792.6**
1. Musicals—Production and direction
ISBN 0-8108-3323-9   LC 97-11996
This is "a handbook for novice directors of the musical. This illustrated nuts-and-bolts compendium includes

22 chapters divided among three major sections addressing preparation, production, and performance. Through
accessible prose and a you-can-do-it tone, the authors
provide an overview of preproduction planning, audition-
ing and casting, blocking, stage composition, rehearsals,
and choreography, as well as the more technical layers
of set design, costumes, and lights." Libr J
Includes bibliographical references

Bordman, Gerald Martin
American musical theatre; a chronicle; [by]
Gerald Bordman. 3rd ed. Oxford Univ. Press
2001 917p $75   **792.6**
1. Musicals
ISBN 0-19-513074-X   LC 00-59812
First published 1978
This book offers "show-by-show, season-by-season descriptions—from the first musical to the 1999/2000
Broadway season. . . . [It] encompasses all musical entertainment from plays, revues, opera bouffe and operet-
tas to one-man and one-woman shows. [It] includes
mini-biographies and . . . song, show and people indexes." Publisher's note

Chapin, Theodore S., 1948-
Everything was possible; the birth of the
musical Follies; by Ted Chapin. Knopf 2003
xxix, 331p il $30   **792.6**
1. Sondheim, Stephen. Follies
ISBN 0-375-41328-6   LC 2002-43291
"Chapin was a gofer for the team that brought Stephen Sondheim's *Follies* to life, and his detailed, I-was-
there chronicle documents the making of a great musical
with unparalleled intimacy." Booklist

Gänzl, Kurt
The encyclopedia of the musical theatre.
2nd ed. Schirmer Bks. 2001 3v il set $295
                   792.6
1. Musicals—Encyclopedias
ISBN 0-02-864970-2   LC 01-18361
First published 1994 in two volumes
This set presents a "collection of information about
people and productions of the 19th and 20th centuries.
The coverage is limited to productions originating in
France, Austria, Britain, the US, and Hungary, is restricted to musical theater, and excludes opera. Each entry includes significant dates and places, as well as logically
arranged biographical and historical details." Choice

The musical; a concise history.
Northeastern Univ. Press 1997 432p il $50
                   792.6
1. Musicals
ISBN 1-555-53311-6   LC 97-3008
This is a "guidebook to 300 years of musicals, both
romantic and comedic, which spans the early 18th to the
late 20th centuries, and covers the theatrical scenes in
America, Europe and Australia." Publ Wkly
Includes discography

Mordden, Ethan, 1947-
Rodgers & Hammerstein. Abrams 1992
224p il hardcover o.p. paperback available
$24.95 **792.6**
1. Rodgers, Richard, 1902-1979 2. Hammerstein, Oscar, 1895-1960 3. Musicals
ISBN 0-8109-8144-0 (pa) LC 91-46586
The author "devotes one chapter each to the Rodgers and Hammerstein musicals—nine for the stage (Oklahoma! through The Sound of Music), one for film (State Fair), and one for television (Cinderella). He describes the genesis of the show, changes occurring during production, and subsequent history (e.g., film versions, revivals)." Choice
"Lovers of the American musical theater will find a treat in . . . [this] lavishly illustrated sort of glorified scrapbook. . . . Mordden's text provides a diverting, informal, and informative backstage tour." Christ Sci Monit
Includes bibliographical references

Norton, Richard C., 1953-
A chronology of American musical theater.
Oxford Univ. Press 2002 3v set $466.50
792.6
1. Musicals—Chronology
ISBN 0-19-508888-3 LC 2001-55710
Contents: v1 1750-1912; v2 1912-1952; v3 1952-2001
"The gorgeous illustrations in this season-by-season chronology of every musical comedy, operetta, comic opera, burlesque, and revue performed on a major New York City stage from 1851 through May 2001 might be enticement enough to acquire this set. Entries for more than 3,000 plays include details such as the full cast, crew, production staff, venues, number of performances, creative personnel, and songs, which are listed as they occur within acts when this information is known. Three indexes cover song titles, show names, and names of principal players and famous chorus menbers. Leaving appraisal and plot summaries to other classic references, these volumes are the most in-depth documentary source on the New York musical stage available, with a chapter that carries the timeline for selected plays back to 1750."—"The Best of the Best Reference Sources." Am Libr
Includes bibliographical references

792.8 Ballet and modern dance

Craine, Debra
The Oxford dictionary of dance; by Debra Craine, Judith Mackrell. Oxford Univ. Press 2000 527p $49.95; pa $16.95 **792.8**
1. Dance—Dictionaries
ISBN 0-19-860106-9; 0-19-860400-9 (pa)
LC 2001-274422
Based on The concise Oxford dictionary of ballet by Horst Kroegler
"The styles covered range from the Brazilian martial art form of *capoeira* to American hip-hop. . . . Most entries are brief, except for those on major individuals, institutions, and works. Some themes are treated (shoes, film, dance notation). Work lists are provided, as well as an extensive bibliography." Choice
For a fuller review see: Booklist, March 1, 2001

International dictionary of ballet; editor, Martha Bremser; assistant editor, Larraine Nicholas; picture editor, Leanda Shrimpton. St. James Press 1993 2v il set $295 **792.8**
1. Ballet—Dictionaries
ISBN 1-55862-084-2 LC 93-25051
"With more than 750 entries, this source covers the major figures in ballet (dancers, choreographers, composers, etc.). Individual ballets, and internationally known ballet companies from the Renaissance to the present. Entries are arranged alphabetically and each includes items such as a list of major roles, premiere performances, a critical essay, biographical or historical information, and a lengthy bibliography. The two-volume work is well-researched and comprehensive." Am Libr

International dictionary of modern dance; with a preface by Don McDonagh; editor, Taryn Benbow-Pfalzgraf; contributing editor, Glynis Benbow-Niemer. St. James Press 1998 xxvi, 891p il $212.50 **792.8**
1. Modern dance—Dictionaries
ISBN 1-55862-359-0 LC 98-9853
"Alphabetically arranged, signed essays treat modern dance schools, artists, companies, periods, works, and performances. A chronology of modern dance opens the work, highlighting important events and people." Libr J

International encyclopedia of dance; a project of Dance Perspectives Foundation, Inc; founding editor, Selma Jeanne Cohen; area editors, George Dorris [et al.] Oxford Univ. Press 1998 6v set $1250 **792.8**
1. Dance—Encyclopedias 2. Ballet—Encyclopedias
ISBN 0-19-509462-X LC 97-36562
This work presents entries on "dances, dancers, and dance topics. . . . Aspects of dance in more than 100 countries are written about by more than 600 writers. . . . Dance as ceremony and ritual in religious as well as social and cultural traditions is covered here, as are the related topics of music, scenic design, dance notation, costumes, aesthetics, and training." Booklist
"In the emerging field of dance scholarship, this set is a milestone." Libr J

Reynolds, Nancy, 1938-
No fixed points; dance in the twentieth century; [by] Nancy Reynolds and Malcolm McCormick. Yale Univ. Press 2003 907p il $50 **792.8**
1. Dance 2. Ballet 3. Modern dance
ISBN 0-300-09366-7 LC 2003-10754
This is a "narrative of the development of ballet, modern dance, and postmodern choreography. Synthesizing a century's worth of observation and opinion, Reynolds and McCormick chart the pendulum swing of styles and isolate individual contributions. . . . They highlight the significance of factors as large as government funding and as small as the depth of Baryshnikov's demi-plié." New Yorker
"Although everyone will be using the book for reference, Reynolds and McCormick have produced a work that is completely unlike a standard reference book; you don't just look things up in it—you read it. Here is a coherent, reasoned and entertaining chronicle of dance performance in the West over the hundred years that are unquestionably the fullest and most complicated in the long history of this fragmented and elusive art." N Y Times
Includes bibliographical references

793.2   Parties and entertainments

Cooke, Courtney
The best baby shower book; a complete guide for party planners. rev ed. Meadowbrook Press 2001 108p il pa $7.95
                              793.2

1. Showers (Parties) 2. Infants
ISBN 0-88166-384-0   LC 00-51132
First published 1986
This is a guide to planning baby showers which includes recipes, decorating ideas, and activities

793.3   Social, folk, national dancing

Soffee, Anne Thomas
Snake hips; belly dancing and how I found true love. Chicago Review Press 2002 xxii, 262p $22.95   **793.3**
1. Belly dancing
ISBN 1-55652-458-7   LC 2002-572
This is the author's story of how she cured a broken heart and changed her life for the better through belly-dancing
"Soffee's witty, flowing prose draws readers into this unlikely but captivating story." Booklist

793.7   Games not characterized by action

Tahan, Malba, 1895-
The man who counted; a collection of mathematical adventures; illustrated by Patricia Reid Baquero & translated by Leslie Clark and Alastair Reid. Norton 1993 244p il hardcover o.p. paperback available $14.95
                                793.7

1. Mathematical recreations
ISBN 0-393-30934-7 (pa)   LC 92-18822
"First published in Brazil in 1949 by the mathematician Julio de Melo e Sousa (Tahan is the imaginary Arab author he claimed to have translated), [this book] is a series of . . . 'Arabian Nights'-style tales, with each story built around a classic mathematical puzzle." Libr J
"This small book is a joy. . . . These are beautifully expressive tales that find mathematical puzzles and numerical intrigue in human situations and speak not just of solving the problems but of the needs we all have for friendship, love, and beauty." Booklist

793.73   Puzzles and puzzle games

Merriam-Webster's crossword puzzle dictionary. 2nd ed. Merriam-Webster 1996 775p $18.95; pa $5.99   **793.73**
1. Crossword puzzles—Dictionaries
ISBN 0-87779-121-X; 0-87779-919-9 (pa)
                              LC 96-24796

First published 1992
This "dictionary is structured in accordance with the way crossword puzzles are constructed and solved. Main entries are in alphabetic order letter-by-letter. If the main entry is a large category, the list of answer words is broken down into alphabetically arranged subcategories. When more than one answer is possible to a clue representing a main entry, the answer words are grouped together according to the number of letters they contain. . . . This dictionary has a broad range of the most current words used in crossword puzzles. The format is easy to use." Am Ref Books Annu, 1997

The **Official** Scrabble players dictionary. 3rd ed. Merriam-Webster 1995 693p $19.95; pa $6.50   **793.73**
1. Scrabble (Game)—Dictionaries
ISBN 0-87779-220-8; 0-87779-915-6 (pa)
                            LC 95-20437

Also available large print edition
First published 1978
This is a dictionary of words which can be used in the game of Scrabble including 100,000 2- to 8- letter words

Pulliam, Tom
The New York times crossword puzzle dictionary; by Tom Pulliam and Clare Grundman. 3rd ed. Times Bks. 1995 656p $27.50; pa $7.99   **793.73**
1. Crossword puzzles—Dictionaries
ISBN 0-8129-2373-1; 0-8129-3122-X (pa)
                            LC 95-11416
"A Hudson Group book"
First published 1977
This dictionary of synonyms for crossword puzzles includes more than 50,000 entries
"One of the more useful works of its kind." Ref Sources for Small & Medium-sized Libr. 6th edition

Random House Webster's crossword puzzle dictionary. 3rd ed. Random House 1998 854p $27.95; pa $18.95   **793.73**
1. Crossword puzzles—Dictionaries
ISBN 0-679-45856-5; 0-375-70624-0 (pa)
                            LC 98-67266
First published 1989 with title: The Random House crossword puzzle dictionary
Each entry lists a variety of terms that may be substituted for the entry term. The arrangement within each term listing is alphabetical and by number of letters
"A useful and entertaining companion for both crossword puzzle and trivia buffs." Ref Sources for Small & Medium-sized Libr. 6th edition

794.1   Chess

Capablanca, José Raúl, 1888-1942
Chess fundamentals. Harcourt Brace & Co. 1921 246p il o.p.; McKay, D. paperback available $14.95   **794.1**
1. Chess
ISBN 0-679-14004-2 (pa)
Explains the general principles of chess through eighteen illustrative games, so that, when grounded in these, the novice may understand the whole elementary science of the game

Fischer, Bobby, 1943-

Bobby Fischer teaches chess; by Bobby Fischer, Stuart Margulies, Donn Mosenfelder. Basic Systems, Inc. 1966 334p il o.p.; Bantam Bks. paperback available $7.99

794.1

1. Chess
ISBN 0-553-26315-3 (pa)
In this book the authors give specific advice and hints aimed at both the beginning and advanced player. Each step-by-step lesson is fully illustrated

United States Chess Federation

U.S. Chess Federation's official rules of chess; compiled and sanctioned by the U.S. Chess Federation; Tim Just, chief editor; Daniel B. Burg, editor. 5th ed. Random House Puzzles & Games 2003 xxxvii, 370p il (McKay chess library) pa $18.95   **794.1**

1. Chess
ISBN 0-8129-3559-4   LC 2003-278349
"This book supersedes the Official rules of chess, first edition, 1974, second edition, 1978, third edition, 1987, and fourth edition, 1993"
This "edition features the latest rules, including guidelines for the popular game of speed chess, an updated quick rating system, and the latest conventions of governing tournaments. It also contains explanations of every legal move, a guide to calculating lifetime rankings, guidelines for sponsoring and running a tournament, and a lesson on how to read and write chess notation." Publisher's note

794.6   Bowling

Anthony, Earl, 1938-2001

Winning bowling; [by] Earl Anthony with Dawson Taylor. Contemporary Bks. 1994 198p il pa $12.95   **794.6**

1. Bowling
ISBN 0-8092-3526-9   LC 94-21344
First published 1977
This is a guide to bowling techniques for beginners

794.7   Indoor ball games

Byrne, Robert, 1930-

Byrne's new standard book of pool and billiards. Harcourt Brace & Co. 1998 xxv, 406p il $35; pa $20   **794.7**

1. Pool (Game) 2. Billiards
ISBN 0-15-100325-4; 0-15-600554-9 (pa)
LC 98-14656
First published 1978 with title: Byrne's standard book of pool and billiards
The author explains the rules of pool and billiards and offers advice on strategy with diagrams of various shots
Includes bibliographical references

McCumber, David

Playing off the rail; a pool hustler's journey. Random House 1996 367p o.p.; Avon Bks. paperback available $13.95 **794.7**

1. Annigoni, Tony 2. Pool (Game)
ISBN 0-380-72923-7 (pa)   LC 95-6955
A "look at the game of pool, which is a gambling sport not yet sanitized by what McCumber calls the 'Fellowship of Christian Athletes types.' He plays financial backer to a sharp-tongued player named Tony Annigoni, and takes him on the road across North America in search of highstakes games. . . . This is a terrific book." New Yorker

Mosconi, Willie, 1913-1993

Willie Mosconi's winning pocket billiards for beginners and advanced players, with a section on trick shots. Crown Trade Paperbacks 1993 140p il pa $9.95   **794.7**

1. Pool (Game)
ISBN 0-5178-8427-5   LC 95-207612
First published 1965 with title: Winning pocket billiards
This book on pocket billiards has more than 100 step-by-step photographs and diagrams to show how shots should be made. With official rules and a section on trick shots

795   Games of chance

Ainslie, Tom

Ainslie's complete Hoyle; illustrated by Jill Schwartz. Simon & Schuster 1975 526p il hardcover o.p. paperback available $18   **795**

1. Games 2. Card games
ISBN 0-671-24779-4 (pa)
Over half of this book is devoted to card games including bridge, rummy, poker, solitaire and related games, as well as children's games. Part two covers board and table games such as backgammon, monopoly, chess, checkers, craps and other dice games, dominoes, mah jong, games of logic, word games (e.g. scrabble, crosswords) and simulation games. Two briefer sections cover gambling-casino games and games suitable for club cars and taverns

Scarne, John, 1903-1985

Scarne's new complete guide to gambling. fully rev expanded updated ed. Simon & Schuster 1973 xxii, 871p il hardcover o.p. paperback available $20   **795**

1. Gambling
ISBN 0-671-63063-6 (pa)
First published 1961 with title: Scarne's complete guide to gambling
The author covers horse racing, dice games, betting on sports, off-track betting, greyhound dog racing, Jai-alai, state lotteries, etc. Rules are given and explanations provided on odds, house percentages and playing strategy
This is "virtually a textbook on gambling." Publ Wkly

795.4　Card games

Bellin, Andy, 1968-

Poker nation; a high stakes, low-life adventure into the heart of a gambling country. HarperCollins Pubs. 2001 258p il hardcover o.p. paperback available $12.95
　　　　　　　　　　　　　　　795.4

1. Card games

ISBN 0-06-095847-2 (pa)　　　LC 2001-42409

The author, "a lapsed astrophysics student who left science for his true calling of professional poker, introduces us to the world of legal and illegal poker games and the cast of strange characters who can be found therein." Libr J

"Bellin offers the best of both worlds, combining detailed advice on how to play the game with engagingly written, humorous stories about those who play it with passion." Booklist

Includes bibliographical references

Gibson, Walter Brown, 1897-1985

Hoyle's modern encyclopedia of card games; rules of all the basic games and popular variations; [by] Walter B. Gibson. Dolphin Bks. (NY) 1974 398p il pa $12.95
　　　　　　　　　　　　　　　795.4

1. Card games

ISBN 0-385-07680-0

"A Dolphin handbook"

This guide to the rules and techniques of various card games includes special sections on pinochle, poker and solitaire

Goren, Charles Henry, 1901-1991

Goren's new bridge complete; [by] Chas H. Goren. rev ed. Doubleday 1985 705p il $34.95　　　　　　　　　　　　　**795.4**

1. Bridge (Game)

ISBN 0-385-23324-8　　　　LC 85-10344

First published 1951 with title: Contract bridge complete

Explanations of basic bridge for beginners as well as data on tournament-winning techniques for advanced players

McManus, James

Positively Fifth Street; murderers, cheetahs, and Binion's World Series of Poker. Farrar, Straus & Giroux 2003 422p il $26　　**795.4**

1. Poker

ISBN 0-374-23648-8　　　　LC 2002-33882

"McManus went to Las Vegas in May 2000 on assignment for *Harper's* to cover the World Series of Poker. . . . He was to throw in coverage of the trial of Sandy Murphy, an ex-stripper, and her boyfriend, Rick Tabish, accused of murdering Ted Binion, the tournament's host. . . . To satisfy his own gambling urge, McManus enter the poker competition and spends 10 days immersed in the culture of Vegas and gambling, rendering a fast-paced, riveting account of his progress through the tournament. . . . A delicious inside look." Booklist

Includes bibliographical references

Patterson, Jerry L.

Blackjack, a winner's handbook; [by] Jerry L. Patterson with Eric Nielsen. Berkley Pub. Group 2001 269p il pa $14.95　　　**795.4**

1. Blackjack (Game)

ISBN 0-399-52683-8　　　　LC 00-51042

First published 1978 by Echelon Enterprises

The author presents rules and strategies for winning at blackjack, including information about card counting and internet casinos

Scarne, John, 1903-1985

Scarne's encyclopedia of card games. Harper & Row 1983 475p il pa $18　**795.4**

1. Card games

ISBN 0-06-091052-6　　　　LC 83-47571

The material in this book has been excerpted, with alterations and additions, from Scarne's encyclopedia of games (1973)

Rules are provided for bridge, pinochle, cribbage, faro and solitaire among many others. In addition the author discusses the histories and variations of the games, odds and probabilities, and how to detect cheating

796　Athletic and outdoor sports and games

Berkow, Ira

The minority quarterback, and other lives in sports. Dee, I.R. 2002 307p $26; pa $16.95
　　　　　　　　　　　　　　　796

1. Sports

ISBN 1-56663-422-9; 1-56663-502-0 (pa)
　　　　　　　　　　　　　　LC 2001-47578

Reprints of columns and feature stories originally published in The New York Times between 1981 and 2000

"Berkow brings together essays on a theme: athletes overcoming hardships. Whether his subject is minority football players struggling to win recognition as quarterbacks—a position once restricted to whites—or baseball pitcher Jim Abbott working past the handicap of having only one arm, he writes with skill, empathy, and insight." Booklist

The **Best** American sports writing. Houghton Mifflin $27.50; pa $13　　　　　**796**

1. Sports

ISSN 1056-8034

Annual. First published 1991. Editors vary

With selections culled from 350 American and Canadian newspapers, this series covers a wide range of sports and sports figures of interest to both the general reader and the die-hard sports fan

The **Best** American sports writing of the century; edited by David Halberstam. Houghton Mifflin 1999 776p $30; pa $18
　　　　　　　　　　　　　　　796

1. Sports

ISBN 0-395-94513-5; 0-395-94514-3 (pa)

"Although there are pieces about mountain climbing, tennis and chess, fully half of the selections are about two sports: baseball and boxing. The book begins with a Best of the Best section led by Gay Talese's 1966 profile of Joe DiMaggio, 'The Silent Season of a Hero.'. . . The final section is a special six-piece tribute to a man who himself claimed to be the best of the best—Muhammad Ali." Publ Wkly

Franck, Irene M.

Famous first facts about sports; [by] Irene M. Franck & David M. Brownstone. Wilson, H.W. 2001 903p $150   **796**
1. Sports
ISBN 0-8242-0973-7   LC 00-43883
"Franck and Brownstone have compiled 5,415 'firsts' covering more than 110 sports. . . . Arranged alphabetically by sport, the concisely described events are listed in chronological order, with headers for time periods. Entries are given consecutive four-digit numbers, which are cited in the five indexes (subjects, years, days, personal names, and geographical locations). . . . The indexes provide essential access and are easy to use. . . . The depth of coverage is impressive." Choice
Includes bibliographical references

Guttmann, Allen

Women's sports; a history. Columbia Univ. Press 1991 339p il hardcover o.p. paperback available $24   **796**
1. Sports 2. Women athletes
ISBN 0-231-06957-X (pa)   LC 90-28692
The author explores "the social and cultural contexts of women's athletics in ancient civilizations, the Middle Ages, and the Renaissance. This lays the groundwork for a subsequent discussion of the subject's current state, in which he . . . exposes controversial issues which threaten the development of women's sports." Libr J
Includes bibliographical references

Hickok, Ralph

The encyclopedia of North American sports history. 2nd ed. Facts on File 2002 594p il $75   **796**
1. Sports—Encyclopedias
ISBN 0-8160-4660-3   LC 2001-55646
First published 1992
"Entries fall into eight categories: sports; general history; biography; sporting events; major awards; cities; stadiums, fields, and arenas; and sports organizations, such as leagues, college conferences, and halls of fame. . . . The importance of this volume is in its coverage of a variety of minor sports, such as women's synchronized swimming, steamboat racing, skin diving, and sled dog racing, for which finding information may be difficult." Booklist

Levine, Peter

Ellis Island to Ebbet's Field; sport and the American-Jewish experience. Oxford Univ. Press 1992 328p il (Sports history and society) hardcover o.p. paperback available $21.50   **796**
1. Jews—United States 2. Sports
ISBN 0-19-508555-8 (pa)   LC 91-42016
The author "explores the importance of sport in transforming Jewish immigrants into American Jews. Drawing on interviews with celebrities as well as lesser-known neighborhood stars, Levine vividly recounts the stories of Red Auerbach, Hank Greenberg, Moe Berg, and many others who became Jewish heroes and symbols of the difficult struggle for American success." Univ Press Books for Public and Second Sch Libr
Includes bibliographical references

Nike is a goddess; the history of women in sports; edited by Lissa Smith; introduction by Mariah Burton Nelson. Atlantic Monthly Press 1998 331p il hardcover o.p. paperback available $14   **796**
1. Sports 2. Women athletes
ISBN 0-87113-761-5 (pa)   LC 98-27049
This "anthology documents the athletic achievements of female athletes during the late-nineteenth and twentieth centuries. Separate chapters written by noted sports journalists (Grace Lichtenstein, Michelle Kaufman, Karen Karbo) cover such disciplines as basketball, soccer, baseball, swimming, horseback riding, tennis, golf, and hockey, among others." Booklist
"The quality of writing in the different sections varies but each writer is well connected with her field and all give a good background history as well as an assessment of current developments in the sport. Controversial issues are not ignored, and lesbianism is addressed." SLJ

Queenan, Joe

True believers; the tragic inner life of sports fans. Holt & Co. 2003 236p $23 **796**
1. Sports
ISBN 0-8050-6979-8   LC 2002-191911
"What does it mean to be the kind of sports fan who roots for teams that perpetually disappoint? Queenan investigates the collective psyche of sports masochists with a thoroughly entertaining mix of sarcasm and self-criticism." Booklist

Sherrow, Victoria

Encyclopedia of women and sports. ABC-CLIO 1996 xxii, 382p il $75   **796**
1. Women athletes—Encyclopedias 2. Sports—Encyclopedias
ISBN 0-87436-826-X   LC 96-19600
"More than 600 alphabetically organized entries highlight key individuals who have participated in or advanced the cause of women in sports and include related topics, such as sexual and racial discrimination, tournaments, organizations, leagues, awards, health issues, segregation, sport history, scholarships, and officiating. The volume not only records athletic achievements but chronicles other accomplishments as well. . . . [It] underscores the progress women have made not only as athletes but as coaches, officials, teachers, administrators, sportscasters, sportswriters, and women's rights advocates. Current as of the 1996 Summer Olympic Games, entries are concise, interesting, and readable." Am Ref Books Annu, 1997

Sports: the complete visual reference; François Fortin {general editor}. Firefly Bks. 2000 372p il $39.95   **796**
1. Sports
ISBN 1-55209-540-1
This is a "reference source on 120 contemporary sports . . . pulling together the history, physical environment for competitions, roles of the players and officials, specific terms and expressions, and dynamics of each. All of this is done with an emphasis on visual presentation, and each entry includes copious illustrations." Booklist
"A sure winner for any sports reference collection." Am Libr

796.323 Basketball

Blais, Madeleine, 1949-

In these girls, hope is a muscle. Atlantic Monthly Press 1995 263p o.p.; Warner Bks. paperback available $13.95 **796.323**

1. Cathedral High School (Springfield, Mass.) 2. Basketball

ISBN 0-446-67210-6 (pa) LC 94-30394

"Weaving accounts of players' personal histories with reportage on their on-court performances, Madeleine Blais recounts the dramatic 1992-93 season of the Lady Hurricanes of Amherst (Mass.) Regional High School." N Y Times Book Rev

"Alternately funny, exciting and moving, the book should be enjoyed not only by girls and women who have played sports but also those who wanted to but let themselves be discouraged." Publ Wkly

Bradley, Bill

Values of the game. Artisan 1998 160p il $30 **796.323**

1. National Basketball Association 2. Basketball

ISBN 1-57965-116-X LC 98-7280

Also available in paperback from Bantam Bks.

In this book, the former senator and New York Knick presents a "blend of sports memoir and inspirational advice interspersed with more than 100 dramatic photos of basketball players past and present. . . . While some may dismiss much of his volume as a collection of copybook maxims, the whole is larger than the sum of its parts, not only because it is so personal but because Bradley moves so deftly from the specific to the general." Publ Wkly

Feinstein, John

A march to madness; the view from the floor in the Atlantic Coast Conference. Little, Brown 1997 464p il hardcover o.p. paperback available $14 **796.323**

1. Atlantic Coast Conference 2. Basketball

ISBN 0-316-27712-6 (pa) LC 97-31060

Feinstein "covers one year with all of the teams in the perennially powerful Atlantic Coast Conference. After introducing each of the schools, their teams, their coaches, and their expectations for the 1996/97 basketball season, the book describes their progress week by week, culminating with Dean Smith's run to the NCAA Final Four. Such a detailed accounting of a sports season could seem interminable to readers, but Feinstein has again produced a narrative that is not only interesting but often exciting." Libr J

Kent, Richard G.

Inside women's college basketball; anatomy of a season; [by] Richard Kent. Taylor, W.T. 2000 222p il $22.95 **796.323**

1. Basketball

ISBN 0-87833-188-3 LC 00-42589

"Kent chronicles the 1999-2000 season as experienced by four top women's programs: Tennessee, Connecticut, Rutgers, and Sacred Heart. . . . This is a fine overview for those looking for insights into the women's game." Booklist

Lynch, Wayne

Season of the 76ers; the story of Wilt Chamberlain and the 1967 NBA champion Philadelphia 76ers; foreword by Billy Cunningham. St. Martin's Press 2002 269p il $24.95 **796.323**

1. Chamberlain, Wilt, 1936-1999 2. Philadelphia 76ers (Basketball team)

ISBN 0-312-28277-X LC 2001-52502

"Lynch chronicles what some say was the greatest season in the National Basketball Association's history in this . . . tale of the 1966-67 Philadelphia team." Libr J

This is an "entertaining tribute to a group that caught lightning in a bottle, if only for a season." Booklist

The **Official** NBA encyclopedia; foreword by Michael Jordan; introduction by David J. Stern; edited by Jan Hubbard. 3rd ed. Doubleday 2000 911p il $50 **796.323**

1. Basketball

ISBN 0-385-50130-7 LC 2001-274272

First published 1989

"Covers history, Hall of Fame, all-time records, all-star games, and official NBA rules. Includes complete statistical profile of every player who has ever appeared in the NBA. Illustrated with photographs; indexed." NY Public Libr Book of How & Where to Look It Up

Shaughnessy, Dan

Ever green: the Boston Celtics; a history in the words of their players, coaches, fans, and foes, from 1946 to the present. St. Martin's Press 1990 259p il hardcover o.p. paperback available $12.95 **796.323**

1. Boston Celtics (Basketball team)

ISBN 0-312-06348-2 (pa) LC 90-37115

The author incorporates recollections of Celtic players and coaches in this history of one of basketball's most successful franchises

Includes bibliographical references

Wolff, Alexander

Big game, small world; a basketball adventure. Warner Bks. 2002 xxiv, 424p il $24.95; pa $15.95 **796.323**

1. Basketball

ISBN 0-446-52601-0; 0-446-67989-5 (pa)

"Wolff traveled to 16 countries and 10 states to assess basketball's impact as a global phenomenon. He profiles a cloistered nun who was once a talented hoopster and investigates the origins of the crossover dribble. Wolff's passion for the game burns feverishly throughout." Booklist

796.332 American football

Bissinger, H. G.

Friday night lights; a town, a team, and a dream. Da Capo Press 2000 367p il pa $15.95 **796.332**

1. Permian High School (Odessa, Tex.) 2. Football

ISBN 0-306-80990-7 LC 00-40510

First published 1990 by Addison-Wesley

In 1988, the author, a "Philadelphia Inquirer editor, left his job to spend a year with a high school sports

Bissinger, H. G.—*Continued*
team. The sport he picked was football, the location, the . . . West Texas oil town of Odessa. . . . Here 20,000 fans turn out regularly to watch their Permian Panthers win." Libr J

"It is a tricky balancing act, but Mr. Bissinger carries it off: 'Friday Night Lights' offers a biting indictment of the sports craziness that grips not only Odessa but most of American society, while at the same time providing a moving evocation of its powerful allure." N Y Times Book Rev

Dent, Jim
The Junction boys; how ten days in hell with Bear Bryant forged a champion team. St. Martin's Press 1999 290p il $24.95; pa $13.95   **796.332**
1. Bryant, Bear 2. Football
ISBN 0-312-19293-2; 0-312-26755-X (pa)
                                        LC 99-22179
"In February 1954, Paul 'Bear' Bryant took the head football coaching position at Texas A & M. The story of his first Aggie team, vividly recounted here by journalist Dent, is a little-known but memorable chapter in the legendary coach's career." Booklist

The undefeated; the Oklahoma Sooners and the greatest winning streak in college football history. St. Martin's Press 2001 288p il $24.95; pa $14.95   **796.332**
1. Oklahoma Sooners (Football team) 2. Football
ISBN 0-312-26656-1; 0-312-30326-2 (pa)
                                        LC 2001-34896
The author recounts how "Oklahoma Sooner football coach Bud Wilkinson won an all-time record 47 straight games over five seasons, which included three undefeated years, from 1954 through 1956. . . . [This] is a fascinating account of an extraordinary athletic achievement that is unlikely to be approached, let alone equaled." Booklist

Includes bibliographical references

Green, Tim
The dark side of the game; my life in the NFL. Warner Bks. 1996 272p hardcover o.p. paperback available $7.50   **796.332**
1. National Football League 2. Football
ISBN 0-446-60520-4 (pa)   LC 95-51000
The author "offers a collection of approximately 70 brief, engagingly written essays on such dark topics as drug use, sex, violence, injuries, cheating, gambling, and money in professional football." Libr J

My greatest day in football; the legends of football recount their greatest moments; edited by Bob McCullough. Thomas Dunne Bks. 2001 269p il $24.95; pa $14.95
                                        796.332
1. Football
ISBN 0-312-27211-1; 0-312-30296-7 (pa)
                                        LC 2001-41975
The author interviews "members of the Pro Football Hall of Fame about their greatest day in football. . . . The personalities of the players take center stage, as many of them discuss not just a single game but their view of the game in general and their lives before, during, and after football." Libr J

Pro football register. Sporting News il pa $16.95   **796.332**
1. Football—Statistics
Annual. First published 1966 with title: Football register

At head of title: The Sporting News

This lists biographical information for National Football league players, including current and past team affiliations and yearly statistics

796.334 Soccer

Araton, Harvey
Alive and kicking; when soccer moms take the field and change their lives forever. Simon & Schuster 2001 253p il $25
                                        796.334
1. Soccer 2. Women athletes
ISBN 0-684-87390-7   LC 2001-31307
"Araton tells the story of a different kind of soccer mom: women over 30 who play in soccer leagues. It's an inspiring tale, written with empathy and emotion." Booklist

Bauer, Gerhard, 1940-
New soccer techniques, tactics & teamwork; [translated by Kelly Ramke and Nicole Franke] Newly rev & updated. Sterling 2002 159p il pa $14.95   **796.334**
1. Soccer
ISBN 1-402-70088-1   LC 2002-7281
First published 1993 with title Soccer techniques, tactics & teamwork
This guide to coaching youth soccer considers "working with the character traits of individual players to developing skills in dribbling, tackling, shooting, and passing. . . . Included is a year-round training schedule that keeps players fit . . . tips for running the most effective practices, and suggestions on getting the greatest results from all players while stressing the importance of teamwork." Publisher's note

Bellos, Alex
Futebol: the Brazilian way of life. Bloomsbury Pub. 2002 407p il maps $25.95; pa $16.95   **796.334**
1. Soccer 2. Brazil—Social life and customs
ISBN 1-58234-250-4; 1-58234-287-3 (pa)
The author aims "to paint a 'portrait of [Brazil], Latin America's largest country, seen through its passion for [soccer]'." Economist
"Compelling. . . . Alternately funny and dark. . . . Bellos offers a cast of characters as colorful as a Carnival parade." Publ Wkly

Hamm, Mia, 1972-
Go for the goal; a champion's guide to winning in soccer and life; [by] Mia Hamm with Aaron Heifetz. HarperCollins Pubs. 1999 222p il hardcover o.p. paperback available $12.95   **796.334**
1. Soccer
ISBN 0-06-093159-0 (pa)   LC 99-19592
Personal anecdotes and both action and instructional photos illustrate soccer skills and techniques

796.342   Tennis

Total tennis: the ultimate tennis encyclopedia; [edited by] Bud Collins. Sport Media Pub. 2003 xxi, 938p il $34.95
796.342
1. Tennis
ISBN 0-9731-4434-3
Collins "integrates, updates, and expands upon material from the previous three editions of his *Tennis Encyclopedia* (o.p.). . . . Easy-to-read charts include biographical data, a year-by-year record of each player's career and year-end rankings, match records in international team events, and the four major tournaments. . . . Thankfully, this book is much more than an array of numbers and the cataloging of records. Several articles . . . complement Collins's own colorful and in-depth player and tournament profiles." Libr J

Wertheim, L. Jon
Venus envy; a sensational season inside the Women's Tour. HarperCollins Pubs. 2001 225p il hardcover o.p. paperback available $14.95
796.342
1. Tennis
ISBN 0-06-095749-2 (pa)   LC 2001-24314
This is the author's "account of a year spent following the superstars and also-rans on the WTA Tour, from the 2000 Australian Open to the 2000 U.S. Open. Wertheim . . . profiles the egos, catty repartee, emotional battering and dysfunctional family relationships that drive Venus and Serena Williams, Lindsay Davenport, Martina Hingis, Anna Kournikova, Monica Seles and some lesser-known professionals." Publ Wkly

796.352   Golf

Andrisani, John
The Tiger Woods way; secrets of Tiger Woods's power swing technique. Crown 1997 153p il hardcover o.p. paperback available $12
796.352
1. Woods, Tiger 2. Golf
ISBN 0-609-80139-2 (pa)   LC 97-6083
The author "shares his discovery of the secrets of Tiger's flawless swing technique to help golfers of all levels learn how to increase their driving distance and improve their game." Publisher's note

Feinstein, John
A good walk spoiled; days and nights on the PGA tour. Little, Brown 1995 xx, 475p il hardcover o.p. paperback available $14.95
796.352
1. PGA Tour Inc. 2. Golf
ISBN 0-316-27737-1 (pa)   LC 94-49552
Along with "profiles of the game's big names—Norman, Price, Watson—Feinstein's sojourn through the 1994 PGA tour also offers remarkable glimpses of the marginal players who struggle to first qualify for the tour and then maintain their tenuous places on it. . . . Golfers of all ages simply won't be able to put this book down." Booklist

The majors: in pursuit of golf's Holy Grail. Little, Brown 1999 480p $25; pa $14.95
796.352
1. Golf
ISBN 0-316-27971-4; 0-316-27795-9 (pa)
LC 99-11390
"Feinstein tackles the sport's four major championships: the Masters, the U.S. Open, the British Open and the PGA, as they were played in 1998." Publ Wkly
"If you want to know how touring pros think, on and off the course but particularly on the courses that are the crucibles of the majors, this is the book. It also tells how golf officials, especially those at the Masters and at the United States Golf Association, think in setting up their courses." N Y Times Book Rev

Open: inside the ropes at Bethpage Black. Little, Brown 2003 368p il $25.95   **796.352**
1. Golf
ISBN 0-316-17003-8   LC 2003-101414
Feinstein "assays the 2002 U.S. Open, which was a historic benchmark as the first time the Open was held on a public golf course, Bethpage Black on Long Island." Libr J
"Amazingly, Feinstein turns the day-to-day operations of the USGA into the stuff of high drama. . . . Feinstein does the impossible here: he writes a blue-collar tearjerker about a purportedly blue-blood sport." Booklist

Frost, Mark
The greatest game ever played; Harry Vardon, Francis Ouimet, and the birth of modern golf. Hyperion 2002 488p il $30
796.352
1. Vardon, Harry, 1870-1937 2. Ouimet, Francis, 1893-1967 3. Golf
ISBN 0-7868-6920-8   LC 2002-68930
The author "tells the story behind the legendary 1913 U.S. Open, in which Francis Ouimet, a 20-year-old golf amateur from Massachusetts, shocked the genteel golf world by defeating British champion Harry Vardon." Publ Wkly
"The climax of the narrative . . . is genuinely exciting, a marvelous re-creation of a signature moment in golf history." Booklist

Martino, Rick
The PGA manual of golf; the professional's way to learn and play better golf; [by] Rick Martino with Don Wade. Rev and updated. Warner Bks. 2002 242p il $34.95   **796.352**
1. Golf
ISBN 0-446-52653-3   LC 2002-101114
First published 1991 by Macmillan under the authorship of Gary Wiren
This golf manual "offers practical programs and exercise regimens to improve performance and flexibility, including graphics that detail stances and body placement, sequence shots of the game's best swings, a history of the sport, and . . . quotes from golf's greatest personalities." Publisher's note

Nicklaus, Jack

Golf my way; by Jack Nicklaus with Ken Bowden; illustrated by Jim McQueen. Simon & Schuster 1974 264p il hardcover o.p. paperback available $15   **796.352**

   1. Golf

   ISBN 0-684-85211-X (pa)

   "This is the only book written by [Jack Nicklaus] that covers in depth his entire technique of the game as he plays it, from top to bottom. The intellectual and scholarly dedication that Nicklaus brings to his game is explained fully." Choice

Player, Gary

The complete golfer's handbook; [by Gary Player, with Chris Whales & Duncan Cruickshank; foreword by Ernie Els] Lyons Press 2000 160p il $24.95; pa $19.95   **796.352**

   1. Golf

   ISBN 1-58574-029-2; 1-58574-765-3 (pa)

   This guide covers "etiquette, equipment, course design, and strategy, in addition to how to swing the club. The material is introductory only, but even experienced golfers will enjoy the graphics and profit from reviewing the concise, clearly presented swing advice." Booklist

Rubenstein, Lorne

A season in Dornoch; golf and life in the Scottish Highlands. Simon & Schuster 2001 242p il o.p.; Citadel Press paperback available $14.95   **796.352**

   1. Golf 2. Scotland—Description

   ISBN 0-8065-2457-X (pa)   LC 2001-47408

   This is "Rubenstein's account of spending an entire summer in the village of Dornoch, living above a bookshop, immersing himself in the rhythms of the community, and playing golf both casually . . . and seriously. . . . Whether Rubenstein is recounting fascinating bits of Highlands history or offering vivid character sketches of Dornoch natives, the prose breathes a kind of atmospheric calm that works on the reader like a mild summer breeze." Booklist

Sampson, Curt

Masters; golf, money, and power in Augusta, Georgia. Villard Bks. 1998 xxxiv, 263p il hardcover o.p. paperback available $14.95   **796.352**

   1. Augusta National Golf Club 2. Golf

   ISBN 0-375-75337-0 (pa)   LC 97-49143

   This history of one of the PGA's most prestigious events "traces the tournament's history since 1933, revealing both the dramatic moments and the controversial secrets, most notably racism—certainly a book to raise eyebrows at the Augusta National Golf Club." Libr J

Snead, Sam

The game I love; wisdom, insight, and instruction from golf's greatest player; [by] Sam Snead with Fran Pirozzolo. Ballantine Bks. 1997 223p $21.95   **796.352**

   1. Golf

   ISBN 0-345-41084-X   LC 97-27232

   This is an anecdotal collection of musings by the American golfing champion. "Included are instructions on the swing, wisdom on putting, and insight on the all-important mental game." Publisher's note

Golf begins at forty; by Sam Snead with Dick Aultman; with illustrations by James McQueen. Dial Press (NY) 1978 175p il o.p.; Doubleday paperback available $14.95   **796.352**

   1. Golf

   ISBN 0-385-27642-7 (pa)   LC 78-5601

   Starting with the attitude of the older, experienced golfer, this book proceeds to practical suggestions for lengthening shots and improving the short game, particularly putting

Whitworth, Kathy, 1939-

Golf for women; [by] Kathy Whitworth with Rhonda Glenn. St. Martin's Press 1990 176p il hardcover o.p. paperback available $14.95   **796.352**

   1. Golf

   ISBN 0-312-06984-7 (pa)   LC 89-78002

   This introductory guide covers grip, stance, body alignment, putting fundamentals, trouble shots, and strategy

   "A splendidly written, detailed, well-illustrated book." Libr J

796.357   Baseball

Angell, Roger

Game time: a baseball companion; edited by Steve Kettmann. Harcourt 2003 398p $25   **796.357**

   1. Baseball

   ISBN 0-15-100824-8   LC 2002-152611

   "A Harvest original"

   Contents: Spring; The old folks behind home; Sunny side of the street; Easy lessons; Takes: waltz of the geezers; Put me in, coach; Takes: digging up Willie; For openers; Takes: pride; Let go, Mets; Summer; Early innings; The companions of the game; Scout; Distance; The web of the game; Takes: penmen; Takes: payback; Wings of fire; The bard in the booth; Style; Takes: three Petes; Fall; Takes: Jacksonian; Blue collar; Takes: the confines; Ninety feet; One for the good guys; Legends of the fens; Can you believe it?; Takes: the purist; Kiss kiss, bang bang

   "Half of the essays in this compilation of highlights from Angell's 40 years of covering baseball for the *New Yorker* have not previously appeared in book form, and even those that have are well worth revisiting. Angell . . . remains the dean of baseball writers." Booklist

Once more around the park. Ballantine Bks. 1991 251p o.p.; Dee, I.R. paperback available $16.95   **796.357**

   1. Baseball

   ISBN 1-56663-371-0 (pa)   LC 90-93223

   A collection of 21 pieces, some from Angell's earlier books and others previously uncollected. "Outstanding among the choices . . . are visits with Hall of Famer Bob Gibson and then-91-year-old Smoky Joe Wood." Libr J

Barra, Allen

Clearing the bases; the greatest baseball debates of the last century; foreword by Bob Costas. St. Martin's Press 2002 xxi, 261p $23.95; pa $13.95 **796.357**

1. Baseball

ISBN 0-312-26556-5; 0-312-30253-3 (pa)

LC 2001-48992

The author "provides considerable insight into many of the most hotly debated topics of baseball's last 100 years." Booklist

Baseball register. Sporting News pa $18.95
796.357

1. Baseball—Statistics

ISSN 0162-542X

Annual. First published 1940. Variant title: Official baseball register

At head of title: The Sporting News

This book gives information, mostly in tabular form, about active players, managers, coaches and recently retired players in major league baseball. Included are place and date of birth; nicknames; whether right or left-handed; height and weight; hobbies; colleges attended; records and awards; yearly statistics for batting, fielding and pitching in the major and minor leagues and major league career totals; and team records of managers. Includes statistics for play in World Series and All-Star games

Bouton, Jim

Ball four; edited by Leonard Shecter. Twentieth-anniversary ed. Collier Bks. 1990 472p il hardcover o.p. paperback available $15.95 **796.357**

1. Baseball

ISBN 0-02-030665-2 (pa) LC 89-49151

Also available in hardcover from Midpoint Trade Bks.

First published 1970 by World

The author offers a behind-the-scenes look at major league baseball, its players and management

Bryant, Howard, 1968-

Shut out; a story of race and baseball in Boston. Routledge 2002 278p il $27.50
796.357

1. Boston Red Sox (Baseball team) 2. Baseball
3. Race discrimination 4. Boston (Mass.)—Race relations

ISBN 0-415-92779-X LC 2002-69950

Also available in paperback from Beacon Press

The author "examines the race relations of one of baseball's most storied teams, the Boston Red Sox, from the early 1930s to the present." Libr J

"Bryant looks at both sides of the race issue, and backs his conclusions with exhaustive research from a variety of sources." Publ Wkly

Includes bibliographical references

Costas, Bob

Fair ball; a fan's case for baseball. Broadway Bks. 2000 179p hardcover o.p. paperback available $12.95 **796.357**

1. Baseball

ISBN 0-7679-0466-4 (pa) LC 99-87992

"The root of baseball's ills, the sports broadcaster Bob Costas argues, lies in how teams like the Yankees and

Atlanta Braves, by virtue of vastly higher revenues than franchises like the Montreal Expos or Kansas City Royals, threaten the game's legitimacy by having 'a monopoly on sustained success.' Costas's solution is for team owners to start meaningful revenue sharing and force a salary cap on the intransigent players union, even if it takes another strike or lockout to do it." N Y Times Book Rev

Geist, Bill

Little League confidential; one coach's completely unauthorized tale of survival. Macmillan 1992 217p o.p.; Dell paperback available $15 **796.357**

1. Little League Baseball, Inc. 2. Baseball

ISBN 0-440-50877-0 (pa) LC 91-37562

The author "relates his decade of service as a little-league baseball coach. He admittedly distills his experiences—and those of others—into a season-long 'docudrama' journal. He tells of pompous coaches lecturing their miniplayers on the subtleties of the infield fly rule; he addresses the question of positioning a player with a personal-injury lawyer for a dad. The book is a wonderful effort filled with empathy for kids, impatience for pushy parents, and a good sense of humor." Booklist

Giamatti, A. Bartlett, 1938-1989

A great and glorious game; baseball writings of A. Bartlett Giamatti; edited by Kenneth S. Robson; foreword by David Halberstam. Algonquin Bks. 1998 121p $15.95 **796.357**

1. Baseball

ISBN 1-56512-192-9 LC 97-32803

Giamatti's "writings make baseball a metaphor for America and Americans. His imagery, in the nine essays in this . . . book, elevates the game from ordinary to beautiful and sometimes humorous." N Y Times Book Rev

Golenbock, Peter, 1946-

Amazin'; the miraculous history of New York's most beloved baseball team. St. Martin's Press 2002 654p il $27.95; pa $18.95 **796.357**

1. New York Mets (Baseball team)

ISBN 0-312-27452-1; 0-312-30992-9 (pa)

LC 2001-48870

This is a history of the New York Mets baseball team

"Golenbock combines his own well-researched commentary with the recollections of eyewitnesses. . . . This is a delightful and painstakingly detailed trip down memory lane that Mets fans will cherish." Publ Wkly

Includes bibliographical references

Gould, Stephen Jay, 1941-2002

Triumph and tragedy in Mudville; a lifelong passion for baseball; foreword by David Halberstam. Norton 2003 342p il $24.95 **796.357**

1. Baseball

ISBN 0-393-05755-0 LC 2002-155523

This is a collection of Gould's "essays about baseball, written over 20 years and published in venues as divergent as the *New York Times* and *Vanity Fair*. . . . The essays are uniformly wonderful. . . . Scientific analysis intersects gently with flat-out fandom. Gould could think, he could write, he was funny, and he loved, loved baseball." Booklist

Halberstam, David, 1934-
Summer of '49. Morrow 1989 304p il o.p.; HarperCollins Pubs. paperback available $13.95 **796.357**
1. New York Yankees (Baseball team) 2. Boston Red Sox (Baseball team)
ISBN 0-06-000781-8 (pa)   LC 89-2886
"This book is ostensibly about the pennant race between the Yankees and Red Sox [in 1949] and the 'rivalry' between Joe DiMaggio and Ted Williams. . . . It is a study of all the elements and personalities that influenced baseball that year and beyond. Halberstam brings them together in such an enjoyable, interesting, and informative manner that a reader needn't be a baseball fan to appreciate the book." Libr J

Joy in Mudville; the big book of baseball humor; edited by Dick Schaap and Mort Gerberg. Doubleday 1992 xx, 424p il hardcover o.p. paperback available $15.95 **796.357**
1. Baseball
ISBN 0-385-46953-5 (pa)   LC 91-42417
"Including articles, book excerpts, and comic strips, this humorous baseball anthology ranges from the familiar 'Casey at the Bat' and Abbott and Costello's hilarious 'Who's on First' routine to selections penned by Garrison Keillor, George Plimpton, and W. P. Kinsella. Suggested for both personal and reference use." Booklist

Kahn, Roger, 1927-
The boys of summer. Harper & Row 1972 xxii, 442p il hardcover o.p. paperback available $15 **796.357**
1. Brooklyn Dodgers (Baseball team) 2. Baseball
ISBN 0-06-091416-5 (pa)
The author describes attending Brooklyn Dodger games as a boy, covering Dodger games as a reporter for the Herald Tribune, and traveling throughout the country to speak with former Dodgers after the team left New York

The head game; baseball seen from the pitcher's mound. Harcourt 2000 xxii, 310p il $25; pa $14 **796.357**
1. Baseball
ISBN 0-15-100441-2; 0-15-601304-5 (pa)
          LC 00-32014
Kahn discusses some pitchers in the history of baseball
"Highly recommended for lovers of literate sports history." Libr J
Includes bibliographical references

Kelly, Jerry, 1953-
Bushville; life and time in amateur baseball. McFarland & Co. 2001 202p il pa $21 **796.357**
1. Baseball
ISBN 0-7864-0979-7   LC 01-31264
Kelly's "reflections on what the game has meant to him—from fascination with baseball's special geometry to the sensual pleasure he takes in its textures of leather and wood—make the perfect antidote to most fans' disgust with the big money and big egos of today's major leaguers." Booklist
Includes bibliographical references

Lewis, Michael
Moneyball; the art of winning an unfair game. Norton 2003 288p $23.95 **796.357**
1. Beane, Billy, 1962- 2. Baseball
ISBN 0-393-05765-8   LC 2003-5089
The author "examines the proceedings of Billy Beane, general manager of the Oakland Athletics, who finished first in the American League West . . . [in 2002] with as many victories as the Yankees despite the third-smallest payroll in the major leagues." N Y Times Book Rev
"With so many baseball books to choose from, it is difficult to single out a few as must-haves, but this one comes pretty close." Booklist

Light, Jonathan Fraser, 1957-
The cultural encyclopedia of baseball. McFarland & Co. 1997 888p il $75 **796.357**
1. Baseball—Encyclopedias
ISBN 0-7864-0311-X   LC 97-763
This work includes "entries for all Hall of Famers, each major league team, and such topics as Bloomer Girls, Bonus Babies, Cuba, Curveballs, Dumbest Players, Home Runs, Length of Games, Racism, Salaries, Sex, and Women in Baseball. Most entries open with an engaging quotation and end with a short bibliography. . . . An entertaining, anecdotal, and informative reference." Libr J

Lupica, Mike
Summer of '98; when homers flew, records fell, and baseball reclaimed America. Putnam 1999 209p $23.95 **796.357**
1. Baseball
ISBN 0-399-14514-1   LC 98-50425
Also available in paperback from McGraw-Hill
"Lupica intersperses stories about the season's highlights—Mark McGwire's and Sammy Sosa's dramatic pursuit of Roger Maris's home run record, rookie Kerry Wood's 20-strikeout game, the New York Yankees phenomenal campaign—with musings about how baseball provides continuity between his relationship with his father and his own experience with his three young sons." Publ Wkly

McCarver, Tim
Tim McCarver's Baseball for brain surgeons and other fans; understanding and interpreting the game so you can watch it like a pro; [by] Tim McCarver with Danny Peary. Villard Bks. 1998 xxi, 344p hardcover o.p. paperback available $12.95 **796.357**
1. Baseball
ISBN 0-375-75340-0 (pa)   LC 97-49301
"This book on the strategy of the diamond sport, covering managing, pitching, catching, batting, fielding and base running, is a discourse that all players could study profitably, from Little Leaguers to major league regulars. It offers well-thought-out positions backed by careful reasoning and broad experience." Publ Wkly

Neft, David S.
The sports encyclopedia: baseball; [by] David S. Neft, Richard M. Cohen. St. Martin's Press pa $22.95 **796.357**
1. Baseball—Statistics
First published 1974 by Grosset & Dunlap. (2003 edition) Periodically revised
Covers baseball from 1876 to the present and contains team statistics, alphabetical registers of batters and pitchers, and summaries of each season

Robinson, Ray, 1920-

Yankee Stadium; 75 years of drama, glamor, and glory; by Ray Robinson and Christopher Jennison. Penguin Studio 1998 182p il $29.95 **796.357**

1. Yankee Stadium (New York, N.Y.)

ISBN 0-670-87093-5   LC 97-48496

"This book is about all the great sporting events—including great boxing matches such as Joe Louis's 1938 demolition of Max Schmeling—and some nonsporting events (such as papal visits and religious revivals) that have occurred at Yankee Stadium over its three-quarters of a century. Baseball does predominate, however, in this tale of 'The House That Ruth Built.' . . . Reminiscences by journalist Pete Hamill, broadcaster Bob Costas, and a few Yankee greats add an extra dimension." Libr J

Smith, Red, 1905-1982

Red Smith on baseball; the game's greatest writer on the game's greatest years; with a foreword by Ira Berkow. Dee, I.R. 2000 363p il $24.95; pa $18.95 **796.357**

1. Baseball

ISBN 1-56663-289-7; 1-56663-415-6 (pa)

LC 99-53675

This volume contains columns written from the 1940s to the early 1980s. "Smith's essays on Bobby Thomson's 'shot heard 'round the world,' Mickey Mantle's first game and Don Larsen's no-hit pitching in the 1956 World Series are all worthy of memorization, and his trenchant views on the reserve clause and the night World Series games are strikes down the middle. As a bonus, the collection offers readers a fascinating look at how baseball writing has changed over the years, as have American attitudes." Publ Wkly

Tofel, Richard J., 1957-

A legend in the making; the New York Yankees in 1939. Dee, I.R. 2002 269p $24.95 **796.357**

1. New York Yankees (Baseball team) 2. Baseball

ISBN 1-56663-411-3   LC 2001-40824

This is the "story of the Yankees' 1939 winning season. . . . The casual racism against Italians and the utter dismissal of black baseball are not ignored, and Tofel grounds the year in events outside of baseball: the *Wizard of Oz* opens, Freud dies, Germany invades Poland. A fine gift for fans." Booklist

Includes bibliographical references

Tygiel, Jules

Baseball's great experiment; Jackie Robinson and his legacy. expanded ed. Oxford Univ. Press 1997 413p il hardcover o.p. paperback available $18.95 **796.357**

1. Robinson, Jackie, 1919-1972 2. Baseball 3. United States—Race relations

ISBN 0-19-510619-9 (pa)   LC 96-38551

First published 1983

A history of the segregation and gradual integration of Afro-American athletes into major league baseball. In addition to Jackie Robinson, the author explores the careers of Larry Doby, Luke Easter, Satchel Paige, and others. Tygiel also notes the vast social and demographic changes wrought by WWII that made integration inevitable

Includes bibliographical references

Ward, Geoffrey C.

Baseball: an illustrated history; narrative by Geoffrey C. Ward; based on a documentary filmscript by Geoffrey C. Ward and Ken Burns; preface by Ken Burns and Lynn Novick; with an introduction by Roger Angell; contributions by John Thorn [et al.] Knopf 1994 xxv, 486p il $65; pa $39.95 **796.357**

1. Baseball

ISBN 0-679-40459-7; 0-679-76541-7 (pa)

LC 93-39809

This "book is the companion to a nine-part PBS television documentary. . . . Each chapter, or 'inning,' proceeds chronologically with a dominant theme and dramatis personae." Libr J

"This lavishly produced, gorgeously illustrated history of the game rises far above the often dreary 'companion volume' genre." Booklist

Will, George F.

Bunts: Curt Flood, Camden Yards, Pete Rose, and other reflections on baseball. Scribner 1998 352p il $25; pa $14 **796.357**

1. Baseball

ISBN 0-684-83820-6; 0-684-85374-4 (pa)

LC 98-23500

A gathering of the author's "uncollected essays on the national pastime. Will holds forth on everything from Pete Rose's ban to the politics of team allegiance (Cubs or White Sox) in Chicago." Libr J

"Will has a passion for the game that he never allows to degenerate into intellectual prattlings or gooey rhapsodies. Indeed, his view of baseball is refreshingly unromantic." Christ Sci Monit

Men at work: the craft of baseball. Macmillan 1990 353p il o.p.; HarperCollins Pubs. paperback available $14 **796.357**

1. Baseball

ISBN 0-06-097372-2 (pa)   LC 89-13265

This book's four chapters cover these "aspects of baseball: The Manager (Tony LaRussa of Oakland), The Pitcher (Orel Hershiser of Los Angeles), The Batter (Tony Gwynn of San Diego), and The Defense [Cal Ripken, Jr., of Baltimore]." Natl Rev

"The author's own devotion to detail in defining the components of the game is sure to instill in readers a greater appreciation of what is required to master the sport at the major league level, thereby providing a deeper understanding of the foundation of the game. Altogether, this is hardcore baseball presented in fluent style." Libr J

796.42   Track and field

Glover, Bob

The runner's handbook; the best-selling classic fitness guide for beginner and intermediate runners; [by] Bob Glover, Jack Shepherd, and Shelly-Lynn Florence Glover. 2nd rev & updated ed. Penguin Bks. 1996 xxvi, 726p pa $17.95 **796.42**

1. Running

ISBN 0-14-046930-3   LC 95-25847

First published 1978

This book covers such topics as how to begin a running program, how to train to become competitive, how to run in races, and health and nutrition for runners

Higdon, Hal

Marathon: the ultimate training guide. [rev ed] Rodale Press 1999 230p pa $15.95

796.42

1. Marathon running

ISBN 1-57954-171-2   LC 99-35214

First published 1993

This "manual includes training schedules designed for busy runners, nutritional information, motivational tips, and race-day guidance to help runners of all experience levels reach the 26.2-mile mark with speed, safety, and great satisfaction." Publisher's note

Runner's world complete book of running; everything you need to know to run for fun, fitness, and competition; edited by Amby Burfoot. Rodale Press 1997 306p il $24.95   **796.42**

1. Running

ISBN 0-87596-354-4   LC 96-53296

Among this volume's contributors are Liz Applegate, Hal Higdon, Joe Henderson and Joan Benoit Samuelson. Topics covered include: nutrition, injury prevention and treatment, shoe selection, mental readiness, and marathon preparation

Scott, Dagny

Runner's world complete book of women's running; the best advice to get started, stay motivated, lose weight, run injury-free, be safe, and train for any distance; [by] Dagny Scott. Rodale 2000 308p il $24.95   **796.42**

1. Running

ISBN 1-57954-118-6   LC 99-59609

Topics covered include racing, nutrition, running during pregnancy, stretching techniques, exercise drills and proper clothing

796.44 Sports gymnastics

Ryan, Joan

Little girls in pretty boxes; the making and breaking of elite gymnasts and figure skaters. Doubleday 1995 243p il o.p.; Warner Bks. paperback available $13.95   **796.44**

1. Gymnastics 2. Ice skating 3. Women athletes

ISBN 0-446-67682-9 (pa)   LC 94-43317

"In an attempt to focus attention on the high price paid through pain, pressure, and humiliation to become an Olympic champion, Ryan has researched the stories behind some of the young female superstar gymnasts and figure skaters. The extraordinary cost to these young women in body, mind, and spirit is dramatized through the intense subculture dominated by gyms, trainers, parents, and sports officials who press for excellence and success without regard to the health and well-being of those involved. . . . A book to be pondered by coaches, parents, and young people." SLJ

796.48 Olympic games

Guttmann, Allen

The Olympics, a history of the modern games. 2nd ed. University of Ill. Press 2002 214p il (Illinois history of sports) $39.95; pa $16.95   **796.48**

1. Olympic games

ISBN 0-252-02725-6; 0-252-07046-1 (pa)

LC 2001-41383

First published 1992

"Guttmann discusses the intended and actual meaning of the modern Olympic Games, from 1896 to 2000. Recounting the memorable and significant athletic events of the Olympics in terms of their social and political impact, Guttmann . . . [attempts to demonstrate] that the modern games were revived to propagate a political message and continue to serve political purposes." Publisher's note

Includes bibliographical references

796.5 Outdoor life

Doan, Marlyn, 1936-

The Sierra Club family outdoors guide; hiking, backpacking, camping, bicycling, water sports, and winter activities with children. Sierra Club Bks. 1995 296p il pa $12   **796.5**

1. Outdoor recreation

ISBN 0-87156-442-4   LC 94-35087

First published 1979 with title: Starting small in the wilderness

This is a guide for adults who want to introduce children to wilderness activities. Besides describing a variety of activities suitable for youngsters of all ages, it includes recommendations for buying, sewing and adapting outdoor gear for children

Includes bibliographical references

McDougall, Len

The outdoors almanac. Burford Bks. 1999 200p il pa $16.95   **796.5**

1. Outdoor life

ISBN 1-58080-035-1   LC 99-28384

The author "has produced a book that is equal parts gear review, tips for experts, reference book, overview for beginners, and anecdotes. . . . The author's writing style is conversational and fun to read, and while his expertise is obvious from the beginning, McDougall patiently explains the hazards and attractions of outdoor exploration." Libr J

Stilwell, Alexander

Encyclopedia of survival techniques; [illustrations, Tony Randall and Anne Cakebread] Lyons Press 2000 192p il maps pa $19.95   **796.5**

1. Wilderness survival

ISBN 1-58574-062-4   LC 2001-271839

This guide covers preparation, basic skills, equipment, various terrains, natural disasters, and first aid

"Campers, scouts, hikers, or anyone interested in outdoor-survival techniques will find easy to use information here." SLJ

796.51   Walking

Randall, Glenn, 1957-
The Outward Bound backpacker's handbook. Lyons Press 2000 222p il pa $14.95   **796.51**
1. Backpacking
ISBN 1-55821-941-2   LC 99-22236
First published 1994 with title The modern backpacker's handbook
This handbook offers advice on backpacking equipment, clothing, planning and preparation, safety, hiking and navigation, and first aid

Solnit, Rebecca
Wanderlust; a history of walking. Viking 2000 326p il hardcover o.p. paperback available $15   **796.51**
1. Walking 2. Hiking 3. Voyages and travels
ISBN 0-14-028601-2 (pa)   LC 99-41153
The author presents a "look at how the act of walking . . . has influenced our history, our science, our literature, and the very way that we see ourselves as human beings. Drawing on a multitude of diverse disciplines, Solnit illustrates that walking has led to some of the best, and worst, incidents in all of history." Booklist
Includes bibliographical references

796.52   Walking and exploring by kind of terrain

Boukreev, Anatoli, d. 1997
The climb; tragic ambitions on Everest; [by] Anatoli Boukreev and G. Weston Dewalt. St. Martin's Press 1997 255p il hardcover o.p. paperback available $6.99   **796.52**
1. Mount Everest Expedition (1996) 2. Mountaineering
ISBN 0-312-96533-8 (pa)   LC 97-23194
"This is a first-person account of the tragic climbing experience in May 1996 on Mount Everest that left eight hikers dead and several others struggling to stay alive. . . . Fast-paced and easy to read, Boukreev's story of adventure and survival will remain in the reader's memory long after the book is finished." Libr J

Coburn, Broughton, 1951-
Everest: mountain without mercy; introduction by Tim Cahill, afterword by David Breashears. National Geographic Soc. 1997 256p il maps $35; pa $24   **796.52**
1. Mount Everest Expedition (1996) 2. Mountaineering
ISBN 0-7922-7014-2; 0-7922-6984-5 (pa)
     LC 97-10765
"Bringing an understated yet powerful Buddhist/Sherpa ethical perspective to the tragedy on Everest chronicled in Jon Krakauer's Into Thin Air, Coburn reports on the IMAX film crew who participated in the rescue effort when the May 1996 expeditions led by guides Rob Hall and Scott Fischer ended in death and crippling injury." Publ Wkly

Krakauer, Jon
Into thin air; a personal account of the Mount Everest disaster. Villard Bks. 1997 xx, 293p il o.p.; Anchor Bks. (NY) paperback available $7.99   **796.52**
1. Mount Everest Expedition (1996) 2. Mountaineering
ISBN 0-385-49208-1 (pa)   LC 96-30031
This is an account of the author's May 1996 Mount Everest climbing expedition in which twelve fellow climbers died during a snow storm
"This tense, harrowing story is as mesmerizing and hard to put down as any well-written adventure novel." SLJ
Includes bibliographical references

Norgay, Jamling Tenzing
Touching my father's soul; a Sherpa's journey to the top of Everest; [by] Jamling Tenzing Norgay with Broughton Coburn. HarperSanFrancisco 2001 316p il map hardcover o.p. paperback available $14.95
     796.52
1. Tenzing Norgay, 1914-1986 2. Mount Everest Expedition (1996) 3. Mountaineering
ISBN 0-06-251688-4 (pa)   LC 00-68723
"Norgay, who led the IMAX *Everest* expedition, is the son of legendary mountaineer Tenzing Norgay, the first Sherpa to conquer Everest with Sir Edmund Hillary in 1953. In this blend of autobiography, family history, and adventure, Norgay describes how he summited Mount Everest in 1996 by following in his father's footsteps." Libr J
This "work has considerably more depth than an exposition of the climb. . . . The son's climb is a pilgrimage exploring his relationship to his father, his Sherpa culture, and Buddhism. It is also a fascinating look into the world of climbers and their relationship to the Sherpas who risk their lives to assist them." Booklist

Taylor, Michael Ray, 1959-
Caves; exploring hidden realms. National Geographic Soc. 2001 216p il maps $35
     796.52
1. Caves
ISBN 0-7922-7904-2   LC 00-52710
This book was produced in conjunction with an IMAX project filming two caver's explorations in the Yucatan, Greenland, and the South-Central United States
"The photographs and the story of the explorations would be sufficient to recommend this work, but it also includes fascinating background material on the history of the caves, their biological diversity, [and] the tools used by spelunkers." Booklist
Includes bibliographical references

796.54   Camping

Guide to summer camps and summer schools. Sargent Pubs. il $35; pa $25
     796.54
1. Camps—Directories 2. Summer schools—Directories
ISSN 0072-8705
First published 1936. (28th edition 2003) Periodically revised. Title varies

Guide to summer camps and summer schools—*Continued*

"This reliable comprehensive source of summer academic and tutorial programs, travel programs, specialized study programs, and recreational camps lists about 1,300 such programs in the U.S. and Canada. An extensive table of contents and an index make it possible to access all of this information." Safford. Guide to Ref Materials For Sch Media Cent. 5th edition

796.6 Cycling and related activities

Bicycling magazine's 900 all-time best tips; top riders share their secrets to maximize fun, safety, and performance; edited by Ed Pavelka. Rodale 2000 138p il pa $9.95
796.6
1. Cycling
ISBN 1-57954-227-1   LC 99-56768
Replaces Bicycling magazine's 600 tips for better bicycling
A collection of information on such topics as bicycle models, accessories, riding styles, and repair techniques

796.72 Automobile racing

Menzer, Joe
The wildest ride; a history of NASCAR (or, How a bunch of good ol' boys built a billion-dollar industry out of wrecking cars). Simon & Schuster 2001 311p il $24; pa $14
796.72
1. National Association for Stock Car Auto Racing
2. Automobile racing
ISBN 0-7432-0507-3; 0-7432-2625-9 (pa)
LC 2001-031088
Also available G.K. Hall large print edition
This history focuses on the "legacy of the founding France family, the evolution of the cars from modified stock cars to purpose-built racers, and the fan-base expansion of the 1980s and 1990s. . . . Highly entertaining and full of facts." Libr J
Includes bibliographical references

Rich, Ronda
My life in the pits; living and learning on the NASCAR Winston Cup circuit; foreword by Richard Childress. HarperEntertainment 2002 255p $24.95   **796.72**
1. National Association for Stock Car Auto Racing
2. Automobile racing
ISBN 0-06-000589-0   LC 2002-510751
This book is "about the author's experiences in racing and her relationships with racing people, which often gave inspiration and meaning to her life. . . . Rich shows a clear passion for the sport, and she offers many moving passages, particularly those dealing with the AIDS-related death of driver Tim Richmond." Libr J

Wright, James D., 1947-
Fixin' to git; one fan's love affair with NASCAR's Winston Cup; [by] Jim Wright. Duke Univ. Press 2002 305p il $26.95; pa $18.95   **796.72**
1. National Association for Stock Car Auto Racing
2. Automobile racing
ISBN 0-8223-2926-3; 0-8223-3220-5 (pa)
LC 2002-485
The author offers his perspectives on NASCAR Winston Cup auto racing "and its significance in modern American culture. . . . [He discusses] a variety of issues, such as fan allegiance, the growth and popularity of NASCAR racing, and the difficulty of setting up a car for the unique conditions of each race track." Libr J
"This is the very best book to surface on auto racing in many years. Informative, entertaining, and eye-opening." Booklist

796.8 Combat sports

Anasi, Robert, 1966-
The gloves; a boxing chronicle. North Point Press 2002 331p $24; pa $14   **796.8**
1. Boxing
ISBN 0-86547-599-7; 0-86547-652-7 (pa)
LC 2001-44111
In this "look at the world of amateur boxing, freelance writer Anasi chronicles how jabbing and jump-roping at a grubby gym in San Francisco's Tenderloin district developed into a life-altering quest to compete, in his early 30s, in New York's storied amateur boxing tournament, the Golden Gloves." Publ Wkly

Cohen, Richard
By the sword; a history of gladiators, musketeers, samurai, swashbucklers, and Olympic champions. Random House 2002 xxiv, 519p il $29.95; pa $15.95   **796.8**
1. Fencing
ISBN 0-375-50417-6; 0-8129-6966-9 (pa)
LC 2002-21309
This is a worldwide history of sword fighting from Ancient Egypt to the present which considers its role in combat and sports, word origins and customs, and the fencing skills of politicians and actors
"A fascinating story told with literary verve and the pride of a longtime practitioner; highly recommended." Libr J
Includes bibliographical references

Jones, Chris, 1973-
Falling hard; a rookie's year in boxing. Arcade Pub. 2002 190p il $23.95   **796.8**
1. Boxing
ISBN 1-55970-621-X   LC 2002-18631
First published 2001 in Canada
"Jones chronicles a year of professional fights and learning the ropes as a neophyte ringside newspaper reporter for the newly formed *National Post*." Publ Wkly
"This is an extraordinary, very personal journey through a world that continues to both fascinate and repel the sporting public." Booklist

Kram, Mark

The ghosts of Manila; the fateful, brutal blood feud between Muhammad Ali and Joe Frazier. HarperCollins Pubs. 2001 232p hardcover o.p. paperback available $12.95

796.8

1. Ali, Muhammad, 1942- 2. Frazier, Joe 3. Boxing
ISBN 0-06-095480-9 (pa)   LC 00-53934
The author "tells the story of Joe Frazier and Muhammad Ali's epic 1975 Manila fight, and the bitter and complex rivalry between the two men that preceded it." Publ Wkly
This is "a fascinating blend of history and biography." Booklist

Ochiai, Hidy

Hidy Ochiai's complete book of self-defense. Contemporary Bks. 1991 340p il pa $18.95   **796.8**

1. Self-defense 2. Karate
ISBN 0-8092-4055-6   LC 90-19279
"The book is loaded with photos that are accompanied by an easy-to-understand text to help guide the reader from the essential basics to the most advanced self-defense moves. It contains an interesting and practical section on self-defense techniques, as well as an absorbing chapter explaining Ochiai's philosophy of the martial arts." Libr J

Park, Yeon Hwan

Black belt tae kwon do; the ultimate reference guide to the world's most popular martial art; by Y.H. Park & Jon Gerrard. Facts on File 2000 272p il $38.50   **796.8**

1. Tae kwon do
ISBN 0-8160-4240-3   LC 99-57876
Coverage includes practice, warm-up, and advanced techniques and forms, sparring strategies, self-defense, and breaking. Over 700 photographs accompany the text. Appendixes cover official competition rules, weight classes, governing bodies, and international organizations and associations. Includes two glossaries, English to Korean and Korean to English

Schulberg, Budd

Sparring with Hemingway and other legends of the fight game. Dee, I.R. 1995 256p $25   **796.8**

1. Boxing
ISBN 1-56663-080-0   LC 94-49153
This is a collection of the author's articles about boxing, originally published between 1954 and 1994
"Included are beautifully crafted portraits of legends such as Benny Leonard, Muhammad Ali, and ageless wonder George Foreman. . . . This literate, entertaining collection represents some of the best writing on any sport." Libr J

Tegnér, Bruce, 1928-1985

Karate: beginner to black belt. Thor 1982 220p il hardcover o.p. paperback available $14   **796.8**

1. Karate
ISBN 0-87407-040-6 (pa)   LC 81-18199
This book contains step-by-step instructions on karate techniques ranging from basic to advanced. Emphasis is on safety, health and fitness

796.9 Ice and snow sports

Bennett, Jeff

The complete snowboarder; [by] Jeff Bennett, Scott Downey and Charles Arnell. 2nd ed. Ragged Mountain Press 2000 148p il pa $14.95   **796.9**

1. Snowboarding
ISBN 0-07-135787-4   LC 00-39059
First published 1994
This offers advice on getting started in snowboarding, equipment, techniques, snowboarding areas and trails, tricks, competitions, safety, and equipment maintenance

Hart, Lowell, 1959-

The snowboard book; a guide for all boarders. Norton 1997 160p il pa $19.95

796.9

1. Snowboarding
ISBN 0-393-31692-0   LC 97-30031
This offers a history of snowboarding, information on equipment, instruction on techniques for various types of terrain and a glossary
Includes bibliographical references

796.91 Ice skating

Brennan, Christine

Inside edge; a revealing journey into the secret world of figure skating. Scribner 1996 319p il o.p.; Anchor Bks. (NY) paperback available $14   **796.91**

1. Ice skating
ISBN 0-385-48607-3 (pa)   LC 95-45697
"A Lisa Drew book"
"Profiling the top-ranked skaters, this book focuses on the 1994-95 season." N Y Times Book Rev

Malone, John Williams

The encyclopedia of figure skating. Facts on File 1998 264p il hardcover o.p. paperback available $18.95   **796.91**

1. Ice skating
ISBN 0-8160-3796-5 (pa)   LC 97-46360
Alphabetical entries cover rules, techniques, competitions, organizations, and individual skaters
"Any source that explains the arcane details of edges, mandatory deductions, judge selection, and how the Zamboni works is a welcome addition to sports reference collections." Booklist

796.962 Ice hockey

Duplacey, James

The official rules of hockey; edited by Dan Diamond. Lyons Press 2001 208p il pa $19.95   **796.962**

1. National Hockey League 2. Hockey
ISBN 1-58574-052-7   LC 00-67176
First published 1996 with title The annotated rules of hockey
"The Official Rules of Hockey is a historical, anecdotal, and illustrated guide to the rules of the world's fastest game. . . . [It includes] rink diagrams, illustrations of officials' signals, and a compendium of milestone moments chronicling the sport's evolving rules of play." Publisher's note

796.98 Winter Olympic games

Wallechinsky, David, 1948-
The complete book of the Winter Olympics. 2002 ed. Overlook Press 2001 xxxviii, 353p il $25.95; pa $15.95   **796.98**
1. Olympic games
ISBN 1-58567-195-9; 1-58567-185-1 (pa)
LC 2001-36018
First published 1984
This compendium of Olympic history provides "backgrounds, stories, and statistics from every Winter Olympics since the Chamonix games of 1924." Publisher's note

797.1 Boating

Conner, Dennis
Learn to sail; [by] Dennis Conner and Michael Levitt; illustrations by Chris Lloyd. St. Martin's Press 1994 240p il $22.95
797.1
1. Sailing
ISBN 0-312-11020-0   LC 94-2611
In this beginner's guide "Conner recommends boats on which to learn, defines sailing etiquette, offers weather analysis, and discusses sailing under adverse conditions and coping with emergencies. . . . This is an excellent introduction to the principles of the sport." Booklist
Includes bibliographical references

Fredston, Jill A.
Rowing to latitude; journeys along the Arctic's edge; [by] Jill Fredston. North Point Press 2001 289p il $24; pa $14   **797.1**
1. Canoes and canoeing 2. Arctic regions—Description
ISBN 0-374-28180-7; 0-86547-655-1 (pa)
LC 2001-30049
The author and her husband, Doug Fesler "canoe the Arctic and sub-Arctic coastlines of Alaska, Canada, Greenland, Norway and Sweden for three months out of each year. . . . Fredston ably describes both the big picture—the coastline, encounters with polar bears, the high-stakes game of second-guessing storms and tides—and the details of their travels. . . . A must-read for armchair travelers, as well as a close and loving look at an intimate relationship." Publ Wkly

Mason, Bill, 1929-
Path of the paddle. rev & updated [ed], by Paul Mason. NorthWord Press 1995 200p il o.p.; Firefly Bks. paperback available $19.95
797.1
1. Canoes and canoeing
ISBN 1-55209-328-X (pa)   LC 94-46399
First published 1980 by Van Nostrand Reinhold
Illustrated with photographs of Canadian rivers, this instructional guide demonstrates that "canoeing isn't just a mellow flatwater pursuit but can be an extremely risky and challenging way to explore some of the world's most rugged back-country." Libr J
Includes bibliographical references

Rousmaniere, John
The illustrated dictionary of boating terms; 2000 essential terms for sailors & powerboaters. [rev ed] Norton 1998 168p il $23.95   **797.1**
1. Boats and boating—Dictionaries
ISBN 0-393-04649-4   LC 97-45938
First published 1976 with title: A glossary of modern sailing terms
"Much of the newer terminology is derived from current boating and sailing magazines and from the author's active participation in boating. The illustrations help clarify definitions. . . . The work is aimed at two audiences, powerboaters and sailors, who do not always speak the same language; variations in terminology are noted. This, and the dictionary's currency, will make it useful for all boat lovers and landlubbers." Choice

797.2 Swimming and diving

Katz, Jane
Swimming for total fitness; a progressive aerobic program; by Jane Katz with Nancy P. Bruning; illustrations by Phillip Jones. updated ed. Doubleday 1992 400p il pa $18.95   **797.2**
1. Swimming 2. Physical fitness
ISBN 0-385-46821-0   LC 92-31877
First published 1981
This introduction to swimming covers basic strokes, kicks, turns, starts, and dives. Progressive training regimens for beginning to advanced swimmers are then presented, followed by a chapter on equipment. A question and answer section concludes the book

Mullen, P. H., Jr.
Gold in the water; the true story of ordinary men and their extraordinary dream of Olympic glory; [by] P.H. Mullen, Jr. Thomas Dunne Bks. 2001 326p il $24.95; pa $14.95   **797.2**
1. Swimming 2. Olympic games, 2000 (Sydney, Australia)
ISBN 0-312-26595-6; 0-312-31116-8 (pa)
LC 2001-31955
"Mullen chronicles the U.S. Olympic swimming team on its journey to the 2000 Summer Games in Sydney. The text moves back and forth in time, giving a sense of the athletes as people and showing what motivates someone to structure his or her whole life toward a single goal." Booklist

798.2 Horsemanship

Price, Steven D., 1940-
Essential riding; a realistic approach to horsemanship. Lyons Press 2000 190p il pa $19.95   **798.2**
1. Horsemanship
ISBN 1-58574-002-0   LC 00-24119
This guide for beginning riders on lesson horses discusses what to wear, what horses wear, how to fall off and how to make the horse go. Also included are chapters on jumping and showing as well as polo and other horse sports
"An excellent book for beginning riders that belongs in all libraries." Booklist
Includes bibliographical references

798.4　Horse racing

Drape, Joe
The race for the Triple Crown; horses, high stakes, and eternal hope. Atlantic Monthly Press 2001 261p hardcover o.p. paperback available $14　　　　　　**798.4**
　1. Horse racing
　ISBN 0-8021-3885-3 (pa)　　　　LC 2001-16044
In this "look at the highest level of horse racing, the author traces the lives of a handful of preeminent horse owners, trainers and jockeys in their preparations for the Kentucky Derby, the Preakness and the Belmont." Publ Wkly

Hillenbrand, Laura
Seabiscuit; an American legend. Random House 2001 399p il $25.95; pa $15.95
　　　　　　　　　　　　　　　　798.4
　1. Horse racing 2. Seabiscuit (Race horse)
　ISBN 0-375-50291-2; 0-449-00561-5 (pa)
　　　　　　　　　　　　　　LC 2001-267852
Hillenbrand tells the story of the race horse who defeated "Triple Crown Winner War Admiral in what [has been] called the greatest horse race of all time [Pimlico, Nov. 1, 1938]." Newsweek
　"This is a remarkable tale well told by a writer who deftly blends history and sport." Economist
　Includes bibliographical references

Mitchell, Elizabeth, 1966-
Three strides before the wire; the dark and beautiful world of horse racing. Hyperion 2002 403p $24.95; pa $14.95　　　**798.4**
　1. Horse racing
　ISBN 0-7868-6723-X; 0-7868-8622-6 (pa)
　　　　　　　　　　　　　　LC 2002-68817
The author "tells the story of Charismatic, who exploded out of the proletarian ranks of claiming horses to come within a stone's throw of sweeping the Triple Crown in 1999 before suffering a career-ending injury in the Belmont Stakes. . . . Mitchell's book possesses an appeal that extends well beyond its subject." Booklist

Squires, James D.
Horse of a different color; a tale of breeding geniuses, dominant females, and the fastest Derby winner since Secretariat; [by] Jim Squires. PublicAffairs 2002 300p il $26; pa $14　　　　　　　　**798.4**
　1. Horse racing 2. Kentucky Derby
　ISBN 1-58648-117-7; 1-58648-180-0 (pa)
　　　　　　　　　　　　　　LC 2001-59602
This is the story of how the author, a former editor of the Chicago Tribune, became a breeder of thoroughbred race horses, including a horse named Monarchos, the champion of the 2001 Kentucky Derby
　This "is fast paced and fun to read. It will appeal not only to horseracing fans but also to people making midlife career changes." Libr J

798.401　Horse race betting

Ainslie, Tom
Ainslie's complete guide to thoroughbred racing. 3rd ed. Simon & Schuster 1986 349p il hardcover o.p. paperback available $14
　　　　　　　　　　　　　　　798.401
　1. Horse racing 2. Gambling
　ISBN 0-671-65655-4 (pa)　　　LC 86-3879
　First published 1968
A guide to the fundamentals of handicapping races including such topics as breeding, judging condition of the horses, calculating speed, track ratings and other tips for successful betting

798.8　Dog racing

Paulsen, Gary
Winterdance; the fine madness of running the Iditarod. Harcourt Brace & Co. 1994 256p il $24; pa $15　　　　　**798.8**
　1. Iditarod Trail Sled Dog Race, Alaska
　ISBN 0-15-126227-6; 0-15-600145-4 (pa)
　　　　　　　　　　　　　　LC 93-42096
　"This book is primarily an account of Paulsen's first Iditarod and its frequent life-threatening disasters. . . . However, the book is more than a tabulation of tribulations; it is a meditation on the extraordinary attraction this race holds for some men and women." Libr J

799.1　Fishing

Frazier, Ian
The fish's eye; essays about angling and the outdoors. Farrar, Straus & Giroux 2002 163p $20; pa $12　　　　　**799.1**
　1. Fishing
　ISBN 0-374-15520-8; 0-312-42169-9 (pa)
　　　　　　　　　　　　　　LC 2001-54451
A compendium of the author's essays written for The New Yorker over the last two decades
　"It's almost impossible to read these heartfelt and lovingly rendered essays without sharing the author's fascination with woods and water and fish." Booklist

Hersey, John, 1914-1993
Blues; with drawings by James Baker. Knopf 1987 205p il hardcover o.p. paperback available $13　　　　　　　**799.1**
　1. Fishing
　ISBN 0-394-75702-5 (pa)　　　LC 86-46008
　"This book about fishing for bluefish off the coast of Cape Cod features a wide array of information about that one group of fish, but not in straightforward fashion. It is written in the form of fictional conversations between the 'fisherman' and 'the stranger,' who discuss everything from the blues' mating habits to recipes for preparing them. They also cover sea lore, fishing, and ecology, with frequent references to literature and poetry." Libr J
　"People who love and care about nature and their place in it, be they fishermen or not, should thoroughly enjoy 'Blues.'" Wilson Libr Bull

Mojetta, Angelo

Simon & Schuster's guide to saltwater fish and fishing. Simon & Schuster 1992 255p il pa $16   **799.1**

1. Fishing 2. Fishes 3. Marine ecology
ISBN 0-671-77947-8   LC 91-45324
"A Fireside book"

This reference guide to more than 150 species of marine fish provides "the essentials for identifying and catching saltwater fish. An overview of angling methods covers equipment, bait, and various fishing techniques. Each entry—complete with a color photograph—provides facts on each specie's habitat, seasonal activity, behavior, distribution, food, and gastronomic value." Publisher's note

Walton, Izaak, 1593-1683

The compleat angler; or, The contemplative man's recreation; [by] Izaak Walton and Charles Cotton; introduction by Howell Raines. Modern Lib. 1996 xxxviii, 416p il hardcover o.p. paperback available $12.95
799.1

1. Fishing
ISBN 0-375-75148-3 (pa)   LC 96-5935
First published 1653

"A treatise on angling with dialogue, which celebrates the countryside and the joys of fishing. It is 'the' classic of piscatory literature." Penguin Companion to Engl Lit
Includes bibliographical references

799.2   Hunting

Jones, Robert F., 1934-

The hunter in my heart; a sportsman's salmagundi. Lyons Press 2002 268p $24.95
799.2

1. Game and game birds 2. Hunting
ISBN 1-58574-465-4

This "is a collection of 30 essays and two short stories. . . . Jones not only tells great outdoor stories but also explores his thoughts on hunting and friendship." Libr J

800   LITERATURE & RHETORIC

801   Literature—Philosophy and theory

Gardner, John, 1933-1982

On moral fiction. Basic Bks. 1978 214p hardcover o.p. paperback available $18   **801**

1. Literature—Philosophy
ISBN 0-465-05226-6 (pa)   LC 77-20409

Gardner "submits that contemporary U.S. art, primarily that of fiction, is generally not of high quality because it is not moral, in that it strives to devalue rather than improve life. Furthermore, Gardner charges that critics have lost track of true, moral art and have failed to denounce that which is false or immoral." Booklist

Kermode, Frank, 1919-

An appetite for poetry. Harvard Univ. Press 1989 242p $32   **801**

1. Poetry—History and criticism 2. Literature—History and criticism 3. Criticism
ISBN 0-674-04093-7   LC 89-31725
Analyzed in Essay and general literature index

This collection contains critical and textual readings of Milton, T. S. Eliot, Wallace Stevens, William Empson and the Bible

"Kermode is not simply a critic but also an artist. . . . In An Appetite for Poetry we encounter writing of balance and decorum, and reading of unflinching audacity." Commonweal

Includes bibliographical references

803   Literature—Encyclopedias and dictionaries

Abrams, M. H. (Meyer Howard), 1912-

A glossary of literary terms. Harcourt Brace & Co. pa $45.95   **803**

1. Literature—Dictionaries
First published 1957. (7th edition, 1999) Periodically revised

In a series of essays, the author discusses literary terms and definitions ranging from the traditional to the avant-garde. Subsidiary terms are included under major or generic terms

Baldick, Chris

The concise Oxford dictionary of literary terms. 2nd ed. Oxford Univ. Press 2001 280p (Oxford paperback reference) pa $14.95   **803**

1. Literature—Dictionaries 2. English language—Terms and phrases
ISBN 0-19-280118-X
First published 1990

This work defines more than 1,000 literary terms. Also provides coverage of traditional drama, rhetoric, literary history, and textual criticism. Includes pronunciation guides on over 200 terms
Includes bibliographical references

Benet's reader's encyclopedia. HarperCollins Pubs. $50   **803**

1. Literature—Dictionaries

First published 1948 under the editorship of William Rose Benet. (4th edition 1996). Periodically revised

Current editor: Bruce Murphy

This encyclopedia contains over 10,000 entries and covers world literature from early times to the present. Includes entries on authors, literary movements, principal characters, plot synopses, terms, awards, myths and legends, etc.

Brewer's dictionary of modern phrase & fable; compiled by Adrian Room. Cassell; [distributed by] Sterling 2000 xx, 773p $39.95   **803**

1. Literature—Dictionaries 2. Allusions
ISBN 0-304-35381-7   LC 2001-369116

This modern version of Brewer's dictionary of phrase and fable "focuses on material from the 20th and 21st centuries. More than 800 entries, arranged alphabetically with cross-references and accompanying quotations, contain insightful and informative descriptions and etymologies. . . . The contemporary phrases contain slang usage as well as technical terms." Choice
For a fuller review see: Booklist, Oct. 1, 2001

Brewer's dictionary of phrase and fable.
HarperResource $50   **803**
1. Literature—Dictionaries 2. Allusions
First published 1870. (16th edition 2000) Periodically
revised
Current editor: Adrian Room
"Over 15,000 brief entries give the meanings and origins of a broad range of terms, expressions, and names of real, fictitious and mythical characters from world history, science, the arts and literature." N Y Public Libr. Ref Books for Child Collect. 2d edition

Carey, Gary
A multicultural dictionary of literary terms;
[by] Gary Carey and Mary Ellen Snodgrass.
McFarland & Co. 1999 184p $35   **803**
1. Literature—Dictionaries
ISBN 0-7864-0552-X   LC 98-35221
"Using the full spectrum of literature, including drama, poetry, and novels, the authors . . . draw from a cross section of works by people of many races and traditions for both literary terms and the examples used to define them." Libr J

Columbia dictionary of modern European literature; Jean-Albert Bédé and William B. Edgerton, general editors. 2d ed fully rev and enl. Columbia Univ. Press 1980 895p $267.50   **803**
1. Literature—Dictionaries 2. Authors, European—Dictionaries
ISBN 0-231-03717-1   LC 80-17082
First published 1947
"Contains signed articles by some 500 contributors on over 1,800 authors who write (or wrote) in European languages other than English from the late 19th century to the present. General articles on individual literatures are also included." Choice

Cuddon, J. A. (John Anthony), 1928-
A dictionary of literary terms and literary theory; revised by C. E. Preston. 4th ed. Blackwell 1998 991p (Blackwell reference) $145.95   **803**
1. Literature—Dictionaries
ISBN 0-631-20271-4   LC 98-9226
Also available in paperback from Penguin Bks. with title: The Penguin dictionary of literary terms
Categories include technical terms, forms, phrases, motifs, concepts, genres, groups, movements, character types, and styles

Cyclopedia of literary characters. rev ed, edited by A. J. Sobczak; original eds edited by Frank N. Magill; associate editor, Janet Alice Long. Salem Press 1998 5v set $368   **803**
1. Literature—Dictionaries 2. Characters and characteristics in literature
ISBN 0-89356-438-9   LC 97-45813
This "edition combines the characters profiled in Cyclopedias of Literary Characters (1963) and Literary Characters II (1990). It also includes all characters that appeared in more recent works of Masterplots II published through 1995." Publisher's note
"Entries are arranged alphabetically by the title of the work. . . . [They] begin with the book's title, foreign title if originally published in a language other than English, author's name with birth and death years, date of first publication, genre, locale, time of action, and plot type. Characters are arranged in order of importance; major characters have 100- to 150-word write-ups. Volume 5 contains three indexes: title, author, and character." Booklist

Encyclopedia of world literature in the 20th century. 3rd ed. St. James Press 1999 4v set $650   **803**
1. Literature—Encyclopedias 2. Literature—Bio-bibliography
ISBN 1-55862-373-6   LC 98-40374
First four volumes originally published 1967-1975 by Unger; a supplementary volume was published 1993 by Continuum
Steven R. Serafin, general editor
This set "provides: more than 2,300 entries on individual authors; approximately 50 national-survey entries that review the literatures of countries around the world; and 50 additional entries that discuss such topics as genres, movements and trends (e.g., deconstruction, feminist criticism, historicism, literature and exile, postmodernism and poststructuralism)." Publisher's note

Harmon, William, 1938-
A handbook to literature. 9th ed. Prentice-Hall 2003 663p pa $56   **803**
1. Literature—Dictionaries
ISBN 0-13-097998-8   LC 2002-23034
First published 1936 by Doubleday under the authorship of William Flint Thrall and Addison Hibbard; later editions by William Harmon and C. Hugh Holman
"This handbook provides an alphabetical listing of more than 2,000 important terms and facts in literature, linguistics, rhetoric, criticism, printing, bookselling, and information technology. Covers a wide range of terms, most centered in literature, but extending into other areas, such as film, radio, TV, printing, linguistics and literary theory, music, graphic arts, classical studies, and computing and information science terms." Publisher's note

Merriam-Webster's encyclopedia of literature. Merriam-Webster 1995 1236p il $45   **803**
1. Literature—Dictionaries
ISBN 0-87779-042-6   LC 94-42741
This work "offers entries on authors, characters, mythological and folkloric figures, scholars, critics, literary styles, movements, terms, landmarks, prizes, and journals. It also has a pronunciation guide for most entries and many photos and illustrations." Libr J

The **Oxford** dictionary of allusions; [edited by] Andrew Delahunty, Sheila Dignen, and Penny Stock. Oxford Univ. Press 2001 453p hardcover o.p. paperback available $16.95   **803**
1. Allusions
ISBN 0-19-860682-6 (pa)   LC 2001-21530
The text "categorizes entries under 190 general headings, ranging from fatness, destruction, and illusion to quest and outlaws. . . . Valuable to students are 22 special entries, nine from Greek mythology and an equal number from the Bible. . . . Selection of cited material is refreshingly unpedantic. Bram Stoker, Saki, V.S. Naipaul, Robertson Davies, Kurt Vonnegut, and Martin

The Oxford dictionary of allusions—*Continued*

Amis are quoted alongside *The Guardian, New Scientist, The Independent*, and *Observer* and lines from classic English writers like Keats, Hardy, Thackeray, Pope, Wilde, and Richardson." Choice

The Oxford dictionary of phrase and fable; edited by Elizabeth Knowles. Oxford Univ. Press 2000 1223p $50   **803**

1. Literature—Dictionaries 2. Allusions
ISBN 0-19-860219-7   LC 2001-274200

This "potpourri of allusive terms includes entries from a broad range of topics, including classical mythology, history, religion, folk customs, superstitions, science and technology, philosophy, and popular culture." Publisher's note

This work "brings together useful information for anyone researching in either the humanities or the social sciences. Futhermore, it reflects the current evolution and state of the methods of scholarly study. This is a title that will not only aid today's students, but will become a touchstone in the history of research itself." Am Ref Books Annu, 2001

Quinn, Edward, 1932-

A dictionary of literary and thematic terms. Facts on File 1999 360p (Facts on File library of American literature) $49.50   **803**

1. Literature—Dictionaries
ISBN 0-8160-3232-7   LC 99-21449

In addition to basic definitions of terms "this general literary dictionary . . . covers common themes in literature such as love, death, alienation, and time. Literary schools are treated with just enough depth to offer a basic understanding of the major tenets." Libr J

Webber, Elizabeth, 1946-

Merriam-Webster's dictionary of allusions; [by] Elizabeth Webber & Mike Feinsilber. Merriam-Webster 1999 592p pa $14.95   **803**

1. Allusions
ISBN 0-87779-628-9   LC 99-33125

"More than 900 entries are listed alphabetically. Each includes a short definition and a longer history of the word or phrase; some also include pronunciation. Length varies from five to six sentences to a page or more, and all include one or more examples of the term in use, complete with date, author (when available), and print or media sources. . . . Almost all of the usage examples are from the late 1980s and 1990s." Booklist

808   Rhetoric

Agress, Lynne, 1941-

Working with words in business and legal writing. Perseus Bks. 2002 123p il pa $13.50   **808**

1. Authorship—Handbooks, manuals, etc.
ISBN 0-7382-0562-1

The author "provides a framework for good writing in business and law. . . . She addresses common failings such as poor grammar, the use of jargon, awkward sentences, excess verbiage, pretentious writing, and poor punctuation, clearly presenting each problem and offering possible solutions." Libr J

The Associated Press stylebook and briefing on media law; with Internet guide and glossary; editor, Norm Goldstein. Perseus Bks. 2002 383p il pa $17.50   **808**

1. Authorship—Handbooks, manuals, etc. 2. Publishers and publishing 3. English language—Usage 4. Libel and slander
ISBN 0-7382-0740-3   LC 2002-105974

First published 1977 under the editorship of Howard Angione with title : The Associated Press stylebook and libel manual

"A guide to usage, this is a manual of style for words and subjects commonly encountered in news writing, designed to help writers make correct choices and instruct users about media law. . . . The stylebook offers information on such thorny matters as military titles, titles of nobility, and metric and temperature conversions. Special sections include an Internet guide with terms for sports and business guidelines and style and a briefing on media law, explaining such things as libel law, fair reporting, the right of privacy, and media applications related to the First Amendment." Choice

The Chicago manual of style. 15th ed. University of Chicago Press 2003 956p il $55   **808**

1. Authorship—Handbooks, manuals, etc. 2. Publishers and publishing—Handbooks, manuals, etc. 3. English language—Usage
ISBN 0-226-10403-6   LC 2003-1860

First published 1906 with title: A manual of style

Updated to reflect current style, technology, and professional practice, this style manual includes journals and electronic publications, descriptive headings on all numbered paragraphs, and reorganized chapters on grammar, usage, and documentation, including guidance on citing electronic sources

Includes bibliographical references

Coles, Robert

The call of stories; teaching and the moral imagination. Houghton Mifflin 1989 xx, 212p hardcover o.p. paperback available $14   **808**

1. Literature—Study and teaching 2. Moral education 3. Books and reading
ISBN 0-395-52815-1 (pa)   LC 88-26659

"A Peter Davison book"

"Using the 'documentary study on psychiatric anthropology' approach of his previous works, Coles presents conversations with college, law, and medical school students that focus on the moral impact of their reading. For Coles, the study of literature is not a purely intellectual exercise but an encounter with exempla that bear on everyday moral dilemmas." Libr J

Conway, Jill K., 1934-

When memory speaks; reflections on autobiography; [by] Jill Ker Conway. Knopf 1998 205p hardcover o.p. paperback available $13   **808**

1. Autobiography 2. Biography as a literary form
ISBN 0-679-76645-6 (pa)   LC 97-49452

In this work Conway "turns her attention to the form of autobiography in general—to 'why readers like to read autobiography, and why individuals are moved to write their life stories'—and to the ways that cultural assumptions, especially those about gender, influence that writing and reading." Libr J

Conway, Jill K., 1934-—*Continued*

"Conway's small gem is a landmark in eliciting fresh contemplation of the inchoate complexity of memory's manifold voices." Publ Wkly

Includes bibliographical references

Fleming, Robert

The African American writer's handbook; how to get in print and stay in print. One World (NY) 2000 339p pa $12   **808**

1. Authorship—Handbooks, manuals, etc. 2. African American authors

ISBN 0-345-42327-5   LC 00-102059

The author "discusses the basics of manuscript submissions, tools of writing, and the publishing world. He speaks of issues that many African-American writers must deal with in producing and marketing their books. He also reveals the importance of self-promotion. In subsequent chapters, Fleming entertains book lovers of any race with a tour of the African-American literary world." Libr J

Includes bibliographical references

Gibaldi, Joseph, 1942-

MLA handbook for writers of research papers. 6th ed. Modern Lang. Assn. of Am. 2003 361p il pa $17   **808**

1. Report writing

ISBN 0-87352-986-3   LC 2002-156363

Also available large print edition

First published 1977 with title: MLA handbook for writers of research papers, theses, and dissertations

This manual discusses research strategies, formatting, documenting sources, writing basics and utilizing electronic sources

Includes bibliographical references

MLA style manual and guide to scholarly publishing. 2nd ed. Modern Lang. Assn. of Am. 1998 xxviii, 343p $25   **808**

1. Authorship—Handbooks, manuals, etc.

ISBN 0-87352-699-6   LC 97-49983

First published 1985 under authorship of Walter S. Achtert and Joseph Gibaldi

This work begins with a "chapter on the publication process, from manuscript to published work, and includes advice for those seeking to publish their articles or books. The second chapter, by the attorney Arthur F. Abelman, reviews legal issues. . . . Subsequent chapters discuss the stylistic conventions and the preparation of manuscripts, theses, and dissertations." Publisher's note

Hodges' Harbrace handbook; [by] Cheryl Glenn [et al.] Heinle & Heinle Pubs. xxxvi, 876p il $49.95   **808**

1. English language—Composition and exercises 2. English language—Grammar

ISBN 0-8384-0345-X   LC 2003-49918

First published 1941 under the authorship of John C. Hodges with title: Harbrace handbook of English. (15th edition 2004) Frequently revised

Variant title: Harbrace college handbook

A guide to the fundamentals of grammar, composition, and usage

Includes bibliographical references

Hooks, Bell

Remembered rapture; the writer at work. Holt & Co. 1999 237p hardcover o.p. paperback available $13   **808**

1. Authorship 2. American literature—African American authors

ISBN 0-8050-5910-5 (pa)   LC 98-7998

"The redoubtable Hooks offers a series of essays on writing, focusing on women, black writers (e.g., why there are so many black women novelists and so few in nonfiction), and what it was like to move to writer-saturated New York." Libr J

McMahan, Elizabeth

The writer's handbook; [by] Elizabeth McMahan, Susan Day. 2nd ed. McGraw-Hill 1988 400p pa $40.31   **808**

1. English language—Grammar 2. Rhetoric

ISBN 0-07-045432-9   LC 87-24160

First published 1980

This guide for acquiring the skills to develop writing proficiency covers grammar, punctuation, style, usage and spelling. A chapter is devoted to business writing

The **New** York Public Library writer's guide to style and usage. HarperCollins Pubs. 1994 838p il $40   **808**

1. Authorship—Handbooks, manuals, etc. 2. English language—Usage

ISBN 0-06-270064-2   LC 93-33255

"A Stonesong Press book"

In five parts, this "guide covers (1) current English usage, with special attention given to bias-free language and commonly misused or confused words; (2) grammar, with an emphasis on controversial issues and with . . . illustrated examples; (3) style, including lists of common abbreviations and a chapter on special characters in 19 different languages; (4) assembling and checking the manuscript, including a discussion of copyright and instructions for indexing; and (5) physical preparation of the manuscript. Information regarding computer-aided writing and production is [included]." Booklist

Includes bibliographical references

O'Neil, Dennis, 1939-

The DC comics guide to writing comics; introduction by Stan Lee. Watson-Guptill 2001 128p il $19.95   **808**

1. Authorship 2. Comic books, strips, etc.

ISBN 0-8230-1027-9   LC 2001-26101

The author "discusses story structure, characterization, script preparation, and other general writing topics. He also covers those more specific to comics writing such as miniseries, maxiseries, and continuity. O'Neil addresses the visual component of the art, the importance of page layout, and the relationship between the writer and the artist." SLJ

"O'Neil addresses the universals of writing in a way that makes the book useful to all aspiring scripters, regardless of their knowledge of comics." Booklist

Rabiner, Susan

Thinking like your editor; how to write serious nonfiction—and get it published; by Susan Rabiner and Alfred Fortunato. Norton 2002 284p $26.95; pa $14 **808**

1. Authorship
ISBN 0-393-03892-0; 0-393-32461-3 (pa)
LC 2001-44551

"In part one, on submissions, the authors discuss how to put together a book proposal and, . . . whether to work through an agent or go solo. In part two, they move to the writing process. . . . Part three discusses how authors and editors (both in-house and freelance) can work together well." Publ Wkly

Siegal, Allan, 1940-

The New York times manual of style and usage; [by] Allan M. Siegal and William G. Connolly. rev and expanded ed. Times Bks. 1999 364p hardcover o.p. paperback available $15 **808**

1. Authorship—Handbooks, manuals, etc.
ISBN 0-8129-6389-X (pa)
LC 99-10630

Replaces the title published 1976 under the editorship of Lewis Jordan

Rules and guidelines observed by The New York Times for consistency of spelling, capitalization, punctuation, abbreviation, and preferred usage

This work "contends with the AP stylebook in authority and usefulness." Columbia J Rev

Stein, Sol

Stein on writing; a master editor of some of the most successful writers of our century shares his craft techniques and strategies. St. Martin's Press 1995 308p $24.95; pa $14.95 **808**

1. Authorship
ISBN 0-312-13608-0; 0-312-25421-0 (pa)
LC 95-31793

The author discusses the process of writing "fiction and nonfiction in terms of characterization, pacing, revision, evoking emotion, and 'liposuctioning flab.' Stein's own writing demonstrates the 'resonance' and 'particularities' he discusses, and his original checklists, writing exercises, and numerous examples encourage the reader/writer to see and do the same. A chapter of help sources and a glossary of terms provide the finishing touch." Libr J

Strunk, William, 1869-1946

The elements of style; with revisions, an introduction, and a chapter on writing by E.B. White. 4th ed. Allyn & Bacon 1999 105p $14.95; pa $7.95 **808**

1. Rhetoric
ISBN 0-205-31342-6; 0-205-30902-X (pa)
LC 99-16419

First privately printed in 1918

This work provides guidelines for proper usage and composition. Misused expressions and commonly misspelled words are discussed. Includes examples

This work is "prescriptive, conservative, and humorous; in sum, it is the best book available on how to write English prose." Nichols. Guide to Ref Books for Sch Media Cent. 4th edition

Turabian, Kate L., 1893-1987

A manual for writers of term papers, theses, and dissertations. University of Chicago Press (Chicago guides to writing, editing, and publishing) $30; pa $14 **808**

1. Report writing 2. Dissertations
First published 1937 with title: A manual for writers of dissertations. (6th edition 1996) Periodically revised

Designed to serve as a guide to suitable style in the presentation of formal papers—term papers, reports, articles, theses, dissertations—both in scientific and in nonscientific fields

Student's guide for writing college papers. 3rd ed. University of Chicago Press 1977 c1976 256p hardcover o.p. paperback available $10 **808**

1. Report writing 2. Dissertations
ISBN 0-226-81623-0 (pa)
LC 76-435

First published 1963

This guide covers selecting a topic, collecting material, planning and writing the paper, and preparing footnotes and bibliographies

United States. Government Printing Office

Style manual. U.S. Govt. Ptg. Office $43, pa $29 **808**

1. Authorship—Handbooks, manuals, etc. 2. Publishers and publishing—Handbooks, manuals, etc. 3. Printing—Style manuals
Also available CD-ROM version

First published 1908 with title: Manual of style. Frequently revised

"A useful and extensive manual giving the practices of the Government Printing Office on copy preparation, with rules for capitalization, punctuation, abbreviations, etc., and information on foreign languages, including alphabets, with pronunciation, special rules, lists of numbers, etc." Guide to Ref Books. 11th edition

Van Wicklen, Janet

The tech writer's survival guide; a comprehensive handbook for aspiring technical writers. Facts on File 2001 269p $35; pa $15.95 **808**

1. Technical writing
ISBN 0-8160-4038-9; 0-8160-4039-7 (pa)
LC 00-62231

First published 1992 with title: The tech writing game

"This guide offers some basic principles of document structure and design for both printed and online media and is full of practical advice on how to glean information from product developers and determine the needs of a document's audience. Van Wicklen draws from her own experience as well as giving testimony from colleagues, demonstrating the wide variability of technical writing jobs. It will be a helpful resource for anyone considering or beginning a career in technical writing." Booklist

Includes bibliographical references

Walker, Janice R.

The Columbia guide to online style; [by] Janice R. Walker and Todd Taylor. Columbia Univ. Press 1998 218p $40.50; pa $19.50

808

1. Authorship—Data processing—Handbooks, manuals, etc. 2. Bibliographical citations
ISBN 0-231-10788-9; 0-231-10789-7 (pa)

LC 98-22875

The authors provide a "manual that not only covers citation of online documents but provides guidelines for producing them. Part 1 presents an adaptable 'citation template' with numerous helpful examples in both a humanities style, based on Modern Language Association form, and a scientific style much like that of the American Psychological Association. Part 2 gives a theoretical rationale for document style and describes standards for producing online documents." Libr J

Includes bibliographical references

Women writers at work; the Paris review interviews; edited by George Plimpton; introduction by Margaret Atwood. Modern Lib. 1998 455p il pa $23   **808**
1. Literature—History and criticism 2. Women authors
ISBN 0-679-77129-8

Revised version of title first published 1989 by Viking

This volume collects sixteen interviews published between 1960 and 1994 in which women writers discuss their work, their lives, and the nature of writing in general. Among the interviewees are: Eudora Welty, Marianne Moore, Susan Sontag and Joyce Carol Oates. Each interview is accompanied by a bio-critical profile, a photograph of the subject and a facsimile manuscript page

The **Writer's** digest guide to good writing; edited by Thomas Clark [et al.] Writer's Digest Bks. 1994 338p hardcover o.p. paperback available $14.99   **808**
1. Authorship—Handbooks, manuals, etc.
ISBN 1-58297-138-2 (pa)   LC 93-43554

This collection of articles culled from issues of Writer's Digest magazine contains "essays on how to write with simplicity, plot and pace a story, build suspense, create characters, and tackle certain genres, including mysteries, horror, romance, and various forms of nonfiction. The selections are organized by decades and include essays by Erle Stanley Gardner, Irving Wallace, Louis L'Amour [and] Allen Ginsberg." Booklist

The **Writer's** handbook. Writer $29.95   **808**
1. Authorship—Handbooks, manuals, etc. 2. Publishers and publishing
ISSN 0084-2710

Annual. First published 1936

Current editor Elfreida Abbe

"A collection of articles, most of which appeared originally in *The writer*, on various phases of professional writing, including fiction, nonfiction, and specialties. Some articles are carried over from earlier editions, some are new, none are dated. The specialties section is a market guide, mainly to the periodical field, giving for each title: address, editor, and type of material accepted with indication of rate of payment. Also has sections for greeting card and drama markets, including regional and university theaters, television, and for book publishers." Guide to Ref Books. 11th edition

The **Writer's** market. Writer's Digest Bks. $29.99   **808**
1. Authorship—Handbooks, manuals, etc. 2. Publishers and publishing
ISSN 0084-2729

Also available CD-ROM version

Annual. First published 1922

"A guide for freelance writers, covering the practical side of writing for publication, including information about book publishers; consumer magazines; trade, technical and a few professional journals; scriptwriting; syndicates; greeting card and gift markets. Provides extensive lists of contests and awards and of relevant organizations and publications. Subject index of book publishers." Guide to Ref Books. 11th edition

Zinsser, William Knowlton

On writing well; the classic guide to writing nonfiction; [by] William Zinsser. 25th anniversary ed. Quill 2001 308p pa $14

808

1. Rhetoric 2. Authorship
ISBN 0-06-000664-1   LC 2001-41623
Among the topics discussed are: style, usage, clutter, imprecision and organization
Includes bibliographical references

Writing to learn. Harper & Row 1988 256p hardcover o.p. paperback available $14   **808**
1. Rhetoric—Study and teaching
ISBN 0-06-272040-6 (pa)   LC 87-45825

"Eschewing theory and philosophical breast-beating, Zinsser uses his own experience to reinforce the fact that clear, eloquent writing can be taught for every subject across the curriculum. A practical manual for teachers and a powerful reminder for everyone that good writing makes possible good thinking." Am Libr

Includes bibliographical referneces

808.06   Writing children's literature

Aiken, Joan, 1924-2004

The way to write for children. St. Martin's Press 1983 93p hardcover o.p. paperback available $8.95   **808.06**
1. Authorship 2. Children's literature—Technique
ISBN 0-312-85840-X (pa)   LC 82-10692
First published 1982 in the United Kingdom

This book is directed to authors who seek to write for children. Aiken's suggestions are intended to aid them "in directing their writing toward specific audiences, beginning with the organization of initial ideas and progressing to the choice of voice, plot, and characters." Publisher's note

"In this crisp, informative and often witty survey of 'the market' Aiken is also giving the customers—teachers, librarians, parents, every one concerned with children's literature of quality—a good general idea of what is available already and of what authors are trying to do." Times Lit Suppl

Seuling, Barbara

How to write a children's book and get it published. rev & expanded ed. Scribner 1991 214p pa $14.95   **808.06**
1. Children's literature—Technique 2. Authorship
ISBN 0-684-19343-4   LC 91-18176
First published 1984

Seuling, Barbara—*Continued*

Presents "five essential steps (from researching the current marketplace to submitting your manuscript) to publishing works for children." Libr J

Includes bibliographical references

Shulevitz, Uri, 1935-

Writing with pictures; how to write and illustrate children's books. Watson-Guptill 1985 271p il hardcover o.p. paperback available $29.95   **808.06**

1. Children's literature—Technique 2. Picture books for children

ISBN 0-8230-5935-9 (pa)   LC 85-15604

"With heavy emphasis on illustration, this detailed book guides aspiring authors/illustrators through telling the story and drawing the pictures to preparing artwork for the printer." Libr J

Includes bibliographical references

808.1   Rhetoric of poetry

Addonizio, Kim, 1954-

The poet's companion; a guide to the pleasures of writing poetry; [by] Kim Addonizio and Dorianne Laux. Norton 1997 284p pa $14.95   **808.1**

1. Poetics

ISBN 0-393-31654-8   LC 96-40451

This work contains "three main sections: 'Subjects for Writing' (e.g. death, the erotic), 'The Poet's Craft' (metaphor, rhyme), and 'The Writing Life' (self-doubt, writer's block); four separate appendixes list other writing texts, anthologies, marketing tips, and electronic resources. . . . Both knowledgeable and practical in their approach, the authors offer everything a poet needs, including . . . a gentle yet insistent lesson on grammar." Libr J

Includes bibliographical references

Aristotle, 384-322 B.C.

Poetics   **808.1**

1. Poetics 2. Aesthetics

Hardcover and paperback editions available from various publishers

In this basic work of literary criticism, Aristotle discusses the fundamental principles of poetry and its various forms, emphasizing tragedy and the epic

Deutsch, Babette, 1895-1982

Poetry handbook: a dictionary of terms. 4th ed. Funk & Wagnalls 1974 203p o.p.; HarperCollins Pubs. paperback available $14   **808.1**

1. Poetics—Dictionaries 2. Poetry—Terminology

ISBN 0-06-463548-1 (pa)

First published 1957

"The craft of verse described in dictionary form. Terms and techniques are defined and illustrated." N Y Public Libr. Ref Books for Child Collect. 2d edition

Higginson, William J., 1938-

The haiku handbook; how to write, share, and teach haiku; [by] William J. Higginson with Penny Harter. McGraw-Hill 1985 331p o.p.; Kodansha Am. paperback available $14   **808.1**

1. Haiku

ISBN 4-770-01430-9 (pa)   LC 84-17174

The author "surveys the original and related forms (renga, haibun, senryu), inventors and developers (Basho, Buson, Issa, Shiki), and the numerous variations that later authors, especially in other languages, have wrought on haiku's simple principles. He discusses the many uses—artistic, personal, psychological—that the mode can serve, encouraging the reader all along the way to use the form, to experiment, and thus to express thoughts and feelings. . . . An extensive reference section gives word lists, a glossary, and good bibliographies." Booklist

Hirsch, Edward

How to read a poem; and fall in love with poetry. Harcourt Brace & Co. 1999 352p $23; pa $15   **808.1**

1. Poetics 2. Poetry—History and criticism

ISBN 0-15-100419-6; 0-15-600566-2 (pa)

LC 98-50065

The author "has gathered an eclectic group of poems from many times and places, with selections as varied as postwar Polish poetry, works by Keats and Christopher Smart, and lyrics from African American work songs. A prolific, award-winning poet in his own right, Hirsch suggests helpful strategies for understanding and appreciating each poem. The book is scholarly but very readable and incorporates interesting anecdotes from the lives of the poets." Libr J

Includes bibliographical references

Myers, Jack Elliott, 1941-

Dictionary of poetic terms; {by} Jack Myers, Don Charles Wukasch. University of N. Tex. Press 2003 434p pa $22.95   **808.1**

1. Poetics—Dictionaries

ISBN 1-57441-166-7   LC 2003-11482

First published 1985 by Longman Press with title: Longman dictionary and handbook of poetry

This volume "contains over 1,600 entries on the devices, techniques, history, theory, and terminology of poetry from the Classical period to the present." Publisher's note

"Particularly useful is the plethora of samples from the works of such greats as James Joyce, Edna St. Vincent Millay, Ezra Pound, and Ogden Nash. Although some of the vocabulary is lofty, the definitions, fascinating history, and brief essays combine to form a useful handbook." Libr J

Includes bibliographical references

Oliver, Mary, 1935-

A poetry handbook. Harcourt Brace & Co. 1994 130p pa $13   **808.1**

1. Poetics 2. Poetry—Marketing

ISBN 0-15-672400-6   LC 93-49676

"A Harvest original"

A "handbook for young poets on the formal aspects and structure of poetry. Oliver excels at explaining the sound and sense of poetry—from scansion to imagery, diction to voice. She stresses the importance of reading poetry, since, in order to write well, 'it is entirely necessary to read widely and deeply.' Sage advice is given in

Oliver, Mary, 1935-—*Continued*
an entire chapter dedicated to revision, wherein Oliver urges poets to consider their first draft 'an unfinished piece of work' that can be polished and improved later. Written in a pleasant and lucid style, this book is a wonderful resource." Libr J

Poet's market. Writer's Digest Bks. $24.99

808.1

ISSN 0883-5470
Annual. First published 1989
"Useful for those aspiring to publish their poems in literary journals and magazines. . . . Entries include a brief journal profile, submission requirements, and contact information. Offers advice to beginning poets on getting published, brief articles by working poets/editors, grant information, contests and awards, poetry readings, writing colonies, organizations and publications useful to poets. Indexes for chapbook publishers, publishers by subject, publishers by state, and a general index." Guide to Ref Books. 11th edition

808.2　Rhetoric of drama

Hauge, Michael
Writing screenplays that sell. McGraw-Hill 1988 xxii, 314p o.p.; HarperPerennial paperback available $17　　　**808.2**
1. Motion picture plays—Technique
ISBN 0-06-272500-9 (pa)　　　LC 88-2688
This book provides a "discussion of the craft—characters, story development, etc.—and industry; lays out the all-important details of format; then tells how to market the finished product. Hauge's volume is a detailed manual offering a step-by-step methodology, a scriptual analysis of a hit film, 'The Karate Kid,' and handy chapter summaries." Libr J

Straczynski, J. Michael, 1954-
The complete book of scriptwriting. rev and expanded [ed] Writer's Digest Bks. 1996 424p il hardcover o.p. paperback available $19.99　　　**808.2**
1. Drama—Technique 2. Television authorship 3. Motion picture plays—Technique 4. Radio authorship
ISBN 1-58297-158-7 (pa)　　　LC 96-30630
First published 1982
This "encyclopedic exploration of writing scripts for TV, motion pictures, animation, radio, and the stage includes examples of actual scripts formatted for each medium." Libr J

808.3　Rhetoric of fiction

Conrad, Barnaby, 1922-
The complete guide to writing fiction; [by] Barnaby Conrad and the staff of the Santa Barbara Writers' Conference. Writer's Digest Bks. 1990 309p $19.99　　　**808.3**
1. Fiction—Technique
ISBN 0-89879-395-5　　　LC 90-12287
"Keynote editorials, gleaned from speeches given at the annual Santa Barbara Writers' Conference, are written by a range of authors, including Danielle Steel, Ray Bradbury, Eudora Welty, and Alice Adams. This nicely organized tutorial on crafting the major elements of a novel features further significant suggestions on revising a manuscript, selling short stories, hiring an agent, marketing the manuscript, and handling rejection." Booklist

Gardner, John, 1933-1982
The art of fiction; notes on craft for young writers. Knopf 1984 224p hardcover o.p. paperback available $12　　　**808.3**
1. Fiction—Technique
ISBN 0-679-73403-1 (pa)　　　LC 83-47850
"This essay distills the late Gardner's ripest thoughts about what fiction is and how to go about learning to write it. The initial section deals with 'literary-aesthetic theory,' the second with 'the fictional process.' . . . The book concludes with two sets of exercises, one for class use and one for individual use. Recommended for any young writer or writing class, and for all readers who care about the craft of fiction." Booklist

On becoming a novelist; foreword by Raymond Carver. Harper & Row 1983 xxv, 150p　　　**808.3**
1. Authorship 2. Fiction—Technique
LC 82-48662
Available in hardcover from P. Smith and in paperback from Norton
The author "explores the dynamic chemistry at the heart of the writer's creative process. Gardner's book is a superbly written, thoroughly original, eminently useful volume." Choice

King, Stephen, 1947-
On writing; a memoir of the craft. Scribner 2000 288p $25; pa $14.95　　　**808.3**
1. Authorship
ISBN 0-684-85352-3; 0-671-02425-6 (pa)
LC 00-30105
The author recounts "his life from early childhood through the aftermath of the 1999 accident that nearly killed him. Along the way, King touts the writing philosophies of William Strunk and Ernest Hemingway, advocates a healthy appetite for reading, expounds upon the subject of grammar, critiques a number of popular writers, and offers the reader a chance to try out his theories. . . . Recommended for anyone who wants to write and everyone who loves to read." Libr J

Lukeman, Noah
The plot thickens; 8 ways to bring fiction to life. St. Martin's Press 2002 221p $19.95; pa $12.95　　　**808.3**
1. Fiction—Technique
ISBN 0-312-28467-5; 0-312-30928-7 (pa)
LC 2001-58564
"Lukeman focuses on the mechanics of storytelling. He introduces budding writers to the techniques of characterization (ask yourself questions about the people you've created), the various ways of generating suspense (danger, a ticking clock), and the importance of conflict." Booklist

Maass, Donald

Writing the breakout novel; winning advice from a top agent and his bestselling client; foreword by Anne Perry. Writer's Digest Bks. 2001 264p hardcover o.p. paperback available $16.99 **808.3**

1. Fiction—Technique
ISBN 1-58297-182-X (pa)   LC 2001-22036

"Using his own clients as case studies, Maass defines the most crucial elements of a breakout novel—a powerful sense of time and place, larger-than-life characters, a high degree of tension, good subplots, and universal themes—and shows the reader how to use these elements efficiently to write a novel that will generate interest and have the potential to hit the best sellers lists. Each section ends with checklists for review." Libr J

Nabokov, Vladimir Vladimirovich, 1899-1977

Lectures on literature; [by] Vladimir Nabokov; edited by Fredson Bowers; introduction by John Updike. Harcourt Brace Jovanovich 1980 xxviii, 385p il hardcover o.p. paperback available $18   **808.3**

1. Fiction—History and criticism
ISBN 0-15-649589-9 (pa)   LC 79-3690

Analyzed in Essay and general literature index
Companion volume to Lectures on Russian literature
"A Bruccoli-Clark book"

In the early 1950s, before Nabokov became a famous writer, he taught literature at Wellesley and Cornell. The editor, with the help of Nabokov's wife and son, has collected seven lectures on "Mansfield Park," "Bleak House," "Madame Bovary," "The Strange Case of Dr. Jekyll and Mr. Hyde," "The Walk by Swann's Place," "The Metamorphosis" and "Ulysses." There are two additional lectures on other topics related to literature. The volume includes a sample examination for the course and pages of original manuscripts with maps and diagrams which the author used to illustrate his lectures

Ramsland, Katherine M., 1953-

The criminal mind; a writer's guide to forensic psychology; by Katherine Ramsland. Writer's Digest Bks. 2002 282p il pa $17.99   **808.3**

1. Criminal psychology 2. Mystery fiction—Technique 3. Forensic sciences
ISBN 1-58297-079-3   LC 2002-16752

The author "examines the fundamentals of psychology and law, theories of criminality, and character disorders that can lead to criminal behavior. . . . Ramsland also explores the legal process, including psychological evaluations, lie detection, insanity pleas and the treatment of criminals and victims." Publisher's note

"The book gives budding writers, and anyone else with an interest in this subject, a solid grounding in the history, terminology, and techniques of forensic psychology." Booklist

Includes bibliographical references

Roberts, Gillian

You can write a mystery. Writer's Digest Bks. 1999 124p il pa $12.99   **808.3**

1. Mystery fiction—Technique
ISBN 0-89879-863-9   LC 99-19316

"Along with analysis of the literary aspects of mystery writing, Roberts also surveys such practical matters as grammar, punctuation, and how to submit the manuscript. If character and setting are what distinguish the best mysteries, failed plot mechanics are invariably what derail the worst. Roberts' basic but too-often-overlooked advice will help keep your story on track." Booklist

Stein, Sol

How to grow a novel; the most common mistakes writers make and how to overcome them. St. Martin's Press 1999 240p $25.95; pa $14.95   **808.3**

1. Fiction—Technique
ISBN 0-312-20949-5; 0-312-26749-5 (pa)
LC 99-36922

"Stein states bluntly right from the beginning that 'liars say they write only for themselves' and that a 'lack of courtesy' toward the reader is one of the chief faults of unsuccessful writing. While this is perhaps a controversial notion, prospective writers will nonetheless be well rewarded by reading this collection of tips, methods, and numerous anecdotes." Libr J

Swain, Dwight V.

Creating characters; how to build story people. Writer's Digest Bks. 1990 195p hardcover o.p. paperback available $14.99   **808.3**

1. Fiction—Technique 2. Characters and characteristics in literature
ISBN 0-89879-662-8 (pa)   LC 90-39640

"Swain talks to his readers in a conversational tone, suggesting techniques, giving examples to illuminate his points, and offering activities for sharpening character development skills. This is a book for those already committed to writing fiction and who want to think about the craft of writing." SLJ

Includes bibliographical references

Techniques of the selling writer. University of Okla. Press 1981 330p $24.95   **808.3**

1. Fiction—Technique
ISBN 0-8061-1191-7

First published 1965 with title: Tricks & techniques of the selling writer

The author offers practical advice for creating and marketing publishable fiction

"Often called 'the bible of fiction writing,' this classic is dated slightly by references to such things as 'carbon copies.' But Swain's tried-and-true scene-and-sequel approach has generated many books and workshops." Libr J

Vargas Llosa, Mario, 1936-

Letters to a young novelist; translated by Natasha Wimmer. Farrar, Straus & Giroux 2002 136p $17   **808.3**

1. Authorship
ISBN 0-374-11916-3   LC 2002-101065

Also available in paperback from Picador USA
Original Spanish edition, 1997

"Mario Vargas Llosa offers less a collection of dictums on the craft of the novel than a tribute to its formal complexities and potential through his admiring comments on works by the likes of Flaubert and Cervantes." N Y Times Book Rev

"Neither a survey course in what to read nor a practical guide to writing, the book finally is a meditation on writing and its proper relationship to life." Publ Wkly

Writing romances; a handbook by the Romance Writers of America; edited by Rita Gallagher and Rita Clay Estrada. Writer's Digest Bks. 1997 209p $18.99

808.3

1. Love stories—Technique
ISBN 0-89879-756-X   LC 96-31927

A "collection of articles by bestselling romance authors, this work covers the business and craft of writing a romance and the requirements of writing for each subgenre." Libr J

808.5   Rhetoric of speech

Detz, Joan
How to write and give a speech; a practical guide for executives, PR people, the military, fund-raisers, politicians, educators, and anyone who has to make every word count. 2nd rev ed. St. Martin's Press 2002 xx, 202p pa $12.95   **808.5**

1. Public speaking
ISBN 0-312-30273-8   LC 2002-67975

First published 1984

Among the various aspects of public speaking discussed are: tips on topic focus, audience assessment, humor, delivery techniques and media coverage

Linklater, Kristin, 1936-
Freeing the natural voice; drawings by Douglas Florian. Drama Bk. Specialists 1976 210p il hardcover o.p. paperback available $19.95   **808.5**

1. Voice
ISBN 0-89676-071-5 (pa)

"Predicated on the basic assumptions that everyone has a voice capable of expressing a full range of emotions within a normal two- to four-octave scale and that daily stress compromises the voice's natural abilities and power {the author} presents a simple and clear narrative, as well as a full set of exercises to cultivate and strengthen the voice." Libr J

Pinsky, Robert
The sounds of poetry; a brief guide. Farrar, Straus & Giroux 1998 129p hardcover o.p. paperback available $11   **808.5**

1. Poetry
ISBN 0-374-52617-6 (pa)   LC 98-18873

Pinsky presents "a manual of proposals on how to read poems—or, more accurately, how to 'hear more of what is going on in poems.' That distinction, in Pinsky's view is vital." Atl Mon

"By bringing his passion for the sound of language—so evident in his own poems—to his expert interpretations of the work of others, Pinsky cracks open the glass case that seems to separate poetry from everyday language, allowing the song of each poem to ring bright and clear." Booklist

Includes bibliographical references

808.8   Literature—Collections

The **Book** of eulogies; a collection of memorial tributes, poetry, essays, and letters of condolence; edited with commentary by Phyllis Theroux. Scribner 1997 400p $26   **808.8**

1. Eulogies 2. Bereavement
ISBN 0-684-82251-2   LC 97-2197

"Theroux has gathered over 100 eulogies delivered in the form of spoken tributes, editorials, letters of condolence, essays, and poetry. Many of these testimonials are eloquently penned by the well known to commemorate the well known (e.g., Thomas Merton on Flannery O'Connor, Robert F. Kennedy on Martin Luther King). Others are equally compelling memorials to unknown souls by everyday people. There are helpful commentaries by the author." Libr J

Into the garden; a wedding anthology: poetry and prose on love and marriage; edited by Robert Hass and Stephen Mitchell. HarperCollins Pubs. 1993 193p hardcover o.p. paperback available $13.95   **808.8**

1. Poetry—Collections 2. Weddings
ISBN 0-06-092469-1 (pa)   LC 92-53339

This anthology of readings suitable for wedding ceremonies contains "American Indian, aboriginal Australian, ancient Egyptian, Buddhist, Hindu, and Sufi poetry and prose in addition to . . . biblical, classical Greek and Roman, European, and American passages. . . . [Also included are] traditional or tradition-respecting ceremonies." Booklist

The **Norton** book of modern war; edited by Paul Fussell. Norton 1991 830p $24.95

808.8

1. Literature—Collections 2. War in literature
ISBN 0-393-02909-3   LC 90-36495

This anthology of 20th century prose and poetry about war covers World War I, the Spanish Civil War, World War II, the Korean War and Vietnam. Authors represented include Heinrich Böll, Marguerite Duras, Ernest Hemingway, Ron Kovic, Norman Mailer, Wilfred Owen and Siegfried Sassoon

Nothing makes you free; writings by descendants of Jewish Holocaust survivors; edited by Melvin Jules Bukiet. Norton 2002 394p $27.95; pa $15.95   **808.8**

1. Holocaust survivors 2. Holocaust, 1933-1945, in literature 3. Literature—Collections
ISBN 0-393-05046-7; 0-393-32425-7 (pa)
     LC 2001-55863

"Excerpts from the works of 30 writers whose parents survived the Holocaust make up this anthology of fiction and memoirs. . . . In these remarkable pieces issues such as guilt, anger, faith, and accountability are explored. They capture not only the experience of the concentration camps but also its powerful legacy, passed down to a new generation through the bond of love that ties parent and child." Booklist

The **Portable** medieval reader; edited, and with an introduction by James Bruce Ross and Mary Martin McLaughlin. Viking 1949 690p hardcover o.p. paperback available $16.95 **808.8**
1. Medieval literature—Collections
ISBN 0-14-015046-3 (pa)
Anthology of "the writings of men and women between the years 1050 and 1500. The aim of the editors is to give, by means of selections from contemporary reports, a picture of the whole structure of the Middle Ages. The less known chronicles have been used whenever possible. The language throughout is modern." Commonweal

Includes bibliographical references

The **Portable** Renaissance reader; edited, and with an introduction by James Bruce Ross and Mary Martin McLaughlin. Viking 1953 756p hardcover o.p. paperback available $16.95 **808.8**
1. Literature—Collections 2. Renaissance
ISBN 0-14-015061-7 (pa)
The editors have covered both the Italian and the North European Renaissance, from about 1400 to 1600. Material is collected under five general headings: An age of gold; The city of man; The study of man; The book of nature; The kingdom of God

Includes bibliographical references

Remembrances and celebrations; a book of eulogies, elegies, letters, and epitaphs; edited by Jill Werman Harris. Pantheon Bks. 1999 xxiii, 308p $25; pa $14 **808.8**
1. Eulogies 2. Bereavement
ISBN 0-375-40123-7; 0-375-70125-7 (pa)
LC 98-32149
"Comprised of eulogies from the 20th century, as well as, poetic elegies, condolence letters and tombstone epitaphs spanning from the 17th century to the present, this eclectic sourcebook offers inspiration for anyone seeking to memorialize a loved one. Since the mourners and the dead in each instance are well-known writers (Lillian Hellman eulogizes Dashiell Hammett) and public figures (Reverend Jesse Jackson lays Jackie Robinson to rest), the collection is a bonanza for the morbidly minded browser as well." Publ Wkly

808.81   Poetry—Collections

Americans' favorite poems; the Favorite Poem Project anthology; edited by Robert Pinsky and Maggie Dietz. Norton 1999 327p $27.50 **808.81**
1. Poetry—Collections
ISBN 0-393-04820-9
LC 99-31979
"People across America, including many teens, share the poetry they love, and talk about what it means in their lives. Their choices—from John Keats to Lucille Clifton—defy stereotypes, and their comments are heartfelt." Booklist

A **Book** of love poetry; edited and with an introduction by Jon Stallworthy. Oxford Univ. Press 1974 c1973 393p hardcover o.p. paperback available $16.95 **808.81**
1. Love poetry
ISBN 0-19-504232-8 (pa)
First published 1973 in the United Kingdom with title: The Penguin book of love poetry
A collection of poems written during the past 2000 years arranged thematically from young love to the "long look back" of the aged
Includes indexes of poets, translators, titles and first lines

A **Book** of lumininous things; an international anthology of poetry; edited and with an introduction by Czeslaw Milosz. Harcourt Brace & Co. 1996 xx, 320p hardcover o.p. paperback available $15 **808.81**
1. Poetry—Collections
ISBN 0-15-600574-3 (pa)
LC 95-38060
"Nobel laureate Milosz states in his introduction that the purpose of this personal and eclectic collection is to present poetry that is 'short, clear, readable, and . . . realistic, that is, loyal toward reality and attempting to describe it as concisely as possible.' . . . Most of the selections are from classical Chinese and 20th-century American and European (primarily Eastern European, Scandinavian, and French) poets." Libr J

City lights pocket poets anthology; edited by Lawrence Ferlinghetti. City Lights Bks. 1995 259p $18.95 **808.81**
1. Poetry—Collections
ISBN 0-87286-311-5
LC 95-31608
"Drawing from the 52 volumes published in the Pocket Poets series since 1956, this selection provides a handy sampler of many of the prominent avant-garde and leftist poets of the post-WW II era. . . . The series' extensive international scope is highlighted in poems culled from German, Russian, Italian, Dutch, Nicaraguan and Spanish poets." Publ Wkly

The **Columbia** Granger's index to poetry in anthologies; edited by Tessa Kale. 12th ed, completely rev indexing anthologies published through Dec. 31, 2001. Columbia Univ. Press 2002 xxvii, 2219p $307 **808.81**
1. Poetry—Indexes
ISBN 0-231-12448-1
LC 2002-17459
Also available as part of Columbia Granger's world of poetry online
First edition, edited by Edith Granger, published 1904 by A. C. McClurg with title: Index to poetry and recitations. Fifth through eighth editions have title Granger's index to poetry
"The selection of some 400 anthologies includes 140 new works published through December 2001. . . . The selection emphasizes poets writing in English and has a US focus, but over 60 anthologies of translations plus many multicultural works create an impressive range and balance, giving access to 81,000 poems by 12,735 poets from 'all parts of the world' and all time periods." Choice
For a fuller review see: Booklist, July 2, 2002

The **Columbia** Granger's Index to poetry in collected and selected works; edited by Keith Newton. 2nd ed, completely rev. Columbia Univ. Press 2004 $225   **808.81**
1. Poetry—Indexes 2. English poetry—Indexes
ISBN 0-231-12528-3   LC 2003-51469
Also available as part of Columbia Granger's world of poetry online

First published 1996

This "edition includes 315 works, by 266 different poets, locating more than 65,000 poems by title, first line, author, and subject. Included . . . are the works of many of the major American and British poets of the last thirty years, such as Robert Pinsky, Seamus Heaney, and Paul Muldoon; important twentieth-century American poets such as Langston Hughes, Dorothy Parker, and Robert Penn Warren; twentieth-century foreign poets in new translations, such as Eugenio Montale and Paul Celan; and diverse poets from all times and places, collected in new editions, such as Cold Mountain, Jones Very, and Guido Cavalcanti." Publisher's note

Holocaust poetry; compiled and introduced by Hilda Schiff. St. Martin's Press 1995 xxiv, 234p $22; pa $14.95   **808.81**
1. Holocaust, 1933-1945—Poetry 2. Poetry—Collections
ISBN 0-312-13086-4; 0-312-14357-5 (pa)
     LC 95-2708
"In English and in translation from many languages, more than 80 poets—including Wiesel, Fink, Brecht, Yevtushenko, Auden, and Sachs—give voice to what seems unspeakable. Schiff points out that compelling historical accounts document the facts and numbers, but a poem, like a story, makes us imagine how it felt for one person. These poems are stark and deceptively simple." Booklist

Includes bibliographical references

Index to children's poetry; a title, subject, author, and first line index to poetry in collections for children and youth; compiled by John E. and Sara W. Brewton. Wilson, H.W. 1942-1965 3v   **808.81**
1. Poetry—Indexes
Basic volume published 1942 $100 (ISBN 0-8242-0021-7); first supplement published 1954 $70 (ISBN 0-8242-0022-5); second supplement published 1965 $70 (ISBN 0-8242-0023-3)
The main volume indexes 15,000 poems by 2,500 authors in 130 collections. The two supplements analyze another 15,000 poems by 2700 authors in 151 collections
"This tool is an invaluable reference source." Peterson. Ref Books for Child

Index to poetry for children and young people; a title, subject, author, and first line index to poetry in collections for children and young people. Wilson, H.W. 1972-1998 6v   **808.81**
1. Poetry—Indexes
A continuation of Index to children's poetry
The volume published 1972 covering 1964-1969 compiled by John E. and Sara W. Brewton and G. Meredith Blackburn III $90 (ISBN 0-8242-0435-2); 1970-1975 published 1978 compiled by John E. Brewton, G. Meredith Blackburn III and Lorraine A. Blackburn $90 (ISBN 0-8242-0621-5); 1976-1981 published 1984 compiled by John E. Brewton, G. Meredith Blackburn III and Lorraine A. Blackburn $90 (ISBN 0-8242-0681-9); 1982-1987 published 1989 compiled by G. Meredith Blackburn III and Lorraine A. Blackburn $95 (ISBN 0-8242-0773-4); 1988-1992 published 1994 compiled by G. Meredith Blackburn III $95 (ISBN 0-8242-0861-7); 1993-1997 published 1998 compiled by G. Meredith Blackburn III $100 (ISBN 0-8242-0939-7)
Each volume analyzes approximately 10,000 poems by some 2,000 authors in more than 110 collections. Over 2,000 subject headings are used in each volume

Music of a distant drum; classical Arabic, Persian, Turkish, and Hebrew poems; translated and introduced by Bernard Lewis. Princeton Univ. Press 2001 222p il $22.95   **808.81**
1. Arabic poetry—Collections 2. Hebrew poetry—Collections 3. Persian poetry—Collections 4. Turkish poetry—Collections
ISBN 0-691-08928-0   LC 2001-19858
"Lewis, one of the foremost scholars of the Middle East, has devoted much of his career to the history of Islam; this volume collects his translations of poems—nearly all appearing in English for the first time—that span eleven centuries and four major Middle Eastern traditions. Many of the most striking works address, in spare, stirring lines, the twin demands of serving the self and serving God." New Yorker

Includes bibliographical references

The **Oxford** book of war poetry; chosen and edited by John Stallworthy. Oxford Univ. Press 1984 xxxi, 358p $30; pa $16.95   **808.81**
1. War poetry 2. Poetry—Collections
ISBN 0-19-214125-2; 0-19-280454-5 (pa)
     LC 83-19303
"This comprehensive anthology focuses on poetic treatment of warfare ranging from the battlefields of ancient history to the conflicts in Vietnam, Northern Ireland, and El Salvador." Univ Press Books for Second Sch Libr
This collection "reminds one of the large numbers and great variety of war poems from many centuries that are very good poems. Mr. Stallworthy's selections include most of the best, at least the best in English." N Y Times Book Rev

Includes bibliographical references

The **Penguin** book of women poets; edited by Carol Cosman, Joan Keefe, Kathleen Weaver; consulting editors, Joanna Banker, Doris Earnshaw, Deirdre Lashgari. Viking 1979 c1978 399p hardcover o.p. paperback available $13.95   **808.81**
1. Poetry—Collections 2. Women poets
ISBN 0-14-058533-8 (pa)   LC 78-26699
First published 1978 in the United Kingdom

This collection "spans 3500 years and 40 literary traditions, from ancient Egypt to modern America. The editors are to be praised for their careful, extensive research." Libr J

Poems for the millennium; the University of California book of modern and postmodern poetry; edited by Jerome Rothenberg and Pierre Joris. University of Calif. Press 1995-1998 2v il **808.81**
1. Poetry—Collections   LC 93-49839

"A Centennial book"

Contents: v1 From fin de siécle to negritude $70; pa $24.95 (ISBN 0-520-07225-1; 0-520-07227-8); v2 From postwar to millennium pa $24.95 (ISBN 0-520-20864-1)

The poetry in this anthology is "often self-referential, certainly aware of its own artistry, embedded in political consciousness, and transgressive. It is the work of more than 100 poets, many little known in the U.S. Rothenberg and Joris see twentieth-century poetics as international and have postwar Japanese poet Fujii Sadakazu rubbing shoulders with Amiri Baraka and Andrei Voznesensky, Tomas Tranströmer and Diane di Prima." Booklist [review of v2]

Poems to read; a new favorite poem project anthology; edited by Robert Pinsky and Maggie Dietz. Norton 2002 xxv, 352p $27.95 **808.81**
1. Poetry—Collections
ISBN 0-393-01074-0   LC 2002-321

This anthology "features works by a wide selection of well-known, mostly American and European writers from throughout the ages: Henry King, Rabindranath Tagore, Gwendolyn Brooks, J.W. von Goethe, Issa, Jorie Graham, Robert Herrick, Dionisio Martínez and Frank O'Hara are just a few of them." Publ Wkly

"A graceful, sometimes jubilant, sometimes lyrical, sometimes brooding, but always welcoming and stirring collection." Booklist

The **Poetry** of our world; an international anthology of contemporary poetry; edited by Jeffrey Paine. HarperCollins Pubs. 2000 xxviii, 511p hardcover o.p. paperback available $18 **808.81**
1. Poetry—Collections
ISBN 0-06-095193-1 (pa)   LC 99-34921

In this global anthology "each section is preceded by a thoughtful introduction of several pages by the selector in that area. . . . A stunning and highly readable anthology." Libr J

Poetry speaks; hear great poets read their work from Tennyson to Plath; editors, Elise Paschen and Rebekah Presson Mosby ; narrator, Charles Osgood. Sourcebooks MediaFusion 2001 336p il $49.95 **808.81**
1. American poetry—Collections 2. English poetry
ISBN 1-570-71720-6   LC 2001-31317

This anthology "comes with three CD's. . . . Each audio selection is prefaced by . . . {an} introduction by Charles Osgood, and the book has an essay on each poet written by a contemporary poet." N Y Times Book Rev

"A cornucopia of pleasurable reading and listening. . . . A must for poetry lovers." SLJ

The **Vintage** book of contemporary world poetry; edited and with an introduction by J.D. McClatchy. Vintage Bks. 1996 xxviii, 654p pa $16 **808.81**
1. Poetry—Collections
ISBN 0-679-74115-1   LC 95-50628

A "varied collection of contemporary poetry from Europe, the Middle East, Africa, Asia, Latin America, and the Caribbean. Here readers will find Nobel laureates and other luminaries, such as Joseph Brodsky, Derek Walcott, Czeslaw Milosz, Octavio Paz, Wole Soyinka, Breyten Breytenbach, and Nguyen Chi Thien, as well as less well known poets. Editor McClatchy has chosen well, selecting poems that illuminate the personal as well as the universal." Booklist

Includes bibliographical references

World poetry; an anthology of verse from antiquity to our time; Katharine Washburn and John S. Major, editors; Clifton Fadiman, general editor. Norton 1998 xxii, 1338p $45 **808.81**
1. Poetry—Collections
ISBN 0-393-04130-1   LC 97-10879

This volume presents poetry "arranged chronologically in eight sections, from the Bronze and Iron Ages to the 20th century, with each time period subdivided by region and language." Christ Sci Monit

The anthology's "stated aim—'to surprise and delight the common reader'—may seem rather quaint; yet it is a worthy one, and is, on the whole, impressively fulfilled." Times Lit Suppl

Includes bibliographical references

808.82   Drama—Collections

The **Best** men's stage monologues of [date]; edited by Jocelyn A. Beard. Smith & Kraus pa $11.95 **808.82**
1. Monologues 2. Acting
ISSN 1067-134X

Annual. First published 1991 for the 1990 theater season

This title and The Best women's stage monologues provide monologues "from contemporary dramatic luminaries, including Charles L. Mee and Daisy Foote. Both volumes offer scenic descriptions and brief leads into the speechs and indicate the tone (dramatic, comic, or seriocomic). In the volume for women, there are no strictly comedic pieces." Libr J [review of 2000 edition]

The **Best** plays of [date]; edited by Jeffrey Eric Jenkins; illustrated with photographs and with drawings by Hirschfeld. Limelight Eds. $47.50 **808.82**
1. Drama—Collections 2. Theater—United States
ISSN 1071-6971

Annual. First published 1920. Variant titles: The Burns Mantle theater yearbook; The Applause/best plays theater yearbook

Some back volumes published by Dodd, Mead available from Applause Theatre Bk. Pubs.; reprints of older annuals available from Ayer; for full information on availability and price contact publishers

The yearbook gives listings of casts and technical personnel for on- and off-Broadway productions, a summary of the season, synopses and lengthy extracts of dialogue from the best plays, and facts and figures on the New York and regional theater

The **Best** stage scenes of [year]; edited by Jocelyn A. Beard. Smith & Kraus pa $14.95   **808.82**
1. Drama 2. Acting
ISSN 1067-3253
Annual. First published 1992
This title culls "selections from recent plays, divided among scenic groupings for men and women, men, and women. . . . The scenes vary in length and intensity, with each scene providing a setting, description, and the number of needed characters." Libr J

The **Best** women's stage monologues of [date]; edited by Jocelyn A. Beard. Smith & Kraus pa $11.95   **808.82**
1. Monologues 2. Acting
ISSN 1067-134X
Annual. First published 1991 for the 1990 theater season
This title and The Best men's stage monologues, provide monologues "from contemporary dramatic luminaries, including Charles L. Mee and Daisy Foote. Both volumes offer scenic descriptions and brief leads into the speechs and indicate the tone (dramatic, comic, or seriocomic). In the volume for women, there are no strictly comedic pieces." Libr J [review of 2000 edition]

Nine plays of the modern theater; with an introduction by Harold Clurman. Grove Press 1981 896p pa $21   **808.82**
1. Drama—Collections
ISBN 0-8021-5032-2   LC 79-52121
This anthology includes plays by Brecht, Beckett, Dürrenmatt, Genet, Pinter, Ionesco, Mrozek, Stoppard, and Mamet

Ottemiller's index to plays in collections; an author and title index to plays appearing in collections published between 1900 and 1985. 7th ed, revised & enlarged by Billie M. Connor and Helene G. Mochedlover. Scarecrow Press 1988 564p $80   **808.82**
1. Drama—Indexes
ISBN 0-8108-2081-1   LC 87-34160
First edition compiled by John H. Ottemiller, published 1943 by H.W. Wilson
This index analyzes 1,350 collections and "covers plays by 2,555 authors. The arrangement is by playwright, with lists of plays and collections in which each is designated by symbols. A list of collections analyzed and key to symbols and a title index complete the volume." Nichols. Guide to Ref Books for Sch Media Cent. 4th edition

Our dramatic heritage; edited by Philip G. Hill. v4-6. Fairleigh Dickinson Univ. Press 1989-1992 3v v4 $65, v5-6 ea $55
808.82
1. Drama—Collections   LC 81-65294
Also available volumes 1-3 covering classical, Renaissance, golden age and eighteenth century drama
Contents: v4 Romanticism and realism (0-8386-3109-6); v5 Reactions to realism (0-8386-3411-7); v6 Expressing the inexpressible (0-8386-3421-4)
Among the dramatists represented are: Goethe, Ibsen, Strindberg, Brecht, Feydeau and Pirandello

Play index. Wilson, H.W. 1953-2003 10v
808.82
1. Drama—Indexes
ISSN 0554-3037
First published 1953 covering the years 1949-1952, and edited by Dorothy Herbert West and Dorothy Margaret Peake $70. Additional volumes: 1953-1960 $70 edited by Estelle A. Fidell and Dorothy Margaret Peake; 1961-1967 $70 edited by Estelle A. Fidell; 1968-1972 $70 edited by Estelle A. Fidell; 1973-1977 $70 edited by Estelle A. Fidell; 1978-1982 $70 edited by Juliette Yaakov; 1983-1987 $190 edited by Juliette Yaakov and John Greenfieldt; 1988-1992 $190 edited by Juliette Yaakov and John Greenfieldt; 1993-1997 edited by Juliette Yaakov and John Greenfieldt $190; 1998-2002 edited by John Greenfieldt $215
Play index indexes plays in collections and single plays; one-act and full-length plays; radio, television, and Broadway plays; plays for amateur production; plays for children, young adults, and adults. It is divided into four parts. Part I is an author, title, and subject index; the author or main entry includes the title of the play, brief synopsis of the plot, number of acts and scenes, size of cast, number of sets, and bibliographic information. Part II is a list of collections indexed, and Part III, a cast analysis, lists plays by the type of cast and number of players required
"This index is an excellent source for locating published plays." Safford. Guide to Ref Materials for Sch Media Cent. 5th edition

The **Ultimate** audition book; 222 monologues, 2 minutes & under; edited by Jocelyn A. Beard. Smith & Kraus 1997-2002 2v (Monologue audition series) ea pa $19.95   **808.82**
1. Monologues 2. Acting
ISBN 1-57525-066-7 (v1); 1-57525-270-8 (v2)
LC 97-10471
Volume 2 edited by John Capecci, Laurie Walker, and Irene Ziegler
Variant title: 222 monologues, 2 minutes & under from literature
This collection draws "upon lesser-known works from significant writers and those of contemporary favorites and reflects a wide range of tone, age, time period, and voice. Divided among female, male, and unisex categories, all meet the obligatory two minutes or less time limit imposed by most directors and auditions." Libr J [review of volume 2]
Includes bibliographical references

808.83   Fiction—Collections

Short story index. Wilson, H.W.   **808.83**
1. Short stories—Indexes
ISSN 0360-9774   LC 75-649762
Also available Short story index: collections indexed 1900-1978 $125 (ISBN 0-8242-0643-6); Also available CD-ROM version and online
Basic volume edited by Dorothy E. Cook and Isabel S. Monro published 1953 $115 (ISBN 0-8242-0384-4); Supplementary volumes: 1950-1954 edited by Dorothy E. Cook and Estelle A. Fidell $115 (ISBN 0-8242-0385-2); 1955-1958 edited by Estelle A. Fidell and Esther V. Flory $115 (ISBN 0-8242-0386-0); 1959-1963 edited by Estelle A. Fidell $115 (ISBN 0-8242-0387-9); 1964-1968 edited by Estelle A. Fidell $115 (ISBN 0-8242-0399-2); 1969-1973 edited by Estelle A. Fidell $115 (ISBN 0-

Short story index—*Continued*

8242-0497-2); 1974-1978 edited by Gary L. Bogart $180; 1979-1983 edited by Juliette Yaakov $180; 1984-1988 edited by Juliette Yaakov $180; 1989-1993 edited by John Greenfieldt and Juliette Yaakov $200; 1994-1998 edited by John Greenfieldt and Juliette Yaakov $200. Beginning 1974 issued annually with five-year cumulations

This index offers a single-alphabet listing of stories by author, title and subject. The List of collections indexed provides full bibliographic information. Includes a Directory of periodicals

"These indexes provide valuable access to short stories in collections published since 1900." Ref Sources for Small & Medium-sized Libr. 6th edition

808.84 Essays—Collections

The **Art** of the personal essay; an anthology from the classical era to the present; selected and with an introduction by Phillip Lopate. Anchor Bks. (NY) 1994 liv, 777p hardcover o.p. paperback available $17.95

808.84

1. Essays
ISBN 0-385-42339-X (pa)   LC 93-29708
"A Teachers & Writers Collaborative book"

Lopate "has selected and introduced some 75 personal essays, covering over 400 years, from East as well as the West, in an attempt to show the development of the genre." Libr J

"Not only are the selections a veritable feast, but Lopate's genre-defining introduction is not to be missed." Booklist

Includes bibliographical references

The **Norton** book of personal essays; edited by Joseph Epstein. Norton 1997 477p $30

808.84

1. Essays
ISBN 0-393-03654-5   LC 96-26975

George Orwell, James Baldwin, Joan Didion, M. F. K. Fisher, Barbara Tuchman and Cynthia Ozick are among the authors chosen by Epstein for inclusion in this collection of "53 personal essays written in English by well-known authors during the past century. They were chosen because he 'found them interesting, touching, pleasing, amusing, delightful—above all, entertaining.' The result is a potpourri of selections that vary widely in subject and style. Topics range from music, racism, and traveling to fathers, children, and childhood." Libr J

808.85 Speeches—Collections

Sutton, Roberta Briggs

Speech index; an index to 259 collections of world famous orations and speeches for various occasions. 4th ed rev & enl. Scarecrow Press 1966 947p $85   **808.85**

1. Speeches—Indexes
ISBN 0-8108-0138-8

Supplement, 1966-1980, by Charity Mitchell, published 1982 $82.50 (ISBN 0-8108-1518-4)

First published 1935 by the H.W. Wilson Company

"Speeches are indexed by orator, type of speech, and by subject, with a selected list of titles given in the appendix. Particularly useful for amateur speakers in locating examples to use in preparing a speech and models they can adapt to their needs." Ref Sources for Small & Medium-sized Libr. 6th edition

The **World's** great speeches; edited by Lewis Copeland, Lawrence W. Lamm, and Stephen J. McKenna. 4th enl 1999 ed. Dover Publs. 1999 xxii, 920p pa $17.95

808.85

1. Speeches
ISBN 0-486-40903-1   LC 99-32880

First published 1942 by Garden City Pub. Co.

An international collection of approximately 300 speeches by over 200 speakers arranged chronologically

Includes a Topical index, Index by nations and Index of speakers

808.88 Collections of miscellaneous writings

African American quotations; [compiled by] Richard Newman; with a foreword by Julian Bond. Oryx Press 1998 504p $59.95

808.88

1. African Americans—Quotations
ISBN 1-57356-118-5   LC 98-19474

Also available in paperback from Checkmark Bks.

"This collection of more than 2500 memorable quotations from African Americans covers a wide range of historical, contemporary, mainstream, and controversial figures from the 18th century to the present. Activists, actors, artists, athletes, clergy, educators, and writers are well represented." Libr J

American Indian quotations; compiled and edited by Howard J. Langer. Greenwood Press 1996 260p il $65.95   **808.88**

1. Native Americans—Quotations
ISBN 0-313-29121-7   LC 95-33151

"This volume offers 800 quotations covering more than four centuries of American life. Arranged chronologically, the quotations include the words of warriors, poets, politicians, doctors, lawyers, athletes, and others. . . . The book provides brief biographical information about those quoted, including both historical and contemporary figures, and cross-references the material through subject, author, and tribal indexes." Publisher's note

Andrews, Robert, 1957-

The Columbia dictionary of quotations. Columbia Univ. Press 1993 1092p $50.95

808.88

1. Quotations
ISBN 0-231-07194-9   LC 93-27305

This work "offers 18,000 quotes arranged alphabetically by speaker under 1500 well-selected topics. Brief citations to original sources are noted, and *See references* guide one to related quotes under other topics. For those who feel most comfortable quoting contemporaries, this sourcebook supplies an ample serving. . . . This should prove a popular general quotation sourcebook for academic, public, and school libraries." Libr J

Andrews, Robert, 1957—— *Continued*

Famous lines; a Columbia dictionary of familiar quotations. Columbia Univ. Press 1997 xxiii, 625p $38.95 **808.88**
1. Quotations
ISBN 0-231-10218-6   LC 96-43879

This work "contains more than 6,000 witticisms, enduring observations, and incendiary statements from all kinds of people from antiquity to yesterday. Besides identifying the source, Andrews . . . provides details of the first publication, specific chapter and scene, and even the character speaking. Besides quotes from Shakespeare and Oscar Wilde, readers will find fascinating quotes from Monty Python, Gloria Steinem, and maybe your favorite author, for example, Agatha Christie. The more than 500 subject headings include homelessness, AIDS, sexual harassment, murder, and war." Booklist

Includes bibliographical references

Bartlett, John, 1820-1905
Familiar quotations. Little, Brown $50
808.88
1. Quotations
First published 1855. (17th edition 2002) Periodically revised. Editors vary

"Arranged chronologically by author, with exact references. Includes many interesting footnotes, tracing history or usage of analogous thoughts, the circumstances under which a particular remark was made, etc. Author and keyword indexes. One of the best books of quotations with a long history." Guide to Ref Books. 11th edition

Biggs, Mary
Women's words; the Columbia book of quotations by women. Columbia Univ. Press 1996 501p $33.95 **808.88**
1. Quotations 2. Women—Quotations
ISBN 0-231-07986-9   LC 95-47973

"Among the 3,000-plus citations, readers will find thought-provoking insights and commentaries from such women as Susan B. Anthony, Hillary Rodham Clinton, Sojourner Truth, Golda Meir, and Queen Elizabeth I, as well as from lesser-known or even anonymous women. Each saying supplies the speaker (if known), birth and death dates, some biographical information, where and when the quotation was spoken, and the context, where applicable." Am Ref Books Annu, 1997

Boller, Paul F.
They never said it; a book of fake quotes, misquotes, and misleading attributions; [by] Paul F. Boller, Jr., and John George. Oxford Univ. Press 1989 xxv, 159p hardcover o.p. paperback available $15.95 **808.88**
1. Quotations 2. Errors 3. Literary forgeries
ISBN 0-19-506469-0 (pa)   LC 88-22115

In an alphabetical list of attributees' names or titles the authors expose the truth behind more than 200 phony quotations

Chambers dictionary of quotations; editor, Alison Jones; with the assistance of Stephanie Pickering [and] Megan Thomson. Chambers; [distributed by] Larousse Kingfisher Chambers 1997 1515p $39.95 **808.88**
1. Quotations
ISBN 0-550-21019-9

"There are more than 20,000 quotations from more than 4,000 sources. Quotations are arranged alphabetically by author, from *Abbott, Diane Julie*, the first black woman member of Parliament; to *Zwerlin, Mike*, U.S. writer and jazz musician. Just these two examples are an indication of the diversity the editors have sought in the people who are represented by quotes." Booklist

The **Columbia** Granger's dictionary of poetry quotations; edited by Edith P. Hazen. Columbia Univ. Press 1992 1132p $131
808.88
1. Quotations
ISBN 0-231-07546-4   LC 91-42240

This work contains the "most memorable lines written by the greatest poets of English. Quotations are organized alphabetically by poet, and coded so one can find full text in hundreds of current anthologies. With keyword and subject indexing." Univ Press Books for Public and Second Sch Libr

The **Concise** Oxford dictionary of quotations; edited by Elizabeth Knowles. 4th ed. Oxford Univ. Press 2001 541p pa $15.95
808.88
1. Quotations
ISBN 0-19-866268-8   LC 2001-36362
First published 1964

Collected here are quotations by about 2,000 authors from around the world ranging in time from the 8th century BC to the present. Arrangement is alphabetical by the names of authors with sections such as Anonymous, Ballads, The Bible, the Mass in Latin, etc. included in the alphabetical order. Foreign quotations are given in the original language followed by the English translation. Indexed by key words

A **New** dictionary of quotations on historical principles from ancient and modern sources; selected and edited by H. L. Mencken. Knopf 1942 1347p $75 **808.88**
1. Quotations
ISBN 0-394-40079-8

Quotations in prose and poetry arranged under subjects. The quotations are dated and names of authors and titles of books quoted are given in full

Nowlan, Robert A.
Born this day; a book of birthdays and quotations of prominent people through the centuries. McFarland & Co. 1996 257p $45
808.88
1. Quotations
ISBN 0-7864-0166-4   LC 96-4189

"Seven individuals are listed for every day of the year, arranged by year of birth. A capsule description of each precedes a quotation that represents the individual's unique outlook. The people selected represent nearly every profession and place. . . . Some quotations will be

Nowlan, Robert A.—*Continued*

familiar, most will not. They cover an enormous array of topics, ranging from politics and philosophy to music and education." Booklist

The **Oxford** book of aphorisms; chosen by John Gross. Oxford Univ. Press 1983 383p hardcover o.p. paperback available $16.96
              808.88
1. Quotations
ISBN 0-19-282015-X (pa)   LC 82-14263

"Aphorisms, maxims, quotations, and pensées from ancient times to the present comprise this volume. Entries, arranged under subjects such as good and evil, provide the originator, source, and date for the sayings (if known)." Nichols. Guide to Ref Books for Sch Media Cent. 4th edition

The **Oxford** book of death; chosen and edited by D.J. Enright. Oxford Univ. Press 1987 351p $30; pa $16.95   **808.88**
1. Death—Quotations
ISBN 0-19-214129-5; 0-19-280380-8 (pa)
                    LC 82-14341

This is a collection of quotations. Enright divides his "subject into 14 parts, beginning with 'Definitons' and ending with 'Epitaphs, Requiems and Last Words.' He introduces each section . . . [and] then presents his selections." Newsweek

"Much work has gone into this compilation, and the individual introductions to the component sections are, as we would expect, elegant, modest and very wise." Times Lit Suppl

Includes bibliographical references

The **Oxford** dictionary of humorous quotations; edited by Ned Sherrin. 2nd ed. Oxford Univ. Press 2001 xxiii, 512p $35; pa $19.95   **808.88**
1. Quotations 2. Wit and humor
ISBN 0-19-860289-8; 0-19-860666-4 (pa)
                    LC 2001-21062
First published 1995

A compilation of nearly 6,000 quotations arranged in themes. Shakespeare, Austen, Groucho Marx, Monty Python and Roseanne are among humorists and pundits represented. Includes author and key word indexes

The **Oxford** dictionary of political quotations; edited by Antony Jay. 2nd ed. Oxford Univ. Press 2001 497p $40   **808.88**
1. Political science—Quotations
ISBN 0-19-863167-7   LC 2001-271051
First published 1996

"This book aims to present 'a bank of political quotations which are part of the currency of political speeches and writings throughout the English-speaking world.' Thus, the primary qualification for a quote's inclusion 'was not its antiquity or profundity, but its familiarity.' The coverage favors the British, but there is ample treatment of Americans as well as politicians from other countries—ranging from Roman times to the present. . . . The 4000-plus quotations are arranged alphabetically by author, with cross references." Libr J [review of 1996 edition]

The **Oxford** dictionary of quotations; edited by Elizabeth Knowles. 5th ed. Oxford Univ. Press 1999 1136p $45   **808.88**
ISBN 0-19-860173-5   LC 99-12096
First published 1941

Some 20,000 "quotations are arranged in one alphabetical sequence of 2,500 English and foreign authors, the Bible, the Book of Common Prayer, and anonymous works. Most quotations from foreign literatures are given both in their original language as well as in an English translation. Exact bibliographical references are provided for known printed sources. Indexed by keyword." Guide to Ref Books. 11th edition [entry for 4th edition]

The **Quotable** woman; the first 5,000 years; compiled and edited by Elaine T. Partnow. Facts on File 2001 974p $75   **808.88**
1. Quotations 2. Women—Quotations
ISBN 0-8160-4012-5   LC 00-37660
Replaces The New quotable woman, published 1992

This is a "collection of notable quotations by women, from Eve to Madeleine Albright. It includes more than 18,000 quotations from more than 3,600 women throughout history, on subjects from friendship and love to politics, religion, art, and women's role in society." Publisher's note

For a review see: Booklist, July 2, 2002

Includes bibliographical references

Quotations for all occasions; compiled by Catherine Frank. Columbia Univ. Press 2000 260p $55; pa $18.95   **808.88**
1. Quotations
ISBN 0-231-11290-4; 0-231-11291-2 (pa)
                    LC 00-24048

This title "organizes its 1500-plus quotes into three sections that cover 150 different occasions. 'Every Year' contains quotes for such annual events as holidays, birthdays, days of the week, and seasons, while 'Occasionally' encompasses quotes for less frequent events, like going back to school, breaking up, quitting smoking, and school reunions. The final section is for 'Once in a Lifetime' experiences, such as turning 16, getting a first car, menopause, and retirement." Libr J

Includes bibliographical references

Random House Webster's quotationary; Leonard Roy Frank, editor. Random House 1999 1039p hardcover o.p. paperback available $27.95   **808.88**
1. Quotations
ISBN 0-375-71968-7 (pa)   LC 98-30433

"The 20,000 quotations in this volume are arranged by subject, from *ability* to *Zen,* and then alphabetically by author. . . . The quotations include factual statements, song lyrics, slogans, titles, and phrases." Booklist

Toasts; over 1,500 of the best toasts, sentiments, blessings, and graces; [compiled by] Paul Dickson; illustrated by Rollin McGrail. Crown 1991 256p il $19 **808.88**
1. Toasts 2. Wit and humor
ISBN 0-517-58412-3   LC 91-6967
Originally published in different form 1981 by Delacorte Press

"Covering traditional occasions such as anniversaries and weddings as well as a variety of other 'toastable'

Toasts—*Continued*

events, this book organizes 1,500 toasts under 75 alphabetically arranged subject headings. Included are ethnic, military, birthday, and holiday toasts. There are also toasts related to sports, aging, food, parents, and even cheese and champagne! The toasts have been gathered from a variety of toast books, many of which date from the late nineteenth and early twentieth centuries. An interesting history of toasting is included." Booklist

Includes bibliographical references

809 Literary history and criticism

Black literature criticism; excerpts from criticism of the most significant works of black authors over the past 200 years; edited by James P. Draper. Gale Res. 1992 3v il set $365   **809**

1. Literature—History and criticism 2. Black authors 3. Blacks in literature

ISBN 0-8103-7929-5   LC 91-33761

Also available supplement $125 (ISBN 0-8103-8574-0)

Contents: v1 Achebe-Ellison; v2 Emechta-Malcolm X; v3 Marshall-Young

This work covers "significant black writers throughout the world, including Chinua Achebe, Toni Morrison, and Wole Soyinka. Selections were made on the basis of scope, quantity of critical information available, recommendations from notable authorities, retrospective evaluations, seminal articles on authors' works, current commentaries offering recent viewpoints, and interviews and authors' statements regarding their works." Libr J

Bloom, Harold, 1930-

The Western canon; the books and school of the ages. Harcourt Brace & Co. 1994 578p o.p.; Riverhead Bks. paperback available $17   **809**

1. Literature—History and criticism

ISBN 1-57322-514-2 (pa)   LC 93-43542

Bloom examines the "question of which books constitute the core of Western literature and are thus the proper object of serious literary study. . . . The twenty-six authors to whom the bulk of 'The Western Canon' is devoted . . . [are] Shakespeare, Dante, Chaucer, Cervantes, Montaigne, Molière, Milton, Johnson, Goethe, Wordsworth, Austen, Whitman, Dickinson, Dickens, George Eliot, Tolstoy, Ibsen, Freud, Proust, Joyce, Woolf, Kafka, Borges, Neruda, Pessoa, and Beckett." New Yorker

The "book succeeds not as a polemic but as a passionate, erudite and highly idiosyncratic series of essays about the literature dearest to one of America's most influential academics." Publ Wkly

Calvino, Italo

Why read the classics? translated from the Italian by Martin McLaughlin. Pantheon Bks. 1999 277p hardcover o.p. paperback available $13   **809**

1. Literature—History and criticism

ISBN 0-679-74349-9 (pa)   LC 99-21535

Analyzed in Essay and general literature index

This is a collection of literary criticism by the Italian author. "Apart from the title essay, all the pieces treat individual authors or works—almost always works." N Y Rev Books

"Calvino celebrates a wide range of great thinkers in these provocative essays. Here are writers from the ancient world, the Renaissance and recent times, and from the old and new worlds. . . . [These essays] are a reminder to us that 'rereading' the classics can amuse as well as reward." New Sci

Contemporary literary criticism. Gale Res.
                                         809

1. Literature—History and criticism

ISSN 0091-3421   LC 76-38938

Irregular. Started publication in 1973

Volumes 1 to 186, 1973-2004, available at $195 each

"Excerpts from criticism of the works of today's novelists, poets, playwrights, short story writers, scriptwriters, and other creative writers." Title page

"This multivolume, ongoing series offers significant passages from contemporary criticism on authors who are now living or who have died since December 31, 1959. . . . Brief author sketches are followed by critical excerpts, presented in chronological order. The number of authors covered in each volume has varied over the years." Ref Sources for Small & Medium-sized Libr. 6th edition

Cyclopedia of literary places; consulting editor, R. Baird Shuman; editor, R. Kent Rasmussen; introduction by Brian Stableford. Salem Press 2003 3v set $305
                                         809

1. Literary landmarks 2. Literature—Encyclopedias

ISBN 1-58766-094-0   LC 2002-156159

"This three-volume set completes Salem's trilogy of reference works analyzing stories (*Masterplots*), characters (*Cyclopedia of Literary Characters*), and now settings in classic works of literature (mostly novels, though a few plays and poems are included). . . . *Literary Places* provides details of both real and imaginary geographic places that serve as settings for approximately 1300 titles covered in the previous works. . . . The entries are alphabetized by title, range in length from 300 to 1000 words, and feature author, type of work, type of plot, time of plot, and a brief synopsis. . . . Well written, easy to use, and fun to read, this set . . . is a valuable addition to all libraries." Libr J

For a fuller review see: Booklist, August 2003

Includes bibliographical references

Encyclopedia of Holocaust literature; edited by David Patterson, Alan L. Berger; and Sarita Cargas. Oryx Press 2002 263p (Oryx Holocaust series) $54.95   **809**

1. Holocaust, 1933-1945, in literature 2. Holocaust, 1933-1945—Personal narratives 3. Holocaust, 1933-1945—Biography

ISBN 1-57356-257-2   LC 2001-36639

The editors provide a "look at 128 authors of Holocaust literature and their works—poems and plays to diaries and memoirs. . . . The alphabetical entries combine biographical information (especially as it pertains to their experience of the Holocaust) and in-depth analysis of their literary works. Entries list a selection of works by the author, sometimes citing further biographical readings about the author." Choice

For a fuller review see Booklist, Sept 1, 2002

Holocaust literature: an encyclopedia of writers and their work; S. Lillian Kremer, editor. Routledge 2002 2v set $250 **809**
1. Holocaust, 1933-1945, in literature
ISBN 0-415-92985-7   LC 2002-23694
"This encyclopedia synthesizes a wide range of literary voices and provides a compelling look at more than 300 novelists, poets, memoirists, dramatists, and other writers who experienced the Holocaust or otherwise integrated the subject into their works." Publisher's note

Holroyd, Michael
Works on paper; the craft of biography and autobiography. Counterpoint 2002 319p $27 **809**
1. Biography as a literary form 2. Autobiography
ISBN 1-58243-150-7   LC 2002-19371
Analyzed in Essay and general literature index
"Holroyd, himself the biographer of Lytton Strachey and George Bernard Shaw, focuses on the struggles of the biographers of Shaw and E. M. Forster, examining certain theoretical and political concerns and the evolution of the genre over the past century. The book also includes essays on autobiography and diaries, and a final section recounts Holroyd's tribulations as a literary figure." N Y Times Book Rev

James, Henry, 1843-1916
Literary criticism. Library of Am. 1984 2v **809**
1. Literature—History and criticism   LC 84-11241
Edited by Leon Edel and Mark Wilson
Contents: v1 Essays on literature, American writers, English writers $40 (ISBN 0-94050-22-4); v2 French writers, other European writers. The prefaces to the New York edition o.p.
"Grouped by nationality, alphabetically by author, and chronologically, the essays provide a kind of critical book within a book on such writers as Balzac, George Eliot, and Hawthorne. These groupings enable the reader to see how James approached a writer and to follow the development of his thinking about particular writers over the years." Publisher's note
Includes bibliographical references

Jarrell, Randall, 1914-1965
No other book; selected essays; edited and introduced by Brad Leithauser. HarperCollins Pubs. 1999 xx, 376p hardcover o.p. paperback available $15 **809**
1. Stead, Christina, 1902-1983. The man who loved children 2. American poetry—History and criticism 3. Literature—History and criticism
ISBN 0-06-095638-0 (pa)   LC 98-55353
"Jarrell taught his peers to appreciate first the young Robert Lowell and W. H. Auden, then Marianne Moore, William Carlos Williams, Elizabeth Bishop, Walt Whitman and Robert Frost. . . . The later Jarrell divided his prose between appreciations of poets, digressions on idiosyncratic passions, and funny or sad indictments of 1950s-style popular culture. . . . As a convincing, above all personal, guide to modern poets, and as a captivating writer of criticism Jarrell has no obvious 20th century equal." Publ Wkly

Kurian, George Thomas
Timetables of world literature. Facts on File 2003 457p $65 **809**
1. Literature—Chronology
ISBN 0-8160-4197-0   LC 2002-3891
Chronicles world literature from the Classical Age through the twentieth century, discussing literary developments and the relationship between literature and the political and social climate of each historical period
"This comprehensive reference . . . helps academic researchers place major works of literature from 58 countries in historical and cultural context." Libr J
Includes bibliographical references

Literary movements for students; presenting analysis, context, and criticism on literary movements; David Galens, project editor. Gale Group 2002 2v il set $185 **809**
1. Literature—History and criticism
ISBN 0-7876-6517-7   LC 2002-10928
Entries provide "historical background information on each movement as well as modern critical interpretation of each movement's characteristic styles and themes. Approximately 25 movements are covered, including absurdism, Greek drama, modernism, science fiction/fantasy, surrealism and many others." Publisher's note
For a review see: Booklist, Feb. 1, 2003
Includes bibliographical references

Literature and its times; profiles of 300 notable literary works and the historical events that influenced them. Gale Res. 1997 5v set $495 **809**
1. Literature—History and criticism
ISBN 0-7876-0606-5   LC 97-34339
Also available supplement $199 (ISBN 0-7876-6550-9)
Edited by Joyce Moss and George Wilson
"The editors chose the selections (fiction, poetry, short stories, plays, biographies, and speeches) with the input of public libraries and secondary-school teachers. . . . Each volume covers a time range subdivided by dates and a general description . . . and begins with a brief overview of the historical events of the era, with a timeline providing a synopsis of each period." Libr J

Masterpieces of world literature; edited by Frank N. Magill. Harper & Row 1989 957p $55 **809**
1. Literature—History and criticism
ISBN 0-06-270050-2   LC 89-45052
"The work, arranged alphabetically by title, contains plot summaries, character portrayals, and critical evaluations of 270 classics of world literature (novels, plays, stories, poems, and essays), all reprints from other Magill guides." Nichols. Guide to Ref Books for Sch Media Cent. 4th edition

Reference guide to world literature; editors, Sara Pendergast, Tom Pendergast. 3rd ed. St. James Press 2003 2v set $350 **809**
1. Literature—History and criticism 2. Literature—Bio-bibliography
ISBN 1-55862-490-2   LC 2002-15410
First published 1984 by St. Martin's Press with title: Great foreign language writers
Contents: v1 Authors; v2 Works, index

Reference guide to world literature—*Continued*

This work "contains 1,100 entries, about equally divided between entries on authors and on literary works. Each author entry in volume 1 includes a short biography, a signed critical essay, and selected lists of works by and about the author. Each literary work entry in volume 2 includes the author and date of publication (if known), a signed critical essay, and a selected list of critical studies. The scope of coverage is major works in languages other than English from the earliest known manuscripts to present day writers. . . . Because of its comprehensiveness and authority, this sturdily bound set is recommended for ready reference in libraries with large world literature sections and for smaller libraries needing more information in this area." Am Ref Books Annu, 2003

Roth, Philip

Shop talk; a writer and his colleagues and their work. Houghton Mifflin 2001 160p $23
809

1. Authors 2. Literature—History and criticism
ISBN 0-618-15314-4   LC 2001-24523

"In this collection of encounters with distinguished minds—unguarded interviews with Primo Levi and Aharon Appelfeld, among others; an odd exchange of letters with Mary McCarthy; fondly contentious portraits of Bernard Malamud and the painter Philip Guston—Roth manages to tease from his subjects the convictions that fuel their work and the vulnerabilities that make them human." N Y Times Book Rev

The **Schomburg** Center guide to black literature from the eighteenth century to the present; Roger M. Valade III, editor, with Denise Kasinec. Gale Res. 1996 xxvi, 545p il $145
809

1. Literature—Bio-bibliography 2. Black authors—Dictionaries 3. Blacks in literature
ISBN 0-7876-0289-2   LC 95-36733

This is a "one-stop guide and ready reference to authors, works, characters, themes, and topics related to black literature. The scope includes both fiction and nonfiction writing from African American authors and international authors whose works have been translated into English. In a dictionary format, it includes biographical entries as well as separate entries for many individual novels, collections of poems, characters, and screenplays. . . . While the scope is defined as from the eighteenth century to the present, the majority of the entries and fuller treatment are given to late-twentieth-century figures." Booklist

Segel, Harold B., 1930-

The Columbia guide to the literatures of Eastern Europe since 1945. Columbia Univ. Press 2003 xxxi, 641p (The Columbia guides to literature since 1945) $95
809

1. East European literature—Bio-bibliography 2. German literature—Bio-bibliography 3. Authors, East European—Dictionaries 4. Authors, German—Dictionaries
ISBN 0-231-11404-4   LC 2002-25661

Segel examines "the literatures of Albania, Bulgaria, Hungary, Romania, and the former states of Czechoslovakia, East Germany, and Yugoslavia. . . . [He] lays out the striking complexity of the region's intellectual life and the lives and work of its writers." Libr J

Includes bibliographical references

Twentieth-century literary criticism. Gale Res. ea volume $195
809

1. Literature—History and criticism
ISSN 0276-8178   LC 76-46132

Irregularly published series which began publication in 1978

"Excerpts from criticism of the works of novelists, poets, playwrights, short story writers, and other creative writers who lived between 1900 and 1999, from the first published critical appraisals to current evaluations." Title page

Twentieth-century literary movements dictionary; Helene Henderson and Jay P. Pederson, editors. Omnigraphics 1999 xxix, 1037p $80
809

1. Literature—History and criticism
ISBN 1-55888-426-2   LC 99-41091

"A compendium to more than 500 literary, critical, and theatrical movements, schools, and groups from more than 80 nations, covering the novelists, poets, short-story writers, dramatists, essayists, theorists, and works, genres, techniques, and terms associated with each movement." Title page

For a review see: Booklist, Feb. 15, 2000

809.1   Poetry—History and criticism

Borges, Jorge Luis, 1899-1986

This craft of verse; edited by Calin-Andrei Mihailescu. Harvard Univ. Press 2000 154p il (Charles Eliot Norton lectures) $25; pa $14.95
809.1

1. Poetry—History and criticism
ISBN 0-674-00290-3; 0-674-00820-0 (pa)
    LC 00-33541

Also available CD-ROM version

This volume is based on the Argentine writer's "Charles Eliot Norton lectures [delivered] at Harvard in 1967-68. . . . [Borges] discusses some of his favorite texts, conducting a literary journey that began in his father's library in Buenos Aires." N Y Times Book Rev

Includes bibliographical references

Gioia, Dana

Can poetry matter? essays on poetry and American culture; Dana Gioia. 10th Anniversary ed. Graywolf Press 2002 231p pa $16
809.1

1. Poetry—History and criticism 2. Criticism
ISBN 1-555-97370-1   LC 2002-102971

First published 1992

In addition to addressing the business of being a poet and the New Formalism the author offers readings of Robinson Jeffers, Weldon Kees, Robert Bly and others

"Gioia makes his case with erudition and skill, and the best essays bring attention to underappreciated poets like Ted Kooser." Libr J

Koch, Kenneth, 1925-2002

Making your own days; the pleasures of reading and writing poetry. Scribner 1998 317p o.p.; Simon & Schuster paperback available $15　　　　　　　　　　**809.1**
1. Poetry—History and criticism 2. Poetry—Collections
ISBN 0-684-82438-8 (pa)　　　　　　LC 98-15810
"This book is divided into two parts: a series of essays on subjects such as meter, rhyme, and personification and an anthology of favorite poems. Most remarkably, non-English poems often appear with several translations, underscoring the flexibility of poetic language. *Making Your Own Days* will be most useful to writers already familiar with the basics." Libr J

Masterplots II, poetry series. rev ed, editor, Philip K. Jason; project editor, Tracy Iron-Georges. Salem Press 2002 8v set $499　　　　　　　　　　　　**809.1**
1. Poetry—History and criticism
ISBN 1-58765-037-1　　　　　　LC 2001-55059
"This set supersedes the six-volume *Masterplots 2: Poetry Series* (1992) and the three-volume *Masterplots 2: Poetry Series Supplement* (1998). It contains 1,385 signed entries written by scholars on individual poems, arranged alphabetically by poem title and ranging in length from three to five pages apiece." Booklist

The **New** Princeton encyclopedia of poetry and poetics; Alex Preminger and T.V.F. Brogan, co-editors; Frank Warnke, O.B. Hardison, Jr., and Earl Miner, associate editors. Princeton Univ. Press 1993 xlvi, 1383p hardcover o.p. paperback available $45　　　　　　　　　　　　**809.1**
1. Poetry—History and criticism 2. Poetry—Dictionaries 3. Poetics—Dictionaries
ISBN 0-691-02123-6 (pa)　　　　　LC 92-41887
First published 1965 with title: Encyclopedia of poetry and poetics
This work deals with the history, forms, genres, movements and critical approaches to oral and written verse. It examines issues in such areas as: hermenuetics, feminist poetics, Chicano poetry, deconstruction, poststructuralism and cultural criticism. Non-Western and emergent poetries are featured and 106 national poetries are covered

Simon, John Ivan

Dreamers of dreams; essays on poets and poetry; {by} John Simon. Dee, I.R. 2001 xxi, 265p $26　　　　　　　　　　　　**809.1**
1. Rilke, Rainer Maria, 1875-1926. Duino elegies 2. Poetry—History and criticism
ISBN 1-56663-413-X　　　　　　LC 2001-32291
In this "collection of reviews and essays about his first love, poetry, Simon includes several appreciative essays on poets he regards as touchstones of modern poetry—Eliot, Mallarmé, Rilke and Rimbaud—and showcases poets he considers unjustly neglected, like Eric Robertson Dodds." N Y Times Book Rev
"More than any other American critic, Simon illuminates the difficulties and convincingly blasts the incompetence too often characteristic of translations." Booklist

809.2　Drama—History and criticism

Bentley, Eric, 1916-

The life of the drama. Applause Theatre Bk. Pubs. 1991 371p pa $12.95　　　**809.2**
1. Drama—History and criticism
ISBN 1-55783-110-6　　　　　　LC 91-28774
Analyzed in Essay and general literature index
First published 1964 by Atheneum
The author discusses plot, character, dialogue, and action in various theatrical genres. Among the dramatists discussed are Aeschylus, Beckett, Brecht, Chekhov, Corneille, Goethe, Ibsen, Ben Jonson, Molière, Pirandello, Racine, Shakespeare, Shaw, and Sophocles
Includes bibliographical references

Critical survey of drama; edited by Carl Rollyson. 2nd rev ed. Salem Press 2003 8v set $499　　　　　　　　　　　　**809.2**
1. Drama—Dictionaries 2. English drama—Dictionaries 3. American drama—Dictionaries
ISBN 1-58765-102-5　　　　　　LC 2003-2190
"Combines, updates, and expands two earlier Salem Press reference sets: Critical survey of drama, revised edition, English language series, published in 1994, and Critical survey of drama, foreign language series, published in 1986." Preface
This set contains "about 630 essays, of which 570 discuss individual dramatists and 60 cover overview topics. . . . Each essay on a dramatist provides . . . material as birth and death dates, lists of the author's major dramatic works (with dates of first production and publication). Each essay opens with a brief survey of the author's publications in literary forms other than drama, a summary of the writer's professional achievements and awards, an extended biographical sketch that centers on the writer's development as a dramatist, and an extensive critical analysis of the writer's major dramatic works. Following this discussion is a list of major publications in fields other than drama and an annotated bibliography of critical works about the author." Publisher's note

Masterplots II, drama series; editor, Christian H. Moe. rev ed. Salem Press 2003 4v set $404　　　　　　　　　　　　**809.2**
1. Drama—Stories, plots, etc. 2. Drama—History and criticism
ISBN 1-58765-116-5　　　　　　LC 2003-12651
First published 1990
The titles included "represent a diverse range of themes, issues, cultures, minority playwrights, and international locales. While the majority of the plays covered in the set are English-language works, plays from such countries as Italy, France, Germany, the Czech Republic, Nigeria, Poland, South Africa, and Sweden are also covered. The vast majority of the plays were first produced during the twentieth century, while a handful were produced earlier." Publisher's note
"This newest addition to a reference standard belongs in most public, academic, and secondary libraries." Booklist

809.3   Fiction—History and criticism

Beacham's encyclopedia of popular fiction; edited by Kirk H. Beetz. Beacham Pub. 1996-2002 19v   **809.3**
1. Fiction—Bio-bibliography   LC 96-20771
This reference work consists of a three volume set of Biography series and sixteen volumes of Analyses series. Available separately or in sets. Apply to publisher for price

Critical survey of long fiction; editor, Carl Rollyson; editor, English edition, English and foreign language series, Frank N. Magill. 2nd rev ed. Salem Press 2000 8v set $499   **809.3**
1. Fiction—History and criticism 2. Fiction—Bio-bibliography
ISBN 0-89356-882-1   LC 00-20195
Also available as separate volumes ea $60
"The current reference work both updates and substantially adds to the previous editions of the Critical survey from which it is partially drawn: the Critical survey of long fiction. English language series, revised edition (1991) and the Critical survey of long fiction. Foreign language series (1984)." pvii
Contents: v1 Chinua Achebe-Karel Capek; v2 Truman Capote-Stanley Elkin; v3 Ralph Ellison-Jamake Highwater; v4 Oscar Hijuelos-Patrick McGinley; v5 Thomas McGuane-J.B. Priestley; v6 V.S. Pritchett-August Strindberg; v7 Jesse Stuart-Emile Zola; v8 Essays, Index
"The first seven volumes contain lengthy essays arranged alphabetically by author. Each essay includes basic biographical information, a bibliography of writings, and a critical analysis of the author's longer works of fiction. In addition, the final volume includes essays that cover topics such as long fiction in various time frames (Greco-Roman through contemporary) in 17 countries, in North America by many different ethnic groups, and in 16 genres, including the detective novel, the novella, and feminist fiction." Libr J

Critical survey of short fiction; editor, Charles E. May. 2nd rev ed. Salem Press 2001 7v il set $473   **809.3**
1. Short stories—History and criticism 2. Short stories—Bio-bibliography
ISBN 0-89356-006-5   LC 00-46384
First published 1981 under the editorship of Frank Magill
"The first six volumes contain 515 author entries arranged alphabetically. . . . They vary in length but have the same items included, beginning with birth and death dates, and a portrait if available, followed by a list of principle works of short fiction. . . . Volume 7 consists of 29 survey essays on history, theory, and genre as well as world cultures. These vary in length from 3,000 to 10,000 words. A new feature, 'Research Tools,' provides lists of award winners as well as a chronology, glossary, and bibliography." Booklist

The **Encyclopedia** of fantasy; edited by John Clute and John Grant; contributing editors, Mike Ashley [et al.]; consultant editors, David G. Hartwell, Gary Westfahl. St. Martin's Griffin 1999 1079p pa $29.95   **809.3**
1. Fantasy fiction—Encyclopedias
ISBN 0-312-19869-8   LC 98-50905
First published 1997
With more than 4,000 signed entries, this volume "documents and surveys the writers, artists, literatures, and media that have used fantasy themes or have fantasy content, from the form's earliest days until the present. Numerous terms and concepts relevant to fantasy are also defined. Entries are clear and well-written and contain bibliographies when appropriate." Am Libr [review of 1997 edition]

Encyclopedia of the novel; editor, Paul Schellinger; assistant editors, Christopher Hudson, Marijke Rijsberman. Fitzroy Dearborn Pubs. 1998 2v set $295   **809.3**
1. Fiction—Encyclopedias 2. Literature—Encyclopedias
ISBN 1-57958-015-7   LC 99-165908
This work's "650 essays are arranged alphabetically and focus on classic novels, great novel writers, types of novels, novels identified with particular countries or regions, technical and formal aspects of novels, theory, influence, and novel criticism. All of the entries are signed and have been contributed by specialists, and conclude with brief biographies, lists of works, and further readings. There are two indexes: a title index and a detailed, general index." Am Libr

Gay, Peter, 1923-
Savage reprisals; Bleak house, Madame Bovary, Buddenbrooks. Norton 2002 192p il $24.95   **809.3**
1. Dickens, Charles, 1812-1870. Bleak House 2. Flaubert, Gustave, 1821-1880. Madame Bovary 3. Mann, Thomas, 1875-1955. Buddenbrooks
ISBN 0-393-05118-8   LC 2002-21874
The premise of this work "is that novels should not be used as factual sources by academics. Gay musters evidence to demonstrate that Dickens was so prejudiced by his own lawsuit that his depiction of the Court of Chancery in 'Bleak House' ignored reforms already in place; that Flaubert's characterization of the bourgeoisie as uncultivated was unfounded; and that Thomas Mann's Buddenbrook family, though true to type in some ways, was the product of authorial ambivalence and guilt." New Yorker
Includes bibliographical references

Great women mystery writers; classic to contemporary; edited by Kathleen Gregory Klein. Greenwood Press 1994 432p $67.95   **809.3**
1. Mystery fiction—Bio-bibliography 2. Women authors
ISBN 0-313-28770-8   LC 94-16123
"In addition to an introductory essay on women mystery writers by the editor, this book contains a collection of essays describing the life and work of 117 women writers of crime fiction. . . . Entries range from critically renowned and popular writers (e.g., Sayers, Christie, Rinehart) to scarcely known writers published by small, specialty presses." Libr J
Includes bibliographical references

Hooper, Brad

The short story readers' advisory; a guide for librarians. American Lib. Assn. 2000 135p pa $32 **809.3**

1. Short stories—History and criticism

ISBN 0-8389-0782-2 LC 99-85751

This work contains over 200 critical essays covering short story authors past and present. A step-by-step guide on how to interview readers in order to match their tastes with appropriate stories is included

Magill's guide to science fiction and fantasy literature; consulting editor, T. A. Shippey; project editor, A. J. Sobczak. Salem Press 1996 4v set $315 **809.3**

1. Science fiction—History and criticism 2. Fantasy fiction—History and criticism

ISBN 0-89356-906-2 LC 96-26261

"These four volumes cover 791 books or series, 238 of them published during the 1980s and 1990s. The entries are 1,000 words long for single books and 1,500 for series, with a one-sentence summary beginning each entry followed by bibliographical information. . . . Volume 4 contains an extensive bibliography of critical works on science fiction and fantasy, a list of major award winners, a genre index." Booklist

Manguel, Alberto

The dictionary of imaginary places; [by] Alberto Manguel & Gianni Guadalupi; illustrated by Graham Greenfield; with additional illustrations by Eric Beddows; maps and charts by James Cook. Newly updated and expanded. Harcourt Brace & Co. 1999 755p il maps $40; pa $24 **809.3**

1. Fantasy fiction—Dictionaries 2. Geographical myths—Dictionaries

ISBN 0-15-100541-9; 0-15-600872-6 (pa)

LC 99-46994

First published 1980 by Macmillan

This resource "contains entries for more than 1,200 imaginary places from literature and folklore. Each entry describes the place, its locale, and history and provides citations to the source work or tale. More than 220 maps and illustrations are included." Booklist

Includes bibliographical references

Mystery and suspense writers; the literature of crime, detection, and espionage; Robin W. Winks, editor in chief; Maureen Corrigan, associate editor. Scribner 1998 2v set $250 **809.3**

1. Mystery fiction—Dictionaries 2. Mystery fiction—Bio-bibliography 3. Spies in literature

ISBN 0-684-80521-9 LC 98-36812

"Articles on 68 mystery writers ranging from Edgar Allen Poe to Sarah Paretsky run from ten to 20 pages and include information on the life and works as well as solid bibliographies for each author." Libr J

Niebuhr, Gary Warren

Make mine a mystery; a reader's guide to mystery and detective fiction. Libraries Unlimited 2003 605p $65 **809.3**

1. Mystery fiction—Bibliography 2. Mystery fiction—History and criticism

ISBN 1-56308-784-7 LC 2003-271056

"The book is divided into two parts. In part 1, 'Introduction to Mystery Fiction,' Niebuhr devotes considerable space to background material: discussion of readers'-advisory service in general and the appeal of mystery fiction in particular and how to build and manage a mystery collection, followed by a history of the genre beginning in 1845. Part 2, 'The Literature,' annotates more than 2,500 titles by more than 200 authors. . . . Among guides to mystery fiction, this one stands out as being thorough and current. Essential for public libraries." Booklist

The **Oxford** companion to crime and mystery writing; editor in chief, Rosemary Herbert; editors, Catherine Aird, John M. Reilly. Oxford Univ. Press 1999 xxiii, 535p $65 **809.3**

1. Mystery fiction—Dictionaries

ISBN 0-19-507239-1 LC 99-21182

"In addition to the usual biographical/critical sketches of major writers [this work] includes many entries on forms ('Ghost Story'), techniques ('Narrative point of view'), crime magazines (*Black Mask*), characters (Mike Hammer), crime writing in regions such as Australia, and histories of various sorts. There is a glossary and a detailed index, and the signed entries generally include bibliographies." Libr J

For a fuller review see: Booklist, May 1, 2000

A **Reader's** companion to the short story in English; edited by Erin Fallon {et al.}; under the auspices of the Society for the Study of the Short Story. Greenwood Press 2001 xxxiv, 432p $105 **809.3**

1. Short stories—History and criticism

ISBN 0-313-29104-7 LC 00-25113

"Although most of the stories covered by Fallon's compilation were written in the later half of the 20th century, the scope is international. . . . Each chapter concisely profiles a writer and contains a biography, a brief review of criticism, a lengthier analysis of specific works, and a bibliography. A section covers the short story genre. This work is extremely important because of the popularity of the genre." Choice

Short story criticism; excerpts from criticism of the works of short fiction writers. Gale Res. $145 **809.3**

1. Short stories—History and criticism

ISSN 0895-9439

Biannual. First published 1988

This "series presents significant critical excerpts on the most important short story writers of all eras and nationalities. Each entry gives a biographical and critical overview, a list of principal works, excerpts of criticism, and a selected bibliography." Ref Sources for Small & Medium-sized Libr. 6th edition

Short story writers; edited by Frank N. Magill; consulting editor, Charles E. May. Salem Press 1997 3v 1007p il (Magill's choice) set $188   **809.3**
1. Short stories—History and criticism
ISBN 0-89356-950-X   LC 97-23079
"The three volumes consist of essays on 102 writers who are arguably the most popular and most acclaimed of the genre. Extracted from among the 363 essays in the 1993 edition of *Critical Survey* [of short fiction], the essays were updated for this edition." Libr J

St. James guide to fantasy writers; editor, David Pringle. St. James Press 1996 711p (St. James guide to writers series) $185
     809.3
1. Fantasy fiction—Bio-bibliography 2. Fantasy fiction—History and criticism
ISBN 1-55862-205-5   LC 95-48783
This volume "offers an A-to-Z compendium of major fantasy writers. Each entry consists of a brief biography, a complete list of published works, a signed critical essay, and comments from some living authors on their work." Libr J

St. James guide to science fiction writers; with a preface by H. Bruce Franklin; editor, Jay P. Pederson; bibliographic editor, Robert Reginald. 4th ed. St. James Press 1996 xxiv, 1175p $185   **809.3**
1. Science fiction—History and criticism 2. Science fiction—Bio-bibliography
ISBN 1-558620-179-2   LC 95-36171
First published 1981 with title: Twentieth-century science-fiction writers
This alphabetically arranged work "lists 649 writers of science fiction—from the early nineteenth to the late twentieth centuries—as well as writers of fantasy, horror, and other forms of speculative fiction that have had an impact on the SF field. Each entry consists of a brief biography, including pseudonyms, nationality, birth and death dates, education, family, career, agent, and address; a complete list of published works; and a signed, critical essay." Am Ref Books Annu, 1996

Supernatural fiction writers; contemporary fantasy and horror; Richard Bleiler, editor. 2nd ed. Scribner 2003 2v (Scribner writers series) set $250   **809.3**
1. Fantasy fiction—History and criticism 2. Fantasy fiction—Bio-bibliography 3. Horror fiction—History and criticism 4. Horror fiction—Bio-bibliography
ISBN 0-684-31250-6   LC 2002-11128
First published 1985
Contents: v1 Peter Ackroyd to Graham Joyce; v2 Guy Gavriel Kay to Roger Zelazny
This edition "is organized alphabetically by writer. Articles range in length from 5 to 12 pages. There is some biographical information but emphasis is on the works, with analysis of important themes, types of work, and, in many cases, individual series and titles. Each article concludes with a selected bibliography of works by the author under discussion, critical and biographical studies, and Web sites if they are available." Booklist

Symons, Julian, 1912-1994
Bloody murder; from the detective story to the crime novel. 3rd rev ed. Mysterious Press 1993 c1992 349p pa $30   **809.3**
1. Mystery fiction—History and criticism
ISBN 0-89296-496-0   LC 92-54127
First published 1972 in the United Kingdom. Present edition first published 1992 in the United Kingdom
A critical survey of crime fiction, including detective stories, psychological crime stories, thrillers, and espionage, covering authors from Poe to the 1990s

810.3   American literature— Encyclopedias and dictionaries

The **Cambridge** handbook of American literature; edited by Jack Salzman. Cambridge Univ. Press 1986 286p $60
     810.3
1. American literature—Dictionaries 2. American literature—Bio-bibliography
ISBN 0-521-30703-1   LC 86-2587
This handbook's "750 entries, two thirds of them about authors, briefly describe the contents and contribution of key works, assess the careers of writers, and explain the tenets and characteristics of literary movements." Wilson Libr Bull

The **Companion** to southern literature; themes, genres, places, people, movements, and motifs; edited by Joseph M. Flora and Lucinda H. MacKethan; associate editor, Todd Taylor. Louisiana State Univ. Press 2001 xxvi, 1054p $69.95   **810.3**
1. American literature—Southern States—Encyclopedias 2. Southern States—Intellectual life
ISBN 0-8071-2692-6   LC 2001-29959
This sourcebook "explores the multifaceted aspects of the 'southern experience as it is depicted in literature.' Focusing on common threads that run through southern writing and set it apart from the literature of other regions, the more than 500 alphabetical entries cover a wide range of topics." Booklist
"This unique compilation [is] . . . an excellent addition to libraries that support studies of Southern literature." Libr J

Encyclopedia of American literature. Facts on File 2002 3v set $225   **810.3**
1. American literature—Encyclopedias
ISBN 0-8160-4121-0   LC 2001-40900
Contents: v1 The colonial and revolutionary era [by] Carol Ruth Berkin; v2 The age of romanticism and realism [by] Lisa Paddock; v3 The modern and post-modern period [by] Carl Rollyson
"All three volumes feature an introductory essay followed by alphabetically arranged entries and a chronology. The entries, which range from literary figures, genres, and literary characters to specific works, topical entries such as 'Lost Generation,' and musicals, provide not just facts but interpretation of the topic's importance as well." Libr J

Encyclopedia of literature in Canada; edited by William H. New. University of Toronto Press 2002 xxii, 1347p $75 **810.3**
1. Canadian literature—Encyclopedias 2. Authors, Canadian—Bio-bibliography
ISBN 0-8020-0761-9

"The diversity of Canadian literature is evident in this volume that examines English, French, native and multicultural works. Also included are articles on authors, literary and social issues, and significant Canadian historical and cultural events." Booklist

HarperCollins Reader's encyclopedia of American literature; edited by George Perkins, Barbara Perkins, and Phillip Leininger. 2nd ed. HarperResource 2002 1126p $49.95 **810.3**
1. American literature—Encyclopedias
ISBN 0-06-019815-X

"Portions of this book appeared in a somewhat modified form in The Reader's Encyclopedia of American Literature published by T.Y. Crowell in 1962 and in Benet's Reader's Encyclopedia, third edition, published by Harper & Row in 1987." Verso of title page

"The bulk of the book consists of entries on authors, titles, characters, literary genres, periodicals, groups and movements, and historical persons and events directly related to literature. The social, political, religious, and philosophical backgrounds of American literature are treated in entries on presidents, political figures, and military personnel who have figured prominently in literature or themselves contributed to it. Many American military actions are given separate entries, as are documents such as the Mayflower Compact, the Declaration of Independence, the Federalist papers, and the Constitution. American Indian tribes receive coverage along with individual entries on Native American writers." Preface

The **Oxford** companion to American literature. Oxford Univ. Press $70 **810.3**
1. American literature—Dictionaries 2. American literature—Bio-bibliography
First published 1941. (6th edition 1995) Periodically revised

In addition to over 2000 entries for individual authors and more than 1,100 for important works this reference includes entries for literary movements, awards, magazines, printers, book collectors and newspapers. A chronological index of literary and social history is appended

The **Oxford** companion to Canadian literature; general editors, Eugene Benson & William Toye. 2nd ed. Oxford Univ. Press 1997 1199p $75 **810.3**
1. Canadian literature—Dictionaries 2. Canadian literature—Bio-bibliography
ISBN 0-19-541167-6   LC 98-162071
First published 1983

More than 1100 signed entries cover Québéçois, Acadian, and English-Canadian literature

"The scope of this volume is impressive. It includes not only information about writers and poets but also publishers, publishing houses, themes and symbols in Canadian literature, and essays on individual works that stand out as landmarks in the field. It is the kind of reference work one can 'dip into' for interest or use as a quick reference tool." Booklist

Snodgrass, Mary Ellen
Encyclopedia of frontier literature. ABC-CLIO 1997 540p il (ABC-CLIO literary companion) $75 **810.3**
1. American literature—Encyclopedias 2. Frontier and pioneer life in literature
ISBN 0-87436-888-X   LC 97-22028

This "reference explores over 400 years worth of the extensive body of literature about the exploration and settlement of North America, presenting dominant themes, literary history, genres, writers, titles, and characters. The alphabetical entries include authors, individuals, peoples, and themes." Book Rep

810.8   American literature— Collections

American nature writing. Fulcrum Pub. pa $17.95 **810.8**
1. Nature 2. American literature—Collections
Annual. First published 1994. Publisher varies

This annual anthology includes "nature writing—creative nonfiction, fiction, and lyric poetry—from both new and seasoned nature writers." Publisher's note

This is an "exemplary series of contemporary nature writing." Booklist

American sea writing; a literary anthology; Peter Neill, editor; foreword by Nathaniel Philbrick. Library of Am. 2000 xxi, 671p $35 **810.8**
1. American literature—Collections 2. Seafaring life in literature
ISBN 1-88301-183-3   LC 00-39106

This anthology "covers the breadth of American writers from the likes of William Bradford and Cotton Mather to such contemporary authors as Peter Matthiessen and John McPhee. Both popular and obscure works are included." Libr J

Includes bibliographical references

Baseball: a literary anthology; edited by Nicholas Dawidoff. Library of Am. 2002 721p $35 **810.8**
1. Baseball 2. American literature—Collections
ISBN 1-931082-09-X   LC 2001-38654

"Beginning with Thayer's *Casey at the Bat* and ending with Buster Olney, there are more than 700 pages of prose and poetry, fiction and sportswriting, writers and players. Scanning the table of contents, it almost seems like *everybody* wrote about baseball: Damon Runyon, Ring Lardner, James Weldon Johnson, William Carlos Williams, James Thurber. But so did Paul Gallico, Nelson Algren, Tallulah Bankhead, and Jacques Barzun. . . . Ineffable, indispensable, inimitable—just like baseball." Booklist

Crossing the danger water; three hundred years of African-American writing; edited and with an introduction by Deirdre Mullane. Anchor Bks. (NY) 1993 xxii, 769p pa $20   **810.8**
1. American literature—African American authors—Collections
ISBN 0-385-42243-1   LC 93-17194

This anthology "includes fiction, autobiography, poetry, songs, and letters by such writers as Frederick Douglass, Sojourner Truth, W.E.B. Du Bois, Zora Neale Hurston, and Richard Wright. Many topics are covered, from slavery, education, the Civil War, Reconstruction, and political issues to spirituals, songs of the Civil Rights movement, and rap music." Libr J

Includes bibliographical references

Growing up Asian American; an anthology; edited and with an introduction by Maria Hong; afterword by Stephen H. Sumida. Morrow 1993 416p o.p.; Avon Bks. paperback available $13.95   **810.8**
1. American literature—Asian American authors—Collections
ISBN 0-380-72418-9 (pa)   LC 93-14033

"Divided into three sections—First Memories, Beginnings of Identity, and Growing Up—this anthology of heartfelt essays, memoirs, and fictional writings by and about Asian Americans is suggested . . . for collections where there is a demand for Asian American literature." Booklist

Includes bibliographical references

I thought my father was God and other true tales from the National Story Project; edited and introduced by Paul Auster; Nelly Reifler, assistant editor. Holt & Co. 2001 xxi, 383p il $25   **810.8**
1. American literature—Collections
ISBN 0-8050-6714-0   LC 00-54397

Also available in paperback from Picador USA

"In 1999, novelist Paul Auster . . . and the hosts of National Public Radio's All Things Considered asked listeners to send in true stories to be read on-air as part of the National Story Project. Auster received more than 4,000 submissions; the 180 best are published here." Publ Wkly

"These are stop-you-in-your-tracks stories about hair-raising coincidences, miracles, tragedies, redemption, and moments of pure hilarity." Booklist

Jewish American literature; a Norton anthology; [compiled and edited by] Jules Chametzky [et al.] Norton 2000 xxiv, 1221p il $39.95   **810.8**
1. American literature—Jewish authors 2. American literature—Collections
ISBN 0-393-04809-8   LC 00-55393

The editors have attempted "to encompass Jewish literature from 1654 to the present in this collection of poems, cartoons, sermons, diaries, letters, stories, speeches, plays, prayers, novel excerpts, and critical writings either translated from Hebrew or Yiddish or written in English. Major sections group the literature chronologically to help identify large movements. . . . This great anthology is essential for Jewish studies and American literature collections." Libr J

Making Callaloo; 25 years of Black literature, 1976-2000; edited by Charles Henry Rowell. St. Martin's Press 2002 xxx, 433p $34.95; pa $17.95   **810.8**
1. American literature—African American authors—Collections 2. Black authors
ISBN 0-312-29021-7; 0-312-28898-0 (pa)
LC 2001-48783

In Callaloo, editor Rowell has published "some of the finest writers in the African diaspora, from the Caribbean and the Americas to Europe. Assembling in this volume an impressive array of short fiction and poetry from the magazine's first 25 years, Rowell showcases the universality of the black aesthetic while celebrating its diverse handling of themes of sexual identity, regional conflicts, racial contradiction, political mayhem and generational issues." Publ Wkly

Modern American memoirs; selected and edited by Annie Dillard and Cort Conley. HarperCollins Pubs. 1995 449p hardcover o.p. paperback available $16   **810.8**
1. American literature—Collections 2. Authors, American
ISBN 0-06-092763-1 (pa)   LC 95-30755

The editors "have collected excerpts from the memoirs of 35 20th-century American authors. The selections represent the best in autobiographical writing published between 1917 and 1992. Included are nine women and 26 men, both black and white, some better known than others, all distinguished writers and wonderful storytellers. . . . The editors precede each entry with a biographical and contextual note. There's an opening essay on the art of the memoirist and an afterword listing additional classics in the genre." Libr J

The **Norton** anthology of African American literature; Henry Louis Gates, Jr., general editor, Nellie Y. McKay, general editor. 2nd ed. Norton 2003 2800p 2 computer laser optical discs pa $70.30   **810.8**
1. American literature—African American authors—Collections
ISBN 0-393-97778-1   LC 2003-66176

First published 1996

"The anthology is divided into seven sections, each with a separate introduction giving the sociopolitical factors that impacted on the material included therein. Featured are 120 writers, 52 of whom are women, richly representing African American vernacular literature, poetry, drama, short stories, novels, slave narratives, and autobiographies." Libr J [review of 1996 edition]

Includes bibliographical references

The **Norton** anthology of American literature; Nina Baym, general editor. Norton 5v maps apply to publisher for price and availability   **810.8**
1. American literature—Collections

First published 1979. (6th edition, 2003) Periodically revised

An anthology of American prose, poetry and drama dating from 1620 to the late 20th century. Includes essays and introductions to authors and works

The **Oxford** book of the American South; testimony, memory, and fiction; edited by Edward L. Ayers, Bradley C. Mittendorf. Oxford Univ. Press 1997 597p hardcover o.p. paperback available $22 **810.8**
1. American literature—Southern States—Collections
ISBN 0-19-512493-6 (pa) LC 96-45135
"Not limiting themselves to fiction (short stories and novels, either in full or in extract), the editors also gather memoirs, diaries, and essays. From both genders and races, from opposite poles on the economic scale, from an eighteenth-century naturalist to a former slave, from Thomas Jefferson to Eudora Welty, these writings give ringing voice to the experiences that have engendered a distinctive southern culture." Booklist

The **Oxford** book of women's writing in the United States; edited by Linda Wagner-Martin, Cathy N. Davidson. Oxford Univ. Press 1995 596p hardcover o.p. paperback available $19.95 **810.8**
1. American literature—Women authors—Collections
ISBN 0-19-513245-9 (pa) LC 95-1499
This anthology provides "samples of the public and private work of 99 women of diverse racial and ethnic backgrounds who write in English and were born in or have lived in the United States over the past four centuries. They include short fiction (almost half of the book), poems, essays, plays, and speeches but have also gone beyond traditional genre categories to include performance pieces, erotica, diaries, letters, and recipes." Libr J

The **Portable** beat reader; edited by Ann Charters. Viking 1992 xxxvi, 642p hardcover o.p. paperback available $17 **810.8**
1. American literature—Collections 2. Bohemianism
ISBN 0-14-243753-0 (pa) LC 91-16155
"Viking portable library"
"The collection proceeds chronologically and from east to west, in effect tracking Kerouac's cross-country journey and linking the East Coast Beats with San Francisco poets such as Kenneth Rexroth, Lawrence Ferlinghetti, Gary Snyder, and Michael McClure. The works of 'second wave' Beat writers Amiri Baraka (LeRoi Jones), Diana DiPrima, Frank O'Hara, Bob Dylan, even Norman Mailer, to name a few, are included, with the connections to the original group discussed." Booklist
"Cutting through bohemian posturing and excess, Charters here reprints much of the most vital, readable and relevant material produced by the Beat generation." Publ Wkly
Includes bibliographical references

The **Portable** Harlem Renaissance reader; edited and with an introduction by David Levering Lewis. Viking 1994 xlvii, 766p hardcover o.p. paperback available $17 **810.8**
1. American literature—African American authors—Collections 2. Harlem Renaissance
ISBN 0-14-017036-7 (pa) LC 93-30233
"General categories include essay, memoir, fiction, poetry, and drama; specific writers include such expected names as Langston Hughes, Zora Neale Hurston, and Claude McKay, but lesser-known names are also represented. There is anger in these pages and also frustration, pride, pain, and elation, but above all there is incredible talent. Reading the collection straight through would be a wonderful education, but most readers will dip in here and there, and that is edifying, too." Booklist

The **Portable** Western reader; edited and with an introduction by William Kittredge. Penguin Bks. 1997 xxi, 600p pa $14.95 **810.8**
1. American literature—West (U.S.)—Collections
ISBN 0-14-023026-2 LC 96-47243
"Viking portable library"
"Part 1, 'Ancient Stories,' shows the evolution of Native American storytelling from the early legends to contemporary stories and includes writings by Catherine McClellan, John Graves, and Louise Erdrich. Parts 2 and 3 contrast the mythology of the 19th-century 'Western' with the actual experience of living in the West. Most of these authors, from Walt Whitman to Larry McMurtry, will be familiar to readers. Part 4, 'Brilliant Possibilities,' showcases the new generation of Western writers, including Gretel Ehrlich, Jimmy Santiago Baca, and Sherman Alexie." Libr J

The **Pushcart** prize . . . : best of the small presses; an annual small press reader. Pushcart Press $35; pa $17 **810.8**
1. American literature—Collections
Some back numbers available in hardcover and paperback from Pushcart Press and Norton
Annual. First published 1976
Edited by Bill Henderson
Each volume "consists of short stories, poems and essays; includes the work of established and beginning writers, and has a faintly subversive character. Its audience would seem to be primarily the young, yet among its contributors are many of the best writers in America. . . . Like all interesting literary journals, 'The Pushcart Prize' is eclectic and uneven. . . . The number and diversity of journals represented and the sheer length of it are impressive." Books of the Times

"The **Real** war will never get in the books"; selections from writers during the Civil War; edited by Louis P. Masur. Oxford Univ. Press 1993 301p il hardcover o.p. paperback available $18.95 **810.8**
1. American literature—Collections 2. United States—History—1861-1865, Civil War
ISBN 0-19-509837-4 (pa) LC 92-24446
This is a collection of excerpts from letters, journal entries, articles, and speeches written during the American Civil War. The fourteen contributors include such writers as Henry Adams, Louisa May Alcott, Frederick Douglass, Nathaniel Hawthorne, Herman Melville, William Gilmore Simms, Harriet Beecher Stowe, and Walt Whitman
"This collection makes available to a wide audience some of the best contemporary writing about the conflict." Libr J
Includes bibliographical references

A **Renaissance** in Harlem; lost voices of an American community; edited by Lionel C. Bascom. Bard 1999 302p $24   **810.8**
1. American literature—African American authors—Collections
ISBN 0-380-97664-1   LC 99-33449
Compiled with manuscripts from the Library of Congress, Manuscript Division, WPA Writer's Project Collection, 1936-1940
This "anthology of Harlem in the 1920s brings together unpublished material by Ralph Ellison and Dorothy West as well as the stirring voices of ordinary people, including peddlers, prostitutes, Pullman porters, and domestic workers." Booklist

Transcendentalism; a reader; [edited by] Joel Myerson. Oxford Univ. Press 2001 xxxvii, 712p $70; pa $32   **810.8**
1. Transcendentalism—Collections 2. New England—Intellectual life
ISBN 0-19-512212-7; 0-19-512213-5 (pa)
LC 00-21484
This reader "draws together in their entirety the essential writings of the Transcendentalist group during its most active period, 1836-1844. It includes the major publications of the *Dial*, the writings on democratic and social reform, the early poetry, nature writings, and all of Emerson's major essays, as well as an . . . introduction and annotations by Myerson." Publisher's note
Includes bibliographical references

Writing New York; a literary anthology; Phillip Lopate, editor. Library of Am. 1998 xxii, 1050p o.p.; Washington Sq. Press paperback available $22.95   **810.8**
1. American literature—Collections 2. New York (N.Y.) in literature
ISBN 0-671-04235-1 (pa)   LC 98-19332
"Essayist Phillip Lopate has assembled a volume of Gotham-related journalism, poetry, fiction, essays, and diaries which is as rich and varied as its subject. . . . The works are arranged chronologically, beginning with Washington Irving and ending with Vivian Gornick, and they serve as a history of the city's allure for writers." New Yorker

810.9 American literature— History and criticism

Aberjhani
Encyclopedia of the Harlem Renaissance; {by} Aberjhani and Sandra L. West; foreword by Clement Alexander Price. Facts on File 2003 xxi, 424p il maps $65; pa $21.95   **810.9**
1. American literature—African American authors—Encyclopedias 2. Harlem Renaissance
ISBN 0-8160-4539-9; 0-8160-4540-2 (pa)
LC 2002-152067
This work includes essays about personalities, places, literary themes, political and sociological movements, newspapers, and discussions that highlighted the Harlem Renaissance
"An appendix of museums and centers that feature works from the Harlem Renaissance round out this indispensable encyclopedia's 350 entries. An excellent and inspiring work of scholarship." Choice
Includes bibliographical references

African American literary criticism, 1773 to 2000; edited by Hazel Arnett Ervin. Twayne Pubs. 1999 xxix, 543p $50   **810.9**
1. American literature—African American authors—History and criticism
ISBN 0-8057-1683-1   LC 99-29491
This resource assembles more than 150 critical statements about African American literature "including public addresses, literary manifestoes, letters, journal entries, reviews, and analytical studies by such authors as W.E.B. Du Bois, Charles Chesnutt, Langston Hughes, Ann Petry, Toni Morrison, Henry Louis Gates, Jr. and many others. Each entry includes a list of sources for further reading." Publisher's note

Asian American literature; reviews and criticism of works by American writers of Asian descent; Lawrence J. Trudeau, editor, with advisors David Henry Hwang, Ravindra N. Sharma, Kenneth Yamashita. Gale Res. 1999 536p il $140   **810.9**
1. American literature—Asian American authors—History and criticism
ISBN 0-7876-0296-5   LC 98-42124
"This reference lists 45 American writers of Asian descent, giving a photo, a short biography, a list of major works, criticism and reviews, and further resource materials." Libr J
Includes bibliographical references

Black women writers (1950-1980); a critical evaluation; edited by Mari Evans. Anchor Press; Doubleday 1984 xxviii, 543p hardcover o.p. paperback available $25
    810.9
1. American literature—African American authors 2. American literature—Women authors 3. American literature—History and criticism
ISBN 0-385-17125-0 (pa)   LC 81-43914
Critical essays on Maya Angelou, Alice Childress, Toni Morisson, Lucille Clifton, and 11 other post World War II Afro-American women writers
"This important work, a tribute to the corpus of literature produced by black women, is an indispensable resource for any serious student, scholar or teacher desiring to probe the depths of the Afro-American literary tradition." Freedomways
Includes bibliographical references

The **Cambridge** history of American literature; general editor, Sacvan Bercovitch; associate editor, Cyrus R.K. Patell. Cambridge Univ. Press 1994-2003 6v   **810.9**
1. American literature—History and criticism
LC 92-42479
First six volumes of a projected eight volume set
Contents: v1 1590-1820 $100, pa $33 (ISBN 0-521-30105-X; 0-521-58571-6); v2 Prose writing 1820-1865 $100 (ISBN 0-521-30106-8); v5 Poetry and criticism, 1900-1950 $95 (ISBN 0-521-30109-2); v6 Prose writing, 1910-1950 $95 (ISBN 0-521-49731-0); v7 Prose writing, 1940-1990 $90 (ISBN 0-521-49732-9); v8 Poetry and criticism, 1940-1995 $100 (ISBN 0-521-49733-7)
Scholars contribute essays assessing major authors, movements and trends in the development of American literature

Chicano literature; a reference guide; edited by Julio A. Martínez and Francisco A. Lomelí. Greenwood Press 1984 492p $95
810.9
1. American literature—Mexican American authors—Bio-bibliography
ISBN 0-313-23691-7   LC 83-22583
"Signed critical essays on the life and works of Chicano authors and on other topics relevant to the history and development of Chicano literature, including articles on the novel, poetry, theater, children's literature, and Chicano philosophy." Ref Sources for Small & Medium-sized Libr. 6th edition
Includes bibliographical references

Columbia literary history of the United States; Emory Elliott, general editor; associate editors, Martha Banta [et al.]; advisory editors, Houston A. Baker [et al.] Columbia Univ. Press 1988 xxviii, 1263p $119
810.9
1. American literature—History and criticism
ISBN 0-231-05812-8   LC 87-14672
This anthology "expands the traditional subjects of literary history by incorporating current theoretical ideas and newly discovered writers. Includes treatment of recently explored subjects, such as the role of women and minorities in U.S. literature. No separate bibliography other than what is found in the text." N Y Public Libr Book of How & Where to Look it Up

Kazin, Alfred, 1915-1998
An American procession; the major writers from 1830-1930. Knopf 1984 408p o.p.; Harvard Univ. Press paperback available $15.95
810.9
1. American literature—History and criticism
ISBN 0-674-03143-1 (pa)   LC 83-26843
Analyzed in Essay and general literature index
This book "starts with Ralph Waldo Emerson in the 1830's and ends a century later with Eliot, Ezra Pound, John Dos Passos, William Faulkner, Ernest Hemingway, and F. Scott Fitzgerald. . . . Between Emerson and the moderns the critical authors . . . are Thoreau, Hawthorne, Poe, Whitman, Melville, Emily Dickinson, Mark Twain, Henry James, Stephen Crane, Theodore Dreiser, and Henry Adams." N Y Times Book Rev
"Over all, 'An American Procession' is a refresher in the best sense: without any fundamental revision of our understanding of our classics, it vivaciously refreshes our awareness of them, and our gratitude for them." New Yorker

Matthiessen, F. O. (Francis Otto), 1902-1950
American renaissance; art and expression in the age of Emerson and Whitman. Oxford Univ. Press 1941 xxiv, 678p il hardcover o.p. paperback available $32.50
810.9
1. American literature—History and criticism
ISBN 0-19-500759-X (pa)
Analyzed in Essay and general literature index
A critical study of works by Emerson, Thoreau, Melville, Hawthorne and Whitman and their impact on American intellectual history

Miles, Barry, 1943-
The Beat Hotel; Ginsberg, Burroughs, and Corso in Paris, 1958-1963. Grove Press 2000 294p il $25; pa $14
810.9
1. American literature—History and criticism 2. Paris (France)—Intellectual life 3. Bohemianism
ISBN 0-8021-1668-X; 0-8021-3817-9 (pa)
LC 00-20187
An exploration of the period three prominent Beat writers "spent living at 9 rue Git-le-Coeur on the Left Bank of Paris. . . . Miles follows what Ginsberg, Burroughs, and Corso did while living at the Beat Hotel, in particular how the experience affected them by providing a productive context for creativity." Booklist
Includes bibliographical references

Modern American literature. 5th ed. St. James Press 1999 3v set $495
810.9
1. American literature—History and criticism
ISBN 1-55862-379-5   LC 98-38952
First published 1960 by Ungar and edited by Dorothy Nyren. The 5th edition incorporates the 3 volumes of the 4th edition and its 3 supplements and adds 70 new entries. Features expanded coverage of black, Hispanic, Native American and women writers

Native North American literature; biographical and critical information on native writers and orators from the United States and Canada from historical times to the present; Janet Witalec, editor; Jeffery Chapman, Christopher Giroux, associate editors. Gale Res. 1994 xlv, 706p il maps $135
810.9
1. American literature—Native American authors—Bio-bibliography 2. Canadian literature—Native American authors—Bio-bibliography
ISBN 0-8103-9898-2   LC 94-32397
"Representing tribal cultures from Canada and the U.S., the 78 individuals included range from well-known historical figures such as Chief Joseph, Sitting Bull, and Tecumseh to such noted contemporary writers as Louise Erdrich, N. Scott Momaday, and James Welch. . . . The entries themselves appear within two major sections, with part 1 devoted to oral literature (subdivided into oral autobiography and oratory) and part 2 focusing on written literature. Each entry consists of a brief overview of the writer's life and career; a list of major writings; lengthy excerpts from book reviews, critical commentary, interviews, etc.; and a bibliography of secondary sources." Booklist

The **Oxford** companion to African American literature; editors, William L. Andrews, Frances Smith Foster, Trudier Harris; foreword by Henry Louis Gates, Jr. Oxford Univ. Press 1997 xxvii, 866p $65   **810.9**
1. American literature—African American authors—History and criticism
ISBN 0-19-506510-7   LC 96-41565
The contributors "have written not just entries but full articles on writers, the works, the subjects and the genres that have formed African American literature." Publ Wkly
"The signed, well-written, and authoritative entries include helpful bibliographies and extensive cross references. A vital reference tool for both general readers and scholars." Libr J

The **Oxford** companion to women's writing in the United States; editors in chief, Cathy N. Davidson, Linda Wagner-Martin; editors, Elizabeth Ammons [et al.] Oxford Univ. Press 1995 xxx, 1021p $60   **810.9**
1. American literature—Women authors—Dictionaries 2. American literature—Women authors—Bio-bibliography
ISBN 0-19-506608-1   LC 94-26359
This "publication consists of over 800 entries that span four centuries of American women's writing. Full biographies and brief bibliographies detail the lives of women from all ethnic groups and regions of the country, including authors as diverse as Willa Cather and Rita Dove. Women who are not known chiefly as writers are also included, i.e., Rachel Carson, Margaret Mead, and Susan B. Anthony." Libr J
"The strength of this desk reference is its forthright language, even tone, and far-ranging bibliographies." Am Ref Books Annu, 1996

Pierpont, Claudia Roth
Passionate minds; women rewriting the world. Knopf 2000 298p il $26.95; pa $13   **810.9**
1. American literature—Women authors—History and criticism 2. English literature—Women authors—History and criticism 3. Women authors—Biography
ISBN 0-679-43106-3; 0-679-75113-0 (pa)
    LC 99-33349
Literary profiles of Gertrude Stein, Mae West, Margaret Mitchell, Zora Neale Hurston, Ayn Rand, Doris Lessing, Anaïs Nin, Eudora Welty, Marina Tsvetaeva, Hannah Arendt, Mary McCarthy, and Olive Schreiner
"A scintillating collection of brief lives of women writers, a book that sparkles with intelligence, wit and human interest. . . . Unfolding with the dramatic élan of a novella, each one is exhaustively researched, sharply focused, convincingly opinionated." N Y Times Book Rev

Roses, Lorraine Elena, 1943-
Harlem Renaissance and beyond: literary biographies of 100 black women writers, 1900-1945; [by] Lorraine Elena Roses, Ruth Elizabeth Randolph. Hall, G.K. & Co. 1989 413p il o.p.; Harvard Univ. Press paperback available $18.95   **810.9**
1. American literature—African American authors—History and criticism 2. Women authors 3. American literature—African American authors—Bio-bibliography
ISBN 0-674-37255-7 (pa)   LC 89-38731
"Included are the major figures, such as Zora Neale Hurston, as well as many writers who have published only two or three pieces but whose work deserves attention. These short sketches, augmented by bibliographical listings and critical commentary, should provide the impetus for further interest and investigation into long-neglected works. A valuable reference tool." Libr J

Wall, Cheryl A.
Women of the Harlem Renaissance. Indiana Univ. Press 1995 246p il (Women of letters) hardcover o.p. paperback available $14.95
   810.9
1. American literature—African American authors 2. Harlem Renaissance
ISBN 0-253-20980-3 (pa)   LC 95-3132
This study of women writers of the Harlem Renaissance begins with an overview: On being young—a woman—and colored, followed by critical and biographical studies of Jessie Redmond Fauset, Nella Larsen, and Zora Neale Hurston
"Wall offers strong critiques of these women's work, uncovering certain similarities, including, most importantly, the travel motif as not only a reflection of the mass migrations of the day but also a larger dislocation." Publ Wkly
Includes bibliographical references

Wilson, Edmund, 1895-1972
Patriotic gore; studies in the literature of the American Civil War. Oxford Univ. Press 1962 xxxii, 816p o.p.; Norton paperback available $19.95   **810.9**
1. American literature—History and criticism 2. United States—History—1861-1865, Civil War
ISBN 0-393-31256-9 (pa)
Analyzed in Essay and general literature index
"A collection of sixteen essays on writing related to the war including the memoirs of Union generals Grant and Sherman and Confederates Mosby and Lee, diaries, political writing, and fiction by writers such as Ambrose Bierce and John De Forest." Benet's Reader's Ency of Am Lit

811   American poetry

Ackerman, Diane
I praise my destroyer; poems. Random House 1998 114p hardcover o.p. paperback available $12   **811**
ISBN 0-679-77134-4 (pa)   LC 97-34464
"All of the poems reflect intelligence, awareness, and the skillful employment of rhyme, meter, alliteration, and other poetic techniques. The book would be especially useful to those interested in bridging the gap between science and art." Libr J

Jaguar of sweet laughter; new & selected poems. Random House 1991 254p hardcover o.p. paperback available $13   **811**
ISBN 0-679-74304-9 (pa)   LC 90-48243
"Ackerman's lyrical voice and her feeling for detail and nuance are omnipresent in this work, assembled from prior books with ten new poems." Libr J

Origami bridges; poems of psychoanalysis and fire. HarperCollins Pubs. 2002 147p $22.95; pa $11.95   **811**
ISBN 0-06-019988-1; 0-06-055529-7 (pa)
    LC 2002-24685
"Sometimes addressed to herself and her personal history, at least as often addressed to 'Dr. B—,' Ackerman's passionate free verse (short, fluent and adorned by irregular rhyme) describes with nearly unmixed awe the relationship she created with her analyst, and the personal transformation she achieved." Publ Wkly

Adair, Virginia Hamilton

Ants on the melon; a collection of poems. Random House 1996 158p hardcover o.p. paperback available $15 **811**

ISBN 0-375-75229-3 (pa)   LC 95-25977

"The appearance of a first collection by a poet now blind and in her 83rd year must be accounted a triumph. . . . [Adair] works with equal daring in free verse and more traditional forms; her subjects include social and religious commentary, but her principal theme is ordinary experience and its resistance to facile interpretation." Libr J

Beliefs and blasphemies; a collection of poems. Random House 1998 109p hardcover o.p. paperback available $15   **811**

ISBN 0-8129-9245-8 (pa)   LC 97-47403

The author presents poems "on God, Jesus, the church, the world as divine creation, experiences of divine immanence, sin, and the afterlife." Booklist

"Adair's searching verses may not always have the ring of the contemporary, and they often stop short here of fully unfurling their insights. But at its best, this collection points the way back to an American tradition of religious poetry understood and cherished by the likes of Elizabeth Bishop and Louise Bogan." Publ Wkly

Alexie, Sherman, 1966-

One stick song. Hanging Loose Press 2000 91p il $25; pa $15   **811**

ISBN 1-88241-377-6; 1-88241-376-8 (pa)   LC 99-58811

"Whether slyly identifying irony as a white man's invention, or deftly moving from prose-like multilayered narratives to formal poetry and song structures, this . . . collection from . . . Alexie demonstrates many of his skills. Most prominent perhaps is his ability to handle multiple perspectives and complex psychological subject matter with a humor that feeds readability." Publ Wkly

Ammons, A. R., 1926-2001

Glare. Norton 1997 294p $25; pa $15   **811**

ISBN 0-393-04096-8; 0-393-31779-X (pa)   LC 96-48506

This volume is divided into two long poems. Written in couplets, Ammons "wants 'Strip' to be akin to litter, however, casually strewn everywhere. . . . 'Scat Scan', the book's shorter poem, is harder to pin down. Again, Ammons is discursive, delighting in wordplay. He sums up his life through twisted proverbs and ingeniously echoes Frost's two most famous poems, 'The Road Not Taken' and 'Stopping by the Woods on a Snowy Evening.' As with all of Ammons's books, this volume is essential." Libr J

Angelou, Maya

The complete collected poems of Maya Angelou. Random House 1994 273p $24.95   **811**

ISBN 0-679-42895-X   LC 94-14501

This volume contains all of Angelou's published poems including her inaugural poem On the pulse of morning

I shall not be moved. Random House 1997 48p $15; pa $9.95   **811**

ISBN 0-679-45708-9; 0-553-35458-3 (pa)

First published 1990

"Angelou's themes include loss of love and youth, human oneness in diversity, the strength of blacks in the face of racism and adversity." Publ Wkly

The author "speaks eloquently of black life, unfolding a significant history in poems that are highly controlled and yet powerful." Libr J

Ashbery, John

Girls on the run; a poem. Farrar, Straus & Giroux 1999 55p hardcover o.p. paperback available $12   **811**

ISBN 0-374-52697-4 (pa)   LC 99-18682

"Based on an enormous illustrated novel by the reclusive artist Henry Darger (1892-1972), who drew from such ephemeral sources as comic strips and coloring books, this splintered narrative recounts the lives of the Vivians, a plucky band of girls who try to create their own Eden while menaced by figures as cartoonish as themselves. Yet the excitement stays just below the level of video-arcade intensity, thanks to the anesthesizing influence of a narrator who is both wide-eyed and disembodied." N Y Times Book Rev

Selected poems. Viking 1985 349p hardcover o.p. paperback available $17.95   **811**

ISBN 0-14-058553-2 (pa)   LC 85-40549

"Elisabeth Sifton books"

"Ashbery's work is seductive precisely because it alludes to shared traditions and assumptions about poetry. His poems attract us with their gestures of 'meaningful' discourse, the meditative pace of their syntax and the memories and expectations of meaningfulness that it evokes, the careful use of qualifiers, and the precisions and surprises of his diction." Benet's Reader's Ency of Am Lit

Your name here; poems. Farrar, Straus & Giroux 2000 127p hardcover o.p. paperback available $13   **811**

ISBN 0-374-52783-0 (pa)   LC 00-39330

"Lines of surreal imagery, bits of dialogue, and dreamlike scenarios rife with synesthetic metaphor, Ashbery writes in a persona that is sometimes bossy, sometimes wistful, often raving and devil-may-care, then tender, ribald, or sly. . . . As wild and arbitrary as these pell-mell performances feel, they are tightly constructed, rhythmic, and sinuous, and underlying their sparkle are musings on memory, time, loss, angst, and desire." Booklist

Atwood, Margaret, 1939-

Morning in the burned house. Houghton Mifflin 1995 127p hardcover o.p. paperback available $15   **811**

ISBN 0-395-82521-0 (pa)   LC 95-22797

"Atwood brings a swift, powerful energy to meditative poems that often begin in domestic settings and then broaden into numinous dialogues. . . . The most vivid poems forge an apprehensible human aspect from scholarly fields of science, history and religion." Publ Wkly

Selected poems. Simon & Schuster 1978 c1976 240p hardcover o.p. paperback available $15   **811**

ISBN 0-395-40422-3 (pa)   LC 77-18042

First published 1976 in Canada

Atwood, Margaret, 1939—*Continued*

"This collection of the best from all of Atwood's published works, dating back to 1966, points out Atwood's progression as a thinker and poet and makes plain her central concern during the years: the transformations that involves us all." Booklist

Selected poems II; poems, selected & new, 1976-1986. Houghton Mifflin 1987 147p hardcover o.p. paperback available $16   **811**
ISBN 0-86547-197-5 (pa)   LC 87-3861
"Tighter, more compactly selected than her previous 'Selected poems' this volume contains material from Atwood's last three collections, as well as a section incorporating previously uncollected 'New Poems (1985-1986).'" Choice

Berry, Wendell, 1934-

Collected poems, 1957-1982. North Point Press 1985 268p hardcover o.p. paperback available $15   **811**
ISBN 0-86547-197-5 (pa)   LC 84-62305
"'What must a man do to be at home in the world?' This is the overriding concern in Wendell Berry's poems, gathered here from eight books from the past 25 years. Though rooted in the rugged rural landscape of Kentucky, the poems ultimately grow from the landscape of the human heart. The interplay of the natural world and the human spirit is the informing principle." Libr J
"As a nature poet Berry has a grass-roots, homespun quality that reminds one of Frost. He moves easily from witty lyrics and graceful elegies to moving love poems, philosophical odes and confessionals." Publ Wkly

A timbered choir; the sabbath poems, 1979-1997. Counterpoint 1998 216p hardcover o.p. paperback available $13.95
811
ISBN 1-58253-006-3 (pa)   LC 98-4925
"Berry has continued periodically to write poems out-of-doors on days of little other work. This book reprints *Sabbaths*, a collection of that writing, adding to it about one and a half times as much new work. . . . Few other poets have such chaste and precise diction or manage line and stanza with such unaffected serenity." Booklist

Berryman, John, 1914-1972

Collected poems, 1937-1971; edited and introduced by Charles Thornbury. Farrar, Straus & Giroux 1989 347p hardcover o.p. paperback available $25   **811**
ISBN 0-374-52281-2 (pa)   LC 89-30944
"Brings together in chronological order for the first time the seven collections of short poems Berryman himself arranged and published. 'Homage to Mistress Bradstreet' is included, though 'The Dream Songs,' as a self-contained work, is excluded." N Y Times Book Rev
"Berryman's poetry, sometimes mannered, elliptical, and convoluted, is distinguished by precise technical control and continued experiments with style." Reader's Ency. 4th edition

The dream songs. Farrar, Straus & Giroux 1969 xx, 427p hardcover o.p. paperback available $18   **811**
ISBN 0-374-51670-7 (pa)
This book contains the author's 385 'dream songs' that originally appeared in various magazines, the Pulit-

zer Prize winning 77 dream songs (1964) and His toy, his dream, his rest (1968). The poet also provides a brief note about Henry, the poems' central character
"Berryman makes brilliant use of his speaker's indiscriminately retentive perception—the patter of jukeboxes, of cocktail parties, of the gutter and the cathedral—to drop us dizzily into an original world where life is lived naked and unashamed." Va Q Rev

Bishop, Elizabeth, 1911-1979

The complete poems, 1927-1979. Farrar, Straus & Giroux 1983 287p hardcover o.p. paperback available $14   **811**
ISBN 0-374-51817-3 (pa)   LC 82-21119
Supersedes the author's Complete poems, published 1969
This volume contains poems from four collections: North & South (1946); A cold spring (1955, winner of Pulitzer prize); Questions of travel (1965); and Geography III (1977). Also included are translations, uncollected poems, and sections entitled "Poems written in youth" and "Occasional poems"
Bishop's "reputation is founded on perhaps 25 poems. . . . Altogether that looks like a modest achievement until one considers that most of the larger poetic reputations of the past century have been founded on similar evidence. The difference is that Bishop's masterpieces stand in a higher ratio to her work as a whole." N Y Times Book Rev

Bly, Robert

Eating the honey of words; new and selected poems. HarperFlamingo 1999 270p hardcover o.p. paperback available $14.95
811
ISBN 0-06-093069-1 (pa)   LC 98-51152
"Collecting over 200 poems from 1950 to 1998, this volume is an appealing poetic sampler, although the ten new poems are unexciting. The poems celebrating discoveries Bly makes when alone and silent are always striking, and his imaginative prose poems radiate witty delight." Libr J

The night Abraham called to the stars; poems. HarperCollins Pubs. 2001 95p hardcover o.p. paperback available $12.95
811
ISBN 0-06-093444-1 (pa)   LC 00-66360
"The book's 48 lyrics are written in a single (here terceted) form, the ghazal, used by such great Islamic poets as Ghalib, and harness high points of Western art and literature to draw general, biblically backed conclusions about the human condition out of the mire." Publ Wkly

Bogan, Louise, 1897-1970

The blue estuaries: poems, 1923-1968. Farrar, Straus & Giroux 1968 136p pa $15
811
ISBN 0-374-52461-0   LC 76-46175
"Influenced by the English metaphysical poets, Bogan's poetry is subtle, restrained, and intellectual." Benet's Reader's Ency of Am Lit

Booth, Philip, 1925-

Lifelines; selected poems, 1950-1999. Viking 1999 291p hardcover o.p. paperback available $18 **811**

ISBN 0-14-058926-0 (pa)   LC 98-46250

"For many readers, the half-century of poetry collected here will recall Robert Frost—the lines are laconic, reflective, and often informed by Booth's New England background (in this case, Maine). Of course, Booth would not be so admirable if he simply waxed poetic about snow falling from the roof. What makes these poems remarkable is the way he calmly looks life—and death—in the eye and doesn't blink." Libr J

Selves; new poems; by Philip Booth. Viking 1990 75p hardcover o.p. paperback available $9.95 **811**

ISBN 0-14-058646-6 (pa)   LC 89-40317

This collection "features contemplative poems born of the observant patience of North country life. The best are based on concrete observation. . . . Booth's strength is that he speaks of significant issues like the ultimate privacy of suffering, the painful hidden destruction of relationships, the coming of aging and death." Libr J

Bowers, Edgar

Collected poems. Knopf 1997 168p hardcover o.p. paperback available $15 **811**

ISBN 0-679-76607-3 (pa)   LC 96-38580

"Surety of rhythm, swiftness of thought, and deftness of phrase animate Bowers' triumphant poems about loss and the struggle to be whole. He is, above all, a delineator—vital, ironic, capable of panoramic sweep—of his transfiguring experiences in Germany during and after the Second World War. His roots are deep in Horace and Pindar, but amid all the eloquent austerity there are blessed moments of unexpected Mozartian lilt and wit." New Yorker

Brodsky, Joseph, 1940-1996

Collected poems in English, 1972-1999; edited by Ann Kjellberg. Farrar, Straus & Giroux 2000 539p $30; pa $18 **811**

ISBN 0-374-12545-7; 0-374-52838-1 (pa)

LC 00-21059

This volume "gathers all the poetry in English Brodsky originally saw through to press in books (or had earmarked for eventual publication), including Russian poems he translated or co-translated. Originally Russian verse from the '60s and '70s gives way to the later, sometimes lighter, work of his last two decades, when he found a second home in the speech of his adoptive country." Publ Wkly

Brooks, Gwendolyn

Selected poems. Harper & Row 1963 127p hardcover o.p. paperback available $12 **811**

ISBN 0-06-093174-4 (pa)   LC 63-16503

"The subject of this poetry is the lives of African American residents of Northern urban ghettos, particularly women, and Brooks has been praised for her depiction of that experience in forms ranging from terza rima to blues meter." Benet's Reader's Ency of Am Lit

Bukowski, Charles

Bone palace ballet; new poems. Black Sparrow Press 1997 363p hardcover o.p. paperback available $17 **811**

ISBN 1-57423-028-X (pa)   LC 97-12731

"This posthumous collection of poems by Bukowski . . . is a wonderful swan song. The settings remain mostly the same—taprooms, race tracks, and back alleys—and the themes largely unchanged—fragile relationships, heavy drinking, and the art of writing. However, one new theme that surfaces in this collection is the acceptance of death and old age." Libr J

Open all night; new poems. Black Sparrow Press 2000 361p $30; pa $17 **811**

ISBN 1-57423-136-7; 1-57423-135-9 (pa)

LC 00-60833

This "volume is chock-full of the kind of alert if grizzled mutterings we've come to expect from Bukowski—about ex-lovers, binge drinking, disillusioned souls and the racetrack. But 'Open All Night' reveals a more wistful Bukowski—an aging writer fearlessly confronting his mortality." N Y Times Book Rev

The roominghouse madrigals; early selected poems, 1946-1966. Black Sparrow Press 1988 256p hardcover o.p. paperback available $15 **811**

ISBN 0-87685-732-2 (pa)   LC 88-10426

The poems are "gathered from the prolific poet's early, out-of-print, and now scarce pamphlets. . . . The language is a bit less ostentatious than in later work, permitting a gentle and often self-mocking humor to emerge." Libr J

What matters most is how well you walk through the fire. Black Sparrow Press 1999 409p hardcover o.p. paperback available $17 **811**

ISBN 1-57423-105-7 (pa)   LC 99-47459

"In subject, treatment, style, etc., there is nothing new in [this posthumous collection] just more conversational free verses about Henry Chinaski, Bukowski's not-very-alter ego: his lousy childhood and lousier youth, the demanding but often slobby dames he gets involved with, his writing and public reading career, his drinking and his gambling at the horse track, and his aging and approaching death. The humor is as raffish and hilarious as ever." Booklist

Campo, Rafael, 1964-

Diva. Duke Univ. Press 1999 98p $49.95; pa $16.95 **811**

ISBN 0-8223-2383-4; 0-8223-2417-2 (pa)

LC 99-18342

A collection by a gay Hispanic physician/poet

"Much contemporary writing described as 'brutally honest' only assumes that stance, not really taking risks, but Campo's heartfelt prose is the real thing. He lays himself bare and in the process creates art." Libr J

Carruth, Hayden, 1921-

Collected longer poems. Copper Canyon Press 1993 205p $25; pa $14 **811**

ISBN 1-55659-058-X; 1-55659-059-8 (pa)

LC 93-11404

"As Carruth admits in his introductory note, not all the pieces here are among his most critically acclaimed,

Carruth, Hayden, 1921—_Continued_

but certainly some are among his best and most ambitious. Few poetic commemorations of a state are as evocative or witty as the plain-spoken 'Vermont,' and 'The Sleeping Beauty,' with its 125 verse paragraphs—by turns lyrical and harrowing, filigreed and abstract—stands as one of the most challenging and rewarding poetic sequences of the last 25 years." Libr J

Collected shorter poems, 1946-1991. Copper Canyon Press 1992 417p $28; pa $18

811

ISBN 1-55659-048-2; 1-55659-049-0 (pa)

LC 92-3389

"This omnibus volume, more than twice the size of _Selected Poetry_ offers a sampling from nearly all of Carruth's prior collections, plus a selection of 32 previously ungathered pieces written over the last five years. Even the new poems are surprisingly eclectic, including rhymed sonnet, Beat litany, Objectivist lyric, and dramatic monolog. Such variety notwithstanding, Carruth's personal blend of wit, _Weltanschauung_, and conscience is indelibly his own, one of the lasting literary signatures of our time." Libr J

Doctor Jazz. Copper Canyon Press 2001 135p $20; pa $15 **811**

ISBN 1-55659-163-2; 1-55659-193-4 (pa)

LC 2001-3556

"A Lannan literary selection"

"An elegy for his daughter grounds the collection, along with powerful poems on the hardships of contemporary rural life, and yet Carruth remains great fun to read. He is as at home with the prison riots of Attica as he is with Odysseus or Jelly Roll Morton—he is the consummate poet of easeful learning and well-tuned orneriness. Perhaps this is why, at eighty, Carruth—unlike his great master, Frost—keeps getting better." New Yorker

Scrambled eggs & whiskey; poems, 1991-1995. Copper Canyon Press 1996 101p hardcover o.p. paperback available $14 **811**

ISBN 1-55659-110-1 (pa)

LC 96-4487

"This is a poet whose virtuosity has often resembled the precision of pure math, a way of ordering a world where 'Truly we are/the wise animals. Just not wise enough.' Sensuality and easeful death remain his later concerns, and these new poems linger tenderly on their subjects with the poise of Horace. That love and irony and poetry persevere even as the body fails occasions the grace of this masterly collection." New Yorker

Carson, Anne, 1950-

Autobiography of red; a novel in verse. Knopf 1998 149p hardcover o.p. paperback available $12 **811**

1. Stesichorus, ca. 640-ca. 550 B.C. 2. Hercules (Legendary character)—Poetry

ISBN 0-375-70129-X (pa)

LC 97-49472

The core of the book is the author's re-interpretation of a lost poem by the Greek poet Stesichoros entitled 'Tale of Geryon'. In the author's recasting, Geryon, "the red giant of myth, has become a small red-winged person of present day life. . . . Geryon is picked on by his schoolmates . . . and bullied by his big brother. His mother seems to be his only refuge. Falling in love at last with the beautiful Herakles . . . their love becomes the centre of Geryon's life until Herakles suddenly leaves him." Quill Quire

"Is it poetry? Is it a novel in verse? A fable? A myth? However you define Carson's distinctive and wildly inventive new work, it is riveting reading. . . . Wistful yet whimsical, offhand yet intense, funky yet erudite . . . this is a reading experience like no other." Libr J

The beauty of the husband; a fictional essay in 29 tangos. Knopf 2001 147p $24; pa $12 **811**

ISBN 0-375-40804-5; 0-375-70757-3 (pa)

LC 00-62002

This poem is "at once the story of a failed marriage and an exploration of Romantic notions of beauty and truth. But Carson's idiosyncratic voice and her punchy declarative style—'You want a clean life I live a dirty one'—quickly make it clear that hers is a thoroughly modern take on the intimate cruelties of married life. And this is the primary pleasure of her writing: it is both entirely new and strangely familiar, like remembering a private language we thought we'd forgotten." New Yorker

Men in the off hours. Knopf 2000 166p il hardcover o.p. paperback available $12 **811**

ISBN 0-375-70756-5 (pa)

LC 00-267850

The author "makes bold references to everyone from Oedipus to Akhamatova, but the effect of these astute, gemlike little poems is less a history lesson than a challenging conversation in a sunlit garden." Libr J

Carver, Raymond

All of us; the collected poems. Knopf 1998 xxx, 386p hardcover o.p. paperback available $14 **811**

ISBN 0-375-70380-2 (pa)

LC 98-15880

"The great short story writer's poems are dark and funny, like the stories, and tell of domestic discord, crazy adventures and sweet intimacies, sometimes with sorrow but more often with thankfulness and affection." Booklist

Includes bibliographical references

A new path to the waterfall; poems; introduction by Tess Gallagher. Atlantic Monthly Press 1989 xxxi, 126p hardcover o.p. paperback available $12 **811**

ISBN 0-87113-374-1 (pa)

LC 88-34989

"In her moving introduction, Carver's widow, writer Tess Gallagher, notes how often a particular poem calls to mind a corresponding story, and the reverse is also true. Indeed, to know Carver by his prose is to know him only partially. Master at illuminating those often mundane moments that starkly dramatize entire lives, Carver was also master at creating mood, and many of those poems have a striking lyrical intensity, especially when Carver unflinchingly faces death while celebrating life. A coda to a remarkable literary career." Libr J

Cherry, Kelly

Rising Venus; poems. Louisiana State Univ. Press 2002 72p $22.95; pa $15.95

811

ISBN 0-8071-2767-1; 0-8071-2768-X (pa)

LC 2001-5168

"Writing from a woman's point of view in poems that are sometimes larky, always precise and stealthily powerful, [Cherry] articulates various stages of a woman's coping with lost love, moving sure-footedly from witticisms to a joltingly candid depiction of depression and madness." Booklist

Ciardi, John, 1916-1986

The collected poems of John Ciardi; compiled and edited by Edward M. Cifelli. University of Ark. Press 1997 xxxii, 618p hardcover o.p. paperback available $34.95
811

ISBN 1-55728-449-0 (pa) LC 96-46331

"This volume supersedes the earlier *Selected Poems* (1984) providing a vastly more comprehensive sampling of Ciardi's work: 450 poems culled from over 20 individual volumes published between 1940 and 1993. In it we find testimony to Ciardi's desire to achieve not 'a voice,' a style formed to forward an author's individuality, but 'voice'—one that is determined by the externals the poet addresses." Libr J

Clifton, Lucille, 1936-

The terrible stories; poems. BOA Eds. 1996 72p (American poets continuum series) hardcover o.p. paperback available $12.50
811

ISBN 1-880238-37-3 (pa) LC 96-84152

"Clifton crafts brief lines and accessible metaphors into a profound and often humorous commentary on the rich survival skills of women, family love and contemporary American—particularly African American—life. Her cogent 10th collection charts a treacherous terrain of personal and historic tragedy." Publ Wkly

Collins, Billy

Nine horses; poems. Random House 2002 120p $21.95; pa $12.95
811

ISBN 1-4000-6177-6; 0-375-75520-9 (pa)
LC 2002-24868

Collins is "often able to proceed unburdened by many of the tools—assonance, alliteration, wordplay, complex metrics—that hang from the poet's belt; he makes his way in the world by being funny." N Y Times Book Rev

Sailing alone around the room; new and selected poems. Random House 2001 171p $21.95; pa $13.95
811

ISBN 0-375-50380-3; 0-375-75519-5 (pa)
LC 99-52861

"Collins will tackle any topic: his subject matter varies from snow days to Aristotle to forgetfulness. The results are accessible but not trite, comical but not laughable, and well crafted but not overly flamboyant. Collins relies heavily on imagery, which becomes the cornerstone of the entire volume." Libr J

Corso, Gregory, 1930-2001

Mindfield; with foreword by William S. Burroughs & Allan Ginsberg; and drawings by the author. Thunder's Mouth Press 1989 268p il hardcover o.p. paperback available $13.95
811

ISBN 0-938410-86-5 (pa) LC 89-5152

Also available limited edition

"This volume includes substantial selections from each of [the author's] six volumes of published poetry and 23 previously unpublished poems. Corso has written a number of the most memorable American poems since WW II. His poetry combines a lyrical directness of speech with a unique blend of surrealism and aphoristic statement." Choice

Creeley, Robert, 1926-

The collected poems of Robert Creeley, 1945-1975. University of Calif. Press 1982 671p hardcover o.p. paperback available $24.95
811

ISBN 0-520-04244-1 (pa) LC 81-19668

Creeley's style is "notably spare and laconic; his primary subject is love and the infinite incongruities that characterize love relationships. There is a distinct dearth of imagery in his poetry; the themes are rendered in a cerebral rather than sensual manner. For Creeley, the intent of the poem is definition, not description." Reader's Ency. 4th edition

Life & death; poems. New Directions 1998 87p $19.95; pa $9.95
811

ISBN 0-8112-1384-6; 0-8112-1449-4 (pa)
LC 97-45805

"Creeley's poems have always been to-the-point, but here they are scrubbed down to the essentials, as befits the theme: Creeley is a mature poet, looking back on life and considering what (little) might lie ahead. Intense, shadowed, and powerfully restrained, these poems are miniatures but hardly small. Creeley has packed them with tremendous vision." Libr J

Selected poems. University of Calif. Press 1991 xxii, 366p $50; pa $19.95
811

ISBN 0-520-06935-8; 0-520-06936-6 (pa)
LC 91-7152

"A Centennial book"

"This new sampling both refines and builds upon its predecessors, *Selected Poems* and *Collected Poems*. From the nearly antagonistic minimalism of 'A Piece' ('One and/one, two,/three') through the philosophical expansiveness of 'Desultory Days' and beyond, it becomes apparent that Creeley's work has not so much opened up over the years as fluctuated in its attentions to self and world." Libr J

Cummings, E. E. (Edward Estlin), 1894-1962

95 poems; edited, with an afterword, by George James Firmage. Liveright 2002 102p pa $13
811

ISBN 0-87140-181-9 LC 2002-72482

This is a reissue with a new afterword of the title first published 1958 in a limited edition by Harcourt Brace & Co.

This poetry collection, the last published in E. E. Cumming's lifetime, celebrates the birds and the flowers, the rain, the snow, the moon, spring and love

Cunningham, J. V. (James Vincent), 1911-1985

The poems of J.V. Cunningham; edited with an introduction & commentary by Timothy Steele. Swallow Press 1997 xxxviii, 215p $32.95; pa $19.95
811

ISBN 0-8040-0997-X; 0-8040-0998-8 (pa)
LC 97-355

"Cunningham is an austere poet with a passion for exact statement in tightly controlled forms, whose ideal poetic models were those of Roman satire and the conceits of the most formal sixteenth- and seventeenth-century poetry. . . . His chosen form is the classical epigram, his elected idiom the satiric and self-parodic, which allows for the play of wit and irony in his commentary on the absurdity of human life." Oxford Companion to 20th Cent Lit in Engl

Di Piero, W. S.

Skirts and slacks; poems. Knopf 2001 66p
hardcover o.p. paperback available $15 **811**
ISBN 0-375-70942-8 (pa)   LC 2001-88080

Di Piero "speaks conversationally but with concentration of loss, displacement and ordinary life, whether in personal relationships or in a kind of celebration of the run-down South Philadelphia of his childhood." N Y Times Book Rev

Dickinson, Emily, 1830-1886

The complete poems of Emily Dickinson;
edited by Thomas H. Johnson. Little, Brown
1960 770p $35; pa $19.95   **811**
ISBN 0-316-18414-4; 0-316-18413-6 (pa)

A chronological arrangement of all known Dickinson poems and fragments

New poems of Emily Dickinson; edited by
William H. Shurr with Anna Dunlap & Emily
Grey Shurr. University of N.C. Press 1993
125p $27.50; pa $13.95   **811**
ISBN 0-8078-2115-2; 0-8078-4416-0 (pa)
            LC 93-20353

This volume increases Dickinson's "body of work by 498 selections. Shurr has accomplished this by combining three volumes of the poet's letters and identifying epigrams, riddles, and various longer lyrical pieces within the prose. These will both challenge and delight serious readers, for wit, unusual rhythms, and musical rhymes predominate." SLJ

Includes bibliographical references

Dillard, Annie

Mornings like this; found poems.
HarperCollins Pubs. 1995 75p hardcover o.p.
paperback available $11.95   **811**
ISBN 0-06-092725-9 (pa)   LC 95-8675

"What Dillard has done is construct poems out of 'bits of broken text'; that is, she's lifted sentences and used them to create original poems on her own themes. So these are language collages, meticulous and surprisingly effective. Dillard found gems embedded in such unlikely and obscure sources as a boys' project manual, nineteenth-century scientific texts, and memoirs, and she has turned them into poems of wonderful resonance, some very moving, others quite funny." Booklist

Dobyns, Stephen, 1941-

Pallbearers envying the one who rides.
Penguin Bks. 1999 149p il pa $15.95   **811**
ISBN 0-14-058916-3   LC 99-18492

In this collection "Dobyns pays complex tribute to admired poets John Berryman, Zbigniew Herbert, and others and in the process mines a new richness for his already skillful verse." Libr J

Dove, Rita

On the bus with Rosa Parks; poems.
Norton 1999 95p hardcover o.p. paperback
available $11   **811**
ISBN 0-393-32026-X (pa)   LC 98-45057

Dove's "poems effortlessly suggest grand narratives and American myths, yet ground themselves tersely in localities, characters, practicalities and particulars. This seventh collection leads off with a Dove specialty, the historical sequence: her 'Cameos' lend broad, social relevance to an intermittently abandoned Depression-era wife and her family." Publ Wkly

Selected poems. Vintage Bks. 1993 xxvi,
210p pa $13   **811**
ISBN 0-679-75080-0   LC 93-26112

"This volume places three previous collections under one cover. . . . The selection begins with *The Yellow House on the Corner,* Dove's first book, most notable for its poems derived from slave narratives. *Museum,* her second book, offers a potpourri of work that ranges over several continents and many millenia; Dove's tirelessly exact language illuminates the lives of saints, contemporary lifestyles, and Greek myths." Booklist

Dugan, Alan, 1923-2003

Poems seven; new and complete poetry.
Seven Stories Press 2001 422p $35; pa
$18.95   **811**
ISBN 1-58322-265-0; 1-58322-512-9 (pa)
            LC 2001-41089

This collection documents "Dugan's project of comic, bleak and formally varied commentary on a dirty, terminally frayed and yet attractive America. . . . This carefully constructed, funny and sometimes unvarying volume combines all six of Dugan's previous books with a decade's worth of new verse." Publ Wkly

Duncan, Robert Edward, 1919-1988

Ground work II; in the dark; [by] Robert
Duncan. New Directions 1987 90p $19.95; pa
$9.95   **811**
ISBN 0-8112-1041-3; 0-8112-1042-1 (pa)
            LC 87-11033

"This, [Duncan's] last volume, at least in part a reflection on that upcoming death, may yet turn out to be his most important. . . . In In the Dark, Robert Duncan dares to address an absolute, where no life stirs, where sleep, waking, and dream all are foreign, where a kind of purity reigns—'And purity begins to flame when we see the word fire in it,' as Duncan wrote in his letter. Duncan's poetry makes its way straight into that flame in the dark." Am Book Rev

Dunn, Stephen, 1939-

Different hours; poems. Norton 2000 121p
$22; pa $12.95   **811**
ISBN 0-393-04986-8; 0-393-32232-7 (pa)
            LC 00-30556

"Stephen Dunn's poetry is strangely easy to like: philosophical but not arid, lyrical but rarely glib, his storytelling balanced effortlessly between the casual and the vivid. But don't mistake that ease for lack of staying power." N Y Times Book Rev

Local visitations; poems. Norton 2003 96p
$21.95   **811**
ISBN 0-393-05200-1   LC 2002-14204

"The opening section of poems recasts Dunn's average American as the mythic Sisyphus, imprisoned by repetitive work ('a repetition/which would never mean more/at the end than at the start') and yet bereft without it ('But more often he finds himself dreaming/of his rock, wishing it back, the better/to defend himself against so many hours'). Nearly half the collection transports 19th-century literary figures to contemporary New Jersey towns ('Mary Shelley in Brigantine,' 'Hawthorne in Tuckerton'), a series of poems more attractive in concept than in practice, where the subjects often fail to transcend the contrivance they inhabit." Libr J

Dunn, Stephen, 1939-—*Continued*

Loosestrife. Norton 1996 96p $19; pa $12
811

ISBN 0-393-03982-X; 0-393-31683-1 (pa)
LC 96-1238

"Dunn understands that there is sorrow in beauty and a 'strange loneliness' even in pleasure, and he examines these dichotomies in language and form as clear and chilling as ice. We feel knocked off balance by the end of one line, then steadied by the beginning of the next." Booklist

Eady, Cornelius, 1954-

Brutal imagination; poems. Putnam 2001 108p $24; pa $13
811

ISBN 0-399-14718-7; 0-399-14720-9 (pa)
LC 00-62674

"A Marian Wood book"

In this "collection of poetry, Eady invokes a chorus of fictional black characters, from Uncle Tom to the invented criminal whom Susan Smith blamed for the kidnapping of her children. A white woman's 'stray thought,' this man haunts the best of these spare, stirring poems. If the poet's premise—the personification of a black figment of the white imagination—is complex, his verse is unsettlingly direct." New Yorker

Eliot, T. S. (Thomas Stearns), 1888-1965

Collected poems, 1909-1962. Harcourt Brace & World 1963 221p $23
811

ISBN 0-15-118978-1

This volume contains the complete text of 'Collected poems, 1909-1935,' the 'Four quartets,' and several other poems accompanied by brief prefatory notes

Inventions of the March Hare; poems 1909-1917; edited by Christopher Ricks. Harcourt Brace & Co. 1997 xlii, 428p $30; pa $15
811

ISBN 0-15-100274-6; 0-15-600587-5 (pa)
LC 96-45399

"Though available in manuscript to scholars since 1968, this is the first appearance—for all but five poems—of Eliot's 'lost' notebook of drafts and fragments. Eliot never intended this unfinished work to see publication, but in page after page his autumnal sensibility, his signature aura of languid urban malaise—however tentative—surfaces unmistakably. . . . For scholars and devotees, Eliot's rehearsals for immortality will yield a cornucopia of delights." Libr J

Emerson, Ralph Waldo, 1803-1882

Collected poems & translations. Library of Am. 1994 637p $35
811

1. Dante Alighieri, 1265-1321. The new life
ISBN 0-940450-28-3
LC 93-40245

Contains Emerson's published poetry, plus selections of his unpublished poetry from journals and notebooks, and some of his translations of poetry from other languages, notably Dante's La vita nuova

Fairchild, B. H. (Bertram H.), 1942-

Early occult memory systems of the Lower Midwest. Norton 2002 125p $22.95
811

ISBN 0-393-05096-3
LC 2002-71886

This poetry "collection journeys through the intersections of imagination and history across the plains of the Midwest." Publisher's note

This is a "strong, compelling collection. . . . If strong emotion courses through Fairchild's work, it never makes it lachrymose, thanks to concrete vocabulary and images, direct syntax, and propulsive rhythms." Booklist

Ferlinghetti, Lawrence

These are my rivers; new & selected poems, 1955-1993. New Directions 1993 308p il hardcover o.p. paperback available $13.95
811

ISBN 0-8112-1273-4 (pa)
LC 93-10383

"Reading this hefty selection from 12 previous volumes, plus 50 pages of new poems, we realize how accurately the poet described himself in 1979: a man who 'thinks he's Dylan Thomas and Bob Dylan rolled together with Charlie Chaplin thrown in.' . . . His style is recognizable throughout—phlegmatic poems running several pages, often lacking stanza breaks, with short lines at the left margin or moving across the page as hand follows eye." Libr J

Gander, Forrest, 1956-

Torn awake. New Directions 2001 95p pa $13.95
811

ISBN 0-8112-1486-9
LC 2001-32657

"There is no solid ground in the world Forrest Gander conjures in his new book of poems, yet his tentativeness is one of this book's essential qualities. . . . The voices vary throughout this book's six highly speculative sequences, . . . yet again and again they call from their spectral airiness a single recurring image, an elemental configuration of man, woman and child." N Y Times Book Rev

Gibbons, Reginald, 1947-

It's time: poems. Louisiana State Univ. Press 2002 64p $22.95; pa $15.95
811

ISBN 0-8071-2814-7; 0-8071-2815-5 (pa)
LC 2002-73076

This collection of poems considers "all manner of things: the migration of birds, the vast variety of hats, and, in a nearly 200-line work called 'Poem Including History' that serves as the volume's centerpiece, Europe itself." Libr J

"If the thoughtful poems in Gibbons' elegant seventh collection were pieces of music, they would be measured piano sonatas, each note, each word, carefully struck, precisely enunciated." Booklist

Gibran, Kahlil, 1883-1931

The Prophet. Knopf 1923 107p il $15
811

ISBN 0-394-40428-9

Also available pocket library editions

A collection of poems by the mystical writer/artist, who was born in Lebanon and died in the United States, in which the prophet Almustafa deals with fundamental aspects of human life such as love, friendship, good and evil, self-knowledge, passion and reason, joy and sorrow, freedom, work, marriage and children, prayer and death

Ginsberg, Allen, 1926-1997

Collected poems, 1947-1980. Harper & Row 1984 xxi, 837p il hardcover o.p. paperback available $24.95
811

ISBN 0-06-091494-7 (pa)
LC 84-47573

A "collection of the poetry of the most celebrated Beat, gathered from the many small-press volumes and magazines in which they have appeared, with sometimes extraordinary notes by the poet." N Y Times Book Rev

Ginsberg, Allen, 1926-1997—*Continued*

Selected poems, 1947-1995. HarperCollins Pubs. 1996 442p il hardcover o.p. paperback available $18 **811**
ISBN 0-06-093376-3 (pa)   LC 96-33824

"Roughly half the size of 1984's *Collected Poems* the selection is nevertheless massive, spanning pieces written in the poet's early twenties to those written just a year or two ago on the threshold of his seventies, an avalanche of songs, rants, and chants. Never less than engaged . . . Ginsberg unleashes tidal celebrations of homoeroticism, leftist politics, Eastern mysticism, and Beat camaraderie." Libr J

Giovanni, Nikki

Blues; for all the changes: new poems. Morrow 1999 100p $15 **811**
ISBN 0-688-15698-3   LC 98-50996

"Giovanni never loses sight of the people in her work. In poems built with broken lines and paragraphs of prose, she spars with the ills that confront us, but every struggle has a human face." Libr J

Love poems. Morrow 1997 96p $14 **811**
ISBN 0-688-14989-8   LC 96-43698

"In one way or another, love shapes most of Giovanni's smart, to-the-point, and emotionally candid poems, but it's wonderful to have a volume devoted strictly to her love poems, especially since it contains 20 new compositions." Booklist

"Funny yet thoughtful, Giovanni celebrates creative energy and the family spirit of African American communities." Libr J

The selected poems of Nikki Giovanni (1968-1995). Morrow 1996 224p $22 **811**
ISBN 0-688-14047-5   LC 95-31646

"Writing as an African American and as a woman, Giovanni speaks with powerful music about politics, love, feminism, and family." Booklist

Glück, Louise, 1943-

Meadowlands. Ecco Press 1996 61p hardcover o.p. paperback available $13 **811**
ISBN 0-88001-506-3 (pa)   LC 95-33526

Glück "interweaves vignettes of the Odyssey and a distressed modern marriage. Grimly serious parables, amusing but disquieting spousal conversations and insightful commentaries written in the voice of Telemachus, Odysseus's son, season the 46 poems. . . . These compressed and tightly focused poems are organized into a short collection of exceptional punch." Publ Wkly

The seven ages. Ecco Press 2001 68p hardcover o.p. paperback available $12.95
811
ISBN 0-06-093349-6 (pa)   LC 00-46654

This is a "book in which repetition functions as incantation, forming a hazy magic that's alternately frightening and beautiful. Whether Glück is talking about her relationship with her sister, a love affair or her own grappling with the passage of time, her insistence on getting at what lies beyond the physical world through seemingly ordinary details produces raw emotion covered with a deceptively simple sheen." N Y Times Book Rev

Goldbarth, Albert

Combinations of the Universe. Ohio State Univ. Press 2003 175p $44.95; pa $19.95
811
ISBN 0-8142-0925-4; 0-8142-5105-6 (pa)
LC 2002-013169

Also available CD-ROM version

"Entranced by life and passionate about the imagination, Goldbarth draws startling comparisons between the visions of myth, art, and science. Exuberant and erudite, he does 'what the brain has been evolved/to do: make wholeness." Booklist

Graham, Jorie, 1951-

The dream of the unified field; selected poems, 1974-1994. Ecco Press 1995 199p hardcover o.p. paperback available $15 **811**
ISBN 0-88001-476-8 (pa)   LC 95-16572

"Combining great vision like Blake's, a Dickinsonian philosophical introspection, and a richly modern sensuality, this selection demonstrates the full range of Graham's poetic gifts." Booklist

Never; poems. Ecco Press 2002 112p $22.95; pa $13.95 **811**
ISBN 0-06-008471-5; 0-06-008472-3 (pa)
LC 2001-51279

"Graham brings such fervor and inquisitiveness to her observation of the living world, she achieves an almost scientific precision as she attempts to describe the sensory totality experienced within a woods or on a stretch of beach. . . . Like Wallace Stevens, Graham is a metaphysical poet who loves landscape and can't help but address a higher power even as she questions every aspect of existence." Booklist

H. D. (Hilda Doolittle), 1886-1961

Collected poems, 1912-1944; edited by Louis L. Martz. New Directions 1983 xxxvi, 629p hardcover o.p. paperback available $21.95 **811**
ISBN 0-8112-0971-7 (pa)   LC 83-6380

This volume includes "H.D.'s poetry, published and unpublished, through her *Trilogy* completed in 1944, excepting her verse dramas and poems in prose works. Also excluded is the late verse in *By Avon River* and *Helen in Egypt*." Libr J

The editor's textual notes "offer valuable and illuminating scholarly commentary and present the most important of the textual variants. An informative and sensitively written introduction discusses aspects of the interpenetration of H.D.'s biography with her poetic sensibility. This volume is an impressive scholarly work." Choice

Hacker, Marilyn, 1942-

Selected poems; 1965-1990. Norton 1994 250p $22; pa $13.95 **811**
ISBN 0-393-03675-8; 0-393-31349-2 (pa)
LC 94-27507

"Few poets have been as successful as Hacker in negotiating the boundary of the feminist and lesbian canon while generating a buzz around their early work. Iambic and readable, the pieces in *Selected Poems*—taken from five previous volumes—use unique inversions to explore self and other through changing situations between friends, lovers, family, and one's surroundings. . . . Often, these are poems of loss, of desire delayed, of pleasure deferred." Libr J

Hacker, Marilyn, 1942-—*Continued*

Squares and courtyards. Norton 2000 107p
$21; pa $12 **811**
ISBN 0-393-04830-6; 0-393-32095-2 (pa)
LC 99-39110
"With customary fortitude and intelligence, Hacker
confronts such sobering subjects as the trauma of her
own chemotherapy and the loss of friends, in poems that
are at once clear-sighted and emotionally full." New
Yorker

Hall, Donald, 1928-

Old and new poems. Ticknor & Fields
1990 244p hardcover o.p. paperback available
$16 **811**
ISBN 0-89919-954-2 (pa) LC 90-31087
This collection "gathers a generous selection of the
work from 1947 to the present. Mr. Hall, as this collection makes clear, has improved with the years. . . . In
the triumphant work of his maturity, in a burly line not
strictly metrical but full-blown in its sonority, Mr. Hall
celebrates with grieving joy the transmutation of matter
into energy and the consumption of life by death, death
seen as the unrefusable essence of life itself." N Y Times
Book Rev

The old life. Houghton Mifflin 1996 134p
hardcover o.p. paperback available $13 **811**
ISBN 0-395-85600-0 (pa) LC 96-1853
"The title poem is a long, autobiographical examination of a life that has embraced the pleasures and pains
of marriage, the ups and downs of a literary career, and
the mistakes of youth and wisdom of old age. . . . The
supporting cast of three other poems reveals Hall's versatility as a poet willing to take linguistic risks without
alienating the reader from the significance of one man's
life. Essential reading." Libr J

The painted bed. Houghton Mifflin 2002
87p $23; pa $14 **811**
ISBN 0-618-18789-8; 0-618-34075-0 (pa)
LC 2001-51620
"In his 1998 collection, 'Without,' Donald Hall had
only one subject, his grief over the death of his wife, the
poet Jane Kenyon. In 'The Painted Bed,' he continues
his grieving and attempts to overcome it in a collection
that combines long, reflective, blank-verse narratives and
brief (and more successful) lyrics. Perhaps only a poet of
Hall's stature and powers could pull off a book like
this—filled with raw sexual disclosures, rowdy anger and
a self-blasting mockery." N Y Times Book Rev

Harjo, Joy, 1951-

A map to the next world; poetry and tales.
Norton 2000 138p hardcover o.p. paperback
available $13 **811**
ISBN 0-393-32096-0 (pa) LC 99-41099
"One of the most significant American Indian poets
here expands her poetic practice to include what she calls
tales but might as easily be considered prose poems.
Harjo's verse has lately taken on a flowing, narrative
quality; these tales, by contrast, take an imagistic,
stream-of-consciousness form. . . . Written with authority and Harjo's trademark exploratory verve, this is fine,
mature work." Booklist

Harrison, Jim, 1937-

The shape of the journey; new & collected
poems. Copper Canyon Press 1998 463p $30;
pa $20 **811**
ISBN 1-55659-095-4; 1-55659-149-7 (pa)
LC 98-25501
"This large collection, which also includes a new grab
bag of nature verse and prose poems called 'Geo-
Bestiary,' has a meandering feel, although Harrison's
concerns—aging, women, eating and drinking, hunting,
the craft of writing and above all the spirit and rhythms
of the natural world—are remarkably constant. . . . Harrison's writing is graceful, direct and muscular, even in
those occasional places where the poems feel like
dashed-off diary entries or, rarer still, when they hit a
mawkish note." N Y Times Book Rev

Hass, Robert, 1941-

Sun under wood; new poems. Ecco Press
1996 77p hardcover o.p. paperback available
$15 **811**
ISBN 0-88001-557-8 (pa) LC 96-19322
The poems in this "collection—artfully assembled
from prose, epigram, conversation, and free verse—prove
both meditative and emotional. Hass is able to
aestheticize loss without succumbing to either nostalgia
or self-consciousness. Ranging widely, from obscure philology to dragonflies mating, his new poems are plangent
and ecstatic." New Yorker

Hayden, Robert Earl, 1913-1980

Collected poems; edited by Frederick
Glaysher. Liveright 1985 205p hardcover o.p.
paperback available $15 **811**
ISBN 0-87140-159-2 (pa) LC 84-28880
"Hayden's poetry is a blend of unrivaled craftsmanship with a sharp, unrestrained vision. His subjects encompass the whole of human experience, from the extremely personal but never obscure ('Approximations') to
the historical but never pedantic ('Belsen, Day of Liberation'). His technique is similarly varied. Hayden is as adept with haiku, imitations of Eskimo song-poems, or sonnets as he is with free verse. A particularly important addition to libraries with black literature collections."
Booklist

Hecht, Anthony, 1923-

The darkness and the light; poems. Knopf
2001 67p $23; pa $15 **811**
ISBN 0-375-41194-1; 0-375-70946-0 (pa)
LC 00-62007
"Hecht knows his classics and uses them, to the extent
of including translations of ancient, medieval, and modern master poets in this book. He appreciates the perdu-
rable forcefulness and relevance of classic situations and
conceits." Booklist

Flight among the tombs; poems; wood
engravings by Leonard Baskin. Knopf 1996
76p il hardcover o.p. paperback available $16
811
ISBN 0-679-76592-1 (pa) LC 96-19619
"The first section, 'Presumptions of Death,' consists of
a collaboration between Hecht and artist Leonard Baskin,
whose wood engravings illustrate a remarkably ironic series of poems written from death's point of view. . . .
The remainder of the book contains new poems on various subjects, but death haunts those pages, too, as Hecht
bids adieu to soul mates James Merrill and Joseph
Brodsky." Booklist

Hillman, Brenda
Cascadia. Wesleyan Univ. Press 2001 77p (Wesleyan poetry) $26; pa $13.95 **811**
ISBN 0-8195-6491-5; 0-8195-6492-3 (pa)
LC 2001-35504
"Geologists know 'Cascadia' as the name for the landmass that became the American West Coast: Hillman's serial mix of long and short poems links Californian geology, geography, history (a Gold Rush-era diarist named Shirley), continental philosophy, and personal experience. . . . Some poems are content with their lyrical verbal effects; others play with typography for effects that are energetic, familiar to readers of Susan Howe and Jorie Graham." Publ Wkly

Hirsch, Edward
Earthly measures; poems. Knopf 1994 93p hardcover o.p. paperback available $18 **811**
ISBN 0-679-76566-2 (pa)
LC 93-26410
"Hirsch contemplates manifestations of the divine in this set of ravishing poems infused with a deeply felt sense of place and history, seeking insights into how instances of spiritual revelation occur in the frequently brutal everyday world." Booklist

Lay back the darkness; poems. Knopf 2003 73p $23 **811**
ISBN 0-375-41521-1
LC 2002-072991
"Sandwiched between two series of classically themed lyrics—the first on Orpheus, the second on Hades—are first-person meditations on life, death, faith, and family, as well as a long poem dedicated to the memory of the 15,000 children who were imprisoned in the Nazi camp at Terezin (Theresienstadt)." Libr J
"Hirsch puts his vaunted formal skills to careful use, creating characters readers will recognize immediately." Publ Wkly

On love; poems. Knopf 1998 86p hardcover o.p. paperback available $15 **811**
ISBN 0-375-70260-1 (pa)
LC 97-49460
"The affirmation of On Love is its language, and the sense it gives that the language of love is inexhaustible. However conversant with the abyss, however true to the devastating logic of desire, the poems ultimately feel triumphant. They are held aloft by nothing but their own joyous artistry." Yale Rev

Hollander, John
Figurehead & other poems. Knopf 1999 89p hardcover o.p. paperback available $15 **811**
ISBN 0-375-70433-7 (pa)
LC 98-14208
Hollander's "justifiably confident in his skills, the solid grace of his constructions, and his ability to make both the light and dark sides of words, thoughts, and even life itself simultaneously visible. It's no wonder that among nimbly philosophic poems about Arachne, Cain, and a painting by Velázquez he disarms, charms, and intrigues his readers with a witty and imaginative tribute to the tabletop sculptures of Saul Steinberg and a bittersweet remembrance of George Moran, an old vaudevillian." Booklist

Selected poetry. Knopf 1993 338p hardcover o.p. paperback available $18 **811**
ISBN 0-679-76198-5 (pa)
LC 92-54789
"Hollander's frequently honored poetry has the gloss of the academy, a European flavor, and a classical con-sciousness. His allusions to ancient Greece and Rome, the Old Testament, and the Talmud forge fresh links to a spiritual and literary past, while his philosophical musings often segue pointedly into sly humor or resigned thoughts of death." Booklist

Howes, Barbara, 1914-1996
Collected poems, 1945-1990. University of Ark. Press 1995 134p hardcover o.p. paperback available $16 **811**
ISBN 0-679-76592-1 (pa)
LC 94-32343
"How often has a forgotten writer been resurrected, heralded as an important voice, only to end up a disap-pointment? All too often, alas. Luckily, this is not the case with Barbara Howes, who . . . is as obscure a worthy poet as I can think of. Her book not only exceeds expectations, but exceeds them in ways I never would have guessed. . . . Certainly there is much in this book for lovers of poetic forms: villanelles, sestinas and a 'Near-Pantoum,' as the poet calls it." N Y Times Book Rev

Hughes, Langston, 1902-1967
The collected poems of Langston Hughes; Arnold Rampersad, editor; David Roessel, associate editor. Knopf 1994 708p $39.95; pa $18 **811**
ISBN 0-679-42631-0; 0-679-76408-9 (pa)
LC 94-14509
"The editors have attempted to collect every poem (860 in all) published by the writer in his lifetime, and have also provided a brief but informative introduction, a detailed chronology and extensive textual notes that include the original date and place of publication for each poem. . . . Although Hughes is best known for his poems celebrating African American life, he was also a passionately political poet." Publ Wkly

Selected poems of Langston Hughes; drawings by E. McKnight Kauffer. Knopf 1959 297p il hardcover o.p. paperback available $13 **811**
ISBN 0-679-72818-X (pa)
This collection represents Langston Hughes' own decisions as to which of his poems he wanted to preserve and reprint

Hugo, Richard F.
Making certain it goes on; the collected poems of Richard Hugo. Norton 1983 xxi, 456p hardcover o.p. paperback available $15.95 **811**
ISBN 0-393-30784-0 (pa)
LC 83-8016
"Though he would never be a serene poet, his collected poems show Hugo turning toward a calm peace that would mark his best work in 'White Center' (1980) and 'The Right Madness On Skye' (1981), and in the 22 new poems in this volume. . . . Among the new poems included [here] Hugo was still driving, looking, and naming. If we had not noticed before that his great gift was the elegy, we see it now." N Y Times Book Rev

Ignatow, David, 1914-1997

I have a name. University Press of New England 1996 75p (Wesleyan poetry) hardcover o.p. paperback available $13.95 **811**

ISBN 0-8195-2240-6 (pa)   LC 96-19350

"Ignatow's words are spare and apparently casual, holding us riveted by the force of what is articulated but not spoken. . . . The subjects are timeless: loss, age, death, the joy of fleeting moments." Booklist

Shadowing the ground. Wesleyan Univ. Press 1991 68p (Wesleyan poetry) hardcover o.p. paperback available $13.95 **811**

ISBN 0-8195-1197-8 (pa)   LC 90-20872

"Here are sixty-five short, spare, untitled poems, their uniformity of appearance (two-thirds of them ten lines or fewer) belying the plural perspectives that David Ignatow brings to his considerations of age and death's imminence. . . . Shadowing the Ground celebrates contrary responses to unplanned obsolescence." World Lit Today

Jackson, Major, 1968-

Leaving Saturn; poems. University of Ga. Press 2002 75p pa $15.95 **811**

ISBN 0-8203-2342-X   LC 2001-43072

"Major Jackson, through both formal and free verse poems, renders visible the spirit of resilience, courage, and creativity he witnessed among his family, neighbors, and friends while growing up in Philadelphia." Publisher's note

Jacobik, Gray

Brave disguises. University of Pittsburgh Press 2002 80p il (Pitt poetry series) pa $12.95 **811**

ISBN 0-8229-5788-4   LC 2003-273029

"Jacobik's multivalent poems of the mind and the body require constant attention to the mental-physical interplay in them, but her skillful prosody, straightforward syntax, and common vocabulary make gratifying work of meeting the poems' demands." Booklist

Jacobsen, Josephine

In the crevice of time; new and collected poems. Johns Hopkins Univ. Press 1995 258p (Johns Hopkins, poetry and fiction) hardcover o.p. paperback available $19.95 **811**

ISBN 0-8018-6339-2 (pa)   LC 95-2798

"In this retrospective spanning nearly six decades of distinguished poetry, the best work comes at the beginning and the end. A contemporary of Robert Penn Warren and Elizabeth Bishop, Jacobsen continues to write stately poems informed by irony, fatalism, and an eloquent appreciation of strength in all its guises, physical and moral. An unabashed formalist, she carefully composes poems that are aggressively metrical . . . and whose surfaces are dense with metaphor, rhyme, assonance, alliteration, and omniscient authority." Libr J

Jarrell, Randall, 1914-1965

The complete poems. Farrar, Straus & Giroux 1969 507p hardcover o.p. paperback available $20 **811**

ISBN 0-374-51305-8 (pa)

Collected here are the entire contents of three published volumes Selected poems (1955), The woman at the Washington Zoo (1960), and The Lost World (1965) plus poems published from 1934 to 1964 but never collected and some never before published

Jeffers, Robinson, 1887-1962

The collected poetry of Robinson Jeffers; edited by Tim Hunt. Stanford Univ. Press 1988-2001 5v set $300 **811**

ISBN 0-8047-4418-1   LC 87-18083

Individual volumes also available ea $75

Contents: v1 1920-1928; v2 1928-1938; v3 1938-1962; v4 Poetry 1903-1920, prose, and unpublished writings; v5 Textual evidence and commentary

"Jeffers' strengths and weaknesses as a poet are inextricable, but he wrote nothing trivial. His narratives owe much to the example of Edward Arlington Robinson, but they surpass the model and have not been equaled since. Their plots and characterizations are repetitive and even obsessive, but the narrative pulse of the ten and five stressed lines is both supple and controlled, while the interspersed authorial commentary varies the cadence and lends shrewd perspective. No reevaluation can ignore them. The shorter poems share the same rhythm of lyric thrust checked by terse observation and dicta." Benet's Reader's Ency of Am Lit

Johnson, James Weldon, 1871-1938

Complete poems; edited with an introduction by Sondra Kathryn Wilson. Penguin Bks. 2000 xxxiii, 202p pa $14 **811**

1. African Americans—Poetry

ISBN 0-14-118545-7   LC 00-39969

This volume contains Fifty years and other poems (1917), God's trombones (1927), Saint Peter relates an incident of the resurrection day (1935), and a number of previously unpublished poems. The editor's introduction considers Johnson's achievements and influence

Justice, Donald Rodney, 1925-

New & selected poems; [by] Donald Justice. Knopf 1995 176p hardcover o.p. paperback available $17 **811**

ISBN 0-679-76598-0 (pa)   LC 95-22618

"This collection features works culled from six previous titles, plus a dozen uncollected poems. . . . Meter and rhyme are featured throughout. If not using—often irregularly—a classic form, Justice improvises one, melding language, meaning and rhythm in a seemingly seamless whole." Publ Wkly

Kenner, Hugh

The Pound era. University of Calif. Press 1971 606p il hardcover o.p. paperback available $24.95 **811**

1. Pound, Ezra, 1885-1972

ISBN 0-520-02427-3 (pa)

"A detailed account of Pound's career from the viewpoint of ideas, movements, and personalities of his age. A main theme of the book is that to Pound and his era, ages and cultures share in a basic continuity. . . . Vorticism, imagism, social credit, China—all receive detailed new treatment as the author probes their impact on Pound's work." Libr J

"As a reader of Pound, Kenner is superb. He moves with ease and authority through the most tangled passages of allusion, ideogram and fragments of Greek and Latin. As an advocate pleading for the 'Cantos' to be recognized as a successful and crucial imaginative achievement, he is perhaps less convincing." N Y Times Book Rev

Includes bibliographical references

Kerouac, Jack, 1922-1969

Book of blues. Penguin Bks. 1995 273p (Penguin poets) pa $13.95   **811**

ISBN 0-14-058700-4   LC 94-45902

A "set of eight previously unpublished 'blues' poems written between 1954 and 1961. These long poems, series of 'choruses' or sketches, resemble, in form and avidity, Kerouac's amazing verse creation *Mexico City Blues* (1959). They are strongly tied to place and are, as the allusion to music implies, boldly improvisational." Booklist

Pomes all sizes; introduction by Allen Ginsberg. City Lights Bks. 1992 175p pa $13.95   **811**

ISBN 0-87286-269-0   LC 92-1204

"This book, which Kerouac prepared for publication before his death in 1969, collects poems written between 1954 and 1965. Most are playful—comments about friends, variations on the sounds of words. Yet a few extremely sensitive longer pieces appear, including 'Caritas,' in which the poet runs after a barefoot beggar boy to give him money for shoes and then begins to doubt the boy's veracity. Other intriguing poems reflect the poet's religious concerns of the moment, running the gamut of Eastern and Western religions." Libr J

Scattered poems. City Lights Bks. 1971 76p pa $7.95   **811**

ISBN 0-87286-064-7

"The Pocket poets series"

This collection "contains poems that either have previously appeared in periodicals or have not appeared in print at all. The poems are delightfully representative of Kerouac: that free and easy style of writing from the music of the imagination, without a score to follow. Those familiar with the San Francisco school of poetry will readily see Kerouac's affinity in style and content with such writers as Rexroth, Everson, Snyder, Ferlinghetti, Ginsberg, et al. . . . Kerouac sings in the American language to an American tune." Libr J

Kinnell, Galway, 1927-

Imperfect thirst. Houghton Mifflin 1994 81p hardcover o.p. paperback available $15   **811**

ISBN 0-395-75528-X (pa)   LC 94-27044

"The language in Kinnell's twelfth collection of poetry is intimate and uninflected, seemingly at the service of nothing more than the precise sensuous detail, the moment of passion or remembrance in which the poem happens to be absorbed. But even readers unfamiliar with this splendid poet's obsessions will sense that his apparent casualness belies a tremendous project." New Yorker

Kizer, Carolyn

Cool, calm & collected; poems 1960-2000. Copper Canyon Press 2000 509p $30; pa $20   **811**

ISBN 1-55659-146-2; 1-55659-181-0 (pa)

LC 00-10243

Kizer "covers civil rights, women's rights and almost everything in between, but even when she's writing about more intimate matters, her underlying concern is freedom. . . . Despite her constant railing against the machine, however, Kizer's poetry remains fundamentally optimistic, perhaps because she seems to love existence almost in spite of herself." N Y Times Book Rev

Koch, Kenneth, 1925-2002

New addresses; poems. Knopf 2000 73p $23; pa $15   **811**

ISBN 0-375-41027-9; 0-375-70912-6 (pa)

LC 99-53978

"Read in one sitting, these enthusiastic apostrophes can be wearyingly whimsical. . . . But the best of the poems, when each is taken on its own terms, bolster the bold belief that underpins much of Koch's career—namely, that to be a continually gracious and grateful writer is not to be a precious or deluded one." N Y Times Book Rev

A possible world; poems. Knopf 2002 96p $24; pa $15   **811**

ISBN 0-375-41492-4; 0-375-71000-0 (pa)

LC 2002-72477

"In his glorious final work, Koch returns to classical forms to express his profound yet bemused gratitude for life, however strange and imperfect. . . . The poet visits the Acropolis, Rome, and Kuala Lumpur, and muses on how varied life is, how quickly the dead are gone, and how long the influence of lovers and friends is felt. Wryly and affectionately reflective, teasingly subversive, and still vitally curious and joyfully creative, Koch brings all his wisdom and artistry to 'A Memoir,' a charming and deeply affecting poem that embraces the dark and the light, a chiming, indelible song of himself, of every self." Booklist

Sun out; selected poems from 1952-1954. Knopf 2002 141p $25; pa $15   **811**

ISBN 0-375-41491-6; 0-375-70999-1 (pa)

LC 2002-20534

This is "a collection of early poems that Koch observed 'are in such a different style . . . that they never seemed to fit into my books.' Koch was hanging out with a lot of painters at the time, and these poems do have more concrete imagery and perhaps tamer lines than his other works, but Koch's classic snap, crackle, and pop are still there." Libr J

Komunyakaa, Yusef

Talking dirty to the gods; poems. Farrar, Straus & Giroux 2000 134p hardcover o.p. paperback available $13   **811**

ISBN 0-374-52793-8 (pa)   LC 00-21277

"Komunyakaa's mournful surrealism seems to have found a perfect mathematical embodiment in this . . . collection, which comprises a hundred and thirty-two poems of four four-line stanzas. These are poems about the uncontrollable human and natural mysteries, and they are made sharper and more mysterious by the eternal recurrence of the stanzaic structure." New Yorker

Thieves of paradise. University Press of New England 1998 128p (Wesleyan poetry) $26; pa $14.95   **811**

ISBN 0-8195-6330-7; 0-8195-6422-2 (pa)

LC 97-40294

"The central subjects of Komunyakaa's poetry—his experiences in the Vietnam War and as an African-American male—have always been made compelling in his hands, and equally compelling has been the moodily energetic, jazz-inspired improvisatory technique that he employs with increasing mastery. But what is most gratifying about Komunyakaa's surrealist riffs, with their almost hallucinatory lushness, is their power to convince us that the individual imagination is more than equal to the most excruciating historical burden." New Yorker

Kumin, Maxine, 1925-
Connecting the dots; poems. Norton 1996
86p $18.95; pa $11.95 **811**
ISBN 0-393-03962-5; 0-393-31695-5 (pa)
LC 95-44441
"Kumin's is a poetry of wide sympathy and tact in which the ecumenical flavor is dominant, starting with the author's description of herself as a 'Jewish agnostic' educated at a convent school. Here both the odd and the even are at home: New Hampshire farm country as well as cosmopolitan Boston, Heidegger and Berlioz interwoven among depictions of spring training, Bosnia, and a New Year's Eve party. This collection is full of generational severance and renewal." New Yorker

The long marriage; poems. Norton 2001
118p $21; pa $12 **811**
ISBN 0-393-04351-7; 0-393-32437-0 (pa)
LC 2001-34553
"Although several of the poems treat Kumin's 50-plus year marriage, one feels that the book's title may refer to 'marriage' as a kind of covenant between the poet and her environment. . . . Divided into seven sections, this collection also includes poems about sociopolitical situations (capital punishment, extinct wildlife, revolutions), considerations of aging and rehabilitation, and tributes to Hopkins, Wordsworth, Rukeyser, and Rilke." Libr J

Selected poems, 1960-1990. Norton 1997
294p $27.50; pa $17.95 **811**
ISBN 0-393-04073-9; 0-393-31836-2 (pa)
LC 96-42433
"A pastoral poet who was strongly influenced by friend and mentor Anne Sexton, Kumin is quite simply one of the very best poets writing today. The present collection represents a lifetime . . . of Kumin's work and includes selections from all her published volumes." Libr J

Kunitz, Stanley, 1905-
The collected poems. Norton 2000 285p
$27.95; pa $15.95 **811**
ISBN 0-393-05030-0; 0-393-32294-7 (pa)
LC 00-41130
In this volume "Kunitz brings together his entire oeuvre, including many unavailable early works and poems from the recent *Passing Through.*" Libr J
"What makes this collection of a lifetime's work so valuable is the way it allows us to perceive the interconnectedness of all Kunitz has written. Each poem stands alone, but each also enriches the others." N Y Times Book Rev

Passing through; the later poems, new and selected. Norton 1995 175p hardcover o.p. paperback available $13 **811**
ISBN 0-393-31615-7 (pa) LC 95-2651
This volume "includes works from three collections published since 1971 as well as nine poems written since 1985. Such longevity has been most kind to Kunitz, who writes in 'The Round': 'I can scarcely wait til tomorrow/when a new life begines for me,/as it does each day,/as it does each day.' And it is this enthusiasm for knowing what's next—mingled with the equally strong drive back through memory and regret—that generates the very particular force and unencumbered immediacy of Kunitz's poems." Libr J

Kyger, Joanne
As ever; selected poems; edited with a foreword by Michael Rothenberg; introduction by David Meltzer. Penguin Bks. 2002 xxi, 306p pa $20 **811**
ISBN 0-14-200112-0 LC 2002-190390
"Though formalists may object to her apparent artlessness, Kyger's obsession for detail draws on a passionate intelligence that is seldom trivial. . . . While many writers have spoken of their work as one continuous project, Kyger's oeuvre actually holds together in this selection from her 20-plus books; throughout, her prosody, both aural and visual, is pitch perfect." Publ Wkly

Laughlin, James, 1914-1997
The secret room; poems. New Directions 1997 184p $22.95; pa $14.95 **811**
ISBN 0-8112-1343-9; 0-8112-1344-7 (pa)
LC 96-26188
Laughlin "shares his thoughts with humor and tenderness as he wades in the waters of his golden years. The speaker in many of these poems admires young women and thinks, 'I could see I was entirely out of/my depth.' He realizes he is not as strong as he once was, but he can still 'make old, sick words sound new.'" Libr J

Levertov, Denise, 1923-1997
Collected earlier poems, 1940-1960. New Directions 1979 133p hardcover o.p. paperback available $10.95 **811**
ISBN 0-8112-0718-8 (pa) LC 78-26199
This collection gathers "together three previously unpublished poems, selections from . . . *The Double Image* (1946) and all the poems from the three following collections, *Here and Now* (1957), *Overland to the Islands* (1958), *With Eyes at the Back of Our Heads* (1960). . . . Poems appear in chronological order with dates and places of composition added." Libr J

Poems, 1960-1967. New Directions 1983 247p hardcover o.p. paperback available
$11.95 **811**
ISBN 0-8112-0859-1 (pa) LC 83-2263
A combined edition of three of the poet's collections The Jacob's ladder, O taste and see, and The sorrow dance, published 1961, 1964, and 1967, respectively
The poet's "concern for quotidian realities and eternal verities gives these poems substance meant to last, expressed in a style that is clear, concise, intense. . . . Lyrical but spare, the lines speak of many things—marriage, rivers, the world that is 'not enough' with us—and the faint sounds of biblical and other literary allusions show a sensibility that has assimilated the great tradition with the urgencies of today. A solid achievement." Booklist

Poems, 1968-1972. New Directions 1987 259p hardcover o.p. paperback available
$14.95 **811**
ISBN 0-8112-1005-7 (pa) LC 86-5389
A combined edition of three of the poet's collections Relearning the alphabet, To stay alive, and Footprints, published 1970, 1971, and 1972, respectively
"Here are love poems, elegies, and poems of natural observations as moving as any in modern American literature, written with the immense craft that distinguishes Levertov's work. A necessity for American poetry collections." Booklist

Levertov, Denise, 1923-1997—*Continued*

This great unknowing; last poems; with a note on the text by Paul A. Lacey. New Directions 1999 68p hardcover o.p. paperback available $9.95   **811**
ISBN 0-8112-1458-3 (pa)   LC 98-51469

"At once as intimate as Creeley and as visionary as Duncan—two Black Mountain poets with whom she is often associated—Levertov has always written a poetry that ranges from the specifically personal to the searchingly mystical. Yet Levertov, from the mid-'60s until her death in 1997, has been one of the few writers of her generation to show that one need not mimic the oracular qualities of the Beats to make a sociopolitical poetry." Publ Wkly

Levine, Philip, 1928-

The mercy; poems. Knopf 1999 81p hardcover o.p. paperback available $15   **811**
ISBN 0-375-70135-4 (pa)   LC 98-43353

"Levine's poetry has been steadily moving to the front rank of American poetry for three decades. . . . If Walt Whitman's vision contained multitudes, and if Emerson's vision of nature transcended what it saw with its own eyes, Levine's poetic vision, nearly religious, transcends class, transcends natural boundaries, and transcends time." Atl Mon

New selected poems. Knopf 1991 292p hardcover o.p. paperback available $20   **811**
ISBN 0-679-74056-2 (pa)   LC 90-53422

This selection contains poems Levine chose for his earlier Selected poems (1984), plus 15 new works

"This is a monumental work that somehow remains wonderfully accessible, largely because Levine has chosen pieces carefully, favoring shorter works and poems that address his staple themes of family (like 'Uncle' and 'My Son and I') and childhood ('Coming Home'). Many of the poems are powerfully imagistic." Libr J

The simple truth; poems. Knopf 1994 69p hardcover o.p. paperback available $16   **811**
ISBN 0-679-76584-0 (pa)   LC 94-14508

This "collection of poetry is largely about the past: friends lost, fates assigned, potatoes eaten, decisions made. . . . Levine's mingling of realism and romanticism, involving many near-meetings between them, produces fascinating, emotionally persuasive shifts and tonal modulations that closely approach a lived truth." Publ Wkly

What work is; poems. Knopf 1991 77p hardcover o.p. paperback available $15   **811**
ISBN 0-679-74058-9 (pa)   LC 90-53421

"This collection amounts to a hymn of praise for all the workers of America. These proletarian heroes, with names like Lonnie, Loo, Sweet Pea, and Packy, work the furnaces, forges, slag heaps, assembly lines, and loading docks at places with unglamorous names like Brass Craft or Feinberg and Breslin's First-Rate Plumbing and Plating. . . . But Levine's characters are also significant for their inner lives, not merely their jobs." Libr J

Longfellow, Henry Wadsworth, 1807-1882

Poems and other writings. Library of Am. 2000 854p $35   **811**
ISBN 1-88301-185-X   LC 00-26678
Edited by J. D. McClatchy

This volume includes "*Hiawatha, Evangeline, The Courtship of Miles Standish* and 'The Midnight Ride of Paul Revere.' Here, too, are some surprisingly powerful lyric and meditative poems—well made, deeply felt, and not much like the schoolhouse favorites." Publ Wkly

Lorde, Audre

The collected poems of Audre Lorde. Norton 1997 489p $35; pa $17.95   **811**
ISBN 0-393-04090-9; 0-393-31972-5 (pa)
     LC 97-10878

"Since her death in 1992, Lorde's reputation has continued to grow. In life a tough, eloquent crusader who demanded that we honor the varieties of human experience, she retained her hold on readers despite the unavailability of much of her work. This edition, then, should be welcomed wherever there is interest in women's, minority, and lesbian literature. It includes Lorde's passionately private early work as well as her later, more obviously political work." Booklist

Lowell, Robert, 1917-1977

Collected poems; edited by Frank Bidart and David Gewanter with the editorial assistance of DeSales Harrison. Farrar, Straus & Giroux 2003 1186p il $45   **811**
ISBN 0-374-12617-8

This collection includes "Lowell's first book, *Land of Unlikeness* (1944); and poems from his 11 ensuing collections, including *Life Studies* (1959) and *The Dolphin* (1973). . . . Substantial notes, a chronology, glossary, and critical essays make this an essential title. Readers who think they know Lowell's work will discover new facets, and readers just venturing into Lowell's potently rendered and ceaselessly evocative poetic universe will find much to contemplate." Booklist
Includes bibliographical references

Lux, Thomas, 1946-

New and selected poems, 1975-1995. Houghton Mifflin 1997 177p $23; pa $15
     811
ISBN 0-395-85832-1; 0-395-92488-X (pa)
     LC 97-430

"With humor, minimalist phrasing, and devotion to everyday language, Lux comments on oddities and trivialities. Reading from cover to cover, one can certainly trace changes in Lux's style, especially by 1986, when he developed lyric and narrative strength and showed an awareness of, and even reverence for, poetry's traditions." Booklist

MacLeish, Archibald, 1892-1982

Collected poems, 1917-1982; with a prefatory note to the newly collected poems by Richard B. McAdoo. Houghton Mifflin 1985 524p hardcover o.p. paperback available $19   **811**
ISBN 0-395-39569-0 (pa)   LC 85-14392

Collects all the known poetry of the author/public servant. As an expatriate in Paris his early work was heavily influenced by Pound and Eliot. After returning to the States his verse concerned itself more with America's political, social, and cultural heritage

Matthews, William, 1942-1997

After all; last poems. Houghton Mifflin 1998 55p hardcover o.p. paperback available $13 **811**

ISBN 0-618-05685-8 (pa)   LC 98-22909

"Since Matthews was one of the few contemporary poets who really knew how to make the vernacular sing, it's sad to think that these are his last poems. Fittingly, some of them are autumnal, but they range widely and brightly from Prague in 1419 to a Caribbean island in 1967 to Martha Mitchell, Finn sheep, and a poetry reading at West Point. A lovely finale." Libr J

Selected poems and translations, 1969-1991. Houghton Mifflin 1992 200p hardcover o.p. paperback available $15 **811**

ISBN 0-395-66993-6 (pa)   LC 91-45716

"This collection brings together more than 100 poems, chosen from eight previously published volumes, and 40 translations from the French, Latin and Bulgarian." Publ Wkly

"Matthews has been widely praised for the solid grounding of his poems, and rightly so. His clear-cut metaphors illuminate the everyday world with the magic of semantic revelation and the grace of othermindedness." Booklist

McClatchy, J. D., 1945-

Hazmat. Knopf 2002 83p $23; pa $15 **811**

ISBN 0-375-41467-3; 0-375-70991-6 (pa)
   LC 2002-20529

"McClatchy continues to explore the connection between the spiritual and the corporeal, seeking 'a desire as yet half-satisfied.' Though he reveres the past and pays tribute to his mentor, James Merrill, the largesse of these poems is the command over craft and language. McClatchy realizes that form and content do matter; what is being said is inherent in *how* it is being said." Libr J

Melville, Herman, 1819-1891

The poems of Herman Melville; edited by Douglas Robillard. rev ed. Kent State Univ. Press 2000 349p pa $29 **811**

ISBN 0-87338-660-4   LC 99-52872

First published 1976 by College and University Press Service

This volume "presents the complete texts of 'Battle-Pieces,' 'John Marr and Other Sailors,' and 'Timoleon,' as well as additional manuscript poems. Also presented are excerpts from the long narrative poem *Clarel* to give the reader a taste of the style and content of this work. The editor's introduction, as well as his notes at the end of each section, are informative as well as appreciative of Melville's status as a poet." Libr J

Meredith, William, 1919-

Effort at speech; new and selected poems. TriQuarterly Bks. 1997 231p $46; pa $17.95 **811**

ISBN 0-8101-5070-0; 0-8101-5071-9 (pa)
   LC 97-9679

Meredith's early poems "are as subtle as aspirin. So easily digestible in their precise meter and perfectly tuned end-rhyme, their power goes virtually unnoticed until the reader lifts his eyes from the page to find himself moved, affected. In work inspired by the poet's service at sea during WWII, devastation comes on the hushed waves of sonnets. . . . The poems in the book's latter half (1970-1987) find formalism surrendering some ground to free verse as Meredith attempts to salve not the sharp pains of war but the blunted ache of aging." Publ Wkly

Merrill, James

The changing light at Sandover; including the whole of The book of Ephraim, Mirabell's books of number, Scripts for the pageant and a new coda, The higher keys. Atheneum Pubs. 1983 560p hardcover o.p. paperback available $25 **811**

ISBN 0-679-74736-2 (pa)   LC 82-72995

This is a "collection, under a new general title, of all three 'divine comedies' unabridged, plus a new, 37-page coda." N Y Times Book Rev

The trilogy "is, surely, an astonishing performance, not a masterpiece, but as near to one, I think, as anything else that American poetry has produced in the last two or three decades." N Y Rev Books

The collected poems of James Merrill; edited by J.D. McClatchy and Stephen Yenser. Knopf 2001 xx, 885p $40; pa $27.50 **811**

ISBN 0-375-41139-9; 0-375-70941-X (pa)
   LC 00-40542

"Excluded are some juvenilia and light verse, as well as Merrill's book-length poem *The Changing Light at Sandover,* in print as a separate volume. Merrill's sonnets, sapphics, longer sequences and sinuous sentences encompass lyric pathos, ebullient comedy, rapt romance and acrid satire. Their formal sophistication can belie their depth of feeling, which is exactly what some readers love best about Merrill's work." Publ Wkly

Merwin, W. S. (William Stanley), 1927-

The folding cliffs; a narrative. Knopf 1998 331p maps $25; $16.95 pa **811**

ISBN 0-375-40148-2; 0-375-70151-6
   LC 98-27434

With this "historical narrative of late-nineteenth-century Hawaii, Merwin restores the epic to our language. When Ko'olau, a cowboy, and his little son, Kaleimanu, contract leprosy, Ko'olau and his wife, Pi'ilani, resist the official policy, which is to remove the sick from their families. Instead, first in company and then on their own, they flee into the wild mountains of Kauai. Merwin's fluid lines transmit with almost hallucinatory beauty this story's dark lessons." New Yorker

The pupil; poems. Knopf 2001 91p $23; pa $15 **811**

ISBN 0-375-41276-X; 0-375-70964-9 (pa)
   LC 2001-33729

This "collection moves in a seasonal progression from spring to winter, covering old and new territory: a difficult clergyman father, a friendship with Ted Hughes, the murder of Matthew Shepard, the horrific practice of bear-baiting in Pakistan, and more recent friendships in Maui, his adopted home. Light is played against darkness as a central metaphor for existence, and there are poems about stars, comets, and the Marfa lights in Texas." Libr J

Merwin, W. S. (William Stanley), 1927—
Continued

The vixen; poems. Knopf 1996 70p
hardcover o.p. paperback available $17 **811**
ISBN 0-679-76601-4 (pa)   LC 95-30283

"Here is a memoryscape of days spent in a remote
part of France: gardens and woods recalled in rich detail,
mist which has 'found/its way without sight into the
hoofprints of cows,' changes of season whence arise a
transcendent fox, a snake reclaiming its skin, an old
woman with a safebox of ash. . . . The present is
stitched tight onto the past, the poems are at once pastoral and narrative, and none comes to a definitive end. Instead, each dissipates, the way a complicated flavor dissolves on the tongue." Publ Wkly

Millay, Edna St. Vincent, 1892-1950

Collected poems; edited by Norma Millay.
Harper & Row 1956 xxi, 738p hardcover o.p.
paperback available $22.50 **811**
ISBN 0-06-090889-0 (pa)

The poems in this collection "are divided into two
separate sections of lyrics and sonnets, arranged
chronologically and printed in groups under the titles of
the original volumes, ranging from 'Renascence' of 1917
to 'Mine the harvest,' published in 1954, four years after
the poet's death." Booklist

Moore, Marianne, 1887-1972

The complete poems of Marianne Moore.
Macmillan; Viking 1981 305p hardcover o.p.
paperback available $16 **811**
ISBN 0-14-018851-7 (pa)   LC 80-13586

This "definitive edition of 'The Complete Poems' was
prepared by Clive Driver and presents all of Moore's final emendations and cuts, punctuation, hyphens, line arrangements, and revised notes (all critical components of
her poetry). It also includes five poems Moore wrote between the publication of the 1967 edition and the time
of her death." Libr J

Morgan, Frederick, 1922-

The one abiding; introduction by Dana
Gioia. Story Line Press 2003 xxiii, 70p pa
$11 **811**
ISBN 1-58654-021-1   LC 2002-7754

Morgan's "collection surveys his . . . long life . . .
but it is personal poetry in the universalizing manner of
Coleridge in 'Frost at Midnight' and of classical Japanese poetry: it discloses transpersonal meaning in individual, autobiographical experiences. . . . Morgan's precision makes the scenes he conjures, even those of
dreams, and the feelings he rouses vivid, affecting, and,
perhaps, indelible." Booklist

Mullen, Harryette Romell

Sleeping with the dictionary; [by] Harryette
Mullen. University of Calif. Press 2002 85p
(New California poetry) hardcover o.p.
paperback available $14.95 **811**
ISBN 0-520-23143-0 (pa)   LC 2001-48050

This collection contains "prose poems, exhaustive alphabetical language-salads . . . Oulipian word-
replacement poems, short stories that recall the quasi-
fantastic realism of John Yau and strange rewrites of
classics. . . . All of the work here is full of such energy,
invention and pleasure that the dictionary surely awoke
refreshed." Publ Wkly

Niedecker, Lorine, 1903-1970

Collected works; edited by Jenny
Penberthy. University of Calif. Press 2002
xxiii, 471p $45 **811**
ISBN 0-520-22433-7   LC 2001-5376

Niedecker "is often likened to Emily Dickinson. She,
too, remained in the backwater where she was born.
Large-scale interest in her work came only years after
her death. Her characteristic poems are, like Dickinson's,
short or in short stanzas, short-lined, and elliptical. But
she wasn't reclusive; she connected with the Objectivists,
New York poets 'led' by Louis Zukofsky. . . . Whereas
Dickinson's poetry is metaphysical, Niedecker's mature
work is profoundly physical, sparked by wry, class-
conscious humor and usually rooted in her Black Lake
Island, Wisconsin, neighborhood." Booklist

Nims, John Frederick, 1913-1999

The powers of heaven and earth; new and
selected poems. Louisiana State Univ. Press
2002 247p $36.95; pa $19.95 **811**
ISBN 0-8071-2826-0; 0-8071-2827-9 (pa)
LC 2002-30055

This is a "collection of the work of one of the foremost formalists and classicists among twentieth-century
American poets: epigrams, odes, sonnets, shaped verse,
and other kinds of poems on life, nature, culture, literature, but first and foremost, on love." Booklist

Norris, Kathleen, 1947-

Journey: new and selected poems,
1969-1999. University of Pa. 2001 131p
hardcover o.p. paperback available $16.95
811
ISBN 0-8229-5761-2 (pa)

A collection of Norris' "poetry spanning 30 years.
Here are poems, arranged chronologically in four sections each beginning with a verse from the *Song of Solomon*, that tenderly describe an event or scene, examine
it, and conclude with a flash of seemingly unrelated insight, leaving profound questions in the reader's heart.
. . . Carrying her readers along on her deeply Christian
journey, Norris avoids spiritual certainty and preachiness,
remaining ever the seeker. Her poems are lyrical, accessible, and hauntingly touching to read and to reread."
Libr J

O'Hara, Frank, 1926-1966

The collected poems of Frank O'Hara;
edited by Donald Allen; with an introduction
by John Ashbery. University of Calif. Press
1995 xxix, 586p pa $24.95 **811**
ISBN 0-520-20166-3   LC 94-24660

A reissue of the title first published 1971 by Knopf

The subjects of this collection "are lunch-time strolls
past construction workers and bargains in wrist watches,
the lives of artists (whether distant heroes or close
friends), the distractions of city life, . . . homosexuality,
. . . headlines glimpsed on newstands. . . . Some [are]
. . . about friendships, occasional pieces written for a
marriage or a departure." Newsweek

Includes bibliographical references

Olds, Sharon

Blood, tin, straw. Knopf 1999 125p
hardcover o.p. paperback available $15 **811**
ISBN 0-375-70735-2 (pa)   LC 99-15602

"Olds has always been a frank and transcendent poet
of the body, and now . . . she expands her profoundly

Olds, Sharon—*Continued*

tactile sensibility to embrace the entire cosmos in poems of powerful female eroticism and emotional acuity that celebrate love both earthly and spiritual." Booklist

The unswept room. Knopf 2002 96p $25; pa $15 **811**
ISBN 0-375-41489-4; 0-375-70998-3 (pa)
LC 2002-18444
"Organized like her previous works, this work begins with poems about her early life and then moves on to grade school, her marriage, and up to the present day. Throughout, Olds re-creates her life, building a scrapbook through words. Although many of her subjects (family, love, sex) stay the same, her tone has shifted from an angry questioning of fate to a passionate acceptance of her own mortality and the experiences she has had." Libr J

The wellspring. Knopf 1996 88p hardcover o.p. paperback available $15 **811**
ISBN 0-679-76560-3 (pa)
LC 95-15835
This collection "takes the form of an intimate family portrait. Olds begins by imagining her parents making love for the first time. This explicitness informs the entire cycle, from poems about her own birth to snapshots of her youth and early sexual experiences, poems remarkable for their integrity, eroticism, tough humor, and unceasing wonder. . . . Olds continues with a series of strikingly original and profoundly moving poems about her children." Booklist

Oliver, Mary, 1935-

The leaf and the cloud; a poem. Da Capo Press 2000 55p hardcover o.p. paperback available $15 **811**
ISBN 0-306-81073-5 (pa)
LC 00-57008
A "book-length poem by a poet devoted to close scrutiny of the natural world and exact, sensuous, and ecstatic description. Lyrical and philosophical in the American transcendental tradition, Oliver addresses her readers directly to ravishing effect." Booklist

New and selected poems. Beacon Press 1992 255p $28.50; pa $16 **811**
ISBN 0-8070-6818-7; 0-8070-6819-5 (pa)
LC 92-7767
This collection "joins together poems written over 30 years. One of the astonishing aspects of Oliver's work is the consistency of tone over this long period. What changes is an increased focus on nature and an increased precision with language that has made her one of the very best poets." N Y Times Book Rev

West wind. Houghton Mifflin 1997 63p hardcover o.p. paperback available $14 **811**
ISBN 0-395-85085-1 (pa)
LC 97-2986
"Although her papers may scatter as the west wind sweeps through her room, Oliver's house is in order. From the chaos of the world, her poems distill what it means to be human and what is worthwhile about life. Echoing the Romantics and Whitman, she affirms the value of aloneness with nature, of watching and listening—not just to get it down as art but simply to live it." Libr J

White pine; poems and prose poems. Harcourt Brace & Co. 1994 55p hardcover o.p. paperback available $14 **811**
ISBN 0-15-600120-9 (pa)
LC 94-20112
"Oliver's simple, beautiful nature and prose poems about spiders, hummingbirds, deer, roses, and all the beauty of the woods have a direct particularity that will appeal to many . . . readers." Booklist

Olson, Charles, 1910-1970

The collected poems of Charles Olson; excluding the Maximus poems; edited by George F. Butterick. University of Calif. Press 1987 xxxvi, 675p hardcover o.p. paperback available $45 **811**
ISBN 0-520-21231-2 (pa)
LC 86-14652
"Perhaps the most important American postmodernist poet, Olson was little published during his life. This work, . . . should solidify his reputation. Olson burst into poetry in his maturity, sure of his instincts. Though his debt to Pound is evident, he went further in exploring both American language and experience. What amazes us now is not just the profundity and erudition of his themes but the variety of ways he expresses his humanity. Ceaselessly experimental, his poems do not lose their intelligence or intelligibility." Libr J

Oppen, George, 1908-1984

New collected poems; edited with an introduction and notes by Michael Davidson; preface by Eliot Weinberger. New Directions 2002 xlv, 433p il $37.95 **811**
ISBN 0-8112-1488-5
LC 2001-44048
Replaces The collected poems of George Oppen (1975)
"Oppen, a Communist and an objectivist poet deeply influenced by Pound and Williams, believed that there were no ideas except in things, but he also believed, fiercely, that our relationship to things was inherently moral. . . . In 1934, he published a book of stunning, elliptical lyrics about 'big-Business' and American capitalism; he then fell silent for the next twenty-five years, during which he struggled to reconcile his fealty to social causes with the demands of aesthetic originality. The culmination of this struggle was his Pulitzer Prize-winning collection 'Of Being Numerous,' published in 1968, which, to a degree unmatched by any book of American poetry since, movingly portrays the individual in a collective world." New Yorker
Includes bibliographical references

Orr, Gregory

The caged owl; new and selected poems. Copper Canyon Press 2002 235p pa $16 **811**
ISBN 1-55659-177-2
LC 2001-6504
"The constraints of personal narrative are stretched to their limits in this summation from Orr, . . . as his poems are often based on tragic experiences occurring to those close to him. Orr's archetypal subject in the new poems and selections from six previous collections . . . is fratricide. As a child, Orr accidentally shot and killed his young brother in a hunting accident." Publ Wkly

Page, P. K. (Patricia Kathleen), 1916-
The hidden room; collected poems; {by}
Patricia Kathleen Page. Porcupine's Quill
1997 2v ea $18.95 **811**
ISBN 0-88984-190-X (v1); 0-88984-193-4 (v2)
LC 98-113870
These two volumes incude the majority of all of the
poet's works published in volume form, from Unit of
five to Hologram, along with some unpublished poems
and poems hitherto published only in magazines

Peacock, Molly, 1947-
Cornucopia; new & selected poems,
1975-2002. Norton 2002 250p $26.95 **811**
ISBN 0-393-05123-4 LC 2002-22884
"Wielding bright metaphors and adeptly combining
story and lyricism, Peacock makes the annealing of the
self in the furnace of family and the fever of erotic love
her signature theme. Her insouciant wit deflects a brooding soul in surprising and gratifyingly lucid poems that
mesh a rich physicality with arresting emotional precision." Booklist

Phillips, Carl, 1959-
Rock Harbor. Farrar, Straus & Giroux 2002
110p $20; pa $12 **811**
ISBN 0-374-25140-1; 0-374-52885-3 (pa)
LC 2002-20588
"Phillips reduces lyric poetry to its bare minimum,
translating complex states of being into spare and clever
syllogisms. His landscapes are stark, singular, and still.
The living entities present, be they bird, tree, horse, or
man, stand alone in wind and shifting light. Monumental
in their carved perfection and deep mystery, they are em-
bodiments of transcendence, objects of desire, instruments of pleasure and pain." Booklist

Pinsky, Robert
The figured wheel; new and collected
poems, 1966-1996. Farrar, Straus & Giroux
1996 303p hardcover o.p. paperback available
$16 **811**
ISBN 0-374-52506-4 (pa) LC 95-47617
"Brought together here are 16 new poems, the work
of Pinsky's four original collections and a sampling of
his fine translations, including a canto from his well-
received version of the Inferno. Taken as a whole, this
is the record of a poet who grows from highly competent
to near-transcendent." Publ Wkly

Jersey rain. Farrar, Straus & Giroux 2000
52p hardcover o.p. paperback available $12
811
ISBN 0-374-52772-5 (pa) LC 99-44209
"The discursive mode suits Pinsky because it allows
his mind to range, to consider, to try out images and
ideas. The pleasure comes less from the poem's perfection as an artifact than from our sense of the poet's sensitive, inquisitive mind at work." N Y Times Book Rev

Plath, Sylvia
The collected poems; edited by Ted
Hughes. Harper & Row 1981 351p hardcover
o.p. paperback available $17.95 **811**
ISBN 0-06-090900-5 (pa)
Also available in hardcover from Buccaneer Bks.

The collection contains "all the poems Plath wrote,
published and unpublished, from 1956 to 1963, as well
as a sample of her early work." Publ Wkly
"Although her best poems deal with suffering and
death, others are exhilarating and affectionate, and her
tone is frequently witty as well as disturbing." Concise
Oxford Companion to Engl Lit

Poe, Edgar Allan, 1809-1849
Complete poems; edited by Thomas Ollive
Mabbott. University of Ill. Press 2000 xxx,
627p il pa $25 **811**
ISBN 0-252-06921-8 LC 00-38639
First published 1969 as volume 1 of: Collected works
of Edgar Allan Poe by Belknap Press of Harvard University Press
This book contains 101 poems and their variants. In
addition to classic poems such as The raven, The bells,
and Annabel Lee, this volume contains previously uncollected poems, fragments, verses published in reviews,
and poems attributed to Poe
Includes bibliographical references

Poems and poetics; Richard Wilbur, editor.
Library of Am. 2003 xxv, 179p (American
poets project) $20 **811**
ISBN 1-931082-51-0 LC 2003-46637
"Wilbur wants Poe to be appreciated as a transcendental cosmic theorist and 'the most difficult of the symbolist writers of his century,' and he appends selections
from Poe's writings about poetics to help understanding
of his cosmology and discusses some of Poe's most intense stories to exemplify his symbolism. The poems,
presented chronologically, show again what a young
prodigy Poe was, formulating his poetic thought while
still in his teens, and what a sonorous Romantic musician
he became." Booklist
Includes bibliographical references

Poets of World War II; Harvey Shapiro,
editor. Library of Am. 2003 xxxii, 262p
(American poets project) $20 **811**
1. World War, 1939-1945—Poetry
ISBN 1-931082-33-2 LC 2002-32125
The editor's "objective is to show that the American
poets of the Second World War were as significant as
their English counterparts in the first one, if different in
tone. Even at their most biting, Siegfried Sassoon and
Wilfred Owen struck a heroic note, penning anthems for
'doomed youth' and the destruction of innocence. . . .
But those who survived battles of the second conflict to
become important poets avoided the attempt to sound noble, or to celebrate fallen comrades. . . . Shapiro, a B-17
gunner, takes pains to show the spectrum of opinion that
actually existed and how it evolved." New Leader
Includes bibliographical references

Ponsot, Marie
Springing; new and selected poems. Knopf
2002 233p $25; pa $16.95 **811**
ISBN 0-375-41389-8; 0-375-70987-8 (pa)
LC 2001-38432
"Ponsot's poems are built around . . . unflinching observations of intimate interactions and misfires, whether
of familial relations ventriloquized through updated
Greek dramatis personae, a French woman's accommodation of her mother's married lover or the self's castings
about the natural world." Publ Wkly

Pound, Ezra, 1885-1972

The cantos of Ezra Pound. New Directions 1970 802p $42; pa $22.95 **811**

ISBN 0-8112-0350-6; 0-8112-1326-9 (pa)

"The first sections of the 'Cantos' were published in magazine form as early as 1917. Pound's conception of his epic changed several times during different phases of his life. Originally intended as a didactic treatise for 'philistine' Americans, it combined elements from classical myth, ancient Oriental poetry, Provençal ballads, and modern economic theory, to create a vast disjointed panorama of the growth of civilization. A monumental work of poetic enterprise." Reader's Ency. 4th edition

Collected early poems of Ezra Pound; edited by Michael John King; with an introduction by Louis L. Martz. New Directions 1982 xxii, 330p hardcover o.p. paperback available $14.95 **811**

ISBN 0-8112-0843-5 (pa) LC 82-8156

The editor "collects all of Pound's early books from 'A Lume Spento' through 'Ripostes,' including the 99 poems Pound excluded from his 1926 collected poems, 'Personae,' as well as 25 poems previously available only in periodicals, and 38 manuscript poems never published before including the complete 'San Trovaso Notebook.'" Libr J

Selected poems. new ed. New Directions 1957 184p pa $8.95 **811**

ISBN 0-8112-0162-7

First published 1949

This "provides a good sampling of the Pound who wrote 'A Virginal,' the latter-day Renaissance poet, as well as the reincarnate Li Po and the other 'personae' that Ezra wore during the years he spent absorbing the styles (and not the political thinking) of other centuries." Saturday Rev

Price, Reynolds, 1933-

The collected poems. Scribner 1997 xxiv, 471p $37.50; pa $20 **811**

ISBN 0-684-83203-8; 0-684-86002-3 (pa)

LC 96-53117

"Price has always stood apart from contemporary movements in poetry, and although it is true that he is not a technical innovator, it would be perilous to ignore him: he has a rare facility for making the strange familiar, and the familiar fresh. Compassionate and candid, Price seems likely to reach an audience unusually wide for contemporary poetry with this generous collection." Libr J

Rexroth, Kenneth, 1905-1982

The collected longer poems. New Directions 1968 307p hardcover o.p. paperback available $12.95 **811**

ISBN 0-8112-0177-5 (pa) LC 68-25549

"Rexroth's pieces proceed with casual narrative, with lumps of prose 'philosophy' barely leavened with syllabics, with lovely lyricism, with engaging romanticism, and overwhelming (at times) pretentiousness." Choice

Selected poems; edited with an introduction by Bradford Morrow. New Directions 1984 152p hardcover o.p. paperback available $10.95 **811**

ISBN 0-8112-0917-2 (pa) LC 84-9972

"This selection retrieves the immensely talented teenager of the early '20s and all the other steps toward the authoritative aged poet of the '70s. We see from Morrow's choices the shape of a career, at once distinctive from, but also exemplary of, the grand sweep of American modernism, which Rexroth very obviously helped—along with Pound and Eliot, Williams and Stevens—to create. Morrow's useful notes illuminate the more arcane allusions." Choice

Rich, Adrienne

Collected early poems, 1950-1970. Norton 1993 xxi, 435p hardcover o.p. paperback available $15 **811**

ISBN 0-393-31385-9 (pa) LC 92-13150

This collection "contains all of the work included in Rich's first six books, and a few previously uncollected pieces as well. Her poetry of the 1950s stems from a strong, mostly male tradition, obviously and intentionally echoing the work of Frost, Williams, Dickinson and Stevens. . . . The poems written in the 1960s are pervaded by the poet's consciousness of the subversive nature of creativity, especially for women, a gift at risk of being suppressed or curtailed at any moment by the self, family or the male-dominated society. In the last poems of the period, Rich's voice is firm and brave, her language still searingly beautiful and individual. This important volume charts the radical transformation of one of America's most significant poets." Publ Wkly

Fox; poems, 1998-2000. Norton 2001 64p $21; pa $12 **811**

ISBN 0-393-04166-2; 0-393-32377-3 (pa)

LC 2001-31240

"Rich's recent style—developed slowly throughout the 1990s—comes to full fruition here, conveying her familiar attentions to social injustice and intense introspection with and a sometimes harsh, fragmented, versatile line whose sources include George Oppen and Anglo-Saxon accentual verse." Publ Wkly

Midnight salvage; poems, 1995-1998. Norton 1999 75p $22; pa $11 **811**

ISBN 0-393-04682-6; 0-393-31984-9 (pa)

LC 98-19293

Rich's "well-known, fiercely held political ideals—her commitments to economic justice, feminism and gay liberation—manifest themselves, now, in her sense of passing the torch, of trying to show the readers and writers who will come after her what she has learned and how she learned it. Her juxtaposed fragments, self-questionings and self-interruptions, and taut, Anglo-Saxonate verse lines, let her sound accessible, democratic, inspiring, while making us work to discover her poems' formal secrets." Publ Wkly

Ríos, Alberto

The smallest muscle in the human body. Copper Canyon Press 2002 107p pa $14 **811**

ISBN 1-55659-173-X LC 2001-6505

Ríos' "concise poems—often stately columns of couplets—drift off regularly into memories of a Mexican-American childhood in Arizona. . . . Whether talking

Ríos, Alberto—*Continued*

about the smell of food, the essence of a crow or a bear's character or of hard-won human wisdom, Ríos writes in a serenely clear manner that enhances the drama in the quick scenes he summons up." N Y Times Bk Rev

Roethke, Theodore, 1908-1963

The collected poems of Theodore Roethke. Doubleday 1966 279p hardcover o.p. paperback available $14.95 **811**

ISBN 0-385-08601-6 (pa)

Roethke's "refreshingly original rhythms are keenly articulated and often hypnotic. Although his work is uneven and he sometimes gives way to self-indulgence or to surprising naiveté, many of his best poems recreate disconcertingly intense psychic or mystical experience. He also had a flair for the seductively lyrical and the brashly irreverent. He ranks as one of the best poets of the first postmodern generation." Benet's Reader's Ency of Am Lit

Salter, Mary Jo, 1954-

A kiss in space. Knopf 1999 84p hardcover o.p. paperback available $15 **811**

ISBN 0-375-70499-X (pa)   LC 98-14210

"Salter's formally polished poems invite the reader into a world of charged discrepancies, where we feel strangely 'giddy, as one is when all is lost.' Her gaze works best when it is recalibrating a familiar perspective with a touch of mild eccentricity—whether it's Chartres from a hot-air balloon, a family's odd home videos, or an embrace at the space station Mir." New Yorker

Sandburg, Carl, 1878-1967

The complete poems of Carl Sandburg. rev and expanded ed. Harcourt Brace Jovanovich 1970 xxxi, 797p $40 **811**

ISBN 0-15-100996-1

First published 1950

Introduction by Archibald MacLeish

A collection of seven of the author's books: Chicago poems, 1916; Cornhuskers, 1918; Smoke and steel, 1920; Slabs of the sunburnt West, 1922; Good morning, America, 1925; The people, yes, 1936; Honey and salt, 1963

"Known for his free verse, written under the influence of Walt Whitman and celebrating industrial and agricultural America, American geography and landscape, figures in American history, and the American common people, [Sandburg] frequently makes use of contemporary American slang and colloquialisms." Herzberg. Reader's Ency of Am Lit

Sarton, May, 1912-1995

Coming into eighty; new poems. Norton 1994 71p $15.95; pa $11 **811**

ISBN 0-393-03689-8; 0-393-31623-8 (pa)
                                    LC 94-18659

"In these sparely fashioned poems Sarton . . . contemplates life from the perspective of 80 years. The book is dedicated to the poet's cat, her muse. This may seem whimsical, and some of the poems are essentially notations ('A Thought'). Others, however, like sudden revelations that occur in the small hours, are distilled and crystalline." Publ Wkly

Schulman, Grace

Days of wonder; new and selected poems. Houghton Mifflin 2002 189p $25; pa $14 **811**

ISBN 0-618-08623-4; 0-618-34082-3 (pa)
                                    LC 2001-39531

"In a characteristic Schulman poem, large, difficult questions resonate in the small, singular moments of appreciation. . . . There are allusions to canonical painters and canonical poems, and a variety of religious references, which engender equal portions of reverence and lament. Many of the poems' small pleasures are found amid sometimes difficult sometimes serene backdrops." Publ Wkly

Schuyler, James

Collected poems. Farrar, Straus & Giroux 1993 429p hardcover o.p. paperback available $32 **811**

ISBN 0-374-52403-3 (pa)   LC 92-40977

"Schuyler's subject is his life, and his poems often read like elegant journal entries. The book presents intimate and conversational accounts of life in the Eastern literary landscape—New York City, New England, Long Island. In urbane free verse, the poet recalls and meditates on music and painting, homosexuality, weekends with friends—John Ashbery and Fairfield Porter among them—deaths, a drive to the Hamptons. . . . Rarely has a poet imparted so much of his experience as honestly and engagingly as Schuyler does here." Publ Wkly

Sexton, Anne

The complete poems; with a foreword by Maxine Kumin. Houghton Mifflin 1981 xxiv, 622p hardcover o.p. paperback available $18 **811**

ISBN 0-395-95776-1 (pa)   LC 81-2482

"This collection contains all the poems in the eight volumes published in Sexton's lifetime, the two published after her death, and seven poems never before in print." Libr J

"Even before her death in 1974, Sexton's work was the subject of critical controversy, often dismissed as mere confessionalism. But, as Maxine Kumin observes in an insightful introductory essay, Sexton 'delineated the problematic position of women—the neurotic reality of the time' and in so doing 'earned her place in the canon.'" Choice

Shapiro, Karl Jay, 1913-2000

Selected poems; [by] Karl Shapiro; John Updike, editor. Library of Am. 2003 xxxi, 197p il (American poets project) $20 **811**

ISBN 1-931082-34-0   LC 2002-32123

"Karl Shapiro, one of the more influential voices of the late 20th century, displayed complex and contrary tendencies in both his life and his poetry. Editor Updike notes that Shapiro's experimentation with voices and forms alienated those who admired the metrical dexterity of his early poems." Libr J

Includes bibliographical references

Sheck, Laurie

Black series; poems. Knopf 2001 100p $23; pa $15 **811**

ISBN 0-375-41279-4; 0-375-70965-7 (pa)
                                    LC 2001-29928

"Sheck's conventions lead her toward extremity and strangeness rather than urbanity and balance, but that

Sheck, Laurie—*Continued*

does not make them less conventional. Like many poets in the modern tradition, she relies on charged words and phrases to create an atmosphere of portent and high emotion rather than attending to precision or sense; she writes vaguely but at a high volume." N Y Times Book Rev

Simic, Charles, 1938-

Jackstraws; poems. Harcourt Brace & Co. 1999 55p $22; pa $13   **811**
  ISBN 0-15-100422-6; 0-15-601098-4 (pa)
                     LC 98-35354
"Simic's sharp and unsparing vision is stereoscopic, uniting, as it so slyly and unnervingly does, haunting memories of and fresh concern about the horrors of Eastern Europe with affectionately sardonic impressions of his second home, America." Booklist

Night picnic; poems. Harcourt 2001 86p $23   **811**
  ISBN 0-15-100630-X   LC 2001-24100
Simic "sees lovers in cemeteries after dark and ponders the secret lives of rats, crows, and worms, yet his noir outlook abates just enough to make room for a new strain of sardonic humor and a keen sense of the entanglement of the erotic and the doomed. . . . Nabokovian in his caustic charm and sexy intelligence, Simic perceives the mythic in the mundane and pinpoints the perpetual suffering that infuses human life with both agony and bliss." Booklist

Selected early poems. Braziller 1999 255p $22; pa $14.95   **811**
  ISBN 0-8076-1456-4; 0-8076-1483-1 (pa)
                     LC 99-34872
First published 1985 with title: Selected poems, 1963-1983
"Charles Simic shows that he is among the very few poets for whom surrealism is a genuine vision, a tool of discovery, rather than a collection of abitrary shocks. . . . His skewed vision manages both to capture the alien concreteness of things and to make them reflect his own consciousness. . . . His skill and sure instinct make this book one of the important poetic achievements of our time." N Y Times Book Rev

The voice at 3:00 a.m; selected late & new poems. Harcourt 2003 177p $25   **811**
  ISBN 0-15-100842-6   LC 2002-38715
This "volume collects outstanding poems from six previous books, beginning with *Unending Blues* (1986) and ending with *Jackstraws* (1999), and presents a sterling set of new poems, each moody, surprising, and tonic." Booklist
"An important purchase for all libraries." Libr J

Walking the black cat; poems. Harcourt Brace & Co. 1996 83p hardcover o.p. paperback available $13   **811**
  ISBN 0-15-600481-X (pa)   LC 96-17064
"The padlocked window of a pawnshop, a woman with the stem of a red rose between her teeth, a blood orange falling off a table with an ominous thud: Simic's poems are crowded with uncanny presences, which he challenges with flirtatious directness." New Yorker

Simpson, Louis Aston Marantz, 1923-

The owner of the house; new collected poems, 1940-2001; [by] Louis Simpson. BOA 2003 407p (American poets continuum series) $30.95; pa $19.95   **811**
  ISBN 1-929918-38-0; 1-929918-39-9 (pa)
                     LC 2003-45241
The author "opens with 42 new poems and continues with selections from his 11 previous books, ending with *There You Are*. This work is filled with evocations of places like Jamaica, Manhattan, Paris, and Venice and range over time from tsarist Russia to World War II to the 1960s. Simpson's obsessive theme is the stultifying effect of middle-class suburban life. . . . The result is a collection both timely and accessible. . . . Highly recommended for all poetry collections." Libr J

Smith, William Jay, 1918-

The world below the window; poems, 1937-1997. Johns Hopkins Univ. Press 1998 240p il (Johns Hopkins, poetry and fiction) hardcover o.p. paperback available $16.95   **811**
  ISBN 0-8018-6783-5 (pa)   LC 97-40731
"Excluding Smith's translations, longer poems, poetry for children and much of his light verse, this . . . volume both slims down and augments 1990's *Collected Poems*. Appearing for the first time, the original, absorbing seven-part series 'Indian Removal' searchingly explores the poet's Choctaw heritage by dramatizing America's shameful past on a hot, tear-laden, swampy Southern stage." Publ Wkly

Snodgrass, W. D. (William De Witt), 1926-

Each in his season; poems. BOA Eds. 1993 126p $25; pa $12.50   **811**
  ISBN 0-918526-98-1; 0-918526-99-X (pa)
                     LC 92-73594
"In 'Each in His Season,' a large-scale, freewheeling roller coaster of a book, W.D. Snodgrass displays his life and art in often contradictory guises, and he is not afraid of risking excess and extreme. . . . Mr. Snodgrass is a reverent and patient observer, and this new collection is a considerable accomplishment." N Y Times Book Rev

Snyder, Gary

Mountains and rivers without end. Counterpoint 1996 165p hardcover o.p. paperback available $14.50   **811**
  ISBN 1-887178-57-0 (pa)   LC 96-26064
"Woven of poems written from 1956 to 1996, this vigorous epic, spanning the landscapes of cities and unsullied nature and covering a period that includes the Beats and their survivors, is rooted in both the American geography and an Eastern spiritual orientation." Publ Wkly

No nature; new and selected poems. Pantheon Bks. 1992 390p hardcover o.p. paperback available $15   **811**
  ISBN 0-679-74252-2 (pa)   LC 92-54110
This is a "selection of the best of Snyder's career, spanning from *Riprap* (1959), published at the time of his involvement with the Beatniks and the San Francisco Renaissance, to a previously unpublished group of sixteen poems entitled 'No Nature.'" Libr J
"There is an understated majesty about the ease with which Mr. Snyder puts the present into perspective." NY Times Book Rev

Soto, Gary

New and selected poems. Chronicle Bks. 1995 177p hardcover o.p. paperback available $14.95 **811**

ISBN 0-8118-0758-4 (pa)   LC 94-27081

"In one of his more striking poems, Soto stares longingly at the unkempt lot in the California slum where his family's house used to be. Elsewhere, a Mexican American simply jogs and laughs after he has been ushered out the back door when immigration officials show up at his workplace. With rare lyricism, gentleness, and a touch of humor, Soto covers the ground that leads many highly touted poets to erupt in pulsating anger. Soto has it all—the learned craft, the intrinsic abilities with language, a fascinating autobiography, and the storyteller's ability to manipulate memories into folklore." Libr J

Stafford, William Edgar, 1914-1993

Even in quiet places; poems; by William Stafford; afterword by Kim Stafford. Confluence Press 1996 120p $20; pa $11 **811**

ISBN 1-88109-019-1; 1-88109-016-7 (pa)
                              LC 95-71021

"A James R. Hepworth book"

"Regardless whether this is the last 'new' collection from Stafford (1914-93), it well demonstrates qualities that made him genuinely beloved by his admirers. . . . His poems are about his own quiet experiences and knowledge. They are often written in the second person . . . a manner that in most poets is annoyingly familiar and abstract at the same time but which Stafford makes personal and concrete." Booklist

The way it is; new & selected poems. Graywolf Press 1998 xx, 268p $24.95; pa $16 **811**

ISBN 1-55597-269-1; 1-55597-284-5 (pa)
                              LC 97-80082

This volume presents "some 400 of Stafford's poems, work gathered from 67 books published between 1960 and 1996, as well as from journals and the poet's Daily Writings." Indep Publ

"Including 71 previously unpublished new poems, among them the poem Stafford wrote the day he died, this collection fully reacquaints us with a quiet, generous presence on the American poetic landscape." Publ Wkly

Stern, Gerald

This time; new and selected poems. Norton 1998 288p hardcover o.p. paperback available $15.95 **811**

ISBN 0-393-31909-1 (pa)   LC 97-43670

"At once self-involved and sympathetic, Stern catalogues with wry dexterity a vast range of sensory data and cultural detritus, always united by 'women and men of all sizes and all ages/living together, without satire.' This healthy collection of new poems and selections from his seven previous volumes . . . is remarkable for its generosity of spirit, manifested in a warm surrealism that is often turned with humor toward his own past." Publ Wkly

Stewart, Susan

Columbarium. University of Chicago Press 2003 122p (Phoenix poets) $22.50; pa $15 **811**

ISBN 0-226-77443-0; 0-226-77444-9 (pa)
                              LC 2003-48354

"Modeled on the seventeenth-century practice of century forms, or books of one hundred pages, *Columbarium* expresses the bond between the living and the dead in voices of parent to child, lover to beloved, and mortal to the gods. . . . Stewart frames her *Columbarium* with four poems paying homage to the elements. . . . The book's center holds an alphabet of 'shadow georgice,' poems of instruction and doubt that link knowledge and the unconscious." Publisher's note

"The poet delves into human universals . . . while constantly attentive to etymology and word choice, and she makes scholarly reference to scores of classical and Biblical figures including Virgil, Hecuba, Peleus, Isaiah, Lot and Lazarus." Publ Wkly

Includes bibliographical references

Stone, Ruth, 1915-

In the next galaxy. Copper Canyon Press 2002 99p $20 **811**

ISBN 1-55659-178-0   LC 2001-7424

"Stone writes conversationally, with lyricism, honesty, wit, and plenty of focus on the passage of time. The suicide of her much-loved husband 40 years ago is a frequent theme, as are observations about aging (which she has achieved with great wisdom), the lives of her young students and neighbors, and ecological and political concerns." Libr J

Strand, Mark, 1934-

Blizzard of one; poems. Knopf 1998 55p $21; pa $15 **811**

ISBN 0-375-40139-3; 0-375-70137-0 (pa)
                              LC 97-49172

"Strand doesn't approach the universal through the particular. He approaches the universal through the universal. In his masterly new collection, 'Blizzard of One,' even the single snowflake that gives the volume its title . . . is a kind of Platonic essence, linked to a continuum of snowflakes out there in the weather and inside, in the reader's consciousness." N Y Times Book Rev

Chicken, shadow, moon and more. Turtle Point Press 2000 91p il $21.95 **811**

ISBN 1-885586-45-X

This volume "is a book of lists that at times sounds like a collection of one-line poems and at other times like a collection of epigrams. Each list is constructed by a repeated use of a single word." N Y Rev Books

"Startling visions, unexpected truths, an aura of wistfulness, and trills of playful humor waft from every page, and always the language is exact, musical, and transcendent." Booklist

Swenson, May, 1919-1989

Nature; poems old and new. Houghton Mifflin 1994 xxiii, 240p hardcover o.p. paperback available $15 **811**

ISBN 0-618-06408-7 (pa)   LC 93-45642

This collection of Swenson's poetry "brings together poems from several earlier books, as well as poems published only in magazines, and introduces us to nine splendid poems published here for the first time. This collection . . . is brought together with special attention

Swenson, May, 1919-1989—*Continued*

to poems describing the environment; poems of tides and the sea, of birds and gardens, of moods and seasons, of self and others. . . . This is a collection to be treasured; it belongs in all libraries with even a modest selection of poetry." Libr J

Tate, James, 1943-

Selected poems. Wesleyan Univ. Press; University Press of New England 1991 239p hardcover o.p. paperback available $17.95

811

ISBN 0-8195-1192-7 (pa)   LC 90-50918

Tate has "created a voice and a kind of poem that no one else could have written. His comedy works not only to entertain, which it does marvelously—he has the rare ability to be very, very funny on the page—but partly to cover and partly to reveal underlying disorientation and angst." N Y Times Book Rev

Shroud of the gnome; poems. Ecco Press 1997 72p hardcover o.p. paperback available $15   **811**

ISBN 0-88001-562-4 (pa)   LC 97-16224

"The master of our idioms takes us on another dizzy, dangerous career through absurd and disintegrating Americana, with his speakers looking on bemusedly as their folk narratives spin out of control. Tate . . . continues to draw on small-town kitsch, haywire nature documentaries and 'a giantess by the name of Anna Swan' to fuel his often hilarious antistories. The joke has not tired." Publ Wkly

Worshipful Company of Fletchers; poems. Ecco Press 1994 82p hardcover o.p. paperback available $13   **811**

ISBN 0-88001-431-8 (pa)   LC 94-9821

The author "offers a collection full of confused narrative voices, prosaic images made startlingly fresh, and landscapes that curve at the sides like hallucinations. . . . Tate is at his best when he weaves into his shimmering language such ordinary objects as toy poodles, crayons, Camp Fire Girls, and gum wrappers. In so doing, he solicits the reader with the familiar, then proceeds to act as trail guide to other worlds." Booklist

Toomer, Jean, 1894-1967

The collected poems of Jean Toomer; edited by Robert B. Jones and Margery Toomer Latimer; with an introduction and textual notes by Robert B. Jones. University of N.C. Press 1988 xxxv, 111p hardcover o.p. paperback aviable $13   **811**

ISBN 0-8078-4209-5 (pa)   LC 87-19203

"This is the only collected edition of poems by Jean Toomer, the enigmatic Afro-American writer, Gurdjieffian guru, and Quaker convert who is perhaps best known for his 1923 lyrical narrative, Cane. The fifty-five poems here—most of them previously unpublished—chart a fascinating evolution of artistic consciousness." Univ Press Books for Public Libr

Troupe, Quincy

Transcircularities; new and selected poems. Coffee House Press 2002 368p $30; pa $17

811

ISBN 1-56689-137-X; 1-56689-135-3 (pa)
LC 2002-71277

Troupe's "verse returns continually to swing, bebop and free-jazz giants, imitating, commemorating or praising Coltrane, Duke, Bud Powell and others in a series of musicianly poems culminating in the recent 'Back to the Dream Time: Miles Speaks from the Dead.' Troupe's forms, driven by performability, range from ecstatic odes to overtly political expostulations." Publ Wkly

Updike, John

Americana and other poems. Knopf 2001 95p $23   **811**

ISBN 0-375-41254-9   LC 2001-88571

This volume "ranges from a number of brilliant, expositional epics that converse as they describe, to shorter works with their quicksilver epiphanies." Christ Sci Monit

Collected poems, 1953-1993. Knopf 1993 xxiv, 387p il hardcover o.p. paperback available $22   **811**

ISBN 0-679-76204-3 (pa)   LC 92-28957

"From the outset Updike's poems are crisp and exact. There is a mock humbleness, ready wit, and divine concreteness to his subjects, an unrelenting curiosity behind his descriptions, and a prodding tension between the tactile and the abstract. . . . From the cocky exuberance of 'Midpoint,' a 1968 autobiographical cycle, to the wry, tender mischief of poems about domesticity, marriage, and aging, Updike's thrill over the unending discovery of poetry inspires images and metaphors of time-stopping perfection as well as humor rich in grace and knowingness." Booklist

Includes bibliographical references

Van Duyn, Mona

Selected poems. Knopf 2002 218p $27.50; pa $16   **811**

ISBN 0-375-41369-3; 0-375-70980-0 (pa)
LC 2001-50672

"Characterized by candor and compassion, Van Duyn's poetry depicts the pleasures and drudgeries of middle-class American life, an approach that at its best becomes an exploration of the spiritual and psychological dimensions of that life. . . . The casually formal surfaces of Van Duyn's poems often resemble those of her model, Elizabeth Bishop, and like Bishop she excels at both formal and free verse." N Y Times Book Rev

Voigt, Ellen Bryant, 1943-

Shadow of heaven; poems. Norton 2002 87p $21; pa $12   **811**

ISBN 0-393-04147-6; 0-393-32464-8 (pa)
LC 2001-44489

"The stark poems that open the volume examine dreams, apple trees, winter fields and (perhaps most impressively) the Himalayas, in a ghazal which is also a tribute to the contemporary poet Agha Shahid Ali." Publ Wkly

"Voigt possesses a gift for lyric poetry that is at once smoothly assured and sometimes overwhelming in its intensity: every tree, bird or insect resonates with symbolism for the life of a relative or a complex emotion." NY Times Book Rev

Walcott, Derek

Collected poems, 1948-1984. Farrar, Straus & Giroux 1986 515p hardcover o.p. paperback available $20 **811**

ISBN 0-374-52025-9 (pa)   LC 85-20688

"It is difficult to think of a poet in our century who—without ever betraying his native sources—has so organically assimilated the evolution of English literature from the Renaissance to the present, who has absorbed the Classical and Judeo-Christian past, and who has mined the history of Western painting as Walcott has. Throughout his entire body of work he has managed to hold in balance his passionate moral concerns with the ideal of art." Poetry

Includes bibliographical references

Omeros. Farrar, Straus & Giroux 1990 325p hardcover o.p. paperback available $15 **811**

ISBN 0-374-52350-9 (pa)   LC 90-33592

This epic poem "follows the wanderings of a present-day Odysseus and the inconsolable sufferings of those who are displaced and traveling with trepidation toward their homes. Written in seven circling books and . . . tercets, the poem illuminates the classical past and its motifs through an extraordinary cast of contemporary characters from the island of Santa Lucia." Publ Wkly

"No poet rivals Mr. Walcott in humor, emotional depth, lavish inventiveness in language or in the ability to express the thoughts of his characters and compel the reader to follow the swift mutations of ideas and images in their minds. This wonderful story moves in a spiral, replicating human thought." N Y Times Book Rev

Warren, Robert Penn, 1905-1989

The collected poems of Robert Penn Warren; edited by John Burt; with a foreword by Harold Bloom. Louisiana State Univ. Press 1998 xxvi, 830p $44.95 **811**

ISBN 0-8071-2333-1   LC 98-26104

"This immense volume gathers 15 books of poetry—as well as uncollected verse from the beginning and end of his writing life—from a formidable American man of letters and our first poet laureate. . . . Scholars will especially cherish the careful, copious textual and explanatory notes provided by Warren's literary executor Burt . . . and fans of American poetry and literary history alike should welcome this opportunity to explore the prodigious oeuvre of one of the New Criticism's most forceful, convincing proponents." Publ Wkly

Whalen, Philip, 1923-2002

Overtime; selected poems; edited by Michael Rothenberg; introduction by Leslie Scalapino. Penguin Bks. 1999 xx, 311p pa $16.95 **811**

ISBN 0-14-058918-X   LC 98-48926

"Palpably realistic, Boswellian in detail, by turns cranky, amused, hungry or sated with experience, Whalen's verse remains uniquely personal, an artifact of one man's creative energy. . . . As many of Whalen's books have dropped out of print, this generous volume, introduced by poet and critic Scalapino, and chronologically organized and selected by poet Rothenberg, is long overdue. It helps reacquaint us with a key figure who continues to work toward social and personal tranformation." Publ Wkly

Wheatley, Phillis, 1753-1784

The poems of Phillis Wheatley; edited with an introduction by Julian D. Mason, Jr. rev & enl ed. University of N.C. Press 1989 235p hardcover o.p. paperback available $18.95 **811**

ISBN 0-8078-4245-1 (pa)   LC 88-23280

First published 1966

This volume contains all of the poems and letters known to have been written by Wheatley, America's first significant black woman writer

Whitman, Walt, 1819-1892

Leaves of grass   **811**

Hardcover and paperback editions available from various publishers

First published 1855

"The book, radical in form and content, takes its title from the themes of fertility, universality, and cyclical life. . . . As he revised and added to the original edition, Whitman arranged the poems in a significant autobiographical order." Reader's Ency. 4th edition

Selected poems; Harold Bloom, editor. Library of Am. 2003 xxxi, 221p (American poets project) $20   **811**

ISBN 1-931082-32-4   LC 2002-32124

The editor "is concerned with Whitman's construction of his all-encompassing persona, and he selects with that in mind. . . . Bloom connects Whitman's project to the thesis of his *The American Religion* (1992) that the tendency of religion in America is to replace God with man, and with the fragments, Bloom presents explicit evidence of the attempt." Booklist

Includes bibliographical references

Wilbur, Richard, 1921-

Mayflies; new poems and translations. Harcourt 2000 80p $22   **811**

ISBN 0-15-100469-2   LC 99-45452

"Wilbur remains America's reigning master of poems in traditional forms, creating flawless, balanced, charming and even profound couplets, sonnets, sapphics, and intricately custom-made stanzas. . . . [This volume] brings together 22 new poems, six renderings of lyric poems from French, Romanian and Bulgarian, and two longer verse translations—from Moliere's *Amphitryon* and Dante's *Inferno*." Publ Wkly

New and collected poems. Harcourt Brace Jovanovich 1988 393p hardcover o.p. paperback available $17   **811**

ISBN 0-15-665491-1 (pa)   LC 87-18175

This "volume includes the complete texts of [the author's] six previous volumes, 23 new poems, three new translations and the text of the cantata 'On Freedom's Ground' (done in collaboration with the composer William Schuman)." N Y Times Book Rev

"Wilbur has done what is most difficult and rare: He has used the full palette of the poetic art to deal with modern experience." Christ Sci Monit

Williams, C. K. (Charles Kenneth), 1936-

Repair. Farrar, Straus & Giroux 1999 69p hardcover o.p. paperback available $12 **811**

ISBN 0-374-52706-7 (pa)   LC 98-51901

Williams "is best known for his breathless, long, and often prosaic line. But in this eighth volume of poetry, he intersperses short-lined poems—perhaps his finest works to date. Focused and lyrical, they include delicate love poems set against precarious backdrops." Libr J

Williams, C. K. (Charles Kenneth), 1936-—
Continued

The singing. Farrar, Straus & Giroux 2003 72p $20 **811**

ISBN 0-374-29286-8   LC 2003-7091

The author focuses on "those aspects of life that haunt and plague us the most: lost love, brute aggression, hate, and death. Williams dissects and ponders these dark mysteries within the contexts of life's implacable organic imperatives and history's compelling yet ineffectual cautionary tales. . . . This is an altogether transfixing and cathartically probing collection, but it reaches its highest peaks in a set of poems in which Williams offers deep and anchoring insights into the time of war that began on September 11, 2001, and in the ravishingly beautiful cycle 'Elegy to an Artist,' a tribute to friendship and ringing testimony to the radiance of the human spirit and the consolation of art." Booklist

The vigil; poems. Farrar, Straus & Giroux 1996 77p hardcover o.p. paperback available $12 **811**

ISBN 0-374-52554-4 (pa)   LC 96-17253

This "collection is in three parts. The first consists of elegies for the dead and for the living but lost and the times that are no more. The second is a set of eight 'Symbols'—poems about the imaginative significance of animals and things. The third begins with the book's title poem; the poems in it are ruefully, wistfully written from the perspective of an incipient old age." Booklist

Williams, William Carlos, 1883-1963

The collected poems of William Carlos Williams. New Directions 1986-1988 2v **811**

LC 86-5448

Contents: v1 1909-1939; ed. by A. Walton Litz and Christopher MacGowan $40, pa $21.95 (ISBN 0-8112-0999-7; 0-8112-1187-8); v2 1939-1962; ed. by Christopher MacGowan $38, pa $21.95 (0-8112-1063-4; 0-8112-1188-6)

"Williams's original approach to poetry, his insistence on the importance of the ordinary, and his successful attempts at making his verse as 'tactile' as the spoken word had a far-reaching effect on American poetry." Reader's Ency. 4th edition

Paterson. rev ed, prepared by Christopher MacGowan. New Directions 1992 311p hardcover o.p. paperback available $14.95 **811**

ISBN 0-8112-1298-X (pa)   LC 92-22956

First published 1963

"Set in Paterson, N.J., the poem is a statement on contemporary civilization. Williams uses one dominant metaphor throughout: the city is the human mind beside the river of time; the language of contemporary events (the waterfall) gives the only kind of meaning possible in the flux of time. The poem is composed of lyrics, narrative episodes, prose interludes, bits of letters, etc., to comprise an ecstatic statement on human life." Herzberg. Reader's Ency of Am Lit

Winters, Yvor, 1900-1968

The selected poems of Yvor Winters; edited by R.L. Barth; introduction by Helen Pinkerton Trimpi. Swallow Press 1999 xlv, 128p $28.95; pa $14.95 **811**

ISBN 0-8040-1012-9; 0-8040-1013-7 (pa)

LC 98-49855

Winters "may still be better known as a notoriously irascible literary critic than as a poet. But he thought poetry was superior to criticism as literature, and he wrote and published it earlier. He abandoned his imagistic early style, however, choosing traditional meters and rhyme for a publicly engaged poetry in which he strove to continue classical Greek and Latin poetry's concern for social and individual virtue, consideration for how the present may affect futurity, and understanding that nothing lasts." Booklist

Wright, C. D.

Steal away; selected and new poems. Copper Canyon Press 2002 235p $25; pa $17 **811**

ISBN 1-55659-172-1; 1-55659-194-2 (pa)

LC 2001-7423

Wright's "poems are crazy quilts constructed out of bits of conversation, a to-do list, dreams, a treatment for a harrowing silent film, and a saxophone solo, but Wright also offers sophisticated readings of the routines and cycle of ordinary life, and ponders the amazing persistence of the ever-hungry body and the tricky mind. It's a boon to have such a wealth of her crackling, intelligent, erotic, 'painfully beautiful,' keep-you-on-your-toes poems in one place. New works accompany selections from nine previous, mostly out of print collections, and all are electrifying in their clear-eyed reports on desire, determination, and survival." Booklist

Wright, Charles, 1935-

Appalachia. Farrar, Straus & Giroux 1998 67p hardcover o.p. paperback available $12 **811**

ISBN 0-374-52624-9 (pa)   LC 98-16803

Wright's "inquisitive poems reside at the crux of faith and art: the realization that no matter how sincerely one prays, or how devotedly one writes, the universe and the divine force that animates it remain out of reach of language, reason, and imagination. . . . Wright tries to connect with the spiritual by conjuring the ancient beaming of stars, winter's starkness, and the valor of flowers. Finally, in sweet, bemused surrender, he acknowledges both the impossibility of certainty, and our insatiable hunger for it." Booklist

Negative blue; selected later poems. Farrar, Straus & Giroux 2000 206p $23; pa $15 **811**

ISBN 0-374-22020-4; 0-374-52773-3 (pa)

LC 99-36987

The author "collects a decade's worth of striking description and laid-back meditation in this sample of work from his last three books. . . . Wright's power lies less in whole poems than in lines within them: those linear strenghts owe something to Ezra Pound, and something more to the antiphonal balances of the Psalms. Wright ends the volume with seven new short poems." Publ Wkly

Wright, James Arlington, 1927-1980

Above the river; the complete poems; [by] James Wright; with an introduction by Donald Hall. Farrar, Straus & Giroux; University Press of New England 1990 xxxvii, 387p hardcover o.p. paperback available $17   **811**

ISBN 0-374-52282-0 (pa)   LC 89-16538

"A Wesleyan University Press edition"

"The narrowed range of Wright's characteristic subjects and format, the very delicacy of his instincts, confine him. But his best poems, with their grace and intelligence, not only stand as a rebuke to most of the glib work of his time, but remain among the finest examples of the midcentury American lyric." N Y Times Book Rev

Wright, Jay

Transfigurations; collected poems. Louisiana State Univ. Press 2000 619p $59.95; pa $24.95   **811**

ISBN 0-8071-2629-2; 0-8071-2630-6 (pa)

LC 00-40560

"Lyric poetry is a way of compressing experience into a heightened moment, but what happens when the experience is one of wanting not to be contained? Wright is an African-American poet who has contended with this dilemma for the last thirty years, and the result is a substantial collection of work. His forcefully musical rhythms drive even poems of everyday experience to a pleasingly contradictory transport. And the later, meditative poems are bound to the world by their attention to the sensual within the spiritual." New Yorker

Zarin, Cynthia

The watercourse: poems. Random House 2002 75p $23; pa $15   **811**

ISBN 0-375-41366-9; 0-375-70977-0 (pa)

LC 2001-38225

"Zarin concentrates on the tiny, inarticulate moments of leisured life, where the pace of childhood stretches into adulthood. . . . This book is firmly in the American light-verse tradition, where serious emotional business gets transacted under the cover of near nursery rhymes." Publ Wkly

811.008 American poetry— Collections

African-American poetry of the nineteenth century; an anthology; edited by Joan R. Sherman. University of Ill. Press 1992 506p hardcover o.p. paperback available $26.95   **811.008**

1. American poetry—African American authors—Collections

ISBN 0-252-06246-9 (pa)   LC 91-41709

Companion to Sherman's Invisible poets (1989)

"The introduction surveys the historical and cultural values of African American poetry. The poems themselves have historical as well as lyric value; unfamiliar as well as familiar poets are included. Though the poems are formal, the rhymes are generally unforced. . . . This anthology also includes an extensive bibliography to help researchers find other resources." Libr J

American poetry: the nineteenth century; edited by John Hollander. Library of Am. 1993 2v ea $35   **811.008**

1. American poetry—Collections

ISBN 0-940450-60-7 (v1); 0-940450-78-X (v2)

LC 93-10702

Volume 1 also available in paperback $14.95 (ISBN 1-88301-136-1)

Contents: v1 Freneau to Whitman; v2 Melville to Stickney; American Indian poetry; Folk songs and spirituals

An anthology of more than 1,000 poems by nearly 150 poets. Arrangement is chronological by poet's date of birth. Biographical sketches of the poets, a chronology of significant events from 1800 to 1900, and an essay on textual selection are included

Hollander has compiled "a selection of nineteenth-century American verse so wonderfully catholic that it not just augments but supersedes every other similar collection." Booklist

American poetry, The twentieth century. Library of Am. 2000 2v ea $35   **811.008**

1. American poetry—Collections

ISBN 1-88301-177-9 (v1); 1-88301-178-7 (v2)

LC 99-43721

The first two volumes of a projected four volume set

Contents: v1 Henry Adams to Dorothy Parker; v2 E.E. Cummings to May Swenson

"Over 200 poets are represented, all born before 1914, and presented in birth-date order." Publ Wkly

These volumes represent a "remarkable feat of assemblage, with excellent capsule biographies and explanatory notes at the end of each volume—the biographies, especially, are well worth reading." N Y Times Book Rev

Includes bibliographical references

The **Best** American poetry. Scribner $30; pa $16   **811.008**

1. American poetry—Collections

ISSN 1040-5763

Series editor: David Lehman

An annual collection of American verse culled from large-circulation magazines and smaller literary reviews

The **Body** electric; America's best poetry from the American poetry review; edited by Stephen Berg, David Bonanno, and Arthur Vogelsang; with an introduction by Harold D. Bloom. Norton 2000 xli, 820p hardcover o.p. paperback available $22.50   **811.008**

1. American poetry—Collections

ISBN 0-393-32170-3 (pa)   LC 99-55513

"Almost every name is familiar—A.R. Ammons, John Ashbery, Lucille Clifton, W.S. Merwin, Adrienne Rich, Charles Simic, Gerald Stern, and Derek Walcott—and some—John Berryman, Robert Lowell, Charles Olson, Frank O'Hara, and Sylvia Plath—are downright monumental. The result is a broad, collective view of the American poet's concerns between the waning of the Vietnam War and the rise of the dot-com day trader." Libr J

The **Columbia** anthology of American poetry; edited by Jay Parini. Columbia Univ. Press 1995 757p $40.95 **811.008**
1. American poetry—Collections
ISBN 0-231-08122-7 LC 94-32423

"Ranging from Anne Bradstreet to Louise Glück, editor Parini aims to represent 'the main schools of poetry that have co-existed in the United States . . . in proportion to their influence,' including more poetry by women and minorities 'than one generally finds' in older anthologies." Libr J

The **Columbia** book of Civil War poetry; Richard Marius, editor; Keith W. Frome, associate editor. Columbia Univ. Press 1994 xxxvi, 543p il $37.95 **811.008**
1. American poetry—Collections 2. United States—History—1861-1865, Civil War—Poetry
ISBN 0-231-10002-7 LC 94-6481

"Bret Harte, Walt Whitman, and Robert Frost are but three of the many writers whose poems about the Civil War fill this noteworthy collection." Booklist

Eight American poets; an anthology: Theodore Roethke, Elizabeth Bishop, Robert Lowell, John Berryman, Anne Sexton, Sylvia Plath, Allen Ginsberg, James Merrill; edited by Joel Conarroe. Random House 1994 xxiv, 306p il hardcover o.p. paperback available $14 **811.008**
1. American poetry—Collections
ISBN 0-679-77643-5 (pa) LC 94-10186

This anthology contains representative work by eight 20th century American confessional poets

Every shut eye ain't asleep; an anthology of poetry by African Americans since 1945; edited by Michael Harper and Anthony Walton. Little, Brown 1994 327p hardcover o.p. paperback available $19 **811.008**
1. American poetry—African American authors—Collections
ISBN 0-316-34710-8 (pa) LC 93-10788

"Using Robert Hayden and Gwendolyn Brooks's poetry as 'emblematic' successes, this anthology selects 35 African American poets (spanning three generations) who were born between 1913 and 1962 and came of age after 1945. Besides the well-known Imamu Baraka, Lucille Clifton, Rita Dove, and Etheridge Knight, the editors feature little-known or younger poets like Elizabeth Alexander, Gerald Barrax, Jayne Cortex, and Dolores Kendrick." Libr J

The **Gift** of tongues; twenty-five years of poetry from Copper Canyon Press; edited and with an introduction by Sam Hamill. Copper Canyon Press 1996 xxvii, 356p $30; pa $16 **811.008**
1. Poetry—Collections
ISBN 1-556-59116-0; 1-556-59117-9 (pa)
LC 96-25337

"The poems range temporally from antiquity to the present and geographically throughout the world. Nobel laureates (Aleixandre, Neruda, Elytis), grand old persons of literary modernism (Rexroth, H.D., Pound), and scads

of senior (Carruth, Levertov, Kizer, etc.) and younger masters are Copper Canyon authors. All appear here, and founder Sam Hamill introduces the poems with the history of Copper Canyon and follows them with a delightfully annotated year-by-year listing of all its titles." Booklist

Includes bibliographical references

Good poems; selected and introduced by Garrison Keillor. Viking 2002 xxvi, 476p $25.95; pa $15 **811.008**
1. American poetry—Collections 2. English poetry—Collections
ISBN 0-670-03126-7; 0-14-200344-1 (pa)
LC 2002-16881

Keillor "has put together a collection of close to 300 poems he has read during . . . [the] PBS broadcast, The Writer's Almanac. . . . Poems are arranged by 19 general themes, such as 'Snow,' 'Failure,' and 'A Good Life.' Authors range from well-known oldies like Emily Dickinson and Robert Frost to unknowns like C.K. Williams. . . . An outstanding feature of this collection is that the selections are all so accessible—even folks who say they don't like poetry can find something here to enjoy." SLJ

Harper's anthology of 20th century Native American poetry; edited by Duane Niatum. Harper & Row 1988 xxxii, 396p hardcover o.p. paperback available $24 **811.008**
1. American poetry—Native American authors
ISBN 0-06-250666-8 (pa) LC 86-45023

This collection "contains the work of 36 native American poets, with hearty selections from each. Among the 36 are poets near the mainstream (Scott Momaday, James Welch, Louise Erdrich); those in academe (Gerald Vizenor, Linda Hogan, Jim Barnes); those writing in the tribal oral tradition (Barney Bush, Peter Blue Cloud, Wendy Rose); and those working in a modernist voice (Gladys Cardiff, Paula Gunn Allen). This book belongs in every collection that claims to represent the multiple voices of American literature today." Booklist

Includes bibliographical references

The **Harvard** book of contemporary American poetry; edited by Helen Vendler. Belknap Press 1985 440p $34 **811.008**
1. American poetry—Collections
ISBN 0-674-37340-5 LC 85-5473

Following an introduction which places recent American poetry in its aesthetic and social contexts, the editor presents a representative selection of the work of thirty-five poets. Among those included are: James Merrill, Elizabeth Bishop, Gary Snyder, Jorie Graham, and Amy Clampitt. Brief biographies of the poets are appended

The **Made** thing; an anthology of contemporary Southern poetry; {edited by} Leon Stokesbury. 2nd ed. University of Ark. Press 1999 xxiii, 379p il $38; pa $22 **811.008**
1. American poetry—Southern States—Collections
ISBN 1-55728-578-0; 1-55728-579-9 (pa)
LC 99-43633

First published 1987

Among the 66 poets included are: Donald Justice, Dave Smith, Pattiann Rogers, Rodney Jones, Wendell Berry, Henry Taylor, Vassar Miller, Robert Penn Warren, and Charles Wright

The **New** American poets; edited by Michael Collier. University Press of New England 2000 xx, 280p il $50; pa $19.95   **811.008**
1. American poetry—Collections
ISBN 0-87451-963-2; 0-87451-964-0 (pa)
       LC 99-56171

"A Bread Loaf anthology"

This anthology includes over 50 poets who are either under 40 or have published a first book within the past five years. D.A. Powell, Mary Jo Bang, Greg Williamson, Pimone Triplett, and Maurice Kilwein Guevara are among the contributors

The **New** Bread Loaf anthology of contemporary American poetry; Michael Collier and Stanley Plumly, editors. University Press of New England 1999 359p hardcover o.p. paperback available $17.95   **811.008**
1. American poetry—Collections
ISBN 0-87451-950-0 (pa)   LC 99-20942

Replaces The Bread Loaf anthology of American poetry, published 1985

"Bread Loaf Writers' Conference and Middlebury College Press"

In this volume, "82 poets select their own work, and the range of voices and styles included is immense: from Agha Shahid Ali, Frank Bidart, and Yusef Komunyakaa to Campbell McGrath, Heather McHugh, Alberto Rios, and more. . . . A superb introduction for the new reader and a splendid handbook for the poet and critic." SLJ

The **New** Oxford book of American verse; chosen and edited by Richard Ellmann. Oxford Univ. Press 1976 liv, 1076p $49.95
       811.008
1. American poetry—Collections
ISBN 0-19-502058-8

Replaces The Oxford book of American verse, edited by F. O. Matthiessen (1950)

"This volume begins with Anne Bradstreet, who died in 1672, and ends with Imamu Amiri Baraka (LeRoy Jones), born in 1934. . . . A few ballads and folk songs, and one hymn, are . . . included. Most of the poets are represented with some amplitude so as to give a sense of their range and variety." Introduction

The **New** young American poets; an anthology; edited by Kevin Prufer; with a foreword by Richard Howard. Southern Ill. Univ. Press 2000 243p hardcover o.p. paperback available $22.50   **811.008**
1. American poetry—Collections
ISBN 0-8093-2309-5 (pa)   LC 99-37043

This anthology contains the "work by 40 poets less than 40 years old. Usually, there are three to five poems per poet, enough to whet a reader's appetite for more. . . . Black, Latino, Asian, and gay voices resound throughout the book." Booklist

The **Poetry** anthology, 1912-2002; ninety years of America's most distinguished verse magazine; edited by Joseph Parisi & Stephen Young; with an introduction by Joseph Parisi. Dee, I.R. 2002 1v, 509p $29.95   **811.008**
1. American poetry—Collections
ISBN 1-56663-468-7   LC 2002-31178

A collection of 600 poems previously published in Poetry magazine, written by such poets as W.H. Auden, Elizabeth Bishop, Sylvia Plath, James Merrill, and Susan Hahn

This is a "comprehensive and thrilling anthology, a veritable history of twentieth-century poetry in English." Booklist

The **Poetry** of black America; anthology of the 20th century; introduction by Gwendolyn Brooks. Harper & Row 1973 xxxi, 552p $25.95   **811.008**
1. American poetry—African American authors—Collections
ISBN 0-06-020089-8   LC 72-76518

A collection of over 600 poems by 145 authors. James Weldon Johnson, Paul Laurence Dunbar, Langston Hughes, Gwendolyn Brooks, Sonia Sanchez, Don Lee and Nikki Giovanni are among the poets represented. Biographical sketches are provided

Postmodern American poetry; a Norton anthology; edited by Paul Hoover. Norton 1994 xxxix, 701p pa $26.95   **811.008**
1. American poetry—Collections
ISBN 0-393-31090-6   LC 93-22753

Hoover "brings together more than 100 writers from the 1950s and since—Olson, Duncan, O'Hara, Ginsberg, Corso, Dorn, Major, Ashbery, Guest—whose adventures with the language renew it for far more than a readymade membership." Publ Wkly

Six American poets; an anthology; edited by Joel Connaroe. Random House 1991 xxxiv, 281p il hardcover o.p. paperback available $14   **811.008**
1. American poetry—Collections
ISBN 0-679-74525-4 (pa)   LC 91-15375

This anthology contains 247 representative poems by Walt Whitman, Emily Dickinson, Wallace Stevens, William Carlos Williams, Robert Frost and Langston Hughes

Songs from this Earth on turtle's back; contemporary American Indian poetry; edited by Joseph Bruchac. Greenfield Review Press 1983 294p il pa $14.95
       811.008
1. American poetry—Native American authors
ISBN 0-912678-58-5   LC 82-82420

"A biographical statement accompanies each sampling from 50 poets representing more than 35 different Native American nations." Libr J

"The collection provides a balance to the volumes of compiled chants and translated (or mistranslated) songs already in most libraries. . . . Writing in English, they display a variety of styles and themes and draw from urban, rural, and reservation backgrounds, yet they share a reverence for the earth and the natural world and a keen understanding of the power of language to create and shape that world." Choice

The **Spoken** word revolution; slam, hip-hop, & the poetry of a new generation; edited by Marc Eleveld; advised by Marc Smith; introduction by Billy Collins. Sourcebooks 2003 241p il $24.95 **811.008**
1. American poetry—Collections 2. American poetry—History and criticism
ISBN 1-4022-0037-4 LC 2003-841

The editors "trace the evolution of spoken-word poetry from the Beats to rap, hip-hop, and performance art. The result is a dynamic and clarifying volume chock-full of fresh and informative commentary by the likes of Billy Collins, Marvin Bell, and Jerry Quickley and an exciting array of knock-out poems by Patricia Smith, Tara Betts, Jeff McDaniel, Roger Bonair-Agard . . . and many more. Eleveld and his contributors not only celebrate the verve, artistry, and significance of performance poetry but also anchor it firmly within the splendid, age-old, and life-sustaining universe of poetry. . . . An accompanying CD presents poets performing their work." Booklist

Unsettling America; an anthology of contemporary multicultural poetry; edited by Maria Mazziotti Gillan and Jennifer Gillan. Penguin Bks. 1994 xxv, 406p hardcover o.p. paperback available $15.95 **811.008**
1. American poetry—Collections
ISBN 0-14-023778-X (pa) LC 94-722

This "anthology provides exposure to poets, emerging and established—Louis Simpson, Rita Dove, Luis Rodriguez—who write directly from the immigrant, ethnic and/or religious experience. . . . This collection is a must for anyone seeking an inclusive, unwincing catalogue of the American experience." Publ Wkly

The **Vintage** book of African American poetry; edited and with an introduction by Michael S. Harper and Anthony Walton. Vintage Bks. 2000 xxxiii, 403p pa $14.95 **811.008**
1. American poetry—African American authors—Collections
ISBN 0-375-70300-4 LC 99-39428

"Included in chronological order here are over two centuries of poets, from Jupiter Hammon (1720-1800) to Reginald Shepherd (b.1963). . . . The editors' eloquent, outspoken vision provides a springboard for further examination of what constitutes the mainstream of American poetry." Libr J

The **World** in us; lesbian and gay poetry of the next wave: an anthology; edited by Michael Lassell and Elena Georgiou. St. Martin's Press 2000 xxi, 392p hardcover o.p. paperback available $17.95 **811.008**
1. American poetry—Collections 2. Homosexuality in literature
ISBN 0-312-27333-9 (pa) LC 99-86683

"A wide variety of form and style is represented, from the hip-hop beat of urban street slang to the steady, studied cadence of more meditative verse. . . . Well-known poets such as Olga Broumas, Alfred Corn, Robert Gluck, and Marilyn Hacker appear alongside new names with equally impressive talents." Libr J

The **Yale** younger poets anthology; edited by George Bradley. Yale Univ. Press 1998 ci, 306p hardcover o.p. paperback available $19 **811.008**
1. American poetry—Collections
ISBN 0-300-07473-5 (pa) LC 97-35444

Founded "in 1919 as a way to exhibit the poetic precocity of Yale students, the *Yale Younger Poets* series has evolved over 78 years into a flagship imprimatur for a poet's first book. . . . As Bradley (a winner himself in 1986) describes in his informative introduction, each of the judges carried out their duties with their own styles, from the distant and difficult Archibald MacLeish and the eccentric classicist Dudley Fitts (who selected James Tate and George Starbuck), to the series' most famous and successful arbiter, W.H. Auden." Publ Wkly

811.009 American poetry— History and criticism

The **Columbia** history of American poetry; Jay Parini, editor; Brett C. Millier, associate editor. Columbia Univ. Press 1993 xxxi, 894p $86.50 **811.009**
1. American poetry—History and criticism
ISBN 0-231-07836-6 LC 92-29399

"These 31 essays by various experts in the field interrogate, dismantle, and ultimately reassemble the history of poetry in the United States, from the work of the slave George Moses Horton . . . to the writings of Beat, Black Arts, and Marxist-oriented Language Poets of today. The great figures of the past—Whitman, Poe, Eliot, and so on—still loom, yet each time we are made to see them in some new way. . . . An essential volume that shows how poetry intersects with our lives and vice versa." Libr J

Includes bibliographical references

Encyclopedia of American poetry, the nineteenth century; edited by Eric L. Haralson; John Hollander, advisory editor. Fitzroy Dearborn Pubs. 1998 536p $100 **811.009**
1. American poetry—Bio-bibliography 2. Poets, American—Dictionaries
ISBN 1-57958-008-4 LC 99-167193

"Entries are substantial, ranging from three pages to more than ten in the case of poets like Emily Dickinson. In addition to furnishing biographical information, each entry is also a critical essay, discussing the poetry as well as the literary and historical significance of the poet. As a companion to the anthology, the essays include specific references to volume and page numbers in the anthology where the reader can find many of the verses under discussion." Booklist

Encyclopedia of American poetry, the twentieth century; edited by Eric L. Haralson. Fitzroy Dearborn Pubs. 2001 846p $125 **811.009**
1. American poetry—Bio-bibliography 2. Poets, American—Dictionaries
ISBN 1-57958-240-0

"The volume features more than 400 entries written by academic contributors on individual poets, landmark poems, and major topics. The poet entries are usually 1,000

Encyclopedia of American poetry, the twentieth century—*Continued*

to 2,000 words long and offer critical treatment of the poet's career and major achievements along with a capsule biography. . . . Approximately one-third of the poet entries include subentries for one or more landmark poems. The 'major topics' entries are longer (around 3,000 words) and include periods or movements (*Black Arts movement, Dada*), verse traditions (often ethnic, such as *Asian American poetry*), and styles and themes (*Confessional poetry, War and antiwar poetry*)." Booklist

812 American drama

Albee, Edward, 1928-

Who's afraid of Virginia Woolf? Scribner Classics 2003 243p $24   **812**
ISBN 0-7432-5525-9   LC 2003-54206
Also available in paperback from Dramatists Play Service and Signet Bks.
A reissue of the title first published 1962 by Atheneum Pubs.
Characters: 2 men, 2 women. 3 acts. First produced at the Billy Rose Theatre, New York City, October 13, 1962
"The play is a virulent unveiling of the relationship between George, a history professor, and his wife, Martha, the college president's daughter. Another couple, Nick and Honey, get caught in the crossfire of George and Martha's verbal and emotional lacerations, and it becomes clear that each character is engaged in an isolated struggle through a personal hell." Reader's Ency. 4th edition

Auburn, David

Proof; a play. Faber & Faber 2001 83p pa $13   **812**
ISBN 0-571-19997-6   LC 00-50284
Also available in paperback from Dramatists Play Service
Characters: 2 men, 2 women. 2 acts, 9 scenes. First produced by the Manhattan Theatre Club, New York City, May 23, 2000
"Twenty-five-year-old Catherine, who sacrificed college to care for her mentally ill father (once a brilliant, much-admired mathematician), is left in a kind of limbo after his death. Socially awkward and a bit of a shut-in, she is gruff with Hal, a former student who shows up even before the funeral wanting to root through the countless notebooks her father kept in the years of his decline, hoping to find mathematical gold. On the heels of his arrival comes Claire, Catherine's cosmopolitan, blandly successful, and pushy sister, with plans to sell their father's house and take Catherine . . . with her back to New York." SLJ

Baraka, Imamu Amiri, 1934-

Dutchman, and The slave; two plays; [by] LeRoi Jones. Morrow 1964 88p hardcover o.p. paperback available $8.95   **812**
ISBN 0-688-21084-8 (pa)
In Dutchman Baraka "explores the revolutionary potential of the educated black middle-class intellectual, represented by the protagonist, Clay, a would-be poet. When Clay is exposed as dangerous—that is, as a latent killer—by white society, seductively imaged as a beautiful white woman named Lula, he is summarily executed by that society. *The Slave* (1964), a fable set in a future of war between the races, continues the theme of black revolutionary militancy." Benet's Reader's Ency of Am Lit

Cruz, Nilo

Anna in the tropics. Theatre Communications Group 2003 84p pa $12.95   **812**

1. Cuban Americans—Drama
ISBN 1-55936-232-4   LC 2003-15859
Characters: 5 men, 3 women. 2 acts, 10 scenes. First produced at the New Theatre, Coral Gables, Florida, October 12, 2002
"Set in a cigar factory in Tampa, Florida, in 1929, where the Cuban-American employees have just hired a new 'lector' to read novels to them while they work, Anna and the Tropics is written in the lyrical, somewhat formalized parlance of a folktale. The play is both a piece of cultural history and a warm-spirited tribute to the transformative power of art." Time

Edson, Margaret

Wit; a play. Faber & Faber 1999 85p pa $13   **812**
ISBN 0-571-19877-5   LC 99-11921
Also available in paperback from Dramatists Play Service
Awarded the Pulitzer Prize, 1999
Characters: 3 men, 3 women, extras. First produced at Long Wharf Theatre, New Haven, Connecticut, October 31, 1997
Drama about English literature professor and Donne scholar hospitalized with advanced ovarian cancer

Foote, Horton

Collected plays. v2. Smith & Kraus 1996 216p hardcover o.p. paperback available $19.95   **812**
ISBN 1-57525-016-0 (pa)
Also available volume I: 4 new plays and volume III: Getting Frankie married—and afterwards, and other plays
"Contemporary playwrights series"
Contents: The trip to Bountiful; The chase; The traveling lady; The roads to home
"Foote's ear for naturalistic dialogue never fails him, and even in the midst of telling an exciting story . . . he never lets the potential for melodrama overwhelm things." Booklist

Getting Frankie married—and afterwards, and other plays. Smith & Kraus 1998 288p (Contemporary playwrights series) hardcover o.p. paperback available $19.95   **812**
ISBN 1-57525-136-1 (pa)
Designated volume III of Horton Foote's collected plays
"Harrison, TX, Foote's imaginary community, is the setting for four plays. The themes of family and community, kinship and friendship in small Southern towns threatened by the oil and gas industries are dramatized with compassion and sensitivity." Libr J

The young man from Atlanta. Dutton 1995 110p il   **812**
Available in paperback from Dramatists Play Service
Awarded the Pulitzer Prize, 1995
Characters: 5 men, 4 women. 6 scenes. First produced by Signature Theatre Company, New York City, January 27, 1995
"The implication is strong that [the title character] was the lover of Will and Lily Dale Kidder's son Bill. He's a needy young man who extracted from Bill thousands

Foote, Horton—*Continued*

of the dollars Will sent him while he floundered about after World War II service. Even after Bill's suicide, which has devastated Will, the young man has importuned Bill's parents, successfully persuading Lily Dale to give him, unbeknownst to Will, half her savings. Now he's back on the Kidders' doorstep in Houston in 1950." Booklist

Gardner, Herb, 1934-2003

Herb Gardner: the collected plays and the screenplay Who is Harry Kellerman and why is he saying those terrible things about me? Applause Theatre Bk. Pubs. 2000 489p il $27.95; pa $16.95 **812**

ISBN 1-55783-394-X; 1-55783-466-0 (pa)

Contents: Thousand clowns; Goodbye people; Thieves; I'm not Rappaport; Conversations with my father; Who is Harry Kellerman and why is he saying those terrible things about me?

These works "have furnished star actors with some of their most memorable roles and star directors with some of their biggest successes. Those favors are returned by the likes of Jason Robards, Judd Hirsch, Elaine May, Charles Grodin, and Dustin Hoffman, who introduce the plays that brightened their reputations." Booklist

Gibson, William, 1914-

The miracle worker; a play for television. Knopf 1957 131p o.p.; Pocket Bks. paperback available $5.99 **812**

1. Keller, Helen, 1880-1968—Drama 2. Sullivan, Anne, 1866-1936—Drama

ISBN 0-7434-5758-7 (pa)

Dramatic portrayal of relationship between Helen Keller and his teacher Anne Sullivan

"The present text is meant for reading, and differs from the telecast version in that I have restored some passages that read better than they play and others omitted in performance for simple lack of time." Author's note

Goodrich, Frances, 1891-1984

The diary of Anne Frank; dramatized by Frances Goodrich and Albert Hackett; based upon the book, Anne Frank: diary of a young girl; with a foreword by Brooks Atkinson. Random House 1956 174p il **812**

1. Netherlands—History—1940-1945, German occupation—Drama 2. World War, 1939-1945—Jews—Drama 3. Jews—Netherlands—Drama

Available in paperback from Dramatists Play Service

Awarded the Pulitzer Prize and the New York Drama Critics Circle Award for 1956

Characters: 5 men, 5 women. 2 acts. First produced at the Cort Theatre, New York City, October 5, 1955

Dramatization of Anne Frank: diary of a young girl, entered in class 92. Portrays ultimately unsuccessful attempt of Jewish family to remain hidden during the German occupation of Holland

Guare, John

Six degrees of separation; a play. Random House 1990 120p hardcover o.p. paperback available $12.95 **812**

ISBN 0-679-73481-3 (pa)   LC 90-53449

Also available in paperback from Dramatists Play Service

Characters: 13 men, 4 women. First produced at the Mitzi Newhouse Theater, New York City, June 1990

Satirical look at contemporary urban America. Upscale, liberal New York City couple is manipulated by young black man

Gurney, A. R. (Albert Ramsdell), 1930-

Nine early plays, 1961-1973. Smith & Kraus 1995 252p (Collected works) $29.95; pa $16.95 **812**

ISBN 1-57525-020-9; 1-880399-88-1 (pa)

LC 95-19638

"Contemporary playwrights series"

"Some of these early plays concern classical material as dealt with by modern characters using modern language. Others deal with WASP culture from the 1930s to today. Electrical language and bare minimum scenic requirements are in all of them." Voice Youth Advocates

Hansberry, Lorraine, 1930-1965

A raisin in the sun. Modern Lib. 1995 xxvi, 135p $14.95 **812**

1. African Americans—Drama

ISBN 0-679-60172-4   LC 95-16074

Also available in paperback from Plume Bks.

Awarded the New York Drama Critics Circle Award for the 1958-1959 season

First published 1959

Characters: 8 men, 3 women. 6 scenes in 3 acts. First produced at the Ethel Barrymore Theatre, New York City, March 11, 1959

"Hansberry's drama focuses on the Youngers, a 1950s African-American working-class family in Chicago striving to realize their individual dreams of prosperity and education, and their collective dream of a better life. It was the first play by an African-American woman to be produced on Broadway." Reader's Ency. 4th edition

Hughes, Langston, 1902-1967

Five plays; edited with an introduction by Webster Smalley. Indiana Univ. Press 1963 258p $29.95; pa $14.95 **812**

ISBN 0-253-32230-8; 0-253-20121-7 (pa)

Contents: Mulatto; Soul gone home; Little Ham; Simply heavenly; Tambourines to glory

Inge, William, 1913-1973

4 plays. Grove Press 1979 c1958 304p $13.50 **812**

ISBN 0-8021-3209-X   LC 78-73032

The author was awarded the Pulitzer Prize, 1953, for Picnic

"A Black cat book"

First published 1958 by Random House

Contents: Come back, Little Sheba; Picnic; Bus stop; The dark at the top of the stairs

Lerner, Alan Jay, 1918-1986

My fair lady; a musical play in two acts. Coward-McCann 1956 186p **812**

Only available with Shaw's Pygmalion, from New Am. Lib. in paperback

Awarded the New York Drama Critics Circle Award for 1956

"Based on 'Pygmalion' by Bernard Shaw; adaptation and lyrics by Alan Jay Lerner; music by Frederick Loewe." Title page

Characters: 28 men, 14 women. First produced at the Mark Hellinger Theatre, New York City, March 15, 1956

A British professor of phonetics transforms a Covent Garden flower girl into a semblance of a duchess

McCullers, Carson, 1917-1967

The member of the wedding; a play. New Directions 1951 118p pa $9.95   **812**

ISBN 0-8112-0093-0

Also available in paperback from Bantam Bks.

Awarded the New York Drama Critics Circle Award for 1950

Characters: 6 men, 7 women. 3 acts with 3 scenes in the last act. First produced at the Empire Theatre, New York City, January 3, 1950

Based on the author's book of the same title, this is "a study of the loneliness of an over-imaginative young Georgian girl." Saturday Rev

Miller, Arthur, 1915-

Broken glass; a play. Penguin Bks. 1994 161p pa $8.95   **812**

ISBN 0-14-024938-9   LC 93-20949

Also available in paperback from Dramatists Play Service

Characters: 3 men, 3 women. 2 acts. First produced at the Booth Theater, New York City, May, 1994

"It's the late 1930s in New York. Phillip Gellburg is an executive and the only Jew among the WASPs at a very Establishment Wall Street bank. His wife, Sylvia, is obsessed with news of Nazi Germany. After seeing a photo of old Jewish men forced to scrub the sidewalk with toothbrushes, she becomes mysteriously paralyzed in the legs. The only one who perceives Sylvia's fears and longings is Dr. Hyman—a man as passionate and empathetic as Phillip is repressed." Publisher's note

The crucible; a play in four acts. Viking 1953 145p hardcover o.p. paperback available $10   **812**

1. Witchcraft—Drama 2. Salem (Mass.)—Drama

ISBN 0-14-048138-9 (pa)

Also available in paperback from Dramatists Play Service

Characters: 11 men, 10 women. First produced at the Martin Beck Theatre in New York City, January 22, 1953

A play based on the Salem witchcraft trials of 1692. It deals particularly with the hounding to death of the nonconformist John Proctor

Death of a salesman; certain private conversations in two acts and a requiem. Viking 1949 139p hardcover o.p. paperback available $10   **812**

ISBN 0-14-048134-6 (pa)

Also available in paperback from Dramatists Play Service

Winner of the New York Drama Critics Circle Award and the Pulitzer Prize, 1949

Characters: 8 men, 5 women. First produced at the Morosco Theatre, New York City, February 10, 1949

"The tragedy of a typical American—a salesman who at the age of sixty-three is faced with what he cannot face: defeat and disillusionment. It is a bitter and moving experience of groping for values and for material success." Wis Libr Bull

A view from the bridge; a play in two acts. Viking 1960 86p hardcover o.p. paperback available $11   **812**

ISBN 0-14-048135-4 (pa)

Also available in paperback from Dramatists Play Service

Characters: 12 men, 3 women. First produced at the Coronet Theatre, New York City, 1955

"Set on the Brooklyn waterfront, the play depicts longshoreman Eddie Carbone's too intense love for his niece Catherine, which causes him to violate the code of the Sicilian community by informing on the illegal immigrant she wants to marry. As narrator Alfieri points out, the play has the primal elements of classical tragedy in the seemingly inevitable course of events that leads to Eddie's destruction." Cambridge Guide To Am Theatre

Norman, Marsha

Collected plays. v1. Smith & Kraus 1998 412p (Contemporary playwrights series) pa $19.95   **812**

ISBN 1-57525-029-2   LC 97-7665

Spine title: Collected works, volume 1

Norman's "characters, whether they be performers in a struggling two-bit circus, women in an all-night laundromat, or a Western outlaw, are ones we can easily identify with and understand." Libr J

O'Neill, Eugene, 1888-1953

Long day's journey into night; a play; with a foreword by Harold Bloom. 2nd ed. Yale Univ. Press 2002 c1989 179p $22.95; pa $12.95   **812**

ISBN 0-300-09410-8; 0-300-09305-5 (pa)

LC 2001-97735

Also available in paperback from Dramatists Play Service

Awarded the Pulitzer Prize, 1957

First published 1956

Characters: 3 men, 2 women. 4 acts, 5 scenes. First produced in Stockholm, Sweden, February, 1956

"Among the papers Eugene O'Neill left when he died in 1953 was the manuscript of an autobiography. Not an autobiography in the usual sense, however. For 'Long Day's Journey Into Night' is in the form of a play—a true O'Neill tragedy, set in 1912 in the summer home of a theatrical family that is isolated from the community by a kind of ingrown misery and a sense of doom." N Y Times Book Rev

Parks, Suzan-Lori

Topdog/underdog. Theatre Communications Group 2001 110p pa $12.95   **812**

ISBN 1-55936-201-4   LC 2001-27316

"Underdog" in the title appears reversed and upside down on the title page

Characters: 2 men. 6 scenes. First produced at The Joseph Papp Public Theater/New York Shakespeare Festival, New York City, July 22, 2001

This is "the story of Lincoln and Booth, two brothers whose names were given to them as a joke foretelling a lifetime of sibling rivalry and resentment. Haunted by the past, the brothers are forced to confront the shattering reality of their future." Publisher's note

Shange, Ntozake

For colored girls who have considered suicide/when the rainbow is enuf; a choreopoem. Macmillan 1977 64p o.p.; Simon & Schuster paperback available $9

812

1. African American women—Drama

ISBN 0-684-84326-9 (pa)   LC 77-3034

Choreopoem performed by seven women exploring the joys and sorrows of being a black woman

Simon, Neil

The collected plays of Neil Simon; with an introduction by Neil Simon. v2-3. Random House 1979-1991 2v v2 $29.95, v3 $34.50
812

ISBN 0-394-50770-3 (v2); 0-679-40889-4 (v3)

Both volumes also available in paperback from New Am. Lib.

Contents v2: Little me; The gingerbread lady; The prisoner of Second Avenue; The Sunshine Boys; The good doctor; God's favorite; California suite; Chaper two; v3: Sweet Charity; They're playing our song; I ought to be in pictures; Fools; The odd couple (female version); Brighton Beach memoirs; Biloxi blues; Broadway bound

Sondheim, Stephen

Sunday in the park with George; music and lyrics by Stephen Sondheim; book by James Lapine; introduction by Andre Bishop. Applause Theatre Bk. Pubs. 1991 218p (Applause musical library) $19.95; pa $14.95
812

1. Seurat, Georges Pierre, 1859-1891—Drama

ISBN 1-55783-067-3; 1-55783-068-1 (pa)

LC 90-981

Awarded the Pulitzer Prize and the New York Drama Critics Circle Award, 1985

Large mixed cast. 2 acts. First presented at the Booth Theatre, New York City, May 2, 1984

Musical inspired by Georges Seurat's painting

"Instead of mimicking reality through a conventional, naturalistic story, the authors of 'Sunday' deploy music and language in nonlinear patterns that, like Seurat's tiny brushstrokes, become meaningful only when refracted through a contemplative observer's mind." N Y Times Mag

Wagner, Jane, 1935-

The search for signs of intelligent life in the universe. Harper & Row 1986 223p il hardcover o.p. paperback available $14 **812**

ISBN 0-06-092071-8 (pa)   LC 86-45435

Characters: 1 woman. 2 acts. First produced at the Plymouth Theater, New York City, September 26, 1985

One woman show. A dozen diverse comic characters reflect eccentricities of American life

Wasserman, Dale, 1917-

Man of La Mancha; a musical play; lyrics by Joe Darion; music by Mitch Leigh. Random House 1966 82p il hardcover o.p. paperback available $9.95   **812**

ISBN 0-394-40619-2 (pa)

Winner of the New York Drama Critics Circle award "Best Musical 1966"

Characters: 14 men, 5 women, extras. First produced at the ANTA Washington Square Theatre, New York City, November 22, 1965

This musical play-adaptation of Don Quixote is built around Cervantes' defense, when imprisoned and held for inquisition. He arranges a mock trial performance to present his case

Wasserstein, Wendy

An American daughter. Harcourt Brace & Co. 1998 105p il hardcover o.p. paperback available $10   **812**

ISBN 0-15-600645-6 (pa)   LC 97-36079

Characters: 6 men, 4 women. 2 acts, 8 scenes. First produced by the Lincoln Center Theater, New York City, April 13, 1997

Satirical drama about intense media scrutiny that woman is subjected to after she is nominated for Surgeon General

The Heidi chronicles, and other plays. Harcourt Brace Jovanovich 1990 252p o.p.; Vintage Bks. paperback available $13   **812**

ISBN 0-679-73499-6 (pa)

Contents: Uncommon women and others; Isn't it romantic; The Heidi chronicles

This collection traces "three decades of changing styles, mores, life objectives, and intellectual challenges. Wasserstein examines her characters and their times with great good humor, complexity, depth of feeling, and a firm refusal to accept trite and easy images." Libr J

The sisters Rosensweig. Harcourt Brace Jovanovich 1993 109p il hardcover o.p. paperback available $11   **812**

ISBN 0-15-600013-X (pa)   LC 93-224

Also available in paperback from Dramatists Play Service

Characters: 4 men, 4 women. 2 acts 7 scenes. First produced at the Mitzi E. Newhouse Theater, New York City, October 22, 1992

This is "a domestic, romantic comedy partly about the three middle-aged sisters of the title and their relations with men and careers and partly about how the eldest sister, international banker Sara, in whose London home the play is set, meets a man who comes to dinner and, through not much effort on her part . . . sweeps him off his feet. Wasserstein's filled the play with the sharp but poignantly revealing developments and dialogue that she writes so well." Booklist

Wilder, Thornton, 1897-1975

Our town; a play in three acts; foreword by Donald Margulies. HarperCollins Pubs. 2003 xx, 181p $19.95; pa $9.95   **812**

ISBN 0-06-053525-3; 0-06-051263-6 (pa)

A reissue with a new foreword of the title first published 1938 by Coward-McCann

Large mixed cast. First produced at McCarter's Theatre, Princeton, N.J., January 22, 1938

"Presented without scenery of any kind, utilizing a narrator and loose episodic form, adventurous and imaginative in style, this unique play . . . is one of the most distinguished in the modern repertoire. It deals with the simplest and most touching aspects of life in a small town." HarperCollins Reader's Ency of Am Lit

Wilson, August

Fences; a play; introduction by Lloyd Richards. New Am. Lib. 1986 101p pa $11   **812**

ISBN 0-452-26401-4   LC 86-5264

Awarded the Pulitzer Prize, 1987

"A Plume book"

Characters: 5 men, 1 woman, 1 girl. 2 acts, 9 scenes. First produced at the Yale Repertory Theatre, New Ha-

Wilson, August—*Continued*
ven, Connecticut, April 30, 1985
Family drama about black experience in America.
1960's spirit of liberation alienates hard-working father
from wife and son

Jitney. Overlook Press 2001 96p hardcover
o.p. paperback available $14.95   **812**
1. African Americans—Drama
ISBN 1-58567-370-6 (pa)   LC 2001-33962
Winner of the New York Drama Critics Circle Award,
2000
Characters: 8 men, 1 woman. 2 acts, 8 scenes. This is
a revised version of a play written 1979
Drama set in 1977 about gypsy cabdrivers who service
Pittsburgh's black Hill District

Joe Turner's come and gone; a play in two
acts. New Am. Lib. 1988 94p pa $11   **812**
1. African Americans—Drama
ISBN 0-452-26009-4   LC 88-1660
"A Plume book"
Characters: 6 men, 5 women. 2 acts, 10 scenes. 1 set-
ting. First produced at the Yale Repertory Theatre, New
Haven, Connecticut, April 29, 1986
This drama looks at life in a Pittsburgh boarding house
for blacks in 1911

Ma Rainey's black bottom; a play in two
acts. New Am. Lib. 1985 111p pa $11 **812**
ISBN 0-452-26113-9   LC 84-27156
"A Plume book"
Characters: 8 men, 2 women. 2 acts. First produced at
the Yale Repertory Theatre, New Haven, Connecticut,
April 6, 1984
Recording session by black blues great Ma Rainey for
white-owned studio, is setting for exploration of racial
relations and conflicts

The piano lesson. New Am. Lib. 1990
108p hardcover o.p. paperback available $11
    812
ISBN 0-452-26534-7 (pa)   LC 90-38734
Awarded the Pulitzer Prize and the New York Drama
Critics Circle Award, 1990
Characters: 5 men, 3 women. 2 acts, 7 scenes. First
presented at the Yale Repertory Theatre, New Haven,
November 26, 1987
Drama set in 1936 Pittsburgh chronicles black experi-
ence in America. Family conflict arises over heirloom pi-
ano

Seven guitars. Dutton 1996 107p hardcover
o.p. paperback available $11   **812**
ISBN 0-452-27692-6 (pa)   LC 95-50536
Also available from French
Winner of the New York Drama Critics Circle award,
1996
Characters: 4 men, 3 women. 2 acts, 9 scenes. First
produced at the Goodman Theater, Chicago, January 21,
1995
"Pittsburgh, summer 1948. Five of his friends gather
after the funeral of Floyd Barton, mysteriously murdered
at 35, just as his first blues record had become a hit. The
sixth play in Wilson's cycle concerned with twentieth-
century African American lives is mostly a flashback.
We learn what happened to Floyd, but before that horrifying climax, Wilson steeps us in the pathos that Floyd
glimpsed a way to escape. . . . As powerful as modern
drama gets." Booklist

Wilson, Lanford, 1937-
5th of July; a play. Hill & Wang 1979
c1978 128p il   **812**
    LC 78-26477
Available in paperback from Dramatists Play Service
"A Mermaid dramabook"
Characters: 4 men, 4 women. 2 acts. First produced by
the Circle Repertory Company, New York City, April
27, 1978
This drama explores "the tenacious links between college friends—a Vietnam veteran, an aspiring country
singer, lovers, ex-lovers—drawn back to an anxious reunion that recalls old wounds and traumas." Booklist

21 short plays. Smith & Kraus 1993 268p
pa $19.95   **812**
ISBN 1-880399-31-8   LC 93-34434
"Contemporary playwrights series"
"The plays range in form from finely crafted one-act
plays to short 'skits' written for various benefits. They
are arranged in chronological order and the collection
spans the years from 1963 to 1991. Wilson's dramatic
style has been characterized by such phrases as 'lyric realism' and 'poetic realism,' but these short plays represent a far greater range of styles." Voice Youth Advocates

The Talley trilogy. Smith & Kraus 1999
272p (Collected works, v3) hardcover o.p.
paperback available $19.95   **812**
ISBN 1-57525-133-7 (pa)
This volume includes Fifth of July, Talley's folly and
Talley & son (1986). A tale told (1981), an early version
of Talley & son is also included
"Wilson didn't begin what became, ultimately, a te-
tralogy with the idea of creating a play cycle. He just
wanted to write a play set in the late 1970s that reflected
in some way the post-Vietnam, post-Watergate letdown
much of young America was feeling. . . . The resultant
four-play cycle captures the Talley's foibles and follies
as thoroughly—and as entertainingly—as J.D. Salinger's
set of stories and short novels did the Glass family."
Booklist

Zindel, Paul
The effect of gamma rays on
man-in-the-moon marigolds; a drama in two
acts; drawings by Dong Kingman. Harper &
Row 1971 108p il o.p.; Bantam Bks.
paperback available $5.99   **812**
ISBN 0-553-28028-7 (pa)
Also available in paperback from Dramatists Play Ser-
vice
Awarded the Pulitzer Prize, 1971, and the 1969-70
New York Drama Critics Circle Award
Characters: 5 women. First produced at the Mercer-
O'Casey Theatre, New York City, April 7, 1970
"The play, in the naturalistic tradition, deals with a
widow and her two daughters, the imagination of one of
whom has been captured by the atom and the possibili-
ties it offers of producing mutations." McGraw-Hill Ency
of World Drama

812.008 American drama— Collections

The **Best** American short plays; edited by Howard Stein and Glenn Young. Applause Theatre Bk. Pubs. $32.95; pa $18.95
812.008
1. Drama—Collections 2. One act plays
ISSN 1062-7561
This series of annual collections was begun in 1937 under the editorship of Margaret Mayorga with title: Best one-act plays, and published by Dodd, Mead through 1955 (starting in 1953 title changed to The best short plays). Beacon Press published the volumes from 1956 through 1961 when publication was suspended. Resumed 1968 under the editorship of Stanley Richards. From 1981 through 1989 edited by Ramon Delgado. Changed to current title and editors with 1990/1991 volume. Volumes prior to 1988 o.p. Apply to publisher for availability and price of retrospective annuals
In addition to the plays each annual contains brief biographical and bibliographical data about dramatists represented

Plays by American women, 1900-1930; edited and with an introduction by Judith E. Barlow. Applause Theatre Bk. Pubs. 1985 xxxiii, 261p hardcover o.p. paperback available $10.95
812.008
1. American drama—Women authors—Collections
ISBN 1-55783-008-8 (pa)
LC 84-24606
Revised edition of Plays by American women: the early years, published 1981 by Avon Books
Contents: A man's world, by R. Crothers; Trifles, by S. Glaspell; Miss Lulu Bett, by Z. Gale; Plumes, by G. D. Johnson; Machinal, by S. Treadwell
Includes bibliographical references

812.009 American drama— History and criticism

Playwrights at work; Paris review; edited by George Plimpton. Modern Lib. 2000 411p il pa $14.95
812.009
1. Dramatists
ISBN 0-679-64021-5
LC 99-44064
A collection of interviews published between 1956 and 1997. Among the interviewees are: Eugene Ionesco, Lillian Hellmann, Wendy Wasserstein, Harold Pinter, and David Mamet
"This is an excellent gathering of brilliant minds in the theater, and these interviews provide significant insight into the works of the writers." Libr J

813.009 American fiction— History and criticism

American women fiction writers; edited and with an introduction by Harold Bloom. Chelsea House 1997 3v (Women writers of English and their works) ea $35.95
813.009
1. American fiction—Women authors 2. American fiction—Bio-bibliography
ISBN 0-7910-4480-7 (v1); 0-7910-4481-5 (v2); 0-7910-4652-4 (v3)
LC 97-6310
Arranged alphabetically by author each entry provides a biographical statement, excerpts of critical opinion, and a bibliography of the writer's works. Carson McCullers, Zona Gale, Margaret Mitchell, Mari Sandoz, and Tess Slesinger are among the thirty-eight authors profiled

Baker, Carlos, 1909-1987
Hemingway: the writer as artist. [4th ed] Princeton Univ. Press 1972 xx, 438p hardcover o.p. paperback available $26.95
813.009
1. Hemingway, Ernest, 1899-1961
ISBN 0-691-01305-5 (pa)
First published 1952
Following a discussion of Hemingway's expatriation and his aesthetic principles, Baker analyzes both the fiction and nonfiction focusing on their texture, structure and symbolism. An annotated checklist of Hemingway's poetry, prose, and journalism is included

Brooks, Cleanth, 1906-1994
William Faulkner: the Yoknapatawpha country. Yale Univ. Press 1963 499p o.p.; Louisiana State Univ. Press paperback available $24.95
813.009
1. Faulkner, William, 1897-1962
ISBN 0-8071-1601-7 (pa)
"Introductory chapters contrast Faulkner with various other regional writers, comment on the social structure in his novels, and discuss his poetic treatment of nature. 'Sanctuary,' 'Light in August,' 'The sound and the fury,' 'Absalom, Absalom!' and other works are analyzed in remaining chapters. Genealogies and a character index are included." Booklist
Includes bibliographical references

The **Columbia** companion to the twentieth-century American short story; Blanche H. Gelfant, editor. Columbia Univ. Press 2000 660p $83.50
813.009
1. Short stories—History and criticism 2. American fiction—History and criticism 3. Short stories—Bio-bibliography 4. American fiction—Bio-bibliography
ISBN 0-231-11098-2
LC 00-31610
"The first 100 pages are devoted to thematic essays that focus on the form of the short story, the development of the genre, several distinct subject types (e.g., short stories of the Holocaust or of the working class), and four different ethnic groups (African American, Asian American, Chicano Latino American, and Native American). . . . The remainder of the book is devoted to over 100 individual author essays that focus on reading for pleasure and understanding rather than critical interpretation. Entries discuss the development of each author and the content and meaning of his or her major short stories." Libr J

Contemporary Jewish-American novelists; a bio-critical sourcebook; edited by Joel Shatzky and Michael Taub; with a foreword by Daniel Walden. Greenwood Press 1997 xxxi, 506p $105 **813.009**
1. American fiction—Jewish authors 2. American fiction—Bio-bibliography
ISBN 0-313-29462-3 LC 96-37047

This "reference work 'includes alphabetically arranged entries for more than 75 Jewish-American novelists whose major works were largely written after World War II.' While major canonical figures such as Norman Mailer and Saul Bellow are profiled, lesser-known novelists—including Judith Katz, Lev Raphael, and Steve Stern—are covered as well. One of the editors' goals is to show the diversity of Jewish-American literature. . . . Each entry includes a biographical section, a cogent discussion of major works and themes, an overview of each novelist's critical reception, and a bibliography of both primary and secondary sources." Booklist

Eble, Kenneth Eugene
F. Scott Fitzgerald; by Kenneth Eble. rev ed. Twayne Pubs. 1977 187p (Twayne's United States authors series) $34 **813.009**
1. Fitzgerald, F. Scott (Francis Scott), 1896-1940
ISBN 0-8057-7183-2 LC 77-429

First published 1963
This assessment of Fitzgerald's oeuvre places particular emphasis on his achievement in the short story format
Includes bibliographical references

The **Facts** on File companion to the American short story; edited by Abby H.P. Werlock. Facts on File 2000 542p $71.50; pa $22.95 **813.009**
1. Short stories—History and criticism
ISBN 0-8160-3164-9; 0-8160-4437-6 (pa)
LC 99-37703

More than 675 alphabetically arranged entries cover authors, characters, and major short stories. Literary terms, themes, and motifs are covered. Winners of prizes and awards are noted

Fargnoli, A. Nicholas
William Faulkner A to Z; the essential reference to his life and work; {by} A. Nicholas Fargnoli and Michael Golay. Facts on File 2001 340p il $65; pa $17.95

813.009
1. Faulkner, William, 1897-1962
ISBN 0-8160-3860-0; 0-8160-4159-8 (pa)
LC 2001-23821

The authors "provide detailed entries on Faulkner, his works, family, friends, contemporaries, and prominent places in his life. The volume also contains entries on publishers, magazines, and other social, historical, and cultural influences on Faulkner's work, including the response from not only critics but also the public. The appendixes are rich in resources, including family trees for Faulkner's family as well as for several families in his books." Voice Youth Advocates
For a fuller review see: Booklist, June 1 & 15, 2002

Gunn, James E., 1923-
Isaac Asimov; the foundations of science fiction; by James Gunn. rev ed. Scarecrow Press 1996 276p $40 **813.009**
1. Asimov, Isaac, 1920-1992 2. Science fiction—History and criticism
ISBN 0-8108-3129-5 LC 96-21068

First published 1982 by Oxford Univ. Press
The author "focuses on Asimov's robots and on the Foundation trilogy, emphasizing throughout Asimov's limited use of background, style, and characterization, and his constantly recurring theme of the rational solution of a problem. The Lucky Starr juveniles get comparatively cursory treatment, but otherwise this is a very fine book indeed—well informed, clearly written, and judicious." Booklist [review of 1982 edition]
Includes bibliographical references

J.D. Salinger; edited and with an introduction by Harold Bloom. Chelsea House 1987 147p (Modern critical views) $37.95

813.009
1. Salinger, J. D. (Jerome David), 1919-
ISBN 0-87754-716-5 LC 86-29941

This collection of nine essays provides a view of Salinger's critical reception. Among the contributors are Alfred Kazin, David Galloway and Gerald Rosen
Includes bibliographical references

John Steinbeck; edited and with an introduction by Harold Bloom. Chelsea House 1987 172p (Modern critical views) $37.95 **813.009**
1. Steinbeck, John, 1902-1968
ISBN 0-87754-635-5 LC 86-29958

A selection of criticism, arranged in chronological order of publication, devoted to the fiction of John Steinbeck
Includes bibliographical references

L'Amour, Louis, 1908-1988
The Sackett companion; a personal guide to the Sackett novels. Bantam Bks. 1988 341p il maps hardcover o.p. paperback available $14.95 **813.009**
ISBN 0-553-37102-9 (pa) LC 88-47530

"Each individual profile of the 17 Sackett novels contains a map, a cover painting, brief plot synopsis, and an annotated list of characters. Sackett enthusiasts will also welcome the inclusion of a detailed Sackett genealogy and family tree." Booklist

Marrs, Suzanne
One writer's imagination; the fiction of Eudora Welty. Louisiana State Univ. Press 2002 xix, 280p il (Southern literary studies) hardcover o.p. paperback available $24.95
813.009
1. Welty, Eudora, 1909-2001
ISBN 0-8071-2841-4 (pa) LC 2002-67133

The author discusses "the intersections between biography and art in the Pulitzer Prize winner's work. . . . Marrs describes the ways Welty's creative process transformed and transfigured fact to serve the purposes of fiction. She points to the sparks that lit Welty's imagination—an imagination that thrived on polarities in her personal life and in society at large." Publisher's note

Marrs, Suzanne—*Continued*

"The best way to appreciate Welty's major place in American literature is to read her books; the next best way is to read Suzanne Marrs's . . . study. . . . Marrs's study illuminates the transformation of life into art while acknowledging the mystery that remains 'at the heart of Eudora Welty's fiction.' . . . Essential." Choice
Includes bibliographical references

Martin, Terence

Nathaniel Hawthorne. rev ed. Twayne Pubs. 1983 221p (Twayne's United States authors series) $34 **813.009**

1. Hawthorne, Nathaniel, 1804-1864
ISBN 0-8057-7384-3   LC 82-23419
First published 1965
A critical introduction to the nature and extent of Hawthorne's achievement in fiction, giving insight into his romances and tales
Includes bibliographical references

Oliver, Charles M.

Ernest Hemingway, A to Z; the essential reference to the life and work. Facts on File 1999 452p il maps $55; pa $17.95 **813.009**

1. Hemingway, Ernest, 1899-1961
ISBN 0-8160-3467-2; 0-8160-3934-8 (pa)
            LC 98-30042
"All things Hemingway here are dissected and rearranged alphabetically, from 'absinthe' to bullfighter 'Zurito'—2500 cross-referenced entries in all. . . . The book also includes several top-notch appendixes of maps, a Hemingway family tree, a chronology and dateline, a bibliography, a complete list of his writings with publication history, and an index. An absolute gold mine for Hemingway aficionados." Libr J

Pritchard, William H.

Updike; America's man of letters. Steerforth Press 2000 351p $27 **813.009**

1. Updike, John
ISBN 1-58642-002-X   LC 00-33835
This study examines Updike's "novels, short stories, poetry, memoirs, and literary criticism, tracing themes, influences, and literary relations, as well as describing characters and situating the works into the larger context of contemporary American literature." Libr J
"All in all, Pritchard's book is a gentle and intelligent request for a little more thought and a little less cranky let's-move-on speed in judging the work of one of America's pre-eminent writers." N Y Times Book Rev
Includes bibliographical references

Richard Wright; critical perspectives past and present; edited by Henry Louis Gates, Jr., and K.A. Appiah. Amistad Press 1993 476p (Amistad literary series) hardcover o.p. paperback available $14.95 **813.009**

1. Wright, Richard, 1908-1960
ISBN 1-56743-027-9 (pa)   LC 92-45757
A collection of critical writings which examine Wright's fiction, nonfiction, and autobiographical works. The volume begins with a selection of reviews, written by such authors as Zora Neale Hurston, Clifton Fadiman, Ralph Ellison, Sinclair Lewis and Irving Howe. The second part consists of twenty-two present-day essays. Also included are a chronology and a bibliography

Richard Wright's Native son; edited and with an introduction by Harold Bloom. Chelsea House 1988 174p (Modern critical interpretations) $37.95 **813.009**

1. Wright, Richard, 1908-1960. Native son
ISBN 1-55546-055-0   LC 87-30402
A collection of critical essays on Wright's classic portrayal of the black experience, arranged chronologically in the order of their original publication
Includes bibliographical references

Sinclair Lewis; edited and with an introduction by Harold Bloom. Chelsea House 1987 144p (Modern critical views) $37.95 **813.009**

1. Lewis, Sinclair, 1885-1951
ISBN 0-87754-628-2   LC 86-29912
A collection of ten critical essays on the novels of Sinclair Lewis which examine their ironic, satiric and moral dimensions
Includes bibliographical references

Skaggs, Peggy

Kate Chopin. Twayne Pubs. 1985 130p (Twayne's United States authors series) $34 **813.009**

1. Chopin, Kate, 1851-1904
ISBN 0-8057-7439-4   LC 84-27977
The author "provides careful analyses of Chopin's two volumes of published short stories ('Bayou Folks' and 'A Night in Arcadie'), the stories of her unpublished volume, 'A Vocation and a Voice,' her uncollected short stories, poems, and essays, as well as her two novels, 'At Fault' and 'The Awakening.' A thorough critical study of interest to both general readers and scholars." Booklist
Includes bibliographical references

The Tales of Poe; edited and with an introduction by Harold Bloom. Chelsea House 1987 167p (Modern critical interpretations) $37.95 **813.009**

1. Poe, Edgar Allan, 1809-1849
ISBN 1-55546-011-9   LC 86-34307
A collection of essays analyzing the themes and styles of Poe's tales of horror
Includes bibliographical references

Tate, Mary Jo

F. Scott Fitzgerald A to Z; the essential reference to his life and work; with a foreword by Matthew J. Bruccoli. Facts on File 1998 340p il $55 **813.009**

1. Fitzgerald, F. Scott (Francis Scott), 1896-1940
ISBN 0-8160-3150-9   LC 97-11321
This "compendium contains alphabetical entries detailing nearly every aspect of the life and work of F. Scott Fitzgerald. Obscure characters who appear in minor works are profiled alongside detailed synopses of Fitzgerald's major novels. Biographical information on extended members of the Fitzgerald clan accompanies exhaustive research documenting Fitzgerald criticism and scholarship." Book Rep

A **Theodore** Dreiser encyclopedia; edited by
Keith Newlin. Greenwood Press 2003 xxiii,
431p il $99.95   **813.009**
1. Dreiser, Theodore, 1871-1945
ISBN 0-313-31680-5   LC 2003-40841

This is a "guide to the essential facts surrounding this
prolific author's life and works. Dreiser's novels and
short stories are covered, as are his plays, which are far
less known. Front matter includes a list of entries, a
chronology, and a preface that analyzes prior contributions to Dreiser scholarship. Alphabetically arranged essays on his books, short stories, and magazine and newspaper pieces make up the book's core. . . . The book
ends with a bibliography arranged by category (books by
Dreiser, critical studies, biographies, etc.). Highly recommended." Choice

814   American essays

Alvarez, Julia
Something to declare; essays. Algonquin
Bks. 1998 300p $20.95   **814**
ISBN 1-56512-193-7   LC 98-20994
Also available in paperback from Plume Bks.

This is a "collection of personal essays by the poet
and novelist Julia Alvarez, who emigrated at the age of
10 from the Dominican Republic to the United States.
With admirable candor and gentle touches of humor, she
describes her struggles with cultural hybridism, historical
and personal memory, the English language and the effects of all these on her literary career." N Y Times
Book Rev

Angelou, Maya
Even the stars look lonesome. Random
House 1997 145p $18; pa $10   **814**
ISBN 0-375-50031-6; 0-553-37972-0 (pa)
    LC 97-17317
Also available large print edition $18 (0-679-77441-6)
Angelou "touches on a number of topics in this brief
collection of essays, including aging, fame, sensuality,
art, and violence. Her opening piece, about the ending of
a long marriage and the beginning of a new life in a new
home, is a winner. Her take on aging is downright amusing; her tribute to sensuality, enlightening; and her salute
to black women, a treasure." Libr J

Wouldn't take nothing for my journey now.
Random House 1993 141p $17; pa $12 **814**
ISBN 0-679-42743-0; 0-553-38017-6 (pa)
    LC 93-5904
Also available in paperback from Bantam Bks.

The author "shares her thoughts about humankind:
how to respect others of different cultures, opinions, and
values as taught by universal philosophies. . . .
Angelou's prose is brisk, fluid, and entrancing. This
work will provide a taste of wisdom to all who read it."
Libr J

Baker, Nicholson
The size of thoughts; essays and other
lumber. Random House 1996 355p hardcover
o.p. paperback available $14   **814**
ISBN 0-679-77624-9 (pa)   LC 95-43667
Analyzed in Essay and general literature index

All but one of these essays "have previously appeared
in publications like the *Atlantic Monthly*, the *New York-*

er, the *New York Review of Books,* and *Esquire* between
1982 and 1995. Their subjects range from changing
one's mind and model airplanes to punctuation and the
books that appear in the pictures of mail-order catalogs.
All the essays are witty, intelligent, thought-provoking,
and a joy to read. A previously unpublished essay, 'Lumber,' which comprises 40 percent of the book, discusses
the meaning of the word *lumber* and traces its use in English literature. It is an example of literary scholarship at
its best: painstakingly thorough and fun to read." Libr J

Baldwin, James, 1924-1987
Collected essays. Library of Am. 1998
869p $35   **814**
ISBN 1-88301-152-3   LC 97-23496

The essays in this volume were selected by Toni Morrison. "Morrison has reprinted all of the material contained in Baldwin's previous collected essays, The Price
of the Ticket (1985). She has added eleven pieces, the
earliest of which dates from 1947—Baldwin's first published review, of a biography of Frederick Douglass, in
the Nation—and the latest from 1984." Times Lit Suppl

The **Beacon** book of essays by contemporary
American women; edited by Wendy
Martin; with the editorial assistance of
Thomas Allen {et al.}. Beacon Press 1996
310p hardcover o.p. paperback available
$16   **814**
1. Women—United States
ISBN 0-8070-6347-9 (pa)   LC 95-21117

This "compilation features essays by women writers of
varying ethnic backgrounds, age, class, sexual orientation
and religion. With the exception of Mary McCarthy's
1951 piece about the significance of names, the contributions were written over the last 30 years and provide an
overview of the cultural impact of the women's liberation movement." Publ Wkly

Includes bibliographical references

Berry, Wendell, 1934-
Home economics; fourteen essays. North
Point Press 1987 192p hardcover o.p.
paperback available $13   **814**
ISBN 0-86547-275-0 (pa)   LC 86-62838

The author writes about what he views as "the passing
of community and farm life, the inherent value of hand
labor and well-made objects, the uses of wild lands, the
decadence of the university, and especially the sacred
economic order of nature, to which human economies
must necessarily be subordinate." Libr J

What are people for? essays. North Point
Press 1990 210p hardcover o.p. paperback
available $13   **814**
ISBN 0-86547-437-0 (pa)   LC 89-29848

These essays describe contemporary ecological problems and present the author's view of how people should
relate to the earth

"Ever thought provoking and always gracefully and
powerfully expressive, Berry, in these essays, proves
himself to be arguably the most essential social and cultural critic of our day." Booklist

The **Best** American essays. Ticknor & Fields
$27.50; pa $13   **814**
ISSN 0888-3742

Annual. First published 1986

Editors vary

The Best American essays—*Continued*

Editors select essays from general interest magazines that touch on topics political, scientific, historical, religious, and sociological, in addition to the personal and literary

The **Best** American essays of the century; Joyce Carol Oates, editor; Robert Atwan, coeditor; with an introduction by Joyce Carol Oates. Houghton Mifflin 2000 596p $30; pa $18 **814**
ISBN 0-618-04370-5; 0-618-15587-2 (pa)

Analyzed in Essay and general literature index

This anthology includes essays "that contemplate diverse worlds, from nature to courtrooms, war and family memories. Race is a pervasive theme, explored with candor and insight by many, including James Baldwin, Zora Neale Hurston, and, in a jolting 1912 condemnation of a Coatesville, Pennsylvania, lynching, John Jay Chapman." Booklist

"Oates has assembled a provocative collection of masterpieces reflecting both the fragmentation and surprising cohesiveness of various American identities." Publ Wkly

Includes bibliographical references

The **Bread** Loaf anthology of contemporary American essays; edited by Robert Pack and Jay Parini. University Press of New England 1989 379p hardcover o.p. paperback available $24.95 **814**
ISBN 0-87451-475-4 (pa)   LC 88-40352

Published for the Bread Loaf Writer's Conference, Middlebury College

This collection "presents 32 essays from diverse authors on varied subjects. Some are by noted scholars and critics, such as Harold Bloom and William Gass, others by familiar authors, such as Joyce Carol Oates and Gore Vidal. The subjects range from Sinclair Lewis and Freud to the Indianapolis 500 and the biology of sex. One might expect a collection like this to be uneven, but the quality of writing is high throughout, and the subjects are not only interesting but educational." Libr J

Includes bibliographical references

Brodsky, Joseph, 1940-1996

Less than one; selected essays. Farrar, Straus & Giroux 1986 501p hardcover o.p. paperback available $18 **814**
ISBN 0-374-52055-0 (pa)   LC 85-15900

Analyzed in Essay and general literature index

The essays in this volume "begin and end with autobiographical pieces; in between there are alternate homages to favorite poets, both Russian and non-Russian, as well as substantial discussions of such topics as geography and history, political force and ethical choice, and literary tradition." N Y Times Book Rev

On grief and reason; essays. Farrar, Straus & Giroux 1996 484p hardcover o.p. paperback available $18 **814**
ISBN 0-374-52509-9 (pa)   LC 94-10872

Analyzed in Essay and general literature index

This volume "collects twenty-one essays, all but one written since 1986." N Y Rev Books

For an "essay on Frost, for an equally probing one on four poems by Thomas Hardy, for an 'Homage to Marcus Aurelius,' for half a hundred pages on an English

translation of a poem Rainer Maria Rilke wrote in German 90 years ago, and for many scattered felicities, this collection is occasion for gratitude. It is rare for someone so advantageously situated, within poetry but both within and outside of American speech, culture and experience, to confide in us with such pedagogic confidence." N Y Times Book Rev

Codrescu, Andrei, 1946-

The Devil never sleeps and other essays. St. Martin's Press 2000 244p il $27.95 **814**
ISBN 0-312-20294-6   LC 99-55765

In this collection "Codrescu takes on the devil, the book of Revelation, the millennium, and Elvis, plus Allen Ginsburg and Lawrence Ferlinghetti. Other sections address innocence, autobiography, politics, and virtuality. . . . The collection includes both brief, personal essays . . . and longer pieces, like Codrescu's 'Notes of a Prodigal Son,' on his return trips to his native Romania." Booklist

The dog with the chip in his neck; essays from NPR and elsewhere. St. Martin's Press 1996 270p il hardcover o.p. paperback available $12 **814**
ISBN 0-312-16819-5 (pa)   LC 96-6428

The pieces in this collection "either have been published previously or were parts of radio broadcasts. The author emigrated to the U.S. in 1966 from Romania, and several of these incisive essays deal with conditions in the post-communist world. . . . He includes entertaining remarks on talk shows, airline travel and the experience of visiting the Coca-Cola Museum. This is informed and entertaining commentary that, despite the humor, makes clear the author's deep concern for his adopted country and for the future of humanity." Publ Wkly

The muse is always half-dressed in New Orleans and other essays. St. Martin's Press 1993 199p hardcover o.p. paperback available $10 **814**
ISBN 0-312-13570-X (pa)   LC 93-7441

"The essays collected here, many previously published or given as speeches, range broadly, from afterthoughts on the fall of Ceauşescu—which Codrescu now sees as staged by the Communists to stay in power—to vegetarian fare on the airlines. Mixing insight with humor, the essays are occasionally repetitious—obviously, they were not originally written to be read together. The result, however, is like a fugue." Libr J

Connell, Evan S., 1924-

The Aztec treasure house; new and selected essays. Counterpoint 2001 470p hardcover o.p. paperback available $17.50 **814**
ISBN 1-58243-253-8 (pa)   LC 2001-28899

Analyzed in Essay and general literature index

Connell "writes about polar exploration; linguistic research; astronomy; preposterous, unkillable fantasies like El Dorado and Prester John; inspired travelers like Ibn Batuta and Mary Kingsley; the insane and tragic Children's Crusade—any subject that illustrates the human urge to strain against physical and mental boundaries. Connell is skeptical, clearheaded and a sworn enemy of all dogma." N Y Times Book Rev

Includes bibliographical references

Davenport, Guy, 1927-

The geography of the imagination; forty essays. North Point Press 1981 384p o.p.; Godine paperback available $18.95   **814**

ISBN 1-56792-080-2 (pa)   LC 91-53116

In addition to essays on modern and classical literature the author also discusses archaeology, biology, lexicography, music and photography. Among his subjects are: Poe, Agassiz, Pound, Ives, Zukofsky, Meatyard, Tchelitchew and Joyce

Includes bibliographical references

Didion, Joan

After Henry. Simon & Schuster 1992 319p o.p.; Vintage Bks. paperback available $14

814

ISBN 0-679-74539-4 (pa)   LC 91-46458

This is a collection of reportorial essays reprinted from The New Yorker, The New York Review of Books and New West. They are arranged in three sections: "Washington," "California," and "New York." Topics include the Reagan presidency, the 1988 political campaign, and the 1989 Central Park jogger rape case

"Readers should welcome the chance to savor the vintage sotto voce style that more than 20 years ago distinguished this careful writer from New Journalism's noisier competition." Time

The white album. Simon & Schuster 1979 222p o.p.; Farrar, Straus & Giroux paperback available $13   **814**

ISBN 0-374-52221-9 (pa)   LC 79-10242

This is a collection of essays about California in the 1960s and 1970s

"All of the essays . . . manifest not only [Miss Didion's] intelligence but an instinct for details that continue to emit pulsations in the reader's memory and a style that is spare, subtly musical in its phrasing and exact." N Y Times Book Rev

Dillard, Annie

For the time being. Knopf 1999 205p $22; pa $12   **814**

ISBN 0-375-40380-9; 0-375-70347-0 (pa)

LC 98-36720

Also available Thorndike Press large print edition

A "meditation on life, death, birth, God, evil, eternity, the nuclear age and the human predicament. This unconventional mosaic, . . . interweaves several disparate topics. . . . Dillard's unifying theme is the congruence of thought she detects in Teilhard, Kabbalists and Gnostics; each impels us to transform, build, complete and grant divinity to the world." Publ Wkly

Ellison, Ralph

Shadow and act. Random House 1964 xxii, 317p hardcover o.p. paperback available $14

814

ISBN 0-679-76000-8 (pa)

Analyzed in Essay and general literature index

This collection of essays is "concerned with three general themes: with literature and folklore, with Negro musical expression—especially jazz and blues—and with the complex relationship between Negro American subculture and North American culture as a whole." Introduction

Epstein, Joseph, 1937-

A line out for a walk; familiar essays. Norton 1991 331p hardcover o.p. paperback available $13.95   **814**

ISBN 0-393-30854-5 (pa)   LC 90-44698

This is a collection of essays on a variety of subjects

"This acknowledged master of the familiar essay will captivate readers who want to escape life momentarily and guide readers who, like Flaubert, want to live more profoundly." Booklist

Fadiman, Anne, 1953-

Ex libris; confessions of a common reader. Farrar, Straus & Giroux 1998 162p hardcover o.p. paperback available $10   **814**

ISBN 0-374-52722-9 (pa)   LC 98-21109

In these "essays, Fadiman confesses her passion for books of all types. She reads Milton's 'On His Blindness' over the phone to her father, whose own sight is failing; assesses the tricky business of 'marrying' her library with her husband's; and admires the distilled beauty of the index to the 1902 Sears, Roebuck catalogue. . . . Each essay is a model of clarity and lightly worn erudition, and speaks volumes about the author's appreciation for people as well as books." New Yorker

Includes bibliographical references

Fiedler, Leslie A.

Fiedler on the roof; essays on literature and Jewish identity; by Leslie Fiedler. Godine 1990 184p $19.95; pa $11.95   **814**

1. Jews in literature

ISBN 0-87923-859-3; 0-87923-949-2 (pa)

LC 90-55282

Analyzed in Essay and general literature index

This volume is a collection of the literary critic's "essays and book reviews since 1970 on more or less Jewish topics. These include: anti-Semitism, the Holocaust, the Book of Job, Isaac Bashevis Singer, Bernard Malamud, . . . and Jewish consciousness in (J.) Joyce's Ulysses." Commentary

"Disturbing, provocative, and brilliant." Libr J

Tyranny of the normal; essays on bioethics, theology & myth; [by] Leslie Fiedler. Godine 1996 155p $22.95   **814**

ISBN 1-56792-003-9   LC 95-34579

Analyzed in Essay and general literature index

"From literature, high and low, Fiedler educes human ambivalences: our simultaneous desire to protect children and to harm them, for example, or our disgust for those we pity or respect. This prolific writer remains as provocative as ever, boldly going where few literary critics dare to venture." New Yorker

Fraser, Kennedy

Ornament and silence; essays on women's lives. Knopf 1996 247p hardcover o.p. paperback available $13   **814**

ISBN 0-375-70112-5 (pa)   LC 96-11479

Analyzed in Essay and general literature index

A collection of fourteen profiles, personal reminiscences and extended reviews of books

"A 'daughter of the paternal old New Yorker' in her youth, Fraser . . . has moved on with time, taking for her more mature role models Nina Berberova, Edith Wharton, and Germaine Greer. Fraser's essays are quiet, thorough, and beautifully paced." Libr J

The **Fun** of it; stories from The talk of the town, The New Yorker; edited by Lillian Ross; introduction by David Remnick. Modern Lib. 2001 xxi, 478p pa $16.95

814

1. New Yorker (Periodical)
ISBN 0-375-75649-3 LC 00-68237
A "selection of stories from 'Talk' in chronologically arranged sections that begin with the 1920s and end in 2000. Many of the early contributions were unsigned, but through archival research Ross ferrets out and reveals the authors of many of those initial pieces. Included in this lively collection are pieces by writers—some of whom became *New Yorker* regulars—such as Robert Benchley, James Thurber, E. B. White, A. J. Liebling, John Updike, Garrison Keillor, Ann Beattie, Bill McKibben, Roger Angell, Steve Martin, and Susan Orlean." Libr J

Gardner, Martin, 1914-
The night is large; collected essays, 1938-1995. St. Martin's Press 1996 586p il hardcover o.p. paperback available $17.95

814

ISBN 0-312-16949-3 (pa) LC 96-10732
Gardner's "essays, collected mainly from Scientific American and The New York Review of Books, exhibit a singular love of discovery; he appears impatient to learn what new truths science may uncover. Mr. Gardner sees the world as a puzzle to be solved, the ultimate brain teaser fabricated by God for our (or His) awe and amusement. So he never shies away from the big questions: Why does the universe exist? Do humans possess free will? Is there a God? These essays serve as his own explorations into the subject matter; he does not set out to convince or cajole." N Y Times Book Rev

Gass, William H., 1924-
Finding a form; essays. Knopf 1996 354p $26 **814**
ISBN 0-679-44662-1 LC 95-49914
Also available in paperback from Cornell Univ. Press
Analyzed in Essay and general literature index
Gass "is 'as obdurate as nails' when it comes to the best possible use of the written word. Each essay in this wide-ranging book (be it titled 'Ezra Pound,' 'Nietzsche: The Polemical Philosopher,' 'Robert Walser,' 'Nature, Culture, and Cosmos,' 'Pulitzer, The People Prize,' or 'The Music of Prose') offers evidence for such a conclusion. Gass is concerned with how best to use a phrase or word and believes we should be tough-minded when it comes to reading. He reveals a sardonic sense of humor as well, for example, in discussing the winners of the Pulitzer prize, and he dislikes the fact that anyone would enjoy his/her own writing." Libr J

Tests of time. Knopf 2002 319p $25 **814**
ISBN 0-375-41257-3 LC 2001-50486
Also available in paperback from University of Chicago Press
Analyzed in Essay and general literature index
"In this collection of fourteen essays, Gass ranges widely across the cultural landscape, offering appreciations of Italo Calvino and Peter Handke, a keen interrogation of the idea of the masterpiece, and a whimsical look at the virtues and vices of lists. Throughout, he keeps returning to what has always been his main theme: the primacy of aesthetic experience." New Yorker

Ginsberg, Allen, 1926-1997
Deliberate prose; selected essays, 1952-1995. HarperCollins Pubs. 2000 xxiv, 536p hardcover o.p. paperback available $17

814

ISBN 0-06-093081-0 (pa) LC 99-41360
This collection of over 100 prose pieces "organizes the material under several general topics: 'Politics and Prophecies,' 'Drug Culture,' 'Manifestations and Spirituality,' 'Censorship and Sex Laws,' 'Autobiographical Fragments,' 'Literary Techniques and the Beat Generation,' 'Writer,' and 'Further Appreciations,' tributes to artistic collaborators and cultural heroes such as Robert Frank, Philip Glass, Andy Warhol, and the Beatles. . . . Taken together, they provide a rare glimpse into Ginsberg's creative practice, a key to sources and influences, and a good overview of his life and art." Libr J

Gordon, Mary, 1949-
Seeing through places; reflections on geography and identity. Scribner 2000 254p hardcover o.p. paperback available $12 **814**
ISBN 0-684-86255-7 (pa) LC 99-22208
Also available Thorndike Press large print edition
Gordon "presents a collection of essays loosely centered around the locations and people that influenced her maturation and shaped her as a writer. . . . These pieces reveal the beginnings of the themes Gordon has developed throughout her writing career—introspection, discontentment, sacrifice, guilt, and bitter redemption." Libr J

Hamill, Pete
Piecework; writings on men and women, fools and heroes, lost cities, vanished friends, small pleasures, large calamities, and how the weather was; foreword by Jimmy Breslin. Little, Brown 1996 432p hardcover o.p. paperback available $16 **814**
ISBN 0-316-34098-7 (pa) LC 95-4738
This is a collection of previously-published essays by the New York newspaper reporter and columnist
"These essays are opinionated, hard-hitting, passionate, and sometimes disturbing. Writing for magazines ranging from Esquire to Art & Antiques, Hamill's writings show readers the decay of New York and other cities, the violence and heartbreak of Lebanon and Nicaragua, and the unraveling of civil life in many parts of our society." Libr J

Hoagland, Edward
Tigers & ice; reflections on nature and life. Lyons Press 1999 206p $22; pa $16.95 **814**
ISBN 1-55821-742-8; 1-58574-182-5 (pa)
LC 98-36477
"Edward Hoagland entered his 60's captivated by sight. After three years of legal blindness, a surgeon restored both his vision and his delight for the tableaux of the natural world. . . . In the 11 essays collected in 'Tigers and Ice,' he considers subjects as varied as suicide, friendship, cowardice, man-made ponds, Indian tigers and Antarctic penguins—all colored by his renewed view of the world." N Y Times Book Rev

Iyer, Pico
Tropical classical; essays from several directions. Knopf 1997 314p hardcover o.p. paperback available $14.95 **814**
ISBN 0-679-77610-9 (pa) LC 96-38578
Analyzed in Essay and general literature index

Iyer, Pico—*Continued*
"As our deputy in far-flung climes like Kathmandu and Ethiopia, Pico Iyer can hardly be surpassed: his métier is journalistic generosity. Through him, the reader has relatives in Bombay, an intimate's knowledge of Nepal, and the chance to drink tea with Norman Lewis. This book is an assortment of short pieces that Iyer wrote during the past two decades. You can open it at random, as you would an atlas, and turn up something fascinating." New Yorker

Kingsolver, Barbara
Small wonder; essays; illustrations by Paul Mirocha. HarperCollins Pubs. 2002 267p $23.95; pa $12.95   **814**
ISBN 0-06-050407-2; 0-06-050408-0 (pa)
LC 2002-276255
"This set of 19 penetrating autobiographical musings on humankind and how we treat each other and the rest of nature coalesced in the stunned aftermath of September 11. . . . Food, motherhood, gardening, literature, television, homelessness, globalization, scientific illiteracy, selfishness, and forgiveness all come under sharp and revelatory scrutiny." Booklist

Kosinski, Jerzy N., 1933-1991
Passing by; selected essays, 1962-1991; [by] Jerzy Kosinski. Random House 1992 256p o.p.; Grove Press paperback available $12   **814**
ISBN 0-8021-3423-8 (pa)   LC 91-51065
"A collection of essays, never published in book form, from the author whose 1991 suicide shocked the literary world." Libr J
"While the selections would be improved by contextualizing introductions, they portray a man who was impassioned about literature and who saw his role as confronting 'life's threatening encounters.'" Publ Wkly

Levertov, Denise, 1923-1997
New & selected essays. New Directions 1992 266p hardcover o.p. paperback available $12.95   **814**
ISBN 0-8112-1218-1 (pa)   LC 92-17887
"This collection of 25 essays, dating from 1965 to 1991, explores several major areas of critical interest to Levertov. . . . Although somewhat uneven and not always convincing, these essays present an opportunity to examine the interests, inspirations, and ideology of one of our most respected poets." Libr J

Lopate, Phillip, 1943-
Portrait of my body; personal essays. Anchor Bks. (NY) 1996 325p hardcover o.p. paperback available $19   **814**
ISBN 0-385-48377-5 (pa)   LC 95-26607
This collection includes "portraits of various individuals, including Lopate's father, a former lover, a conceptual artist, and several colleagues, most memorably the late Donald Barthelme. Lopate also writes with startling originality and verve about going to the movies, teaching, dating, marriage, Buddhism, and, in perhaps his boldest essay, the Holocaust. These are entertaining and revelatory compositions by virtue of their candor, exactitude, and implicit faith in confession." Booklist

Lynch, Thomas, 1948-
The undertaking; life studies from the dismal trade. Norton 1997 xx, 202p il $23   **814**
1. Death 2. Undertakers and undertaking
ISBN 0-393-04112-3   LC 96-40900
Also available in paperback from Penguin Bks.
"Like his father and most of his siblings, Michigan poet Lynch . . . runs a funeral home, 'a kind of family farm, working the back forty of the emotional register.' In this superb collection of essays, he melds poetic language, resonant anecdotes and meditative musings, about the rights/rites of passage." Publ Wkly

Mamet, David
Make-believe town; essays and remembrances. Little, Brown 1996 207p hardcover o.p. paperback available $15.99   **814**
ISBN 0-316-55035-3 (pa)   LC 95-53147
Mamet's book "is a miscellaneous collection of short essays dealing with a variety of topics from his gambling experiences to his impressions of London, from his view of screenwriting to his opinion of the media's treatment of Nixon's death." Libr J
"Most of these pieces evaporate rather quickly and a few sound self-important, but Mamet's writing remains spare and lucid." Publ Wkly

Manguel, Alberto
Into the looking-glass wood; essays on books, reading, and the world. Harcourt 2000 272p pa $13   **814**
ISBN 0-15-601265-0   LC 99-55234
First published 1998 in Canada
Manguel "recalls incidents both literary and political from his early years in Buenos Aires, and portrays Borges, Julio Cortázar, and Che Guevara. He also analyzes what it means to be a Jew, and the implications of creating categories such as 'gay literature.' With the entire literary universe at his fingertips, Manguel always has just the right quote or anecdote to illustrate his supple and unpredictable lines of reasoning." Booklist

McPhee, John A.
Irons in the fire; [by] John McPhee. Farrar, Straus & Giroux 1997 215p $22; pa $14   **814**
ISBN 0-374-17726-0; 0-374-52545-5 (pa)
LC 96-32358
The title essay of this "collection of *New Yorker* pieces is . . . [an] account of cattle rustling in Nevada that harks back to the Wild West. In California, McPhee ponders an environmental disaster in the making as he inspects the world's largest mountain of scrapped automobile tires. Other pieces deal with a blind professor of English who uses a talking computer and forensic geologists who sift sand, pebbles, microfossils and mineral grains to solve murders, track down terrorists and pinpoint remote geographies." Publ Wkly
"John McPhee's essays are proof that the kind of journalism that can effortlessly put a topic into perfect perspective will never go out of style." N Y Times Book Rev

Miller, Arthur, 1915-
Echoes down the corridor; collected essays,
1947-1999; edited by Stephen R. Centola.
Viking 2000 332p hardcover o.p. paperback
available $15   **814**
ISBN 0-14-200005-1 (pa)   LC 00-40427
Analyzed in Essay and general literature index
"The 50 essays collected here range from atmospheric
reminiscences of his childhood in Brooklyn and studies
at the University of Michigan, to accounts of visits to
China, the Soviet Union and Turkey as an advocate for
victims of governmental persecution. Deeply influenced
by the radical culture of the 1930s and by his youth during the depression, Miller has always been firmly on the
political left." Publ Wkly
"This collection is not to be missed." Libr J

Ozick, Cynthia
Quarrel & quandary; essays. Knopf 2000
247p hardcover o.p. paperback available $13
                                             814
1. Literature—History and criticism
ISBN 0-375-72445-1 (pa)   LC 99-89889
Among the topics discussed in this collection of personal and literary essays are Henry James, Anne Frank,
Kafka, poetry, and public intellectuals
"All the essays collected here began life elsewhere as
reviews and higher journalism. This kind of gathering of
literary leftovers is usually not worth reprinting. Ozick's
work is an exception. Her pieces have genuine durability.
They are great essays." N Y Times Book Rev

Price, Reynolds, 1933-
Feasting the heart; fifty-two commentaries
for the air. Scribner 2000 178p $22; pa $12
                                             814
ISBN 0-7432-0369-0; 0-7432-0370-4 (pa)
                                    LC 00-47008
These commentaries from NPR's All things considered voice "Price's thoughts on topics ranging from the
movies to the writing life to family relations. Recurring
themes that he explores with particularly compelling insight include the cultural and emotional blessings of a
small-town Southern boyhood, the difficulties—and surprising advantages—of being physically disabled . . .
and the richness of his experiences as both a student and
a teacher." Publ Wkly

Rich, Adrienne
Blood, bread, and poetry; selected prose,
1979-1985. Norton 1986 238p hardcover o.p.
paperback available $11.95   **814**
1. Feminism
ISBN 0-393-31162-7 (pa)   LC 86-5452
Analyzed in Essay and general literature index
This work "includes radical feminist philosophy, literary criticism, and personal history—all approached from
her white, Jewish, lesbian, middle-class American 'location.'" Booklist

Said, Edward W.
Reflections on exile and other essays.
Harvard Univ. Press 2000 xxxv, 617p
(Convergences) $36.95; pa $19.95   **814**
1. Melville, Herman, 1819-1891. Moby Dick 2. Conrad, Joseph, 1857-1924. Nostromo 3. Politics in literature 4. Literature—History and criticism 5. Criticism
ISBN 0-674-00302-0; 0-674-00997-5 (pa)
                                    LC 00-44996
"Written between 1967 and the present by a literary
critic and advocate for the Palestinian cause, these pieces
often deal with the self-deceiving fictions of the colonizers about the people they oppress; others deplore some
fashionable critical theories as unengaged with real life
and history." N Y Times Book Rev
Includes bibliographical references

Snyder, Gary
The practice of the wild; essays. North
Point Press 1990 190p o.p.; Shoemaker &
Heard paperback available $15   **814**
ISBN 1-59376-016-7 (pa)   LC 90-7590
"Poet Snyder's tough, beautiful essays combine native
American lore, Confucian/Zen philosophy, and a loving
respect for the wilderness." Booklist

Sontag, Susan, 1933-
Styles of radical will. Farrar, Straus &
Giroux 1969 274p o.p.; Picador paperback
available $14   **814**
ISBN 0-312-42021-8 (pa)
Analyzed in Essay and general literature index
"The book contains essays, some previously published,
arranged in groups. The first group of three is aesthetic
and philosophical; three deal with film; and the last set
is . . . a reply to a Partisan Review questionnaire about
America and an . . . essay on a trip to North Vietnam."
Libr J

Where the stress falls; essays. Farrar,
Straus & Giroux 2001 351p $25; pa $14
                                             814
1. Gombrowicz, Witold. Ferdydurke 2. Zagajewski,
Adam, 1945- Another beauty 3. Wescott, Glenway,
1901-1987. The pilgrim hawk
ISBN 0-374-28917-4; 0-312-42131-1 (pa)
                                    LC 2001-33704
The essays in this collection "are organized into three
categories. 'Reading' encompasses Sontag's erudite, critical renderings on autobiography and the works and influence of international literary figures such as Machado de
Assis, Roland Barthes, Danilo Kiš, Marina Tsvetaeva,
and Robert Walser. In the middle section, 'Seeing,'
Sontag is more approachable, expressing her perceptive
and provocative opinions on cinema, garden history, photography, painting, opera, drama, and dance. Finally, in
'There and Now,' Sontag recounts her experiences in Sarajevo and her feelings regarding travel, activism, writing, and translations." Libr J

Updike, John
More matter; essays and criticism. Knopf
1999 xxiii, 897p $35; pa $19.95   **814**
ISBN 0-375-40630-1; 0-449-00628-X (pa)
                                    LC 98-43124
"Updike gathers eight years' worth of occasional
pieces, book, reviews, awards speeches, autobiographical
ruminations, and cultural criticism. He plies his well-
honed literary craftsmanship on subjects ranging from the

Updike, John—*Continued*
Danish philosopher Kierkegaard and the quasi-American rodent Mickey Mouse to photography, cartooning, and his favorite author, Henry Green." Libr J

Vidal, Gore, 1925-
The last empire; essays 1992-2000. Doubleday 2001 465p hardcover o.p. paperback available $16 **814**
ISBN 0-375-72639-X (pa)   LC 00-52320
Analyzed in Essay and general literature index
This collection of forty-eight essays deals with figures literary, historical and political
This anthology "shows the mandarin populist to be at the height of his powers of both vituperation and sagacity." Publ Wkly

United States—essays, 1952-1992. Random House 1992 1295p hardcover o.p. paperback available $24.95 **814**
ISBN 0-7679-0806-6 (pa)   LC 91-39743
Analyzed in Essay and general literature index
These "essays span Vidal's writing life, falling into three sections: literature (both whom he likes and doesn't like), politics (ranging from pornography to Lincoln), and personal concerns (his own past and tastes, his involvement in the movies, etc.). What's wonderful about Vidal as essayist is not only his erudition but also his appreciation of aesthetic and behavioral standards while at the same time remaining open-minded about variations on those standards." Booklist

Wallace, David Foster
A supposedly fun thing I'll never do again; essays and arguments. Little, Brown 1997 353p hardcover o.p. paperback available $14.95 **814**
ISBN 0-316-92528-4 (pa)   LC 96-42528
This collection includes essays about tennis, state fairs, cruises, Dostoyevsky, David Lynch and the scholar H. L. Hix
"Mr. Wallace's distinctive and infectious style, an acrobatic cartwheeling between high intellectual discourse and vernacular insouciance, makes him tremendously entertaining to read, whatever his subject." N Y Times Book Rev

White, E. B. (Elwyn Brooks), 1899-1985
Essays of E. B. White. Harper & Row 1977 277p hardcover o.p. paperback available $15 **814**
ISBN 0-06-093223-6 (pa)   LC 77-7717
Also available in hardcover from P. Smith
Analyzed in Essay and general literature index
Most of the essays first appeared in The New Yorker. "They range from a 1934 piece on the St. Nicholas Magazine 'League' and the distinguished writers who were members of it as children, to a 1975 report from Allen Cove, Maine, where White had retreated from the bedlam of the city." Publ Wkly

Writings from the New Yorker. Harper & Row 1990 244p hardcover o.p. paperback available $14 **814**
ISBN 0-06-092123-4 (pa)   LC 89-46564
"Wide-ranging in subject matter, these essays tackle such diverse subjects as Krushchev, Senator McCarthy, revolving doors, and Sunday drivers in New York, all with a sense of humor." Libr J

Williams, William Carlos, 1883-1963
In the American grain. Boni & Liveright 1925 235p o.p.; New Directions paperback available $11.95 **814**
ISBN 0-8112-0230-5 (pa)
Williams portrays "the developing American conscience in sketches of such major figures as Columbus, Cotton Mather, Washington, Franklin, and Poe, and such minor ones as Champlain, Thomas Morton, Père Sebastian Rasles, and Jacataqua. He sought the grain of American character especially in homely, rather than heroic, incidents of national history." Benet's Reader's Ency of Am Lit

815.008 American speeches— Collections

In our own words; extraordinary speeches of the American century; edited by Robert G. Torricelli and Andrew Carroll. Kodansha Int. 1999 xxx, 450p $28 **815.008**
1. American speeches
ISBN 1-56836-291-9   LC 99-29995
Also available in paperback from Washington Sq. Press
"Arranged by decade from the Progressive Era to the '90s Technological Revolution, this book includes eulogies, sermons, fireside chats, public tributes, commencement addresses, and more. . . . Entries are attributed to Jane Addams, Clarence Darrow, Al 'Scarface' Capone, General George S. Patton, Jack Kerouac, Vince Lombardi, Jane Fonda, Ronald Reagan, and others." SLJ
Includes bibliographical references

Representative American speeches. Wilson, H.W. (Reference shelf) pa $50 **815.008**
1. American speeches
Also available Representative American speeches, 1937-1997 $90 (ISBN 0-8242-0931-1)
Annual. First published 1937-1938
Editors vary
A compilation containing a selection of speeches of the year made by eminent men and women on major trends and events. Each speech is prefaced by a note about the speaker and the occasion. The appendix in each volume contains biographical notes

Voices of multicultural America; notable speeches delivered by African, Asian, Hispanic, and Native Americans, 1790-1995; Deborah Gillan Straub, editor. Gale Res. 1996 lii, 1372p il $185 **815.008**
1. American speeches 2. Ethnic groups
ISBN 0-8103-9378-6   LC 95-31473
This is a collection of "230 speeches by 130 persons. . . . The entries are arranged in one alphabet by name, each beginning with an approximately two-page biographical sketch. The historical context of the speech and the specific occasion provide perspective. Following the speech, which is usually presented in its entirety, a brief paragraph describes its aftermath. . . . The book represents a remarkably diverse range of political and social viewpoints." Booklist
Includes bibliographical references

816   American letters

Letters of a nation; a collection of extraordinary American letters; edited by Andrew Carroll. Kodansha Int. 1997 xlviii, 446p o.p.; Broadway Bks. paperback available $16.95   **816**
1. American letters
ISBN 0-7679-0331-5 (pa)   LC 97-25510
An anthology of "letters that chronicle American life over the entire course of our turbulent history. Letters from presidents alternate with letters from immigrants struggling against prejudice; letters from Native Americans and whites reveal both sides of the conquest; black activists write about racism and inequality; and a World War II ambulance driver describes the unmitigated horror of a concentration camp. Carroll has also selected letters full of joy and wonder, as well as hilarious letters by Groucho Marx and E. B. White. There simply isn't a dull passage to be found in this mind-opening, heart-stretching volume." Booklist

Letters of the century; America, 1900-1999; edited by Lisa Grunwald and Stephen J. Adler. Dial Press (NY) 1999 741p il $35
816
1. American letters 2. United States—Civilization
ISBN 0-385-31590-2   LC 99-16808
This anthology "contains four hundred and twelve letters arranged chronologically to demonstrate the effects of war, the Depression, demographic change, scientific innovation, medical discovery, and artistic experimentation on American life." New Yorker
Among the letter writers gathered are "Carl Van Doren, Huey Long, Franklin D. Roosevelt, Lillian Hellman and a Vietnam soldier named Dusty. This is one of the most original literary tributes to the closing century." Publ Wkly

817   American humor and satire

Allen, Woody
Side effects. Random House 1980 149p o.p.; Ballantine Bks. paperback available $6.99   **817**
ISBN 0-345-34335-2 (pa)   LC 79-5549
"The sixteen sketches—which {are concerned with themes} of love and death, angst and despair, bagels and lox—appeared originally in magazines." Commonweal

Without feathers. Random House 1975 210p o.p.; Ballantine Bks. paperback available $6.99   **817**
ISBN 0-345-33697-6 (pa)
A collection of sixteen satirical sketches, most of which previously appeared in The New Yorker and other periodicals, and two one-act plays: God, and Death. The sketches include "take-offs on other writers (Kafka, Bellow, Strindberg), and several 'intellectual' dissertations on such topics as the Irish genius, the origins of slang, the lesser ballets, psychic phenomena, etc." Libr J

Barry, Dave
Dave Barry does Japan. Random House 1992 210p il o.p.; Fawcett Bks. paperback available $13.95   **817**
ISBN 0-449-90810-0 (pa)   LC 92-53634
This collection of humor is based on the author's three week trip to Japan
"There are a few sensitive moments in his comical tour, but Barry does not stray long from his typical, sarcastic self, so fans should be delighted." Booklist

Dave Barry hits below the Beltway; a vicious and unprovoked attack on our most cherished political institutions. Random House 2001 180p il $24.95; pa $14.95   **817**
ISBN 0-375-50219-X; 0-345-43248-7 (pa)
LC 2001-31661
Also available large print edition $24.95 (ISBN 0-375-43139-X)
"The Declaration of Independence and the Constitution were never meant to tickle the funny bone, but when rewritten by Barry they do just that. With his keen sense of the ridiculous he has great fun frolicking with people such as Al Gore, George W. Bush, and Pat Robertson; in places such as D.C., South Florida, and Austin; and with subjects such as the Palm Beach ballot, political campaigns, and social security. Barry even succeeds in the improbable task of writing amusing footnotes." Libr J

Dave Barry in cyberspace. Crown 1996 215p hardcover o.p. paperback available $12.95   **817**
ISBN 0-449-91230-2 (pa)   LC 96-22316
A "tongue-in-cheek guide to computing. . . . Designed to look like a user's manual, complete with section tabs and a mock glossary, it offers a wryly skeptical tour of the digital world with outrageously irreverent commentary on word-processing applications, software installation and use, Windows 95, Comdex trade shows, technical support services and much more." Publ Wkly

Dave Barry is from Mars and Venus. Crown 1997 269p il hardcover o.p. paperback available $12.95   **817**
ISBN 0-345-42578-2 (pa)   LC 97-10698
In this collection Barry "joins a team of future Olympic synchronized swimmers in the pool in response to a challenge; checks out laser tag; appears on *Wheel of Fortune*; runs for president; and expresses himself on history, politics, culture, various insects, and the aforementioned war between the sexes in pungent prose, plus occasional poetry and drama." Booklist

Dave Barry is not making this up. Crown 1994 244p hardcover o.p. paperback available $12.50   **817**
ISBN 0-449-90973-5 (pa)   LC 94-8341
"From 'Father Faces Life: A Long-Overdue Attack on Natural Childbirth,' which first earned him visibility, through off-kilter takes on sneakers, UFOs, ubiquitous health hazards, 'Consumers from Mars,' and radio's not-so-golden oldies, Barry blends fact and fiction, family frustrations and cultural anomalies, sarcasm and sentimentality." Booklist

Barry, Dave—*Continued*
Dave Barry is not taking this sitting down!
Crown 2000 229p il hardcover o.p. paperback
available $12.95   **817**
ISBN 0-345-44410-8 (pa)   LC 00-31415
"The title represents Barry's rage not only about toilets but about airline 'bistro service' meals, television ads
for pharmaceuticals, and the general moral decay confronting America today. Fans will not be disappointed
with Barry's forays into proper word usage when he
dons his 'Mr. Language Person' hat. And they will certainly rally around him on issues concerning the IRS,
college dormitories, and Internet millionaires." Libr J

Dave Barry talks back; cartoons by Jeff
MacNelly. Crown 1991 285p il hardcover
o.p. paperback available $12   **817**
ISBN 0-517-58868-4 (pa)   LC 91-11139
A collection of the humorist's newspaper columns.
Topics range from politics to popular culture

Dave Barry turns 40. Crown 1990 179p
o.p.; Fawcett Bks. paperback available $12.95
               817
ISBN 0-449-90587-X (pa)   LC 90-1621
Humorist Dave Barry writes about the onset of middle
age and its effects, both physical and mental

Dave Barry turns 50. Crown 1998 219p
hardcover o.p. paperback available $13.95
               817
ISBN 0-345-43169-3 (pa)   LC 98-18978
"Tracing the history of boomers, Barry measures some
of the greatest achievements of our time, like the introduction of the first major TV jingle. . . . Other topics
include politics, highlighted by Watergate, and inventions
of concern to baby boomers such as Oreos, Silly Putty,
long-playing records, and espresso makers." Libr J

Dave Barry's complete guide to guys; a
fairly short book. Random House 1995 xxv,
189p il hardcover o.p. paperback available
$11   **817**
ISBN 0-449-91026-1 (pa)   LC 94-41080
"After presenting a scientific quiz with which a male
can assess his 'guyness quotient,' the author treats the biological nature, social development, medical concerns
and domestic side of guys. He even provides a chapter
for the woman who is contemplating having a relationship with such a creature." Publ Wkly

Dave Barry's greatest hits. Crown 1988
287p hardcover o.p. paperback available $12
               817
ISBN 0-449-90406-7 (pa)   LC 88-3822
Humor and commentary by the Pulitzer Prize winning
columnist

Dave Barry's only travel guide you'll ever
need. Fawcett Columbine 1991 171p il maps
hardcover o.p. paperback available $12.95
               817
1. Travel
ISBN 0-449-90759-7 (pa)   LC 91-70649
"The popular humor columnist's take on traveling
again showcases his scattergun style, which is really best

indulged in smaller doses than a whole book's worth.
. . . Folks like Barry's farrago of non sequiturs, deliberate stupidity, heavy-handed ironies, flippancy, and
lampshade-hat silliness." Booklist

Bombeck, Erma
Forever, Erma; best-loved writing from
America's favorite humorist. Andrews &
McMeel 1996 273p hardcover o.p. paperback
available $12.95   **817**
ISBN 0-8362-3673-4 (pa)   LC 96-33986
This Bombeck "compilation, put together by the editors of her syndicated pieces, is intended to represent the
best of a writing career that spanned more than 30 years.
All the familiar characters of Bombeck's columns are
here: the ungrateful kids, the husband behind the newspaper, the competitive friends. . . . [Bombeck] is eulo-
gized here by two fellow columnists, Ellen Goodman and
Art Buchwald. There is also a touching goodbye from
her husband, Bill. A fitting finale for the much-loved humorist." Booklist

A marriage made in heaven—; or, Too
tired for an affair. HarperCollins Pubs. 1993
256p hardcover o.p. paperback available
$6.99   **817**
ISBN 0-06-109202-9 (pa)   LC 92-56207
The author, who was married in 1949, discusses her
own marriage and the institution of matrimony in the
United States during the same period
Bombeck "devotes chapters to such serious episodes
as her early difficulties conceiving children, a miscarriage at the age of 40 and, more recently, a mastectomy.
But even these jolts are leavened with Mrs. Bombeck's
brand of self-deprecatory wit." N Y Times Book Rev

Carlin, George, 1937-
Brain droppings. Hyperion 1997 258p
hardcover o.p. paperback available $12.95
               817
ISBN 0-7868-8321-9 (pa)   LC 96-52373
"Carlin, the thinking man's comedian, is known for
his fresh and weirdly funny take on life. This book's title
accurately describes what's inside; these bits seem to
have come tumbling out of Carlin's brain in random order. Some are laugh-out-loud funny and some are . . .
well, just droppings. . . . Bad words, by the way,
abound, but if you know Carlin's work, you'd expect
that." Booklist

Napalm & silly putty. Hyperion 2001 269p
$22.95; pa $12.95   **817**
ISBN 0-7868-6413-3; 0-7868-8758-3 (pa)
               LC 00-54055
The comedian "covers a wide range of issues from
rape and religion to the homeless. . . . And any topic is
fair game: abortion, airport security, cars, funerals, language, organ donors, sports, technology, TV and war.
. . . Over 100 scintillating short pieces are interrupted
by loony lists and hundreds of clever one-liners." Publ
Wkly

Frazier, Ian
Coyote v. Acme. Farrar, Straus & Giroux
1996 117p hardcover o.p. paperback available
$11   **817**
ISBN 0-374-52491-2 (pa)   LC 95-26360
This collection "contains 22 pieces spoofing a wide
range of subjects from Wylie Coyote to Joseph Stalin,

Frazier, Ian—*Continued*

from aggressive New Yorkers to the all-powerful Internal Revenue Service." Libr J

"The title essay, with its exposition, in deadly legalese, of one Wile E. Coyote's complaints against a generic purveyor of explosive devices, shows Frazier's great comic range, however trite the subject. Although this book is not Frazier at full-bore, readers of his generation will find an occasional cultural reference long thought lost, and find themselves oddly beholden to a fellow who can resurrect Billy Joe McCallister from beneath the Tallahatchie Bridge." Publ Wkly

Grizzard, Lewis

It wasn't always easy, but I sure had fun; the best of Lewis Grizzard. Villard Bks. 1994 311p o.p.; Ballantine Bks. paperback available $7.50   **817**
ISBN 0-345-40001-1 (pa)   LC 94-18337
A representative selection of satirical pieces on contemporary life by the late southern humorist

Ivins, Molly

Molly Ivins can't say that, can she? Random House 1991 284p hardcover o.p. paperback available $13   **817**
ISBN 0-679-74183-6 (pa)   LC 91-52662
This is a "collection of previously published pieces from The Progressive, Ms., The Nation and other magazines. . . . Country music, Nancy Reagan's wardrobe, national political conventions, the Iran-contra affair, the Dallas Cowboys cheerleaders, football as the established religion in Texas, the differences between Southerners and other Americans and also the differences between Texans and other Southerners—on all these matters and many others, she has wise and often hilarious things to say." N Y Times Book Rev

Nothing but good times ahead. Random House 1993 255p hardcover o.p. paperback available $13   **817**
ISBN 0-679-75488-1 (pa)   LC 93-10401
A collection of the author's newspaper columns and magazine pieces written between 1991 and 1993

Keillor, Garrison

We are still married; stories & letters. Viking 1989 330p hardcover o.p. paperback available $15   **817**
ISBN 0-14-013156-6 (pa)   LC 88-40283
The "poems, opinions, stories, letters and whatnots in this collection ponder the meaning and nuance of yard sales, sneezes, Woodlawn Cemetery, the last surviving cigarette smokers . . . and traveling with teen-age children." N Y Times Book Rev

Martin, Steve, 1945?-

Pure drivel. Hyperion 1998 104p $19.95; pa $10.95   **817**
ISBN 0-7868-6467-2; 0-7868-8505-X (pa)
LC 98-28739
Also available G.K. Hall large print edition
"The short essays, conversations, and proclamations collected here are relayed in a slyly deadpan Valley voice that belies the coiled craziness of their content. Martin also brings his gift for comedic timing to these creations, setting a quirky beat that perfectly sets off their ironic wiles." Booklist

McManus, Patrick F.

Into the twilight, endlessly grousing. Simon & Schuster 1997 221p hardcover o.p. paperback available $12   **817**
ISBN 0-684-84799-X (pa)   LC 97-23502
McManus presents a "collection of columns, most of them reprinted from *Outdoor Life*. His humor recalls Thurber's dictum about scenes of chaos and confusion that are remembered in moments of calm. . . . Also included are parodies of the private-eye genre and a profusion of pithy one-liners." Publ Wkly

Mirth of a nation; the best contemporary humor; edited by Michael J. Rosen. HarperPerennial 2000 619p pa $15.95 **817**
1. American wit and humor
ISBN 0-06-095321-7   LC 99-44293
An anthology of more than 50 contributors, "most represented by two or three short works. Included are veterans like Dave Barry, Roy Blount Jr., and Fran Lebowitz, and rising stars like David Sedaris, Sandra Tsing Loh, Patricia Marx, and David Rakoff. Though many of the pieces have been published or broadcast previously, some appear in this volume for the first time." Booklist

Moore, Michael

Downsize this! Crown 1996 278p il hardcover o.p.; Perennial Bks. paperback available $13   **817**
ISBN 0-06-097733-7 (pa)   LC 96-201764
A collection of humorous essays about American political, corporate and social life
"Mr. Moore has a real talent for cutting through the garbage, digging out the important points and serving them up in delightful, outrageous, sometimes irrefutable ways. He is at his absolute best when confronting his enemies head on, asking the questions everyone else would love to put directly to the people in charge." N Y Times Book Rev

Nilsen, Alleen Pace

Encyclopedia of 20th century American humor; [by] Alleen Pace Nilsen and Don L. F. Nilsen. Oryx Press 2000 360p il $73.95
                    817
1. American wit and humor—Encyclopedias
ISBN 1-57356-218-1   LC 99-47257
This "is a 98-entry reference work. A bibliography that includes scholarly works on humor, biographies, and joke books stretches over 20 pages and rounds out the text. Arranged alphabetically, articles vary in length from one to five pages. A few are illustrated with cartoons and photographs. Some longer articles are broken down into subtopics." Booklist

O'Rourke, P. J.

Eat the rich. Atlantic Monthly Press 1998 246p il hardcover o.p. paperback available $13   **817**
1. Economics—Humor 2. Wit and humor
ISBN 0-87113-760-7 (pa)   LC 98-27100
In this book the American humorist surveys "practical economics by means of trips to places that exemplify different economic practices and their good and bad outcomes." Booklist
This "is a delightful collection of anecdotes and one-liners." N Y Times Book Rev

O'Rourke, P. J.—*Continued*

Parliament of whores; a lone humorist attempts to explain the entire U.S. government. Atlantic Monthly Press 1991 xx, 233p hardcover o.p. paperback available $13   **817**

ISBN 0-8021-3970-1 (pa)   LC 91-8416

"A Morgan Entrekin book"

"In a manner that is more likely to grab a reader by the lapels and throttle him into hysterics than your average high school civics textbook, O'Rourke deftly skewers our three branches of government." Libr J

Peter, Laurence J.

The Peter Principle; by Laurence J. Peter & Raymond Hull. Morrow 1969 179p il   **817**

1. Management—Anecdotes

Available in hardcover from Buccaneer Bks.

"In a delightful spoof of administrative inefficiency in both public and private enterprise, the authors expound their theory known as the Peter Principle—'in a hierarchy every employee tends to rise to his level of incompetence.' From this they develop their science of hierarchiology." Cincinnati Public Libr

Seinfeld, Jerry

Sein language. Bantam Bks. 1993 180p il $19.95; pa $7.50   **817**

ISBN 0-553-09606-0; 0-553-56915-5 (pa)
        LC 93-14467

Comedian Seinfeld "ruminates on fish and their fear of driving, childhood pony rides with depressed ponies, One-Second Martinizing and the fact that 'your hair freaks out when it wakes up at somebody else's house.' Viewers of 'Seinfeld' should enjoy this compilation of monologues." N Y Times Book Rev

Trillin, Calvin

Family man. Farrar, Straus & Giroux 1998 184p hardcover o.p. paperback available $11   **817**

ISBN 0-374-52583-8 (pa)   LC 97-48296

In this collection of essays on family life, Trillin discusses such topics as "zipping and unzipping a snowsuit, changing diapers, celebrating Halloween, and eating Thanksgiving dinner." Libr J

"Trillin has a gift for intelligent humor couched in a felicitous style, appealing to a wide range of readers." Booklist

Travels with Alice. Ticknor & Fields 1989 195p o.p.; Farrar, Straus & Giroux paperback available $12   **817**

ISBN 0-374-52600-1 (pa)   LC 89-32735

"In this gathering of 15 recollections of holidays . . . Trillin offers himself as essayist rather than descriptive writer, interpreter rather than guide. With him most of the time were his wife Alice and two daughters, and their experiences—renting a house in the south of France, shopping at the Central Market in Florence, and hanging around the small French town of Uzés—provide the themes of a readable, unexacting book of pleasant rambles and a multiplicity of small happenings and human stories." Libr J

Wyse, Lois

Funny, you don't look like a grandmother; illustrated by Lilla Rogers. Crown 1989 111p il $14   **817**

ISBN 0-517-57157-9   LC 88-20387

Also available in paperback from Avon Bks.

A collection of anecdotes which describe what it is like to be a contemporary grandmother

817.008   American humor and satire—Collections

Honey, hush! an anthology of African American women's humor; edited by Daryl Cumber Dance; foreword by Nikki Giovanni. Norton 1997 xxxix, 673p il hardcover o.p. paperback available $17.95   **817.008**

1. American wit and humor 2. African American women

ISBN 0-393-31818-4 (pa)   LC 97-6772

The editor "has collected folktales, proverbs, slave narratives, and cartoons reflecting the humor of African American women. Among those included are authors Audre Lorde and Toni Morrison and comedian Whoopi Goldberg." Libr J

Includes bibliographical references

The **Penguin** book of women's humor; edited with an introduction by Regina Barreca. Penguin Bks. 1995 xxxviii, 657p pa $16.95   **817.008**

1. Wit and humor 2. Women authors

ISBN 0-14-017294-7   LC 95-9009

Contributors to this anthology range "from Aphra Behn to Elayne Boosler, from Erma Bombeck to Roz Chast and Nicole Hollander (yes, cartoonists are represented too). . . . Selections range from one-liners to longer excerpts from books. Most of these examples are just long enough to pique the reader's interest to seek out the source volume." Libr J

Roy Blount's book of Southern humor; edited by Roy Blount, Jr. Norton 1994 668p $27.50   **817.008**

1. Southern States—Humor 2. American wit and humor

ISBN 0-393-03695-2   LC 94-18611

"Close to 150 selections from 114 writers run the gamut of genres from essays to country/western lyrics. Authors, many of whom are not generally considered humorists, range from Edgar Allen Poe to Dave Barry. . . . There is something here for everyone." Libr J

Russell Baker's book of American humor; edited by Russell Baker. Norton 1993 598p il $30   **817.008**

1. American wit and humor

ISBN 0-393-03592-1   LC 93-22733

"Two hundred years of American humor have gone into the making of this anthology. . . . In the lineup are many of the old pros—Mark Twain, Fred Allen, James Thurber—and several relative newcomers—Fran Lebowitz, Nora Ephron, P.J. O'Rourke, and Dave Barry. The selections are nicely assorted in substance and are arranged by theme rather than chronology." Libr J

Includes bibliographical references

818 American miscellany

Abbey, Edward, 1927-1989

The serpents of paradise; a reader; edited by John Macrae. Holt & Co. 1995 400p hardcover o.p. paperback available $16 **818**
    ISBN 0-8050-3133-2 (pa)   LC 94-44065
"A John Macrae book"
The editor has organized these "essays, travel pieces, and works of fiction to parallel events in Abbey's unusual life. Since everything Abbey wrote was autobiographical no matter what literary form it took, a biographical structure is the ideal context for a sampling of his work. His fiction is represented by excerpts from several of his novels, . . while his nonfiction, usually considered his strongest and most influential writing, is culled from many sources." Booklist
Includes bibliographical references

Alcott, Louisa May, 1832-1888

The sketches of Louisa May Alcott; with an introduction by Gregory Eiselein. Ironweed Press 2001 283p (Ironwood American classics) pa $22.95 **818**
    ISBN 0-9655309-8-1   LC 00-57259
"Grouped into five categories ('Hospital sketches,' 'Letters from the Mountains,' 'Sketches of Europe,' 'Concord, Massachusetts,' and 'From *The Youth's Companion* and *Merry's Museum*)', these by turns frank, witty, ironic, charming and pensive pieces were almost all written when Alcott was between the ages of 28 and 43." Publ Wkly
Includes bibliographical references

Amory, Cleveland

The cat and the curmudgeon; illustrations by Lisa Adams. Little, Brown 1990 295p il hardcover o.p. paperback available $15.99 **818**
    ISBN 0-316-03745-1 (pa)   LC 90-6419
This installment in the "saga of how a mature curmudgeon copes with the tribulations of, as the author would say, being owned by a cat who, truth be told, is a curmudgeon himself: administering pills, trips to and visits from the vet, walks in the park and romance (human curmudgeon to woman, not cat to cat), to name a few." N Y Times Book Rev

The cat who came for Christmas; illustrations by Edith Allard. Little, Brown 1987 240p il hardcover o.p. paperback available $12.95 **818**
    ISBN 0-316-05821-1 (pa)   LC 87-3258
This is the "story of a white cat rescued by Amory one Christmas Eve. Struggling to understand his feline friend, he becomes devoted to a degree that not everyone will understand. An animal rights activist, Amory shares his feelings about veterinarians, airlines, hotels, human and animal natures, and the complexities of modern life." Libr J

Baraka, Imamu Amiri, 1934-

The LeRoi Jones/Amiri Baraka reader; by Amiri Baraka; edited by William Harris in collaboration with Amiri Baraka. 2nd ed. Thunder's Mouth Press 2000 xxxiii, 586p pa $16.95 **818**
    1. Blues music
    ISBN 1-56025-238-3   LC 99-32364
First published 1991
A collection of Baraka's poems, plays, and other writings. "The selections included are arranged chronologically in four distinct periods: The Beat Period (1957-62), The Transitional Period (1963-65), The Black Nationalist Period (1965-74), and The Third World Marxist Period (1974-present)." Libr J [review of 1991 edition]
Includes bibliographical references

Bierce, Ambrose, 1842-1914?

The collected writings; with an introduction by Clifton Fadiman. Citadel Press 1946 810p pa $19.95 **818**
    ISBN 0-8065-0180-4
Also available in hardcover from Replica Bks.
Collected works of the American journalist, aphorist, poet, and short story writer. Fadiman's introduction locates Bierce's place and influence in the American literary tradition

Bishop, Elizabeth, 1911-1979

The collected prose; edited, with an introduction, by Robert Giroux. Farrar, Straus & Giroux 1984 xxii, 278p hardcover o.p. paperback available $16 **818**
    ISBN 0-374-51855-6 (pa)   LC 83-16418
A collection of Bishop's autobiographical sketches and short stories
"Whether she is discussing the sensuous joys and dark fears of childhood or diamond mining and the preparation of food in Brazil, Elizabeth Bishop provides warm, unforced revelations on an array of topics. . . . A book to relish as well as to read." Choice
Includes bibliographical references

Capote, Truman, 1924-1984

Music for chameleons; new writing. Random House 1980 262p hardcover o.p. paperback available $13 **818**
    ISBN 0-679-74566-1 (pa)   LC 79-5532
"There are three sections: one of short stories, or something like; one consisting of the 'In cold blood'-like 'short novel, Handcarved coffins;' and one called 'Conversational portraits,' which is precisely that." Choice

Cather, Willa, 1873-1947

Stories, poems, and other writings. Library of Am. 1992 1039p $35 **818**
    ISBN 0-940450-71-2   LC 91-62294
This volume contains the novels Alexander's bridge (1912) and My mortal enemy (1926); the poetry collection April twilights, and other poems (1923); the essay collection Not under forty (1936); and the following short story collections: Youth and the bright Medusa (1920); Obscure destinies (1932); The old beauty, and others (1948); and uncollected stories from 1892-1929

Cooper, Robert Leon, 1931-
Around the world with Mark Twain. Arcade Pub. 2000 420p il maps $27.95 **818**

1. Twain, Mark, 1835-1910 2. Voyages around the world

ISBN 1-55970-522-1   LC 00-25045

"In 1895, nearly 60 years old, plagued by ill health, and $70,000 in debt, Samuel Clemens took his wife and his daughter Clara and set out on a year-long speaking tour of the Pacific Northwest, Fiji, Australia, New Zealand, India, Ceylon, Mauritius, and South Africa. . . . Exactly 100 years later, Cooper, . . . and his wife, Alice, followed Twain's footsteps as exactly as the passage of a century would allow. The result is an unusually informative blend of biography (of an underexamined segment of Twain's life), 19th-century colonial history, and travel to spots steamy and remote." Libr J

Includes bibliographical references

Crane, Stephen, 1871-1900
Prose and poetry. Library of Am. 1984 1379p $40; pa $15.95   **818**

ISBN 0-940450-17-8; 1-883011-39-6 (pa)

LC 83-19908

Edited by J. C. Levenson

"Maggie: a girl of the streets; The red badge of courage; Stories, sketches, and journalism; Poetry." Title page

"This collection also includes both Crane's collections of epigrammatic free verses—'The Black Riders' and 'War is kind'—and selections from his uncollected poems." Publisher's note

Includes bibliographical references

Day, Clarence, 1874-1935
Life with father   **818**

Various editions available

First published 1935 by Knopf

Humourous essays on the life of a New York family, during the Brownstone front era. Although most of the members of the Day family come into the picture, it is the author's dominating and very forceful father who occupies center stage

Delany, Sadie
The Delany sisters' book of everyday wisdom; [by] Sarah and A. Elizabeth Delany, with Amy Hill Hearth. Kodansha Am. 1994 133p il hardcover o.p. paperback available $8.95   **818**

ISBN 1-56836-166-1 (pa)   LC 94-34144

The authors' "homespun, plucky advice—exercise regularly, don't smoke or drink, shun credit cards, spend more time with family—reflects their perception that people today are too rushed, self-centered, overworked, lack consideration and 'rot their brains' watching TV. Interspersed with family photographs and documents, recipes and numbered lists of pointers for right living." Publ Wkly

Dickey, James
The James Dickey reader; edited by Henry Hart. Simon & Schuster 1999 350p pa $23.95   **818**

ISBN 0-684-86435-5   LC 99-23976

"A Touchstone book"

Hart "has assembled excerpts from all of Dickey's novels, along with his yearning, provocative essays and 116 pages of Dickey's poems." Publ Wkly

This collection reveals "a writer whose mastery of the trials of instinct remains a vital source of energy in a literature weighed down by its genteel literary traditions." N Y Times Book Rev

Dillard, Annie
The Annie Dillard reader. HarperCollins Pubs. 1994 455p hardcover o.p. paperback available $15   **818**

ISBN 0-06-092660-0 (pa)   LC 94-19482

This reader includes Holy the firm; excerpts from Pilgrim at Tinker Creek, An American childhood, and Teaching a stone to talk; and a reworked version of her 1978 short story The living

"This selection of writings, chosen by Dillard herself, provides a perfect sampling of her incisive, versatile, and impeccable achievements." Booklist

Teaching a stone to talk; expeditions and encounters. Harper & Row 1982 177p hardcover o.p. paperback available $13   **818**

1. Natural history

ISBN 0-06-091541-2 (pa)   LC 82-47520

"In the fourteen pensées that make up this book [the author] bears witness, reflects on her observations of the order and disorder, the splendor and horror of the natural world." New Yorker

Du Bois, W. E. B. (William Edward Burghardt), 1868-1963
Writings. Library of Am. 1986 1334p $40; pa $15.95   **818**

ISBN 0-940450-33-X; 1-883011-31-0 (pa)

LC 86-10565

Edited by Nathan Huggins

Contents: The suppression of the African slave-trade; The souls of black folk; Dusk of dawn; Essays; Articles from The crisis

Includes bibliographical references

Einstein, Albert, 1879-1955
Ideas and opinions; with an introduction by Alan Lightman; based on Mein weltbild, edited by Carl Seelig, and other sources; new translations and revisions by Sonja Bargmann. Modern Lib. 1994 418p $16.95; pa $13   **818**

ISBN 0-679-60105-8; 0-517-88440-2 (pa)

LC 94-2115

A reissue of the title first published 1954 by Crown

This is a collection of the scientist's general writings on such subjects as freedom, education, religion, politics and government, the Jewish people, and Germany

Eiseley, Loren C., 1907-1977
The night country; [by] Loren Eiseley; illustrated by Leonard Everett Fisher. Scribner 1971 240p il o.p.; University of Neb. Press paperback available $16.95   **818**

ISBN 0-8032-6735-5 (pa)

These poetically expressed reflections "evoke a sense of wonder and appreciation of nature and man's place in the universe. The striking black-and-white illustrations preceding each chapter contribute to the mood and tone." Booklist

Includes bibliographical references

Eiseley, Loren C., 1907-1977—*Continued*

The star thrower; introduction by W. H. Auden. Times Bks. 1978 319p o.p.; Harcourt paperback available $14 **818**
ISBN 0-15-684909-7 (pa)   LC 77-87827
A collection of the late scientist's essays and poems. "The materials are arranged in three categories, 'Nature and Autobiography,' 'Early Poems,' and 'Science and Humanism'." Christ Sci Monit
"To read this collection is to see the things he points out to us refracted, transmuted, and clarified through the prism of his poetic imagination and literate style." Libr J

Eliot, T. S. (Thomas Stearns), 1888-1965

The complete poems and plays, 1909-1950. Harcourt Brace & Co. 1952 392p $35 **818**
ISBN 0-15-121185-X
This book is made up of six individual titles formerly published separately: Collected poems (1909-1935); Four quartets; Old Possum's book of practical cats; Murder in the cathedral; Family reunion; Cocktail party

Ellison, Ralph

Going to the territory. Random House 1986 338p hardcover o.p. paperback available $14
818
ISBN 0-394-75062-4 (pa)   LC 85-28117
Analyzed in Essay and general literature index
"This collection of essays, addresses, and reviews deals with topics in literature, music, and race relations. . . . Ellison tries to view American culture as a cloth of one piece. His analysis of the growth of the culture, and of the dynamic interaction of the diverse elements within it, is perceptive and convincing." Libr J

Emerson, Ralph Waldo, 1803-1882

Essays & lectures. Library of Am. 1983 1321p $35 **818**
ISBN 0-940450-15-1   LC 83-5447
Edited by Joel Porte
Contents: Nature; Addresses and lectures; Essays, first and second series; Representative men; English traits; The conduct of life; Uncollected prose
Includes bibliographical references

The portable Emerson. [rev ed], edited by Carl Bode in collaboration with Malcolm Cowley. Penguin Bks. 1981 xxxix, 670p pa $16.95 **818**
ISBN 0-14-015094-3   LC 81-4047
"The Viking portable library"
First published 1946 by Viking and analyzed in Essay and general literature index
The editors have provided the following selections: essays, including History, Self-reliance, The over-soul, Circles and The poet; The complete texts of Nature and English traits; biographical essays on Plato, Napoleon, Henry David Thoreau, Thomas Carlyle, and others as well as twenty-two poems
Includes bibliographical references

Foster, David R.

Thoreau's country; journey through a transformed landscape. Harvard Univ. Press 1999 270p $30; pa $16 **818**
1. Thoreau, Henry David, 1817-1862
ISBN 0-674-88645-3; 0-674-00668-2 (pa)
LC 98-39531
"Henry David Thoreau's lifework was his journals, which were approximately two million words in length, and for years editors have quarried various selections from this mass of prose. Here Foster. . . . chooses passages that reveal the actual nature of the terrain he inhabited. . . . What emerges from this compilation is both a fresh awareness of Thoreau as a writer and an account, shaped partly by Foster's elegant interpretation, of how landscapes change and change again." New Yorker
Includes bibliographical references

Franklin, Benjamin, 1706-1790

Writings. Library of Am. 1987 1605p $45
818
ISBN 0-940450-29-1   LC 87-3303
Edited by J. A. Leo Lemay
This volume contains the text of Franklin's Autobiography "as well as 57 new attributions. Also included are all prefaces and maxims from the full run of Poor Richard's Almanack, plus a . . . selection of other writings, both personal and public. The material is arranged by the eras of Franklin's [life]." Libr J
Includes bibliographical references

Frost, Robert, 1874-1963

Collected poems, prose, & plays. Library of Am. 1995 1036p $35 **818**
ISBN 1-883011-06-X   LC 94-43693
This volume contains "all of the plays, a generous selection of prose, all collected poems, and 94 uncollected poems, as well as 17 poems that were previously unpublished." Libr J

Fulk, Mark K., 1968-

Understanding May Sarton. University of S.C. Press 2001 186p (Understanding contemporary American literature) $34.95
818
1. Sarton, May, 1912-1995
ISBN 1-570-03422-2   LC 2001-1661
"This overview of the writings of May Sarton . . . devotes two chapters to Sarton's poetry, two to her novels, one each to her autobiography and her journals, and one section to . . . *Mrs. Stevens Hears the Mermaids Singing*. Fulk argues that both Sarton's writing and her life can be characterized as 'candor to the point of pain and a search for an intimacy that is seldom achieved.' . . . A valuable addition to all collections supporting American literature and women's studies." Choice
Includes bibliographical references

Hawthorne, Nathaniel, 1804-1864

The portable Hawthorne; edited by Malcolm Cowley. rev. and expanded ed. Viking 1969 698p hardcover o.p. paperback available $16.95 **818**
1. Short stories
ISBN 0-14-015038-2 (pa)
"The Viking portable library"
First published 1948

Hawthorne, Nathaniel, 1804-1864—*Continued*

This anthology contains the complete text of The scarlet letter with Hawthorne's introduction "The custom house." Thirteen of Hawthorne's stories are also included as are passages from his American notebook plus sections from his European journals and letters and excerpts from his novel The house of the seven gables

Includes bibliographical references

Hemingway, Ernest, 1899-1961

The Fifth Column, and four stories of the Spanish Civil War. Scribner 1969 151p hardcover o.p. paperback available $11   **818**

1. Spain—History—1936-1939, Civil War—Drama
2. Spain—History—1936-1939, Civil War—Fiction

ISBN 0-684-83926-1 (pa)

"The Scribner library of contemporary classics"

First published 1962

The Fifth Column, Hemingway's only full-length play, was first published in 1938. Set in Madrid under siege during The Spanish Civil War, it deals with an American's involvement in counter-espionage activities against the Fascists. The stories included are: The denunciation; The butterfly and the tank; Night before battle; Under the ridge

Henry David Thoreau; edited and with an introduction by Harold Bloom. Chelsea House 1987 276p (Modern critical views) $37.95   **818**

1. Thoreau, Henry David, 1817-1862

ISBN 0-87754-697-5   LC 86-31020

Stanley Cavell, Loren Eiseley and Walter Ben Michaels are among the contributors who discuss Thoreau's language, narrative technique and philosophy

Includes bibliographical references

Henry David Thoreau's Walden; edited and with an introduction by Harold Bloom. Chelsea House 1987 150p (Modern critical interpretations) $37.95   **818**

1. Thoreau, Henry David, 1817-1862

ISBN 1-55546-012-7   LC 87-9306

A collection of eight critical essays on Thoreau's Walden arranged in chronological order of publication

Includes bibliographical references

Hodder, Alan D.

Thoreau's ecstatic witness. Yale Univ. Press 2001 346p $40   **818**

1. Thoreau, Henry David, 1817-1862

ISBN 0-300-08959-7   LC 2001-33320

The author examines "what he considers the religious expression in Thoreau's work. . . . Hodder believes that much of that expression has been overlooked, with disproportionate critical attention being paid to Thoreau's literary, philosophical, and political concerns. He makes a . . . case that Thoreau's various designations . . . come into better focus once his religious sensibility is factored into his character and work. . . . This work is not always an easy read—it demands some knowledge of the writings of Thoreau and other Transcendentalists—but it is certainly worth the effort." Libr J

Includes bibliographical references

Hurston, Zora Neale, 1891-1960

Folklore, memoirs, and other writings. Library of Am. 1995 1001p il $35   **818**

ISBN 0-940450-84-4   LC 94-21384

Companion volume to Novels and stories (1995)

"This is the first time the unexpurgated version of Hurston's 1942 autobiography, *Dust Tracks on the Road*, is being published; sections deemed too provocative (dealing with politics, race, and sex) have been restored. *Mules and Men* (1935) is a collection of African American folklore she gleaned on travels in the South, while *Tell My Horse* (1938) tenders her personal findings on African-based religion in Jamaica and Haiti. Additionally, 22 magazine and book articles with anthropological themes . . . that have never been gathered into book form are corralled here." Booklist

James, Henry, 1843-1916

The portable Henry James; edited and with an introduction by Morton Dauwen Zabel. rev ed, revised by Lyell H. P. Powers. Viking 1968 696p hardcover o.p. paperback available $18   **818**

ISBN 0-14-243767-0 (pa)

"The Viking portable library"

First published 1951 and analyzed in Essay and general literature index

Included are three complete novelettes (The pupil, The beast in the jungle, and The beach of desolation) as well as a number of short stories. There is also a selection of essays, critical writings, letters, and passages from James' autobiographical writings

Includes bibliographical references

Jefferson, Thomas, 1743-1826

The life and selected writings of Thomas Jefferson; edited and with an introduction by Adrienne Koch and William Peden. Modern Lib. 1993 xlii, 691p hardcover o.p. paperback available $15.95   **818**

ISBN 0-375-75218-8 (pa)

First published 1944

Contents: Autobiography, including the Declaration of Independence; The anas; Travel journals; Essay on Anglo-Saxon; Biographical sketches; Notes on Virginia; Public papers; Letters

Writings. Library of Am. 1984 1600p $35   **818**

ISBN 0-940450-16-X   LC 83-19917

Edited by Merrill D. Peterson

"Autobiography—A summary view of the rights of British America—Notes on the State of Virginia—Public papers—Addresses, messages, and replies—Miscellany—Letters." Title page

This is "the largest and most skillfully edited single-volume Jefferson ever published." N Y Times Book Rev

Includes bibliographical references

Keeley, Edmund

Inventing paradise; the Greek journey, 1937-1947. Farrar, Straus & Giroux 1999 289p o.p.; Northwestern Univ. Press paperback available $22.95   **818**

1. Miller, Henry, 1891-1980 2. Greece—Description

ISBN 0-8101-1939-0 (pa)   LC 98-51340

"In July, 1939, Henry Miller arrived in Greece during a heat wave and was befriended by Lawrence Durrell,

Keeley, Edmund—*Continued*
the poet George Seferis, and the poet's friend George Katsimbalis, the title character of Miller's book about his Greek adventure, 'The Colossus of Maroussi.' In this masterly weave of scholarship and personal experience, Keeley, a renowned translator of modern Greek poetry, uses letters, journals, poems, and his own lucid prose to recreate the world of Miller's 'little band of friends' and track them through the war." New Yorker
Includes bibliographical references

Kerouac, Jack, 1922-1969
Atop an Underwood; early stories and other writings; edited with an introduction and commentary by Paul Marion. Viking 1999 249p hardcover o.p. paperback available $13
818
ISBN 0-14-029639-5 (pa)   LC 99-20052
This volume collects 60 examples "of Kerouac's juvenilia. These fugitive pieces, previously unpublished, provide a tantalizing glimpse of the future Beat generation originator, spanning Kerouac's adolescence and his first years in New York." Publ Wkly

The portable Jack Kerouac; edited by Ann Charters. Viking 1995 xxv, 625p hardcover o.p. paperback available $15.95   **818**
ISBN 0-14-017819-8 (pa)   LC 94-20120
"Charters has chosen selections from each of Kerouac's 14 novels, which comprise a complex and evocative autobiographical series Kerouac called the Legend of Duluoz. . . . Charters has also included poetry from *San Francisco Blues* and *Book of Haikus*, as well as a group of essays that cover Kerouac's main passions and interests: writing, traveling, jazz, and Buddhism." Booklist
Includes bibliographical references

Kincaid, Jamaica
Talk stories; foreword by Ian Frazier. Farrar, Straus & Giroux 2001 xx, 247p hardcover o.p. paperback available $13 **818**
ISBN 0-374-52791-1 (pa)   LC 00-42684
A collection of Kincaid's unsigned pieces from New Yorker's Talk of the Town. "Many pieces feature black musicians, one reports on a charm school for young black women, another describes a very feisty Miss Jamaica, and all capture the aura of New York in a far funkier time than the present. . . . Great fun to read and an invaluable addition to an important writer's oeuvre." Booklist

King, Florence
The Florence King reader. St. Martin's Press 1995 xxvii, 417p hardcover o.p. paperback available $13.95   **818**
ISBN 0-312-14337-0 (pa)   LC 94-37898
"Among the pieces selected here are King's novel in its entirety, a chapter of her uncompleted, savagely funny, 'heaving-bosom historical,' book reviews, and excerpts from essay collections on any and all topics in American life. A reader to be relished." Booklist

King, Stephen, 1947-
Stephen King's danse macabre. Everest House 1981 400p il o.p.; Berkley Pub. Group paperback available $14.95   **818**
1. Horror fiction—History and criticism
ISBN 0-425-18160-X (pa)   LC 79-28056
King includes "childhood reminiscences, anecdotes about fellow writers, plot synopses of favorite films, novels, stories and television programs, a selected reading list, even a quiz—that deals with the genre in which he has so far chosen to work." N Y Times Book Rev

Langston Hughes; critical perspectives past and present; edited by Henry Louis Gates, Jr., and K.A. Appiah. Amistad Press 1993 255p (Amistad literary series) hardcover o.p. paperback available $14.95   **818**
1. Hughes, Langston, 1902-1967
ISBN 1-56743-029-5 (pa)   LC 92-45756
A collection of critical writings about Hughes's poetry, novels, short stories and other works. The first part contains reviews by Countee Cullen, Richard Wright, James Baldwin, and others. The second part of the book consists of ten critical essays
Includes bibliographical references

Lowell, Robert, 1917-1977
Collected prose; edited and introduced by Robert Giroux. Farrar, Straus & Giroux 1987 377p $25; pa $30   **818**
ISBN 0-374-12625-9; 0-374-52267-7 (pa)
LC 86-29098
Analyzed in Essay and general literature index
This "collection of Robert Lowell's prose ranges in time from an essay on the Iliad written in 1935 at St. Mark's to the unfinished study, 'New England and Further,' on which he was working when he died in 1977." Publisher's note
"Lowell's attention to tradition, social issues and the subtleties of craft gives his Collected Prose energy and lasting value." Nation
Includes bibliographical references

MacDonald, Betty, 1908-1958
The egg and I   **818**
1. Farm life
Hardcover and paperback editions available from various publishers
First published 1946 by Lippincott
These are the reminiscences of the author's life with her husband on a chicken farm in the state of Washington
This is "sprightly, diverting, and excellent entertainment. The whole book crackles with innocent deviltry of acorns hitting the roof-tops." Saturday Rev

Mailer, Norman
The time of our time. Random House 1998 1286p hardcover o.p. paperback available $24.95   **818**
ISBN 0-375-75491-1 (pa)   LC 97-44879
In addition to his novels, Mailer's "accounts of political conventions, prize fights, demonstrations, and moon landings effected a sea-change in magazine journalism, launching a thousand self-referential copycats. . . . Mailer doesn't need to stake his claim as a novelist or social critic: This sprawling reader does both, following Mailer's two careers by presenting novel excerpts set chronologically and thematically among his most memorable nonfiction, right up to his account of the 1996 campaign." Libr J

The **Mark** Twain encyclopedia; editors, J.R. LeMaster, James D. Wilson; editorial and research assistant, Christie Graves Hamric. Garland 1993 xxx, 848p (Garland reference library of the humanities) $155 **818**
1. Twain, Mark, 1835-1910
ISBN 0-8240-7212-X   LC 92-45662
This "reference guide consists of approximately 740 signed articles by noted authorities. The articles cover all aspects of Twain's life. . . . Each article includes a bibliography. There are a detailed chronology of Twain's life and a lengthy Clemens genealogy." Am Libr

Matthiessen, Peter
The Peter Matthiessen reader; nonfiction 1959-1991; edited with an introduction by McKay Jenkins. Vintage Bks. 2000 359p pa $14 **818**
ISBN 0-375-70272-5   LC 99-35246
Excerpts and essays highlighting the spiritual, literary, and political aspects of Matthiessen's work from Wildlife in America to Men's lives

McPhee, John A.
The second John McPhee reader; selected by David Remnick and Patricia Strachan; edited by Patricia Strachan; with an introduction by David Remnick. Farrar, Straus & Giroux 1996 393p il $27.50; pa $14 **818**
ISBN 0-374-25686-1; 0-374-52463-7 (pa)
LC 95-33519
"This collection picks up where the first *McPhee Reader* (1977) left off and gathers selections from 11 books published since 1975. Whether describing plate tectonics, marching with the Swiss army, or exploring the wilds of Alaska, McPhee draws the reader into the scene. Like a carpenter constructing a fine house, he selects his building materials carefully so that each part supports the others and contributes to the overall structure of the piece. The lifeblood of his writing comes, as in a novel, from his profiles of people and the stories spoken in their own voices." Libr J

Mencken, H. L. (Henry Louis), 1880-1956
A second Mencken chrestomathy; selected, revised, and annotated by the author; edited and with an introduction by Terry Teachout. Knopf 1995 xxvi, 491p $30 **818**
ISBN 0-679-42829-1   LC 94-12087
"Mencken edited the first [Chrestomathy] himself in 1948. He called it 'a sort of Mencken Encyclopedia,' but noted that he had 'an excess of copied material about equal in bulk to the matter now in the book.' Mr. Teachout . . . has organized the unused material into discrete sections and provided titles and chapter headings—as well as performing a substantial amount of copy editing." Booklist

Miller, Henry, 1891-1980
Henry Miller on writing; selected by Thomas H. Moore from the published and unpublished works of Henry Miller. New Directions 1964 216p pa $11.95 **818**
ISBN 0-8112-0112-0
The author discusses the art and practice of writing with insights on how he set his goals, how he discovered the excitement of using words, how the books he read influenced him, and how he learned to draw on his own experiences

Miller, R. Baxter
The art and imagination of Langston Hughes. University Press of Ky. 1989 149p $30 **818**
1. Hughes, Langston, 1902-1967
ISBN 0-8131-1662-7   LC 89-5645
The author "offers a biocritical reading of Hughes' writings. This literary analysis delves into the conditions of Hughes' own experiences to explore the characteristic themes of the writer's art and to examine how his imagination was fired by black folk culture and his memories of the women in his life." Booklist
Includes bibliographical references

Oliver, Mary, 1935-
Winter hours; prose, prose poems, and poems. Houghton Mifflin 1999 109p $22; pa $14 **818**
ISBN 0-395-85084-3; 0-395-85087-8 (pa)
LC 99-19141
"Oliver has set aside the frames of form and the mask of her poetic persona to share memories and meditations in essays made of both poetry and prose. Writing with the knowingness born of many years of devotion to observation and expression, Oliver declares her unceasing love of nature, the source of her art, and her willingness to embrace what most people resent: the shift in tone and meter age brings." Booklist

Osgood, Charles
See you on the radio. Putnam 1999 xx, 249p **818**
LC 99-26958
Available Thorndike Press large print edition
A collection of "100-odd commentaries (often culminating in verse) recorded for CBS Radio over the past eight years. . . . Osgood generally works from a small wire story—usually one that exhibits what he calls HPF, or Human Perversity Factor—or a scientific/medical study that proves the glaringly obvious. Sometimes, though, he weighs in lightly but sensitively on current events." Publ Wkly

The **Oxford** companion to Mark Twain; editor, Gregg Camfield. Oxford Univ. Press 2003 xxi, 767p il $75 **818**
1. Twain, Mark, 1835-1910
ISBN 0-19-510710-1   LC 2002-151880
Contents: Censorship, by N. Hentoff; Critical reception, by D. L. Smith; The dream of domesticity, by S. K. Harris; Etiquette, by J. Martin; Performance, by A. Miller; Realism, by F. Pohl; Mark Twain's reputation, by L. J. Budd; Technology, by B. Michelson; Researching Mark Twain; A bibliography of works, by S. L. Clemens; A chronology of Samuel Clemens's life, work, and times

This volume "begins with 300 alphabetically arranged entries of varying lengths devoted to all [Twain's] works, places and people related to his life, and analyses of his views on a variety of topics, from animals to spiritualism. Next come a bibliography of his published works collated from other bibliographies, a chronology, and a general index." Choice

Ozick, Cynthia

A Cynthia Ozick reader; edited by Elaine M. Kauvar. Indiana Univ. Press 1996 xxix, 322p hardcover o.p. paperback available $19.95 **818**

ISBN 0-253-21053-4 (pa)   LC 95-39500

"Besides seven poems and seven fiction pieces, including a selection from Ozick's epic novel, *Trust,* there are eight provocative essays taken from her previous collections, focusing on the secret humanness underlying the literary lives of Virginia Woolf and Edith Wharton, the demise of a literary culture, classical vs. modern feminism, and her cherished Henry James. This anthology is a good introduction to the range of styles, themes, and ideas in her writing." Libr J

Includes bibliographical references

Parker, Dorothy, 1893-1967

The poetry and short stories of Dorothy Parker. Modern Lib. 1994 457p $17.95 **818**

ISBN 0-679-60132-5

This collection contains all of Parker's published poetry and twenty-four short stories. A biographical note is included

The portable Dorothy Parker; with a new introduction by Brendan Gill. rev and enl ed. Viking 1973 xxvii, 610p hardcover o.p. paperback available $14.95 **818**

ISBN 0-14-015074-9 (pa)

"The Viking portable library"

First published 1944 with title: Dorothy Parker

This collection contains: thirty-two short stories; poems; drama reviews; book reviews, including the entire text of Constant reader; and miscellaneous articles

"It is hard to imagine a library that would not want this book." Choice

Percy, Walker, 1916-1990

Lost in the cosmos; the last self-help book. Picador 2000 262p pa $14 **818**

ISBN 0-312-25399-0   LC 99-87846

A reissue of the title first published 1983 by Farrar, Straus & Giroux

"The book consists of a mock self-help quiz. Percy poses 20 questions with didactic overtones. . . . Lost in the Cosmos contains essays, science fiction, one-liners, charts, a script for 'The Last Donahue Show,' and letters to 'Dear Abby.'" Christ Today

"The whole is brought off with that sly humor and intellectual verve that have made the author's novels exceptional." Natl Rev

Signposts in a strange land; edited with an introduction by Patrick Samway. 1st Picador USA ed. Picador 2000 428p pa $15 **818**

ISBN 0-312-25419-9   LC 99-89573

A reissue of the title first published 1991 by Farrar, Straus & Giroux

This collection's "speeches, interviews, and essays (some published for the first time) investigate various aspects of Percy's lifelong interests: the South; science, language, and literature; and morality and religion." Booklist

Includes bibliographical references

Plimpton, George

The best of Plimpton. Atlantic Monthly Press 1990 368p il hardcover o.p. paperback available $15 **818**

ISBN 0-87113-503-5 (pa)   LC 90-42037

"A Morgan Entrekin book"

This "volume collects Plimpton pieces from the last 35 years. Included are the articles that served as the basis for his well-known books—e.g., *Paper Lion, The Bogey Man*—and a wealth of other sport and nonsport accounts. Plimpton watches a World Series game with poet Marianne Moore; probes the enigma that was football legend Vince Lombardi; profiles actor Warren Beatty, novelist William Styron, and . . . provides portraits of places he's known and loved (Newport Beach, Elaine's Restaurant in New York, Norfolk, Nebraska)." Booklist

Poe, Edgar Allan, 1809-1849

The collected tales and poems of Edgar Allan Poe. Modern Lib. 1992 1026p $20 **818**

ISBN 0-679-60007-8   LC 92-50231

A reissue of The complete tales and poems of Edgar Allan Poe published 1938

This volume contains short stories, poems, and a sampling of Poe's essays, criticism and journalistic writings

Essays and reviews. Library of Am. 1984 1544p $40 **818**

ISBN 0-940450-19-4   LC 83-19923

Edited by G. R. Thompson

This volume is divided into six main divisions: Theory of poetry, Reviews of British and Continental authors; Reviews of American authors and American criticism; Magazines and criticism; The literary and social scene; and Articles and marginalia

Includes bibliographical references

Poetry and tales. Library of Am. 1984 1408p $37.50 **818**

ISBN 0-940450-18-6   LC 83-19931

Edited by Patrick F. Quinn

This volume contains 70 stories and Poe's poetic work in its entirety

Includes bibliographical references

Rasmussen, R. Kent

Mark Twain A to Z; the essential reference to his life and writings; foreword by Thomas A. Tenney. Facts on File 1995 xxiv, 552p il maps $65 **818**

1. Twain, Mark, 1835-1910

ISBN 0-8160-2845-1   LC 94-39156

"The nearly 1,300 entries are devoted primarily to proper names relating to Twain, including titles of all of his major and many of his minor works; characters and fictional locales; his family, friends, and associates; places he lived or visited; publishers and illustrators of his works; and periodicals in which he published. . . . The most extensive entries are those devoted to Twain's more widely read works. Each of these provides an introduction to the work (including a word count), a chapter-by-chapter synopsis, and a publication history." Booklist

Includes bibliographical references

Rich, Adrienne

Arts of the possible; essays and conversations. Norton 2001 190p $23.95; pa $13.95   **818**
ISBN 0-393-05045-9; 0-393-32312-9 (pa)
           LC 00-51522
Analyzed in Essay and general literature index
This volume "collects Rich's best-known prose from the 1970s and 1980s, with new writing that extends through the 1990s. In letters such as 'Why I Refused the National Medal for the Arts,' and through complaints about feminism as the cult of the personal and a renewed call for a collective global vision, she delights, and is by turns lyrical and polemical." Ms

Rooney, Andrew A.

Sincerely, Andy Rooney. PublicAffairs 1999 325p $23; pa $13   **818**
ISBN 1-891620-34-7; 1-58648-045-6 (pa)
           LC 99-43726
Among the topics discussed in this collection of letters are World War II, football, lawyers, woodworking, taxes, homosexuality, racism, heroism, 60 Minutes, and the existence of God

Royko, Mike, 1932-1997

For the love of Mike; more of the best of Mike Royko; foreword by Roger Ebert. University of Chicago Press 2001 xxi, 270p $22; pa $13   **818**
ISBN 0-226-73073-5; 0-226-73074-3 (pa)
           LC 00-50303
This second collection of Royko's best columns follows One more time, published 1999. This "volume brings together more than 100 additional selections chosen from over 7000 pieces. The collection is organized around some of Royko's favorite themes, ranging from the affliction of being a Cubs fan to his passionate concern for civil rights. His columns cover all types of issues, from the distress of short-legged male dogs in a Chicago winter to the need for stricter handgun regulations." Libr J

One more time; the best of Mike Royko; commentaries by Lois Wille; with a foreword by Studs Terkel. University of Chicago Press 1999 275p il $22; pa $12   **818**
ISBN 0-226-73071-9; 0-226-73072-7 (pa)
           LC 98-46699
"Insider politics and historical events like the 1968 Democratic convention, the assassinations of JFK and King, and the war in Vietnam are all covered in this selection of columns from Royko's 34 years at the *Daily News, Chicago Sun-Times* and *Chicago Tribune*." Publ Wkly

Sedaris, David

Me talk pretty one day. Little, Brown 2000 272p $22.95; pa $14.95   **818**
ISBN 0-316-77772-2; 0-316-77696-3 (pa)
           LC 00-25052
Also available G. K. Hall large print edtion
"In this collection of 27 fairly short essays, some of which appeared in *Esquire* and *The New Yorker*, Sedaris gives the impression of ease and naturalness. Whether he is writing about overcoming a lisp, learning to play the guitar, trying to master French, or taking an IQ test, whether the locales are North Carolina, New York, or France, the author is both amused and amusing." Libr J

Silko, Leslie, 1948-

Storyteller; [by] Leslie Marmon Silko. Seaver Bks. 1981 278p il o.p.; Arcade Pub. paperback available $17.95   **818**
ISBN 1-55970-005-X (pa)   LC 80-20251
This "consists of short stories, anecdotes, folktales, poems, historical and autobiographical notes, and photographs." N Y Times Book Rev
"Memory and invention are the stuff of Silko's storytelling. Although many of her stories traverse familiar territory—the dislocation of a disinherited people—her perceptions are acute, and her style reflects the breadth, the texture, the mortality of her subjects." Saturday Rev

Sova, Dawn B.

Edgar Allan Poe, A-Z; the essential reference to his life and work. Facts on File 2001 310p il $65; pa $17.95   **818**
1. Poe, Edgar Allan, 1809-1849
ISBN 0-8160-3850-3; 0-8160-4161-X (pa)
           LC 00-61039
This "reference work, consisting of some 3400 entries and illustrated with 50 black-and-white illustrations, treats all of the author's work—some 350 stories, poems, essays, and articles. Together with the entries covering Poe's literary works . . . are factual treatments of the people, places, and events associated with him. . . . The encyclopedia contains chronologies of the author's life and work, a directory of 'Poe Research Collections,' and a selective bibliography." Libr J

Stein, Gertrude, 1874-1946

Selected writings; edited with an introduction and notes by Carl Van Vechten and with an essay on Gertrude Stein by F. W. Dupee. Modern Lib. 1962 706p hardcover o.p. paperback available $18   **818**
ISBN 0-679-72464-8 (pa)
Also available in hardcover from P. Smith
In addition to the autobiography of Alice B. Toklas and the libretto Four saints in three acts, this volume contains representative selections of Stein's poetry, prose, drama, and criticism

Writings, 1903-1932. Library of Am. 1998 941p $40   **818**
ISBN 1-883011-40-X   LC 97-28915
Contents: Q.E.D.; Three lives; Portraits and other short works; The autobiography of Alice B. Toklas

Writings, 1932-1946. Library of Am. 1998 844p $40   **818**
ISBN 1-88301-141-8   LC 97-28916
Contents: Stanzas in meditation; Lectures in America; The geographical history of America; Ida; Brewsie and Willie; Other works
In addition to theater pieces, fiction, and poetry "memoir, philosophical speculation, literary criticism and theory, all sorts of briefer forms that are hard to account for but easy to marvel at and even to delight in, pack these volumes, and constitute, as the editors surely intended us to discover, the most consistently achieved representation of new ways of responding to life and new possibilities of getting experience into words that American literature has to show." N Y Times Book Rev

Steinbeck, John, 1902-1968

Working days; the journals of The grapes of wrath, 1938-1941; edited by Robert DeMott. Viking 1989 lvii, 180p il hardcover o.p. paperback available $15   **818**
1. Steinbeck, John, 1902-1968. The grapes of wrath
ISBN 0-14-014457-9 (pa)   LC 88-40276
This is the diary the American novelist kept while he was writing The grapes of wrath. The volume "covers the period of actual composition, from May to October, 1938, followed by a few post-production entries from the period October 1939 to January 1941." San Francisco Rev Books
This book "will provide a field day for Steinbeck aficionados, but for its insights into the creative mind it is also a valuable book for writers, aspiring or arrived." N Y Times Book Rev

Stevens, Wallace, 1879-1955

Collected poetry and prose. Library of Am. 1997 xxii, 1032p $35   **818**
ISBN 1-88301-145-0   LC 97-7023
Having all of Stevens' "poems—especially all the late poems—in one volume is a great thing (previously, one had to seek them out in three different books); the 'Adagia' and his replies to questionnaires are marvelous; and even in the somewhat turgid prose pieces, he sometimes expresses himself with exemplary force and concision." N Y Times Book Rev

Opus posthumous; poems, plays, prose. rev enl & corr ed, edited by Milton J. Bates. Knopf 1989 334p hardcover o.p. paperback available $19   **818**
ISBN 0-679-72534-2 (pa)   LC 88-46045
Companion volume to The collected poems of Wallace Stevens
First published 1957 under the editorship of Samuel French Morse
This is a collection of the author's poetry, drama, aphorisms, and essays
This volume provides a "marvelous chance to discover again the unity in diversity of Stevens's mind. . . . The accumulation of verse and prose makes it a paradoxically good introduction to Stevens's work, even though it was first published after his death." Times Lit Suppl

Sullivan, Rosemary

Labyrinth of desire; women, passion, and romantic obsession. Counterpoint 2002 178p $22; pa $13.95   **818**
1. Women—Psychology 2. Women in literature
ISBN 1-58243-177-9; 1-58243-287-2 (pa)
    LC 2001-47244
First published 2001 in Canada
"This book about love and addictive relationships begins with a fable about one woman's experience with obsession, and succeeding chapters also use fables to explore the various components of obsession." Libr J
"Sullivan's cultural references—Frida Kahlo, Sylvia Plath, Virginia Woolf, Marguerite Duras—are right on target for any woman who's ready to (re)question the role of love in her life." Publ Wkly

Theroux, Paul

Fresh air fiend; travel writings, 1985-2000. Houghton Mifflin 2000 466p $27; pa $15
   818
ISBN 0-618-03406-4; 0-618-12693-7 (pa)
    LC 99-58521
"A collection of previously published essays, articles, book introductions, and short stories." Libr J
"Although somewhat uneven, perhaps because they were originally written for different audiences, almost every piece in this collection is informative, insightful, and evocative." Christ Sci Monit
Includes bibliographical references

Thompson, Hunter S.

The great shark hunt; strange tales from a strange time. Summit Bks. 1979 602p hardcover o.p. paperback available $16   **818**
ISBN 0-7432-5045-1 (pa)   LC 79-831
"A Rolling Stone Press book"
"A retrospective in journalistic theater, this gathers together excerpts from Thompson's 'Fear and Loathing in Las Vegas' and 'Fear and Loathing on the Campaign Trail,' plus his reportage from such diverse journals as 'Rolling Stone,' 'Playboy,' 'The New York Times,' etc., going back to 1962." Publ Wkly
Includes bibliographical references

Thoreau, Henry David, 1817-1862

Collected essays and poems. Library of Am. 2001 703p $35   **818**
ISBN 1-88301-195-7   LC 00-46234
Edited by Elizabeth Hall Witherell
Among the 27 essays included are Civil disobedience, Walking, Martyrdom of John Brown, A Yankee in Canada, and Life without principle. Many of the poems were taken from Thoreau's journals and manuscripts
Includes bibliographical references

The portable Thoreau; edited and with an introduction by Carl Bode. rev ed. Viking 1964 698p hardcover o.p. paperback available $15.95   **818**
ISBN 0-14-015031-5 (pa)
"The Viking portable library"
First published 1947 and analyzed in Essay and general literature index
This volume contains the complete text of Walden and a large portion of A week on the Concord and Merrimack Rivers as well as selections from The Maine Woods, Cape Cod and Excursions. Some of Thoreau's poems, essays and a portion of his Journal are also included
Includes bibliographical references

Walden and other writings of Henry David Thoreau; edited by Brooks Atkinson. Modern Lib. 1992 769p $19.95; pa $10.95   **818**
ISBN 0-679-60004-3; 0-679-78334-2 (pa)
    LC 92-50225
First Modern Library edition, 1950
In addition to Walden, this collection of Thoreau's prose includes: A week on the Concord and Merrimack Rivers; Cape Cod; The Allegash and East Branch; Walking; Civil disobedience; Slavery in Massachusetts; A plea for Captain John Brown; Life without principle

Thoreau, Henry David, 1817-1862—*Continued*

A week on the Concord and Merrimack rivers; Walden, or, Life in the woods; The Maine woods; Cape Cod. Library of Am. 1985 1114p il $35 **818**
ISBN 0-940450-27-5   LC 85-5175
Edited by Robert F. Sayre
"Politically the most conscious of the Transcendentalists, an acute observer of natural and social facts, Thoreau was an outstanding prose stylist." Reader's Ency
Includes bibliographical references

Thurber, James, 1894-1961

The dog department; James Thurber on hounds, scotties, and talking poodles; edited by Michael J. Rosen. HarperCollins Pubs. 2001 285p il $32 **818**
1. Dogs
ISBN 0-06-019656-4   LC 00-59789
This collection of Thurber's magazine articles and cartoons "includes pieces from the classic and hugely popular *Thurber's Dogs* (1955), which is now out of print, along with some previously unpublished materials and a large selection of 'Talk of the Town' miniatures from the *New Yorker*." Booklist

People have more fun than anybody; a centennial celebration of drawings and writings by James Thurber; edited by Michael J. Rosen. Harcourt Brace & Co. 1994 169p il hardcover o.p. paperback available $15 **818**
ISBN 0-15-600235-3 (pa)   LC 93-37922
"Being a hundred or so never before collected drawings and writings, a veritable kennel of good dogs, celebrity guests, a thousand or more laughs, several poignant revelations, and Thurber's favorite birthday cake." Title page
The editor has collected 18 comic prose pieces and over 75 cartoons mostly from Thurber's work for the New Yorker

Trillin, Calvin

Too soon to tell. Farrar, Straus & Giroux 1995 292p o.p.; Warner Bks. paperback available $12.95 **818**
ISBN 0-446-67230-0 (pa)   LC 94-24629
"In this collection of nearly 100 syndicated columns, Calvin Trillin holds forth on everything from the animal kingdom . . . to the possibility of being labeled a member of the cultural elite. . . . 'Too Soon to Tell' abounds with Mr. Trillin's self-deprecating humor and slyly acerbic insights, not to mention invaluable homespun wisdom." N Y Times Book Rev

Twain, Mark, 1835-1910

The portable Mark Twain; edited by Bernard De Voto. Viking 1946 786p hardcover o.p. paperback available $15.95 **818**
ISBN 0-14-015020-X (pa)
Analyzed in Essay and general literature index
"The Viking portable library"
Contains the following complete works: Notorious jumping frog of Calavaras County; Private history of a campaign that failed; Adventures of Huckleberry Finn;

Fenimore Cooper's literary offenses; Mysterious stranger. Also comprehensive selections from: A tramp abroad; Old times on the Mississippi; Connecticut Yankee in King Arthur's court; Pudd'n-head Wilson; Following the equator; Mark Twain in eruption; Mark Twain's autobiography. Twenty-eight of Twain's letters are also included

The wit and wisdom of Mark Twain; edited by Alex Ayres. Harper & Row 1987 265p o.p.; Plume Bks. paperback available $13.95 **818**
ISBN 0-452-01058-6 (pa)   LC 87-45020
The editor "provides systematic access to plenty of Twain's bon mots by arranging them in a dictionary of topics from *Adam* to *youth*. . . . Where background is needed, Ayres supplies it succinctly and, as an afterword, proffers 'What Mark Twain might say today' on such ponderables as communism, extraterrestrial intelligence, the national debt, terrorism, and the unborn. Much to Ayres' credit, many of these approximations sound markedly Twainian." Booklist
Includes bibliographical references

Updike, John

Hugging the shore; essays and criticism. Knopf 1983 xx, 919p $30 **818**
ISBN 0-394-53179-5   LC 83-47957
In addition to miscellaneous essays, this volume contains pieces on "classic nineteenth-century figures (Flaubert, Hawthorne), and twentieth-century authors." N Y Rev Books
"These reviews are models of craft—and something more. Updike summarizes expertly and quotes tellingly, and takes care to seek out the true thematic and moral center of whatever book he's analyzing." Christ Sci Monit

Vonnegut, Kurt, 1922-

Fates worse than death; an autobiographical collage of the 1980s. Putnam 1991 237p il o.p.; Berkley Pub. Group paperback available $13.95 **818**
ISBN 0-425-13406-7 (pa)   LC 91-10691
In this book the author "applies an apocalyptic eye to everything from global starvation to censorship. In this collection of speeches, essays and memoirs, linked together by reflective passages, Mr. Vonnegut is perhaps more intimate with the reader than ever. He reveals a tortured family life and tells stories of alcoholism and insanity and of deep grief and, sometimes, reconciliation." N Y Times Book Rev

Palm Sunday; an autobiographical collage. Delacorte Press 1981 330p il hardcover o.p. paperback available $13.95 **818**
ISBN 0-385-33426-5 (pa)   LC 80-27322
This is a collection of the author's letters, reviews, speeches, memoirs, a "self-interview," a short story, a play and a sermon he delivered on Palm Sunday

Walker, Alice, 1944-

Anything we love can be saved; a writer's activism: essays, speeches, statements & letters. Random House 1997 xxv, 225p hardcover o.p. paperback available $13.95
818

ISBN 0-345-40796-2 (pa)   LC 96-41159
Walker has assembled a "wide-ranging collection of personal essays, remarks, letters, speeches and statements, many previously published. . . . Constantly testing and stretching her readers' imaginations and boundaries, Walker expresses her warmth, her anger, her optimism in this provocative, lively collection." Publ Wkly

In search of our mothers' gardens; womanist prose. Harcourt Brace Jovanovich 1983 397p hardcover o.p. paperback available $15
818
ISBN 0-15-644544-1 (pa)   LC 83-8584
"Novelist and poet Walker brings together assorted essays and reviews that refocus attention on her own life and literary work. By 'womanist,' Walker means an extended concept of black feminism, and this dual minority consciousness informs the basic ideas and themes behind all of her writing." Booklist

Includes bibliographical references

Living by the word; selected writings, 1973-1987. Harcourt Brace Jovanovich 1988 196p hardcover o.p. paperback available $9
818
ISBN 0-15-652865-7 (pa)   LC 87-29615
The author "presents a collection of miscellaneous essays, speeches, and journal entries that encapsulates the concerns of her writings and her life. Minorities, whether racial or sexual, figure prominently in these pieces as Walker discusses her own identity as a black American woman." Booklist

Wharton, Edith, 1862-1937

Edith Wharton abroad; selected travel writings, 1888-1920; edited by Sarah Bird Wright. St. Martin's Press 1995 216p hardcover o.p. paperback available $15.95
818
ISBN 0-312-16120-4 (pa)   LC 95-3119
"From her first unpublished diary of a Mediterranean cruise to the accomplished later studies of the art, architecture, and culture of Italy, France, and Morocco, this collection is a useful introduction to the travel writings of Wharton." Libr J
Includes bibliographical references

White, E. B. (Elwyn Brooks), 1899-1985

One man's meat. new and enl ed. Harper & Row 1944 350p o.p.; Tilbury House paperback available $14.95
818
ISBN 0-88448-192-1 (pa)
Analyzed in Essay and general literature index
First published 1942
Fifty-five essays, on a variety of themes, in which the author's memories of his life in New York blend with the everyday life on his salt water farm in Maine. Many of the articles have appeared in Harpers, or the New Yorker

Whitman, Walt, 1819-1892

Complete poetry and collected prose. Library of Am. 1982 1380p $35; pa $17.95
818

ISBN 0-940450-02-X; 1-883011-35-3 (pa)
LC 81-20768
Edited by Justin Kaplan
Contents: Leaves of grass (1855); Leaves of grass (1891-92); Complete prose works (1892); Supplementary prose

Wilson, Edmund, 1895-1972

The fifties; from notebooks and diaries of the period; edited with an introduction by Leon Edel. Farrar, Straus & Giroux 1986 xxxii, 663p il hardcover o.p. paperback available $40
818
ISBN 0-374-52066-6 (pa)   LC 86-9997
This installment of the American writer's journals records his travels, family matters, research on literary and historical subjects, and meetings with other writers
Includes bibliographical references

The forties; from notebooks and diaries of the period; edited with an introduction by Leon Edel. Farrar, Straus & Giroux 1983 xxviii, 369p il hardcover o.p. paperback available $30
818
ISBN 0-374-51835-1 (pa)   LC 82-21028
This book records Wilson's assignments for the New Yorker during the decade. Included are notes taken for his travel books as well as more personal reflections

Upstate; records and recollections of northern New York. Farrar, Straus & Giroux 1971 386p il o.p.; Syracuse Univ. Press paperback available $19.95
818
1. Wilson family 2. New York (State)
ISBN 0-8156-2499-9 (pa)
This book opens with historical anecdotes and family reminiscences about persons connected with the development of the area surrounding literary critic Edmund Wilson's ancestral home in the upper New York State community of Talcottville. It continues with selections from his diary-notebook from 1950 to 1970

Wolfe, Tom

Hooking up. Farrar, Straus & Giroux 2000 293p $25; pa $13
818
ISBN 0-374-10382-8; 0-312-42023-4 (pa)
LC 00-58748
This collection "provides a great introduction to Wolfe the nonfiction stylist: the peerless portraitist (Robert Noyce, Frederick Hart), the contrarian social critic ('In the Land of the Rococo Marxists') and the literary bomb thrower ('My Three Stooges')." Newsweek
Includes bibliographical references

820.3 English literature— Encyclopedias and dictionaries

The **Cambridge** guide to literature in English; [edited by] Ian Ousby; foreword by Doris Lessing. new ed. Cambridge Univ. Press 1993 1054p il $50   **820.3**
1. English literature—Dictionaries 2. English literature—Bio-bibliography 3. American literature—Dictionaries 4. American literature—Bio-bibliography
ISBN 0-521-44086-6   LC 93-7941
First published 1988

"A handbook to the literature in English produced by all English speaking cultures. . . . Includes entries for authors, major individual works, and genres, movements, groups, critical concepts, etc. Attempts to be very current and includes a number of living authors. Also has black-and-white illustrations." Guide to Ref Books. 11th edition

The **Oxford** companion to English literature; edited by Margaret Drabble. 6th ed. Oxford Univ. Press 2000 1172p $75   **820.3**
1. English literature—Dictionaries 2. English literature—Bio-bibliography 3. American literature—Dictionaries 4. American literature—Bio-bibliography
ISBN 0-19-866244-0   LC 00-36741
First published 1932 under the editorship of Sir Paul Harvey

Includes entries for literary authors, works, critics, movements, terminology, fictional characters, significant non literary figures and important periodicals. A literary chronology is appended
This is "a valuable, reliable, and readable guide to the entire spectrum of English literature from its beginnings through the twentieth century." Booklist

Wilde, W. H. (William Henry), 1923-
The Oxford companion to Australian literature; [by] William H. Wilde, Joy Hooton, Barry Andrews. 2nd ed. Oxford Univ. Press 1994 833p $90   **820.3**
1. Australian literature—Dictionaries 2. Australian literature—Bio-bibliography
ISBN 0-19-553381-X   LC 94-235762
First published 1985

Alphabetical entries provide information on authors, literary works, journals, awards, movements, societies, important literary characters and relevant historical events
This is a "splendid companion not just to Australian literature, but to many other aspects of Australian culture and history as well. . . . This volume is so easy to use that the lack of an index is no handicap at all." Am Ref Books Annu, 1996

820.8 English literature— Collections

Mirrorwork; 50 years of Indian writing, 1947-1997; edited by Salman Rushdie and Elizabeth West. Holt & Co. 1997 xx, 553p hardcover o.p. paperback available $15   **820.8**
1. Indic literature—Collections
ISBN 0-8050-5710-2 (pa)   LC 97-19595
Published in the United Kingdom with title: The Vintage book of Indian writing, 1947-1997

"Here the editors present extracts from the writings of 32 postindependence writers. The selections include chapters from novels and memoirs, short stories, and speeches. The authors, spanning four generations, range from the celebrated (Jawaharlal Nehru, R.K. Narayan, Rushdie, Arundhati Roy) to the lesser known. Author biographies are included. The book is valuable as an introduction to Indo-Anglican writing." Libr J

The **Norton** anthology of English literature; M. H. Abrams, general editor [et al.] Norton 2v + computer optical discs apply to publisher for price and availablility   **820.8**
1. English literature—Collections
Also available in six paperback volumes accompanied by media companions
First published 1962. (7th edition 2000) Periodically revised

Contains representative writings of authors which convey the tone and trends of specific literary movements and periods. Both volumes contain explanatory footnotes, selected bibliographies, notes on literary forms and usage, an author-title index, and marginalia glossaries

The **Norton** anthology of literature by women; the traditions in English; [compiled by] Sandra M. Gilbert, Susan Gubar. 2nd ed. Norton 1996 xxxviii, 2452p pa $61.25   **820.8**
1. American literature—Women authors—Collections 2. English literature—Women authors—Collections
ISBN 0-393-96825-1   LC 96-5751
First published 1985

The editors provide representative selections of prose and poetry by women. Period introductions, biographical headnotes and bibliographies are provided

The **Oxford** anthology of English literature; general editors: Frank Kermode and John Hollander. Oxford Univ. Press 1973 6v in 2 il maps   **820.8**
1. English literature—Collections
Each of the six parts collected here were published separately and are available in paperback. Apply to publisher for prices and availability

Contents: v1 The Middle Ages through the eighteenth century: Medieval English literature, edited by J. B. Trapp; The literature of Renaissance England, edited by John Hollander and Frank Kermode; The Restoration and the eighteenth century, edited by Martin Price; v2 1800 to the present: Romantic poetry and prose, edited by Harold Bloom and Lionel Trilling; Victorian prose and poetry, edited by Lionel Trilling and Harold Bloom; Modern British literature, edited by Frank Kermode and John Hollander

820.9 English literature—History and criticism

Backgrounds to English literature. Facts on File 2002 5v set $150   **820.9**
1. English literature—History and criticism 2. Great Britain—Civilization
ISBN 0-8160-5125-9   LC 2002-71284
Also available separately ea $27

Backgrounds to English literature—*Continued*

Contents: v1 The Renaissance, by P. Lee-Browne; v2 The romantics, by N. King; v3 The Victorians, by A. Cruttenden; v4 The modernist period, 1900-1945, by P. Lee-Browne; v5 Post-war literature 1945 to the present, by C. Merz and P. Lee-Browne

This set provides "the historical, cultural, and social background of each major period. Each volume is a basic introduction to the period: its history, leaders, important laws, social and religious movements, scientific developments, and details of daily life in different regions and classes within Great Britain. The set summarizes the literary genres of each period and discusses representative writers and works." Publisher's note

"Will be useful for students studying the social, historical, and cultural influences on authors of the post-war period." SLJ

Includes bibliographical references

The **Cambridge** guide to women's writing in English; [edited by] Lorna Sage; advisory editors, Germaine Greer, Elaine Showalter. Cambridge Univ. Press 1999 696p il $80; pa $29   **820.9**
1. English literature—Women authors—Dictionaries
ISBN 0-521-49525-3; 0-521-66813-1 (pa)
LC 98-50778

A "guide to women writers in the English language. The coverage is thorough, crossing historical, national, and generic boundaries as it ranges from Julian of Norwich to Terry Macmillan [sic], from M.F.K. Fisher to Pauline Kael, from Ghanaian playwright Ama Ata Aidoo to Native American writer Mourning Dove. There are also articles on selected titles and themes. The entries, which range from 160 to 500 words, are informative, critical, and jargon-free." Libr J

For a fuller review see: Booklist, March 1, 2000

Encyclopedia of British writers, 19th and 20th centuries; [written and developed by Book Builders LLC] Facts on File 2003 2v set $150   **820.9**
1. Authors, English—Dictionaries 2. English literature—Bio-bibliography 3. English literature—History and criticism
ISBN 0-8160-4670-0   LC 2002-33920

Contents: v1 19th-century British writers; v2 20th-century British writers

This work includes "a range of authors and genres, obscure to celebrated, famous and notorious, from the opening of the period to authors active today, novelists, poets, critics, playwrights. Entries are clear and concise, consisting of brief but informative biographical sketches. For key figures . . . entries include a critical analysis of the author's works, a list of major works, and a brief bibliography of further readings. The critical appraisal that is part of the biographical sketches increases the volumes' usefulness. . . . Entries include a somewhat esoteric selection of literary movements, e.g., 'Georgian Poetry,' 'Sensation Fiction,' 'Aestheticism,' 'Oxford Movement.' Both volumes include a brief contextualizing introduction and useful time line." Choice

Gilbert, Sandra M.

No man's land; the place of the woman writer in the twentieth century; [by] Sandra M. Gilbert and Susan Gubar. v3: Letters from the front. Yale Univ. Press 1994 476p il $55; pa $21   **820.9**
1. English literature—Women authors—History and criticism 2. American literature—Women authors—History and criticism
ISBN 0-300-05631-1; 0-300-06660-0 (pa)
LC 87-10560

The third and final volume of a set begun with: The war of the words (1988) and Sexchanges (1988)

In this volume the authors "read women's 20th-century literary productions as letters from the shifting fronts of the 'sex war.' Within this framework, they undertake a broad chronological survey of English and American poets and novelists that includes Virginia Woolf; Marianne Moore and Edna St. Vincent Millay; three prominent novelists of the Harlem Renaissance, Jessie Redmon Fauset, Nella Larsen and Zora Neale Hurston; H. D., Sylvia Plath and Anne Sexton." N Y Times Book Rev

Includes bibliographical references

Heilbrun, Carolyn G., 1926-2003

Hamlet's mother and other women. Columbia Univ. Press 1990 266p (Gender and culture) hardcover o.p. paperback available $21   **820.9**
1. English literature—Women authors—History and criticism 2. American literature—Women authors—History and criticism 3. Feminism 4. Women in literature
ISBN 0-231-07177-9 (pa)   LC 89-49208

Analyzed in Essay and general literature index

"In this collection of essays and speeches advocating the application of feminist criticism to the canon of English literature, Heilbrun . . . also offers an acute view of the politics of academia. . . . Calling upon such related fields as psychology and semiotics, she focuses on the lives and writings of Virginia Woolf and James Joyce, E.M. Forster, Vera Brittain, May Sarton and others." Publ Wkly

Includes bibliographical references

The **Oxford** companion to Irish literature; edited by Robert Welch, assistant editor, Bruce Stewart. Oxford Univ. Press 1996 xxv, 614p maps $55   **820.9**
1. Irish literature—Dictionaries 2. Irish literature—Bio-bibliography
ISBN 0-19-866158-4   LC 95-44943

Encompassing "Ireland's literary heritage from the bardic poets and Celtic sagas to twentieth-century authors like Brian Friel, Edna O'Brien, and Nuala Ní Dhomhnaill, the more than 2,000 unsigned entries cover writers, titles of major works, literary genres and motifs, folklore, mythology, periodicals, associations, and historical figures and events." Booklist

The **Oxford** guide to literature in English translation; edited by Peter France. Oxford Univ. Press 2000 xxii, 656p hardcover o.p. paperback available $29.95 **820.9**
1. Literature—History and criticism 2. Translating and interpreting
ISBN 0-19-924784-6 (pa)   LC 99-28791
This "guide emphasizes 'high-culture' books in translation that have had the most lasting impact on English-speaking culture since the Middle Ages. . . . The first 116 pages cover translation theory and history, while the heart of this guide is the 17 geographic sections that follow, starting with African languages, moving through Latin, and ending with the West Asian languages. There are excellent bibliographies and an author index." Libr J

The **Oxford** illustrated history of English literature; edited by Pat Rogers. Oxford Univ. Press 1987 528p il maps hardcover o.p. paperback available $24.95 **820.9**
1. English literature—History and criticism
ISBN 0-19-285437-2 (pa)   LC 86-8507
"Covers the whole range of English literature from Anglo-Saxon times to the present day. Contributors are eminent scholars and writers in their respective periods. It is generously illustrated in color and black-and-white, with pictures chosen to illuminate and supplement the text, and includes suggestions for further reading, maps, and a table of important dates." Univ Press Books for Public Libr

Pool, Daniel
What Jane Austen ate and Charles Dickens knew; from fox hunting to whist: the facts of daily life in nineteenth-century England. Simon & Schuster 1993 416p il maps hardcover o.p. paperback available $14
820.9
1. English literature—History and criticism 2. England—Social life and customs
ISBN 0-671-88236-8 (pa)   LC 93-16240
"Modern American readers of 19th-century English novels are often brought up short by bizarre references and puzzling words that did not need explaining when the books were written. Now they do, and Daniel Pool does a charming job of clearing things up in a witty, informal survey of daily life in the Hanoverian-Victorian era." N Y Times Book Rev
Includes bibliographical references

Ricks, Christopher
Reviewery. Handsel Bks. 2002 c2001 386p $30   **820.9**
1. English literature—History and criticism 2. American literature—History and criticism 3. Books—Reviews
ISBN 1-59051-019-4   LC 2002-24389
Analyzed in Essay and general literature index
This collection of the author's literary and cultural reviews from newspapers and journals range around the twentieth century, taking on major figures in biography, poetry, fiction, sociology and cultural studies as well as various non-literary arts
"Ricks takes seriously his duties as a sentinel of literature and wields his pen with determined force." N Y Times Book Rev

Sanders, Andrew
The short Oxford history of English literature. 2nd ed. Oxford Univ. Press 2000 732p pa $18.95   **820.9**
1. English literature—History and criticism
ISBN 0-19-818697-5   LC 00-21242
Also available in hardcover 1996 revised edition
First published 1994
"The *History* provides detailed discussion of Old and Middle English literature, the Renaissance, Shakespeare, the seventeenth and eighteenth centuries, the Romantics, Victorian and Edwardian literature, Modernism, and post-war writing. Discussions of key writers and works are combined with analysis of the impact on literature of contemporary political, social, and intellectual developments. The book includes Scottish, Irish, and Welsh writers, and it asks about the future of the canon in the light of the fragmented condition of British writing in the post-imperial period." Publisher's note
Includes bibliographical references

Vendler, Helen Hennessy
Coming of age as a poet; Milton, Keats, Eliot, Plath; [by] Helen Vendler. Harvard Univ. Press 2003 174p il $22.95   **820.9**
1. English poetry—History and criticism 2. American poetry—History and criticism
ISBN 0-674-01024-8   LC 2002-27287
Contents: John Milton: the elements of happiness; John Keats: perfecting the sonnet; T.S. Eliot: inventing Prufrock; Sylvia Plath: reconstructing the Colossus
"Milton's *L'Allegro*, Keats's *On First Looking into Chapman's Homer*, Eliot's *The Love Song of J. Alfred Prufrock*, and Plath's *The Colossus* are the poems that Helen Vendler considers, exploring each as an accession to poetic confidence, mastery, and maturity." Publisher's note
Vendler "succeeds in revealing the aesthetic power and technical beauty of great poetry." N Y Times Book Rev
Includes bibliographical references

Woolf, Virginia, 1882-1941
The second common reader. Harcourt Brace & Co. 1932 295p hardcover o.p. paperback available $13   **820.9**
1. English literature—History and criticism
ISBN 0-15-602816-6 (pa)
Analyzed in Essay and general literature index
Published in the United Kingdom with title: The common reader. Second series
Twenty-two essays on a variety of books and their authors—from William Hazlitt to Thomas Hardy, from John Donne to Robinson Crusoe

Women and writing; edited and with an introduction by Michèle Barrett. Harcourt Brace & Co. 1980 c1979 198p pa $13
820.9
1. English literature—Women authors—History and criticism
ISBN 0-15-602806-9   LC 79-3371
First published 1979 in the United Kingdom
"The selection of essays, reviews, and extracts from longer works presented here manifests the effortless, light intelligence that has awed and enthralled readers since the early decades of this century. The introduction by Michèle Barrett is interesting." Booklist

Wullschläger, Jackie

Inventing wonderland; the lives and fantasies of Lewis Carroll, Edward Lear, J.M. Barrie, Kenneth Grahame, and A.A. Milne. Free Press 1996 228p il hardcover o.p. paperback available $19.95 **820.9**

1. Children's literature—History and criticism 2. Fantasy fiction—History and criticism 3. Authors, English
ISBN 0-7432-2892-8 (pa)   LC 95-49924
First published 1995 in the United Kingdom
Wullschläger "examines the authors of five classics of British children's literature and offers shrewd assessments of those profoundly eccentric men and their great works." N Y Times Book Rev
Includes bibliographical references

821   English poetry

Auden, W. H. (Wystan Hugh), 1907-1973

Collected poems; edited by Edward Mendelson. Vintage Bks. 1991 xxvii, 926p pa $24   **821**
ISBN 0-679-73197-0   LC 91-158031
Originally published in hardcover in different form by Random House in 1976
A compilation of all the poems Auden wished to preserve, in his final revisions. Previous collected editions and later shorter poems are included. There is also an absurdist play written 1928: Paid on both sides

Blake, William, 1757-1827

The complete writings of William Blake; with variant readings; edited by Geoffrey Keynes. [new ed] Oxford Univ. Press 1966 944p (Oxford standard authors) hardcover o.p. paperback available $26   **821**
ISBN 0-19-281050-2 (pa)
First published 1957
Blake's "poetry deals in the subtlest kind of symbolism with a skill that cannot be matched. His philosophy is a series of intuitive flights into the realm of the Absolute, soaring with tranquil and imperious assurance; to our minds they are presented as a group of strange, complicated symbols, which to Blake are the clearest, most familiar realities." Legouis and Cazamian's Hist of Eng Lit

The essential Blake; selected and with an introduction by Stanley Kunitz. Ecco Press 1987 92p (Essential poets, v4) hardcover o.p. paperback available $11.95   **821**
ISBN 0-88001-502-0 (pa)   LC 86-24087
The editor has selected the poems he feels provide the best introduction to Blake's craft

Songs of innocence and of experience; shewing the two contrary states of the human soul 1789-1794; [by] W. Blake. Oxford Univ. Press 1977 155p il hardcover o.p. paperback available $15.95   **821**
ISBN 0-19-281089-8 (pa)   LC 78-300013
Also available CD-ROM version
Songs of innocence was first published 1789; Songs of experience 1794

"Two series of poems. . . . The first group exults in the omnipresence of divine love and sympathy, even in face of sorrow; the second group, gloomy in tone, opposes the first and deals with the power of evil. Innocence and experience are two opposing states of the human soul; the poems of one group are set against the poems of the other. . . . Often the same subject is treated in each group, as in 'The Chimney Sweeper' and 'A Little Boy Lost.'" Reader's Ency. 4th edition

Boland, Eavan

Against love poetry. Norton 2001 53p $21; pa $12   **821**
ISBN 0-393-02042-8; 0-393-32424-9 (pa)
LC 2001-30698
"Poems consistently feminist, domestic and devoted to the poet's native Ireland; Boland argues that the sweet, icky stuff that passes for love poetry is no such thing. Her concern is with polarities of love and control, against thoughtless submission but much in favor of sacrifices in partnership." N Y Times Book Rev

Brontë, Emily, 1818-1848

The complete poems of Emily Jane Brontë; edited from the manuscripts by C. W. Hatfield. Columbia Univ. Press 1941 xxi, 262p $65; pa $20   **821**
ISBN 0-231-01222-5; 0-231-10347-6 (pa)
A re-editing of the complete poems of Emily Brontë, based on all the known manuscripts. About half of the 193 poems are those belonging to the so-called Gondal cycle

Browning, Elizabeth Barrett, 1806-1861

Sonnets from the Portuguese   **821**
Hardcover and paperback editions available from various publishers
A series of sonnets which "were written during a period of seven years and are considered by some scholars to have been inspired by her love for her husband [poet Robert Browning]." New Century Handb of Engl Lit

Browning, Robert, 1812-1889

Robert Browning's poetry; authoritative texts, criticism; selected and edited by James F. Loucks. Norton 1980 c1979 604p hardcover o.p. paperback available $18.15
821
ISBN 0-393-09092-2 (pa)   LC 79-10295
"A Norton critical edition"
"Editor Loucks has chosen wisely from Browning's prodigious output (filling 12 volumes in the 'complete' edition), with selections covering the early 'experimental phase' as well as the interesting, though less studied, years of 'later achievement,' but with a greater part of his emphasis upon the poet's middle and major period (1855-69)." Booklist
Includes bibliographical references

Byron, George Gordon Byron, 6th Baron, 1788-1824

Don Juan   **821**
Hardcover and paperback editions available from various publishers
"'Don Juan,' begun in 1819, was still unfinished when Byron died. This sixteen-thousand-line poem in sixteen cantos was continually added to by the poet, and as such it can be read as a contemporary account of the au-

Byron, George Gordon Byron, 6th Baron, 1788-1824—*Continued*

thor's moods and feelings. Byron used 'Don Juan' as a platform to express many of his sardonic opinions of people and events. The protagonist is, of course, Byron himself, only thinly disguised as the famous Spanish rake." Reader's Ency. 4th edition

Chaucer, Geoffrey, d. 1400

The Canterbury tales   **821**
Hardcover and paperback editions available from various publishers
"A collection of twenty-four stories, all but two of which are in verse, written by Geoffrey Chaucer mainly between 1386 and his death in 1400. The stories are supposed to be related by members of a company of thirty-one pilgrims (including the poet himself) who are on their way to the shrine of St. Thomas at Canterbury. The prologue which tells of their assembly at the Tabard Inn in Southwark and their arrangement that each shall tell two stories on the way to Canterbury and two on the return journey, is a remarkable picture of English social life in the fourteenth century, inasmuch as every class is represented from the gentlefolks to the peasantry." Keller. Reader's Dig of Books

The complete poetry and prose of Geoffrey Chaucer; edited by John H. Fisher. 2nd ed. Harcourt Brace & Co. 1989 1040p il $105.95
821
ISBN 0-03-028612-3   LC 88-29400
First published 1977
Contents: Canterbury tales; Troylus and Criseyde; Book of the Duchess; Parliament of fowls; House of fame; Legend of good women; Short poems; Romaunt of the rose; Boece; Treatise on the astrolabe, and Equatorie of the planets
Includes bibliographical references

The portable Chaucer; selected, translated and edited by Theodore Morrison. rev ed. Viking 1975 611p hardcover o.p. paperback available $15.95   **821**
ISBN 0-14-015081-1 (pa)
"The Viking portable library"
First published 1949
Contains Troilus and Cressida, The Canterbury tales, selections from The book of the duchess and The bird's parliament, and some short verse
Includes bibliographical references

Davis, Dick, 1945-

Belonging; poems. Swallow Press 2002 54p $24.95; pa $14.95   **821**
ISBN 0-8040-1042-0; 0-8040-1043-9 (pa)
LC 2002-17749
Davis' "poems are full of fine emotion, intelligence, wit, and multinational culture. He lithely celebrates the legendary rake Casanova; poignantly conjures 'Kipling's Kim, Thirty Years On'; economically reports a father's aching futility in comforting his child ('A Bit of Paternity'); deftly valorizes the power of art ('Just So'); and often muses on the shortness of life and the limitations of being human, so cogently that a single quatrain can take one's breath away." Booklist

Gardner, John, 1933-1982

The poetry of Chaucer. Southern Ill. Univ. Press 1977 xxxv, 408p hardcover o.p. paperback available $22.50   **821**
1. Chaucer, Geoffrey, d. 1400
ISBN 0-8093-0871-1 (pa)   LC 76-22713
Gardner "surveys Chaucer's verse from the early Book of the Duchess, moving chronologically through the 'minor poems' and Troilus, and ending with five chapters on the Canterbury Tales." Libr J
Includes bibliographical references

Gunn, Thom

Boss Cupid. Farrar, Straus & Giroux 2000 111p hardcover o.p. paperback available $13
821
ISBN 0-374-52771-7 (pa)   LC 99-57739
"Boss Cupid offers a splendid introduction for the uninitiated. Almost all of Gunn's virtues are on display here: his playful, metrical dexterity, his unflinching celebration both of beauty and of transience. . . . Advancing age and the AIDS-related deaths of friends—'my everpresent dead'—figure prominently in these poems, but so does Gunn's humorous touch." Time

Heaney, Seamus

Electric light. Farrar, Straus & Giroux 2001 98p $20; pa $13   **821**
ISBN 0-374-14683-7; 0-374-52841-1 (pa)
LC 00-67278
Heaney's "book of poems is a compendium of poetic genres set in an array of forms and tuned to many kinds of experience, the work of a mature poet and world citizen, aware of his cultural authority as a public man and of the rights and responsibilities that go with it." N Y Times Book Rev

Finders keepers; selected prose 1971-2001. Farrar, Straus & Giroux 2002 452p $30; pa $15   **821**
1. Poetry—History and criticism
ISBN 0-374-15496-1; 0-374-52878-0 (pa)
Analyzed in Essay and general literature index
This collection "gathers Heaney's occasional prose from four decades, much of it meditating upon other poets who have moved him, including familiar members of the canon, such as Eliot and Yeats and Auden, and lesser-known and newer moderns, such as Hugh MacDiarmid, Thomas Kinsella, and Norman MacCaig, whose work draws his interest. Not surprisingly for a poet from a war-wracked land, Heaney comes back again and again to the question of how poetry can matter against human savagery." Booklist

Opened ground; selected poems, 1966-1996. Farrar, Straus & Giroux 1998 443p hardcover o.p. paperback available $16
821
ISBN 0-374-52678-8 (pa)   LC 98-4331
"The best of nobel laureate Heaney's poems, gathered from 12 previous collections, create a substantial volume that charts the course of one man's thoroughly examined personal life and reflects a volatile era in the life of his troubled country, Northern Ireland, though the particulars Heaney renders so vibrantly become archetypal and unbounded in their tragedy and bliss." Booklist

Heaney, Seamus—*Continued*

The spirit level. Farrar, Straus & Giroux 1996 81p hardcover o.p. paperback available $12 **821**

ISBN 0-374-52511-0 (pa)   LC 95-42585

Heaney's "poems, resting at the balance points between what we see as opposites, can make us realize that at times our vision utterly deceives us. They will last. Anyone who reads poetry has reason to rejoice at living in the age when Seamus Heaney is writing." N Y Times Book Rev

Hill, Geoffrey

The orchards of Syon. Counterpoint 2002 72p $24 **821**

ISBN 1-58243-166-3   LC 2001-47245

"Cast as a sequence of 72 uniform blank-verse soliloquies compounded out of a dissonant amalgam of demotic jabber and oracular utterance, 'The Orchards of Syon' confirms that Hill, for all his newfound volubility, can be as refractory as ever. . . . But for readers with the patience and stamina to stick with it, Hill's brooding meditations on his ancestral countryside's 'wintry swamp-thickets, brush-heaps of burnt light' or 'the burring air of the fell' carry the haunting force of a last will and testament." N Y Times Book Rev

The triumph of love. Houghton Mifflin 1998 82p hardcover o.p. paperback available $13 **821**

ISBN 0-618-00183-2 (pa)   LC 98-19502

This book-length poem "ends up so much more satisfying than much of Hill's recent work because there is so much more of Hill in it. . . . When we have read [the book] a few times (no one should read it just once) we know, more than we could from his previous work, what vexes and distresses, what heartens and cheers Hill, what gives him his grim satisfactions and how." Yale Rev

Hopkins, Gerard Manley, 1844-1889

The poems of Gerard Manley Hopkins. 4th ed. Oxford Univ. Press 1967 lxvi, 362p hardcover o.p. paperback available $19.95 **821**

ISBN 0-19-281094-4 (pa)

First published 1918 in the United Kingdom; 1948 in the United States

"Based on the first edition of 1918 and enlarged to incorporate all known poems and fragments; edited with additional notes, a foreword on the revised text, and a new biographical and critical introduction by W. H. Gardner and N. H. Mackenzie." Title page

This book brings together all the poems, including the early verses first published in the poet's "Journals and Papers" (1959), the remainder of his Latin verse together with translations into English of all the Latin poems which are entirely original compositions

Housman, A. E. (Alfred Edward), 1859-1936

The collected poems of A. E. Housman. Holt & Co. 1965 254p pa $16 **821**

ISBN 0-8050-0547-1

Also available in hardcover from Buccaneer Bks.

This anthology "constitutes the authorized canon of A. E. Housman's verse as established in 1939." Note on the text

Hughes, Ted, 1930-1998

Birthday letters. Farrar, Straus & Giroux 1998 197p hardcover o.p. paperback available $12 **821**

ISBN 0-374-52581-1 (pa)   LC 98-122533

Hughes offers a collection of poems written over 25 years. They examine his "seven-year marriage to Sylvia Plath, which ended with their separation, and in 1963, with Plath's suicide." Times Lit Suppl

"Some of the poems are direct responses to specific poems by Plath. The sequence thus becomes the most sustained and harrowing domestic conflict ever written." Newsweek

Selected poems, 1957-1994. Farrar, Straus & Giroux 2002 333p $35; pa $15 **821**

ISBN 0-374-25875-9; 0-374-52864-0 (pa)   LC 2002-21603

"With poems that are characteristically alert to the processes of creation as well as self-destruction, this selection displays Hughes's mighty, even terrifying, talent." N Y Times Book Rev

Jonson, Ben, 1573?-1637

The complete poems; edited by George Parfitt. Yale Univ. Press 1982 634p (English poets, 12) o.p.; Penguin Bks. paperback available $14.95 **821**

ISBN 0-14-042277-3 (pa)   LC 81-15948

Jonson's "poetry, notable for its balance, its control, its unadorned simplicity that is not without lyricism, prefigured the later lyrics of the 17th-century Cavalier poets, the 'sons of Ben.'" Reader's Ency. 3d edition

Keats, John, 1795-1821

The complete poems of John Keats. Modern Lib. 1994 398p $19.95 **821**

ISBN 0-679-60108-2   LC 94-4339

The works in this compilation include Lamia, Isabella, The Eve of St. Agnes', Endymion, and La Belle Dame sans Merci

Poems. Knopf 1994 253p (Everyman's library pocket poets) $12.50 **821**

ISBN 0-679-43319-8   LC 94-2495

A representative collection by the influential English romantic

Includes bibliographical references

Kennelly, Brendan, 1936-

The little book of Judas. Bloodaxe Bks.; [distributed by] Dufour Eds. 2002 224p pa $21.95 **821**

ISBN 1-85224-584-0   LC 2002-416947

"Kennelly condenses and extends his epic meditation on the theme of betrayal, The Book of Judas (1992), plumbing deeper than ever into treachery in love, politics, poetry—everything—as he transforms Judas into the complementary trickster every savior needs and demands." Booklist

Kipling, Rudyard, 1865-1936

Complete verse; definitive edition. Doubleday 1989 c1940 850p hardcover o.p. paperback available $20 **821**

ISBN 0-385-26089-X (pa)   LC 88-7364

Replaces Rudyard Kipling's verse: definitive edition, published 1940

Kipling, Rudyard, 1865-1936—*Continued*

This edition includes all of Kipling's published poetry and, in addition, more than 20 poems which have not previously appeared in the inclusive edition of his verse

Langland, William, 1330?-1400?

Piers Plowman   **821**

Hardcover and paperback editions available from various publishers

This Middle English poem is "written in 'Alliterative Verse' like Old English poetry and uses a deliberately rustic and archaic dialect. It is an allegorical moral and social satire, written as a 'vision' of the common medieval type." Reader's Ency. 4th edition

Larkin, Philip

Collected poems; edited with an introduction by Anthony Thwaite. Farrar, Straus & Giroux 1989 330p hardcover o.p. paperback available $18   **821**

ISBN 0-374-52275-8 (pa)   LC 88-83528

"'Larkin's poetry is a bit too easily resigned to grimness don't you think?' Elizabeth Bishop once wrote to Robert Lowell. It is true that his range is narrow, but within its confines is a beguiling variety of tones and forms. He never repeats himself to make the same point, and his poems are more readily memorized than those of almost any other postwar poet. . . . And when most of the flashier, more blustery contemporary literature has passed away, his poetry—ghostly, heartbreaking, exhilarating—will continue to haunt." N Y Times Book Rev

Lasdun, James

Landscape with chainsaw; poems. Norton 2001 80p hardcover o.p. paperback available $11   **821**

ISBN 0-393-32370-6 (pa)   LC 2001-18007

"The poems in this collection accomplish an extraordinary deconstruction and reconstruction of landscapes, both natural and interior. At their center stands the poet, like a latter-day Everyman—part Thoreau, part Hendrix, part John Deere—wielding his axe against the recalcitrant forests of upstate New York. . . . Lasdun's clear-cutting takes in everything from Celan to Arthurian legend, laying bare the complexities of the poet's own background as an English Jew and his sense, expressed as 'clean-etched, irreducible unillusion,' of being forever a colonist or a refugee, never a native." New Yorker

Lewis, C. S. (Clive Staples), 1898-1963

Narrative poems; edited by Walter Hooper. Harcourt Brace Jovanovich 1972 c1969 hardcover o.p. paperback available $12   **821**

ISBN 0-15-602798-4 (pa)

First published 1969 in the United Kingdom

"The four long narrative poems which comprise this collection reveal the romantic longing that Lewis says in the preface haunted him from the age of six. *Dymer*, nearly 100 pages in length, recounts the story of a monster who murders his father and becomes a god. The subjects of the other poems reflect Lewis' attachment to Arthurian legend, to Utopias, and to the techniques of Anglo-Saxon verse." Libr J

Mahon, Derek, 1941-

Selected poems. New enl ed. Penguin Bks. 2000 213p pa $17   **821**

ISBN 0-14-118233-4

First published 1991

This collection includes "portions of two earlier volumes, The Hudson Letter and The Yellow Book, and concludes with . . . more recent work. Mahon blends a respect for structure with a modernist style in evocative verses that are abstract yet substantial and combines solid images from nature with elusive, complex human thoughts." Publisher's note

Marvell, Andrew, 1621-1678

The complete poems; edited by George de F. Lord. Knopf 1993 lxv, 275p $15   **821**

ISBN 0-679-42038-X   LC 92-54301

This volume contains all of the metaphysical poet's lyric and satiric verse

Includes bibliographical references

Milton, John, 1608-1674

The Riverside Milton; edited by Roy Flannagan. Houghton Mifflin 1998 xxxii, 1213p il $79.16   **821**

ISBN 0-395-80999-1   LC 97-72469

This anthology of Milton's poetry and prose includes an "index designed to help students from undergraduate to graduate levels conceive paper topics; . . . introductions; . . . annotations with references; margin definitions; and a chronology." Publisher's note

Muldoon, Paul

Moy sand and gravel. Farrar, Straus & Giroux 2002 107p $22; pa $12   **821**

ISBN 0-374-21480-8; 0-374-52884-5 (pa)

LC 2002-20129

This collection "shimmers with play, the play of mind, the play of recondite information over ordinary experience, the play of observation and sensuous detail, of motion upon custom, of Irish and English languages and landscapes, of meter and rhyme. Sure enough, everything Muldoon thinks of makes him think of something else, and poem after poem takes the form of linked association." N Y Times Book Rev

Poems, 1968-1998. Farrar, Straus & Giroux 2001 479p $35; pa $19   **821**

ISBN 0-374-12543-0; 0-374-52844-6 (pa)

LC 00-45607

"Language is heightened, experimental, and also utterly mundane, even coarse. His subjects match the language, what with trips on mescaline chockablock with bucolic landscapes. The luck of this collection is that it is long and dense enough to show the poet wrestling not only with craft—his intricate and often hidden rhymes show, right from the start, his obsession with form—but also with the reason for poetry in a technological age." Booklist

Murray, Les A., 1938-

Conscious and verbal; [by] Les Murray. Farrar, Straus & Giroux 2001 94p $23; pa $13   **821**

ISBN 0-374-12882-0; 0-374-52860-8 (pa)

LC 2001-40222

"The poet became a minor celebrity when he awoke from a three-week coma and was pronounced 'conscious and verbal,' but this new volume is more concerned with his familiar Australian topography: dead dogs, the 'Internationale,' oysters, soil, the color yellow. Murray sticks to the cheerfully formal lines that distinguish his work while letting his voice shift between chestnuts of local dialect and a brawny but humble standard English." New Yorker

Pope, Alexander, 1688-1744
Selected poetry; edited with an introduction and notes by Pat Rogers. Oxford Univ. Press 1998 xxiii, 226p pa $11.95   **821**
   ISBN 0-19-283494-0   LC 98-230887
   "Oxford world's classics"
   The works in this compilation of poems by the 18th century satirist include The Rape of the Lock, An Essay on Criticism, Windsor Forest, and The Dunciad
   Includes bibliographical references

Rossetti, Christina Georgina, 1830-1894
The complete poems of Christina Rossetti; edited, with textual notes and introductions, by R. W. Crump. a variorum ed. Louisiana State Univ. Press 1979-1990 3v il v1 $50; v2 $75; v3 $100   **821**
   ISBN 0-8071-0358-6 (v1); 0-8071-1246-1 (v2); 0-8071-1530-4 (v3)   LC 78-5571
   This set includes three types of material "poems published in various collections of hers; uncollected, individually published verse; and work that has remained in manuscript form. For the first time, the poetry will appear in critical texts, with a full list of variants, including punctuation, from all authoritative sources." Choice
   Rossetti is "known for her ballads and her mystic religious lyrics, marked by symbolism, vividness of detail, and intensity of feeling." Reader's Ency. 4th edition

Rossignol, Rosalyn
Chaucer A to Z; the essential reference to his life and works. Facts on File 1999 432p il $55   **821**
   1. Chaucer, Geoffrey, d. 1400
   ISBN 0-8160-3296-3   LC 98-51842
   "Entries include all of Chaucer's characters or people mentioned in his writing; historical background on people, places, and events; synopses of all his works; and summaries of the major critical approaches to his writing. Appendixes provide a list of all Chaucer's known works, a chronology of his life, and a short bibliography listing basic works for further reading." Libr J

Shakespeare, William, 1564-1616
Poems. Knopf 1994 252p (Everyman's library pocket poets) $12.50   **821**
   ISBN 0-679-43320-1   LC 94-2494
   Also available CD-ROM version
   A representative selection of Shakespeare's verse

Sonnets   **821**
   Hardcover and paperback editions available from various publishers; also available CD-ROM version
   "A series of 154 sonnets by Shakespeare. Probably composed between 1593 and 1601, they are written in the form of three quatrains and a couplet that has come to be known as Shakespearean. Influenced by, and often reacting against, the popular sonnet cycles of the time, notably Sir Philip Sidney's 'Astrophel and Stella', Shakespeare's sonnets are among the finest examples of their kind." Reader's Ency. 4th edition

Shelley, Percy Bysshe, 1792-1822
The complete poems of Percy Bysshe Shelley; with notes by Mary Shelley. Modern Lib. 1994 xxv, 914p $25.95   **821**
   ISBN 0-679-60111-2   LC 94-3320
   This volume collects Shelley's political epics, hymns, satires, odes, elegies, lyrical dramas and verse epistles

Shelley's poetry and prose; authoritative texts, criticism; selected and edited by Donald H. Reiman and Neil Fraistat. 2nd ed. Norton 2002 c2001 xxii, 786p il pa $18.75   **821**
   ISBN 0-393-97752-8   LC 2001-30903
   "A Norton critical edition"
   First published 1977
   "This edition includes all of Shelley's greatest poetry and other poems frequently taught or discussed . . . as well as three of his most important prose works." Preface
   Includes bibliographical references

Smith, Stevie, 1902-1971
Collected poems; edited with a preface by James MacGibbon. New Directions 1983 591p il pa $19.95   **821**
   ISBN 0-8112-0882-6   LC 83-43008
   First published 1975 in the United Kingdom
   Smith "wrote three novels, but has been more widely recognized for her witty, caustic, and enigmatic verse, much of it illustrated by her own comic drawings." Concise Oxford Companion to Engl Lit

Spenser, Edmund, 1552?-1599
The faerie queene   **821**
   Hardcover and paperback editions available from various publishers
   "The greatest work of Spenser, of which the first three books were entrusted to the printer in Nov. 1589, and the second three were published in 1596." Oxford Companion to Engl Lit
   "An epic to compare with the great epics of the classical world and of Renaissance Italy, The Faerie Queene is simultaneously a nationalistic paean to the greatness of Elizabeth and her England, an imaginative romance, and a moral allegory of the soul in quest of salvation." Reader's Ency. 4th edition

Thomas, Dylan, 1914-1953
Selected poems, 1934-1952. rev ed. New Directions 2003 214p pa $14.95   **821**
   ISBN 0-8112-1542-3   LC 2002-155792
   First published 1953 with title: The collected poems of Dylan Thomas
   "The prologue in verse, written for this collected edition of my poems, is intended as an address to my readers, the strangers. This book contains most of the poems I have written, and all, up to the present year, that I wish to preserve. Some of them I have revised a little." Preface [of 1953 edition]

Vendler, Helen Hennessy
Seamus Heaney; [by] Helen Vendler. Harvard Univ. Press 1998 188p $25; pa $12.95   **821**
   1. Heaney, Seamus
   ISBN 0-674-79611-X; 0-674-00205-9 (pa)   LC 98-12413
   It is "useful to have Vendler's sympathetic commentary—by far the best introduction to the poet's work. She describes a poem in ways that take one constantly by surprise, raising issues one had not thought existed." Nation

Wordsworth, William, 1770-1850

Selected poetry of William Wordsworth; edited by Mark Van Doren; introduction by David Bromwich. Modern Library ed. Modern Lib. 2001 xxii, 687p $24.95; pa $11.95   **821**

ISBN 0-679-64224-2; 0-375-75941-7 (pa)
                        LC 00-66444

This collection "represents Wordsworth's prolific output, from the poems first published in Lyrical Ballads in 1798 . . . to the late 'Yarrow Revisited.' Wordsworth's poetry is celebrated for its deep feeling, its use of ordinary speech, the love of nature it expresses, and its representation of commonplace things and events." Publisher's note

William Wordsworth; the major works; edited with an introduction and notes by Stephen Gill. Oxford Univ. Press 2000 xxxii, 752p pa $16.95   **821**

ISBN 0-19-284044-4   LC 83-17278

"Oxford world's classics"

A reissue of the title first published 1984 in the Oxford authors series

"This volume presents the poems in their order of composition and in their earliest completed state, enabling the reader to trace Wordsworth's poetic development and to share the experience of his contemporaries. It includes a . . . sample of . . . lyrics, and also longer narratives such as The Ruined Cottage, Home at Grasmere, Peter Bell, and the autobiographical masterpiece, The Prelude (1805)." Publisher's note

Includes bibliographical references

821.008   English poetry— Collections

The **Best** loved poems of the American people; selected by Hazel Felleman. Doubleday 1936 xxxv, 670p $19.95
                    821.008
1. English poetry—Collections 2. American poetry—Collections
ISBN 0-385-00019-7

First published by Garden City Publishing Company

Poems are grouped under the following headings: Love and friendship; Inspiration; Poems that tell a story; Faith and reverence; Home and mother; Childhood and youth; Patriotism and war; Humor and whimsey; Memory and grief; Nature; Animals; Various themes

British women poets of the Romantic era; an anthology; edited by Paula R. Feldman. Johns Hopkins Univ. Press 1997 xxxvi, 879p hardcover o.p. paperback available $29.95   **821.008**
1. English poetry—Women authors—Collections
ISBN 0-8018-6640-5 (pa)   LC 96-47417

An "anthology of works by 62 British women poets writing between 1770 and 1840. . . . The poets are presented in alphabetical order, with each entry including a brief biography with birth and death dates, sample poems, major works, selected works, and the source of the poetry. The result is a singular resource providing information found in no other reference work." Libr J

Includes bibliographical references

Christmas poems; selected and edited by John Hollander and J.D. McClatchy. Knopf 1999 254p (Everyman's library pocket poets) $12.50   **821.008**
1. Christmas—Poetry 2. English poetry—Collections 3. American poetry—Collections
ISBN 0-375-40789-8   LC 99-36265

Contributors to this collection of Christmas poetry include Milton, Tennyson, Rossetti, Thackeray, Eliot, McGinley, Morris, Bishop and Geoffrey Hill

The **Columbia** anthology of British poetry; edited by Carl Woodring and James Shapiro. Columbia Univ. Press 1995 xxxi, 891p $41   **821.008**
1. English poetry—Collections
ISBN 0-231-10180-5   LC 94-46333

This anthology "contains major British poetry from Beowulf to the present day. Poets receive a short biographical introduction along with their poetry. . . . It includes more female poets than most comparable anthologies, and is conducive to browsing. Major poems such as Coleridge's 'Rime of the Ancient Mariner,' Britain's best-loved poems, and newly rediscovered poems are part of this collection." SLJ

Inventions of farewell; a book of elegies; edited and with an introduction by Sandra M. Gilbert. Norton 2001 478p $25.95
                    821.008
1. American poetry—Collections 2. English poetry—Collections
ISBN 0-393-04972-8   LC 00-48954

This collection includes "Milton's 'Lycidas' and Shelley's 'Adonais,' Donne's 'Death, be not proud,' John Crowe Ransom's 'Elegy for Jane, my student thrown from a horse,' and A. E. Housman's 'With Rue My Heart Is Laden.' If this book gathered only all those together with Shakespeare's sonnets and Dickinson's lyrics, it would have been enough. But Gilbert . . . gathers such contemporary work as searing selections from *Without*, Donald Hall's book-length elegy for his wife, poet Jane Kenyon; Ruth Stone's hallucinatory yet ordinary memories; and Tess Gallagher's devouring grief for Raymond Carver." Booklist

The **Making** of a poem; a Norton anthology of poetic forms; edited by Mark Strand and Eavan Boland. Norton 2000 xxxi, 366p hardcover o.p. paperback available $15.95
                    821.008
1. English poetry—Collections 2. American poetry—Collections
ISBN 0-393-32178-9 (pa)   LC 99-55233

A "collection of villanelles, sestinas, sonnets, elegies, pastorals, ballads, pantoums, odes, and other familiar structures that have shaped English poetry since Beowulf. Each chapter focuses on a single form. . . . Most useful are the selections themselves, which illustrate how particular forms have been employed over time, from canonical classics by Chaucer, Shelley, and Elizabeth Bishop through newer pieces by Hayden Carruth, Michael Palmer, and Thylias Moss." Libr J

The **New** Oxford book of eighteenth century verse; chosen and edited by Roger Lonsdale. Oxford Univ. Press 1984 xlii, 870p hardcover o.p. paperback available $21.50   **821.008**
1. English poetry—Collections
ISBN 0-19-282054-0 (pa)   LC 83-17477
Replaces The Oxford Book of eighteenth century verse, edited by David Nicol Smith (1926)
This anthology "will be welcome to anyone interested in the poetry of the period. The casual reader will find a goodly selection of the familiar . . . [and] a number of unfamiliar works, since about 25 percent of the inclusions are of such obscure writers as John Hawthorn, J. Wilde, and that most prolific of authors, Anonymous. . . . Indexed by first line and author, with brief biographical and historical notes." Libr J

The **New** Oxford book of Irish verse; edited, with translations, by Thomas Kinsella. Oxford Univ. Press 2001 xxx, 423p pa $16.95   **821.008**
1. Irish poetry—Collections
ISBN 0-19-280192-9   LC 2001-278442
Replaces The Oxford Book of Irish verse, XVIIth century-XXth century, chosen by Donagh MacDonagh and Lennox Robinson (1958); this is a reissue of the 1986 edition
"This selection is divided into three parts. Book I opens with the earliest pre-Christian poetry in Old Irish and ends in the fourteenth century with the first Irish poetry in the English language. Book II covers the fourteenth to the eighteenth centuries and Book III the nineteenth and twentieth centuries." Publisher's note

The **New** Oxford book of Victorian verse; edited by Christopher Ricks. Oxford Univ. Press 1987 xxxiv, 654p hardcover o.p. paperback available $19.95   **821.008**
1. English poetry—Collections
ISBN 0-19-284084-3 (pa)   LC 86-23701
Replaces The Oxford Book of Victorian verse, edited by Sir Arthur Quiller-Couch (1912)
An anthology of 19th century English poetry. Among the poets prominently featured are: Clough, Morris, Arnold, the Decadents, Emily Brontë, Clare, Barnes, and Christina Rossetti
"While general collections should all add Ricks, those retaining [the Quiller-Couch edition] should dust him off and keep him available in order to represent fully Victorian verse and changing attitudes toward it." Libr J

The **Norton** anthology of modern and contemporary poetry; edited by Jahan Ramazani, Richard Ellmann, Robert O'Clair. 3rd ed. Norton 2003 2v set $75   **821.008**
1. English poetry—Collections 2. American poetry—Collections   LC 2002-37990
First published 1973 with title: The Norton anthology of modern poetry
Contents: v1 Modern poetry; v2 Contemporary poetry
This volume includes "1596 poems by 195 poets. . . . The anthology includes the works of such masters as Walt Whitman, Ezra Pound, Dylan Thomas, Langston Hughes, Gertrude Stein, Lucille Clifton, Louise Erdrich, and Allen Ginsberg. . . . Extensive, and beautifully com-

posed introductions provide insight, observations, and historical context for the selections. . . . This ambitious, highly successful work is a veritable tribute to the enduring power of literature and language." SLJ
Includes bibliographical references

The **Norton** book of light verse; edited by Russell Baker; with the assistance of Kathleen Leland Baker. Norton 1986 447p $29.95   **821.008**
1. English poetry—Collections 2. American poetry—Collections 3. Humorous poetry
ISBN 0-393-02366-4   LC 86-18172
Arranged by subject, this anthology presents some four hundred British and American light verse selections. The poems date from the sixteenth-century to the present

The **Oxford** book of comic verse; edited by John Gross. Oxford Univ. Press 1994 xxxiv, 512p hardcover o.p. paperback available $16.95   **821.008**
1. English poetry—Collections 2. American poetry—Collections 3. Humorous poetry
ISBN 0-19-284086-X (pa)   LC 94-656
The editor "defines comic verse as primarily meant to amuse. From this bland definition he delves his principles of inclusion: funny poems that do not exceed the boundaries of good taste. No bawdy lyrics, no skewering satire here. Within these limits, he surveys the field from Chaucer to Glyn Maxwell (1962-)." Publ Wkly
Includes bibliographical references

The **Oxford** book of English verse; edited by Christopher Ricks. Oxford Univ. Press 1999 xxxii, 690p $39.95   **821.008**
1. English poetry—Collections
ISBN 0-19-214182-1   LC 99-20831
First published 1900 under the editorship of Sir Arthur Quiller-Couch with title: The Oxford book of English verse, 1250-1900. Present edition replaces The New Oxford book of English verse, 1250-1950, edited by Helen Gardner published 1972
This collection "starts with anonymous 13th-century lyric and ends with Seamus Heaney; in between are seven centuries' worth of poems in English from Britain and Ireland. . . . Ricks brings in plenty of dialect verse, excerpts from long poems and verse plays, and a few translations into English. . . . Long after reviewers stop debating how Ricks chose each item, readers will keep returning to these pages to find yet another good poem they've not before seen." Publ Wkly

The **Oxford** book of garden verse; edited by John Dixon Hunt. Oxford Univ. Press 1993 xxxv, 341p $43   **821.008**
1. Gardens—Poetry 2. Gardening—Poetry 3. English poetry—Collections 4. American poetry—Collections
ISBN 0-19-214196-1   LC 92-32260
"The collection spans 700 years, beginning with an extract from Chaucer's Parliament of Fowls and ending with Reginald Arkell's 'What is a garden?' Hunt has arranged the poems chronologically. . . . There have been other collections of garden verse, but it would be difficult to find one as thorough, intelligent, and satisfying as this." Times Lit Suppl

The **Oxford** book of sonnets; edited by John Fuller. Oxford Univ. Press 2000 xxxiv, 362p $25; pa $15.95   **821.008**
1. English poetry—Collections 2. American poetry—Collections
ISBN 0-19-214267-4; 0-19-280389-1 (pa)
LC 00-36757
"Indisputable masterpieces appear plentifully, but Fuller's determination to present a large number of distinguished practitioners assures that there are also many superb poems by virtual unknowns. And Fuller's introduction is a sharp-witted miracle of concise comprehensiveness." Booklist
Includes bibliographical references

The **Penguin** book of the sonnet; 500 years of a classic tradition in English; edited by Phillis Levin. Penguin Bks. 2001 419p pa $18   **821.008**
1. English poetry—Collections 2. American poetry—Collections
ISBN 0-14-058929-5   LC 00-62350
In an introductory essay, Levin "discusses the sonnet's origins, history, traditions, and possibilities. . . . Interwoven with the history are approaches to interpreting and criticizing this poetic form. The bulk of the text is an anthology of over 600 sonnets composed by more than 230 poets. Over 150 of the poets represented wrote during the 20th century." Libr J
Includes bibliographical references

Poems that live forever; compiled by Hazel Felleman. Doubleday 1965 xxiv, 454p $18.95   **821.008**
1. English poetry—Collections 2. American poetry—Collections
ISBN 0-385-00358-7
An anthology of favorite poetry largely by English and American authors
"Arrangement is by subject under such headings as stories and ballads, love, friendship, home and family, patriotism and war, humor, death, faith and inspiration, others." Publ Wkly

Verses of the poets Laureate; from John Dryden to Andrew Motion; collected by Hilary Laurie; introduced by Andrew Motion. Orion Media (London); [distributed by] Trafalgar Sq. 2000 c1999 207p il pa $17.95   **821.008**
1. English poetry—Collections
ISBN 0-75281-859-7
First published 1999 in the United Kingdom
"Nineteen men have been England's poet laureate since Charles II created the post in 1668. . . . Editor Laurie presents work by all of them." Booklist

821.009   English poetry—History and criticism

Brooks, Cleanth, 1906-1994
The well wrought urn; studies in the structure of poetry. Reynal 1947 o.p.; Harcourt paperback available $14   **821.009**
1. English poetry—History and criticism
ISBN 0-15-695705-1 (pa)
Analyzed in Essay and general literature index

"Essays in criticism for critics, in which a theory of poetic structure is explored by analyses of great poems from Donne and Shakespeare to William Butler Yeats. Author dwells on the devices of paradox, irony and metaphor and finally examines the approach to poetry made by other modern critics." Libr J

The **Columbia** history of British poetry; Carl Woodring, editor; James Shapiro, associate editor. Columbia Univ. Press 1993 732p $83   **821.009**
1. English poetry—History and criticism
ISBN 0-231-07838-2   LC 93-18226
David Daiches, Jerome McGann, Calvin Bedient and Margaret Anne Doody are among the contributors to this "overview of British poetry. The 26 essays succeed in placing the rich poetry of the British Isles in a historical perspective that takes into account the theological, economical, cultural, and aesthetic influences of each major period." Libr J

Heaney, Seamus
The redress of poetry. Farrar, Straus & Giroux 1995 211p hardcover o.p. paperback available $12   **821.009**
1. English poetry—History and criticism 2. American poetry—History and criticism 3. Irish poetry—History and criticism
ISBN 0-374-52488-2 (pa)   LC 95-19556
Ten lectures elucidating the works of George Herbert, Christopher Marlowe, Brian Merriman, Dylan Thomas, Philip Larkin, Hugh MacDiarmid, John Clare, Oscar Wilde, W. B. Yeats and Elizabeth Bishop
"Heaney's lectures offer the reader a brimming metaphoric energy, a fine-tuned analytic vocabulary, a buoyant vivacity of description, a reflective humor, an ethical awareness, a capaciousness of mind, and imaginative penetration that are unequalled in contemporary critical prose." New Yorker

Pritchard, William H.
Lives of the modern poets. Oxford Univ. Press 1980 316p o.p.; University Press of New England paperback available $27
821.009
1. American poetry—History and criticism 2. English poetry—History and criticism
ISBN 0-87451-787-7 (pa)   LC 79-17615
Analyzed in Essay and general literature index
"This collection of nine critical essays provides introductions and evaluations for the poets Pritchard sees as the most interesting of those writing in English in the early 20th Century: Thomas Hardy, W. B. Yeats, E. A. Robinson, Robert Frost, Ezra Pound, T. S. Eliot, Wallace Stevens, Hart Crane, and William Carlos Williams." Libr J

Schmidt, Michael, 1947-
Lives of the poets. Knopf 1999 975p hardcover o.p. paperback available $20
821.009
1. English poetry—History and criticism 2. American poetry—History and criticism 3. Poets, English—Biography 4. Poets, American—Biography
ISBN 0-375-70604-6 (pa)   LC 98-51913
First published 1998 in the United Kingdom
In this "survey of poetry in English, Schmidt . . . enthuses about more than 250 poets whose work dates from

Schmidt, Michael, 1947—*Continued*

the 14th century to 1998. More than a critical essay, this friendly and accessible history embodies the life of poetry and conveys its changeable, subjective beauty." Libr J

Includes bibliographical references

822 English drama

Behan, Brendan, 1923-1964

The complete plays; introduced by Alan Simpson; with a bibliography by E. H. Mikhail. Grove Weidenfeld 1991 384p pa $15 **822**
ISBN 0-8021-3070-4 LC 78-53931
"An Evergreen book"
First published 1978
Contents: The quare fellow; The hostage; Richard's cork leg; Moving out; A garden party; The big house

Besier, Rudolf, 1878-1942

The Barretts of Wimpole Street; a comedy in five acts. Little, Brown 1930 165p **822**
1. Browning, Elizabeth Barrett, 1806-1861—Drama
2. Browning, Robert, 1812-1889—Drama
Available in paperback from Dramatists Play Service
Characters: 13 men, 4 women. First produced in England at the Malvern Festival, August 20, 1930
"The long-famous courtship and elopement of Elizabeth Barrett and Robert Browning furnish the theme for this drama. . . . The author has followed the known facts faithfully and yet has succeeded in creating a play which is of commanding interest in itself." Carnegie Libr. of Pittsburgh

Bolt, Robert

A man for all seasons; a play in two acts. Random House 1962 xxv, 163p il hardcover o.p. paperback available $9.50 **822**
1. More, Sir Thomas, Saint, 1478-1535—Drama
2. Great Britain—History—1485-1603, Tudors—Drama
ISBN 0-679-72822-8 (pa)
Characters: 11 men, 2 women. First produced in the United States at the ANTA Theatre, New York City, November 22, 1961
A play set in sixteenth century England about Sir Thomas More, a devout Catholic, and his conflict with Henry VIII

Christie, Agatha, 1890-1976

The mousetrap and other plays; introduction by Ira Levin. HarperPaperbacks 1993 c1978 742p o.p.; Signet Bks. paperback available $7.99 **822**
ISBN 0-451-20114-0 (pa)
First published 1978 by Dodd, Mead
Includes the following plays: Ten little Indians; Appointment with death; The hollow; The mousetrap; Witness for the prosecution; Towards zero; Verdict; Go back for murder

Churchill, Caryl

Far away. Theatre Communications Group 2001 44p pa $11.95 **822**
ISBN 1-55936-199-9 LC 2001-27317
First published 2000 in the United Kingdom

Characters: 1 man, 2 women. 3 acts. First produced at the Royal Court Theatre Upstairs, London, November 24, 2000
"At the beginning of *Far Away*, we see a girl questioning her aunt after having seen her uncle hitting people with an iron bar. Many years later when the whole world is at war, including the birds and the animals, the girl returns to take refuge with her aunt." Publisher's note

Mad forest; a play from Romania. Theatre Communications Group 1996 87p pa $9.95 **822**
ISBN 1-55936-114-X LC 96-12875
First published 1991 in the United Kingdom
Large mixed cast. 3 acts. First performed at the New York Theater Workshop, New York, December 4, 1991
This play "explores the reactions of two ordinary families to the confused events of the Romanian revolution: the dreadful damage done to people's lives by years of repression, and the painful difficulties of sudden but lasting change." Publisher's note

Coward, Noel

Three plays; Blithe spirit, Hay fever, Private lives; introduction by Philip Hoare. Vintage Bks. 1999 254p pa $13 **822**
ISBN 0-679-78179-X LC 98-47414
First published 1965 by Dell
Contents: Blithe spirit; Hay fever; Private lives

Dryden, John, 1631-1700

All for love; edited by David M. Vieth. University of Neb. Press 1972 xxxiv, 146p (Regents Restoration drama series) hardcover o.p. paperback available $24.95 **822**
1. Cleopatra, Queen of Egypt, d. 30 B.C.—Drama
ISBN 0-8032-5379-6 (pa)
Also available in paperback from Norton
An English Restoration tragedy which is an adaptation of Shakespeare's "Antony and Cleopatra" done in blank verse

Fugard, Athol

"Master Harold"—and the boys. Knopf 1982 60p o.p.; Penguin Bks. paperback available $10 **822**
1. South Africa—Race relations—Drama
ISBN 0-14-048187-7 (pa) LC 82-48027
Characters: 3 men. 1 act. First produced at the Yale Repertory theatre, New Haven, Connecticut, 1982
Drama with racial overtones set in Port Elizabeth tea room focuses on precocious white South African teenager's relationship with two black men who work for his family, both old enough to be his father

Sorrows and rejoicings. Theatre Communications Group 2002 54p il pa $11.95 **822**
ISBN 1-55936-208-1 LC 2001-45683
Also available in paperback from French
Characters: 1 man, 3 women. First produced at the McCarter Theatre, Princeton, 2002
"The play tells the story of a dying white poet, Dawid Olivier, who has gone back to his village after 16 years of political exile in London to reconnect with his liberated homeland and with his black mistress, Marta, and their light-skinned teenage daughter, Rebecca." New Yorker

Fugard, Athol—*Continued*

Valley song. Theatre Communications Group 1996 60p il pa $10.95   **822**
ISBN 1-55936-119-0   LC 96-7091
Also available in paperback from French

Characters: 1 man, 1 woman. First produced at The Manhattan Theater Club, New York, December 12, 1995

This post-apartheid play "is a coming-of-age story about a young girl seeking the courage to embrace the future while her grandfather searches for the wisdom to let go of the past." Publisher's note

Gay, John, 1685-1732

The beggar's opera; edited by Edgar V. Roberts; music edited by Edward Smith. University of Neb. Press 1969 xxix, 238p music (Regents Restoration drama series) hardcover o.p. paperback available $17.95   **822**

ISBN 0-8032-5361-3 (pa)
Also available in paperback from Dramatists Play Service and Penguin Bks.

First published 1728

A ballad opera, this is a rogues' comedy satirizing corrupt politics in 18th century England

Goldsmith, Oliver, 1728-1774

She stoops to conquer   **822**
Available in paperback from various publishers

18th century social comedy about love affairs of two cousins

"The author's masterpiece. A delightful example of the best type of English society comedy." Pratt Alcove

Marlowe, Christopher, 1564-1593

Doctor Faustus   **822**
Available in hardcover and paperback editions from various publishers

"A drama in blank verse and prose . . . published apparently in 1604, though entered in the Stationer's Register in 1601, and probably produced in 1588. It is perhaps the first dramatization of the medieval legend of a man who sold his soul to the Devil, and who became identified with a Dr. Faustus, a necromancer of the 16th cent." Oxford Companion to Engl Lit

Osborne, John, 1929-1994

Look back in anger. Criterion Bks. 1957 96p o.p.; Penguin Bks. paperback available $10   **822**
ISBN 0-14-048175-3 (pa)
Characters: 3 men, 2 women. First produced at the Royal Court Theatre, London, May 8, 1956

This play "introduced a new strain of realism to British theatre and set the tone for the generation of anti-Establishment writers who became known as the Angry Young Men. Osborne described his own parents as 'impoverished middle class,' but his play deals with the frustrations, crude language, and squalid conditions of working-class life." Reader's Ency. 4th edition

Pinter, Harold, 1930-

Betrayal. Grove Press 1979 c1978 138p pa $12.50   **822**
ISBN 0-8021-3080-1   LC 78-65251
Also available in paperback from Dramatists Play Service

First published 1978 in the United Kingdom

Characters: 3 men, 1 woman. 9 scenes. First produced at the National Theatre, London, November 15, 1978

The development of an adulterous love affair, between a woman and her husband's best friend, is portrayed from 1977 backwards in time to its inception in 1968

Complete works; with an introduction, Writing for the theatre. Grove Weidenfeld 1990 4v v1 $14.50; v2 $13.50; v3 $14; v4 $13.50   **822**
ISBN 0-8021-5096-9 (v1); 0-8021-3237-5 (v2); 0-8021-5049-7 (v3); 0-8021-5050-0 (v4)
       LC 90-13933
Also available in paperback from French

"An Evergreen book"

First Grove Press edition published 1977-1981

Plays included are: v1 The birthday party; The room; The dumb waiter; A slight ache; A night out; v2 The caretaker; The dwarfs; The collection; The lover; Night school; Trouble in the works; The black and white [revue sketch]; Request stop; Last to go; Special offer; v3 The homecoming; Tea party; The basement; Landscape; Silence; Night; That's your trouble; That's all; Applicant; Interview; Dialogue for three; v4 Old times; No man's land; Betrayal; Monologue; Family voices

The homecoming. Grove Press 1966 c1965 82p pa $13   **822**
ISBN 0-8021-5105-1
Also available in paperback from French

First published 1965 in the United Kingdom

Characters: 5 men, 1 woman. First American production at the Music Box, New York City, January 5, 1967

Professor living in America visits family in London where he introduces his wife to menacing all-male household

Rostand, Edmond, 1868-1918

Cyrano de Bergerac; translated and adapted for the modern stage by Anthony Burgess. Applause Theatre & Cinema Bks. 1998 175p pa $6.95   **822**
1. Cyrano de Bergerac, 1619-1655—Drama
ISBN 1-55783-230-7   LC 96-2545
A reissue of the title first published 1971 by Knopf

This version was commissioned for production at the Tyrone Guthrie Theater in Minneapolis. It is adapted and translated from the French play originally produced in 1897. Cyrano, the hero, a Gascon poet and swordsman notorious for his long nose, is in love with Roxana

Shaffer, Peter

Equus. Atheneum Pubs. 1974 211p o.p.; Penguin Bks. paperback available $10   **822**
ISBN 0-14-026070-6 (pa)
Characters: 5 men, 4 women. 1 act, 35 scenes. First produced by the National Theater, London, July 26, 1973

Drama about "a jolting confrontation between a psychiatrist and a 17-year-old boy who has blinded six horses from the stable where he is employed. As the probe into the boy's attitudes and behavior deepens, this criminal act is revealed to have been a result of his notions of a sexual/religious spirit in horses." Booklist

Lettice & lovage; a comedy. Harper & Row 1990 100p   **822**
       LC 88-45724
Available in paperback from French

Shaffer, Peter—*Continued*

"A Cornelia & Michael Bessie book"

First published 1988 in the United Kingdom

Characters: 2 men, 3 women, extras. 3 acts. 3 settings. First produced at the Theatre Royal, Bath, October 6, 1987

This play is "about the initially chilly, ultimately warm relationship between two middle-aged women rather bogged down in life. Lettice is the daughter of a female theatrical entrepreneur from whom she imbibed a love of history and histrionics. Lotte, daughter of an art-book publisher, is a former student of architecture with a historical turn of mind herself. . . . Both women's parts, written for star turns, are full of comic invention based upon credible, though eccentric, characterization." Booklist

Peter Shaffer's Amadeus; with an introduction by the director Sir Peter Hall and a wholly new preface by the author. Perennial Bks. 2001 xxxiv, 124p pa $15   **822**

1. Mozart, Wolfgang Amadeus, 1756-1791—Drama 2. Salieri, Antonio, 1750-1825—Drama

ISBN 0-06-093549-9   LC 2001-278382

First published 1980 in the United Kingdom

Characters: 9 men, 1 woman, extras. 2 acts. First produced at the National Theater of Great Britain, November 1979

Explores relationship between Austrian court composer Antonio Salieri and the divinely gifted young Wolfgang Amadeus Mozart

Stoppard, Tom

Arcadia. Faber & Faber 1993 97p hardcover o.p. paperback available $13   **822**

ISBN 0-571-16934-1 (pa)   LC 94-103754

Also available in paperback from French; Awarded the New York Drama Critics Circle Award for Best Play, 1995

Characters: 8 men, 3 women. 2 acts, 7 scenes. First produced at the Royal National Theatre, London, 1993. In the U.S., first produced at the Lincoln Center Theater, New York City, March 30, 1995

Dramatic comedy set in English country house concurrently in present day and 1809. Landscape gardening, poetry, chaos theory, sex, and the end of the world are among topics discussed in exploration of clash between classical order and romantic ardor

The invention of love. Grove Press 1998 102p pa $12   **822**

1. Housman, A. E. (Alfred Edward), 1859-1936—Drama

ISBN 0-8021-3581-1   LC 98-28331

Also available in paperback from French

Characters: 19 men, 1 woman, extras. 2 acts. First performed at the American Conservatory Theater, San Francisco, January 14, 2000

Scenes from life of homosexual poet and classical scholar A. E. Housman

Rosencrantz and Guildenstern are dead. Grove Press 1967 126p hardcover o.p. paperback available $12   **822**

1. Shakespeare, William, 1564-1616—Parodies, imitations, etc.

ISBN 0-8021-3275-8 (pa)

Characters: 13 men, 2 women, extras. First produced in this form April 11, 1967 in London

This play "took the theatre world on both sides of the Atlantic by storm. The originality of the idea which put Hamlet's two insignificant friends centerstage was matched by the brilliance of the dialogue between these bewildered nonentities." Reader's Ency. 4th edition

Travesties. Grove Press 1975 99p pa $13   **822**

ISBN 0-8021-5089-6

Characters: 5 men, 2 women. Prologue, 2 acts. First produced at the Aldwych Theatre, London, June 10, 1974

Satire on politics, literature and art. James Joyce, Lenin and Dadaist Tristan Tzara come together in memories of obscure English diplomat in Zurich. Song and dance routines

Synge, J. M. (John Millington), 1871-1909

The complete plays. Vintage Bks. 1960 268p pa $10   **822**

ISBN 0-394-70178-X

Also available in hardcover from Amereon and in paperback from Heinemann Educ. Bks.

Contents: In the shadow of the glen; Riders to the sea; The tinker's wedding; The well of the saints; The playboy of the Western world; Deirdre of the sorrows

Thomas, Dylan, 1914-1953

Under milk wood; a play for voices. New Directions 1954 107p music pa $8.95   **822**

ISBN 0-8112-0209-7

"A radio play for voices. Written in poetic, inventive prose, this play is full of humor, a joyful sense of the goodness of life and love, and a strong Welsh flavor. It is an impression of a spring day in the lives of the people of Llareggub, a Welsh village situated under Milk Wood. It has no plot, but a wealth of characters who dream aloud, converse with one another, and speak in choruses of alternating voices." Reader's Ency. 4th edition

Wilde, Oscar, 1854-1900

The importance of being Earnest   **822**

Hardcover and paperback editions available from various publishers

Written in 1895

Drawing room comedy exposing quirks and foibles of Victorian society with plot revolving around amorous pursuits of two men who face social obstacles when they woo young ladies of quality

This play "is noted for its witty lines, its clever situations, and its satire on the British nobility and clergy." Reader's Ency. 4th edition

822.008   English drama— Collections

Everyman, and medieval miracle plays; edited with an introduction by A. C. Cawley. Dent o.p.; Tuttle paperback available $6.95   **822.008**

1. Mysteries and miracle plays

ISBN 0-460-87280-X (pa)

"Everyman's library"

First Everyman's library edition published 1909 with title: Everyman, with other interludes including eight miracle plays

In addition to Everyman, this collection includes plays from the Towneley, Coventry, York and Chester cycles

Restoration plays; with an introduction by Brice Harris. Modern Lib. 1953 xx, 674p o.p.; McGraw-Hill paperback available $11.25   822.008

1. English drama—Collections
ISBN 0-07-553658-7 (pa)

Contents: The rehearsal, by G. Villiers; The country wife, by W. Wycherley; The man of mode, by G. Etherege; All for love, by J. Dryden; Venice preserved, by T. Otway; The relapse, by J. Vanbrugh; The way of the world, by W. Congreve; The beaux' stratagem, by G. Farquhar

822.3 William Shakespeare

Bloom, Harold, 1930-
Shakespeare: the invention of the human. Riverhead Bks. 1998 xx, 745p hardcover o.p. paperback available $18   822.3

1. Shakespeare, William, 1564-1616—Criticism
ISBN 1-57322-751-X (pa)   LC 98-21325

In this critical study, Bloom argues "that the plays and poems of Shakespeare are not just 'the center of the Western canon'; they are nothing less than 'secular scripture'. . . . Bloom's book proceeds through genre groupings in rough chronological order." Commentary

"The passion and obsessiveness of Bloom's approach are its greatest recommendation." N Y Rev Books

Boyce, Charles
Shakespeare A to Z; the essential reference to his plays, his poems, his life and times, and more; David White, editorial consultant; foreword by Terry Hands. Facts on File 1990 742p il $75   822.3

1. Shakespeare, William, 1564-1616
ISBN 0-8160-1805-7   LC 90-31239
Also available in paperback from Delta
"A Roundtable Press book"

This book has "synopses of all of Shakespeare's plays by act and scene; sketches of all of his characters, as well as the historic personages on whom some of them were based; biographies of his contemporaries in the Elizabethan theater; portraits of many of the actors who achieved fame in his plays; and mentions of many modern theatrical works that have been influenced by him." SLJ

Includes bibliographical references

Chute, Marchette Gaylord, 1909-1994
Stories from Shakespeare; [by] Marchette Chute. World Pub. Services 1956 351p il o.p.; New Am. Lib. paperback available $11.95   822.3

1. Shakespeare, William, 1564-1616—Adaptations
ISBN 0-452-01061-6 (pa)

A retelling of the plays, comedies, tragedies, and histories included in Shakespeare's First folio. "Its purpose is to give the reader a preliminary idea of each of the thirty-six plays by telling the stories and explaining in a general way the intentions and points of view of the characters." Introduction

Coye, Dale F.
Pronouncing Shakespeare's words; a guide from A to zounds. Greenwood Press 1998 724p $125.95   822.3

1. Shakespeare, William, 1564-1616—Dictionaries
ISBN 0-313-30655-9   LC 97-44868
Also available in paperback from Routledge

This work provides the correct pronunciation of over 300 words from Shakespeare's plays and poems. An "introduction precedes a phonetic pronunciation guide that includes definitions. Organized by play or poem, words are given in the order in which they appear in a linear reading. Lists at the beginning of each work contain pronunciation guides for place and proper names, the most common 'hard' words, and the most common reduced forms." Libr J

Includes bibliographical references

Frye, Northrop
Northrop Frye on Shakespeare; edited by Robert Sandler. Yale Univ. Press 1986 186p hardcover o.p. paperback available $17

822.3

1. Shakespeare, William, 1564-1616—Criticism
ISBN 0-300-04208-6 (pa)   LC 86-50485

Shakespeare scholar Frye provides in-depth analyses of ten plays

"Frye's work is completely accessible, its style crisp and engaging. Most of all, it is full of basic 'good sense' about our most abused literary figure." Libr J

Gollob, Herman
Me and Shakespeare; adventures with the Bard. Doubleday 2002 341p $26; pa $15

822.3

1. Shakespeare, William, 1564-1616
ISBN 0-385-49817-9; 0-385-49818-7 (pa)
                               LC 2001-53799

Retired book editor Gollob "decided to become a 'Shakespeare maven' in his Lear years. Gollob voraciously read Shakespeare's plays and criticism. He journeyed to Stratford-on-Avon, and began teaching a course on Shakespeare for college seniors, seeking in his pursuit of a deeper knowledge of Shakespeare a deeper understanding of his own life. . . . A robust extrovert, Gollob is frank and funny, and ardent in his enthusiasm for books, boxing and acting." N Y Times Book Rev

Holden, Anthony, 1947-
William Shakespeare; the man behind the genius: a biography. Little, Brown 2000 367p il $29.95   822.3

1. Shakespeare, William, 1564-1616
ISBN 0-316-51849-2   LC 99-89806
First published 1999 in the United Kingdom

"The liveliness of Holden's narrative indeed owes much to his shrewd reading of Shakespeare's drama and poetry, mined for clues as to the poet's religious beliefs, romantic entanglements, and political alliances. But the literature provides only hints: for more substantive evidence, Holden ferrets out the biographical implications of church registers, commercial accounts, and legal documents." Booklist

Includes bibliographical references

Honan, Park

Shakespeare; a life. Oxford Univ. Press 1998 479p il hardcover o.p. paperback available $17.95 **822.3**

1. Shakespeare, William, 1564-1616—Biography
ISBN 0-19-282527-5 (pa)   LC 98-22114

The author presents an "account of Shakespeare's life from birth to death, with some attention paid to the historical, political, and social world Shakespeare inhabited. Extensive notes and a study of the biographical writings on Shakespeare to date conclude the work." Libr J

Kermode, Frank, 1919-

Shakespeare's language. Farrar, Straus & Giroux 2000 324p hardcover o.p. paperback available $15   **822.3**

1. Shakespeare, William, 1564-1616—Language
ISBN 0-374-52774-1 (pa)   LC 99-55846

Kermode "devotes particular attention to the four great tragedies written at the height of Shakespeare's powers: *Hamlet, Othello, King Lear* and *Macbeth*. While Kermode's concern is with the Bard's verse, he betrays no simplistic notions about literary language operating in a vacuum. A careful, close analysis of passages in each play is informed by a breathtaking knowledge of Elizabethan history and culture, as well as by the entire history of Shakespeare criticism from Coleridge to Eliot and the new historicists." Publ Wkly

Includes bibliographical references

Lamb, Charles, 1775-1834

Tales from Shakespeare; by Charles and Mary Lamb   **822.3**

1. Shakespeare, William, 1564-1616—Adaptations

Hardcover and paperback editions available from various publishers

First published 1807

A now classic collection of twenty plays by Shakespeare adapted as prose stories—the comedies by Mary Lamb, the tragedies by Charles Lamb

Norwich, John Julius, 1929-

Shakespeare's kings; the great plays and the history of England in the Middle Ages, 1337-1485. Scribner 2000 401p il hardcover o.p. paperback available $16   **822.3**

1. Shakespeare, William, 1564-1616—Histories
ISBN 0-7432-0031-4 (pa)   LC 99-58271

The author offers "overviews of *Edward III; Richard II; Henry IV*, parts 1 and 2; *Henry V; Henry VI*, parts 1, 2, and 3; and *Richard III*, examining each play through the lens of history. In addition to providing the necessary historical commentary, he also fills in the gaps between the plays, enabling readers to thoroughly comprehend the entire series in the proper historical context." Booklist

Olsen, Kirstin

All things Shakespeare; an encyclopedia of Shakespeare's world. Greenwood Press 2002 2v il maps set $150   **822.3**

1. Shakespeare, William, 1564-1616
ISBN 0-313-31503-5   LC 2002-69732

This "encyclopedia describes Shakespeare's physical environment, including common objects, daily activities, and popular beliefs and attitudes. Information is grouped into general topic clusters such as 'Behavior,' 'Clothing and Dress,' 'Furniture,' 'Fire,' and 'War and Peace.' . . . Within the 200-plus entries, references are made to the play, act, and scene in which Shakespeare mentions the item or activity being discussed." Libr J

The **Oxford** companion to Shakespeare; general editor, Michael Dobson; associate general editor, Stanley Wells. Oxford Univ. Press 2001 xxix, 541p il maps $60 **822.3**

1. Shakespeare, William, 1564-1616
ISBN 0-19-811735-3   LC 2001-277478

This volume "illuminates not only Shakespeare's life and works but also the many forms that interpretation of Shakespeare has taken in the centuries since his death." Booklist

Shakespeare, William, 1564-1616

The Columbia dictionary of quotations from Shakespeare; {selected by} Mary and Reginald Foakes. Columbia Univ. Press 1998 516p $63   **822.3**

1. Shakespeare, William, 1564-1616—Quotations
2. Quotations
ISBN 0-231-10434-0   LC 97-44894

"The book is organized by topics ('Age,' 'Duplicity,' 'Fish'), followed by passages of about five or six lines. After each selection, the citation, the character, and usually the context of the lines are given. If a reference is obscure, the explanation is more elaborate. Indexes provide access by play and poem, by character, and by keyword." SLJ

The complete works of William Shakespeare   **822.3**

Hardcover and paperback editions available from various publishers

For a comparison of most of the editions of Shakespeare see: The Reader's Adviser

A dictionary of quotations from Shakespeare; a topical guide to over 3,000 great passages from the plays, sonnets, and narrative poems; selected by Margaret Miner and Hugh Rawson. Dutton 1992 368p o.p.; New Am. Lib. paperback available $14.95   **822.3**

1. Shakespeare, William, 1564-1616—Quotations
2. Quotations
ISBN 0-452-01127-2 (pa)   LC 92-1354

The focus of this "dictionary, the authors say, is on 'quotations that are likely to be of practical use for writers and speakers today . . . [and] relevant to modern times and present-day problems.' Consequently, among the 400 categories are such headings as democracy, media, public relations, and *Star Wars*. Nearly half the quotations are annotated, with useful information about meaning and context." Libr J

The Norton Shakespeare; based on the Oxford edition; Stephen Greenblatt, general editor [et al.]; with an essay on the Shakespearean stage by Andrew Gurr. Norton 1997 3420p il $62.50   **822.3**

ISBN 0-393-97087-6   LC 97-7083

The editors' "mission is to make Shakespeare accessible to modern readers. With lengthy introductions providing insight into Shakespeare's life and times as well as textual notes, marginal glosses, footnotes, and bibliographies, they more than achieve their aim . . . [Includes] an illustrated chronology of Shakespeare's life, and over 150 illustrations. The result is a work of immense scope, scholarship, and richness." Libr J

Vendler, Helen Hennessy

The art of Shakespeare's sonnets; [by] Helen Vendler. Harvard Univ. Press 1997 672p hardcover o.p. paperback available $18.95   **822.3**

1. Shakespeare, William, 1564-1616. Sonnets
ISBN 0-674-63712-7 (pa)   LC 97-15306
An "examination of the sonnets in the light of the rhetorical conventions whose passing has left many readers alienated from these difficult poems." N Y Times Book Rev

"Helen Vendler, who in her homely and uncombative but uncompromising way has produced here what is probably the least irrelevant and most critically illuminating of all extended commentaries on the Sonnets, in the end more or less agrees with that plain and pungent poet's judgment." N Y Rev Books
Includes bibliographical references

Wells, Stanley W., 1930-

Shakespeare: for all time; [by] Stanley Wells. Oxford Univ. Press 2003 xxi, 442p il $40   **822.3**

1. Shakespeare, William, 1564-1616
ISBN 0-19-516093-2   LC 2002-27412
First published 2002 in the United Kingdom
"Chapters on Shakespeare's life in Stratford and in London offer a . . . view of the development of the writer's career and personality. At the core of the book lies a . . . study of the writings themselves—how Shakespeare set about writing a play, his relationships with the company of actors with whom he worked, his developing mastery of the literary and rhetorical skills that he learned at the Stratford grammar school, the essentially theatrical quality of the structure and language of his plays. Subsequent chapters trace the fluctuating fortunes of his reputation and influence." Publisher's note
Includes bibliographical references

823.009   English fiction—History and criticism

Bunson, Matthew

The complete Christie; an Agatha Christie encyclopedia. Pocket Bks. 2000 454p hardcover o.p. paperback available $23.95   **823.009**

1. Christie, Agatha, 1890-1976
ISBN 0-671-02831-6 (pa)   LC 00-42793
This volume offers a biography of Christie that includes new theories about her 1926 disappearance. The text consists of plot synopses, alphabetical character entries, and listings of films, television programs, radio shows, and documentaries. Illustrated with book covers and productions stills

The **Cambridge** companion to Jane Austen;

edited by Edward Copeland and Juliet McMaster. Cambridge Univ. Press 1997 251p (Cambridge companions to literature) $65; pa $23   **823.009**

1. Austen, Jane, 1775-1817
ISBN 0-521-49517-2; 0-521-49867-8 (pa)
      LC 96-23387
Scholars assess "Jane Austen's works in the contexts of her contemporary world, and of present-day critical discourse. Besides discussions of Austen's novels and

letters, there are essays on religion, politics, class consciousness, publishing practices, domestic economy, style in the novels and the significance of her juvenile works. A chronology provides biographical information." Publisher's note

The **Columbia** history of the British novel;

John Richetti, editor; John Bender, Deirdre David, Michael Seidel, associate editors. Columbia Univ. Press 1994 xxix, 1064p $95   **823.009**

1. English fiction—History and criticism
ISBN 0-231-07858-7   LC 92-35749
In this chronologically arranged volume, scholars provide 39 essays surveying the history of the British novel. "Some essays are devoted to individual authors (e.g., Austen, Dickens), others to several authors (e.g., Amis, Snow, and Wilson), and still others to such topics as 'The Gothic Novel, 1764-1824.' Each essay has a brief selected bibliography; an appendix includes thumbnail sketches of 100 of the British novelists discussed." Libr J

Davis, Paul B. (Paul Benjamin), 1934-

Charles Dickens A-Z; the essential reference to the life and work; [by] Paul Davis. Facts on File 1998 432p il $55; pa $17.95   **823.009**

1. Dickens, Charles, 1812-1870
ISBN 0-8160-2905-9; 0-8160-4087-7 (pa)
      LC 97-26237
"The more than 2500 entries cover the significant elements of Dickens's life, synopses of his works, 'biographies' of his characters, descriptions of the novels' settings, and relevant historical information. The body of Dickensian criticism is also summarized." Libr J

Fargnoli, A. Nicholas

James Joyce A to Z; the essential reference to the life and work; [by] A. Nicholas Fargnoli and Michael Patrick Gillespie. Facts on File 1995 304p $55   **823.009**

1. Joyce, James, 1882-1941
ISBN 0-8160-2904-0   LC 94-34660
Also available in paperback from Oxford Univ. Press
The main portion of this compendium "is an A-Z listing of all things Joyce, from 'Abbey Theatre' to 'Works in Progress,' and most things in between. The several appendixes that follow offer a marvelous list of Joycean arcanum, including a time line from Ulysses, the text of Judge Woolsey's 1933 decision to lift the ban on the book in the United States, and a working outline of Finnigans Wake. Overall, this is a delightful and helpful volume." Libr J
Includes bibliographical references

Ford, Paul F.

Companion to Narnia; illustrated by Lorinda Bryan Cauley. Harper & Row 1980 xxxii, 313p il hardcover o.p. paperback available $18   **823.009**

1. Lewis, C. S. (Clive Staples), 1898-1963. Chronicles of Narnia
ISBN 0-06-251136-X (pa)   LC 80-7734
C. S. Lewis wrote seven books of fantasy that are collectively called The Chronicles of Narnia. This book "is an encyclopedia of Narnian names and terms and related matters, with . . . footnoted articles, page references to American and British hardcover editions, cross-references, and a running footline for quick location of materials in the alphabet." Choice

Head, Dominic
The Cambridge introduction to modern British fiction, 1950-2000. Cambridge Univ. Press 2002 307p $65; pa $22 **823.009**
1. English fiction—History and criticism
ISBN 0-521-66014-9; 0-521-66966-9 (pa)
LC 2001-43261
This study "includes chapters on the state and the novel, class and social change, gender and sexual identity, national identity, and multiculturalism." Publisher's note
"Anyone with an interest in the contemporary novel, not just British fiction, will appreciate this outstanding survey and analysis. . . . The quality of discussion is admirably consistent within and between each chapter, the prose as carefully crafted as the judgments are measured. . . . This book should become a standard reference work for its subject." Choice
Includes bibliographical references

James Joyce's Ulysses; edited and with an introduction by Harold Bloom. Chelsea House 1987 168p (Modern critical interpretations) $37.95 **823.009**
1. Joyce, James, 1882-1941. Ulysses
ISBN 1-55546-021-6
LC 87-5830
Critical essays assessing Joyce's modernist masterpiece
Includes bibliographical references

The **Oxford** reader's companion to Conrad; edited by Owen Knowles and Gene Moore. Oxford Univ. Press 2000 xxxii, 429p il maps hardcover o.p. paperback available $16.95 **823.009**
1. Conrad, Joseph, 1857-1924
ISBN 0-19-860421-1 (pa)
LC 00-698346
This "reference is concerned with seven broad areas: biography, places associated with the life and writings, literary life, reputation, the works, influences and sources, and historical and cultural contexts." Libr J
For a fuller review see: Booklist, Nov. 15, 2000

Oxford reader's companion to Dickens; edited by Paul Schlicke. Oxford Univ. Press 1999 xxiii, 654p $55; pa $16.95
823.009
1. Dickens, Charles, 1812-1870
ISBN 0-19-866213-0; 0-19-866253-X (pa)
"Brief but substantive articles, arranged alphabetically, cover Charles Dickens's life; work; critical reception; historical, social, and cultural contexts; geography; and illustrations. The treatment is comprehensive. Each of Dickens's works, including his journalism, is summarized and evaluated, reflecting a balanced range of contemporary critical perspectives. At the same time, the articles are accessible to the general reader." Libr J

The **Oxford** reader's companion to Hardy; edited by Norman Page. Oxford Univ. Press 2000 xx, 528p il maps hardcover o.p. paperback available $16.95 **823.009**
1. Hardy, Thomas, 1840-1928
ISBN 0-19-860419-X (pa)
LC 00-699687
This companion is "concerned with seven broad areas: the works, people, places, contexts, publishing, criticism and scholarship, and miscellaneous topics. Both a biogra-

phy and a chronology are included. Long discussions of the novels are divided into sections (e.g., composition, illustrations, plot, reception, and critical approaches), while the essays on the poetry collections are not." Libr J
For a fuller review see: Booklist, Nov. 15, 2000

Oxford reader's companion to Trollope; edited by R. C. Terry. Oxford Univ. Press 1999 xxiv, 624p il maps hardcover o.p. paperback available $16.95 **823.009**
1. Trollope, Anthony, 1815-1882
ISBN 0-19-860420-3 (pa)
"In more than 500 alphabetical listings (in eight subject areas), 36 Trollope scholars profile his private and public life, his life as a writer, his characters, locations, and associations, and his literary and social contexts. Particularly noteworthy are their discussions of—and annotated entries about—each of Trollope's 47 novels, characters, and locations." Libr J

Poplawski, Paul
A Jane Austen encyclopedia. Greenwood Press 1998 411p il $95 **823.009**
1. Austen, Jane, 1775-1817
ISBN 0-313-30017-8
LC 97-44880
This volume "examines the life, works, characters, and minutiae of Austeniana. The alphabetically arranged entries include extensive plot summaries that end with lists of major and minor characters, brief character descriptions, and short articles on the author's family and friends." SLJ

Sova, Dawn B.
Agatha Christie A to Z; the essential reference to her life and writings; [by] Dawn Sova; foreword by David Suchet; introduction by Mathew Prichard. Facts on File 1996 384p il $55; pa $17.95 **823.009**
1. Christie, Agatha, 1890-1976
ISBN 0-8160-3018-9; 0-8160-4311-6 (pa)
LC 95-48326
This compendium of over 2,500 entries includes synopsis, publishing (or dramatization) history, character and setting descriptions for every work. Information on key associates, relatives, agents, and others who played a part in Christie's life is also included

Thornton, Weldon
D.H. Lawrence; a study of the short fiction. Twayne Pubs. 1993 174p (Twayne's studies in short fiction) $31 **823.009**
1. Lawrence, D. H. (David Herbert), 1885-1930
ISBN 0-8057-0862-6
LC 93-25540
This study of Lawrence's short stories is divided into three parts. Part one, The short fiction, examines nine separate stories. Part two, The writer, includes excerpts from Lawrence's essays, letters and other writings in which he discusses his own short stories and those of others. The third part, The critics, contains excerpts from critical essays
Includes bibliographical references

824   English essays

Amis, Martin
The war against cliché; essays and reviews, 1971-2000. Hyperion 2001 352p $35   **824**
1. Bellow, Saul. The adventures of Augie March 2. Nabokov, Vladimir Vladimirovich, 1899-1977. Lolita
ISBN 0-7868-6674-8   LC 2002-279116
Also available in paperback from Vintage Bks.
"Talk Miramax books"
Analyzed in Essay and general literature index
"Strong opinions and easily ignited aggression by an energetic stylist who mounts a powerful defense of Philip Larkin and declares 'The Adventures of Augie March' his second-favorite novel ever." N Y Times Book Rev

Barnes, Julian
Something to declare; essays on France. Knopf 2002 295p il $25; pa $14   **824**
ISBN 0-375-41513-0; 1-4000-3087-0 (pa)
LC 2002-109567
Analyzed in Essay and general literature index
Articles previously published in various publications between 1982 and 2000
This is a collection of essays which were previously published in various periodicals. They "are mostly about men and women in French arts and letters (a full half of the book is devoted to Flaubert and those who surrounded him) or about Anglophone writers in France like Edith Wharton or Elizabeth David." N Y Times Book Rev

Berger, John, 1926-
Selected essays; edited by Geoff Dyer. Pantheon Bks. 2001 588p $35; pa $18   **824**
ISBN 0-375-42156-4; 0-375-71318-2 (pa)
LC 2001-36673
Analyzed in Essay and general literature index
This volume "selects essays from previous volumes, including *The Sense of Sight* and *Keeping a Rendezous*. They include terse meditations on painters like Picasso, Matisse, Pollock, Goya, Poussin and Gauguin, as well as sculptors like Lipschitz, Brancusi and Zadkine. . . . Piles and piles of prejudices here wind up being eminently readable because they're expressed without ornate flourishes and in a plain-spoken (sometimes overly so) stance." Publ Wkly
Includes bibliographical references

Carlyle, Thomas, 1795-1881
Past and present; edited with an introduction and notes by Richard D. Altick. New York Univ. Press 1977 294p hardcover o.p. paperback available $20   **824**
ISBN 0-8147-0562-6 (pa)
First published 1843
In this work Carlyle's "attack on the contemporary failure of democracy, as he saw it, was presented poetically as an account of the ordered life at the medieval abbey of St Edmund's, Bury. Labour and duty are the true ends of life (the 'gospel of work'), and the many voluntarily submit to the leadership of the superior few, such as Abbott Sampson." Penguin Companion to Engl Lit

Sartor resartus; edited with an introduction and notes by Kerry McSweeney and Peter Sabor. Oxford Univ. Press 1987 xlii, 273p (The World's classics) pa $11.95   **824**
ISBN 0-19-283673-0   LC 87-5753
First published 1833-1834, Sartor resartus contains the germ of Carlyle's philosophy. It purports to be an interpretation of the work of an erudite German professor but is really the story of Carlyle's own fierce spiritual conflict between doubt and faith. It presents a philosophy of clothes, or the outward forms of things
Includes bibliographical references

De Quincey, Thomas, 1785-1859
The confessions of an English opium-eater   **824**
1. Drug abuse
Hardcover and paperback editions available from various publishers
First published 1822
This famous account of the English author's ecstasies and sufferings until his drug habit was brought under control "attracted attention, not simply by its personal disclosures, but by the extraordinary power of its dreampainting." Ency Britannica

Naipaul, V. S. (Vidiadhar Surajprasad), 1932-
The writer and the world; essays. Knopf 2002 524p $30; pa $15   **824**
ISBN 0-375-40739-1; 0-375-70730-1 (pa)
LC 2002-20813
Analyzed in Essay and general literature index
"The election campaign is a recurring theme in this comprehensive collection of essays spanning four decades and scattered about the globe: India, Zaire, Grenada, Anguilla, the Americas. . . . Naipaul deconstructs the mythologized—among them Eva Peron, Mobutu Sese Seko, John Steinbeck, Eldridge Cleaver, the American Dream—and how progress falters in the face of ritualism and single-mindedness. Revolutionary movements often fall prey to these, and Naipaul analyzes those derailments, particularly in postcolonial society. While some of his travelogues date back to the early 1960s, they nonetheless seem fresh, speaking to Naipaul's astute and prescient powers of observation." Publ Wkly

Rushdie, Salman
Step across this line; collected nonfiction 1992-2002. Random House 2002 402p $25.95; pa $15.95   **824**
ISBN 0-679-46334-8; 0-679-78349-0 (pa)
LC 2002-21314
Rushdie's collection includes "essays about his harrowing, often surreal life in the wake of the *fatwa*, and sharp editorials on Kashmir, northern Ireland, Kosovo, and Islam and the West before and after September 11. But he has also composed an enrapturing essay about the film that made him a writer, *The Wizard of Oz*, and incisive looks at rock and roll, reading, artistic influence, photography, and commercial hype, as well as inspiring discussions of why literature and freedom of speech matter." Booklist

Woolf, Virginia, 1882-1941
Essays of Virginia Woolf; edited by Andrew McNeillie. Harcourt Brace Jovanovich 1987-1989 3v   **824**
Volume 4 covering years 1925-1928 (1994) published in the United Kingdom

Woolf, Virginia, 1882-1941—*Continued*

Contents: v1 1904-1912 pa $23 (ISBN 0-15-629054-5); v2 1912-1918 o.p.; v3 1919-1924 pa $28 (ISBN 0-15-629056-1)

The first three volumes of a projected six-volume collection of Woolf's critical reviews, art and drama notices, travel pieces and extended ruminations on subjects ranging from character in fiction to the social status of women

826   English letters

The **Oxford** book of letters; edited by Frank and Anita Kermode. Oxford Univ. Press 1995 559p hardcover o.p. paperback available $16.95   **826**

1. English letters 2. American letters
ISBN 0-19-280490-1 (pa)   LC 94-36412

"This volume includes more than 300 letters that document the concerns of writers, political leaders, and ordinary citizens over the period 1535-1985. Each letter is accompanied by an explanatory note identifying the writer and establishing the context. The correspondents, some more skilled than others, pursue a range of topics, including an account of a public execution, gossip about friends and relatives, and the hardships of moving to a new land in search of a better life." Libr J

827   English humor and satire

The **Oxford** book of humorous prose; William Caxton to P.G. Wodehouse: a conducted tour; [chosen and edited] by Frank Muir. Oxford Univ. Press 1990 xxxiv, 1162p hardcover o.p. paperback available $21.50   **827**

1. English wit and humor 2. American wit and humor
ISBN 0-19-280379-4 (pa)   LC 89-9242

"A sprinkling of American contributors join British humorists in this selection of pieces ranging from the gently witty to the irreverent, the bawdy, and the sexy." Booklist

"Selections are generally very short, with bridges, often fairly humorous of themselves, by Muir. The humor ranges from the broad to the subtle and, in fact, in any other way that humor might range; there's something in here for everyone." Libr J

Swift, Jonathan, 1667-1745

A tale of a tub, and other work; edited with an introduction by Angus Ross and David Woolley. Oxford Univ. Press 1986 xxviii, 237p (The World's classics) pa $8.95   **827**

ISBN 0-19-283593-9   LC 85-5072

Includes the Battle of the books and the Mechanical operation of the spirit

A tale of a tub, The battle of the books, and A discourse concerning the mechanical operation of the spirit, were first published together in 1704. The first is an allegorical satire ridiculing the corruptions of religion and learning by extremists and pedants. The second is a mock heroic satire on squabbles concerning the relative merits of ancient and modern authors presented as an account of the battle between ancient and modern books in St James Library. The third ridicules the manner of worship and preaching of religious enthusiasts of the period

828   English miscellany

Achebe, Chinua, 1930-

Home and exile. Oxford Univ. Press 2000 110p $18.95   **828**

ISBN 0-19-513506-7   LC 99-462124

Also available in paperback from Anchor Bks.

This volume consists of "Achebe's ruminations (both serious and humorous) on empire, post-colonialism, Western writers (e.g., Joseph Conrad, Graham Greene, and Elspeth Huxley) on Africa, universal culture, and expatriation and exile." Libr J

"This slim volume—told in Achebe's subtle, witty and gracious style—is one of those small gems of literary and historical analysis that readers will treasure and reread over the years." Publ Wkly

Includes bibliographical references

Adams, Douglas, 1952-2001

The salmon of doubt; hitchhiking the universe one last time. Harmony Bks. 2002 xxxvi, 299p $24; pa $13.95   **828**

ISBN 1-4000-4508-8; 0-345-46095-2 (pa)
LC 2002-22798

This "collection comprises letters, fragments of ideas for books, films and TV, ruminations on a diverse array of subjects and a good bit of a final unfinished novel by the author of The Hitchhiker's Guide to the Galaxy series." Publ Wkly

"It is plain from the editing that [Christopher] Cerf had to extract nuggets from fragments, but even minor Adams seems like a message from an old friend." Booklist

Blake, William, 1757-1827

The complete poetry and prose of William Blake; edited by David V. Erdman; commentary by Harold Bloom. newly rev ed. University of Calif. Press 1982 xxvi, 990p $65   **828**

ISBN 0-520-04473-8   LC 81-40323

Also available in paperback from Anchor Bks.

First published 1965 with title: Poetry and prose of William Blake

This collection contains the complete poetry and prose of Blake, including his letters, as well as critical commentary

Coleridge, Samuel Taylor, 1772-1834

The portable Coleridge; edited and with an introduction by I. A. Richards. Viking 1950 630p hardcover o.p. paperback available $16.95   **828**

ISBN 0-14-015048-X (pa)

"The Viking portable library"

Includes: The rime of the ancient mariner (1875); Christabel; Kubla Khan; and most of the shorter poems; ample representation of the "Biographia literaria," generous selections from the other literary criticism, political essays, notebooks, and letters; also a lengthy biographical introduction

Includes bibliographical references

Conrad, Joseph, 1857-1924

The portable Conrad; edited and with an introduction and notes by Morton Dauwen Zabel. rev ed, [edited] by Frederick R. Karl. Viking 1969 762p hardcover o.p. paperback available $18   **828**

ISBN 0-14-015033-1 (pa)
"The Viking portable library"
First published 1947
Contains two novels: The Nigger of the Narcissus and Typhoon; three long stories; six shorter stories; and a selection from Conrad's prefaces, letters and autobiographical writings
Includes bibliographical references

Donne, John, 1572-1631

The complete poetry and selected prose of John Donne; edited by Charles M. Coffin; introduction by Denis Donoghue; notes by W. T. Chmielewski. Modern Library pa. ed. Modern Lib. 2001 xxxii, 697p pa $14.95
   828

ISBN 0-375-75734-1   LC 2001-30077
A reissue of the Modern Library edition published 1994
This volume contains Donne's love poetry, satires, epigrams, verse letters and holy sonnets. Also includes selected prose and a sampling of private letters

Hitchens, Christopher

Why Orwell matters. Basic Bks. 2002 211p $24; pa $14.95   **828**
1. Orwell, George, 1903-1950
ISBN 0-465-03049-1; 0-465-03050-5 (pa)
    LC 2002-8035
Hitchens "defends a great writer from attacks by both right and left, though he also refutes those fans who proclaim his sainthood. George Orwell (1903-1950), a socialist who abhorred all forms of totalitarianism, was, as Hitchens points out, prescient about the 'three great subjects of the twentieth century:' imperialism, fascism, and Stalinism. In all things, Orwell's feelings were every bit as visceral as intellectual, and Hitchens devotes some of his best writings to describing Orwell's first-hand experiences with empire in Burma." Publ Wkly

Hussey, Mark, 1956-

Virginia Woolf A-Z; a comprehensive reference for students, teachers, and common readers to her life, work, and critical reception. Facts on File 1995 452p il $55
   828

1. Woolf, Virginia, 1882-1941
ISBN 0-8160-3020-0   LC 94-36500
This work provides: synopses and publishing histories of works; discussions of intellectual and literary influences on Woolf; biographical entries on important people in her life, including family and friends; and an overview of the critical reception to her work
Includes bibliographical references

Huxley, Aldous, 1894-1963

Brave new world, and Brave new world revisited; with a foreword by the author; introduction by Martin Green. Harper & Row 1965 c1960 2v in 1 pa $16   **828**
ISBN 0-06-090101-2
Partially analyzed in Essay and general literature index

"HarperColophon books"
First published 1960; a combined edition of the two titles published 1932 and 1958 respectively
Brave new world is a satirical novel "set in the year 632 AF (After Ford), it is a grim picture of the world which Huxley thinks our scientific and social developments have already begun to create." Reader's Ency. 4th edition

Orwell, George, 1903-1950

The Orwell reader; fiction, essays, and reportage; with an introduction by Richard H. Rovere. Harcourt, Brace & Co. 1956 456p hardcover o.p. paperback available $17   **828**
ISBN 0-15-670176-6 (pa)
Analyzed in Essay and general literature index
"Twenty-five or so selections from the works of George Orwell, including among other things, generous chunks of all five of his novels, sections of 'Homage to Catalonia,' 'The Road to Wigan Pier,' and 'The Lion and the Unicorn,' and, in their entirety, his essays on Kipling, Tolstoy, and Swift, as well as the autobiographical pieces 'Why I Write' and 'Such Were the Joys.'" New Yorker

Sisman, Adam

Boswell's presumptuous task; the making of the life of Dr. Johnson. Farrar, Straus & Giroux 2001 xxii, 351p il o.p.; Penguin Bks. paperback available $15   **828**
1. Boswell, James, 1740-1795. Life of Samuel Johnson
ISBN 0-14-200175-9 (pa)   LC 00-67699
First published 2000 in the United Kingdom
James Boswell's The Life of Samuel Johnson was published in 1791, six years after the death of its subject. In this book, Sisman chronicles Boswell's motives for writing his biography and the techniques he adopted
"Mr. Sisman's book is illuminating both of Boswell's character and of all aspects of his authorship." Economist
Includes bibliographical references

Spenser, Edmund, 1552?-1599

The works of Edmund Spenser. Variorum ed, edited by Edwin Greenlaw, Charles Grosvenor Osgood [and] Frederick Morgan Padelford. Johns Hopkins Univ. Press 2002 11v il maps pa   **828**
ISBN 0-8018-6989-7
Available paperback edition; for price and availability see publisher
First published 1932-1945
v5-v11 have additional editor, Ray Heffner
Contents: v1-v6 The faerie queene; v7-v8 The minor poems; v9 Index to the poetry; v10 The prose works; v11 The life of Edmund Spenser by Alexander C. Judson
"The bibliography is useful; the index full; and the illustrations are appropriately chosen and excellently reproduced. Altogether, this is a work which literary scholarship will receive with acclaim and to which American humanists can point with pride." Christ Sci Monit [review of v11, 1945 edition]
Includes bibliographical references

Thomas, Dylan, 1914-1953

A child's Christmas in Wales   **828**
1. Christmas—Wales
Hardcover and paperback editions available from various publishers
First published 1954 by New Directions

Thomas, Dylan, 1914-1953—*Continued*

A portrait of Christmas Day in a small Welsh town and of the author's childhood there

For any season of the year "the language is enchanting and the poetry shines with an unearthly radiance." N Y Times Book Rev

Woolf, Virginia, 1882-1941

Flush; a biography. Harcourt Brace & Co. 1933 185p il hardcover o.p. paperback available $12 **828**

1. Browning, Elizabeth Barrett, 1806-1861
ISBN 0-15-631952-7 (pa)

A fanciful look at Elizabeth Browning through the eyes of her cocker spaniel Flush

"With wit, audacity and penetration Virginia Woolf gives us, as it were, the pre-primitive mind. The result is a poetic biography which awakens in the reader an acute delight in all the physical senses, a renewed knowledge of the way in which concepts may first take shape in a consciousness interpreting entirely through instincts and sensations." N Y Times Book Rev

The Virginia Woolf reader; edited by Mitchell A. Leaska. Harcourt Brace Jovanovich 1984 371p hardcover o.p. paperback available $16 **828**

ISBN 0-15-693590-2 (pa)   LC 84-4478

"A Harvest book"

Excerpts from Woolf's "novels form less than 20 percent of a reader whose selections of short stories, essays, letters, and diary entries are excellent. This collection will be useful to those already familiar with Woolf's novels and seeking an introductory selection of her other writings." Libr J

829   Old English (Anglo-Saxon)

Beowulf

Beowulf; [translated by] Seamus Heaney. Farrar, Straus & Giroux 1999 220p $25 **829**

ISBN 0-374-11119-7   LC 99-23209

This edition also available in paperback from Norton; other verse and prose translations available from various publishers

"Much that seemed off-putting about Beowulf to modern readers becomes, in Heaney's retelling, eerily intriguing instead. . . . Beowulf may, by modern standards, seem bloodthirsty and deluded, but Heaney's poetry makes eloquently persuasive the hero's tragic stature." Time

830.3   German literature— Encyclopedias and dictionaries

Encyclopedia of German literature; Matthias Konzett, editor. Fitzroy Dearborn Pubs. 2000 2v set $175 **830.3**

1. German literature—Encyclopedias 2. German literature—Bio-bibliography
ISBN 1-57958-138-2

"Essay-like entries cover three main categories: authors, works (novels, books of poetry, and essays), and topics, the last encompassing everything from literary terms and movements, artistic forums, cities, and historical eras to the key legacy of the Frankfurt School and its members. Rather lengthy lists for further reading are provided with each essay." Libr J

For a fuller review see: Booklist, Oct. 1, 2000

Garland, Henry B. (Henry Burnand)

The Oxford companion to German literature; by Henry and Mary Garland. 3rd ed, by Mary Garland. Oxford Univ. Press 1997 951p maps $95 **830.3**

1. German literature—Dictionaries 2. German literature—Bio-bibliography
ISBN 0-19-815896-3   LC 96-53309

First published 1976

Entries include biographies, synopses of important works, literary terms and movements, historical events and figures, and material relevant to the social and intellectual background of German literature from the earliest records to the present

830.9   German literature— History and criticism

The **Cambridge** history of German literature; edited by Helen Watanabe-O'Kelly. Cambridge Univ. Press 1997 613p $90; pa $32 **830.9**

1. German literature—History and criticism
ISBN 0-521-43417-3; 0-521-78573-1 (pa)
          LC 95-52412

This work provides a history of German literature "up to the Unification of Germany in 1990. It is a history for our times: well-known authors and movements are set in a wider literary, cultural and political context, standard judgments are reexamined where appropriate, and a new prominence is given to writing by women. . . . Titles and quotations are translated, and there is an extensive bibliography." Publisher's note

A "briskly written survey of German literature that grounds literary practice in the social and historical context of each period and yet does not shortchange the aesthetic qualities of the representative works discussed." Choice

831   German poetry

Celan, Paul

Poems of Paul Celan; translated by Michael Hamburger. Rev and expanded. Persea Bks. 2002 xxxiv, 366p $35; pa $18.95 **831**

1. Bilingual books—English-German
ISBN 0-89255-275-1; 0-89255-276-X (pa)
          LC 2001-59341

First published 1980 with title: Paul Celan: poems

"This bilingual German-English selection culled from [the poet's] nine collections reveals that his is a poetry of darkness: anguish over what life offers and denies; the ever-present shadow of death that shades each breath. . . . Yet it also expresses an undefined, perhaps undefinable, joy." Booklist [review of 1989 edition]

Selected poems and prose of Paul Celan; translated by John Felstiner. Norton 2000 xxxvi, 426p il $29.95; pa $17.95 **831**

ISBN 0-393-04999-X; 0-393-32224-6 (pa)
          LC 00-41849

Celan biographer Felstiner's "collection usefully gathers poems from all periods of Celan's life as well as his sparse but illuminating prose pieces; it should prove invaluable for classroom use and for all readers interested in the full range of Celan's writing." N Y Times Book Rev

Grass, Günter, 1927-

Novemberland; selected poems, 1956-1993; translated from the German by Michael Hamburger. Harcourt Brace & Co. 1996 163p hardcover o.p. paperback available $15　**831**
　　ISBN 0-15-600331-7 (pa)　　　　LC 95-38418
"A Helen and Kurt Wolff book"

"This anthology contains 54 poems in the original German with facing page translations by the esteemed Hamburger, whose published translations of Grass poems began more than 30 years ago. This volume includes selections from all of Grass's major collections. . . . Grass's poems treat many of the same motifs as his novels, and all document his fascination with Poland, Danzig, and recent German history." Libr J

Rilke, Rainer Maria, 1875-1926

Duino elegies　　　　　　　　**831**
Available in paperback from various publishers
First English translation published 1939

"These elegies, the last great work of the poet, were named for the castle of Duino on the Adriatic, where they were first conceived." New Statesman (1913)

New poems; selected and translated by Edward Snow. rev bilingual ed. North Point Press 2001 329p pa $15　　　　**831**
　　1. Bilingual books—English-German
　　ISBN 0-86547-612-8　　　　LC 2001-42714

"The translations in this book were originally published in two separate volumes: New poems (Neue Gedichte) in 1984 and New poems: the other part (Der neuen Gedichte anderer Teil) in 1987." Preface

In this "translation, Edward Snow renders into believable English the complete text of Rilke's work of early maturity. . . . Maintaining fidelity to Rilke's idiosyncratic and problematic German, Snow does not reproduce his formal structures but does capture the rhythms, tone shifts, and overall feel of the poems to an admirable degree. Bilingual edition." Booklist [review of 1984 edition of New poems (1907)]

Sonnets to Orpheus　　　　　　**831**
　　　　　　　　　　　　LC 87-6146
Available in paperback from various publishers
First English translation 1936 in the United Kingdom; 1942 in the United States by Norton

"Deeply rooted in the symbolist tradition, the 'Sonnets' collapse the barriers that exist between the inner and the outer world and celebrate the inherently musical quality of language. In his masterful translation of the 'Sonnets', Young captures the fluidity of the original with sensitivity and precision." Libr J

Uncollected poems; selected and translated by Edward Snow. Bilingual ed. North Point Press 1995 265p hardcover o.p. paperback available $15　　　　**831**
　　ISBN 0-86547-513-X (pa)　　　　LC 94-24438

This volume includes poems "written between 1908, the year Rilke published New Poems, and 1923, when Duino Elegies and Sonnets to Orpheus appeared." Libr J

"Snow is particularly adept at capturing what one might call the non-Orphic side of Rilke's voice. Even in the most complex and rhetorically charged pieces, however, Snow is careful never to simplify Rilke. . . . Most important of all, these translations . . . let us get beyond the simplifications of the Rilke legend with its cycles of transcendent inspiration and imaginative paralysis." New Repub

832　German drama

Dürrenmatt, Friedrich

The visit; a tragi-comedy; translated from the German by Patrick Bowles. Grove Press 1962 109p pa $12　　　　　**832**
　　ISBN 0-8021-3066-6
"An Evergreen original"
Characters: 28 men, 6 women, extras. 3 acts. First produced in the United States at the Lunt-Fontaine Theatre, New York City, May 5, 1958

This play "concerns millionaire Claire Zachanassian's return to her small home town where, in her youth, she was seduced and abandoned by III. She seeks revenge and, to get it, she bribes the entire population: every man, woman and child will be rich for the rest of their lives if they agree to put III to death. After a feeble moral struggle and a travesty of a trial, the people of Güllen condemn and execute the erstwhile lover. In so doing they condemn themselves and Dürrenmatt condemns society as a whole." Cambridge Guide to World Theatre

Goethe, Johann Wolfgang von, 1749-1832

Faust　　　　　　　　　　**832**
Available in hardcover and paperback from various publishers

In this epic drama "Mephistopheles makes a bargain with the aged Faust. If Faust is granted one moment of complete contentment, he loses his soul. Faust regains his youth and with Mephistopheles he travels about enjoying every form of earthly pleasure." Haydn. Thesaurus of Book Dig

Weiss, Peter, 1916-1982

The persecution and assassination of Jean-Paul Marat as performed by the inmates of the Asylum of Charenton under the direction of the Marquis de Sade; English version by Geoffrey Skelton; verse adaptation by Adrian Mitchell; introduction by Peter Brook. Atheneum Pubs. 1965 117p hardcover o.p. paperback available $6.95　　　**832**
　　1. Marat, Jean Paul, 1743-1793—Drama 2. Sade, marquis de, 1740-1814—Drama
　　ISBN 0-689-70568-9 (pa)
Original German edition, 1964
Characters: 20 men, 7 women. 2 acts, 33 divisions. First produced in the United States at the Martin Beck Theatre, New York City, December 27, 1965

"This play within a play, which contains elements associated with both the 'Theatre of the Absurd' and the 'Theatre of Cruelty', consists of a debate, set in a lunatic asylum, between the French revolutionary 'Marat' and the eccentric individualist the Marquis de Sade." Reader's Ency. 4th edition

833.009　German fiction—History and criticism

Franz Kafka's The metamorphosis; edited and with an introduction by Harold Bloom. Chelsea House 1988 149p (Modern critical interpretations) $37.95　　　**833.009**
　　1. Kafka, Franz, 1883-1924. The metamorphosis
　　ISBN 1-55546-070-4　　　　LC 87-17827

Martin Greenberg, Stanley Corngold and Evelyn Torton Beck are among the contributors to this collection of critical assessments of Kafka's classic

Includes bibliographical references

838   German miscellany

Dürrenmatt, Friedrich
Plays and essays; edited by Volkmar Sander; foreword by Martin Esslin. Continuum 1982 xxii, 312p (German library) $39.50; pa $19.95   **838**
ISBN 0-8264-0257-7; 0-8264-0267-4 (pa)
LC 81-22184
"The volume contains two of Dürrenmatt's most popular and important plays ('Romulus the Great,' 1948, and 'The Visit,' 1956); rules (a set of theses) for his famous 1962 play, 'The Physicists,' a novella titled 'The Judge and His Hangman;' an essay on the problem of modern theater; and a hypothetical lecture intended 'only as a rough outline of several of [the world's political] laws.'" Booklist

Rilke, Rainer Maria, 1875-1926
Rilke on love and other difficulties; translations and considerations of Rainer Maria Rilke; [edited by] John J. L. Mood. Norton 1975 117p hardcover o.p. paperback available $12.95   **838**
ISBN 0-393-31098-1 (pa)
A collection of Rilke's letters, prose, poetry and critical essays, which reveals his insight into the human condition, especially the juxtaposition of male and female

839   Other Germanic literatures

The **Sagas** of Icelanders; a selection; preface by Jane Smiley; introduction by Robert Kellogg. Viking 2000 lxvi, 782p il maps (World of the sagas) hardcover o.p. paperback available $20   **839**
1. Sagas 2. Old Norse literature
ISBN 0-14-100003-1 (pa)   LC 99-44111
A selection from the 5 volume Complete sagas of Icelanders, published 1997 in the United Kingdom
"The Icelandic Sagas are among the masterpieces of world literature whose composition stretches from about the year 1000 to 1500. Presenting the adventures of Norse and Viking heroes, the sagas are told with ritual simplicity and a realism that anticipate the modern novel." Libr J
Includes bibliographical references

839.3   Dutch, Flemish, Afrikaans literatures

Frank, Anne, 1929-1945
Anne Frank's Tales from the secret annex; with translations by Ralph Manheim and Michel Mok. Doubleday 1984 c1983 136p hardcover o.p. paperback available $4.95
839.3
ISBN 0-553-58638-6 (pa)   LC 82-45871
Original Dutch edition copyrighted 1949. First English translation published 1960 in the United Kingdom with title: Tales from the house behind
This volume presents all of Anne Frank's existing stories, sketches and drafts as well as her personal reminiscences and essays
"The themes and plots of her brief fables are not extraordinary. But their very ordinariness reminds readers that the writer who kept one of the world's most widely read diaries was an ordinary child." Horn Book

839.7   Swedish literature

Hammarskjöld, Dag, 1905-1961
Markings; translated from the Swedish by Leif Sjöberg & W. H. Auden; with a foreword by W. H. Auden. Knopf 1964 xxiii, 221p pa $29.95   **839.7**
1. Spiritual life
ISBN 0-394-43532-X
Also available in paperback from Ballantine Bks.
Original Swedish edition, 1963
The author described this account as a sort of white book concerning his negotiations with himself and with God. A record of his inner life, it opens with a poem he wrote around 1925; most of the entries were made during the nineteen forties and fifties—and the book ends with a poem written only a few weeks before his plane crashed

Strindberg, August, 1849-1912
Strindberg: five plays; translated, with an introduction by Harry G. Carlson. University of Calif. Press 1983 297p hardcover o.p. paperback available $19.95   **839.7**
ISBN 0-520-04698-6 (pa)   LC 82-15882
Contents: The father; Miss Julie; The dance of death; A dream play; The ghost sonata

839.8   Danish and Norwegian literatures

Ibsen, Henrik, 1828-1906
The complete major prose plays; translated and introduced by Rolf Fjelde. Farrar, Straus & Giroux 1978 1143p o.p.; New Am. Lib. paperback available $28   **839.8**
ISBN 0-452-26205-4 (pa)   LC 77-28349
Contents: Pillars of society; A doll house; Ghosts; An enemy of the people; The wild duck; Rosmersholm; The lady from the sea; Hedda Gabler; The master builder; Little Eyolf; John Gabriel Borkman; When we dead awaken
Includes bibliographical references

Ibsen: four plays; translated by Brian Johnston. Smith & Kraus 1996 295p (Great translations for actors) pa $19.95   **839.8**
ISBN 1-57525-064-0   LC 96-36230
Designated v2 on title page
Contents: Pillars of society; The wild duck; Rosmersholm; The master builder

Ibsen: four plays; translated by Brian Johnston with Rick Davis. Smith & Kraus 1998 235p (Great translations for actors) pa $19.95   **839.8**
ISBN 0-57525-145-0
Designated v3 on title page

Ibsen, Henrik, 1828-1906—Continued
    Contents: The lady from the sea; Little Eyolf; John Gabriel Borkman; When we dead awaken

Ibsen: four major plays; translated by Rick Davis and Brian Johnston. Smith & Kraus 1995 286p (Great translations for actors) pa $19.95   **839.8**
    ISBN 1-880399-67-9   LC 95-13632
    Designated v1 on cover
    Contents: A doll house; Ghosts; An enemy of the people; Hedda Gabler

"All four of these versions have been 'production-tested,' which shows in their graceful and believable dialogue and their sheer theatricality. Davis and Johnston have unlocked the power in Ibsen's works and made it clear why Ibsen was once *the* playwright for firebrands, Fabians, and other progressives throughout the world." Booklist

Jacobsen, Rolf, 1907-1994
The roads have come to an end now; selected and last poems of Rolf Jacobsen; translated by Robert Bly, Roger Greenwald, and Robert Hedin. Copper Canyon Press 2001 168p pa $16   **839.8**
    1. Bilingual books—English-Norwegian
    ISBN 1-55659-165-9   LC 2001-4488
    "A Kage-an book"

"This bilingual (Norwegian-English) edition of 73 poems demonstrates a poet whose vision of the natural world and humanity's place in it is cosmically penetrative. Jacobsen regards the world as filled with an essential energy, animated by what must be God, and reading his work induces a certain calm ecstasy about everyday existence." Booklist

840.3   French literature— Encyclopedias and dictionaries

The **New** Oxford companion to literature in French; edited by Peter France. Oxford Univ. Press 1995 li, 865p maps $80 **840.3**
    1. French literature—Dictionaries 2. French literature—Bio-bibliography
    ISBN 0-19-866125-8

First published 1959 with title: The Oxford companion to French literature

"This work views literature from the perspective of its greater cultural context. Accordingly, topics discussed go beyond the poets, novelists, and dramatists of the traditional French canon, and include philosophy, science, art, history, linguistics, and cinema. Even strip cartoons and pamphlets are treated. . . . The more than 3,000 entries are written by approximately 130 international experts. In addition to brief entries, there are long articles on general topics, such as Québec, feminism, Occitan literature, and the history of the French language." Am Ref Books Annu, 1996

841   French poetry

Baudelaire, Charles, 1821-1867
Les fleurs du mal; the complete text of The flowers of evil; in a new translation by Richard Howard; illustrated with nine original monotypes by Michael Mazur. Godine 1982 xxxii, 365p il hardcover o.p. paperback available $18.95   **841**
    ISBN 0-87923-462-8 (pa)   LC 81-13283
    Original French edition, 1857
"Howard puts the original's rhymed alexandrines primarily into iambic pentameter blank verse, which allows him to capture the immediate, concrete, visceral quality of Baudelaire's imagery." Choice

The flowers of evil; selected and edited by Marthiel and Jackson Mathews. rev ed. New Directions 1963 c1962 xxxi, 448p pa $19.95   **841**
    ISBN 0-8112-1117-7
A previous selection of poems translated from the 1857 French work by Geoffrey Wagner was published in 1947 by New Directions. This selection contains translations by various translators. Texts are given in both English and the original French
"Faced with the conflict of good and evil, Baudelaire discards conventional dualities and finds beauty or good also manifested in the perverse, the grotesque, and the morbid. Baudelaire had an ability to discern the sinister in nature; the poems show an acutely, even painfully sensitive mind, and the characteristically modern emphasis on subjective experience." Reader's Ency. 4th edition

Poems. Knopf 1993 256p (Everyman's library pocket poets) $12.50   **841**
    ISBN 0-679-42910-7   LC 93-14363
A representative selection of poetry by the French symbolist

Beckett, Samuel, 1906-1989
Collected poems in English and French. Grove Press 1977 147p hardcover o.p. paperback available $13   **841**
    ISBN 0-8021-3096-8 (pa)   LC 77-77855
This work contains poems written by Beckett in English and French along with his translations and bilingual versions of poems by Eluard, Rimbaud, Apollinaire, and Chamfort

Chanson de Roland
The song of Roland   **841**
    1. Roland (Legendary character)—Poetry
Available in hardcover and paperback from various publishers
"This heroic poem celebrates the mighty feats of Roland, the great French hero in the time of Charlemagne. The medieval legend has replaced and transformed the actual facts of history to a great extent but the epic poem has continued in popularity." Bookman's Manual

Mallarmé, Stéphane, 1842-1898

Collected poems; translated and with a commentary by Henry Weinfield. University of Calif. Press 1994 282p hardcover o.p. paperback available $24.95   **841**

ISBN 0-520-20711-4 (pa)   LC 94-26794

"This collection, put together and translated by poet/scholar Weinfield, makes the poems of Mallarmé accessible to late 20th-century readers for the first time. This hefty volume contains Weinfield's introduction; the poems and prose poems themselves, with English and French versions *en face*; and a meticulous poem-by-poem critique and commentary. By staying close to the language and meter of the originals, Weinfield has artfully retained their flavor." Libr J

Rimbaud, Arthur, 1854-1891

Illuminations, and other prose poems; translated by Louise Varèse. rev ed. New Directions 1957 xxxv, 182p pa $10.95   **841**

ISBN 0-8112-0184-8

This translation first published 1946

These prose poems of the French Symbolist are given in both their original texts and in English translations. This edition also contains two other series of prose poems, together with an introduction in which the translator discusses the complicated ins and outs of 'Rimbaudien' scholarship and the special qualities of Rimbaud's writing

A season in hell & The drunken boat; English translation by Louise Varèse. New Directions 1961 xx, 108p pa $9.95   **841**

ISBN 0-8112-0185-6

Title page and text in French and English

Although he stopped writing at the age of nineteen, Arthur Rimbaud (1854-1891) possessed a revolutionary talent and his poetry and prose have increasingly influenced the major writers of our century. To his A season in hell is here added Rimbaud's longest and possibly greatest single poem The drunken boat

Includes bibliographical references

Tristan

The romance of Tristan and Isolt; translated from the Old French by Norman B. Spector; with a foreword by Eugène Vinaver. Northwestern Univ. Press 1973 91p hardcover o.p. paperback available $13.95   **841**

ISBN 0-8101-0767-8 (pa)

"The earliest, but incomplete, extant version of this medieval romance was that written in Anglo-Norman French verse by Thomas of Britain about 1185. . . . The story is laid in Ireland and Cornwall with some versions adding details from Brittany. Sir Tristram is sent to Ireland to bring Isolde to Cornwall to be the bride of King Mark. A love potion causes Tristram and Isolde to fall in love and after many trysts and separations each dies of love of the other." Reader's Adviser

Verlaine, Paul, 1844-1896

Selected poems; translated by C. F. MacIntyre. University of Calif. Press 1948 xx, 228p il pa $15.95   **841**

ISBN 0-520-01298-4

Eighty poems, chosen from Verlaine's first six books. French originals and translations are on facing pages.

Contains a preface by the translator

The translator "has done Verlaine a gracious courtesy, and American readers a great kindness. The charm, verbal fireworks, sympathy and nostalgia of this major French poet are Englished with color and convictions." Chicago Sunday Trib

Includes bibliographical references

Villon, François, b. 1431

The poems of François Villon; translated and with an introduction and notes by Galway Kinnell. Houghton Mifflin 1977 xxiii, 246p o.p.; University Press of New England paperback available $17.95   **841**

ISBN 0-87451-236-0 (pa)   LC 77-12999

This translation first published 1965 by New American Library

French text (based on the Longnon-Foulet edition of 1932) and English translation on facing pages. Includes a critical introduction and explanatory notes

"Using standard academic texts of the medieval French poet, Kinnell exceeds a transliteration of the originals. . . . Villon's ribaldry and humorous despair sparkle throughout." Booklist

Includes bibliographical references

842   French drama

Beckett, Samuel, 1906-1989

Ends and Odds; eight new dramatic pieces. Grove Press 1977 c1976 128p hardcover o.p. paperback available $8.95   **842**

ISBN 0-8021-5046-2 (pa)

Contents: Ends: Not I; That time; Footfalls; Ghost trio; Odds: Theatre I; Theatre II; Radio I; Radio II

"Ends and Odds proclaim imaginary worlds as dense as any [Beckett] has made before. A head, a hand, a lonely voice, or even a faint footfall is filled with as much intensity as silence and darkness itself. . . . It is a tiring style . . . but it does not tire the mind." New Repub

Waiting for Godot; tragicomedy in 2 acts. Grove Press 1954 60p il hardcover o.p. paperback available $12   **842**

ISBN 0-8021-3034-8 (pa)

Translated from the French by the author

Originally written in French. The play was first produced in Paris during the winter of 1952

"There are strong biblical references throughout, but Beckett's powerful and symbolic portrayal of the human condition as one of ignorance, delusion, paralysis, and intermittent flashes of human sympathy, hope, and wit has been subjected to many varying interpretations. The theatrical vitality and versatility of the play have been demonstrated by performances throughout the world." Oxford Companion to Engl Lit. 5th edition

Camus, Albert, 1913-1960

Caligula & three other plays; translated from the French by Stuart Gilbert; with a preface written specially for this edition and translated by Justin O'Brien. Knopf 1958 302p hardcover o.p. paperback available $8.76   **842**

ISBN 0-394-70207-7 (pa)

"Four of the author's best-known plays, written between 1938 and 1950. 'Caligula,' about the infamous emperor's self-destroying rebellion against fate; 'The Misunderstanding,' about the murder of a man by his ghoulish mother and sister,' 'The Just Assassins,' on the self-questionings of terrorists; and 'State of Siege,' an allegory about the refusal of one individual in a plague-stricken city to compromise with evil." Publ Wkly

Genet, Jean, 1910-1986

The blacks: a clown show; translated from the French by Bernard Frechtman. Grove Press 1960 128p pa $13   **842**

ISBN 0-8021-5028-4

"An Evergreen book"

Original French edition, 1958

"Drama in which a group of bizarrely dressed Negroes give a performance for another group of Negroes who wear white masks and represent the major figures of white society's established authority." McGraw-Hill Ency of World Drama

The maids [and] Deathwatch; two plays; with an introduction by Jean-Paul Sartre; translated from the French by Bernard Frechtman. Grove Press 1954 166p hardcover o.p. paperback available $13   **842**

ISBN 0-8021-5056-X (pa)

Deathwatch, a one-act play written 1947 and first produced 1949 "deals with an insignificant criminal who tries to assume the highly desirable and prestigious role of murderer. . . . In 'The Maids (Les bonnes),' produced in 1947, . . . two servant girls have created an elaborate ritual in which they impersonate their mistress and finally murder her symbolically." McGraw-Hill Ency of World Drama

Ionesco, Eugène

Rhinoceros, and other plays; translated by Derek Prouse. Grove Press 1960 141p pa $10   **842**

ISBN 0-8021-3098-4

Also available in hardcover from P. Smith

"An Evergreen book"

Contents: Rhinoceros; The future is in eggs; The leader

Three satirical comedies by a leading dramatist of the "theater of the absurd." In Rhinoceros, one man resists the pressure to conform as everyone about him accepts their transformation into rhinoceroses and he finds himself socially isolated. In The future is in eggs, a couple must produce eggs destined to become intellectuals. The leader is a satire on the mass adulation of political figures in which the leader turns out to be a headless figure

Molière, 1622-1673

The misanthrope, and other plays; translated and with an introduction by Donald M. Frame. New Am. Lib. 1968 512p pa $6.95   **842**

ISBN 0-451-52415-2

"A Signet classic"

Contents: The misanthrope; The doctor in spite of himself; The miser; The would-be gentleman; The mischievous machinations of Scapin; The learned women; The imaginary invalid

Tartuffe, and other plays; translated with an introduction by Donald M. Frame. New Am. Lib. 1967 384p pa $6.95   **842**

ISBN 0-451-52454-3

Contents: The ridiculous précieuses; The school for husbands; The school for wives; The critique of the school for wives; The Versailles impromptu; Tartuffe; Don Juan

Includes bibliographical references

Sartre, Jean Paul, 1905-1980

No exit, and three other plays. Vintage Bks. 1989 275p pa $12   **842**

ISBN 0-679-72516-4   LC 89-40097

Contents: No exit; The flies; Dirty hands; The respectful prostitute

No exit is a modern morality play; The flies is a reworking of the Orestes-Electra story. The third play concerns a young Communist intellectual's attempt to maintain his integrity as party line changes and personal relationships alter perceptions of his murder of a party boss who had fallen out of favor, but whose memory is later rehabilitated. The last play concerns a prostitute's involvement in false charges of rape against a murdered black man and his companion in a town in the American South

843.009   French fiction—History and criticism

Shattuck, Roger

Proust's way; a field guide to In search of lost time. Norton 2000 xxiv, 290p hardcover o.p. paperback available $14.95   **843.009**

1. Proust, Marcel, 1871-1922

ISBN 0-393-32180-0 (pa)   LC 99-58472

Shattuck "explains the major settings of the work, summarizes character and plot, and discusses central themes. Shattuck acknowledges that there is no one right interpretation of In Search of Lost Time but succeeds in providing a framework to help readers get through it. He addresses readers coming to the work for the first time." Libr J

Includes bibliographical references

844   French essays

Camus, Albert, 1913-1960

The myth of Sisyphus, and other essays; translated from the French by Justin O'Brien. Knopf 1955 212p hardcover o.p. paperback available $12   **844**

ISBN 0-679-73373-6 (pa)

Analyzed in Essay and general literature index

Personal reflections on the meaning of life and the philosophical questions surrounding suicide

Resistance, rebellion, and death; translated from the French and with an introduction by Justin O'Brien. Knopf 1961 c1960 271p hardcover o.p. paperback available $13   **844**

ISBN 0-679-76401-1 (pa)

Analyzed in Essay and general literature index

Camus, Albert, 1913-1960—*Continued*

"A selection of forthright essays on contemporary world politics, on capital punishment and the relations of the state and the individual, and on art, chosen from the three volumes of 'Actuelles,' published in France between 1950 and 1958." Publ Wkly

848 French miscellany

Rimbaud, Arthur, 1854-1891

Arthur Rimbaud: complete works; translated from the French by Paul Schmidt. Harper & Row 1975 309p hardcover o.p. paperback available $15   **848**

ISBN 0-06-095550-3 (pa)

This is a compilation of Rimbaud's "poetry, prose, and selected letters and documents. Translator Schmidt has divided the works into chronological segments corresponding to periods in Rimbaud's life, prefacing each division with biographical background. Original French versions not provided." Booklist

Complete works, selected letters; translation, introduction and notes by Wallace Fowlie. University of Chicago Press 1966 370p hardcover o.p. paperback available $14   **848**

ISBN 0-226-71973-1 (pa)

In this bilingual edition of Rimbaud's work the original French texts are accompanied by English prose translations. In addition to the complete poetic works there are two prose fragments, a short story in the form of a seminarian's journal, and a selection of letters chosen to illustrate biographical details and Rimbaud's credo as a poet

Valéry, Paul, 1871-1945

Selected writings. New Directions 1950 256p hardcover o.p. paperback available $12.95   **848**

ISBN 0-8112-0213-5 (pa)

"Seventeen poems are translated by eighteen translators, including Denis Devlin, Léonie Adams, and C. Day Lewis. . . . The rest of the book is composed of the French love miscellanies, essays, dialogues, and critiques." New Yorker

Voltaire, 1694-1778

The portable Voltaire; edited, and with an introduction by Ben Ray Redmen. Viking 1949 569p hardcover o.p. paperback available $17   **848**

ISBN 0-14-015041-2 (pa)

"The Viking portable library"

The selections from Voltaire's works include: Candide, part one; Three stories: Zadig, Micromegas, and Story of a good Brahmin; Letters, and selections from the Philosophical Dictionary and other works. The editor's introduction gives a biographical sketch of Voltaire

850.3 Italian literature— Encyclopedias and dictionaries

Dictionary of Italian literature; Peter Bondanella and Julia Conaway Bondanella, editors-in-chief; Jody Robin Shiffman, associate editor. rev expanded ed. Greenwood Press 1996 716p $125.95

850.3

1. Italian literature—Dictionaries
ISBN 0-313-27745-1   LC 95-33077
First published 1979

This dictionary "provides some 400 alphabetically arranged entries on Italian writers, periods, literary movements, and versification, and on critical problems related to literary history." Publisher's note

The **Oxford** companion to Italian literature; edited by Peter Hainsworth and David Robey. Oxford Univ. Press 2002 xli, 644p maps $95   **850.3**

1. Italian literature—Dictionaries 2. Italian literature—Bio-bibliography
ISBN 0-19-818332-1   LC 2001-59301

This reference work features "assessments of Italy's writers, famous and not-so-famous, from 1200 to 2000. It covers writers who wrote in Italian, dialect, or Latin, and offers . . . background information on historical events, regional culture, and the other arts." Publisher's note

"A magisterial addition to the Oxford companions to literature, this volume goes far beyond its core subject of Italian literature to cover its substrate and context. . . . An excellent ready-reference companion for readers seeking less an introduction to the summits of the literature . . . but a reminder of relevant details." Choice

For a review see: Booklist, Sept. 15, 2003

Includes bibliographical references

850.9 Italian literature—History and criticism

The **Cambridge** history of Italian literature; edited by Peter Brand and Lino Pertile. rev ed. Cambridge Univ. Press 1999 xxii, 699p map pa $33   **850.9**

1. Italian literature—History and criticism
ISBN 0-521-66622-8   LC 00-265436
First published 1996

Scholars analyze and describe the works of writers who have added to Italy's literary tradition from its origins to today. The editors provide translations, maps, bibliographies, and chronological charts

"Contemporary readers will no doubt be delighted to learn more about such topics as the evolution of opera, compositions by Italian women writers, and the development of feminism." Choice

851   Italian poetry

Dante Alighieri, 1265-1321

Dante's Inferno; translations by twenty contemporary poets; introduced by James Merrill; with an afterword by Giuseppe Mazzotta; edited by Daniel Halpern. Ecco Press 1993 199p hardcover o.p. paperback available $13.95   **851**

ISBN 0-88001-373-7 (pa)   LC 92-28061

In this "experiment in translation, . . . the 34 cantos of the *Inferno* are shared among 20 poets all known for their strong original work in English, and some, too, for their distinguished accomplishments as translators. The effect of the book is to summon a multiplicity of voices from the one, and to direct readers not only back to the source but to the varying tempos and temperaments of modern poetry in English." Publ Wkly

The divine comedy   **851**

Available in hardcover and paperback from various publishers

An epic poem, completed in 1321, in which the poet describes his visionary spiritual journey through Hell, Purgatory and Paradise—guided first by the classical poet Vergil and then by his beloved Beatrice—which results in a purification of his religious faith

The divine comedy of Dante Alighieri; edited and translated by Robert M. Durling; introduction and notes by Ronald L. Martinez and Robert M. Durling; illustrations by Robert Turner. Oxford Univ. Press 1996-2003 2v il map   **851**

1. Bilingual books—English-Italian   LC 95-12740

The first two volumes of Dante's epic poem

Contents: v1 Inferno $39.95; pa $17.95 (ISBN 0-19-508740-2; pa 0-19-508744-5); v2 Purgatorio $45 (ISBN 0-19-508741-0)

An epic poem, completed in 1321, in which the poet describes his visionary spiritual journey through Hell, Purgatory and Paradise—guided first by the classical poet Vergil and then by his beloved Beatrice—which results in a purification of his religious faith

"Durling bases his translation on the Petrocchi edition of Dante, with occasional nods to the variant readings of Antonio Lanza and Federico Sanguineti. . . . This . . . translation suggests Dante's verse form without actually using terza rima. This bilingual edition includes the Italian on the facing page and textual and historical notes at the end of each canto." Libr J

Includes bibliographical references

The portable Dante; translated, edited, and with an introduction and notes by Mark Musa. Penguin Bks. 1995 xliii, 654p pa $17   **851**

ISBN 0-14-243754-9   LC 94-15988

First published 1947

This book "contains complete verse translations of Dante's two masterworks, The Divine Comedy and La Vita Nuova, as well as a bibliography, notes, and an introduction by . . . Mark Musa." Publisher's note

Contains complete verse translations of The Divine comedy and La vita nuova

Includes bibliographical references

Purgatorio; a new verse translation by W.S. Merwin. Knopf 2000 xxix, 359p $30; pa $19.95   **851**

ISBN 0-375-40921-1; 0-375-70839-1 (pa)

LC 99-40708

A translation of the central section of The divine comedy. "The 'Purgatorio' is the only section to take place on Earth, and it is also the most human and hopeful. In his introduction, Merwin confides that he has been reading Dante since his adolescence, and his reverence for the poet, his erudition, and the incredible elasticity and naturalness of his translation render this masterpiece (presented in its original Italian on facing pages) fresh and radiant." Booklist

Vita nuova   **851**

Available in paperback from Oxford University Press in a translation by Mark Musa; also available bilingual edition translated by Dino S. Cervigni in hardcover and paperback from Notre Dame Press

Written ca. 1292

A series of autobiographical poems in which Dante tells the story of his love for Beatrice

Montale, Eugenio, 1896-1981

Collected poems, 1920-1954; translated and annotated by Jonathan Galassi. rev ed. Farrar, Straus & Giroux 2000 625p pa $18   **851**

ISBN 0-374-52625-7   LC 00-35456

First published 1997

Contents: Ossi di seppia = Cuttlefish bones; Le occasioni = The occasions; La bufera e altro = The storm, etc

"It is generally agreed that the core of Montale's work consists of three major collections: Cuttlefish Bones (1925), The Occasions (1939), and The Storm, etc. (1956). Galassi chooses to publish all three together, separating them from a body of work of almost equal length that came later. He defends this decision in a brilliant afterword that offers the best short account I have yet come across of the nature, import, and elusive content of Montale's work." N Y Rev Books [review of 1997 edition]

Includes bibliographical references

852   Italian drama

Pirandello, Luigi, 1867-1936

Naked masks; five plays; edited by Eric Bentley. Dutton 1952 xxvii, 386p o.p.; Meridian Bks. paperback available $13.95

852

ISBN 0-452-01082-9 (pa)

Contents: Liolã; It is so! (If you think so); Henry IV; Six characters in search of an author; Each in his own way

854   Italian essays

Eco, Umberto

How to travel with a salmon & other essays; translated from the Italian by William Weaver. Harcourt Brace & Co. 1994 248p il hardcover o.p. paperback available $15   **854**

ISBN 0-15-600125-X (pa)   LC 94-10340

"A Helen and Kurt Wolff book"

Eco, Umberto—*Continued*

"In this collection of parodies, satires and whimsical mini-essays written over the last 30 years, Italian novelist/critic Eco . . . takes readers on a delightful romp through the absurdities of modern life." Publ Wkly

860.3 Spanish literature— Encyclopedias and dictionaries

Concise encyclopedia of Latin American literature; editor, Verity Smith. Fitzroy Dearborn Pubs. 2000 xxi, 678p $75 **860.3**

1. Latin American literature—Encyclopedias 2. Latin American literature—Bio-bibliography

ISBN 1-57958-252-4

Based on the Encyclopedia of Latin American literature (1997)

Contains entries on 50 leading writers and 50 important works of Latin American and Caribbean literature. Also includes survey articles on the literature of individual countries and topical essays. Bibliographies of primary and secondary sources are listed

860.9 Spanish literature— History and criticism

The **Cambridge** history of Latin American literature; edited by Roberto González Echevarría and Enrique Pupo-Walker. Cambridge Univ. Press 1996 3v ea $110 **860.9**

1. Latin American literature—History and criticism

LC 93-37750

Contents: v1 Discovery to modernism (ISBN 0-521-34069-1); v2 The twentieth century (ISBN 0-521-34070-5); v3 Brazilian literature. Bibliographies (ISBN 0-521-41035-5)

"These volumes span from pre-Columbian times to the present and include chapters on Latin American writing in the United States. Some 40 international scholars trace the development of Latin American literature in essay form. The bibliography in Volume 3 consumes 455 pages." Libr J

"The editors have added an interdisciplinary dimension to their work by incorporating the materials and methodologies proper to history. . . . [This] will become a classic in the field." Choice

Hispanic literature criticism; Jelena Krstovic, editor. Gale Res. 1994 2v il set $250 **860.9**

1. Latin American literature—History and criticism 2. Spanish literature—History and criticism 3. American literature—Hispanic American authors—History and criticism 4. Authors, Latin American

ISBN 0-8103-9145-7 LC 94-76177

Contents: v1 Allende to Jimenez; v2 Lorca to Zamora

This reference work "focuses on the major literary figures of the Spanish- and Portuguese-speaking world. It offers a brief biographical sketch, a list of principal works, numerous critical essays, and a short bibliography of additional articles about 71 prominent authors from Spain, Portugal, Latin America, and Latino United States." Libr J

Moss, Joyce, 1951-

Latin American literature and its times; [by] Joyce Moss, Lorraine Valestuk. Gale Group 1999 xxxix, 562p il (World literature and its times) $125 **860.9**

1. Latin American literature—History and criticism

ISBN 0-7876-3726-2 LC 99-29292

"Highlights Latin American literature and Latino works 'produced in the United States.' Arrangement is alphabetical by title. Lengthy, informative essays discuss individual poems and fiction and nonfiction titles with a focus on the political, economical, social contexts in which the pieces were written. . . . Each essay concludes with a list 'For More Information.' Black-and-white photographs, movie stills, and reproductions are sprinkled throughout." SLJ

For a fuller review see: Booklist, Jan. 1 & 15, 2000

861 Spanish poetry

Borges, Jorge Luis, 1899-1986

Selected poems; edited by Alexander Coleman. Viking 1999 477p hardcover o.p. paperback available $19 **861**

ISBN 0-14-058721-7 (pa) LC 99-10318

"Poetry is the heart of Borges' metaphysical, mythical, and cosmopolitan oeuvre. . . . Editor Coleman commissioned a wealth of new translations for this unprecedented and invaluable collection, and the roster of translators includes such luminaries as Robert S. Fitzgerald, W.S. Merwin, Mark Strand, and John Updike." Booklist

Cid, ca. 1043-1099

The poem of the Cid **861**

Paperback editions available from various publishers

"The poem is based on the exploits of Rodrigo or Ruy Díaz de Bivar (c.1043-1099), who was known as 'el Cid.' . . . Similar in form to the 'Chanson de Roland,' the poem is notable for its simplicity and directness and for its exact, picturesque detail. Despite the inclusion of much legendary material, the figure of the Cid who is depicted as the model Castilian warrior, is not idealized to an extravagant degree." Reader's Ency. 4th edition

García Lorca, Federico, 1898-1936

Selected poems; edited by Francisco García Lorca and Donald M. Allen. New Directions 1955 180p hardcover o.p. paperback available $10.95 **861**

ISBN 0-8112-0091-4 (pa)

The poet's brother, in his preface "clearly traces the line of development in Lorca's work from the early lyrics and ballads to the later lyric dramas. The English versions of the poems, by eighteen translators, bring out the contrast and color of the originals, which are included, and there is a chronology of the poet's life." New Yorker

Juana Inés de la Cruz, 1651-1695

A Sor Juana anthology; translated by Alan S. Trueblood; with a foreword by Octavio Paz. Harvard Univ. Press 1988 248p hardcover o.p. paperback available $18.95 **861**

ISBN 0-674-82121-1 (pa) LC 87-27693

This volume "offers a useful sampling and English rendition of Sor Juana's work. Poetry predominates

Juana Inés de la Cruz, 1651-1695—*Continued*

among the selections. . . . Given the difficulty of Mr. Trueblood's task—attempting to capture in English the voice of a poet who herself mastered many poetic languages—his translations are admirable." N Y Times Book Rev

Includes bibliographical references

Neruda, Pablo, 1904-1973

Five decades; a selection (poems: 1925-1970); edited and translated by Ben Belitt. Grove Press 1974 xxii, 431p hardcover o.p. paperback available $15   **861**

ISBN 0-8021-3035-6 (pa)

Bilingual selection of poems from twenty-one books published between 1925 and 1970. Text in Spanish and English

"Belitt's insight into the intricate metaphysical imagery of Neruda's poetry is quite apparent in these translations." Choice

Includes bibliographical references

Late and posthumous poems, 1968-1974; introduction by Manuel Duran; edited and translated by Ben Belitt. Grove Press 1988 239p hardcover o.p. paperback available $13   **861**

ISBN 0-8021-3145-X (pa)   LC 88-11290

"With the exception of the darker surrealism of the 1930s, Nobel Prize-winning poet Neruda's work was consistently life-affirming, even to his last days. Translated by Belitt, no stranger to Neruda, the 'late and posthumous poems' display an exhilarating variety. These poems attest to Neruda's warmth, profundity, and humility." Libr J

Selected odes of Pablo Neruda; translated, with an introduction by Margaret Sayers Peden. University of Calif. Press 1990 375p (Latin American literature and culture) hardcover o.p. paperback available $16.95   **861**

ISBN 0-520-22708-5 (pa)   LC 90-10707

"With the Spanish text and the English translation on facing pages, the beautiful odes of the great Chilean poet pay tribute to simple things in simple words, from bicycles and birds to his suit." Booklist

Stones of the sky; translated by James Nolan. 2nd ed. Copper Canyon Press 2002 70p pa $14   **861**

1. Bilingual books—English-Spanish
ISBN 1-556-59170-5   LC 2002-278427

"A Kage-an book"

First published 1987

"In this bilingual collection, the late Nobel laureate establishes immediate intimacy with poems that are at once deeply personal, expansive and universal. Neruda does not embellish but keeps the purity of his emotions intact, lending the verses majestic and understated beauty." Publ Wkly

Paz, Octavio, 1914-1998

The collected poems of Octavio Paz, 1957-1987; edited & translated by Eliot Weinberger; with additional translations by Elizabeth Bishop [et al.] New Directions 1987 669p il hardcover o.p. paperback available $23.95   **861**

ISBN 0-8112-1173-8 (pa)   LC 87-23989

"Dense, weighty, and miraculous, this bilingual edition compresses into one volume all the poems published in book form since 1957. Nearly 200 poems, some newly translated, many new to an English-language edition, conclusively demonstrate Paz's power." Libr J

Includes bibliographical references

Selected poems; edited by Eliot Weinberger; translated from the Spanish by G. Aroul [et al.] New Directions 1984 147p hardcover o.p. paperback available $10.95   **861**

ISBN 0-8112-0899-0 (pa)   LC 84-9856

"The 67 well-chosen selections show Paz in his several phases and guises—in lyrics and prose poems, in long, free-form pieces and short, impressionistic works—a range of styles representing the best modes of East and West as practiced South over the last half-century. Many of the translations are by his peers (Elizabeth Bishop, Mark Strand, W. C. Williams)." Booklist

A tale of two gardens; poems from India, 1952-1995; edited and translated by Eliot Weinberger; with additional translations by Elizabeth Bishop [et al.] New Directions 1997 111p pa $8   **861**

1. India—Poetry
ISBN 0-8112-1349-8   LC 96-38111

This volume "collects the poetry from over 40 years of Nobel Prize winner Octavio Paz's many and various commitments to India—as Mexican ambassador, student of Indian philosophy, and above all, as poet. . . . [Verse included ranges] from the long work 'Mutra,' written in 1952 and accompanied here by a new commentary by the author, to the celebrated poems of *East Slope*, and his recent adaptations from the classical Sanskrit." Publisher's note

Reversible monuments; contemporary Mexican poetry; edited by Mónica de la Torre and Michael Wiegers. Copper Canyon Press 2002 675p pa $20   **861**

1. Mexican poetry—Collections 2. Bilingual books—English-Spanish
ISBN 1-55659-159-4   LC 2002-6189

This bilingual anthology includes 31 contributors, "most writing in Spanish but some in indigenous languages. Spacious and accommodating, this work presents a generous number of gracefully translated poems by each poet, a felicitous in-depth approach that makes this much more than a sampler, and a sound decision given the poet's propensity for long, dreamy poems. Sensuality is ever-present, as is an intimate connection with nature. . . . This is without doubt a landmark volume." Booklist

Twentieth century Latin American poetry; a bilingual anthology; edited by Stephen Tapscott. University of Tex. Press 1996 xxii, 418p il (Texas Pan American series) hardcover o.p. paperback available $26.95 **861**

1. Latin American poetry—Collections
ISBN 0-292-78140-7 (pa)   LC 95-40288
This anthology "samples the works of more than 75 poets, including such giants as Neruda, Dario, Reyes, Vallejo, Borges and Paz. With original-language versions and translations set side by side, the collection is arranged in order of the poets' dates of birth from José Marti, born in Cuba in 1853, to Marjorie Agosín, born in the U.S. 102 years later. Tapscott's well-conceived and lucid introduction is expanded in concise individual introductions that provide basic information and some evaluation." Publ Wkly
Includes bibliographical references

862 Spanish drama

García Lorca, Federico, 1898-1936
Five plays; comedies and tragicomedies; translated by James Graham-Lujan and Richard L. O'Connell. New Directions 1963 246p music hardcover o.p. paperback available $11.95 **862**
ISBN 0-8112-0090-6 (pa)
Also available in hardcover from Greenwood Press
Contents: The billy-club puppets; The shoemaker's prodigious wife; The love of Don Perlimplin and Belisa in the garden; Dōna Rosita, the spinster; The butterfly's evil spell

Three tragedies; translated by James Graham-Luján and Richard L. O'Connell; introduced by Francisco García Lorca. Greenwood Press 1977 212p $65.95 **862**
ISBN 0-8371-9578-0   LC 77-3056
Also available in paperback from New Directions
First published 1947 by New Directions
Contents: Blood wedding; Yerma; Bernarda Alba
A dramatic trilogy comprised of three tragedies of Spanish peasant life

864 Spanish essays

Borges, Jorge Luis, 1899-1986
Selected non-fictions; edited by Eliot Weinberger; translated by Esther Allen, Suzanne Jill Levine & Eliot Weinberger. Viking 1999 559p hardcover o.p. paperback available $18 **864**
ISBN 0-14-029011-7 (pa)   LC 99-12386
"Shifting effortlessly from Homer to Hitler, from Kafka to King Kong, these hundred and sixty-one essays, appreciations, prologues, and philosophical investigations are dizzying in scope and dazzling in execution. But it is Borges's dogged pursuit of familiar themes—infinity and eternity, reflexivity and recurrence—which gives this collection its unusual unity and depth." New Yorker

Fuentes, Carlos, 1928-
Myself with others; selected essays. Farrar, Straus & Giroux 1988 214p $19.95; pa $18 **864**
ISBN 0-374-21750-5; 0-374-52237-5 (pa)
LC 87-7448
Essays by the Mexican writer on subjects ranging from the cinema of Buñuel to the literary output of Cervantes, Borges and Garcia Marquez

Paz, Octavio, 1914-1998
The labyrinth of solitude; The other Mexico, Return to the labyrinth of solitude, Mexico and the United States, The philanthropic ogre. Grove Press 1985 398p hardcover o.p. paperback available $14.50 **864**
1. Mexico—Civilization 2. Mexican national characteristics
ISBN 0-8021-5042-X (pa)   LC 82-47999
The labyrinth of solitude and The other Mexico were first published 1961 and 1972 respectively
In this collection of essays and one interview, Paz explorers the cultural and historical influences on the social behavior of his countrymen

Vargas Llosa, Mario, 1936-
The language of passion; translated by Natasha Wimmer. Farrar, Straus & Giroux 2003 292p $24; pa $14 **864**
ISBN 0-374-18326-0; 0-312-42254-7 (pa)
LC 2002-37909
"This collection focuses on the essays that appeared during the 1990s, most of which are imbued with a wit and an intellect that make them instantly engaging." Libr J
Includes bibliographical references

868 Spanish miscellany

Allende, Isabel
Aphrodite; a memoir of the senses; drawings, Robert Shekter; recipes, Panchita Llona; translated from the Spanish by Margaret Sayers Peden. HarperCollins Pubs. 1998 315p il $26; pa $19.95 **868**
ISBN 0-06-017590-7; 0-06-093017-9 (pa)
LC 97-40274
"With her 'sole focus on the sensual art of food and its effects on amorous performance,' this distinguished Latin American writer wanders delectably through the ways food arouses the senses, citing tales and truths, folklore and science, and drawing into her fascinating discussions such topics as the role of language in seduction and the need for physical touch." Booklist

Borges, Jorge Luis, 1899-1986
Labyrinths; selected stories & other writings; edited by Donald A. Yates & James E. Irby; preface by André Maurois. New Directions 1962 248p il hardcover o.p. paperback available $12.95 **868**
ISBN 0-8112-0012-4 (pa)
A collection of tales, literary and metaphysical essays, and parables

869   Portuguese literature

Lispector, Clarice, 1925-1977
Selected cronicas; translated by Giovanni
Pontiero. New Directions 1996 212p pa
$12.95   **869**
    ISBN 0-8112-1340-4   LC 96-23768
    "In these crônicas—part anecdote, memoir, observa-
tion, essay—the late avante-garde writer shows herself to
have been as adept at short nonfiction as she was at
short fiction. Based on a column she began writing at the
behest of Brazil's leading newspaper in 1967, these
pieces bring together the lyricism of poetry to everyday
reality." Publ Wkly

Pessoa, Fernando, 1888-1935
Fernando Pessoa & Co; selected poems;
edited and translated from the Portuguese by
Richard Zenith. Grove Press 1998 290p
hardcover o.p. paperback available $14   **869**
    ISBN 0-8021-3627-3 (pa)   LC 97-50201
    "Pessoa developed his poetic opus through the mouth-
pieces of distinct and separate literary personalities called
heteronyms. . . . This collection includes selections from
three of those alter egos—the bucolic pagan Caeiro, the
Epicurean classicist Reis, and the sensational modernist
Campos—plus the 'real' Pessoa." Libr J
    Includes bibliographical references

870.8   Latin literature— Collections

The **Portable** Roman reader; edited, and with
an introduction by Basil Davenport. Viking
1951 656p hardcover o.p. paperback
available $18   **870.8**
    1. Latin literature—Collections
    ISBN 0-14-015056-0 (pa)
    "The Viking portable library"
    This anthology includes selections from Plautus, Ter-
ence, Caesar, Virgil, Seneca, Juvenal as well as complete
plays by Plautus and Terence and the anonymous poem
Vigil of Venus

870.9   Latin literature—History and criticism

Hamilton, Edith, 1867-1963
The Roman way. Norton 1932 281p
hardcover o.p. paperback available $11.95
                         870.9
    1. Latin literature—History and criticism 2. Rome—
Civilization
    ISBN 0-393-31078-7 (pa)
    Companion volume to The Greek way
    An interpretation of Roman life from the descriptions
in the works of great writers from Plautus and Terence
to Virgil and Juvenal

871.008   Latin poetry— Collections

The **Roman** poets; selected and edited by
Peter Washington. Knopf 1997 253p il
(Everyman's library pocket poets) $12.50
                      871.008
    1. Rome—Poetry 2. Latin poetry
    ISBN 0-375-40071-0   LC 98-124022
    A representative selection of classical Latin verse

872   Latin dramatic poetry and drama

Terence
Terence, the comedies; translations by
Palmer Bovie, Constance Carrier, and
Douglass Parker; edited by Palmer Bovie.
Johns Hopkins Univ. Press 1992 xxi, 398p
(Complete Roman drama in translation)
hardcover o.p. paperback available $22.95
                        872
    ISBN 0-8018-4354-5 (pa)   LC 91-33984
    First published 1974 by Rutgers University Press with
title: The complete comedies of Terence
    Includes the following plays: The brothers (Adelphoe);
The eunuch (Eunouchus); The girl from Andros (Andria);
Her husband's mother (Hecyra); Phormio; The self-
tormentor (Heautontimorumenos)

873   Latin epic poetry and fiction

Ovid, 43 B.C.-17 or 18
Metamorphoses   **873**
Hardcover and paperback editions available from various publishers
    "A series of tales in Latin verse. . . . Dealing with
mythological, legendary, and historical figures, they are
written in hexameters, in fifteen books, beginning with
the creation of the world and ending with the deification
of Caesar and the reign of Augustus." Reader's Ency. 4th
edition

Tales from Ovid; [translated by] Ted
Hughes. Farrar, Straus & Giroux 1997 257p
hardcover o.p. paperback available $14   **873**
    ISBN 0-374-52587-0 (pa)   LC 97-36061
    Hughes retells 24 Greco-Roman myths from Ovid's
Latin epic
    This is "an inspired act of translation that stands as
vigorous poetry in its own right." N Y Times Book Rev
    Includes bibliographical references

Virgil
The Aeneid of Virgil   **873**
Hardcover and paperback editions available from various publishers
    "The Aeneid is in twelve books: the first six in imita-
tion of the Odyssey; the last six, of the Iliad. The Trojan
hero is led to Italy, where he is to be the father of a race
and of an empire supreme among nations. On his way
thither he tarries at Carthage, whose queen, Dido, loves

Virgil—*Continued*

him as with the first love of a virgin. To her he tells the story of Troy. For love of him she slays herself when the gods lead him from her shores. Arrived in Italy he seeks the underworld, under the protection of the Sibyl of Cumæ. He emerges thence to overcome his enemies." Keller. Reader's Dig of Books

874 Latin lyric poetry

Horace

The Odes and Epodes; with an English translation by C. E. Bennett. rev ed. Harvard Univ. Press 1927 430p $21.50   **874**
ISBN 0-674-99037-4
"The Loeb classical library"
This edition first published 1918
English prose translations of the Odes and Epodes, opposite the original Latin. There is a short introductory chapter on the life and works of Horace, followed by a chapter on the meters he used. An index of proper names refer to the Latin originals by number and line
Includes bibliographical references

877 Latin satire and humor

Erasmus, Desiderius, 1466?-1536

The praise of folly   **877**
Hardcover and paperback editions available from various publishers
A "satirical monologue in Latin. . . . Folly praises herself and proclaims her superiority over Wisdom. The author's argument, of course, is 'that it is folly not to see things as they really are; scholars should not abandon ideals just because they cannot be fully realized but should apply their learning and reason as best they can to daily living.'" Reader's Adviser

Juvenal

Satires   **877**
Hardcover and paperback editions available from various publishers
"The sixteen 'Satires' of Juvenal, which contain a vivid picture of contemporary Rome under the Empire, have seldom been equalled as biting diatribes. . . . Juvenal's invectives in powerful hexameters, exact and epigrammatic, were aimed at lax and luxurious society, tyranny, criminal excesses, and the immorality of women." Reader's Adviser

878 Latin miscellany

Caesar, Julius, 100-44 B.C.

The Gallic War; with an English translation by H. J. Edwards. Harvard Univ. Press 1958 xxii, 616p il maps $21.50   **878**
1. Rome—History
ISBN 0-674-99080-3
"The Loeb classical library"
Caesar's account of his campaign (58-50 B.C.) to bring the province of Gaul (France) under his control

Horace

Satires, Epistles and Ars poetica; with an English translation by H. Rushton Fairlough. Harvard Univ. Press 1926 xxx, 508p $21.50   **878**
ISBN 0-674-99214-8
"The Loeb classical library"

Latin and English on opposite pages
Horace's Satires sketch boldly but good-humoredly the social life of his day. The Epistles are simple, friendly correspondence, in which we find the man Horace, without a trace of the moral teacher or censor. His "Art of poetry," a brief and apparently casual letter, has had great influence on modern literature

Martial

Epigrams; edited and translated by D.R. Shackleton Bailey. Harvard Univ. Press 1993 3v ea $21.50   **878**
1. Epigrams
ISBN 0-674-99555-4 (v1); 0-674-99556-2 (v2); 0-674-99529-5 (v3)   LC 92-8234
"Loeb classical library"
Latin and English on opposite pages
"Martial's twelve books of 'Epigrams' are written for the most part in elegiac couplets modelled on Ovid and Catullus. They show his acute observation of Roman life in the last third of the first century and were often brutally insulting or grossly obscene." Bookman's Manual
Includes bibliographical references

Suetonius Tranquillus, C., ca. 69-ca. 122

The twelve Caesars; [by] Gaius Suetonius Tranquillus; translated by Robert Graves; revised with an introduction by Michael Grant. Penguin Bks. 2003 363p maps pa $14   **878**
1. Emperors—Rome 2. Rome—History
ISBN 0-14-044921-3   LC 2003-267782
A reissue with new Chronology and updated further reading of the translation published 1957
"A detailed account of the life and times of the first twelve emperors from Caesar to Domitian." Reader's Ency. 4th edition
Includes bibliographical references

Tacitus, Cornelius

The complete works of Tacitus; translated from the Latin by Alfred John Church and William Jackson Brodribb; edited and with an introduction by Moses Hadas. Modern Lib. 1942 xxv, 773p il o.p.; McGraw-Hill paperback available $11.25   **878**
1. Rome—History
ISBN 0-07-553639-0 (pa)
Contains: The annals; The history; The life of Cnaeus Julius Agricola; Germany and its tribes; A dialogue on oratory

880.3 Classical Greek literature—Encyclopedias and dictionaries

The **Oxford** companion to classical literature; edited by M. C. Howatson. 2nd ed. Oxford Univ. Press 1989 615p il maps $65 **880.3**
1. Classical literature—Dictionaries
ISBN 0-19-866121-5   LC 88-27330
First published 1937 under the editorship of Sir Paul Harvey
This work "covers classical literature from the appearance of the Greeks, around 2200 B.C., to the close of the

The Oxford companion to classical literature—*Continued*

Athenian philosophy schools in A.D. 529. It includes articles on authors, major works, historical notables, mythological figures, and topics of literary significance. Short summaries of major works, chronologies, charts, and maps are special features." Nichols. Guide to Ref Books for Sch Media Cent. 4th edition

880.8   Classical Greek literature—Collections

The **Classical** Greek reader; edited by Kenneth J. Atchity; associate editor, Rosemary McKenna. Holt & Co. 1996 xxxiv, 442p il (Henry Holt reference book) o.p. paperback available $22.50   **880.8**
1. Greek literature—Collections 2. Greece—Civilization
ISBN 0-19-512303-4 (pa)   LC 96-10180
This reader provides excerpts from the works of classical Greek writers
"Across the centuries, ranging from the Homeric poets to Graeco-Roman writers of the third century A.D., we find ourselves in the company of physicians and storytellers, herbalists and romance writers—and women. Atchity is mining a tradition of inexhaustible riches: the voices we encounter here offer passage to the literary, artistic, social, political, religious, scientific and philosophical texts that underlie Western intellectual tradition." Smithsonian

The **Norton** book of classical literature; edited by Bernard Knox. Norton 1993 866p $29.95   **880.8**
1. Greek literature—Collections 2. Latin literature—Collections
ISBN 0-393-03426-7   LC 92-10378
"A comprehensive volume of more than 300 pieces of classical literature, primarily Greek but also some Roman." Booklist

880.9   Classical Greek literature—History and criticism

Hamilton, Edith, 1867-1963
The echo of Greece. Norton 1957 224p hardcover o.p. paperback available $12.95   **880.9**
1. Greek literature—History and criticism 2. Greece—Civilization
ISBN 0-393-00231-4 (pa)
An interpretive essay on the Greek way of life during the fourth century B.C. It deals particularly with the political philosophies of Greek teachers and leaders—Isocrates, Plato, Aristotle, Demosthenes, and Alexander the Great

The Greek way. Norton 1943 347p hardcover o.p. paperback available $12.95   **880.9**
1. Greek literature—History and criticism 2. Greece—Civilization
ISBN 0-393-31077-9 (pa)
Companion volume to The Roman way

First published 1930. Variant title: The great age of Greek literature
An account of writers and literary forms of the Periclean Age including discussions of Pindar, Aristophanes, Aeschylus, tragedy, Greek religion and philosophy

881.008   Classical Greek poetry—Collections

The **Oxford** book of classical verse in translation; edited by Adrian Poole and Jeremy Maule. Oxford University Press 1995 xlix, 606p $45   **881.008**
1. Classical poetry—Collections
ISBN 0-19-214209-7
A "collection of classical verse from Homer to Boethius. Translations, modern and older, are brought together in a rich blending of Greek and Latin writings. Some of the greatest poets in the English language—Dryden, Pope, Tennyson, Poe, Byron, Yeats, Browning, Houseman, Wilde, Shelley, and Pound are among the translators. They emphasize the debt English poetry owes to the classics." SLJ

882   Classical Greek dramatic poetry and drama

Aeschylus
The Oresteia   **882**
Hardcover and paperback editions available from various publishers
The only extant Greek dramatic trilogy. It includes Agamemnon, The libation bearers, and The Eumenides

Aristophanes
The complete plays of Aristophanes; edited and with an introduction by Moses Hadas. Bantam Bks. 1962 501p pa $5.95   **882**
ISBN 0-553-21343-1
"A Bantam classic"
Includes the following plays: Acharnians; Knights; Clouds; Wasps; Peace; Birds; Lysistrata; Thesmophoriazusae; Frogs; Ecclesiazusae; Plutus

Euripides, ca. 485-ca. 406 B.C.
Ten plays; translated by Moses Hadas and John McLean; with an introduction by Moses Hadas. Bantam Bks. 1981 c1960 358p pa $6.95   **882**
ISBN 0-553-21363-6
"A Bantam classic"
A reissue of the 1960 Bantam edition; first published 1936 by Dial Press
Contents: Alcestis; Medea; Hippolytus; Andromache; Ion; Trojan women; Electra; Iphigenia among the Taurians; The Bacchants; Iphigenia at Aulis

Sophocles
Antigone   **882**
Hardcover and paperback editions available from various publishers
Disaster follows the refusal of King Creon of Thebes to allow the burial of his nephew, whom he had declared a traitor. When the dead man's sister, Antigone, who is

Sophocles—*Continued*

engaged to Creon's son, defies the tyrant, she is condemned to death. Warned of the god's displeasure by the prophet Tiresias, Creon relents too late, for Antigone has already hanged herself. Her suicide is followed by those of Creon's son and his wife

The complete plays of Sophocles; translated by Sir Richard Claverhouse Jebb; edited with an introduction by Moses Hadas. Bantam Bks. 1982 c1967 261p pa $5.99 **882**

ISBN 0-553-21354-7

"A Bantam classic"

A reissue of the 1967 Bantam edition

Contents: Ajax; Electra; Oedipus the King; Antigone; Trachinian women; Philoctetes; Oedipus at Colonus

Oedipus the King **882**

Hardcover and paperback editions available from various publishers

This classical tragedy deals with the fulfillment of a prophecy as it is revealed that Oedipus has unwittingly killed his father, married his mother and brought the plague to Thebes. He blinds himself in horror and becomes an outcast

883 Classical Greek epic poetry and fiction

Finley, M. I. (Moses I.), 1912-1986

The world of Odysseus; introduction by Bernard Knox. New York Review of Bks. 2002 xxi, 205p maps (New York Review Books classics) pa $12.95 **883**

1. Greece—Civilization 2. Troy (Extinct city)

ISBN 1-59017-017-2   LC 2002-2882

A reissue of the title first published 1954 by Viking Press

The author attempts to present the reader with a picture of Greek society based on a close reading of the Iliad and Odyssey

Includes bibliographical references

Homer

The Iliad **883**

1. Trojan War—Poetry

Hardcover and paperback editions available from various publishers

A "Greek epic poem (8th century B.C.?) attributed to Homer. In twenty-four books of dactylic hexameter verse, it details the events of the few days near the end of the Trojan War, focusing on the withdrawal of Achilles from the contest and the disastrous effects of this act on the Greek campaign." Reader's Ency. 4th edition

The odyssey; a modern translation of Homer's classic tale; by R.L. Eickhoff. Forge 2001 512p $25.95 **883**

ISBN 0-312-86669-0   LC 2001-41819

"A Tom Doherty Associates book"

This version of the classic "is more a close but highly embroidered paraphrase than a prose translation. . . . Eickhoff's novelized *Odyssey* is both vigorous and readable, but it does not supersede the verse translations of Robert Fagles or Robert Fitzgerald." Libr J

884 Classical Greek lyric poetry

Pindar

The odes of Pindar **884**

Hardcover and paperback editions available from various publishers

The Odes (Epinicia) celebrated victories in the great national games, and were accompanied by music, which is lost to us. The fragments represent almost every kind of lyric poem

"Since Pindar's Epinicia are generally concerned with mythical subjects, reserving praise of the mortal victor for the end of the ode, his works are a fine source of legend." Reader's Ency. 4th edition

Sappho

If not, winter; fragments of Sappho; translated by Anne Carson. Knopf 2002 397p $27.50; pa $14 **884**

ISBN 0-375-41067-8; 0-375-72451-6 (pa)   LC 2001-50247

"Carson's translation follows Sappho's diction and form . . . closely and includes the Greek original on the facing page. Much of what survives of Sappho are fragments, often just a stray word, phrase, or even a few letters. Like many modern poets, Carson deploys these on the blank page, letting their suggestiveness fill the gaps and create whole lyrics in the imagination of the readers." Libr J

888 Classical Greek miscellany

Aristotle, 384-322 B.C.

The basic works of Aristotle; edited, and with an introduction by Richard McKeon. Random House 1941 xxxix, 1487p $49.95; pa $19.95 **888**

ISBN 0-394-41610-4; 0-375-75799-6 (pa)

Follows the Oxford translation of 1931

Contains entire texts of the following: Physica; De generatione et corruptione; De anima; Parva naturalia; Metaphysica; Ethica Nicomachea; Politica; De poetica

Some chapters have been omitted from the following included works: Organon; De caelo; Historia animalium; De partibus animalium; De generatione animalium; Rhetorica

Includes bibliographical references

Introduction to Aristotle; with a new general introduction and new introductions to the particular works, by Richard McKeon. 2nd ed rev and enl. University of Chicago Press 1974 c1973 lii, 759p $23 **888**

ISBN 0-226-56032-5

Also available in paperback from McGraw-Hill

First published 1947 by Modern Library

Contents: Analytics posteriora (Posterior analytics); Physica (Physics) the second of the eight books; De anima (On the soul); De partibus animalium (On the parts of animals) book I, chapter I; Metaphysica (Metaphysics) the first and twelfth of the fourteen books; Ethica Nicomachea (Nicomachean ethics); Politica (Politics) the first and third of the eight books; Poetica (Poetics); Rhetorica (Rhetoric) book I, chapters 1-4, book II, chapters 18-22

Plato

The dialogues of Plato; Apology, Crito, Phaedo, Symposium, Republic; Jowett translation edited and with introductory notes by J. D. Kaplan. Washington Sq. Press 1950 386p pa $5.99 **888**

ISBN 0-671-52524-7

The dialogues "chosen for this edition are the best-known of Plato's writings and also the most influential. They are valuable both as literature and as the major statements of his philosophy." Introduction

The portable Plato; edited with an introduction by Scott Buchanan. Viking 1948 696p hardcover o.p. paperback available $17 **888**

ISBN 0-14-015040-4 (pa)

"The Viking portable library"

"Protagoras, Symposium, Phaedo, and the Republic, complete, in the English translation of Benjamin Jowett." Title page

Includes bibliographical references

The republic; edited by G.R.F. Ferrari; translated by Tom Griffith. Cambridge Univ. Press 2000 xlviii, 382p (Cambridge texts in the history of political thought) $38; pa $11 **888**

1. Utopias 2. Political science
ISBN 0-521-48173-2; 0-521-48443-X (pa)
LC 00-24471

Griffith's "aim was to translate the Greek text as if it were a conversation, and he has succeeded admirably. The text does indeed flow like a conversation, with the entire back-and-forth interaction that such exchanges involve. . . . {He} has also written a very useful introduction that places the work in a historical context and provides a glossary that will help readers identify individuals and places mentioned in the work." Libr J

889 Modern Greek literature

Cavafy, Constantine P., 1863-1933

The complete poems of Cavafy; translated by Rae Dalven; with an introduction by W. H. Auden. Expanded ed. Harcourt Brace Jovanovich 1976 xxiv, 311p pa $17 **889**

ISBN 0-15-619820-7 LC 76-22804

"A Harvest book"

First published 1961

Contains translations of poems, chronologically arranged, which have never before appeared in book form in English or in Greek. Auden's introduction analyzes Cavafy's poetry

Includes bibliographical references

Elytês, Odysseus, 1911-1996

The collected poems of Odysseus Elytis; translated by Jeffrey Carson and Nikos Sarris; introduction and notes by Jeffrey Carson. Johns Hopkins Univ. Press 1997 xlii, 595p $56 **889**

ISBN 0-8018-4924-1 LC 96-44514

"The work of 1979 Nobel Prize winner Elytis (1911-96) has the quality of a cathedral or epic—vast in scope yet richly decorated. This excellent 'complete' collected edition (it omits unpublished poems) testifies to the bountiful, sincere nature of Elytis's voice as patriot and poet. . . . Containing informative annotations, a chronology, an autobiographical essay, and the author's Nobel address, this work is a valuable resource on international poetry." Libr J

Seferis, George, 1900-1971

Collected poems; translated, edited, and introduced by Edmund Keeley and Philip Sherrard. rev ed. Princeton Univ. Press 1995 296p (Lockert library of poetry in translation) hardcover o.p. paperback available $17.95 **889**

ISBN 0-691-01491-4 (pa) LC 92-10552

First published 1967

Nobel laurete Seferis' "verse is spare, hernetic, and characterized by a profound knowledge of Greek history and classical mythology and a deep understanding of Greece's past and its relevance to her present and future." Reader's Ency. 4th edition

Includes bibliographical references

891 East-Indo European literatures

Mahābhārata

Mahābhārata. **891**

Hardcover and paperback editions available from various publishers

"One of the two great epic poems of ancient India (the other being the 'Rāmāyana'), about eight times as long as the 'Iliad' and 'Odyssey' together. It is a great compendium, added to as late as AD 600, although it had very nearly acquired its present form by the 4th century. Covering an enormous range of topics, the *Mahābhārata*, with its famous interpolation, the 'Bhagavadgītā', has as its central theme the great war between the sons of two royal brothers, in a struggle for succession." Reader's Ency. 4th edition

Mahābhārata. Bhagavadgītā

The Bhagavad Gita **891**

Hardcover and paperback editions available from various publishers

"An eighteen-part discussion between the god Krishna, an avatar of Vishnu appearing as a charioteer, and Arjuna, a warrior about to enter battle, on the nature and meaning of life. Sometimes called the New Testament of Hinduism, it is an interpolation in the great Hindu epic the Mahābhārata." Reader's Ency. 4th edition

Narayan, R. K., 1906-2001

The Ramayana; a shortened modern prose version of the Indian epic: (suggested by the Tamil version of Kamban). Viking 1972 171p hardcover o.p. paperback available $11 **891**

ISBN 0-14-018700-6 (pa)

A retelling of Prince Rama's courtship of the fourteen-year-old Sita, their exile, Sita's abduction, the search, and the great battle with her abductor Ravana, involving a pantheon of gods, heroes, and evil spirits

Narayan "has not produced a scholarly translation but rather, by using his skills as a novelist, has given us a short and readable modern version." Libr J

Omar Khayyam

Rubáiyát of Omar Khayyám. **891**

Hardcover and paperback editions available from various publishers

"The Rubáiyát' (Quatrains) of Omar the Tentmaker, of Persia, is composed of a series of stanzas forming 'a medley of love and tavern songs, tinged with Sufi mysticism, and with the melancholy of Eastern fatalism.'" Dickinson. Best Books Ser

891.7   East Slavic literatures. Russian

Akhmatova, Anna Andreevna, 1889-1966

The complete poems of Anna Akhmatova; [by] Anna Akhmatova; translated by Judith Hemschemeyer; edited and with an introduction by Roberta Reeder. Zephyr Press (Somerville) 1990 c1989 2v il hardcover o.p. paperback available $29   **891.7**

ISBN 0-939010-27-5 (pa)   LC 88-51831

"Anna Akhmatova—the high priestess of Russian poetry—saw her husband shot, her son imprisoned twice by Stalin, her work banned in the 1930's and late 40's. . . . Sonorous, calm, deliberate in movement, her Russian has no English equivalent, but in this admirably restrained and accurate translation, sense and message strike with all the weight of the original." N Y Times Book Rev

The **Cambridge** history of Russian literature; edited by Charles A. Moser. rev ed. Cambridge Univ. Press 1992 709p hardcover o.p. paperback available $55   **891.7**

1. Russian literature—History and criticism
ISBN 0-521-42567-0 (pa)   LC 91-38275

This volume presents "a survey of Russian literature from the beginnings to this decade, in sufficient but not overwhelming detail.' Ten chapters by specialists elucidate this history from 988 to approximately 1980, with a lengthy bibliography at the end of the volume." Sheehy. Guide to Ref Books. 10th edition. suppl

Chekhov, Anton Pavlovich, 1860-1904

The plays of Anton Chekhov; a new translation by Paul Schmidt. HarperCollins Pubs. 1997 387p hardcover o.p. paperback available $14.95   **891.7**

ISBN 0-06-092875-1 (pa)   LC 96-42456

Available in hardcover from P. Smith

Contents: Swan song; The bear; The proposal; Ivanov; The seagull; A reluctant tragic hero; The wedding reception; The festivities; Uncle Vanya; Three sisters; The dangers of tobacco; The cherry orchard

The **portable** Chekhov; edited and with an introduction by Avrahm Yarmolinsky. Viking 1947 631p hardcover o.p. paperback available $17   **891.7**

ISBN 0-14-015035-8 (pa)

"The Viking portable Library"

This collection contains "two plays, 'The Cherry Orchard' and 'The Boor,' 28 short stories and selections from Chekhov's letters." Publ Wkly

Malcolm, Janet

Reading Chekhov; a critical journey. Random House 2001 209p $23.95   **891.7**

1. Chekhov, Anton Pavlovich, 1860-1904
ISBN 0-375-50668-3   LC 2001-19585

"The author's pilgrimage to Chekhov's Russia—Moscow, St. Petersburg, the gardens of his villa in Yalta—is a reunion with this most reticent of literary fathers. Malcolm analyzes the transformations that Chekhov grants his redeemable roués and guileless heroines, and illuminates the hidden surreality and waywardness of his realism." New Yorker

Nabokov, Vladimir Vladimirovich, 1899-1977

Lectures on Russian literature; edited with an introduction by Fredson Bowers. Harcourt Brace Jovanovich 1981 324p il hardcover o.p. paperback available $16   **891.7**

1. Russian literature—History and criticism
ISBN 0-15-602776-3 (pa)

Analyzed in Essay and general literature index

Companion volume Lectures on literature

This book is "derived from notes Nabokov made for his literature classes at Wellesley and Cornell. Included are chapters on Gogol, Turgenev, Dostoevsky, Tolstoy, Chekhov, and Gorki, as well as several miscellaneous essays on censorship and the art of translation." Libr J

Reference guide to Russian literature; editor, Neil Cornwell; associate editor, Nicole Christian. Fitzroy Dearborn Pubs. 1998 xl, 972p $160   **891.7**

1. Russian literature—Dictionaries 2. Russian literature—Bio-bibliography
ISBN 1-88496-410-9   LC 97-169924

A guide to approximately 270 writers and their works "author entries include telegraphic biographical sketches, detailed bibliographies of Russian- and English-language sources and critical studies, and, in many cases, 1000-word entries for specific novels, plays, and stories. There are alphabetical and chronological lists, 13 introductory essays on various aspects of Russian literature, and a Russian/English title index." Libr J

Terras, Victor

A history of Russian literature. Yale Univ. Press 1991 654p hardcover o.p. paperback available $35   **891.7**

1. Russian literature—History and criticism
ISBN 0-300-05934-5 (pa)   LC 91-13337

This history of Russian literature begins with a chapter on folklore and then presents a chronological account covering Old Russian literature (eleventh to sixteenth centuries); the seventeenth century; the eighteenth century; the Romantic period; the age of the novel; the Silver Age, and the Soviet period

"The book's minor shortcomings are overshadowed by its numerous merits; its accuracy, keenness of observation, subtle comments, vivid quotations, erudition. . . . Almost every page of the book invites one to read and re-read Russian literature." Times Lit Suppl

Includes bibliographical references

TŠvetaeva, Marina Ivanovna, 1892-1941

Selected poems [of] Marina Tsvetayeva; translated by Elaine Feinstein, with literal versions provided by Angela Livingstone [et al.] rev and enl ed. Oxford Univ. Press 1981 108p o.p.; Penguin Bks. paperback available $15 **891.7**

ISBN 0-14-018759-6 (pa)   LC 80-41681

Also available another edition translated by David McDuff from Bloodaxe Bks.

This translation first published 1971

"As a poet Tsvetayeva impresses with her psychic energy, she is on fire with poetry, and nothing is put in perspective, everything is immediate, emotional in the best sense." N Y Times Book Rev

Includes bibliographical references

Turgenev, Ivan Sergeevich, 1818-1883

A month in the country; a comedy in five acts; by Ivan Turgenev; translated and introduced by Isaiah Berlin. Viking 1982 127p **891.7**

LC 81-52222

Available in paperback from Dramatists Play Service

Characters: 7 men, 5 women, 1 boy. 5 acts. First produced at the Maly Theatre, Moscow, January 13, 1872

Month spent by young German tutor on 19th century Russian estate sparks rivalry between bored wife and her young ward

891.8   Slavic (Slavonic) literatures

Čapek, Karel, 1890-1938

R.U.R. and The insect play; by the Brothers Čapek. Oxford Univ. Press 1961 179p pa $15.95 **891.8**

ISBN 0-19-281010-3

Translated from the Czech by Paul Selver

"R.U.R." is a fantasy in which robots revolt against their human masters. In "The insect play," a dying tramp dreams about insect life

Miłosz, Czesław

The collected poems, 1931-1987. Ecco Press 1988 511p hardcover o.p. paperback available $20 **891.8**

ISBN 0-88001-174-2 (pa)   LC 87-24479

"Nobel Prize winner Milosz here includes most works from his four books of poetry available in English, plus 50 pages of new poems and numerous older poems never before translated, yet excludes poems not translated to his satisfaction." Libr J

"Milosz is a poet of memory, a witness; his real heroes are the dead to whom his poems make reparation. . . . Like other major witnesses of this century—Primo Levi, Zbigniew Herbert—Milosz is a moralist: his work does not pronounce or make judgments; it simply takes as its criterion human decency—disinterested, modes, and not willingly misled." N Y Rev Books

The history of Polish literature. 2nd ed. University of Calif. Press 1983 583p il hardcover o.p. paperback available $21.95 **891.8**

1. Polish literature—History and criticism

ISBN 0-520-04477-0 (pa)   LC 82-20227

"This edition reproduces the original hardcover edition published by The Macmillan Company and Collier Macmillan Ltd., London, in 1969. The book was completed a couple of years earlier, so the material it covered did not extend beyond the middle 1960s. In order to give the reader some idea of later developments in contemporary Polish literature, a brief epilogue has been added to this edition. The bibliography has also been considerably updated." Preface

Milosz's ABCs; translated from the Polish by Madeline G. Levine. Farrar, Straus & Giroux 2001 313p hardcover o.p. paperback avaialble $13 **891.8**

ISBN 0-374-52795-4 (pa)   LC 00-42176

"The short prose entries in this quiet book take note of some of the people and places and ideas that contributed to the making of Milosz. The subjects of his sketches range from Alchemy and Curiosity to Rimbaud and Whitman, from childhood friends to Polish intellectuals little known in the West. But what could have been no more than a light memory work becomes almost a registry of gratitude: a meditation on the obligations of having lived a life and the responsibilities inherent in its particulars." New Yorker

Includes bibliographical references

New and collected poems 1931-2001. HarperCollins Pubs. 2001 xxi, 776p $45; pa $19.95 **891.8**

ISBN 0-06-019667-X; 0-06-051448-5 (pa)

LC 2001-50123

"Milosz has stated repeatedly in his poems his belief in the power of language to rescue from the void all he has seen and all the people he has known in a long life. But beneath this belief, it now appears, was the deeper belief that none of this was possible because of the inadequacy of language to capture reality, though he maintains this always has to be the poet's goal. . . . Throughout his career and throughout this vast collection, Milosz argues with himself about his poetics." N Y Times Book Rev

A roadside dog. Farrar, Straus & Giroux 1998 208p hardcover o.p. paperback available $13 **891.8**

ISBN 0-374-52623-0 (pa)   LC 98-14026

This "book is a collection of reflections, a few dreams, some poems, and . . . 'Subjects to Let'—ideas and plots that Milosz, at 87, feels he will never develop and presents for others to flesh out. Two themes recur in many of these little writings: the opposition of the inner life of the mind and emotions and the outer life of the body and communication; and the occasionally paradoxical nature of personality." Booklist

"Even if this book turns out to have less linguistic sticking power than earlier collections, Milosz makes a wise, wryly humane fin de siècle companion." Publ Wkly

Miłosz, Czesław—*Continued*
To begin where I am; selected essays; edited and with an introduction by Bogdana Carpenter and Madeline G. Levine. Farrar, Straus & Giroux 2001 462p hardcover o.p. paperback available $15 **891.8**
ISBN 0-374-52859-4 (pa)   LC 2001-33356
Analyzed in Essay and general literature index
A retrospective of Milosz's "prose works, in which he weaves autobiography and portraits of people, famous and otherwise, who have influenced him into graceful and provocative musings on time, history, religion, science, and art." Booklist

Szymborska, Wisława, 1923-
Poems, new and collected, 1957-1997; translated from the Polish by Stanisław Barańczak and Clare Cavanagh. Harcourt Brace & Co. 1998 273p $27; pa $17 **891.8**
ISBN 0-15-100353-X; 0-15-601146-8 (pa)
LC 97-32277
This career-spanning collection by the 1996 Nobel Prize winner includes her Nobel lecture
Szymborska's "work is ultimately wisdom literature, written in a first person that expresses a universal humanity that American poets—lockstep individualists all—haven't dared essay since early in this century." Booklist

View with a grain of sand; selected poems; translated from the Polish by Stanisław Barańczak and Clare Cavanagh. Harcourt Brace & Co. 1995 214p $20; pa $14 **891.8**
ISBN 0-15-100153-7; 0-15-600216-7 (pa)
LC 94-36112
This collection by Poland's Nobel laureate "selects work from seven volumes of poetry that span nearly 40 years. Her eye is sharp and her wit wonderfully wicked. . . . It is about time more readers found the poetry of Szymborska, and this collection gives them the opportunity." Libr J

Zagajewski, Adam, 1945-
Mysticism for beginners; translated from the Polish by Clare Cavanagh. Farrar, Straus & Giroux 1997 71p hardcover o.p. paperback available $12 **891.8**
ISBN 0-374-52687-7 (pa)   LC 97-9097
"Contemplative and grimly ironic, with a metaphysical sense of metaphor, Zagajewski is considered the leading poet of a generation of postwar Polish writers, and these heart-staggering poems should only widen his reputation." New Yorker

Without end; new and selected poems; translations by Clare Cavanagh [et al.] Farrar, Straus & Giroux 2002 285p $30; pa $15
891.8
ISBN 0-374-22096-4; 0-374-52861-6 (pa)
LC 2001-40252
"Zagajewski's poetic evolution is clearly charted in 'Without End,' a new anthology of his work that is made up of his three English-language collections—'Tremor' (1985), 'Canvas' (1991) and 'Mysticism for Beginners' (1997)—as well as his most recent work and new translations of some early poems. . . . Zagajewski's poems pull us from whatever routine threatens to dull our senses, from whatever might lull us into mere existence. This is an astonishing book." N Y Times Book Rev

892 Afro-Asiatic literatures. Semitic literatures

Amichai, Yehuda
Open closed open; poems; translated from the Hebrew by Chana Bloch and Chana Kronfeld. Harcourt Brace & Co. 2000 184p $25 **892**
ISBN 0-15-100378-5   LC 00-23537
Original Hebrew edition, 1998
"Constructing a lineage in which to place himself, Amichai begins these verses of personal and cultural history with a stone from a destroyed Jewish graveyard; and moves on to enact the story of David, recall poems by Ibn Ezra, and even consider Jesus as an instance of 'Jewish Travel.' Within this vast context, the 25 longish poems of the collection, originally written in Hebrew, offer everyday acts of alternately joyous and sober reverence for God." Publ Wkly
Amichai "writes with the casual wisdom and generous humor of a master." Booklist

Poems of Jerusalem; and, Love poems; a bilingual edition. Sheep Meadow Press 1992 265p pa $16.95 **892**
1. Love poetry 2. Jerusalem—Poetry
ISBN 1-87881-819-8   LC 92-31558
Poems of Jerusalem first published 1988 by Perennial Lib.; Love poems first published 1981 by Harper & Row
This work is "actually drawn from eight previous works and boasts an even larger array of translators (including Stephen Mitchell, David Rosenberg, Ted Hughes, and the poet himself). The thematic arrangement deftly emphasizes the Israeli poet's constant preoccupation with both Jerusalem and love." Libr J

The selected poetry of Yehuda Amichai; edited and translated from the Hebrew by Chana Bloch and Stephen Mitchell. newly rev & expanded ed. University of Calif. Press 1996 195p pa $16.95 **892**
ISBN 0-520-20538-3   LC 96-18580
First published 1986
"Although much of Amichai's poetry focuses on war, he is able to describe its horrors by maintaining a clear distance between himself and his subject. The result is a finely controlled emotional pitch that allows the poet to convey his sense of pain and outrage without pathos or sentimentality. He writes colloquially, in language that is always commensurate with emotional experience." Reader's Ency. 4th edition

Anthology of modern Palestinian literature; edited and introduced by Salma Khadra Jayyusi. Columbia Univ. Press 1992 xxxiii, 744p $65; pa $29 **892**
1. Arabic literature—Collections
ISBN 0-231-07508-1; 0-231-07509-X (pa)
LC 92-5189
"Presented here are translations of poems, stories, and excerpts from novels, as well as works by Palestinian poets who write in English. Also included are personal narratives by Palestinian writers depicting the varied aspects of Palestinian life from the turn of the century to the present. . . . Biographical sketches introduce the authors, and a chronology of modern Palestinian history provides background for some of the events and places referred to

Anthology of modern Palestinian literature—*Continued*

in the selections. The introduction by the editor provides a concise but comprehensive political history of Palestinian literature during the twentieth century." Publisher's note

Includes bibliographical references

Encyclopedia of Arabic literature; edited by Julie Scott Meisami and Paul Starkey. Routledge 1998 2v set $345   **892**

1. Arabic literature—Dictionaries 2. Arabic literature—Bio-bibliography

ISBN 0-415-06808-8   LC 96-47907

"This encyclopedia contains generally brief biographical articles on writers . . . as well as longer ones on literary genres, prosody, writing techniques, and related topics such as censorship and literary patronage. A brief bibliography of primary sources and secondary material follows each article. The encyclopedia has a wide scope, covering Arabic writing (and the oral tradition, too) from ancient and pre-Islamic times to the present and including not only Muslim writers but Christians, Jews, and others who made significant contributions to Arabic literature." Libr J

Gilgamesh

Gilgamesh   **892**

Hardcover and paperback editions available from various publishers

Variant title: The epic of Gilgamesh

"A Babylonian poem. One of the oldest and most important major epics in literature, it was first discovered on clay tablets in the library of 'Assur-Bani-Pal' (668-626 BC). . . . The epic includes stories, originally separate, of 'Gilgamesh', a legendary king of Sumerian origin; 'Enkidu', a sort of primeval man; Utnapishtim, the Babylonian 'Noah'; and several other tales." Reader's Ency. 4th edition

Kovner, Abba, 1918-1987

Sloan Kettering; poems; translated from the Hebrew by Eddie Levenston; foreword by Leon Wieseltier. Schocken Bks. 2002 134p $17; pa $120   **892**

ISBN 0-8052-4198-1; 0-8052-1145-4 (pa)

LC 2002-70692

"Kovner, an Israeli writer and resistance fighter, led the famous Vilna ghetto uprising in Lithuania during the Second World War, in these plainspoken poems he writes about his hospitalization for cancer, which killed him in 1987." New Yorker

Night and horses and the desert; an anthology of classical Arabic literature. Overlook Press 2000 462p o.p.; Anchor Bks. paperback available $16   **892**

1. Arabic literature—Collections 2. Arabic literature—History and criticism

ISBN 0-385-72155-2 (pa)   LC 00-42738

This "anthology presents a wide range of classical Arabic poetry and prose, covering the fifth to the 16th centuries from Afghanistan to Andalusia, Spain." Libr J

"The chapter on the Qur'an is perhaps the most essential as it examines just how vital the dogma of Islam has been for the Arabic understanding of culture and art. . . . This persuasive work will surely fill in the gap in the study of Arabic literature in this country." Publ Wkly

Includes bibliographical references

895.1   Chinese literature

Anthology of Chinese literature; compiled and edited by Cyril Birch. Grove Weidenfeld 1987 2v   **895.1**

1. Chinese literature—Collections

"UNESCO collection of representative works: Chinese series"

Reprint of the 1965-1972 edition

Contents: {v1} From early times to the 14th century; Donald Keene, associate editor (ISBN 0-8021-5038-1); v2 From the 14th century to the present day (ISBN 0-8021-5090-X)

This "set is likely to remain for years to come the best introductory sampler to the literature of China, a model of the anthologizer's art." Choice

Includes bibliographical references

An **Anthology** of Chinese literature: beginnings to 1911; edited and translated by Stephen Owen. Norton 1996 xlviii, 1212p hardcover o.p. paperback available $59.65   **895.1**

1. Chinese literature—Collections

ISBN 0-393-97106-6 (pa)   LC 95-11409

"In a book that moves roughly chronologically through the tradition, Owen gathers texts according to genres, themes, forms, and other groupings to show the way essential texts build off each other and how the tradition echoes itself. Included are a range of forms . . . presented . . . [with] commentary to provide a . . . view of the interplay between Chinese literature, culture, and history." Publisher's note

Includes bibliographical references

Anthology of modern Chinese poetry; edited and translated by Michelle Yeh. Yale Univ. Press 1993 245p hardcover o.p. paperback available $19   **895.1**

1. Chinese poetry—Collections

ISBN 0-300-05947-7 (pa)   LC 92-16322

Published with assistance from Mary Cady Tew Memorial Fund

"Arranged chronologically, this selection of twentieth-century poetry from China and Taiwan offers a few poems by each of 67 poets born between 1891 and 1963. Its scope is enormous, its range impressive. Editor Yeh's translations are accessible and fluid; her introduction and notes are helpful without being overbearingly scholarly." Booklist

Includes bibliographical references

The **Columbia** book of Chinese poetry; from early times to the thirteenth century; translated and edited by Burton Watson. Columbia Univ. Press 1984 385p il (Translations from the Oriental classics) $69; pa $27   **895.1**

1. Chinese poetry—Collections

ISBN 0-231-05682-6; 0-231-05683-4 (pa)

LC 83-26182

This anthology's "arrangement is historical, beginning with selections from a first millenium BC collection of Chinese verse (the Shih ching), and ending with tz'u lyrics from the Sung period (AD 960-1279). The 12 selections [are] each prefaced with a two- or three-page introduction." Choice

Includes bibliographical references

The **Columbia** history of Chinese literature; Victor H. Mair, editor. Columbia Univ. Press 2001 xx, 1342p $78 **895.1**
1. Chinese literature—History and criticism
ISBN 0-231-10984-9 LC 2001-28236
This "history explores a wide range of Chinese literature, from the classics to humor to folk tales to oral traditions, and moves from ancient times to the end of the 20th century. . . . Mair has overseen a host of excellent scholars writing on a vast subject." Libr J
Includes bibliographical references

One hundred poems from the Chinese; [edited and translated] by Kenneth Rexroth. New Directions 1956 159p hardcover o.p. paperback available $10.95 **895.1**
1. Chinese poetry—Collections
ISBN 0-8112-0180-5 (pa)
"Nine poets, who lived centuries ago, speak with the poignancy of understatement of unchanging things; the brevity of life, the richness of friendship, the beauties of nature, the inevitability of old age and death." Booklist
Includes bibliographical references

The **Shorter** Columbia anthology of traditional Chinese literature; Victor H. Mair, editor. Columbia Univ. Press 2000 xxx, 741p map (Translations from the Asian classics) $65; pa $26 **895.1**
1. Chinese literature—Collections
ISBN 0-231-11998-4; 0-231-11999-2 (pa)
LC 00-35878
Abridged version of Columbia anthology of traditional Chinese literature, published 1994
This "abridged volume, which, like the original includes selections of Chinese literature from the beginnings to 1919 . . . retains the characteristics of the original in that it is arranged according to genre rather than chronology and interprets 'literature' very broadly to include not just literary fiction, poetry, and drama, but folk and popular literature, lyrics and arias, elegies and rhapsodies, biographies, autobiographies and memoirs, letters, criticism and theory, and travelogues and jokes. It also contains fresh translations by newer voices in the field." Publisher's note
Includes bibliographical references

895.6 Japanese literature

Keene, Donald, 1922-
The pleasures of Japanese literature. Columbia Univ. Press 1988 133p il (Companion to Asian studies) $60; pa $19.50 **895.6**
1. Japanese literature—History and criticism
ISBN 0-231-06736-4; 0-231-06737-2 (pa)
LC 88-18069
The author discusses Japanese aesthetics, poetry, fiction and drama, focusing on works of the premodern period
"If your library has no other introduction to the Japanese classics, nor any need for another, this is the one it ought to include." Booklist
Includes bibliographical references

Seeds in the heart; Japanese literature from earliest times to the late sixteenth century. Holt & Co. 1993 1265p o.p.; Columbia Univ. Press paperback available $37 **895.6**
1. Japanese literature—History and criticism
ISBN 0-231-11441-9 (pa) LC 93-1082
This volume completes the author's history of Japanese literature begun with: World within walls (1977) and Dawn to the West (1984)
"The first half of 'Seeds in the Heart' encompasses everything from the myths, legends, songs and poems of the eighth-century 'Kojiki' ('Record of Ancient Matters') and 'Manyoshu,' a collection of 4,500 poems, to the 'The Tale of Genji' and later works of fiction. . . . During Japan's middle ages (1185-1600), Buddhism and popular (rather than aristocratic) forms of storytelling and theater generated a repertory of characters and genres that would eventually form the country's first broadly based, national culture. The literature of these centuries has rarely attracted the scholarly attention paid to the earlier 'high' classical tradition. So Mr. Keene's attention to this period makes the second half of 'Seeds in the Heart' especially valuable." N Y Times Book Rev
Includes bibliographical references

Modern Japanese literature; an anthology; compiled and edited by Donald Keene. Grove Press 1960 c1956 440p hardcover o.p. paperback available $15.95 **895.6**
1. Japanese literature—Collections
ISBN 0-8021-5095-0 (pa)
"The selections give a representative sampling of the poetry, prose, and drama from the 1870's through the 1940's. Short enlightening notes on the writers or background for the text are added unobtrusively." Booklist

One hundred poems from the Japanese; [edited and translated] by Kenneth Rexroth. New Directions 1956 143p hardcover o.p. paperback available $10.95 **895.6**
1. Japanese poetry—Collections
ISBN 0-8112-0181-3 (pa)
Also available: One hundred more poems from the Japanese pa $8.95 (ISBN 0-8112-0619-X)
A bilingual collection of poems drawn chiefly from the traditional Manyōshu, Kokinshū, and Hyakunin Isshu collections and also containing examples of haiku and other later forms. The translator's introduction provides background information on the history and nature of Japanese poetry
Includes bibliographical references

Waley, Arthur, 1889-1966
The Nō plays of Japan; with letters by Oswald Sickert. Grove Press 1957 319p o.p.; Dover Publs. paperback available $12.95 **895.6**
1. Nō plays
ISBN 0-486-40156-1 (pa)
"An Evergreen book"
First published 1921 in the United Kingdom; first United States edition published 1922 by Knopf
Contains translation of 20 Nō plays and summaries of 16 more. In his introduction Mr. Waley gives a brief history of the Nō drama, its origin, the text of the plays, and the chief playwrights. He also tells about the stage settings, costumes and properties used in the production of these plays. The greatest representation is given to the works of Seami and Zenchiku Ujinobu
Includes bibliographical references

896   African literatures

African writers; C. Brian Cox, editor.
Scribner 1997 2v set $250   **896**
1. African literature—Bio-bibliography 2. African literature—Dictionaries
ISBN 0-684-19651-4   LC 96-16128

"Sixty-five authors from throughout the African continent are included. The entries, which are written by an impressive array of contributors, generally provide a solid overview of the author's life and works and include a bibliography of primary and secondary sources." Libr J

Heinemann book of African women's poetry; edited by Stella Chipasula and Frank Chipasula. Heinemann (Portsmouth) 1995 230p pa $11.95   **896**
1. African poetry—Collections 2. Women poets
ISBN 0-435-90680-1

The editors "have selected work by women poets from 18 African countries, from Algeria to Senegal, Mauritius, and Zimbabwe. This broad geographical and cultural spectrum highlights Africa's considerable diversity while, simultaneously, affirming the shared experiences and perspectives of African women writers." Booklist

The **New** African poetry; an anthology; edited by Tanure Ojaide, Tijan M. Sallah. Lynne Rienner Pubs. 1999 253p hardcover o.p. paperback available $17.95   **896**
1. African poetry—Collections
ISBN 0-89410-891-3 (pa)   LC 99-29889

"A Three continents book"

In this anthology the editors "group poets by region. . . . Most of these 62 well-educated postcolonial poets more willingly embrace the ancestral 'oratory' tradition of the African continent than poets with a Western literary orientation of the era of Leopold Senghor and Wole Soyinka. Instead of anti-colonialism, these poets focus on women's roles, rural life, and the need for creativity despite economic hardships. Realistic criticism of patriarchies and traditional taboos arises from a strong attachment to homeland. Overall, regional diversity seems to have replaced defensiveness of Pan-African unity." Libr J

The **Penguin** book of modern African poetry; edited by Gerald Moore and Ulli Beier. 4th ed. Penguin Bks. 1999 xxvi, 448p pa $15.95   **896**
1. African poetry—Collections
ISBN 0-14-118100-1

First published 1963 in the United Kingdom with title: Modern poetry from Africa

"The poems are organized by country. . . . The poets are organized by age, from oldest to youngest. . . . Their writing has an urgency that derives from the sense, . . . that there is much to be done and all of it important." N Y Times Book Rev [review of 1988 edition]

Includes bibliographical references

897   North American native literatures

American Indian literature; an anthology; edited and with an introduction by Alan R. Velie. rev ed. University of Okla. Press 1991 373p il hardcover o.p. paperback available $27.95   **897**
1. Native American literature 2. American literature—Native American authors—Collections
ISBN 0-8061-2345-1 (pa)   LC 90-50700

First published 1979

An illustrated anthology of Native American tales, songs, memoirs, oratory, poetry and fiction. The editor provides critical introductions to each section

Includes bibliographical references

Coltelli, Laura, 1941-
Winged words: American Indian writers speak; {reported by} Laura Coltelli. University of Neb. Press 1990 211p il (American Indian lives) hardcover o.p. paperback available $9.95   **897**
1. American literature—Native American authors
ISBN 0-8032-6351-1 (pa)   LC 89-39323

A compilation of interviews with Louise Erdrich, N. Scott Momaday, James Welch and eight other Native American writers

"Coltelli's questions probe the writers' sources of inspiration, methods of composition, and perceptions of their own and their works' relationship to tribal culture, among other broad areas. But it's the questions Coltelli has tailored to each individual that hit pay dirt and result in some illuminating moments." Booklist

Includes bibliographical references

The **Portable** North American Indian reader; edited and with an introduction by Frederick W. Turner III. Viking 1974 628 hardcover o.p. paperback available $17   **897**
1. Native American literature 2. American literature—Native American authors—Collections
ISBN 0-14-015077-3 (pa)

"The Viking portable library"

This introduction to the traditions and history of the North American Indian includes: myths, tales, poetry, oratory, and autobiography from the Iroquois, Cherokee, Winnebago, Sioux, and many other tribes

Includes bibliographical references

900 GEOGRAPHY & HISTORY

901 History—Philosophy and theory

Berlin, Sir Isaiah
The sense of reality; studies in ideas and their history; edited by Henry Hardy; with an introduction by Patrick Gardiner. Farrar, Straus & Giroux 1997 xx, 278p hardcover o.p. paperback available $13   **901**
1. History—Philosophy
ISBN 0-374-52569-2 (pa)   LC 96-39829
Analyzed in Essay and general literature index
First published 1996 in the United Kingdom
Berlin maintains that "the great goods of human life are diverse and conflicting. . . . Values like self-realization and social cohesion, economic progress and settled communities cannot always be made compatible. Sometimes we must choose between them. In the nine seminal essays collected in 'The Sense of Reality' ranging over such diverse subjects as the Romantic movement, Marxism, Kant's influence on nationalism and the thought of Rabindranath Tagore, Berlin argues with rare wisdom and passion that every such choice entails a loss." N Y Times Book Rev
Includes bibliographical references

Gaddis, John Lewis
The landscape of history; how historians map the past. Oxford Univ. Press 2002 192p il $25   **901**
1. History—Philosophy
ISBN 0-19-506652-9   LC 2002-10392
This book began as a series of lectures the author gave as a visiting professor at Oxford University. It addresses questions about the philosophy and methodology of the historian
"Mr. Gaddis's learned and graceful reflections . . . are deeply humane, propelled by the conviction that only by sustaining a historical consciousness can we know where we should want to go. They will also never allow either the reader of history or the writer of it to think about the past in quite the same way again." N Y Times (Late N Y Ed)
Includes bibliographical references

Gould, Stephen Jay, 1941-2002
Questioning the millennium; a rationalist's guide to a precisely arbitrary countdown. Rev ed. Harmony Bks. 1999 221p il $17.95   **901**
1. Millennium 2. Calendars—Social aspects
ISBN 0-609-60541-0
First published 1997
"New preface for 2000." Jacket
In this work, "Gould explores the evolution and anomalies of our present-day calendar and offers [a] . . . survey of millennial, apocalyptic crazes throughout history." Publ Wkly
"Gould in conclusion says that he has 'always and dearly loved calendrical questions because they display all our foibles in revealing miniature'—our foible, that is, of looking to nature for anthropocentric order and, not finding it there, seeking to impose it. Gould's ability to empathize with failed science, to retrace its awkward but earnest steps, is perhaps his outstanding quality as an essayist." New Yorker

Hobsbawm, E. J. (Eric J.), 1917-
On history. New Press (NY) 1997 305p $25; pa $15.95   **901**
1. Historiography
ISBN 1-56584-393-2; 1-56584-468-8 (pa)
"In these collected pieces—articles, lectures and reviews—Eric Hobsbawm surveys the writings of modern historians with the magisterial gaze of a man who has seen both the rise of Hitler and the fall of Communism. He notes how the discipline has changed in the last century: how social history and economic history have come of age, how modern historians speak of change and forces where Victorians spoke of ideas and progress. He rejects postmodernist claims that history can be freely revised because all facts are merely intellectual constructions." N Y Times Book Rev

Spengler, Oswald, 1880-1936
The decline of the West. new rev ed. Knopf 1945 2v v1 $45; v2 $50   **901**
1. History—Philosophy 2. Civilization—History
Also available from Kessinger Pub. and in an abridged paperback edition from Oxford Univ. Press
First published 1926-1928
Translated from the German by C. F. Atkinson
Contents: v1 Form and actuality (ISBN 0-394-42179-5); v2 Perspectives of world-history (ISBN 0-394-42176-0)
This work "reflects the pessimistic atmosphere in Germany after World War I. Spengler maintained that history has a natural development, in which every culture is a distinct organic form that grows, matures, and decays." Reader's Ency. 4th edition

902 History—Miscellany. Chronologies

Aron, Paul, 1956-
Unsolved mysteries of history; an eye-opening investigation into the most baffling events of all time. Wiley 2000 225p il hardcover o.p. paperback available $15.95   **902**
1. History—Miscellanea 2. Curiosities and wonders
ISBN 0-471-44257-7 (pa)   LC 00-43463
"Weighs conflicting views on the issues involved in answering such chapter-entitling queries as 'Who Was King Arthur?' or 'Did Jesus Die on the Cross?' or 'Was Gorbachev Part of the August Coup?' In most cases, the answer Aron arrives at is a suitable 'nobody knows for sure,' but the brief summaries of the issues and the brisk examinations of competing claims and theories about them afford readers more information and insight about some delicious historical riddles." Booklist
Includes bibliographical references

Grun, Bernard, 1901-1972
The timetables of history; a horizontal linkage of people and events. new 3rd rev ed. Simon & Schuster 1991 724p hardcover o.p. paperback available $22   **902**
1. Historical chronology
ISBN 0-671-74271-X (pa)   LC 92-100939
"A Touchstone book"
First published 1975
Based on Werner Stein's Kulturfahrplan

Grun, Bernard, 1901-1972—*Continued*

"These clearly laid-out timetales relate significant events occuring in various fields of endeavor to their historical and political milieu. Daily life as well as science, literature, religion, the arts, and music are charted in a two-page format that facilitates an easy comparison. More recent times are covered in greater detail." Ref Sources for Small & Medium-sized Libr. 6th edition

Shenkman, Richard

Legends, lies & cherished myths of world history; illustrations by George J. McKeon. HarperCollins Pubs. 1993 301p il hardcover o.p. paperback available $14   **902**
 1. History—Miscellanea
 ISBN 0-06-092255-9 (pa)   LC 92-56210
 The author "offers what he says is the truth behind popular misconceptions on events such as the Trojan War (there was none), the Spanish Inquisition (they weren't so bad), and the Black Hole of Calcutta (he doesn't know whether to believe the English or the Indians), as well as on people such as Napoleon (he really wasn't short, just average)." Book Rep
 Includes bibliographical references

The **Timetables** of American history; Laurence Urdang, editor. Simon & Schuster il pa $23   **902**
 1. Historical chronology
 "A Touchstone book"
 First published 1982. (2001 edition) Periodically revised
 Presents information chronologically in tabular form. Each double-page spread has columns for history and politics, the arts, science and technology, and miscellaneous

The **Wilson** calendar of world history; edited by John Paxton and Edward W. Knappman; contributors: Rodney Carlisle [et al.] Wilson, H.W. 1999 460p il $100   **902**
 1. Historical chronology 2. Calendars
 ISBN 0-8242-0937-0   LC 98-50998
 "A New England Publishing Associates book"
 "Based on S.H. Steinberg's Historical table." Title page
 This successor to Steinberg's chronology reports on 25,000 historical events and includes expanded coverage of the arts and sciences as well as events in Latin America, Asia, and Africa. Includes index for people, places, events, concepts, inventions, discoveries, and titles of works
 Includes bibliographical references

903   History—Encyclopedias and dictionaries

Encyclopedia of world history. Facts on File 2000 524p il maps $93.50   **903**
 1. World history—Encyclopedias 2. History—Outlines, syllabi, etc.
 ISBN 0-8160-4249-7   LC 00-34721
 Editorial Board: Patrick K. O'Brien
 "The 6,500 entries are alphabetical with cross-references and include colored maps, paintings, photographs, charts, and tables. Difficult-to-find topics, such as regions of Russia and the Balkans, Africa, and Oceania, are covered through the year 2000. The article on former President Bill Clinton discusses his full term. Interesting quotes from famous people accompany the articles, usually with illustrations." Voice Youth Advocates

904   Collected accounts of events

Davis, Lee Allyn

Man-made catastrophes; [by] Lee Davis. rev ed. Facts on File 2002 402p il $60   **904**
 1. Disasters
 ISBN 0-8160-4418-X   LC 2001-54324
 "Facts on File science library"
 First published 1993
 This describes man-made disasters "from the burning of Babylon in 538B.C. to the 2001 terrorist attack on the World Trade Center in New York City. . . . [The entries] are organized by disaster type: air crashes, civil unrest and terrorism, explosions, maritime disasters, nuclear and industrial accidents, railway disasters, and space disasters." Publisher's note
 For a review see: Booklist, Nov. 1, 2002
 Includes bibliographical references

Davis, Paul K., 1952-

100 decisive battles; from ancient times to the present. ABC-CLIO 1999 462p il maps o.p.; Oxford Univ. Press paperback available $18.95   **904**
 1. Battles 2. Military history
 ISBN 0-19-514366-3 (pa)   LC 99-47618
 Surveys the one hundred most decisive battles in world history from the Battle of Megiddo in 1469 B.C. to Desert Storm, 1991. "Entries are approximately two thousand words long, limiting background details and confining the descriptions to the combatants, the historical setting, the battle itself, and the results. Each entry ends with a list of references used by the author in his research." Voice Youth Advocates

Hanson, Victor Davis

Carnage and culture; landmark battles in the rise of Western power. Doubleday 2001 492p il hardcover o.p. paperback available $16   **904**
 1. Battles 2. Military history
 ISBN 0-385-72038-6 (pa)   LC 00-65582
 The author analyzes nine battles and "maintains that Western nations are the world's best when it comes to waging war. From Salamis in 480 B.C.E. to the Tet offensive in 1968, Western forces have prevailed." Libr J
 "This provocative work is likely to engender controversy." Booklist
 Includes bibliographical references

907 History—Education and related topics

Nash, Gary B.

History on trial; culture wars and the teaching of the past; by Gary B. Nash, Charlotte Crabtree, and Ross E. Dunn. Knopf 1997 318p il hardcover o.p. paperback available $15   **907**

1. History—Study and teaching 2. Culture conflict
ISBN 0-679-76750-9 (pa)   LC 97-2819

This book "is divided into two distinct, but related parts. The first is a survey of how history has been taught in American schools over the years. . . . The second part is more polemical, focusing on the 'culture wars' over the controversial national history standards developed and published in 1994. The authors were deeply involved in writing, revising, and defending the standards." Book Rep

The authors offer "an important resource to parents, teachers, administrators, government officials, or anyone trying to understand how history can be most effectively taught in the 1990s." Christ Sci Monit

Schama, Simon

Dead certainties; unwarranted speculations. Knopf 1991 333p hardcover o.p. paperback available $16   **907**

1. Historiography
ISBN 0-679-73613-1 (pa)   LC 90-52902

This exploration of the nature of historical writing consists of two stories. The first one "is concerned with the battlefield death of James Wolfe, British commander in the North American campaign of the Seven Years' War; the second with the murder ninety years later of a Harvard Medical School professor, George Parkman." New Repub

Tuchman, Barbara Wertheim

Practicing history; selected essays; by Barbara W. Tuchman. Knopf 1981 306p hardcover o.p. paperback available $14.95   **907**

1. Historiography 2. Modern history
ISBN 0-345-30363-6 (pa)   LC 81-47509

A collection of essays on the nature, methodology and writing of history

909 World history. Civilization

Africana; the encyclopedia of the African and African American experience; editors, Kwame Anthony Appiah, Henry Louis Gates. Basic Civitas Bks. 1999 2095p il maps $59.95   **909**

1. Blacks—Encyclopedias 2. African Americans—Encyclopedias 3. Africa—Civilization—Encyclopedias
ISBN 0-465-00071-1   LC 99-37834

This encyclopedia covers "prominent individuals, events, trends, places, political movements, art forms, business and trade, religions, ethnic groups, organizations, and countries on both sides of the ocean. . . . There are articles on contemporary nations of sub-Saharan Africa, ethnic groups from various regions of Africa, African American Academy award winners, Caribbean musical styles, African religions in Brazil, and European colonial powers." Booklist

Boorstin, Daniel J., 1914-2004

The creators. Random House 1992 811p il hardcover o.p. paperback available $18   **909**

1. Civilization 2. Arts 3. Creation (Literary, artistic, etc.)
ISBN 0-679-74375-8 (pa)   LC 91-39948

In this volume "Boorstin undertakes an interpretive history of creativity in Western civilization. Packed with shrewd, entertaining profiles of Dante, Goethe, Benjamin Franklin and dozens of others, this stimulating synthesis sets the achievements of individual geniuses into a coherent narrative of humanity's advance from ignorance." Publ Wkly

Includes bibliographical references

The discoverers. Random House 1983 745p hardcover o.p. paperback available $17.95   **909**

1. Civilization 2. Exploration 3. Science—History
ISBN 0-394-72625-1 (pa)   LC 83-42766

The author "leads his reader through . . . anecdotal information of the discoveries of timekeeping, mapmaking, observations of nature, both large and small, and of insights into human social organizations, past and present, in this popularized, general history of @mankind's need to know.'" Choice

The seekers; the story of man's continuing quest to understand his world. Random House 1998 298p hardcover o.p. paperback available $15   **909**

1. Civilization—History
ISBN 0-375-70475-2 (pa)   LC 98-15430

Concluding volume of author's trilogy begun with The discoverers and The creators

"This is an account, generally chronological, of how the Western world's heritage of ideas of meaning and purpose was shaped by the thinking of the great philosophers and religious leaders from ancient times to the present. Until the rise of scientific thinking in the 17th century, Boorstin observes, answers were sought from history and human events, but in modern times, ideologies and dogmas overcame that way of thinking." Libr J

Includes bibliographical references

Braudel, Fernand

A history of civilizations; translated by Richard Mayne. Allen Lane/The Penguin Press 1993 xl, 600p maps hardcover o.p. paperback available $16.95   **909**

1. Civilization—History
ISBN 0-14-012489-6 (pa)   LC 93-30639

Original French edition, 1962

This "history of the world takes a deliberately anti-ethnocentric approach. Beginning with Islam, black Africa, China, India, Japan, Korea and Southeast Asia, the [author] . . . delineates in quick strokes the religions, politics, social structures, arts, economics and ethos of each civilization. Only then does he move on to Europe, the U.S., Latin America and the U.S.S.R. . . . Marked by flashes of illumination and cross-cultural parallels, the book is inevitably out-of-date in many areas, yet also surprisingly current." Publ Wkly

Cahill, Tom

The gifts of the Jews; how a tribe of desert nomads changed the way everyone thinks and feels; [by] Thomas Cahill. Talese 1998 291p (Hinges of history) $23.50; pa $14   **909**
1. Bible. O.T.—History of Biblical events 2. Judaism—History 3. Jews—History
ISBN 0-385-48248-5; 0-385-48249-3 (pa)
           LC 97-45139
In this colloquial look at the influence of the Hebrew Bible on civilization, the author gives "the Jews credit for revolutionizing the concepts of democracy, universal law, monotheism, linear time, personal vocation, destiny, self-improvement and the belief in the equality of all humans. He stumbles on the odd aside and occasionally is surprisingly insensitive. . . Still, his passion and breadth of knowledge are admirable." N Y Times Book Rev
Includes bibliographical references

The **Cambridge** illustrated history of the Islamic world; edited by Francis Robinson. Cambridge Univ. Press 1996 xxiii, 328p il maps hardcover o.p. paperback available $35   **909**
1. Islamic countries—History
ISBN 0-521-66993-6 (pa)   LC 95-37562
"Facts about Islam's history and practice are presented, along with its economic, societal, and intellectual structures. Excellent graphics support the text. Maps are extensive and exact." SLJ
Includes bibliographical references

Cocker, Mark

Rivers of blood, rivers of gold; Europe's conquest of indigenous peoples. Grove Press 2000 416p il hardcover o.p. paperback available $16   **909**
1. Imperialism 2. Genocide 3. Colonies
ISBN 0-8021-3801-2 (pa)   LC 99-87927
The author "looks in detail at the Spanish conquest of Mexico, the British near-extermination of the Tasmanian Aborigines, the white settlers' dispossession of the Apaches, and the German subjugation of the Herero and Nama of South-West Africa. Cocker shows that European imperialism involved the deaths of millions and the complete extinction of numerous distinct peoples." Booklist
Includes bibliographical references

Cultures of the Jews; a new history; edited with an introduction by David Biale. Schocken Bks. 2002 xxxiii, 1196p il $45   **909**
1. Jews—History 2. Jewish civilization
ISBN 0-8052-4131-0   LC 2002-23008
"The book is split into three main sections: 'Ancient Mediterranean Origins,' 'Diversities of Diaspora,' and 'Modern Encounters.' Within this framework, leading scholars such as Isaiah Gafni, Aron Rodrigue, and Stephen Whitfield contribute broad essays examining the development of Jewish culture in different contexts. Interactions between Jewish and non-Jewish cultures form an important subtext for the essays, as scholars outline the latest thinking about gender, language, religion, drama, and literature in Jewish history. The book pays equal attention to the Sephardic and Ashkenazic experiences and finishes with significant essays on American, European, and non-European Jewries." Choice

"The book is truly one of the most important works on the subject ever published." Booklist
Includes bibliographical refernces

Fargues, Philippe

The atlas of the Arab world; [by] Philippe Fargues & Rafic Boustani. Facts on File 1991 144p il maps $55   **909**
1. Arab countries
ISBN 0-8160-2346-8   LC 89-675447
"A wealth of information presented in colorful maps, graphs, diagrams, and charts. Arranged by broad cultural topics such as ethnic groups and religions, society, cities, oil and industry, facts not readily available in standard resources are presented and compared." SLJ

Freeman, Charles, 1947-

Egypt, Greece, and Rome; civilizations of the ancient Mediterranean. 2nd ed. Oxford Univ. Press 2004 688p $29.95   **909**
1. Mediterranean civilization
ISBN 0-19-926364-7   LC 2004-41505
First published 1996
Freeman's "introduction to the ancient Mediterranean adds Egypt to the standard Greco-Roman nexus. Covering an immense variety of material with competence and sensitivity to nuance, Freeman relates the familiar parts of the classical story, but his is no mere rehash of the Persian War or the fall of the Roman Republic. He analytically recounts political events, religious movements, and society, with steady awareness of the fragmented character of the surviving evidence." Booklist [review of 1996 edition]
Includes bibliographical references

Gilbert, Martin, 1936-

The Jews in the twentieth century; an illustrated history. Schocken Bks. 2001 376p il $50   **909**
1. Jews—History
ISBN 0-8052-4190-6   LC 2001-20633
This is a "100-year chronicle of Jewish history, practice, culture, art and survival . . . [that] intertwines an enormous range of people, events, themes and ideas." Publ Wkly
"This meticulously researched book is indispensable to anyone interested in the history of the Jews." Booklist
Includes bibliographical references

A **Historical** atlas of the Jewish people; from the time of the patriarchs to the present; general editor, Eli Barnavi; English edition editor, Miriam Eliav-Feldon; cartography, Michel Opatowski; new edition revised by Denis Charbit. new ed. Schocken Bks. 2002 321p il maps $45   **909**
1. Jews—History—Maps
ISBN 0-8052-4226-0   LC 2003-279553
First published 1992 by Knopf
"Covering three millennia of Jewish history and culture through a combination of concise text, accurate and well-drawn maps, and a sumptuous array of photographs, diagrams, and reproductions of paintings, this atlas succeeds in covering all the main themes of the Jewish experience. The material is arranged chronologically and systematically. . . . The result is a reference that will profit both scholars and lay readers." Libr J [review of 1992 edition]

A **History** of civilization. Prentice-Hall il maps $116 **909**

1. Civilization—History

First published 1955. (9th edition 1996) Periodically revised

This illustrated survey of the history of Western civilization includes chapters on the Renaissance, the Protestant Reformation, the Enlightenment, the two World Wars, and 20th century thought and letters. Non-Western contributions to the West are discussed

Includes bibliographical references

A **History** of private life; Philippe Ariès and Georges Duby, general editors. Harvard Univ. Press 1987-1991 5v il **909**

1. Civilization 2. Manners and customs 3. Family life
LC 86-18286

Translated by Arthur Goldhammer

Contents: v1 From pagan Rome to Byzantium; Paul Veyne, editor $52.50; pa $24.95 (ISBN 0-674-39975-7; 0-674-39974-9); v2 Revelations of the medieval world; Georges Duby, editor hc op; pa $24.95 (ISBN 0-674-40001-1); v3 Passions of the Renaissance; Roger Chartier, editor hc op; pa $24.95 (ISBN 0-674-40002-4); v4 From the fires of revolution to the Great War; Michelle Perrot, editor $48.95; pa $24.95 (ISBN 0-674-39978-1; 0-674-40003-8); v5 Riddles of identity in modern times; Antoine Prost and Gérard Vincent, editors $52.50; pa $19.95 (ISBN 0-674-39979-X; 0-674-40004-6)

"An extraordinarily rich compendium of information on virtually all aspects of life in all social classes. . . . The lucid style should appeal to the general reader, for whom the book is intended." Libr J [review of v1]

Includes bibliographical references

Hourani, Albert Habib

A history of the Arab peoples; with a new afterword by Malise Ruthven. 2nd ed. Belknap Press 2002 xx, 565p il maps $39.95 **909**

1. Arab countries—History 2. Arab civilization
ISBN 0-674-01017-5   LC 2003-269357
First published 1991

This history of the Arab peoples is divided into five parts: The making of a world (seventh-tenth century); Arab Muslim societies (eleventh-fifteenth century); The Ottoman age (sixteenth-eighteenth century); The age of European empires (1800-1939); The age of nation-states (since 1939). Includes a 2002 afterword, genealogies and dynasties

Includes bibliographical references

The **Illustrated** history of the Jewish people; edited by Nicholas De Lange. Harcourt Brace & Co. 1997 $36 **909**

1. Jews—History
ISBN 0-15-100302-5

This is "a collection of eight essays . . . that chronologically survey Jewish history from biblical times to Prime Minister Rabin's assassination." Libr J

The editor "has assembled an unimpeachable group of historians, whose eight chronologically and thematically organized essays are models of contemporary scholarship. The narrative is lucid and lively, as faithful to traditional sources as it is aware of their fallibility" N Y Times Book Rev

James, Lawrence

The rise and fall of the British Empire. St. Martin's Press 1995 704p il hardcover o.p. paperback available $19.95 **909**

1. Great Britain—Colonies 2. Commonwealth countries—History
ISBN 0-312-16985-X (pa)   LC 95-38774
First published 1994 in the United Kingdom

The author "surveys the major periods and events in Britain's rise and decline as a global power without attempting to be the definitive study of any one of those periods or events. . . . James' focus rests primarily on individuals—those who built the British Empire, those who maintained it, and those who, when it came time, eased it out of existence." Booklist

Johnson, Paul, 1928-

A history of the Jews. Harper & Row 1987 644p hardcover o.p. paperback available $17 **909**

1. Jews—History
ISBN 0-06-091533-1 (pa)   LC 85-42575

This narrative attempts to cover the "interplay between Jewish history and Western history, and between the philosophical, ethical, religious, social and political notions of Judaic culture and those of Western culture." Publisher's note

This "is an absorbing, provocative, well-written, often moving book, an insightful and impassioned blend of history and myth, story and interpretation." Christ Sci Monit

Includes bibliographical references

Lamb, David

The Arabs; journeys beyond the mirage. 2nd Vintage Books ed, rev and updated. Vintage Bks. 2002 348p map pa $15 **909**

1. Arab countries
ISBN 1-4000-3041-2   LC 2002-524048
First published 1987 by Random House

The author "explores the Arabs' religious, political, and cultural views, noting the differences and key similarities between the many segments of the Arab world. He explains Arab attitudes and actions toward the West, including the growth of terrorism, and situates current events in a larger historical backdrop that goes back more than a thousand years." Publisher's note

"Intelligent and incisive . . . Mr. Lamb has the first-rate reporter's tools, and he uses them to relate, with compelling detail, who the Arabs are." N Y Times Book Rev

Includes bibliographical references

Ortega y Gasset, José, 1883-1955

The revolt of the masses; translated, annotated, and with an introduction by Anthony Kerrigan; edited by Kenneth Moore; with a foreword by Saul Bellow. University of Notre Dame Press 1985 xxxi, 192p o.p.; Norton paperback available $13.95 **909**

1. Civilization 2. Europe—Civilization 3. Proletariat
ISBN 0-393-31095-7 (pa)   LC 81-40457
Original Spanish edition, 1930; first English translation, 1932

A collection of essays by the Spanish intellectual in which he analyzes the dangers of control of government by the masses. He sees Bolshevism and Fascism as particularly threatening to civilization

The **Oxford** history of the British Empire;
Wm. Roger Lewis, editor-in-chief. Oxford
Univ. Press 1998-1999 5v maps   **909**
1. Imperialism 2. Great Britain—Colonies
LC 97-36299
Contents: v1 The origins of empire, ed. by Nicholas
Canny $55; pa $22 (ISBN 0-19-820562-7; 0-19-
924676-9); v2 The eighteenth century, ed. by P. J. Marshall hc op; pa $22 (ISBN 0-19-924677-7); v3 The nine-
teenth century, ed. by Andrew Porter $55; pa $21.95
(ISBN 0-19-820565-1; 0-19-924678-5); v4 The twentieth
century, ed. by Judith M. Brown and Wm. Roger Louis
$55; pa $19.95 (ISBN 0-19-820564-3; 0-19-924679-3);
v5 Historiography, ed. by Robin W. Winks $100; pa
$24.95 (ISBN 0-19-820566-X; 0-19-924680-7)
In these volumes "over three dozen scholars examine
both major and minor aspects of the modern imperial experience. The chronological focus develops from the 16th
century, when Ireland was the starting point of the empire to the end of the 18th, when the 13 American Colonies were lost." [review of v1-2] Libr J

Pagden, Anthony
Peoples and empires; a short history of
European migration, exploration, and
conquest from Greece to the present. Modern
library ed. Modern Lib. 2001 xxv, 206p
$19.95; pa $10.95   **909**
1. World history 2. Colonies 3. Immigration and emigration
ISBN 0-679-64096-7; 0-8129-6761-5 (pa)
LC 00-66204
"A Modern chronicles book"
This "overview of European empire building and colonization commences with the diffusion of Greek civilization and traces the subsequent evolution of the ensuing
Roman, Spanish, French, and British empires. More interesting than how those empires physically expanded is
the insightful discussion on what motivated individual
men and entire nations to migrate and conquer." Booklist
Includes bibliographical references

Potok, Chaim, 1929-2002
Wanderings; Chaim Potok's history of the
Jews. Knopf 1978 431p il maps o.p.; Fawcett
Bks. paperback available $7.99   **909**
1. Jews—History
ISBN 0-449-21582-2 (pa)   LC 78-54915
This informal history of the Jewish people emphasizes
the themes of wandering and persecution
Includes bibliographical references

Roberts, J. M. (John Morris), 1928-2003
The new history of the world. {4th rev ed}.
Oxford Univ. Press 2003 1232p il map $40
909
1. World history
ISBN 0-19-521927-9   LC 2003-270110
First published 1976 in the United Kingdom with title:
The Hutchinson history of the world; first published
1976 in the United States in a slightly different form by
Knopf with title: History of the world; this edition first
published 2002 in the United Kingdom with title: The
New Penguin history of the world
This overview of history from prehistoric times to the
effects of the September 11, 2001 attacks is divided into
eight sections: Before history--beginnings; The first civilizations; The classical Mediterranean; The age of diverging traditions; The making of the European age; The
great acceleration; The end of the Europeans' world; The
latest age

Toynbee, Arnold, 1852-1883
A study of history; abridgement of volumes
I-X; by D. C. Somervell. Oxford Univ. Press
1946-1957 2v   **909**
1. Civilization—History 2. History—Philosophy
Contents: v1 Abridgement of volumes I-VI, pa $19.95
(ISBN 0-19-505080-0); v2 Abridgement of volumes
VII-X $35; pa $18.95 (ISBN 0-19-500199-0, 0-19-
505081-9)
An abridgment of the first ten volumes of Toynbee's
twelve-volume study on the rise and fall of civilizations.
The editor has followed the pattern of the original work
and has added a final chapter on how this book came to
be written and a summary of the ten volumes

Tye, Larry
Home lands; portrait of the renewed Jewish
diaspora. Holt & Co. 2001 336p il hardcover
o.p. paperback available $16   **909**
1. Jews—Identity
ISBN 0-8050-6591-1   LC 2001-16918
"This book portrays a heterogeneous people who
thrive in secular societies as far-flung as the former Soviet Union and Argentina but continue to embrace beliefs
and practices that define them as Jews. . . . In this perceptive (and probably controversial) book, Tye outlines
the basis for a new, more nuanced relationship between
Israel and the diaspora." Booklist
Includes bibliographical references

Wells, H. G. (Herbert George), 1866-1946
The outline of history; being a plain history
of life and mankind; revised and brought up
to date by Raymond Postgate and G. P.
Wells; with maps and plans by J. F.
Horrabin. Doubleday 1971 xxii, 1103p il
maps   **909**
Available in hardcover from Somerset Pubs.
First published 1920 by Macmillan
"Beginning with the postition of the earth in space it
covers geologic time and human history down to the
present." Wis Libr Bull

909.07   World history — ca. 500-1450/1500

Burns, Thomas S.
A history of the Ostrogoths. Indiana Univ.
Press 1984 299p il hardcover o.p. paperback
available $19.95   **909.07**
1. Medieval civilization 2. Teutonic peoples
ISBN 0-253-20600-6 (pa)   LC 83-49286
This "study of the Ostrogoths . . . explores the interaction between Rome and her eastern Germanic neighbors with the focus on the Ostrogothic experience. Traditional literary sources are looked at with a fresh eye, and
new archaeological materials are thoroughly explored."
Libr J
Includes bibliographical references

The **Cambridge** illustrated history of the Middle Ages; edited by Robert Fossier; translated by Janet Sondheimer. Cambridge Univ. Press 1986-1997 3v il set $160
909.07

ISBN 0-521-59078-7   LC 85-21268

Volume two translated by Stuart Airlie and Robyn Marsack; volume three translated by Sarah Hanbury-Tension

Contents: v1 350-950 (1989); v2 950-1250 (1997); v3 1250-1520 (1986)

This illustrated historical overview explores the social, political, economic, religious, demographic, intellectual, and military aspects of the medieval world

The **Encyclopedia** of the Middle Ages; Norman F. Cantor, general editor. Viking 1999 464p il maps $45
909.07

1. Middle Ages—Encyclopedias

ISBN 0-670-10011-0   LC 99-14265

This reference "covers North and South America, China, Japan, India, and Africa, in addition to Western Europe. Geared to reflect the latest scholarship and theories on the Middle Ages, this work is alphabetically arranged with generous cross-references. . . . The lavish color illustrations add an attractive dimension to the work. More than 25 color maps are included. Drawings of people, photographs of buildings, and the use of artwork all combine to make this a visually exciting reference work." Booklist

The **Oxford** illustrated history of the Crusades; edited by Jonathan Riley-Smith. Oxford Univ. Press 1995 436p il maps hardcover o.p. paperback available $24.95
909.07

1. Crusades

ISBN 0-19-285294-9 (pa)   LC 94-24229

Scholars explore the complex religious, economic, and military aspects of the Crusades

Includes bibliographical references

909.08   Modern history, 1450/1500-

Herman, Arthur, 1956-
The idea of decline in Western history. Free Press 1996 521p $30   **909.08**
1. Western civilization

ISBN 0-684-82791-3   LC 96-36285

"Herman recaps the two-century-long tradition of criticism of Western civilization. . . . He covers two historians most closely identified with predicting decline, Oswald Spengler and Arnold Toynbee, and also brings forth less famous prognosticators of the doom of the West. . . . An accessible survey for the serious nonacademic." Booklist

Includes bibliographical references

Kennedy, Paul M., 1945-
The rise and fall of the great powers; economic change and military conflict from 1500 to 2000; [by] Paul Kennedy. Random House 1988 xxv, 677p maps hardcover o.p. paperback available $17   **909.08**

1. Modern history 2. Economic conditions 3. Balance of power

ISBN 0-679-72019-7 (pa)   LC 87-9690

The author "assesses the interaction between economics and strategy of the past five centuries; the correlation between productive and revenue-sharing capacities on the one hand and military strength on the other." Publ Wkly

"Kennedy's great achievement is that he makes us see our current international problems against a background of empires that have gone under because they were unable to sustain the material cost of greatness; and he does so in a universal historical perspective." N Y Rev Books

Includes bibliographical references

The **New** Cambridge modern history. Cambridge Univ. Press 1957-1979 14v apply to publisher for availability and price
909.08

1. Modern history

This 14-volume set replaces The Cambridge modern history, first published 1902-1912 by Macmillan in thirteen volumes

Contents: v1 The Renaissance, 1493-1520; v2 The Reformation, 1520-1559; v3 The Counter-Reformation and the price of revolution, 1559-1610; v4 The decline of Spain and the Thirty-Years' War, 1609-48/59; v5 The ascendency of France, 1648-88; v6 The rise of Great Britain and Russia, 1688-1715/25; v7 The old regime, 1713-63; v8 The American and French revolutions, 1763-93; v9 War and peace in an age of upheaval, 1793-1830; v10 The zenith of European power, 1830-70; v11 Material progress and world-wide problems, 1870-1898; v12 The shifting balance of world forces, 1893-1945 (originally titled: The era of violence); v13 Companion volume; v14 Atlas

"The most important general modern history, useful for reference purposes because of its high authority." Sheehy. Guide to Ref Books. 10th edition

Tuchman, Barbara Wertheim
The march of folly; from Troy to Vietnam; [by] Barbara W. Tuchman. Knopf 1984 447p il o.p.; Ballantine Bks. paperback available $16   **909.08**

1. Modern history

ISBN 0-345-30823-9 (pa)   LC 83-22206

The author analyzes examples of governmental bumbling including the Trojan horse, the U.S. involvement in Vietnam, and the British loss of the American colonies

Includes bibliographical references

909.81 World history—19th century, 1800-1899

Bernier, Olivier
The world in 1800. Wiley 2000 452p il $40   **909.81**
1. Modern civilization
ISBN 0-471-30371-2   LC 99-32208
The author "surveys the globe at the turn of the 19th century and finds there the key to modern culture and politics. . . . He argues that the palaces and performance halls, salons and Senate chambers, colleges and churches of 1800 were home to great transformations that not only shaped the 19th century but the 20th as well." Publ Wkly
Includes bibliographical references

909.82 World history—20th century, 1900-1999

Brendon, Piers
The dark valley: a panorama of the 1930s. Knopf 2000 795p il hardcover o.p. paperback available $19   **909.82**
1. World politics 2. Europe—History—1918-1945
ISBN 0-375-70808-1 (pa)   LC 00-34918
The author analyzes the 1930s "from the start of the Depression to the eve of WWII, a period of economic collapse in the democracies and aggressive totalitarianism in the nations that would ultimately form the Axis. Brendon traces how each of seven nations (the U.S., Britain, France, Spain, Italy, Russia and Japan) responded to the era's economic upheavals." Publ Wkly
"This book is a superb achievement. The author is at his best in his writing on Japan." Eng Hist Rev
Includes bibliographical references

The **Columbia** history of the 20th century; [edited by] Richard W. Bulliet. Columbia Univ. Press 1998 651p $62; pa $29   **909.82**
1. World history—20th century
ISBN 0-231-07628-2; 0-231-07629-0 (pa)
                                      LC 97-39426
Scholars contribute chapters on topics ranging "from 'Ethnicity and Racism,' to 'Nationalism,' 'Communications,' 'Industry and Business,' and others. The idea is for readers to peruse those chapters that appeal to them. Articles average under 25 pages, so content is quite broad. While the level of scholarship varies a bit, overall quality is good." Libr J

Conquest, Robert
Reflections on a ravaged century. Norton 1999 317p hardcover o.p. paperback available $15.95   **909.82**
1. World history—20th century
ISBN 0-393-32086-3 (pa)   LC 99-31980
The author takes "stock of the bloody fruit of 20th-century political ideology. . . . Accordingly, he offers withering critiques of Marx, Lenin and anybody who took seriously the idea that the complexities of human social life could be adequately explained by any one theory." Publ Wkly
Includes bibliographical references

Encyclopedia of conflicts since World War II; editor, James Ciment; contributors, Kenneth L. Hill, David MacMichael, Carl Skutsch. Sharpe Ref. 1999 4v il set $399
                                                       909.82
1. World politics—1945-—Encyclopedias 2. Military history—Encyclopedias
ISBN 0-7656-8004-1   LC 98-28374
Discusses the roots of war, various alliances and summit meetings meant to forestall conflict, and the background and events connected with numerous specific conflicts in the second half of the twentieth century

Facts on file; world news digest with cumulative index. Facts on File News Services apply to publisher for price
                                                       909.82
1. World history—20th century—Periodicals
ISSN 0014-6641
Also available CD-ROM version and online
Started publication 1940. Looseleaf with annual cumulations and five-year indexes
"A weekly classified digest of news arranged under mainly geographical headings: United States, Europe, Other world news, Sports, Obituaries, Miscellaneous, etc. Indexes are published twice monthly and are cumulative throughout the year." Guide to Ref Books. 11th edition

Gilbert, Martin, 1936-
History of the twentieth century. Morrow 2001 783p maps hardcover o.p. paperback available $19.95   **909.82**
1. World history—20th century
ISBN 0-06-050594-X (pa)   LC 2001-32612
Condensed version of the three-volume work first published 1997-1999
Contents: The first decade, 1900-09; The paths to war, 1910-14; First World War, 1914-18; Aftermath of Armageddon, 1919-25; Between two storms, 1926-32; Towards the abyss, 1933-39; Second World War, 1939-45; Recovery and relapse, 1946-56; Hopes raised, hopes dashed, 1957-67; Challenges of modernity, 1968-79; Renewed expectations, 1980-89; Brave new world, 1990-99
The author "chronicles world events year by year, from the dawn of aviation to the flourishing technology age, taking us through World War I to the inauguration of Franklin Roosevelt as president of the United States and Hitler as chancellor of Germany. He continues on to document wars in South Africa, China, Ethiopia, Spain, Korea, Vietnam, and Bosnia, as well as apartheid, the arms race, the moon landing, and the beginnings of the computer age, while interspersing the influence of art, literature, music, and religion." Publisher's note

Glover, Jonathan, 1941-
Humanity; a moral history of the twentieth century. Yale Univ. Press 2000 464p $27.95; pa $15.95   **909.82**
1. World history—20th century 2. Ethics
ISBN 0-300-08700-4; 0-300-08715-2 (pa)
                                      LC 00-36500
First published 1999 in the United Kingdom
"In this 'moral history of the 20th century,' Glover . . . analyzes some of its real and terrible moral dilemmas. Is the bombing of civilians ever justified if it would shorten a dreadful war? Should the Allies have accepted Adolf Eichmann's offer to trade a million Jews for 10,000 trucks? What kind of risk to self and family

Glover, Jonathan, 1941-—*Continued*
should a moral person be expected to take in opposing
a terrifying regime." N Y Times Book Rev
Includes bibliographical references

Huntington, Samuel P.
The clash of civilizations and the remaking
of world order. Simon & Schuster 1996 367p
il maps hardcover o.p. paperback available
$15   **909.82**
1. World politics—1965- 2. Modern civilization—
1950-
ISBN 0-684-84441-9 (pa)   LC 96-31492
Huntington posits "a paradigm for post-Cold War international politics in which the principal source of conflict will be cultural divisions among competing civilizations. Prophesying an assault on Western interests,
values, and power from a Confucian-Islamic connection,
he . . . [enjoins] Western governments to reconcile
themselves to new global realities and [offers] recommendations for prescriptive action." Libr J
"The Huntington argument that the West should stop
intervening in civilizational conflicts it doesn't understand makes a powerful claim that internationalists cannot easily ignore." N Y Times Book Rev

Junger, Sebastian
Fire. Norton 2001 224p $24.95   **909.82**
1. Disasters 2. World politics—1991- 3. Terrorism
4. War
ISBN 0-393-01046-5   LC 2001-45236
This is a collection of previously published magazine
articles. "Two [pieces] deal with the dangerous work of
firefighting . . . in the American West. . . . [Another]
chronicles the author's travels with the anti-Taliban
forces in northern Afghanistan a year or so ago, and contains a . . . portrait of Gen. Ahmed Shah Massoud, the
Northern Alliance's longtime military leader, who was
assassinated . . . by agents reportedly linked to Osama
bin Laden." N Y Times (Late N Y Ed)
The stories are "all told with Junger's unfailing eye
for detail, which often lends the pieces a disturbing authenticity." Libr J

National Geographic eyewitness to the 20th
century. National Geographic Soc. 1998
400p il $40   **909.82**
1. World history—20th century
ISBN 0-7922-7049-5   LC 98-22756
"Chapters are arranged thematically by decade and
open with a six-page essay discussing each era. . . .
Most useful of all are the double-page spreads for each
year presenting events, people, and themes in short paragraph entries. Brief trends and trivia are listed vertically.
A time line appears along the bottom of the pages. Photographs bring the discussions to life and sidebars present
interesting developments and people." SLJ

The **Oxford** history of the twentieth century;
edited by Michael Howard and Wm. Roger
Louis. Oxford Univ. Press 1998 xxii, 458p
il hardcover o.p. paperback available
$22.50   **909.82**
1. World history—20th century
ISBN 0-19-285370-8 (pa)   LC 98-12861
"Besides global wars hot and cold, population explosion and urbanization impacted the entire century, as one
of 27 articles in *Twentieth Century* underscores. Embracing nonpolitical topics in areas such as physics, modern-

ism in art, and international economics, this work exposes the interested reader to developments that have affected most people." Booklist
Includes bibliographical references

Reynolds, David, 1952-
One world divisible; a global history since
1945. Norton 2000 861p il (Global century
series) $35; pa $19.95   **909.82**
1. World history—1945-
ISBN 0-393-04821-7; 0-393-32108-8 (pa)
                                   LC 99-33903
This world history focuses on the "concept of state-
building, within the contexts of the competing trends of
globalization and fragmentation. Writing with great economy but without compromising essential insights, Reynolds brings forth the forces at work—as often as not determined or fanatical individuals—in shaping a country's
government and foreign policy. Whether assessing Nasser
in Egypt, Jinnah in Pakistan, or Mao in China, Reynolds
injects the account with fresh explanations of events."
Booklist
Includes bibliographical references

Roberts, J. M. (John Morris), 1928-2003
Twentieth century; the history of the world,
1901 to 2000. Viking 1999 xx, 905p maps
hardcover o.p. paperback available $20
                                   909.82
1. World history—20th century
ISBN 0-14-29656-5 (pa)   LC 99-41833
An "examination of the world during the 20th century.
. . . To be fair, the 20th century is indeed complex, and
giving each potential topic the attention it deserves
would be impossible. And, although Roberts gives issues
such as the cause of the Holocaust a facile treatment, his
effort and his writing are magnificent. Perhaps the best
facet of this book is its treatment of the world beyond
Europe and North America. Roberts's philosophical and
thought-provoking asides also enhance the book." Libr J
Includes bibliographical references

Shawcross, William
Deliver us from evil; peacekeepers,
warlords, and a world of endless conflict.
Simon & Schuster 2000 447p hardcover o.p.
paperback available $16   **909.82**
1. World politics—1965- 2. Military history
ISBN 0-7432-0028-4 (pa)   LC 99-58915
The author "takes inventory of a decade's worth of
conflict, ranging from Cambodia to Rwanda, Croatia to
East Timor, and assesses the reactions of governments,
the U.N. and humanitarian agencies to the carnage." Publ
Wkly
Includes bibliographical references

Tuchman, Barbara Wertheim
The proud tower; a portrait of the world
before the war, 1890-1914; [by] Barbara W.
Tuchman. Macmillan 1966 528p il o.p.;
Ballantine Bks. paperback available $15.95
                                   909.82
1. World history—20th century 2. World history—
19th century 3. Europe—Social conditions 4. United
States—Social conditions
ISBN 0-345-40501-3 (pa)
The author describes pre-war social conditions in the
U.S., France, England and Germany
Includes bibliographical references

Walker, Martin, 1947-

The Cold War; a history. Holt & Co. 1994
392p hardcover o.p. paperback available $16
909.82

1. World politics—1945-1991 2. Cold war
ISBN 0-8050-3454-4 (pa) LC 94-5152
"A John Macrae book"
First published 1993 in the United Kingdom

The author "traces the course of the Cold War from
Yalta in 1945 through the Korean War, the Kennedy-
Khrushchev confrontations, Vietnam, the 'New Cold
War' during the Reagan administration, the advent of
glasnost and perestroika under Gorbachev and the 'year
of miracles' (1989) which brought down the Berlin
Wall." Publ Wkly

"Mr. Walker avoids the tangled debates over which
side started the conflict and which did the most to sustain it. His analysis is broader, and with lively prose and
well-chosen anecdotes, he deftly traverses a half-century
of fascinating material." N Y Times Book Rev

Includes bibliographical references

Watson, Peter, 1943-

The modern mind; an intellectual history of
the 20th century. HarperCollins Pubs. 2001
847p $40; pa $19.95 **909.82**

1. Modern civilization 2. Intellectual life 3. Modern
philosophy
ISBN 0-06-019413-8; 0-06-008438-3 (pa)
LC 00-63166

Watson examines "the history of ideas in the 20th
century. . . . He contends that the century has been
'dominated intellectually by a coming to terms with science.' He claims that science has not only changed the
things we think about but also the ways we think about
those things." Christ Sci Monit

"This book will be read and consulted for many
years." Libr J

Includes bibliographical references

909.83 World history—21st century, 2000-2099

The **21st** century; edited by Hilary D.
Claggett. Wilson, H.W. 1999 185p
(Reference shelf) pa $50 **909.83**

1. Millennium 2. Forecasting
ISBN 0-8242-0966-4 LC 99-462343

A collection of articles focusing on the millenial years
1000 and 2000. The Y2K scare is discussed and contributors speculate on the future of the planet

Includes bibliographical references

910 Geography and travel

The **National** Geographic desk reference; a
geographical reference with hundreds of
photographs, maps, charts, and graphs.
National Geographic Soc. 1999 699p il $40
910

1. Geography
ISBN 0-7922-7082-7 LC 99-23549

This reference provides the "basics of geography and
maps, physical geography (such as information on climate, geology, and soils), human geography, an alphabetical listing of the world's 191 nations, 80 maps, a glossary, and an index." Libr J

Includes bibliographical references

National geographic index, 1888-1988.
National Geographic Soc. 1989 1215p il
maps $29.95 **910**

1. National geographic (Periodical)—Indexes 2. Geography—Periodicals—Indexes
ISBN 0-87044-764-5 LC 88-33086

Also available volume covering 1989-1998 pa $15.95.
Coverage continues with annual volumes each pa $6

Complete National Geographic Magazine 32-disk set
available on CD-ROM

This index to National Geographic magazine "indexes
some 7,000 articles published in the 1,148 issues of the
magazine over the last 100 years. Articles may be located by subject, title, author, or photographer." Booklist

Points unknown; a century of great
exploration; edited by David Roberts.
Norton 2000 608p $29.95 **910**

1. Voyages and travels 2. Explorers 3. Adventure and
adventurers
ISBN 0-393-05000-9 LC 00-32915
"An Outside book"

"Collection of excerpts from mostly first-person narratives of adventure travel and exploration from the beginning of the century until today. Each selection is preceded by a short introductory passage written by well-known
writers and adventurers . . . as well as the lesser known.
. . . At times the narratives focus on the challenge of the
individual vs. nature, at others on the difficulty of teamwork when the struggle becomes overwhelming." Libr J

"A mesmerizing display of the pull adventure exerts."
Booklist

910.2 Geography—Miscellany. Travel guides

Baedeker guides; [distributed by] Random
House il maps prices vary **910.2**

Available guides cover countries, regions and major
cities. Periodically revised

"Baedeker is one of the classic names in the field of
travel literature." Am Ref Books Annu, 1983

Eyewitness travel guides. DK Pub. prices
vary **910.2**

Started publication in 1993. Frequently revised and
updated

This series includes about 70 guidebooks to countries,
cities and regions

"As elegant as they are informative, these exceptionally attractive guides are a pleasure to have along during
the trip and will be treasured long afterward as important
reminders of time well spent." Booklist

Fodor's travel guides. Fodor's Travel Publs.
prices vary **910.2**

Formerly: Fodor's modern guides, published by Mc-
Kay

Revised annually, "Fodor's offers more than 300
guides to the world's nations, regions, and cities—from
Acapulco to Williamsburg. The books give details on
how to get to all these places and where to stay, where
to eat, and what to see once you get there." N Y Public
Libr Book of How & Where to Look It Up

"These guides are always reliable for clear, concise,
easily accessible information." Booklist

Insight guides. Langenscheidt prices vary
910.2

Also available Insight compact guides and Insight pocket guides

This series of travel guides covers countries and international cities

"Luxurious but hefty guides brimming with information as well as luscious illustrations entice readers to travel to domestic and foreign locations; best for pretravel study and posttrip remembrances." Booklist

Lonely Planet guides. Lonely Planet prices vary
910.2

This series includes over 600 guide books in different languages covering countries, cities and regions as well as specialist activity guides, shoestring guides and world food guides

"Handy, striking, and packed with relevant information, these guides continue to be among the best and most widely esteemed in the business." Booklist

Michelin guides. Michelin Travel Publs. prices vary
910.2

The Michelin Red guides issued annually deal primarily with accomodations and restaurants, garages and service stations. Text is in French, English, Italian and German. The Michelin Green guides are mainly concerned with sightseeing, places of interest and suggested itineraries and routes

The **Rough** guides. Rough Guides prices vary
910.2

This series has over one hundred titles covering destinations from Amsterdam to Zimbabwe

"Especially now in their beautiful new physical look and feel, these remain hard to beat in terms of comprehensive coverage, upbeat attitude and portability." Booklist

910.3 Geography—Dictionaries, encyclopedias, gazetteers

Cities of the world. Gale Res. 4v il maps set $370
910.3

1. Cities and towns
ISSN 0889-2741

First published 1982. (6th edition 2002) Periodically revised

Contents v1 Africa; v2 The Western Hemisphere (excluding U.S.); v3 Europe and the Mediterranean Middle East; v4 Asia, the Pacific, and the Asiatic Middle East

"Organized alphabetically by country, then by city, coverage includes geography and climate, population, government, arts and education, transportation and much more. Profiles are based on U.S. State Department Post Reports." Publisher's note

The **Columbia** gazetteer of the world; edited by Saul B. Cohen. Columbia Univ. Press 1998 3v set $780
910.3

1. Gazetteers
ISBN 0-231-11040-5   LC 98-71262

Also available online

First published 1952 with title: The Columbia Lippincott gazetteer of the world

The 165,000 entries in this gazetteer "include information on the following, where appropriate: demography; physical geography; political boundaries; industry, trade, and service activities; agriculture; cultural, historical, and archeological points of interest; transportation lines; longitude, latitude, and elevations; distance to relevant places; pronunciations; official local government place names; and changed or variant names and spellings." Booklist

Merriam-Webster's geographical dictionary. 3rd ed. Merriam-Webster 1997 26a, 1361p maps $32.95
910.3

1. Geography—Dictionaries
ISBN 0-87779-546-0   LC 96-52365

First published 1949 with title: Webster's geographical dictionary

This guide contains data about countries, cities, and physical features. More than 48,000 entries and over 250 maps provide population, size, economic data and historical notes. Pronunciations are included and a table of foreign terms used in English is provided

Worldmark encyclopedia of the nations. Gale Res. 5v il maps set $425
910.3

1. Geography—Dictionaries 2. World history—Dictionaries 3. World politics—Encyclopedias

First published 1960. (11th edition 2003) Periodically revised

"Factual and statistical information on the countries of the world, exhibited in uniform format under such rubrics as topography, population, public finance, language, and ethnic composition. Country articles appear in volumes 2 through 5, arranged geographically by continent. Volume 1 is devoted to the United Nations and its affiliated agencies. Illustrations, maps." Ref Sources for Small & Medium-sized Libr. 6th edition

910.4 Accounts of travel. Seafaring life. Buried treasure

Ashcraft, Tami Oldham, 1960-

Red sky in mourning; a true story of love, loss, and survival at sea; [by] Tami Oldham Ashcraft with Susea McGearhart. Hyperion 2002 232p $23.95; pa $14.95
910.4

1. Shipwrecks 2. Survival after airplane accidents, shipwrecks, etc.
ISBN 0-7868-6737-X; 0-7868-8676-5 (pa)
                        LC 2001-39922

Also available Thorndike Press large print edition

The author recounts how in 1983 the boat she was sailing from Tahiti was wrecked in a hurricane, killing her fiancé, and how she survived after a 41 day solo journey

"Tragic, depressing, and yet inspiring, the contrast between the idealized past and the horrific present is stark, making Ashcraft's story of survival and perseverance all the more memorable and profound." Booklist

Ballard, Robert D.

The discovery of the Titanic; [by] Robert D. Ballard, with Rick Archbold; introduction by Walter Lord; illustrations of the Titanic by Ken Marschall. new & updated [ed] Madison Press Bks. 1995 287, liiip il pa $13.99

910.4

1. Titanic (Steamship) 2. Shipwrecks 3. Underwater exploration
ISBN 0-446-67174-6   LC 95-226990
"A Warner/Madison Press book"
First published 1987 by Warner Bks.
An account of the discovery and exploration of the sunken ocean liner by the leader of the joint French/American expedition

Bawlf, R. Samuel

The secret voyage of Sir Francis Drake, 1577-1580; [by] Samuel Bawlf. Walker & Co. 2003 400p il maps $28   **910.4**
1. Drake, Sir Francis, 1540?-1596 2. Northwest Coast of North America
ISBN 0-8027-1405-6   LC 2002-193383
Also available in paperback from Penguin Bks.
The author argues "that, during a mysteriously unaccounted-for six months, in 1579, of Sir Francis Drake's 1577-80 round-the-world voyage, Drake, in essence, rewrote the history of exploration by sailing as far as latitude 57 degrees (present-day Alaska) in a secret search for a western entrance to the Northwest Passage. . . . Bawlf presents an admirably clear and well-documented account of the life and times of one of 16th-century England's most daring adventurers." Libr J
Includes bibliographical references

The **Best** American travel writing. Houghton Mifflin $27.50; pa $13   **910.4**
1. Travel
ISSN 1530-1516
Annual. First published 2000
Editors vary
A selection of travel writing from various American publications
"The book's loose definition of the travel genre means it will appeal to any reader who enjoys high-quality nonfiction." Publ Wkly [review of 2003 edition]

Butler, Daniel Allen

Unsinkable: the full story of the RMS Titanic. Stackpole Bks. 1998 292p il $19.95
910.4
1. Titanic (Steamship) 2. Shipwrecks
ISBN 0-8117-1814-X   LC 98-9294
Also available in paperback from Da Capo Press
This is a history "of the disaster and aftermath, drawing on first-person accounts and solid secondary sources." Libr J
Includes bibliographical references

Cahill, Tim

Pass the butterworms; remote journeys oddly rendered. Villard Bks. 1997 283p hardcover o.p. paperback available $13

910.4

1. Voyages and travels 2. Adventure and adventurers
ISBN 0-375-70111-7 (pa)   LC 96-33142
The author describes his travel experiences, including "a trip to Mongolia, a . . . pleasure cruise to the North

Pole on a Russian icebreaker, and an experimental trip to Honduras to explore the likelihood of arranging trip packages for travelers wishing to go off the beaten track." Libr J
"Mr. Cahill's strength as a travel-writer is a detached irony, an ability to see his predicaments—and they are often insoluble—as farcical and self-induced. . . . He is also politically engaged; a substantial chapter, investigating the killing of a young human-rights activist on an obscure stretch of a Peruvian river, is provocative journalism." Economist

Clifford, Barry

The lost fleet; the discovery of a sunken armada from the golden age of piracy. Morrow 2002 287p il $27.95; pa $13.95

910.4

1. Shipwrecks 2. Pirates 3. Naval history
ISBN 0-06-019818-4; 0-06-095779-4 (pa)
     LC 2001-28758
The author "attempts to weave together two stories: the . . . 1678 wreck of the French West Indies fleet, under the command of Jean Comte d'Estrées, on the treacherous reef of Las Aves off the coast of Venezuela and Clifford's 1997-98 expedition to explore the site of the catastrophe and document the remains of the lost fleet." Libr J
Clifford's "present-day descriptions of the wreck site will inspire the reader's imagination, and his contagious enthusiasm for underwater archaeology makes this a thoroughly enjoyable and aptly recommended read." Booklist

Cordingly, David, 1938-

Under the black flag; the romance and the reality of life among the pirates. Random House 1996 296p maps o.p.; Harcourt Brace & Co. paperback available $14   **910.4**
1. Pirates
ISBN 0-15-600549-2 (pa)   LC 95-41414
"This succinct history is full of unexpected revelations about the facts and myths of piracy; a typical seventeenth-century Western pirate vessel, for example, was run democratically long before the French Revolution, and one of the most successful pirates of all time was a nineteenth-century Chinese woman who controlled some fifty thousand seagoing outlaws." New Yorker
Includes bibliographical references

Women sailors and sailors' women; an untold maritime history. Random House 2001 286p il hardcover o.p. paperback available $14.95   **910.4**
1. Voyages and travels 2. Adventure and adventurers 3. Women
ISBN 0-375-75872-0 (pa)   LC 00-62762
A look at "the lives of the intrepid women who went to sea during the great age of sail. Countless females set sail for reasons of adventure, romance, or duty in the seventeenth, eighteenth, and nineteenth centuries. Included among their numbers were the wives or mistresses of ships' officers, prostitutes, female pirates, and women disguised as male sailors. . . . A significant contribution to both women's history and maritime scholarship." Booklist
Includes bibliographical references

Dana, Richard Henry, 1815-1882

Two years before the mast **910.4**

1. Seafaring life 2. Voyages and travels

Hardcover and paperback editions available from various publishers

First published anonymously in 1840

The author "shipped out of Boston in 1834 on the *Pilgrim* and sailed around the Horn to California on a hide-trading expedition. The book is based on the journal he kept during the voyage. Horrified by the brutal captain's mistreatment of the sailors, and shocked by their lack of legal redress, Dana wrote with a burning indignation that did much to rouse the public to the mariners' plight." HarperCollins Reader's Ency of Am Lit. 2d edition

Dash, Mike

Batavia's graveyard; the true story of the mad heretic who led history's bloodiest mutiny. Crown 2002 381p maps $25; pa $14.95 **910.4**

1. Batavia (Ship) 2. Shipwrecks

ISBN 0-609-60766-9; 0-609-80716-1 (pa)

LC 2001-54775

"In 1629 the *Batavia* a 160-foot merchant ship launched by the Dutch East India Company, was carrying silver to East India when it ran upon coral atolls northwest of Australia and coughed up its passengers. . . . Officers set out in life boats to Java for help, leaving Jeronimus Corneliszoon, a failed apothecary and heretic, in charge; he began terrorizing his own crewmen, then the other marooned passengers. Within two months, 115 of the survivors (including 30 women and children) had murdered each other with swords, pikes, daggers and by drowning." Publ Wkly

"Dash astutely incorporates material on ships, navigation, law, theology, and psychology. An extraordinarily riveting narrative." Booklist

Includes bibliographical references

Dolan, Brian

Ladies of the Grand Tour; British women in pursuit of enlightenment and adventure in eighteenth-century Europe. HarperCollins Pubs. 2002 337p il $27 **910.4**

1. Voyages and travels 2. Women—Great Britain—History

ISBN 0-06-018543-0 LC 2001-24916

First published 2001 in the United Kingdom

This study of British women travelers in the 18th century discusses how travel afforded them opportunities that may have been "denied to them at home: freedom from a narrowly defined femininity, the chance to develop and exercise their intelligence, an escape from an abusive marriage or, occasionally, a career as a travel writer or political correspondent. . . . This book is richly detailed and immensely entertaining." Publ Wkly

Includes bibliographical references

García Márquez, Gabriel, 1928-

The story of a shipwrecked sailor; who drifted on a life raft for ten days without food or water, was proclaimed a national hero, kissed by beauty queens, made rich through publicity, and then spurned by the government and forgotten for all time; translated from the Spanish by Randolph Hogan. Knopf 1986 106p hardcover o.p. paperback available $11 **910.4**

1. Velasco, Luis Alejandro, d. 2000 2. Survival after airplane accidents, shipwrecks, etc.

ISBN 0-679-72205-X (pa) LC 85-45673

Original Spanish edition, 1970

"In 1955 Garcia Marquez was working as a reporter in Colombia. One of his stories was a serialized account of a sailor who was swept overboard with seven other crew members of a Colombian destroyer and who was the only one to survive. This book presents Garcia Marquez' version of the sailor's first-person narrative." Booklist

Heyerdahl, Thor

Kon-Tiki: across the Pacific by raft; translated by F.H. Lyon. Rand McNally 1950 304p il o.p.; Simon & Schuster paperback available $5.99 **910.4**

1. Kon-Tiki Expedition (1947) 2. Pacific Ocean 3. Ethnology—Polynesia

ISBN 0-671-72652-8 (pa)

Original Norwegian edition, 1948

The "story of the six men who crossed the Pacific from Peru to the Polynesians on a primitive balsa-log raft such as Peruvian natives of the fifth century used, to prove that it was possible that the legendary race that came to Easter Island and the Polynesians could have come from Peru." Wis Libr Bull

Hill, A. J.

Under pressure; the final voyage of Submarine S-5. Free Press 2002 239p il $25 **910.4**

1. Cooke, Charles Maynard 2. S-5 (Submarine) 3. Submarines 4. Rescue work

ISBN 0-7432-3677-7 LC 2002-71271

Also available in paperback from New Am. Lib.

"In 1920 U.S.S. S-5, practicing crash dives off the Atlantic coast, sank due to a combination of negligence and poor mechanical design. . . . The compressed air remaining in the vessel was sufficient to raise only the submarine's stern to the surface. The crew then began a daylong struggle to endure foul air and unnaturally tilted quarters until they could cut a hole in the exposed stern. From there they signaled a passing ship, whose engineers cut another hole through which the crew was rescued." Booklist

Horwitz, Tony, 1958-

Blue latitudes; boldly going where Captain Cook has gone before. Holt & Co. 2002 480p $26 **910.4**

1. Cook, James, 1728-1779 2. Voyages and travels

ISBN 0-8050-6541-5 LC 2002-24133

Also available Thorndike Press large print edition and in paperback from Picador

"Journeying to key Cook sites, Horwitz retells the sailor's story and tries to re-create first contacts from the point of view of the locals—Tahitians, Maoris, Aleuts,

Horwitz, Tony, 1958-—*Continued*
Hawaiians, and others—and judge the legacy of his landing. This thought-provoking travelogue brims with insight." Booklist
Includes bibliographical references

Iyer, Pico
The global soul; jet lag, shopping malls,
and the search for home. Knopf 2000 303p
$25; pa $13   **910.4**
1. Voyages and travels 2. Popular culture
ISBN 0-679-45433-0; 0-679-77611-7 (pa)
LC 99-35758
This book "comprises a series of linked journalistic
essays, each of which attempts in a different way to address the phenomenon of worldwide displacement and its
consequences. The book is bracketed by two personal accounts. The first, of seeing his house in the Los Angeles
foothills burned down by wildfire, is about the process
of detaching. The other . . . concerns his life in a Japanese community where he doesn't speak much of the
language. . . . In the intervening five chapters Iyer travels, and finds places that function as metaphors." N Y
Times Book Rev

Jessop, Violet, 1887-1971
Titanic survivor; the newly discovered
memoirs of Violet Jessop who survived both
the Titanic and Britannic disasters;
introduced, edited, and annotated by John
Maxtone-Graham. Sheridan House 1997 238p
il $23.95   **910.4**
1. Titanic (Steamship) 2. Britannic (Ship) 3. Shipwrecks
ISBN 1-57409-035-6   LC 97-14210
Not only did Jessop serve as stewardess "on the ill-
fated maiden voyage of the *Titanic*, but after surviving
the horror of that tragedy, she was serving on the
Titanic's sister ship, the *Britannic*, when, during World
War I, it hit a mine in the Aegean Sea and sank. Jessop
reentered service after the war and died in 1971, leaving
behind this manuscript, which has been informatively
annotated by editor John Maxtone-Graham. . . . An important contribution to the growing body of 'Titanic literature.'" Booklist
Includes bibliographical references

Junger, Sebastian
The perfect storm; a true story of men
against the sea. Norton 1997 226p il map
$23.95   **910.4**
1. Storms 2. Shipwrecks
ISBN 0-393-04016-X   LC 96-42412
Also available in paperback from HarperCollins Pubs.
"With waves as high as a hundred feet and winds so
strong that anemometers were torn from their moorings,
the storm of the title struck unsuspecting mariners off the
coast of Nova Scotia in October, 1991. Junger traces the
last voyage of the Andrea Gail—a commercial swordfishing boat that was lost, with all six hands, in the
storm—and his account is relentlessly suspenseful." New
Yorker

Kaplan, Robert D.
The ends of the earth; a journey at the
dawn of the 21th century. Random House
1996 476p maps hardcover o.p. paperback
available $16   **910.4**
1. Asia—Description 2. West Africa—Description
3. Middle East—Description
ISBN 0-679-75123-8 (pa)   LC 95-24653
Also available in hardcover from P. Smith
"Kaplan's book takes the form of a travelogue, beginning with his tour of West Africa, and continuing . . .
[through] countries in the Near East and Central, South
and Southeast Asia." New Yorker
"Readers looking for an easy ride had better fasten
their seat belts, for the author treats us to all sorts of
speculation on the condition of humankind as the century
is about to turn, along with generous dollops of history.
Intermingled with graphic descriptions of exotic locales
are highly personal ruminations. . . . A challenging and
engrossing read." Publ Wkly
Includes bibliographical references

Kinder, Gary
Ship of gold in the deep blue sea. Atlantic
Monthly Press 1998 507p o.p.; Vintage Bks.
paperback available $14.95   **910.4**
1. Central America (Steamship) 2. Shipwrecks
ISBN 0-375-70337-3 (pa)   LC 97-49812
"On September 12, 1857, the steamship *Central America* sank in a great storm off the coast of South Carolina
and settled a mile and a half beneath the waves. Most of
the 423 souls on board perished. Lost, too, was
$2,189,000 (now worth $1 billion) in California gold.
. . . In 1989, a group of investors and treasure salvagers
equipped with the latest underwater equipment was able
to bring back much of the cargo, including the largest
treasure ever recorded. The discovery of this vessel and
its riches led to protracted litigation between various
claimants, and the case is still in the courts. Kinder has
followed the story from its beginning." Libr J

Konstam, Angus
The history of pirates. Lyons Press 1999
192p il maps hardcover o.p. paperback
available $19.95   **910.4**
1. Pirates
ISBN 1-58574-516-2 (pa)
The author "chronicles the evolution of piracy from
antiquity to the present. . . . Konstam profiles individual
pirates, explores infamous vessels, and compares and
contrasts various pirate regions and eras. He does a commendable job of separating fact from fiction." Booklist

The history of shipwrecks. Lyons Press
1999 192p il maps $35; pa $19.95   **910.4**
1. Shipwrecks
ISBN 1-55821-970-6; 1-58574-620-7 (pa)
In this illustrated volume "both the prelude to and the
aftermath of each notable shipwreck are explored in
depth. Especially interesting is the space devoted to daring sea rescues, painstaking salvage efforts, and the
fledgling science of underwater archaeology. While most
readers are familiar with the tragic tale of the *Titanic*,
Konstam introduces a host of equally compelling maritime disasters that will enthrall serious students and casual browsers." Booklist

Krieger, Michael J.

All the men in the sea; the untold story of one of the greatest rescues in history; [by] Michael Krieger. Free Press 2002 222p il maps $25; pa $6.99 **910.4**
1. Rescue work 2. Shipwrecks
ISBN 0-7432-2708-5; 0-7434-7091-5 (pa)
LC 2002-72204
This is an account "of the disaster that befell pipelaying divers and attendant seamen aboard barge 269 during a hurricane. Floating 60 miles off the coast of Yucatan Peninsula, 269 was moored to two tugboats in October 1995 when Hurricane Roxanne moved in. . . . In the second part of the book, Krieger examines the . . . suit brought against the Mexican-U.S. company that owned the barge by various parties who are still plagued by choking memories of a debacle so viscerally recaptured." Publ Wkly

Lord, Walter, 1917-2002

A night to remember. Holt & Co. 1955 209p il **910.4**
1. Titanic (Steamship) 2. Shipwrecks
Available Niagra large print edition and in paperback from Bantam Bks.
A detailed account of "the tragic drama of that terrible night—April 4, 1912—when the 'Titanic,' the unsinkable ship, struck an iceberg and went down in the icy waters of the Atlantic." Libr J

Mackintosh-Smith, Tim, 1961-

Travels with a tangerine; a journey in the footnotes of Ibn Battutah. Welcome Rain 2002 351p il maps $30 **910.4**
1. Ibn Battuta, 1304-1377 2. Voyages and travels 3. Middle East—Description 4. North Africa—Description 5. Turkey—Description
ISBN 1-56649-247-5 LC 2002-16821
First published 2001 in the United Kingdom
Ibn Battuta "grew up in Tangier. . . . At the age of 21, he embarked on a pilgrimage to Mecca and spent the next 30 years traveling throughout the Middle and Far East. . . . This volume covers only the first part of Battutah's path, from Tangier to Constantinople." Publ Wkly
"Mackintosh-Smith writes with a delectable wit, offering a fascinating glimpse into both the present-day and 14th-century Islamic worlds." Libr J
Includes bibliographical references

McPhee, John A.

Looking for a ship. Farrar, Straus & Giroux 1990 241p $18.95; pa $15 **910.4**
1. Stella Lykes (Freighter) 2. Seafaring life
ISBN 0-374-19077-1; 0-374-52319-3 (pa)
LC 90-3311
In this book McPhee focuses on the "plight of the U.S. merchant marine. Accompanying Second Mate Andy Chase on a 42-day run down the west coast of South America aboard the S.S. *Stella Lykes,* McPhee provides the reader with stories and tales of modern seafaring life and the problems of making a living as a merchant mariner. . . . An engrossing tale of the sea, with excellent detail and humanity." Libr J

Milton, Giles, 1966-

The riddle and the knight; in search of Sir John Mandeville, the world's greatest traveler. Farrar, Straus & Giroux 2001 230p il hardcover o.p. paperback available $14 **910.4**
1. Mandeville, Sir John 2. Pilgrims and pilgrimages 3. Voyages and travels
ISBN 0-312-42129-X (pa) LC 2001-33644
First published 1996 in the United Kingdom
"After embarking on a pilgrimage to Jerusalem in 1322, Sir John Mandeville did not return to his native England until 34 years later. Milton follows Mandeville's original route, resulting in a delightful travelogue and a long-overdue resurrection of an intriguing figure." Booklist
Includes bibliographical references

National Geographic expeditions atlas; foreword by Peter H. Raven. National Geographic Soc. 2000 310p il maps $40 **910.4**
1. Voyages and travels
ISBN 0-7922-7616-7 LC 99-86883
"Organized into seven topical sections, this book . . . includes time lines, more than 220 vibrant photographs and illustrations, 60 maps recounting National Geographic's 112-year history of exploration, and first-hand accounts that introduce the reader to some of the bravest adventurers of our time, such as Jacques Cousteau, Richard Byrd, Amelia Earhart, Jane Goodall, and many more." Libr J
Includes bibliographical references

O'Donnell, Edward T., 1963-

Ship ablaze; the tragedy of the steamboat General Slocum. Broadway Bks. 2003 332p il map $24.95 **910.4**
1. Fires 2. New York (N.Y.)—History
ISBN 0-7679-0905-4 LC 2002-33008
"In New York City on June 15, 1904 a terrible fire on the steamboat *General Slocum* took the lives of more than 1000 people. . . . O'Donnell . . . vividly recounts the fear and crushing panic on the boat that day. . . . [He] skillfully sets forth the background of the event and the city." Libr J

Pellegrino, Charles R.

Ghosts of the Titanic; new discoveries from the depths of the ocean floor; [by] Charles Pellegrino; foreword by James Cameron. Morrow 2000 293p il hardcover o.p. paperback available $7.50 **910.4**
1. Titanic (Steamship) 2. Shipwrecks 3. Underwater exploration
ISBN 0-380-72472-3 (pa) LC 00-24552
Pellegrino presents an account of "the shipwreck and the nightmarish human dramas of survivors, reconstructed from letters, diaries and oral histories. . . . Contrary to the popular notion that the ship succumbed to a gigantic gash after it hit an iceberg, he shows that the *Titanic,* which sank on its maiden voyage in 1912, was felled by a series of ice stabs and bullet-hole-like punctures adding up to just 12 square feet of openings through which tons of water poured." Publ Wkly

Perrottet, Tony
Route 66 A.D.; on the trail of ancient Roman tourists. Random House 2002 391p il maps **910.4**
1. Mediterranean region—Description 2. Mediterranean region—Antiquities   LC 2001-48539
Available in paperback with title: Pagan holiday $12.95 (ISBN 0-375-75639-6)
"Embarking on an intercontinental odyssey encompassing stops in Greece, Turkey, and Egypt, Perrottet interweaves and contrasts his modern-day experiences with those of the ancient Romans. Brimming with humor, adventure, anecdotal tidbits, and fascinating historical information, this delightful travelogue offers a unique twist on some classic journeys." Booklist
Includes bibliographical references

Philbrick, Nathaniel
In the heart of the sea; the tragedy of the whaleship Essex. Viking 2000 302p il hardcover o.p. paperback available $14
910.4
1. Essex (Whale-ship) 2. Shipwrecks
ISBN 0-14-100182-8 (pa)   LC 99-53740
"On November 20, 1820, the Nantucket whaleship Essex was rammed by a large sperm whale and sank in the Pacific, 'just about as far from land as it was possible to be anywhere on earth.' The episode inspired Melville, but this climactic moment proves less interesting than the story of the survivors' voyage in the ship's whaleboats, a months-long ordeal that included madness and cannibalism. Philbrick nicely links the experiences aboard ship with the values of Nantucket society." New Yorker

Read, Piers Paul, 1941-
Alive; the story of the Andes survivors. Lippincott 1974 352p il maps o.p.; Avon Bks. paperback available $7.99   **910.4**
1. Survival after airplane accidents, shipwrecks, etc. 2. Andes
ISBN 0-380-00321-X (pa)
The author describes the extraordinary hardships endured by the survivors of a horrific plane crash in the Andes

Ritchie, David, 1952-
Shipwrecks; an encyclopedia of the world's worst disasters at sea. Facts on File 1996 292p il $44   **910.4**
1. Shipwrecks—Encyclopedias
ISBN 0-8160-3163-0   LC 95-15664
In this volume the author "lists several hundred shipwrecks alphabetically by ship name; vessels named after people are in last name order. The greatest number of wrecks he includes date from the middle 1800s to the 1940s. Specifically excluded are ships sunk during combat. Some wrecks are given page-long coverage and contain many colorful anecdotes. . . . Ritchie gives good, balanced accounts of such controversial wrecks as the *Mary Celeste, SS Waratah, Lusitania,* and *Titanic.*" Libr J

Salak, Kira, 1971-
The four corners; one woman's solo journey into the heart of Papua New Guinea. Counterpoint 2001 401p $26   **910.4**
1. Papua New Guinea—Description
ISBN 1-58243-165-5   LC 2001-28894
The author discusses her experiences "when she set out to become the first woman to traverse Papua New Guinea." N Y Times Book Rev
This is a "consistently interesting and well-written memoir." Publ Wkly

Shaw, David W., 1961-
The sea shall embrace them; the tragic story of the steamship Arctic. Free Press 2002 241p $25; pa $14   **910.4**
1. Arctic (Steamship) 2. Shipwrecks
ISBN 0-7432-2217-2; 0-7432-3503-7 (pa)
LC 2001-40956
"On September 27, 1854, the Collins steamer *Arctic* collided with the French ship *Vesta* in dense fog. . . . The *Arctic* sank, killing every woman and child aboard. . . . Extensively researched, Shaw's reconstruction of the tragedy exposes the villains, praises the heroes, and makes a grim yet gripping story." Booklist
Includes bibliographical references

Slung, Michele B., 1947-
Living with cannibals and other women's adventures; [by] Michele Slung; foreword by Reeve Lindbergh. National Geographic Soc. 2000 243p il map $22; pa $14   **910.4**
1. Explorers 2. Voyages and travels 3. Women—Biography
ISBN 0-7922-7686-8; 0-7922-7676-0 (pa)
LC 99-87458
"This is a collection of short biographies of spirited women who have undertaken physical adventures and explorations from the eighteenth century to the present. . . . Among the famous women profiled are astronaut Shannon Lucid, mountain climber Catherine Destivelle, Arctic explorer Louise Arner Boyd, and gorilla specialist Dian Fossey." Booklist

Theroux, Paul
The Pillars of Hercules; a grand tour of the Mediterranean. Putnam 1995 509p o.p.; Fawcett Bks. paperback available $14.95
910.4
1. Mediterranean region—Description
ISBN 0-449-91085-7 (pa)   LC 95-32786
"On this grand tour, the reader travels with Theroux from the Rock of Gibraltar to Jebel Musa in Morocco, stopping in Alexandria to philosophize with Naguib Mahfouz and in Morocco to talk to Paul Bowles and reflecting along the way on historical events and great writings about the Mediterranean." Booklist

To the ends of the earth; the selected travels of Paul Theroux. Random House 1991 xxi, 342p il o.p.; Ivy Bks. (NY) paperback available $6.99   **910.4**
1. Voyages and travels
ISBN 0-8041-1122-7 (pa)   LC 91-9533
First published in different form 1990 in the United Kingdom with title: Traveling the world

Theroux, Paul—*Continued*

This volume contains the author's own selection of what he considers to be his best travel writing. Pieces have been chosen from: The great railway bazaar; The old Patagonian express; The kingdom by the sea; Sunrise with seamonsters and Riding the iron rooster

Thorpe, I. J.

8 men and a duck; an improbable voyage by reed boat to Easter Island; by Nick Thorpe. Free Press 2002 240p il maps $24; pa $13 **910.4**

1. Voyages and travels 2. Pacific Ocean
ISBN 0-7432-1928-7; 0-7432-4309-9 (pa)
LC 2002-19715

"Thorpe's chance encounter with a sailor on a bus in Bolivia led him to join an eight-man, two-duck crew of a reed boat on a voyage across the Pacific. They were attempting to replicate Thor Heyerdahl's sea voyage on the *Kon-Tiki*." Booklist

The "narrative is witty, sad and as brave and daft as those who sail." Publ Wkly

Williams, Glyn, 1932-

Voyages of delusion; the quest for the Northwest Passage. Yale Univ. Press 2003 xx, 467p il maps $29.95 **910.4**

1. Northwest Passage 2. Arctic regions—Exploration
ISBN 0-300-09866-9
LC 2002-109284

First published 2002 in the United Kingdom

"Williams chronicles the ill-advised expeditions of several eighteenth-century explorers attempting to find the Northwest Passage." Booklist

"Students of maritime exploration and 18th-century British politics will find this work engrossing, especially the detailed notes on sources." Publ Wkly

Yeager, Jeana

Voyager; {by} Jeana Yeager and Dick Rutan with Phil Patton. Adventure Lib. 2001 358p il $40 **910.4**

1. Voyager (Airplane) 2. Aeronautics—Flights
ISBN 1-88528-324-5
LC 2001-91291

A reissue with a new introduction of the title first published 1987 by Knopf

Relates the story behind "the *Voyager's* nine-day epic flight around the world without refueling. . . . The demanding physical requirements of the flight and the setbacks in its preparation represent a pinnacle of endurance by Yeager and Rutan, who spent six years designing, building, and testing the aircraft." Libr J

911 Historical geography

Atlas of world history; Patrick O'Brien, general editor. Oxford Univ. Press 1999 367p il maps $85 **911**

1. Historical atlases
ISBN 0-19-521567-2

Also available concise edition $45 (ISBN 0-19-521921-X)

Published in the United Kingdom with title: Philip's atlas of world history

"The volume is divided into five main chronological sections, from 'The Ancient World' to 'The Twentieth Century.' Each of these sections contains numerous two-page spreads featuring maps and accompanying essays.

Following the maps are a 24-page 'Timechart,' a 32-page section called 'Events, People and Places' that features brief entries on major subjects within the maps, a 24-page index, and a 4-page bibliography." Booklist

Beck, Warren A.

Historical atlas of the American West; by Warren A. Beck and Ynez D. Haase. University of Okla. Press 1989 xlii, 78p maps hardcover o.p. paperback available $24.95 **911**

1. West (U.S.)—Historical geography—Maps 2. Historical atlases
ISBN 0-8061-2456-3 (pa)
LC 88-40540

"Defining the West as that part of the United States lying west of the 100th meridian, Beck and Haase provide a cartographic survey of the history of the region. In addition to maps illustrating such standard themes as natural resources, exploration and travel routes, the growth of the transportation network, and Indian tribal lands, the authors have included detailed maps on such topics as the Spanish-Mexican land grants and the Mt. St. Helens's eruption. . . . This atlas is an essential purchase for most libraries." Libr J

Gilbert, Martin, 1936-

The Routledge atlas of American history. 4th ed. Routledge 2003 176p maps $75; pa $19.95 **911**

1. United States—Historical geography—Maps
ISBN 0-415-28151-2; 0-415-28152-0 (pa)

First published 1968 by Weidenfeld & Nicolson. Variant titles: American history atlas; Dent atlas of American history

This includes 320 maps relating to American political, military, social, transport, and economic history

Hammond atlas of world history; edited by Geoffrey Barraclough. 5th ed, edited by Richard Overy. Hammond 1999 375p il maps $95 **911**

1. Historical atlases
ISBN 0-8437-1120-5

First published 1978 with title: The Times atlas of world history

Contents: Section 1. Human origins and early cultures; section 2. The first civilizations; section 3. The classical civilizations of Eurasia; section 4. The world of divided regions; section 5. The world of the emerging West; section 6. The age of European dominance; section 7. The age of global civilization

This historical "atlas contains more than 600 . . . maps, color photographs, illustrations, a 300,000 word narrative, a 7,500-entry index, and a 100,000-word glossary of individuals, peoples, events, and treaties. It also includes . . . [a] 12-page chronology of world history from 9000 BC to 1999 AD." Publisher's note

Historical atlas of the United States; [edited by] Mark C. Carnes; cartography, Malcolm A. Swanston. Routledge 2003 304p maps $125 **911**

1. United States—Historical geography—Maps
ISBN 0-415-94111-3
LC 2002-31764

"More than 300 maps divided into 21 chronologically arranged parts cover the history of the U.S. from the formation of the North American continent to the September 11, 2001, attacks. There are special sections for presidential elections and territorial growth. . . . Overall, this atlas is a useful companion to the study of American history." Booklist

Magocsi, Paul R.

Historical atlas of Central Europe; [by] Paul Robert Magocsi. rev and expanded ed. University of Wash. Press 2002 274p maps (History of East Central Europe) $75; pa $45
911

1. Central Europe—Historical geography—Maps
ISBN 0-295-98193-8; 0-295-98146-6 (pa)
LC 2001-27907

First published 1993 with title: Historical atlas of East Central Europe

"The volume is arranged chronologically, with coverage beginning about A.D. 400 (roughly the time of the demise of the Roman Empire) and continuing through the end of the 20th century. The maps and tables provide information on military affairs; population and population movements; economy; ethnolinguistic distributions; and religious, cultural, and educational institutions. All are extremely well done." SLJ

Oxford atlas of exploration; foreword by John Hemming. Oxford Univ. Press 1998 c1997 unp il $45   **911**

1. Exploration—Atlases
ISBN 0-19-521353-X

"Beginning with the expeditions of the Egyptian nobleman Harkhuf to the upper Nile c.2300 B.C.E., the editors of this work chronicle humanity's quest to explore the unknown through 100 original color maps and 300 mostly color illustrations. Coverage includes Muslim, Chinese, and Polynesian explorers and scientific, commercial, and military expeditions. The very informative text is divided into ten primarily geographical sections. The atlas's value as a reference tool is greatly enchanced by an additional section of 'Biographical Details' featuring 210 explorers, geographers, and cartographers." Libr J

912   Atlases. Maps

Aczel, Amir D.

The riddle of the compass; the invention that changed the world. Harcourt 2001 178p il maps $23; pa $13   **912**

1. Compass
ISBN 0-15-100506-0; 0-15-600753-3 (pa)
LC 00-47153

This book tracks "down the roots of the compass and tells the story of navigation through the ages." Publisher's note

Includes bibliographical references

Goode's world atlas; John C. Hudson, editor; Edward B. Espenshade, Jr., editor emeritus. Rand McNally il maps $35.95; pa $29.95
912

1. Atlases

First published 1922 with title: Goode's school atlas. (20th edition revised 2000) Periodically revised

"Contains thematic maps and tables showing distribution of population, minerals, manufacturing, and other subjects. Also included are metropolitan-area maps, physical-political maps of regions, geographic tables, and ocean-floor maps showing earth movement. Pronouncing index included." N Y Public Libr Book of How & Where to Look It Up

Hammond world atlas. 4th ed. Hammond 2002 287p il maps $75   **912**

1. Atlases
ISBN 0-8437-1836-6   LC 2002-68882

Also available print and CD-ROM edition $95 (ISBN 0-8437-1838-2)

First published 1992 with title: Hammond atlas of the world

Contents: Thematic section; Satellite section; Map section: Europe; Asia; Africa; Australia, New Zealand, and Central Pacific; North and Middle America; South American and polar regions; Statistical tables and index

"The fourth edition of the *Hammond World Atlas* is recommended as a first purchase among medium-sized atlases for academic, public, and high school libraries. It is a complete revision with new material, and, most importantly, the maps are fantastic." Booklist

National Geographic atlas of the world. National Geographic Soc. il maps $150
912

First published 1963. (7th edition 1999) Periodically revised

"More than 75 large-format color maps grouped by continent portray the world with detailed, digitally painted terrain modeling. Each continent is introduced by satellite, political, and physical maps and a section with country summaries. . . . [Also included are] thematic maps treating environmental issues, natural resources, and human culture. . . . This outstanding publication is highly recommended for all reference collections." Libr J

Oxford atlas of the world. 11th ed. Oxford Univ. Press 2004 various paging il maps $80   **912**

1. Atlases
ISBN 0-19-521986-4

Also available Oxford new concise world atlas $35 (ISBN 0-19-521983-X)

First published 1992

"The major elements of the atlas include satellite images, brief summaries of history and statistics for the world's nations, world thematic maps and text, city maps (four per page), 176 pages of physical/political maps (the heart of the atlas), and a gazetteer. While the pagination is almost exactly the same as in the tenth edition (2002), the maps have been updated (e.g., the map of New York City is now post-9/11)." Libr J

"The Oxford Atlas of the World is one of the best atlases available and is highly recommended for all reference collections." Am Ref Books Annu, 2003 [entry for 10th edition]

Rand McNally commercial atlas & marketing guide. Rand McNally maps $395   **912**

1. Atlases
ISSN 0361-9723

Annual. First published 1876

"Primarily an atlas of the United States, with large, detailed, clear maps. Includes many statistical tables of population, business and manufacturers, agriculture, and other commercial features, such as indicators of market potential." Ref Sources for Small & Medium-sized Libr. 6th edition

Rand McNally road atlas; United States, Canada, & Mexico. Rand McNally maps pa $8 **912**
1. United States—Maps 2. Road maps
Also available in spiral-binding $18
Annual. First published 1924
"Road maps of each state in the United States, Canada, and Mexico. Distances shown on the maps. Index of place names and mileage charts included." Ref Sources for Small & Medium-sized Libr. 6th edition

The **Times** atlas of the world. comprehensive ed. Times Bks. il maps $250 **912**
1. Atlases
First published 1967. (10th edition 1999) Periodically revised
"The classic atlas. Very detailed with listings for most geographic and urban locations. Index gives longitude and latitude as well as map reference. Contains 123 plates and a 222-page index-gazetteer." Ref Sources for Small & Medium-sized Libr. 6th edition

World atlas of the oceans; more than 200 maps and charts of the ocean floor; edited by Manfred Leier. Firefly Bks. 2001 264p il maps $50 **912**
1. Ocean—Maps 2. Marine biology
ISBN 1-55209-585-1
"This work begins with several sections about oceans in general, including relief maps as well as chapters on 'How the Oceans Were Formed' and 'The Ocean as a Habitat and Commercial Area.' The section that follows contains bathymetric charts documenting the levels of individual oceans and basins. . . . The habitats and commerce section is extensive and covers many fascinating topics such as ocean currents and tides, hurricane formation, sea life, sea trade, oil and mineral deposits, and canals and ports. There is even information on sunken ships and treasure and shipwrecks of the twentieth century. Each topic warrants a two-page spread with photographs, maps, tables, or all of the above." Booklist

914.1 Geography of and travel in the British Isles

Bryson, Bill
Notes from a small island. Morrow 1996 324p hardcover o.p. paperback available $14 **914.1**
1. Great Britain—Civilization 2. Great Britain—Description
ISBN 0-380-72750-1 (pa)   LC 95-43437
"Before his return to the U.S. after a 20-year residence in England, journalist Bryson . . . embarked on a farewell tour of his adopted homeland. His trenchant, witty and detailed observations of life in a variety of towns and villages will delight Anglophiles." Publ Wkly

Theroux, Paul
The kingdom by the sea; a journey around Great Britain. Houghton Mifflin 1983 353p **914.1**
1. Great Britain—Description   LC 83-10838
Available in paperback from Penguin Bks.
"Theroux depicts a declining and dreary Britain as he circles its coastlines on foot and by local bus and train.

He finds dilapidated and near-empty resorts, tired old people, skinheads and other unsavory young people, closed factories, chronic unemployment, boredom, and hopelessness. . . . But it is a valid and perceptive set of impressions by a skillful writer who wants to like the country." Libr J

914.11 Geography of and travel in Scotland

Boswell, James, 1740-1795
The journal of a tour to the Hebrides with Samuel Johnson **914.11**
1. Johnson, Samuel, 1709-1784 2. Hebrides (Scotland)—Description 3. Scotland—Description
Available in paperback editions from various publishers
First published 1785
The renowned biographer here recounts the daily events of a tour which he took in 1773 with Johnson

914.2 Geography of and travel in England and Wales

Herriot, James
James Herriot's Yorkshire; photographs by Derry Brabbs. St. Martin's Press 1979 223p il hardcover o.p. paperback available $19.95 **914.2**
1. Yorkshire (England)—Description
ISBN 0-312-43971-7 (pa)   LC 79-5339
Noted veterinarian Herriot conducts a guided tour of Yorkshire, England. Color photographs accompany the anecdotal text

914.6 Geography of and travel in the Iberian Peninsula

Michener, James A., 1907-1997
Iberia; Spanish travels and reflections; photographs by Robert Vavra. Random House 1968 818p il maps hardcover o.p. paperback available $7.99 **914.6**
1. Spain—Description
ISBN 0-449-20733-1 (pa)
The author presents his impressions of Spain based on visits to ten of its cities

915 Geography of and travel in Asia

Jensen, Carsten
I have seen the world begin; translated from the Danish by Barbara Haveland. Harcourt 2002 337p maps $28 **915**
1. Asia—Description
ISBN 0-15-100768-3   LC 2001-39736
First published 2000 in the United Kingdom
On cover: Travels through China, Cambodia, and Vietnam
This "travelogue recounts the author's journey by way of stirring word-pictures of the things he saw and precise portraits of the people he met." Booklist

Polo, Marco, 1254-1323?
The travels of Marco Polo   **915**
1. Asia—Description 2. Voyages and travels
Hardcover and paperback editions available from various publishers
An autobiographical account of Marco Polo's thirteenth century travels in Asia

Theroux, Paul
The great railway bazaar: by train through Asia. Houghton Mifflin 1975 342p   **915**
1. Asia—Description 2. Railroads—Asia
Available in paperback from Penguin Bks.
The author "took a four-month solitary lecture tour of Asia in 1973, traveling by train wherever possible. His route was through Turkey, Iran, India, Southeast Asia, Japan, and back to London via the Soviet Union. He writes of conversations and impressions of the people encountered." Libr J

915.1   Geography of travel in China and adjacent areas

Ma Jian
Red dust; a path through China; translated from the Chinese by Flora Drew. Pantheon Bks. 2001 324p maps hardcover o.p. paperback available $14   **915.1**
1. China—Description
ISBN 0-385-72023-8 (pa)   LC 2001-21575
"Faced with imprisonment, Jian fled to the Chinese countryside, eventually making his way to Tibet. His journey is presented as a combination travelogue and a narrative of sheer poetry and spirituality." Booklist

Salzman, Mark
Iron & silk. Random House 1987 c1986 211p hardcover o.p. paperback available $12
      915.1
1. China—Description 2. Martial arts
ISBN 0-394-75511-1 (pa)   LC 86-11846
The author tells of his two years teaching English to medical students in China's Hunan Province following his graduation from Yale University in 1982
This book is "not so much a treatise on modern Chinese mores as a series of telling vignettes. . . . [The author] describes his encounter with Pan Qingfu, the country's foremost master of wushu, the traditional Chinese martial art." Time

Theroux, Paul
Riding the iron rooster; by train through China. Putnam 1988 480p o.p.; Ivy Bks. (NY) paperback available $7.50   **915.1**
1. China—Description 2. Railroads—China
ISBN 0-8041-0454-9 (pa)   LC 87-31574
This is an account of the author's year-long rail journey through China
"For Theroux, traveling is both about people—their thoughts, customs, and peculiarities—and a form of autobiography, and here we learn as much about his own quirks and fancies as we do about the intriguing world of contemporary China." Libr J

915.4   Geography of and travel in South Asia. India

Matthiessen, Peter
The snow leopard. Viking 1978 338p hardcover o.p. paperback available $15
      915.4
1. Himalaya Mountains—Description 2. Natural history—Himalaya Mountains 3. Zen Buddhism
ISBN 0-14-025508-7 (pa)   LC 78-5
Companion volume Nine-headed dragon river (1986)
This book "is based on the journal Matthiessen kept during his trek with the field biologist George Schaller to the Crystal Mountain, in upper Nepal, in 1973. The trek took them 250 miles to the Land of Dolpo, on the Tibetan plateau. . . . The purpose: to observe the November rut of the Himalayan blue sheep in order to determine whether this little-known species is related to the extinct common ancestor of the goat and the sheep." Saturday Rev
Includes bibliographical references

915.6   Geography of and travel in the Middle East

Feiler, Bruce S.
Walking the Bible; a journey by land through the five books of Moses; by Bruce Feiler. Morrow 2001 451p $26; pa $14.95
      915.6
1. Bible. O.T. Pentateuch—Geography 2. Middle East—Description
ISBN 0-380-97775-3; 0-380-80731-9 (pa)
      LC 00-56076
"Determined to connect more deeply with his religious roots, Feiler joined an archaeologist in a trek through the Middle East, visiting the sites mentioned in the Pentateuch, the first five books of the Hebrew Bible. A book full of wonder and awe and personal enlightenment." Booklist
Includes bibliographical references

Horwitz, Tony, 1958-
Baghdad without a map, and other misadventures in Arabia. Dutton 1991 276p map o.p.; New Am. Lib. paperback available $15   **915.6**
1. Middle East—Description
ISBN 0-452-26745-5 (pa)   LC 90-46653
This is an account of the author's travels in Egypt, Libya, the Sudan, Lebanon, Iraq, Iran and other countries in the Middle East. Horwitz accompanied his wife to the region "in the late 1980s and returned to Baghdad in August 1990 following the invasion of Kuwait." Libr J
"Horwitz mixes insight and humor in these observations that illustrate on an everyday level both the contradictions and the idiosyncrasies of the Arab world." Booklist

915.9 Geography of and travel in Southeast Asia

Gargan, Edward A.
A river's tale; a year on the Mekong. Knopf 2002 332p il maps hardcover o.p. paperback available $14 **915.9**
1. Southeast Asia—Description 2. Mekong River—Description
ISBN 0-375-70559-7 (pa) LC 2001-38056
"A chronicle of a year-long journey along the nearly 3,000 miles of the Mekong River as it descends from the Tibetan plateau through southern Asia, Gargan's book is a vivid look at the disparate peoples [that] settled the length of the river's path." Publ Wkly
Includes bibliographical references

916 Geography of and travel in Africa

Matthiessen, Peter
African silences. Random House 1991 225p maps hardcover o.p. paperback available $13 **916**
1. Natural history—Africa 2. Africa—Description
ISBN 0-679-73102-4 (pa) LC 90-52893
"In this account of three trips to Central and Western Africa, Matthiessen reports on the almost total devastation of wildlife in Senegal, Gambia, and the Ivory Coast and describes an expedition searching for the rare Congo peacock and gorillas in the Virunga Mountains of Zaire." Libr J

Theroux, Paul
Dark star safari; overland from Cairo to Cape Town. Houghton Mifflin 2003 472p maps $28 **916**
1. Africa—Description
ISBN 0-618-13424-7 LC 2002-32710
This book's "itinerary is Africa, from Cairo to Cape Town: down the Nile, through Sudan and Ethiopia, to Kenya, Uganda, and ultimately to the tip of South Africa." Publisher's note
"Where Theroux sees Africa uncluttered by preconceived notions, his writing can be brilliant. . . . But where Theroux has traveled before—40 years ago, as first a Peace Corps teacher, then a lecturer at Uganda's Makerere University in the golden years just after the country's independence—he sees Africa not for what it is, but for what it might have been." Christ Sci Monit

917 Geography of and travel in North America

The **Columbia** gazetteer of North America; edited by Saul B. Cohen. Columbia Univ. Press 2000 1157, 24p il $156 **917**
1. North America—Gazetteers
ISBN 0-231-11990-9 LC 00-27512
"This work includes more than 50,000 entries covering every incorporated place and country in the United States, along with many unincorporated places and physical features throughout North America. Arranged alphabetically, each entry includes a pronunciation guide, loca-

tion information, and longitude and latitude where appropriate. If the listing is a municipality, brief population figures are provided as well. . . . Color maps of the physical regions of North America, along with political maps of the region, are included as reference points." Am Ref Books Annu, 2001

917.3 Geography of and travel in the United States

American guide series il **917.3**
All state and city guides are available from Somerset Pubs. at various prices. Some titles are also available from other publishers
Compiled by the Federal Writers' Project (later called the Writers' Program) of the Works Progress Administration, these guides were originally published 1937-1949 by various publishers. Since then they have been reprinted, many in revised editions, by several different publishers
"Includes guides to each state, (of the 48 that then made up the U.S.) many cities and regions, and some special subjects. The state guidebooks are particularly useful, giving accurate information about points of interest with some historical and background material and sidelights on the unusual features." Guide to Ref Books. 11th edition

Beatty, Michael A., 1935-
County name origins of the United States. McFarland & Co. 2001 665p $195 **917.3**
1. Geographic names—United States 2. United States—Local history
ISBN 0-7864-1025-6 LC 2001-18034
Arranged alphabetically by state, this study shows "how each county in the United States was named. Dates and circumstances under which counties were named or renamed are provided, including brief biographical, geographical, and other relevant historical information. In cases where name derivations are unknown or disputed, an informed discussion gives probable origins." Libr J
For a fuller review see: Booklist, Nov. 15, 2001
Includes bibliographical references

Cantor, George, 1941-
Historic landmarks of black America; foreword by Robert L. Harris, Jr. Gale Res. 1991 372p il maps $75 **917.3**
1. Historic sites 2. African Americans—History 3. United States—Local history 4. United States—Description
ISBN 0-8103-7809-4 LC 91-12543
This is a guide "to over 300 sites in the U.S. and Canada for travelers or students seeking information on landmarks in African-American history. . . . Arranged by region, then by state, entries include a summary of the history and significance of the landmark, exact location, and in most cases, hours and admission charge." SLJ

The **Complete** guide to America's national parks; the official visitor's guide of the National Park Foundation. Fodor's Travel Pubs. il maps pa $19 **917.3**
1. National parks and reserves—United States
First published 1979. (11th edition 2001) Periodically revised. Publisher varies

The Complete guide to America's national parks—*Continued*

This park visitors' guide also covers national monuments, military parks, seashores and lakeshores, historic sites, and battlefields. Entries are listed by State, and include contact information, activities and facilities, travel directories, and nearby attractions and points of interest

Cronkite, Walter

Around America; a tour of our magnificent coastline; drawings by David Canright. Norton 2001 211p il maps $23.95; pa $13.95   **917.3**

1. United States—Description 2. United States—Local history

ISBN 0-393-04083-6; 0-393-32335-8 (pa)

LC 00-69563

In this "rumination on the people and places along America's seashores, Cronkite shows his reverence for the country's coastal means of travel. Starting in the Northeast, working south, then circling around to the West Coast, the book reads like a lively but laid-back cruise." Publ Wkly

Curtis, Nancy C.

Black heritage sites; an African American odyssey and finder's guide. American Lib. Assn. 1996 677p il $75   **917.3**

1. Historic sites 2. African Americans—History

ISBN 0-8389-0643-5   LC 95-5788

Also available in a two volume paperback edition from New Press

This "guide locates significant places in African-American history and supplies . . . recent addresses, phone numbers, and visitors' information. . . . Organized by region, a historical essay introduces each section, presenting the culture and history in that area." Publisher's note

Ferris, Gary W.

Presidential places; a guide to the historic sites of U.S. presidents; [by] Gary Ferris. Blair 1999 284p il pa $15.95   **917.3**

1. Presidents—United States—Homes 2. Historic sites 3. United States—Description

ISBN 0-89587-176-9   LC 98-50395

This is a "guide to historic places of interest relating to all the American presidents. Included are, among other things, presidential birthplaces, where they lived, where they went to school, the churches they attended, where they are buried, and the monuments, museums, and libraries dedicated to their lives and administrations." Libr J

Includes bibliographical references

Heat Moon, William Least

Blue highways; a journey into America; photographs by the author; with a new afterword by the author. Back Bay Bks. 1999 429p il $29.95; pa $14.95   **917.3**

1. United States—Description

ISBN 0-316-35391-4; 0-316-35329-9 (pa)

LC 00-265444

A reissue of the title first published 1982 by Little, Brown

An account of the author's journey across the U.S. in a van taking only secondary roads

River horse; the logbook of a boat across America. Houghton Mifflin 1999 506p il o.p.; Penguin Bks. paperback available $14   **917.3**

1. Inland navigation 2. Boats and boating 3. United States—Description

ISBN 0-14-029860-6 (pa)   LC 99-31517

"A Peter Davison book"

The author sets out across the United States "propelled chiefly by a dual-outboard dubbed *Nikawa*, 'River Horse' in Osage. In this hardy craft, he and a small crew attempt to travel more than 5000 miles by inland waterways from the Atlantic to the Pacific in a single season." Publ Wkly

Heat-Moon's "journey becomes a living history of the U.S. as the well-read author refers to numerous historical events that took place along his route, quoting at length from other writers and adventurers who preceded him." Booklist

Jenkins, Peter, 1951-

A walk across America. Morrow 1979 288p il maps hardcover o.p. paperback available $6.99   **917.3**

1. United States—Description

ISBN 0-06-095955-X (pa)   LC 78-10320

This book chronicles the author's journey with his dog from New York to the Gulf of Mexico

Kane, Joseph Nathan, 1899-2002

Nicknames and sobriquets of U.S. cities, states, and counties. 3rd ed, [by] Joseph Nathan Kane & Gerard L. Alexander. Scarecrow Press 1979 429p $45   **917.3**

1. Geographic names—United States 2. Nicknames

ISBN 0-8108-1255-X   LC 79-20193

First published 1965 with title: Nicknames of cities and states of the U.S.

An enlargement of a section of Kane's "1000 facts worth knowing" plus Alexander's "Nicknames of American cities, towns and villages (past and present)"

"Comprehensive listing of nicknames of cities, counties, and states. Indexed geographically by city and state, and alphabetically by nickname." Ref Sources for Small & Medium-sized Libr. 6th edition

McMurtry, Larry

Roads; driving America's great highways. Simon & Schuster 2000 206p hardcover o.p. paperback available $13   **917.3**

1. Roads 2. United States—Description

ISBN 0-684-86885-7 (pa)   LC 00-27889

Also available Thorndike Press large print edition

In this volume McMurtry provides "reminiscence and commentary on whatever pops up in the windows or in his mind as he crisscrosses the country: enigmatic glances at the Western past, salutes to hundreds of literary and historical figures." N Y Times Book Rev

Mobil travel guides. Globe Pequot Press maps   **917.3**

1. United States—Description

Annual. First published by Simon & Schuster. Publisher varies

These "regional guides to the United States contain information about points of interest, annual or seasonal events, restaurant and lodging facilities (with ratings), and suggested auto tours. Organized by state and city. A good basic reference collection." Ref for Small & Medium-sized Public Libr. 6th edition

National Geographic guide to America's historic places; prepared by the Book Division, National Geographic Society. National Geographic Soc. 1996 384p il maps pa $24   **917.3**
1. Historic sites 2. United States—Description
ISBN 0-7922-3415-4   LC 96-38536
Arranged by state this guide to more than 2,500 historical sights includes: battlefields, wild west towns, colonial villages, historic districts, Indian dwellings and pioneer trails. Includes driving and walking tours, maps and 250 photographs

National Geographic guide to the national parks of the United States; {Caroline Hickey, project manager}. 4th ed. National Geographic Soc. 2003 464p il maps pa $25
                                                917.3
1. National parks and reserves—United States
ISBN 0-7922-6972-1   LC 2003-269667
First published 1989
Previous ed.: 2001
This guide provides information on each of the fifty national parks, including things to do, campgrounds and accommodations, and facilities for the disabled

National Geographic guide to the state parks of the United States; prepared by the Book Division, National Geographic Society. 2nd ed. National Geographic Soc. 2004 384p il maps pa $24   **917.3**
1. Parks—United States
ISBN 0-7922-6628-5   LC 2003-61515
First published 1997
A guide to more than 200 parks in all 50 states. Each entry provides information on: outstanding scenery and nature; historic and cultural sites; recreational activities; wildlife watching; camping and lodging. 32 maps and 250 color photographs accompany the text

Parks directory of the United States; Darren L. Smith, editor. Omnigraphics maps $165
                                                917.3
1. Parks—United States 2. Historic sites
First published 1992. Frequently revised
"A guide to more than 4,700 national and state parks, recreation areas, historic sites, battlefields, monuments, forests, preserves, memorials, seashores, trails, urban parks, wildlife refuges, and other designated recreation areas in the United States administered by national and state park agencies." Title page

Paterniti, Michael
Driving Mr. Albert; a trip across America with Einstein's brain. Dial Press (NY) 2000 211p hardcover o.p. paperback available $10.95   **917.3**
1. Harvey, Thomas S., 1912- 2. Einstein, Albert, 1879-1955 3. United States—Description
ISBN 0-385-33303-X (pa)   LC 00-24030
Also available G. K. Hall large print edition
This is an account of Paterniti's meeting with Dr. Thomas Stoltz Harvey and of his travels across America. Harvey is the pathologist who performed Einstein's autopsy and took home portions of the scientist's brain
"A splendid peek into the weird side of American life where, often as not, things simply do not add up. 'Driving Mr. Albert' is a work of—OK, maybe not genius, but certainly uncommon intelligence." Newsweek

Stone, Nathaniel
On the water; discovering America in a rowboat; illustrations by Elizabeth Stone. Broadway Bks. 2002 323p il $21.95; pa $12.95   **917.3**
1. Boats and boating 2. United States—Description
ISBN 0-7679-0841-4; 0-7679-0842-2 (pa)
                                     LC 2002-18489
"Pushing off from New York City's Hudson River, [the author] rowed to the Erie Canal, down to Ohio, onward to the Mississippi, across the Gulf to Key West, and back up along the coastline of the Atlantic to Maine. It was a 6,000-mile journey, and it took him 10 months to complete. This is the chronicle of his adventure, his voyage into and around America, the story of the people he met and the places he saw. . . . It's a straightforward, crisply written memoir." Booklist

917.4 Geography of and travel in New England

Bryson, Bill
A walk in the woods; rediscovering America on the Appalachian Trail. Broadway Bks. 1998 276p hardcover o.p. paperback available $14.95   **917.4**
1. Appalachian region—Description
ISBN 0-7679-0252-1 (pa)   LC 97-32627
"After living abroad, Bryson decided to reacquaint himself with America by walking the famed Appalachian Trail, which traverses 14 states and stretches 2,100 miles." Booklist
"Bryson's breezy, self-mocking tone may turn off readers who hanker for another 'Into Thin Air' or 'Seven Years in Tibet.' Others, however, may find themselves turning the pages with increasing amusement and anticipation as they discover that they're in the hands of a satirist of the first rank, one who writes (and walks) with Chaucerian brio." N Y Times Book Rev
Includes bibliographical references

917.41 Geography of and travel in Maine

Thoreau, Henry David, 1817-1862
The Maine woods   **917.41**
1. Maine—Description
Available in hardcover and paperback from Princeton Univ Press
First published 1864
This account of the author's rambles around the lakes and woods of Maine "records three different excursions: Thoreau's trip to Mount Katahdin (which he called 'Ktaadn'), published in the 'Union Magazine' in 1848; 'Chesuncook,' which appeared in the 'Atlantic Monthly' in the same year; and 'The Allegash and the East Branch,' which is a marvel of precise observation." Herzberg. Reader's Ency of Am Lit

917.44 Geography of and travel in Massachusetts

Thoreau, Henry David, 1817-1862
Cape Cod   **917.44**
1. Cape Cod (Mass.)—Description
Available in hardcover from Princeton Univ. Press and in paperback from Penguin Bks.

Thoreau, Henry David, 1817-1862—Continued

First published 1865

This "account is based on the author's experiences during the three short visits to Cape Cod (Oct. 1849; June 1850; July 1855), and includes ten essays on the history and character of the inhabitants, 'The Highland Light,' Nantucket, the sea, the beach, and other aspects of the Cape." Oxford Companion to Am Lit

917.8 Geography of and travel in Western United States

Wallis, Michael, 1945-

Route 66: the mother road. St. Martin's Griffin 2001 276p il maps $35; pa $19.95
             917.8

1. West (U.S.)—Description
ISBN 0-312-28167-6; 0-312-28161-7 (pa)
          LC 2001-31944

This is a reissue of the title first published 1990

"75th anniversary edition"

The author examines the highway's history, roadside diners, towns, motels, and people

Includes bibliographical references

917.91 Geography and travel in Arizona

Fletcher, Colin, 1922-

The man who walked through time; with photographs taken en route by the author. Knopf 1967 o.p.; Vintage Bks. paperback available $13   **917.91**

1. Grand Canyon (Ariz.)
ISBN 0-679-72306-4 (pa)

An account of the author's journey on foot through the Grand Canyon National Park

River; one man's journey down the Colorado, source to sea. Knopf 1997 400p il maps hardcover o.p. paperback available $16
             917.91

1. Colorado River (Colo.-Mexico)—Description
ISBN 0-375-70182-6 (pa)   LC 96-13220

"Fletcher recounts his attempt to traverse the Colorado River from its source in the mountains of Wyoming to the Gulf of California. Traveling by raft when possible and backpacking the nonnavigable stretches, he embraced six months of solitude in spectacular scenery and gained an appreciation of the river. The reclusive author also offers some personal history and reflections on topics ranging from religion to environmentalism." Libr J

918 Geography of and travel in South America. Latin America

Theroux, Paul

The old Patagonian express; by train through the Americas. Houghton Mifflin 1979 404p hardcover o.p. paperback available $15
             918

1. America—Description 2. Railroads—Latin America
ISBN 0-395-52105-X (pa)   LC 79-15353

The author describes his journey from Boston to Patagonia by train

918.2 Geography of and travel in Argentina

Chatwin, Bruce

In Patagonia. Summit Bks. 1977 205p map o.p.; Penguin Bks. paperback available $14
             918.2

1. Patagonia (Argentina and Chile)—Description
ISBN 0-14-243719-0 (pa)   LC 78-885
First published 1977 in the United Kingdom

This travelogue "captures the exotic characters and scenery Chatwin encountered in the southern tip of South America on a search for an important prehistoric artifact." Booklist

919 Geography of and travel in Pacific Ocean Islands

Theroux, Paul

The happy isles of Oceania; paddling the Pacific. Putnam 1992 528p maps o.p.; Ballantine Bks. paperback available $14.95
             919

1. Oceania—Description
ISBN 0-449-90858-5 (pa)   LC 91-39687

The author "spent 18 months in a one-man collapsible kayak exploring such exotic Pacific islands as New Zealand, Australia, the Soloman and Cook Islands, Fiji, Samoa, Tahiti, Easter Island, and Hawaii. . . . A brilliant storyteller with an eye for the absurd, Theroux takes the reader to little-known places where time seems to have stood still and people lead simple lives totally unrelated to 20th-century America." Libr J

919.4 Geography of and travel in Australia

Chatwin, Bruce

The songlines. Viking 1987 293p hardcover o.p. paperback available $13.95   **919.4**

1. Australia—Description 2. Australian aborigines
ISBN 0-14-009429-6 (pa)   LC 86-40512

"An Elisabeth Sifton book"

The author's travels in this book were organized around the concept of "'Songlines'—the invisible pathways along which aboriginal Australians travel to perform their central cultural activities." Publ Wkly

"This is an important book and a challenging one. . . . It is full of odd characters, bizarre incidents, moments of poetry—some of them comic—that spring as much from the writer's own generosity of spirit as from the richness of things." Times Lit Suppl

920 Biography

Books of biography are arranged as follows: 1. Biographical collections (920) 2. Biographies of individuals alphabetically by name of biographee (92)

Abdul-Jabbar, Kareem, 1947-
Black profiles in courage; a legacy of African American achievement; [by] Kareem Abdul-Jabbar and Alan Steinberg; foreword by Henry Louis Gates, Jr. Morrow 1996 xxiv, 232p il o.p.; Avon Bks. paperback available $13   **920**
   1. African Americans—Biography
   ISBN 0-308-81341-6 (pa)   LC 96-26245
   This book "profiles the historical achievements of 11 historical black figures from Estevanico de Dorantes to Rosa Parks." Libr J
   The authors have provided "interesting and nuanced accounts of heroic African Americans whose accomplishments changed U.S. history. . . . Although Abdul-Jabbar is highly critical of past and present racism in the U.S., he gives credit to the abolitionist movement and leaders such as William Lloyd Garrison for their efforts toward ending slavery." Publ Wkly
   Includes bibliographical references

The **American** Heritage illustrated history of the presidents; Michael Beschloss, general editor. Crown 2000 528p il $35   **920**
   1. Presidents—United States
   ISBN 0-8129-3249-8   LC 99-462173
   "A Byron Preiss book"
   "Historians analyze the incidents, problems, and milestones of each leader from Washington to Clinton. . . . The bibliography includes a dozen related Web sites. An excellent resource." SLJ

Angelo, Bonnie
First mothers; the women who shaped the presidents. Morrow 2000 451p il o.p.; Perennial Bks. paperback available $15.95
     920
   1. Presidents—United States—Mothers
   ISBN 0-06-093711-4 (pa)   LC 00-56636
   Starting with Sara Delano Roosevelt, the author explores the influence of 11 women, each of whom raised a boy that would become president
   "This is an enthralling look at the women who've raised the men who've run the country." Booklist

Anthony, Carl Sferrazza
America's first families; an inside view of 200 years of private life in the White House. Touchstone 2000 411p il hardcover o.p. paperback available $18   **920**
   1. White House (Washington, D.C.) 2. Presidents—United States—Family
   ISBN 0-684-86442-8 (pa)   LC 00-64936
   "A Lisa Drew book"
   "Anthony's book records the behind-the-scene lives of American presidents and their families with photographs, drawings, and letters from newspapers, library archives, and private collections." Booklist
   "This close-up look at the lives of White House residents offers an intimate and objective perspective on the fish-bowl life most First Families have experienced." Libr J
   Includes bibliographical references

First ladies; the saga of the presidents' wives and their power. Morrow 1990-1991 2v il hardcover o.p. paperbacks available v1 $17.95; v2 $17   **920**
   1. Presidents' spouses—United States
                       LC 90-5858
   Contents: v1 1789-1961 (ISBN 0-688-11272-2); v2 1961-1990 (ISBN 0-688-12575-1)
   This work combines political analysis, social history, and biography in examining the White House years of the First Ladies
   "Exhaustively researched and meticulously presented, these sensitive and insightful portraits contain a wealth of invaluable biographical material." Booklist
   Includes bibliographical references

Baker, Jean H.
The Stevensons; a biography of an American family. Norton 1996 577p il hardcover o.p. paperback available $16.95
     920
   1. Stevenson, Adlai E. (Adlai Ewing), 1900-1965
   2. Stevenson family
   ISBN 0-393-31598-3   LC 95-5823
   This work "traces the story of Illinois's most prominent political dynasty. Despite the distinguished careers of the eldest Adlai Stevenson (1835-1914), who was Grover Cleveland's second Vice President, and former Senator Adlai Stevenson 3d (born in 1930), the clan remains overshadowed by *the* Adlai Stevenson, Adlai 2d (1900-65): lawyer, diplomat, reform governor, two-time Presidential candidate and an eloquent, untarnished standard bearer for American liberalism. Ms. Baker, . . . has a sharp eye for theme and irony." N Y Times Book Rev
   Includes bibliographical references

Ball, Edward, 1959-
The sweet hell inside; a family history. Morrow 2001 384p il o.p.; Perennial Bks. paperback available $13.95   **920**
   1. Harleston family 2. African Americans
   ISBN 0-06-050590-7 (pa)   LC 2001-30880
   "The Harlestons of South Carolina were descended from a slave woman and her master, the start of a line of fair-skinned blacks who rose to prominence in the state through commerce, social service, and the arts. . . . [The author] was approached by Edwina Harleston Whitlock, a distant black relative (a sixth cousin, twice removed), to take a storehouse of genealogical material she had about her family and to write its history. The result is a stunning look at a fascinating family and the history of blacks in the U.S. from the 1800s to the 1960s." Booklist

Bell, Eric Temple, 1883-1960
Men of mathematics; [by] E. T. Bell. Simon & Schuster 1937 xxi, 592p il hardcover o.p. paperback available $17   **920**
   1. Mathematicians
   ISBN 0-671-62818-6 (pa)
   Analyzed in Essay and general literature index
   This volume looks at the lives and contributions of 35 pioneers of modern mathematics

Biography index; a cumulative index to biographical material in books and magazines. Wilson, H.W. annual subscription $280   **920**
1. Biography—Indexes 2. Biography—Bibliography
ISSN 0006-3053
Also available CD-ROM version and online
First issued September 1946
Published quarterly, November, February, May, and August, with bound annual and permanent two-year cumulations. Permanent volumes $305 each
"Indexes biographical articles published in . . . periodicals, current books of individual and collected biography, obituaries, letters, diaries, memoirs, and incidental biographical material in otherwise nonbiographical books. Includes an index by professions and occupations. Annual and three-year cumulations." Ref Sources for Small & Medium-sized Libr. 6th edition

Boller, Paul F.
Presidential wives; [by] Paul F. Boller, Jr. 2nd, rev ed. Oxford Univ. Press 1998 553p pa $17.95   **920**
1. Presidents' spouses—United States
ISBN 0-19-512142-2   LC 98-3480
First published 1988
This collection covers every First Lady from Martha Washington to Hillary Rodham Clinton. The author devotes a chapter to each of his subjects featuring a biographical essay followed by anecdotes
Includes bibliographical references

Booknotes: life stories; notable biographers on the people who shaped America; [complied by] Brian Lamb. Times Bks. 1999 xxiii, 471p il hardcover o.p. paperback available $16.95   **920**
1. Biography
ISBN 0-8129-3339-7 (pa)   LC 98-41374
"Lamb, host of C-SPAN's *Booknotes,* has compiled an anthology of interviews focusing on the lives of 75 prominent people from the 1700s to the present. The result is chatty and informal." Libr J

Brennan, Richard P.
Heisenberg probably slept here; the lives, times, and ideas of the great physicists of the 20th century. Wiley 1997 274p il (Wiley popular science) $22.95; pa $14.95   **920**
1. Physicists
ISBN 0-471-15709-0; 0-471-29585-X (pa)
LC 96-42935
The author "offers biographical sketches of physicists Isaac Newton, Albert Einstein, Max Planck, Ernest Rutherford, Niels Bohr, Werner Heisenberg, Richard Feynman, and Murray Gell-Mann, along with an explanation of the contribution each made to physics." Libr J
"Brennan provides an accessible view of some tough areas of science by knowing what to leave out, and the way he links the continuing quest of physics through the century is admirable." New Sci
Includes bibliographical references

Brightman, Carol
Sweet chaos: the Grateful Dead's American adventure. Potter 1998 356p il $27.50   **920**
1. Grateful Dead (Musical group)
ISBN 0-517-59448-X   LC 98-11826
Also available in paperback from Pocket Bks.

The author "explores the Grateful Dead's place in American culture, considering the influence of the beat generation, the @acid tests' of Ken Kesey's Merry Pranksters, the student protest movement, and the ever-present drug culture." Libr J
"Brightman's is an engrossing treatment of the Dead and their times. . . . She offers fresh perspectives and insights and captures the flavor of the band." Booklist
Includes bibliographical references

The **Brontës**; a life in letters; [compiled and introduced by] Juliet Barker. Overlook Press 1998 xxx, 414p il $35; pa $19.95
     920
1. Brontë family
ISBN 0-87951-838-3; 1-58567-152-5 (pa)
LC 97-24201
"Brontë chroniclers have always been simultaneously fascinated by the family's remarkable letters and frustrated by the Victorian horror of personal publicity. Much of the correspondence was dispersed, defaced, or burned, and until this decade the only collection was a haphazard and sprawling affair. Barker's judicious scholarship finally clears the way for us to hear the Brontës tell their own tales." New Yorker
Includes bibliographical references

Brookhiser, Richard
America's first dynasty; the Adamses, 1735-1918. Free Press 2002 244p il $25; pa $14   **920**
1. Adams family 2. Adams, John, 1735-1826 3. Adams, John Quincy, 1767-1848 4. Adams, Charles Francis, 1807-1886 5. Adams, Henry, 1838-1918
ISBN 0-684-86881-4; 0-684-86864-4 (pa)
LC 2001-51276
Also available Thorndike Press large print edition
An "account of the lives of John, John Quincy, Charles Francis and Henry, four generations of men often brilliant but often shortsighted as well: two presidents, one diplomat and, finally, a historian who felt he had failed the ancestors." N Y Times Book Rev
Includes bibliographical references

Burt, Daniel S.
The biography book; a reader's guide to nonfiction, fictional, and film biographies of the 500 most fascinating individuals of all time. Oryx Press 2001 629p $83.95   **920**
1. Biography—Bibliography
ISBN 1-57356-256-4   LC 00-10116
This "book provides annotated bibliographies of works on international historical figures. Entries are arranged alphabetically by person and begin with a paragraph on the individual's life and significance. Each entry contains a birth and death date, and recommended autobiographical and biographical studies. Primary sources include letters, memoirs, diaries, interviews, etc. Biographical novels, fictional portraits, films, documentaries, and theatrical performances are also identified. . . . A wonderful resource for students, biography lovers, and librarians." SLJ
For a fuller review see: Booklist, Sept 1, 2001

Carey, Charles W.

American inventors, entrepreneurs, and business visionaries; [by] Charles W. Carey, Jr. Facts on File 2002 xx, 410p il (American biographies) $65   **920**
1. Inventors 2. Businesspeople 3. United States—Biography
ISBN 0-8160-4559-3   LC 2001-53252
"More than 280 individuals from the seventeenth through twentieth centuries who helped change the American economy are profiled here. . . . Each entry provides birth date (and death date where applicable), followed by a page or two on the person's life and innovations, and concludes with a brief further reading list. . . . This volume is worthy of inclusion in reference collections of public, academic, and high-school libraries. Its content is wide-ranging and its entries provide interesting reading." Booklist

Caroli, Betty Boyd

First ladies. Expanded and updated ed. Oxford Univ. Press 2003 xxii, 447p pa $17.95   **920**
1. Presidents' spouses—United States
ISBN 0-19-516676-0   LC 2002-41655
First published 1987
Subtitle on cover: From Martha Washington to Laura Bush
In addition to profiling each woman who has served as First Lady the author examines the ways the role has evolved over the years
Includes bibliographical references

The Roosevelt women; a portrait in five generations. Basic Bks. 1998 511p il hardcover o.p. paperback available $22   **920**
1. Roosevelt family
ISBN 0-465-07134-1 (pa)   LC 98-37072
In this look at the influence and accomplishments of Edith, Eleanor and Corinne Roosevelt, as well as Alice Roosevelt Longworth, the author "not only discusses the achievements of these women but also gives the reader a personal view of the Roosevelt family." Libr J
Includes bibliographical references

Chernow, Ron

The Warburgs; the twentieth-century odyssey of a remarkable Jewish family. Random House 1993 820p il hardcover o.p. paperback available $21   **920**
1. Warburg family
ISBN 0-679-74359-6 (pa)   LC 93-16599
The author "chronicles the saga of [one] of the world's most powerful and oldest banking families. In telling this monumental tale of the Warburgs, Chernow offers a panoramic view of nearly 500 years of world history, concentrating on the role of Jews in German business, culture, and politics from the time of Kaiser Wilhelm to that of Adolf Hitler. He also explains how the Warburgs extended their influence to America by marrying into two influential families." Booklist
Includes bibliographical references

Collier, Peter, 1939-

The Roosevelts; an American saga; [by] Peter Collier with David Horowitz. Simon & Schuster 1994 542p il hardcover o.p. paperback available $17   **920**
1. Roosevelt family
ISBN 0-684-80140-X (pa)   LC 94-5729
The authors "treat briefly the earlier history of the family that produced the famous Roosevelts—Theodore, Franklin and Eleanor—and the division of the clan into the Oyster Bay and Hyde Park branches. It also describes the early life of the famous three and offers vivid and persuasive analyses of their personalities. . . . [This book does not discuss] the Roosevelts' accomplishments as public servants. Rather it is what Mr. Collier . . . calls an account of the 'generational inheritance' of their children and grandchildren. . . . The complicated way these children were affected by their upbringing makes fascinating reading." N Y Times Book Rev
Includes bibliographical references

Colt, George Howe

The big house; a century in the life of an American summer home. Scribner 2003 327p $25   **920**
1. Colt family 2. Vacation homes 3. Cape Cod (Mass.)—Social life and customs
ISBN 0-684-84517-2   LC 2002-191138
The author details the history of his Boston Brahmin family and the . . . Cape Cod summer house that brought them together--and in some cases, divided them--for five generations. . . . The Big House, as it is known, is too costly to maintain. After spending 42 summers there, Colt brings his wife and children for a final stay before the house is sold. Libr J
Colt's account, like the house that lies at its center, is full of surprises and contains more than seems humanly possible: a family memoir, a brief history of the Cape, an investigation of nostalgia, a catalogue of local fauna, a study of class, and a meditation on the privileges and burdens of the past. New Yorker
Includes bibliographical references

Dance, Stanley

The world of Count Basie. Da Capo Press 1985 c1980 xxi, 399p il pa $18   **920**
1. Jazz musicians
ISBN 0-306-80245-7   LC 85-12901
A reprint of the title first published 1980 by Scribner
This book "consists of numerous tape-recorded and edited interviews with musicians and vocalists associated with Basie, and each gets to tell his own story. Many overlap and there are interesting confirmations and disputes over details. The language has been polished (and no doubt in some cases cleaned up), but Dance does not noticeably impose his own views on others. There are good photographs." Choice
Includes discography and bibliographical references

Davis, John H., 1929-

The Guggenheims (1848-1988); an American epic. Shapolsky Pubs. 1988 512p il hardcover o.p. paperback available $14.99   **920**
1. Guggenheim family
ISBN 0-56171-072-5 (pa)   LC 88-39902
First published 1978 by Morrow
This book provides a look at the Guggenheim family, from the patriarch Meyer to the present-day generation

Davis, Peter G.

The American opera singer; the lives and adventures of America's great singers in opera and concert, from 1825 to the present. Doubleday 1997 626p il hardcover o.p. paperback available $19.95   **920**
1. Singers
ISBN 0-385-42174-5 (pa)   LC 97-9123
"This book records the emergence of American opera singers and the development of musical institutions to train and support them. It also traces the evolution of musical styles, which from 1825 on have placed new demands on the voice." New Yorker
"Davis tells anecdotes and presents essential details of his subjects' personal lives in biographical sketches ranging from a paragraph to several pages in length." Booklist
Includes bibliographical references

Davis, Stephen, 1947-

Old gods almost dead: the 40-year odyssey of the Rolling Stones. Broadway Bks. 2001 xxx, 590p il $27.50; pa $15.95   **920**
1. Rolling Stones
ISBN 0-7679-0312-9; 0-7679-0313-7 (pa)
LC 2001-35683
This chronicle of the rock band describes "their changes, from blues purists disdainful of rock 'n' roll to R & B proselytizers to pop-music magicians to satanic rockers to media stars on a long downhill slide." Booklist
"There's enough sex, drugs, and debauchery here to titillate most readers, but Davis remains neutral, letting his audience make their own judgments." Libr J
Includes bibliographical references

Donn, Linda

The Roosevelt cousins; growing up together, 1882-1924. Knopf 2001 237p il $30
          920
1. Roosevelt family 2. Roosevelt, Theodore, 1858-1919 3. Longworth, Alice Roosevelt, 1884-1980 4. Roosevelt, Franklin D. (Franklin Delano), 1882-1945 5. Roosevelt, Eleanor, 1884-1962
ISBN 0-679-44637-0   LC 2001-33893
"Keen competitive spirits between the Oyster Bay and Hyde Park Roosevelts colored personal relationships among famous cousins that were played out publicly in the national political arena between the two most prominent females, Alice and Eleanor. . . . In her narrative of the Roosevelt clan, Donn . . . draws on her training in clinical psychology to create an insightful, nuanced view of the main characters and their relationships." Libr J
Includes bibliographical references

Encyclopedia of archaeology: The great archaeologists; edited by Tim Murray. ABC-CLIO 1999 2v set $150   **920**
ISBN 1-57607-199-5   LC 99-52159
Companion set to Encyclopedia of archaeology: History and discoveries
"There are 58 entries arranged chronologically from William Camden (1551-1623) to David Clarke (1938-1976). . . . Each entry begins with an italicized summary of the individual's main contributions to the discipline. The evolution of archaeological practice and theory becomes a fascinating story as the work of many individuals, largely unknown to the general public, is traced through their biographies." Booklist

Feather, Leonard

From Satchmo to Miles; new foreword by the author. Da Capo Press 1984 c1972 258p il (Roots of jazz) hardcover o.p. paperback available $15   **920**
1. Jazz musicians 2. African American musicians
ISBN 0-306-80302-X (pa)   LC 83-15223
First published 1972 by Stein & Day
A collection of profiles of jazz musicians including Count Basie, Lester Young, Oscar Peterson, Ray Charles, Don Ellis, Duke Ellington, Billie Holiday, Ella Fitzgerald, Louis Armstrong, Dizzy Gillespie, Norman Granz, Miles Davis and Charlie Parker

Fox, James, 1945-

Five sisters; the Langhornes of Virginia. Simon & Schuster 2000 496p il $30; pa $16
          920
1. Langhorne family 2. Astor, Nancy Witcher Langhorne, Viscountess, 1879-1964 3. Brand, Phyllis, 1880-1937
ISBN 0-684-80812-9; 0-7432-0042-X (pa)
          LC 99-41815
First published 1998 in the United Kingdom with title: The Langhorne sisters
"Irene Langhorne, the last great Southern belle, moved North in 1895, when she married Charles Dana Gibson, creator of the Gibson girl. In her wake, three younger sisters (her elder, Lizzie, was already married) burst onto the glittering society stage. Nancy, the most famous, married Waldorf Astor and threw herself into English political activism; Phyllis, the author's grandmother, was more introverted; Nora, with 'a heart like a hotel,' repeatedly led the family to the brink of scandal. Fox brings intimacy to these semi-public personalities, elevating a century's gossip and legend into absorbing history." New Yorker
Includes bibliographical references

Fraser, Antonia, 1932-

The warrior queens. Knopf 1989 c1988 383p il hardcover o.p. paperback available $16   **920**
1. Women—Biography 2. Kings and rulers 3. Women soldiers
ISBN 0-679-72816-3 (pa)   LC 88-45778
First published 1988 in the United Kingdom with title: Boadicea's chariot
The author "covers 17 women, from Queen Boadicea to Margaret Thatcher, who have ruled, specifically in time of war. Her character vignettes are sharp and incisive, and along the way she offers some intriguing thoughts on how societies through time have reacted to females cast in a role of military leadership. . . . Highly recommended." Libr J
Includes bibliographical references

The wives of Henry VIII. Knopf 1993 c1992 479p il hardcover o.p. paperback available $17   **920**
1. Henry VIII, King of England, 1491-1547 2. Great Britain—History—1485-1603, Tudors
ISBN 0-679-73001-X (pa)   LC 92-52950
First published 1992 in the United Kingdom with title: The six wives of Henry VIII
This work examines the lives of the six women—Catherine of Aragon, Anne Boleyn, Jane Seymour, Anna of Cleves, Katherine Howard, and Catherine Parr—who became Queens of England between 1509 and 1547. The

Fraser, Antonia, 1932-—*Continued*
author discusses their marriages to Henry VIII
"Fraser's readable style, empathy for her subjects, and piquant use of historical details and anecdotes make this a satisfying addition to the history shelves." Libr J
Includes bibliographical references

Gallagher, Winifred
Spiritual genius; the mastery of life's meaning. Random House 2002 292p $24.95
920
1. Spiritual life
ISBN 0-375-50310-2   LC 2001-41905
The author reports on her interviews and time spent with a variety of religious figures. "From a goddess on an obscure Indian island to passionate scholars (Huston Smith), community activists (Tony Campolo), hermits and healing doctors, the individuals she highlights are deeply religious men and women with a gift for 'combining mysticism and activism.'" Publ Wkly
"Gallagher is to be commended for her deft and respectful treatment of so many traditions." N Y Times Book Rev
Includes bibliographical references

Gates, Henry Louis
The African-American century; how Black Americans have shaped our country; [by] Henry Louis Gates, Jr. and Cornel West. Free Press 2000 414p il $30; pa $16   **920**
1. African Americans 2. African Americans—Intellectual life
ISBN 0-684-86414-2; 0-684-86415-0 (pa)
LC 00-63596
"Gates and West have listed and written biographies of their choices of the 100 most important and influential [African Americans] of the . . . twentieth century. In their opinion the subjects that they have selected have made significant impacts and contributions to American society. . . . The entries are arranged by decade and by the person's period of prominence in society, 1900-1909 through 1990-1999. Profiles include Madame C.J. Walker, Langston Hughes, Carter G. Woodson, Paul Robeson, Thurgood Marshall, and Colin Powell." MultiCult Rev

Thirteen ways of looking at a black man. Random House 1997 xxvii, 226p hardcover o.p. paperback available $12   **920**
1. African Americans—Biography
ISBN 0-679-77666-4 (pa)   LC 96-33138
A "collection of essays about contemporary African Americans. . . . Each essay focuses on a noted cultural figure: James Baldwin, Albert Murray, Bill T. Jones, Colin Powell, O. J. Simpson, Louis Farrakhan, Harry Belafonte, and Anatole Broyard; however, the effect of each essay goes beyond its primary subject by illuminating society at large." Booklist
"Mr. Gates's strong suit is finding the common man in uncommon figures, without losing sight of the ways in which race, class and personal experience have shaped each life." N Y Times Book Rev

Green, Stanley, 1923-1990
The world of musical comedy; the story of the American musical stage as told through the careers of its foremost composers and lyricists. 4th ed rev and enl. Da Capo Press 1984 c1980 480p il pa $35   **920**
1. Composers—United States 2. Librettists 3. Musicals
ISBN 0-306-80207-4   LC 83-26340
First published 1960 by Ziff-Davis; this is a reprint of the 1980 edition published by A. S. Barnes supplemented with author corrections
"From Victor Herbert to Marvin Hamlisch, Green gives us a classic history of the genre. . . . Thirty-one chapters tell the tale of some 70 individuals or teams that have had a lasting effect on the musical theater. . . . The appendix gives the vitals on every major production of the past 85 years." Booklist

Greenstein, George, 1940-
Portraits of discovery; profiles in scientific genius. Wiley 1997 c1998 232p il $24.95
920
1. Scientists
ISBN 0-471-19138-8   LC 97-6048
The author examines the interaction between the personal and professional in the lives of: Annie Jump Cannon, Cecilia Helena Payne Gaposchkin, Ludwig Boltzman, George Gamow, Homi Jehangir Bhaba, Luis W. Alvarez, Richard Phillips Feynman, Martin L. Perl, Margaret J. Geller, and John Huchra
Greenstein's "portraits are at least as interesting in what they reveal about the blemishes on the face of great scientists: The eccentricities and idiosyncrasies that energize many scientists' work also may accentuate their human flaws." Sci Books & Film
Includes bibliographical references

Halberstam, David, 1934-
The teammates. Hyperion 2003 217p il $22.95   **920**
1. Boston Red Sox (Baseball team) 2. Baseball—Biography
ISBN 1-401-30057-X   LC 2003-42334
This is an "account of the lives and friendships of four legendary Boston Red Sox: Ted Williams, Dominic DiMaggio, Johnny Pesky and Bobby Doerr; the story unfolds in a series of flashbacks as DiMiggio and Pesky drive 1,300 miles to Florida to visit the ailing Williams." N Y Times Book Rev
"This account of good people living full lives and appreciating the experience will move readers." Booklist

Haley, Alex
Roots. Doubleday 1976 587p $30   **920**
1. Haley family 2. Kinte family
ISBN 0-385-03787-2
Also available in paperback from Dell
This book details Haley's "search for the genealogical history of his family. He describes his trip to Gambia, the African homeland of his ancestors, and recounts the lives of his forebears." Benet's Reader's Ency of Am Lit

Harrison, Daphne Duval, 1932-

Black pearls; blues queens of the 1920s.
Rutgers Univ. Press 1988 295p il hardcover
o.p. paperback available $20 **920**
1. Blues music 2. African American singers
ISBN 0-8135-1280-8 (pa) LC 87-14084
"This book tells the cultural and social impact of the
blues during the 1920s when the genre was dominated by
women, both on stage and on record. Harrison . . .
writes with authority, focusing particularly on Sippie
Wallace, Edith Wilson, Victoria Spivey, and Alberta
Hunter as she analyzes the music and the collective black
experience out of which it grew. A significant book."
Libr J
Includes bibliographical references

Herken, Gregg, 1947-

Brotherhood of the bomb; the tangled lives
and divided loyalties of Robert Oppenheimer,
Ernest Lawrence, and Edward Teller. Holt &
Co. 2002 448p il $30; pa $16 **920**
1. Oppenheimer, J. Robert, 1904-1967 2. Lawrence,
Ernest Orlando, 1901-1958 3. Teller, Edward, 1908-
2003 4. Atomic bomb 5. Nuclear physics
ISBN 0-8050-6588-1; 0-8050-6589-X (pa)
LC 2002-17219
This "tells the story of the birth of the nuclear age
through the biographies of the era's most influential
physicists—Robert Oppenheimer, Ernest Lawrence, and
Edward Teller." New Yorker
"Meticulous and authoritative, Herken's revisitation of
the J. Robert Oppenheimer cause célèbre of 1954 might
supersede every previous account of how the physicist
was humiliated by having his security clearance revoked
amid Red-baiting innuendo." Booklist
Includes bibliographical references

Hibbert, Christopher, 1924-

The House of Medici; its rise and fall.
Morrow 1975 c1974 364p il maps hardcover
o.p. paperback available $16 **920**
1. House of Medici 2. Florence (Italy)—History
ISBN 0-688-05339-4 (pa)
First published 1974 in the United Kingdom with title:
The rise and fall of the House of Medici
This book is concerned with "heads of the Medici
family [who] directed the government of the Florentine
state from 1434, with Cosimo's return from exile, until
the death of the Grand Duke Giovanni Gastone in 1737."
Times Lit Suppl
Includes bibliographical references

Jackson-Laufer, Guida M. (Guida Myrl)

Women rulers throughout the ages; an
illustrated guide; [by] Guida M. Jackson.
ABC-CLIO 1999 xlvi, 469p il $75 **920**
1. Heads of state 2. Queens
ISBN 1-57607-091-3 LC 99-22705
First published 1990 with title: Women who ruled
This resource "presents female queens, empresses,
prime ministers, rulers, presidents, constitutional monarchs, de facto and regent rulers—in fact, any verifiable
female ruler, and in some cases, legendary rulers. Arranged alphabetically by the names used during their
reigns, the women from virtually every nationality and
culture are presented in straightforward prose, without
bias or flattery. . . . All include the date of the reign and
a short bibliography." SLJ

Kane, Joseph Nathan, 1899-2002

Facts about the presidents; Janet Podell &
Steven Anzovin [editors] 7th ed. Wilson,
H.W. 2001 721p il $110 **920**
1. Presidents—United States
ISBN 0-8242-1007-7 LC 2001-26261
First published 1959
The main part of this work provides an individual
chapter on each President, from Washington through
George W. Bush, presenting such information as family,
education, election, Vice President, main events and ac-
complishments of his administration, and First Lady. Part
two contains tables and lists presenting comparative data
on all the Presidents
Includes bibliographical references

Kennedy, John F. (John Fitzgerald), 1917-1963

Profiles in courage. HarperCollins Pubs.
2003 xxii, 245p $19.95 **920**
1. Politicians—United States 2. Courage
ISBN 0-06-053062-6 LC 2003-40676
A reissue of the title first published 1956
This series of profiles of Americans who took coura-
geous stands at crucial moments in public life includes
John Quincy Adams, Daniel Webster, Thomas Hart Ben-
ton, Sam Houston, Edmund G. Ross, Lucius Q. C.
Lamar, George Norris, Robert A. Taft and others
Includes bibliographical references

Kingston, Maxine Hong

China men. Knopf 1980 308p o.p.; Vintage
Bks. paperback available $13.95 **920**
1. Chinese Americans—Biography
ISBN 0-679-72328-5 (pa) LC 79-3469
This book "paints a rich picture of the writer's male
family members, but those portraits of her grandfathers,
father, and brothers are interspersed with fascinating bits
of historical data. . . . The whole is held together by
pieces of folklore that one feels compelled to go back to
and reread." Libr J

Klein, Maury, 1939-

The change makers; from Carnegie to
Gates: how the great entrepreneurs
transformed ideas into industries. Times Bks.
2003 318p $26; pa $15 **920**
1. Entrepreneurship 2. Business enterprises 3. Creative ability 4. Businesspeople—Biography
ISBN 0-8050-6914-3; 0-8050-7518-6 (pa)
LC 2002-32439
"Klein profiles 26 famous industrialists, from Andrew
Carnegie to Warren Buffet, and discovers money to be
merely a by-product of their efforts. They all possess
masterful creativity and often exhibit flaws as great as
the results achieved." Booklist
Includes bibliographical references

Kunhardt, Philip B., 1928-

The American president; [by] Philip Kunhardt, Jr., Philip Kunhardt III, and Peter W. Kunhardt; foreword by Stephen Skowroneck; introduction by Richard E. Neustadt. Riverhead Bks. 1999 481p il $50; pa $13.95   **920**

1. Presidents—United States
ISBN 1-57322-149-X; 1-57322-832-X (pa)
LC 99-30869

In this companion volume to a PBS series the arrangement is thematic rather than chronological. "One category groups Presidents by their heroic reputations, while other categories take into account the President's political circumstances, the expanding power of the office, and the officeholders' individual mindsets. The book is profusely illustrated, and each President receives a two- to three-page discussion and an 'In His Words' section." Libr J

Includes bibliographical references

Leamer, Laurence

The Kennedy men; 1901-1963: the laws of the father. Morrow 2001 882p il o.p.; Perennial Bks. paperback available $17.95
920

1. Kennedy family 2. Kennedy, Joseph P., 1888-1969 3. Kennedy, John F. (John Fitzgerald), 1917-1963
ISBN 0-06-050288-6 (pa)   LC 2001-31689

This is a biography of Joseph P. Kennedy and his sons from the beginning of the last century through the assassination of John F. Kennedy

"Leamer's writing is impressive throughout, regularly catching the reader up with a felicitous phrase or a surprising insight." Booklist

Includes bibliographical references

The Kennedy women; the saga of an American family. Villard Bks. 1994 933p il o.p.; Fawcett Bks. paperback available $18.95
920

1. Kennedy family
ISBN 0-449-91171-3 (pa)   LC 94-15361

This is the chronicle of "all the Kennedy women, from the grandmothers of Rose and Joe Kennedy onward. Even those readers convinced they know all they want to know about America's first family will find themselves forced to admit that Leamer does a splendid job of weaving together the stories of six generations of women into a highly readable, compelling saga." Booklist

Includes bibliographical references

Lee, Helie

In the absence of sun; a Korean American woman's promise to reunite three lost generations of her family. Harmony Bks. 2002 342p il maps hardcover o.p. paperback available $18.95   **920**

1. Lee family 2. Korean Americans 3. Korea (North)
ISBN 0-449-91171-3 (pa)   LC 2002-1680

"Lee's *Still Life with Rice* (1996) was a novelized account of her grandmother's life and escape from what would become North Korea. As she now recounts her and her father's struggles to get other people out of the North, she continues to wrestle with her own Korean heritage—in particular, the paternalistic and patronizing attitudes toward women." Booklist

Lees, Gene

You can't steal a gift; Dizzy, Clark, Milt, and Nat; foreword by Nat Hentoff. Yale Univ. Press 2001 269p il $27.95   **920**

1. Jazz musicians
ISBN 0-300-08965-1   LC 2001-3444

Lees discusses the lives and careers of four jazz musicians: Dizzy Gillespie, Terry Clark, Milt Hinton, and Nat King Cole. A theme of the book is how these artists were affected by race relations in the United States

The author "has a natural ease with words and a graceful prose style that captures the reader's attention." Booklist

Life stories; profiles from The New Yorker; edited by David Remnick. Random House 2000 480p $26.95   **920**

1. United States—Biography
ISBN 0-375-50355-2   LC 99-53712

An assemblage of 25 biographical profiles spanning the years 1927 to 1999 "with subjects ranging from Ernest Hemingway and Marlon Brando to a fake prince, a pair of eccentric mathematicians, and Biff the show dog." Booklist

Louvish, Simon

Monkey business; the lives and legends of the Marx brothers: Groucho, Chico, Harpo, Zeppo with added Gummo. St. Martin's Press 2000 471p il o.p. Warner Bks. paperback available $13.95   **920**

1. Marx Brothers
ISBN 0-446-67695-0 (pa)   LC 00-302623

First published 1999 in the United Kingdom

In addition to Groucho, the author "expands the canvas to appraise the contributions of the other brothers, plus Margaret Dumont, a regular target of the brothers' mayhem. . . . Louvish does a solid job of separating fact from fiction and includes a family tree and a discussion of the FBI's file on the group." Libr J

Lovell, Mary S.

The sisters: the saga of the Mitford family. Norton 2002 c2001 611p il $29.95; pa $18.95
920

1. Mitford family 2. Mitford, Nancy, 1904-1973 3. Mitford, Jessica, 1917-1996 4. Mitford, Unity, 1914-1948
ISBN 0-393-01043-0; 0-393-32414-1 (pa)
LC 2001-44942

First published 2001 in the United Kingdom with title: The Mitford girls

"The story of the six high-spirited, aristocratic, amusing and amusable sisters who did as they pleased, mostly, and captured the imagination of Britain for about half the 20th century; the author takes no sides and, what is truly remarkable, keeps track of all six lives at once." NY Times Book Rev

Includes bibliographical references

Malone, John Williams

It doesn't take a rocket scientist; great amateurs of science; [by] John Malone. Wiley 2002 232p $24.95   **920**

1. Scientists
ISBN 0-471-41431-X   LC 2003-269159

This examines the lives and work of ten amateur scientists, including Gregor Mendel, David H. Levy, Henri-

Malone, John Williams—*Continued*

etta Swan Leavitt, Joseph Priestley, Michael Faraday, Grote Reber, Arthur C. Clarke, Thomas Jefferson, Susan Hendrickson, and Felix d'Herelle

Includes bibliographical references

Marton, Kati

Hidden power; presidential marriages that shaped our recent history. Pantheon Bks. 2001 414p il hardcover o.p. paperback available $14 **920**

1. Presidents—United States 2. Presidents' spouses—United States

ISBN 0-385-72188-9 (pa)

This book provides a "survey of a dozen First Couples, from Edith and Woodrow Wilson to Laura and George Bush. Marton mixes some good history with a lot of pop marriage psychology to show the part that patience, tolerance, insight, determination, sex and occasionally even love have played in the pursuit and exercise of presidential power." Time

Includes bibliographical references

McBrien, Richard P.

Lives of the popes; the pontiffs from St. Peter to John Paul II. HarperSanFrancisco 1997 520p hardcover o.p. paperback available $18 **920**

1. Popes—Biography 2. Papacy

ISBN 0-06-065304-3 (pa)   LC 97-21897

The author provides biographical sketches of all the popes since the Apostle Peter. He also offers an "overview of the evolution of the Roman Catholic Church, ponders the probable future of the papacy, reviews the rules governing both the election and the removal of a pope, furnishes . . . outlines of key papal encyclicals, rates the popes, and includes a time line of significant papal, ecclasiastical, and secular events." Booklist

McBrien offers "plenty of historical facts and sobering, valuable judgments." N Y Times Book Rev

Includes bibliographical references

McNally, Dennis

A long strange trip; the inside history of the Grateful Dead. Broadway Bks. 2002 684p il $30; pa $18.95 **920**

1. Grateful Dead (Musical group)

ISBN 0-7679-1185-7; 0-7679-1186-5 (pa)

LC 2002-25561

A history of the rock music group led by Jerry Garcia which first became popular in the 1960's

"As the Dead's publicist for more than 20 years, McNally packs this . . . full of intimate details otherwise unavailable. . . . The most exhaustively researched book on the band to date." Publ Wkly

Includes bibliographical references

Mikaelian, Allen

Medal of honor; profiles of America's military heroes from the Civil War to the present; with commentary by Mike Wallace. Hyperion 2002 xxviii, 300p $25.95; pa $14.95 **920**

1. Soldiers—United States 2. United States—Military history

ISBN 0-7868-6662-4; 0-7868-8576-9 (pa)

The author "portrays eleven recipients of the award, from each branch of the military, and examines what

drove them to go so far above and beyond the call of duty. They include Leopold Karpeles, a Union colorbearer during the horrifically chaotic Civil War Battle of the Wilderness; Vernon Baker, who single-handedly destroyed three German machine-gun nests during a fierce World War II engagement; and Thomas Kelley, who, during a river battle in Vietnam, continued to protect a disabled troop transport even after sustaining a severe head wound from the blast of an enemy rocket." Publisher's note

"This absorbing set of accounts should appeal to military history enthusiasts and anyone interested in the heroic exploits of ordinary Americans." Publ Wkly

Nagel, Paul C.

The Adams women; Abigail and Louisa Adams, their sisters and daughters. Oxford Univ. Press 1987 310p il o.p.; Harvard Univ. Press paperback available $16.50 **920**

1. Adams, Abigail, 1744-1818 2. Adams, Louisa Catherine, 1775-1852 3. Adams family

ISBN 0-674-00410-8 (pa)   LC 86-31262

The author describes "the lives of the Adams wives and daughters as women in the society where the Adams men were so prominent. Using their letters and journals as his principal source, and quoting from them liberally, he has brought these strong and intelligent women to the center of the stage." Wilson Libr Bull

Includes bibliographical references

Nash, Jay Robert

Bloodletters and badmen; a narrative encyclopedia of American criminals from the Pilgrims to the present. completely rev updated & expanded. Evans & Co. 1995 698p il pa $19.95 **920**

1. Criminals

ISBN 0-87131-777-X   LC 94-49585

First published 1973 by Lippincott

Among the notorious Americans profiled are Charles Whitman, David Berkowitz, Charlie Starkweather, Richard Speck, Lee Harvey Oswald, Al Capone, Dutch Schultz, Bonnie Parker, Clyde Barrow, Frank and Jesse James, and the Wild Bunch

Includes bibliographical references

The **Norton** book of American autobiography; edited and introduced by Jay Parini and with a preface by Gore Vidal. Norton 1999 711p $32.50 **920**

1. United States—Biography 2. Autobiography

ISBN 0-393-04677-X   LC 98-43398

"Parini has compiled over 60 selections from autobiographies and memoirs published since the 17th century. . . . [He] includes works by such diverse writers as Henry David Thoreau, U.S. Grant, Gertrude Stein, Malcom X, Mary McCarthy, and Richard Rodriguez. . . . The selections are arranged chronologically, and each is prefaced by an introduction on its author and its merit." Libr J

Includes bibliographical references

O'Neill, Joseph, 1964-

Blood-dark track; a family history. Granta Bks. 2001 338p il maps $27.95 **920**

1. O'Neill, James, 1909-1973

ISBN 1-86207-288-4   LC 2001-431289

"A smart, diligent inquiry into the World War II era and the (possibly culpable) activities of the author's

O'Neill, Joseph, 1964-—*Continued*
grandfathers, one a Turk interned by the British in Palestine, the other an I.R.A. officer, perhaps a murderer." NY Times Book Rev

Perry, Mark, 1950-
Lift up thy voice; the Grimké family's journey from slaveholders to civil rights leaders. Viking 2001 xxiii, 406p hardcover o.p. paperback available $15   **920**
1. Grimké family
ISBN 0-14-200103-1 (pa)   LC 2001-17594
The author discusses "the Grimke family of South Carolina. . . . John Faucherand Grimke . . . was a slaveholding aristocrat who spawned two internationally known abolitionist daughters, who in turn nurtured their biracial nephews, . . . Archibald and Francis, [who] . . . carried on their aunts' legacy of pursuing racial justice through their leadership in the National Association for the Advancement of Colored People, and the Harlem Renaissance." Women's Rev Books
This book "provides an important and highly readable narrative." N Y Times Book Rev
Includes bibliographical references

Plutarch, ca. 46-ca. 120
Plutarch: the lives of the noble Grecians and Romans; the Dryden translation; edited and revised by Arthur Hugh Clough. Modern Lib. 1992 2v ea $23.95   **920**
1. Greece—Biography 2. Rome—Biography
ISBN 0-679-60008-6 (v1); 0-679-60009-4 (v2)
    LC 92-50223
First Modern Library edition published 1932
This work is "arranged mainly in pairs in which a Greek and a Roman are contrasted. His subjects, who include Demosthenes and Cicero, were statesmen or generals. In the process of writing about them, he invents dialogue and describes the emotions of the personages involved." Reader's Ency. 4th edition

Prose, Francine, 1947-
The lives of the muses; nine women & the artists they inspired. HarperCollins Pubs. 2002 419p il $25.95   **920**
1. Creation (Literary, artistic, etc.) 2. Women—Biography
ISBN 0-06-019672-6   LC 2002-24682
The author examines the lives of "Hester Thrale, Dr. Johnson's guiding light; Alice Liddell, the inspiration for *Alice in Wonderland*; Elizabeth Siddal, prey to the morbid Dante Gabriel Rosetti; Lou Andreas-Salome . . . who entranced Nietzsche, Rilke, and Freud; the dreadful Gala Dali; the photographer Lee Miller, who 'graduated from being seen to seeing'; Charis Weston, a muse demoted to 'art wife'; dancer Suzanne Farrell, whose artistry suggests that choreographer George Balanchine was as much her muse as she was his; and the 'reviled and despised' Yoko Ono." Booklist
Includes bibliographical references

Reynolds, Moira Davison
American women scientists; 23 inspiring biographies, 1900-2000. McFarland & Co. 1999 149p il $35   **920**
1. Women scientists
ISBN 0-7864-0649-6   LC 99-14603
"Four-to-six page profiles of 23 of the century's premier women scientists, representing a wide variety of

disciplines. The entries are arranged chronologically beginning with Cornelia Clapp (1849-1934) and ending with Mary Good (1931-). . . . Each entry includes a black-and-white portrait." SLJ
Includes bibliographical references

Richardson, John, 1924-
Sacred monsters; profiles of friends and foes: Capote, Garbo, Braque, and others. Random House 2001 363p il $27.95   **920**
1. Arts—Biography 2. Celebrities
ISBN 0-679-42490-3   LC 2001-31623
Each of the biographical essays collected here "is a portrait of an intriguing art world figure whom Richardson either knew personally or felt compelled to rescue from oblivion, and his subjects span twentieth-century art, from the Sitwells and Picasso's surrogate mother, trendsetter Eugenia Errazuriz, to Warhol and Brice Marden. In between, Richardson, whose dry wit is as delectable as fine wine, tells riveting, sexually candid tales about peculiar but gratifying relationships." Booklist

Ritter, Lawrence S.
The glory of their times; the story of the early days of baseball told by the men who played it. new enl ed. Morrow 1984 360p il hardcover o.p. paperback available $14.95
    920
1. Baseball—Biography
ISBN 0-688-11273-0 (pa)   LC 84-221549
First published 1966 by Macmillan
A collection of 26 oral histories of baseball's early days by veteran players

Rubin, Louis Decimus, 1923-
My father's people; a family of Southern Jews; [by] Louis D. Rubin Jr. Louisiana State Univ. Press 2002 139p il $22.50   **920**
1. Rubens family
ISBN 0-8071-2808-2   LC 2002-454
The author "tells the stories of Hyman and Fannie Rubin, his grandparents, and their seven children. . . . Rubin's descriptions are affectionate, yet he doesn't gloss over their flaws, and as a result, those he knows best come alive for readers." Publ Wkly

Russell, Dick
Black genius and the American experience. Carroll & Graf Pubs. 1997 497p il hardcover o.p. paperback available $16.95   **920**
1. African Americans—Intellectual life 2. African Americans—Biography
ISBN 0-7867-0573-6 (pa)   LC 97-34048
Russell "focuses on 24 men and nine women, some well known and many lesser known—among them Duke Ellington, Romare Bearden, Ralph Ellison, Cheryl McAfee, Paul Robeson, Gordon Parks, Cornel West, Toni Morrison, Bob Moses, Elma Lewis, and Albert Murray—in a refreshingly atypical narrative style of juxtapositions rather than linearity." Libr J
Includes bibliographical references

Salley, Columbus
The black 100; a ranking of the most influential African-Americans, past and present. rev and updated. Carol Pub. Group 1999 384p il pa $21.95   **920**
1. African Americans—Biography
ISBN 0-8065-2048-5   LC 98-47713
"A Citadel Press book"

Salley, Columbus—*Continued*

First publishd 1993

The author profiles 100 black men and women and ranks them, based upon his subjective evaluation of their contributions to black American society. They include Dr. Martin Luther King, Jr., Malcolm X, Zora Neale Hurston, Paul Robeson, Muhammad Ali, Arthur Ashe, Toni Morrison, Oprah Winfrey, and August Wilson

Includes bibliographical references

Schonberg, Harold C.

The great pianists. rev and updated. Simon & Schuster 1987 525p il hardcover o.p. paperback available $18   **920**

1. Pianists

ISBN 0-671-63837-8 (pa)   LC 87-341

"A Fireside book"

First published 1963

Beginning with the Bach family, the author describes the personal lives and careers of outstanding pianists from the eighteenth century to the present

The lives of the great composers. 3rd ed. Norton 1997 653p il $35   **920**

1. Composers

ISBN 0-393-03857-2   LC 96-13308

First published 1970

This book traces the lives of important musical figures from Monteverdi to Ives and includes information on the serialists, minimalist composers and the new tonalists of the 1990s

"Schonberg writes for the lay reader. His intention is to humanize the composers and the writing, always highly readable, emphasizes biographical information rather than musical analysis." Libr J

Includes bibliographical references

Sifters: Native American women's lives; edited by Theda Perdue. Oxford Univ. Press 2001 260p (Viewpoints on American culture) $55; pa $19.95   **920**

1. Native American women

ISBN 0-19-513080-4; 0-19-513081-2 (pa)

LC 00-39950

"From Pocahontas, a Powhatan woman of the seventeenth century, to Ada Deer, the Menominee woman who headed the Bureau of Indian Affairs in the 1990s, the essays span four centuries. Each one recounts the experiences of women from vastly different cultural traditions. . . . Contributors focus on the ways in which different women have fashioned lives that remain firmly rooted in their identity as Native women." Publisher's note

Includes bibliographical references

Starkey, David

Six wives: the queens of Henry VIII. HarperCollins Pubs. 2003 xxvii, 852p il $29.95   **920**

1. Henry VIII, King of England, 1491-1547 2. Great Britain—History—1485-1603, Tudors

ISBN 0-694-01043-X

The author covers each of Henry's six wives, "their personalities, their place in the family networks and religious currents at court and the overall patterns of the king's infatuations and disillusionments." Publ Wkly

"Solidly researched and delightfully told, this is highly recommended." Libr J

Includes bibliographical references

Steinhardt, Arnold, 1937-

Indivisible by four; a string quartet in pursuit of harmony. Farrar, Straus & Giroux 1998 308p hardcover o.p. paperback available $15   **920**

1. Guarneri String Quartet

ISBN 0-374-52700-8 (pa)   LC 98-7978

"Having been together for 35 years, the Guarneri quartet, with John Dalley, Michael Tree, David Soyer and Steinhardt as first violin, is the oldest American group to have preserved the same membership. With self-effacing modesty, . . . Steinhardt describes both his own career and that of the group." Publ Wkly

Terkel, Studs, 1912-

My American century. New Press 1997 xxiii, 532p hardcover o.p. paperback available $14.95   **920**

1. United States—Biography

ISBN 1-56584-469-6 (pa)   LC 96-52779

This volume gathers "the introductions Terkel wrote for his eight oral-history books (and the fiftieth anniversary edition of Steinbeck's *The Grapes of Wrath*) with 40-odd interviews: Terkel's conversations with gangsters and grandmothers, authors and executives, photographers and farmers, cabbies and crusaders. . . . A superb introduction to Terkel's work (or to oral history) and a trip down memory lane for his fans." Booklist

Thomas, Robert McG., Jr.

52 McGs; the best obituaries from legendary New York Times writer Robert McG. Thomas Jr.; edited by Chris Calhoun; foreword by Thomas Mallon. Scribner 2001 192p il $20   **920**

1. Obituaries

ISBN 0-7432-1562-1   LC 2001-42952

Also available in paperback from Citadel Press

Thomas chose "as his subjects unsung characters who had died in unremarkable ways. His obituaries, which became known simply as McG.s, focused on such marginal celebrities as the inventor of Kitty Litter, a traveling goat man, and a champion duckpins player." Libr J

"This highly browsable collection of 52 obits shows Thomas at his deadline best." Publ Wkly

Tillyard, Stella K.

Aristocrats; Caroline, Emily, Louisa, and Sarah Lennox, 1740-1832; [by] Stella Tillyard. Farrar, Straus & Giroux 1994 406p il hardcover o.p. paperback available $17

920

1. Aristocracy 2. Great Britain—Social life and customs

ISBN 0-374-52447-5 (pa)   LC 94-9799

This is an account of four 18th-century society women. They "are Caroline, Emily, Louisa and Sarah Lennox, daughters of the second Duke of Richmond, the grandson of Charles II and his mistress Louise de Kéroualle. The main story starts with the birth of Caroline in 1723 and ends with the death of Sarah in 1826." London Rev Books

The Lennox sisters "were born into the highest reaches of eighteenth-century society; their letters, spanning nearly a century, give a panoramic view of aristocratic Georgian life. Drawing on their correspondence and a wealth of supporting material, Stella Tillyard brings them together in a richly detailed group biography that reads as satisfyingly as any family chronicle in fiction." Times Lit Suppl

To the best of my ability; the American presidents; James McPherson, editor. DK Pub. 2000 480p il map hardcover o.p. paperback available $19.95   **920**
1. Presidents—United States
ISBN 0-7894-8156-1 (pa)   LC 00-21569
The first half of this heavily illustrated book summarizes the "lives and administrations of the 42 men who have held the presidency. Each has a chapter generally running between six to eight pages . . . written by one of 32 contributing historians or biographers. . . . The second half of the book contains chapters on each election campaign, including very short essays describing issues, tables of results, and the full text of each president's inaugural address." Libr J

Truman, Margaret, 1924-
First ladies. Random House 1995 368p il o.p.; Fawcett Bks. paperback available $13.95   **920**
1. Presidents' spouses—United States
ISBN 0-449-22323-X (pa)   LC 95-9713
"Truman's look at the nation's first ladies features capsule accounts of a selective number of women who have shared the White House with their husbands. She includes the obvious subjects such as Martha Washington, Dolley Madison, Mary Todd Lincoln, Eleanor Roosevelt and all the modern presidents' wives, along with lesser-known first ladies as Julia Grant and Julia Tyler." Publ Wkly
"Written in a chatty, gossipy, easy-to-read style, the book offers thumbnail sketches that are insightful, amusing, factual, personal, and sometimes colored by [the author's] own experiences in the White House." SLJ

Uglow, Jennifer S.
The lunar men; five friends whose curiosity changed the world; [by] Jenny Uglow. Farrar, Straus & Giroux 2002 xx, 588p il $30; pa $15   **920**
1. Darwin, Erasmus, 1731-1802 2. Priestley, Joseph, 1733-1804 3. Watt, James, 1736-1819 4. Wedgwood, Josiah, 1730-1795 5. Boulton, Matthew, 1728-1809 6. Lunar Society of Birmingham (England) 7. Inventors 8. Scientists
ISBN 0-374-19440-8; 0-374-52888-8 (pa)
        LC 2002-72353
The author discusses the friends who in the 1760s founded a discussion club called the Lunar Society that met once a month in Birmingham, England. Among them were the "toymaker Matthew Boulton and his partner James Watt, of steam-engine fame; the potter Josiah Wedgwood; . . . [and] Erasmus Darwin, physician, poet, inventor, and theorist of evolution (a forerunner of his grandson Charles). Later came Joseph Priestley, discoverer of oxygen and fighting radical." Publisher's note
"Uglow has given us a remarkable story of remarkable men, richly detailed and brilliantly told. She has mined the archives with telling effect, and if she gives us the Lunars in the round, she has not neglected their science. It is an exemplary work." N Y Times Book Rev

Walker-Hill, Helen
From spirituals to symphonies; African-American women composers and their music. Greenwood Press 2002 401p il $94.95   **920**
1. African American women 2. Composers
ISBN 0-313-29947-1   LC 2001-40600
This profiles the lives and works of Undine Smith Moore, Julia Perry, Margaret Bonds, Irene Britton Smith, Dorothy Rudd Moore, Valerie Capers, Mary Watkins, and Regina Harris Baiocchi
This is "an accessible, thoughtful, and humanist study. . . . Detailed works lists and an appendix enumerating other black women composers add reference value." Libr J

Ward-Royster, Willa, 1922-
How I got over; Clara Ward and the world-famous Ward Singers; {by} Willa Ward-Royster; as told to Toni Rose; foreword by Horace Clarence Boyer. Temple Univ. Press 1997 263p $51.50   **920**
1. Clara Ward Singers 2. Gospel music
ISBN 1-56639-489-9   LC 96-5943
"Ward-Royster relates the rise of her family's world-renowned gospel group, formed by her mother and headlined by her sister. . . . The book contains details on everything from successful performances on the stage of the Apollo, major TV variety shows, and international tours to top sales of hit recordings and friendships with such luminaries as Mahalia Jackson." Libr J

Ware, Susan, 1950-
Letter to the world; seven women who shaped the American century. Norton 1998 xxiv, 344p il $25.95   **920**
1. Women—Biography
ISBN 0-393-04652-4   LC 97-45923
Also available in paperback from Harvard Univ. Press
The author "considers the lives of seven women who had an exceptional impact on 20th-century American culture and society's perception of the role of women: Eleanor Roosevelt, Dorothy Thompson, Margaret Mead, Katharine Hepburn, Babe Didrikson Zaharias, Martha Graham, and Marian Anderson. In addition to focusing on outstanding achievements in their chosen fields, Ware looks at their often unconventional private lives." Libr J
Includes bibliographical references

Warner, Ezra J.
Generals in blue; lives of the Union commanders. Louisiana State Univ. Press 1964 xxiv, 679p il $39.95   **920**
1. Generals 2. United States—History—1861-1865, Civil War—Biography
ISBN 0-8071-0822-7
This book contains biographical sketches of the 583 men who attained the rank of general during the Civil War years. A photograph of each man is also included
Includes bibliographical references

Warner, Ezra J.—*Continued*

Generals in gray; lives of the Confederate commanders. Louisiana State Univ. Press 1959 xxvii, 420p il $39.95   **920**
1. Generals 2. United States—History—1861-1865, Civil War—Biography 3. Confederate States of America—Biography
ISBN 0-8071-0823-5

"Biographical sketches of the Confederate generals; concise outlines of their military careers, also giving dates of birth and death and places of burial. The product of ten years of research, much of it done in interviews with descendants. Illustrated with 425 portraits." Publ Wkly

Includes bibliographical references

Weir, Alison

The children of Henry VIII. Ballantine Bks. 1996 385p il hardcover o.p. paperback available $15   **920**
1. Great Britain—History—1485-1603, Tudors
ISBN 0-345-40786-5 (pa)   LC 96-14849
Published in the United Kingdom with title: Children of England

This "book covers the lives of Henry's children Mary Tudor and Edward VI, but it only takes Elizabeth up to her accession, and it also includes the entire short life of Jane Grey, the granddaughter of Henry's sister Mary. When Henry died in 1547, he left a country embroiled in several social problems brought about by the enclosure of common lands, the high cost of his European wars, and the closure of monasteries. How his heirs dealt with these problems, along with their relationships, makes interesting reading." Libr J

Includes bibliographical references

The six wives of Henry VIII. Grove Weidenfeld 1992 643p il hardcover o.p. paperback available $15   **920**
1. Henry VIII, King of England, 1491-1547 2. Great Britain—History—1485-1603, Tudors
ISBN 0-8021-3683-4 (pa)   LC 91-29522
First published 1991 in the United Kingdom

This is a collective biography of the wives of the Tudor king of England

"Wonderfully detailed, extensively researched. . . . The narrative is free flowing, humorous, informative, and readable." SLJ

Includes bibliographical references

Zwonitzer, Mark

Will you miss me when I'm gone? the Carter Family and their legacy in American music; {by} Mark Zwonitzer with Charles Hirshberg. Simon & Schuster 2002 417p il $25   **920**
1. Carter family (Musical group)
ISBN 0-684-85763-4   LC 2002-22395
The author "follows the Carter family's history from the 1891 birth of A.P. Carter, the musical founder, up through the late 1970s, offering background on the social, economic and technological developments that spawned American folk, country and rock music. . . . Zwonitzer writes with flair, weaving anecdotes into a compelling study that will intrigue historians and music lovers alike." Publ Wkly

920.003   Biographical reference works

Abrams, Irwin

The Nobel Peace Prize and the laureates; an illustrated biographical history, 1901-2001. Centennial ed. Science Hist. Publs. 2001 350p il pa $35   **920.003**
1. Nobel Prizes 2. Biography—Dictionaries
ISBN 0-88135-388-4   LC 2001-49554
First published 1988 by G.K. Hall & Co.

This reference work "provides a biography with bibliographic references (and a photograph) of each individual winner of the Nobel Peace Prize from its inception in 1901 through the 2001 award. . . . The introductory material and all the biographical entries are concise, well-written, meet high academic standards, and are enjoyable as well." Choice

Adamson, Lynda G.

Notable women in American history; a guide to recommended biographies and autobiographies. Greenwood Press 1999 450p $52.95   **920.003**
1. Women—Biography—Dictionaries 2. Autobiography—Bibliography 3. Diaries—Bibliography 4. United States—Biography—Dictionaries
ISBN 0-313-29584-0   LC 98-55350
Companion volume to Notable women in world history

This volume "concentrates on women who made contributions to U.S. history from the colonial period through 1998. The 500 women covered were born in America or became naturalized citizens; had a full-length biography or autobiography published since 1970; and, in the case of twentieth-century actors, authors, and poets, have been recognized by their peers." Booklist

Notable women in world history; a guide to recommended biographies and autobiographies. Greenwood Press 1998 401p $52.95   **920.003**
1. Women—Biography—Dictionaries
ISBN 0-313-29818-1   LC 97-33136

"The entries are arranged alphabetically by last name with appropriate cross-references for alternative designations. Each contains the woman's name, key dates, occupation or avocation, and birthplace. A short biographical sketch about parents, education, general achievement, and recognition or awards follows. Women of all time periods are included. . . . Because it includes only those born outside the U.S., it complements sources on American women. *Notable Women in World History* is a useful addition to academic, public, and high-school libraries. It would be especially useful for women's studies collections." Booklist

Allaby, Michael, 1933-

Makers of science; [by] Michael Allaby & Derek Gjertsen. Oxford Univ. Press 2002 5v il maps set $185   **920.003**
1. Scientists 2. Science—History
ISBN 0-19-521680-6   LC 2001-48396
"This set incorporates the political and social setting as well as the scientific achievements of each scientist. Volumes are arranged chronologically, beginning with Aristotle and ending with Stephen Hawking. In between

Allaby, Michael, 1933-—_Continued_

are biographies of more than 40 European and U.S. scientists 'whose discoveries were crucial to the development of science,' ranging in length from 8 to 16 pages. . . . Scientific principles are clearly explained, often with diagrams. Intriguing personal stories are also woven in." Booklist

American authors, 1600-1900; a biographical dictionary of American literature; edited by Stanley J. Kunitz and Howard Haycraft. Wilson, H.W. 1938 846p il (Authors series) $115 **920.003**

1. Authors, American—Dictionaries 2. American literature—Bio-bibliography

ISBN 0-8242-0001-2

"Complete in one volume with 1300 biographies and 400 portraits." Title page

"This volume contains biographies of 1,300 authors who contributed to the development of American literature, from the founding of Jamestown (1607) to the end of the nineteenth century. Each essay describes the author's life, discusses past and present significance, and evaluates principal works." Safford. Guide to Ref Materials for Sch Media Cent. 5th edition

American men & women of science; a biographical directory of today's leaders in physical, biological and related sciences. Gale Group 8v set $975 **920.003**

1. Scientists—Dictionaries

ISSN 0192-8570

Also available CD-ROM version

Irregular. First published 1906 by Science Press with title: American men of science. Some editions were divided into two sections: Physical and biological sciences and Social sciences

"Brief biographical sketches of . . . scientists and engineers active in the United States and Canada. Arranged alphabetically, with discipline index." Ref Sources for Small & Medium-sized Libr. 6th edition

American national biography; general editors, John A. Garraty, Mark C. Carnes. Oxford Univ. Press 1999 24v set $795 **920.003**

1. United States—Biography—Dictionaries

ISBN 0-19-520635-5 LC 98-20826

Also available online

Also available Supplement 1 published 2002 $150 (ISBN 0-19-515063-5), the first in an ongoing series of Supplements

Conceived as the successor to the Dictionary of American biography, first published between 1926 and 1937

Published under the auspices of the American Council of Learned Societies

"ANB defines 'American' broadly as a person whose significance, achievement, fame, or influence occurred during residence within what is now the US, or whose life or career directly influenced the course of US history. Subjects must have died before 1996. . . . Subjects are arranged alphabetically. The typical entry, 750 to 7,500 words in length, proceeds chronologically, following the major personal and professional events of the subject's life, birth to death. The concluding paragraph attempts to assess the subject's contributions from today's perspective. A brief bibliography after each entry, not meant to be comprehensive, lists major sources, including locations of archives and collections of personal papers." Choice

American political leaders, 1789-2000. CQ Press 2000 546p $60 **920.003**

1. Politicians—United States—Dictionaries 2. United States—Biography—Dictionaries

ISBN 1-56802-562-9 LC 00-25223

First published 1987 with title: American leaders, 1789-1987

A compilation of biographical information on presidents, vice-presidents, state governors, cabinet officers, members of Congress, and Supreme Court justices

American writers; a collection of literary biographies; Leonard Unger, editor in chief. Scribner 1974-1998 4v + supplement I-IV (in 8v) + retrospective supplement 1 set $1845 **920.003**

1. Authors, American—Dictionaries 2. American literature—Bio-bibliography 3. American literature—History and criticism

ISBN 0-684-80586-3

Continued by ongoing series of supplementary volumes each $145

"Signed essays on the life and works of selected American authors; selective bibliographies by and about each author. The basic set (1974. 4 v.) contains 97 essays originally published in the University of Minnesota pamphlets on American writers series; some have been revised and updated. Each of the 2-v. supplements covers 29 writers not included in the parent series; the supplements give greater attention to women and minorities." Guide to Ref Books. 11th edition

American writers: selected authors; a three volume set containing sixty-four essays from the parent publication is available $325 (ISBN 0-684-80604-5)

Ancell, R. Manning, 1942-

The biographical dictionary of World War II generals and flag officers; the U.S. Armed Forces; [by] R. Manning Ancell with Christine M. Miller. Greenwood Press 1996 706p $130.95 **920.003**

1. World War, 1939-1945—Biography—Dictionaries 2. United States—Armed Forces—Biography—Dictionaries 3. Generals—Dictionaries 4. Admirals—Dictionaries

ISBN 0-313-29546-8 LC 95-50450

"The nearly 2,400 entries, which, according to the preface, represent 99 percent of the total number who served, are listed in alphabetical order in six chapters: 'Army,' 'Army Air Force,' 'National Guard,' 'Navy,' 'Marine Corps,' and 'Coast Guard.' . . . The volume concludes with two appendixes (state-by-state and service-by-service summary of birthplaces and birth dates; generals and flag officers who died during World War II) and an alphabetical index to all biographees." Booklist

Includes bibliographical references

Attwater, Donald, 1892-1977

The Penguin dictionary of saints; [by] Donald Attwater, with Catherine Rachel John. 3rd ed. Penguin Bks. 1995 381p pa $15.95 **920.003**

1. Christian saints—Dictionaries

ISBN 0-14-051312-4 LC 96-165638

First published 1965

"Information includes classification of saints (martyr, confessor, and so on); date of existence; their circumstances in becoming a saint; and their feast day. It also

Attwater, Donald, 1892-1977—*Continued*
provides a glossary and lists of further reading, some patron saints, some emblems that identify specific saints, and feast days in the order that they arrive within the calendar year." Am Ref Books Annu, 1997

Bailey, Martha J., 1929-
American women in science: 1950 to the present; a biographical dictionary. ABC-CLIO 1998 xxxiii, 455p il $75   **920.003**
1. Women scientists—Dictionaries
ISBN 0-87436-921-5   LC 98-22433
Companion volume American women in science: a biographical dictionary (1994)
This work focuses "on individuals, mostly in the United States, who were born in 1920 or after and/or started their careers after 1950. The fields of engineering, physics, anthropology, medicine, computer science, psychology, and chemistry are the best represented. . . . An accurate, well-written, and useful resource." SLJ

Baker's biographical dictionary of musicians. Schirmer Bks. 6v set $675   **920.003**
1. Music—Bio-bibliography 2. Musicians—Dictionaries
First published 1900 in one volume under the authorship of Theodore Baker. (Centennial 9th edition 2001) Periodically revised

Nicolas Slonimsky, editor emeritus
"Brief articles about composers, performers, critics, conductors, and teachers arranged alphabetically under surname with pronunciation, list of musical works, and a bibliography of print sources. Includes classical, jazz, rock, country, blues, and other popular musicians." Ref Sources for Small & Medium-sized Libr. 6th edition
"This monumental work collocates information from classical, popular, and jazz music on a scale greater than any other source. Essential for all libraries." Choice

Baker's biographical dictionary of popular musicians since 1990; introduction by David Freeland. Schirmer Ref. 2003 2v il set $195   **920.003**
1. Popular music—Dictionaries
ISBN 0-02-865799-3   LC 2003-13956
This dictionary includes more than 500 artists and groups active from 1990-2000. Rock, rhythm and blues, rap, country, classical, and jazz are among the popular styles covered. Select discographies, bibliographies, and a glossary of musical terms are provided
"An excellent companion to the 2001 expansion of *Baker's Biographical Dictionary of Musicians.* . . . Given the broad spectrum of musical styles covered here, this would make an excellent reference for public and academic libraries." Libr J

Baker's biographical dictionary of twentieth-century classical musicians; edited by Laura Kuhn; associate editor, Dennis McIntire. Schirmer Bks. 1997 1595p $130   **920.003**
1. Music—Bio-bibliography
ISBN 0-02-871271-4   LC 96-6515
Based on Baker's biographical dictionary of musicians
"This is the first single-volume work on twentieth-century classical composers and musicians. . . . Composers and performers who are known primarily for jazz but made a contribution to classical music are included, such

as George Gershwin, Duke Ellington, Irving Berlin, Max Roach, and Wynton Marsalis. There are brief entries for Richard Rodgers and Frederick Loewe, but not George M. Cohan. . . . This volume will undoubtedly be an essential resource for study of twentieth-century classical musicians." Am Ref Books Annu, 1998

The **Biographical** dictionary of scientists. 3rd ed, consultant editors, Roy Porter, Marilyn Ogilvie. Oxford Univ. Press 2000 2v il set $125   **920.003**
1. Scientists—Dictionaries
ISBN 0-19-521663-6   LC 00-36752
First published 1983-1985 in the United Kingdom; first United States edition edited by David Abbott published 1984-1986 by Bedrick Books
This reference offers over 1,280 entries for men and women in all fields of science ranging in length from 500 to 1,200 words, with 150 illustrations, chronologies, quotations, tables of scientific discoveries and Nobel Prize Winners

Includes bibliographical references

Breton, Mary Joy, 1924-
Women pioneers for the environment. Northeastern Univ. Press 1998 322p il hardcover o.p. paperback available $18.95   **920.003**
1. Environmentalists 2. Women—Biography 3. Environmental movement
ISBN 1-55553-426-0 (pa)   LC 98-16439
The author presents "profiles of 42 women environmentalists from the last two centuries who have addressed myriad environmental issues all around the world. Her chronicling of the valor and intelligence of activists who have risked all to protect threatened species, wilderness areas, and humankind is as riveting as it is informative." Booklist
Includes bibliographical references

British authors of the nineteenth century; edited by Stanley J. Kunitz; associate editor: Howard Haycraft; complete in one volume with 1000 biographies and 350 portraits. Wilson, H.W. 1936 677p il (Authors series) $105   **920.003**
1. Authors, English—Dictionaries 2. English literature—Bio-bibliography
ISBN 0-8242-0007-1
"More than a thousand authors of the British Empire (including Canada, Australia, South Africa, and New Zealand) are represented by sketches varying in length from approximately 100 to 2500 words, roughly proportionate to the importance of the subjects." Preface

Butler, Alban, 1711-1773
Butler's Lives of the saints; complete edition; edited, revised and supplemented by Herbert Thurston and Donald Attwater. Christian Classics 1956 4v set $149.95; pa $109.95   **920.003**
1. Christian saints—Dictionaries
ISBN 0-87061-045-7; 0-87061-137-2 (pa)
Also available in a concise edition, edited by Michael Walsh, in paperback from HarperSanFrancisco
A reprint of the four volume set published 1956 by Kenedy

Butler, Alban, 1711-1773—*Continued*

New edition of a work first published 1756-1759. The calendar arrangement is retained, but the number of entries has almost doubled and many of the entries have been rewritten in whole or part

"The biographies of the saints and beati are arranged by their feast days with each of the four volumes containing three months. . . . Each volume has a table of contents arranged by the days of the month with a list of the feasts for each day." Booklist

The **Cambridge** dictionary of scientists; [by] David Millar [et al.] 2nd ed. Cambridge Univ. Press 2002 464p il hardcover o.p. paperback available $20   **920.003**
1. Scientists—Dictionaries
ISBN 0-521-00062-9 (pa)   LC 2002-512240
First published 1996 as a revision of: Chambers concise dictionary of scientists

"The alphabetically organized, illustrated biographical dictionary . . . [covers] over 1,500 key scientists . . . from 40 countries. Physics, chemistry, biology, geology, astronomy, mathematics, medicine, meteorology and technology are all represented and special attention is paid to pioneer women." Publisher's note

Carlin, Richard

The big book of country music; a biographical encyclopedia. Penguin Bks. 1995 526p o.p.; Leonard, H. paperback available $19.95   **920.003**
1. Country music—Dictionaries
ISBN 0-7935-7564-8 (pa)   LC 94-39275
This volume examines "artists and personnel, musical instruments, and musical forms related to the indigenous American music we call country. The 600 entries offer an overview of the evolution of country music that can be appreciated by novices and devotees alike." Libr J
Includes bibliographical references

Country music: a biographical dictionary. Routledge 2003 497p il $125   **920.003**
1. Country music—Dictionaries
ISBN 0-415-93802-3   LC 2002-3451
"Portions of this book originally appeared as The big book of country music: a biographical encyclopedia, by Richard Carlin (Penguin, 1995)." Verso of title page

The author "presents an authoritative and acerbically opinionated A-Z guide to 700 country western solo artists and groups. Each article consists of a brief biography, career highs and lows, and select discographies." Libr J

Includes bibliographical references

Concise dictionary of American biography. 5th ed complete to 1980. Scribner 1997 2v set $250   **920.003**
1. United States—Biography—Dictionaries
ISBN 0-684-80549-9   LC 97-34104
First published 1964
Published under the auspices of the American Council of Learned Societies

"This edition contains all 19,173 entries from the base set in abridged form. Some 1,063 new biographies, covering people who died between 1971-1980, have been added since the 4th edition." Publisher's note

"The occupations index, listing such colorful categories as adventuress, racketeer, mercantry, and mystic, reflects the diversity of those represented. A good choice for reference collections lacking the full DAB." Libr J

Contemporary artists; editors, Sara Pendergast and Tom Pendergast; advisers, Jean-Christophe Ammann {et al.}. 5th ed. St. James Press 2001 2v il set $265   **920.003**
1. Artists—Dictionaries
ISBN 1-55862-407-4   LC 2001-48443
First one volume edition published 1977

In this reference nearly 850 prominent artists (those who have exhibited works in major galleries or museums) are listed. . . . Alphabetic entries provide biographical information (e.g., nationality, education, address), individual and select group exhibitions, collections in which the artist's work is contained, publications by or about the individual, a critical essay or essays, and occasionally a statement by the artist. The essays highlight the artist's achievements and offer insight into their work. . . . As a reference tool, this publication remains a classic, indispensable part of every art library's collection and is highly recommended." Am Ref Books Annu, 2003

Contemporary authors. Gale Res. apply to publisher for price and availability   **920.003**
1. Authors—Dictionaries   2. Literature—Bio-bibliography
Started publication 1967. Frequency varies. Indexes cumulate at frequent intervals. Editors vary
Revised and updated biographies from this series are: 1st revision, Permanent series, and New revision series

"A bio-bibliographical guide to current writers in fiction, general nonfiction, poetry, journalism, drama, motion pictures, television, and other fields." Title page

"Published to give an up-to-date source of biographical information on current authors in many fields—humanities, social sciences, and sciences—and from many countries. Sketches attempt to give, as pertinent: personal facts (including names of parents, children, etc.), career, writings (as complete a bibliography as possible), work in progress, sidelights, and occasional biographical sources." Guide to Ref Books. 11th edition

Contemporary black biography; profiles from the international black community. Gale Res. il $99   **920.003**
1. African Americans—Biography
ISSN 1058-1316
Started publication 1992. Editors vary

"Included in each volume are biographies of innovators in the black global community who are currently living and/or who have had a lasting impact on society. Every field of endeavor imaginable is represented, from science, politics, and creative arts to sports. . . . This . . . title will be useful for its coverage of current people in the news who are not as easy to find elsewhere." Booklist

Contemporary dramatists. St. James Press $175   **920.003**
1. Dramatists, English—Dictionaries 2. Dramatists, American—Dictionaries 3. English drama—Bio-bibliography 4. American drama—Bio-bibliography
First published 1972 by St. Martin's Press. (6th edition 1998) Periodically revised

"Biographies, published work, and critical essays on living dramatists, with supplements for screen, radio, and television writers, musical librettists, and theater groups." N Y Public Libr. Book of How & Where to Look It Up

Contemporary poets. St. James Press $190
920.003

1. Poets, English—Dictionaries 2. Poets, American—Dictionaries 3. English poetry—Bio-bibliography 4. American poetry—Bio-bibliography

First published 1970 with title: Contemporary poets of the English language. (7th edition 2000) Periodically revised. Editors vary

"A biographical handbook of contemporary poets, arranged alphabetically. Entries consist of a short biography, full bibliography, comments by many of the poets, and a signed critical essay." Ref Sources for Small & Medium-sized Libr. 6th edition

Contemporary Southern writers; guest foreword by Thomas M. Carlson; editor, Roger Matuz. St. James Press 1999 xxvii, 442p $185
920.003

1. Authors, American—Dictionaries 2. American literature—Southern States—Bio-bibliography

ISBN 1-55862-370-1 LC 98-35875

"Each of the 244 entries provides the author's career highlights, awards, and a contact address, as well as a complete bibliography, including uncollected short works, media adaptations, and critical studies. . . . The authors covered represent nearly all categories—poetry, fiction, plays, humor, children's literature, genres, criticism, and nonfiction—and their reputations range from up-and-coming to legendary." Libr J

Contemporary women artists; editors, Laurie Collier Hillstrom, Kevin Hillstrom; with a preface by Lucy R. Lippard. St. James Press 1999 760p $175
920.003

1. Women artists—Dictionaries

ISBN 1-558-62372-8 LC 99-10053

This work "covers 350 women artists, mostly US painters and sculptors. Entries are helpfully indexed by nationality and medium and include photographers, performance and video artists, ceramicists, filmmakers, textile artists, and weavers from countries in Latin America and western and eastern Europe." Choice

Includes bibliographical references

Contemporary women poets; introductory forwords by Elizabeth M. Mills, Diane Wakosi; editor, Pamela L. Shelton. St. James Press 1997 xxi, 400p (Contemporary writers) $175
920.003

1. American poetry—Women authors—Bio-bibliography 2. English poetry—Women authors—Bio-bibliography 3. American poetry—Women authors—Dictionaries 4. English poetry—Women authors—Dictionaries

ISBN 1-55862-356-6 LC 97-38406

This volume provides coverage of "250 modern women poets writing in English. . . . Each entry includes a biography, a listing of works both by and about the poet, a personal statement when available from the poet about her work and influences, and a critical essay." Libr J

Contemporary world writers; preface, Susan Bassnett; editor, Tracy Chevalier. 2nd ed. St. James Press 1993 686p $175
920.003

1. Authors—Dictionaries 2. Literature—Bio-bibliography

ISBN 1-55862-200-4 LC 93-5352

First published 1984 by St. Martin's Press with title: Contemporary foreign language writers

"A biobibliography of approximately 340 living authors from 60 countries, whose works have been translated in whole or in part into English. For each writer, a biographical sketch is followed by a bibliography of works (with translated English language titles or publications), a section of secondary studies in English if available, and a signed critical essay reviewing the author's work." Guide to Ref Books. 11th edition

Cummings, Paul, 1933-1997
Dictionary of contemporary American artists. Palgrave Macmillan il $115 920.003

1. Artists—United States—Dictionaries

First published 1966. (6th edition 1994) Periodically revised

"Information on more than 900 artists: birth and death dates and places, where they studied art and with whom, teaching positions, memberships, commissions, awards and scholarships won, dealers, exhibitions and collections of work, addresses, and extensive bibliographical information. Supplemented with cross-references to artists who appeared in the previous five editions, black-and-white illustrations, a pronunciation guide to names, and a general bibliography." Ref Sources for Small & Medium-sized Libr. 6th edition

Current biography yearbook. Wilson, H.W. il $130
920.003

1. Biography—Periodicals

ISSN 0084-9499

Also available CD-ROM version and online

Current biography: cumulated index, 1940-2000 available $60 (ISBN 0-8242-0997-4)

Annual. First published 1940 with title: Current biography

Also issued monthly except December at a subscription price of $130 per year (ISSN 0011-3344). Yearbooks 1940-2002 available ea $120

"Biographies of prominent people written in lively, popular prose. Emphasis is on entertainers, star athletes, politicians, and other celebrities. Series is cumulative, with biographies revised and updated occasionally. Each volume has seven-year index." N Y Public Libr Book of How & Where to Look It Up

Dictionary of American biography. Scribner 1946 c1927-c1936 10v + supplement 1-10 + comprehensive index set $2930 920.003

1. United States—Biography—Dictionaries

ISBN 0-684-80540-5

First published 1928-1936 as 20 volume set plus index. Supplements 1-10 covering 1931-1980 published 1944-1995. Comprehensive index complete through supplement ten published 1996

Set and first eight supplements published under the auspices of the American Council of Learned Societies Editors vary

"The scholarly American biographical dictionary designed on the lines of the English 'Dictionary of national biography' . . . with signed articles and bibliographies. . . . More than 13,600 biographies in the basic set. Does not include living persons." Guide to Ref Books. 11th edition

Dictionary of Hispanic biography; Joseph C. Tardiff & L. Mpho Mabunda, editors; foreword by Rudolfo Anaya. Gale Res. 1996 xxv, 1011p il $150   **920.003**
1. Hispanic Americans—Dictionaries 2. Spain—Biography—Dictionaries 3. Latin America—Biography—Dictionaries
ISBN 0-8103-8302-0   LC 95-38261
"Ranging from the 'period of discovery' to the present (70 percent of the entries are from the contemporary period), this work covers some 471 notable Hispanics of Spain, Spanish America, and the United States. Virtually all vocations are represented." Libr J

The **Dictionary** of national biography; edited by Sir Leslie Stephen and Sir Sidney Lee. Oxford Univ. Press 1908-1909 22v set $2400 + supplementary volumes at various prices   **920.003**
1. Great Britain—Biography—Dictionaries
ISBN 0-19-865101-5
Also available CD-ROM version
A sixty-volume new edition in preparation
Second supplement, 1901-1911 Edited by Sir Sidney Lee (ISBN 0-19-865201-1); Third supplement, 1912-1921 Edited by H. W. C. Davis and J. R. H. Weaver (ISBN 0-19-865202-X); Fourth supplement, 1922-1930 Edited by J. R. H. Weaver (ISBN 0-19-865203-8); Fifth supplement, 1931-1940 Edited by L. G. Wickham Legg (ISBN 0-19-865204-6); Sixth supplement, 1941-1950 Edited by L. G. Wickham Legg and E. T. Williams (ISBN 0-19-865205-4); Seventh supplement, 1951-1960 Edited by E. T. Williams and Helen M. Palmer (ISBN 0-19-865206-2); Eighth supplement, 1961-1970 Edited by E. T. Williams and C. S. Nicholls (ISBN 0-19-865207-0); Ninth supplement, 1971-1980 Edited by Lord Blake and C. S. Nicholls (ISBN 0-19-865208-9) op; Tenth supplement, 1981-1985 Edited by Lord Blake and C. S. Nicholls (ISBN 0-19-865210-0) op; Eleventh supplement, 1986-1990 Edited by C. S. Nicholls (ISBN 0-19-865212-7) op
"Founded in 1882 by George Smith. From the earliest times to 1900." Title page
The main work and first supplement were originally published in sixty-six volumes, in 1885-1901, and reissued 1908-1909 in twenty-two volumes
"Authoritative and comprehensive British biography. Well-documented and signed biographies of notable inhabitants of the British Isles and colonies. Each article includes a bibliography, and every supplement has a cumulative index to all entries beginning from 1901 in one alphabetical sequence." Ref Sources for Small & Medium-sized Libr. 6th edition

Dictionary of scientific biography; Charles Coulston Gillispie, editor in chief. Scribner 1981 c1980-c1990 18v in 10 set $1800   **920.003**
ISBN 0-684-80558-X
This is a reprint of the title published 1970-1980 in 16 volumes. Volumes 15-18 are Supplements
Published under the auspices of the American Council of Learned Societies
This "biographical dictionary covers over forty-five hundred people ranging from Einstein, Newton, and Pasteur to Marx, Columbus, and Abailard. Its focus is on the biographee's place in the history of science, rather than on his or her life story. The signed entries run from part of a page to many pages and include excellent bibliographies." RQ

Dictionary of women artists; editor, Delia Gaze; picture editors, Maja Mihajlovic, Leanda Shrimpton. Fitzroy Dearborn Pubs. 1997 2v il set $310   **920.003**
1. Women artists—Dictionaries
ISBN 1-88496-421-4   LC 97-206872
"The chronological coverage extends from 975 A.D. to artists born in 1945. Each of the alphabetically arranged entries includes a brief biography, information about the genre of art produced, and an example of the artist's work. These volumes also present 20 introductory surveys on such topics as 'Court Artists' and 'Training and Professionalism,' and include an overview of women's art in the 19th and 20th centuries by country. Together with their chronological list of artists, the volumes include a range of information not ordinarily found in a resource of this type." Am Libr

Dictionary of world biography; Frank N. Magill, editor; Christina J. Moose, managing editor; Alison Aves, researcher and bibliographer. Salem Press 1998-1999 10v il set $926   **920.003**
1. Biography—Dictionaries 2. Ancient history
    LC 97-51154
Contents: v1 The ancient world; v2 The Middle Ages; v3 The Renaissance; v4 The 17th and 18th centuries; v5-6 The nineteenth century; v7-9 The 20th century; v10 Index
A revision and reordering, with new entries added, of the material in the thirty volumes comprising the various subsets designated "series" published under the collective title: Great lives from history, 1987-1995

Encyclopedia of American war heroes; Bruce H. Norton, editor and compiler. Facts on File 2002 xxvii, 292p il $60; pa $19.95   **920.003**
1. Heroes and heroines 2. United States—Military history
ISBN 0-8160-4637-9; 0-8160-4638-7 (pa)
    LC 2001-57517
"This volume includes almost 400 entries featuring men and women who fought and, in most cases, died during military service to the U.S. Many of the individuals profiled were awarded one or more citations for their heroic achievements. . . . An introduction, which describes the criteria the editor used for selecting entrants, is followed by a section explaining the different citations. Coverage is extensive, going back to 1675 and extending to the present." Booklist

Encyclopedia of artists; {consulting editor, William Vaughan; contributors, Christopher Ackroyd, et al.}. Oxford Univ. Press 2000 6v il set $195   **920.003**
1. Artists—Dictionaries 2. Art—Dictionaries
ISBN 0-19-521572-9   LC 00-27167
"The first five volumes of this set alphabetically profile more than two hundred artists, covering western art from the Middle Ages to the present. Each artist is accorded a two-page spread consisting of three parts. The main introductory section details the artist's life and work. . . . Each entry then provides a data file that lists the major facts about each artist: nationality, style, dates, key works with dates, things to look for in the art, comparable artists, and related glossary terms. . . . Volume six consists of articles on art movements and styles men-

Encyclopedia of artists—_Continued_
tioned in the other volumes." Voice Youth Advocates

"This set is beautifully written and illustrated. It will not only provide reliable information for researchers but will also entertain the interested browser. It is most appropriate for high school, public, and undergraduate libraries." Am Ref Books Annu, 2001

Encyclopedia of world biography. 2nd ed. Gale Res. 1998 17v il set $1095   **920.003**
1. Biography—Dictionaries
ISBN 0-7876-2221-4   LC 97-42327

Also available CD-ROM version

Kept up-to-date by yearly supplements. Volumes available 1998-2003 designated volumes 18-23 at $125 ea

First published 1973 with title: McGraw-Hill encyclopedia of world biography

Presents brief biographical sketches which provide vital statistics as well as information on the importance of the person listed. Volumes 1-16 are arranged alphabetically; volume 17 is the index

European authors, 1000-1900; a biographical dictionary of European literature; edited by Stanley J. Kunitz and Vineta Colby; complete in one volume with 967 biographies and 309 portraits. Wilson, H.W. 1967 1016p il (Authors series) $115   **920.003**
1. Authors, European—Dictionaries 2. Literature—Bio-bibliography
ISBN 0-8242-0013-6

Includes continental European writers born after the year 1000 and dead before 1925. Nearly a thousand major and minor contributors to thirty-one different literatures are discussed

"These biographies provide quick, satisfactory introductions to a staggering variety of authors and literatures." Choice

Ewen, David, 1907-1985
American songwriters; an H. W. Wilson biographical dictionary. Wilson, H.W. 1987 489p il $105   **920.003**
1. Composers—United States—Dictionaries
ISBN 0-8242-0744-0   LC 86-24654

Replaces Popular American composers and Popular American composers: First supplement, published 1962 and 1972 respectively

Arranged alphabetically, this reference volume includes 146 biographical entries on American lyricists and composers. Ragtime, minstrel, Tin Pan Alley, Broadway, rock, jazz, blues, folk, country and western, and soul are among the styles represented. Biographies range from Eubie Blake, George Gershwin and George M. Cohan to Chuck Berry, Carole King and Bob Dylan

Explorers and discoverers of the world; edited by Daniel B. Baker. Gale Res. 1993 xli, 637p il maps $99   **920.003**
1. Explorers—Dictionaries
ISBN 0-8103-5421-7   LC 92-055094

"Exploration and discovery are conceived in the broadest sense in this work, encompassing all chronological periods with articles on aviators, mountaineers, underwater and space explorers as well as those who promoted exploration. Lesser known individuals, including women and non-Europeans, make up the 320 biographical profiles." Libr J

Farmer, David Hugh
The Oxford dictionary of saints. 5th ed. Oxford Univ. Press 2003 xxiv, 579p maps pa $15.95   **920.003**
1. Christian saints—Dictionaries
ISBN 0-19-860629-X   LC 2003-269437

First published 1978

This biographical dictionary profiles the lives, cults, and artistic associations of over 1,000 saints, from the famous to the obscure. An appendix on pilgrimage sights in Europe is also included

"Even those who do not believe in the saints ... will be able to enjoy and to profit from this splendid book." Economist

Includes bibliographical references

Feather, Leonard
The biographical encyclopedia of jazz; {by} Leonard Feather and Ira Gitler, with the assistance of Swing journal, Tokyo. Oxford Univ. Press 1999 xx, 718p $49.95   **920.003**
1. Jazz musicians
ISBN 0-19-507418-1   LC 98-15485

This book is based in part on Leonard Feather's Encyclopedia of jazz, The new encyclopedia of jazz, The encyclopedia of jazz in the sixties, and on a subsequent work by Mr. Feather and Ira Gitler, The encyclopedia of jazz in the seventies

This reference source "is made up of more than 3,000 biographies, listed in alphabetical order. Musicians, singers, songwriters, and producers are included. Each entry begins with birth and death information, instruments played, and music-education information. This is followed by a listing of groups each individual played with for significant periods of time. Concluding each entry are lists of recordings, broadcast appearances, and record labels. . . . An indispensable reference source for its comprehensiveness and quality of scholarship." Booklist

Includes discographies

Fredriksen, John C.
American military leaders; from colonial times to the present. ABC-CLIO 1999 2v il set $175   **920.003**
1. Soldiers—United States—Biography 2. United States—Military history
ISBN 1-57607-001-8   LC 99-27929

"Prominent men and women of the military are the scope of this reference work. Coverage includes the most famous of leaders such as Grant, Patton, and Schwarzkopf; but what makes the source so outstanding is its inclusion of forgotten leaders such as Native American Stand Watie, aviator Jackie Cochran, and army educator Alden Partridge. Biographies range from two to three pages, concluding with a bibliography. Photographs and illustrations are included, and both a subject index and a list of leaders organized by their military titles can be found at the end of volume two." Am Libr

America's military adversaries; from colonial times to the present. ABC-CLIO 2001 621p il $85   **920.003**
1. Spies—Dictionaries 2. Heads of state—Dictionaries 3. United States—Military history—Dictionaries
ISBN 1-57607-603-2   LC 2001-5293

This is a "biographical encyclopedia of the various military adversaries (naval, air, and land) America has faced since colonial times. . . . The material is divided into a preface, 223 entries for military adversaries of the

Fredriksen, John C.—*Continued*

United States, an appendix listing all by occupation, and an appendix divided by conflict. Additionally, a 50-page bibliography is provided as well as a useful index. . . . This well-done work is especially useful for those looking to begin research into those who led America's military adversaries. It should be included in all libraries." Recomm Ref Books for Small & Medium-sized Libr & Media Cent, 2003

Gates, Alexander E.

A to Z of earth scientists. Facts on File 2002 336p il (Notable scientists) $45

920.003

1. Earth sciences 2. Scientists—Dictionaries
ISBN 0-8160-4580-1   LC 2002-14616

This "profiles the lives of 192 people who devoted their careers to the disciplines and subdisciplines of the earth sciences during the 18th century to the present. . . . Entries appear in alphabetical order under the name by which the scientist is most commonly known. Also included are birth date, date of death (if applicable), nationality, and earth science specialty. An essay containing more personal data, including an emphasis on the scientist's main work and contributions to the field follows this information." Am Ref Books Annu, 2003

Grant, Michael, 1914-

Greek and Latin authors, 800 B.C.-A.D. 1000; a biographical dictionary. Wilson, H.W. 1980 490p il (Authors series) $105   **920.003**

1. Authors, Greek—Dictionaries 2. Authors, Latin—Dictionaries 3. Classical literature—Bio-bibliography
ISBN 0-8242-0640-1   LC 79-27446

Covers more than 370 classical authors. Each entry includes "the pronunciation of the author's name, biographical background, an overview of major works with critical commentary on the nature and quality of those works, and, where relevant, a brief discussion of the influence of the author's works on later literature." Ref Sources for Small & Medium-sized Libr. 5th edition

Gubert, Betty Kaplan, 1934-

Distinguished African Americans in aviation and space science; [by] Betty Kaplan Gubert, Miriam Sawyer, and Caroline M. Fannin. Oryx Press 2002 319p il (Distinguished African Americans series) $64.95   **920.003**

1. African American pilots 2. Astronauts
ISBN 1-57356-246-7   LC 2001-34821

This profiles 80 men and 20 women in aviation and space science covering 80 years of the 20th century

"Public and school libraries should not hesitate to add this title to their collections." Booklist

Includes bibliographical references

Guiley, Rosemary Ellen

The encyclopedia of saints. Facts on File 2001 419p il $82.50; pa $24.95   **920.003**

1. Christian saints—Dictionaries
ISBN 0-8160-4133-4; 0-8160-4134-2 (pa)
                              LC 00-69176

This volume offers "accounts of the lives and experiences of more than 400 principal saints, from early martyrs such as Lucy of Syracuse to recently canonized saints such as Katherine Drexel. Entries provide a biographical overview, a record of the saint's religious jour-

neys and mystical experiences, a discussion of personal philosophies and important theological influences, as well as his or her patronage, feast days and popular role within the Church." Publisher's note

For a review see: Booklist, Feb, 1, 2002

Hall, Timothy L.

American religious leaders. Facts on File 2003 430p il (American biographies) $65

920.003

1. Religious biography
ISBN 0-8160-4534-8   LC 2002-2454

"Facts on File library of American history"

This reference "traces the history of American religion through the lives of its leaders. More than 250 entries explore America's religious and spiritual leaders from colonial times to today. The book focuses on those who have occupied the spotlight of historical attention in one way or another: the founders, the pioneers, the heretics, and the saints, among others. . . . Notable figures and leaders from many of the major churches and religious groups in America are covered, including Episcopalians, Presbyterians, Methodists, Catholics, Black Muslims, Jews, and Mormons along with leaders from smaller and lesser-known but no less important religions." Publisher's note

"This is a perfect source for fast, basic information for anyone who wishes a two-minute reading synopsis on an American religious leader. It should be within arms reach of any reference librarian working an information desk or a telephone." Am Ref Books Annu, 2003

Includes bibliographical references

Supreme Court justices; a biographical dictionary. Facts on File 2001 566p $65

920.003

1. United States. Supreme Court 2. Judges—Dictionaries
ISBN 0-8160-4194-6   LC 00-65415

"Facts on File library of American history"

This work offers "sketches of the lives of members of the Court through the Clinton presidency. . . . Includes a wide array of appendixes that would be valuable at a reference desk. . . . Of greatest interest is the excellent bibliography, grouped by general works, then by justice in alphabetical order. . . . This book would be useful in any public or academic library." Choice

The **Harvard** biographical dictionary of music; edited by Don Michael Randel. Belknap Press 1996 1013p il $39.95

920.003

1. Music—Bio-bibliography
ISBN 0-674-37299-9   LC 96-16456

Companion volume to The New Harvard dictionary of music

"International in scope and covering all eras of music from the ancient to the present, this important new reference source has information concerning 5,500 individuals. Most are associated with classical concert music, although prominent jazz, rock, folk, and popular personalities are also represented: Madonna, Mozart, Zoot Sims, Mick Jagger, and Dolly Parton are included. Musicologists, educators, teachers, and reviewers, no matter how influential, are excluded. Entries consist of brief to long paragraphs that may include a bibliography or a list of compositions. . . . This is an authoritative and significant new reference work which all libraries must purchase." Choice

Havlice, Patricia Pate
Index to artistic biography. Scarecrow Press 1973 2v set $135   **920.003**
1. Artists—Indexes
ISBN 0-8108-0540-5
First supplementary volume (published 1981) available for $115.50 (ISBN 0-8108-1446-3); second supplementary volume (published 2002 in two volumes) available for set $195 (ISBN 0-8108-4062-6)
The first two volumes list some 70,000 artists' biographies found in sixty-four reference works. The first supplement covers seventy titles and lists around 47,000 names. The second supplement covers 131 titles published from 1980 through 1999

The **International** who's who. Europa Publs.; [distributed by] Gale Res. $450   **920.003**
1. Biography—Dictionaries
ISSN 0074-9613
Annual. First published 1935
"Offers brief biographical data on prominent persons throughout the world." Guide to Ref Books. 11th edition

Jewish women in America; an historical encyclopedia; edited by Paula E. Hyman and Deborah Dash Moore. Routledge 1997 2v xxxi, 1770p set $275   **920.003**
1. Jewish women—Dictionaries
ISBN 0-415-91936-3   LC 97-26842
This work contains 800 "biographies and 110 topical essays on subjects ranging from cookbooks to vaudeville. . . . [It provides] encyclopedic coverage of the many varied roles that Jewish women have occupied in America, from the earliest days until the present. All articles are signed and written with attention to detail by noted scholars; 500 period photographs are well-chosen and supplement the text." Am Libr

Kelly, J. N. D. (John Norman Davidson)
The Oxford dictionary of popes. Oxford Univ. Press 1986 347p hardcover o.p. paperback available $15.95   **920.003**
1. Popes—Dictionaries
ISBN 0-19-282085-0 (pa)   LC 85-15599
"An excellent source of information, arranged chronologically with an alphabetical index. Includes popes, antipopes, and an appendix on Pope Joan." Ref Sources for Small & Medium-sized Libr. 6th edition

Kort, Carol
A to Z of American women in the visual arts; [by] Carol Kort and Liz Sonneborn. Facts on File 2002 258p il (Facts on File library of American history) $44   **920.003**
1. American art—Dictionaries 2. Women artists—Dictionaries
ISBN 0-8160-4397-3   LC 2001-40231
At head of title: A to Z of women
This "profiles 130 American women artists who work in a variety of visual mediums, among them painting, sculpture, printmaking, graphic arts, photography, architecture, and quilting." Booklist
A "handy, well-written volume. . . . The biographical entries are filled with interesting personal and career details that make for absorbing reading." Voice Youth Advocates
Includes bibliographical references

Kuhlman, Erika A., 1961-
A to Z of women in world history; [by] Erika Kuhlman. Facts on File 2002 452p il $49.50   **920.003**
1. Women—Biography—Dictionaries
ISBN 0-8160-4334-5   LC 2001-54327
"Facts on File library of world history"
"The 260 women who are profiled here have not only made a mark on their own cultures but have also 'influenced other women from diverse cultures and different historical periods pursuing the same goals.'. . . Entries are organized first under 14 areas of accomplishment, from 'Adventurers and Athletes' to 'Writers.'. . . Entries are generally around two pages in length, and each offers suggestions for further reading. . . . *A to Z of Women in World History* is a good place to start for researchers who are taking a sphere-of-activity approach to women's history. This highly readable volume is recommended for high-school, public, and academic libraries." Booklist

Latin American writers; Carlos A. Solé, editor in chief; Maria Isabel Abreu, associate editor. Scribner 1989 3v set $350   **920.003**
1. Authors, Latin American 2. Latin American literature—History and criticism
ISBN 0-684-18463-X   LC 88-35481
Also available Supplement 1 $130 (ISBN 0-684-80599-5)
This work "provides a scholarly overview of Latin American literature from the colonial period to the present. Entries are lengthy and cover 176 writers of Spanish America and Brazil and include a signed biographical and critical essay, followed by a selected bibliography of primary and secondary sources." Ref Sources for Small & Medium-sized Libr. 6th edition

Leaders of the American Civil War; a biographical and historiographical dictionary; edited by Charles F. Ritter and Jon L. Wakelyn. Greenwood Press 1998 xxxiv, 465p $85   **920.003**
1. United States—History—1861-1865, Civil War—Biography—Dictionaries
ISBN 0-313-29560-3   LC 98-12156
This dictionary "includes 47 articles on outstanding military and civilian Union and Confederate leaders as well as entries for other significant figures, including Frederick Douglass, Clara Barton, Dorothea Dix, and even Walt Whitman." Libr J

Lester, Patrick D.
The biographical directory of Native American painters. SIR Publs.; [distributed by] University of Okla. Press 1995 701p $59.95   **920.003**
1. Native American artists—Directories 2. Native American art
ISBN 0-8061-9936-9 (University of Okla. Press)   LC 95-69012
"Listing more than 3,000 Native American painters and graphic artists from the US and Canada, Lester's book uses survey forms sent to the painters or their families to expand and update Jeanne O. Snodgrass's American Indian Painters (1968), which had 1,188 entries. Coverage is from earliest times to the present. . . . Entries vary in size according to the available information. Most include statistics, education, location of work,

Lester, Patrick D.—*Continued*
and other occupations." Choice
"This useful compendium includes both major and obscure painters and is highly recommended for public and academic libraries." Libr J

McBrien, Richard P.
Lives of the saints; from Mary and Francis of Assisi to John XXIII and Mother Teresa. HarperSanFrancisco 2001 xxiii, 646p il hardcover o.p. paperback available $19.95
920.003
1. Christian saints—Dictionaries
ISBN 0-06-065341-8 (pa)   LC 00-53933
"This work goes beyond the Roman Catholic Church's list of saints to include those of the Orthodox, Anglican, and Lutheran churches. Concise and well-researched biographical sketches are arranged by feast days, with access provided by indexes for saints, personal names, and subjects. Complementing the biographies are thoughtful essays on the history of saints, their place in religious history, and canonization; a series of seven tables on feast days, patron saints, iconography, and papal canonization." Libr J
Includes bibliographical references

Meier, Matt S.
Notable Latino Americans; a biographical dictionary; [by] Matt S. Meier with Conchita Franco Serri and Richard A. Garcia. Greenwood Press 1997 431p il $73.95
920.003
1. Hispanic Americans—Dictionaries
ISBN 0-313-29105-5   LC 96-27392
This dictionary "offers 127 biographies of men and women of Latino descent who were born in or immigrated to the United States and have made a noteworthy impact. The majority of those profiled are writers, sports figures, actors, or political activists, though some lesser-known personalities in the sciences, education, and the arts are also included. The entries average three pages and generally include a picture and a short bibliography of additional sources." Libr J

Merriam-Webster's biographical dictionary. Merriam-Webster 1995 1170p $27.95
920.003
1. Biography—Dictionaries
ISBN 0-87779-743-9   LC 94-43025
Replaces Webster's new biographical dictionary
This work "chronicles the lives of more than 34,000 celebrated, important, and notorious men and women from all parts of the world, all eras, and all fields of endeavor. . . . [Arranged alphabetically, the] entries provide birth and death dates, nationality or ethnic origin, pronunciations, pseudonyms, variant spellings, pertinent information about the individual's career, and more." Publisher's note

Merriam-Webster's dictionary of American writers. Merriam-Webster 2001 536p il $24.95   **920.003**
1. American literature—Bio-bibliography 2. Authors, American—Dictionaries 3. American literature—History and criticism
ISBN 0-87779-022-1   LC 2001-30046
"The bulk of the work consists of 1000 biographical articles on influential American authors. Following is a section of briefer descriptive entries on over 500 literary works, including important novels, poems, plays, essays, and histories. The dictionary ends with a section that lists and describes 75 of the groups, movements, and periodicals that have shaped American literature. . . . This is a wonderful book, to be used for reference and read for enrichment." Libr J

Modern Japanese writers; Jay Rubin, editor. Scribner 2000 434p $130   **920.003**
1. Authors, Japanese 2. Japanese literature—History and criticism
ISBN 0-684-80598-7   LC 00-63505
"This handbook is a collection of alphabetically arranged articles on 23 twentieth-century Japanese writers and one literary genre, written by noted scholars in the field. Entries are generally around 18 pages in length. Each author entry treats a writer's life and work and is accompanied by a selected bibliography of primary and secondary sources. Most of the writers included have been translated into English, and two of them, Kawabata Yasunari and Oe Kenzaburo, are Nobel Prize winners." Booklist

Musicians since 1900; performers in concert and opera; compiled and edited by David Ewen. Wilson, H.W. 1978 974p il $120
920.003
1. Musicians—Dictionaries
ISBN 0-8242-0565-0   LC 78-12727
"Replaces @Living musicians' and its supplement (1940-57). Gives @detailed biographical, critical and personal information about 432 of the most distinguished performing musicians in concert and opera since 1900.'—*Introd.*' . . . A few bibliographical references are given at the end of each biography; a classified list of musicians concludes the volume." Sheehy. Guide to Ref Books. 10th edition

Nobel Prize winners; an H.W. Wilson biographical dictionary; editor, Tyler Wasson; consultants, Gert H. Brieger [et al.] Wilson, H.W. 1987 xxxiv, 1165p il $145   **920.003**
1. Nobel Prizes 2. Biography—Dictionaries
ISBN 0-8242-0756-4   LC 87-16468
Also available 1987-1991 supplement $60 (ISBN 0-8242-0834-X) and 1992-1996 supplement $60 (ISBN 0-8242-0906-0); 1997-2001 supplement $70 (ISBN 0-8242-1018-2)
This reference book "begins with an alphabetical listing of winners, a listing of prize categories (broken down chronologically by years), an article on Alfred Nobel, and another on the process by which the prizes are awarded. . . . Included are all winners (persons and institutions) from 1901-1986 in entries of 1200-1500 words." SLJ

North American women artists of the twentieth century; a biographical dictionary; edited by Jules Heller and Nancy G. Heller. Garland 1995 xxii, 612p il (Garland reference library of the humanities) hardcover o.p. paperback available $41.95
920.003
1. Women artists—Dictionaries
ISBN 0-8153-2584-3 (pa)   LC 94-49710
This is a "guide to more than 1500 Canadian, Mexican, and United States women artists born between 1850

North American women artists of the twentieth century—*Continued*

and 1960. Artists are listed alphabetically, and each artist . . . is briefly treated in several paragraphs that end with bibliographical citations, often to important journal articles. More than 100 illustrations provide a small sampling of their work. . . . An essential acquisition for all art reference libraries." Libr J

The **Norton/Grove** dictionary of women composers; edited by Julie Anne Sadie & Rhian Samuel. Norton 1995 xliii, 548p il $45   920.003
1. Women composers—Dictionaries
ISBN 0-393-03487-9

First published 1994 in the United Kingdom with title: The New Grove dictionary of women composers

This "provides detailed biographies of more than 1,000 creators of Western classical music. In signed articles, the Dictionary chronicles the lives and works of women composers from all corners of the world." Publisher's note

"This important volume does not merely recycle material from the 1980 *New Grove* but collects 900 newly written articles, the longer ones signed." Libr J

Notable American women: the modern period; a biographical dictionary; edited by Barbara Sicherman [et al.] Harvard Univ. Press 1980 xxii, 773p hardcover o.p. paperback available $41.50   920.003
1. Women—United States—Biography 2. United States—Biography—Dictionaries
ISBN 0-674-62733-4 (pa)   LC 80-18402

Also available Notable American women, 1607-1950 pa $57.50 (ISBN 0-674-62734-2)

This set provides "1 1/2- to 2-page biographies and references for 442 American women. Women were chosen from science, business, and engineering as well as from such traditional fields as education, entertainment, and social work, with a wide variety of 'career patterns, philosophical outlooks and personal styles' represented. . . . Entries describe the life and personality of the individual, evaluate her career, and place it in an historical context. Special emphasis is given to the conflicting demands of her public and personal lives." Choice

Notable black American men; Jessie Carney Smith, editor. Gale Res. 1998 xxxiv, 1365p il $150   920.003
1. African Americans—Biography—Dictionaries 2. United States—Biography—Dictionaries
ISBN 0-7876-0763-0   LC 98-38166

Companion to Notable black American women

This work "profiles 500 men, from poet Jupiter Hammon (b. 1711) to Tiger Woods. . . . Each entry begins with birth and death dates and a few words describing the subject's major fields of endeavor, followed by a biographical essay, a list of references, and, in some cases, a note on collections of source material." Booklist

Notable black American scientists; Kristine M. Krapp, editor. Gale Res. 1999 xxvi, 349p il $125   920.003
1. Scientists—Dictionaries 2. African Americans—Biography—Dictionaries
ISBN 0-7876-2789-5   LC 98-36338

The "contributors to this compilation of 254 bibliographic profiles emphasize the achievements of black scientists and physicians, men and women, from Colonial times to the present, in the territory that is now the US. . . . Each entry begins with basic information about each subject—name, year of birth and death (if deceased), and specialty. A biographical essay follows." Choice

Notable black American women [bk I-III]; Jessie Carney Smith, editor. Gale Res. 1992-2002 3v il bk I $160; bk II-III ea $130   920.003
1. African American women—Dictionaries 2. United States—Biography—Dictionaries
ISBN 0-8103-4749-0 (bk I); 0-8103-9177-5 (bk II); 0-7876-6494-4 (bk III)   LC 91-35074

"This biographical encyclopedia documents the achievements of 500 African-American women who have made significant contributions to American culture from the colonial era to the present. . . . Subjects include women active in all fields of endeavor, from education, science, and the arts, to business, law and politics. . . . Authoritative and entertaining at the same time, these sketches are appropriate for high school and college students as well as the general reader." Am Libr [review of first volume]

Notable mathematicians; from ancient times to the present; Robyn V. Young, editor; Zoran Minderovic, associate editor. Gale Res. 1998 xxi, 612p il $105   920.003
1. Mathematicians—Dictionaries
ISBN 0-7876-3071-3   LC 97-33662

This work profiles "300 mathematicians chosen for their historical importance, discoveries, familiarity to the public, awards and prizes, and involvement in mathematics education. . . . Female and minority mathematicians have been expressly represented." Libr J

Includes bibliographical references

Notable native Americans; Sharon Malinowski, editor; George H.J. Abrams, consulting editor and author of foreword. Gale Res. 1995 xliv, 492p il $105
                920.003
1. Native Americans—Biography—Dictionaries
ISBN 0-8103-9638-6   LC 94-36202

This is a "compilation of biographical and bibliographical information on more than two hundred and sixty-five notable Native North American men and women throughout history, from all fields of endeavor. . . . Approximately thirty percent of the entries focus on historical figures and seventy percent on contemporary or twentieth-century individuals. Signed narrative essays, ranging from one to three pages in length, include Indian names and their English translations as well as name variants." Preface

Notable scientists from 1900 to the present; Brigham Narins, editor. [Updated 2nd ed] Gale Group 2001 5v il set $395 **920.003**
1. Scientists—Dictionaries 2. Engineers—Dictionaries
ISBN 0-7876-1751-2 LC 00-110113
First published 1995 with title Notable twentieth-century scientists

This reference profiles "approximately 1,600 scientists active in the twentieth century in the various fields of natural, physical, and applied sciences. More recent fields, such as computer science, ecology, engineering, and environmental science, are represented. The work is international in scope and includes entries for women and minority scientists. . . . The entries begin with the scientist's name, birth and death dates, nationality, and primary field of specialization. This information is followed by a 400- to 2,500-word biographical essay, a list of selected writings by the scientist, and a list of sources for further reading. A photograph of the scientist also accompanies more than 400 of the entries." Am Ref Books Annu, 2002

Notable U.S. ambassadors since 1775; a biographical dictionary; edited by Cathal J. Nolan. Greenwood Press 1997 430p $109.95 **920.003**
1. Diplomats—Dictionaries 2. United States—Foreign relations—Dictionaries
ISBN 0-313-29195-0 LC 96-50291
This work contains historical-biographical profiles of 58 architects of U.S. foreign policy. "Following a preface that describes the editor's selection criteria, each entry begins with full birth and death dates and locations, education, family background, and career progression. The larger issues during diplomatic assignments are described fully, as well as the difficulties in achieving success." Booklist

Notable women in mathematics; a biographical dictionary; edited by Charlene Morrow and Teri Perl. Greenwood Press 1998 302p il $52.95 **920.003**
1. Women mathematicians—Dictionaries
ISBN 0-313-29131-4 LC 97-18598
"This book features five-to-six page profiles of 59 mathematicians and scientific computing researchers from around the world. Each profile describes the woman's major life events and educational and career milestones, includes a discussion of her areas of mathematical research in nontechnical terms, and lists works by and about that person. All entries have an accompanying black-and-white photograph. The majority of essays are based on interviews by the authors." SLJ

Notable women in the physical sciences; a biographical dictionary; edited by Benjamin F. Shearer and Barbara S. Shearer. Greenwood Press 1997 479p il $55
920.003
1. Women scientists—Dictionaries
ISBN 0-313-29303-1 LC 96-9024
"Featuring biographical essays on 96 world and U.S. women scientists, this volume includes women who made a significant contribution to the physical sciences from antiquity to the present, though the emphasis is on 20th-century women. . . . Disciplines include astronomy, astrophysics, biochemistry, chemistry, and physics. The essays average five pages in length and describe obsta-

cles encountered and achievements experienced by each scientist. Each entry provides a chronology, a descriptive essay, and a bibliography." Choice

Oakes, Elizabeth H., 1951-
A to Z of chemists. Facts on File 2002 276p il $45 **920.003**
1. Chemists—Dictionaries
ISBN 0-8160-4579-8 LC 2002-68685
"Facts on File science library"
At head of title: Notable scientists
"This title includes 152 biographies of chemists, including 23 women. . . . The entries run between 750 and 1200 words (one to one and one-half pages apiece). They all begin with a summary of the subject's major contribution, followed by a chronological biography of their personal and professional life. Appendixes list the birthplace and country of activity of the chemists as well as a chart of their life spans." Libr J
For a fuller review see: Booklist, Feb. 1, 2003

International encyclopedia of women scientists. Facts on File 2002 448p il $82.50
920.003
1. Women scientists—Dictionaries
ISBN 0-8160-4381-7 LC 2001-23100
This volume "covers more than 500 scientists. Dating back to 400 BCE, it treats current, historical, and minority women scientists. The entries . . . include biographical information that provides detailed descriptions of education, research, and notable accomplishments. Oakes also supplies an impressive, expansive set of indexes: general alphabetical, field of specialization, country of birth, country of major scientific activity, and year of birth." Choice
Includes bibliographical references

Photographers and filmmakers. Macmillan Ref. USA 2001 452p il (Macmillan profiles) $90 **920.003**
1. Motion picture producers and directors—Dictionaries 2. Photographers—Dictionaries
ISBN 0-02-865635-0 LC 2001-30185
This reference "considers 125 film animators, movie directors, photographers, and video artists. . . . The collection features alphabetically arranged articles incorporating sidebars, inserts, time lines, pull quotes, definitions, and a glossary. An international roster of artists represents a variety of specializations that chronicle technical developments. . . . Overall the articles are accessible and insightful." Booklist
Includes bibliographical references

Religious leaders of the world. Macmillan Ref. USA 2000 449p il (Macmillan profiles) $90 **920.003**
1. Religious biography
ISBN 0-02-865492-7 LC 00-101564
This volume, profiling more than 150 subjects, "treats biblical, historical, and contemporary figures, including saints and popes. Major world religions and religious movements are represented, as are some smaller sects such as Shakers and Jehovah's Witnesses and African and Native American beliefs." Booklist

Rittner, Don

A to Z of scientists in weather and climate. Facts on File 2003 256p il (Notable scientists) $45　　　　　**920.003**

1. Scientists 2. Meteorology

ISBN 0-8160-4797-9　　　　LC 2002-152435

This reference "includes 115 biographical sketches of individuals throughout history, around the world, and working in a variety of disciplines, who have contributed to an understanding of climate and weather. Entries, informative and clearly written . . . consist of a text of 750 to 2,000 words that includes the subject's early history, educational background, positions held, prizes and awards, and major contributions to weather and climate studies." Choice

Includes bibliographical references

Schneider, Dorothy

First ladies; a biographical dictionary; [by] Dorothy Schneider and Carl J. Schneider. Facts on File 2001 406p il $65; pa $19.95
920.003

1. Presidents' spouses—United States

ISBN 0-8160-4195-4; 0-8160-4196-2 (pa)

　　　　　　　　　　　LC 00-68130

This reference work begins with a study of "the evolution of the role of first lady. Presented chronologically, each biography contains a preface that discusses background information about the first lady, followed by a four to 20 page biography and an evaluation of each woman's impact on the role. . . . Several appendices cover presidential spouses who did not live to be first ladies, White House hostesses, and a list of first lady firsts. . . . The subject is entertaining and this volume invites browsing and research." Book Rep

Includes bibliographical references

The **Scribner** encyclopedia of American lives; Kenneth T. Jackson, editor in chief; Karen Markoe, general editor; Arnold Markoe, executive editor. Scribner 1998-2003 6v il set $540　　　**920.003**

1. United States—Biography—Dictionaries

ISBN 0-684-31292-1　　　　LC 98-33793

Individual volumes also available ea $140

Contents: v1 1981-1985; v2 1986-1990; v3 1991-1993; v4 1994-1996; v5 1997-1999; v6 2000-2002

"Scribner envisions SEAL as the continuation of the *Dictionary of American Biography* (DAB). . . . Selection criteria are that the biographees made significant contributions to American life and culture. . . . An appreciable number of women and people of color are recognized. All biographies are signed contributions by 332 scholars." Libr J [review of first two volumes]

The **Scribner** encyclopedia of American lives, The 1960s; William L. O'Neill, volume editor. Scribner 2003 2v il set $250
920.003

1. United States—Biography—Dictionaries

ISBN 0-684-80666-5　　　　LC 2002-12581

"Thematic series." Cover

"The two alphabetically arranged volumes in SEAL 1960s contain biographical sketches, usually between 1,000 and 2,000 words, of 647 figures who 'defined the decade, or who were influential at the time.' Americans from different races, socioeconomic groups, classes, and regions of the U.S. are included, along with the occa-sional person of another nationality who had long periods of residence in the U.S. and was an influence on American culture. The signed entries, written by scholars, begin with a brief summary of the person's chronology and important accomplishments. This is followed by a narrative of the subject's life. . . . In many cases, a black-and-white photograph accompanies the narrative, which concludes with an assessment of the subject's overall contribution and a brief bibliography listing a few key sources. . . . Recommended for all high-school, public, and academic libraries wanting complete SEAL coverage or libraries wanting to supplement their collection of 1960s resources with a purely biographical approach." Booklist

Sonneborn, Liz

A to Z of American women in the performing arts. Facts on File 2001 264p il $44　　　　　　　　**920.003**

1. Entertainers 2. Women—United States—Biography

ISBN 0-8160-4398-1　　　　LC 2001-23580

This "book profiles 150 female performers, with entries for performing categories that range from actresses, dancers, and singers to circus and Wild West show performers. The book covers women of numerous ethnic groups from the early 1800s to the present. The women are listed alphabetically by their professional names and entries average about a page in length. . . . Each entry concludes with suggestions for further reading and research, and a list of recommended performances available on tape or disc." Book Rep

St. James guide to Black artists; editor, Thomas Riggs. St. James Press 1997 xxiv, 625p il $218　　　　　　**920.003**

1. Black artists—Dictionaries

ISBN 1-55862-220-9　　　　LC 97-3068

This "dictionary provides information concerning approximately 400 artists, nearly 300 of whom were living at the time of publication. . . . An index of nationalities lists 26 groups from Europe, Africa, and the Caribbean, but US artists predominate. . . . The signed entries profile the artist and list the artist's exhibitions, the institutions holding the artist's work, and the artist's publications. Many entries provide photographs of the artists or examples of their work." Choice

St. James guide to Hispanic artists; profiles of Latino and Latin American artists; editor, Thomas Riggs. St. James Press 2002 xx, 682p il $195　　　　　　　**920.003**

1. Hispanic American art 2. Artists—United States

ISBN 1-55862-470-8　　　　LC 2001-41935

"Published in association with the Association of Hispanic Arts, Association for Latin American Art"

This "guide profiles some 375 of the most prominent Hispanic artists of the past century. The entries include basic biographical information, critical commentary, and lists of exhibitions, publications, and collections holding their works." Libr J

Includes bibliographical references

St. James guide to native North American artists; with a preface by Rick Hill; and introduction by W. Jackson Rushing; editor, Roger Matuz. St. James Press 1997 xxxii, 691p il $155   **920.003**
1. Native American artists—Dictionaries 2. Native American art
ISBN 1-55862-221-7   LC 97-18453
"This guide highlights just fewer than 400 twentieth-century North American Indian artists, many of whom are still active in their fields. The artists have worked or are currently working in a variety of genres: painting, fabric arts, jewelry, drawing, photography, sculpture, beadwork, carving, architecture, mixed media, basketry, pottery, performance art, and printmaking. Each entry includes basic biographical information, a list of exhibitions and galleries housing them, a bibliography of books and articles by and about the artist, and a critical appraisal written by a specialist in the field." Booklist

The **Supreme** Court justices: a biographical dictionary; edited by Melvin I. Urofsky. Garland 1994 570p il (Garland reference library of the humanities) $85   **920.003**
1. United States. Supreme Court 2. Judges—Dictionaries
ISBN 0-8153-1176-1   LC 94-10028
"Alphabetically arranged, each entry begins with life dates, the date of nomination to the Court, the name of the president who nominated the justice, and the date he or she was seated. The contributors . . . provide facts and context along with analysis of the important cases in the individual justice's career." Libr J

Vigué, Jordi
Great women masters of art. Watson-Guptill 2003 480p il (Great masters of art series) pa $21.95   **920.003**
1. Women artists—Dictionaries
ISBN 0-8230-2114-9   LC 2002-109821
This is a "guide featuring the life and work of the greatest women painters of Western art—from the 15th century to the present day. . . . Each artist is represented by several . . . reproductions of her most significant works, alongside a biographical timeline and brief history of her life and career." Publisher's note

Waldman, Carl
Biographical dictionary of American Indian history to 1900. Facts on File 2001 506p il map $71.50; pa $24.95   **920.003**
1. Native Americans—Biography—Dictionaries
ISBN 0-8160-4252-7; 0-8160-4253-5 (pa)
LC 00-49027
First published 1989 with title: Who was who in Native American history
This includes "entries on approximately 1,000 notable Native and non-Native people in the U.S. and Canada from precontact until the end of the nineteenth century. . . . The entries are well written and informative. This is a good first source for quick, accurate, ready-reference information." Booklist

Waldrup, Carole Chandler, 1925-
The vice presidents; biographies of the 45 men who have held the second highest office in the United States. McFarland & Co. 1996 271p il $45   **920.003**
1. Vice-presidents—United States
ISBN 0-7864-0179-6   LC 96-30538
This work "presents biographical portraits of the 45 individuals who have theoretically been 'a heartbeat from the presidency.' These portraits are presented in chronological order of service, from John Adams to Albert Gore Jr." Am Ref Books Annu, 1997
"Well-written with clear, precise language and vocabulary, this informative book will be useful in either the reference section or with the collective biographies." Book Rep
Includes bibliographical references

Who was who; a companion to Who's who. St. Martin's Press 1920-1996 10v v1-7 op; v8 & v9 ea $125; v10 $140   **920.003**
1. Great Britain—Biography—Dictionaries
A cumulated index to volumes 1-10 is available for $150 (ISBN 0-312-29364-X)
Contents: v1 1897-1915 (ISBN 0-312-87570-3); v2 1916-1928 (ISBN 0-312-87605-X); v3 1929-1940 (ISBN 0-312-87640-8); v4 1941-1950 (ISBN 0-312-87675-0); v5 1951-1960 (ISBN 0-312-87710-2); v6 1961-1970 (ISBN 0-312-87745-5); v7 1971-1980 (ISBN 0-312-87746-3); v8 1981-1990 (ISBN 0-312-06818-2); v9 1991-1995 (ISBN 0-312-16246-4); v10 1996-2000 (ISBN 0-312-29366-6)
"For the most part the original sketches as they last appeared in 'Who's who' are reprinted with the date of death added, but in a few instances additional information has been incorporated." Guide to Ref Books. 11th edition

Who was who in America; with world notables. Marquis Who's Who 1942-2002 14v & Index v1-13 ea $90; v14 & Index ea $149.95   **920.003**
1. United States—Biography—Dictionaries
Also available online
Also available historical volume 1607-1896 $90 (ISBN 0-8379-0236-3); Complete 16-volume set $999.95 (ISBN 0-8379-0242-8)
Contents: v1 1897-1942 (ISBN 0-8379-0201-0); v2 1943-1950 (ISBN 0-8379-0206-1); v3 1951-1960 (ISBN 0-8379-0203-7); v4 1961-1968 (ISBN 0-8379-0204-5); v5 1969-1973 (ISBN 0-8379-0205-3); v6 1974-1976 (ISBN 0-8379-0207-X); v7 1977-1981 (ISBN 0-8379-0210-X); v8 1982-1985 (ISBN 0-8379-0214-2); v9 1985-1989 (ISBN 0-8379-0217-7); v10 1989-1993 (ISBN 0-8379-0220-7); v11 1993-1996 (ISBN 0-8379-0225-8); v12 1996-1998; v13 1998-2000; v14 2000-2002 and Index volume (1607-2002) (ISBN 0-8379-0245-2)
"Includes sketches removed from 'Who's who in America' because of death of the biographee; date of death and, often, interment location is added. With the 'Historical volume' these volumes form a series entitled 'Who's who in American history.'" Guide to Ref Books. 11th edition

Who was who in the Greek world, 776 BC-30 BC; edited by Diana Bowder. Cornell Univ. Press 1982 227p il $52.50   **920.003**

1. Greece—Biography—Dictionaries 2. Greece—History

ISBN 0-8014-1538-1   LC 82-71594

Companion volume to Who was was who in the Roman world, 753 BC-AD 476 (1980)

"A Phaidon book"

"More than 750 entries, arranged alphabetically, give brief but readable biographical data about notable Greeks (and non-Greeks important in Greek history). . . . Specialized, but a worthwhile addition to the reference shelf." Booklist

Who's who; an annual biographical dictionary. St. Martin's Press $300   **920.003**

1. Great Britain—Biography—Dictionaries
ISSN 0083-937X

"The pioneer work of the who's who type and still one of the most important. Until 1897, it was the handbook of titled and official classes and included lists of names rather than biographical sketches. . . . It is principally British, but a few prominent names of other nationalities are included. Biographies are reliable and fairly detailed; they give main facts, addresses, often telephone numbers and in case of authors, lists of works." Guide to Ref Books. 11th edition

Who's who among African Americans. Gale Res. $210   **920.003**

1. African Americans—Biography—Dictionaries

First published 1976 by Educational Communications with title: Who's who among black Americans. Biennial schedule after 5th edition

"Short entries focusing on career achievements and positions. Indexes list entries by place of birth and profession." N Y Public Libr Book of How & Where to Look It Up

Who's who in America. Marquis Who's Who 3v $749   **920.003**

1. United States—Biography—Dictionaries
ISSN 0083-9396

Also available online

Annual. First published 1899

"The standard dictionary of contemporary biography, containing concise biographical data, prepared according to established practices, with addresses and, in the case of authors, lists of works. . . . Each edition is thoroughly revised, new biographies added, and others dropped. For names of persons dropped because of death, see 'Who was who in America'." Guide to Ref Books. 11th edition

Who's who in American art. Marquis Who's Who $295   **920.003**

1. Artists—United States—Dictionaries
ISSN 0000-0191

Also available online

Companion volume to American art directory

Biennial. First published 1936 by American Federation of Arts as part of American art annual

"Profiles representatives of all segments of the art world including artists, administrators, and librarians. En-

tries give vital statistics, professional education and training, commissions and exhibitions, and membership in art societies. Includes geographic and professional classification indexes and cumulative necrology." N Y Public Libr Book of How & Where to Look It Up

Who's who in American politics. Marquis Who's Who 2v set $345   **920.003**

1. Politicians—United States—Dictionaries
ISSN 0000-0205

Biennial. First published 1967 by Bowker

"Biographical directory of political leaders in the Congress, the executive branch of the federal government, state legislatures, state executive branches, mayors of cities with populations over 50,000, national and state party chairs, national party committee members, county chairs, and state supreme court justices. Entries are arranged by state, then alphabetically by name. Indexed by name." Ref Sources for Small & Medium-sized Libr. 6th edition

Who's who in art. Art Trade Press; [distributed by] Gale Res. $184.75   **920.003**

1. Artists, British—Dictionaries

Biennial. First published 1927. Subtitle varies

"Includes primarily British artists, designers, craftsmen, critics, writers, teachers, collectors, and curators, with appendixes of monograms and signatures, and obituary, and acronyms. Includes a list of academies, groups, and societies." Guide to Ref Books. 11th edition

Who's who in British history; beginnings to 1901; general editor, Geoffrey Treasure; authors and contributors, Ian Dawson [et al.] Fitzroy Dearborn Pubs. 1998 2v maps set $325   **920.003**

1. Great Britain—Biography—Dictionaries
ISBN 1-884964-90-7

"The length of entries varies from many pages (Henry VIII) to a column for most persons. . . . The choice of entries (ending with 1901) reflects the traditional emphasis of history teaching, with heavy representation of statemen, royalty, military persons, diplomats, major writers, and leading ladies of the stage and aristocracy." Choice

Who's who in finance and industry. Marquis Who's Who $325   **920.003**

1. Business—Biography—Dictionaries
ISSN 0083-9523

Also available online

Biennial. First published 1936 with title: Who's who in commerce and industry

"Gives international coverage of businessmen. Includes index of firms with references to personnel for whom sketches are included." Guide to Ref Books. 11th edition

Who's who of American women. Marquis Who's Who $279   **920.003**

1. Women—United States—Biography 2. United States—Biography—Dictionaries
ISSN 0083-9841

Also available online

Biennial. First published for 1958/1959

"This title provides information on women who are successful in a variety of professions, including business,

Who's who of American women—*Continued*

government, education, art and culture, and those who have received prestigious honors or have been selected for honorary institutions. The biographical data are provided by the women themselves so the quality varies. In general it includes name, occupation, birth date, education, career history, publications, professional activities, awards, and home and office addresses. This has long been a standard source in many public and academic libraries." Am Ref Books Annu, 2003

Women in world history; a biographical encyclopedia; Anne Commire, editor, Deborah Klezmer, associate editor. Gale Res. 1999-2002 17v set $1,495 **920.003**
1. Women—History—Encyclopedias 2. Women—Biography
ISBN 0-7876-3736-X   LC 99-24692

"The editors researched wives, daughters, mothers, and other women who were not documented in traditional, male-oriented sources, especially history books. . . . Some entries are only a sentence or two because of lack of information, but the majority include most or all of the following: dates, if known, or time of flourishing; an identifying summary of life and achievements; a personal profile with vital statistics and names of family members; events in the life of the biographee; vitae listing such things as works for authors or winning records for athletes; a quotation by or about the individual; and bibliographical references." Booklist

World artists, 1950-1980; an H.W. Wilson biographical dictionary; [edited] by Claude Marks. Wilson, H.W. 1984 912p il $130
                                                      920.003
1. Artists—Dictionaries
ISBN 0-8242-0707-6   LC 84-13152

"The 312 painters, sculptors, and graphic artists in this biographical dictionary were selected from the outstanding artistic figures in the US, Europe, and Latin America. . . . The biographical information includes family, working background, and aesthetic beliefs. There are many quotations from the artist and from critics. Also included is a list of significant collections and a bibliography." Choice

World artists, 1980-1990; an H.W. Wilson biographical dictionary; edited by Claude Marks. Wilson, H.W. 1991 413p il $95
                                                      920.003
1. Artists—Dictionaries
ISBN 0-8242-0827-7   LC 91-13183

This volume contains brief biographies of 118 artists from around the world who have been influential in the 1980's

World authors, 1900-1950; editors, Martin Seymour-Smith and Andrew Kimmens. Wilson, H.W. 1996 4v il (Authors series) set $590   **920.003**
1. Authors—Dictionaries 2. Literature—Biography
ISBN 0-8242-0899-4   LC 96-16380

Replaces Twentieth century authors (1942) and its First supplement (1955)

Contents: v1 Abbot-Doyle; v2 Dreiser-Ledwidge; v3 Lee-Saintsbury; v4 Saki-Zweig

Provides almost 2700 articles on twentieth-century authors from all over the world who wrote in English or whose works are available in English translation

World authors, 1950-1970; a companion volume to Twentieth century authors; edited by John Wakeman; editorial consultant: Stanley J. Kunitz. Wilson, H.W. 1975 1594p il (Authors series) $150
                                                      920.003
1. Authors—Dictionaries   2. Literature—Bio-bibliography
ISBN 0-8242-0419-0

This volume includes 959 "authors who came into prominence between 1950 and 1970. . . . Authors were chosen for literary importance or outstanding popularity." Wilson Libr Bull

World authors, 1970-1975; editor, John Wakeman; editorial consultant, Stanley J. Kunitz. Wilson, H.W. 1980 894p il (Authors series) $130   **920.003**
1. Authors—Dictionaries   2. Literature—Bio-bibliography
ISBN 0-8242-0641-X   LC 79-21874

This volume provides biographical or autobiographical sketches for 348 of the most influential and popular men and women of letters who have come into prominence between 1970 and 1975

World authors, 1975-1980; editor, Vineta Colby. Wilson, H.W. 1985 829p il (Authors series) $130   **920.003**
1. Authors—Dictionaries   2. Literature—Bio-bibliography
ISBN 0-8242-0715-7   LC 85-10045

This work profiles the lives and works of 379 writers

World authors, 1980-1985; editor, Vineta Colby. Wilson, H.W. 1990 938p il (Authors series) $130   **920.003**
1. Authors—Dictionaries   2. Literature—Bio-bibliography
ISBN 0-8242-0797-1   LC 90-49782

This volume covers 320 contemporary writers

World authors, 1985-1990; a volume in the Wilson authors series; editor, Vineta Colby. Wilson, H.W. 1995 970p il (Authors series) $130   **920.003**
1. Authors—Dictionaries   2. Literature—Bio-bibliography
ISBN 0-8242-0875-7   LC 95-41656

This volume covers 345 novelists, playwrights, poets, and other authors who have risen to prominence in the late 1980s

World authors, 1990-1995; editor, Clifford Thompson. Wilson, H.W. 1999 863p il $145   **920.003**
1. Authors—Dictionaries   2. Literature—Bio-bibliography
ISBN 0-8242-0956-7   LC 99-48161

The 317 authors treated in this volume include novelists, playwrights, and poets who have published significant work in the early 1990s. Also covers essayists, historians, biographers, critics, philosophers, and social scientists who have made exceptional contributions to the literature of our time

World authors, 1995-2000; editors, Clifford Thompson, Mari Rich {et al.}. Wilson, H.W. 2003 872p il $150   **920.003**
1. Authors—Dictionaries   2. Literature—Bio-bibliography
ISBN 0-8242-1032-8   LC 2003-45062

This reference includes 320 novelists, poets, dramatists, essayists, social scientists, and biographers who have published significant works from 1995 through 2000. Each profile details the author's life and career, the circumstances under which their works were produced, and their literary significance

World explorers and discoverers; editor, Richard E. Bohlander; consultants, John L. Allen [et al.] Macmillan 1991 531p il maps o.p.; Da Capo Press paperback available $25.95   **920.003**
1. Explorers—Dictionaries
ISBN 0-306-80824-2 (pa)   LC 91-23156

"Over 300 explorers and discoverers are featured in this attractive compilation that covers exploration from ancient times to the present and includes such notable moderns as Jacques Cousteau and Edmund Hillary." Am Libr

World musicians; edited by Clifford Thompson; staff contributors: Denise Bonilla {et al.}; consultants: Justin Dello Joio, Lewis Porter. Wilson, H.W. 1999 1181p il $115   **920.003**
1. Musicians—Dictionaries
ISBN 0-8242-0940-0   LC 98-29205

International in coverage, this volume profiles "contemporary musicians whose specialties range from classical to pop, opera to rap, bluegrass to rock. . . . Written in a lively style and ranging in length from 500 to 3,500 words, the articles cover each musician's personal and professional life and are frequently spiced with quotations from published interviews with the subject and excerpts from critical commentary. Many entries include a black-and-white photo of the musician, and all conclude with a selected bibliography of additional publications and recordings." Booklist

World poets; Ron Padgett, editor in chief. Scribner 2000 3v il set $295   **920.003**
1. Poetry—Bio-bibliography 2. Poets—Dictionaries
ISBN 0-684-80591-X   LC 00-24801

"This resource examines the lives and works of 110 poets often studied in high school. The individuals included represent writers from all over the world, from prehistory to the present time. . . . Following the entries on the individual poets are 15 thematic essays covering such topics as the troubadours, the poetry of the Harlem Renaissance, and Asian-American poetry. Appendixes include information on poetic meter and lists of major prizewinners. This useful set concludes with a comprehensive index." SLJ

Writers for young adults; Ted Hipple, editor. Scribner 1997 3v il set $295   **920.003**
1. Authors, American—Dictionaries 2. Authors, English—Dictionaries 3. Young adult literature
ISBN 0-684-80474-3   LC 97-6890

Also available Writers for young adults, supplement I $100 (ISBN 0-684-80618-5)

Contains articles on writers whose works are popular with young adults, including contemporary authors, such as Francesca Lia Block and Maya Angelou, and classic authors, such as Sir Arthur Conan Doyle and Louisa May Alcott

"This set is an extremely valuable tool for every reference librarian serving young adults or those who teach and care for them." Libr J

Yount, Lisa
A to Z of biologists. Facts on File 2003 390p il (Notable scientists) $45   **920.003**
1. Biologists—Dictionaries
ISBN 0-8160-4541-0   LC 2002-13816

"Facts on File science library"

"Each profile focuses on a particular biologist's research and contributions to the field and his or her effect on scientists whose work followed. Their lives and personalities are also discussed through incidents, quotations, and photographs. The profiles are culturally inclusive and span a range of biologists from ancient times to the present day." Publisher's note

92   Individual biography

Acheson, Dean, 1893-1971
Chace, James. Acheson; the Secretary of State who created the American world. Simon & Schuster 1998 512p o.p.; Harvard Univ. Press paperback available $18.50   **92**
1. United States—Foreign relations
ISBN 0-674-00081-1 (pa)   LC 98-3801

"Dean Acheson was Truman's Secretary of State from 1949 to 1953, and today's world, as Chace shows in this lucid biography, was shaped in no small degree by his efforts." New Yorker

Includes bibliographical references

Adams, Ansel, 1902-1984
Adams, Ansel. Ansel Adams, an autobiography; {by} Ansel Adams with Mary Street Alinder. Little, Brown 1985 400p il $65; pa $14.95   **92**
ISBN 0-8212-1596-5; 0-8212-2241-4 (pa)
     LC 85-8135

A New York Graphic Society book

The American photographer's "autobiography moves from family reminiscences to his experiences with Edward Weston, Paul Strand, Dorothea Lange, the Newhalls, Georgia O'Keefe, Steiglitz, and Steichen, giving Adams's perspective on developments in the visual arts." Libr J

"Consisting of an almost perfect mix of interacting text and images, including some unexpected candid snapshops of Adams himself, this work is an outstanding document of 20th-century American photography." Choice

Includes bibliographical references

Alinder, Mary Street. Ansel Adams; a biography. Holt & Co. 1996 xx, 489p il hardcover o.p. paperback available $17.95
   92
ISBN 0-8050-5835-4 (pa)   LC 95-44741

"As Alinder traces the straightforward course of Adams' dazzling career . . . she emphasizes the connection between his stunning landscape photography and his

Adams, Ansel, 1902-1984—*Continued*

zealous work with the Sierra Club. Alinder is as lucid on the topic of Adams' technical mastery as on his environmentalism and aesthetics, and she also tackles the muddle of his contentious private life with aplomb and candor." Booklist

Includes bibliographical references

Adams, Henry, 1838-1918

Adams, Henry. The education of Henry Adams **92**

Hardcover and paperback editions available from various publishers

First published in a popular edition 1918

"Henry Adams was the son of Charles Francis Adams, U.S. Minister to Britain during the Civil War, and a grandson of John Quincy Adams. His 'education' consists of everything that happened to him or about him from his birth to his death." St Louis Public Libr

"The book omits any mention of the thirteen years of Adams's marriage and the seven years following his wife's suicide. It does, however, present a vivid picture of the people and places the author knew." Reader's Ency. 4th edition

Adams, John, 1735-1826

McCullough, David G. John Adams; [by] David McCullough. Simon & Schuster 2001 751p il maps $35; pa $18.95 **92**

1. United States—Politics and government—1775-1783, Revolution

ISBN 0-684-81363-7; 0-7432-2313-6 (pa)

LC 2001-27010

Also available Thorndike Press large print edition

"In tracing Adam's life from childhood through his many critical, heroic, and selfless acts during the Revolution, his vice presidency under Washington, and his own term as president, the full measure of Adams—a man widely regarded in his time as the equal of Jefferson, Hamilton, and all of the other Founding Fathers—is revealed." Libr J

"This is a wonderfully stirring biography; to read it is to feel as if you are witnessing the birth of a country firsthand." Booklist

Includes bibliographical references

Adams, John Quincy, 1767-1848

Nagel, Paul C. John Quincy Adams; a public life, a private life. Knopf 1997 432p il map o.p.; Harvard Univ. Press paperback available $18.95 **92**

ISBN 0-674-47940-8 (pa)

LC 96-49640

The author traces the life and career of the sixth president of the United States "utilizing diary entries to provide keen insight into this extraordinary man, who often suffered from severe depression. The result is a fascinating psychobiography." Libr J

Includes bibliographical references

Remini, Robert Vincent. John Quincy Adams; [by] Robert V. Remini. Times Bks. 2002 172p (American presidents series) $20 **92**

1. United States—Politics and government—1783-1865

ISBN 0-8050-6939-9

LC 2002-24210

"Remini focuses on important incidents throughout Adams's life, demonstrating that he was not the failure he would have been if judged only by his presidential

years." Libr J

The author's "judicious, eloquent survey of the sixth president's life and career intends not to proffer new and explosive ideas but to fashion recent scholarship into a highly readable overview for the general reader." Booklist

Includes bibliographical references

Addams, Jane, 1860-1935

Elshtain, Jean Bethke. Jane Addams and the dream of American democracy; a life. Basic Bks. 2001 xxii, 329p il hardcover o.p. paperback available $20 **92**

ISBN 0-465-01913-7 (pa)

LC 2001-43493

In this biography of the founder of the settlement-house movement, "Elshtain gives a moving account of a stunningly creative woman occupied cognitively, emotionally and spiritually with the ways an elite in a cosmopolitan society riven by inequality might offer succor to others." N Y Times Book Rev

Includes bibliographical references

Albee, Edward, 1928-

Gussow, Mel. Edward Albee; a singular journey: a biography. Simon & Schuster 1999 448p o.p.; Applause Theatre Bk. Pubs. paperback available $16.95 **92**

ISBN 1-55783-447-4 (pa)

LC 99-26558

"Albee regained his position as one of America's greatest playwrights with the 1994 production of 'Three Tall Women,' achieving a level of theatrical mastery and critical acclaim that he hadn't seen since 'Who's Afraid of Virginia Woolf' and 'A Delicate Balance,' almost two decades earlier. The years in between were marked by excessive drinking, outrageous behavior, inferior work, and a diminished career, but Gussow, with a light and generous touch, shows us the strengths of an artist whose core of resilience ultimately insured his survival." New Yorker

Includes bibliographical references

Albert, Prince Consort of Victoria, Queen of Great Britain, 1819-1861

Weintraub, Stanley. Uncrowned king: the life of Prince Albert. Free Press 1997 478p il map hardcover o.p. paperback available $25 **92**

ISBN 0-7432-0609-6 (pa)

LC 96-37752

The author contends that "Albert, far from being a minor German princeling, was in fact a conscientious, well-informed administrator who essentially acted as England's king while married to Victoria. . . . While reviled by many of his wife's subjects as a foreigner and worse yet, a German, Albert fought valiantly to improve British education and single-handedly pulled together the Great Exhibition of 1851." Publ Wkly

Weintraub "defends his stand with knowledge, reason, and writerly savoir faire." Booklist

Albright, Madeleine Korbel, 1937-

Albright, Madeleine Korbel. Madam Secretary; a memoir; [by] Madeleine Albright with Bill Woodward. Macmillan 2003 562p il $27.95 **92**

ISBN 1-40503-369-X

"Albright came to the U.S. as a young Czech refugee, and braved all the demands that working mothers face, first as ambassador to the UN, then as the first woman secretary of state. Refreshingly frank, she expertly explicates the most intense global conflicts of the last decade." Booklist

Alexander, Jane

Alexander, Jane. Command performance; an actress in the theatre of politics. PublicAffairs 2000 335p $25; pa $16.50　**92**

ISBN 1-891620-06-1; 0-306-81044-1 (pa)

LC 00-23375

This is a chronicle of Alexander's four-year tenure as chairman of the National Endowment for the Arts

"Alexander's liberal activism long predates her chairmanship, and her analysis of politicians' evolution from public servants to interest-group stooges is as strong as her defense of the arts." Publ Wkly

Alexandra, Empress, consort of Nicholas II, Emperor of Russia, 1872-1918

Massie, Robert K. Nicholas and Alexandra. See entry under Nicholas II, Emperor of Russia, 1868-1918　**92**

Alfred, the Great, King of England, 849-899

Duckett, Eleanor Shipley. Alfred the Great. University of Chicago Press 1956 220p hardcover o.p. paperback available $16　**92**

1. Great Britain—History—0-1066

ISBN 0-226-16779-8 (pa)

"The life of Alfred the Great set against the social and political background of ninth-century England. King Alfred's accomplishments as soldier, ruler, translator, and author show him to be a many-sided man who, despite his prowess on the battlefield, loved the serenity and the solitude of the scholarly life." Booklist

Algren, Nelson, 1909-1981

Beauvoir, Simone de. A transatlantic love affair: letters to Nelson Algren. See entry under Beauvoir, Simone de, 1908-1986　**92**

Ali, Muhammad, 1942-

Remnick, David. King of the world: Muhammad Ali and the rise of an American hero. Random House 1998 326p il hardcover o.p. paperback available $14　**92**

1. African American athletes

ISBN 0-375-70229-6 (pa)　　LC 98-24539

This book focuses on Ali's career "in the early sixties—roughly, late 1962 to late 1965. . . . Five heavyweight title fights are dealt with in depth: the first Patterson-Liston fight on September 25, 1962, and their rematch on July 22, 1963: the first Liston-Ali fight on February 25, 1964, and their rematch on May 25, 1965: and the first Ali-Patterson fight on November 22, 1965." Nation

"This is the best book ever on Muhammad Ali and one of the best on America in the 1960s." Booklist

Includes bibliographical references

Allen, Woody

Meade, Marion. The unruly life of Woody Allen; a biography. Scribner 2000 384p il o.p.; Cooper Sq. Pubs. paperback available $18.95　**92**

ISBN 0-8154-1149-9 (pa)　　LC 99-45482

This biography examines Allen's "career as a writer, director and actor, and as an extremely funny spokesman

for an emerging cultural trend toward openness about one's own neuroses and one's own sexual foibles." N Y Times Book Rev

Includes bibliographical references

Allende, Isabel

Allende, Isabel. Paula; translated from the Spanish by Margaret Sayers Peden. HarperCollins Pubs. 1995 330p hardcover o.p. paperback available $13.95　**92**

1. Allende family

ISBN 0-06-092721-6 (pa)　　LC 95-2452

Allende "interweaves the story of her own life with the slow dying of her 28-year-old daughter, Paula." Publ Wkly

This "is a deeply affecting tale, written in the rich, luminous prose typical of Allende's novels, that investigates the sources of her writing as it paints a vivid portrait of Chile." Libr J

Amis, Kingsley, 1922-1995

Amis, Kingsley. The letters of Kingsley Amis; edited by Zachary Leader. Hyperion 2001 lvi, 1212p il $40　**92**

ISBN 0-7868-6757-4

"Talk Miramax books"

First published 2000 in the United Kingdom

"More than a thousand delicious pages of uncharitable observations by the author of 'Lucky Jim' and many other fine surly novels . . . his letters to Philip Larkin are particularly funny, despite the absence of Larkin's letters to him." N Y Times Book Rev

Includes bibliographical references

Bradford, Richard. Lucky him: the life of Kingsley Amis. Owen, P.; [distributed by] Dufour Eds. 2001 432p il $44.95　**92**

ISBN 0-7206-1117-2　　LC 2001-431013

This is a biography of the English novelist, best known for such works as Lucky Jim, The old devils, and Difficulties with girls

"The writing is consistently clear and the insights—literary and biographical—are formidable." Publ Wkly

Includes bibliographical references

Amis, Martin

Amis, Martin. Experience. Hyperion 2000 406p il $23.95; pa $14　**92**

1. Amis, Kingsley, 1922-1995

ISBN 0-7868-6652-7; 0-375-72683-7 (pa)

LC 00-699777

This is an "account of a literary life with an extraordinary father. Even by English standards Kingsley Amis, whom his son rightly sees as the finest comic novelist of his generation, was a highly eccentric figure." Publ Wkly

This is a "portmanteau of personal history, ancestor worship and promiscuous opinionizing, and a piñata of literary gossip that Amis beats with a stick, causing many names to drop. . . . And if we stay put till the last 100 pages, it will break our heart." N Y Times Book Rev

Andersen, Hans Christian, 1805-1875

Wullschläger, Jackie. Hans Christian Andersen; the life of a storyteller. Knopf 2001 489p il maps o.p.; University of Chicago Press paperback available $19 **92**

ISBN 0-226-91747-9 (pa)   LC 00-62003

This is a biography of the "Danish fairy-tale writer, who came out of more impoverished circumstances than did any other literary titan, retained peasantlike gaucheness and servility throughout his life, and whose neuroses and repressed bisexuality influenced his stories as much as his ugly-duckling success." Booklist

"Wullschlager succeeds brilliantly at portraying Andersen's inner mind and uncovering his hopes and fears and details the historical context that served to produce such a grand body of literature. . . . [This biography] will be a standard study for years to come." Libr J

Includes bibliographical references

Anderson, Marian, 1897-1993

Keiler, Allan. Marian Anderson; a singer's journey. Scribner 2000 447p il o.p.; University of Ill. Press paperback available $21.95   **92**

ISBN 0-252-07067-4 (pa)   LC 99-43319

"A Lisa Drew book"

"Keiler offers an assessment of the great contralto, the first African American soloist at the Metropolitan Opera." Libr J

The author's "clear, succinct prose, initially lacking narrative coherence, gains strength and momentum as his subject matures from a young and struggling artist into one of the enduring voices of our century." Publ Wkly

Includes discography and bibliographical references

Angelou, Maya

Angelou, Maya. I know why the caged bird sings. Random House 1970 c1969 281p $20; pa $13   **92**

ISBN 0-394-42986-9; 0-553-38001-X (pa)

Also available in paperback from Bantam Bks.

The first volume in the author's autobiographical series covers her childhood and adolescence in rural Arkansas, St. Louis, and San Francisco

"Angelou is a skillful writer; her language ranges from beautifully lyrical prose to earthy metaphor, and her descriptions have power and sensitivity." Libr J

Followed by Gather together in my name (1974); Singin' and swingin' and gettin' merry like Christmas (1976); The heart of a woman (1981); All God's children need traveling shoes (1986); A song flung up to heaven (2002)

Angelou, Maya. A song flung up to heaven. Random House 2002 212p $23.95; pa $13   **92**

ISBN 0-375-50747-7; 0-553-38203-9 (pa)

LC 2001-34914

"This sixth installment in Angelou's autobiographical works begins in 1964 as Angelou returned to the U.S. from Ghana. . . . She worked in Watts at the time of the riots, and Malcolm X and Martin Luther King Jr. were both assassinated just before she was to begin working with them. . . . She moved to New York, where she rejoined a vibrant group of famous writers, intellectuals, and friends; worried about her young-adult son; and understood the humor and heartache of a painful love affair. . . . Spiced with her mother's aphorisms, her often-poetic prose is best at the end, as she muses on the condition of black women and sitting at her mother's table, begins to write I Know Why the Caged Bird Sings." Booklist

Anthony, Susan B., 1820-1906

Anthony, Susan B. Failure is impossible; Susan B. Anthony in her own words; [edited by] Lynn Sherr. Times Bks. 1995 xxviii, 384p il hardcover o.p. paperback available $23   **92**

1. Feminism

ISBN 0-8129-2718-4 (pa)   LC 94-29913

This is a collection of Susan B. Anthony's journal entries, correspondence, speeches, interviews, and published writings. The author has arranged the selections by topic and chronologically within topics

Includes bibliographical references

Ward, Geoffrey C. Not for ourselves alone: the story of Elizabeth Cady Stanton and Susan B. Anthony. See entry under Stanton, Elizabeth Cady, 1815-1902   **92**

Arana, Marie

Arana, Marie. American chica; two worlds, one childhood. Dial Press (NY) 2001 309p hardcover o.p. paperback available $12.95   **92**

ISBN 0-385-31963-0 (pa)   LC 00-47529

The author, born to a Peruvian father and an American mother, writes of her childhood in Peru

Arana "blends a journalist's dedication to research with a style that sings with humor. Her memoir is an outstanding contribution to the growing shelf of Latina literature." Publ Wkly

Armstrong, Lance

Armstrong, Lance. It's not about the bike; my journey back to life; [by] Lance Armstrong with Sally Jenkins. Putnam 2000 275p il $24.95; pa $14   **92**

ISBN 0-399-14611-3; 0-425-17961-3 (pa)

LC 00-35612

Armstrong describes his early years growing up in Plano, Texas, his rise through the sports world as a champion American cyclist, his diagnosis and recovery from testicular cancer, and his triumph in the 1999 Tour de France

"Readers will respond to the inspirational recovery story, and they will appreciate the behind-the-scenes cycling information." Booklist

Armstrong, Louis, 1900-1971

Armstrong, Louis. Louis Armstrong, in his own words; selected writings; edited and with an introduction by Thomas Brothers; annotated index by Charles Kinzer. Oxford Univ. Press 1999 xxvii, 255p il hardcover o.p. paperback available $14.95   **92**

ISBN 0-19-514046-X (pa)   LC 99-17040

In this collection Armstrong "recounts episodes from his childhood in New Orleans, pays tribute to other musicians, and extolls the virtues of marijuana, laxatives, and rice and beans while speaking candidly about race relations, the music business, and his extramarital affairs. The joy he took in expressing himself on paper is abundantly evident." New Yorker

Includes bibliographical references

Armstrong, Louis, 1900-1971—*Continued*

Collier, James Lincoln. Louis Armstrong, an American genius. Oxford Univ. Press 1983 383p il hardcover o.p. paperback available $21.50 **92**

    ISBN 0-19-503727-8 (pa)   LC 83-11378

The author tells the story of Armstrong's life and evaluates his musical contributions

"Collier's scholarship is impeccable, his note-by-note musical analysis razor sharp, and his conclusions about Armstrong's place in American music expertly defended. In all respects, a biography worthy of its subject." Booklist

Augustine, Saint, Bishop of Hippo

Wills, Garry. Saint Augustine. Viking 1999 xx, 152p (Penguin lives series) $19.95 **92**

    ISBN 0-670-88610-6   LC 98-50317

Wills begins "by addressing centuries of misconceptions. Though his admiration for the saint is occasionally tainted by defensiveness, his account of Augustine's search for a faith and a philosophy engages our sympathy. He also conveys the turbulence of the era, when the Roman Empire was beleaguered by barbarians and the Catholic Church by heretics, and shows how Augustine's responses to the troubles of his time have shaped Christianity down to our own." New Yorker

Austen, Jane, 1775-1817

Nokes, David. Jane Austen; a life. Farrar, Straus & Giroux 1997 578p o.p.; University of Calif. Press paperback available $21.95
92

    ISBN 0-520-21606-7 (pa)   LC 97-24768

"Eschewing the biographer's usual perspective of omniscient foreknowledge in favor of a novelistic perspective of ambiguous immediacy, Nokes allows us to see Austen's talent as a mystery unfolding, not a fact explained. We thus witness the emergence of a personality sufficiently subtle and complex to produce *Sense and Sensibility, Pride and Prejudice*, and *Emma*. Readers of Austen's fiction will rejoice at having a biography so carefully nuanced, so refreshingly candid." Booklist

Shields, Carol. Jane Austen. Viking 2001 185p (Penguin lives series) $19.95 **92**

    ISBN 0-670-89488-5   LC 00-43807

Also available Thorndike Press large print edition

"In chronicling her subject's life and personality, Shields emphasizes Austen's keen ability to listen, observe, and capture clearly the social mores of her time and explore human nature in her writing. Shields contends that historical references are behind many of the scenes and characters in Austen's novels, and as a way of more clearly personalizing Austen's experiences or feelings, she interjects commentary regarding writing and publishing that is presumably based on personal experience." Libr J

Tomalin, Claire. Jane Austen; a life. Knopf 1997 341p il hardcover o.p. paperback available $14 **92**

    ISBN 0-679-76676-6 (pa)   LC 97-36887

Tomalin's "biography of the great novelist reveals that Austen developed her skill in creating fascinating fictional lives while living a life that was more eventful—and far more traumatic—than her official biographers have previously acknowledged." Booklist

The author "has produced a portrait of remarkable subtlety. The light Ms. Tomalin casts on her subject is strong but oblique: the profile of the novelist appears surrounded by her friends and neighbours and by her energetic and beloved family." Economist

Awee

Nasdijj. The boy and the dog are sleeping. See entry under Nasdijj **92**

Bach, Johann Sebastian, 1685-1750

Wolff, Christoph. Johann Sebastian Bach; the perfect musician. Norton 2000 599p il hardcover o.p. paperback available $18.95
92

    ISBN 0-393-32256-4 (pa)   LC 99-54364

"Bach's professional life and continual development as a composer are described in chronological order; a separate chapter discusses his domestic life." Libr J

This work "is likely to be the standard one-volume Bach biography for some time to come. It is a solid, richly informative treatment, presenting the copious details of Bach's life in a coherent, readable narrative." N Y Rev Books

Includes bibliographical references

Baker, Chet

Gavin, James. Deep in a dream: the long night of Chet Baker. Knopf 2002 430p il $26.95 **92**

    ISBN 0-679-44287-1   LC 2001-43379

This is a biography of the trumpet player and vocalist who gained fame in the 1950s and "found himself the heartthrob of female jazz fans and the winner of numerous polls for favorite trumpet player." Booklist

Gavin "has constructed a meticulous account of Baker's life in and out of music, and he lets the facts fall where they may." N Y Times Book Rev

Baker, Russell, 1925-

Baker, Russell. Growing up. Congdon & Weed 1982 278p il o.p.; New Am. Lib. paperback available $15 **92**

    ISBN 0-452-25550-3 (pa)   LC 82-12534

This book "recounts the first 24 years of [Baker's] life as the son of an independent and deep-rooted Virginian family." Natl Rev

Baldrige, Letitia

Baldrige, Letitia. A lady, first; my life in the Kennedy White House and the American embassies of Paris and Rome. Viking 2001 292p il hardcover o.p. paperback available $15 **92**

    ISBN 0-14-200159-7 (pa)   LC 2001-26544

In this autobiography Baldrige recalls "her White House years and the Kennedy family and relates many details of her subsequent career in public relations and publishing." Libr J

"A life lived so fully and at such a frenetic pace is scarcely to be believed at first, until one takes into account Baldrige's spirited will and work ethic. . . . Baldrige is an exemplary role model for women because she opened doors by refusing to accept that they were closed." Publ Wkly

Ballmer, Steven

Maxwell, Fredric Alan. Bad boy Ballmer; the man who now runs Microsoft. Morrow 2002 278p $26.95; pa $14.95 **92**

1. Microsoft Corporation
ISBN 0-06-621014-3; 0-06-093541-3 (pa)
LC 2002-21918

This book is "about Bill Gates' go-to guy and the current CEO of Microsoft, Steve Ballmer. Maxwell casts Ballmer as so maniacal and driven that his ruthless management earned him the nickname 'The Embalmer.' A penetrating biography of one of business' key players." Booklist

Balzac, Honoré de, 1799-1850

Robb, Graham. Balzac; a life. Norton 1994 521p il hardcover o.p. paperback available $15 **92**

ISBN 0-393-31387-5 (pa) LC 94-18614

This is a biography of the nineteenth-century French novelist whose work includes the "nearly 100 interlinked novels and stories grouped under the collective heading 'La Comédie Humaine.'" Christ Sci Monit

"Balzac's life was more cause for incredulity than anything he wrote, and Robb compellingly sets out the documentable facts against and within the world Balzac created from them. . . . The result is nearly a novel, although Robb does not fictionalize with re-created dialogs and hypothetical events. He has in fact produced an extensive traditional biography . . . not a critical reassessment." Libr J

Includes bibliographical references

Bandele, Asha

Bandele, Asha. The prisoner's wife; a memoir. Scribner 1999 219p hardcover o.p. paperback available $12.95 **92**

ISBN 0-671-02148-6 (pa) LC 99-12117

"Poet asha bandele writes of her relationship with Rashid, a man serving 20-to-life for murder. She tells of how she met this man while she was visiting the prison to read her poetry; of how she visited him as a friend/lover, waiting five years before she married him; of waiting the long months after the marriage before they were granted a conjugal visit; of love letters, long collect phone calls, and the horror and indignity of their prison situation." Booklist

"The author has a poet's fluid skill with language and maintains a lyrical tone throughout." Libr J

Barkley, Charles

Barkley, Charles. I may be wrong but I doubt it; edited and with an introduction by Michael Wilbon. Random House 2002 245p $22.95; pa $12.95 **92**

ISBN 0-375-50883-X; 0-8129-6628-7 (pa)
LC 2002-29169

The retired NBA champion "explores a wide range of interests. Each chapter has a theme, and Barkley has no problem speaking his mind on any topic, whether it is politics . . . or lack of minority control in sports. . . . In between these chapters are other sections that retell some of the great and not-so-great moments in his career. . . . This is a very entertaining look at one of the most intelligent minds in pro sports, and like Barkley's career, it's bound to produce fierce arguments." Publ Wkly

Barnum, P. T. (Phineas Taylor), 1810-1891

Saxon, A. H. P.T. Barnum: the legend and the man. Columbia Univ. Press 1989 437p il hardcover o.p. paperback available $22.50 **92**

ISBN 0-231-05687-7 (pa) LC 89-982

"Working primarily from Barnum's letters, business papers, family members' and associates' diaries, and legal documents, Saxon has pieced together a picture of the legendary circus owner. Saxon's detailed coverage of Barnum's life . . . is rich with anecdotes yet scholarly enough to please any researcher. Saxon succeeds admirably in capturing the essence of Barnum." Booklist

Includes bibliographical references

Barthelme, Frederick

Barthelme, Frederick. Double down; reflections on gambling and loss; [by] Frederick and Steven Barthelme. Houghton Mifflin 2000 198p $24 **92**

1. Barthelme, Steven
ISBN 0-395-95429-0 LC 99-23957

Also available in paperback from Harvest Bks.

"In the space of a couple of . . . years, the brothers Frederick and Steven Barthelme . . . managed to [lose] more than a quarter of a million dollars in the Mississippi gambling boats. Double Down is their account of how this happened, what led up to it and spurred them on, and how it ended in tears when . . . the casino which had taken their money charged them with conspiracy to cheat." N Y Rev Books

"Beautifully evoking the gamblers' addiction, their mesmerizing account is best read as a novel Camus might have imagined, with the writer/protagonists as their own lost characters. A work of high art; enthusiastically recommended." Libr J

Barthelme, Steve

Barthelme, Frederick. Double down. See entry under Barthelme, Frederick **92**

Bartoli, Cecilia, 1966-

Chernin, Kim. Cecilia Bartoli; the passion of song; [by] Kim Chernin with Renate Stendhal. HarperCollins Pubs. 1997 232p il o.p.; Women's Press paperback available $24.95 **92**

ISBN 0-7043-4623-0 (pa) LC 96-34343

This profile of the Italian opera singer is divided into two parts. "Chernin reviews five Bartoli performances in Berkeley and transcribes a conversation with her in Houston. . . . Stendhal contributes a guide to some 10 years of Bartoli's opera performances; it consists mostly of plot summaries with commentary on Bartoli's interpretations. . . . Altogether, [Stendhal] and Chernin give us not a biography but two adoring fans' personal perspectives on a most promising singer." Booklist

Barton, Clara, 1821-1912

Oates, Stephen B. A woman of valor: Clara Barton and the Civil War. Free Press 1994 527p il map hardcover o.p. paperback available $16.95 **92**

1. United States—History—1861-1865, Civil War
ISBN 0-02-874012-2 (pa) LC 93-38830

The author "uses both primary and secondary sources in addressing the Civil War career of Clara Barton. . . .

Barton, Clara, 1821-1912—*Continued*

An 'angel of the battlefield' who succored the wounded while under fire, Barton also raised funds and supplies through a network of women's support groups, while challenging the conventional belief that nursing was inappropriate for respectable women." Publ Wkly

"This is a carefully written and researched work that brings to life both the Civil War and a period of Barton's life that was to affect her forever." Libr J

Includes bibliographical references

Basie, Count, 1904-1984

Basie, Count. Good morning blues: the autobiography of Count Basie; as told to Albert Murray. Da Capo Press 1995 399p il pa $17.95   **92**

    ISBN 0-306-81107-3   LC 94-44697

    First published 1985 by Random House

"Basie pays tribute to his colleagues and managers (and to John Hammond for 'discovering' him), but does not hesitate to discuss their weaknesses and shortcomings; his language is direct and earthy. Although some of the book reads more like a catalogue or itinerary than an autobiography, it will have strong appeal for jazz buffs and fans of the late bandleader." Publ Wkly

Baum, L. Frank (Lyman Frank), 1856-1919

Rogers, Katharine M. L. Frank Baum, creator of Oz; [a biography] St. Martin's Press 2002 318p il $27.95   **92**

    ISBN 0-312-30174-X   LC 2002-69826

    Also available in paperback from Da Capo Press

    "Works by L. Frank Baum"

Rogers "correlates the events of Baum's life to his literary output, showing readers how his belief in feminism, concern for animal rights, and interest in technology produced a fairyland where all the heroes are women and girls, animals talk, and machinelike creations such as Tik-Tok and the Tin Woodman hold their own with the brightest and best humans." Libr J

"Rogers' meticulously researched and documented biography draws generously on original and secondary sources, affording a detailed account that is more scholarly than popular." Booklist

Includes bibliographical references

Bayley, John, 1925-

Bayley, John. Elegy for Iris. St. Martin's Press 1999 275p il hardcover o.p. paperback available $13   **92**

    1. Murdoch, Iris 2. Alzheimer's disease

    ISBN 0-312-42111-7 (pa)   LC 98-40895

"Iris Murdoch is best known for her novels, which are filled with characters embroiled in philosophical conflicts. In this memoir, her husband, a renowned literary critic, presents his insights into her creativity, her personality, and their relationship. . . . Reminiscences of the past are juxtaposed with the reality of the present, in which Bayley tries to cope with the daily frustrations of caring for Murdoch now that she has Alzheimer's disease." Libr J

"This splendid book enlarges our imagination of the range and possibilities of love." N Y Times Book Rev

Bayley, John. Iris and her friends; a memoir of memory and desire. Norton 1999 275p il hardcover o.p. paperback available $13.95   **92**

    1. Murdoch, Iris 2. Alzheimer's disease

    ISBN 0-393-32079-0 (pa)   LC 99-33124

Bayley follows Elegy for Iris "with more memories of his own life and his time with his wife, Iris Murdoch, who was living through the final stages of Alzheimer's disease as he wrote this. Bayley's eye for what is not obvious glimmers. . . . He revisits favorite books, places, and people, exposing the human scale of the courage it takes to keep to the demands of a home." Libr J

Beauvoir, Simone de, 1908-1986

Bair, Deirdre. Simone de Beauvoir; a biography. Summit Bks. 1990 718p il hardcover o.p. paperback available $31.95

                                              92

    ISBN 0-671-74180-2 (pa)   LC 89-22029

"Bair's biography of the French author, philosopher, and feminist aims to restore the balance between interest in de Beauvoir's personal life—as the lifelong companion of Jean-Paul Sartre and sometime lover of Nelson Algren—and the question of her achievements as a writer and thinker." Booklist

Includes bibliographical references

Beauvoir, Simone de. A transatlantic love affair: letters to Nelson Algren; compiled and annotated by Sylvie Le Bon de Beauvoir; translations from the French by Ellen Gordon Reeves; notes by Vanessa King. New Press 1998 559p il hardcover o.p. paperback available $18.95   **92**

    1. Algren, Nelson, 1909-1981

    ISBN 1-56584-560-9 (pa)   LC 97-53085

"Compiled by de Beauvoir's adopted daughter and literary executor, this is an engrossing collection of passionate, compassionate, and historical letters from de Beauvoir to her beloved, the American writer Nelson Algren. . . . Readers will be absorbed in the joys and disappointments of [her] relationship with Algren and fascinated by her accounts of the activities surrounding her, including the political situation in France, and of her friends and acquaintances, including Richard Wright, Albert Camus, Truman Capote, Margaret Mead, Charlie Chaplin, and Arthur Koestler." Libr J

Beckett, Samuel, 1906-1989

Gordon, Lois G. The world of Samuel Beckett, 1906-1946; [by] Lois Gordon. Yale Univ. Press 1996 250p il $50; pa $16.95

                                              92

    ISBN 0-300-06409-8; 0-300-07495-6 (pa)

                                    LC 95-22851

Gordon "examines the first 40 years of the playwright/novelist's 83-year life, which includes periods in Ireland, where he was born; in Paris, where he spent much of his life; and in London, Germany, and other parts of France. . . . Gordon has been thorough in her research and careful in her presentation." Choice

Includes bibliographical references

Beckwith, Jonathan R., 1935-

Beckwith, Jonathan R. Making genes, making waves; a social activist in science; [by] Jon Beckwith. Harvard Univ. Press 2002 242p il $27.95 **92**
ISBN 0-674-00928-2   LC 2002-22747
"The text traces Beckwith's development as both a scientist and an activist, essentially in a chronological narrative form, with a few chapters providing expanded coverage of specific examples of the interaction between scientific research and societal effects. Those working in scientific fields or students who plan to pursue such a career would enjoy this book." Sci Books Films
Includes bibliographical references

Beethoven, Ludwig van, 1770-1827

Lockwood, Lewis. Beethoven: the music and the life. Norton 2002 c2003 604p il music $39.95 **92**
ISBN 0-393-05081-5   LC 2002-75397
The author "concentrates primarily on his subject's music and development as a composer before dedicating separate chapters to biography and the historical, political, and cultural milieus. . . . All of Lockwood's narrative, including the discussion of specific compositions, will be accessible to serious music lovers with only a modest technical background. This results partly from an interesting innovation . . . 100 additional musical examples are available on a companion web site. . . . Lockwood's study offers a new and authoritative interpretation of a prodigiously gifted and complex man and artist." Libr J
Includes bibliographical references

Solomon, Maynard. Beethoven. 2nd rev ed. Schirmer Bks. 1998 554p hardcover o.p. paperback available $19.95 **92**
ISBN 0-8256-7268-6 (pa)   LC 97-51363
First published 1977
In this revision, "Solomon approaches his subject from myriad different angles—historical, psychological, sociological, and aesthetic—to treat the reader to a view of Beethoven, his music, and his era that answers longstanding questions and reveals new ways of considering the composer, his works, and his motivation." Libr J

Bell, Gertrude Margaret Lowthian, 1868-1926

Wallach, Janet. Desert queen; the extraordinary life of Gertrude Bell: adventurer, adviser to kings, ally of Lawrence of Arabia. Talese 1996 xxv, 419p hardcover o.p. paperback available $15.95 **92**
ISBN 0-385-49575-7 (pa)   LC 95-44868
"High-spirited, outspoken, and self-reliant, . . . [Bell] was the first woman to earn a degree in history at Oxford, a skilled mountain climber and equestrienne, and an avid and fearless traveler who found her spiritual home in the deserts of Iraq and Arabia. . . . Fluent in Arabic and on good terms with powerful men, Bell became an invaluable asset to British intelligence and was drafted as a spy during World War I. . . . Wallach . . . brings the resolute Bell and her complex world vividly to life." Booklist
Includes bibliographical references

Belli, Gioconda, 1948-

Belli, Gioconda. The country under my skin; a memoir of love and war; translated by Kristina Cordero with the author. Knopf 2002 380p il $25; pa $14 **92**
ISBN 0-375-40370-1; 1-4000-3216-4 (pa)
The Nicaraguan poet relates the "story of her life as a privileged young wife and mother, advertising and media executive, gun-running revolutionary, and exiled enemy of the state." Booklist
"This excellent autobiography . . . is a fascinating literary and political memoir. . . . Enjoyable reading for its descriptions of a woman coming to grips with her feminism, political activities, and move to the United States, it will also be of value to scholars looking at Nicaragua or to collections in Latin America or literature in general." Libr J

Bellow, Saul

Atlas, James. Bellow; a biography. Random House 2000 686p il hardcover o.p. paperback available $16.95 **92**
ISBN 0-375-75958-1 (pa)   LC 00-42529
The author "traces Bellow's life from his birth in 1915 through his student years to his mature development as a novelist." Libr J
"Atlas shares his subject's devotion to literature, intimacy with Chicago (the city Bellow immortalized), and Jewishness, and he succeeds brilliantly in chronicling and interpreting Bellow's very full life, difficult personality, and powerful work." Booklist
Includes bibliographical references

Bellow, Saul. Conversations with Saul Bellow; edited by Gloria L. Cronin and Ben Siegel. University Press of Miss. 1994 xx, 303p (Literary conversations series) hardcover o.p. paperback available $20 **92**
ISBN 0-87805-718-8 (pa)   LC 94-19474
A collection of interviews with the Nobel laureate in which he discusses his life and work as well as his social, political and religious views

Benjamin, Judah Philip, 1811-1884

Evans, Eli N. Judah P. Benjamin, the Jewish Confederate. Free Press 1988 xxi, 469p il hardcover o.p. paperback available $17 **92**
ISBN 0-02-909911-0 (pa)   LC 87-19256
"Judah Benjamin served in the Confederate cabinet as secretary of state and of war, as well as attorney general; he sat at President Jefferson Davis' right hand. But, as he wished it, little information about him exists in the history books. Evans rectifies the situation and does it well. . . . Evans places particular focus on the nature of that relationship with Jefferson Davis, as well as on Benjamin's sense of himself as a Jew in the nineteenth-century South." Booklist
Includes bibliographical references

Berezovsky, Boris A.

Klebnikov, Paul. Godfather of the Kremlin; Boris Berezovsky and the looting of Russia. Harcourt 2000 400p il hardcover o.p. paperback available $14   **92**

1. Russia (Federation)—Economic conditions
ISBN 0-15-601330-4 (pa)   LC 99-462183

This biography tells the story of one of Russia's wealthiest and most powerful businessmen, who transformed his obscure auto dealership into an empire that included Russia's largest TV network, its largest automobile manufacturer, the national airline, and one of the world's biggest oil companies

Includes bibliographical references

Bergman, Ingrid, 1915-1982

Spoto, Donald. Notorious: the life of Ingrid Bergman. HarperCollins Pubs. 1997 xx, 474p o.p.; Da Capo Press paperback available $19   **92**

ISBN 0-306-81030-1 (pa)   LC 97-3455

Spoto traces Bergman's life "from her difficult childhood in Sweden . . . through her early career as a Swedish film star, to her ascension to Hollywood stardom as the leading lady of such actors as Spencer Tracy, Humphrey Bogart and Cary Grant. Particular attention is given to her work with Alfred Hitchcock." Publ Wkly

The author's "perceptions about Bergman personally and professionally are keen, and the narrative reads like a full-bodied story, not just a listing of professional credits and personal landmarks." Booklist

Includes bibliographical references

Berlin, Irving, 1888-1989

Furia, Philip. Irving Berlin; a life in song; [by] Philip Furia, with the assistance of Graham Wood; Irving Berlin songography compiled by Ken Bloom. Schirmer Bks. 1998 323p il $25   **92**

ISBN 0-02-864815-3   LC 98-15486

The author "portrays Berlin as a lonely, hardworking dynamo who composed almost until the day he died, yet who spent his last years as a bitter recluse, and convincingly identifies his broader achievements: completing the Americanization of the Broadway musical with *Annie Get Your Gun* (1946), revitalizing Tin Pan Alley and shepherding songwriting from Broadway to Hollywood." Publ Wkly

Includes bibliographical references

Hamm, Charles. Irving Berlin; songs from the melting pot: the formative years, 1907-1914. Oxford Univ. Press 1996 292p il $42.50   **92**

ISBN 0-19-507188-3   LC 96-6335

"Hamm explores the influence of pre-World War I culture on Berlin's output as it changed from ethnic novelty songs to songs for the stage influenced by European styles." Booklist

The author "shows an informed sensitivity for the social and historical atmosphere in which these songs were produced, and . . . makes effective use of period recordings . . . in an effort to understand how they were meant to play to their first listeners." N Y Times Book Rev

Includes discography and bibliographical references

Berlioz, Hector, 1803-1869

Holoman, D. Kern. Berlioz. Harvard Univ. Press 1989 687p il $36   **92**

ISBN 0-674-06778-9   LC 88-35788

This is a biography of the nineteenth-century composer, conductor, and music critic

"There may be aspects of Berlioz's life which Holoman has not fathomed, but he paints as full a picture as has yet been attempted." New Statesman (1913)

Includes bibliographical references

Bernays, Anne

Bernays, Anne. Back then; two lives in 1950's New York; [by] Anne Bernays and Justin Kaplan. Morrow 2002 309p il $25.95; pa $13.95   **92**

1. Kaplan, Justin
ISBN 0-06-019855-9; 0-06-095805-7 (pa)
   LC 2001-59031

Pulitzer Prize-winner Kaplan and novelist Bernays, a married couple, recount "their remarkably parallel lives in 1950s New York City. Both grew up in well-to-do Jewish families, she on Manhattan's Upper East Side, he on the Upper West Side; both went away to college, majored in English and returned to New York to work in publishing. What makes this book successful is the way both writers capture the diverse sounds and sense of various subcultures in the city: bohemian, literary, Jewish, upper-crust, etc." Publ Wkly

Bernhardt, Sarah, 1844-1923

Bernhardt, Sarah. My double life: the memoirs of Sarah Bernhardt; translated by Victoria Tietze Larson. State Univ. of N.Y. Press 1999 345p $26.50; pa $25.95   **92**

ISBN 0-7914-4053-2; 0-7914-4054-0 (pa)
   LC 98-30036

This is a newly translated abridgment of Bernhardt's autobiography originally published 1907

"The most tempestuous and possibly the most famous actress of her time, Bernhardt . . . is presented as both melodramatic and frustratingly discreet." Publ Wkly

Includes bibliographical references

Bettelheim, Bruno

Raines, Theron. Rising to the light: a portrait of Bruno Bettelheim. Knopf 2002 xx, 518p $35   **92**

ISBN 0-679-40196-2   LC 2001-54536

This biography "tries to restore the controversial psychologist's celebratory status as therapist, writer, and teacher. The focus is on Bettelheim's many years as principal of the residential Orthogenic School for troubled children in Chicago. . . . Most interesting is the discussion of Bettelheim's life before he came to the U.S. in 1939, especially his Holocaust survivor experience. . . . This is sure to continue the passionate debate." Booklist

Includes bibliographical references

Bierce, Ambrose, 1842-1914?

Morris, Roy. Ambrose Bierce; alone in bad company. Crown 1995 306p o.p.; Oxford Univ. Press paperback available $19.95   **92**

ISBN 0-19-512628-9 (pa)   LC 95-30281

This "study of Bierce (1842-1914), a journalist and short-story writer, draws a parallel between the sardonic writer's dark vision and his unhappy life. According to

Bierce, Ambrose, 1842-1914?—*Continued*

Morris the depression Bierce developed during a lonely and unhappy Indiana childhood intensified after his Civil War experiences." Publ Wkly

"Mr. Morris's disturbing, vividly realized biography brings to life a haunted writer whose private torments mirrored a turbulent era." N Y Times Book Rev

Includes bibliographical references

Billy, the Kid

Utley, Robert Marshall. Billy the Kid; a short and violent life; [by] Robert M. Utley. University of Neb. Press 1989 302p il hardcover o.p. paperback available $16   **92**

ISBN 0-8012-9558-8 (pa)   LC 89-30022

Examines the career of the young outlaw whose life and death were an expression of the violence prevalent on the American frontier

"Robert M. Utley does what countless books, movies, television shows, musical compositions, and paintings have failed to do: he successfully strips off the veneer of legendry to expose the reality of Billy the Kid." Univ Press Books for Public Libr

Includes bibliographical references

Bird, Larry

Bird, Larry. Bird watching; on playing and coaching the game I love; [by] Larry Bird with Jackie MacMullan; foreword by Pat Riley. Warner Bks. 1999 318p hardcover o.p. paperback available $7.99   **92**

ISBN 0-446-60888-2 (pa)   LC 99-18906

In this memoir Bird "discusses, for example, his disdain for coaches who are screamers; his admiration for fellow coach Pat Riley . . . and his overwhelming affection for his hometown of French Lick, Indiana. There are anecdotes from his playing days, insights into his coaching philosophy, and even some details of life in French Lick." Booklist

This is "an endearingly honest self-portrait of a humble man who has made the most of his opportunities." Publ Wkly

Birkeland, Kristian, 1867-1917

Jago, Lucy. The northern lights; the true story of the man who unlocked the secrets of the Aurora borealis. Knopf 2001 297p hardcover o.p. paperback available $14   **92**

ISBN 0-375-70882-0 (pa)   LC 2001-29895

This is a "biography of Kristian Birkeland, a Norwegian scientist who discovered the origins of the aurora borealis." Economist

"Instead of a stiff, scholarly biography, British journalist Jago has written a poignantly human story filled with minute, extensively researched details." Libr J

Includes bibliographical references

Black Elk, 1863-1950

Black Elk. Black Elk speaks; being the life story of a holy man of the Oglala Sioux; as told through John G. Neihardt (Flaming Rainbow); introduction by Vine Deloria, Jr.; illustrated with drawings by Standing Bear and a portfolio of photographs. University of Neb. Press 1979 299p il $50; pa $14.95

92

1. Oglala Indians
ISBN 0-8032-1309-3; 0-8032-6170-5 (pa)
      LC 79-12367

A reprint of the title first published 1932 by Morrow

The Indian whose life story this is, was born in 1863. He was a famous warrior and hunter in his youth, and became a practicing medicine man among his people. Of him Neihardt says, "As an indubitable seer, he seemed to represent the consciousness of the Plains Indian more fully than any other I had ever known."

This "is about as near as you can get to seeing life and death, war and religion, through an Indian's eyes." Outlook

Steltenkamp, Michael F. Black Elk, holy man of the Oglala. University of Okla. Press 1993 xxiii, 211p il maps hardcover o.p. paperback available $17.95   **92**

1. Oglala Indians
ISBN 0-8061-2988-3 (pa)   LC 93-22089

This "is the story of Black Elk's later years, when the holy man converted to Roman Catholicism and worked actively as a catechist, converting the Lakota to his new religion." Antioch Rev

Includes bibliographical references

Blackwood, Caroline

Schoenberger, Nancy. Dangerous muse: the life of Lady Caroline Blackwood. Talese 2001 377p il $27.50   **92**

ISBN 0-385-48979-X   LC 00-53508

Also available in paperback from Da Capo Press

This is a biography of the English novelist and socialite who was also an heir to the Guinness fortune and "best known for marrying painter Lucian Freud, then Aaron Copland's prize student Israel Citkowitz, then patrician poet Robert Lowell." Publ Wkly

"'Dangerous Muse' is not so much a literary biography as a fable for our own times—dramatic, chilling and suggestive." N Y Times Book Rev

Includes bibliographical references

Blake, William, 1757-1827

Bentley, G. E. (Gerald Eades). The stranger from paradise: a biography of William Blake. Yale Univ. Press 2001 xxvii, 532p il maps $39.95; pa $24.95   **92**

ISBN 0-300-08939-2; 0-300-10030-3 (pa)

The author "traces Blake from his natal landscape, youth, marriage, and apprenticeship through to his later years as a working engraver, poet, and radical visionary. Bentley is academic and thorough, and this is more of a straight biography than an analysis." Libr J

Includes bibliographical references

Blakelock, Ralph Albert, 1847-1919

Vincent, Glyn. The unknown night: the madness and genius of R. A. Blakelock, an American painter. Grove Press 2003 362p il $27.50 **92**
ISBN 0-8021-1734-1 LC 2002-29747
A biography of the 19th century American landscape painter who suffered from schizophrenia
"An arresting and ultimately haunting portrait of an intrepid and besieged artist." Booklist
Includes bibliographical references

Blount, Roy

Blount, Roy. Be sweet; a conditional love story; [by] Roy Blount, Jr. Knopf 1998 289p o.p.; Harcourt paperback available $13 **92**
ISBN 0-15-600682-0 (pa) LC 97-49352
"Blount figures that at age 57 he has lived long enough to hunt for life-defining moments among sundry episodes, including his stint as coeditor of his college paper with presidential wanna-be Lamar Alexander, his days smokin' dope with '70s slugger Richie Allen when Blount was a *Sports Illustrated* reporter, and a slew of childhood memories." Booklist

Blunt, Anthony, 1907-1983

Carter, Miranda. Anthony Blunt: his lives. Farrar, Straus & Giroux 2001 590p il $30; pa $18 **92**
ISBN 0-374-10531-6; 0-312-42146-X (pa)
LC 2001-50135
In 1979 "the noted British art expert Anthony Blunt was revealed to have been a spy for the Soviet Union. This meticulous book traces Blunt's career: his early school days, his association with the Bloomsbury group, his membership in a 'secret debating society' known as the Apostles, his recruitment into the spy game as a 'talent spotter,' his time spent in MI5 (he started passing documents to the Russians in 1941), and beyond." Booklist
"Thoroughly researched and carefully crafted, this is sure to be the definitive biography." Publ Wkly

Blunt, Judy, 1954-

Blunt, Judy. Breaking clean. Knopf 2002 303p hardcover o.p. paperback available $13 **92**
ISBN 0-375-70130-3 (pa) LC 2001-29861
The author chronicles the hardships she endured as a ranch wife, mother, and laborer in rural Montana, and how she left it all, including her marriage, to get herself a college education and become a writer
Blunt has a "keen and poetic awareness, steely candor, and commanding storytelling skills." Booklist

Boone, Daniel, 1734-1820

Faragher, John Mack. Daniel Boone; the life and legend of an American pioneer. Holt & Co. 1992 429p il maps hardcover o.p. paperback available $18 **92**
ISBN 0-8050-3007-7 (pa) LC 92-21873
"The popular image of Daniel Boone is that of an unlettered backwoodsman, skilled hunter and Indian fighter. But evidence argues that he was reasonably well educated for his time and place, that he was a landowner, businessman and a respected leader of frontier society. Faragher . . . has sifted through folklore and fact to reconstruct a realistic portrait of Boone and the expanding frontier. . . . Faragher has written an absorbing, definitive biography." Publ Wkly
Includes bibliographical references

Boswell, James, 1740-1795

Martin, Peter. A life of James Boswell. Yale Univ. Press 2000 613p $35; pa $18.95 **92**
ISBN 0-300-08489-7; 0-300-09312-8 (pa)
This is a biography of the diarist and author of The life of Samuel Johnson
"Martin has written the best biography of the greatest biographer in the English language. . . . One of the many virtues of Martin's work is his successful synthesis of Boswell's life story with a keen analysis of Boswell's artistry." Atl Mon

Brady, Mathew B., ca. 1823-1896

Panzer, Mary. Mathew Brady and the image of history; with an essay by Jeana K. Foley. Smithsonian Institution Press 1997 xxiii, 232p il $44.95 **92**
ISBN 1-56098-793-6 LC 97-9493
In this reassessment of the life and work of the iconic 19th-century photographer, the author "points out that Brady seldom stood behind the camera, preferring the role of studio chief executive officer and entrepreneur to that of a mere 'operator.'. . . Moreover, Brady was an incompetent businessman, often leaving his creditors in the lurch, and ended his career in bankruptcy. This is enough to make us think twice about Brady, but Panzer's most audacious assertion is that we also need to think twice about the meaning of the pictures attributed to him." N Y Times Book Rev
Includes bibliographical references

Bragg, Rick

Bragg, Rick. All over but the shoutin'. Pantheon Bks. 1997 xxii, 329p hardcover o.p. paperback available $14 **92**
ISBN 0-679-77402-5 (pa) LC 97-9918
"Honest, unsentimental, and so elegantly spare it nearly hurts to read, this memoir by Pulitzer Prize-winning journalist Bragg recounts a dirt-poor childhood in Alabama and the debt he owes his mother." Libr J

Brahe, Tycho, 1546-1601

Ferguson, Kitty. Tycho & Kepler; the unlikely partnership that forever changed our understanding of the heavens. Walker & Co. 2002 402p il maps $27; pa $15 **92**
1. Kepler, Johannes, 1571-1630
ISBN 0-8027-1390-4; 0-8027-7688-4 (pa)
LC 2002-27445
This book follows "the lives of two of the greatest astronomers of all time—the eminent, arrogant Danish stargazer Tycho Brahe and the passionate, young Austrian mathematician Johannes Kepler. In what Ferguson sees as an almost mystical turn of fate, the dynamic duo were brought together in Prague, where Kepler became Brahe's combative assistant." Astronomy
"Ferguson has a wonderful ability not only to explain her topic and its significance but also to render the historical background in such a way that the participants do not seem to be either incredibly farsighted prophets or quaint characters fumbling for explanations. Highly recommended for academic and public libraries." Libr J
Includes bibliographical references

Brahms, Johannes, 1833-1897

MacDonald, Malcolm. Brahms. Oxford Univ. Press 2001 490p il music (Master musicians series) pa $19.95   **92**
ISBN 0-19-816484-X   LC 2002-280636
First published 1990 by Schirmer Bks.

The author "relates all known facts about the composer, his relationship with friends and acquaintances, and his music. Biography and creative output are interwoven throughout the book, as the author rather laboriously discusses each composition in chronological order. It is assumed that the reader has a fair knowledge of Brahms' works and can read music, for MacDonald includes 68 musical examples that are important to the discussion. MacDonald's verbose style may put off the casual reader, but for a real Brahms lover, the book is a treat." Libr J

Includes bibliographical references

Swafford, Jan. Johannes Brahms; a biography. Knopf 1997 xxii, 699p il hardcover o.p. paperback available $19   **92**
ISBN 0-679-74582-3 (pa)   LC 97-29308

This book traces the composer's "early life playing piano in the brothels of Hamburg, through his middle years performing his chamber music and conducting his choral works, to his late years directing Vienna's Gesellschaft der Musikfreunde in his orchestral music." Booklist

"Swafford's study, clearly a labor of profound affection, is a model biography: eloquent, clear-sighted and often moving." Publ Wkly

Includes bibliographical references

Brando, Marlon, 1924-

Bosworth, Patricia. Marlon Brando. Viking 2001 228p il (Penguin lives series) $21.95   **92**
ISBN 0-670-88236-4   LC 00-68591

Also available Thorndike Press large print edition

This biography presents "the personal and professional highlights of Brando's life, including his disastrous marriage to Anna Kashfi and its effect on his son, and how he resurrected his career (which had barely survived 10 flops) with Francis Ford Coppola's *The Godfather.*" Publ Wkly

"Bosworth, a gifted writer, has a clean, spare, but witty style, which helps her pack much more than one might expect into this tiny volume." Booklist

Includes filmography

Brasillach, Robert, 1909-1945

Kaplan, Alice Yaeger. The collaborator: the trial & execution of Robert Brasillach; [by] Alice Kaplan. University of Chicago Press 2000 308p $25; pa $15   **92**
ISBN 0-226-42414-6; 0-226-42415-4 (pa)
    LC 99-48291

Kaplan details "the life of Robert Brasillach, a prolific and controversial French critic who was executed for treason, at age 35, after France's liberation from the Nazis. A fascist-leaning writer known for his defense of Nazi crimes . . . Brasillach was the only distinguished writer put to death by the postwar French government." Publ Wkly

This "is one of the best-written, most absorbing pieces of literary history in years." N Y Times Book Rev

Includes bibliographical references

Brecht, Bertolt, 1898-1956

Fuegi, John. Brecht and company; sex, politics, and the making of the modern drama. Grove Press 1994 xx, 732p il hardcover o.p. paperback available $20   **92**
ISBN 0-8021-3910-8 (pa)   LC 93-23051

The author "believes Brecht wrote very little in the dramas that made him famous; rather, he systematically plagiarized and 'collaborated' with lovers and colleagues by signing his name to plays they essentially wrote. . . . Fuegi's massive effort examines every aspect of Brecht's career and personality, and ranges from his childhood in Augsburg through his early successes and his exile to his return to East Germany." Booklist

Includes bibliographical references

Breslin, Jimmy

Breslin, Jimmy. I want to thank my brain for remembering me; a memoir. Little, Brown 1996 219p hardcover o.p. paperback available $12.95   **92**
ISBN 0-316-11879-6 (pa)   LC 96-10488

"Confronting the possibility of death just past age 65 . . . Breslin memory-surfs through a troubled childhood and a lifetime in various journalistic trenches, from copyboy to columnist. . . . The book is full of family stories, political stories, and classic Breslin street stories, plus lots of details about brain operations from both patient's and surgeon's point of view." Booklist

Brokaw, Tom

Brokaw, Tom. A long way from home; growing up in the American heartland. Random House 2002 272p $24.95; pa $12.95   **92**
ISBN 0-375-50763-9; 0-375-75935-2 (pa)
    LC 2002-31865

Also available large print edition $26.95 (ISBN 0-375-43185-3)

News anchor Brokaw "shares the events, tone, and tenor of his midwestern upbringing." Booklist

"Peppered with photographs . . . this tribute to an idyllic childhood should please Brokaw's loyal fans." Publ Wkly

Brombert, Victor H.

Brombert, Victor H. Trains of thought; memories of a stateless youth; [by] Victor Brombert. Norton 2002 334p il $25.95   **92**
ISBN 0-393-05115-3   LC 2002-67081

"The author considers his life from early youth until young adulthood. . . . The child of Russian émigrés, Brombert grew up in Paris during the roiling events of the 1930s; he eventually escaped to America only to return to Europe as a soldier, participating in the final months of World War II." Libr J

"Evocative and luminous, a book to be savored." Booklist

Brontë, Charlotte, 1816-1855

Gaskell, Elizabeth Cleghorn. The life of Charlotte Brontë; [by] Elizabeth C. Gaskell; with an introduction by Clement Shorter   **92**

Hardcover and paperback editions available from various publishers

First published 1857

Brontë, Charlotte, 1816-1855—*Continued*

"Mrs. Gaskell was herself a popular novelist, who commanded a very wide audience. She brought to bear upon the biography of Charlotte Brontë all those literary gifts which had made the charm of her seven volumes of romance . . . . It is quite certain that Charlotte Brontë would not stand on so splendid a pedestal today but for the single-minded devotion of her accomplished biographer." Clement K. Shorter

Gordon, Lyndall. Charlotte Brontë; a passionate life. Norton 1995 418p il hardcover o.p. paperback available $17   **92**

ISBN 0-393-31448-0 (pa)

First published 1994 in the United Kingdom

The author "dismantles once and for all the image of Charlotte Brontë as a figure of pathos and presents, instead, a courageous survivor, a determined writer, and a woman of volcanic emotion. . . . Gordon, as skilled at literary analysis as at chronicling a life, approaches Brontë's tragic and enduringly relevant story from several angles, carefully identifying all the autobiographical elements of her novels and contrasting her commitment to writing and her independent spirit to her era's strict and pitiless code of behavior for women." Booklist

Includes bibliographical references

Brown, Claude, 1937-2002

Brown, Claude. Manchild in the promised land. Macmillan 415p o.p.; Touchstone Bks. paperback available $14   **92**

ISBN 0-684-86418-5 (pa)

"Hudson River editions"

First published 1965

This is "the autobiography of a young black man raised in Harlem. [It is] a realistic description of life in the ghetto. . . . The core of the book concerns the 'plague' of heroin addiction that swept through Harlem in the 1950s taking the lives of many of Brown's contemporaries." Publ Wkly

Brown, James

Brown, James. James Brown, the godfather of soul; [by] James Brown, with Bruce Tucker. Macmillan 1986 336p il o.p.; Thunder's Mouth Press paperback available $14.95   **92**

ISBN 1-56025-115-8 (pa)   LC 86-12715

"Brown's musical career spans four decades and his style defines the genre called soul. He has chronicled his life, from his birth in 1933 through a troubled youth, prison, and the ups and downs of a spiraling career." Libr J

This "is a solid, informative autobiography, and fans will welcome its vast discography." N Y Times Book Rev

Broyard, Anatole

Broyard, Anatole. Kafka was the rage; a Greenwich Village memoir. Carol Southern Bks. 1993 149p hardcover o.p. paperback available $12   **92**

1. Greenwich Village (New York, N.Y.)—Intellectual life

ISBN 0-679-78126-9 (pa)   LC 93-7830

"The late *New York Times* critic revisits Greenwich Village in the late 1940s, which was 'like Paris in the twenties, with the difference that it was *our* city.'" Libr

J

"In this lovely memoir of youth, Broyard has captured the special feel and ambiance of the Village in a more innocent era—a time fraught with exhilarations, adventures, discoveries and hope." Publ Wkly

Brundtland, Gro Harlem

Brundtland, Gro Harlem. Madame Prime Minister; a life in power and politics. Farrar, Straus & Giroux 2002 485p il $35   **92**

1. Norway—Politics and government

ISBN 0-374-16716-8   LC 2002-19925

A memoir of the first female prime minister of Norway and director-general of the World Health Organization

"The writing style is plain and direct. . . . Brundtland is thoughtful, straightforward and unflinching, even when describing heartbreaking family tragedies. There are occasional flashes of self-deprecatory humor and much introspection." Publ Wkly

Buber, Martin, 1878-1965

Friedman, Maurice S. Encounter on the narrow ridge: a life of Martin Buber; [by] Maurice Friedman. Paragon House 1991 496p il $22.95; pa $18.95   **92**

ISBN 1-55778-453-1; 1-55778-596-1 (pa)

LC 90-44502

This biography (based on the author's three volume Martin Buber's life and work) "traces Buber's career showing the pivotal events in his life as well as the influences of Judaism, Christianity, general philosophical thought, and linguistics on his writings and lectures. Friedman analyzes succinctly, but with great care, Buber's responses to the important events of the 20th century." Libr J

Includes bibliographical references

Buckley, William F. (William Frank), 1925-

Buckley, William F. (William Frank). Nearer, my God; an autobiography of faith; by William F. Buckley, Jr. Doubleday 1997 xx, 313p o.p.; Harcourt paperback available $14   **92**

ISBN 0-15-600618-9 (pa)   LC 97-6219

Buckley's book is "part memoir, part commentary on religious issues past and present." Time

"As we might expect, Nearer My God is rich in anecdote, witty, and animated by what Buckley refers to as his 'polemical inclinations.'. . . But what gives it unity as a book, and not just a loose collection of pieces bound in cloth, is the warmth and the depth of Buckley's faith, at once complex and many-sided." Christ Today

Buffalo Bill, 1846-1917

Carter, Robert A. Buffalo Bill Cody; the man behind the legend. Wiley 2000 496p il $30; pa $18.95   **92**

ISBN 0-471-31996-1; 0-471-07780-1 (pa)

LC 00-20368

The author "explores Buffalo Bill's life, moving from his childhood to his marriage to his years as a scout, expert marksman, peerless Buffalo hunter, and, finally, entrepreneur-entertainer to the world." Libr J

This is "a stolid sifting of facts from fiction." Booklist

Includes bibliographical references

Bundrum, Charlie, d. 1958

Bragg, Rick. Ava's man. Knopf 2001 259p
$25; pa $13 **92**
ISBN 0-375-41062-7; 0-375-72444-3 (pa)
LC 2001-32677
Also available large print edition $25 (ISBN 0-375-43120-9)
In this account of his maternal grandfather's life as a roofer and bootlegger in Appalachia, the author "creates a soulful, poignant portrait of working-class Southern life." Publ Wkly

Burney, Fanny, 1752-1840

Harman, Claire. Fanny Burney; a biography. Knopf 2001 xxviii, 430p il $30 **92**

ISBN 0-679-44658-3
In this biography of the author of Evelina, Harman "moves back and forth between Burney's version of events and a historian's perspective, zestfully chronicling and assessing Burney's hectic family life, unique wit and literary gifts, fear and pride over her novels, suffering in the court of Mad King George, late marriage, and, most resoundingly, her many-faceted significance in the history of literature." Booklist

Burroughs, Augusten

Burroughs, Augusten. Running with scissors; a memoir. St. Martin's Press 2002 304p $23.95; pa $14 **92**
ISBN 0-312-28370-9; 0-312-42227-X (pa)
LC 2001-58857
In this memoir the author recalls his youth with a mentally ill mother, living with his mother's psychiatrist in a chaotic household, and his early homosexual experiences
"Burroughs tempers the pathos with sharp, riotous humor in stories that are self-deprecating, raunchy, sexually explicit." Booklist

Burton, Isabel, Lady, 1831-1896

Lovell, Mary S. A rage to live: a biography of Richard and Isabel Burton. See entry under Burton, Sir Richard Francis, 1821-1890 **92**

Burton, Sir Richard Francis, 1821-1890

Lovell, Mary S. A rage to live: a biography of Richard and Isabel Burton. Norton 1998 910p il hardcover o.p. paperback available $19.95 **92**
1. Burton, Isabel, Lady, 1831-1896
ISBN 0-393-32039-1 (pa) LC 98-29886
This is a "dual biography of Victorian explorer/author Richard Burton and his equally adventurous wife, Isabel, using research materials not previously available." Libr J
This is "a readable narrative of great verve and passion." N Y Rev Books
Includes bibliographical references

Bush, Barbara, 1925-

Bush, Barbara. Barbara Bush; a memoir. Scribner 1994 575p il $25; pa $16 **92**
1. Bush, George, 1924-
ISBN 0-02-519635-9; 0-7432-5447-3 (pa)
LC 94-13829
Also available in paperback from St. Martin's Press
"A Lisa Drew book"

The former "First Lady, one of the most popular in modern history, gives the reader a tour through her life story and the parallel universe of the political spouse." NY Times Book Rev

Bush, George, 1924-

Bush, George. All the best, George Bush; my life in letters and other writings. Scribner 1999 640p il $30; pa $16 **92**
ISBN 0-684-83958-X; 0-7432-0041-1 (pa)
LC 99-40440
"A Lisa Drew book"
The former president presents his autobiography in the form of annotated letters, memos, journal entries, and speeches written between 1942 and March 1999
This work "is refreshing and, in many ways, will shed more light on the man's personal character and public persona than any memoir or biography could. It offers an intriguing picture of a man who takes fierce pride in his modesty." Publ Wkly

Parmet, Herbert S. George Bush; the life of a Lone Star Yankee. Scribner 1997 576p il o.p.; Transaction Pubs. paperback available $29.95 **92**
ISBN 0-7658-0730-0 (pa) LC 97-33616
This biography of the forty-first president of the United States details his "climb up the business and political ladder in Texas . . . [then focuses on his] first runs for office, in 1964, when he faced a problem that dogged him his entire career: convincing right-wing Republicans that he was a true-blue Goldwater conservative. But he wasn't, and Parmet astutely analyzes both the contributors to and the forces within the Republican Party with which the unideological Bush had to contend." Booklist
Includes bibliographical references

Bush, George W.

Andersen, Christopher P. George and Laura; portrait of an American marriage; [by] Christopher Andersen. Morrow 2002 307p il $25.95; pa $7.99 **92**
1. Bush, Laura
ISBN 0-06-621370-3; 0-06-103224-7 (pa)
LC 2002-33776
This is an account of the marriage of President George W. Bush and Laura Welch Bush
This is "a largely respectful rehash of familiar tales. As cut and pasted by Christopher Andersen, the author of other tell-all political-couple books, the story of the Bush marriage has neither fireworks nor glamour. What he depicts is an attraction of opposites based on love and commitment. . . . Whatever the provenance of the anecdotes, Mrs. Bush does emerge as more complicated than her public image." N Y Times Book Rev
Includes bibliographical references

Bruni, Frank. Ambling into history: the unlikely odyssey of George W. Bush. HarperCollins Pubs. 2002 278p hardcover o.p. paperback available $12.95 **92**
ISBN 0-06-093782-3 (pa)
Also available Thorndike Press large print edition
The author, who covered Bush's 2000 presidential campaign for the New York Times, focuses on Bush's personality and mannerisms as well as his basic interactions with family, friends, and the public
"Given [Bruni's] familiarity with Bush, one would expect his book to contain revealing insights, and this superb, incisive, and surprising account does not disappoint." Booklist

Bush, George W.—*Continued*

Minutaglio, Bill. First son: George W. Bush and the Bush family dynasty. Times Bks. 1999 371p il hardcover o.p. paperback available $14 **92**

ISBN 0-609-80867-2 (pa)   LC 99-16462

In this political biography the "author traces the Bush family history from Prescott to George to First Son. This family dynasty has been of great assistance to George W. as he is called, in his rise in business and politics. While giving surprisingly little attention to George W.'s performance as governor of Texas . . . the author focuses on his development as a young man and emergence into the national political limelight." Libr J

Bush, Laura

Andersen, Christopher P. George and Laura. See entry under Bush, George W.

92

Byron, George Gordon Byron, 6th Baron, 1788-1824

Eisler, Benita. Byron—child of passion, fool of fame. Knopf 1999 837p il hardcover o.p. paperback available $18 **92**

ISBN 0-679-74085-6 (pa)   LC 98-35261

Eisler's "biography portrays Byron as a restless, brilliant man in thrall: he is, in her view, the puppet of his own extravagant passions and even in his lifetime was so fictionalized and mythologized by others that he found it hard to maintain his own sense of self." Publ Wkly

"This is a splendidly readable biography of a perpetually fascinating genius." Atl Mon

Includes bibliographical references

MacCarthy, Fiona. Byron: life and legend. Farrar, Straus & Giroux 2002 674p il $35

92

ISBN 0-374-18629-4   LC 2002-111340

"Beginning with his childhood and the sexual abuse that he likely suffered in the care of his nurse, MacCarthy . . . here offers an evenhanded portrait of the legendary Byron. She chronicles a life filled with tempestuous relationships . . . and affairs . . . and documents how Byron's appreciation of the East during his early travels through Greece and Turkey influenced both his life and his writing. . . . This work is first-rate, offering a detailed account while refusing to judge its subject. Highly recommended for academic and public libraries." Libr J

Includes bibliographical references

Cage, John

Revill, David. The roaring silence: John Cage, a life. Arcade Pub. 1992 375p il $27.95 **92**

ISBN 1-55970-166-8   LC 92-5917

This is a biography of the twentieth-century American composer

"The biography is thoroughly researched and generally sprightly in tone, and risks the occasional reproof to Cage. . . . But Revill's thrust is inevitably to take Cage on his own terms." London Rev Books

Includes bibliographical references

Cagney, James, 1899-1986

McCabe, John. Cagney. Knopf 1997 439p il o.p.; Carroll & Graf Pubs. paperback available $14.95 **92**

ISBN 0-7867-0580-9 (pa)   LC 97-5067

"The author traces Cagney's life from his poor beginnings with an alcoholic father but fiercely determined mother through his unexpected drift into vaudeville and the theater to his slow but inevitable rise to film stardom." Libr J

This work "exceeds the typical standards of celebrity biography because McCabe is fully attentive to the many dimensions of his subject's artistry." Commonweal

Includes bibliographical references

Callas, Maria, 1923-1977

Gage, Nicholas. Greek fire; the story of Maria Callas and Aristotle Onassis. Knopf 2000 xxi, 422p il $26.95; pa $7.99 **92**

1. Onassis, Aristotle Socrates, 1906-1975

ISBN 0-375-40244-6; 0-446-61076-3 (pa)

    LC 00-40553

The author traces "Onassis's and Callas's pasts, their relationship, and the Jackie Kennedy years." Libr J

This "biography is perhaps the most understanding of La Callas yet to be published, and its appeal will extend beyond opera lovers to anyone with an interest in the lives of the rich and famous." Booklist

Includes bibliographical references

Scott, Michael. Maria Meneghini Callas. Northeastern Univ. Press 1992 372p il $29.95 **92**

ISBN 1-55553-146-6   LC 92-17103

The author "traces the career of the controversial diva from her teenage appearances as a budding prima donna through the triumphs of the early 1950s to later years when Callas's voice was increasingly frail." Publ Wkly

"We come away from this critical biography with a sound understanding of Callas' complicated personal life and her total commitment to her instrument and career." Booklist

Includes bibliographical references

Camus, Albert, 1913-1960

Todd, Olivier. Albert Camus; a life; translated by Benjamin Ivry. abr & ed English version. Knopf 1997 434p il $30

92

ISBN 0-679-42855-0   LC 97-2991

Also available in paperback from Carroll & Graf Pubs.

Original French edition, 1996

This is a biography of the French novelist, playwright, literary editor, and philosopher

"Todd's exhaustive biography, which aims—and succeeds—in presenting 'the man' and not just the writer, has been shortened for its English translation, which refers readers to the French edition for notes, sources and bibliography." Publ Wkly

Capone, Al, 1899-1947

Bergreen, Laurence. Capone; the man and the era. Simon & Schuster 1994 701p il hardcover o.p. paperback available $19 **92**

ISBN 0-684-82447-7 (pa)   LC 94-5941

Bergreen "traces Capone's childhood in Brooklyn, his entry into organized crime and his violent rise to the top

Capone, Al, 1899-1947—*Continued*

of the Chicago crime world. He focuses on Capone's battles with law-enforcement agencies that eventually resulted, in 1931, in his conviction on tax evasion charges and imprisonment at Alcatraz." Publ Wkly

"Mr. Bergreen has written a book objective and rigorous enough to meet scholarly standards, yet colorful enough to engross the general reader." N Y Times Book Rev

Includes bibliographical references

Capote, Truman, 1924-1984

Plimpton, George. Truman Capote; in which various friends, enemies, acquaintances, and detractors recall his turbulent career. Talese 1997 498p il hardcover o.p. paperback available $16.95

92

ISBN 0-385-49173-5 (pa)   LC 97-14792

This book of recollections of the American writer "proceeds more or less chronologically, from Capote's Alabama childhood in the 1920s to his . . . death in Los Angeles in 1984." Times Lit Suppl

"The book is an intoxicating swirl of contradictory stories, serious analysis and rumors, adroitly edited in chapters arranged like those of a picaresque novel." Publ Wkly

Caravaggio, Michelangelo Merisi da, 1573-1610

Langdon, Helen. Caravaggio; a life. Farrar, Straus & Giroux 1999 463p il map o.p.; Westview Press paperback available $22

92

ISBN 0-8133-3794-1 (pa)   LC 98-51195

First published 1998 in the United Kingdom

In this study of the Renaissance painter, "Langdon's masterly achievement is to integrate Caravaggio's art and life in a convincing and vividly delineated re-creation of his world." Libr J

Robb, Peter. M: the man who became Caravaggio. Holt & Co. 2000 570p il o.p.; Picador USA paperback available $18   **92**

ISBN 0-312-27474-2 (pa)   LC 99-43576

"A John Macrae book"

First published 1998 in Australia

The author examines the life and work of the Italian painter

Robb's "mettlesome assertions regarding M's ruthlessness, 'hairtriggered touchiness,' resiliency, and homosexuality, as well as his confident theories regarding his crimes and punishments, make for great narrative vitality and drama." Booklist

Includes bibliographical references

Carmichael, Hoagy, 1899-1982

Sudhalter, Richard. Stardust melody: the life and music of Hoagy Carmichael; [by] Richard M. Sudhalter. Oxford Univ. Press 2002 432p il $35; pa $18.95   **92**

ISBN 0-19-513120-7; 0-19-516898-4 (pa)

LC 2001-34612

"Among the legends of American popular music, Carmichael, composer of such standards as 'Star Dust' and 'Skylark,' is not getting his due, argues the author, who intends to rectify this injustice. The result is a thorough and engaging profile of the great American composer and performer." Booklist

Includes bibliographical references

Carnegie, Andrew, 1835-1919

Krass, Peter. Carnegie. Wiley 2002 612p il $35; pa $19.95   **92**

ISBN 0-471-38630-8; 0-471-46883-5 (pa)

LC 2002-10162

"From bobbin boy in a cotton mill to one of American history's most famous characters, Carnegie's life was one of contradictions. In his lifetime, Carnegie gave away a staggering $350 million, setting a standard for social conscience. Krass used original sources such as letters, diaries, and other writings by primary and peripheral characters in Carnegie's life to penetrate the public persona and show the man who crusaded for universal literacy and world peace." Booklist

Wall, Joseph Frazier. Andrew Carnegie. University of Pittsburgh Press 1989 1137p il hardcover o.p. paperback available $22.50

92

ISBN 0-8229-5904-6 (pa)   LC 88-38160

A reissue of the title first published 1970 by Oxford University Press

This biography follows Carnegie from his boyhood in Scotland through his emigration to America, his rise in the business world, and his early ventures in oil, railroads, telegraphy, and the iron and steel industries

Includes bibliographical references

Caroline Amelia Elizabeth, Queen, consort of George IV, King of Great Britain, 1768-1821

Fraser, Flora. The unruly queen: the life of Queen Caroline. Knopf 1996 xxi, 537p il maps o.p.; University of Calif. Press paperback available $19.95   **92**

ISBN 0-520-21275-4 (pa)   LC 95-49297

This biography is "about a very odd couple—Caroline of Brunswick and the Prince of Wales—whose incompatibility became entangled with public policy during the Regency, when Great Britain fought Napoleon and confronted the dislocations of the Industrial Revolution." New Yorker

"In reconstructing a life that easily could be ridiculed or pitied, Fraser does neither; instead, she sympathizes without whitewashing. Lovers of history and biography will find this an excellent book." Booklist

Carreras, José, 1946-

Carreras, José. Singing from the soul; an autobiography. Y.C.P. Publs. 1991 280p il (Library of courage) $30.95   **92**

ISBN 1-878756-89-3   LC 90-71130

"The Spanish tenor begins his life story with an account of his diagnosis, treatment, and recovery from leukemia in 1987 and 1988. His return to the concert and operatic stages in the following year provides a triumphant and emotional climax midway through the book. . . . The second half of the book then sketches in Carreras' previous life and career." Booklist

Includes discography

Carroll, Lewis, 1832-1898

Cohen, Morton Norton. Lewis Carroll; a biography; by Morton N. Cohen. Knopf 1995 xxiii, 577p il hardcover o.p. paperback available $14.36 **92**

ISBN 0-679-74562-9 (pa)   LC 95-2663

Cohen begins by "tracing Dodgson's early years up through his most productive decade, the 1860s, . . . then retraces his steps in order to examine Dodgson's achievements and personality." Booklist

"Delightfully illustrated with photographs and Carroll's drawings woven throughout, this extraordinary, meticulous biography gives us a sharper and deeper picture of Carroll than any before, presenting a many-sided man." Publ Wkly

Carson, Rachel, 1907-1964

Lear, Linda J. Rachel Carson; witness for nature; [by] Linda Lear. Holt & Co. 1997 634p il hardcover o.p. paperback available $20 **92**

ISBN 0-8050-3428-5 (pa)   LC 97-8324

"Lear traces the path of Carson's determined, self-sacrificing life from her nature-struck youth to her dream of becoming a writer, her focus on science instead of literature in college, her unusual career as a government scientist, and, coming full circle, her transformation into a 'literary sensation.'" Booklist

This "is the most exhaustive account so far of Carson's private, professional and public lives." N Y Times Book Rev

Includes bibliographical references

Carter, Jimmy, 1924-

Carter, Jimmy. Everything to gain; making the most of the rest of your life; [by] Jimmy and Rosalynn Carter. Random House 1987 198p o.p.; University of Ark. Press paperback available $21.95 **92**

ISBN 1-55728-388-5 (pa)   LC 86-27885

"The former president and First Lady alternate first-person reminiscences with sections written jointly to tell the story of their lives after leaving the White House in 1980. Frankly acknowledging the trauma of the lost election, the Carters record their efforts to overcome the difficulties of making a fresh start while deeply in debt, adjusting to life in a small house in Plains, Ga., and other challenges." Publ Wkly

Carter, Jimmy. An hour before daylight; memories of my rural boyhood. Simon & Schuster 2001 284p il $26; pa $15 **92**

1. Carter family 2. Georgia—Social life and customs

ISBN 0-7432-1193-6; 0-7432-1199-5 (pa)

LC 00-48248

Also available large print edition $26 (0-7432-1220-7)

In this memoir, the thirty-ninth president of the United States remembers his childhood in rural Georgia

This "is social and agricultural history as plain and honest as one of the tables the author makes in his workshop—an American classic." New Yorker

Carter, Jimmy. Keeping faith: memoirs of a president. University of Ark. Press 1995 633p il pa $34.95 **92**

ISBN 1-55728-330-3   LC 95-9691

A reissue of the title first published 1982 by Bantam Bks.

These memoirs treat such matters as "improving relations with China; enacting energy legislation; negotiating the second Strategic Arms Limitation treaty (SALT II); concluding the Panama Canal treaties; and convincing Menachem Begin and Anwar Sadat to reach agreement at Camp David. Carter also devotes more than a quarter of the book to the frustrations arising from the capture of hostages in Tehran." N Y Rev Books

Carter, Jimmy. Living faith. Times Bks. 1996 256p hardcover o.p. paperback available $13 **92**

ISBN 0-8129-3034-7 (pa)   LC 96-20993

Also available large print edition $14.95 (ISBN 0-679-75902-6)

In this "spiritual autobiography, the former president . . . traces the growth and development of his faith through his career in the Navy and various political offices, and through his work with Habitat for Humanity (which builds housing for poor Americans) and the Carter Center (an international peacemaking organization). Carter also discusses the impact that Soren Kierkegaard and Reinhold Niebuhr have had on his life." Publ Wkly

Morris, Kenneth Earl. Jimmy Carter, American moralist; [by] Kenneth E. Morris. University of Ga. Press 1996 397p il $29.95; pa $19.95 **92**

ISBN 0-8203-1862-0; 0-8203-1949-X (pa)

LC 96-6350

The author asserts that "the Carter family is not quite the downhome, folksy clan of campaign advertising; they were actually rural gentry perched atop their county's segregated social pyramid. Members of the family were internally estranged, according to Morris, and Jimmy was a loner—a persona confirmed at Annapolis, where he left no discernible impression besides good grades. Yet Carter surmounted these aspects of himself and his background to become a gregarious integrationist, an indefatigable campaigner, and after a 1966 electoral defeat, a born-again Christian." Booklist

Includes bibliographical references

Carter, Rubin

Hirsch, James S. Hurricane: the miraculous journey of Rubin Carter. Houghton Mifflin 2000 358p il $25; pa $14 **92**

ISBN 0-395-97985-4; 0-618-08728-1 (pa)

LC 99-52703

"In 1967, Rubin 'Hurricane' Carter, a black boxing champion and high-profile citizen of Paterson, New Jersey, and his friend John Artis were falsely convicted of the triple murders of three white people in a local bar. Each man spent almost 20 years in prison before being exonerated. . . . [This biography] briefly recounts Carter's youth and his boxing career before settling into the nightmare that began on that fateful night in 1967." Booklist

"Scrupulously researched and expertly crafted, Hirsch's updated account of Carter's life is both a rich portrait of a complex man and a clear-eyed telling of a remarkable life." Publ Wkly

Carver, Raymond

Halpert, Sam. Raymond Carver; an oral biography. University of Iowa Press 1995 196p $32.95; pa $17.95   **92**
ISBN 0-87745-502-3; 0-87745-503-1 (pa)
LC 94-46555
This is a "remembrance of Carver by his family, friends, and fellow writers. . . . These reminiscences include many insights into the sources and literary qualities of his writings. This highly readable oral biography is an expanded and rearranged version of *When We Talk About Raymond Carver* (Gibbs Smith, 1991)." Libr J

Cash, Johnny

Ring of fire: the Johnny Cash reader; edited by Michael Streissguth. Da Capo Press 2002 xxvi, 310p $26; pa $16.95   **92**
ISBN 0-306-81122-7; 0-306-61225-8 (pa)
Streissguth "here compiles biography, autobiography, and articles on Cash, archiving his career avatars over the years." Libr J
Includes bibliographical references

Cassatt, Mary, 1844-1926

Mathews, Nancy Mowll. Mary Cassatt; a life. Villard Bks. 1994 383p il o.p.   **92**
LC 93-22148
Yale Univ. Press paperback available $19.95 (ISBN 0-300-07754-8)
"Mathews presents the little-known facts of Cassatt's very private life and answers the question: Why did Cassatt, single and childless, choose to make motherhood her 'signature theme'?" Publ Wkly
This "is an evenly written, well-documented, and sympathetic—but not patronizing—biography that should be acquired by most libraries." Libr J

Castro, Fidel, 1927-

Quirk, Robert E. Fidel Castro. Norton 1993 898p il maps hardcover o.p. paperback available $19.95   **92**
1. Cuba—Politics and government
ISBN 0-393-31327-1 (pa)
LC 92-39300
The author provides "a historian's interpretation of the Cuban leader's complex life and times. . . . Quirk offers detailed interpretations of Castro's personal rise to power, the failures of the Cuban Revolution, and the regime's recent difficulties." Libr J
"Quirk's richly detailed, psychologically acute portrait reveals more about Castro's unique personality and character than do previous biographies." Publ Wkly
Includes bibliographical references

Szulc, Tad. Fidel; a critical portrait. Morrow 1986 703p o.p.; Avon Bks. paperback available $18.95   **92**
1. Cuba—History
ISBN 0-380-80888-9 (pa)
LC 86-16460
The author "devotes the greater part of this book to Castro's early, formative years and the forging and triumph of his revolutionary movement. The years of Castro's rule after the Bay of Pigs invasion receive briefer treatment. Well written and very readable." Choice
Includes bibliographical references

Cather, Willa, 1873-1947

Lee, Hermione. Willa Cather; double lives. Pantheon Bks. 1989 410p il hardcover o.p. paperback available $23   **92**
ISBN 0-679-73649-2 (pa)
LC 89-43233
Also available in paperback from Little, Brown
"This interpretive biography . . . examines the relationship between Cather's work and her personal life." Booklist
The author's "discussion of Cather's 12 novels and numerous stories is so absorbing that it provokes a re-reading of the work, which makes it a valuable critical study." N Y Times Book Rev
Includes bibliographical references

Woodress, James Leslie. Willa Cather; a literary life; [by] James Woodress. University of Neb. Press 1987 xx, 583p il hardcover o.p. paperback available $29.95   **92**
ISBN 0-8032-9708-4 (pa)
LC 86-30894
The author "does a fine job of describing Willa Cather's colorful public life and of piecing together the puzzle of her unconventional private life. . . . Mr. Woodress does not try to superimpose on Cather's life any theories—feminist, Freudian, Lacanian, or otherwise. Instead, he recounts in straightforward and lively prose the life of a remarkable woman." N Y Times Book Rev
Includes bibliographical references

Catherine II, the Great, Empress of Russia, 1729-1796

Erickson, Carolly. Great Catherine. Crown 1994 392p il o.p.; St. Martin's Press paperback available $17.95   **92**
1. Russia—History
ISBN 0-312-13503-3 (pa)
LC 93-44164
The author portrays Catherine as "a shrewd, headstrong, cultivated woman, a political reformer and supporter of education and the arts, who codified laws, built schools and asserted her independence in a land where women had low status." Publ Wkly
"Erickson's fluid, captivating portrait of Catherine the Great reads like a first-rate historical novel." Booklist
Includes bibliographical references

Troyat, Henri. Catherine the Great; translated by Joan Pinkham. Dutton 1980 377p il hardcover o.p. paperback available $16.95   **92**
ISBN 0-452-01120-5 (pa)
LC 79-25613
Original French edition, 1977
"Relying heavily on Catherine's own memoirs, plus her correspondence with her Western idolaters-publicists, such as Friedrich Grimm, Voltaire and Diderot, Troyat gives us a portrait the Empress herself might have decreed for posterity." Publ Wkly
Includes bibliographical references

Cayce, Edgar, 1877-1945

Cayce, Edgar. My life as a seer; the lost memoirs; compiled and edited by A. Robert Smith. St. Martin's Press 1999 xxvii, 365p il $25.95; pa $7.99   **92**
ISBN 0-312-20419-1; 0-312-97144-3 (pa)
LC 99-31180
First published 1997 by A.R.E. Press with title: The lost memoirs of Edgar Cayce

Cayce, Edgar, 1877-1945—*Continued*
"These memoirs give the reader insight into Cayce's childhood, his values and beliefs, and how he viewed his gift." Libr J

Kirkpatrick, Sidney. Edgar Cayce; an American prophet. Riverhead Bks. 2000 564p il hardcover o.p. paperback available $16
92
ISBN 1-57322-896-6 (pa)   LC 00-27975
"Born in 1877 in rural Christian County, Kentucky, Cayce became a professional portrait photographer, but he regularly gave 'trance readings' for the sick on the side. These readings, in which he made accurate medical diagnoses and prescribed effective treatments for thousands of patients, eventually made him famous." New Yorker
This is a "fair, fascinating, and well-researched biography of one of 20th-century America's most famous psychics." Libr J

Chambers, Whittaker
Chambers, Whittaker. Witness. Random House 1952 808p o.p.; Regnery Pub. paperback available $19.95   **92**
1. Communist Party (U.S.) 2. Communism—United States
ISBN 0-89526-789-6 (pa)
Available in hardcover from Amereon
Whittaker Chambers' own account of his life, his connection with the Communist Party and his repudiation of it, and his role in the Hiss-Chambers trial

Chandler, Raymond, 1888-1959
Hiney, Tom. Raymond Chandler; a biography. Atlantic Monthly Press 1997 310p il hardcover o.p. paperback available $14
92
ISBN 0-8021-3637-0 (pa)   LC 97-264
"Hiney traces the writer's nomadic childhood from pre-Mafia Chicago to pre-telephone Nebraska, from Quaker Ireland and Edwardian England to his education south of London at Dulwich College and his 1913 arrival in the 'mean streets' of Los Angeles, the later setting for his crime fiction. . . . Living at over 100 addresses, he sustained no long friendships, and was 'variously rich, poor, drunk, teetotal, sacked, married and suicidal.'. . . No rough edges have been filed off for this revealing, well-written biography." Publ Wkly
Includes bibliographical references

Channing, Carol
Channing, Carol. Just lucky I guess; a memoir of sorts. Simon & Schuster 2002 262p il $24.95   **92**
ISBN 0-7432-1606-7   LC 2002-26994
Also available Thorndike Press large print edition
"Broadway legend Channing recounts her magical life in this . . . memoir. Widely known for her portrayal of Dolly Levi, the title character from the popular Broadway musical Hello, Dolly!, and for her performance as Lorelei Lee in Gentlemen Prefer Blondes. Channing has spent more than five decades in show business." Booklist
"Channing's memories are refreshingly upbeat; her frequent digressions are detours worth taking." N Y Times Book Rev

Chaplin, Charlie, 1889-1977
Lynn, Kenneth S. Charlie Chaplin and his times. Simon & Schuster 1997 604p il o.p.; Cooper Sq. Pubs. paperback available $19.95
92
ISBN 0-8154-1255-X (pa)   LC 96-30978
The author "interweaves Chaplin's life with the events and personalities of his era, including British music hall impresario Fred Karno, silent screen star and pal Douglas Fairbanks, numerous lovers and wives, brother Sydney, and Adolf Hitler. . . . Lynn addresses his subject's leftist views and makes sense of the House Committee on Un-American Activities investigations of 1947 that led to Chaplin's European exile until 1973. All a biography should be, this is enthusiastically recommended." Libr J
Includes bibliographical references

Milton, Joyce. Tramp: the life of Charlie Chaplin. HarperCollins Pubs. 1996 578p il o.p.; Da Capo Press paperback available $20
92
ISBN 0-306-80831-5 (pa)   LC 95-48438
The author "shows how Chaplin, brought up in London's East End culture, was instilled with a class consciousness that later resonated in his Communist sympathies and his creation of the lumpenproletariat icon of the 'Little Guy'—the celluloid role he could never eclipse." Libr J
"Milton presents a well-researched, evenhanded portrait of a troubled entertainment genius." Publ Wkly
Includes bibliographical references

Chaplin, Oona
Scovell, Jane. Oona; living in the shadows: a biography of Oona O'Neill Chaplin. Warner Bks. 1998 354p il hardcover o.p. paperback available $14.99   **92**
1. Chaplin, Charlie, 1889-1977
ISBN 0-446-67541-5 (pa)   LC 98-21592
A "biography of Oona O'Neill Chaplin, daughter of playwright Eugene O'Neill and wife of film legend Charlie Chaplin." Publ Wkly
Includes bibliographical references

Chatwin, Bruce
Shakespeare, Nicholas. Bruce Chatwin. Talese 2000 618p il $35; pa $18   **92**
ISBN 0-385-49829-2; 0-385-49830-6 (pa)
LC 99-36474
"This life of the author of 'The Songlines', who died of AIDS in 1989, portrays a man, beset with an almost biological lust for loneliness, whose singular genius was for passionate transitory connection." N Y Times Book Rev
Includes bibliographical references

Chaucer, Geoffrey, d. 1400
West, Richard. Chaucer, 1340-1400; the life and times of the first English poet. Carroll & Graf Pubs. 2000 302p il map hardcover o.p. paperback available $14   **92**
1. Great Britain—History—1154-1399, Plantagenets
ISBN 0-7867-0925-1 (pa)   LC 00-712752
West's biography "combines history and literary criticism. He places Chaucer within his historical context and examines his life and writings." Libr J

Chekhov, Anton Pavlovich, 1860-1904

Callow, Philip. Chekhov, the hidden ground; a biography. Dee, I.R. 1998 428p il $30; pa $18.95 **92**

ISBN 1-56663-187-4; 1-56663-395-8 (pa)

LC 97-46679

"Callow sees Chekhov as distant in virtually all his relationships, with romantic disillusionment and the search for intimacy recurring themes in his writing. He argues persuasively that while Chekhov's art is resplendent with human emotion, his own life was strangely cold and remote. . . . Not strictly a literary biography, this book is particularly effective in discussing Chekhov's work as it relates to his life." Libr J

Includes bibliographical references

Chen, Da, 1962-

Chen, Da. Colors of the mountain. Random House 1999 310p hardcover o.p. paperback available $13 **92**

1. China—History—1949-

ISBN 0-385-72060-2 (pa)

This is a memoir of the author's childhood. "Chen, 38, was born in a tiny village on the southeastern tip of China during the 'Year of the Great Starvation.' Because his grandfather was a wealthy landowner, his family was a prime target during the Cultural Revolution." Newsweek

"Despite the devastating circumstances of his childhood and adolescence, Chen recounts his coming of age with arresting simplicity." Publ Wkly

Chen, Da. Sounds of the river; a memoir. HarperCollins Pubs. 2002 307p hardcover o.p. paperback available $12.95 **92**

1. China—History—1949-

ISBN 0-06-095872-3 (pa)   LC 2001-39215

"This book begins where Chen's . . . memoir, *Colors of the Mountain* left off. Coming from the small town of Yellow Stone in the southern province of Fujian, 16-year-old Chen moves to early 1980's Beijing to study English at the university." Publ Wkly

"Da Chen once again describes his past with fondness and buoyancy." N Y Times Book Rev

Cheng, Nien, 1915-

Cheng, Nien. Life and death in Shanghai. Grove Press 1987 c1986 547p hardcover o.p. paperback available $16 **92**

1. China—History—1949-1976

ISBN 0-14-010870-X (pa)   LC 86-45254

First published 1986 in the United Kingdom

"For six and a half years, from 1966 until 1973, Nien Cheng, an upper-class Chinese widow . . . was held in solitary confinement at Shanghai Detention House No. 1, charged with espionage, but never tried. Her book . . . [is an] account of that experience and its aftermath." Ms

This "is a volume that belongs on the shelf alongside the writings of Primo Levi, Elie Wiesel, Dith Pran, and other chroniclers of ideological fanaticism, its dehumanizing consequences, and its all too rare resisters." Christ Sci Monit

Child, Julia

Fitch, Noel Riley. Appetite for life; the biography of Julia Child. Doubleday 1997 569p il hardcover o.p. paperback available $16.95 **92**

ISBN 0-385-49383-5 (pa)   LC 97-11061

This biography details the private life and professional career of PBS' The French chef, whose Mastering the art of French cooking (1961) revolutionized the American kitchen

"Fitch not only richly details Child's personal life but also effectively places her writing and television shows within the context of work by other cooking luminaries of the time. Entertaining and informative." Libr J

Includes bibliographical references

Churchill, Lady Clementine, 1885-1977

Churchill, Sir Winston. Winston and Clementine. See entry under Churchill, Sir Winston, 1874-1965 **92**

Churchill, Sir Winston, 1874-1965

Churchill, Sir Winston. Winston and Clementine; the personal letters of the Churchills; edited by their daughter Mary Soames. Houghton Mifflin 1999 732p il $35; pa $16 **92**

1. Churchill, Lady Clementine, 1885-1977

ISBN 0-395-96319-2; 0-618-08251-4 (pa)

LC 99-18699

First published 1998 in the United Kingdom with title: Speaking for themselves

"Throughout their life together Sir Winston and Lady Churchill exchanged letters whenever they were separated. These private letters, expertly edited by their youngest daughter, evoke times and places and people, the characters of both correspondents, and above all a warm and lasting love. . . . The notes and connecting passages by Ms. Soames do effective service and are often sharp and funny. They should not be skipped." Atl Mon

Includes bibliographical references

Jenkins, Roy, Baron. Churchill; a biography. Farrar, Straus & Giroux 2001 xxi, 1002p il $40 **92**

1. Great Britain—Politics and government—20th century

ISBN 0-374-12354-3   LC 2001-40560

Also available in paperback from Plume Bks.

In this biography Jenkins "concentrates on analyzing Churchill's evolution as a political animal; within those confines this work is a mighty accomplishment. Jenkins illustrates eloquently how Churchill, perhaps to serve his insatiable ambition, learned to play the game of democratic electoral politics, despite his own aristocratic inclinations." Booklist

Includes bibliographical references

Manchester, William. The last lion: Winston Spencer Churchill. Little, Brown 1983-1988 2v il maps ea $50 **92**

1. Great Britain—Politics and government—20th century

LC 82-24972

Both volumes also available in paperback from Dell

Contents: v1 Visions of glory, 1874-1932 (ISBN 0-316-54503-1); v2 Alone, 1932-1940 (ISBN 0-316-54512-0)

Churchill, Sir Winston, 1874-1965—Continued

The first two volumes of a projected three volume biography cover the life of the British statesman from birth to the Nazi blitzkrieg and Churchill's appointment as prime minister

"Manchester is not only master of detail, anecdote, and setpiece, but also of 'the big picture'. . . . Some critics may find his prose rather purple, but his style is entirely appropriate to his subject, and the panoramic sweep of his work." Natl Rev

Includes bibliographical references

Cicero, Marcus Tullius, 106-43 B.C.

Everitt, Anthony. Cicero; the life and times of Rome's greatest politician. Random House 2002 c2001 359p il maps hardcover o.p. paperback available $14.95   92
  1. Rome—History
  ISBN 0-375-75895-X (pa)   LC 2001-48531

The author presents the Roman orator as "a product of his age. . . . [He] scrutinizes Roman society in discussing events of the orator's life and, when describing Cicero's marriage, acquaints the reader with various aspects of that institution and the home of the era." Libr J

This "masterful biography draws on Cicero's letters to his friend Atticus to give a clear picture of the famous Roman orator, noting both his brilliance and his faults." Booklist

Includes bibliographical references

Cid, ca. 1043-1099

Fletcher, R. A. (Richard A.). The quest for El Cid; [by] Richard Fletcher. Knopf 1990 c1989 217p il maps o.p.; Oxford Univ. Press paperback available $15.95   92
  1. Spain—History
  ISBN 0-19-506955-2 (pa)   LC 89-43289

First published 1989 in the United Kingdom

This is an attempt to examine the historical realities behind the legend of Rodrigo Diaz de Vivar, a medieval warrior who became the hero of the Spanish national epic poem El Poema de Mio Cid

"Beginning students, sophisticated scholars, and the general reader interested in Spanish medieval history will benefit from this provocative, learned, and elegantly written study." Libr J

Includes bibliographical references

Clancy, Liam

Clancy, Liam. The mountain of the women; memoirs of an Irish troubadour. Doubleday 2002 294p il $24.95   92
  1. Singers
  ISBN 0-385-50204-4   LC 2001-28450

A memoir of the Irish folk singer and member of the popular group the Clancy Brothers and Tommy Makem

"This is an endearing and lively memoir." Booklist

Clapton, Eric

Schumacher, Michael. Crossroads: the life and music of Eric Clapton. Hyperion 1995 387p il o.p.; Citadel Press paperback available $15.95   92
  ISBN 0-8065-2466-9 (pa)   LC 94-39436

The author "chronicles the life and career of the reclusive British blues performer. . . . Schumacher covers a tale of unhappy personal relationships, a failed marriage,

drug and alcohol addiction and the tragic death of the performer's infant son, while giving full account of Clapton's significant accomplishments as guitarist and vocalist, his forays into rock and his performances and recordings." Publ Wkly

Includes discography

Clare, John, 1793-1864

Bate, Jonathan. John Clare: a biography. Farrar, Straus & Giroux 2003 648p il map $40   92
  ISBN 0-374-17990-5   LC 2003-44063

This is a "biography of the farm laborer who is now considered the peer of his fellow second-generation British Romantic poets, Byron, Shelley, and Keats." Booklist

This biography "succeeds splendidly . . . not only making generous use of Clare's own wonderful prose and verse but adding historical perspective and a constant, intelligent probing which amount almost to a dialogue with Clare's view of himself." Times Lit Suppl

Includes bibliographical references

Clark, James H., 1944-

Lewis, Michael. The new new thing; a Silicon Valley story. Norton 1999 268p $25.95   92
  ISBN 0-393-04813-6   LC 99-43412

Also available in paperback from Penguin Bks.

The author offers a "look at the life and career of Dr. Jim Clark, the eccentric but brilliant visionary who thus far has created three multi-billion-dollar ground-breaking enterprises—Silicon Graphics, Netscape, and Healtheon." Libr J

This "is a splendid, entirely satisfying book, intelligent and fun and revealing and troubling in the correct proportions, resolutely skeptical but not at all cynical, brimming with fabulous scenes as well as sharp analysis." NY Times Book Rev

Claudel, Camille, 1864-1943

Ayral-Clause, Odile. Camille Claudel; a life. Abrams 2002 279p il $29.95   92
  ISBN 0-8109-4077-9   LC 2001-46507

This is a biography of the "nineteenth-century French sculptor who worked with Auguste Rodin, became his lover, and then left him to gain recognition for herself in the art world. . . . Eventually, however, she crumbled beneath the combined weight of social reproof, deprivation, and art-world prejudices. Her family, distraught by her unconventional behavior as well as her delusions and paranoia, had her committed to a mental asylum, where she died thirty years later." Publisher's note

"Fair and precise, Ayral-Clause's clarion biography arouses the only reasonable response to Claudel's saga: outrage." Booklist

Includes bibliographical references

Cleveland, Grover, 1837-1908

Brodsky, Alyn. Grover Cleveland; a study in character. St. Martin's Press 2000 496p il $35   92
  ISBN 0-312-26883-1   LC 00-40258

"Truman Talley books"

This is a biography of America's 22nd and 24th president

"This is a useful and well-researched work that makes a strong case that Cleveland was a scrupulously honest politician and an effective president who resisted the entrenched power of railroad magnates and land developers to protect the public interest." Booklist

Includes bibliographical references

Cleveland, Grover, 1837-1908—*Continued*

Graff, Henry F. (Henry Franklin). Grover Cleveland. Times Bks. 2002 154p il (American presidents series) $20　　**92**
ISBN 0-8050-6923-2　　LC 2002-20315
A biography of the only American president to serve two nonconsecutive terms
This "volume is a valuable addition to the literature on the Presidency and is a compelling argument for taking Cleveland seriously as a President." Libr J
Includes bibliographical references

Clinton, Bill, 1946-

Maraniss, David. First in his class: a biography of Bill Clinton. Simon & Schuster 1995 512p il hardcover o.p. paperback available $15　　**92**
ISBN 0-684-81890-6 (pa)　　LC 94-48245
The author "offers a heavily documented (nearly 400 interviews), unauthorized biography that ends with Clinton's announcement for the presidency. Maraniss writes, 'My goal was for this book to be neither pathography nor hagiography, but a fair-minded examination of a complicated human being and the forces that shaped him and his generation.' He has achieved his goal. . . . All in all, *First in His Class* is solid journalism that thoughtfully evokes the tumultuous times—desegregation, assassinations, Vietnam—that shaped Clinton." Booklist
Includes bibliographical references

Sheehy, Gail. Hillary's choice. See entry under Clinton, Hillary Rodham, 1947-

92

Clinton, Hillary Rodham, 1947-

Brock, David. The seduction of Hillary Rodham. Free Press 1996 452p il hardcover o.p. paperback available $23.95　　**92**
ISBN 0-684-83770-6 (pa)　　LC 96-36030
The author "recounts Hillary Rodham's transformation from campus radical to Watergate investigator, legal services activist, Rose law firm partner, Governor's wife and, ultimately, co-Presidential candidate and First Lady." N Y Times Book Rev
Includes bibliographical references

Clinton, Hillary Rodham. Living history. Simon & Schuster 2003 562p il $28　　**92**
ISBN 0-7432-2224-5　　LC 2003-276264
Also available Thorndike Press large print edition
This is the former First Lady's "memoir of life through the White House years. It is also her chronicle of living history with Bill Clinton." Publisher's note
"This book is important not because of the history Senator Clinton records, but because of the history she doesn't record, and what that airbrushing tells us about the history she aspires to shape." N Y Times Book Rev

Sheehy, Gail. Hillary's choice. Random House 1999 389p il hardcover o.p. paperback available $16　　**92**
1. Clinton, Bill, 1946-
ISBN 0-345-43636-3 (pa)　　LC 99-52279
Also available large print edition $21.95 (ISBN 0-375-40851-7)
Sheehy examines Hillary's childhood, education, career, her subsequent marriage to Bill Clinton and the role she played in the early years of his administration
Includes bibliographical references

Clooney, Rosemary

Clooney, Rosemary. Girl singer; an autobiography; [by] Rosemary Clooney with Joan Barthel. Doubleday 1999 336p il hardcover o.p. paperback available $15.95

92
ISBN 0-7679-0555-5 (pa)　　LC 99-24342
Also available Random House large print edition
Clooney discusses her life and career as a singer
"Clooney's writing conveys the same kind of honesty as her singing. A rich, complicated life is evoked in a voice that filters strong emotion through a hard-earned commonsensical wisdom." N Y Times Book Rev
Includes discography

Cobain, Kurt, 1967-1994

Cross, Charles R. Heavier than heaven: a biography of Kurt Cobain. Hyperion 2001 381p il $24.95; pa $14.95　　**92**
ISBN 0-7868-6505-9; 0-7868-8402-9 (pa)
　　LC 2001-24187
This is a biography of Kurt Cobain, the lead singer of the rock group Nirvana, who committed suicide in 1994 at the age of 27
"Cross followed the Nirvana juggernaut from the beginning, and though he nearly bludgeons the reader with tales of Cobain's debauched excesses, one is still drawn to the artist's forceful personality." Libr J

Cobb, Ty, 1886-1961

Stump, Al. Cobb; a biography; with a foreword by Jimmie Reese. Algonquin Bks. 1994 436p il hardcover o.p. paperback available $15.95　　**92**
ISBN 1-56512-144-9 (pa)　　LC 94-26122
The author, who collaborated with Cobb on his 1961 autobiography (My life in baseball), here presents his own version of the life and times of the baseball player
"Emphasizing Cobb's bitter final days, Stump's portrait of the splenetic Hall of Famer is both chilling and oddly moving." Am Libr
Includes bibliographical references

Coetzee, J. M., 1940-

Coetzee, J. M. Youth; scenes from Provincial Life II. Viking 2002 169p $22.95

92
ISBN 0-670-03102-X　　LC 2002-16879
Sequel to Boyhood
"John, the narrator of 'Youth', is a misfit in 1950s South Africa. . . . He believes he must flee an impending revolution and discover real life. . . . [John] settles on London with youthful hopes for life and love and art. Instead he finds himself in a city of 'low, grey, wet weather' where he . . . is a gauche colonial, neither refugee nor tourist." Economist
Coetzee's "artistry allows him to write about his youthful self from the vantage point of adult knowledge while reflecting on his self-involved intellectual and social gaucheries with detached, wry humor." Publ Wkly

Colby, William E.

Prados, John. Lost crusader: the secret wars of CIA director William Colby. Oxford Univ. Press 2003 380p il $35　　**92**
1. United States. Central Intelligence Agency
ISBN 0-19-512847-8　　LC 2002-25794
"The book focuses on key moments in Colby's career, which spanned from his early days in the office of the

Colby, William E.—*Continued*
OSS in the 1940s to his replacement as head of the CIA by George Bush in 1975." Publ Wkly
This "should stand the test of time as a high-quality contribution. For academic and large public libraries." Libr J
Includes bibliographical references

Cole, Nat King, 1919?-1965
Epstein, Daniel Mark. Nat King Cole. Farrar, Straus & Giroux 1999 433p il o.p.; Northeastern Univ. Press paperback available $20 **92**

ISBN 1-55553-469-4 (pa)   LC 99-32940
This biography of the African American vocalist, jazz pianist and composer "depicts a multitalented musician who—whether contending with racism, with black leaders criticizing his lack of activism or with jazz critics who believed he had 'sold out'—maintained an implacable, dignified demeanor." Publ Wkly
"The biographer sometimes digs too deep into esoterica, spending pages analyzing the lyrics of Straighten Up and Fly Right, for example. But when he recounts the singer's personal struggles, including a shocking 1956 onstage kidnapping attempt by Alabama racists, the human drama is, well unforgettable." Time

Cole, Natalie
Cole, Natalie. Angel on my shoulder; an autobiography; written with Digby Diehl. Warner Bks. 2000 353p il hardcover o.p. paperback available $7.99 **92**
ISBN 0-446-61207-3 (pa)   LC 00-61455
In this memoir by the daughter of the late Nat King Cole, the Grammy Award-winning songstress recalls her childhood, her personal battle and victory over drugs and alcohol, and the legal battles with her mother and siblings over her father's estate
"Although she concentrates mostly on the good times, Cole isn't shy about the bad times, which makes this intriguing, engaging, and inspirational life story worthy of attention." Booklist

Coleridge, Samuel Taylor, 1772-1834
Holmes, Richard. Coleridge: darker reflections, 1804-1834. Pantheon Bks. 1999 622p il hardcover o.p. paperback available $18 **92**
ISBN 0-375-70838-3 (pa)   LC 98-30501
Sequel to Coleridge: early visions, 1772-1804 (1990)
In this "concluding volume of a two-volume biography, Holmes recounts the poet's troubled later years." New Yorker
This volume and its predecessor "make up one of the great literary biographies of the late twentieth century." Booklist
Includes bibliographical references

Colette, 1873-1954
Thurman, Judith. Secrets of the flesh: a life of Colette. Knopf 1999 592p il hardcover o.p. paperback available $18.95 **92**
ISBN 0-345-37103-8 (pa)   LC 99-18959
Thurman focuses on the "morally subversive Colette in the social milieu of early-20th-century Paris. . . . [She] does not hesitate to expose the dishonest, selfish, exploitive facets of the feminist icon who wrote articles for Occupation newspapers and sometimes behaved

heartlessly toward lovers. Nevertheless, her Colette comes off as an appealing, even heroic, figure." Publ Wkly
Includes bibliographical references

Columbus, Christopher
Morison, Samuel Eliot. Admiral of the ocean sea: a life of Christopher Columbus; maps by Erwin Raisz; drawings by Bertram Greene. Little, Brown 1942 xx, 680p il maps hardcover o.p. paperback available $28.99 **92**

ISBN 0-316-58478-9 (pa)
"An Atlantic Monthly Press book"
A condensation of the author's two-volume work with same title also published in 1942 but now o.p.
"An authoritative . . . biography of Columbus which is also decidedly original in its emphasis on the ability of Columbus as seaman and navigator and in the amount of space given to tracing the routes of the voyages and landings." Libr J

Conroy, Pat
Conroy, Pat. My losing season. Talese 2002 402p $27.95; pa $14.95 **92**
ISBN 0-385-48912-9; 0-553-38190-3 (pa)
LC 2002-66212
Also available Random House large print edition $29.95 (ISBN 0-375-43179-9)
"Novelist Conroy ruminates on the profound effect of his final year as a point guard for the Citadel's basketball team, interweaving stories about the years leading up to college, his abusive father, his love-hate relationship with his school, and his growing fondness for books and writing." Booklist
"A wonderfully rich, informative, and well-researched reminiscence." Libr J

Constance, Empress, consort of Henry VI, Holy Roman Emperor, 1154-1198
Simeti, Mary Taylor. Travels with a medieval queen. Farrar, Straus & Giroux 2001 318p il $30 **92**
ISBN 0-374-27878-4   LC 2001-23826
This is the story of the medieval Queen "Constance of Hauteville, daughter of the Norman King Roger II of Sicily, wife of the Holy Roman Emperor Henry VI, and mother to the Emperor Frederick II. In 1194, at the age of forty, Constance journeyed from Germany south to reconquer her father's throne. On the way she discovered that she was pregnant for the first time and decided to give birth in public so that the world would know the child was truly hers. . . . [The author] retraces Constance's route from Germany to Sicily." Publisher's note
"An intriguing combination of travelogue, cultural history, and biography." Booklist
Includes bibliographical references

Conway, Jill K., 1934-
Conway, Jill K. True north; a memoir. Knopf 1994 250p hardcover o.p. paperback available $13 **92**
ISBN 0-679-74461-4 (pa)   LC 93-45302
This continuation of the author's memoir begun in The road from Coorain covers "the period from her departure from Australia for the U.S. to enter graduate school in 1960 through her appointment as Smith College president in 1975." Publ Wkly
"Conway analyzes her own experiences in the U.S.

Conway, Jill K., 1934-—*Continued*

and Canada just as thoughtfully and penetratingly as her academic work investigates the lives of several previous generations of American women." Booklist

Cook, James, 1728-1779

Hough, Richard Alexander. Captain James Cook; [by] Richard Hough. Norton 1995 398p il hardcover o.p. paperback available $18.95 **92**

ISBN 0-393-31519-3 (pa)   LC 94-35998
Available in hardcover from Replica Bks.
First published 1994 in the United Kingdom
This is a "narrative of the life of the great 18th-century navigator, explorer, and cartographer." Libr J
"Hough's easygoing, thorough treatment . . . spotlights a proud, determined man." Booklist
Includes bibliographical references

Copland, Aaron, 1900-1990

Pollack, Howard. Aaron Copland; the life and work of an uncommon man. Holt & Co. 1999 690p il o.p.; University of Ill. Press paperback available $24.95 **92**

ISBN 0-252-06900-5 (pa)   LC 98-29179
In this biography "Pollack devotes single chapters to topics that include Copland's standing among his peers, his identities, and his contributions as a citizen. . . . In this honest, exhaustive, well-written, and loving biography, Copland appears as the quintessentially American composer." Booklist

Cotton, Eddy Joe

Cotton, Eddy Joe. Hobo: a young man's thoughts on trains and tramping in America. Harmony Bks. 2002 xxix, 285p il maps $22; pa $12 **92**

ISBN 0-609-60738-3; 1-400-04809-5 (pa)
LC 2002-17191
This is a memoir of the author's six years as a hobo traveling across America
"Cotton's life has been chaotic, aimless, interesting, dangerous, and daring, and this book mirrors all of those qualities." Libr J

Coward, Noel

Hoare, Philip. Noël Coward; a biography. Simon & Schuster 1996 605p il o.p.; University of Chicago Press paperback available $18 **92**

ISBN 0-226-34512-2 (pa)   LC 96-25923
First published 1995 in the United Kingdom
In this biography of the playwright and songwriter, the author "shows Coward as not only a witty charmer but also the ruthless self-made man. . . . Hoare also provides details of the sex lives of the rich and famous in Coward's circle of friends and acquaintances, as well as his longer-lasting personal and professional relationships." Libr J
"The author's prose can be stilted, and his prolix plot summaries of Coward's plays could be tighter. Nonetheless, Hoare has profiled vividly and in depth a complex legend who had a talent for creating and recreating both himself and his works." Publ Wkly
Includes bibliographical references

Crane, Hart, 1899-1932

Mariani, Paul L. The broken tower: a life of Hart Crane; [by] Paul Mariani. Norton 1999 492p il hardcover o.p. paperback available $15.95 **92**

ISBN 0-393-32041-3 (pa)   LC 98-37726
"Using unpublished letters, manuscripts, and photographs [Mariani] pieces together the life and passions of this brilliant yet tormented man whose creative genius left us 'The Bridge' and whose influence still reverberates among poets today." Libr J
Includes bibliographical references

Crane, Stephen, 1871-1900

Davis, Linda H. Badge of courage: the life of Stephen Crane. Houghton Mifflin 1998 414p il $35 **92**

ISBN 0-89919-934-8   LC 98-11870
In this biography "Davis traces Crane's development as a writer and the many chronic illnesses that eventually led to this early death at 28." Libr J
"Davis has a more stimulating objective than the revival of a literary reputation. It is the man himself who fills up her capacious book." New Yorker
Includes bibliographical references

Crazy Horse, Sioux Chief, ca. 1842-1877

McMurtry, Larry. Crazy Horse. Viking 1999 148p (Penguin lives series) $19.95
92

ISBN 0-670-88234-8   LC 98-26644
Also available Thorndike Press large print edition
"Though essentially a loner and devoid of political ambition, Crazy Horse was a respected military tactician, equally feared and admired for the strength and the intensity of his convictions. Rather than merely attempting to sort out fact from fiction, McMurtry incorporates conjecture and legend into this philosophical portrait of both the man and the myth." Booklist

Cronkite, Walter

Cronkite, Walter. A reporter's life. Knopf 1997 384p il $26.95; pa $15 **92**

ISBN 0-394-57879-1; 0-345-41103-X (pa)
LC 96-21053
In this memoir the news broadcaster writes "about his midwestern childhood, marriage, and family and . . . [the] stories he's covered." Booklist
Cronkite's "memoir is a short course on the flow of events in the second half of this century—events the world knows more about because of Walter Cronkite's work, and some of which might not have happened without it." N Y Times Book Rev

Crosby, Bing, 1904-1977

Giddins, Gary. Bing Crosby: a pocketful of dreams: the early years, 1903-1940. Little, Brown 2001 728p il $30; pa $17.95 **92**

ISBN 0-316-88188-0; 0-316-88645-9 (pa)
LC 00-44403
This "work chronicles Crosby's life as well as his singing, recording, radio, and film careers up to 1940, the year of the first of his popular 'Road' movies with Bob Hope." Libr J
"Giddins has contributed a landmark study of popular singing in the first half of the twentieth century." Booklist
Includes bibliographical references

Curie, Marie, 1867-1934

Dry, Sarah. Curie; with an essay by Sabine Seifert. Haus 2003 170p il (Life & times) pa $15.95 **92**

ISBN 1-904341-29-2

This is a biography of the first woman to win two Nobel Prizes, one for physics and the other for chemistry

"Concise and engaging, this amply illustrated history of Madame Curie . . . makes an excellent introduction to the feminist icon and scientific pioneer. Dry does an excellent job of delineating the major events of Curie's life, including her early education in the underground schools of the 19th-century Polish resistance movement, her heady intellectual courtship with Pierre Curie in France, and later their discovery of radioactivity in 1898. Sidebars on topics such as the invention of the laboratory, and the inclusion of Seifert's essay on Irène Joliot-Curie, Marie Curie's less famous daughter and co-worker, make this pocket sized book especially comprehensive, and a wonderful introduction to a fascinating and inspiring career." Publ Wkly

Includes bibliographical references

Quinn, Susan. Marie Curie; a life. Simon & Schuster 1995 509p il o.p.; Addison-Wesley paperback available $20 **92**

ISBN 0-201-88794-0 (pa)   LC 94-43517

This is a biography of the Polish-born scientist who was twice the recipient of the Nobel Prize for her work with radium

"A well-written, evenhanded story of dedication, disappointment, tragedy, and extraordinary achievement." Booklist

Includes bibliographical references

Curzon, George Nathaniel Curzon, 1st Marquis, 1859-1925

Gilmour, David. Curzon: imperial statesman. Farrar, Straus & Giroux 2003 684p il maps $45 **92**

ISBN 0-374-13356-5   LC 2002-116618

First published 1994 in the United Kingdom

In this biography of the last viceroy of India, the author's aim "is to rescue Curzon from his critics. A person's lack of manners, he argues, should not condemn him to perpetual derision. Curzon was undoubtedly annoying, but he also restored India's greatest monuments; rationalized its police; reformed its currency, universities and railways; and reorganized its irrigation system." N Y Times Book Rev

"This is a superbly written account of a proud, talented, but rather tragic figure." Booklist

Includes bibliographical references

Custer, Elizabeth Bacon, 1842-1933

Custer, Elizabeth Bacon. Boots and saddles; or, Life in Dakota with General Custer **92**

1. Custer, George Armstrong, 1839-1876

Hardcover and paperback editions available from various publishers

First published 1885 by Harper

Written partly to protect her husband's memory against detractors, this memoir by George Armstrong Custer's wife deals primarily with their life in the Dakota Territory in the 1870's, just prior to the fatal Battle of the Little Big Horn

Custer, George Armstrong, 1839-1876

Wert, Jeffry D. Custer; the controversial life of George Armstrong Custer. Simon & Schuster 1996 462p il maps hardcover o.p. paperback available $20 **92**

ISBN 0-684-83275-5 (pa)   LC 96-7290

"Focusing on Custer's Civil War actions, Wert methodically examines a man often considered an enigma in American history. Clear writing and excellent use of primary source materials demonstrate how history should be written." Booklist

Dalai Lama XIV, 1935-

Dalai Lama XIV. Freedom in exile; the autobiography of the Dalai Lama. HarperCollins Pubs. 1990 288p il maps hardcover o.p. paperback available $15 **92**

ISBN 0-06-098701-4 (pa)   LC 89-46523

"A Cornelia & Michael Bessie book"

"The Dalai Lama's story is, in part, a chapter in the 2,500-year history of Buddhism as well as a testament to the 'mendacity and barbarity' of Communist China. He shares the details of his amazing life, a glimpse at some of the mysteries of Tibetan Buddhism, and his unshakable belief in the basic good of humanity." Booklist

Daley, Richard J., 1902-1976

Cohen, Adam. American pharaoh: Mayor Richard J. Daley: his battle for Chicago and the nation; [by] Adam Cohen and Elizabeth Taylor. Little, Brown 2000 614p map hardcover o.p. paperback available $16.95

92

1. Chicago (Ill.)—Politics and government

ISBN 0-316-83489-0 (pa)   LC 99-42157

This is a biography of the man who was "mayor of Chicago from 1955 until his death in 1976. His command extended far beyond the boundaries of Cook County, where he greatly influenced such decisive events of the Sixties as Kennedy's election in 1960, Martin Luther King's ill-fated Chicago campaign for civil rights, and the notorious '68 Democratic Convention." Libr J

"Penetrating, nonsensationalistic and exhaustive, this is an impressive and important biography." Publ Wkly

Includes bibliographical references

Dalí, Salvador, 1904-1989

Gibson, Ian. The shameful life of Salvador Dalí. Norton 1998 798p il $45 **92**

ISBN 0-393-04624-9   LC 97-46707

First published 1997 in the United Kingdom

In this biography of the Spanish surrealist painter "Gibson's central thesis is that Dalí was motivated largely by sexual shame and selfishness." Libr J

"Meticulously researched and compulsively readable, Gibson's narrative benefits from sturdy readings of the paintings and an in-depth knowledge of the artist's milieu." Publ Wkly

Includes bibliographical references

Dante Alighieri, 1265-1321

Hollander, Robert. Dante; a life in works. Yale Univ. Press 2001 222p $30 **92**

ISBN 0-300-08494-3   LC 00-49539

Original Italian version, 2000

Hollander aims to produce an "evaluation of Dante's progress as writer and thinker, through analysis of his work, both poetry and prose, whether written in Italian

Dante Alighieri, 1265-1321—*Continued*

or Latin. This is preceded by a four-page summary of the events of Dante's life." N Y Rev Books

The author "writes with brevity, clarity, and a confidence that comes from his mastery of the vast scholarship and a lifetime of reflection. An important contribution to scholarship, yet readily accessible to the general reader." Libr J

Includes bibliographical references

Lewis, R. W. B. (Richard Warrington Baldwin). Dante. Viking 2001 203p (Penguin lives series) $19.95   92
ISBN 0-670-89909-7   LC 00-43600

Also available Thorndike Press large print edition

This is a biography of the Italian poet who wrote "extensively about politics, philosophy, science and especially literature, including commentary on his own work. As . . . Lewis demonstrates in this brief, loving and unassumingly learned biography, Dante wrote the story of his own life, presenting not the enigma of silence but the greater mystery that grows from knowledge of a life." N Y Times Book Rev

Darnley, Henry Stewart, Lord, 1545-1567

Weir, Alison. Mary, Queen of Scots, and the murder of Lord Darnley. See entry under Mary, Queen of Scots, 1542-1587   92

Darwin, Charles, 1809-1882

Browne, Janet. Charles Darwin: a biography. Random House 1995-2002 2v il
92
LC 94-006598

Both volumes available in paperback from Princeton Univ. Press

Contents: v1 Voyaging o.p. (ISBN 0-3945-7942-9); v2 The power of place $37.50 (ISBN 0-6794-2932-8)

Volume one of this biography focuses on his early years, leading up to his marriage and his moving out of London to the countryside of Kent. Volume two focuses on the second half of his life, during which he published On the origin of species (1859) and The descent of man (1871)

"This biography is matchless in detail and compass, and one feels an abiding gratitude that Browne was willing to sacrifice so many years of her life to reconstruct Darwin's." N Y Times Book Rev

Desmond, Adrian J. Darwin; [by] Adrian Desmond & James Moore. Warner Bks. 1992 c1991 808p il o.p.; Norton paperback available $23.95   92
ISBN 0-393-31150-3 (pa)   LC 91-50412

First published 1991 in the United Kingdom

The authors portray "Darwin as a freethinking agnostic fearful of being labeled an anarchist, a scientific titan trapped on a literary treadmill, a voyager on the *Beagle* appalled at 'low' races of savages, and a paterfamilias who subordinated women but was completely dependent on his wife." Publ Wkly

"No other biography of Darwin has anywhere near the density of detail this book has. This rich tapestry, supplemented with 91 fine illustrations, is intended to provide the basis for relating Darwin the creative scientist to his social and political milieu." N Y Times Book Rev

Includes bibliographical references

Davis, Jefferson, 1808-1889

Cooper, William J. Jefferson Davis, American. Knopf 2000 757p il maps $35; pa $18   92
1. United States—History—1861-1865, Civil War
ISBN 0-394-56916-4; 0-375-72542-3 (pa)
LC 00-62006

In this biography of the president of the Confederacy, the author traces Davis' political career and personal life, including his days at West Point, as Secretary of War in the Mexican War, and as U.S. senator from Mississippi

"In the already cluttered field of Civil War history, Cooper's is the definitive biography; readers will be particularly pleased to discover the compelling power of his narrative." Publ Wkly

Includes bibliographical references

Davis, Miles

Davis, Miles. Miles, the autobiography; [by] Miles Davis with Quincy Troupe. Simon & Schuster 1989 431p il hardcover o.p. paperback available $15   92
ISBN 0-671-72582-3 (pa)   LC 89-19652

"The legendary jazz musician Miles Davis . . . takes us on a historical journey that begins with his growing up in the mid-1920s in East St. Louis, then moves on to New York City in the 1940s, where he was a student at the Julliard School of Music, and to his encounters with other jazz greats like Charlie Parker, Dizzy Gillespie, Billie Holiday, Herbie Hancock, and George Duke." Libr J

This book "is profusely detailed, exceedingly candid and eminently readable—by any criterion a major addition to the literature of jazz." N Y Times Book Rev

Troupe, Quincy. Miles and me: biography of Miles Davis. University of Calif. Press 2000 189p il $25; pa $12.95   92
ISBN 0-520-21624-5; 0-520-23471-5 (pa)
LC 99-54370

"In the late 1970s, Troupe met Davis in New York, became friends with him, and eventually collaborated with him on Miles' autobiography. This slim memoir tells the intimate story of their unlikely friendship. . . . This is both a revealing look at a musical genius and a tender, surprisingly sweet remembrance of a good but demanding friend." Booklist

Dean, James, 1931-1955

Alexander, Paul. Boulevard of broken dreams: the life, times, and legend of James Dean. Viking 1994 314p il o.p.; NAL/Dutton paperback available $15   92
ISBN 0-452-27840-6 (pa)   LC 93-42180

"The interesting thing about James Dean is the fact that, almost 40 years after his death, he remains an icon of American pop culture. In the last chapter of this tell-all biography, Alexander takes a stab at accounting for Dean's continuing popularity, but his real interest throughout the book is in the actor's sex life. Although he devotes some attention to Dean's work as an actor and to his heterosexual liaisons, Alexander's contribution to the Dean legend is to label him as homosexual." Booklist

Dean, James, 1931-1955—*Continued*

Holley, Val. James Dean; the biography. St. Martin's Press 1995 324p il hardcover o.p. paperback available $15.95 **92**

ISBN 0-312-15156-X (pa) LC 95-20000

The author bases his profile of the actor on "100 or so interviews with people who have never before spoken on record. His presentation of Dean's career in New York onstage is surprising in that for most people his image is filmic. But, like Brando, he worked well on the stage, gained notoriety, and became a member of the Actors Studio. Holley reveals that Dean's television work was extensive and continued after he became a Hollywood star. It seemed before that James Dean came from nowhere, a total myth, who in the last 18 months of his life acted in three films—*East of Eden, Rebel without a Cause,* and *Giant,* and only *East of Eden* had been released when he crashed. Now it's different; an icon has human dimensions." Booklist

Includes bibliographical references

Delany, Bessie

Delany, Sadie. Having our say. See entry under Delany, Sadie **92**

Delany, Sadie

Delany, Sadie. Having our say; the Delany sisters' first 100 years; [by] Sarah and A. Elizabeth Delany; with Amy Hill Hearth. Kodansha Int. 1993 210p il $20 **92**

1. Delany, Bessie 2. Delany family

ISBN 1-56836-010-X LC 93-23890

Also available in paperback from Dell

"The Delany sisters' story is a collective meditation on American life since Sadie's birth in 1889 and Bessie's in 1891 in Raleigh, North Carolina. . . . The sisters migrated to New York City's Harlem in the 1910s and in the 1950s to the suburb of Mt. Vernon, New York. The assertive Bessie battled racism and sexism as the only black female member of her Columbia University Dental School class in the 1920s. The more reticent Sadie became the first black domestic science teacher in the New York City high schools." Libr J

"The combination of the two voices, beautifully blended by Ms. Hearth, evokes an epic history, often cruel and brutal, but always deeply humane in their spirited telling of it." N Y Times Book Rev

Dempsey, Jack, 1895-1983

Kahn, Roger. A flame of pure fire: Jack Dempsey and the roaring '20s. Harcourt Brace & Co. 1999 474p il hardcover o.p. paperback available $15 **92**

ISBN 0-15-601414-9 (pa) LC 99-15382

This biography details the life and career of heavyweight boxer William Harrison "Jack" Dempsey

"In graceful and fluid prose, Kahn presents the con men, gangsters, prostitutes and starlets who inhabited the turbulent, Prohibition-era story of Jack Dempsey." Publ Wkly

Includes bibliographical references

Descartes, René, 1596-1650

Watson, Richard A. Cogito ergo sum: the life of René Descartes; [by] Richard Watson. Godine 2002 375p $35 **92**

ISBN 1-56792-184-1 LC 2001-40858

In this biography the author "is less interested in the revered philosopher and mathematician than in the diminutive, arrogant Frenchman who fathered a child out of wedlock, probably dabbled in drugs, and practiced vivisection on animals." New Yorker

"For all of his puckish delight in a juicy anecdote, Watson recognizes and carefully explicates the cultural centrality of Descartes' intellectual legacy. That legacy ensures numerous readers sure to praise a biographer who delivers both the philosopher's cerebral doctrines and his unmistakably human conduct." Booklist

Includes bibliographical references

Devonshire, Georgiana Spencer Cavendish, Duchess of, 1757-1806

Foreman, Amanda. Georgiana, Duchess of Devonshire. Random House 2000 454p hardcover o.p. paperback available $15.95 **92**

ISBN 0-375-75383-4 (pa) LC 99-23580

Also available Thorndike Press large print edition

Georgiana "was the society leader of her day. Daughter of the fabulously wealthy Earl Spencer (and ancestor of the late princess of Wales) and married to the even more wealthy duke of Devonshire, Georgiana was watched, adored, and imitated. But she evolved herself into more than just a fashionable hostess; she got involved in Whig politics, to an extent unprecedented for women. . . . The tenor of the subject's time and place—in this instance, aristocratic Britain in the late 1700s and early 1800s—is both colorfully and meaningfully realized." Booklist

Includes bibliographical references

Diamant, Dora, d. 1952

Diamant, Kathi. Kafka's last love; the mystery of Dora Diamant. Basic Bks. 2002 402p il $30 **92**

1. Kafka, Franz, 1883-1924

ISBN 0-465-01550-6 LC 2002-153099

"A bright and intrepid Polish Jewish refugee who fled her Orthodox family [Dora Diamant] met Kafka by the Baltic Sea, and it was love at first sight. . . . Kathi's captivating account of their brief but intense time together illuminates both Kafka's genius and Dora's joie de vivre." Booklist

"Unlike Kafka's previous lovers, Dora has been little more than a footnote to his life, and virtually ignored by Kafka scholars. Diamant's biography will change all that. It is a moving and generous account—not just of that fateful last year of Kafka's life, but of the remarkable woman who shared it and whose devotion survived some of 20th-century Europe's worst excesses." New Statesman (1913)

Includes bibliographical references

Dickens, Charles, 1812-1870

Kaplan, Fred. Dickens; a biography. Morrow 1988 607p il o.p.; Johns Hopkins Univ. Press paperback available $20.95 **92**

ISBN 0-8018-6018-0 (pa) LC 88-12859

"In tracing Dickens's career from 'boy prodigy' to grizzled Victorian giant of letters . . . Kaplan covers his roles as journalist, novelist, social reformer and businessman." Publ Wkly

"Kaplan has synthesized the vast amount of biodata into a coherent account of Dickens's public and private selves. . . . Important to Dickens scholars while accessible to the general public." Libr J

Dickens, Charles, 1812-1870—*Continued*

Smiley, Jane. Charles Dickens. Viking 2002 212p (Penguin lives series) $19.95
92

ISBN 0-670-03077-5   LC 2001-45607

Also available Thorndike Press large print edition

This "biography examines Dickens' life through his work, starting not with his birth but rather the beginnings of his literary career. After writing short essays for a monthly magazine, Dickens began the serialization of his first novel, *The Pickwick Papers*. Dickens quickly became both a best-selling novelist and a famous man, who had to contend with both the envy of other authors and, much later on, the very public dissolution of his marriage. . . . Smiley's superb and thoughtful analysis should appeal to anyone familiar with the great author's work." Booklist

Dickinson, Emily, 1830-1886

Habegger, Alfred. My wars are laid away in books: the life of Emily Dickinson. Random House 2001 764p il hardcover o.p. paperback available $16.95   **92**

ISBN 0-8129-6601-5 (pa)   LC 2001-19429

The author "traces Dickinson's evolution as a writer from her early childhood in the 1830s to her poetry of sex, isolation, and death in the 1860s and 1870s." Libr J

"Weaving together a chronologically integrated reading of Emily Dickinson's poetry and correspondence, Habegger has written the most complete and satisfying biography to date of a poet long shrouded in myth and illusion." Booklist

Includes bibliographical references

Dierker, Larry, 1946-

Dierker, Larry. This ain't brain surgery; how to win the pennant without losing your mind. Simon & Schuster 2003 289p il $25
92

1. Houston Astros (Baseball team)

ISBN 0-7432-0400-X   LC 2003-52809

"Dierker, a pitcher and then radio commentator for the Houston Astros, stepped out of the announcer's booth to become the Astros' manager in 1997. . . . Baseball and the Houston Astros have been Dierker's professional adult life, but unlike many baseball lifers, he has a healthy perspective about the game and his role in it, as reflected in the title of this literate, humorous, and entertaining memoir." Booklist

Dietrich, Marlene, 1901-1992

Riva, Maria. Marlene Dietrich; by her daughter. Knopf 1993 789p il hardcover o.p. paperback available $18   **92**

ISBN 0-345-38645-0 (pa)   LC 92-54288

"Using her mother's diary, radiograms, and letters, [Riva] gives proper weight to Dietrich's youth, her experience with the Berlin stage, her collaboration with director Josef Von Sternberg (*The Blue Angel*, 1930; *Morocco*, 1930), and her latter day triumphs on stage and as a chanteuse. There are arresting tales here (father and stepfather killed in World War I; a stint entertaining of U.S. troops during the Battle of the Bulge; affairs with legends of the screen and other arts) that give the reader a true grasp of both biographer and subject." Libr J

Dillard, Annie

Dillard, Annie. An American childhood. Harper & Row 1987 255p hardcover o.p. paperback available $14   **92**

ISBN 0-06-091518-8 (pa)   LC 87-45042

In this autobiography, Dillard presents as account of her life from her childhood in Pittsburgh until her entrance into college

"Dillard's luminous prose painlessly captures the pain of growing up in this wonderful evocation of childhood. . . . The events of childhood often loom larger than life; the magic of Dillard's writing is that she sets down typical childhood happenings with their original immediacy and force." Publ Wkly

Dillard, Annie. The writing life. Harper & Row 1989 111p hardcover o.p. paperback available $11   **92**

ISBN 0-06-091988-4 (pa)   LC 89-45034

The author "probes the sorcery that levitates her own writing, discussing with clear eye and wry wit how, where and why she writes." Publ Wkly

DiMaggio, Joe

Cramer, Richard Ben. Joe DiMaggio; the hero's life. Simon & Schuster 2000 546p $28; pa $16   **92**

ISBN 0-684-85391-4; 0-684-86547-5 (pa)

LC 00-49232

In this biography of the baseball player, "Cramer taps every plank in the wall that DiMaggio erected around himself and that protected him from inquiry. In the wall's hollow spots, Cramer locates the girls, finds the Mob guys, and behind the legend of grace and elegance on and off the field discovers a legend who in reality was more often than not graceless and inelegant." New Yorker

Dinesen, Isak, 1885-1962

Dinesen, Isak. Letters from Africa, 1914-1931; edited for the Rungstedlund Foundation by Frans Lasson; translated by Anne Born. University of Chicago Press 1981 xli, 474p il hardcover o.p. paperback available $22   **92**

ISBN 0-226-15311-8 (pa)   LC 80-25856

Original Danish edition, 1978

"Isak Dinesen (Baroness Karen Blixen) kept up a lively correspondence with Danish relatives and friends throughout her 17 years on a Kenyan coffee farm—the period that was to form the basis of her *Out of Africa*. . . . The range and depth of these letters . . . provide deep insight into the popular Danish writer, as well as a wealth of precise details concerning her years in Africa." Booklist

Includes bibliographical references

Thurman, Judith. Isak Dinesen; the life of a storyteller. St. Martin's Press 1982 495p il hardcover o.p. paperback available $18   **92**

ISBN 0-312-13525-4 (pa)   LC 82-5573

This biography traces Dinesen's life from her childhood in Denmark through her years in Kenya and her return to Denmark to focus on her literary career

"With great insight and a novelist's gift for nuance and narrative sweep, Thurman shows the extraordinary degree to which Dinesen's life and art meshed. In addition, Thurman's sensitive criticism of Dinesen's work reveals exceptional artistry in its own right." Booklist

Includes bibliographical references

Doolittle, James Harold, 1896-1993

Doolittle, James Harold. I could never be so lucky again; an autobiography; by General James H. "Jimmy" Doolittle, with Carroll V. Glines. Bantam Bks. 1991 574p il   **92**

LC 91-3353

Available from Schiffer

In this "memoir, World War II flying ace Doolittle . . . recalls his sterling military career and the importance of his family." Booklist

"The book recalls vividly Doolittle's days as an aviation pioneer—and retells the exciting story of the Tokyo raid." Publ Wkly

Includes bibliographical references

Dostoyevsky, Fyodor, 1821-1881

Frank, Joseph. Dostoevsky. Princeton Univ. Press 1976-1995 5v il   **92**

Volumes 4 & 5 also available in paperback

Contents: {v1} The seeds of revolt, 1821-1849 pa $19.95 (ISBN 0-691-01355-1); {v2} The years of ordeal, 1850-1859 pa $19.95 (ISBN 0-691-01422-1); {v3} The stir of liberation, 1860-1865 pa $19.95 (ISBN 0-691-01452-3); {v4} The Miraculous Years, 1865-1871 $70 (ISBN 0-691-04364-7); {v5} The mantle of the prophet, 1871-1881 $45 (ISBN 0-691-08665-6)

The five volume biography of Dostoyevsky, these volumes trace his life from his boyhood to 1881. His writings are discussed in relation to influences and themes which recur in his greatest works

Includes bibliographical references

Douglas, Kirk, 1916-

Douglas, Kirk. My stroke of luck. Morrow 2002 196p il hardcover o.p. paperback available $12.95   **92**

ISBN 0-06-001404-0 (pa)   LC 2002-727755

Also available large print edition $22.95 (ISBN 0-06-008333-6)

"Douglas reflects on his 1995 stroke, the flubbed suicide attempt that followed, and celebrity friends who have had battles of their own." Libr J

"Entertaining and uplifting, Douglas's story is a lesson in survival, one that will entice readers whether or not they have had similar illnesses. . . . This book is a natural for the 65-plus crowd." Publ Wkly

Douglas, William O. (William Orville), 1898-1980

Murphy, Bruce Allen. Wild Bill: the legend and life of William O. Douglas. Random House 2003 716p il $35   **92**

ISBN 0-394-57628-4   LC 2002-23114

This is an "accounting of the multiple political and legal careers pursued by William O. Douglas, who, as the high court's longest-serving jurist, survived four attempted impeachments. Murphy's . . . research uncovers new dimensions of Douglas and his connected political and judicial activities." Libr J

The author "does a wonderful job of providing just enough historical context to allow general readers to appreciate the complexity of his brilliant, but flawed, subject without bogging down his narrative in a crush of detail. Douglas's biography is as much a history of American politics in the mid-20th century as it is a portrayal of the man himself." Publ Wkly

Includes bibliographical references

Douglass, Frederick, 1817?-1895

Douglass, Frederick. Autobiographies. Library of Am. 1994 1126p $35; pa $13.95   **92**

1. Abolitionists

ISBN 0-940450-79-8; 1-883011-30-2 (pa)

LC 93-24168

Contents: Narrative of the life of Frederick Douglass, an American slave; My Bondage and my freedom; Life and times of Frederick Douglass

"This one volume containing Douglass's seminal works is highly recommended for black history collections." Libr J

Includes bibliographical references

Douglass, Frederick. My bondage and my freedom   **92**

1. Abolitionists

Hardcover and paperback editions available from various publishers

First published 1855 by Orton & Mulligan

In this autobiography Douglass tells of his life as a slave and his early years in the abolitionist movement

Douglass, Frederick. Narrative of the life of Frederick Douglass, an American slave; written by himself   **92**

1. Abolitionists

Hardcover and paperback editions available from various publishers

Originally published 1845 by the Boston Anti-slavery office

"Frederick Douglass became famous as a slave who escaped to the North and spent his life-time in the abolitionist movement. His 'Narrative,' one of three autobiographical works written by the self-taught slave, is the story of his life up to his escape to freedom." Libr J

Doyle, Sir Arthur Conan, 1859-1930

Stashower, Daniel. Teller of tales: the life of Arthur Conan Doyle. Holt & Co. 1999 472p il hardcover o.p. paperback available $16   **92**

ISBN 0-8050-6684-5 (pa)   LC 98-35059

"Best known for creating Sherlock Holmes, Sir Arthur Conan Doyle . . . led a turbulent life as a doctor, playwright, avid sportsman, and crusader for hopeless or unpopular causes." Libr J

"Stashower has done an admirable job in creating both a general, well-researched biography of a complex literary giant and in providing insights into the origins and apparent contradictions of his later beliefs." Publ Wkly

Includes bibliographical references

Drake, Sir Francis, 1540?-1596

Cummins, John G. Francis Drake; the lives of a hero; [by] John Cummins. St. Martin's Press 1995 348p il maps hardcover o.p. paperback available $16.95   **92**

ISBN 0-312-16365-7 (pa)   LC 95-43509

"The author reexamines the myth of Francis Drake the Elizabethan adventurer in order to present a truly balanced chronicle of Francis Drake the man. . . . As Cummins recounts Drake's humble origins and meteoric rise, a full-bodied portrait of a brilliant but flawed hero emerges. Fueled by a dazzling combination of luck, talent, and ambition, Drake parlayed a successful career as a navigator and a profiteer into a formidable legend that has survived centuries of scrutiny." Booklist

Includes bibliographical references

Du Bois, W. E. B. (William Edward Burghardt), 1868-1963

Lewis, David Levering. W.E.B. DuBois; biography of a race, 1868-1919. Holt & Co. 1993 735p il hardcover o.p. paperback available $20 **92**
1. African Americans—Civil rights
ISBN 0-8050-3568-0 (pa) LC 93-16617
In this first volume of a two-volume set, "the first 50 years of DuBois's life are detailed, not only on a personal level but also in the context of American history. This exhaustive study includes an in-depth analysis of the civil rights movement of the 19th and early 20th centuries. . . . A magnificent resource." SLJ
Includes bibliographical references

Du Pré, Jacqueline, 1945-1987

Wilson, Elizabeth. Jacqueline du Pré; her life, her music, her legend. Arcade Pub. 1999 466p il $27.95; pa $14.95 **92**
ISBN 1-55970-490-X; 1-55970-519-1 (pa)
LC 98-49664
This is a biography of "the classical cellist, who flourished briefly as the brightest young star in the firmament in the 1960s and early '70s, only to see her career ended before she was 30 by multiple sclerosis." Publ Wkly
"Wilson, a professional cellist, has given priority to the music. Her method is discreet, methodical, informed and accurate. Above all it is measured in its tone." N Y Times Book Rev
Includes bibliographical references

Dubner, Stephen J.

Dubner, Stephen J. Turbulent souls; a Catholic son's return to his Jewish family. Morrow 1998 320p il hardcover o.p. paperback available $14 **92**
1. Dubner family
ISBN 0-380-72930-X (pa) LC 98-34077
"Beginning with the journey of his grandparents from Russia and Poland to the United States, Dubner continues with that of his parents from Judaism to Catholicism. . . . We read here of people whose lives are suffused with religion. It is religion that brings color and stability to their lives, but it is also religion that brings turbulence, especially when one leaves one faith for another." Libr J

Duchamp, Marcel, 1887-1968

Tomkins, Calvin. Duchamp; a biography. Holt & Co. 1996 550p il map hardcover o.p. paperback available $20 **92**
ISBN 0-8050-5789-7 (pa) LC 96-3080
"A John Macrae book"
"Tomkins organizes the facts of Duchamp's life and work into a sober, coherent whole, and for this alone his book makes valuable reading for anyone seeking to understand how art's cutting edge was honed." New Repub
Includes bibliographical references

Dulles, Allen Welsh, 1893-1969

Grose, Peter. Gentleman spy: the life of Allen Dulles. Houghton Mifflin 1994 641p il o.p.; University of Mass. Press paperback available $24.95 **92**
1. United States. Central Intelligence Agency
ISBN 1-55849-044-2 (pa) LC 94-22677
"A Richard Todd book"

This biography of the CIA director under Eisenhower and Kennedy "renders the interplay of person and public event and allows readers to enter the dark world of US-sponsored terror and covert paramilitary operations. . . . Grose sets forth in fascinating and often unfamiliar detail the spectacular CIA covert operations: in Iran, Guatemala, Indonesia; the U-2 incident; the Bay of Pigs." Choice
Includes bibliographical references

Duncan, Isadora, 1878-1927

Kurth, Peter. Isadora; a sensational life. Little, Brown 2001 652p il $29.95; pa $17.95 **92**
ISBN 0-316-50726-1; 0-316-05713-4 (pa)
LC 2001-38064
The author recounts the life and career of the modern dance legend through "her own writings, recollections of her contemporaries and press coverage of the day." Libr J
Kurth "diligently tracks Duncan's every triumph and tragedy . . . and sets her entire complex milieu in motion." Booklist
Includes bibliographical references

Durrell, Gerald M., 1925-1995

Botting, Douglas. Gerald Durrell; the authorized biography. Carroll & Graf Pubs. 1999 xx, 644p il $29.95; pa $16.95 **92**
ISBN 0-7867-0655-4; 0-7867-0796-8 (pa)
LC 00-268642
A biography of the naturalist, writer, and founder of the Jersey Zoo
"Given full access to Durrell's personal and professional papers, Botting clearly admires his subject yet presents an evenhanded account." Libr J
Includes bibliographical references

Duse, Eleonora, 1858-1924

Sheehy, Helen. Eleonora Duse; a biography. Knopf 2003 380p il $32.50 **92**
ISBN 0-375-40017-6
"As Sheehy tells the entire remarkable story of the 'first modern actor,' she discloses how Duse not only advanced acting but also 'expanded the very idea of woman' through her magnetic artistry; her revolutionary productions of plays by Zola, Ibsen, and Gabriele d'Annunzio (her most notorious and inspiring lover); and her work as director and manager of her own company." Booklist
"Sheehy's astute analyses and well-chosen quotes make this book valuable to acting students, as well as those fascinated by the internal contradictions that torture and uplift creative geniuses." Publ Wkly
Includes bibliographical references

Dylan, Bob, 1941-

Shelton, Robert. No direction home: the life and music of Bob Dylan. Morrow 1986 573p il o.p.; Da Capo Press paperback available $18.95 **92**
ISBN 0-306-80782-3 (pa) LC 85-26781
This is a "biography recounting Dylan's life, analyzing his music, and attempting to place Dylan against the background of his times." Choice
"Descriptions of Dylan's family background, his adolescence in Hibbing, Minnesota, and brief university career are without peer. In many respects, [this] supersedes all previous books on Dylan." New Statesman (1913)
Includes discography and bibliographical references

Dylan, Bob, 1941-——*Continued*

Sounes, Howard. Down the highway: the life of Bob Dylan. Grove Press 2001 527p il $27.50; pa $16   **92**

ISBN 0-8021-1686-8; 0-8021-3891-8 (pa)

LC 00-69463

This biography traces Dylan's "career: the early days as a struggling folksinger, the rise to the forefront of the early-'60s folk scene, the controversial switch to rock, the motorcycle accident and the subsequent retreat from public view, and the latter-day de-emphasis of recording and concentration on the concert series known as the Never Ending Tour." Booklist

"Through extensive interviews Sounes aptly captures the contradictory facets of an American folk legend." Publ Wkly

Includes bibliographical references

Spitz, Bob. Dylan; a biography. McGraw-Hill 1989 639p il o.p.; Norton paperback available $19.95   **92**

ISBN 0-393-30769-7 (pa)   LC 88-12912

"Lamenting the impenetrable mythology that surrounds singer/songwriter Bob Dylan . . . Spitz accomplishes his demystification through a sometimes fanciful reconstruction of Dylan's life, replete with sordid examples of his reputedly capricious personality. Although the relevance of such treatment is questionable and his often lurid prose will be objectionable to some, Spitz gives a fascinating portrayal of one of the most influential and complex figures in popular music." Choice

Earhart, Amelia, 1898-1937

Butler, Susan. East to the dawn; the life of Amelia Earhart. Addison-Wesley 1997 489p il map o.p.; Da Capo Press paperback available $17.95   **92**

ISBN 0-306-80887-0 (pa)   LC 97-19123

In this biography of the pilot and women's rights advocate "Butler shows a mastery of aviation history, and considerable sophistication about the technology of flight and navigation . . . The mountain of new material it marshals guarantees 'East to the Dawn' a permanent place on the shelf of Amelia Earhart references." N Y Times Book Rev

Includes bibliographical references

Rich, Doris L. Amelia Earhart; a biography. Smithsonian Institution Press 1989 321p il hardcover o.p. paperback available $16.95   **92**

ISBN 1-56098-725-1 (pa)   LC 89-32181

"Rich emphasizes Earhart's flying career and the stories and personalities behind her accomplishments. It is a scholarly account of her life, highlighting her goals, enthusiasm, and competitive pioneer spirit." Libr J

A "fast-paced, richly detailed biography." Publ Wkly

Includes bibliographical references

Ware, Susan. Still missing: Amelia Earhart and the search for modern feminism. Norton 1993 304p il hardcover o.p. paperback available $13.95   **92**

1. Feminism

ISBN 0-393-31255-0 (pa)   LC 93-9468

"A biography of the first woman to fly solo across the Atlantic. While the facts of Earhart's life have been told

both by herself and numerous others, this book's unique approach emphasizes their significant impact on women's history. This is a scholarly portrait of a person who was not only America's best-known woman aviator but also a nurse, settlement worker, author, lecturer, and even clothing designer—a woman whose life and ideas epitomized liberal feminism before the philosophy was fully articulated." Libr J

Earp, Wyatt, 1848-1929

Barra, Allen. Inventing Wyatt Earp; his life and many legends. Carroll & Graf Pubs. 1998 432p hardcover o.p. paperback available $15.95   **92**

ISBN 0-7867-0685-6 (pa)

This is a "biographical and historical study of the legend of Wyatt Earp as it occurs in text and film." Libr J

"Barra is at his best in describing the efforts of assorted Hollywood icons, including John Ford, John Sturges, and Kevin Costner, to depict the 'real' Earp." Booklist

Tefertiller, Casey. Wyatt Earp; the life behind the legend. Wiley 1997 403p $45; pa $19.95   **92**

ISBN 0-471-18967-7; 0-471-28362-2 (pa)

LC 97-2932

This is an account "of the storied life of lawman Wyatt Earp—a villain and a hero in Tombstone, Arizona, both before and after his death in 1929. Portrayed by novelists, historians, and filmmakers, the Earp brothers—especially Wyatt—became the stuff of legends. Attempting to uncover what really happened in Tombstone, Tefertiller draws on newspaper articles and personal accounts by Earp's friends, enemies, and acquaintances." Libr J

"An engrossing, satisfying inspection of a quintessential figure in American popular culture." Booklist

Includes bibliographical references

Eastwood, Clint

Schickel, Richard. Clint Eastwood; a biography. Knopf 1996 557p il hardcover o.p. paperback available $15   **92**

ISBN 0-679-74991-8 (pa)   LC 96-32836

Schickel examines the life and career of the actor-director

"No mere celebrity bio, this is a beautifully written, comprehensive and astonishingly insightful study of a man who, seemingly against all odds, has achieved world renown as both a pop culture icon and an accomplished film artist." Publ Wkly

Includes bibliographical references

Eddy, Mary Baker, 1821-1910

Gill, Gillian. Mary Baker Eddy. Perseus Bks. 1998 xxxv, 713p il hardcover o.p. paperback available $24   **92**

1. Christian Science

ISBN 0-7382-0227-4 (pa)   LC 98-86397

A Merloyd Lawrence book

This "biography of Christian Science's founder offers detailed depictions of her early years of obscurity, her multiple marriages, the controversies she endured, and the inspiration that sustained her." Libr J

Includes bibliographical references

Edelman, Marian Wright

Edelman, Marian Wright. Lanterns; a memoir of mentors. Beacon Press 1999 xxi, 180p il o.p.; Perennial Bks. paperback available $14   **92**
ISBN 0-06-095859-6 (pa)   LC 99-44228
This is "Edelman's account of how a diverse group of mentors, ranging from Martin Luther King Jr. and Robert Kennedy to the women of her South Carolina hometown, influenced her to dedicate her life to securing a future for America's children. Upon graduating from Yale Law School in the 1960's, Edelman became an attorney at the NAACP Legal Defense and Educational Fund Inc., . . . where she fought to integrate the schools." N Y Times Book Rev
"Throughout this absorbing memoir, Edelman's voice resounds with spirituality, a reliance on her faith, and a belief in equality." Booklist
Includes bibliographical references

Edison, Thomas A. (Thomas Alva), 1847-1931

Israel, Paul. Edison; a life of invention. Wiley 1998 552p il $50; pa $18.95   **92**
ISBN 0-471-52942-7; 0-471-36270-0 (pa)
                                LC 98-10105
This biography focuses on Edison's technical work, experiments, and business dealings
"Dozens of facsimiles of his original drawings are reproduced, which fortify the impression of Edison's meticulousness, as do Israel's accounts of his business ventures." Booklist
Includes bibliographical references

Edwards, Jonathan, 1703-1758

Marsden, George M. Jonathan Edwards; a life. Yale Univ. Press 2003 xx, 615p $35
                                            92
ISBN 0-300-09693-3   LC 2002-013611
"In the first full critical biography of Edwards in 60 years, the author humanizes America's greatest colonial clergyman." Booklist
"Clearly sympathetic to his subject without ever becoming an outright apologist for either his character or his theology, Marsden . . . writes with such verve that he has given us not only the definitive biography but also a narrative that reads like a novel—that most appropriate art form for examining the interior drama of the soul." Commonweal
Includes bibliographical references

Ehrlich, Gretel

Ehrlich, Gretel. A match to the heart; one woman's story of being struck by lightning. Pantheon Bks. 1994 200p o.p.; Penguin Bks. paperback available $14   **92**
1. Lightning
ISBN 0-14-017937-2 (pa)   LC 93-34981
"Hit by lightning on a stormy August afternoon in 1991, Ms. Ehrlich was left with damage to her nervous system that resulted in constant fainting spells. . . . This eclectic chronicle of recovery offers excursions into neurobiology, cardiology, the lore and science of lightning and the medical literature of lightning injury, as well as musings on the Tibetan Book of the Dead and the healing power of the ocean." N Y Times Book Rev

Einstein, Albert, 1879-1955

Bjerknes, Christopher Jon. Albert Einstein; the incorrigible plagiarist. XTX 2002 408p pa $19.95   **92**
1. Relativity (Physics)
ISBN 0-9719629-8-7   LC 2002-5657
Contents: The priority myth; Space-time, or is it "time-space"?; "Theory of relativity" or "pseudorelativism"?; Hero worship; E=mc²; Einstein's modus operandi; History; Mileva Einstein-Marity; Politics and anecdotes
The author argues that Einstein plagiarized his theory of relativity from several of his contemporaries, including Poincare, Lorentz, and Gerber
Includes bibliographical references

Einstein, Albert. Dear Professor Einstein; Albert Einstein's letters to and from children; edited by Alice Calaprice; foreword by Evelyn Einstein; with an essay by Robert Schulmann. Prometheus Bks. 2002 232p il $24   **92**
ISBN 1-591-02015-8   LC 2002-73570
This is a collection of over 60 letters to Einstein from children all around the world, as well as his responses
Includes bibliographical references

Fölsing, Albrecht. Albert Einstein; a biography; translated from the German by Ewald Osers. Viking 1997 882p il hardcover o.p. paperback available $20   **92**
ISBN 0-14-023719-4 (pa)   LC 96-26341
This biography traces "Einstein's life from early childhood through his final years at Princeton's Institute for Advanced Study. It gives equal detail to his technical accomplishments and personal life, including his role as an international spokesman for Zionism and pacifism. It also includes a more honest picture of his relationships with women." Libr J
Includes bibliographical references

Eire, Carlos M. N.

Eire, Carlos M. N. Waiting for snow in Havana; confessions of a Cuban boy; [by] Carlos Eire. Free Press 2003 383p il $25
                                            92
ISBN 0-7432-1965-1   LC 2002-73875
"From 1960 through 1962, some fourteen thousand Cuban children were airlifted—unaccompanied—to the United States by Operation Pedro (Peter) Pan. Once here, they were farmed out to CIA-funded refugee camps, then to foster homes. Many never saw their island parents again. Carlos Eire, now a Yale professor of history and religious studies, was a Peter Pan. [This memoir] tells mostly of Eire's privileged boyhood during the pre-Castro 1950s." Commonweal
The author "looks beyond the literal to see the mythological themes inherent in the epic struggle for identity that each of our lives represents. . . . As painful as Eire's journey has been, his ability to see tragedy and suffering as a constant source of redemption is what makes this book so powerful." Publ Wkly

Eisenhower, Dwight D. (Dwight David), 1890-1969

Ambrose, Stephen E. Eisenhower; soldier and president. Simon & Schuster 1990 635p il hardcover o.p. paperback available $18

              92

    ISBN 0-671-74758-4 (pa)   LC 90-9701

Condensed version of a two volume work published 1983-1984

"Tracing Eisenhower's family background, education, military and political careers, and influence as elder statesman, the author chronicles Eisenhower's triumphs and failures and at the same time provides a vivid picture of the off-duty Ike. . . . This is the definitive one-volume biography of Eisenhower." Publ Wkly

Includes bibliographical references

Wicker, Tom. Dwight D. Eisenhower. Times Bks. 2002 158p (American presidents series) $20   **92**

    1. United States—Politics and government—1953-1961

    ISBN 0-8050-6907-0   LC 2002-20397

This volume "holds Eisenhower's accomplishments up against the two major issues of his time: the cold war and civil rights. Wicker . . . likes the man more than his policies." N Y Times Book Rev

This work "captures the key events of the Eisenhower presidency in a way that is highly accessible and intellectually compelling." Libr J

Includes bibliographical references

Eisenhower, Mamie Doud, 1896-1979

Eisenhower, Susan. Mrs. Ike: memories and reflections on the life of Mamie Eisenhower. Farrar, Straus & Giroux 1996 392p il o.p.; Capital Bks. (Dulles) paperback available $16.95   **92**

    ISBN 1-93186-804-2 (pa)   LC 96-25019

This biography "follows Mamie Doud from the proper, functional, socially conscious family environment into which she was born, to her early married years to Ike Eisenhower . . . to the war years as home-front wife of the Allied commander, and to her years in the White House, where she functioned as the perfect 1950s First Lady." Booklist

"Enhanced by unpublished letters . . . this work is a good attempt at exploring a woman of another time who lived in a different state of grace." Libr J

Eleanor, of Aquitaine, Queen, consort of Henry II, King of England, 1122?-1204

Weir, Alison. Eleanor of Aquitaine; a life. Ballantine Bks. 2000 xxi, 441p il maps $28; pa $15.95   **92**

    ISBN 0-345-40540-4; 0-345-43487-0 (pa)

                    LC 99-54785

First published 1999 in the United Kingdom

A biography of the twelfth-century queen, first of France, then of England, the consort of Henry II and mother of Richard the Lionhearted

"In approaching as complex a subject as feudalism, Weir wears her learning lightly and has a pleasant habit of anticipating all the questions of a curious reader." Publ Wkly

Includes bibliographical references

Elijah Muhammad, 1897-1975

Evanzz, Karl. The messenger: the rise and fall of Elijah Muhammad. Pantheon Bks. 1999 667p hardcover o.p. paperback available $18   **92**

    ISBN 0-679-77406-8 (pa)   LC 99-11826

A "critical biography of one of America's leading black nationalists of the 20th century. One of the founders of the Nation of Islam (NOI), Muhammad helped convert thousands of African Americans to the religion popularly known as the Black Muslims. Evanzz concludes that Muhammad was essentially a con man who used his considerable powers of persuasion to get rich and seduce women. Especially fascinating is Evanzz's extensive use of FBI files to make his case." Libr J

Includes bibliographical references

Eliot, George, 1819-1880

Hughes, Kathryn. George Eliot; the last Victorian. Farrar, Straus & Giroux 1999 383p il o.p.; Cooper Sq. Pubs. paperback available $19.95   **92**

    ISBN 0-8154-1121-9 (pa)   LC 98-42926

First published 1998 in the United Kingdom

In this biography Hughes "shows how George Eliot (née Mary Anne Evans, 1819-80), in spite of her outwardly anti-Victorian lifestyle, was in fact a true Victorian. . . . A solitary, ascetic child and young woman, she was raised in an upwardly mobile country family. . . . In 1852 she met the married writer and editor George Henry Lewes, with whom she lived until his death in 1878." Libr J

Includes bibliographical references

Eliot, T. S. (Thomas Stearns), 1888-1965

Gordon, Lyndall. T.S. Eliot; an imperfect life. Norton 1999 721p $35; pa $18.95   **92**

    ISBN 0-393-04728-8; 0-393-32093-6 (pa)

                    LC 98-46864

First published 1998 in the United Kingdom

"The present volume combines material from Gordon's previous award-winning works, *Eliot's Early Years* [1977] and *Eliot's New Life* [1988], with extensive additional research. Subjects covered in depth include Eliot's complex relationships with women and the Americanness of his work despite his near-obsession with things British." Libr J

"Gordon's book is the most authoritative life of Eliot thus far, and is certain to spark new controversies." Publ Wkly

Includes bibliographical references

Elizabeth I, Queen of England, 1533-1603

Hibbert, Christopher. The virgin queen: Elizabeth I; genius of the Golden Age. Addison-Wesley 1991 287p il maps hardcover o.p. paperback available $22   **92**

    1. Great Britain—History—1485-1603, Tudors

    ISBN 0-201-60817-0 (pa)   LC 90-23275

First published 1990 in the United Kingdom

In this biography of Elizabeth I "Hibbert goes for personality and colour. He has the good gossip writer's nose for human foibles. . . . A wonderfully rich and interesting personality emerges from Mr. Hibbert's pages and he parades [the Queen's] whims, wisely without trying to reconcile them." Hist Today

Includes bibliographical references

Elizabeth I, Queen of England, 1533-1603—*Continued*

Strachey, Lytton. Elizabeth and Essex; a tragic history. Harcourt Brace & Co. 1928 296p il hardcover o.p. paperback available $14   **92**
1. Essex, Robert Devereux, 2nd Earl of, 1566-1601
2. Great Britain—History—1485-1603, Tudors
ISBN 0-15-602761-5 (pa)

The story "begins where the conventional biography recedes, when the queen at fifty-three falls in love with a lad of twenty—a favorite whom she forgives again and again and sends at last to the scaffold." Chicago Public Libr

Includes bibliographical references

Weir, Alison. The life of Elizabeth I. Ballantine Bks. 1998 532p il hardcover o.p. paperback available $15.95   **92**
1. Great Britain—History—1485-1603, Tudors
ISBN 0-345-42550-2 (pa)   LC 98-34917

First published 1998 in the United Kingdom

This is a biography of "Elizabeth Tudor, the second of the three surviving children of the great English king Henry VIII." Booklist

"Weir brings a fine sense of selection and considerable zest to her portrait of the self-styled Virgin Queen." Publ Wkly

Includes bibliographical references

Elizabeth II, Queen of Great Britain, 1926-

Pimlott, Ben. The Queen: a biography of Elizabeth II. Wiley 1997 651p il hardcover o.p. paperback available $24.95   **92**
1. Great Britain—History—1952-
ISBN 0-471-28330-4 (pa)   LC 97-21270

First published 1996 in the United Kingdom

The author explores "the role of the queen and how the events of the past few decades have changed it. Is the monarch just a figurehead, or are there specific governmental actions she can take? How did the royal family lose its privacy, along with much public respect? Pimlott tackles these questions and other historical, psychological, and sociological issues surrounding the queen and her family." Libr J

"One of the many merits of Ben Pimlott's superbly judicious biography of Elizabeth II is that it understands this connection between monarchy and masses, and carefully evokes its political importance." N Y Times Book Rev

Includes bibliographical references

Shawcross, William. Queen and country: the fifty-year reign of Elizabeth II. Simon & Schuster 2002 240p il $35   **92**
1. Great Britain—History—1952-
ISBN 0-7432-2676-3   LC 2002-17579

Portraying both the personal and public duties of the monarch since her reign, Shawcross also "details the British tabloid wars that have raged since the 1980s and tells how the royal family has increasingly been the subject of invasive and titillating press scrutiny. . . . This rather reverential biography should please fans of the British monarchy." Publ Wkly

Ellington, Duke, 1899-1974

Ellington, Duke. Music is my mistress; by Edward Kennedy Ellington. Doubleday 1973 522p il o.p.; Da Capo Press paperback available $18.50   **92**
ISBN 0-306-80033-0 (pa)

"After a prologue there are eight acts unfolding in chronological order—all dealing with Duke Ellington's life. . . . The book is complete with abundant pictures of family, friends, and influential people the composer-bandleader-pianist has met and played with." Best Sellers

Includes discography and bibliographical references

Nicholson, Stuart. Reminiscing in tempo: a portrait of Duke Ellington. Northwestern Univ. Press 1999 538p il $42.50   **92**
ISBN 1-55553-380-9   LC 99-10873

The author "presents Ellington's life through block quotes, arranging bits and pieces of some 70 years' worth of painstakingly gathered interviews, *Variety* articles, press releases, handbills and even declassified FBI files into a composite narrative of the Duke's life." Publ Wkly

Includes discography and bibliographical references

Emerson, Ralph Waldo, 1803-1882

Richardson, Robert D. Emerson; the mind on fire: a biography; by Robert D. Richardson, Jr.; with a frontispiece by Barry Moser. University of Calif. Press 1995 671p il $50; pa $21.95   **92**
ISBN 0-520-08808-5; 0-520-20689-4 (pa)
LC 94-36008

"A Centennial book"

"Richardson focuses principally on his subject's inner life, the life of his mind and spirit. But in this subtle portrayal of Emerson the thinker, the reader also sees the clearly limned portrait of Emerson the social activist. . . . A masterful work, this biography will attract the attention of scholars and serious general readers for decades." Booklist

Includes bibliographical references

Epstein, Sir Jacob, 1880-1959

Rose, June. Demons and angels: a life of Jacob Epstein. Carroll & Graf Pubs. 2002 300p il $28   **92**
ISBN 0-7867-1000-4   LC 2002-67253

A biography of the American sculptor who made his home in England, was reviled in the popular press for his early controversial work, and was knighted in 1954

"A solid and often compelling work that strikes an excellent balance between the artist's work and his tempestuous and confusing personal life." Libr J

Includes bibliographical references

Erikson, Erik H. (Erik Homburger), 1902-1994

Friedman, Lawrence Jacob. Identity's architect: a biography of Erik H. Erikson; [by] Lawrence J. Friedman. Scribner 1999 592p il $35   **92**
ISBN 0-684-19525-9   LC 98-50266

Also available in paperback from Harvard Univ. Press

The author "portrays Erikson as an artistic, somewhat insecure, courageous, upbeat, wise, and perhaps tragic figure. Trained in Vienna by Anne Freud, Erikson had no

Erikson, Erik H. (Erik Homburger), 1902-1994—*Continued*

academic degree yet became a professor at Harvard." Libr J

"Friedman's biography is lucidly written, extensively researched and covers both Erikson's rise to celebrity in the 1950s and 1960s and the attacks on his reputation from feminist and New Left critics in the 1970s." Publ Wkly

Includes bibliographical references

Essex, Robert Devereux, 2nd Earl of, 1566-1601

Strachey, Lytton. Elizabeth and Essex. See entry under Elizabeth I, Queen of England, 1533-1603   **92**

Evans, Walker, 1903-1975

Rathbone, Belinda. Walker Evans; a biography. Houghton Mifflin 1995 358p il hardcover o.p. paperback available $15   **92**

ISBN 0-6180-5672-6 (pa)   LC 95-3711

This is a biography of the photographer whose "documentary studies of the rural South during the Depression evoke the dark side of the American dream." Publ Wkly

"Rathbone does a superb job of describing Evans' elusive personality and unique vision." Booklist

Includes bibliographical references

Exley, Frederick

Yardley, Jonathan. Misfit: the strange life of Frederick Exley. Random House 1997 xxx, 255p il o.p.; Rowman & Littlefield paperback available $18.95   **92**

ISBN 0-7425-1159-6 (pa)   LC 96-51737

"Exley, best known for his 1968 cult classic, *A Fan's Notes,* was indeed a misfit. He managed to sponge off his family and friends successfully throughout his life, believing it was beneath him to earn a living by conventional means. Yardley . . . demonstrates that Exley's great interest in life was himself and that the three novels he wrote were all strongly autobiographical." Libr J

"Exley's short, unhappy life wouldn't support a traditional biography, and Yardley's mix of reporting, reminiscing, and reflecting works just fine. He draws no dramatic conclusions but muses thoughtfully on Exley's many contradictions." Booklist

Fanon, Frantz, 1925-1961

Macey, David. Frantz Fanon; a biography. Picador 2001 640p maps $40; pa $20   **92**

ISBN 0-312-27550-1; 0-312-30042-5 (pa)
     LC 2001-21807

A biography "of the psychiatrist from Martinique who propagandized for Algerian independence in the 1950's and sought to justify violence not only as a tactic but also as therapy for the oppressed." N Y Times Book Rev

"Macey's writing and research is rich with historical context and personal information that both Fanon loyalists and general readers will appreciate." Libr J

Includes bibliographical references

Farrakhan, Louis

Levinsohn, Florence Hamlish. Looking for Farrakhan. Dee, I.R. 1997 305p $25   **92**

ISBN 1-56663-157-2   LC 97-11335

Levinsohn's "biography, which reflects on the black experience and how it changed young Eugene Walcott

into Louis Farrakhan, leader of the Nation of Islam, attempts to make sense of this prominent figure in American politics." Libr J

Fernández Revuelta, Alina

Fernández Revuelta, Alina. Castro's daughter; an exile's memoir of Cuba; [by] Alina Fernández; translated by Dolores M. Koch. St. Martin's Press 1998 259p il hardcover o.p. paperback available $13.95   **92**

ISBN 0-312-24293-X (pa)   LC 98-22370

Original Spanish edition, 1997

This is an autobiography by the daughter of the Cuban leader. She discusses her relationship with Castro, "her childhood, her adolescence and eventual marriage, and the birth of her daughter." Booklist

"Fernandez is certainly among Castro's harshest critics, and her story is both intriguing and valuable for its insights into everyday life in revolutionary Cuba." Libr J

Feynman, Richard Phillips

Gleick, James. Genius: the life and science of Richard Feynman. Pantheon Bks. 1992 532p hardcover o.p. paperback available $16   **92**

ISBN 0-679-74704-4 (pa)   LC 92-6577

"Although it would be hard to relate personal stories about Feynman more engagingly than Feynman himself did in *What Do You Care What Other People Think?* the late Nobelist could not hope for better than his biographer here delivers—a portrait in which the physicist remains a person and is not reduced to an icon of science." Publ Wkly

Includes bibliographical references

Filar, Marian, 1917-

Filar, Marian. From Buchenwald to Carnegie Hall; [by] Marian Filar and Charles Patterson. University Press of Miss. 2002 231p il $30   **92**

1. Holocaust, 1933-1945—Personal narratives

ISBN 1-57806-419-8   LC 2001-26907

"Born in 1917, the youngest of seven children in a musical family, Filar was a soloist prodigy with the Warsaw Philharmonic when he was 12. . . . Then came the war and his first cattle-car deportation with other Warsaw Ghetto rebels who were marked for special cruelty. . . . By 1950, Filar was a refugee on a displaced person's ship passing the Statue of Liberty, and in 1952 he debuted at Carnegie Hall." Publ Wkly

"Among the many astonishing accounts of Holocaust survival, this is one of the most remarkable." Booklist

Fisher, Eddie

Fisher, Eddie. Been there, done that; [by] Eddie Fisher, with David Fisher. St. Martin's Press 1999 341p il $24.95; pa $7.99   **92**

ISBN 0-312-20972-X; 0-312-87558-9 (pa)
     LC 99-27236

"Thomas Dunne books"

"Fisher tells the story of his rise from poverty to 1950s crooner stardom and beyond." Publ Wkly

"What makes this memoir engaging is Fisher's sharp, often self-deprecating wit and his willingness to dish about his cohorts and conquests." N Y Times Book Rev

Fitzgerald, Ella

Fidelman, Geoffrey Mark. First lady of song: Ella Fitzgerald for the record. Carol Pub. Group 1994 xx, 379p il o.p.; Replica Bks. paperback available $32   **92**
ISBN 0-7351-0096-9 (pa)   LC 94-17470
"A Birch Lane Press book"
In this "biography of legendary singer Ella Fitzgerald . . . Fidelman provides a year-by-year account of her career from her debut at the Apollo Theater in Harlem in 1934 to her 1993 retirement because of failing health. He emphasizes Fitzgerald's complex relationship with Norman Granz, her longtime manager and producer, and her dedication to her art at the expense of her close friendships and health." Publ Wkly
Includes discography

Fitzgerald, F. Scott (Francis Scott), 1896-1940

Bruccoli, Matthew Joseph. Fitzgerald and Hemingway; a dangerous friendship; [by] Matthew J. Bruccoli. Carroll & Graf Pubs. 1994 236p il o.p.; Bruccoli Clark paperback available $11.95   **92**
1. Hemingway, Ernest, 1899-1961
ISBN 0-89723-053-1 (pa)   LC 94-4669
"Drawing heavily from his subjects' letters to each other and their joint editor, Max Perkins, Bruccoli . . . endeavors to separate fact from fiction in this analysis of the legendary Hemingway/Fitzgerald relationship. . . . Bruccoli's style, while scholarly, is quite readable, making for a pleasant sojourn through the chaotic lives of the celebrated duo." Libr J
Includes bibliographical references

Fitzgerald, F. Scott (Francis Scott). A life in letters; edited by Matthew J. Bruccoli; with the assistance of Judith S. Baughman. Scribner 1994 xxiii, 503p $30; pa $18   **92**
ISBN 0-684-19570-4; 0-684-80153-1 (pa)
    LC 93-31011
"Early letters to his editor, Maxwell Perkins, and friends, Edmund Wilson and Ernest Hemingway, document Fitzgerald's devotion to craft, exemplified by *The Great Gatsby* (1925), as well as the novelist's ever-present financial problems. . . . Letters to his wife, Zelda—when she was hospitalized for mental illness—detail the destruction of their marriage." Publ Wkly
"Essential reading for a full understanding of Fitzgerald as an artist and a man." Libr J

Fitzgerald, Zelda, 1900-1948

Cline, Sally. Zelda Fitzgerald; her voice in paradise. Arcade Pub. 2003 c2002 xx, 492p il $27.95   **92**
1. Fitzgerald, F. Scott (Francis Scott), 1896-1940
ISBN 1-55970-688-0   LC 2002-43649
First published 2002 in the United Kingdom
This "biography reveals Zelda Fitzgerald's life as a complexity of 'voices,' from Southern belle who married F. Scott Fitzgerald and was taken to New York where suddenly she was living in the shadow of a famous and egotistical husband, to life in Paris, return to New York, and hospitalization for mental illness." Libr J
"Cline not only clarifies many heretofore misunderstood aspects of Zelda's life, she also celebrates her unique style of whimsical and sardonic artistic expression." Booklist
Includes bibliographical references

Foner, Moe, 1915-2002

Foner, Moe. Not for bread alone; a memoir; by Moe Foner with Dan North; foreword by Ossie Davis. Cornell Univ. Press 2002 142p $25   **92**
ISBN 0-8014-4061-0   LC 2002-5100
This memoir focuses on Foner's work on behalf of "the union of New York City hospital and healthcare workers, best known by its number—1199." Nation
Foner's "memoir is a unique window into the evolution of 1199 SEIU from its origins as a tiny conglomeration of drugstore employees into the country's largest healthcare union." Libr J
Includes bibliographical references

Fontana, Lavinia, 1552-1614

Murphy, Caroline P. Lavinia Fontana; a painter and her patrons in sixteenth-century Bologna. Yale Univ. Press 2003 236p il $60   **92**
ISBN 0-300-09913-4   LC 2002-13591
The author "assesses the relation of Fontana's native city Bologna to the artist's work and career. . . . The book discusses sixteenth-century Bologna's economics and emergent artistic culture, how and why Fontana became an artist, her crucial relationship with the noblewomen who became her most loyal patrons . . . and the portraits and religious works she created for Bolognese children." Publisher's note
"Murphy is the first to write an in-depth, English-language treatise on heretofore overlooked Fontana and her world, and the resulting finely illustrated volume is exhilarating." Booklist
Includes bibliographical references

Foote, Horton

Foote, Horton. Beginnings; a memoir. Scribner 2001 270p il $24; pa $14   **92**
ISBN 0-7432-1115-4; 0-7432-1116-2 (pa)
    LC 2001-47088
Sequel to Farewell
Foote "chronicled his Wharton, TX, childhood in *Farewell*. . . . Now he continues his story where he left off, leaving Wharton at 17 to study to become an actor. He travels to theater school in Pasadena but eventually makes it to New York by way of Martha's Vineyard, where he soon discovers his talent for writing and hobnobs with the likes of Martha Graham, Tennessee Williams, and Agnes de Mille." Libr J

Foote, Horton. Farewell; a memoir of a Texas childhood. Scribner 1999 287p il hardcover o.p. paperback available $13   **92**
ISBN 0-684-86570-X (pa)   LC 99-10227
In this memoir the award-winning screenwriter/playwright "recalls his small-town Texas childhood, from his birth in 1916 to his departure . . . 17 years later." Libr J
"Foote draws no conclusions about himself or his origins at the end of the warm, spare chronicle, but it provides a key to the birth of his distinctive sensibility." N Y Times Book Rev

Ford, Henry, 1863-1947

Baldwin, Neil. Henry Ford and the Jews; the mass production of hate. PublicAffairs 2001 416p il $27.50; pa $16   **92**

1. Antisemitism
ISBN 1-891620-52-5; 1-58648-163-0 (pa)
LC 2001-41679

"Baldwin reveals the complex tale of how 'Heinrich' Ford promoted a virulent brand of antisemitism, disseminating his point of view through a privately-published newspaper, *The Dearborn Independent*—and how the Jewish American community responded with alarm and courage." Publisher's note

"The strength of this biography lies in context: by emphasizing Ford's background, influences and the world around the auto manufacturer, Baldwin . . . brings a fresh approach to what has long been known about one of America's most famous anti-Semites." Publ Wkly

Ford, John, 1894-1973

Davis, Ronald L. John Ford; Hollywood's old master. University of Okla. Press 1995 383p il (Oklahoma western biographies) hardcover o.p. paperback available $21.95   **92**

ISBN 0-8061-2916-6 (pa)   LC 94-25178

In this study of the influential filmmaker, "Davis draws on the recollections of the actors who worked frequently with Ford, including John Wayne, Henry Fonda and Maureen O'Hara, to document Ford's tyranny on the set, which intimidated his cast but wrung brilliant performances from them." Publ Wkly

Includes bibliographical references

Eyman, Scott. Print the legend: the life and times of John Ford. Simon & Schuster 1999 656p il o.p.; Johns Hopkins Univ. Press paperback available $23.50   **92**

ISBN 0-8018-6560-3 (pa)   LC 99-37046

This is a biography chronicling the life and career of the director of "such classics as *The grapes of wrath, The searchers* and *The man who shot Liberty Valance.* . . . Eyman has written a quietly magnificent biography of an American original who has shaped our perception of movies as serious art." Publ Wkly

Includes bibliographical references

Forrest, Nathan Bedford, 1821-1877

Hurst, Jack. Nathan Bedford Forrest; a biography. Knopf 1993 433p maps hardcover o.p. paperback available $15   **92**

1. United States—History—1861-1865, Civil War
ISBN 0-679-74830-X (pa)   LC 92-54383

In this study of the Confederate Civil War general, Hurst "devotes the first part of the book to Forrest's pre-war occupation as a slave trader, and the last part to Forrest's involvements with the Ku Klux Klan and state politics as well as his attempts to regain the fortune that was lost during the war. The author presents a detailed study of Forrest's wartime campaigns, from his brilliant exploits in battle to his controversies with his commanding officers and the debacle at Fort Pillow." Libr J

"Hurst, to his credit, doesn't arbitrate the truth, but lets the known facts and contemporary news accounts battle among themselves over Forrest's legendary exploits in the Lost Cause, as well as his postwar resistance to Radical Reconstruction." Booklist

Forten, James, 1766-1842

Winch, Julie. A gentleman of color: the life of James Forten. Oxford Univ. Press 2002 501p il $35; pa $18.95   **92**

ISBN 0-19-508691-0; 0-19-516340-0 (pa)
LC 2001-36215

This is "a life-and-times biography of James Forten (1766-1842), an entrepreneur, social reformer, Revolutionary War patriot, and gentleman, who stood as one of the most influential and well-known African Americans of his day." Libr J

The author "has done a masterful job of researching and piecing together Forten's life. . . . But the strength of the book—aside from rediscovering Forten—is the careful and often surprising research into the complexity of African-American life in the 18th and early 19th centuries." Publ Wkly

Includes bibliographical references

Fossey, Dian

Mowat, Farley. Woman in the mists: the story of Dian Fossey and the mountain gorillas of Africa. Warner Bks. 1987 380p il hardcover o.p. paperback available $19.99   **92**

1. Gorillas
ISBN 0-446-38720-7 (pa)   LC 87-40166

The author has "organized Fossey's journals into a biography that quotes her writings so heavily as to be autobiographical. Much of the text parallels material in Fossey's Gorillas in the Mist but provides additional insights into her personal life, difficulties in maintaining funding, and the continuation of her work up to her death in 1985. This gripping, action-packed story is essential reading for all who understand the sacrifice of self for the preservation of other species." Libr J

Foster, Stephen Collins, 1826-1864

Emerson, Ken. Doo-dah!: Stephen Foster and the rise of American popular culture. Da Capo Press 1998 400p il pa $16.50   **92**

ISBN 0-306-80852-8   LC 98-15480

First published 1997 by Simon & Schuster

The author "explores the roots of early popular music while tracing the tragic life of composer Stephen Collins Foster. . . . He also aims his spotlight at other musical personalities of the period, and provides further illumination of how Foster's songs have been incorporated into popular contemporary melodies. . . . Emerson's exhaustive research . . . has been meticulously worked into a vivid portrait of 19th-century America." Publ Wkly

Includes discography and bibliographical references

Foucault, Michel, 1926-1984

Macey, David. The lives of Michel Foucault; a biography. Pantheon Bks. 1994 c1993 xxiii, 599p hardcover o.p. paperback available $25   **92**

ISBN 0-679-75792-9 (pa)   LC 93-28220

First published 1993 in the United Kingdom

Macey "traces Foucault's constantly evolving thought against the backdrop of his political activism and travels, draws on interviews with friends and colleagues and on the cooperation of Foucault's former lover, Daniel Defert. Details of Foucault's experimentation with LSD and opium, his near-death experience after being hit by a car, and his activism against racism, the Vietnam War and prison conditions round out a portrait of a versatile thinker who remains a personal enigma." Publ Wkly

Includes bibliographical references

Fox, Michael J.

Fox, Michael J. Lucky man; a memoir. Hyperion 2002 304p $22.95; pa $12.95 **92**
ISBN 0-7868-6764-7; 0-7868-8874-1 (pa)
Also available Random House large print edition
In this autobiography the actor discusses his professional career in feature films and television. He also "writes of the last 10 years, during which--with the unswerving support of his wife, family, and friends--he has dealt with his illness. He talks about what Parkinson's has given him: the chance to appreciate a wonderful life and career, and the opportunity to help search for a cure and spread public awareness of the disease." Publisher's note

Fox, Paula

Fox, Paula. Borrowed finery; a memoir. Holt & Co. 2001 210p hardcover o.p. paperback available $12 **92**
ISBN 0-8050-7184-9 (pa)　　　　LC 00-54398
The author of Desperate characters (1970), Monkey Island (1991), and The Widow's children (1999) "recounts the chaotic and often traumatic circumstances of her childhood. With parents too unstable and self-absorbed to care for her, she was shuffled from doorstep to boarding school, from New York to Cuba to Montreal. . . . Fox tells her stories with no trace of self pity. Her style is honest without being laborious, and her recollections bear the unmistakable mark of uncontrived innocence." Libr J

Francis, of Assisi, Saint, 1182-1226

Martin, Valerie. Salvation: scenes from the life of St. Francis. Knopf 2001 268p hardcover o.p. paperback available $13 **92**
ISBN 0-375-70883-9 (pa)　　　　LC 00-44361
"This is a series of 31 frescolike word panels on the radical popular stigmatist and founder of the Franciscan Order. . . . The scenes begin with Francis's death and end with his encounter with a leper. The use of the present tense draws one into the joy and suffering of Francis and the barbarity of his age." Libr J
"This portrait will be most interesting to readers who are already familiar with the basic facts of Francis's life and remain open to exploring a new, gritty interpretation of them." Publ Wkly
Includes bibliographical references

Frank, Anne, 1929-1945

Frank, Anne. The diary of a young girl: the definitive edition; edited by Otto H. Frank and Mirjam Pressler; translated by Susan Massotty. Doubleday 1995 340p $27.50; pa $12.95 **92**
1. World War, 1939-1945—Jews 2. Netherlands—History—1940-1945, German occupation 3. Jews—Netherlands 4. Holocaust, 1933-1945
ISBN 0-385-47378-8; 0-385-42360-8 (pa)
　　　　　　　　　　　　　　LC 94-41379
Hardcover and paperback editions available from various publishers
"This new translation of Frank's famous diary includes material about her emerging sexuality and her relationship with her mother that was originally excised by Frank's father, the only family member to survive the Holocaust." Libr J

Frank, Anne. The diary of Anne Frank: the critical edition. rev Critical ed. Doubleday 2003 851p il $75 **92**
1. World War, 1939-1945—Jews 2. Netherlands—History—1940-1945, German occupation 3. Jews—Netherlands 4. Holocaust, 1933-1945
ISBN 0-385-50847-6　　　　LC 2003-269527
First published 1989
"Prepared by the Netherlands State Institute for War Documentation; introduced by Harry Paape, Gerrold van der Stroom, and David Barnouw; with a summary of the report by the Netherlands Forensic Institute; compiled by H.J.J. Hardy; edited by David Barnouw and Gerrold van der Stroom; translated by Arnold J. Pomerans, B.M. Mooyaart-Doubleday and Susan Massotty." Title page
This volume brings together "the three known versions of Frank's diary—the original, a self-edited version . . . [and] another edited by her father. It also contains . . . handwriting and paper analyses, new documentation regarding the Frank family's arrest, and . . . information about the diary's troubled publication history." Libr J [review of 1989 edition]
Includes bibliographical references

Müller, Melissa. Anne Frank; the biography; translated by Rita and Robert Kimber. Holt & Co. 1998 330p $23; pa $14 **92**
1. World War, 1939-1945—Jews 2. Netherlands—History—1940-1945, German occupation 3. Jews—Netherlands 4. Holocaust, 1933-1945
ISBN 0-8050-5996-2; 0-8050-5997-0 (pa)
　　　　　　　　　　　　　　LC 98-22923
This biography covers Anne Frank's life from her childhood to her last days in Bergen-Belsen concentration camp
"Müller includes a family tree; a family history; and considerable insight into the character, personality, and quality of life of Anne's parents, relatives, and friends. Interviews with many of these surviving people give a clearer idea of the situation and Anne's reactions to it." SLJ

Frankel, Max, 1930-

Frankel, Max. The times of my life and my life with the Times. Random House 1999 546p il map $29.95; pa $15.95 **92**
1. New York times
ISBN 0-679-44824-1; 0-385-33498-2 (pa)
　　　　　　　　　　　　　　LC 98-16831
This is an autobiography by the former editor of The New York Times. "The book is organized chronologically, and [moves] . . . back and forth between Frankel's personal and professional life." Commentary
"Every reader will learn a very great deal about how a newspaper works, how an editor dances with a publisher, and who has the final say and why. On that level, this memoir is one of the most elegant ever composed by a newspaperman." N Y Times Book Rev

Frankenthaler, Helen, 1928-

Elderfield, John. Frankenthaler. Abrams 1987 448p il $150 **92**
ISBN 0-8109-0916-2　　　　LC 87-1118
This is a study of the life and work of American abstract artist Helen Frankenthaler
The author "writes with confidence and authority, drawing upon extensive interviews with the artist. With

Frankenthaler, Helen, 1928-—Continued

its 262 color and 138 black-and-white illustrations, detailed chronologies, and lengthy bibliography, this superb critical account is highly recommended." Libr J
Includes bibliographical references

Franklin, Benjamin, 1706-1790

Brands, H. W. The first American: the life and times of Benjamin Franklin. Doubleday 2000 759p hardcover o.p. paperback available $17　　　　**92**
ISBN 0-385-49540-4 (pa)　　　　LC 00-27930
"Brands fills in disparate pockets of history (the importance of Cotton Mather in Boston, the intellectual enthusiasms of the Royal Society in London) with readable, unobtrusive scholarship. Perhaps he took as his model his unassuming subject, who treated his extraordinary achievements in fields as diverse as science and diplomacy as if they were ordinary. Franklin emerges as a man with a passion to add to human happiness." New Yorker
Includes bibliographical references

Franklin, Benjamin. The autobiography of Benjamin Franklin　　　　**92**
Hardcover and paperback editions available from various publishers

Written between 1771 and 1788

"Franklin's account of his life, written for his son William. . . . During the Revolutionary War, the manuscript was put aside. . . . Franklin later more than doubled the length . . . but still took the story only to 1757-1759, ending before the period of his greatest public service. Still, the book remains the first undisputed classic of American literature and one of the most interesting autobiographies in English." Benet's Reader's Ency of Am Lit

Jennings, Francis. Benjamin Franklin, politician. Norton 1996 240p $27.50　　　**92**
ISBN 0-393-03983-8　　　　LC 96-3377
This study "focuses on Franklin's political career from 1744 to 1775, before the American Revolution. The author traces the bitter struggle between Franklin, who served as master of the Pennsylvania Assembly, and the Penn family, who attempted to control the assembly by feudal rule. Many details of this political battle, which included Franklin's resentment of and revenge against Pennsylvania's Quakers and his prejudice toward German immigrants, were omitted from his *Autobiography*." Publ Wkly
"This interesting and idiosyncratic portrait of Franklin . . . reads in part more like a polemic than history. It does, however, provide a counterpoint to more sympathetic views of Franklin." Libr J
Includes bibliographical references

Morgan, Edmund Sears. Benjamin Franklin; [by] Edmund S. Morgan. Yale Univ. Press 2002 339p il $24.95; pa $16　　　**92**
ISBN 0-300-09532-5; 0-300-10162-7 (pa)
　　　　LC 2002-1143
Also available Thorndike Press large print edition
"Morgan adopts a chronological approach from which he often departs for expansive discussions of Franklin's occupational arenas—printing, morals, science, politics, and diplomacy—through which Franklin expressed his attitude toward life." Booklist
"The general reader will find this book to be a well-

written, thoughtful appreciation of one of the Founding Fathers who did the most to shape his era and our own." Libr J
Includes bibliographical references

Franklin, Rosalind, 1920-1958

Maddox, Brenda. Rosalind Franklin: the dark lady of DNA. HarperCollins Pubs. 2002 380p il $29.95; pa $15.95　　　**92**
ISBN 0-06-018407-8; 0-06-098508-9 (pa)
　　　　LC 2002-68898
This "biography elucidates the vital role that Franklin played in the discovery of DNA's structure and the evolution of virology, and dispels the myths that surround this gifted biophysicist, who fought sexism for most of her all-too-brief life." Booklist
The author "does an excellent job of revisiting Franklin's scientific contributions . . . while revealing Franklin's complicated personality." Libr J
Includes bibliographical references

Frederick II, King of Prussia, 1712-1786

MacDonogh, Giles. Frederick the Great; a life in deed and letters. St. Martin's Press 2000 436p il hardcover o.p. paperback available $16.95　　　**92**
ISBN 0-312-27266-9 (pa)　　　　LC 00-24799
First published 1999 in the United Kingdom
This biography portrays Frederick II of Prussia "as a sensitive young man who plots an escape from his father's tyrannical control, and later . . . as an accomplished diplomat, strategist and military leader." Publ Wkly
"Both general readers and those with a strong background in European history will find great value in this outstanding biography." Booklist
Includes bibliographical references

Freud, Sigmund, 1856-1939

Breger, Louis. Freud; darkness in the midst of vision; an analytical biography. Wiley 2000 480p il $30; pa $18.95　　　**92**
ISBN 0-471-31628-8; 0-471-07858-1 (pa)
　　　　LC 99-59994
The author "deconstructs the myth Freud fabricated of himself, comparing Freud's self-analysis with the actual events of his life. . . . This groundbreaking work is more than just plain biography; it is Freudian analysis (literally) at its best." Booklist
Includes bibliographical references

Freud, Sigmund. The Freud/Jung letters; the correspondence between Sigmund Freud and C. G. Jung; edited by William McGuire; translated by Ralph Manheim and R. F. C. Hull. Princeton Univ. Press 1974 xlii, 650p $99.50　　　**92**
1. Jung, C. G. (Carl Gustav), 1875-1961
ISBN 0-691-09890-5
"Bollingen series"
"The birth, nurturing, and ultimate termination of friendship pervades the 360 letters written between 1906 and 1914, and the early twentieth-century psychological concepts exposed are enlivened by case histories and personal sidelights." Booklist
Includes bibliographical references

Freud, Sigmund, 1856-1939—*Continued*

Gay, Peter. Freud; a life for our time. Norton 1988 xx, 810p il hardcover o.p. paperback available $19.95   **92**
ISBN 0-393-31826-5 (pa)   LC 87-20454

This biography provides an "updating of our knowledge of the life of the founder of psychoanalysis . . . and it also delineates the continuing impact of Freud's thought on modern endeavors in a number of fields." Sci Books Films

"The book is beautifully written. Gay's approach is to try to understand Freud and his alliances and environment rather than to worship or challenge him." Choice

Includes bibliographical references

Friedan, Betty

Friedan, Betty. Life so far. Simon & Schuster 2000 399p il $26   **92**
ISBN 0-684-80789-0   LC 00-23920

In this memoir, "Friedan reminisces over a life of social activism that has included helping to found the National Organization for Women, the National Abortion and Reproductive Rights Action League, and the National Women's Political Caucus, as well as writing the pivotal *The Feminine Mystique*." Libr J

Frost, Robert, 1874-1963

Parini, Jay. Robert Frost; a life. Holt & Co. 1999 514p il $35; pa $16   **92**
ISBN 0-8050-3181-2; 0-8050-6341-2 (pa)
          LC 98-26690

This biography of the American poet has "its focus on the internal realm where, in Frost's case, creativity and madness fought a battle royal." Booklist

"Rarely has Frost's story been told this dexterously, or with a better understanding of the relation of Frost's personal crises to his accomplishment as a poet." Publ Wkly
Includes bibliographical references

Fuller, Alexandra, 1969-

Fuller, Alexandra. Don't let's go to the dogs tonight; an African childhood. Random House 2002 301p il $24.95; pa $13.95   **92**
ISBN 0-375-50750-7; 0-375-75899-2 (pa)
          LC 2001-41752

"Fuller grew up in Rhodesia (now Zimbabwe) during the civil war, and she watched her parents fight against the local Africans to keep their farm. In a memoir powerful in its frank straightforwardness, she neither apologizes for nor champions her family's views and actions. Instead she gives us an honest, moving portrait of one family struggling to survive tumultuous times." Booklist

Fuller, Margaret, 1810-1850

Von Mehren, Joan. Minerva and the muse: a life of Margaret Fuller. University of Mass. Press 1995 398p il $40; pa $20.95   **92**
ISBN 0-87023-941-4; 1-55849-015-9 (pa)
          LC 94-18663

The author "details Fuller's evolution from child prodigy to leading New England intellectual." Publ Wkly

"Von Mehren is sympathetic to Fuller's lifelong struggle to achieve fame and public acclamation for her views on Transcendentalism and feminism, but she balances her sympathy with objectivity and distance." Libr J
Includes bibliographical references

Fulton, Robert, 1765-1815

Sale, Kirkpatrick. The fire of his genius: Robert Fulton and the American dream. Free Press 2001 242p il $24; pa $13   **92**
ISBN 0-684-86715-X; 0-7432-2321-7 (pa)
          LC 2001-23064

Sale examines the life of the American inventor, "explaining how his North River steamboat opened up the North American continent to settlement and how it became the key factor that influenced the beginnings of the American industrial revolution. . . . This is an informative, moving story that personalizes the relatively obscure life of a self-taught tinkerer who had a genius for self-promotion and exploiting the discoveries of others." Libr J

Includes bibliographical references

Gandhi, Indira, 1917-1984

Frank, Katherine. Indira: the life of Indira Nehru Gandhi. Houghton Mifflin 2001 567p $35   **92**
1. India—Politics and government
ISBN 0-395-73097-X   LC 2001-24526

This biography examines the life of India's third prime minister within "the context of the Congress Party prior to independence and in the first four decades afterward. With impressive sensitivity and insight, Frank probes Indira's relationships with her dynamic and demanding father, Jawaharlal Nehru; her dying mother; a flamboyant, unfaithful husband; and her two divergent sons. These often intimate personal revelations are adroitly presented against the backdrop of Indira's public life." Libr J
Includes bibliographical references

Gandhi, Mahatma, 1869-1948

Chadha, Yogesh. Gandhi; a life. Wiley 1998 c1997 546p il hardcover o.p. paperback available $19.95   **92**
1. India—Politics and government
ISBN 0-471-35062-1 (pa)   LC 97-37406

First published 1997 in the United Kingdom with title: Rediscovering Gandhi

"Chadha reexamines Gandhi's life with an eye to restoring its complications and contradictions, noting that 'to suppress his weaknesses would be to undermine his strengths.' And he succeeds in his mission, presenting the great leader not as a holy man but as a humanist and politician." Booklist
Includes bibliographical references

Wolpert, Stanley A. Gandhi's passion; the life and legacy of Mahatma Gandhi; [by] Stanley Wolpert. Oxford Univ. Press 2001 308p il $35; pa $17.95   **92**
1. India—Politics and government
ISBN 0-19-513060-X; 0-19-515634-X (pa)
          LC 00-45298

"From his pampered childhood to his ascetic final years, the text follows the Mahatma ('Great Soul') on a paradoxical pilgrimage in which the deliberate acceptance of suffering endowed him with the power he needed to challenge the leading politicians of Europe, Africa, and Asia." Booklist

"This accessible account of Gandhi's life is an excellent introduction to the work of the most compelling of 20th-century leaders." Christ Century
Includes bibliographical references

Garcia, Jerry

Greenfield, Robert. Dark Star: an oral biography of Jerry Garcia. Morrow 1996 374p il o.p.; Broadway Bks. paperback available $16.95　**92**
　1. Grateful Dead (Musical group)
　ISBN 0-7679-0035-9 (pa)　　LC 96-13314
This "life of the Grateful Dead guitarist and cultural icon features reminiscences from over 60 people who knew him, from his boyhood in Menlo Park, Calif., to his death." Publ Wkly
"The last half dwells painfully on Garcia's heroin addiction, his 1986 lapse into a diabetic coma, and his fatal 1995 heart attack, but readers will finish with a better understanding of this charismatic musician." Libr J

Jackson, Blair. Garcia; an American life. Viking 1999 497p hardcover o.p. paperback available $15.95　**92**
　ISBN 0-14-029199-7 (pa)　　LC 99-28775
"As the front man for the Grateful Dead, the band that epitomized the '60s hippie counterculture, Jerry Garcia's place in music history is assured. Yet, Jackson asserts in this . . . biography, Garcia's genius as a guitarist and songwriter has often been overlooked." Publ Wkly
"Jackson has written a wonderful account of the beginnings of the band . . . in the mid-1960's, their relationship with Ken Kesey and his Merry Pranksters, their embrace of psychedelic drugs and the adoration and obsession of Deadheads throughout the country." N Y Times Book Rev
Includes bibliographical references

García Lorca, Federico, 1898-1936

Gibson, Ian. Federico García Lorca: a life. Pantheon Bks. 1989 xxii, 551p il hardcover o.p. paperback available $18　**92**
　ISBN 0-679-77401-7 (pa)　　LC 88-28871
Loosely based on the two-volume Spanish work published 1985-1987
This is a biography of the Spanish writer who was assassinated during the Spanish Civil War
"Gibson's sense of place is equalled by his sense of person. His re-creation of the teeming artistic talent and the café life of Spain in the 1930s is superb. So effective is Gibson's account of Lorca's vitality and fecundity that along with admiration for the poet's opulent talent, he provokes a fierce outrage at his ultimate fate." Times Lit Suppl
Includes bibliographical references

García Márquez, Gabriel, 1928-

García Márquez, Gabriel. Living to tell the tale; translated by Edith Grossman. Knopf 2003 483p maps $26.95　**92**
　ISBN 1-4000-4134-1　　LC 2003-58924
"García Márquez tells the entrancing story of his remarkable family, chronicles the turbulence of his troubled country, Colombia, and offers a piquant portrait of himself as a struggling young writer. A resplendent memoir written with compassion and artistry." Booklist

Garland, Judy

Clarke, Gerald. Get happy: the life of Judy Garland. Random House 2000 510p il hardcover o.p. paperback available $15.95
　92
　ISBN 0-385-33515-6 (pa)　　LC 99-36285
Also available Thorndike Press large print edition

Clarke reexamines the life of the singer and actress who "began her career as a toddler in vaudeville, went on to movies, radio, TV, and concert tours, and experienced more than the average number of reversals, love affairs, and suicide attempts." New Yorker
"This exhaustively researched and illuminating biography . . . is as compassionate as it is wrenching." Publ Wkly
Includes bibliographical references

Gates, Henry Louis

Gates, Henry Louis. Colored people; a memoir; [by] Henry Louis Gates, Jr. Knopf 1994 216p hardcover o.p. paperback available $13　**92**
　ISBN 0-679-73919-X (pa)　　LC 93-12256
The author presents a "memoir of growing up in a West Virginia mill town during the 1950s and '60s." Time
"As Gates traces his evolution from 'Negro' to Afrowearing 'black,' he also traces the evolution of Piedmont (and, by extension, of much of America) at a time when the relationship between the races was being redefined." Newsweek

Gatzoyiannis, Eleni

Gage, Nicholas. Eleni. Random House 1983 470p hardcover o.p. paperback available $14　**92**
　1. Greece—History—20th century
　ISBN 0-345-41043-2 (pa)　　LC 82-42803
"On August 28, 1948, a Greek peasant woman, Eleni Gatzoyiannis, was executed by guerrillas in her village of Lia. Some 30 years later, her son . . . wrote this book . . . weaving together three stories: World War II and the civil war in Greece; Eleni's life and how the catastrophic events in Greece smashed her world; and his own search for vengeance." Libr J
"The separate strands lead to an intensely moving climax, making Eleni one of the rare books in which the power of art re-creates the full historical truth." NY Rev Books

Gauguin, Paul, 1848-1903

Druick, Douglas W.
　Art Institute of Chicago. Van Gogh and Gauguin. See entry under Gogh, Vincent van, 1853-1890　**92**

Thomson, Belinda. Gauguin. Thames & Hudson 1987 215p il (World of art) pa $14.95　**92**
　ISBN 0-500-20220-6　　LC 87-50203
This "covers the artist's private life and professional development in great detail and captures the dramatic appeal inherent in both these areas. Some of the controversies of Gauguin's life are also clarified." Booklist
Includes bibliographical references

Gaulle, Charles de, 1890-1970

Williams, Charles. The last great Frenchman; a life of General de Gaulle. Wiley 1995 544p il $30; pa $19.95　**92**
　ISBN 0-471-11711-0; 0-471-18071-8 (pa)
　　LC 94-42881
The author offers "appraisals of de Gaulle's career as soldier, politician and head of state. Williams contrasts

Gaulle, Charles de, 1890-1970—*Continued*

the infuriatingly obstinate public figure with the private man, emotional and affectionate in the bosom of his family. Especially interesting is the account of de Gaulle's tender relationship with his retarded daughter. . . . The author also sheds light on de Gaulle's determined anti-Americanism during his final years." Publ Wkly

Includes bibliographical references

Gay, Peter, 1923-

Gay, Peter. My German question; growing up in Nazi Berlin. Yale Univ. Press 1998 208p il $40; pa $11.95   **92**

1. Jews—Germany 2. Jews—Persecutions
ISBN 0-300-07670-3; 0-300-08070-0 (pa)
                                        LC 98-26686

Gay writes of his childhood in pre-World War II Berlin. He reflects that "his family was fortunate to emigrate from Germany to America shortly after the 1938 Kristallnacht, the 'Night of Broken Glass' when Nazi-sponsored riots destroyed synagogues and Jewish stores. But Gay . . . takes issue with the suggestion that German Jews should have fled when Hitler came to power in 1933." Libr J

"A searching, sensitive portrait of Gay's youth, as crystalline as memory can be made." Booklist

Gearin-Tosh, Michael

Gearin-Tosh, Michael. Living proof; a medical mutiny. Scribner 2002 327p $25
                                              92

1. Cancer—Personal narratives
ISBN 0-7432-2517-1   LC 2002-17739

The author describes how he rejected chemotherapy for his cancer of the bone marrow, and opted "for a course of treatment including frequent coffee enemas and plenty of freshly prepared vegetable juices; acupuncture helped, too. His cancer seemed in remission when he wrote this book. . . . Gearin-Tosh provides pertinent information about unusual treatment of a devastating malady in a context that resembles a good novel." Booklist

Includes bibliographical reference

Gehrig, Lou, 1903-1941

Robinson, Ray. Iron horse: Lou Gehrig in his time. Norton 1990 300p il o.p.; Perennial Bks. paperback available $13.50   **92**

ISBN 0-06-097408-7 (pa)   LC 89-29272

"Playing in the considerable shadow of Babe Ruth, Lou Gehrig's accomplishments as baseball's 'Iron Horse' include a legendary record of 2,130 consecutive games played. . . . Robinson's narrative not only traces Gehrig's life and career but also provides an insightful look at baseball in the 1920s and the Depression years." Libr J

Gell-Mann, Murray, 1929-

Johnson, George. Strange beauty: Murray Gell-Mann and the revolution in twentieth-century physics. Knopf 1999 434p il hardcover o.p. paperback available $15
                                              92

ISBN 0-679-75688-4 (pa)   LC 99-19952

This is a biography of the American physicist who was awarded the Nobel prize in 1969 for his work on the interaction of elementary particles and their classification

"While it is necessarily dense in parts, this book is free of mathematics and is accessible to the advanced lay reader." Libr J

Includes bibliographical references

Gellhorn, Martha

Moorehead, Caroline. Gellhorn: a twentieth-century life. Holt & Co. 2003 463p il $27.50   **92**

ISBN 0-8050-6553-9   LC 2003-47755

This is a biography "of Martha Gellhorn, intrepid world traveler, war correspondent, and true free spirit, who covered the twentieth century's most horrific conflicts, married and divorced Ernest Hemingway, and devoted herself to bearing witness to life on the edge." Booklist

Moorehead "tells this sad story with historical command and psychological insight. . . . Not blind to the faults of her subject—which included blatantly partial reporting—Moorehead displays Gellhorn's saving grace: unflinching candor." N Y Times Book Rev

Includes bibliographical references

Genghis Khan, 1162-1227

Ratchnevsky, Paul. Genghis Khan: his life and legacy; translated and edited by Thomas Nivison Haining. Blackwell 1992 313p il hardcover o.p. paperback available $27.95
                                              92

ISBN 0-631-18949-1 (pa)   LC 91-2295
Original German edition, 1983

This is a biography of "the man responsible for unifying the scattered Mongol tribes into an empire-building nation." Libr J

"This is an outstanding piece of historical writing that will enthrall both specialists and those with a more casual interest in the field." Booklist

Includes bibliographical references

Geronimo, Apache Chief, 1829-1909

Debo, Angie. Geronimo; the man, his time, his place. University of Okla. Press 1976 xx, 480p il maps (Civilization of the American Indian series) hardcover o.p. paperback available $24.95   **92**

1. Apache Indians
ISBN 0-8061-1828-8 (pa)   LC 76-13858

The author "interviewed people who knew Geronimo, who fought with him and lived with him in captivity. She has written a colorful narrative of revenge and raids, of escape, pursuit and surrender. . . . Her portrait of Geronimo the old celebrity is touching, and a tribute to an exceptional leader." Publ Wkly

Includes bibliographical references

Gershwin, George, 1898-1937

Gilbert, Steven E. The music of Gershwin. Yale Univ. Press 1995 255p music (Composers of the twentieth century) $47
                                              92

ISBN 0-300-06233-8   LC 95-12086

This book analyzes major musical works of George Gershwin including Rhapsody in Blue, Concerto in F, An American in Paris, Porgy and Bess, and some of his popular songs and lesser known works

"With this book, Gershwin's music finally gets the attention it deserves. . . . Gilbert's book is not for the casual reader, since it requires an understanding of music theory and notation." Libr J

Includes bibliographical references

Gielgud, Sir John, 1904-2000

Croall, Jonathan. Gielgud; a theatrical life, 1904-2000. Continuum 2001 579p il $35; pa $24.95 **92**

ISBN 0-8264-1333-1; 0-8264-1403-6 (pa)
LC 2001-28019

Croall examines the life and career of the British actor, director, and producer

"Witty and well-written as well as well-researched, Croall's fine and complete portrait of the man and his endearing charm often reads more like a novel than like nonfiction." Booklist

Includes bibliographical references

Gielgud, Sir John. An actor and his time. Applause Theatre Bk. Pubs. 1997 333p $21.95; pa $16.95 **92**

ISBN 1-55783-299-4; 1-55783-415-6 (pa)
LC 97-31701

First published 1979 in the United Kingdom

This autobiography chronicles Gielgud's work in the theatre and motion pictures. Includes his personal reminiscences of Ellen Terry, Sarah Bernhardt, Mrs. Patrick Campbell, Bernard Shaw and Ralph Richardson, among others

Gielgud "proves himself to be a storyteller of the highest order, making this essential reading for theater lovers." Libr J

Gilbreth, Frank Bunker, 1868-1924

Gilbreth, Frank B. Cheaper by the dozen; [by] Frank B. Gilbreth, Jr. and Ernestine Gilbreth Carey; drawings by Vasiliu. [updated ed] Crowell 1963 245p il o.p.; Perennial Bks. paperback available $9.95 **92**

1. Gilbreth family
ISBN 0-06-008460-X (pa)

First published 1948

This biographical portrait of family life highlights the reminiscences of the twelve Gilbreth children and their adventures with their father, whose time and efficiency studies were applied to domestic life

Ginsberg, Allen, 1926-1997

Ginsberg, Allen. Family business; selected letters between a father and son; by Allen Ginsberg and Louis Ginsberg; edited by Michael Schumacher. Bloomsbury Pub. 2001 xxxi, 412p il $37.50; pa $16.95 **92**

1. Ginsberg, Louis, 1895-1976
ISBN 1-58234-107-9; 1-58234-216-4 (pa)
LC 2001-35431

"Like many fathers and sons, Louis and Allen Ginsberg had their differences, but they were united by their affection for each other and their love of poetry. In this judicious selection of letters written between 1944 and 1976, Schumacher . . . reprints *My Son the Poet*, an article Louis wrote for the *Chicago Sun Times Book World*. A postscript contains several of Allen's poems to his father." Libr J

"Anyone interested in either Ginsberg, the beats, American poetry or the '60s should not miss this ferociously tender and comical collection." Publ Wkly

Includes bibliographical references

Ginsberg, Allen. Spontaneous mind; selected interviews, 1958-1996; with a preface by Václav Havel; edited by David Carter. HarperCollins Pubs. 2001 601p hardcover o.p. paperback available $17.95 **92**

ISBN 0-06-093082-9 (pa)
LC 00-40849

"The bulk of the collection [of interviews] dates from 1965-72, Ginsberg's years as countercultural symbol and spokesman: dialogues at demonstrations and on the road, transcripts from 'Firing Line' and the Chicago Seven trial." N Y Times Book Rev

Includes bibliographical references

Ginsberg, Louis, 1895-1976

Ginsberg, Allen. Family business. See entry under Ginsberg, Allen, 1926-1997 **92**

Giovanni, Nikki

Giovanni, Nikki. Gemini: an extended autobiographical statement on my first twenty-five years of being a black poet. Bobbs-Merrill 1972 c1971 149p o.p.; Penguin Bks. paperback available $12 **92**

ISBN 0-14-004264-4 (pa)

These autobiographical essays trace Giovanni's life from her early years in Cincinnati to her years as successful poet and black activist

Giuliani, Rudolph W.

Kirtzman, Andrew. Rudy Giuliani; emperor of the city. Morrow 2000 333p il hardcover o.p. paperback available $13.95 **92**

1. New York (N.Y.)—Politics and government
ISBN 0-06-009389-7 (pa)

This political biography follows Giuliani from 1989 when he first set out to capture New York's City's mayoralty to his withdrawal from the 2000 senate race for medical and personal reasons

Gladstone, W. E. (William Ewart), 1809-1898

Jenkins, Roy, Baron. Gladstone; a biography. Random House 1997 xxvii, 698p il hardcover o.p. paperback available $16.95 **92**

ISBN 0-8129-6641-4 (pa)
LC 96-49632

First published 1995 in the United Kingdom

The author provides "insights into Gladstone's political achievements, failures, and personal eccentricities. . . . Jenkins is at his best tracing the major issues Gladstone attempted to ameliorate in his four premierships— extending the franchise, giving home rule to Ireland, and opposing imperialism." Booklist

This "book is a very decent try at an immensely difficult subject, encompassing an enormous amount of material. Lord Jenkins goes through the sources with commendable zeal. He also writes well." N Y Times Book Rev

Includes bibliographical references

Glenn, John, 1921-

Glenn, John. John Glenn; a memoir; [by] John Glenn with Nick Taylor. Bantam Bks. 1999 422p il $27; pa $7.99 **92**

1. United States. Congress. Senate 2. Astronauts

ISBN 0-553-11074-8; 0-553-58157-0 (pa)

LC 99-42672

Also available large print edition $13.95 (ISBN 0-375-70785-9)

This is Glenn's account of how a "small-town Ohio boy weathers the Depression nurtured by conservative patriotic values, marries his high school sweetheart, flies combat missions in two wars, is selected as one of the original Mercury astronauts, becomes an instant national hero as the first American to orbit the earth, is elected to the Senate, and, after serving for four terms . . . returns to space aboard the Shuttle at age 77." Libr J

Gogh, Vincent van, 1853-1890

Druick, Douglas W. Van Gogh and Gauguin; the studio of the south; [by] Douglas W. Druick and Peter Kort Zegers in collaboration with Britt Salvesen; with contributions to the text by Kristin Hoermann Lister and the assistance of Mary C. Weaver. Thames & Hudson 2001 418p il maps $65 **92**

1. Gauguin, Paul, 1848-1903

ISBN 0-500-51054-7 LC 2001-37695

Published in conjunction with an exhibition held at the Art Institute of Chicago, Sept 22, 2001-Jan. 13, 2002 and the Van Gogh Museum, Amsterdam, Feb. 2-June 2, 2002

This describes the relationship of the two artists who shared a studio in the south of France in 1888 and their influence on each other's work

"Journals, letters, maps, and personal histories are interwoven compellingly, leaving the reader with a real feel for the artist's perceptions. Current, highly informative, and scholarly in scope yet accessible." Libr J

Includes bibliographical references

Goldwater, Barry M., 1909-1998

Goldberg, Robert Alan. Barry Goldwater. Yale Univ. Press 1995 463p il $45 **92**

ISBN 0-300-06261-3 LC 94-46848

This is a biography of the Arizona senator and 1964 Republican presidential candidate

"Goldberg does a fine job of placing Goldwater where he always belonged, as a libertarian conservative, not a traditional one. Beautifully written, contextually rich." Libr J

Includes bibliographical references

Goodall, Jane, 1934-

Goodall, Jane. Beyond innocence; an autobiography in letters: the later years; edited by Dale Peterson. Houghton Mifflin 2001 418p il $28; pa $15 **92**

1. Women scientists

ISBN 0-618-12520-5; 0-618-25734-9 (pa)

LC 00-54124

This second volume of Goodall's correspondence follows Africa in my blood

In this "volume of Goodall's letters, a lively portrait is formed through her missives as the young woman rose to the height of her scientific contributions and fame. She became a mother, divorced her first husband, married her second, and lost him to cancer. She was also the

first to observe cannibalism in chimps, lost many of her study troop during a polio epidemic, and weathered the kidnapping of a group of her students. . . . This illuminating glimpse into the mind, emotions, and philosophy of an important scientist who also happens to be a celebrated figure will be requested in all libraries." Booklist

Goodall, Jane. Africa in my blood; an autobiography in letters: the early years, 1934-1966; edited by Dale Peterson. Houghton Mifflin 2000 386p il map $28; pa $15 **92**

ISBN 0-395-85404-0; 0-618-12735-6 (pa)

LC 99-86680

This collection of "Goodall's early letters shows how the dauntless field naturalist came to her career almost by chance: while visiting a school friend in Kenya, in 1957, Goodall met the anthropologist Louis Leakey, who decided she would make an excellent primate researcher and wangled her a grant to observe chimpanzees on a remote reserve." New Yorker

Goodall, Jane. Reason for hope; a spiritual journey; [by] Jane Goodall with Phillip Berman. Warner Bks. 1999 282p $26.95; pa $14.95 **92**

ISBN 0-446-52225-2; 0-446-67613-6 (pa)

LC 99-25611

Primatologist Goodall "offers this autobiography as a meditation on how her spiritual beliefs evolved in response to major events of her lifetime, including her childhood in World War II-era England; early days at Gombe with the chimpanzees; rearing her only child, Grub; divorce, remarriage, and the loss of her second husband to cancer, and the turning point in her career when she dedicated herself to the plight of chimpanzees held in captivity for biomedical research." Libr J

Goodwin, Doris Kearns

Goodwin, Doris Kearns. Wait till next year; a memoir. Simon & Schuster 1997 261p il hardcover o.p. paperback available $14 **92**

ISBN 0-684-84795-7 (pa) LC 97-39766

The author, a Brooklyn Dodger fan, discusses "the remarkable '50s in New York baseball, together with the rituals of her church and the universal preoccupations of childhood." Booklist

"For self-esteem-building female role models, for baseball lore and inning-by-inning action and for a lively trip into the recent American past, you could hardly do better." N Y Times Book Rev

Goodyear, Charles, 1800-1860

Korman, Richard. The Goodyear story; an inventor's obsession and the struggle for a rubber monopoly. Encounter Bks. 2002 230p il $25.95; pa $16.95 **92**

1. Goodyear Tire & Rubber Company 2. Rubber

ISBN 1-89355-437-6; 1-89355-482-1 (pa)

LC 2001-55635

"Charles Goodyear began his obsessive quest to find the recipe for making rubber in the 1830s and ended up becoming an American industrial legend. Besides tracing the life of this inspiring entrepreneur, Korman's social history of factory life and debtors prison in the early to mid-1800s is exceedingly well drawn." Booklist

Includes bibliographical references

Goodyear, Charles, 1800-1860—*Continued*

Slack, Charles. Noble obsession; Charles Goodyear, Thomas Hancock, and the race to unlock the greatest industrial secret of the nineteenth century. Hyperion 2002 274p il $24.95; pa $14.95   **92**

1. Hancock, Thomas, 1786-1865 2. Goodyear Tire & Rubber Company

ISBN 0-7868-6789-2; 0-7868-8856-3 (pa)

         LC 2002-68932

This is the story of how Charles Goodyear discovered the process of vulcanization of rubber, making possible the manufacture of rubber tires carried out by Thomas Hancock and the company which bears Goodyear's name

"Slack brings Charles Goodyear back to life and redeems the man who gave up everything to give his gift to the world." Booklist

Includes bibliographical references

Gordimer, Nadine, 1923-

Gordimer, Nadine. Conversations with Nadine Gordimer; edited by Nancy Topping Bazin and Marilyn Dallman Seymour. University Press of Miss. 1990 xxiv, 321p (Literary conversations series) $46   **92**

ISBN 0-87805-444-8   LC 90-12556

This is a collection of interviews in which Gordimer talks "about her life as a white South African, about her fiction, and about writers she admires." Booklist

Includes bibliographical references

Gore, Albert, Jr.

Zelnick, Bob. Gore: a political life. Regnery Pub. 1999 384p $29.95; pa $16.95   **92**

ISBN 0-89526-326-2; 0-89526-241-X (pa)

         LC 99-194035

Zelnick examines the life and career of Al Gore, the former senator from Tennessee and Vice President of the United States

The author provides "a useful and comprehensive survey of the highs and lows of Gore's political career." NY Times Book Rev

Gorey, Edward, 1925-2000

Ross, Clifford. The world of Edward Gorey; by Clifford Ross and Karen Wilkin. Abrams 1996 190p il hardcover o.p. paperback available $19.95   **92**

ISBN 0-8109-9083-0 (pa)   LC 95-47900

This book includes an "interview with Mr. Ross, [in which] Edward Gorey speaks of his likes and dislikes and aspects of his career. . . . Ms. Wilkin discusses Gorey's work as illustrator, author, stage designer, and miscellaneous creator." Atl Mon

Includes bibliographical references

Gorky, Arshile, 1904-1948

Matossian, Nouritza. Black angel: the life of Arshile Gorky. Overlook Press 2000 576p il map hardcover o.p. paperback available $24.95   **92**

ISBN 1-58567-285-8 (pa)   LC 99-59584

"Matossian follows Gorky from the village of his birth to his lonely suicide 44 years later, concentrating less on his art than his oft-strained relationships." Libr J

"Little space is devoted to describing the art, but by bringing us closer to Gorky the man, this book makes his life's tragedies all the more immediate and appalling." Publ Wkly

Includes bibliographical references

Spender, Matthew. From a high place; a life of Arshile Gorky. Knopf 1999 xxiii, 417p il map o.p.; University of Calif. Press paperback available $19.95   **92**

ISBN 0-520-22548-1 (pa)   LC 99-61595

"Spender, a sculptor and writer and the husband of Gorky's daughter, provides a personal and intimate biography of the Armenian American abstract expressionist." Libr J

Gould, Glenn, 1932-1982

Ostwald, Peter F. Glenn Gould; the ecstasy and tragedy of genius. Norton 1997 368p il hardcover o.p. paperback available $16.95

         92

ISBN 0-393-31847-8 (pa)   LC 96-43854

This biography examines the life and career of the pianist, and attempts to explain his psychosomatic illnesses

"Ostwald's analyses of Gould's musicianship and discussions of his radio broadcasts and TV documentaries are illuminating, and his writing has an intimacy that makes you feel you've actually been in the same room with the pianist." Publ Wkly

Includes bibliographical references

Goya, Francisco, 1746-1828

Blackburn, Julia. Old man Goya. Pantheon Bks. 2002 239p il $23; pa $13   **92**

ISBN 0-375-40611-5; 0-375-70579-1 (pa)

         LC 2002-280534

The author "focuses on the second half of Goya's long and amazingly productive life, beginning with the devastating illness that left him deaf at age 47. . . . [She] not only empathetically imagines the sea change caused by Goya's abrupt sensory loss, and convincingly assesses its impact on his work, she also conjures up the artists's mise-en-scène, from the frenetic streets of Madrid to the sanctuary of the studio, the bizarreness of the court of Charles IV, the horrors of famine and war, Goya's long marriage, and, after his wife's death, late-life relationship with a much younger woman. . . . [This is a] vital, inventively participatory portrait of a master portraitist and observer of life." Booklist

Includes bibliographical references

Hughes, Robert. Goya. Knopf 2003 429p il $40   **92**

ISBN 0-394-58028-1   LC 2002-43281

This is the "story of an artist whose life and work bridged the transition from the eighteenth-century reign of the old masters to the early days of the nineteenth-century moderns. . . . Hughes tracks Goya's development, as man and artist . . . from the early works commissioned by the Church, through his long, productive, and tempestuous career at court, to the darkly sinister and cryptic work he did at the end of his life." Publisher's note

This is "a remarkably vital, delectably discursive, and deeply affecting study." Booklist

Includes bibliographical references

Graham, Billy, 1918-

Graham, Billy. Just as I am; the autobiography of Billy Graham. HarperSanFrancisco; Zondervan 1997 xxiii, 760p il maps $28.50; pa $18 **92**
ISBN 0-06-063387-5 (Zondervan); 0-06-063392-1 (pa Zondervan) LC 97-605
Also available Walker & Co. large print edition
"In this memoir, Graham looks back at age 78 on his lifetime of personal relationships, ministry, leadership, and experiences. He chronicles such events and stories as his boyhood in North Carolina, his first steps in ministry, details of evangelistic trips and revivals, and meetings with world and local leaders. . . . All libraries would do well to stock this readable title by an important national figure." Libr J

Graham, Katharine

Graham, Katharine. Personal history. Knopf 1997 642p il $35; pa $15.95 **92**
1. Washington post
ISBN 0-394-58585-2; 0-375-70104-4 (pa)
LC 96-49638
"In 1963, Graham took over as publisher of the *Washington Post* as a classic grieving widow. Her husband, Phil, had shot himself at their country estate. . . . The first half of her story centers around life with Phil, the second on three pivotal events at the *Post*: the publication of the Pentagon Papers, the Watergate scandal and the prolonged pressman's strike of 1975." Publ Wkly
"Throughout this easy-to-read story, Graham writes about her personal life and the lives of others, ranging from presidents to household help, with sympathy and grace." Libr J

Grant, Cary, 1904-1986

McCann, Graham. Cary Grant; a class apart. Columbia Univ. Press 1997 346p il hardcover o.p. paperback available $19.95 **92**
ISBN 0-231-10885-0 (pa) LC 96-38577
First published 1996 in the United Kingdom
"McCann's biography shows how working-class Archie Leach transformed himself into Cary Grant. Unlike many self-made successes, Grant never renounced his humble origins but incorporated them into his persona. As a result, he became, McCann says, a 'democratic gentleman,' at ease in any element, who shone in both serious dramas and screwball comedies and, unlike most male stars, appealed equally to men and women." Booklist
Includes bibliographical references

Grant, Ulysses S. (Ulysses Simpson), 1822-1885

Catton, Bruce. Grant moves south; with maps by Samuel H. Bryant. Little, Brown 1960 564p maps hardcover o.p. paperback available $24.99 **92**
1. United States—History—1861-1865, Civil War—Campaigns
ISBN 0-316-13244-6 (pa)
"Grant's development as a man and leader is brilliantly shown in this reconstruction of his Mississippi campaign." Booklist
Includes bibliographical references

Catton, Bruce. Grant takes command; with maps by Samuel H. Bryant. Little, Brown 1969 556p maps hardcover o.p. paperback available $24.99 **92**
1. United States—History—1861-1865, Civil War—Campaigns
ISBN 0-316-13240-3 (pa)
This sequel to Grant moves south "takes up Ulysses S. Grant's career just after his capture of Vicksburg in 1863. . . . It carries the action right up to Richmond and Lee's surrender at Appomattox." Publ Wkly
Includes bibliographical references

Grant, Ulysses S. (Ulysses Simpson). Memoirs and selected letters; personal memoirs of U.S. Grant, selected letters, 1839-1865. Library of Am. 1990 2v in 1 il maps $35 **92**
1. United States—History—1861-1865, Civil War
ISBN 0-940450-58-5 LC 90-60013
This volume includes Grant's personal memoirs, first published in 1885 and 175 letters written between 1839 and 1865
Includes bibliographical references

Simpson, Brooks D. Ulysses S. Grant; triumph over adversity, 1822-1865. Houghton Mifflin 2000 533p $35 **92**
1. United States—History—1861-1865, Civil War
ISBN 0-395-65994-9 LC 99-43518
In this first volume of a planned two-volume biography, Simpson's main focus is on Grant's Civil War years. He had resigned from the army in 1854, charged with drunkenness. "The outbreak of war in 1861 found the thirty-nine-year-old Grant working as a salesman in his father's leather store at Galena, Illinois. . . . [Simpson analyzes] Grant's rise in three years from store clerk to commander of the armies of the United States." New Repub
"A detailed and exciting narrative of how one man succeeded, where so many others had failed, in pinning the Union back together again, albeit with a bloody bayonet." N Y Times Book Rev
Includes bibliographical references

Smith, Jean Edward. Grant. Simon & Schuster 2001 781p il $35; pa $20 **92**
1. United States—History—1861-1865, Civil War
ISBN 0-684-84926-7; 0-684-84927-5 (pa)
LC 00-53794
This biography surveys the career and achievements of the 18th U.S. president, from his days at West Point to the Civil War campaigns and his subsequent elevation to the presidency
"While he acknowledges Grant's failure to rein in his 'friends' and cabinet members as president, Smith convincingly illustrates how Grant's backbone and political skills were used to advance the cause of former slaves in the South. This is an outstanding and long overdue reevaluation of the life and career of a great American." Booklist
Includes bibliographical references

Greenspan, Alan

Martin, Justin. Greenspan; the man behind money. Perseus Bks. 2000 284p il hardcover o.p. paperback available $17.50   **92**

ISBN 0-7382-0524-9 (pa)

In this biography the author "shows how Alan Greenspan's early experiences have shaped his tenure as chairman of the Federal Reserve Board." N Y Times Book Rev

Includes bibliographical references

Griffin, Joseph Howard, b. 1888

Pearson, Hugh. Under the knife; how a wealthy Negro surgeon wielded power in the Jim Crow South. Free Press 2000 249p il hardcover o.p. paperback available $18.95   **92**

ISBN 0-7432-4257-2 (pa)   LC 99-39636

The author examines the life and career of his great-uncle Joseph Griffin who was "a physician, surgeon, and hospital founder in Bainbridge, Georgia, during the Jim Crow era. . . . This is not rah-rah history: Griffin built his fortune and reputation in a dangerous world where even his right to life was not guaranteed, and the corners he cut and the compromises he struck challenge the modern reader's empathy." Booklist

Groves, Leslie R., 1896-1970

Norris, Robert S. Racing for the bomb: General Leslie R. Groves, the Manhattan Project's indispensable man. Steerforth Press 2002 xxi, 722p hardcover o.p. paperback available $24.95   **92**

1. Manhattan Project

ISBN 1-58642-067-4 (pa)   LC 2001-57629

This is a biography of the military engineer in charge of the Manhattan Project, which developed the atomic bomb

This "work will not only serve scholars and general readers equally well but also take its place among the handful of best books about the birth of the atomic age." Booklist

Includes bibliographical references

Guevara, Ernesto, 1928-1967

Anderson, Jon Lee. Che Guevara; a revolutionary life. Grove Press 1997 814p il maps hardcover o.p. paperback available $20   **92**

ISBN 0-8021-3558-7 (pa)   LC 97-3993

This is a "biography of the life and death of the larger-than-life revolutionary Ernesto 'Che' Guevara, the Argentine doctor who joined with Castro to overturn Fulgencio Batista's reign in Cuba. . . . This book, with its 89 photographs, will be an invaluable addition to the literature of American revolutionaries." Booklist

Includes bibliographical references

Taibo, Paco Ignacio. Guevara, also known as Che; [by] Paco Ignacio Taibo II; translated by Martin Michael Roberts. St. Martin's Press 1997 691p hardcover o.p. paperback available $17.95   **92**

ISBN 0-312-20652-6 (pa)   LC 97-15343

"A Thomas Dunne book"

Original Spanish edition published 1996 in Mexico

This is a biography of "the Argentine-born revolutionary who helped Fidel Castro overthrow the Cuban dictator Fulgencio Batista in 1959. Three decades after he was captured and killed by the Bolivian Army on still another revolutionary mission, Guevara remains an icon of leftist idealism and subversive mystique." N Y Times Book Rev

Includes bibliographical references

Guggenheim, Peggy, 1898-1979

Gill, Anton. Art lover: a biography of Peggy Guggenheim. HarperCollins Pubs. 2002 480p il $29.95; pa $15.95   **92**

ISBN 0-06-019697-1; 0-06-095681-X (pa)

LC 2001-51731

A biography of the art collector who "championed the work of Kandinsky, Tanguy, Pollock, Rothko and the New York School. Gill traces her evolution from 'belle-laide' to 'grande dame' of the modern art world." N Y Times Book Rev

Guggenheim "was known as much for her sexual exploits as for her championing of modern art, a fact Gill . . . examines with candor, sensitivity, and mellifluous grace." Booklist

Includes bibliographical references

Guinness, Alec

Guinness, Alec. My name escapes me; the diary of a retiring actor; with a preface by John le Carré. Viking 1997 214p hardcover o.p. paperback available $14   **92**

ISBN 0-14-027745-5 (pa)   LC 97-3670

Companion volume to Blessings in disguise (1986)

Guinness's diary "entries run from January 1995 to June 1996. For the most part, they're surprisingly ordinary, the pleasantly grumpy ruminations of an articulate and self-deprecating Bristish retiree: haggling with British Rail over his senior citizen discount, playing the National Lottery . . . getting fitted for hearing aids, registering horror at the atrocities on the nightly news, watching films on the telly. . . . The mix of wit, sentiment and quotidian detail makes for an engaging . . . substantial, read." Publ Wkly

Guinness, Alec. A positively final appearance; a journal 1996-98. Viking 1999 245p $24.95; pa $14   **92**

ISBN 0-670-88800-1; 0-14-029964-5 (pa)

LC 99-14264

"This sequel to *My name escapes me,* written in the form of a diary from the summer of 1996 through 1998, comprises the distinguished actor's celebrations of life's pleasures great (the solace of Catholicism; a loving marriage) and small (a good meal, a devoted pet). . . . The book is shadowed with dark ruminations about the rise of germ warfare, the ethics of abortion and the arms race between Pakistan and India." Publ Wkly

Gunther, John, 1929-1947

Gunther, John. Death be not proud; a memoir. Harper & Row 1949 261p il hardcover o.p. paperback available $11.95   **92**

ISBN 0-06-092989-8 (pa)

Also available in hardcover from Buccaneer Bks.

A memoir of John Gunther's seventeen-year-old son, who died after a series of operations for a brain tumor. Not only a tribute to a remarkable boy but an account of a brave fight against disease

Gurewitsch, A. David, 1902-1974

Gurewitsch, Edna. Kindred souls: the friendship of Eleanor Roosevelt and David Gurewitsch. See entry under Roosevelt, Eleanor, 1884-1962 **92**

Gutierrez, Eduardo, 1978-1999

Breslin, Jimmy. The short sweet dream of Eduardo Gutierrez. Crown 2002 213p hardcover o.p. paperback available $12 **92**

ISBN 1-400-04682-3 (pa)   LC 2001-47283

"A true-life account of an illegal Mexican immigrant who died on a New York construction site, and of the dreary lives and modest ambitions common to Mexicans in this country." N Y Times Book Rev

Haffner, Sebastian

Haffner, Sebastian. Defying Hitler; a memoir; translated from the German by Oliver Pretzel. Farrar, Straus & Giroux 2002 309p il $24; pa $14 **92**

1. Germany—History—1918-1933

ISBN 0-374-16157-7; 0-312-42113-3 (pa)
                   LC 2002-17058

"In August 1938 a young German lawyer and journalist with the . . . name of Raimund Pretzel arrived in England. . . . Pretzel, a non-Jew, was fleeing to join and marry a Jewish woman pregnant with their first child. . . . Choosing a new name—Sebastian Haffner—to keep the Nazis from retaliating against his relatives, he went on to a . . . career as a journalist and historian in England, where he died in 1999. Afterward, while perusing his father's papers, Oliver Pretzel . . . found a . . . typescript in German. It was Haffner's unfinished memoir about his early years, begun in 1939, that sought through autobiography to understand how Hitler came to power." New Leader

"This is a small masterpiece." Booklist

Hamilton, Alexander, 1757-1804

Brookhiser, Richard. Alexander Hamilton, American. Free Press 1999 240p il hardcover o.p. paperback available $14 **92**

1. United States—Politics and government—1783-1809

ISBN 0-684-86331-6 (pa)   LC 98-46846

Also available Thorndike Press large print edition

This is a biography of the Secretary of the Treasury. Brookhiser discusses Hamilton's life, from his "teenage years in St. Croix and youth in Manhattan, through his formative years as Washington's aide during the Revolutionary War, to his role in the writing of the Constitution and the Federalist Papers, to his later careers as Secretary of the Treasury, lawyer, politician, and journalist." Natl Rev

Includes bibliographical references

Hamilton, Ann

Simon, Joan. Ann Hamilton. Abrams 2001 280p il $75 **92**

1. Installations (Art)

ISBN 0-8109-4160-0   LC 00-64284

"Hamilton's site-specific, multimedia installation pieces involve stunning arrangements and quantities of materials. . . . These major works of art are almost always space-and time-sensitive. . . . Simon combines biographical information and interviews with discussions about the making of these pieces as well as their meaning. Her inviting introduction offers a succinct discussion of installation art, both in general and in relation to Hamilton's work, followed by a chronological presentation of her pieces." Libr J

Simon "does an outstanding, even exhilarating job of chronicling the evolution of Hamilton's sophisticated ideas, assessing her extraordinary range and 'massive quantities' of materials and intricacy of construction, and describing the 'uncanny' experience of entering each unique space." Booklist

Includes bibliographical references

Hammer, Armand, 1898-1990

Epstein, Edward Jay. Dossier: the secret history of Armand Hammer. Random House 1996 418p il o.p.; Carroll & Graf Pubs. $15.99 **92**

ISBN 0-7867-0677-5 (pa)   LC 95-43146

"Epstein follows Hammer from his dealings with Lenin in the 1920s to his rise to the top of the corporate world in the 1970s. Along the way, Epstein provides many lurid details, concerning Hammer's dealings with wives, lovers, family members, fellow board members, foreign heads of state, and every president since FDR." Libr J

The author employs a "wealth of primary sources he tapped in Soviet archives and elsewhere. . . . It is hard to imagine a sharper picture of how a tycoon is both born and made and how the power game is played." NY Times Book Rev

Includes bibliographical references

Hancock, Thomas, 1786-1865

Slack, Charles. Noble obsession. See entry under Goodyear, Charles, 1800-1860 **92**

Handel, George Frideric, 1685-1759

Hogwood, Christopher. Handel; chronological table by Anthony Hicks. Thames & Hudson 1985 c1984 312p il maps music hardcover o.p. paperback available $18.95 **92**

ISBN 0-500-27498-3 (pa)   LC 85-203040

First published 1984 in the United Kingdom

The author "addresses his book to the serious layman. The composer's comings and goings are documented as accurately as possible, and Mr. Hogwood has added terse critical commentary about the music in sophisticated language but without musical examples." N Y Times Book Rev

Includes bibliographical references

Hansberry, Lorraine, 1930-1965

Hansberry, Lorraine. To be young, gifted and black; Lorraine Hansberry in her own words; adapted by Robert Nemiroff; with original drawings and art by Miss Hansberry; and an introduction by James Baldwin. Prentice-Hall 1969 xxii, 266p il o.p.; Random House paperback available $13 **92**

ISBN 0-679-76415-1 (pa)

Also available in paperback from New Am. Lib.

Work on this book and on the script for the play of the same title, which was presented at New York's Cherry Lane Theatre in 1969, "proceeded concurrently, each drawing upon the experiences and creative discoveries of the other, but ultimately diverging quite drastically." Postscript

Harrington, Michael, 1928-1989

Isserman, Maurice. The other American: the life of Michael Harrington. PublicAffairs 2000 449p $28.50; pa $14   **92**

ISBN 1-89162-030-4; 1-58648-036-7 (pa)
                                              LC 99-56654

This biography of the leftist social critic and author of the influential The other America (1962) is "also a veritable Zagat's guide through the left sectarian factions of the last three-quarters of the 20th century." N Y Times Book Rev

Includes bibliographical references

Harrison, Jim, 1937-

Harrison, Jim. Off to the side; a memoir. Atlantic Monthly Press 2002 313p $25; pa $14   **92**

ISBN 0-87113-860-3; 0-8021-4030-0 (pa)
                                              LC 2002-26051

"Harrison reflects on how childhood tragedies and a profound involvement with nature gave rise to . . . [his] passion for writing. . . . A mesmerizing storyteller and down-to-earth philosophizer, Harrison explicates his 'seven obsessions,' which include alcohol, strip clubs, hunting, fishing, and dogs, and offers compelling ruminations on the splendor of nature and the crimes of man, the mysteries of spirit and the revelations of art." Booklist

Hart, Moss, 1904-1961

Bach, Steven. Dazzler: the life and times of Moss Hart. Knopf 2001 462p il o.p.; Da Capo Press paperback available $19   **92**

ISBN 0-306-81135-9 (pa)   LC 2001-87954

This biography of the actor, director, and playwright chronicles "Hart's life, his early successes, his artistic missteps in middle age, and his later-life triumphs in the 1950s and 1960s." Booklist

"In narrating its subject's life, Dazzler is both gossipy and credible, a relatively rare and laudable combination." New Leader

Hawking, S. W. (Stephen W.)

White, Michael. Stephen Hawking; a life in science; [by] Michael White and John Gribbin. New updated ed. Joseph Henry Press 2002 348p pa $17.95   **92**

1. Astrophysics
ISBN 0-309-08410-5   LC 2002-11961
First published 1992 by Dutton

Contents: The day Galileo died; Classical cosmology; Going up; Doctors and doctorates; From black holes to the big bang; Marriage and fellowship; Singular solutions; The breakthrough years; When black holes explode; The foothills of fame; Back to the beginning; Science celebrity; When the universe has babies; A brief history of time; The end of physics?; Hollywood, fame and fortune; A brief history of time travel; Stephen Hawking, superstar

This book "sets out to show how natural talent combined with immense willpower have enabled Hawking to live a surprisingly active and interesting life and at the same time be a distinguished astrophysicist. It tries hard to express abstract concepts in ordinary language and tells enough about Hawking's relations with the world for readers to grasp that living close to such determination is not always easy. . . . Highly recommended." Choice

Includes bibliographical references

Hawthorne, Nathaniel, 1804-1864

Miller, Edwin Haviland. Salem is my dwelling place: a life of Nathaniel Hawthorne. University of Iowa Press 1991 596p il $39.95; pa $24.95   **92**

ISBN 0-87745-332-2; 0-87745-381-0 (pa)
                                              LC 91-14543

This is a biography of the 19th century American novelist

"Psychologically probing (but free of all jargon), Miller's elegantly written study gives us a fresh, sympathetic picture of an immensely complex, repressed man. . . . A masterful work, wholly satisfying." Libr J

Includes bibliographical references

Haydn, Joseph, 1732-1809

Geiringer, Karl. Haydn: a creative life in music; by Karl Geiringer in collaboration with Irene Geiringer. 3rd rev & enl ed. University of Calif. Press 1982 403p il hardcover o.p. paperback available $21.95

                                              92

ISBN 0-520-04317-0 (pa)   LC 82-2821
First published 1946

The author is "one of the few scholars who have devoted themselves almost exclusively to the study of this great master. He has not only collected all the new data that have cast light on Haydn research . . . he has also contributed many valuable observations and ideas." Saturday Rev

Includes bibliographical references

Hearst, William Randolph, 1863-1951

Nasaw, David. The chief: the life of William Randolph Hearst. Houghton Mifflin 2000 687p il $35; pa $16   **92**

ISBN 0-395-82759-0; 0-618-15446-9 (pa)
                                              LC 99-462122

"Few publishers have loomed as large in their lifetimes, or cast as long a shadow after death, as William Randolph Hearst. . . . Nasaw's judicious and comprehensive biography sensibly seeks to understand its subject, not to judge him." New Yorker

Includes bibliographical references

Hellman, Lillian, 1906-1984

Hellman, Lillian. Pentimento. Little, Brown 1973 297p hardcover o.p. paperback available $14.95   **92**

ISBN 0-316-35288-8 (pa)

This continuation of An unfinished woman—a memoir (1969) offers sketches of events and people from the author's past. She reminisces about her childhood in the South, some of her eccentric relatives including Cousin Bethe and Uncle Willy, Julia, her childhood friend who was trapped by the Nazis, Dashiell Hammett, who was her lover, and her experiences in the theater

"Pentimento is valuable as a picture of a woman and writer in the making." New Repub

Helms, Richard

Helms, Richard. A look over my shoulder; a life in the Central Intelligence Agency; [by] Richard Helms with William Hood. Random House 2003 478p il $35 **92**

1. United States. Central Intelligence Agency
ISBN 0-375-50012-X   LC 2002-35262

In this memoir the Director of Central Intelligence Agency from 1966 to 1973 "offers an insider's defense—and occasionally critique—of the frequently maligned agency's performance during the turbulent 1950s, '60s and early '70s. He argues that criticisms of the CIA are misdirected because the agency made no policy and had no agenda of its own—it merely did the president's bidding. . . . The strength of the book is in the breadth of history it encompasses." Publ Wkly

Includes bibliographical references

Hemings, Sally, 1773-1835

Gordon-Reed, Annette. Thomas Jefferson and Sally Hemings. See entry under Jefferson, Thomas, 1743-1826 **92**

Hemingway, Ernest, 1899-1961

Bruccoli, Matthew Joseph. Fitzgerald and Hemingway. See entry under Fitzgerald, F. Scott (Francis Scott), 1896-1940 **92**

Kert, Bernice. The Hemingway women. Norton 1983 555p il hardcover o.p. paperback available $16.95 **92**

ISBN 0-393-31835-4 (pa)   LC 82-18988

The author "examines the lives of Ernest Hemingway's mother, sisters, wives, and other female friends and lovers—the influential nature of their relationships with him and their lives apart from him." Booklist

"Comprehensive and well researched, Kert's book will be of interest to scholars, undergraduate students, and general readers." Choice

Includes bibliographical references

Lynn, Kenneth S. Hemingway. Simon & Schuster 1987 702p il o.p.; Harvard Univ. Press paperback available $22.50 **92**

ISBN 0-674-38732-5 (pa)   LC 87-82

"Taking as his premise Hemingway's glib assertion that the only analyst he relied upon was his 'portable Corona Number 3,' Lynn tracks the exploration of a disordered inner world as Hemingway sought to find some sort of resolution to the agony of his personal conflicts through 'his cunningly wrought fiction.' The man who emerges from Lynn's biography is a vastly more complex and compelling figure than the white-bearded, pontificating 'Papa' of myth." Publ Wkly

Includes bibliographical references

Mellow, James R. Hemingway: a life without consequences. Houghton Mifflin 1992 704p il o.p.; Addison-Wesley paperback available $26 **92**

ISBN 0-201-62620-9 (pa)   LC 92-9549

"In sheer number of pages, Mr. Mellow's version of the life is most heavily weighed toward the years 1921 to 1930, when Hemingway lived in Paris during his first two marriages and published the novels and stories that built his early reputation as one of this country's most

important writers. Mr. Mellow seems in a hurry to get through the rest of the story, but he does dutifully summarize Hemingway's childhood, adolescence and the major events of the later years. . . . Mr. Mellow takes careful note of Hemingway's publications in the context of his life and gives sensitive readings, both biographical and critical, to them all." N Y Times Book Rev

Includes bibliographical references

Reynolds, Michael S. Hemingway; [by] Michael Reynolds. Blackwell 1989-1997 3v il maps **92**

Contents: [v2] The Paris years pa $15.95 (0-393-31879-6); [v3] The American homecoming (op); [v4] The 1930s pa $14.95 (ISBN 0-393-31778-1); [v5] The final years pa $15.95 (ISBN 0-393-32047-2)

These volumes continue the author's study of Hemingway's life begun with The young Hemingway. The Paris years covers the period from 1922 to 1925, while The American homecoming discusses Hemingway's experiences and works from 1926 to 1929. The 1930s focuses on the civil war in Spain and Hemingway's life on Key West

Includes bibliographical references

Hendrix, Jimi

Murray, Charles Shaar. Crosstown traffic: Jimi Hendrix and the post-war rock'n'roll revolution. St. Martin's Press 1990 c1989 247p il hardcover o.p. paperback available $12 **92**

ISBN 0-312-06324-5 (pa)   LC 89-77681

First published 1989 in the United Kingdom

"The book is a broad-based study of African-American music—blues, jazz, rhythm and blues, and soul—and how the music influenced, and was influenced by, Hendrix." Libr J

"This informed, textured account will be irresistible to devotees of Hendrix and psychedelic rock as well as fans of blues, funk, jazz and rock 'n' roll." Booklist

Includes discography and bibliographical references

Henry VIII, King of England, 1491-1547

Weir, Alison. Henry VIII; the king and his court. Ballantine Bks. 2001 632p il $28; pa $16.95 **92**

1. Great Britain—History—1485-1603, Tudors
ISBN 0-345-43659-8; 0-345-43708-X (pa)
LC 2001-116042

In this biography of the Tudor king, the author "examines the minutiae of his daily life and gives prominence to the background players of his court. . . . At times, the weighty detail and numerous characters will make the work inaccessible; however, as a scholarly study it is a significant achievement." Libr J

Includes bibliographical references

Hepburn, Audrey, 1929-1993

Walker, Alexander. Audrey; her real story. St. Martin's Press 1995 319p il hardcover o.p. paperback available $16.95 **92**

ISBN 0-312-18046-2 (pa)   LC 94-33716

The author "recounts his subject's childhood in war-torn Europe and her early stage and film career. . . . Both the narrative and the writing itself become more lively as he discusses the heyday of her career, her sometimes turbulent love life and her work with Third World children for UNICEF." Publ Wkly

Hepburn, Katharine, 1907-2003

Berg, A. Scott (Andrew Scott). Kate remembered. Putnam 2003 370p il $25.95
92

ISBN 0-399-15164-8   LC 2003-545232

Also available Thorndike Press large print edition

In this posthumous biography, the author reveals "details about such pivotal events as the death of her brother by hanging, her relationships with powerful men like Howard Hughes and John Ford, and her slow, sad decline. . . . Berg's writing is so intimate that readers may feel they are hiding behind a curtain as they listen to the stories he elicits from his subject. Kate herself comes across pretty much the way she did on screen: bossy, courageous, and self-involved." Booklist

Hepburn, Katharine. Me; stories of my life. Knopf 1991 420p il hardcover o.p. paperback available $15.95
92

ISBN 0-345-41009-2 (pa)   LC 90-50805

Also available large print edition $16.95 (ISBN 0-679-74245-X)

This book "sounds just like its author—lots of cropped sentences, dashes, Hepburnian phrasing. But it's not a full-dress autobiography; as the subtitle proclaims, this is a collection of stories. . . . Still, fans will not be disappointed. Beginning with her early years . . . and concluding with her relationship with Tracy, Hepburn delivers all kinds of wry moments and, of course, a most interesting cast of characters." Booklist

Leaming, Barbara. Katharine Hepburn. Limelight Eds. 2000 549p il $23.95   **92**

ISBN 0-87910-293-4   LC 00-25227

A reissue of the title first published 1995 by Crown

This biography begins with a "portrait of the entire Hepburn clan, stressing the effect of the suicides that ran through Kate's maternal and paternal families. This is, in fact, a family biography, with at least half the book devoted to Hepburn's grandmother and mother. . . . By the time Kate enters the story, readers will be thoroughly caught up in a tale that already has delivered a full measure of intrigue, romance, and scandal. The book has been prodigiously researched (Leaming's source notes make fascinating reading on their own), and her access to various, previously unavailable papers not only makes possible the family history, but also paves the way for startling new revelations about Hepburn's life." Booklist [review of 1995 edition]

Herriot, James

Herriot, James. All creatures great and small. 20th anniversary ed. St. Martin's Press 1992 442p $21.95; pa $7.99   **92**

1. Veterinary medicine

ISBN 0-312-08498-6; 0-312-96578-8 (pa)

LC 92-18975

First published 1972

The first volume of Herriot's autobiographical account of the practice of veterinary medicine in Yorkshire, England in the 1930s

Followed by All things bright and beautiful (1974), All things wise and wonderful (1977), and The Lord God made them all (1981)

Wight, Jim. The real James Herriot; a memoir of my father. Ballantine Bks. 2000 371p il hardcover o.p. paperback available $14.95   **92**

ISBN 0-345-43490-0 (pa)

"The Yorkshire veterinarian Alf Wight, known to the world as James Herriot, won international acclaim for the wry, observant stories of his life as a simple country animal doctor. His son, Jim Wight, also a veterinary surgeon, now tells the story behind the stories. . . . The real-life models for the colorful characters and incidents in the Herriot books are lovingly explained throughout." N Y Times Book Rev

Hewitt, Don, 1922-

Hewitt, Don. Tell me a story; 50 years and 60 minutes in television. PublicAffairs 2001 272p il $26; pa $15   **92**

ISBN 1-58648-017-0; 1-58648-141-X (pa)

LC 2001-16222

Also available Thorndike Press large print editon

"Beginning in 1948 as producer-director of [CBS Television's] first nightly newscast with Douglas Edwards and then with Walter Cronkite, [Hewitt] also worked with Edward R. Murrow. . . . He has presided over '60 Minutes' since he developed the program in 1968. . . . [This book] traces Hewitt's life and provides observations on news, politics and his signature show." N Y Times Book Rev

"Hewitt has positive things to say about most of the reporters and anchors he discusses, but his comments about the several generations of CBS executives and owners for whom he has worked are less consistently sunny. At 78, Hewitt remains blunt, opinionated, and full of ideas about where TV news has been and where it's going. His life may be one of the more interesting stories the veteran newsman has ever told." Booklist

Hickam, Homer H., 1943-

Hickam, Homer H. The Coalwood way; by Homer H. Hickam, Jr. Delacorte Press 2000 318p $23.95; pa $6.99   **92**

ISBN 0-385-33516-4; 0-440-23716-5 (pa)

LC 00-35884

Also available Random House large print edition

This sequel to Rocket boys "continues the author's life story with his senior year in high school, 1959, in the declining West Virginia mining town of Coalwood. The rocket club, featured in the last book, is pushed to the periphery, and the focus shifts to Hickam's teenage problems, which include his parents, girls, and a sadness whose cause he cannot divine." Booklist

Hickam, Homer H. Rocket boys; a memoir; [by] Homer H. Hickam, Jr. Delacorte Press 1998 368p $25.95; pa $14   **92**

ISBN 0-385-33320-X; 0-385-33321-8 (pa)

LC 98-19304

"Raised in Appalachian coal country, Homer H. Hickam, Jr., might well have followed his father and grandfather into the mine. But when he was 14, his life was changed by a space launch on the other side of the world. Hickam's story of how a teenage boy's handmade rockets lifted the hopes of a hardscrabble town is told in his [memoir]." Smithsonian

"Even if Hickam stretched the strict truth to metamorphose his memories into Stand By Me-like material for Hollywood . . . the embellishing only converts what is a good story into an absorbing, rapidly readable one that is unsentimental but artful about adolescence, high school, and family life." Booklist

Hillerman, Tony

Hillerman, Tony. Seldom disappointed; a memoir. HarperCollins Pubs. 2001 341p il hardcover o.p. paperback available $13.95
92

ISBN 0-06-050586-9 (pa)   LC 2001-24160
Also available large print edition $26 (ISBN 0-06-621399-1)
In this memoir Hillerman "relates his childhood in Oklahoma during the Depression, his service in World War II, his university education, his career in journalism and academia, and his eventual turn to writing mysteries. The entire book will appeal to his fans, but the first half is intensely gripping." Libr J

Him, Chanrithy, 1965-

Him, Chanrithy. When broken glass floats; growing up under the Khmer Rouge. Norton 2000 330p il map hardcover o.p. paperback available $13.95
92

1. Cambodia—History
ISBN 0-393-32210-6 (pa)   LC 99-58417
Him "was 10 in 1975 when the Khmer Rouge overtook her country in what she calls the time of broken glass. Feeling a survivor's responsibility to do so, Him vividly recalls the brutality of the camps, the strict social control, and alienation from family that the Khmer Rouge enforced." Booklist

Himes, Chester, 1909-1984

Sallis, James. Chester Himes; a life. Walker & Co. 2000 368p il $28; pa $18.95
92
ISBN 0-8027-1362-9; 0-8027-7639-6 (pa)
LC 00-63328
This is a biography of the African-American crime novelist. "Sentenced to 25 years in prison for armed robbery when he was 19, he turned to writing while behind bars and, when released after serving eight years, published two novels. Their poor reception by the white establishment only confirmed Himes's beliefs about racism in America. He eventually moved to Paris, spending most of the rest of his life abroad. . . . The author succeeds splendidly in fleshing Himes out in this riveting biography." Libr J
Includes bibliographical references

Himmler, Heinrich, 1900-1945

Breitman, Richard. The architect of genocide: Himmler and the final solution. Knopf 1991 335p o.p.; University Press of New England paperback available $24.95
92

1. National socialism 2. Germany—Politics and government—1933-1945
ISBN 0-87451-596-3 (pa)   LC 90-52956
The author "focuses on Himmler's role in the decision making of the final solution, on how Himmler and the SS gained control of Nazi Germany's Jewish policy, and on other related World War II activities." Booklist
"This engrossing, detailed study constitutes a powerful refutation of revisionist scholars who claim that Hitler did not plan the Final Solution in advance but instead improvised it out of either military or political frustration." Publ Wkly
Includes bibliographical references

Hirohito, Emperor of Japan, 1901-1989

Bix, Herbert P. Hirohito and the making of modern Japan. HarperCollins Pubs. 2000 800p il maps hardcover o.p. paperback available $18
92
1. Japan—Politics and government
ISBN 0-06-093130-2 (pa)   LC 99-89427
"In 1945, fearing that the Japanese would resist American occupation unless the Emperor ordered them to obey, General MacArthur colluded with Hirohito in maintaining that the sovereign had been powerless to control Japan's military leaders. . . . [Bix], uses newly available sources to argue that Hirohito was a war criminal. An imperialist whose policies reflected his belief in the racial superiority of the Japanese, Hirohito governed by manipulation for almost two decades, and used the threat of Soviet Communism to justify domestic repression and soaring military budgets. The author's virtuoso scholarship and accessible narrative invite us into Hirohito's world." New Yorker
Includes bibliographical references

Hiss, Alger

Hiss, Tony. The view from Alger's window. See entry under Hiss, Tony   **92**

Hiss, Tony

Hiss, Tony. The view from Alger's window; a son's memoir. Knopf 1999 241p il hardcover o.p. paperback available $13
92

1. Hiss, Alger
ISBN 0-375-70128-1 (pa)   LC 98-50911
Companion volume to the author's Laughing last (1977)
This memoir "revolves around the 445 previously unpublished letters that 'Alger'. . . wrote home from federal prison in Lewisburg, Pa., where he served nearly four years for perjury." Publ Wkly
"A poignant, wonderfully written and deeply troubling memoir." N Y Times Book Rev

Hitchcock, Alfred, 1899-1980

Spoto, Donald. The dark side of genius; the life of Alfred Hitchcock; [with a new introduction by the author] Centennial ed. Da Capo Press 1999 594p il pa $22   **92**
ISBN 0-306-80932-X   LC 99-37941
This is a reissue of the title first published 1983 by Little, Brown
This is a biography of the director of such films as The man who knew too much, The thirty-nine steps, The lady vanishes, Rebecca, Spellbound, Strangers on a train, Rear window, and Psycho
This "is a vivid and perceptive portrait of a man whose character was as strange and shadowed as his films. . . . Hitchcock's final obsession was secretiveness, but he has been well served by a knowledgeable and revealing biography." Time
Includes bibliographical references

Hitler, Adolf, 1889-1945

Bullock, Alan. Hitler and Stalin; parallel lives. Knopf 1992 c1991 1081p il maps hardcover o.p. paperback available $25   **92**
1. Stalin, Joseph, 1879-1953 2. Germany—Politics and government—1933-1945 3. Soviet Union—Politics and government
ISBN 0-679-72994-1 (pa)   LC 91-52711
First published 1991 in the United Kingdom

Hitler, Adolf, 1889-1945—*Continued*

This biography of Hitler and Stalin "places the lives of the dictators side by side and follows them from beginning to end." Christ Sci Monit

"The twentieth century cannot be understood without close examination of the work of Stalin and Hitler. It is particularly important to note what their regimes and aims had in common and where they differed. Alan Bullock has put us all in his debt by placing their actions side by side, in enormous detail, and in chronological sequence to make the comparison easy." Times Lit Suppl

Includes bibliographical references

Hitler, Adolf. Mein Kampf; translated by Ralph Manheim. Houghton Mifflin 1943 xxi, 694p $40; pa $22   **92**

1. National socialism 2. Germany—Politics and government—1918-1933

ISBN 0-395-95105-4; 0-395-92503-7 (pa)

"Hitler's steady rise to power was interrupted only by the Beer Hall Putsch (1923), an unsuccessful attempt to overthrow the Weimar Republic. . . . During the nine months of imprisonment that followed he wrote 'Mein Kampf' (1924; tr. 'My struggle,' 1940). This book contained autobiographical and reflective passages, rife with hysterical anti-Semitism and paranoia, as well as the program he intended to implement; for the West it was a warning that went unheeded." Reader's Ency. 3d edition

Kershaw, Ian. Hitler. Norton 1999-2000 2v il ea $35; pa $21.95   **92**

1. Germany—Politics and government—1918-1933
2. Germany—Politics and government—1933-1945

ISBN 0-393-04671-0 (v1); 0-393-04994-9 (v2); 0-393-32035-9 (v1 pa); 0-393-32252-1 (v2 pa)

LC 98-29569

Contents: [v1] 1889-1936, hubris; [v2] 1936-1945, nemesis

"Kershaw provides an examination based on a number of archival sources not used by previous biographers. . . . More than a chronicle of Hitler's life, this is an analysis of the major historiographical issues, the circumstances that shaped his personality, and the historical events that enabled Hitler to rise to power." Libr J

Includes bibliographical references

Rosenbaum, Ron. Explaining Hitler; the search for the origins of his evil. Random House 1998 xlvi, 444p o.p.; Perennial Bks. paperback available $16   **92**

1. National socialism 2. Germany—Politics and government—1933-1945

ISBN 0-06-095339-X (pa)   LC 97-34468

This book examines interpretations of Hitler made by his contemporaries and by historians

"In this brilliantly skeptical inventory of the world's Hitler-thinking, Rosenbaum analyzes not only the multiple Hitler theories but also the agendas and fantasies that the theorizers bring to their subject." Time

Toland, John. Adolf Hitler. Anchor Bks. (NY) 1992 xx, 1035p il pa $24   **92**

1. Germany—Politics and government—1933-1945
2. National socialism

ISBN 0-385-42053-6   LC 91-31242

A reissue of the title first published 1976

This biography is based on more than 250 interviews with people acquainted with Hitler and materials from U.S. and British archives

"In the course of detailed and painstaking investigations [Toland] has disposed of a number of myths." N Y Times Book Rev

Includes bibliographical references

Ho, Chí Minh, 1890-1969

Duiker, William J. Ho Chi Minh; by William Duiker. Hyperion 2000 695p il maps $35; pa $16.95   **92**

ISBN 0-7868-6387-0; 0-7868-8701-X (pa)

LC 00-26757

In this biography the author "examines Ho's life primarily in the context of his political activity in Paris, Moscow, southern China, and Vietnam, occasionally spiced with anecdotes of Ho's highly secretive personal life. . . . Duiker handles the complicated political and diplomatic issues with ease, and his narrative, though it sometimes strays from Ho's life to fill in the bigger picture, never bogs down." Booklist

Includes bibliographical references

Hoffa, Jimmy

Russell, Thaddeus. Out of the jungle: Jimmy Hoffa and the remaking of the American working class. Knopf 2001 272p il o.p.; Temple Univ. Press paperback available $18.95   **92**

ISBN 1-59213-027-5 (pa)   LC 2001-29927

In this chronicle of the life and career of Hoffa, "the author presents new interpretations of how the Depression, the New Deal, World War II, and Robert F. Kennedy's crusade against organized crime affected not only Hoffa and the Teamsters but also the American labor movement as a whole." Publisher's note

"Russell makes good use of a range of primary-source materials plus period newspaper accounts and other materials to highlight this story." Libr J

Hogan, Linda

Hogan, Linda. The woman who watches over the world; a native memoir. Norton 2001 224p $24.95; pa $13.95   **92**

ISBN 0-393-05018-1; 0-393-32305-6 (pa)

LC 00-49005

In this memoir the author chronicles "her difficult childhood, alcoholism, the anguish of her two psychologically damaged adopted children, and struggles with a neuromuscular disease. She also expresses a lacerating yet crucial vision of the tragic legacies of the U.S. government's brutal war on Native Americans." Booklist

Hogarth, William, 1697-1764

Uglow, Jennifer S. Hogarth; a life and a world; {by} Jenny Uglow. Farrar, Straus & Giroux 1997 794p il hardcover o.p. paperback available $30   **92**

ISBN 0-374-52851-9 (pa)   LC 97-6624

This biography is "a study as much literary and social as artistic of 18th-century England and of the hard-nosed, vespine little genius who depicted mainly its corruptions." N Y Times Book Rev

"The work has been carefully researched, and the insights are illuminating. Fascinating and very rewarding reading for both art and social historians of England, this volume is recommended for every public and academic library." Libr J

Includes bibliographical references

Holiday, Billie, 1915-1959

Clarke, Donald. Wishing on the moon: the life and times of Billie Holiday. Viking 1994 468p il o.p.; Da Capo Press paperback available $18 **92**
ISBN 0-306-81136-7 (pa)   LC 94-8881
This biography "not only chronicles every phase of Holiday's ascent from the streets of Baltimore to the stages of New York's hottest nightclubs and most prestigious concert halls, but also documents every significant recording session, performance, and tour. . . . Clarke's portrait embraces every facet of Holiday's paradoxical nature, from her fierceness to her vulnerability, her childlikeness to her innate elegance and amazing strength." Booklist

Griffin, Farah Jasmine. If you can't be free, be a mystery: in search of Billie Holiday. Free Press 2001 240p o.p.; Ballantine Bks. paperback available $13 **92**
ISBN 0-345-44973-8 (pa)   LC 2001-18962
In this biography Griffin places Billie Holiday "in the musical and political context of her time and explores the myths she and others manufactured about her life." Booklist
"While Griffin's book isn't the last word on Holiday, it does prove to be an excellent antidote to the often ridiculous material that has been written about Lady Day over the years." Libr J
Includes discography and bibliographical references

Nicholson, Stuart. Billie Holiday. Northeastern Univ. Press 1995 311p il $42.50; pa $18.95 **92**
ISBN 1-55553-248-9; 1-55553-303-5 (pa)
LC 95-16155
"Nicholson's fact-filled biography conveys not only the details of African American jazz singer Holiday's stormy life, but also a sense of the musical and social environments that produced her." Booklist
Includes discography and bibliographical references

O'Meally, Robert G. Lady Day: the many faces of Billie Holiday; produced by Toby Byron/Multiprises. Arcade Pub. 1991 207p il o.p.; Da Capo Press paperback available $20 **92**
ISBN 0-306-80959-1 (pa)   LC 91-16218
"Narcotics, jail, sexual abuse, and prejudice are often our first associations concerning the life of the great jazz singer, but this biography recalls only Holiday as artist. O'Meally . . . puts her tragedy and talent into perspective, and what emerges is a critique of a singer. The book's first section is outstanding in this regard, employing stories, quotes, and interviews in describing Holiday's technique." Libr J
Includes bibliographical references

Holroyd, Michael

Holroyd, Michael. Basil Street blues. Norton 2000 306p il $24.95; pa $13.95 **92**
ISBN 0-393-04850-0; 0-393-32174-6 (pa)
LC 99-56057
"This 'vicarious autobiography' by a well-known biographer takes the form of a family history with Holroyd's parents as the main characters. Both were lifelong optimists, flitting glamorously from marriage to marriage, but both ended up alone, poor, and bewildered by misfortune. Holroyd's eye for absurd details . . . brightens and enriches a potentially bleak tale." New Yorker

Hooks, Bell

Hooks, Bell. Wounds of passion; a writing life. Holt & Co. 1997 xxiii, 260p hardcover o.p. paperback available $13 **92**
ISBN 0-8050-5722-6 (pa)   LC 97-23506
In this continuation of the author's autobiography, Hooks chronicles "her rigorous education, both in a long, complicated relationship with a fellow writer and as a college and graduate student, experiences that led her away from poetry (her first literary love) to groundbreaking prose that expressed her feminist convictions and views on the status of black women in America." Booklist

Hoover, J. Edgar (John Edgar), 1895-1972

Gentry, Curt. J. Edgar Hoover; the man and the secrets. Norton 1991 846p il hardcover o.p. paperback available $17.95 **92**
1. United States. Federal Bureau of Investigation
ISBN 0-393-32128-2 (pa)   LC 90-30576
Also available in paperback from New Am. Lib.
The author "has based his account of Hoover on more than 300 interviews and on access to previously classified FBI documents. . . . Gentry paints a portrait of Hoover as the 'indispensable man,' with many provocative revelations about his political dealings." Libr J
Includes bibliographical references

Hope, Bob, 1903-2003

Quirk, Lawrence J. Bob Hope: the road well-traveled. Applause Theatre Bk. Pubs. 1998 327p il $26.95; pa $14.95 **92**
ISBN 1-55783-353-2; 1-55783-450-4 (pa)
LC 98-87957
Also available Thorndike Press large print edition
"Quirk recaps Hope's life and surveys his relationships with myriad entertainment personalities. . . . This is a good, solid Hollywood bio by a veteran Tinseltown observer." Booklist
Includes filmography and bibliographical references

Houdini, Harry, 1874-1926

Brandon, Ruth. The life and many deaths of Harry Houdini. Random House 1994 355p il hardcover o.p. paperback available $14.95 **92**
1. Magicians
ISBN 0-8129-7042-X (pa)   LC 94-4080
The author provides a psychological "portrait of the great and enigmatic escape artist Harry Houdini. She not only reveals Houdini's impressive technical secrets but also identifies the sources of his unabashed melodramatics and puzzling innocence. . . . Houdini was one of the most compelling 'idols of popular culture' in the early years of this mass-appeal century, and he still works his magic through the medium of Brandon's bold and magnetic interpretation." Booklist
Includes bibliographical references

Hoving, Thomas, 1931-

Hoving, Thomas. Making the mummies dance; inside the Metropolitan Museum of Art. Simon & Schuster 1993 447p il hardcover o.p. paperback available $21.95   **92**

1. Metropolitan Museum of Art (New York, N.Y.)—Management

ISBN 0-671-88075-6 (pa)   LC 92-31460

"As director of Manhattan's Metropolitan Museum of Art from 1967 to 1977 . . . Hoving transformed a stodgy, elitist institution into a bottomline-oriented business enterprise, a modernized, expansive museum that actively engages the public. In this ebullient memoir, Hoving, who is preening and amusingly self deprecating at once, provides a rare behind-the-scenes peek at turf wars, intrigues, fabulous acquisitions and stormy managerial battles." Publ Wkly

Hudson, Jeffrey, 1619-1681

Page, Nick. Lord Minimus; the extraordinary life of Britain's smallest man. St. Martin's Press 2002 c2001 261p il $16.95; pa $11.95   **92**

ISBN 0-312-29161-2; 0-312-31619-4 (pa)
     LC 2002-24860

First published 2001 in the United Kingdom

"Standing only 18 inches tall, Jeffrey Hudson—later dubbed Lord Minimus—caught the eye and captured the heart of Queen Henrietta Maria, after he was presented to her baked in a pie at a royal banquet hosted by the duke of Buckingham in honor of King Charles I. . . . Brimming with action and adventure, this off-beat biography reads like fiction." Booklist

Includes bibliographical references

Hughes, Langston, 1902-1967

Hughes, Langston. I wonder as I wander; an autobiographical journey; introd. by Arnold Rampersad. 2nd Hill and Wang ed. Hill & Wang 1993 xxii, 405p (American century series) pa $16   **92**

ISBN 0-8090-1550-1   LC 92-39307

First published 1956 by Rinehart

Continuing the autobiography begun in The big sea (1940), this volume contains an account of Hughes' journeys through Russia, Spain, China, and Japan, as well as some incidents of his poetry readings in this country

Hughes, Langston. Remember me to Harlem: the letters of Langston Hughes and Carl Van Vechten, 1925-1964; edited by Emily Bernard. Knopf 2001 xxxix, 356p il hardcover o.p. paperback available $15   **92**

1. Van Vechten, Carl, 1880-1964

ISBN 0-375-72707-8 (pa)   LC 00-62929

"In these letters, poet Hughes and his white mentor, Van Vechten . . . discuss literature and politics while gossiping about other literary figures like James Baldwin, W.E.B. Du Bois, and Ralph Ellison." Libr J

"Bernard's painstakingly assembled edition provides comprehensive background notes and a complete guide to the procession of famous and obscure personages appearing in the letters, as well as a graceful introduction briefly sketching the correspondents' lives and the arc of the Harlem Renaissance." Publ Wkly

Includes bibliographical references

Rampersad, Arnold. The life of Langston Hughes. 2nd ed. Oxford Univ. Press 2002 2v 528p il set $79.90   **92**

     LC 2001-58766

Both volumes also available in paperback

First published 1986-1988

Contents: v1 1902-1941, I, too, sing America (ISBN 0-19-515160-7); v2 1941-1967, I dream a world (ISBN 0-19-515161-5)

"Rampersad is an unsparing but sympathetic analyst of Hughes's life and work; he has written an absorbing critical biography that is also a deft social history of black America in the 20th century." Publ Wkly {review of 1986-1988 edition}

Includes bibliographical references

Hughes, Ted, 1930-1998

Feinstein, Elaine. Ted Hughes; the life of a poet. Norton 2001 273p il $29.95; pa $15.95   **92**

ISBN 0-393-04967-1; 0-393-32362-5 (pa)
     LC 2001-44925

This biography of the English poet examines Hughes's relationship with "his first wife, Sylvia Plath, who committed suicide in 1963 during the acrimonious breakup of their marriage, . . . [and with] Assia Wevill, the woman for whom Hughes left Plath, and who later killed herself and their child." Economist

Includes bibliographical references

Hurston, Zora Neale, 1891-1960

Boyd, Valerie. Wrapped in rainbows; the life of Zora Neale Hurston. Scribner 2003 527p il $30   **92**

ISBN 0-684-84230-0   LC 2002-17011

"A Lisa Drew book"

This is a biography of the folklorist and author of Their Eyes Were Watching God (1937), Tell My Horse (1938), Dust Tracks on a Road (1942) and Seraph on the Suwanee (1948)

"As the author adeptly and passionately analyzes Hurston's revolutionary books, intense spirituality, and myriad adventures, Hurston emerges in all her splendor—not only smarter, tougher, and more dazzlingly alive than most people but also freer." Booklist

Includes bibliographical references

Hurston, Zora Neale. Dust tracks on a road; with a new foreword by Maya Angelou. HarperCollins Pubs. 1991 277p hardcover o.p. paperback available $14   **92**

ISBN 0-06-092168-4 (pa)   LC 90-55501

Also available G.K. Hall large print edition

First published 1942 by Lippincott

The author describes her wanderings in and out of schools and jobs as a young girl, finishing her course work at Barnard, and beginning her life's work

Includes bibliographical references

Hurston, Zora Neale. Zora Neale Hurston: a life in letters; collected and edited by Carla Kaplan. Doubleday 2002 880p il $40; pa $19.95   **92**

ISBN 0-385-49035-6; 0-385-49036-4 (pa)
     LC 00-65671

A collection of over 500 letters by the Harlem Renaissance author

Hurston, Zora Neale, 1891-1960—*Continued*

These letters reveal "a gifted yet complex personality at once humorous, cynical, and analytical." Libr J
Includes bibliographical references

Huxley, Aldous, 1894-1963

Murray, Nicholas Russell. Aldous Huxley; a biography; [by] Nicholas Murray. Thomas Dunne Bks. 2003 496p il $29.95   **92**
   ISBN 0-312-30237-1   LC 2002-35426
  First published 2002 in the United Kingdom
  This is the portrait of a significant figure of twentieth-century English writing, who pursued careers as a novelist, poet, biographer, philosopher, and socialist and political thinker
  "[A] generous and intelligent biography" Guardian
  Includes bibliographical references

Huxley, Elspeth, 1907-1997

Huxley, Elspeth. The flame trees of Thika; memories of an African childhood. Morrow 1959 288p il o.p.; Penguin Bks. paperback available $14   **92**
  1. Kenya—Social life and customs
  ISBN 0-14-118378-0 (pa)
  This is an account of the author's childhood on a coffee plantation in Kenya. She describes the landscape, the Kikuya peoples, the European settlers and the difficulties her parents faced adjusting to life in the bush

Isabella, Queen, consort of Edward II, King of England, 1292-1358

Doherty, P. C. Isabella and the strange death of Edward II; [by] Paul Doherty. Carroll & Graf Pubs. 2003 262p $25   **92**
  1. Great Britain—History—1154-1399, Plantagenets
  ISBN 0-7867-1193-0   LC 2003-43568
  This is a biography of the French princess who was married to Edward II at the age of thirteen, and with her lover Sir Roger Mortimer, ruled over England following the murder of her husband
  Includes bibliographical references

Isherwood, Christopher, 1904-1986

Isherwood, Christopher. Diaries; edited by Katherine Bucknell. v1: 1939-1960. HarperCollins Pubs. 1997 1047p hardcover o.p. paperback available $20   **92**
  ISBN 0-06-118018-1 (pa)   LC 97-5501
  "Michael di Capua books"
  First published 1996 in the United Kingdom
  "This volume spans the period from 1939, when Isherwood left England for good to live in the U.S., to his sixty-fifth birthday in 1960, when he was in permanent residence in California. . . . His entries are stylish but not studied, spontaneous but not slapdash. And as diaries should be if published for public reading, his are analytical and not strictly narrative; one can learn what he thought and not simply what he observed." Booklist

Ishi

Kroeber, Theodora. Ishi in two worlds; a biography of the last wild Indian in North America. University of Calif. Press 1976 262p il $50; pa $16.95   **92**
  1. Yana Indians
  ISBN 0-520-00674-7; 0-520-22940-1 (pa)
  First published 1961

An account "of the life of the sole survivor of a California Indian tribe. The author, wife of the famed anthropologist, reconstructs the decimation of Ishi's [Yana] people and his reluctant entry in 1911 into the world of his conquerors." Booklist

Ives, Charles Edward, 1874-1954

Swafford, Jan. Charles Ives; a life with music. Norton 1996 525p il hardcover o.p. paperback available $16.95   **92**
  ISBN 0-393-31719-6 (pa)   LC 95-22549
  "Ives was a professional organist, a successful insurance executive, a political idealist, and an immensely prolific composer. The author believes that Ives's transcendentalism was central to his identity, ceaselessly inspiring him while also spurring him on to an inevitable physical collapse. Swafford—a composer himself—intersperses his biography with valuable 'entr'actes' of approachable musical analysis, and ends with a ringing endorsement of Ives as an ideal composer for a democratic society." New Yorker
  Includes bibliographical references

Jackson, Andrew, 1767-1845

Booraem, Hendrik. Young Hickory: the making of Andrew Jackson. Taylor Pub. Co. 2001 318p il maps $26.95   **92**
  ISBN 0-87833-263-4   LC 00-48820
  This biography of the seventh president of the United States covers "the first 21 years of Jackson's life, taking him up to the time when he moved to what later became Tennessee. Using published works as well as numerous previously neglected archival materials, Booraem provides a thorough and fascinating account of life in the Carolina backcountry." Libr J
  Includes bibliographical references

Jackson, Joe, 1887 or 8-1951

Fleitz, David L. Shoeless; the life and times of Joe Jackson. McFarland & Co. 2001 314p il pa $29.95   **92**
  1. Chicago White Sox (Baseball team)
  ISBN 0-7864-0978-9   LC 2001-18318
  "Shoeless Joe Jackson, banned from baseball for his alleged involvement in the 1919 World Series gambling scandal, is viewed by many as an illiterate phenom hustled by city slickers. Fleitz shows it ain't so, Joe, in this provocative biography." Booklist
  Includes bibliographical references

James, Etta, 1938-

James, Etta. Rage to survive: the Etta James story; [by] Etta James, with David Ritz. Villard Bks. 1995 271p il o.p.; Da Capo Press paperback available $16.50   **92**
  ISBN 0-306-80812-9 (pa)   LC 94-23759
  "Born to a 14-year-old mother and raised by surrogate parents, blues and R&B star James started singing gospel in church at five, was discovered at 14 and had a rapid rise to fame. Nevertheless, her story is a disturbing saga of drug addiction, jail sentences for writing bad checks and stealing prescription drugs, involvements with the wrong men and anger at a disruptive and unstable mother who has refused to reveal who her daughter's father is." Publ Wkly
  "With a supporting cast resembling the roster of the Rock Hall of Fame, this autobiography reads as its author sings—rough, gritty, and brutally honest." Libr J

James, Henry, 1811-1882

Habegger, Alfred. The father: a life of Henry James, Sr. Farrar, Straus & Giroux 1994 578p il o.p.; University of Mass. Press paperback available $21.95   **92**
  1. James family
  ISBN 1-55849-331-X (pa)   LC 93-41823
James "was the father of five children, including William, the psychologist and philosopher; Henry Jr., the novelist; and Alice, a diarist. To his contemporaries, he was 'Absolute James,' a passionate and outspoken religious and philosophical writer. In this eloquent and imposing book Habegger . . . gives protracted attention to James's writings on the utopian doctrines of Fourier and the abstruse mysticism of Swedenborg." Publ Wkly
Includes bibliographical references

James, Jesse, 1847-1882

Stiles, T. J. Jesse James; last rebel of the Civil War. Knopf 2002 510p il maps $27.50; pa $16   **92**
  ISBN 0-375-40583-6; 0-375-70558-9 (pa)
                   LC 2002-25493
This is a "revisionist biography of Jesse James, one that takes issue with the traditional image of the Wild West outlaw . . . and with the folk-hero notion of James as a prairie Robin Hood. . . . Mr. Stiles presents James as a Confederate terrorist caught up in the wild political turbulence of his times." N Y Times Book Rev
"This is a well-written and often surprising reinterpretation of the life of a legendary and enigmatic figure." Booklist
Includes bibliographical references

James, P. D.

James, P. D. Time to be in earnest; a fragment of autobiography. Knopf 2000 269p hardcover o.p. paperback available $12.95
                                 92
  ISBN 0-345-44212-1 (pa)   LC 99-57603
"In 1997, on the eve of her 77th birthday noted mystery novelist James . . . decided to keep a diary for the first time ever, recording one year in her life. The result is this 'fragment of autobiography,' a mix of memoir, ruminations on everything from her writing career to Princess Diana's death, and literary criticism." Libr J

Jefferson, Thomas, 1743-1826

Adams, William Howard. The Paris years of Thomas Jefferson; original photography by Adelaide de Menil. Yale Univ. Press 1997 354p il $42; pa $19   **92**
  1. Paris (France)—Intellectual life
  ISBN 0-300-06903-0; 0-300-08261-4 (pa)
                   LC 97-12330
Adams chronicles the five years Thomas Jefferson spent in Paris as the American minister to the court of France
"This book is a fresh treatment of the transition in Jefferson's head and heart, the defining experience that challenged and mellowed his conceptions of society, culture, and mores." Choice
Includes bibliographical references

Ellis, Joseph J. American sphinx: the character of Thomas Jefferson. Knopf 1997 365p $29.95; pa $15   **92**
  ISBN 0-679-44490-4; 0-679-76441-0 (pa)
                        LC 96-26171
This biography focuses on "various important junctures of Jefferson's life (his tenures as minister to France, secretary of state, and, of course, president, among others) and major aspects of his personal consciousness (from his conduct of romance to his attitude toward slavery)." Booklist
"Penetrating Jefferson's placid, elegant facade, this extraordinary biography brings the sage of Monticello down to earth without either condemning or idolizing him." Publ Wkly

Gordon-Reed, Annette. Thomas Jefferson and Sally Hemings; an American controversy. University Press of Va. 1997 xx, 288p hardcover o.p. paperback available $14.95
                                 92
  1. Hemings, Sally, 1773-1835
  ISBN 0-8139-1833-2 (pa)   LC 96-34550
"Hemings, a slave who was one-quarter African, was also a half sister of Jefferson's deceased wife, and she lived at Monticello for many years. In this understated, brilliant study an African-American law professor examines the allegation that Jefferson was the father of Hemings' children." New Yorker
Includes bibliographical references

Randall, Willard Sterne. Thomas Jefferson; a life. Holt & Co. 1993 708p o.p.; HarperCollins Pubs. paperback available $20
                                 92
  ISBN 0-06-097617-9 (pa)   LC 93-2057
"A John Macrae book"
This biography focuses on Jefferson's "youthful lawyering on the frontier, his political eclipse as Virginia's ineffectual war governor, and his ambassadorship to France." Booklist
"Randall's substantial, balanced biography will be valuable for general readers who seek a one-volume work on one of the leading Founding Fathers." Libr J
Includes bibliographical references

Joan, of Arc, Saint, 1412-1431

Gordon, Mary. Joan of Arc. Viking 2000 xxv, 180p (Penguin lives series) $19.95   **92**
  ISBN 0-670-88537-1   LC 99-55678
"A Lipper/Viking book"
"This biography rehearses the well-known highlights in Joan's short life: the voices she heard who charged her with the mission to save France, her participation in the Battle of Orléans and the coronation of King Charles VII; her trial by an ecclesiastical court, where she was charged with witchcraft, heresy and idolatry. . . . The strength of this 'biographical meditation' lies in the penultimate chapter, in which Gordon investigates the numerous re-creations of Joan on stage and screen." Publ Wkly
Includes bibliographical references

Joan, of Arc, Saint, 1412-1431—*Continued*

Pernoud, Régine. Joan of Arc; her story; [by] Régine Pernoud, Marie-Véronique Clin; translated and revised by Jeremy duQuesnay Adams; edited by Bonnie Wheeler. St. Martin's Press 1999 xxii, 304p il maps o.p.; Palgrave paperback available $16.95   **92**

1. France—History—1328-1589, House of Valois

ISBN 0-312-22730-2 (pa)   LC 98-45059

Original French edition, 1986

This work "traces the appearance of Joan as a documented historical character rather than adhering to a standard chronological sequence. Informing the narrative is a novel interpretation of Joan as a political prisoner. Moving beyond the narrative, the American translator . . . has added a series of appendixes containing valuable contextual material. . . . These materials discuss key historical events, provide biographical information on Joan's contemporaries, and discuss Joan's afterlife in history, literature, folklore, art, and iconography." Libr J

Includes bibliographical references

John, Gwen, 1876-1939

Roe, Sue. Gwen John; a painter's life. Farrar, Straus & Giroux 2001 xx, 364p il $30   **92**

ISBN 0-374-11317-3   LC 2001-40549

The author "balances biography with a critical analysis of John's work. She also considers John's own virtues as an artist well beyond her secondary roles as the sister of painter Augustus John, Rodin's model and mistress, and Whistler's student. . . . Roe's blend of insight and eloquent narrative merges into a thoughtful, enduring masterpiece." Libr J

Includes bibliographical references

John Paul II, Pope, 1920-

Buttiglione, Rocco. Karol Wojtyła; the thought of the man who became Pope John Paul II; translated by Paolo Guietti and Francesca Murphy. Eerdmans 1997 384p $35   **92**

ISBN 0-8028-3848-0   LC 97-23188

Original Italian edition, 1982

The author traces the Pope's "intellectual development, offering a critique of his literary works and a detailed analysis of how he was influenced by Thomism and phenomenology, which he sought to reconcile while emphasizing individual freedom of conscience. . . . Recommended for general collections for its broad sweep complementary to other biographies on the pope." Libr J

Flynn, Raymond. John Paul II; a personal portrait of the pope and the man. St. Martin's Press 2001 204p il hardcover o.p. paperback available $14.95   **92**

ISBN 0-312-28328-8 (pa)   LC 00-45965

Flynn, the "former mayor of Boston and ex-ambassador to the Vatican, tells us . . . what his book is not: It is not a biography, or an analysis. . . . Flynn views it, rather, as a profile based on his own experiences with Pope John Paul II, dating back to a 1969 visit to Boston of then-Cardinal Karol Wojtyla." Natl Rev

Kwitny, Jonathan. Man of the century: the life and times of Pope John Paul II. Holt & Co. 1997 754p $30   **92**

ISBN 0-8050-2688-6   LC 97-6532

The author "follows the pope's life, from when he was Karol Wojtyla, a young man caught between his love for theater and his call to the priesthood, through his support as bishop of Krakow for Poland's Solidarity movement and his election and subsequent work as Pope John Paul II. . . . Kwitny's lively journalistic style make this book, in spite of its great detail, an accessible story of one of the century's most important religious leaders." Publ Wkly

Weigel, George. Witness to hope: the biography of Pope John Paul II. Cliff St. Bks. 1999 992p il $35; pa $20   **92**

ISBN 0-06-018793-X; 0-06-093286-4 (pa)

LC 99-26340

Weigel "focuses on John Paul's trademark ideas: Christian humanism, the inner connection between freedom and truth, and culture as the driving force of history. As a guide to the pope's thought, *Witness to Hope* is invaluable." Publ Wkly

Includes bibliographical references

Johnson, Joyce, 1935-

Kerouac, Jack. Door wide open. See entry under Kerouac, Jack, 1922-1969   **92**

Johnson, Lyndon B. (Lyndon Baines), 1908-1973

Caro, Robert A. The years of Lyndon Johnson. Knopf 1982-2002 3v il v1-v2 ea $45; v3 $35   **92**

1. United States—Politics and government—20th century   LC 82-47811

Also available in paperback from Vintage Bks.

Contents: v1 The path to power (ISBN 0-394-49973-5); v2 Means of ascent (ISBN 0-394-52835-2); v3 Master of the Senate (ISBN 0-394-52836-0)

These are the first three volumes in a projected four-volume biography of President Johnson. The path to power covers the years 1908-1941, Means of ascent continues from 1941 to Johnson's election to Congress in 1948, and Master of the Senate covers Johnson's Senate career from 1950-1960

Includes bibliographical references

Dallek, Robert. Lone star rising: Lyndon Johnson and his times, 1908-1960. Oxford Univ. Press 1991 721p il $40   **92**

1. United States—Politics and government—20th century

ISBN 0-19-505435-0   LC 90-39830

This first volume of Dallek's biographical study chronicles Johnson's formative years, his congressional tenure, and his nomination for vice-president in 1960

"The author combines painstaking historical research with acute sociological insight, producing a fascinating and balanced account of the life and times of one of the most influential legislators of the twentieth century." Booklist

Includes bibliographical references

Johnson, Samuel, 1709-1784

Boswell, James. The life of Samuel Johnson   **92**

Hardcover and paperback editions available from various publishers

Johnson, Samuel, 1709-1784—*Continued*
First published 1791
Variant title: The life of Johnson
"The most famous biography in the English language. It is an intimate and minute delineation of the great lexicographer's life, character and person, enlivened with small-talk, gossip and bits of familiar correspondence. It is also an admirable portrayal of the society of which Johnson was the outstanding figure." Pratt Alcove

Jones, Mother, 1830-1930
Gorn, Elliott J. Mother Jones; the most dangerous woman in America. Hill & Wang 2001 408p il hardcover o.p. paperback available $14 **92**
ISBN 0-8090-7094-4 (pa)   LC 00-44997
This is a biography of union organizer and labor leader Mary Harris Jones, known more popularly as Mother Jones
Gorn "has successfully separated fact from myth . . . situating Jones's story within a wider cultural frame." Publ Wkly
Includes bibliographical references

Jones, John Paul, 1747-1792
Morison, Samuel Eliot. John Paul Jones; a sailor's biography; with an introduction by James C. Bradford; charts and diagrams by Erwin Raisz. Naval Inst. Press 1989 xxvi, 537p il (Classics of naval literature) hardcover o.p. paperback available $24.95
92
1. United States—Naval history
ISBN 1-55750-410-5 (pa)   LC 89-13423
A reissue with a new introduction of the title first published 1959 by Little, Brown
This "documented chronicle of the American sea captain's life . . . is particularly concerned with his ability as a seaman and with the naval engagements in which he took part." Booklist
"Morison has destroyed the myth of John Paul Jones but has left us a more human, more understandable character." Best Sellers
Includes bibliographical references

Jones, Quincy
Jones, Quincy. Q: the autobiography of Quincy Jones. Doubleday 2001 412p il $26; pa $15.95 **92**
ISBN 0-385-48896-3; 0-7679-0510-5 (pa)
LC 2001-28151
"With some chapters written by Jones, and others by his family and friends . . . this (auto)biography full of behind-the-scenes anecdotes has an improvisational feel that suits its subject: a jazz musician and superstar composer. . . . Jones has composed a life story that gives much more than the typical celebrity memoir." Publ Wkly
Includes discography and filmography

Joplin, Scott, 1868-1917
Berlin, Edward A. King of ragtime: Scott Joplin and his era. Oxford Univ. Press 1994 334p il hardcover o.p. paperback available $21.50 **92**
ISBN 0-19-510108-1 (pa)   LC 93-28318
The author "shows how Joplin launched his career in the black social clubs of Sedalia, Mo.; achieved success

with the *Maple Leaf Rag*; and went on to win the respect of whites as well as his fellow African Americans, composing numerous rags and two operas." Publ Wkly
"Essential in any library concerned with American music." Booklist
Includes bibliographical references

Curtis, Susan. Dancing to a black man's tune: a life of Scott Joplin. University of Mo. Press 1994 xx, 265p il (Missouri biography series) $29.95 **92**
ISBN 0-8262-0949-1   LC 93-46116
A "study of the life and world of ragtime creator Scott Joplin (1868-1917). Lapsing only occasionally into academic jargon, the author ably places Joplin in the context of an emerging biracial society and culture as a man who was denied rights because of his color yet applauded as a musician." Publ Wkly
Includes bibliographical references

Jordan, Michael
Halberstam, David. Playing for keeps: Michael Jordan and the world he made. Random House 1999 426p hardcover o.p. paperback available $15.95 **92**
1. African American athletes
ISBN 0-7679-0444-3 (pa)   LC 98-49964
Halberstam presents a biography of basketball player Michael Jordan
"What's particularly effective about Halberstam's storytelling is that he follows Jordan's athletic trajectory, not in chronological order but through juxtaposed images of a hot-blooded college player with an as-yet unpolished game and an even-tempered 30-year-old at the height of his career. Jordan was not born a flawless pro, but developed his gifts by working tirelessly and intensely." Natl Rev

Joyce, James, 1882-1941
Ellmann, Richard. James Joyce. new and rev ed. Oxford Univ. Press 1982 887p il hardcover o.p. paperback available $27.50
92
ISBN 0-19-503381-7 (pa)   LC 81-22455
First published 1959
This biography describes "Joyce's working methods, views on life and literature, political opinions, familial relationships and problems, and incessant struggle against poverty and threatening blindness." Publ Wkly
This "is a vast undertaking and continuing achievement—massive, masterly, and definitive, rich in anecdote and detail. It is also extremely readable; the easy, often sympathetic style communicates gracefully not only facts but analysis." Choice
Includes bibliographical references

McCourt, John. James Joyce; a passionate exile. St. Martin's Press 2001 112p il $22.95
92
ISBN 0-312-26941-2
First published 2000 in the United Kingdom
This biography of the Irish novelist explores "the places that inspired and are reflected in *Ulysses* and *Finnegans Wake*. . . . Historical photos and reproductions of paintings of the era bring alive the well-known journey of the exile who famously never stopped writing about home." Booklist

Joyce, James, 1882-1941—*Continued*

O'Brien, Edna. James Joyce. Viking 1999
179p (Penguin lives series) $19.95   **92**
ISBN 0-670-88230-5   LC 99-23214
"A Lipper/Viking book"
O'Brien "tells the story of the aspiring young writer
and his downwardly mobile family, his escape to Europe,
the constant struggle to scrape together enough money to
live on, and finally his relative comfort, thanks to patrons, once *Ulysses* was published. She also provides
thoughtful appreciations of Joyce's major works." Booklist

Joyner-Kersee, Jackie

Joyner-Kersee, Jackie. A kind of grace; the
autobiography of the world's greatest female
athlete; [by] Jackie Joyner-Kersee with Sonja
Steptoe. Warner Bks. 1997 310p il $28   **92**
1. African American athletes
ISBN 0-446-52248-1   LC 97-14966
This memoir recounts the Olympic gold medalist's
"triumphs over poverty, family tragedy, and near-fatal
asthma attacks." Libr J
"A competent account of an admirable life." Booklist

Jung, C. G. (Carl Gustav), 1875-1961

Freud, Sigmund. The Freud/Jung letters.
See entry under Freud, Sigmund, 1856-1939
    92

Hayman, Ronald. A life of Jung. Norton
2001 xxi, 522p il hardcover o.p. paperback
available $18.95   **92**
ISBN 0-393-32322-6 (pa)   LC 00-54802
First published 1999 in the United Kingdom
In this exploration of the life and career of the Swiss
psychologist, "Hayman ferrets out the childhood beginnings of schizophrenic tendencies, chronicles his descent
into near insanity, documents his flirtation with fascism,
and details his abusive treatment of women." Booklist
"One of the many strengths of this candid and dis-
cerning biography is that Hayman enlists . . . provocative, alarming material to build a careful, nuanced portrait of his subject that neither excuses nor excoriates his
actions and words." Publ Wkly
Includes bibliographical references

Jung, C. G. (Carl Gustav). Memories,
dreams, reflections; recorded and edited by
Aniela Jaffé; translated from the German by
Richard and Clara Winston. rev ed. Vintage
Bks. 1989 c1963 430p pa $14   **92**
ISBN 0-679-72395-1   LC 88-37040
First published 1963 by Pantheon Bks.
"This volume of recollections reveals the intellectual
and spiritual development of an eminent Swiss psycholo-
gist and psychiatrist while only touching upon the out-
ward events of his long and productive life. . . . An im-
portant, firsthand document for readers who wish to un-
derstand this seminal writer and thinker." Booklist
Includes bibliographical references

Kahlo, Frida, 1907-1954

Herrera, Hayden. Frida: a biography of
Frida Kahlo. Harper & Row 1983 507p il
hardcover o.p. paperback available $24.95
    92
ISBN 0-06-008589-4 (pa)   LC 80-8688
This biography of the Mexican painter and wife of Diego Rivera "is a mesmerizing story of radical art, romantic politics, bizarre loves and physical suffering. . . .
Herrera resolves Kahlo the public figure and Kahlo the
artist in a perceptive portrait of a woman who rose above
a circumscribed content with a grand style." Time
Includes bibliographical references

Kahlo, Frida. The diary of Frida Kahlo; an
intimate self-portrait; introduction by Carlos
Fuentes; essay and commentaries by Sarah
M. Lowe. Abrams 1995 295p il   **92**
    LC 94-45994
Available Abradale Press reprint $19.98 (ISBN 0-
8109-8195-5)
This is "a facsimile of a journal {the artist Frida
Kahlo} wrote in longhand in the last decade of her life.
The diary {is} supplemented by a translation of her
Spanish entries. . . . {It includes} drawings and water-
colors." N Y Times Book Rev
"Sprinkled with irony, black humor, even gaiety . . .
this volume is a testament to Kahlo's resilience and cour-
age." Publ Wkly
Includes bibliographical references

Zamora, Martha. Frida Kahlo; the brush of
anguish; abridged and translated by Marilyn
Sode Smith. Chronicle Bks. 1990 143p il
hardcover o.p. paperback available $24.95
    92
ISBN 0-8118-0485-2 (pa)   LC 90-33874
This biography of the Mexican painter is an abridgment and translation of a title originally published in
Mexico in 1987
Most "important here is the collection of 75 color
plates of the artist's original works. Of interest to the initiated because they comprise largely seldom-seen works
in various Mexican collections, these plates represent the
best collection now available of Kahlo's work." Libr J
Includes bibliographical references

Kandinsky, Wassily, 1866-1944

Hahl-Koch, Jelena. Kandinsky. Rizzoli Int.
Publs. 1993 431p il $150   **92**
ISBN 0-8478-1404-1   LC 91-52769
Translated from the German by Karin Brown, Ralph
Harratz and Katharine Harrison
The author discusses the life and art of the Russian
abstract painter
"Doubtless some will be disturbed and others uplifted
by the material contained in Ms. Hahl-Koch's dense and
physically beautiful volume. Most will find it stimulating
and utterly engrossing." N Y Times Book Rev
Includes bibliographical references

Kaplan, Cynthia

Kaplan, Cynthia. Why I'm like this; true stories. Morrow 2002 212p $23.95; pa $12.95 **92**

ISBN 0-688-17850-2; 0-06-051261-X (pa)
LC 2001-58657

"Kaplan's book consists of 21 loosely connected essays, mostly about her family. . . . [Topics include] summer camp, headaches, a stylish mother, a sick grandmother, a reliable husband and a cute baby." N Y Times Book Rev

"Kaplan consistently amuses while cutting surprisingly deep." Booklist

Kaplan, Jonathan, 1954-

Kaplan, Jonathan. The dressing station; a surgeon's chronicle of war and medicine. Grove Press 2001 407p $25; pa $14 **92**

ISBN 0-8021-1707-4; 0-8021-3962-0 (pa)
LC 2001-51241

A physician trained in South Africa and London, the author recounts his experiences "as an emergency field surgeon on the front lines of apartheid in Nambia and Zululand, as well as in Kurdistan, Mozambique, Burma, and Eritrea. Between stints on those horrific battlefields, Kaplan served as a hospital surgeon, flying doctor, ship's medical officer, journalist, and documentary filmmaker." Libr J

"Remarkably engaging, though at times horrifying." Booklist

Kaplan, Justin

Bernays, Anne. Back then. See entry under Bernays, Anne **92**

Karajan, Herbert von

Osborne, Richard. Herbert von Karajan; a life in music. Northeastern Univ. Press 2000 851p il $37.50 **92**

ISBN 1-55553-425-2
LC 99-59108

First published 1998 in the United Kingdom

"Because Karajan's career developed in Nazi Germany, Osborne dwells at length . . . on Karajan's involvement with the regime and his postwar exoneration. Drawing on a vast variety of source materials and quoting some in full, Osborne takes us on the enthralling musical journey that was the life of one of the greatest of conductors." Booklist

Includes bibliographical references

Keaton, Buster, 1895-1966

Meade, Marion. Buster Keaton: cut to the chase. HarperCollins Pubs. 1995 440p il o.p.; Da Capo Press paperback available $18 **92**

ISBN 0-306-80802-1 (pa)
LC 95-21390

The author "paints a moving and loving portrait of a comic genius, mechanical thinker, and superb athlete. The book provides the context of family and friends, (including Charlie Chaplin and Fatty Arbuckle) behind Keaton's career, and in doing so adds flesh and humanity to the funny bones and gags that have entertained and marveled audiences for decades. A remarkably gentle and insightful story of a silent comic riddle." Choice

Includes filmography and bibliographical references

Keats, John, 1795-1821

Motion, Andrew. Keats. Farrar, Straus & Giroux 1998 636p il o.p.; University of Chicago Press paperback available $18 **92**

ISBN 0-226-56240-8 (pa)
LC 97-76775

First published 1997 in the United Kingdom

"Motion emphasizes that Keats was no other-worldly creature of exquisite sensibilities but a man whose liberal politics and commitment to medicine animated his aesthetics and enlightened his poetry." Booklist

Includes bibliographical references

Keller, Helen, 1880-1968

Herrmann, Dorothy. Helen Keller; a life. Knopf 1998 394p il o.p.; University of Chicago Press paperback available $20 **92**

1. Blind 2. Deaf

ISBN 0-226-32763-9 (pa)
LC 98-14556

The author "takes us beyond the image of Helen Keller portrayed in *The Miracle Worker* to unearth a passionate, politically radical woman whose inspiration and teacher, Annie Sullivan, is equally fiery and brilliant. Herrmann brings us into the every day lives of the famous pair, but the story is hardly mundane. . . . Herrmann gives us fascinating details via archives and unpublished memoirs to show how society's view of disabled people was greatly shaped by Keller and Sullivan." Libr J

Includes bibliographical references

Keller, Helen. The story of my life. Doubleday 1954 382p il **92**

1. Blind 2. Deaf

Hardcover and paperback editions available from various publishers

First published 1903

This biography of the inspirational Keller contains accounts of her home life and her relationship with her devoted teacher Anne Sullivan

Lash, Joseph P. Helen and teacher; the story of Helen Keller and Anne Sullivan Macy. AFB Press 1997 811p il $49.95 **92**

1. Sullivan, Anne, 1866-1936 2. Blind 3. Deaf

ISBN 0-89128-289-0
LC 96-45300

Also available in paperback

A reissue of the title first published 1980 by Delacorte Press

The author addresses "such subjects as Sullivan's incredible possessiveness toward Keller and whether Sullivan's famous association with her student came at a high personal price." Libr J

"This is a deeply absorbing portrait of two intertwined lives whose meanings can't be understood separately." NY Times Book Rev

Includes bibliographical references

Kemble, Adelaide, 1814?-1879

Blainey, Ann. Fanny and Adelaide: the lives of the remarkable Kemble sisters. See entry under Kemble, Fanny, 1809-1893 **92**

Kemble, Fanny, 1809-1893

Blainey, Ann. Fanny and Adelaide: the lives of the remarkable Kemble sisters. Dee, I.R. 2001 339p $27.50   **92**
1. Kemble, Adelaide, 1814?-1879
ISBN 1-56663-372-9   LC 00-50440
"Fanny Kemble was one of Europe's most celebrated actresses; her sister, Adelaide, one of its greatest opera singers. Blainey's dual biography of those two spirited women draws heavily on letters the sisters wrote one another, including a set discovered quite recently, to give us a good look at the inner workings of English theater of the late 1700s through the mid-1800s and the role that women played in the arts then." Booklist
Includes bibliographical references

Clinton, Catherine. Fanny Kemble's civil wars. Simon & Schuster 2000 302p il o.p.; Oxford Univ. Press paperback available $15.95   **92**
ISBN 0-19-514815-0 (pa)   LC 30-30097
This is the biography of the English actress, author, and abolitionist who "commanded center stage in the American drama over slavery and in her much-publicized personal civil wars of marriage to one of America's wealthiest slaveholders, bitter divorce, and publication of her private letters and her antislavery journal describing life on a Georgia plantation." Libr J
"This biography is every bit as sharp, evocative and eloquent as Kemble's *Journal*." Publ Wkly
Includes bibliographical references

Kennan, George Frost, 1904-

Kennan, George Frost. Sketches from a life; [by] George F. Kennan. Pantheon Bks. 1989 365p o.p.; Norton paperback available $14.95   **92**
1. United States—Foreign relations
ISBN 0-393-32139-8 (pa)   LC 88-43282
"This is a collection of very private reflections spanning some 60 years of foreign service in Nazi Germany, the Baltic states, the Low Countries, the Soviet Union, as well as nonofficial travels covering the entire globe. Kennan has marvelous insight into his ever-changing surroundings—an insight that is always sharp, sometimes melancholy, and punctuated frequently by dry, Midwestern wit." Libr J

Kennedy, John F. (John Fitzgerald), 1917-1963

Dallek, Robert. An unfinished life: John F. Kennedy, 1917-1963. Little, Brown 2003 838p il $30   **92**
ISBN 0-316-17238-3   LC 2002-116388
Also available Thorndike Press large print edition
This is a biography of the thirty-fifth president of the United States
The author "has written the most accessible, balanced, and scholarly biography yet of JFK. . . . It is the Kennedy biography against which others will be measured." Libr J
Includes bibliographical references

Kenney, Charles. John F. Kennedy; the presidential portfolio: history as told through the collection of the John F. Kennedy Library and Museum; introduction by Michael Beschloss. PublicAffairs 2000 241p il $35   **92**
1. United States—Politics and government—1961-1974
ISBN 1-891620-36-3   LC 00-57581
Includes computer optical disc
This volume features approximately 250 photos and documents and highlights "the many remarkable events of Kennedy's life and his presidency." Publisher's note
"The text is less detailed (and less focused on controversy) than a full-scale biography, but it emphasizes what most would consider the key elements of JFK's presidency . . . while also devoting chapters to Jacqueline and Robert F. Kennedy. Likely to appeal to Kennedy fans and to others seeking a sense of the period." Booklist

Mahoney, Richard D. Sons and brothers: the days of Jack and Bobby Kennedy. Arcade Pub. 1999 441p il $27.95; pa $14.95   **92**
1. Kennedy, Robert F., 1925-1968 2. Kennedy, Joseph P., 1888-1969 3. United States—Politics and government—1961-1974
ISBN 1-55970-480-2; 1-55970-534-5 (pa)
     LC 99-25681
This study "of the brothers' relationship chronicles its evolution, its mutual dependencies, and the wide-ranging effect that the actions of the brothers' father, Joe, had on Jack's and Bobby's political lives." Booklist
"Writing in a steady, almost relentlessly elegiac tone, Mahoney proves that the lives and deaths of John F. and Robert F. Kennedy remain as compelling now as they were throughout the turbulent 1960s." Publ Wkly
Includes bibliographical references

Reeves, Richard. President Kennedy; profile of power. Simon & Schuster 1993 798p il hardcover o.p. paperback available $22   **92**
1. United States—Politics and government—1961-1974
ISBN 0-671-89289-4 (pa)   LC 93-24805
This is an account "of John F. Kennedy's three years as president, with an emphasis on leadership techniques." Choice
"Reeves doesn't try to soft-pedal the distasteful, but his account of the Kennedy presidency is resolutely matter of fact and not an indictment." Time
Includes bibliographical references

Kennedy, Joseph P., 1888-1969

Kennedy, Joseph P. Hostage to fortune; the letters of Joseph P. Kennedy; edited by Amanda Smith. Viking 2000 xxxvi, 764p il hardcover o.p. paperback available $20   **92**
ISBN 0-14-200037-X (pa)   LC 00-36786
This collection of Joseph P. Kennedy's personal papers is supplemented with "other family correspondence and documentation, including Rose Kennedy's letters to the children and their own school compositions and diaries." N Y Times Book Rev
"Libraries with active history collections will want this weighty collection." Booklist
Includes bibliographical references

Kennedy, Robert F., 1925-1968

Mahoney, Richard D. Sons and brothers: the days of Jack and Bobby Kennedy. See entry under Kennedy, John F. (John Fitzgerald), 1917-1963   **92**

Schlesinger, Arthur M. Robert Kennedy and his times; [by] Arthur M. Schlesinger, Jr. Houghton Mifflin 1978 1066p il o.p.; Ballantine Bks. paperback available $16.95
92

1. United States—Politics and government—20th century
ISBN 0-345-41061-0 (pa)   LC 78-8469
"A highly sympathetic and readable political biography covering in depth Robert Kennedy's tenure in public life. At times extremely partisan, at times dispassionate, Schlesinger's study effectively captures Kennedy's impact on national politics and the main currents of American politics during the 1950s and 1960s." Choice
Includes bibliographical references

Thomas, Evan. Robert Kennedy; his life. Simon & Schuster 2000 509p il hardcover o.p. paperback available $15   **92**
ISBN 0-7432-0329-1 (pa)   LC 00-41995
This biography "reveals a very human Kennedy struggling to come to terms with his brother's assassination, his role in wiretapping Martin Luther King Jr., and his fatal decision to take on Eugene McCarthy and Hubert Humphrey in the 1968 Democratic primary." Libr J
"A solid, judicious life of a politician whose tragic death inspired a generation of what-if history." Booklist
Includes bibliographical references

Kepler, Johannes, 1571-1630

Ferguson, Kitty. Tycho & Kepler. See entry under Brahe, Tycho, 1546-1601   **92**

Kerouac, Jack, 1922-1969

Kerouac, Jack. Door wide open; a beat love affair in letters, 1957-1958; [by] Jack Kerouac and Joyce Johnson; with introduction and commentary by Joyce Johnson. Viking 2000 xxvi, 182p hardcover o.p. paperback available $13   **92**
1. Johnson, Joyce, 1935-
ISBN 0-14-100187-9 (pa)   LC 99-53219
"In a hip, literate correspondence marked by high diction and '50s slang, 21-year-old Johnson (born Glassman) and 35-year-old Kerouac chart the flowering of the Beats and their complicated love affair." Publ Wkly

Kerouac, Jack. Selected letters, 1940-1956; edited with an introduction and commentary by Ann Charters. Viking 1995 xxvi, 629p hardcover o.p. paperback available $16.95
92

ISBN 0-14-023444-6 (pa)   LC 94-12911
"These letters, addressed to the likes of William Burroughs, Allen Ginsberg, and publisher Robert Giroux, take Kerouac from his early years up to the publication of On the Road." Libr J
The editor "made two very wise decisions here: she supplied continuity and context for the letters, and she included significant letters from the correspondents. The frustration of the long-rejected writer is doubly felt by the reader, since this selection ends on the eve of the big Beat breakthrough." Choice
Includes bibliographical references

Kerouac, Jack. Selected letters, 1957-1969; edited with an introduction and commentary by Ann Charters. Viking 1999 xxvii, 514p hardcover o.p. paperback available $17   **92**
ISBN 0-14-029615-8 (pa)   LC 99-17374
This volume "starts with the publication of On the Road and continues almost to the day Kerouac died. The years 1957-1960, the height of Kerouac's career, occupy more than half the volume. Later letters record his struggle to care for his ailing mother, his efforts to finish his later books and his troubles with money and health. . . . Frequent addressees and subjects include Gary Snyder, Philip Whalen, Lawrence Ferlinghetti, William Burroughs and Allen Ginsberg." Publ Wkly

Kerrey, Robert

Kerrey, Robert. When I was a young man; a memoir; [by] Bob Kerrey. Harcourt 2002 270p il $26; pa $14   **92**
ISBN 0-15-100474-9; 0-15-602743-7 (pa)
LC 2002-764
The former Nebraska governor and senator recounts his childhood in Lincoln, Nebraska, dashed plans for a career in pharmacology, and his involvement, and subsequent wounding, in Vietnam
"Kerrey's deceptively simple writing style has great strength, and he presents his personal memories against the larger backdrop of antiwar protesters and other events of the period." Publ Wkly

Keynes, John Maynard, 1883-1946

Skidelsky, Robert Jacob Alexander. John Maynard Keynes. v3: Fighting for freedom, 1937-1946. Viking 2001 576p hardcover o.p. paperback available $20   **92**
ISBN 0-14-200167-8 (pa)
This last installment of Skidelsky's biographical study of Keynes' life follows Hopes betrayed, 1883-1920 (1986) and The economist as savior, 1920-1937 published 1994. Volume one available in paperback
"Depression, war, and the new postwar world form the backdrop for the final volume in this comprehensive three-volume Keynes biography." Booklist

Khrushchev, Nikita Sergeevich, 1894-1971

Nikita Khrushchev; edited by William Taubman, Sergei Khrushchev, and Abbott Gleason; translated by David Gehrenbeck, Eileen Kane, and Alla Bashenko. Yale Univ. Press 2000 391p $45   **92**
1. Soviet Union—Politics and government
ISBN 0-300-07635-6   LC 99-51323
A collection of essays re-evaluating aspects of Khrushchev's political career. Topics include his rise to power and his domestic, foreign, and military policy. Two essays compare Khrushchev and Gorbachev

King, B. B.
King, B. B. Blues all around me; the autobiography of B.B. King; [by] B.B. King with David Ritz. Avon Bks. 1996 336p il hardcover o.p. paperback available $14 **92**
ISBN 0-380-80760-2 (pa)   LC 96-27773
King recounts his humble beginnings and his career as a prominent blues guitarist
"This is one of the best recent pop-music bios. King speaks straight from the soul, it seems, just like he plays the guitar." Booklist

King, Martin Luther, 1929-1968
Bennett, Lerone. What manner of man: a biography of Martin Luther King, Jr.; by Lerone Bennett, Jr.; with an introduction by Benjamin E. Mays. [3rd rev ed] Johnson 1968 251p il $19.95 **92**
1. African Americans—Civil rights
ISBN 0-87485-027-4
First published 1964
The author traces King's life from his childhood, education, accomplishments as a Baptist minister, his leadership in the black Civil Rights movement, his winning the 1964 Nobel Peace Prize to the tragic end of his life in 1968

Dyson, Michael Eric. I may not get there with you: the true Martin Luther King, Jr. Free Press 2000 404p $25; pa $15 **92**
1. African Americans—Civil rights
ISBN 0-684-86776-1; 0-684-83037-X (pa)
                            LC 99-40478
In this work of biocriticism, the author "argues that we have tarnished King's true legacy by translating it into a cliché." N Y Times Book Rev
Dyson "believes that the ministry fostered King's rhetorical gifts but also encouraged his authoritarian personality. We learn much about his flaws, and about conflict, dissent, and generational differences within the black community, as Dyson insists that King, properly understood, remains a controversial figure." New Yorker
Includes bibliographical references

Frady, Marshall. Martin Luther King, Jr. Penguin Bks. 2002 216p (Penguin lives series) $19.95 **92**
1. African Americans—Civil rights
ISBN 0-670-88231-3   LC 2002-77730
Also available Thorndike Press large print edition
"A Lipper/Viking book"
The author examines the life of Martin Luther "King from his rise to national notice in the Montgomery, AL, bus boycott of 1955-56 to his 1968 murder on a motel balcony in Memphis, TN." Libr J
"Frady's sensitive, succinct presentation never lets King's foibles obscure his tremendous contributions to American life." Publ Wkly

King, Martin Luther. The autobiography of Martin Luther King, Jr; edited by Clayborne Carson. Warner Bks. 1998 400p il $25; pa $15.95 **92**
1. African Americans—Civil rights
ISBN 0-446-52412-3; 0-446-67650-0 (pa)
                            LC 98-35704
"Carson, director of Martin Luther King Jr. Papers Project, brings together selections from King's writings, speeches, and recordings to create this fascinating 'autobiography' of the famed civil rights leader and Nobel Peace Prize winner. The writings trace King's struggles with religion, philosophy, and the racial politics of the U.S." Booklist
Includes bibliographical references

Kipling, Rudyard, 1865-1936
Gilmour, David. The long recessional: the imperial life of Rudyard Kipling. Farrar, Straus & Giroux 2002 351p il maps $26; pa $15 **92**
ISBN 0-374-18702-9; 0-374-52896-9 (pa)
                            LC 2002-100585
This biography focuses on Kipling's social and political views in relation to the British Empire, especially as expressed in his fiction and poetry
The author "offers a brief, sympathetic, well-informed, and highly readable account of Kipling." Libr J
Includes bibliographical references

Ricketts, Harry. Rudyard Kipling; a life. Carroll & Graf Pubs. 2000 c1999 434p il hardcover o.p. paperback available $16 **92**
ISBN 0-7867-0830-1 (pa)
First published 1999 in the United Kingdom with title: The unforgiving minute: a life of Rudyard Kipling
This work "succeeds in disentangling some of the political muddle of Kipling's life. Ricketts' literary analysis is competent, if unsophisticated. Most valuably, he traces the debt to Browning and the many other resonant literary allusions in Kipling's work, thus undermining the charges of philistinism . . . levelled against it." New Statesman (Engl)

Kissinger, Henry, 1923-
Kissinger, Henry. Years of renewal. Simon & Schuster 1999 1151p il maps hardcover o.p. paperback available $24 **92**
1. United States—Foreign relations
ISBN 0-684-85572-0 (pa)   LC 98-41038
This concluding volume of Kissinger's memoirs "starts with Nixon's resignation and continues through the two years of the Ford administration. . . . As Kissinger explains China policy, Soviet policy, Middle East diplomacy and various crises (in Cyprus, Angola and elsewhere), his insight extends not only to explanations of policy but also to accounts of bureaucratic infighting and turf battles—as well as to relations between the executive branch and Congress." Publ Wkly
"Statecraft defies simple solutions, and one of the merits of Kissinger's memoir—especially this somber and reflective third volume—is that he so rarely provides them." N Y Times Book Rev
Includes bibliographical references

Klemperer, Victor, 1881-1960
Klemperer, Victor. I will bear witness; a diary of the Nazi years, 1933-1941; translated by Martin Chalmers. Random House 1998 556p hardcover o.p. paperback available $15.95 **92**
1. Germany—History—1933-1945
ISBN 0-375-75378-8 (pa)   LC 98-15429
Also available volume covering years 1941-1945 pa $14.95 (ISBN 0-375-75697-3)
"Klemperer, a professor at the University of Dresden, was a Jew by birth. He managed to survive the war, liv-

Klemperer, Victor, 1881-1960—*Continued*
ing relatively unscathed with his Aryan wife in Dresden.
After his death in 1960, a former student discovered his
wartime diaries, and this is the first volume to be published in the U.S." Booklist
"Never has the isolation of living in a world that
wishes one's people dead been rendered with greater pathos. Every act of cruelty as well as every gesture of
kindness is scrupulously recorded." Nation

Knight, Bobby
Knight, Bobby. Knight: my story; [by] Bob
Knight with Bob Hammel. Thomas Dunne
Bks. 2002 387p il $25.95; pa $14.95   **92**
ISBN 0-312-28257-5; 0-312-31117-6 (pa)
                                    LC 2001-48990
Also available Thorndike Press large print edition
Knight, fired after 29 years as the basketball coach of
Indiana University, "displays here his palpable affection
for his players and his reverence for the game and the
great coaches who preceded him—Joe Lapchick and
Henry Iba, among others." Booklist
"College hoops fans can learn more about the game
from this book than from most instructional guides."
Publ Wkly

Koppel, Ted, 1940-
Koppel, Ted. Off camera; private thoughts
made public. Knopf 2000 320p hardcover o.p.
paperback available $14   **92**
ISBN 0-375-72708-6 (pa)   LC 00-34919
The television journalist of *Nightline* presents a daily
diary for 1999 chronicling "the controversial events from
the century's last year, such as the Clinton impeachment
trial and the Columbine High School shootings. . . . The
subtitle of the book may lead some readers to expect a
bit of muckraking, but they will be disappointed. . . .
Yet one does not get the sense that Koppel is restraining
himself or hiding anything, merely that this is a person
who lives his life with integrity so that his private
thoughts are full of the same." Libr J

Koufax, Sandy, 1935-
Gruver, Ed. Koufax; by Edward Gruver.
Taylor Pub. Co. 2000 264p il $24.95; pa
$16.95   **92**
ISBN 0-87833-157-3; 0-87833-294-4 (pa)
                                    LC 99-56763
"This is the biography of legendary L.A. Dodgers
pitcher Sandy Koufax, who for half a decade mesmerized
hitters as few have ever done. . . . Drawing on child-
hood friends, teammates, opponents, journalists, and
Dodger management, Gruver has written a compelling
story, complete with appendix of notable statistics." Libr
J

Leavy, Jane. Sandy Koufax; a lefty's
legacy. HarperCollins Pubs. 2002 xxii, 282p
$23.95; pa $13.95   **92**
ISBN 0-06-019533-9; 0-06-093329-1 (pa)
                                    LC 2002-68722
In this biography of the Dodgers pitcher "Levy also
uses his career to examine the changes baseball has undergone in the last four decades." Booklist
The author "delivers an honest and exquisitely detailed
examination of a complex man." Publ Wkly

Koul, Sudha
Koul, Sudha. The tiger ladies; a memoir of
Kashmir. Beacon Press 2002 218p $25; pa
$15   **92**
ISBN 0-8070-5918-8; 0-8070-5919-6 (pa)
                                    LC 2001-5970
The author recalls her childhood in Kashmir in a Hin-
du Brahmin family
Kohl calls her "book 'an epitaph to a way of life.'
Many readers, too, will mourn the loss of her Kashmir
when they finish this simple, resonant tale." Publ Wkly

Kübler-Ross, Elisabeth
Kübler-Ross, Elisabeth. The wheel of life;
a memoir of living and dying. Scribner 1997
286p il hardcover o.p. paperback available
$13   **92**
ISBN 0-684-84631-4 (pa)   LC 97-6435
In this autobiography "Kübler-Ross describes her
growing-up years in Switzerland as one of a set of triplet
sisters, her fight to become a doctor, and later, the even
stronger opposition she met when she began her research
on death and dying. Despite the weightiness inherent in
working with and writing about mortality, the book has
a light, almost airy feel to it, which goes along with the
author's central theme that death is merely a transformation." Booklist

Kubrick, Stanley
LoBrutto, Vincent. Stanley Kubrick; a
biography. Fine, D.I. 1996 579p il o.p.; Da
Capo Press paperback available $20   **92**
ISBN 0-306-80906-0 (pa)   LC 96-35737
"LoBrutto traces Kubrick's career from his high-
school days as a photographer for *Look* magazine to the
decade of inactivity since *Full Metal Jacket.*" Booklist
"For the true film buff, there's an astonishing amount
of technical information, but there's also a good deal of
illuminating backstage human interest." Publ Wkly
Includes bibliographical references

Walker, Alexander. Stanley Kubrick,
director; a visual analysis by Sybil Taylor
and Ulrich Ruchti. rev and expanded. Norton
1999 376p il $35; pa $25   **92**
ISBN 0-393-04601-X; 0-393-32119-3 (pa)
                                    LC 98-24086
First published 1998 in the United Kingdom
"Walker describes Kubrick as a guarded, suspicious,
obsessive, controlling, paranoid workaholic, and makes
us feel that he's bestowing a compliment. Each movie is
given a thorough analysis, reinforced by the extensive
use of stills in each case." Publ Wkly
Includes bibliographical references

Kumin, Maxine, 1925-
Kumin, Maxine. Always beginning; essays
on a life in poetry. Copper Canyon Press
2000 256p pa $17   **92**
1. Poetics 2. Poetry
ISBN 1-556-59141-1   LC 00-9936
"This prose collection traces parallel developments in
Kumin's career. First, and most effective, are her memoirs of cultivating her New Hampshire farm, with diary
entries devoted to vegetable beds and rearing foals.
Alongside these versions of the pastoral, she charts her
growth as a writer." N Y Times Book Rev

Kurosawa, Akira, 1910-1998

Kurosawa, Akira. Something like an autobiography; translated by Audie E. Bock. Knopf 1982 205p il hardcover o.p. paperback available $15　　**92**

1. Motion picture industry
ISBN 0-394-71439-3 (pa)　　LC 81-48100
These are the memoirs of the Japanese filmmaker, covering his life up to 1951-52, when his film Rashōmon won international awards
This "is a fascinating, moving record of one man's pursuit of excellence in a single art." N Y Times Book Rev

Lancaster, Burt, 1913-1994

Buford, Kate. Burt Lancaster; an American life. Knopf 2000 447p il o.p.; Da Capo Press paperback available $18　　**92**
ISBN 0-306-81019-0 (pa)　　LC 99-37351
Also available Thorndike Press large print edition
"Lancaster's decades-long political involvement with liberal causes (and his constant run-ins with the House Un-American Activities Committee in the 1950s) are a central theme in this well-researched and engaging biography, which also details the artist's acting career, his turns as a producer and his personal life." Publ Wkly
Includes bibliographical references

Lardner, Ring, 1915-2000

Lardner, Ring. I'd hate myself in the morning; a memoir; [by] Ring Lardner, Jr. Thunder's Mouth Press 2000 198p il $22.95; pa $14.95　　**92**
ISBN 1-56025-296-0; 1-56025-338-X (pa)
LC 00-44298
"Lardner was a two-time Academy Award winner . . . and a member of the 'Hollywood Ten,' the group of writers and directors who went to jail rather than name names to the House Un-American Activities Committee (HUAC). In this book, he easily blends sketches of his famous father . . . with those of his student days in Moscow and anecdotes of his Hollywood and blacklist years." Booklist
"Of interest to cultural historians as well as general readers, this book belongs in both academic and public libraries." Libr J

Lauren, Ralph

McDowell, Colin. Ralph Lauren; the man, the vision, the style. Rizzoli Int. Publs. 2003 203p il $40　　**92**
ISBN 0-8478-2524-8　　LC 2002-111923
"The book covers Lauren's Bronx childhood (he was born Ralph Lifshitz and changed his name in his teens) and the path to his fashion empire, which now brings in $2 billion a year. . . . A fine tribute to the man who made it cool for guys to wear pink." Publ Wkly

Lawrence, D. H. (David Herbert), 1885-1930

Ellis, David. D.H. Lawrence, dying game, 1922-1930. Cambridge Univ. Press 1998 xxx, 780p il maps (The Cambridge biography— D.H. Lawrence, 1885-1930) $70　　**92**
ISBN 0-521-25421-3　　LC 96-52443
"The final volume of the Cambridge Biography of D. H. Lawrence chronicles his progress from leaving Europe

in 1922 to his death in Venice in 1930. . . . It describes his travels in Ceylon, Australia, the USA and Mexico in an increasingly desperate search for an ideal community. With his return to Europe in 1925, there is a detailed account of his rediscovery of painting, his battle against censorship, and the vitality with which he resisted the debilitating effects of tuberculosis." Publisher's note
Includes bibliographical references

Kinkead-Weekes, Mark. D.H. Lawrence, triumph to exile, 1912-1922. Cambridge Univ. Press 1996 xlv, 943p il maps (The Cambridge biography—D.H. Lawrence, 1885-1930) $65　　**92**
ISBN 0-521-25420-5　　LC 95-36102
"This second volume of the . . . Cambridge Biography of D. H. Lawrence covers the years 1912-22, the period in which Lawrence forged his reputation as one of the greatest and most controversial writers of the twentieth century." Publisher's note
Includes bibliographical references

Worthen, John. D.H. Lawrence, the early years, 1885-1912. Cambridge Univ. Press 1991 626p il (The Cambridge biography— D.H. Lawrence, 1885-1930) hardcover o.p. paperback available $30　　**92**
ISBN 0-521-43772-5 (pa)　　LC 90-23423
This "first volume of Cambridge's three-volume life of Lawrence, . . . takes the young writer through his elopement with Frieda. . . . This persuasive biography is compulsive good reading from cover to cover. A major event in modern literary studies." Libr J
Includes bibliographical references

Lawrence, T. E. (Thomas Edward), 1888-1935

Asher, Michael. Lawrence, the uncrowned king of Arabia. Overlook Press 1999 418p il maps $37.95　　**92**
ISBN 0-87951-712-3　　LC 99-37255
The author "personally retraces the footsteps of Lawrence, as recounted in his classic Seven Pillars of Wisdom. . . . Asher's Lawrence is a flawed man thrust by events into the forefront of history. Asher recounts Lawrence's exploits in the Arab Revolt in a fast-paced narrative style. . . . The book presents an excellent analysis of the personal demons that plagued Lawrence throughout his life, his revulsion over the horrors of war and the torment of reconciling his strict religious upbringing with his homosexuality." Publ Wkly
Includes bibliographical references

Leadbelly, 1885-1949

Wolfe, Charles K. The life and legend of Leadbelly; by Charles Wolfe and Kip Lornell. HarperCollins Pubs. 1992 333p il o.p.; Da Capo Press paperback available $15.95　　**92**
ISBN 0-306-80896-X (pa)　　LC 92-52606
"Drawing on a variety of primary and secondary sources, including numerous interviews, Wolfe and Lornell attempt to separate fact from fiction. . . . Photographs, informative notes, and a full discography are valuable additions." Choice
Includes bibliographical references

Lee, Robert E. (Robert Edward), 1807-1870

Fellman, Michael. The making of Robert E. Lee. Random House 2000 xx, 360p il $29.95   **92**

1. United States—History—1861-1865, Civil War
ISBN 0-679-45650-3   LC 99-44062
Also available in paperback from Johns Hopkins Univ. Press

"Struggling to subdue his ambitions and passions in a peacetime military career whose monotony was only momentarily breached by the Mexican American War and at Harpers Ferry, Lee found in the Civil War a chance to express himself fully. In a study rich with discussions of Lee's religious beliefs and political opinions, the author skewers previous efforts to detach Lee from slavery, racism, and the mentality of the Lost Cause. Sure to arouse debate, this book challenges and delights." Libr J
Includes bibliographical references

Freeman, Douglas Southall. Lee; an abridgment in one volume, by Richard Harwell, of the four-volume R. E. Lee; with a new foreword by James M. McPherson. Scribner 1991 xxiii, 601p il maps hardcover o.p. paperback available $18   **92**
1. United States—History—1861-1865, Civil War
ISBN 0-684-82953-3 (pa)   LC 91-20088
First published 1961

"Students of history will continue to want and to use the original four-volume work but most general readers will find this abridgment more convenient and adequate to their interest. All footnotes and all of the appendix have been omitted as well as details of Civil War action that are not necessary to show the main course of Lee's life and action." Booklist

Nolan, Alan T. Lee considered; General Robert E. Lee and Civil War history. University of N.C. Press 1991 231p il $29.95; pa $16.95   **92**
1. United States—History—1861-1865, Civil War
ISBN 0-8078-1956-5; 0-8078-4587-6 (pa)
      LC 90-48296

In this biography of the Confederate Civil War general, the author contends "that Lee the slaveholder was not antislavery, that the reluctant secessionist endorsed Southern independence, that the general lost the war by his repeated offensive thrusts and provincial vision—and more." Libr J
"Nolan uses sources cleverly to build his case and adroitly pits this new 'truth' against the words of Lee's historically staunchest promoters." Booklist
Includes bibliographical references

Thomas, Emory M. Robert E. Lee; a biography. Norton 1995 472p il maps paperback available $17.95   **92**
ISBN 0-393-31631-9 (pa)   LC 95-10522
"Civil War historian Thomas presents Lee as neither an icon nor a flawed figure, but rather as a man who made the best of his lot, whose comic vision of life ultimately shaped him into an individual who was both more and less than his legend." Publ Wkly
Includes bibliographical references

Lenin, Vladimir Il'ich, 1870-1924

Service, Robert. Lenin—a biography. Harvard Univ. Press 2000 xxv, 561p il maps $38.95; pa $19.95   **92**
ISBN 0-674-00330-6; 0-674-00828-6 (pa)
      LC 00-21394
This biography focuses "on Lenin the man. It draws on a wealth of new material to provide a subtle and complex portrait. . . . In particular, Service's account adds much to our knowledge of Lenin's early years and his final years as a man cut down by a series of strokes. . . . It is lucidly written, sharply observed, full of good sense, packed with vivid anecdote and, above all, succeeds—where so many have failed—in creating a Lenin who is believably human." Hist Today
Includes bibliographical references

Volkogonov, Dmitriĭ Antonovich. Lenin; a new biography; [by] Dmitri Volkogonov; translated and edited by Harold Shukman. Free Press 1994 xxxix, 529p il $30   **92**
ISBN 0-02-933435-7   LC 94-31752
A condensed English version of the two-volume Russian edition published in 1994

The author argues "that Lenin, far from having laid the foundations for a more liberal form of socialism, was the true progenitor of Stalinism; and . . . that in his personality and philosophy Lenin was hostile to the interests of Russia." Economist
"The author draws heavily on newly declassified KGB archives that he oversees as special assistant to President Boris Yeltsin. . . . Volkogonov's narrative is indispensable for understanding the Bolshevik coup, their crushing of the democratic opposition and the tragic aftermath." Publ Wkly
Includes bibliographical references

Leonardo, da Vinci, 1452-1519

Bramly, Serge. Leonardo; discovering the life of Leonardo da Vinci; translated by Siân Reynolds. HarperCollins Pubs. 1991 493p il o.p.; Penguin Bks. paperback available $24   **92**
ISBN 0-14-023175-7 (pa)   LC 90-56356
"An Edward Burlingame book"
Original French edition, 1988
In this account Bramly "sheds light on the more personal aspects of Leonardo. . . . As he follows da Vinci's often frustrating career and ever-widening sphere of inquiries, inventions, and discoveries, he also patches together overlooked clues about his private life, causing us to marvel anew at Leonardo's fertile and versatile mind while acquiring a sharper image of Leonardo the man. A richly detailed, expansive, and thoroughly enjoyable portrait." Booklist
Includes bibliographical references

Nuland, Sherwin B. Leonardo da Vinci. Viking 2000 170p il (Penguin lives series) $19.95   **92**
ISBN 0-670-89391-9   LC 00-32061
"Nuland devotes the first 120 pages . . . to Leonardo's pursuit of life as what we would call a scientist. The remaining 50 pages are focused specifically on his works as an anatomist. Nuland chronicles Leonardo's insights and mistakes and discusses his place in the history of anatomical studies." Libr J
"Nuland . . . elegantly sketches Leonardo's life of

Leonardo, da Vinci, 1452-1519—*Continued*

constant employment by noblemen eager to enjoy the prestige he reflected on them and of even more constant curiosity, which drove him to become the greatest anatomist before Vasari. . . . A scintillating addition." Booklist

White, Michael. Leonardo; the first scientist. St. Martin's Press 2000 370p il $27.95; pa $16.95   **92**
ISBN 0-312-20333-0; 0-312-27026-7 (pa)
The author "focuses on the scientific creations of da Vinci, emphasizing his notebooks, which had been lost for 200 years and only portions of which have been recovered. White describes how da Vinci's personal life affected his scientific discoveries and predictions, and vice versa." Booklist

Leonowens, Anna Harriette, 1834-1914

Landon, Margaret. Anna and the King of Siam; illustrated by Margaret Ayer. Harper & Row 1944 391p il map hardcover o.p. paperback available $14.95   **92**
1. Mongkut, King of Siam, 1804-1868 2. Thailand—Social life and customs
ISBN 0-06-095488-4 (pa)
Also available in hardcover from Buccaneer Bks.
Anna Leonowens' experiences at the Siamese court in the 1860's. From her experiences she wrote two books, "The English governess at the Siamese court," and "The romance of the harem." The author has put these two books into one story with additions to make a complete tale

Leopold, Aldo, 1886-1948

Lorbiecki, Marybeth. Aldo Leopold; a fierce green fire. Oxford Univ. Press 1999 212p il maps pa $16.95   **92**
ISBN 0-19-512966-0   LC 98-52349
A reissue of the title first published 1996 by Falcon
This is a biography of the conservationist "who developed the country's first wildlife management department at the University of Wisconsin in 1934." Sci Books Films
"Sufficient facts and context are provided to leave the reader informed yet not overburdened with detail. . . . This highly readable, lavishly illustrated biography is recommended for all environmental collections." Libr J
Includes bibliographical references

Lessing, Doris May, 1919-

Lessing, Doris May. Under my skin; volume one of my autobiography, to 1949; [by] Doris Lessing. HarperCollins Pubs. 1994 419p il hardcover o.p. paperback available $15   **92**
ISBN 0-06-092664-3 (pa)   LC 94-20051
This autobiography "covers the first 30 years of Doris Lessing's life, from her birth to British expatriate parents then living in Persia, through her girlhood growing up on a farm in Southern Rhodesia, up until 1949, the year she departed for England." Christ Sci Monit
"In this immediate, vivid, beautifully paced memoir, Doris Lessing sets the individual against history, the personal against the general, and shows, by the example of her own life set down honestly, how biography and fiction mesh, how fiction transmutes the personal to the general, how the particular experience illuminates the universe." London Rev Books

Levant, Oscar, 1906-1972

Kashner, Sam. A talent for genius: the life and times of Oscar Levant; [by] Sam Kashner and Nancy Schoenberger. Villard Bks. 1994 512p il o.p.; Silman-James Press paperback available $17.95   **92**
ISBN 1-879505-39-8 (pa)   LC 93-40647
The life and career of the celebrity "known for his quick wit, acerbic tongue, and neurotic disposition . . . . Kashner and Schoenberger painstakingly define the demons that stalked Levant throughout his life, creating a wonderfully illuminating portrait of this decidedly complex man." Booklist
Includes bibliographical references

Levi, Primo, 1919-1987

Angier, Carole. The double bond: Primo Levi, a biography. Farrar, Straus & Giroux 2002 xxvi, 898p il $40; pa $20   **92**
ISBN 0-374-11315-7; 0-374-52898-5 (pa)
This is a biography of the Italian Jewish chemist and writer. Levi was the author of The Periodic Table, Survival in Auschwitz, The Drowned and the Saved and Other People's Trades
"Angier's long, gripping narrative of Levi's time in Auschwitz synthesizes the best of his memoirs, poetry, fiction, essays, and scientific writing. . . . A compelling biography and a must for all Holocaust collections." Booklist
Includes bibliographical references

Anissimov, Myriam. Primo Levi; tragedy of an optimist. Overlook Press 1998 452p il $37.95; pa $18.95   **92**
1. Auschwitz (Poland: Concentration camp)
ISBN 0-87951-806-5; 1-58567-020-0 (pa)
    LC 97-9904
"A serious, lively, conscientiously researched biography of the distinguished Italian writer whose optimism and rationalism were not totally suppressed by his experience as an inmate of Auschwitz." N Y Times Book Rev
Includes bibliographical references

Levi, Primo. The periodic table; translated from the Italian by Raymond Rosenthal. Schocken Bks. 1984 233p hardcover o.p. paperback available $12   **92**
ISBN 0-8052-1041-5 (pa)   LC 84-5453
Available in hardcover from Random House
Original Italian edition, 1975
"This curious memoir, organized in 21 chapters from Argon to Zinc, ransacks the periodic table of the elements for strained metaphors as it traces one adolescent's search for identity. Levi ironically portrays himself as a young aspiring chemist eager to fathom nature's secrets." Publ Wkly

Lewis, C. S. (Clive Staples), 1898-1963

Downing, David C. The most reluctant convert: C. S. Lewis's journey to faith. InterVarsity Press 2002 191p $16   **92**
ISBN 0-8308-2311-5   LC 2001-51941
The author "traces Lewis' early life chronologically, discriminating its periods according to the state of Lewis' belief in God. . . . Drawing cogently upon Lewis' and his associates' writings and other recollections, Downing

Lewis, C. S. (Clive Staples), 1898-1963—
Continued
creates an intellectual biography that seizes and sustains interest as though it were a spellbinding suspense thriller." Booklist
Includes bibliographical references

Wilson, A. N. (Andrew Norman). C.S. Lewis; a biography. Norton 1990 334p il hardcover o.p. paperback available $15.95
                                                        92
ISBN 0-393-32340-4 (pa)   LC 89-27361
This biography "brings to light the most important episodes and aspects of Lewis' life: for instance, his curious and longstanding relationship with Janie ('Minto') Moore, his troubled friendship with J. R. R. Tolkien, his secret marriage to Joy Gresham, his conversion to Christianity, and his unending and increasingly subtle scrutiny of what it meant to be a Christian." Booklist
"The mixture presented in Wilson's biography of the life of learning, the college life at Magdalen where he taught, of domestic drama and bad temper, religion, and sex, is irresistible." N Y Rev Books
Includes bibliographical references

Lewis, Sinclair, 1885-1951
Lingeman, Richard R. Sinclair Lewis; rebel from Main Street; [by] Richard Lingeman. Random House 2002 xxiii, 659p il $35   **92**
ISBN 0-679-43823-8   LC 2001-19782
A biography of "America's first Nobel laureate in literature (1930), whose posthumous reputation has gone into undeserved decline." N Y Times Book Rev
Lingeman "succeeds in capturing the giddy, forward progression of Lewis's life, full of obsessions and accidents; it's only at the end that one realizes that one had finished a tragedy. Although relatively few readers may set out to read a life of Sinclair Lewis, this well-crafted biography holds many rewards for those who find it." Publ Wkly
Includes bibliographical references

Lin, Maya Ling
Lin, Maya Ying. Boundaries; [by] Maya Lin. Simon & Schuster 2000 unp il $40
                                                        92
ISBN 0-684-83417-0   LC 00-28026
"The designer of The Vietnam Veterans Memorial discusses her memorial building and how it had a profound impact on her maturity." Libr J

Lincoln, Abraham, 1809-1865
Donald, David Herbert. Lincoln. Simon & Schuster 1995 714p il maps hardcover o.p. paperback available $18   **92**
ISBN 0-684-82535-X   LC 95-4782
This biography examines: "Lincoln's relationship with his father; his romance with Ann Rutledge; his bouts of 'hypo,' which amounted at times almost to clinical depression; his marriage; his political ambition; his attitudes toward slavery and black people; his relations with radical Republicans during the Civil War; the mistakes and successes of his wartime leadership." Atl Mon
Includes bibliographical references

Miller, William Lee. Lincoln's virtues; an ethical biography. Knopf 2002 515p $32.50; pa $15   **92**
ISBN 0-375-40158-X; 0-375-70173-7 (pa)
                                   LC 2001-38099
The author's "project to chronicle man rather than myth is explicitly concerned with the evolution of Lincoln's character, motivations and ideals." Publ Wkly
"Miller delivers a still-enigmatic Lincoln, possessed of the steely but subtle personality that makes him one of the most, if not the most, read-about figures in history." Booklist
Includes bibliographical references

Morris, Jan. Lincoln, a foreigner's quest. Simon & Schuster 2000 205p o.p.; Da Capo Press paperback available $13.50   **92**
ISBN 0-306-81032-8 (pa)   LC 99-48516
This book conveys "through the narrative device of a travelog Morris's reflections about Abraham Lincoln, his America, and the nation he helped refashion in the crucible of war." Libr J
"A marvelously compressed and persuasive portrayal of this most iconic of American presidents." N Y Times Book Rev

Neely, Mark E., Jr. The last best hope of earth: Abraham Lincoln and the promise of America. Harvard Univ. Press 1993 214p il hardcover o.p. paperback available $17.95
                                                        92
ISBN 0-674-51126-3 (pa)   LC 93-22863
"Relying on the writings and speeches of Lincoln, Neely . . . has in effect composed a political biography. By using Lincoln's own words, he shows us the greatness, fears, and pettiness of the man. Intensely nationalistic, Lincoln had a strong faith in the Constitution and an intuitive understanding of our forefathers' ideas. Neely demonstrates Lincoln's grasp of military strategy, extension of presidential power, restrictions on civil liberties, and the realization that the Constitution would survive during the Civil War." Libr J
Includes bibliographical references

Sandburg, Carl. Abraham Lincoln: The prairie years and The war years. illustrated ed. Harcourt Brace Jovanovich 1970 c1954 640p il maps hardcover o.p. paperback available $26   **92**
1. Frontier and pioneer life 2. United States—History—1861-1865, Civil War
ISBN 0-15-602752-6 (pa)
First published 1954
A condensation of the two volumes of "The prairie years" (1926) and the four volumes of "The war years" (1939). The author has taken advantage of material made available since the original volumes were published to include in this edition of his lifetime study of Lincoln
"A biography that as a whole is superior to the longer life. This one volume has a form which the six lacked. It is a tighter and tidier book. It retains the superb qualities of the original work without the faults of the latter." Saturday Rev
Includes bibliographical references

Lincoln, Mary Todd, 1818-1882

Baker, Jean H. Mary Todd Lincoln; a biography. Norton 1987 429p il hardcover o.p. paperback available $17.95   **92**

ISBN 0-393-30586-4 (pa)   LC 86-23757

The author "portrays Mrs. Lincoln as a woman tortured by a series of family bereavements and thwarted from developing her natural talents by a patriarchal society that branded as 'unwomanly' her involvement in her husband's political career. Ms. Baker establishes her first argument with a lengthy investigation of Mary Todd's early family history in Lexington, Ky., and sustains the second by enlarging upon such topics as 19th-century domesticity, childbirth, mourning customs, spiritualism and America's deplorable insanity laws." NY Times Book Rev

Includes bibliographical references

Lindbergh, Anne Morrow, 1906-2001

Hertog, Susan. Anne Morrow Lindbergh; a biography. Talese 1999 561p il hardcover o.p. paperback available $17   **92**

ISBN 0-385-72007-6 (pa)   LC 99-28759

After her marriage to Charles Lindbergh, Anne Morrow "soon recognized the difficulty of reconciling her literary ambitions with accompanying her husband as copilot, navigator and radio operator. After the tragic kidnapping and death of their first child, which they blamed in part on dogged press coverage of their personal life, the Lindberghs moved abroad. They became embroiled with the leaders of Nazi Germany, according to Hertog, because Charles believed that the democratic system was weak and ineffectual. . . . This sympathetic portrayal of Anne as a wife, mother, poet and feminist may well find a readership more interested in a talented woman's creative struggle than in the oft-told Lindbergh story." Publ Wkly

Includes bibliographical references

Lindbergh, Reeve. No more words: a journal of my mother, Anne Morrow Lindbergh. Simon & Schuster 2001 174p $24; pa $12   **92**

ISBN 0-7432-0313-5; 0-7432-0314-3 (pa)
     LC 2001-49196

"Challenged by the perils of old age and a series of strokes, Mrs. Lindbergh made her final home on a farm in Vermont, in a house adjacent to her daughter's. . . . Her retreat into silence and varying stages of dementia distressed Reeve, who longed to communicate with her once eloquent mother. Reeve writes fluidly about her mother's fading, expressing herself poignantly and posing powerful questions about life, death, and the depth of silence." Booklist

Lindbergh, Reeve. Under a wing. See entry under Lindbergh, Charles, 1902-1974   **92**

Lindbergh, Charles, 1902-1974

Berg, A. Scott (Andrew Scott). Lindbergh. Putnam 1998 628p il $30; pa $16   **92**

1. Air pilots

ISBN 0-399-14449-8; 0-425-17041-1 (pa)
     LC 98-18548

"The first biographer to be granted unfettered access to Lindbergh's private papers, Berg provides enough fresh detail to trace the roots of Lindbergh's personality, its strengths as well as its maddening flaws, all the way back to his turbulent boyhood." N Y Times Book Rev

Lindbergh, Reeve. Under a wing; a memoir. Simon & Schuster 1998 223p il o.p.; Delta Bks. paperback available $13.95   **92**

1. Lindbergh, Anne Morrow, 1906-2001

ISBN 0-385-33444-3 (pa)   LC 98-30111

From the "perspective of a woman in her early fifties, the youngest child of aviator and American hero Charles Lindbergh and beloved writer Anne Morrow Lindbergh tellingly reflects on the foibles, as well as the strength of character of those two well-known figures." Booklist

"A rare memoir whose goal is not to expose but finally to understand." Libr J

Linné, Carl von, 1707-1778

Blunt, Wilfrid. Linnaeus, the compleat naturalist; with an introduction by William T. Stearn. Princeton Univ. Press 2002 264p il maps $35   **92**

ISBN 0-691-09636-8

First published 1971 by Viking with title: The compleat naturalist: a life of Linnaeus

This biography traces the Swedish scientist's life from his days as a poor student at Lund University through his scientific achievements and academic career at Uppsala

Includes bibliographical references

Lively, Penelope, 1933-

Lively, Penelope. A house unlocked. Grove Press 2002 c2001 225p il $23; pa $13   **92**

ISBN 0-8021-1712-0; 0-8021-4007-6 (pa)
     LC 2001-55745

First published 2001 in the United Kingdom

"The British novelist Penelope Lively spent her early childhood in Egypt, but it was her school holidays at Golsoncott—a manor house that her grandparents bought in the wilds of Somerset, in 1923—that shaped her life. In this slim, beguiling book, Lively describes the contents and customs of the house. . . . By meticulously tracing the provenance of these objects, she re-creates the life they once furnished." New Yorker

Includes bibliographical references

Livingstone, David, 1813-1873

Dugard, Martin. Into Africa; the epic adventures of Stanley & Livingstone. Doubleday 2003 340p il maps $24.95   **92**

1. Stanley, Henry M. (Henry Morton), 1841-1904

ISBN 0-385-50451-9   LC 2002-31374

This is a "history focusing on the famous meeting of Dr. David Livingstone and Henry Morton Stanley in east Africa. . . . Dugard details how the expeditions were conceived and equipped, the land through which they traveled, the tribes they encountered, the horrific evidence of the slave trade, and the myriad dangers experienced, such as sleeping sickness, malaria, carnivorous animals, snakes, war, hunger, and dehydration. Following the two men's journeys in alternating chapters, Dugard offers a text that is lively, enthralling, and informative." Libr J

Includes bibliographical references

Lloyd Webber, Andrew, 1948-

Citron, Stephen. Sondheim and Lloyd-Webber. See entry under Sondheim, Stephen   **92**

Lombardi, Vince

Maraniss, David. When pride still mattered: a life of Vince Lombardi. Simon & Schuster 1999 541p il hardcover o.p. paperback available $16 **92**

ISBN 0-684-77018-5 (pa) LC 99-37859

"From Lombardi's formative years as a player and coach at Fordham University through assistantships with West Point and the Giants and, finally, to his tenure as head coach of the Packers, Maraniss presents a portrait of a complicated human being who was a great teacher but a mediocre listener, an effective psychologist despite being rife with flaws." Publ Wkly

Includes bibliographical references

Long, Huey Pierce, 1893-1935

Hair, William Ivy. The Kingfish and his realm: the life and times of Huey P. Long. Louisiana State Univ. Press 1991 406p il map hardcover o.p. paperback available $21.95 **92**

1. Louisiana—Politics and government
ISBN 0-8071-2124-X (pa) LC 91-18546

This is a biography of the man who was governor of Louisiana from 1928 to 1932 and senator from 1932 until his assassination in 1935

"Written with passion and mordant wit, the book is literally hard to put down; the Kingfish seems to stimulate good writing. Overall, [this] is one of the more convincing negative biographies of recent years." Rev Am Hist

Includes bibliographical references

Loomis, Alfred Lee, 1887-1975

Conant, Jennet. Tuxedo Park; a Wall Street tycoon and the secret palace of science that changed the course of World War II. Simon & Schuster 2002 330p il $26; pa $14 **92**

1. Atomic bomb
ISBN 0-684-87287-0; 0-684-87288-9 (pa)
LC 2002-21001

Also available Thorndike Press large print edition

In 1928 Alfred Loomis, a wealthy financier and amateur physicist, "established a premier research facility in Tuxedo Park, N.Y., that attracted such brilliant minds as Einstein, Bohr and Fermi and became instrumental in the Allies' WWII victory. Conant . . . draws on studies, family papers and interviews with Loomis's friends, family and colleagues . . . to trace the story of the tycoon's professional and social life." Publ Wkly

"Conant displays a real feel for the personal lives and sensibilities of the era's leading scientists and industrialists in a fascinating, never-before-told bit of American history." Booklist

Includes bibliographical references

Lowell, Robert, 1917-1977

Mariani, Paul L. Lost puritan: a life of Robert Lowell. Norton 1994 527p il hardcover o.p. paperback available $15 **92**

ISBN 0-393-31374-3 (pa) LC 93-48018

This biography "of a protean confessional poet uses letters and diaries to reveal a writer whose fascination with preachers, statesmen and generals hints at restlessness with his own art." N Y Times Book Rev

"Mariani, for all his moment-by-moment acuteness and lucidity, offers no radically new insights into Lowell's life or art, nor does he provide those powerfully developed thematic and narrative lines that distinguish the greatest literary biographies. Still, this remains an impressive piece of writing and documentation." Choice

Luce, Clare Boothe, 1903-1987

Morris, Sylvia Jukes. Rage for fame: the ascent of Clare Boothe Luce. Random House 1997 561p il hardcover o.p. paperback available $27 **92**

ISBN 0-8129-9249-0 (pa) LC 96-43084

This first of a projected two-volume biography "describes how the future congresswoman and second wife of *Time* magazine founder Henry Luce, bedded her way upward while career-climbing in New York journalism and writing a stage mega-hit, *The Women*. . . . By 1942—at age 39—she turned to politics and was elected a Republican representative from Connecticut." Publ Wkly

Includes bibliographical references

Luther, Martin, 1483-1546

Bainton, Roland Herbert. Here I stand: a life of Martin Luther. Abingdon Press 1950 422p il music hardcover o.p. paperback available $7 **92**

1. Europe—Church history 2. Reformation
ISBN 0-687-16895-3 (pa)

Also available paperback from NAL/Dutton

This biography of Martin Luther interprets his work, writings, and lasting contributions. It recreates the spiritual setting of the sixteenth century and shows Luther's place within it

Includes bibliographical references

Erikson, Erik H. (Erik Homburger). Young man Luther; a study in psychoanalysis and history. Norton 1958 hardcover o.p. paperback available $13.95 **92**

ISBN 0-393-31036-1 (pa)

"This study of Martin Luther as a young man was planned as a chapter in a book on emotional crises in late adolescence and early adulthood. But Luther proved too bulky a man to be merely a chapter." Preface

Oberman, Heiko Augustinus. Luther: man between God and the Devil; [by] Heiko A. Oberman; translated by Eileen Walliser-Schwarzbart. Yale Univ. Press 1990 c1989 xx, 380p il o.p.; Doubleday paperback available $16.95 **92**

1. Europe—Church history 2. Reformation
ISBN 0-385-42278-4 (pa) LC 89-5747

Original German edition, 1982

The author "posits that to understand Luther the reformer is to first realize he was a medieval man for whom Satan was as real as God and human. By placing Luther back into the context of his own age, Oberman strips away any simplistic, post-Enlightenment notions of Luther as the savior of humanity from the darkest obscurantism of the Catholic Church. . . . A triumph of scholarship that brings Luther to life in all of his furious, outspoken, and violent passion." Booklist

Includes bibliographical references

Lynn, Loretta

Lynn, Loretta. Loretta Lynn: coal miner's daughter; [by] Loretta Lynn with George Vecsey. Da Capo Press 1996 204p il pa $16 **92**

ISBN 0-306-80680-0 LC 95-46394

"A Bernard Geis Associates book"

Lynn, Loretta—*Continued*

First published 1976 by Regnery

The author "tells in her own words of her youth in Butcher Holler, Kentucky, her marriage at 14 to Doolittle 'Mooney' Lynn, being a grandmother at age 29, and her rise to country music's Best Female Vocalist. . . . The book seems an honest account of her career and marriage." Libr J

Lynn, Loretta. Still woman enough; a memoir; [by] Loretta Lynn with Patsi Bale Cox. Hyperion 2002 244p il $24.95; pa $7.99
92

ISBN 0-7868-6650-0; 0-7868-8987-X (pa)

Also available Thorndike Press large print edition

In this sequel to Coal miner's daughter, "Lynn mostly focuses on her marriage and the trials and pleasures of Nashville stardom, including fond recollections of friends like Conway Twitty and Tammy Wynette. . . . Though her grammar may make purists flinch . . . Lynn's literary voice is as natural and endearing as her songs." Publ Wkly

MacCready, Paul B.

Ciotti, Paul. More with less; Paul MacCready and the dream of efficient flight. Encounter Bks. 2002 259p il $26.95; pa $16.95
92

ISBN 1-89355-450-3; 1-89355-490-2 (pa)
LC 2002-72464

This is a "biography of MacCready, who built not only the Gossamer Condor, an award-winning man-powered plane, but also solar-powered planes and cars. . . . [The author] traces the sources of MacCready's inspiration and describes the community of maverick engineers and designers concentrated in Southern California (where MacCready worked). Threaded through the book are interviews with MacCready himself, who continues to work today and is particularly interested in renewable-resource technology." Publ Wkly

Includes bibliographical references

Machiavelli, Niccolò, 1469-1527

Viroli, Maurizio. Niccolò's smile: a biography of Machiavelli; translated from the Italian by Antony Shugaar. Farrar, Straus & Giroux 2000 271p maps hardcover o.p. paperback available $13
92

ISBN 0-374-52800-4 (pa)
LC 00-29380

This biography of the Italian political philosopher traces his life "from respected secretary of the Florentine republic, dispatched on crucial diplomatic missions to Europe's most illustrious courts, to forgotten commoner. . . . Viroli provides a detailed, historical background for Machiavelli's personal triumphs and woes. But the strength of this work lies in his ceaseless concentration on Machiavelli the man, who comes alive on each page." Publ Wkly

Includes bibliographical references

MacLaine, Shirley

MacLaine, Shirley. The Camino; a journey of the spirit. Pocket Bks. 2000 307p hardcover o.p. paperback available $13.95
92

ISBN 0-7434-0073-9 (pa)
LC 00-28347

"Following a centuries-old tradition, entertainer MacLaine walked nearly 500 miles across northern

Spain's Camino Santiago de Compostela. . . . An effort to 'feel human again,' her physical feat was daunting: she hiked for 10 hours a day on her own, often in intense heat, and slept in *refugios*—crowded, dirty shelters. Though she observes the small villages, historic cathedrals and other trekkers along the way, MacLaine is most interested in her interior journey." Publ Wkly

MacLeish, Archibald, 1892-1982

MacLeish, Archibald. Archibald MacLeish: reflections; edited by Bernard A. Drabeck and Helen E. Ellis; foreword by Richard Wilbur. University of Mass. Press 1986 291p il $40; pa $18.95
92

ISBN 0-87023-511-7; 0-87023-623-7 (pa)
LC 85-28912

"In these long interviews, conducted during the last five years of his life, a noted writer talks about his professional life as a poet, playwright, lawyer, editor of 'Fortune,' Librarian of Congress and Harvard professor." Publ Wkly

"In this genial, relaxed book we have a golden view of the candidly retrospective statesman-poet in his old age as he really was, with most pretension and all rhetoric abandoned." N Y Times Book Rev

Includes bibliographical references

Madison, James, 1751-1836

Wills, Garry. James Madison. Times Bks. 2002 xx, 184p (American presidents series) $20
92

ISBN 0-8050-6905-4
LC 2002-19692

The author "maintains that Madison possessed qualities that served him well early in his career but proved to be a handicap during his Presidency. . . . Written with flair, this clear and balanced account is based on a sure handling of the material." Libr J

Mah, Adeline Yen, 1937-

Mah, Adeline Yen. Falling leaves; a true story of an unwanted Chinese daughter. Wiley 1998 278p il $22.95
92

ISBN 0-471-24742-1
LC 97-40144

Also available in paperback from Broadway Bks.

First published 1997 in the United Kindgom with title: Falling leaves return to their roots

"Although the focus of this memoir is the author's struggle to be loved by a family that treated her cruelly, it is more notable for its portrait of the domestic affairs of an immensely wealthy, Westernized Chinese family in Shanghai as the city evolved under the harsh strictures of Mao and Deng. . . . In recounting this painful tale, Yen Mah's unadorned prose is powerful, her insights keen and her portrait of her family devastating." Publ Wkly

Maḥfūẓ, Najīb, 1912-

Maḥfūẓ, Najīb. Echoes of an autobiography; [by] Naguib Mahfouz; translated by Denys Johnson-Davies. Doubleday 1997 118p hardcover o.p. paperback available $12
92

ISBN 0-385-48556-5 (pa)
LC 96-12386

Originally serialized 1994 in an Arabic newspaper

"Mahfouz's first nonfiction book to be published in English, this mosaic of autobiographical vignettes, reflections, allegories, childhood memories, dream visions and Sufi-like spiritual maxims and paradoxes is a deep pool of wisdom that confirms his stature as a writer of universal appeal." Publ Wkly

Mailer, Norman

Dearborn, Mary V. Mailer; a biography. Houghton Mifflin 1999 478p il $30; pa $15
92

ISBN 0-395-73655-2; 0-618-15460-4 (pa)

LC 99-32214

"Dearborn supplies a close reading of one of the most controversial American writers of the postwar era. Mailer's body of work, beginning with his career-defining first novel, *The Naked and the Dead* (1948), is analyzed with remarkable insight. Mailer's notorious personal life is also examined, as Dearborn sorts through the various preoccupations that have obsessed the writer over five decades in the literary spotlight." Booklist

Includes bibliographical references

Malcolm X, 1925-1965

Carson, Clayborne. Malcolm X: the FBI file; introduction by Spike Lee; edited by David Gallen. Carroll & Graf Pubs. 1991 514p il hardcover o.p. paperback available $13.95
92

ISBN 0-88184-758-5 (pa)   LC 91-26697

"This is a collection of declassified documents from the FBI surveillance of the orator and religious (later political) leader that, with historian Carson's studious commentary, focuses less on Malcolm's relation to the FBI and more on that to the larger civil rights movement. These excerpts . . . follow his travels and speeches, media interviews and FBI interviews, oftentimes including transcripts as written or summarized by Gallen and Carson." Booklist

Malcolm X. The autobiography of Malcolm X; with the assistance of Alex Haley; introduction by M. S. Handler; epilogue by Alex Haley; afterword by Ossie Davis. Ballantine Bks. 1992 500p $25.95; pa $15
92

1. Black Muslims
ISBN 0-345-37975-6; 0-345-37671-4 (pa)

LC 92-52659

Also available in hardcover from Amereon

First published 1965 by Grove Press

Based on tape-recorded conversations with Alex Haley, this account of the life of the Black Muslim leader was completed shortly before his murder

Alex Haley "did his job with sensitivity and with devotion. . . . [The book] will have a permanent place in the literature of the Afro-American struggle." N Y Rev Books

The Malcolm X encyclopedia; edited by Robert L. Jenkins, co-edited by Mfanya Donald Tryman. Greenwood Press 2002 643p il $74.95
92

ISBN 0-313-29264-7   LC 2001-23318

"The major section of the volume consists of 500 essays that create a cross-disciplinary, textured description of the man, his life, his times, and events. . . . Topics include *African nationalism, Civil rights movement, Police brutality, Socialism*, and *White liberals*, among others. Also included are a detailed chronology as well as several thematic essays that provide a framework for the entries that follow. . . . All encyclopedia entries have a short bibliography, but there is an extensive bibliography of books, articles, newspapers, electronic resources, and oral interviews included as a separate section in the vol-

ume. . . . The encyclopedia would add a first-stop resource for library users seeking information on this important figure of contemporary American history." Booklist

Perry, Bruce. Malcolm; the life of a man who changed black America. Station Hill Press 1991 542p il hardcover o.p. paperback available $14.95
92

ISBN 0-88268-121-4 (pa)   LC 90-23350

"Perry traces Malcolm X's footsteps from birth in 1925 to death in 1965, using several hundred interviews to fill in detail and correct the autobiography Alex Haley edited. Probing what he labels as the deep-seated and hidden causes that made Malcolm who and what he was, Perry produces a portrait of an emotionally abused and abandoned boy who grew to manipulate his fearful helplessness into emotional and political power." Libr J

Includes bibliographical references

Mandela, Nelson

Mandela, Nelson. Long walk to freedom: the autobiography of Nelson Mandela. Little, Brown 1994 558p il hardcover o.p. paperback available $16.95
92

1. South Africa—Politics and government
ISBN 0-316-54818-9 (pa)   LC 94-79980

This is an account of Nelson "Mandela's life from his 'country childhood' following his birth on July 18, 1918 to his inauguration as president of South Africa on May 10, 1994." Libr J

This book "provides important new evidence to the forty-year story of apartheid, as seen by its most formidable opponent. And there is enough candour to provide insights into the nature of leadership." Times Lit Suppl

Mandela, Nelson. Mandela; an illustrated autobiography. Little, Brown 1996 208p il map $29.95
92

1. South Africa—Politics and government
ISBN 0-316-55038-8   LC 96-77497

"This is an illustrated and abridged edition of Long walk to freedom: the autobiography of Nelson Mandela." Verso of title page

"The photos, from a variety of archives and journalistic sources, ably illustrate Mandela and, even more so, the South Africa around him." Libr J

Sampson, Anthony. Nelson Mandela; the authorized biography. Knopf 1999 xxvi, 672p hardcover o.p. paperback available $19   **92**

1. South Africa—Politics and government
ISBN 0-679-78178-1 (pa)   LC 99-18498

Sampson traces "the course of Nelson Mandela's life, from his birth in 1918 in the Transkei region of South Africa, to his retirement from the presidency in 1999, at the end of his first and only term." Commonweal

"While not neglecting the personality of the man, Mr. Sampson has concentrated on the politics, and, for an authorised life, it can be treated as definitive." Economist

Includes bibliographical references

Manet, Édouard, 1832-1883

Brombert, Beth Archer. Edouard Manet; rebel in a frock coat. Little, Brown 1995 xxii, 505p il o.p.; University of Chicago Press paperback available $19.95 **92**

ISBN 0-226-07544-3 (pa)   LC 94-45881

This biography of the French painter discusses "Manet's world and the importance of 19th-century Paris to the formation of Manet's personal and artistic life." Libr J

"To recount Manet's life, as Brombert has done in this elegant biography, is to tell the story of an enormously influential artist struggling to paint what he called 'the spirit of contemporaneity' while remaining committed to the conservative institutions of civil life—the very same institutions that shunned him." New Yorker

Mankiller, Wilma

Mankiller, Wilma. Mankiller: a chief and her people; [by] Wilma Mankiller and Michael Wallis. St. Martin's Press 1993 xxiv, 292p il hardcover o.p. paperback available $14.95 **92**

1. Cherokee Indians
ISBN 0-312-20662-3 (pa)   LC 93-25698

This "account of the first woman principal chief of the Cherokee Nation describes . . . [her] childhood spent on an allotment farm in Mankiller Flat, Oklahoma, her teenage years in the 1960s as an 'urban Indian,' a near brush with death, and a life of solid accomplishment in service and tribal leadership rooted in Cherokee culture." Libr J

"A must-read for everyone interested in, specifically, the history of Native Americans and women and, in general, tales of exceptional people." Booklist

Mann, Thomas, 1875-1955

Heilbut, Anthony. Thomas Mann; eros and literature. Knopf 1995 636p il o.p.; University of Calif. Press paperback available $19.95 **92**

ISBN 0-520-20911-7 (pa)   LC 94-37034

"This biography covers Mann's life and work up to his late fifties, the period succeeding The Magic Mountain. . . . A postscript covers his years in America and his final return to Europe." Introduction

"Heilbut's breezy, impressionistic book—not so much a biography as a free-ranging thematic essay—will be controversial for its insistent concentration on sexuality. Mann is presented, more or less, as an author of homoerotic fiction." New Yorker

Includes bibliographical references

Kurzke, Hermann. Thomas Mann; life as a work of art: a biography; translated by Leslie Willson. Princeton Univ. Press 2002 581p il $35 **92**

ISBN 0-691-07069-5   LC 2002-23665

This biography of the German author focuses on "Mann's homosexuality, his relations to Jews and Judaism, the canny construction of the persona of Great Author, and how Mann transformed everything around him into art." Libr J

"A major achievement in literary biography." Booklist

Mao Zedong, 1893-1976

Short, Philip. Mao; a life. Holt & Co. 2000 782p il maps hardcover o.p. paperback available $20 **92**

1. China—Politics and government
ISBN 0-8050-6638-1 (pa)   LC 99-41839
"A John Macrae book"

This biography "takes Mao from his 1893 birth in the village of Shaoshan to school in Changsha, where he trained to be a teacher, and then into revolutionary activity, the long fight with Chiang Kai-shek, and leadership of the most populous nation on Earth." Booklist

Includes bibliographical references

Spence, Jonathan D. Mao Zedong; [by] Jonathan Spence. Viking 1999 188p map (Penguin lives series) $19.95 **92**

1. China—Politics and government
ISBN 0-670-88669-6   LC 99-27739
"A Lipper/Viking book"

"This specialist's book for nonspecialists concisely recounts the life of the Communist leader who revolutionized China. Ideas travel fast: Mao, a peasant son born in 1893, was able to read Darwin and Marx in translation and add Western ideas to his heritage of classical Chinese thought, and Spence helps us understand why he eventually embraced Communism. What is less clear is why a gifted, high-minded youth became a ruthless, crackpot tyrant." New Yorker

Includes bibliographical references

Maria Celeste, 1600-1634

Sobel, Dava. Galileo's daughter; a historical memoir of science, faith, and love. Walker & Co. 1999 420p $27 **92**

1. Galilei, Galileo, 1564-1642
ISBN 0-8027-1343-2   LC 99-23885
Also available in paperback from Penguin Bks.

This book "is organized around a series of letters that Suor Maria Celeste wrote to Galileo from May 1623, when Galileo was 59 and already celebrated throughout Europe, until April 1634, when she died of dysentary. . . . For the most part they deal with the daughter's concern for her father's constant illnesses and difficulties with his enemies, expressions of love and devotion, requests for money, details of the brutally spare life in the convent of San Matteo and routine household matters while Galileo was on trial in Rome." N Y Times Book Rev

"Sobel has a remarkable ability to explain technical subjects without being simplistic or pedantic. There is a tremendous amount of fascinating detail in this work, and yet it reads as smoothly and compellingly as fiction." Libr J

Includes bibliographical references

Marie Antoinette, Queen, consort of Louis XVI, King of France, 1755-1793

Fraser, Antonia. Marie Antoinette; the journey. Talese 2001 xxii, 512p il $35; pa $16.95 **92**

1. France—History—1589-1789, Bourbons
ISBN 0-385-48948-X; 0-385-48949-8 (pa)
    LC 2001-23493
Also available Thorndike Press large print edition

The author portrays the Austrian-born Queen consort of Louis XVI of France as "neither heroine nor villain, but a young wife and mother who, in her journey into maturity, finds herself caught in a deadly vise." Publ

Marie Antoinette, Queen, consort of Louis XVI, King of France, 1755-1793—*Continued*

Wkly
"A well-researched biography that may cause one to rethink the role in which history has cast Marie Antoinette." Libr J
Includes bibliographical references

Lever, Evelyne. Marie Antoinette; the last queen of France; translated from the French by Catherine Temerson. Farrar, Straus & Giroux 2000 357p il hardcover o.p. paperback available $16.95   **92**
   1. France—History—1589-1789, Bourbons
   ISBN 0-312-28333-4 (pa)   LC 00-28763
   The author examines "the opulent Versailles subculture and the queen whose royal excesses served as a major catalyst for the revolutionary upheaval of 1789. Through the skillful use of memoirs and other primary documents, Lever creates an empathic picture of Louis XVI's headstrong wife." Libr J
   Includes bibliographical references

Marion, Frances, d. 1973

Beauchamp, Cari. Without lying down; Frances Marion and the powerful women of early Hollywood. University of Calif. Press 1997 475p il pa $19.95   **92**
   ISBN 0-520-21492-7   LC 97-44800
   First published 1997 in hardcover by Scribner
   "From 1916 to 1946, Frances Marion was the highest-paid screenwriter in Hollywood. She wrote hundreds of scripts. . . . She won two Academy Awards. . . . Beauchamp pored over unpublished manuscripts, diaries, appointment books, letters, and studio contracts for this extremely well documented biography, which will delight movie fans with its insider's view of early Hollywood." Booklist
   Includes filmography and bibliographical references

Markham, Beryl, 1902-1986

Trzebinski, Errol. The lives of Beryl Markham; Out of Africa's hidden free spirit and Denys Finch Hatton's last great love. Norton 1993 396p il maps hardcover o.p. paperback available $12   **92**
   ISBN 0-393-31252-6 (pa)   LC 93-9919
   This is a biography of the aviator who was the first woman to fly solo across the Atlantic. "Markham was born in 1902 to British parents and grew up on her father's farm in Kenya." Libr J
   The author offers "confirmation of the rumor that Beryl's third husband actually wrote her best-selling memoir, West with the Night." Booklist
   Includes bibliographical references

Marlborough, Sarah Jennings Churchill, Duchess of, 1660-1744

Field, Ophelia. Sarah Churchill, Duchess of Marlborough; the queen's favourite. St. Martin's Press 2003 560p il $35   **92**
   ISBN 0-312-31466-3   LC 2003-46543
   "Sarah's intimate relationship with Queen Anne serves as the natural centerpiece of this biography. One of the queen's most favored companions for a great number of years, Sarah . . . used any backdoor source available to

her as a woman to wield social, political, and economic power in a man's world. Married to one of England's greatest generals, she exploited whatever and whomever possible in order to advance the Whig party or to increase her already immense fortune. . . . Field paints a fascinating portrait of an influential woman." Booklist
Includes bibliographical references

Marlowe, Christopher, 1564-1593

Nicholl, Charles. The reckoning: the murder of Christopher Marlowe. Harcourt Brace & Co. 1994 c1992 413p il o.p.; University of Chicago Press paperback available $17   **92**
   1. Great Britain—History—1485-1603, Tudors
   ISBN 0-226-58024-5 (pa)   LC 94-138154
   First published 1992 in the United Kingdom
   The author argues that the Elizabethan playwright, who is believed to have been stabbed in a dispute over the bill ('recknynge') at Eleanor Bull's victualling house in 1593, was in fact murdered with government complicity as part of a plot against Sir Walter Raleigh
   "A remarkable piece of scholarship, this work carefully reconstructs the events leading up to the murder with all the excitement and suspense of a modern mystery novel; at the same time it vividly conveys the energy and color of Elizabethan England." Libr J
   Includes bibliographical references

Marshall, John, 1755-1835

Smith, Jean Edward. John Marshall; definer of a nation. Holt & Co. 1996 736p il hardcover o.p. paperback available $22   **92**
   ISBN 0-8050-5510-X (pa)   LC 96-15072
   "A Marian Wood book"
   Smith presents a "portrait of the most significant and influential jurist in U.S. history. Appointed chief justice of the Supreme Court in 1801, John Marshall, farmer, soldier, lawyer, diplomatic envoy, and politician, served as the nation's premier legal authority and moral barometer for 35 years." Booklist
   "Mr. Smith's splendid biography deserves a large readership mostly because it has recovered Marshall the man." N Y Times Book Rev
   Includes bibliographical references

Marshall, Thurgood

Ball, Howard. A defiant life: Thurgood Marshall and the persistence of racism in America. Crown 1999 428p il hardcover o.p. paperback available $23   **92**
   1. African Americans—Civil rights
   ISBN 0-676-80666-X (pa)   LC 98-23031
   "Ball parallels Marshall's personal life with the Supreme Court cases he judged, providing operational context, both on and off the bench, for Marshall's quest for racial and civil justice. This book is an invaluable read for those interested in U.S. social and legal history." Booklist

Marshall, Thurgood—*Continued*

Marshall, Thurgood. Thurgood Marshall; his speeches, writings, arguments, opinions, and reminiscences; edited by Mark Tushnet; foreword by Randall Kennedy. Hill Bks. 2001 xxvi, 548p (Library of Black America) $40; pa $24.95 **92**
1. African Americans—Civil rights
ISBN 1-55652-385-8; 1-55652-386-6 (pa)
LC 2001-16793

This is a collection of speeches and writings by the first African American member of the U.S. Supreme Court

"In a career ranging from his trial and appellate work for the NAACP to his tenure as an associate justice of the Court, Marshall wrought revolutionary changes in U.S. law and politics, and this collection of his legal briefs, writings, speeches, and judicial opinions, plus a never-before-published oral interview, gives us a superior analysis of the advocate, the democrat, the dissenter, and the unflagging fighter for equality." Libr J

Includes bibliographical references

Rowan, Carl Thomas. Dream makers, dream breakers: the world of Justice Thurgood Marshall; [by] Carl T. Rowan. Little, Brown 1993 475p il o.p.; Welcome Rain paperback available $18.95 **92**
1. United States. Supreme Court
ISBN 1-56649-235-1 (pa)
LC 92-29892

The author "offers a no-holds barred account of one of the most influential and controversial figures in American law and jurisprudence of this century. His work brings to life Marshall, the Surprene Court, U.S. law and modern America itself. Particularly effective is Rowan's account of the innovative legal arguments Marshall and his colleagues employed to win the now-famous *Brown v. Board of Education* case of 1954." Libr J

Includes bibliographical references

Williams, Juan. Thurgood Marshall; American revolutionary. Times Bks. 1998 459p il hardcover o.p. paperback available $16 **92**
1. United States. Supreme Court
ISBN 0-8129-3299-4 (pa)
LC 98-9735

"Williams presents Marshall as a revolutionary 'of grand vision,' but this well-rounded portrait of the man also addresses his vanities and warts, from his ascension to his deflation and subsequent redemption. This is a must read for all Americans concerned with the struggle for civil and individual rights." Booklist

Marx, Groucho, 1891-1977

Kanfer, Stefan. Groucho: the life and times of Julius Henry Marx. Knopf 2000 465p il hardcover o.p. paperback available $15 **92**
ISBN 0-375-70207-5 (pa)
LC 99-54002

"Plagued by nagging financial insecurities, partly realized literary ambitions, and difficult, unsatisfying relations with his wives, lovers, and daughters, Groucho was a 'depressive clown,' notes Kanter. . . . The book also details Groucho's ambivalent relations with his son, Arthur; his brothers; New Deal liberals; intellectuals and collaborators like S. J. Perelman; and his custodian, Erin Fleming." Libr J

Includes bibliographical references

Marx, Karl, 1818-1883

Wheen, Francis. Karl Marx; a life. Norton 2000 431p il $27.95; pa $14.95 **92**
1. Communism
ISBN 0-393-04923-X; 0-393-32157-6 (pa)
LC 99-87466

First published 1999 in the United Kingdom

"Following Marx from his childhood in Trier, Germany, through his exile in London, Wheen . . . takes readers from hovel to grand house, from the International Working Man's Association to *Capital*, from obscurity to notoriety and back again." Publ Wkly

Includes bibliographical references

Mary, Queen of Scots, 1542-1587

Fraser, Antonia. Mary Queen of Scots. illustrated abridged ed. Delacorte Press 1978 208p il hardcover o.p. paperback available $19.95 **92**
1. Great Britain—History—1485-1603, Tudors
2. Scotland—History—16th century
ISBN 0-380-31129-X (pa)
LC 78-703

A condensation of the title first published 1969

A look at the tragic life of Mary Stuart, the 16th century Catholic ruler of Protestant Scotland, and her incessant struggle with political and religious opponents

Includes bibliographical references

Weir, Alison. Mary, Queen of Scots, and the murder of Lord Darnley. Ballantine Bks. 2003 670p il map $27.95; pa $16.95 **92**
1. Darnley, Henry Stewart, Lord, 1545-1567 2. Scotland—History—16th century
ISBN 0-345-43658-X; 0-8129-7151-5 (pa)
LC 2002-34467

The author "sets out to prove that contrary to supposition Mary, Queen of Scots, was innocent of the murder of her husband, Lord Darnley." Libr J

"No stone is left unturned in {Weir's} investigation, and despite its detail, her book is as dramatic as witnessing firsthand the most riveting court case." Booklist

Mather, Increase, 1639-1723

Hall, Michael G. (Michael Garibaldi). The last American Puritan: the life of Increase Mather, 1639-1723. Wesleyan Univ. Press 1988 438p il maps hardcover o.p. paperback available $29.95 **92**
1. Puritans
ISBN 0-8195-6238-6 (pa)
LC 87-7367

This "biography of an important colonial clergyman is based on a thorough mastery of primary sources. In addition to serving as Harvard's president, Mather was active in politics and religion, and he demonstrated an active interest in science. Since Mather was a prolific author as well, his life can serve to document the intellectual history of his generation." Libr J

Includes bibliographical references

Matisse, Henri

Spurling, Hilary. The unknown Matisse; a life of Henri Matisse. v1: The early years, 1869-1908. Knopf 1998 xxv, 480p il $40 **92**

ISBN 0-679-43428-3
LC 97-46816

Also available in paperback from University of Calif. Press

Matisse, Henri—_Continued_

In this first volume of the author's biography of the French artist, Spurling focuses on Matisse's training as an art student in Paris

This volume "makes for a gripping read and reveals much about the artist's early development." Publ Wkly

Includes bibliographical references

Maxwell, William, 1908-2000

Warner, Sylvia Townsend. The element of lavishness: letters of Sylvia Townsend Warner and William Maxwell, 1938-1978. See entry under Warner, Sylvia Townsend, 1893-1978   **92**

McBride, James

McBride, James. The color of water. See entry under McBride-Jordan, Ruth, 1921-   **92**

McBride-Jordan, Ruth, 1921-

McBride, James. The color of water; a black man's tribute to his white mother. Riverhead Bks. 1996 228p il $23.95; pa $14   **92**

1. McBride, James

ISBN 1-57322-022-1; 1-57322-578-9 (pa)

LC 95-37243

This volume combines accounts of McBride's childhood in a mixed-race family and of his mother's life history, in alternating chapters. "Ruth McBride recounts fleeing the rural South and her Orthodox Jewish family to live in Harlem, cofound a Baptist church, and twice survive widowhood to raise 12 children." Booklist

"Told with humor and clear-eyed grace, McBride's memoir is not only a terrific story, it's a subtle contribution to the current debates on race and identity. . . . The sheer strength of spirit, pain and humor of McBride and his mother as they wrestled with different aspects of race and identity is vividly told." Nation

McCain, John S., 1936-

Drew, Elizabeth. Citizen McCain. Simon & Schuster 2002 181p $23   **92**

ISBN 0-7432-3002-7   LC 2002-20761

Also available Thorndike Press large print edition

This biography follows Arizona "Senator John McCain through the 2001 legislative session as he maneuvers toward his goal of campaign finance reform. . . . In the midst of her narrative, Drew is forced to change her focus from the battle over campaign finance reform to the events of September 11. In Drew's view, McCain provides a rare example of leadership as he makes numerous media appearances . . . designed to reassure the public after the terrorist attacks." Publ Wkly

"This is a valentine to McCain, who comes across as decent, understanding, and friendly—there's none of that hair-trigger McCain who sometimes appeared during his presidential campaign." Booklist

McCain, John S. Faith of my fathers; [by] John McCain with Mark Salter. Random House 1999 349p $25   **92**

1. McCain, John Sidney, 1884-1945 2. McCain, John S., 1911-1981

ISBN 0-375-50191-6   LC 99-13496

Also available large print edition $25 (ISBN 0-375-40847-9) and in paperback from HarperPerennial

"McCain examines the lives of his grandfather and father—both four-star admirals—and shows how their lessons helped him through his years as a prisoner of war in Vietnam." Booklist

This is a "serious, utterly engrossing account of faith, fathers and military tradition." Publ Wkly

McCall, Nathan

McCall, Nathan. Makes me wanna holler; a young black man in America. Random House 1994 404p hardcover o.p. paperback available $13   **92**

ISBN 0-679-74070-8 (pa)   LC 93-30654

The author relates the "story of his rise from poverty to success as a journalist at the _Washington Post_. He uses graphic language, blunt descriptions, honest expression, introspection, and careful observation to describe his early years in Portsmouth, Virginia, as a young black male, the recipient of a 12-year prison sentence for armed robbery, whose life was dangerously out of control. Insensitivity, alienation, racial hatred, drugs (especially crack), guns, rape, robbery, the black American as an endangered species—McCall covers it all in a depressing yet spellbinding documentary." Libr J

McCarthy, Joseph, 1908-1957

Herman, Arthur. Joseph McCarthy; reexamining the life and legacy of America's most hated senator. Free Press 2000 404p il $26   **92**

ISBN 0-684-83625-4   LC 99-37011

This is a biographical study of Joseph McCarthy, Republican Senator from Wisconsin, and the anticommunist movement which he led

Herman "has filed a brief for the defense that is simultaneously audacious in its argument and painstaking in its scholarship." Natl Rev

Includes bibliographical references

McCarthy, Mary, 1912-1989

Brightman, Carol. Writing dangerously: Mary McCarthy and her world. Potter 1992 714p il o.p.; Harcourt Brace & Co. paperback available $18.95   **92**

ISBN 0-15-600067-9 (pa)   LC 92-7180

"This book considers McCarthy's career as reviewer, critic, editor, author, investigative journalist, and political commentator. . . . The author's approach has been to analyze the provocative elements in McCarthy's temperament, which led to promiscuity, radical politics, character assassinations, and feuds with other writers." Libr J

"The achievement of [this book] is Ms. Brightman's placement of McCarthy's personal and literary selves in historical, intellectual and social contexts, and her willingness to explore her subject's multiplicity." N Y Times Book Rev

Includes bibliographical references

Kiernan, Frances. Seeing Mary plain: a life of Mary McCarthy. Norton 2000 845p il $35; pa $25   **92**

ISBN 0-393-03801-7; 0-393-32307-2 (pa)

LC 99-41098

Kiernan uses "her interviews with more than 200 sources to provide multiple points of view on McCarthy's life and work. McCarthy knew most of her generation's literary leading lights, from the _Partisan Review_ crowd to anti-Vietnam activists. . . . Each chapter includes commentary by McCarthy, friends, ex-lovers, admirers, and adversaries." Booklist

Includes bibliographical references

McCarthy, Mary, 1912-1989—*Continued*

McCarthy, Mary. How I grew. Harcourt Brace Jovanovich 1987 278p il hardcover o.p. paperback available $8.95   **92**
ISBN 0-15-642185-2 (pa)   LC 86-29480
In this memoir, a continuation of Memories of a Catholic girlhood, the author writes about her life and intellectual development from ages thirteen to twenty-one

McClellan, George Brinton, 1826-1885

Sears, Stephen W. George B. McClellan; the young Napoleon. Ticknor & Fields 1988 482p il o.p.; Da Capo Press paperback available $16.95   **92**
1. United States—History—1861-1865, Civil War
ISBN 0-306-80913-3 (pa)   LC 88-2138
This biography of the Civil War general "covers both the awkward character traits that led to McClellan's incompetence and the battlefield actions that he regularly bungled. In addition to its merit as Civil War history, the book is of great interest as the portrait of an intelligent man working at what he failed to realize was the wrong profession." Atlantic
Includes bibliographical references

McCourt, Frank

McCourt, Frank. Angela's ashes; a memoir. Scribner 1996 364p il $25; pa $14   **92**
ISBN 0-684-87435-0; 0-684-84267-X (pa)
    LC 96-5335
"Frank McCourt, a teacher, grandfather and occasional actor, was born in New York City, but grew up in the Irish town of Limerick during the grim 1930's and 40's before he came back here as a teen-ager. His recollections of childhood are mournful and humorous, angry and forgiving." N Y Times Book Rev

McCourt, Frank. 'Tis; a memoir. Scribner 1999 367p hardcover o.p. paperback available $14   **92**
ISBN 0-684-86574-2 (pa)   LC 99-31280
Also available Simon & Schuster large print edition $26 (ISBN 0-684-86449-5)
Sequel to Angela's ashes
This volume "takes McCourt from his arrival in America and subsequent service in the Korean War through the mid-1980s. . . . This memoir features a mesmerizing narrative fraught with sufferings. It triumphs by effecting a genuinely comic meditation upon human frailty, grace and possibility." Publ Wkly

McCourt, Malachy, 1931-

McCourt, Malachy. A monk swimming. Hyperion 1998 290p $23.95; pa $14   **92**
ISBN 0-7868-6398-6; 0-7868-8414-2 (pa)
    LC 97-46720
The author recounts stories of his "serendipitous success as an actor and a bar owner after arriving in New York penniless and uneducated." Booklist
"The memoir, which covers ground through 1963, will have readers smiling and laughing constantly." Publ Wkly

McCourt, Malachy. Singing my him song. HarperCollins Pubs. 2000 242p hardcover o.p. paperback available $14   **92**
ISBN 0-06-095548-1 (pa)   LC 00-59774
In this sequel to A monk swimming, "McCourt tells us the rest of his story; how he got from there to here, how he went from living the headlong and heedless life of a world-class drunk to becoming a sober, loving father and grandfather, still happily married after thirty-five years." Publisher's note

McCullers, Carson, 1917-1967

Savigneau, Josyane. Carson McCullers; a life; translated by Joan E. Howard. Houghton Mifflin 2001 370p il $30   **92**
ISBN 0-395-87820-9   LC 00-46547
In this biography the author explores "McCuller's life as a writer and on the 'adolescent spirit' that she says not only permeated McCuller's work but also characterized her personal relationships with fellow writers like Tennessee Williams and Truman Capote as well as with members of her family." N Y Times Book Rev
This is a "heartfelt, honest portrait of one of the great novelists of the American South." Libr J
Includes bibliographical references

McDaniel, Hattie, 1895-1952

Jackson, Carlton. Hattie: the life of Hattie McDaniel. Madison Bks. 1989 220p il hardcover o.p. paperback available $12.95   **92**
ISBN 1-56833-004-9 (pa)   LC 89-30903
"For those of us who knew her only as 'Mammy' in *Gone with the Wind,* Hattie McDaniel's life story holds lots of surprises. She was also a singer, songwriter, and radio, stage, and TV performer. With an anecdotal style, the author clears up a lot of errors concerning her career." Booklist
Includes bibliographical references

McDermott, Mickey, 1928-2003

McDermott, Mickey. A funny thing happened on the way to Cooperstown; [by] Mickey McDermott with Howard Eisenberg. Triumph 2003 270p il $24.95   **92**
1. Baseball—Biography
ISBN 1-57243-532-1   LC 2002-45573
McDermott "won 18 games for the Boston Red Sox in 1951 and seemed a sure thing, but he finished a lackluster career with 69 wins and 69 losses. . . . After leaving baseball, McDermott struggled at various jobs until, unbelievably, he won $7 million in the Arizona state lottery in 1991. With the help of coauthor Eisenberg, he tells the story of his life and wild times in this thoroughly engaging memoir." Booklist

McEnroe, John

McEnroe, John. You cannot be serious; [by] John McEnroe with Jams Kaplan. Putnam 2002 342p il $25.95; pa $14   **92**
ISBN 0-399-14858-2; 0-425-19008-0 (pa)
    LC 2002-23875
Tennis star McEnroe's "recollections fall into three categories: accounts of key matches, life as a jet-setting celebrity, and reflections on the emotional roller coaster that has been his personal life." Booklist

McGhee, Fredrick L., 1861-1912

Nelson, Paul David. Fredrick L. McGhee; a life on the color line, 1861-1912; {by} Paul D. Nelson; foreword by David Levering Lewis. Minnesota Hist. Soc. Press 2002 xxvi, 234p il $29.95   **92**

ISBN 0-87351-425-4   LC 2001-58689

"McGhee, born a slave but later able to achieve a substantial career as an attorney and civil rights activist, was a contemporary of Booker T. Washington and W. E. B. DuBois. . . . Nelson explores the life of this extraordinary man and the reasons for his obscurity. . . . A very fascinating read." Booklist

Includes bibliographical references

McGinn, Colin, 1950-

McGinn, Colin. The making of a philosopher; my journey through twentieth century philosophy. HarperCollins Pubs. 2002 241p $25.95; pa $12.95   **92**

ISBN 0-06-019792-7; 0-06-095760-3 (pa)
                                            LC 2001-39502

"In recounting his career as an academic philosopher in England and the U.S., McGinn often ventures outside the lecture hall, recounting time spent cruising Sunset Boulevard, video gaming in Westwood Village, and hobnobbing with the glitterati at movie premiere parties. The liveliness of his narrative won't keep the uninitiated from being baffled when the topic turns to 'truth conditions' in Davidsonian semantics of 'indexicals' in Kaplarian reference theory, but even so, McGinn manages to restore a fundamental equality between the Oxford don and the California video gamer. Both will probably enjoy reading his book." Booklist

McLuhan, Marshall, 1911-1980

Gordon, W. Terrence. Marshall McLuhan; escape into understanding. Basic Bks. 1997 465p il   **92**
                                            LC 97-224018

Available in hardcover and paperback from Gingko Press

The author begins this biography with "McLuhan's childhood, Cambridge years, marriage, and conversion to Catholicism; later he turns to view the man who coined the term *global village* and became a pop icon with the publication of *The Medium Is the Message* through a detailed analysis of his work. Gordon provides a straightforward and lucid account of McLuhan's life and ideas, at times defending the media guru against detractors." Libr J

Includes bibliographical references

McMurtry, Larry

McMurtry, Larry. Walter Benjamin at the Dairy Queen; reflections at sixty and beyond. Simon & Schuster 1999 204p il hardcover o.p. paperback available $12   **92**

ISBN 0-684-87019-3 (pa)   LC 99-19346

Also available Thorndike Press large print edition

"When McMurtry recalls reading 'Don Quixote' as a thirteen-year-old on a Texas ranch and imagining himself as a character in the novel, other obsessional readers will immediately feel a kinship with this author. His appealing ruminations about his life and work as a reader, writer, and bookseller explore the differences between 'dense and empty, open and closed, new country and old cities, no society and old society'—the bare land in which he was reared and the crowded universe of literature." New Yorker

McPherson, Aimee Semple, 1890-1944

Epstein, Daniel Mark. Sister Aimee: the life of Aimee Semple McPherson. Harcourt Brace Jovanovich 1993 475p il hardcover o.p. paperback available $18   **92**

ISBN 0-15-600093-8 (pa)   LC 92-23324

This is a biography of the American evangelist and faith healer

"Any secular treatment of a subject who claims divine inspiration must sooner or later confront The Question: did God actually speak to her? Epstein's hedge is that Sister Aimee believed He did. . . . On the whole, however, the book is a lively read. That it is neither hagiography nor exposé is its strength as well as its weakness. Sister Aimee emerges as an unlikely yet compelling heroine." Natl Rev

Includes bibliographical references

McQueen, Steve, 1930-1980

Terrill, Marshall. Steve McQueen; portrait of an American rebel. Fine, D.I. 1993 463p il o.p.; Plexus Pub. paperback available $19.95   **92**

ISBN 0-85965-231-9 (pa)   LC 93-072577

For this biography "Terrill interviewed dozens of people from McQueen's past, including all his ex-wives and a number of costars, such as James Coburn, Robert Vaughn, and Suzanne Pleshette. . . . Included is a McQueen filmography and a fascinating section on films McQueen turned down. Terrill's writing style is unremarkable, but the glitzy, behind-the-scenes Hollywood subject matter makes this long book quick reading." Booklist

Includes bibliographical references

McVeigh, Timothy J.

Michel, Lou. American terrorist: Timothy McVeigh and the Oklahoma City bombing; [by] Lou Michel and Dan Herbeck. ReganBooks 2001 xxi, 426p il hardcover o.p. paperback available $7.99   **92**

1. Oklahoma City (Okla.) bombing, 1995
ISBN 0-06-106518-8 (pa)   LC 2001-16094

This account of McVeigh's life describes "his relationship with Terry Nichols and Michael Fortier and the consuming distrust of the government shared by the three. [Details] of the bombing itself is reconstructed, from the origins of the plot to the moment of detonation and McVeigh's aborted getaway." Publisher's note

Mead, Margaret, 1901-1978

Mead, Margaret. Blackberry winter; my earlier years. Morrow 1972 305p il o.p.; Kodansha Am. paperback available $15   **92**

ISBN 1-56836-069-X (pa)

Available in hardcover from P. Smith

"About one-third of Mead's autobiography covers the years before she became an anthropologist and another third her field work in Samoa, in New Guinea, among the Omaha Indians, and in Bali. . . . The concluding chapters . . . describe in subjective detail her role as mother and grandmother." Choice

Mehta, Ved, 1934-

Mehta, Ved. All for love. Thunder's Mouth Press 2001 345p $24.95   **92**

ISBN 1-56025-321-5   LC 2001-27050

In this "autobiographical work, author Mehta conducts an exquisite exploration of his love life as a young man,

Mehta, Ved, 1934-—*Continued*

attempting to focus an objective lens on the most subjective of matters. The volume, the ninth in Mehta's Continents of Exile series, examines the blind writer's pathos-laden involvement with four different women while living in New York City in the 1960s and 1970s and working at the *New Yorker*." Publ Wkly

"Mehta's moving confessions reveal much about the will, the many ways we 'see,' and the many obstacles to love we contrive and overcome." Booklist

Meiji, Emperor of Japan, 1852-1912

Keene, Donald. Emperor of Japan: Meiji and His world, 1852-1912. Columbia Univ. Press 2002 922p il $41.50   **92**

1. Japan—History—1868-1945

ISBN 0-231-12340-X   LC 2001-28826

This is a "biography-cum-history of Emperor Meiji and his times. . . . Meiji's reign saw Japan become fully industrialized under a brand new constitution, and with new economic and educational systems adopted. Despite the book's massive scale, Keene's graceful writing holds the reader's interest throughout." Booklist

Melville, Herman, 1819-1891

Hardwick, Elizabeth. Herman Melville. Viking 2000 161p (Penguin lives series) $19.95   **92**

ISBN 0-670-89158-4   LC 00-36510

"A Lipper/Viking book"

"Interweaving critical readings of his fiction and poetry with events in Melville's life, Hardwick offers glimpses into his tortured writing career, his sometimes difficult family life, and his ambivalent relationship with his friend Nathaniel Hawthorne." Libr J

Includes bibliographical references

Parker, Hershel. Herman Melville; a biography. Johns Hopkins Univ. Press 1996-2002 2v il maps ea $45   **92**

LC 96-18984

Contents: v1 1819-1851 (ISBN 0-8018-5428-8); v2 1851-1891 (ISBN 0-8018-6892-0)

"Volume I ends with . . . Friday, 14 November 1851, the day he presented Hawthorne with a copy of the novel dedicated to him, Moby-Dick, in the dining-room of Curtis's Hotel in Lenox, Massachusetts. Volume II chronicles Melville's long, painful decline, marked by misfortune and miscalculation." London Review of Bks.

This is "a highly detailed, beautifully written, and moving portrait of a great writer." Libr J

Includes bibliographical references

Robertson-Lorant, Laurie. Melville; a biography. Potter 1996 xxv, 710p il o.p.; University of Mass. Press paperback available $24.95   **92**

ISBN 1-55849-145-7 (pa)   LC 95-30235

"With access to more than 500 recently discovered Melville family letters, which show Melville to have been a functioning member of a problem-torn extended family, Robertson-Lorant corrects our traditional view of the older Melville as *isolato*. Instead, he appears here to represent the social consciousness of 19th century America. Together with jargon-free, user-friendly commentary on all Melville's major works, Robertson-Lorant offers an array of historical phenomena . . . that provide an invaluable context for Melville's life and art." Libr J

Mencken, H. L. (Henry Louis), 1880-1956

Mencken, H. L. (Henry Louis). My life as author and editor; edited and with an introduction by Jonathan Yardley. Knopf 1993 xxi, 449p $30; pa $25   **92**

ISBN 0-679-41315-4; 0-679-74102-X (pa)

LC 92-4496

Mencken's "memoir, which he set aside in 1948 following a severe stroke and ordered locked away for 35 years after his death, covers his literary apprenticeship, his co-editorship of *The Smart Set* and his feuds and friendships with Theodore Dreiser, Sinclair Lewis, F. Scott Fitzgerald, Ezra Pound, Alfred Knopf and others." Publ Wkly

An "absorbing memoir that anyone who cares about modern American literature will want to read." N Y Times Book Rev

Teachout, Terry. The skeptic: the life of H.L. Mencken. HarperCollins Pubs. 2002 410p il $29.95; pa $15.95   **92**

ISBN 0-06-050528-1; 0-06-050529-X (pa)

LC 2002-24953

"This biography copes with Mencken's crankiness, his provinciality and his inability to believe Germany was doing wrong in the 20th century by placing them in contemporary contexts." N Y Times Book Rev

This is "an engrossing, sympathetic biography." Booklist

Includes bibliograpical references

Mendel, Gregor, 1822-1884

Henig, Robin Marantz. The monk in the garden: how Gregor Mendel and his pea plants solved the mystery of inheritance. Houghton Mifflin 2000 292p il $24; pa $14   **92**

ISBN 0-395-97765-7; 0-618-12741-0 (pa)

LC 00-24341

The author explores "Mendel's personality and experiments. The latter lasted but a few years in the 1850s and 1860s, ending when Mendel became the abbot of his monastery in what is now Brno in the Czech Republic. Henig crisply conveys how the laws of inheritance that Mendel derived from his statistical analysis remained unnoticed until several botanists who discovered them independently in 1900 also learned that Mendel found them first. This biography itself rediscovers a scientist often mentioned but insufficiently known." Booklist

Mendelssohn, Felix, 1809-1847

Mercer-Taylor, Peter Jameson. The life of Mendelssohn; [by] Peter Mercer-Taylor. Cambridge Univ. Press 2000 238p il (Musical lives) hardcover o.p. paperback available $20   **92**

ISBN 0-521-63972-7 (pa)   LC 99-58441

A study of "the composer and his music, family history, cultural setting, and creative aspirations. . . . The book contains no musical examples but plentiful allusions to monumental works in the Western art music tradition. . . . The author describes pieces in ways music lovers can appreciate and places the composer in the context of his times for historians who seek breadth in biographies. The bibliographic essay . . . guides readers to other sources." Libr J

"The book is well written, carefully produced, and a pleasure to read." Choice

Merton, Thomas, 1915-1968

Merton, Thomas. Intimate Merton; his life from his journals; edited by Patrick Hart and Jonathan Montaldo. HarperSanFrancisco 1999 374p il hardcover o.p. paperback available $16   **92**

    ISBN 0-06-251629-9 (pa)   LC 99-33239

"This is a one-volume condensation of Merton's journals, which have been published over the last few years; its seven chapters correspond to the seven volumes of Merton's complete journals. . . . [The editors] have maintained all of Merton's central themes—including controversial ones, like the relationship with the nurse identified as 'M.' and Merton's doubts about his vocation." Libr J

Merton, Thomas. The seven storey mountain. Fiftieth anniversary edition. Harcourt Brace & Co. 1998 467p $35; pa $16   **92**

    ISBN 0-15-100413-7; 0-15-601086-0 (pa)

    LC 98-198169

First published 1948. This edition "includes an introduction by Merton's editor, Robert Giroux, and a reader's note by biographer and Thomas Merton Society Founder Fr. William Shannon." Libr J

"The autobiography of a poet who became a convert to Catholicism and at the age of 26 after a full and traveled world career as student and teacher, entered a Trappist monastery." Publ Wkly

Mill, John Stuart, 1806-1873

Mill, John Stuart. Autobiography   **92**

Available in paperback from Houghton Mifflin, Penguin Bks. and Kessinger

Written 1873

"A human document of unusual interest. Mill, a noble spirit educated by a narrow-minded pedant, shut off from all normal contact, developed an egotism that makes this book so completely an autobiography that besides his father and [his] wife he seems to exist alone in a world of which he has both center and circumference." Pratt Alcove

Millay, Edna St. Vincent, 1892-1950

Milford, Nancy. Savage beauty: the life of Edna St. Vincent Millay. Random House 2001 550p il $29.95; pa $14.95   **92**

    ISBN 0-394-57589-X; 0-375-76081-4 (pa)

    LC 2001-18598

Also available Thorndike Press large print edition

"In 1923, Edna St. Vincent Millay became the first woman to win the Pulitzer Prize for poetry. To write her biography, Milford . . . persuaded Millay's younger sister and sole heir, Norma, to give her access to hundreds of Millay's personal papers, letters, and notebooks. Selecting from 'this extraordinary collection,' Milford meticulously integrates Millay's major poems, letters received and sent, reactions of friends, and comments from extensive interviews with Norma into an orderly and affecting narrative." Libr J

Includes bibliographical references

Miller, Emmett

Tosches, Nick. Where dead voices gather. Little, Brown 2001 330p $24.95; pa $14.95   **92**

    ISBN 0-316-89507-5; 0-316-89537-7 (pa)

    LC 2001-18608

This book "attempts to rescue from obscurity the blackface performer and minstrel singer Emmett Miller, who gained brief fame in the twenties and thirties, and who left behind only a handful of recordings at his death, in 1962." New Yorker

"As engrossing as a great mystery novel, this is essential for libraries with a focus on American popular culture." Libr J

Min, Anchee, 1957-

Min, Anchee. Red azalea. Pantheon Bks. 1994 306p o.p.; Berkley Pub. Group paperback available $14   **92**

    1. China—History—1949-1976

    ISBN 0-425-16687-2 (pa)   LC 93-9038

"In this memoir of growing up in China during the Cultural Revolution, sexual freedom becomes a powerful political as well as literary statement." N Y Times Book Rev

Mingus, Charles, 1922-1979

Mingus, Sue. Tonight at noon. See entry under Mingus, Sue   **92**

Santoro, Gene. Myself when I am real: the life and music of Charles Mingus. Oxford Univ. Press 2000 452p $30; pa $17.95   **92**

    ISBN 0-19-509733-5; 0-19-514711-1 (pa)

    LC 99-46734

The author "has attempted not only to capture the complex, contradictory character of jazz bassist and composer Mingus, but also to assert his music's towering significance in American culture as a whole." Publ Wkly

Includes discography and bibliographical references

Mingus, Sue

Mingus, Sue. Tonight at noon; a love story; {by} Sue Graham Mingus. Pantheon Bks. 2002 266p il $24   **92**

    1. Mingus, Charles, 1922-1979

    ISBN 0-375-42115-7   LC 2001-56042

Also available in paperback from Da Capo Press

"A memoir (by a onetime Milwaukee debutante) of ll years and numerous tumults with a very difficult man, the jazz composer, bandleader and double-bass virtuoso Charles Mingus, the last three as his wife until his death in 1979." N Y Times Book Rev

"This is a powerful and moving book, unsparing in its portrayal of the devastation caused by Lou Gehrig's disease and charged with insight into the personality of a jazz great." Publ Wkly

Modigliani, Amedeo, 1884-1920

Wayne, Kenneth. Modigliani & the artists of Montparnasse. Abrams 2002 223p il $60   **92**

    ISBN 0-8109-3247-4   LC 2002-18228

Catalog of an exhibition held at the Albright-Knox Gallery, Buffalo, N.Y., Oct. 18, 2002-Jan. 12, 2003, the Kimball Art Museum, Fort Worth, Tex., Feb. 9-May 25, 2003, and the Los Angeles County Museum of Art, Los Angeles, Calif., June 29-Sept. 28, 2003

Published in association with the Albright-Knox Art Gallery, Buffalo, N.Y.

Modigliani, Amedeo, 1884-1920—*Continued*
"The book explores Modigliani's relationships with peers (such as Archipenko, de Chirico, Brancusi, Leger, Picasso, and Rivera) as well his relation with the Paris neighborhood. Essays by curators are flawlessly researched and approachable, and the simple, full-page color presentation of the paintings and sculpture make this a complete reference for one of the most important periods in modern art." Libr J
Includes bibliographical references

Monk, Thelonious, 1917-1982
Gourse, Leslie. Straight, no chaser; the life and genius of Thelonious Monk. Schirmer Bks. 1997 340p il hardcover o.p. paperback available $15 **92**
ISBN 0-8256-7229-5 (pa)   LC 97-10509
This biography "focuses on the composer's personality and erratic behavior (probably due to a combination of depression and drugs) and shows how people who believed in him, such as his companion, Nellie Smith, and his manager, Harry Colomby, supported him despite his eccentricities and made it possible for him to develop his revolutionary musical ideas." Publ Wkly
Includes discography, videography, and bibliographical references

Monroe, Bill, 1911-1996
Smith, Richard D. Can't you hear me callin': the life of Bill Monroe, father of bluegrass. Little, Brown 2000 365p il $25.95 **92**
ISBN 0-316-80381-2   LC 99-54372
Also available in paperback from Da Capo Press
The author traces Monroe's "life from a music-rich but isolated childhood in the pastoral backroads of Kentucky to his early years as a struggling professional musician to his well-deserved status as an acclaimed elder statesman and musical ambassador. . . . A sensitive, tasteful, well-balanced portrait of a complicated man." Booklist
Includes discography, videography and bibliographical references

Monroe, Marilyn, 1926-1962
Leaming, Barbara. Marilyn Monroe. Crown 1998 464p il hardcover o.p. paperback available $16 **92**
ISBN 0-609-80553-3 (pa)   LC 98-18738
In this biography the film star "emerges as a smart perfectionist riddled with self-doubt and self-destructive tendencies. . . . The story of Monroe's life reads tragically from day one. . . . It was a life that despite the bright light of fame shining on it for many years could only be described as one long downward spiral." Booklist
Learning "has a sure dramatic instinct for illuminating overlooked material and re-examining the most interesting episodes." N Y Times Book Rev

Moore, Marianne, 1887-1972
Molesworth, Charles. Marianne Moore; a literary life. Atheneum Pubs. 1990 xxii, 472p il o.p.; Northeastern Univ. Press paperback available $20 **92**
ISBN 1-55553-115-6 (pa)   LC 90-709
"Molesworth charts the growth of a major modernist through careful critical readings of her poetry and prose,

her work as an editor of the *Dial*, and an examination of Moore as an active, social New York literary figure whose colleagues and admirers included T.S. Eliot and Ezra Pound." Publ Wkly
Includes bibliographical references

Moore, Marianne. The selected letters of Marianne Moore; Bonnie Costello, general editor; Cleste Goodridge, and Cristanne Miller, associate editors. Knopf 1997 597p il $35 **92**
ISBN 0-679-43909-9   LC 96-52200
Also available in paperback from Penguin Bks.
"Moore wrote some 30,000 letters; the prevailing tone of this selection is excitement at coming of age in the era of Pound, Eliot, H.D. and Williams." N Y Times Book Rev
Moore's "letters are jaunty and self-possessed in tone, probing and uncompromising in content, and absolutely magnetic." Booklist

More, Sir Thomas, Saint, 1478-1535
Moynahan, Brian. God's bestseller: William Tyndale, Thomas More, and the writing of the English Bible. See entry under Tyndale, William, d. 1536   **92**

Morgan, J. Pierpont (John Pierpont), 1837-1913
Strouse, Jean. Morgan; American financier. Random House 1999 796p il o.p.; Perennial paperback available $18 **92**
ISBN 0-06-095589-9 (pa)   LC 98-35028
This biography "focuses on the accomplishments and failures of Morgan as financier, art collector, and American." Libr J
"Strouse is in full command of Pierpont Morgan's personal life, his financial operations, his collecting, and his benefactions, and presents a rich, vivid picture of the background against which they took place. . . . She has written a magnificent biography, which illuminates her subject and his world." N Y Rev Books
Includes bibliographical references

Morgan, Robert, 1918-2004
Morgan, Robert. The man who flew the Memphis Belle; memoir of a WWII bomber pilot; [by] Robert Morgan with Ron Powers. Dutton 2001 388p il hardcover o.p. paperback available $14 **92**
ISBN 0-451-20594-4 (pa)   LC 00-65857
In this memoir Morgan traces his life and focuses on his wartime experiences when he flew the Memphis Belle on 25 combat missions over Europe and then "transferred to the Pacific theater and flew 26 missions over Japan in a newly developed B-29 bomber, named *Dauntless Dotty*. . . . Written in a chatty style that is easy and exciting to read, this book is recommended for all public and most academic libraries." Libr J
Includes bibliographical references

Morisot, Berthe, 1841-1895
Higonnet, Anne. Berthe Morisot. Harper & Row 1990 240p il o.p.; University of Calif. Press paperback available $24.95 **92**
ISBN 0-520-20156-6 (pa)   LC 89-45669
"An Edward Burlingame Bk."

Morisot, Berthe, 1841-1895—*Continued*

In this biography of the Impressionist artist the author "argues that Morisot developed a strategy to portray 'a feminine visual culture' in an 'extremely daring unfeminine career while making minimal personal sacrifices'. . . . Overall this is a well argued and convincing study." Libr J

Includes bibliographical references

Morris, Willie

Morris, Willie. My dog Skip. Random House 1995 122p il hardcover o.p. paperback available $10   **92**

1. Dogs

ISBN 0-679-76722-3 (pa)   LC 94-41637

"Morris remembers back to the boy-and-his-dog days in his small hometown in the Deep South, where Skip was involved in all of his pranks and escapades. Poignancy rather than humor is the pervading tone of this ode to a steadfast presence." Booklist

Morrison, Jim, 1943-1971

Hopkins, Jerry. No one here gets out alive; by Jerry Hopkins and Daniel Sugerman. Warner Bks. 1980 387p il hardcover o.p. paperback available $7.99   **92**

1. Doors (Musical group)

ISBN 0-446-60228-0 (pa)   LC 79-26611

This biography of rock musician Jim Morrison gives "an idea of how profoundly Morrison, as lyricist and lead singer of the Doors, affected the youth of America in the late 1960s. . . . The book includes a list of the Doors' records, books, and films." Booklist

Riordan, James. Break on through: the life and death of Jim Morrison; [by] James Riordan and Jerry Prochnicky. Morrow 1991 544p il hardcover o.p. paperback available $15   **92**

ISBN 0-688-11915-8 (pa)   LC 90-26580

This look at the life and work of Jim Morrison is "well documented and avoids unfounded speculation and unnecessary tales of debauchery common to many other rock 'n' roll biographies. . . . An excellent biography of a true rock icon." Choice

Includes discography and bibliographical references

Morse, Samuel Finley Breese, 1791-1872

Silverman, Kenneth. Lightning man: the accursed life of Samuel F.B. Morse. Knopf 2003 503p il $35   **92**

ISBN 0-375-40128-8   LC 2002-43613

This is a "biography of Samuel F.B. Morse, the inventor of the Morse code and the disputed inventor of the electromagnetic telegraph. . . . Silverman shows how Morse's never-ending battle with negative self-image, a result of his strict Calvinist upbringing, was the common thread that tied together the disparate events of his life. And Silverman's well-paced, character-driven storytelling brings Morse's raw, emotional persona to life. Strongly recommend for public libraries and for academic library collections at all levels." Libr J

Mortimer, John Clifford, 1923-

Mortimer, John Clifford. The summer of a dormouse; [by] John Mortimer. Viking 2001 191p hardcover o.p. paperback available $13   **92**

ISBN 0-14-200126-0 (pa)   LC 00-68525

Also available Thorndike Press large print edition

This third volume of Mortimer's autobiography follows *Clinging to the Wreckage* (1987) and *Murderers and Other Friends* (1996)

In this installment Mortimer "writes tenderly about his childhood years in England during World War I. He vividly describes Tuscany, where he collaborated with Franco Zeffirelli on the screenplay of *Tea with Mussolini,* and summer afternoons spent sitting on the terrace drinking Chianti and discussing opera. . . . Mortimer spares no expense when it comes to telling a good tale." Libr J

Moses, Robert, 1888-1981

Caro, Robert A. The power broker: Robert Moses and the fall of New York. Knopf 1974 1246, xxxivp il $50; pa $21.95   **92**

ISBN 0-394-48076-7; 0-394-72024-5 (pa)

This is a biographical critique of the man who in four decades as a public official "built most of the parks, bridges and highways in and around New York City." Newsweek

Includes bibliographical references

Mowat, Farley

Mowat, Farley. Born naked. Houghton Mifflin 1994 c1993 256p il maps hardcover o.p. paperback available $13   **92**

ISBN 0-395-73528-9 (pa)   LC 93-23702

"A Peter Davison book"

First published 1993 in Canada

The "renowned naturalist and writer gives us a glimpse of his parents, his growing up in Canada, and the roots of his love for animals." Booklist

"There are no dull pages here; every man, woman, child, and animal mentioned even casually makes an impression. . . . Highly recommended to all those who like good writing." Libr J

Moynihan, Daniel Patrick, 1927-2003

Hodgson, Godfrey. The gentleman from New York: Daniel Patrick Moynihan: a biography. Houghton Mifflin 2000 452p il $38   **92**

ISBN 0-395-86042-3   LC 00-38921

"A cold war liberal, more of a regular Democrat than a reformer, Moynihan will no doubt be remembered as one of the smarter, more thoughtful elected officials of the late twentieth century. Others will probably produce more critical biographies, but, for now, Hodgson has supplied a fairly balanced overview." Booklist

Includes bibliographical references

Mozart, Wolfgang Amadeus, 1756-1791

Einstein, Alfred. Mozart; his character, his work; translated by Arthur Mendel and Nathan Broder. Oxford Univ. Press 1945 492p il music hardcover o.p. paperback available $22.50   **92**

ISBN 0-19-500732-8 (pa)

The author's "examination of the events of Mozart's life in relation to his character, and even more, his analysis of the sources, models, and methods of the musician's creative processes are penetrating and illuminating." Christ Sci Monit

Mozart, Wolfgang Amadeus, 1756-1791—
Continued

Gutman, Robert W. Mozart; a cultural biography. Harcourt Brace & Co. 1999 839p hardcover o.p. paperback available $20   **92**
ISBN 0-15-601170-9 (pa)   LC 99-31953
The author interweaves "the chronology of Mozart's life and musical compositions with essays on the social, political, and religious fabrics of the 18th century, offering extended discourses on the Enlightenment, *Sturm und Drang*, Freemasonry, and other movements that influenced the composer both personally and in his works." Libr J
Includes bibliographical references

Solomon, Maynard. Mozart; a life. HarperCollins Pubs. 1995 640p il hardcover o.p. paperback available $22   **92**
ISBN 0-06-092692-9 (pa)   LC 94-42277
"The author explores Mozart's life and works with a wealth of facts that were culled from 18th-century sources as well as from the most recent scholarship. Mozart and his family emerge in a new light from this mass of well-chosen detail through Solomon's own convincing interpretation of events and relationships. Appropriate musical and pictorial examples, which will appeal to both scholarly and casual readers, accompany the text." Libr J
Includes bibliographical references

Muir, John, 1838-1914

Ehrlich, Gretel. John Muir; nature's visionary. National Geographic Soc. 2000 240p il map $35   **92**
1. Naturalists
ISBN 0-7922-7954-9   LC 00-60944
The author chronicles Muir's "life—from his self-education as a boy in Scotland and Wisconsin to his solitary cross-country treks, fruitful mountain hermitage, and cofounding of the Sierra Club. . . . Ehrlich beautifully captures Muir's essence and clearly defines the ongoing significance of his accomplishments. Lynn Johnson's gorgeous landscape photography and a wealth of wonderful archival images provide the perfect accompaniment." Booklist

Muir, John. Nature writings; the story of my boyhood and youth, my first summer in the Sierra, the mountains of California, Stickeen, selected essays. Library of Am. 1997 888p il $35   **92**
ISBN 1-88301-124-8   LC 96-9664
This compilation of Muir's writings "combines The Story of My Boyhood and Youth, My First Summer in the Sierra, The Mountains of California, Stickeen, and a number of his essays along with illustrations, a chronology of his life, and scholarly notes." Libr J
Muir "is at his best . . . when he is looking intently at something, walking around it, sniffing the air, looking again. As a writer he is a kind of visionary sensualist, a seer who reveals what lies in plain sight." Commentary

Muir, John. The story of my boyhood and youth   **92**
Available in paperback from University of Wis. Press
First published 1913 by Houghton Mifflin

"The naturalist's childhood in a strict Presbyterian home in Scotland, his boyhood experiences of the privations and out-of-door delights of pioneer life on a Wisconsin farm, and his shifts and contrivances while earning his way through the state university." Cleveland Public Libr

Wilkins, Thurman. John Muir; apostle of nature. University of Okla. Press 1995 xxvii, 302p il maps (Oklahoma western biographies) hardcover o.p. paperback available $19.95   **92**
ISBN 0-8061-2797-X (pa)   LC 95-11426
"Wilkins follows Muir from his Scottish boyhood, clouded by a harsh, fundamentalist father, to an adolescence of arduous farmwork in Wisconsin to a lifelong career of exploration and study of wildernesses, particularly those of the western U.S., and vividly relates some of Muir's more perilous adventures on cliffside and snowfield. . . . An affectionate, uncluttered tale of an American folk hero." Booklist
Includes bibliographical references

Munch, Edvard, 1863-1944

Tøjner, Poul Erik. Munch: in his own words. Prestel 2003 213p il pa $39.95   **92**
ISBN 3-7913-2883-2   LC 2002-116746
First published 2000 by Forlaget Press
This biography of the Norwegian artist traces his "artistic development through the examination of his personal papers, including sketches, diaries, and letters that are here translated into English for the first time. These writings also show how Munch was affected by the early loss of his mother, his love affairs, and his interaction with friends and fellow artists, as well as by the literary trends and philosophy of pre-World War I Europe. This highly personal approach allows us to see the forces at work on Munch and how they were expressed in his art. This beautifully produced and well-illustrated book belongs in most art libraries." Libr J

Murdoch, Iris

Bayley, John. Elegy for Iris. See entry under Bayley, John, 1925-   **92**
Bayley, John. Iris and her friends. See entry under Bayley, John, 1925-   **92**

Conradi, Peter. Iris Murdoch; a life; [by] Peter J. Conradi. Norton 2001 xxix, 706p il $35; pa $19.95   **92**
ISBN 0-393-04875-6; 0-393-32401-X (pa)
          LC 2001-32972
The author chronicles the personal, professional, and literary life of the philosopher and novelist, "documenting Murdoch's eccentricities and legendary kindnesses." Publ Wkly
"Rich footnoting leads the reader to expansions on the narrative as well as to the authority behind the biographer's statements. Scholars need this text, but it will also intrigue lay readers." Libr J
Includes bibliographical references

Murphy, Gerald, 1888-1964

Vaill, Amanda. Everybody was so young: Gerald and Sara Murphy, a lost generation love story. Houghton Mifflin 1998 470p il o.p.; Broadway Bks. paperback available $16 **92**

1. Murphy, Sara, 1883-1975
ISBN 0-7679-0370-6 (pa)   LC 97-49149
"Often considered minor Lost Generation celebrities, the Murphys were in fact much more than legendary party givers. Vaill's compelling biography unveils their role in the European avant-garde movement of the 1920s." Libr J
Includes bibliographical references

Murphy, Sara, 1883-1975

Vaill, Amanda. Everybody was so young: Gerald and Sara Murphy, a lost generation love story. See entry under Murphy, Gerald, 1888-1964   **92**

Murrow, Edward R.

Sperber, Ann M. Murrow, his life and times; [by] A. M. Sperber; with a preface by Neil Hickey. Fordham Univ. Press 1998 xxvi, 795p il $35; pa $25   **92**
ISBN 0-8232-1881-3; 0-8232-1882-1 (pa)
LC 98-52507
A reissue of the title first published 1986 by Freundlich Bks.
This "is the biography of America's foremost broadcast journalist, Edward R. Murrow. At twenty-nine, he was the prototype of a species new to communications— an eyewitness to history with power to reach millions. His wartime radio reports from London rooftops brought the world into American homes for the first time. His legendary television documentary See it Now exposed us to the scandals and injustices within our own country." Publisher's note
This "ambitious exploration of Murrow's life places his story in the foreground of what is, as well, a panorama of the years 1935-65." N Y Times Book Rev
Includes bibliographical references

Mussolini, Benito, 1883-1945

Bosworth, R. J. B. (Richard J. B.). Mussolini. Oxford Univ. Press 2002 584p il $35; pa $14.95   **92**
1. Fascism 2. Italy—Politics and government
ISBN 0-340-73144-3; 0-340-80988-4 (pa)
LC 2002-283267
"While Bosworth does not demonize Mussolini, he views him as an extreme example of an ego-driven personality incapable of divorcing his own self-gratifying impulses from the best interests of his people. . . . The author also . . . asserts that, as a political force, Mussolini was not an aberration." Booklist
This is "the definitive study of the Italian dictator and belongs in every public and academic library with a strong European history collection." Libr J
Includes bibliographical references

Nabokov, Vladimir Vladimirovich, 1899-1977

Boyd, Brian. Vladimir Nabokov. Princeton Univ. Press 1990-1991 2v il   **92**
Contents: {v1} The Russian years pa $49 (ISBN 0-691-02470-7); {v2} The American years pa $29.95 (ISBN 0-691-02471-5)

This biography follows the life of the novelist and poet from his childhood in czarist Russia and European exile to his final years in the United States. The author provides extensive critical analysis of Nabokov's literary output
Includes bibliographical references

Johnson, Kurt. Nabokov's Blues; the scientific odyssey of a literary genius; by Kurt Johnson and Steven L. Coates. Zoland Bks. 1999 372p il o.p.; McGraw-Hill paperback available $16.95   **92**
1. Butterflies
ISBN 0-07-137330-6 (pa)   LC 99-23648
The authors examine "both the role that lepidopterology played in Nabokov's life as well as Nabokov's contributions to science. Nabokov, it turns out, was both passionate and serious in his study of butterflies." Booklist
"Like Nabokov himself, this volume exemplifies some of the virtues shared by art and science: wit, intelligence, and, above all, meticulousness." New Yorker
Includes bibliographical references

Nabokov, Vladimir Vladimirovich. Speak, memory; an autobiography revisited; [by] Vladimir Nabokov; with an introduction by Brian Boyd. Knopf 1999 xxxv, 268p il map $17; pa $14   **92**
ISBN 0-375-40553-4; 0-679-72339-0 (pa)
LC 98-49237
A revised version of the memoir first published 1951 in the United States with title: Conclusive evidence
These recollections of the author's youthful years give an account of a vanishing world. They offer a picture of the author's family, their flight from Russia, education in England, and émigré life in Paris and Berlin
Includes bibliographical references

Naipaul, V. S. (Vidiadhar Surajprasad), 1932-

Naipaul, V. S. (Vidiadhar Surajprasad). Between father and son; selected correspondence of V.S. Naipaul and his family, 1949-1953; edited by Gillon Aitken. Knopf 2000 297p $26; pa $13   **92**
ISBN 0-375-40730-8; 0-375-70726-3 (pa)
LC 99-31089
"In 1950, at the age of 17, famous-writer-in-the-making V. S. Naipaul ventured to Oxford University in England on a scholarship supplied by the government of his native Trinidad. He and his father maintained a rich, full correspondence during his time away, and these letters fortunately have been gathered into book form." Booklist
Include bibliographical references

Naipaul, V. S. (Vidiadhar Surajprasad). Reading & writing; a personal account. New York Review of Bks. 2000 64p $16.95   **92**
ISBN 0-940322-38-2   LC 99-49615
Naipaul writes about his experiences growing up as an Indian living in Trinidad, his travels in India, his education at Oxford, and his struggles as a young writer in London
The author "elegantly expresses hard-earned wisdom about literature and culture, the political stakes of history and the relationship between the writer and the world." N Y Times Book Rev

Napoleon I, Emperor of the French, 1769-1821

Johnson, Paul. Napoleon. Viking 2002 190p (Penguin lives series) $19.95 **92**
ISBN 0-670-03078-3   LC 2001-45605

Also available Thorndike Press large print edition

Johnson "presents a concise appraisal of Napoleon's career and a precise understanding of his enigmatic character. The author views Napoleon, not as an 'idea man' whose ideology was the ladder by which he propelled himself to heights of power, but as an opportunist who took advantage of a series of events and situations he could manipulate into achieving supreme control." Booklist

Includes bibliographical references

McLynn, F. J. Napoleon; a biography; [by] Frank McLynn. Arcade Pub. 2002 739p il maps $32.95; pa $18.95 **92**
ISBN 1-55970-631-7; 1-55970-670-8 (pa)
    LC 2002-18632

First published 1997 in the United Kingdom

In this biography "McLynn is hard on Napoleon both as general and as statesman, and faults his failures to rein in his openly 'venal' marshals, treacherous administrative elite and astonishingly rapacious siblings." Publ Wkly

"Written with great stylistic flourish, McLynn's full embrace of his subject's life, which benefits from exhaustive research resulting in a comprehensive picture of the Napoleonic era, is a rich reading experience." Booklist

Schom, Alan. Napoleon Bonaparte; a life. HarperCollins Pubs. 1997 xxii, 888p hardcover o.p. paperback available $23.95 **92**
ISBN 0-06-092958-8 (pa)   LC 97-5805

The author's aim in this study of Napoleon's life is to offer a "one-volume biography in English covering all aspects of his life." N Y Times Book Rev

"Schom's judgments have all the more impact for being brief and infrequent. What really interests him is telling the story of the man who made universal rules for others but recognized none for himself. He tells it straightforwardly and well; and not, thankfully, at the multi-volume length he believes the subject still really requires." Times Lit Suppl

Includes bibliographical references

Nasdijj

Nasdijj. The blood runs like a river through my dreams; a memoir. Houghton Mifflin 2000 216p $23; pa $13 **92**
ISBN 0-618-04892-8; 0-618-15448-5 (pa)
    LC 00-38916

"Born on the Navajo reservation in 1950 to migrant workers (a Navajo storytelling mother and a white cowboy father) . . . Nasdijj writes about the life and death of his son, Tommy Nothing Fancy, their fishing trips, his travails as a committed but unpublished writer, life on the reservation, homelessness, ethnic cleansing in America, love, survival, hope. Illuminating both the comic and the tragic, his writing is a striking blend of 'tell it like it is' truths that hit right between the eyes and sensuous, expressive, poetic passages that urgently bid the reader to reread, linger, share, and appreciate. The stories and their implications are heartbreaking; but more importantly, they are heart expanding." Booklist

Nasdijj. The boy and the dog are sleeping. Ballantine Bks. 2003 324p $22.95 **92**
1. Awee
ISBN 0-345-45389-1   LC 2002-28157

Companion volume to The blood runs like a river through my dreams

The author "describes his experiences as the adoptive parent of a dying son. This is the story of Awee, an 11-year-old Navajo boy with AIDS, who finds himself nestled under Nasdijj's wing when his own parents are no longer able—or willing—to care for him because they, too, have the disease. Nasdijj's poetic writing style results in a narrative that is an often overwrought stream-of-consciousness grab bag of the mundane and the eloquent." N Y Times Book Rev

Nelson, Horatio Nelson, Viscount, 1758-1805

Hibbert, Christopher. Nelson; a personal history. Addison-Wesley 1994 472p il hardcover o.p. paperback available $22 **92**
ISBN 0-201-40800-7 (pa)   LC 94-39545

This biography of Horatio Nelson concentrates mostly on the "admiral's life ashore, especially his liaison with Emma, Lady Hamilton." Choice

The book "succeeds admirably in presenting a vivid and intimate picture of Nelson and Lady Hamilton together, helped by numerous and apt illustrations, half of them in colour. . . . The result is essentially a book of domestic detail, told with charm and perception." Times Lit Suppl

Includes bibliographical references

Newton, Sir Isaac, 1642-1727

Berlinski, David. Newton's gift: how Sir Isaac Newton unlocked the system of the world. Free Press 2000 217p il $24; pa $14 **92**
ISBN 0-684-84392-7; 0-7432-1776-4 (pa)
    LC 00-34724

Berlinski presents a "review of the development of Sir Isaac Newton's classical mechanics. He also provides selected . . . biographical sections that highlight Newton's . . . personality and his work methods." Libr J

"Berlinski does not presuppose much mathematical sophistication on the part of his readers, and he illustrates every technical idea with words, with symbols, and with pictures. The result is a bright and engaging introduction to Isaac Newton that . . . succeeds in conveying a sense of the man while whetting the appetite of the ambitious reader for a more bracing encounter with Newton's formidable achievements." Commentary

Fara, Patricia. Newton: the making of genius. Columbia Univ. Press 2002 347p il $29.95 **92**
ISBN 0-231-12806-1   LC 2003-265510

This "social history examines the reasons behind Isaac Newton's canonization as scientific genius. . . . Fara contributes to Newton's biography by focusing on the roots of Newton's apotheosis. She examines how idealized portraits propagated Newton's public image, and how the marketing of Newtonian images outside academic circles commercialized science in the same way Einstein's face sells today. Throughout, Fara, . . . effectively employs the words and imagery of religious discourse to characterize the idealization and commercialization of Newton in the service of emerging secular politics and culture." Publ Wkly

Includes bibliographical references

Newton, Sir Isaac, 1642-1727—*Continued*

Gleick, James. Isaac Newton. Pantheon Bks. 2003 272p il $22.95   **92**
ISBN 0-375-42233-1   LC 2002-192696

In this biography Gleick presents "his subject in his scientific glory and in his less well known roles of heretic, alchemist, and recluse; he also reveals how Newton's mathematical ideas were instrumental in creating what we now call the scientific worldview." Libr J

This "is now the biography of choice for the interested layman. Gleick copes with the complex tapestry of Newton's interests by teasing them apart into individual chapters, assembled into a smooth chronological flow. . . . Newton the man emerges from the shadows." N Y Times Book Rev

Includes bibliographical references

Westfall, Richard S. The life of Isaac Newton. Cambridge Univ. Press 1993 328p il hardcover o.p. paperback available $16   **92**
ISBN 0-521-47737-9 (pa)   LC 92-33777

In this book the author has "reduced his longer 1980 biography of Newton *(Never at Rest)* to a size that is more suitable for general audiences. The result is a work whose faults lie only in the paucity of source materials that all Newton biographers face. . . . Westfall's book comes as close to presenting the man as the impersonal evidence allows without undue extrapolation." Sci Books Films

Includes bibliographical references

Nicholas II, Emperor of Russia, 1868-1918

Ferro, Marc. Nicholas II; the last of the tsars; translated by Brian Pearce. Oxford Univ. Press 1993 305p il map hardcover o.p. paperback available $19.95   **92**
1. Russia—History
ISBN 0-19-509382-8 (pa)   LC 92-41440

"The last Tsar, as this fluently written biography makes abundantly clear, was largely to blame for the demise of the monarchy. Ferro is concerned to illuminate the personality of the Tsar, his relationship with his wife and Rasputin and to look again at the circumstances surrounding his death." Hist Today
Includes bibliographical references

Massie, Robert K. Nicholas and Alexandra. Atheneum Pubs. 1967 584p il o.p.; Dell paperback available $18   **92**
1. Alexandra, Empress, consort of Nicholas II, Emperor of Russia, 1872-1918 2. Russia—History
ISBN 0-345-43831-0 (pa)

This study provides an intimate account of the Romanov family and the coming of the Russian Revolution. Kerensky, Lenin and Rasputin are among the personalities profiled

This book, "solid with research, reads as lightly as a novel, as authoritatively as a textbook. Dialogue and lively description lend a sense of immediacy, but his notes, discreetly relegated to the back of the book, show how carefully he has avoided slipping into fiction." Christ Sci Monit

Includes bibliographical references

Nicklaus, Jack

Nicklaus, Jack. Jack Nicklaus; my story; with Ken Bowden. Simon & Schuster 1997 505p il $30; pa $24.95   **92**
ISBN 0-684-83628-9; 0-684-83870-2 (pa)
                    LC 97-3824

This "is both Nicklaus's autobiography and a history of modern golf, for the subjects are wholly intertwined. The book begins with Nicklaus's first national accomplishment, winning the United States Amateur at the age of 19 in 1959. It concludes with Nicklaus winning the Masters for the sixth time in 1986." N Y Times Book Rev

"What comes across most forcibly in this fine book is Nicklaus' respect for the complexity of golf and the never-ending challenges it affords players at every level." Booklist

Nietzsche, Friedrich Wilhelm, 1844-1900

Safranski, Rüdiger. Nietzsche; a philosophical biography; translated by Shelley Frisch. Norton 2001 409p $29.95; pa $18.95   **92**
ISBN 0-393-05008-4; 0-393-32380-3 (pa)
                    LC 2001-52130

This biography of the German philosopher focuses "on the temporal course of Nietzsche's inner life and his self-transformation through thought and writing." New Rep

"With brilliant insights and impressive scholarship, Safranski . . . here makes a major contribution to understanding and appreciating the lasting significance of Friedrich Nietzsche." Libr J
Includes bibliographical references

Nightingale, Florence, 1820-1910

Small, Hugh. Florence Nightingale; avenging angel. St. Martin's Press 1999 221p il $45   **92**
ISBN 0-312-22699-3   LC 99-32306
First published 1998 in the United Kingdom

"Nightingale took to her bed for many years after her famous Crimean War service. Small argues that the reason for her invalidism was not neurosis but overwhelming guilt when Nightingale realized that 14,000 British soldiers had died in the wartime hospitals because doctors and nurses failed to practice elementary sanitary procedures that she should have enforced." Booklist

"This book should reestablish Nightingale as a major figure in 19th-century health reform." Libr J
Includes bibliographical references

Nin, Anaïs, 1903-1977

Nin, Anaïs. The diary of Anaïs Nin. Harcourt Brace & Co. 1966-1980 7v il hardcover o.p. paperbacks available   **92**
Published in the United Kingdom with title: The journals of Anaïs Nin

Contents: v1 1931-1934 $14 (ISBN 0-15-626025-5); v2 1934-1939 $20 (ISBN 0-15-626026-3); v3 1939-1944 o.p.; v4 1944-1947 $16 (ISBN 0-15-626028-X); v5 1947-1955 $17 (ISBN 0-15-626030-1); v6 1955-1966 o.p.; v7 1966-1974 $20 (ISBN 0-15-626035-2)

"A record of avant-garde life in Paris and New York, with portraits of friends like Henry Miller and Lawrence Durrell, the diaries essentially chronicle a woman's coming to terms with her identity as a woman." Reader's Ency. 4th edition

Nixon, Richard M. (Richard Milhous), 1913-1994

Reeves, Richard. President Nixon; alone in the White House. Simon & Schuster 2001 702p il $35; pa $16   92
1. United States—Politics and government—1961-1974
ISBN 0-684-80231-7; 0-7432-2719-0 (pa)
LC 2001-34417

This narrative "is chronological, from Nixon's inauguration in January 1969 to April 1973, when he realized that he had lost control over the Watergate scandals. . . . In between are Vietnam and crime in the streets, affirmative action and the end of the gold standard, Chile and the antiballistic missile treaty, the opening to China and, of course, Watergate. A fascinating study of the brilliant, profoundly flawed man elected to lead the nation through a troubled time." Booklist
Includes bibliographical references

Summers, Anthony. The arrogance of power: the secret world of Richard Nixon; [by] Anthony Summers with Robbyn Swan. Viking 2000 640p il hardcover o.p. paperback available $16   92
1. United States—Politics and government—20th century
ISBN 0-14-026078-1 (pa)   LC 00-60012

The author investigates controversial issues surrounding Nixon's life and career
This is "the most thorough case against Nixon yet, reminding us both how complex our 37th president was and how much damage he ultimately did." Publ Wkly
Includes bibliographical references

Novacek, Michael J.

Novacek, Michael J. Time traveler; in search of dinosaurs and ancient mammals from Montana to Mongolia; [by] Michael Novacek. Farrar, Straus & Giroux 2002 368p il $26; pa $15   92
ISBN 0-374-27880-6; 0-374-52876-4 (pa)
LC 2001-40438

"The author first describes the youthful experiences that inspired him to become a paleontologist. . . . Then Novacek launches into his various expeditions. . . . Interweaving his adventures with explanations of where his finds fit into the geologic past, Novacek has combined the comedic with the informative in this entertaining survey of his career." Booklist
Includes bibliographical references

Novarro, Ramon, 1899-1968

Soares, André. Beyond paradise: the life of Ramon Novarro. St. Martin's Press 2002 400p il $27.95   92
ISBN 0-312-28231-1   LC 2002-68125

"One of the most popular leading men of the 1920s, Metro-Goldwyn-Mayer player Novarro had a dark secret: he was gay. . . . With this carefully researched, well-balanced, and intelligently written book, screenwriter Soares has probably produced the definitive Novarro biography." Libr J
Includes bibliographical references

Nudelman, Meyer

Nuland, Sherwin B. Lost in America. See entry under Nuland, Sherwin B.   92

Nuland, Sherwin B.

Nuland, Sherwin B. Lost in America; a journey with my father. Knopf 2003 209p $24; pa $12   92
1. Nudelman, Meyer
ISBN 0-375-41294-8; 0-375-75722-1 (pa)
LC 2002-40795

This is a "memoir about becoming an assimilated second-generation American from a home dominated by his angry, altogether unassimilable Orthodox Jewish father." N Y Times Book Rev
"Written with enormous empathy, yet without a hint of sentimentality, Nuland's memoir is both heartbreaking and breathtaking." Publ Wkly

Nur el Hussein, Queen, consort of Hussein, King of Jordan

Nur el Hussein, Queen, consort of Hussein, King of Jordan. Leap of faith; memoirs of an unexpected life; [by] Queen Noor. Weidenfeld & Nicolson 2003 467p il $25.95   92

ISBN 0-297-64664-8

"The American-born widow of the late king Hussein of Jordan brings a unique perspective to Middle East politics." Booklist

Nuwere, Ejovi

Nuwere, Ejovi. Hacker cracker: a journey from the mean streets of Brooklyn to the frontiers of cyberspace; [by] Ejovi Nuwere with David Chanoff. Morrow 2002 258p $24.95; pa $12.95   92
ISBN 0-06-621079-8; 0-06-093581-2 (pa)
LC 2002-69611

"By age 21, Nuwere had grown from a precocious child in Brooklyn's embattled Bed-Stuy neighborhood to a well-established Internet security specialist for a major investment bank. In between, he served a long stint as a renegade though ultimately benign hacker, an experience that gave him much-needed background for his professional career. Written with Chanoff, his memoir is . . . [a] primer to hacker culture matched with the personal story of being raised by an extended family (due to Nuwere's mother's death from AIDS) in an impoverished environment. . . . This is an empathetic, revealing account of a new breed of insurgents." Publ Wkly

Oakley, Annie, 1860-1926

Kasper, Shirl. Annie Oakley. University of Okla. Press 1992 288p il $29.95; pa $19.95   92

ISBN 0-8061-2418-0; 0-8061-3244-2 (pa)
LC 91-50864

This biography of the legendary sharpshooter "not only paints a picture of a woman with an unusual occupation for her time; it also colors the whole era of Wild West performers from Buffalo Bill to Will Rogers." Booklist
Includes bibliographical references

Oakley, Annie, 1860-1926—*Continued*

Riley, Glenda. The life and legacy of Annie Oakley. University of Okla. Press 1994 252p il (Oklahoma western biographies) hardcover o.p. paperback available $17.95

92

ISBN 0-8061-3506-9 (pa)   LC 94-10260

"To provide a factual and intimate biography of Annie Oakley, the legendary female sharpshooter and star of Buffalo Bill Cody's Wild West Show, Riley attempts to place her seemingly mythical subject firmly into historical, cultural, and sociological contexts. . . . What emerges is a multidimensional portrait of an entertainer and a businesswoman whose enduring fame and popularity both reflected and defied the conventions of her era." Booklist

Includes bibliographical references

O'Brian, Patrick

King, Dean. Patrick O'Brian; a life revealed. Holt & Co. 2000 397p il hardcover o.p. paperback available $15   **92**

ISBN 0-8050-5977-6 (pa)   LC 99-48495

"This is exactly the sort of literary biography that O'Brian, the author of the celebrated Aubrey/Maturin naval novels, hoped to avoid. Reluctant to provide facts about himself, and often untruthful when he did so, O'Brian . . . had much in his past that he wanted buried. He walked away from his first marriage, changed his name from Russ to O'Brian, and pretended Anglo-Irish ancestry. King's diligent research yields pleasing details." New Yorker

Includes bibliographical references

O'Connor, Flannery

O'Connor, Flannery. The habit of being; letters; edited and with an introduction by Sally Fitzgerald. Farrar, Straus & Giroux 1979 617p hardcover o.p. paperback available $20   **92**

ISBN 0-374-52104-2 (pa)   LC 78-11559

This collection includes letters to friends in the literary establishment: Robert Lowell and Elizabeth Hardwick, Caroline Gordon Tate, Robert and Sally Fitzgerald and others

Odum, Eugene Pleasants, 1913-2002

Craige, Betty Jean. Eugene Odum: ecosystem ecologist & environmentalist. University of Ga. Press 2001 xxii, 226p il hardcover o.p. paperback available $17.95

92

ISBN 0-8203-2473-6 (pa)   LC 00-56826

"Odum wrote the groundbreaking, now classic *Fundamentals of Ecology*; brought *ecosystem* into the popular lexicon, and taught a holistic view of nature. As Craige . . . covers his life as teacher, theorist, and activist, she reveals just how pivotal Odum was in the advancement of ecological science and environmental ethics." Booklist

"A captivating biography of one of the most influential ecologists of the twentieth century. . . . An enjoyable book for both the professional interested in the history of modern ecology and the layperson interested in the impact Odum's vision of ecology has had on environmentalism." Choice

Includes bibliographical references

O'Faolain, Nuala

O'Faolain, Nuala. Almost there; the onward journey of a Dublin woman. Riverhead Bks. 2003 275p $24.95; pa $14   **92**

ISBN 1-57322-241-0; 1-57322-374-3 (pa)

LC 2002-36722

In this autobiography the author "reveals the emotional damage she still suffers from being raised in a large family by an alcoholic mother and a remote father." Booklist

This "is a thought-provoking work that differs markedly from the self-serving memoirs we frequently see." Libr J

O'Faolain, Nuala. Are you somebody; the accidental memoir of a Dublin woman. Holt & Co. 1998 c1996 215p hardcover o.p. paperback available $13   **92**

ISBN 0-8050-5664-4 (pa)   LC 97-29725

First published 1996 in Ireland

In this memoir O'Faolain "describes growing up in the kind of poverty that had her mother raiding the gas meter for shillings while her father ignored his nine children and kept a mistress on the other side of town. The nascent women's movement and O'Faolain's expansive love of reading kept her afloat: she made it to college, rubbed elbows with literary Dublin, and became a BBC producer in London." New Yorker

This is a "moving and painfully honest memoir." Libr J

O'Hair, Madalyn Murray, 1919-1995

Dracos, Ted. Ungodly: the passions, torments, and murder of atheist Madalyn Murray O'Hair. Free Press 2003 291p il $25

92

ISBN 0-7432-2833-2   LC 2003-049303

"Madalyn Murray O'Hair, the notorious atheist who launched the Supreme Court case taking prayer out of America's public schools, was also the victim (along with her son and granddaughter) in a brutal Texas murder that went unsolved for years. Dracos . . . reviews the case in full-true-crime mode, the prose purpler with every page." Publ Wkly

O'Hara, John, 1905-1970

Wolff, Geoffrey. The art of burning bridges: a life of John O'Hara. Knopf 2003 xxii, 373p $30   **92**

ISBN 0-679-42771-6   LC 2002-43095

The author "shows us O'Hara growing up in Pottstown, PA, the region made prosperous by the world's richest coal deposit, where, as a doctor's son in a Catholic family, he learned to live as a well-to-do social outsider. Conscientious as a writer, O'Hara, as Wolff shows, secluded himself in a hotel room to write novels but at other times abused liquor and women uncontrollably, seriously jeopardizing, for instance, his lucrative relationship with *The New Yorker*. . . . Written with considerable verve, this literary biography is highly recommended for large public libraries with patrons who remember our recent cultural history." Libr J

Includes bibliographical references

O'Keeffe, Georgia, 1887-1986

Robinson, Roxana. Georgia O'Keeffe: a life; Roxana Robinson. University Press of New England 1999 639p il pa $22.95   **92**
ISBN 0-87451-906-3   LC 98-30944

A reissue of the title first published 1989 by Harper & Row

"This biography, the first to draw on sources unavailable during O'Keeffe's lifetime—and the first to be granted her family's cooperation—offers a persuasive feminist analysis of the life and work of an iconic figure in American art. . . . {The author's} detailed, sensitive critique of O'Keeffe's work . . . alternates with an absorbing, intimate narrative of O'Keeffe's personal life." Publ Wkly

Includes bibliographical references

Olivier, Fernande, 1881-1966

Olivier, Fernande. Loving Picasso: the private journal of Fernande Olivier; translated from the French by Christine Baker and Michael Raeburn; foreword and notes by Marilyn McCully; epilogue by John Richardson. Abrams 2001 296p il $35   **92**
1. Picasso, Pablo, 1881-1973
ISBN 0-8109-4251-8   LC 00-57628

These are the recollections of Fernande Olivier, Picasso's first mistress. The present work is "a retranslation of two works, her 'Picasso et Ses Amis,' published in the 1930's, and 'Souvenirs Intimes,' based on her childhood diaries, now lost, and published after her death." N Y Times Book Rev

"Olivier's insightful and detailed commentary on the mores and people of Paris and the Bateau Lavoir—the studio where she lived with Picasso—offer an astute insider's perspective and are invaluable to art scholarship and to anyone seeking to understand this period in modern art." Libr J

Includes bibliographical references

Olivier, Laurence, 1907-1989

Lewis, Roger. The real life of Laurence Olivier. Applause Theatre Bk. Pubs. 1997 272p il $25.95; pa $18.95   **92**
ISBN 1-55783-298-6; 1-55783-413-X (pa)
     LC 97-31702

First published 1996 in the United Kingdom

This is a life of the English stage and screen actor

"Lewis enjoys exploring the details that make up such a rich life—Olivier seemed to have met everyone, known everyone, and played every major role in existence. The indexing and photographs are quite good." Libr J

Olmsted, Frederick Law, 1822-1903

Rybczynski, Witold. A clearing in the distance: Frederick Law Olmsted and America in the nineteenth century. Scribner 1999 480p il $28; pa $15.95   **92**
ISBN 0-684-82463-9; 0-684-86575-0 (pa)
     LC 99-18094

"A portrait of Olmsted not just as landscape architect but as cultural figure." Libr J

"Rybczynski, celebrated for his sparkling prose as well as for his deep knowledge of architectural history, adeptly chronicles the life of the man who 'was a landscape architect before that profession was founded.'" Booklist

Includes bibliographical references

Onassis, Aristotle Socrates, 1906-1975

Gage, Nicholas. Greek fire. See entry under Callas, Maria, 1923-1977   **92**

Onassis, Jacqueline Kennedy

Andersen, Christopher P. Jackie after Jack; a portrait of the lady; [by] Christopher Andersen. Morrow 1998 472p il o.p.; Warner Bks. paperback available $7.50   **92**
ISBN 0-446-60743-6 (pa)   LC 97-49673

Also available Thorndike Press large print edition

An account of Jacqueline Kennedy Onassis' life after the death of President John F. Kennedy

Includes bibliographical references

Bowles, Hamish. Jacqueline Kennedy; the White House Years: selections from the John F. Kennedy Library and Museum; [compiled and edited by] Hamish Bowles; with essays by Arthur Schlesinger, Jr., Hamish Bowles, and James Wagner. Bulfinch Press 2001 198p il $50   **92**
ISBN 0-8212-2745-9   LC 00-66237

Also available in hardcover and paperback from the Metropolitan Museum of Art

This "book accompanies a summer 2001 Metropolitan Museum of Art exhibition of the same name, curated by Bowles. . . . The focus here is Jackie's famous and much emulated wardrobe. Each gown, suit, and accessory has an informational entry that includes a photograph of Jackie wearing the item." Libr J

The selections "examine in detail different aspects of Jackie's life, including the inauguration, her White House style, her travels, and her hats, as well as other topics. . . . Viewers can expect a sense of nostalgia, a swelling of pride, and a tightening of the throat. A time line of Jackie's life is appended." Booklist

Davis, John H. Jacqueline Bouvier; an intimate memoir; [by] John Davis. Wiley 1996 208p il $24.95; pa $14.95   **92**
ISBN 0-471-12945-3; 0-471-24944-0 (pa)
     LC 96-4332

This "book by the late Mrs. Onassis's cousin is as much a nostalgic look at a vanished way of life as it is a memoir of Jacqueline Bouvier from her birth in 1929 until her marriage to Senator John F. Kennedy in September 1953. The author's access to family papers helped fill in the details of an enormously privileged yet often unhappy childhood." Libr J

"Davis is an engaging writer, and although many of the facts of his story will be known by Kennedy aficionados, there is a wistful sweetness to his writing that captures both the woman and the era of privileged upbringings." Booklist

Leaming, Barbara. Mrs. Kennedy; the missing history of the Kennedy years. Free Press 2001 406p il $25; pa $14   **92**
ISBN 0-684-86209-3; 0-7432-2749-2 (pa)
     LC 2001-40442

Also available Thorndike Press large print edition

"Asserting that Jacqueline Kennedy's role in shaping her husband's presidency has been under-examined, Leaming . . . offers a corrective in this intimate look at a very private woman. Initially inclined to keep herself as much in the background as possible, says Leaming,

Onassis, Jacqueline Kennedy—*Continued*
Jacqueline Kennedy became an increasingly visible and vocal first lady as she realized how effective she could be as an image maker. It's in this capacity that Leaming convincingly depicts her as being instrumental in shaping the course of her husband's administration." Publ Wkly

O'Neill, Eugene, 1888-1953
Black, Stephen A. (Stephen Ames). Eugene O'Neill; beyond mourning and tragedy. Yale Univ. Press 1999 xxiv, 543p $45; pa $17.95
92

ISBN 0-300-07676-2; 0-300-09399-3 (pa)
LC 99-33897
When Black "tracks down correspondences between O'Neill's life and art he adds zip to the life but depersonalizes the art. Still, as he brings the life and the art into apposition, new coloring is cast on a number of the plays. His observations will prove enlightening." New Leader
Includes bibliographical references

O'Neill, Tip, 1912-1994
Farrell, John A. Tip O'Neill and the Democratic century. Little, Brown 2001 776p il hardcover o.p. paperback available $17.95
92

1. United States—Politics and government—20th century
ISBN 0-316-18570-1 (pa)   LC 00-58005
This is a biography of the Boston Democrat "who rose through the ranks to serve as Speaker of the House during the Carter and Reagan administrations." Booklist
"Farrell's long, detailed and fascinating book is more than the definitive biography of a flawed but startlingly successful old-fashioned political leader. It's also a guided tour through American governmental history from the beginning of the New Deal through the Reagan years." N Y Times Book Rev
Includes bibliographical references

Orwell, George, 1903-1950
Meyers, Jeffrey. Orwell; wintry conscience of a generation. Norton 2000 380p il maps hardcover o.p. paperback available $16.95
92

ISBN 0-393-32263-7 (pa)   LC 00-38020
In this biography Meyers "writes about the aristocratic air Orwell cultivated at Eton; his devotion to social justice and instinct for self-punishment (which led him to live with the destitute and take a bullet in the Spanish Civil War); his steadfast socialism and hatred of totalitarianism; his mix of politeness and prickliness; his sadistic streak . . . and his desperate need for love, exhibited in his various affairs." Publ Wkly
"With wit and acumen, Meyers portrays a complex, eccentric, intelligent, and unbending man hard on family and friends, a writer of singular gifts, and a 'prophetic moralist' whose vision continues to illuminate society's dark side." Booklist
Includes bibliographical references

Palmer, Arnold, 1929-
Palmer, Arnold. A golfer's life; [by] Arnold Palmer with James Dodson. Ballantine Bks. 1999 420p il hardcover o.p. paperback available $15   **92**
ISBN 0-345-41482-9 (pa)   LC 98-51681
Also available Random House large print edition

Palmer's "immense popularity is widely credited with rescuing professional golf in the late 1950s and 1960s. Written with humor and candor, the book recounts Palmer's friendships and rivalries with the greats of the game, his enduring marriage to Winnie Palmer, his legendary triumphs and disasters, and his battle against cancer." Libr J

Parcells, Bill
Gutman, Bill. Parcells; a biography. Carroll & Graf Pubs. 2000 304p il hardcover o.p. paperback available $14   **92**
ISBN 0-7867-0934-0 (pa)
The author "tracks Parcells's rise from a star New Jersey athlete to a head coach in the NFL, first with the New York Giants, then the New England Patriots and finally the New York Jets." Publ Wkly

Parish, Sister, 1910-1994
Bartlett, Apple Parish. Sister: the life of legendary American interior decorator Mrs. Henry Parish II; [by] Apple Bartlett and Susan Bartlett Crater. St. Martin's Press 2000 xxiii, 357p il $35   **92**
ISBN 0-312-24240-9   LC 00-27968
"An oral history, compiled by the daughter and granddaughter of the formidably descended aristocrat who went into the decorating business in 1933 and lived a life characterized by robust frivolity and lots of hard work." N Y Times Book Rev
Includes bibliographical references

Parker, Dorothy, 1893-1967
Meade, Marion. Dorothy Parker; what fresh hell is this? Villard Bks. 1988 c1987 459p il o.p.; Penguin Bks. paperback available $17.95
92

ISBN 0-14-011616-8 (pa)   LC 87-40189
"The author has written a disturbing story of a writer whose life was marked by endless disturbances and self-depreciation, and who left behind no correspondence, manuscripts, or private papers. Under the circumstances, Ms. Meade has brilliantly reconstructed her subject's life. . . . The book is a tribute to a woman who left her mark on the literary history of her times and whose coruscating wit is still remembered." West Coast Rev Books
Includes bibliographical references

Parks, Rosa, 1913-
Brinkley, Douglas. Rosa Parks. Viking 2000 246p (Penguin lives series) $19.95
92

ISBN 0-670-89160-6   LC 00-35916
"A Lipper/Viking book"
"Rosa Parks' story takes readers from rural Alabama to the Montgomery Industrial School for Girls, marriage to barber Raymond Parks, quiet activism in the '30s and '40s, a first experience of integration at the Highlander Folk School, arrest in 1955 and the bus boycott, a move to Detroit, and more than 20 years on the staff of Rep. John Conyers (D-Mich.)." Booklist

Parks, Rosa, 1913-——*Continued*

Parks, Rosa. Quiet strength; the faith, the hope, and the heart of a woman who changed a nation; reflections by Rosa Parks with Gregory J. Reed. Zondervan 1994 93p il hardcover o.p. paperback available $9.99

92

ISBN 0-310-23587-1 (pa)   LC 94-46141

"Parks, one of the U.S.' authentic living legends, is the black lady who on December 1, 1955, refused to surrender her bus seat to a white man, was arrested under the Jim Crow law that required blacks to make way for whites, and thereby launched the yearlong bus boycott by blacks in Birmingham, Alabama, which led to the national overturning of that city's and similar segregation laws across the nation. In this tiny collection of what seem like outtakes from oral-history tapes, she rehearses her great day." Booklist

Includes bibliographical references

Patton, George S. (George Smith), 1885-1945

D'Este, Carlo. Patton; a genius for war. HarperCollins Pubs. 1995 977p il maps hardcover o.p. paperback available $21   **92**

ISBN 0-06-092762-3 (pa)   LC 95-38433

In this biography of the World War II general the author "provides new information from family archives and other sources about Patton's ancestry, childhood and pre-WW II military career. . . . The account of Patton's campaigns from North Africa through Sicily, Normandy and the Ardennes enables the reader to understand why the general is regarded as one of the great military leaders. This is a major biography of a major American military figure." Publ Wkly

Includes bibliographical references

Hirshson, Stanley P. General Patton: a soldier's life. HarperCollins Pubs. 2002 xxii, 826p il maps $34.95; pa $18.95   **92**

ISBN 0-06-000982-9; 0-06-000983-7 (pa)
LC 2002-68881

The author attempts "to round out the unknown familial aspects of Patton's life and [provide a] . . . context for understanding the enigmatic commander. . . . Those interested in Patton will find Hirshson's book valuable reading." Libr J

Includes bibliographical references

Paul VI, Pope, 1897-1978

Hebblethwaite, Peter. Paul VI; the first modern Pope. Paulist Press 1993 749p il $29.95   **92**

ISBN 0-8091-0461-X   LC 93-6475

This is a "biography of Giovanni Battista Montini, who followed John XXIII as Pope Paul VI (1963-78)." Libr J

This book is in no "sense an attempt to whitewash Paul, and its factual descriptions of the working of the Roman Curia are perturbing. But the portrait of the inner man is beautifully done." Times Lit Suppl

Includes bibliographical references

Paul, the Apostle, Saint

Murphy-O'Connor, J. (Jerome). Paul; a critical life; [by] Jerome Murphy-O'Connor. Clarendon Press 1996 416p maps hardcover o.p. paperback available $21   **92**

ISBN 0-19-285342-2 (pa)   LC 95-49173

This biography of the apostle Paul is based on an "analysis of his letters. . . . The first chapter of the book, 'The Chronological Framework,' compares evidence from the Pauline corpus with that of Luke's Acts and extant extrabiblical archaeological evidence. . . . The remaining 13 chapters, based on information extracted from the authentic Pauline letters, discuss in more detail specific events in Paul's life. . . . In addition to Paul's biography, Murphy-O'Connor also treats the development in Paul's theological thought." Libr J

"This is likely to become the standard work on Paul's life for the next generation and is warmly recommended as such." Choice

Includes bibliographical references

Wilson, A. N. (Andrew Norman). Paul: the mind of the Apostle. Norton 1997 273p hardcover o.p. paperback available $16.95

92

ISBN 0-393-31760-9 (pa)   LC 96-47834

The author gives "an explanation of the abiding influence of the apostle Paul in Western culture. He accomplishes this . . . by profiling Paul against the social context of the Greco-Roman world in which the apostle lived." Choice

"Wilson's insights fascinate and provoke. Even as rich and incisive a portrait as this one cannot provide a complete understanding of Paul or the turbulent time in which he lived, but readers will come away seeing the enigmatic apostle as an imaginative transformer who shaped a worldwide religious movement." Booklist

Includes bibliographical references

Pauling, Linus C., 1901-1994

Pauling, Linus C. Linus Pauling in his own words; selections from his writings, speeches, and interviews; edited by Barbara Marinacci; introduction by Linus Pauling. Simon & Schuster 1995 320p hardcover o.p. paperback available $20   **92**

ISBN 0-684-81387-4 (pa)   LC 95-31123

"A Touchstone book"

This book "attempts to follow the life and career of Dr. Pauling through his own writings, interspersed with narrative by the editor. The book succeeds wonderfully. Linus Pauling is unique among modern scientists, both for winning two Nobel Prizes and for his political and social views. Through his writings, the breadth and depth of his work become clear to the reader." Sci Books Films

Includes bibliographical references

Pei, I. M., 1917-

Wiseman, Carter. I.M. Pei: a profile in American architecture. Rev ed. Abrams 2001 340p il $65   **92**

ISBN 0-8109-3477-9   LC 2001-18904

First published 1990

The author presents "discussions of a handful of the most conspicuous works produced by one of American's foremost practicing architects. Beautifully illustrated (with many color photographs), handsomely produced,

Pei, I. M., 1917-—*Continued*

well written, highly informative, and aptly subtitled, this volume makes the works easily accessible to the general reading public." Choice [review of 1990 edition]

Pépin, Jacques

Pépin, Jacques. The apprentice: my life in the kitchen. Houghton Mifflin 2003 318p il $26   **92**

ISBN 0-618-19737-0   LC 2002-192158

Also available Thorndike Press large print edition

"Pépin recounts his journey from the kitchen of his mother's humble restaurant in rural France after World War II to his current position as author of 21 cookbooks, star of 13 PBS cooking shows and dean of special programs at the French Culinary Institute in New York City. . . . Each chapter concludes with one or two recipes." Publ Wkly

"Pépin relates how his interest in food and culinary techniques developed into passions for cooking and teaching. He does this deftly, neatly capturing personalities and events with clear, concise writing." Libr J

Pepys, Samuel, 1633-1703

Pepys, Samuel. The diary of Samuel Pepys. University of Calif. Press 1970-1983 11v il maps Apply to publisher for price and availability   **92**

1. Great Britain—History—1603-1714, Stuarts
2. Great Britain—Social life and customs

"Written in shorthand between 1660 and 1669 and not deciphered until 1825, when it was published in part, the Diary was never intended for the public eye. It not only presents a vivid picture of an age, but is also a uniquely uninhibited and spontaneous revelation of its author's life and character." Reader's Ency. 4th edition

Tomalin, Claire. Samuel Pepys; the unequalled self. Knopf 2002 xxiii, 470p il $30; pa $16.95   **92**

1. Great Britain—History—1603-1714, Stuarts
2. Great Britain—Social life and customs

ISBN 0-375-41143-7; 0-375-72553-9 (pa)

      LC 2002-75701

A biography of the government official whose diary vividly described life in Restoration London

"Tomalin mines the diary, and she also expands upon the characters and events, great and small, that affected Pepys' life and livelihood to bring the man and his milieu to life—pungently as well as vibrantly." Booklist

Includes bibliographical references

Peterson, Oscar, 1925-

Peterson, Oscar. A jazz odyssey: the life of Oscar Peterson; editor & consultant, Richard Palmer. Continuum 2002 382p il $29.95

    92

ISBN 0-8264-5807-6   LC 2002-73362

This is a memoir of the Canadian jazz pianist

"Peterson's discussion of the dynamics of the jazz trio and, in particular, the styles of the many outstanding bassists with whom he has played is a particular highlight." Booklist

Petit, Philippe, 1949-

Petit, Philippe. To reach the clouds; my high wire walk between the Twin Towers. North Point Press 2002 244p il $30   **92**

ISBN 0-86547-651-9   LC 2002-23520

"On August 7, 1974, French funambulist Petit, then 24, performed an astonishing high-wire act on a cable that he and his accomplices had surreptitiously rigged between the north and south towers of the World Trade Center. . . . Petit details the entire adventure." Libr J

"The way in which the walk itself stopped traffic and galvanized the city is captured in Petit's descriptions and the 140 b&w photos (including Petit's notebook sketches)." Publ Wkly

Petroski, Henry

Petroski, Henry. Paperboy; confessions of a future engineer. Knopf 2002 364p il maps hardcover o.p. paperback available $14   **92**

ISBN 0-375-71898-2 (pa)   LC 2001-38100

In this "memoir, Petroski reminisces about his idyllic 1950s Catholic boyhood in Cambria Heights, Queens, as a member of a guild of paperboys. . . . Petroski gives readers a warm, nostalgic riding tour of his youth and foreshadows the engineer-to-be in the boy." Publ Wkly

Philip II, King of Spain, 1527-1598

Kamen, Henry. Philip of Spain. Yale Univ. Press 1997 384p il maps $40; pa $18.95

    92

1. Spain—History

ISBN 0-300-07081-0; 0-300-07800-5 (pa)

      LC 96-52421

The author "offers the most favorable major assessment of Philip ever written in English. . . . The reason he has fared so badly until lately, Kamen . . . suggests, is that he 'failed to project his image', disdaining the visual and literary propaganda mastered by his rivals, especially Elizabeth of England." Atl Mon

"Kamen's prose is lucid, succinct, and thorough. . . . In humanizing a man too often viewed as a cardboard tyrant, Kamen has made a valuable contribution to European historiography." Booklist

Includes bibliographical references

Picasso, Pablo, 1881-1973

Léal, Brigitte. The ultimate Picasso; {by} Brigitte Léal, Christine Piot, Marie-Laure Bernadac; preface by Jean Leymarie. Abrams 2000 535p il hardcover o.p. paperback available $35   **92**

ISBN 0-8109-9114-4 (pa)

These "essays detail events in Picasso's life and the circumstances surrounding the creation of his art, his influences, and world events. This lavish, handsome book contains more than 1200 reproductions, nearly 800 in full color." SLJ

Includes bibliographical references

Penrose, Sir Roland. Picasso: his life and work. 3rd ed. University of Calif. Press 1981 517p il hardcover o.p. paperback available $21.95   **92**

ISBN 0-520-04207-7 (pa)   LC 80-54015

First published 1958 by Harper

The author "has produced a painstaking, comprehensive biography . . . and, what is more, a pop-

Picasso, Pablo, 1881-1973—*Continued*

ular biography, assuming neither knowledge of nor sympathy with twentieth-century art on the part of the reader." Times Lit Suppl [review of 1958 edition]

Includes bibliographical references

Pickford, Mary, 1893-1979

Whitfield, Eileen. Pickford; the woman who made Hollywood. University Press of Ky. 1997 441p il $27.50 **92**

ISBN 0-8131-2045-4   LC 97-29312

"Silent screen star Mary Pickford was 'America's Sweetheart,' capturing the imagination of the public as 'Little Mary,' the adolescent with spunk. She married swashbuckler Douglas Fairbanks, and with Charlie Chaplin and D.W. Griffith they formed United Artists, the first production company run by people who acted and directed. . . . Though it does include delicious anecdotes from those who were there, this is not simply a typical celebrity biography but a 'biography' of the times." Libr J

Includes bibliographical references

Pinchot, Gifford, 1865-1946

Miller, Char. Gifford Pinchot and the making of modern environmentalism. Island Press (Washington, D.C.) 2001 458p il $28 **92**

ISBN 1-55963-822-2   LC 2001-5665

"Charismatic, progressive, and controversial, Gifford Pinchot (1865-1946) established and directed the Forest Service under Theodore Roosevelt, lobbied hard for responsible logging practices, expressed prescient warnings about pollution, and called for sustainable energy. Miller's animated biography portrays Pinchot in all his fervor, and environmentalism in all its complexity." Booklist

Includes bibliographical references

Pinkerton, Allan, 1819-1884

Mackay, James A. (James Alexander). Allan Pinkerton; the first private eye; [by] James Mackay. Wiley 1997 256p il $35 **92**

1. Pinkerton's National Detective Agency

ISBN 0-471-19415-8   LC 97-21271

"Though Pinkerton started the first U.S. detective agency after successfully uncovering a counterfeit ring, little was known about him. The author does an excellent job of tracing Pinkerton's early life and his arrival in the United States from Scotland. Then he examines better-known aspects of Pinkerton's career—his part in Lincoln's train ride through Baltimore, investigation of the Confederate spy Rose Greenhow, and association with Gen. George McClellan, his mentor and hero." Libr J

Includes bibliographical references

Pirsig, Robert M., 1928-

Pirsig, Robert M. Zen and the art of motorcycle maintenance; an inquiry into values. Morrow 1974 412p $26; pa $13 **92**

ISBN 0-688-00230-7; 0-688-05230-4 (pa)

A collection of the author's philosophical musings inspired by a motorcycle trip with his son

Pius XII, Pope, 1876-1958

Cornwell, John. Hitler's pope: the secret history of Pius XII. Viking 1999 430p il hardcover o.p. paperback available $15 **92**

ISBN 0-14-029627-1 (pa)   LC 99-28311

"Relying on exclusive access to Vatican and Jesuit archives, . . . [the author] argues that through a 1933 Concordat with Hitler, Pope Pius XII facilitated the dictator's rise—and, ultimately, the Holocaust." Libr J

Includes bibliographical references

Plath, Sylvia

Plath, Sylvia. The unabridged journals of Sylvia Plath, 1950-1962; edited by Karen V. Kukil. Anchor Press 2000 732p il pa $18 **92**

ISBN 0-385-72025-4   LC 00-42024

First published 2000 in the United Kingdom with title: Journals of Sylvia Plath, 1950-1962

Kukil presents diaries written by the poet Sylvia Plath. "This edition includes two journals written between August 1957 and November 1959 that [her husband Ted] Hughes ordered to be unsealed in 1997 shortly before his death." Christ Sci Monit

"This is essential for anyone engaged in Plath studies." Libr J

Includes bibliographical references

Wagner-Martin, Linda. Sylvia Plath; a literary life. St. Martin's Press 1999 172p (Literary lives) $45; pa $19.95 **92**

ISBN 0-312-22323-4; 1-40391-653-5 (pa)   LC 99-12184

First published 1998 in the United Kingdom

The author "begins by summarizing Plath's childhood, which was marked by her educator parents' deep involvement with books, and her father's unexpected death when she was eight. . . . Wagner-Martin works strictly by the light of Plath's writings as she spins the oft-told tale of Plath's blazing creativity and fatal despair, and what emerges is a tragic tale of an artist envied and mistreated by those closest to her, and of a poet far more artistic than her reputation for being confessional implies." Booklist

Includes bibliographical references

Poe, Edgar Allan, 1809-1849

Silverman, Kenneth. Edgar A. Poe; mournful and never-ending remembrance. HarperCollins Pubs. 1991 564p il hardcover o.p. paperback available $18 **92**

ISBN 0-06-092331-8 (pa)   LC 90-56397

The author explains "how Poe's early life influenced his work. He details Poe's turbulent career as poet, short story writer, and editor . . . and traces his literary development through bouts of alcoholism and hallucinations and disputes with literary rivals. An excellent addition to the literature that furthers understanding of America's gothic tale-teller." Libr J

Includes bibliographical references

Walsh, John Evangelist. Midnight dreary: the mysterious death of Edgar Allan Poe. Rutgers Univ. Press 1998 199p il $25 **92**

ISBN 0-8135-2605-1   LC 98-24043

Also available in paperback from Palgrave

Poe, Edgar Allan, 1809-1849—*Continued*
This is an account of the "circumstances leading to Poe's death in Baltimore, in October 1849." Publ Wkly
Walsh "has undertaken a superbly informed speculation on the week proceeding the mysterious death of Edgar Allan Poe 150 years ago." Libr J
Includes bibliographical references

Poitier, Sidney
Poitier, Sidney. The measure of a man; a spiritual autobiography. HarperSanFrancisco 2000 255p il hardcover o.p. paperback available $16 **92**
ISBN 0-06-251608-6 (pa)   LC 99-88322
Also available large print edition $26 (ISBN 0-06-019717-X)
"Poitier attempts to unravel for himself his own remarkable life story, looking at early life experiences, his family, and various themes that he believes have contributed to his success. *Measure* is not a chronological autobiography; the book emphasizes themes that have shaped his life. . . . Poitier's tale is an affirmation of the value of morality and personal integrity in leading a successful, fulfilling life." Booklist

Pompadour, Jeanne Antoinette Poisson, marquise de, 1721-1764
Lever, Evelyne. Madame de Pompadour; translated from the French by Catherine Temerson. Farrar, Straus & Giroux 2002 310p il $26; pa $16.95 **92**
1. France—History—1589-1789, Bourbons
ISBN 0-374-11308-4; 0-312-31050-1 (pa)
LC 2002-22811
Original French edition, 2000
This is a biography of "Madame de Pompadour, official 'favorite' of France's handsome but moody Louis XV." Booklist
"Lever has crafted a detailed and fascinating portrait of the woman who pretty well ran France from 1745 to 1764." Publ Wkly
Includes bibliographical references

Porter, Cole, 1891-1964
McBrien, William. Cole Porter; a biography. Knopf 1998 459p il hardcover o.p. paperback available $15 **92**
ISBN 0-679-72792-2 (pa)   LC 97-46116
In this biography of the American songwriter, the author "weaves a complex and groundbreaking portrait of Porter, interspersed with lyrics and 72 illustrations, recounting his affluent upbringing in Peru, Ind., and his emergence in the 1930s as the musical theater's reigning sophisticate. . . . This astute biography will help to create a standard-setting portrait of Porter as a homosexual artist in a heterosexual world." Publ Wkly
Includes bibliographical references

Potemkin, Grigoriĭ Aleksandrovich, kníàz, 1739-1791
Montefiore, Sebag. Prince of princes: the life of Potemkin. Thomas Dunne Bks. 2001 634p il $45 **92**
ISBN 0-312-27815-2   LC 2001-42382
First published 2000 in the United Kingdom
A "biography of Prince Grigory Alexandrovich Potemkin . . . who served as Catherine the Great's military strategist, diplomat, literary adviser, art collector and lov-

er." N Y Times Book Rev
"The palace intrigue is . . . magnified by this well-documented work. . . . Montefiore's job as biographer is to aggrandize his subject, and so Potemkin here assumes nearly mythical stature in 18th-century history." Libr J
Includes bibliographical references

Pound, Ezra, 1885-1972
Tytell, John. Ezra Pound; the solitary volcano. Anchor Press 1987 368p il hardcover o.p. paperback available $19 **92**
ISBN 0-385-19870-1 (pa)   LC 86-25912
"In this incisive interpretative biography, based on interviews with those who knew him and a mass of published and unpublished Poundiana, Tytell examines the circumstances behind the poems and thereby generates new understanding of the man." Publ Wkly
Includes bibliographical references

Powell, Colin L.
Powell, Colin L. My American journey; [by] Colin L. Powell, with Joseph E. Persico. Random House 1995 643p il $26.95; pa $14.95 **92**
ISBN 0-679-43296-5; 0-345-46641-1 (pa)
LC 95-17119
Also available large print edition $16.95 (ISBN 0-679-76511-5)
"This is the 'story so far,' as General Powell tells it, from the Bronx to Vietnam to the White House, from the common to the regal. His account is one of . . . extremes, tales that span from peeling potatoes with the Soviet General Staff to conversing with the Queen of England." Libr J
This "is an endearing and well-written book. It will make you like Colin Powell." N Y Times Book Rev

Presley, Elvis, 1935-1977
Guralnick, Peter. Careless love: the unmaking of Elvis Presley. Little, Brown 1999 767p il $27.95; pa $17.95 **92**
ISBN 0-316-33222-4; 0-316-33297-6 (pa)
LC 98-25778
This second and concluding volume of Guralnick's biography of the rock star covers "Elvis's hitch in the army through his death in 1977. . . . The breadth of Guralnick's research is nothing short of amazing, and his lyrical narrative presents an empathetic portrait of a man struggling with drugs, sex, family, personal eccentricities, money, and the delicate web of relationships surrounding any famous figure." Libr J
Includes bibliographical references

Guralnick, Peter. Last train to Memphis: the rise of Elvis Presley. Little, Brown 1994 560p il $27.95; pa $17.95 **92**
ISBN 0-316-33220-8; 0-316-33225-9 (pa)
LC 94-10763
The first of a two volume biography of the rock pioneer
The author "depicts Elvis as a naive yet extremely talented boy whose dream of stardom came true, leaving him a virtual prisoner of his own success. . . . Taking pains to keep the story fresh and flowing and refraining from foreshadowing and editorializing, Guralnick lets the facts speak for themselves." Booklist
Includes bibliographical references

Price, Reynolds, 1933-

Price, Reynolds. Clear pictures; first loves, first guides. Atheneum Pubs. 1989 304p il $26 **92**

ISBN 0-684-84752-3   LC 88-34395

North Carolina novelist Price "trains his lenses on family, neighbors, rural surroundings, and a few significant 'snapshot' scenes that provide a kind of narrative continuity to a sensitive, much-loved and loving, child's slow realization of himself. . . . The achievements of the autobiography are multiple, among them a clear-sighted chronicle of the rural South in the Thirties and Forties." Libr J

Price, Reynolds. A whole new life. Atheneum Pubs. 1994 213p $23; pa $13

92

1. Cancer—Personal narratives
ISBN 0-684-87255-2; 0-7432-3854-0 (pa)
LC 93-35967

Price gives an "account of his 'mid-life collision with cancer and paralysis.' In 1984, he was found to have a malignant tumor of the spinal cord, and three surgeries and radiation therapy arrested the growth but left him unable to walk. Although he has not written an essay on illness per se, he embraces elements of an essay as he pauses to ponder nature's systemic breakdowns, the importance of friendships in times of stress, or how to handle pain psychologically. His book is primarily a chronological narrative of events in the treatment of his disease and his rehabilitation." Booklist

Prokofiev, Sergey, 1891-1953

Nice, David. Prokofiev: from Russia to the West, 1891-1935. Yale Univ. Press 2003 390p il music $35 **92**

ISBN 0-300-09914-2

First of a projected two volume work

"Part 1 chronicles Prokofiev's childhood, family relationships, and training at the St. Petersburg Conservatoire, while Part 2 covers his concert tours in America, France, and Germany and prodigious compositional output, beginning with the fairy tale opera, *The Love of Three Oranges*. . . . Nice embeds many musical examples in the body of the text and writes cogently about them. . . . Overall, the writing is fluid and unencumbered by excessive analytical detail, and at times witty. . . . Throughout, the composer's outsized personality and compositional brilliance shine through." Libr J

Includes discography and bibliographical references

Proust, Marcel, 1871-1922

Carter, William C. Marcel Proust; a life. Yale Univ. Press 2000 946p $45; pa $18.95

92

ISBN 0-300-08145-6; 0-300-09400-0 (pa)
LC 99-53701

"Excavating biographic details out of such material as untranslated memoirs and recently collected letters, Carter . . . accounts for the daily affairs of this social butterfly-turned-hypochondriac and shut-in. Proust's romances and infatuations, his political action during the Dreyfus affair, and his literary runs-ins with Anatole France and André Gide, as well as larger issues such as his homosexuality, all receive lengthy treatment." Publ Wkly

Includes bibliographical references

Tadié, Jean-Yves. Marcel Proust; translated by Euan Cameron. Viking 2000 xx, 986p hardcover o.p. paperback available $20 **92**

ISBN 0-14-100203-4 (pa)   LC 00-20565

Original French edition, 1996

In this "biography of Proust, Tadie measures his subject's life by focusing steadily on the influences that shaped his seven-volume masterpiece, *Remembrance of Things Past*." Booklist

"The sheer breadth of Tadie's research can occasionally feel overwhelming, but at the same time his familiarity with Proust's life and work enables him to reject the *idées reçues* that have shaped his subject's legend." New Yorker

Includes bibliographical references

Puccini, Giacomo, 1858-1924

The Puccini companion; edited by William Weaver and Simonetta Puccini. Norton 1994 436p il hardcover o.p. paperback available $19.95 **92**

ISBN 0-393-32052-9 (pa)   LC 93-27718

This is a "collection of articles by an assortment of top musicologists, music critics, and opera lovers whose coverage ranges from Puccini's early efforts at a symphonic style to the modernist implications of his final opus, the aforementioned *Turandot*. All the essays are thoroughgoing yet unpedantic. . . . The editors conclude the volume with useful bibliographies, chronologies, plot summaries of individual works, and a directory of people involved with Puccini." Booklist

Puig, Manuel

Levine, Suzanne Jill. Manuel Puig and spider woman; his life and fictions. Farrar, Straus & Giroux 2000 446p il o.p.; University of Wis. Press paperback available $19.95 **92**

ISBN 0-299-17574-X (pa)   LC 99-39130

"Born and raised in a small provincial town in Argentina, Puig connected with the outside world through film. Eventually, though, he sought a wider world, finding it first in Buenos Aires and later abroad. Levine, who translated Puig's novels into English, knew the man personally and brings great psychological depth to her portrait, especially in her treatment of his novels and the role of the cinema in both his life and work." Booklist

Includes bibliographical references

Pulitzer, Joseph, 1885-1955

Pfaff, Daniel W. Joseph Pulitzer II and the Post-dispatch; a newspaperman's life. Pennsylvania State Univ. Press 1991 455p il $54.50 **92**

1. St. Louis post-dispatch (Newspaper)
ISBN 0-271-00748-6   LC 90-49036

The author examines Joseph Pulitzer's tenure as editor of the St. Louis Post-Dispatch and his uneasy relationship with his legendary father

The author "has written an outstanding biography, one that may set students of journalistic history to wondering whether Pulitzer II was not a better newsman than his revered father." Publ Wkly

Includes bibliographical references

Puller, Lewis B., 1945-1994

Puller, Lewis B. Fortunate son; the autobiography of Lewis B. Puller, Jr. Grove Weidenfeld 1991 389p hardcover o.p. paperback available $13 **92**
1. Vietnam War, 1961-1975—Personal narratives
ISBN 0-8021-3690-7 (pa) LC 91-4463

This is a "Vietnam memoir by a veteran who survived a truly horrifying array of wounds (the loss of both legs, one hand, and most of the remaining hand), then went on to survive a bout with alcoholism, earn a law degree, preserve his marriage, and become active in veterans affairs. Puller managed all this in the long shadow of his father, the legendary marine general Chesty Puller." Booklist

Putin, Vladimir

Putin, Vladimir. First person: an astonishingly frank self-portrait; by Russia's president Vladimir Putin with Nataliya Gevorkyan, Natalya Timakova, and Andrei Kolesnikov; translated by Catherine A. Fitzpatrick. PublicAffairs 2000 206p il pa $15 **92**
ISBN 1-58648-018-9 LC 00-132549

This volume is "the product of some 24 hours of interviews with Putin conducted by three Russian journalists, with brief comments from other sources, including Putin's family, friends, teachers, and some associates. . . . The approach is chronological, describing Putin as son, schoolboy, university student, young intelligence specialist, spy, democrat, bureaucrat, family man, and politician." Booklist

Pyle, Ernie, 1900-1945

Tobin, James. Ernie Pyle's war; America's eyewitness to World War II. Free Press 1997 312p il $25 **92**
ISBN 0-684-83642-4 LC 97-6165

Also available in paperback from University Press of Kan.

"This is the portrait of a complex, enormously gifted but tortured writer, entrapped and ultimately driven to death by a sense of obligation to the image he inadvertently created of himself." N Y Times Book Rev

"Living and working among the troops he so vividly chronicled, Pyle offered a unique insider's perspective of the harsh reality experienced by the common soldier during World War II. . . . A respectful and insightful biography of a giant among journalists." Booklist
Includes bibliographical references

Rabin, Yitzhak, 1922-1995

Kurzman, Dan. Soldier of peace: the life of Yitzhak Rabin. HarperCollins Pubs. 1998 555p $30 **92**
1. Israel—Politics and government
ISBN 0-06-018684-4 LC 97-51898

A review of the life and political career of the late Israeli leader
Includes bibliographical references

Shalom, friend: the life and legacy of Yitzhak Rabin; the Jerusalem Report staff; edited by David Horovitz; prologue by Hirsch Goodman. Newmarket Press 1996 314p il maps $24.95 **92**
ISBN 1-55704-287-X LC 96-5146

"This is a collaborative effort by more than a dozen writers and editors of the Jerusalem Report, a prestigious Israeli newsmagazine, all of whom had close personal and professional knowledge of the former prime minister, assassinated in November 1995. Their views are supplemented by numerous interviews with knowledgeable people." Libr J
Includes bibliographical references

Raleigh, Elizabeth Throckmorton, Lady, d. 1647

Beer, Anna R. My just desire; the life of Bess Ralegh, wife to Sir Walter; [by] Anna Beer. Ballantine Bks. 2003 xx, 292p il $24.95 **92**
ISBN 0-345-45290-9 LC 2003-51845

This is an account of the life of Bess Ralegh, courtier to Queen Elizabeth I and wife of Sir Walter. "During her nearly three decades of marriage to Sir Walter, he was largely absent because of expeditions or long stints in the Tower of London, and Bess was compelled to wear a number of 'manly' hats: business manager, political infighter and guardian of her husband's reputation." Publ Wkly

"Beer's 'revisionist' biography . . . fascinates with its vivid re-creation of the tangled interrelationships, jealousies, alliances, and betrayals of English court life. . . . This insightful work is recommended for libraries." Libr J
Includes bibliographical references

Ramanujan Aiyangar, Srinivasa, 1887-1920

Kanigel, Robert. The man who knew infinity: a life of the genius, Ramanujan. Scribner 1991 438p il maps o.p.; Washington Sq. Press paperback available $15 **92**
ISBN 0-671-75061-5 (pa) LC 90-49788

This biography traces the life of the Indian mathematician. "Working alone in relative obscurity and lacking the usual academic credentials [Ramanujan] could easily have passed unnoticed. However, with the help of a handful of friends and the ultimate support of renowned English mathematician G.H. Hardy, his work was brought to the attention of the world." Libr J

"Kanigel deserves high praise for a work of arduous research and rare insight." Booklist
Includes bibliographical references

Rand, Ayn, 1905-1982

Rand, Ayn. Journals of Ayn Rand; edited by David Harriman; foreword by Leonard Peikoff. Dutton 1997 727p il hardcover o.p. paperback available $22 **92**
ISBN 0-452-27887-2 (pa) LC 97-12737

"This work offers almost everything the author ever wrote to herself. As intriguing yet sometimes numbing as her fiction, the book, which covers the years from 1927 to the mid-1970s, contains her first philosophical stabs, notes on her novels, HUAC testimony against alleged Hollywood communists, and her unfinished projects." Publ Wkly

Rand, Ayn, 1905-1982—*Continued*

Rand, Ayn. Letters of Ayn Rand; edited by Michael S. Berliner; introduction by Leonard Peikoff. Dutton 1995 xxi, 681p il hardcover o.p. paperback available $20   **92**
ISBN 0-452-27404-4 (pa)   LC 94-23646

"Sprinkled with critiques of liberals, leftists and others whom she saw as corrupted by collectivist thinking, the voluminous correspondence reflects Rand's desperate concerns for her parents and sisters, trapped under Stalinism in her native Russia (which she left for Hollywood in 1926), and includes her analyses of her novels' plots as well as pessimistic cultural commentary on an America she considered to be in decline." Publ Wkly

"Imbued with her fiercely held beliefs, the letters most devoted to politics and philosophy fairly blaze off the page. . . . Regardless of one's opinion of her thinking, her letters add greatly to our understanding of a most exceptional woman of letters." Booklist

Ray, Man, 1890-1976

Lottman, Herbert R. Man Ray's Montparnasse. Abrams 2001 261p il $29.95   **92**

ISBN 0-8109-4333-6   LC 2001-633
Lottman presents a "snapshot of Man Ray between the two world wars, emphasizing the 1920s, with the developing Montparnasse section of Paris as the backdrop. Here are the cutting-edge dadaists and surrealists flanking Man Ray and his unerring camera eye, along with poets and artists, collectors, lovers, and other assorted characters. . . . Lottman's vivid exploration of 20th-century art events will serve the art historian and student of Paris very well in documenting an essential epoch and place." Libr J
Includes bibliographical references

Reagan, Nancy, 1923-

Edwards, Anne. The Reagans: portrait of a marriage. See entry under Reagan, Ronald, 1911-2004   **92**

Reagan, Ronald, 1911-2004

D'Souza, Dinesh. Ronald Reagan; how an ordinary man became an extraordinary leader. Free Press 1997 292p hardcover o.p. paperback available $13   **92**
1. United States—Politics and government—1974-1989
ISBN 0-684-84823-6 (pa)   LC 97-31396
In this study of the fortieth president of the United States, D'Souza "argues that Reagan earned presidential stature comparable with that of Washington, Lincoln, and Roosevelt." Booklist
The author's "provocative argument for Reagan's greatness opens a necessary and complicated debate." Commentary
Includes bibliographical references

Edwards, Anne. The Reagans: portrait of a marriage. St. Martin's Press 2003 420p il $27.95; pa $16.95   **92**
1. Reagan, Nancy, 1923-
ISBN 0-312-28500-0; 0-312-33117-7 (pa)
LC 2003-46684
This biography examines the personal and political relationship of the fortieth president of the United States and his wife, Nancy

"While Edwards celebrates the Reagans' achievements, she does not shy away from presenting the darker, grimmer side of their life and does a wonderful job of fully fleshing out the convoluted and tortured emotions that define this famous family. In all, she offers an engaging yet honest look at the human experience played out on the public stage." Publ Wkly

Includes bibliographical references

Redding, Otis, 1941-1967

Freeman, Scott. Otis!: the Otis Redding story. St. Martin's Press 2001 261p il hardcover o.p. paperback available $14.95
  92

ISBN 0-312-30297-5 (pa)   LC 2001-41976
A biography of the African American singer whose recording of "(Sittin' on) The Dock of the Bay" became a mainstream hit after his death in an airplane crash in 1967
"This is a fine and vital pop-music book." Booklist

Reeve, Christopher

Reeve, Christopher. Still me. Random House 1998 309p il hardcover o.p. paperback available $7.99   **92**
1. Physically handicapped
ISBN 0-345-43241-X (pa)   LC 98-10223
Also available large print edition $14.95 (ISBN 0-375-70234-2)
This autobiography begins with Reeve's "riding accident and relates in almost slow-motion detail what happened before and after the near-fatal spill in 1995. His remembrances then move back and forth in time. Reeve's early life, his complex relationships, and his career are juxtaposed against the life he leads now as filmmaker, husband and father, and spokesman for those with spinal-cord injuries." Booklist

Reichl, Ruth

Reichl, Ruth. Comfort me with apples; more adventures at the table. Random House 2001 302p $24.95; pa $13.95   **92**
ISBN 0-375-50195-9; 0-375-75873-9 (pa)
LC 00-53355
Also available G.K. Hall large print edition
Sequel to Tender at the bone (1998)
"In this second installment of her memoirs, [Reichl] retraces her route from married life on a commune in late-seventies Berkeley to her first job as a food critic, dining at expensive restaurants in Los Angeles with her glamorous editor. . . . Reichl writes with gusto, and her story has all the ingredients of a modern fairy tale: hard work, weird food, and endless curiosity." New Yorker

Rembrandt Harmenszoon van Rijn, 1606-1669

Schama, Simon. Rembrandt's eyes. Knopf 1999 640p il $50; pa $35   **92**
ISBN 0-679-40256-X; 0-375-70981-9 (pa)
LC 99-19971
Schama's prose unfurls the life of Rembrandt in all its pathos. From prodigy to pauper, the troubled genius of 17th century Dutch painting is intricately conceived as he rises and falls in a world of war, plague and stolid bourgeois comfort. . . . Schama's book is a marvel of storytelling: sometimes heart pounding, always sympathetic and coolly reasoned. Seamlessly joining social history and art, what a triumph of scholarship and imagination. Time

Remington, Frederic, 1861-1909

Dippie, Brian W. The Frederic Remington
Art Museum collection. Abrams 2000 264p il
$49.50   **92**
1. West (U.S.) in art
ISBN 0-8109-6711-1   LC 00-49339
This biography examines the artist's life and work and
follows his evolution from illustrator to artist
"Photographs and comparative images enhance the au-
thor's discussions of Remington himself and of the indi-
vidual paintings, drawings, and sculptures." Libr J
Includes bibliographical references

Renoir, Auguste, 1841-1919

Renoir, Jean. Renoir: my father;
introduction by Robert Herbert; translated by
Randolph and Dorothy Weaver. New York
Review of Bks. 2001 437p il pa $17.95
                                              92
ISBN 0-940322-77-3   LC 2001-2539
A reissue of the title first published 1962 by Little,
Brown
The author "tells the life story of his father, Pierre
Auguste Renoir, the great Impressionist painter. Recount-
ing Pierre-Auguste's extraordinary career, beginning as a
painter of fans and porcelain, recording the rules of
thumb by which he worked, and capturing his unpreten-
tious and wonderfully engaging talk and personality. . . .
[This volume] includes 12 pages of color plates and 18
pages of black and white images." Publisher's note

Reston, James, 1909-1995

Stacks, John F. Scotty: James B. Reston
and the rise and fall of American journalism.
Little, Brown 2003 373p il $29.95   **92**
ISBN 0-316-80985-3   LC 2002-20776
"The life of a journalist who joined The New York
Times in 1939 and came to personify it; his access to the
powerful, who came to trust his balance and propriety,
served him well in the 1950's, less well in the age of
Vietnam and Watergate." N Y Times Book Rev
"This is a straightforward biography, well researched
and competently written." Publ Wkly
Includes bibliographical references

Rich, Buddy, 1917-1987

Tormé, Mel. Traps, the drum wonder: the
life of Buddy Rich. Oxford Univ. Press 1991
233p il   **92**
                                      LC 90-22594
Available in hardcover and paperback from Hal Leonard Pub. Corp.
"Singer Tormé here celebrates his friend, the late
Rich, who was one of the most famous and explosive
jazz drummers." Libr J
"Mr. Tormé's account of Rich's struggle with the
brain tumor that killed him at the age of 69 is clear-eyed,
understated and powerful. Rich was brave, and prickly,
to the end. His biographer has managed to present a
sympathetic portrait of a difficult person. One comes
away from this very touching book with a palpable sense
of Buddy Rich's complexity, and with admiration for
Mel Tormé's accomplishment." N Y Times Book Rev

Richardson, John, 1924-

Richardson, John. The sorcerer's
apprentice; Picasso, Provence, and Douglas
Cooper. Knopf 1999 318p o.p.; University of
Chicago Press paperback available $17   **92**
1. Cooper, Douglas, 1911-1984
ISBN 0-226-71245-1 (pa)   LC 99-27200
Picasso biographer John Richardson "has written a
concise account of the first half of his own life and notably of his long relationship as a young man with the
Cubist art historian and collector Douglas Cooper. The
account concentrates on the dozen years, from early 1949
to the end of 1960, when Richardson lived with Cooper,
visiting museums and monuments all over Europe, meeting the great artists and other personalities of the day,
and restoring the colonnaded Château de Castille in the
south of France." N Y Times Book Rev
Includes bibliographical references

Richelieu, Armand Jean du Plessis, Cardinal, duc de, 1585-1642

Levi, Anthony. Cardinal Richelieu and the
making of France. Carroll & Graf Pubs. 2000
327p il $26   **92**
1. France—History—1589-1789, Bourbons
ISBN 0-7867-0778-X   LC 2001-267748
In this biography of the first minister to King Louis
XIII, the author "narrates how Richelieu brought about
financial, military, administrative, and cultural centralization." Libr J
"Levi gives Richelieu well-deserved credit for molding
France into a modern nation-state. . . . This is an interesting portrait of an admirable, but not very lovable his-
torical giant." Booklist
Includes bibliographical references

Richthofen, Manfred von, Freiherr, 1892-1918

Kilduff, Peter. Richthofen; beyond the
legend of the Red Baron. Wiley 1994 c1993
256p il maps hardcover o.p. paperback
available $19.95   **92**
1. World War, 1914-1918—Aerial operations
ISBN 0-471-12033-2 (pa)   LC 93-240935
First published 1993 in the United Kingdom
In this biography of the WWI flying ace "Kilduff focuses on details, clarifying Richthofen's victory list and
analyzing the circumstances of how he was shot down."
Publ Wkly
"Together with diary entries, letters, and archival materials, these descriptions form a vivid picture of World
War I air combat. A valuable treatment of a remarkable
life." Libr J
Includes bibliographical references

Rilke, Rainer Maria, 1875-1926

Rilke, Rainer Maria. Diaries of a young
poet; translated and annotated by Edward
Snow and Michael Winkler. Norton 1997 xxi,
306p il hardcover o.p. paperback available
$15.95   **92**
ISBN 0-393-31850-8 (pa)
"Three diaries reveal three Rilkes. The Florence Diary,
which he began at twenty-two, is a kind of open letter
to his then love, Lou Andreas-Salomé, full of youthful
ardor and sublime observations of art and nature. . . .
The Schmargendorf Diary reveals the virtuoso at play,
with slender fragments of stories, fairy tales, and poems

Rilke, Rainer Maria, 1875-1926—*Continued*
following each other in dazzling succession. The last diary, written during his stay in Worpswede, is the most rewarding, for the chance to watch Rilke's rich friendships with other artists ripen alongside the growing authority of his poetic voice." New Yorker

Rivera, Diego, 1886-1957
Hamill, Pete. Diego Rivera. Abrams 1999 207p il $49.50; pa $24.95 **92**
  ISBN 0-8109-3234-2; 0-8109-9082-2 (pa)
                  LC 99-28100
The author examines "Rivera's work and diverse styles. He also describes the pivotal role Rivera's art played in Mexico's development." N Y Times Book Rev
Includes bibliographical references

Marnham, Patrick. Dreaming with his eyes open: a life of Diego Rivera. Knopf 1998 350p il o.p.; University of Calif. Press paperback available $24.95 **92**
  ISBN 0-520-22408-6 (pa)   LC 98-6145
  "Retracing the steps of writers who've tackled Rivera's life and times before him, Marnham attempts to separate the facts from the fables surrounding the man." Publ Wkly
  "For the browsing public as well as specialists in European, Latin American, and American modern art, this book is not to be overlooked." Libr J
Includes bibliographical references

Robeson, Paul, 1898-1976
Robeson, Paul, Jr. The undiscovered Paul Robeson; the early years (1898-1939); [by] Paul Robeson, Jr. Wiley 2001 383p il $30
                              92
  ISBN 0-471-24265-9   LC 2001-17656
This is the first volume of a biography of the African American actor, singer and political activist by his son. It covers the years from Robeson's birth in Princeton, N.J., through the 1930s
  "Extensively illustrated with personal photographs, this is a unique account of a brilliant but troubled man." Libr J

Robinson, Jackie, 1919-1972
Falkner, David. Great time coming: the life of Jackie Robinson, from baseball to Birmingham. Simon & Schuster 1995 382p il hardcover o.p. paperback available $18.95
                                92
  ISBN 0-684-82348-9 (pa)   LC 94-44876
This is a biography of the baseball player and civil rights activist. In addition to covering Robinson's professional career, the book focuses attention on his life after baseball
  "Falkner has written a very balanced account—neither muckraking nor fawning—of a fascinating and complex figure, one whose importance and interest reaches well beyond his exploits as an athlete." Christ Sci Monit
Includes bibliographical references

Rockefeller, David, 1915-
Rockefeller, David. Memoirs. Random House 2002 517p $35; pa $17.95 **92**
  1. Chase Manhattan Bank, N.A.
  ISBN 0-679-40588-7; 0-8129-6973-1 (pa)
                 LC 2002-24800
"This autobiography by the youngest son of John D. Rockefeller Jr. and Abby Aldrich Rockefeller is also a history of 20th-century America and its influence in the world order." Libr J
"Rockefeller's style is restrained and self-deprecating; the account of his attempts to modernize and globalize Chase makes for excellent business history, and his sketch of his complicated relationship with his brother is especially convincing." New Yorker

Rockefeller, John D. (John Davison), 1839-1937
Chernow, Ron. Titan: the life of John D. Rockefeller, Sr. Random House 1998 xxii, 774p il $30; pa $18 **92**
  ISBN 0-679-43808-4; 0-679-75703-1 (pa)
                 LC 97-33117
This is a biography of the industrialist who created Standard Oil. "Chernow presents Rockefeller as a principled, enterprising monopolist whose philanthropic abilities rivaled his knack for making money." Publ Wkly
"This book is a triumph of the art of biography. Unflaggingly interesting, it brings John D. Rockefeller Sr. . . to life through sustained narrative portraiture of the large-scale, 19th-century kind." N Y Times Book Rev
Includes bibliographical references

Rockne, Knute, 1888-1931
Robinson, Ray. Rockne of Notre Dame; the making of a football legend. Oxford Univ. Press 1999 290p il hardcover o.p. paperback available $16.95 **92**
  ISBN 0-19-515792-3 (pa)   LC 99-13712
  "After a childhood sketch, Robinson briefly touches on Rockne's playing career before devoting most of the book to a game-by-game description of Rockne's 12 years as coach, during which his Notre Dame teams, with the help of Rockne's motivational techniques and coaching tactics, won an astounding 105 games while losing only 12. To Robinson's credit, the book is cleanly written and mainly free of sports jargon." Publ Wkly

Rockwell, Norman, 1894-1978
Claridge, Laura P. Norman Rockwell; a life; [by] Laura Claridge. Random House 2001 546p il hardcover o.p. paperback available $16.95 **92**
  ISBN 0-8129-6723-2 (pa)   LC 2001-19784
  "Claridge peers beyond the idyllic public image that Rockwell himself helped to perpetuate to find the insecure, impulsive artist underneath." Libr J
  The author "isn't overwhelmed by the complexities and contradictions of Rockwell's temperament, relationship, and oeuvre but rather is invigorated by them, and her insightful portrait matches Rockwell's paintings in its judicious detail, layers of perception, delight in discovery, and reflections on 'the slippery nature of truth in art' and life." Booklist
Includes bibliographical references

Rodgers, Richard, 1902-1979

The Richard Rodgers reader; edited by Geoffrey Block. Oxford Univ. Press 2002 356p il music (Readers on American musicians) $32.50   **92**

ISBN 0-19-513954-2   LC 2001-37505

"This reader depicts Rodgers as methodical, versatile, outgoing, and a family man—'the most successful, productive, diverse, and influential American composer for the musical stage of the twentieth century.'" Booklist

"A fine combination of anecdote, music criticism, and biography, this is recommended for all libraries interested in American popular culture and American musical theater." Libr J

Includes bibliographical references

Secrest, Meryle. Somewhere for me: a biography of Richard Rodgers. Knopf 2001 457p il $30   **92**

ISBN 0-375-40164-4   LC 2001-29873

Also available in paperback from Hal Leonard

This is a biography of the composer of The King and I, South Pacific, Carousel, and Oklahoma! "Rodgers wrote 39 musicals and more than 900 songs during his career." N Y Times

"This deeply researched and moving critical biography covers the composer's long life and career . . . with astute analysis of his work and sympathetic, but not hagiographic, insights into the man." Publ Wkly

Includes bibliographical references

Rodriguez, Richard, 1944-

Rodriguez, Richard. Hunger of memory; the education of Richard Rodriguez; an autobiography. Godine 1982 195p o.p.; Bantam Bks. paperback available $14   **92**

ISBN 0-553-38251-9 (pa)   LC 81-81810

An account "of the coming of age of a person of Mexican descent and culture in American society and the inevitable transition in the private life of his family. Rodriguez focuses on his educational experiences, from his parochial elementary school . . . to his university years and subsequent experience as an educator." Libr J

Rogers, Will, 1879-1935

Robinson, Ray. American original: a life of Will Rogers. Oxford Univ. Press 1996 288p il $34   **92**

ISBN 0-19-508693-7   LC 95-31578

In this biography of the American humorist, Robinson attempts "to separate fact from legend and build up a composite portrait of the man. As such, the book is so complete and thorough that until, if ever, new material comes to light, it can scarcely be superseded. Robinson's admiration for Rogers is evident on every page, but that does not blind him to Rogers's faults." Libr J

Yagoda, Ben. Will Rogers; a biography. Knopf 1993 409p il o.p.; University of Okla. Press paperback available $22.95   **92**

ISBN 0-8061-3238-8 (pa)   LC 92-40177

This is a biography of "the rope-twirling vaudeville monologist, salty political commentator, silent film actor and *New York Times* columnist. . . . [This is] a resonant portrait imbued with Rogers's irreverent spirit, yet attuned to both the strengths and limitations of his commonsense, crackerbarrel world view." Publ Wkly

Includes bibliographical references

Roiphe, Anne Richardson, 1935-

Roiphe, Anne Richardson. 1185 Park Avenue; a memoir; [by] Anne Roiphe. Free Press 1999 257p il hardcover o.p. paperback available $13   **92**

ISBN 0-684-85732-4 (pa)   LC 98-51939

The author "dissects her childhood family, depicting as well a grim view of growing up rich and Jewish on Upper Park Avenue in the 1940s and 1950s. The daughter of a wealthy, frightened, chain-smoking mother and a handsome, philandering, cold, immigrant father who rejected his past, Roiphe watched her parents savage each other daily." Libr J

"Roiphe's devastating memoir fully engages the reader in her painful story of hatred and betrayal." Publ Wkly

Rommel, Erwin, 1891-1944

Fraser, David. Knight's cross: a life of Field Marshal Erwin Rommel. HarperCollins Pubs. 1994 c1993 601p il maps hardcover o.p. paperback available $21.95   **92**

ISBN 0-06-092597-3 (pa)   LC 93-43832

First published 1993 in the United Kingdom

This is a biography of the general who commanded German troops in World War II

"Fraser presents what definitely will become the standard biography . . . as the author astutely traces the qualities of leadership which Rommel embodied." Booklist

Includes bibliographical references

Rooney, Andrew A.

Rooney, Andrew A. My war; [by] Andy Rooney. PublicAffairs 2000 333p il $20; pa $14   **92**

ISBN 1-58648-010-3; 1-58648-159-2 (pa)
     LC 00-59228

A reissue of the title first published 1995 by Random House

The author "relates how he became a notable combat journalist in WW II, a war he calls 'the ultimate experience for anyone in it.' For the Army newspaper *Stars and Stripes,* he covered the air war over Germany, the D-Day invasion of Normandy and the Allied drive into Germany. Rooney's simple, ruminative style . . . grips the reader as he describes famous events of the war." Publ Wkly

Roosevelt, Eleanor, 1884-1962

Cook, Blanche Wiesen. Eleanor Roosevelt. Viking 1992-1999 2v il hardcover o.p. paperback available v1 $16.95; v2 $17.95   **92**

ISBN 0-14-009460-1 (v1); 0-14-017894-5 (v2)
     LC 87-40632

Contents: v1: 1884-1933; v2: 1933-1938

"A feminist biography that regards its subject not only as a mostly 19th-century woman who invented her own life with very little help, but also as a self-created political figure of considerable significance." N Y Times Book Rev [review of v1]

Includes bibliographical references

Roosevelt, Eleanor, 1884-1962—*Continued*

The Eleanor Roosevelt encyclopedia; edited by Maurine H. Beasley, Holly C. Shulman, and Henry R. Beasley; foreword by Blanche Wiesen Cook; introduction by James McGregor Burns. Greenwood Press 2000 xxvi, 628p il $73.95 **92**
1. United States—Politics and government—1933-1945
ISBN 0-313-30181-6   LC 00-23530
This reference work "examines the many roles of our foremost First Lady. Given Roosevelt's significance and appeal, this volume is an exception to the rule that encyclopedic treatments of single individuals belong only in larger collections." Booklist

Goodwin, Doris Kearns. No ordinary time. See entry under Roosevelt, Franklin D. (Franklin Delano), 1882-1945   **92**

Gurewitsch, Edna. Kindred souls: the friendship of Eleanor Roosevelt and David Gurewitsch; [by] Edna P. Gurewitsch; introduction by Geoffrey C. Ward. St. Martin's Press 2002 296p il $27.95   **92**
1. Gurewitsch, A. David, 1902-1974
ISBN 0-312-28698-8   LC 2001-48653
"Gurewitsch writes that her husband and Mrs. Roosevelt first met in 1944. Shortly thereafter, David became her personal physician, and a friendship blossomed that endured until Mrs. Roosevelt's death in 1962. . . . With admiration for her subject, Gurewitsch has significantly expanded our understanding of the last years of the 20th century's great American woman." Publ Wkly
Includes bibliographical references

Roosevelt, Franklin D. (Franklin Delano), 1882-1945

Black, Conrad M. Franklin Delano Roosevelt: champion of freedom. PublicAffairs 2003 1,280p il $39.95   **92**
ISBN 1-58648-184-3   LC 2003-47054
The author "makes the case that FDR was the most important person of the twentieth century, transforming his nation and the world through his unparalleled skill as a domestic politician, war leader, strategist, and global visionary—all of which he accomplished despite a physical infirmity that could easily have ended his public life at age thirty-nine. Black also takes on the great critics of FDR, especially those who accuse him of betraying the West at Yalta." Publisher's note
"The sweeping and persuasive impact of this . . . big book makes it not only the best one-volume life of the 32nd president but the best at any length, bound to be widely read and discussed." Publ Wkly
Includes bibliographical references

Davis, Kenneth Sydney. FDR, into the storm, 1937-1940; a history; [by] Kenneth S. Davis. Random House 1993 691p hardcover o.p. paperback available $29   **92**
1. United States—Politics and government—1933-1945
ISBN 0-8129-8205-9 (pa)   LC 92-21640
This is the fourth volume of a five-volume biography begun with FDR, the beckoning destiny, 1882-1928 (1972); FDR, the New York years, 1928-1933 (1985);

FDR, the New Deal years, 1933-1937 (1986)
In this study "particular emphasis is laid on Roosevelt's attempt to 'pack' the Supreme Court, his response to the growing threat of fascism in Europe, and the unexpectedly strong challenge by Republican Wendell Wilkie in the 1940 presidential campaign." Publ Wkly
Includes bibliographical references

Fried, Albert. F.D.R. and his enemies. St. Martin's Press 1999 261p hardcover o.p. paperback available $15.95   **92**
1. United States—Politics and government—1933-1945
ISBN 0-312-23827-4 (pa)   LC 98-56141
The author "examines Roosevelt's conflict with and victory over varied critics, including Al Smith, Huey Long, Charles Lindbergh, and Charles Coughlin. Fried convincingly asserts that Roosevelt defeated his critics primarily because he was a superb pragmatist who refused to be hindered by an ideological straightjacket." Booklist
Includes bibliographical references

Goodwin, Doris Kearns. No ordinary time; Franklin and Eleanor Roosevelt: the home front in World War II. Simon & Schuster 1994 759p il hardcover o.p. paperback available $18   **92**
1. Roosevelt, Eleanor, 1884-1962 2. World War, 1939-1945—United States 3. United States—History—1933-1945
ISBN 0-684-80448-4 (pa)   LC 94-28565
"This is a nearly day-by-day account of the doings of Franklin and Eleanor Roosevelt during the Second World War. While Eleanor was championing the rights of female munitions workers and of Negroes in segregated Army barracks, her husband was making and breaking policy." New Yorker
Includes bibliographical references

Roosevelt, Theodore, 1858-1919

Cooper, John Milton. The warrior and the priest: Woodrow Wilson and Theodore Roosevelt. See entry under Wilson, Woodrow, 1856-1924   **92**

Dalton, Kathleen. Theodore Roosevelt; a strenuous life. Knopf 2002 708p il $35   **92**
ISBN 0-679-44663-X   LC 2002-22857
A biography of the 26th President of the United States
Dalton's "stunning portrayal presents a realistic and balanced view that challenges traditional interpretations. . . . This book is certain to intrigue both scholars and the public." Libr J
Includes bibliographical references

McCullough, David G. Mornings on horseback; [by] David McCullough. Simon & Schuster 1981 445p il hardcover o.p. paperback available $16   **92**
1. Roosevelt family
ISBN 0-671-44754-8 (pa)   LC 81-1697
This biography follows Theodore Roosevelt from his childhood to his defeat for mayor of New York and marriage to Edith Carow in 1886
"Based on diligent and thorough research, with em-

Roosevelt, Theodore, 1858-1919—*Continued*

phasis on family, physical ailments, and friends, and written with verve and color, this is a stimulating book that will appeal to the general reader." Libr J

Includes bibliographical references

Morris, Edmund. The rise of Theodore Roosevelt. Modern Library pa. ed. Modern Lib. 2001 xxxiv, 920p il pa $17.95   **92**

ISBN 0-375-75678-7   LC 2001-30520

A reissue of the title first published 1979 by Coward, McCann & Geoghegan

"Revised and updated." Cover

This first volume of a projected three volume study of the life and times of Theodore Roosevelt "covers Roosevelt's life up to the age of 42, when an assassin's bullet elected him the youngest president in the nation's history." Booklist

Includes bibliographical references

Morris, Edmund. Theodore Rex. Random House 2001 772p il map $35; pa $16.95

                                                    92
ISBN 0-394-55509-0; 0-8129-6600-7 (pa)
                                    LC 2001-19366
Sequel to The rise of Theodore Roosevelt

"The second entry in Morris's projected three-volume life of Theodore Roosevelt focuses on the presidential years 1901 through early 1909." Publ Wkly

"Morris excels at placing TR in the context of his time, showing how he out maneuvered powerful but ossified opponents from the Gilded Age and trumped isolationists by averting war, in the process winning the first Nobel Peace Prize." Libr J

Includes bibliographical references

Ross, Lillian, 1927-

Ross, Lillian. Here but not here; a love story. Random House 1998 240p il o.p.; Counterpoint paperback available $15   **92**

1. Shawn, William
ISBN 1-58243-110-8 (pa)   LC 97-43669

"*New Yorker* writer Ross on her intimate relationship with the magazine's famed editor, William Shawn." Libr J

"Ross writes directly and with great feeling about her years with Shawn. . . . It is a remarkable and very moving love story, composed like most great love stories of both passion and regret." Booklist

Roth, Herman, 1901-1989

Roth, Philip. Patrimony; a true story. Simon & Schuster 1991 238p il o.p.; Vintage Bks. paperback available $12   **92**

1. Roth, Philip
ISBN 0-679-75293-5 (pa)   LC 90-35891

This "is an account of how Roth cared for his eighty-six-year-old father during the last stages of the parent's incurable brain tumor." Time

This "ordinary, crucial story is well suited to a comic master, and Mr. Roth brings to the tale his gift for attention, his worldly, vernacular heart and the tremendous inventive force that here he keeps largely in check." N Y Times Book Rev

Roth, Philip

Roth, Philip. The facts; a novelist's autobiography. Farrar, Straus & Giroux 1988 195p o.p.; Vintage Bks. paperback available $12   **92**

ISBN 0-679-74905-5 (pa)   LC 88-14187

Following a prologue about his parents, Roth recounts "five stages of his life: his New Jersey youth; his college days at Bucknell; meeting his wife-to-be while an instructor at the University of Chicago; his early writing days, including [his conflict with] . . . the Jewish community; and his life in the sixties." Libr J

"The Facts is a lively and serious version of a novelist's life, but it seems even more interesting as a new way of formulating the questions about the imagination that Roth has been pursuing with increasing complication in the Zuckerman novels." N Y Rev Books

Rothko, Mark, 1903-1970

Breslin, James E. B. Mark Rothko; a biography. University of Chicago Press 1993 700p il $45; pa $27.50   **92**

ISBN 0-226-07405-6; 0-226-07406-4 (pa)
                                    LC 93-14966

This biography covers "Rothko's personal and artistic relationships, as well as the changing cultural and philosophical forces that shaped his life and art. Breslin also considers Rothko's attitude toward the role of the self in the paintings." Libr J

This book "is painstakingly researched, fluently written and unfailingly intelligent in tracing the tragic course of its subject's tormented character." N Y Times Book Rev

Includes bibliographical references

Rousseau, Jean-Jacques, 1712-1778

Cranston, Maurice. Jean-Jacques: the early life and work of Jean-Jacques Rousseau, 1712-1754. University of Chicago Press 1991 382p il map pa $23   **92**

ISBN 0-226-11862-2   LC 90-45994
First published 1983 by Norton

This first volume of Cranston's biographical study of the life and work of the French philosopher "traces the evolution of Rousseau's attitudes through the influence of that . . . Calvinist citystate, Geneva, his refuge in Catholic Savoy, and his introduction to the new 'scientific' ideology of the French Enlightenment." Publisher's note

"Cranston presents Rousseau's work in the context of his life. He proceeds impartially but not dispassionately; his scholarship is impeccable but not obtrusive. The result is a most readable narrative that has something for readers at all levels of sophistication." Choice

Includes bibliographical references

Cranston, Maurice. The noble savage: Jean-Jacques Rousseau, 1754-1762. University of Chicago Press 1991 399p il $45; pa $20   **92**

ISBN 0-226-11863-0; 0-226-11864-9 (pa)
                                    LC 90-28111

This second volume of the trilogy "covers the most productive, turbulent, and controversial eight years of Rousseau's life. His *Discourse on Inequality, Letter to Voltaire on Providence, Letter to d'Alembert, La Nouvelle Héloise, The Social Contract*, and *Emile* emerge from this period." Choice

"Cranston offers the finest and most richly detailed

Rousseau, Jean-Jacques, 1712-1778—Continued

portrait ever assembled of these vagabond years." New Statesman Soc

Includes bibliographical references

Cranston, Maurice. The solitary self: Jean-Jacques Rousseau in exile and adversity; with a foreword by Sanford Lakoff. University of Chicago Press 1997 247p il $35; pa $20   **92**

ISBN 0-226-11865-7; 0-226-11866-5 (pa)

LC 96-12922

"This final volume in Cranston's definitive trilogy chronicles Rousseau's last turbulent years as an outcast in England and Neuchatel, after the burning of *Émile* and the order for his arrest. . . . This is a scholarly yet ingratiating portrayal of a man whose last years found him battling sciatica and Voltaire, enjoying botany and Boswell. Cranston's authoritative work has given us an invaluable account of the paradoxical life of an emotionally devoted yet tactlessly demanding man." Booklist

Includes bibliographical references

Rousseau, Jean-Jacques. Confessions; edited and introduced by P. N. Furbank. Knopf 1992 2v in 1 $20   **92**

ISBN 0-679-40998-X   LC 91-53194

Also available in paperback from Penguin Bks. and Oxford Univ. Press

"Everyman's library"

First Everyman's library edition, 1931

"An autobiography by Jean-Jacques Rousseau. The twelve volumes, written between 1766 and 1770, were published posthumously (I-VI, 1781; VII-XII, 1788). In this work, Rousseau 'frankly and sincerely' reveals the details of his erratic and rebellious life. Scholars find, however, that his unconscious motivation was to justify himself in the eyes of his supposedly numerous persecutors." Reader's Ency. 4th edition

Russell, Bertrand, 1872-1970

Monk, Ray. Bertrand Russell; the spirit of solitude, 1872-1921. Free Press 1996 695p $35   **92**

ISBN 0-684-82802-2   LC 96-15103

This first volume of a two-part biography chronicles Russell's "loss of religious faith, numerous romantic liaisons, two marriages, a desire to reunite philosophy and science, chronic emotional problems and a fear of madness, pacifism, imprisonment, a brush with death, and the birth of a son. . . . A rigorous, compelling portrait." Booklist

Includes bibliographical references

Rustin, Bayard, 1910-1987

Anderson, Jervis. Bayard Rustin; troubles I've seen: a biography. HarperCollins Pubs. 1997 418p il o.p.; University of Calif. Press paperback available $21.95   **92**

ISBN 0-520-21418-8 (pa)   LC 96-25003

"This noted African-American reformer, who died in 1987, was a courageous man of multiple gifts and charismatic personality. He organized the famous March on Washington and tutored civil-rights protesters in the techniques of Gandhian non-violence, but he was denied the prominence his achievements merited because he was openly homosexual. Rustin was astute, charming, and dedicated, and Anderson . . . captures him in all his variety, bringing to the task his own familiarity with the African-American, pacifist, and labor movements, in which Rustin played a part." New Yorker

D'Emilio, John. Lost prophet: the life and times of Bayard Rustin. Free Press 2003 568p il $35   **92**

ISBN 0-684-82780-8   LC 2003-52771

The author "believes the lack of attention paid to Rustin in 1960s history books is tragic, and he examines . . . the reasons behind the snub, most notably Rustin's 1953 arrest for lewd vagrancy in Pasadena, Calif. Drawing on interviews with Rustin's colleagues, friends and lovers, D'Emilio explores all facets of the activists life, from his Quaker upbringing and early imprisonment for draft dodging to his close but tenuous relationship with Martin Luther King Jr." Publ Wkly

"D'Emilio illuminates the connections and contexts of Rustin's work and sexuality. . . . Highly recommended for African American, civil rights, and 20th-century U.S. history and biography collections." Libr J

Includes bibliographical references

Ruth, Babe, 1895-1948

Creamer, Robert W. Babe; the legend comes to life. Simon & Schuster 1974 443p il hardcover o.p. paperback available $14   **92**

ISBN 0-671-76070-X (pa)

This biography covers Babe Ruth's personal life and his sports career

Ryan, Evelyn, d. 1998

Ryan, Terry. The prize winner of Defiance, Ohio; how my mother raised 10 kids on 25 words or less; foreword by Suze Orman. Simon & Schuster 2001 351p il $24; pa $13   **92**

1. Ryan family

ISBN 0-7432-1122-7; 0-7432-1123-5 (pa)

LC 2001-18379

The author recounts the life of her mother, "a small-town Ohio housewife in the nineteen-fifties who lived on the brink of dire poverty, thanks to a brood of ten kids and an ineffectual drunk of a husband. Since Evelyn couldn't work outside her home, she worked inside it, penning hundreds of product jingles and entering them in the national contests that drove the advertising industry of the day." New Yorker

Sacagawea, b. 1786

Clark, Ella Elizabeth. Sacagawea of the Lewis and Clark expedition; {by} Ella E. Clark and Margot Edmonds. University of Calif. Press 1979 171p il hardcover o.p. paperback available $16.95   **92**

1. Lewis and Clark Expedition (1804-1806)

ISBN 0-520-05060-6 (pa)   LC 78-65466

"Sacagawea, the Shoshone Indian woman who accompanied the Lewis and Clark expedition, has been a regional heroine and a feminist celebrity for most of this century. But, as these writers show, her role as 'the guide' was more fictive than actual. . . . Based on careful interpretation of the explorer's journals, this revisionist study does a good job of redefining her actual contributions." Booklist

Includes bibliographical references

Sacks, Oliver W.

Sacks, Oliver W. Uncle Tungsten; memories of a chemical boyhood; [by] Oliver Sacks. Knopf 2001 337p il $25; pa $14
                                                            92

ISBN 0-375-40448-1; 0-375-70404-3 (pa)
                            LC 2001-33738
Also available Thorndike Press large print edition
"Sacks' first scientific love was chemistry, and he presents an avid history of the field within a memoir that pays tribute to his uncle, who welcomed Sacks into his lab, thus encouraging his passion for chemistry and learning." Booklist

Sade, marquis de, 1740-1814

Gray, Francine du Plessix. At home with the Marquis de Sade; a life. Simon & Schuster 1998 491p il o.p.; Penguin Bks. paperback available $14.95   **92**
1. Sade, Renée Pélagie de Montreuil, marquise de, d. 1810
ISBN 0-14-028677-2 (pa)   LC 98-34224
This biography "looks at Sade from the perspective of his remarkably loyal female companions, particularly his long-suffering first wife." Booklist
"The effect is an original, absorbing and readable account of Sade, his family, and his world." Libr J
Includes bibliographical references

Sagan, Carl, 1934-1996

Davidson, Keay. Carl Sagan; a life. Wiley 1999 xx, 540p hardcover o.p. paperback available $24.95   **92**
ISBN 0-471-39536-6 (pa)   LC 99-36206
The author profiles the life and scientific career of the influential American astronomer
"Sagan is presented in such a way that readers can decide whether to view him admirably or with a dose of skepticism." Booklist
Includes bibliographical references

Sage, Lorna

Sage, Lorna. Bad blood. Morrow 2002 281p $24.95; pa $13.95   **92**
ISBN 0-06-621443-2; 0-06-093808-0 (pa)
                            LC 2001-51190
"This posthumous memoir by a distinguished critic and reviewer looks at her own early life for the connections between social forces and their consequences, happy or otherwise, for individuals; it discovers en route that estrangement and rebellion are not, as we often think, limited to ourselves." N Y Times Book Rev
"This wry family memoir . . . serves as a corrective to anyone harboring romantic notions about growing up in rural Britain." New Yorker

Said, Edward W.

Said, Edward W. Out of place; a memoir. Knopf 1999 295p il $26.95; pa $14   **92**
ISBN 0-394-58739-1; 0-679-73067-2 (pa)
                            LC 99-31106
In this memoir Said offers an "account of his intellectual and moral development. At the heart of Said's story is the sense of dislocation experienced by a boy whose father was a Palestinian-born American citizen, whose mother was Lebanese, and who was raised in Egypt under the colonial rule of the British. This is the moving tale of a man who is always an outsider." Publ Wkly

Sakharov, Andreï Dmitrievich, 1921-1989

Lourie, Richard. Sakharov; a biography. University Press of New England 2002 465p il $35   **92**
ISBN 1-58465-207-1   LC 2001-5246
A biography "of Andrei Sakharov, the nuclear physicist who developed into an authentic apostle of humanity and democracy in the former Soviet Union." N Y Times Book Rev
"Utilizing newly accessible KGB files as well as Sakharov's personal correspondence, Lourie provides a revealing portrait of an extraordinary man to whom the world owes a great debt." Booklist
Includes bibliographical references

Salzman, Mark

Salzman, Mark. Lost in place; growing up absurd in suburbia. Random House 1995 273p hardcover o.p. paperback available $13
                                                            92
ISBN 0-679-76778-9 (pa)   LC 95-7847
In this "memoir about his 'existential angst' as a slightly off-center teenager, . . . writer Salzman vividly recalls his unconventional friends, frugal parents, and other memorable characters from his freewheeling, Connecticut youth." Booklist

Sand, George, 1804-1876

Jack, Belinda Elizabeth. George Sand; a woman's life writ large; [by] Belinda Jack. Knopf 2000 395p il hardcover o.p. paperback available $16   **92**
ISBN 0-679-77918-3 (pa)   LC 99-40857
"Prodigious author, cross-dresser, lover of Chopin and Alfred de Musset, intimate of (among others) Liszt, Balzac, Dumas (père and fils), Turgenev, and Flaubert (who cried twice at her funeral), Sand was both before her time and quintessentially of it. Jack's nuanced, moving assessment of the writer's early years . . . is the strongest section of this packed life. When Sand moves onto a larger stage, Jack's style becomes breathless, as if she could barely keep up with her flamboyant subject." New Yorker

Saroyan, William, 1908-1981

Leggett, John. A daring young man: a biography of William Saroyan. Knopf 2002 462p il $30   **92**
ISBN 0-375-41301-4   LC 2002-67149
The author "traces the development of Saroyan's writerly gifts from his childhood to his death. . . . His fame rose meteorically, and he published his best plays, stories, and novels . . . before he was 30. His fame then faded as he descended into an inferno of gambling debts and failed relationships that marred his writing. . . . Leggett's thoughtful, critical readings provide a definitive and lucid portrait of the tragicomedy of Saroyan's life." Libr J
Includes bibliographical references

Sartre, Jean Paul, 1905-1980

Gerassi, John. Jean-Paul Sartre; hated conscience of his century. v1: Protestant or protester? University of Chicago Press 1989 213p il $30   **92**
ISBN 0-226-28797-1   LC 88-27945
This first volume of a biography of the French philosopher and writer covers the years from his birth through

Sartre, Jean Paul, 1905-1980—*Continued*

the end of World War II

"A dazzlingly original work. . . . 'Jean-Paul Sartre'is an intellectual biography that effectively explores the complexities of Sartre's thinking and the successive philosophical and political positions he espoused and publicized." N Y Times Book Rev

Includes bibliographical references

Sartre, Jean Paul. The words; translated from the French by Bernard Frechtman. Braziller 1964 255p o.p.; Vintage Bks. paperback available $11   **92**

ISBN 0-394-74709-7 (pa)

The French existentialist writer "examines the formation of his character during his childhood years, which were passed in a completely adult world between his widowed mother and her parents. The central event of his childhood was the discovery of the world of words, of language." Libr J

Sayre, Nora

Sayre, Nora. On the wing; a young American abroad. Counterpoint 2001 216p il hardcover o.p. paperback available $15   **92**

ISBN 1-58243-214-7 (pa)   LC 00-65861

"The late journalist and critic recalls her days in London in the 1950's with the likes of Cyril Connolly, Arthur Koestler and Tyrone Power." N Y Times Book Rev

Sayre "presents an entertaining and fluent coming-of-age story that will delight literary enthusiasts both young and old." Publ Wkly

Schaap, Dick, 1934-2001

Schaap, Dick. Flashing before my eyes; 50 years of headlines, datelines & punchlines; by Dick Schaap as told to Dick Schaap; introduction by Mitch Albom. Morrow 2001 300p il $25   **92**

ISBN 0-380-97512-2   LC 00-48971

Also available Thorndike Press large print edition

In this memoir Schaap chronicles his career in journalism

"This autobiography superbly illustrates Schaap's gift for getting to know newsmakers, both famous and obscure, and presenting them through the amusing and/or telling anecdote. A valuable addition to all sports and journalism collections." Libr J

Schlesinger, Arthur M., 1917-

Schlesinger, Arthur M. A life in the twentieth century; innocent beginnings, 1917-1950; {by} Arthur M. Schlesinger, Jr. Houghton Mifflin 2000 557p il $28.95; pa $15   **92**

ISBN 0-395-70752-8; 0-618-21925-0 (pa)

LC 00-61322

This first volume of Schlesinger's autobiography covers the author's life through the publication of The Age of Jackson and The Vital Center

Schlesinger's "autobiography, skillfully interweaving the personal and the historical, is elegantly simple and marvellously clear. Complex thoughts are set forth with a lucidity that conceals the depth of the intellectual analysis. Wit, humour and the resources of a natural storyteller sweep the reader along." Economist

Schoenberg, Arnold, 1874-1951

Shawn, Allen. Arnold Schoenberg's journey. Farrar, Straus & Giroux 2001 xx, 340p il $26   **92**

ISBN 0-374-10590-1   LC 2001-23807

Also available in paperback from Harvard Univ. Press

This biography "discusses each of Schoenberg's works in chronological order, always within the larger context of his life and times. . . . Intended for the lay reader, the book is written in engagingly direct prose, and the few musical examples presented are not overlaid with obfuscating technical analyses." Libr J

Includes bibliographical references

Schorr, Daniel, 1916-

Schorr, Daniel. Staying tuned; a life in journalism. Pocket Bks. 2001 354p il hardcover o.p. paperback available $14   **92**

ISBN 0-671-02088-9 (pa)   LC 2001-21014

Schorr tells of his life as a reporter for CBS, CNN and National Public Radio

"Schorr's memoir is as much an inside look at the famous world figures of the latter half of the twentieth century as it is the story of one man's life and career." Booklist

Schroeder, Patricia

Schroeder, Patricia. 24 years of House work—and the place is still a mess; my life in politics; [by] Pat Schroeder. Andrews McMeel Pub. 1998 244p il   **92**

LC 98-12336

Available in G.K. Hall large print edition

The former Congresswoman from Colorado presents an account of her career in the House of Representatives from 1972 to 1996

"A better guide may never have been written about how a woman politician successfully balanced her political and personal lives." N Y Times Book Rev

Schubert, Franz, 1797-1828

Newbould, Brian. Schubert, the music and the man. University of Calif. Press 1997 465p il $55   **92**

ISBN 0-520-21065-4   LC 96-49876

This study focuses on the composer's music. "Biography is not ignored, however. Newbould presents a thorough, cautious accounting of Schubert's life, dealing sensitively and soberly with such controversial issues as the composer's self-destructive behavior and his ambivalent sexuality." Libr J

Includes bibliographical references

Schwartz, Morris

Albom, Mitch. Tuesdays with Morrie; an old man, a young man, and life's greatest lesson. Doubleday 1997 192p $22.95; pa $12.95   **92**

ISBN 0-385-48451-8; 0-7679-0592-X (pa)

LC 96-52535

"As a student at Brandeis University in the late 1970s, Albom was especially drawn to his sociology professor, Morris Schwartz. On graduation he vowed to keep in touch with him, which he failed to do until 1994, when he saw a segment about Schwartz on the TV program *Nightline*, and learned that he had just been diagnosed with Lou Gehrig's disease. By then a sports columnist for the *Detroit Free Press* . . . Albom was idled by the

Schwartz, Morris—*Continued*

newspaper strike in the Motor City and so had the opportunity to visit Schwartz in Boston every week until the older man died. Their dialogue is the subject of this moving book." Publ Wkly

Schwarzkopf, H. Norman

Cohen, Roger. In the eye of the storm: the life of General H. Norman Schwarzkopf; [by] Roger Cohen, Claudio Gatti. Farrar, Straus & Giroux 1991 342p il maps hardcover o.p. paperback available $28   **92**

ISBN 0-374-52826-8 (pa)   LC 91-15581

This biography of the U.S. general covers his life in the military, his family, and his role in the Persian Gulf War

"On the whole it is a rather serious and highly readable book that provides important insights into the general, especially into his origins, character and psychology." N Y Times Book Rev

Schwarzkopf, H. Norman. It doesn't take a hero: General H. Norman Schwarzkopf; the autobiography; written with Peter Petre. Bantam Bks. 1992 530p il maps hardcover o.p. paperback available $7.99   **92**

1. Persian Gulf War, 1991

ISBN 0-553-56338-6 (pa)   LC 92-20762

"The whole book is a description of General Schwarzkopf's relations with people. It is remarkably emotional. To an unusual degree he sees events as secondary to the personalities he has been affected by. He emphasizes his sensitive side. . . . 'It Doesn't Take a Hero' is not a military record. . . . It covers the gulf war, of course, but General Schwarzkopf devotes so much space to his life before that event that he has produced two books in one." N Y Times Book Rev

Includes bibliographical references

Schweitzer, Albert, 1875-1965

Schweitzer, Albert. Out of my life and thought; an autobiography; translated by Antje Bultmann Lemke; foreword by Jimmy Carter; preface by Rhena Schweitzer Miller and Antje Bultmann Lemke. Johns Hopkins Univ. Press 1998 272p il (Albert Schweitzer library) pa $18.95   **92**

ISBN 0-8018-6097-0   LC 98-28166

First English translation by C. T. Campion published 1933; this translation first published 1990 by Holt

This is "the autobiography of the world-famous missionary doctor, organist, philosopher, theologian, and Nobel Peace Prize winner." Booklist

Includes bibliographical references

Seeger, Pete

Dunaway, David King. How can I keep from singing: Pete Seeger. Da Capo Press 1990 388p il pa $17   **92**

ISBN 0-306-80399-2   LC 89-71394

A reprint with a new preface of the title first published 1981 by McGraw-Hill

"The focus of Seeger's life has been on using music as a force for social change. . . . But he is perhaps best known as the major banjo-playing folksinger who pioneered the folk music revival that flowered in the 1960s. This excellent book provides a well-written and exten-

sively researched account, not only of Seeger's life, but also of the social and political movements of the times in which he lived. An extensive bibliography and discography add to the book's usefulness." Libr J

Serkin, Rudolf, 1903-1991

Lehmann, Stephen. Rudolf Serkin; a life; [by] Stephen Lehmann and Marion Faber. Oxford Univ. Press 2003 344p il + 1 sound disc $35   **92**

ISBN 0-19-513046-4   LC 2002-2384

Contents: Beginnings: Eger and Vienna; "The venerable firm of Busch and Serkin"; American pianist; Performing; Voices: Richard Goode, Thomas Frost, Claude Frank, and Lilian Kallir; Teaching; Voices: Eugege Istomin, Seymour Lipkin, Lee Luvisi, Ruth Laredo; Marlboro; Voices: Philipp Naegele, Blanche Moyse, Arnold Steinhardt; Epilogue: 1991; Carnegie Hall recitals, 1937-1987

"Lehmann and Faber's three-part commemoration of the great pianist's centenary recounts his life and career, proffers lengthy reminiscences by his pupils and associates, and describes his performing, teaching, and direction of the summer Marlboro Festival." Booklist

Includes discography and bibliographical references

Seuss, Dr.

Morgan, Judith. Dr. Seuss & Mr. Geisel; a biography; [by] Judith & Neil Morgan. Random House 1995 345p il o.p.; Da Capo Press paperback available $18   **92**

ISBN 0-306-80736-X (pa)   LC 94-17817

"Fans of *The Cat in the Hat, The Grinch Who Stole Christmas* and other classics may be surprised to learn that Dr. Seuss was terrified of children and had none of his own, and that writing verse was a supreme effort for him. While children's literature is Ted Geisel's principal claim to fame, his creative life was multifarious, including an apprenticeship with film director and army major Frank Capra during WW II and stints in advertising. The authors deftly evoke the settings where Geisel lived and worked." Publ Wkly

Sexton, Anne

Middlebrook, Diane Wood. Anne Sexton; a biography. Houghton Mifflin 1991 xxiii, 488p il o.p.; Vintage Bks. paperback available $17   **92**

ISBN 0-679-74182-8 (pa)   LC 91-13701

"A Peter Davison book"

For this biography of the troubled American confessional poet the author "plumbed psychiatric records, including tapes made of therapy sessions; interviewed family members, fellow poets, friends and lovers; and closely read the poems themselves to reconstruct Sexton's life—its interior sequences and external chronology." Publ Wkly

"Ms. Middlebrook has written a wonderful book: just, balanced, insightful, complex in its sympathies and in its judgment of Sexton both as a person and as a writer." N Y Times Book Rev

Includes bibliographical references

Shabazz, Betty

Rickford, Russell John. Betty Shabazz: a remarkable story of survival and faith before and after Malcolm X; foreword by Myrlie Evers-Williams. Sourcebooks 2003 xxii, 633p il $35   **92**

ISBN 1-4022-0171-0   LC 2002-003447

"Just as the achievements of her husband, Malcolm X, were overshadowed by those of Martin Luther King Jr., Betty Shabazz's accomplishments have been overshadowed by those of King's widow. [The author] corrects that imbalance with this penetrating biography." Booklist

Includes bibliographical references

Shakur, Tupac

Dyson, Michael Eric. Holler if you hear me: searching for Tupac Shakur. Basic Bks. 2001 292p il $24; pa $15   **92**

ISBN 0-465-01755-X; 0-465-01756-8 (pa)
     LC 2001-36564

In this biography of the late rapper, Dyson "examines Tupac both culturally and spiritually through a loosely organized series of meditations that begin in Tupac's childhood . . . and move through his manhood." New Yorker

"Dyson's discussion goes beyond slogans and poses to the actualities of 'thug life' and the consequences of Shakur's passions and allegiances. Piquant and analytical." Booklist

Includes bibliographical references

Shaw, Bernard, 1856-1950

Peters, Sally. Bernard Shaw; the ascent of the superman. Yale Univ. Press 1996 328p il $45; pa $22   **92**

ISBN 0-300-06097-1; 0-300-07500-6 (pa)
     LC 95-37248

An "exploration of the ambiguities and passions that formed this great playwright and thinker. Shaw's sexuality, always a good topic of speculation, is studied here, but one wishes for more insights and in-depth analysis. Peters does devote a chapter to Shaw's close relationship with the actor and playwright Harley Granville Barker, mainly from Shaw's point of view. One may not agree with Peter's conclusions, but they will prove to be of interest to anyone studying Shaw." Libr J

Includes bibliographical references

Shelley, Mary Wollstonecraft, 1797-1851

Seymour, Miranda. Mary Shelley. Grove Press 2001 655p il $35; pa $20   **92**

ISBN 0-8021-1702-3; 0-8021-3948-5 (pa)
     LC 2001-35094

First published 2000 in the United Kingdom

"Born to two of the most famous parents in 19th-century England—philosopher and novelist William Godwin and political activist Mary Wollstonecraft, who died ten days after giving birth to Mary—the young girl inherited their intellectual perspicacity. When she was 16, she eloped with Percy Bysshe Shelley, and by the time she was 24, she had been widowed, lost three of her four children in infancy, and written what was to become her most famous book, *Frankenstein*." Libr J

"A convincing and memorable portrait." Booklist

Includes bibliographical references

Sunstein, Emily W. Mary Shelley; romance and reality. Little, Brown 1989 478p il o.p.; Johns Hopkins Univ. Press paperback available $19.95   **92**

ISBN 0-8018-4218-2 (pa)   LC 88-12990

A "revisionist account of a woman who 'literally embodies the English Romantic movement'. . . . Sunstein provides substantial documentation of the breadth of Shelley's education and the extent of her writing. . . . Most rewarding, perhaps, are Sunstein's astute insights into Shelley's emotional life." Choice

Includes bibliographical references

Sheppard, William Henry, 1865-1927

Kennedy, Pagan. Black Livingstone; a true tale of adventure in the nineteenth-century Congo. Viking 2002 237p il hardcover o.p. paperback available $14   **92**

ISBN 0-14-200176-7 (pa)   LC 2001-26096

The author presents "the incredible life and adventures of William Henry Sheppard, a submissively complex African American missionary funded by the segregated Southern Presbyterian Church in 1890 to explore unmapped regions of the Congo and win converts. When he returned to the United States, he was nicknamed 'Black Livingstone' in reference to David Livingstone and spoke all over the country to raise funds for the church." Libr J

"Kennedy is an engaging writer and ably captures the undercurrent of horror found everywhere in the late 19th-century Congo while honoring Sheppard's accomplishments, heroism and character." Publ Wkly

Includes bibliographical references

Sheridan, Peter, 1952-

Sheridan, Peter. 44, Dublin made me; a memoir. Viking 1999 278p hardcover o.p. paperback available $12.95   **92**

ISBN 0-14-028641-1 (pa)   LC 98-48568

Also available Thorndike Press large print edition

The author "recalls life at his home at 44 Seville Place during the 1960s, when he came of age, the Beatles made Sgt. Pepper's Lonely Hearts Club Band and the Americans walked on the moon. . . . With his brother, film director Jim Sheridan, he well represents the current cultural explosion in Ireland, and communicates the experiences and values that fuel today's rich artistic scene. Readers of this friendly, direct book will easily be able to picture the author telling his tales in a cozy Dublin pub." Publ Wkly

Sheridan, Peter. 47 roses. Viking 2002 214p $24.95; pa $14   **92**

ISBN 0-670-03100-3; 0-14-200286-0 (pa)
     LC 2001-57470

In this "sequel to his childhood memoir, '44: Dublin Made Me,' the Irish theatre impresario Peter Sheridan revisits his parents' marriage and discovers, after his father's death, that an Englishwoman whom he had known as a family friend was also his father's mistress on and off for almost fifty years. Sheridan's prose style is Chekhov by way of Monty Python and Rabelais, and this extravagantly sympathetic portrait of all the parties involved—including the ferocious, torch-bearing Doris—is hilarious." New Yorker

Sherman, William T. (William Tecumseh), 1820-1891

Fellman, Michael. Citizen Sherman: a life of William Tecumseh Sherman. Random House 1995 486p il o.p.; University Press of Kan. paperback available $19.95   **92**

   ISBN 0-7706-0840-0 (pa)   LC 94-41087

"Using Sherman's personal correspondence as well as that of his friends and family, Fellman . . . examines the private thoughts and life of the Union general." Libr J

"This superb biography gives as full a portrait of nineteenth-century family dynamics as of the dynamics of the battlefield. Fellman's Sherman is not a lovable man, but he is a complete one." New Yorker

Includes bibliographical references

Kennett, Lee B. Sherman; a soldier's life; [by] Lee Kennett. HarperCollins Pubs. 2001 426p il maps hardcover o.p. paperback available $14.95   **92**

   1. United States—History—1861-1865, Civil War
   ISBN 0-06-093074-8 (pa)   LC 2001-16687

The author presents a "consideration of Sherman's personality and character . . . as well as a thoughtful reconsideration of Sherman's views on a number of issues (including his relationship with Ulysses S. Grant) and his wartime performance." Libr J

This is a "well-balanced analytical biography." Publ Wkly

Includes bibliographical references

Sickles, Daniel E., 1825-1914

Keneally, Thomas. American scoundrel: the life of the notorious Civil War General Dan Sickles. Talese 2002 397p $27.50; pa $15   **92**

   ISBN 0-385-50139-0; 0-385-72225-7 (pa)
      LC 2001-43078

A "biography of Tammany politician and Civil War general Dan Sickles. Sickles was famous in his time both as the cold-blooded killer of his wife's lover, the son of Francis Scott Key, and as the insubordinate commander who defied orders at Cemetery Ridge." Publ Wkly

"A frequently spellbinding recitation of the career of a totally awful politician, crook, adulterer and murderer who was no good as a general either." N Y Times Book Rev

Simon, Neil

Simon, Neil. The play goes on; a memoir. Simon & Schuster 1999 348p il hardcover o.p. paperback available $14   **92**

   ISBN 0-684-86980-2 (pa)   LC 99-36449

Sequel to Rewrites

This memoir "recounts the second half of Simon's life, starting with the life-shattering impact of the death of his first wife, Joan, of cancer at 40, and proceeding through the ensuing 30 years, during which Simon had periods of incredible fertility and others in which his creativity dried up and he feared he would never write again." Booklist

Simon, Neil. Rewrites; a memoir. Simon & Schuster 1996 397p hardcover o.p. paperback available $14   **92**

   ISBN 0-684-83562-2 (pa)   LC 96-13691

This first volume of the dramatist's memoirs focuses on his career as it evolved from writing high school skits

to TV programs to Broadway

"This is a gentleman's autobiography, and Simon never stoops to dishing the dirt on his show biz cronies." Libr J

Sinatra, Frank, 1915-1998

Friedwald, Will. Sinatra! the song is you; a singer's art. Da Capo Press 1997 559p il pa $18.50   **92**

   ISBN 0-306-80742-4   LC 96-43855

A reprint of the title first published 1995 by Scribner

This work "details Sinatra's musical legacy, from his start as a big band vocalist and his early Columbia recordings, through his Capital Records triumphs of the 1950s and his not always successful 1960s and 1970s experiments on the Reprise label, to his commercial pinnacle but aesthetic nadir, the recent Duets." Booklist

Friedwald's "commentary is alert and perceptive, and even more valuable is the wealth of pointed reminiscence drawn from interviews he has done with musicians who worked closely with Mr. Sinatra." N Y Times Book Rev

Includes discography and bibliographical references

Hamill, Pete. Why Sinatra matters. Little, Brown 1998 185p il hardcover o.p. paperback available $12.95   **92**

   ISBN 0-316-73886-7 (pa)   LC 98-67480

A "reminiscence of Sinatra after hours serves as the frame for shrewd reflections on the singer's art ('as an artist, Sinatra had only one basic subject: loneliness'), his personality, his audience and—most interesting—his ethnicity, a subject about which Hamill, against all odds, contrives to say fresh and persuasive things." N Y Times Book Rev

Includes filmography and bibliographical references

Zehme, Bill. The way you wear your hat; Frank Sinatra and the lost art of livin'; photo editor, Vincent Virga; photographs by Phil Stern unless otherwise indicated. HarperCollins Pubs. 1997 245p il hardcover o.p. paperback available $15.95   **92**

   ISBN 0-06-093175-3 (pa)   LC 97-37597

This biography, published in tribute of Sinatra's 82nd birthday, examines his career, lifestyle, and personal philosophy

Singer, Isaac Bashevis, 1904-1991

Singer, Isaac Bashevis. More stories from my father's court; translated by Curt Leviant. Farrar, Straus & Giroux 2000 216p hardcover o.p. paperback available $12   **92**

   1. Jews—Poland
   ISBN 0-374-52798-9 (pa)   LC 00-37583

Sequel to In my father's court

These pieces were first published in Yiddish in the Jewish daily Forward from 1955-1960

These autobiographical sketches depict the workings of the beth din, the rabbinical court that met in the Singer's Warsaw home

"This book is a portrait of the artist as a voyeuristic yeshiva boy, someone who assimilated into his soul the weird contradictions of modern Jewish life and, half chronicler and half creator, spun them into lasting stories." N Y Times Book Rev

Sitting Bull, Dakota Chief, 1831-1890

Utley, Robert Marshall. The lance and the shield: the life and times of Sitting Bull; [by] Robert M. Utley. Holt & Co. 1993 413p il o.p.; Ballantine Bks. paperback available $16.95 **92**
ISBN 0-345-38938-7 (pa)   LC 92-42681
"A John Macrae book"
"Born in 1831 on the great Plains, son of a chief, Sitting Bull was a seasoned warrior by the age of 15; at 26, he was tribal war chief. As the conflicts with the U.S. Army began in the 1850s, Sitting Bull represented the spirit of resistance among his people. Utley follows the increasing hostilities of succeeding years and gives a vivid account of the Battle of the Little Big Horn in 1876." Publ Wkly
"This book is well written, strongly documented, and fairly reasoned to satisfy even specialists within the field. It surpasses all previous biographies of Sitting Bull." Choice
Includes bibliographical references

Skinner, B. F. (Burrhus Frederic), 1904-1990

Bjork, Daniel W. B.F. Skinner; a life. American Psychological Assn. 1997 298p il pa $19.95   **92**
ISBN 1-55798-416-6   LC 96-40385
A reissue of the title first published 1993 by Basic Bks.
This is a biography of the psychologist known for his utopian novel Walden Two, his book Beyond freedom and dignity, and his behaviorist theories
"Bjork places Skinner squarely in the context of the US social, technological, and political history. . . . Although heavily documented, Bjork's book is very readable because documentation is in endnotes. A handsome, well-indexed work, with an excellent bibliography." Choice

Smith, Alfred Emanuel, 1873-1944

Finan, Christopher M. Alfred E. Smith, the happy warrior. Hill & Wang 2002 396p il $26; pa $16   **92**
1. United States—Politics and government
ISBN 0-8090-3033-0; 0-8090-1632-X (pa)
LC 2002-19476
This is a biography of the "governor of New York and the first Catholic candidate for president, trounced by Herbert Hoover in the 1928 election amidst a torrent of anti-Catholic bigotry." Booklist
"Finan writes well, but for an occasional lapse into anachronism." NY Times Book Rev
Includes bibliographical references

Slayton, Robert A. Empire statesman: the rise and redemption of Al Smith. Free Press 2001 480p il maps $30   **92**
ISBN 0-684-86302-2   LC 00-60011
A biography of the Catholic son of Irish immigrants who became Governor of New York State and ran for president in 1928
"Slayton's biography of Smith is valuable because it describes the vitriolic mood of much of the nation during the 1928 campaign." N Y Times Book Rev
Includes bibliographical references

Smith, Bob, 1941-

Smith, Bob. Hamlet's dresser; a memoir. Scribner 2002 287p $24; pa $14   **92**
ISBN 0-684-85269-1; 0-684-85270-5 (pa)
LC 2002-510935
This memoir describes the author's youth in a dysfunctional family with a profoundly retarded sister, and his lifelong love of Shakespeare as a teacher and as a dresser for the American Shakespeare Festival in Stratford, CT.
This is a "beautiful, sad, and wonderful story. . . . [The] anecdotal tales of theater legends like John Houseman, Morris Carnovsky, Katharine Hepburn, and Bert Lahr are priceless." Libr J

Smith, Joseph, 1805-1844

Brodie, Fawn McKay. No man knows my history: the life of Joseph Smith, the Mormon prophet; by Fawn M. Brodie. 2nd ed rev and enl. Knopf 1971 499, xxp il hardcover o.p. paperback available $18   **92**
1. Mormons
ISBN 0-679-73054-0 (pa)
First published 1945
Taking as her title a phrase from a sermon by Joseph Smith himself, the author has attempted to discover as much of the truth concerning Joseph Smith and the beginnings of Mormonism, as can be found in an intensive research into documents, diaries, unpublished manuscripts, etc.
Includes bibliographical references

Remini, Robert Vincent. Joseph Smith. Viking 2002 190p (Penguin lives series) $19.95   **92**
1. Mormons
ISBN 0-670-03083-X   LC 2001-56762
Also available Thorndike Press large print edition
In this biography of the founder of the Mormon Church, the author "places Smith in the context of his time in terms of the broader social, political, and economic events that influenced him and his church." Libr J
"A masterful evenhanded précis that will engross history and religion readers alike." Booklist
Includes bibliographical references

Smith, Liz

Smith, Liz. Natural blonde. Hyperion 2000 460p il $25.95; pa $7.99   **92**
ISBN 0-7868-6325-0; 0-7868-9012-6 (pa)
LC 00-33457
Also available Random House large print edition
Smith describes her childhood and college years in Texas, then "offers a unique history of gossip reporting during the past five decades, emphasizing the ascendance in columns of film stars over bluebloods." Publ Wkly

Smith, William, 1769-1839

Winchester, Simon. The map that changed the world; William Smith and the birth of modern geology; illustrations by Soun Vannithone. HarperCollins Pubs. 2001 329p il map $26; pa $13.95   **92**

1. Stratigraphic geology
ISBN 0-06-019361-1; 0-06-093180-9 (pa)
                   LC 2001-16603

"In the early years of the nineteenth century, William Smith created the first geological map of Great Britain, a time-consuming, solitary project that helped establish geology as one of the 'fundamental fields of study.' . . . Winchester tells Smith's story, including the dramatic ups and downs of his personal life. . . . This is just the kind of creative nonfiction that elevates a seemingly arcane topic into popular fare." Booklist

Snyder, Don J.

Snyder, Don J. The cliff walk; a memoir of a lost job and a life found. Little, Brown 1997 265p $23.95; pa $12.95   **92**

ISBN 0-316-80308-1; 0-316-80348-0 (pa)
                   LC 96-51163

"When the author is fired by Colgate University, he never doubts that his brilliance and charm will soon gain him entrance to a new ivory tower. Instead, he is forced to move his family of five to Maine in the off season. With his pride and his checking account steadily eroding, he concocts wild schemes—stealing golf balls from a nearby course with his son, and secretly contemplating selling his unborn child. Finally, Snyder gives his last seventeen hundred dollars to a dying woman so she can take her children to Disney World. This dire act propels him into a real job—building a house—and toward a vision of self that depends more on strength than on prestige." New Yorker

Solzhenitsyn, Aleksandr, 1918-

Solzhenitsyn, Aleksandr. Invisible allies; translated from the Russian by Alexis Klimoff and Michael Nicholson. Counterpoint Bks. 1995 344p hardcover o.p. paperback available $22.50   **92**

ISBN 1-887178-42-2 (pa)   LC 95-33079

"A Cornelia and Michael Bessie book"

The author's "best-known works, including the *Gulag Archipelago* . . . were written in secret, circulated only as underground typescripts (samizdat), and eventually smuggled out of the Soviet Union for publication in the West. This current work details how all that occurred and thanks the more than 100 individuals who typed manuscripts, microfilmed them, stored copies, and transported them." Libr J

Includes bibliographical references

Sondheim, Stephen

Citron, Stephen. Sondheim and Lloyd-Webber; the new musical. Oxford Univ. Press 2001 425p il $39.95   **92**

1. Lloyd Webber, Andrew, 1948-
ISBN 0-19-509601-0   LC 2001-31408

In this volume Citron profiles the two composers, highlighting their personal lives and tracing "their creative development from tentative neophytes to much-feted giants, integrating the various directions that musical theater has taken." Libr J

Includes bibliographical references

Secrest, Meryle. Stephen Sondheim; a life. Knopf 1998 461p il o.p.; Delta Bks. paperback available $14.95   **92**

ISBN 0-385-33412-5 (pa)   LC 98-14258

This biography was "written with considerable cooperation from its subject and his friends. The composer-lyricist's personal demons—his overbearing mother, his intolerance of his homosexuality—have darkened the tone of a brilliant series of American musicals, each of which is richly described." New Yorker

Includes bibliographical references

Sontag, Susan, 1933-

Rollyson, Carl E. (Carl Edmund). Susan Sontag; the making of an icon; [by] Carl Rollyson and Lisa Paddock. Norton 2000 370p il $29.95   **92**

ISBN 0-393-04928-0   LC 00-20402

The authors "have unearthed a deluge of information on Sontag's personal life—on her early years and family life, her lesbianism. . . her relationship with son David Rieff and her battles with breast cancer. While the authors provide an intelligent, though not strikingly original, analysis of her work, they are best at detailing how Sontag and her publishers have marketed her image as much as her thought." Publ Wkly

Includes bibliographical references

Soto, Hernando de, ca. 1500-1542

Duncan, David Ewing. Hernando de Soto; a savage quest in the Americas. Crown 1995 xxxvii, 570p il maps o.p.; University of Okla. Press paperback available $29.95   **92**

ISBN 0-8061-2977-8 (pa)   LC 95-663

This is a "biography of the conquistador who from 1539 to his death in 1543 was 'the first European to penetrate deeply into the interior of our continent.'" Libr J

"Duncan's scholarship and documentation are impeccable, and his chronology unfolds like a superbly crafted novel." Booklist

Includes bibliographical references

Speer, Albert, 1905-1981

Fest, Joachim C. Speer: the final verdict; [by] Joachim Fest; translated from the German by Ewald Osers and Alexandra Dring. Harcourt 2002 419p il $30; pa $15

    92

ISBN 0-15-100556-7; 0-15-602874-3 (pa)
                   LC 2002-6074

One of the "defendants at Nuremberg . . . was armaments minister Albert Speer. . . . [He projected] the image of himself as the apolitical 'outsider' at the heart of the Nazi regime—as the person who accepted moral responsibility for its crimes but first came to hear of them at the end of the war. . . . [This is a] biographical study [of Speer]." Hist Today

"This is a valuable, important biography, but perhaps it is an effort to explain the unexplainable." Booklist

Includes bibliographical references

Speer, Albert, 1905-1981—*Continued*

Sereny, Gitta. Albert Speer; his battle with truth. Knopf 1995 757p il hardcover o.p. paperback available $25 **92**
1. National socialism 2. Germany—Politics and government—1933-1945
ISBN 0-679-76812-2 (pa)   LC 94-19764

The author of this biography of the Nazi war criminal "conducted intensive and protracted interviews with Speer . . . and many of the people who were close to him. Along with the interviews and analysis are good descriptions of what was happening in Germany throughout the Third Reich. Sereny's clear and concise prose makes this book suitable for both the scholar and the lay reader. She has produced what will become one of the standard works in Holocaust studies." Libr J

Includes bibliographical references

Van der Vat, Dan. The good Nazi: the life and lies of Albert Speer. Houghton Mifflin 1997 406p il $30 **92**
1. National socialism 2. Germany—Politics and government—1933-1945
ISBN 0-395-65243-X   LC 97-39924

In this biography the author sets out "to prove that Speer was as implicated in the Holocaust as the first-rank Nazis he served as Hitler's minister of wartime production, despite his repeated denials and Nuremberg's verdict on that subject." Libr J

"Not a repentant sinner to Van der Vat, Speer is a professional thug and trickster with no claim 'to a share of the moral high ground' onto which he tried to pen himself. Van der Vat's well-documented book is so convincing it imparts a hollow ring to Speer's self-serving apologias." Publ Wkly

Includes bibliographical references

Stalin, Joseph, 1879-1953

Bullock, Alan. Hitler and Stalin. See entry under Hitler, Adolf, 1889-1945 **92**

Conquest, Robert. Stalin; breaker of nations. Viking 1991 346p il hardcover o.p. paperback available $14.95 **92**
1. Soviet Union—Politics and government
ISBN 0-14-016953-9 (pa)   LC 91-28782

The author "portrays the Soviet dictator as an insufferably rude husband, a Georgian who hated his roots and Russified himself, a crude boor who yearned to be a backslapping man to the people." Publ Wkly

"Intended for the general reader, [this work] provides a superb portrait of the man who terrorized his country for 30 years. . . . Briskly written, authoritative yet not pedantic, filled with interesting incidents and anecdotes, [it] makes for fascinating reading." N Y Times Book Rev

Includes bibliographical references

Radzinsky, Edvard. Stalin; the first in-depth biography based on explosive new documents from Russia's secret archives; translated by H.T. Willetts. Doubleday 1996 607p il hardcover o.p. paperback available $16.95 **92**
ISBN 0-385-47954-9 (pa)   LC 95-4495

For this biography of the Soviet ruler the author "has examined mountains of rare archival sources and inter-

viewed many who lived through decades of Stalinist (mis)rule. The result is the best general biography of Stalin to date. Radzinsky strips away layer after layer of myth, falsehood, and enigma to produce a riveting portrait of a man whose primary role model was Ivan the Terrible." Libr J

Includes bibliographical references

Stanley, Henry M. (Henry Morton), 1841-1904

Dugard, Martin. Into Africa. See entry under Livingstone, David, 1813-1873 **92**

Stanton, Elizabeth Cady, 1815-1902

Ward, Geoffrey C. Not for ourselves alone: the story of Elizabeth Cady Stanton and Susan B. Anthony; an illustrated history; based on a documentary film by Ken Burns, written by Geoffrey C. Ward; with a preface by Ken Burns; introduction by Paul Barnes; and contributions by Martha Saxton, Ann D. Gordon, Ellen Carol DuBois. Knopf 1999 240p $35; pa $19.95 **92**
1. Anthony, Susan B., 1820-1906
ISBN 0-375-40560-7; 0-375-70969-X (pa)
LC 99-31056

This biographical study of Cady and Anthony, leaders of the women's rights movement in the United States, was published to accompany a television film by Ken Burns

"Ward writes beautifully, and he knows how to weigh evidence and how to assess the salience of events. He quotes shrewdly from the words of his protagonists. Although the interpretation is far from exciting or original, he freshens his material by including new essays by scholars." New Repub

Includes bibliographical references

Stavans, Ilan

Stavans, Ilan. On borrowed words; a memoir of language. Viking 2001 263p $23.95; pa $15 **92**
ISBN 0-670-87763-8; 0-14-20094-9 (pa)
LC 00-68586

"As a white-skinned Mexican Jew for whom Yiddish, not Spanish, is his mother tongue, literary and social critic Stavans . . . has never felt truly Mexican. As he explores his feelings about his youth in Mexico City, he considers the connection between identity and language and recounts the history of the city's insular Jewish community. Guided by his love of literature, he soon found his spiritual home in New York." Booklist

"The best and most original parts of this book are Stavans's insights into the intersections of language, geography and culture." N Y Times Book Rev

Steffens, Lincoln, 1866-1936

Steffens, Lincoln. The autobiography of Lincoln Steffens. Harcourt Brace & Co. 1931 2v il **92**
v1 o.p.; v2 available in paperback for $10.95 (ISBN 0-15-609396-0)

The life of an American reporter, journalist, student of ethics and politics

"Here is a text-book on journalism; a treasure house for the historian of that wave of social idealism that shook the United States from 1900 to 1917; a casebook for the psychologist of political types. Above all it is the vivid diary of a bold and humane pilgrim." Survey

Stegner, Wallace Earle, 1909-1993

Benson, Jackson J. Wallace Stegner; his life and work. Viking 1996 xx, 472p il hardcover o.p. paperback available $20   **92**

ISBN 0-14-024796-3 (pa)   LC 96-12757

"The son of a sometime 'whiskey-runner,' Stegner became a Pulitzer Prize-winning author, founder of the writing program at Stanford University, and devoted family man who admitted he did not 'wake up' to writing until after he had earned his Ph.D. In this engrossing work, Benson offers a portrait of a resilient truth-seeker, steadfast moralist, obsessive realist, and compassionate humanist who became the standard-bearer for western regionalist writing." Booklist

Stein, Gertrude, 1874-1946

Stein, Gertrude. The autobiography of Alice B. Toklas. Modern Lib. 1993 342p $15.50; pa $13   **92**

1. Toklas, Alice B. 2. Paris (France)—Intellectual life
ISBN 0-679-60081-7; 0-679-72463-X (pa)
LC 93-15339

First published 1933 by Harcourt Brace & Co.

"The book is really Stein's autobiography, presented as though written by her secretary, Alice Toklas. The book provoked a rejoinder from various Parisian artists and writers, *Testimony Against Gertrude Stein* (1935). . . . For the average reader, however, Stein's book holds much fascination in its views of Parisian life and personalities, and the whole is offered in a genuinely witty style." Benet's Reader's Ency of Am Lit

Steinbeck, John, 1902-1968

Steinbeck, John. Conversations with John Steinbeck; edited by Thomas Fensch. University Press of Miss. 1988 xxi, 116p (Literary conversations series) hardcover o.p. paperback available $18   **92**

ISBN 0-87805-360-3 (pa)   LC 88-17538

"This collection of Steinbeck's interviews allows him to speak on his own behalf in an illuminating expression of his intentions, goals, and achievements. From the beginning of his career through his last years the interviews reveal a fascinating, controversial, and captivating personality." Univ Press Books for Second Sch Libr

Includes bibliographical references

Steinberg, Saul, 1914-1999

Steinberg, Saul. Reflections and shadows; [by] Saul Steinberg with Aldo Buzzi; translated from the Italian by John Shepley. Random House 2002 100p il $24.95   **92**

ISBN 0-375-50571-7   LC 2001-48696

A collection of autobiographical vignettes by the artist best known for his cartoons in the New Yorker magazine, based on taped conversations recorded and edited by Aldo Buzzi

"This slender volume is crammed full of wit, charm, and astute observations that should leave every reader . . . wishing for more." Libr J

Includes bibliographical references

Steinem, Gloria

Heilbrun, Carolyn G. The education of a woman: the life of Gloria Steinem. Dial Press (NY) 1995 xxv, 451p il o.p.; Ballantine Bks. paperback available $23   **92**

ISBN 0-345-40621-4 (pa)   LC 95-19683

The author "offers a study of Steinem that takes into account both her feminine and feminist appeal." Libr J

"The portrait that results is nuanced and thoughtful. . . . Heilbrun's goal is at once to understand how Steinem became the woman she is, and what her life can teach us about childhood and family, self and society. Slow at the start, but Heilbrun soon captures readers' interest and imagination." Booklist

Includes bibliographical references

Stengel, Casey

Creamer, Robert W. Stengel; his life and times. University of Neb. Press 1996 349p il pa $18.95   **92**

ISBN 0-8032-6367-8   LC 95-40143

First published 1984 by Simon & Schuster

"Casey Stengel is remembered as either the shrewd, innovative New York Yankee manager who won 10 pennants and seven World Series from 1949 to 1960 or as the seemingly senile, aged master of malaprop who (mis)-managed the legendarily inept New York Mets in the early 1960s. Creamer . . . dissolves the apparently disparate images and melds them into an inclusive vision of an unexpectedly complex man." Booklist

Stern, Isaac

Stern, Isaac. My first 79 years; [by] Isaac Stern written with Chaim Potok. Knopf 1999 317p il o.p.; Da Capo Press paperback available $18   **92**

ISBN 0-306-81006-9 (pa)   LC 99-30918

In this memoir Stern discusses his musical career, his efforts on behalf of arts funding, his support of the state of Israel, and his participation in the 1959 campaign to save Carnegie Hall from demolition

"This is a sensitive and engrossing history of a man and an era." Libr J

Stewart, Martha

Byron, Christopher. Martha Inc.; the incredible story of Martha Stewart Living Omnimedia; [by] Christopher M. Byron. Wiley 2002 405p il $27.95; pa $14.95   **92**

ISBN 0-47112-300-5; 0-471-42958-9 (pa)

In this biography of Martha Stewart, Byron "is most persuasive when he describes her professional maneuverings—particularly her genius for using any partnership to her advantage, from her marriage to her Kmart deal. Byron sifts the now familiar elements of Stewart's personal life—impoverished upbringing, bullying dad, cohorts of betrayed friends—and arrives at the plausible if predictable conclusion that character problems like ruthless egotism are at the root of her business success." New Yorker

Includes bibliographical references

Stowe, Harriet Beecher, 1811-1896

Hedrick, Joan D. Harriet Beecher Stowe; a life. Oxford Univ. Press 1994 507p il hardcover o.p. paperback available $19.95

92

ISBN 0-19-509639-8 (pa)   LC 93-16610

This biography "brings to life not just the complex and fascinating woman and writer but also the 19th-century America that shaped her and was in turn shaped by her. Hedrick manages to weave into his immensely readable biography a history teeming with the domestic detail of the famous Beecher clan, the settling of the West, and the impact of the Civil War and the abolition movement." Libr J

Includes bibliographical references

Stravinsky, Igor, 1882-1971

Joseph, Charles M. Stravinsky inside out. Yale Univ. Press 2001 xx, 320p il $29.95

92

ISBN 0-300-07537-5   LC 2001-913

This study "reveals a . . . flawed and fragile human being, who craved approval, dealt ungenerously with colleagues, loved James Bond movies, and tried hard to further his son's musical career. Although the aged Stravinsky's eagerness to play the role of celebrity composer for the golden age of television . . . was an embarrassment, most of these episodes testify to the protean survival skills of an artist whose sense of identity was always in flux and whose cunning was commensurate with his talent." New Yorker

Includes bibliographical references

Walsh, Stephen. Stravinsky; a creative spring: Russia and France, 1882-1934. Knopf 1999 698p il o.p.; University of Calif. Press paperback available $24.95   **92**

ISBN 0-520-22749-2 (pa)   LC 99-462433

"In this reference-oriented biography, Walsh uses diaries, press clippings, and other materials to probe in detail the life of a man kept very busy with effectively dividing his time between performance, composition, family, and mistress." Booklist

Includes bibliographical references

Strayhorn, Billy, 1915-1967

Hajdu, David. Lush life: a biography of Billy Strayhorn. Farrar, Straus & Giroux 1996 305p il o.p.; North Point Press paperback available $15   **92**

ISBN 0-86547-512-1 (pa)   LC 95-44707

"In 1939, when Billy Strayhorn, a young pianist and composer, was invited to visit Duke Ellington in Harlem, he put together a tune to mark the occasion: 'Take the 'A' Train.' That tune became the Ellington Orchestra's theme, and began a collaboration that sustained both musicians throughout their interwoven careers. Hajdu invests his biography of Strayhorn with the kind of sensitivity and clarity which is the mark of his subject's best work, and shows that Strayhorn managed to thrive in Ellington's considerable shadow." New Yorker

Includes bibliographical references

Sullivan, Anne, 1866-1936

Lash, Joseph P. Helen and teacher. See entry under Keller, Helen, 1880-1968   **92**

Tallchief, Maria

Tallchief, Maria. Maria Tallchief; America's prima ballerina; [by] Maria Tallchief with Larry Kaplan. Holt & Co. 1997 351p il $30   **92**

ISBN 0-8050-3302-5   LC 96-45271

"A John Macrae book"

In this memoir Tallchief focuses "on her remembrances of her years with choreographer George Balanchine. . . . She met Balanchine at the start of her career, when she was with the Ballet Russe de Monte Carlo and Balanchine was about to form a company that would become a precursor to the New York City Ballet. Tallchief subsequently became Balanchine's wife, muse, and prima ballerina, and, though the marriage was short-lived, their artistic partnership endures in Balanchine's works created for Tallchief. She also writes about other stars, but the memoir sparkles when she recalls the subtlety and detail of a movement or the beauty of a musical phrase." Libr J

Tecumseh, Shawnee Chief, 1768-1813

Eckert, Allan W. A sorrow in our heart: the life of Tecumseh. Bantam Bks. 1992 862p maps hardcover o.p. paperback available $7.99   **92**

1. Shawnee Indians

ISBN 0-553-56174-X (pa)   LC 91-31858

This is a "narrative biography of Tecumseh, the remarkable Shawnee warrior and statesman who succeeded in organizing a group of disparate tribes into a cohesive confederacy of nations. . . . Eckert places his subject firmly within his proper social and historical context by providing a tremendous amount of meticulously researched and authenticated background information, including illuminating details of tribal life and Shawnee culture." Booklist

Includes bibliographical references

Teller, Edward, 1908-2003

Teller, Edward. Memoirs; a twentieth-century journey in science and politics; [by] Edward Teller with Judith Shoolery. Perseus Bks. 2001 628p il hardcover o.p. paperback available $18.95

92

ISBN 0-7382-0778-0 (pa)

This memoir, by the nuclear physicist who worked to develop the hydrogen bomb, recounts his origins in the scientific community in Germany prior to the Nazi takeover and describes his "work on safe proliferation of nuclear energy, the so-called Stars Wars defense system and the early detection of earth-crossing objects. . . . Readers can enjoy these panoramic and beautifully written recollections of one of the great scientific, if controversial, figures of all time." Publ Wkly

Teresa, Mother, 1910-1997

Spink, Kathryn. Mother Teresa; a complete authorized biography. HarperSanFrancisco 1997 306p il hardcover o.p. paperback available $15.95   **92**

1. Missionaries of Charity 2. Missions—India

ISBN 0-06-251553-5 (pa)   LC 97-41349

"Spink's biography benefits from her own 18-year involvement with the work of the Missionaries of Charity Order as well as from the intimate relationship she developed over the years with Mother Teresa. . . . A final

Teresa, Mother, 1910-1997—*Continued*

chapter in the book provides glimpses of Mother Teresa's affection for Princess Diana, a brief description of Mother Teresa's funeral and a short account of the election of Sister Nirmal as her successor." Publ Wkly

Teresa, of Avila, Saint, 1515-1582

Medwick, Cathleen. Teresa of Avila; the progress of a soul. Knopf 1999 282p hardcover o.p. paperback available $12.95   **92**

ISBN 0-385-50129-3 (pa)   LC 99-18921

In this biography of the sixteenth-century Spanish nun, "Medwick traces Teresa's early years, her entrance into the genteel life of the Convent of the Incarnation in Avila, her second conversion as a person of prayer, and her subsequent trials as a founder of reformed monasteries of women under the austere rule of Mount Carmel." Commonweal

Includes bibliographical references

Thomas, Helen

Thomas, Helen. Front row at the White House; my life and times. Scribner 1999 415p il $26; pa $14   **92**

ISBN 0-684-84911-9; 0-684-86809-1 (pa)

       LC 99-13787

"A Lisa Drew book"

Thomas' "memoir blends commentary on the men (and women) of 1600 Pennsylvania Avenue with more personal reminiscences as well as broader judgments about how politics, the media, and American society have changed over the years." Booklist

Includes bibliographical references

Thompson, Hunter S.

Thompson, Hunter S. Fear and loathing in America; the brutal odyssey of an outlaw journalist, 1968-1976; foreword by David Halberstam; edited by Douglas Brinkley. Simon & Schuster 2000 xxv, 756p il $30; pa $15   **92**

ISBN 0-684-87315-X; 0-684-87316-8 (pa)

       LC 00-47012

This is the second volume of a projected three volume edition of Thompson's letters; earlier volume The proud highway published 1997 by Villard Books

"During the period covered in this collection, Thompson was a vital, deliriously erratic force in journalism, covering the turbulent 1968 Democratic National Convention in Chicago, the 1968 election of Richard M. Nixon, the 1972 campaign, Watergate, the falls of Nixon and Saigon." N Y Times Book Rev

Thompson, Jim

Philpott, Tom. Glory denied; the saga of Jim Thompson, America's longest-held prisoner of war. Norton 2001 457p $26.95   **92**

1. Vietnam War, 1961-1975
ISBN 0-393-02012-6   LC 00-66993

Also available in paperback from Plume Bks.

This is a biography of a Green Beret held prisoner in Vietnam from 1964 until 1973. It "is told to Philpott in the form of an oral history, and it includes Jim's story as told by him, his wife and other family members, friends back home, his fellow prisoners, and those who knew him when he finally got out." Booklist

"Philpott's well-researched biography is a remarkable story of survival that will take its place among the testimonies of other POWs." Libr J

Thurber, James, 1894-1961

Grauer, Neil A. Remember laughter: a life of James Thurber. University of Neb. Press 1994 xxii, 204p il hardcover o.p. paperback available $10   **92**

ISBN 0-8032-7056-9 (pa)   LC 94-2945

In this assessment of the humorist, the author "manages to offer a writer's life with a balance that is often lost in contemporary biography. Expedient, germane and selective, the book maintains an interest in the subject's personal life and development only to illuminate Thurber's work, which is what warranted the biography in the first place." N Y Times Book Rev

Includes bibliographical references

Thurmond, Strom, 1902-2003

Cohodas, Nadine. Strom Thurmond & the politics of southern change. Mercer Univ. Press 1994 574p il pa $18.95   **92**

ISBN 0-86554-446-8   LC 94-15867

A reissue of the title first published 1993 by Simon & Schuster

This "biography traces South Carolina Senator Thurmond's career from his status as a 'consummate white reactionary' to that of a savvy politician who courts black voters." Publ Wkly

This is "a readable, well-documented account of the Southern battle over integration from the perspective of one of its most highly visible conservative opponents." Libr J

Includes bibliographical references

Tiffany, Louis Comfort, 1848-1933

Loring, John. Louis Comfort Tiffany at Tiffany & Co. Abrams 2002 255p il $60   **92**

1. Tiffany & Co.
ISBN 0-8109-3288-1   LC 2002-5145

This examines the life and work of the late 19th and early 20th century designer of Art Nouveau jewelry, enamels, blown glass and other objets d'art and his relationship to his family's company, illustrated with 350 color images

Timerman, Jacobo, 1923-1999

Timerman, Jacobo. Prisoner without a name, cell without a number; translated from the Spanish by Toby Talbot. Knopf 1981 164p o.p.; University of Wis. Press paperback available $17.95   **92**

ISBN 0-299-18244-4 (pa)   LC 80-2715

The author "an outspoken Zionist and formerly a newspaper publisher in Buenos Aires, relates his 30-month political incarceration—torture and isolation in a clandestine prison, then detention in an official penal institution—which preceded his expulsion from [Argentina] in 1979." Publ Wkly

Tipton, Billy, 1914-1989

Middlebrook, Diane Wood. Suits me: the double life of Billy Tipton. Houghton Mifflin 1998 326p il maps hardcover o.p. paperback available $14   **92**

ISBN 0-395-95789-3 (pa)   LC 97-42466

"A Peter Davison book"

Tipton, Billy, 1914-1989—*Continued*

This is a biography of the "jazz singer Tipton, a woman who passed as a man and even married five women." Libr J

"Always scintillating, Middlebrook vividly describes the jazz scene Tipton reveled in and captures the energy and the enigma of Tipton's brilliant if confounding improvisational life." Booklist

Includes bibliographical references

Tito, Josip Broz, 1892-1980

West, Richard. Tito; and the rise and fall of Yugoslavia. Carroll & Graf Pubs. 1995 436p il hardcover o.p. paperback available $15.95

92

1. Yugoslavia—Politics and government

ISBN 0-7867-0332-6 (pa)   LC 95-10404

First published 1994 in the United Kingdom

This biography "describes Tito's rise to power, his creation of the Partisan Army during the Axis occupation, his consolidation of southern Slavs after the war and establishment of a Communist Yugoslavia, the break with Stalin in 1948, Tito's subsequent rivalry with the Soviet bloc and his leadership of nonaligned states. . . . The book also clarifies the present three-way conflict among Serbs, Croats and Muslims." Publ Wkly

"This combination of history and biography is based on a sympathetic attitude toward its subject, a relaxed style of writing, and a good command of published sources." Libr J

Includes bibliographical references

Tolkien, J. R. R. (John Ronald Reuel), 1892-1973

Hammond, Wayne G. J.R.R. Tolkien, artist & illustrator; [by] Wayne G. Hammond, Christina Scull. Houghton Mifflin 1995 207p il hardcover o.p. paperback available $25

92

ISBN 0-618-08361-8 (pa)   LC 96-105237

Along with biographical material and text describing his artwork, this book reproduces more than 200 drawings, sketches and paintings Tolkien made throughout his life. Included are the "Father Christmas" letters to his children and images created in connection with The Hobbit and The Lord of the Rings

"The open and inviting format and the reproductions of his art make this a Tolkien lover's dream, and the insightful text will quickly capture attention as well." Booklist

Includes bibliographical references

Toulouse-Lautrec, Henri de, 1864-1901

Frey, Julia. Toulouse-Lautrec; a life. Viking 1994 xxii, 595p il o.p.; Phoenix Press paperback available $27.50   **92**

ISBN 1-85799-363-2 (pa)   LC 94-20407

The author chronicles Toulouse-Lautrec's "transformation from a pampered invalid into one of the most radical of the fin de siècle artists. . . . Her sensitive, eloquent, and richly illustrated biography has brought the real Toulouse-Lautrec out from behind the scrim of myth." Booklist

Trotsky, Leon, 1879-1940

Volkogonov, Dmitrii Antonovich. Trotsky; the eternal revolutionary; [by] Dmitri Volkogonov; translated and edited by Harold Shukman. Free Press 1996 xxxvi, 524p il map $32.50   **92**

ISBN 0-684-82293-8   LC 95-42315

"The book consists of two roughly equal parts. The first chronicles Trotsky's youth, pre-1917 revolutionary career and accomplishments as one of Soviet Russia's leaders; the second, his remarkably swift fall from power followed by years of wanderings as an exile and Stalin's relentlessly hunted quarry." N Y Times Book Rev

"Whatever Trotsky's ultimate historical status may be, Volkogonov has made a valiant effort to bring him back to living history." N Y Rev Books

Includes bibliographical references

Truman, Harry S., 1884-1972

McCullough, David G. Truman; [by] David McCullough. Simon & Schuster 1992 1117p il $40; pa $22   **92**

ISBN 0-671-45654-7; 0-671-86920-5 (pa)

LC 92-5245

This biography of the 33rd president "not only conveys in rich detail Truman's accomplishments as a politician and statesman, but also reveals the character and personality of this constantly-surprising man—as schoolboy, farmer, soldier, merchant, county judge, senator, vice president and chief executive. The book relates how Truman overcame the stigma of business failure and debt . . . and acquired a reputation for honesty, reliability and common sense." Publ Wkly

Includes bibliographical references

Truth, Sojourner, d. 1883

Painter, Nell Irvin. Sojourner Truth; a life, a symbol. Norton 1996 370p il $28; pa $15.95   **92**

ISBN 0-393-02739-2; 0-393-31708-0 (pa)

LC 95-47595

"Sojourner Truth's remarkable career as a powerful, impassioned speaker and advocate of abolitionism and women's rights spanned more than 30 years. Painter . . . traces Truth's life and legacy using a variety of sources, including her many photographs." Libr J

"Painter persuasively offers us the real woman behind the myth." Publ Wkly

Includes bibliographical references

Turner, J. M. W. (Joseph Mallord William), 1775-1851

Hamilton, James. Turner. Random House 2003 xxv, 461p il $35   **92**

ISBN 1-400-06015-X   LC 2002-36991

First published 1997 in the United Kingdom

The author "contends that painter J.W.M. Turner . . . was a prodigy who first exhibited his work in his father's barber shop and owed his fame to innate opportunism as much as to matchless talent." Publ Wkly

"Through in-depth and thoroughly enjoyable analyses of Turner's many travel sketchbooks, Hamilton provides a wealth of information and insights." Booklist

Includes bibliographical references

Turner, Tina

Turner, Tina. I, Tina; [by] Tina Turner, with Kurt Loder. Morrow 1986 236p il o.p.; Avon Bks. paperback available $6.99   **92**

ISBN 0-380-70097-2 (pa)   LC 86-16455

"Born Anna Mae Bullock in 1939 in Nut Bush, Tennessee, Tina Turner is now—after a fantastic comeback—one of the hottest acts in rock music. . . . The path that Tina . . . followed to pull herself out of sleepy Nut Bush and eventually to gain international stardom is traced here." Booklist

"Kurt Loder has edited I, Tina nicely, letting [Turner's] narrative take center stage, punctuating it with the voices of friends, colleagues, and family." Nation

Twain, Mark, 1835-1910

Emerson, Everett. Mark Twain; a literary life. University of Pa. Press 1999 386p il $34.95   **92**

ISBN 0-8122-3516-9   LC 99-34173

Emerson "portrays a man who, in mid-life, had trouble reconciling his rough-and-tumble, Western persona with a proper Eastern rustyle. Emerson argues convincingly that Twain spent too much time trying both to write sequels to his most lucrative works and to establish himself as a dramatist and let himself be distracted by his social life and star-crossed business ventures." Libr J

Includes bibliographical references

Twain, Mark. The autobiography of Mark Twain; as arranged and edited with an introduction and notes, by Charles Neider. Harper & Row 1959 xxvi, 388p il hardcover o.p. paperback available $15   **92**

ISBN 0-06-095542-2 (pa)

The editor "has arranged the selections in coordinated chronological order, ending with the death of Clemens' daughter Jean in December, 1909." Booklist

Tynan, Kenneth, 1927-1980

Tynan, Kenneth. The diaries of Kenneth Tynan; edited by John Lahr. Bloomsbury Press 2001 439p il $32.95; pa $16.95   **92**

ISBN 1-58234-160-5; 1-58234-245-8 (pa)

LC 2001-35274

Tynan "was one of Britain's foremost drama critics; here, he spent two seasons as theater critic for the *New Yorker*. Along with Laurence Olivier, he helped found London's National Theater, where he functioned as literary manager for 10 years. Not surprisingly, Tynan dissects theatrical foibles and politicking with a keen inside perspective; he can also discourse on the European common market, Spaniards' attitudes toward homosexuality, cricket, French cuisine, Ethel Merman and much more. . . . Celebrated names are not merely dropped (from Katharine Hepburn and Princess Margaret to W.H. Auden and Jerry Lewis), but integral to his revelatory anecdotes." Publ Wkly

Tynan, Ronan, 1960-

Tynan, Ronan. Halfway home: my life 'til now. Scribner 2002 238p il $24   **92**

ISBN 0-7432-2291-1   LC 2001-49662

Also available in paperback from Citadel Press

"A Lisa Drew book"

An autobiography by a member of the Irish Tenors, who, though born with a congenital deformity and despite the amputation of both legs, became a winner in the Disabled Olympics, competed in horse shows and races, and became the first disabled person ever admitted to the National College of Physical Education

"Readers expecting the usual singer biography will be delighted and transfixed by Tynan's extraordinary life story." Libr J

Tyndale, William, d. 1536

Moynahan, Brian. God's bestseller: William Tyndale, Thomas More, and the writing of the English Bible; a story of martyrdom and betrayal. St. Martin's Press 2003 xxv, 422p il $27.95   **92**

1. More, Sir Thomas, Saint, 1478-1535 2. Bible—Versions 3. Bible—History

ISBN 0-312-31486-8   LC 2003-43124

First published 2002 in the United Kingdom with title: If God spare my life

"In telling the compelling saga of how William Tyndale defied church and king, at the final cost of his life, to publish Holy Writ in English, Moynahan accentuates the contrast between Tyndale, fearless champion of individual conscience, and his ferocious, antiheretical foe, Thomas More, who eventually fell to the executioner's ax himself." Booklist

Includes bibliographical references

Typhoid Mary, d. 1938

Bourdain, Anthony. Typhoid Mary; an urban historical. Bloomsbury Pub. 2001 148p $19.95   **92**

ISBN 1-58234-133-8   LC 2001-18444

The subject of Bourdain's book is the cook "Mary Mallon, who became known as Typhoid Mary after infecting 33 people with typhoid fever . . . in turn-of-the-century New York." N Y Times Book Rev

"Investing a tragic tale with a new twist, Bourdain plays historical detective, providing an entertaining and suspenseful evocation of turn-of-the-century New York." Booklist

Includes bibliographical references

Valentino, Rudolph, 1895-1926

Leider, Emily Wortis. Dark lover: the life and death of Rudolph Valentino; [BY] Emily W. Leider. Farrar, Straus & Giroux 2003 514p il $35; pa $16   **92**

ISBN 0-374-28239-0; 0-571-21114-3 (pa)

LC 2002-29779

This is a "study of the movie star and his era, and of how he altered forever the electric charges of both men and women in 1921 with 'The Sheik.'" N Y Times Book Rev

"A comprenhensive . . . portrait of the great screen lover." Booklist

Includes bibliographical references

Van Vechten, Carl, 1880-1964

Hughes, Langston. Remember me to Harlem: the letters of Langston Hughes and Carl Van Vechten, 1925-1964. See entry under Hughes, Langston, 1902-1967   **92**

Velázquez, Diego, 1599-1660

Brown, Jonathan. Velázquez, painter and courtier. Yale Univ. Press 1986 322p il hardcover o.p. paperback available $39.95
92

ISBN 0-300-03894-1 (pa)   LC 85-14234

"The life of the great Spanish painter Diego de Velázquez was extraordinary, and Jonathan Brown has made it enthralling. The painter's astonishing ability to paint directly from life manifested itself when he was still a youth, and he quickly became not only the court painter to King Philip IV but the master of the King's collections. . . . Read in context, the pictures, often interpreted by critics and artists but never so well as by Mr. Brown, mean far more than ever before." N Y Times Book Rev

Includes bibliographical references

Verdi, Giuseppe, 1813-1901

Berger, William. Verdi with a vengeance; an energetic guide to the life and complete works of the king of opera. Vintage Bks. 2000 497p il pa $15   **92**

ISBN 0-375-70518-X   LC 00-42261

The author "provides a brief overview of the composer's life and times and examines the connections between contemporary politics and Verdi's creative output. . . . A glossary and recommended recordings, films, and soundtracks are included. Informative and eminently readable for the novice and scholar alike." Libr J

Includes bibliographical references

Vermeer, Johannes, 1632-1675

Bailey, Anthony. Vermeer; a view of Delft. Holt & Co. 2001 272p il map hardcover o.p. paperback available $16   **92**

ISBN 0-8050-6930-5 (pa)   LC 00-66366

"A John Macrae book"

Published in the United Kingdom with title: A view of Delft: Vermeer then and now

Bailey presents a "depiction of the painter's world, both the city of Delft and his chaotic household, musing on the mystery of how Vermeer achieved the quiet, even holy, perfection of his paintings with 11 young children underfoot." Booklist

Includes bibliographical references

Victoria, Queen of Great Britain, 1819-1901

Erickson, Carolly. Her little majesty: the life of Queen Victoria. Simon & Schuster 1997 304p il hardcover o.p. paperback available $19.95   **92**

ISBN 0-7432-3657-2 (pa)   LC 96-35041

This is a biography of the British monarch

"Erickson has a knack for plucking pithy quotes, and the essentials of the queen's life are often deftly set out." Publ Wkly

Includes bibliographical references

Hibbert, Christopher. Queen Victoria; a personal history. Basic Bks. 2000 557p il hardcover o.p. paperback available $21   **92**

1. Great Britain—History—19th century

ISBN 0-306-81085-9 (pa)   LC 2001-269136

Hibbert explores the life and reign of the British monarch based on "primary sources, particularly the 60 million words of Victoria's letters and journals. As a result,

he renders Victoria and her familial and political relationships with deliciously gossipy and often touching intimacy." N Y Times Book Rev

Includes bibliographical references

Strachey, Lytton. Queen Victoria. Harcourt Brace & Co. 1921 434p il hardcover o.p. paperback available $16   **92**

1. Great Britain—History—19th century

ISBN 0-15-602756-9 (pa)

Also available in paperback from Penguin Bks.

"Harbrace modern classics"

This portrait of Queen Victoria and her time, includes characterizations of Lord Melbourne, Palmerston, Gladstone, Disraeli, and the prince consort

Includes bibliographical references

Vallone, Lynne. Becoming Victoria. Yale Univ. Press 2001 256p il $26.95   **92**

1. Great Britain—History—19th century

ISBN 0-300-08950-3   LC 00-68561

"Analyzing Victoria's girlhood diaries, drawings and fiction, as well as records of her education and scores of accounts of her childhood, Valone . . . constructs a revisionist account of the princess's youthful persona but also traces the process by which Victoria was molded into the 'right' kind of adult: capable of assuming the throne and also a clear embodiment of all that was womanly and pure. . . . Well-researched, and with sophisticated cultural criticism, this sound scholarship will engage the interest of academics and nonacademics alike." Publ Wkly

Includes bibliographical references

Vidal, Gore, 1925-

Kaplan, Fred. Gore Vidal; a biography. Doubleday 1999 850p il hardcover o.p. paperback available $19   **92**

ISBN 0-385-47704-X (pa)   LC 99-14828

This "portrait of one of America's most accomplished writers demonstrates veteran biographer Kaplan's ability to weave masses of information into a smooth, interpretive account. Vidal's twin obsessions—writing and politics—surfaced early, and Kaplan tracks his subject's many contributions in both arenas." Booklist

Includes bibliographical references

Villa, Pancho, 1878-1923

Katz, Friedrich. The life and times of Pancho Villa. Stanford Univ. Press 1998 985p hardcover o.p. paperback available $30.95
92

1. Mexico—History

ISBN 0-8047-3046-6 (pa)   LC 97-47271

The author "traces Pancho Villa's rise from relatively obscure outlaw to national leader of the Mexican Revolution (1910-20) and his subsequent decline to guerrilla leader. . . .[This] is likely to be the definitive account of Villa for years to come." Libr J

Includes bibliographical references

Wałęsa, Lech, 1943-

Wałęsa, Lech. The struggle and the triumph; an autobiography; by Lech Walesa with the collaboration of Arkadiuz Rybicki; translated by Franklin Philip in collaboration with Helen Mahut. Arcade Pub. 1992 330p il hardcover o.p. paperback available $16.95

92

1. Solidarity (Labor union) 2. Poland—Politics and government
ISBN 1-55970-221-4 (pa)   LC 91-35875
In this sequel to A way of hope (1987), Walesa "continues his autobiography from 1983 to his election to the Polish presidency in 1990. . . . From his power base in Solidarity, Walesa portrays his maturing role as a national and international leader and his commitment to nonviolence to achieve political and economic reform." Libr J

Walker, Alice, 1944-

Walker, Alice. The same river twice; honoring the difficult: a meditation on life, spirit, art, and the making of the film The color purple, ten years later. Scribner 1996 302p il hardcover o.p. paperback available $14   **92**

ISBN 0-671-00377-1 (pa)   LC 95-30056
This "book finds the Pulitzer Prize-winning author still grappling with criticism of the film version of her novel The Color Purple. . . . Walker's memoir pieces together assorted journal entries, magazine clippings, occasional photographs and even her original screenplay to form an intimate scrapbook of the period." Publ Wkly
Includes bibliographical references

Walker, C. J., Madame, 1867-1919

Lowry, Beverly. Her dream of dreams: the rise and triumph of Madam C.J. Walker. Knopf 2003 481p il map $27.50   **92**
ISBN 0-679-44642-7   LC 2002-27494
This biography describes the "journey of Sarah Breedlove (Walker's original name) from abject poverty through virulent racism and Jim Crow laws to the height of business success with her hair-care products for black women." Booklist
This "is a vividly told story that will appeal to general readers and scholars alike." Libr J
Includes bibliographical references

Walton, Sam

Walton, Sam. Sam Walton, made in America; my story; by Sam Walton with John Huey. Doubleday 1992 269p il o.p.; Bantam Bks. paperback available $7.99   **92**
1. Wal-Mart Stores, Inc.
ISBN 0-553-56283-5 (pa)   LC 92-18874
The founder of Wal-Mart Stores, the largest retail chain in the world, recounts how he made his fortune
"Readers will enjoy the folksy narrative of the small-town millionaire who revolutionized retail distribution. . . . Coauthor Huey does a fine job of incorporating candid testimonials from family members and associates." Libr J
Includes bibliographical references

Warhol, Andy, 1928?-1987

Koestenbaum, Wayne. Andy Warhol. Viking 2001 224p il (Penguin lives series) $21.95   **92**
ISBN 0-670-03000-7   LC 2001-17986
Koestenbaum offers an analysis of the "artist's early-1950s line drawings, through his filmic output, to his work after his near-fatal shooting by a disgruntled acquaintance. . . . The text is constructed not only from a scholarly examination of the work but also from the obscure but fascinating aphorisms and insights of Warhol's personal acquaintances." Libr J

Warhol, Andy. The Andy Warhol diaries; edited by Pat Hackett. Warner Bks. 1989 807p il hardcover o.p. paperback available $25.95   **92**
ISBN 0-446-39138-7 (pa)   LC 88-40565
The entries included in this edition of the American artist's diaries were originally "phoned in each morning (from 1976 to his death in 1987) to his associate Pat Hackett." Newsweek
"Despite their virtuoso triviality, their naïve snobbery and their incredible length, the diaries of Andy Warhol are not without a certain charm. . . . Ms. Hackett's editing, one feels, is affectionate and scrupulous, yet correctly unprotective." N Y Times Book Rev

Warner, Sylvia Townsend, 1893-1978

Warner, Sylvia Townsend. The element of lavishness: letters of Sylvia Townsend Warner and William Maxwell, 1938-1978; edited by Michael Steinman. Counterpoint 2001 xxvii, 356p il $27.50; pa $18   **92**
1. Maxwell, William, 1908-2000
ISBN 1-58243-118-3; 1-58243-247-3 (pa)
LC 00-64459
"Between 1936 and 1977, Sylvia Townsend Warner published more than a hundred and fifty stories in The New Yorker. Almost from the start, the writer William Maxwell was her editor. They hardly ever met (Maxwell lived in New York and Warner in Dorset), but they recognized in each other a kindred spirit, and their formal epistolary relationship soon quickened into deep, abiding love." New Yorker

Washington, Booker T., 1856-1915

Harlan, Louis R. Booker T. Washington: the making of a black leader, 1856-1901. Oxford Univ. Press 1972 379p il hardcover o.p. paperback available $21.50   **92**
ISBN 0-19-501915-6 (pa)
This book "covers Washington's life from his birth as a slave in western Virginia up to [the year 1901, when he died] with Theodore Roosevelt at the White House, an event signifying white recognition of Washington as the chief spokesman for black interests in the period before World War I." Libr J

Harlan, Louis R. Booker T. Washington: the wizard of Tuskegee, 1901-1915. Oxford Univ. Press 1983 548p il hardcover o.p. paperback available $24.95   **92**
1. Tuskegee Institute
ISBN 0-19-504229-8 (pa)   LC 82-14547
This is the second and concluding volume of a life of the black educator and founder of Tuskegee Institute

Washington, Booker T., 1856-1915—*Continued*

"Having avoided the pitfalls of white guilt and black rage and the temptation to judge the past by standards of the present, Mr. Harlan deserves honors for his remarkable achievement." N Y Times Book Rev

Includes bibliographical references

Washington, Booker T. Up from slavery; an autobiography 92

1. Tuskegee Institute

Hardcover and paperback editions available from various publishers

First published 1901

"The classic autobiography of the man who, though born in slavery, educated himself and went on to found Tuskegee Institute." N Y Public Libr

Washington, George, 1732-1799

Brookhiser, Richard. Founding father: rediscovering George Washington. Free Press 1996 230p hardcover o.p. paperback available $14 92

ISBN 0-684-83142-2 (pa)   LC 95-50650

The author presents what he calls a "'moral biography' of the first president. He explores Washington's role as a general, his part in the writing of the Constitution, and his years as president. Brookhiser then turns to Washingon's private life, examining his character, his strong sense of duty, and his constant struggle to hold his temper in check so he could be an effective leader. Finally, the author describes Washington's role as the father of his country." Libr J

"Brookhiser's slim, graceful volume is readable in one sitting. His style is muscular and discursive, yet unaffectedly erudite." Christ Sci Monit

Includes bibliographical references

Ferling, John E. The first of men: a life of George Washington. University of Tenn. Press 1988 598p il maps hardcover o.p. paperback available $26 92

1. United States—History

ISBN 0-87049-628-X (pa)   LC 87-26037

The author "probes the contradictions and complexities of character that led to Washington's success." Publ Wkly

Ferling "incorporates a wealth of traditional primary material. . . . This is a well-documented, gracefully written and engaging history." Choice

Includes bibliographical references

Flexner, James Thomas. George Washington. Little, Brown 1965-1972 4v il 92

1. United States—History

Contents: {v1} The forge of experience (1732-1775) $40 (ISBN 0-316-28597-8); {v2} George Washington in the American Revolution (1775-1783) o.p. (ISBN 0-316-28595-1); {v3} George Washington and the new nation (1783-1793) $42 (ISBN 0-316-28600-1); {v4} Anguish and farewell (1793-1799) o.p. (ISBN 0-316-28602-8)

Includes bibliographical references

Grizzard, Frank E., Jr. George Washington: a biographical companion; [by] Frank E. Grizzard, Jr. ABC-CLIO 2002 437p il map (ABC-CLIO biographical companion) $55 92

ISBN 1-57607-082-4   LC 2001-6957

Contents: Introduction; George Washington; Selected writings; Chronology

"In approximately 200 articles ranging from one paragraph to several pages and covering everything from John Adams to the Whiskey Rebellion, Grizzard . . . gives us anyone, anyplace, or anything at all relevant to George Washington. Each of the alphabetically arranged entries includes the topic or name, the date, the significance to Washington, cross references to related entries in the book, and a short bibliography; sometimes, extensive background information is given that thoroughly explains the topic's place in Washington's life. . . . More than a companion for those reading about Washington's life, this work is also an interesting and sometimes detailed reference work on Colonial and Revolutionary America." Libr J

Randall, Willard Sterne. George Washington; a life. Holt & Co. 1997 548p hardcover o.p. paperback available $18 92

1. United States—History

ISBN 0-8050-5992-X (pa)   LC 97-19125

"A John Macrae book"

"Chronicling less the adaptive leader of the struggling rebellion or the persuasive conciliator of the infant republic, Randall . . . portrays instead the vain, restless, ambitious provincial who got 'tremendously lucky'. . . . Altogether human, Randall's demythologized Washington comes vividly to life." Publ Wkly

Includes bibliographical references

Smith, Richard Norton. Patriarch: George Washington and the new American nation. Houghton Mifflin 1993 xxi, 424p hardcover o.p. paperback available $16 92

1. United States—History

ISBN 0-395-85512-8 (pa)   LC 92-21732

"A Richard Todd book"

In this study the author "argues that Washington was not the mere figurehead that other historians have portrayed, but a canny politician who mastered and controlled his brilliant subordinates, Alexander Hamilton and Thomas Jefferson. In a lively and engaging style, the author describes Washington's world in New York, Philadelphia, and Mt. Vernon, and the major policy issues of the 1790s, especially the vituperative politics of the era." Libr J

Includes bibliographical references

Washington, George. The diaries of George Washington; Donald Jackson, editor; Dorothy Twohig, associate editor. University Press of Va. 1976-1979 6v il maps v3, 5 ea $65; v4, 6 $60 92

Contents: v1 1748-65 o.p.; v2 1766-70 o.p.; v3 1771-75, 1780-81 (ISBN 0-8139-0721-7); v4 1784-June 1786 (ISBN 0-8139-0722-5); v5 July 1786-December 1789 (ISBN 0-8139-0801-9); v6 January 1790-December 1799 (ISBN 0-8139-0807-8)

"Here is the little-known Washington: the adventurer, surveyor, novice soldier, slave-owner, experimental farm-

Washington, George, 1732-1799—*Continued*
er. And here, too—beautifully illustrated—are the routine and rhythm of life in 18th-century Virginia." Choice

Includes bibliographical references

Wasserman, Lew R., 1913-2002
Bruck, Connie. When Hollywood had a king; the reign of Lew Wasserman, who leveraged talent into power and influence. Random House 2003 512p il $29.95   **92**
ISBN 0-375-50168-1   LC 2003-41418
The author "shows how Lew Wasserman managed both to end the era of movie moguls (by freeing the stars of the 1940s from their studio contracts) and then to become the greatest mogul of them all (by realizing that television was an opportunity not a threat)." Booklist
"Those who are interested in comprehensive details about the inner workings of the entertainment industry—its history, business, customs, people, and gossip—will find this a fascinating read and a solid resource." Libr J

Includes bibliographical references

Waters, Muddy, 1915-1983
Gordon, Robert. Can't be satisfied: the life and times of Muddy Waters. Little, Brown 2002 xx, 408p il $25.95; pa $15.95   **92**
ISBN 0-316-32849-9; 0-316-16494-1 (pa)
                                   LC 2001-50473
In this biography of the blues musician "Gordon details the gritty life reflected in Muddy's lyrics. . . . He makes Muddy the musician, Muddy the man, Muddy the parent, and Muddy the tool of the (not so) sainted Chess brothers come alive. . . . Packed with facts, copiously referenced, and featuring a foreword by . . . Keith Richards, this book is absolutely essential for any popular music collection worthy of the name." Booklist

Includes bibliographical references

Watson, James D., 1928-
Watson, James D. Genes, girls, and Gamow; after the double helix. Knopf 2002 xxix, 259p il $26; pa $14   **92**
ISBN 0-375-41283-2; 0-375-72715-9 (pa)
                                   LC 2001-38543
"In 1953, Watson, then 25, and colleague Francis Crick discovered the structure of DNA. . . . Here Watson . . . gives a detailed, journal-writer's account of the aftermath, recalling . . . his younger self's professional and—equally pressing—amorous ambitions. . . . Reading Watson is a delight, an opportunity to breathe the rarefied air of his generation's greatest scientists and to crash a faculty cocktail party or two along the way." Publ Wkly

Webster, Daniel, 1782-1852
Remini, Robert Vincent. Daniel Webster; the man and his time; [by] Robert V. Remini. Norton 1997 796p il $26; pa $14   **92**
1. United States—Politics and government—1815-1861
ISBN 0-393-04552-8; 0-375-72715-9 (pa)
                                   LC 97-24371
This work explores the life and times of the influential politician and statesman of antebellum America
"Remini tends to exaggerate Webster's personal peccadilloes, but it cannot be said that he underestimates his subject's importance to American political culture. For Remini, Webster's muscular nationalism, embroidered with Lincoln's democratic eloquence, provided the foundation for a strong and enduring union." Choice

Includes bibliographical references

Weil, Simone, 1909-1943
Gray, Francine du Plessix. Simone Weil. Viking 2001 248p il (Penguin lives series) $19.95   **92**
ISBN 0-670-89998-4   LC 00-51367
The author "recounts the chronology of Weil's short life, all the while interweaving Weil's emerging political, philosophical, and spiritual ideas into the biographical narrative." Libr J
"Part intellectual primer and part case study, this slim, sympathetic biography makes us question whether we value Weil's thinking despite the example of her punishing, courageous, profoundly exasperating life, or because of it." New Yorker

Includes bibliographical references

Weill, Kurt, 1900-1950
Hirsch, Foster. Kurt Weill on stage; from Berlin to Broadway. Knopf 2002 403p il $35
                                             92
ISBN 0-375-40375-2   LC 2002-18450
Also available in paperback from Limelight Editions
"This biography traces Weill's career from his satirical Weimar collaborations with Brecht to the musicals he created for Broadway after fleeing the Nazis in 1933." Publ Wkly
This is "a clear, careful, reasoned analysis of its subject's work—his music—and its evolution." Booklist

Includes bibliographical references

Schebera, Jürgen. Kurt Weill; an illustrated life; translated by Caroline Murphy. Yale Univ. Press 1995 381p il $50   **92**
ISBN 0-300-06055-6   LC 94-41444
Original German edition, 1990
"Published with the assistance of the Kurt Weill Foundation for Music"
"Schebera makes wonderful use of archival illustrations: concert programs, advertisements, photos, even a few record labels from the Twenties and Thirties. This is a scholarly work, but the appealing subject, complete with the drama of Nazi persecution and flight from prewar Germany, makes it a good choice for most music collections." Libr J

Includes discography and bibliographical references

Welles, Orson, 1915-1985
Thomson, David. Rosebud: the story of Orson Welles. Knopf 1996 463p il hardcover o.p. paperback available $16   **92**
ISBN 0-679-77283-9 (pa)   LC 95-44216
In this examination of Welles, "Thomson trots out the myths and reinterprets them in Welles' favor, which he fits into his ingenious conceit of Welles as the antihero Kane. . . . Throughout, Thomson is engaging and humorous, particularly in working with another masterful conceit. On a controversial interpretation or on an exquisite insight, the publisher enters the narrative and converses with the author. Prettily done. Thomson summarizes that Welles was, at once, 'magnificent *and* a poor bastard.' And this is, at once, a brilliant and maddening inquiry." Booklist

Includes bibliographical references

Wellington, Arthur Wellesley, Duke of, 1769-1852

Hibbert, Christopher. Wellington; a personal history. Addison-Wesley 1997 460p il maps o.p.; Da Capo Press paperback available $21   **92**

1. Great Britain—History—19th century
ISBN 0-7382-0148-0 (pa)   LC 97-17285

In this biography of Arthur Wellesley, the author "emphasizes the duke of Wellington's personality, family, and friendships." Booklist

"Altogether, Wellington does not quite pass the 'niceness' test. . . . He was a difficult man, a major military figure, a minor Prime Minister and in sum a historically important legend. Hibbert skillfully brings out all these characteristics." N Y Times Book Rev

Includes bibliographical references

Welty, Eudora, 1909-2001

Waldron, Ann. Eudora; a writer's life. Doubleday 1998 398p il hardcover o.p. paperback available $23   **92**

ISBN 0-385-47648-5 (pa)   LC 98-5708

This is a biography of the writer from Mississippi

"Waldron's biography of Welty is the first to be written and, until the definitive treatment arrives, will satisfy readers curious to know details about the life of this much loved figure." Booklist

Includes bibliographical references

Welty, Eudora. One writer's beginnings. Harvard Univ. Press 1984 104p il (William E. Massey, Sr. lectures in the history of American civilization) $20.95; pa $12   **92**

ISBN 0-674-63925-1; 0-674-63927-8 (pa)   LC 83-18638

A series of lectures in which the author reflects on her Southern heritage and her early artistic influences

Wesley, John, 1703-1791

Tomkins, Stephen. John Wesley; a biography. Eerdmans 2003 208p pa $20   **92**

1. Methodist Church
ISBN 0-8028-2499-4   LC 2003-54328

In this biography of the founder of the Methodist religion "Tomkins presents a keenly engaging portrait of a great man full of contradictoriness. Wesley insisted he was loyal to the Church of England yet consented to his followers setting up establishments and engaging in practices that flouted Anglican authority. . . . He altered the face of Christianity in the West by inspiring modern evangelicalism and Pentecostalism. A fascinating figure, fascinatingly limned." Booklist

Includes bibliographical references

West, Mae, 1892-1980

Leider, Emily Wortis. Becoming Mae West. Farrar, Straus & Giroux 1997 431p il o.p.; Da Capo Press paperback available $18   **92**

ISBN 0-306-80951-6 (pa)   LC 96-43803

This exploration of the West persona "focuses on the first four decades of West's career, up to 1938. Yet Leider's biography is also a portrait of an era: she devotes a great deal of the book to rendering the historical context, particularly the moral landscape, of the early 1900's, in order to more clearly define West's place in it and ultimately her mastery of it." N Y Times Book Rev

White, E. B. (Elwyn Brooks), 1899-1985

Elledge, Scott. E.B. White; a biography. Norton 1984 400p il hardcover o.p. paperback available $15.95   **92**

ISBN 0-393-30305-5 (pa)   LC 83-4032

This biography "follows White from his birth in Mount Vernon, N.Y. to his . . . octogenarian retreat in Maine." Libr J

The author is "fair, respectful, thorough, entertaining, skillful and unpedantic. He has performed a splendid exercise in scholarship and literary analysis, and the result is fun." N Y Times Book Rev

Includes bibliographical references

Whitman, Walt, 1819-1892

Callow, Philip. From noon to starry night: a life of Walt Whitman. Dee, I.R. 1992 394p il $28.50; pa $14.95   **92**

ISBN 0-929587-95-2; 1-56663-133-5 (pa)   LC 92-5311

The author "attempts to illuminate Walt Whitman's life . . . by focusing primarily on the poet's experiences before the Civil War. . . . Callow adds a historical sketch of early-19th-century America to show how the nation Whitman celebrated so eloquently in *Leaves of Grass* formed his complex personality." Publ Wkly

"Infused with tenderness and respect, this fine biography deciphers the complexity of Whitman's sexuality and passionate creativity while celebrating his abiding compassion and grandeur of spirit." Booklist

Includes bibliographical references

Morris, Roy. The better angel: Walt Whitman in the Civil War; [by] Roy Morris, Jr. Oxford Univ. Press 2000 270p hardcover o.p. paperback available $15.95   **92**

1. United States—History—1861-1865, Civil War
ISBN 0-19-514709-X (pa)   LC 99-86210

"Morris reveals the Civil War's transformative effect on Whitman: the anxious journeys to find his brother (who eventually became a prisoner of war), the shocking confrontation with the injuries and conditions of the wounded men, the frustration with doctors' attitudes, and the experience of affection for the wounded." Booklist

Includes bibliographical references

Wideman, John Edgar

Wideman, John Edgar. Hoop roots. Houghton Mifflin 2001 242p $24; pa $13   **92**

ISBN 0-395-85731-7; 0-618-25775-6 (pa)   LC 2001-26455

Wideman "examines his lifelong relationship with basketball. He argues that basketball first allowed him to set his own standard in a white world that often imposes definitions of success on black people. A poignant, thought-provoking memoir." Booklist

Wiesel, Elie, 1928-

Wiesel, Elie. All rivers run to the sea; memoirs. Knopf 1995 432p il $35; pa $15   **92**

1. Holocaust, 1933-1945—Personal narratives
ISBN 0-679-43916-1; 0-8052-1028-8 (pa)   LC 95-17607

Original French edition, 1994

Wiesel "begins with his boyhood in the Carpathian Mountains of Central Europe and his uprooting and

Wiesel, Elie, 1928——*Continued*

transport by cattle car to the barbed wire infernos of Auschwitz and Buchenwald. Here Wiesel describes the horror of being among Jews bound for the death camps as the war was drawing to a close. . . . He describes in following chapters his schooling in postwar France, his decision to become a journalist, and his travels to Israel and throughout the world." Libr J

"Wiesel's immensely moving, unforgettable memoir has the searing intensity of his novels and autobiographical tales." Publ Wkly

Wiesel, Elie. And the sea is never full; memoirs, 1969-; translated from the French by Marion Wiesel. Knopf 1999 429p hardcover o.p. paperback available $15   **92**

1. Holocaust, 1933-1945
ISBN 0-8052-1029-6 (pa)   LC 99-15604

Continues the author's memoirs begun in All the rivers run to the sea

Original French edition, 1996

"This concluding volume begins when the author is age 40. He continues his travels . . . and he continues to write, his books including *Souls on fire*, *Four Hasidic Masters*, *Twilight*, and more. . . . Wiesel is the most significant writer to have made the Holocaust the major theme of his work, just as it has been of major importance to his life. The horror of the Holocaust can be felt in this memoir with an intensity beyond words." Booklist

Wiesenthal, Simon

Pick, Hella. Simon Wiesenthal; a life in search of justice. Northeastern Univ. Press 1996 349p il $35   **92**

ISBN 1-55553-273-X   LC 96-11808

"Simon Wiesenthal, a survivor of Auschwitz, Gross-Rosen, and Mauthausen concentration camps, has spent his life searching for Nazis suspected of participation in the Holocaust. Pick, who lost close relatives in the Holocaust, [interviewed] . . . Wiesenthal and was allowed unrestricted access to . . . his archives and files." Booklist

This biography "has interesting things to say about forgiveness, including an extraordinary hallucinogenic encounter with a dying SS officer, and conveys a broadly sympathetic picture of a man capable of distinguishing between individuals and their political rhetoric." Times Lit Suppl

Includes bibliographical references

Wilde, Oscar, 1854-1900

Belford, Barbara. Oscar Wilde; a certain genius. Random House 2000 381p il hardcover o.p. paperback available $23   **92**

ISBN 0-8129-9261-X (pa)   LC 00-26827

Belford presents a "psychological portrait of Oscar Wilde, from precocious schoolboy to pampered, talented adult to literary lion undone by a reactionary, moralistic society. She writes frankly of his sexual adventures and in so doing impresses us with how contemporary Wilde remains, 100 years after his death." Booklist

Includes bibliographical references

Ellmann, Richard. Oscar Wilde. Knopf 1988 c1987 680p il hardcover o.p. paperback available $19.95   **92**

ISBN 0-394-75984-2 (pa)   LC 87-45354

First published 1987 in the United Kingdom

"Wilde's life epitomizes the classic formula for a tragic history, the man who, by hubris, falls from greatness. In Mr. Ellmann's hands, the story becomes as compelling as fiction while never deviating from the facts. Humour and elegance illuminate the accounts of Wilde's family, his friends and the enemies he earned." Economist

Includes bibliographical references

Wilder, Billy, 1906-2002

Sikov, Ed. On Sunset Boulevard: the life and times of Billy Wilder. Hyperion 1998 675p il hardcover o.p. paperback available $17.95   **92**

ISBN 0-7868-8503-3 (pa)   LC 98-23504

This biography of the filmmaker concentrates "on Wilder's movies and their humorous cynicism and sullied idealism about life and love." Booklist

"Sikov has painted as good a portrait of Billy Wilder, the man, the artist, the showman, the self-promoter, the profitably prescient art collector and the successful businessman, as we are likely to get from the outside." N Y Times Book Rev

Includes filmography

Wilder, Laura Ingalls, 1867-1957

Anderson, William T. Laura Ingalls Wilder country; text by William Anderson; color photography by Leslie A. Kelly. HarperPerennial 1990 119p il hardcover o.p. paperback available $24.95   **92**

1. Literary landmarks—United States
ISBN 0-06-097346-3 (pa)   LC 89-46512

Cover subtitle: The people and places in Laura Ingalls Wilder's life and books

"Contemporary and period photographs of the places in the Laura Ingalls Wilder books have been combined with a narrative about the actual historical settings." Horn Book

Williams, Hank, 1923-1953

Escott, Colin. Hank Williams; the biography; [by] Colin Escott with George Merritt and William MacEwen. Little, Brown 1994 307p il hardcover o.p. paperback available $19.99   **92**

ISBN 0-316-24938-6 (pa)   LC 93-48092

A look at the career of the influential country singer/songwriter. Williams' self-destructive behavior and turbulent personal life are also examined

Includes discography and bibliographical references

Williams, Ted, 1918-2002

Linn, Edward. Hitter: the life and turmoils of Ted Williams; [by] Ed Linn. Harcourt Brace Jovanovich 1993 437p il hardcover o.p. paperback available $16   **92**

1. Boston Red Sox (Baseball team)
ISBN 0-15-600091-1 (pa)   LC 92-41870

"Linn's book is not a typical game-by-game baseball biography, but a series of snapshots of Williams's career. The [author] . . . touches on the many high points, but does not neglect Williams's warts, including his constant battle with Boston baseball writers. The product of an unhappy childhood, Williams formed close friendships with the 'underdogs,' and gave unsparingly of himself to a charity for combatting cancer in children." Libr J

Williams, Ted, 1918-2002—*Continued*

Williams, Ted. Ted Williams; my life in pictures; [by] Ted Williams with David Pietrusza. Total Sports 2001 201p il $45
92

ISBN 1-930844-07-7   LC 2001-23360

Featuring over 300 photographs, this pictorial autobiography recounts Williams's life on and off the field, "many from his personal collection and never before published." Publisher's note

Williams, Tennessee, 1911-1983

Leverich, Lyle. Tom: the unknown Tennessee Williams. Crown 1995 xxvi, 644p il o.p.; Norton paperback available $18   **92**

ISBN 0-393-31663-7 (pa)   LC 95-6038

This is the first installment of a projected two-volume biography of the American dramatist. Coverage begins with Williams' birth in 1911 and extends to the opening of The Glass Menagerie in 1945

"The book is a tremendous accomplishment, and Leverich is an appealing biographer: modest, thorough, balanced, and passionate. In prose that is clear—if not scintillating—he bushwhacks a path through a morass of gossip and myth, and prepares the way for a more subtle interpretation of the man and his plays." New Yorker

Spoto, Donald. The kindness of strangers: the life of Tennessee Williams. Da Capo Press 1997 409p il pa $18.50   **92**

ISBN 0-306-80805-6   LC 97-8428

First published 1985 by Little, Brown

"Based on hundreds of interviews with those who knew him and on other previously unpublished material, [the author] presents a portrait of Tennessee Williams which is both respectful and sensitive." Wilson Libr Bull

Includes bibliographical references

Wilson, Edith Bolling Galt, 1872-1961

Levin, Phyllis Lee. Edith and Woodrow: the Wilson White House. See entry under Wilson, Woodrow, 1856-1924   **92**

Wilson, Woodrow, 1856-1924

Auchincloss, Louis. Woodrow Wilson. Viking 2000 128p (Penguin lives series) $19.95   **92**

ISBN 0-670-88904-0   LC 99-46890

Also available Thorndike Press large print edition

"A Lipper/Viking book"

"Auchincloss visits Wilson's relationships with his two wives, his adviser Colonel House, and his archenemy, Henry Cabot Lodge, while analyzing Wilson's successes and failures at Princeton, as governor of New Jersey, as president, and as world leader. Auchincloss sees Wilson as admirable but flawed." Libr J

Includes bibliographical references

Cooper, John Milton. The warrior and the priest: Woodrow Wilson and Theodore Roosevelt; [by] John Milton Cooper, Jr. Belknap Press 1983 442p il hardcover o.p. paperback available $20.95   **92**

1. Roosevelt, Theodore, 1858-1919 2. United States—Politics and government—1898-1919

ISBN 0-674-94751-7 (pa)   LC 83-6021

This "book is divided into four sections dealing respectively with the origins and early careers of both men, the parallel presidencies of Theodore Roosevelt (US) and Woodrow Wilson (Princeton), the election of 1912, and WW I." Choice

The author's "distinctions are sharp, his insights original, his judgments balanced and his narrative unfailingly graceful." N Y Times Book Rev

Includes bibliographical references

Levin, Phyllis Lee. Edith and Woodrow: the Wilson White House. Scribner 2001 606p il $35   **92**

1. Wilson, Edith Bolling Galt, 1872-1961 2. United States—Politics and government—1898-1919

ISBN 0-7432-1158-8   LC 2001-41109

"A Lisa Drew book"

Levin discusses the White House during the incumbency of Woodrow and Edith Wilson

"This detailed, highly readable marital case study is recommended for public and academic libraries." Libr J

Includes bibliographical references

Winchell, Walter, 1897-1972

Gabler, Neal. Winchell; gossip, power, and the culture of celebrity. Knopf 1994 681p il hardcover o.p. paperback available $17   **92**

ISBN 0-679-76439-9 (pa)   LC 93-44259

"At the peak of his career during the 1930s and 1940s, Walter Winchell was America's most powerful and feared journalist; when he died in 1972, he had been long forgotten. Gabler's biography brings back to life the man credited with inventing the gossip column and with creating today's celebrity culture." Libr J

Includes bibliographical references

Winner, Lauren F.

Winner, Lauren F. Girl meets God; on the path to a spiritual life. Algonquin Bks. 2002 303p $23.95   **92**

ISBN 1-56512-309-3   LC 2002-74508

Also available in paperback from Shaw

Winner's autobiography is an " account of her odyssey from Orthodox Judaism to evangelical Christianity." Christ Century

The author "reveals herself through abundant, concrete and often funny descriptions of her life, inner and outer." Publ Wkly

Includes bibliographical references

Wolff, Tobias, 1945-

Wolff, Tobias. This boy's life: a memoir. Atlantic Monthly Press 1989 288p o.p.; Grove/Atlantic paperback available $13   **92**

ISBN 0-8021-3668-0 (pa)   LC 88-17600

The novelist and short story writer "offers an engrossing and candid look into his childhood and adolescence in his first book of nonfiction. In unaffected prose he recreates scenes from his life that sparkle with the immediacy of narrative fiction. The result is an intriguingly guileless book, distinct from the usual reflective commentary of autobiography." Libr J

Woodhull, Victoria C., 1838-1927

Goldsmith, Barbara. Other powers: the age of suffrage, spiritualism, and the scandalous Victoria Woodhull. Knopf 1998 531p il o.p.; Perennial Lib. paperback available $16   **92**

1. Feminism 2. Women—Suffrage

ISBN 0-06-095332-2 (pa)   LC 97-49464

"Victoria Woodhull was a charismatic and notorious figure in the struggle for women's rights in the years following the Civil War. She was the first woman to address Congress and the first woman to run for president. Goldsmith . . . has successfully woven together a history of Woodhull's life with the lives of the powerful she touched." Libr J

Includes bibliographical references

Woolf, Virginia, 1882-1941

Gordon, Lyndall. Virginia Woolf, a writer's life. Norton 1985 c1984 341p il hardcover o.p. paperback available $14.95   **92**

ISBN 0-393-32205-X (pa)   LC 84-25424

First published 1984 in the United Kingdom

"Gordon combines literary criticism with biographical investigation in her life of Virginia Woolf. . . . Using the major novels *To the Lighthouse* and *The Waves,* Gordon explores in detail the autobiographical ramifications of these works as she traces Woolf's childhood, marriage, and literary career." Booklist

Includes bibliographical references

Lee, Hermione. Virginia Woolf. Knopf 1997 893p il hardcover o.p. paperback available $20   **92**

ISBN 0-375-70136-2 (pa)   LC 97-71155

First published 1996 in the United Kingdom

Lee "re-creates the world Woolf was born into in 1882, a maze of formalities and reticences, and then leads us through changes that, slow in coming but shocking in effect, made all that seem light-years away by the time Woolf was 50. She convinces us that Woolf, contrary to previous assumptions, reveled in a deep intimacy with her husband, Leonard. Finally, she makes a persuasive case for the underlying sanity of this woman as she battled her own madness and shows the brilliant literary uses she made of her instability." N Y Times Book Rev

Includes bibliographical references

Woolf, Virginia. A moment's liberty: the shorter diary; abridged and edited by Anne Olivier Bell; introduction by Quentin Bell. Harcourt Brace Jovanovich 1990 516p $22.95; pa $20   **92**

ISBN 0-15-161894-1; 0-15-661912-1 (pa)

     LC 90-33428

An abridged edition of the five volumes of Woolf's Diary, published 1977-1984

"The diaries here may appeal to a larger audience, not least because each year represented is prefaced by a wonderfully succinct overview. Here are Woolf's superbly drawn portraits of Max Beerbohm, T.S. Eliot, John Maynard Keynes, Katherine Mansfield—and her occasionally acerbic remarks on what they said and did. But the diaries are also a repository for luminous thoughts on birds and weather, the pleasures of walking or listening to music." Publ Wkly

Woolf, Virginia. Moments of being; edited, with an introduction and notes, by Jeanne Schulkind. 2nd ed. Harcourt Brace Jovanovich 1985 230p pa $14   **92**

ISBN 0-15-661918-0   LC 85-8521

"A Harvest/HBJ book"

First published 1976

This volume consists of unpublished autobiographical writings, including several "Reminiscences" written at the start of Woolf's career, a piece entitled "A sketch of the past" written shortly before her suicide, and papers read to the Memoir Club

Includes bibliographical references

Wordsworth, William, 1770-1850

Johnston, Kenneth R. The hidden Wordsworth; poet, lover, rebel, spy. Norton 1998 965p il $45; pa $24.95   **92**

ISBN 0-393-04623-0; 0-393-32159-2 (pa)

     LC 97-40317

This "volume focuses on the poet's first thirty-six years, the tumultuous decades immortalized in 'The Prelude.' Johnston's spacious, absorbing argument—that Wordsworth's moments of emotion recollected in tranquillity were themselves rather less than tranquil—is amply supported by a thorough documentation of the multifarious life and times of the young poet, at Hawkshead, at Cambridge, in Grasmere, and abroad." New Yorker

Includes bibliographical references

Wright, Frank Lloyd, 1867-1959

Secrest, Meryle. Frank Lloyd Wright; a biography. University of Chicago Press 1998 634p il pa $20   **92**

ISBN 0-226-74414-0   LC 97-51590

First published 1992 in the United Kingdom; first United States edition published 1993 by Knopf

A portrait of a "complex, often contradictory architect. . . . Secrest writes with authority and compassion about Wright's long and turbulent career. Her exhaustive scholarship provides fresh insights into Wright's personality." Libr J

Includes bibliographical references

Wright, Orville, 1871-1948

Adams, Noah. The flyers. See entry under Wright, Wilbur, 1867-1912   **92**

Wright, Richard, 1908-1960

Rowley, Hazel. Richard Wright; the life and times. Holt & Co. 2001 626p il hardcover o.p. paperback available $18   **92**

ISBN 0-8050-7088-5 (pa)   LC 00-54249

In this biography Rowley chronicles Wright's "journey from the South to Chicago, New York, and Paris—and from *Native Son,* the novel that made him famous, to his scorchingly honest books about Africa and Spain." Booklist

"The strength of [this book] is [the] painstaking research. Rowley . . . has a daunting dedication to primary sources and her documentation is meticulous." N Y Times Book Rev

Includes bibliographical references

Wright, Richard, 1908-1960—*Continued*

Wright, Richard. Black boy; a record of childhood and youth. Harper & Row 1964 c1945 285p hardcover o.p. paperback available $13 **92**
1. African Americans—Social conditions
ISBN 0-06-092978-2 (pa)

Also available in hardcover from Buccaneer Bks.

A reissue of the title first published 1945 by World Publishing Company

This autobiographical work concludes with Wright "newly arrived in Chicago in 1927 as a fugitive from the white South that never knew him. [It] relates his nomadic life in Tennessee, Arkansas, and Mississippi, abandoned by his father and with his mother working at menial jobs or incapacitated by illness." Benet's Reader's Ency of Am Lit

Wright, Richard. Conversations with Richard Wright; edited by Keneth Kinnamon and Michel Fabre. University Press of Miss. 1993 xxi, 253p il (Literary conversations series) hardcover o.p. paperback available $20 **92**
ISBN 0-87805-633-5 (pa)   LC 93-13938

In this collection of interviews, "the author of *Native Son*, *Black Boy*, and *Uncle Tom's Children* expounds on topics not only of literature but of politics, race, and society." Booklist

Wright, Wilbur, 1867-1912

Adams, Noah. The flyers; in search of Wilbur and Orville Wright. Crown 2003 221p il $22 **92**
1. Wright, Orville, 1871-1948
ISBN 1-400-04912-1   LC 2003-15011

The author highlights "the triumphs and quixotic personalities of his subjects and their nuclear family at the expense of setbacks in the field and dry laboratory experiments." Libr J

"The most appealing part of the book is the look at the close relationship between Orville, Wilbur and their sister Katherine. . . . Adams uses letters and diaries to describe the lives of the Wrights; some of these details are not widely included in other books that focus on their inventions and accomplishments. . . . In the end, he's a personable guide into the Wright Brothers' world, offering a refreshing look at these aviation pioneers." Publ Wkly
Includes bibliographical references

Wyeth, Andrew, 1917-

Wyeth, Andrew. Andrew Wyeth, autobiography; introduction by Thomas Hoving; with commentaries by Andrew Wyeth. Little, Brown 1995 168p il $50; pa $29.95 **92**
ISBN 0-8212-2159-0; 0-8212-2569-3 (pa)
LC 94-48305

"A Bulfinch Press book"

Published in conjunction with a retrospective exhibit, this book reproduces 137 paintings. "Each painting is accompanied by commentary from the artist that lends insight into his life and character. Several nude studies are included." Booklist
Includes bibliographical references

Wyeth, N. C. (Newell Convers), 1882-1945

Michaelis, David. N.C. Wyeth; a biography. Knopf 1998 555p il o.p.; HarperCollins Pubs. paperback available $24.95 **92**
ISBN 0-06-008926-1 (pa)   LC 98-6143

This biography "explores not only the destiny of a ferociously disciplined and conflicted patriarch but the lives of four generations of an American artistic dynasty." New Yorker

"Michaelis's work is an outstanding example of the biographer's art. Integrating Wyeth's complex personal and psychological life with his artistic oeuvre, Michaelis creates a portrait of both the artist and the man." Libr J
Includes bibliographical references

Yeats, W. B. (William Butler), 1865-1939

Brown, Terence. The life of W.B. Yeats; a critical biography. Blackwell 1999 410p il (*Blackwell critical biographies*) $66.95; pa $29.95 **92**
ISBN 0-631-18298-5; 0-631-22851-9 (pa)
LC 99-28388

In this biography Brown places "Yeats's work as poet and dramatist in its political and social—as well as personal and erotic—context." N Y Times Book Rev
Includes bibliographical references

Foster, R. F. (Robert Fitzroy). W.B. Yeats; a life. Oxford Univ. Press 1997-2003 2v il v1 op; v2 $45 **92**
ISBN 0-19-818465-4 (v2)   LC 96-31671

Contents: v1 The apprentice mage, 1865-1914; v2 The arch-poet, 1915-1939

This two volume biography "focuses on what Yeats *did* rather than on what he *wrote*. . . . Driven by an almost ruthless need to dominate events, Yeats imposed himself at the center of cultural, literary and political controversy, making important friends (and enemies) in all walks of life. This meticulously researched 'authorized' biography, prepared with the cooperation of Yeats's children, lets the facts speak for themselves." Publ Wkly

Includes bibliographical references

Young, Lester

Daniels, Douglas Henry. Lester leaps in: the life and times of Lester "Pres" Young. Beacon Press 2002 524p il hardcover o.p. paperback available $22 **92**
ISBN 0-8070-7125-0 (pa)   LC 2001-37387

This "biography of legendary tenor saxophonist Lester Young celebrates the jazzman's musical genius while shedding significant light on his myth-shrouded personal life. . . . This is an important biography, both to jazz history and to American cultural studies." Booklist
Includes bibliographical references

Young, Neil

McDonough, Jimmy. Shakey: Neil Young's biography. Villard Bks. 2002 786p il $29.95; pa $16.95 **92**
ISBN 0-679-42772-4; 0-679-75096-7 (pa)
LC 2001-43528

This biography of the rock musician "follows Mr. Young from his Canadian childhood through the nearly 50 albums he has made." N Y Times (Late N Y Ed)

"When Young talks, the book sparkles and offers a warm, engaging portrait of the man who keeps on rockin' in the free world." Libr J

Young, Toby, 1963-

Young, Toby. How to lose friends and alienate people. Da Capo Press 2002 xxvii, 340p hardcover o.p. paperback available $14.95   **92**

ISBN 0-306-81227-4 (pa)

British writer Young describes his experiences working for Vanity Fair magazine in New York

"This thoroughly humorous memoir provides a scathing portrait of the egomaniacal world of New York media and an insightful look at modern American celebrity culture." Booklist

Zanichkowsky, Stephen

Zanichkowsky, Stephen. Fourteen; growing up alone in a crowd. Basic Bks. 2002 xxv, 261p $25; pa $15.95   **92**

ISBN 0-465-09400-7; 0-465-09401-5 (pa)
                                              LC 2002-1518

This is the author's memoir of growing up eighth of fourteen children in a dysfunctional family

"Written in a straightforward, unadorned style, this unusual memoir generates an emotional intensity almost imperceptibly, until we feel utterly caught up in the chaos of Zanichkowsky's very big family. . . . An unsentimental and unflinchingly honest memoir." Booklist

Zappa, Frank

Zappa, Frank. The real Frank Zappa book; [by] Frank Zappa, with Peter Occhiogrosso. Poseidon Press 1989 352p il hardcover o.p. paperback available $14   **92**

ISBN 0-671-70572-5 (pa)   LC 89-3470

"The outspoken Zappa, one of the most inventive and controversial artists of the past 20 years, is frank, often disgusting, and always entertaining in describing his life. . . . Zappa also relates his opinions about the music performing and recording industries, but then rattles on about a myriad of things: church, drugs, yuppies, politics." Libr J

929   Genealogy, names, insignia

Baxter, Angus, 1912-

In search of your European roots; a complete guide to tracing your ancestors in every country in Europe. 3rd ed. Genealogical 2001 315p pa $18.95   **929**

1. Genealogy
ISBN 0-8063-1657-8   LC 00-136383
First published 1985

This work covers the various types of genealogical records available in approximately 30 European countries. Archival resources from the national to local level are described. Also included are telephone numbers, e-mail addresses, fax numbers, and URL's for various European archives and organizations

Includes bibliographical references

Bentley, Elizabeth Petty

Directory of family associations; [by] Elizabeth Petty Bentley, & Deborah Ann Carl. 4th ed. Genealogical 2001 320p $34.95
                                              929

1. Genealogy
ISBN 0-8063-1679-9   LC 2001-131456
First published 1991

Contains information on approximately 6,000 family name associations in the United States; lists addresses, phone numbers, contact persons, and publications (if any)

The genealogist's address book. Genealogical pa $39.95   **929**

1. Genealogy

First published 1991. (4th edition 1998) Periodically revised

A "source for names, addresses, phone numbers, hours, and publications for national and state genealogical institutions and organizations. Included are ethnic and religious organizations that can help with genealogical research, as well as research centers and lineage societies. Special sections address adoption research and the use of computers." Libr J [review of 1992 edition]

Carmack, Sharon DeBartolo, 1956-

Organizing your family history search; efficient & effective ways to gather and protect your genealogical research. Betterway Bks. 1999 150p il pa $17.99   **929**

1. Genealogy
ISBN 1-55870-511-2   LC 99-21643

Aspects covered range "from organizing and filing maps to making provisions in your will for your research. . . . Organizing tips from well-known researchers are scattered throughout, and the appendix includes contacts for archival supplies and genealogical societies and publishers. Carmack's solutions are inventive and flexible enough to fit any researcher." Libr J

Includes bibliographical references

Croom, Emily Anne

The genealogist's companion and sourcebook. 2nd ed. Betterway Bks. 2003 454p il map pa $19.99   **929**

1. Genealogy
ISBN 1-55870-651-8   LC 2003-50017
First published 1994

This how-to genealogy handbook seeks to explore "collections and libraries within the U.S. and the records that may be found within them. . . . In addition to covering government records, cemetery records, newspapers, city directories, and other sources, there are chapters of African American and Native American genealogy. . . . Because the volume is easy reading and instructive at the same time, it will be a very popular choice for public libraries." Booklist [review of 1994 edition]

Greenwood, Val D.

The researcher's guide to American genealogy. 3rd ed. Genealogical 2000 662p il $29.95   **929**

1. Genealogy 2. Archives—United States
ISBN 0-8063-1621-7   LC 99-73349
First published 1973

"This classic textbook for the more experienced researcher gives detailed answers to questions about primary records, including vital, census, probate, land, court (including adoption), church, military, cemetery, and wills. Completely updated, it remains the outstanding text and reference book in American genealogy and the benchmark against which others must be judged." Libr J [review of 1990 edition]

Includes bibliographical references

Kemp, Thomas Jay

Virtual roots 2.0; a guide to genealogy and local history on the World Wide Web. rev and updated. Scholarly Resources 2003 311p $75; pa $29.95 **929**
1. Genealogy 2. World Wide Web
ISBN 0-8420-2922-2; 0-8420-2923-0 (pa)
LC 2002-154366
First published 1997
Accompanied by computer laser optical disc
The more than 1,000 "Web sites in this directory are arranged into four primary categories—general subjects, U.S., international, and family associations—each of which is further subdivided by topic, state, country, or family name. Web site entries include organization name, address, telephone number(s), Internet and e-mail addresses, and, where appropriate, other Web links that open even more doorways." Booklist [review of 1997 edition]
Includes bibliographical references

Kovacs, Diane K.

Genealogical research on the Web. Neal-Schuman 2002 194p (Neal-Schuman netguide series) pa $59.95 **929**
1. Genealogy—Internet resources
ISBN 1-55570-430-1
LC 2001-59644
"The first section of this book . . . addresses the basics of using the Internet for genealogical research. Next is a discussion of the top 10 genealogical tools on the Internet, followed by a chapter on networking with other genealogists. . . . Each chapter ends with a tutorial composed of several activities, typically involving visits to Web sites. . . . This is one work that serves a variety of users as well as uses and should be of interest wherever genealogists are to be found." Booklist
Includes bibliographical references

Moore, Dahrl Elizabeth

The librarian's genealogy notebook; a guide to resources. American Lib. Assn. 1998 142p il map pa $35 **929**
1. Genealogy
ISBN 0-8389-0744-X
LC 98-19110
"Moore shows librarians how to mine their own libraries for reference sources that might already be available, offers useful advice on obtaining information from external sources, and also includes general sources to which libraries may want to provide access or own." Publisher's note
Includes bibliographical references

Neagles, James C.

The Library of Congress; a guide to genealogical and historical research; by James C. Neagles, assisted by Mark C. Neagles. Ancestry 1990 381p il $39.95 **929**
1. Library of Congress 2. Genealogy 3. United States—Local history
ISBN 0-916489-48-5
LC 89-18594
"This book describes significant materials in the Local History and Genealogy Reading Room as well as other areas of the Library of Congress. It is divided into three sections. Part 1 is an introduction to the Library, its divisions, services, and catalogs. Part 2 discusses categories of records and publications pertinent to genealogy, while part 3, which makes up more than half the book, describes key source materials by region and state." Booklist
Includes bibliographical references

Printed sources; a guide to published genealogical records; edited by Kory L. Meyerink. Ancestry 1998 840p $49.95
929
1. Genealogy—Bibliography 2. United States—History—Bibliography
ISBN 0-916489-70-1
LC 98-10852
The book opens with an "introductory chapter that highlights categories of research, the evaluation of records, interlibrary loan, and even the Dewey Decimal system. Editor Meyerink then divides the book into four sections encompassing background information (how-to-books, atlases), finding aids, printed original records, and compiled records (family histories, periodicals)." Libr J

Roberts, Ralph, 1945-

Genealogy via the Internet; tracing your family roots quickly and easily: computerized genealogy in plain English. 2nd ed. Alexander Bks. 2003 288p il $24.95 **929**
1. Genealogy—Internet resources
ISBN 1-57090-129-5
First published 1998
The author "explains about personal computers, the basics of genealogy and how to go about combining the two for online searching. He provides several pages of possible web sites a searcher might explore, and an index for easy location of topics." Book Rep [review of 1998 edition]
Includes bibliographical references

929.4   Personal names

Dictionary of American family names; Patrick Hanks, editor. Oxford Univ. Press 2003 3v set $295 **929.4**
1. Personal names—United States
ISBN 0-19-508137-4
LC 2003-3844
This is a guide to 70,000 of the most frequently found surnames in the United States. Based on an 88.7 million-name sample culled from a commercial telephone database, the entries indicate the frequency of the name within the sample, plus an explanation of the name. Libr J
This set will be useful for genealogists, historians, and others curious about their family roots. SLJ
Includes bibliographical references

Lansky, Bruce

The very best baby name book in the whole wide world. Meadowbrook Press 1996 1995 358p il hardcover o.p. paperback available $8 **929.4**
1. Personal names
ISBN 0-671-56113-8 (pa)
LC 95-46292
First published 1982 with title: The best baby name book in the whole wide world
This work offers parents advice on choosing a name and provides lists of over 13,000 names

Latham, Edward

A dictionary of names, nicknames, and surnames of persons, places, and things. Omnigraphics 1990 334p $48 **929.4**
1. Names—Dictionaries 2. Nicknames 3. Personal names—Dictionaries
ISBN 1-55888-901-9
LC 89-26513
A reissue of the title first published 1904 by Dutton

Latham, Edward—*Continued*

Compiled as a supplement to the "ordinary dictionaries of biography, geography, mythology, etc. [wherein] a person or place is often alluded to by means of a surname or nickname without any clue being given to the reader, who does not happen to be aware of the actual name of the person or place." Preface

Room, Adrian

Dictionary of first names. New ed. Cassell 2002 368p pa $14.95   **929.4**

1. Personal names—Dictionaries

ISBN 0-304-36226-3

First published 1995

Cover title: Cassell's dictionary of first names

This offers information about more than 2000 personal names, including definitions, origin, history, and development, people real and fictional who shared particular names and lists the top five personal names given to children each year over the past 50 years

Shankle, George Earlie

American nicknames; their origin and significance. 2nd ed. Wilson, H.W. 1955 524p $70   **929.4**

1. Nicknames 2. Personal names—United States 3. Geographic names—United States

ISBN 0-8242-0004-7

First published 1937

"Not limited to nicknames of persons, but includes also those applied to places, institutions, or objects, arranged by real names with cross-references from nicknames. Information under the real names includes some explanation of the nicknames and their origin, and gives references to sources of information in footnotes." Guide to Ref Books. 11th edition

Twentieth century American nicknames; edited by Laurence Urdang; compiled by Walter C. Kidney and George C. Kohn; with a foreword by Leslie Alan Dunkling. Wilson, H.W. 1979 398p $70   **929.4**

1. Nicknames 2. Personal names—United States 3. Geographic names—United States

ISBN 0-8242-0642-8   LC 79-23390

"Nicknames and the real names of persons, places, etc., are listed in a single alphabet. Includes variant nicknames. Editor attempted to avoid duplication of nicknames appearing in Shankle's *American nicknames*." Ref Sources for Small & Medium-sized Libr. 5th edition

929.9   Flags

Sedeen, Margaret

Star-spangled banner; our nation and its flag; prepared by the Book Division, National Geographic Society. National Geographic Soc. il   **929.9**

1. Flags—United States

Available in various bindings and editions

First published 1993. (2001 edition) Periodically revised

"Sections deal with the invention of this national symbol, its wartime and diplomatic uses, its appearance in exploration of earth and space, and its role in everyday American life." Libr J

"With enough history for student researchers and lots of pictures for browsers, this attractive book about the flag is recommended for most collections." Booklist

Shearer, Benjamin F.

State names, seals, flags, and symbols; a historical guide. 3rd ed, rev and expanded. Greenwood Press 2001 495p il $69.95   **929.9**

1. Geographic names—United States 2. Seals (Numismatics) 3. Flags—United States

ISBN 0-313-31534-5   LC 2001-23525

First published 1987

"Chapters on mottoes, flowers, trees, birds, songs, holidays, and license plates are just a sampling of what is covered, and the format is such that the concisely written material can be found as expeditiously as possible. Even though the book is touted predominantly as a reference tool, the information provided makes fascinating and enlightening reading." Libr J [review of 1994 edition]

Includes bibliographical references

930   History of ancient world to ca.499

The **Cambridge** ancient history. Cambridge Univ. Press 1970-2001 il maps apply to publisher for price and availability   **930**

1. Ancient history

Original 12 volume set published 1923-1939 with 5 volumes of plates

Contents: v1, pt 1 Prolegomena and prehistory 3rd ed. 1970; v1, pt 2 Early history of the Middle East 3rd ed. 1971; v2, pt 1 History of the Middle East and the Aegean Region, ca. 1800-1380 B.C. 3rd ed. 1973; v2, pt 2 History of the Middle East and the Aegean Region, ca. 1380-1000 B.C. 3rd ed. 1975; v3, pt 1 The prehistory of the Balkans; the Middle East and the Aegean world, tenth to eighth centuries B.C. 2nd ed. 1982; v3, pt 2 The Assyrian and Babylonian Empires and other states of the Near East, from the eighth to the sixth centuries B.C. 2nd ed. 1992; v3, pt3 The expansion of the Greek world, eighth to sixth centuries B.C. 2nd ed. 1982; v4 Persia, Greece and the Western Mediterranean, ca. 525 to 479 B.C. 2nd ed. 1988; v5 The Fifth Century B.C. 2nd ed. 1992; v6 The Fourth Century B.C. 2nd ed. 1994; v7, pt 1 The Hellenistic World 2nd ed. 1984; v7, pt 2 The rise of Rome to 220 B.C. 2nd ed. 1990; v8 Rome and the Mediterranean to 133 B.C. 2nd ed. 1990; v9 The last age of the Roman Republic, 146-43 B.C. 2nd ed. 1994; v10 The Augustan Empire, 43 B.C.-A.D. 69 2nd ed. 1996; v11 The imperial peace, A.D. 70-192; v13 The late empire, A.D. 337-425; v14 Late antiquity: empire and successors, A.D. 425-600

Available volumes of plates illustrating v1-2, v3, v4, v5-6, v7 pt 1

"An excellent reference history. Each chapter has been written by a specialist, with full bibliographies at the end of each volume." Guide to Ref Books. 11th edition

Encyclopedia of the ancient world; editor, Thomas J. Sienkewicz. Salem Press 2002 3v il maps set $341   **930**

1. Ancient civilization—Encyclopedias

ISBN 0-89356-038-3   LC 2001-49896

Contents: v1 Overviews, 'Abd al-Malik-Corinthian War; v2 Coriolanus, Gnaeus Marcius-Pharsalus, Battle of; v3 Phidias-Zurvanism indexes

This reference work encompasses "not only Greece and Rome but also 'the civilizations, cultures, traditions, monuments and artifacts, significant wars and battles, and important personages of the rest of the world: Europe (outside Greece and Rome), Africa, the Americas, Asia, and Oceania.' The time span is from prehistory to approximately 700 C.E." Booklist

Ryan, William B. F.

Noah's flood; the new scientific discoveries about the event that changed history; [by] William Ryan and Walter Pitman; illustrations by Anastasia Sotiropoulos; maps by William Haxby. Simon & Schuster 1999 319p il maps $25; pa $14   **930**
1. Floods
ISBN 0-684-81052-2; 0-684-85920-3 (pa)
LC 98-45384

The authors present "evidence that there really was a flood of biblical proportions 7000 years ago, one that destroyed a civilization and doubled the capacity of the Black Sea." Libr J

This is "an interesting and provocative story . . . that incorporates archeology, oceanography, biblical studies, anthropology (not to mention archeobotany, paleopathology and archeozoology) and, one must conclude, a healthy portion of imagination." N Y Times Book Rev

Includes bibliographical references

930.1   Archaeology

Ceram, C. W., 1915-1972

Gods, graves, and scholars; the story of archaeology; translated from the German by E. B. Garside and Sophie Wilkins. 2nd rev and substantially enl ed. Knopf 1967 441p il maps hardcover o.p. paperback available $14   **930.1**
1. Archeology
ISBN 0-394-74319-9 (pa)
Original German edition, 1949; first English language edition, 1951

"The story of Champollion and the reading of the Rosetta Stone, the decipherment of the inscriptions on the monument of Darius the Great, Leonard Woolley's famous excavations at Ur, and John Lloyd Stephens' discovery of the ruins of a great Mayan city are . . . told in this book." Doors to More Mature Read

Includes bibliographical references

Darvill, Timothy

The concise Oxford dictionary of archaeology. Oxford Univ. Press 2002 506p il maps $60   **930.1**
1. Archeology—Dictionaries   2. Antiquities—Dictionaries
ISBN 0-19-211649-5   LC 2002-283530

This volume includes "more than 4000 entries arranged alphabetically and coded by type, e.g., artifact; biographical; cultural phase or period; deity; document; equipment; general term; legal term; material; monument class or category; site; monument, or area of archaeological importance; and technique." Libr J

This "is quite possibly one of the finest single-volume reference works in the field of archaeology currently available. . . . It covers a wide array of archaeological topics in comfortably sized, easy-to-understand entries. The coverage is very broad. . . . [This reference] will be useful in all sorts of libraries for all sorts of patrons, from children writing book reports to university students preparing research papers to readers of historical fiction curious about terminology and authenticity. It is recommended as a vital reference resource for all types of libraries." Am Ref Books Annu, 2003

Includes bibliographical references

Encyclopedia of archaeology: History and discoveries; edited by Tim Murray. ABC-CLIO 2001 3v il maps set $285   **930.1**
1. Archeology—Encyclopedias
ISBN 1-57607-198-7   LC 2001-2617
Companion set to Encyclopedia of archaeology: The great archaeologists

This set includes "entries covering the history of archaeology in specific countries or regions as well as 'the histories of significant sites, debates, techniques, methods and issues that are central to the global practice of the discipline.' . . . The national and regional surveys are the most valuable aspect of this resource. . . . Entries here on Egypt, Mexico, and Maya civilization, to name a few, provide useful synthesis for the general reader." Booklist

Encyclopedia of underwater and maritime archaeology; edited by James P. Delgado. Yale Univ. Press 1998 493p il $75   **930.1**
1. Underwater exploration—Encyclopedias   2. Shipwrecks—Encyclopedias
ISBN 0-300-07427-1   LC 97-61536
First published 1997 in the United Kingdom with title: British Museum encyclopaedia of underwater and maritime archaeology

"The volume's 450 alphabetically arranged entries cover sites from prehistory to the modern era (including *Titanic*), legislation and legal issues, organizations, nations and regions, research themes, and technology and techniques. . . . More than 100 illustrations in color are complemented by more than 200 black-and-white drawings and photos." Booklist

The **Oxford** companion to archaeology; editor in chief, Brian M. Fagan; editors, Charlotte Beck [et al.] Oxford Univ. Press 1996 xx, 844p il maps $75   **930.1**
1. Archeology—Dictionaries
ISBN 0-19-507618-4   LC 96-30792

"In addition to broad discussions of specific civilizations such as Islamic, Olmec, and African, there are entries on theories (post processual), ethics, processes (lithics), dating techniques, pop culture (archaeology in film and television), specific sites and site management, plantation archaeology, and human evolution." Booklist

932   Egypt to 640 A.D.

Aldred, Cyril, 1914-1991

Akhenaten: King of Egypt. Thames & Hudson 1988 320p il hardcover o.p. paperback available $26.95   **932**
1. Akhenaton, King of Egypt, fl. ca. 1388-1358 B.C.   2. Egypt—Antiquities
ISBN 0-500-27621-8 (pa)   LC 87-51153

The author "relates the archaeological processes whereby Akhenaten's existence and his impact on Egyptian life were reconstructed through unearthed physical evidence." Booklist

Aldred "ranges over archaeology, art-history, morbid pathology, social and political history and the evolution of ideas. This is a book to which one will return, and gain each time one does so." Times Lit Suppl

Includes bibliographical references

Assmann, Jan

The mind of Egypt; history and meaning in the time of the Pharaohs; translated by Andrew Jenkins. Metropolitan Bks. 2002 513p il $35   **932**

1. Historiography 2. Egypt—Civilization 3. Egypt—History

ISBN 0-8050-5462-6   LC 2001-44504

Also available in paperback from Harvard Univ. Press

The author "attempts to portray and illustrate the development of a uniquely Egyptian mindset by exploring the ideals, emotions, politics, legal system, religious beliefs, and moral codes that defined and characterized antiquity's most technologically advanced and psychologically complex civilization. . . . An examination of this mentality provides an original twist on the well-documented events that shaped Egyptian history." Booklist

Includes bibliographical references

Brier, Bob

Egyptian mummies; unraveling the secret of an ancient art. Morrow 1994 352p il hardcover o.p. paperback available $15   **932**

1. Mummies 2. Egypt—Antiquities

ISBN 0-688-14624-4 (pa)   LC 94-14227

The author "discusses Egyptian religion and funerary practice and the burials of pharaohs and priests, nobles and commoners, pets and sacred animals. He describes desecrations by grave robbers, ancient and modern, and shows how Napoleon's invasion of Egypt—not only with soldiers but also with scholars and scientists—brought into being the field of Egyptology. A fascinating study." Libr J

Includes bibliographical references

The murder of Tutankhamen; a true story. Putnam 1998 xx, 264p il hardcover o.p. paperback available $14   **932**

1. Tutankhamen, King of Egypt 2. Egypt—History

ISBN 0-425-16689-9 (pa)   LC 97-49193

By "combining known historical events with evidence gathered by advanced technologies, Brier has re-created the suspenseful story of religious upheaval and political intrigue that likely resulted in the murder of the teenage King Tutankhamen." Booklist

"Brier obviously knows his subject and is impassioned by it. Readers who enjoy history or true-crime stories will be intrigued by this work." SLJ

Includes bibliographical references

Bunson, Margaret R.

Encyclopedia of ancient Egypt. rev ed. Facts on File 2002 462p il maps $70   **932**

1. Egypt—Civilization—Dictionaries 2. Egypt—Antiquities—Dictionaries

ISBN 0-8160-4563-1   LC 2002-3550

First published 1991

This work consists of "alphabetically arranged entries covering Egypt from around 3200 B.C. to the fall of the New Kingdom in 1070 B.C. There are several broad entries such as *Egypt, Agriculture, and Religion*. The bulk of the book, however, consists of specific entries for kings and queens, gods and goddesses, cities, important documents, etc." Booklist [review of 1991 edition]

David, A. Rosalie (Ann Rosalie)

Handbook to life in ancient Egypt; [by] Rosalie David. rev ed. Facts on File 2003 417p il maps $50   **932**

1. Egypt—Civilization

ISBN 0-8160-5034-1   LC 2002-35229

"Facts on File library of world history"

First published 1998

This covers such topics as the geography of Ancient Egypt, society and government, religion, funerary beliefs and customs, architecture, trade and transport, the army and navy, economy and industry, and everyday life

For a review see: Booklist, Nov. 15, 2003

Includes bibliographical references

Hawass, Zahi

Valley of the golden mummies. Abrams 2000 224p il $49.50   **932**

1. Mummies 2. Egypt—Antiquities

ISBN 0-8109-3942-8   LC 00-26628

The author describes the 1999 discovery and excavation of over a hundred Egyptian mummies at the Bahariya Oasis

"Fabulous color photographs of the remote and serene excavation site and detailed pictures of the various finds grace Hawass's informative text." Publ Wkly

Includes bibliographical references

Lepre, J. P.

The Egyptian pyramids; a comprehensive, illustrated reference. McFarland & Co. 1990 341p il $65   **932**

1. Egypt—Antiquities 2. Pyramids

ISBN 0-89950-461-2   LC 89-43623

This "study of the pyramids built during the reigns of 42 different pharaohs, incorporates details pertaining to the history of each of the pharaohs who constructed a pyramid, concise chronological listings of the pyramids, relevant textual studies from the ancient Egyptian sources, and a review of the material remains associated with the pyramids." Choice

Includes bibliographical references

The **Oxford** encyclopedia of ancient Egypt; Donald B. Redford, editor in chief. Oxford Univ. Press 2001 3v set $450   **932**

1. Egypt—Civilization—Encyclopedias 2. Egypt—Antiquities—Encyclopedias

ISBN 0-19-510234-7   LC 99-54801

This reference work covers "archaeology, biography, history, language, social history, and more. . . . [It features] essays from more than 250 contributors from various countries and scholarly pursuits, all with solid academic credentials. . . . One is not likely to encounter another work of this magnitude on a subject of such universal interest for some time." Booklist

Tyldesley, Joyce A.

Nefertiti; Egypt's sun queen; [by] Joyce Tyldesley. Viking 1999 232p il $27.95; pa $14.95   **932**

1. Egypt—History

ISBN 0-670-86998-8; 0-14-025820-5 (pa)

     LC 98-35469

"Born in approximately 1350 B.C., Nefertiti was the wife of Akhenaten, an eighteenth-dynasty pharaoh who initiated a radical religious revolution in his kingdom. . . . Adored by the masses, Nefertiti was elevated to semidivine status and adopted a dynamic political and

Tyldesley, Joyce A.—*Continued*
cultural role. . . . Tyldesley manages to do an admirable job re-creating the exquisite opulence of palace life and piecing together Nefertiti's early public years." Booklist
Includes bibliographical references

Verner, Miroslav
The pyramids; the mystery, culture, and science of Egypt's great monuments; translated from the German by Steven Rendall. Grove Press 2001 495p il map hardcover o.p. paperback available $17.50
932
1. Pyramids 2. Egypt—Antiquities
ISBN 0-8021-3935-3 (pa)   LC 2001-35084
In this study, the author "focuses on research of the last decade and excavations over the past 20 years. Verner divides his book into chapters according to pharaonic dynasty, spotlighting individual pharaohs' pyramids. He not only explains the layout of each pyramid but also presents various theories on how each pyramid was built and tells stories about the people that were buried there." Booklist
Includes bibliographical references

936 Europe north and west of Italian peninsula to ca. 499 A.D.

Cunliffe, Barry
The ancient Celts. Oxford Univ. Press 1997 324p il maps $55   **936**
1. Celts
ISBN 0-19-815010-5   LC 96-53308
Also available in paperback from Penguin Bks.
This is a "survey of the origins of the Celts and their expansion during the Iron Age through their largely successful subjection by the Romans. . . . [Cunliffe] has written a readable and informative book with many attractive illustrations." Libr J
Includes bibliographical references

North, John David
Stonehenge; a new interpretation of prehistoric man and the cosmos; [by] John North. Free Press 1997 609p il maps $35
936
1. Stonehenge (England) 2. Prehistoric peoples 3. Astronomy
ISBN 0-684-84512-1   LC 97-31439
North applies his "background in astronomy to this study of Neolithic monuments. His aim is 'to discover certain patterns of intellectual and religious behavior through a study of archaelogical remains that seem to have been deliberately directed in some way towards phenomena in the heavens.'" Libr J
The author "is writing for the serious student of the place, who will gobble up the inventory of its angles, its sight lines, and its stellar orientation." Booklist
Includes bibliographical references

937 Roman Empire

Bunson, Matthew
Encyclopedia of the Roman Empire. rev ed. Facts on File 2002 636p il maps $75   **937**
1. Rome—History—Encyclopedias
ISBN 0-8160-4562-3   LC 2001-53253
First published 1994

This reference work provides information on the key places, people, events, and culture of Roman history, from the reign of Julius Caesar to the fall of the last Roman emperor in 476 A.D.
"An excellent ready-reference source." Booklist [review of 1994 edition]

Connolly, Peter, 1935-
The ancient city; life in classical Athens & Rome; [by] Peter Connolly, Hazel Dodge. Oxford Univ. Press 1998 256p il maps $35; pa $21.95   **937**
1. Classical civilization 2. Rome—Civilization 3. Athens (Greece) 4. Greece—Civilization
ISBN 0-19-917242-0; 0-19-521582-6 (pa)
LC 98-201131
The authors "focus specifically on city life in two 'golden ages' of ancient times: Athens in fifth-century B.C. and Rome in second-century A.D. [They] place each city in its historical and geographical perspective, and then highlight how people really lived in those times and places. Detailed color drawings, cutaways, photographs, and maps make this an extremely useful as well as an outstandingly attractive book." Voice Youth Advocates
Includes bibliographical references

Fowler, Brenda
Iceman; uncovering the life and times of a prehistoric man found in an alpine glacier. Random House 2000 313p il o.p.; University of Chicago Press paperback available $15
937
1. Mummies 2. Italy—Antiquities 3. Prehistoric peoples
ISBN 0-226-25823-8 (pa)   LC 99-39878
"In September 1991, hikers in the Alps discovered a well-preserved frozen corpse; nearby lay a stone ax and swatches of leather and fur. The man turned out to have died in the early Bronze Age, making him an incalculable treasure for students of early human beings. Fowler . . . offers a brisk and easy-to-follow narrative, first of the great discovery, then of the personal and political struggles for control of the frozen body." Publ Wkly

Gibbon, Edward, 1737-1794
The decline and fall of the Roman Empire
937
1. Rome—History 2. Byzantine Empire
Hardcover and paperback editions available from various publishers
First published 1776-1788 in the United Kingdom with title: The history of the decline and fall of the Roman Empire
"In this substantial history of the Roman Empire, Gibbon bridges the abyss between the ancient and the modern world. It is the one historical work of the eighteenth century that is still accepted as authoritative. It covers thirteen centuries of history, during which time paganism was breaking down and Christianity was taking its place." Reader's Adviser

Grant, Michael, 1914-
Collapse and recovery of the Roman Empire. Routledge 1999 123p $34.95   **937**
1. Emperors—Rome 2. Rome—History
ISBN 0-415-17323-X   LC 98-8222
"Grant examines the causes for the near disintegration of the empire in the mid-third century A.D., including

Grant, Michael, 1914-—*Continued*

the problems of imperial succession, Germanic encroachments on the frontiers, and chronic conflicts with the Persians in the East. . . . This work is a worthy and necessary addition to both academic and public library collections on classical history." Booklist

Includes bibliographical references

The **Oxford** history of the Roman world; edited by John Boardman, Jasper Griffin, Oswyn Murray. Oxford Univ. Press 1991 518p il maps hardcover o.p. paperback available $17.95 **937**

1. Rome—History

ISBN 0-19-280203-8 (pa) LC 91-11763

"The text ... first published 1986 ... in The Oxford history of the classical world." Verso of title page

This "work tells the story of the rise of Rome from its origins as a cluster of villages to the foundation of the Roman Empire by Augustus, to its consolidation in the first two centuries CE. It also discusses aspects of the later Empire and its influence on Western civilization." Publisher's note

Includes bibliographical references

938 Greece to 323 A.D.

Adkins, Lesley

Handbook to life in ancient Greece; [by] Lesley Adkins and Roy A. Adkins. Facts on File 1997 472p il maps $50 **938**

1. Greece—Civilization

ISBN 0-8160-3111-8 LC 96-42111

Also available in paperback from Oxford Univ. Press

This work covers "life in ancient Greece from the Minoan period to the Roman conquest. Ten thematic chapters cover history and government, biographies, military affairs, geography, economy, towns and rural areas, fine arts and literature, religion and mythology, science and philosophy, as well as everyday life. A profusion of fine-lined drawings, maps, lists, charts, and b&w photos enhance the textbook format." Book Rep

Includes bibliographical references

Burckhardt, Jacob, 1818-1897

The Greeks and Greek civilization; translated by Sheila Stern; edited with an introduction by Oswyn Murray. St. Martin's Press 1998 449p hardcover o.p. paperback available $16.95 **938**

1. Greece—Civilization

ISBN 0-312-24447-9 (pa) LC 98-30107

Translation of selected lectures on ancient Greece delivered by the German cultural historian in the 1870s

"These lectures provide not only a rich overview of Burckhardt's learning but a precious glimpse into the intellectual world of the late nineteenth century. . . . Here his topics range from the importance of the 'agon' in forging individualism to the pessimism and violence that underlay much of Greek culture." New Yorker

Includes bibliographical references

Levi, Peter, 1931-

Atlas of the Greek world. Facts on File 1981 c1980 239p il maps (Historical atlas series) $45 **938**

1. Greece—Maps 2. Greece—Civilization 3. Greece—Antiquities

ISBN 0-87196-448-1 LC 81-122477

First published 1980 in the United Kingdom

"After a part on 'the land in context,' the material is arranged chronologically: the ages of Bronze, of tyranny, of Pericles, and of Alexander. A final part on 'the fate of Hellenism' deals with Greece's influence on later Western civilization." Libr J

"A great deal of information is presented in a generally attractive manner. Recommended for public and undergraduate libraries." Choice

Martin, Thomas R., 1947-

Ancient Greece; from prehistoric to Hellenistic times. Yale Univ. Press 1996 252p il maps $45; pa $16 **938**

1. Greece—History

ISBN 0-300-06767-4; 0-300-08493-5 (pa)

LC 95-26690

The author "blends social, cultural, political, and military data to create a panoramic view of the Greek world. He moves chronologically from prehistory through the end of the Hellenistic era to 30 B.C." Libr J

"Free of suffocating scholasticism, this stolid narrative is well suited for a small library needing an overview of ancient Greece." Booklist

Includes bibliographical references

Robinson, Cyril Edward, b. 1884

Everyday life in ancient Greece; [by] C. E. Robinson. Oxford Univ. Press 1933 159p il maps o.p.; Greenwood Press reprint available $62.95 **938**

1. Greece—Civilization 2. Greece—Social life and customs

ISBN 0-8371-9078-9 (lib bdg)

The development of Greek society is traced from its origins to the end of the classical age. Special focus is on Athens and its economy, politics, art, religion and education

Thucydides

The history of the Peloponnesian War **938**

1. Greece—History—431-404 B.C., Peloponnesian War

Hardcover and paperback editions available from various publishers

Variant title: The Peloponnesian War

Thucydides' "chosen subject was the Peloponnesian War, which covered 27 years of his own lifetime, 431-404 B.C., and in which he fought as a commander of the Athenian troops in Thrace. His ideal of history is said to have been first accuracy, and then relevancy. . . . He rarely digressed. His history is unfinished, breaking off in the middle of the year 411 B.C." Reader's Adviser

Wood, Michael, 1948-

In the footsteps of Alexander the Great; a journey from Greece to Asia. University of Calif. Press 1997 256p il maps hardcover o.p. paperback available $18.95 **938**

1. Alexander, the Great, 356-323 B.C. 2. Historic sites 3. Asia—Description

ISBN 0-520-23192-9 (pa) LC 97-19188

Based on the PBS series, this "book recreates Alexander's 22,000 mile, ten-year expedition from Greece to India, following as much as possible the actual route of his journey." Publisher's note

This book is "illustrated with a mixture of Alexandrine art from a variety of cultures, landscapes that capture the wide range of geographies through which Alexander and his imperial armies passed, and portraits of cultures . . . in which the influence of that long-ago juggernaut is still visible." Booklist

Includes bibliographical references

938.003   Classical dictionaries

Grant, Michael, 1914-

A guide to the ancient world; a dictionary of classical place names. Wilson, H.W. 1986 728p maps $105 **938.003**

1. Classical dictionaries 2. Mediterranean region—Gazetteers

ISBN 0-8242-0742-4 LC 86-15785

"This dictionary provides background for about nine hundred places important to an understanding of the cultures of the ancient Greeks, Etruscans, and Romans. . . . The time period covered is from the first millennium B.C. until the fall of the Roman empire in the fifth century A.D. Depending on the subject, a typical entry includes information about history, geography, archaeology, and sometimes art and mythology." Am Ref Books Annu, 1987

The **Oxford** classical dictionary; edited by Simon Hornblower and Antony Spawforth. 3rd rev ed. Oxford Univ. Press 2003 1v, 1640p $110 **938.003**

1. Classical dictionaries

ISBN 0-19-860641-9

First published 1949 under the editorship of M. Cary and others

This reference includes over 6,000 entries about the ancient Greco-Roman world, covering such topics as politics, government and economy, religion and mythology, law and philosophy, science and geography, languages, literature, art and architecture, archeology, historical writing, military history, social history, sex, and gender

"This is a work that makes a fascinating world of learning accessible to a broad audience." Booklist

Includes bibliographical references

Sacks, David

Encyclopedia of the ancient Greek world. Facts on File 1995 306p il $49.50 **938.003**

1. Greece—History—Dictionaries

ISBN 0-8160-2323-9 LC 94-33229

Also available in paperback from Oxford Univ. Press with title: A dictionary of the ancient Greek world

This "source features articles ranging from 100 to 3,000 words on all aspects of the Greek world. . . . The 525 articles are accompanied by line drawings that generally reproduce famous artwork. A bibliography and index conclude the work. Sacks covers almost every topic of interest, ranging from mythological figures (*Cassandra, Paris*), historical people (*Arion, Sappho*), events (*Peloponnesian War*—the longest entry in the work), and places (*Argos, Megara*) to general topics (*Clothing, Ships and Seafaring*)." Booklist

939   Other parts of ancient world to ca. 640

Civilizations of the ancient Near East; Jack M. Sasson, editor in chief. Scribner 1995 4v il maps set $500 **939**

1. Middle East—Civilization

ISBN 0-684-19279-9 LC 95-1712

This "work concentrates on the Near East, broadly defined to include a region from Northeast Africa to India, Pakistan, and Burma, with principal focus on the core areas of Egypt, Syro-Palestine, Mesopotamia, and Anatolia. The time span ranges from the third millennium B.C.E., when writing was invented, to 330 B.C.E., when Alexander triumphed over the Persian Empire. The 189 contributors from five continents and 16 countries include some of the world's finest scholars." Libr J

Wood, Michael, 1948-

In search of the Trojan War. University of Calif. Press 1998 288p il pa $19.95 **939**

1. Trojan War 2. Troy (Extinct city) 3. Turkey—Antiquities 4. Bronze Age

ISBN 0-520-21599-0 LC 98-4958

A reissue of the title first published 1985 by Facts on File

The author "outlines the path the legend took through medieval, Renaissance and modern society. The bulk of this . . . book is devoted to archeological efforts to prove the truth of Homer's epic and confirm that Troy was actually at Hissarlik. Mr. Wood also describes the history and archeology of Mycenae." N Y Times Book Rev [review of 1985 edition]

"This is a first-rate book. . . . The book makes a readable and clear approach to some of the knottiest problems of Bronze Age archaeology." Choice [review of 1985 edition]

Includes bibliographical references

940   General history of Europe

Encyclopedia of European social history from 1350 to 2000; Peter N. Stearns, editor-in-chief. Scribner 2000 6v set $700 **940**

1. Europe—Social conditions—Encyclopedias

ISBN 0-684-80582-0 LC 00-46376

This reference includes over 200 articles on topics ranging from serfdom and the economy to witchcraft and public health. The set includes some 700 pictures and maps as well as biographies of prominent Europeans and a comprehensive index

Sachar, Howard Morley, 1928-

Dreamland; Europeans and Jews in the aftermath of the Great War; [by] Howard M. Sachar. Knopf 2002 385p map hardcover o.p. paperback available $15　　　**940**

1. Jews—Europe 2. Europe—History—1918-1945
ISBN 0-375-70829-4 (pa)　　　LC 2001-38471

An overview of Jewish life in Europe during the three decades before the Holocaust

"This scholarly analysis provides a completely original slant on the much-studied interwar period." Booklist

Includes bibliographical references

940.1　Europe—Early history to 1453

Dictionary of the Middle Ages; Joseph R. Strayer, editor in chief. Scribner 1982-1989 12v + index il maps set $1,625　　**940.1**

1. Middle Ages—Dictionaries
ISBN 0-684-19073-7　　　LC 82-5904

Also available supplement published 2003 $130 (ISBN 0-684-80642-8)

"Authoritative and modern, this interdisciplinary dictionary spans the years from A.D. 500 to 1500, taking cognizance of the Byzantine, Islamic, and Jewish contributions to medieval life as well as the European. . . . The contents are in alphabetical sequence, some articles providing brief definitions or identifications, others offering extensive background and analysis." Ref Sources: a brief guide

Gies, Frances

Life in a medieval village; [by] Frances and Joseph Gies. Harper & Row 1990 257p il maps hardcover o.p. paperback available $14　　　**940.1**

1. Medieval civilization 2. Middle Ages—History
ISBN 0-06-092046-7 (pa)　　　LC 89-33759

"Elton, England, is the focal point of the authors' efforts to portray the everyday life and social structure of the High Middle Ages. After giving a brief summary of Elton's origins and development in the Roman and Anglo-Saxon periods, the book examines just how the residents lived and worked within the feudal structure at the beginning of the fourteenth century." Booklist

Includes bibliographical references

Gies, Joseph

Life in a medieval city; [by] Joseph and Frances Gies. Crowell 1969 274p il maps o.p.; HarperCollins Pubs. paperback available $13.50　　　**940.1**

1. Medieval civilization 2. Middle Ages—History
ISBN 0-06-090880-7 (pa)

"A portrait of a medieval city [Troyes], a flourishing settlement of a type not known in Europe before the Middle Ages." Cincinnati Public Libr

Herlihy, David, 1930-1991

The black death and the transformation of the west; edited and with an introduction by Samuel K. Cohn, Jr. Harvard Univ. Press 1997 117p hardcover o.p. paperback available $12　　　**940.1**

1. Plague 2. Europe—History—476-1492 3. Medieval civilization 4. Renaissance
ISBN 0-674-07613-3 (pa)　　　LC 96-54637

These "essays redefine the historical study of the Black Death. . . . Herlihy's contention is that we can learn from this 'devastating natural disaster': for example, parallels can be drawn to today's pandemic of AIDS, especially in the resultant bigotries that both engendered. Cohn introduces the lectures, admirably setting the scene. This book, which opens a new chapter on the history and implications of the plague, is essential for all readers of medieval history." Libr J

Includes bibliographical references

The **New** Cambridge medieval history. Cambridge Univ. Press 1995- il maps ea $140　　　**940.1**

1. Middle Ages—History

This set replaces the Cambridge medieval history, published 1929-1967

Contents: v2 c. 700-c. 900; v3 c. 900-c. 1024; v5 c. 1198-c. 1300; v6 c. 1300-c. 1415; v7 c. 1415-c. 1500

"An excellent reference history, written by specialists, with full bibliographies at the end of each volume." Guide to Ref Books. 11th edition [entry for Cambridge medieval history]

The **Oxford** history of medieval Europe; edited by George Holmes. Oxford Univ. Press 2001 395p il maps pa $16.95　**940.1**

1. Europe—History—476-1492
ISBN 0-19-280133-3　　　LC 2002-281715

This is an abridged edition of The Oxford illustrated history of medieval Europe, published 1988

This compact edition covers such subjects as the chivalric code of knights, popular festivals, new art forms, the Black Death, the fall of Rome, and the emergence of the Reformation

Includes bibliographical references

Reston, James, Jr.

The last apocalypse; Europe at the year 1000 A.D. Doubleday 1998 299p il maps hardcover o.p. paperback available $14.95　　　**940.1**

1. Europe—History—476-1492
ISBN 0-385-48336-8 (pa)　　　LC 97-18812

The author "theorizes that the year A.D. 999 . . . was a turning point in history, marking the Christian West's joining of forces against the triple heathen threat of Vikings, Hungarian Magyar tribes and the Moors in Spain." Publ Wkly

"Reston's seemingly encyclopedic knowledge of the tenth century, combined with his disarming interpretations of the period's events, makes for fascinating reading." Booklist

Includes bibliographical references

940.2 Europe—1453-

Barzun, Jacques, 1907-
From dawn to decadence; 500 years of Western cultural life, 1500 to the present. HarperCollins Pubs. 2000 877p hardcover o.p. paperback available $20 **940.2**
1. Western civilization 2. Europe—Intellectual life 3. Europe—Civilization
ISBN 0-06-092883-2 (pa)   LC 99-16194
"Barzun recounts the religious, political, artistic, and social revolutions that shaped Western culture." Booklist
"Encyclopedic without being discontinuous, the book hardly seems as long, as carefully constructed or as densely packed as it is. Though the ideas it explains are often complicated, the explanations it offers are limpidly clear, sparkling with biographical anecdote and counter-canonical observations." N Y Times Book Rev
Includes bibliographical references

Campbell, Gordon
The Oxford dictionary of the Renaissance. Oxford Univ. Press 2003 xlvi, 862p il $150
940.2
1. Renaissance—Dictionaries
ISBN 0-19-860175-1   LC 2002-42560
"The entries range from Aachen to Zwingli and cover all aspects of the European Renaissance, from the early 14th century in Italy to the Second Defenestration of Prague in 1618, which led to the Thirty Years War. Campbell emphasizes cultural history, though he includes science, theology, medicine, and law under this heading and places a strong emphasis on central and eastern Europe as well as Spain." Libr J
For a fuller review see: Booklist, Jan. 1 & 15, 2004
Includes bibliographical references

Durant, William James, 1885-1981
The age of Louis XIV; by Will and Ariel Durant. Simon & Schuster 1963 802p il (Story of civilization, pt8) $40   **940.2**
1. Europe—Civilization 2. Europe—History—1492-1789
ISBN 0-671-01215-0
"A history of European civilization in the period of Pascal, Molière, Cromwell, Milton, Peter the Great, Newton and Spinoza: 1648-1715." Title page
Includes bibliographical references

Encyclopedia of the Enlightenment; Alan Charles Kors, editor in chief. Oxford Univ. Press 2003 4v il set $495   **940.2**
1. Enlightenment—Encyclopedias 2. Philosophy—Encyclopedias
ISBN 0-19-510430-7   LC 2002-3766
Contents: v1 Abbadie-Enlightenment studies; v2 Enthusiasm-Lyceums and museums; v3 Mably-Ruysch; v4 Sade-Zoology
This reference includes over 700 articles about "philosophic and social changes engendered by the Enlightenment. It {covers} . . . not only France, England, Scotland, the Low Countries, Italy, English-speaking North America, the German states, and Hapsburg Austria but also Iberian, Ibero-American, Jewish, Russian, and Eastern European cultures." Publisher's note
Includes bibliographical references

Encyclopedia of the Renaissance; Paul F. Grendler, editor in chief. Scribner 1999 6v set $750   **940.2**
1. Renaissance—Encyclopedias
ISBN 0-684-80514-6   LC 99-48290
Contents: v1 Abrabanel-civility; v2 Class-Furió Ceriol; v3 Galen-Lyon; v4 Machiavelli-Petrarchism; v5 Peucer-Sforza; v6 Shakespeare-Zwingli
This set covers "aspects of the Renaissance from the origins of humanism in Italy (ca. 1350) through 1750. . . . The encyclopedia's strength lies in its scholarship and in the comprehensiveness and diversity of its scope." Booklist

Hobsbawm, E. J. (Eric J.), 1917-
The age of revolution, 1789-1848. World Pub. Co. 1962 356p il maps (World histories of civilization) o.p.; Vintage Bks. paperback available $15   **940.2**
1. Europe—History—1789-1900 2. Industries—History
ISBN 0-679-77253-7 (pa)
"This book traces the transformation of the world between 1789 and 1848 insofar as it was due to what is here called the 'dual revolution'—the French Revolution of 1789 and the contemporaneous (British) Industrial Revolution." Preface
Includes bibliographical references

Johnson, Paul, 1928-
The Renaissance. Modern Lib. 2000 196p (Modern Library chronicles) $19.95; pa $9.95
940.2
1. Renaissance
ISBN 0-679-64086-X; 0-8129-6619-8 (pa)
LC 00-35491
The author "assesses the historic and economic background of the period and then examines the Renaissance in literature and scholarship, the anatomy of Renaissance sculpture, Renaissance buildings, the evolution of painters and paintings of the period, and, finally, the dissemination and decline of the Renaissance." Libr J
Includes bibliographical references

Manchester, William
A world lit only by fire; the medieval mind and the Renaissance: portrait of an age. Little, Brown 1992 318p il maps hardcover o.p. paperback available $15.95   **940.2**
1. Renaissance
ISBN 0-316-54556-2 (pa)   LC 91-39928
The author covers "the tumultuous span from the Dark Ages to the dawn of the Renaissance. He delineates an age when invisible spirits infested the air, when tolerance was seen as treachery and 'a mafia of profane popes desecrated Christianity.' Besides re-creating the arduous lives of ordinary people, . . . [Manchester] peoples his tapestry with such figures as Leonardo, Machiavelli, Lucrezia Borgia, Erasmus, Luther, Henry VIII and Anne Boleyn." Publ Wkly
Includes bibliographical references

Pope, Stephen
Dictionary of the Napoleonic wars. Facts on File 2000 572p $71.50   **940.2**
1. Europe—History—1789-1815—Dictionaries
ISBN 0-8160-4243-8   LC 99-48829
Pope "has produced more than 1000 alphabetical entries, supplemented by 30 maps, detailing nearly every

Pope, Stephen—*Continued*
aspect of Napoleonic warfare. From broad subjects such as strategy, tactics, diplomacy, and propaganda to specific battles, treaties, weapons, naval warfare, and myriad colorful personalities, the book offers a wealth of succinct information." Libr J

Urban, Mark, 1961-
The man who broke Napoleon's codes. HarperCollins Pubs. 2002 c2001 348p il hardcover o.p. paperback available $13.95
940.2
1. Scovell, George, 1774-1861 2. Cryptography 3. Europe—History—1789-1815 4. Great Britain—Military history
ISBN 0-06-093455-7 (pa)   LC 2001-39284
First published 2001 in the United Kingdom
This book "introduces readers to George Scovell, an engraver's apprentice who stumbled into a job as the Duke of Wellington's decoder and managed to unravel Bonaparte's legendary Great Paris Cipher, which contained 1,400 coded elements. Mark Urban . . . chronicles Wellington's campaigns against the French from the battle of Corunna in 1809 to the 1815 victory at Waterloo, showing how Scovell's decoding of enemy communiques was pivotal to Napoleon's defeat." Publ Wkly
The author "has combined the fast-paced narrative of a spy novel with colorful period detail describing the inner workings of an army staff at war." Libr J
Includes bibliographical references

Wilson, Ellen Judy
Encyclopedia of the Enlightenment; Peter Hanns Reill, consulting editor; Ellen Judy Wilson, principal author. Facts on File 1996 485p il $55   **940.2**
1. Enlightenment—Encyclopedias 2. Philosophy—Encyclopedias 3. Europe—Intellectual life
ISBN 0-8160-2989-X   LC 95-11962
This work identifies and discusses the "key people, subject fields, terms, styles, works, and European locations important in history from the late 1600s to 1800. Americans such as Franklin, Jefferson, and Paine are included." SLJ

940.3   World War I, 1914-1918

Burg, David F.
Almanac of World War I; [by] David F. Burg and L. Edward Purcell; introduction by William Manchester. University Press of Ky. 1998 320p il maps $24.95   **940.3**
1. World War, 1914-1918
ISBN 0-8131-2072-1   LC 98-26625
"The bulk of the text is arranged chronologically by year and date, listing almost daily occurrences from 1914 through 1918. . . . The work is international in scope, covering political and military happenings from around the world. . . . There is really nothing comparable to this volume." Booklist

Gilbert, Martin, 1936-
The First World War; a complete history. Holt & Co. 1994 xxiv, 615p il maps hardcover o.p. paperback available $21.95
940.3
1. World War, 1914-1918
ISBN 0-8050-4734-4 (pa)   LC 94-27268
This work "covers WW I on all major fronts—domestic, diplomatic, military—as well as such bloody preludes as the Armenian massacre of 1915." Publ Wkly
"What Mr. Gilbert seeks to do, and frequently succeeds in doing, is to humanize, indeed to personalize, World War I. His effort and accomplishment make this a rewarding and significant book." N Y Times Book Rev
Includes bibliographical references

Keegan, John, 1934-
The First World War. Knopf 1999 475p il maps $35; pa $16   **940.3**
1. World War, 1914-1918
ISBN 0-375-40052-4; 0-375-70045-5 (pa)
LC 98-31826
In this study of the first World War, Keegan discusses "the strategy and tactics, the fighting, and the morale. . . . World War I, he says, remains a mystery, in its origins, its course, and above all in the courage and stamina of its combatants." Natl Rev
This history is "elegantly written, clear, detailed and omniscient. As a narrative it is outstanding." N Y Times Book Rev
Includes bibliographical references

An illustrated history of the First World War. Knopf 2001 429p il $50   **940.3**
1. World War, 1914-1918
ISBN 0-375-41259-X   LC 2001-41410
The text is an abridgment of the author's The First World War. For this illustrated volume the text is complemented by "almost 500 photographs, posters, drawings and maps, a cross-section of material produced by all the major combatants and clarified by Keegan's extensive captions." Publ Wkly
Includes bibliographical references

MacMillan, Margaret
Paris 1919; six months that changed the world. Random House 2002 560p $35; pa $16.95   **940.3**
1. Wilson, Woodrow, 1856-1924 2. Paris Peace Conference (1919-1920) 3. World War, 1914-1918—Peace 4. Germany—History—1918-1933
ISBN 0-375-50826-0; 0-375-76052-0 (pa)
LC 2002-23707
First published 2001 in the United Kingdom with title: Peacemakers
The author examines the Paris Peace Conference of 1919. Economist John Maynard Keynes blamed "the failure of the conference on the vindictiveness of the French in general and of Clemenceau in particular. Margaret MacMillan . . . argues that the conference has been blamed for many disasters that were, in fact, determined either by events that took place before it began or by later troubles." Economist
"MacMillan's lucid prose brings her participants to colorful and quotable life, and the grand sweep of her narrative encompasses all the continents the peacemakers vainly carved up." Publ Wkly
Includes bibliographical references

Massie, Robert K., 1929-
Dreadnought; Britain, Germany, and the coming of the great war. Random House 1991 xxxi, 1007p il map o.p.; Ballantine Bks. paperback available $18.95 **940.3**
1. World War, 1914-1918—Causes 2. Germany—History—1866-1918 3. Great Britain—History—20th century
ISBN 0-345-37556-4 (pa) LC 91-52672
The author discusses the race for naval superiority between Great Britain and Germany leading up to the First World War
"Dreadnought is history in the grand manner, as most readers prefer it: how people shaped, or were shaped by, events that consensus has declared to be landmarks. At his vivid best, Massie does not simply retell the past. He allows one, in a way, to relive it." Time
Includes bibliographical references

Stokesbury, James L.
A short history of World War I. Morrow 1981 348p maps hardcover o.p. paperback available $14.95 **940.3**
1. World War, 1914-1918
ISBN 0-688-00129-7 (pa) LC 80-22206
This chronologically arranged history of World War I presents both the political and military perspectives
Includes bibliographical references

Tuchman, Barbara Wertheim
The guns of August; [by] Barbara W. Tuchman. anniversary ed. Macmillan 1988 c1962 511p il maps o.p.; Bantam Bks. paperback available $14.95 **940.3**
1. World War, 1914-1918
ISBN 0-345-38623-X (pa) LC 88-29330
A reissue with a new preface by the author of the title first published 1962
A history of the negotiations that preceded World War I and the course of the war's first month
Includes bibliographical references

The Zimmermann telegram; [by] Barbara W. Tuchman. [new ed] Macmillan 1966 244p il hardcover o.p. paperback available $14 **940.3**
1. World War, 1914-1918—Causes
ISBN 0-345-32425-0 (pa)
First published 1958
The author discusses the German plan to induce Mexico to attack the U.S. during World War I
Includes bibliographical references

The **United** States in the First World War; an encyclopedia; editor, Anne Cipriano Venzon; consulting editor, Paul L. Miles. Garland 1995 xx, 830p maps (Garland reference library of the humanities) $155 **940.3**
1. World War, 1914-1918
ISBN 0-8240-7055-0 LC 95-1782
"Biography, economics, civil rights, women's issues, foreign relations, battles, armaments, and conferences are among the topics included. Arrangement is alphabetical, and most articles are brief—between one column and a page. . . . Most articles include brief bibliographies. There are six maps, but no other illustrations." Libr J

World War I; a history; edited by Hew Strachan. Oxford Univ. Press 1999 356p il maps $45 **940.3**
1. World War, 1914-1918
ISBN 0-19-820614-3 LC 97-44997
First published 1998 in the United Kingdom with title: The Oxford illustrated history of the First World War
"Strachan has commissioned 20 historians to summarize present thought about the July 1914 crisis, the military course of the war, the social and economic strains it exerted in all the belligerents, and its conclusion in revolutions and treaties. . . . Readers will find this comprehensive work a captivating introduction to the Great War." Booklist
Includes bibliographical references

940.4 World War I, 1914-1918 (Military conduct of the war)

Dallas, Gregor
1918: war and peace. Overlook Press 2001 616p $40; pa $19.95 **940.4**
1. World War, 1914-1918—Peace
ISBN 1-58567-157-6; 1-58567-319-6 (pa)
LC 2001-21104
The author discusses how the First World War ended. He examines "how the ceasefire was arranged, who the major participants were, and how the general population learned about the armistice." Libr J
Dallas "provides a meticulously detailed and intensive study of the years 1918-1919." Publ Wkly
Includes bibliographical references

Eisenhower, John S. D., 1922-
Yanks: the epic story of the American Army in World War I; [by] John S. D. Eisenhower with Joanne Thompson Eisenhower. Free Press 2001 353p il maps hardcover o.p. paperback available $16
940.4
1. United States. Army 2. World War, 1914-1918—Campaigns
ISBN 0-7432-2385-3 (pa) LC 2001-23124
"This history focuses entirely on the challenges, victories, sacrifices . . . and long-term consequences of the American Expeditionary Force (AEF) in Europe during World War I." Libr J
"This is an important work that should help alter the historical picture of the American role in the conflict." Booklist
Includes bibliographical references

Farwell, Byron
Over there; the United States in the Great War, 1917-1918. Norton 1999 336p $27.95; pa $15.95 **940.4**
1. World War, 1914-1918—United States
ISBN 0-393-04698-2; 0-393-32028-6 (pa)
LC 98-35705
This history of American intervention in World War I focuses primarily on the military aspects of the war but also discusses its social and economic impact
"This title does provide good coverage on the intervention in Russia and the role of women in the war, notably the 'Hello Girls.'" Libr J
Includes bibliographical references

Groom, Winston, 1944-

A storm in Flanders; the Ypres salient, 1914-1918: tragedy and triumph on the Western Front. Atlantic Monthly Press 2002 276p il $27.50; pa $14   **940.4**
1. World War, 1914-1918—Campaigns
ISBN 0-87113-842-5; 0-8021-3998-1 (pa)
                  LC 2002-19433
This is an account of the four year World War I battle for the Ypres Salient in Belgian Flanders
"This is an important and brilliantly written work that is a vital addition to twentieth-century history collections." Booklist
Includes bibliographical references

Harries, Meirion, 1951-

The last days of innocence; America at war, 1917-1918; [by] Meirion and Susie Harries. Random House 1997 573p il hardcover o.p. paperback available $16
                           940.4
1. World War, 1914-1918—United States
ISBN 0-679-74376-6 (pa)   LC 96-21756
The authors first "treat the details of America's entrance into the war and the agonizing months of war preparation; they then visit the fighting and the peace efforts." Libr J
"This is an excellent study of US participation in WWI. The research is in far greater depth than the usual 'popular history,' the analysis is sharp and informative, and the writing is clear and a pleasure to read. The authors strike an even balance between necessity for condensation and the accuracy that comes from detailed treatment." Choice
Includes bibliographical references

Lawrence, T. E. (Thomas Edward), 1888-1935

Seven pillars of wisdom; a triumph. Doubleday 1935 672p il maps hardcover o.p. paperback available $19.95   **940.4**
1. World War, 1914-1918—Middle East 2. Arabs 3. Bedouins 4. Wahhabis
ISBN 0-385-41895-7 (pa)
"Not only a history of the Arab revolt during the [First] World War, but a commentary on the national characteristics, and political policies of Arabs, Turks and British." Cleveland Public Libr

Liddell Hart, Sir Basil Henry, 1895-1970

The real war, 1914-1918; with twenty-five maps; by B. H. Liddell Hart. Little, Brown 1930 508p maps hardcover o.p. paperback available $23.99   **940.4**
1. World War, 1914-1918
ISBN 0-316-52505-7 (pa)
A short history of World War I in which the action of the book ranges wherever Germany and the Allies locked in combat: Poland, Mesopotamia, Gallipoli, Caporetto, Baghdad, the North Sea, and the Mediterranean
Includes bibliographical references

Macintyre, Ben, 1963-

The Englishman's daughter; a true story of love and betrayal in World War I. Farrar, Straus & Giroux 2001 254p il maps $24
                           940.4
1. World War, 1914-1918—France
ISBN 0-374-12985-1   LC 2001-33477
This "is the story of seven British soldiers, separated from their units, . . . who hid in an occupied French village for most of [World War I]." N Y Times (Late N Y Ed)
"The book has some surprising twists that include such pure examples of love, betrayal, honor, and sacrifice that it is easy to forget that the story is absolutely true." Libr J
Includes bibliographical references

Mosier, John, 1944-

The myth of the Great War; a new military history of World War I. HarperCollins Pubs. 2001 381p il hardcover o.p. paperback available $14.95   **940.4**
1. World War, 1914-1918—Campaigns
ISBN 0-06-008433-2 (pa)   LC 00-46103
"After dissecting the major campaigns on the western front, Mosier concludes that Germany's ultimate defeat was the direct result of the influx of American soldiers into France in 1917 and 1918. . . . This is revisionist history that convincingly smashes the myths that Allied governments, leaders, and propagandists worked so hard to promulgate. Mosier's masterful account is a welcome addition." Booklist
Includes bibliographical references

Ousby, Ian

The road to Verdun; World War I's most momentous battle and the folly of nationalism. Doubleday 2002 393p il maps $30; pa $16   **940.4**
1. World War, 1914-1918—Campaigns
ISBN 0-385-50393-8; 0-385-72173-0 (pa)
                  LC 2002-19475
This is a study of the Battle of Verdun which "killed 700,000 French and German soldiers, 10% of all those killed in the war. Yet a sense of glory was maintained, however inappropriately, amid the gore: the road leading to the battlefield was called the Sacred Way, and the French General Neville gained immortality by his brave statement, 'They [the Germans] shall not pass.'" Publ Wkly

Preston, Diana

Lusitania; an epic tragedy. Walker & Co. 2002 532p il maps $28   **940.4**
1. Lusitania (Steamship) 2. World War, 1914-1918—Naval operations
ISBN 0-8027-1375-0   LC 2001-56767
Also available in paperback from Berkley Pub. Group
This is the "tale of the May 1915 sinking of the *Lusitania* . . . during a crossing from New York to Liverpool. Hit by a German submarine's torpedo, it sank in 18 minutes, with 1,200 casualties." Publ Wkly
The author's "thorough research is elegantly conveyed by a humanizing narrative that covers everyone involved. . . . A captivating and conscientious narrative of the disaster and its consequences." Booklist
Includes bibliographical references

Weintraub, Stanley, 1929-
Silent night; the story of the World War I Christmas truce. Free Press 2001 206p il $25
940.4

1. World War, 1914-1918—Armistices
ISBN 0-684-87281-1   LC 2001-33423
Also available in paperback from Penguin Bks.
Weintraub argues that "the Christmas truce of 1914 . . . was actually World War I's greatest missed opportunity. Started by Saxons and Bavarians who felt more solidarity with the English than with their own Prussian commanders, informal cease-fires broke out on Christmas Eve and spread along much of the Western Front." N Y Times Book Rev
Includes bibliographical references

940.53   World War II, 1939-1945

Ambrose, Stephen E.
The American Heritage new history of World War II; [by] Stephen E. Ambrose with C. L. Sulzberger. Viking 1997 640p $60
940.53

1. World War, 1939-1945
ISBN 0-670-87474-4   LC 97-18678
First published 1966 under the authorship of C. L. Sulzberger with title: The American Heritage picture history of World War II
This study presents "the war as a three-way ideological struggle among fascism, communism and democracy, with the 'grand alliance' against Hitler being essentially a relationship of convenience. Victory over the Axis, Ambrose and Sulzberger demonstrate, was assisted by a series of avoidable Japanese and German mistakes, but it was by no means assured. . . . While of limited use to scholars and specialists, for general readers this was, and still is, a solid introduction to an enormously complex subject." Publ Wkly

Art from the ashes; a Holocaust anthology; edited by Lawrence L. Langer. Oxford Univ. Press 1995 689p il hardcover o.p. paperback available $47.95   **940.53**

1. Holocaust, 1933-1945—Personal narratives 2. Holocaust, 1933-1945, in literature
ISBN 0-19-507732-6 (pa)   LC 94-11446
This collection "includes both fiction and nonfiction, as well as drama and poetry. Among the nonfiction pieces are excerpts from the ghetto diaries of Abraham Lewin (Warsaw) and Avraham Tory (Kovno), an essay from Primo Levi's The Drowned and the Saved, and an essay from Elie Wiesel's Legends of Our Time." Booklist
A "remarkable volume, perfectly suited for anyone studying the Holocaust. . . . Compared with [the] firsthand accounts, fiction could be, one would think, only a pallid version of reality. Yet the fiction Mr. Langer collects . . . highlights the reality of the Holocaust with stunning intensity." N Y Times Book Rev

Ba'u, Yosef, 1920-
Dear God, have you ever gone hungry? memoirs; by Joseph Bau; translated from the Hebrew by Sam Yurman. Arcade Pub. 1998 228p il $24.95; pa $13.95   **940.53**

1. Jews—Persecutions 2. Holocaust, 1933-1945—Personal narratives
ISBN 1-55970-431-4; 1-55970-540-X (pa)
LC 98-17133
Bau's "memoir recounts the love story depicted so movingly in the film Schindler's List. Bau fell in love with and married Rebecca Tannenbaum in the Plaszów concentration camp in Poland during World War II. Anxious to save her husband at whatever cost, Rebecca placed Joseph's name on the list of Jews that Oskar Schindler would be allowed to take with him to his new factory in Brinnlitz, Czechoslovakia. She herself was sent to Auschwitz, where she was selected for the gas chamber three times but each time managed to elude death. Amazingly, both survived the Holocaust." Libr J

Berenbaum, Michael, 1945-
The world must know; the history of the Holocaust as told in the United States Holocaust Memorial Museum; Arnold Kramer, editor of photographs. Little, Brown 1993 240p il hardcover o.p. paperback available $24.95   **940.53**

1. United States Holocaust Memorial Museum 2. Holocaust, 1933-1945
ISBN 0-316-09134-0 (pa)   LC 92-32813
This work was written to commemorate the opening of the U.S. Holocaust Memorial Museum in April 1993 on the fiftieth anniversary of the Warsaw Ghetto uprising. Berenbaum uses the museum's photographs and documents to "chronicle the Holocaust's four historical participants: the victims, the perpetrators, the bystanders, and the rescuers." Booklist
"Visually evocative and unsettling, the book, supplemented with a useful bibliography, is an excellent choice for those with little acquaintance of the subject or those needing a concise synopsis." Libr J

Beschloss, Michael R., 1955-
The conquerors: Roosevelt, Truman, and the destruction of Hitler's Germany, 1941-1945; [by] Michael Beschloss. Simon & Schuster 2002 377p il maps $26.95; pa $15
940.53

1. Roosevelt, Franklin D. (Franklin Delano), 1882-1945 2. Truman, Harry S., 1884-1972 3. World War, 1939-1945—Germany 4. Reconstruction (1939-1951) 5. United States—Foreign relations—Germany 6. Germany—Foreign relations—United States
ISBN 0-684-81027-1; 0-7432-4454-0 (pa)
LC 2002-30331
"As German forces were driven back in 1943-45, American leaders were anxious that in 20 years, just as it had done after its defeat in 1918, a vengeful Germany would start another world war. To prevent this, two schools of thought flowed through DC's salons of power: punishment or rehabilitation. . . . Beschloss covers the meeting-by-meeting, memo-by-memo political battle between the two approaches. . . . Beschloss' comprehensive research and narration into every nuance opens a significant perspective on bureaucratic politics' effect on the Germany that eventually formed in the early cold war." Booklist
Includes bibliographical references

The **Buchenwald** report; translated, edited, and with an introduction by David A. Hackett; foreword by Frederick A. Praeger. Westview Press 1995 397p map hardcover o.p. paperback available $28   **940.53**
1. Holocaust, 1933-1945—Personal narratives 2. Buchenwald (Germany: Concentration camp)
ISBN 0-8133-3363-6 (pa)   LC 94-39714

"This seminal document, published here in its entirety for the first time, is a report compiled for the Allied Army from interviews with the inmates of the Buchenwald concentration camp, located near Weimar, Germany in April 1945, shortly after the camp's liberation. . . . It is immediate, direct, and, as the product of the testimony of many people, more inclusive and wide-ranging than any single individual's personal testament. A classic of Holocaust literature that should be in any library that covers European history." Libr J

Includes bibliographical references

Carley, Michael Jabara, 1945-
1939; the alliance that never was and the coming of World War II. Dee, I.R. 1999 xxv, 321p maps $28.95   **940.53**
1. World War, 1939-1945—Diplomatic history 2. World War, 1939-1945—Causes
ISBN 1-56663-252-8   LC 99-24873

Carley "asserts that reflexive and extreme anti-Communist paranoia on the part of British and French politicians and diplomats prevented a very achievable alliance against Hitler." Booklist

The author "provides a detailed and fascinating perspective on one of the major causes of World War II." Libr J

Includes bibliographical references

Chesnoff, Richard Z., 1937-
Pack of thieves; how Hitler and Europe plundered the Jews and committed the greatest theft in history. Doubleday 1999 325p il hardcover o.p. paperback available $14   **940.53**
1. Holocaust, 1933-1945 2. Jews—Persecutions
ISBN 0-385-72064-5 (pa)   LC 99-33257

The author outlines the "Nazi plot to segregate Jews from the economic mainstream by expropriating their businesses, savings accounts, jewelry, art collections, and other personal belongings. What is startling, though, is not the fact that many Germans supported and profited from this plan, but that large numbers of government officials and private citizens in conquered and neutral European nations enthusiastically jumped on the bandwagon." Booklist

Children in the Holocaust and World War II; their secret diaries; [compiled by] Laurel Holliday. Pocket Bks. 1995 xxi, 409p il map hardcover o.p. paperback available $15
940.53
1. Holocaust, 1933-1945—Personal narratives 2. World War, 1939-1945—Children
ISBN 0-671-52055-5 (pa)   LC 95-3211

"Diary entries written by young people in ghettos, concentration camps, cities, and a Copenhagen prison camp offer . . . glimpses of life during World War II. Each selection is introduced by a brief biography that includes the author's name, country, age, family circumstances before and during the war, and concludes with

circumstances of death or postwar life. Nine girls and 14 boys, Jews and gentiles, aged 10 to 18, are featured." SLJ

"This anthology is a haunting reminder of the impact of war on children. The powerful images will long be remembered." Voice Youth Advocates

Includes bibliographical references

Churchill, Sir Winston, 1874-1965
Closing the ring. Houghton Mifflin 1951 749p maps (Second World War, v5) hardcover o.p. paperback available $18

940.53
1. World War, 1939-1945 2. World War, 1939-1945—Great Britain
ISBN 0-395-41059-2 (pa)

"'Closing the Ring' sets forth the year of conflict from June 1943 to June 1944. Aided by the command of the oceans, the mastery of the U-boats, and our ever growing superiority in the air, the Western Allies were able to conquer Sicily and invade Italy, with the result that Mussolini was overthrown and the Italian nation came over to our side." Preface

The gathering storm. Houghton Mifflin 1948 784p maps (Second World War, v1) hardcover o.p. paperback available $19

940.53
1. World War, 1939-1945 2. World War, 1939-1945—Great Britain
ISBN 0-395-41055-X (pa)

The first volume of Churchill's monumental history of the Second World War describes the days between the false peace and Hitler's near-victory just before Dunkirk

The grand alliance. Houghton Mifflin 1950 903p maps (Second World War, v3) hardcover o.p. paperback available $18

940.53
1. World War, 1939-1945 2. World War, 1939-1945—Great Britain
ISBN 0-395-41057-6 (pa)

This volume begins with the German drive in the East, covers the War in Africa and describes the entrance into the war of Russia and, after Pearl Harbor, the United States

The hinge of fate. Houghton Mifflin 1950 1000p maps (Second World War, v4) hardcover o.p. paperback available $18

940.53
1. World War, 1939-1945 2. World War, 1939-1945—Great Britain
ISBN 0-395-41058-4 (pa)

Describing events leading to the invasion of Sicily, warfare in Africa, the discouragingly slow job of reconquest in Europe, meetings with Roosevelt, and efforts at collaboration with Stalin, this volume covers the period from January 1942 to May 1943

Churchill, Sir Winston, 1874-1965—*Continued*

Their finest hour. Houghton Mifflin 1949 751p maps (Second World War, v2) hardcover o.p. paperback available $19
940.53
1. World War, 1939-1945 2. World War, 1939-1945—Great Britain
ISBN 0-395-41056-8 (pa)
This volume starts with the problems confronting Churchill as he assumed the office of Prime Minister in 1940 and continues with accounts of the Battle of Britain, the Battle of France and Dunkirk

Triumph and tragedy. Houghton Mifflin 1953 800p maps (Second World War, v6) hardcover o.p. paperback available $18
940.53
1. World War, 1939-1945 2. World War, 1939-1945—Great Britain
ISBN 0-395-41060-6 (pa)
The concluding volume of Churchill's history of World War II begins with D-Day and covers campaigns leading to the defeat of Germany and Japan

Clendinnen, Inga

Reading the Holocaust. Cambridge Univ. Press 1999 227p il map $45; pa $15 **940.53**
1. Holocaust, 1933-1945—Historiography
ISBN 0-521-64174-8; 0-521-64597-2 (pa)
LC 98-53636
In this reexamination of the Holocaust Clendinnen "first considers the problematic nature of eyewitness accounts, then turns to an unflinching inquiry into the Nazi mentality and finally takes on the tough question of artistic representation. . . . This slim, powerful book forces a reader to re-examine almost all the assumptions we've accepted since the Holocaust occurred." N Y Times Book Rev
Includes bibliographical references

Cohen, Rich

The avengers. Knopf 2000 261p il hardcover o.p. paperback available $13
940.53
1. Kovner, Abba, 1918-1987 2. Korczak-Marla, Rozka, 1921-1988 3. Kempner, Vitka 4. World War, 1939-1945—Underground movements 5. Holocaust, 1933-1945
ISBN 0-375-70529-5 (pa)
LC 00-21062
Cohen chronicles the resistance efforts of a small group of European Jews during the Second World War. Attention is focused primarily on the activities of three individuals: Rozka Korczak, Vitka Kempner, and Abba Kovner
"Cohen is a skilled writer. His language is spare and muscular, his descriptions evocative, his technique suspenseful." N Y Times Book Rev

Daniels, Roger

Prisoners without trial; Japanese Americans in World War II; consulting editor, Eric Foner. Hill & Wang 1993 146p il (Critical issue series) hardcover o.p. paperback available $11
940.53
1. Japanese Americans—Evacuation and relocation, 1942-1945 2. World War, 1939-1945—United States
ISBN 0-0890-1553-6 (pa)
LC 92-27144
An account of "the relocation of Japanese Americans during World War II, an injustice prompted not by military necessity but by political and racial motivations. The purpose of this volume is to tell the story in light of the redress legislation enacted in 1988." Libr J

Dawidowicz, Lucy S.

The war against the Jews, 1933-1945. 10th anniversary ed. Free Press 1986 c1975 xxxx, 466p maps o.p.; Bantam Bks. paperback available $18.95
940.53
1. Holocaust, 1933-1945 2. Jews—Europe
ISBN 0-553-34532-X (pa)
LC 86-6516
A reissue with new introduction and supplementary bibliography of the title first published 1975 by Holt, Rinehart & Winston
"One of the best histories of the mass murder of Jews in World War II. Argues for the centrality of anti-Semitism in Hitler's program." Reader's Adviser

Denes, Magda, 1934-1996

Castles burning; a child's life in war. Norton 1997 384p $24
940.53
1. Holocaust, 1933-1945—Personal narratives
ISBN 0-393-03966-8
LC 96-16311
"Denes was five years old in 1939 when her father, a wealthy Hungarian Jewish publisher, left Hungary after his newspaper was seized by the authorities, leaving Magda, her 12-year-old brother, Ivan, and their mother to cope with wartime conditions in Budapest and, ultimately, the German takeover in March 1944. The author recounts . . . how she and her family survived years of hiding in Hungary and, later, lived as displaced persons in Germany." Publ Wkly

Dwork, Deborah

Holocaust: a history; [by] Deborah Dwork, Robert Jan Van Pelt. Norton 2002 xx, 444p il $27.95; pa $15.95
940.53
1. Holocaust, 1933-1945 2. Jews—Germany 3. Germany—Politics and government—1933-1945
ISBN 0-393-05188-9; 0-393-32524-5 (pa)
LC 2002-23565
"The authors examine such issues as the historic relationship between Jews, gentiles, and Germans; World War I and its consequences; National Socialism in the Weimar Republic; the Third Reich and its anti-Semitic measures; worldwide refugee policies that became a disaster for the Jews; and Jewish and gentile life under German occupation. They also examine the efforts by Allied nations to help the Jews. . . . This is a monumental work of impeccable scholarship." Booklist
Includes bibliographical references

Encyclopedia of Jewish life before and during the Holocaust; edited by Shmuel Spector and Geoffrey Wigoder. New York Univ. Press 2001 3v il maps set $99

940.53

1. Jews—Europe 2. Holocaust, 1933-1945—Encyclopedias

ISBN 0-8147-9356-8

"These three volumes are an abridgment of the multivolume Encyclopedia of Jewish Communities published in Hebrew by Yad Vashem" Verso of title page

"Each entry provides vital information on the town's Jewish inhabitants on the eve of German occupation, gives the dates of Jewish roundups and mass executions and estimates how many Jews from that community survived the war." Publ Wkly

For a fuller review see: Booklist, Oct. 1, 2001

Encyclopedia of the Holocaust; Israel Gutman, editor in chief. complete and unabridged ed. Macmillan Lib. Ref. USA 1995 c1990 2v set $295   **940.53**

1. Holocaust, 1933-1945

ISBN 0-0286-4527-8

A reissue of the 1990 edition

"This set provides a wealth of information about a major event in the history of Western civilization. More than 1,000 entries treat countries, people, reflections in the arts and theology, sites of camps and massacres, and contemporary documentation centers." Ref Sources for Small & Medium-sized Libr. 6th edition

Encyclopedia of the Holocaust; Schmuel Spector, Robert Rozett, editors. Facts on File 2000 528p il $93.50   **940.53**

1. Holocaust, 1933-1945—Encyclopedias

ISBN 0-8160-4333-7   LC 00-30917

Following several introductory essays are "alphabetical entries on people, places, events, organizations, laws, and concepts. The language is clear, but more important is the authenticity of the information and the refusal to surrender to a simplification of issues. There are ample good-quality, black-and-white photographs, some unfamiliar, and also maps and tables. A detailed chronology and a thematic bibliography conclude the volume." SLJ

For a fuller review see: Booklist, March 1, 2001

Epstein, Eric Joseph, 1959-

Dictionary of the Holocaust; biography, geography, and terminology; [by] Eric Joseph Epstein and Philip Rosen; foreword by Henry R. Huttenbach. Greenwood Press 1997 416p $67.95   **940.53**

1. Holocaust, 1933-1945—Dictionaries

ISBN 0-313-30355-X   LC 97-8779

The nearly 2,000 alphabetically arranged entries cover people, places and events related to the Holocaust. "Among the personalities profiled here are Dietrich Bonhoeffer, Anne Frank, Primo Levi, Oskar Schindler, Harry S. Truman, and Elie Wiesel. Place entries include references to well-known locations, the number of prewar Jewish inhabitants, the date of liberation, and the number of Jews left after liberation. Entries dealing with concentration camps are generally the longest and identify camps by location, type, when opened and liberated, nationalities incarcerated, numbers murdered, other victimization, and camp commandants. Among the terms that are defined are many foreign expressions." Booklist

Evans, Richard J.

Lying about Hitler; history, Holocaust, and the David Irving trial; [by] Richard Evans. Basic Bks. 2001 318p hardcover o.p. paperback available $16   **940.53**

1. Irving, David John Cawdell, 1938- 2. Lipstadt, Deborah E. 3. Trials 4. Holocaust, 1933-1945—Historiography

ISBN 0-465-02153-0 (pa)   LC 00-140130

Evans writes of the unsuccessful libel suit brought by English historian "David Irving against Deborah Lipstadt. . . . In her book, 'Denying the Holocaust,' Lipstadt called Irving 'one of the most dangerous spokespersons for Holocaust denial.'" New Yorker

Evans's "superb [book], . . . is never less than absorbing. A sure-footed writer, he allows the story to tell itself, eschewing rhetorical flourishes in favor of a clinical dissection of Irving's works and statements." Natl Rev

Includes bibliographical references

Fogelman, Eva

Conscience & courage; rescuers of the Jews during the Holocaust. Anchor Bks. (NY) 1994 xx, 393p hardcover o.p. paperback available $16   **940.53**

1. Holocaust, 1933-1945 2. World War, 1939-1945—Jews—Rescue

ISBN 0-385-42028-5 (pa)   LC 93-34021

The author "attempts to explain why the rescuers of Holocaust victims acted as they did. . . . Fogelman emphasizes the ordinary rescuer but also discusses better-known people like Oskar Schindler, Raoul Wallenberg, and Miep Gies. Besides offering a psychological reason for the rescuers' sacrifices, Fogelman tells the fascinating stories of people who risked their lives to help individuals in trouble." Libr J

Includes bibliographical references

Friedländer, Saul, 1932-

Nazi Germany and the Jews. v1: The years of persecution, 1933-1939. HarperCollins Pubs. 1997 436p hardcover o.p. paperback available $17.95   **940.53**

1. Jews—Germany 2. Jews—Persecutions 3. Holocaust, 1933-1945 4. Germany—History—1933-1945

ISBN 0-06-092878-6 (pa)   LC 96-21915

This is the first of a projected two volume study

The author examines "the segregation of the Jewish communities in both Germany and Austria in the period between 1933-1939. The author argues that Hitler was driven by a fanatical hatred of Jews, which he labeled 'redemptive anti-Semitism.' . . . Friedländer argues, however, that Hitler's fanaticism was not shared by most Germans, although antisemitism was endemic throughout Germany." Choice

"Not the least impressive aspect of Friedländer's book is the skill with which he juxtaposes different levels of reality within an overall chronological frame, moving from high-level Nazi debates on Jewish policy to the routine brutalities of the SA and SS, and from the perceptions of the average German citizen to those of the victims." N Y Rev Books

Includes bibliographical references

Gies, Miep, 1909-

Anne Frank remembered; the story of the woman who helped to hide the Frank family; [by] Miep Gies with Alison Leslie Gold. Simon & Schuster 1987 252p il maps hardcover o.p. paperback available $14

940.53

1. Frank family 2. Netherlands—History—1940-1945, German occupation 3. Holocaust, 1933-1945
ISBN 0-671-66234-1 (pa)   LC 86-25991

"A memoir by the courageous Dutch woman who helped to hide the Frank family, this book augments the Anne Frank story. Perceptive characterizations, with insight into life in Amsterdam during the Nazi occupation." SLJ

Gilbert, Martin, 1936-

The boys; the untold story of 732 young concentration camp survivors. Holt & Co. 1997 511p il maps hardcover o.p. paperback available $16.95   **940.53**

1. Holocaust, 1933-1945—Personal narratives 2. Holocaust survivors 3. Jews—Great Britain
ISBN 0-8050-4403-5 (pa)   LC 96-50910

"The title refers to a group of 732 mostly Polish Jews who somehow remained alive after terrible wartime ordeals. Most were in their middle or late teens, but some were as young as 12. Tracked by death for five years, they saw the destruction of their prewar communities, witnessed the massacre of family members and close acquaintances, and suffered unimaginable physical and mental torment. . . . Martin Gilbert seldom intrudes, and lets the survivors speak for themselves. To be sure, he is always there, assembling the thousands of scraps of memory into a coherent, compelling, moving narrative." N Y Times Book Rev

The Holocaust; a history of the Jews of Europe during the Second World War. Holt & Co. 1986 c1985 959p il maps hardcover o.p. paperback available $24   **940.53**

1. Holocaust, 1933-1945
ISBN 0-8050-0348-7 (pa)   LC 85-5523

"Proceeding chronologically from Hitler's rise to power in 1933 to Germany's surrender and the liberation of the concentration camps, [the author] documents the countless horrors of this 'unprecedented explosion of evil over good,' drawing extensively on records and testimonies of those who survived (as well as some who eventually perished)." Booklist

Includes bibliographical references

Holocaust journey; traveling in search of the past. Columbia Univ. Press 1997 480p il $60; pa $20.95   **940.53**

1. Holocaust, 1933-1945 2. Concentration camps 3. Jews—Europe
ISBN 0-231-10964-4; 0-231-10965-2 (pa)
LC 97-15895

The author chronicles "a tour of Holocaust sites that he conducted with a dozen students and friends; the text of documents they studied at each stop is included. Gilbert not only describes their itinerary and the problems of conducting a tour but integrates the history of European Jewry into his narrative. He then details the specific events of the Holocaust associated with each location." Libr J

Includes bibliographical references

Never again; a history of the Holocaust. Universe Pub. 2000 192p il maps $32.50

940.53

1. Holocaust, 1933-1945
ISBN 0-7893-0409-0

The author "arranges the principal events of the Holocaust into illustrated, two-page layouts per topic, such as Kristallnacht." Booklist

The Routledge atlas of the Holocaust. 3rd ed. Routledge 2002 282p il maps $75; pa $19.95   **940.53**

1. Holocaust, 1933-1945
ISBN 0-415-28145-8; 0-415-28146-6 (pa)

First published 1982 in the United Kingdom with title: The Dent atlas of the Holocaust

The author "uses 317 maps, text, and photographs to document Hitler's attempt to destroy Europe's Jews. . . . Commentary offers statistical information, historical background, and something about the people of the area. Archival photographs bring the events to life. . . . This small but effective work demonstrates the magnitude of the Nazi terror by bringing it down to a personal level." Am Ref Books Annu, 2003

Includes bibliographical references

The Second World War; a complete history. Holt & Co. 1989 846p il maps hardcover o.p. paperback available $25

940.53

1. World War, 1939-1945
ISBN 0-8050-1788-7 (pa)   LC 89-11129

The author begins this study "with the invasion of Poland. Gilbert's flowing narrative is spiced with anecdotal details culled from diaries, memoirs and official documents. He is especially skillful at interweaving summaries of military strategy with vignettes of civilian suffering—the genocide of the Jews is never far from view." Newsweek

Includes bibliographical references

Glass, James M.

Life unworthy of life; racial phobia and mass murder in Hitler's Germany. Basic Bks. 1997 252p hardcover o.p. paperback available $23   **940.53**

1. Holocaust, 1933-1945 2. Antisemitism 3. Eugenics
ISBN 0-465-09846-0 (pa)   LC 97-20118

The author's "thesis is that the Holocaust was possible because the German scientific community supported the genocidal actions against the Jews. {According to Glass}, the German public health profession {taught} . . . that Jews possessed innate criminal tendencies. . . . It also disseminated the belief that Jewish flesh and blood polluted the health of the German nation, its genes, and its culture." Choice

"Forcefully argued and well documented, this work is a must for any Holocaust collection." Booklist

Includes bibliographical references

Goldhagen, Daniel

Hitler's willing executioners; ordinary Germans and the Holocaust; [by] Daniel Jonah Goldhagen. Knopf 1996 622p il maps $35; pa $16   **940.53**

1. Holocaust, 1933-1945 2. Germany—History—1933-1945 3. Antisemitism 4. National socialism
ISBN 0-679-44695-8; 0-679-77268-5 (pa)

LC 95-38591

The author "endeavors to show that the common apologia for the Germans—that Hitler 'brainwashed' them—is nonsense and that most Germans gave their active assent to genocide. An ordinary German commander, for example, might feel himself bound by a strict code of conduct yet not be at all averse to murdering Jews. The book ends with a detailed notes section and an appendix that explains the correct methodology for studying the Nazi period." Libr J

A moral reckoning; the role of the Catholic Church in the Holocaust and its unfulfilled duty of repair; [by] Daniel Jonah Goldhagen. Knopf 2002 362p il $25; pa $16   **940.53**

1. Pius XII, Pope, 1876-1958 2. Catholic Church—Relations—Judaism 3. Holocaust, 1933-1945 4. Antisemitism
ISBN 0-375-41434-7; 0-375-71417-0 (pa)

LC 2002-16264

The author "addresses a series of questions about the behavior of the Roman Catholic Church during the Holocaust." N Y Times (Late N Y Ed)

This is "a landmark work. . . . This volume is recommended for all libraries and essential for those supporting a Holocaust studies program." Libr J

Includes bibliographical references

Goldsmith, Martin

The inextinguishable symphony; a true story of music and love in Nazi Germany. Wiley 2000 346p il $24.95; pa $15.95

     940.53

1. Goldsmith, George 2. Goldsmith, Rosemarie, 1917-1984 3. Jews—Germany 4. Holocaust, 1933-1945
ISBN 0-471-35097-4; 0-471-07864-6 (pa)

LC 00-25955

The author "tells the story of his parents, musicians who played in the orchestra of the Jewish Kulturbund, which was established by the Nazis as a propaganda tool." Libr J

Goldsmith's "weaving together of cultural and personal history constitutes a gripping tale of persecution, intrigue, and love and an insider's—or two insiders'—view of a dark time." Booklist

Includes bibliographical references

Guttenplan, D. D.

The Holocaust on trial. Norton 2001 328p il hardcover o.p. paperback available $15.95

     940.53

1. Irving, David John Cawdell, 1938- 2. Lipstadt, Deborah E. 3. Trials 4. Holocaust, 1933-1945—Historiography
ISBN 0-393-32292-0 (pa)   LC 2001-30370

The author chronicles the "libel trial in Britain brought by historian David Irving. Irving, widely viewed as an apologist for Hitler, sued American scholar Deborah Lipstadt, whose *Denying the Holocaust* (1993) had labeled Irving as a right-wing extremist. . . . Interspersing

essayistic diversions, the author presents a thoughtful work as well as a courtroom thriller." Booklist

"Interspersing essayistic diversions, the author presents a thoughtful work as well as a courtroom thriller." Booklist

Includes bibliographical references

The **Holocaust** and history; the known, the unknown, the disputed, and the reexamined; edited by Michael Berenbaum and Abraham J. Peck. Indiana Univ. Press 1998 836p $58.71; pa $35   **940.53**

1. Holocaust, 1933-1945
ISBN 0-253-33374-1; 0-253-21529-3 (pa)

LC 97-40030

Published in association with the United States Holocaust Memorial Museum, Washington, D.C.

"Papers collected here originated at a 1993 conference organized by the US Holocaust Memorial Museum's Research Institute. . . . The 50 contributors treat the subject from every conceivable angle: the role of antisemitism and racism; the politics of 'racial hygiene'; Nazi leadership and bureaucracy; the complicity of 'ordinary' people; the experiences of Gypsies, homosexuals, and blacks; the concentration camps; the Holocaust as reflected in international relations; the response of Jews, rescuers, and survivors. Recognizing the passionately controversial nature of the field, the editors have opted for variety over unanimity." Choice

The **Holocaust** encyclopedia; Walter Laqueur, editor; Judith Tydor Baumel, associate editor. Yale Univ. Press 2001 xxxix, 765p il maps $60   **940.53**

1. Holocaust, 1933-1945—Encyclopedias
ISBN 0-300-08432-3   LC 00-106567

This "encyclopedia provides fresh and lengthy articles on such topics as antisemitism, historiography, Jewish women, memorials, and resistance, just to brush the surface." Choice

For a fuller review see: Booklist, Oct. 1, 2001

Japanese Americans, from relocation to redress; edited by Roger Daniels, Sandra C. Taylor, Harry H.L. Kitano; contributions by Leonard J. Arrington [et al.] rev & updated ed. University of Wash. Press 1991 xxi, 242p il pa $25   **940.53**

1. Japanese Americans—Evacuation and relocation, 1942-1945 2. World War, 1939-1945—Reparations
ISBN 0-295-97117-7   LC 91-2892

First published 1986 by University of Utah Press

A collection of essays on Japanese Americans focusing on their wartime relocation and their efforts to seek reparations

Includes bibliographical references

Johnson, Eric A. (Eric Arthur), 1948-

Nazi terror; the Gestapo, Jews and ordinary Germans. Basic Bks. 2000 xx, 636p il hardcover o.p. paperback available $21

     940.53

1. Germany. Gestapo 2. Holocaust, 1933-1945—Historiography 3. Germany—History—1933-1945 4. Jews—Germany 5. National socialism
ISBN 0-465-04908-7 (pa)   LC 00-269061

The author contends "that the reasons ordinary Germans joined the Gestapo were varied and multifaceted,

Johnson, Eric A. (Eric Arthur), 1948-—
Continued

not simply owing to 'eliminationist anti-Semitism'." Libr J

"The great virtue of 'Nazi Terror' is the high degree of levelheadness and common sense, backed by painstaking research, it brings to questions that unfailingly provoke agitated debate." N Y Times Book Rev

Keegan, John, 1934-

The Second World War. Viking 1990 c1989 608p il maps hardcover o.p. paperback available $20.95   **940.53**

    1. World War, 1939-1945
    ISBN 0-14-011341-X (pa)   LC 89-16682
    First published 1989 in the United Kingdom

This military and stategic history contains sections covering the Eastern and Western fronts and the war in the Pacific

"Keegan accompanies his narrative with a series of set battlepieces, of strategic analyses, and of 'themes of war'. . . . [The book] is beautifully ordered and . . . a pleasure to read." New Statesman Soc

Includes bibliographical references

Kelly, Clara Olink

The flamboya tree; memories of a mother's wartime courage. Random House 2002 204p il hardcover o.p. paperback available $12.95
    940.53

    1. World War, 1939-1945—Personal narratives
    2. World War, 1939-1945—Prisoners and prisons
    ISBN 0-8129-6685-6 (pa)   LC 2001-41906

Kelly recounts how she "spent nearly four years in a brutal Japanese concentration camp in Indonesia during WWII. She survived because of her mother, who cared for her three children (including a newborn baby), found them food and shelter, nurtured them with unwavering love under appalling conditions, and insisted on honesty, decency, even good manners, as they coped with filth, hunger, and disease. The child's-eye view of her brave parent makes this memoir a moving, immediate account of a relatively unknown wartime drama." Booklist

Kruk, Herman, 1897-1944

The last days of the Jerusalem of Lithuania; chronicles from the Vilna ghetto and the camps, 1939-1944; edited and introduced by Benjamin Harshav; translated by Barbara Harshav. Yivo Inst. for Jewish Res. 2002 732p il maps $45   **940.53**

    1. Jews—Lithuania   2. Holocaust, 1933-1945
    3. World War, 1939-1945—Underground movements
    ISBN 0-300-04494-1   LC 2002-16736

This a collection of Kruk's journals and other writings from the Jewish ghetto of Vilna and a labor camp in Estonia

This "is a major addition to Holocaust literature and Jewish history. In 1961 a Yiddish edition of the Vilna diaries was published. This larger new edition has been painstakingly assembled from those diaries and other documents and writings by Kruk that were widely scattered and only found since the 1961 edition; Harshav has also added a wealth of new footnotes." Publ Wkly

Includes bibliographical references

Langer, Lawrence L.

Admitting the Holocaust; collected essays. Oxford Univ. Press 1995 202p hardcover o.p. paperback available $14.95   **940.53**

    1. Holocaust, 1933-1945 2. Holocaust, 1933-1945, in literature
    ISBN 0-19-510648-2 (pa)   LC 94-13368
    Analyzed in Essay and general literature index

In these essays Langer examines how "Western intellectuals and writers have sought to come to terms with the Holocaust. He argues that they have created, in their novels, stories, and films, a morally manageable version of the Holocaust rather than an unadorned yet honest view of mass murder without historical parallel." Libr J

"A horribly bleak, undeniably important book." Booklist

Includes bibliographical references

Levi, Primo, 1919-1987

The drowned and the saved; translated from the Italian by Raymond Rosenthal. Summit Bks. 1988 203p o.p.; Vintage Bks. paperback available $12   **940.53**

    1. Holocaust, 1933-1945—Personal narratives
    2. Auschwitz (Poland: Concentration camp)
    ISBN 0-679-72186-X (pa)   LC 87-18052
    Original Italian edition, 1986

Auschwitz survivor Levi, an Italian Jewish chemist from Turin, wrote this final contemplation of the Holocaust before his suicide in 1987

"If the unending tragedy of the Holocaust can ever be said to make sense, then it does so in these pages." New Yorker

Survival in Auschwitz; and, The reawakening; two memoirs; translated by Stuart Woolf. Summit Bks. 1986 c1985 397p map   **940.53**

    1. World War, 1939-1945—Personal narratives
    2. Holocaust, 1933-1945—Personal narratives
    3. Auschwitz (Poland: Concentration camp)
    LC 85-27618

Both works available separately in paperback from Simon & Schuster

Survival in Auschwitz originally published 1958 in Italy; first United States edition published 1959 by Orion Press with title: If this is a man. The reawakening originally published 1963 in Italy; first United States edition published 1965 by Little, Brown

This volume brings together two memoirs that tell of the Italian Jewish chemist's ten months as a concentration camp inmate and of his liberation and return journey home through the Soviet Union, Hungary and Romania

"These books are at one time powerful and understated, offered without a whisper of self-pity, even quite frequently with humor." America

Lewy, Guenter, 1923-

The Nazi persecution of the gypsies. Oxford Univ. Press 2000 306p il hardcover o.p. paperback available $15.95   **940.53**

    1. Gypsies 2. World War, 1939-1945—Atrocities
    3. National socialism
    ISBN 0-19-514240-3 (pa)   LC 98-52545

The author "begins with a brief history of the maltreatment of Gypsies all over Europe, from the fifteenth century onward; then, by dint of exhaustive research, Lewy documents the horrors of their expulsions, detentions, deportations, and deaths during the systematic madness of the Holocaust." Booklist

Includes bibliographical references

Life: World War 2; history's greatest conflict in pictures; edited by Richard B. Stolley. Little, Brown 2001 351p il $60   **940.53**
1. World War, 1939-1945—Pictorial works 2. World history—20th century—Pictorial works
ISBN 0-8212-2771-8   LC 2001-93633
"A Bulfinch Press book"
This "album of 665 photographs taken from the archives of *Life* magazine and other collections begins with the years 1919 to 1939, the two decades leading up to World War II. Editor Stolley then proceeds to chronicle the war, year by year through 1945, and ends with what he calls 'the war's aftermath,' 1946 to 2001. . . . For World War II buffs, the book is a natural treasure." Booklist

Lifton, Robert Jay, 1926-
The Nazi doctors; medical killing and the psychology of genocide. Basic Bks. 1986 561p hardcover o.p. paperback available $23   **940.53**
1. Holocaust, 1933-1945 2. World War, 1939-1945—Atrocities 3. Concentration camps
ISBN 0-465-04905-2 (pa)   LC 85-73874
"How could German physicians trained as scientist-healers carry out Nazi orders for mass killings? . . . Lifton, an American Jewish physician, seeks answers through interviews with surviving doctors, family members, and victims and by painstakingly gleaning Holocaust archives." Sci Books Films
Includes bibliographical references

Lindwer, Willy
The last seven months of Anne Frank; translated from the Dutch by Alison Meersschaert. Pantheon Bks. 1991 204p il o.p.; Anchor Bks. (NY) paperback available $12.95   **940.53**
1. Frank, Anne, 1929-1945 2. Holocaust, 1933-1945—Personal narratives 3. Netherlands—History—1940-1945, German occupation
ISBN 0-385-42360-8 (pa)   LC 90-53437
"Six Dutch Jewish women who survived the concentration camps in the last months of the war bear witness to the kind of suffering that Anne Frank endured before she died." Booklist

Linenthal, Edward Tabor, 1947-
Preserving memory; the struggle to create America's Holocaust Museum. Viking 1995 336p il o.p.; Columbia Univ. Press paperback available $18.50   **940.53**
1. United States Holocaust Memorial Museum 2. Holocaust, 1933-1945
ISBN 0-231-12407-4 (pa)   LC 94-23410
The author "describes the 15-year effort to create a national museum commemorating the Holocaust. He begins with the creation in May 1978 of the President's Commission on the Holocaust during the Carter administration. He then covers issues related to the location, design, and construction of the museum building. Linenthal's most significant contribution is the chapter on defining and representing the horror of the Holocaust." Libr J
Includes bibliographical references

Lipstadt, Deborah E.
Denying the Holocaust; the growing assault on truth and memory. Free Press 1993 278p o.p.; Plume Bks. paperback available $15   **940.53**
1. Holocaust,   1933-1945—Historiography 2. Antisemitism
ISBN 0-452-27274-2 (pa)   LC 93-9952
This is an "account of the antecedents, origins, and development of the . . . movement to deny that the [Nazi] destruction of European Jewry ever took place at all." Commentary
"Lipstadt has written a disturbing book that deserves a wide readership." Libr J
Includes bibliographical references

Lukacs, John, 1924-
Five days in London, May 1940. Yale Univ. Press 1999 236p $19.95; pa $11.95   **940.53**
1. Halifax, Edward Frederick Lindley Wood, 1st Earl of, 1881-1959 2. Churchill, Sir Winston, 1874-1965 3. World War, 1939-1945—Diplomatic history 4. World War, 1939-1945—Great Britain 5. Great Britain—Politics and government
ISBN 0-300-08030-1; 0-300-08466-8 (pa)
     LC 99-27583
This work focuses on the "chaotic few days during which, according to the author, Hitler came closest to winning the war. . . . Lukacs concentrates on the struggle within the British War Cabinet, which pitted the Prime Minister, Winston Churchill, against the Foreign Secretary, Lord Halifax, a Tory idol and a friend of the King. The point of contention was Halifax's belief that England should attempt to negotiate a general European settlement with Hitler. Churchill's stubborn refusal won out. The author's equally stubborn digging uncovered a stunning amount of defeatism and intrigue against Churchill by contemporary statesmen." New Yorker
Includes bibliographical references

Murray, Williamson
A war to be won; fighting the Second World War, 1937-1945; [by] Williamson Murray, Allan R. Millett. Harvard Univ. Press 2000 656p il $37.50; pa $18.95   **940.53**
1. World War, 1939-1945
ISBN 0-674-00163-X; 0-674-00680-1 (pa)
     LC 99-86624
The authors "juggle various aspects of the conflict—air, naval and ground operations, changes in tactics, partisan resistance and military technology, to name a few—as well as its various theaters and campaigns, including Russia, the North Atlantic, Western Europe, the Pacific, China, North Africa, Italy, the Balkans and Burma. And, unlike many of their peers, they bind these narrative strands together instead of considering them in isolation." N Y Times Book Rev
Includes bibliographical references

Ng, Wendy L.
Japanese American internment during World War II; a history and reference guide; [by] Wendy Ng. Greenwood Press 2002 xxvi, 204p $45   **940.53**
1. Japanese Americans—Evacuation and relocation, 1942-1945
ISBN 0-313-31375-X   LC 00-69128
Contents: Chronology of events in Japanese American history: the Japanese in America before World War II;

Ng, Wendy L.—*Continued*

Evacuation; Life within barbed wire; The question of loyalty: Japanese Americans in the military and draft resisters; Legal challenges to the evacuation and internment; After the war: resettlement and redress; Photographic essay

"The combination of historical facts as presented in the essays and the ideas and sentiments expressed in the primary documents gives readers a vivid sense of this period in history. This readable book would be a solid addition to high school, public, and academic libraries." Voice Youth Advocates

Includes bibliographical references

Novick, Peter

The Holocaust in American life. Houghton Mifflin 1999 373p $27; pa $15   **940.53**
1. Holocaust, 1933-1945 2. Jews—United States
ISBN 0-395-84009-0; 0-618-08232-8 (pa)
                                      LC 99-20074

Novick "examines how a variety of domestic and foreign events have moved Holocaust consciousness to the center of American life and kept it there." Booklist

"A measured, thorough investigation of the process by which the collective memory of the Holocaust has evolved, and a plea to more consciously shape that memory in the future, Novick's study will be a benchmark in Holocaust studies for years to come." Publ Wkly

Includes bibliographical references

Overy, R. J. (Richard James), 1947-

The road to war; [by] Richard Overy with Andrew Wheatcroft. Random House 1990 c1989 364p il maps o.p.; Penguin Bks. paperback available $14.95   **940.53**
1. World War, 1939-1945—Causes
ISBN 0-14-028530-X (pa)   LC 89-10435
First published 1989 in the United Kingdom

"Overy presents the 1920s and 1930s as perceived by the major powers at the time without the benefit of hindsight. There are no 'pure knights' here preparing for the 'good war,' only paranoid politicians haunted by the effects of World War I, the Russian Revolution, and the Great Depression." Libr J

"The book is a concise, highly readable account of how WW II came about." Publ Wkly

Includes bibliographical references

Why the Allies won; [by] Richard Overy. Norton 1996 396p il maps hardcover o.p. paperback available $17.95   **940.53**
1. World War, 1939-1945 2. Strategy
ISBN 0-393-31619-X (pa)   LC 95-52444

"Eschewing the belief that the Allies won solely because of their prodigious production of weapons and equipment, Mr. Overy points out that in the early stages of the war, before the Allies were fully mobilized, the Axis countries held the production advantage, yet failed to achieve victory because Germany's management of supply logistics was far inferior to that of the Allies—frequently as a result of Hitler's wrongheaded interference. . . . Assiduously researched and concisely written, this is a highly perceptive study." N Y Times Book Rev

Includes bibliographical references

The **Oxford** companion to World War II; general editor, I.C.B. Dear; consultant editor, M.R.D. Foot. Oxford Univ. Press 1995 xxii, 1343p il maps hardcover o.p. paperback available $24.95   **940.53**
1. World War, 1939-1945—Encyclopedias
ISBN 0-19-860446-7 (pa)   LC 95-148182

"Nearly 1800 A-Z entries describe key political and military leaders, battles and campaigns, weapons and inventions, alliances and diplomatic efforts, and events and phenomena. . . . Enhanced by 3900 illustrations and maps, the volume boasts well over 100 contributors." Libr J

Reporting World War II. Library of Am. 1995 2v set $70   **940.53**
1. World War, 1939-1945 2. Reporters and reporting
ISBN 1-883011-12-4   LC 94-45463

Also available separately each $35 (v1 ISBN 1-883011-04-3; v2 ISBN 1-883011-05-1)

Contents: v1 American journalism, 1938-1944; v2 American journalism, 1944-1946

This "collection of some 200 entries by nearly 90 writers, drawn from newspapers, magazine articles, broadcast transcripts and book excerpts, recalls WW II campaigns and battles in all theaters but pays attention to the home front as well. It begins with an excerpt from William L. Shirer's *Berlin Diary* and ends with one from John Hersey's *Hiroshima*. . . . This is a treasure trove of war reporting, featuring writing of the highest order." Publ Wkly

Rhodes, Richard, 1937-

Masters of death; the SS-Einsatzgruppen and the invention of the Holocaust. Knopf 2002 335p il maps $27.50; pa $14.95
                                      940.53
1. Holocaust, 1933-1945 2. Germany—History—1933-1945
ISBN 0-375-40900-9; 0-375-70822-7 (pa)
                                      LC 2001-38898

This is an account of "the mass murders of Jews perpetrated by the Einsatzgruppen—special task forces—organized by the SS commanders Himmler and Heydrich before the gruesome death camps industrialized the Final Solution." Publ Wkly

This is "a grotesquely fascinating chronicle. . . . Reading this book is an ordeal, but it is a necessary trial if one is to grasp the full scope of the war against the Jews." Booklist

Ryback, Timothy W.

The last survivor; in search of Martin Zaidenstadt; [by] Timothy Ryback. Pantheon Bks. 1999 195p hardcover o.p. paperback available $12   **940.53**
1. Zaidenstadt, Martin 2. Holocaust, 1933-1945 3. Dachau (Germany: Concentration camp) 4. Dachau (Germany)—Social life and customs
ISBN 0-679-75826-7 (pa)   LC 98-52319

Ryback explores "how the modern inhabitants of Dachau cope with living in the shadow of the infamous Nazi concentration camp. The central figure in the story . . . is the enigmatic figure of Martin Zaidenstadt. A former Polish soldier and inmate of the camp, Zaidenstadt now spends his days sitting in Dachau and lecturing about the camp and his personal history." Libr J

This study "is elegantly written without ever neglecting the magnitude of horror that underlies every gesture, breath and nuance in Dachau." N Y Times Book Rev

Shermer, Michael

Denying history; who says the Holocaust never happened and why do they say it? {by} Michael Shermer, Alex Grobman; foreword by Arthur Hertzberg. University of Calif. Press 2000 312p hardcover o.p. paperback available $16.95   940.53
1. Holocaust, 1933-1945
ISBN 0-520-23469-3 (pa)   LC 00-28690
The authors "respond to specific attacks that have been made over the years against the veracity of the accepted 'facts' of the Holocaust;. . .[they also] discuss historical truth, how we know it, and what motivates some people to become deniers." New Leader
"Using the deniers' own words to tear down their arguments, Shermer and Grobman provide a clear method for determining the reality of past events and supply a powerful weapon for anyone who cares about learning from the credible historical record." Publ Wkly
Includes bibliographical references

Sorel, Nancy Caldwell

The women who wrote the war. Arcade Pub. 1999 458p il $27.95   940.53
1. World War, 1939-1945—Journalists 2. Women journalists
ISBN 1-55970-493-4   LC 99-16177
Also available in paperback from HarperCollins Pubs
Sorel provides "information about the women reporters who covered World War II. Though numbering fewer than 100, these women were extremely dedicated to overcoming the bias of their employers, who often felt that the front was no place for a woman, and of the military itself. The stories of these women reporters—e.g., Lee Miller, Martha Gelhorn—are at once inspiring, frustrating, and sad, and most are certainly worth knowing." Libr J
Includes bibliographical references

Spiegelman, Art

Maus; a survivor's tale. Pantheon Bks. 1996 2v in 1 il $35   940.53
1. Spiegelman, Vladek 2. Holocaust, 1933-1945
ISBN 0-679-40641-7   LC 96-32796
Also available CD-ROM version, The complete Maus; available paperback boxed set edition $28 (ISBN 0-679-74840-7)
A combined edition of Maus (1986) and Maus II (1991)
Contents: My father bleeds history; And here my troubles began
In this work "Spiegelman takes the comic book to a new level of seriousness, portraying Jews as mice and Nazis as cats. Depicting himself being told about the Holocaust by his Polish survivor father, Spiegelman not only explores the concentration-camp experience, but also the guilt, love, and anger between father and son." Rochman. Against borders

Takaki, Ronald T., 1939-

Double victory; a multicultural history of America in World War II; [by] Ronald Takaki. Little, Brown 2000 282p il hardcover o.p. paperback available $15.95   940.53
1. World War, 1939-1945—United States 2. United States—Race relations
ISBN 0-316-83156-5 (pa)   LC 99-40374
"Takaki discusses the experiences of African Americans, Indians, Chicanos, Asian Americans from several

nations, German and Italian Americans, and Jewish Americans. . . . Despite Jim Crow, internment camps, neglected slums, barrios, reservations, and rejection of Jewish refugees, the nation's not-quite-Americans fought bravely in World War II." Booklist

Todorov, Tzvetan, 1939-

Facing the extreme; moral life in the concentration camps; translated by Arthur Denner and Abigail Pollak. Metropolitan Bks. 1996 307p hardcover o.p. paperback available $14.95   940.53
1. Holocaust, 1933-1945 2. Concentration camps 3. Totalitarianism 4. Good and evil
ISBN 0-8050-4264-4 (pa)   LC 95-32056
Original French edition, 1991
An "analysis of what constitutes moral living in the Nazi concentration camps and in the Soviet gulag. The author begins by using the Warsaw Ghetto uprising as an example of classical heroism. He then asserts that although concentration camp life was too oppressive to allow heroic acts like the uprising, it did not mean that living a moral life was impossible in the camps. With insight and precision, Todorov carefully examines such 'everyday' virtues as caring, dignity, and the life of the mind, which helped prisoners preserve their humanity under the most inhumane conditions." Libr J
Includes bibliographical references

Weinberg, Gerhard L.

A world at arms; a global history of World War II. Cambridge Univ. Press 1994 1178p maps $45; pa $25   940.53
1. World War, 1939-1945
ISBN 0-521-44317-2; 0-521-55879-4 (pa)
LC 92-37637
"Beginning with the German invasion of Poland and concluding with the Japanese surrender, this . . . overview of WW II concentrates on the tactical decisions made by Allied and Axis leaders and the interrelationship among the various theaters." Publ Wkly
"Weinberg's unrivaled command of archival sources combine with a smooth writing style to produce a definitive one-volume history of World War II." Libr J
Includes bibliographical references

Witness; voices from the Holocaust; edited by Joshua M. Greene and Shiva Kumar in consultation with Joanne Weiner Rudof; foreword by Lawrence L. Langer; in association with the Fortunoff Video Archive for Holocaust Testimonies, Yale University. Free Press 2000 xxx, 270p il hardcover o.p. paperback available $15

940.53
1. Holocaust, 1933-1945—Personal narratives
ISBN 0-684-86526-2 (pa)   LC 99-58401
In this companion to the PBS series the editors "have woven together the testimonies of 27 individuals into an unforgettable narrative of the Holocaust: starting with pre-WWII Jewish life, they go on to describe the war's out-break, ghettos, resistance and hiding, death camps, death marches, liberation and life after the Holocaust." Publ Wkly
Includes bibliographical references

The **World** reacts to the Holocaust; David S. Wyman, editor; Charles H. Rosenzveig, project director. Johns Hopkins Univ. Press 1996 xxiii, 981p $80   **940.53**
1. Holocaust, 1933-1945
ISBN 0-8018-4969-1   LC 96-15395
This is a "country-by-country chronicle of the impact of the Holocaust on world history. Covering 22 countries and the United Nations, the volume carefully traces the contentions and controversies involved in coming to terms with the events leading up to the Holocaust, from prewar attitudes and perceptions to the political, economic, and cultural legacies in the 1990s." Univ Press Books for Public and Second Sch Libr
Includes bibliographical references

World War II; an encyclopedia of quotations; compiled and edited by Howard J. Langer. Greenwood Press 1999 449p il $83.95
                                         940.53
1. World War, 1939-1945—Quotations 2. Quotations
ISBN 0-313-30018-6   LC 98-26436
This is a collection of 1,554 "quotations dealing with World War II. . . . The first 12 chapters are arranged by type of person quoted . . . and then alphabetically by name. A typical entry has a short introductory paragraph providing biographical and historical information including birth and death years of persons. The remaining chapters cover other sources, including movies and songs." Booklist

Wyman, David S.
The abandonment of the Jews; America and the Holocaust, 1941-1945. Pantheon Bks. 1984 444p o.p.; New Press paperback available $18.95   **940.53**
1. Holocaust, 1933-1945 2. World War, 1939-1945—United States
ISBN 1-56584-415-7 (pa)   LC 84-42711
"Wyman identifies three factors which led the United States to abandon the Jews in Europe (despite full knowledge of what that abandonment would mean): anti-Semitism; a sense of helplessness; and . . . fear of being branded as pro-Jewish." Nation
"A first-rate book for both specialists and generalists." Choice
Includes bibliographical references

Yahil, Leni
The Holocaust; the fate of European Jewry, 1932-1945; translated from the Hebrew by Ina Friedman and Haya Galai. Oxford Univ. Press 1990 808p il maps (Studies in Jewish history) hardcover o.p. paperback available $29.95   **940.53**
1. Holocaust, 1933-1945 2. Jews—Europe
ISBN 0-19-504523-8 (pa)   LC 89-37750
Original Hebrew edition, 1987
This volume "covers all aspects of the subject, such as Jewish resistance and emigration, and the various worldwide efforts, successful and otherwise, at rescue. . . . The most important original contribution to the study of the Holocaust made by Ms. Yahil is that she places it in the political context of that era." N Y Times Book Rev
Includes bibliographical references

Ziegler, Jean, 1934-
The Swiss, the gold, and the dead; translated from the German by John Brownjohn. Harcourt Brace & Co. 1998 322p $27   **940.53**
1. World War, 1939-1945—Destruction and pillage 2. Holocaust, 1933-1945 3. Banks and banking—Corrupt practices 4. World War, 1939-1945—Reparations 5. Germany—Foreign relations—Switzerland 6. Switzerland—Foreign relations—Germany
ISBN 0-15-100334-3   LC 97-36497
"Ziegler details how top Swiss bankers fenced and laundered the gold that the Germans stole from conquered nations' central banks, from Jewish businesses and homes, even from Holocaust victims' teeth." Publ Wkly
"Masterfully translated, this is the most readable book available about the Swiss scandals." Libr J
Includes bibliographical references

Zuccotti, Susan, 1940-
Under his very windows; the Vatican and the Holocaust in Italy. Yale Univ. Press 2000 408p il $29.95; pa $16.95   **940.53**
1. Pius XII, Pope, 1876-1958 2. Jews—Italy 3. Holocaust, 1933-1945 4. Catholic Church—Relations—Judaism
ISBN 0-300-08487-0; 0-300-09310-1 (pa)
                                         LC 00-43307
Zuccotti's "aim is to show that whatever help was given to the Jews by the Catholic Church during the war resulted almost entirely from spontaneous acts by courageous individuals—priests, monks and nuns, and occasionally prelates—and not from any interventions by the Vatican. . . . Zuccotti makes her case strongly. . . . This is a serious and well-researched book." N Y Times Book Rev
Includes bibliographical references

940.54   World War II, 1939-1945 (Military conduct of the war)

Alperovitz, Gar
The decision to use the atomic bomb and the architecture of an American myth; [by] Gar Alperovitz with the assistance of Sanho Tree [et al.] Knopf 1995 843p hardcover o.p. paperback available $18   **940.54**
1. World War, 1939-1945—United States 2. Hiroshima (Japan)—Bombardment, 1945 3. United States—Foreign relations
ISBN 0-679-76285-X (pa)   LC 95-8778
"Alperovitz is the dean of revisionist scholars who argue that the nuclear bombing of Japan was unnecessary and that America bears a hefty responsibility for the cold war. . . . His main and probably most controversial contention is that certain documents pertaining to the decision were doctored, some by none other than Truman himself. Further, Alperovitz sees James Byrnes, Truman's Mephistophelian secretary of state, as a furtive player who nixed such alternative plans as modifying the unconditional-surrender demand and encouraging a Russian declaration of war." Booklist
Includes bibliographical references

Ambrose, Stephen E.

Band of brothers; E Company, 506th Regiment, 101st Airborne from Normandy to Hitler's Eagle's Nest; [by] Stephen Ambrose. Simon & Schuster 2001 333p il maps $25; pa $16   **940.54**

1. United States. Army. Parachute Infantry Regiment, 506th. Company E 2. World War, 1939-1945—Europe

ISBN 0-7432-1638-5; 0-7432-2454-X (pa)

LC 2001-20134

A reissue of the title first published 1992

"Here is the story of the daring E Company, which began the war by parachuting into France on D-Day and ended it by capturing Eagle's Nest, Hitler's outpost in Bavaria." Libr J

"Moving, poignant, and uplifting, this book is highly recommended for medium and large World War II collections." Booklist

Includes bibliographical references

Citizen soldiers; the U.S. Army from the Normandy beaches to the Bulge to the surrender of Germany, June 7, 1944-May 7, 1945. Simon & Schuster 1997 512p il maps hardcover o.p. paperback available $17

940.54

1. World War, 1939-1945—Campaigns—France

ISBN 0-684-84801-5 (pa)   LC 97-23876

This continuation of D-Day focuses on the front-line experiences of American soldiers who fought in northwestern Europe in the war's last years

"These events have all been well documented, but in Ambrose's capable hands, the bloody and dramatic battles fought in northwest Europe in 1944-45 come alive as never before." N Y Times Book Rev

Includes bibliographical references

D-Day, June 6, 1944; the climactic battle of World War II. Simon & Schuster 1994 655p il maps $30; pa $17   **940.54**

1. World War, 1939-1945—Campaigns—France 2. Normandy (France), Attack on, 1944

ISBN 0-671-88403-4; 0-684-80137-X (pa)

LC 93-40353

This is an account of the Allied invasion of Normandy in 1944. The author argues "that the invasion represented a triumph of the old United States Army, whose officers had transformed millions of civilians into a cohesive, highly trained and motivated mass army that, backed by a united nation, won with relative ease." Christ Sci Monit

"Mr. Ambrose wonderfully illuminates the mind of the very young soldier of any nation anywhere who has never been in fighting before." N Y Times Book Rev

Includes bibliographical references

The victors; Eisenhower and his boys, the men of World War II. Simon & Schuster 1998 396p hardcover o.p. paperback available $16   **940.54**

1. Eisenhower, Dwight D. (Dwight David), 1890-1969 2. United States. Army 3. World War, 1939-1945—Campaigns

ISBN 0-684 85629-8 (pa)   LC 98-37808

This work "follows the World War II Allied campaign in Europe from the appointment of Gen. Dwight D.

Eisenhower as commander of the European Theater of Operations to the final surrender of Germany, seven days after Hitler's suicide." N Y Times Book Rev

"The author is a master of letting his subjects tell the story, of standing back and allowing the large lessons to unfold. The result is history with lasting impact." SLJ

Includes bibliographical references

The wild blue; the men and boys who flew the B-24s over Germany 1944-45. Simon & Schuster 2001 299p il $26; pa $16   **940.54**

1. McGovern, George S. (George Stanley), 1922- 2. B-24 bomber 3. Air pilots 4. World War, 1939-1945—Aerial operations

ISBN 0-7432-0339-9; 0-7432-2309-8 (pa)

LC 2001-20563

Ambrose presents profiles of American pilots who flew B-24 bombers focusing on the Dakota Queen piloted by future senator and presidential candidate George McGovern

"Ambrose's narrative flows smoothly, even as he manages to cover each man's story." Libr J

Includes bibliographical references

Astor, Gerald, 1926-

A blood-dimmed tide; the Battle of the Bulge by the men who fought it. Fine, D.I. 1992 532p il maps o.p.; Dell paperback available $6.99   **940.54**

1. Ardennes, Battle of the, 1944-1945 2. World War, 1939-1945—Personal narratives

ISBN 0-440-21574-9 (pa)   LC 91-58657

"Interviewing more than 50 veterans from both sides of the Bulge, Astor . . . has written an objective account of the Ardennes campaign that delineates a complex mix of cowardice and courage, stupidity and brilliance, brutality and grace under fire." Libr J

Includes bibliographical references

Crisis in the Pacific; the battles for the Philippine Islands by the men who fought them—an oral history. Fine, D.I. 1996 478p il o.p.; Dell paperback available $6.99

940.54

1. World War, 1939-1945—Campaigns—Philippines 2. World War, 1939-1945—Personal narratives

ISBN 0-440-23695-9 (pa)   LC 95-50032

This is a study of the "crucial Pacific campaign from the viewpoint of both the individual soldier and military leaders. Astor expresses opinions on many topics, such as Douglas MacArthur as a military leader, the American war plan for the Pacific, and Japanese policy toward POWs." Libr J

Includes bibliographical references

The greatest war; Americans in combat, 1941-1945. Presidio Press 1999 1033p o.p.; Warner Bks. paperback available $6.99

940.54

1. World War, 1939-1945—Personal narratives 2. United States—Armed forces

ISBN 0-446-61047-X (pa)   LC 99-43632

"Beginning with Pearl Harbor and proceeding chronologically to the dropping of the atomic bomb, this book describes army, navy, and marine corps actions through the eyes of the participants. The entries are well chosen, and Astor has arranged them in a fast-paced, smoothly flowing narrative." Libr J

Includes bibliographical references

Astor, Gerald, 1926-—*Continued*

Operation Iceberg; the invasion and conquest of Okinawa in World War II. Fine, D.I. 1995 480p il maps o.p.; Dell paperback available $6.99   **940.54**
1. World War, 1939-1945—Campaigns—Okinawa Island 2. World War, 1939-1945—Personal narratives
ISBN 0-440-22178-1 (pa)   LC 94-68093
In this oral history of the Okinawa campaign Astor provides "a masterful account of the battle as seen through the eyes of both American and Japanese survivors." Libr J

Atkinson, Rick

An army at dawn; the war in North Africa, 1942-1943. Holt & Co. 2002 681p il maps $30; pa $16   **940.54**
1. World War, 1939-1945—Campaigns—North Africa 2. World War, 1939-1945—North Africa
ISBN 0-8050-6288-2; 0-8050-7448-1 (pa)
                                 LC 2002-24130
This is the first volume of a projected World War II trilogy
This "volume covers the conception of Operation Torch through the German surrender in Tunisia in May 1943. . . . An exemplary work that feeds anticipation of the succeeding volumes." Booklist
Includes bibliographical references

Ballard, Robert D.

Return to Midway; [by] Robert D. Ballard and Rick Archbold; principal photography by David Doubilet. . . . National Geographic Soc. 1999 191p il maps $40   **940.54**
1. Midway, Battle of, 1942 2. Shipwrecks 3. World War, 1939-1945—Naval operations
ISBN 0-7922-7500-4   LC 99-10831
In this narrative, Ballard "intersperses chapters on the Battle of Midway with a fascinating account of his search for the U.S.S. *Yorktown*, which was sunk by a Japanese destroyer on June 7, 1942. Period photographs from the battle are combined with those of the *Yorktown* as she rests today, and paintings by marine artist Ken Marschall add detail to complete the record. The lively narrative is punctuated with two Japanese and two American oral history accounts of the battle." Libr J
Includes bibliographical references

Beevor, Antony, 1946-

The fall of Berlin 1945. Viking 2002 xxxvii, 489p il maps $29.95; pa $16 **940.54**
1. Berlin, Battle of, 1945 2. World War, 1939-1945—Germany
ISBN 0-670-03041-4; 0-14-200280-1 (pa)
                                 LC 2002-510674
This narrative covers "the months from January to May in 1945, as Soviet and other Allied troops advanced to Berlin." Publ Wkly
The author "relies on material from American, German, British, French, and Swedish archives and documents from former Soviet files, making the book an invaluable and meticulous account." Booklist

Stalingrad. Viking 1998 493p il maps hardcover o.p. paperback available $16.95
                                     940.54
1. Stalingrad, Battle of, 1942-1943
ISBN 0-14-028458-3 (pa)   LC 98-19346
This study of the Battle of Stalingrad relies on "previously published firsthand accounts in German and Russian along with newly available Soviet archival sources and caches of letters from the front." Publ Wkly
"Beevor has composed a history of Stalingrad unlikely to be bettered." Booklist
Includes bibliographical references

Blair, Clay, 1925-1998

Hitler's U-boat war. Random House 1996-1998 2v il maps hardcover o.p. paperbacks available ea $19.95   **940.54**
1. World War, 1939-1945—Naval operations—Submarine 2. World War, 1939-1945—Atlantic Ocean
                                 LC 96-2275
Contents: v1 The hunters, 1939-1942 (ISBN 0-679-64032-0); v2 The hunted, 1942-1945 (ISBN 0-679-64033-9)
This is a history of the German submarine campaign against Allied forces during the Second World War
This is "the most thorough study of the U-Boat campaign available; it includes a massive amount of detailed statistics." Libr J [review of volume 1]
Includes bibliographical references

Blum, Howard, 1948-

The brigade; an epic story of vengeance, salvation, and World War II. HarperCollins Pubs. 2001 326p il hardcover o.p. paperback available $13.95   **940.54**
1. Carmi, Israel 2. Pinchuk, Arie 3. Peltz, Johanan 4. Great Britain. Army. Jewish Brigade 5. World War, 1939-1945—Personal narratives
ISBN 0-06-093283-X (pa)   LC 2001-24324
This is an account of three members of the Jewish Brigade who fought with the British Army during World War II
"This book is not a standard military history, but is written more like a novel. It is packed with detail but moves along quickly." SLJ

Boyne, Walter J., 1929-

Clash of Titans; World War II at sea. Simon & Schuster 1995 381p il maps hardcover o.p. paperback available $16
                                     940.54
1. World War, 1939-1945—Naval operations
ISBN 0-684-83914-8 (pa)   LC 95-5432
This volume covers "the great naval campaigns from 1939 to 1945. Boyne vividly depicts all the pivotal battles and skillfully analyzes each nation's naval tactics and strategy as he explains how seapower shaped and changed the course of the war." Libr J
Includes bibliographical references

Clash of wings; World War II in the air. Simon & Schuster 1994 415p il hardcover o.p. paperback available $16   **940.54**
1. World War, 1939-1945—Aerial operations
ISBN 0-684-83915-6 (pa)   LC 93-46526
"A one-volume overview of the leaders, aircraft, technology, tactics, and strategy as well as the events of the

Boyne, Walter J., 1929——*Continued*
aerial side of World War II. Knowledgeable and literate,
Boyne is more successful than most at covering so large
a topic." Booklist

Includes bibliographical references

Bradley, James
Flags of our fathers; [by] James Bradley
with Ron Powers. Bantam Bks. 2000 376p
$24.95; pa $13.95   **940.54**
1. Rosenthal, Joe, 1911- 2. United States. Marine
Corps 3. Iwo Jima, Battle of, 1945
ISBN 0-553-11133-7; 0-553-38029-X (pa)
                                    LC 00-25803
This is the "story of the most famous photograph to
come out of World War II, the flag-raising on Mount Su-
ribachi during the Battle of Iwo Jima in February 1945.
Bradley is the son of one of the six men immortalized
in that remarkable photo, and his gripping narrative, vivid descriptions, and heartfelt style make this a powerful
story of courage, humility, and tragedy." Libr J

Includes bibliographical references

Breitman, Richard, 1947-
Official secrets; what the Nazis planned,
what the British and Americans knew. Hill &
Wang 1998 325p hardcover o.p. paperback
available $22   **940.54**
1. World War, 1939-1945—Atrocities 2. Holocaust,
1933-1945 3. Germany—Politics and government—
1933-1945
ISBN 0-8090-0184-5 (pa)   LC 98-7997
Breitman sheds new light on "evidence that Britain's
top intelligence analysts knew, as early as September
1941, that the Germans were systematically carrying out
mass murder of Jews in Nazi-occupied Soviet territories
and planning their liquidation in the lands they conquered." Publ Wkly
This "is a remarkable study, concise yet carefully nuanced." N Y Times Book Rev

Brokaw, Tom
An album of memories; personal histories
from the greatest generation. Random House
2001 314p il maps $29.95; pa $14.95
                                        940.54
1. World War, 1939-1945—Personal narratives
ISBN 0-375-50581-4; 0-375-76041-5 (pa)
                                  LC 2001-273436
Also available large print edition $29.95 (ISBN 0-375-
43134-9)
This volume "gathers letters written to Brokaw by
Americans who lived through the Depression and World
War II and, in some cases, letters written by their children. Brokaw provides a brief introduction and a time
line for each chapter; these cover the Depression, the war
in Europe and in the Pacific, and the wartime 'home
front,' closing with 'Reflections.' The book is lavishly illustrated with reproductions of photographs, drawings,
documents, and other memorabilia of the era." Booklist

The greatest generation. Random House
1998 412p il $24.95; pa $13.95   **940.54**
1. World War, 1939-1945—Personal narratives
ISBN 0-375-50202-5; 0-385-33462-1 (pa)
                                    LC 98-44267
Also available large print edition pa $24.95 (ISBN 0-
375-70569-4)

Brokaw presents profiles of some fifty men and wom-
en who came of age during the Depression and World
War II, focusing particularly on their experiences of the
war
"If not the greatest, all Brokaw's heroes—tall and
short, famous and obscure—are part of the great generation that turned the old Chinese curse 'May you live in
interesting times' into a blessing." Time

Budiansky, Stephen
Battle of wits; the complete story of
codebreaking in World War II. Free Press
2000 436p il hardcover o.p. paperback
available $16   **940.54**
1. World War, 1939-1945—Secret service 2. Cryptography
ISBN 0-7432-1734-9 (pa)   LC 00-28418
In this account of cryptography in World War II, the
author "recounts the code breakers' battles with the enci-
phering schemes and technical designs of Germany's and
Japan's coding machines." Booklist
"Budiansky is a master at interweaving the science of
code breaking within its cultural and historical contexts."
Publ Wkly

Includes bibliographical references

Childers, Thomas
Wings of morning; the story of the last
American bomber shot down over Germany
in World War II. Addison-Wesley 1995 276p
il hardcover o.p. paperback available $18
                                        940.54
1. World War, 1939-1945—Aerial operations
ISBN 0-201-40722-1 (pa)   LC 94-24296
"This outstanding remembrance, possibly the most
original title among this year's World War II anniversary
works, was reconstructed from the 'last American bomber's' letters home." Booklist

Includes bibliographical references

Clayton, Tim
Finest hour; the battle of Britain; [by] Tim
Clayton and Phil Craig. Simon & Schuster
2000 349p il hardcover o.p. paperback
available $14   **940.54**
1. Britain, Battle of, 1940 2. World War, 1939-
1945—Aerial operations 3. World War, 1939-1945—
Great Britain
ISBN 0-684-86931-4 (pa)   LC 00-33904
Companion volume to PBS television documentary
"This volume about Britain's defiance of the seemingly victorious Nazis in 1940 combines a chronicle of
meta-events, such as the French surrender, Churchill's
speeches, and Roosevelt's hand-wringing, with the personal experiences of several British soldiers, pilots, and
sailors as well as some U.S. correspondents thrown in for
good measure." Booklist

Costello, John, 1943-1995
The Pacific War. Rawson, Wade 1981
742p il maps o.p.; Quill paperback available
$21.95   **940.54**
1. World War, 1939-1945—Pacific Ocean
ISBN 0-688-01620-0 (pa)   LC 81-7381
A "history of World War II as it was played out in
the Pacific theater. . . . Emphasizing the role played by
Allied intelligence sources during the early period of the
war, Costello analyzes the actual battles from Pearl Harbor to the atomic bombing of Japan." Booklist

Includes bibliographical references

Daws, Gavan

Prisoners of the Japanese; POWs of World War II in the Pacific. Morrow 1994 462p il map hardcover o.p. paperback available $16
940.54

1. World War, 1939-1945—Prisoners and prisons 2. Prisoners of war 3. World War, 1939-1945—Pacific Ocean

ISBN 0-688-14370-9 (pa) LC 93-49363

This is an "account of the treatment that more than 140,000 American, Australian, British and Dutch prisoners of war . . . [received] at the hands of the Japanese in World War II." N Y Times Book Rev

"Daws offers a well-written thoroughly researched account of these POWs. . . . An exceptionally worthwhile addition to the literature on the war in the Pacific." Booklist

Includes bibliographical references

Dunnigan, James F.

The Pacific War encyclopedia; [by] James F. Dunnigan and Albert A. Nofi. Facts on File 1998 2v il maps set $137.50 **940.54**

1. World War, 1939-1945—Encyclopedias

ISBN 0-8160-3439-7 LC 97-15634

"Entries are arranged alphabetically and include . . . (military personnel and politicos from all sides, as well as persons such as Charles Lindbergh and Ernie Pyle), places (Manchukuo, Melbourne, Nagasaki, Timor, etc.) and events (Battle of Iwo Jima, Port Chicago mutiny)." Booklist

This work "is lively as well as informative, and . . . will be attractive to military buffs while still useful to more serious researchers." Libr J

Victory at sea; World War II in the Pacific; [by] James F. Dunnigan and Albert A. Nofi. Morrow 1995 612p hardcover o.p. paperback available $17 **940.54**

1. World War, 1939-1945—Campaigns—Pacific Ocean 2. World War, 1939-1945—Naval operations

ISBN 0-688-14947-2 (pa) LC 94-41232

This "is a collection of hundreds of facts on the Pacific War divided into 11 chapters that cover the campaigns, ships, and aircraft of both sides. There is a biographical chapter, a gazeteer, and a chronology." Libr J

Ford, Daniel

Flying Tigers; Claire Chennault and the American Volunteer Group. Smithsonian Institution Press 1991 450p il (Smithsonian history of aviation series) hardcover o.p. paperback available $17.09 **940.54**

1. Chennault, Claire Lee, 1890-1958 2. China. Air Force. American Volunteer Group 3. World War, 1939-1945—Aerial operations

ISBN 1-56098-541-0 (pa) LC 90-26953

This is a study of Claire Chennault and the American Volunteer Group aviators who flew for China early in World War II

"Myths and exaggerations that surround the Flying Tigers create a difficult task for any author seeking truth. Based on careful research that includes documents, diaries, and interviews, Ford's book appears to come close to the actual facts." Choice

Includes bibliographical references

Frank, Richard B.

Downfall; the end of the Imperial Japanese Empire. Random House 1999 484p il o.p.; Penguin Bks. paperback available $16
940.54

1. World War, 1939-1945—Japan 2. World War, 1939-1945—Aerial operations 3. Japan—History—1868-1945

ISBN 0-14-100146-1 (pa) LC 99-11838

"Weaving together the strands of military and diplomatic events, Frank contends that absent the bombings of Hiroshima and Nagasaki the war would have continued for at least several more months, at a cost in Japanese and Allied civilian and combatant lives far in excess of the admittedly awful toll that the atomic bombs exacted. A powerful work of history." Libr J

Includes bibliographical references

Fussell, Paul, 1924-

Wartime: understanding and behavior in the Second World War. Oxford Univ. Press 1989 330p il $35; pa $16.95 **940.54**

1. World War, 1939-1945—United States 2. World War, 1939-1945—Great Britain 3. World War, 1939-1945—Propaganda

ISBN 0-19-503797-9; 0-19-506577-8 (pa)

LC 89-2875

In this book Fussell "seeks to evoke the psychological and emotional culture of Americans and Britons during the Second World War." Newsweek

"Fussell's version of the war doesn't, perhaps, exactly 'balance the scales,' but it is a useful corrective. Nobody who reads it will come away thinking about the war complacently." New Repub

Includes bibliographical references

Goldstein, Donald M.

D-Day Normandy; the story and photographs; by Donald M. Goldstein, Katherine V. Dillon, and J. Michael Wenger. Pergamon-Brassey's 1994 180p il maps hardcover o.p. paperback available $19.95
940.54

1. Normandy (France), Attack on, 1944 2. World War, 1939-1945—Campaigns—France

ISBN 1-57488-023-3 (pa) LC 93-35473

This volume "chronicles the events in picture form, with newly released information from the British and American archives." Libr J

Includes bibliographical references

The way it was; Pearl Harbor, the original photographs; {by} Donald M. Goldstein, Katherine V. Dillon and J. Michael Wenger. Pergamon-Brassey's 1991 181p il maps hardcover o.p. paperback available $19.95
940.54

1. Pearl Harbor (Oahu, Hawaii), Attack on, 1941—Pictorial works

ISBN 1-57488-359-3 (pa) LC 90-49572

This is a collection of photographs of the Japanese attack on Pearl Harbor in 1941

"The 430 prints in this . . . collection were gathered from various Japanese and U.S. sources, and most have never been seen by the general public. The majority were taken during the height of the air raid itself, many from Japanese cockpits. . . . The overall effect is to give the reader an uncanny sense of being present at the battle." Libr J

Greene, Bob, 1947-

Duty; a father, his son, and the man who won the war. Morrow 2000 295p $25; pa $14
940.54

1. Tibbets, Paul W. 2. Hiroshima (Japan)—Bombardment, 1945 3. World War, 1939-1945
ISBN 0-380-97849-0; 0-380-81411-0 (pa)
LC 00-710184
Also available large print edition pa $25 (ISBN 0-06-019755-2)
Greene, a columnist for the Chicago Tribune, returns to his hometown to see his dying father. He "decides to seek out his father's longtime hero—an 83-year-old fellow WWII vet and Ohioan named Paul Tibbets. Tibbets was the man who, as a 29-year-old lieutenant colonel, piloted the *Enola Gay*, the plane that dropped the atomic bomb on Hiroshima. Combining excerpts from his father's wartime journals, interviews with Tibbets and his own personal recollections, Greene pays homage to the ideals of his father and conveys successfully what WWII meant to men of that generation." Publ Wkly

Hastings, Max

Overlord: D-Day and the battle for Normandy. Simon & Schuster 1984 368p il maps hardcover o.p. paperback available $22.95
940.54

1. Operation Overlord 2. Normandy (France), Attack on, 1944
ISBN 0-671-55435-2 (pa)
LC 83-20439
Hastings presents an "analysis of the Normandy campaign. He . . . {considers} the limits of the Allied armies' fighting power compared to the Wehrmacht." Libr J
"Hastings' reportage of the battle is not unworthy to stand with that of the best journalists and writers who witnessed it. . . . He has managed to recreate what it was like for almost everyone who was there." N Y Times Book Rev
Includes bibliographical references

Hersey, John, 1914-1993

Hiroshima; a new edition with a final chapter written forty years after the explosion. Knopf 1985 196p il $26; pa $6.50
940.54

1. Hiroshima (Japan)—Bombardment, 1945 2. Atomic bomb 3. World War, 1939-1945—Japan
ISBN 0-394-54844-2; 0-679-72103-7 (pa)
LC 85-40346
First published 1946
An account of the aftermath of the first atomic bomb as reflected in the lives of six survivors

Hicks, George, 1936-

The comfort women; Japan's brutal regime of enforced prostitution in the Second World War. Norton 1995 c1994 303p il maps hardcover o.p. paperback available $14.95
940.54

1. Comfort women 2. World War, 1939-1945—Women 3. Sino-Japanese Conflict, 1937-1945
ISBN 0-393-31694-7 (pa)
LC 95-2162
The author begins his "report with a historical survey of wartime sexual exploitation of women, then narrows the focus to the 'comfort women' system developed by the Japanese. The copious testimony of victims is shockingly graphic. . . . This significant addition to 'the poor record of mankind to womankind, especially in war,'

properly approaches the subject as a human-rights issue tied to the rise of feminism in Asia." Publ Wkly
Includes bibliographical references

Howarth, David Armine, 1912-

We die alone; by David Howarth. Adventure Lib. 1996 218p il $40
940.54

1. Baalsrud, Jan 2. Escapes 3. World War, 1939-1945—Prisoners and prisons 4. Prisoners of war 5. Norway—History
ISBN 1-88528-306-7
LC 96-83530
Also available in paperback from Lyons Press
A reissue of the title first published 1955
"An ambush by Nazi soldiers kills all but one of the commandos on a mission in Norway. Wounded Jan Baalsrud survives blinding snow, frostbite, delirium, and self-amputation before escaping to freedom." Booklist

Hoyt, Edwin Palmer

The GI's war; the story of American soldiers in Europe in World War II; [by] Edwin P. Hoyt. McGraw-Hill 1988 620p il maps o.p.; Cooper Sq. Pubs. paperback available $16.95
940.54

1. World War, 1939-1945—Campaigns 2. Soldiers—United States
ISBN 0-8154-1031-X (pa)
LC 87-29868
The author "uses simple, almost stark, stories to establish the matter-of-fact attitude of rank-and-file American soldiers who fought the Germans. A reporter and foxhole-level narrator, he relies heavily on letters, tapes, and interviews from junior officers and enlisted men who served in the U.S. Army's combat arms in the European theater." Libr J
Includes bibliographical references

Irwin, John P., 1926-

Another river, another town; a teenage tank gunner comes of age in combat, 1945. Random House 2002 176p $21.95; pa $11.95
940.54

1. World War, 1939-1945—Personal narratives 2. World War, 1939-1945—Campaigns—Germany
ISBN 0-375-50775-2; 0-375-75963-8 (pa)
LC 2001-48482
This "memoir of an 18-year-old GI tank gunner on the German front in 1945 conveys the romance of combat as well as the fear and slaughter with a wry honesty and with no slick talk of innocence lost. . . . Military buffs will appreciate Irwin's ironic detachment, which still never denies the righteousness of the cause and the courage of those suddenly at war." Booklist

Keil, Sally Van Wagenen

Those wonderful women in their flying machines; the unknown heroines of World War II. rev and expanded ed. Four Directions Press 1990 418p il $24.95
940.54

1. Women Airforce Service Pilots (U.S.) 2. World War, 1939-1945—Women 3. World War, 1939-1945—Aerial operations
ISBN 0-9627659-0-2
LC 90-84246
First published 1979 by Rawson, Wade
"Using a narrative approach, Keil views the courageous endeavors of World War II women flyers who served in a division of the U.S. Army Air Force as Women's Airforce Service Pilots (WASPs)." Booklist

Knox, Donald, 1936-

Death march; the survivors of Bataan. Harcourt Brace Jovanovich 1981 xxv, 482p il maps hardcover o.p. paperback available $18

940.54

1. World War, 1939-1945—Prisoners and prisons
2. World War, 1939-1945—Campaigns—Philippines
3. Prisoners of war—United States
ISBN 0-15-625224-4 (pa)   LC 81-47555
The author records "recollections of some 68 survivors of the Japanese capture of Bataan. . . . Some of these soldiers, nurses, pilots, sailors, and others went to prison camp, some escaped to join guerrilla bands, some ended the war working in Japan and Manchuria as slave labor." Libr J

Lamb, Richard

War in Italy, 1943-1945; a brutal story. St. Martin's Press 1994 c1993 335p o.p.; Da Capo Press paperback available $18.50

940.54

1. World War, 1939-1945—Italy 2. Italy—History—1914-1945
ISBN 0-306-80688-6 (pa)   LC 94-1116
"A Thomas Dunne book"
First published 1993 in the United Kingdom
"Based in part on newly opened Italian archives, Lamb's review of the final two years of WW II from the Italian viewpoint offers several surprises. Chronicling the atrocities perpetrated by the Nazis against Italian civilians, the persecution of Italian Jews and the widespread slaughter of surrendering Italian soldiers, he also dwells on the attempted annexation of northwest Italy by de Gaulle and of northeast Italy by Tito." Publ Wkly

Leckie, Robert

Okinawa; the last battle of World War II. Viking 1995 220p il hardcover o.p. paperback available $13.95   **940.54**

1. World War, 1939-1945—Campaigns—Okinawa Island
ISBN 0-14-017389-7 (pa)   LC 94-39145
In this history of the Battle of Okinawa "Leckie supplies an accessible historical overview of a perplexing war tactic, the kamikaze attack." Booklist

Lee, Bruce

Marching orders; the untold story of World War II. Crown 1995 608p il maps o.p.; Da Capo Press paperback available $20   **940.54**

1. World War, 1939-1945—Secret service 2. Cryptography 3. World War, 1939-1945—Japan
ISBN 0-306-81036-0 (pa)   LC 94-41998
This "study argues that the U.S. breaking of Japanese diplomatic and military codes played a major role as well in the defeat of Nazi Germany. Lee . . . suggests that intercepts expressing Germany's commitment to world conquest helped determine the Allied policy of unconditional surrender." Publ Wkly
"Many of the mysteries that have eluded historians since the end of the war are much clarified. . . . This is the most significant publication about World War II since the recent series of books on the Ultra revelations and should be purchased by all libraries." Libr J
Includes bibliographical references

Lifton, Robert Jay, 1926-

Hiroshima in America; fifty years of denial; {by} Robert Jay Lifton & Greg Mitchell. Putnam 1995 425p il o.p.; Avon Bks. paperback available $18.95   **940.54**

1. Atomic bomb 2. Hiroshima (Japan)—Bombardment, 1945
ISBN 0-380-72764-1 (pa)   LC 95-13734
"A Grosset/Putnam book"
Lifton and Mitchell examine "the reaction of the American people to the bombing of Hiroshima in 1945 and its domestic aftermath. The authors examine what they perceive to be a conspiracy by the government to mislead and suppress information about the actual bombing, Truman's decision to drop the bomb, and the birth and mismanagement of the beginning of the nuclear age." Libr J
Includes bibliographical references

Linderman, Gerald F.

The world within war; America's combat experience in World War II. Free Press 1997 408p o.p.; Harvard Univ. Press paperback available $19.95   **940.54**

1. Soldiers—United States 2. World War, 1939-1945—Campaigns
ISBN 0-674-96202-8 (pa)   LC 97-36361
"Linderman considers the various experiences affecting soldiers, principally infantrymen, during the course of the war." Booklist
This "is destined to rank among the finest books about the American fighting experience in World War II." N Y Times Book Rev
Includes bibliographical references

Manchester, William

Goodbye, darkness; a memoir of the Pacific War. Little, Brown 1980 401p il hardcover o.p. paperback available $16.95   **940.54**

1. World War, 1939-1945—Pacific Ocean 2. World War, 1939-1945—Personal narratives
ISBN 0-316-50111-5 (pa)   LC 80-17310
This memoir arises from a 1978 trip the author made "to Pacific battlefields, seeking to exorcise three decades of nightmares dating to wartime days as a Marine Corps sergeant. . . . First tracing his family background, youth, enlistment, training, and embarkation from San Diego, Manchester unravels a memoir featuring historical reconstruction, disjointed flash-forwards, shocking vignettes, [and] redoubtable vocabulary." Choice

Marks, Leo

Between silk and cyanide; a codemaker's war, 1941-1945. Free Press 1999 613p il hardcover o.p. paperback available $17

940.54

1. Great Britain. Special Operations Executive 2. World War, 1939-1945—Secret service 3. World War, 1939-1945—Personal narratives
ISBN 0-684-86780-X (pa)   LC 99-17581
The author chronicles his "career as a cryptologist with British Intelligence during World War II. As a codemaker and codebreaker for the super-secret Special Operations Executive (SOE) in London, Marks played a major role in the handling of covert operations throughout Occupied Europe." Libr J
This "is essential reading, not just for students of secret warfare, but for everyone who values the human spirit and the power of a writer to bear witness to it." New Leader

May, Ernest R.

Strange victory; Hitler's conquest of France. Hill & Wang 2000 594p il maps hardcover o.p. paperback available $15

940.54

1. World War, 1939-1945—France 2. France—History—1940-1945, German occupation
ISBN 0-8090-8854-1 (pa)   LC 99-53619

This is an analysis of "the defeat of France in 1940. . . . [May argues that] France misjudged German intentions. If the French had anticipated the Ardennes offensive, it is doubtful that they would have been defeated when and as they were." N Y Times Book Rev

"Military and history buffs should find this work especially attractive, but the smoothly flowing narrative and avoidance of overly technical jargon will allow general readers to appreciate this fresh look at an old controversy." Booklist

Miller, Nathan, 1927-

War at sea; a naval history of World War II. Scribner 1995 592p il maps o.p.; Oxford Univ. Press paperback available $29.95

940.54

1. World War, 1939-1945—Naval operations
ISBN 0-19-511038-2 (pa)   LC 95-8484

"A Lisa Drew book"

The author "relates the history of the last great sea war for the general reader, from the sinking of the passenger ship *Athenia* on September 2, 1939, to the surrender ceremony aboard the USS *Missouri* on September 2, 1945." Publ Wkly

"Miller's research—primarily on the Royal Navy—and a reading of hundreds of pertinent monographs has enabled him to fashion a briskly paced narrative that will both inform and entertain." Choice

Includes bibliographical references

Morison, Samuel Eliot, 1887-1976

History of United States naval operations in World War II; introduction by Dudley Wright Knox. University of Ill. Press 2001-2002 15v il maps apply to publisher for price and availability

940.54

1. World War, 1939-1945—Naval operations
LC 00-64840

A reissue of the title first published 1947-1962 by Little, Brown

Contents: v1 The Battle of the Atlantic, September 1939-May 1943; v2 Operations in North African Waters, October 1942-June 1943; v3 The rising sun in the Pacific, 1931-April 1942; v4 Coral Sea, Midway, and submarine actions, May 1942-August 1942; v5 The struggle for Guadalcanal, August 1942-February 1943; v6 Breaking the Bismarcks barrier, 22 July 1942-1 May 1944; v7 Aleutians, Gilberts and Marshalls, June 1942-April 1944; v8 New Guinea and the Marianas, March 1944-August 1944; v9 Sicily, Salerno, Anzio, January 1943-June 1944; v10 The Atlantic Battle won, May 1943-May 1945; v11 The invasion of France and Germany, 1944-1945; v12 Leyte, June 1944-January 1945; v13 The liberation of the Philippines, Luzon, Mindanao, the Visayas, 1944-1945; v14 Victory in the Pacific, 1945; v15 Supplement and general index

Includes bibliographical references

Moskin, J. Robert

Mr. Truman's war; the final victories of World War II and the birth of the postwar world. Random House 1996 411p il o.p.; University Press of Kan. paperback available $19.95

940.54

1. Truman, Harry S., 1884-1972 2. World War, 1939-1945—United States
ISBN 0-7006-1184-3 (pa)   LC 95-46449

Just hours after Roosevelt's death, Truman "began to deal with Churchill, Stalin, and de Gaulle to win the war and shape the postwar world. In five short months, Truman faced more difficult and more world-altering decisions than any other president before him. . . . [The author] provides rich detail of this brief period." Libr J

Includes bibliographical references

Nelson, Craig

The first heroes; the extraordinary story of the Doolittle Raid—America's first World War II victory. Viking 2002 430p il $27.95; pa $15

940.54

1. Doolittle, James Harold, 1896-1993 2. United States. Army Air Forces 3. World War, 1939-1945—Japan 4. World War, 1939-1945—Aerial operations
ISBN 0-670-03087-2; 0-14-200341-7 (pa)
LC 2002-28092

"The Doolittle Raid in April 1942 consisted of 16 B-25 bombers, crewed by 80 volunteers, who made the first air raid on the home islands of Japan. Four months after Pearl Harbor, they struggled off the USS *Hornet*, flew halfway across the Pacific, bombed Tokyo, and carried on into China." Libr J

"The most interesting part of the book is the harrowing story of survival as crew members are forced to ditch their planes on the Asian mainland. This is a thrilling real-life saga that both informs and inspires." Booklist

Includes bibliographical references

No end save victory; perspectives on World War II; essays by Stephen E. Ambrose [et al.] ; edited by Robert Cowley. Putnam 2001 688p il maps o.p.; Berkley Pub. Group paperback available $16.95 **940.54**

1. World War, 1939-1945—Campaigns
ISBN 0-425-18338-6 (pa)   LC 00-45694

This collection of essays called from MHQ: the quarterly journal of military history includes articles by Caleb Carr, Stanley Weintraub and Stephen Ambrose

Norman, Elizabeth M.

We band of angels; the untold story of American nurses trapped on Bataan by the Japanese. Random House 1999 327p il maps o.p.; Atria Bks. paperback available $14.95

940.54

1. World War, 1939-1945—Medical care 2. World War, 1939-1945—Prisoners and prisons 3. Prisoners of war 4. Nurses
ISBN 0-671-78718-7 (pa)   LC 98-45998

The author relates the experiences of 77 American Army and Navy nurses who were taken prisoner on Bataan

Norman "tells their harrowing story through survivor interviews as well as letters and journals kept by the nurses during this time. Her book is a well-written account of an obscure piece of World War II history." Libr J

Includes bibliographical references

Nossiter, Adam

The Algeria Hotel; France, memory, and the Second World War. Houghton Mifflin 2001 302p il maps $26 **940.54**

1. World War, 1939-1945—France 2. France—History—1940-1945, German occupation

ISBN 0-395-90245-2   LC 00-69458

"The rationalizations that let the French dispose of the past are the subject of this sensitive book, which covers the trial of a former cabinet minister, the Vichy memory hole and the interpretation of a Nazi atrocity." N Y Times Book Rev

"This is a powerfully revealing and important contribution to a continuing controversy." Booklist

Includes bibliographical references

Overy, R. J. (Richard James), 1947-

The Battle of Britain; the myth and the reality; by Richard Overy. Norton 2001 177p maps hardcover o.p. paperback available $13.95   **940.54**

1. Britain, Battle of, 1940

ISBN 0-393-32297-1 (pa)   LC 00-69249

First published 2000 in the United Kingdom with title: The Battle

This is an "account of the battle, its effects on the civilian population and its current place in history." N Y Times Book Rev

Includes bibliographical references

Patton, George S. (George Smith), 1885-1945

War as I knew it; by George S. Patton, Jr.; annotated by Paul D. Harkins. Houghton Mifflin 1947 425p il maps hardcover o.p. paperback available $18   **940.54**

1. World War, 1939-1945—Campaigns

ISBN 0-395-73529-7 (pa)

Edited by Beatrice Ayer Patton

An account of the General's WWII European campaigns from the fight for Sicily to the conquest of Germany based on a series of "open letters" written to his wife

Persico, Joseph E.

Roosevelt's secret war; FDR and World War II espionage. Random House 2001 xxiv, 564p il map hardcover o.p. paperback available $15.95   **940.54**

1. Roosevelt, Franklin D. (Franklin Delano), 1882-1945 2. World War, 1939-1945—Secret service

ISBN 0-375-76126-8 (pa)   LC 2001-19106

This is an "account of [Franklin Delano] Roosevelt's experiences with World War II intelligence operations." N Y Times (Late N Y Ed)

"World War II historians and military buffs will welcome this extremely well-written book." Libr J

Includes bibliographical references

Prange, Gordon William, 1910-1980

At dawn we slept; the untold story of Pearl Harbor; [by] Gordon W. Prange in collaboration with Donald M. Goldstein and Katherine V. Dillon. Viking 1991 889p il hardcover o.p. paperback available $20.95   **940.54**

1. Pearl Harbor (Oahu, Hawaii), Attack on, 1941

ISBN 0-14-015734-4 (pa)   LC 91-50176

First published 1981 by McGraw-Hill

The author "offers a comprehensive account of Japanese preparations for the attack, the origins and extent of American unpreparedness, and the aftermath of the attack on both sides." Booklist

Includes bibliographical references

Miracle at Midway; [by] Gordon W. Prange, Donald M. Goldstein and Katherine V. Dillon. McGraw-Hill 1982 469p il maps o.p.; Penguin Bks. paperback available $20   **940.54**

1. Midway, Battle of, 1942

ISBN 0-14-006814-7 (pa)   LC 82-4691

This is an account of the American victory over the Japanese at Midway in June 1942

"The authors present a clear, balanced, technically accurate account with penetrating insights into the nature of military command as well as the battle's lessons for naval warfare." America

Includes bibliographical references

Read, Anthony

The fall of Berlin; [by] Anthony Read and David Fisher. Norton 1993 513p il maps o.p.; Da Capo Press paperback available $18.50   **940.54**

1. Berlin, Battle of, 1945 2. World War, 1939-1945—Germany 3. Germany—History—1933-1945

ISBN 0-306-80619-3 (pa)   LC 92-28641

A description of "the bombing of Berlin by the British and Americans and how the Russian Army fought its way toward and through Berlin in 1945. The authors intend no startling new interpretations or profound analysis. Instead, they offer vignettes, often based on diaries, to describe life in Berlin late in the war. They also retell the story of fanatical Nazi leaders and of the Wehrmacht's desperate efforts to defend the city. The result is a highly readable and, at the same time, sophisticated and reliable narrative history." Libr J

Includes bibliographical references

Rees, Laurence, 1957-

War of the century; when Hitler fought Stalin. Norton 2000 256p il $27.95   **940.54**

1. World War, 1939-1945—Soviet Union

ISBN 1-56584-599-4

First published 1999 in the United Kingdom

The author argues that the "Russo-German War of 1941-1945 was a one-of-a-kind death struggle between two ruthless dictatorships, as well as an ideological conflict that gave neither combatant any room for compromise." Publ Wkly

"This well-illustrated companion volume to the BBC-TV series outlines the major events and historical threads of the period and uses, to good effect, recently released Soviet information as well as the recollections of surviving participants from all sides." Libr J

Sandler, Stanley, 1937-

Segregated skies; all-black combat squadrons of WW II. Smithsonian Institution Press 1992 217p il (Smithsonian history of aviation series) hardcover o.p. paperback available $17.95   **940.54**

1. United States. Army Air Forces 2. World War, 1939-1945—Aerial operations 3. World War, 1939-1945—African Americans

ISBN 1-56098-917-3 (pa)   LC 91-39452

The author "details the World War II experiences of blacks in the three fighter groups that shattered the U.S. Army Air Corps' all-white policy. He begins with the government's 1940 decision to develop 'colored personnel for the aviation service' by training them in isolation outside Tuskegee, Alabama, and concludes with descriptions of combat in North Africa and southern Europe." Libr J

Includes bibliographical references

Sebag-Montefiore, Hugh

Enigma: the battle for the code. Wiley 2000 422p il $30; pa $16.95   **940.54**

1. Cryptography 2. World War, 1939-1945—Secret service

ISBN 0-471-40738-0; 0-471-49035-0 (pa)

     LC 00-43920

This is the story of the German Enigma code

"Describing the breaking of the German naval code during World War II, is both engrossing and exciting. Much of the information presented here is based on recently declassified documents." Booklist

Includes bibliographical references

Sides, Hampton, 1962-

Ghost soldiers; the forgotten epic story of World War II's most dramatic mission. Doubleday 2001 342p il maps $24.95

     940.54

1. United States. Army. Ranger Battalion, 6th 2. World War, 1939-1945—Campaigns—Philippines 3. World War, 1939-1945—Prisoners and prisons

ISBN 0-385-49564-1   LC 2001-17337

Also available Random House large print edition $24.95 (ISBN 0-375-43110-1)

Sides presents an account of a military operation in the Pacific during World War II. "A force of 121 soldiers from the invading United States Army's Sixth Ranger Battalion was ordered to liberate a prisoner of war camp near the town of Cabanatuan. With the aid of a group of Filipino guerrillas, the mission was accomplished." N Y Times Book Rev

"The author's excellent grasp of human emotions and bravery makes this a compelling book hard to put down." Publ Wkly

Smith, Jim B.

The last mission; the secret story of World War II's final battle; [by] Jim B. Smith and Malcolm McConnell. Broadway Bks. 2002 346p il $24.95; pa $14.95   **940.54**

1. World War, 1939-1945—Aerial operations 2. Hiroshima (Japan)—Bombardment, 1945

ISBN 0-7679-0778-7; 0-7679-0779-5 (pa)

     LC 2002-22336

An expanded and revised version of Jim B. Smith's 1st person account: The last mission, published 1995

"Smith was a radio operator on the crew of the B-29 bomber *Boomerang* in the Pacific theater of World War

II. His plane, along with the others in the 315th Bomb Wing, 20th Air Force, was assigned to bomb strategic targets in the Japanese home islands. . . . On their return from one mission, they passed three Superforts flying toward Japan and learned only later that one was the *Enola Gay* on its mission to drop the first atomic bomb on Hiroshima. . . . More than a fascinating firsthand report of the last bombing mission over Japan, this book is an account of the last days of World War II in the Pacific." Libr J

Includes bibliographical references

Smith, Michael, 1952-

Station X; decoding Nazi secrets. TV Bks. 1999 247p il $24.95   **940.54**

1. Great Britain. Government Communications Headquarters 2. World War, 1939-1945—Great Britain 3. World War, 1939-1945—Secret service 4. Cryptography

ISBN 1-57500-094-6   LC 99-51598

This companion volume to a PBS Nova documentary "is an account of Britain's defeat of the German Enigma ciphers." Booklist

"On one level, this page-turner is a deeply satisfying parable of the power of humane intellect to defeat evil; it's also a stunning re-creation of one of the most important chapters in the war." Publ Wkly

Includes bibliographical references

Spector, Ronald

Eagle against the sun; the American war with Japan; {by} Ronald H. Spector. Free Press 1985 589p il hardcover o.p. paperback available $18   **940.54**

1. World War, 1939-1945—Campaigns—Pacific Ocean 2. World War, 1939-1945—United States 3. World War, 1939-1945—Japan

ISBN 0-394-74101-3 (pa)   LC 84-47888

Also available in paperback from Vintage Bks.

This is a "one-volume history of the American-Japanese conflict during WW II." Choice

While "policy, strategy and military operations are emphasized . . . Mr. Spector makes a real attempt to give readers some idea of what the war was like for the men and women who fought it. It is here that the book is at its best." N Y Times Book Rev

Includes bibliographical references

Stafford, David, 1942-

Roosevelt and Churchill; men of secrets. Overlook Press 2000 xxiv, 359p il $32.50; pa $16.95   **940.54**

1. Roosevelt, Franklin D. (Franklin Delano), 1882-1945 2. Churchill, Sir Winston, 1874-1965 3. World War, 1939-1945—Diplomatic history 4. World War, 1939-1945—Secret service 5. United States—Foreign relations—Great Britain 6. Great Britain—Foreign relations—United States

ISBN 1-58567-068-5; 1-58567-249-1 (pa)

     LC 00-55750

An "account of the crucial wartime relationship between two statesman who appreciated the importance of their intelligence-gathering services yet at times also guarded what they knew from each other if they believed it would benefit them politically." Libr J

"Stafford is a superb researcher and has a feel for when 'secret' meant 'significant' and when it did not." N Y Times Book Rev

Includes bibliographical references

Stanton, Doug

In harm's way; the sinking of the USS Indianapolis and the extraordinary story of its survivors. Holt & Co. 2001 333p il $25; pa $14 **940.54**

1. Indianapolis (Cruiser) 2. World War, 1939-1945—Naval operations 3. Shipwrecks

ISBN 0-8050-6632-2; 0-8050-7366-3 (pa)

LC 00-68254

Stanton discusses the loss of the USS Indianapolis, which was given the "job of carrying components of the Hiroshima bomb from San Francisco to Tinian. . . . The Indianapolis (then) headed for Leyte in the Philippines. . . . On July 30, 1945, the Indianapolis was cruising, unescorted, west of Guam when two torpedoes struck it, sinking the ship in a few minutes. An estimated 300 men were killed by the blast or entombed below. About 900 went into the Pacific. . . . Only 321 survived; of these, some died later in the hospital." Natl Rev

"Illuminating and emotional without being maudlin, Stanton's book helps explain what many have long considered an inexplicable catastrophe." Publ Wkly

Stevenson, William, 1924 or 5-

A man called Intrepid; the secret war. Harcourt Brace Jovanovich 1976 xxv, 486p il maps o.p.; Lyons Press paperback available $18.95 **940.54**

1. Stephenson, Sir William Samuel, 1896-1989 2. World War, 1939-1945—Secret service

ISBN 1-58574-154-X (pa)

An examination of World War II Allied secret intelligence operation coordinated by William Stephenson a.k.a. Intrepid

Stinnett, Robert B.

Day of deceit; the truth about FDR and Pearl Harbor. Free Press 1999 386p il maps hardcover o.p. paperback available $16

940.54

1. Roosevelt, Franklin D. (Franklin Delano), 1882-1945 2. Pearl Harbor (Oahu, Hawaii), Attack on, 1941 3. Intelligence service—United States

ISBN 0-7432-0129-9 (pa)

LC 99-38402

The author addresses the question of whether the U.S. had knowledge of the impending Japanese attack on Pearl Harbor

"Although Stinnett's accusatory light doesn't definitively fall on FDR, it illuminates fishy aspects of the case. . . . Whether the result of simple dereliction or sinister dereliction of duty, Pearl Harbor holds fewer secrets because of Stinnett's research." Booklist

Includes bibliographical references

Takaki, Ronald T., 1939-

Hiroshima; why America dropped the atomic bomb; [by] Ronald Takaki. Little, Brown 1995 193p il hardcover o.p. paperback available $14.95 **940.54**

1. World War, 1939-1945—United States 2. Atomic bomb 3. Hiroshima (Japan)—Bombardment, 1945

ISBN 0-316-83124-7 (pa)

LC 95-13546

This study of the bombings of Hiroshima and Nagasaki focuses on the psychological motivations of the American decision-makers, especially Harry Truman

"Right or wrong, the study is a provocative addition to the unresolved debate over the dropping of the atomic bombs." Publ Wkly

Includes bibliographical references

Thompson, Robert Smith

Empires on the Pacific; World War II and the struggle for the mastery of Asia. Basic Bks. 2001 434p $30; pa $18.95 **940.54**

1. World War, 1939-1945—Asia

ISBN 0-465-08575-X; 0-465-08576-8 (pa)

LC 2001-36561

In this study, Thompson asserts that "the U.S. had strong political and economic interests in East Asia and saw Japan as a danger to those interests. . . . The author makes his points by telling only one side of the story, but his alternate view of our 'last good war' is bound to attract attention and may generate controversy." Booklist

Includes bibliographical references

940.55 Europe—1945-

Garton Ash, Timothy

History of the present; essays, sketches, and dispatches from Europe in the 1990s. Random House 2000 c1999 448p hardcover o.p. paperback available $15 **940.55**

1. Europe—Politics and government

ISBN 0-375-72762-0 (pa)

LC 00-62553

First published 1999 in the United Kingdom

The essays collected here "deal with events that the author witnessed such as the East German vote for reunification or the tragedy of Kosovo. Throughout, a detailed chronology of events in both Eastern and Western Europe frames the essays to maintain their chronological order and establish points of reference. Topics range widely, from the European Union and the single currency integration to Poland, the former Czechoslovakia, and troubles in the former Yugoslavia. This collection will appeal to informed lay readers." Libr J

Mazower, Mark

Dark continent: Europe's twentieth century. Knopf 1999 487p il maps hardcover o.p. paperback available $16 **940.55**

1. Europe—History—20th century

ISBN 0-679-75704-X (pa)

LC 98-15886

Mazower shapes his "history of Europe's 20th century as a struggle among liberal democracy, communism and fascism." Publ Wkly

The author's "relative unconcern with international and great-power politics probably accounts for a rather intra-European perspective . . . just as it contributes to some exaggeration of the points of comparison and convergence in East and West European economic history. . . . But these are minor defects, the price to be paid for a confident and unconventional work of historical interpretation." N Y Times Book Rev

Includes bibliographical references

941 British Isles

Black, Jeremy

A history of the British Isles. 2nd ed. Palgrave Macmillan 2003 xxxi, 352p il maps (Palgrave essential histories) pa $19.95 **941**

1. Great Britain—History 2. Ireland—History

ISBN 1-40390-043-4

LC 2002-28675

First published 1996 by St. Martin's Press

This is a political, social, economic, and cultural history of the British Isles from pre-Roman times to the present

Includes bibliographical references

Buruma, Ian

Anglomania; a European love affair. Random House 1999 304p hardcover o.p. paperback available $14   **941**

1. Great Britain—Civilization 2. British national characteristics

ISBN 0-375-70536-6 (pa)   LC 98-27387

First published 1998 in the United Kingdom with title: Voltaire's coconuts; or, Anglomania in Europe

The author "addresses the issue of England's place in Europe by examining the long-standing European fascination with England. . . . Integrating discussions of diverse figures such as Voltaire and Theodor Herzl, the founder of Zionism, Buruma shows how various continental Anglophiles projected onto England whatever they wished—and what they wished for, mostly, was enlightened, liberal rationalism." Publ Wkly

"A historically significant scrutiny of Anglophilia rife with compelling contemporary implications." Booklist

The **Cambridge** historical encyclopedia of Great Britain and Ireland; editor, Christopher Haigh. Cambridge Univ. Press 1985 392p il maps hardcover o.p. paperback available $33   **941**

1. Great Britain—History—Dictionaries

ISBN 0-521-39552-6 (pa)   LC 85-47568

"Broad chronological overview of seven themes ranging from government to culture. The essays on topics such as government and politics, warfare, society, the economy, and international relations are supported by short identification paragraphs in the margins. The time period covered extends from 100 B.C. to 1975. There is a biographical section with about 800 entries." Ref Sources for Small & Medium-sized Libr. 5th edition

Cannon, John, 1926-

The Oxford illustrated history of the British monarchy; [by] John Cannon and Ralph Griffiths. Oxford Univ. Press 1988 727p il $55; pa $27.50   **941**

1. Great Britain—Kings and rulers 2. Great Britain—Politics and government

ISBN 0-19-822786-8; 0-19-289328-9 (pa)

     LC 88-5172

"A dynastic account of the history, public and private, of the British monarchy. Augmented by many illustrations that show the visual magnificence that is a part of the monarchy." N Y Public Libr Book of How & Where to Look It Up

Includes bibliographical references

The **Columbia** companion to British history; edited by Juliet Gardiner & Neil Wenborn. Columbia Univ. Press 1997 840p maps $63   **941**

1. Great Britain—History—Encyclopedias

ISBN 0-231-10792-7   LC 96-23774

First published 1995 in the United Kingdom with title: The History today companion to British history

This reference work contains "more than 4,500 dictionary entries that not only cover political and constitutional history, but also provide information on social, economic, religious, military, naval, legal, and cultural history. . . . The entries . . . [cover topics such as] blasphemy, divorce, and homosexuality, as well as the historical events and rulers that are standard for any encyclopedia. In addition, the encyclopedia seems to be strong on entries for Scotland and Ireland." Booklist

Davies, Norman

The Isles; a history. Oxford Univ. Press 1999 xlii, 1222p il hardcover o.p. paperback available $24.95   **941**

1. Great Britain—History 2. Ireland—History

ISBN 0-19-514831-2 (pa)   LC 99-29052

"Davies examines how the various component parts of @the Isles'—England, Scotland, Ireland, and Wales—interacted with one another and the rest of the world. Consequently, a great deal of attention is given to the English colonization of Ireland, Scotland's relationship with England before and after union, and the creation of empire." Libr J

"Bursting with fresh insights on nearly every page, this magisterial narrative, scholarly yet down-to-earth and engrossing, reveals Davies at his iconoclastic best." Publ Wkly

Includes bibliographical references

Johnson, Paul, 1928-

Castles of England, Scotland and Wales. Harper & Row 1989 215p il map o.p.; Seven Dials $16.95   **941**

1. Castles 2. Great Britain—Description

ISBN 1-84188-088-4 (pa)   LC 89-45046

First published 1978 in the United Kingdom with title: The National Trust book of British castles

Johnson's survey of castle-building and restoration leads the reader through the architectural, military, and political history of England, Wales, and Scotland. . . . Johnson provides a fascinating tour, via excellent color photographs and sharp diagrams, of these surviving structures and their historical importance." Booklist

The **Oxford** companion to British history; edited by John Cannon. Oxford Univ. Press 1997 1044p maps $70; pa $29.95   **941**

1. Great Britain—History—Encyclopedias

ISBN 0-19-866176-2; 0-19-860514-5 (pa)

     LC 97-27598

"Covering more than 2,000 years of British history, this one-volume historical dictionary includes social, political, military, cultural, economic, scientific, and biographical events. . . . Entries cover the range of history from major political figures, such as Disraeli and Elizabeth I, to music, literature, and science, with entries for the Beatles, Mary Shelley, and Sir Isaac Newton." Booklist

The **Oxford** history of Britain; edited by Kenneth O. Morgan. rev ed, updated ed. Oxford Univ. Press 2001 780p maps pa $18.95   **941**

1. Great Britain—History

ISBN 0-19-280135-X   LC 2001-271568

Also available The Oxford illustrated history of Britain $26.50 (ISBN 0-19-289326-2)

Text based on: The Oxford illustrated history of Britain, published 1984

"Covering two thousand years of British history, the book tells the story of Britain and her peoples from the coming of the Roman legions to the present day. Here ten . . . contributors including Peter Salway, John Blair, John S. Morrill, and Paul Langford offer essays on everything from the Anglo-Saxon period to the Stuarts to the Liberal Age and the twentieth century." Publisher's note

Includes bibliographical references

Schama, Simon

A history of Britain. Hyperion 2000-2003
3v ea $40   **941**
1. Great Britain—History
ISBN 0-7868-6675-6 (v1); 0-7868-6752-3 (v2);
0-7868-6899-6 (v3)   LC 00-61442
"Talk Miramax books"
Contents: [v1] At the edge of the world, 3500 B.C.-
1603 A.D.; v2 The wars of the British, 1603-1776; v3
The fate of empire, 1776-2000
Schama "writes wonderfully, in an easygoing yet ele-
gant manner, with an eye for the telling aesthetic detail,
and throughout brimming with intelligence and passion."
N Y Times Book Rev
Includes bibliographical references

941.06   British Isles—Stuart and Commonwealth periods, 1603-1714

Macleod, John, 1966-

Dynasty: the Stuarts, 1560-1807. St.
Martin's Press 2001 386p il $27.50   **941.06**
1. House of Stuart 2. Great Britain—History—1603-
1714, Stuarts
ISBN 0-312-27206-5   LC 2001-34909
First published 1999 in the United Kingdom
In MacLeod's "survey of Stuart monarchs and pretenders, he acknowledges their destructive hubris and
outright incompetence. But he also shows that the Britain
they presided over nurtured cultural brilliance and critical
political evolution that led to a more broadly based society. The author effectively weaves his portraits of individual Stuarts into the broader milieu of social and political turmoil. This is a fast-paced and easily digestible
popular history." Booklist
Includes bibliographical references

941.07   British Isles—Period of House of Hanover, 1714-1837

Brewer, John, 1947-

The pleasures of the imagination; English
culture in the eighteenth century. Farrar,
Straus & Giroux 1997 xxx, 721p il o.p.;
University of Chicago Press paperback
available $20   **941.07**
1. Great Britain—Civilization 2. Great Britain—So-
cial life and customs 3. Great Britain—Intellectual life
ISBN 0-226-67419-6 (pa)   LC 97-60984
The author "examines the evolution of the visual arts,
literature, music and theater in 18th-century England."
Publ Wkly
"A remarkable feat of scholarship, this volume will
quickly establish itself as an indispensable reference."
Booklist
Includes bibliographical references

941.08   British Isles—Period of Victoria and House of Windsor, 1837-

The **Cambridge** illustrated history of the
British Empire; edited by P.J. Marshall.
Cambridge Univ. Press 1996 400p il maps
$55; pa $35   **941.08**
1. Great Britain—Colonies 2. Commonwealth countries—History 3. Imperialism
ISBN 0-521-43211-1; 0-521-00254-0 (pa)
    LC 95-14535
"This book examines the experience of colonialism in
North America, India, Africa, Australia and the Caribbean, giving a brief history of the British imperial territories and looking at slavery, trade, religion, art, transportation, and the development of new ideas." Book Rep
Includes bibliographical references

McKillop, A. B., 1946-

The spinster & the prophet; H.G. Wells,
Florence Deeks, and the case of the
plagiarized text. Four Walls Eight Windows
2002 477p il $26.95   **941.08**
1. Wells, H. G. (Herbert George), 1866-1946
2. Deeks, Florence Amelia 3. Plagiarism 4. Historiography
ISBN 1-56858-236-6   LC 2002-71292
"When, in 1920, Florence Deeks finally received her
rejected manuscript—a feminist history of the world—
from Macmillan after eight months, she couldn't understand why it appeared in such bad condition. . . . Later
that year, when she read H.G. Wells's new book, *The
Outline of History*, published by Macmillan, she felt a
chill. There were so many similarities to her own work:
shared themes, organization, word choice, even the same
mistakes. Florence made a dramatic decision—she would
sue Wells and his publisher for plagiarism. . . . The author handles the dual story line brilliantly, weaving together two opposing characters into one altogether gripping tale of literary theft." Publ Wkly
Includes bibliographical references

941.1   Scotland

Devine, T. M. (Thomas Martin)

The Scottish nation 1700-2000. Viking
1999 xxiii, 695p il maps hardcover o.p.
paperback available $20   **941.1**
1. Scotland—History
ISBN 0-14-100234-4 (pa)   LC 99-29866
"The author divides the book into chronological periods to cover Scottish economic, military, and social history; regional differences in the Highlands and Lowlands;
and the development of Scottish identity." Libr J
Includes bibliographical references

Herman, Arthur, 1956-

How the Scots invented the modern world; the true story of how western Europe's poorest nation created our world & everything in it. Crown 2001 392p $25.95; pa $14.95   **941.1**

1. Scotland—Civilization 2. Scottish national characteristics

ISBN 0-609-60635-2; 0-609-80999-7 (pa)

LC 2001-28951

The author discusses Scottish "contributions to education, science, history, and political thought." Libr J

"This is a worthwhile book for the general reader." Publ Wkly

Includes bibliographical references

Nicolson, Adam, 1957-

Sea room: an island life in the Hebrides. North Point Press 2002 391p il maps $27; pa $14   **941.1**

1. Hebrides (Scotland)—Social life and customs

ISBN 0-86547-636-5; 0-86547-667-5 (pa)

LC 2002-19816

First published 2001 in the United Kingdom

The author is the owner "of three remote Scottish islands, the Shiants, located in the Hebrides and purchased by Nicolson's father through a 1937 newspaper advertisement. . . . Nicolson's book offers as much information about the geological origins of the islands, the seasonal details of the flora and fauna, and the melding of Norse language into the culture as it does about the author's solitary boat rides and peaceful beachcombing adventures." Libr J

"Magnificent and poetic, this is a literary and ecological masterpiece." Booklist

Includes bibliographical references

941.5   Ireland

Ardagh, John, 1928-

Ireland and the Irish; portrait of a changing society. Penguin Bks. 1995 479p maps pa $13.95   **941.5**

1. Ireland—Social conditions 2. Irish national characteristics

ISBN 0-14-017160-6   LC 96-151596

First published 1994 in the United Kingdom

The author surveys political, social and economic conditions in contemporary Ireland

"Ardagh is a gifted writer with a lucid style and a perceptive grasp of the ironies inherent in a nation seeking to transform itself while striving to hold onto (or to reconstruct) a treasured past. His chapters on the Irish diaspora and the surprisingly vibrant efforts to revive the Gaelic language are particularly enlightening." Booklist

Cahill, Tom

How the Irish saved civilization; the untold story of Ireland's heroic role from the fall of Rome to the rise of medieval Europe; [by] Thomas Cahill. Talese 1995 246p il maps $27.50; pa $12.95   **941.5**

1. Ireland—Civilization 2. Learning and scholarship 3. Medieval civilization

ISBN 0-385-41848-5; 0-385-41849-3 (pa)

LC 94-28130

This book describes the part played by Irish scribal scholars during the Dark Ages "in preserving and trans-

mitting the classical literature of both Greece and Rome." Booklist

"Highly literate and affectionate, if somewhat rambling and indulgent. . . . As a freewheeling, witty popular history of Irish Christianity in the Dark Ages, this will amuse and enlighten." Libr J

Includes bibliographical references

Moorhouse, Geoffrey, 1931-

Sun dancing; a vision of medieval Ireland. Harcourt Brace & Co. 1997 284p maps hardcover o.p. paperback available $13

    941.5

1. Skellig Michael (Monastery: Ireland) 2. Monasticism and religious orders 3. Ireland—History

ISBN 0-15-600602-2 (pa)   LC 97-8748

"In the first half of his book, Moorhouse recreates fictionally the lives of monks on the Skelligs—14 rocky, wind-lashed islands off Ireland's west coast, on which a monastic tradition thrived from the sixth through the thirteenth centuries. . . . In the book's second half, Moorhouse explains . . . the major figures, traditions, and controversies of Irish Christianity, especially in its monastic form." Booklist

"A useful introduction to Irish monasticism for general and informed lay readers." Libr J

Includes bibliographical references

The Oxford companion to Irish history; edited by S.J. Connolly. 2nd ed. Oxford Univ. Press 2002 650p maps $60   **941.5**

1. Ireland—History—Encyclopedias

ISBN 0-19-866270-X   LC 2002-284352

First published 1998

"Connolly and the contributors of this work cover every aspect of Irish life in this compact volume: political, social, religious, economic, and intellectual. Entries are compact as well, generally ranging from half a page to just over one page. . . . Most medium and large public and academic libraries with an interest in Irish history will want to add this title to their collection." Am Ref Books Annu, 2003

The Oxford illustrated history of Ireland; edited by R.F. Foster. Oxford Univ. Press 1989 382p il maps $55; pa $24.95   **941.5**

1. Ireland—History

ISBN 0-19-822970-4; 0-19-285245-0 (pa)

LC 89-16168

This illustrated history includes "six essays by Irish scholars, five covering chronological periods in Irish history and the sixth a . . . discussion of the interplay between Irish literature and history." Libr J

"A thoughtful and highly informative volume that manages to underscore the ancient and rooted aspects of Irish culture, even while it explores in depth the mobility and shifting of the Irish people into 'fractured and sometimes unexpected patterns.'" Booklist

Includes bibliographical references

941.6   Ulster. Northern Ireland

Coogan, Tim Pat, 1935-

The troubles; Ireland's ordeal, 1966-1995, and the search for peace. Roberts Rinehart Pubs. 1996 c1995 460p il maps o.p.; Palgrave Macmillan paperback available $22.95 **941.6**

1. Northern Ireland—History

ISBN 0-312-29418-2 (pa)

First published 1995 in the United Kingdom

Coogan, Tim Pat, 1935-—*Continued*

In this political history the author "examines all parties to the struggle. . . . He reconstructs the past 30 years, from the 1969 marching and riots to the H-Block protests, the MacBride Principles, the Anglo-Irish agreement, and the recent paramilitary cease-fire. Coogan traces the current peace process, stalled by Great Britain's insistence that the IRA hand in its weapons, to the 1979 visit of Pope John Paul II." Libr J

Includes bibliographical references

Mitchell, George J., 1933-

Making peace. Knopf 1999 191p il o.p.; University of Calif. Press paperback available $18.95   **941.6**

1. International arbitration 2. Northern Ireland—Politics and government

ISBN 0-520-22523-6 (pa)   LC 99-61004

The author, the former Senate majority leader, helped broker "a peace settlement in Northern Ireland. This is his account of his role as chairman of the interparty negotiations and of how the major nationalist and unionist political parties—and the British and Irish governments—managed to forge the 1998 Good Friday peace agreement." Publ Wkly

Mitchell "presents a readable, illuminating portrait of the negotiation process, offering vivid snapshots of the key players and the high and low points of the whole affair." Libr J

Toolis, Kevin

Rebel hearts; journeys within the IRA's soul. St. Martin's Press 1996 384p hardcover o.p. paperback available $15.95   **941.6**

1. Irish Republican Army 2. Northern Ireland—History

ISBN 0-312-15632-4 (pa)   LC 96-35

"A Thomas Dunne book"

The author "draws together many facets of militant IRA republicanism. Weaving together the history of the troubles in Northern Ireland with the stories of families and individuals, he looks into the 'rebel hearts' of these partisans and offers reasons for their joining the IRA. His portraits of brothers Dermot and Martin Finucane, Chieftain Martin McGuinness, and informer Patty Flood are compelling. But no less important is the historical detail of a quarter-century of violence, reprisal, loss, and sadness." Libr J

942 England and Wales

Medieval England; an encyclopedia; editors: Paul E. Szarmach, M. Teresa Tavormina, Joel T. Rosentha. Garland 1998 lxiv, 882p il maps $155   **942**

1. Great Britain—History—Encyclopedias 2. Medieval civilization—Encyclopedias

ISBN 0-8240-5786-4   LC 97-35523

"Containing more than 700 entries by more than 300 international scholars, the volume encompasses the fields of Old English and Middle English language and literature, music and liturgy, history, and history of art. . . . The A-Z entries are supported by lists of kings and queens of England, archbishops of Canterbury and York, and popes, 590-1502, as well as a glossary of musical and liturgical terms." Booklist

Roberts, Jane, 1949-

Royal landscape; the gardens and parks of Windsor. Yale Univ. Press 1997 596p il maps $150   **942**

1. Windsor Castle 2. Gardens

ISBN 0-300-07079-9   LC 97-15718

This is a study of the gardens and parks of Windsor Castle, in Berkshire, England. "The first section is a chronological examination of the royals and their gardeners, architects, and farmers. The second section examines the parks from a topological point of view, discussing the flora and fauna . . . agricultural experiments, and potential land uses." Libr J

"A truly grand document offering a sweeping perspective on the development of a renowned royal locale." Booklist

Includes bibliographical references

942.01 England—Early history to 1066

Goodrich, Norma Lorre

King Arthur. Watts 1986 406p il maps o.p.; HarperCollins Pubs. paperback available $17   **942.01**

1. Arthur, King 2. Great Britain—History—0-1066

ISBN 0-06-097182-7 (pa)   LC 85-22558

The author examines historical and literary materials relating to Arthur as both an actual and legendary figure

Includes bibliographical references

King Arthur in legend and history; edited by Richard White; foreword by Allan Massie. Routledge 1998 xxv, 570p il maps hardcover o.p. paperback available $34.95   **942.01**

1. Arthur, King 2. Great Britain—History—0-1066

ISBN 0-415-92063-9 (pa)   LC 97-47726

First published 1997 in the United Kingdom

"This book is a compilation of source material excerpted primarily from longer works. . . . The documents themselves are arranged in roughly chronological and geographical order, ranging from *Gildas* (c. 548) to *The Buik of the Chronicles of Scotland* (1535). The anthology presents both historical and literary works and draws from French and German as well as English sources." Libr J

Includes bibliographical references

Lacey, Robert

The year 1000; what life was like at the turn of the first millennium: an Englishman's world; {by} Robert Lacey, Danny Danziger. Little, Brown 1999 230p hardcover o.p. paperback available $12.95   **942.01**

1. Great Britain—History—0-1066

ISBN 0-316-51157-9 (pa)   LC 98-31254

Lacey and Danziger "have set out to capture what life was like in Anglo-Saxon England at the end of the first millennium. The framework for their story was provided by a priceless written work from that period, 'The Julius Work Calendar.'" Libr J

"This is a superb time capsule, and the authors distill a wealth of historical information into brightly entertaining reading." Publ Wkly

Includes bibliographical references

942.04 England—Period of Houses of Lancaster and York, 1399-1485

Weir, Alison
The Wars of the Roses. Ballantine Bks. 1995 462p il hardcover o.p. paperback available $14.95   **942.04**
1. Great Britain—History—1455-1485, War of the Roses
ISBN 0-345-40433-5 (pa)
This is an account "of the first phase of the War of the Roses. Accepting the Tudor view that the conflict originated with Richard II's deposition, [the author] devotes half of the book to relations between Lancaster and York from 1399 to 1455. The second half deals with the period from the first Battle of St. Albans (1455) to the Battle of Tewkesbury (1471)." Libr J
"No history collection should do without this perfectly focused and beautifully unfolded account." Booklist

942.05 England—Tudor period, 1485-1603

Martin, Colin, 1939-
The Spanish Armada; [by] Colin Martin, Geoffrey Parker. 2nd. rev ed. Mandolin; [distributed by] St. Martin's Press 1999 xx, 295p il maps $69.95; pa $22.95   **942.05**
1. Spanish Armada, 1588
ISBN 0-7190-5810-4; 1-901341-14-3 (pa)
    LC 99-44272
First published 1988 by Norton
This "interpretation of why Philip II's great Armada of 1588 failed so disastrously is based on a fresh examination of archival sources across Europe combined with the archaeological investigation of some of its wrecked ships off the coasts of Scotland and Ireland." Publisher's note
Includes bibliographical references

Mattingly, Garrett, 1900-1962
The Armada. Houghton Mifflin 1988 c1959 443p il maps hardcover o.p. paperback available $17   **942.05**
1. Spanish Armada, 1588
ISBN 0-395-08366-4 (pa)   LC 87-26210
A reissue of the title first published 1959; 1984 edition had title: The defeat of the Spanish Armada
This account of the defeat of the Spanish Armada by the British in 1588 describes in detail the "military measures and actions, the sentiments and passions of the public, political intrigue, and the motives and maneuvering of the royal figures involved, notably Elizabeth." Publ Wkly
Includes bibliographical references

Watkins, Susan
The public and private worlds of Elizabeth I; photographs by Mark Fiennes. Thames & Hudson 1998 208p il $40   **942.05**
1. Elizabeth I, Queen of England, 1533-1603
ISBN 0-500-01869-3   LC 98-60339
This account "outlines the details of court life and analyzes Elizabeth's life-long obsession with her public persona." Booklist
"The text is informative and well written, but it is the photographs, of architecture, landscapes, jewelry, clothing, furniture, and more, that will attract and hold readers. Anyone who wonders what daily life looked like (for the upper classes, at least) need look no further." Libr J
Includes bibliographical references

942.06 England—Stuart and Commonwealth periods, 1603-1714

Fraser, Antonia, 1932-
Faith and treason; the story of the Gunpowder Plot. Doubleday 1996 xxxv, 347p il hardcover o.p. paperback available $16   **942.06**
1. Fawkes, Guy, 1570-1606 2. Gunpowder plot, 1605 3. Great Britain—History—1603-1714, Stuarts
ISBN 0-385-47190-4 (pa)   LC 96-21709
"A Nan A. Talese book"
"A small group of Roman Catholics planned to blow up Parliament on its opening day in 1605, when the Protestant King James and his older son would be present, and to proclaim the nine-year-old princess Elizabeth queen, raise her as a Catholic, and so restore Catholicism as the state religion. . . . The Gunpowder Plot was both cruel and crackpot, but Fraser does a wonderful job of conveying to the modern reader just why a few Catholics felt that it was justified and also was likely to succeed." New Yorker
Includes bibliographical references

Trevelyan, George Macaulay, 1876-1962
The English Revolution, 1688-1689. Holt & Co. 1939 c1938 281p o.p.; Oxford Univ. Press paperback available $16.95   **942.06**
1. Great Britain—History—1603-1714, Stuarts
ISBN 0-19-500263-6 (pa)
First published 1938 in the United Kingdom
This study covers not only the revolution itself but also the events of the reign of James II, which led up to it and the political changes which followed
Includes bibliographical references

942.08 England—Period of Victoria and House of Windsor, 1837-

Taylor, A. J. P. (Alan John Percivale), 1906-1990
English history, 1914-1945. Oxford Univ. Press 1965 xxvii, 708p maps (Oxford history of England) $100; pa $19.95   **942.08**
1. Great Britain—History—20th century
ISBN 0-19-821715-3; 0-19-285268-X (pa)
A study of the political, economic, and social changes in England over a thirty year span

942.1 London

Ackroyd, Peter
London: the biography. Talese 2001 c2000
xxvi, 801p il $45; pa $18.95 **942.1**
1. London (England)—History
ISBN 0-385-49770-9; 0-385-49771-7 (pa)
LC 2001-27153
First published 2000 in the United Kingdom
Ackroyd's social history of London is organized the-
matically with "essays on such topics as drinking, natural
history, suicide, crowds, ghosts, rivers, prostitution, the-
atres, murder, sounds and children." London Rev Books
"A sweeping, highly readable account of London's
colorful and complicated history." Libr J
Includes bibliographical references

Porter, Roy, 1946-2002
London, a social history. Harvard Univ.
Press 1995 431p il maps $33; pa $17.84
942.1
1. London (England)—History 2. London (England)—Social conditions
ISBN 0-674-53838-2; 0-674-53839-0 (pa)
LC 94-33025
This is a social history of London from Roman times
through the regime of Prime Minister Margaret Thatcher
"Roy Porter's eloquent synthesis of London's history
is a remarkable achievement. . . . Perhaps the best-
researched part of a well-researched book is the section
on the nineteenth and twentieth centuries. . . . But while
he depicts the advances in social and economic conditions, Porter is not blind to its deficiences and never ro-
manticizes the past." Times Lit Suppl
Includes bibliographical references

942.9 Wales

Davies, John, 1938-
A history of Wales. Allen Lane/The
Penguin Press 1993 718p maps hardcover o.p.
paperback available $18 **942.9**
1. Wales—History
ISBN 0-14-014581-8 (pa)
"Davies unearths the evidence of prehistoric hill forts
and Roman ruins; he delineates the feudal wars, the 1536
union with England and the ensuing Reformation; and he
explains the transformations of the Industrial Revolution.
Accurate in all details, using meaningful modern maps,
balanced where doubts exist, this impressive history
could be criticized as a labor of patriotic love, if not for
the visibly high professional standard to which Davies
adheres." Booklist

Morris, Jan, 1926-
A writer's house in Wales. National
Geographic Soc. 2002 143p (National
Geographic directions) $25 **942.9**
1. Wales
ISBN 0-7922-6523-8 LC 2001-44731
The author "reflects on her home in Wales, its beautiful setting and the nature of being Welsh. . . . This slim
and charming volume offers a crisp account of the turbulent history of the Welsh and their battle to maintain
their language and culture in the shadow of their more
powerful neighbor." Publ Wkly

943 Central Europe. Germany

Blumenthal, W. Michael
The invisible wall; Germans and Jews: a
personal exploration. Counterpoint 1998 444p
il hardcover o.p. paperback available $21
943
1. Blumenthal family 2. Jews—Germany
ISBN 1-58243-012-8 (pa) LC 97-47735
"A Cornelia and Michael Bessie book"
"Blumenthal, U.S. secretary of the Treasury under
President Carter, traces the historical trajectory of German Jewry, from medieval ghetto to the Holocaust,
through the lives of six of his ancestors." Publ Wkly
The author's "writing style is reflective and thorough,
and his overriding passion for these stories is felt
throughout." Booklist
Includes bibliographical references

Craig, Gordon Alexander, 1913-
The Germans; [by] Gordon A. Craig.
Putnam 1982 350p maps o.p.; New Am. Lib.
paperback available $15.95 **943**
1. Germany—Civilization 2. Germany—History
ISBN 0-452-01085-3 (pa) LC 81-8650
This work examining the social history of Germany
contains "chapters on religion, money, Germans and
Jews, women, professors and students, romantics, litera-
ture and society, soldiers, Berlin—and an appendix called
'The Awful German Language.'" Publisher's note
Includes bibliographical references

Elon, Amos
The pity of it all; a history of the Jews in
Germany, 1743-1933. Metropolitan Bks. 2002
446p il $30; pa $15 **943**
1. Jews—Germany 2. Germany—Civilization
ISBN 0-8050-5964-4; 0-312-42281-4 (pa)
LC 2002-67833
The author argues "that the underlying tragedy of both
peoples was the German failure, unlike what happened in
the rest of Europe, to throw off the shackles of an authoritarianism that existed apart from anti-Semitism but
fed off it and intensified it as well." NY Times (Late N
Y Ed)
"Covering two centuries, Elon gives us a broad picture
of an uncannily productive population—German Jews,
for whom religious and national identity coexisted in a
uniquely uneasy fashion. Their struggle is given human
dimension through a series of remarkable portraits ranging from Moses Mendelssohn to Albert Einstein to Hannah Arendt." Libr J
Includes bibliographical references

Fulbrook, Mary, 1951-
A concise history of Germany. Cambridge
Univ. Press 1991 c1990 263p il maps
(Cambridge concise histories) hardcover o.p.
paperback available $22 **943**
1. Germany—History
ISBN 0-521-36836-7 (pa) LC 90-32506
First published 1990 in the United Kingdom
"Covering German history from the medieval period
to the nation's current reunification, the book examines
the political, social, and cultural context. . . . Major figures on the German scene such as Martin Luther, Immanuel Kant, and Adolf Hitler are given appropriate attention in Fulbrook's account, but her main emphasis is
. . . on broader historical currents." Booklist
Includes bibliographical references

Gay, Ruth

The Jews of Germany; a historical portrait; with an introduction by Peter Gay. Yale Univ. Press 1992 297p il maps $50; pa $35

943

1. Jews—Germany
ISBN 0-300-05155-7; 0-300-06052-1 (pa)

LC 91-30235

This is a history of Germany's Jews from the first century to the Holocaust

"Illustrated sumptuously with paintings, photographs and excerpts from letters and historical documents, . . . this affirming history survives the sad end of the centuries-old German Jewish way of life." N Y Times Book Rev

Ozment, Steven E.

Flesh and spirit; private life in early modern Germany; [by] Steven Ozment. Viking 1999 348p il map hardcover o.p. paperback available $15   **943**

1. Behaim family 2. Family life 3. Nuremberg (Germany)—Social life and customs 4. Germany—Social life and customs
ISBN 0-14-029198-9 (pa)   LC 99-20914

A "portrayal of German family life in the sixteenth and early seventeeth centuries. . . . By focusing on episodes in the domestic lives of five families (four merchant and one clerical), Ozment opens to our view the emotional dynamics of courtship and marriage, of parenthood and child-rearing, in post-Reformation Nurnberg." Booklist

The narrative "is informative, and Ozment's profiles are almost novelistic in their specificity. . . . All Ozment's subjects appear more exceptional than representative—and all the more interesting for it." Publ Wkly

Schulze, Hagen

Germany; a new history; translated by Deborah Lucas Schneider. Harvard Univ. Press 1998 356p il maps hardcover o.p. paperback available $16.95   **943**

1. Germany—History
ISBN 0-674-00545-7 (pa)   LC 98-23629

Schulze provides "a concise overview of 2,000 years of German history. . . . This is a fast-moving survey that manages to touch most of the critical bases—from Charlemagne to Frederick the Great to Hitler—without concentrating on any one particular historical era." Booklist

Includes bibliographical references

943.08   Germany since 1866

Craig, Gordon Alexander, 1913-

Germany, 1866-1945; by Gordon A. Craig. Oxford Univ. Press 1978 825p (Oxford history of modern Europe) hardcover o.p. paperback available $41.95   **943.08**

1. Germany—History
ISBN 0-19-502724-8 (pa)   LC 78-58471

"A Clarendon Press book"

A "predominantly military and political history of modern Germany." Libr J

"An impressive . . . survey of modern German history, this book is an indispensable reference." New Statesman (1913)

Includes bibliographical references

Smith, Helmut Walser, 1962-

The butcher's tale; murder and anti-semitism in a German town. Norton 2002 270p il maps $25.95; pa $14.95   **943.08**

1. Antisemitism 2. Homicide 3. Germany—Ethnic relations
ISBN 0-393-05098-X; 0-393-32505-9 (pa)

LC 2002-22883

"In 1900, in Konitz, a small town in the Eastern reaches of the German Empire, a Christian boy was found murdered. . . . Though the Konitz police never caught their killer, they scrupulously recorded each indictment, . . . [including] the long disclosure, published in a local newspaper, of Gustav Hoffmann, the town's Christian butcher, in which he accused his next-door neighbor, the Jewish butcher Adolph Lewy, of conspiring with other Jews of the town to commit the crime. . . . [Smith reconstructs the] crime, the ensuing investigation, and the anti-Semitic mob violence that obscured the identity of the real killer." Publisher's note

The author "does a masterful job exploring the history of the blood libel . . . as well as of community and how people band together to bring about great good or in the case of Konitz genuine evil. . . . Although classed by the publisher as history/Judaica, this powerful volume will also appeal to true-crime readers and anyone interested in the dynamics that can turn a peaceful community into a place of hatred and violence." Publ Wkly

Includes bibliographical references

943.086   Germany—Period of Third Reich, 1933-1945

Ayçoberry, Pierre

The social history of the Third Reich; 1933-1945; translated from the French by Janet Lloyd. New Press 2000 380p $30; pa $15.95   **943.086**

1. National socialism 2. Germany—Politics and government—1933-1945 3. Germany—Social conditions
ISBN 1-56584-549-8; 1-56584-635-4 (pa)

LC 99-14059

"In examining the actions of individuals and social groups, [the author] illustrates that German citizens' response to the Nazi regime varied wildly. Some resisted bravely; others saw an opportunity for advancement. Most people sought merely to survive. In fact, what is extremely unsettling is how so many could maintain a semblance of normalcy in their lives. Ayçoberry does not attempt to answer the unanswerable questions posed by the Nazi era, but his disturbing, brutally honest, and scrupulously fair work may be a landmark in the field." Booklist

Includes bibliographical references

Burleigh, Michael, 1955-

The Third Reich; a new history. Hill & Wang 2000 xxv, 965p il maps hardcover o.p. paperback available $18   **943.086**

1. Germany—History—1933-1945
ISBN 0-8090-9326-X (pa)   LC 00-31838

This account of Germany under National Socialism "focuses on the moral breakdown that gave Hitler control of an industrial society, which then, along with the rest of the world, suffered the catastrophic consequences." Publ Wkly

"This brilliant and unique view of a great tyranny is an important addition to our understanding of the first half of the twentieth century." Booklist

Includes bibliographical references

Fest, Joachim C., 1926-

Plotting Hitler's death; the story of the German resistance, 1933-1945; [by] Joachim Fest; translated by Bruce Little. Holt & Co. 1996 419p il hardcover o.p. paperback available $16.95   **943.086**

1. Hitler, Adolf, 1889-1945 2. Germany—History—1933-1945

ISBN 0-0850-5648-3 (pa)   LC 96-7306

The author "covers the whole sweep of resistance from the beginning of the Third Reich to its destruction. Adding greatly to the work for the general reader is a section of short biographies of the major people involved in the resistance and a list of books that are cited in the original German edition that are available in English." Libr J

Fischer, Klaus P., 1942-

Nazi Germany; a new history. Continuum 1995 734p il hardcover o.p. paperback available $32.95   **943.086**

1. Hitler, Adolf, 1889-1945 2. National socialism 3. Germany—History—1933-1945

ISBN 0-8264-0906-7 (pa)   LC 94-41796

This is an "analysis of the Third Reich from its late-19th-century origins to its apocalyptic collapse." Libr J

"An indispensable, compellingly readable political, military and social history of the Third Reich." Publ Wkly

Includes bibliographical references

Fleming, Gerald

Hitler and the final solution; with an introduction by Saul Friedlander. University of Calif. Press 1984 xxxvi, 219p il hardcover o.p. paperback available $18.95   **943.086**

1. Hitler, Adolf, 1889-1945 2. Holocaust, 1933-1945

ISBN 0-520-06022-9 (pa)   LC 83-24352

Original German edition, 1982

This work attempts to prove "that the Final Solution was deliberately designed and personally willed and ordered by Hitler. Fleming reveals the elaborate precautions taken not only to disguise the nature of the operation but also to ensure that it could not be connected with Hitler." Publisher's note

Includes bibliographical references

Hay, Jeff

A history of the Third Reich; by Jeff T. Hay; Christopher R. Browning, consulting editor. Greenhaven Press 2003 4v il maps set $299.80   **943.086**

1. National socialism 2. Germany—History—1933-1945

ISBN 0-7377-1283-X   LC 2002-33900

Contents: v1 A-L; v2 M-Z; v3 Personalities; v4 Primary sources/index

"Combines A-Z articles, biographical profiles, and primary source material to help high-school students understand the social and political forces that shaped, or were shaped by, the Third Reich. An accessible, reliable source." Booklist

Michael, Robert

Nazi-Deutsch/Nazi-German; an English lexicon of the language of the Third Reich; [by] Robert Michael and Karin Doerr; forewords by Paul Rose, Leslie Morris and Wolfgang Mieder. Greenwood Press 2002 xx, 480p $79.95   **943.086**

1. German language—Dictionaries 2. National socialism 3. Germany—History—1933-1945

ISBN 0-313-32106-X   LC 2001-42328

"This lexicon serves as a dictionary of the terminology and specialized vocabulary of Nazi ideology. It covers hundreds of propaganda slogans, military terms, abbreviations and acronyms, euphemisms, and code names. It also defines ranks and offices in the Nazi Party, the German Reich government, and the armed forces. An appendix includes lists of concentration camps, Nazi songs, the Nazi Party Program, the Hitler oaths, and examples of Nazi material included in children's textbooks. . . . This compilation will be a strong research tool for academic, public, and high-school libraries." Booklist

Includes bibliographical references

Pool, James, 1948-

Hitler and his secret partners; contributions, loot and rewards, 1933-1945. Pocket Bks. 1997 415p il hardcover o.p. paperback available $14   **943.086**

1. Hitler, Adolf, 1889-1945 2. Germany—Politics and government—1933-1945 3. World War, 1939-1945—Destruction and pillage

ISBN 0-671-76082-3 (pa)   LC 97-15506

The author examines the way German industrialists and financiers backed Hitler and how the Nazis received material support from abroad. Pool alleges that Henry Ford, Edward VIII and Joe Kennedy assisted the Nazi regime

This book "is a reminder that the worst-kept secret of WWII is that so many malefactors emerged little the worse." Publ Wkly

Includes bibliographical references

Rempel, Gerhard

Hitler's children; the Hitler youth and the SS. University of N.C. Press 1989 354p il hardcover o.p. paperback available $24.95
    943.086

1. Germany—History—1933-1945 2. National socialism

ISBN 0-8078-4299-0 (pa)   LC 88-28036

The author examines the alliance between the Nazi SS and the Hitler Youth

"Rempel's objective work brings into focus one aspect of the sordid history of the Third Reich." Booklist

Includes bibliographical references

Shirer, William L. (William Lawrence)

The rise and fall of the Third Reich; a history of Nazi Germany; with a new afterword by the author. Simon & Schuster 1990 1249p hardcover o.p. paperback available $25   **943.086**

1. Germany—History—1933-1945

ISBN 0-671-72868-7 (pa)   LC 90-221762

"A Touchstone book"

First published 1960

This is a comprehensive, documented history of Germany from the beginning of the Nazi party in 1918 to

Shirer, William L. (William Lawrence)—
Continued
the World War II defeat of Germany in 1945. Here is a detailed account of the events, and the leading figures of the Nazi era, especially Adolf Hitler
Includes bibliographical references

Speer, Albert, 1905-1981
Inside the Third Reich; memoirs; translated from the German by Richard and Clara Winston; introduction by Eugene Davidson. Macmillan 1970 596p il o.p.; Simon & Schuster paperback available $18   **943.086**
1. Hitler, Adolf, 1889-1945 2. Germany—History—1933-1945 3. World War, 1939-1945—Germany
ISBN 0-684-82949-5 (pa)
Original German edition, 1969
The author, Hitler's "architect and later his armaments minister, was in the dictator's inner circle for almost 12 years. . . . [After the war] Speer used the enforced leisure of his 20 prison years as a war criminal to plan and write these memoirs." Libr J
Includes bibliographical references

Turner, Henry Ashby
Hitler's thirty days to power; January 1933; [by] Henry Ashby Turner, Jr. Addison-Wesley 1996 255p il hardcover o.p. paperback available $16   **943.086**
1. Hitler, Adolf, 1889-1945 2. National socialism 3. Germany—Politics and government—1918-1933
ISBN 0-201-32800-3 (pa)   LC 96-20012
The author explores "the fateful 30 days before Hitler became chancellor of Germany in January 1933. Although many of the facts are known, this study reveals that the Nazi dictator did not come to power as the result of 'impersonal forces.' The slender, analytical volume indicates that rather, at a time of mortal peril for Germany—and the world—intrigue was the order of the day in Berlin. . . . Students of German history and extremist movements should enjoy this fast-paced narrative." Publ Wkly
Includes bibliographical references

943.087   Germany—1945-1999

Brenner, Michael
After the Holocaust; rebuilding Jewish lives in postwar Germany; translated from the German by Barbara Harshav. Princeton Univ. Press 1997 196p il $47.50; pa $19.95
943.087
1. Jews—Germany 2. Holocaust survivors 3. Germany—History—1945-1990
ISBN 0-691-02665-3; 0-691-00679-2 (pa)
LC 97-1149
Original German edition, 1995
This introduction to German Jewry since 1945 consists of two essays by Brenner and 15 short autobiographical statements by Jewish communal, religious, and cultural leaders
"If the middle section of interviews seems redundant, it is only because Brenner has covered the material so well and so succinctly elsewhere." Publ Wkly
Includes bibliographical references

Darnton, Robert
Berlin journal, 1989-1990. Norton 1991 352p il hardcover o.p. paperback available $12.95   **943.087**
1. Germany (East)—Politics and government 2. Berlin (Germany)
ISBN 0-393-31018-3 (pa)   LC 90-19745
"Darnton spent parts of 1989 and 1990 in Germany, witnessing the end of that country's division into East and West as the Berlin Wall fell. . . . [He] focuses more on events and aftereffects in East Germany as experienced by ordinary citizens, rather than trying to write a definitive study. Darnton talks with workers, bureaucrats, and government officials and describes what was happening and what the people understood about these momentous events." Booklist

Grass, Günter, 1927-
Two states—one nation? translated from the German by Krishna Winston with A.S. Wensinger. Harcourt Brace Jovanovich 1990 123p hardcover o.p. paperback available $14
943.087
1. German reunification question (1949-1990) 2. Germany—Politics and government
ISBN 0-15-692060-3 (pa)   LC 90-42125
"A Helen and Kurt Wolff book"
A collection of the author's speeches, essays, and newspaper interviews on the subject of German reunification dating from 1961 to the spring of 1990

943.7   Czech Republic and Slovakia

Demetz, Peter, 1922-
Prague in black and gold; scenes from the life of a European city. Hill & Wang 1997 411p maps hardcover o.p. paperback available $15   **943.7**
1. Prague (Czech Republic)—History
ISBN 0-8090-1609-5 (pa)   LC 96-52216
The author presents an "account of the city's history and culture by focusing on epic events as well as heroes, villains and martyrs throughout the millennia of its existence. . . . A highly literate panorama of a focal point of European culture." Publ Wkly
Includes bibliographical references

943.8   Poland

The **Chronicle** of the Łódź ghetto, 1941-1944; edited by Lucjan Dobroszycki; translated by Richard Lourie [et al.] Yale Univ. Press 1984 lxviii, 551p il hardcover o.p. paperback available $37   **943.8**
1. Jews—Poland 2. Holocaust, 1933-1945 3. Łódź (Poland)—Social conditions
ISBN 0-300-03924-7 (pa)   LC 84-3614
"This English edition comprises about one fourth of the original surviving German and Polish manuscript. Day-by-day entries of one to ten pages recorded events and living conditions from January 1941 to the ghetto's liquidation in July 1944. The chronicle was composed by a team of writers, employees of the Jewish ghetto administration." Libr J
"The record is made more profoundly melancholic by the restrained archivist style employed by the chroniclers." New Statesman (1913)

943.9 Hungary

Michener, James A., 1907-1997
The bridge at Andau. Random House 1957
270p map o.p.; Fawcett Bks. paperback
available $6.99   **943.9**
1. Hungary—History—1956, Revolution 2. Hungarian
refugees
ISBN 0-449-21050-2 (pa)
"The heroism, horror and tragedy of the 1956 Hungarian revolt is revealed through interviews with many refugees [who crossed the bridge at Andau to freedom]."
Cleveland Public Libr

944 France and Monaco

Kanigel, Robert
High season; how one French Riviera town
has seduced travelers for two thousand years;
[by] Rob Kanigel. Viking 2002 309p il
$25.95   **944**
1. Nice (France)
ISBN 0-670-89988-7   LC 2001-43786
The author "tells the story of how Nice became the
prototypical French Riviera resort it is today." N Y
Times Book Rev
This is "an ardently researched, enlightening report on
a city that becomes, through the course of this study, a
marker for change, an indicator of social mores and fashions and a case study for the rise of tourism as an industry and an art form." Publ Wkly

Karnow, Stanley
Paris in the fifties; illustrations by Annette
Karnow. Times Bks. 1997 352p il hardcover
o.p. paperback available $14   **944**
1. French national characteristics 2. Paris (France)—
Social life and customs 3. France—Politics and government
ISBN 0-8129-3137-8 (pa)   LC 97-18521
"Karnow chronicles his early years in Paris, where he
worked as a young reporter for Time magazine (1950-
59). . . . [His book] closes with the collapse of the
Fourth Republic in 1958 and the recall to power of
Charles de Gaulle." Libr J
"Not content with simply ensconcing himself in the
Time bureau offices, . . . Karnow created a personal life
for himself and took in all that Paris and the provinces
had to offer. And now he offers this succulent book,
which Francophiles will devour." Booklist

Merriman, John M.
The stones of Balazuc; a French village in
time; [by] John Merriman. Norton 2002 422p
il maps $27.95   **944**
1. France—History
ISBN 0-393-05113-7   LC 2002-515
This is a history of Balazuc, a village above the
Ardèche River in south-central France
The author "has written an exhaustively researched
and valuable chronicle. . . . While some of Balazuc's
history is unique, much of it reflects on larger themes of
French history. As such, Merriman's vivid account
should appeal to those with an interest in French history,
especially its rural aspects." Publ Wkly
Includes bibliographical references

Tuchman, Barbara Wertheim
A distant mirror; the calamitous 14th
century; [by] Barbara W. Tuchman. Knopf
1978 xx, 677p il maps hardcover o.p.
paperback available $17.95   **944**
1. Coucy, Enguerrand de, 1340-1397 2. France—History—1328-1589, House of Valois 3. World history—
14th century 4. Medieval civilization
ISBN 0-345-34957-1 (pa)   LC 78-5985
The author traces the history of the fourteenth century
by following the career of a "feudal lord, Enguerrand de
Coucy VII, the seigneur of some 150 towns and villages
in Picardy. He was born in 1340, and he died in captivity in 1397, having been made a prisoner by the Turks."
Time
Includes bibliographical references

White, Edmund, 1940-
The flaneur; a stroll through the paradoxes
of Paris. Bloomsbury Pub. 2001 211p maps
$16.95   **944**
1. Paris (France)—Description
ISBN 1-58234-135-4   LC 00-46812
Also available G. K. Hall large print edition
"White defines the *flâneur* of his title as an 'aimless
stroller who loses himself in the crowd, who has no destination and goes wherever caprice or curiosity direct his
or her step.' White assumes the role of *flâneur* to perambulate the narrow streets and grand boulevards of Paris,
to gather impressions of people and places." Booklist
"White is richly informed, and his evocative writing
should appeal to both armchair travelers and visitors to
Paris." Libr J

944.04 France—Revolutionary period, 1789-1804

Burke, Edmund, 1729?-1797
Reflections on the Revolution in France
                                         944.04
1. France—History—1789-1799, Revolution
Hardcover and paperback editions available from various publishers
First published 1790
"A treatise by Edmund Burke, written in the form of
a letter to a Frenchman. It attacks the leaders and principles of the French Revolution for their violence and excesses, and urges reform, rather than rebellion, as a
means of correcting social and political abuses." Benet's
Reader's Ency. 4th edition

Lefebvre, Georges, 1874-1959
The French Revolution. Columbia Univ.
Press 1962-1964 2v hardcover o.p.
paperbacks available ea $25   **944.04**
1. France—History—1789-1799, Revolution
Original French edition, 1930; this translation is based
on 1957 reprintings
Contents: v1 From its origins to 1793, translated by
Elizabeth Moss Evanson (ISBN 0-231-08598-2); v2
From 1793 to 1799, translated by John Hall Stewart and
James Friguglietti (ISBN 0-231-08599-0)
An account of the political, military, social, economic
and intellectual aspects of the French Revolution
Includes bibliographical references

Schama, Simon

Citizens: a chronicle of the French Revolution. Knopf 1989 xx, 948p il maps hardcover o.p. paperback available $28

944.04

1. France—History—1789-1799, Revolution
ISBN 0-679-72601-1 (pa)   LC 88-45320
The author "offers a narrative in the form of a nine-teenth-century chronicle that delves into the events and meaning of that momentous series of historical events." Booklist
"Baroque eloquence and rococo sparkle make the book long but never long-winded. All in all, it is an intelligent book for intelligent readers that is also a delight to read." N Y Times Book Rev
Includes bibliographical references

944.05   France—Period of First Empire, 1804-1815

Hamilton-Williams, David

The fall of Napoleon; the final betrayal. Wiley 1994 352p il maps hardcover o.p. paperback available $35   **944.05**
1. Napoleon I, Emperor of the French, 1769-1821
2. France—History—1799-1815
ISBN 0-471-16077-6 (pa)
"This second volume in a trilogy following *Waterloo: New Perspectives* [1994] explores the political and diplomatic intrigues carried out by France's enemies—Britain, Russia, Austria, and Prussia—while at the same time describing the military campaigns of 1813, 1814, and 1815 and the deceit and treachery of those surrounding Napoleon himself." Libr J
The author "is always sympathetic, indeed almost Bonapartist, toward Napoleon. . . . The sections dealing with covert operations make particularly gripping reading." Booklist

Schom, Alan

One hundred days; Napoleon's road to Waterloo. Atheneum Pubs. 1992 398p il maps o.p.; Oxford Univ. Press paperback available $21.50   **944.05**
1. Napoleon I, Emperor of the French, 1769-1821
2. Waterloo, Battle of, 1815
ISBN 0-19-508177-3 (pa)   LC 92-4249
This is an account of "Napoleon's escape from Elba in February 1815 and his return . . . to France. Rallying the nation behind him, he mustered his army and marched off to meet Wellington at Waterloo. . . . This is a first-class reconstruction of Napoleon's final campaign." Publ Wkly
Includes bibliographical references

944.081   France—Period of Third Republic, 1870-1945

Bredin, Jean-Denis

The affair; the case of Alfred Dreyfus; translated from the French by Jeffrey Mehlman. Braziller 1986 628p il hardcover o.p. paperback available $19.95   **944.081**
1. Dreyfus, Alfred, 1859-1935 2. Antisemitism
3. France—Politics and government—1815-1914
ISBN 0-8076-1175-1 (pa)   LC 85-22374
Original French edition, 1983

In his examination of the case, the author seeks to "set the affair within the . . . currents of French history and the rising tide of anti-Semitism." Choice
"That Bredin manages to be both passionate and exact is his first outstanding virtue. He is admirably free of the baroque conspiracy theories that sprout so luxuriantly on both sides of this case." N Y Rev Books
Includes bibliographical references

Derfler, Leslie

The Dreyfus affair. Greenwood Press 2002 xxii, 167p il (Greenwood guides to historic events, 1500-1900) $44.95   **944.081**
1. Dreyfus, Alfred, 1859-1935 2. France—Politics and government—1815-1914 3. Antisemitism
ISBN 0-313-31791-7   LC 2001-38365
"Following a chronology is a @Historical Overview' containing several chapters of background and analysis. These chapters provide context for what is commonly known as the Dreyfus affair, discuss how anti-Semitism and socialism played into and were affected by the affair, and summarize how the affair has been viewed through history. The next section is an A-Z collection of biographies of almost 20 key individuals. . . . Primary documents comprise the next chapter and most documents are accompanied by short explanations. . . . This guide is useful for researchers who need more information than they can find in an encyclopedia." Booklist
Includes bibliographical references

944.083   France—Period of Fifth Republic, 1958-

Fenby, Jonathan

France on the brink. Arcade Pub. 1999 449p il map $27.95; pa $16.95   **944.083**
1. France—Civilization 2. French national characteristics
ISBN 1-55970-488-8; 1-55970-524-8 (pa)
    LC 98-49658
The author contends that France is a "'nation at risk' whose decline he traces over the last three decades. Fenby provides a wealth of examples: a criminal justice system in crisis, the waning of country customs, changing demographics, an aging population, the plummeting status of politicians, and a debilitating nostalgia for the past." Libr J
"Fenby is critical but not hostile; his firsthand experience, both as a reporter and as an in-law, enlivens his book even as it deepens our understanding." New Yorker
Includes bibliographical references

Mayle, Peter

Encore Provence; new adventures in the south of France. Knopf 1999 226p $23; pa $12   **944.083**
1. Provence (France)—Social life and customs
ISBN 0-679-44124-7; 0-679-76269-8 (pa)
    LC 99-62335
Companion volume to Toujours Provence (1991) and A year in Provence (1995)
Also available large print edition pa $23 (ISBN 0-375-70683-6)
Mayle's "book is all about the renewal of his acquaintance with the land he so loves. Essays range widely over Provençal life. . . . His observations and commentaries are laced with humor but encompass true respect and admiration for his adopted homeland." Booklist

945   Italian Peninsula and adjacent islands. Italy

Barzini, Luigi Giorgio, 1908-1984
The Italians; by Luigi Barzini. Atheneum Pubs. 1964 352p maps hardcover o.p. paperback available $14   **945**
1. Italian national characteristics 2. Italy—Civilization
ISBN 0-689-70540-9 (pa)
Also available in hardcover from P. Smith
"The Italians as they are and as foreigners think they are . . . described by an Italian journalist whose probing examination of national life and character does not over-simplify a society webbed with contradiction and incongruity." Booklist

Epstein, Alan, 1949-
As the Romans do; the delights, dramas, and daily diversions of life in the eternal city. Morrow 2000 287p hardcover o.p. paperback available $13   **945**
1. Rome (Italy)—Social life and customs
ISBN 0-06-093395-X (pa)   LC 99-42763
Based on his day-to-day observations, Epstein examines contemporary Italian views on religion, marriage, and family. He also discusses such traditional activities as baking bread, playing bocci, and eating in Trattorias

Levey, Sir Michael, 1927-
Florence; a portrait. Harvard Univ. Press 1996 xxix, 498p il hardcover o.p. paperback available $22.95   **945**
1. Florence (Italy)—History
ISBN 0-674-30658-9 (pa)   LC 95-31215
This is an analysis of "Florence's political and artistic history from earliest times through the nineteenth century." Booklist
"If at times the detail overwhelms the big picture, the 150 illustrations (50 in color) and Levey's excellent artistic counsel make this a worthy guide for anyone seriously seeking Florence." Publ Wkly
Includes bibliographical references

Lewis, R. W. B. (Richard Warrington Baldwin), 1917-2002
The city of Florence; historical vistas and personal sightings. Farrar, Straus & Giroux 1995 351p il o.p.; Holt & Co. paperback available $16   **945**
1. Florence (Italy)—History
ISBN 0-8050-4630-5 (pa)   LC 94-20160
"Part history, part art appreciation, and part love letter, this enchanting book describes how Florentines of the past made their city splendid; tells how its great works of art and architecture have withstood war, weather, and urban renewal; and records how the author and his family have experienced this magnetic place from the nineteen-forties to the nineteen-nineties." New Yorker
Includes bibliographical references

Mayes, Frances
Bella Tuscany; the sweet life in Italy. Broadway Bks. 1999 286p $25; pa $15   **945**
1. Tuscany (Italy)—Social life and customs
ISBN 0-7679-0283-1; 0-7679-0284-4 (pa)
LC 99-24880
"This book follows *Under the Tuscan Sun*, Mayes's popular account of falling in love with Tuscany and purchasing an old villa for her summer vacations. Now Mayes, on sabbatical from her teaching position in San Francisco, is experiencing Italy in the early spring with her friend and soon-to-be-spouse, Ed." Libr J

Under the Tuscan sun; at home in Italy. Chronicle Bks. 1996 280p $22.95   **945**
1. Tuscany (Italy)—Social life and customs
ISBN 0-8118-0842-4   LC 96-15137
Also available in paperback from Broadway Bks.
The author "recounts the purchase and renovation of an abandoned Tuscan villa." Libr J
"Casual and conversational, {Ms. Mayes's} chapters are filled with craftsmen and cooks, with exploratory jaunts into the countryside—but what they all boil down to is an intense celebration of what she calls 'the voluptuousness of Italian life.' Occasionally, this leads to the sort of gushy observations you might expect from a besotted lover. But more often it produces an appealing and very vivid snapshot imagery." N Y Times Book Rev

Morris, Jan, 1926-
Trieste and the meaning of nowhere. Simon & Schuster 2001 203p il o.p.; Da Capo Press paperback available $15   **945**
1. Trieste (Italy)—Description
ISBN 0-306-81180-4 (pa)   LC 2001-31356
Morris discusses "Trieste's modern history—from the long period of wealth and stability under the Habsburgs, through the ambiguities of Fascism and the hardships of the Cold War." Publisher's note
"Morris is not only skilled at vividly describing townspeople and buildings in a way that brings Trieste to life, but she also successfully balances the personal with the historical by providing references to both history and literature." Libr J

Norwich, John Julius, 1929-
A history of Venice. Knopf 1982 xxiv, 673p il maps hardcover o.p. paperback available $25   **945**
1. Venice (Italy)—History
ISBN 0-679-72197-5 (pa)   LC 81-48116
First published 1977-1981 in the United Kingdom in two volumes with title: Venice
"An account of the Venetian Republic, from its obscure 5th century origins to its demise in 1797. . . . This is largely a political history, the greater part of which concentrates on Venice's prime between the 13th and 16th centuries." Libr J
This "history is complete, accurate, elegantly written, and easily readable by nonspecialists." N Y Times Book Rev
Includes bibliographical references

The **Oxford** history of Italy; edited by George Holmes. Oxford Univ. Press 1997 386p il maps hardcover o.p. paperback available $27.50   **945**
1. Italy—History
ISBN 0-19-285444-5 (pa)   LC 98-100006
Twelve scholars survey Italian social, political and cultural history from the time of the Roman Empire to the present
"An excellent choice for readers wanting either a refresher course on Italian history or those who have no background whatsoever in the subject but have a desire to learn the basics." Booklist

Parks, Tim

An Italian education; the further adventures of an expatriate in Verona. Grove Press 1995 338p o.p.; Avon Bks. paperback available $12.95   **945**

1. Italy—Social life and customs
ISBN 0-380-72760-9 (pa)   LC 95-1699

This book "has a simple premise: a description of the world and upbringing of Mr. Parks's children and others around them in Montecchio, the small village near Verona in northern Italy where he has lived with his Italian wife for almost a decade and a half." N Y Times Book Rev

"Parks has made a wry, thoughtful, and often hilarious book from his experience of shepherding his offspring through their 'foreign' childhood—a parable of how our children, no matter what, are other than ourselves." New Yorker

Prose, Francine, 1947-

Sicilian odyssey. National Geographic Soc. 2003 186p il (National Geographic directions) $20   **945**

1. Sicily (Italy)—Description
ISBN 0-7922-6535-1   LC 2002-44379

This is an account of Prose's month-long sojourn on the Mediterranean island of Sicily in 2002

"This penetrating and quick-witted novelist and critic proves to be an agile, philosophical, and entrancing travel writer as she explores the narrow roads of medieval mountaintop towns, mosaic-adorned churches, and the noisy streets of Palermo." Booklist

Robb, Peter

Midnight in Sicily; on art, food, history, travel, and la Cosa Nostra. Faber & Faber 1998 326p o.p.; Vintage Bks. paperback available $14   **945**

1. Andreotti, Giulio 2. Political corruption 3. Mafia 4. Italy—Politics and government
ISBN 0-375-70158-2 (pa)   LC 97-41778

The author "tells the story of the Mafia, from its peasant origins to the 1990's and the continuing trials of Giulio Andreotti, a seven-time Prime Minister of Italy who was accused of Mafia association and commissioning the murder of a journalist." N Y Times Book Rev

"This is an epic study, told with flair." Publ Wkly
Includes bibliographical references

Rotella, Mark, 1967-

Stolen figs and other adventures in Calabria. North Point Press 2003 310p il map $25   **945**

1. Calabria (Italy)—Description
ISBN 0-86547-627-6   LC 2003-42052

"Rotella introduces the world of contemporary Calabria, the southernmost tip of Italy and his ancestral home. . . . Stories flow easily from his pen, and his portrait of Calabrese life will no doubt encourage more to visit the south of Italy." Booklist
Includes bibliographical references

Wills, Garry, 1934-

Venice: lion city; the religion of empire. Simon & Schuster 2001 415p il $35   **945**

1. Venice (Italy)—History
ISBN 0-684-87190-4   LC 2001-32232

Also available in paperback from Washington Sq. Press

This is a "history of Venice during its golden age of empire in the fifteenth and sixteenth centuries. . . . The uniqueness of Venetian civilization has never been more richly and astutely explained." Booklist
Includes bibliographical references

946   Iberian Peninsula and adjacent islands. Spain

Fuentes, Carlos, 1928-

The buried mirror; reflections on Spain and the New World. Houghton Mifflin 1992 399p il hardcover o.p. paperback available $28   **946**

1. Spain—Civilization 2. Latin America—Civilization
ISBN 0-395-92499-5 (pa)   LC 91-34312

Also available in hardcover from P. Smith

The author "believes that a common cultural heritage can help the countries of Latin America transcend disunity and fragmentation. . . . He . . . explores Spanish America's love-hate relationship with Spain and its search for an identity in its multicultural roots." Publ Wkly

"Every page in this lapidary essay offers profound insight into the Spanish American psyche." Libr J
Includes bibliographical references

Hughes, Robert

Barcelona. Knopf 1992 573p il hardcover o.p. paperback available $18   **946**

1. Barcelona (Spain)—History
ISBN 0-679-74383-9 (pa)   LC 91-53179

The author discusses the history, art, architecture, culture and politics of the Catalan capital from Roman times to the twentieth century

"The great distinction of Hughes' approach is that he can move, commandingly, from a Miró canvas to transvestite hookers in the street without missing a beat—and bring to both the same kind of rigorous attention and full-bodied sensibility." Time
Includes bibliographical references

Kurlansky, Mark

The Basque history of the world. Walker & Co. 1999 387p il $25   **946**

1. Basque Provinces (France and Spain)
ISBN 0-8027-1349-1   LC 99-26808

Also available in paperback from Penguin Bks.

"This book traces the history of the Basques from their mysterious origins to their politically fraught existence in this century. . . . [Kurlansky] shows how Basques, famed for their geographic and linguistic isolation, have played significant roles in world history—as mercenaries in ancient Greece, whalers in the Middle Ages, explorers in the Americas, and even cautious supporters of modern European integration." New Yorker

Spain: a history; edited by Raymond Carr. Oxford Univ. Press 2000 318p il $45 **946**

1. Spain—History
ISBN 0-19-820619-4   LC 99-42639

The essays in this volume present a journey through Spain's "entire history: from its prehistoric settlement through Roman, Visigothic, and Islamic rule, and from its golden age of exploration to the Spanish Civil War in the 1930s, Franco's resulting rule, the monarchy's reestablishment, Basque separatists, and modern Spain's political unrest." Booklist

Includes bibliographical references

Stewart, Chris

Driving over lemons; an optimist in Andalucía. Pantheon Bks. 2000 248p il maps hardcover o.p. paperback available $12 **946**

1. Spain—Description 2. Spain—Social life and customs
ISBN 0-375-41028-7 (pa)   LC 99-56675

"Stewart, one of the founders and the first drummer of the rock band Genesis . . . sets out for Spain from England. He buys a sheep farm in the Alpujarra Mountains in Andalucia, and, accompanied by wife Ana and his young daughter, learns to survive without running water, electricity, or roads. Along the way, Stewart forges some solid friendships with neighboring peasants and farmers, travelers, and expatriates." Libr J

"The ability to write hilarious travelogues featuring excruciating scenes of discomfort may well be a [British] national characteristic. It's certainly possessed by Chris Stewart." N Y Times Book Rev

Vincent, Mary

Cultural atlas of Spain and Portugal; [by] Mary Vincent and R.A. Stradling. Facts on File 1994 240p il maps $45   **946**

1. Spain 2. Portugal
ISBN 0-8160-3014-6   LC 94-31211

This volume explores the cultural history of the Iberian peninsula. "The text and maps are complemented by 240 beautiful color photographs that highlight many important historical and cultural events. These encompass features on art, palaces, buildings, artists, posters, food, and even Expo'92 in Seville. A chronology, dynastic chart, glossary, short bibliography, and gazetteer complete the volume." Am Ref Books Annu, 1996

946.9   Portugal

Saramago, José

Journey to Portugal; translated from the Portuguese and with notes by Amanda Hopkinson and Nick Caistor. Harcourt 2001 452p il maps $35; pa $16   **946.9**

1. Portugal—Description
ISBN 0-15-100587-7; 0-15-600713-4 (pa)
          LC 00-53613

"This Portuguese Nobel Prize winner takes a lengthy and wide-ranging sojourn through his beloved homeland, and his superbly written narrative of the journey gives the reader not only an appreciation for the current lay of the Portuguese land but also a very edifying course in the history of a proud nation." Booklist

947   Eastern Europe. Russia

Drakulić, Slavenka

Café Europa; life after communism. Norton 1997 213p $21   **947**

1. Eastern Europe—Social conditions 2. Eastern Europe—Politics and government
ISBN 0-393-04012-7   LC 96-46010

First published 1996 in the United Kingdom

The author of these pieces is "at once critical of a culture that remains bleakly conformist in the aftermath of Communist rule and empathetic for its having known nothing else. With consistent equanimity, she examines the frustrating plight of the novice Balkan democracies. On a more quotidian level, too, she finds that much is

wanting, measured against Western standards of *richesse*, congeniality, and even taxi service. Owing largely to Drakulić's knack for drawing humor from an abundance of anecdotes—whether about a toothpaste monopoly or the bureaucratic cartwheels required to purchase a vacuum cleaner—these essays read like stories." New Yorker

Encyclopedia of Eastern Europe; from the Congress of Vienna to the fall of communism; edited by Richard Frucht. Garland 2000 958p (Garland reference library of social science) $160   **947**

1. Eastern Europe
ISBN 0-8153-0092-1   LC 00-21517

"Alphabetically arranged entries include many biographies as well as issues (*Bessarabian question*), geographic entities, military events (*Brusilov Offensive June-August 1916*), literature, historical events, movements, etc. There are long articles on the history of the seven primary countries of the region: Albania, Bulgaria, Czechoslovakia, Hungary, Poland, Romania, and Yugoslavia. Separate articles cover a nation's geography, art, culture, language, literature, and émigrés. All entries include a bibliography and *see also* references." Booklist

Figes, Orlando

Natasha's dance; a cultural history of Russia. Metropolitan Bks. 2002 xxxiii, 728p il maps $35   **947**

1. Russia—Civilization
ISBN 0-8050-5783-8   LC 2002-71881

Also available in paperback from Picador

The author "describes the twists and turns of Russian history through cultural and artistic events from the founding of Rus in the 12th century through the Soviet era." Libr J

"Figes succeeds in describing the extraordinary scope and power of Russian culture—and in outlining its great themes and issues—in a way that gives the reader a far better understanding of Russia than any history focusing solely on the progression of autocrats, wars and conquests." N Y Times Book Rev

Includes bibliographical references

Hosking, Geoffrey A., 1942-

Russia and the Russians; a history; {by} Geoffrey Hosking. Belknap Press 2001 718p il map $35; pa $18.95   **947**

1. Russia—History 2. Soviet Union—History
ISBN 0-674-00473-6; 0-674-01114-7 (pa)
          LC 00-65085

Hosking argues "that Russia was far more successful in constructing an imperial identity than in envisioning a nation evolving from its diversity." New Leader

"This is a high-quality overview, suitable for all libraries." Booklist

Russia: people and empire, 1552-1917; [by] Geoffrey Hosking. Harvard Univ. Press 1997 548p maps $33; pa $15.16   **947**

1. Russian national characteristics 2. Russia—History
ISBN 0-674-78118-X; 0-674-78119-8 (pa)
          LC 97-5069

The author explores the question "of how and why the Russians never developed a sense of nation. He argues that the Russian monarchy and aristocracy were always more interested in building an expansive empire than in promoting the belief in nationhood, something understood by the powerless peasantry. The expensive and in-

Hosking, Geoffrey A., 1942-—*Continued*
efficient bureaucracy that emerged over the centuries
weighed against any possibility of community, and in the
end this tottering edifice was unable to withstand the cat-
aclysm of World War I. Hosking has brought a powerful
intellect and great erudition to this work." Libr J
Includes bibliographical references

Kaufman, Jonathan
A hole in the heart of the world; being
Jewish in Eastern Europe. Viking 1997 328p
il hardcover o.p. paperback available $16
947
1. Jews—Eastern Europe 2. Holocaust survivors
3. Eastern Europe—History
ISBN 0-14-025453-6 (pa)   LC 96-25656
This work "traces the lives of five Holocaust survivors
who continued to live in Eastern Europe after WWII.
Four of the survivors were Jewish and, in addition to being hunted by Nazis during the war, they and their children endured intermittent waves of postwar anti-
Semitism." Publ Wkly
This book "becomes much more than just a sketch of
a few Eastern European Jewish survivors; it becomes a
window into the history of 20th-century Eastern European Jewry. And since no ethnic minority was more a part
of European intellectual and cultural life than the Jews,
Kaufman is also able to provide more general glimpses
into the area's recent history." New Leader

Massie, Suzanne
Land of the firebird; the beauty of old
Russia. Simon & Schuster 1980 493p o.p.;
HeartTree Press paperback available $32
947
1. Russia—Civilization 2. Russian art
ISBN 0-9644184-1-X (pa)   LC 80-12860
"A Touchstone book"
The author's intent "is to give 'a sense of the whole,
now-vanished culture of old Russia . . . to describe that
beauty which the Russians once knew how to create,
what they loved, and admired and how they once lived
and rejoiced.'" N Y Times Book Rev
Includes bibliographical references

Milner-Gulland, R. R.
Cultural atlas of Russia and the former
Soviet Union; by Robin Milner-Gulland with
Nikolai Dejevsky. rev ed. Checkmark Bks.
1998 240p il maps $50   **947**
1. Russia—Civilization 2. Former Soviet republics
ISBN 0-8160-3815-5   LC 98-29263
"An Andromeda book"
First published 1989 with title: Cultural atlas of Russia
and the Soviet Union
This survey of the civilizations of Russia and the for-
mer Soviet republics is divided into three parts: The geographical background, History, and Regions and countries
of the former Soviet Union
"Aimed at the general reader, the atlas is easy to use,
informative, and entertaining." Choice [review of 1989
edition]
Includes bibliographical references

Riasanovsky, Nicholas Valentine, 1923-
A history of Russia; [by] Nicholas V.
Riasanovsky. 6th ed. Oxford Univ. Press
2000 xx, 726p il maps $59.95   **947**
1. Russia—History 2. Soviet Union—History
ISBN 0-19-512179-1   LC 98-56640
First published 1963

This volume covers "the social, economic, cultural,
political, and military events of Russia's past. It includes
a . . . chapter on the post-Gorbachev era. . . . [It exam-
ines] the rise of Yeltsin, the nationalities question, and
Russia's attempts to adapt to market capitalism." Publisher's note
Includes bibliographical references

Rosenberg, Tina
The haunted land; facing Europe's ghosts
after communism. Random House 1995 xxiv,
437p hardcover o.p. paperback available $16
947
1. Eastern Europe—Politics and government 2. Communism
ISBN 0-679-74499-1 (pa)   LC 94-24750
This is a "report on the moral, political and legal dilemmas confronting Germany, Poland, the Czech Republic and Slovakia as they face their Communist pasts."
Publ Wkly
"In describing the predicaments and yearnings of people poised between easy-to-repress memories and hard-
to-fulfill dreams, Ms. Rosenberg shows shrewd understanding. She has talked boldly to everyone, listened well
and written a sad and important story." N Y Times Book
Rev
Includes bibliographical references

Schmemann, Serge
Echoes of a native land; two centuries of a
Russian village. Knopf 1997 350p il
hardcover o.p. paperback available $15   **947**
1. Osorgin family 2. Koltsovo (Russia)—History
ISBN 0-679-75707-4 (pa)   LC 96-52205
"Schmemann reports on two centuries of his family
lineage in [the village of Sergiyevskoye], . . . known today as Koltsovo. He begins . . . [in] the 19th century,
describing estate life and the people's devotion to the
czar. He continues with the Russian Revolution, which
drove his family out of the area and eventually to
France. Finally, Schmemann discusses the transition to
communism and its effects on the region." Libr J
Includes bibliographical references

Stokes, Gale
The walls came tumbling down; the
collapse of communism in Eastern Europe.
Oxford Univ. Press 1993 319p hardcover o.p.
paperback available $26.95   **947**
1. Communism 2. Eastern Europe—Politics and government
ISBN 0-19-506645-6 (pa)   LC 92-44862
The author "deals with all the formerly Communist
countries in Eastern Europe except Albania, and he
traces the history of the collapse of the Soviet-type regimes rather than concentrating . . . on their evolution
since the collapse." N Y Times Book Rev
This book "can be recommended as a coherent, well-
written history that defines its time frame well, provides
sound coverage, makes prudent judgments, and wears its
analysis lightly. . . . Stokes's overview traces the ebb
and flow of personalities and events in a manner that is
both accessible to lay readers and informative to scholars." Libr J

Volkov, Solomon

St. Petersburg; a cultural history; translated by Antonina W. Bouis. Free Press 1995 598p il hardcover o.p. paperback available $26.50
947

1. Saint Petersburg (Russia)—History
ISBN 0-684-83296-8 (pa)   LC 95-24116
The author offers an "overview of the traditions and individuals responsible for the great cultural evolution of St. Petersburg (Leningrad) and its ever-shifting mythos—from Pushkin to Chagall, from Gogol to Stravinsky and on to the cultural diaspora of the late 20th century." Libr J

Four of Volkov's "six very long chapters revolve around figures representative of certain periods or trends in the evolution of the St. Petersburg myth: Akhmatova, Balanchine, Shostakovich and Brodsky. Aspects of these central biographical and cultural portraits lead him . . . into countless mini-biographies of related figures." N Y Times Book Rev

Warnes, David

Chronicle of the Russian tsars; the reign-by-reign record of the rulers of imperial Russia. Thames & Hudson 1999 224p il $34.95
947

1. Russia—Kings and rulers 2. Russia—History
ISBN 0-500-05093-7   LC 98-61289
The introduction provides a "historical overview of how Tsarism came into being. The succeeding chapters are divided by major political events and social upheaval. . . . The reign of each tsar is analyzed within this framework, highlighting major events, but also giving abundant personal details such as marriages, children, etc." SLJ
Includes bibliographical references

947.08   Russia since 1855

Kurth, Peter

Tsar: the lost world of Nicholas and Alexandra; photographs by Peter Christopher. Little, Brown 1995 229p il hardcover o.p. paperback available $29.95
947.08

1. Nicholas II, Emperor of Russia, 1868-1918 2. Alexandra, Empress, consort of Nicholas II, Emperor of Russia, 1872-1918 3. Russia—History
ISBN 0-316-55788-9 (pa)   LC 95-12820
In text and photographs, this volume examines the lives of Tsar Nicholas II, the Empress Alexandra, and the Russian Imperial family
"A large format and a profusion of illustrations ostensibly mark it a picture book; instead it is a remarkably comprehensive overview of the reign of the last czar and his consort. . . . Kurth sensitively documents the imperial family's suffering as prisoners of the Bolsheviks and their eventual execution." Booklist
Includes bibliographical references

Massie, Robert K., 1929-

The Romanovs; the final chapter. Random House 1995 308p il hardcover o.p. paperback available $14.95
947.08

1. Nicholas II, Emperor of Russia, 1868-1918 2. House of Romanov 3. Russia—Kings and rulers
ISBN 0-345-40640-0 (pa)   LC 95-4718
This book "is divided into three major parts. The first segment—by far the most fascinating and original—fo-

cuses on the complex scientific process used in identifying the Romanovs' remains. . . . The second part concerns the various impostors who have claimed to be members of the Russian imperial family. . . . [The] third segment [is] a report on those Romanov émigrés—close relatives of the Czar's—who survived the Bolsheviks' persecution." N Y Times Book Rev
Includes bibliographical references

Moynahan, Brian

The Russian century; a photographic history of Russia's 100 years; text by Brian Moynahan; foreward by Yevgeny Yevtushenko; photographs researched by Annabel Merullo and Sarah Jackson. Random House 1994 320p il hardcover o.p. paperback available $16.95
947.08

1. Russia—History—Pictorial works
ISBN 0-679-76436-4 (pa)   LC 94-15256
An "overview of Russia's tragic history in the 20th century. The photographs were culled from numerous Russian archives, most previously sealed, and the result is a fresh and startling view of an embattled nation. . . . The text is as good as the photos. . . . Moynahan neatly condenses Russia's history while retaining a flair for the telling anecdote." Libr J

Pipes, Richard

A concise history of the Russian Revolution. Knopf 1995 431p il maps hardcover o.p. paperback available $16
947.08

1. Russia—History
ISBN 0-679-74544-0 (pa)   LC 95-3127
A one volume condensation of the author's The Russian Revolution and Russia under the Bolshevik regime
"Forcefully showing why the 70-year-old Communist experiment failed [Pipes] provides the nonacademic reader with accurate historical events in a highly readable format." Libr J
Includes bibliographical references

The Russian Revolution. Knopf 1990 xxiv, 944p il maps hardcover o.p. paperback available $25
947.08

1. Russia—History
ISBN 0-679-73660-3 (pa)   LC 89-35129
The author provides a "history of great turmoil, from the last decade of the nineteenth century, when student ferment reached troublesome proportions, to the Bolshevik takeover in October 1917 and the party's subsequent establishment of its own authoritarian regime." Booklist
This is a "massive, wonderfully vivid, gripping chronicle. . . . No other book so brilliantly clarifies the inner dynamics of the Russian Revolution." Publ Wkly
Includes bibliographical references

947.084   Russia (Soviet Union)— 1917-1991

Amis, Martin

Koba the dread; laughter and the twenty million. Hyperion 2002 306p il $24.95
947.084

1. Stalin, Joseph, 1879-1953 2. Soviet Union—Politics and government
ISBN 0-7868-6876-7
Also available in paperback from Vintage Bks.

Amis, Martin—Continued

This book "evokes a terrible crime, in fact several million crimes. Koba is Joseph Stalin, the 20 million his victims. Interwoven with [the author's] impressionistic narrative . . . are details of Amis's family history, along with his sparring with the memory of his late father, Kingsley, and a close friend, the English journalist Christopher Hitchens, both one-time defenders of Soviet rule." Libr J

"Amis create[s] a compelling narrative, summarizing vast amounts of information and presenting it in a lucid, accessible form." New York Times

Figes, Orlando

A people's tragedy; the Russian Revolution, 1891-1924. Viking 1997 xx, 923p hardcover o.p. paperback available $25

947.084

1. Soviet Union—History—1917-1921, Revolution
ISBN 0-14-024364-X (pa)   LC 96-36761
First published 1996 in the United Kingdom
This is a "history of the Russian Revolution from 1917 to Lenin's death in 1924." Choice
The author has "produced an engagingly written and well-researched book that will leave few readers with any doubts that the Bolsheviks, and especially their leader, Lenin, were ruthless killers, willing to sacrifice millions of lives for the sake of power and their own personal ambitions." N Y Times Book Rev
Includes bibliographical references

Hochschild, Adam, 1942-

The unquiet ghost; Russians remember Stalin. Viking 1994 xxvii, 304p il maps o.p.; Mariner Bks. paperback available $14

947.084

1. Stalin, Joseph, 1879-1953 2. Soviet Union—History
ISBN 0-618-25747-0 (pa)   LC 93-27473
In this look at Stalin's legacy the author "visits the ruins of the old prison camps of Kazakhstan and Kolyma, digs through the K.G.B. archives and spends a night at Stalin's seaside retreat. Most important, he interviews camp survivors, camp guards and the children of both. The questions he asks are of universal significance. . . . By asking these questions while traveling through today's Russia, Mr. Hochschild effectively places Stalinism in a modern context." N Y Times Book Rev
Includes bibliographical references

Medvedev, Roy Aleksandrovich, 1925-

Let history judge; the origins and consequences of Stalinism; [by] Roy Medvedev. rev and expanded ed, edited and translated by George Shriver. Columbia Univ. Press 1989 xxi, 903p $104; pa $35 **947.084**

1. Stalin, Joseph, 1879-1953 2. Soviet Union—Politics and government
ISBN 0-231-06350-4; 0-231-06351-2 (pa)
LC 89-758
Original Russian edition copyrighted 1967; first United States edition published 1972 by Knopf
"Never have Stalin's crimes against humanity been more forcefully or more thoroughly documented than in . . . [this book, which] distills firsthand testimonies of the mass arrests, torture, imprisonment and executions that befell millions of innocent Soviet citizens." Publ Wkly
Includes bibliographical references

Pipes, Richard

Russia under the Bolshevik regime. Knopf 1993 587p il o.p.; Vintage Bks. paperback available $21 **947.084**

1. Lenin, Vladimir Il'ich, 1870-1924 2. Soviet Union—History
ISBN 0-679-76184-5 (pa)   LC 92-42710
"In this sequel to *The Russian Revolution* Pipes persuasively argues that Lenin's one-party dictatorship, through its terrorizing, suppression of the press, censorship and monopolistic control of cultural organizations, set the stage for Stalin's genocidal totalitarianism. . . . Pipes shows how both Hitler and Mussolini drew on Lenin's tyrannical methods, and he perceptively analyzes the mind-set of Western fellow-travelers who wove fantasies of the U.S.S.R. as an egalitarian Eden while rationalizing its evils." Publ Wkly
Includes bibliographical references

Reed, John, 1887-1920

Ten days that shook the world   **947.084**

1. Soviet Union—History—1917-1921, Revolution
Available in paperback from Penguin Bks.
First published 1919 by International Pubs.
"A reportorial, firsthand, and sympathetic account of the November Revolution in Russia (1917). . . . After prefatory explanation of political groups and other organizations, and of the background of the uprising, the work tells with graphic detail of the fall of the provisional government, the revolution and counterrevolution, the solidifying of power, and the resultant congress." Oxford Companion to Am Lit. 5th edition

947.085   Russia (Soviet Union)—1953-1991

Coleman, Fred

The decline and fall of the Soviet Empire; forty years that shook the world, from Stalin to Yeltsin. St. Martin's Press 1996 459p hardcover o.p. paperback available $19.95

947.085

1. Soviet Union—History
ISBN 0-312-16816-0 (pa)   LC 96-1658
"Arguing that Soviet communism was doomed by its own internal weaknesses, Coleman asserts that the empire was never as powerful as the West thought, and that the U.S. could have hastened its demise had we been more astute in watching for cracks in the armor. He also warns against the resurgence of a revitalized KGB, if not now, then under a future authoritarian regime. Although at times readers may unavoidably sense that Coleman is writing with the advantage of hindsight, he marshals his evidence to make a convincing case." Publ Wkly

Gorbachev, Mikhail

On my country and the world; [by] Gorbachev. Columbia Univ. Press 1999 300p $50; pa $17.95 **947.085**

1. World politics—1965- 2. Soviet Union—Politics and government 3. Russia (Federation)—Politics and government
ISBN 0-231-11514-8; 0-231-11515-6 (pa)
LC 99-31273
The former Soviet leader presents an analysis of his country's Communist past and an account of his role in government in the 1980s. Gorbachev also includes ideas

Gorbachev, Mikhail—*Continued*
for political change
Gorbachev is "fresh and candid in its initial section on the pluses and minuses of the Revolution of 1917." Nation

Remnick, David
Lenin's tomb; Russia and the fall of Communism. Random House 1993 576p hardcover o.p. paperback available $15.95
947.085
1. Soviet Union—Politics and government
ISBN 0-679-75125-4 (pa)　　　　LC 92-56841
"This book is a record of almost four years beginning in 1988 when David Remnick, a Washington Post reporter, was assigned to Moscow. . . . He argues convincingly that what did in the old Soviet leadership, right down through Mikhail Gorbachev, was its unending assault not only on people but on memory. By making a secret of history, it made its people increasingly distracted, and desperate, until they overthrew it." N Y Times Book Rev

Satter, David
Age of delirium; the decline and fall of the Soviet Union. Knopf 1996 424p o.p.; Yale Univ. Press paperback available $17.95
947.085
1. Soviet Union—History
ISBN 0-300-08705-5　　　　LC 95-38592
The author "appraises the Russians by writing about the travails of average people in the last decade of Soviet rule. Objects of the Communist ideology's enforced unanimity, his subjects include dissidents sent to psychiatric wards, persecuted religious people, a TASS journalist learning how to write the party line, and miners exploited by the workers' state. . . . An insightful from-the-ground-up view of typical Russians whom the top-down politicians are now courting." Booklist

947.086　Russia—1991-

Lieven, Anatol
Chechnya; tombstone of Russian power; with photographs by Heidi Bradner. Yale Univ. Press 1998 436p il $50　　**947.086**
1. Chechnya (Russia)
ISBN 0-300-07398-4　　　　LC 98-84479
This is an account of "Chechnya's strategic and symbolic significance, the breakdown of legitimacy, mismanagement and pervasive corruption within the Russian state, from Yeltsin down, which destroyed public and military morale." Publ Wkly
"The book is a great, ostentatiously erudite festival of ideas, sometimes brilliant, sometimes dubious, but never less than interesting." N Y Times Book Rev

Remnick, David
Resurrection; the struggle for a new Russia. Random House 1997 398p hardcover o.p. paperback available $15　　**947.086**
1. Russia (Federation)—Politics and government
ISBN 0-375-75023-1 (pa)　　　　LC 96-47360
In this companion volume to Lenin's tomb, "Remnick concentrates on the post-Soviet scene and its prospects. . . . Chaotic uncertainty, massive corruption, and crime are notoriously present, yet the possibility of a different, better life also beckons. . . . This is an interesting, highly informative portrait of a country struggling toward a fateful future." Libr J
Includes bibliographical references

Service, Robert
A history of twentieth-century Russia. Harvard Univ. Press 1998 xxxiii, 653p il maps $32.50; pa $20.95　　**947.086**
1. Soviet Union—History 2. Russia (Federation)—History
ISBN 0-674-40347-9; 0-674-40348-7 (pa)
LC 97-37440
In this "survey of recent Russian history, Robert Service spans the . . . era from the rise of communism in the first decade of this century to the aftermath of its collapse in 1991." Economist
"A perceptive, judicious appraisal." Booklist
Includes bibliographical references

947.5　Caucasus

Baiev, Khassan
The Oath; a surgeon under fire; [by] Khassan Baiev; with Ruth and Nicholas Daniloff. Walker & Co. 2003 xxii, 376p il $26　　**947.5**
1. Chechnya (Russia)
ISBN 0-8027-1404-8　　　　LC 2003-52502
This "memoir tells the story of a surgeon in Chechnya who, through two invasions of his homeland, refused to take up arms, choosing instead to treat civilians and soldiers on both sides, even as he was targeted for death by both Russian and Chechen leaders." Booklist
The author "is modest, which only adds to his heroism. But more than that, he has humanized the Chechens, whom others have portrayed as terrorists. Russian president Vladimir Putin has tried to equate Russia's fight against the Chechens with the U.S. battle against al-Qaida. Those who read this stirring memoir will be hard-pressed to see the situation so simply." Publ Wkly

948　Scandinavia

The **Oxford** illustrated history of the Vikings; edited by Peter Sawyer. Oxford Univ. Press 1997 298p il maps hardcover o.p. paperback available $24.95　　**948**
1. Vikings
ISBN 0-19-285434-8 (pa)　　　　LC 97-16649
This illustrated collection of articles includes discussion of the Vikings' impact on England, Iceland, Greenland, Russia, and the Frankish and Danish Empires; Viking ships and ship-building; Viking religion; and the ways in which Vikings have been portrayed throughout history. Significant archaeological finds are featured
Includes bibliographical references

Roesdahl, Else
The Vikings; translated by Susan M. Margeson and Kirsten Williams. Allen Lane 1991 322p il maps o.p.; Viking paperback available $15.95　　**948**
1. Vikings
ISBN 0-14-025282-7 (pa)
Original Danish edition, 1987
A survey of Viking civilization from c.750-c.1050. "About one-third of the book deals with Viking expansion into Russia, Normandy, the British Isles, Iceland, Greenland, etc. . . . Most of the book surveys the geography, people, society, religion, art, etc., of the Vikings' Scandinavian homelands." Libr J
Includes bibliographical references

948.97 Finland

Beach, Hugh
A year in Lapland; guest of the reindeer herders. Smithsonian Institution Press 1993 227p il o.p.; University of Wash. Press paperback available $19.95   **948.97**
1. Lapland
ISBN 0-295-98037-0 (pa)   LC 92-30436
The author "tells of his first year among the Saami reindeer herders of Swedish Lapland. His narrative interweaves adventure, descriptions of the harsh beauty of the landscape, supernatural tales and ancient myths. Beach also explores topics of change in the lives of the herders brought on by laws requiring village groups to move and by adaptations to new items such as rubber boots, seaplanes, and appliances." Libr J

949.2 Netherlands

Schama, Simon
The embarrassment of riches; an interpretation of Dutch culture in the Golden Age. Knopf 1987 698p il maps hardcover o.p. paperback available $23   **949.2**
1. Netherlands—Civilization
ISBN 0-679-78124-2 (pa)   LC 86-45418
The author aims to show "how, in the seventeenth century, a modest assortment of farming, fishing and shipping communities, without shared language, religion or government, transformed themselves into a formidable world empire—the Dutch Republic." Publisher's note
"Delving into customs, beliefs, popular art and quirks of behavior, Schama has fashioned a tour de force, a profound, unconventional and rewarding portrait of a people." Publ Wkly
Includes bibliographical references

949.5 Greece

Clogg, Richard, 1939-
A concise history of Greece. 2nd ed. Cambridge Univ. Press 2002 291p il maps (Cambridge concise histories) $53; pa $19   **949.5**
1. Greece—History
ISBN 0-521-80872-3; 0-521-00479-9 (pa)
            LC 2002-725551
First published 1992
This is an illustrated introduction to the history of modern Greece from the late eighteenth century to the present
Includes bibliographical references

Norwich, John Julius, 1929-
Byzantium. Knopf 1989-1996 c1988-c1995 3v il maps ea $45   **949.5**
1. Byzantine Empire   LC 88-45508
Volume one and two first published 1988-1991 in the United Kingdom
Contents [v1] The early centuries (ISBN 0-394-53778-5); [v2] The apogee (ISBN 0-394-53779-3); [v3] The decline and fall (ISBN 0-679-41650-1)
This is a history of the Byzantine Empire from its foundation by Constantine the Great through its conquest by the Ottoman Turks
Includes bibliographical references

A short history of Byzantium. Knopf 1997 430p il maps hardcover o.p. paperback available $17   **949.5**
1. Byzantine Empire
ISBN 0-679-77269-3 (pa)   LC 96-44458
"In his shorter telling of the history between the founding of Constantinople in 330 and its fall in 1453, Lord Norwich has sacrificed none of the virtues of the longer work: lively narration and a taste for the eccentric anecdote and revelatory detail." N Y Times Book Rev

949.6 Balkan Peninsula

Glenny, Misha
The Balkans; nationalism, war, and the Great Powers, 1804-1999. Viking 2000 xxvi, 726p il maps hardcover o.p. paperback available $20   **949.6**
1. Balkan Peninsula—History
ISBN 0-14-023377-6 (pa)   LC 99-89564
According to Glenny, "Europe's Great Powers have rearranged the Balkan states to suit their own purposes three times during the past 200 years: at the Congress of Berlin in 1878, at the Paris Peace Conference following World War I, and during the 1940s, when the USSR came to influence much of the region. . . . This exhaustive and thoroughly researched history covers the breakup of the 19th-century empires and the formation and subsequent demise of the 20th-century ones." Libr J
Includes bibliographical references

Kaplan, Robert D.
Balkan ghosts; a journey through history. St. Martin's Press 1993 xxvii, 307p o.p.; Vintage Bks. paperback available $14 **949.6**
1. Balkan Peninsula—History
ISBN 0-679-74981-0 (pa)   LC 92-43300
"Focusing on the former Yugoslavia and on Rumania, Bulgaria, and Greece, Kaplan takes the reader on a . . . tour through the peninsula, using as his own guides the writings of John Reed, C.L. Sulzberger, and Rebecca West." Libr J
"Mr. Kaplan occasionally falls prey to gullibility, but the fantastic stories he gathers bring one closer to understanding the real history of the Balkans." N Y Times Book Rev

Mazower, Mark
The Balkans: a short history. Modern Lib. 2000 xliii, 188p maps (Modern Library chronicles) $19.95; pa $11.95   **949.6**
1. Balkan Peninsula—History
ISBN 0-679-64087-8; 0-8129-6621-X (pa)
            LC 00-56244
Mazower "has written a concise history of Europe's troubled southeastern corner that is both sympathetic to the region's never-ending struggle for identity and freedom from invaders and critical of its inhabitants' recurring failure to reconcile the religious and cultural differences imposed on them by the powers of the West and the East." Publ Wkly
This "is an excellent primer on the region's history, especially the growth of the nation-state in the 19th century." Economist
Includes bibliographical references

949.7 Yugoslavia, Croatia, Slovenia, Bosnia and Hercegovina, Macedonia

Clark, Wesley K.

Waging modern war; Bosnia, Kosovo, and the future of combat. PublicAffairs 2001 xxxi, 479p il hardcover o.p. paperback available $18 **949.7**
1. Yugoslav War, 1991-1995 2. Kosovo (Serbia)—History
ISBN 1-58648-139-8 (pa)   LC 01-19717
This is an account of the former Supreme Allied Commander's experiences during the Kosovo crises. "Clark tells a story of frustration with NATO allies, who had to approve each operation and target selection, and with U.S. policymakers as he tried to formulate a strategy that would achieve his military goals." Libr J

Cohen, Roger

Hearts grown brutal; sagas of Sarajevo. Random House 1998 xlix, 523p il maps hardcover o.p. paperback available $25
949.7
1. Yugoslavia—History 2. Yugoslav War, 1991-1995 3. Sarajevo (Bosnia and Hercegovina)
ISBN 0-8129-9178-8 (pa)   LC 99-204500
"Cohen draws on Bosnia's history as well as on the personal stories of four 'typical' families—Serb, Muslim, Croat and Jew—to illustrate the area's inextricable tangle of identity." Publ Wkly
Cohen "has written a lyrical, but also embittered and anti-historical account of the siege of Sarajevo. . . . Though he pays an occasional homage to the past, he is essentially present-minded, concerned largely with the here and now." Christ Sci Monit
Includes bibliographical references

Donia, Robert J.

Bosnia and Hercegovina; a tradition betrayed; [by] Robert J. Donia, John V.A. Fine Jr.; with maps by John C. Hamer. Columbia Univ. Press 1994 318p il maps $50.50; pa $23   **949.7**
1. Bosnia and Hercegovina 2. Yugoslavia—History
ISBN 0-231-10160-0; 0-231-10161-9 (pa)
LC 94-16223
This book "at once interprets the region's complex religious history, defends its distinctiveness against claims of Serbia and Croatia, and demonstrates its people's use of religion as a 'code' of identity rather than as a source of conflict. . . . [This book's] purpose and clarity assure it a secure place in the literature of southeastern Europe." Libr J
Includes bibliographical references

Hall, Brian, 1959-

The impossible country; a journey through the last days of Yugoslavia. Godine 1994 335p $23.95   **949.7**
1. Yugoslavia—History
ISBN 1-56792-000-4   LC 93-38896
Also available in paperback from Penguin Bks.
The author "was one of the last outsiders permitted to travel freely in Yugoslavia during the final days of its existence. From early May to mid-September 1991 he questioned members of the various Balkan 'tribes' in Zagreb, Belgrade, Sarajevo and points in between, listening to comments on their history, prejudices, superstitions, fears, aspirations and opinions of other ethnic and national groups. . . . Hall's account, which he modestly calls a travel book, is an excellent source for understanding the complications and contradictions of the current Balkan crisis." Publ Wkly
Includes bibliographical references

Ignatieff, Michael

Virtual war; Kosovo and beyond. Holt & Co. 2000 246p il o.p.; Picador paperback available $14   **949.7**
1. Kosovo (Serbia)—History
ISBN 0-312-27835-7 (pa)   LC 00-20015
"In essays about NATO's air war against Serbia, Ignatieff describes the roles of central figures in it: diplomat Richard Holbrooke, General Wesley Clark, and prosecutor Louise Arbour, the indictor of Serb leader Slobodan Milosevic. Ignatieff tosses in vignettes of his visit to an Albanian Kosovar refugee camp, his postwar sojourn to friends in Belgrade, and his debate-by-letter with economist Robert Skidelsky over the morality of waging war for human rights." Booklist
Includes bibliographical references

Judah, Tim, 1962-

Kosovo; war and revenge. Yale Univ. Press 2000 xx, 348p $45; pa $19.95   **949.7**
1. Kosovo (Serbia)—History
ISBN 0-300-08313-0; 0-300-08354-8 (pa)
LC 99-89404
Judah presents an account of the war in Kosovo, on which he reported from the refugee camps. After the Serb withdrawal, he went into Kosovo with NATO forces and reported from Pristina and Belgrade
The author "describes events in modern Kosovo in thorough detail and with a serious attempt at fairness to all parties." Atl Mon
Includes bibliographical references

Maass, Peter, 1960-

Love thy neighbor; a story of war. Knopf 1996 305p hardcover o.p. paperback available $14   **949.7**
1. Yugoslav War, 1991-1995 2. Bosnia and Hercegovina
ISBN 0-679-76389-9 (pa)   LC 95-39250
This book on the Yugoslav conflict is based on Maass's experiences as the Washington Post's reporter in Bosnia
"Maass was only in Bosnia for about a year, from 1992 to 1993, but he saw a great deal. And he displays extraordinary sensitivity to the ambiguities of his position." Nation
Includes bibliographical references

McAllester, Matthew, 1969-

Beyond the Mountains of the Damned; the war inside Kosovo. New York Univ. Press 2002 227p il $30; pa $17.95   **949.7**
1. Kosovo (Serbia)—History
ISBN 0-8147-5660-3; 0-8147-5661-1 (pa)
LC 2001-4370
This is an account of the war in Kosovo. McAllester "tells the story of Pec, Kosovo's most destroyed city and the site of the earliest and worst atrocities of the war, through the lives of two men—one Serb and one Kosovar." Publisher's note

McAllester, Matthew, 1969-—*Continued*

"McAllester's spare, understated prose . . . is potent, as is his exploration of the human side of geopolitics and war." Publ Wkly

Includes bibliographical references

Rieff, David

Slaughterhouse; Bosnia and the failure of the West. Simon & Schuster 1995 240p hardcover o.p. paperback available $18.95

949.7

1. Yugoslav War, 1991-1995 2. Bosnia and Hercegovina

ISBN 0-684-81903-1 (pa)   LC 94-40148

This account of the war in the former Yugoslavia grew out of Rieff's travels in the region from 1992 through 1994

"*Slaughterhouse* is perhaps the most powerful, passionate, and penetrating dissection of a Westerner of the ongoing Bosnian tragedy." Booklist

Rohde, David

Endgame; the betrayal and fall of Srebrenica, Europe's worst massacre since World War II. Farrar, Straus & Giroux 1997 440p o.p.; Westview Press paperback available $20   **949.7**

1. Yugoslav War, 1991-1995 2. Srebrenica (Bosnia and Hercegovina)

ISBN 0-8133-3533-7 (pa)   LC 96-51729

This "is an account of the capture of the small Bosnian town of Srebrenica in July 1995 and the subsequent killing by the conquering Serbs of around 7,000 of its people. The massacre gnaws at the Western conscience not just because of its coldbloodedness and size, but because in April 1993 Srebrenica had become the first place in the world to be declared a 'safe area' by the United Nations." N Y Times Book Rev

"Rohde argues that the fall of Srebrenica could have been prevented, but he is ultimately unable to explain the 'collective failure' of the United States, the United Nations, and NATO in stopping the massacre. His investigation is carefully documented by over 300 footnotes. This is an important and revealing book." Libr J

Silber, Laura

Yugoslavia; death of a nation; [by] Laura Silber and Allan Little. rev and updated ed. Penguin Bks. 1997 403p il maps pa $15

949.7

1. Yugoslav War, 1991-1995 2. Yugoslavia—Politics and government

ISBN 0-14-026263-6   LC 96-36086

First published 1995 in the United Kingdom with title: The death of Yugoslavia; first United States edition published 1996 by TV Books

This book, a companion volume to a BBC television series called The Death of Yugoslavia, chronicles the disintegration of the Socialist Federal Republic of Yugoslavia in 1991 and charts the development of the ensuing conflict

This is "an impressive achievement. Strong on characters, regional nuances, and the 'inner' diplomatic game, 'Yugoslavia' is a work of depth and breadth that will be hard to eclipse. It answers many perplexities left from five years of Balkan intrigues and war." Christ Sci Monit [review of 1996 edition]

950   Asia. Orient. Far East

Fallows, James M.

Looking at the sun; [by] James Fallows. Pantheon Bks. 1994 517p hardcover o.p. paperback available $15   **950**

1. East Asia

ISBN 0-679-76162-4 (pa)   LC 93-38367

The author discusses the "culture, government and economic development of 11 East Asian nations. . . . Mr. Fallows's central thesis is that Western societies, especially the United States, 'have been using the wrong mental tools to classify, shape and understand the information they receive about Asia.'" N Y Times Book Rev

"A fascinating, fresh, and potentially controversial contemplation of the global market." Booklist

Levinson, David, 1947-

Encyclopedia of modern Asia; [by] David Levinson, Karen Christensen. Scribner 2002 6v il maps set $695   **950**

1. Asia—Encyclopedias

ISBN 0-684-80617-7   LC 2002-8712

This "set is alphabetically arranged by topic. Volume 6 provides the index for the set. . . . The topics cover the 33 Asian countries' geography, economics, politics, human rights, cultures and languages, and biographies. Sidebars derived from primary source materials and black-and-white illustrations are interspersed throughout the text." Am Ref Books Annu, 2003

Includes bibliographical references

951   China and adjacent areas

Blunden, Caroline

Cultural atlas of China; by Caroline Blunden and Mark Elvin. rev ed. Checkmark Bks. 1998 240p il maps $50   **951**

1. China—Civilization

ISBN 0-8160-3814-7   LC 98-34322

First published 1983

"The first part of the book covers geography and patterns of settlement. The second discusses the politics, society, and art of China from prehistory to the present day. The third part consists of thematic essays on subjects such as religion, calligraphy, and poetry. . . . Although coverage is strongest in history and art, the complex present is not neglected. The maps are superb and the illustrations exceptional." Booklist [review of 1983 edition]

Includes bibliographical references

The **Cambridge** encyclopedia of China; editor, Brian Hook; consultant editor, Denis Twitchett. 2nd ed. Cambridge Univ. Press 1991 502p il maps $75   **951**

1. China—Encyclopedias

ISBN 0-521-35594-X   LC 91-18600

First published 1982

"Topics cover history, law, medicine, religion, literature, and architecture, with less emphasis on social conditions. . . . A useful purchase, especially for smaller libraries." Libr J

The **Cambridge** history of China; general editors, Denis Twitchett and John K. Fairbank. Cambridge Univ. Press 1978-2002 12v apply to publisher for price and availability **951**

1. China—History   LC 76-29852

Twelve volumes of a projected fifteen volume set

Contents: v1 The Ch'in and Han Empires, 221 B.C.-A.D. 220 (ISBN 0-521-24327-0); v3 Sui and T'ang China, 589-906, pt.1 (ISBN 0-521-21446-7); v6 Alien regimes and border states, 907-1368 (ISBN 0-521-24331-9); v7 The Ming Dynasty, 1368-1644, pt.1 (ISBN 0-521-24332-7); v8 The Ming Dynasty, 1368-1644, pt.2 (ISBN 0-521-24333-5); v9 The Ch'ing Empire to 1800, pt.1 (ISBN 0-521-24334-3); v10 Late Ch'ing, 1800-1911, pt.1 (ISBN 0-521-21447-5); v11 Late Ch'ing, 1800-1911, pt.2 (ISBN 0-521-22029-7); v12 Republican China, 1912-1949, pt.1 (ISBN 0-521-23541-3); v13 Republican China, 1912-1949, pt.2 (ISBN 0-521-24338-6); v14 The People's Republic, pt.1 (ISBN 0-521-24336-X); v15 The People's Republic, pt.2: Revolutions within the Chinese Revolution, 1966-1982 (ISBN 0-521-24337-8)

"An important series for scholars, this is also a valuable reference tool for general collections." Libr J

Includes bibliographical references

Dalai Lama XIV, 1935-

My Tibet; text by His Holiness the fourteenth Dalai Lama of Tibet; photographs and introduction by Galen Rowell. University of Calif. Press 1990 162p il hardcover o.p. paperback available $34.95   **951**

1. Tibet (China)—Pictorial works
ISBN 0-520-08948-0 (pa)   LC 90-10868

"A Mountain Light Press book"

This is "a volume of photographs taken in recent years by Galen Rowell, with a text drawn from interviews with the Dalai Lama or essays written previously by him." N Y Times Book Rev

"Nowhere has the logic of merging Buddhist philosophy and environmentalism received a clearer and more compelling expression than in My Tibet. . . . It is a model of the kind of chemistry that can develop when both a wonderful photographer and a thoughtful writer care deeply about their subject." Nat Hist

Dong, Stella

Shanghai, 1842-1949; the rise and fall of a decadent city. Morrow 2000 318p il hardcover o.p. paperback available $15   **951**

1. Shanghai (China)
ISBN 0-06-093481-6 (pa)   LC 99-41902

An "account of a city legendary for decadence, violence, and greedy imperialism. Dong meticulously details the European commercial interests that deliberately promoted opium trafficking and exploited the land and people of Shanghai with every conceivable vice for nearly 100 years." Booklist

Fairbank, John King, 1907-1991

China; a new history; [by] John King Fairbank and Merle Goldman. enl ed. Belknap Press 1998 546p il maps hardcover o.p. paperback available $19.95   **951**

1. China—History
ISBN 0-674-11673-9 (pa)   LC 98-9474

First published 1992

Fairbank covers the history of China from paleolithic cultures of 400,000 B.C. up to 1989. Goldman adds a chapter on events in the post-Mao period and a new preface and epilogue

Includes bibliographical references

China: tradition & transformation; [by] John K. Fairbank, Edwin O. Reischauer. rev ed. Houghton Mifflin 1989 551p il pa $41.96   **951**

1. China—History
ISBN 0-395-49692-6   LC 88-83732

First published 1978

Also issued as part of East Asia: tradition & transformation, by John Fairbank, Edwin O. Reischauer, Albert Craig

This study of the history and culture of China focuses on the traditions of the Chinese people and the changes imposed on the country by foreign influences

The great Chinese revolution: 1800-1985. Harper & Row 1986 396p maps hardcover o.p. paperback available $16   **951**

1. China—History
ISBN 0-06-039076-X (pa)   LC 86-665

"A Cornelia & Michael Bessie book"

Contents: Late imperial China: growth and change, 1800-1895; The transformation of the late imperial order, 1895-1911; The era of the first Chinese Republic, 1912-1949; The Chinese People's Republic, 1949-1985

"The book is never pedantic, but gathers together a lifetime of scholarship plus a true gift for presentation of complex issues and a fine eye for telling illustration." Libr J

Includes bibliographical references

Hessler, Peter, 1969-

River town; two years on the Yangtze. HarperCollins Pubs. 2001 402p maps hardcover o.p. paperback available $13.95   **951**

1. Yangtze River valley (China)—Description
ISBN 0-06-095374-8 (pa)   LC 00-49872

Hessler recounts his experiences living and teaching in the small Sichuanese city of Fuling, which is located in the Yangtze River valley. "Hessler arrived in Fuling in 1996 to teach English classes at the local college, as one of the first two Peace Corps volunteers to serve there." N Y Times Book Rev

"This touching memoir . . . transcends the boundaries of the travel genre and will appeal to anyone wanting to learn more about the heart and soul of the Chinese people." Libr J

Hsü, Immanuel Chung-yueh, 1923-

The rise of modern China; [by] Immanuel C.Y. Hsü. Oxford Univ. Press il maps $51.95   **951**

1. China—History

First published 1970. (6th edition 2000) Periodically revised

An examination of China's social, economic, intellectual, and political history, from 1600 to the present

Includes bibliographical references

Kemenade, Willem van

China, Hong Kong, Taiwan, Inc.; translated from the Dutch by Diane Webb. Knopf 1997 444p hardcover o.p. paperback available $16   **951**

1. China—Politics and government 2. Hong Kong (China) 3. Taiwan

ISBN 0-679-77756-3 (pa)   LC 97-71923

This is an "analysis of China's recent past and reflections on its future direction. Van Kemenade explores the anticipated political and economic fallout from the mainland's absorption of capitalist Hong Kong . . . and the possibility of its eventual takeover of Taiwan. He projects a foreseeable confrontation with Japan over Asian hegemony, ethnic and economic upheavals on China's 'wild' western border that abutts former Soviet republics and a political backlash from the fast-growing middle class, which in its pursuit of wealth seems no longer loyal to socialist ideals." Publ Wkly

Nomachi, Kazuyoshi, 1946-

Tibet; introduction by Robert A.F. Thurman; foreword by the 14th Dalai Lama. Shambhala Publs. 1997 198p il maps $55

951

1. Buddhism 2. Tibet (China)—Pictorial works

ISBN 1-57062-256-6   LC 97-3533

Pictured in this collection of photographs "are sacred mountains, rivers, and immense expanses of open land and sky. . . . Attuned to Tibet's intrinsic spirituality, Nomachi also photographed the ancient temples, weathered stupas, and intricate mandalas. . . . And then there are the people: villagers and nomads bundled up against the cold; young monks wrapped in jewel-hued Buddhist robes." Booklist

Perkins, Dorothy

Encyclopedia of China; the essential reference to China, its history and culture. Facts on File 1999 662p il $104.50   **951**

1. China—Encyclopedias

ISBN 0-8160-2693-9   LC 97-52622

"A Roundtable Press book"

"Entries are arranged alphabetically and cover a broad range of topics, including religion, politics, Westerners prominent in Chinese history, cities, regions, the arts, and history. Copious cross-references facilitate browsing." Booklist

Prager, Emily

Wuhu diary; on taking my adopted daughter back to her hometown in China. Random House 2001 238p il hardcover o.p. paperback available $13   **951**

1. China—Description 2. Adoption

ISBN 0-385-72199-4 (pa)   LC 2001-19104

Prager discusses bringing her adopted daughter on a visit back to China. The book "chronicles mother and daughter's seven-week journey to Wuhu, a small city in the southern Chinese province of Anhui, where LuLu eventually celebrates her fifth birthday." Christ Sci Monit

"For anyone considering multicultural adoption or already involved in one, this compelling work offers encouragement and an example of how to help an adopted child get acquainted with her roots and build her sense of self. For others, it provides a wonderful view of a part of China seldom written about." Libr J

Preston, Diana

The Boxer Rebellion; the dramatic story of China's war on foreigners that shook the world in the summer of 1900. Walker & Co. 2000 xxvii, 436p il maps $28   **951**

1. China—History

ISBN 0-8027-1361-0   LC 00-39243

Also available in paperback from Berkley Pub. Group

"The Boxers, Chinese peasants who blamed foreigners for the dislocation of their lives, began by murdering missionaries and converts and destroying railroad and telegraph lines in the countryside. Gaining strength, they besieged the foreign quarters of Tientsin and Peking until European and Japanese troops came to the rescue." New Yorker

"Preston's account, compiled from the many letters, diaries, and memoirs by European survivors of the siege, captures an odd strain of mordant humor." N Y Times Book Rev

Includes bibliographical references

Schell, Orville

Virtual Tibet; searching for Shangri-la from the Himalayas to Hollywood. Metropolitan Bks. 2000 340p $26; pa $15   **951**

1. Tibet (China) 2. Tibet (China) in motion pictures

ISBN 0-8050-4381-0; 0-8050-4382-9 (pa)

LC 99-88146

Schell examines romanticized visions of Tibet in Western travel accounts and films

The author is a "seasoned traveler in China, . . . and his book has the bracing air about it of disenchantment. The fact that he was a bit of a seeker once himself, mesmerized by the idea of Tibet, and of Communist China, makes him the perfect chronicler of such afflictions in others." N Y Rev Books

Seagrave, Sterling

The Soong dynasty. Harper & Row 1985 532p il hardcover o.p. paperback available $18   **951**

1. Sung family 2. China—History—1912-1949

ISBN 0-06-091318-5 (pa)   LC 83-48802

The author examines the impact that the influential Soong family had on modern China. One of T.V. Soong's daughters married Sun Yat-sen and the other Chiang Kai-shek

Includes bibliographical references

Spence, Jonathan D.

The Chan's great continent; China in Western minds. Norton 1998 279p hardcover o.p. paperback available $14.95   **951**

1. China—Civilization

ISBN 0-393-31989-X (pa)   LC 98-10823

"Spence follows the ways that China has been 'refracted over time in Western minds.' . . . In analyzing Western reactions to China from the thirteenth century to the present, reactions ranging from imaginative to stereotypical to informed, Spence [covers] . . . diplomatic reports, correspondence, travelogues, novels, drama, poetry, and film." Booklist

"Spence's book will appeal not only to those interested in history and literature, but to anyone looking for a perspective on contemporary discourse about China." Publ Wkly

Includes bibliographical references

Spence, Jonathan D.—*Continued*

God's Chinese son; the Taiping Heavenly Kingdom of Hong Xiuquan. Norton 1996 400p il maps hardcover o.p. paperback available $15.95   **951**

1. Hung, Hsiu-ch'üan, 1814-1864 2. China—History—1850-1864, Taiping Rebellion
ISBN 0-393-31556-8 (pa)   LC 95-17245

"In 1836, twenty-two-year-old Hong Xiuquan failed the civil-service examinations in Canton and came across some Christian tracts. When he later fell sick and had visions, he became convinced that he was the Christian God's second son, destined to rule a 'heavenly kingdom' on earth. Many were attracted to Hong's egalitarian policies—despite his enforced separation of the sexes—and his sect prospered. But its attempts to overthrow the Qing dynasty resulted in unprecedented bloodshed: twenty million people died before the uprising was defeated, in 1864. Spence's present-tense narrative is riveting." New Yorker

Includes bibliographical references

The search for modern China. Norton 1990 xxv, 876p il maps hardcover o.p. paperback available $27.70   **951**

1. China—History
ISBN 0-393-30780-8 (pa)   LC 89-9241

"Beginning with the decline of the Ming dynasty and ending with the Tiananmen Square massacre, Spence chronicles the cultural and social transformations of the country, concentrating on the many wars and rebellions." Booklist

Spence's "own sense of China's past is so vivid, his understanding so sure and his writer's skill so powerful that the reader apprehends distant events as if they were contemporary." New Statesman (1913)

Includes bibliographical references

Treason by the book; [by] Jonathan Spence. Viking 2001 300p map $24.95; pa $14   **951**

1. Tseng, Ch'ing, 1568-1650 2. China—History 3. China—Politics and government
ISBN 0-670-89292-0; 0-14-200041-8 (pa)
    LC 00-43805

"In early-eighteenth-century China, Emperor Yongzheng deployed his vast bureaucracy to ferret out the origins of certain slanderous statements. The gossip proved to be part of a disinformation campaign run by rebels bent on overthrowing his dynasty. He quashed it by publishing a volume of some of the rebellious writings that had inspired the malcontents, along with rebuttals by a team of scholars, and then distributed it throughout his enormous empire as compulsory reading." New Yorker

"Spence's story of emperor, officials, and conspirators is both rousingly unlikely and highly informative." Libr J

Studwell, Joe

The China dream; the quest for the last untapped market on earth. Atlantic Monthly Press 2002 xx, 359p o.p.; Grove Press paperback available $15   **951**

1. China—Economic conditions
ISBN 0-8021-3975-2 (pa)   LC 2001-58996

This "account of the many attempts to capitalize on 'the last big market in the world' is an excellent examination of the political and economic history of China." Booklist

"This book is a well-written, informative introduction to business in China, albeit from a relentlessly downbeat perspective." Publ Wkly

Includes bibliographical references

Tsering Shakya

The dragon in the land of snows; a history of modern Tibet since 1947. Columbia Univ. Press 1999 574p il $32.50   **951**

1. Tibet (China)
ISBN 0-231-11814-7   LC 99-14020

Also available in paperback from Penguin Bks.

This history "explains what has happened to Tibet since the Chinese military invasion of 1950." Publ Wkly

"Drawing on Tibetan, Chinese, British, Indian and American sources, Shakya weaves an authoritative and easily readable narrative. 'The Dragon in the Land of Snows' is likely to be the definitive history of modern Tibet for a generation or more." N Y Times Book Rev

Includes bibliographical references

Winchester, Simon

The river at the center of the world; a journey up the Yangtze and back in Chinese time. Holt & Co. 1996 xx, 410p maps hardcover o.p. paperback available $16   **951**

1. Yangtze River valley (China)
ISBN 0-8050-5508-8 (pa)   LC 96-12399

In 1994, the author followed the Yangtze's "course from the East China Sea to Tibet by boat, car, train, plane, bus and foot; but this is more than an ordinary account of a traveler's pilgrimage, although it is a must for any visitor to China. Wryly humorous, gently skeptical, immensely knowledgeable as he wends his way along the 3900 miles of the great river, Winchester provides an irresistible feast of detail about the character of the river itself, the landscape, the cities, villages and people along its banks." Publ Wkly

Includes bibliographical references

951.04   China—Period of Republic, 1912-1949

Chang, Iris

The rape of Nanking; the forgotten holocaust of World War II. Basic Bks. 1997 290p il maps o.p.; Penguin Bks. paperback available $14.95   **951.04**

1. Nanjing (Jiangsu Province, China) massacre, 1937 2. Sino-Japanese Conflict, 1937-1945
ISBN 0-14-027744-7 (pa)   LC 97-24137

This is an account of the massacre in Nanking "of at least 250,000 Chinese civilians by invading Japanese troops in 1937." Libr J

"Chang's book is a memorial to the victims of Nanking, a damning indictment of Japanese political historiography, a valuable addition to Pacific war literature, and a literary model of how to speak about the unspeakable." Booklist

951.05   China—Period of People's Republic, 1949-

Becker, Jasper

The Chinese. Free Press 2000 464p il $27.50   **951.05**

1. China—Economic conditions 2. China—Social conditions

ISBN 0-684-84412-5   LC 00-42167

Also available in paperback from Oxford Univ. Press

This account of China and the Chinese "conveys the sense of a country out of control: political corruption endangers economic development, ecological disaster looms, and a chasm grows between the powerful rich and the underrepresented poor. As Becker shows, China today is emerging from its Maoist past, which created a new nation and a Leninist bureaucracy but not a democracy, and from Deng Xiaoping's reforms, which unleashed market forces without waiting for the development of a legal system, public culture, or institutional transformation." Libr J

This "is a captivating and enlightening read for anyone interested in Asian or cultural studies." Booklist

Includes bibliographical references

Buruma, Ian

Bad elements; Chinese rebels from Los Angeles to Beijing. Random House 2001 xxv, 367p hardcover o.p. paperback available $15   **951.05**

1. Dissent 2. Human rights 3. China—Politics and government

ISBN 0-679-78136-6 (pa)   LC 2001-19365

The author interviews Chinese dissidents in the United States, Asia, and Europe "to find out what happened to them and how they feel about the future of human rights in China. Buruma's study is both engaging and deeply informed." Libr J

Includes bibliographical references

Chang, Jung, 1952-

Wild swans; three daughters of China. Simon & Schuster 1991 524p il hardcover o.p. paperback available $15   **951.05**

1. China—History 2. Women—China

ISBN 0-7432-4698-5 (pa)   LC 91-20696

Also available in paperback from Anchor Bks.

The author "tells the harrowing life stories of her maternal grandmother, her mother, and herself. Their tales span a period of radical change in China that has touched every aspect of life." Booklist

Fang Lizhi

Bringing down the Great Wall; writing on science, culture, and democracy in China; introduction by Orville Schell; editor and principal translator, James H. Williams. Knopf 1991 c1990 xlviii, 336p o.p.; Norton paperback available $10.95   **951.05**

1. Human rights 2. China—Politics and government

ISBN 0-393-30885-5 (pa)   LC 90-53064

Analyzed in Essay and general literature index

"A comprehensive selection of the written (and spoken) words of the witty, passionate, tenacious and articulate Chinese scientist and dissident who at present is living in the United States." N Y Times Book Rev

Lord, Bette Bao

Legacies: a Chinese mosaic. Knopf 1990 245p hardcover o.p. paperback available $19   **951.05**

1. China—Social life and customs 2. China—Politics and government

ISBN 0-449-90620-5 (pa)   LC 89-43452

The author lived in China from 1985 to 1989. Her book is based on interviews with Chinese people, including an actress, a teacher, a veteran of the Long March, an artist, a journalist, a peasant, an entrepreneur and a Communist Party cadre, who recount their experiences of persecution during the Cultural Revolution. The author also describes her own experiences and her family history

"A vivid and startling mosaic of the political struggles that foreshadowed the Tiananmen Square uprising." Time

Schoppa, R. Keith, 1943-

The Columbia guide to modern Chinese history. Columbia Univ. Press 2000 356p il map (Columbia guides to Asian history) $49   **951.05**

1. China—History

ISBN 0-231-11276-9   LC 99-53420

This narrative overview of Chinese history focuses on five areas: domestic politics, society, the economy, culture, and relations with the outside world. Contains approximately 500 annotated entries for further research in English as well as electronic resources and films. A chronology, excerpts from primary documents, and numerous graphs and tables are appended

Wei Jingsheng

The courage to stand alone; letters from prison and other writings; edited and translated by Kristina M. Torgeson. Viking 1997 xxxiv, 283p il hardcover o.p. paperback available $13.95   **951.05**

1. China—Politics and government 2. Human rights 3. Political prisoners

ISBN 0-14-027535-5 (pa)   LC 96-50179

"Chinese political dissident Jingsheng was arrested in 1979 for demanding democratic reforms from the Communist Party and, except for a brief period of freedom in 1993, has been in prison ever since. This collection of letters to friends, family, and party officials shows a political system bent on control and a man who rejects its tyranny." Booklist

Includes bibliographical references

Wu, Harry

Bitter winds; a memoir of my years in China's Gulag; [by] Harry Wu and Carolyn Wakeman. Wiley 1993 290p il $35; pa $19.95   **951.05**

1. Political prisoners 2. China—Politics and government

ISBN 0-471-55645-9; 0-471-11425-1 (pa)

LC 93-15799

In this "memoir, Wu recalls his 19 years in Chinese labor camps. Though a middle-class college student, he was initially a patriotic Communist, but he soon ran afoul of the thought police. Hoping to flee the country in 1959, he was denounced as an 'enemy of the revolution.' The book . . . focuses primarily on Wu's first decade as a prisoner struggling against starvation, seeing others succumb and learning a brutal survival ethic from fellow inmates. It is an intimate story of bravery and tragedy." Publ Wkly

Wu, Harry—*Continued*

Troublemaker; one man's crusade against China's cruelty; [by] Harry Wu with George Vecsey. Times Bks. 1996 328p il o.p.; Newsmax.com paperback available $24.95

951.05

1. China—Politics and government 2. Human rights 3. Political prisoners
ISBN 0-9704029-9-6 (pa)   LC 96-20956

Wu "chronicles his recent campaign to expose China's slave-labor camp system—six to eight million inmates in 1155 camps rife with beatings, torture, murders and near starvation conditions. He also presents shocking evidence that China is executing prisoners to harvest their organs for transplants, and that China's prison-made goods— everything from shoes to tea to tools—are exported to the U.S." Publ Wkly

"Denounced in China as a 'traitor' and 'spy,' Wu is hailed as a hero in the West and has received many human rights awards. This book meticulously unveils the dramatic story of his 'crusade' against the Chinese government. . . . An interesting but disturbing book." Libr J

951.9   Korea

Brady, James, 1928-

The coldest war: a memoir of Korea. Orion Bks. (NY) 1990 248p il o.p.; Griffin paperback available $14.95   **951.9**

1. Korean War, 1950-1953—Personal narratives
ISBN 0-312-26511-5 (pa)   LC 89-28348
Also available G. K. Hall large print edition

"From November 1951 to July 1952, the author was a marine lieutenant who frequently found himself called upon to fight and kill Chinese and North Korean soldiers on the battlefields of Korea. His memoir of that experience is a well-crafted piece told in a voice that skillfully mixes the sardonic insight of an older man looking back on a highly extraordinary episode of his past with the naïveté of the young warrior he once was." Booklist

Breen, Michael, 1952-

The Koreans; who they are, what they want, where their future lies. St. Martin's Press 1999 276p hardcover o.p. paperback available $14.95   **951.9**

1. Korean national characteristics 2. Korea—History
ISBN 0-312-32609-2 (pa)   LC 99-45599
First published 1998 in the United Kingdom

In this survey of Korea's culture, the author "probes such diverse topics as the status of civil liberties, generational social strains within families, and the massive corruption that permeates Korean society. He writes with a snappy, readable style." Booklist
Includes bibliographical references

Catchpole, Brian

The Korean War, 1950-53. Carroll & Graf Pubs. 2000 372p il maps $26; pa $14 **951.9**

1. Korean War, 1950-1953
ISBN 0-7867-0780-1; 0-7867-0924-3 (pa)

This "account covers the conflict from North Korea's early victories and attempts to penetrate the Pusan defense line and MacArthur's amphibious assault at Inchon, which reversed the tide of the war, drawing in the Chi-nese People's Liberation Army, all the way up to the 10-minute Battle in the Yellow Sea just two years ago. Writing from the British perspective, Catchpole naturally highlights British involvement in this unpopular war, which was the first to take place under United Nations auspices." Publ Wkly
Includes bibliographical references

Connor, Mary E.

The Koreas; a global studies handbook. ABC-CLIO 2002 305p il (Global studies, Asia) $55   **951.9**

1. Korea
ISBN 1-57607-277-0   LC 2001-8670

This volume "has two parts, a narrative section and a reference materials section. The narrative section provides information on Korea's geography and history from earliest times, its economic and political developments since 1945, and contemporary culture and social problems. The reference section contains a chronology; significant people, places, and events; Korean language, food, and etiquette; organizations; and an annotated bibliography." Choice

Cumings, Bruce, 1943-

Korea's place in the sun; a modern history. Norton 1997 527p il maps hardcover o.p. paperback available $20.60   **951.9**

1. Korea—History
ISBN 0-393-31681-5 (pa)   LC 96-15398

This history of Korea from 1860 focuses primarily on the post-1945 period

"Mr. Cumings has pored over the historical documents and he argues intelligently. His book is important precisely because he marshals considerable evidence to challenge conventional understanding." N Y Times Book Rev
Includes bibliographical references

Edwards, Paul M., 1933-

The Korean War; a historical dictionary. Scarecrow Press 2003 xxxix, 367p il maps (Historical dictionaries of war, revolution, and civil unrest) $75   **951.9**

1. Korean War, 1950-1953—Dictionaries
ISBN 0-8108-4479-6   LC 2002-70848

"This reference is designed to provide brief . . . information about all aspects of the war including units involved, the United Nations, political and military actions, significant sites and operations, and weapons used." Publisher's note
Includes bibliographical references

Encyclopedia of the Korean War; a political, social, and military history; Spencer C. Tucker, editor. ABC-CLIO 2000 3v set $275   **951.9**

1. Korean War, 1950-1953—Encyclopedias
ISBN 1-57607-029-8   LC 00-9036
Also available in paperback from Checkmark Bks.

This reference work covers "personalities, events, technical and military information, political and social background, and battles and campaigns." Libr J

Hickey, Michael, 1929-

The Korean War; the West confronts communism. Overlook Press 2000 397p il maps hardcover o.p. paperback available $19.95 **951.9**
1. United Nations—Armed Forces—Korea 2. Korean War, 1950-1953
ISBN 1-58567-179-7 (pa)　　　LC 00-27692
First published 1999 in the United Kingdom
An "analysis of both the military and political factors that caused the war and the conduct on all sides. . . . The author does not mince words when criticizing General MacArthur and other UN commanders. Using declassified documents as well as regimental and personal diaries, he wades through political intrigue and military disasters and triumphs to give us a memorable account." Libr J
Includes bibliographical references

Knox, Donald, 1936-

The Korean War; an oral history. Harcourt Brace Jovanovich 1985-1988 2v il hardcover o.p. paperback available ea $22　　**951.9**
1. Korean War, 1950-1953　　　LC 85-8567
Contents: v1 Pusan to Chosin (ISBN 0-15-602792-5;); v2 Uncertain victory, with additional text by Alfred Coppel (ISBN 0-15-602793-3)
The first volume "covers the conflict in 1950; the second part continues through the armistice in 1953. There are excerpts from books and battle diaries, and occasional discussions of events in wider context, but it is the front-line soldiers who tell the story." Libr J
Includes bibliographical references

Oberdorfer, Don

The two Koreas; a contemporary history. New ed. Basic Bks. 2001 521p il map pa $21
951.9
1. Korea—History
ISBN 0-465-05162-6　　　LC 2001-43486
First published 1997 by Addison-Wesley
This is a study of North and South Korean politics and an analysis of U.S. policy from the 1970s to the present
Includes bibliographical references

Tomedi, Rudy, 1951-

No bugles, no drums; an oral history of the Korean War. Wiley 1993 259p il hardcover o.p. paperback available $19.95　　**951.9**
1. Korean War, 1950-1953—Personal narratives
ISBN 0-471-10573-2 (pa)　　　LC 93-10569
Tomedi "has gathered a group of articulate veterans and arranged their oral histories to cover the major events of the war. What makes this oral history so valuable is the wide variety of accounts. There are, for example, the observations of Lewis Millet, who led the last American bayonet charge, and the details given by Nick Tosques of his years as a prisoner of war. This . . . will undoubtedly become a standard work on the Korean War." Libr J

Weintraub, Stanley, 1929-

MacArthur's war; Korea and the undoing of an American hero. Free Press 1999 385p il $27.50　　**951.9**
1. MacArthur, Douglas, 1880-1964 2. Korean War, 1950-1953
ISBN 0-684-83419-7　　　LC 99-35870
This work "covers the early Korean War, from June 1950 to April 1951, when Truman removed Douglas MacArthur from command. Journalistic accounts, memoirs, papers and previous histories let Weintraub cover the backroom, high-level maneuvering, the evolving public relations of the conflict and the dismaying and bloody facts on the ground." Publ Wkly
"Full of salient insights, this is a memorable, comprehensive history of the first 10 months of the 'forgotten war.'" Booklist
Includes bibliographical references

952　Japan

Beasley, W. G. (William G.), 1919-

The rise of modern Japan. 3rd ed. St. Martin's Press 2000 322p maps $21.95　**952**
1. Japan—History
ISBN 0-312-23373-6
First published 1990
This is a history of Japan from the 19th century to the end of the 20th century

Benedict, Ruth, 1887-1948

The chrysanthemum and the sword; patterns of Japanese culture. Houghton Mifflin 1946 324p hardcover o.p. paperback available $15　　**952**
1. Japan—Civilization 2. Japan—Social life and customs 3. Japanese national characteristics
ISBN 0-395-50075-3 (pa)
In this book an anthropologist writes of the Japanese view of life and of themselves. She sketches in the main outlines of their society and then describes their system of practical ethics, their ideas of good and evil and the disciplines which make them able to live according to their code

The **Cambridge** encyclopedia of Japan; editors, Richard Bowring, Peter Kornicki. Cambridge Univ. Press 1993 400p il maps $70　　**952**
1. Japan
ISBN 0-521-40352-9　　　LC 92-8167
This volume is divided "into eight categories: geography, history, language, thought and religion, arts and crafts, society, politics, and the economy. Each of these categories is further divided into 7-11 subjects that deal with numerous topics, such as the physical structure of the country, climate, education, family, judicial system, cinema, products, foreign policy, and important historical figures." Am Ref Books Annu, 1994

Downer, Lesley

Women of the pleasure quarters; the secret history of the geisha. Broadway Bks. 2001 288p il hardcover o.p. paperback available $14.95 **952**

1. Geishas 2. Japan—Social life and customs
ISBN 0-7679-0490-7 (pa) LC 00-49409
Downer's "book is a combination of the history of the geisha and a study of the contemporary world of the geisha." Booklist

The author "skillfully intertwines her profiles of Kyoto personalities and tea-house customs with a fluidly written geisha history that's unabashedly aimed at a Western audience. . . . Written in dynamic, highly readable prose, the book is supported by exhaustive research and a lengthy bibliography." Publ Wkly

Jansen, Marius B.

The making of modern Japan. Belknap Press 2000 871p il maps $35; pa $18.95 **952**

1. Japan—History
ISBN 0-674-00334-9; 0-674-00991-6 (pa)
LC 00-41352
"Roughly a third of the book deals with Tokugawa politics, culture, and society before the 'opening to the world' in the mid-19th century; fewer than 100 pages cover the period since 1945; and the balance treats the crucial 1868-1945 period of modernization and war." Libr J

"Jansen has produced what is sure to become the standard narrative history of modern Japan. . . . In every way this is a remarkable book . . . and no reference collection on Japan can pretend to be complete without it." Choice

Includes bibliographical references

McClain, James L., 1944-

Japan, a modern history. Norton 2001 xxiii, 632, 92p il maps $35; pa $31.25 **952**

1. Japan—History
ISBN 0-393-04156-5; 0-393-97720-X (pa)
LC 2001-34545
In this study McClain "analyzes major trends in politics, the economy, society, culture and the arts, foreign affairs, and almost every other conceivable aspect of Japanese society." Libr J

"This is a well-written, well-researched, and easily readable survey of the modern history of a fascinating and important nation." Booklist

Includes bibliographical references

Perez, Louis G.

The history of Japan. Greenwood Press 1998 244p maps (Greenwood histories of the modern nations) $45 **952**

1. Japan—History
ISBN 0-313-30296-0 LC 97-45657
This history covers prehistoric and early feudal Japan through 1997. Cultural aspects examined include theater and cinema, marriage customs as well as the women's movement and political scandals. Includes chronology, glossary of selected terms, and a bibliographic essay

Reischauer, Edwin O. (Edwin Oldfather), 1910-1990

Japan: the story of a nation. 4th ed. Knopf 1989 375p il o.p.; McGraw-Hill paperback available $52.55 **952**

1. Japan—History
ISBN 0-07-557074-2 (pa)
First published 1970
This history of the Japanese people from their origins to the present examines their civilization, cultural heritage, militarism, and economy
Includes bibliographical references

Japan, tradition & transformation; [by] Edwin O. Reischauer, Albert M. Craig. rev ed. Houghton Mifflin 1989 352p il hardcover o.p. paperback available $61.56 **952**

1. Japan—History
ISBN 0-395-49696-9 (pa) LC 88-83734
First published 1978
This text on the history and culture of Japan examines the traditions of the Japanese people and analyzes the changes wrought by foreign influences

The Japanese today; change and continuity. Belknap Press 1988 426p il maps hardcover o.p. paperback available $21.50 **952**

1. Japan 2. Japanese national characteristics
ISBN 0-674-47182-2 (pa) LC 87-14904
First published 1977 with title: The Japanese
The author "shows how change within continuity has been the most enduring characteristic of the Japanese experience—throughout the nation's history. He analyzes and explains in detail the government, education, business, and social structure of the country in modern times." Christ Sci Monit
Includes bibliographical references

Seagrave, Sterling

The Yamato dynasty; the secret history of Japan's Imperial family; [by] Sterling Seagrave and Peggy Seagrave. Broadway Bks. 2000 394p il hardcover o.p. paperback available $23 **952**

1. Japan—Politics and government 2. Japan—Kings and rulers
ISBN 0-7679-0497-4 (pa) LC 99-49888
This "history of Japan from the mid-19th century to the present weaves together an iconoclastic historical narrative with a mostly caustic view of Japan's imperial family. The Seagraves depict modern Japan as a country consistently dominated by a closed financial oligarchy in league with politicians, bureaucrats, the imperial family, and underworld bosses." Libr J
Includes bibliographical references

Smith, Patrick L.

Japan; a reinterpretation. Pantheon Bks. 1997 385p hardcover o.p. paperback available $14 **952**

1. Japan—Civilization 2. Japan—History
ISBN 0-679-74511-4 (pa) LC 96-39220
This study focuses on events after World War II. Smith examines the U.S. role in post-war Japan, and the social structure of Japanese society
"In his sweeping analysis of the country's history, economy, politics and culture, Smith has produced a new

Smith, Patrick L.—*Continued*
startlingly clear-sighted vision of the often misunderstood Japanese." Publ Wkly
Includes bibliographical references

952.03   Japan—1868-1945

Pleshakov, Konstantin
The Tsar's last armada; the epic journey to the Battle of Tsushima; [by] Constantine Pleshakov. Basic Bks. 2002 xx, 396p il maps hardcover o.p. paperback available $17.50
                   952.03
1. Russo-Japanese War, 1904-1905
ISBN 0-465-05792-6 (pa)   LC 2001-52532
This is an account of events leading to the Russo-Japanese War and the defeat of the Russian fleet in the Tsushima Straits in 1905
"A compulsively readable account told from the Russian viewpoint." Booklist
Includes bibliographical references

952.04   Japan—1945-

Dower, John W.
Embracing defeat; Japan in the wake of World War II; by John Dower. Norton 1999 676p il $29.95; pa $17.95   **952.04**
1. Japan—History—1945-1952, Allied occupation
ISBN 0-393-04686-9; 0-393-32027-8 (pa)
                   LC 98-22133
This "account of Japan between August 1945 and April 1952 assesses the impact of Allied activity on modern Japanese history." N Y Times Book Rev
"Dower demonstrates an impressive mastery of voluminous sources, both American and Japanese, and he deftly situates the political story within a rich cultural context." Publ Wkly
Includes bibliographical references

Encyclopedia of contemporary Japanese culture; edited by Sandra Buckley. Routledge 2001 xxix, 634p $140   **952.04**
1. Japan—Civilization
ISBN 0-415-14344-6   LC 2001-19655
This reference includes "more than 750 topical and biographical entries exploring the 'lived experience of everyday Japanese life' for the postwar period. . . . {It includes} articles on minorities in Japan and the Japanese Diaspora in the Americas. Most notably . . . {this} features excellent coverage of Japanese women and consistently introduces critical feminist perspectives that are rarely seen in other reference works on Japan. . . . {This} is eminently readable . . . an ideal reference tool." Am Ref Books Annu, 2003

Iyer, Pico
The lady and the monk; four seasons in Kyoto. Knopf 1991 337p hardcover o.p. paperback available $14   **952.04**
1. Kyoto (Japan)—Description
ISBN 0-679-73834-7 (pa)   LC 91-413
"British born and Harvard educated, Iyer arrived in Japan in 1987 with no organized plans, contacts, or living arrangements. This poetic account of his yearlong sojourn offers fascinating insight into Japanese culture and the people he met." Booklist

953   Arabian Peninsula and adjacent areas

Theroux, Peter
Sandstorms: days and nights in Arabia. Norton 1990 281p hardcover o.p. paperback available $13.95   **953**
1. Arab countries—Description
ISBN 0-393-30797-2 (pa)   LC 89-28609
The author "recounts his experiences in the Middle East of the 1980s. The author went to Egypt to teach English and wound up chronicling the disappearance of Lebanon's Shia Iman Moussa Sadr. But *Sandstorms* is the human side of an American in Arabia. . . . Theroux's Arabia is rough but undeniably real, poignant and elemental." Libr J

953.8   Saudi Arabia

Aburish, Said K.
The rise, corruption, and coming fall of the House of Saud. St. Martin's Press 1995 328p il hardcover o.p. paperback available $17.95
                   953.8
1. Saudi Arabia—History
ISBN 0-312-16119-0 (pa)   LC 95-10197
First published 1994 in the United Kingdom
In this "account, the author contends that the members of the royal house are ruining the country with their self-indulgent spending and unnecessary military 'toys.' He states that the West must stop tolerating the Saudi persistence in maintaining the status quo." Libr J
"A well-researched and provocative exposé/denunciation of Arabia's powerful ruling clan." Publ Wkly
Includes bibliographical references

954   South Asia. India

Davidson, Robyn, 1950-
Desert places. Viking 1996 279p il maps hardcover o.p. paperback available $13.95
                   954
1. Rabaris (Indic people) 2. Nomads 3. India—Description
ISBN 0-14-026797-2 (pa)   LC 96-21394
"In this work, Davidson, an author and Australian journalist who resides in England, . . . recounts her stay among the Rabari, sheep- and camel-herding nomads in northwestern India." Libr J
This book "is dazzling. Ms. Davidson travelled in Rajasthan for months and grew up, quite violently, in the process. She starts as a romantic; a dreamer haunted by schlock images of sunsets on rippling desert sands; she ends shriven, with new stature as a person and as a writer." Economist

Keay, John
India: a history. Atlantic Monthly Press 2000 xviii, 576p il maps o.p.; Grove Press paperback available $19.95   **954**
1. India—History
ISBN 0-8021-3797-0 (pa)   LC 99-53417
This history ranges "from the ancient brick cities of Mohenjo-daro and Harappa, built in the Indus Valley

Keay, John—*Continued*

around 2000 B.C., to modern India's urban middle class." Publ Wkly

Keay's "history exhibits the complete panoply of cultures that have arisen on, or arrived at, the plain of the Ganges River. . . . Within this mix of cultures, Keay avers, Indian historiography is afflicted with the selective interpretations of nationalist writers: he corrects the defect by example in this evenhanded, informed, and enthusiastic illumination of the vastness of Indian history." Booklist

Includes bibliographical references

Lapierre, Dominique

The City of Joy; translated from the French by Kathryn Spink. Doubleday 1985 464p o.p.; Warner Bks. paperback available $7.99
954
1. Calcutta (India)—Social conditions
ISBN 0-446-35556-9 (pa)   LC 85-10128
An account of life in the most squalid of Calcutta's slums, Anand Nagar (The City of Joy). The author focuses on the lives of a rickshaw driver, a Polish Catholic priest, an American doctor and an Assamese nurse

McLeod, John

The history of India. Greenwood Press 2002 xx, 223p (Greenwood histories of the modern nations) $39.95
954
1. Mogul Empire 2. India—History—1526-1765
ISBN 0-313-31459-4   LC 2002-276829
The author presents "in broad outlines some of the major events and episodes that make up India's history. . . . This is a useful compilation of important facts relating to Indian history. Its strength lies primarily in the last six chapters in which brief narratives of the struggle for independence and post-independence India down to the close of the twentieth century are nicely presented. All in all, this is a book that all libraries should have." Recomm Ref Books for Small & Medium-sized Libr & Media Cent, 2003

Includes bibliographical references

Singh, Patwant, 1925-

The Sikhs. Knopf 2000 276p il $27.50; pa $14
954
1. Sikhs
ISBN 0-375-40728-6; 0-385-50206-0 (pa)
LC 99-31807
The author "traces Sikh history from its origins in the 15th century through Indira Gandhi's 1984 storming of the Golden Temple. . . . Sikhs, he argues, have for centuries been an embattled people because their culture and religion defy the predominant religions in the region, as well as the Indian caste system with its ruling elite." Publ Wkly

Includes bibliographical references

Tharoor, Shashi, 1956-

India; from midnight to the millennium. Arcade Pub. 1997 392p map o.p.; HarperCollins Pubs. paperback available $14.95
954
1. India—History
ISBN 0-06-097753-1 (pa)   LC 97-8376
This is an "economic, political, and sociological study of India since independence in 1947, considering such issues as centralization vs. federalism and pluralism vs. fundamentalism." Libr J

"Each telling anecdote illuminates some aspect of Indian culture, from politics to religion, creating a mosaic that reflects India's endless variations on the theme of life." Booklist

Wolpert, Stanley A., 1927-

A new history of India; [by] Stanley Wolpert. Oxford Univ. Press il maps $55; pa $34.95
954
1. India—History
First published 1977. (7th edition 2003) Periodically revised

A comprehensive survey of Indian history from its early beginnings to the present. Includes discussion of the assassination of Rajiv Gandhi; violence in Kashmir, Punjab, and Assam; and the effects of rural development

Includes bibliographical references

954.03 India—Period of British rule, 1785-1947

Keay, John

The honourable company; a history of the English East India Company. Macmillan 1994 c1991 xxii, 474p il maps o.p.; HarperCollins Pubs. paperback available $17.95   **954.03**
1. East India Company 2. Great Britain—Commerce 3. India—History
ISBN 0-00-638072-7 (pa)   LC 93-33587
First published 1991 in the United Kingdom
The author "deals with his subject from its inception as the East Indies Company, a monopoly of a few merchants trading in spices from the vaguely defined Indies, to its demise more than two centuries later as the East India Company, an administrative service that ruled India from Britain. The changing nature of the company affected the history of Britain; Keay brings in all the factors that affected the role of the company, such as wars, politics, personal interests, relations with local rulers, competition, and fights over internal control." Libr J

Includes bibliographical references

Read, Anthony

The proudest day; India's long road to independence; [by] Anthony Read and David Fisher. Norton 1998 xxv, 565p il maps hardcover o.p. paperback available $17.50
954.03
1. India—History 2. India—Politics and government 3. Great Britain—Colonies
ISBN 0-393-31898-2 (pa)   LC 98-10707
This British writing team presents "the story of India's advance to independence from the founding of the Indian National Congress in 1885, under . . . Allan Octavian Hume, to Independence Day on Aug. 15, 1947, under . . . Viscount Mountbatten." N Y Times Book Rev

"Scrupulously researched from Indian and British sources, this sweeping history portrays the 250-year British occupation as a struggle between liberals—those who sought to prepare India for early self-government—and imperialists (like Churchill) who viewed the vast subcontinent as Britain's feudal property." Publ Wkly

Includes bibliographical references

954.05   India—1971-

Bumiller, Elisabeth
May you be the mother of a hundred sons;
a journey among the women of India.
Random House 1990 306p il hardcover o.p.
paperback available $13.95   **954.05**
1. Women—India 2. India—Social life and customs
ISBN 0-449-90614-0 (pa)   LC 89-27120
"In addition to the usual discussion of arranged marriages, movie stars, and Indira Gandhi, India's late prime
minister, Bumiller portrays a wide cross section of Indian
society. Her discussion of bride burning, family planning,
village health programs, the outlook of village women,
and female infanticide will generate much comment and
discussion. Essential for libraries with women's studies
and Third World collections." Libr J
Includes bibliographical references

955   Iran

Follett, Ken, 1949-
On wings of eagles. Morrow 1983 444p il
maps o.p.; New Am. Lib. paperback available
$7.99   **955**
1. Iran hostage crisis, 1979-1981
ISBN 0-451-16353-2 (pa)   LC 83-9328
The author "recounts the efforts of successful Texas
industrialist Ross Perot to rescue from a Teheran jail two
senior corporate executives arrested during the anti-
American and revolutionary period in Iran in 1979." Libr
J

Hiro, Dilip
The longest war; the Iran-Iraq military
conflict. Routledge 1991 xxiv, 323p il maps
hardcover o.p. paperback available $27.95
     955
1. Iran-Iraq War, 1980-1988
ISBN 0-415-904-07-2 (pa)   LC 90-45641
First published 1989 in the United Kingdom
This is an account of the 1980-1988 war between Iran,
under the rule of the Ayatollah Khomeini and Iraq, under
the rule of Saddam Hussein
The author "writes clearly and, although the style is
somewhat journalistic, the end product is balanced, well
researched, and carefully done." Choice
Includes bibliographical references

Mackey, Sandra, 1937-
The Iranians; Persia, Islam, and the soul of
a nation; W. Scott Harrop, research assistant.
Dutton 1996 xxii, 426p maps hardcover o.p.
paperback available $15.95   **955**
1. Iran—Politics and government
ISBN 0-452-27563-6 (pa)   LC 95-44135
The author presents "information on Iranian civilization from Cyrus the Great to the present. Throughout this
turbulent history of invasions and conquerors, the Persian
soul, with its foundations in the Zoroastrian concept of
justice overlaid with Shia Islam, has steadfastly endured.
Since many Westerners had little familiarity with Iran
until the overthrow of the Shah in 1979, this very readable book provides a perspective on what led up to those
events, what is happening in Iran today, and how the
current situation is likely to affect the future of Iran and
its relationship with the West." Libr J

Molavi, Afshin
Persian pilgrimages; journeys across Iran.
Norton 2002 xx, 315p il $25.95   **955**
1. Iran
ISBN 0-393-05119-6   LC 2002-69211
The author "reveals Iran and its history through the
voices of the people he interviewed, including merchants,
students, feminists, traditionalists, children and revolutionaries, as they speak on such subjects as poetry, campus politics, personal appearance, democracy, religion,
war and the West. In addition to his descriptions of landmarks and monuments, Molavi makes comparisons to
other writings on Iran." Publ Wkly
"Molavi packs a lot of information into this work, but
his readable prose makes this an appealing journey."
Booklist

Wright, Robin
The last great revolution; turmoil and
transformation in Iran. Knopf 2000 xxiv,
339p il hardcover o.p. paperback available
$14   **955**
1. Iran—Politics and government
ISBN 0-375-70630-5 (pa)   LC 99-27798
The author "talks to journalists, educators, politicians,
entertainers, and others to present a picture of the cultural and political changes in Iran: the softening of cultural
restrictions, the empowerment of women, and the modernization of industry and the economy." Booklist
Includes bibliographical references

956   Middle East

The **Continuum** political encyclopedia of the
Middle East; Avraham Sela, editor. rev and
updated ed. Continuum 2002 944p maps
$175   **956**
1. Middle East—Politics and government 2. Middle
East—History
ISBN 0-8264-1413-3   LC 2001-8542
First published 1999 with title: The political encyclopedia of the Middle East
This "contains entries on countries ranging from Afghanistan to Yemen; political movements and leaders;
major foreign nations that impact this area, such as the
United States and Russia; religions and religious movements; and regional topics of concern including 'Oil,'
'Terrorism,' 'Water Politics,' and 'Women, Gender and
Politics.'. . . Alphabetical entries range from a few paragraphs to lengthy commentaries. . . . Large libraries
serving older students will find this a useful . . . source
of objective information on the history and issues affecting the contemporary Middle East." SLJ

Friedman, Thomas L.
From Beirut to Jerusalem. Farrar, Straus &
Giroux c1990 541p il maps $32   **956**
1. Middle East—Politics and government 2. Jewish-
Arab relations 3. Lebanon—History 4. Israel—Politics
and government
ISBN 0-374-15895-9   LC 92-148666
Also available in paperback from Anchor Bks.
First published 1989
The author presents an account of the political situa-
tion in the Middle East as he witnessed it in his years
as a reporter in Lebanon and Jerusalem
"When recounting his frequently harrowing experi-
ences in that troubled region, Friedman can be absolutely

Friedman, Thomas L.—*Continued*

riveting; similarly, his historical insights, his explanation of the root causes of the Arab-Israeli conflict, and his impressions of people and places in the Holy Land never fail to fascinate." Booklist

Herzog, Chaim, 1918-1997

The Arab-Israeli wars; war and peace in the Middle East. Random House 1982 392p il maps hardcover o.p. paperback available $16 **956**

1. Jewish-Arab relations
ISBN 0-394-71746-5 (pa)   LC 80-5291
This book traces "the Arab-Israeli wars and military conflicts from the 1948 War of Independence through the 1973 Yom Kippur War." Libr J
Includes bibliographical references

Hiro, Dilip

A dictionary of the Middle East. St. Martin's Press 1996 367p il map o.p.; Carroll & Graf Pubs. paperback available $17.95 **956**

1. Middle East—Dictionaries
ISBN 0-7867-1269-4 (pa)   LC 96-4395
"In more than 1,000 alphabetically arranged entries, varying in length from a few lines to a few pages, Hiro covers more than 150 personalities in politics, business, culture, and religion; places of religious and cultural significance; oil and other minerals; political and religious sects; economic infrastructure; and political and religious ideologies." Booklist

Lewis, Bernard

The Middle East; a brief history of the last 2,000 years. Scribner 1995 433p il $30; pa $16 **956**

1. Middle East—History
ISBN 0-684-80712-2; 0-684-83280-1 (pa)
LC 96-4384
"Lewis has chosen to accentuate the social, economic, and cultural changes that have occurred over 20 centuries. He ranges from seemingly trivial concerns (changes in dress and manners in an Arab coffeehouse) to earth-shaking events (the Mongol conquest of Mesopotamia) in painting a rich, varied, and fascinating portrait of a region that is steeped in traditionalism while often forced by geography and politics to accept change." Booklist
Includes bibliographical references

What went wrong? Western impact and Middle Eastern response. Oxford Univ. Press 2002 180p il $23 **956**

1. Middle East—History
ISBN 0-19-514420-1   LC 2001-36214
Also available in paperback from HarperCollins Pubs.
The author's "fundamental argument is that Muslims became accustomed in the early centuries of their history to perceiving themselves as the bearers of the final and true faith, and so never came to understand or accept the Christian civilization of Western Europe that he maintains has surpassed and humbled them." N Y Times (Late N Y Ed)
"Like many of Lewis's previous writings on this subject . . . this book will undoubtedly generate significant debate and disagreement among scholars regarding the author's analysis of Islamic responses to modernity and Westernization." Libr J
Includes bibliographical references

The **Middle** East. CQ Press il maps $55; pa $39.95 **956**

1. Middle East—Politics and government
First published 1974. (9th edition 2000) Periodically revised
Covers topics such as oil, Islam, the Arab-Israeli conflict, the Persian Gulf, and the arms trade in the Middle East. Also presents profiles of Middle Eastern nations and twentieth-century leaders and includes documents such as UN resolutions and peace treaties
Includes bibliographical references

Miller, Judith, 1948-

God has ninety-nine names; reporting from a militant Middle East. Simon & Schuster 1996 574p hardcover o.p. paperback available $15 **956**

1. Islam and politics 2. Middle East—Politics and government
ISBN 0-684-83228-3 (pa)   LC 96-4179
In this study of the Middle East, Miller "examines micro sociopolitical issues affecting everyday life in the region. It offers astute critical commentary on the state of affairs in ten Middle Eastern countries. The strength of Miller's book lies in the author's ability to give non-specialists an appreciation of the complexities of the contemporary Middle East while eschewing the esotericism of scholarly books about the region." Libr J

Morris, Benny, 1948-

Righteous victims; a history of the Zionist-Arab conflict, 1881-1998. Knopf 1999 751p hardcover o.p. paperback available $18 **956**

1. Israel-Arab conflicts 2. Jewish-Arab relations
ISBN 0-679-74475-4 (pa)   LC 98-42774
Morris traces the history of Arab-Israeli conflicts and examines major events and their aftereffects
"The author displays a remarkable grasp of the history of the Zionist-Arab conflict and an analytical style that is devoid of the polemics that have characterized so many books on this subject." Libr J
Includes bibliographical references

Said, Edward W.

The end of the peace process; Oslo and after. Pantheon Bks. 2000 345p $27.50; pa $14 **956**

1. Israel-Arab conflicts 2. Jewish-Arab relations
ISBN 0-375-40930-0; 0-375-72574-1 (pa)
LC 99-44765
The author provides "analysis of the pitfalls of the Oslo agreement. Most of the essays in this collection have appeared in Cairo's *al-Ahram Weekly* and *al-Hayat*, London's Arabic-language daily. Each essay is Said's reflection on a dimension of the Palestinian predicament. . . . He is as critical of the corruption, incompetence, and authoritarianism of the Palestinian Authority as he is of American and Israeli postures." Libr J

Wheatcroft, Andrew

The Ottomans. Viking 1994 c1993 xxix, 322p il hardcover o.p. paperback available $14.95 **956**

1. Turkey—History
ISBN 0-14-016879-6 (pa)   LC 94-147252
First published 1993 in the United Kingdom

Wheatcroft, Andrew—*Continued*

"To show us the Ottoman world, Wheatcroft brings us to the great capital of Stamboul, with its mosques, palaces, marketplaces, barracks, and slums. We see sultans and viziers, beys and pashas, janissaries and sipahis, eunuchs and slaves. We observe Ottoman politics, military practice, and social customs. Sometimes the narrative pace slows amid the plentiful detail, but this is a small criticism. The work is well illustrated and offers an up-to-date bibliography." Libr J

956.04   Middle East—1945-1980

Oren, Michael

Six days of war; June 1967 and the making of the modern Middle East; [by] Michael B. Oren. Oxford Univ. Press 2002 446p il $30

956.04

1. Israel-Arab War, 1967
ISBN 0-19-515174-7   LC 2001-58823
Also available in paperback from Presidio Press
This is a history of the June 1967 Arab-Israeli War
"What makes this book important is the breadth and depth of the research. Oren draws on archives, newly declassified documents, memoirs and interviews from Israel, America, Britain and what was then the Soviet Union." N Y Times Book Rev
Includes bibliographical references

956.1   Turkey

Goodwin, Jason, 1964-

Lords of the horizons; a history of the Ottoman Empire. Holt & Co. 1999 351p il map hardcover o.p. paperback available $15

956.1

1. Turkey—History
ISBN 0-312-42066-8 (pa)   LC 98-41601
"A John Macrae book"
In this study of the Ottoman Empire, the chapters "each have a theme: the importance of the annual campaign to capture new territory, for example, and the part played in the Ottoman psyche by the concept of borderlands, the absence of clock-time, [and] the role of the city or of the sea." Natl Rev
"A history of distinctive originality, Goodwin's account imbibes deeply of traveler's impressions and seeks to see and describe, rather than explain and judge. A valuable synthesis." Booklist
Includes bibliographical references

Kinzer, Stephen

Crescent and star; Turkey between two worlds. Farrar, Straus & Giroux 2001 252p hardcover o.p. paperback available $14

956.1

1. Turkey—Politics and government
ISBN 0-374-52866-7 (pa)   LC 2001-23298
The author "gives a concise introduction to Turkey: Kemal Atatürk's post-WWI establishment of the modern secular Turkish state; the odd makeup of contemporary society, in which the military enforces Atatürk's reforms. In stylized but substantive prose, he devotes chapters to the problems he sees plaguing Turkish society: Islamic fundamentalism, frictions regarding the large Kurdish minority and the lack of democratic freedoms." Publ Wkly

Pope, Hugh

Turkey unveiled; a history of modern Turkey; [by] Hugh and Nicole Pope. Overlook Press 1998 373p il maps $29.95; pa $16.95

956.1

1. Turkey—Politics and government
ISBN 0-87951-898-7; 1-58567-096-0 (pa)

LC 98-16616

The authors present a study of "Turkish governments and political leaders over the past seventy years, with particular emphasis on the . . . reforms of . . . President Turgut Özal." Times Lit Suppl
"The Popes have written a deeply revealing guide to modern Turkish culture and politics that fills a wide gap in our cultural knowledge." N Y Times Book Rev
Includes bibliographical references

956.7   Iraq

Atkinson, Rick

Crusade; the untold story of the Persian Gulf War. Houghton Mifflin 1993 575p il maps hardcover o.p. paperback available $17

956.7

1. Persian Gulf War, 1991
ISBN 0-395-71083-9 (pa)   LC 93-14388
The author provides an "account of the actions and utterances of those who directed and fought in the Persian Gulf War. He also provides a thorough analysis of diplomatic and political aspects of the conflict. Rich in pertinent details, the powerful narrative leaps nimbly from Washington to Riyadh, from Baghdad to Kuwait City, and to various battle sites across the sands. Expectedly, the book's dominant personality is General H. Norman Schwarzkopf." Publ Wkly
Includes bibliographical references

Clancy, Tom, 1947-

Into the storm; a study in command; [by] Tom Clancy with Fred Franks, Jr. Putnam 1997 531p il maps hardcover o.p. paperback available $16.95

956.7

1. Persian Gulf War, 1991
ISBN 0-425-16308-3 (pa)   LC 96-38068
This history of the Persian Gulf War focuses on the command of General Frederick M. Banks
Includes bibliographical references

Friedman, Norman, 1946-

Desert victory; the war for Kuwait. Naval Inst. Press 1991 435p il $46.95; pa $26.95

956.7

1. Persian Gulf War, 1991
ISBN 1-55750-254-4; 1-55750-255-2 (pa)

LC 91-21088

"The narrative deals with the background of the conflict, the buildup of the war, and the blockade of Iraq, and outlines the main naval, air, and ground operations." Choice
"A thoughtful book, almost certainly of permanent value." Booklist

Gordon, Michael R.

The generals' war; the inside story of the conflict in the Gulf; by Michael R. Gordon and Bernard E. Trainor. Little, Brown 1994 551p il map hardcover o.p. paperback available $18.95   **956.7**
   1. Persian Gulf War, 1991
   ISBN 0-316-32100-1 (pa)   LC 94-27144
   This book examines the strategy of "U.S. command officers in the conflict with Iraq. . . . [It asks the question] Why didn't the generals press on to dismantle the Republican Guard of Saddam Hussein, and what were the consequences of their decision against such an act?" Booklist
   "This cogent analysis provides several disturbing answers worthy of our attention." Libr J
   Includes bibliographical references

Grossman, Mark

Encyclopedia of the Persian Gulf War. ABC-CLIO 1995 522p il maps   **956.7**
   1. Persian Gulf War, 1991   LC 95-38945
   Available CD-ROM version
   "Through entries on Iraq, Kuwait, and other involved nations, as well as an extensive timeline, Grossman explores the conflict's underpinnings and beginnings. Articles on aircraft and countless other subjects are included, such as the antiwar movement, summits and charters, chemical and biological warfare, Congressional debates, economic and environmental effects of the war on Iraq, prisoners of war, the Gulf War syndrome, and scud missiles." SLJ

Kelly, Michael, 1957-2003

Martyrs' Day; chronicle of a small war. 2nd Vintage Books ed, [with a new foreword and afterword] Vintage Bks. 2001 365p pa $14   **956.7**
   1. Persian Gulf War, 1991—Personal narratives
   ISBN 1-4000-3036-6   LC 2002-524049
   First published 1993 by Random House
   "This eyewitness account differs from the many other books on the Persian Gulf War in that it deals primarily with the human-interest elements rather than military matters. Kelly, a journalist who traveled extensively in the countries that were affected by the Gulf conflict, chronicles the vagaries of the war and its impact on the lives of the people in a revealing and disturbing text." Libr J

Mackey, Sandra, 1937-

The reckoning; Iraq and the legacy of Saddam Hussein. Norton 2002 415p il maps $27.95; pa $16.95   **956.7**
   1. Hussein, Ṣaddām 2. Iraq—Politics and government
   ISBN 0-393-05141-2; 0-393-32428-1 (pa)
                      LC 2002-16611
   The author offers a "history of Iraq and its early Mesopotamian civilization with . . . biographies of all of its historical figures through the ages, shedding perspective on the current regime of Saddam Hussein and looking ahead to what an Iraq without Hussein might resemble. . . . An extremely thorough appraisal." Booklist
   Includes bibliographical references

Newell, Clayton R., 1942-

Historical dictionary of the Persian Gulf War, 1990-1991. Scarecrow Press 1998 lix, 363p maps (Historical dictionaries of war, revolution, and civil unrest) $65   **956.7**
   1. Persian Gulf War, 1991
   ISBN 0-8108-3511-8   LC 98-18944
   The author attempts "to help the reader understand the Gulf War and its background. He includes several pages of abbreviations and acronyms along with pages of maps, all . . . describing what happened and why during the 1991 conflict. There is . . . a 30-page introduction that describes the political developments that led up to the war and a much-needed chronology of events. . . . The dictionary entries average about a paragraph and cover the war's personalities as well as its combat equipment." Libr J

Schwartz, Richard Alan, 1951-

Encyclopedia of the Persian Gulf War. McFarland & Co. 1998 216p il maps $45
                             956.7
   1. Persian Gulf War, 1991
   ISBN 0-7864-0451-5   LC 97-51886
   "Beginning with a seven-page overview, this encyclopedia presents alphabetically arranged entries that describe the conflict, including key figures, places, battles, diplomacy, and more." SLJ

Swofford, Anthony

Jarhead: a Marine's chronicle of the Gulf War and other battles. Scribner 2003 260p $25   **956.7**
   1. United States. Marine Corps 2. Persian Gulf War, 1991—Personal narratives
   ISBN 0-7432-3535-5   LC 2002-30866
   The author, "who served in a United States Marine Corps Surveillance and Target Acquisition/Scout-Sniper platoon during the [1991 Gulf War] operation known as Desert Storm [presents an account of his experiences]." N Y Times (Late NY Ed)
   This book offers "an unflinching portrayal of the loneliness and brutality of modern warfare and sophisticated analyses of—and visceral reactions to—its politics." Publ Wkly

Tripp, Charles

A history of Iraq. 2nd ed. Cambridge Univ. Press 2002 324p il maps $60; pa $20 **956.7**
   1. Iraq—History
   ISBN 0-521-82148-7; 0-521-52900-X (pa)
                      LC 2002-511523
   First published 2000
   This "book traces Iraq's political history from its nineteenth-century roots in the Ottoman empire, to the development of the state, its transformation from monarchy to republic and the rise of the Ba'th party and the ascendancy . . . of Saddam Husain." Publisher's note
   Includes bibliographical references

956.94 Palestine. Israel

Armstrong, Karen

Jerusalem; one city, three faiths. Knopf 1996 xxi, 471p il maps hardcover o.p. paperback available $17.95   **956.94**

1. Jerusalem—History
ISBN 0-345-39168-3 (pa)   LC 96-75888

Armstrong's "overarching theme, that Jerusalem has been central to the experience and 'sacred geography' of Jews, Muslims and Christians and thus has led to deadly struggles for dominance, is a familiar one, yet she brings to her sweeping, profusely illustrated narrative a grasp of sociopolitical conditions seldom found in other books." Publ Wkly

Blumenfeld, Laura R.

Revenge; a story of hope. Simon & Schuster 2002 382p il $25   **956.94**

1. Jewish-Arab relations 2. Israel-Arab conflicts
ISBN 0-684-85316-7   LC 2002-17552

Also available in paperback from Washington Sq. Press

"When her father, an American rabbi, was shot in the Old City of Jerusalem, Blumenfeld ingratiated herself with the Palestinian gunman's family, planning the disclosure of her identity as a form of revenge; Blumenfeld . . . explores the mechanics and psychology of vengeance and creates a subtle portrait of the gunman himself." Booklist

Collins, Larry, 1929-

O Jerusalem! [by] Larry Collins and Dominique Lapierre. Simon & Schuster 1972 637p il maps hardcover o.p. paperback available $17   **956.94**

1. Jerusalem—History—1948, Siege 2. Israel-Arab War, 1948-1949
ISBN 0-671-66241-4 (pa)

This is an account of the struggle for the city of Jerusalem during the Israel-Arab War of 1948

Includes bibliographical references

Farsoun, Samih K.

Palestine and the Palestinians; [by] Samih K. Farsoun with Christina E. Zacharia. Westview Press 1997 375p maps hardcover o.p. paperback available $29   **956.94**

1. Palestinian Arabs 2. Israel-Arab conflicts
ISBN 0-8133-2773-3 (pa)   LC 97-21954

This study of the Palestinian peoples covers their economic and social conditions, their political activity and national aspirations

"This is an excellent introduction to the modern history of the Palestinians, the transformations of their troubled land, and the prospects of both." Choice

Includes bibliographical references

Gilbert, Martin, 1936-

Jerusalem in the twentieth century. Wiley 1996 412p il maps $30; pa $16.95   **956.94**

1. Jerusalem 2. Palestine—History 3. Israel—History
ISBN 0-471-16308-2; 0-471-28328-2 (pa)
     LC 96-18458

This political, social and military history of Jerusalem "concentrates on the return of the Jews to Jerusalem in the 20th century. They find a squalid city badly governed by the Turks and inaugurate the cultural, intellectual, so-

cial (hospitals, etc.), and economic rejuvenation in the city. What ensues is a continual record of conflict among the inhabitants of the region." Libr J

"Gilbert's history is heavily Zionist. . . . Nonetheless, despite his tilt, Gilbert is well worth reading. He has an unrivalled ability to tell a story through the eyes of (some of) those taking part and his book is good popular history." London Rev Books

Includes bibliographical references

Gordis, Daniel

If a place can make you cry; dispatches from an anxious state. Crown 2002 xxiii, 279p maps $24   **956.94**

1. Israel—Social conditions 2. Jewish-Arab relations
ISBN 1-4000-4613-0   LC 2002-23725

This is a collection of e-mails, some of which appeared in the New York Times magazine, by a rabbi from Los Angeles who settled in Israel in 1998. "He explains how his family must balance their love of Israel with the fear of living in a land torn by strife." Booklist

"Gordis is a provocative and penetrating observer." Publ Wkly

Hazony, Yoram

The Jewish state; the struggle for Israel's soul. Basic Bks. 2000 433p hardcover o.p. paperback available $18   **956.94**

1. Zionism 2. Israel—Politics and government
ISBN 0-465-02902-7 (pa)   LC 00-21814

The author "asserts that 'the idea of the Jewish state'—and the future of the state—is under fervent attack from its own intellectual and cultural establishment. These 'post-Zionists' advocate, for example, the dejudaization of the public school curriculum and the repeal the Law of Return . . . in order to create a more secular and equitable 'post-Jewish' state." Publ Wkly

"An extremely well-thought-out treatise, *The Jewish State* screams out for attention and is strongly recommended for anyone interested in contemporary Israeli politics." Libr J

Horovitz, David Phillip

A little too close to God; the thrills and panic of a life in Israel; [by] David Horovitz. Knopf 2000 311p $27.50   **956.94**

1. Israel—Politics and government 2. Israel—Social conditions 3. Israeli national characteristics
ISBN 0-375-40381-7

The author, editor of the Jerusalem Report, argues "that in recent years the conservative Netanyahu government and the continued influence of extreme Orthodox Jews have done little except complicate daily life in Israel and prevent serious peace negotiations from taking place. He presents a highly informative history and current-events narrative in a manner that makes it personal and relevant to Jews and non-Jews alike." Libr J

Laqueur, Walter, 1921-

A history of Zionism; with a new preface by the author. Schocken Bks. 1989 xxii, 639p il hardcover o.p. paperback available $16.95
     956.94

1. Zionism
ISBN 0-8052-1149-7 (pa)   LC 88-38221

A reissue with new introduction of the title first published 1972 by Holt, Rinehart & Winston

The author examines the history of Zionism over the past three centuries from its European roots to the establishment of the state of Israel

Includes bibliographical references

Peres, Shimon, 1923-
The imaginary voyage; with Theodor Herzl in Israel; in collaboration with Patrick Girard. Arcade Pub. 1999 256p $23.95   **956.94**
1. Herzl, Theodor, 1860-1904 2. Zionism 3. Israel—History
ISBN 1-55970-468-3   LC 99-24365
Peres "takes the reader on an imaginary journey around present-day Israel with Theodor Herzl (1860-1904), the father of modern Zionism. The imaginary Herzl proves a good foil to whom Peres explains concisely how Israel has evolved." Publ Wkly

Sachar, Howard Morley, 1928-
A history of Israel; from the rise of Zionism to our time. 2nd ed rev & updated. Knopf 1996 xx, 1153p pa $30   **956.94**
1. Israel—History 2. Zionism
ISBN 0-679-76563-8   LC 95-23908
First published in two volumes 1976-1987. Volume two published by Oxford University Press
This is a history of the state of Israel. "When first published in 1976, this truly monumental history was hailed as a definitive work. . . . As extraordinarily stimulating as the first edition." Booklist
Includes bibliographical references

Shipler, David K.
Arab and Jew; wounded spirits in a promised land. rev ed. Penguin Bks. 2002 xxxix, 565p maps pa $17   **956.94**
1. Jewish-Arab relations 2. Israel-Arab conflicts 3. Israel—Social conditions 4. Palestinian Arabs
ISBN 0-14-200229-1   LC 2001-54862
First published 1986 by Times Bks.
The author examines the stereotypes that Arabs and Jews have of one another and "the origins of the prejudices that have been intensified by war, terrorism, and nationalism. . . . Shipler examines the process of indoctrination that begins in schools; he discusses the far-ranging effects of socioeconomic differences, historical conflicts between Islam and Judaism, attitudes about the Holocaust, and much more." Publisher's note
Includes bibliographical references

Shlaim, Avi
The iron wall; Israel and the Arab world since 1948. Norton 1999 704p il hardcover o.p. paperback available $17.95   **956.94**
1. Israel-Arab conflicts 2. Jewish-Arab relations 3. Israel—Foreign relations
ISBN 0-393-32112-6 (pa)   LC 99-23121
"The title of Shlaim's book is an allusion to an article called 'On the Iron Wall' by Zeev Jabotinsky. . . . Jabotinsky argued, the only path forward for the Zionist project was the path of force: to erect an 'iron wall' in the form of a Jewish battalion in the British army. . . . [Shlaim uses] the concept of the 'iron wall' as an organizing paradigm to explain the evolution of the politics of the Yishuv and the state of Israel from the 1920s to the 1980s." New Repub
"A thorough analysis of Israel's relationships with the West as well as its neighbors from a controversial but thoughtful point of view." Booklist
Includes bibliographical references

956.95   West Bank and Jordan

Grossman, David
The yellow wind; translated from the Hebrew by Haim Watzman; {with a new afterword by the author}. Picador; Farrar, Straus & Giroux 2002 222p map pa $13   **956.95**
1. Palestinian Arabs 2. West Bank 3. Jewish-Arab relations
ISBN 0-312-42098-6   LC 2002-67325
Original Hebrew edition, 1987; this translation first published 1988
"Grossman was assigned to report for a weekly newspaper on life for both occupied and occupier on the West Bank during the 20th anniversary of its conquest. With an eye and ear for revealing detail, he argues that the Jews are now doing to Palestinians what has been done to them through the ages." Libr J

957   Siberia

Thubron, Colin, 1939-
In Siberia. HarperCollins Pubs. 2000 287p hardcover o.p. paperback available $14   **957**
1. Siberia (Russia)—Description
ISBN 0-06-095373-X (pa)   LC 99-41346
The author "traverses all points of the compass in Russia's vast, sparsely settled Wild East. Thubron journeys into what 'seems less a country than a region in people's minds,' encountering people in search of explanations for past atrocities and ways to live through current hardships—all the while finding solace in science or religion." Libr J
"Thubron elegantly encompasses both awe-inspiring landscapes and their dark histories as well as immersing himself in local eccentricities." Times Lit Suppl

958.1   Afghanistan

Anderson, Jon Lee
The lion's grave; dispatches from Afghanistan; photographs by Thomas Dworzak. Grove Press 2002 244p il $23; pa $13   **958.1**
1. Afghanistan
ISBN 0-8021-1723-6; 0-8021-4025-4 (pa)
LC 2002-70659
In this "account, which includes his diary entries. Anderson recounts the arduous task of developing sources and reporting on the complexities of a nation caught up in its own ethnic and religious conflicts and its place in the new war on terrorism." Booklist
"The author's reporting reflects an astute understanding of the constellation of sociopolitical forces in today's Afghanistan. Anderson's penetrating observations and his ability to bring life to his subject—the fall of Kandahar and Kunduz, the dangerous search of the Tora Bora caves—are admirable." Libr J

Ansary, Mir Tamim

West of Kabul, East of New York; an Afghan American story. Farrar, Straus & Giroux 2002 292p $22; pa $13   **958.1**

1. Afghanistan—Social conditions 2. Islamic civilization

ISBN 0-374-28757-0; 0-312-42151-6 (pa)

The author, an Afghan American, reflects on his dual heritage. In light of the events of September 11, he focuses particular attention on the relationship between Islam and the West

"While Ansary's political insights can be detached or perhaps purposefully aloof his descriptions of having lived in and identified alternately with the West and the Islamic world are utterly compelling." Publ Wkly

Benard, Cheryl, 1953-

Veiled courage; inside the Afghan women's resistance; [by] Cheryl Benard in cooperation with Edit Schlaffer. Broadway Bks. 2002 293p $23.95   **958.1**

1. Revolutionary Association of the Women of Afghanistan 2. Women—Afghanistan 3. Afghanistan—Politics and government 4. Resistance to government

ISBN 0-7679-1301-9   LC 2002-20657

This history of the Revolutionary Association of the Women of Afghanistan "describe how individuals, including indigent refugees, joined RAWA and became strong, clandestine freedom fighters against the oppressive rule of first the Soviet Communist invaders, then the Northern Alliance, and, finally, the Taliban." SLJ

"This essential book will be sought out by those curious about resistance in that country." Booklist

Bergen, Peter L.

Holy war, Inc.; inside the secret world of Osama bin Laden. Free Press 2001 242p $26; pa $14   **958.1**

1. Terrorism

ISBN 0-7432-0502-2; 0-7432-3495-2 (pa)

         LC 2001-54732

Also available G.K. Hall large print edition

The author was a member of the CNN team that interviewed Saudi terrorist Osama bin Laden in 1997. Here he discusses "the history of Al Qaeda as a terrorist organization, profiles its leaders and more prominent members and examines its evolution as a global network." NY Times

"Although it may be impossible to fully understand bin Laden, Bergen does an admirable job of portraying him as a person, not just the face of terrorism. Readers will come away from this book understanding why bin Laden has been successful and how difficult it will be to dismantle his organization of terror." Booklist

Includes bibliographical references

Corwin, Phillip

Doomed in Afghanistan; a UN officer's memoir of the fall of Kabul and Najibullah's escape, 1992. Rutgers Univ. Press 2003 xx, 241p il $28   **958.1**

1. Najibullah, Mohammed 2. United Nations—Afghanistan 3. Afghanistan—History—Soviet occupation, 1979-1989

ISBN 0-8135-3171-3   LC 2002-24831

This book "focuses on the period after the Soviets left the country in 1988, when the UN was given the task of establishing a broad-based regime that would have included the communists. Thanks to the intrigues of the

US and its clients, Pakistan and Saudi Arabia, the UN team, of which the author was a member, failed to effect the escape of Najibullah, the leftist president of Afghanistan, from Kabul. As a result, there could be no broad-based coalition that might have prevented the rise of the Taliban and the country's decline into barbarism. . . . This engaging and sympathetic essay enables readers to understand the country's tragic recent past and the failure of diplomacy . . . which paved the way for civil war and the rise of 'Islamic fundamentalism.'" Choice

Includes bibliographical references

Elliot, Jason, 1965-

An unexpected light; travels in Afghanistan. St. Martin's Press 2001 473p map hardcover o.p. paperback available $18   **958.1**

1. Afghanistan—Description

ISBN 0-312-28846-8 (pa)   LC 2001-50036

This "is an account of Elliot's two visits to Afghanistan. The first occurred when he joined the mujaheddin circa 1979 and was smuggled into Soviet-occupied Afghanistan; the second happened nearly ten years later, when he returned to the still war-torn land. The skirmishes that Elliot painstakingly describes here took place between the Taliban and the government of Gen. Ahmad Shah Massoud in Kabul. . . . Elliot traveled widely in the hinterland, visiting Faizabad in the north and Herat in the west. The result is some of the finest travel writing in recent years." Libr J

Ewans, Martin

Afghanistan; a short history of its people and politics. HarperCollins Pubs. 2002 244p il maps hardcover o.p. paperback available $13.95   **958.1**

1. Afghanistan—History

ISBN 0-06-050508-7 (pa)   LC 2002-17342

"Ewans shows how centuries of invasions, fierce tribal rivalries, and powerful dynasties led to the creation of an Afghan empire during the eighteenth century. . . . The ruling Afghan dynasty was overthrown by a communist coup in the 1970s, which was answered in turn by a Soviet invasion in 1979. Roughly a decade later, the Soviet Union was forced to withdraw and left Afghanistan with a civil war that was to tear apart the nation's last remnants of religious and ethnic unity. It was into this climate that the Taliban was born." Publisher's note

"This is a fascinating story and the best book-length examination of Afghanistan's history we're likely to have for some time." Booklist

Includes bibliographical references

Rashid, Ahmed

Taliban: militant Islam, oil, and fundamentalism in Central Asia. Yale Univ. Press 2000 274p maps $40; pa $14.95 **958.1**

1. Taliban (Afghanistan) 2. Afghanistan—Politics and government 3. Islamic fundamentalism

ISBN 0-300-08340-8; 0-300-08902-3 (pa)

         LC 99-68718

Also available Thorndike Press large print edition

The author "covers the origin and rise of the Taliban, its concepts of Islam on questions of gender roles and drugs, and the importance of the country to the development of energy resources in the region. . . . A lucid and thoroughly researched account." Libr J

Zoya

Zoya's story; an Afghan woman's struggle for freedom; {by} Zoya with John Follain and Rita Cristofari. HarperCollins Pubs. 2002 239p $24.95; pa $12.95 **958.1**

1. Afghanistan 2. Women—Afghanistan
ISBN 0-06-009782-5; 0-06-009783-3 (pa)

"After both her parents were killed by the Mujahideen, Zoya took up her mother's work in the Revolutionary Association of the Women of Afghanistan and, with her grandmother, journeyed to Pakistan, where she could receive an education. A few years later, Zoya returned to Afghanistan, where she witnessed public executions but also saw heartening displays of courage. A stirring memoir by an uncompromisingly brave woman." Booklist

959 Southeast Asia

Somers Heidhues, Mary F.

Southeast Asia: a concise history. Thames & Hudson 2000 192p il maps hardcover o.p. paperback available $18.95 **959**

1. Southeast Asia—History
ISBN 0-500-28303-6 (pa)   LC 99-66014

This "history ranges from Southeast Asia's prehistoric times to the most recent political developments in Indonesia. Heidhues . . . divides her study into seven well-balanced chapters, touching on the political history, economics, society, and culture of Burma, Thailand, Cambodia, Vietnam, Malaysia, Singapore, Brunei, Indonesia, and the Philippines." Libr J

959.1 Myanmar (Burma)

Aung San Suu Kyi

Freedom from fear, and other writings; edited with an introduction by Michael Aris; foreword to the first edition by Vaclav Havel, foreword to the second edition by Archbishop Desmond Tutu. rev ed. Penguin Bks. 1995 xxxi, 374p il pa $14.95 **959.1**

1. Myanmar—Politics and government
ISBN 0-14-025317-3   LC 96-902734

First published 1991

This is a collection of essays, letters, speeches, and other writings by the Burmese opposition leader, Winner of the 1991 Nobel Peace Prize

"Mrs. Aung San Suu Kyi's excellent book offers inspiration to many other peoples in the region as much as it reflects Myanmar's own desire for change." N Y Times Book Rev [review of 1991 edition]

Includes bibliographical references

Marshall, Andrew

The trouser people; a story of Burma—in the shadow of the Empire. Counterpoint 2002 307p il maps hardcover o.p. paperback available $16 **959.1**

1. Scott, Sir James George, 1851-1935 2. Myanmar
ISBN 1-58243-242-2 (pa)   LC 2001-47246

"Marshall recounts his adventures in Burma over a five-year period, inspired by the diaries of late-19th-century Scottish adventurer Sir George Scott. . . . Scott furthered the interests of the British colonials (aka the trouser people) by mapping and photographing remote areas of Burma. . . . This is a valuable firsthand look at areas and living conditions in a country relatively unknown in the West." Publ Wkly

959.3 Thailand

Wyatt, David K.

Thailand: a short history. 2nd ed. Yale Univ. Press 2003 352p il maps pa $20 **959.3**

1. Thailand—History
ISBN 0-3000-8475-7

First published 1984

This volume provides a general history of Thailand beginning with the migrations of the Tai peoples from southern China, examining the social and economic changes to the present

Includes bibliographical references

959.6 Cambodia

Bizot, François

The gate; translated from the French by Euan Cameron; with a preface by John Le Carré. Knopf 2003 275p $24; pa $14 **959.6**

1. Bizot, François 2. Communism—Cambodia 3. Atrocities 4. Cambodia—History—1970-1975, Civil War
ISBN 0-375-41293-X; 0-375-72723-X (pa)
    LC 2002-69428

Original French edition, 2000

The author, who was "seized by Cambodian rebels in 1971, recalls peculiar daily chat sessions over politics and philosophy with his chief captor, an obviously dangerous man who later ran one of the Khmer Rouge's ghastliest killing fields." N Y Times Book Rev

Bizot's "tale of his experiences, both in the camp and as translator at the gate of the French embassy, leaves readers with haunting images of the doomed." Booklist

Chandler, David P.

The tragedy of Cambodian history; politics, war, and revolution since 1945. Yale Univ. Press 1991 396p il maps hardcover o.p. paperback available $25 **959.6**

1. Cambodia—History
ISBN 0-300-05752-0 (pa)   LC 91-17074

The author "examines Cambodia's five governments from the end of WW II to the beginning of the Vietnamese protectorate in 1979." Publ Wkly

"Mr. Chandler's spadework in French, American and British archives, the multitude of interviews he conducted with participants and observers of many nationalities, and his readings in the largely French-language Cambodian press going back to colonial days have enabled him to construct as complete a historical narrative as has ever been compiled." N Y Times Book Rev

Includes bibliographical references

Kamm, Henry

Cambodia: report from a stricken land. Arcade Pub. 1998 xxiv, 262p il maps $25.95 **959.6**

1. Cambodia—History
ISBN 1-55970-433-0   LC 98-22707

This is an account of events in Cambodia since the 1970s. Kamm argues that these "events were man-made and avoidable, the consequence of cynical and callous decisions by rival Cambodian leaders and by foreign powers, including the United States. . . . Guiltiest by far were the Khmer Rouge, who made Cambodia a killing

Kamm, Henry—_Continued_

field while their . . . regime under Pol Pot held power between 1975 and 1979." N Y Times Book Rev

"Sober yet passionate, Kamm's well-informed survey is an excellent introduction to a country that the world has all but abandoned." Libr J

Kiernan, Ben

The Pol Pot regime; race, power, and genocide in Cambodia under the Khmer Rouge, 1975-79. 2nd ed. Yale Univ. Press 2002 xxiii, 477p il map (Yale Nota bene) pa $19.95   **959.6**

1. Communism—Cambodia 2. Atrocities 3. Cambodia—Politics and government

ISBN 0-300-09649-6   LC 2002-100979

First published 1996

This is an account of "the Cambodian catastrophe; the significant internal resistance to the Khmer Rouge; and the racialist and totalitarian attitudes by which Pol Pot's regime justified the death, by starvation and disease as well as torture and murder, of some 1.5 million of their 8 million countrymen." Booklist {review of 1996 edition}

Includes bibliographical references

Ung, Loung, 1970-

First they killed my father; a daughter of Cambodia remembers. HarperCollins Pubs. 2000 240p il $23.95; pa $13   **959.6**

1. Cambodia—History

ISBN 0-06-019332-8; 0-06-093138-8 (pa)

LC 99-34707

The author's father was a "high-ranking government official in Phnom Penh. She was only five when the Khmer Rouge stormed the city and her family was forced to flee. They sought refuge in various camps, hiding their wealth and education, always on the move and ever fearful of being betrayed. After 20 months, Ung's father was taken away, never to be seen again. Her story of starvation, forced labor, beatings, attempted rape, separations, and the deaths of her family members is one of horror and brutality." SLJ

959.7   Vietnam

Sachs, Dana

The house on Dream Street; memoir of an American woman in Vietnam. Algonquin Bks. 2000 348p o.p.; Seal Press paperback available $15.95   **959.7**

1. Vietnam—Description

ISBN 1-58005-100-6 (pa)   LC 00-44191

This is an American journalist's account of her visits to Vietnam. "Her memoir covers the time from her initial plunge into the country, as a touring backpacker in 1989, to her triumphant return in 1998 with . . . [her] husband and son." Publ Wkly

"Sachs is an engaging and sensitive writer who tells her story ably." Libr J

959.704   Vietnam—1949-

The **American** experience in Vietnam; a reader; edited by Grace Sevy. University of Okla. Press 1989 319p hardcover o.p. paperback available $24.95   **959.704**

1. Vietnam War, 1961-1975

ISBN 0-8061-2390-7 (pa)   LC 89-40222

"Thirty essays, speeches, and interviews on the subject of America's involvement in the Vietnam War. The selections . . . include sections on American policy, the nature of the war and the soldiers who fought it, the role of the press, and the antiwar movement. The writers hail from all points on the political spectrum, but mostly from the center and the left; among their number are Norman Podhoretz, Martin Luther King, Jr., Paul Goodman, and John Kerry." Booklist

Includes bibliographical references

Anderson, David L.

The Columbia guide to the Vietnam War. Columbia Univ. Press 2002 308p maps (Columbia guides to American history and cultures) $47; pa $22.50   **959.704**

1. Vietnam War, 1961-1975

ISBN 0-231-11492-3; 0-231-11493-1 (pa)

LC 2002-20143

"The first part of the book contains a historical narrative. The rest consists of a 'mini-encyclopedia' listing events, individuals, and military operations; a brief chronology; an annotated bibliography of books, feature films, documentaries, and electronic resources; a collection of mostly excerpted documents; and an appendix of pertinent statistics." Booklist

"Anderson's guide successfully compresses the copiously documented, labyrinthine history of the Vietnamese conflict into a single economical volume. In five parts, the guide's narrative and encyclopedia sections provide a fascinating survey of the war, while the remaining elements of the work link modern researchers to a host of richly documented resources. . . . The guide will become an important resource for those seeking a historical overview as well as direction for further research. Strongly recommended." Choice

Includes bibliographical references

Berman, Larry

No peace, no honor; Nixon, Kissinger, and betrayal in Vietnam. Free Press 2001 334p $27.50; pa $14   **959.704**

1. Nixon, Richard M. (Richard Milhous), 1913-1994 2. Kissinger, Henry, 1923- 3. Vietnam War, 1961-1975 4. United States—Politics and government—1961-1974

ISBN 0-684-84968-2; 0-7432-2349-7 (pa)

LC 2001-23904

Berman "navigates recently declassified records to show that Nixon never sought a peaceful solution to the war. Instead, the Paris Peace Treaty, which ended U.S. involvement in 1973 after five years of tortured negotiations between Kissinger and his North Vietnam counterpart Le Duc Tho, was so deliberately ambiguous that Nixon believed he would be able to return with U.S. air power to avoid being blamed for the loss of the war." Libr J

"In the endless flow of assessments, reassessments and re-reassessments of the war in Vietnam, a study occasionally appears that goes beyond a rehash of the polemics that have marked that tragic experience. Larry

Berman, Larry—*Continued*

Berman's 'No Peace, No Honor' belongs in that select category." N Y Times Book Rev
Includes bibliographical references

Bilton, Michael

Four hours in My Lai; [by] Michael Bilton and Kevin Sim. Viking 1992 430p il maps hardcover o.p. paperback available $17

959.704

1. Mỹ Lai Massacre, Vietnam, 1968
ISBN 0-14-017709-4 (pa)   LC 91-47651

The authors "have reconstructed perhaps the ugliest day in recent American history: March 16, 1968, when 105 soldiers of Charlie Company, 11th Brigade, Americal Division . . . massacred approximately 500 children, women and old men in the Vietnamese hamlet of My Lai. . . . The authors . . . recount circumstances leading up to the massacre, the horrific event itself and the subsequent cover-up and investigation." N Y Times Book Rev

"Any collection organized around the Vietnam War that does not carry this work is not complete." Libr J
Includes bibliographical references

Bloods: an oral history of the Vietnam War by black veterans; [edited by] Wallace Terry. Random House 1984 311p il o.p.; Ballantine Bks. paperback available $6.99

959.704

1. Vietnam War, 1961-1975—Personal narratives 2. African American soldiers
ISBN 0-345-31197-3 (pa)   LC 83-42775

Black Vietnam War veterans discuss their experiences in battle and stateside

This is "an intimate overview that often makes the reader stop, sit back, and think about this war that tore at America. . . . The accounts are moving, powerful and offer several views." Voice Youth Advocates
Includes bibliographical references

Burrows, Larry, 1926-1971

Vietnam; introduction by David Halberstam. Knopf 2002 243p il $50

959.704

1. Vietnam War, 1961-1975—Pictorial works
ISBN 0-375-41102-X   LC 2002-19100

This volume presents the work of Larry Burrows, who "photographed the conflict in Vietnam from 1962, the earliest days of American involvement, until 1971, when he died in a helicopter shot down on the Vietnam/Laos border. . . . [It includes] unpublished images from the Burrows archive." Publisher's note

This "confirms that [Burrows] was an artist as well as a journalist, capable of arousing the great tragic emotions, pity and terror." Booklist
Includes bibliographical references

Caputo, Philip

A rumor of war. Holt, Rinehart & Winston 1977 346p o.p.; Holt & Co. paperback available $15   **959.704**

1. Vietnam War, 1961-1975—Personal narratives
ISBN 0-8050-4695-X (pa)   LC 76-29900

These are "the combat recollections of a very young Marine officer in Vietnam in 1965-1966. Caputo later became a newspaperman. . . . He remembers himself as a patriotic youngster, eager to prove his manhood, and

then . . . he takes us through his step-by-step discovery that war and manhood and their interrelation are more complicated than he had dreamed." New Yorker

Ellsberg, Daniel, 1931-

Secrets: a memoir of Vietnam and the Pentagon papers. Viking 2002 498p il $29.95; pa $16   **959.704**

1. Pentagon Papers 2. Vietnam War, 1961-1975
ISBN 0-670-03030-9; 0-14-200342-5 (pa)
LC 2002-16874

Ellsberg recalls how he leaked "the Pentagon Papers, which documented U.S. foreign-policy failures and deceit in Vietnam from 1945 to 1968. . . . Ellsberg's autobiographical account provides insight into the disturbing abuses of presidential power that plagued the Vietnam/Watergate era." Libr J
Includes bibliographical references

Encyclopedia of the Vietnam War; a political, social, and military history; Spencer C. Tucker, editor. ABC-CLIO 1998 3v il maps set $275   **959.704**

1. Vietnam War, 1961-1975—Encyclopedias
ISBN 0-87436-983-5   LC 98-4184

Also available CD-ROM version and in an abridged one volume edition in paperback from Oxford University Press

"The first two volumes contain more than 900 signed articles ranging in length from several paragraphs to several pages. Volume three provides a representative selection of documents pertaining to the war, beginning with a speech by Ho Chi Minh in 1920 and ending with President Clinton's announcement of normalization of diplomatic relations with Vietnam in 1995. These primary sources add enormous value to the set." SLJ

FitzGerald, Frances, 1940-

Fire in the lake; the Vietnamese and the Americans in Vietnam. Little, Brown 1972 491p maps hardcover o.p. paperback available $16.95   **959.704**

1. Vietnam War, 1961-1975 2. Vietnam—Politics and government
ISBN 0-316-15919-0 (pa)

"An Atlantic Monthly Press book"

This book looks at the effects American intervention had on the Vietnamese social and intellectual landscape
Includes bibliographical references

Franklin, H. Bruce (Howard Bruce), 1934-

M.I.A.; or, Mythmaking in America. Hill Bks. 1992 225p o.p.; Rutgers Univ. Press paperback available $13   **959.704**

1. Vietnam War, 1961-1975—Missing in action
ISBN 0-8135-2001-0 (pa)   LC 91-34068

"Franklin reviews the astonishing numbers games the Pentagon and POW/MIA activists have played, traces the deliberate manipulation of this issue by a generation of self-serving politicians . . . analyzes the roles of groups like the National League of Families and VIVA and of individuals like Henry Kissinger and H. Ross Perot in developing and sustaining true believers' faith, and reveals the interplay between life and art in POW/MIA books and films, from *The Deerhunter* to *Rambo* and beyond." Booklist
Includes bibliographical references

Glasser, Ronald J.

365 days. Braziller 1971 292p hardcover
o.p. paperback available $14.95   **959.704**
1. Vietnam War, 1961-1975—Personal narratives
2. Vietnam War, 1961-1975—Medical care
ISBN 0-8076-1527-7 (pa)
The author, a military doctor who was stationed in Japan, recounts his experiences treating wounded American military personnel during the Vietnam War

Goldstein, Donald M.

The Vietnam war: the story and
photographs; by Donald M. Goldstein,
Katherine V. Dillon, and J. Michael Wenger.
Brassey's 1997 179p il maps hardcover o.p.
paperback available $19.95   **959.704**
1. Vietnam War, 1961-1975
ISBN 1-57488-210-4 (pa)   LC 97-11574
This history of the Vietnam War "proceeds both chronologically and thematically, beginning with the French colonial era and the Indochina War, then covering successive stages of the U.S. involvement. The text is sufficiently detailed, clear, and balanced to serve as a narrative introduction to the subject, but the real strength lies in the photographs. They cover the subject with admirable thoroughness. . . . They do not include too many chestnuts, and they adequately cover the Vietnamese, the navy, and other subjects relatively neglected in the literature thus far." Booklist
Includes bibliographical references

Hendrickson, Paul

The living and the dead; Robert McNamara
and five lives of a lost war. Knopf 1996 427p
il hardcover o.p. paperback available $15
    959.704
1. McNamara, Robert S., 1916- 2. Vietnam War,
1961-1975
ISBN 0-679-78117-X (pa)   LC 96-7445
In this look at the Vietnam War, the author "probes the histories of several men and women whose lives were irreversibly altered by the war: an Army nurse, a Quaker protester who immolated himself outside the Pentagon, a Marine helicopter gunner, and a Vietnamese politician. But the main exhibit here is the life and conscience of Robert McNamara." New Yorker
"Exhaustively researched, probing, important contribution to the annals of American history." Publ Wkly
Includes bibliographical references

Isaacs, Arnold R.

Vietnam shadows; the war, its ghosts, and
its legacy. Johns Hopkins Univ. Press 1997
236p hardcover o.p. paperback available
$19.95   **959.704**
1. Vietnam War, 1961-1975 2. United States—Civilization
ISBN 0-8018-6344-9 (pa)   LC 97-10823
This overview of the Vietnam War explores the political, social, cultural and military dimensions of the conflict
The author's "range is impressive. He comments on everything from the moral opacity of Robert McNamara to American 'escape-goating'—his neologism for the impulse to produce counterfactual histories in which we win the war after all. Isaacs's basic judgments are sound, and his exquisite nose for detecting self-deception leads him to some awkward truths about the wartime mythologies that have become encased in middle-aged amber." NY Times Book Rev
Includes bibliographical references

Kaiser, David E., 1947-

American tragedy; Kennedy, Johnson, and
the origins of the Vietnam War; [by] David
Kaiser. Harvard Univ. Press 2000 566p il
$36; pa $18.95   **959.704**
1. Kennedy, John F. (John Fitzgerald), 1917-1963
2. Johnson, Lyndon B. (Lyndon Baines), 1908-1973
3. Vietnam War, 1961-1975 4. United States—Politics and government—1961-1974
ISBN 0-674-00225-3; 0-674-00672-0 (pa)
    LC 99-52925
The author argues that "a cautious President Kennedy consistently resisted the entreaties of State and Defense Department professionals (many of them Eisenhower holdovers) to dramatically expand our commitment in Vietnam. Unfortunately, Kaiser asserts, President Johnson was far more willing to accept the advice of those same men." Booklist
"The first-rate research is complemented by an intriguing model of intergenerational policy-making." Libr J
Includes bibliographical references

Karnow, Stanley

Vietnam; a history. 2nd rev & updated ed.
Penguin Bks. 1997 768p il maps pa $17.95
    959.704
1. Vietnam War, 1961-1975 2. Vietnam—History
ISBN 0-14-026547-3
First published 1983
A summation "of over two centuries of conflict in Indochina. Chronicling a tragic history, Karnow presents a balanced and sympathetic view of Vietnamese aspirations and the mishaps that led to American involvement in a 'war nobody won.'" Voice Youth Advocates [review of 1983 edition]
Includes bibliographical references

Langguth, A. J., 1933-

Our Vietnam; the war, 1954-1975. Simon
& Schuster 2000 766p il maps hardcover o.p.
paperback available $20   **959.704**
1. Vietnam War, 1961-1975
ISBN 0-7432-1231-2 (pa)   LC 00-57384
The author tells the story of the Vietnam War "mainly through the actions of key personalities. Each of his chapters is titled for one of the principal characters, . . . among them presidents and other . . . American officials of the era, as well as figures like Daniel Ellsberg, who leaked the Pentagon Papers. The list also includes the names of . . . Vietnamese leaders on both sides." N Y Times Book Rev
This book "is unique in its perspective of the major players on both sides." Booklist
Includes bibliographical references

Lind, Michael, 1962-

Vietnam, the necessary war; a
reinterpretation of America's most disastrous
military conflict. Free Press 1999 314p $25;
pa $14   **959.704**
1. Vietnam War, 1961-1975 2. United States—Foreign relations
ISBN 0-684-84254-8; 0-684-87027-4 (pa)
    LC 99-28449
The author "argues that the war in Vietnam, however horrifying, had to be fought not to extend ideology but to preserve the military and diplomatic credibility of the United States." Libr J
"Lind's arguments, if not always persuasive, are always provocative." Publ Wkly
Includes bibliographical references

Mann, Robert, 1958-

A grand delusion; America's descent into Vietnam. Basic Bks. 2000 821p il $35; pa $22 **959.704**
1. Vietnam War, 1961-1975 2. Vietnam—Politics and government 3. United States—Politics and government—20th century
ISBN 0-465-04369-0; 0-465-04370-4 (pa)
LC 00-49824
This account of the United States involvement in the Vietnam War focuses on the political causes and "collision of personalities throughout the White House, Congress, and elsewhere during that era. Mann's history concentrates on seven American leaders in the halls of power rather than on the battlefield." Libr J
Includes bibliographical references

McCloud, Bill, 1948-

What should we tell our children about Vietnam? University of Okla. Press 1989 155p hardcover o.p. paperback available $14.95 **959.704**
1. Vietnam War, 1961-1975
ISBN 0-8061-3240-X (pa)
LC 89-40218
"President Bush, William Westmoreland, Gary Trudeau, and Philip Caputo are among some of the best known of 128 individuals who gave their views when McCloud, a junior high school teacher and veteran, wrote to ask them what young people should understand about the war." Booklist
Includes bibliographical references

McNamara, Robert S., 1916-

In retrospect; the tragedy and lessons of Vietnam; {by} Robert S. McNamara with Brian VanDeMark. Times Bks. 1995 414p il o.p.; Vintage Bks. paperback available $16 **959.704**
1. Vietnam War, 1961-1975
ISBN 0-679-76749-5 (pa)
LC 94-40088
"Former defense secretary McNamara seeks 'to put Vietnam in context' and counter 'the cynicism and even contempt with which so many people view our political institutions and leaders.' . . . He identifies 'eleven major causes for our disaster in Vietnam' and six points when the U.S. could legitimately have withdrawn. Certainly not the last word on this still-controversial subject but an essential acquisition for most libraries." Booklist
Includes bibliographical references

Moore, Harold G., 1922-

We were soldiers once—and young; Ia Drang: the battle that changed the war in Vietnam; [by] Harold G. Moore and Joseph L. Galloway. Random House 1992 412p il maps $26.95; pa $7.50 **959.704**
1. Vietnam War, 1961-1975—Personal narratives
ISBN 0-679-41158-5; 0-345-47264-0 (pa)
LC 92-53642
"On Nov. 14, 1965, the 1st Battalion of the 7th Cavalry, commanded by Col. Moore and accompanied by UPI reporter Galloway, helicoptered into Vietnam's remote Ia Drang Valley and found itself surrounded by a numerically superior force of North Vietnamese regulars. Moore and Galloway here offer a detailed account, based on interviews with participants and on their own recollections, of what happened during the four-day battle." Publ Wkly
Includes bibliographical references

Prochnau, William W., 1937-

Once upon a distant war. Times Bks. 1995 546p il o.p.; Vintage Bks. paperback available $16 **959.704**
1. Vietnam War, 1961-1975—Journalists
ISBN 0-679-77265-0 (pa)
LC 95-7327
This is a study of American journalists who reported on the Vietnam War, focusing on the years between 1961 and 1963. The author discusses the activities of reporters and photographers such as Peter Arnett, Homer Bigart, Malcolm Browne, Horst Fass, David Halberstam, Marguerite Higgins, Charley Mohr, and Neil Sheehan
Prochnau's "thesis is hardly new—Vietnam has long been seen as the lesson that taught reporters to stop automatically believing government handout—but Prochnau illustrates it in fresh, interesting ways." Time

Reporting Vietnam. Library of Am. 1998 2v il map ea $35 **959.704**

1. Vietnam War, 1961-1975 2. Reporters and reporting
ISBN 1-883011-58-2 (v1); 1-883011-59-0 (v2)
LC 98-12267

Also available in paperback
Contents: Pt.1 American journalism, 1959-1969; pt.2 American journalism, 1969-1975

This collection includes "newspaper, magazine, book excerpts, and one TV commentary, Walter Cronkite's post-Tet report concluding that the United States should quickly negotiate its way out." Commonweal
"This book will help readers understand better what it was like to live through that tumultuous period of American history." Publ Wkly

Sheehan, Neil

A bright shining lie: John Paul Vann and America in Vietnam. Random House 1988 861p il hardcover o.p. paperback available $18 **959.704**
1. Vann, John Paul 2. Vietnam War, 1961-1975
ISBN 0-679-72414-1 (pa)
LC 87-43330
The author "tells the story of the war through the focus of John Paul Vann, an army officer who faced down South Vietnamese politicians and American generals to expose the corruption that undermined our efforts and later was President Nixon's civilian adviser in Vietnam until he was killed in a helicopter crash in 1972. It is a dramatic device that lets Mr. Sheehan bring the very palpable feel of the war to us with passionate power." N Y Times Book Rev
Includes bibliographical references

Sherwood, John Darrell, 1966-

Fast movers; America's jet pilots and the Vietnam experience. Free Press 2000 268p il o.p.; St. Martin's Press paperback available $6.99 **959.704**
1. Vietnam War, 1961-1975—Aerial operations
ISBN 0-312-97962-2 (pa)
LC 99-27744
The author discusses aerial operations during the Vietnam War and profiles about a dozen fliers. He describes "the specs of their jets, their ordnance, and the dogfighting dangers encountered on specific missions. These war stories propel the text." Booklist
Includes bibliographical references

Shultz, Richard H., 1947-

The secret war against Hanoi; Kennedy and Johnson's use of spies, saboteurs, and covert warriors in North Vietnam; [by] Richard H. Shultz, Jr. HarperCollins Pubs. 1999 408p il hardcover o.p. paperback available $15

959.704

1. United States. Military Assistance Command, Vietnam. Studies and Observations Group 2. Vietnam War, 1961-1975—Secret service 3. Subversive activities 4. United States—Politics and government—1961-1974

ISBN 0-06-093253-8 (pa)   LC 99-44524

"Organized in a military entity euphemistically named the Studies and Observation Group (SOG), the covert war, it was hoped, would annoy Hanoi enough to force it to scale back its war in the south. . . . Schultz was given access to SOG archives and veterans and has produced a professional volume on how SOG originated and operated over its eight-year existence." Booklist

Includes bibliographical references

Summers, Harry G.

Vietnam War almanac; [by] Harry G. Summers, Jr. Facts on File 1985 414p il o.p.; Presidio Press paperback available $18.95

959.704

1. Vietnam War, 1961-1975

ISBN 0-8914-1692-7 (pa)   LC 83-14054

"Provides a clear, accessible, and objective look at the conflict that shaped a generation. Includes an introductory history of the country and a description of the physical and historical conditions that shaped American policy there; a chronology of events, both in Vietnam and in the United States; and 500 articles." N Y Public Libr Book of How & Where to Look It Up

The **Vietnam** War; editor, Mark Lawrence; introduction by David K. Shipler. Fitzroy Dearborn Pubs. 2001 2v il maps (New York Times 20th century in review) set $150   **959.704**

1. Vietnam War, 1961-1975

ISBN 1-57958-368-7   LC 2002-726953

Contents: v1 1945-1969; v2 1969-2000

Articles and photos from The New York Times trace "the origins, the strategies, the successes, the failures, and the bitter legacy of this war for the United States, Vietnam, and the world." Publisher's note

"A must-have for all libraries." Recomm Ref Books for Small & Medium-sized Libr & Media Cent, 2003

959.9   Philippines

Hemley, Robin, 1958-

Invented Eden; the elusive, disputed history of the Tasaday. Farrar, Straus & Giroux 2003 339p il maps $25   **959.9**

1. Tasaday (Philippine people) 2. Impostors and imposture

ISBN 0-374-17716-3   LC 2002-32547

"Hemley revisits an infamous and persistently enigmatic chapter in the long and harrowing conflict between traditional cultures and industrialized societies in this compelling and exacting inquiry into the 1971 'discovery' of the Tasaday, allegedly a band of Stone Age people living in the Philippines." Booklist

Includes bibliographical references

Karnow, Stanley

In our image; America's empire in the Philippines. Random House 1989 494p il maps hardcover o.p. paperback available $27

959.9

1. Philippines—History

ISBN 0-345-32816-7 (pa)   LC 88-42676

A history of American involvement in the Philippines from 1898 to the present

The author's "treatment of the indecisiveness of President McKinley over the issue of empire and of the egotistical General MacArthur make the work a definite purchase for libraries. . . . Those who love swashbuckling history will enjoy this work." Libr J

Includes bibliographical references

960   Africa

Africa: an encyclopedia for students; John Middleton, editor. Scribner 2002 4v il maps set $395   **960**

1. Africa—Encyclopedias

ISBN 0-684-80650-9   LC 2001-49348

A comprehensive look at the continent of Africa and the countries that comprise it, including peoples and cultures, the land and its history, art and architecture, and daily life

Cultural atlas of Africa; edited by Jocelyn Murray. rev ed. Checkmark Bks. 1998 240p il maps $50   **960**

1. Africa—Civilization

ISBN 0-8160-3813-9

"An Andromeda book"

First published 1981

This survey of African civilization is divided into three parts. Part One: The physical background, describes the geography of the continent. Part Two: The Cultural background, includes such topics as languages, religions, early man, history, the arts, and education. Part Three: The Nations of Africa, offers information about individual countries divided by region

This "is an important contribution to our understanding of the African continent." Booklist [review of 1981 edition]

Includes bibliographical references

Davidson, Basil, 1914-

Africa in history; themes and outlines. rev and expanded ed. Collier Bks. 1991 425p o.p.; Simon & Schuster paperback available $16   **960**

1. Africa—History

ISBN 0-684-82667-4 (pa)   LC 90-23905

First published 1966 with title: Africa: history of a continent

Among the topics discussed are Africa's diverse regional differences, apartheid, the rise of Islam, tribal mores, slavery and colonization

Includes bibliographical references

Encyclopedia of African peoples; by the Diagram Group. Facts on File 2000 400p il $75   **960**

1. Africans—Encyclopedias

ISBN 0-8160-4099-0   LC 99-55125

Repackaging, with some updating, of the six-volume Peoples of Africa (1997)

Encyclopedia of African peoples—*Continued*

This work covers more than 1,000 ethnic groups. Entries discuss each major groups' history, language, religion, social structure, and cultural traditions. Africa's regions and nations are described in terms of population, geography, climate, economy and recent historical events. More than 300 thumbnail biographies are included

"The beautifully rendered two-color illustrations depict people, material culture, and historical events; maps and charts are included." Libr J

Falola, Toyin

Key events in African history; a reference guide. Greenwood Press 2002 xxiii, 347p il maps $64.95   **960**
1. Africa—History
ISBN 0-313-31323-7   LC 2001-58644
"An Oryx book"

"Falola surveys the . . . history of the African continent by focusing on 36 pivotal events that either caused or led to significant changes and developments in African social, political, and cultural life from around 40,000 B.C.E. to the collapse of apartheid in the 1990s. . . . Following a detailed time line of historical events, each topic is highlighted in an individual chapter including cross-references, historical and political maps, illustrations, a notes section, and a suggested list for further reading." Booklist

Gates, Henry Louis

Wonders of the African world; {by} Henry Louis Gates, Jr. Knopf 1999 275p il map hardcover o.p. paperback available $24.95
    960
1. Africa—Civilization
ISBN 0-375-70948-7 (pa)   LC 99-18496

"In conjunction with the PBS television series of the same title, Gates offers a 12-nation reprise of the magnificence of ancient African civilizations . . . {moving} in clusters—from the black gods and kings of Nubia, to Ethiopia's links to the Holy Land and the Lost Ark of the Covenant, to Timbuktu's commercial and intellectual center, to the slave kingdoms, and to the Lost Cities of Great Zimbabwe." Libr J

"Gates writes with concentration and clarity, and anticipates the questions that arise in the wary reader's mind, delivering the answers at just the right time." N Y Times Book Rev

Includes bibliographical references

Kapuściński, Ryszard

The shadow of the sun; translated from the Polish by Klara Glowczewska. Knopf 2001 325p $25; pa $14   **960**
1. Africa—Description
ISBN 0-679-45491-8; 0-679-77907-8 (pa)
     LC 2001-88076
Original Polish edition, 1988

This is "a collection of reminiscences by a Polish journalist on his 40-year career of covering the third world." N Y Times Book Rev

"This lyrically evocative patchwork quilt of memories, experiences, and adventures provides an intimate portrait of the dazzling mystery that is Africa." Booklist

Lefkowitz, Mary R., 1935-

Not out of Africa; how "Afrocentrism" became an excuse to teach myth as history; [by] Mary Lefkowitz. Basic Bks. 1996 222p il map hardcover o.p. paperback available $19
    960
1. Africa—Historiography 2. History—Study and teaching
ISBN 0-465-09838-X (pa)   LC 95-49109
"A New Republic book"

"Those classicists who believe there are Egyptian antecedents for Greek philosophy are known as Afrocentrists. . . . Lefkowitz claims that the Afrocentrists are perpetuating myths and that they protect their claims by labeling those who question those claims as narrow-minded or racist." Libr J

"The book is a case study in historical methods, the value and limits of scholarship, and the preciousness of hard-bitten reason and objectivity. The book is also lucid and accessible." Christ Sci Monit

Includes bibliographical references

Page, Willie F., 1929-

The encyclopedia of African history and culture. Facts on File 2001 3v il map set $247.50   **960**
1. Africa—Encyclopedias
ISBN 0-8160-4472-4   LC 00-63613
"A Learning Source book"
Contents: v1 Ancient Africa; v2 African kingdoms; v3 From conquest to colonialization

"This survey of African history from the earliest stages to 1850 fills a gap in the reference collection, especially for students and general readers." Booklist

Pakenham, Thomas, 1933-

The scramble for Africa, 1876-1912. Random House 1991 xxv, 738p il maps o.p.; Avon Bks. paperback available $22.95   **960**
1. Africa—History
ISBN 0-380-71999-1 (pa)   LC 91-52681
This book is an account of the colonization and conquest of Africa by five European nations—Great Britain, France, Belgium, Germany, and Italy

This is a "sweeping narrative, refreshingly old fashioned in its appreciation of the fact that imperialism did have some virtues, which offers as good an introduction to the 'scramble' as has ever been written." Libr J

Includes bibliographical references

Reader, John, 1937-

Africa: a biography of the continent. Knopf 1998 801p il maps hardcover o.p. paperback available $18   **960**
1. Africa—History
ISBN 0-679-73869-X (pa)   LC 97-36892
First published 1997 in the United Kingdom

This book discusses "the paleontology of the early African continent, covering a period of approximately three billion years. [Reader] then traces the history of human origins in Africa and proceeds to track the imprint of that beginning on human evolution, staying grounded in Africa as he marks the immigration of humans to other continents." Booklist

Reader "writes with sweeping historical perspective and an engaging familiarity with the continent and its people." Publ Wkly

Includes bibliographical references

962   Egypt and Sudan

Egypt: ancient culture, modern land; general editor: Jaromir Malek. University of Okla. Press 1993 192p il maps (Cradles of civilization) $34.95   **962**
1. Egypt—History 2. Egypt—Civilization
ISBN 0-8061-2526-8   LC 92-50718
"This book considers Egypt's natural environment, culture, leadership, economy, religious beliefs, and everyday life during the last five thousand years, from ancient times to the present." Publisher's note

Ghosh, Amitav
In an antique land. Knopf 1993 393p o.p.; Vintage Bks. paperback available $15   **962**
1. Ben Yijû, Abraham, 12th cent. 2. Egypt—Social life and customs 3. Jews—Egypt
ISBN 0-679-72783-3 (pa)   LC 92-54276
The author describes his sojourn in rural Egypt as a student of social anthropology. Ghosh sought to reconstruct the life of Bomma, the Indian slave of a twelfth-century Egyptian Jewish merchant named Abraham Ben Yijû, mentioned in a Cairo manuscript
The author "offers an enchanting, subtle glimpse into ordinary life in contemporary rural Egypt, in a manner that at times rivals anything by the masters of social realism in modern Egyptian literature." N Y Times Book Rev

Rodenbeck, Max, 1962-
Cairo; the city victorious. Knopf 1999 300p map hardcover o.p. paperback available $14
962
1. Cairo (Egypt)
ISBN 0-679-76727-4 (pa)   LC 98-14214
First published 1998 in the United Kingdom
The author "combines historical scholarship and personal narrative to introduce readers to a city that has long been regarded as the heart of Arab culture and civilization." Libr J
This is "a remarkable volume, both for its insights into Cairo's current perplexities and for its rich chronicle of her past glories." Booklist
Includes bibliographical references

962.4   Sudan

Scroggins, Deborah
Emma's war. Pantheon Bks. 2002 389p il $25; pa $15   **962.4**
1. McCune, Emma 2. Sudan—History—Civil War, 1983-
ISBN 0-375-40397-3; 0-375-70377-2 (pa)
LC 2002-22033
"In 1991, in the middle of a refugee crisis in southern Sudan, a twenty-seven-year-old British aid worker named Emma McCune scandalized the relief community by marrying a local guerrilla leader. . . . Scroggins, a veteran reporter on Sudan, uses Emma's story to examine the failure of Western idealism in Africa." New Yorker
"A difficult book to read at times, it takes a focused look at the politics in and surrounding Sudan, as well the common people and warriors caught up in the daily struggle to survive. To call it powerful is an understatement." Booklist
Includes bibliographical references

966   West Africa and offshore islands

Langewiesche, William
Sahara unveiled; a journey across the desert. Pantheon Bks. 1996 301p il hardcover o.p. paperback available $14   **966**
1. Sahara Desert
ISBN 0-679-75006-1 (pa)   LC 95-48864
"Besides evoking the Sahara's power, majesty, emptiness, heat, beauty and terrors and describing its ecology and meteorology, Langewiesche adds details that may astonish armchair travelers who still think of the desert as populated by camels and Bedouins. . . . He is knowledgeable about the imprint of French colonialism on North African economy and politics, and about Muslim beliefs in practice. Throughout this vivid account, he scatters many charming native folktales." Publ Wkly

Palin, Michael
Sahara; photographs by Basil Pao. Thomas Dunne Bks. 2003 256p il map $29.95   **966**
1. West Africa—Description 2. Sahara Desert
ISBN 0-312-30541-9   LC 2002-192805
First published 2002 with title: Inside Sahara
"Palin takes the reader on an adventurous tour through Gibraltar, nine African countries, and the non-self-governing territory of Western Sahara. . . . [This] is an enjoyable and original travelog. . . . The photographs are beautiful and plentiful." Libr J

966.4   Sierra Leone

Campbell, Greg
Blood diamonds; tracing the deadly path of the world's most precious stones. Westview Press 2002 xxv, 251p maps $26; pa $15.95
966.4
1. Diamonds 2. Sierra Leone
ISBN 0-8133-3939-1; 0-8133-4220-1 (pa)
LC 2002-4931
"Campbell explores the significance of the diamond trade in Sierra Leone. . . . He recounts the horrors of this war-torn nation. . . . The underlying motivation for the violence and strife of Sierra Leone is centered in the diamond trade, much of it illegal smuggling sanctioned by the cartel DeBeers." Booklist
"This focused study of the catastrophic effect of blood diamonds on Sierra Leone belongs in all libraries." Libr J

Voeten, Teun
How de body? one man's terrifying journey through an African war; translated from the Dutch by Roz Vatter-Buck. Thomas Dunne Bks. 2002 308p il $24.95   **966.4**
1. Insurgency 2. Sierra Leone—History—Civil War, 1991-
ISBN 0-312-28219-2   LC 2001-58496
Original Dutch edition, 2000
"Voeten, a Dutch photojournalist, went to Sierra Leone on assignment to chronicle the child soldiers, as young as eight years old, who were forced to engage in that nation's civil war. When he is caught in rebel territory, Voeten is confronted with the gigantic contradictions of Western indifference and compassion and of

Voeten, Teun—*Continued*

atrocities beyond imagination. . . . He has written an exciting adventure that educates the West to one of the many wars about which we cannot afford to be indifferent." Booklist

Includes bibliographical references

966.9 Nigeria

Maier, Karl

This house has fallen; midnight in Nigeria. PublicAffairs 2000 xxxvii, 327p hardcover o.p. paperback available $18   **966.9**

1. Nigeria—Politics and government
ISBN 0-8133-4045-4 (pa)   LC 00-28199

The author "explores the promise and paradox of Nigeria. [He] . . . recounts the history of this nation cobbled together from British colonial interests in its formative years and dominated by international oil interests in more recent years." Booklist

Includes bibliographical references

Soyinka, Wole

The open sore of a continent; a personal narrative of the Nigerian crisis. Oxford Univ. Press 1996 170p hardcover o.p. paperback available $13.95   **966.9**

1. Nigeria—Politics and government
ISBN 0-19-511921-5 (pa)   LC 96-8757

Soyinka begins with the "1995 murder of dissident writer Ken Saro-Wiwa and works his way back through the grim, almost unbelievable history of Nigeria's brutal despots. As he describes various forms of systematic humiliation, torture, murder, 'ethnic cleansing,' greed, ecological destruction, and all the other 'spoils of power,' Soyinka interprets his personal experiences of protest, harassment, incarceration, and exile within a broad framework of historical and literary references." Booklist

967 Central Africa and offshore islands

Encyclopedia of Africa, south of the Sahara; John Middleton, editor in chief; J.F. Ade. Ajayi [et al.], editorial board. Scribner 1997 4v il maps set $500   **967**

1. Sub-Saharan Africa—Encyclopedias
ISBN 0-684-80466-2   LC 97-31364

"In addition to individual entries for countries, there is coverage of prehistory and archaeology, ecology, traditional and modern arts, and major language families." Libr J

O'Hanlon, Redmond

No mercy: a journey to the heart of the Congo. Knopf 1997 461p il maps hardcover o.p. paperback available $15   **967**

1. Congo (Republic)—Description
ISBN 0-699-73732-4 (pa)   LC 96-36677

First published 1996 in the United Kingdom with title: Congo journey

The author sets out to catch a glimpse "of the African version of the Loch Ness monster: the legendary Mokélémbembe dinosaur residing in the unreachable depths of Lake Télé, deep in the northern Congo forests." Libr J

"O'Hanlon is consciously creating a tale for us with a quest, a hero and funny foreigners along the way. But he does it so skillfully that, delighted, we skip along beside him. All demands for authenticity are suspended. This is not a report, it's a yarn." New Statesman (1913)

967.5 Zaire, Rwanda, Burundi

Hochschild, Adam, 1942-

King Leopold's ghost; a story of greed, terror, and heroism in Colonial Africa. Houghton Mifflin 1998 366p il map $26; pa $15   **967.5**

1. Congo (Republic)—History 2. Belgium—Colonies 3. Atrocities
ISBN 0-395-75924-2; 0-618-00190-5 (pa)
                LC 98-16813

The author "focuses on King Leopold's reign of terror in the Belgian Congo and the unswerving efforts by human rights activists (Sir Roger Casement, E.D. Morel, and others) and the Congo Reform Association to raise awareness of the enslavement, mutilation, and murder of millions of Congolese." Libr J

"Hochschild's impressively researched history records the roles of the famous and obscure, missionaries, journalists, opportunists, politicians, and royalty in this long-forgotten drama." Booklist

Includes bibliographical references

967.571 Rwanda

Carr, Rosamond Halsey

Land of a thousand hills; my life in Rwanda; [by] Rosamond Halsey Carr with Ann Howard Halsey. Viking 1999 248p il maps hardcover o.p. paperback available $15   **967.571**

1. Rwanda—Description
ISBN 0-452-28202-0 (pa)   LC 99-13132

"Carr, then a young New York fashion illustrator, moved to Africa with her hunter husband in 1954. After their divorce, she took a job as a plantation manager and eventually became a plantation owner—the last foreign owner in Rwanda. In her 45 years in the Congo and Rwanda, she saw the fight for independence and then the rise of ethnic unrest and genocidal conflict in the 1990s. She now runs an orphanage on her plantation." Libr J

Gourevitch, Philip

We wish to inform you that tomorrow we will be killed with our families; stories from Rwanda. Farrar, Straus & Giroux 1998 355p hardcover o.p. paperback available $15
                967.571

1. Rwanda—Politics and government 2. Genocide
ISBN 0-312-24335-9 (pa)   LC 98-22132

"In 1994, the world was informed of the inexplicable mass killings in Rwanda, in which over 800,000 were killed in 100 days. Gourevitch . . . spent over three years putting together an oral history of the mass killing that occurred in this small country." Libr J

This work is "readable and moving, Gourevitch is an impassioned and thoughtful observer. But this is not a work that gives much pleasure or comfort. Nor are its arguments fool-proof, its evidence complete, or its documentation thorough. . . . Still Gourevitch does struggle to come close to a great mystery of evil, and he makes us attend to great crimes." Commonweal

Keane, Fergal

Season of blood; a Rwandan journey. Viking 1995 198p hardcover o.p. paperback available $14   **967.571**

1. Rwanda—Politics and government

ISBN 0-14-024760-2 (pa)   LC 96-156637

First published 1995 in the United Kingdom

This is an account of journalist Keene's observations of the war in Rwanda in 1994 in which majority Hutus hunted down minority Tutsis

"A brief and highly personal account, Mr. Keane's book does not attempt to present an exhaustive study of the genocide or its aftermath. Rather, it offers the eloquence of unrehearsed eyewitness testimony." N Y Times Book Rev

967.62   Kenya

Dinesen, Isak, 1885-1962

Out of Africa. Modern Lib. 1992 399p $16.95   **967.62**

1. Kenya

ISBN 0-679-60021-3   LC 92-50213

A reissue of the title first published 1938 by Random House

A record of the author's life on a Kenya coffee plantation, and of the natives and their primitive festivals, of big game and of Lulu the gazelle who came to live at the farm

Out of Africa and Shadows on the grass. Vintage Bks. 1989 462p pa $13.95   **967.62**

1. Kenya

ISBN 0-679-72475-3   LC 89-40144

Out of Africa is a recording of the author's life on a Kenya coffee plantation. Shadows on the grass consists of four short essays which present the author's recollections of her servants in Africa

967.73   Somalia

Bowden, Mark, 1951-

Black Hawk down; a story of modern war. Atlantic Monthly Press 1999 386p il maps $25; pa $13.95   **967.73**

1. Somalia

ISBN 0-87113-738-0; 0-14-028850-3 (pa)

LC 98-46688

Also available G. K. Hall large print edition

The author describes "both sides of the October 1993 raid into the heart of Mogadishu, Somalia, a raid that quickly became the most intensive close combat Americans have engaged in since the Vietnam War. But Bowden's gripping narrative of the fighting is only a framework for an examination of the internal dynamics of America's elite forces and a critique of the philosophy of sending such high-tech units into combat with minimal support." Publ Wkly

968   Southern Africa. Republic of South Africa

Thompson, Leonard Monteath

A history of South Africa; [by] Leonard Thompson. 3rd ed. Yale Univ. Press 2001 xxiv, 358p il maps hardcover o.p. paperback available $17.95   **968**

1. South Africa—History

ISBN 0-300-08776-4 (pa)   LC 00-32101

First published 1990

This is an exploration of South Africa's "history, from the earliest known human inhabitation of the region to the present, focusing primarily on the experiences of its black inhabitants." Publisher's note

Includes bibliographical references

968.06   Period as Republic, 1961-

Tutu, Desmond

No future without forgiveness; [by] Desmond Mpilo Tutu. Doubleday 1999 287p hardcover o.p. paperback available $14.95

968.06

1. South Africa. Commission for Truth and Reconciliation 2. South Africa—Race relations

ISBN 0-385-49690-7 (pa)   LC 99-34451

The author reflects on his role "as chairman of the Truth and Reconciliation Commission. Tutu speaks frankly of . . . the struggle that preceded it and of the betrayals and jubilations of this unique commission. The TRC's work was unprecedented not only in its emphasis on restorative over retributive justice but in the spirituality that permeated its work, the bulk of which constituted hearings from the 'victims' and 'perpetrators' of apartheid." Publ Wkly

Includes bibliographical references

The rainbow people of God; the making of a peaceful revolution; edited by John Allen. Doubleday 1994 xxii, 281p il hardcover o.p. paperback available $15.95   **968.06**

1. South Africa—Race relations 2. Sermons

ISBN 0-385-48374-0 (pa)   LC 94-16011

This collection of Tutu's "speeches, letters, and sermons—from the time of the 1976 Soweto Uprising, through the long years of repression and defiance, up to the triumph of the democratic election—serves as an immediate contemporary history of South Africa. Tutu's media secretary, John Allen, provides a general historical introduction and a connecting narrative that places the individuals pieces in dramatic context." Booklist

Includes bibliographical references

Waldmeir, Patti

Anatomy of a miracle; the end of apartheid and the birth of the new South Africa. Norton 1997 303p il $27.50   **968.06**

1. South Africa—Politics and government 2. South Africa—Race relations

ISBN 0-393-03997-8   LC 96-21150

Also available in paperback from Rutgers Univ. Press

Waldmeir traces the political and personal struggles that ultimately contributed to the dismantling of apartheid in South Africa

"Although Mandela attributes greatness to de Klerk

Waldmeir, Patti—*Continued*
for his courage, it is Mandela's own character that domi-
nates this history. . . . Engrossing in its sweep, this account also describes the obstacles facing the regime."
Publ Wkly
Includes bibliographical references

968.91 Zimbabwe

Lessing, Doris May, 1919-
African laughter; four visits to Zimbabwe;
[by] Doris Lessing. HarperCollins Pubs. 1992
442p hardcover o.p. paperback available $15
968.91

1. Zimbabwe
ISBN 0-06-092433-0 (pa)   LC 92-52590
"After the wars fought by black nationalists for the
liberation of Rhodesia ended in 1980 and the nation of
Zimbabwe came into being, Lessing was able to return
to the homeland that had officially exiled her 25 years
earlier because of her opposition to the white government. The distinguished novelist . . . details four trips
she made to Zimbabwe in 1982, 1988, 1989, and 1992
in a series of haunting vignettes dealing with facets of
life there." Publ Wkly

970 North America

Morgan, Ted, 1932-
Wilderness at dawn; the settling of the
North American continent. Simon & Schuster
1993 541p il maps hardcover o.p. paperback
available $20   **970**
1. North America—History 2. United States—History—1600-1775, Colonial period 3. Canada—History—0-1763 (New France)
ISBN 0-671-88237-6 (pa)   LC 93-2628
The author discusses "movements of people into what
is today the US, from the arrival of the earliest hunters
approximately 15,000 years ago to the colonists of the
late 18th century." Choice
Morgan "tells a good story, emphasizing the ordinary
people who did the actual settlement. . . . A useful survey of the colonial frontier." Libr J
Includes bibliographical references

Purcell, L. Edward
Encyclopedia of battles in North America,
1517 to 1916; [by] L. Edward Purcell and
Sarah J. Purcell. Facts on File 2000 383p
maps (Facts on File library of American
history) $66; pa $24.95   **970**
1. Battles 2. United States—Military history 3. Canada—Military history
ISBN 0-8160-3350-1; 0-8160-4402-3 (pa)
LC 99-38634
"Entries are in alphabetical order by battle name, from
Adobe Walls to Yorktown, each one with bibliographic
references. Many were from wars that are vaguely remembered today, if at all (e.g., the Pequot War of 1637
or the Russian-Indian War of 1804 in Alaska). There are
cross references to alternate names, a comprehensive bibliography, a glossary, 50 maps, and indexes by war, year,
and geographic area." Libr J
For a fuller review see Booklist, Nov. 1, 2000

970.004 North American native peoples

American encounters; natives and newcomers
from European contact to Indian removal,
1500-1850; edited by Peter C. Mancall and
James H. Merrell. Routledge 2000 594p il
$105; pa $39.95   **970.004**
1. Native Americans—History
ISBN 0-415-92374-3; 0-415-92375-1 (pa)
LC 99-28708
This anthology "consolidates 25 influential essays that
have been previously published in peer-reviewed academic journals such as *Ethnohistory, William & Mary Quarterly,* and *American Indian Culture and Research Journal.* While not interrelated, these articles provide insight
into various contact points throughout North America."
Libr J

Includes bibliographical references

American Indians; consulting editor, Harvey
Markowitz. Salem Press 1995 3v il maps
(Ready reference) set $331   **970.004**
1. Native Americans—Encyclopedias 2. Native Americans—Mexico—Encyclopedias
ISBN 0-89356-757-4   LC 94-47633
"A Magill book"
"This set contains 1,129 articles ranging in length
from 200 to 3,000 words. The entries cover a wide range
of persons, tribes, organizations, cultural and historical
events, and contemporary issues of U.S., Canadian, and
some Mesoamerican Indian groups. Individual entries appear for 275 North American tribes. Entries are arranged
alphabetically and are illustrated with 250 black-and-
white photographs, maps, charts, tables, and drawings."
Booklist

American nations; encounters in Indian
country, 1850 to the present; [edited by]
Frederick E. Hoxie, Peter C. Mancall, and
James H. Merrell. Routledge 2001 519p il
maps $100; pa $34.95   **970.004**
1. Native Americans—History
ISBN 0-415-92749-8; 0-415-92750-1 (pa)
LC 00-68420
This is a "collection of 23 articles that illuminate the
experiences of different tribes as they have maintained
their unique ethnic identities while dealing with the U.S.
government." Libr J

Includes bibliographical references

Archaeology of the Appalachian highlands;
edited by Lynne P. Sullivan and Susan C.
Prezzano. University of Tenn. Press 2001
xxxiii, 410p il maps $55   **970.004**
1. Native Americans—Antiquities 2. Appalachian region
ISBN 1-57233-142-9   LC 2001-2744
"The essays here examine the many ways that the cultures of the native people living in the Appalachian region were shaped by their mountainous environment."
Libr J

Bordewich, Fergus M.

Killing the white man's Indian; the reinvention of Native Americans at the end of the 20th century. Doubleday 1996 400p hardcover o.p. paperback available $15

970.004

1. Native Americans
ISBN 0-385-42036-6 (pa)   LC 95-23069

In separate chapters the author examines "historic Indian-white relations, modern Indian identity, the revival of tribal authority, Indians and environmentalism, conflicts between reinvigorated Indian property rights and archaeological research, new Indian claims to lands said to be sacred, Indian alcoholism, the reservation-based system of Indian colleges, and the promise and perils of growing economic and political cooperation with the world beyond the reservation." Booklist

Boyer, Ruth McDonald, 1918-

Apache mothers and daughters; four generations of a family; [by] Ruth McDonald Boyer and Narcissus Duffy Gayton. University of Okla. Press 1992 xx, 393p il maps hardcover o.p. paperback available $19.95   **970.004**

1. Apache Indians
ISBN 0-8061-2922-0 (pa)   LC 92-54149

A family history of four generations of Chiricahua Apache women. "Woven into this account are factual details about the Apaches." Publisher's note

"The voice throughout the narrative is an Apache one, emphasizing the continuation of Chiricahua culture. . . . It's a treat for anyone interested in cultural change and persistence." Libr J

Includes bibliographical references

Bragdon, Kathleen J.

The Columbia guide to American Indians of the Northeast. Columbia Univ. Press 2001 292p il maps (Columbia guides to American Indian history and culture) $47   **970.004**

1. Native Americans
ISBN 0-231-11452-4   LC 2001-47341

This handbook "includes not only a broad overview of the history of Native Americans in the Northeast but also a partially annotated listing of materials for further research including published primary sources, oral traditions, films, and Internet sites." Libr J

Brown, Dee Alexander

Bury my heart at Wounded Knee; an Indian history of the American West; [by] Dee Brown. Thirtieth anniversary ed. Holt & Co. 2001 487p il $35; pa $16   **970.004**

1. Native Americans—West (U.S.) 2. Native Americans—Wars 3. West (U.S.)—History
ISBN 0-8050-6634-9; 0-8050-6669-1 (pa)
LC 00-40958

First published 1970

This is an account of the experience of the American Indian during the white man's expansion westward

Includes bibliographical references

Chatters, James

Ancient encounters; Kennewick Man and the first Americans; [by] James C. Chatters. Simon & Schuster 2001 303p il maps $26; pa $15   **970.004**

1. Kennewick Man 2. Native Americans—Antiquities
ISBN 0-684-85936-X; 0-684-85937-8 (pa)
LC 00-54754

Anthropologist and forensic consultant Chatters gives his account of the discovery, scientific investigation, and ensuing controversy surrounding Kennewick Man, a 9,500 year old skeleton found near Kennewick (Wa.), in 1996

Includes bibliographical references

A **Companion** to American Indian history; edited by Philip J. Deloria and Neal Salisbury. Blackwell 2001 513p maps (Blackwell companions to American history) $131.95   **970.004**

1. Native Americans—History
ISBN 0-631-20975-1   LC 2001-18461

"This collection of 25 authoritative historiographical essays examines the current state of scholarship on the history of Native American peoples. In addition to providing an overview, it charts new directions for future research." Libr J

Includes bibliographical references

Crow Dog, Leonard, 1942-

Crow Dog; four generations of Sioux medicine men; [by] Leonard Crow Dog and Richard Erdoes. HarperCollins Pubs. 1995 243p il hardcover o.p. paperback available $13   **970.004**

1. American Indian Movement 2. Dakota Indians
ISBN 0-06-092682-1 (pa)   LC 94-40695

Erdoes has recorded Leonard Crow Dog's oral narrative of the history of his family and his people, the Lakota. Mr. Crow Dog discusses "the generations of his family who have carried the name Crow Dog since the American government told them it would be their family name. . . . He tells of his involvement as the spiritual leader of the American Indian Movement and the occupation of Wounded Knee in the early 1970's." Booklist

Deloria, Vine

Custer died for your sins; an Indian manifesto; by Vine Deloria, Jr. Macmillan 1969 279p o.p.; University of Okla. Press paperback available $19.95   **970.004**

1. Native Americans
ISBN 0-8061-2129-7 (pa)

The author examines how anthropologists, missionaries, and government agencies have mistreated American Indians

Documents of American Indian diplomacy; treaties, agreements, and conventions, 1775-1979; [compiled by] Vine Deloria, Jr., and Raymond J. DeMallie; with a foreword by Daniel K. Inouye. University of Okla. Press 1999 2v (Legal history of North America) set $125   **970.004**
1. Native Americans—Government relations 2. Treaties
ISBN 0-8061-3118-7   LC 98-45365

This is a collection of hundreds of treaties and agreements made by American Indian nations with the Continental Congress, England, Spain, and other foreign countries, the Confederacy, the Republic of Texas, railroad companies, other Indian nations, and the U.S. government, with chapter introductions which put them in historical and political context

"A must for all libraries." Libr J

Includes bibliographical references

Encyclopedia of North American Indians; Frederick E. Hoxie, editor. Houghton Mifflin 1996 756p il maps $45   **970.004**
1. Native Americans—Encyclopedias
ISBN 0-395-66921-9   LC 96-21411

"More than 260 authorities, many of whom are Indian, contributed to this single-volume work. It includes four types of entries: descriptions of tribes; biographical sketches selected to provide regional representation; overview interpretive essays on cultural and historical topics; and definitions for often misunderstood terms." Libr J

Fenton, William Nelson, 1908-
The Great Law and the Longhouse; a political history of the Iroquois Confederacy; {by} Willam N. Fenton. University of Okla. Press 1998 xxii, 786p il map (Civilization of the American Indian series) $75   **970.004**
1. Iroquois Indians—History
ISBN 0-8061-3003-2   LC 97-19842

This is a history of the Iroquois Confederacy of the Six Nations "from the mid-sixteenth century to the Canandaigua treaty of 1794." Publisher's note

"If a library has only one book about the Iroquois . . . it should be this title." Libr J

Includes bibliographical references

Fowler, Loretta, 1944-
The Columbia guide to American Indians of the Great Plains. Columbia Univ. Press 2003 283p il maps (Columbia guides to American Indian history and culture) $45   **970.004**
1. Native Americans—Great Plains
ISBN 0-231-11700-0   LC 2002-73708

"This work is divided into four parts: a general survey of the history and cultures of the native peoples of the region; alphabetically arranged entries focusing on individuals, places, and events; a chronology; and a listing of resources for further research that includes published primary sources, oral traditions, films, and Internet sites. . . . Highly recommended." Libr J

Frazier, Ian
On the rez. Farrar, Straus & Giroux 2000 311p il $25; pa $14   **970.004**
1. War Lance, Le 2. Oglala Indians 3. Pine Ridge Indian Reservation (S.D.)
ISBN 0-374-22638-5; 0-312-27859-4 (pa)
   LC 99-28353

Frazier discusses the history of the Oglala Sioux and the Indians that he met on the Pine Ridge Reservation in South Dakota, including his friend Le War Lance

"As Frazier serendipitously shuttles his narrative between Pine Ridge visits and snippets of Indian history, a fascinating picture emerges of a people struggling with the consequences of old wrongs and human orneriness." Time

The **Gale** encyclopedia of Native American tribes; edited by Sharon Malinowski [et al.] Gale Res. 1998 4v il maps set $450
   970.004
1. Native Americans—Encyclopedias
ISBN 0-7876-1085-2   LC 97-36848

Contents: v1 Northeast, Southeast Caribbean; v2 Great Basin, Southwest Middle America; v3 Arctic, Subarctic, Great Plains, Plateau; v4 California, Pacific Northwest, Pacific Islands

This set provides historical, cultural and current information on Native American tribes

Garrison, Tim Alan, 1961-
The legal ideology of removal; the southern judiciary and the sovereignty of Native American nations. University of Ga. Press 2002 331p (Studies in the legal history of the South) $39.95   **970.004**
1. Native Americans—Claims 2. State rights
ISBN 0-8203-2212-1   LC 2001-52260

This study attempts "to show how state courts enabled the mass expulsion of Native Americans from their southern homelands in the 1830s." Publisher's note

Includes bibliographical references

Handbook of North American Indians; William C. Sturtevant, general editor. Smithsonian Institution Press 1978- il maps apply to publisher for price and availability
   970.004
1. Native Americans   LC 77-17162

Also available in hardcover from U.S. Government Printing Office, Superintendent of Documents

Volumes published to date are: v4 History of Indian-white relations; Wilcomb E. Washburn, volume editor (ISBN 0-87474-184-X); v5 Arctic; David Damas, volume editor (ISBN 0-87474-185-8); v6 Subarctic; June Helm, volume editor (ISBN 0-87474-186-6); v7 Northwest coast; Wayne Suttles, volume editor (ISBN 0-87474-187-4); v8 California; Robert F. Heizer, volume editor (ISBN 0-87474-188-2); v9-10 Southwest; Alfonso Ortiz, volume editor (ISBN 0-87474-189-0; 0-87474-190-4); v11 Great Basin; Warren L. D'Azevedo, volume editor (ISBN 0-87474-191-2); v12 Plateau; Deward E. Walker, Jr., volume editor (ISBN 0-87474-192-0); v13 Plains; Raymond J. Demallie, volume editor pa (ISBN 0-87474-193-9); v15 Northeast; Bruce G. Trigger, volume editor (ISBN 0-87474-195-5); v17 Languages; Ives Goddard, volume editor (ISBN 0-87474-197-1)

"This projected twenty-one volume set . . . . gives an encyclopedic summary of current historical-cultural

Handbook of North American Indians—
Continued

knowledge of North American Indians. Extensively re-searched, readable essays are accompanied by illustra-tions, maps, and bibliographies." Ref Sources for Small & Medium-sized Libr. 6h edition

Harmon, Alexandra, 1945-

Indians in the making; ethnic relations and Indian identities around Puget Sound. University of Calif. Press 1998 393p il maps (American crossroads) hardcover o.p. paperback available $21.95   **970.004**

1. Native Americans—Northwest Coast of North America 2. Washington (State)—History

ISBN 0-520-22685-2 (pa)   LC 98-17665

The author "examines how both the federal govern-ment and the native peoples of western Washington were constantly redefining Indian identity to their advantage over a 150-year period. Harmon's examination of the na-tive fishing rights controversy of the 1960s and 1970s is particularly useful." Libr J

Includes bibliographical references

Hirschfelder, Arlene B.

Native American; [by] Arlene Hirschfelder. DK Pub. 2000 192p il $24.95   **970.004**

1. Native Americans

ISBN 0-7894-5162-X   LC 99-49061

This "heavily pictorial book resembles a stop-frame documentary film. Historic photos crowd its pages, showing American Indian life from ancestral times to the present. Excerpts from Indian autobiographies offer the voices of Black Elk, Tecumseh, Louis Riel, Sarah Winnemucca, and others, and Hirschfelder's own text is concise and comprehensive." Booklist

Includes bibliographical references

Iverson, Peter

We are still here; American Indians in the twentieth century. Davidson, H. 1998 255p il (American history series) pa $14.95 **970.004**

1. Native Americans

ISBN 0-88295-940-9   LC 97-38321

The author "begins at Wounded Knee and tells the stories of Indian communities throughout the United States, including not only political leaders and activists, but also professionals, artists, soldiers and athletes." Pub-lisher's note

Includes bibliographical references

Johnson, Michael, 1937-

Macmillan encyclopedia of Native American tribes. 2nd US ed. Macmillan Lib. Ref. USA 1999 288p il maps $150 **970.004**

1. Native Americans—Encyclopedias

ISBN 0-00-286349-9   LC 99-30114

First published 1994 with title: The native tribes of North America

This reference "arranges Native American tribes ac-cording to geographic culture regions and then by lan-guage families. . . . Within chapters extensive detail is given to where tribes are located. A limited description of cultural characteristics, such as dress, housing, and politics, follows. Each tribal entry ends with census in-formation on population trends. The strength of this ref-erence lies in its illustrations." Voice Youth Advocates

Josephy, Alvin M., 1915-

500 nations; an illustrated history of North American Indians; [by] Alvin M. Josephy, Jr. Gramercy Bks. 2001 468p il maps $39.99   **970.004**

1. Native Americans—History

ISBN 0-517-16394-2   LC 2001-23623

A reissue of the title first published 1994 by Knopf

"Based on a documentary filmscript by Jack Leustig, Roberta Grossman, Lee Miller, and William Morgan with contributions by John M.D. Pohl."

A "chronological overview of the history of North American Indians from the ancient legends of the peo-ples' origins to the problems faced during the Western expansion to the present. . . . The narrative is brought to life by excerpts from journals and diaries as well as through contemporary interviews. The book is beautifully and colorfully illustrated with 485 paintings, drawings, prints, historical photographs, and artifacts." SLJ

Includes bibliographical references

The Nez Perce Indians and the opening of the Northwest; {by} Alvin M. Josephy, Jr. Houghton Mifflin 1997 xx, 705p il map pa $19   **970.004**

1. Nez Percé Indians 2. Pacific Northwest

ISBN 0-395-85011-8   LC 96-54278

"A Mariner book"

First published 1965 by Yale University Press

This history of the Nez Perce tribe traces its contact with white settlers from Lewis and Clark to Chief Joseph and war in 1877

Includes bibliographical references

Now that the buffalo's gone; a study of today's American Indians; by Alvin M. Josephy, Jr. Knopf 1982 300p il o.p.; University of Okla. Press paperback available $24.95   **970.004**

1. Native Americans 2. Native Americans—Govern-ment relations

ISBN 0-8061-1915-2 (pa)   LC 82-47797

This look at American Indians focuses primarily on the Seminoles, the Pequots, the Senecas, and the Taos Pueblo Indians

Includes bibliographical references

Keoke, Emory Dean

Encyclopedia of American Indian contributions to the world; 15,000 years of inventions and innovations; {by} Emory Dean Keoke and Kay Marie Porterfield. Facts on File 2002 384p il $65   **970.004**

1. Native Americans—Encyclopedias 2. Inventions

ISBN 0-8160-4052-4   LC 00-49034

This "volume describes more than 450 inventions and innovations that originated with indigenous peoples of North, Middle, and South America." Booklist

"This volume provides comprehensive coverage of the often-underreported contributions and achievements of the Indians of the western hemisphere." Book Rep

Matthiessen, Peter

Indian country. Viking 1984 338p hardcover o.p. paperback available $14.95

970.004

1. Native Americans—Claims 2. Human ecology
ISBN 0-14-013023-3 (pa)   LC 83-47996

This "is a collection of essays about various 'traditional' Indians who are seeking to preserve their old ways and beliefs in the face of the destructive exploitation of their environment by large energy, mining, and lumber companies, backed by the U.S. government." Sci Books Films

McLoughlin, William Gerald

After the Trail of Tears; the Cherokees' struggle for sovereignty, 1839-1880; [by] William G. McLoughlin. University of N.C. Press 1993 439p maps hardcover o.p. paperback available $21.95   **970.004**

1. Cherokee Indians
ISBN 0-8078-4433-0 (pa)   LC 93-18532

The author "recounts the tragedy that continued to afflict the Cherokee Nation after their forced removal from their traditional home to Oklahoma during the 1820s and 1830s. In Oklahoma the Cherokee Nation set out to reconstruct their society, reestablishing their newspaper, which published in the Cherokee language, and governing themselves according to a constitution modeled on that of the United States. . . . McLoughlin vividly depicts the conflicts between 'full-bloods,' who sought to live by more traditional ways, and Cherokees of mixed ancestry who favored assimilation into the dominant culture." Publ Wkly

Includes bibliographical references

McReynolds, Edwin C.

The Seminoles. University of Okla. Press 1957 397p il maps (Civilization of the American Indian series) hardcover o.p. paperback available $21.95   **970.004**

1. Seminole Indians
ISBN 0-8061-1255-7 (pa)

"This is almost strictly a military and political history, in great detail, spiced with a few incidents which reveal the courageous character of the Seminoles, and stressing their relations with the Creeks." Libr J

Includes bibliographical references

Nabokov, Peter

A forest of time; American Indian ways of history. Cambridge Univ. Press 2002 246p $60; pa $22   **970.004**

1. Native Americans
ISBN 0-521-56024-1; 0-521-56874-9 (pa)
        LC 2001-25955

"This multidisciplinary intellectual history describes the many ways that individual Native American groups have defined their histories for their own purposes. By bringing these varying Native perspectives to the fore, Nabokov has performed a service that will only enrich future research into the history of Native American groups." Libr J

Includes bibliographical references

Nagel, Joane

American Indian ethnic renewal; Red power and the resurgence of identity and culture. Oxford Univ. Press 1996 298p il hardcover o.p. paperback available $21.95

970.004

1. Native Americans
ISBN 0-19-512063-9 (pa)   LC 94-23948

The author "argues that American Indian political activism, especially the Red Power movement of the 1970s, was directly responsible for both a cultural renaissance among Indian peoples and major changes in federal Indian policy." Libr J

Includes bibliographical references

Native America in the twentieth century; an encyclopedia; edited by Mary B. Davis; assistant editors, Joan Berman, Mary E. Graham, Lisa A. Mitten. Garland 1994 xxxvii, 787p il maps (Garland reference library of social science) hardcover o.p. paperback available $50   **970.004**

1. Native Americans—Encyclopedias
ISBN 0-8153-2583-5 (pa)   LC 94-768

This volume offers "tribal-specific information on the art, daily life, economic development, and religion of 20th-century American Indians and Alaskan Natives and the government policy that affects them." Libr J

Native American testimony; a chronicle of Indian-white relations from prophecy to the present, 1492-2000; edited by Peter Nabokov; with a foreword by Vine Deloria, Jr. Rev and updated ed. Penguin Bks. 1999 xxiii, 506p il maps pa $16.95   **970.004**

1. Native Americans—Government relations 2. Native Americans—History—Sources
ISBN 0-14-028159-2

First published 1978 by Crowell with subtitle: An anthology of Indian and white relations, first encounter to dispossession

"A collection of primary-source material, grouped by key issues that arose during 500 years of Indian and white encounters in North America. Nabokov uses traditional narratives, old government transcripts, reservation newspapers, and firsthand interviews to highlight this chronological volume. Photographs appear throughout." SLJ [review of 1991 edition]

Includes bibliographical references

The **Native** North American almanac; a reference work on Native North Americans in the United States and Canada; Duane Champagne, editor. 2nd ed. Gale Res. 2001 xxvii, 1472p il maps $150   **970.004**

1. Native Americans
ISBN 0-7876-1655-9

First published 1994

This book "covers the civilization and culture of the indigenous peoples of the U.S. and Canada—both historic and contemporary. Included are signed essays, annotated directories, excerpts and biographies. Each chapter contains a subject-specific bibliography, photographs, maps and charts—400 illustrations in all." Publisher's note

Includes bibliographical references

Perdue, Theda, 1949-

The Columbia guide to American Indians of the Southeast; [by] Theda Perdue and Michael D. Green. Columbia Univ. Press 2001 325p il maps (Columbia guides to American Indian history and culture) $47

970.004

1. Native Americans—Southern States
ISBN 0-231-11570-9   LC 2001-35338
"The first half of the text focuses on the history and culture of the region's native groups. This includes not only the Mississippian Moundbuilder cultures that arose between 800 and 1000 C.E. but also well-known native groups such as the Cherokee and Creeks. . . . Immediately following the survey are alphabetically arranged entries focusing on individuals, places, and events. The final two sections are a chronology and a listing of resources for further research, which include published primary sources, oral traditions, films, and Internet sites. . . . An essential purchase for all libraries collecting books about Native Americans." Libr J

Prehistoric culture change on the Colorado plateau; ten thousand years on Black Mesa; edited by Shirley Powell and Francis E. Smiley. University of Ariz. Press 2002 221p il maps $50   **970.004**

1. Native Americans—Antiquities
ISBN 0-8165-1439-9   LC 2001-6425
This summarizes the results of the Black Mesa Archaeological Project which studies the evolution of Native American cultures in the American Southwest

This work's "examination of the evolution of Native American cultures in the Southwest is first-rate and unsurpassed." Libr J

Includes bibliographical references

Pritzker, Barry

A Native American encyclopedia; history, culture, and peoples; [by] Barry M. Pritzker. Oxford Univ. Press 2000 591p il $55; pa $29.95   **970.004**

1. Native Americans—Encyclopedias
ISBN 0-19-513897-X; 0-19-513877-5 (pa)
LC 99-53677
First published 1998 by ABC-CLIO as a two-volume set with title: Native Americans

"Organized geographically, each section begins with an introduction to the area and its original inhabitants. Tribal entries follow, with some smaller related groups discussed together. Each article includes sections on location, population, language, history, religion, government, customs, dwellings, diet, key technology, trade, notable arts, transportation, dress, and war/weapons. A contemporary section follows, with information on government/reservations, economy, legal status, and daily life." Libr J [review of 1998 edition]

Includes bibliographical references

Prucha, Francis Paul

The great father; the United States government and the American Indians. University of Neb. Press 1984 2v il hardcover o.p. paperback available $60   **970.004**

1. Native Americans—Government relations
ISBN 0-8032-8734-8 (pa)   LC 83-16837
"Beginning with the American Revolution and continuing to 1980, Prucha . . . brilliantly chronicles the his-

tory of relations between the federal government and Native Americans, in a work that belongs in all public and academic libraries." Libr J

Includes bibliographical references

Rajtar, Steve, 1951-

Indian war sites; a guidebook to battlefields, monuments, and memorials, state by state with Canada and Mexico. McFarland & Co. 1999 330p $39.95   **970.004**

1. Native Americans—Wars
ISBN 0-7864-0710-7   LC 99-25893
This is a "reference to hundreds of conflicts, both major and minor, between American Indians and Europeans. Divided alphabetically by state and then chronologically within each, entries include name and date, a nonspecific location (e.g., Spring River), a brief description, and bibliographic sources. If the battle was a part of a larger war Rajtar also gives the name of the war; and if there is a monument, he tells its location and briefly describes what's there." Libr J

Includes bibliographical references

Richter, Daniel K.

Facing east from Indian country; a Native history of early America. Harvard Univ. Press 2001 317p il maps $27.50; pa $15.95

970.004

1. Native Americans
ISBN 0-674-00638-0; 0-674-01117-1 (pa)
LC 2001-24997
The author "recasts early American history from the Native American point of view and in doing so illuminates as much about the Europeans as about the original Americans. . . . Exploring the varying complexities of different native people's relationships with England, France and Spain, he argues that the Native Americans were safer during the colonial era than after the Revolution. . . . Gracefully written and argued, Richter's compelling research and provocative claims make this an important addition to the literature for general readers of both Native American and U.S. studies." Publ Wkly

Includes bibliographical references

Roberts, David, 1943-

In search of the old ones; exploring the Anasazi world of the Southwest. Simon & Schuster 1996 271p il map hardcover o.p. paperback available $14   **970.004**

1. Pueblo Indians—Antiquities 2. Southwestern States—Antiquities
ISBN 0-684-83212-7 (pa)   LC 95-46218
Roberts "chronicles the search for clues to the mystery of the Anasazi's abandonment of their extraordinary cliff dwellings some 700 years ago. Roberts blends accounts of his hiking adventures in the glorious canyon country of the Southwest with a chronicle of Anglos of the nineteenth century who shared his passion for studying the elusive Anasazi, especially the cowboy-archaeologist Richard Wetherell." Booklist

Includes bibliographical references

Roberts, David, 1943-—*Continued*

Once they moved like the wind; Cochise, Geronimo, and the Apache wars. Simon & Schuster 1993 368p il hardcover o.p. paperback available $22 **970.004**

1. Cochise, Apache Chief, d. 1874 2. Geronimo, Apache Chief, 1829-1909 3. Apache Indians 4. Native Americans—Wars

ISBN 0-671-88556-1 (pa)   LC 93-7112

The author "tells the story of the Chiricahua Apache resistance to the encroachments of the whites in post-Civil War frontier America. Using contemporary letters and reminiscences, he relates the story from the Apache point of view, focusing on the leadership of Cochise and Geronimo." Libr J

"The book is history at its most engrossing." Publ Wkly

Includes bibliographical references

Taylor, Colin F.

Native American weapons. University of Okla. Press 2001 128p il $24.95 **970.004**

1. Native Americans 2. Weapons

ISBN 0-8061-3346-5   LC 00-66959

"With more than 150 photographs and illustrations, many of them in color, this work surveys the types of weapons used by native groups throughout North America. Taylor . . . includes not only combat weapons but also those used for ceremonial purposes." Libr J

Includes bibliographical references

Waldman, Carl

Atlas of the North American Indian; illustrations by Molly Braun. rev ed. Facts on File 2000 385p maps $49.50; pa $21.95 **970.004**

1. Native Americans

ISBN 0-8160-3974-7; 0-8160-3975-5 (pa)
           LC 99-23678

First published 1985

"Details the migration of prehistoric tribes to North America from Asia. A unique section on 'Lifeways' provides information on all socioeconomic and religious aspects of Native American cultures, both pre- and post-contact with European Americans. Covers the Indian Wars, the Land Cessions, and contemporary Native American conditions." N Y Public Libr. Book of How & Where to Look It Up

Encyclopedia of Native American tribes; illustrations by Molly Braun. rev ed. Facts on File 1999 xxiii, 312p il maps $71.50; pa $19.95 **970.004**

1. Native Americans—Encyclopedias

ISBN 0-8160-3963-1; 0-8160-3964-X (pa)
           LC 98-50263

"Facts on File library of American history"

First published 1988

This "gives an overview of the history and culture of tribes and peoples from Abenaki to Zuni. Focus is on U.S. North American tribes, but there is also coverage of cultural groupings in Canada and Central America. The volume is notable for its ease of use, its wonderful illustrations, and the great starting point it provides." Booklist

Includes bibliographical references

Wallace, Anthony F. C., 1923-

The long bitter trail; Andrew Jackson and the Indians; consulting editor, Eric Foner. Hill & Wang 1993 143p maps (Critical issue series) hardcover o.p. paperback available $11 **970.004**

1. Jackson, Andrew, 1767-1845 2. Native Americans—Government relations

ISBN 0-8090-1552-8 (pa)   LC 92-32609

A "retelling of the story of the Trail of Tears. This refers to the forced removal in the 1830s of thousands of Indians, particularly the Cherokee and the Choctaw, from the American east to west of the Mississippi River. The author expands his focus to examine the relocation of numerous Indian groups. Central to the story is Andrew Jackson, who assumed the presidency confronted with a government divided over the question of Indian removal and who soon became one of its major proponents." Publ Wkly

Weatherford, J. McIver

Native roots; how the Indians enriched America; [by] Jack Weatherford. Crown 1991 310p il o.p.; Fawcett Bks. paperback available $12.95 **970.004**

1. Native Americans

ISBN 0-449-90713-9 (pa)   LC 91-6520

The author "writes about some 20 different aspects of the material and intellectual culture of Native Americans, in . . . [an attempt] to show how present-day America was built on Indian foundations." Voice Lit Suppl

"A valuable corrective to the sentimentality with which we regard the first U.S. settlers and developers." Booklist

Includes bibliographical references

Wilson, James, 1949-

The earth shall weep; the history of Native Americans. Atlantic Monthly Press 1999 xxix, 466p maps hardcover o.p. paperback available $16 **970.004**

1. Native Americans

ISBN 0-8021-3680-X (pa)   LC 99-13098

"Wilson begins with the first English settlements on the Atlantic coast in the 1500s and moves from century to century, focusing on various geographic areas through the massacre at Wounded Knee in 1890. He then addresses today's social, political, and economic issues while trying to examine the legacy of ignorance and misunderstanding." Libr J

"Employing elegiac prose and steady narrative momentum, Wilson has written a richly informative history that places Native Americans 'at the center of the historical stage.'" Publ Wkly

Includes bibliographical references

970.01 North America—Early history to 1599

Adovasio, J. M. (James M.), 1944-

The first Americans; in pursuit of archaeology's greatest mystery; [by] J.M. Adovasio with Jake Page. Random House 2002 328p il maps hardcover o.p. paperback available $14.95   **970.01**

1. Native Americans—Origin 2. America—Antiquities

ISBN 0-375-75704-X (pa)   LC 2002-69766

"In 1974, Adovasio stepped into a roiling debate about the first human presence in the Americas when he unearthed materials suggesting that we were here 4000 years earlier than commonly believed." Libr J

"Readers get a lively, close-up view of how archaeologists study America's original discoverers." Booklist

Includes bibliographical references

America in 1492; the world of the Indian peoples before the arrival of Columbus; edited and with an introduction by Alvin Josephy, Jr.; developed by Frederick E. Hoxie. Knopf 1992 477p il maps hardcover o.p. paperback available $20   **970.01**

1. Native Americans—History 2. Native Americans—Antiquities 3. America—Exploration 4. America—Antiquities

ISBN 0-679-74337-5 (pa)   LC 90-26222

These essays depict "the diverse lives of the approximately 75 million people living in the Americas around the turn of the fifteenth century. Geography guides the first section. . . . Another section focuses on languages, spiritual beliefs and customs, art, and 'systems of knowledge.'" Booklist

Includes bibliographical references

Archaeology of prehistoric native America; an encyclopedia; editor, Guy Gibbon; associate editors, Kenneth M. Ames {et al.}. Garland 1998 lxxvii, 941p il map (Garland reference library of the humanites) $205   **970.01**

1. Native Americans—Antiquities—Encyclopedias 2. North America—Antiquities—Encyclopedias

ISBN 0-8153-0725-X   LC 98-11443

This encyclopedia includes alphabetically arranged entries covering North American prehistory and archaeology

"This superb reference source . . . has no equal in its coverage of Native American cultures in North America prior to European contact." Libr J

Dillehay, Tom D.

The settlement of the Americas; a new prehistory; [by] Thomas D. Dillehay. Basic Bks. 2000 xxi, 371p il hardcover o.p. paperback available $22   **970.01**

1. America—Exploration 2. America—Antiquities

ISBN 0-465-07669-6 (pa)   LC 00-27572

Dillehay "pushes back by at least 1,000 years our estimates of when the New World was first settled. He challenges a long-held belief—that the first inhabitants of the Americas were the so-called Clovis people, a big-game-hunting culture who came through North America starting 11,200 years ago and reached South America even

later. Drawing on his 20-plus years of research at Monte Verde, in Chile, he argues that South America was inhabited by 12,500 years ago." Publ Wkly

This "is a seminal work in the field that is accessible to lay readers." Libr J

Includes bibliographical references

Schobinger, Juan

The ancient Americans; a reference guide to the art, culture, and history of pre-Columbian North and South America; translation, Carys Evans-Corrales; consultant, Susan Kart. Sharpe, M.E. 2000 2v il maps set $159   **970.01**

1. Native Americans—Antiquities 2. America—Antiquities

ISBN 0-7656-8034-3   LC 00-56280

Original Spanish language edition, 1997

This reference "surveys the entire Western Hemisphere prior to the arrival of Europeans in the Americas. This copiously illustrated work is especially notable for its numerous full-color plates of Native American rock art." Libr J

Includes bibliographical references

Vikings: the North Atlantic saga; edited by William W. Fitzhugh and Elisabeth I. Ward. Smithsonian Institution Press 2000 432p il maps $60; pa $34.95   **970.01**

1. Vikings 2. America—Exploration

ISBN 1-56098-970-X; 1-56098-995-5 (pa)

LC 99-57983

Catalog of an exhibition at the National Museum of Natural History, Smithsonian Institution, Washington, D.C., April 29, 2000-September 5, 2000

"While the book concentrates on the New World, there are also chapters on the Vikings in Iceland, Greenland, and France and along the coasts of Britain and the rivers of Russia. The contributors discuss the Viking saga from the perspectives of natural science, archaeology, history, oral tradition, and early writings." Libr J

This book is "well designed, heavily illustrated and almost encyclopedic in scope and detail." Publ Wkly

Includes bibliographical references

971 Canada

The **Canadian** encyclopedia; [editor-in-chief, James H. Marsh] McClelland & Stewart 2000 lxvi, 2573p il maps $64.99   **971**

1. Canada—Encyclopedias

ISBN 0-7710-2099-6   LC 00-302429

Also available CD-ROM version and online

First published 1985 in three volumes by Hurtig

"This volume contains 10,000 articles written 'from the Canadian point of view.' Special features include maps and comparative statistics of Canada's major cities. Entries cover many features of Canadian culture, history, sports, and politics and quintessential Canadian interests and personalities such as hockey, the beaver, and Céline Dion." Booklist

Riendeau, Roger E., 1950-

A brief history of Canada; by Roger Riendeau. Facts on File 2000 310p il maps $45   **971**

1. Canada—History
ISBN 0-8160-3157-6   LC 99-23494
Also available in paperback from Fitzhenry & Whiteside

Topics covered in this history include "geographical features, the Norse discovery, the fall of New France, nationhood, and finally, the modern era. Riendeau has written a good text enriched by photos, maps, and a bibliography for further reading." Libr J

Weihs, Jean Riddle

Facts about Canada, its provinces and territories; [by] Jean Weihs; illustrations by Cameron Riddle. Wilson, H.W. 1995 246p il maps $60   **971**

1. Canada
ISBN 0-8242-0864-1   LC 94-23275
Coverage includes "geography and climate, parks and historic sites, demography, government and politics, financial and economic information, history, culture and education, motor vehicle use statistics, trivia about the 'first, biggest and best,' information sources and a selected bibliography. Weihs provides very current information and has clearly researched her topic extensively." Voice Youth Advocates

971.3   Ontario

Berton, Pierre, 1920-

Niagara; a history of the Falls. Kodansha Am. 1997 371p il maps $27   **971.3**

1. Niagara Falls (N.Y. and Ont.)
ISBN 1-56836-154-8   LC 96-44821
This "book is less a history of the falls than a chronicle of those who have measured themselves against its prodigious force. Niagara has gradually become a tourist center and an invaluable source of hydroelectric power for the continent, but Berton's hairraising accounts of the daredevils who have tested its power confirm the religious sense of awe that the first European explorers felt in the presence of the great cataract. The terrifying tale of Love Canal is only the most recent example of Niagara's impressive ability to bite back at the civilization that is continually tempted to exploit it." New Yorker
Includes bibliographical references

972   Middle America. Mexico

Coe, Michael D.

The Maya. 6th ed, fully rev and expanded. Thames & Hudson 1999 256p il maps (Ancient peoples and places) pa $18.95   **972**

1. Mayas
ISBN 0-500-28066-5   LC 98-60191
First published 1966 by Praeger
An illustrated survey of the Maya civilization, focusing on the achievements of the Classic Period, A.D. 300-900
Includes bibliographical references

Díaz del Castillo, Bernal, 1496-1584

The discovery and conquest of Mexico, 1517-1521. Farrar, Straus & Giroux 1956 xxxi, 478p il map o.p.; Da Capo Press paperback available $21   **972**

1. Mexico—History
ISBN 0-306-81319-X (pa)
"Edited from the only exact copy of the original MS (and published in Mexico) by Genaro Garcia. Translated with an introduction and notes by A. P. Maudslay. Introduction to the American edition by Irving A. Leonard." Title page
"The memoirs of an old man, who began to write of his experiences half a century after they occurred and completed his account at the age of 84, they are not free from minor inaccuracies, but they are the most reliable narrative that exists." Chicago Sunday Trib

Foster, Lynn V.

A brief history of Mexico. rev ed. Facts on File 2004 320p $45   **972**

1. Mexico—History
ISBN 0-8160-5057-0   LC 2003-54269
First published 1997
An overview of Mexican history covering pre-Columbian civilizations and contemporary indigenous cultures. Language, art, religion, politics and economics are discussed. A chronology and bibliography are included

Guillermoprieto, Alma, 1949-

Looking for history; dispatches from Latin America. Pantheon Bks. 2001 303p il $25   **972**

1. Mexico—Politics and government 2. Cuba—Politics and government 3. Colombia—Politics and government
ISBN 0-375-42094-0   LC 00-62382
The author discusses conditions in Latin America, focusing particularly on Mexico, Colombia, and Cuba. "The essays . . . have been adapted from work which first appeared in the New Yorker and the New York Review of Books." Economist
"Among the stories, book reviews, and descriptions are perceptive and insightful observations of Latin American politics and society that help illuminate this important part of the world. This volume will be of interest to Latin American collections as well as current affairs libraries." Libr J

Kirkwood, Burton

The history of Mexico. Greenwood Press 2000 245p (Greenwood histories of the modern nations) $45   **972**

1. Mexico—History
ISBN 0-313-30351-7   LC 99-33688
A historical survey of Mexico and its people from the arrival of the first humans in the Western Hemisphere to the end of the 20th century. Topics range from Mexico's cultural past to current issues such as the war on drugs and the North American Free Trade Agreement
Includes bibliographical references

Meyer, Michael C.

The course of Mexican history; [by] Michael C. Meyer, William L. Sherman. Oxford Univ. Press $79.95; pa $52.95   **972**

1. Mexico—History
First published 1979. (7th edition 2002) Periodically revised

Meyer, Michael C.—*Continued*
A chronologically arranged survey of the political, economic, social, and cultural history of Mexico, ranging from the pre-Columbian period to the present

The **Oxford** history of Mexico; edited by Michael C. Meyer and William H. Beezley. Oxford Univ. Press 2000 709p il maps $45
972

1. Mexico—History
ISBN 0-19-511228-8   LC 99-56044
The editors "have compiled 20 previously unpublished essays by experts who explore Mexico from precolonial times to the present. . . . Examining the country with new and different approaches, the contributors challenge traditional historical concepts on a variety of issues." Libr J

Includes bibliographical references

Prescott, William Hickling, 1796-1859
History of the conquest of Mexico. Modern Lib. 1998 xxvi, 1005p hardcover o.p. paperback available $17.95   **972**
1. Cortés, Hernán, 1485-1547 2. Mexico—History 3. Aztecs
ISBN 0-375-75803-8 (pa)   LC 98-10173
Also available in edition with History of the conquest of Peru from Cooper Sq. Press
First published 1843 in three volumes
This is a history of the subjugation of the Aztec people by Hernan Cortez and his soldiers between 1519 and 1522

Smith, Michael Ernest, 1953-
The Aztecs; [by] Michael E. Smith. 2nd ed. Blackwell 2003 c2002 367p il maps (Peoples of America) hardcover o.p. paperback available $27.95   **972**
1. Aztecs 2. Mexico—Antiquities
ISBN 0-631-23016-5 (pa)   LC 2001-6950
First published 1996
The author "summarizes the results of archaeological research conducted largely in the past 30 years into the everyday lives of ordinary people in the villages, hamlets, and farmsteads from many regions of central Mexico. His method permits a fresh view of such topics as agricultural methods, population size, market system, relations between city-states and the empire, and even human sacrifice. Smith carries his social account of these people through transformation under Spanish rule and their legacy in modern Mexico." Libr J [review of 1996 edition]
Includes bibliographical references

Townsend, Richard F.
The Aztecs. rev ed, 2nd ed. Thames & Hudson 2000 232p il maps (Ancient peoples and places) pa $18.95   **972**
1. Aztecs
ISBN 0-500-28132-7   LC 99-70847
First published 1992
"In addition to analyzing the advancement and eventual dissolution of the extensive Aztec empire, the author also provides a fascinating record of the minutiae of daily life. . . . A compact introduction to the historical and sociological evolution of a prominent Meso-American civilization." Booklist [review of 1992 edition]
Includes bibliographical references

972.08   Mexico since 1867

Fuentes, Carlos, 1928-
A new time for Mexico; translated from the Spanish by Marina Gutman Castañeda and the author. Farrar, Straus & Giroux 1996 216p o.p.; University of Calif. Press paperback available $16.95   **972.08**
1. Mexico—Politics and government
ISBN 0-520-21183-9 (pa)   LC 96-10540
In these essays "Fuentes calls on Mexican president Ernesto Zedillo to take definitive steps toward a full democracy—electoral reform; equal access of candidates to the media; independent, aggressive labor unions; and, above all, true separation between the ruling party and the government. . . . Offering lapidary, lyrical meditations on Mexico as a land of continual metamorphosis, Fuentes nostalgically reminisces about his home in Veracruz, whose port his father defended against a Yankee invasion in 1914." Publ Wkly

Lewis, Oscar, 1914-1970
The children of Sánchez; autobiography of a Mexican family. Random House 1961 xxxi, 499p hardcover o.p. paperback available $17
972.08
1. Mexico City (Mexico)—Social conditions 2. Poor—Mexico City (Mexico) 3. Family
ISBN 0-394-70280-8 (pa)
"First-person autobiographical narratives by the members of a poor family in Mexico City. One by one, the father and his four grown children told the anthropologist author their stories of fights, sex, struggles for jobs, bitterness, hate, sickness, death, and only a little happiness." Publ Wkly
"Oscar Lewis has made something brilliant and of singular significance, a work of such unique concentration and sympathy." N Y Times Book Rev

Riding, Alan
Distant neighbors; a portrait of the Mexicans. Knopf 1984 385p hardcover o.p. paperback available $14   **972.08**
1. Mexico—Social life and customs 2. Mexican national characteristics
ISBN 0-679-72441-9 (pa)   LC 84-47811
This is an examination of Mexico's economy, society, and politics, and of the relationship between the United States and Mexico
Includes bibliographical references

Womack, John
Zapata and the Mexican Revolution. Knopf 1969 c1968 435p il hardcover o.p. paperback available $17   **972.08**
1. Zapata, Emiliano, 1879-1919 2. Mexico—History
ISBN 0-394-70853-9 (pa)
The author reconstructs the "history of the agrarian revolution in southern Mexico from the late Díaz period to about 1920. The work is well written [and] carefully conceived." Choice

972.8 Central America

Pérez-Brignoli, Héctor
A brief history of Central America; translated by Ricardo B. Sawrey A. and Susana Stettri de Sawrey. University of Calif. Press 1989 223p maps hardcover o.p. paperback available $18.97   **972.8**
1. Central America—History
ISBN 0-520-06832-7 (pa)   LC 89-31889
This book presents the economic, political and cultural history of Guatemala, Honduras, El Salvador, Nicaragua and Costa Rica, the five national states of Central America
"For interested laypersons, this is an excellent introduction with an accurate sense of the region." Libr J
Includes bibliographical references

972.81 Guatemala

Wilkinson, Daniel, 1970-
Silence on the mountain; stories of terror, betrayal, and forgetting in Guatemala. Houghton Mifflin 2002 373p $24   **972.81**
1. Guatemala 2. Terrorism
ISBN 0-618-22139-5   LC 2002-75936
This "book traces the history of Guatemala's 36-year internal struggle through personal interviews that recount the . . . stories of plantation owners, army officials, guerrillas and the wretchedly poor peasants stuck in the middle." Publ Wkly
"The author's style is taut and precise, but it is the Guatemalans themselves who speak with the greatest eloquence." New Yorker
Includes bibliographical references

972.87 Panama

McCullough, David G., 1933-
The path between the seas; the creation of the Panama Canal, 1870-1914; [by] David McCullough. Simon & Schuster 1977 698p il maps hardcover o.p. paperback available $18   **972.87**
1. Panama Canal
ISBN 0-671-24409-4 (pa)   LC 76-57967
This is a "history of the canal project, beginning with de Lesseps' bold and ultimately disastrous investment and ending with the triumph of American enterprise in 1914." Libr J
"Not only is this a well-told story of the building of the Panama Canal but it also supplies welcome background for the . . . debate on the canal's role in inter-American relations." Booklist
Includes bibliographical references

972.91 Cuba

Bardach, Ann Louise
Cuba confidential; love and vengeance in Miami and Havana. Random House 2002 xxi, 417p il $25.95; pa $15.95   **972.91**
1. González, Elián 2. Cuban refugees 3. Cuban Americans 4. United States—Foreign relations—Cuba 5. Cuba—Foreign relations—United States
ISBN 0-375-50489-3; 0-385-72052-1 (pa)
LC 2002-17887
"The 2000 custody battle between little Elián González's father, acting, according to Bardach, as the surrogate for the Cuban government, and his exiled Miami relatives, the surrogate anti-Castro forces, became a relentless media event and international affair. . . . [The author] uses the Elián story as a starting place to examine the larger issues that have roiled Cuba-U.S. politics for four decades." Publ Wkly
"This compact volume offers clear explanations of events, individuals and dynamics since the Cuban Revolution." Libr J
Includes bibliographical references

Codrescu, Andrei, 1946-
Ay, Cuba! a socio-erotic journey; photographs by David Graham. St. Martin's Press 1999 206p il map hardcover o.p. paperback available $18   **972.91**
1. Cuba
ISBN 0-312-27471-8 (pa)   LC 98-40545
The author spent time "interviewing and photographing Cubans from all walks of life, from artists and administrators to hustlers and working people. The result is a lively, tragicomic look at Cuba, enriched by insights gleaned from Codrescu's own experience with communism in his native Romania." Libr J
Includes bibliographical references

Encyclopedia of Cuba; people, history, culture; edited by Luis Martínez-Fernández {et al.}. Greenwood Press 2003 2v il maps set $174.95   **972.91**
1. Cuba—Encyclopedias
ISBN 1-57356-334-X   LC 2002-70030
"An Oryx book"
"The editors intend this work to be a non-politicized look at Cuban people, politics, history, and culture. Chapters cover topics such as history, government, and popular culture. Within each chapter, entries are in alphabetical order. An excellent introduction to a colorful and important nation." Booklist
Includes bibliographical references

Gimbel, Wendy
Havana dreams; a story of Cuba. Knopf 1998 234p il hardcover o.p. paperback available $13   **972.91**
1. Revuelta, Naty, 1925- 2. Cuba—History
ISBN 0-679-75070-3 (pa)   LC 98-14571
At the center of this personal "history of modern Cuba is a brief affair between a married Havana socialite named Naty Revuelta and Fidel Castro, carried out mostly in love letters written in 1953-54 while the future dictator was in jail. The affair fizzled, but not before Castro supposedly left his paramour with a daughter, Alina." Publ Wkly
Gimbel "succeeds in showing the complexity of family relationships resulting from the Cuban revolution, which extends into two countries." Libr J

Harvey, David Alan, 1944-
Cuba; photographs by David Alan Harvey; essays by Elizabeth Newhouse. National Geographic Soc. 1999 215p il $50   **972.91**
1. Cuba
ISBN 0-7922-7501-2   LC 99-32488
This collection of Harvey's photographs depicts "the effects of Cuba's totalitarian government and dire economy upon its remarkably resilient population. . . . These images are matched with staff writer Newhouse's historical overview, which discusses the country's rich architectural heritage, culture, and social conditions. Together these add up to a sympathetic understanding of what the island is like today." Libr J

Pérez, Louis A., 1943-
Cuba; between reform and revolution. 2nd ed. Oxford Univ. Press 1995 539p maps $70; pa $28.95   **972.91**
1. Cuba—History
ISBN 0-19-509481-6; 0-19-509482-4 (pa)
         LC 95-14801
First published 1988
"A narrative history that emphasizes the antecedents of the Cuban revolution and concludes with an analysis of Fidel Castro's successes and failures." N Y Public Libr Book of How & Where to Look It Up [entry for 1988 edition]
Includes bibliographical references

Suchlicki, Jaime
Cuba; from Columbus to Castro and beyond; [by] James Suchlicki. 5th ed. Brassey's 2002 285p pa $24.95   **972.91**
1. Cuba—History
ISBN 1-57488-436-0   LC 2002-3953
First published 1997
A summary of Cuba's development, with emphasis on the twentieth century and the factors that led to the Cuban revolution
Includes bibliographical references

972.94   Haiti

Shacochis, Bob
The immaculate invasion. Viking 1999 408p map $27.95; pa $14.95   **972.94**
1. Haiti
ISBN 0-670-86304-1; 0-14-024895-1 (pa)
         LC 98-11693
This book examines events following the arrival of American soldiers in "Haiti in 1994 to return exiled President Jean-Bertrand Aristide to power." New Leader
"Bob Shacochis proves that he is a writer of rare grace and intuition (though when he lapses into macho military jargon, his fine writing is diminished)." N Y Times Book Rev

972.97   Leeward Islands

Kincaid, Jamaica
A small place. Farrar, Straus & Giroux 1988 81p hardcover o.p. paperback available $11   **972.97**
1. Antigua and Barbuda
ISBN 0-374-52707-5 (pa)   LC 88-376
Antiguan Kincaid addresses foreign visitors to her country. In this essay, she discusses the poverty and political corruption of the island, which she views as a legacy of British colonialism and also as a result of an economy controlled by tourism

973   United States

American eras. Gale Res. 1997-1998 8v il set $825   **973**
1. United States—Civilization 2. United States—History
Also available separately for $115
Contents: Early American civilizations (prehistory to 1600); The Colonial era (1600-1754); The Revolutionary era (1754-1783); Development of a nation (1783-1815); The reform era and eastern U.S. development (1815-1850); Westward expansion (1801-1861); Civil War and Reconstruction (1850-1877); Development of the industrial U.S. (1877-1900)
This reference set "provides information on U.S. history, including social history, prior to the twentieth century. Each era-specific volume includes an introductory essay describing the time period to provide context and an overview, 150 illustrations, an index of photographs, a bibliography, a subject index and a list of contributors." Publisher's note

Anzovin, Steven, 1954-
Famous first facts about American politics; [by] Steven Anzovin & Janet Podell. Wilson, H.W. 2001 756p $150   **973**
1. United States—Politics and government 2. United States—History
ISBN 0-8242-0971-0   LC 00-49960
This offers over 5,000 entries of firsts in national, state, and local U.S. politics from the founding of the nation through the 2000 election and includes five indexes: subject, name, year, day, and place

Appleby, Joyce Oldham
Inheriting the revolution; the first generation of Americans; [by] Joyce Appleby. Belknap Press 2000 322p il $28.50; pa $16   **973**
1. United States—History—1783-1865 2. United States—Social conditions
ISBN 0-674-00236-9; 0-674-00663-1 (pa)
         LC 99-49787
The author "deals with two themes in this book: the historical experience of the generation after the American Revolution and conflicts within American identity." N Y Times Book Rev
"This book provides a splendid introduction to the period for students and general readers." Libr J
Includes bibliographical references

Boller, Paul F.

Presidential inaugurations; [by] Paul F. Boller, Jr. Harcourt 2001 298p $25; pa $14

973

1. Presidents—United States—Inauguration 2. Washington (D.C.)—Social life and customs
ISBN 0-15-100546-X; 0-15-600759-2 (pa)

LC 00-49893

The author "examines the events and controversies surrounding Presidential inaugurations. . . . Written with elegance and wit, this is a wonderful addition to the very thin literature available on Presidential inaugurations." Libr J

Includes bibliographical references

Boorstin, Daniel J., 1914-2004

The Americans: The democratic experience. Random House 1973 717p hardcover o.p. paperback available $19

973

1. United States—Civilization 2. United States—Social conditions 3. United States—Economic conditions
ISBN 0-394-71011-8 (pa)

Concluding volume of the author's trilogy which began with The Americans: The colonial experience and continued with The Americans: The national experience

This volume is concerned with the democratization of the national character over the past hundred years and the growth of technology

Includes bibliographical references

The Americans: The national experience. Random House 1965 517p hardcover o.p. paperback available $16

973

1. United States—Civilization 2. American national characteristics 3. United States—Intellectual life
ISBN 0-394-70358-8 (pa)

This is the second volume of the author's trilogy

A cultural interpretation of American history, this book traces "the roots of contemporary American life to the years between the Revolution and the Civil War." Booklist

Includes bibliographical references

Hidden history; selected and edited by Daniel J. Boorstin and Ruth F. Boorstin. Harper & Row 1987 xxv, 332p o.p.; Vintage Bks. paperback available $14

973

1. United States—Civilization
ISBN 0-679-72223-8 (pa)

LC 87-45023

"A Cornelia & Michael Bessie book"

"A collection of essays and abridgments from [Boorstin's] books that investigates certain overlooked or disregarded corners of history. . . . History engagingly written, deeply felt, widely appealing." Booklist

Churchill, Sir Winston, 1874-1965

The great republic; a history of America; edited by Winston S. Churchill. Random House 1999 454p hardcover o.p. paperback available $14.95

973

1. United States—History
ISBN 0-375-40856-8 (pa)

LC 99-28511

Also available large print edition $25.95 (ISBN 0-375-40856-8)

"The first half of the volume offers an old-fashioned narrative history of America's political development, from the age of exploration to the 1880s. The second

half reprints articles that Churchill penned for English publications on such themes as Prohibition, the muckracking of Upton Sinclair, and the death of Franklin Delano Roosevelt." Libr J

Commager, Henry Steele, 1902-1998

The American mind; an interpretation of American thought and character since the 1880's. Yale Univ. Press 1950 476p hardcover o.p. paperback available $22 **973**

1. United States—Civilization 2. American national characteristics 3. United States—Intellectual life
ISBN 0-300-00046-4 (pa)

Analyzed in Essay and general literature index

Partial contents: John Fiske and the evolutionary philosophy; William James and the impact of pragmatism; Determinism in literature; Religious thought and practice; Lester Ward and the science of society; Thorstein Veblen and the new economics; Innovators in historical interpretation; Applications of political theory; Evolution of American law; Architecture and society; Bibliography

Dallek, Robert

Hail to the chief; the making and unmaking of American presidents. Hyperion 1996 xx, 232p o.p.; Oxford Univ. Press paperback available $15.95

973

1. Presidents—United States 2. United States—Politics and government
ISBN 0-19-514582-8 (pa)

LC 96-8033

"Dallek offers anecdotes about success and failure in the presidency. He groups the stories around five qualities presidents must exhibit before historians will grant them greatness: the 'vision thing,' practical politicking, consensus building, charisma, and credibility." Booklist

"The book is a model of clarity, conciseness, balance, and insight." Libr J

Includes bibliographical references

Eyewitness to America; 500 years of America in the words of those who saw it happen; edited by David Colbert. Pantheon Bks. 1997 xxx, 599p hardcover o.p. paperback available $16.95

973

1. United States—History—Sources
ISBN 0-679-76724-X (pa)

LC 96-24150

This volume contains a "panorama of first-person accounts of moments in the country's story that stretch from an October 10, 1492, diary entry by one of Columbus's crewmen to a 1994 e-mail message from Bill Gates. The nearly 300 entries tend to be short, preceded by informative introductions. The result is a feeling for history that is both immediate and dramatic." Publ Wkly

Includes bibliographical references

Facts about the states; editors, Joseph Nathan Kane, Janet Podell, Steven Anzovin. 2nd ed. Wilson, H.W. 1994 c1993 624p il $100

973

1. United States—Local history 2. State governments
ISBN 0-8242-0849-8

LC 93-30328

First published 1989

Provides geographic, demographic, economic, political, and cultural facts about the fifty states, Puerto Rico, and the District of Columbia. Part I presents state entries in alphabetical order. Part II provides comparative tables that rank states in categories such as population, geography, education, and finance

Hakim, Joy

Freedom; a history of US. Oxford Univ. Press 2002 406p il $40   **973**

1. American national characteristics 2. United States—History

ISBN 0-19-515711-7   LC 2002-29016

"Hakim divides American history into 16 parts, from the time of independence to a final chapter that chronicles the years from 1968, when Nixon was elected president, to the present. In between, she offers a lucid picture of the events and people that shaped our country. . . . With more than 400 illustrations, the book's theme—our continuous struggle for freedom—is explored visually as well as through the author's fluid narrative." Booklist

Includes bibliographical references

Hofstadter, Richard, 1916-1970

The American political tradition, and the men who made it; with a foreword by Christopher Lasch. 25th anniversary ed. Knopf 1973 xxxiii, 378p hardcover o.p. paperback available $14   **973**

1. United States—Politics and government

ISBN 0-679-72315-3 (pa)

First published 1948 and analyzed in Essay and general literature index

This volume contains twelve essays, ten of which analyze the political careers of Lincoln, Jefferson, Jackson, Calhoun, Wendell Phillips, Bryan, Theodore Roosevelt, Wilson, Hoover and Franklin D. Roosevelt

Includes bibliographical references

Kammen, Michael G.

In the past lane; historical perspectives on American culture; [by] Michael Kammen. Oxford Univ. Press 1997 277p il hardcover o.p. paperback available $25   **973**

1. United States—Civilization 2. Popular culture—United States 3. United States—Historiography

ISBN 0-19-513091-X (pa)   LC 97-21613

Analyzed in Essay and general literature index

These essays "range from the influence of the personal experiences of prominent historians on their work to the changing attitudes toward the 'unique' aspects of American history as reflected in the views of historians, past and present. For professional historians or serious students of history, Kammen's essays provide an excellent opportunity to gauge how those who chronicle our past both influence and are influenced by national and personal experiences." Booklist

Includes bibliographical references

Keegan, John, 1934-

Fields of battle; the wars for North America. Knopf 1996 c1995 348p il maps hardcover o.p. paperback available $15   **973**

1. North America—Military history

ISBN 0-679-74664-1 (pa)   LC 96-154385

First published 1995 in the United Kingdom with title: Warpaths: travels of a military historian in North America

The author "demonstrates how North America's geography has influenced its history: how its mountain chains and river systems have determined where people fought, and fought repeatedly. For example, the defenses that Cornwallis built at Yorktown to deter American forces were improved and reused by the Confederates almost a century later. Keegan's tour of the continent skips the

Mexican War, and his book is atypically discursive. For Americans, the charm is the familiarity of its sites—Brooklyn, Pittsburgh, Laramie, and other home towns." New Yorker

Linklater, Andro

Measuring America; how an untamed wilderness shaped the United States and fulfilled the promise of democracy. Walker & Co. 2002 310p il maps $26   **973**

1. United States—Geography 2. Public lands—United States 3. United States—Territorial expansion 4. Surveying

ISBN 0-8027-1396-3   LC 2002-73573

Also available in paperback from Plume

"The American innovation of individual land ownership got a great boost when, in 1784, the indebted young republic began to parcel up for sale wilderness west of the Ohio River based on a new standard system of measurement—one that imprints every corner of American life to this day." Libr J

The author "has the talent not just to let us know how things work, but to make us want to know. Discussing this and other technologies with an enthusiast's detailed passion, he engages himself in a great deal more." N Y Times (Late N Y Ed)

Includes bibliographical references

Loewen, James W.

Lies across America; what our historic sites get wrong. New Press 1999 480p il $26.95   **973**

1. Historic sites 2. Monuments

ISBN 1-56584-344-4   LC 99-14212

Also available in paperback from Touchstone Bks.

"The book consists of 95 brief commentaries on specific sites from Alaska to Florida to Maine, sandwiched between essays that offer advice on how to interpret what you read or are told at historic sites." N Y Times Book Rev

Includes bibliographical references

Morison, Samuel Eliot, 1887-1976

A concise history of the American Republic; [by] Samuel Eliot Morison, Henry Steele Commager, William E. Leuchtenburg. 2nd ed. Oxford Univ. Press 1983 765p il maps hardcover o.p. paperback available $58.95   **973**

1. United States—History

ISBN 0-19-503180-6 (pa)   LC 82-3621

Also available in a two volume paperback edition, each $39.95: v1 To 1877 (ISBN 0-19-503181-4); v2 Since 1865 (ISBN 0-19-503182-2)

First published 1977

"An abbreviated and revised edition of The growth of the American Republic." Title page

Includes bibliographical references

The growth of the American Republic; [by] Samuel Eliot Morison, Henry Steele Commager, and William E. Leuchtenburg. 7th ed. Oxford Univ. Press 1980 2v il maps ea $59.95   **973**

1. United States—History

ISBN 0-19-502593-8 (v1); 0-19-502594-6 (v2)

    LC 79-52432

First published 1930 in a single volume

Morison, Samuel Eliot, 1887-1976—*Continued*

A history of the United States that deals with military, political, economic, social, literary and spiritual aspects of the nation's development

"A good general history, well-written." Sheehy. Guide to Ref Books. 10th edition

The Oxford history of the American people. Meridian 1994 3v il maps **973**
1. United States—History   LC 94-14636

First published 1965 by Oxford University Press

Contents: v1 Prehistory to 1789 pa $15.95 (ISBN 0-452-01130-2); v2 1789 through Reconstruction pa o.p.; v3 1869-1963 pa $17 (ISBN 0-452-01132-9)

A political, social, and military history of the United States from prehistoric man to President Kennedy's assassination, including such aspects of American life as sports, science, art, and music. Also includes comments on Canadian history

Osborn, William M.

The wild frontier; atrocities during the American-Indian War from Jamestown Colony to Wounded Knee. Random House 2000 363p hardcover o.p. paperback available $19 **973**
1. Native Americans—Wars 2. Native Americans—Government relations 3. Frontier and pioneer life
ISBN 0-375-75856-9 (pa)   LC 00-27171

"Characterizing the years between 1622 and 1890 as the era of the American-Indian War, Osborn provides a balanced analysis of the vicious atrocities committed by white settlers and Native Americans during the prolonged period of westward expansion. . . . Laden with stark, unsparing descriptions . . . the detailed narrative retains an admirable objectivity." Booklist

Includes bibliographical references

The **Reader's** companion to the American presidency; edited by Alan Brinkley and Davis Dyer. Houghton Mifflin 2000 566p il $40 **973**
1. Presidents—United States 2. United States—Politics and government
ISBN 0-395-78889-7   LC 99-59638

"Essays written by professors and historians present an overview of each administration through factual details, anecdotes, and analysis. The amount of criticism in each article varies depending on the writer and the president. The text is academic but readable. . . . A detailed time line runs along the bottom of the pages and includes other important political and cultural events." SLJ

Includes bibliographical references

Schlesinger, Arthur M., 1917-

The cycles of American history; [by] Arthur M. Schlesinger, Jr. Houghton Mifflin 1986 498p hardcover o.p. paperback available $16 **973**
1. United States—History 2. United States—Foreign relations 3. United States—Politics and government
ISBN 0-395-95793-1 (pa)   LC 86-7706

"For this volume, Schlesinger has revised and updated papers, reviews, and essays that have appeared in various forms over the past quarter-century. . . . Each of the 14 essays that make up the book offers a fresh, demanding, and lively argument about important issues in American intellectual, political, or diplomatic history." Choice

Includes bibliographical references

The disuniting of America; reflections on a multicultural society. rev & enl ed. Norton 1998 208p $21.95; pa $12.95 **973**
1. Multiculturalism 2. Multicultural education 3. United States—Historiography 4. United States—Civilization
ISBN 0-393-04580-3; 0-393-31854-0 (pa)
LC 97-25124

First published 1992

The author argues against radical multiculturalism, bilingual education, and the influence of ethnic, political, and religious pressure groups on the teaching of history. Includes an epilogue that assesses the impact of radical multiculturalism and radical monoculturalism on the Bill of Rights and concludes with an annotated reading list of titles essential for understanding the American experience

Steinbeck, John, 1902-1968

Travels with Charley; in search of America. Viking 1962 246p **973**
1. United States—Civilization 2. United States—Description
Available various paperback editions

The Nobel laureate recounts his impressions and observations of America gathered during a trip through forty states in the company of his French poodle Charley

Virga, Vincent

Eyes of the nation; a visual history of the United States; by Vincent Virga and curators of the Library of Congress; historical commentary by Alan Brinkley. Knopf 1997 399p il $75 **973**
1. United States—History—Pictorial works
ISBN 0-679-44330-4   LC 97-36603

This visual history "showcases more than 500 illustrations, manuscripts, engravings, prints, movie stills and other artifacts stretching back to the 15th century. The accompanying text by the historian Alan Brinkley rolls through the high and low points of the nation's history, but it is the captions that sparkle the brightest, adding context while offering surprising information." N Y Times Book Rev

Wetterau, Bruce

Congressional Quarterly's desk reference on the Presidency. CQ Press 2000 311p il (Desk reference series) $49.95 **973**
1. Presidents—United States
ISBN 1-56802-589-0   LC 00-63024

Over 500 questions and answers on the organization, procedures, and history of the office and on the presidents and their wives. Topics covered include scandals, elections, the White House, and the executive branch

Includes bibliographical references

Wilkins, Roger W., 1932-

Jefferson's pillow; the founding fathers and the dilemma of Black patriotism; [by] Roger Wilkins. Beacon Press 2001 163p hardcover o.p. paperback available $14 **973**
1. Mason, George, 1725-1792 2. Washington, George, 1732-1799 3. Jefferson, Thomas, 1743-1826 4. Madison, James, 1751-1836 5. United States—History 6. United States—Race relations
ISBN 0-8070-0957-1 (pa)   LC 2001-25117

Also available G. K. Hall large print edition

Wilkins, Roger W., 1932-—*Continued*

"Wilkins returns to America's beginnings and the lives of the founding fathers to explore how . . . race and slavery still impede our progress. In . . . [an] analysis of the lives of George Washington, George Mason, James Madison, and . . . Thomas Jefferson, he explores how class, education, and personality allowed for the institution of slavery in a nation conceived under the premise that all men are created equal." Publisher's note

"This is an important look at the essential and ongoing contradictions at the heart of American ideals of liberty and patriotism." Booklist

Includes bibliographical references

Wills, Garry, 1934-

A necessary evil; a history of American distrust of government. Simon & Schuster 1999 365p hardcover o.p. paperback available $15 **973**

1. United States—Politics and government 2. Resistance to government

ISBN 0-684-87026-6 (pa) LC 99-35879

This "analysis of the distorted mythology that has grown up around government in the U.S. takes on hot-button issues from the Second Amendment and term limits to the idea that the Founders sought to create an inefficient government. Provocative and enlightening." Booklist

Includes bibliographical references

Witness to America; an illustrated documentary history of the United States from the Revolution to today; Stephen Ambrose and Douglas Brinkley, editors. HarperCollins Pubs. 1999 605p il $39.95 **973**

1. United States—History—Sources 2. United States—History—Pictorial works

ISBN 0-06-271611-5 LC 99-23797

"A Lou Reda book"

A revised and updated edition of The heritage of America edited by Henry Steele Commager and Allan Nevins, first published 1939

The editors provide a collection of primary source material on pivotal moments in American history. Includes audio CD containing dramatizations and actual clips of events included in text

Includes bibliographical references

Zimmermann, Warren, 1934-2004

First great triumph; how five Americans made their country a world power. Farrar, Straus & Giroux 2002 562p il $30; pa $15 **973**

1. United States—History—1898-1919 2. Spanish-American War, 1898

ISBN 0-374-17939-5; 0-374-52893-4 (pa) LC 2002-25015

The author credits five men "for the vision, determination and political skill that first gave the United States its global ambition. His book is a history of the American rise to power and a collective biography of [his] five heroes: Theodore Roosevelt, the assistant secretary of the Navy and later president; Alfred T. Mahan, the naval strategist; Senator Henry Cabot Lodge of Massachusetts; Secretary of State John Hay; and the first American colonial administrator, Elihu Root." N Y Times (Late N Y Ed)

Includes bibliographical references

973.02 United States—History—Miscellany. Chronologies

The **New** encyclopedia of American scandal; George Childs Kohn, editor. Facts on File 2001 455p il (Facts on File library of American history) $71.50; pa $24.95 **973.02**

1. United States—History—Miscellanea

ISBN 0-8160-4225-X; 0-8160-4420-1 (pa) LC 00-34099

First published 1989 under the authorship of George C. Kohn with title: Encyclopedia of American scandal

This compendium includes "more than 450 people and incidents from the 1600s to the present, surveying episodes of graft, bribery, deception, and outrage by people in high places. Although the tragic, career-derailing impact of historic humiliations cannot be denied, this frank book entertains as well as informs." Choice

The **New** York Public Library American history desk reference. 2nd ed. Hyperion 2003 576p il maps pa $21.95 **973.02**

1. United States—History—Dictionaries

ISBN 0-7868-6847-3 LC 2003-56655

"A Stonesong Press book"

First published 1997 by Macmillan

This book includes "information on a variety of topics from military and foreign affairs to education and science. Information is organized into . . . timelines highlighting events throughout America's history, along with numerous sidebars, photos, maps, brief biographies, and trivia tidbits." Publisher's note

"[This is a] well-designed, convenient-size volume filled with lists, charts, tables, and short articles. . . . [This] volume should be [a] useful ready-reference compilation for public and academic libraries." Booklist [review of 1997 edition]

Shenkman, Richard

Legends, lies, and cherished myths of American history. Morrow 1988 202p o.p.; HarperCollins Pubs. paperback available $13 **973.02**

1. United States—History—Miscellanea

ISBN 0-06-097261-0 (pa) LC 88-9293

The author "debunks a host of popular myths associated with U.S. history. From the Founding Fathers to the Reagan presidency, heretofore undisputed facts are exposed as fiction. Misquotes, misinterpretations, and downright fabrications are all duly recorded in an amusing and illuminating fashion. An irresistible browsing item." Booklist

Includes bibliographical references

973.03 United States—History—Encyclopedias and dictionaries

Dictionary of American history; Stanley I. Kutler, editor in chief. 3rd ed. Scribner 2003 10v il map set $1,050 **973.03**

1. United States—History—Dictionaries

ISBN 0-684-80533-2 LC 2002-12433

First published 1940 in 5 volumes edited by James Truslow Adams

Dictionary of American history—*Continued*

"This set provides 4,434 entries pertaining to American history. . . . Volumes 1-8 provide an alphabetic listing of key events, while volume 9 offers primary documents and archival maps and volume 10 offers a research guide and index to the set. Each article runs several paragraphs to several pages in length and each have a bibliography and *see also* references." Am Ref Books Annu, 2003

Includes bibliographical references

Encyclopedia of American cultural and intellectual history; edited by Mary Kupiec Cayton and Peter W. Williams. Scribner 2000 3v il set $400 **973.03**
1. United States—Civilization—Encyclopedias
2. United States—Intellectual life—Encyclopedias
ISBN 0 684-80561-8   LC 2001-20005

Art movements, education and academia, the counterculture, the sciences, domestic life, social classes, Hollywood, and post-structuralism are among the topics covered. Each article includes illustrations, boxed biographies, or documentary excerpts

Encyclopedia of American history; Gary B. Nash, general editor. Facts on File 2003 11v il maps set $935 **973.03**
1. United States—History—Encyclopedias
ISBN 0-8160-4371-X   LC 2001-51278

Contents: v1 Three worlds meet beginnings to 1607; v2 Colonization and settlement 1608 to 1760; v3 Revolution and new nation 1761 to 1812; v4 Expansion and reform 1813 to 1855; v5 Civil War and Reconstruction 1856 to 1869; v6 The development of the industrial United States 1870 to 1899; v7 The emergence of modern America 1900 to 1928; v8 The Great Depression and World War II 1929 to 1945; v9 Postwar United States 1946 to 1968; v10 Contemporary United States 1969 to the present; v11 Comprehensive index

"The volumes are organized chronologically, but the entries within each volume are alphabetical. Each book begins with a contents list, and there are copious see and cross-references. Essays of varying length cover events; 'major categories of the American experience' (education, urbanization, etc.); people, places, concepts, and more. At the end of each entry, one or more suggestions for further reading (generally adult titles) are offered. . . . This encyclopedia is a valuable resource for students of American history and can be used to support any classroom text, offering students ample opportunity for fuller exploration of topics of interest." SLJ

For a fuller review see: Booklist, May 15, 2003

The **Encyclopedia** of American political history; edited by Paul Finkelman, Peter Wallenstein. CQ Press 2001 xxxii, 494p il map $140 **973.03**
1. United States—Politics and government—Encyclopedias
ISBN 1-56802-511-4   LC 00-66812

This reference tool covers "significant events, people [and] concepts in U.S. political history. Organized alphabetically, the 225 entries vary in length from a few paragraphs to several pages. The book opens with a descriptive time line of political events and ends with an appendix of acronyms and abbreviations used in U.S. history." Libr J

Encyclopedia of American social history; Mary Kupiec Cayton, Elliott J. Gorn, Peter W. Williams, editors. Scribner 1993 3v il map set $400 **973.03**
1. United States—Social conditions—Encyclopedias
2. United States—Social life and customs—Encyclopedias
ISBN 0-684-19246-2   LC 92-10577

"The encyclopedia is divided into a number of thematic sections with clusters of lengthy signed essays exploring such issues as the interaction between diverse groups; it concludes with essays about how groups lead their lives and how work and social problems affect the fabric of American society." Libr J

Encyclopedia of American studies; edited by George T. Kurian {et al.}. Grolier Educ. 2001 4v il set $399 **973.03**
1. United States—Civilization—Encyclopedias
ISBN 0-7172-9222-3   LC 2001-23415

"Published under the sponsorship of the American Studies Association"

This work "brings together a range of topics related to the culture of the US, from political movements, arts, and religion to wars, landmark legal rulings, and technology. The preface explains the concept and discipline of @American studies.' A table of contents groups by subject the 660 entries, nearly all written by academics. . . . Entries are clearly written with enough interesting detail to inspire high school or undergraduate students to conduct further research." Choice

For a fuller review see: Booklist, Jan. 1 & 15, 2001

Encyclopedia of rural America; the land and people; Gary A. Goreham, editor. ABC-CLIO 1997 2v il map set $175 **973.03**
1. Country life—United States 2. United States—Rural conditions—Encyclopedias 3. United States—Geography—Encyclopedias
ISBN 0-87436-842-1   LC 97-23320

"This encyclopedia covers a broad range of topics, such as agriculture, the arts, economics, the environment, health, humanities, and political and social science. The 230 alphabetically arranged entries, from *addiction* to *worker's compensation*, are listed in the front of each volume for handy reference." Booklist

Olson, James Stuart, 1946-

Encyclopedia of the industrial revolution in America; [by] James S. Olson; technical editor: Robert L. Shadle. Greenwood Press 2002 xxv, 313p il $69.95 **973.03**
1. Industrial revolution—Encyclopedias 2. United States—History—Encyclopedias
ISBN 0-313-30830-6   LC 00-52129

This encyclopedia offers "coverage of the economic, political, and social developments of the Industrial Revolution in the United States from 1750 to 1920. . . . Highlights of the work include . . . entries on developments in water and rail transportation, agriculture, manufacturing, mass production, the labor movement, big government, and the key inventions that changed the American economy." Publisher's note

"A well-organized and comprehensive ready reference." Voice Youth Advocates

The **Oxford** companion to United States history; editor in chief, Paul S. Boyer; editors, Melvyn Dubofsky [et al.] Oxford Univ. Press 2001 xliv, 940p il maps $75
973.03

1. United States—History—Dictionaries
ISBN 0-19-508209-5   LC 00-55801
First published 1966 under the authorship of Thomas A. Johnson with title: The Oxford companion to American history

This reference work contains 1,400 alphabetically arranged signed entries. See and see also references are provided. Coverage starts with the colonial period and examines notable men and women and major events in U.S. history

For a review see: Booklist, Dec. 1, 2001

The **Reader's** companion to American history; Eric Foner and John A. Garraty, editors; sponsored by the Society of American Historians. Houghton Mifflin 1991 xxii, 1226p $45   **973.03**

1. United States—History—Encyclopedias
ISBN 0-395-51372-3   LC 91-19508

"The nearly 1000 entries, ranging from concise explanations to multipage essays, are all equally well written, crisp, and entertaining. Most entries are signed by the nearly 400 contributors, many of whom are acknowledged experts in their fields. . . . Brief bibliographies and thorough 'See also' references to related articles follow each entry." Libr J

973.06   United States—History— Organizations

Directory of historical organizations in the United States and Canada. American Assn. for State & Local Hist. pa $149.95
973.06

1. United States—History—Societies—Directories
2. Canada—History—Societies—Directories
ISSN 0070-5659
First published 1956 with title: Directory of historical societies and agencies in the United States and Canada. (2001 edition) Periodically revised

"Libraries should acquire the latest edition of this publication, which lists historical societies geographically, giving mailing address, number of members, museums, hours and size of library, publication program, etc." Ref Sources for Small & Medium-sized Libr. 5th edition

973.2   United States—Colonial period, 1607-1775

Anderson, Fred, 1949-
The crucible of war; the Seven Years' War and the fate of empire in British North America, 1754-1766; with illustrations from the William L. Clements Library. Knopf 2000 862p il hardcover o.p. paperback available $21   **973.2**

1. Seven Years' War, 1756-1763 2. United States—History—1600-1775, Colonial period
ISBN 0-375-70636-4 (pa)   LC 99-18512
The author "demonstrates that the conflict was more than just a peripheral squabble that anticipated the American Revolution. Not only did the war decisively alter relations among the French, the English and the Native American allies of the two powers, who for decades had played the English and French off one another to their own advantage, but just as critical, argues Anderson, the war also changed the character of British imperialism, with the mother country trying to reshape the terms of empire and the colonists' place in it." Publ Wkly

Bailyn, Bernard
The peopling of British North America; an introduction. Knopf 1986 177p hardcover o.p. paperback available $12   **973.2**

1. United States—History—1600-1775, Colonial period
ISBN 0-394-75779-3 (pa)   LC 85-82144
In this introductory volume of a projected multivolume work, the author "gives first airing to his overall argument on settling patterns in history. Though designed to introduce the subsequent volumes, this superbly articulate study is understandable on its own." Booklist
Includes bibliographical references

Boorstin, Daniel J., 1914-2004
The Americans: The colonial experience. Random House 1958 434p hardcover o.p. paperback available $15   **973.2**

1. United States—Civilization 2. United States—History—1600-1775, Colonial period 3. American national characteristics 4. United States—Intellectual life
ISBN 0-394-70513-0 (pa)
The first volume of the author's trilogy entitled: The Americans

"This study of colonial America attempts to show that it was not merely an offshoot of the mother country, but a new civilization. . . . The author centers his highly informative work on colonial education, the special qualities of American speech, and the growth of a distinct culture." Booklist
Includes bibliographical references

Demos, John, 1937-

The unredeemed captive; a family story from early America. Knopf 1994 315p maps hardcover o.p. paperback available $14

973.2

1. Williams, Eunice, 1696-1786 2. Williams family 3. Williams, John, 1664-1729 4. Mohawk Indians 5. Massachusetts—History—1600-1775, Colonial period

ISBN 0-679-75961-1 (pa)   LC 93-23907

John Williams, "a Puritan minister, and his family were captured in 1704 in their Massachusetts home by a group of Frenchmen and Native Americans, and forced to march to Canada. Although he and four of his children were later released, his wife died on the march and his daughter, Eunice, became a convert to Catholicism and married a Native American. Despite the ongoing attempts of her father and brother to persuade Eunice to return to Massachusetts, she would agree only to brief visits and lived in a Native American settlement until her death at the age of 95." Publ Wkly

This "is a lively introduction to an authentically multicultural colonial North America." N Y Times Book Rev

Earle, Alice Morse, 1851-1911

Child life in colonial days   **973.2**

1. United States—Social life and customs—1600-1775, Colonial period 2. Children—United States

Hardcover and paperback editions available from various publishers

Companion volume to Home life in colonial days (1898)

First published 1899 by Macmillan

An account of how children spent their days in school and at home

Hawke, David Freeman

Everyday life in early America. Harper & Row 1988 195p il (Everyday life in America) hardcover o.p. paperback available $13

973.2

1. United States—History—1600-1775, Colonial period 2. United States—Social life and customs

ISBN 0-06-091251-0 (pa)   LC 87-17667

The author "provides enlightening and colorful descriptions of early Colonial Americans and debunks many widely held assumptions about 17th century settlers." Publ Wkly

Includes bibliographical references

Lepore, Jill, 1966-

The name of war; King Philip's War and the origins of American identity. Knopf 1998 xxviii, 337p il maps hardcover o.p. paperback available $15   **973.2**

1. King Philip's War, 1675-1676 2. Native Americans—Wars 3. Great Britain—Colonies—America

ISBN 0-375-70262-8 (pa)   LC 97-2820

"Lepore's history of King Philip's War, deals with what happened in New England and what sense the participants and their heirs have made of it over the years." N Y Times Book Rev

"This is a powerful book that doesn't shy away from depicting the sheer horror of what must be termed a race war." Booklist

Includes bibliographical references

Schultz, Eric B., 1957-

King Philip's War; the history and legacy of America's forgotten conflict; [by] Eric B. Schultz, Michael J. Tougias. Countryman Press 1999 416p il maps hardcover o.p. paperback available $18.95   **973.2**

1. King Philip's War, 1675-1676 2. Native Americans—Government relations 3. New England—History—1600-1775, Colonial period

ISBN 0-88150-483-1 (pa)   LC 99-23481

The first part of this volume provides a "chronological retelling of the war. The second part, organized geographically and the heart of the volume, takes readers through New England to various sites associated with the conflict. . . . The third part offers three contemporary narratives reflecting the significance of the war on the people of the era. Useful maps assist the reader throughout." Libr J

Includes bibliographical references

973.3 United States—Periods of Revolution and Confederation, 1775-1789

The **American** Revolution; writings from the War of Independence. Library of Am. 2001 878p $40   **973.3**

1. United States—History—1775-1783, Revolution

ISBN 1-88301-191-4   LC 00-45373

This collection includes "over 120 pieces by more than 70 Revolution-era writers from both sides of the War of Independence. The book begins with Paul Revere's personal account of his famous ride in April 1775 and ends with a description of George Washington's resignation from the command of the Continental Army in December 1783. . . . At the book's end one can find a long section that includes a chronology, biographical sketches of the authors, and other notes on the texts." Libr J

"This work will serve as a marvelous research tool for specialists, but general readers with an interest in American history will also find fascinating gems." Booklist

Becker, Carl, 1873-1945

The Declaration of Independence; a study in the history of political ideas. Knopf 1942 286p hardcover o.p. paperback available $11

973.3

1. Jefferson, Thomas, 1743-1826 2. United States. Declaration of Independence 3. United States—Politics and government—1775-1783, Revolution

ISBN 0-394-70060-0 (pa)

A reprint, with a new preface, of a book first published 1922 by Harcourt Brace & Co.

"A study of the Declaration, the philosophy that lay behind it, the history of its several drafts, an estimate of its literary quality." Wis Libr Bull

Includes bibliographical references

Bobrick, Benson, 1947-

Angel in the whirlwind; the triumph of the American Revolution. Simon & Schuster 1997 553p o.p.; Penguin Bks. paperback available $15.95   **973.3**

1. United States—History—1775-1783, Revolution

ISBN 0-14-027500-2 (pa)   LC 97-11320

This survey of the American Revolution ranges "from the end of the French and Indian War to the end of the Revolutionary War, with brief coverage of the framing of the Constitution and the inauguration of Washington." Libr J

"Many of the stories are familiar—Paul Revere's ride, Arnold's descent into infamy—but the book's strength lies in its many lesser-known details on the battlefield and beyond. . . . Though the format demands only brief treatment of complicated issues, what emerges is a highly impressive show of exhaustive research and engaging storytelling." Publ Wkly

Includes bibliographical references

Calloway, Colin G. (Colin Gordon), 1953-

The American Revolution in Indian country; crisis and diversity in Native American communities. Cambridge Univ. Press 1995 xxiii, 327p il maps (Cambridge studies in North American Indian history) $55; pa $21   **973.3**

1. Native Americans—History 2. United States—History—1775-1783, Revolution

ISBN 0-521-47149-4; 0-521-47569-4 (pa)

LC 94-28669

This study presents "coverage of Indian experiences in the American Revolution. . . . Calloway focuses on eight Indian communities." Publisher's note

"This elegantly written and well-documented work's emphasis on Indian communities, rather than the exploits of native warriors on the battlefield, illuminates a theater of conflict that has largely been ignored in monographs about the American Revolution." Libr J

Cohen, I. Bernard, 1914-2003

Science and the founding fathers; science in the political thought of Jefferson, Franklin, Adams and Madison. Norton 1995 368p il hardcover o.p. paperback available $15.95

973.3

1. Franklin, Benjamin, 1706-1790 2. Jefferson, Thomas, 1743-1826 3. Madison, James, 1751-1836 4. Adams, John Quincy, 1767-1848 5. Political science 6. Science—United States—History

ISBN 0-393-31510-X (pa)   LC 94-26731

The author "analyzes how Thomas Jefferson, Benjamin Franklin, John Adams, and James Madison incorporated their scientific beliefs and knowledge into their political lives. Cohen examines each man's scientific education and then searches for examples of how that knowledge was expressed in their published works. He looks closely at phrases from the Declaration of Independence and the Constitution and shows that they have a Newtonian basis." Libr J

Draper, Theodore, 1912-

A struggle for power; the American Revolution. Times Bks. 1996 544p hardcover o.p. paperback available $13.56   **973.3**

1. United States—History—1775-1783, Revolution

ISBN 0-679-77642-7 (pa)   LC 95-11605

The author "maintains that the Revolution was really a power struggle spawned by the British system of chartering colonies, which placed fiscal control of public funds with the colonial assemblies." Libr J

This is an "elegantly written, masterful study. . . . Drawing freely on period pamphlets, letters, petitions, travelogues and assembly minutes, [the author] vividly evokes the populist discontent, intellectual gymnastics and mob violence that led to revolution." Publ Wkly

Includes bibliographical references

Dunn, Susan, 1945-

Sister revolutions; French lightning, American light. Faber & Faber 1999 258p il hardcover o.p. paperback available $14

973.3

1. United States—History—1775-1783, Revolution 2. France—History—1789-1799, Revolution

ISBN 0-571-19989-5 (pa)   LC 99-18178

"The American Revolution, according to Dunn, was more peaceful and practical, in part because its leaders were both intellectuals and men of political experience. The French Revolution, on the other hand, veered into extravagant abstractions because its leaders were intellectuals with litttle or no previous political experience. This book is clearly written and should appeal particularly to undergraduate students and members of the general public." Choice

Includes bibliographical references

Ferling, John E.

Setting the world ablaze; Washington, Adams, and Jefferson and the American Revolution; [by] John Ferling. Oxford Univ. Press 2000 xxiv, 392p il maps hardcover o.p. paperback available $19.95   **973.3**

1. Washington, George, 1732-1799 2. Adams, John, 1735-1826 3. Jefferson, Thomas, 1743-1826 4. United States—History—1775-1783, Revolution

ISBN 0-19-515084-8 (pa)   LC 99-89686

In this history Ferling profiles "the three men who were, in his view, the most important leaders of the American Revolution. Thomas Jefferson was the 'pen,' John Adams the 'tongue,' and George Washington the 'sword.' Ferling's command of the material is sure-footed, though not everyone will agree with his views." Libr J

Includes bibliographical references

Fischer, David Hackett

Paul Revere's ride. Oxford Univ. Press 1994 445p il maps $37.50; pa $19.95 **973.3**

1. Revere, Paul, 1735-1818 2. Lexington (Mass.), Battle of, 1775 3. Concord (Mass.), Battle of, 1775

ISBN 0-19-508847-6; 0-19-509831-5 (pa)

LC 93-25739

"Fischer's solid study of Paul Revere and his infamous ride debunks the myths surrounding the event, reconstructing the circumstances leading to the Battle of Lexington and Concord. Fischer's extensive use of primary sources affords an intimate glimpse of the participants' thoughts and feelings." Booklist

Includes bibliographical references

Foner, Eric

Tom Paine and Revolutionary America. Oxford Univ. Press 1976 xx, 326p il maps hardcover o.p. paperback available $26.95

973.3

1. Paine, Thomas, 1737-1809 2. United States—Politics and government—1775-1783, Revolution 3. United States—Economic conditions—1775-1783, Revolution 4. United States—Social conditions
ISBN 0-19-502182-7 (pa)   LC 75-25456
The author examines the roots of Paine's thought within the social, economic and political context of colonial America
Includes bibliographical references

Hibbert, Christopher, 1924-

Redcoats and rebels; the American Revolution through British eyes. Norton 1990 xx, 375p il maps hardcover o.p. paperback available $16.95   **973.3**

1. United States—History—1775-1783, Revolution
ISBN 0-393-32293-9 (pa)   LC 90-31753
Beginning with the Stamp Act of 1765 "the author interprets the War for Independence as viewed by the mother country: more a dirty insurrection than the sacred pursuit of liberty." Booklist
"Mr. Hibbert has an eye for the telling anecdote and the graphic quotation, and his bibliography indicates that he has consulted a wealth of manuscript material as well as research published during the last 30 years that illuminates what lay behind the British defeat." N Y Times Book Rev

Ketchum, Richard M., 1922-

Saratoga; turning point of America's Revolutionary War. Holt & Co. 1997 545p il maps hardcover o.p. paperback available $18   **973.3**

1. Saratoga Campaign, 1777
ISBN 0-8050-6123-1 (pa)   LC 97-2773
A "narrative account of the Saratoga campaign of 1777. . . . Ketchum provides the full political context within which the fighting took place while penning dozens of colorful portraits of the principal characters. The author also succeeds in his goal of telling the story from the perspective of the participants, illustrating what the American Revolution in upstate New York meant for soldiers and civilians alike." Libr J
Includes bibliographical references

Maier, Pauline, 1938-

American scripture; making the Declaration of Independence. Knopf 1997 xxi, 304p hardcover o.p. paperback available $14

973.3

1. United States. Declaration of Independence 2. United States—Politics and government—1775-1783, Revolution
ISBN 0-679-77908-6 (pa)   LC 97-2769
"In the spring of 1776, with a British invasion fleet on its way, the Second Continental Congress appointed a committee to compose a statement explaining America's decision to seek independence. Thomas Jefferson was the principal drafter of the statement, but Maier makes it clear that his task was to express the sentiments of the Congress, not his personal views, and she shows that when the congressmen edited his draft they improved it greatly (rather than 'mangling' it, as Jefferson ever after

maintained). The Declaration of Independence is, she argues, a profoundly collective document, both in its origins and in our still-evolving interpretation of its self-evident truths." New Yorker

Morgan, Edmund Sears

The birth of the Republic, 1763-89; [by] Edmund S. Morgan. 3rd ed. University of Chicago Press 1992 206p (Chicago history of American civilization) hardcover o.p. paperback available $13   **973.3**

1. United States—History—1775-1783, Revolution 2. United States—History—1783-1809
ISBN 0-226-53757-9 (pa)   LC 92-8871
First published 1956
A brief study of the American revolutionary period from 1763 to 1789
Includes bibliographical references

Raphael, Ray

A people's history of the American Revolution; how common people shaped the fight for independence. New Press 2001 386p $25.95   **973.3**

1. United States—History—1775-1783, Revolution
ISBN 1-56584-653-2   LC 00-62039
Also available in paperback from Perennial Bks.
This volume "collects the experiences of ordinary people during the American Revolution and sutures them into a story. And that story is that the rebellion and war inescapably influenced everyone—farmers, townspeople, women, Indians, free blacks and enslaved blacks, plutocrats and proletarians." Booklist
"Moving from broad overviews to stories of small groups or individuals, Raphael's study is impressive in both its sweep and its attention to the particular." Publ Wkly
Includes bibliographical references

Tuchman, Barbara Wertheim

The first salute; [by] Barbara W. Tuchman. Knopf 1988 347p il maps hardcover o.p. paperback available $14.95   **973.3**

1. United States—History—1775-1783, Revolution
ISBN 0-345-33667-4 (pa)   LC 88-45216
"'The first salute' accorded to the striped flag of the thirteen States was given by a Dutch colony, St. Eustatius, in November, 1776. The subject of this study is the contribution of the Dutch and the French, to the independence of the United States." West Coast Rev Books
"The book is a tightly woven narrative, ingeniously structured. It is not a blow-by-blow account of the conflict; familiarity with issues and events is assumed. Instead, Tuchman takes a specific incident and through it elucidates the course and outcome of the war." Christ Sci Monit
Includes bibliographical references

Wood, Gordon S.

The radicalism of the American Revolution. Knopf 1992 447p hardcover o.p. paperback available $16   **973.3**

1. United States—Politics and government—1775-1783, Revolution 2. United States—History—1775-1783, Revolution 3. United States—Social life and customs
ISBN 0-679-73688-3 (pa)   LC 91-19719
"Under the broad categories of monarchy, republicanism, and democracy, Wood explains how the US was

Wood, Gordon S.—*Continued*

transformed from a society that took for granted a nonworking elite and a dependent servile underclass to one in which the free-standing individualist, who worked for a living, became the norm. . . . [A] readable book based on hundreds of primary and secondary sources." Choice

Includes bibliographical references

973.4 United States—Constitutional period, 1789-1809

Ellis, Joseph J.

Founding brothers; the revolutionary generation. Knopf 2000 288p $26.95; pa $14   **973.4**

1. United States—History—1783-1809 2. United States—Politics and government—1783-1809 3. Presidents—United States 4. United States—Biography

ISBN 0-375-40544-5; 0-375-70524-4 (pa)

LC 99-59304

This study looks at the intertwined lives of "Benjamin Franklin, Thomas Jefferson, John Adams, Alexander Hamilton, James Madison and Aaron Burr. . . . As Ellis sees it, the founding brethren not only 'created the American republic' but 'held it together throughout the volatile and vulnerable early years by sustaining their presence until national habits and customs took root.'" NY Times Book Rev

"Ellis' essays are angled, fascinating, and perfect for general-interest readers." Booklist

Includes bibliographical references

Freeman, Joanne B.

Affairs of honor; national politics in the new republic. Yale Univ. Press 2001 xxiv, 376p $29.95; pa $16.95   **973.4**

1. United States—Politics and government—1783-1865

ISBN 0-300-08877-9; 0-300-09755-7 (pa)

LC 2001-915

According to Freeman, an "honor culture" structured the American founders' "political status before political parties developed. In those early years, she argues, 'the culture of honor met with a burgeoning democracy and an ambiguous egalitarian ethic of republicanism; the former questioned assumptions about political leadership, the latter renounced the trappings of aristocracy without offering a defined alternative.' . . . [Freeman describes] national politics in the new nation, devotes chapters to three major techniques wielded by political players—political gossip, 'a paper war,' and dueling—and then examines, as a case study, the 1800 presidential election." Booklist

"Freeman's prose is lively, and she balances entertaining narrative with sharp analysis." Publ Wkly

Includes bibliographical references

Hamilton, Alexander, 1757-1804

Writings. Library of Am. 2001 1108p $40   **973.4**

1. United States—Politics and government—1775-1783, Revolution 2. United States—Politics and government—1783-1809

ISBN 1-931082-04-9   LC 2001-23043

"The text consists of more than 170 letters, speeches, essays, reports, and memoranda written between 1769 and 1804, including all of Hamilton's material presented in The Federalist. This additionally sports several conflicting eyewitness accounts of Hamilton's lethal duel with Aaron Burr." Libr J

Includes bibliographical references

The **Louisiana** Purchase; a historical and geographical encyclopedia; Junius P. Rodriguez, editor. ABC-CLIO 2002 xxxv, 513p il maps $95   **973.4**

1. Louisiana Purchase 2. United States—History—1783-1809

ISBN 1-57607-188-X   LC 2002-3228

"The reasons for as well as the immediate and historical repercussions of the purchase are explored in nearly 300 articles written by 85 distinguished scholars. Coverage includes native peoples, noteworthy personalities, and geographical areas associated with a land acquisition that nearly doubled the size of our nation. An extensive bibliography, 49 pertinent documents, a chronology, and an index round out this excellent volume." Libr J

Miller, John Chester, 1907-1991

The Federalist era, 1789-1801. Harper & Row 1960 304p il map (New American nation series) o.p.; Waveland Press paperback available $15.50   **973.4**

1. Federal Party (U.S.) 2. United States—History—1783-1809

ISBN 1-57766-031-5 (pa)

A chronicle of the administrations of George Washington and John Adams, concentrating on the politics and diplomacy

Includes bibliographical references

Washington, George, 1732-1799

Writings. Library of Am. 1997 xxiii, 1149p $40   **973.4**

1. Virginia—History 2. United States—Politics and government—1775-1783, Revolution 3. United States—Politics and government—1783-1809

ISBN 1-883011-23-X   LC 96-9665

This "selection of Washington's letters, speeches, diary entries, maxims and military orders reveals a writer of surprising versatility and a statesman consciously involved with the forging of our national character." Publ Wkly

973.5 United States—1809-1845

Encyclopedia of the United States in the nineteenth century; Paul Finkelman, editor in chief. Scribner 2001 3v il maps set $400   **973.5**

1. United States—History—19th century—Encyclopedias

ISBN 0-684-80500-6   LC 00-45811

In this historical overview: "population, politics and government, economy and work, society and culture, religion, social problems and reform, everyday life, and foreign policy are explored in more than 600 A-to-Z articles. Complete with more than 400 illustrations and maps, this set includes . . . [a] year-by-year chronology, original documents [and] tables." Publisher's note

Miller, William Lee

Arguing about slavery; the great battle in the United States Congress. Knopf 1996 577p hardcover o.p. paperback available $17

973.5

1. Adams, John Quincy, 1767-1848 2. United States. Congress 3. Slavery—United States 4. United States—Politics and government—1815-1861
ISBN 0-679-76844-0 (pa) LC 95-35075
"In tracing the growing hostility between North and South over the extension of slavery into the Western territories, Miller pays special attention to the so-called gag rule, in force from 1834 to 1844, which blocked discussion of antislavery proposals in the House of Representatives. The central figure in Miller's study is John Quincy Adams, in his second career as U.S. representative from Massachusetts, and his heroic fight for repeal of the gag rule and for the right to petition Congress for the abolition of slavery." Publ Wkly
"Miller lays out the arcane workings of the proceedings with admirable detail, clarity, and verve." Christ Sci Monit
Includes bibliographical references

Molotsky, Irvin

The flag, the poet & the song; the story of the Star-Spangled Banner. Dutton 2001 240p il o.p.; Plume Bks. paperback available $13

973.5

1. Star spangled banner (Song) 2. Flags—United States 3. War of 1812
ISBN 0-452-28345-0 (pa) LC 2001-17325
Molotsky traces "the evolution of the song from an old English drinking song to its adoption in 1931 as the national anthem. And he gives us facts about the flag that challenge our long-held understanding of its genesis. . . . Personalities play a big part in Molotsky's treatment, with President and Dolly Madison, Francis Scott Key, and Mary Pickersgill (the real Betsy Ross) taking major roles. The War of 1812 gets well-deserved coverage as the historical scene for the unfolding of the anthem." Libr J
"Chock-full of humor, irony, and fun facts, this delightful tribute to the flag will appeal to a variety of inquisitive readers." Booklist
Includes bibliographical references

Oates, Stephen B., 1936-

The approaching fury; voices of the storm, 1820-1861; Buz Wyeth, editor. HarperCollins Pubs. 1997 495p hardcover o.p. paperback available $15

973.5

1. United States—History—1815-1861 2. United States—History—1861-1865, Civil War—Causes
ISBN 0-06-092885-9 (pa) LC 96-31965
Companion volume to The whirlwind of war
This work consists of a "series of dramatic autobiographical monologs relating 13 different voices and viewpoints on the coming of the Civil War, from Jefferson Davis's and Lincoln's agonizing over disunion in 1860-61. Turner, Harriet Beecher Stowe, Frederick Douglass, Mary Chestnut, and others make cameo appearances, but Henry Clay, John Calhoun, Stephen A. Douglas, Davis, and Lincoln dominate the discussion." Libr J
"Taken on its own terms, this book powerfully recreates some of the momentous events that produced the catastrophe of 1861. Mr. Oates succeeds in bringing his characters alive and in creating highly dramatic scenes for them to act out." N Y Times Book Rev
Includes bibliographical references

Remini, Robert Vincent, 1921-

Andrew Jackson & his Indian wars; [by] Robert V. Remini. Viking 2001 347p il maps hardcover o.p. paperback available $15

973.5

1. Jackson, Andrew, 1767-1845 2. Native Americans—Wars 3. Native Americans—Government relations 4. United States—Politics and government—1815-1861
ISBN 0-14-200128-7 (pa) LC 2001-17903
Remini's critical study of Andrew Jackson is offered as a "response to scholars who deplore Jackson's treatment of Indians. . . . Remini sees Jackson as 'a patriot' who did good as well as 'supposed evil.'" N Y Times Book Rev
"This provocative book is sure to create controversy for scholars, the Native American community and lay historians, among others." Publ Wkly
Includes bibliographical references

The Battle of New Orleans; [by] Robert V. Remini. Viking 1999 226p il maps hardcover o.p. paperback available $14 **973.5**

1. New Orleans (La.), Battle of, 1815
ISBN 0-14-100179-8 (pa) LC 99-19837
This "book establishes the War of 1812 historically as our second War of Independence, and describes its climactic battle in the maze of cypress swamps and bayous along the winding Mississippi. Remini, . . . unforgettably portrays individuals on both sides, and provides good maps to help us follow the action." New Yorker
Includes bibliographical references

Tocqueville, Alexis de

Democracy in America **973.5**

1. United States—Social conditions 2. United States—Politics and government 3. Democracy 4. American national characteristics
Hardcover and paperback editions available from various publishers
First part originally published in France, 1835; the second in 1840
Based partly on the French author's observations of American political and social conditions during a visit in 1831-1832. "It remains the best philosophical discussion of Democracy illustrated by the experience of the United States, up to the time when it was written, which can be found in any language." Pratt Alcove

973.7 United States—Administration of Abraham Lincoln, 1861-1865. Civil War

Blanton, DeAnne, 1964-

They fought like demons; women soldiers in the American Civil War; [by] DeAnne Blanton and Lauren M. Cook. Louisiana State Univ. Press 2002 277p il (Conflicting worlds) $29.95 **973.7**

1. Women soldiers 2. United States—History—1861-1865, Civil War
ISBN 0-8071-2806-6 LC 2002-4441
Also available in paperback from Vintage Bks.
"The authors reconstruct the reasons why women entered the armed forces: many were simply patriotic, while others followed their husbands or lovers and yet

Blanton, DeAnne, 1964-—*Continued*
others yearned to break free from the constraints that
Victorian society had laid on them as women. Blanton
and Cook detail women soldiers in combat, on the
march, in camp and in the hospital, where many were
discovered after getting sick. Some even wound up in
grim prisons kept by both sides, while a few hid pregnancies and were only discovered after giving birth. . . .
Solid research by the authors, including a look at the careers of a few women soldiers after the war, makes this
a compelling book that belongs in every Civil War library." Publ Wkly
Includes bibliographical references

Boatner, Mark Mayo, 1921-
The Civil War dictionary; by Mark Mayo
Boatner III; maps and diagrams by Allen C.
Northrop and Lowell I. Miller. rev ed.
McKay, D. 1988 974p maps o.p.; Vintage
Bks. paperback available $22   **973.7**
1. United States—History—1861-1865, Civil War—
Dictionaries
ISBN 0-679-73392-2 (pa)   LC 87-40599
First published 1959
"With more than 4,000 entries . . . this dictionary re-
mains the most comprehensive and consistently accurate
reference tool on the American Civil War. In addition to
the biographical sketches there are entries relating to
campaigns and battles, naval engagements, weapons, issues and incidents, military terms and definitions, politics, literature, and statistics." Choice
Includes bibliographical references

Catton, Bruce, 1899-1978
A stillness at Appomattox. Doubleday 1953
438p maps hardcover o.p. paperback available
$14.95   **973.7**
1. Appomattox Campaign, 1865 2. United States—
History—1861-1865, Civil War—Campaigns
ISBN 0-385-04451-8 (pa)
Also available in hardcover from P. Smith
Concluding volume of trilogy which began with Mr.
Lincoln's army (1951) and Glory road (1952). This final
volume of the author's study of the Army of the Poto-
mac covers the period from early 1864 to April, 1865
The author's "approach is judicious, his interpretation
unbiased and his coverage comprehensive." N Y Times
Book Rev
Includes bibliographical references

The **Causes** of the Civil War; edited by
Kenneth M. Stampp. 3rd rev ed. Simon &
Schuster 1991 255p pa $14   **973.7**
1. United States—History—1861-1865, Civil War—
Causes 2. United States—History—1861-1865, Civil
War—Sources
ISBN 0-671-75155-7   LC 91-36819
"A Touchstone book"
First published 1959 by Prentice-Hall
This book integrates the conclusions of various post-
war historians with the thoughts of contemporary com-
mentators like Jefferson Davis, Horace Greeley, and Lin-
coln. Political, cultural and economic aspects are empha-
sized
Includes bibliographical references

Coombe, Jack D.
Gunsmoke over the Atlantic; first naval
actions of the Civil War. Bantam Bks. 2002
268p il maps hardcover o.p. paperback
available $13.95   **973.7**
1. United States—History—1861-1865, Civil War—
Naval operations
ISBN 0-553-38073-7 (pa)   LC 2001-52677
The author "details selected maritime events that
aimed to enforce the Union blockade and combat the
weak but developing Confederate navy." Libr J
Includes bibliographical references

Daniel, Larry J., 1947-
Shiloh; the battle that changed the Civil
War. Simon & Schuster 1997 430p il map
hardcover o.p. paperback available $14

                                    973.7
1. Shiloh (Tenn.), Battle of, 1862
ISBN 0-684-83857-5 (pa)   LC 96-51539
"Before Antietam, Shiloh stood as the bloodiest engagement of the Civil War. The April 1862 battle did not
decide the war, as Daniel . . . recognizes, but it almost
ruined Gen. U.S. Grant, shook up the commands of both
Union and Confederate armies, and left the West open to
Union advances." Libr J
The author "has crafted a superbly researched volume
that will appeal to both the beginning Civil War reader
as well as those already familiar with the course of fighting in the wooded terrain bordering the Tennessee River." Publ Wkly
Includes bibliographical references

Davis, Burke, 1913-
Sherman's march. Random House 1980
335p il maps hardcover o.p. paperback
available $14   **973.7**
1. Sherman, William T. (William Tecumseh), 1820-
1891 2. United States—History—1861-1865, Civil
War—Campaigns
ISBN 0-394-75763-7 (pa)   LC 79-5550
The author "reconstructs Sherman's infamous, but
vastly consequential march through Georgia and the Carolinas, which sent the Confederacy into its death throes.
Basing his narrative on eyewitness accounts, Davis
brings the event down to a personal level." Booklist
Includes bibliographical references

To Appomattox; nine April days, 1865.
Rinehart 1959 433p il maps o.p.; Burford
Bks. paperback available $18.95   **973.7**
1. United States—History—1861-1865, Civil War
2. Appomattox Campaign, 1865
ISBN 1-58080-097-1 (pa)
"The story of the last nine days of the Civil War from
the march on Richmond to the surrender at Appomattox.
Quotations from diaries, letters, newspapers and military
reports create a sense of immediacy as the reader follows
each day's events in the city, in the Confederate camp,
and with the Union Army." Publ Wkly
Includes bibliographical references

Davis, William C., 1946-

Battle at Bull Run; a history of the first major campaign of the Civil War. Doubleday 1977 298p il maps o.p.; Louisiana State Univ. Press paperback available $17.95 **973.7**
1. Bull Run, 1st Battle of, 1861
ISBN 0-8071-0867-7 (pa)   LC 76-42322
In this account of the war's first major engagement Davis' "sketches of the commanders, which will particularly delight Civil War enthusiasts, delve into the officer's backgrounds and unusual characteristics and include critical appraisals of their leadership capabilities. In addition, Davis includes fascinating human interest stories about the troops." Libr J
Includes bibliographical references

An honorable defeat; the last days of the Confederate government. Harcourt 2001 496p il maps $30; pa $16   **973.7**
1. Davis, Jefferson, 1808-1889 2. Breckinridge, John Cabell, 1821-1875 3. Confederate States of America
ISBN 0-15-100564-8; 0-15-600748-7 (pa)
LC 00-46143
This is an account of "the contentious relationship of two men . . . Jefferson Davis, the stubborn, imperious, and delusional leader of the Rebel forces, and the sensible and personable John C. Breckenridge, Davis's Secretary of War." Libr J
Davis "knows his two principal players well, and a marvelous supporting cast of politicians and soldiers helps him to fashion a story rich in pathos and humor." N Y Times Book Rev
Includes bibliographical references

Eicher, David J., 1961-

The longest night; a military history of the Civil War; foreword by James M. McPherson; maps by Lee Vande Visse. Simon & Schuster 2001 990p maps $40; pa $22   **973.7**
1. United States—History—1861-1865, Civil War—Campaigns
ISBN 0-684-84944-5; 0-684-84945-3 (pa)
LC 2001-34153
An account of battles and military strategies in the Civil War
"Civil War buffs and military history scholars will find Eicher's superb analyses and original insights into oft-neglected theaters of operations extremely valuable. An important work that will be an essential component of Civil War collections." Booklist
Includes bibliographical references

Encyclopedia of the American Civil War; a political, social, and military history; David S. Heidler and Jeanne T. Heidler, editors; foreword by James W. McPherson; David J. Coles, associate editor; Gary W. Gallagher, James M. McPherson, Mark E. Neely, Jr., editorial board. ABC-CLIO 2000 5v il maps set $425   **973.7**
1. United States—History—1861-1865, Civil War—Encyclopedias
ISBN 1-57607-066-2   LC 00-11195
Also available in a one-volume edition from Norton
"The editors have compiled a comprehensive source that provides a first-stop reference on broad areas or specific topics on the Civil War. The contemporary photographs and lithographs bring the human element into the encyclopedia, a type of reference known more for facts and figures than emotions. The primary-source-documents volume brings obscure resources together, which will further illumine the period for students."—"Outstanding Reference Sources." American Libraries, May 2001

Faust, Drew Gilpin

Mothers of invention; women of the slaveholding South in the American Civil War. University of N.C. Press 1996 326p il $37.50   **973.7**
1. United States—History—1861-1865, Civil War—Women 2. Women—Southern States
ISBN 0-8078-2255-8   LC 95-8896
Also available in paperback from Vintage Bks.
Based on journals, letters and memoirs, this is an "analysis of the impact of secession, invasion and conquest on Southern white women. Antebellum images based on helplessness and dependence were challenged as women assumed an increasing range of social and economic responsibilities. . . . Faust's provocative analysis of a complex subject merits a place in all collections of U.S. history." Publ Wkly
Includes bibliographical references

Foote, Shelby

The Civil War; a narrative. Random House 1958-1974 3v maps set $165; pa $75   **973.7**
1. United States—History—1861-1865, Civil War
ISBN 0-394-49517-9; 0-394-74913-8
Volumes also available separately
Contents: v1 Fort Sumter to Perryville; v2 Fredericksburg to Meridian; v3 Red River to Appomattox
"In objectivity, in range, in mastery of detail, in beauty of language and feeling for the people involved, this work surpasses anything else on the subject." New Repub
Includes bibliographical references

Freeman, Douglas Southall, 1886-1953

Lee's lieutenants; a study in command. Scribner Classics 1997 3v il maps ea $40   **973.7**
1. United States—History—1861-1865, Civil War—Campaigns 2. United States—History—1861-1865, Civil War—Biography 3. Confederate States of America
ISBN 0-684-83783-8 (v1); 0-684-83784-6 (v2); 0-684-83785-4 (v3)   LC 97-151696
Also available in a one-volume abridged edition in hardcover and paperback
Reissue of the set first published 1942-1944
Contents: v1 Manassas to Malvern Hill; v2 Cedar Mountain to Chancellorsville; v3 Gettysburg to Appomattox
A "detailed treatment of the military history of the Civil War as seen through the performance of the Confederate officers. The clarity of Freeman's description of battles lies in his use of only the information known to the Confederate officers at the time of the battle." Enoch Pratt Free Libr
Includes bibliographical references

Furgurson, Ernest B., 1929-

Chancellorsville, 1863; the souls of the brave. Knopf 1992 405p il maps hardcover o.p. paperback available $16   **973.7**
1. Chancellorsville (Va.), Battle of, 1863
ISBN 0-679-72831-7 (pa)   LC 91-47059
Furgurson presents an account of "the battle's separate phases, the strategic thinking on both sides, the confusion and hesitation in Richmond and Washington, and the events surrounding Stonewall Jackson's death." Choice
"Mr. Furgurson has written what should become the standard account of the battle. He is especially good at discussing both larger tactical issues and the experiences of ordinary soldiers. He is also evenhanded." N Y Times Book Rev
Includes bibliographical references

Not war but murder; Cold Harbor, 1864. Knopf 2000 328p il maps hardcover o.p. paperback available $14   **973.7**
1. Cold Harbor (Va.), Battle of, 1864
ISBN 0-679-78139-0 (pa)   LC 99-37147
"On June 3, 1864, the Union Second, Sixth, and Eighteenth Corps assaulted Confederate breastworks at Cold Harbor outside Richmond, VA. The resulting bloodbath amounted to U.S. Grant's worst defeat and 'Bobby' Lee's final great victory. . . . [Furgurson] re-tells the well-known story of how the friction between Grant and his insecure direct subordinate, George Meade, poisoned the Army of the Potomac's whole chain of command." Libr J
The author's "engagement with the people he writes about comes through in every line, making one of the most wrenching incidents of the war grimly immediate." Publ Wkly
Includes bibliographical references

Gallagher, Gary W.

The Confederate War. Harvard Univ. Press 1997 218p il hardcover o.p. paperback available $15.95   **973.7**
1. United States—History—1861-1865, Civil War
2. Confederate States of America
ISBN 0-674-16056-8 (pa)   LC 97-2495
This is a "historiographical study of the arguments over why the South lost the Civil War. [Gallagher] ad-dresses various explanations—lack of a sense of national-ity, guilt over slavery, low morale (especially among women), and the heavy casualties caused by Lee's offen-sive strategy." Booklist
This book "is the best thing that has happened to Con-federate historiography in many years. Gallagher has a more thorough command of the sources for Confederate history than any other historian I have read and he brings that mastery to bear in a concise, hard-hitting book." NY Rev Books
Includes bibliographical references

Horwitz, Tony, 1958-

Confederates in the attic; dispatches from the unfinished Civil War. Pantheon Bks. 1998 406p map hardcover o.p. paperback available $14.95   **973.7**
1. United States—History—1861-1865, Civil War
ISBN 0-679-75833-X (pa)   LC 97-26759
According to Horwitz's "chronicle of his tour of the Old South, many people have yet to make peace with the past. In a South Carolina town, whites relate to Horwitz their pride in the 'lost cause,' even equating southern

valor with the courage of Martin Luther King; a black preacher explains that affection for the 'cause' strikes him as an endorsement of slavery. Esteemed Civil War scholar Shelby Foote strives to explain the origins of the Klan as the reaction to a perceived foreign occupation." Booklist
This "is the work of a skilled journalist looking at how—and why—the War Between the States continues to live in so many issues still with us." Libr J

Klein, Maury, 1939-

Days of defiance; Sumter, secession, and the coming of the Civil War. Knopf 1997 496p il hardcover o.p. paperback available $16   **973.7**
1. United States—History—1861-1865, Civil War
ISBN 0-679-76882-3 (pa)   LC 96-39156
This is "a study of the months between Abraham Lin-coln's election and the outbreak of hostilities at Fort Sumter on April 12, 1861." New Leader
"With a novelist's skill, Klein has crafted an engross-ing portrait of the nation's descent into chaos and war." Publ Wkly
Includes bibliographical references

Leckie, Robert

None died in vain; the saga of the American Civil War. HarperCollins Pubs. 1990 682p maps hardcover o.p. paperback available $20   **973.7**
1. United States—History—1861-1865, Civil War
ISBN 0-06-092116-1 (pa)   LC 89-45832
This account of the Civil War examines contributing social, political and economic causes, recounts major and minor battles, and provides biographical information about key people
Includes bibliographical references

Leonard, Elizabeth D.

All the daring of the soldier; women of the Civil War armies. Norton 1999 368p il o.p.; Penguin Bks. paperback available $15   **973.7**
1. Women soldiers 2. United States—History—1861-1865, Civil War
ISBN 0-14-029858-4 (pa)   LC 98-52304
The author presents "stories of dozens of women who served in both the Union and Confederacy during the Civil War. Some were spies, but many more adopted men's names, dressed in men's clothes and lived and fought and died alongside mostly unsuspecting men." Publ Wkly
Includes bibliographical references

The **Library** of Congress Civil War desk reference; Margaret E. Wagner, Gary W. Gallagher, and Paul Finkelman, editors; foreword by James M. McPherson. Simon & Schuster 2002 xxv, 949p il maps $45   **973.7**
1. United States—History—1861-1865, Civil War
ISBN 0-684-86350-2   LC 2002-75465
"A Grand Central Press book"
"Beginning with the antebellum period, the 13 chap-ters cover topics such as 'Wartime Politics,' 'Battles and Battlefields,' 'Medical Care and Medicine,' 'The Home Front,' and 'The Civil War in Literature and the Arts.'. . . The chapters end with bibliographies of sources, and a massive bibliography provides even more

The Library of Congress Civil War desk reference—*Continued*

resources. . . . With its solid scholarship, informative approach, and broad sweep, [this] is an excellent source for school, academic, and public libraries. . . . Highly recommended for all Civil War collections." Booklist

Lincoln, Abraham, 1809-1865

Speeches and writings; speeches, letters, and miscellaneous writings. Library of Am. 1989 2v ea $35   **973.7**
1. United States—Politics and government—1861-1865 2. United States—Politics and government—1815-1861

Also available in an abridged one-volume paperback edition from Vintage Bks. with title: Selected speeches and writings

Contents: v1 1832-1858 (ISBN 0-940450-43-7); v2 1859-1865 (ISBN 0-940450-63-1)

These volumes are based upon The collected works of Abraham Lincoln (1953). Included are all seven of the Lincoln-Douglas debates, political speeches, business and personal letters, poems, and telegrams to generals in the field

"Replete with extremely helpful notes on the texts and an extensive chronology, this edition makes a momentous and thrilling addition to any . . . library." N Y Times Book Rev

Macdonald, John, 1945-

Great battles of the Civil War; foreword by John Keegan. Macmillan 1988 200p il maps $39.95   **973.7**
1. United States—History—1861-1865, Civil War—Campaigns

ISBN 0-02-577300-3   LC 88-1782

The author "has selected 17 crucial Civil War engagements and applied computer mapping to their geography. . . . The cartography is accompanied by an intelligent text, clear graphs of force and loss ratios, and well-chosen illustrations. This unique Civil War atlas is valuable, if not indispensable, for library collections." Libr J

McPherson, James M.

Abraham Lincoln and the second American Revolution. Oxford Univ. Press 1991 173p hardcover o.p. paperback available $13.95   **973.7**
1. Lincoln, Abraham, 1809-1865 2. United States—History—1861-1865, Civil War

ISBN 0-19-507606-0 (pa)   LC 90-6885

The author "examines Lincoln's role in the transformation wrought by the Civil War—the liberation of four million slaves, the overthrow of the social and political order of the South." Publ Wkly

Includes bibliographical references

Battle cry of freedom; the Civil War era. Oxford Univ. Press 1988 904p il maps (Oxford history of the United States) $47.50; pa $18.95   **973.7**
1. United States—History—1861-1865, Civil War

ISBN 0-19-503863-0; 0-19-516895-X (pa)
     LC 87-11045

A narrative history of events from the Mexican War through Appomattox. The author describes military campaigns, tactics and leaders. How the war changed the American political, social and economic landscape is explored

This volume "is comprehensive yet succinct, scholarly without being pedantic, eloquent but unrhetorical. It is compellingly readable." N Y Times Book Rev

Includes bibliographical references

Drawn with the sword; reflections on the American Civil War. Oxford Univ. Press 1996 258p hardcover o.p. paperback available $16.95   **973.7**
1. Stowe, Harriet Beecher, 1811-1896. Uncle Tom's cabin 2. United States—History—1861-1865, Civil War

ISBN 0-19-511796-4 (pa)   LC 95-38107

A collection of "essays on some of the most thought-provoking questions of the Civil War. All of the essays were published earlier but have been updated and revised for this compilation. The topics deal with such subjects as the origins of the Civil War, the slavery question in both North and South, why the North won the war and why the South lost, President Abraham Lincoln, and the change in historical writing." Libr J

"These pieces provide a lively reminder that the best scholarship is also often a pleasure to read." N Y Times Book Rev

For cause and comrades; why men fought in the Civil War. Oxford Univ. Press 1997 237p $25; pa $15.95   **973.7**
1. Soldiers—United States 2. United States—History—1861-1865, Civil War

ISBN 0-19-509023-3; 0-19-512499-5 (pa)
     LC 96-24760

"Volumes have been written on the causes of the Civil War, but less has been written on what caused soldiers to risk their lives on the battlefield. McPherson . . . fills the gap. After studying thousands of letters and diaries, he discusses what really led soldiers to enlist, what kept them in the army, and what led them to the front lines." Libr J

Includes bibliographical references

Oates, Stephen B., 1936-

The whirlwind of war; voices of the storm, 1861-1865. HarperCollins Pubs. 1998 846p hardcover o.p. paperback available $18.95   **973.7**
1. United States—History—1861-1865, Civil War

ISBN 0-06-093092-6 (pa)   LC 97-51171

Companion volume to The approaching fury

Oates "tells the conflict's story through reconstructed first-person narratives, . . . writing in the voices and from the viewpoints of 10 well-known figures." Publ Wkly

Paludan, Phillip S., 1938-

The presidency of Abraham Lincoln; [by] Phillip Shaw Paludan. University Press of Kan. 1994 xx, 384p (American presidency series) $29.95; pa $15.95   **973.7**
1. Lincoln, Abraham, 1809-1865 2. United States—Politics and government—1861-1865

ISBN 0-7006-0671-8; 0-7006-0745-5 (pa)
     LC 93-46830

The author "traces the year-by-year chronology of a Presidency engaged with recruiting, placating, appeasing and coercing the various and competing factions of the war years, and sees in Lincoln 'a commitment to the po-

Paludan, Phillip S., 1938-—_Continued_

litical-constitutional system that would itself move the nation toward its highest ambitions.' . . . Equally interesting is Mr. Paludan's depiction of how the war transformed the national Government, not only establishing the foundations for the Gilded Age but more subtly strengthening and enriching the role of government." NY Times Book Rev

Includes bibliographical references

Perry, Mark, 1950-

Conceived in liberty; Joshua Chamberlain, William Oates, and the American Civil War. Viking 1997 500p il maps hardcover o.p. paperback available $15.95   **973.7**

1. Chamberlain, Joshua Lawrence, 1828-1914 2. Oates, William C., 1835-1910 3. Gettysburg (Pa.), Battle of, 1863 4. United States—History—1861-1865, Civil War

ISBN 0-14-024797-1 (pa)   LC 97-24284

The author "presents the life and times of two men who met in battle at Little Round Top on Gettysburg's second day. . . . The account of the two officers' pre- and postwar careers is strong and gripping. That, and a look at the prevalent trends of the time that shaped Oates and Chamberlain, makes this a worthwhile purchase and enjoyable reading for Civil War buffs." Libr J

Includes bibliographical references

Sears, Stephen W.

Chancellorsville. Houghton Mifflin 1996 593p hardcover o.p. paperback available $17   **973.7**

1. Chancellorsville (Va.), Battle of, 1863

ISBN 0-395-87744-X (pa)   LC 96-31220

In this history of the campaign that ended in Chancellorsville, the author argues that "a chain of errors, assumptions, and communications failures combined with the genuine brilliance and good luck of the Confederates to lead to a stinging if indecisive Union defeat." Booklist

Includes bibliographical references

Landscape turned red; the Battle of Antietam. Ticknor & Fields 1983 431p il maps o.p.; Mariner Bks. paperback available $16   **973.7**

1. Antietam (Md.), Battle of, 1862

ISBN 0-618-34419-5 (pa)   LC 82-19519

This "account of the Battle of Antietam, the bloodiest day of the Civil War, is wide-ranging, detailed, and copiously documented. Stephen Sears . . . describes the tension-filled days preceding September 17, 1862, especially the political climate of Union pessimism and Confederate optimism. . . . The battle itself is then exhaustively recounted." Booklist

Includes bibliographical references

To the gates of Richmond; the Peninsula Campaign. Ticknor & Fields 1992 468p il maps o.p.; Mariner Bks. paperback available $16   **973.7**

1. Peninsular Campaign, 1862

ISBN 0-618-12713-5 (pa)   LC 92-6923

"The campaign on the peninsula between the James and York rivers in Virginia in the spring of 1862 was McClellan's major strategic effort and the first major Union offensive in the East. . . . Sears does an outstanding job in making intelligible an extremely complex campaign." Booklist

Includes bibliographical references

Tobin, Jacqueline, 1950-

Hidden in plain view; the secret story of quilts and the underground railroad; [by] Jacqueline L. Tobin and Raymond G. Dobard. Doubleday 1999 208p il map $27.50; pa $14   **973.7**

1. Underground railroad 2. Ciphers 3. Quilts

ISBN 0-385-49137-9; 0-385-49767-9 (pa)

LC 98-49804

The authors present the "theory that slaves created quilts coded with patterns to help one another flee to freedom." N Y Times Book Rev

This is "a needed and valuable contribution to the literature of African American culture." Libr J

Includes bibliographical references

Trudeau, Noah Andre, 1949-

Gettysburg: a testing of courage. HarperCollins Pubs. 2002 xx, 694p maps $34.95; pa $18.95   **973.7**

1. Gettysburg (Pa.), Battle of, 1863

ISBN 0-06-019363-8; 0-06-093186-8 (pa)

LC 2002-514159

This history of the Battle of Gettysburg "begins on May 15, 1863, and describes in minute detail the events leading up to the battle, the battle itself (often hour by hour), and Lee's retreat in the early hours of July 4. Trudeau . . . intertwines his narrative with firsthand accounts using letters, diaries, memoirs, and after-action reports from local residents, soldiers, and officers. . . . A monumental work, thoroughly researched and well written, this is the best recent single-volume history of the campaign." Libr J

Includes bibliographical references

Like men of war; black troops in the Civil War, 1862-1865. Little, Brown 1998 xxii, 548p il maps $29.95; pa $18   **973.7**

1. African American soldiers 2. United States—History—1861-1865, Civil War

ISBN 0-316-85325-9; 0-316-85344-5 (pa)

LC 97-15380

A "study of the battlefield experiences of black Union regiments. Some 60 maps help the reader make sense of famous engagements (Fort Wagner and the Crater) and notorious incidents (Fort Pillow) in which black soldiers fought, as well as scores of lesser-known clashes. Rich archival research is integrated into a lively narrative that places the raising and deployment of black regiments in broader contexts. This book will become a basic source of information on the subject." Libr J

Includes bibliographical references

Ward, Geoffrey C.

The Civil War; an illustrated history; [by] Geoffrey C. Ward with Ken Burns and Ric Burns. Knopf 1990 425p il maps $75; pa $29.95   **973.7**

1. United States—History—1861-1865, Civil War

ISBN 0-394-56285-2; 0-679-74277-8 (pa)

LC 89-43475

The authors aim to "present the war as the central defining event of American history and of the lives of those Americans caught up in it. In four separate, additional essays, professional historians briefly discuss the causes of the war, emancipation, the politics of the war, and its long-term meaning." Libr J

"A companion to a nine-part Public Broadcasting System documentary, this superbly designed book easily stands on its own." N Y Times Book Rev

Includes bibliographical references

Wert, Jeffry D.

Gettysburg, day three. Simon & Schuster 2001 448p il maps $27.50; pa $16 **973.7**
1. Gettysburg (Pa.), Battle of, 1863
ISBN 0-684-85914-9; 0-684-85915-7 (pa)
LC 2001-31071
The author re-creates "the confusing vortex of battle as he shifts his descriptions from sector to sector. He interweaves experiences of individual soldiers with the broader tactical moves of the familiar command icons such as Lee, Longstreet, Hancock, and Meade. . . . This work will be an excellent addition to Civil War collections." Booklist
Includes bibliographical references

Mosby's Rangers. Simon & Schuster 1990 384p il hardcover o.p. paperback available $14 **973.7**
1. Confederate States of America. Army. Virginia Cavalry Battalion, 43rd 2. United States—History—1861-1865, Civil War
ISBN 0-671-74745-2 (pa)
LC 90-37917
In this "history of Mosby's Rangers, one of the most successful irregular army units to operate during the Civil War, Wert details the guerrilla group's exploits which provided Jeb Stuart and Robert E. Lee with valuable intelligence on the enemy's movements." Booklist
"Well-researched, objectively written, this is a first-class history." Publ Wkly
Includes bibliographical references

White, Ronald C. (Ronald Cedric), 1939-

Lincoln's greatest speech; the second inaugural; {by} Ronald C. White Jr. Simon & Schuster 2002 254p il hardcover o.p. paperback available $14 **973.7**
1. Lincoln, Abraham, 1809-1865 2. Presidents—United States—Inaugural addresses
ISBN 0-7432-1299-1 (pa)
LC 2001-54234
"White breaks down the speech phrase by phrase, then integrates it according to its rhetorical framework of past, present, and future. He seeks sources for the speech's ideas in Lincoln's ambiguous stance toward organized religion, in the sermons of preachers he listened to, and in his Bible-reading habit. . . . Must-have Lincolnalia." Booklist
Includes bibliographical references

Wiley, Bell Irvin, 1906-

The life of Billy Yank; the common soldier of the Union. Bobbs-Merrill 1952 454p il **973.7**
1. United States. Army—Military life 2. United States—History—1861-1865, Civil War
Available in hardcover and paperback from Louisiana State Univ. Press
"The soldiers' own writings—their letters and diaries—are . . . used as chief source for a picture of the response of the Union men to the call to arms, their training, army life, reactions to Southerners they encountered, opinions of Negroes, and comments on their Reb counterparts." Booklist
Includes bibliographical references

The life of Johnny Reb; the common soldier of the Confederacy. Bobbs-Merrill 1943 444p **973.7**
1. Confederate States of America. Army—Military life 2. United States—History—1861-1865, Civil War
Available in hardcover and paperback from Louisiana State Univ. Press

"Composite biography of the ordinary soldier of the Confederacy—his behavior in camp and under fire, his food, clothing, weapons, religion, amusements, attitude toward women, and so on. Taken mostly from firsthand accounts in letters, diaries, and records." New Yorker
Includes bibliographical references

Wills, Garry, 1934-

Lincoln at Gettysburg; the words that remade America. Simon & Schuster 1992 317p hardcover o.p. paperback available $14 **973.7**
1. Lincoln, Abraham, 1809-1865
ISBN 0-671-86742-3 (pa)
LC 92-3546
Also available G. K. Hall large print edition
The author "argues that in the Gettysburg Address Abraham Lincoln, with consummate skill, changed the Constitution from within, making the hope it embodies triumph over its words by insinuating the ringing affirmation of equality from the Declaration of Independence into people's minds as the foundation of the American Government." N Y Times Book Rev
This is a "tour de force that will cause much discussion and argument." Libr J
Includes bibliographical references

Winik, Jay, 1957-

April 1865; the month that saved America. HarperCollins Pubs. 2001 461p il maps $32.50; pa $14.95 **973.7**
1. United States—History—1861-1865, Civil War
ISBN 0-06-018723-9; 0-06-093088-8 (pa)
LC 2001-336531
Also available G. K. Hall large print edition
Winik reflects on the significance of three pivotal events in April 1865: the fall of Richmond, the surrender at Appomattox, and the assassination of Abraham Lincoln
Winik "has written a provocative account. . . . He suggests that the assassination of Lincoln could have triggered a coup in the North, and his insights into the on-again, off-again 'peace' negotiations are incisive. Scholars and Civil War buffs may disagree with some of his assertions, but this fast moving, well-written chronicle will highlight obscure aspects of the war and stimulate further controversy." Booklist
Includes bibliographical references

973.8 United States—Reconstruction period, 1865-1901

Connell, Evan S., 1924-

Son of the Morning Star. North Point Press 1984 441p il hardcover o.p. paperback available $16 **973.8**
1. Custer, George Armstrong, 1839-1876 2. Little Bighorn, Battle of the, 1876
ISBN 0-86547-510-5 (pa)
LC 84-60681
The author "explores the whole context of the defeat of General Custer at the Battle of the Little Bighorn." Booklist
This book is "impressive in its massive presentation of information, and in the conclusions it draws about the probable events that led to the fracas on the banks of the Little Bighorn. But its strength lies in the way the author has shaped his material." N Y Times Book Rev
Includes bibliographical references

Diner, Steven J., 1944-

A very different age; Americans of the progressive era. Hill & Wang 1997 320p hardcover o.p. paperback available $14

973.8

1. Progressivism (United States politics) 2. United States—History—20th century

ISBN 0-8090-1611-7 (pa)   LC 97-3801

The author examines the "social, economic, political, and other changes experienced by Americans during the first two decades of the 20th century. . . . The writing is succinct and fluid. . . . This rewarding social history is an excellent book for both experienced historians and novices." Libr J

Includes bibliographical references

Foner, Eric

Reconstruction; America's unfinished revolution, 1863-1877. HarperCollins Pubs. 1988 xxvii, 690p il maps hardcover o.p. paperback available $23.95   **973.8**

1. Reconstruction (1865-1876) 2. United States—History—1865-1898

ISBN 0-06-093716-5 (pa)   LC 87-45615

Also available in hardcover from P. Smith

"Incorporating much eyewitness material, this book emphasizes the centrality of the Black experience. The book also examines the themes of race and class, the remodeling of Southern society, and the national context. A complete, modern, scholarly text." N Y Public Libr Book of How & Where to Look It Up

Includes bibliographical references

Franklin, John Hope, 1915-

Reconstruction after the Civil War. 2nd ed. University of Chicago Press 1994 265p (Chicago history of American civilization) hardcover o.p. paperback available $16

973.8

1. Reconstruction (1865-1876) 2. United States—History—1865-1898

ISBN 0-226-26079-8 (pa)   LC 94-27366

First published 1961

This is an "account of American life in a time of great challenge, unfamiliar problems, and uncertain leadership. Discusses the Radicals' effort to secure racial justice in the South, the fact that corruption existed not only in the South, and that some worthwhile measures emerged from 'carpetbag' legislatures." Guide to Read in Am Hist [review of 1961 edition]

Includes bibliographical references

Sandoz, Mari, 1896-1966

The Battle of the Little Bighorn. Lippincott 1966 191p maps (Great battles of history series) o.p.; University of Neb. Press paperback available $9.95   **973.8**

1. Custer, George Armstrong, 1839-1876 2. Little Bighorn, Battle of the, 1876

ISBN 0-8032-9100-0 (pa)

"An account of the United States Army expedition against the Sioux Nation with emphasis on the political motives and ambitions of General Custer." Publ Wkly

Includes bibliographical references

Schlereth, Thomas J.

Victorian America; transformations in everyday life, 1876-1915. HarperCollins Pubs. 1991 363p (Everyday life in America) hardcover o.p. paperback available $15

973.8

1. United States—Social life and customs

ISBN 0-06-092160-9 (pa)   LC 89-46555

The author surveys the objects, events, experiences, products and tastes that comprised what he terms America's Victorian culture (1876-1915) and shows how its values shaped modern life

"What a wonderful book. . . . Schlereth is no wry compiler of trivia. His analysis of social context reveals truly profound, intangible transformations in how and where Americans spent their time during four pivotal decades." Booklist

Includes bibliographical references

Stampp, Kenneth M. (Kenneth Milton)

The era of reconstruction, 1865-1877. Knopf 1965 228p o.p.; Random House paperback available $9.56   **973.8**

1. Reconstruction (1865-1876) 2. United States—Politics and government—1865-1898

ISBN 0-394-70388-X (pa)

A political history of the brief "radical" rule in the post Civil War South

Includes bibliographical references

Utley, Robert Marshall, 1929-

Custer: cavalier in buckskin; {by} Robert M. Utley. rev ed. University of Okla. Press 2001 176p il map $29.95; pa $17.95   **973.8**

1. Custer, George Armstrong, 1839-1876 2. Native Americans—Wars 3. West (U.S.)—History

ISBN 0-8061-3347-3; 0-8061-3387-2 (pa)

                       LC 2001-27356

First published 1988 with title: Cavalier in buckskin

The author offers theories and facts regarding the mythology surrounding Custer, telling how he promoted himself as an American hero in an effort to increase his rank in the army

This "is a fair and full-bodied account that cogently interprets the facts, provides the proper psychological analysis, and offers solid grounding for the development of the considerable myth." Booklist {review of 1988 edition}

Includes bibliographical references

Welch, James, 1940-2003

Killing Custer; the Battle of the Little Bighorn and the fate of the Plains Indians; by James Welch with Paul Stekler. Norton 1994 320p il $25   **973.8**

1. Little Bighorn, Battle of the, 1876 2. Native Americans—Wars

ISBN 0-393-03657-X   LC 94-5617

Also available in paperback from Penguin Bks.

"Welch produced this history of the Indian wars of the northern plains as a by-product of his work scripting a television documentary on the Battle of the Little Bighorn. In addition to military history, it contains long sections describing the life of the Plains Indians, accounts of contemporary Indian radical groups, and Welch's reactions while visiting the various historic sites in the area." Libr J

Includes bibliographical references

973.9 United States—1901-

American decades. Gale Res. 1994-2000 10v
set $995   **973.9**
1. United States—Civilization 2. United States—History—20th century
ISBN 0-7876-5076-5
Also available CD-ROM version
"A Manly, Inc. book"
The set is divided as follows: 1900-1909 (ISBN 0-8103-5722-4); 1910-1919 (ISBN 0-8103-5723-2); 1920-1929 (ISBN 0-8103-5724-0); 1930-1939 (ISBN 0-8103-5725-9); 1940-1949 (ISBN 0-8103-5726-7); 1950-1959 (ISBN 0-8103-5727-5); 1960-1969 (ISBN 0-8103-8883-9); 1970-1979 (ISBN 0-8103-8882-0); 1980-1989 (ISBN 0-8103-8881-2); 1990-1999 (ISBN 0-7876-4030-1)
"A series of volumes covering the twentieth century by decades. . . . Fun to browse, each volume is divided into 13 sections covering topics such as the arts, government and politics, lifestyles and social trends, medicine and health, and sports. Each section opens with a chronology and overview and closes with short biographies, deaths, and a bibliography of important books published in the decade. Sidebars highlight events and prominent individuals." Am Libr

Evans, Harold
The American century; by Harold Evans with Gail Buckland and Kevin Baker. Knopf 1998 xxiii, 710p il $60; pa $35   **973.9**
1. United States—History—20th century 2. United States—Politics and government—20th century
ISBN 0-679-41070-8; 0-375-70938-X (pa)
LC 96-7449
This narrative history of the United States spans the years 1889-1989
This "compilation is a family album for all Americans to ponder; it smartly emphasizes the contributions of men and women other than presidents and top politicians, although these leaders are not slighted. The chapters are thematic, forthrightly exploring such overarching ideas as capitalism vs. communism, the contributions of immigrants, the struggle for civil rights, and the rise of conservatism at the century's close. Accompanying the text are 900 unforgettable (and many rarely seen) photographs." Libr J
Includes bibliographical references

Galbraith, John Kenneth, 1908-
Name-dropping; from F.D.R. on. Houghton Mifflin 1999 194p $26; pa $14   **973.9**
1. Politicians—United States 2. United States—Politics and government—20th century
ISBN 0-395-82288-2; 0-618-15453-1 (pa)
LC 99-20070
The author "reminisces about important figures with whom he has been involved in his long and distinguished life in the public arena. Among the brief portraits are those of Franklin and Eleanor Roosevelt, Harry Truman, JFK, LBJ, Nehru, and others. More than the self-effacing title indicates, this book offers important insights into the people and times on which its author reflects. Galbraith writes with a wit, style, and elegance few can match." Libr J

Kort, Michael
The Columbia guide to the Cold War. Columbia Univ. Press 1998 366p (Columbia guides to American history and cultures) $60; pa $19.50   **973.9**
1. Cold war 2. United States—Foreign relations 3. United States—History—1945-
ISBN 0-231-10772-2; 0-231-10773-0 (pa)
LC 98-7154
The author begins "with a narrative survey of the Cold War which explains some of the historiographical debates that have occupied historians for more than 50 years. Following this section is a mini-encyclopedia consisting of one- or two-page essays on a wide range of Cold War topics. The book concludes with a concise chronology and a comprehensive bibliography of books, films, novels, journal articles, and archival sources. Finally . . . Kort points out some of the relevant current websites and CD-ROM products." Libr J

Menand, Louis
The Metaphysical Club. Farrar, Straus & Giroux 2001 546p il $30; pa $15   **973.9**
1. Holmes, Oliver Wendell, 1841-1935 2. James, William, 1842-1910 3. Peirce, Charles S. (Charles Sanders), 1839-1914 4. Dewey, John, 1859-1952 5. United States—Intellectual life 6. Metaphysics
ISBN 0-374-19963-9; 0-374-52849-7 (pa)
LC 00-66279
In this book Menand "provides a panorama of American post-Civil War thought . . . focusing on the lives and thinking of 'four giants': William James, Charles Sanders Peirce, Oliver Wendell Holmes Jr., and John Dewey. . . . The 'club' of the title, with the four giants as its core, actually only existed for about nine months in 1872, but its members influenced the culture for decades to come." Booklist
"Menand brings rare common sense and graceful, witty prose to his richly nuanced reading of American intellectual history." N Y Times Book Rev
Includes bibliographical references

Slotkin, Richard, 1942-
Gunfighter nation; the myth of the frontier in twentieth-century America. Atheneum Pubs. 1992 850p o.p.; University of Okla. Press paperback available $31.95   **973.9**
1. Frontier and pioneer life—West (U.S.) 2. Popular culture—United States
ISBN 0-8061-3031-8 (pa)
LC 92-4446
This is the final volume of Slotkin's trilogy on the influence of the frontier on the American character begun with Regeneration through violence (1973) and The fatal environment (1985)
"On the premise that myth is spread by mass media, Slotkin examines numerous elements of popular culture ranging from James Fenimore Cooper's Hawkeye in *The last of the Mohicans* to John Wayne's *Green Berets* film to demonstrate how the myth affects American perceptions regarding foreign and domestic issues." Libr J
Includes bibliographical references

St. James encyclopedia of popular culture; editors, Tom Pendergast and Sara Pendergast; with an introduction by Jim Cullen. St. James Press 1999 c2000 5v il set $695   **973.9**
1. Popular culture—United States—Encyclopedias 2. United States—Civilization—Encyclopedias
ISBN 1-55862-400-7   LC 99-46540

This is an "overview of popular culture in twentieth-century America with a particular emphasis on the second half of the century. In more than 2,700 entries, the nearly 450 contributors attempt to cover the major personalities, productions, products, events, and developments from film, music, print culture, social life, sports, television and radio, art, and performances (which include theater, dance, stand-up comedy, and other live performances). . . . The entries seldom sink to trivialization. They are generally thoughtful and well written, providing information and insight. . . . The editors have done a masterful job of providing something for nearly everyone." Am Ref Books Annu, 2001

Includes bibliographical references

Terkel, Studs, 1912-
American dreams; lost and found. New Press 2003 xxv, 470p pa $16.95   **973.9**
1. United States—Civilization 2. United States—Social conditions
ISBN 1-56584-545-5   LC 2003-276288

A reissue of the title first published 1980 by Pantheon Bks.

A collection of statements by individual Americans expressing their personal aspirations and disappointments and feelings about the American dream, gathered by Terkel in his travels around the country

973.91   United States—1901-1953

Allen, Frederick Lewis, 1890-1954
Only yesterday; an informal history of the 1920's. Wiley 1997 285p (Wiley investment classics) $21.95   **973.91**
1. United States—History—1919-1933 2. United States—Social conditions 3. United States—Economic conditions—1919-1933
ISBN 0-471-18952-9   LC 97-19930

Also available in paperback from HarperCollins Pubs.

A reissue of the title first published 1931 by Harper and Brothers

"An account of the years from the spring of 1919 to . . . [1931]. It is a kaleidoscopic picture of American politics, society, manners, morals, and economic conditions." Booklist

Includes bibliographical references

Since yesterday; the nineteen-thirties in America, September 3, 1929-September 3, 1939. HarperCollins Pubs. 1940 362p il hardcover o.p. paperback available $14
     973.91
1. United States—History—1919-1933 2. United States—History—1933-1945 3. United States—Social conditions 4. United States—Economic conditions
ISBN 0-06-091322-3 (pa)

A retrospective of the decade from September 3, 1929, when the great bull market reached its peak, to September 3, 1939, when England declared war on Germany. Since the years covered are those of the Great Depression, the chronicle focuses more politics and economics than manners, customs and the arts

Burns, James MacGregor
The three Roosevelts; patrician leaders who transformed America; by James MacGregor Burns & Susan Dunn. Atlantic Monthly Press 2001 678p il $37.50; pa $18   **973.91**
1. Roosevelt, Theodore, 1858-1919 2. Roosevelt, Franklin D. (Franklin Delano), 1882-1945 3. Roosevelt, Eleanor, 1884-1962 4. United States—Politics and government—20th century
ISBN 0-87113-780-1; 0-8021-3872-1 (pa)
     LC 00-60896

Burns and Dunn "present an analysis of the Roosevelts that [aims to] establish the connections among their careers, ideas and values. . . . Theodore, Franklin and Eleanor not only changed the very nature of American society, [the authors argue], they also altered the history of the rest of the world." America

Burns and Dunn "succeed in approaching their subjects with grace, respect and insight. In the end, they do great justice to three remarkable lives." Publ Wkly

Includes bibliographical references

Hofstadter, Richard, 1916-1970
The age of reform from Bryan to F.D.R. Knopf 1955 328, xxp hardcover o.p. paperback available $12.95   **973.91**
1. United States—Politics and government—20th century
ISBN 0-394-70095-3 (pa)

This analysis of the reform movements in American politics from 1890-1940 reviews: The agrarian uprising that found its expression in the Populist movement of the 1890's; The Progressive movement from about 1900-1914; The New Deal of the 1930's. Emphasis is placed upon the ideas of the leading political reformers

Includes bibliographical references

Kennedy, David M., 1941-
Freedom from fear; the American people in depression and war, 1929-1945. Oxford Univ. Press 1999 936p il maps (Oxford history of the United States) $39.95; pa $22.50 **973.91**
1. United States—History—1919-1933 2. United States—History—1933-1945
ISBN 0-19-503834-7; 0-19-514403-1 (pa)
     LC 98-49580

Also available in a two-volume paperback edition

This narrative history of the United States spans the period from the Great Depression to the end of the Second World War

"Rarely does a work of historical synthesis combine such trenchant analysis and elegant writing. For its scope, its insight and its purring narrative engine, Kennedy's book will stand for years to come as the definitive account of the critical decades of the American century." Publ Wkly

Includes bibliographical references

Schlesinger, Arthur M., 1917-
The crisis of the old order, 1919-1933; {by} Arthur M. Schlesinger, Jr. Houghton Mifflin 2003 557p (Age of Roosevelt) pa $17
     973.91
1. Roosevelt, Franklin D. (Franklin Delano), 1882-1945 2. United States—History—1919-1933
ISBN 0-618-34085-8   LC 2003-47884
"A Mariner book"

A reissue of the title first published 1957

Schlesinger, Arthur M., 1917-—*Continued*

This is the first of three volumes which interpret the political, economic, social, and intellectual life of the United States during the time when Franklin D. Roosevelt was in office. This volume covers the years preceding his first term

Includes bibliographical references

Followed by The coming of the New Deal, and The politics of upheaval

Terkel, Studs, 1912-

Hard times; an oral history of the great depression. Norton 2000 462p pa $14.95

973.91

1. Great Depression, 1929-1939 2. United States—Social conditions 3. United States—Economic conditions—1919-1933 4. United States—Economic conditions—1933-1945

ISBN 1-56584-656-7   LC 2003-389318

A reissue of the title first published 1970 by Pantheon Bks.

"Persons of all ages, occupations, and classes scattered across the U.S. remember what they experienced or were told about the economic crisis of the 1930's. The result is a social document of immense interest." Booklist

Watkins, T. H. (Tom H.), 1936-2000

The hungry years; a narrative history of the Great Depression in America. Holt & Co. 1999 587p il hardcover o.p. paperback available $17   **973.91**

1. Great Depression, 1929-1939 2. United States—Economic conditions—1919-1933 3. United States—Economic conditions—1933-1945

ISBN 0-8050-6506-7 (pa)   LC 99-10391

"A Marian Wood book"

"This book explores how everyday Americans across the country coped with economic disaster." Libr J

"The vignettes Watkins selects are gritty, visceral, and seamlessly sutured to the federal programs that rolled out in the course of the decade, making this a signal addition to the rich historiography of the Depression." Booklist

973.917 United States—Administration of Franklin D. Roosevelt, 1933-1945

Encyclopedia of the Great Depression and the New Deal. Sharpe Ref. 2001 2v il maps set $199   **973.917**

1. Great Depression, 1929-1939—Encyclopedias 2. New Deal, 1933-1939—Encyclopedias 3. United States—History—1933-1945—Encyclopedias

ISBN 0-7656-8033-5   LC 00-56285

This reference is divided into "six parts: thematic essays, general entries, separate entries for government and international affairs, biographies, and historical documents. . . . The final section includes legislation, court cases, presidential papers, and a variety of other pertinent documents, either in full or in part." Libr J

This "is an exceptional piece of work—lavishly laid out with easily understood graphs and maps, which are beautifully rendered with large illustrations, and, most importantly, a comprehensive array of lucid entries with up-to-date bibliographies. . . . This is a superb reference tool that should be in all libraries." Am Ref Books Annu, 2002

Includes bibliographical references

Leuchtenburg, William Edward, 1922-

Franklin D. Roosevelt and the New Deal, 1932-1940; {by} William E. Leuchtenburg. Harper & Row 1963 393p il (New American nation series) hardcover o.p. paperback available $16   **973.917**

1. Roosevelt, Franklin D. (Franklin Delano), 1882-1945 2. New Deal, 1933-1939 3. United States—History—1933-1945

ISBN 0-06-133025-6 (pa)

This treatment of Roosevelt's first two terms in office emphasizes the economic crisis and New Deal reforms. The author shows how social forces influenced government action: the San Francisco strike in 1934, the careers of Huey Long and Father Coughlin, the sharecroppers' revolt, and unemployment

This book "is comprehensive, logically organized, and written with clarity and detachment." Am Hist Rev

Includes bibliographical references

Schlesinger, Arthur M., 1917-

The coming of the New Deal, 1933-1935; [by] Arthur M. Schlesinger, Jr. Houghton Mifflin 2003 669p (Age of Roosevelt) pa $17   **973.917**

1. Roosevelt, Franklin D. (Franklin Delano), 1882-1945 2. New Deal, 1933-1939 3. United States—History—1933-1945

ISBN 0-618-34086-6   LC 2003-47859

"A Mariner book"

A reissue of the title first published 1959

"This second volume of 'The Age of Roosevelt' continues the work begun with 'The Crisis of the Old Order, 1919-1933'. . . . The dramatic story of how representative democracy began the battle to conquer economic collapse is followed through the first two years of the New Deal." Libr J

Includes bibliographical references

Followed by The politics of upheaval

The politics of upheaval, 1935-1936; [by] Arthur M. Schlesinger, Jr. 1st Mariner Books ed. Houghton Mifflin 2003 749p (Age of Roosevelt) pa $17   **973.917**

1. Roosevelt, Franklin D. (Franklin Delano), 1882-1945 2. New Deal, 1933-1939 3. United States—History—1933-1945

ISBN 0-618-34087-4   LC 2003-47889

"A Mariner book"

A reissue of the title first published 1960

This third volume of The age of Roosevelt "concentrates on the turbulent concluding years of Franklin D. Roosevelt's first term." Publisher's note

Includes bibliographical references

973.92 United States—1953-

Atlas of American politics, 1960-2000; [by] Fred M. Shelley [et al.] CQ Press 2002 242p maps $156.25   **973.92**

1. United States—Politics and government—Maps

ISBN 1-56802-665-X   LC 2001-18267

This work "examines U.S. government and politics at the congressional district, state, and national levels from a combined historical, geographical, and political perspective. More than 200 maps from a variety of gov-

Atlas of American politics, 1960-2000—
Continued

ernment and private sources show the relationship between the nation's geography and its political life. . . .
This book provides a unique look at U.S. politics during
the last 40 years and will be useful to students and researchers from the high-school level up." Booklist

Bloom, Allan David
The closing of the American mind. Simon
& Schuster 1987 392p hardcover o.p.
paperback available $14   **973.92**
    1. Higher education 2. United States—Intellectual life
    ISBN 0-671-65715-1 (pa)   LC 86-24768
    This is the author's assessment of liberal arts educa-
tion today. "In essence, he argues that over the last 25
years the academy has all but abandoned the intellectual
and moral principles that have traditionally informed and
given substance to liberal education, becoming prey to
the enthusiasms—increasingly politicized—of the moment." N Y Times Book Rev

Bowden, Charles, 1945-
Blues for cannibals; the notes from
underground. North Point Press 2002 293p
$24; pa $14   **973.92**
    1. American national characteristics 2. United
States—Description 3. United States—Social conditions 4. United States—Moral conditions
    ISBN 0-86547-624-1; 0-86547-653-5 (pa)
                 LC 2001-31721
    In this look at the underbelly of American society
Bowden "profiles rapists, drunks, outlaws, a suicidal artist, ne'er-do-wells, and do-gooders; suffers grievously
over tortured and murdered children; brilliantly links the
story of an institutionalized self-taught artist and convicted killer who obsessively paints pictures of presidents
with a blazing reassessment of Lyndon Johnson; chronicles an execution; mourns the death of four friends; and
vividly portrays the mighty nineteenth-century Yaqui war
leader Cajeme. As furious, wounded, lustful, and compelling as Algren and Miller." Booklist

Bryson, Bill
I'm a stranger here myself; notes on
returning to America after 20 years away.
Broadway Bks. 1999 288p hardcover o.p.
paperback available $14.95   **973.92**
    1. United States—Description 2. United States—So-
cial life and customs
    ISBN 0-7679-0382-X (pa)   LC 99-18074
    Also available Thorndike Press large print edition
    The author collects "columns on America he wrote
weekly, while living in New Hampshire in the mid-to-
late 1990s, for a British Sunday newspaper. Although he
happily describes himself as dazzled by American ease,
friendliness and abundance, Bryson has no trouble finding comic targets, among them fast food, computer efficiency and, ironically, American friendliness and putative
convenience." Publ Wkly

The **Columbia** guide to America in the
1960s; David Farber and Beth Bailey,
editors. Columbia Univ. Press 2001 508p il
map (Columbia guides to American history
and cultures) $60; pa $25   **973.92**
    1. United States—History—1961-1974 2. United
States—Social conditions
    ISBN 0-231-11372-2; 0-231-11373-0 (pa)
                LC 00-65577
    This reference work includes "a dictionary, an exten-
sive annotated bibliography, a chronology of the era, and
statistical information [and] two extraordinary bonuses: a
section 'Debating the Sixties,' which includes ten essays
by prominent historians . . . and an excellent 77-page
history of the 1960s. This book is a fine addition to any
library's collection." Choice

Fariello, Griffin
Red scare; memories of the American
inquisition: an oral history. Norton 1995 575p
                              973.92
    1. Anticommunist movements 2. Internal security—
United States   LC 94-25859
    Available in hardcover from Replica Bks.
    "Here, in some 70 narratives, are the stories of the fa-
mous and the obscure who were the victims of McCarthyism—its indiscriminate allegations and unsubstantiated
charges—as well as the stories of high government officials, FBI agents, and informers paid to finger Communists. A useful addition to the literature of the period."
Libr J
    Includes bibliographical references

Frum, David, 1960-
How we got here; the 70's: the decade that
brought you modern life (for better or worse).
Basic Bks. 2000 xxiv, 418p il hardcover o.p.
paperback available $16   **973.92**
    1. United States—Civilization—1970-
    ISBN 0-465-04196-5 (pa)
    The author "aims 'to describe—and to judge' the
transformation of American values during the '70s. Surveying politics, legal cases and opinion polls as well as
popular culture, he links what he sees as America's loss
of faith in government, the rise of 'sourness and cynicism' and the culture of licentiousness and divorce,
among other social changes, to events in that decade."
Publ Wkly
    Includes bibliographical references

Gitlin, Todd
The sixties; years of hope, days of rage.
Bantam Bks. 1987 513p hardcover o.p.
paperback available $19.95   **973.92**
    1. United States—History—1961-1974 2. United
States—Social conditions 3. Students—Political activity
    ISBN 0-553-37212-2 (pa)   LC 87-47575
    "Though ex-SDS leader Gitlin occasionally falls prey
to the self-indulgence that snares most sixties' commentators, his analysis of the decade's politics is thought-
provoking and clearheaded. Rather than singing the familiar hymn of praise to youthful idealism, Gitlin carefully dissects why the activist spirit developed when it
did and what its legacy has been." Am Libr
    Includes bibliographical references

Gregory, Ross

Cold War America, 1946 to 1990; Richard Balkin, general editor. Facts on File 2003 670p il map (Almanacs of American life) $105 **973.92**

1. Cold war 2. United States—History—1945- 3. United States—Social conditions

ISBN 0-8160-3868-6   LC 2001-51136

"This is a treasure trove of statistical information documenting the enormous changes in American life from 1945 to 1990. . . . Found herein are data on everything from the population by sex . . . region, and race, business formations and failures, bull and bear markets, and operations of the postal service to the federal debt, high school seniors and drugs, executions by gender and race, and recipients of National Book Awards and Pulitzer Prizes. . . . Enhancing the work's appeal are photographs throughout the text and an exhaustive index." Am Ref Books Annu, 2003

Includes bibliographical references

Halberstam, David, 1934-

The fifties. Villard Bks. 1993 800p il o.p.; Fawcett Bks. paperback available $17.95
973.92

1. United States—Social life and customs 2. United States—Politics and government—20th century 3. Popular culture—United States

ISBN 0-449-90933-6 (pa)   LC 92-56815

This is a social history of the United States during the 1950s

The author's "sources are secondary and derivative, but his instinct for the revealing anecdote, his ear for the memorable quote, and his awesome powers of organization add up to a variegated overview that moves seamlessly between the serious shenanigans of Chief Justice Earl Warren and the frivolous ones of . . . Grace Metalious." Natl Rev

Includes bibliographical references

Kuralt, Charles, 1934-1997

Charles Kuralt's America. Putnam 1995 279p il o.p.; Anchor Bks. (NY) paperback available $14 **973.92**

1. United States—Description 2. United States—Social life and customs

ISBN 0-385-48510-7 (pa)   LC 95-34785

Also available Thorndike Press large print edition

"After serving 37 years as a reporter at CBS, Kuralt retired and set out on a trip to see his favorite American locations. . . . In this journal, the author records the people, places, and pets he encountered." Libr J

"Kuralt is not in search of crises or epiphanies; he values nature and good food, neighborliness and craftsmanship, quaintness and quirkiness. Though no literary match for American chroniclers like Calvin Trillin, the effable Kuralt does, in un-fancy style, convey his enthusiasm and his engagement." Publ Wkly

Charles Kuralt's American moments; edited and with a preface by Peter Freundlich; foreword by Charles Osgood. Simon & Schuster 1998 255p il **973.92**

1. United States—Description 2. United States—Social life and customs   LC 98-40627

Available Thorndike Press large print edition

This work is based on Kuralt's televised "series of 90-second slices of life. This volume collects those vignettes' verbal transcripts [and] illustrates each with one or more frames from their visual continuities." Booklist

"This may be a different format than Kuralt's other books, but it is just as powerful, capturing those moments that Americans hold dear." Libr J

On the road with Charles Kuralt. Putnam 1985 316p il o.p.; Fawcett Bks. paperback available $19 **973.92**

1. United States—Social life and customs 2. United States—Description

ISBN 0-449-00740-5 (pa)   LC 85-6330

"As a CBS reporter specializing in 'soft' news, Kuralt has been roaming around the U.S. since 1967 in search of 'just plain folks.' Some 100 of the television interviews that resulted from that search have been transcribed for this collection. Loosely organized by themes emphasizing the individuality, altruism, and humor that characterize small town and rural Americans, the interviews and anecdotes are consistently entertaining." Booklist

Leebaert, Derek

The fifty-year wound; the true price of America's Cold War victory. Little, Brown 2002 750p il hardcover o.p. paperback available $16.95 **973.92**

1. Cold war 2. United States—Foreign relations 3. United States—Politics and government—1945- 4. United States—Social conditions

ISBN 0-316-16496-8 (pa)   LC 2001-34452

The author considers how the Cold War affected the U.S., addressing such questions as "Why did the conflict drag on for decades? What did the Cold War do to the country, and how? What was lost while victory was gained?" Publisher's note

"In the most important work on the Cold War to come out in years, Leebaert makes us contemplate what we lost while winning the Cold War." Libr J

Includes bibliographical references

Marling, Karal Ann

As seen on TV; the visual culture of everyday life in the 1950s. Harvard Univ. Press 1994 328p il map $27.50; pa $20.50
973.92

1. Television broadcasting 2. Popular culture—United States 3. United States—Social life and customs

ISBN 0-674-04882-2; 0-674-04883-0 (pa)

     LC 94-2814

"Marling highlights the impact of television's first influential decade. From Mamie Eisenhower's apparel to the aesthetics of food advertising and cookbooks, she [aims to] demonstrate the extent to which Americans began to measure their personal lives against what was seen on television." Christ Sci Monit

"A nostalgic, informative and sometimes funny view of 1950's American culture." Publ Wkly

Includes bibliographical references

O'Reilly, Bill

The no-spin zone; confrontations with the powerful and famous in America; afterword by James Ellroy. Broadway Bks. 2001 190p $24.95; pa $14 **973.92**

1. Celebrities 2. United States—Politics and government—1989- 3. United States—Social conditions

ISBN 0-7679-0848-1; 0-7679-0849-X (pa)

     LC 2001-43031

Also available large print edition $24.95 (ISBN 0-375-43126-8)

O'Reilly, Bill—*Continued*

The author includes excerpts from his TV talk show interviews, including "James Carville (on Bill Clinton), Dr. Laura (on working mothers), former surgeon general Dr. Jocelyn Elders (on sex education), Puff Daddy (on rap), Susan Sarandon (on police brutality), Al Sharpton (on boycotts)—and insightfully introduces each, mulling over the issue or providing background." Publ Wkly

Phillips, Kevin P.

Arrogant capital; Washington, Wall Street, and the frustration of American politics; [by] Kevin Phillips. Little, Brown 1994 231p hardcover o.p. paperback available $18.99

973.92

1. United States—Politics and government—20th century 2. Political corruption
ISBN 0-316-70602-7 (pa)   LC 94-10035

This book "suggests that Bill Clinton's early successes and later failures were both symptoms of a deeper political and economic shift. That shift . . . is the collapse of the capacity of the US economy to sustain growth in jobs and income for the middle class. The 'arrogant capital' of Phillips's title means both Washington, DC, with its lobbyists and warring interest groups, and the financial capital that flows through brokerages and investment banks without creating an adequate base for middle-class employment." N Y Rev Books

Phillips "makes a convincing case that voters see Washington as the enemy because they can't crack the interlock between interest-group power and the political system." N Y Times Book Rev
Includes bibliographical references

Rather, Dan

The American dream; stories from the heart of our nation. Morrow 2001 xxii, 266p hardcover o.p. paperback available $12.95

973.92

1. American national characteristics 2. United States—Social life and customs 3. United States—Social conditions
ISBN 0-06-093770-X (pa)   LC 2001-30031
Also available large print edition $25 (ISBN 0-06-620964-1)

In this book Rather tells stories of individual Americans and their dreams. He "groups his material into chapters that focus on elements of our national aspirations: liberty, enterprise, pursuit of happiness, family, fame, education, innovation, and 'giving back.' The Americans that Rather describes are a diverse group but, he urges, their stories are an inspirational reminder of the power of the nation's fundamental ideas to motivate a wide range of people." Booklist

Schulman, Bruce J.

The seventies; the great shift in American culture, society, and politics. Free Press 2001 334p il o.p.; Da Capo Press paperback available $17   **973.92**

1. United States—Civilization—1970-
ISBN 0-306-81126-X (pa)   LC 2001-23238

Schulman explores developments in American politics and culture during "the years between Woodstock and Reagan. . . . 'The great shift' [he sees] is away from the public-spirited universalism that gave America the New Deal and the civil rights movement, and toward the sovereignty of the free market and private life." N Y Times Book Rev

"This is an important contribution to modern American social history and the literature of popular culture." Publ Wkly
Includes bibliographical references

Schwartz, Richard Alan, 1951-

Cold War culture; media and the arts, 1945-1990; [by] Richard A. Schwartz. Facts on File 1998 376p il (Cold War America) $60.50; pa $24.95   **973.92**

1. Popular culture—United States 2. United States—Civilization
ISBN 0-8160-3104-5; 0-8160-4264-0 (pa)

LC 96-29642

This work "covers the various influences on American culture during the years 1945 to 1990. Schwartz organizes Cold War culture alphabetically within the following broad categories: art, cartoons, consumer goods, dance, film, games and toys, television and theater. . . . This reference source is easy to read and hard to put down as a browsing item." SLJ

Smith, Hedrick

The power game; how Washington works. Random House 1988 xxii, 793p o.p.; Ballantine Bks. paperback available $16.95

973.92

1. United States—Politics and government—1974-1989 2. Power (Social sciences)
ISBN 0-345-41048-3 (pa)   LC 87-42669

The author "relies primarily on anecdotes and case studies from the Reagan era to illustrate how the use of power determines the effectiveness of government." Libr J

Smith "has an insider's awareness of the alliances, machinations and turf-battles that make the capital work; he knows what he is talking about." Economist
Includes bibliographical references

Witcover, Jules

The year the dream died; revisiting 1968 in America. Warner Bks. 1997 544p $25; pa $16   **973.92**

1. United States—History—1961-1974
ISBN 0-446-51849-2; 0-446-67471-0 (pa)

LC 96-42017

Political columnist Witcover reviews "the tumultuous year in which the nation came 'unglued.' Nixon and Agnew vie for the villain's role, although neither would have been significant, contends the author, had LBJ not eroded his Kennedy legacy by escalating American involvement in Vietnam. . . . This backward look is enriched by the 20/20 hindsight of surviving participants, some still prominent in public life." Publ Wkly

Woodward, Bob, 1943-

Shadow; five presidents and the legacy of Watergate. Simon & Schuster 1999 592p il hardcover o.p. paperback available $16

973.92

1. Presidents—United States 2. Watergate Affair, 1972-1974 3. United States—Politics and government—1974-1989 4. United States—Politics and government—1989-
ISBN 0-684-85263-2 (pa)   LC 99-37045

Woodward examines the long-term effect of the Watergate Affair on the presidencies of Gerald Ford, Jimmy Carter, Ronald Reagan, George Bush, and Bill

Woodward, Bob, 1943—*Continued*

Clinton

The author is an "effective investigative journalist. These skills are on full display in Shadow. . . . [The book] is most interesting as a reconstruction of the many scandals that have troubled the Clinton Administration." Nation

Includes bibliographical references

973.921 United States—Administration of Dwight D. Eisenhower, 1953-1961

Branch, Taylor

Parting the waters: America in the King years, 1954-63. Simon & Schuster 1988 1064p il hardcover o.p. paperback available $20 **973.921**

1. King, Martin Luther, 1929-1968 2. United States—History—1953-1961 3. African Americans—Civil rights

ISBN 0-671-68742-5 (pa)   LC 88-24033

This history of the American civil rights movement from 1954 to 1963 focuses on the life of Dr. Martin Luther King

The author "has searched out the hidden reality and often tragic human drama of the King years. On his best pages, the past, miraculously, seems to spring back to life. King himself appears human, all too human. Yet when the reader is done, his remarkable virtues and ordinary vices seem of a piece, the component parts of a coherent, towering personality." Newsweek

Includes bibliographical references

973.922 United States—Administration of John F. Kennedy, 1961-1963

Benson, Michael

The encyclopedia of the JFK assassination. Facts on File 2002 348p il map (Facts on File library of American history) $75; pa $21.95 **973.922**

1. Kennedy, John F. (John Fitzgerald), 1917-1963—Assassination

ISBN 0-8160-4476-7; 0-8160-4477-5 (pa)
     LC 2001-53212

"This volume provides a listing of people, places, and events related (however slightly) to November 22 to 24, 1963. Following an introduction that describes the events and summarizes conspiracy theories are hundreds of entries. . . . These range from a paragraph to identify people and groups . . . to 4 or 5 pages. . . . This volume is readable and intriguing." Booklist

Branch, Taylor

Pillar of fire; America in the King years, 1963-65. Simon & Schuster 1998 746p il hardcover o.p. paperback available $17 **973.922**

1. King, Martin Luther, 1929-1968 2. United States—History—1961-1974 3. African Americans—Civil rights

ISBN 0-684-84809-0 (pa)   LC 97-46076

Second volume in the author's proposed trilogy about the civil rights movement, begun with: Parting the waters: America in the King years, 1954-1963

This volume covers "the years of Birmingham, Freedom Summer, the Nobel Peace Prize award to Martin Luther King Jr., and countless other public and private campaigns, conflicts, episodes, and incidents." Libr J

"Branch's research is impeccable and his knowledge of his material solid. . . . The book is significant for marshaling so much information, particularly the profiles of all the many individuals involved in the race issues of that time." Booklist

Includes bibliographical references

Freedman, Lawrence

Kennedy's wars; Berlin, Cuba, Laos, and Vietnam. Oxford Univ. Press 2000 xx, 528p il $35; pa $18.95 **973.922**

1. Kennedy, John F. (John Fitzgerald), 1917-1963 2. United States—Foreign relations 3. Military policy—United States

ISBN 0-19-513453-2; 0-19-515243-3 (pa)
     LC 99-87898

The author examines how President Kennedy's "time in office was occupied with a series of confrontations with communism. . . . [He contends that] in each of the four cases under review Kennedy resisted pressure from his staff and advisers, not to mention from the Pentagon, to take drastic action, . . . and that he left the cold war in a far less dangerous state than he found it." Economist

"Lawrence's book is an excellent treatment of U.S. foreign policy during this dynamic era and an insightful portrait of John F. Kennedy as a leader." Libr J

Includes bibliographical references

Fursenko, A. V. (Aleksandr Vasil´evich)

"One hell of a gamble"; Khrushchev, Castro, and Kennedy, 1958-1964; [by] Aleksandr Fursenko and Timothy Naftali. Norton 1997 420p il hardcover o.p. paperback available $15.95 **973.922**

1. Cuban Missile Crisis, 1962 2. United States—Foreign relations—Soviet Union 3. Soviet Union—Foreign relations—United States

ISBN 0-393-31790-0 (pa)   LC 97-1022

For this diplomatic history of the Cuban Missile Crisis, the authors were granted "permission to review Khrushchev's papers; they were also able to draw on archival material from other official Soviet sources." N Y Times Book Rev

Includes bibliographical references

Halberstam, David, 1934-

The best and the brightest; foreword by John McCain. Modern Library ed. Modern Lib. 2001 xxviii, 780p $24.95; pa $16,95 **973.922**

1. United States—Politics and government—1961-1974 2. United States—Foreign relations—Vietnam 3. Vietnam—Foreign relations—United States

ISBN 0-679-64099-1; 0-449-90870-4 (pa)
     LC 2001-31261

A reissue of the title first published 1972

"The author describes analytically rather than narratively, how the Kennedy-Johnson intellectual (McNamara, Bundy, Rusk, Ball, Taylor, et al.) men praised as 'the best and the brightest' men of this century, became the architects of the disastrous American policy of Indochina." Libr J

Includes bibliographical references

Kennedy, Robert F., 1925-1968

Make gentle the life of this world; the vision of Robert F. Kennedy; edited and with an introduction by Maxwell Taylor Kennedy. Harcourt Brace & Co. 1998 188p il $20

973.922

1. Quotations
ISBN 0-15-100356-4   LC 97-45018
Also available in paperback from Broadway Bks.

This is a collection of quotations by Robert F. Kennedy and the authors who inspired him

"Chapters are arranged by issues that were most important to Kennedy and remain timely today—the responsibilities of citizens to their government, the tragedy of poverty in the midst of plenty, the importance of dissent in a democratic society, and work as the solution for the welfare crises. The book's haunting photos convey Kennedy's spirit as successfully as the words." Libr J

Thirteen days; a memoir of the Cuban missile crisis; with introductions by Robert S. McNamara and Harold Macmillan. Norton 1969 224p il hardcover o.p. paperback available $12.95   **973.922**

1. Cuban Missile Crisis, 1962 2. United States—Politics and government—1961-1974 3. United States—Foreign relations—Soviet Union 4. Soviet Union—Foreign relations—United States
ISBN 0-393-31834-6 (pa)

Also available in paperback from G. K. Hall large print edition

A behind-the-scenes account of the Cuban Missile Crisis of 1962. Includes reproductions of pertinent documents and speeches by both President Kennedy and Nikita Khrushchev

The **Kennedy** tapes; inside the White House during the Cuban Missile Crisis; edited by Ernest R. May and Philip D. Zelikow. Belknap Press 1997 728p il $35; pa $16.95

973.922

1. Kennedy, John F. (John Fitzgerald), 1917-1963 2. Cuban Missile Crisis, 1962
ISBN 0-674-17926-9; 0-674-17927-7 (pa)
LC 97-14216

This volume is based on tape recordings made during White House deliberations at the time of the Cuban Missile Crisis

"An incredible resource for determining not only how the Cuban Missile Crisis was debated but also how JFK and his most trusted advisers handled themselves during those desperate hours. . . . This volume will provide scholars with data to analyze for years to come." Libr J

Includes bibliographical references

Matthews, Chris, 1945-

Kennedy & Nixon; the rivalry that shaped postwar America; [by] Christopher Matthews. Simon & Schuster 1996 377p il hardcover o.p. paperback available $14   **973.922**

1. Kennedy, John F. (John Fitzgerald), 1917-1963 2. Nixon, Richard M. (Richard Milhous), 1913-1994 3. United States—Politics and government—20th century
ISBN 0-684-83246-1 (pa)   LC 96-15677

This exploration of the rift between Kennedy and Nixon "shows how these two anti-New Dealers, anti-

Communists, and freshmen members of Congress in 1946 became enemies as their political careers advanced." Libr J

Includes bibliographical references

Posner, Gerald L.

Case closed; Lee Harvey Oswald and the assassination of JFK. Random House 1993 607p il o.p.; Anchor Bks. paperback available $16.95   **973.922**

1. Kennedy, John F. (John Fitzgerald), 1917-1963—Assassination 2. Oswald, Lee Harvey
ISBN 1-4000-3462-0 (pa)   LC 93-12821

In this book Posner argues that Lee Harvey Oswald was solely responsible for the assassination of President Kennedy and that none of the theories alleging conspiracy is valid

"One of the strongest and most important features of the book, indeed, is Posner's painstaking dissection of each and every one of the competing conspiracy theories. None of them stands up under scrutiny." Natl Rev

Includes bibliographical references

973.923 United States— Administration of Lyndon B. Johnson, 1963-1969

Reaching for glory; Lyndon Johnson's secret White House tapes, 1964-1965; edited and with commentary by Michael Beschloss. Simon & Schuster 2001 475p il $30; pa $15   **973.923**

1. Johnson, Lyndon B. (Lyndon Baines), 1908-1973 2. United States—Politics and government—1961-1974
ISBN 0-684-80408-5; 0-7432-2714-X (pa)
LC 2001-49661

Companion volume to Taking charge: the Johnson White House tapes, 1963-1964

"Political skill, ruthlessness and paranoia distinguish Johnson's talks covering the period in 1964 and 1965 when he got his Great Society programs through Congress and plunged this country into war in Vietnam." New York Times Book Rev

Includes bibliographical references

Taking charge; the Johnson White House tapes, 1963-1964; edited and with commentary by Michael R. Beschloss. Simon & Schuster 1997 591p il hardcover o.p. paperback available $16   **973.923**

1. Johnson, Lyndon B. (Lyndon Baines), 1908-1973 2. United States—Politics and government—1961-1974
ISBN 0-684-84792-2 (pa)   LC 97-26749

This book is a "selection of conversations taped by Lyndon B. Johnson during the first nine months of his Presidency—beginning on the day of the Kennedy assassination and continuing through the close of the Democratic National Convention in 1964. . . . There are no stunning revelations and no recorded moments of epochal importance. But 'Taking Charge' is a riveting book nevertheless. This is partly because it has been superbly edited and annotated by the historian Michael R. Beschloss, who has made everything—even the most arcane references—accessible to ordinary readers." N Y Times Book Rev

The **Times** were a changin'; the sixties reader; edited by Irwin Unger and Debi Unger. Three Rivers Press (NY) 1998 355p hardcover o.p. paperback available $16

973.923

1. United States—History—1961-1974
ISBN 0-609-80337-9 (pa)   LC 97-39844

The Ungers have compiled "an anthology illustrating the social, cultural, and political events that made the 1960s distinctive in American history. [They] present nearly 60 letters, manifestos, reports, speeches, essays, articles, and court decisions . . . arranged in 12 chapters." Libr J

"The broad range of viewpoints and the easy access to such an array of primary sources make the book a powerful adjunct for study of the sixties, as well as an interesting book for browsing." Book Rep

973.924 United States— Administration of Richard Nixon, 1969-1974

Abuse of power; the new Nixon tapes; edited with an introduction and commentary by Stanley I. Kutler. Free Press 1997 xxiii, 675p hardcover o.p. paperback available $30.95   **973.924**

1. Nixon, Richard M. (Richard Milhous), 1913-1994
2. Watergate Affair, 1972-1974 3. United States— Politics and government—1961-1974
ISBN 0-684-85187-3 (pa)   LC 97-32096

"This is an edited collection of transcripts of President Nixon's Watergate-related conversations made available under a 1974 Congressional directive covering tapes related to 'abuse of governmental power.' More than 90 percent of the volume covers the year after the June 1972 break-in and focuses on Watergate." Choice

Bernstein, Carl
All the president's men; [by] Carl Bernstein, Bob Woodward. Simon & Schuster 1999 349p il $26; pa $14   **973.924**

1. Washington post 2. Watergate Affair, 1972-1974
ISBN 0-684-86355-3; 0-671-89441-2 (pa)
          LC 98-54773

A reissue of the title first published 1974

The two Washington Post reporters whose investigative journalism first revealed the Watergate scandal tell the way it happened from the first suspicions, through the trail of false leads, lies, secrecy, and high-level pressure, to the final moments when they were able to put the pieces of the puzzle together and write the series that won the Post a Pulitzer Prize

Emery, Fred
Watergate; the corruption of American politics and the fall of Richard Nixon. Times Bks. 1994 555p il o.p.; Simon & Schuster paperback available $25.95   **973.924**

1. Nixon, Richard M. (Richard Milhous), 1913-1994
2. Watergate Affair, 1972-1974
ISBN 0-684-81323-8 (pa)   LC 93-44736

"In addition to an introductory section on the cast of characters involved, Emery provides a detailed examination of the Committee To Re-elect the President (CRP) and its dirty tricks: wire-tapping, money laundering campaigns, and the infamous burglary of Democratic National Committee headquarters. Unlike much of the psychopersonal material that has come out on Nixon, Emery's book focuses on the tough political problems, documenting the need for impeachment and ultimately endorsing it. Riveting reading that is based on an unprecedented combing of the primary sources." Libr J

Includes bibliographical references

Woodward, Bob, 1943-
The final days; [by] Bob Woodward, Carl Bernstein. Simon & Schuster 1976 476p il hardcover o.p. paperback available $15

973.924

1. Nixon, Richard M. (Richard Milhous), 1913-1994
2. Watergate Affair, 1972-1974 3. United States— Politics and government—1961-1974
ISBN 0-671-89440-4 (pa)

The title refers to the final days of the Nixon Presidency. The authors have "constructed a two-part narrative, the first half covering the period from April 30, 1973—the day John Dean was fired as White House counsel—until late July 1974, and the second half covering the last two weeks in detail." N Y Times Book Rev

973.927 United States— Administration of Ronald Reagan, 1981-1989

FitzGerald, Frances, 1940-
Way out there in the blue; Reagan, Star Wars, and the end of the Cold War. Simon & Schuster 2000 592p hardcover o.p. paperback available $17   **973.927**

1. Reagan, Ronald, 1911-2004 2. Strategic Defense Initiative 3. Cold war 4. United States—Politics and government—1974-1989
ISBN 0-7432-0023-3 (pa)   LC 99-59913

Fitzgerald offers a history of U.S. missile-defense programs over the last two decades, focusing particular attention on the Strategic Defense Initiative (SDI) supported by President Reagan

"Explaining the Star Wars saga, Fitzgerald delivers all the information that any nonexpert could absorb." Booklist

Includes bibliographical references

The **Iran-Contra** scandal; the declassified history; edited by Peter Kornbluh and Malcolm Byrne. New Press 1993 xxxiii, 412p hardcover o.p. paperback available $24.95   **973.927**

1. Iran-Contra Affair, 1985-1990
ISBN 1-56584-047-X (pa)   LC 92-53732

"A National Security Archive Documents reader"

This volume contains "one hundred documents concerning the Iran-Contra Scandal, covering the period from Reagan's original presidential finding of Dec. 1, 1981 to Bush's grant of executive clemency of Dec. 24, 1992. With a helpful chronology of key events and a glossary of major participants, the volume sets forth with contextual introductions the documents, the paper trail of this major controversy in contemporary American politics." Libr J

Includes bibliographical references

Johnson, Haynes Bonner, 1931-

Sleepwalking through history; America in the Reagan years; {by} Haynes Johnson. Norton 1991 524p il hardcover o.p. paperback available $15.95   **973.927**

1. Reagan, Ronald, 1911-2004 2. United States—Politics and government—1974-1989 3. United States—History—1974-1989

ISBN 0-393-32434-6 (pa)   LC 90-38623

This is a study of American politics, history, and culture during the 1980s

The author "concentrates on major events like the Iran-contra affair and the Wall street scene, and briefly touches on other domestic scandals. . . . Not the definitive history of the 1980s, but recommended as an important book by an important author." Libr J

Includes bibliographical references

Reagan, Ronald, 1911-2004

Reagan, in his own hand; edited, with an introduction and commentary by Kiron K. Skinner, Annelise Anderson, Martin Anderson; with a foreword by George P. Schultz. Free Press 2001 xxvi, 549p il $30; pa $16   **973.927**

1. United States—Politics and government—1989-

ISBN 0-7432-0123-X; 0-7432-1938-4 (pa)

    LC 00-66304

"A collection of . . . manuscripts is presented here, just as Reagan wrote them, including his corrections and notes. With a few exceptions, they are very short radio commentaries delivered during the pre-presidential period (1975-1979), focusing mostly on foreign policy and the economy." Publ Wkly

This collection provides "an excellent glimpse into Reagan the man and the thinker." Libr J

973.928 United States—Administration of George Bush, 1989-1993

Schell, Jonathan, 1943-

Writing in time; a political chronical. Moyer Bell 1997 303p hardcover o.p. paperback available $14.95   **973.928**

1. United States—Politics and government—1989-

ISBN 1-55921-295-0 (pa)   LC 96-8516

This volume "traces the 1992 Presidential campaign, the election and President Clinton's first term through Jonathan Schell's columns for Newsday. This chronicle is a distinctly partisan one: Schell's views of the White House and its wannabes are seen strictly from the left. But the author's eye for issues and motives is so sure that even those who detest his opinions will find 'Writing in Time' a lively refresher course on five years of American history." N Y Times Book Rev

Woodward, Bob, 1943-

The commanders. Simon & Schuster 1991 398p il hardcover o.p. paperback available $16   **973.928**

1. Bush, George, 1924- 2. United States. Dept. of Defense 3. United States—Foreign relations 4. Persian Gulf War, 1991

ISBN 0-7432-3475-8 (pa)   LC 91-13037

This book discusses "top-level White House {and} Pentagon decisionmaking, first in the attack on Panama,

and then in the 5½ months of diplomatic and especially military maneuvering that preceded the [1991] war with Iraq." Christ Sci Monit

973.929 United States—Administration of Bill Clinton, 1993-

Applebome, Peter

Dixie rising; how the South is shaping American values, politics, and culture. Times Bks. 1996 385p il o.p.; Harvest Bks. paperback available $13   **973.929**

1. Southern States—Politics and government 2. Southern States—Civilization

ISBN 0-15-600550-6 (pa)   LC 96-16080

The author explores the "contradictions of the modern South. Not only does the South exercise disproportionate political power (Dixie now claims leadership of Congress as well as the White House); most of our serious conflicts over race and religion continue to play out dramatically in the old Confederacy. Applebome's unusual historical literacy helps him understand a region drenched in the tradition and legends of the Civil War, racist demagoguery and the battles over integration." Publ Wkly

Bennett, William John, 1943-

The death of outrage: Bill Clinton and the assault on American ideals; [by] William J. Bennett. Free Press 1998 154p hardcover o.p. paperback available $12.50   **973.929**

1. United States—Politics and government—1989-

ISBN 0-684-86403-7 (pa)   LC 98-36055

Bennett examines the scandals that have plagued the Clinton presidency

"His partisanship notwithstanding, Bennett's slim volume is useful in recounting—and then ridiculing—the sometimes ludicrous rationales and excuses advanced by Democrats he repeatedly describes as Clinton 'apologists.'" N Y Times Book Rev

Conason, Joe

The hunting of the President; the ten-year campaign to destroy Bill and Hillary Clinton; by Joe Conason and Gene Lyons. St. Martin's Press 2000 413p $25.95; pa $14.95   **973.929**

1. Clinton, Bill, 1946- 2. Clinton, Hillary Rodham, 1947- 3. United States—Politics and government—1989-

ISBN 0-312-24547-5; 0-312-27319-3 (pa)

    LC 00-40527

The authors argue "that, although the conspiracy may not have been vast, a group of dedicated anti-Clintonites was determined to bring his presidency down." Booklist

"The story of the Clinton scandals is a tortuous, labyrinthine puzzle, and Conason and Lyons do their best to simplify it. But their cast of characters is enormous, and their research overwhelming." Publ Wkly

Johnson, Haynes Bonner, 1931-

The best of times; America in the Clinton years; [by] Haynes Johnson. Harcourt 2001 610p $27; pa $16   **973.929**

1. Clinton, Bill, 1946- 2. United States—Politics and government—1989- 3. United States—History—1989-

ISBN 0-15-100445-5; 0-15-602701-1 (pa)

    LC 2001-24753

"A James H. Silberman book"

Johnson, Haynes Bonner, 1931-—*Continued*

"A near-fanatical public demand for scandals was the most distinguishing trait of the Nineties, states Johnson. . . . Ultimately, the Nineties, according to Johnson, will be remembered as a time of squandered opportunities despite U.S. global preeminence and a booming economy." Libr J

"A magnetic book that every thoughtful American will want to read." Publ Wkly

Includes bibliographical references

Klein, Joe, 1946-

The natural: the misunderstood presidency of Bill Clinton. Doubleday 2002 230p $22.95; pa $14   **973.929**

1. Clinton, Bill, 1946- 2. United States—Politics and government—1989-
ISBN 0-385-50619-8; 0-7679-1412-0 (pa)
                                        LC 2001-47428

Also available Thorndike Press large print edition

The author discusses Bill Clinton's character, the accomplishments and problems of his administration, the making of policy and the workings of the White House

"This book is more readable than . . . others, dense but tight, funny, adroitly written and, in sum, the first savvy synthesis of the Clinton Age." N Y Times Book Rev

Reich, Robert B.

Locked in the cabinet. Knopf 1997 338p hardcover o.p. paperback available $15
                                            973.929

1. United States. Dept. of Labor 2. United States—Politics and government—1989-
ISBN 0-375-70061-7 (pa)   LC 97-71921

The author writes about his tenure as Secretary of Labor in the first Clinton administration

"Reich has an acid pen, and he is by turns witty, churlish, and plain vulgar. . . . The specificity of detail in this book adds up not only to an absorbing accounting of failed service in the Cabinet but also to a powerful indictment of the Clinton Presidency." New Leader

Stephanopoulos, George

All too human; a political education. Little, Brown 1999 456p $32; pa $14.95   **973.929**

1. Clinton, Bill, 1946- 2. Presidents—United States 3. United States—Politics and government—1989-
ISBN 0-316-92919-0; 0-316-93016-4 (pa)
                                        LC 99-13817

This is a political memoir by a former senior advisor to President Clinton

"A fascinating if controversial insiders account of life inside the Clinton pressure cooker administration during its early years." Libr J

Includes bibliographical references

Toobin, Jeffrey R.

A vast conspiracy; the real story of the sex scandal that nearly brought down a president. Random House 2000 422p o.p.; Touchstone Bks. paperback available $14   **973.929**

1. Clinton, Bill, 1946- 2. United States—Politics and government—1989-
ISBN 0-7432-0413-1 (pa)   LC 99-53869

"Toobin's thesis is that the real vast conspiracy wasn't the right-wing one . . . [Hillary Clinton] charged was behind the scandal, but a more subtle attempt by the legal system to circumvent the political process through an

'after the fact election.'" Time

"Even for those who disagree with [Toobin's] assessment, the book is still hugely entertaining. There are plenty of scandal pellets to be found scattered throughout the analysis." Christ Sci Monit

Will, George F.

With a happy eye but . . . America and the world, 1997-2002. Free Press 2002 367p il $27; pa $15   **973.929**

1. World politics—1991- 2. United States—Politics and government—1989- 3. United States—Foreign relations
ISBN 0-684-83821-4; 0-7432-4384-6 (pa)
                                        LC 2002-72206

In this collection of columns, essays, and addresses, Will addresses a broad range of topics, such as "civil liberties, fast food, P.D. James, the G.I. Bill of Rights, Enron, the European Union, the careers of James Madison, Don Zimmer and the Unabomber, and the fate of Governors Island." N Y Times Book Rev

Includes bibliographical references

The woven figure; conservatism and America's fabric, 1994-1997. Scribner 1997 384p hardcover o.p. paperback available $21.95   **973.929**

1. Conservatism 2. United States—Politics and government—1989-
ISBN 0-684-84820-1 (pa)   LC 97-34731

This is a collection of previously published newspaper columns presenting the author's views on such topics as affirmative action, abortion, welfare reform, the Clinton administration, multiculturalism, and campaign finance reform

973.931 Administration of George W. Bush

Bernstein, Richard

Out of the blue; the story of September 11, 2001, from Jihad to Ground Zero; [by] Richard Bernstein and the staff of the New York Times. Times Bks. 2002 287p il $25; pa $15   **973.931**

1. September 11 terrorist attacks, 2001 2. Terrorism
ISBN 0-8050-7240-3; 0-8050-7410-4 (pa)
                                        LC 2002-20396

This account of the September 11, 2001 terrorist attacks focuses "on the personal—the victims, the perpetrators and heroes whose lives became tangled in catastrophe. . . . It uses these stories as a jumping-off point for a comprehensive look at the terror attacks—the reactions of New Yorkers, the nation and the world; the criticism of U.S. government agencies; the lingering effects of the tragedy. While some of this information has been published elsewhere, it has not been gathered so comprehensively—nor has it been written so well." Publ Wkly

Friedman, Thomas L.

Longitudes and attitudes; exploring the world after September 11. Farrar, Straus & Giroux 2002 383p $23   **973.931**

1. September 11 terrorist attacks, 2001 2. Terrorism 3. United States—Politics and government—1989- 4. United States—Foreign relations
ISBN 0-374-19066-6   LC 2002-74321

Also available in paperback from Anchor Bks.

Friedman, Thomas L.—*Continued*

This is a collection "of Friedman's *New York Times* columns from September 2001 through June 2002, with a lengthy postscript describing Friedman's travels and interviews throughout this period." Booklist

"Unapologetically pro-American, Friedman's deliberation on what changed on September 11 outside of the U.S. ultimately centers on the strength of American society and our place in the world." Publ Wkly

Includes bibliographical references

Miller, John

The cell: inside the 9/11 plot and why the FBI and CIA failed to stop it; [by] John Miller and Michael Stone, with Chris Mitchell. Hyperion 2002 336p $24.95; pa $13.95 **973.931**

1. September 11 terrorist attacks, 2001 2. Terrorism 3. Intelligence service—United States

ISBN 0-7868-6900-3; 0-7868-8782-6 (pa)

LC 2002-27322

Also available Thorndike Press large print edition

The authors analyze the circumstances inside and outside the United States that culminated in the September 11 terrorist attack. Included is an account of Miller's face-to-face meeting with Osama bin Laden in Afghanistan in 1998

This is a "frightening and important book." Publ Wkly

Woodward, Bob, 1943-

Bush at war; inside the Bush White House. Simon & Schuster 2002 400p $28 **973.931**

1. Bush, George W. 2. Large print books 3. September 11 terrorist attacks, 2001 4. Military policy—United States

ISBN 0-7432-0473-5

Also available Thorndike Press large print edition

Woodward discusses "how President George W. Bush and his top national security advisers, after the initial shock of the September 11 attacks, led the nation to war." Publisher's note

"While at times relying a bit too heavily on transcribed conversations, Woodward nonetheless offers one of the first truly insightful and informative accounts of the decision making process in the war on terror" Publ Wkly

974 Northeastern United States

Ulrich, Laurel

The age of homespun; objects and stories in the creation of an American myth; [by] Laurel Thatcher Ulrich. Knopf 2001 501p il maps $35; pa $16 **974**

1. Textile industry—History 2. American national characteristics 3. United States—Social life and customs

ISBN 0-679-44594-3; 0-679-76644-8 (pa)

LC 2001-29862

Ulrich attempts to demonstrate "how early Americans and their descendants made, used, sold, and saved textiles in order to assert identities, shape relationships, and create history." Publisher's note

This "is an edifying, entertaining voyage for any reader." Booklist

974.4 Massachusetts

Bradford, William, 1588-1657

Of Plymouth Plantation, 1620-1647; the complete text, with notes and an introduction by Samuel Eliot Morison. Knopf 1952 xliii, 448p maps $25 **974.4**

1. Massachusetts—History—1600-1775, Colonial period 2. Pilgrims (New England colonists)

ISBN 0-394-43895-7

Also available in paperback from McGraw-Hill

Written between 1630 and 1650; first published 1856 with title: History of Plymouth Plantation

"The opening book sketches the origin of the Separatist movement, the flight from England to Holland, the settlement at Leiden, the plans for the settlement in New England, and the *Mayflower* voyage. The second book, which includes the major part of the history, is in the form of annals from 1620 to 1646, and describes every aspect of the life of the Pilgrims. Besides being a primary historical source, the work has artistic value because of its dignified, sonorous style, deriving from the Geneva Bible." Oxford Companion to Am Lit. 5th edition

Kidder, Tracy

Home town. Random House 1999 349p o.p.; Washington Sq. Press paperback available $14.95 **974.4**

1. Northampton (Mass.) 2. City and town life

ISBN 0-671-78521-4 (pa) LC 99-13614

Kidder presents a portrait of the town of Northampton, Massachusetts. He "surveys Northampton through several sets of eyes. . . . But the observer who tells most of the story . . . [is a] town cop named Tommy O'Connor. . . . O'Connor was born in town—his father Bill was the county treasurer—played Little League here, has seen jobs dry up and the downtown decay, and then . . . has seen the . . . town center yuppified." Time

This "acutely observed, crisply written, and utterly absorbing documentary proves that there is nothing on this spinning earth more amazing and full of grace than everyday life." Booklist

Includes bibliographical references

974.6 Connecticut

O'Nan, Stewart, 1961-

The circus fire; a true story. Doubleday 2000 370p il hardcover o.p. paperback available $14 **974.6**

1. Ringling Bros.-Barnum & Bailey Combined Shows, Inc. 2. Fires—Hartford (Conn.)

ISBN 0-385-49685-0 (pa) LC 99-42051

"On a hot day in July 1944, some 9000 people were attending the Ringling Bros. Barnum & Bailey Circus in Hartford when a fire broke out. Mayhem and panic separated parents from children, some people were forced to crawl past the big cats in order to escape, and, in the end, many animals and 167 people died. Although O'Nan doesn't really solve the mystery of the origin of the fire, his attempt to identify the culprit makes a riveting side story." Libr J

974.7 New York

Bloom, Ken

Broadway; its history, people, and places: an encyclopedia. 2nd ed. Routledge 2003 679p il $95   **974.7**
1. Theater—New York (N.Y.)
ISBN 0-415-93704-3   LC 2003-2692
First published 1991

"Following a brief historical overview, . . . [the author] presents 394 alphabetical entries with multiple cross references for easy browsing. The most substantial entries cover theaters, playwrights, composers, directors, performers, and producers, with a special emphasis on composers and lyricists. . . . Bloom adds a touch of atmosphere with entries on critics, restaurants, publicity stunts, nightclubs, and other periphery characters and incidents that are so much a part of the Great White Way. As much a storyteller as a chronicler, he uses anecdotes and a plethora of black-and-white photographs, many never before published, to produce an entertaining as well as an informative work. Highly recommended for all theater collections." Libr J
Includes bibliographical references

Burrows, Edwin G., 1943-

Gotham; a history of New York City to 1898; [by] Edwin G. Burrows and Mike Wallace. Oxford Univ. Press 1998 xxiv, 1383p il maps hardcover o.p. paperback available $29.95   **974.7**
1. New York (N.Y.)—History
ISBN 0-19-514049-4 (pa)   LC 97-39308

This history "begins with the Indian settlements and the subsequent seizure of the city by the Dutch in 1626 and continues up to the consolidation of the five boroughs in 1898. The authors . . . cover an extraordinary range of topics, including religion, race, gender and class, architecture, society and the arts, noted personalities, sports and the special customs immigrants brought with them." America
Includes bibliographical references

The Encyclopedia of New York City; edited by Kenneth T. Jackson. Yale Univ. Press 1995 1350p il $65   **974.7**
1. New York (N.Y.)—Encyclopedias
ISBN 0-300-05536-6   LC 95-2811

This volume "serves up 4,300 articles by 680 authors, along with tables, lists, charts, and 688 illustrations. . . . Survey-articles take on the large conceptual subjects, like government and politics, architecture, education, immigration and science. Major articles are devoted to the history of each borough. Smaller entries deal with neighborhoods past and present, institutions (banks, advertising agencies, churches, labor unions, charities), historical events, local foods and folkways, ethnic groups, religions, newspapers, magazines, writers, [and] painters." NY Times Book Rev

Homberger, Eric

The historical atlas of New York City; a visual celebration of nearly 400 years of New York City's history; Alice Hudson, cartographic consultant. Holt & Co. 1994 192p il maps (Henry Holt reference book) hardcover o.p. paperback available $22   **974.7**
1. New York (N.Y.)—History
ISBN 0-8050-6004-9 (pa)   LC 94-18992

This is an "encyclopedic overview of the history of New York City. . . . Detailed color maps abound, accompanied by a running commentary of major historical and cultural eras. Many of the most detailed maps are rendered schematically for easier reading. Each period treated features historical photos and illustrations along with accompanying map(s). . . . A visual delight." Libr J

Langewiesche, William

American ground, unbuilding the World Trade Center. North Point Press 2002 205p $22; pa $13   **974.7**
1. World Trade Center (New York, N.Y.) 2. September 11 terrorist attacks, 2001
ISBN 0-86547-582-2; 0-86547-675-6 (pa)
LC 2002-75153

First published as a three part series of articles in Atlantic Monthly

This is an account "of the cleanup operation at ground zero—the 'unbuilding,' as he puts it, of the World Trade Center." N Y Times (Late N Y Ed)

"This is a genuinely monumental story, told without melodrama, an intimate depiction of ordinary Americans reacting to grand-scale tragedy at their best—and sometimes their worst." Publ Wkly

New York September 11; by Magnum photographers; introduction by David Halberstam. PowerHouse Bks. 2001 140p il $29.95   **974.7**
1. World Trade Center terrorist attack, 2001 2. Documentary photography
ISBN 1-57687-130-4   LC 2001-52330

This collection of photographs documents the attack on the World Trade Center on September 11, 2001. The book is organized essentially as a series of picture essays by individual photographers

Picciotto, Richard

Last man down; a New York City firefighter's story of survival and escape from the World Trade Center; by Richard Picciotto with Daniel Paisner. Berkley Bks. 2002 243p $24.95; pa $7.99   **974.7**
1. World Trade Center (New York, N.Y.) 2. New York (N.Y.). Fire Dept. 3. September 11 terrorist attacks, 2001
ISBN 0-425-18677-6; 0-425-18988-0 (pa)
LC 2002-19522

This "first-person account of a 9-11 survivor provides a firefighter's view of the World Trade Center catastrophe. An invaluable eyewitness to history as well as a professional just doing his job, Battalion Commander Richard Picciotto was inside the North Tower when it collapsed." Booklist

Schneider, Paul

The Adirondacks; a history of America's first wilderness. Holt & Co. 1997 368p il maps hardcover o.p. paperback available $16

974.7

1. Adirondack Mountains (N.Y.)—History

ISBN 0-8050-5990-3 (pa)   LC 96-39844

"A John Macrae book"

The author presents a "history of New York State's Adirondack region. He relates here the life and lore of these scenic mountains and lakes (Whiteface, Mt. Marcy, Fulton Chain Lakes) from the region's earliest inhabitants (Haudenosaunce/Iroquois) through the advent of Henry Hudson (1609), the Revolutionary War, abolitionists (John Brown), 19th-century homesteaders, Hudson River School artists, tuberculosis patients to Melville Dewey's Lake Placid Club, the Adirondack Mountain Club, and the present environmental conservation efforts." Libr J

Von Drehle, Dave

Triangle: the fire that changed America. Atlantic Monthly Press 2003 340p il $25

974.7

1. Triangle Shirtwaist Company, Inc. 2. Fires 3. New York (N.Y.) 4. Clothing industry 5. Factories

ISBN 0-87113-874-3   LC 2003-41835

Also available Thorndike Press large print edition

"The tragic conflagration at the Triangle Shirtwaist Factory in March 1911 resulted in the deaths of 123 women (most of them young immigrants), caused widespread public outrage, and set in motion a wave of reform. Drehle's vivid retelling of this horrifying event begins with the strike that immediately preceded it and then examines the terrible fire, the unsuccessful prosecution of the factory owners, and the fight to prevent similar tragedies in the future." Libr J

"Von Drehle's engrossing account, which emphasizes the humanity of the victims and the theme of social justice, brings us of the pivotal and most shocking episodes of American labor history to life." Publ Wkly

Includes bibliographical references

Wetzsteon, Ross

Republic of dreams; Greenwich Village, the American Bohemia, 1910-1960. Simon & Schuster 2001 615p il $35; pa $19.95 **974.7**

1. Greenwich Village (New York, N.Y.)—Intellectual life 2. New York (N.Y.)—Social life and customs

ISBN 0-684-86995-0; 0-684-86996-9 (pa)

LC 2001-34229

Wetzsteon chronicles the cultural and artistic life of New York City's Greenwich Village. "His story begins around 1910, about the time the term 'Village' entered the lexicon. It ends around 1960, when bohemianism had spread well beyond the neighborhood's confines." N Y Times (Late N Y Ed)

"This collection of affectionate set pieces truly approximates the free-wheeling Village spirit." Publ Wkly

Includes bibliographical references

White, Shane

Stories of freedom in Black New York. Harvard Univ. Press 2002 260p il $27.95

974.7

1. African Company (Theater company) 2. African Americans—New York (N.Y.) 3. New York (N.Y.)—Race relations 4. New York (N.Y.)—Intellectual life

ISBN 0-674-00893-6   LC 2002-68540

"The early nineteenth century was turbulent in New York, as the state dealt with the end of slavery. Focusing especially on a black theater group, its leading actor, and a Jewish newspaper editor, White examines the black theater, balls, cotillions, and other social expressions that provoked virulent attacks and editorials from whites." Booklist

The author "makes a persuasive case for the company's cultural importance, particularly as a forerunner of the Harlem Renaissance that was still a century away." Publ Wkly

Includes bibliographical references

974.8   Pennsylvania

Longman, Jere

Among the heroes; United Flight 93 and the passengers and crew who fought back. HarperCollins Pubs. 2002 288p il $24.95; pa $13.95 **974.8**

1. Hijacking of airplanes 2. September 11 terrorist attacks, 2001

ISBN 0-06-009908-9; 0-06-009909-7 (pa)

LC 2002-68530

This is an account of the United Airlines flight which was hijacked on September 11, 2001 and crashed in Pennsylvania before reaching its intended target

This book "gives us an incredibly detailed and personal tale of that horrific episode." Booklist

Includes bibliographical references

974.9   New Jersey

Sheehy, Gail

Middletown, America; one town's passage from trauma to hope. Random House 2003 xxv, 412p il map $24.95 **974.9**

1. September 11 terrorist attacks, 2001 2. Middletown (N.J.)

ISBN 0-375-50862-7   LC 2003-46694

This is an "examination of the traumatic impact of 9/11 on Middletown, New Jersey, which suffered 'the largest concentrated death toll' from the terrorist attacks." Booklist

"Among the growing body of 9/11 literature, this title stands out and should find a place in all libraries." Libr J

975   Southeastern United States. Southern States

Cash, Wilbur Joseph, 1900-1941

The mind of the South; with a new introduction by Bertram Wyatt-Brown. Vintage Bks. 1991 xliv, 444p pa $16 **975**

1. Southern States—Civilization

ISBN 0-679-73647-6   LC 91-50042

First published 1941 by Knopf

Cash, Wilbur Joseph, 1900-1941—*Continued*

A psychological, cultural, and social history of the old South

Dent, Tom, 1932-1998

Southern journey; a return to the civil rights movement. Morrow 1997 400p il o.p.; University of Ga. Press paperback available $18.95 **975**

1. Southern States—Race relations 2. African Americans—Civil rights

ISBN 0-8203-2291-1 (pa)   LC 96-28395

This book examines race relations in the American South. "To collect impressions of what has changed, and what hasn't since the 1960s, Dent traveled the back roads of a half-dozen Southern states for nearly a year, talking with 140 Southerners, black and white." Christ Sci Monit

"Dent compellingly reveals that ordinary Southerners fundamentally changed the region and are poised to make more substantive changes." Libr J

Wiencek, Henry

The Hairstons; an American family in black and white. St. Martin's Press 1999 xx, 361p il map hardcover o.p. paperback available $14.95 **975**

1. Hairston family 2. African Americans—Southern States 3. Slavery—United States 4. United States—Race relations

ISBN 0-312-25393-1 (pa)   LC 98-44014

Wiencek tells the "story of the Hairston family, the largest slaveholders in the South and one of the wealthiest families in the U.S. Wiencek details the race mixing that occured between master and slave and the family's efforts to keep its dark-skinned members enslaved and to maintain wealth only for its white members. A fascinating book that explores the complexity of family and racial relationships in the U.S." Booklist

Includes bibliographical references

975.3 District of Columbia (Washington)

Allen, Thomas B., 1929-

The Washington Monument; it stands for all. Discovery Bks. (NY) 2000 172p il $29.95 **975.3**

1. Washington Monument (Washington, D.C.)

ISBN 1-56331-921-7   LC 00-25608

"Allen provides a brief biographical sketch of Washington; a chronology of the construction of the monument, which took almost 100 years; and background on events centering on and around the monument, Pierre Charles L'Enfant's plans for the city, and the evolution of the monument itself." Libr J

Katharine Graham's Washington; {compiled by} Katharine Graham. Knopf 2002 813p il $30; pa $16.95 **975.3**

1. Washington (D.C.)

ISBN 0-375-41471-1; 1-4000-3059-5 (pa)
        LC 2002-111640

"The late newspaper publisher's posthumous legacy is a delightful and insightful anthology of writings on the city that formed so much of her personality and her professional life. She draws from her personal collection of writings by a range of writers, many of them personal friends." Booklist

Monkman, Betty C.

The White House; its historic furnishings and first families; principal photography by Bruce White. Abbeville Press 2000 320p il $65 **975.3**

1. White House (Washington, D.C.)

ISBN 0-7892-0624-2   LC 00-27085

"Monkman, the White House curator, documents the furnishings and decorative objects as well as the metamorphoses of White House interiors. The impact of the presidents and first ladies is particularly intriguing." Libr J

Includes bibliographical references

The **White** House; actors and observers; edited by William Seale. Northeastern Univ. Press 2002 xxii, 214p il $40 **975.3**

1. White House (Washington, D.C.) 2. Presidents—United States

ISBN 1-55553-547-X   LC 2002-9087

Essays derived from papers delivered at a 200th anniversary symposium sponsored by the White House Historical Association

Contents: Introduction: like no other house, by W. Steele; Abigail Adams as first lady, by E. B. Gelles; Dolley Madison creates the White House, by C. Allgor; The earliest photographs of the White House, 1840s, by C. Krainik; The Lincoln White House: stage for the Republic's survival, by J. Baker; Images of the Executive Mansion, 1861-1865, by B. C. Monkman; The gold in the Gilded Age, by R. N. Smith; Frances Benjamin Johnston's White House, by W. B. Bushong; Images of the White House, 1890-1910, by L. B. Tederick; Theodore Roosevelt's White House, by J. A. Gable; Eleanor Roosevelt and Franklin Roosevelt: partnership in politics and crises, by A. Black; White House news photographers and the White House, by D. Brack; Presidential reality: "if it hasn't happened on television, it hasn't happened", by M. J. Kumar

This is "a pictorial history of the presidential residence. Accompanied by a succession of essays presented at a symposium honoring the 200th anniversary of the White House, this stunning collection of paintings, drawings, and photographs chronicles two centuries of presidential history. . . . This irresistible gallery of pictures will appeal to scholars and browsers alike." Booklist

Includes bibliographical references

975.5 Virginia

Furgurson, Ernest B., 1929-

Ashes of glory; Richmond at war. Knopf 1996 419p il maps hardcover o.p. paperback available $16 **975.5**

1. Richmond (Va.)—History 2. United States—History—1861-1865, Civil War—Campaigns

ISBN 0-679-74660-9 (pa)   LC 95-49591

The author "tells the story of a city that between 1861 and 1865 epitomized the experience of the Civil War as a revolutionary one. Capital of a state that had long opposed secession, Richmond now became the symbol of Southern independence. It also remained a center of clandestine Unionism that hosted a struggle between espionage networks matching anything seen in Cold War Berlin." Publ Wkly

Includes bibliographical references

Milton, Giles, 1966-

Big Chief Elizabeth; the adventures and fate of the First English Colonists in America. Farrar, Straus & Giroux 2000 358p il maps hardcover o.p. paperback available $14   **975.5**

1. Elizabeth I, Queen of England, 1533-1603 2. Virginia—History 3. Great Britain—Colonies—America 4. Native Americans 5. America—Exploration

ISBN 0-312-42018-8 (pa)   LC 00-31522

"Nearly 500 years ago, a small group of white men landed on the shores of North America and named it Virginia (for the Virgin Queen [Elizabeth]). Their purpose was to capture some natives and bring them to England to learn their language and everything else they could about the country they wished to colonize. . . . [Milton] chronicles the century-long battle to establish a permanent settlement in Virginia." Christ Sci Monit

Noël Hume, Ivor, 1927-

The Virginia adventure; Roanoke to James Towne: an archaeological and historical odyssey. Knopf 1994 xxviii, 491p il maps o.p.; University Press of Va. paperback available $19.95   **975.5**

1. Roanoke Island (N.C.)—History 2. Jamestown (Va.)—History

ISBN 0-8139-1758-1 (pa)   LC 93-33213

The author discusses "the historical archaeology of the Roanoke and James Fort (later James Towne) settlements. Drawing extensively on firsthand accounts and other textual sources, he conjures up the feel of the Elizabethan experience that gave life to these settlements. . . . Hume also includes masterly and generous accounts of the history of the excavation of these sites and offers his well-informed views on where future work needs to be done. Written with wit, compassion, and tremendous attention to detail, this is historical archaeology at its best." Libr J

Includes bibliographical references

975.7   South Carolina

Ball, Edward, 1959-

Slaves in the family. Farrar, Straus & Giroux 1998 540p il maps o.p.; Ballantine Bks. paperback available $16.95   **975.7**

1. Ball family 2. Plantation life 3. Slavery—United States 4. South Carolina 5. United States—Race relations

ISBN 0-345-43105-7 (pa)   LC 97-34640

"For nearly a hundred and seventy years before the Civil War, members of the Ball family owned a string of plantations worked by slaves along South Carolina's Cooper River. After the war, the author's ancestors lost or sold their land and scattered to make new lives, but he wondered what happened to the slaves. This book, a brilliant blend of archival research and oral history, tells what he found." New Yorker

975.8   Georgia

Berendt, John

Midnight in the garden of good and evil; a story of Savannah. Random House 1994 388p $25; pa $14   **975.8**

1. Savannah (Ga.)—Social life and customs

ISBN 0-679-42922-0; 0-679-75152-1 (pa)

    LC 93-3955

Also available large print edition $20 (ISBN 0-679-76283-3)

On one level, this book is a "travelog, recounting former *New York* magazine editor Berendt's eight years in Savannah, Georgia, that beautifully preserved hothouse of a Southern city where eccentric characters like black drag queen Lady Chablis and charming con man Joe Odom blossom in rich profusion. It is also a tale of true crime, the saga of antiques dealer Jim Williams whose 1981 shooting of his sometime lover Danny Hansford in the historic Mercer House obsesses Savannah denizens." Libr J

"Berendt has fashioned a Baedeker to Savannah that, while it flirts with condescension, is always contagiously affectionate. Few cities have been introduced more seductively." Newsweek

Carter, Jimmy, 1924-

Turning point; a candidate, a state, and a nation come of age. Times Bks. 1992 xxv, 223p il o.p.; Random House paperback available $14   **975.8**

1. Georgia—Politics and government

ISBN 0-8129-2299-9 (pa)   LC 92-53671

The former president gives an account of his first political campaign, in which he successfully challenged the old regime for a seat in the Georgia State Senate in 1962

"The story of how Carter and a few loyal friends saw this episode through to success is good reading for anyone who cares about democracy. It's a simply told tale, but the author acknowledges the complexities of the experience." Christ Sci Monit

Foxfire [1]-11. Doubleday 1972-1993 11v il pa ea $16.95   **975.8**

1. Country life—Georgia 2. Appalachian region—Social life and customs 3. Handicraft

Editors: v1-6 Eliot Wigginton; v7 Paul F. Gillespie; v8-9 Eliot Wigginton and Margie Bennett; v10 George P. Reynolds and Susan Walker; v11 Kaye Carver Collins and Lacy Hunter

First book in series has title: The Foxfire book

"A chronicle of the economic, historic, and cultural changes of an Appalachian village as perceived through the inquisitive minds of its younger generation. . . . Begun . . . as an experiment in getting students more directly involved in their classwork, the 'Foxfire' volumes have developed into an enduring example of a practical and effective educational philosophy." Booklist

976.1 Alabama

Agee, James, 1909-1955
Let us now praise famous men; three tenant families; [by] James Agee, Walker Evans; with an introduction to the new edition by John Hersey. Houghton Mifflin 1988 c1941 liv, 471p il hardcover o.p. paperback available $16.95   **976.1**
1. Alabama—Social conditions 2. Farm tenancy
ISBN 0-395-48897-4 (pa)   LC 88-18110
First published 1941
This republication of the classic work based on a 1936 journalistic assignment contains "about twice as many photographs [by Evans] as the original contained." Best Sellers
This work documents "the ways of life of three Alabama tenant-farming families. . . . [It] is a unique and complex book, deeply honest and compassionate, and remarkable for its extraordinary descriptive, lyric, and meditative prose." Benet's Reader's Ency of Am Lit

McWhorter, Diane
Carry me home; Birmingham, Alabama: the climactic battle of the civil rights revolution. Simon & Schuster 2001 701p il $35; pa $17
976.1
1. African Americans—Civil rights 2. Birmingham (Ala.)—Race relations
ISBN 0-684-80747-5; 0-7432-1772-1 (pa)
LC 00-53827
McWhorter presents an account of the struggle for civil rights in Birmingham, Ala., both from a personal and societal perspective
"A daughter of Birmingham's privileged elite, McWhorter weaves a personal narrative through this startling account of the history, events, and major players on both sides of the civil rights battle in that city." Booklist
Includes bibliographical references

976.2 Mississippi

Rubin, Richard
Confederacy of silence; a true tale of the new old South. Atria Bks. 2002 438p $26; pa $14
976.2
1. Mississippi—Race relations
ISBN 0-671-03666-1; 0-671-03667-X (pa)
LC 2002-510321
"Rubin, an Ivy League-educated New Yorker, went to work as a sportswriter in Greenwood, Mississippi. Almost in spite of himself, he came to love Greenwood, even as he remained aware of the ways in which the New South resembled the old. He also befriended a black high-school quarterback who he believed would become an N.F.L. star. Five years after Rubin left town, though, he heard that the player had been indicted for murder, and he returned to find out what had gone wrong." New Yorker
"Rubin's memoir exposes the racial polarity of the Delta in clear, effective prose." Publ Wkly

Welty, Eudora, 1909-2001
One time, one place; Mississippi in the Depression : a snapshot album. rev ed. University Press of Miss. 1996 115p il $35
976.2
1. Mississippi—Pictorial works
ISBN 0-87805-866-4   LC 95-46057
First published 1971 by Random House
This is a "collection of photographs of Mississippians that Welty took in the 1930s, when she worked for the Works Progress Administration (WPA). This Silver Anniversary Edition contains a great foreword by William Maxwell that absolutely nails the importance of the book for many readers." Booklist

976.4 Texas

Davis, William C., 1946-
Three roads to the Alamo; the lives and fortunes of David Crockett, James Bowie and William Barret Travis. HarperCollins Pubs. 1998 791p il hardcover o.p. paperback available $20   **976.4**
1. Crockett, Davy, 1786-1836 2. Bowie, James, 1799?-1836 3. Travis, William Barret, 1809-1836 4. Texas—History 5. Alamo (San Antonio, Tex.)
ISBN 0-06-093094-2 (pa)   LC 97-43815
Davis provides portraits of the three frontiersmen "showing both the differences and similarities that propelled them into a remote Spanish mission in Mexican Texas for a fatal confrontation with the Mexican President, Santa Anna and his troops in March 1836." N Y Times Book Rev
This "is a readable, stimulating, and exceptionally well-researched narrative history." Libr J
Includes bibliographical references

Larson, Erik
Isaac's storm; a man, a time, and the deadliest hurricane in history. Crown 1999 323p $25; pa $13   **976.4**
1. Cline, Isaac Monroe, 1861-1955 2. Hurricanes 3. Floods 4. Galveston (Tex.)—History
ISBN 0-609-60233-0; 0-375-70827-8 (pa)
LC 99-25515
"The hurricane that struck Galveston, Texas, on September 8, 1900, was the nation's deadliest natural disaster; it destroyed much of the city and killed thousands of people. Larson relates the tragedy in several layers, centering on the personal and professional story of Isaac Cline, head of the U.S. Weather Bureau's Galveston office." Voice Youth Advocates
"Larson expertly captures the power of the storm itself and the ironic, often catastrophic consequences of the unpredictable intersection of natural force and human choice." Publ Wkly

Robinson, Charles M., 1949-
The men who wear the star; the story of the Texas Rangers; [by] Charles M. Robinson III. Random House 2000 xxi, 352p hardcover o.p. paperback available $14.95   **976.4**
1. Texas Rangers 2. Frontier and pioneer life—Texas 3. Texas—History
ISBN 0-375-75748-1 (pa)   LC 99-27160
An "account of the Rangers from their beginnings—10 men mustered to defend against Indian depredations in

Robinson, Charles M., 1949-—*Continued*
1823—to the early 20th century, when the automobile re-placed the horse as the rangers' mount of choice." N Y Times Book Rev

Robinson "has done a good job of covering the his-tory of the Rangers. . . . He evenhandedly shows both their virtues and flaws and helps one to understand the foundations underlying the modern image." Libr J
Includes bibliographical references

976.6   Oklahoma

Hirsch, James S.
Riot and remembrance; the Tulsa race war and its legacy. Houghton Mifflin 2002 358p
il $25; pa $14   **976.6**
1. African Americans—Tulsa (Okla.) 2. Riots 3. Tul-sa (Okla.)—Race relations
ISBN 0-618-10813-0; 0-618-34076-9 (pa)
LC 2001-51615
"James S. Hirsch's history of the Tulsa, Okla., race riot in 1921 places the incident in a national debate on race and reparations." N Y Times Book Rev
"Hirsch unearths an important episode in U.S. history with verve, intelligence and compassion." Publ Wkly
Includes bibliographical references

Madigan, Tim
The burning; massacre, destruction, and the Tulsa race riot of 1921. Thomas Dunne Bks.
2001 297p il $24.95; pa $13.95   **976.6**
1. African Americans—Tulsa (Okla.) 2. Riots 3. Tul-sa (Okla.)—Race relations
ISBN 0-312-27283-9; 0-312-30247-9 (pa)
LC 2001-41811
This is an account of the 1921 attack by whites on Greenwood, the black district of Tulsa, Oklahoma
"Madigan's skill at description, dialogue and pacing keeps the reader's interest at peak levels, and he does not gloss over brutal scenes of murder, arson and torture." Publ Wkly
Includes bibliographical references

Wickett, Murray R., 1965-
Contested territory; whites, Native Americans, and African Americans in Oklahoma, 1865-1907. Louisiana State Univ.
Press 2000 240p il $59.95; pa $26.95 **976.6**
1. Oklahoma—History 2. Native Americans—History 3. African Americans—History 4. United States—Race relations
ISBN 0-8071-2584-9; 0-8071-2647-0 (pa)
LC 00-32122
"This monograph is an examination of race relations in the Oklahoma Territory during the period between the conclusion of the Civil War and the granting of Oklaho-ma statehood. Though its subject matter is extremely complex . . . the information is presented in a manner that is accessible to educated readers." Libr J
Includes bibliographical references

977   North Central United States. Lake states

Barry, John M.
Rising tide; the great Mississippi flood of 1927 and how it changed America. Simon & Schuster 1997 524p il maps hardcover o.p. paperback available $16   **977**
1. Floods—Mississippi River 2. Mississippi River val-ley—History
ISBN 0-684-84002-2 (pa)   LC 96-40077
This is the "story of human defeat by a savage, unpre-dictable river. . . . The flood of 1927, three times great-er than the flood of 1993, was an unprecedented disaster that spurred a political innovation. Congress's agreement to rebuild the Mississippi's shattered flood-control sys-tem marked the federal government's first assumption of full financial responsibility for a regional calamity. Much of the book recounts how the greed of New Orleans bankers and Delta planters increased the sufferings of the rural poor. . . . Barry's book is a virtuoso piece of expo-sition." New Yorker
Includes bibliographical references

977.1   Ohio

Frazier, Ian
Family. Farrar, Straus & Giroux 1994 386p
il maps hardcover o.p. paperback available
$16   **977.1**
1. Frazier family 2. City and town life 3. Ohio—So-cial life and customs
ISBN 0-312-42059-5 (pa)   LC 94-14730
"An extraordinary history of an ordinary family, in which the author plays the roles of gossip, pedant and loyal member, yielding a reunion strangers are wel-come—and fortunate—to attend." N Y Times Book Rev

977.3   Illinois

Miller, Donald L., 1944-
City of the century; the epic of Chicago and the making of America; [by] Donald Miller. Simon & Schuster 1996 704p il maps hardcover o.p. paperback available $18
977.3
1. Chicago (Ill.)—History
ISBN 0-684-83138-4 (pa)   LC 96-4018
In this account of Chicago's history in the nineteenth century "Miller tells of Chicago's historical and literary figures, reform leaders, architects, industrialists, and en-trepreneurs." Libr J

Tintori, Karen
Trapped: the 1909 Cherry Mine disaster. Simon & Schuster 2002 273p il $25; pa $14
977.3
1. Coal mines and mining—Accidents
ISBN 0-7434-2194-9; 0-7434-2195-7 (pa)
LC 2002-104596
"On November 13, 1909, a fire trapped 480 coal min-ers . . . 400 feet below ground in a mine at Cherry, Illi-nois. Only 221 escaped. . . . Tintori describes the life-and-death struggle of the miners below ground and the terror of the women and children gathered at the mine's entrance. . . . Tintori's graphic account of this tragedy is a sad but gripping story." Booklist

978 Western United States

Ambrose, Stephen E.

Lewis & Clark; voyage of discovery; [photographs by] Sam Abell. National Geographic Soc. 2002 255p il maps $35

978

1. Lewis and Clark Expedition (1804-1806) 2. West (U.S.)—Exploration 3. West (U.S.)—Description

ISBN 0-7922-6473-8   LC 2002-727771

First published 1998

Bicentennial edition

"Ambrose, drawing on his hikes and canoe trips to all the monuments between St. Louis and Fort Clatsop associated with the explorers, melds his memories and own journal entries with a . . . Lewis and Clark narrative spiced by entries from their journals." Booklist

"In addition to the superb writing, the book has stunning, full-color photographs of the places that Lewis and Clark so vividly described. . . . This combination of easy-to-read writing, high-quality photographs, and period artwork makes this book appealing to a wide range of readers." SLJ

Includes bibliographical references

Undaunted courage; Meriwether Lewis, Thomas Jefferson, and the opening of the American West. Simon & Schuster 1996 511p il maps $30; pa $17

978

1. Lewis, Meriwether, 1774-1809 2. Lewis and Clark Expedition (1804-1806) 3. West (U.S.)—Exploration

ISBN 0-684-81107-3; 0-684-82697-6 (pa)

LC 95-37146

This treatment of the Lewis and Clark Expedition "is essentially a biography of Lewis, although the bulk of it is a lively retelling of the journey of the two captains—together with their party of soldiers and frontiersmen, Clark's black slave, York, and the legendary Shoshone Indian woman, Sacagawea, and her infant son—conveyed with passionate enthusiasm by Mr. Ambrose and sprinkled liberally with some of the most famous and vivid passages from the travelers' journals." N Y Times Book Rev

Includes bibliographical references

Brown, Dee Alexander

The American West; photos edited by Martin F. Schmitt. Scribner 1994 461p il maps hardcover o.p. paperback available $15

978

1. West (U.S.)—History

ISBN 0-684-80441-7 (pa)   LC 94-37444

"This narrative history of westward expansion paints a vivid portrait of the settlers, pioneers, entrepreneurs, and Native Americans of the old West. Useful as collateral research material and for recreational reading." Booklist

Includes bibliographical references

Brown, Kenneth A.

Four corners; history, land, and people of the desert Southwest. HarperCollins Pubs. 1995 372p il maps hardcover o.p. paperback available $14

978

1. Southwestern States

ISBN 0-06-092759-3 (pa)   LC 95-40208

"With its spectacular ancient rock formations, high plateaus and desert valleys, its Native American multistory cliff dwellers, its confluence of Mormon, Spanish, Navajo, Ute, Anglo and other cultures, the Four Corners region—the intersection of Arizona, New Mexico, Colorado and Utah—is a world unto itself. Nature writer Brown takes readers on a wondrous odyssey through this sparsely inhabited region in a seamless mix of travelogue, geology, biology and history." Publ Wkly

Dary, David

The Santa Fe Trail; its history, legends, and lore. Knopf 2000 368p il maps $30   **978**

1. Santa Fe Trail

ISBN 0-375-40361-2   LC 00-23276

Also available in paperback from Penguin Bks.

This is a history of the Santa Fe Trail, a route in the Southwestern United States "employed for commercial and emigrant traffic for nearly six decades, beginning in 1822, . . . after New Spain declared independence from Spain and renamed itself Mexico." N Y Times Book Rev

"This is a solid account, grounded in available original sources. . . . Far from writing a dry business history, Dary has an engaging style that allows him to relate some of the lore and legends and show that they are just lore and legends." Libr J

Seeking pleasure in the Old West. Knopf 1995 352p il o.p.; University Press of Kan. paperback available $14.95   **978**

1. West (U.S.)—Social life and customs 2. Amusements

ISBN 0-7006-0828-1 (pa)   LC 95-2709

This book relates the "many ways people in the American West sought pleasure in the nineteenth century. It describes both the how and why of those diversions that Americans spent their nonworking hours pursuing, often amid adversity and hardship. Those activities ranged from the simple and homespun to the bawdy and elaborate. . . . Whenever possible, journals, diaries, newspapers, and first-person recollections are employed to capture the flavor of activities in the participants' own words." Booklist

Duncan, Dayton

Lewis & Clark; the journey of the Corps of Discovery; based on a documentary film by Ken Burns, written by Dayton Duncan; with a preface by Ken Burns and contributions by Stephen E. Ambrose, Erica Funkhouser, William Least Heat-Moon. Knopf 1997 248p il maps hardcover o.p. paperback available $25

978

1. Lewis and Clark Expedition (1804-1806) 2. West (U.S.)—Exploration

ISBN 0-375-70652-6 (pa)   LC 97-73823

This is a companion volume to PBS television film 'Lewis and Clark: The journey of the Corps of Discovery,' by Ken Burns

An "attractive book with a well-written text and an excellent presentation of historic paintings, photographs, maps, and original quotations from various of Lewis and Clark's journals." Sci Books Films

Frazier, Ian

Great Plains. Farrar, Straus & Giroux 1989 290p il maps hardcover o.p. paperback available $13 **978**

1. Great Plains—Description 2. West (U.S.)—Description

ISBN 0-312-27850-0 (pa)   LC 88-31106

The author recounts his experiences and observations traveling in the Western United States

"This is a colorful and engaging blend of travelogue, local color, geography and folklore." Publ Wkly

Lewis, Meriwether, 1774-1809

The essential Lewis and Clark; Landon Y. Jones, editor. Ecco Press 2000 xx, 203p $24; pa $13.95 **978**

1. Lewis and Clark Expedition (1804-1806) 2. West (U.S.)—Exploration

ISBN 0-06-019600-9; 0-06-001159-9 (pa)

LC 99-86335

Excerpts from the 1904-05 version of: Original journals of the Lewis and Clark expedition, 1804-1806; edited by Reuben Gold Thwaites

In this volume the editor presents excerpts from the journals of Lewis and Clark "that focus on the seminal junctures of the journey, including their reactions to the breathtaking physical majesty of the West, their initial encounters with various Native American tribes, and their fascinating accounts of the physical and moral courage of their fellow travelers." Booklist

The **Lewis** and Clark journals; an American epic of discovery: the abridgment of the definitive Nebraska edition; [by] Meriwether Lewis, William Clark, and members of the Corps of Discovery; edited and with an introduction by Gary E. Moulton. University of Neb. Press 2003 lviii, 413p il maps $29.95 **978**

1. Lewis, Meriwether, 1774-1809 2. Lewis and Clark Expedition (1804-1806) 3. West (U.S.)—Exploration

ISBN 0-8032-2950-X   LC 2002-28526

"Moulton presents an abridged version of the Journals of the Lewis and Clark Expedition . . . that celebrates the Corps of Discovery's landmark journey 200 years ago. What makes this single volume of journal selections more powerful than its contemporaries is the use of other corps members' diaries to provide further details about the journey. Major themes include anthropological observations about the Native Americans the corps encountered, their relations with these tribes, and the natural history work of Lewis and Clark. The expedition is broken down into 12 chronological chapters, and notes defining 19th-century vocabulary, shifting geographic place names, and events requiring editorial explanation are included alongside the text. This book will bring the expedition alive to a new generation of readers. Recommended for all libraries." Libr J

"This is a very smooth abridgment of the 13-volume edition of the explorers' journals. Suited to the general reader, this edition is an invaluable and easily digested account of the epic journey." Booklist

Luchetti, Cathy, 1945-

Children of the West; family life on the frontier. Norton 2001 253p il $39.95 **978**

1. Children—West (U.S.) 2. Frontier and pioneer life—West (U.S.) 3. West (U.S.)—Social life and customs

ISBN 0-393-04913-2   LC 00-53287

"In the nineteenth and early twentieth centuries, the children who resided in the sparsely populated plains and prairies of the western U.S. were subject to a unique variety of hardships and joys. . . . Utilizing more than 100 vintage photographs and excerpts from letters, diaries, and journals, Luchetti examines aspects of childbearing, child rearing, childhood, and adolescence on the American frontier." Booklist

Includes bibliographical references

Morgan, Ted, 1932-

A shovel of stars; the making of the American West, 1800 to the present. Simon & Schuster 1995 559p il maps hardcover o.p. paperback available $25 **978**

1. West (U.S.)—History 2. Frontier and pioneer life—West (U.S.)

ISBN 0-684-81492-7 (pa)   LC 94-43838

Companion volume Wilderness at dawn

Morgan "looks at the settlement of each state during its territorial period from the Louisiana Purchase in 1803 to the admission of Alaska and Hawaii in 1959." Libr J

"This grandly inspired work—a completely satisfying read—embraces the texture and the drama of the West in all its heartbreak and heroism." Booklist

Includes bibliographical references

The **Oxford** history of the American West; edited by Clyde A. Milner II, Carol A. O'Connor, Martha A. Sandweiss. Oxford Univ. Press 1994 872p il maps hardcover o.p. paperback available $29.95 **978**

1. West (U.S.)—History

ISBN 0-19-511212-1 (pa)   LC 93-38829

"This book surveys the area's history and development from the time of the early natives up to the current day. The first three sections chronicle political, social, and economic history in roughly chronological order. . . . The final section examines how the West has been interpreted in art, literature, and popular entertainment. All the authors of the various chapters focus on the major events with just the right amount of interpretation and case-study illustration to give the reader a good sense of how the West developed." Libr J

Includes bibliographical references

Parkman, Francis, 1823-1893

The Oregon Trail **978**

1. Oregon Trail 2. West (U.S.)—Description 3. Native Americans 4. Frontier and pioneer life—West (U.S.)

Hardcover and paperback editions available from various publishers

Originally published serially in Knickerbocker Magazine; first published in book form, 1849, with title: The California and Oregon Trail

"An account of a trip made in 1846 by the author and his cousin Quincy Adams Shaw. They traveled together from St. Louis to Fort Laramie; there they separated, Parkman going to live for some weeks with a tribe of Sioux Indians. *The Oregon Trail* provides valuable descriptions of the prairies at the most fascinating period of their history and a remarkable ethnological study of the Indians." Benet's Reader's Ency of Am Lit

Includes bibliographical references

Raban, Jonathan

Bad land; an American romance. Pantheon Bks. 1996 324p hardcover o.p. paperback available $14 **978**
1. Frontier and pioneer life—West (U.S.) 2. West (U.S.)—History
ISBN 0-679-75906-9 (pa)   LC 96-13432
This "book about Montana examines the present remains and historical origins of the last great wave of American western settlement, the migration of homesteaders to eastern Montana in the first decade of this century." London Rev Books
Raban "turns Montana into a profound symbol for America's sense of displacement; for its tragic romance with rootlessness, its search for identity under that big blue sky." New Statesman (1913)

Schlissel, Lillian

Far from home; families of the westward journey; [by] Lillian Schlissel, Byrd Gibbens, Elizabeth Hampsten; foreword by Robert Coles. Schocken Bks. 1989 264p il o.p.; University of Neb. Press paperback available $14.95 **978**
1. Frontier and pioneer life—West (U.S.) 2. West (U.S.)—Social life and customs
ISBN 0-8032-9295-3 (pa)   LC 88-42685
"The authors relate the story of three pioneering families—largely through the words of mothers and daughters preserved in old correspondence and later autobiographical writings." Christ Sci Monit
"An immensely readable book that peers closely into the lives of ordinary American frontier families." Booklist
Includes bibliographical references

Schmidt, Thomas, 1959-

The Lewis & Clark Trail; foreword by Stephen E. Ambrose. Bicentennial ed completely rev. National Geographic Soc. 2002 192p il maps pa $16 **978**
1. Lewis and Clark Expedition (1804-1806) 2. West (U.S.)—Description
ISBN 0-7922-6471-1   LC 2001-7003
First published 1998
Color photographs and maps provide a guide to the Lewis and Clark National Historic Trail

Shoumatoff, Alex

Legends of the American desert; sojourns in the greater Southwest. Knopf 1997 533p o.p.; Perennial Bks. paperback available $15 **978**
1. Southwestern States—History
ISBN 0-06-097769-8 (pa)
"Shoumatoff focuses on past and present conditions of human, animal, and plant habitation—all in the face of the need to adapt to the scarcity of water. Elevating his account to superior travel writing, Shoumatoff smoothly blends geology, geography, history, economics, and even paleontology into a complete course in the American desert's story from the time of immigrant Native Americans coming over from Asia on the frozen Bering Sea to the kingdom of the cowboys in the nineteenth century to today's influx of retirees." Booklist

Slaughter, Thomas P.

Exploring Lewis and Clark; reflections on men and wilderness. Knopf 2003 231p il maps $24; pa $14 **978**
1. Lewis, Meriwether, 1774-1809 2. Clark, William, 1770-1838 3. Sacagawea, b. 1786 4. York, ca. 1775-ca. 1815 5. Lewis and Clark Expedition (1804-1806) 6. West (U.S.)—Exploration
ISBN 0-375-40078-8; 0-375-70071-4 (pa)
          LC 2002-69376
The author "utilizes the journals of explorers Lewis and Clark to investigate their epic journey and its subsequent mythical status. What becomes quickly apparent is that these were imperfect men who have become legends." Libr J
"It may be easy to dismiss as a nitpicking revisionist potshot at our beloved heroes, but as the expedition's bicentennial approaches, this book's perspective will help keep our understanding well nuanced and grounded in fact." Booklist
Includes bibliographical references

Ward, Geoffrey C.

The West; an illustrated history; narrative by Geoffrey C. Ward; based on a documentary film script by Geoffrey C. Ward and Dayton Duncan; with a preface by Stephen Ives and Ken Burns; and contributions by Dayton Duncan [et al.] Little, Brown 1996 445p il hardcover o.p. paperback available $24.95 **978**
1. West (U.S.)—History
ISBN 0-316-73589-2 (pa)   LC 96-4323
"The book's eight chapters, each written by a different historian, are arranged according to the corresponding PBS series. Beginning with Western America in the 1500s, the work presents all aspects of Western culture from the reality to the myth, moving chronologically from the Spanish exploration of the West, Native Americans, Hispanic Westerners, women in the West, and the Gold Rush, and ending with Buffalo Bill's Wild West Show. If one is looking for an in-depth, comprehensive history of the westward movement, this is not it, but as an introduction, this work is an enjoyable and interesting place to start." Libr J

West, Elliott, 1945-

The contested plains; Indians, goldseekers, & the rush to Colorado. University Press of Kan. 1998 xxiv, 422p il maps $34.95; pa $16.95 **978**
1. Native Americans—Great Plains 2. Great Plains—History 3. Colorado—Gold discoveries
ISBN 0-7006-0891-5; 0-7006-1029-4 (pa)
          LC 97-36478
This "monograph synthesizes the history of native peoples on the Plains with an emphasis on the nomadic lifestyles that developed with the arrival of horses. It was a way of life adversely affected by both military campaigns launched by the United States and the arrival of large numbers of gold-seekers bent on exploiting natural resources during the Colorado Gold Rush." Libr J
Includes bibliographical references

Zeman, Scott C.
Chronology of the American West; from 23,000 B.C.E. through the twentieth century; foreword by Peter Iverson. ABC-CLIO 2002 381p il $85   **978**
1. West (U.S.)—History
ISBN 1-57607-207-X   LC 2002-3372
"Zeman breaks the time line into four unequal but natural divisions: 23,000 B.C.E.-1502, 1502-1840, 1840-1932, and 1932-2000. . . . Within this framework, events are listed year by year and briefly annotated. Black-and-white illustrations and full-page sidebars on events, people, or places pepper the chronology and bring the history to life. Sidebar articles have further reading lists attached, and an extensive bibliographic essay follows the main text. Zeman has produced a balanced, well-rounded chronology." Booklist
Includes bibliographical references

978.03   Western United States— Encyclopedias and dictionaries

The **New** encyclopedia of the American West; edited by Howard R. Lamar. Yale Univ. Press 1998 1324p il maps $60
      978.03
1. Frontier and pioneer life—West (U.S.)—Encyclopedias 2. West (U.S.)—Encyclopedias
ISBN 0-300-07088-8   LC 98-6231
First published 1977 by Crowell with title: The Reader's encyclopedia of the American West
This reference work covers "the history, geography, culture, literature, art, and natural history of both the real and the imaginary West. . . . [Coverage spans] prehistory to the present, and . . . [includes] events in the history of the trans-Mississippi West . . . [as well as] the frontier or 'western' stage of all 50 American states. Entries range from important events in the expansion of the U.S. . . . to the first European and American discoverers, among them Coronado, LaSalle, and Lewis and Clark." Publisher's note

Slatta, Richard W., 1947-
The cowboy encyclopedia. ABC-CLIO 1994 474p il o.p.; Norton paperback available $17   **978.03**
1. Cowhands—Encyclopedias 2. West (U.S.)—Encyclopedias 3. Frontier and pioneer life—Encyclopedias
ISBN 0-393-31473-1 (pa)   LC 94-19824
"Focusing on the cowboy experience in North and South America, *The Cowboy Encyclopedia* provides history, definitions, and commentary in an A-to-Z arrangement with major topics such as saddles and cowboy films receiving longer topical entries. Excellent cross-references and an extensive index provide easy access to all aspects of a topic. Appendixes cover cowboy films and videotape sources, museums, periodicals, and western cultural happenings." Am Libr

978.1   Kansas

Stratton, Joanna L.
Pioneer women; voices from the Kansas frontier; introduction by Arthur M. Schlesinger, Jr. Simon & Schuster 1981 319p il hardcover o.p. paperback available $12.95
      978.1
1. Women—Kansas 2. Frontier and pioneer life—Kansas 3. Kansas—History
ISBN 0-671-44748-3 (pa)   LC 80-15960
"A unique book based on the memoirs of nearly 800 pioneer women who lived in Kansas between 1854 and 1890. . . . The book presents personal and detailed accounts of life inside homes, the schools, and the social organizations of early Kansas." Choice
Includes bibliographical references

979   Great Basin and Pacific Coast states

Durham, Michael S., 1935-
Desert between the mountains; Mormons, miners, padres, mountain men, and the opening of the Great Basin, 1772-1869. Holt & Co. 1997 336p il o.p.; University of Okla. Press paperback available $19.95   **979**
1. Frontier and pioneer life—West (U.S.) 2. Mormons 3. Great Basin—History
ISBN 0-8061-3186-1 (pa)   LC 97-13619
This is a history of the settlement of the Great Basin area in what is now Utah and Nevada
"This is well-written history at its most easy-going." Publ Wkly
Includes bibliographical references

979.1   Arizona

Dolnick, Edward, 1952-
Down the great unknown; John Wesley Powell's 1869 journey of discovery and tragedy through the Grand Canyon. HarperCollins Pubs. 2001 367p il maps $27.50; pa $13.95   **979.1**
1. Powell, John Wesley, 1834-1902 2. Grand Canyon (Ariz.) 3. Colorado River (Colo.-Mexico)
ISBN 0-06-019619-X; 0-06-095586-4 (pa)
      LC 2001-24819
Also available Thorndike Press large print edition
This book recounts "the adventures of the 19th-century explorer. Powell, who had lost an arm during the Civil War, set out in early 1869 with a team of nine other men in the first endeavor to map the Green and Colorado Rivers, along with the canyons that cradle them." NY Times Book Rev
"Dolnick, a science journalist who has rafted down the Grand, turns in a most estimable rendition of that storied expedition. It skillfully integrates the notes and journals of expedition members with technical insight about the perils of roiling whitewater." Booklist
Includes bibliographical references

979.3 Nevada

Denton, Sally

The money and the power; the making of Las Vegas and its hold on America, 1947-2000; by Sally Denton and Roger Morris. Knopf 2001 479p hardcover o.p. paperback available $15 **979.3**

1. Las Vegas (Nev.) 2. Organized crime 3. Political corruption

ISBN 0-375-70126-5 (pa)   LC 00-62011

The authors contend that "modern Las Vegas enjoys a thriving economy dependent on gambling, greed, political corruption, and drugs that mirrors what is practiced throughout America." Libr J

"The idea of Las Vegas as the epitome of crass American pop culture has become at least a surface truism in most circles. But Denton and Morris . . . go much deeper than the surface in this sobering account of the famous Nevada resort town." Booklist

Includes bibliographical references

Martin, Gregory, 1971-

Mountain City. North Point Press 2000 193p hardcover o.p. paperback available $12 **979.3**

1. Mountain City (Nev.)

ISBN 0-86547-616-0 (pa)   LC 99-56160

The author "portrays life in remote Mountain City, 84 miles from Elko. He centers his telling around Tremewan's store, where his Basque uncle Mel and aunt Lou Basañez, Grandma and Gramps Tremewan, and cousin Mitch sell groceries to the town's 33 residents, area miners and ranchers, and the Indians from the nearby Duck Valley Reservation." Libr J

Martin "maintains an immediacy that highlights the humanity of his subjects and frames the steady press of time that is forcing an era of the American West deep into memory." Publ Wkly

979.4 California

Cannon, Lou

Official negligence; how Rodney King and the riots changed Los Angeles and the LAPD. Times Bks. 1998 c1997 xxi, 698p il o.p.; Westview Press paperback available $20 **979.4**

1. King, Rodney 2. Los Angeles (Calif.). Police Dept. 3. Riots 4. Los Angeles (Calif.)—Race relations

ISBN 0-8133-3725-9 (pa)   LC 97-21982

This is an account of the riots in Los Angeles in 1992 that were the aftermath of the beating "of a black motorist, Rodney King, by four white police officers." Economist

This work represents "the best kind of reportage—meticulous, unbiased and complete." Publ Wkly

Includes bibliographical references

Didion, Joan

Where I was from. Knopf 2003 226p $23 **979.4**

1. American national characteristics 2. California—History 3. California—Social conditions

ISBN 0-679-43332-5   LC 2002-43325

In this "assessment of her home and her opinions, Didion gives up on California and its inhabitants, including her own pioneer family; she now sees the state's history as a fiasco, a saga of advancement with other people's money, chiefly the government's spent on behalf of business interests." N Y Times Book Rev

This "is a complex and challenging memoir, difficult to enter into but just as difficult to put down. . . . Those who have long admired the clarity and precision of her prose will not be disappointed with this partly autobiographical, partly historical, but fully engrossing account." Libr J

Fradkin, Philip L.

The seven states of California; a natural and human history. Holt & Co. 1995 474p il maps o.p.; University of Calif. Press paperback available $19.95 **979.4**

1. California—Description

ISBN 0-520-20942-7 (pa)   LC 94-39984

"A John Macrae book"

The author "attempts to define California . . . by dividing it into seven ecological provinces. He examines each region by choosing a representative story illustrating how people are influenced by the landscape they inhabit. Fradkin's background as a newspaper reporter is evident throughout, and much of this work reflects his concern for the state's history of mistreating minorities. An interesting look at how California has evolved." Libr J

Includes bibliographical references

Kurzman, Dan

Disaster! the great San Francisco earthquake and fire of 1906. Morrow 2001 xxiv, 296p il map hardcover o.p. paperback available $13.95 **979.4**

1. Earthquakes—California 2. San Francisco (Calif.)—History

ISBN 0-06-008432-4 (pa)   LC 00-53321

The author's account of the San Francisco earthquake "focuses on the human drama, following more than 100 different characters over several days, to illustrate the extremes of courage and cowardice that tragedy can evoke." Publ Wkly

"Working from diaries and papers that survived the fires, Kurzman brings history alive. . . . This riveting history belongs in public and academic libraries." Libr J

Includes bibliographical references

Muir, John, 1838-1914

The Yosemite; the original John Muir text; illustrated with photographs by Galen Rowell; each photograph accompanied by an excerpt from the works of John Muir and an annotation by Galen Rowell; introduction by the photographer. Sierra Club Bks. 1989 218p il hardcover o.p. paperback available $14.95 **979.4**

1. Yosemite National Park (Calif.)

ISBN 0-87156-782-2 (pa)   LC 88-34919

"A Yolla Bolly Press book"

New photographs complement Muir's classic 1912 natural history of the national park

Includes bibliographical references

979.7   Washington

Harden, Blaine

A river lost; the life and death of the Columbia. Norton 1996 271p maps $25; pa $14.95   **979.7**

1. Columbia River

ISBN 0-393-03936-6; 0-393-31690-4 (pa)

          LC 95-38618

In this look at the development of Columbia River region, the author "examines the changes—sociological, environmental, economic and aesthetic—that the taming of this great river wrought. His wonderful account touches on the destruction of Native American cultures dependent on the river and its salmon, and on the near extinction of the salmon themselves. Also fairly portrayed are the people and industries currently dependent on both the managed river and massive government subsidies." Publ Wkly

Includes bibliographical references

979.8   Alaska

Borneman, Walter R., 1952-

Alaska: saga of a bold land. HarperCollins Pubs. 2003 608p il maps $34.95; pa $16.95

          979.8

1. Alaska—History

ISBN 0-06-050306-8; 0-06-050307-6 (pa)

          LC 2002-27271

"Separated into nine chronologically based chapters, the text explores a recurring theme in Alaska's development: conflict among disparate groups over how the land would be used for personal enrichment. . . . Engaging chapters detail the important events and those who helped shape Alaska's history. . . . This expansive, comprehensive history is recommended for all libraries." Libr J

Includes bibliographical references

Jenkins, Peter, 1951-

Looking for Alaska. St. Martin's Press 2002 434p il $25.95; pa $14.95   **979.8**

1. Alaska—Description 2. Alaska—Social life and customs

ISBN 0-312-26178-0; 0-312-30289-4 (pa)

          LC 2001-48871

This is the author's "account of eighteen months spent traveling over twenty thousand miles in tiny bush planes, on snow machines and snowshoes, in fishing boats and kayaks, on the Alaska Marine Highway and the Haul Road, searching for what defines Alaska." Publisher's note

This book "sparkles with adventure, quirky characters, unbelievable hardships, and indescribable beauty." Libr J

McPhee, John A.

Coming into the country; [by] John McPhee. Farrar, Straus & Giroux 1977 438p maps hardcover o.p. paperback available $15

          979.8

1. Alaska—Description

ISBN 0-374-52287-1 (pa)   LC 77-12249

This book "is actually three lengthy bulletins about Alaska. . . . The first describes a canoe trip that McPhee and four companions took. . . . Second, McPhee tells of a helicopter ride with a committee looking for a site on which to build a new state capital. The last and longest section covers some wintry months spent in Eagle, a tiny settlement on the Yukon River." Time

Raban, Jonathan

Passage to Juneau; a sea and its meanings. Pantheon Bks. 1999 435p $26.50; pa $15

          979.8

1. Northwest Coast of North America—Description 2. Pacific Northwest—Description 3. Alaska—Description

ISBN 0-679-44262-6; 0-679-77614-1 (pa)

          LC 99-28777

"Long fascinated by the Inside Passage (the protected waterway that runs from Washington State up to Alaska), Raban casts off in his 35'ketch from his home port in Seattle to follow in the wake of generations of salmon fishermen. He draws a rather dark portrait of the region as he fills out its history, through the cranky journals of Captain Vancouver and others, and meditates on the beautiful but threatening and lonesome landscape, with its struggling communities, submerged mountains, tricky waters, and names like Deception Pass and Desolation Sound." Libr J

980   South America. Latin America

The **Cambridge** history of Latin America; edited by Leslie Bethell. Cambridge Univ. Press 1984-1995 10v in 11   **980**

1. Latin America—History

First ten volumes of a projected eleven volume set

Contents: v1-2 Colonial Latin America v1 $170, v2 $180 (ISBN 0-521-23223-6; 0-521-24516-8); v3 From independence to c.1870 $190 (ISBN 0-521-23224-4); v4-5 c.1870 to 1930 v4 $170, v5 $180 (ISBN 0-521-23225-2; 0-521-24517-6); v6 pt1-pt 2 Latin America Since 1930: Economy, society, and politics pt1 Economy and society $130, pt2 Politics and society $130 (ISBN 0-521-23226-0; 0-521-46556-7); v7 Latin America since 1930, Mexico, Central America and the Caribbean $170 (ISBN 0-521-24518-4); v8 Latin America since 1930 $170 (ISBN 0-521-26652-1); v10 Latin America since 1930: Ideas, culture, and society $130 (ISBN 0-521-19594-6); v11 Bibliographical essays $150 (ISBN 0-521-39525-9)

"History of the areas south of the United States from just prior to the European invasions to the present. . . . Covers general themes in Latin American history with chronological accounts of the individual countries. Bibliographical essays are appended to each chapter." NY Public Libr Book of How & Where to Look It Up

Chasteen, John Charles, 1955-

Born in blood and fire; a concise history of Latin America. Norton 2000 352p il maps hardcover o.p. paperback available $39.05

          980

1. Latin America—History

ISBN 0-393-97613-0 (pa)   LC 00-41868

"Chasteen focuses on major political, social and economic topics and trends that helped shape Latin America, including liberalism, the caste system, the mixing of races, nationalism and the Western notion of 'Progress'; he also examines the role that Europe and the United States played in the development of these phenomena. Also refreshing is Chasteen's examination of the periods he covers from the perspective of women." Publ Wkly

Includes bibliographical references

The **South** American handbook. Passport Bks. maps $39.95 **980**

1. Latin America 2. South America

Annual. First published 1924 by Rand McNally

"For each country, brief historical and socioeconomic information is followed by detailed descriptions of individual cities—their museums, libraries, art exhibitions, hotels (with rates), shops, transportation, etc. Though chiefly used for up-to-date travel information, the series has historical value in libraries." Booklist

Williamson, Edwin

The Penguin history of Latin America. Allen Lane 1992 o.p.; Penguin Bks. paperback available $18 **980**

1. Latin America—History

ISBN 0-14-012559-0 (pa)

"The book is organized topically, rather than by country, and the author wisely selected regional examples of his major themes, rather than attempting a detailed analysis of each country. The work ends with an unusual exploration of literature and culture in relation to identity and modernization, followed by a helpful bibliographic essay." Libr J

981 Brazil

Page, Joseph A.

The Brazilians. Addison-Wesley 1995 540p il map hardcover o.p. paperback available $22.50 **981**

1. Brazilian national characteristics 2. Brazil

ISBN 0-201-44191-8 (pa)   LC 94-45812

The author "probes deep into the layers of Spanish, Portuguese, Dutch, African and Indian heritage that make Brazil so alluring and paradoxical. . . . In this magnetizing study, Page also explores the meld of Catholicism and Pentecostalism, of native Indian healers and modern medicine, of African rhythms and Western music. He discusses the environmental and investment scenes as well as the addiction to soccer and to the *telenovelas* of the powerful Globus media empire." Publ Wkly

Includes bibliographical references

Skidmore, Thomas E.

Brazil; five centuries of change. Oxford Univ. Press 1999 254p maps hardcover o.p. paperback available $28.95 **981**

1. Brazil

ISBN 0-19-505810-0 (pa)   LC 98-23122

Skidmore explores the country's "history, its political and economic development, and social and racial relationships. . . . This is a well-researched look at a fascinating country." Booklist

Includes bibliographical references

982 Argentina

Brown, Jonathan C.

A brief history of Argentina. Facts on File 2002 324p il maps $45 **982**

1. Argentina—History

ISBN 0-8160-4959-9   LC 2002-6459

Contents: Ancient Argentina and the European Encounter; The Colonial Rio de la Plata; Imperial Reform and Conflict in the Rio de la Plata; Crisis of the Colonial Order and Revolution; Agrarian Expansion and Nation Building, 1820-1880; The Liberal Age, 1880-1916; The Decline of Liberalism, 1916-1930; The Rise of Populism, 1930-1955; The Failure of De-Peronization, 1955-1983; The Neo-Liberal Age Begins

This "reference focuses on such key events as the arrival of European colonialists, the struggle for independence, the era of Juan and Eva Peron, and the period known as the Dirty War. Special attention is given to: the culture and history of Argentina's indigenous population; how the area became one of Spain's most commercially successful colonies; the historic, social, and political conditions that led to the Dirty War {and} the conflict of political power and economic privilege in modern Argentina." Publisher's note

Includes bibliographical references

985 Peru

Bingham, Hiram, 1875-1956

Lost city of the Incas; the story of Machu Picchu and its builders; with an introduction by Hugh Thomson; photographs by Hugh Thomson. Sterling 2002 274p il $35; pa $12.95 **985**

1. Machu Picchu (Peru) 2. Peru—Antiquities 3. Incas

ISBN 0-2976-0759-6; 1-84212-585-0 (pa)

LC 2002-483039

A reissue of the title first published 1948 by Duell

"In 1911 Bingham, an American explorer, found the Inca city of Machu Picchu, which had been lost for 300 years. In this volume he tells of its origin, how it came to be lost and how it was finally discovered." Libr J

Includes bibliographical references

Hemming, John, 1935-

The conquest of the Incas. Harcourt Brace Jovanovich 1970 641p il maps hardcover o.p. paperback available $25 **985**

1. Incas 2. Peru—History

ISBN 0-15-602826-3 (pa)

"This [study] focuses on relations of Spaniards and Incas during the Spanish conquest of Peru launched by Pizarro and partners. Spaniards and Incas speak frequently in their own words as preserved in Spanish documents. . . . Inca ways and achievements, the empire's tragic vulnerability because of rivalrous leaders and civil war, and conquest aftermath are made sharply manifest." Booklist

Includes bibliographical references

Moseley, Michael Edward

The Incas and their ancestors; the archaeology of Peru. rev ed. Thames & Hudson 2001 288p il maps $27.50 **985**

1. Incas 2. Peru—Antiquities

ISBN 0-500-28277-3   LC 00-108866

First published 1992

This account of Andean prehistory and archaeology takes us from the first settlement of 10,000 years ago to the Spanish conquest

"Clearly presented, with a generous ration of maps and illustrations, [the volume] is thoughtful and welcome." Times Lit Suppl [review of 1992 edition]

Includes bibliographical references

Prescott, William Hickling, 1796-1859
History of the conquest of Peru. Modern
Lib. 1998 xxiii, 705p   **985**
1. Peru—History 2. Incas   LC 98-10174
Only available in edition with History of the conquest
of Mexico from Cooper Sq. Press
First published 1847
This is a history of the subjugation of the Inca people
by Francisco Pizarro and his soldiers
Includes bibliographical references

986.6   Ecuador

Kane, Joe
Savages. Knopf 1995 273p il map
hardcover o.p. paperback available $14
                                        986.6
1. Waorani Indians 2. Amazon River valley 3. Human ecology
ISBN 0-679-74019-8 (pa)   LC 95-4258
"In the Ecuadorian Amazon the author befriends Moi,
a Huaorani warrior who is learning new strategies in his
fight to keep American oil companies from destroying
his homeland. Moi not only smuggles Kane past Ecuadorian military check-points into Huaorani territory but
also returns with him to confront the savages in the conference halls of Washington." New Yorker
Includes bibliographical references

990   Other parts of world. Pacific Ocean islands

Michener, James A., 1907-1997
Return to paradise. Random House 1951
437p hardcover o.p. paperback available
$7.99   **990**
1. Islands of the Pacific
ISBN 0-449-20650-5 (pa)
Partially analyzed in Essay and general literature index
Essays included are: The atoll; Polynesia; Fuji; Guadalcanal; Espiritu Santo; New Zealand; Australia; New
Guinea; Rabaul; What I learned. Short stories included
are: Mr. Morgan; Povenaa's daughter; Mynah birds; The
story; Good life; Until they sail; The jungle; The
fossickers
"Alternate chapters describe each island followed by
a short story set against the region described." Ont Libr
Rev

994   Australia

The **Australian** people; an encyclopedia of
the nation, its people and their origins;
edited by James Jupp. Cambridge Univ.
Press 2001 xx, 940p il maps $150   **994**
1. Australia—Encyclopedias 2. Australia—Race relations 3. Australian aborigines—Social conditions
ISBN 0-521-80789-1   LC 2001-37896
First published 1988 in Australia
This "documents the dramatic history of Australian
settlement and describes the rich ethnic and cultural inheritance of the nation through the contributions of its
people." Publisher's note
Includes bibliographical references

Bryson, Bill
In a sunburned country. Broadway Bks.
2000 307p il maps hardcover o.p. paperback
available $14.95   **994**
1. Australia—Description
ISBN 0-7679-0386-2 (pa)   LC 00-25566
Also available large print edition $25 (ISBN 0-375-43056-3)
In this book, Bryson "chronicles his exploration of
Australia, he introduces us to a town that went without
electricity until the early 1990s, a former high-ranking
politician who hawks his own autobiography to passersby, an assortment of coffee shops and restaurants, . . .
a type of giant worm, and the world's most poisonous
creature, the box jellyfish." Booklist
Includes bibliographical references

Clarke, F. G. (Francis Gordon)
The history of Australia. Greenwood Press
2002 236p (Greenwood histories of the
modern nations) $45   **994**
1. Australia—History
ISBN 0-313-31498-5   LC 2001-54704
This volume "begins with a timeline of historical
events. The first chapter is a very short overview of Australia (geography, climate, culture, and so on). The rest
of the text is a chronological study in short, concise
chapters beginning 60,000 years ago with Aboriginal
Australia and ending with 2001 and beyond. Each chapter is broken down into smaller sections, with headings,
covering such essential topics as colonization, war, government, and politics. The work ends with smaller sections for notable people, notes, a bibliographic essay, and
an index." Recomm Ref Books for Small & Medium-sized Libr & Media Cent, 2003
Includes bibliographical references

Hughes, Robert
The fatal shore. Knopf 1987 688p il maps
hardcover o.p. paperback available $18   **994**
1. Australia—History 2. Penal colonies
ISBN 0-394-75366-6 (pa)   LC 86-45272
"This epic account chronicles the history of Australia
during the 80 years (1788-1868) of England's convict
transportation system, when some 160,000 convicts
reached 'the fatal shore.' Interweaving his own lucid narrative with untapped original sources—including the diaries and letters of the prisoners themselves—Hughes
shows the evolution of the system and of the fledgling
nation that emerged from the brutal penal colony." Libr
J
Includes bibliographical references

995.3   Papua New Guinea. New Guinea region

Flannery, Tim F. (Tim Fridjof), 1956-
Throwim way leg; tree-kangaroos, possums,
and penis gourds—on the track of unknown
mammals in wildest New Guinea; {by} Tim
Flannery. Atlantic Monthly Press 1998 326p
il map hardcover o.p. paperback available $14
                                        995.3
1. Ethnology—New Guinea 2. New Guinea—Description
ISBN 0-8021-3665-6 (pa)   LC 98-38435
Flannery chronicles "his scientific and cross-cultural
adventures during 15 expeditions of New Guinea—

Flannery, Tim F. (Tim Fridjof), 1956-—
Continued
undertaken in order to research the many species of mammals that exist on this large island, which he refers to as @one of the world's last frontiers.'" Publ Wkly

This "is more than an account of {the author's} fieldwork. It is an enthralling introduction to the mountain people of New Guinea." N Y Times Book Rev

996 Polynesia and Micronesia

Severin, Timothy
In search of Robinson Crusoe. Basic Bks. 2002 333p il hardcover o.p. paperback available $16.95   **996**
  1. Selkirk, Alexander, 1676-1721 2. Defoe, Daniel, 1661?-1731. Robinson Crusoe 3. Survival after airplane accidents, shipwrecks, etc.
ISBN 0-465-07699-8 (pa)   LC 2002-71661
The author examines "the fictional Crusoe alongside the historic realities of colonization and human ingenuity. . . . Readers learn about the history of marooning among plunderers, blockade navies and other piratical sailors, as well as the ethnography of the so-called 'Moskito Man' (aka Man Friday) and all the ways to provide for oneself on a deserted island. . . . The work is energetic and Severin is an ideal guide to the world behind the word. This will surely appeal to the lovers of maritime history." Publ Wkly

Souhami, Diana
Selkirk's Island; the true and strange adventures of the real Robinson Crusoe. Harcourt 2002 c2001 246p $24; pa $13   **996**
  1. Selkirk, Alexander, 1676-1721 2. Defoe, Daniel, 1661?-1731. Robinson Crusoe 3. Survival after airplane accidents, shipwrecks, etc. 4. Islands of the Pacific
ISBN 0-15-100526-5; 0-15-602717-8 (pa)
                 LC 01-24979
Also available Thorndike Press large print edition
First published 2001 in the United Kingdom
"Daniel Defoe based his 1719 novel *Robinson Crusoe* on the trials and tribulations of Scottish seaman Alexander Selkirk. Souhami . . . draws on journals, maritime histories and ship and parish records to detail his . . . [story]. Complete with detailed comparisons between Defoe's novel and Selkirk's life, Souhami's account is a well-researched investigation of a forgotten anti-hero." Publ Wkly
Includes bibliographical references

998 Arctic islands and Antarctica

Alexander, Caroline, 1956-
The Endurance; Shackleton's legendary Antarctic expedition. Knopf 1998 211p il $29.95   **998**
  1. Shackleton, Sir Ernest Henry, 1874-1922 2. Endurance (Ship) 3. Imperial Trans-Antarctic Expedition (1914-1917) 4. Antarctica—Exploration
ISBN 0-375-40403-1
Published in association with the American Museum of Natural History

In 1914, Sir Ernest Shackleton "sailed to Antarctica with 27 men in hopes of being the first human to transverse the continent. But his ship, the *Endurance,* was trapped, then crushed, by ice in the Weddell Sea, propelling the party into a nightmare of cold and near starvation. Alexander, relying extensively on journals by crew members, some never published, as well as on myriad other sources, delivers a spellbinding story of human courage. . . . What makes this book especially exciting, however, are the 170 previously unpublished photos by the expedition's photographer, Frank Hurley." Publ Wkly

Antarctica: an encyclopedia from Abbott Ice Shelf to zooplankton; edited by Mary Trewby. Firefly Bks. 2002 208p il maps $35   **998**
  1. Antarctica—Encyclopedias
ISBN 1-55297-590-8   LC 2002-514992
This "guide to Antarctica features a true encyclopedia layout, with over 1000 concise, alphabetically arranged entries and 250 photographs that cover natural history, climate, geology, tourism, and more. . . . The entries in this book are easily accessible and particularly useful for quick reference." Libr J

Cookman, Scott, 1952-
Ice blink; the mysterious fate of Sir John Franklin's lost polar expedition. Wiley 2000 244p il maps $24.95; pa $15.95   **998**
  1. Franklin, Sir John, 1786-1847 2. Northwest Passage 3. Arctic regions—Exploration
ISBN 0-471-37790-2; 0-471-40420-9 (pa)
                 LC 99-47620
In this "account of the fabled 1845 Franklin expedition in search of the Northwest Passage, Cookman inculpates a novel malefactor in the tragedy: botulism. In the 1980s, three frozen corpses of expedition members were found and exhumed. . . . Autopsies revealed lead, fingering lead-soldered cans from the provisions. . . . Adventure readers will flock to this fine regaling of the enduring mystery surrounding the best-known disaster in Arctic exploration." Booklist
Includes bibliographical references

Ehrlich, Gretel
This cold heaven; seven seasons in Greenland. Pantheon Bks. 2001 377p il maps $27.50; pa $14   **998**
  1. Greenland
ISBN 0-679-44200-6; 0-679-75852-6 (pa)
                 LC 00-69277
"Ehrlich began traveling to Greenland during her recovery from a nearly fatal lightning strike, and her keen, often poetic responses to the beauty of the frigid landscape and the warmth of Inuit families, combined with a profound immersion in Greenland history, infuse her captivating account with both drama and reflection." Booklist
Includes bibliographical references

Fleming, Fergus, 1959-
Ninety degrees North; the quest for the North Pole. Grove Press 2002 c2001 xxi, 470p il maps $26; pa $15   **998**
  1. Arctic regions—Exploration 2. North Pole
ISBN 0-8021-1725-2; 0-8021-4036-X (pa)
               LC 2002-21469
Companion volume to Barrow's boys (2000)
First published 2001 in the United Kingdom

Fleming, Fergus, 1959-—*Continued*

Fleming presents a historical "narrative of the late 19th-century Arctic exploration and the quest for the North Pole." New Sci

"The book is fascinating for how Fleming renders the haughty, post-Enlightenment brio of the principal adventurers and the extreme, often fatal ends toward which it pushed them." Publ Wkly

Includes bibliographical references

Lopez, Barry Holstun, 1945-

Arctic dreams; imagination and desire in a northern landscape; [by] Barry Lopez. Scribner 1986 xxix, 464p maps o.p.; Vintage Bks. paperback available $15   998

1. Arctic regions 2. Natural history—Arctic regions
ISBN 0-375-72748-5 (pa)   LC 85-24979

Based on his experiences in the region Lopez discusses "Arctic exploration, geography, weather, animal migration, and behavior." Libr J

"What compels the reader to enter this frozen world of the far north is Lopez's beautiful prose style and the breadth and strength of his understanding. He lavishes attention on and achieves precise expression of this world." Choice

Includes bibliographical references

McGonigal, David

Antarctica and the Arctic; the complete encyclopedia; [by] David McGonigal, Lynn Woodworth. Firefly Bks. 2001 608p il maps $60   998

1. Antarctica 2. Arctic regions
ISBN 1-55297-545-2

"The book covers the environment of the poles, polar geophysics and weather patterns, ecology, wildlife and flora, polar exploration, and working in the polar environments. . . . The last section contains additional resources such as the Antarctic Treaty, wildlife conservation status, a vocabulary, a list of museums and research institutes with strong Antarctic collections, and recommended Antarctic links on the web. . . . In addition, there is a CD-ROM, which is fully searchable." Libr J

"This encyclopedia, replete with more than 1,000 stunning color photographs and more than 80 thematic maps, will surprise, delight and educate anyone who wishes to know more about Antarctica." Booklist

Mikkelsen, Ejnar, 1880-1971

Two against the ice; translated from the Danish by Maurice Michael. Steerforth Press 2003 206p il map pa $14.95   998

1. Greenland 2. Arctic regions—Exploration
ISBN 1-58642-057-7   LC 2002-151150

Original Danish editon, 1955; this translation first published 1957 in the United Kingdom

"Mikkelsen and lver Iversen, a ship's mechanic, set off sledging across Greenland to retrieve the diaries of three other Danish explorers who perished during a previous expedition. . . . Amazingly, both he and Iversen survive the two-year jaunt despite frostbite, scurvy, and near-starvation. Readers will be amazed and amused by the way the two explorers keep their spirits about them and downplay the terrifying dangers as though it were all in good fun. Fascinating and fun reading." Booklist

Preston, Diana

A first rate tragedy; Robert Falcon Scott and the race to the South Pole. Houghton Mifflin 1998 269p il map hardcover o.p. paperback available $14   998

1. Scott, Robert Falcon, 1868-1912 2. British Antarctic ("Terra Nova") Expedition (1910-1913) 3. Antarctica—Exploration 4. South Pole
ISBN 0-618-00201-4 (pa)   LC 98-47411

"In 1912, Robert Scott and four members of his Antarctic expedition reached the South Pole only to find a Norwegian flag planted by Roald Amundsen. The returning party of Englishmen perished, . . . failing in the attempt to be first to the Pole and sending their country into mourning but making a legend of Scott." Libr J

"A whole generation was brought up on the legend of Scott of the Antarctic. Diana Preston successfully explains why and how this came about. . . . {She} has written a first-rate book retelling the familiar tale in compulsive terms and adding a thoughtful twist of her own." Times Lit Suppl

Includes bibliographical references

Solomon, Susan, 1956-

The coldest March. Yale Univ. Press 2001 xxii, 383p il maps $29.95; pa $16.95   998

1. Scott, Robert Falcon, 1868-1912 2. British Antarctic ("Terra Nova") Expedition (1910-1913) 3. Antarctica—Exploration 4. South Pole
ISBN 0-300-08967-8; 0-300-09921-5 (pa)

          LC 00-54996

"In November 1911, Capt. Robert Falcon Scott and his British team set out to be the first to reach the South Pole. Battling the brutal weather of Antarctica, they reached the pole in January 1912 only to discover that a Norwegian team had beat them there by nearly a month. On their return from the Pole, Scott and four of his companions died in harsh conditions. Ever since, history has not known whether to label them heroes or bunglers. Solomon . . . analyzes all the factors present during Scott's expedition in an attempt to explain that his failure was due not to incompetence but to a combination of unpredictable weather, erroneous choices and bad luck." Libr J

Includes bibliographical references

Waterman, Jonathan

Arctic crossing; a journey through the Northwest Passage and Inuit culture. Knopf 2001 354p il o.p.; Lyons Press paperback available $16.95   998

1. Northwest Passage 2. Inuit
ISBN 1-58574-730-0 (pa)

Waterman "chronicles his three-year attempt to kayak, ski, and dogsled the 2,000 miles of the Northwest Passage." Quill Quire

"His encounters with the Inuit and his candid observations of their culture and poverty-stricken, often brutal lifestyle provide the most interesting passages." Publ Wkly

Includes bibliographical references

AUTHOR, TITLE, SUBJECT, AND ANALYTICAL INDEX

This index to the books in the Classified Catalog includes author, title, subject, and analytical entries; added entries for joint authors, and for editors of works entered under title; and name and subject cross-references; all arranged in one alphabet.

The number in bold face type at the end of each entry refers to the Dewey Decimal Classification where the main entry for the book will be found. Works classed in 92 are arranged by the name of the person written about. Biographies of artists and musicians, formerly classed in 709.2 and 780.92, are now classed in 920 and 92.

For further information about this index and for examples of entries, see Directions for Use of the Catalog.

4 plays. Inge, W. **812**
5th of July. Wilson, L. **812**
8 men and a duck. Thorpe, I. J. **910.4**
20 best garden designs. Newbury, T. **712**
20th-century fashion. Peacock, J. **391**
21 short plays. Wilson, L. **812**
The **21st** century **909.83**
24 years of House work—and the place is still a mess. Schroeder, P. **92**
25 gorgeous sweaters for the brand new knitter. Ham, C. **746.43**
The **36-hour** day. Mace, N. L. **618.97**
40 nights to knowing the sky. Schaaf, F. **520**
44, Dublin made me. Sheridan, P. **92**
47 roses. Sheridan, P. **92**
50 simple things you can do to improve your personal finances. Glink, I. R. **332.024**
50 wonderful ways to be a single-parent family. Ginsberg, B. G. **649**
52 McGs. Thomas, R. M., Jr. **920**
60 minutes (Television program)
See/See also pages in the following book(s):
Hewitt, D. Tell me a story **92**
60 years of the Oscar. See Osborne, R. A. 75 years of the Oscar **791.43**
75 years of the Oscar. Osborne, R. A. **791.43**
76ers (Basketball team) *See* Philadelphia 76ers (Basketball team)
95 poems. Cummings, E. E. **811**
100 days. See Schom, A. One hundred days **944.05**
100 decisive battles. Davis, P. K. **904**
100 flowers and how they got their names. Wells, D. **582.13**
The **100** most influential books ever written. Seymour-Smith, M. **028**
100 one-night reads. Major, D. C. **028**
100 questions & answers about Parkinson [sic] disease. Lieberman, A. **616.8**
100 suns, 1945-1962. Light, M. **623.4**
175 high-impact cover letters. Beatty, R. H. **650.14**
200 of nothing. Dewdney, A. K. **510**
222 monologues, 2 minutes & under from literature. See The Ultimate audition book **808.82**
365 days. Glasser, R. J. **959.704**
401(k) plan
Wolman, W. The great 401(k) hoax **332.024**
500 nations. Josephy, A. M. **970.004**
The 529 College Savings Plan. Feigenbaum, R. A. **378.3**
1,001 ingenious gardening ideas **635**
1001 legal words you need to know **349**

1089 and all that. Acheson, D. J. **510**
1185 Park Avenue. Roiphe, A. R. **92**
1918: war and peace. Dallas, G. **940.4**
1939. Carley, M. J. **940.53**
20,000 years of fashion. Boucher, F. **391**

A

A.I.D.S. (Disease) *See* AIDS (Disease)
A is for American. Lepore, J. **306.44**
A to Z of American women in the performing arts. Sonneborn, L. **920.003**
A to Z of American women in the visual arts. Kort, C. **920.003**
A to Z of chemists. Oakes, E. H. **920.003**
A to Z of earth scientists. Gates, A. E. **920.003**
A to Z of scientists in weather and climate. Rittner, D. **920.003**
A to Z of women in world history. Kuhlman, E. A. **920.003**
An **A-Z** of food and drink. Ayto, J. **641.03**
AACR *See* Anglo-American cataloguing rules
Abadi, Jennifer Felicia
A fistful of lentils **641.5**
Abadie, Daniel
(ed) Magritte, R. Magritte **759.9493**
The **abandonment** of the Jews. Wyman, D. S. **940.53**
Abanes, Richard
One nation under gods **289.3**
Abate, Frank R.
(ed) The New Oxford American dictionary. See The New Oxford American dictionary **423**
Abbey, Edward, 1927-1989
The serpents of paradise **818**
Abbott, Jack Henry, 1944-2002
In the belly of the beast **365**
Abbreviations
Dictionaries
Acronyms, initialisms, & abbreviations dictionary **421.03**
Guinagh, K. Dictionary of foreign phrases and abbreviations **422.03**
Stahl, D. Abbreviations dictionary **421.03**
Abbreviations dictionary. Stahl, D. **421.03**
ABC of architecture. O'Gorman, J. F. **720**
Abdul-Jabbar, Kareem, 1947-
Black profiles in courage **920**
Abegg, Martin
(tr) Dead Sea scrolls. The Dead Sea scrolls **296.1**
Abel, Niels Henrik, 1802-1829
See/See also pages in the following book(s):
Bell, E. T. Men of mathematics p307-26 **920**

Abell, Sam
  (jt. auth) Ambrose, S. E. Lewis & Clark   978
Aberjhani
  Encyclopedia of the Harlem Renaissance   810.9
Ability
  Fisher, H. E. The first sex   305.4
Testing
  Gould, S. J. The mismeasure of man   153.9
ABMS compendium of certified medical specialists. See
  The Official ABMS directory of board certified med-
  ical specialists   610.69
Abner, Allison, 1959-
  (jt. auth) Beal, A. C. The black parenting book
                                                649
Abnormalities, Human See Birth defects
Abolitionists
  Douglass, F. Autobiographies   92
  Douglass, F. My bondage and my freedom   92
  Douglass, F. Narrative of the life of Frederick Doug-
  lass, an American slave   92
Aborigines, Australian See Australian aborigines
Abortion
  Abortion wars   363.46
  Reagan, L. J. When abortion was a crime   363.46
  Solinger, R. Beggars and choosers   363.46
  Tribe, L. H. Abortion: the clash of absolutes
                                                363.46
  Weddington, S. R. A question of choice   363.46
Law and legislation
  Hull, N. E. H. Roe v. Wade   344
Abortion, Spontaneous See Miscarriage
Abortion rights movement See Pro-choice movement
Abortion wars   363.46
About behaviorism. Skinner, B. F.   150.19
About face. Mann, J.   327.73
About time. Davies, P. C. W.   530.1
About town. Yagoda, B.   051
Above the river. Wright, J. A.   811
Abraham (Biblical figure)
About
  Feiler, B. S. Abraham   222
Abraham Lincoln and the second American Revolution.
  McPherson, J. M.   973.7
Abraham Lincoln: The prairie years and The war years.
  Sandburg, C.   92
Abram, David
  The spell of the sensuous   128
Abram, Norm
  Measure twice, cut once   684
Abrams, Irwin
  The Nobel Peace Prize and the laureates   920.003
Abrams, M. H. (Meyer Howard), 1912-
  A glossary of literary terms   803
  (ed) The Norton anthology of English literature. See
  The Norton anthology of English literature
                                                820.8
Abrams, Meyer Howard See Abrams, M. H. (Meyer
  Howard), 1912-
Abramson, Albert
  The history of television, 1942 to 2000   621.388
Abridged Dewey decimal classification and relative in-
  dex. Dewey, M.   025.4
Absolute zero and the conquest of cold. Shachtman, T.
                                                536
The **absorbent** mind. Montessori, M.   155.4
Abstinence. Wilson, L.
  In Wilson, L. 21 short plays p235-41   812
Abstract art
  See also Cubism
Aburish, Said K.
  The rise, corruption, and coming fall of the House of
  Saud   953.8
Abuse of children See Child abuse
Abuse of power   973.924
Abuse of wives See Wife abuse

Academic dissertations See Dissertations
Academic libraries
Periodicals
  Choice   028.1
Academic Press dictionary of science and technology
                                                503
Academy Awards (Motion pictures)
  Osborne, R. A. 75 years of the Oscar   791.43
Accadians (Sumerians) See Sumerians
Accident insurance
  Matthews, J. L. How to win your personal injury claim
                                                346.03
Accidents
  See also types of accidents and subjects with the
  subdivision Accidents
Prevention
  Hutton, J. T. Preventing falls   618.97
  Shore, K. Keeping kids safe   649
Acclimatization See Adaptation (Biology)
Accountability See Liability (Law)
Accounting
  Century 21 accounting: advanced course   657
  Century 21 accounting: first-year course   657
  Siegel, J. G. Accounting handbook   657
Accounting handbook. Siegel, J. G.   657
Acculturation
  See also Socialization
  Handlin, O. The uprooted   325.73
Ace the IT job interview!. Moreira, P.   650.14
Acharnians. Aristophanes
  In Aristophanes. The complete plays of Aristophanes
  p13-51   882
Achebe, Chinua, 1930-
  Home and exile   828
Acheson, D. J.
  1089 and all that   510
Acheson, David See Acheson, D. J.
Acheson, Dean, 1893-1971
About
  Chace, J. Acheson   92
  See/See also pages in the following book(s):
  Halberstam, D. The best and the brightest
                                                973.922
Achmatova, Anna See Akhmatova, Anna Andreevna,
  1889-1966
Achord, James L.
  Understanding hepatitis   616.3
Achtemeier, Paul J.
  (ed) The HarperCollins Bible dictionary. See The
  HarperCollins Bible dictionary   220.3
Ackerman, Diane
  Cultivating delight   508
  Deep play   155.6
  I praise my destroyer   811
  Jaguar of sweet laughter   811
  A natural history of love   152.4
  A natural history of the senses   152.1
  Origami bridges   811
  The rarest of the rare   578.68
  A slender thread   362.28
Ackroyd, Peter
  London: the biography   942.1
ACLU See American Civil Liberties Union
Acoustics See Sound
Acquired immune deficiency syndrome See AIDS (Dis-
  ease)
Acquired tastes. Mayle, P.   305.5
Acronyms
Dictionaries
  Acronyms, initialisms, & abbreviations dictionary
                                                421.03
  Stahl, D. Abbreviations dictionary   421.03
Acronyms, initialisms, & abbreviations dictionary
                                                421.03

ACT assessment
How to prepare for the ACT, American College Testing Assessment Program **378.1**
Actes and monuments of these latter and perilous days. See Foxe, J. Foxe's Book of martyrs **272**
Acting
Adler, S. Stella Adler: the art of acting **792**
The Best men's stage monologues of [date] **808.82**
The Best stage scenes of [year] **808.82**
The Best women's stage monologues of [date] **808.82**
Chekhov, M. To the actor **792**
Hagen, U. Respect for acting **792**
Harold, M. An actor's guide to performing Shakespeare **792**
Mamet, D. True and false **792**
Moore, S. The Stanislavski system **792**
Rodenburg, P. Speaking Shakespeare **792**
Stanislavsky, K. An actor prepares **792**
Stanislavsky, K. Building a character **792**
Stanislavsky, K. Creating a role **792**
The Ultimate audition book **808.82**
Costume
See Costume
Actions and defenses *See* Litigation
Active living every day **613.7**
Activism, Social *See* Social action
An **actor** and his time. Gielgud, Sir J. **92**
An **actor** prepares. Stanislavsky, K. **792**
Actors
Vanity Fair's Hollywood **791.43**
The **Actor's** book of movie monologues **791.43**
An **actor's** guide to performing Shakespeare. Harold, M. **792**
Actresses *See* Actors
Actual innocence. Dwyer, J. **347**
Aczel, Amir D.
Entanglement **530.1**
Fermat's last theorem **512**
God's equation **523.1**
The riddle of the compass **912**
Adair, Virginia Hamilton
Ants on the melon **811**
Beliefs and blasphemies **811**
Adair-Hoy, Angela
(jt. auth) Rose, M. J. How to publish and promote online **070.5**
Adam, Judith
Landscape planning **635**
Adam, Eve, and the serpent. Pagels, E. H. **241**
Adamantius *See* Origen
Adams, Abigail, 1744-1818
About
Nagel, P. C. The Adams women **920**
Adams, Ansel, 1902-1984
Ansel Adams, an autobiography **92**
About
Alinder, M. S. Ansel Adams **92**
See/See also pages in the following book(s):
Bustard, B. I. Picturing the century **779**
Adams, Charles Francis, 1807-1886
About
Brookhiser, R. America's first dynasty **920**
Adams, Douglas, 1952-2001
The salmon of doubt **828**
Adams, Francis V.
The breathing disorders sourcebook **616.2**
Adams, Fred C.
The five ages of the universe **523.1**
Origins of existence **576.8**
Adams, George Martin
Birdscaping your garden **598**

Adams, Harriet Chalmers, 1875-1937
See/See also pages in the following book(s):
Slung, M. B. Living with cannibals and other women's adventures **910.4**
Adams, Henry, 1838-1918
The education of Henry Adams **92**
Mont-Saint-Michel and Chartres **726**
About
Brookhiser, R. America's first dynasty **920**
See/See also pages in the following book(s):
Kazin, A. An American procession p3-21, 245-52, 277-310 **810.9**
Vidal, G. United States—essays, 1952-1992 p1251-71 **814**
Adams, Jody
In the hands of a chef **641.5**
Adams, John, 1735-1826
About
Brookhiser, R. America's first dynasty **920**
Ferling, J. E. Setting the world ablaze **973.3**
McCullough, D. G. John Adams **92**
See/See also pages in the following book(s):
Ellis, J. J. Founding brothers **973.4**
Adams, John Quincy, 1767-1848
About
Brookhiser, R. America's first dynasty **920**
Cohen, I. B. Science and the founding fathers **973.3**
Miller, W. L. Arguing about slavery **973.5**
Nagel, P. C. John Quincy Adams **92**
Remini, R. V. John Quincy Adams **92**
See/See also pages in the following book(s):
Kennedy, J. F. Profiles in courage **920**
Adams, Louisa Catherine, 1775-1852
About
Nagel, P. C. The Adams women **920**
Adams, Marcia
New recipes from quilt country **641.5**
Adams, Noah
The flyers **92**
Adams, Robert Lang
(ed) The Adams cover letter almanac & disk. See The Adams cover letter almanac & disk **650.14**
Adams, Scott
The Dilbert principle **650.1**
Adams, William Howard
The Paris years of Thomas Jefferson **92**
The **Adams** cover letter almanac & disk **650.14**
Adams family
About
Brookhiser, R. America's first dynasty **920**
Nagel, P. C. The Adams women **920**
See/See also pages in the following book(s):
Vidal, G. United States—essays, 1952-1992 p644-63 **814**
The **Adams** resume almanac **650.14**
The **Adams** women. Nagel, P. C. **920**
Adamson, Joy, 1910-1980
Born free **599.75**
Adamson, Lynda G.
American historical fiction **016.813**
Notable women in American history **920.003**
Notable women in world history **920.003**
World historical fiction **016.8**
The **adaptable** house. Friedman, A. **728**
Adaptation (Biology)
Boaz, N. T. Evolving health **616.07**
See/See also pages in the following book(s):
Toffler, A. Future shock p289-326 **303.4**
Adaptations, Film *See* Film adaptations
ADD *See* Attention deficit disorder
Addams, Jane, 1860-1935
About
Elshtain, J. B. Jane Addams and the dream of American democracy **92**

Addiction to alcohol *See* Alcoholism
Addiction to work *See* Workaholism
Addictive behavior *See* Compulsive behavior
Adding to a house. Wenz, P. S.   **690**
Addonizio, Kim, 1954-
    The poet's companion   **808.1**
Addresses *See* Speeches
Adirondack Mountains (N.Y.)
History
    Schneider, P. The Adirondacks   **974.7**
The **Adirondacks**. Schneider, P.   **974.7**
Adjustment (Psychology)
    Brehony, K. A. After the darkest hour   **155.9**
Adkins, Denice
    (jt. auth) Sauers, M. Using the Internet as a reference tool   **025.04**
Adkins, Lesley
    Handbook to life in ancient Greece   **938**
Adkins, Roy
    (jt. auth) Adkins, L. Handbook to life in ancient Greece   **938**
Adler, Dennis, 1948-
    The art of the sports car   **629.222**
Adler, Jerry
    (jt. auth) Gerson, A. The price of terror   **363.1**
Adler, Kraig
    (ed) Firefly encyclopedia of reptiles and amphibians. See Firefly encyclopedia of reptiles and amphibians   **597.9**
Adler, Margot
    Drawing down the moon   **133.4**
Adler, Mortimer J., 1902-2001
    Aristotle for everybody   **185**
    How to read a book   **028**
    How to speak, how to listen   **302.2**
    How to think about God   **212**
    How to think about the great ideas   **080**
    (ed) Great treasury of Western thought. See Great treasury of Western thought   **080**
Adler, Robert E., 1946-
    Science firsts: from the creation of science to the science of creation   **509**
Adler, Stella, 1901-1992
    Stella Adler: the art of acting   **792**
Administration *See* Management
Administration of criminal justice
    Dwyer, J. Actual innocence   **347**
    Encyclopedia of crime & justice   **364.03**
    Encyclopedia of crime and punishment   **364.03**
    Geoghegan, T. In America's court   **345**
Administrative ability *See* Executive ability
Administrative agencies
    See also Executive departments
Administrative assistant's & secretary's handbook. Stroman, J.   **651.3**
Administrators and executors *See* Executors and administrators
Admiral of the ocean sea: a life of Christopher Columbus. Morison, S. E.   **92**
Admirals
Dictionaries
Ancell, R. M. The biographical dictionary of World War II generals and flag officers   **920.003**
Admissions applications *See* College applications
Admissions confidential. Toor, R.   **378.1**
Admitting the Holocaust. Langer, L. L.   **940.53**
Adolescence
    Feig, P. Kick me   **305.23**
    The "Go ask Alice" book of answers   **613**
    Hine, T. The rise and fall of the American teenager   **305.23**
    Mead, M. Coming of age in Samoa   **306**
    See/See also pages in the following book(s):
    Pollack, W. S. Real boys p145-80   **305.23**

Encyclopedias
    Adolescence in America   **305.23**
Adolescence in America   **305.23**
Adolescent depression. Mondimore, F. M.   **616.85**
Adolescent psychology
    See also Boys—Psychology
    Di Prisco, J. Field guide to the American teenager   **305.23**
    Jackson, L. Freaks, geeks and asperger syndrome   **618.92**
    Mondimore, F. M. Adolescent depression   **616.85**
    Your adolescent   **155.5**
Adolescents *See* Teenagers
Adoptable dog. Ross, J.   **636.7**
Adoption
    Gilman, L. The adoption resource book   **362.7**
    Prager, E. Wuhu diary   **951**
    See/See also pages in the following book(s):
    Bartholet, E. Nobody's children   **362.7**
Adoption, Interracial *See* Interracial adoption
The **adoption** resource book. Gilman, L.   **362.7**
Adovasio, J. M. (James M.), 1944-
    The first Americans   **970.01**
Adovasio, James M. *See* Adovasio, J. M. (James M.), 1944-
Adrian, Jane *See* Leach, Penelope
Adrouny, A. Richard, 1952-
    Understanding colon cancer   **616.99**
Adult child sexual abuse victims
    Bass, E. The courage to heal   **362.83**
Adult survivors of child sexual abuse *See* Adult child sexual abuse victims
Adultery
    Barash, D. P. The myth of monogamy   **306.7**
Adulthood
    Sheehy, G. New passages   **305.24**
Adults sexually abused as children *See* Adult child sexual abuse victims
Advanced digital photography. Ang, T.   **775**
The **advent** of the algorithm. Berlinski, D.   **511**
Adventure and adventurers
    Cahill, T. Pass the butterworms   **910.4**
    Cordingly, D. Women sailors and sailors' women   **910.4**
    Points unknown   **910**
Adventure fiction
    See also Science fiction
The **adventures** of Amos 'n' Andy. Ely, M. P.   **791.44**
The **adversary**. Carrère, E.   **364.1**
Advertising
    See/See also pages in the following book(s):
    Boorstin, D. J. The Americans: The democratic experience   **973**
Directories
Standard directory of advertisers   **659.1**
Standard directory of advertising agencies   **659.1**
Encyclopedias
The Advertising age encyclopedia of advertising   **659.1**
The **Advertising** age encyclopedia of advertising   **659.1**
Aeken, Hieronymus van *See* Bosch, Hieronymus, d. 1516
Aeneas (Legendary character)
    See/See also pages in the following book(s):
    Hamilton, E. Mythology p319-42   **292**
The **Aeneid** of Virgil. Virgil   **873**
Aerial reconnaissance
    Burrows, W. E. By any means necessary   **327.12**
Aeronautics
    See also Airplanes; Airships; Flight; Rocketry; Rockets (Aeronautics)
    Gorn, M. H. Expanding the envelope   **629.13**
    Jane's all the world's aircraft   **629.133**

Aeronautics—*Continued*
Flights
Botting, D. Dr. Eckener's dream machine   **629.133**
Lindbergh, C. The spirit of St. Louis   **629.13**
Yeager, J. Voyager   **910.4**
History
Chant, C. A century of triumph   **629.13**
Demetz, P. The air show at Brescia, 1909   **629.13**
Grant, R. G. Flight: 100 years of aviation   **629.13**
Heppenheimer, T. A. First flight   **629.13**
Tobin, J. To conquer the air   **629.13**
Aeronautics, Commercial *See* Commercial aeronautics
Aeronautics, Military *See* Military aeronautics
Aeschylus
Agamemnon
In Aeschylus. The Oresteia   **882**
The Eumenides
In Aeschylus. The Oresteia   **882**
The libation bearers
In Aeschylus. The Oresteia   **882**
The Oresteia   **882**
See/See also pages in the following book(s):
Hamilton, E. The Greek way p239-57   **880.9**
Aesthetics
See also Art appreciation
Aristotle. Poetics   **808.1**
See/See also pages in the following book(s):
Gay, P. The Enlightenment: an interpretation   **190**
Keene, D. The pleasures of Japanese literature p3-22   **895.6**
Sontag, S. Styles of radical will p3-34   **814**
Encyclopedias
Encyclopedia of aesthetics   **111**
AFDC (Aid to families with dependent children) *See* Child welfare
Affairs of honor. Freeman, J. B.   **973.4**
Affirmative action programs
Carter, S. L. Reflections of an affirmative action baby   **342**
Cose, E. Color-blind   **305.8**
See/See also pages in the following book(s):
Pipes, R. Property and freedom p266-78   **323.4**
The **affluent** society. Galbraith, J. K.   **330**
Afghanistan
Anderson, J. L. The lion's grave   **958.1**
Zoya. Zoya's story   **958.1**
Description
Elliot, J. An unexpected light   **958.1**
History
Ewans, M. Afghanistan   **958.1**
History—Soviet occupation, 1979-1989
Corwin, P. Doomed in Afghanistan   **958.1**
Politics and government
Benard, C. Veiled courage   **958.1**
Rashid, A. Taliban: militant Islam, oil, and fundamentalism in Central Asia   **958.1**
Social conditions
Ansary, M. T. West of Kabul, East of New York   **958.1**
Africa
Civilization
Cultural atlas of Africa   **960**
Gates, H. L. Wonders of the African world   **960**
See/See also pages in the following book(s):
Achebe, C. Home and exile   **828**
Civilization—Encyclopedias
Africana   **909**
Description
Kapuściński, R. The shadow of the sun   **960**
Matthiessen, P. African silences   **916**
Theroux, P. Dark star safari   **916**
Encyclopedias
Africa: an encyclopedia for students   **960**
Page, W. F. The encyclopedia of African history and culture   **960**

Historiography
Lefkowitz, M. R. Not out of Africa   **960**
History
Davidson, B. Africa in history   **960**
Falola, T. Key events in African history   **960**
Pakenham, T. The scramble for Africa, 1876-1912   **960**
Reader, J. Africa: a biography of the continent   **960**
Natural history
See Natural history—Africa
Africa, North *See* North Africa
Africa, South *See* South Africa
Africa, Sub-Saharan *See* Sub-Saharan Africa
Africa, West *See* West Africa
Africa: an encyclopedia for students   **960**
The **Africa** cookbook. Harris, J. B.   **641.5**
Africa in history. Davidson, B.   **960**
Africa in my blood. Goodall, J.   **92**
The **African** American almanac   **305.8**
African American art
Patton, S. F. African-American art   **704**
African-American art. Patton, S. F.   **704**
African American artists
Harlem Renaissance: art of black America   **709.73**
Henkes, R. The art of black American women   **709.73**
African American arts
Murray, A. The blue devils of Nada   **700**
African American athletes
Halberstam, D. Playing for keeps: Michael Jordan and the world he made   **92**
Joyner-Kersee, J. A kind of grace   **92**
Remnick, D. King of the world: Muhammad Ali and the rise of an American hero   **92**
The **African-American** atlas. Asante, M. K.   **305.8**
African American authors
Fleming, R. The African American writer's handbook   **808**
The **African-American** century. Gates, H. L.   **920**
African American children
Beal, A. C. The black parenting book   **649**
Canada, G. Reaching up for manhood   **305.23**
African American cooking
Harris, J. B. The welcome table   **641.5**
Randall, J. A taste of heritage   **641.5**
White, J. Soul food   **641.5**
The **African** American encyclopedia   **305.8**
African American firsts in science and technology. Webster, R. B.   **509**
African American folklore *See* African Americans—Folklore
African-American heritage cooking. See Harris, J. B. The welcome table   **641.5**
African American inventors
Webster, R. B. African American firsts in science and technology   **509**
African American literary criticism, 1773 to 2000   **810.9**
African American literature *See* American literature—African American authors
African American music
See also Gospel music; Rap music
Floyd, S. A. The power of black music   **780.89**
Lomax, A. The land where the blues began   **781.643**
See/See also pages in the following book(s):
Baraka, I. A. The LeRoi Jones/Amiri Baraka reader   **818**
Gioia, T. The history of jazz   **781.65**
African American musicians
Feather, L. From Satchmo to Miles   **920**
African American photographers
Willis, D. Reflections in Black   **770**

African American pilots
  Gubert, B. K. Distinguished African Americans in aviation and space science   **920.003**
African American poetry *See* American poetry—African American authors
African-American poetry of the nineteenth century
    811.008
African American quotations   **808.88**
African American singers
  Harrison, D. D. Black pearls   **920**
African American soldiers
  Bloods: an oral history of the Vietnam War by black veterans   **959.704**
  Buckley, G. L. American patriots   **355**
  Trudeau, N. A. Like men of war   **973.7**
  Wright, K. Soldiers of freedom   **355**
The **African** American woman's guide to successful makeup and skincare. Fornay, A.   **646.7**
African American women
  Honey, hush!   **817.008**
  Jones, J. Labor of love, labor of sorrow   **305.4**
  Olson, L. Freedom's daughters   **323.1**
  Overcoming the odds   **649**
  Richardson, B. L. What mama couldn't tell us about love   **158**
  Walker-Hill, H. From spirituals to symphonies
    920
  Zucchino, D. Myth of the welfare queen   **362.5**
Dictionaries
  Notable black American women [bk I-III]
    920.003
Drama
  Shange, N. For colored girls who have considered suicide/when the rainbow is enuf   **812**
Health and hygiene
  The Black women's health book   **613**
  Essence total makeover   **646.7**
  Ferrell, P. Let's talk hair   **646.7**
  Fornay, A. The African American woman's guide to successful makeup and skincare   **646.7**
The **African** American writer's handbook. Fleming, R.
    808
African Americans
  The African American almanac   **305.8**
  Ball, E. The sweet hell inside   **920**
  Cleaver, E. Soul on ice   **305.8**
  Cose, E. The envy of the world   **305.8**
  Du Bois, W. E. B. The Oxford W. E. B. Du Bois reader   **305.8**
  Du Bois, W. E. B. The souls of black folk   **305.8**
  Gates, H. L. The African-American century   **920**
  Kennedy, R. Nigger   **305.8**
  Lasch-Quinn, E. Race experts   **305.8**
Biography
  Abdul-Jabbar, K. Black profiles in courage   **920**
  Contemporary black biography   **920.003**
  Gates, H. L. Thirteen ways of looking at a black man
    920
  Russell, D. Black genius and the American experience
    920
  Salley, C. The black 100   **920**
Biography—Dictionaries
  Notable black American men   **920.003**
  Notable black American scientists   **920.003**
  Who's who among African Americans   **920.003**
Civil rights
  Ball, H. A defiant life: Thurgood Marshall and the persistence of racism in America   **92**
  Bennett, L. What manner of man: a biography of Martin Luther King, Jr.   **92**
  Branch, T. Parting the waters: America in the King years, 1954-63   **973.921**
  Branch, T. Pillar of fire   **973.922**
  Civil rights in the United States   **323.1**
  Dent, T. Southern journey   **975**

  Dyson, M. E. I may not get there with you: the true Martin Luther King, Jr   **92**
  Egerton, J. Speak now against the day   **323.1**
  The Eyes on the prize civil rights reader   **323.1**
  Fairclough, A. Better day coming   **323.1**
  Frady, M. Martin Luther King, Jr.   **92**
  Halberstam, D. The children   **323.1**
  King, M. L. The autobiography of Martin Luther King, Jr   **92**
  King, M. L. The papers of Martin Luther King, Jr.
    323.1
  King, M. L. A testament of hope   **323.1**
  King, M. L. Why we can't wait   **323.1**
  Lewis, D. L. W.E.B. DuBois   **92**
  Marshall, T. Thurgood Marshall   **92**
  McDonald, L. The rights of racial minorities   **342**
  McWhorter, D. Carry me home   **976.1**
  Olson, L. Freedom's daughters   **323.1**
  Reporting civil rights   **323.1**
  Robeson, P. Here I stand   **305.8**
  Voices in our blood   **323.1**
  Williams, J. Eyes on the prize: America's civil rights years, 1954-1965   **323.1**
  See/See also pages in the following book(s):
  Foner, E. The story of American freedom   **323.44**
  Rickford, R. J. Betty Shabazz: a remarkable story of survival and faith before and after Malcolm X
    92
  Williams, J. Thurgood Marshall   **92**
Civil rights—Encyclopedias
  Encyclopedia of African-American civil rights
    305.8
Drama
  Hansberry, L. A raisin in the sun   **812**
  Wilson, A. Jitney   **812**
  Wilson, A. Joe Turner's come and gone   **812**
Economic conditions
  Loury, G. C. The anatomy of racial inequality
    305.8
Education
  Kozol, J. Death at an early age   **306.43**
  McWhorter, J. H. Losing the race   **305.8**
  Overcoming the odds   **649**
Encyclopedias
  The African American encyclopedia   **305.8**
  Africana   **909**
  Encyclopedia of African-American culture and history
    305.8
  The New York Public Library African American desk reference   **305.8**
Folklore
  From my people   **398.2**
Health and hygiene
  Reed, J. The black man's guide to good health
    613
History
  Asante, M. K. The African-American atlas   **305.8**
  Black firsts: 4,000 ground-breaking and pioneering historical events   **305.8**
  Cantor, G. Historic landmarks of black America
    917.3
  Curtis, N. C. Black heritage sites   **917.3**
  Franklin, J. H. From slavery to freedom   **305.8**
  Harley, S. The timetables of African-American history
    305.8
  Johnson, C. R. Africans in America: America's journey through slavery   **326**
  Wickett, M. R. Contested territory   **976.6**
  Williams, J. This far by faith   **200**
History—Sources
  Remembering slavery   **326**
Intellectual life
  Gates, H. L. The African-American century   **920**
  Gates, H. L. The future of the race   **305.8**

African Americans—Intellectual life—*Continued*
Russell, D. Black genius and the American experience
    920

Music
See African American music

Poetry
Johnson, J. W. Complete poems   811
See/See also pages in the following book(s):
Jackson, M. Leaving Saturn   811

Quotations
African American quotations   808.88

Race identity
Tatum, B. D. "Why are all the Black kids sitting together in the cafeteria?" and other conversations about race   305.8

Religion
Cone, J. H. A black theology of liberation   261.8
Lincoln, C. E. The black church in the African American experience   277.3
Williams, J. This far by faith   200
See/See also pages in the following book(s):
Boorstin, D. J. The Americans: The national experience p190-99   973

Religion—Encyclopedias
Encyclopedia of African American religions   200.9
The Encyclopedia of African and African-American religions   299

Segregation
Packard, J. M. American nightmare   305.8
Remembering Jim Crow   305.8
Woodward, C. V. The strange career of Jim Crow   305.8

Social conditions
Berlin, I. Many thousands gone   326
Dash, L. Rosa Lee   305.8
Gates, H. L. The future of the race   305.8
Graham, L. O. Our kind of people   305.8
Loury, G. C. The anatomy of racial inequality   305.8
McWhorter, J. H. Losing the race   305.8
West, C. Restoring hope   305.8
Wright, R. Black boy   92

Social life and customs
Hooks, B. Salvation   306.7

Mississippi
Hendrickson, P. Sons of Mississippi   305.8
Lomax, A. The land where the blues began   781.643

New York (N.Y.)
White, S. Stories of freedom in Black New York   974.7

Southern States
Dray, P. At the hands of persons unknown   364.1
Griffin, J. H. Black like me   305.8
King, J. Hate crime: the story of a dragging in Jasper, Texas   364.1
Remembering Jim Crow   305.8
Wiencek, H. The Hairstons   975

Tulsa (Okla.)
Hirsch, J. S. Riot and remembrance   976.6
Madigan, T. The burning   976.6

African Americans in art
Willis, D. Reflections in Black   770

African Americans in literature
The Coretta Scott King Awards book, 1970-1999   028.5
Richards, P. Best literature by and about Blacks   016.8

African Americans in motion pictures
George, N. Blackface: reflections on African-Americans and the movies   791.43
Jones, G. W. Black cinema treasures   791.43

African Americans on television
Bogle, D. Primetime blues   791.45

Ely, M. P. The adventures of Amos 'n' Andy   791.44

African art
An Anthology of African art: the twentieth century   709.6
A History of art in Africa   709.6

African civilization *See* Africa—Civilization

African Company (Theater company)
White, S. Stories of freedom in Black New York   974.7

African cooking
Harris, J. B. The Africa cookbook   641.5
Stow, J. The African kitchen   641.5
African exodus. Stringer, C. B.   599.93
The **African** kitchen. Stow, J.   641.5
African laughter. Lessing, D. M.   968.91

African literature
Bio-bibliography
African writers   896
Dictionaries
African writers   896

African mythology
Dictionaries
Scheub, H. A dictionary of African mythology   299

African poetry
Collections
Heinemann book of African women's poetry   896
The New African poetry   896
The Penguin book of modern African poetry   896
The **African** prayer book   242
African silences. Matthiessen, P.   916
African writers   896
Africana   909

Africans
Encyclopedias
Encyclopedia of African peoples   960
Africans in America: America's journey through slavery. Johnson, C. R.   326
Africa's vanishing wildlife. Stuart, C.   591.9
After all. Matthews, W.   811
After heaven. Wuthnow, R.   200.9
After Henry. Didion, J.   814
After the dance. Danticat, E.   394.25
After the darkest hour. Brehony, K. A.   155.9
After the death of a child. Finkbeiner, A. K.   155.9
After the Holocaust. Brenner, M.   943.087
After the Trail of Tears. McLoughlin, W. G.   970.004
Against love poetry. Boland, E.   821
Against the tide. Dean, C.   333.91
Agamemnon. Aeschylus
    In Aeschylus. The Oresteia   882
Agatha Christie A to Z. Sova, D. B.   823.009
Age *See* Old age
Age and employment
    See also Teenagers—Employment
The **Age** of Beethoven, 1790-1830
    In New Oxford history of music v8   780.9
The **age** of chivalry. Bulfinch, T.
    In Bulfinch, T. Bulfinch's mythology   291.1
Age of delirium. Satter, D.   947.085
The **Age** of enlightenment, 1745-1790
    In New Oxford history of music v7   780.9
The **age** of fable. Bulfinch, T.
    In Bulfinch, T. Bulfinch's mythology   291.1
The **age** of homespun. Ulrich, L.   974
The **Age** of humanism, 1540-1630
    In New Oxford history of music v4   780.9
The **age** of Louis XIV. Durant, W. J.   940.2
The **age** of reform from Bryan to F.D.R. Hofstadter, R.   973.91
The **age** of revolution, 1789-1848. Hobsbawm, E. J.   940.2
The **age** of sacred terror. Benjamin, D.   303.6

The **age** of science. Piel, G. 509
The **age** of spiritual machines. Kurzweil, R. 006.3
Aged *See* Elderly
Agee, James, 1909-1955
Let us now praise famous men 976.1
Ageless body, timeless mind. Chopra, D. 612.6
Ageless: take control of your age and stay youthful for
life. Schneider, E. L. 612.6
Ageless yoga. Reichmann, R. 613.7
The **ages** of Gaia. Lovelock, J. 570.1
Aggressiveness (Psychology)
Lamb, S. The secret lives of girls 305.23
Simmons, R. Odd girl out 305.23
Aging
See also Menopause
Atkins, R. C. Dr. Atkins' age-defying diet revolution
613
Carter, J. The virtues of aging 305.26
Chopra, D. Ageless body, timeless mind 612.6
Dollemore, D. The doctors book of home remedies for
seniors 613
Fitness over fifty 613
Goldman, B. Brain fitness 153.1
Greer, G. The change 618.1
Hillman, J. The force of character 155.67
Kirkwood, T. Time of our lives 612.6
Looking after your body 613
Medina, J. The clock of ages 612.6
Peck, B. The baby boomer body book 613
The Practical guide to aging 305.26
Rowe, J. W. Successful aging 612.6
Sheehy, G. New passages 305.24
Vaillant, G. E. Aging well 305.26
Victoroff, J. I. Saving your brain 612.8
Williamson, M. L. Great sex after 40 306.7
See/See also pages in the following book(s):
Cohen, G. D. The creative age 305.24
Encyclopedias
Encyclopedia of aging 305.26
The Encyclopedia of aging: a comprehensive resource
in gerontology and geriatrics 305.26
Aging parents
Pipher, M. B. Another country 306.8
Aging well. Vaillant, G. E. 305.26
Agnew, Connie L., 1957-
Twins! 649
Agnosticism
See/See also pages in the following book(s):
Turner, J. Without God, without creed 211
Agrarian question *See* Agriculture—Government policy
Agress, Lynne, 1941-
Working with words in business and legal writing
808
Agricola, Gnaeus Julius, 40-93
See/See also pages in the following book(s):
Tacitus, C. The complete works of Tacitus p677-706
878
Agricultural industry
Charles, D. Lords of the harvest 664
Agricultural policy *See* Agriculture—Government policy
Agricultural products *See* Farm produce
Agriculture
See also Food supply; Livestock industry
See/See also pages in the following book(s):
Emerson, R. W. The portable Emerson p558-68
818
Tudge, C. The time before history p264-79
599.93
Dictionaries
Hortus third 635
Economic aspects
See also Agricultural industry
Hurt, R. D. Problems of plenty 630
Environmental aspects
Berry, W. Citizenship papers 338.1

Fatal harvest 630
Stoll, S. Larding the lean Earth 631.4
Government policy
Berry, W. Citizenship papers 338.1
Hurt, R. D. Problems of plenty 630
United States
Hurt, R. D. Problems of plenty 630
Agriculture and the environment *See* Agriculture—En-
vironmental aspects
Ahearn, Allen
Collected books 002.075
Ahearn, Patricia
(jt. auth) Ahearn, A. Collected books 002.075
AHS garden problem solver. Greenwood, P. 635
AI (Artificial intelligence) *See* Artificial intelligence
AIA *See* American Institute of Architects
Aid to families with dependent children *See* Child wel-
fare
Aidells, Bruce
The complete meat cookbook 641.6
AIDS (Disease)
AIDS sourcebook 362.1
Fisher, M. Sleep with the angels 362.1
Gallo, R. C. Virus hunting 616.97
Grmek, M. D. History of AIDS 616.97
Monette, P. Borrowed time 362.1
Null, G. AIDS: a second opinion 616.97
Shilts, R. And the band played on 362.1
See/See also pages in the following book(s):
Garrett, L. The coming plague p281-389 614.4
Oldstone, M. B. A. Viruses, plagues, and history
614.4
Dictionaries
Watstein, S. B. The encyclopedia of HIV and AIDS
616.97
Encyclopedias
Encyclopedia of AIDS 362.1
Law and legislation
Rubenstein, W. B. The rights of people who are HIV
positive 344
The **AIDS** dictionary. See Watstein, S. B. The encyclo-
pedia of HIV and AIDS 616.97
AIDS sourcebook 362.1
Aiken, Joan, 1924-2004
The way to write for children 808.06
AIM *See* American Indian Movement
Ainslie, Tom
Ainslie's complete guide to thoroughbred racing
798.401
Ainslie's complete Hoyle 795
Ainslie's complete guide to thoroughbred racing. Ainslie,
T. 798.401
Ainslie's complete Hoyle. Ainslie, T. 795
Ainsworth, Maryan Wynn
From Van Eyck to Bruegel. See From Van Eyck to
Bruegel 759.9493
Ainsworth, Patricia, 1932-
Understanding depression 616.85
Ain't it cool? Knowles, H. 791.43
Air and space. Chaikin, A. 629.13
Air apparent. Monmonier, M. S. 551.6
Air carriers *See* Airlines
Air conditioning
Kittle, J. L. Home heating and air conditioning systems
697
Air lines *See* Airlines
Air pilots
See also African American pilots; Women air pi-
lots
Ambrose, S. E. The wild blue 940.54
Berg, A. S. Lindbergh 92
See/See also pages in the following book(s):
Morgan, R. The man who flew the Memphis Belle
92
The **air** show at Brescia, 1909. Demetz, P. 629.13

Air warfare *See* Military aeronautics

The **airline** encyclopedia, 1909-2000. Smith, M. J.
387.7

Airlines

Encyclopedias

Smith, M. J. The airline encyclopedia, 1909-2000
387.7

Airplane hijacking *See* Hijacking of airplanes

Airplanes

Blatner, D. The flying book   387.7

Wright, O. How we invented the airplane   629.13

See/See also pages in the following book(s):

Ciotti, P. More with less   92

Airplanes, Military *See* Military airplanes

Airships

Botting, D. Dr. Eckener's dream machine   629.133

Aiyangar, Srinivasa Ramanujan *See* Ramanujan
Aiyangar, Srinivasa, 1887-1920

Ajax. Sophocles

In Sophocles. The complete plays of Sophocles p1-
35   882

AKC *See* American Kennel Club

Akera, Atsushi

(ed) From 0 to 1: an authoritative history of modern
computing. See From 0 to 1: an authoritative history
of modern computing   004

Akhenaton, King of Egypt, fl. ca. 1388-1358 B.C.

About

Aldred, C. Akhenaten: King of Egypt   932

Akhmatova, Anna Andreevna, 1889-1966

The complete poems of Anna Akhmatova   891.7

See/See also pages in the following book(s):

Simon, J. I. Dreamers of dreams   809.1

Volkov, S. St. Petersburg   947

Akkadians (Sumerians) *See* Sumerians

ALA *See* American Library Association

Alabama

Social conditions

Agee, J. Let us now praise famous men   976.1

Alamo (San Antonio, Tex.)

Davis, W. C. Three roads to the Alamo   976.4

Alaska

Description

Jenkins, P. Looking for Alaska   979.8

McPhee, J. A. Coming into the country   979.8

Raban, J. Passage to Juneau   979.8

Schooler, L. The blue bear   599.78

History

Borneman, W. R. Alaska: saga of a bold land
979.8

Social life and customs

Jenkins, P. Looking for Alaska   979.8

Albatrosses

Safina, C. Eye of the albatross   598

Albee, Edward, 1928-

Who's afraid of Virginia Woolf?   812

About

Gussow, M. Edward Albee   92

See/See also pages in the following book(s):

Playwrights at work   812.009

**Albert, Prince Consort of Victoria, Queen of Great
Britain, 1819-1861**

About

Weintraub, S. Uncrowned king: the life of Prince Albert   92

See/See also pages in the following book(s):

Strachey, L. Queen Victoria p134-203, 253-96   92

Albom, Mitch, 1958-

Tuesdays with Morrie [biography of Morris Schwartz]
92

Albright, Madeleine Korbel, 1937-

Madam Secretary   92

Albrizio, Ann

Classic millinery techniques   646.5

An **album** of memories. Brokaw, T.   940.54

Alcestis. Euripides

In Euripides. Ten plays p3-80   882

Alchemy

Greenberg, A. The art of chemistry   540

See/See also pages in the following book(s):

Connell, E. S. The Aztec treasure house p412-32
814

The **alchemy** of the heavens. Croswell, K.   523.1

Alcindor, Lew *See* Abdul-Jabbar, Kareem, 1947-

Alcock, John, 1942-

In a desert garden   595.7

Alcoholism

Dorris, M. The broken cord   362.292

West, J. W. The Betty Ford Center book of answers
616.86

Alcoran *See* Koran

Alcott, Louisa May, 1832-1888

The sketches of Louisa May Alcott   818

Alder, Ken

The measure of all things   526

Aldred, Cyril, 1914-1991

Akhenaten: King of Egypt   932

Alemán, Ana M. Martínez *See* Martínez Alemán, Ana
M.

Alexander, the Great, 356-323 B.C.

About

Wood, M. In the footsteps of Alexander the Great
938

See/See also pages in the following book(s):

Hamilton, E. The echo of Greece p115-37   880.9

Alexander, Caroline, 1956-

The Endurance   998

Alexander, Gerard

(jt. auth) Kane, J. N. Nicknames and sobriquets of U.S.
cities, states, and counties   917.3

Alexander, Jane

Command performance   92

Alexander, Margaret Walker *See* Walker, Margaret,
1915-1998

Alexander, Paul, 1955-

Boulevard of broken dreams: the life, times, and legend of James Dean   92

Alexander, Shana

The astonishing elephant   599.67

Alexander Hamilton, American. Brookhiser, R. 92

**Alexandra, Empress, consort of Nicholas II, Emperor
of Russia, 1872-1918**

About

Kurth, P. Tsar: the lost world of Nicholas and
Alexandra   947.08

Massie, R. K. Nicholas and Alexandra   92

Alexie, Sherman, 1966-

One stick song   811

Alfred, the Great, King of England, 849-899

About

Duckett, E. S. Alfred the Great   92

Algae

Barker, R. And the waters turned to blood   615.9

Algar, Ayla Esen

Classical Turkish cooking   641.5

Algeria

Church history

Kiser, J. W. The monks of Tibhirine   271

The **Algeria** Hotel. Nossiter, A.   940.54

Algorithms

Berlinski, D. The advent of the algorithm   511

Algren, Nelson, 1909-1981

About

Beauvoir, S. de. A transatlantic love affair: letters to
Nelson Algren   92

Ali, Muhammad, 1942-

About

Kram, M. The ghosts of Manila   796.8

Remnick, D. King of the world: Muhammad Ali and
the rise of an American hero   92

Alice Neel. Neel, A.   **759.13**

Aliens

  See also Immigrants

United States

  See also United States—Immigration and emigration

  Lewis, L. N. How to get a green card   **342**

Alighieri, Dante *See* Dante Alighieri, 1265-1321

Alinder, Mary Street, 1946-

  Ansel Adams   **92**

  (jt. auth) Adams, A. Ansel Adams, an autobiography   **92**

Alinsky, Saul

  Rules for radicals   **322.4**

Alive. Read, P. P.   **910.4**

Alive and kicking. Araton, H.   **796.334**

Alkoran *See* Koran

All creatures great and small. Herriot, J.   **92**

All for love. Dryden, J.   **822**

  also in Restoration plays   **822.008**

All for love. Mehta, V.   **92**

All God's children. Butterfield, F.   **364.1**

All music guide   **781.64**

All music guide to country   **781.642**

All music guide to jazz   **781.65**

All-new hints from Heloise. Heloise   **640**

All of the women of the Bible. Deen, E.   **220.9**

All of us. Carver, R.   **811**

All over but the shoutin'. Bragg, R.   **92**

All rivers run to the sea. Wiesel, E.   **92**

All the best, George Bush. Bush, G.   **92**

All the daring of the soldier. Leonard, E. D.   **973.7**

All the laws but one. Rehnquist, W. H.   **342**

All the men in the sea. Krieger, M. J.   **910.4**

All the president's men. Bernstein, C.   **973.924**

All things Shakespeare. Olsen, K.   **822.3**

All too human. Stephanopoulos, G.   **973.929**

Allaby, Michael, 1933-

  The Facts on File weather and climate handbook   **551.6**

  Makers of science   **920.003**

Allen, Charlotte, 1943-

  The human Christ   **232.9**

Allen, Frederick Lewis, 1890-1954

  Only yesterday   **973.91**

  Since yesterday   **973.91**

Allen, Paula Gunn

  See/See also pages in the following book(s):

  Coltelli, L. Winged words: American Indian writers speak   **897**

Allen, Stewart Lee

  In the devil's garden   **641**

Allen, Thomas B., 1929-

  The shark almanac   **597**

  The Washington Monument   **975.3**

Allen, Woody

  Death [play]

    In Allen, W. Without feathers   **817**

  God [play]

    In Allen, W. Without feathers   **817**

  Side effects   **817**

  Without feathers   **817**

  Woody Allen on Woody Allen   **791.43**

About

  Meade, M. The unruly life of Woody Allen   **92**

Allende, Isabel

  Aphrodite   **868**

  Paula   **92**

Allende family

About

  Allende, I. Paula   **92**

Allergies, Food *See* Food allergy

Allergies A-Z. See Lipkowitz, M. Encyclopedia of allergies   **616.97**

Allergy

  See also Food allergy

  Brody, J. E. Jane Brody's allergy fighter   **616.2**

  Pescatore, F. The allergy and asthma cure   **616.97**

  Walsh, W. E. Food allergies   **616.97**

  Young, S. Allergies   **616.97**

Encyclopedias

  Lipkowitz, M. Encyclopedia of allergies   **616.97**

The **allergy** and asthma cure. Pescatore, F.   **616.97**

Allison, Kathleen Cahill

  American Medical Association complete guide to women's health   **613**

Allison, Nancy, 1954-

  (ed) The Illustrated encyclopedia of body-mind disciplines. See The Illustrated encyclopedia of body-mind disciplines   **615.5**

Allocation of time *See* Time management

Allport, Gordon, 1897-1967

  Becoming   **155.2**

  The nature of prejudice   **152.4**

Allusions

  Brewer's dictionary of modern phrase & fable   **803**

  Brewer's dictionary of phrase and fable   **803**

  Cole, S. The Facts on File dictionary of cultural and historical allusions   **031.02**

  The Oxford dictionary of allusions   **803**

  The Oxford dictionary of phrase and fable   **803**

  Webber, E. Merriam-Webster's dictionary of allusions   **803**

The **almanac** of American politics. Barone, M.   **328.73**

Almanac of World War I. Burg, D. F.   **940.3**

Almanacs

  See also Nautical almanacs

  Barone, M. The almanac of American politics   **328.73**

  Canadian almanac & directory   **317.1**

  Catholic almanac   **282**

  Chase's calendar of events   **394.26**

  CQ almanac plus   **328.73**

  Encyclopaedia Britannica almanac   **031.02**

  The New York Times almanac   **031.02**

  The Time almanac   **031.02**

  The World almanac and book of facts   **031.02**

Almost everyone's guide to science. Gribbin, J. R.   **500**

Almost like a whale. See Jones, S. Darwin's ghost   **576.8**

Almost there. O'Faolain, N.   **92**

Alopecia areata. Thompson, W. J. A.   **616.5**

Alper, Joseph S., 1946-

  (ed) The Double-edged helix. See The Double-edged helix   **599.93**

Alper, Michael M., 1953-

  (jt. auth) Turkington, C. The encyclopedia of fertility and infertility   **616.6**

Alperovitz, Gar

  The decision to use the atomic bomb and the architecture of an American myth   **940.54**

Alschuler, William R.

  The science of UFOs   **001.9**

The **alternative** health & medicine encyclopedia. Marti, J.   **615.5**

Alternative medicine

  See also Holistic medicine; Naturopathy; Osteopathic medicine

  American Cancer Society's Guide to complementary and alternative cancer methods   **616.99**

  Blackwell complementary and alternative medicine   **615.5**

  Breast cancer   **616.99**

  Buhner, S. H. Vital man   **613**

  Cassileth, B. R. The alternative medicine handbook   **615.5**

Alternative medicine—*Continued*
The Illustrated encyclopedia of body-mind disciplines
 615.5
Maleskey, G. Nature's medicines **615.5**
Marti, J. The alternative health & medicine encyclopedia **615.5**
McTaggart, L. The field: the quest for the secret force of the universe **615.5**
The New York Times guide to alternative health
 615.5
Null, G. For women only! **613**
Pelletier, K. R. The best alternative medicine
 615.5
Weil, A. Eight weeks to optimum health **613**
Whorton, J. C. Nature cures **615.5**
 See/See also pages in the following book(s):
Gearin-Tosh, M. Living proof **92**
McLanahan, S. A. Surgery and its alternatives
 617
The **alternative** medicine handbook. Cassileth, B. R.
 615.5
Altman, Adelaide, 1925-
Elderhouse: planning your best home ever **728**
Alvarez, A. (Alfred), 1929-
Night **154.6**
Alvarez, Alfred *See* Alvarez, A. (Alfred), 1929-
Alvarez, Julia
Something to declare **814**
Alvarez, Luis W.
 See/See also pages in the following book(s):
Greenstein, G. Portraits of discovery p92-110 **920**
Alvarez, Walter, 1940-
T. rex and the Crater of Doom **551.7**
Always beginning. Kumin, M. **92**
Alzheimer's disease
Bayley, J. Elegy for Iris **92**
Bayley, J. Iris and her friends **92**
Cutler, N. R. Understanding Alzheimer's disease
 616.8
Kuhn, D. Alzheimer's early stages **616.8**
Mace, N. L. The 36-hour day **618.97**
Mayo Clinic on Alzheimer's disease **616.8**
Shenk, D. The forgetting: Alzheimer's, portrait of an epidemic **616.8**
Tanzi, R. E. Decoding darkness **616.8**
Victoroff, J. I. Saving your brain **612.8**
Warner, M. L. The complete guide to Alzheimer's-proofing your home **362.1**
   Encyclopedias
Moore, E. A. Encyclopedia of Alzheimer's disease
 616.8
Turkington, C. The encyclopedia of Alzheimer's disease **616.8**
Alzheimer's early stages. Kuhn, D. **616.8**
AMA *See* American Medical Association
The **AMA** handbook of business letters. Seglin, J. L.
 651.7
Amadeus, Peter Shaffer's. Shaffer, P. **822**
The **Amateur** astronomer **520**
Amateur radio stations
   Handbooks, manuals, etc.
The ARRL handbook for radio amateurs
 621.3841
Amazin'. Golenbock, P. **796.357**
Amazing grace. Kozol, J. **362.7**
Amazon.com Inc.
Spector, R. Amazon.com **338.7**
Amazon River valley
Kane, J. Savages **986.6**
Montgomery, S. Journey of the pink dolphins
 599.5
 See/See also pages in the following book(s):
Davis, W. One river **581.6**
Amazons to fighter pilots **355**
Ambassadors *See* Diplomats

Amber
Poinar, G. O. The quest for life in amber **560**
Ambling into history: the unlikely odyssey of George W. Bush. Bruni, F. **92**
Ambrose, Stephen E.
The American Heritage new history of World War II
 940.53
Band of brothers **940.54**
Citizen soldiers **940.54**
Comrades **302.3**
D-Day, June 6, 1944 **940.54**
Eisenhower **92**
Lewis & Clark **978**
Nothing like it in the world **385**
Undaunted courage **978**
The victors **940.54**
The wild blue **940.54**
(ed) Witness to America. See Witness to America
 973
Amelia Earhart's daughters. Haynsworth, L. **629.13**
Amen, Daniel
Change your brain, change your life **616.89**
Amenhotep IV, King of Egypt *See* Akhenaton, King of Egypt, fl. ca. 1388-1358 B.C.
America
 See also Latin America; North America; South America
   Antiquities
Adovasio, J. M. The first Americans **970.01**
America in 1492 **970.01**
Dillehay, T. D. The settlement of the Americas
 970.01
Schobinger, J. The ancient Americans **970.01**
   Description
Theroux, P. The old Patagonian express **918**
   Exploration
America in 1492 **970.01**
Dillehay, T. D. The settlement of the Americas
 970.01
Milton, G. Big Chief Elizabeth **975.5**
Vikings: the North Atlantic saga **970.01**
 See/See also pages in the following book(s):
Boorstin, D. J. The Americans: The national experience p223-41 **973**
Connell, E. S. The Aztec treasure house p58-82, 294-345 **814**
America in 1492 **970.01**
America in so many words. Barnhart, D. K. **422**
America Online for dummies. See Kaufeld, J. AOL for dummies **025.04**
America Online Inc.
Kaufeld, J. AOL for dummies **025.04**
America votes **324.6**
American Academy of Child and Adolescent Psychiatry
Your adolescent. See Your adolescent **155.5**
American Academy of Child Psychiatry
 See also American Academy of Child and Adolescent Psychiatry
American Academy of Pediatrics guide to your child's sleep **618.92**
American Airlines Flight 11 hijacking, 2001 *See* World Trade Center terrorist attack, 2001
American architecture *See* Architecture—United States
American architecture since 1780. Whiffen, M.
 720.973
American art
Avery, K. J. American drawings and watercolors in the Metropolitan Museum of Art v1 **759.13**
Discovered lands, invented pasts **759.13**
Harlem Renaissance: art of black America **709.73**
Haskell, B. The American century **709.73**
Henkes, R. The art of black American women
 709.73
Hughes, R. American visions **709.73**

American art—*Continued*
See/See also pages in the following book(s):
Boorstin, D. J. The Americans: The democratic experience 973
Dictionaries
Kort, C. A to Z of American women in the visual arts 920.003
Directories
American art directory 702.5
American art annual. See American art directory 702.5
American art annual. See Who's who in American art 920.003
American art directory 702.5
American artists *See* Artists—United States
American arts *See* Arts—United States
American authors, 1600-1900 920.003
American ballads
Sandburg, C. The American songbag 782.42
The **American** Bar Association guide to family law 346.01
The **American** Bar Association guide to home ownership 346.04
The **American** Bar Association guide to wills and estates 346.05
The **American** Bar Association guide to workplace law 344
The **American** Bar Association legal guide for older Americans 346.01
The **American** Bar Association legal guide for small business 343
American bison *See* Bison
American bison. Lott, D. F. 599.64
The **American** book of days 394.26
American book prices current 018
American book trade directory 070.5025
American Bookworks Corporation
Turkington, C. The encyclopedia of learning disabilities 371.9
American buffalo. Mamet, D.
In Nine plays of the modern theater p791-896 808.82
American Cancer Society's Guide to complementary and alternative cancer methods 616.99
The **American** century. Evans, H. 973.9
The **American** century. Haskell, B. 709.73
American chica. Arana, M. 92
An **American** childhood. Dillard, A. 92
American Civil Liberties Union
McDonald, L. The rights of racial minorities 342
O'Neil, R. M. The rights of public employees 342
Outten, W. N. The rights of employees and union members 344
The Rights of women. See The Rights of women 346.01
Rubenstein, W. B. The rights of people who are HIV positive 344
American College of Physicians complete home medical guide 616.02
American College Testing Program examination *See* ACT assessment
American colonies *See* United States—History—1600-1775, Colonial period
American composers *See* Composers—United States
American cookery, James Beard's. Beard, J. 641.5
American cooking *See* Cooking
American decades 973.9
American Diabetes Association complete guide to diabetes 616.4
American dialects. Herman, L. 427
American Dietetic Association complete food and nutrition guide. Duyff, R. L. 613.2

American drama
Bio-bibliography
Contemporary dramatists 920.003
Dictionaries
Bordman, G. M. The Oxford companion to American theatre 792.03
Critical survey of drama 809.2
History and criticism
Bordman, G. M. American theatre: a chronicle of comedy and drama, 1869-1914 792
Bordman, G. M. American theatre: a chronicle of comedy and drama, 1914-1930 792
Bordman, G. M. American theatre: a chronicle of comedy and drama, 1930-1969 792
Hischak, T. American theatre: a chronicle of comedy and drama, 1969-2000 792
Women authors—Collections
Plays by American women, 1900-1930 812.008
American drawings and watercolors in the Metropolitan Museum of Art v1. Avery, K. J. 759.13
The **American** dream. Rather, D. 973.92
American dreams. Terkel, S. 973.9
American electricians' handbook 621.3
American encounters 970.004
American eras 973
American espionage
Burrows, W. E. By any means necessary 327.12
Laird, T. Into Tibet 327.12
American exorcism. Cuneo, M. W. 265
The **American** experience in Vietnam 959.704
American fiction
Bibliography
Adamson, L. G. American historical fiction 016.813
Bio-bibliography
American women fiction writers 813.009
The Columbia companion to the twentieth-century American short story 813.009
Contemporary Jewish-American novelists 813.009
History and criticism
The Columbia companion to the twentieth-century American short story 813.009
Jewish authors
Contemporary Jewish-American novelists 813.009
Women authors
American women fiction writers 813.009
American folk music *See* Folk music—United States
American folklore 398.03
American foreign relations since 1600 016.327
American furniture
Kirk, J. T. American furniture 749.2
American ground, unbuilding the World Trade Center. Langewiesche, W. 974.7
American guide series 917.3
American Heart Association
American Heart Association low-fat, low-cholesterol cookbook. See American Heart Association low-fat, low-cholesterol cookbook 641.5
American Heart Association cookbook 641.5
American Heart Association low-fat & luscious desserts 641.8
American Heart Association low-fat, low-cholesterol cookbook 641.5
The **American** Heart Association low-salt cookbook 641.5
American Heart Association meals in minutes 641.5
American Heart Association quick-and-easy cookbook 641.5
The **American** Heritage college dictionary 423
The **American** Heritage dictionary. See The American Heritage college dictionary 423
The **American** Heritage dictionary of idioms. Ammer, C. 427

The **American** Heritage dictionary of the English language   **423**

The **American** Heritage illustrated history of the presidents   **920**

The **American** Heritage new history of World War II. Ambrose, S. E.   **940.53**

The **American** Heritage Spanish dictionary   **463**

American historical fiction. Adamson, L. G.   **016.813**

American history atlas. See Gilbert, M. The Routledge atlas of American history   **911**

The **American** history cookbook. Zanger, M. H.   **641.5**

American home cooking. Jamison, C. A.   **641.5**

American homelessness. Hombs, M. E.   **362.5**

American Horticultural Society
Greenwood, P. AHS garden problem solver   **635**
Pruning & training. See Pruning & training   **635.9**

The **American** Horticultural Society A-Z encyclopedia of garden plants   **635.9**

The **American** Horticultural Society complete guide to water gardening. Robinson, P.   **635.9**

The **American** Horticultural Society encyclopedia of garden plants. See The American Horticultural Society A-Z encyclopedia of garden plants   **635.9**

American Horticultural Society encyclopedia of gardening   **635**

American Horticultural Society encyclopedia of plants and flowers   **635.9**

The **American** Horticultural Society gardening manual   **635**

American hostages
Iran
See also Iran hostage crisis, 1979-1981

American hymns old and new   **782.27**

American Indian ethnic renewal. Nagel, J.   **970.004**

American Indian literature   **897**

American Indian Movement
Crow Dog, L. Crow Dog   **970.004**

American Indian myths and legends   **398.2**

American Indian quotations   **808.88**

American Indians *See* Native Americans

American Indians   **970.004**

American Institute of Architects
Architectural graphic standards   **692**

American inventors, entrepreneurs, and business visionaries. Carey, C. W.   **920**

American Jewish Historical Society
American Jewish history. See American Jewish history   **305.8**

American Jewish history   **305.8**

American Jewish year book   **296**

American jihad   **297**

American Judaism. Glazer, N.   **296**

American Kennel Club
The complete dog book   **636.7**

The **American** language. Mencken, H. L.   **427**

American law in the 20th century. Friedman, L. M.   **349**

American letters
Letters of a nation   **816**
Letters of the century   **816**
The Oxford book of letters   **826**

American library annual. See The Bowker annual library and book trade almanac   **020.5**

American Library Association
See also Joint Steering Committee for Revision of AACR; Young Adult Library Services Association; Anglo-American cataloguing rules. See Anglo-American cataloguing rules   **025.3**

American Library Association. Coretta Scott King Award Task Force
The Coretta Scott King Awards book, 1970-1999. See The Coretta Scott King Awards book, 1970-1999   **028.5**

American Library Association. Social Responsibilities Round Table. Coretta Scott King Award Task Force *See* American Library Association. Coretta Scott King Award Task Force

American Library Association. Young Adult Services Division
See also Young Adult Library Services Association

American Library Association publications
Anglo-American cataloguing rules   **025.3**
Booklist   **028.1**
Bouricius, A. The romance readers' advisory   **016.8**
Carter, B. Best books for young adults   **028.1**
The Coretta Scott King Awards book, 1970-1999   **028.5**
Crews, K. D. Copyright essentials for librarians and educators   **346.04**
Gorman, M. The concise AACR2, 1998 revision   **025.3**
Guide to reference books   **011**
Hooper, B. The short story readers' advisory   **809.3**
Intellectual freedom manual   **323.44**
Jones, B. M. Libraries, access, and intellectual freedom   **025.2**
Moore, D. E. The librarian's genealogy notebook   **929**
The Newbery & Caldecott medal books, 1986-2000   **028.5**
Norlin, E. Usability testing for library websites   **025.04**
Reference sources for small and medium-sized libraries   **011**
Saricks, J. G. The readers' advisory guide to genre fiction   **025.5**
Saricks, J. G. Readers' advisory service in the public library   **025.5**
Steele, A. T. Bare bones children's services   **027.62**
Vaillancourt, R. J. Bare bones young adult services   **027.62**
Willis, M. R. Dealing with difficult people in the library   **025.5**

American library directory   **027**

American literature
See also various forms of American literature, e.g. American poetry
African American authors
Black women writers (1950-1980)   **810.9**
The Coretta Scott King Awards book, 1970-1999   **028.5**
Hooks, B. Remembered rapture   **808**
Wall, C. A. Women of the Harlem Renaissance   **810.9**

See/See also pages in the following book(s):
Black literature criticism   **809**
African American authors—Bibliography
Richards, P. Best literature by and about Blacks   **016.8**
African American authors—Bio-bibliography
Roses, L. E. Harlem Renaissance and beyond: literary biographies of 100 black women writers, 1900-1945   **810.9**
African American authors—Collections
Crossing the danger water   **810.8**
Making Callaloo   **810.8**
The Norton anthology of African American literature   **810.8**
The Portable Harlem Renaissance reader   **810.8**
A Renaissance in Harlem   **810.8**
African American authors—Encyclopedias
Aberjhani. Encyclopedia of the Harlem Renaissance   **810.9**

American literature—*Continued*
African American authors—History and criticism
African American literary criticism, 1773 to 2000
810.9
The Oxford companion to African American literature
810.9
Roses, L. E. Harlem Renaissance and beyond: literary biographies of 100 black women writers, 1900-1945
810.9
Asian American authors—Collections
Growing up Asian American 810.8
Asian American authors—History and criticism
Asian American literature 810.9
Bio-bibliography
American authors, 1600-1900 920.003
American writers 920.003
The Cambridge guide to literature in English
820.3
The Cambridge handbook of American literature
810.3
Merriam-Webster's dictionary of American writers
920.003
The Oxford companion to American literature
810.3
The Oxford companion to English literature 820.3
Black authors
See American literature—African American authors
Collections
American nature writing 810.8
American sea writing 810.8
Baseball: a literary anthology 810.8
I thought my father was God and other true tales from the National Story Project 810.8
Jewish American literature 810.8
Modern American memoirs 810.8
The Norton anthology of American literature
810.8
The Portable beat reader 810.8
The Pushcart prize . . . : best of the small presses
810.8
"The Real war will never get in the books"
810.8
Writing New York 810.8
Dictionaries
The Cambridge guide to literature in English
820.3
The Cambridge handbook of American literature
810.3
The Oxford companion to American literature
810.3
The Oxford companion to English literature 820.3
Encyclopedias
Encyclopedia of American literature 810.3
HarperCollins Reader's encyclopedia of American literature 810.3
Snodgrass, M. E. Encyclopedia of frontier literature
810.3
Hispanic American authors—History and criticism
Hispanic literature criticism 860.9
History and criticism
American writers 920.003
Black women writers (1950-1980) 810.9
The Cambridge history of American literature
810.9
Columbia literary history of the United States
810.9
Kazin, A. An American procession 810.9
Matthiessen, F. O. American renaissance 810.9
Merriam-Webster's dictionary of American writers
920.003
Miles, B. The Beat Hotel 810.9
Modern American literature 810.9
Ricks, C. Reviewery 820.9
Wilson, E. Patriotic gore 810.9

Jewish authors
Jewish American literature 810.8
Mexican American authors—Bio-bibliography
Chicano literature 810.9
Native American authors
Coltelli, L. Winged words: American Indian writers speak 897
Native American authors—Bio-bibliography
Native North American literature 810.9
Native American authors—Collections
American Indian literature 897
The Portable North American Indian reader 897
Women authors
Black women writers (1950-1980) 810.9
Women authors—Bio-bibliography
The Oxford companion to women's writing in the United States 810.9
Women authors—Collections
The Norton anthology of literature by women
820.8
The Oxford book of women's writing in the United States 810.8
Women authors—Dictionaries
The Oxford companion to women's writing in the United States 810.9
Women authors—History and criticism
Gilbert, S. M. No man's land v3 820.9
Heilbrun, C. G. Hamlet's mother and other women
820.9
Pierpont, C. R. Passionate minds 810.9
New England
See/See also pages in the following book(s):
Lowell, R. Collected prose p179-212 818
Southern States—Bio-bibliography
Contemporary Southern writers 920.003
Southern States—Collections
The Oxford book of the American South 810.8
Southern States—Encyclopedias
The Companion to southern literature 810.3
West (U.S.)—Collections
The Portable Western reader 810.8
American Lung Association 7 steps to a smoke-free life. Fisher, E. B. 616.86
American Medical Association
Directory of physicians in the United States. See Directory of physicians in the United States
610.69
American Medical Association complete guide to children's health 618.92
American Medical Association complete guide to women's health. Allison, K. C. 613
American Medical Association complete medical encyclopedia 610.3
American Medical Association family medical guide
616.02
American medical directory. See Directory of physicians in the United States 610.69
American men & women of science 920.003
American military leaders. Fredriksen, J. C.
920.003
The **American** mind. Commager, H. S. 973
American Museum of Natural History
Alexander, C. The Endurance 998
Wallace, J. A gathering of wonders 508
American music
Dictionaries
The New Grove dictionary of American music
780.973
Encyclopedias
Women and music in America since 1900 780.9
History and criticism
Crawford, R. America's musical life 780.973
Hall, C. J. A chronicle of American music, 1700-1995
780.973

The **American** musical film song encyclopedia. Hischak, T.   **782.42**
American musical theatre. Bordman, G. M.   **792.6**
American musical traditions   **781.62**
American national biography   **920.003**
American national characteristics
   Boorstin, D. J. The Americans: The colonial experience   **973.2**
   Boorstin, D. J. The Americans: The national experience   **973**
   Bowden, C. Blues for cannibals   **973.92**
   Commager, H. S. The American mind   **973**
   Didion, J. Where I was from   **979.4**
   Hakim, J. Freedom   **973**
   Rather, D. The American dream   **973.92**
   Tocqueville, A. de. Democracy in America   **973.5**
   Ulrich, L. The age of homespun   **974**
American nations   **970.004**
American nature writing   **810.8**
American nicknames. Shankle, G. E.   **929.4**
American nightmare. Packard, J. M.   **305.8**
American normal. Osborne, L.   **616.89**
The **American** opera singer. Davis, P. G.   **920**
American orations *See* American speeches
American original: a life of Will Rogers. Robinson, R.   **92**
American painting
   Cohen-Solal, A. Painting American   **759.13**
   Gerdts, W. H. California impressionism   **759.13**
   Marin, C. Chicano visions   **709.73**
   Wilton, A. American sublime   **759.13**
American patriots. Buckley, G. L.   **355**
American pharaoh: Mayor Richard J. Daley: his battle for Chicago and the nation. Cohen, A.   **92**
American philosophy
   Rand, A. The voice of reason; essays in objectivist thought   **191**
American photography. Goldberg, V.   **770**
American poetry
   African American authors—Collections
   African-American poetry of the nineteenth century   **811.008**
   Every shut eye ain't asleep   **811.008**
   The Poetry of black America   **811.008**
   The Vintage book of African American poetry   **811.008**
   Bio-bibliography
   Contemporary poets   **920.003**
   Encyclopedia of American poetry, the nineteenth century   **811.009**
   Encyclopedia of American poetry, the twentieth century   **811.009**
   Collections
   American poetry: the nineteenth century   **811.008**
   American poetry, The twentieth century   **811.008**
   The Best American poetry   **811.008**
   The Best loved poems of the American people   **821.008**
   The Body electric   **811.008**
   Christmas poems   **821.008**
   The Columbia anthology of American poetry   **811.008**
   The Columbia book of Civil War poetry   **811.008**
   Eight American poets   **811.008**
   Good poems   **811.008**
   The Harvard book of contemporary American poetry   **811.008**
   Inventions of farewell   **821.008**
   The Making of a poem   **821.008**
   The New American poets   **811.008**
   The New Bread Loaf anthology of contemporary American poetry   **811.008**
   The New Oxford book of American verse   **811.008**
   The New young American poets   **811.008**

The Norton anthology of modern and contemporary poetry   **821.008**
The Norton book of light verse   **821.008**
The Oxford book of comic verse   **821.008**
The Oxford book of garden verse   **821.008**
The Oxford book of sonnets   **821.008**
The Penguin book of the sonnet   **821.008**
Poems that live forever   **821.008**
The Poetry anthology, 1912-2002   **811.008**
Poetry speaks   **808.81**
Postmodern American poetry   **811.008**
Six American poets   **811.008**
The Spoken word revolution   **811.008**
Unsettling America   **811.008**
The World in us   **811.008**
The Yale younger poets anthology   **811.008**
   History and criticism
The Columbia history of American poetry   **811.009**
Heaney, S. The redress of poetry   **821.009**
Jarrell, R. No other book   **809**
Pritchard, W. H. Lives of the modern poets   **821.009**
Schmidt, M. Lives of the poets   **821.009**
The Spoken word revolution   **811.008**
Vendler, H. H. Coming of age as a poet   **820.9**
   Native American authors
Harper's anthology of 20th century Native American poetry   **811.008**
Songs from this Earth on turtle's back   **811.008**
   Women authors—Bio-bibliography
Contemporary women poets   **920.003**
   Women authors—Dictionaries
Contemporary women poets   **920.003**
   Southern States—Collections
The Made thing   **811.008**
American poetry: the nineteenth century   **811.008**
American poetry, The twentieth century   **811.008**
American political leaders, 1789-2000   **920.003**
The **American** political tradition, and the men who made it. Hofstadter, R.   **973**
The **American** president. Kunhardt, P. B.   **920**
American presidential campaigns and elections   **324**
American prisoners of war *See* Prisoners of war—United States
An **American** procession. Kazin, A.   **810.9**
American reference books annual   **011**
American religions. Melton, J. G.   **200.9**
American renaissance. Matthiessen, F. O.   **810.9**
The **American** Revolution   **973.3**
The **American** Revolution in Indian country. Calloway, C. G.   **973.3**
American roots music   **781.62**
American science *See* Science—United States
American scripture. Maier, P.   **973.3**
American sea writing   **810.8**
American sermons   **252**
American Sign Language. Sternberg, M. L. A.   **419**
The **American** Sign Language handshape dictionary. Tennant, R. A.   **419**
American skin. Wynter, L. E.   **305.8**
American Society of Mechanical Engineers. History and Heritage Committee
   Landmarks in mechanical engineering. See Landmarks in mechanical engineering   **621**
American soldiers. Kindsvatter, P. S.   **355**
The **American** songbag. Sandburg, C.   **782.42**
American songs
   See also Folk songs—United States; Spirituals (Songs)
   Porter, C. The complete lyrics of Cole Porter   **782.42**
American speeches
   In our own words   **815.008**
   Representative American speeches   **815.008**

American speeches—*Continued*
Voices of multicultural America   **815.008**
American sphinx: the character of Thomas Jefferson. El-
lis, J. J.   **92**
American sublime. Wilton, A.   **759.13**
American surgery. Rutkow, I. M.   **617**
American terrorist: Timothy McVeigh and the Oklahoma
City bombing. Michel, L.   **92**
American theatre: a chronicle of comedy and drama,
1869-1914. Bordman, G. M.   **792**
American theatre: a chronicle of comedy and drama,
1914-1930. Bordman, G. M.   **792**
American theatre: a chronicle of comedy and drama,
1930-1969. Bordman, G. M.   **792**
American theatre: a chronicle of comedy and drama,
1969-2000. Hischak, T.   **792**
American tragedy. Kaiser, D. E.   **959.704**
American universities and colleges   **378.73**
American visions. Hughes, R.   **709.73**
The **American** way of death revisited. Mitford, J.
     393
The **American** West. Brown, D. A.   **978**
American wit and humor
Honey, hush!   **817.008**
Mirth of a nation   **817**
The Oxford book of humorous prose   **827**
Roy Blount's book of Southern humor   **817.008**
Russell Baker's book of American humor
     817.008

Encyclopedias
Nilsen, A. P. Encyclopedia of 20th century American
humor   **817**
American women fiction writers   **813.009**
American women in science: 1950 to the present. Bai-
ley, M. J.   **920.003**
American women scientists. Reynolds, M. D.   **920**
The **American** woodland garden. Darke, R.   **635.9**
American workers, American unions. Zieger, R. H.
     331.8
American writers   **920.003**
American writers: selected authors. See American writ-
ers   **920.003**
American Youth Hostels, Inc.
Hostelling North America. See Hostelling North Amer-
ica   **647.9**
Americana and other poems. Updike, J.   **811**
Americanisms
Ammer, C. The American Heritage dictionary of idi-
oms   **427**
Barnhart, D. K. America in so many words   **422**
Bartlett's Roget's thesaurus   **423**
Bryson, B. Made in America   **420**
Dalzell, T. Flappers 2 rappers   **427**
Dictionary of American regional English   **427**
Dictionary of American slang   **427**
The Doubleday Roget's thesaurus in dictionary form
     423
Garner, B. A. Garner's modern American usage
     423
Hendrickson, R. The Facts on File dictionary of
American regionalisms   **427**
Herman, L. American dialects   **427**
Lepore, J. A is for American   **306.44**
Lutz, W. The Cambridge thesaurus of American En-
glish   **423**
McWhorter, J. H. Doing our own thing   **306.44**
Mencken, H. L. The American language   **427**
Metcalf, A. A. How we talk   **427**
The New Oxford American dictionary   **423**
The Oxford American dictionary and language guide
     423
The Oxford American dictionary of current English
     423
Random House historical dictionary of American slang
     427

Spears, R. A. NTC's dictionary of American slang and
colloquial expressions   **427**
Wilson, K. G. The Columbia guide to standard
American English   **428**
Young, S. The new comprehensive American rhyming
dictionary   **423**
See/See also pages in the following book(s):
Boorstin, D. J. The Americans: The colonial experi-
ence   **973.2**
Boorstin, D. J. The Americans: The democratic experi-
ence   **973**
Boorstin, D. J. The Americans: The national experi-
ence p275-98   **973**
Americanos. Olmos, E. J.   **305.8**
Americans' favorite poems   **808.81**
The **Americans:** The colonial experience. Boorstin, D. J.
     973.2
The **Americans:** The democratic experience. Boorstin, D.
J.   **973**
The **Americans:** The national experience. Boorstin, D. J.
     973
Americans with Disabilities Act handbook. Perritt, H.
H., Jr.   **344**
America's art museums. Loebl, S.   **708**
America's fastest growing jobs   **331.7**
America's favorite backyard birds. Harrison, K.
     598
America's federal jobs. See Guide to America's federal
jobs   **351.076**
America's first dynasty. Brookhiser, R.   **920**
America's first families. Anthony, C. S.   **920**
America's library. Conaway, J.   **027.5**
America's military adversaries. Fredriksen, J. C.
     920.003
America's most wanted (Television program)
Walsh, J. Public enemies   **364.1**
America's musical life. Crawford, R.   **780.973**
America's top doctors   **610.69**
America's working women   **331.4**
Amery, Colin
Vanishing histories   **363.6**
Ames, Kenneth M.
Archaeology of prehistoric native America. See Ar-
chaeology of prehistoric native America   **970.01**
Ames, Louise Bates
Your eight-year-old   **649**
Your five-year-old   **649**
Your four-year-old   **649**
Your one-year-old   **649**
Your seven-year-old   **649**
Your six-year-old   **649**
Your three-year-old   **649**
Your two-year-old   **649**
Amichai, Yehuda
Open closed open   **892**
Poems of Jerusalem; and, Love poems   **892**
The selected poetry of Yehuda Amichai   **892**
Amihai, Yehuda *See* Amichai, Yehuda
Amini, Fari
(jt. auth) Lewis, T. A general theory of love
     152.4
Amis, Kingsley, 1922-1995
The letters of Kingsley Amis   **92**
About
Amis, M. Experience   **92**
Bradford, R. Lucky him: the life of Kingsley Amis
     92
Amis, Martin
Experience   **92**
Koba the dread   **947.084**
The war against cliché   **824**
Amish
Adams, M. New recipes from quilt country   **641.5**
Amish roots   **289.7**
Hostetler, J. A. Amish society   **289.7**

Amish—_Continued_
Kraybill, D. B. On the backroad to heaven   289.7
Kraybill, D. B. The riddle of Amish culture
    289.7
Amish roots   289.7
Ammann, Othmar Hermann, 1879-1965
    See/See also pages in the following book(s):
Petroski, H. Engineers of dreams   624
Ammer, Christine
The American Heritage dictionary of idioms   427
Ammons, A. R., 1926-2001
Glare   811
Ammons, Elizabeth
(ed) The Oxford companion to women's writing in the United States. See The Oxford companion to women's writing in the United States   810.9
Among grizzlies. Treadwell, T.   599.78
Among the believers. Naipaul, V. S.   297
Among the heroes. Longman, J.   974.8
Amory, Cleveland
The cat and the curmudgeon   818
The cat who came for Christmas   818
Amos 'n' Andy (Radio program)
Ely, M. P. The adventures of Amos 'n' Andy
    791.44
Amos 'n' Andy (Television program)
Ely, M. P. The adventures of Amos 'n' Andy
    791.44
Amphibians
    See also Frogs
Amphibians: the world of frogs, toads, salamanders and newts   597.8
Conant, R. A field guide to reptiles & amphibians
    597.9
Firefly encyclopedia of reptiles and amphibians
    597.9
Stebbins, R. C. A field guide to Western reptiles and amphibians   597.9
Tyning, T. F. A guide to amphibians and reptiles
    597.9
Amphibians: the world of frogs, toads, salamanders and newts   597.8
Amphitryon. Plautus, T. M.
    _In_ The Portable Roman reader p22-74   870.8
Amster, Linda
(ed) The New York Times Passover cookbook. See The New York Times Passover cookbook   641.5
Amundsen, Darrel W.
(ed) The History of science and religion in the western tradition. See The History of science and religion in the western tradition   291.1
Amundsen, Roald, 1872-1928
    See/See also pages in the following book(s):
Connell, E. S. The Aztec treasure house p96-122
    814
Amusements
Dary, D. Seeking pleasure in the Old West   978
Amusing ourselves to death. Postman, N.   302.23
The **Amy** Vanderbilt complete book of etiquette. Tuckerman, N.   395
Anacondas
Murphy, J. C. Tales of giant snakes   597.9
Anaesthetics _See_ Anesthetics
The **analects** of Confucius. Confucius   181
Anarchism and anarchists
    See/See also pages in the following book(s):
Tuchman, B. W. The proud tower p63-113
    909.82
Anasazi culture _See_ Pueblo Indians
Anasi, Robert, 1966-
The gloves   796.8
Anatomica's body atlas   611

Anatomy
    See also Musculoskeletal system; Physiology
    Encyclopedias
World of anatomy and physiology   612
Anatomy, Artistic _See_ Artistic anatomy
Anatomy, Human _See_ Human anatomy
Anatomy of a miracle. Waldmeir, P.   968.06
Anatomy of greed. Cruver, B.   333.79
The **anatomy** of prejudices. Young-Bruehl, E.
    303.3
The **anatomy** of racial inequality. Loury, G. C.
    305.8
An **anatomy** of thought. Glynn, I.   612.8
Ancell, R. Manning, 1942-
The biographical dictionary of World War II generals and flag officers   920.003
The **Anchor** Bible. Bible   220.5
The **Anchor** Bible dictionary   220.3
The **ancient** Americans. Schobinger, J.   970.01
Ancient and oriental music
    _In_ New Oxford history of music v1   780.9
Ancient art
    See also Byzantine art; Greek art
Frankfort, H. The art and architecture of the ancient Orient   709.39
The **ancient** Celts. Cunliffe, B.   936
The **ancient** city. Connolly, P.   937
Ancient civilization
    See also Classical civilization
Hancock, G. Underworld: the mysterious origins of civilization   551.7
The Oxford history of the biblical world   220.9
Teresi, D. Lost discoveries   509
    Encyclopedias
Encyclopedia of the ancient world   930
Salisbury, J. E. Encyclopedia of women in the ancient world   305.4
Ancient encounters. Chatters, J.   970.004
Ancient Greece. Martin, T. R.   938
Ancient history
    See also Classical dictionaries
The Cambridge ancient history   930
Dictionary of world biography   920.003
Ancient light. Lightman, A. P.   523.1
Ancient philosophy
Plato. Complete works   184
    Encyclopedias
Encyclopedia of classical philosophy   180
—and never let her go. Rule, A.   364.1
And the band played on. Shilts, R.   362.1
And the sea is never full. Wiesel, E.   92
And the waters turned to blood. Barker, R.   615.9
Andau, The bridge at. Michener, J. A.   943.9
Andersen, Christopher P.
George and Laura [Bush]   92
Jackie after Jack [biography of Jacqueline Kennedy Onassis]   92
Andersen, Hans Christian, 1805-1875
    About
Wullschläger, J. Hans Christian Andersen   92
Anderson, Anna, d. 1984
    See/See also pages in the following book(s):
Massie, R. K. The Romanovs   947.08
Anderson, David L.
The Columbia guide to the Vietnam War   959.704
Anderson, Edward F., 1932-2001
The cactus family   583
Anderson, Fred, 1949-
The crucible of war   973.2
Anderson, Jean, 1929-
The food of Portugal   641.5
The new German cookbook   641.5
Anderson, Jervis
Bayard Rustin   92

Anderson, Jon Lee
Che Guevara 92
The lion's grave 958.1
Anderson, Margo J., 1945-
(ed) Encyclopedia of the U.S. Census. See Encyclopedia of the U.S. Census 304.6
Anderson, Marian, 1897-1993
About
Keiler, A. Marian Anderson 92
See/See also pages in the following book(s):
Ware, S. Letter to the world 920
Anderson, Pam
How to cook without a book 641.5
Anderson, Sean, 1952-
Historical dictionary of terrorism 303.6
Anderson, Sherry Ruth
The feminine face of God 291
Anderson, Terry H., 1946-
The movement and the sixties 303.4
Anderson, William T., 1952-
Laura Ingalls Wilder country 92
Anderton, Stephen
Urban sanctuaries 635.9
Andes
Read, P. P. Alive 910.4
Andreas-Salomé, Lou, 1861-1937
See/See also pages in the following book(s):
Prose, F. The lives of the muses 920
Andreasen, Nancy C.
Brave new brain 616.89
Andreotti, Giulio
About
Robb, P. Midnight in Sicily 945
Andrew Jackson & his Indian wars. Remini, R. V. 973.5
Andrews, Barry G., 1943-
(jt. auth) Wilde, W. H. The Oxford companion to Australian literature 820.3
Andrews, Cecily Isabel Fairfield See West, Dame Rebecca, 1892-1983
Andrews, Robert, 1957-
The Columbia dictionary of quotations 808.88
Famous lines 808.88
Andrisani, John
The Tiger Woods way 796.352
Andromache. Euripides
In Euripides. Ten plays p101-29 882
Andrzejewski, Jerzy, 1910-1983
See/See also pages in the following book(s):
Miłosz, C. To begin where I am p116-41, 189-201 891.8
The **Andy** Warhol diaries. Warhol, A. 92
Anecdotes
See also Wit and humor
Anesthetics
See/See also pages in the following book(s):
Friedman, M. Medicine's 10 greatest discoveries 610.9
Ang, Tom
Advanced digital photography 775
Digital photographer's handbook 775
Silver pixels 778.3
Angel in the whirlwind. Bobrick, B. 973.3
Angel on my shoulder. Cole, N. 92
Angela's ashes. McCourt, F. 92
Angell, Roger
Game time: a baseball companion 796.357
Once more around the park 796.357
Angelo, Bonnie
First mothers 920
Angelo, Joseph A.
Encyclopedia of space exploration 629.4
The Facts on File dictionary of space technology 629.4

The Facts on File space and astronomy handbook 520
Angelou, Maya
The complete collected poems of Maya Angelou 811
Even the stars look lonesome 814
I know why the caged bird sings 92
I shall not be moved 811
A song flung up to heaven 92
Wouldn't take nothing for my journey now 814
See/See also pages in the following book(s):
Black women writers (1950-1980) 810.9
Women writers at work p285-306 808
Anger
Tavris, C. Anger 152.4
See/See also pages in the following book(s):
Amen, D. Change your brain, change your life 616.89
Angier, Bradford
Field guide to edible wild plants 581.6
Angier, Carole
The double bond: Primo Levi, a biography 92
Angier, Natalie
Woman 612.6
Angina pectoris See Heart diseases
Anglo-American cataloguing rules
Gorman, M. The concise AACR2, 1998 revision 025.3
Anglo-American cataloguing rules 025.3
Anglomania. Buruma, I. 941
Anichkov, N. N. (Nikolai Nikolaevich), 1885-1964
See/See also pages in the following book(s):
Friedman, M. Medicine's 10 greatest discoveries 610.9
Anichkov, Nikolai Nikolaevich See Anichkov, N. N. (Nikolai Nikolaevich), 1885-1964
Animal abuse See Animal welfare
Animal attacks
Capuzzo, M. Close to shore 597
Animal attractions. Hanson, E. 590.73
Animal behavior
See also Sexual behavior in animals
Avise, J. C. Genetics in the wild 591.3
Bagemihl, B. Biological exuberance 591.56
Bekoff, M. Minding animals 591.5
Dugatkin, L. A. Cheating monkeys and citizen bees 591.56
Griffin, D. R. Animal minds 591.5
Hauser, M. D. Wild minds 591.5
Linden, E. The octopus and the orangutan 591.5
Masson, J. M. When elephants weep 591.5
Waal, F. de. The ape and the sushi master 156
Animal communication
Fouts, R. Next of kin 156
Animal ER. Tufts University. School of Veterinary Medicine 636.089
Animal experimentation
See also Animal welfare
Blum, D. The monkey wars 179
Greek, C. R. Sacred cows and golden geese 179
Preston, R. The hot zone 614.5
Rudacille, D. The scalpel and the butterfly 179
Animal husbandry See Livestock industry
Animal intelligence
Hauser, M. D. Wild minds 591.5
Linden, E. The octopus and the orangutan 591.5
Masson, J. M. When elephants weep 591.5
Page, G. Inside the animal mind 591.5
Yoerg, S. Clever as a fox 591.5
Animal introduction
Todd, K. Tinkering with Eden 591.6
Animal lore See Animals—Folklore
Animal minds. Griffin, D. R. 591.5
Animal painting and illustration
See also Animals in art

Animal rights
See also Animal welfare
Blum, D. The monkey wars   **179**
Coetzee, J. M. The lives of animals   **179**
Goodall, J. The ten trusts   **333.95**
Wise, S. M. Drawing the line   **179**
    Encyclopedias
Encyclopedia of animal rights and animal welfare
    179
Animal tracks
Elbroch, M. Mammal tracks & sign   **599**
Murie, O. J. A field guide to animal tracks   **599**
Animal welfare
Coetzee, J. M. The lives of animals   **179**
Fox, M. W. Inhumane society   **179**
Goodall, J. The ten trusts   **333.95**
Rudacille, D. The scalpel and the butterfly   **179**
    Encyclopedias
Encyclopedia of animal rights and animal welfare
    179
Animals
See also Dangerous animals; Game and game birds; Invertebrates; Pets; Predatory animals; Rare animals; Zoology; names of orders and classes of the animal kingdom; kinds of animals characterized by their environments; and names of individual species
Lavers, C. Why elephants have big ears   **590**
    Folklore
See also Dragons; Monsters; Mythical animals
    Folklore—Encyclopedias
Sax, B. The mythical zoo   **398.03**
    Pictorial works
See also Animals in art
Mitchell, J. G. National Geographic, the wildlife photographs   **779**
    Sexual behavior
See Sexual behavior in animals
    Africa
Stuart, C. Africa's vanishing wildlife   **591.9**
    Antarctica
Matthiessen, P. End of the earth   **508**
Animals, Domestic See Domestic animals
Animals, Extinct See Extinct animals
Animals, Fossil See Fossils
Animals, Habits and behavior of See Animal behavior
Animals, Mythical See Mythical animals
Animals in art
Germond, P. An Egyptian bestiary   **709.32**
Animals in literature
Sax, B. The mythical zoo   **398.03**
Animals' rights See Animal rights
Animated films
Barrier, J. M. Hollywood cartoons   **791.43**
Kanfer, S. Serious business   **741.5**
Animation (Cinematography)
See also Computer animation
Anissimov, Myriam
Primo Levi   **92**
Anna and the King of Siam [biography of Anna Harriette Leonowens] Landon, M.   **92**
Anna in the tropics. Cruz, N.   **812**
The **annals**. Tacitus, C.
In Tacitus, C. The complete works of Tacitus p3-416
    878
Annals of the former world. McPhee, J. A.   **557**
Anne Boleyn, Queen, consort of Henry VIII, King of England, 1507-1536
See/See also pages in the following book(s):
Fraser, A. The wives of Henry VIII p113-223
    920
Starkey, D. Six wives: the queens of Henry VIII
    920
Anne Frank remembered. Gies, M.   **940.53**
Anne Frank's Tales from the secret annex. Frank, A.
    839.3

Anne of Cleves, Queen, consort of Henry VIII, King of England, 1515-1557
See/See also pages in the following book(s):
Fraser, A. The wives of Henry VIII p287-354
    920
Starkey, D. Six wives: the queens of Henry VIII
    920
The **Annie** Dillard reader. Dillard, A.   **818**
Annigoni, Tony
    About
McCumber, D. Playing off the rail   **794.7**
Anno, Mitsumasa, 1926-
See/See also pages in the following book(s):
Marcus, L. S. Ways of telling   **741.6**
The **annotated** rules of hockey. See Duplacey, J. The official rules of hockey   **796.962**
Annuals (Plants)
Armitage, A. M. Armitage's manual of annuals, biennials, and half-hardy perennials   **635.9**
Ellis, B. W. Taylor's guide to annuals   **635.9**
Phillips, R. Annuals and biennials   **635.9**
Rice, G. Discovering annuals   **635.9**
Annuals and biennials. Phillips, R.   **635.9**
Anorexia nervosa
Hornbacher, M. Wasted: a memoir of anorexia and bulimia   **616.85**
Anosike, Benji O.
Immigration manual   **342**
Another country. Pipher, M. B.   **306.8**
Another river, another town. Irwin, J. P.   **940.54**
Anouilh, Jean, 1910-1987
Thieves' carnival
In Our dramatic heritage v6   **808.82**
Ansary, Mir Tamim
West of Kabul, East of New York   **958.1**
Ansary, Tamim See Ansary, Mir Tamim
Ansary, Tamin See Ansary, Mir Tamim
Anselm, Saint, Archbishop of Canterbury, 1033-1109
See/See also pages in the following book(s):
Jaspers, K. The great philosophers   **109**
Answers to frequently asked questions in Parkinson's disease. Cram, D. L.   **616.8**
Antarctica
See also South Pole
McGonigal, D. Antarctica and the Arctic   **998**
    Encyclopedias
Antarctica: an encyclopedia from Abbott Ice Shelf to zooplankton   **998**
    Exploration
Alexander, C. The Endurance   **998**
Matthiessen, P. End of the earth   **508**
Preston, D. A first rate tragedy   **998**
Solomon, S. The coldest March   **998**
Antarctica: an encyclopedia from Abbott Ice Shelf to zooplankton   **998**
Antarctica and the Arctic. McGonigal, D.   **998**
An **Anthology** of African art: the twentieth century
    709.6
Anthology of Chinese literature   **895.1**
An **Anthology** of Chinese literature: beginnings to 1911
    895.1
Anthology of modern Chinese poetry   **895.1**
Anthology of modern Palestinian literature   **892**
Anthony, Carl Sferrazza
America's first families   **920**
First ladies   **920**
Anthony, Earl, 1938-2001
Winning bowling   **794.6**
Anthony, Susan B., 1820-1906
Failure is impossible   **92**
    About
Ward, G. C. Not for ourselves alone: the story of Elizabeth Cady Stanton and Susan B. Anthony   **92**

Anthrax
See/See also pages in the following book(s):
Frist, W. H. When every moment counts   613.6
Anthropogeography *See* Human geography
An **anthropologist** on Mars. Sacks, O. W.   616.8
Anthropology
See also Forensic anthropology; Physical anthropology
Lévi-Strauss, C. The savage mind   155.8
Anti-war poetry *See* War poetry
Antibiotics
See/See also pages in the following book(s):
Palumbi, S. R. The evolution explosion   576.8
The **antichrist**. Nietzsche, F. W.
In Nietzsche, F. W. The portable Nietzsche   193
Anticommunist movements
Fariello, G. Red scare   973.92
From the secret files of J. Edgar Hoover   363.2
The **antidepressant** sourcebook. Morrison, A. L.   616.85

Antidepressants
Glenmullen, J. Prozac backlash   616.85
Morrison, A. L. The antidepressant sourcebook   616.85

Antietam (Md.), Battle of, 1862
Sears, S. W. Landscape turned red   973.7
Antigone. Sophocles   882
also in Sophocles. The complete plays of Sophocles p115-47   882

Antigua and Barbuda
Kincaid, J. A small place   972.97
Antiques
Keno, L. Hidden treasures   749.2
Kovel, R. M. Kovels' antiques and collectibles price list   745.1
Kovel, R. M. Kovels' know your antiques   745.1
Kovel, R. M. Kovel's know your collectibles   745.1
Maloney, D. J. Maloney's antiques & collectibles resource directory   745.1
Prisant, C. Antiques roadshow primer   745.1
Conservation and restoration
Miller, J. Care and repair of everyday treasures   745.1

Antiques roadshow (Television program)
Prisant, C. Antiques roadshow primer   745.1
Antiques roadshow primer. Prisant, C.   745.1
Antiquities
See also Archeology
Collection and preservation
Stille, A. The future of the past   303.4
Dictionaries
Darvill, T. The concise Oxford dictionary of archaeology   930.1
Antiquity of man *See* Human origins
Antisemitism
See also Jews—Persecutions
Arendt, H. Origins of totalitarianism   321.9
Baldwin, N. Henry Ford and the Jews   92
Bredin, J.-D. The affair   944.081
Derfler, L. The Dreyfus affair   944.081
Dershowitz, A. M. The vanishing American Jew   305.8
Gager, J. G. The origins of anti-Semitism   296.3
Glass, J. M. Life unworthy of life   940.53
Goldhagen, D. Hitler's willing executioners   940.53
Goldhagen, D. A moral reckoning   940.53
Kertzer, D. I. The Popes against the Jews   261.2
Lipstadt, D. E. Denying the Holocaust   940.53
Smith, H. W. The butcher's tale   943.08
See/See also pages in the following book(s):
Craig, G. A. The Germans p126 46   943
Crossan, J. D. Who killed Jesus?   232.9
Kamen, H. The Spanish Inquisition   272

Antoninus, Marcus Aurelius *See* Marcus Aurelius, Emperor of Rome, 121-180
Ants
Hölldobler, B. The ants   595.7
Hölldobler, B. Journey to the ants   595.7
Ants on the melon. Adair, V. H.   811
Anxiety
Hallowell, E. M. Worry   616.85
Root, B. A., Jr. Understanding panic and other anxiety disorders   616.85
Tillich, P. The courage to be   179
See/See also pages in the following book(s):
Amen, D. Change your brain, change your life   616.89
Anybody's sports medicine book. Garrick, J. G.   617.1
Anything we love can be saved. Walker, A.   818
Anzovin, Steven, 1954-
Famous first facts about American politics   973
(ed) Facts about the states. See Facts about the states   973
(ed) Famous first facts, international edition. See Famous first facts, international edition   031.02
(jt. auth) Kane, J. N. Famous first facts   031.02
AOL for dummies. Kaufeld, J.   025.04
Aoyagi, Akiko, 1950-
(jt. auth) Shurtleff, W. The book of tofu   641.6
Apache Indians
Boyer, R. M. Apache mothers and daughters   970.004
Debo, A. Geronimo   92
Roberts, D. Once they moved like the wind   970.004
See/See also pages in the following book(s):
Brown, D. A. The American West p124-31   978
Brown, D. A. Bury my heart at Wounded Knee   970.004
Josephy, A. M. Now that the buffalo's gone p101-13   970.004
Apache mothers and daughters. Boyer, R. M.   970.004
The **apartment** book. See Michael, M. The new apartment book   747
The **ape** and the sushi master. Waal, F. de   156
Aperture (Periodical)
Photography past forward: Aperture at 50   770.9
Apes
See also Chimpanzees; Gorillas; Orangutan
Waal, F. de. Bonobo   599.8
Aphrodite. Allende, I.   868
Apiculture *See* Bees
Apocalypses. Weber, E. J.   291
Apocrypha (Old Testament) *See* Bible. O.T. Apocrypha
The **Apocrypha**. Bible. O.T. Apocrypha   229
Apollo project
Chaikin, A. A man on the moon   629.45
Reynolds, D. W. Apollo: the epic journey to the moon   629.45
Schefter, J. L. The race   629.45
Zimmerman, R. Genesis   629.45
Apollo: the epic journey to the moon. Reynolds, D. W.   629.45
Apologetics
John Paul II, Pope. Crossing the threshold of hope   282
Apology. Plato
In Plato. The dialogues of Plato p4-40   888
Apoplexy *See* Stroke
Apostolic Church *See* Church history—30-600, Early church
Appalachia. Wright, C.   811
Appalachian Mountain region *See* Appalachian region
Appalachian region
Archaeology of the Appalachian highlands   970.004

Appalachian region—*Continued*
Description
Bryson, B. A walk in the woods   917.4
Social life and customs
Foxfire [1]-11   975.8
The **appearance** of impropriety. Morgan, P. W.   306

Appel, Alfred
Jazz modernism   781.65
Appelbaum, Judith
How to get happily published   070.5
Appelfeld, Aharon *See* Appelfeld, Aron
Appelfeld, Aron
See/See also pages in the following book(s):
Langer, L. L. Admitting the Holocaust p125-37   940.53

Appetite disorders *See* Eating disorders
Appetite for life. Fitch, N. R.   92
An **appetite** for poetry. Kermode, F.   801
Appetizers
Stewart, M. Martha Stewart's hors d'oeuvres handbook   641.8
Appiah, Anthony
(ed) Africana. See Africana   909
(ed) Richard Wright. See Richard Wright [critical essays]   813.009
Appiah, Kwame Anthony *See* Appiah, Anthony
The **Applause/best** plays theater yearbook. See The Best plays of [date]   808.82
Apple, Hope
(jt. auth) Jacob, M. To be continued   016.8
Applebaum, Anne, 1964-
Gulag   365
Applebaum, Wilbur
(ed) Encyclopedia of the scientific revolution. See Encyclopedia of the scientific revolution   509
Applebome, Peter
Dixie rising   973.929
Appleby, Joyce Oldham
Inheriting the revolution   973
Apples
See/See also pages in the following book(s):
Hubbell, S. Shrinking the cat   660.6
Pollan, M. The botany of desire   581.6
Appleton, George, 1902-
(ed) The Oxford book of prayer. See The Oxford book of prayer   291.4
Applicant. Pinter, H.
In Pinter, H. Complete works v3   822
Applications for college *See* College applications
Applications for positions
The Adams cover letter almanac & disk   650.14
The Adams resume almanac   650.14
Beatty, R. H. 175 high-impact cover letters   650.14
Beatty, R. H. The interview kit   650.14
Bolles, R. N. What color is your parachute?   331.7
Enelow, W. S. Cover letter magic   650.14
Jackson, T. The new perfect resume   650.14
Resumes and cover letters that have worked   650.14
Rosenberg, A. D. The resume handbook   650.14
Yate, M. J. Cover letters that knock 'em dead   650.14
Yate, M. J. Knock 'em dead   650.14
Yate, M. J. Resumes that knock 'em dead   650.14
Applied arts *See* Decorative arts
Applied psychology
See also Negotiation
Beattie, M. Beyond codependency   616.86
Bloomfield, H. H. Making peace with your past   158
Carnegie, D. How to win friends and influence people   158
Klauser, H. A. Write it down, make it happen   158
May, R. Freedom and destiny   158
Peale, N. V. The power of positive living   248
Peale, N. V. The power of positive thinking   253.5
Peck, M. S. Further along the road less traveled   158
Peck, M. S. The road less traveled   158
Peck, M. S. The road less traveled and beyond   158
Appointment with death. Christie, A.
In Christie, A. The mousetrap and other plays   822
Appomattox Campaign, 1865
Catton, B. A stillness at Appomattox   973.7
Davis, B. To Appomattox   973.7
The **apprentice:** my life in the kitchen. Pépin, J.   92
The **approaching** fury. Oates, S. B.   973.5
April 1865. Winik, J.   973.7
April twilights, and other poems. Cather, W.
In Cather, W. Stories, poems, and other writings   818
Aptitude testing *See* Ability—Testing
Aquanauts *See* Underwater exploration
Aquarian Age movement *See* New Age movement
Aquarium fish. Mills, D.   639.34
Aquariums
Mills, D. Aquarium fish   639.34
Sandford, G. Aquarium: owner's manual   639.34
Aquatic animals *See* Marine animals
Aquinas, Thomas *See* Thomas, Aquinas, Saint, 1225?-1274
Arab and Jew. Shipler, D. K.   956.94
Arab civilization
Hourani, A. H. A history of the Arab peoples   909
Arab countries
Fargues, P. The atlas of the Arab world   909
Lamb, D. The Arabs   909
Description
Theroux, P. Sandstorms: days and nights in Arabia   953
History
Hourani, A. H. A history of the Arab peoples   909
Arab-Israel War, 1948-1949 *See* Israel-Arab War, 1948-1949
Arab-Israel War, 1967 *See* Israel-Arab War, 1967
Arab-Israeli conflicts *See* Israel-Arab conflicts
The **Arab-Israeli** wars. Herzog, C.   956
Arab-Jewish relations *See* Jewish-Arab relations
Arabic language
Dictionaries
The Oxford English-Arabic dictionary of current usage   492
Arabic literature
Bio-bibliography
Encyclopedia of Arabic literature   892
Collections
Anthology of modern Palestinian literature   892
Night and horses and the desert   892
Dictionaries
Encyclopedia of Arabic literature   892
History and criticism
Night and horses and the desert   892
Arabic poetry
Collections
Music of a distant drum   808.81
Arabs
See also Bedouins
Lawrence, T. E. Seven pillars of wisdom   940.4
Palestine
See Palestinian Arabs

The **Arabs**. Lamb, D.   **909**

Arachnida *See* Spiders; Ticks

Arana, Marie
  American chica   **92**

Araton, Harvey
  Alive and kicking   **796.334**

Arbitration, International *See* International arbitration

Arbitration and award
  See also Litigation

Arblay, Frances Burney d' *See* Burney, Fanny, 1752-1840

Arcadia. Stoppard, T.   **822**

Archaeology *See* Archeology

Archaeology of prehistoric native America   **970.01**

Archaeology of the Appalachian highlands   **970.004**

Archaeopteryx
  Shipman, P. Taking wing   **568**

Archambault, Ariane
  (jt. auth) Corbeil, J.-C. The Firefly visual dictionary   **423**

Archbold, Rick, 1950-
  (jt. auth) Ballard, R. D. The discovery of the Titanic   **910.4**
  (jt. auth) Ballard, R. D. Return to Midway   **940.54**

Archeological specimens *See* Antiquities

Archeology
  See also Antiquities; Excavations (Archeology); Prehistoric peoples; Rock drawings, paintings, and engravings; names of extinct cities; and names of groups of people and of cities (except extinct cities), countries, regions, etc., with the subdivision Antiquities
  Ceram, C. W. Gods, graves, and scholars   **930.1**
      Dictionaries
  Darvill, T. The concise Oxford dictionary of archaeology   **930.1**
  The Oxford companion to archaeology   **930.1**
      Encyclopedias
  Encyclopedia of archaeology: History and discoveries   **930.1**

Archimedes, ca. 287-212 B.C.
  See/See also pages in the following book(s):
  Bell, E. T. Men of mathematics p19-34   **920**

The **architect** of genocide: Himmler and the final solution. Breitman, R.   **92**

Architects
  Wiseman, C. Shaping a nation   **720.973**

Architectural carving. Burton, M.   **736**

Architectural engineering *See* Building

Architecture
  Harwood, B. Architecture and interior design through the 18th century   **729**
  Langmead, D. Encyclopedia of architectural and engineering feats   **721**
  O'Gorman, J. F. ABC of architecture   **720**
  Palladio, A. The four books on architecture   **720**
  Rybczynski, W. The look of architecture   **721**
  The Seventy wonders of the modern world   **720.9**
      20th century
  Gropius, W. The new architecture and the Bauhaus   **724**
  Wiseman, C. Shaping a nation   **720.973**
      15th and 16th centuries
  Rybczynski, W. The perfect house: a journey with the Renaissance architect Andrea Palladio   **724**
      Conservation and restoration
  Stewart, M. Martha Stewart's new old house   **728**
      Details
  See also Woodwork
  American Institute of Architects. Architectural graphic standards   **692**
  The Elements of style   **721**
  Maliszewski-Pickart, M. Architecture and ornament   **721**

      Dictionaries
  Ching, F. A visual dictionary of architecture   **720.3**
  Curl, J. S. Oxford dictionary of architecture   **720.3**
  Dictionary of architecture & construction   **720.3**
  The Penguin dictionary of architecture and landscape architecture   **720.3**
      History
  Fletcher, Sir B. F. Sir Banister Fletcher's A history of architecture   **720.9**
  Glancey, J. The story of architecture   **720.9**
  Trachtenberg, M. Architecture, from prehistory to post-modernity   **720.9**
      United States
  LeBlanc, S. The architecture traveler   **720.973**
  McAlester, V. A field guide to American houses   **728**
  Whiffen, M. American architecture since 1780   **720.973**
  Wiencek, H. National Geographic guide to America's great houses   **728.8**
  Wiseman, C. Shaping a nation   **720.973**

Architecture, Domestic *See* Domestic architecture
      Designs and plans
  See Domestic architecture—Designs and plans

Architecture, Ecclesiastical *See* Church architecture

Architecture, Medieval *See* Medieval architecture

Architecture, Renaissance *See* Architecture—15th and 16th centuries

Architecture and interior design through the 18th century. Harwood, B.   **729**

Architecture and ornament. Maliszewski-Pickart, M.   **721**

Architecture, from prehistory to post-modernism. See Trachtenberg, M. Architecture, from prehistory to postmodernity   **720.9**

Architecture, from prehistory to postmodernity. Trachtenberg, M.   **720.9**

Architecture in the garden. Van Sweden, J. A.   **712**

The **architecture** traveler. LeBlanc, S.   **720.973**

Archives
      United States
  Greenwood, V. D. The researcher's guide to American genealogy   **929**

Arctic (Steamship)
  Shaw, D. W. The sea shall embrace them   **910.4**

Arctic crossing. Waterman, J.   **998**

Arctic dreams. Lopez, B. H.   **998**

Arctic regions
  See also North Pole
  Lopez, B. H. Arctic dreams   **998**
  Mangelsen, T. D. Polar dance   **599.78**
  McGonigal, D. Antarctica and the Arctic   **998**
      Description
  Fredston, J. A. Rowing to latitude   **797.1**
      Exploration
  Cookman, S. Ice blink   **998**
  Fleming, F. Ninety degrees North   **998**
  Mikkelsen, E. Two against the ice   **998**
  Williams, G. Voyages of delusion   **910.4**
      Natural history
  See Natural history—Arctic regions

Ardagh, John, 1928-
  Ireland and the Irish   **941.5**

Arden, Lynie, 1949-
  Work-at-home sourcebook   **338.7**

Ardennes, Battle of the, 1944-1945
  Astor, G. A blood-dimmed tide   **940.54**

Ardley, Neil, 1937-
  (jt. auth) Macaulay, D. The new way things work   **600**

Arduini, Paolo
  Simon & Schuster's guide to fossils   **560**

Are we hardwired? Clark, W. R.   **155.7**

Are you somebody. O'Faolain, N.   **92**

Arem, Arnold
In our hands   617
Arendt, Hannah
The life of the mind   153
On revolution   303.6
Origins of totalitarianism   321.9
Thinking
   In Arendt, H. The life of the mind   153
Willing
   In Arendt, H. The life of the mind   153
   See/See also pages in the following book(s):
Pierpont, C. R. Passionate minds   810.9
Argentina
       History
Brown, J. C. A brief history of Argentina   982
      Politics and government
   See/See also pages in the following book(s):
Naipaul, V. S. The writer and the world p346-437
                                     824
Argentini, Paul, 1926-
(jt. auth) Boland, R. Musicals!   792.6
Argonauts (Greek mythology)
   See/See also pages in the following book(s):
Hamilton, E. Mythology p159-79   292
Arguing about slavery. Miller, W. L.   973.5
Ariès, Philippe, 1914-1984
(ed) A History of private life. See A History of private life   909
Aristocracy
Tillyard, S. K. Aristocrats   920
Aristocrats. Tillyard, S. K.   920
Aristophanes
Acharnians
   In Aristophanes. The complete plays of Aristophanes p13-51   882
Birds
   In Aristophanes. The complete plays of Aristophanes p229-86   882
Clouds
   In Aristophanes. The complete plays of Aristophanes p101-41   882
The complete plays of Aristophanes   882
Ecclesiazusae
   In Aristophanes. The complete plays of Aristophanes p417-62   882
Frogs
   In Aristophanes. The complete plays of Aristophanes p367-415   882
Knights
   In Aristophanes. The complete plays of Aristophanes p53-100   882
Lysistrata
   In Aristophanes. The complete plays of Aristophanes p287-328   882
Peace
   In Aristophanes. The complete plays of Aristophanes p185-227   882
Plutus
   In Aristophanes. The complete plays of Aristophanes p463-501   882
Thesmophoriazusae
   In Aristophanes. The complete plays of Aristophanes p329-66   882
Wasps
   In Aristophanes. The complete plays of Aristophanes p143-83   882
   See/See also pages in the following book(s):
Hamilton, E. The Greek way p126-58   880.9
Aristotle, 384-322 B.C.
The basic works of Aristotle   888
Ethics   170
   also in Aristotle. The basic works of Aristotle p927-1112   888
   also in Aristotle. Introduction to Aristotle p337-581   888

Introduction to Aristotle   888
Metaphysics
   In Aristotle. The basic works of Aristotle p689-926   888
On generation and corruption
   In Aristotle. The basic works of Aristotle p470-531   888
On the soul
   In Aristotle. The basic works of Aristotle p535-603   888
   In Aristotle. Introduction to Aristotle p153-245   888
Organon
   In Aristotle. The basic works of Aristotle p1-212   888
Parva naturalia
   In Aristotle. The basic works of Aristotle p607-30   888
Physica
   In Aristotle. The basic works of Aristotle p213-394   888
Poetics   808.1
   also in Aristotle. The basic works of Aristotle p1455-87   888
   also in Aristotle. Introduction to Aristotle p668-713   888
Politics   320
   also in Aristotle. The basic works of Aristotle p1127-1316   888
Posterior analytics
   In Aristotle. Introduction to Aristotle p8-111   888
         About
Adler, M. J. Aristotle for everybody   185
Rubenstein, R. E. Aristotle's children   189
   See/See also pages in the following book(s):
Durant, W. J. The story of philosophy p41-74   109
Hamilton, E. The echo of Greece p94-103   880.9
Jaspers, K. The great philosophers   109
The Renaissance philosophy of man p47-133   189
Russell, B. A history of Western philosophy p159-207   109
Aristotle for everybody. Adler, M. J.   185
Aristotle's children. Rubenstein, R. E.   189
Arius, d. 336
         About
Rubenstein, R. E. When Jesus became God   273
Armada, 1588 *See* Spanish Armada, 1588
The **Armada**. Mattingly, G.   942.05
Armaments *See* Military weapons
Armaments race *See* Arms race
The **armchair** James Beard. Beard, J.   641.5
Armed forces
   See also Navies
Armesto, Felipe Fernández- *See* Fernández-Armesto, Felipe
Armitage, Allan M.
Armitage's manual of annuals, biennials, and half-hardy perennials   635.9
Armitage's manual of annuals, biennials, and half-hardy perennials. Armitage, A. M.   635.9
Armored cars (Tanks) *See* Military tanks
Armour-Hileman, Victoria, 1958-
Singing to the dead   261
Arms and armor *See* Weapons
Arms and the man. Shaw, B.
   In Our dramatic heritage v5   808.82
Arms control
   See also Arms race
Arms race
   See/See also pages in the following book(s):
Rhodes, R. Dark sun   623.4
Armstrong, Helen Joseph
Patternmaking for fashion design   646.4

Armstrong, Karen
The battle for God 291
Buddha 294.3
A history of God 291
In the beginning 222
Islam 297
Jerusalem 956.94
Visions of God 248.2
Armstrong, Lance
It's not about the bike 92
Armstrong, Louis, 1900-1971
Louis Armstrong, in his own words 92
About
Collier, J. L. Louis Armstrong, an American genius 92

See/See also pages in the following book(s):
Feather, L. From Satchmo to Miles 920
Russell, D. Black genius and the American experience 920
Armstrong, Nancy
(jt. auth) Friedman, V. M. Field guide to stains 648
Army Air Forces (U.S.) *See* United States. Army Air Forces
An **army** at dawn. Atkinson, R. 940.54
Army life *See* Soldiers
Arnell, Charles
(jt. auth) Bennett, J. The complete snowboarder 796.9
Arnold, Emily *See* McCully, Emily Arnold
Arnold, Roseanne *See* Barr, Roseanne
Arnold Schoenberg's journey. Shawn, A. 92
Arnot, Bob
The breast cancer prevention diet 616.99
The breast health cookbook 616.99
Arnot, Robert Burns *See* Arnot, Bob
Aron, Paul, 1956-
Unsolved mysteries of history 902
Aronson, Emily
(ed) The New cooks' catalogue. See The New cooks' catalogue 683
Around America. Cronkite, W. 917.3
Around the world with Mark Twain. Cooper, R. L. 818
Arousal, the secret logic of sexual fantasies. Bader, M. J. 306.7
Arrington, Leonard J.
Japanese Americans, from relocation to redress. See Japanese Americans, from relocation to redress 940.53
The **ARRL** handbook for radio amateurs 621.3841
The **arrogance** of power: the secret world of Richard Nixon. Summers, A. 92
Arrogant capital. Phillips, K. P. 973.92
Ars nova and the Renaissance
In New Oxford history of music v3 780.9
Ars poetica. Horace
In Horace. Satires, Epistles and Ars poetica 878
Arson
Wambaugh, J. Fire lover 364.1
Art
See also Artistic anatomy; Decoration and ornament; Installations (Art); New York (N.Y.) in art; Symbolism in art
Kampen O'Riley, M. Art beyond the west 709
15th and 16th centuries
Campbell, T. Tapestry in the Renaissance 746
Graham-Dixon, A. Renaissance 709.02
The Medici, Michelangelo, & the art of late Renaissance Florence 709.45
19th century
See also Impressionism (Art)
Craske, M. Art in Europe, 1700-1830 709.03

Kostenevich, A. G. French art treasures at the Hermitage 709.44
Schapiro, M. Impressionism 709.44
20th century
Barnitz, J. Twentieth-century art of Latin America 709
Blistène, B. A history of 20th-century art 709.04
Designed for delight 745
Fineberg, J. D. Art since 1940 709.04
Kostenevich, A. G. French art treasures at the Hermitage 709.44
Lippard, L. R. Overlay 709
Lucie-Smith, E. Art today 709.04
Lucie-Smith, E. Visual arts in the twentieth century 709.04
Rowell, M. Objects of desire 758
20th century—Encyclopedias
Dempsey, A. Art in the modern era 709.04
Bibliography
Art index 705
Collectors and collecting
Feigen, R. Tales from the art crypt 708
Dictionaries
The Concise Oxford dictionary of art and artists 703
Encyclopedia of artists 920.003
Frazier, N. The Penguin concise dictionary of art history 703
Langmuir, E. Yale dictionary of art and artists 703
The Oxford companion to western art 703
The Oxford dictionary of art 703
Directories
American art directory 702.5
Encyclopedias
Metzger, P. W. The artist's illustrated encyclopedia 703
Forgeries
Hoving, T. False impressions 702.8
History
Art: a world history 709
Beckett, W. Sister Wendy's American collection 709
Borzello, F. A world of our own 704
Fenton, J. Leonardo's nephew 709
Gardner's art through the ages 709
Gombrich, E. H. The story of art 709
Janson, H. W. History of art 709
The Oxford history of western art 709
Stokstad, M. Art history 709
Marketing—Directories
Artist's & graphic designer's market 702.5
Museums
See Art museums
Periodicals—Indexes
Art index 705
Philosophy
See/See also pages in the following book(s):
Hamilton, E. The Greek way p53-69 880.9
Psychology
See/See also pages in the following book(s):
Jung, C. G. Man and his symbols p230-71 150.19
Technique
Metzger, P. W. The artist's illustrated encyclopedia 703

Art, African *See* African art
Art, African American *See* African American art
Art, American *See* American art
Art, Ancient *See* Ancient art
Art, Asian *See* Asian art
Art, Baroque *See* Baroque art
Art, Buddhist *See* Buddhist art
Art, Byzantine *See* Byzantine art
Art, Canadian *See* Canadian art

Art, Chinese *See* Chinese art
Art, Christian *See* Christian art
Art, Egyptian *See* Egyptian art
Art, French *See* French art
Art, Greek *See* Greek art
Art, Hispanic American *See* Hispanic American art
Art, Indian *See* Native American art
Art, Islamic *See* Islamic art
Art, Italian *See* Italian art
Art, Latin American *See* Latin American art
Art, Medieval *See* Medieval art
Art, Modern *See* Modern art
Art, Prehistoric *See* Prehistoric art
Art, Renaissance *See* Art—15th and 16th centuries
Art, Russian *See* Russian art
The **art** & elegance of beadweaving. Wells, C. W.   **745.58**
Art: a world history   **709**
Art and architecture in Italy, 1600-1750. Wittkower, R.   **709.45**
The **art** and architecture of ancient Egypt. Smith, W. S.   **709.32**
The **art** and architecture of Russia. Hamilton, G. H.   **709.47**
The **art** and architecture of the ancient Orient. Frankfort, H.   **709.39**
The **art** and craft of papermaking. Dawson, S.   **676**
The **art** and imagination of Langston Hughes. Miller, R. B.   **818**
Art and music
   Appel, A. Jazz modernism   **781.65**
Art and mythology
   See/See also pages in the following book(s):
   Carr-Gomm, S. Hidden symbols in art   **704.9**
       Dictionaries
   Impelluso, L. Gods and heroes in art   **700**
Art and religion
   Silverman, D. Van Gogh and Gauguin   **759.4**
Art appreciation
   Beckett, W. Sister Wendy's 1000 masterpieces   **759**
   Beckett, W. Sister Wendy's American collection   **709**
   Kimmelman, M. Portraits   **701**
   Manguel, A. Reading pictures   **750**
Art beyond the west. Kampen O'Riley, M.   **709**
Art criticism
   Berger, J. The shape of a pocket   **701**
   Gombrich, E. H. The preference for the primitive   **709**
   Manguel, A. Reading pictures   **750**
Art deco
   Art deco 1910-1939   **709.04**
Art deco 1910-1939   **709.04**
Art from the ashes   **940.53**
Art history. Stokstad, M.   **709**
Art in Europe, 1700-1830. Craske, M.   **709.03**
Art in the modern era. Dempsey, A.   **709.04**
Art index   **705**
Art industries and trade *See* Decorative arts
Art lover: a biography of Peggy Guggenheim. Gill, A.   **92**
Art museums
   See also names of individual art museums
   Kimmelman, M. Portraits   **701**
   Loebl, S. America's art museums   **708**
Art nouveau   **709.03**
The **art** of ancient Egypt. Robins, G.   **709.32**
The **art** of black American women. Henkes, R.   **709.73**
The **art** of burning bridges: a life of John O'Hara. Wolff, G.   **92**
The **art** of calligraphy. Harris, D.   **745.6**
The **art** of chemistry. Greenberg, A.   **540**
The **art** of dying. Weenolsen, P.   **155.9**

The **art** of fiction. Gardner, J.   **808.3**
The **art** of hand reading. Reid, L.   **133.6**
The **art** of knotting & splicing. Day, C. L.   **623.88**
The **art** of loving. Fromm, E.   **152.4**
The **art** of National Geographic. Carter, A. A.   **741.6**
The **Art** of natural building   **690**
The **art** of Peter Max. Riley, C. A.   **760**
The **art** of quick breads. See Hensperger, B. The best quick breads   **641.8**
The **art** of Shakespeare's sonnets. Vendler, H. H.   **822.3**
The **art** of spelling. Vos Savant, M. M.   **421**
Art of the basket. Sentance, B.   **746.41**
The **art** of the infinite. Kaplan, R.   **515**
The **Art** of the personal essay   **808.84**
The **art** of the sports car. Adler, D.   **629.222**
Art since 1940. Fineberg, J. D.   **709.04**
Art thefts
   Harclerode, P. The lost masters   **709**
   Petropoulos, J. The Faustian bargain   **709**
   The Spoils of war   **709**
Art today. Lucie-Smith, E.   **709.04**
Arthritis
   Arthritis sourcebook . . .   **616.7**
   Lawrence, R. M. Preventing arthritis   **616.7**
Arthritis sourcebook . . .   **616.7**
Arthur, King
       About
   Goodrich, N. L. King Arthur   **942.01**
   King Arthur in legend and history   **942.01**
   Malory, Sir T. Le morte d'Arthur   **398.2**
Arthur Rimbaud: complete works. Rimbaud, A.   **848**
Artificial intelligence
   Brooks, R. A. Flesh and machines   **629.8**
   Kurzweil, R. The age of spiritual machines   **006.3**
   Menzel, P. Robo sapiens: evolution of a new species   **629.8**
   Moravec, H. P. Robot   **629.8**
   Wood, G. Edison's Eve   **629.8**
   See/See also pages in the following book(s):
   Devlin, K. J. Goodbye, Descartes p143-207   **128**
Artificial satellites
   Dickson, P. Sputnik: the shock of the century   **629.46**
The **artist** blacksmith. Parkinson, P.   **682**
Artistic anatomy
   See also Figure drawing
   Hart, C. Human anatomy made amazingly easy   **743**
Artistic photography
   Coles, R. When they were young   **779**
   Homer, W. I. Stieglitz and the Photo-Secession, 1902   **779**
   Icons of photography   **779**
   Photography past forward: Aperture at 50   **770.9**
   Smith, J. Edward Steichen: the early years   **779**
   Steichen, E. Steichen's legacy   **779**
   Struth, T. Thomas Struth, 1977-2002   **779**
Artists
   See also African American artists; Architects; Illustrators; Native American artists; Women artists
   Kimmelman, M. Portraits   **701**
       Dictionaries
   The Concise Oxford dictionary of art and artists   **703**
   Contemporary artists   **920.003**
   Encyclopedia of artists   **920.003**
   Langmuir, E. Yale dictionary of art and artists   **703**
   World artists, 1950-1980   **920.003**
   World artists, 1980-1990   **920.003**
       Indexes
   Havlice, P. P. Index to artistic biography   **920.003**

Artists—*Continued*
United States
Henkes, R. The art of black American women
709.73
St. James guide to Hispanic artists　920.003
United States—Dictionaries
Cummings, P. Dictionary of contemporary American
artists　920.003
Who's who in American art　920.003
Artists, British
Dictionaries
Who's who in art　920.003
Artist's & graphic designer's market　702.5
The **artist's** handbook of materials and techniques.
Mayer, R.　751.2
The **artist's** illustrated encyclopedia. Metzger, P. W.
703
Artist's market. See Artist's & graphic designer's market
702.5
Artists' materials
Mayer, R. The artist's handbook of materials and tech-
niques　751.2
Metzger, P. W. The artist's illustrated encyclopedia
703
Arts
See also Surrealism
Barzun, J. The use and abuse of art　701
Boorstin, D. J. The creators　909
Reid, J. D. The Oxford guide to classical mythology in
the arts, 1300-1990s　700
Biography
Richardson, J. Sacred monsters　920
History
Ochoa, G. The Wilson chronology of the arts
700
Philosophy
Berlin, Sir I. The roots of romanticism　141
Steiner, W. Venus in exile　700
United States
Haskell, B. The American century　709.73
Arts, African American *See* African American arts
Arts, Applied *See* Decorative arts
Arts, Decorative *See* Decoration and ornament; Decora-
tive arts
Arts and crafts *See* Handicraft
Arts of the possible. Rich, A.　818
As ever. Kyger, J.　811
As good as I could be. Cheever, S.　306.8
As seen on TV. Marling, K. A.　973.92
As the Romans do. Epstein, A.　945
Asahara, Shoko
About
Lifton, R. J. Destroying the world to save it　299
Asante, Molefi K., 1942-
The African-American atlas　305.8
The **ascent** of science. Silver, B. L.　509
Ash, Timothy Garton *See* Garton Ash, Timothy
Ashbery, John
Girls on the run　811
Selected poems　811
Your name here　811
Ashby, Bonnie
(jt. auth) Turkington, C. The encyclopedia of infectious
diseases　616.9
Ashcraft, Tami Oldham, 1960-
Red sky in mourning　910.4
Ashe, Geoffrey
Encyclopedia of prophecy　133.3
Asher, Donald
The overnight résumé　650.14
Asher, Michael, 1953-
Lawrence, the uncrowned king of Arabia　92
Ashes of glory. Furgurson, E. B.　975.5
Ashes to ashes. Kluger, R.　394.1

Asia
See also names of individual countries, e.g. China
Description
Jensen, C. I have seen the world begin　915
Kaplan, R. D. The ends of the earth　910.4
Polo, M. The travels of Marco Polo　915
Theroux, P. The great railway bazaar: by train through
Asia　915
Wood, M. In the footsteps of Alexander the Great
938
Encyclopedias
Levinson, D. Encyclopedia of modern Asia　950
Religion—Dictionaries
Leeming, D. A. A dictionary of Asian mythology
291.103
Asia, East *See* East Asia
Asia, Southeast *See* Southeast Asia
Asian American literature *See* American literature—
Asian American authors
Asian American literature　810.9
Asian Americans
History
Avakian, M. Atlas of Asian-American history
305.8
Takaki, R. T. Strangers from a different shore
305.8
Asian art
Lee, S. E. A history of Far Eastern art　709.5
The **Asian** journal of Thomas Merton. Merton, T.
248
Asian mythology
Dictionaries
Leeming, D. A. A dictionary of Asian mythology
291.103
Asian philosophy *See* Oriental philosophy
Asimov, Isaac, 1920-1992
Atom　539.7
Isaac Asimov's guide to earth & space　520
About
Gunn, J. E. Isaac Asimov　813.009
Asleson, Robyn, 1961-
Albert Moore　759.2
Asma, Stephen T.
Stuffed animals & pickled heads　508
ASPCA complete cat care manual. Edney, A. T. B.
636.8
ASPCA complete dog care manual. Fogle, B.　636.7
ASPCA complete dog training manual. See Fogle, B.
New complete dog training manual　636.7
ASPCA complete guide to cats. Richards, J. R.
636.8
Asperger's syndrome
Attwood, T. Asperger's syndrome　616.89
Bashe, P. R. The oasis guide to asperger syndrome
618.92
Hewetson, A. The stolen child　616.89
Jackson, L. Freaks, geeks and asperger syndrome
618.92
Osborne, L. American normal　616.89
Asperger's syndrome. Attwood, T.　616.89
Asquith, H. H. (Herbert Henry), 1852-1928
See/See also pages in the following book(s):
Massie, R. K. Dreadnought p563-80　940.3
Asquith, Herbert Henry *See* Asquith, H. H. (Herbert
Henry), 1852-1928
Assisted suicide *See* Euthanasia
Assmann, Jan
The mind of Egypt　932
The **Associated** Press stylebook and briefing on media
law　808
The **Associated** Press stylebook and libel manual. See
The Associated Press stylebook and briefing on me-
dia law　808
Associations
See also Societies

Associations, International See International agencies
Asteroids
  Norton, O. R. Rocks from space   523.5
  Peebles, C. Asteroids   523.4
Asthma
  Freedman, M. R. Living well with asthma   616.2
  Pescatore, F. The allergy and asthma cure   616.97
  Wray, B. B. Taking charge of asthma   616.2
    See/See also pages in the following book(s):
  Brazelton, T. B. To listen to a child p145-55
        155.4
The **astonishing** elephant. Alexander, S.   599.67
Astor, Gerald, 1926-
  A blood-dimmed tide   940.54
  Crisis in the Pacific   940.54
  The greatest war   940.54
  Operation Iceberg   940.54
**Astor, Nancy Witcher Langhorne, Viscountess, 1879-
1964**
        About
  Fox, J. Five sisters   920
Astrology
  Goodman, L. Linda Goodman's star signs   133
  Goodman, L. Linda Goodman's sun signs   133.5
  Miller, S. Planets and possibilities   133.5
  Parker, J. KISS guide to astrology   133.5
  Snodgrass, M. E. Signs of the zodiac   133.5
        Encyclopedias
  Lewis, J. R. The astrology book   133.5
The **astrology** book. Lewis, J. R.   133.5
The **astrology** encyclopedia. See Lewis, J. R. The astrol-
  ogy book   133.5
Astronautics
    See also Space flight
  Burrows, W. E. This new ocean   629.4
  Dickson, P. Sputnik: the shock of the century
        629.46
  Dyson, G. Project Orion   629.47
  Heppenheimer, T. A. Countdown   629.4
  Launius, R. D. Frontiers of space exploration
        629.45
  Schefter, J. L. The race   629.45
  Zimmerman, R. The chronological encyclopedia of dis-
  coveries in space   629.4
        Dictionaries
  Angelo, J. A. The Facts on File dictionary of space
  technology   629.4
  Williamson, M. The Cambridge dictionary of space
  technology   629.4
        United States
  Kranz, E. F. Failure is not an option   629.45
  Space exploration   629
  Walsh, P. J. Echoes among the stars   629.4
  Wolfe, T. The right stuff   629.45
Astronauts
    See also Women astronauts
  Glenn, J. John Glenn   92
  Gubert, B. K. Distinguished African Americans in avi-
  ation and space science   920.003
  Wolfe, T. The right stuff   629.45
Astronomers
  Ferris, T. Seeing in the dark   520
  Lightman, A. P. Ancient light   523.1
The **Astronomical** almanac   528
Astronomy
    See also Constellations; Stars
  The Amateur astronomer   520
  Angelo, J. A. The Facts on File space and astronomy
  handbook   520
  Asimov, I. Isaac Asimov's guide to earth & space
        520
  Berman, B. Secrets of the night sky   520
  Chartrand, M. R. The Audubon Society field guide to
  the night sky   523
  Cosmic dispatches   520

  Dickinson, T. The backyard astronomer's guide
        522
  Dickinson, T. From the big bang to Planet X   520
  Ferris, T. Seeing in the dark   520
  Jastrow, R. God and the astronomers   523.1
  Moore, P. Atlas of the universe   523
  North, J. D. Stonehenge   936
  On the shoulders of giants   520
  Panek, R. Seeing and believing   522
  Plait, P. C. Bad astronomy   520
  Raymo, C. An intimate look at the night sky   520
  Ridpath, I. Stars and planets   520
  Sagan, C. Cosmos   520
  Schaaf, F. 40 nights to knowing the sky   520
  The Universe revealed   523
  Upgren, A. R. The turtle and the stars   520
    See/See also pages in the following book(s):
  Connell, E. S. The Aztec treasure house p167-219
        814
  Sagan, C. Broca's brain p250-67   500
        Atlases
    See Stars—Atlases
        Dictionaries
  Mitton, J. Cambridge dictionary of astronomy
        520.3
  Williamson, M. The Cambridge dictionary of space
  technology   629.4
        Encyclopedias
  Astronomy encyclopedia   520
  Encyclopedia of astronomy and astrophysics   520.3
        History
  The Cambridge illustrated history of astronomy
        520
        History—Encyclopedias
  History of astronomy   520.3
Astronomy encyclopedia   520
Astrophysics
  Barrow, J. D. The origin of the universe   523.1
  Davies, P. C. W. About time   530.1
  Goodstein, D. L. Feynman's lost lecture   521
  Hawking, S. W. The nature of space and time
        530.1
  Thorne, K. S. Black holes and time warps   530.1
  White, M. Stephen Hawking   92
        Encyclopedias
  Encyclopedia of astronomy and astrophysics   520.3
Astros (Baseball team) See Houston Astros (Baseball
  team)
At dawn we slept. Prange, G. W.   940.54
At home in the world. Pearl, D.   070.4
At home with the Marquis de Sade. Gray, F. du P.
        92
At the hands of persons unknown. Dray, P.   364.1
Atchity, Kenneth John
  (ed) The Classical Greek reader. See The Classical
  Greek reader   880.8
Ath, Rand Flem- See Flem-Ath, Rand
Athanasius, Saint, Patriarch of Alexandria, d. 373
        About
  Rubenstein, R. E. When Jesus became God   273
Atheism
    See also Agnosticism
  Gay, P. A Godless Jew   150.19
    See/See also pages in the following book(s):
  Turner, J. Without God, without creed   211
Athens, Lonnie H.
        About
  Rhodes, R. Why they kill   364.3
Athens (Greece)
  Connolly, P. The ancient city   937
Athletes
    See also African American athletes; Women ath-
  letes
        Drug use
  Kuhn, C. Pumped   617.1

Athletic medicine *See* Sports medicine
Athletics
  See also Sports
Atkins, P. W. (Peter William), 1940-
  The periodic kingdom   541.2
Atkins, Peter William *See* Atkins, P. W. (Peter William), 1940-
Atkins, Robert C.
  Dr. Atkins' age-defying diet revolution   613
  Dr. Atkins' new diet revolution   613.2
Atkins, Stephen E.
  Encyclopedia of modern American extremists and extremist groups   322.4
Atkinson, Rick
  An army at dawn   940.54
  Crusade   956.7
Atlanta (Ga.)
Race relations
  Brown, E. The condemnation of Little B   364.1
Atlantic Coast Conference
  Feinstein, J. A march to madness   796.323
Atlantis
  Ellis, R. Imagining Atlantis   001.9
  Wilson, C. The Atlantis blueprint   001.9
The **Atlantis** blueprint. Wilson, C.   001.9
Atlas, James
  Bellow   92
Atlas of American politics, 1960-2000   973.92
Atlas of Asian-American history. Avakian, M.   305.8
The **atlas** of holy places & sacred sites. Wilson, C.   291.3
Atlas of human anatomy. Netter, F. H.   611
The **atlas** of the Arab world. Fargues, P.   909
Atlas of the Greek world. Levi, P.   938
Atlas of the North American Indian. Waldman, C.   970.004
Atlas of the universe. Moore, P.   523
Atlas of world history   911
Atlases
  Goode's world atlas   912
  Hammond world atlas   912
  Oxford atlas of the world   912
  Rand McNally commercial atlas & marketing guide   912
  The Times atlas of the world   912
Atlases, Historical *See* Historical atlases
Atmosphere
Encyclopedias
  Encyclopedia of atmospheric sciences   551.5
Atom. Krauss, L. M.   523.1
Atomic bomb
  Conant, J. Tuxedo Park   92
  Herken, G. Brotherhood of the bomb   920
  Hersey, J. Hiroshima   940.54
  Lifton, R. J. Hiroshima in America   940.54
  Rhodes, R. The making of the atomic bomb   623.4
  Takaki, R. T. Hiroshima   940.54
  Walker, M. Nazi science   509
Atomic weapons *See* Nuclear weapons
Atoms
  Asimov, I. Atom   539.7
  See/See also pages in the following book(s):
  Feynman, R. P. Six easy pieces   530
Dictionaries
  The Facts on File dictionary of atomic and nuclear physics   539.7
Atonement, Day of *See* Yom Kippur
Atop an Underwood. Kerouac, J.   818
Atrocities
  Bizot, F. The gate   959.6
  Hochschild, A. King Leopold's ghost   967.5
  Kiernan, B. The Pol Pot regime   959.6
  Sontag, S. Regarding the pain of others   303.6

Atsumori. Zeami
  In Waley, A. The Nō plays of Japan   895.6
Attacks by animals *See* Animal attacks
Attenborough, David, 1926-
  The life of birds   598
Attention deficit disorder
  Barkley, R. A. Taking charge of ADHD   618.92
  DeGrandpre, R. J. Ritalin nation   618.92
  Diller, L. H. Running on Ritalin   618.92
  Hallowell, E. M. Driven to distraction   616.85
  Maté, G. Scattered   616.85
  Solden, S. Journeys through ADDulthood   616.85
  Stein, D. B. Ritalin is not the answer   618.92
Attig, Thomas, 1945-
  The heart of grief   155.9
  How we grieve   155.9
Attitude (Psychology)
  Viscott, D. S. Emotional resilience   158
Attridge, Harold W.
  (ed) The HarperCollins encyclopedia of Catholicism. See The HarperCollins encyclopedia of Catholicism   282
Attucks, Crispus, d. 1770
  See/See also pages in the following book(s):
  Abdul-Jabbar, K. Black profiles in courage p35-42   920
Attwater, Donald, 1892-1977
  The Penguin dictionary of saints   920.003
  (ed) Butler, A. Butler's Lives of the saints   920.003
Attwood, Tony, 1952-
  Asperger's syndrome   616.89
Atwan, Robert
  (ed) The Best American essays of the century. See The Best American essays of the century   814
Atwood, Craig D.
  (ed) Mead, F. S. Handbook of denominations in the United States   280
Atwood, Margaret, 1939-
  Morning in the burned house   811
  Selected poems   811
  Selected poems II   811
Auburn, David
  Proof   812
Auca Indians (Ecuador) *See* Waorani Indians
Auchincloss, Louis
  Woodrow Wilson   92
Auden, W. H. (Wystan Hugh), 1907-1973
  Collected poems   821
  See/See also pages in the following book(s):
  Brodsky, J. Less than one p304-19   814
  Heaney, S. Finders keepers p209-19   821
  Jarrell, R. No other book   809
Auden, Wystan Hugh *See* Auden, W. H. (Wystan Hugh), 1907-1973
Audi, Robert, 1941-
  (ed) The Cambridge dictionary of philosophy. See The Cambridge dictionary of philosophy   103
Audio cassettes *See* Sound recordings
Audio video market place. See AV market place   371.3025
Audiovisual materials
Directories
  AV market place   371.3025
Audubon Society *See* National Audubon Society
The **Audubon** Society field guide to North American butterflies. Pyle, R. M.   595.7
The **Audubon** Society field guide to North American fishes, whales, and dolphins   597
The **Audubon** Society field guide to North American fossils. Thompson, I.   560
The **Audubon** Society field guide to North American insects and spiders. Milne, L. J.   595.7
The **Audubon** Society field guide to North American mushrooms. Lincoff, G.   579.6

The **Audubon** Society field guide to North American rocks and minerals. Chesterman, C. W.   **549**

The **Audubon** Society field guide to North American trees. Little, E. L.   **582.16**

The **Audubon** Society field guide to North American weather. Ludlum, D. M.   **551.6**

The **Audubon** Society field guide to the night sky. Chartrand, M. R.   **523**

Auerbach, Susan, 1956-
(ed) Encyclopedia of multiculturalism. See Encyclopedia of multiculturalism   **305.8**

Augusta National Golf Club
Sampson, C. Masters   **796.352**

Augustine, Saint, Bishop of Hippo
The confessions of St. Augustine   **242**
About
Wills, G. Saint Augustine   **92**
See/See also pages in the following book(s):
Jaspers, K. The great philosophers   **109**
Küng, H. Great Christian thinkers p69-98   **230**
Russell, B. A history of Western philosophy p352-66   **109**

Augustus, Emperor of Rome, 63 B.C.-14 A.D.
See/See also pages in the following book(s):
Suetonius Tranquillus, C. The twelve Caesars   **878**

Auiler, Dan
Vertigo   **791.43**

Aultman, Dick
(jt. auth) Snead, S. Golf begins at forty   **796.352**

Aum Shinrikyō
Lifton, R. J. Destroying the world to save it   **299**
Murakami, H. Underground   **364.1**

Aum Supreme Truth *See* Aum Shinrikyō

Aung San Suu Kyi
Freedom from fear, and other writings   **959.1**

Auroras
Savage, C. Aurora   **538**

Auschwitz (Poland: Concentration camp)
Anissimov, M. Primo Levi   **92**
Levi, P. The drowned and the saved   **940.53**
Levi, P. Survival in Auschwitz; and, The reawakening   **940.53**

Aust, Tracy DiSabato- *See* DiSabato-Aust, Tracy

Austen, Jane, 1775-1817
Mansfield Park; criticism
In Nabokov, V. V. Lectures on literature p9-61   **808.3**
About
The Cambridge companion to Jane Austen   **823.009**
Nokes, D. Jane Austen   **92**
Poplawski, P. A Jane Austen encyclopedia   **823.009**
Shields, C. Jane Austen   **92**
Tomalin, C. Jane Austen   **92**
See/See also pages in the following book(s):
Bloom, H. The Western canon   **809**
Woolf, V. Women and writing p109-20   **820.9**

Auster, Paul, 1947-
I thought my father was God and other true tales from the National Story Project. See I thought my father was God and other true tales from the National Story Project   **810.8**

Australia
Description
Bryson, B. In a sunburned country   **994**
Chatwin, B. The songlines   **919.4**
Encyclopedias
The Australian people   **994**
History
Clarke, F. G. The history of Australia   **994**
Hughes, R. The fatal shore   **994**
Race relations
The Australian people   **994**

Australian aborigines
Chatwin, B. The songlines   **919.4**
Social conditions
The Australian people   **994**

Australian Committee on Cataloguing
See also Joint Steering Committee for Revision of AACR

Australian literature
Bio-bibliography
Wilde, W. H. The Oxford companion to Australian literature   **820.3**
Dictionaries
Wilde, W. H. The Oxford companion to Australian literature   **820.3**

The **Australian** people   **994**

Authoritarianism *See* Totalitarianism

Authors
See also Literature—Bio-bibliography; Women authors
Bloom, H. Genius   **153.9**
Gillespie, J. T. The Newbery companion   **028.5**
Marcus, L. S. Ways of telling   **741.6**
The Newbery & Caldecott medal books, 1986-2000   **028.5**
Newbery and Caldecott Medal books, 1966-1975   **028.5**
Newbery and Caldecott Medal books, 1976-1985   **028.5**
Newbery Medal books, 1922-1955   **028.5**
Roth, P. Shop talk   **809**
Dictionaries
Contemporary authors   **920.003**
Contemporary world writers   **920.003**
World authors, 1900-1950   **920.003**
World authors, 1950-1970   **920.003**
World authors, 1970-1975   **920.003**
World authors, 1975-1980   **920.003**
World authors, 1980-1985   **920.003**
World authors, 1985-1990   **920.003**
World authors, 1990-1995   **920.003**
World authors, 1995-2000   **920.003**
Homes and haunts
See Literary landmarks

Authors, African American *See* African American authors

Authors, American
Modern American memoirs   **810.8**
Dictionaries
American authors, 1600-1900   **920.003**
American writers   **920.003**
Contemporary Southern writers   **920.003**
Merriam-Webster's dictionary of American writers   **920.003**
Writers for young adults   **920.003**

Authors, Black *See* Black authors

Authors, Canadian
Bio-bibliography
Encyclopedia of literature in Canada   **810.3**

Authors, East European
Dictionaries
Segel, H. B. The Columbia guide to the literatures of Eastern Europe since 1945   **809**

Authors, English
Wullschläger, J. Inventing wonderland   **820.9**
See/See also pages in the following book(s):
Woolf, V. The second common reader p127-55   **820.9**
Dictionaries
British authors of the nineteenth century   **920.003**
Encyclopedia of British writers, 19th and 20th centuries   **820.9**
Writers for young adults   **920.003**

Authors, European
Dictionaries
Columbia dictionary of modern European literature
803
European authors, 1000-1900 920.003
Authors, German
Dictionaries
Segel, H. B. The Columbia guide to the literatures of Eastern Europe since 1945 809
Authors, Greek
Dictionaries
Grant, M. Greek and Latin authors, 800 B.C.-A.D. 1000 920.003
Authors, Japanese
Modern Japanese writers 920.003
Authors, Latin
Dictionaries
Grant, M. Greek and Latin authors, 800 B.C.-A.D. 1000 920.003
Authors, Latin American
Hispanic literature criticism 860.9
Latin American writers 920.003
Authors and publishers
Appelbaum, J. How to get happily published
070.5
Germano, W. P. Getting it published 070.5
Herman, J. Jeff Herman's guide to book publishers, editors, & literary agents 070.5
Directories
Guide to literary agents 070.5
Authorship
See also Journalism; Radio authorship
Aiken, J. The way to write for children 808.06
Gardner, J. On becoming a novelist 808.3
Hooks, B. Remembered rapture 808
King, S. On writing 808.3
O'Neil, D. The DC comics guide to writing comics
808
Rabiner, S. Thinking like your editor 808
Seuling, B. How to write a children's book and get it published 808.06
Stein, S. Stein on writing 808
Vargas Llosa, M. Letters to a young novelist
808.3
Zinsser, W. K. On writing well 808
Data processing—Handbooks, manuals, etc.
Walker, J. R. The Columbia guide to online style
808
Handbooks, manuals, etc.
Agress, L. Working with words in business and legal writing 808
The Associated Press stylebook and briefing on media law 808
The Chicago manual of style 808
Fleming, R. The African American writer's handbook
808
Gibaldi, J. MLA style manual and guide to scholarly publishing 808
The New York Public Library writer's guide to style and usage 808
Siegal, A. The New York times manual of style and usage 808
United States. Government Printing Office. Style manual 808
The Writer's digest guide to good writing 808
The Writer's handbook 808
The Writer's market 808
Internet resources
Rose, M. J. How to publish and promote online
070.5
Autism
Attwood, T. Asperger's syndrome 616.89
Bashe, P. R. The oasis guide to asperger syndrome
618.92
Children with autism 618.92

Cohen, S. Targeting autism 618.92
Frith, U. Autism: explaining the enigma 618.92
Harris, S. L. Siblings of children with autism 649
Hewetson, A. The stolen child 616.89
Ives, M. Caring for a child with autism 618.92
Jackson, L. Freaks, geeks and asperger syndrome
618.92
Karasik, J. The ride together 618.92
Ozonoff, S. A parent's guide to asperger syndrome and high-functioning autism 618.92
Park, C. C. Exiting nirvana 616.89
Richman, S. Raising a child with autism 618.92
Seroussi, K. Unraveling the mystery of autism and pervasive developmental disorder 618.92
Siegel, B. Helping children with autism learn
371.9
Waltz, M. Autistic spectrum disorders 618.92
Wing, L. The autistic spectrum 618.92
The **autistic** spectrum. Wing, L. 618.92
Autistic spectrum disorders. Waltz, M. 618.92
Auto repair manual, Chilton's 629.28
Autobiographies. Douglass, F. 92
Autobiography
Conway, J. K. When memory speaks 808
Holroyd, M. Works on paper 809
The Norton book of American autobiography 920
Bibliography
Adamson, L. G. Notable women in American history
920.003
Technique
See Biography as a literary form
Autobiography. Mill, J. S. 92
Autobiography as a literary form *See* Biography as a literary form
The **autobiography** of Alice B. Toklas. Stein, G.
92
also in Stein, G. Selected writings p1-237 818
also in Stein, G. Writings, 1903-1932 818
The **autobiography** of Benjamin Franklin. Franklin, B.
92
also in Franklin, B. Writings 818
The **autobiography** of Lincoln Steffens. Steffens, L.
92
The **autobiography** of Malcolm X. Malcolm X 92
The **autobiography** of Mark Twain. Twain, M. 92
The **autobiography** of Martin Luther King, Jr. King, M. L. 92
Autobiography of red. Carson, A. 811
The **autobiography** of Thomas Jefferson. Jefferson, T.
In Jefferson, T. The life and selected writings of Thomas Jefferson p3-104 818
In Jefferson, T. Writings 818
Autographs
Prices
American book prices current 018
Automata *See* Robots
Automobile industry
Bradsher, K. High and mighty 629.2
Brinkley, D. Wheels for the world 338.7
See/See also pages in the following book(s):
Baldwin, N. Henry Ford and the Jews 92
Boorstin, D. J. The Americans: The democratic experience 973
Automobile racing
Menzer, J. The wildest ride 796.72
Rich, R. My life in the pits 796.72
Wright, J. D. Fixin' to git 796.72
Automobiles
See also Sport utility vehicles
Standard guide to American muscle cars 629.222
Encyclopedias
The Beaulieu encyclopedia of the automobile
629.222

Automobiles—*Continued*

History

Kimes, B. R. Standard catalog of American cars, 1805-1942   **629.222**

Maintenance and repair

Chilton's auto repair manual   **629.28**

Kachur, B. Every woman's quick & easy car care   **629.28**

Volpe, R. The lady mechanic's total car care for the clueless   **629.28**

Automobiles, Foreign *See* Foreign automobiles

Maintenance and repair

See Foreign automobiles—Maintenance and repair

AV market place   **371.3025**

Avakian, Monique

Atlas of Asian-American history   **305.8**

Ava's man [Bundrum, Charlie] Bragg, R.   **92**

The **avengers**. Cohen, R.   **940.53**

Aveni, Anthony F.

Empires of time   **529**

Avery, Byllye Y.

See/See also pages in the following book(s):

Russell, D. Black genius and the American experience   **920**

Avery, Kevin J.

American drawings and watercolors in the Metropolitan Museum of Art v1   **759.13**

Avery-Peck, Alan J. (Alan Jeffery), 1953-

The Encyclopedia of Judaism. See The Encyclopedia of Judaism [Continuum]   **296.03**

Aviation *See* Aeronautics

Aviators *See* Air pilots

Avise, John C.

Genetics in the wild   **591.3**

Awakening the mind. Wise, A.   **615.8**

Awards

Awards, honors, & prizes   **001.4**

Kohn, A. Punished by rewards   **153.8**

Awards, honors, & prizes   **001.4**

Awee

About

Nasdijj. The boy and the dog are sleeping   **92**

Axelrod, Alan, 1952-

(ed) Van Nostrand's concise encyclopedia of science. See Van Nostrand's concise encyclopedia of science   **503**

Ay, Cuba!. Codrescu, A.   **972.91**

Ayçoberry, Pierre

The social history of the Third Reich   **943.086**

Aycock, Wendell M.

(jt. auth) Walker, W. S. Twentieth century short story explication: new series   **016.8093**

Ayer directory of publications. See Gale directory of publications and broadcast media   **070.025**

Ayral-Clause, Odile

Camille Claudel   **92**

Ayto, John

An A-Z of food and drink   **641.03**

(comp) The Oxford dictionary of slang. See The Oxford dictionary of slang   **427**

Azarian, Mary

See/See also pages in the following book(s): '

The Newbery & Caldecott medal books, 1986-2000 p306-16   **028.5**

The **Aztec** treasure house. Connell, E. S.   **814**

Aztecs

Prescott, W. H. History of the conquest of Mexico   **972**

Smith, M. E. The Aztecs   **972**

Townsend, R. F. The Aztecs   **972**

See/See also pages in the following book(s):

Ceram, C. W. Gods, graves, and scholars p323-47   **930.1**

Religion

Miller, M. E. The gods and symbols of ancient Mexico and the Maya   **299**

B

B-24 bomber

Ambrose, S. E. The wild blue   **940.54**

Baalsrud, Jan

About

Howarth, D. A. We die alone   **940.54**

Baars, Bernard J.

In the theater of consciousness   **153**

Babel, Tower of

See/See also pages in the following book(s):

Ceram, C. W. Gods, graves, and scholars p279-96   **930.1**

Babies *See* Infants

Baboons

Sapolsky, R. M. A primate's memoir   **599.8**

Baby and child. See Leach, P. Your baby & child   **649**

The **Baby** book   **649**

The **baby** boomer body book. Peck, B.   **613**

Baby care *See* Infants—Care

Baby catcher. Vincent, P.   **618.2**

The **Bacchants.** Euripides

In Euripides. Ten plays p281-312   **882**

Bach, Johann Sebastian, 1685-1750

About

Wolff, C. Johann Sebastian Bach   **92**

See/See also pages in the following book(s):

Grout, D. J. A history of Western music   **780.9**

Bach, Steven

Dazzler: the life and times of Moss Hart   **92**

Bach family

See/See also pages in the following book(s):

Schonberg, H. C. The great pianists   **920**

Bachman, Richard *See* King, Stephen, 1947-

Back then. Bernays, A.   **92**

Backgrounds to English literature   **820.9**

Backpacking

Randall, G. The Outward Bound backpacker's handbook   **796.51**

The **backyard** astronomer's guide. Dickinson, T.   **522**

The **backyard** bird feeder's bible. Roth, S.   **598**

Bacon, Francis, 1561-1626

See/See also pages in the following book(s):

Durant, W. J. The story of philosophy p75-112   **109**

Bacon, Tony

The ultimate guitar book   **787.87**

Bacteria

Bakalar, N. Where the germs are   **616**

Bacteriology

See also Germ theory of disease

See/See also pages in the following book(s):

Friedman, M. Medicine's 10 greatest discoveries   **610.9**

The **bad** & the beautiful. Kashner, S.   **791.43**

Bad astronomy. Plait, P. C.   **520**

Bad blood. Sage, L.   **92**

Bad boy Ballmer. Maxwell, F. A.   **92**

Bad elements. Buruma, I.   **951.05**

Bad land. Raban, J.   **978**

Bader, Michael J.

Arousal, the secret logic of sexual fantasies   **306.7**

Badge of courage: the life of Stephen Crane. Davis, L. H.   **92**

Badger, David

Snakes   **597.9**

Baedeker guides   **910.2**

Bagemihl, Bruce
Biological exuberance   591.56
Baghdad without a map, and other misadventures in Arabia. Horwitz, T.   915.6
Bahn, Paul G.
The Cambridge illustrated history of prehistoric art   709.01
Baiev, Khassan
The Oath   947.5
Baigrie, Brian S. (Brian Scott)
(ed) History of modern science and mathematics. See History of modern science and mathematics   509
Bailey, Anthony
Vermeer   92
Bailey, Beth L., 1957-
(ed) The Columbia guide to America in the 1960s. See The Columbia guide to America in the 1960s   973.92
Bailey, Colin B., 1955-
Renoir's portraits   759.4
Bailey, Covert
Smart exercise   613.7
Bailey, Ethel Zoe
(comp) Hortus third. See Hortus third   635
Bailey, Jill
(ed) The Facts on File dictionary of botany. See The Facts on File dictionary of botany   580
Bailey, Liberty Hyde, 1820-1912
(comp) Hortus third. See Hortus third   635
Bailey, Martha J., 1929-
American women in science: 1950 to the present   920.003
Bailey, Rebecca Anne, 1952-
Easy to love, difficult to discipline   649
Bailey Hortorium See Cornell University. Bailey Hortorium
Bailyn, Bernard
The peopling of British North America   973.2
Bain, David Haward
Empire express   385
Bainton, Roland Herbert, 1894-1984
Here I stand: a life of Martin Luther   92
Baiocchi, Regina A. Harris, 1956-
See/See also pages in the following book(s):
Walker-Hill, H. From spirituals to symphonies   920
Bair, Deirdre
Simone de Beauvoir   92
Bakalar, Nick
Where the germs are   616
Baker, Beth A., 1964-
(ed) Holidays and anniversaries of the world. See Holidays and anniversaries of the world   394.26
Baker, Carlos, 1909-1987
Hemingway: the writer as artist   813.009
Baker, Chet
About
Gavin, J. Deep in a dream: the long night of Chet Baker   92
Baker, Daniel B.
(ed) Explorers and discoverers of the world. See Explorers and discoverers of the world   920.003
Baker, Florence von Sass, 1841-1916
See/See also pages in the following book(s):
Slung, M. B. Living with cannibals and other women's adventures   910.4
Baker, Jean H.
Mary Todd Lincoln   92
The Stevensons   920
Baker, Kevin, 1958-
(jt. auth) Evans, H. The American century   973.9
Baker, Nicholson
Double fold   025.2
The size of thoughts   814

Baker, Russell, 1925-
Growing up   92
(ed) The Norton book of light verse. See The Norton book of light verse   821.008
(ed) Russell Baker's book of American humor. See Russell Baker's book of American humor   817.008
Baker, Theodore, 1851-1934
Baker's biographical dictionary of musicians. See Baker's biographical dictionary of musicians   920.003
Baker's biographical dictionary of twentieth-century classical musicians. See Baker's biographical dictionary of twentieth-century classical musicians   920.003
Baker, Vernon, 1919-
See/See also pages in the following book(s):
Mikaelian, A. Medal of honor   920
Baker's biographical dictionary of musicians   920.003
Baker's biographical dictionary of popular musicians since 1990   920.003
Baker's biographical dictionary of twentieth-century classical musicians   920.003
Baker's dictionary of music. Slonimsky, N.   780.3
Baker's dictionary of opera   792.5
Bakich, Michael E.
The Cambridge guide to the constellations   523.8
The Cambridge planetary handbook   523.4
Baking
See also Bread; Cake
Beranbaum, R. L. The pie and pastry bible   641.8
Cunningham, M. The Fannie Farmer baking book   641.8
Greenspan, D. Baking with Julia   641.8
Malgieri, N. How to bake   641.8
Nathan, J. The Jewish holiday baker   641.8
Patent, G. Baking in America   641.8
Walter, C. Great pies & tarts   641.8
Baking in America. Patent, G.   641.8
Baking with Julia. Greenspan, D.   641.8
Bakker, Rosemary
Elderdesign   728
Bakos, Susan Crain
(jt. auth) Block, J. D. Sex over 50   613.9
Balaban, Naomi E.
(ed) The Handy science answer book. See The Handy science answer book   500
Balance of power
Kennedy, P. M. The rise and fall of the great powers   909.08
Balanchine, George, 1904-1983
See/See also pages in the following book(s):
Volkov, S. St. Petersburg   947
Balay, Robert
(ed) Guide to reference books. See Guide to reference books   011
The **balcony**. Genet, J.
In Nine plays of the modern theater p293-394   808.82
Bald eagle
Beans, B. E. Eagle's plume   598
Baldick, Chris
The concise Oxford dictionary of literary terms   803
Baldrige, Letitia
A lady, first   92
Letitia Baldrige's more than manners!   649
Letitia Baldrige's new complete guide to executive manners   395
Letitia Baldrige's new manners for new times   395
Baldwin, James, 1924-1987
Collected essays   814

Baldwin, James, 1924-1987—*Continued*
  See/See also pages in the following book(s):
  Gates, H. L. Thirteen ways of looking at a black man
      920
  Russell, D. Black genius and the American experience
      920
Baldwin, Jan
  (jt. auth) Stow, J. The African kitchen   641.5
Baldwin, Neil, 1947-
  Henry Ford and the Jews   92
Balkan ghosts. Kaplan, R. D.   949.6
Balkan Peninsula
History
  Glenny, M. The Balkans   949.6
  Kaplan, R. D. Balkan ghosts   949.6
  Mazower, M. The Balkans: a short history   949.6
  The **Balkans**. Glenny, M.   949.6
  The **Balkans**: a short history. Mazower, M.   949.6
Ball, Edward, 1959-
  Slaves in the family   975.7
  The sweet hell inside   920
Ball, George W.
  See/See also pages in the following book(s):
  Galbraith, J. K. Name-dropping   973.9
Ball, Howard, 1937-
  A defiant life: Thurgood Marshall and the persistence
      of racism in America   92
Ball, Liz
  Step-by-step yard & garden basics. See Step-by-step
      yard & garden basics   635
Ball, Philip, 1962-
  Bright earth   701
  Life's matrix   553.7
  Stories of the invisible   541.2
Ball family
About
  Ball, E. Slaves in the family   975.7
  Ball four. Bouton, J.   796.357
Ballard, Robert D.
  The discovery of the Titanic   910.4
  The eternal darkness   551.46
  Return to Midway   940.54
Ballet
  De Vonyar, J. Degas and the dance   759.4
  Reynolds, N. No fixed points   792.8
Dictionaries
  International dictionary of ballet   792.8
Encyclopedias
  International encyclopedia of dance   792.8
Ballmer, Steven
About
  Maxwell, F. A. Bad boy Ballmer   92
Balloons, Dirigible *See* Airships
Balmer, Randall Herbert
  Religion in twentieth century America   200.9
  (jt. auth) Butler, J. Religion in American life
      200.9
Balter, Lawrence
  (ed) Parenthood in America. See Parenthood in Ameri-
      ca   306.8
Baltsan, Hayim
  Webster's New World Hebrew dictionary   492.4
Balzac, Honoré de, 1799-1850
About
  Robb, G. Balzac   92
Bambach, Carmen
  (ed) Leonardo, da Vinci. Leonardo da Vinci, master
      draftsman   741
Bambara, Toni Cade
  See/See also pages in the following book(s):
  Black women writers (1950-1980)   810.9
Bamford, Lawrence von, 1937-
  (ed) Small house designs. See Small house designs
      728

Ban Breathnach, Sarah
  A man's journey to simple abundance   158
Band of brothers. Ambrose, S. E.   940.54
Bandele, Asha
  The prisoner's wife   92
Banes, Helen
  Fiber & bead jewelry   745.59
Banes, Sally
  (jt. auth) Banes, H. Fiber & bead jewelry   745.59
Banham, Martin
  (ed) The Cambridge guide to theatre. See The Cam-
      bridge guide to theatre   792.03
Bankruptcy
  How to file for chapter 7 bankruptcy   346.07
Banks, Arthur S.
  (ed) Political handbook of the world. See Political
      handbook of the world   324.025
Banks and banking
Corrupt practices
  Ziegler, J. The Swiss, the gold, and the dead
      940.53
United States
  Greider, W. Secrets of the temple   332.1
Banned books *See* Books—Censorship
Banned in the U.S.A. Foerstel, H. N.   025.2
Banneker, Benjamin, 1731-1806
  See/See also pages in the following book(s):
  Russell, D. Black genius and the American experience
      920
Baptists
  See also Mennonites
Baraka, Amiri *See* Baraka, Imamu Amiri, 1934-
Baraka, Imamu Amiri, 1934-
  Dutchman
    In Baraka, I. A. Dutchman, and The slave p1-38
      812
    In Baraka, I. A. The LeRoi Jones/Amiri Baraka read-
      er   818
  Dutchman, and The slave   812
  The LeRoi Jones/Amiri Baraka reader   818
  Primitive world: an anti-nuclear jazz musical
    In Baraka, I. A. The LeRoi Jones/Amiri Baraka read-
      er   818
  The slave
    In Baraka, I. A. Dutchman, and The slave p39-88
      821
  What was the relationship of the Lone Ranger to the
      means of production
    In Baraka, I. A. The LeRoi Jones/Amiri Baraka read-
      er   818
Barash, David P.
  The myth of monogamy   306.7
Baratay, Eric, 1960-
  Zoo: a history of zoological gardens in the West
      590.73
Barbarians at the gate: the fall of RJR Nabisco.
      Burrough, B.   338.8
Barbary States *See* North Africa
Barbash, Thomas *See* Barbash, Tom
Barbash, Tom
  (jt. auth) Lutnick, H. On top of the world   332.6
Barbecue cooking
  Schlesinger, C. The thrill of the grill   641.7
Barbed wire
  Razac, O. Barbed wire   323.4
Barber, Nigel
  Encyclopedia of ethics in science and technology
      174
Barbour, Ian G.
  When science meets religion   291.1
Barbour, Julian B.
  The end of time   530.1
Barboza, Steven
  (ed) American jihad. See American jihad   297

Barcelona (Spain)
History
Hughes, R. Barcelona   946
Barclay, Donald A., 1958-
Managing public-access computers   025
Bardach, Ann Louise
Cuba confidential   972.91
Bardo thödol *See* Tibetan book of the dead
Bare bones children's services. Steele, A. T.
  027.62
Bare bones young adult services. Vaillancourt, R. J.
  027.62
Barefield, Eddie, 1909-1991
See/See also pages in the following book(s):
Dance, S. The world of Count Basie   920
Barefoot Contessa family style. Garten, I.   641.5
Barfield, Thomas
(ed) The Dictionary of anthropology. See The Dictionary of anthropology   306
Bargaining *See* Negotiation
Barkas, Janet L. *See* Yager, Jan
Barker, Juliet R. V.
(comp) The Brontës. See The Brontës   920
Barker, Rodney, 1946-
And the waters turned to blood   615.9
Barker, Teresa
(jt. auth) Deak, J. Girls will be girls   649
Barkley, Charles
I may be wrong but I doubt it   92
Barkley, Russell A., 1949-
Taking charge of ADHD   618.92
Barkus, Philip
Comprehensive postal exam   383
Barlow, Connie C.
Green space, green time   291.1
Barlow, Judith E.
(ed) Plays by American women, 1900-1930. See Plays by American women, 1900-1930   812.008
Barlow, Maude
Blue gold: the fight to stop the corporate theft of the world's water   333.91
Barlow, Philip L.
(jt. auth) Gaustad, E. S. New historical atlas of religion in America   200.9
The **barmaid's** brain and other strange tales from science. Ingram, J.   500
Barnavi, Eli
(ed) A Historical atlas of the Jewish people. See A Historical atlas of the Jewish people   909
Barnes, Christine
Color   746.46
Barnes, Djuna, 1892-1982
See/See also pages in the following book(s):
American women fiction writers   813.009
Barnes, Julian
Something to declare   824
Barnes, Myra Edwards
(jt. auth) Bushart, H. L. Soldiers of God   322.4
Barnes, Robert D.
Invertebrate zoology   592
Barnet, Ann B.
The youngest minds   155.4
Barnet, Richard J.
(jt. auth) Barnet, A. B. The youngest minds
  155.4
Barnett, Jo Ellen
Time's pendulum   529
Barnett, Paul, 1949-
See also Grant, John, 1949-
Barnhart, David K.
America in so many words   422
Barnhart, Robert K.
(ed) The Barnhart dictionary of etymology. See The Barnhart dictionary of etymology   422.03
The **Barnhart** dictionary of etymology   422.03

Barnitz, Jacqueline
Twentieth-century art of Latin America   709
Barnouw, David
(ed) Frank, A. The diary of Anne Frank: the critical edition   92
Barnum, P. T. (Phineas Taylor), 1810-1891
About
Saxon, A. H. P.T. Barnum: the legend and the man
  92
Barnum, Phineas Taylor *See* Barnum, P. T. (Phineas Taylor), 1810-1891
Barone, Michael
The almanac of American politics   328.73
Baroque art
Careri, G. Baroques   709
Wittkower, R. Art and architecture in Italy, 1600-1750
  709.45
Baroudi, Carol
(jt. auth) Levine, J. R. The Internet for dummies
  004.6
Barr, Roseanne
See/See also pages in the following book(s):
Life stories   920
Barr, Stephen M., 1953-
Modern physics and ancient faith   291.1
Barra, Allen
Clearing the bases   796.357
Inventing Wyatt Earp   92
Barraclough, Geoffrey, 1908-1984
(ed) Hammond atlas of world history. See Hammond atlas of world history   911
Barreca, Regina
(ed) The Penguin book of women's humor. See The Penguin book of women's humor   817.008
Barrenechea, Teresa, 1956-
The Basque table   641.5
Barrett, David B.
(ed) World Christian encyclopedia. See World Christian encyclopedia   230.003
Barrett, Sara J. Berman- *See* Berman-Barrett, Sara J., 1964-
Barrett, William, 1913-1992
Irrational man   142
The **Barretts** of Wimpole Street. Besier, R.   822
Barrie, J. M. (James Matthew), 1860-1937
See/See also pages in the following book(s):
Wullschläger, J. Inventing wonderland   820.9
Barrie, James Matthew *See* Barrie, J. M. (James Matthew), 1860-1937
Barrier, J. Michael
Hollywood cartoons   791.43
Barringer, T. J. (Tim J.)
(jt. auth) Wilton, A. American sublime   759.13
Barringer, Tim J. *See* Barringer, T. J. (Tim J.)
Barron, Neil, 1934-
What do I read next? See What do I read next?
  016.8
(ed) Fantasy and horror. See Fantasy and horror
  016.8
Barron's finance & investment handbook. Downes, J.
  332.6
Barron's guide to law schools   378.73
Barron's guide to medical & dental schools. Wischnitzer, S.   610.69
Barron's how to prepare for the American College Testing Program (ACT). See How to prepare for the ACT, American College Testing Assessment Program   378.1
Barron's how to prepare for the ASVAB Armed Forces test. See How to prepare for the Armed Forces test—ASVAB   355
Barron's profiles of American colleges   378.73
Barron's SAT I. See How to prepare for SAT I
  378.1

Barrow, John D., 1952-
The book of nothing   111
The origin of the universe   523.1
Barry, Dave
Dave Barry does Japan   817
Dave Barry hits below the Beltway   817
Dave Barry in cyberspace   817
Dave Barry is from Mars and Venus   817
Dave Barry is not making this up   817
Dave Barry is not taking this sitting down!   817
Dave Barry talks back   817
Dave Barry turns 40   817
Dave Barry turns 50   817
Dave Barry's complete guide to guys   817
Dave Barry's greatest hits   817
Dave Barry's only travel guide you'll ever need   817
Barry, John M.
Rising tide   977
Barry, Marion, 1936-
See/See also pages in the following book(s):
Halberstam, D. The children   323.1
Barth, Karl, 1787-1853
See/See also pages in the following book(s):
Küng, H. Great Christian thinkers p185-212   230
Barthel, Joan
(jt. auth) Clooney, R. Girl singer   92
Barthelme, Frederick
Double down   92
Barthelme, Steve
(jt. auth) Barthelme, F. Double down   92
Barthes, Roland
See/See also pages in the following book(s):
Sontag, S. Where the stress falls   814
Bartholet, Elizabeth
Nobody's children   362.7
Bartle, Lisa R.
(jt. auth) Burgess, M. Reference guide to science fiction, fantasy, and horror   016.8
Bartlett, Apple Parish
Sister: the life of legendary American interior decorator Mrs. Henry Parish II   92
Bartlett, John, 1820-1905
Familiar quotations   808.88
Bartlett's Roget's thesaurus   423
Bartoli, Cecilia, 1966-
About
Chernin, K. Cecilia Bartoli   92
Barton, Clara, 1821-1912
About
Oates, S. B. A woman of valor: Clara Barton and the Civil War   92
Barton, John, 1948-
(ed) Oxford Bible commentary. See Oxford Bible commentary   220.7
Baryshnikov, Mikhail, 1948-
See/See also pages in the following book(s):
Life stories   920
Barzini, Luigi Giorgio, 1908-1984
The Italians   945
Barzun, Jacques, 1907-
Begin here   371.1
From dawn to decadence   940.2
The use and abuse of art   701
Basbanes, Nicholas A., 1943-
Patience & fortitude   002
Bascom, Lionel C.
(ed) A Renaissance in Harlem. See A Renaissance in Harlem   810.8
Baseball
Angell, R. Game time: a baseball companion   796.357
Angell, R. Once more around the park   796.357
Barra, A. Clearing the bases   796.357
Baseball: a literary anthology   810.8

Bouton, J. Ball four   796.357
Bryant, H. Shut out   796.357
Costas, B. Fair ball   796.357
Geist, B. Little League confidential   796.357
Giamatti, A. B. A great and glorious game   796.357
Gould, S. J. Triumph and tragedy in Mudville   796.357
Joy in Mudville   796.357
Kahn, R. The boys of summer   796.357
Kahn, R. The head game   796.357
Kelly, J. Bushville   796.357
Lewis, M. Moneyball   796.357
Lupica, M. Summer of '98   796.357
McCarver, T. Tim McCarver's Baseball for brain surgeons and other fans   796.357
Smith, R. Red Smith on baseball   796.357
Tofel, R. J. A legend in the making   796.357
Tygiel, J. Baseball's great experiment   796.357
Ward, G. C. Baseball: an illustrated history   796.357
Will, G. F. Bunts: Curt Flood, Camden Yards, Pete Rose, and other reflections on baseball   796.357
Will, G. F. Men at work: the craft of baseball   796.357
Biography
Halberstam, D. The teammates   920
McDermott, M. A funny thing happened on the way to Cooperstown   92
Ritter, L. S. The glory of their times   920
Encyclopedias
Light, J. F. The cultural encyclopedia of baseball   796.357
Statistics
Baseball register   796.357
Neft, D. S. The sports encyclopedia: baseball   796.357
Baseball: a literary anthology   810.8
Baseball for brain surgeons and other fans, Tim McCarver's. McCarver, T.   796.357
Baseball register   796.357
Baseball's great experiment. Tygiel, J.   796.357
The **basement**. Pinter, H.
In Pinter, H. Complete works v3   822
Basham, Arthur Llewellyn
The origins and development of classical Hinduism   294.5
Bashe, Patricia Romanowski
The oasis guide to asperger syndrome   618.92
Bashe, Philip
(jt. auth) McFarlane, R. The complete bedside companion   649.8
(jt. auth) Teeley, P. The complete cancer survival guide   616.99
The **basic** book of photography. Grimm, T.   770.2
Basic book repair methods. Schechter, A. A.   025.7
Basic economics. Sowell, T.   330
Basic electronics. Grob, B.   621.381
Basic Japanese-English dictionary   495.6
Basic life skills *See* Life skills
Basic rights *See* Civil rights; Human rights
The **basic** works of Aristotle. Aristotle   888
Basic writings. Heidegger, M.   193
The **basic** writings of C. G. Jung. Jung, C. G.   150.19
Basic writings of Kant. Kant, I.   193
Basic writings of Nietzsche. Nietzsche, F. W.   193
The **basic** writings of Sigmund Freud. Freud, S.   150.19
Basie, Count, 1904-1984
Good morning blues: the autobiography of Count Basie   92
About
Dance, S. The world of Count Basie   920

Basie, Count, 1904-1984—About—*Continued*
  See/See also pages in the following book(s):
  Feather, L. From Satchmo to Miles   **920**
Basie, William *See* Basie, Count, 1904-1984
Basil Street blues. Holroyd, M.   **92**
Basketball
  Blais, M. In these girls, hope is a muscle
    796.323
  Bradley, B. Values of the game   **796.323**
  Feinstein, J. A march to madness   **796.323**
  Kent, R. G. Inside women's college basketball
    796.323
  The Official NBA encyclopedia   **796.323**
  Wolff, A. Big game, small world   **796.323**
  See/See also pages in the following book(s):
  Knight, B. Knight: my story   **92**
Basketwork
  Sentance, B. Art of the basket   **746.41**
Baskin, Yvonne
  A plague of rats and rubbervines   **577**
Basque cooking
  Barrenechea, T. The Basque table   **641.5**
The **Basque** history of the world. Kurlansky, M.
    946
Basque Provinces (France and Spain)
  Kurlansky, M. The Basque history of the world
    946
The **Basque** table. Barrenechea, T.   **641.5**
Bass, Ellen
  The courage to heal   **362.83**
Bastianich, Lidia
  Lidia's Italian-American kitchen   **641.5**
  Lidia's Italian table   **641.5**
Batavia (Ship)
  Dash, M. Batavia's graveyard   **910.4**
Batavia's graveyard. Dash, M.   **910.4**
Batcheller, Robert
  (jt. auth) Thomas, L. Homebuilding pitfalls   **690**
Batchelor, Mary
  (ed) The Doubleday prayer collection. See The
    Doubleday prayer collection   **242**
Bate, Jonathan
  John Clare: a biography   **92**
Bathsheba's breast. Olson, J. S.   **616.99**
Bathurst, Bella
  The lighthouse Stevensons   **623.89**
Batson, Raymond M.
  (jt. auth) Greeley, R. The compact NASA atlas of the
    solar system   **523.2**
Batstone, David B., 1958-
  Saving the corporate soul & (who knows?) maybe your
    own   **658.4**
Battered children *See* Child abuse
The **batterer**. Dutton, D. G.   **362.82**
Battering of wives *See* Wife abuse
The **Battle**. See Overy, R. J. The Battle of Britain
    940.54
Battle at Bull Run. Davis, W. C.   **973.7**
Battle cries and lullabies. De Pauw, L. G.   **355**
Battle cry of freedom. McPherson, J. M.   **973.7**
The **battle** for God. Armstrong, K.   **291**
Battle of Britain, 1940 *See* Britain, Battle of, 1940
The **Battle** of Britain. Overy, R. J.   **940.54**
The **Battle** of New Orleans. Remini, R. V.   **973.5**
Battle of Stalingrad *See* Stalingrad, Battle of, 1942-
  1943
Battle of the Bulge *See* Ardennes, Battle of the, 1944-
  1945
The **Battle** of the Little Bighorn. Sandoz, M.   **973.8**
Battle of Waterloo *See* Waterloo, Battle of, 1815
Battle of wits. Budiansky, S.   **940.54**
Battles
  Davis, P. K. 100 decisive battles   **904**
  Hanson, V. D. Carnage and culture   **904**

  Purcell, L. E. Encyclopedia of battles in North Ameri-
    ca, 1517 to 1916   **970**
Battleships *See* Warships
Ba'u, Yosef, 1920-
  Dear God, have you ever gone hungry?   **940.53**
Baudelaire, Charles, 1821-1867
  Les fleurs du mal   **841**
  The flowers of evil   **841**
  Poems   **841**
Bauer, Gerhard, 1940-
  New soccer techniques, tactics & teamwork
    796.334
Bauhaus
  Gropius, W. The new architecture and the Bauhaus
    724
Baum, L. Frank (Lyman Frank), 1856-1919
      About
  Rogers, K. M. L. Frank Baum, creator of Oz   **92**
  See/See also pages in the following book(s):
  Vidal, G. United States—essays, 1952-1992 p1094-
    1119   **814**
Baum, Lyman Frank *See* Baum, L. Frank (Lyman
  Frank), 1856-1919
Baumann, Martin
  (ed) Religions of the world. See Religions of the world
    291
Baumfree, Isabella *See* Truth, Sojourner, d. 1883
Bawer, Bruce, 1956-
  Stealing Jesus   **277.3**
Bawlf, R. Samuel
  The secret voyage of Sir Francis Drake, 1577-1580
    910.4
Baxandall, Rosalyn Fraad, 1939-
  (ed) America's working women. See America's work-
    ing women   **331.4**
Baxter, Angus, 1912-
  In search of your European roots   **929**
Bayless, Deann Groen
  (jt. auth) Bayless, R. Rick Bayless's Mexican kitchen
    641.5
Bayless, Rick
  Rick Bayless's Mexican kitchen   **641.5**
Bayley, Iris *See* Murdoch, Iris
Bayley, John, 1925-
  Elegy for Iris   **92**
  Iris and her friends   **92**
Baym, Nina
  (ed) The Norton anthology of American literature. See
    The Norton anthology of American literature
    810.8
Be sweet. Blount, R.   **92**
Beach, Hugh
  A year in Lapland   **948.97**
Beacham, Walton, 1943-
  (ed) Beacham's guide to the endangered species of
    North America. See Beacham's guide to the endan-
    gered species of North America   **578.68**
Beacham's encyclopedia of popular fiction   **809.3**
Beacham's guide to the endangered species of North
  America   **578.68**
Beaches
  Dean, C. Against the tide   **333.91**
The **Beacon** book of essays by contemporary American
  women   **814**
Beaconsfield, Benjamin Disraeli, Earl of *See* Disraeli,
  Benjamin, Earl of Beaconsfield, 1804-1881
Beading for the first time. Benson, A.   **745.58**
Beads. Coles, J.   **745.58**
Beadwork
  Banes, H. Fiber & bead jewelry   **745.59**
  Benson, A. Beading for the first time   **745.58**
  Coles, J. Beads   **745.58**
  Wells, C. W. The art & elegance of beadweaving
    745.58

Beagle Expedition (1831-1836)
Darwin, C. The voyage of the Beagle 508
Keynes, R. D. Fossils, finches, and Fuegians 508
The **beak** of the finch. Weiner, J. 598
Beal, Anne C.
The black parenting book 649
Beall, Julianne, 1946-
(ed) Dewey, M. Dewey decimal classification and relative index 025.4
Beane, Billy, 1962-
About
Lewis, M. Moneyball 796.357
Beans, Bruce E.
Eagle's plume 598
The **bear.** Chekhov, A. P.
In Chekhov, A. P. The plays of Anton Chekhov p19-33 891.7
Beard, James, 1903-1985
The armchair James Beard 641.5
Beard on bread 641.8
James Beard's American cookery 641.5
Beard, Jocelyn
(ed) The Best men's stage monologues of [date] See The Best men's stage monologues of [date] 808.82
(ed) The Best stage scenes of [year] See The Best stage scenes of [year] 808.82
(ed) The Best women's stage monologues of [date] See The Best women's stage monologues of [date] 808.82
(ed) The Ultimate audition book. See The Ultimate audition book 808.82
Beard, Ray O.
(ed) Day, C. L. The art of knotting & splicing 623.88
Beard on bread. Beard, J. 641.8
Bearden, Romare, 1914-1988
See/See also pages in the following book(s):
Ellison, R. Going to the territory p227-38 818
Russell, D. Black genius and the American experience 920
Beardslee, William R.
Out of the darkened room 616.85
Bears
See also Grizzly bear; Polar bear
Craighead, L. Bears of the world 599.78
Montgomery, S. Search for the golden moon bear 599.78
Schooler, L. The blue bear 599.78
Bears of the world. Craighead, L. 599.78
Beaser, Richard S.
The Joslin guide to diabetes 616.4
Beasley, Henry R., 1929-
(ed) The Eleanor Roosevelt encyclopedia. See The Eleanor Roosevelt encyclopedia 92
Beasley, Maurine Hoffman
(ed) The Eleanor Roosevelt encyclopedia. See The Eleanor Roosevelt encyclopedia 92
Beasley, Ruth
(jt. auth) Reinisch, J. The Kinsey Institute new report on sex 306.7
Beasley, W. G. (William G.), 1919-
The rise of modern Japan 952
Beasley, William G. See Beasley, W. G. (William G.), 1919-
The **Beat** Hotel. Miles, B. 810.9
Beatles
The Beatles anthology 781.66
The **Beatles** anthology 781.66
Beattie, Melody
Beyond codependency 616.86
Codependents' guide to the twelve steps 616.86
Beatty, Michael A., 1935-
County name origins of the United States 917.3

Beatty, Richard H., 1939-
175 high-impact cover letters 650.14
The interview kit 650.14
Beauchamp, Cari
Without lying down 92
The **Beaulieu** encyclopedia of the automobile 629.222
Beautiful child. Hayden, T. L. 371.9
Beauty, Personal See Personal grooming
The **beauty** myth. Wolf, N. 305.4
The **beauty** of the husband. Carson, A. 811
Beauty: the new basics. Berg, R. 646.7
Beauvoir, Simone de, 1908-1986
The second sex 305.4
A transatlantic love affair: letters to Nelson Algren 92
About
Bair, D. Simone de Beauvoir 92
See/See also pages in the following book(s):
Women writers at work p138-56 808
The **beaux'** stratagem. Farquhar, G.
In Restoration plays 822.008
Becher, Anne
Biodiversity 333.95
Beck, Simone
(jt. auth) Child, J. Mastering the art of French cooking 641.5
Beck, Warren A.
Historical atlas of the American West 911
Becker, Carl, 1873-1945
The Declaration of Independence 973.3
Becker, Charlotte B., 1944-
(ed) Encyclopedia of ethics. See Encyclopedia of ethics [Routledge] 170
Becker, Jasper
The Chinese 951.05
Becker, Lawrence C.
(ed) Encyclopedia of ethics. See Encyclopedia of ethics [Routledge] 170
Becker, Marion Rombauer, 1903-1976
(jt. auth) Rombauer, I. von S. Joy of cooking 641.5
Becker, Norman
The complete book of home inspection 643
Becker, Patricia C.
(ed) A Statistical portrait of the United States. See A Statistical portrait of the United States 317.3
Beckett, Kenneth A.
Gardening basics. See Gardening basics 635
Beckett, Samuel, 1906-1989
Collected poems in English and French 841
Ends and Odds 842
Footfalls
In Beckett, S. Ends and Odds p39-49 842
Ghost trio
In Beckett, S. Ends and Odds p51-65 842
Not I
In Beckett, S. Ends and Odds p11-23 842
Radio I
In Beckett, S. Ends and Odds p103-12 842
Radio II
In Beckett, S. Ends and Odds p113-28 842
That time
In Beckett, S. Ends and Odds p25-37 842
Theatre I
In Beckett, S. Ends and Odds p69-80 842
Theatre II
In Beckett, S. Ends and Odds p81-101 842
Waiting for Godot 842
also in Nine plays of the modern theater p115-97 808.82
About
Gordon, L. G. The world of Samuel Beckett, 1906-1946 92

Beckett, Samuel, 1906-1989—About—*Continued*
See/See also pages in the following book(s):
Bloom, H. The Western canon   **809**
Playwrights at work   **812.009**
Beckett, Wendy
Sister Wendy's 1000 masterpieces   **759**
Sister Wendy's American collection   **709**
The story of painting   **759**
Beckmann, Max, 1884-1950
Max Beckmann   **769**
Beckstrom, Robert J.
Ortho's home repair problem solver   **643**
Beckwith, Jon *See* Beckwith, Jonathan R., 1935-
Beckwith, Jonathan R., 1935-
Making genes, making waves   **92**
Becoming. Allport, G.   **155.2**
Becoming Mae West. Leider, E. W.   **92**
Becoming Mona Lisa. Sassoon, D.   **759.5**
Becoming Victoria. Vallone, L.   **92**
Bed & breakfast encyclopedia. Sakach, D.   **647.9**
Bed & breakfasts, country inns. Sakach, D.   **647.9**
A **bed** for the night. Rieff, D.   **361.2**
Bedard, Claire
(jt. auth) Garbarino, J. Parents under siege   **649**
Bédé, Jean Albert
(ed) Columbia dictionary of modern European litera-
ture. See Columbia dictionary of modern European
literature   **803**
Bednar, Nancy
The encyclopedia of sewing machine techniques
    646.2
Bedouins
Lawrence, T. E. Seven pillars of wisdom   **940.4**
Beebe, Reta F.
Jupiter   **523.4**
Been there, done that. Fisher, E.   **92**
Beer, Anna R., 1964-
My just desire   **92**
Beers, Mark H.
(ed) The Merck manual of medical information. See
The Merck manual of medical information
    616.02
Bees
Hubbell, S. A book of bees—and how to keep them
    638
Beethoven, Ludwig van, 1770-1827
About
Lockwood, L. Beethoven: the music and the life
    92
Rosen, C. The classical style   **780.9**
Solomon, M. Beethoven   **92**
See/See also pages in the following book(s):
Grout, D. J. A history of Western music   **780.9**
Schonberg, H. C. The great pianists   **920**
Beetles
Evans, A. V. An inordinate fondness for beetles
    595.7
Beetz, Kirk H., 1952-
(ed) Beacham's encyclopedia of popular fiction. See
Beacham's encyclopedia of popular fiction
    809.3
Beevor, Antony, 1946-
The fall of Berlin 1945   **940.54**
Stalingrad   **940.54**
Beezley, William H.
(ed) The Oxford history of Mexico. See The Oxford
history of Mexico   **972**
Before you hire a contractor. Gonzalez, S.   **690**
Beggars and choosers. Solinger, R.   **363.46**
The **beggar's** opera. Gay, J.   **822**
also in The Oxford anthology of English literature
v1   **820.8**
Begin here. Barzun, J.   **371.1**
Beginners' guide to herb gardening. Cuthbertson, Y.
    635

Beginner's guide to TV repair. See Davidson, H. L. TV
repair for beginners   **621.388**
Beginnings. Foote, H.   **92**
Begoun, Paula, 1953-
Don't go to the cosmetics counter without me
    646.7
Behaim family
About
Ozment, S. E. Flesh and spirit   **943**
Behan, Brendan, 1923-1964
The big house
In Behan, B. The complete plays   **822**
The complete plays   **822**
A garden party
In Behan, B. The complete plays   **822**
The guare fellow
In Behan, B. The complete plays   **822**
The hostage
In Behan, B. The complete plays   **822**
Moving out
In Behan, B. The complete plays   **822**
Richard's cork leg
In Behan, B. The complete plays   **822**
Behavior *See* Human behavior
Behavior, Compulsive *See* Compulsive behavior
Behavior, Sexual *See* Sexual behavior
Behavior genetics
Clark, W. R. Are we hardwired?   **155.7**
Hamer, D. H. Living with our genes   **155.2**
Weiner, J. Time, love, memory   **591.5**
Behaviorism
Kohn, A. Punished by rewards   **153.8**
Skinner, B. F. About behaviorism   **150.19**
Watson, J. B. Behaviorism   **150.19**
Behe, Michael J., 1952-
Darwin's black box   **576.8**
Behind the screen. Mann, W. J.   **791.43**
Behnke, Robert J.
Trout and salmon of North America   **597**
Behr, Edward, 1926-
Prohibition   **363.4**
Beier, Ulli
(ed) The Penguin book of modern African poetry. See
The Penguin book of modern African poetry
    896
Being a widow. Caine, L.   **306.8**
Being and nothingness. Sartre, J. P.   **142**
Being and time. Heidegger, M.   **111**
Being Jewish. Goldman, A. L.   **296.4**
Beisner, Robert L.
(ed) American foreign relations since 1600. See
American foreign relations since 1600   **016.327**
Bekoff, Marc
Minding animals   **591.5**
(ed) Encyclopedia of animal rights and animal welfare.
See Encyclopedia of animal rights and animal wel-
fare   **179**
(jt. auth) Goodall, J. The ten trusts   **333.95**
Belafonte, Harry
See/See also pages in the following book(s):
Gates, H. L. Thirteen ways of looking at a black man
    920
Belford, Barbara
Oscar Wilde   **92**
Belgium
Colonies
Hochschild, A. King Leopold's ghost   **967.5**
Religion
Harline, C. E. Miracles at the Jesus Oak   **231.7**
Belief and doubt
Shermer, M. Why people believe weird things
    001.9
See/See also pages in the following book(s):
Lewis, C. S. The world's last night, and other essays
p13-30   **230**

Belief beyond boundaries   **291.9**

Beliefs and blasphemies. Adair, V. H.   **811**

Beling, Stephanie

Powerfoods   **613.2**

Bell, Alexander Graham, 1847-1922

See/See also pages in the following book(s):

Lepore, J. A is for American   **306.44**

Bell, Catharine E.

(ed) Encyclopedia of the world's zoos. See Encyclopedia of the world's zoos   **590.73**

Bell, Clare

Hirschfeld's New York   **741.5**

Bell, Currer *See* Brontë, Charlotte, 1816-1855

Bell, Ellis *See* Brontë, Emily, 1818-1848

Bell, Eric Temple, 1883-1960

Men of mathematics   **920**

Bell, Gertrude Margaret Lowthian, 1868-1926

About

Wallach, J. Desert queen   **92**

Bella Tuscany. Mayes, F.   **945**

Bellamy, Charles L.

(jt. auth) Evans, A. V. An inordinate fondness for beetles   **595.7**

Bellamy, Edward, 1850-1898

Looking backward, 2000-1887; criticism

In Mumford, L. The story of utopias p159-69   **321**

Bellenir, Karen

(ed) Breast cancer sourcebook. See Breast cancer sourcebook   **616.99**

(ed) Cancer sourcebook. See Cancer sourcebook   **616.99**

(ed) Diet and nutrition sourcebook . . . See Diet and nutrition sourcebook . . .   **613.2**

(ed) Drug abuse sourcebook. See Drug abuse sourcebook   **362.29**

(ed) Substance abuse sourcebook. See Substance abuse sourcebook   **616.86**

Belli, Gioconda, 1948-

The country under my skin   **92**

Bellin, Andy, 1968-

Poker nation   **795.4**

Bellos, Alex

Futebol: the Brazilian way of life   **796.334**

Bellow, Saul

The adventures of Augie March; criticism

In Amis, M. The war against cliché   **824**

Conversations with Saul Bellow   **92**

About

Atlas, J. Bellow   **92**

See/See also pages in the following book(s):

Langer, L. L. Admitting the Holocaust p75-87   **940.53**

Belly dancing

Soffee, A. T. Snake hips   **793.3**

Belonging. Davis, D.   **821**

Ben-Gurion, David, 1886-1973

See/See also pages in the following book(s):

Cohen, E. A. Supreme command   **355**

Ben Jelloun, Tahar, 1944-

Islam explained   **297**

Ben Yijû, Abraham, 12th cent.

About

Ghosh, A. In an antique land   **962**

Benard, Cheryl, 1953-

Veiled courage   **958.1**

Benbow-Pfalzgraf, Taryn

(ed) Contemporary fashion. See Contemporary fashion   **391**

(ed) International dictionary of modern dance. See International dictionary of modern dance   **792.8**

Benchley, Peter

Shark trouble   **597**

Benecke, Mark

The dream of eternal life   **612.6**

Benedict, Ruth, 1887-1948

The chrysanthemum and the sword   **952**

Benet's reader's encyclopedia   **803**

Benet's reader's encyclopedia of American literature. See HarperCollins Reader's encyclopedia of American literature   **810.3**

Benjamin, Daniel, 1961-

The age of sacred terror   **303.6**

Benjamin, Joan

(ed) Great garden formulas. See Great garden formulas   **635**

Benjamin, Judah Philip, 1811-1884

About

Evans, E. N. Judah P. Benjamin, the Jewish Confederate   **92**

Benjamin, Paul *See* Auster, Paul, 1947-

Benjamin Franklin, politician. Jennings, F.   **92**

Benkei on the bridge. Hiyoshi, Y.

In Waley, A. The Nō plays of Japan   **895.6**

Bennett, James S.

The complete motorcycle book   **629.28**

Bennett, Jeff

The complete snowboarder   **796.9**

Bennett, Lerone, 1928-

What manner of man: a biography of Martin Luther King, Jr.   **92**

Bennett, William John, 1943-

The death of outrage: Bill Clinton and the assault on American ideals   **973.929**

Benson, Ann

Beading for the first time   **745.58**

Benson, Eugene, 1928-

(ed) The Oxford companion to Canadian literature. See The Oxford companion to Canadian literature   **810.3**

Benson, Jackson J.

Wallace Stegner   **92**

Benson, Michael

The encyclopedia of the JFK assassination   **973.922**

Benson, Sonia

(ed) The Hispanic American almanac. See The Hispanic American almanac   **305.8**

Bentley, Elizabeth Petty

Directory of family associations   **929**

The genealogist's address book   **929**

Bentley, Eric, 1916-

The life of the drama   **809.2**

Bentley, G. E. (Gerald Eades), 1930-

The stranger from paradise: a biography of William Blake   **92**

Bentley, Gerald Eades *See* Bentley, G. E. (Gerald Eades), 1930-

Bentley, P. J.

Digital biology   **570.1**

Benton, Charlotte

(ed) Art deco 1910-1939. See Art deco 1910-1939   **709.04**

Benton, Thomas Hart, 1782-1858

See/See also pages in the following book(s):

Kennedy, J. F. Profiles in courage   **920**

Benton, Tim

(ed) Art deco 1910-1939. See Art deco 1910-1939   **709.04**

Bentonville (N.C.), Battle of, 1865

See/See also pages in the following book(s):

Davis, B. Sherman's march p231-40   **973.7**

Benvie, Sam

The encyclopedia of North American trees   **582.16**

Benzer, Seymour, 1921-

About

Weiner, J. Time, love, memory   **591.5**

Beowulf

Beowulf   **829**

Beowulf—*Continued*

  also in The Oxford anthology of English literature
    v1   **820.8**

Beranbaum, Rose Levy
  The cake bible   **641.8**
  The pie and pastry bible   **641.8**

Berberova, Nina
  See/See also pages in the following book(s):
  Fraser, K. Ornament and silence   **814**

Bercovitch, Sacvan
  (ed) The Cambridge history of American literature. See
    The Cambridge history of American literature
     810.9

Bereavement
  Attig, T. The heart of grief   **155.9**
  Attig, T. How we grieve   **155.9**
  The Book of eulogies   **808.8**
  Edelman, H. Motherless daughters   **155.9**
  Emswiler, M. A. Guiding your child through grief
     155.9
  Finkbeiner, A. K. After the death of a child
     155.9
  Kohn, I. A silent sorrow   **618.3**
  Levy, A. The orphaned adult   **155.9**
  Levy, N. To begin again   **296.7**
  Remembrances and celebrations   **808.8**
  Sife, W. The loss of a pet   **155.9**

Berenbaum, Michael, 1945-
  The world must know   **940.53**
  (ed) The Holocaust and history. See The Holocaust and
    history   **940.53**

Berendt, John
  Midnight in the garden of good and evil   **975.8**

Berezovsky, Boris A.
    About
  Klebnikov, P. Godfather of the Kremlin   **92**

Berg, A. Scott (Andrew Scott)
  Kate remembered [a biography of Katharine Hepburn]
     92
  Lindbergh   **92**

Berg, Andrew Scott *See* Berg, A. Scott (Andrew Scott)

Berg, Paul, 1926-
  Dealing with genes   **576.5**

Berg, Rona
  Beauty: the new basics   **646.7**

Berg, Stephen
  (ed) The Body electric. See The Body electric
     811.008

Bergen, Peter L.
  Holy war, Inc.   **958.1**

Berger, Alan L., 1939-
  (ed) Encyclopedia of Holocaust literature. See Encyclo-
    pedia of Holocaust literature   **809**

Berger, John, 1926-
  Selected essays   **824**
  The shape of a pocket   **701**

Berger, Lisa
  (jt. auth) Goldman, B. Brain fitness   **153.1**

Berger, William, 1961-
  Verdi with a vengeance   **92**

Bergerac, Cyrano de *See* Cyrano de Bergerac, 1619-
  1655

Bergman, Ingmar, 1918-
  See/See also pages in the following book(s):
  Sontag, S. Styles of radical will p123-45   **814**

Bergman, Ingrid, 1915-1982
    About
  Spoto, D. Notorious: the life of Ingrid Bergman
     92

Bergman, Paul, 1943-
  Represent yourself in court   **347**

Bergreen, Laurence
  Capone   **92**

Bergson, Henri, 1859-1941
  See/See also pages in the following book(s):
  Durant, W. J. The story of philosophy p338-50
     109
  Russell, B. A history of Western philosophy p791-810
     109

Berihah (Organization)
  Szulc, T. The secret alliance   **325**

Berkeley, George, 1685-1753
  See/See also pages in the following book(s):
  Russell, B. A history of Western philosophy p647-59
     109

Berkin, Carol
  A brilliant solution   **342**
  Encyclopedia of American literature. See Encyclopedia
    of American literature   **810.3**

Berkow, Ira
  The minority quarterback, and other lives in sports
     796

Berley, Peter
  The modern vegetarian kitchen   **641.5**

Berlin, Edward A.
  King of ragtime: Scott Joplin and his era   **92**

Berlin, Ira, 1941-
  Many thousands gone   **326**

Berlin, Irving, 1888-1989
    About
  Furia, P. Irving Berlin   **92**
  Hamm, C. Irving Berlin   **92**
  See/See also pages in the following book(s):
  Green, S. The world of musical comedy   **920**

Berlin, Sir Isaiah
  The roots of romanticism   **141**
  The sense of reality   **901**

Berlin, Battle of, 1945
  Beevor, A. The fall of Berlin 1945   **940.54**
  Read, A. The fall of Berlin   **940.54**

Berlin (Germany)
  Darnton, R. Berlin journal, 1989-1990   **943.087**
  See/See also pages in the following book(s):
  Craig, G. A. The Germans p261-86   **943**
  Herrington, S. A. Traitors among us p1-62
     327.12

Berlin journal, 1989-1990. Darnton, R.   **943.087**

Berlin Wall (1961-1989)
  See/See also pages in the following book(s):
  Freedman, L. Kennedy's wars   **973.922**

Berlinski, David, 1942-
  The advent of the algorithm   **511**
  Newton's gift: how Sir Isaac Newton unlocked the sys-
    tem of the world   **92**
  A tour of the calculus   **515**

Berlioz, Hector, 1803-1869
    About
  Holoman, D. K. Berlioz   **92**

Berlioz, Louis Hector *See* Berlioz, Hector, 1803-1869

Berlo, Janet Catherine
  Native North American art   **709.01**

Berlow, Lawrence H., 1945-
  The reference guide to famous engineering landmarks
    of the world   **620**

Berman, Bob
  Secrets of the night sky   **520**

Berman, Larry
  No peace, no honor   **959.704**

Berman, Phillip L.
  (jt. auth) Goodall, J. Reason for hope   **92**

Berman-Barrett, Sara J., 1964-
  (jt. auth) Bergman, P. Represent yourself in court
     347

Bernadac, Marie-Laure
  (jt. auth) Léal, B. The ultimate Picasso   **92**

Bernadette, Saint, 1844-1879
    About
  Harris, R. Lourdes   **232.91**

Bernard, Jami
  Breast cancer, there and back   **616.99**
Bernays, Anne
  Back then   **92**
Bernhardt, Sarah, 1844-1923
  My double life: the memoirs of Sarah Bernhardt
        92
Bernier, Olivier
  The world in 1800   **909.81**
Bernoulli, Daniel, 1700-1782
  See/See also pages in the following book(s):
  Guillen, M. Five equations that changed the world
        530.1
Bernoulli family
  See/See also pages in the following book(s):
  Bell, E. T. Men of mathematics p131-38   **920**
Bernstein, Carl
  All the president's men   **973.924**
  (jt. auth) Woodward, B. The final days   **973.924**
Bernstein, Leonard, 1918-1990
  See/See also pages in the following book(s):
  Green, S. The world of musical comedy   **920**
Bernstein, Nina
  The lost children of Wilder   **362.7**
Bernstein, Peter L.
  The power of gold   **398**
Bernstein, Richard
  The coming conflict with China   **327.73**
  Out of the blue   **973.931**
  Ultimate journey   **294.3**
Bernstein, William
  The four pillars of investing   **332.6**
Berra, Kathy
  Heart attack! See Heart attack!   **616.1**
Berry, Andrew
  (jt. auth) Watson, J. D. DNA: the secret of life
        576.5
Berry, Charles W.
  Computer and Internet dictionary for ages 9 to 99
        004
Berry, Wendell, 1934-
  Citizenship papers   **338.1**
  Collected poems, 1957-1982   **811**
  Home economics   **814**
  A timbered choir   **811**
  What are people for?   **814**
Berryman, John, 1914-1972
  Collected poems, 1937-1971   **811**
  The dream songs   **811**
  See/See also pages in the following book(s):
  Lowell, R. Collected prose p104-18   **818**
Berthe Morisot. Higonnet, A.   **92**
Bertholle, Louisette
  (jt. auth) Child, J. Mastering the art of French cooking
        641.5
Berton, Pierre, 1920-
  Niagara   **971.3**
Beschloss, Michael R., 1955-
  The conquerors: Roosevelt, Truman, and the destruction of Hitler's Germany, 1941-1945   **940.53**
  (ed) The American Heritage illustrated history of the presidents. See The American Heritage illustrated history of the presidents   **920**
  (ed) Reaching for glory. See Reaching for glory
        973.923
  (ed) Taking charge. See Taking charge   **973.923**
Besier, Rudolf, 1878-1942
  The Barretts of Wimpole Street   **822**
The **best** alternative medicine. Pelletier, K. R.
        615.5
Best American crime reporting. See Best American crime writing   **364.1**
Best American crime writing   **364.1**
The **Best** American essays   **814**
The **Best** American essays of the century   **814**

The **Best** American poetry   **811.008**
The **Best** American recipes   **641.5**
The **Best** American science and nature writing **500**
The **Best** American science writing   **500**
The **Best** American short plays   **812.008**
The **Best** American sports writing   **796**
The **Best** American sports writing of the century
        796
The **Best** American travel writing   **910.4**
The **best** and the brightest. Halberstam, D. **973.922**
The **best** baby shower book. Cooke, C.   **793.2**
Best books
  Best books for young adult readers   **011.6**
  Booklist   **028.1**
  Carter, B. Best books for young adults   **028.1**
  Ellington, E. A year of reading   **028**
  Fadiman, C. The new lifetime reading plan **028**
  Fiction catalog   **016.8**
  Helbig, A. Dictionary of American children's fiction, 1995-1999   **028.5**
  Lesher, L. P. The best novels of the nineties
        016.8
  Lipson, E. R. The New York Times parent's guide to the best books for children   **011.6**
  Major, D. C. 100 one-night reads   **028**
  Pearl, N. Now read this II   **016.8**
  The Reader's adviser   **011**
  Required reading   **301**
  Seymour-Smith, M. The 100 most influential books ever written   **028**
Best books for young adult readers   **011.6**
Best books for young adults. Carter, B.   **028.1**
The **Best** business stories of the year   **070.4**
Best literature by and about Blacks. Richards, P.
        016.8
The **Best** loved poems of the American people
        821.008
The **Best** men's stage monologues of [date] **808.82**
The **best** novels of the nineties. Lesher, L. P. **016.8**
The **best** of Abbie Hoffman. Hoffman, A.   **303.4**
The **best** of Plimpton. Plimpton, G.   **818**
The **best** of times. Johnson, H. B.   **973.929**
Best one-act plays. See The Best American short plays
        812.008
The **Best** plays of [date]   **808.82**
The **best** quick breads. Hensperger, B.   **641.8**
Best short plays. See The Best American short plays
        812.008
The **Best** stage scenes of [year]   **808.82**
The **Best** women's stage monologues of [date]
        808.82
Bethell, Leslie
  (ed) The Cambridge history of Latin America. See The Cambridge history of Latin America   **980**
Betrayal. Pinter, H.   **822**
  also in Pinter, H. Complete works v4   **822**
Betrayal of trust. Garrett, L.   **362.1**
The **betrayal** of work. Shulman, B.   **331.2**
A **betrothal**. Wilson, L.
  In Wilson, L. 21 short plays p219-34   **812**
Bettelheim, Bruno
  Freud and man's soul   **150.19**
        About
  Raines, T. Rising to the light: a portrait of Bruno Bettelheim   **92**
The **better** angel: Walt Whitman in the Civil War. Morris, R.   **92**
Better day coming. Fairclough, A.   **323.1**
Better Homes and Gardens decorating basics. See Decorating basics   **747**
Better Homes and Gardens new complete guide to home repair & improvement   **643**
Better Homes and Gardens new cook book **641.5**

Better Homes and Gardens step-by-step yard & garden basics. See Step-by-step yard & garden basics 635

Better living. See Kingwell, M. In pursuit of happiness 170

Betting See Gambling

Betty Crocker's best loved recipes 641.5

Betty Crocker's cooking basics 641.5

The **Betty** Ford Center book of answers. West, J. W. 616.86

Betty Shabazz: a remarkable story of survival and faith before and after Malcolm X. Rickford, R. J. 92

Between father and son. Naipaul, V. S. 92

Between friends. Lyons, C. 745.5

Between silk and cyanide. Marks, L. 940.54

Betzina, Sandra
Fabric savvy 646.2
Power sewing step-by-step 646.4
Sandra Betzina sews for your home 646.2

Bevan, A. W. R.
Meteorites: a journey through space and time 523.5

Bevan, Alex See Bevan, A. W. R.

Bevel, James Luther, 1936-
See/See also pages in the following book(s):
Halberstam, D. The children 323.1

Beverages
Ayto, J. An A-Z of food and drink 641.03

Beyond belief. Naipaul, V. S. 297

Beyond belief. Pagels, E. H. 229

Beyond bok choy. Ross, R. L. S. 641.6

Beyond codependency. Beattie, M. 616.86

Beyond evolution. Fox, M. W. 174

Beyond numeracy. Paulos, J. A. 510

Beyond paradise: the life of Ramon Novarro. Soares, A. 92

Beyond personality. Lewis, C. S.
In Lewis, C. S. Mere Christianity 230

Beyond the melting pot. Glazer, N. 305.8

Beyond the Mountains of the Damned. McAllester, M. 949.7

Beyond the wild blue. Boyne, W. J. 358.4

Bhabha, Homi Jehangir, 1909-1966
See/See also pages in the following book(s):
Greenstein, G. Portraits of discovery p68-91 920

Bhagavadgītā See Mahābhārata. Bhagavadgītā

Bhopal Union Carbide Plant Disaster, Bhopal, India, 1984
Lapierre, D. Five past midnight in Bhopal 363.1

Biale, David, 1949-
(ed) Cultures of the Jews. See Cultures of the Jews 909

Bias crimes See Hate crimes

Bible

History

Moynahan, B. God's bestseller: William Tyndale, Thomas More, and the writing of the English Bible 92

Bible
The Anchor Bible 220.5
Good news Bible 220.5
The HarperCollins study Bible 220.5
The Holy Bible [King James Bible. Oxford Univ. Press] 220.5
The Holy Bible: new revised standard version 220.5
Holy Bible: the new King James Version 220.5
The new American Bible 220.5
New American standard Bible 220.5
The new Jerusalem Bible 220.5
The new Oxford annotated Bible 220.5
The revised English Bible 220.5

Antiquities
Sheler, J. L. Is the Bible true? 220.1

Biography
Calvocoressi, P. Who's who in the Bible 220.9
Deen, E. All of the women of the Bible 220.9
Women in scripture 220.9

Commentaries
Bowker, J. The complete Bible handbook 220.6
The HarperCollins Bible commentary 220.7
The New Interpreter's Bible 220.7
Oxford Bible commentary 220.7
Reader's digest complete guide to the Bible 220.7

Concordances
Cruden, A. Cruden's Complete concordance to the Old and New Testaments 220.5
Strong, J. The strongest Strong's exhaustive concordance of the Bible 220.5

Criticism
Gomes, P. J. The good book 220.1
Murphy, C. The Word according to Eve 220.8

Dictionaries
The Anchor Bible dictionary 220.3
Eerdmans dictionary of the Bible 220.3
The HarperCollins Bible dictionary 220.3
The Oxford companion to the Bible 220.3
The Oxford guide to ideas & issues of the Bible 220.3

Encyclopedias
The Interpreter's dictionary of the Bible 220.3

Geography
The HarperCollins concise atlas of the Bible 220.9

History
Bobrick, B. Wide as the waters 220.5
McGrath, A. E. In the beginning 220.5
Nicolson, A. God's secretaries: the making of the King James Bible 220.5
The Oxford illustrated history of the Bible 220

History of Biblical events
The Cambridge companion to the Bible 220.9
The HarperCollins concise atlas of the Bible 220.9
The Oxford history of the biblical world 220.9

History of contemporary events
Sheler, J. L. Is the Bible true? 220.1

Meditations
Carter, J. Sources of strength 248.4

Study and teaching
Davis, K. C. Don't know much about the Bible 220.6

Versions
Bobrick, B. Wide as the waters 220.5
McGrath, A. E. In the beginning 220.5
Moynahan, B. God's bestseller: William Tyndale, Thomas More, and the writing of the English Bible 92
Nicolson, A. God's secretaries: the making of the King James Bible 220.5

Bible. N.T.

Criticism
Brown, R. E. An introduction to the New Testament 225
Johnson, L. T. The real Jesus 232.9
Miles, J. Christ: a crisis in the life of God 232

Bible. N.T. Apocryphal books. Gospel of Thomas See Gospel of Thomas

Bible. N.T. Gospels
The five Gospels 226
The three Gospels 226

Criticism
Bonhoeffer, D. The cost of discipleship 226
Crossan, J. D. Excavating Jesus 225.9
Crossan, J. D. Who killed Jesus? 232.9
Pagels, E. H. The origin of Satan 235

Bible. N.T. John
Pagels, E. H. Beyond belief 229

Bible. New Testament *See* Bible. N.T.
Bible. O.T.
  The Old Testament: King James Version   221.5
  The Song of songs   223
  Tanakh   221.5
Criticism
  Bible. O.T. Pentateuch. The book of J   222
  Miles, J. God: a biography   231
  Pagels, E. H. Adam, Eve, and the serpent   241
  Telushkin, J. Biblical literacy   221.6
History of Biblical events
  Cahill, T. The gifts of the Jews   909
Bible. O.T. Apocrypha
  The Apocrypha   229
Bible. O.T. Genesis
Criticism
  Armstrong, K. In the beginning   222
  Dershowitz, A. M. The Genesis of justice   222
  Kushner, H. S. How good do we have to be?   296.7
  Moyers, B. Genesis: a living conversation   222
Bible. O.T. Pentateuch
  The book of J   222
  The five books of Moses   222
  Satinover, J. Cracking the Bible code   222
  The Torah: the five books of Moses   222
Criticism
  Friedman, R. E. Who wrote the Bible?   222
  Kugel, J. L. The Bible as it was   222
Geography
  Feiler, B. S. Walking the Bible   915.6
Bible. O.T. Prophets
Criticism
  Heschel, A. J. The prophets   224
Bible. Old Testament *See* Bible. O.T.
Bible and science
  Schroeder, G. L. The science of God   261.5
The **Bible** as it was. Kugel, J. L.   222
Biblical literacy. Telushkin, J.   221.6
Bibliographic index   011
Bibliographical citations
  Walker, J. R. The Columbia guide to online style   808
Bibliography
  See also Bibliographical citations; Books
  Books in print   015.73
  Forthcoming books   015.73
Best books
  See Best books
Bibliography
  Bibliographic index   011
Indexes
  Bibliographic index   011
Bicycle repair step by step. Plas, R. van der   629.28
Bicycles
  See also Cycling
  Sloane, E. A. Sloane's complete book of bicycling   629.227
Maintenance and repair
  Bicycling magazine's basic maintenance and repair   629.28
  Langley, J. Bicycling magazine's complete guide to bicycle maintenance and repair for road and mountain bikes   629.28
  Plas, R. van der. Bicycle repair step by step   629.28
Bicycles and bicycling *See* Cycling
Bicycling magazine's 900 all-time best tips   796.6
Bicycling magazine's basic maintenance and repair   629.28
Bicycling magazine's complete guide to bicycle maintenance and repair for road and mountain bikes. Langley, J.   629.28

Biddle, Flora Miller
  The Whitney women and the museum they made   708
Biddle, Wayne
  A field guide to germs   616
  A field guide to the invisible   500
Biedermann, Hans, 1930-
  Dictionary of symbolism   302.2
Bienen, Leigh B.
  (jt. auth) Geis, G. Crimes of the century   345
Bienvenu, Marcelle
  (jt. auth) Lagasse, E. Every day's a party   642
Bierce, Ambrose, 1842-1914?
  Can such things be?
    In Bierce, A. The collected writings   818
  The collected writings   818
  The Devil's dictionary
    In Bierce, A. The collected writings   818
  Fantastic fables
    In Bierce, A. The collected writings   818
  In the midst of life
    In Bierce, A. The collected writings   818
  The monk and the hangman's daughter
    In Bierce, A. The collected writings   818
About
  Morris, R. Ambrose Bierce   92
  See/See also pages in the following book(s):
  Wilson, E. Patriotic gore p617-34   810.9
Big bang cosmology *See* Big bang theory
Big bang theory
  Rees, M. J. Just six numbers   523.1
The **big** book of country music. Carlin, R.   920.003
The **big** book of gardening secrets. Smith, C. W. G.   635
Big book of knitting. Buss, K.   746.43
The **big** book of preserving the harvest. Costenbader, C. W.   641.4
The **big** book of small household repairs. Wing, C.   643
The **big** book of soups & stews. Vollstedt, M.   641.8
Big Chief Elizabeth. Milton, G.   975.5
Big game hunting *See* Hunting
Big game, small world. Wolff, A.   796.323
The **big** house. Behan, B.
  In Behan, B. The complete plays   822
The **big** picture. Jacobs, L.   770
The **big** questions. Morris, R.   501
Big red book of resumes, McGraw-Hill's   650.14
The **big** red fez. Godin, S.   005.7
The **big** splat; or, How our moon came to be. Mackenzie, D.   523.3
Bigg, Patricia Nina *See* Ainsworth, Patricia, 1932-
The **biggest** bangs. Katz, J. I.   522
Biggie Smalls *See* Notorious B.I.G. (Musician)
Biggs, Emma, 1956-
  The encyclopedia of mosaic techniques   738.5
Biggs, Mary
  Women's words   808.88
Bigotry *See* Toleration
Bilingual books
English-German
  Celan, P. Poems of Paul Celan   831
  Rilke, R. M. New poems   831
English-Italian
  Dante Alighieri. The divine comedy of Dante Alighieri   851
English-Norwegian
  Jacobsen, R. The roads have come to an end now   839.8
English-Spanish
  Neruda, P. Stones of the sky   861
  Reversible monuments   861
Bill, Buffalo *See* Buffalo Bill, 1846-1917

The **Billboard** book of number 1 hits. Bronson, F.
    781.64

The **Billboard** book of top 40 hits. Whitburn, J.
    781.64

Billiards
  Byrne, R. Byrne's new standard book of pool and billiards   **794.7**

Billions and billions. Sagan, C.   **500**

Billy, the Kid
About
  Utley, R. M. Billy the Kid   **92**
  See/See also pages in the following book(s):
  Brown, D. A. The American West p301-09   **978**

The **billy-club** puppets. García Lorca, F.
  In Garcia Lorca, F. Five plays p13-55   **862**

Biloxi blues. Simon, N.
  In Simon, N. The collected plays of Neil Simon v3 p595-691   **812**

Bilton, Michael
  Four hours in My Lai   **959.704**

Bing, Stanley
  Throwing the elephant   **650.1**

Bing Crosby: a pocketful of dreams: the early years, 1903-1940. Giddins, G.   **92**

Binge-purge behavior *See* Bulimia

Bingham, Clara
  Class action   **342**

Bingham, Hiram, 1875-1956
  Lost city of the Incas   **985**

Biochemistry
Dictionaries
  The Facts on File dictionary of biochemistry   **572**
Research
  Watson, J. D. The double helix   **572.8**

Biodiversity. Becher, A.   **333.95**

Bioengineered foods *See* Food—Biotechnology

Bioethics
  Clones and clones   **174**
  The Double-edged helix   **599.93**
  Fox, M. W. Beyond evolution   **174**
  Fukuyama, F. Our posthuman future   **174**
  Human cloning and human dignity   **174**

Biographical dictionary of American Indian history to 1900. Waldman, C.   **920.003**

The **Biographical** dictionary of scientists   **920.003**

The **biographical** dictionary of World War II generals and flag officers. Ancell, R. M.   **920.003**

The **biographical** directory of Native American painters. Lester, P. D.   **920.003**

Biographical directory of the American Congress, 1774-1996   **328.73**

The **biographical** encyclopedia of jazz. Feather, L.   **920.003**

Biography
  Booknotes: life stories   **920**
Bibliography
  Biography index   **920**
  Burt, D. S. The biography book   **920**
Dictionaries
  Abrams, I. The Nobel Peace Prize and the laureates   **920.003**
  Dictionary of world biography   **920.003**
  Encyclopedia of world biography   **920.003**
  The International who's who   **920.003**
  Merriam-Webster's biographical dictionary   **920.003**
  Nobel Prize winners   **920.003**
Indexes
  Biography index   **920**
Periodicals
  Current biography yearbook   **920.003**
Technique
  See Biography as a literary form

Biography as a literary form
  See also Autobiography
  Conway, J. K. When memory speaks   **808**
  Holroyd, M. Works on paper   **809**
  See/See also pages in the following book(s):
  Gass, W. H. Finding a form p177-96   **814**

The **biography** book. Burt, D. S.   **920**

Biography index   **920**

Biography of a germ. Karlen, A.   **579.3**

Biological diversity
  Becher, A. Biodiversity   **333.95**
  Buchmann, S. The forgotten pollinators   **577**
  Margulis, L. What is life?   **570.1**
  Tudge, C. The variety of life   **578**
  See/See also pages in the following book(s):
  Wilson, E. O. In search of nature   **113**
Encyclopedias
  Encyclopedia of biodiversity   **333.95**
  Life on earth   **333.95**

Biological exuberance. Bagemihl, B.   **591.56**

Biological hazards. Callahan, J. R.   **615.9**

Biological invasions
  Baskin, Y. A plague of rats and rubbervines   **577**
  Bright, C. Life out of bounds   **577**

Biological warfare
  Frist, W. H. When every moment counts   **613.6**
  Miller, J. Germs   **358**
  Preston, R. The demon in the freezer   **616.9**

Biologists
Dictionaries
  Yount, L. A to Z of biologists   **920.003**

Biology
  See also Adaptation (Biology); Biochemistry; Gaia hypothesis; Life (Biology); Marine biology; Microbiology
  Goodwin, B. C. How the leopard changed its spots   **576**
  Gould, S. J. An urchin in the storm   **570**
  Margulis, L. Five kingdoms   **570**
  Mayr, E. This is biology   **570**
  Serafini, A. The epic history of biology   **570**
Classification
  Tudge, C. The variety of life   **578**
Computer simulation
  Bentley, P. J. Digital biology   **570.1**
Dictionaries
  McGraw-Hill dictionary of bioscience   **570.3**
Philosophy
  Keller, E. F. Making sense of life   **570.1**
  Lovelock, J. The ages of Gaia   **570.1**
  Margulis, L. What is life?   **570.1**
  Thomas, L. The lives of a cell   **570.1**
  Watson, L. Dark nature   **111**
Social aspects
  See Sociobiology

Biology, Molecular *See* Molecular biology

Biomechanics *See* Human engineering

Biosphere
  Lovelock, J. The ages of Gaia   **570.1**
  Smil, V. The earth's biosphere   **577**

The **biotech** century. Rifkin, J.   **303.4**

Biotechnology
  See also Food—Biotechnology; Reproductive technology
  Fukuyama, F. Our posthuman future   **174**
  Rifkin, J. The biotech century   **303.4**
Dictionaries
  Steinberg, M. L. The Facts on File dictionary of biotechnology and genetic engineering   **660.6**

The **bipolar** child. Papolos, D. F.   **618.92**

Biracial people *See* Racially mixed people

Bird, Isabella L., 1831-1904
  See/See also pages in the following book(s):
  Slung, M. B. Living with cannibals and other women's adventures   **910.4**

Bird, Larry
Bird watching   92
Bird, Lonnie
The complete illustrated guide to shaping wood
    684
The **bird-catcher** in hell. Enami, S.
    In Waley, A. The Nō plays of Japan   895.6
The **bird** feeder book. Stokes, D. W.   598
The **bird** garden. Kress, S. W.   598
Bird watching
Adams, G. M. Birdscaping your garden   598
Cocker, M. Birders   598
Sibley, D. Sibley's birding basics   598
Stokes, D. W. The bird feeder book   598
    See/See also pages in the following book(s):
Carson, R. Lost woods   570
Bird watching. Bird, L.   92
Bird Woman *See* Sacagawea, b. 1786
Birders. Cocker, M.   598
The **birder's** handbook. Ehrlich, P. R.   598
Birds
    See also Albatrosses; Finches; Game and game
    birds
Attenborough, D. The life of birds   598
Firefly encyclopedia of birds   598
Roth, S. The backyard bird feeder's bible   598
Sibley, D. Sibley's birding basics   598
        Flight
Shipman, P. Taking wing   568
        Migration
Weidensaul, S. Living on the wind   598
        Protection
Beans, B. E. Eagle's plume   598
        Europe
Peterson, R. T. A field guide to the birds of Britain
    and Europe   598
        Great Britain
Peterson, R. T. A field guide to the birds of Britain
    and Europe   598
        North America
Book of North American birds   598
Bull, J. L. The National Audubon Society field guide
    to North American birds, Eastern region   598
Cokinos, C. Hope is the thing with feathers   598
Dunn, E. H. Birds at your feeder   598
Ehrlich, P. R. The birder's handbook   598
Field guide to the birds of North America   598
Kaufman, K. Birds of North America   598
Kress, S. W. The bird garden   598
Peterson, R. T. A field guide to the birds of eastern
    and central North America   598
Robbins, C. S. Birds of North America   598
Sibley, D. The Sibley field guide to birds of eastern
    North America   598
Sibley, D. The Sibley field guide to birds of western
    North America   598
Sibley, D. The Sibley guide to bird life & behavior
    598
Sibley, D. The Sibley guide to birds   598
Stokes, D. W. Stokes field guide to birds: Eastern re-
    gion   598
Stokes, D. W. Stokes field guide to birds: Western re-
    gion   598
Udvardy, M. D. F. National Audubon Society field
    guide to North American birds, Western region
    598
        United States
Harrison, K. America's favorite backyard birds
    598
        West (U.S.)
Peterson, R. T. A field guide to western birds
    598
Birds. Aristophanes
    In Aristophanes. The complete plays of Aristophanes
    p229-86   882

Birds at your feeder. Dunn, E. H.   598
The **birds** of heaven. Matthiessen, P.   598
Birds of North America. Kaufman, K.   598
Birds of North America. Robbins, C. S.   598
Birdscaping your garden. Adams, G. M.   598
Birkeland, Kristian, 1867-1917
        About
Jago, L. The northern lights   92
Birmingham (Ala.)
        Race relations
King, M. L. Why we can't wait   323.1
McWhorter, D. Carry me home   976.1
Birth *See* Childbirth
Birth control
Family planning sourcebook   363.9
Tone, A. Devices and desires   363.9
Birth control pills *See* Oral contraceptives
Birth defects
Hallman, T. Sam: the boy behind the mask   362.1
Birth injuries *See* Birth defects
The **birth** of bebop. DeVeaux, S. K.   781.65
The **birth** of pleasure. Gilligan, C.   152.4
The **birth** of the Republic, 1763-89. Morgan, E. S.
    973.3
The **birth** of time. Gribbin, J. R.   523.1
Birth rate
    See also Population
Birth without violence. Leboyer, F.   618.4
Birthday letters. Hughes, T.   821
The **birthday** party. Pinter, H.
    In Nine plays of the modern theater p395-470
    808.82
    In Pinter, H. Complete works v1   822
Bishop, Elizabeth, 1911-1979
The collected prose   818
The complete poems, 1927-1979   811
    See/See also pages in the following book(s):
Heaney, S. Finders keepers p361-77   821
Heaney, S. The redress of poetry   821.009
Rich, A. Blood, bread, and poetry p124-35   814
Women writers at work p181-207   808
Bishop, Isabella Lucy Bird *See* Bird, Isabella L., 1831-
    1904
Bishop, Jack
The complete Italian vegetarian cookbook   641.5
Biskind, Peter
Easy riders, raging bulls   791.43
Bismarck, Otto, Fürst von, 1815-1898
    See/See also pages in the following book(s):
Fulbrook, M. A concise history of Germany p126-37
    943
Kissinger, H. Diplomacy p103-36   327.73
Massie, R. K. Dreadnought p48-103   940.3
Bison
Lott, D. F. American bison   599.64
    See/See also pages in the following book(s):
Brown, D. A. Bury my heart at Wounded Knee
    970.004
Bissinger, Buzz *See* Bissinger, H. G.
Bissinger, H. G.
Friday night lights   796.332
Bitter winds. Wu, H.   951.05
Bittman, Mark
How to cook everything   641.5
Bix, Herbert P.
Hirohito and the making of modern Japan   92
Bizot, François
The gate   959.6
        About
Bizot, F. The gate   959.6
Bjerknes, Christopher Jon, 1965-
Albert Einstein   92
Bjork, Daniel W.
B.F. Skinner   92

Björkman, Stig, 1938-
(jt. auth) Allen, W. Woody Allen on Woody Allen
791.43
Blachford, Stacey
(ed) Drugs and controlled substances. See Drugs and controlled substances **616.86**
Black, Conrad M.
Franklin Delano Roosevelt: champion of freedom
92
Black, Henry Campbell, 1860-1927
Black's law dictionary **340.03**
Black, Jeremy
A history of the British Isles **941**
Black, Margaret J.
(jt. auth) Mitchell, S. A. Freud and beyond
150.19
Black, Stephen A. (Stephen Ames)
Eugene O'Neill **92**
Black & white photography for 35mm. Mizdal, R.
770
The **black** 100. Salley, C. **920**
Black Americans See African Americans
The **black** and white [revue sketch] Pinter, H.
In Pinter, H. Complete works v2 **822**
Black angel: the life of Arshile Gorky. Matossian, N.
92
Black art (Magic) See Witchcraft
Black artists
Dictionaries
St. James guide to Black artists **920.003**
Black authors
See also African American authors
Black literature criticism **809**
Making Callaloo **810.8**
Dictionaries
The Schomburg Center guide to black literature from the eighteenth century to the present **809**
Black belt tae kwon do. Park, Y. H. **796.8**
Black boy. Wright, R. **92**
The **black** church in the African American experience. Lincoln, C. E. **277.3**
Black cinema treasures. Jones, G. W. **791.43**
Black death See Plague
The **black** death and the transformation of the west. Herlihy, D. **940.1**
Black Elk, 1863-1950
Black Elk speaks **92**
About
Steltenkamp, M. F. Black Elk, holy man of the Oglala
92
Black firsts: 4,000 ground-breaking and pioneering historical events **305.8**
Black genius and the American experience. Russell, D.
920
Black Hawk down. Bowden, M. **967.73**
Black heritage sites. Curtis, N. C. **917.3**
Black holes (Astronomy)
Ferguson, K. Prisons of light **523.8**
Schilling, G. Flash! **522**
Thorne, K. S. Black holes and time warps **530.1**
Black holes and baby universes and other essays. Hawking, S. W. **523.1**
Black holes and time warps. Thorne, K. S. **530.1**
Black Kettle, Cheyenne Chief, 1803?-1868
See/See also pages in the following book(s):
Brown, D. A. The American West p100-09 **978**
Black like me. Griffin, J. H. **305.8**
Black literature (American) See American literature—African American authors
Black literature criticism **809**
Black Livingstone [biography of William Henry Sheppard] Kennedy, P. **92**
Black magic (Witchcraft) See Magic
The **black** man's guide to good health. Reed, J.
613

Black music
See also African American music
Black musicians
See also African American musicians
Black Muslims
American jihad **297**
Gardell, M. In the name of Elijah Muhammad
297
Malcolm X. The autobiography of Malcolm X **92**
See/See also pages in the following book(s):
Levinsohn, F. H. Looking for Farrakhan **92**
The Malcolm X encyclopedia **92**
Black noise. Rose, T. **781.64**
The **black** one hundred. See Salley, C. The black 100
920
The **black** parenting book. Beal, A. C. **649**
Black pearls. Harrison, D. D. **920**
Black poetry (American) See American poetry—African American authors
Black profiles in courage. Abdul-Jabbar, K. **920**
Black series. Sheck, L. **811**
A **black** theology of liberation. Cone, J. H. **261.8**
Black women writers (1950-1980) **810.9**
The **Black** women's health book **613**
Blackberry winter. Mead, M. **92**
Blackburn, G. Meredith
(comp) Index to poetry for children and young people. See Index to poetry for children and young people
808.81
Blackburn, Julia
Old man Goya **92**
Blackburn, Lorraine A.
(comp) Index to poetry for children and young people. See Index to poetry for children and young people
808.81
Blackburn, Simon
The Oxford dictionary of philosophy **103**
Think: a compelling introduction to philosophy
100
Blackface: reflections on African-Americans and the movies. George, N. **791.43**
Blackjack (Game)
Patterson, J. L. Blackjack, a winner's handbook
795.4
Blackjack, a winner's handbook. Patterson, J. L.
795.4
Blacks
Biography
See also African Americans—Biography
Encyclopedias
Africana **909**
Race identity
See also African Americans—Race identity
Religion
The Encyclopedia of African and African-American religions **299**
United States
See African Americans
The **blacks:** a clown show. Genet, J. **842**
Blacks in art
See also African Americans in art
Blacks in literature
See also African Americans in literature
Black literature criticism **809**
The Schomburg Center guide to black literature from the eighteenth century to the present **809**
Black's law dictionary. Black, H. C. **340.03**
Black's veterinary cyclopedia. See Black's veterinary dictionary **636.089**
Black's veterinary dictionary **636.089**
Blacksmithing
Parkinson, P. The artist blacksmith **682**
Blackwell complementary and alternative medicine
615.5

Blackwood, Caroline
About
Schoenberger, N. Dangerous muse: the life of Lady Caroline Blackwood   **92**
Bladder control disease *See* Urinary incontinence
Blaikie, Tim
(jt. auth) Troubridge, E. Scenic art and construction   **792**
Blainey, Ann, 1935-
Fanny and Adelaide: the lives of the remarkable Kemble sisters   **92**
Blair, Clay, 1925-1998
Hitler's U-boat war   **940.54**
Blair, Eric *See* Orwell, George, 1903-1950
Blair, Steven N.
Active living every day. See Active living every day   **613.7**
Blais, Madeleine, 1949-
In these girls, hope is a muscle   **796.323**
Blake, Anthony
(jt. auth) Collister, L. The bread book   **641.8**
Blake, Marie, d. 1993
You can paint pastels   **741.2**
Blake, William, 1757-1827
The complete poetry and prose of William Blake   **828**
The complete writings of William Blake   **821**
The essential Blake   **821**
Songs of innocence and of experience   **821**
About
Bentley, G. E. The stranger from paradise: a biography of William Blake   **92**
Blake-Krebs, Barbara
(ed) When Parkinson's strikes early. See When Parkinson's strikes early   **616.8**
Blakelock, Ralph Albert, 1847-1919
About
Vincent, G. The unknown night: the madness and genius of R. A. Blakelock, an American painter   **92**
Blakeslee, Sandra
(jt. auth) Wallerstein, J. S. Second chances   **306.89**
Blanchard, Margaret A.
(ed) History of the mass media in the United States. See History of the mass media in the United States   **302.23**
Blanchfield, Deirdre S.
(ed) Gale encyclopedia of medicine. See Gale encyclopedia of medicine   **610.3**
The **blank** slate. Pinker, S.   **155.2**
Blanton, DeAnne, 1964-
They fought like demons   **973.7**
Blass, Steve, 1942-
See/See also pages in the following book(s):
Life stories   **920**
Blatner, David
The flying book   **387.7**
The joy of π   **516.2**
Blau, Melinda, 1943-
(jt. auth) Taffel, R. The second family   **306.8**
Bleiler, Richard
Reference guide to mystery and detective fiction   **016.8**
(ed) Supernatural fiction writers. See Supernatural fiction writers   **809.3**
Blenkinsopp, Joseph, 1927-
(ed) The HarperCollins Bible commentary. See The HarperCollins Bible commentary   **220.7**
Blessed Virgin Mary, Saint *See* Mary, Blessed Virgin, Saint
Blimps *See* Airships
Blind
Herrmann, D. Helen Keller   **92**
Keller, H. The story of my life   **92**

Lash, J. P. Helen and teacher   **92**
Dictionaries
The Encyclopedia of blindness and vision impairment   **362.4**
The **blind**. Maeterlinck, M.
In Our dramatic heritage v6   **808.82**
Blind eye. Stewart, J. B.   **364.1**
Blind watchers of the sky. Kolb, R.   **523.1**
Blistène, Bernard
A history of 20th-century art   **709.04**
Blithe spirit. Coward, N.
In Coward, N. Three plays   **822**
Blizzard of one. Strand, M.   **811**
Bloch, Lisa Friedman
(jt. auth) Marrs, R. P. Dr. Richard Marr's fertility book   **616.6**
Block, Geoffrey Holden
(ed) The Richard Rodgers reader. See The Richard Rodgers reader   **92**
Block, Joel D.
Sex over 50   **613.9**
Blofeld, John Eaton Calthorpe, 1913-1987
Taoism: the road to immortality   **299**
Blood
Circulation
See also Cardiovascular system
See/See also pages in the following book(s):
Friedman, M. Medicine's 10 greatest discoveries   **610.9**
Blood and guts. Porter, R.   **610.9**
Blood, bread, and poetry. Rich, A.   **814**
Blood-dark track. O'Neill, J.   **920**
Blood diamonds. Campbell, G.   **966.4**
A **blood-dimmed** tide. Astor, G.   **940.54**
Blood evidence. Lee, H. C.   **614**
The **blood** runs like a river through my dreams. Nasdijj   **92**
Blood, tin, straw. Olds, S.   **811**
Blood wedding. García Lorca, F.
In García Lorca, F. Three tragedies   **862**
In Our dramatic heritage v6   **808.82**
Bloodletters and badmen. Nash, J. R.   **920**
Bloods: an oral history of the Vietnam War by black veterans   **959.704**
Bloody murder. Symons, J.   **809.3**
Bloom, Allan David
The closing of the American mind   **973.92**
Bloom, Harold, 1930-
Genius   **153.9**
How to read and why   **028**
Shakespeare: the invention of the human   **822.3**
The Western canon   **809**
(ed) Bible. O.T. Pentateuch. The book of J   **222**
(ed) Franz Kafka's The metamorphosis. See Franz Kafka's The metamorphosis   **833.009**
(ed) Henry David Thoreau. See Henry David Thoreau [critical essays]   **818**
(ed) Henry David Thoreau's Walden. See Henry David Thoreau's Walden   **818**
(ed) J.D. Salinger. See J.D. Salinger [critical essays]   **813.009**
(ed) James Joyce's Ulysses. See James Joyce's Ulysses   **823.009**
(ed) John Steinbeck. See John Steinbeck [critical essays]   **813.009**
(ed) Richard Wright's Native son. See Richard Wright's Native son   **813.009**
(ed) Romantic poetry and prose. See Romantic poetry and prose   **820.8**
(ed) Sinclair Lewis. See Sinclair Lewis [critical essays]   **813.009**
(ed) The Tales of Poe. See The Tales of Poe   **813.009**
(ed) Whitman, W. Selected poems   **811**

Bloom, Howard, 1943-
The Lucifer principle 128
Bloom, Ken
Broadway 974.7
Bloom, Miriam, 1934-
Understanding sickle cell disease 616.1
Bloomfield, Harold H., 1944-
Making peace with your past 158
Bloomfield, Louis
How things work 530
Blouin, Jacques
(jt. auth) Peynaud, E. The taste of wine 641.2
Blount, Roy
Be sweet 92
(ed) Roy Blount's book of Southern humor. See Roy Blount's book of Southern humor 817.008
The **blue** bear. Schooler, L. 599.78
Blue collar workers See Working class
The **blue** devils of Nada. Murray, A. 700
The **blue** estuaries: poems, 1923-1968. Bogan, L. 811
Blue Ginger. Tsai, M. 641.5
Blue gold: the fight to stop the corporate theft of the world's water. Barlow, M. 333.91
Blue highways. Heat Moon, W. L. 917.3
Blue latitudes. Horwitz, T. 910.4
Blue Sky. Weishar, P. 778.5
Blues. Giovanni, N. 811
Blues. Hersey, J. 799.1
Blues all around me. King, B. B. 92
Blues for cannibals. Bowden, C. 973.92
Blues music
    See also Jazz music
Baraka, I. A. The LeRoi Jones/Amiri Baraka reader 818
Harrison, D. D. Black pearls 920
Lomax, A. The land where the blues began 781.643
Murray, A. The blue devils of Nada 700
Nothing but the blues 781.643
    See/See also pages in the following book(s):
King, B. B. Blues all around me 92
Blum, Deborah
Love at Goon Park 150.19
The monkey wars 179
Sex on the brain 612.6
Blum, Howard, 1948-
The brigade 940.54
Blumenfeld, Laura R.
Revenge 956.94
Blumenthal, Betsy, 1943-
Hands on dyeing 746.1
Blumenthal, W. Michael
The invisible wall 943
Blumenthal family
                About
Blumenthal, W. M. The invisible wall 943
Blunden, Caroline
Cultural atlas of China 951
Blunt, Anthony, 1907-1983
                About
Carter, M. Anthony Blunt: his lives 92
Blunt, Judy, 1954-
Breaking clean 92
Blunt, Wilfrid, 1901-1987
Linnaeus, the compleat naturalist 92
Bly, Robert
Eating the honey of words 811
Iron John 305.31
The night Abraham called to the stars 811
    See/See also pages in the following book(s):
Gioia, D. Can poetry matter? 809.1
BNA's directory of state and federal courts, judges, and clerks 347

Boadicea, Queen, d. 62
    See/See also pages in the following book(s):
Fraser, A. The warrior queens 920
Boadicea's chariot. See Fraser, A. The warrior queens 920
Board of Governors of the Federal Reserve System (U.S.) See Federal Reserve System (U.S.). Board of Governors
Boardman, John, 1927-
Greek art 709.38
(ed) The Oxford history of the Roman world. See The Oxford history of the Roman world 937
Boatner, Mark Mayo, 1921-
The Civil War dictionary 973.7
Boats, Submarine See Submarines; Submersibles
Boats and boating
    See also Sailing
Heat Moon, W. L. River horse 917.3
Stone, N. On the water 917.3
                Dictionaries
Rousmaniere, J. The illustrated dictionary of boating terms 797.1
Boaz, Noel Thomas
Evolving health 616.07
Bob Hope: the road well-traveled. Quirk, L. J. 92
Bob Vila's complete guide to remodeling your home. Vila, B. 643
Bobbi Brown beauty evolution. Brown, B. 646.7
Bobbitt, Philip
The shield of Achilles 327
Bobby Fischer teaches chess. Fischer, B. 794.1
Bobick, James E.
(ed) The Handy science answer book. See The Handy science answer book 500
Bobrick, Benson, 1947-
Angel in the whirlwind 973.3
Wide as the waters 220.5
Bodanis, David
E=mc^2 530.1
Bodmer, W. F. (Walter Fred), 1936-
The book of man 572.8
Bodmer, Walter Fred See Bodmer, W. F. (Walter Fred), 1936-
Body and mind See Mind and body
Body atlas, Anatomica's 611
The **Body** electric 811.008
Body language See Nonverbal communication
Body language. Fast, J. 153.6
Boehm, Arthur
(jt. auth) Tsai, M. Blue Ginger 641.5
Boehme, Jacob See Böhme, Jakob, 1575-1624
Boese, Alex
The museum of hoaxes 001.9
Bogan, Louise, 1897-1970
The blue estuaries: poems, 1923-1968 811
Bogdanov, Vladimir, 1965-
(ed) All music guide. See All music guide 781.64
(ed) All music guide to country. See All music guide to country 781.642
(ed) All music guide to jazz. See All music guide to jazz 781.65
Bogle, Donald
Primetime blues 791.45
Bohemianism
Miles, B. The Beat Hotel 810.9
The Portable beat reader 810.8
Bohlander, Richard E.
(ed) World explorers and discoverers. See World explorers and discoverers 920.003
Böhme, Jakob, 1575-1624
    See/See also pages in the following book(s):
Jaspers, K. The great philosophers 109

Bohr, Niels Henrik David, 1885-1962
See/See also pages in the following book(s):
Brennan, R. P. Heisenberg probably slept here
    920
    Flowers, C. Instability rules   **509**
Boigny, Félix Houphouët- *See* Houphouët-Boigny, Félix
The **boilerplate** rhino. Quammen, D.   **508**
Bok, Derek Curtis
    The trouble with government   **306**
Bok, Sissela
    Mayhem   **302.23**
Boland, Eavan
    Against love poetry   **821**
    (ed) The Making of a poem. See The Making of a
    poem   **821.008**
Boland, Mary L.
    Your right to child custody, visitation, and support
    346.01
Boland, Robert, 1925-
    Musicals!   **792.6**
Boldt, Laurence G.
    Zen and the art of making a living   **331.7**
Boleyn, Anne *See* Anne Boleyn, Queen, consort of Henry VIII, King of England, 1507-1536
Bollard, John K.
    (ed) Pronouncing dictionary of proper names. See Pronouncing dictionary of proper names   **423**
Boller, Paul F.
    Presidential inaugurations   **973**
    Presidential wives   **920**
    They never said it   **808.88**
Bolles, Richard Nelson
    Job-hunting on the Internet   **025.04**
    What color is your parachute?   **331.7**
Bollinger, Don
    Hardwood floors   **694**
Bolshevism *See* Communism
Bolt, Robert
    A man for all seasons   **822**
Boltzmann, Ludwig, 1844-1906
    See/See also pages in the following book(s):
    Greenstein, G. Portraits of discovery p31-51   **920**
Bombeck, Erma
    Forever, Erma   **817**
    A marriage made in heaven—; or, Too tired for an affair   **817**
Bonanno, Bill
    Bound by honor   **364.1**
Bonanno, David
    (ed) The Body electric. See The Body electric
    811.008
Bonaparte, Napoleon *See* Napoleon I, Emperor of the French, 1769-1821
Bond, Otto Ferdinand, b. 1885
    (comp) The University of Chicago Spanish dictionary. See The University of Chicago Spanish dictionary
    463
Bond, Robert E. Bond's franchise guide. See Bond's franchise guide   **381**
Bondanella, Julia Conaway
    (ed) Dictionary of Italian literature. See Dictionary of Italian literature   **850.3**
Bondanella, Peter E., 1943-
    (ed) Dictionary of Italian literature. See Dictionary of Italian literature   **850.3**
Bonds, Margaret, 1913-1972
    See/See also pages in the following book(s):
    Walker-Hill, H. From spirituals to symphonies
    920
Bond's franchise guide   **381**
Bone palace ballet. Bukowski, C.   **811**
Bone wars. Rea, T.   **560**
The **bonehunters'** revenge. Wallace, D. R.   **560**
Bones of the master. Crane, G.   **294.3**

Bonhoeffer, Dietrich, 1906-1945
    The cost of discipleship   **226**
    A testament to freedom   **230**
Bonner, Lonnice Brittenum
    Good hair   **646.7**
    Plaited glory   **646.7**
Bonney, William H. *See* Billy, the Kid
Bonobo. Waal, F. de   **599.8**
Bontekoe, Ronald, 1954-
    (ed) A Companion to world philosophies. See A Companion to world philosophies   **109**
Book business. Epstein, J.   **070.5**
Book collecting
    Ahearn, A. Collected books   **002.075**
    American book trade directory   **070.5025**
    Basbanes, N. A. Patience & fortitude   **002**
Book industry
    See also Publishers and publishing
    American book trade directory   **070.5025**
    The Bowker annual library and book trade almanac
    020.5
Book of American humor, Russell Baker's   **817.008**
Book of American verse, The New Oxford   **811.008**
A **book** of bees—and how to keep them. Hubbell, S.
    638
Book of blues. Kerouac, J.   **811**
Book of changes *See* I ching
The **book** of common prayer. Episcopal Church
    264
Book of counsel *See* Popol vuh
The **Book** of eulogies   **808.8**
Book of great cookies. See Heatter, M. Maida Heatter's brand-new book of great cookies   **641.8**
The **Book** of heaven   **291**
Book of honor. Gup, T.   **327.12**
The **book** of J. Bible. O.T. Pentateuch   **222**
The **book** of Judas [abridgement] See Kennelly, B. The little book of Judas   **821**
The **book** of Klezmer. Strom, Y.   **781.62**
A **Book** of love poetry   **808.81**
A **Book** of luminous things   **808.81**
The **book** of man. Bodmer, W. F.   **572.8**
Book of martyrs, Foxe's. Foxe, J.   **272**
A **book** of Middle Eastern food. See Roden, C. The new book of Middle Eastern food   **641.5**
The **book** of miracles. Woodward, K. L.   **291.1**
Book of Mormon
    The Book of Mormon   **289.3**
    Givens, T. By the hand of Mormon   **289.3**
Book of North American birds   **598**
The **book** of nothing. Barrow, J. D.   **111**
The **book** of numbers. Conway, J. H.   **512**
The **book** of old silver: English, American, foreign. Wyler, S. B.   **739.2**
Book of Southern humor, Roy Blount's   **817.008**
The **Book** of the cosmos   **523.1**
Book of the Duchess. Chaucer, G.
    In Chaucer, G. The complete poetry and prose of Geoffrey Chaucer   **821**
Book of the people *See* Popol vuh
The **Book** of the states   **352.13**
The **book** of tofu. Shurtleff, W.   **641.6**
The **Book** of war   **355**
Book repair. Lavender, K.   **025.7**
Book review digest   **028.1**
Book trade *See* Book industry; Booksellers and bookselling
Bookbinding
    Fox, G. The essential guide to making handmade books   **686.3**
Bookkeeping
    Century 21 accounting: advanced course   **657**
    Century 21 accounting: first-year course   **657**
Booklist   **028.1**
Bookman's price index   **018**

Booknotes: life stories   920
Books
  See also Printing
Censorship
Foerstel, H. N. Banned in the U.S.A   025.2
Classification
  See Classified catalogs
Conservation and restoration
Lavender, K. Book repair   025.7
Schechter, A. A. Basic book repair methods
   025.7
Handbooks, manuals, etc.
Fox, G. The essential guide to making handmade books   686.3
Prices
Ahearn, A. Collected books   002.075
American book prices current   018
Bookman's price index   018
Reviews
Book review digest   028.1
Booklist   028.1
Choice   028.1
Perrin, N. A child's delight   028.5
Ricks, C. Reviewery   820.9
Books, Filmed *See* Film adaptations
Books, Rare *See* Rare books
Books and reading
Adler, M. J. How to read a book   028
Basbanes, N. A. Patience & fortitude   002
Bloom, H. How to read and why   028
Coles, R. The call of stories   808
Ellington, E. A year of reading   028
Fadiman, C. The new lifetime reading plan   028
Herald, D. T. Genreflecting   016.8
Lesser, W. Nothing remains the same   028
Major, D. C. 100 one-night reads   028
Quindlen, A. How reading changed my life   028
Seymour-Smith, M. The 100 most influential books ever written   028
Szymborska, W. Nonrequired reading   028.1
Trelease, J. The read-aloud handbook   028.5
  See/See also pages in the following book(s):
Woolf, V. The second common reader p224-45
   820.9
Best books
  See Best books
Books and reading for children *See* Children—Books and reading
Books for children *See* Children's literature
Books in print   015.73
The **Books** of the American Negro spirituals   782.42
Booksellers and bookselling
Spector, R. Amazon.com   338.7
Boole, George, 1815-1864
  See/See also pages in the following book(s):
Bell, E. T. Men of mathematics p433-47   920
Boone, Daniel, 1734-1820
About
Faragher, J. M. Daniel Boone   92
  See/See also pages in the following book(s):
Williams, W. C. In the American grain p130-39
   814
The **boor**. Chekhov, A. P.
  In Chekhov, A. P. The portable Chekhov   891.7
Booraem, Hendrik, 1939-
Young Hickory: the making of Andrew Jackson
   92
Boorstin, Daniel J., 1914-2004
The Americans: The colonial experience   973.2
The Americans: The democratic experience   973
The Americans: The national experience   973
The creators   909
The discoverers   909
Hidden history   973
The seekers   909

Booth, Martin, 1944-
Opium   615
Booth, Philip, 1925-
Lifelines   811
Selves   811
Boothe, Clare *See* Luce, Clare Boothe, 1903-1987
Boots and saddles. Custer, E. B.   92
Bordewich, Fergus M.
Killing the white man's Indian   970.004
Bordman, Gerald Martin
American musical theatre   792.6
American theatre: a chronicle of comedy and drama, 1869-1914   792
American theatre: a chronicle of comedy and drama, 1914-1930   792
American theatre: a chronicle of comedy and drama, 1930-1969   792
The Oxford companion to American theatre
   792.03
Bordo, Susan, 1947-
The male body   305.31
Borges, Jorge Luis, 1899-1986
Labyrinths   868
Selected non-fictions   864
Selected poems   861
This craft of verse   809.1
  See/See also pages in the following book(s):
Bloom, H. The Western canon   809
Borgia, Cesare, 1476?-1507
  See/See also pages in the following book(s):
Wills, G. Certain trumpets p227-46   303.3
Bork, Robert H., 1927-
Slouching towards Gomorrah   306
Born free. Adamson, J.   599.75
Born in blood and fire. Chasteen, J. C.   980
Born naked. Mowat, F.   92
Born this day. Nowlan, R. A.   808.88
Borneman, Walter R., 1952-
Alaska: saga of a bold land   979.8
Borneo
Description
Galdikas, B. Reflections of Eden   599.8
  See/See also pages in the following book(s):
Galdikas, B. Orangutan odyssey   599.8
Borrowed finery. Fox, P.   92
Borrowed time. Monette, P.   362.1
Bortman, Marci
(ed) Environmental encyclopedia. See Environmental encyclopedia   363.7
Borzello, Frances
A world of our own   704
Bosch, Hieronymus, d. 1516
Hieronymus Bosch   759.9492
Boschung, Herbert T., Jr.
The Audubon Society field guide to North American fishes, whales, and dolphins. See The Audubon Society field guide to North American fishes, whales, and dolphins   597
Bosket family
About
Butterfield, F. All God's children   364.1
Bosnia and Hercegovina
  See also Sarajevo (Bosnia and Hercegovina); Srebrenica (Bosnia and Hercegovina)
Donia, R. J. Bosnia and Hercegovina   949.7
Maass, P. Love thy neighbor   949.7
Rieff, D. Slaughterhouse   949.7
Boss Cupid. Gunn, T.   821
Bossidy, Lawrence A.
Execution: the discipline of getting things done
   658.4
Boston (Mass.)
Race relations
Bryant, H. Shut out   796.357
Lukas, J. A. Common ground   305.8

Boston Celtics (Basketball team)
Shaughnessy, D. Ever green: the Boston Celtics
 796.323
Boston Museum of Fine Arts *See* Museum of Fine Arts
 (Boston, Mass.)
Boston Red Sox (Baseball team)
Bryant, H. Shut out **796.357**
Halberstam, D. Summer of '49 **796.357**
Halberstam, D. The teammates **920**
Linn, E. Hitter: the life and turmoils of Ted Williams
 92

Boston Women's Health Book Collective
Our bodies, ourselves for the new century. See Our
 bodies, ourselves for the new century **613**
Boswell, James, 1740-1795
The journal of a tour to the Hebrides with Samuel
 Johnson **914.11**
The life of Samuel Johnson **92**
In Sisman, A. Boswell's presumptuous task **828**
 About
Martin, P. A life of James Boswell **92**
Boswell's presumptuous task. Sisman, A. **828**
Bosworth, Patricia
Marlon Brando **92**
Bosworth, R. J. B. (Richard J. B.), 1943-
Mussolini **92**
Bosworth, Richard J. B. *See* Bosworth, R. J. B. (Rich-
 ard J. B.), 1943-
Botanical chemistry
Beling, S. Powerfoods **613.2**
Botany
 See also Plants
The Brooklyn Botanic Garden gardener's desk refer-
 ence **635.9**
Sabbagh, K. A Rum affair **580**
 Dictionaries
The Facts on File dictionary of botany **580**
Hortus third **635**
 Terminology
 See also Popular plant names
Botany, Medical *See* Medical botany
The **botany** of desire. Pollan, M. **581.6**
Botox *See* Botulinum toxin
The **Botox** miracle. Mitchell, D. R. **615.8**
Botting, Douglas
Dr. Eckener's dream machine **629.133**
Gerald Durrell **92**
Botulinum toxin
Mitchell, D. R. The Botox miracle **615.8**
Boucher, François, b. 1885
20,000 years of fashion **391**
Boudicca *See* Boadicea, Queen, d. 62
Bouknight, Joanne Kellar
The kitchen idea book **643**
Boukreev, Anatoli, d. 1997
The climb **796.52**
Boulder (Colo.). Police Dept.
Schiller, L. Perfect murder, perfect town **364.1**
Boulevard of broken dreams: the life, times, and legend
 of James Dean. Alexander, P. **92**
Boulter, Michael Charles
Extinction: evolution and the end of man **576.8**
Boulton, Matthew, 1728-1809
 About
Uglow, J. S. The lunar men **920**
Bound by honor. Bonanno, B. **364.1**
Boundaries. Lin, M. Y. **92**
Bourdain, Anthony
A cook's tour **641**
Typhoid Mary **92**
Bouricius, Ann
The romance readers' advisory **016.8**
Bourne, Jennie, 1951-
DSL: a Wiley tech brief **621.382**

Bourne, Russell
Gods of war, gods of peace **200.9**
Boustani, Rafic
(jt. auth) Fargues, P. The atlas of the Arab world
 909
Bouton, Jim
Ball four **796.357**
Bowden, Charles, 1945-
Blues for cannibals **973.92**
Bowden, Ken
(jt. auth) Nicklaus, J. Golf my way **796.352**
(jt. auth) Nicklaus, J. Jack Nicklaus **92**
Bowden, Mark, 1951-
Black Hawk down **967.73**
Bowder, Diana
(ed) Who was who in the Greek world, 776 BC-30
 BC. See Who was who in the Greek world, 776 BC-
 30 BC **920.003**
Bower, Lynn Marie
Creating a healthy household **643**
Bowers, Edgar
Collected poems **811**
Bowie, James, 1799?-1836
 About
Davis, W. C. Three roads to the Alamo **976.4**
Bowker, John, 1935-
The complete Bible handbook **220.6**
World religions **200**
(ed) The Cambridge illustrated history of religions. See
 The Cambridge illustrated history of religions
 200.9
(ed) The Oxford dictionary of world religions. See The
 Oxford dictionary of world religions **200.3**
The **Bowker** annual library and book trade almanac
 020.5
Bowles, Chester, 1901-1986
 See/See also pages in the following book(s):
Galbraith, J. K. Name-dropping **973.9**
Bowles, Hamish
Jacqueline Kennedy **92**
Bowles, Jane Auer, 1917-1973
 See/See also pages in the following book(s):
American women fiction writers **813.009**
Bowling
Anthony, E. Winning bowling **794.6**
Bowman, Carl F.
(jt. auth) Kraybill, D. B. On the backroad to heaven
 289.7
Bowman, John Stewart, 1931-
(ed) Facts about the American wars. See Facts about
 the American wars **355**
Bown, Deni
New encyclopedia of herbs & their uses **581.6**
Bowring, Richard John, 1947-
(ed) The Cambridge encyclopedia of Japan. See The
 Cambridge encyclopedia of Japan **952**
The **Boxer** Rebellion. Preston, D. **951**
Boxing
Anasi, R. The gloves **796.8**
Jones, C. Falling hard **796.8**
Kram, M. The ghosts of Manila **796.8**
Schulberg, B. Sparring with Hemingway and other leg-
 ends of the fight game **796.8**
Boxshall, Geoffrey Allan
(jt. auth) Lincoln, R. J. The Cambridge illustrated dic-
 tionary of natural history **508**
The **boy** and the dog are sleeping. Nasdijj **92**
The **boy** genius and the mogul. Stashower, D.
 791.45
Boyatzis, Richard E.
(jt. auth) Goleman, D. Primal leadership **658.4**
Boyce, Charles
Shakespeare A to Z **822.3**
Boyd, Brian, 1952-
Vladimir Nabokov **92**

Boyd, Louise Arner, 1887-1972
See/See also pages in the following book(s):
Slung, M. B. Living with cannibals and other women's
  adventures   **910.4**
Boyd, Valerie
Wrapped in rainbows   **92**
Boyden, Matthew
The Rough Guide to opera   **792.5**
Boyer, Carl B. (Carl Benjamin), 1906-
A history of mathematics   **510**
Boyer, Paul S., 1935-
(ed) The Oxford companion to United States history.
  See The Oxford companion to United States history
      973.03
Boyer, Ruth McDonald, 1918-
Apache mothers and daughters   **970.004**
Boyle, Kay, 1902-1992
See/See also pages in the following book(s):
American women fiction writers   **813.009**
Boyne, Walter J., 1929-
Beyond the wild blue   **358.4**
Clash of Titans   **940.54**
Clash of wings   **940.54**
Boys
Feig, P. Kick me   **305.23**
Pollack, W. S. Real boys   **305.23**
Pollack, W. S. Real boys' voices   **305.23**
      Employment
    See Child labor
      Psychology
Canada, G. Reaching up for manhood   **305.23**
Boys, Teenage *See* Teenagers
The **boys.** Gilbert, M.   **940.53**
The **boys** of summer. Kahn, R.   **796.357**
Brabec, Jeffrey
Music, money, and success   **780**
Brabec, Todd
(jt. auth) Brabec, J. Music, money, and success
      780
Bradford, Richard
Lucky him: the life of Kingsley Amis   **92**
Bradford, William, 1588-1657
Of Plymouth Plantation, 1620-1647   **974.4**
Bradley, Bill
Values of the game   **796.323**
Bradley, Fern Marshall
(ed) Rodale's all-new encyclopedia of organic garden-
  ing. See Rodale's all-new encyclopedia of organic
  gardening   **635**
Bradley, George, 1953-
(ed) The Yale younger poets anthology. See The Yale
  younger poets anthology   **811.008**
Bradley, James
Flags of our fathers   **940.54**
Bradley, Lloyd
This is reggae music   **781.646**
Bradshaw-Isherwood, Christopher William *See* Isher-
  wood, Christopher, 1904-1986
Bradsher, Keith
High and mighty   **629.2**
Brady, George S. (George Stuart)
Materials handbook   **620.1**
Brady, James, 1928-
The coldest war: a memoir of Korea   **951.9**
Brady, Mathew B., ca. 1823-1896
      About
Panzer, M. Mathew Brady and the image of history
      92
Bragdon, Kathleen J.
The Columbia guide to American Indians of the North-
  east   **970.004**
Bragg, Rick
All over but the shoutin'   **92**
Ava's man [Bundrum, Charlie]   **92**

Brahe, Tycho, 1546-1601
      About
Ferguson, K. Tycho & Kepler   **92**
Brahms, Johannes, 1833-1897
      About
MacDonald, M. Brahms   **92**
Swafford, J. Johannes Brahms   **92**
Brain, Marshall
Marshall Brain's more how stuff works   **600**
Brain
Amen, D. Change your brain, change your life
      616.89
Calvin, W. H. How brains think   **153.9**
Deacon, T. W. The symbolic species   **153.6**
Dowling, J. E. Creating mind   **612.8**
Eliot, L. What's going on in there?   **612.8**
Glynn, I. An anatomy of thought   **612.8**
Greenfield, S. The private life of the brain   **612.8**
Pinker, S. How the mind works   **153**
Ratey, J. J. A user's guide to the brain   **612.8**
Restak, R. M. Mozart's brain and the fighter pilot
      612.8
Restak, R. M. Mysteries of the mind   **612.8**
Sagan, C. The dragons of Eden   **153**
Schacter, D. L. Searching for memory   **153.1**
The Scientific American book of the brain   **612.8**
Victoroff, J. I. Saving your brain   **612.8**
Wise, A. Awakening the mind   **615.8**
      Diseases
    See also Stroke
      Encyclopedias
Turkington, C. The encyclopedia of the brain and brain
  disorders   **612.8**
Brain droppings. Carlin, G.   **817**
The **brain** encyclopedia. See Turkington, C. The ency-
  clopedia of the brain and brain disorders   **612.8**
Brain fitness. Goldman, B.   **153.1**
Brainwashing
Huxley, A. Brave new world revisited   **303.3**
Bramly, Serge, 1949-
Leonardo   **92**
Branch, Taylor
Parting the waters: America in the King years, 1954-63
      973.921
Pillar of fire   **973.922**
Branch Davidians
Tabor, J. D. Why Waco?   **291.9**
Brand, Peter
(ed) The Cambridge history of Italian literature. See
  The Cambridge history of Italian literature
      850.9
Brand, Phyllis, 1880-1937
      About
Fox, J. Five sisters   **920**
Brand name products
    See also Trademarks
Brand-new book of great cookies, Maida Heatter's.
  Heatter, M.   **641.8**
Brando, Marlon, 1924-
      About
Bosworth, P. Marlon Brando   **92**
See/See also pages in the following book(s):
Life stories   **920**
Brandon, Ruth
The life and many deaths of Harry Houdini   **92**
Surreal lives   **709.04**
Brands, H. W.
The first American: the life and times of Benjamin
  Franklin   **92**
What America owes the world   **327.73**
Brantley, Ben
(ed) The New York Times book of Broadway. See The
  New York Times book of Broadway   **792**

Branton, Ann
(comp) The Children's song index, 1978-1993. See
The Children's song index, 1978-1993   **782.42**
Brasher, Brenda E., 1952-
(ed) Encyclopedia of fundamentalism. See Encyclope-
dia of fundamentalism   **200.9**
Brasillach, Robert, 1909-1945
About
Kaplan, A. Y. The collaborator: the trial & execution
of Robert Brasillach   **92**
Brass culture: when reggae was king. See Bradley, L.
This is reggae music   **781.646**
Braudel, Fernand
A history of civilizations   **909**
Brave disguises. Jacobik, G.   **811**
Brave new brain. Andreasen, N. C.   **616.89**
Brave new world revisited. Huxley, A.   **303.3**
   also in Huxley, A. Brave new world and Brave new
   world revisited   **828**
Braving the elements. Laskin, D.   **551.6**
Bravo, Charles Delaunay Turner, 1845-1876
About
Ruddick, J. Death at the priory   **364.1**
Bravo, Florence, 1845-1878
About
Ruddick, J. Death at the priory   **364.1**
Brazelton, T. Berry, 1918-
The earliest relationship   **155.4**
The irreducible needs of children   **155.4**
To listen to a child   **155.4**
Touchpoints   **649**
Touchpoints three to six   **649**
Brazil
Page, J. A. The Brazilians   **981**
Skidmore, T. E. Brazil   **981**
Social life and customs
Bellos, A. Futebol: the Brazilian way of life
   796.334
Veloso, C. Tropical truth   **781.64**
Brazil body & soul   **709.8**
Brazilian national characteristics
Page, J. A. The Brazilians   **981**
The **Brazilians**. Page, J. A.   **981**
Bread
Beard, J. Beard on bread   **641.8**
Collister, L. The bread book   **641.8**
Hensperger, B. The best quick breads   **641.8**
Hensperger, B. The bread lover's bread machine cook-
book   **641.8**
The **bread** book. Collister, L.   **641.8**
The **Bread** Loaf anthology of American poetry. See The
New Bread Loaf anthology of contemporary
American poetry   **811.008**
The **Bread** Loaf anthology of contemporary American
essays   **814**
The **bread** lover's bread machine cookbook. Hensperger,
B.   **641.8**
Break on through: the life and death of Jim Morrison.
Riordan, J.   **92**
Breakfast at the track. Wilson, L.
   In Wilson, L. 21 short plays p189-93   **812**
Breakfasts
Jamison, C. A. A real American breakfast   **641.5**
Breaking clean. Blunt, J.   **92**
Breaking faith. Cornwell, J.   **282**
Breaking the deadlock. Posner, R. A.   **324**
Breast
Love, S. M. Dr Susan Love's breast book   **618.1**
Breast cancer
Arnot, B. The breast cancer prevention diet
   616.99
Arnot, B. The breast health cookbook   **616.99**
Bernard, J. Breast cancer, there and back   **616.99**
Breast cancer   **616.99**
Breast cancer sourcebook   **616.99**

Halpin, B. It takes a worried man   **362.1**
Leopold, E. A darker ribbon   **616.99**
Lerner, B. H. The breast cancer wars   **616.99**
Link, J. The breast cancer survival manual
   616.99
Link, J. Take charge of your breast cancer
   616.99
Olson, J. S. Bathsheba's breast   **616.99**
Breast cancer   **616.99**
The **breast** cancer prevention diet. Arnot, B.   **616.99**
Breast cancer sourcebook   **616.99**
The **breast** cancer survival manual. Link, J.   **616.99**
Breast cancer, there and back. Bernard, J.   **616.99**
The **breast** cancer wars. Lerner, B. H.   **616.99**
Breast feeding
Huggins, K. The nursing mother's companion   **649**
The Nursing mother's problem solver   **649**
Pryor, G. Nursing mother, working mother   **649**
Steingraber, S. Having faith   **618.2**
The Womanly art of breastfeeding   **649**
The **breast** health cookbook. Arnot, B.   **616.99**
Breath sweeps mind   **294.3**
The **breathing** disorders sourcebook. Adams, F. V.
   616.2
Breathnach, Sarah Ban See Ban Breathnach, Sarah
Brecher, John
(jt. auth) Gaiter, D. J. The Wall Street journal guide to
wine   **641.2**
Brecht, Bertolt, 1898-1956
The caucasian chalk circle
   In Nine plays of the modern theater p1-115
   808.82
Galileo
   In Our dramatic heritage v5   **808.82**
The threepenny opera
   In Our dramatic heritage v5   **808.82**
About
Fuegi, J. Brecht and company   **92**
Brecht and company. Fuegi, J.   **92**
Breckinridge, John Cabell, 1821-1875
About
Davis, W. C. An honorable defeat   **973.7**
Bredin, Alice, 1962-
The virtual office survival handbook   **658**
Bredin, Jean-Denis
The affair   **944.081**
Breeding
Hubbell, S. Shrinking the cat   **660.6**
Breedlove, Sarah See Walker, C. J., Madame, 1867-
1919
Breen, Jon L., 1943-
Novel verdicts   **016.8**
Breen, Michael, 1952-
The Koreans   **951.9**
Breger, Louis, 1935-
Freud   **92**
Brehony, Kathleen A.
After the darkest hour   **155.9**
Breiter, Barbara
The complete idiot's guide to knitting and crocheting
   746.43
Breitman, Richard, 1947-
The architect of genocide: Himmler and the final solu-
tion   **92**
Official secrets   **940.54**
Bremner, J. Douglas, 1961-
Does stress damage the brain?   **616.85**
Bremser, Martha
(ed) International dictionary of ballet. See International
dictionary of ballet   **792.8**
Brendon, Piers
The dark valley: a panorama of the 1930s   **909.82**
Brennan, Christine
Inside edge   **796.91**

Brennan, Richard P.
Heisenberg probably slept here   920

Brenner, Joël Glenn
The emperors of chocolate   338.7

Brenner, Michael
After the Holocaust   943.087

Brenner, Robert C.
(jt. auth) Capelo, G. R. VCR troubleshooting & repair   621.388

Brescia (Italy)
       History
Demetz, P. The air show at Brescia, 1909   629.13

Breslin, James E. B., 1935-1996
Mark Rothko   92

Breslin, Jimmy
I want to thank my brain for remembering me   92
The short sweet dream of Eduardo Gutierrez   92

Breslow, Lester
(ed) Encyclopedia of public health. See Encyclopedia of public health   362.1

Breton, Mary Joy, 1924-
Women pioneers for the environment   920.003

Brewer, Ebenezer Cobham, 1810-1897
Brewer's dictionary of phrase and fable. See Brewer's dictionary of phrase and fable   803

Brewer, John, 1947-
The pleasures of the imagination   941.07

Brewer's dictionary of modern phrase & fable   803
Brewer's dictionary of phrase and fable   803

Brewton, John Edmund, 1898-
(comp) Index to poetry for children and young people. See Index to poetry for children and young people   808.81

Brewton, Sara Westbrook
(comp) Index to poetry for children and young people. See Index to poetry for children and young people   808.81

Brickell, Christopher
American Horticultural Society encyclopedia of gardening. See American Horticultural Society encyclopedia of gardening   635
(ed) The American Horticultural Society A-Z encyclopedia of garden plants. See The American Horticultural Society A-Z encyclopedia of garden plants   635.9
(ed) American Horticultural Society encyclopedia of plants and flowers. See American Horticultural Society encyclopedia of plants and flowers   635.9
(ed) Pruning & training. See Pruning & training   635.9

Bridal customs See Marriage customs and rites
Bride's book of etiquette   395

Bridge (Game)
Goren, C. H. Goren's new bridge complete   795.4
The **bridge** at Andau. Michener, J. A.   943.9

Bridges
Brown, D. J. Bridges   624
Graf, B. Bridges that changed the world   624
Petroski, H. Engineers of dreams   624

Bridges that changed the world. Graf, B.   624
A **brief** history of Argentina. Brown, J. C.   982
A **brief** history of Canada. Riendeau, R. E.   971
A **brief** history of Central America. Pérez-Brignoli, H.   972.8
A **brief** history of Mexico. Foster, L. V.   972
A **brief** history of science. Crump, T.   509
A **brief** history of the future. Naughton, J.   621.382
A **brief** history of thyme and other herbs. Seymour, M.   635
A **brief** history of time. Hawking, S. W.   523.1

Brier, Bob
Egyptian mummies   932
The encyclopedia of mummies   393
The murder of Tutankhamen   932

Brier, Robert See Brier, Bob

The **brigade**. Blum, H.   940.54
Briggs, Jody, 1945-
Encyclopedia of stage lighting   792

Briggs, Nancy
(jt. auth) Galdikas, B. Orangutan odyssey   599.8

Bright, Chris
Life out of bounds   577

Bright, William, 1928-
International encyclopedia of linguistics. See International encyclopedia of linguistics   410

Bright earth. Ball, P.   701
A **bright** shining lie: John Paul Vann and America in Vietnam. Sheehan, N.   959.704

Brightman, Carol
Sweet chaos: the Grateful Dead's American adventure   920
Writing dangerously: Mary McCarthy and her world   92

Brighton Beach memoirs. Simon, N.
In Simon, N. The collected plays of Neil Simon v3 p479-593   812

Brignoli, Héctor Pérez- See Pérez-Brignoli, Héctor

Brigstocke, Hugh
(ed) The Oxford companion to western art. See The Oxford companion to western art   703

Brill, A. A. (Abraham Arden), 1874-1948
(ed) Freud, S. The basic writings of Sigmund Freud   150.19

Brill, Abraham Arden See Brill, A. A. (Abraham Arden), 1874-1948

Brill, Steve
The wild vegetarian cookbook   641.5
A **brilliant** madness. Duke, P.   616.89
A **brilliant** solution. Berkin, C.   342
Bringing down the Great Wall. Fang Lizhi   951.05

Brinkley, Alan
(ed) The Reader's companion to the American presidency. See The Reader's companion to the American presidency   973
(jt. auth) Virga, V. Eyes of the nation   973

Brinkley, Douglas
Rosa Parks   92
Wheels for the world   338.7
(ed) Witness to America. See Witness to America   973

Bristow, M. J.
(ed) National anthems of the world. See National anthems of the world   782.42

Britain, Battle of, 1940
Clayton, T. Finest hour   940.54
Overy, R. J. The Battle of Britain   940.54

Britannic (Ship)
Jessop, V. Titanic survivor   910.4

Britannica concise encyclopedia   031

British Antarctic ("Terra Nova") Expedition (1910-1913)
Preston, D. A first rate tragedy   998
Solomon, S. The coldest March   998

British artists See Artists, British
British authors of the nineteenth century   920.003
British Commonwealth countries See Commonwealth countries
British East India Company See East India Company
British Empire See Great Britain—Colonies

British Library
See also Joint Steering Committee for Revision of AACR

British Museum encyclopaedia of underwater and maritime archaeology. See Encyclopedia of underwater and maritime archaeology   930.1

British national characteristics
Buruma, I. Anglomania   941
See/See also pages in the following book(s):
Emerson, R. W. The portable Emerson p395-518   818

British philosophy
See/See also pages in the following book(s):
Durant, W. J. The age of Louis XIV p548-97
    940.2
British pottery
Godden, G. A. Encyclopaedia of British pottery and
  porcelain marks   **738**
British women poets of the Romantic era   **821.008**
Brittain, Vera, 1893-1970
See/See also pages in the following book(s):
Heilbrun, C. G. Hamlet's mother and other women
  p38-49   **820.9**
Britton, Lesley
Montessori play & learn   **371.3**
Broad, William, 1951-
The universe below   **551.46**
(jt. auth) Miller, J. Germs   **358**
Broadcast journalism
See also Television broadcasting of news
Garner, J. We interrupt this broadcast   **070.1**
Broadcast talks. Lewis, C. S.
In Lewis, C. S. Mere Christianity   **230**
Broadcasting
See also Television broadcasting
Broadcasting & cable yearbook   **384.54**
Broadway. Bloom, K.   **974.7**
Broadway bound. Simon, N.
In Simon, N. The collected plays of Neil Simon v3
  p693-803   **812**
Broca's brain. Sagan, C.   **500**
Brock, David
The seduction of Hillary Rodham   **92**
Brockett, Oscar Gross, 1923-
History of the theatre   **792.09**
Broder, David S.
Democracy derailed   **328.73**
Broderick, Robert C., 1913-
(ed) The Catholic encyclopedia. See The Catholic en-
  cyclopedia   **282**
Brodie, Carolyn S., 1958-
(jt. auth) Latrobe, K. H. The children's literature dic-
  tionary   **028.5**
Brodie, Fawn McKay, 1915-1981
No man knows my history: the life of Joseph Smith,
  the Mormon prophet   **92**
Brodsky, Alyn
Grover Cleveland   **92**
Brodsky, Joseph, 1940-1996
Collected poems in English, 1972-1999   **811**
Less than one   **814**
On grief and reason   **814**
See/See also pages in the following book(s):
Simon, J. I. Dreamers of dreams   **809.1**
Volkov, S. St. Petersburg   **947**
Brody, Jane E.
Jane Brody's allergy fighter   **616.2**
Jane Brody's good seafood book   **641.6**
Brody, Lora, 1945-
The kitchen survival guide   **641.5**
Broenkow, William W., 1939-
(ed) Interdisciplinary encyclopedia of marine sciences.
  See Interdisciplinary encyclopedia of marine sciences
    551
Brogan, T. V. F. (Terry V. F.)
(ed) The New Princeton encyclopedia of poetry and
  poetics. See The New Princeton encyclopedia of po-
  etry and poetics   **809.1**
Brogan, Terry V. F. *See* Brogan, T. V. F. (Terry V. F.)
Brognart, Gilbert
See/See also pages in the following book(s):
Miłosz, C. To begin where I am p102-15   **891.8**
Brokaw, Tom
An album of memories   **940.54**
The greatest generation   **940.54**
A long way from home   **92**

The **broken** cord. Dorris, M.   **362.292**
Broken glass. Miller, A.   **812**
The **broken** tower: a life of Hart Crane. Mariani, P. L.
    92
Brombert, Beth Archer
Edouard Manet   **92**
Brombert, Victor H.
Trains of thought   **92**
Bromiley, Geoffrey William
(ed) The Encyclopedia of Christianity. See The Ency-
  clopedia of Christianity   **230.003**
Bronowski, Jacob, 1908-1974
Science and human values   **500**
Bronson, Fred
The Billboard book of number 1 hits   **781.64**
Brontë, Charlotte, 1816-1855
About
Gaskell, E. C. The life of Charlotte Brontë   **92**
Gordon, L. Charlotte Brontë   **92**
Brontë, Emily, 1818-1848
The complete poems of Emily Jane Brontë   **821**
Brontë family
About
The Brontës   **920**
The **Brontës**   **920**
Brontosaurus. Wilson, L.
In Wilson, L. 21 short plays p153-68   **812**
Bronx (New York, N.Y.)
Social conditions
Kozol, J. Ordinary resurrections   **305.23**
Bronze Age
Wood, M. In search of the Trojan War   **939**
Brook, Peter, 1925-
The empty space   **792**
Brookes, John, 1933-
Garden masterclass   **712**
John Brookes' natural landscapes   **635.9**
Brookhiser, Richard
Alexander Hamilton, American   **92**
America's first dynasty   **920**
Founding father: rediscovering George Washington
    92
Brooklyn (New York, N.Y.)
Social conditions
Salamon, J. Facing the wind   **364.1**
The **Brooklyn** Botanic Garden gardener's desk reference
    635.9
Brooklyn Dodgers (Baseball team)
Kahn, R. The boys of summer   **796.357**
See/See also pages in the following book(s):
Goodwin, D. K. Wait till next year   **92**
Gruver, E. Koufax   **92**
Brooks, Cleanth, 1906-1994
The well wrought urn   **821.009**
William Faulkner: the Yoknapatawpha country
    813.009
Brooks, Geraldine
Nine parts of desire   **305.4**
Brooks, Gwendolyn
Selected poems   **811**
See/See also pages in the following book(s):
Black women writers (1950-1980)   **810.9**
Brooks, Robert B.
Raising resilient children   **649**
Brooks, Rodney Allen
Flesh and machines   **629.8**
Brooks, Tim
The complete directory to prime time network and ca-
  ble TV shows, 1946-present   **791.45**
Brotherhood of the bomb. Herken, G.   **920**
Brothers
Ambrose, S. E. Comrades   **302.3**
The **brothers.** Terence
In Terence. Terence, the comedies   **872**
Brothers and sisters *See* Siblings; Twins

Brothers Grimm
 See also Grimm, Jacob, 1785-1863; Grimm, Wilhelm, 1786-1859
Brown, Bobbi
 Bobbi Brown beauty evolution   646.7
Brown, Claude, 1937-2002
 Manchild in the promised land   92
Brown, David Alan, 1942-
 Leonardo da Vinci   759.5
 Virtue & beauty. See Virtue & beauty   757
Brown, David E.
 Inventing modern America   609
Brown, David J., 1946-
 Bridges   624
Brown, Dee Alexander
 The American West   978
 Bury my heart at Wounded Knee   970.004
Brown, Edward Espe
 (jt. auth) Madison, D. The Greens cook book   641.5
Brown, Elaine
 The condemnation of Little B   364.1
Brown, James
 James Brown, the godfather of soul   92
Brown, Jim, 1950-
 (ed) American roots music. See American roots music   781.62
Brown, John Russell
 (ed) The Oxford illustrated history of theatre. See The Oxford illustrated history of theatre   792.09
Brown, Jonathan
 Velázquez, painter and courtier   92
Brown, Jonathan C.
 A brief history of Argentina   982
Brown, Kenneth A.
 Four corners   978
Brown, Marianne Gluszak
 (jt. auth) Tennant, R. A. The American Sign Language handshape dictionary   419
Brown, Nancy, 1940-
 (jt. auth) Saricks, J. G. Readers' advisory service in the public library   025.5
Brown, Rachel
 The weaving, spinning, and dyeing book   746.1
Brown, Raymond Edward
 An introduction to the New Testament   225
Brown, Sarah
 The vegetarian bible   641.5
Brown, Terence
 The life of W.B. Yeats   92
Brown: the last discovery of America. Rodriguez, R.   305.8
Brown v. Board of Education
 Irons, P. H. Jim Crow's children   344
Browne, E. J. *See* Browne, Janet, 1950-
Browne, Janet, 1950-
 Charles Darwin: a biography   92
Browne, Joy
 The nine fantasies that will ruin your life and the eight realities that will save you   158
Browne, Malcolm W.
 See/See also pages in the following book(s):
 Prochnau, W. W. Once upon a distant war   959.704
Browne, Patrick Lee- *See* Lee-Browne, Patrick
Browning, Elizabeth Barrett, 1806-1861
 Sonnets from the Portuguese   821
   About
 Woolf, V. Flush   828
   Drama
 Besier, R. The Barretts of Wimpole Street   822
Browning, Michael
 (jt. auth) Maples, W. R. Dead men do tell tales   614

Browning, Robert, 1812-1889
 Robert Browning's poetry   821
   Drama
 Besier, R. The Barretts of Wimpole Street   822
Brownlee, Don
 (jt. auth) Ward, P. D. Rare earth   576.8
Brownlow, Kevin
 Mary Pickford rediscovered   791.43
Brownmiller, Susan
 In our time   305.4
Brownson, JeanMarie
 (jt. auth) Bayless, R. Rick Bayless's Mexican kitchen   641.5
Brownstone, David M.
 Facts about American immigration   325.73
 (jt. auth) Franck, I. M. Famous first facts about sports   796
 (jt. auth) Franck, I. M. The Wilson chronology of women's achievements   305.4
Broyard, Anatole
 Kafka was the rage   92
 See/See also pages in the following book(s):
 Gates, H. L. Thirteen ways of looking at a black man   920
 Life stories   920
Brubaker, Melinda
 (jt. auth) Mailhot, C. B. Surgery: a patient's guide from diagnosis to recovery   617
Bruccoli, Matthew Joseph, 1931-
 Fitzgerald and Hemingway   92
Bruce, Anthony
 An encyclopedia of naval history   359
Bruce, Debra Fulghum, 1951-
 Making a baby   618.2
Bruce, Evangeline
 See/See also pages in the following book(s):
 Heymann, C. D. The Georgetown ladies' social club   305.4
Bruchac, Joseph, 1942-
 (ed) Songs from this Earth on turtle's back. See Songs from this Earth on turtle's back   811.008
Bruck, Connie
 When Hollywood had a king   92
Bruderhof communities *See* Hutterian Brethren
Bruehl, Elisabeth Young- *See* Young-Bruehl, Elisabeth
Bruemmer, Fred
 (jt. auth) Mangelsen, T. D. Polar dance   599.78
Bruer, John T., 1949-
 The myth of the first three years   155.4
Brundtland, Gro Harlem
 Madame Prime Minister   92
Brunelleschi, Filippo, 1377-1446
   About
 King, R. Brunelleschi's dome   726
Brunelleschi's dome. King, R.   726
Bruni, Frank
 Ambling into history: the unlikely odyssey of George W. Bush   92
Bruning, Nancy
 (jt. auth) Katz, J. Swimming for total fitness   797.2
Bruno, Giordano, 1548-1600
 See/See also pages in the following book(s):
 Jaspers, K. The great philosophers   109
Bruno, Leonard C.
 Science & technology firsts   609
Bruno, Richard L.
 The polio paradox   616.8
Brunvand, Jan Harold
 The choking Doberman and other "new" urban legends   398.2
 Encyclopedia of urban legends   398.2
 Too good to be true   398.2
 The vanishing hitchhiker   398.2

Brunvand, Jan Harold—*Continued*
(ed) American folklore. See American folklore
398.03
Brushwork essentials. Weber, M. C.   751.4
Brutal imagination. Eady, C.   811
Bruun, Bertel
(jt. auth) Robbins, C. S. Birds of North America
598
Bruyère, Christian, 1944-
(jt. auth) Inwood, R. Creative country construction
690
Bryan, Ashley, 1923-
See/See also pages in the following book(s):
Marcus, L. S. Ways of telling   741.6
Bryan, Betsy Morrell
(ed) The Quest for immortality. See The Quest for immortality   709.32
Bryan, William Jennings, 1860-1925
See/See also pages in the following book(s):
Hofstadter, R. The American political tradition, and the men who made it p183-202   973
Bryant, Bear
About
Dent, J. The Junction boys   796.332
Bryant, Howard, 1968-
Shut out   796.357
Bryant, Paul W. *See* Bryant, Bear
Bryce, Robert
Pipe dreams   333.79
Bryson, Bill
I'm a stranger here myself   973.92
In a sunburned country   994
Made in America   420
The mother tongue: English & how it got that way
420
Notes from a small island   914.1
A short history of nearly everything   500
A walk in the woods   917.4
Bstan-'dzin-rgya-mtsho *See* Dalai Lama XIV, 1935-
Buber, Martin, 1878-1965
I and thou   181
About
Friedman, M. S. Encounter on the narrow ridge: a life of Martin Buber   92
See/See also pages in the following book(s):
Tillich, P. Theology of culture   230
Buber, Mordekhai Martin *See* Buber, Martin, 1878-1965
Bubonic plague *See* Plague
Buchanan, Edna
See/See also pages in the following book(s):
Life stories   920
Buchanan, Mark
Nexus: small worlds and the groundbreaking science of networks   530
Buchanan, Rita
Taylor's master guide to landscaping   712
(ed) Taylor's master guide to gardening. See Taylor's master guide to gardening   635.9
Buchenwald (Germany: Concentration camp)
The Buchenwald report   940.53
The **Buchenwald** report   940.53
Bucher, Julia A.
(ed) Caregiving: a step-by-step resource for caring for the person with cancer at home. See Caregiving: a step-by-step resource for caring for the person with cancer at home   649.8
Buchholz, Barbara Ballinger
Successful homebuilding and remodeling   690
Buchholz, Ester Schaler
The call of solitude   155.9
Buchmann, Stephen
The forgotten pollinators   577

Büchner, Georg, 1813-1837
Woyzeck
In Our dramatic heritage v4   808.82
Buck, Craig
(jt. auth) Forward, S. Toxic parents: overcoming their hurtful legacy and reclaiming your life   362.82
Buck, Pearl S. (Pearl Sydenstricker), 1892-1973
See/See also pages in the following book(s):
American women fiction writers   813.009
Buckingham, George Villiers, 2nd Duke of, 1628-1687
The rehearsal
In Restoration plays   822.008
Buckland, Gail
(jt. auth) Evans, H. The American century   973.9
Buckley, Gail Lumet, 1937-
American patriots   355
Buckley, Sandra, 1954-
Encyclopedia of contemporary Japanese culture. See Encyclopedia of contemporary Japanese culture
952.04
Buckley, William F. (William Frank), 1925-
Buckley, the right word   422
Nearer, my God   92
Buckley, the right word. Buckley, W. F.   422
Bud, Robert
(ed) Instruments of science. See Instruments of science
502.8
Budd, Ann, 1956-
The knitter's handy book of patterns   746.43
Buddha, Gautama *See* Gautama Buddha
Buddha. Armstrong, K.   294.3
Buddhism
See also Zen Buddhism
Bernstein, R. Ultimate journey   294.3
Breath sweeps mind   294.3
Buddhism: the illustrated guide   294.3
Crane, G. Bones of the master   294.3
Dalai Lama XIV. Violence and compassion   294.3
Dalai Lama XIV. The way to freedom   294.3
Keown, D. A dictionary of Buddhism   294.3
Kerouac, J. Some of the dharma   294.3
Nomachi, K. Tibet   951
Ross, N. W. Buddhism, a way of life and thought
294.3
Smith, H. Buddhism: a concise introduction   294.3
Sogyal, Rinpoche. The Tibetan book of living and dying   294.3
Thondup, T. Enlightened journey   294.3
Tibetan book of the dead. The Tibetan book of the dead   294.3
See/See also pages in the following book(s):
Dalai Lama XIV. Freedom in exile   92
Dalai Lama XIV. My Tibet   951
Dictionaries
Prebish, C. S. Historical dictionary of Buddhism
294.3
Buddhism: the illustrated guide   294.3
Buddhist art
See/See also pages in the following book(s):
Suzuki, D. T. Manual of Zen Buddhism p153-86
294.3
Buderi, Robert
The invention that changed the world   621.3848
Budgets, Personal *See* Personal finance
Budiansky, Stephen
Battle of wits   940.54
The truth about dogs   636.7
Budwig, Robert
(jt. auth) Coles, J. Beads   745.58
Buffalo, American *See* Bison
Buffalo Bill, 1846-1917
About
Carter, R. A. Buffalo Bill Cody   92
Kasson, J. S. Buffalo Bill's Wild West   791.8
Buffalo Bill's Wild West. Kasson, J. S.   791.8

Buffett, Warren E.
About
Hagstrom, R. G. The Warren Buffett way   332.6
See/See also pages in the following book(s):
Klein, M. The change makers   920
Buford, Kate
Burt Lancaster   92
The **bug** in her ear. Feydeau, G.
In Our dramatic heritage v6   808.82
Bugialli, Giuliano
Bugialli's Italy   641.5
Bugialli's Italy. Bugialli, G.   641.5
Bugliosi, Vincent
Helter skelter   364.1
Buhle, Mari Jo, 1943-
Feminism and its discontents   150.19
Buhner, Stephen Harrod
Vital man   613
Build your dream home for less. Woodson, R. D.
   690
Building
See also Carpentry; House construction
The Art of natural building   690
Eck, J. The distinctive home   728
Scutella, R. M. How to plan, contract, and build your own home   690
Spence, W. P. Encyclopedia of construction methods & materials   690
Woodson, R. D. Build your dream home for less   690
Details
See Architecture—Details
Dictionaries
Dictionary of architecture & construction   720.3
Means illustrated construction dictionary   690
Building a character. Stanislavsky, K.   792
Building a great résumé. Wendleton, K.   650.14
Building and designing decks. Schuttner, S.   690
Building blocks of matter   539.7
Building failures
Levy, M. Why buildings fall down   690
Building materials
The Art of natural building   690
Encyclopedias
Brady, G. S. Materials handbook   620.1
Building the Getty. Meier, R.   708
Buildings
See also Church buildings; Houses
Bukiet, Melvin Jules
(ed) Nothing makes you free. See Nothing makes you free   808.8
Bukowski, Charles
Bone palace ballet   811
Open all night   811
The roominghouse madrigals   811
What matters most is how well you walk through the fire   811
Bukowski, Steven J.
Flooring instant answers   690
Bulbs
Bulbs of North America   635.9
Ellis, B. W. Taylor's guide to bulbs   635.9
Hill, L. Bulbs   635.9
Bulbs of North America   635.9
Bulfinch, Thomas, 1796-1867
Bulfinch's mythology   291.1
Bulfinch's mythology. Bulfinch, T.   291.1
Bulge, Battle of the *See* Ardennes, Battle of the, 1944-1945
Bulimia
Hornbacher, M. Wasted: a memoir of anorexia and bulimia   616.85
Bull, John L.
The National Audubon Society field guide to North American birds, Eastern region   598

Bull Run, 1st Battle of, 1861
Davis, W. C. Battle at Bull Run   973.7
Bullard, Sara
Teaching tolerance   649
Bullfights
Hemingway, E. The dangerous summer   791.8
Hemingway, E. Death in the afternoon   791.8
Bulliet, Richard W.
(ed) The Columbia history of the 20th century. See The Columbia history of the 20th century   909.82
Bullock, Alan
Hitler and Stalin   92
Bulls (Basketball team) *See* Chicago Bulls (Basketball team)
Bully for brontosaurus. Gould, S. J.   508
Bülow, Hans von, 1830-1894
See/See also pages in the following book(s):
Schonberg, H. C. The great pianists   920
Bumiller, Elisabeth
May you be the mother of a hundred sons   954.05
Bunch, Bryan H.
The kingdom of infinite number   513
The Penguin desk encyclopedia of science and mathematics   503
Bundrum, Charlie, d. 1958
About
Bragg, R. Ava's man   92
Bundy, McGeorge
See/See also pages in the following book(s):
Halberstam, D. The best and the brightest   973.922
Bunson, Margaret R.
Encyclopedia of ancient Egypt   932
Bunson, Matthew
The complete Christie   823.009
Encyclopedia of the Roman Empire   937
The vampire encyclopedia   398
Bunts: Curt Flood, Camden Yards, Pete Rose, and other reflections on baseball. Will, G. F.   796.357
Buonarroti, Michel Angelo *See* Michelangelo Buonarroti, 1475-1564
Burch, Monte, 1943-
Complete guide to building log homes   694
Burchfield, R. W. (Robert W.)
(ed) Fowler, H. W. The new Fowler's modern English usage   428
Burchfield, Robert W. *See* Burchfield, R. W. (Robert W.)
Burck, Charles
(jt. auth) Bossidy, L. A. Execution: the discipline of getting things done   658.4
Burckhardt, Jacob, 1818-1897
The Greeks and Greek civilization   938
The **burden** of our time. See Arendt, H. Origins of totalitarianism   321.9
The **bureau** and the mole. Vise, D. A.   327.12
Bureaucracy
Howard, P. The death of common sense   348
Burfoot, Amby
(ed) Runner's world complete book of running. See Runner's world complete book of running   796.42
Burg, David F.
Almanac of World War I   940.3
Burgess, Anthony, 1917-1993
See/See also pages in the following book(s):
Amis, M. The war against cliché   824
Burgess, Mary A. *See* Burgess, Mary Wickizer, 1938-
Burgess, Mary Wickizer, 1938-
(ed) Reginald, R. Science fiction and fantasy literature, 1975-1991   016.8

Burgess, Michael, 1948-
Reference guide to science fiction, fantasy, and horror
016.8
Burgess Shale and the nature of history. See Gould, S. J. Wonderful life: the Burgess Shale and the nature of history **560**
The **buried** mirror. Fuentes, C. **946**
Burke, Edmund, 1729?-1797
Reflections on the Revolution in France **944.04**
Burke, James, 1936-
Circles: 50 round trips through history, technology, science, culture **609**
The knowledge web **609**
Burkholder, JoAnn M., 1953-
About
Barker, R. And the waters turned to blood **615.9**
Burleigh, Michael, 1955-
The Third Reich **943.086**
Burleson, Mark
The ceramic glaze handbook **738.1**
Burma See Myanmar
Burney, Charles, 1726-1814
See/See also pages in the following book(s):
Woolf, V. The second common reader p97-112
820.9
Burney, Fanny, 1752-1840
About
Harman, C. Fanny Burney **92**
Burnham, James, 1905-1987
See/See also pages in the following book(s):
Orwell, G. The Orwell reader p335-54 **828**
The **burning**. Madigan, T. **976.6**
Burns, David D.
Feeling good **158**
Burns, Deborah
(ed) Storey's horse-lover's encyclopedia. See Storey's horse-lover's encyclopedia **636.1**
Burns, James MacGregor
The three Roosevelts **973.91**
Burns, Ken
(jt. auth) Duncan, D. Lewis & Clark **978**
(jt. auth) Ward, G. C. Baseball: an illustrated history **796.357**
(jt. auth) Ward, G. C. The Civil War **973.7**
(jt. auth) Ward, G. C. Jazz **781.65**
Burns, Kristine Helen
(ed) Women and music in America since 1900. See Women and music in America since 1900
780.9
Burns, Ric
(jt. auth) Ward, G. C. The Civil War **973.7**
Burns, Robert, 1759-1796
See/See also pages in the following book(s):
Heaney, S. Finders keepers p378-95 **821**
Burns, Thomas S.
A history of the Ostrogoths **909.07**
Burns and scalds
Burns sourcebook . . . **617.1**
The **Burns** Mantle theater yearbook. See The Best plays of [date] **808.82**
Burns sourcebook . . . **617.1**
Burpee complete gardener **635**
Burr, Aaron, 1756-1836
See/See also pages in the following book(s):
Ellis, J. J. Founding brothers **973.4**
Williams, W. C. In the American grain p188-207
814
Burr, Brooks M.
(jt. auth) Page, L. M. A field guide to freshwater fishes: North America north of Mexico **597**
Burrell, C. Colston
(jt. auth) Phillips, E. Rodale's illustrated encyclopedia of perennials **635.9**
Burros, Marian Fox
The new elegant but easy cookbook **641.5**

Burrough, Bryan, 1961-
Barbarians at the gate: the fall of RJR Nabisco
338.8
Burroughs, Augusten
Running with scissors **92**
Burroughs, William S., 1914-1997
See/See also pages in the following book(s):
Miles, B. The Beat Hotel **810.9**
Burrows, Edwin G., 1943-
Gotham **974.7**
Burrows, Larry, 1926-1971
Vietnam **959.704**
Burrows, William E.
By any means necessary **327.12**
This new ocean **629.4**
Burstein, Dave, 1951-
(jt. auth) Bourne, J. DSL: a Wiley tech brief
621.382
Burstiner, Irving
The small business handbook **658.1**
Bursts, Cosmic gamma ray See Gamma ray bursts
Burt, Daniel S.
The biography book **920**
Burt, William Henry, 1903-1987
A field guide to the mammals **599**
Burton, Isabel, Lady, 1831-1896
About
Lovell, M. S. A rage to live: a biography of Richard and Isabel Burton **92**
Burton, Mike, 1944-
Architectural carving **736**
Burton, Sir Richard Francis, 1821-1890
About
Lovell, M. S. A rage to live: a biography of Richard and Isabel Burton **92**
Burton, Sharon
Procedures for the automated office **651.3**
Buruma, Ian
Anglomania **941**
Bad elements **951.05**
Bury my heart at Wounded Knee. Brown, D. A.
970.004
Bus stop. Inge, W.
In Inge, W. 4 plays p149-219 **812**
Buscaglia, Leo F.
Loving each other **158**
Busch, Robert
The grizzly almanac **599.78**
The wolf almanac **599.77**
Bush, Barbara, 1925-
Barbara Bush **92**
Bush, Dorothy, 1901-1992
See/See also pages in the following book(s):
Angelo, B. First mothers **920**
Bush, George, 1924-
All the best, George Bush **92**
About
Bush, B. Barbara Bush **92**
Halberstam, D. War in a time of peace **327.73**
Parmet, H. S. George Bush **92**
Woodward, B. The commanders **973.928**
See/See also pages in the following book(s):
Mann, J. About face **327.73**
Woodward, B. Shadow **973.92**
Bush, George W.
About
Andersen, C. P. George and Laura **92**
Bruni, F. Ambling into history: the unlikely odyssey of George W. Bush **92**
Dershowitz, A. M. Supreme injustice **324**
Minutaglio, B. First son: George W. Bush and the Bush family dynasty **92**
Posner, R. A. Breaking the deadlock **324**
Woodward, B. Bush at war **973.931**

Bush, Laura
About
Andersen, C. P. George and Laura   92
Bush at war. Woodward, B.   973.931
Bushart, Howard L.
Soldiers of God   322.4
Bushman, Richard L., 1931-
Joseph Smith and the beginnings of Mormonism
          289.3
Bushville. Kelly, J.   796.357
Business
See also Small business
Adams, S. The Dilbert principle   650.1
The Best business stories of the year   070.4
Bing, S. Throwing the elephant   650.1
Camp, J. Start with no   658.4
Bibliography
Pagell, R. A. International business information
          650
Biography—Dictionaries
Who's who in finance and industry   920.003
Corrupt practices
Bryce, R. Pipe dreams   333.79
Cruver, B. Anatomy of greed   333.79
Dictionaries
Folsom, W. D. Understanding American business jar-
gon   650
Encyclopedias
Encyclopedia of busine$$ and finance   650
Information services
Encyclopedia of business information sources   650
Pagell, R. A. International business information
          650
Periodicals—Indexes
Business periodicals index   650
Business and politics
See/See also pages in the following book(s):
Friedman, T. L. The Lexus and the olive tree
          337
Business depression, 1929-1939 *See* Great Depression,
1929-1939
Business education
See also Keyboarding (Electronics)
Business enterprises
See also Corporations
Klein, M. The change makers   920
Business ethics
Batstone, D. B. Saving the corporate soul & (who
knows?) maybe your own   658.4
Morgan, P. W. The appearance of impropriety
          306
Business etiquette
Baldrige, L. Letitia Baldrige's new complete guide to
executive manners   395
Business failures
Bryce, R. Pipe dreams   333.79
Cruver, B. Anatomy of greed   333.79
Business letters
Phillips, E. H. Shocked, appalled, and dismayed!
          651.7
Seglin, J. L. The AMA handbook of business letters
          651.7
Business periodicals index   650
Business: the ultimate resource   658
Businesspeople
Carey, C. W. American inventors, entrepreneurs, and
business visionaries   920
Biography
Klein, M. The change makers   920
Busing (School integration)
Lukas, J. A. Common ground   305.8
Busoni, Ferruccio, 1866-1924
See/See also pages in the following book(s):
Schonberg, H. C. The great pianists   920

Buss, Katharina
Big book of knitting   746.43
Bustard, Bruce I., 1954-
Picturing the century   779
Buster Keaton remembered. Keaton, E.   791.43
The **butcher's** tale. Smith, H. W.   943.08
Butler, Alban, 1711-1773
Butler's Lives of the saints   920.003
Butler, Daniel Allen
Unsinkable: the full story of the RMS Titanic
          910.4
Butler, Jon, 1940-
Religion in American life   200.9
Butler, Susan
East to the dawn   92
Butler's Lives of the saints. Butler, A.   920.003
Butterfield, Fox
All God's children   364.1
Butterflies
Johnson, K. Nabokov's Blues   92
Pyle, R. M. The Audubon Society field guide to North
American butterflies   595.7
Schappert, P. A world for butterflies   595.7
Stokes, D. W. The butterfly book   595.7
The **butterfly** book. Stokes, D. W.   595.7
The **butterfly's** evil spell. García Lorca, F.
In Garcia Lorca, F. Five plays p191-236   862
Butterworth, Rod R.
Signing made easy   419
Buttiglione, Rocco
Karol Wojtyła   92
Buttrick, George A.
(ed) The Interpreter's dictionary of the Bible. See The
Interpreter's dictionary of the Bible   220.3
Bütz, Richard
How to carve wood   731.4
Buying *See* Consumer education
Buzzed. Kuhn, C.   615
Buzzi, Aldo, 1910-
(jt. auth) Steinberg, S. Reflections and shadows
          92
By any means necessary. Burrows, W. E.   327.12
By hand. Kilby, J. E.   745
By the hand of Mormon. Givens, T.   289.3
By the sword. Cohen, R.   796.8
Byrd, James, Jr.
About
King, J. Hate crime: the story of a dragging in Jasper,
Texas   364.1
Byrne, Malcolm
(ed) The Iran-Contra scandal. See The Iran-Contra
scandal   973.927
Byrne, Robert, 1930-
Byrne's new standard book of pool and billiards
          794.7
Byrne's new standard book of pool and billiards. Byrne,
R.   794.7
Byrne's standard book of pool and billiards. See Byrne,
R. Byrne's new standard book of pool and billiards
          794.7
Byron, Christopher
Martha Inc.   92
Byron, George Gordon Byron, 6th Baron, 1788-1824
Don Juan   821
About
Eisler, B. Byron—child of passion, fool of fame
          92
MacCarthy, F. Byron: life and legend   92
Byron: life and legend. MacCarthy, F.   92
Byzantine art
Lowden, J. Early Christian & Byzantine art
          709.02
Byzantine Empire
Gibbon, E. The decline and fall of the Roman Empire
          937

Byzantine Empire—*Continued*
Norwich, J. J. Byzantium 949.5
Norwich, J. J. A short history of Byzantium
949.5
Byzantium. Norwich, J. J. 949.5

C

C.A.T.V. *See* Cable television
C.L.E.P. *See* College Level Examination Program
Cabinetwork
See/See also pages in the following book(s):
Underhill, R. The woodwright's apprentice 684
Cabins *See* Log cabins and houses
Cable, George Washington, 1844-1925
See/See also pages in the following book(s):
Wilson, E. Patriotic gore p549-87, 593-604 810.9
Cable television
Broadcasting & cable yearbook 384.54
Cables, Submarine *See* Submarine cables
Cachin, Françoise
(jt. auth) Cézanne, P. Cézanne 759.4
Cactus
Anderson, E. F. The cactus family 583
Hewitt, T. The complete book of cacti & succulents
635.9
The **cactus** family. Anderson, E. F. 583
Cadavers *See* Dead
Cadillac desert. Reisner, M. P. 333.91
Caeiro, Alberto *See* Pessoa, Fernando, 1888-1935
Caesar, Caius, 20 B.C.-4 A.D.
See/See also pages in the following book(s):
Suetonius Tranquillus, C. The twelve Caesars 878
Caesar, Julius, 100-44 B.C.
The Gallic War 878
See/See also pages in the following book(s):
Hamilton, E. The Roman way 870.9
Café Europa. Drakulić, S. 947
Cage, John
About
Revill, D. The roaring silence: John Cage, a life
92
The **caged** owl. Orr, G. 811
Cagney, James, 1899-1986
About
McCabe, J. Cagney 92
Cahill, Susan Neunzig
(ed) Wise women: over two thousand years of spiritual writing by women. See Wise women: over two thousand years of spiritual writing by women 200
Cahill, Tim
Pass the butterworms 910.4
Cahill, Tom
Desire of the everlasting hills 232
The gifts of the Jews 909
How the Irish saved civilization 941.5
Caine, Lynn
Being a widow 306.8
Cairo (Egypt)
Rodenbeck, M. Cairo 962
Cairo Museum *See* Egyptian Museum
The **Cairo** Museum. See Egyptian treasures from the Egyptian Museum in Cairo 709.32
Cake
Beranbaum, R. L. The cake bible 641.8
Dalsass, D. The new good cake book 641.8
Desaulniers, M. Death by chocolate cakes 641.8
Malgieri, N. Perfect cakes 641.8
The **cake** bible. Beranbaum, R. L. 641.8
Cake decorating
Peters, C. Colette's cakes 641.8

Calabria (Italy)
Description
Rotella, M. Stolen figs and other adventures in Calabria 945
Calaprice, Alice
(ed) Einstein, A. Dear Professor Einstein 92
Calasibetta, Charlotte Mankey
The Fairchild dictionary of fashion 391
Calculus
Berlinski, D. A tour of the calculus 515
Calcutta (India)
Social conditions
Lapierre, D. The City of Joy 954
Caldecott Medal
The Newbery & Caldecott medal books, 1986-2000
028.5
Newbery and Caldecott Medal books, 1966-1975
028.5
Newbery and Caldecott Medal books, 1976-1985
028.5
Calendars
Chase's calendar of events 394.26
Duncan, D. E. Calendar 529
Religious holidays and calendars 291.3
Richards, E. G. Mapping time 529
The Wilson calendar of world history 902
Social aspects
Gould, S. J. Questioning the millennium 901
Calhoun, Craig J., 1952-
(ed) Dictionary of the social sciences. See Dictionary of the social sciences 300.3
Calhoun, John C. (John Caldwell), 1782-1850
See/See also pages in the following book(s):
Hofstadter, R. The American political tradition, and the men who made it p67-91 973
McPherson, J. M. Drawn with the sword 973.7
California
Description
Fradkin, P. L. The seven states of California
979.4
History
Didion, J. Where I was from 979.4
Social conditions
Didion, J. Where I was from 979.4
The **California** and Oregon Trail. See Parkman, F. The Oregon Trail 978
California impressionism. Gerdts, W. H. 759.13
California suite. Simon, N.
In Simon, N. The collected plays of Neil Simon v2 p549-632 812
Caligula, Emperor of Rome, 12-41
See/See also pages in the following book(s):
Suetonius Tranquillus, C. The twelve Caesars 878
Caligula. Camus, A.
In Camus, A. Caligula & three other plays p1-74
842
Caligula & three other plays. Camus, A. 842
Calisthenics *See* Gymnastics
The **call** of solitude. Buchholz, E. S. 155.9
The **call** of stories. Coles, R. 808
Callahan, Joan R.
Biological hazards 615.9
Callahan, Lisa
The fitness factor 613.7
Callas, Maria, 1923-1977
About
Gage, N. Greek fire 92
Scott, M. Maria Meneghini Callas 92
Calligraphy
Child, H. Calligraphy today 745.6
Harris, D. The art of calligraphy 745.6
Lovett, P. Calligraphy and illumination 745.6
Shepherd, M. Learn calligraphy 745.6
Calligraphy and illumination. Lovett, P. 745.6
Calligraphy today. Child, H. 745.6

Callow, Philip
Chekhov, the hidden ground 92
From noon to starry night: a life of Walt Whitman 92
Calloway, Colin G. (Colin Gordon), 1953-
The American Revolution in Indian country 973.3
Calories and carbohydrates. Kraus, B. 613.2
Calvin, William H., 1939-
How brains think 153.9
Calvino, Italo
Invisible cities; criticism
In Gass, W. H. Tests of time p37-68 814
Why read the classics? 809
See/See also pages in the following book(s):
Gass, W. H. Tests of time p37-68 814
Vidal, G. United States—essays, 1952-1992 p476-95 814
Calvocoressi, Peter
Who's who in the Bible 220.9
Cambodia
Communism
See Communism—Cambodia
Description
See/See also pages in the following book(s):
Jensen, C. I have seen the world begin 915
History
Chandler, D. P. The tragedy of Cambodian history 959.6
Him, C. When broken glass floats 92
Kamm, H. Cambodia: report from a stricken land 959.6
Ung, L. First they killed my father 959.6
History—1970-1975, Civil War
Bizot, F. The gate 959.6
Politics and government
Kiernan, B. The Pol Pot regime 959.6
The **Cambridge** ancient history 930
The **Cambridge** companion to Jane Austen 823.009
The **Cambridge** companion to Newton 530
The **Cambridge** companion to singing 782
The **Cambridge** companion to the Bible 220.9
Cambridge dictionary of astronomy. Mitton, J. 520.3
The **Cambridge** dictionary of philosophy 103
The **Cambridge** dictionary of scientists 920.003
The **Cambridge** dictionary of space technology. Williamson, M. 629.4
The **Cambridge** dictionary of statistics. Everitt, B. 519.5
The **Cambridge** encyclopedia of China 951
The **Cambridge** encyclopedia of human evolution 599.93
The **Cambridge** encyclopedia of Japan 952
The **Cambridge** encyclopedia of language. Crystal, D. 400
The **Cambridge** encyclopedia of meteorites. Norton, O. R. 523.5
The **Cambridge** encyclopedia of the English language. Crystal, D. 420
The **Cambridge** grammar of the English language. Huddleston, R. D. 425
Cambridge guide to American theatre 792.03
The **Cambridge** guide to children's books in English 028.5
The **Cambridge** guide to literature in English 820.3
The **Cambridge** guide to the constellations. Bakich, M. E. 523.8
Cambridge guide to the weather. Reynolds, R. 551.5
The **Cambridge** guide to theatre 792.03
The **Cambridge** guide to women's writing in English 820.9
The **Cambridge** guide to world theatre. See The Cambridge guide to theatre 792.03

The **Cambridge** handbook of American literature 810.3
The **Cambridge** historical encyclopedia of Great Britain and Ireland 941
The **Cambridge** history of American literature 810.9
The **Cambridge** history of China 951
The **Cambridge** history of German literature 830.9
The **Cambridge** history of Italian literature 850.9
The **Cambridge** history of Judaism 296
The **Cambridge** history of Latin America 980
The **Cambridge** history of Latin American literature 860.9
The **Cambridge** history of Russian literature 891.7
The **Cambridge** illustrated dictionary of natural history. Lincoln, R. J. 508
The **Cambridge** illustrated history of astronomy 520
The **Cambridge** illustrated history of medicine 610.9
The **Cambridge** illustrated history of prehistoric art. Bahn, P. G. 709.01
The **Cambridge** illustrated history of religions 200.9
The **Cambridge** illustrated history of the British Empire 941.08
The **Cambridge** illustrated history of the Islamic world 909
The **Cambridge** illustrated history of the Middle Ages 909.07
The **Cambridge** introduction to modern British fiction, 1950-2000. Head, D. 823.009
The **Cambridge** modern history. See The New Cambridge modern history 909.08
The **Cambridge** planetary handbook. Bakich, M. E. 523.4
The **Cambridge** star atlas. Tirion, W. 523.8
Cambridge star atlas 2000.0. See Tirion, W. The Cambridge star atlas 523.8
The **Cambridge** thesaurus of American English. Lutz, W. 423
The **Cambridge** world history of food 641.3
Cameron, Angus
The L.L. Bean game and fish cookbook 641.6
Camfield, Gregg
(ed) The Oxford companion to Mark Twain. See The Oxford companion to Mark Twain 818
The **Camino**. MacLaine, S. 92
Camp, Jim
Start with no 658.4
Campaign funds
United States
See/See also pages in the following book(s):
Drew, E. The corruption of American politics 364.1
Campbell, Ballard C., 1940-
(ed) American presidential campaigns and elections. See American presidential campaigns and elections 324
Campbell, Don G.
The Mozart effect 615.8
Campbell, Gordon
The Oxford dictionary of the Renaissance 940.2
Campbell, Greg
Blood diamonds 966.4
Campbell, Jeremy, 1931-
The liar's tale 177
Campbell, Joseph, 1904-1987
The masks of God 291.1
The power of myth 291.1
Transformations of myth through time 291.1
Campbell, Keith, 1938-
(jt. auth) Wilmut, I. The second creation 174
Campbell, Thomas
Tapestry in the Renaissance 746

Campbell, Tom *See* Campbell, Thomas
Campo, Rafael, 1964-
Diva 811
Campos, Alvaro de *See* Pessoa, Fernando, 1888-1935
Camps
Directories
Guide to summer camps and summer schools
796.54
Camus, Albert, 1913-1960
Caligula
In Camus, A. Caligula & three other plays p1-74
842
Caligula & three other plays 842
The just assassins
In Camus, A. Caligula & three other plays p233-302
842
The misunderstanding
In Camus, A. Caligula & three other plays p75-134
842
The myth of Sisyphus, and other essays 844
The rebel 303.6
Resistance, rebellion, and death 844
State of siege
In Camus, A. Caligula & three other plays p135-232
842
About
Todd, O. Albert Camus 92
Can poetry matter? Gioia, D. 809.1
Can such things be? Bierce, A.
In Bierce, A. The collected writings 818
Canada, Geoffrey
Fist, stick, knife, gun 305.23
Reaching up for manhood 305.23
Canada
Weihs, J. R. Facts about Canada, its provinces and territories 971
Directories
Canadian almanac & directory 317.1
Encyclopedias
The Canadian encyclopedia 971
History
Riendeau, R. E. A brief history of Canada 971
History—0-1763 (New France)
Morgan, T. Wilderness at dawn 970
History—Societies—Directories
Directory of historical organizations in the United States and Canada 973.06
Military history
Purcell, L. E. Encyclopedia of battles in North America, 1517 to 1916 970
Social conditions—Encyclopedias
Encyclopedia of social issues 306
Canadian almanac & directory 317.1
Canadian art
Directories
American art directory 702.5
Canadian authors *See* Authors, Canadian
Canadian Committee on Cataloguing
See also Joint Steering Committee for Revision of AACR
The Canadian encyclopedia 971
Canadian literature
Bio-bibliography
The Oxford companion to Canadian literature
810.3
Dictionaries
The Oxford companion to Canadian literature
810.3
Encyclopedias
Encyclopedia of literature in Canada 810.3
Native American authors—Bio-bibliography
Native North American literature 810.9
Canby, Vincent
The New York times guide to the best 1,000 movies ever made 791.43

Cancer
See also Breast cancer; Lung cancer
Adrouny, A. R. Understanding colon cancer
616.99
American Cancer Society's Guide to complementary and alternative cancer methods 616.99
The Cancer pain sourcebook 616.99
Cancer sourcebook 616.99
Caregiving: a step-by-step resource for caring for the person with cancer at home 649.8
Childhood cancer 618.92
Coleman, C. N. Understanding cancer 616.99
Everyone's guide to cancer therapy 616.99
Gordon, J. S. Comprehensive cancer care 616.99
Hall, S. S. A commotion in the blood 616.07
Harpham, W. S. Diagnosis, cancer 616.99
Informed decisions 616.99
Janes-Hodder, H. Childhood cancer 618.92
Pediatric cancer sourcebook 618.92
Teeley, P. The complete cancer survival guide
616.99
See/See also pages in the following book(s):
Gallo, R. C. Virus hunting p59-115 616.97
Diet therapy
Arnot, B. The breast cancer prevention diet
616.99
Arnot, B. The breast health cookbook 616.99
Personal narratives
Gearin-Tosh, M. Living proof 92
Price, R. A whole new life 92
The Cancer pain sourcebook 616.99
Cancer sourcebook 616.99
Candlemaker's companion. Oppenheimer, B.
745.59
Candles
Oppenheimer, B. Candlemaker's companion
745.59
Canfield, Dorothy *See* Fisher, Dorothy Canfield, 1879-1958
Canning and preserving
Costenbader, C. W. The big book of preserving the harvest 641.4
Shephard, S. Pickled, potted, and canned 641.4
Ziedrich, L. The joy of pickling 641.4
Cannon, Annie Jump, 1863-1941
See/See also pages in the following book(s):
Greenstein, G. Portraits of discovery p7-30 920
Cannon, John, 1926-
The Oxford illustrated history of the British monarchy
941
(ed) The Oxford companion to British history. See The Oxford companion to British history 941
Cannon, Lou
Official negligence 979.4
Canoes and canoeing
Fredston, J. A. Rowing to latitude 797.1
Mason, B. Path of the paddle 797.1
Can't be satisfied: the life and times of Muddy Waters. Gordon, R. 92
Can't you hear me callin': the life of Bill Monroe, father of bluegrass. Smith, R. D. 92
The Canterbury tales. Chaucer, G. 821
also in Chaucer, G. The complete poetry and prose of Geoffrey Chaucer 821
also in Chaucer, G. The portable Chaucer 821
Cantor, Georg, 1845-1918
See/See also pages in the following book(s):
Bell, E. T. Men of mathematics p555-79 920
Cantor, George, 1941-
Historic landmarks of black America 917.3
Cantor, Norman F.
In the wake of the plague 614.5
(ed) The Encyclopedia of the Middle Ages. See The Encyclopedia of the Middle Ages 909.07

Cantor Fitzgerald LP
Lutnick, H. On top of the world   **332.6**
The **cantos** of Ezra Pound. Pound, E.   **811**
Capablanca, José Raúl, 1888-1942
Chess fundamentals   **794.1**
Capano, Thomas J., 1949-
     About
Rule, A. —and never let her go   **364.1**
Cape, Judith *See* Page, P. K. (Patricia Kathleen), 1916-
Cape Cod (Mass.)
     Description
Thoreau, H. D. Cape Cod   **917.44**
     Social life and customs
Colt, G. H. The big house   **920**
Cape Cod. Thoreau, H. D.
    also in Thoreau, H. D. A week on the Concord and
     Merrimack rivers; Walden; The Maine woods;
     Cape Cod   **818**
Čapek, Josef, 1887-1945
(jt. auth) Čapek, K. R.U.R. and The insect play
   891.8
Čapek, Karel, 1890-1938
The insect play
   In Čapek, K. R.U.R. and The insect play   **891.8**
R.U.R. and The insect play   **891.8**
R.U.R. (Rossum's Universal Robots)
   In Čapek, K. R.U.R. and The insect play   **891.8**
Capelo, Gregory R.
VCR troubleshooting & repair   **621.388**
Capers, Valerie
    See/See also pages in the following book(s):
Walker-Hill, H. From spirituals to symphonies
   920
Capital
Marx, K. Capital   **330.1**
Capital punishment
Henderson, H. Capital punishment   **364.66**
Solotaroff, I. The last face you'll ever see   **364.66**
Capitalism
    See also Entrepreneurship
Friedman, M. Free to choose   **330.1**
Greider, W. The soul of capitalism   **330.1**
McMillan, J. Reinventing the bazaar   **330.1**
Soto, H. de. The mystery of capital   **330.1**
    See/See also pages in the following book(s):
Heilbroner, R. L. The worldly philosophers   **330.1**
Caplan, Arthur L.
(ed) The Ethics of organ transplants. See The Ethics of
   organ transplants   **174**
Capone, Al, 1899-1947
     About
Bergreen, L. Capone   **92**
Capote, Truman, 1924-1984
In cold blood   **364.1**
Music for chameleons   **818**
     About
Plimpton, G. Truman Capote   **92**
Cappella Sistina (Vatican) *See* Vatican. Cappella Sistina
Capra, Fritjof
The web of life   **570.1**
Captain Jack *See* Kintpuash, Modoc Chief, 1837?-1873
Caputo, Philip
Ghosts of Tsavo   **599.75**
A rumor of war   **959.704**
Capuzzo, Mike
Close to shore   **597**
Caravaggio, Michelangelo Merisi da, 1573-1610
     About
Langdon, H. Caravaggio   **92**
Robb, P. M: the man who became Caravaggio   **92**
Carbon dioxide greenhouse effect *See* Greenhouse effect
Card games
    See also Bridge (Game); Poker
Ainslie, T. Ainslie's complete Hoyle   **795**

Bellin, A. Poker nation   **795.4**
Gibson, W. B. Hoyle's modern encyclopedia of card
   games   **795.4**
Scarne, J. Scarne's encyclopedia of card games
   795.4
The **cardiovascular** cure. Cooke, J. P.   **616.1**
Cardiovascular system
     See also Blood—Circulation
     Diseases
Cooke, J. P. The cardiovascular cure   **616.1**
DeBakey, M. E. The new living heart   **616.1**
Care, Medical *See* Medical care
Care and repair of everyday treasures. Miller, J.
   745.1
Care of children *See* Child care
Care of the dying *See* Terminal care
Career changes
Wendleton, K. Building a great résumé   **650.14**
Career comeback. Richardson, B. G.   **650.14**
Career guidance *See* Vocational guidance
Careers *See* Occupations
Caregivers
Caregiving: a step-by-step resource for caring for the
   person with cancer at home   **649.8**
Carter, R. Helping yourself help others   **649.8**
McFarlane, R. The complete bedside companion
   649.8
Caregiving: a step-by-step resource for caring for the
   person with cancer at home   **649.8**
Careless love: the unmaking of Elvis Presley. Guralnick,
   P.   **92**
Careri, Giovanni, 1958-
Baroques   **709**
The **caretaker.** Pinter, H.
   In Pinter, H. Complete works v2   **822**
Carey, Charles W.
American inventors, entrepreneurs, and business
   visionaries   **920**
Carey, Ernestine Gilbreth
(jt. auth) Gilbreth, F. B. Cheaper by the dozen
   92
Carey, Gary
A multicultural dictionary of literary terms   **803**
Cargas, Sarita
(ed) Encyclopedia of Holocaust literature. See Encyclo-
   pedia of Holocaust literature   **809**
Caribbean region
     Politics and government
    See/See also pages in the following book(s):
Naipaul, V. S. The writer and the world p73-140
   824
Caricatures *See* Cartoons and caricatures
Caring for a child with autism. Ives, M.   **618.92**
Caring for your school-age child   **649**
Carl, Deborah Ann
(jt. auth) Bentley, E. P. Directory of family associa-
   tions   **929**
Carle, Eric
    See/See also pages in the following book(s):
Marcus, L. S. Ways of telling   **741.6**
Carley, Michael Jabara, 1945-
1939   **940.53**
Carlin, Bob
(ed) American musical traditions. See American musi-
   cal traditions   **781.62**
Carlin, George, 1937-
Brain droppings   **817**
Napalm & silly putty   **817**
Carlin, Richard
The big book of country music   **920.003**
Country music: a biographical dictionary   **920.003**
Carlson, Charles B.
The smart investor's survival guide   **332.6**
Carlson, Laurie M., 1952-
A fever in Salem   **133.4**

Carlson, Liisa
(jt. auth) Giffin, J. M. Dog owner's home veterinary handbook **636.7**
Carlson, Shawn
(ed) The Amateur astronomer. See The Amateur astronomer **520**
Carlyle, Jane Welsh, 1801-1866
See/See also pages in the following book(s):
Woolf, V. The second common reader p167-81 **820.9**
Carlyle, Thomas, 1795-1881
Past and present **824**
Sartor resartus **824**
Carmack, Sharon DeBartolo, 1956-
Organizing your family history search **929**
Carmi, Israel
About
Blum, H. The brigade **940.54**
Carmichael, Hoagy, 1899-1982
About
Sudhalter, R. Stardust melody: the life and music of Hoagy Carmichael **92**
Carnage and culture. Hanson, V. D. **904**
Carnegie, Andrew, 1835-1919
About
Krass, P. Carnegie **92**
Rea, T. Bone wars **560**
Wall, J. F. Andrew Carnegie **92**
See/See also pages in the following book(s):
Klein, M. The change makers **920**
Carnegie, Dale, 1888-1955
How to win friends and influence people **158**
Carnegie Library of Pittsburgh. Science and Technology Dept.
The Handy science answer book. See The Handy science answer book **500**
Science and technology desk reference. See Science and technology desk reference **500**
Carnes, Mark C. (Mark Christopher), 1950-
(ed) American national biography. See American national biography **920.003**
(ed) Historical atlas of the United States. See Historical atlas of the United States **911**
Carnival
Danticat, E. After the dance **394.25**
Caro, Robert A.
The power broker: Robert Moses and the fall of New York **92**
The years of Lyndon Johnson **92**
Caroli, Betty Boyd
First ladies **920**
The Roosevelt women **920**
Caroline, Queen, consort of George IV, King of Great Britain, 1768-1821 *See* Caroline Amelia Elizabeth, Queen, consort of George IV, King of Great Britain, 1768-1821
Caroline Amelia Elizabeth, Queen, consort of George IV, King of Great Britain, 1768-1821
About
Fraser, F. The unruly queen: the life of Queen Caroline **92**
Carols
The New Oxford book of carols **782.28**
Carpentry
Abram, N. Measure twice, cut once **684**
Carpetbag rule *See* Reconstruction (1865-1876)
Carpets *See* Weaving
Carr, Anna, 1955-
Rodale's illustrated encyclopedia of herbs. See Rodale's illustrated encyclopedia of herbs **635**
Carr, Caleb, 1955-
The lessons of terror **303.6**
Carr, Joseph J.
Old time radios! **621.384**

Carr, Raymond
(ed) Spain: a history. See Spain: a history **946**
Carr, Rosamond Halsey
Land of a thousand hills **967.571**
Carr-Gomm, Sarah
Hidden symbols in art **704.9**
Carreras, José, 1946-
Singing from the soul **92**
Carrère, Emmanuel, 1957-
The adversary **364.1**
Carrière, Jean-Claude
(jt. auth) Dalai Lama XIV Violence and compassion **294.3**
Carroll, Andrew
(ed) Letters of a nation. See Letters of a nation **816**
Carroll, James
Constantine's sword **261.2**
Toward a new Catholic Church **282**
Carroll, Lewis, 1832-1898
About
Cohen, M. N. Lewis Carroll **92**
See/See also pages in the following book(s):
Wullschläger, J. Inventing wonderland **820.9**
Carruth, Hayden, 1921-
Collected longer poems **811**
Collected shorter poems, 1946-1991 **811**
Doctor Jazz **811**
Scrambled eggs & whiskey **811**
Carry me home. McWhorter, D. **976.1**
Cars (Automobiles) *See* Automobiles
Carson, Anne, 1950-
Autobiography of red **811**
The beauty of the husband **811**
Men in the off hours **811**
(tr) Sappho. If not, winter **884**
Carson, Clayborne, 1944-
Malcolm X: the FBI file **92**
(ed) The Eyes on the prize civil rights reader. See The Eyes on the prize civil rights reader **323.1**
Carson, Johnny, 1925-
See/See also pages in the following book(s):
Life stories **920**
Carson, Rachel, 1907-1964
The edge of the sea **577.7**
Lost woods **570**
The sea around us **551.46**
Under the sea wind **577.7**
About
Lear, L. J. Rachel Carson **92**
See/See also pages in the following book(s):
Leopold, E. A darker ribbon **616.99**
Carson, Rob, 1950-
Mount St. Helens: the eruption and recovery of a volcano **551.2**
Carter, Alice A.
The art of National Geographic **741.6**
The Red Rose girls **759.13**
Carter, Betty, 1944-
Best books for young adults **028.1**
Carter, Bill, 1939-
Latitude **526**
Carter, Bruce *See* Hough, Richard Alexander, 1922-1999
Carter, Graydon
(ed) Vanity Fair's Hollywood. See Vanity Fair's Hollywood **791.43**
Carter, Gregg Lee, 1951-
(ed) Guns in American society. See Guns in American society **363.3**
Carter, Hurricane *See* Carter, Rubin
Carter, James Earl *See* Carter, Jimmy, 1924-
Carter, Jimmy, 1924-
Everything to gain **92**
An hour before daylight **92**

Carter, Jimmy, 1924——_Continued_
Keeping faith: memoirs of a president   92
Living faith   92
Sources of strength   248.4
Turning point   975.8
The virtues of aging   305.26
About
Morris, K. E. Jimmy Carter, American moralist
                                            92
See/See also pages in the following book(s):
Woodward, B. Shadow   973.92
Carter, Lillian, 1898-1983
See/See also pages in the following book(s):
Angelo, B. First mothers   920
Carter, Merri Sue, 1964-
(jt. auth) Carter, B. Latitude   526
Carter, Miranda, 1965-
Anthony Blunt: his lives   92
Carter, Rita
Exploring consciousness   153
Carter, Robert A.
Buffalo Bill Cody   92
Carter, Rosalynn
Helping someone with mental illness   616.89
Helping yourself help others   649.8
(jt. auth) Carter, J. Everything to gain   92
Carter, Rubin
About
Hirsch, J. S. Hurricane: the miraculous journey of
Rubin Carter   92
Carter, Stephen L.
God's name in vain   322
Integrity   170
Reflections of an affirmative action baby   342
Carter, Steve, 1956-
Men like women who like themselves   158
Carter, William C.
Marcel Proust   92
Carter family (Musical group)
Zwonitzer, M. Will you miss me when I'm gone?
                                            920
Carter family
About
Carter, J. An hour before daylight   92
Cartooning for the beginner. Hart, C.   741.5
Cartoons, Animated _See_ Animated films
Cartoons and caricatures
See also Comic books, strips, etc.
Hart, C. Cartooning for the beginner   741.5
Hirschfeld, A. Hirschfeld on line   741.5
McCloud, S. Reinventing comics   741.5
Carvajal, Carol Styles
(ed) The Oxford Spanish dictionary. See The Oxford
Spanish dictionary   463
Carver, Raymond
All of us   811
A new path to the waterfall   811
About
Halpert, S. Raymond Carver   92
Carving, Wood _See_ Wood carving
Carwardine, Mark
(ed) Whales, dolphins, and porpoises. See Whales, dol-
phins, and porpoises   599.5
Cascadia. Hillman, B.   811
Case closed. Posner, G. L.   973.922
The **case** for marriage. Waite, L. J.   306.8
The **casebook** of forensic detection. Evans, C.   614
The **cases** that haunt us. Douglas, J. E. 364.1
Casey, Winifred Rosen _See_ Rosen, Winifred, 1943-
Cash, Johnny
About
Ring of fire: the Johnny Cash reader   92
Cash, Wilbur Joseph, 1900-1941
The mind of the South   975

Caspari, Rachel, 1957-
(jt. auth) Wolpoff, M. H. Race and human evolution
                                            599.97
Cassanelli, Roberto
Houses and monuments of Pompeii. See Houses and
monuments of Pompeii   709.38
Cassatt, Mary, 1844-1926
Mary Cassatt, modern woman   759.13
About
Mathews, N. M. Mary Cassatt   92
Cassedy, James H.
Medicine in America: a short history   610.9
Cassel, Gary H., 1953-
The eye book   617.7
The **Cassell** dictionary of English idioms 423
Cassell dictionary of proverbs. Pickering, D.   398.9
The **Cassell** dictionary of slang. Green, J.   427
Cassell's dictionary of first names. See Room, A. Dictio-
nary of first names   929.4
Cassell's French dictionary   443
Cassell's German dictionary   433
Cassell's Italian dictionary   453
Cassell's Spanish-English, English-Spanish dictionary
                                            463
Cassette tape recordings, Video _See_ Videotapes
Cassette tapes, Audio _See_ Sound recordings
Cassidy, Frederic Gomes, 1907-2000
(ed) Dictionary of American regional English. See Dic-
tionary of American regional English   427
Cassidy, John
Dot.con   381
Cassidy, Joseph Edward
About
Wise, D. Cassidy's run   327.12
Cassidy's run. Wise, D.   327.12
Cassileth, Barrie R.
The alternative medicine handbook   615.5
Cassin-Scott, Jack
The illustrated encyclopaedia of costume and fashion
from 1066 to the present   391
Cassirer, Ernst, 1874-1945
(ed) The Renaissance philosophy of man. See The Re-
naissance philosophy of man   189
Cassirer, Nadine Gordimer _See_ Gordimer, Nadine,
1923-
Castaneda, Carlos
The teachings of Don Juan   299
Castillo, Bernal Díaz del _See_ Díaz del Castillo, Bernal,
1496-1584
Castillo, Carlos, 1890-
(comp) The University of Chicago Spanish dictionary.
See The University of Chicago Spanish dictionary
                                            463
Castle, David
(ed) Genetically modified foods. See Genetically modi-
fied foods   363.1
Castles
Johnson, P. Castles of England, Scotland and Wales
                                            941
Castles burning. Denes, M.   940.53
Castro, Fidel, 1927-
About
Quirk, R. E. Fidel Castro   92
Szulc, T. Fidel   92
See/See also pages in the following book(s):
Fernández Revuelta, A. Castro's daughter   92
Gimbel, W. Havana dreams   972.91
Castronova, Frank V.
(ed) Beacham's guide to the endangered species of
North America. See Beacham's guide to the endan-
gered species of North America   578.68
Castro's daughter. Fernández Revuelta, A.   92
The **cat** and the curmudgeon. Amory, C.   818
Cat watching. Morris, D.   636.8
The **cat** who came for Christmas. Amory, C.   818

Cataloging
  Anglo-American cataloguing rules   **025.3**
  Gorman, M. The concise AACR2, 1998 revision
     025.3
  Intner, S. S. Standard cataloging for school and public
  libraries   **025.3**
Catalogs *See* Classical mythology—Catalogs; Firearms—
  Catalogs; High school libraries—Catalogs; Kitchen
  utensils—Catalogs; School libraries—Catalogs
Catastrophes (Geology)
  Alvarez, W. T. rex and the Crater of Doom
     551.7
  Dauber, P. M. The three big bangs   **523.1**
  Powell, J. L. Night comes to the Cretaceous
     576.8
  Rubin, A. E. Disturbing the solar system   **521**
Catastrophic extinction of species *See* Mass extinction
  of species
Catching cold. See Davies, P. The devil's flu
     614.5
Catching the light. Zajonc, A.   **535**
Catchpole, Brian
  The Korean War, 1950-53   **951.9**
Cateforis, David
  (jt. auth) Stokstad, M. Art history   **709**
**Catharine Howard, Queen, consort of Henry VIII,
  King of England, d. 1542**
  See/See also pages in the following book(s):
  Fraser, A. The wives of Henry VIII p287-354
     920
  Starkey, D. Six wives: the queens of Henry VIII
     920
**Catharine Parr, Queen, consort of Henry VIII, King
  of England, 1512-1548**
  See/See also pages in the following book(s):
  Fraser, A. The wives of Henry VIII p355-414
     920
  Starkey, D. Six wives: the queens of Henry VIII
     920
Cathedral High School (Springfield, Mass.)
  Blais, M. In these girls, hope is a muscle
     796.323
Cathedrals
  Prache, A. Cathedrals of Europe   **726**
Cathedrals of Europe. Prache, A.   **726**
Cather, Willa, 1873-1947
  April twilights, and other poems
  In Cather, W. Stories, poems, and other writings
     818
  Not under forty
  In Cather, W. Stories, poems, and other writings
     818
  Stories, poems, and other writings   **818**
  About
  Lee, H. Willa Cather   **92**
  Woodress, J. L. Willa Cather   **92**
  See/See also pages in the following book(s):
  American women fiction writers   **813.009**
Catherine II, the Great, Empress of Russia, 1729-1796
  About
  Erickson, C. Great Catherine   **92**
  Troyat, H. Catherine the Great   **92**
**Catherine, of Aragon, Queen, consort of Henry VIII,
  King of England, 1485-1536**
  See/See also pages in the following book(s):
  Fraser, A. The wives of Henry VIII p7-111   **920**
  Starkey, D. Six wives: the queens of Henry VIII
     920
Catherine Howard *See* Catharine Howard, Queen, con-
  sort of Henry VIII, King of England, d. 1542
Catherine Parr *See* Catharine Parr, Queen, consort of
  Henry VIII, King of England, 1512-1548
Catholic almanac   **282**

Catholic Church
  See also Inquisition
  Carroll, J. Toward a new Catholic Church   **282**
  Collins, P. The modern Inquisition   **282**
  Cornwell, J. Breaking faith   **282**
  Harline, C. E. Miracles at the Jesus Oak   **231.7**
  John Paul II, Pope. Crossing the threshold of hope
     282
  New Catholic encyclopedia: jubilee volume, the
  Wojtyla years   **282**
  Reese, T. J. Inside the Vatican   **282**
  Wills, G. Papal sin   **262**
  Wills, G. Why I am a Catholic   **282**
  Woodward, K. L. Making saints   **282**
  See/See also pages in the following book(s):
  Russell, B. A history of Western philosophy p301-487
     109
  Directories
  Catholic almanac   **282**
  The Official Catholic directory   **282**
  Encyclopedias
  The Catholic encyclopedia   **282**
  The HarperCollins encyclopedia of Catholicism
     282
  New Catholic encyclopedia   **282**
  History
  Duffy, E. Saints & sinners   **282**
  Küng, H. The Catholic Church   **282**
  Maxwell-Stuart, P. G. Chronicle of the popes   **282**
  Liturgy
  Norris, K. The cloister walk   **255**
  Relations—Judaism
  Carroll, J. Constantine's sword   **261.2**
  Goldhagen, D. A moral reckoning   **940.53**
  Kertzer, D. I. The Popes against the Jews   **261.2**
  Zuccotti, S. Under his very windows   **940.53**
  United States
  Gillis, C. Roman Catholicism in America   **282**
  Greeley, A. M. The Catholic myth   **282**
  Saints and sinners   **282**
  The **Catholic** encyclopedia   **282**
  The **Catholic** myth. Greeley, A. M.   **282**
Catholics
  United States
  Greeley, A. M. The Catholic myth   **282**
  Saints and sinners   **282**
Catron, Louis E.
  Theatre sources dot com   **025.04**
Cats
  The Doctor's book of home remedies for dogs and cats
     636.7
  Edney, A. T. B. ASPCA complete cat care manual
     636.8
  Fogle, B. The new encyclopedia of the cat   **636.8**
  Herriot, J. James Herriot's cat stories   **636.8**
  Masson, J. M. The nine emotional lives of cats
     636.8
  McGinnis, T. The well cat book   **636.8**
  Morris, D. Cat watching   **636.8**
  Petspeak   **636.089**
  Richards, J. R. ASPCA complete guide to cats
     636.8
  Thomas, E. M. The tribe of tiger   **599.75**
  Wilbourn, C. The total cat   **636.8**
  See/See also pages in the following book(s):
  Hubbell, S. Shrinking the cat   **660.6**
  Diseases
  The Cornell book of cats   **636.8**
  McGinnis, T. The well cat book   **636.8**
Cats, Wild *See* Wild cats
Cats' paws and catapults. Vogel, S.   **571.4**
Cattle
  Lovenheim, P. Portrait of a burger as a young calf
     636.2

Catton, Bruce, 1899-1978
Grant moves south — 92
Grant takes command — 92
A stillness at Appomattox — 973.7
The **caucasian** chalk circle. Brecht, B.
In Nine plays of the modern theater p1-115 — 808.82
Cauchy, Augustin Louis, Baron, 1789-1857
See/See also pages in the following book(s):
Bell, E. T. Men of mathematics p270-93 — 920
Cauldwell, Rex
Safe home wiring projects — 621.319
The **Causes** of the Civil War — 973.7
Cavafy, Constantine P., 1863-1933
The complete poems of Cavafy — 889
See/See also pages in the following book(s):
Brodsky, J. Less than one p53-68 — 814
Cavalier in buckskin. See Utley, R. M. Custer: cavalier in buckskin — 973.8
Cave, Yvonne
Succulents for the contemporary garden — 635.9
Cave drawings and paintings
See also Rock drawings, paintings, and engravings
Cavendish, Georgiana Spencer, Duchess of Devonshire
See Devonshire, Georgiana Spencer Cavendish, Duchess of, 1757-1806
Cavendish, Margaret *See* Newcastle, Margaret Cavendish, Duchess of, 1624?-1674
Caves
Taylor, M. R. Caves — 796.52
Cawley, A. C. (Arthur Clare)
(ed) Everyman, and medieval miracle plays. See Everyman, and medieval miracle plays — 822.008
Cawley, Arthur Clare *See* Cawley, A. C. (Arthur Clare)
Cayce, Edgar, 1877-1945
My life as a seer — 92
About
Kirkpatrick, S. Edgar Cayce — 92
Cayley, Arthur, 1821-1895
See/See also pages in the following book(s):
Bell, E. T. Men of mathematics p378-405 — 920
Cayton, Mary Kupiec
Encyclopedia of American cultural and intellectual history. See Encyclopedia of American cultural and intellectual history — 973.03
Encyclopedia of American social history. See Encyclopedia of American social history — 973.03
CD-ROMs
American decades — 973.9
The American Heritage dictionary of the English language — 423
American Institute of Architects. Architectural graphic standards — 692
American library directory — 027
American men & women of science — 920.003
The ARRL handbook for radio amateurs — 621.3841
Bibliographic index — 011
Biography index — 920
Blake, W. Songs of innocence and of experience — 821
The Book of the states — 352.13
Book review digest — 028.1
Books in print — 015.73
Borges, J. L. This craft of verse — 809.1
Business periodicals index — 650
Canadian almanac & directory — 317.1
CD-ROMs in print — 025.3
Choice — 028.1
County and city data book — 317.3
CRC handbook of chemistry and physics — 540
Current biography yearbook — 920.003
Current medical diagnosis and treatment — 610.3
Current surgical diagnosis & treatment — 617

Darke, R. The color encyclopedia of ornamental grasses — 635.9
The Dictionary of national biography — 920.003
Directory of physicians in the United States — 610.69
Dorland's illustrated medical dictionary — 610.3
Education index — 370.5
Encyclopedia of African-American culture and history — 305.8
The Encyclopedia of religion — 200.3
Encyclopedia of the Vietnam War — 959.704
Encyclopedia of world biography — 920.003
Essay and general literature index — 080
Facts on file — 909.82
The Foundation directory — 061.025
General science index — 505
Goldbarth, A. Combinations of the Universe — 811
Grossman, M. Encyclopedia of the Persian Gulf War — 956.7
Hawley's condensed chemical dictionary — 540.3
Humanities index — 050
I ching. The classic of changes — 299
Jane's all the world's aircraft — 629.133
Jane's fighting ships — 623.8
Kane, J. N. Famous first facts — 031.02
Library literature & information science index — 020
Manual of mineral science — 549
Marks' standard handbook for mechanical engineers — 621
The Merck index — 615
Merriam-Webster's collegiate dictionary — 423
Merriam-Webster's collegiate thesaurus — 423
Monthly catalog of United States Government publications — 015.73
National Electrical Code handbook — 621.3
National geographic index, 1888-1988 — 910
Netter, F. H. Atlas of human anatomy — 611
The New Encyclopaedia Britannica — 031
The New Oxford American dictionary — 423
The New York Times Index — 071
The Official ABMS directory of board certified medical specialists — 610.69
The Oxford English dictionary — 423
Random House Webster's unabridged dictionary — 423
Readers' guide to periodical literature — 051
Shakespeare, W. Poems — 821
Shakespeare, W. Sonnets — 821
Short story index — 808.83
Shorter Oxford English dictionary on historical principles — 423
Social sciences index — 300.5
Spiegelman, A. Maus — 940.53
Standard and Poor's register of corporations, directors, and executives — 338.7
Standard directory of advertisers — 659.1
Standard directory of advertising agencies — 659.1
Taber's cyclopedic medical dictionary — 610.3
Ulrich's periodicals directory — 011
United Nations. Statistical Office. Statistical yearbook — 310.5
United States. Bureau of Labor Statistics. Occupational outlook handbook — 331.7
United States. Bureau of the Census. Statistical abstract of the United States — 317.3
United States. Government Printing Office. Style manual — 808
Webster's third new international dictionary of the English language, unabridged — 423
The World Book encyclopedia — 031
The Writer's market — 808
Directories
CD-ROMs in print — 025.3
CD-ROMs in print — 025.3

Cecil, Robert Arthur Talbot Gascoyne- *See* Salisbury, Robert Arthur Talbot Gascoyne-Cecil, 3rd Marquis of, 1830-1903

CEEB *See* College Entrance Examination Board

Celan, Paul
Poems of Paul Celan   831
Selected poems and prose of Paul Celan   831
See/See also pages in the following book(s):
Simon, J. I. Dreamers of dreams   809.1

Celebrate the world. MacDonald, M. R.   398.2

Celebrate with chocolate. Desaulniers, M.   641.6

Celebration & renewal   296.4

Celebrities
O'Reilly, B. The no-spin zone   973.92
Richardson, J. Sacred monsters   920

Cells
Harold, F. M. The way of the cell   571.6
Loewenstein, W. R. The touchstone of life   571.6
Rensberger, B. Life itself   571.6
    Dictionaries
The Facts on File dictionary of cell and molecular biology   571.6

The **cellular** connection. Steuernagel, R.   621.385

Cellular telephones
Murray, J. B., Jr. Wireless nation   384.5
Steuernagel, R. The cellular connection   621.385

Celtic mythology
    Dictionaries
MacKillop, J. Dictionary of Celtic mythology   299

Celtics (Basketball team) *See* Boston Celtics (Basketball team)

Celts
Cunliffe, B. The ancient Celts   936

Censorship
DelFattore, J. What Johnny shouldn't read   379
See/See also pages in the following book(s):
Bok, S. Mayhem   302.23
Gass, W. H. Tests of time p179-95   814
    Encyclopedias
Censorship: a world encyclopedia   363.3
Censorship: a world encyclopedia   363.3

Census
    See also United States—Census

Census Bureau (U.S.) *See* United States. Bureau of the Census

Center for Public Integrity
Fagin, D. Toxic deception   615.9

Central America
    History
Pérez-Brignoli, H. A brief history of Central America   972.8

Central America (Steamship)
Kinder, G. Ship of gold in the deep blue sea   910.4

Central cities *See* Inner cities

Central Europe
    Historical geography—Maps
Magocsi, P. R. Historical atlas of Central Europe   911

Central Intelligence Agency (U.S.) *See* United States. Central Intelligence Agency

Central Pacific Railroad
Ambrose, S. E. Nothing like it in the world   385
See/See also pages in the following book(s):
Bain, D. H. Empire express   385

Century 21 accounting: advanced course   657
Century 21 accounting: first-year course   657
Century 21 keyboarding & information processing   652.3

A **century** of recorded music. Day, T.   780
The **century** of the gene. Keller, E. F.   576.5
A **century** of triumph. Chant, C.   629.13

Ceram, C. W., 1915-1972
Gods, graves, and scholars   930.1

The **ceramic** glaze handbook. Burleson, M.   738.1

Ceramics
Karmason, M. G. Majolica: a complete and illustrated survey   738
    Dictionaries
Hamer, F. The potter's dictionary of materials and techniques   738.1
Ceramics. Nelson, G. C.   738.1

Cerebrovascular disease *See* Stroke

Ceremonies *See* Rites and ceremonies

Certain trumpets. Wills, G.   303.3

Cervantes Saavedra, Miguel de, 1547-1616
Don Quixote de la Mancha; dramatization. See Wasserman, D. Man of La Mancha   812
See/See also pages in the following book(s):
Bloom, H. The Western canon   809

Césaire, Aimé
See/See also pages in the following book(s):
Baraka, I. A. The LeRoi Jones/Amiri Baraka reader   818

Cézanne, Paul, 1839-1906
Cézanne   759.4

Chace, James
Acheson   92

Chadha, Yogesh
Gandhi   92

Chadwick, Bruce
The reel Civil War   791.43

Chadwick, Douglas H.
The company we keep   591.68

Chadwick, Owen
A history of Christianity   270

Chadwick, Ruth F.
(ed) Encyclopedia of applied ethics. See Encyclopedia of applied ethics   170

Chadwick, William Owen *See* Chadwick, Owen

Chaikin, Andrew, 1956-
Air and space   629.13
A man on the moon   629.45

Chaisson, Eric
The Hubble wars   522

Chalker, Sylvia
The Oxford dictionary of English grammar   428

Chalmers, David Mark
Hooded Americanism: the history of the Ku Klux Klan   322.4

Chamberlain, Joshua Lawrence, 1828-1914
    About
Perry, M. Conceived in liberty   973.7

Chamberlain, Wilt, 1936-1999
    About
Lynch, W. Season of the 76ers   796.323

Chambers, Diane P., 1959-
Communicating in sign   419

Chambers, John Whiteclay
(ed) The Oxford companion to American military history. See The Oxford companion to American military history   355

Chambers, Whittaker
Witness   92

Chambers concise dictionary of scientists. See The Cambridge dictionary of scientists   920.003

Chambers dictionary of quotations   808.88

Chametzky, Jules
(ed) Jewish American literature. See Jewish American literature   810.8

Champagne, Duane
(ed) The Native North American almanac. See The Native North American almanac   970.004

Chance
Orkin, M. What are the odds?   519.2

Chancellorsville (Va.), Battle of, 1863
Furgurson, E. B. Chancellorsville, 1863   973.7
Sears, S. W. Chancellorsville   973.7

Chandler, David P.
The tragedy of Cambodian history   959.6

Chandler, Raymond, 1888-1959
About
Hiney, T. Raymond Chandler   92
Chandler, Seth Carlo, 1846-1913
About
Carter, B. Latitude   526
Chang, Iris
The Chinese in America   305.8
The rape of Nanking   951.04
Chang, Jung, 1952-
Wild swans   951.05
Change, Social *See* Social change
The **change**. Greer, G.   618.1
The **change** in the weather. Stevens, W. K.   551.5
The **change** makers. Klein, M.   920
Change of life in women *See* Menopause
Change of sex *See* Transsexualism
Change your brain, change your life. Amen, D.
    616.89
Change your looks, change your life. Copeland, M.
    617.9
Changing careers *See* Career changes
The **changing** faces of Jesus. Vermès, G.   232
The **changing** light at Sandover. Merrill, J.   811
Channing, Carol
Just lucky I guess   92
Chanoff, David
(jt. auth) Nuwere, E. Hacker cracker: a journey from the mean streets of Brooklyn to the frontiers of cyberspace   92
The **Chan's** great continent. Spence, J. D.   951
Chanson de Roland
The song of Roland   841
Chant, Christopher
A century of triumph   629.13
Chantrell, Glynnis
(ed) The Oxford dictionary of word histories. See The Oxford dictionary of word histories   422.03
Chants (Plain, Gregorian, etc.)
See/See also pages in the following book(s):
Grout, D. J. A history of Western music   780.9
Chanukah *See* Hanukkah
Chaos (Science)
Peat, F. D. From certainty to uncertainty   530
Chaotic behavior in systems *See* Chaos (Science)
Chapin, Theodore S., 1948-
Everything was possible   792.6
Chaplin, Charlie, 1889-1977
About
Lynn, K. S. Charlie Chaplin and his times   92
Milton, J. Tramp: the life of Charlie Chaplin   92
Scovell, J. Oona   92
Chaplin, Oona
About
Scovell, J. Oona   92
Chapman, Richard
The complete guitarist   787.87
Chapman, Robert L.
(ed) Dictionary of American slang. See Dictionary of American slang   427
(ed) Roget's international thesaurus. See Roget's international thesaurus   423
Chapter two. Simon, N.
In Simon, N. The collected plays of Neil Simon v2 p635-737   812
Character
Hillman, J. The force of character   155.67
Schlessinger, L. C. How could you do that?!   170
Characters and characteristics in literature
Cyclopedia of literary characters   803
Swain, D. V. Creating characters   808.3
Charan, Ram
(jt. auth) Bossidy, L. A. Execution: the discipline of getting things done   658.4

Chardin, Pierre Teilhard de *See* Teilhard de Chardin, Pierre
Charette, William
See/See also pages in the following book(s):
Mikaelian, A. Medal of honor   920
Chariots of the damned. McKinney, M.   356
Charitable institutions *See* Charities
Charities
Directories
The Foundation directory   061.025
Charlemagne, Emperor, 742-814
See/See also pages in the following book(s):
Bulfinch, T. Bulfinch's mythology   291.1
Charles, Daniel
Lords of the harvest   664
Charles, Ray
See/See also pages in the following book(s):
Feather, L. From Satchmo to Miles   920
Charles Dickens A-Z. Davis, P. B.   823.009
Charles Kuralt's America. Kuralt, C.   973.92
Charles Kuralt's American moments. Kuralt, C.
    973.92
Charles the Great *See* Charlemagne, Emperor, 742-814
Charlesworth, James H.
Jesus and the Dead Sea scrolls   232
Charlie Chaplin and his times. Lynn, K. S.   92
Charters, Ann, 1936-
(ed) The Portable beat reader. See The Portable beat reader   810.8
Chartrand, Mark R.
The Audubon Society field guide to the night sky
    523
The **chase**. Foote, H.
In Foote, H. Collected plays v2 p61-111   812
Chase Manhattan Bank, N.A.
Rockefeller, D. Memoirs   92
Chase's annual events. See Chase's calendar of events
    394.26
Chase's calendar of events   394.26
Chasing science. Pohl, F.   500
Chasing spies. Theoharis, A. G.   327.12
Chasteen, John Charles, 1955-
Born in blood and fire   980
Chatters, James
Ancient encounters   970.004
Chatwin, Bruce
In Patagonia   918.2
The songlines   919.4
About
Shakespeare, N. Bruce Chatwin   92
Chaucer, Geoffrey, d. 1400
Book of the Duchess
In Chaucer, G. The complete poetry and prose of Geoffrey Chaucer   821
The Canterbury tales   821
also in Chaucer, G. The complete poetry and prose of Geoffrey Chaucer   821
also in Chaucer, G. The portable Chaucer   821
The complete poetry and prose of Geoffrey Chaucer
    821
Equatorie of the planets
In Chaucer, G. The complete poetry and prose of Geoffrey Chaucer   821
House of fame
In Chaucer, G. The complete poetry and prose of Geoffrey Chaucer   821
Legend of good women
In Chaucer, G. The complete poetry and prose of Geoffrey Chaucer   821
Parliament of fowls
In Chaucer, G. The complete poetry and prose of Geoffrey Chaucer   821
The portable Chaucer   821

Chaucer, Geoffrey, d. 1400—*Continued*
Treatise on the astrolabe
In Chaucer, G. The complete poetry and prose of
Geoffrey Chaucer   **821**
Troilus and Cressida
In Chaucer, G. The complete poetry and prose of
Geoffrey Chaucer   **821**
In Chaucer, G. The portable Chaucer   **821**
About
Gardner, J. The poetry of Chaucer   **821**
Rossignol, R. Chaucer A to Z   **821**
West, R. Chaucer, 1340-1400   **92**
See/See also pages in the following book(s):
Bloom, H. The Western canon   **809**
Chaucer, 1340-1400. West, R.   **92**
Chaucer A to Z. Rossignol, R.   **821**
Chaves, Mark
Ordaining women   **262**
Cheaper by the dozen. Gilbreth, F. B.   **92**
Chearney, Lee Ann, 1959-
(jt. auth) Chambers, D. P. Communicating in sign
   419
Cheating monkeys and citizen bees. Dugatkin, L. A.
   591.56
Chechnya (Russia)
Baiev, K. The Oath   **947.5**
Lieven, A. Chechnya   **947.086**
Cheever, Susan
As good as I could be   **306.8**
Chef Paul Prudhomme's Louisiana kitchen. Prudhomme,
P.   **641.5**
Chef Paul Prudhomme's Louisiana tastes. Prudhomme,
P.   **641.5**
Chekhov, Anton Pavlovich, 1860-1904
The bear
In Chekhov, A. P. The plays of Anton Chekhov p19-
33   **891.7**
The boor
In Chekhov, A. P. The portable Chekhov   **891.7**
The cherry orchard
In Chekhov, A. P. The plays of Anton Chekhov
p331-87   **891.7**
In Chekhov, A. P. The portable Chekhov   **891.7**
In Our dramatic heritage v4   **808.82**
The dangers of tobacco
In Chekhov, A. P. The plays of Anton Chekhov
p323-29   **891.7**
The festivities
In Chekhov, A. P. The plays of Anton Chekhov
p191-205   **891.7**
Ivanov
In Chekhov, A. P. The plays of Anton Chekhov p51-
108   **891.7**
The plays of Anton Chekhov   **891.7**
The portable Chekhov   **891.7**
The proposal
In Chekhov, A. P. The plays of Anton Chekhov p35-
49   **891.7**
A reluctant tragic hero
In Chekhov, A. P. The plays of Anton Chekhov
p165-73   **891.7**
The seagull
In Chekhov, A. P. The plays of Anton Chekhov
p109-64   **891.7**
Swan song
In Chekhov, A. P. The plays of Anton Chekhov p9-
17   **891.7**
Three sisters
In Chekhov, A. P. The plays of Anton Chekhov
p257-322   **891.7**
Uncle Vanya
In Chekhov, A. P. The plays of Anton Chekhov
p207-55   **891.7**

The wedding
In Chekhov, A. P. The plays of Anton Chekhov
p175-89   **891.7**
About
Callow, P. Chekhov, the hidden ground   **92**
Malcolm, J. Reading Chekhov   **891.7**
See/See also pages in the following book(s):
Nabokov, V. V. Lectures on Russian literature
   891.7
Chekhov, Michael, 1891-1955
To the actor   **792**
Chemical elements
Atkins, P. W. The periodic kingdom   **541.2**
Strathern, P. Mendeleyev's dream   **540.9**
Chemical engineering
See also Biotechnology
The Chemical formulary   **660**
The **Chemical** formulary   **660**
Chemical industry
See also Pesticides industry
Fagin, D. Toxic deception   **615.9**
Chemical pollution *See* Pollution
Chemical reactions
Rabinow, P. Making PCR   **572.8**
Chemical warfare
See/See also pages in the following book(s):
Frist, W. H. When every moment counts   **613.6**
Chemicals
Fagin, D. Toxic deception   **615.9**
Chemistry
See also Biochemistry; Botanical chemistry
Ball, P. Stories of the invisible   **541.2**
Dictionaries
Hawley's condensed chemical dictionary   **540.3**
History
Cobb, C. Creations of fire   **540**
Greenberg, A. The art of chemistry   **540**
Salzberg, H. W. From caveman to chemist   **540**
Strathern, P. Mendeleyev's dream   **540.9**
Tables
CRC handbook of chemistry and physics   **540**
Lange's handbook of chemistry   **540**
The **chemistry** professor [play] Vonnegut, K.
In Vonnegut, K. Palm Sunday p260-90   **818**
Chemists
Dictionaries
Oakes, E. H. A to Z of chemists   **920.003**
Chen, Da, 1962-
Colors of the mountain   **92**
Sounds of the river   **92**
Cheng, Nien, 1915-
Life and death in Shanghai   **92**
Chennault, Claire Lee, 1890-1958
About
Ford, D. Flying Tigers   **940.54**
Chepesiuk, Ronald
The war on drugs   **363.45**
Chergé, Christian de
See/See also pages in the following book(s):
Kiser, J. W. The monks of Tibhirine   **271**
Chernin, Kim
Cecilia Bartoli   **92**
Chernow, Ron
Titan: the life of John D. Rockefeller, Sr.   **92**
The Warburgs   **920**
Cherokee Indians
Mankiller, W. Mankiller: a chief and her people
   92
McLoughlin, W. G. After the Trail of Tears
   970.004
Cherry, Kelly
Rising Venus   **811**
Cherry Mine disaster. See Tintori, K. Trapped: the 1909
Cherry Mine disaster   **977.3**

The **cherry** orchard. Chekhov, A. P.
  In Chekhov, A. P. The plays of Anton Chekhov
    p331-87 **891.7**
  In Chekhov, A. P. The portable Chekhov **891.7**
  In Our dramatic heritage v4 **808.82**
Chesnoff, Richard Z., 1937-
  Pack of thieves **940.53**
Chess
  Capablanca, J. R. Chess fundamentals **794.1**
  Fischer, B. Bobby Fischer teaches chess **794.1**
  United States Chess Federation. U.S. Chess Federation's official rules of chess **794.1**
Chess fundamentals. Capablanca, J. R. **794.1**
Chesterman, Charles W.
  The Audubon Society field guide to North American rocks and minerals **549**
Chevalier, Tracy, 1962-
  (ed) Contemporary world writers. See Contemporary world writers **920.003**
Chevallier, Andrew
  Encyclopedia of herbal medicine **615**
Chevannes, Barry
  Rastafari: roots and ideology **299**
Cheyenne Indians
  See/See also pages in the following book(s):
  Brown, D. A. The American West p100-09, 215-40 **978**
  Brown, D. A. Bury my heart at Wounded Knee **970.004**
Chez Panisse (Berkeley, Calif.: Restaurant)
  Waters, A. Chez Panisse vegetables **641.6**
Chez Panisse vegetables. Waters, A. **641.6**
Chiang, Kai-shek, 1887-1975
  See/See also pages in the following book(s):
  Tuchman, B. W. Stilwell and the American experience in China, 1911-45 p90-122 **327.73**
Chiappe, Luis M.
  Walking on eggs **567.9**
Chicago (Ill.)
                    History
  Miller, D. L. City of the century **977.3**
            Politics and government
  Cohen, A. American pharaoh: Mayor Richard J. Daley: his battle for Chicago and the nation **92**
Chicago Bulls (Basketball team)
  See/See also pages in the following book(s):
  Halberstam, D. Playing for keeps: Michael Jordan and the world he made **92**
The **Chicago** manual of style **808**
Chicago poems. Sandburg, C.
  In Sandburg, C. Complete poems of Carl Sandburg p3-76 **811**
Chicago White Sox (Baseball team)
  Fleitz, D. L. Shoeless **92**
Chicano literature *See* American literature—Mexican American authors
Chicano literature **810.9**
Chicano visions. Marin, C. **709.73**
Chicanos *See* Mexican Americans
Chicken, shadow, moon and more. Strand, M. **811**
Chickens
  Grimes, W. My fine feathered friend **636.5**
Chidester, David
  Christianity **270**
Chief Joseph *See* Joseph, Nez Percé Chief, 1840-1904
The **chief:** the life of William Randolph Hearst. Nasaw, D. **92**
Child, Heather
  Calligraphy today **745.6**
Child, Julia
  From Julia Child's kitchen **641.5**
  Julia and Jacques cooking at home **641.5**
  Julia's kitchen wisdom **641.5**
  Mastering the art of French cooking **641.5**
  The way to cook **641.5**

Greenspan, D. Baking with Julia **641.8**
                    About
  Fitch, N. R. Appetite for life **92**
Child abuse
  See also Child sexual abuse
  Domestic violence & child abuse sourcebook **362.82**
  Forward, S. Toxic parents: overcoming their hurtful legacy and reclaiming your life **362.82**
  See/See also pages in the following book(s):
  Bartholet, E. Nobody's children **362.7**
Child-adult relationship
  See also Conflict of generations
Child and father *See* Father-child relationship
Child and mother *See* Mother-child relationship
Child and parent *See* Parent-child relationship
The **child** and the curriculum. Dewey, J.
  In Dewey, J. The school and society, and The Child and the curriculum **372**
Child care
  See also Child rearing; Infants—Care
  Caring for your school-age child **649**
  Leach, P. Your baby & child **649**
  Spock, B. Dr. Spock's the first two years **649**
  Spock, B. Dr. Spock's the school years **649**
  Stoppard, M. Complete baby and child care **649**
Child custody
  Boland, M. L. Your right to child custody, visitation, and support **346.01**
Child development
  Barnet, A. B. The youngest minds **155.4**
  Blum, D. Love at Goon Park **150.19**
  Brazelton, T. B. The irreducible needs of children **155.4**
  Brazelton, T. B. To listen to a child **155.4**
  Brazelton, T. B. Touchpoints **649**
  Brazelton, T. B. Touchpoints three to six **649**
  Bruer, J. T. The myth of the first three years **155.4**
  The Children's Hospital guide to your child's health and development **618.92**
  Coles, R. The moral intelligence of children **155.4**
  Gilbert, S. A field guide to boys and girls **305.23**
  Gopnik, A. The scientist in the crib **155.4**
  Leach, P. Your baby & child **649**
  Levine, M. D. A mind at a time **370.15**
  Mayes, L. C. The Yale Child Study Center guide to understanding your child **649**
  Montessori, M. The absorbent mind **155.4**
  Spock, B. Dr. Spock's the first two years **649**
  Spock, B. Dr. Spock's the school years **649**
  Stoppard, M. Complete baby and child care **649**
A **child** is born. Nilsson, L. **612.6**
Child labor
  Levine, M. J. Children for hire **331.3**
Child life in colonial days. Earle, A. M. **973.2**
Child molesting *See* Child sexual abuse
Child psychiatry
  See also Autism
Child psychology
  See also Child rearing
  Barnet, A. B. The youngest minds **155.4**
  Brazelton, T. B. The earliest relationship **155.4**
  Brazelton, T. B. The irreducible needs of children **155.4**
  Brazelton, T. B. To listen to a child **155.4**
  Gardner, R. A. The parents book about divorce **306.89**
  Greenspan, S. I. The child with special needs **362.1**
  Kübler-Ross, E. On children and death **155.9**
  Montessori, M. The absorbent mind **155.4**
  Papolos, D. F. The bipolar child **618.92**
  Piaget, J. The moral judgment of the child **155.4**

Child psychology—*Continued*
Sears, W. Parenting the fussy baby and high-need child
649
Seligman, M. E. P. The optimistic child   **155.4**
Shapiro, L. E. How to raise a child with a high EQ
649
White, B. L. The new first three years of life
155.4
Child rearing
See also Parenting; Socialization
American Medical Association complete guide to children's health   **618.92**
Ames, L. B. Your eight-year-old   **649**
Ames, L. B. Your five-year-old   **649**
Ames, L. B. Your four-year-old   **649**
Ames, L. B. Your one-year-old   **649**
Ames, L. B. Your seven-year-old   **649**
Ames, L. B. Your six-year-old   **649**
Ames, L. B. Your three-year-old   **649**
Ames, L. B. Your two-year-old   **649**
Bailey, R. A. Easy to love, difficult to discipline
649
Baldrige, L. Letitia Baldrige's more than manners!
649
Barkley, R. A. Taking charge of ADHD   **618.92**
Beal, A. C. The black parenting book   **649**
Brazelton, T. B. The irreducible needs of children
155.4
Brazelton, T. B. Touchpoints   **649**
Brazelton, T. B. Touchpoints three to six   **649**
Brooks, R. B. Raising resilient children   **649**
Caring for your school-age child   **649**
Deak, J. Girls will be girls   **649**
Deutsch, F. Halving it all   **649**
Dosick, W. D. Golden rules   **649**
Edelman, M. W. The measure of our success   **170**
Eisenberg, A. What to expect the toddler years
649
Elias, M. J. Emotionally intelligent parenting   **649**
Emswiler, M. A. Guiding your child through grief
155.9
Füredi, F. Paranoid parenting   **649**
Garbarino, J. Parents under siege   **649**
Garber, S. W. Monsters under the bed and other childhood fears   **649**
Gilbert, S. A field guide to boys and girls   **305.23**
Karp, H. The happiest baby on the block   **649**
Mayes, L. C. The Yale Child Study Center guide to understanding your child   **649**
Medved, M. Saving childhood   **305.23**
Murkoff, H. E. What to expect the first year   **649**
Pollack, W. S. Real boys   **305.23**
Rosenfeld, A. A. Hyper-parenting   **649**
Spock, B. Dr. Spock's the first two years   **649**
Spock, B. Dr. Spock's the school years   **649**
Stoppard, M. Complete baby and child care   **649**
White, B. L. Raising a happy, unspoiled child
649
Child sexual abuse
See also Adult child sexual abuse victims
Bass, E. The courage to heal   **362.83**
See/See also pages in the following book(s):
Levine, J. Harmful to minors   **306.7**
Child support
Boland, M. L. Your right to child custody, visitation, and support   **346.01**
Child welfare
See also Child support
Bartholet, E. Nobody's children   **362.7**
Bernstein, N. The lost children of Wilder   **362.7**
The **child** with special needs. Greenspan, S. I.
362.1
Childbirth
See also Natural childbirth
Douglas, A. The mother of all baby books   **649**

Kitzinger, S. The complete book of pregnancy and childbirth   **618.2**
Lees, C. C. Pregnancy and birth   **618.2**
Mayo Clinic complete book of pregnancy & baby's first year   **618.2**
Murkoff, H. E. What to expect when you're expecting
618.2
Nilsson, L. A child is born   **612.6**
Sears, W. The pregnancy book   **618.2**
Wolf, N. Misconceptions   **618.2**
Childers, Thomas
Wings of morning   **940.54**
Childhood cancer   **618.92**
Childhood cancer. Janes-Hodder, H.   **618.92**
Childhood diseases *See* Children—Diseases
Childlessness
See also Infertility
Children
See also African American children; Boys; Exceptional children; Girls; Handicapped children; Infants; Only child
Bullard, S. Teaching tolerance   **649**
Canada, G. Fist, stick, knife, gun   **305.23**
Jones, G. Killing monsters   **302.23**
Kozol, J. Ordinary resurrections   **305.23**
See/See also pages in the following book(s):
Toffler, A. Future shock p212-28   **303.4**
Abuse
See Child abuse
Adoption
See Adoption
Books and reading
Perrin, N. A child's delight   **028.5**
Care
See Child care
Development
See Child development
Diseases
See also Children—Health and hygiene
American Medical Association complete guide to children's health   **618.92**
Childhood cancer   **618.92**
The Children's Hospital guide to your child's health and development   **618.92**
Janes-Hodder, H. Childhood cancer   **618.92**
Pediatric cancer sourcebook   **618.92**
Selikowitz, M. Down syndrome   **618.92**
Thompson, C. E. Raising a child with a neuromuscular disorder   **618.92**
Employment
See Child labor
Health and hygiene
See also Children—Diseases; Children—Nutrition
American Academy of Pediatrics guide to your child's sleep   **618.92**
American Medical Association complete guide to children's health   **618.92**
The Children's Hospital guide to your child's health and development   **618.92**
Diller, L. H. Running on Ritalin   **618.92**
First aid for children fast   **618.92**
Martin, K. L. Does my child have a speech problem?
618.92
Micheli, L. J. The sports medicine bible for young athletes   **617.1**
Stein, D. B. Ritalin is not the answer   **618.92**
See/See also pages in the following book(s):
Brazelton, T. B. To listen to a child p81-122
155.4
History
Orme, N. Medieval children   **305.23**

Children—*Continued*
Hygiene
See Children—Health and hygiene
Institutional care
See/See also pages in the following book(s):
Bartholet, E. Nobody's children   362.7
Language
Golinkoff, R. M. How babies talk   401
Management
See Child rearing
Nutrition
Sears, W. The family nutrition book   613.2
The Yale guide to children's nutrition   613.2
Pictorial works
Coles, R. When they were young   779
Psychology
See Child psychology
Religious life
Coles, R. The spiritual life of children   291.4
Socialization
See Socialization
Training
See Child rearing
United States
Coles, R. Children of crisis   305.23
Earle, A. M. Child life in colonial days   973.2
Medved, M. Saving childhood   305.23
West (U.S.)
Luchetti, C. Children of the West   978
Children, Emotionally disturbed *See* Emotionally disturbed children
The **children**. Halberstam, D.   323.1
Children and adults *See* Child rearing
Children for hire. Levine, M. J.   331.3
Children in the Holocaust and World War II   940.53
Children of crisis. Coles, R.   305.23
Children of divorced parents
Wallerstein, J. S. Second chances   306.89
Children of England. See Weir, A. The children of Henry VIII   920
The **children** of Henry VIII. Weir, A.   920
The **children** of Sánchez. Lewis, O.   972.08
Children of single parents *See* Single parent family
Children of the West. Luchetti, C.   978
Children with autism   618.92
Children with spina bifida   618.92
Children's catalog   011.6
Children's companion, Mary Engelbreit's. Engelbreit, M.   645
Children's diseases *See* Children—Diseases
The **Children's** Hospital guide to your child's health and development   618.92
Children's libraries
See also Young adults' libraries
Cullum, C. N. The storytime sourcebook   027.62
Steele, A. T. Bare bones children's services   027.62
Children's literature
See also Caldecott Medal; Coretta Scott King Award; Fairy tales; Newbery Medal; Picture books for children
Bibliography
Children's catalog   011.6
Lipson, E. R. The New York Times parent's guide to the best books for children   011.6
Trelease, J. The read-aloud handbook   028.5
Bio-bibliography
The Continuum encyclopedia of children's literature   028.5
Helbig, A. Dictionary of American children's fiction, 1995-1999   028.5
Dictionaries
Helbig, A. Dictionary of American children's fiction, 1995-1999   028.5

Latrobe, K. H. The children's literature dictionary   028.5
Encyclopedias
The Cambridge guide to children's books in English   028.5
The Continuum encyclopedia of children's literature   028.5
History and criticism
The Coretta Scott King Awards book, 1970-1999   028.5
Gillespie, J. T. The Newbery companion   028.5
The Newbery & Caldecott medal books, 1986-2000   028.5
Newbery and Caldecott Medal books, 1966-1975   028.5
Newbery and Caldecott Medal books, 1976-1985   028.5
Newbery Medal books, 1922-1955   028.5
Perrin, N. A child's delight   028.5
Wullschläger, J. Inventing wonderland   820.9
Stories, plots, etc.
Masterplots II, juvenile and young adult fiction series   028.5
Technique
Aiken, J. The way to write for children   808.06
Seuling, B. How to write a children's book and get it published   808.06
Shulevitz, U. Writing with pictures   808.06
The **children's** literature dictionary. Latrobe, K. H.   028.5
Children's poetry
See also Nursery rhymes
The **Children's** song index, 1978-1993   782.42
Childress, Alice, 1920-1994
See/See also pages in the following book(s):
Black women writers (1950-1980)   810.9
Childs, Lucinda
See/See also pages in the following book(s):
Sontag, S. Where the stress falls   814
A **child's** Christmas in Wales. Thomas, D.   828
A **child's** delight. Perrin, N.   028.5
Chilies to chocolate   641.3
Chilton, Bruce
Rabbi Jesus   232.9
Chilton's auto repair manual   629.28
Chilton's import car repair manual   629.28
Chilvers, Ian
A dictionary of twentieth-century art   709.04
(ed) The Concise Oxford dictionary of art and artists. See The Concise Oxford dictionary of art and artists   703
(ed) The Oxford dictionary of art. See The Oxford dictionary of art   703
Chimpanzees
Fouts, R. Next of kin   156
Goodall, J. In the shadow of man   599.8
Goodall, J. Through a window   599.8
China
Civilization
Blunden, C. Cultural atlas of China   951
Spence, J. D. The Chan's great continent   951
Description
Ma Jian. Red dust   915.1
Prager, E. Wuhu diary   951
Salzman, M. Iron & silk   915.1
Theroux, P. Riding the iron rooster   915.1
See/See also pages in the following book(s):
Jensen, C. I have seen the world begin   915
Economic conditions
Becker, J. The Chinese   951.05
Studwell, J. The China dream   951
Encyclopedias
The Cambridge encyclopedia of China   951
Perkins, D. Encyclopedia of China   951

China—*Continued*
Foreign relations—United States
Bernstein, R. The coming conflict with China
327.73
Laird, T. Into Tibet 327.12
Mann, J. About face 327.73
Tuchman, B. W. Stilwell and the American experience
in China, 1911-45 327.73
See/See also pages in the following book(s):
Tuchman, B. W. Practicing history p188-207 907
History
The Cambridge history of China 951
Chang, J. Wild swans 951.05
Fairbank, J. K. China 951
Fairbank, J. K. China: tradition & transformation
951
Fairbank, J. K. The great Chinese revolution: 1800-
1985 951
Hsü, I. C.-Y. The rise of modern China 951
Preston, D. The Boxer Rebellion 951
Schoppa, R. K. The Columbia guide to modern Chi-
nese history 951.05
Spence, J. D. The search for modern China 951
Spence, J. D. Treason by the book 951
History—1850-1864, Taiping Rebellion
Spence, J. D. God's Chinese son 951
History—1912-1949
Seagrave, S. The Soong dynasty 951
History—1949-
Chen, D. Colors of the mountain 92
Chen, D. Sounds of the river 92
History—1949-1976
Cheng, N. Life and death in Shanghai 92
Min, A. Red azalea 92
Politics and government
Bernstein, R. The coming conflict with China
327.73
Buruma, I. Bad elements 951.05
Fang Lizhi. Bringing down the Great Wall
951.05
Kemenade, W. van. China, Hong Kong, Taiwan, Inc.
951
Lord, B. B. Legacies: a Chinese mosaic 951.05
Short, P. Mao 92
Spence, J. D. Mao Zedong 92
Spence, J. D. Treason by the book 951
Wei Jingsheng. The courage to stand alone
951.05
Wu, H. Bitter winds 951.05
Wu, H. Troublemaker 951.05
Social conditions
Becker, J. The Chinese 951.05
Social life and customs
Lord, B. B. Legacies: a Chinese mosaic 951.05
See/See also pages in the following book(s):
Mah, A. Y. Falling leaves 92
China. Air Force. American Volunteer Group
Ford, D. Flying Tigers 940.54
China (Porcelain) *See* Porcelain
China (Republic of China, 1949-) *See* Taiwan
The **China** dream. Studwell, J. 951
China, Hong Kong, Taiwan, Inc. Kemenade, W. van
951
China men. Kingston, M. H. 920
China: tradition & transformation. Fairbank, J. K.
951
The **Chinese.** Becker, J. 951.05
Chinese Americans
Biography
Kingston, M. H. China men 920
History
Chang, I. The Chinese in America 305.8
Chinese art
Hearn, M. K. Splendors of Imperial China 709.51

Sickman, L. The art and architecture of China
709.51
Tregear, M. Chinese art 709.51
Chinese civilization *See* China—Civilization
Chinese cooking
Lo, E. Y.-F. The Chinese kitchen 641.5
Chinese ethics
Confucius. The analects of Confucius 181
Confucius. The wisdom of Confucius 181
The **Chinese** in America. Chang, I. 305.8
The **Chinese** kitchen. Lo, E. Y.-F. 641.5
Chinese language
Dictionaries
The Oxford starter Chinese dictionary 495.1
Chinese literature
Collections
Anthology of Chinese literature 895.1
An Anthology of Chinese literature: beginnings to
1911 895.1
The Shorter Columbia anthology of traditional Chinese
literature 895.1
History and criticism
The Columbia history of Chinese literature 895.1
Chinese philosophy
Confucius. The analects of Confucius 181
Confucius. The wisdom of Confucius 181
Chinese poetry
Collections
Anthology of modern Chinese poetry 895.1
The Columbia book of Chinese poetry 895.1
One hundred poems from the Chinese 895.1
Ching, Frank, 1943-
A visual dictionary of architecture 720.3
Chipasula, Frank
(ed) Heinemann book of African women's poetry. See
Heinemann book of African women's poetry
896
Chipasula, Stella
(ed) Heinemann book of African women's poetry. See
Heinemann book of African women's poetry
896
Chitty, A. B.
(jt. auth) Murolo, P. From the folks who brought you
the weekend 331
Chivalry
See also Medieval civilization
Bulfinch, T. Bulfinch's mythology 291.1
Chocolate
See also Cooking—Chocolate
Brenner, J. G. The emperors of chocolate 338.7
Chocolate to morphine. See Weil, A. From chocolate to
morphine 616.86
Choice (Psychology)
See also Decision making
Choice 028.1
Choice of college *See* College choice
Choice theory. Glasser, W. 150
The **choking** Doberman and other "new" urban legends.
Brunvand, J. H. 398.2
Cholesterol
See/See also pages in the following book(s):
Friedman, M. Medicine's 10 greatest discoveries
610.9
Chomsky, Noam
See/See also pages in the following book(s):
Devlin, K. J. Goodbye, Descartes p96-142 128
Choose the right word 423
Chopin, Frédéric, 1810-1849
See/See also pages in the following book(s):
Schonberg, H. C. The great pianists 920
Chopin, Kate, 1851-1904
About
Skaggs, P. Kate Chopin 813.009
Chopra, Deepak
Ageless body, timeless mind 612.6

Chopra, Deepak—*Continued*
Overcoming addictions   **616.86**
Chopra, Jo Mcgowan *See* McGowan Chopra, Jo
Chorionitis *See* Scleroderma (Disease)
Chown, Marcus
The universe next door   **523.1**
Christ *See* Jesus Christ
Christ: a crisis in the life of God. Miles, J.   **232**
Christ and culture. Niebuhr, H. R.   **261**
Christ-Janer, Albert
(comp) American hymns old and new. *See* American hymns old and new   **782.27**
Christensen, Karen
(jt. auth) Levinson, D. Encyclopedia of modern Asia   **950**
Christian art
Lowden, J. Early Christian & Byzantine art   **709.02**
Snyder, J. Medieval art   **709.02**
See/See also pages in the following book(s):
Hamilton, G. H. The art and architecture of Russia   **709.47**
Christian behavior. Lewis, C. S.
In Lewis, C. S. Mere Christianity   **230**
Christian civilization
Niebuhr, H. R. Christ and culture   **261**
Christian Coalition (Organization)
See/See also pages in the following book(s):
Martin, W. C. With God on our side   **261.8**
Christian doctrine *See* Doctrinal theology
Christian ethics
See/See also pages in the following book(s):
Bonhoeffer, D. A testament to freedom p361-91   **230**
Christian fundamentalism
Bawer, B. Stealing Jesus   **277.3**
Utter, G. H. The religious right   **277.3**
See/See also pages in the following book(s):
Armstrong, K. The battle for God   **291**
Christian life
Carter, J. Sources of strength   **248.4**
Girzone, J. F. A portrait of Jesus   **232.9**
John Paul II, Pope. Crossing the threshold of hope   **282**
Lewis, C. S. Letters to Malcolm: chiefly on prayer   **248**
Lewis, C. S. The Screwtape letters   **248**
Christian missions
Armour-Hileman, V. Singing to the dead   **261**
Christian philosophy
Lewis, C. S. Mere Christianity   **230**
Lewis, C. S. The world's last night, and other essays   **230**
Teilhard de Chardin, P. The divine milieu   **230**
Tillich, P. Theology of culture   **230**
Christian saints
Woodward, K. L. Making saints   **282**
Dictionaries
Attwater, D. The Penguin dictionary of saints   **920.003**
Butler, A. Butler's Lives of the saints   **920.003**
Farmer, D. H. The Oxford dictionary of saints   **920.003**
Guiley, R. E. The encyclopedia of saints   **920.003**
McBrien, R. P. Lives of the saints   **920.003**
Christian Science
Eddy, M. B. Science and health, with key to the Scriptures   **289.5**
Fraser, C. God's perfect child   **289.5**
Gill, G. Mary Baker Eddy   **92**
Schoepflin, R. B. Christian Science on trial   **289.5**
Christian Science on trial. Schoepflin, R. B.   **289.5**
Christian sociology
Chaves, M. Ordaining women   **262**
Niebuhr, H. R. Christ and culture   **261**

Christian symbolism
See/See also pages in the following book(s):
Carr-Gomm, S. Hidden symbols in art   **704.9**
Christianity
See also Christian civilization
Bawer, B. Stealing Jesus   **277.3**
Chidester, D. Christianity   **270**
Jenkins, P. The next Christendom   **270**
Pagels, E. H. Beyond belief   **229**
Ward, K. Christianity   **230**
See/See also pages in the following book(s):
Armstrong, K. A history of God   **291**
Dictionaries
The Oxford dictionary of the Christian Church   **230.003**
Encyclopedias
The Encyclopedia of Christianity   **230.003**
Encyclopedia of early Christianity   **230.003**
World Christian encyclopedia   **230.003**
Evidences
See Apologetics
History
See Church history
Christianity and evolution *See* Creationism
Christianity and evolution. Teilhard de Chardin, P.   **231.7**
Christianity and other religions
Carroll, J. Constantine's sword   **261.2**
Cox, H. G. Many mansions   **261.2**
Gager, J. G. The origins of anti-Semitism   **296.3**
Christianity and politics
Martin, W. C. With God on our side   **261.8**
Utter, G. H. The religious right   **277.3**
Christiansen, Donald
(ed) Electronics engineers' handbook. *See* Electronics engineers' handbook   **621.381**
Christiansen, Keith
From Van Eyck to Bruegel. *See* From Van Eyck to Bruegel   **759.9493**
Christianson, Gale E.
Greenhouse   **363.7**
Christianson, Stephen G.
(ed) The American book of days. *See* The American book of days   **394.26**
Christie, Agatha, 1890-1976
Appointment with death
In Christie, A. The mousetrap and other plays   **822**
Go back for murder
In Christie, A. The mousetrap and other plays   **822**
The hollow
In Christie, A. The mousetrap and other plays   **822**
The mousetrap
In Christie, A. The mousetrap and other plays   **822**
The mousetrap and other plays   **822**
Ten little Indians
In Christie, A. The mousetrap and other plays   **822**
Towards zero
In Christie, A. The mousetrap and other plays   **822**
Verdict
In Christie, A. The mousetrap and other plays   **822**
Witness for the prosecution
In Christie, A. The mousetrap and other plays   **822**
About
Bunson, M. The complete Christie   **823.009**
Sova, D. B. Agatha Christie A to Z   **823.009**

Christmas
Gulevich, T. Encyclopedia of Christmas and New Year's celebrations   **394.26**
Marling, K. A. Merry Christmas!   **394.26**
Poetry
Christmas poems   **821.008**
Wales
Thomas, D. A child's Christmas in Wales   **828**
Christmas carols *See* Carols
Christmas decorations
Stewart, M. Handmade Christmas   **745.59**
Christmas poems   **821.008**
Christopher, Thomas
(jt. auth) Van Sweden, J. A. Architecture in the garden   **712**

Chromosome mapping *See* Gene mapping
The **chronic** pain solution. Dillard, J.   **616**
A **chronicle** of American music, 1700-1995. Hall, C. J.   **780.973**
The **Chronicle** of the Łódź ghetto, 1941-1944   **943.8**
Chronicle of the popes. Maxwell-Stuart, P. G.   **282**
Chronicle of the Russian tsars. Warnes, D.   **947**
The **chronicle** of Western fashion. Peacock, J.   **391**
The **chronological** encyclopedia of discoveries in space. Zimmerman, R.   **629.4**
Chronology, Historical *See* Historical chronology
A **chronology** of American musical theater. Norton, R. C.   **792.6**
The **Chronology** of science   **509**
Chronology of the American West. Zeman, S. C.   **978**
Chronology of Western classical music. Hall, C. J.   **780.9**
The **chrysanthemum** and the sword. Benedict, R.   **952**

Chudnovsky, D. (David), 1947-
See/See also pages in the following book(s):
Life stories   **920**
Chudnovsky, David *See* Chudnovsky, D. (David), 1947-
Chudnovsky, G. (Gregory), 1952-
See/See also pages in the following book(s):
Life stories   **920**
Chudnovsky, Gregory *See* Chudnovsky, G. (Gregory), 1952-
Church, Sally K.
(ed) The Oxford starter Chinese dictionary. See The Oxford starter Chinese dictionary   **495.1**
Church
See also Christianity
Church and race relations
Cone, J. H. A black theology of liberation   **261.8**
Church and social problems
See also Christian sociology
Church and state
See also Christianity and politics
Carter, S. L. God's name in vain   **322**
Church architecture
See/See also pages in the following book(s):
Hamilton, G. H. The art and architecture of Russia   **709.47**
Church buildings
King, R. Brunelleschi's dome   **726**
Church history
See also United States—Church history
Chadwick, O. A history of Christianity   **270**
Chidester, D. Christianity   **270**
Foxe, J. Foxe's Book of martyrs   **272**
See/See also pages in the following book(s):
Potok, C. Wanderings p279-322   **909**
30-600, Early church
Riley, G. J. The river of God   **270**
Rubenstein, R. E. When Jesus became God   **273**

600-1500, Middle Ages
See also Inquisition
See/See also pages in the following book(s):
Tuchman, B. W. A distant mirror p25-37, 320-39   **944**

1517-1648, Reformation
See Reformation
Dictionaries
The Oxford dictionary of the Christian Church   **230.003**
Encyclopedias
Encyclopedia of early Christianity   **230.003**
Church music
See also Gospel music
See/See also pages in the following book(s):
Grout, D. J. A history of Western music   **780.9**
Church of Christ, Scientist *See* Christian Science
Church of Jesus Christ of Latter-day Saints
Abanes, R. One nation under gods   **289.3**
Bushman, R. L. Joseph Smith and the beginnings of Mormonism   **289.3**
Ostling, R. N. Mormon America   **289.3**
Churchill, Caryl
Far away   **822**
Mad forest   **822**
Churchill, Lady Clementine, 1885-1977
About
Churchill, Sir W. Winston and Clementine   **92**
Churchill, Sarah Jennings *See* Marlborough, Sarah Jennings Churchill, Duchess of, 1660-1744
Churchill, Sir Winston, 1874-1965
Closing the ring   **940.53**
The gathering storm   **940.53**
The grand alliance   **940.53**
The great republic   **973**
The hinge of fate   **940.53**
Their finest hour   **940.53**
Triumph and tragedy   **940.53**
Winston and Clementine   **92**
About
Jenkins, R., Baron. Churchill   **92**
Lukacs, J. Five days in London, May 1940   **940.53**
Manchester, W. The last lion: Winston Spencer Churchill   **92**
Stafford, D. Roosevelt and Churchill   **940.54**
See/See also pages in the following book(s):
Cohen, E. A. Supreme command   **355**
Kissinger, H. Diplomacy p394-422   **327.73**
Massie, R. K. Dreadnought p748-89   **940.3**
Chute, Marchette Gaylord, 1909-1994
Stories from Shakespeare   **822.3**
CIA *See* United States. Central Intelligence Agency
Ciardi, John, 1916-1986
The collected poems of John Ciardi   **811**
Cicala, Roger
(ed) The Cancer pain sourcebook. See The Cancer pain sourcebook   **616.99**
Cicero, Marcus Tullius, 106-43 B.C.
About
Everitt, A. Cicero   **92**
See/See also pages in the following book(s):
Hamilton, E. The Roman way   **870.9**
Cid, ca. 1043-1099
The poem of the Cid   **861**
About
Fletcher, R. A. The quest for El Cid   **92**
Cid Campeador *See* Cid, ca. 1043-1099
Cikovsky, Nicolai, Jr.
Winslow Homer   **759.13**
Ciment, James
(ed) Encyclopedia of conflicts since World War II. See Encyclopedia of conflicts since World War II   **909.82**

Ciment, James—*Continued*
(ed) Encyclopedia of the Great Depression and the New Deal. See Encyclopedia of the Great Depression and the New Deal   **973.917**
Ciment, Michel, 1938-
Kubrick   **791.43**
Cinematography
Netzley, P. D. The encyclopedia of movie special effects   **778.5**
Solnit, R. River of shadows   **778.5**
Cinque, 1811?-1879
See/See also pages in the following book(s):
Abdul-Jabbar, K. Black profiles in courage p46-50; 57-67   **920**
Cioran, E. M. (Emile M.), 1911-1995
See/See also pages in the following book(s):
Sontag, S. Styles of radical will p74-95   **814**
Cioran, Emile M. *See* Cioran, E. M. (Emile M.), 1911-1995
Ciotti, Paul
More with less   **92**
Cipher and telegraph codes
See/See also pages in the following book(s):
Silverman, K. Lightning man: the accursed life of Samuel F.B. Morse   **92**
Ciphers
Satinover, J. Cracking the Bible code   **222**
Tobin, J. Hidden in plain view   **973.7**
The **circle** of innovation. Peters, T. J.   **658.4**
Circles: 50 round trips through history, technology, science, culture. Burke, J.   **609**
Circulatory system *See* Cardiovascular system
Circumcision
Gollaher, D. Circumcision   **392**
Circumnavigation *See* Voyages around the world
The **circus** at the edge of the earth. Wilkins, C.   **791.3**
The **circus** fire. O'Nan, S.   **974.6**
Cirincione, Diane V.
(jt. auth) Jampolsky, G. G. Love is the answer: creating positive relationships   **152.4**
Citations, Bibliographical *See* Bibliographical citations
Cities, Imaginary *See* Geographical myths
Cities and towns
See also Inner cities
Cities of the world   **910.3**
Duany, A. Suburban nation   **307.7**
Kunstler, J. H. The city in mind   **307.7**
Mumford, L. The culture of cities   **307.7**
      Encyclopedias
Encyclopedia of urban cultures   **307.7**
      Growth
See also Urbanization
      History
Mumford, L. The city in history   **307.7**
      United States
County and city data book   **317.3**
Savageau, D. Places rated almanac   **307.7**
See/See also pages in the following book(s):
Boorstin, D. J. The Americans: The democratic experience   **973**
Cities of the world   **910.3**
Citizen McCain [biography of John McCain] Drew, E.   **92**
Citizen Sherman: a life of William Tecumseh Sherman. Fellman, M.   **92**
Citizen soldiers. Ambrose, S. E.   **940.54**
Citizens: a chronicle of the French Revolution. Schama, S.   **944.04**
Citizenship papers. Berry, W.   **338.1**
Citron, Stephen
Sondheim and Lloyd-Webber   **92**
City and town life
Frazier, I. Family   **977.1**
Kidder, T. Home town   **974.4**

Mumford, L. The city in history   **307.7**
The **city** in history. Mumford, L.   **307.7**
The **city** in mind. Kunstler, J. H.   **307.7**
City lights pocket poets anthology   **808.81**
The **city** of Florence. Lewis, R. W. B.   **945**
The **City** of Joy. Lapierre, D.   **954**
City of the century. Miller, D. L.   **977.3**
City planning
Duany, A. Suburban nation   **307.7**
Mumford, L. The culture of cities   **307.7**
Civil disobedience *See* Resistance to government
Civil disorders *See* Riots
Civil engineering
See also Mechanical engineering; Water supply engineering
Petroski, H. Engineers of dreams   **624**
Civil rights
See also African Americans—Civil rights; Handicapped—Civil rights; Right of privacy; Women's rights
Civil rights in the United States   **323.1**
Dershowitz, A. M. Shouting fire   **323**
Rehnquist, W. H. All the laws but one   **342**
Civil rights (International law) *See* Human rights
Civil rights in the United States   **323.1**
Civil service
      Examinations
Civil service arithmetic and vocabulary   **351.076**
Civil service handbook   **351.076**
      United States
Civil service handbook   **351.076**
Federal civil service jobs   **351.076**
Guide to America's federal jobs   **351.076**
Civil service arithmetic and vocabulary   **351.076**
Civil service handbook   **351.076**
Civil War
      United States
See United States—History—1861-1865, Civil War
The **Civil** War. Foote, S.   **973.7**
The **Civil** War. Ward, G. C.   **973.7**
The **Civil** War dictionary. Boatner, M. M.   **973.7**
Civilization
See also names of continents, countries, states, etc., with the subdivision *Civilization,* e.g. United States—Civilization
Boorstin, D. J. The creators   **909**
Boorstin, D. J. The discoverers   **909**
Fromm, E. To have or to be?   **302**
A History of private life   **909**
Ortega y Gasset, J. The revolt of the masses   **909**
Wright, R. NonZero   **303.4**
      Dictionaries
Hirsch, E. D. The new dictionary of cultural literacy   **031**
      History
Boorstin, D. J. The seekers   **909**
Braudel, F. A history of civilizations   **909**
A History of civilization   **909**
Mumford, L. The city in history   **307.7**
Spengler, O. The decline of the West   **901**
Toynbee, A. A study of history   **909**
Civilization, Ancient *See* Ancient civilization
Civilization, Arab *See* Arab civilization
Civilization, Christian *See* Christian civilization
Civilization, Classical *See* Classical civilization
Civilization, Islamic *See* Islamic civilization
Civilization, Jewish *See* Jewish civilization
Civilization, Medieval *See* Medieval civilization
Civilization, Mediterranean *See* Mediterranean civilization
Civilization, Modern *See* Modern civilization
Civilization, Sumerian *See* Sumerians
Civilization, Western *See* Western civilization
Civilization and science *See* Science and civilization

Civilization and technology *See* Technology and civilization

Civilizations of the ancient Near East   **939**

Claflin, Victoria *See* Woodhull, Victoria C., 1838-1927

Claggett, Hilary D., 1964-
  (ed) The 21st century. See The 21st century
                      909.83

Claiborne, Craig
  The New York Times cook book   **641.5**

Clancy, Liam
  The mountain of the women   **92**

Clancy, Tom, 1947-
  Into the storm   **956.7**
  Special forces   **356**

Clapton, Eric
                   About
  Schumacher, M. Crossroads: the life and music of Eric Clapton   **92**

Clara Ward Singers
  Ward-Royster, W. How I got over   **920**

Clare, John, 1793-1864
                   About
  Bate, J. John Clare: a biography   **92**
  See/See also pages in the following book(s):
  Heaney, S. Finders keepers p300-18   **821**
  Heaney, S. The redress of poetry   **821.009**

Claridge, Laura P.
  Norman Rockwell   **92**

Clark, Cathy Scott- *See* Scott-Clark, Cathy

Clark, Duncan
  Classical music: the rough guide. See Classical music: the rough guide   **781.6**

Clark, Ella Elizabeth, 1896-
  Sacagawea of the Lewis and Clark expedition   **92**

Clark, James H., 1944-
                   About
  Lewis, M. The new new thing   **92**

Clark, Jerome
  Encyclopedia of strange and unexplained physical phenomena   **001.9**

Clark, Jim *See* Clark, James H., 1944-

Clark, John O. E. (John Owen Edward), 1937-
  (ed) The Facts on File dictionary of earth science. See The Facts on File dictionary of earth science
                   550.3

Clark, M. (Michael)
  (ed) The Oxford-Duden German dictionary. See The Oxford-Duden German dictionary   **433**

Clark, Melissa
  (jt. auth) Berley, P. The modern vegetarian kitchen
                   641.5

Clark, Michael *See* Clark, M. (Michael)

Clark, Thomas
  (ed) The Writer's digest guide to good writing. See The Writer's digest guide to good writing   **808**

Clark, Wesley K.
  Waging modern war   **949.7**

Clark, William, 1770-1838
  The Lewis and Clark journals. See The Lewis and Clark journals   **978**
  (jt. auth) Lewis, M. The essential Lewis and Clark   **978**
                   About
  Slaughter, T. P. Exploring Lewis and Clark   **978**

Clark, William R., 1938-
  Are we hardwired?   **155.7**

Clark, William S., 1937-
  A field guide to hawks of North America   **598**

Clarke, Arthur C., 1917-
  Greetings, carbon-based bipeds!   **500**
  See/See also pages in the following book(s):
  Malone, J. W. It doesn't take a rocket scientist
                   920

Clarke, Donald, 1940-
  Wishing on the moon: the life and times of Billie Holiday   **92**

Clarke, F. G. (Francis Gordon)
  The history of Australia   **994**

Clarke, Francis Gordon *See* Clarke, F. G. (Francis Gordon)

Clarke, Frank G. *See* Clarke, F. G. (Francis Gordon)

Clarke, Gerald
  Get happy: the life of Judy Garland   **92**

Clarke, Graham
  (jt. auth) Courtier, J. Indoor plants   **635.9**

Clarke, Tony
  (jt. auth) Barlow, M. Blue gold: the fight to stop the corporate theft of the world's water   **333.91**

The **clash**. LaFeber, W.   **327.73**

The **clash** of civilizations and the remaking of world order. Huntington, S. P.   **909.82**

Clash of Titans. Boyne, W. J.   **940.54**

Clash of wings. Boyne, W. J.   **940.54**

Class action. Bingham, C.   **342**

Classic hand tools. Hack, G.   **621.9**

The **classic** Italian cookbook. See Hazan, M. Essentials of classic Italian cooking   **641.5**

Classic millinery techniques. Albrizio, A.   **646.5**

The **classic** of changes. I ching   **299**

Classic Russian cooking. Molokhovets, E.   **641.5**

The **classic** tales. Frankel, E.   **296.1**

Classical antiquities
  See also Greece—Antiquities
                   Dictionaries
  See Classical dictionaries

Classical civilization
  See also Rome—Civilization
  Connolly, P. The ancient city   **937**

Classical dictionaries
  Grant, M. A guide to the ancient world   **938.003**
  The Oxford classical dictionary   **938.003**

The **Classical** Greek reader   **880.8**

Classical literature
  See also Greek literature; Latin literature
                   Bio-bibliography
  Grant, M. Greek and Latin authors, 800 B.C.-A.D. 1000   **920.003**
                   Dictionaries
  The Oxford companion to classical literature
                   880.3

Classical music *See* Music

Classical music 101. Plotkin, F.   **781.6**

Classical music for dummies. Pogue, D.   **781.6**

Classical music: the listener's companion   **781.6**

Classical music: the rough guide   **781.6**

Classical mythology
  Graves, R. Greek myths   **292**
  Hamilton, E. Mythology   **292**
  Vernant, J. P. The universe, the gods, and men
                   292
                   Catalogs
  Reid, J. D. The Oxford guide to classical mythology in the arts, 1300-1990s   **700**
                   Dictionaries
  Grimal, P. The dictionary of classical mythology
                   292
  Impelluso, L. Gods and heroes in art   **700**

Classical poetry
                   Collections
  The Oxford book of classical verse in translation
                   881.008

The **classical** style. Rosen, C.   **780.9**

Classical Turkish cooking. Algar, A. E.   **641.5**

Classification
                   Books
  See Library classification

Classification, Dewey Decimal *See* Dewey Decimal Classification

Classified catalogs
Children's catalog   011.6
Middle and junior high school library catalog
                                                             011.6
Senior high school library catalog   011.6
Claude-Pierre, Peggy
The secret language of eating disorders   616.85
Claudel, Camille, 1864-1943
About
Ayral-Clause, O. Camille Claudel   92
Claudius, Emperor of Rome, 10 B.C.-54
See/See also pages in the following book(s):
Suetonius Tranquillus, C. The twelve Caesars   878
Clause, Odile Ayral- *See* Ayral-Clause, Odile
Clausen, Ruth Rogers, 1938-
Dreamscaping   712
Clauser, Henry R.
(jt. auth) Brady, G. S. Materials handbook   620.1
Clausewitz, Carl von, 1780-1831
On war   355
Clausius, Rudolf Julius Emmanuel, 1822-1888
See/See also pages in the following book(s):
Guillen, M. Five equations that changed the world
                                                             530.1
Clavell, Maria Collazo- *See* Collazo-Clavell, Maria
Clawson, Calvin C.
Mathematical mysteries   512
Clawson, Dan
(ed) Required reading. See Required reading   301
Clay, Cassius *See* Ali, Muhammad, 1942-
Clayman, Charles B.
(ed) American Medical Association family medical
guide. See American Medical Association family
medical guide   616.02
(ed) The Human body. See The Human body
                                                             612
Clayton, Buck, 1911-1991
See/See also pages in the following book(s):
Dance, S. The world of Count Basie   920
Clayton, Jade
McGraw-Hill illustrated telecom dictionary
                                                             621.382
Clayton, Tim
Finest hour   940.54
Cleaning
Friedman, V. M. Field guide to stains   648
How to clean practically anything   648
Clear pictures. Price, R.   92
A **clearing** in the distance: Frederick Law Olmsted and
America in the nineteenth century. Rybczynski, W.
                                                             92
Clearing the bases. Barra, A.   796.357
Cleaver, Eldridge, 1935-1998
Soul on ice   305.8
Clemenceau, Georges, 1841-1929
See/See also pages in the following book(s):
Cohen, E. A. Supreme command   355
Clemens, Samuel Langhorne *See* Twain, Mark, 1835-
1910
Clement, Mary, 1943-
(jt. auth) Humphry, D. Freedom to die   179.7
Clementi, Muzio, 1752-1832
See/See also pages in the following book(s):
Schonberg, H. C. The great pianists   920
Clendinnen, Inga
Reading the Holocaust   940.53
Cleopatra, Queen of Egypt, d. 30 B.C.
Drama
Dryden, J. All for love   822
CLEP *See* College Level Examination Program
CLEP: Master the College-Level Examination Program.
See Master the CLEP   378.1
Clerical employees *See* Office workers

Cleveland, Grover, 1837-1908
About
Brodsky, A. Grover Cleveland   92
Graff, H. F. Grover Cleveland   92
Clever as a fox. Yoerg, S.   591.5
Clicking. Popcorn, F.   650.1
Cliff, Stafford
(jt. auth) Slesin, S. Japanese style   747.2
Cliff dwellers and cliff dwellings
See/See also pages in the following book(s):
Connell, E. S. The Aztec treasure house p433-53
                                                             814
The **cliff** walk. Snyder, D. J.   92
Clifford, Barry
The lost fleet   910.4
Clifford, Denis
Make your own living trust   346.05
Nolo's simple will book   346.05
Plan your estate   346.05
Quick & legal will book   346.05
Clifton, Lucille, 1936-
The terrible stories   811
See/See also pages in the following book(s):
Black women writers (1950-1980)   810.9
Climacteric, Female *See* Menopause
Climate
See also Greenhouse effect; Meteorology; United
States—Climate; Weather
Allaby, M. The Facts on File weather and climate
handbook   551.6
Encyclopedia of climate and weather   551.6
Stevens, W. K. The change in the weather   551.5
Weather   551.5
The **climb.** Boukreev, A.   796.52
Climbing Mount Improbable. Dawkins, R.   576
Climbing plants
Michener, D. Taylor's guide to ground covers
                                                             635.9
Clin, Marie-Véronique
(jt. auth) Pernoud, R. Joan of Arc   92
Cline, Isaac Monroe, 1861-1955
About
Larson, E. Isaac's storm   976.4
Cline, Sally
Zelda Fitzgerald   92
Clinton, Bill, 1946-
About
Bennett, W. J. The death of outrage: Bill Clinton and
the assault on American ideals   973.929
Conason, J. The hunting of the President   973.929
Halberstam, D. War in a time of peace   327.73
Johnson, H. B. The best of times   973.929
Klein, J. The natural: the misunderstood presidency of
Bill Clinton   973.929
Maraniss, D. First in his class: a biography of Bill
Clinton   92
Sheehy, G. Hillary's choice   92
Stephanopoulos, G. All too human   973.929
Talbott, S. The Russia hand   327.73
Toobin, J. R. A vast conspiracy   973.929
See/See also pages in the following book(s):
Mann, J. About face   327.73
Woodward, B. Shadow   973.92
Clinton, Catherine, 1952-
Fanny Kemble's civil wars   92
Clinton, Hillary Rodham, 1947-
Living history   92
About
Brock, D. The seduction of Hillary Rodham   92
Conason, J. The hunting of the President   973.929
Sheehy, G. Hillary's choice   92
Clinton, William Jefferson *See* Clinton, Bill, 1946-
The **clock** of ages. Medina, J.   612.6
Clogg, Richard, 1939-
A concise history of Greece   949.5

The **cloister** walk. Norris, K.   255

Clones and clones   174

Cloning
    Clones and clones   174
    Flesh of my flesh   174
    Fukuyama, F. Our posthuman future   174
    Human cloning and human dignity   174
    Kolata, G. Clone   174
    Wilmut, I. The second creation   174

Clooney, Rosemary
    Girl singer   92

Close, F. E.
    The particle odyssey   539.7

Close to shore. Capuzzo, M.   597

The **closing** of the American mind. Bloom, A. D.
    973.92

Closing the ring. Churchill, Sir W.   940.53

Cloth See Fabrics

Clothing and dress
    See also Costume; Fashion; Men's clothing
    Morris, M. Every sewer's guide to the perfect fit
    646.4

Clothing industry
    Contemporary fashion   391
    In an influential fashion   391
    Von Drehle, D. Triangle: the fire that changed America
    ca   974.7

Clouds
    Hamblyn, R. The invention of clouds   551.57

Clouds. Aristophanes
    In Aristophanes. The complete plays of Aristophanes
    p101-41   882

Clown act omnibus. McVicar, W.   791.3

Clowns
    McVicar, W. Clown act omnibus   791.3

Clubs
    See also Societies

Clute, John
    (ed) The Encyclopedia of fantasy. See The Encyclopedia of fantasy   809.3

Coakes, Michelle
    Creative pottery   738

Coal
    Freese, B. Coal: a human history   553.2

Coal: a human history. Freese, B.   553.2

Coal miner's daughter. See Lynn, L. Loretta Lynn: coal miner's daughter   92

Coal mines and mining
Accidents
    Tintori, K. Trapped: the 1909 Cherry Mine disaster
    977.3

The **Coalwood** way. Hickam, H. H.   92

Coastal landforms See Coasts

Coasts
    Dean, C. Against the tide   333.91

Coates, Steven L., 1955-
    (jt. auth) Johnson, K. Nabokov's Blues   92

Cobain, Kurt, 1967-1994
About
    Cross, C. R. Heavier than heaven: a biography of Kurt Cobain   92

Cobb, Cathy
    Creations of fire   540

Cobb, Geraldyn M., 1931-
    See/See also pages in the following book(s):
    Haynsworth, L. Amelia Earhart's daughters
    629.13

Cobb, Jerrie See Cobb, Geraldyn M., 1931-

Cobb, Ty, 1886-1961
About
    Stump, A. Cobb   92

Coburn, Broughton, 1951-
    Everest: mountain without mercy   796.52
    (jt. auth) Norgay, J. T. Touching my father's soul
    796.52

Coburn, Katharine M., 1962-
    (jt. auth) Poirier, L. M. Women & diabetes   616.4

Cocaine
    Streatfeild, D. Cocaine   362.29

Cochise, Apache Chief, d. 1874
About
    Roberts, D. Once they moved like the wind
    970.004
    See/See also pages in the following book(s):
    Brown, D. A. The American West p124-31   978
    Brown, D. A. Bury my heart at Wounded Knee
    970.004

Cochran, Jacqueline, 1910?-1980
    See/See also pages in the following book(s):
    Haynsworth, L. Amelia Earhart's daughters
    629.13

Cocina de la familia. Tausend, M.   641.5

Cocker, Mark
    Birders   598
    Rivers of blood, rivers of gold   909

Cocktail party. Eliot, T. S.
    In Eliot, T. S. The complete poems and plays, 1909-
    1950 p295-388   818

Cocteau, Jean, 1889-1963
    Orphée
    In Our dramatic heritage v6   808.82

Cod. Kurlansky, M.   639.2

The **code** book. Singh, S.   652

Code deciphering See Cryptography

Code name Kindred Spirit. Trulock, N.   327.12

Codependents' guide to the twelve steps. Beattie, M.
    616.86

Codes See Ciphers

Codes, Penal See Criminal law

Codfish
    Kurlansky, M. Cod   639.2

Codina, Carles
    The complete book of jewelry making   739.27

Codrescu, Andrei, 1946-
    Ay, Cuba!   972.91
    The Devil never sleeps and other essays   814
    The dog with the chip in his neck   814
    The muse is always half-dressed in New Orleans and other essays   814

Cody, William Frederick See Buffalo Bill, 1846-1917

Coe, Michael D.
    The Maya   972

Coelacanth
    Thomson, K. S. Living fossil   597
    Weinberg, S. A fish caught in time   597

Coelho, Daniel H.
    (ed) The Ethics of organ transplants. See The Ethics of organ transplants   174

Coetzee, J. M., 1940-
    The lives of animals   179
    Youth   92

Coffey, Michael, 1954-
    Days of infamy   355

Coffey, Timothy
    The history and folklore of North American wildflowers   582.13

Coffin, Charles M.
    (ed) Donne, J. The complete poetry and selected prose of John Donne   828

Coffin, Tristram Potter, 1922-
    (ed) The Folklore of the American holidays. See The Folklore of the American holidays   394.26

A **coffin** in Egypt. Foote, H.
    In Foote, H. Getting Frankie married—and afterwards, and other plays   812

Cogeval, Guy
    Edouard Vuillard. See Edouard Vuillard   759.4

Cogito ergo sum: the life of René Descartes. Watson, R. A.   92

Cognition See Theory of knowledge

Cohan, George M., 1878-1942
See/See also pages in the following book(s):
Green, S. The world of musical comedy   920
Cohen, A. (Abraham), b. 1887
Everyman's Talmud   296.1
Cohen, Abraham *See* Cohen, A. (Abraham), b. 1887
Cohen, Adam
American pharaoh: Mayor Richard J. Daley: his battle
for Chicago and the nation   92
Cohen, Carl, 1931-
(jt. auth) Copi, I. M. Introduction to logic   160
Cohen, Donald J., 1940-2001
(jt. auth) Mayes, L. C. The Yale Child Study Center
guide to understanding your child   649
Cohen, Eliot A.
Supreme command   355
Cohen, Gene D.
The creative age   305.24
Cohen, George J.
(ed) American Academy of Pediatrics guide to your
child's sleep. See American Academy of Pediatrics
guide to your child's sleep   618.92
Cohen, Hennig
(ed) The Folklore of the American holidays. See The
Folklore of the American holidays   394.26
Cohen, I. Bernard, 1914-2003
Science and the founding fathers   973.3
(ed) The Cambridge companion to Newton. See The
Cambridge companion to Newton   530
Cohen, Isaac
(ed) Breast cancer. See Breast cancer   616.99
Cohen, Lawrence J.
Playful parenting   649
Cohen, Lizabeth
A consumer's republic   339.4
Cohen, Morton Norton, 1921-
Lewis Carroll   92
Cohen, Randy
The good, the bad & the difference   170
Cohen, Rich
The avengers   940.53
Cohen, Richard
By the sword   796.8
Cohen, Richard M., 1938-
(jt. auth) Neft, D. S. The sports encyclopedia: baseball
                                               796.357
Cohen, Roger
Hearts grown brutal   949.7
In the eye of the storm: the life of General H. Norman
Schwarzkopf   92
Cohen, Saul Bernard, 1925-
(ed) The Columbia gazetteer of North America. See
The Columbia gazetteer of North America   917
Cohen, Shirley
Targeting autism   618.92
Cohen, Stephen F.
Failed crusade   327.73
Cohen-Solal, Annie
Painting American   759.13
Cohn, Lawrence, 1932-
(ed) Nothing but the blues. See Nothing but the blues
                                               781.643
Cohodas, Nadine
Strom Thurmond & the politics of southern change
                                               92
Coile, D. Caroline
Encyclopedia of dog breeds   636.7
Coins
A Guide book of United States coins   737.4
Handbook of United States coins   737.4
Krause, C. L. Standard catalog of world coins
                                               737.4
Official know-it-all guide: coins   737.4
Cokinos, Christopher
Hope is the thing with feathers   598

Cola di Rienzi *See* Rienzo, Cola di, ca. 1313-1354
Colamosca, Anne
(jt. auth) Wolman, W. The great 401(k) hoax
                                               332.024
Colbert, David
(ed) Eyewitness to America. See Eyewitness to America
                                               973
Colby, Vineta
(ed) European authors, 1000-1900. See European authors, 1000-1900   920.003
(ed) World authors, 1975-1980. See World authors,
1975-1980   920.003
(ed) World authors, 1980-1985. See World authors,
1980-1985   920.003
(ed) World authors, 1985-1990. See World authors,
1985-1990   920.003
Colby, William E.
About
Prados, J. Lost crusader: the secret wars of CIA director William Colby   92
Colchie, Elizabeth Schneider *See* Schneider, Elizabeth, 1943-
Cold
See also Low temperatures
A cold case. Gourevitch, P.   364.1
Cold Harbor (Va.), Battle of, 1864
Furgurson, E. B. Not war but murder   973.7
Cold war
Burrows, W. E. By any means necessary   327.12
FitzGerald, F. Way out there in the blue   973.927
Gates, R. M. From the shadows   327.73
Gregory, R. Cold War America, 1946 to 1990
                                               973.92
Grose, P. Operation Rollback   327.12
Heppenheimer, T. A. Countdown   629.4
Kort, M. The Columbia guide to the Cold War
                                               973.9
Leebaert, D. The fifty-year wound   973.92
Schweizer, P. Reagan's War   327.73
Walker, M. The Cold War   909.82
See/See also pages in the following book(s):
Foner, E. The story of American freedom p246-73
                                               323.44
Kissinger, H. Diplomacy   327.73
Rhodes, R. Dark sun   623.4
Cold War America, 1946 to 1990. Gregory, R.
                                               973.92
Cold War culture. Schwartz, R. A.   973.92
Cold zero. Whitcomb, C.   363.2
The **coldest** March. Solomon, S.   998
The **coldest** war: a memoir of Korea. Brady, J.
                                               951.9
Cole, K. C.
First you build a cloud   530
The hole in the universe   530
The universe and the teacup   510
Cole, Nat King, 1919?-1965
About
Epstein, D. M. Nat King Cole   92
See/See also pages in the following book(s):
Lees, G. You can't steal a gift   920
Cole, Natalie
Angel on my shoulder   92
Cole, Simon A., 1967-
Suspect identities   363.2
Cole, Sylvia
The Facts on File dictionary of cultural and historical
allusions   031.02
Cole, Trevor
(ed) American Horticultural Society encyclopedia of
plants and flowers. See American Horticultural Society encyclopedia of plants and flowers   635.9
Colegate, Isabel
A pelican in the wilderness   291.4

Coleman, C. Norman
Understanding cancer   **616.99**
Coleman, Edward, 1968-
(jt. auth) Seglin, J. L. The AMA handbook of business letters   **651.7**
Coleman, Fred
The decline and fall of the Soviet Empire   **947.085**
Coleridge, Samuel Taylor, 1772-1834
The portable Coleridge   **828**
The rime of the ancient mariner
In Coleridge, S. T. The portable Coleridge   **828**
About
Holmes, R. Coleridge: darker reflections, 1804-1834   **92**

See/See also pages in the following book(s):
Alvarez, A. Night p181-92   **154.6**
Coles, David J.
(ed) Encyclopedia of the American Civil War. See Encyclopedia of the American Civil War   **973.7**
Coles, Janet
Beads   **745.58**
Coles, Robert
The call of stories   **808**
Children of crisis   **305.23**
Lives of moral leadership   **170**
The moral intelligence of children   **155.4**
Old and on their own   **305.26**
The secular mind   **291.1**
The spiritual life of children   **291.4**
When they were young   **779**
Colet, Louise, 1810-1876
See/See also pages in the following book(s):
Fraser, K. Ornament and silence   **814**
Colette, 1873-1954
About
Thurman, J. Secrets of the flesh: a life of Colette   **92**
Colette's cakes. Peters, C.   **641.8**
The **collaborator:** the trial & execution of Robert Brasillach. Kaplan, A. Y.   **92**
Collapse and recovery of the Roman Empire. Grant, M.   **937**

Collapse of structures *See* Structural failures
Collazo-Clavell, Maria
(ed) Mayo Clinic on managing diabetes. See Mayo Clinic on managing diabetes   **616.4**
Collected books. Ahearn, A.   **002.075**
Collected earlier poems, 1940-1960. Levertov, D.   **811**
Collected early poems, 1950-1970. Rich, A.   **811**
Collected early poems of Ezra Pound. Pound, E.   **811**
Collected essays. Baldwin, J.   **814**
Collected essays and poems. Thoreau, H. D.   **818**
Collected longer poems. Carruth, H.   **811**
The **collected** longer poems. Rexroth, K.   **811**
Collected plays v1. Norman, M.   **812**
Collected plays v2. Foote, H.   **812**
The **collected** plays of Neil Simon v2-3. Simon, N.   **812**
Collected plays, volume III. See Foote, H. Getting Frankie married—and afterwards, and other plays   **812**
Collected poems. Auden, W. H.   **821**
Collected poems. Bowers, E.   **811**
Collected poems. Hayden, R. E.   **811**
The **collected** poems. Kunitz, S.   **811**
Collected poems. Larkin, P.   **821**
Collected poems. Lowell, R.   **811**
Collected poems. Mallarmé, S.   **841**
Collected poems. Millay, E. S.   **811**
The **collected** poems. Plath, S.   **811**
The **collected** poems. Price, R.   **811**
Collected poems. Schuyler, J.   **811**

Collected poems. Smith, S.   **821**
Collected poems & translations. Emerson, R. W.   **811**
Collected poems (1909-1935). Eliot, T. S.
In Eliot, T. S. The complete poems and plays, 1909-1950   **818**
Collected poems, 1909-1962. Eliot, T. S.   **811**
Collected poems, 1912-1944. H. D.   **811**
Collected poems, 1917-1982. MacLeish, A.   **811**
Collected poems, 1920-1954. Montale, E.   **851**
Collected poems, 1937-1971. Berryman, J.   **811**
Collected poems, 1945-1990. Howes, B.   **811**
Collected poems, 1947-1980. Ginsberg, A.   **811**
Collected poems, 1948-1984. Walcott, D.   **811**
Collected poems, 1953-1993. Updike, J.   **811**
Collected poems, 1957-1982. Berry, W.   **811**
Collected poems in English, 1972-1999. Brodsky, J.   **811**
Collected poems in English and French. Beckett, S.   **841**
The **collected** poems of A. E. Housman. Housman, A. E.   **821**
The **collected** poems of Audre Lorde. Lorde, A.   **811**
The **collected** poems of Charles Olson. Olson, C.   **811**
The **collected** poems of George Oppen. See Oppen, G. New collected poems   **811**
The **collected** poems of James Merrill. Merrill, J.   **811**
The **collected** poems of Jean Toomer. Toomer, J.   **811**
The **collected** poems of John Ciardi. Ciardi, J.   **811**
The **collected** poems of Langston Hughes. Hughes, L.   **811**
The **collected** poems of Octavio Paz, 1957-1987. Paz, O.   **861**
The **collected** poems of Odysseus Elytis. Elytēs, O.   **889**
The **collected** poems of Robert Creeley, 1945-1975. Creeley, R.   **811**
The **collected** poems of Robert Penn Warren. Warren, R. P.   **811**
The **collected** poems of Theodore Roethke. Roethke, T.   **811**
The **collected** poems of William Carlos Williams. Williams, W. C.   **811**
Collected poems, prose, & plays. Frost, R.   **818**
The **collected** poetry of Robinson Jeffers. Jeffers, R.   **811**
The **collected** prose. Bishop, E.   **818**
Collected prose. Lowell, R.   **818**
Collected shorter poems, 1946-1991. Carruth, H.   **811**
The **collected** tales and poems of Edgar Allan Poe. Poe, E. A.   **818**
Collected works. Niedecker, L.   **811**
The **collected** writings. Bierce, A.   **818**
The **collection.** Pinter, H.
In Pinter, H. Complete works v2   **822**
Collection development (Libraries) *See* Libraries—Collection development
Collectors and collecting
Kovel, R. M. Kovels' antiques and collectibles price list   **745.1**
Kovel, R. M. Kovel's know your collectibles   **745.1**
Maloney, D. J. Maloney's antiques & collectibles resource directory   **745.1**
Mauriès, P. Cabinets of curiosities   **069**
College and university libraries *See* Academic libraries
College applications
See also Colleges and universities—Entrance requirements
Steinberg, J. The gatekeepers   **378.1**

College applications—*Continued*
Toor, R. Admissions confidential   378.1
The **College** blue book   378.73
College Board *See* College Entrance Examination Board
College choice
Fiske, E. B. The Fiske guide to colleges   378.73
Fiske, E. B. The Fiske guide to getting into the right college   378
The **college** cost book. See College Entrance Examination Board. The college costs & financial aid handbook   378.3
College costs
   See also Student aid
College Entrance Examination Board. The college costs & financial aid handbook   378.3
Feigenbaum, R. A. The 529 College Savings Plan   378.3
Peterson's college money handbook   378.3
College Entrance Examination Board
The college costs & financial aid handbook   378.3
The college handbook   378.73
Index of majors and graduate degrees   378.73
College entrance requirements *See* Colleges and universities—Entrance requirements
The **college** handbook. College Entrance Examination Board   378.73
The **college** handbook index of majors. See College Entrance Examination Board. Index of majors and graduate degrees   378.73
College Level Examination Program
Master the CLEP   378.1
Colleges and universities
   See also Higher education
         Curricula
College Entrance Examination Board. Index of majors and graduate degrees   378.73
         Directories
The World of learning   060.25
         Entrance examinations
   See also ACT assessment; Scholastic Aptitude Test
         Entrance requirements
Fiske, E. B. The Fiske guide to getting into the right college   378
How to prepare for SAT I   378.1
How to prepare for the ACT, American College Testing Assessment Program   378.1
         Finance
   See also College costs
   See/See also pages in the following book(s):
Fiske, E. B. The Fiske guide to getting into the right college   378
         Selection
   See College choice
         United States
   See/See also pages in the following book(s):
Boorstin, D. J. The Americans: The colonial experience   973.2
Boorstin, D. J. The Americans: The national experience p152-61   973
         United States—Directories
American universities and colleges   378.73
Barron's guide to law schools   378.73
Barron's profiles of American colleges   378.73
The College blue book   378.73
College Entrance Examination Board. The college handbook   378.73
College Entrance Examination Board. Index of majors and graduate degrees   378.73
Fiske, E. B. The Fiske guide to colleges   378.73
Peterson's colleges with programs for students with learning disabilities or attention deficit disorders   378.73
Peterson's competitive colleges   378.73
Peterson's guide to four-year colleges   378.73
Peterson's guide to two-year colleges   378.73

Collegiate dictionary, Merriam-Webster's   423
Collier, James Lincoln, 1928-
Louis Armstrong, an American genius   92
Collier, Michael, 1953-
(ed) The New American poets. See The New American poets   811.008
Collier, Peter, 1939-
The Roosevelts   920
Collins, Billy
Nine horses   811
Sailing alone around the room   811
Collins, Bud
(ed) Total tennis: the ultimate tennis encyclopedia. See Total tennis: the ultimate tennis encyclopedia   796.342
Collins, Francis S.
   See/See also pages in the following book(s):
Davies, K. Cracking the genome   599.93
Collins, James C.
Good to great   658
Collins, John B.
(jt. auth) Bailey, C. B. Renoir's portraits   759.4
Collins, Joseph T.
(jt. auth) Conant, R. A field guide to reptiles & amphibians   597.9
Collins, Larry, 1929-
O Jerusalem!   956.94
Collins, Paul
The modern Inquisition   282
Collins, Victoria F. (Victoria Felton), 1942-
(jt. auth) Woodhouse, V. Divorce and money   346.01
Collins German-English, English-German dictionary   433
Collister, Linda
The bread book   641.8
Colman, Andrew M.
A dictionary of psychology   150.3
Colombia
         Politics and government
Guillermoprieto, A. Looking for history   972
Colombo, Cristoforo *See* Columbus, Christopher
Colon (Anatomy)
Adrouny, A. R. Understanding colon cancer   616.99
The **colonial** experience. See Boorstin, D. J. The Americans: The colonial experience   973.2
Colonialism *See* Imperialism
Colonies
Cocker, M. Rivers of blood, rivers of gold   909
Pagden, A. Peoples and empires   909
Color
Pyle, D. What every artist needs to know about paints & colors   752
Color. Barnes, C.   746.46
Color-blind. Cose, E.   305.8
Color blindness
Sacks, O. W. The island of the colorblind   617.7
The **color** encyclopedia of ornamental grasses. Darke, R.   635.9
Color for adventurous gardeners. Lloyd, C.   635.9
Color in art
Ball, P. Bright earth   701
The **color** of water [biography of Ruth McBride-Jordan] McBride, J.   92
Color purple (Motion picture)
   See/See also pages in the following book(s):
Walker, A. The same river twice   92
Colorado
         Gold discoveries
West, E. The contested plains   978
Colorado River (Colo.-Mexico)
Dolnick, E. Down the great unknown   979.1
         Description
Fletcher, C. River   917.91

Colored people. Gates, H. L.   92
Colors of the mountain. Chen, D.   92
Colt, George Howe
   The big house   920
Colt family
          About
   Colt, G. H. The big house   920
Coltelli, Laura, 1941-
   Winged words: American Indian writers speak
       897
Coltrane, John, 1926-1967
   Love supreme; criticism
   In Kahn, A. A love supreme   781.65
Columbarium. Stewart, S.   811
The **Columbia** anthology of American poetry
       811.008
The **Columbia** anthology of British poetry   821.008
The **Columbia** book of Chinese poetry   895.1
The **Columbia** book of Civil War poetry   811.008
The **Columbia** companion to British history   941
The **Columbia** companion to the twentieth-century
   American short story   813.009
Columbia dictionary of modern European literature
       803
The **Columbia** dictionary of quotations. Andrews, R.
       808.88
The **Columbia** dictionary of quotations from Shake-
   speare. Shakespeare, W.   822.3
The **Columbia** encyclopedia   031
The **Columbia** gazetteer of North America   917
The **Columbia** gazetteer of the world   910.3
The **Columbia** Granger's dictionary of poetry quotations
       808.88
The **Columbia** Granger's index to poetry in anthologies
       808.81
The **Columbia** Granger's Index to poetry in collected
   and selected works   808.81
The **Columbia** guide to America in the 1960s
       973.92
The **Columbia** guide to American Indians of the Great
   Plains. Fowler, L.   970.004
The **Columbia** guide to American Indians of the North-
   east. Bragdon, K. J.   970.004
The **Columbia** guide to American Indians of the South-
   east. Perdue, T.   970.004
The **Columbia** guide to digital publishing   070.5
The **Columbia** guide to modern Chinese history.
   Schoppa, R. K.   951.05
The **Columbia** guide to online style. Walker, J. R.
       808
The **Columbia** guide to standard American English. Wil-
   son, K. G.   428
The **Columbia** guide to the Cold War. Kort, M.
       973.9
The **Columbia** guide to the literatures of Eastern Europe
   since 1945. Segel, H. B.   809
The **Columbia** guide to the Vietnam War. Anderson, D.
   L.   959.704
The **Columbia** history of American poetry   811.009
The **Columbia** history of British poetry   821.009
The **Columbia** history of Chinese literature   895.1
The **Columbia** history of the 20th century   909.82
The **Columbia** history of the British novel   823.009
The **Columbia** history of Western philosophy   190
The **Columbia** Lippincott gazetteer of the world. See
   The Columbia gazetteer of the world   910.3
Columbia literary history of the United States
       810.9
Columbia River
   Harden, B. A river lost   979.7
Columbia University. Health Service
   The "Go ask Alice" book of answers. See The "Go ask
   Alice" book of answers   613
Columbian Exposition (1893: Chicago, Ill.) *See*
   World's Columbian Exposition (1893: Chicago, Ill.)

Columbus, Christopher
          About
   Morison, S. E. Admiral of the ocean sea: a life of
   Christopher Columbus   92
   See/See also pages in the following book(s):
   Connell, E. S. The Aztec treasure house p294-318
       814
   Williams, W. C. In the American grain p7-26
       814
Combinations of the Universe. Goldbarth, A.   811
Combs, Cindy C.
   Encyclopedia of terrorism   303.6
Come back, Little Sheba. Inge, W.
   In Inge, W. 4 plays p1-69   812
The **comeback**. Gurney, A. R.
   In Gurney, A. R. Nine early plays, 1961-1973 p1-26
       812
Comedy
   See/See also pages in the following book(s):
   Hamilton, E. The Greek way p126-58   880.9
Comets
   See also Halley's comet
   Levy, D. H. Comets   523.6
   Norton, O. R. Rocks from space   523.5
   Sagan, C. Comet   523.6
Comfort, Alex, 1920-2000
   The joy of sex   613.9
Comfort me with apples. Reichl, R.   92
Comfort women
   Hicks, G. The comfort women   940.54
Comic book nation. Wright, B. W.   741.5
Comic books, strips, etc.
   See also Cartoons and caricatures
   Daniels, L. Marvel   741.5
   McCloud, S. Reinventing comics   741.5
   O'Neil, D. The DC comics guide to writing comics
       808
   The World encyclopedia of comics   741.5
   Wright, B. W. Comic book nation   741.5
The **coming** conflict with China. Bernstein, R.
       327.73
Coming into eighty. Sarton, M.   811
Coming into the country. McPhee, J. A.   979.8
Coming of age as a poet. Vendler, H. H.   820.9
Coming of age in Samoa. Mead, M.   306
The **coming** of the New Deal, 1933-1935. Schlesinger,
   A. M.   973.917
The **coming** plague. Garrett, L.   614.4
Coming to America. Daniels, R.   325.73
Commager, Henry Steele, 1902-1998
   The American mind   973
   (jt. auth) Morison, S. E. A concise history of the
   American Republic   973
   (jt. auth) Morison, S. E. The growth of the American
   Republic   973
Command performance. Alexander, J.   92
The **commanders**. Woodward, B.   973.928
Commerce
   See also Electronic commerce
Commercial aeronautics
   See also Airlines
   Blatner, D. The flying book   387.7
          Hijacking
   See Hijacking of airplanes
Commercial fishing
   Kurlansky, M. Cod   639.2
Commercial photography
   See also Photojournalism
   Jacobs, L. The big picture   770
Commercial products
   Bower, L. M. Creating a healthy household   643
   How products are made   670
          Encyclopedias
   Brady, G. S. Materials handbook   620.1

Commire, Anne
(ed) Women in world history. See Women in world history   **920.003**
Commission for Truth and Reconciliation (South Africa) *See* South Africa. Commission for Truth and Reconciliation
Common ground. Lukas, J. A.   **305.8**
Common phrases and where they come from. Korach, M.   **422**
Common poisonous plants and mushrooms of North America. Turner, N. J.   **581.6**
Common sense. Paine, T.   **320**
The **common** thread. Sulston, J.   **572.8**
Commoner, Barry, 1917-
Making peace with the planet   **304.2**
Commonsense copyright. Talab, R. S.   **346.04**
Commonwealth countries
See also Great Britain—Colonies
History
The Cambridge illustrated history of the British Empire   **941.08**
James, L. The rise and fall of the British Empire   **909**
Commonwealth of Independent States
See also Former Soviet republics; Russia (Federation); Soviet Union
Commonwealth of Nations *See* Commonwealth countries
A **commotion** in the blood. Hall, S. S.   **616.07**
Communicable diseases
See also Epidemiology; Prion diseases; Sexually transmitted diseases; Smallpox
Callahan, J. R. Biological hazards   **615.9**
Drexler, M. Secret agents   **614.4**
Epidemic! the world of infectious diseases   **614.4**
Garrett, L. The coming plague   **614.4**
Karlen, A. Man and microbes   **614.4**
Oldstone, M. B. A. Viruses, plagues, and history   **614.4**
Ryan, F. Virus-X   **614.4**
Stoffman, P. The family guide to preventing and treating 100 infectious illnesses   **616**
Wills, C. Yellow fever, black goddess   **614.4**
Encyclopedias
Turkington, C. The encyclopedia of infectious diseases   **616.9**
Prevention
See/See also pages in the following book(s):
Peters, C. J. Virus hunter   **614.5**
Communicating in sign. Chambers, D. P.   **419**
Communication
See also Nonverbal communication; Telecommunication
Adler, M. J. How to speak, how to listen   **302.2**
Donovan, D. M. What did I just say!?!   **649**
King, L. How to talk to anyone, anytime, anywhere   **302.3**
Locke, J. L. The de-voicing of society   **302.3**
Stone, D. Difficult conversations   **158**
Tannen, D. I only say this because I love you   **306.8**
Encyclopedias
The Encyclopedia of new media   **302.23**
Communication among animals *See* Animal communication
Communication systems, Computer *See* Computer networks
Communism
See also Anticommunist movements
Marx, K. The Communist manifesto of Karl Marx and Friedrich Engels   **335.4**
Pipes, R. Communism: a history   **335.4**
Rosenberg, T. The haunted land   **947**
Stokes, G. The walls came tumbling down   **947**
Wheen, F. Karl Marx   **92**

See/See also pages in the following book(s):
Berlin, Sir I. The sense of reality p116-67   **901**
Cambodia
Bizot, F. The gate   **959.6**
Kiernan, B. The Pol Pot regime   **959.6**
United States
Chambers, W. Witness   **92**
Haynes, J. E. Venona   **327.12**
Communism and literature
See/See also pages in the following book(s):
Nabokov, V. V. Lectures on Russian literature   **891.7**
The **Communist** manifesto of Karl Marx and Friedrich Engels. Marx, K.   **335.4**
Communist Party (U.S.)
Chambers, W. Witness   **92**
Haynes, J. E. Venona   **327.12**
Community development
See also City planning
Etzioni, A. The spirit of community   **307**
Community organization
Alinsky, S. Rules for radicals   **322.4**
Community quilts. Kavaya, K.   **746.46**
The **compact** NASA atlas of the solar system. Greeley, R.   **523.2**
Companies *See* Business enterprises; Corporations
A **Companion** to American Indian history   **970.004**
Companion to Narnia. Ford, P. F.   **823.009**
The **Companion** to southern literature   **810.3**
A **Companion** to world philosophies   **109**
The **company** we keep. Chadwick, D. H.   **591.68**
Comparative philology *See* Linguistics
Comparative physiology
Hughes, H. C. Sensory exotica   **573.8**
Widmaier, E. P. Why geese don't get obese (and we do)   **571**
Comparative psychology
Calvin, W. H. How brains think   **153.9**
Waal, F. de. The ape and the sushi master   **156**
Comparative religion *See* Christianity and other religions; Religions
Compass
Aczel, A. D. The riddle of the compass   **912**
Competitive colleges, Peterson's   **378.73**
The **compleat** angler. Walton, I.   **799.1**
The **complete** antiques price list. See Kovel, R. M. Kovels' antiques and collectibles price list   **745.1**
The **complete** aquarium handbook. See Sandford, G. Aquarium: owner's manual   **639.34**
Complete baby and child care. Stoppard, M.   **649**
Complete basements, attics & bonus rooms   **643**
The **complete** bedside companion. McFarlane, R.   **649.8**
The **complete** Bible handbook. Bowker, J.   **220.6**
The **complete** book of bicycling. See Sloane, E. A. Sloane's complete book of bicycling   **629.227**
The **complete** book of cacti & succulents. Hewitt, T.   **635.9**
The **complete** book of decorative painting. Leigh, T.   **745.7**
Complete book of dreams, Parkers'. Parker, J.   **154.6**
The **complete** book of food. See Rinzler, C. A. The new complete book of food   **641.3**
The **Complete** book of garden projects   **712**
The **complete** book of hairstyling. Worthington, C.   **646.7**
The **complete** book of herbs, spices, and condiments. See Rinzler, C. A. The new complete book of herbs, spices, and condiments   **641.3**
The **complete** book of home design. Gilliatt, M.   **747**
The **complete** book of home inspection. Becker, N.   **643**

The **complete** book of jewelry making. Codina, C.
    739.27

The **Complete** book of pasta and noodles   **641.8**

The **complete** book of pottery making. Kenny, J. B.
    738.1

The **complete** book of pregnancy and childbirth. Kitzinger, S.   **618.2**

The **complete** book of scriptwriting. Straczynski, J. M.
    808.2

The **Complete** book of sewing   **646.4**

The **complete** book of t'ai chi. McFarlane, S.
    613.7

The **complete** book of the Winter Olympics. Wallechinsky, D.   **796.98**

Complete book of walking, Prevention's. See Spilner, M. Prevention's complete book of walking
    613.7

Complete book of women's running, Runner's world. Scott, D.   **796.42**

The **Complete** book of woodworking   **684**

The **complete** cancer survival guide. Teeley, P.
    616.99

Complete cat care manual. See Edney, A. T. B. ASPCA complete cat care manual   **636.8**

The **complete** Christie. Bunson, M.   **823.009**

The **complete** collected poems of Maya Angelou. Angelou, M.   **811**

The **complete** comedies of Terence. See Terence. Terence, the comedies   **872**

The **complete** Dead Sea scrolls in English. Dead Sea scrolls   **296.1**

The **Complete** directory of large print books and serials
    015.73

The **complete** directory to prime time network and cable TV shows, 1946-present. Brooks, T.   **791.45**

Complete do-it-yourself manual. See New complete do-it-yourself manual   **643**

The **complete** dog book. American Kennel Club
    636.7

Complete dog training manual. See Fogle, B. New complete dog training manual   **636.7**

Complete drug reference. See Consumer drug reference
    615

The **Complete** encyclopedia of trees and shrubs
    635.9

The **complete** film dictionary. Konigsberg, I.
    791.4303

The **complete** gods and goddesses of ancient Egypt. Wilkinson, R. H.   **299**

The **complete** golfer's handbook. Player, G.
    796.352

The **complete** guide to Alzheimer's-proofing your home. Warner, M. L.   **362.1**

The **Complete** guide to America's national parks
    917.3

Complete guide to building log homes. Burch, M.
    694

Complete guide to cats, ASPCA. Richards, J. R.
    636.8

The **complete** guide to factory-made houses. See Watkins, A. M. Manufactured houses   **693**

Complete guide to sewing. See New complete guide to sewing   **646.2**

Complete guide to the Bible, Reader's digest   **220.7**

Complete guide to water gardening, The American Horticultural Society. Robinson, P.   **635.9**

The **complete** guide to writing fiction. Conrad, B.
    808.3

The **complete** guitarist. Chapman, R.   **787.87**

The **complete** history of costume and fashion. Cosgrave, B.   **391**

The **complete** home learning sourcebook. Rupp, R.
    371.04

The **complete** home veterinary guide. Pinney, C. C.
    636.089

The **complete** how to figure it. Huff, D.   **640**

The **complete** idiot's guide to knitting and crocheting. Breiter, B.   **746.43**

The **complete** illustrated guide to shaping wood. Bird, L.
    684

The **complete** Italian vegetarian cookbook. Bishop, J.
    641.5

The **complete** lyrics of Cole Porter. Porter, C.
    782.42

The **complete** major prose plays. Ibsen, H.   **839.8**

The **complete** meat cookbook. Aidells, B.   **641.6**

The **complete** motorcycle book. Bennett, J. S.
    629.28

Complete office handbook. Jaderstrom, S.   **651.8**

The **complete** operas of Mozart. Osborne, C.   **792.5**

The **complete** operas of Puccini. Osborne, C.   **792.5**

The **complete** operas of Richard Wagner. Osborne, C.
    792.5

The **complete** pig. Rath, S.   **636.4**

The **complete** plays. Behan, B.   **822**

The **complete** plays. Synge, J. M.   **822**

The **complete** plays of Aristophanes. Aristophanes
    882

The **complete** plays of Sophocles. Sophocles   **882**

The **complete** poems. Jarrell, R.   **811**

The **complete** poems. Jonson, B.   **821**

The **complete** poems. Marvell, A.   **821**

Complete poems. Poe, E. A.   **811**

The **complete** poems. Sexton, A.   **811**

The **complete** poems, 1927-1979. Bishop, E.   **811**

The **complete** poems and plays, 1909-1950. Eliot, T. S.
    818

The **complete** poems of Anna Akhmatova. Akhmatova, A. A.   **891.7**

The **complete** poems of Carl Sandburg. Sandburg, C.
    811

The **complete** poems of Cavafy. Cavafy, C. P.   **889**

The **complete** poems of Christina Rossetti. Rossetti, C. G.   **821**

The **complete** poems of Emily Dickinson. Dickinson, E.
    811

The **complete** poems of Emily Jane Brontë. Brontë, E.
    821

The **complete** poems of John Keats. Keats, J.   **821**

The **complete** poems of Marianne Moore. Moore, M.
    811

The **complete** poems of Percy Bysshe Shelley. Shelley, P. B.   **821**

Complete poetry and collected prose. Whitman, W.
    818

The **complete** poetry and prose of Geoffrey Chaucer. Chaucer, G.   **821**

The **complete** poetry and prose of William Blake. Blake, W.   **828**

The **complete** poetry and selected prose of John Donne. Donne, J.   **828**

The **complete** serger handbook. James, C.   **646.2**

The **complete** single mother. Engber, A.   **306.8**

The **complete** snowboarder. Bennett, J.   **796.9**

The **complete** tales and poems of Edgar Allan Poe. See Poe, E. A. The collected tales and poems of Edgar Allan Poe   **818**

Complete verse. Kipling, R.   **821**

Complete works. Pinter, H.   **822**

Complete works. Plato   **184**

The **complete** works of Tacitus. Tacitus, C.   **878**

The **complete** works of William Shakespeare. Shakespeare, W.   **822.3**

Complete works, selected letters. Rimbaud, A.   **848**

The **complete** writings of William Blake. Blake, W.
    821

Composers
    See also Women composers
    Classical music: the rough guide   **781.6**

Composers—*Continued*
Hall, C. J. Chronology of Western classical music
780.9
Schonberg, H. C. The lives of the great composers
920
Slonimsky, N. The great composers and their works
780.9
Steinberg, M. The symphony **784.2**
Walker-Hill, H. From spirituals to symphonies
920

See/See also pages in the following book(s):
Grout, D. J. A history of Western music **780.9**
Siepmann, J. The piano **786.2**
United States
Green, S. The world of musical comedy **920**
United States—Dictionaries
Ewen, D. American songwriters **920.003**
Composition (Rhetoric) *See* Rhetoric
Composition as explanation. Stein, G.
In Stein, G. Selected writings p511-23 **818**
Comprehensive cancer care. Gordon, J. S. **616.99**
Comprehensive postal exam. Barkus, P. **383**
Compulsion (Psychology) *See* Compulsive behavior
Compulsive behavior
See also Workaholism
Henderson, E. C. Understanding addiction **362.29**
Compulsive working *See* Workaholism
Compulsory labor *See* Slavery
Computer and Internet dictionary for ages 9 to 99. Berry, C. W. **004**
Computer animation
Weishar, P. Blue Sky **778.5**
Computer-based information systems *See* Information systems
Computer crimes
See also Computer security
Computer industry
Gerstner, L. V., Jr. Who says elephants can't dance?
338.7
Zygmont, J. Microchip: an idea, its genesis, and the revolution it created **338.7**
Computer jargon *See* Computer science—Dictionaries
Computer keyboarding *See* Keyboarding (Electronics)
Computer networks
See also Internet
Bourne, J. DSL: a Wiley tech brief **621.382**
Lowe, D. Networking for dummies **004.6**
Sauers, M. Using the Internet as a reference tool
025.04
Law and legislation
Gelman, R. B. Protecting yourself online **342**
Computer programming
See also Computer software
Farrell, M. Learning computer programming **005**
Computer-readable databases. See Gale directory of databases **025.04**
Computer science
Computer sciences **004**
Dictionaries
The Facts on File dictionary of computer science
004
Encyclopedias
Encyclopedia of computer science **004**
Henderson, H. Encyclopedia of computer science and technology **004**
World of computer science **004**
Computer sciences **004**
Computer security
Gelman, R. B. Protecting yourself online **342**
Jennings, C. The hundredth window **005.8**
Speed, T. The personal Internet security guidebook
005.8

See/See also pages in the following book(s):
Nuwere, E. Hacker cracker: a journey from the mean streets of Brooklyn to the frontiers of cyberspace
92
Computer software
From 0 to 1: an authoritative history of modern computing **004**
Computer software industry
See/See also pages in the following book(s):
Lewis, M. The new new thing **92**
Computers
See also Data processing; Macintosh (Computer); Microcomputers
Barclay, D. A. Managing public-access computers
025
From 0 to 1: an authoritative history of modern computing **004**
Johnson, G. A shortcut through time **004**
Kurzweil, R. The age of spiritual machines **006.3**
Access control
See Computer security
Dictionaries
See Computer science—Dictionaries
Berry, C. W. Computer and Internet dictionary for ages 9 to 99 **004**
Downing, D. Dictionary of computer and Internet terms **004**
Encyclopedias
Henderson, H. Encyclopedia of computer science and technology **004**
History
Ifrah, G. The universal history of computing **004**
Jargon
See Computer science—Dictionaries
Comrades. Ambrose, S. E. **302.3**
Comrie, Bernard, 1947-
(ed) The World's major languages. See The World's major languages **400**
Comte-Sponville, André
A small treatise on the great virtues **179**
Conant, Jennet
Tuxedo Park [biography of Alfred Lee Loomis]
92
Conant, Roger, 1909-
A field guide to reptiles & amphibians **597.9**
Conarroe, Joel, 1934-
(ed) Eight American poets. See Eight American poets
811.008
Conason, Joe
The hunting of the President **973.929**
Conaway, James, 1941-
America's library **027.5**
Conceived in liberty. Perry, M. **973.7**
Concentration camps
See also Auschwitz (Poland: Concentration camp); Buchenwald (Germany: Concentration camp); Dachau (Germany: Concentration camp); Holocaust, 1933-1945; Japanese Americans—Evacuation and relocation, 1942-1945
Applebaum, A. Gulag **365**
Gilbert, M. Holocaust journey **940.53**
Lifton, R. J. The Nazi doctors **940.53**
Todorov, T. Facing the extreme **940.53**
Conception
Prevention
See Birth control
Concert music, 1630-1750
In New Oxford history of music v6 **780.9**
The **concise** AACR2, 1998 revision. Gorman, M.
025.3
The **Concise** American Heritage Spanish dictionary
463
The **concise** book of lying. Sullivan, E. E. **177**
Concise dictionary of American biography **920.003**

The **concise** encyclopedia of fibromyalgia and myofascial pain. Patarca, R.   **616.7**

Concise encyclopedia of Islam   **297**

Concise encyclopedia of Latin American literature   **860.3**

A **concise** history of costume. See Laver, J. Costume and fashion   **391**

A **concise** history of Germany. Fulbrook, M.   **943**

A **concise** history of Greece. Clogg, R.   **949.5**

A **concise** history of the American Republic. Morison, S. E.   **973**

A **concise** history of the Russian Revolution. Pipes, R.   **947.08**

The **concise** Oxford dictionary of archaeology. Darvill, T.   **930.1**

The **Concise** Oxford dictionary of art and artists   **703**

The **Concise** Oxford dictionary of English etymology   **422.03**

The **concise** Oxford dictionary of literary terms. Baldick, C.   **803**

The **Concise** Oxford dictionary of proverbs   **398.9**

The **Concise** Oxford dictionary of quotations   **808.88**

The **Concise** Oxford Russian dictionary   **491.7**

The **concise** Oxford thesaurus. See The Oxford American thesaurus of current English   **423**

Concise Routledge encyclopedia of philosophy   **103**

Conclusive evidence. See Nabokov, V. V. Speak, memory   **92**

Concord (Mass.), Battle of, 1775
Fischer, D. H. Paul Revere's ride   **973.3**

Concordances See Bible—Concordances

The **condemnation** of Little B. Brown, E.   **364.1**

Condensed chemical dictionary, Hawley's   **540.3**

Condiments
Rinzler, C. A. The new complete book of herbs, spices, and condiments   **641.3**

Conduct of life
Ban Breathnach, S. A man's journey to simple abundance   **158**

Browne, J. The nine fantasies that will ruin your life and the eight realities that will save you   **158**

Carter, S. L. Integrity   **170**

Coles, R. Lives of moral leadership   **170**

Covey, S. R. First things first   **158**

Dowrick, S. Forgiveness and other acts of love   **248.4**

Gaines, P. Moments of grace   **170**

Kübler-Ross, E. Life lessons   **170**

Lunden, J. Wake-up calls   **155.2**

Schlessinger, L. C. How could you do that?!   **170**

Woodruff, P. Reverence   **170**

Cone, James H.
A black theology of liberation   **261.8**

Confederacy of silence. Rubin, R.   **976.2**

Confederate States of America
Davis, W. C. An honorable defeat   **973.7**

Freeman, D. S. Lee's lieutenants   **973.7**

Gallagher, G. W. The Confederate War   **973.7**
See/See also pages in the following book(s):
Cooper, W. J. Jefferson Davis, American   **92**

Biography
Warner, E. J. Generals in gray   **920**

Confederate States of America. Army
See/See also pages in the following book(s):
Leonard, E. D. All the daring of the soldier   **973.7**

Military life
Wiley, B. I. The life of Johnny Reb   **973.7**

Confederate States of America. Army. Virginia Cavalry Battalion, 43rd
Wert, J. D. Mosby's Rangers   **973.7**

The **Confederate** War. Gallagher, G. W.   **973.7**

Confederates in the attic. Horwitz, T.   **973.7**

Confessions. Rousseau, J.-J.   **92**

Confessions of a street addict. Cramer, J. J.   **332.6**

The **confessions** of an English opium-eater. De Quincey, T.   **824**

The **confessions** of St. Augustine. Augustine, Saint, Bishop of Hippo   **242**

Conflict, Ethnic *See* Ethnic relations

Conflict of cultures *See* Culture conflict

Conflict of generations
Lancaster, L. C. When generations collide   **658.3**

Confronting fear   **303.6**

Confucius
The analects of Confucius   **181**
The wisdom of Confucius   **181**
See/See also pages in the following book(s):
Jaspers, K. The great philosophers   **109**

Congenital diseases *See* Medical genetics

Conglomerate corporations
Burrough, B. Barbarians at the gate: the fall of RJR Nabisco   **338.8**

Congo (Brazzaville) *See* Congo (Republic)

Congo (Republic)
Description
O'Hanlon, R. No mercy: a journey to the heart of the Congo   **967**

History
Hochschild, A. King Leopold's ghost   **967.5**

Congo journey. See O'Hanlon, R. No mercy: a journey to the heart of the Congo   **967**

Congregationalism
See/See also pages in the following book(s):
Marsden, G. M. Jonathan Edwards   **92**

Congress (U.S.) *See* United States. Congress

Congress A to Z   **328.73**

Congress and the Nation   **328.73**

Congressional Quarterly, Inc.
Congress and the Nation. See Congress and the Nation   **328.73**

CQ's politics in America. See CQ's politics in America   **328.73**

The Middle East. See The Middle East [CQ Press]   **956**

Congressional Quarterly almanac. See CQ almanac plus   **328.73**

Congressional Quarterly guide to Congress. See Guide to Congress   **328.73**

Congressional Quarterly's desk reference on the Presidency. Wetterau, B.   **973**

Congressional Quarterly's guide to the presidency. See Guide to the presidency   **352.23**

Congreve, William, 1670-1729
The way of the world
In The Oxford anthology of English literature v1   **820.8**

In Restoration plays   **822.008**

Conklin, Barbara Gardner
Encyclopedia of forensic science   **363.2**

Conley, Cort, 1944-
(ed) Modern American memoirs. See Modern American memoirs   **810.8**

Connaroe, Joel
(ed) Six American poets. See Six American poets   **811.008**

Connaughton, Dennis
American Medical Association complete guide to children's health. See American Medical Association complete guide to children's health   **618.92**

Connect. Hallowell, E. M.   **158**

Connecting the dots. Kumin, M.   **811**

Connell, Evan S., 1924-
The Aztec treasure house   **814**
Son of the Morning Star   **973.8**

Connelly, Owen
On war and leadership   **355.3**

Conner, Dennis
Learn to sail   797.1
Conniff, Richard
The natural history of the rich   305.5
Connolly, Peter, 1935-
The ancient city   937
Connolly, S. J. (Sean J.)
(ed) The Oxford companion to Irish history. See The
Oxford companion to Irish history   941.5
Connolly, Sean J. See Connolly, S. J. (Sean J.)
Connolly, William G.
(jt. auth) Siegal, A. The New York times manual of
style and usage   808
Connor, Billie M., 1934-
(ed) Ottemiller's index to plays in collections. See
Ottemiller's index to plays in collections   808.82
Connor, Mary E.
The Koreas   951.9
Connors, Joseph
(jt. auth) Wittkower, R. Art and architecture in Italy,
1600-1750   **709.45**
The **conquerors:** Roosevelt, Truman, and the destruction
of Hitler's Germany, 1941-1945. Beschloss, M. R.
    940.53
Conquest, Robert
Reflections on a ravaged century   **909.82**
Stalin   92
The **conquest** of the Incas. Hemming, J.   985
Conrad, Barnaby, 1922-
The complete guide to writing fiction   808.3
Conrad, Clyde Lee
See/See also pages in the following book(s):
Herrington, S. A. Traitors among us p63-173, 375-98
    327.12
Conrad, Joseph, 1857-1924
Nostromo; criticism
In Said, E. W. Reflections on exile and other essays
p276-81   814
The portable Conrad   828
About
The Oxford reader's companion to Conrad
    823.009
Conradi, Peter, 1945-
Iris Murdoch   92
Conroy, John, 1951-
Unspeakable acts, ordinary people   323.4
Conroy, Pat
My losing season   92
Conscience & courage. Fogelman, E.   940.53
Conscious and verbal. Murray, L. A.   821
Consciousness
Baars, B. J. In the theater of consciousness   153
Carter, R. Exploring consciousness   153
Damasio, A. R. The feeling of what happens   153
Glynn, I. An anatomy of thought   612.8
See/See also pages in the following book(s):
May, R. The courage to create   153.3
Consciousness expanding drugs See Hallucinogens
Conservation movement See Environmental movement
Conservation of energy See Energy conservation
Conservation of natural resources
See also Nature conservation; Soil conservation;
Wildlife conservation
See/See also pages in the following book(s):
Crawford, M. Habitats and ecosystems   578.68
Conservatism
Martin, W. C. With God on our side   261.8
Podhoretz, N. My love affair with America   320.5
Utter, G. H. The religious right   277.3
Will, G. F. The woven figure   **973.929**
See/See also pages in the following book(s):
Emerson, R. W. The portable Emerson p92-110
    818
Foner, E. The story of American freedom p307-32
    323.44

Considine, Glenn D.
(ed) Van Nostrand's scientific encyclopedia. See Van
Nostrand's scientific encyclopedia   503
Consilience. Wilson, E. O.   121
Conspiracies
Ronson, J. Them: adventures with extremists
    322.4
The **conspiracy** of ignorance. Gross, M. L.   371
Constance, Empress, consort of Henry VI, Holy Roman Emperor, 1154-1198
About
Simeti, M. T. Travels with a medieval queen   92
Constantine's sword. Carroll, J.   261.2
Constellations
See also Astrology
Bakich, M. E. The Cambridge guide to the constellations   523.8
Constitution annotated. See United States. Constitution.
The Constitution of the United States of America
    342
The **Constitution** of the United States of America. United States. Constitution   342
Constitutional history
United States
Berkin, C. A brilliant solution   342
The Debate on the Constitution   342
Garbus, M. Courting disaster   347
Maddex, R. L. The U.S. Constitution A to Z   342
Simon, J. F. What kind of nation   342
Vile, J. R. Encyclopedia of constitutional amendments,
proposed amendments, and amending issues, 1789-
2002   342
See/See also pages in the following book(s):
Boorstin, D. J. The Americans: The national experience p406-16   973
Constitutional law
United States
Encyclopedia of the American Constitution   342
Finkelman, P. Landmark decisions of the United States
Supreme Court   347
Lively, D. E. Landmark Supreme Court cases
    342
Maddex, R. L. The U.S. Constitution A to Z   342
The Oxford guide to United States Supreme Court decisions   342
Rabban, D. M. Free speech in its forgotten years
    342
Renstrom, P. G. Constitutional rights sourcebook
    342
United States. Constitution. The Constitution of the
United States of America   342
Vile, J. R. Encyclopedia of constitutional amendments,
proposed amendments, and amending issues, 1789-
2002   342
Constitutional rights See Civil rights
Constitutional rights sourcebook. Renstrom, P. G.
    342
Construction See Building
Construction, House See House construction
Consuls See Diplomats
Consumer credit
Leonard, R. Credit repair   332.7
Consumer drug reference   615
Consumer education
Begoun, P. Don't go to the cosmetics counter without
me   **646.7**
Consumer reports complete guide to health services for
seniors   **362.6**
Gonzalez, S. Before you hire a contractor   690
The New York Times guide to alternative health
    615.5
Reconstructive and cosmetic surgery sourcebook
    617.9
Sleep disorders sourcebook . . .   **616.8**
West, S. The hysterectomy hoax   **618.1**

Consumer goods *See* Commercial products
Consumer health information source book   **016.613**
Consumer protection
  Bradsher, K. High and mighty   **629.2**
  Consumer sourcebook   **381**
Consumer Reports Books (Firm)
  Consumer drug reference. See Consumer drug reference   **615**
  How to clean practically anything. See How to clean practically anything   **648**
Consumer reports complete guide to health services for seniors   **362.6**
Consumer sourcebook   **381**
Consumers
  Cohen, L. A consumer's republic   **339.4**
  Underhill, P. Why we buy   **658.8**
A **consumer's** dictionary of cosmetic ingredients. Winter, R.   **668**
A **consumer's** dictionary of food additives. Winter, R.   **664**
The **consumer's** guide to herbal medicine. Karch, S. B.   **615**
Consumers' guide to hospitals   **362.1**
A **consumer's** republic. Cohen, L.   **339.4**
Consumption (Economics)
  Cohen, L. A consumer's republic   **339.4**
Contagious diseases *See* Communicable diseases
Container gardening
  See also House plants
  Hillier, M. Container gardening through the year   **635.9**
Container gardening through the year. Hillier, M.   **635.9**
Contemporary American religion   **200.9**
Contemporary artists   **920.003**
Contemporary authors   **920.003**
Contemporary black biography   **920.003**
Contemporary dramatists   **920.003**
Contemporary fashion   **391**
Contemporary foreign language writers. See Contemporary world writers   **920.003**
Contemporary Jewish-American novelists   **813.009**
Contemporary literary criticism   **809**
Contemporary poets   **920.003**
Contemporary Southern writers   **920.003**
Contemporary women artists   **920.003**
Contemporary women poets   **920.003**
Contemporary world writers   **920.003**
The **contested** plains. West, E.   **978**
Contested territory. Wickett, M. R.   **976.6**
Continental drift
  See/See also pages in the following book(s):
  Tudge, C. The time before history p41-55   **599.93**
The **Continuum** encyclopedia of children's literature   **028.5**
The **Continuum** political encyclopedia of the Middle East   **956**
Contra-Iran Affair, 1985-1990 *See* Iran-Contra Affair, 1985-1990
Contraception *See* Birth control
Contract bridge complete. See Goren, C. H. Goren's new bridge complete   **795.4**
Controversies in food and nutrition. Goldstein, M. C.   **641.3**
Convenience cookery *See* Quick and easy cooking
Convenience foods
  Schlosser, E. Fast food nation   **394.1**
A **convenient** spy. Stober, D.   **327.12**
Conversation
  King, L. How to talk to anyone, anytime, anywhere   **302.3**
  Locke, J. L. The de-voicing of society   **302.3**
  Martin, J. Miss Manners' basic training: the right thing to say   **395**
  Tannen, D. You just don't understand   **302.2**

Conversations on the dark secrets of physics. Teller, E.   **530**
Conversations with John Steinbeck. Steinbeck, J.   **92**
Conversations with my father. Gardner, H.
  In Gardner, H. Herb Gardner: the collected plays and the screenplay Who is Harry Kellerman and why is he saying those terrible things about me?   **812**
Conversations with Nadine Gordimer. Gordimer, N.   **92**
Conversations with Richard Wright. Wright, R.   **92**
Conversations with Saul Bellow. Bellow, S.   **92**
Conversion
  Gaines, P. Moments of grace   **170**
  James, W. The varieties of religious experience   **210**
Convict labor
  Applebaum, A. Gulag   **365**
Convicts *See* Prisoners
Conway, Jill K., 1934-
  True north   **92**
  When memory speaks   **808**
Conway, John Horton
  The book of numbers   **512**
Coogan, Michael David
  (ed) The Illustrated guide to world religions. See The Illustrated guide to world religions   **291**
  (ed) The Oxford companion to the Bible. See The Oxford companion to the Bible   **220.3**
  (ed) The Oxford guide to ideas & issues of the Bible. See The Oxford guide to ideas & issues of the Bible   **220.3**
  (ed) The Oxford history of the biblical world. See The Oxford history of the biblical world   **220.9**
Coogan, Tim Pat, 1935-
  The troubles   **941.6**
Cook, Allan R.
  (ed) Arthritis sourcebook . . . See Arthritis sourcebook . . .   **616.7**
  (ed) Burns sourcebook . . . See Burns sourcebook . . .   **617.1**
  (ed) Men's health concerns sourcebook. See Men's health concerns sourcebook   **613**
  (ed) Skin disorders sourcebook. See Skin disorders sourcebook   **616.5**
Cook, Blanche Wiesen
  Eleanor Roosevelt   **92**
Cook, David
  Robot building for beginners   **629.8**
Cook, David A.
  A history of narrative film   **791.43**
Cook, Edward M.
  (tr) Dead Sea scrolls. The Dead Sea scrolls   **296.1**
Cook, James, 1728-1779
  About
  Horwitz, T. Blue latitudes   **910.4**
  Hough, R. A. Captain James Cook   **92**
Cook, Lauren M.
  (jt. auth) Blanton, D. They fought like demons   **973.7**
Cook, Thomas H.
  (ed) Best American crime writing. See Best American crime writing   **364.1**
Cook, Will Marion, 1869-1944
  See/See also pages in the following book(s):
  Russell, D. Black genius and the American experience   **920**
Cook-Deegan, Robert M.
  The gene wars   **572.8**
Cooke, Charles Maynard
  About
  Hill, A. J. Under pressure   **910.4**
Cooke, Courtney
  The best baby shower book   **793.2**

Cooke, Jacob Ernest, 1924-
(ed) The Federalist. See The Federalist   342
Cooke, John P.
The cardiovascular cure   616.1
Cookery, Oriental *See* Oriental cooking
Cookies
  Heatter, M. Maida Heatter's brand-new book of great cookies   641.8
  Pillsbury best cookies cookbook   641.8
Cooking
  See also Baking; Southern cooking; Vegetarian cooking
  Adams, J. In the hands of a chef   641.5
  Adams, M. New recipes from quilt country   641.5
  Allen, S. L. In the devil's garden   641
  American Heart Association cookbook   641.5
  American Heart Association low-fat, low-cholesterol cookbook   641.5
  The American Heart Association low-salt cookbook   641.5
  American Heart Association meals in minutes   641.5
  American Heart Association quick-and-easy cookbook   641.5
  Anderson, P. How to cook without a book   641.5
  Ayto, J. An A-Z of food and drink   641.03
  Beard, J. The armchair James Beard   641.5
  Beard, J. James Beard's American cookery   641.5
  The Best American recipes   641.5
  Better Homes and Gardens new cook book   641.5
  Betty Crocker's best loved recipes   641.5
  Betty Crocker's cooking basics   641.5
  Bittman, M. How to cook everything   641.5
  Bourdain, A. A cook's tour   641
  Brody, L. The kitchen survival guide   641.5
  Burros, M. F. The new elegant but easy cookbook   641.5
  Child, J. Julia's kitchen wisdom   641.5
  Child, J. The way to cook   641.5
  Claiborne, C. The New York Times cook book   641.5
  David, E. Is there a nutmeg in the house?   641.5
  Dojny, B. The New England cookbook   641.5
  Farmer, F. M. The Fannie Farmer cookbook   641.5
  Fussell, B. H. Home bistro   641.5
  Garten, I. Barefoot Contessa family style   641.5
  Gibbons, E. Stalking the wild asparagus   581.6
  Giedt, F. T. The Joslin Diabetes great chefs cook healthy cookbook   641.5
  The Good Housekeeping step-by-step cookbook   641.5
  Griffith, L. Garlic, garlic, garlic   641.6
  Haber, B. From hardtack to home fries   394.1
  Jamison, C. A. American home cooking   641.5
  Jamison, C. A. A real American breakfast   641.5
  Kafka, B. Party food   641.5
  Kafka, B. Roasting   641.7
  Kamman, M. The new making of a cook   641.5
  Lagasse, E. Every day's a party   642
  Lanza, L. Totally dairy-free cooking   641.5
  Larousse gastronomique   641.03
  Madison, D. Local flavors   641.5
  The Martha Stewart Living cookbook   641.5
  Mercuri, B. Food festival, U.S.A.   641.5
  Parsons, R. How to read a french fry   641.5
  Pépin, J. Jacques Pépin celebrates   641.5
  Pépin, J. Jacques Pépin's simple and healthy cooking   641.5
  Rombauer, I. von S. Joy of cooking   641.5
  Smith, C. Cooking with the diabetic chef   641.5
  Stewart, M. Great parties   642
  Stewart, M. The Martha Stewart cookbook   641.5
  Stewart, M. Martha Stewart's healthy quick cook   641.5

  Stewart, M. Martha Stewart's menus for entertaining   642
  Stewart, M. Special occasions   641.5
  Tsai, M. Blue Ginger   641.5
  Weil, A. The healthy kitchen   641.5
  Zanger, M. H. The American history cookbook   641.5
  See/See also pages in the following book(s):
  The New living heart diet   616.1
  Pépin, J. The apprentice: my life in the kitchen   92
Chocolate
  Desaulniers, M. Celebrate with chocolate   641.6
  Desaulniers, M. Death by chocolate cakes   641.8
Dictionaries
  International dictionary of food & cooking   641.03
Fish
  Cameron, A. The L.L. Bean game and fish cookbook   641.6
  Kurlansky, M. Cod   639.2
Game
  Cameron, A. The L.L. Bean game and fish cookbook   641.6
Meat
  Aidells, B. The complete meat cookbook   641.6
  Schlesinger, C. How to cook meat   641.6
Mushrooms
  Czarnecki, J. A cook's book of mushrooms   641.6
Natural foods
  See also Natural foods
Pasta products
  The Complete book of pasta and noodles   641.8
  Puck, W. Wolfgang Puck's pizza, pasta and more!   641.8
Potatoes
  Marshall, L. A passion for potatoes   641.6
Poultry
  Fowler, D. L. Fried chicken   641.6
Seafood
  Brody, J. E. Jane Brody's good seafood book   641.6
  Peterson, J. Fish & shellfish   641.6
Tofu
  Shurtleff, W. The book of tofu   641.6
Vegetables
  Morash, M. The victory garden cookbook   641.6
  Peterson, J. Vegetables   641.6
  Ross, R. L. S. Beyond bok choy   641.6
  Schneider, E. Vegetables from amaranth to zucchini   641.6
  Waters, A. Chez Panisse vegetables   641.6
  Willinger, F. H. Red, white, and greens   641.6
Louisiana
  Prudhomme, P. Chef Paul Prudhomme's Louisiana kitchen   641.5
  Prudhomme, P. Chef Paul Prudhomme's Louisiana tastes   641.5
Cooking, Barbecue *See* Barbecue cooking
Cooking for the sick
  See also Diet therapy
Cooking the Roman way. Downie, D.   641.5
Cooking utensils *See* Kitchen utensils
Cooking with the diabetic chef. Smith, C.   641.5
Cookman, Scott, 1952-
  Ice blink   998
A **cook's** book of mushrooms. Czarnecki, J.   641.6
Cooks' catalogue. See The New cooks' catalogue   683
A **cook's** tour. Bourdain, A.   641
Cool, calm & collected. Kizer, C.   811
Coombe, Jack D.
  Gunsmoke over the Atlantic   973.7
Cooper, Douglas, 1911-1984
About
  Richardson, J. The sorcerer's apprentice   92

Cooper, Howard
(jt. auth) Diamant, A. Living a Jewish life   **296.7**
Cooper, John Julius *See* Norwich, John Julius, 1929-
Cooper, John Milton
The warrior and the priest: Woodrow Wilson and Theodore Roosevelt   **92**
Cooper, Lorraine, 1905-1985
See/See also pages in the following book(s):
Heymann, C. D. The Georgetown ladies' social club   **305.4**
Cooper, Robert Leon, 1931-
Around the world with Mark Twain   **818**
Cooper, William J., 1940-
Jefferson Davis, American   **92**
Cope, E. D. (Edward Drinker), 1840-1897
About
Wallace, D. R. The bonehunters' revenge   **560**
Cope, Edward Drinker *See* Cope, E. D. (Edward Drinker), 1840-1897
Copeland, Edward
(ed) The Cambridge companion to Jane Austen. See The Cambridge companion to Jane Austen   **823.009**
Copeland, Lewis
(ed) The World's great speeches. See The World's great speeches   **808.85**
Copeland, Mary Ellen
(jt. auth) Starlanyl, D. Fibromyalgia & chronic myofascial pain syndrome   **616.7**
Copeland, Michelle
Change your looks, change your life   **617.9**
Copeland, Peter
(jt. auth) Hamer, D. H. Living with our genes   **155.2**
Copi, Irving M.
Introduction to logic   **160**
Coping with psoriasis. Cram, D. L.   **616.5**
Copland, Aaron, 1900-1990
Music and imagination   **781.1**
About
Pollack, H. Aaron Copland   **92**
Coppel, Alfred, 1921-
(jt. auth) Knox, D. The Korean War   **951.9**
Coppinger, Lorna
(jt. auth) Coppinger, R. Dogs   **636.7**
Coppinger, Raymond
Dogs   **636.7**
Copyright
Crews, K. D. Copyright essentials for librarians and educators   **346.04**
Elias, S. Patent, copyright & trademark   **346.04**
Fishman, S. The copyright handbook   **346.04**
Hoffmann, G. M. Copyright in cyberspace   **346.04**
Lessig, L. The future of ideas   **346.04**
Talab, R. S. Commonsense copyright   **346.04**
Music
Krasilovsky, M. W. This business of music   **780**
Copyright essentials for librarians and educators. Crews, K. D.   **346.04**
The **copyright** handbook. Fishman, S.   **346.04**
Copyright in cyberspace. Hoffmann, G. M.   **346.04**
Corbeil, Jean-Claude
The Firefly visual dictionary   **423**
Corcoran, James
(jt. auth) Dees, M. S., Jr. Gathering storm   **322.4**
Cordell, Linda S.
(ed) Chilies to chocolate. See Chilies to chocolate   **641.3**
Cordingly, David, 1938-
Under the black flag   **910.4**
Women sailors and sailors' women   **910.4**
Cordry, Harold V., 1943-
The multicultural dictionary of proverbs   **398.9**
Coren, Stanley
The left-hander syndrome   **152.3**

Why we love the dogs we do   **636.7**
Coretta Scott King Award
The Coretta Scott King Awards book, 1970-1999   **028.5**
The **Coretta** Scott King Awards book, 1970-1999   **028.5**
Corey, Melinda
(jt. auth) Ochoa, G. The Wilson chronology of science and technology   **502**
(jt. auth) Ochoa, G. The Wilson chronology of the arts   **700**
The **cormorant-fisher**. Enami, S.
In Waley, A. The Nō plays of Japan   **895.6**
Corn
See/See also pages in the following book(s):
Hubbell, S. Shrinking the cat   **660.6**
The **Cornell** book of cats   **636.8**
Cornell Feline Health Center
The Cornell book of cats. See The Cornell book of cats   **636.8**
Cornell University. Bailey Hortorium
Hortus third. See Hortus third   **635**
Cornhuskers. Sandburg, C.
In Sandburg, C. Complete poems of Carl Sandburg p79-147   **811**
Cornucopia. Peacock, M.   **811**
Cornwell, John, 1940-
Breaking faith   **282**
Hitler's pope: the secret history of Pius XII   **92**
Cornwell, Neil
(ed) Reference guide to Russian literature. See Reference guide to Russian literature   **891.7**
Cornwell, Patricia Daniels
Portrait of a killer   **364.1**
Coronado, Francisco Vázquez de *See* Vázquez de Coronado, Francisco, 1510-1549
Corporate mergers and acquisitions
See also Conglomerate corporations
Corporations
Drucker, P. F. Managing the non-profit organization   **658**
Directories
Krantz, L. Job finder's guide   **331.7**
Standard and Poor's register of corporations, directors, and executives   **338.7**
Corporations, Conglomerate *See* Conglomerate corporations
Corpses *See* Dead
Corréard, Marie-Hélène
(ed) The Oxford-Hachette French dictionary. See The Oxford-Hachette French dictionary   **443**
Correspondence schools and courses
The Independent study catalog   **374**
Corrigan, John
Religion in America   **200.9**
Corruption, Police *See* Police corruption
The **corruption** of American politics. Drew, E.   **364.1**
The **Corsini** encyclopedia of psychology and behavioral science   **150.3**
Corso, Gregory, 1930-2001
Mindfield   **811**
See/See also pages in the following book(s):
Miles, B. The Beat Hotel   **810.9**
Corson, Richard
Stage makeup   **792**
Cortés, Hernán, 1485-1547
About
Prescott, W. H. History of the conquest of Mexico   **972**
See/See also pages in the following book(s):
Williams, W. C. In the American grain p27-38   **814**
Corwin, Phillip
Doomed in Afghanistan   **958.1**

Cosa nostra *See* Mafia
Cosby, Bill, 1937-
   Fatherhood   306.8
   Love and marriage   306.8
Cose, Ellis
   Color-blind   305.8
   The envy of the world   305.8
Cosgrave, Bronwyn
   The complete history of costume and fashion   391
Cosloy, Sharon
   (jt. auth) Steinberg, M. L. The Facts on File dictionary of biotechnology and genetic engineering   660.6
Cosman, Carol
   (ed) The Penguin book of women poets. See The Penguin book of women poets   808.81
Cosmetic surgery *See* Plastic surgery
Cosmetics
   See also Theatrical makeup
   Begoun, P. Don't go to the cosmetics counter without me   646.7
   DuPriest, L. Natural beauty   646.7
   Gross, K. J. Woman's face   646.7
   Peiss, K. L. Hope in a jar   391
   Dictionaries
   Winter, R. A consumer's dictionary of cosmetic ingredients   668
Cosmic dispatches   520
Cosmic gamma ray bursts *See* Gamma ray bursts
Cosmology
   See also Big bang theory
   Aczel, A. D. God's equation   523.1
   Adams, F. C. The five ages of the universe   523.1
   Barrow, J. D. The origin of the universe   523.1
   The Book of the cosmos   523.1
   Chown, M. The universe next door   523.1
   Cosmic dispatches   520
   Croswell, K. The universe at midnight   523.1
   Dauber, P. M. The three big bangs   523.1
   Davies, P. C. W. The last three minutes   523.1
   Deutsch, D. The fabric of reality   530
   Ferguson, K. Measuring the universe   523.1
   Ferris, T. The whole shebang   523.1
   Gleiser, M. The prophet and the astronomer   523.1
   Gribbin, J. R. The birth of time   523.1
   Guth, A. H. The inflationary universe   523.1
   Hawking, S. W. Black holes and baby universes and other essays   523.1
   Hawking, S. W. A brief history of time   523.1
   Jastrow, R. God and the astronomers   523.1
   Kolb, R. Blind watchers of the sky   523.1
   Lightman, A. P. Ancient light   523.1
   Rees, M. J. Just six numbers   523.1
   Rees, M. J. Our cosmic habitat   523.1
   Siegfried, T. Strange matters   523.1
   Smoot, G. Wrinkles in time   523.1
   Trefil, J. S. Other worlds   523.2
   Tyson, N. D. G. Universe down to Earth   523.1
   See/See also pages in the following book(s):
   Greene, B. R. The elegant universe   539.7
Cosmos. Sagan, C.   520
The **cost** of discipleship. Bonhoeffer, D.   226
Costas, Bob
   Fair ball   796.357
Costello, Elaine
   Random House Webster's American sign language dictionary   419
Costello, John, 1943-1995
   The Pacific War   940.54
Costenbader, Carol W.
   The big book of preserving the harvest   641.4
Costume
   See also Clothing and dress; Fashion; Theatrical makeup

Dictionaries
Calasibetta, C. M. The Fairchild dictionary of fashion   391
History
Boucher, F. 20,000 years of fashion   391
Cassin-Scott, J. The illustrated encyclopaedia of costume and fashion from 1066 to the present   391
Cosgrave, B. The complete history of costume and fashion   391
De Marly, D. Dress in North America v1   391
Hunnisett, J. Period costume for stage & screen   391
Laver, J. Costume and fashion   391
Nunn, J. Fashion in costume, 1200-2000   391
Peacock, J. 20th-century fashion   391
Peacock, J. The chronicle of Western fashion   391
Peacock, J. Men's fashion   391
Costume and fashion. Laver, J.   391
Côté, Lucien J.
   (ed) Parkinson's disease and quality of life. See Parkinson's disease and quality of life   616.8
Cott, Nancy F.
   (ed) No small courage. See No small courage   305.4
Cottage industry *See* Home-based business
Cottage industry, Electronic *See* Telecommuting
Cotterell, Arthur
   A dictionary of world mythology   291.103
Cotton, Charles, 1630-1687
   (jt. auth) Walton, I. The compleat angler   799.1
Cotton, Eddy Joe
   Hobo: a young man's thoughts on trains and tramping in America   92
Couch, Dick, 1943-
   The warrior elite   359.9
Coucy, Enguerrand de, 1340-1397
   About
   Tuchman, B. W. A distant mirror   944
Counseling
   See also Marriage counseling
Countdown. Heppenheimer, T. A.   629.4
Counted thread embroidery
   See also Cross-stitch
Counter-Reformation
   See also Reformation
Counties USA   352.13
Counting
   See also Numbers
Country and western music *See* Country music
Country life
   Georgia
   Foxfire [1]-11   975.8
   United States
   Encyclopedia of rural America   973.03
Country music
   Dawidoff, N. In the country of country   781.642
   Hentoff, N. Listen to the stories   781.65
   Wolff, K. Country music: the rough guide   781.642
   Dictionaries
   Carlin, R. The big book of country music   920.003
   Carlin, R. Country music: a biographical dictionary   920.003
   Encyclopedias
   The Encyclopedia of country music   781.642
   Stambler, I. Country music: the encyclopedia   781.642
The **country** under my skin. Belli, G.   92
The **country** wife. Wycherley, W.
   In Restoration plays   822.008
County and city data book   317.3
County government
   Counties USA   352.13

County government—*Continued*
Directories
Government phone book USA   320.025
County name origins of the United States. Beatty, M. A.
   917.3
Couples, Married *See* Married people
Courage
Kennedy, J. F. Profiles in courage   920
Tillich, P. The courage to be   179
   See/See also pages in the following book(s):
May, R. The courage to create   153.3
The **courage** to be. Tillich, P.   179
The **courage** to create. May, R.   153.3
The **courage** to heal. Bass, E.   362.83
The **courage** to stand alone. Wei Jingsheng   951.05
The **course** of Mexican history. Meyer, M. C.   972
Courthion, Pierre
Georges Seurat   759.4
Courtier, Jane
Indoor plants   635.9
Courting disaster. Garbus, M.   347
Courts
United States—**Directories**
BNA's directory of state and federal courts, judges, and clerks   347
Courts and courtiers
See also Queens
Courtwright, David T., 1952-
Forces of habit   362.29
Cover letter magic. Enelow, W. S.   650.14
Cover letters that knock 'em dead. Yate, M. J.
   650.14
Coverlets *See* Quilts
Covey, Stephen R.
First things first   158
Covington, Melody Mauldin
(jt. auth) Downing, D. Dictionary of computer and Internet terms   004
Covington, Michael A., 1957-
(jt. auth) Downing, D. Dictionary of computer and Internet terms   004
Coward, Noel
Blithe spirit
   In Coward, N. Three plays   822
Hay fever
   In Coward, N. Three plays   822
Private lives
   In Coward, N. Three plays   822
Three plays   822
About
Hoare, P. Noël Coward   92
The **cowboy** encyclopedia. Slatta, R. W.   978.03
Cowhands
   See/See also pages in the following book(s):
Brown, D. A. The American West p59-76   978
Encyclopedias
Slatta, R. W. The cowboy encyclopedia   978.03
Cowley, Robert
(ed) No end save victory. See No end save victory
   940.54
Cowling, Elizabeth
Matisse, Picasso. See Matisse, Picasso   759.4
Picasso: style and meaning   759.4
Cows *See* Cattle
Cox, Brian, 1928-
(ed) African writers. See African writers   896
Cox, C. B. *See* Cox, Brian, 1928-
Cox, Harvey Gallagher
Many mansions   261.2
Cox, Jeff, 1940-
Landscape with roses   635.9
Perennial all-stars   635.9
Cox, Patsi Bale
(jt. auth) Lynn, L. Still woman enough   92

Cox, Peter, 1955-
You don't need meat   613.2
Coye, Dale F.
Pronouncing Shakespeare's words   822.3
Coyote v. Acme. Frazier, I.   817
CQ *See* Congressional Quarterly, Inc.
CQ almanac plus   328.73
CQ's politics in America   328.73
CQ's state fact finder   317.3
Crab wars. Sargent, W.   333.95
Crabs
Sargent, W. Crab wars   333.95
Crabtree, Charlotte
(jt. auth) Nash, G. B. History on trial   907
Cracking the Bible code. Satinover, J.   222
Cracking the genome. Davies, K.   599.93
Cradle of life. Schopf, J. W.   576.8
Crafts (Arts) *See* Handicraft
Craig, Albert M.
(jt. auth) Reischauer, E. O. Japan, tradition & transformation   952
Craig, Gordon Alexander, 1913-
The Germans   943
Germany, 1866-1945   943.08
Craig, John R.
(jt. auth) Bushart, H. L. Soldiers of God   322.4
Craig, Phil
(jt. auth) Clayton, T. Finest hour   940.54
Craige, Betty Jean
Eugene Odum: ecosystem ecologist & environmentalist
   92
Craighead, Lance
Bears of the world   599.78
Craighead, W. Edward
(ed) The Corsini encyclopedia of psychology and behavioral science. See The Corsini encyclopedia of psychology and behavioral science   150.3
Craine, Debra
The Oxford dictionary of dance   792.8
Cram, David L. (David Lee), 1934-
Answers to frequently asked questions in Parkinson's disease   616.8
Coping with psoriasis   616.5
Cramer, Bertrand G.
(jt. auth) Brazelton, T. B. The earliest relationship
   155.4
Cramer, James J.
Confessions of a street addict   332.6
Cramer, Richard Ben
Joe DiMaggio   92
Cran, William
(jt. auth) McCrum, R. The story of English   420
Crane, George
Bones of the master   294.3
Crane, Hart, 1899-1932
About
Mariani, P. L. The broken tower: a life of Hart Crane
   92
   See/See also pages in the following book(s):
Pritchard, W. H. Lives of the modern poets p235-62
   821.009
Crane, Margaret
(jt. auth) Buchholz, B. B. Successful homebuilding and remodeling   690
Crane, Stephen, 1871-1900
Prose and poetry   818
About
Davis, L. H. Badge of courage: the life of Stephen Crane   92
   See/See also pages in the following book(s):
Kazin, A. An American procession p256-74   810.9
Cranes (Birds)
Matthiessen, P. The birds of heaven   598

Cranston, Maurice
Jean-Jacques: the early life and work of Jean-Jacques Rousseau, 1712-1754   92
The noble savage: Jean-Jacques Rousseau, 1754-1762   92
The solitary self: Jean-Jacques Rousseau in exile and adversity   92
Craske, Matthew
Art in Europe, 1700-1830   709.03
Crater, Susan Bartlett
(jt. auth) Bartlett, A. P. Sister: the life of legendary American interior decorator Mrs. Henry Parish II   92
Craven, Toni
(ed) Women in scripture. See Women in scripture   220.9
Crawford, Dorothy H.
The invisible enemy   616
Crawford, Mark
Habitats and ecosystems   578.68
Crawford, Richard, 1935-
America's musical life   780.973
Crawshaw, Alwyn
You can paint watercolors   751.42
Crazy Horse, Sioux Chief, ca. 1842-1877
About
McMurtry, L. Crazy Horse   92
CRC handbook of chemistry and physics   540
CRC standard mathematical tables and formulae   510
Creamer, Robert W.
Babe [Ruth]   92
Stengel   92
The **created** self. Weber, R. J.   155.2
Creating a healthy household. Bower, L. M.   643
Creating a role. Stanislavsky, K.   792
Creating characters. Swain, D. V.   808.3
Creating mind. Dowling, J. E.   612.8
Creating minds. Gardner, H.   153.3
Creating the not so big house. Susanka, S.   728
Creation
Study and teaching
See Creationism
Creation (Literary, artistic, etc.)
Boorstin, D. J. The creators   909
Prose, F. The lives of the muses   920
Creationism
See also Evolution
Deloria, V. Evolution, creationism, and other modern myths   291.1
Pennock, R. T. Tower of Babel   576.8
Creations of fire. Cobb, C.   540
Creative ability
Cohen, G. D. The creative age   305.24
Csikszentmihalyi, M. Creativity   153.3
Gardner, H. Creating minds   153.3
Heskett, J. Toothpicks and logos   745.2
Klein, M. The change makers   920
May, R. The courage to create   153.3
The **creative** age. Cohen, G. D.   305.24
Creative cardboard. Ragsdale, L.   745.54
Creative country construction. Inwood, R.   690
The **creative** jeweler. McSwiney, S.   739.27
Creative mythology. Campbell, J.
In Campbell, J. The masks of God v4   291.1
Creative pottery. Coakes, M.   738
Creative thinking
Csikszentmihalyi, M. Creativity   153.3
Sternberg, R. J. Successful intelligence   153.9
Creativity. Csikszentmihalyi, M.   153.3
The **creators**. Boorstin, D. J.   909
Credit
See also Consumer credit
Credit repair. Leonard, R.   332.7

Creech, Sharon
See/See also pages in the following book(s):
The Newbery & Caldecott medal books, 1986-2000 p227-38   028.5
Creeley, Robert, 1926-
The collected poems of Robert Creeley, 1945-1975   811
Life & death   811
Selected poems   811
Cremation
See/See also pages in the following book(s):
Mitford, J. The American way of death revisited   393
Crenshaw, Mary Ann, 1929-
(jt. auth) Dibra, B. Dogspeak   636.7
Crescent and star. Kinzer, S.   956.1
Crete (Greece)
See/See also pages in the following book(s):
Ceram, C. W. Gods, graves, and scholars p56-72   930.1
Crews, Kenneth D.
Copyright essentials for librarians and educators   346.04
Crick, Francis, 1916-
See/See also pages in the following book(s):
Flowers, C. Instability rules   509
Friedman, M. Medicine's 10 greatest discoveries   610.9
Horvitz, L. A. Eureka!: scientific breakthroughs that changed the world   509
Crile, George, 1907-1992
See/See also pages in the following book(s):
Leopold, E. A darker ribbon   616.99
Crime
See also Criminal law; Hate crimes; Homicide; Trials
Best American crime writing   364.1
Walsh, J. Public enemies   364.1
Encyclopedias
Encyclopedia of crime & justice   364.03
Encyclopedia of crime and punishment   364.03
United States
Geis, G. Crimes of the century   345
Crime syndicates *See* Organized crime
Crimes of the century. Geis, G.   345
Criminal investigation
See also Forensic anthropology; Forensic sciences
Conklin, B. G. Encyclopedia of forensic science   363.2
Evans, C. The casebook of forensic detection   614
Criminal justice, Administration of *See* Administration of criminal justice
Criminal law
See also Insanity defense
Mack, R. L. A layperson's guide to criminal law   345
The **criminal** mind. Ramsland, K. M.   808.3
Criminal psychology
Douglas, J. E. The cases that haunt us   364.1
Kirwin, B. The mad, the bad, and the innocent   614
Ramsland, K. M. The criminal mind   808.3
Rhodes, R. Why they kill   364.3
Criminalistics *See* Forensic sciences
Criminals
Best American crime writing   364.1
Jones, A. Women who kill   364.1
Maas, P. Manhunt   364.1
Nash, J. R. Bloodletters and badmen   920
Rhodes, R. Why they kill   364.3
Walsh, J. Public enemies   364.1
Encyclopedias
Encyclopedia of crime & justice   364.03
Newton, M. The encyclopedia of serial killers   364.03

Criminals—*Continued*
Identification
See also Fingerprints
Cole, S. A. Suspect identities   363.2
Crisis centers
Ackerman, D. A slender thread   362.28
Crisis in the Pacific. Astor, G.   940.54
Crisis intervention telephone service *See* Hotlines (Telephone counseling)
Cristofari, Rita
(jt. auth) Zoya Zoya's story   958.1
Critical survey of drama   809.2
Critical survey of long fiction   809.3
Critical survey of short fiction   809.3
Criticism
See also Art criticism
Gioia, D. Can poetry matter?   809.1
Kermode, F. An appetite for poetry   801
Said, E. W. Reflections on exile and other essays   814
Critique of pure reason. Kant, I.   193
The **critique** of the school for wives. Molière
In Molière. Tartuffe, and other plays   842
Crito. Plato
In Plato. The dialogues of Plato p44-62   888
Critser, Greg
Fat land   613.2
Crittenden, Ann
The price of motherhood   306.8
Croall, Jonathan
Gielgud   92
Croce, Benedetto, 1866-1952
See/See also pages in the following book(s):
Durant, W. J. The story of philosophy p350-57   109
Crochet your way. Tracy, G.   746.43
Crocheting
Breiter, B. The complete idiot's guide to knitting and crocheting   746.43
Tracy, G. Crochet your way   746.43
Turner, P. How to crochet   746.43
Crocker, Betty
Betty Crocker cookie book   641.8
Crockett, Davy, 1786-1836
About
Davis, W. C. Three roads to the Alamo   976.4
Crohn's disease *See* Inflammatory bowel diseases
Croke, Vicki
Tufts University. School of Veterinary Medicine. Animal ER   636.089
Cronin, Gloria L., 1947-
(ed) Bellow, S. Conversations with Saul Bellow   92
Cronin, Isaac, 1948-
(ed) Confronting fear. See Confronting fear   303.6
Cronkite, Walter
Around America   917.3
A reporter's life   92
Croom, Emily Anne
The genealogist's companion and sourcebook   929
Crops *See* Farm produce
Crosby, Bing, 1904-1977
About
Giddins, G. Bing Crosby: a pocketful of dreams: the early years, 1903-1940   92
Cross, Charles R.
Heavier than heaven: a biography of Kurt Cobain   92
Cross, Mary Ann Evans *See* Eliot, George, 1819-1880
Cross cultural conflict *See* Culture conflict
Cross-stitch
Greenoff, J. The cross stitcher's bible   746.44
The **cross** stitcher's bible. Greenoff, J.   746.44
Crossan, John Dominic
Excavating Jesus   225.9

Jesus   232.9
Who killed Jesus?   232.9
Crossing the danger water   810.8
Crossing the threshold of hope. John Paul II, Pope   282
Crossroads: the life and music of Eric Clapton. Schumacher, M.   92
Crosstown traffic: Jimi Hendrix and the post-war rock'n'roll revolution. Murray, C. S.   92
Crossword puzzles
Dictionaries
Merriam-Webster's crossword puzzle dictionary   793.73
Pulliam, T. The New York times crossword puzzle dictionary   793.73
Random House Webster's crossword puzzle dictionary   793.73
Crosswy, Tiffany
(jt. auth) Sakach, D. Bed & breakfast encyclopedia   647.9
Croswell, Ken
The alchemy of the heavens   523.1
Planet quest   523
The universe at midnight   523.1
Crothers, Rachel, 1878-1958
A man's world
In Plays by American women, 1900-1930   812.008
Crow Dog, Leonard, 1942-
Crow Dog   970.004
The **crucible.** Miller, A.   812
The **crucible** of war. Anderson, F.   973.2
Cruden, Alexander, 1701-1770
Cruden's Complete concordance to the Old and New Testaments   220.5
Cruden's Complete concordance to the Old and New Testaments. Cruden, A.   220.5
Cruelty to animals *See* Animal welfare
Cruickshank, Duncan
(jt. auth) Player, G. The complete golfer's handbook   796.352
Crump, Thomas
A brief history of science   509
Crusade. Atkinson, R.   956.7
Crusades
The Oxford illustrated history of the Crusades   909.07
Read, P. P. The Templars   271
See/See also pages in the following book(s):
Tuchman, B. W. A distant mirror p545-63   944
Cruttenden, Aidan
The Victorians
In Backgrounds to English literature v3   820.9
Cruver, Brian
Anatomy of greed   333.79
Cruz, Juana Inés de la *See* Juana Inés de la Cruz, 1651-1695
Cruz, Nilo
Anna in the tropics   812
Crying
Lutz, T. Crying   152.4
Cryogenics *See* Low temperatures
Cryptography
Budiansky, S. Battle of wits   940.54
Lee, B. Marching orders   940.54
Sebag-Montefiore, H. Enigma: the battle for the code   940.54
Singh, S. The code book   652
Smith, M. Station X   940.54
Urban, M. The man who broke Napoleon's codes   940.2
Crystal, David, 1941-
The Cambridge encyclopedia of language   400
The Cambridge encyclopedia of the English language   420

Crystal, David, 1941—_Continued_
A dictionary of language | 410
English as a global language | 420
Language and the Internet | 400
Crystallography _See_ Crystals
Crystals
Holden, A. Crystals and crystal growing | 548
Johnsen, O. Minerals of the world | 549
Crystals and crystal growing. Holden, A. | 548
Csikszentmihalyi, Mihaly
Creativity | 153.3
Cuba
Codrescu, A. Ay, Cuba! | 972.91
Harvey, D. A. Cuba | 972.91
See/See also pages in the following book(s):
Baraka, I. A. The LeRoi Jones/Amiri Baraka reader | 818
Fernández Revuelta, A. Castro's daughter | 92
Encyclopedias
Encyclopedia of Cuba | 972.91
Foreign relations—United States
Bardach, A. L. Cuba confidential | 972.91
History
Gimbel, W. Havana dreams | 972.91
Pérez, L. A. Cuba | 972.91
Suchlicki, J. Cuba | 972.91
Szulc, T. Fidel [Castro] | 92
Politics and government
Guillermoprieto, A. Looking for history | 972
Quirk, R. E. Fidel Castro | 92
Cuba confidential. Bardach, A. L. | 972.91
Cuban Americans
Bardach, A. L. Cuba confidential | 972.91
Drama
Cruz, N. Anna in the tropics | 812
Cuban Missile Crisis, 1962
Fursenko, A. V. "One hell of a gamble" | 973.922
Kennedy, R. F. Thirteen days | 973.922
The Kennedy tapes | 973.922
See/See also pages in the following book(s):
Freedman, L. Kennedy's wars | 973.922
Cuban refugees
Bardach, A. L. Cuba confidential | 972.91
Cubism
Krauss, R. E. The Picasso papers | 759.4
Staller, N. A sum of destructions | 759.4
Cuddon, J. A. (John Anthony), 1928-
A dictionary of literary terms and literary theory | 803
Cuddon, John Anthony _See_ Cuddon, J. A. (John Anthony), 1928-
Culbert, David Holbrook
(jt. auth) Cull, N. J. Propaganda and mass persuasion | 303.3
Culinary Institute of America
Kolpan, S. Exploring wine | 641.2
Cull, Nicholas John
Propaganda and mass persuasion | 303.3
Cullen-DuPont, Kathryn
Encyclopedia of women's history in America | 305.4
Cullinan, Bernice E.
(ed) The Continuum encyclopedia of children's literature. See The Continuum encyclopedia of children's literature | 028.5
Cullum, Carolyn N.
The storytime sourcebook | 027.62
Cullum, Paul
(jt. auth) Knowles, H. Ain't it cool? | 791.43
Cultivated plants _See_ Annuals (Plants); House plants; Ornamental plants
Cultivating delight. Ackerman, D. | 508
Cults
See also Satanism; Sects
Belief beyond boundaries | 291.9
Jenkins, P. Mystics and messiahs | 200.9
Lewis, J. R. Cults in America | 291.9
Lifton, R. J. Destroying the world to save it | 299
Melton, J. G. Encyclopedic handbook of cults in America | 291.9
Tabor, J. D. Why Waco? | 291.9
See/See also pages in the following book(s):
Atkins, S. E. Encyclopedia of modern American extremists and extremist groups | 322.4
Encyclopedias
The encyclopedia of cults, sects, and new religions | 200.3
Cults in America. Lewis, J. R. | 291.9
Cultural anthropology _See_ Ethnology
Cultural atlas of Africa | 960
Cultural atlas of China. Blunden, C. | 951
Cultural atlas of Russia and the former Soviet Union. Milner-Gulland, R. R. | 947
Cultural atlas of Russia and the Soviet Union. See Milner-Gulland, R. R. Cultural atlas of Russia and the former Soviet Union | 947
Cultural atlas of Spain and Portugal. Vincent, M. | 946
The **cultural** encyclopedia of baseball. Light, J. F. | 796.357
Cultural pluralism _See_ Multiculturalism
Culturally deprived children _See_ Socially handicapped children
Culture
Bloom, H. The Lucifer principle | 128
Huxley, A. Brave new world revisited | 303.3
Klein, R. G. The dawn of human culture | 599.93
Niebuhr, H. R. Christ and culture | 261
Tillich, P. Theology of culture | 230
See/See also pages in the following book(s):
Lewis, C. S. The world's last night, and other essays p31-49 | 230
Culture, Popular _See_ Popular culture
Culture conflict
Nash, G. B. History on trial | 907
The **culture** of cities. Mumford, L. | 307.7
Culture shock _See_ Culture conflict
Cultures of the Jews | 909
Cumings, Bruce, 1943-
Korea's place in the sun | 951.9
Cummings, E. E. (Edward Estlin), 1894-1962
95 poems | 811
Cummings, Edward Estlin _See_ Cummings, E. E. (Edward Estlin), 1894-1962
Cummings, Paul, 1933-1997
Dictionary of contemporary American artists | 920.003
Cummins, John G., 1937-
Francis Drake | 92
Cummins, Ronnie
Genetically engineered food | 363.1
Cuneiform inscriptions
See/See also pages in the following book(s):
Ceram, C. W. Gods, graves, and scholars p223-42 | 930.1
Cuneo, Michael W.
American exorcism | 265
Cunliffe, Barry
The ancient Celts | 936
Cunningham, Bradley Morris
About
Rule, A. Dead by sunset | 364.1
Cunningham, J. V. (James Vincent), 1911-1985
The poems of J.V. Cunningham | 811
Cunningham, James Vincent _See_ Cunningham, J. V. (James Vincent), 1911-1985
Cunningham, Marion
The Fannie Farmer baking book | 641.8
(ed) Farmer, F. M. The Fannie Farmer cookbook | 641.5

Cunningham, Rosa Lee
About
Dash, L. Rosa Lee   305.8
Curie, Marie, 1867-1934
About
Dry, S. Curie   92
Quinn, S. Marie Curie   92
Curiosities and wonders
See also Monsters
Aron, P. Unsolved mysteries of history   902
Clark, J. Encyclopedia of strange and unexplained physical phenomena   001.9
Guinness book of records   032.02
Jay, R. Jay's journal of anomalies   791
The Seventy wonders of the modern world   720.9
Collectors and collecting
Mauriès, P. Cabinets of curiosities   069
Curl, James Stevens, 1937-
Oxford dictionary of architecture   720.3
Curly girl. Massey, L.   646.7
Curran, Brian
(jt. auth) Amery, C. Vanishing histories   363.6
Current biography yearbook   920.003
Current diagnosis & treatment. See Current medical diagnosis and treatment   610.3
Current medical diagnosis and treatment   610.3
Current surgical diagnosis & treatment   617
Curricula (Courses of study) *See* Education—Curricula
Currie, Philip J.
(ed) Encyclopedia of dinosaurs. See Encyclopedia of dinosaurs   567.9
Curry, Judith A.
(ed) Encyclopedia of atmospheric sciences. See Encyclopedia of atmospheric sciences   551.5
A **cursing** brain? Kushner, H. I.   616.8
Curtin, Sharon R.
(jt. auth) Gordon, J. S. Comprehensive cancer care   616.99
Curtis, Christopher Paul
See/See also pages in the following book(s):
The Newbery & Caldecott medal books, 1986-2000 p343-58   028.5
Curtis, Garniss H., 1919-
(jt. auth) Swisher, C. C. Java man   599.93
Curtis, Nancy C.
Black heritage sites   917.3
Curtis, Susan, 1956-
Dancing to a black man's tune: a life of Scott Joplin   92
Curzon, George Nathaniel Curzon, 1st Marquis, 1859-1925
About
Gilmour, D. Curzon: imperial statesman   92
Cusanus, Nicolaus *See* Nicholas, of Cusa, Cardinal, 1401-1464
Cushman, Karen
See/See also pages in the following book(s):
The Newbery & Caldecott medal books, 1986-2000 p245-55   028.5
Cusk, Rachel, 1967-
A life's work   306.8
Custer, Elizabeth Bacon, 1842-1933
Boots and saddles   92
Custer, George Armstrong, 1839-1876
About
Connell, E. S. Son of the Morning Star   973.8
Custer, E. B. Boots and saddles   92
Sandoz, M. The Battle of the Little Bighorn   973.8
Utley, R. M. Custer: cavalier in buckskin   973.8
Wert, J. D. Custer   92
Custer died for your sins. Deloria, V.   970.004
Customer relations
Phillips, E. H. Shocked, appalled, and dismayed!   651.7

Customs, Social *See* Manners and customs
Cutcliffe, Stephen H.
(ed) Technology & American history. See Technology & American history   609
Cuthbertson, Yvonne, 1944-
Beginners' guide to herb gardening   635
Cutler, Neal R.
Understanding Alzheimer's disease   616.8
Cutting your family's hair. Handel, G.   646.7
Cvetaeva, Marina Ivanovna *See* T͡Svetaeva, Marina Ivanovna, 1892-1941
Cyber commerce *See* Electronic commerce
Cycad island. See Sacks, O. W. The island of the colorblind   617.7
The **cycles** of American history. Schlesinger, A. M.   973
Cycling
See also Bicycles; Motorcycles
Bicycling magazine's 900 all-time best tips   796.6
Sloane, E. A. Sloane's complete book of bicycling   629.227
Cyclones
See also Hurricanes
Longshore, D. Encyclopedia of hurricanes, typhoons and cyclones   551.55
Cyclopedia of literary characters   803
Cyclopedia of literary places   809
A **Cynthia** Ozick reader. Ozick, C.   818
Cyrano de Bergerac, 1619-1655
Drama
Rostand, E. Cyrano de Bergerac   822
Cyrano de Bergerac. Rostand, E.
also in Our dramatic heritage v4   808.82
Cytology *See* Cells
Czarnecki, Jack
A cook's book of mushrooms   641.6

D

D Day *See* Normandy (France), Attack on, 1944
D-Day, June 6, 1944. Ambrose, S. E.   940.54
D-Day Normandy. Goldstein, D. M.   940.54
D.H. Lawrence, dying game, 1922-1930. Ellis, D.   92
D.N.A. *See* DNA
Da Vinci, Leonardo *See* Leonardo, da Vinci, 1452-1519
Dachau (Germany)
Social life and customs
Ryback, T. W. The last survivor   940.53
Dachau (Germany: Concentration camp)
Ryback, T. W. The last survivor   940.53
Daintith, John
The Facts on File dictionary of computer science. See The Facts on File dictionary of computer science   004
(ed) The Facts on File dictionary of biochemistry. See The Facts on File dictionary of biochemistry   572
Dairy-free diet *See* Milk-free diet
Dakad, Joseph
About
O'Neill, J. Blood-dark track   920
Dakota Indians
See also Oglala Indians
Crow Dog, L. Crow Dog   970.004
See/See also pages in the following book(s):
Brown, D. A. The American West p78-98   978
Brown, D. A. Bury my heart at Wounded Knee   970.004
Josephy, A. M. Now that the buffalo's gone p243-54   970.004
Dalai Lama XIV, 1935-
Freedom in exile   92

Dalai Lama XIV, 1935——*Continued*
My Tibet — 951
Violence and compassion — 294.3
The way to freedom — 294.3
About
The Dalai Lama — 294.3
The **Dalai** Lama — 294.3
Dalby, Andrew
Dictionary of languages — 410
Daley, Richard J., 1902-1976
About
Cohen, A. American pharaoh: Mayor Richard J. Daley: his battle for Chicago and the nation — 92
Daley, Rosie
(jt. auth) Weil, A. The healthy kitchen — 641.5
Dalí, Gala, d. 1982
See/See also pages in the following book(s):
Prose, F. The lives of the muses — 920
Dalí, Salvador, 1904-1989
About
Gibson, I. The shameful life of Salvador Dalí — 92
Lubar, R. S. Dali: the Salvador Dali Museum collection — 759.6
Dallas, Gregor
1918: war and peace — 940.4
Dallek, Robert
Hail to the chief — 973
Lone star rising: Lyndon Johnson and his times, 1908-1960 — 92
An unfinished life: John F. Kennedy, 1917-1963 — 92
Dalsass, Diana
The new good cake book — 641.8
Dalton, Katharina, 1916-
Depression after childbirth — 616.85
Dalton, Kathleen
Theodore Roosevelt — 92
D'Aluisio, Faith, 1957-
(jt. auth) Menzel, P. Robo sapiens: evolution of a new species — 629.8
Dalzell, Tom, 1951-
Flappers 2 rappers — 427
Damasio, Antonio R.
The feeling of what happens — 153
Looking for Spinoza — 152.4
The **damask** drum. Zeami
In Waley, A. The Nō plays of Japan — 895.6
The **damn** good resume guide. Parker, Y. — 650.14
Damon Lee Fowler's new southern kitchen. Fowler, D. L. — 641.5
Damp, Dennis V.
Post Office jobs — 383
Dams, Bernd H.
(jt. auth) Zega, A. Palaces of the Sun King — 728
Dana, Richard Henry, 1815-1882
Two years before the mast — 910.4
Dana's manual of mineralogy. See Manual of mineral science — 549
Dance, Daryl Cumber
(ed) From my people. See From my people — 398.2
(ed) Honey, hush! See Honey, hush! — 817.008
Dance, Stanley
The world of Count Basie — 920
Dance
See also Ballet; Belly dancing; Modern dance
Reynolds, N. No fixed points — 792.8
Dictionaries
Craine, D. The Oxford dictionary of dance — 792.8
Encyclopedias
International encyclopedia of dance — 792.8
Internet resources
Catron, L. E. Theatre sources dot com — 025.04
The **dance** of death. Strindberg, A.
In Strindberg, A. Strindberg: five plays p113-204 — 839.7

The **dance** of deception. Lerner, H. G. — 155.3
The **dance** of intimacy. Lerner, H. G. — 155.6
Danchin, Antoine
The Delphic boat — 572.8
Dancing *See* Dance
Dangerous animals
See also Animal attacks
Quammen, D. Monster of God — 591.6
Dangerous muse: the life of Lady Caroline Blackwood. Schoenberger, N. — 92
The **dangerous** summer. Hemingway, E. — 791.8
The **dangers** of tobacco. Chekhov, A. P.
In Chekhov, A. P. The plays of Anton Chekhov p323-29 — 891.7
Daniel, Larry J., 1947-
Shiloh — 973.7
Daniel, Margaret Truman *See* Truman, Margaret, 1924-
Daniels, Douglas Henry
Lester leaps in: the life and times of Lester "Pres" Young — 92
Daniels, Les, 1943-
Marvel — 741.5
Daniels, Roger
Coming to America — 325.73
Prisoners without trial — 940.53
(ed) Japanese Americans, from relocation to redress. See Japanese Americans, from relocation to redress — 940.53
Danielson, Dennis Richard, 1949-
(ed) The Book of the cosmos. See The Book of the cosmos — 523.1
Daniloff, Nicholas
(jt. auth) Baiev, K. The Oath — 947.5
Daniloff, Ruth
(jt. auth) Baiev, K. The Oath — 947.5
Dante Alighieri, 1265-1321
Dante's Inferno — 851
The divine comedy — 851
also in Dante Alighieri. The portable Dante — 851
The divine comedy of Dante Alighieri — 851
The new life; criticism
In Emerson, R. W. Collected poems & translations — 811
The portable Dante — 851
Purgatorio — 851
Vita nuova — 851
also in Dante Alighieri. The portable Dante — 851
About
Emerson, R. W. Collected poems & translations — 811
Hollander, R. Dante — 92
Lewis, R. W. B. Dante — 92
See/See also pages in the following book(s):
Bloom, H. The Western canon — 809
Dante's Inferno. Dante Alighieri — 851
Danticat, Edwidge, 1969-
After the dance — 394.25
D'Antonio, Michael
(jt. auth) Spielman, A. Mosquito — 595.7
Danziger, Danny
(jt. auth) Lacey, R. The year 1000 — 942.01
D'Arblay, Frances Burney *See* Burney, Fanny, 1752-1840
Dare to repair. Sussman, J. — 643
A **daring** young man: a biography of William Saroyan. Leggett, J. — 92
Darion, Joe, 1917-2001
Wasserman, D. Man of La Mancha — 812
Dark Ages *See* Middle Ages
The **dark** at the top of the stairs. Inge, W.
In Inge, W. 4 plays p221-304 — 812
Dark continent: Europe's twentieth century. Mazower, M. — 940.55

Dark lover: the life and death of Rudolph Valentino. Leider, E. W. **92**

Dark nature. Watson, L. **111**

The **dark** side of genius. Spoto, D. **92**

The **dark** side of the game. Green, T. **796.332**

Dark Star: an oral biography of Jerry Garcia. Greenfield, R. **92**

Dark star safari. Theroux, P. **916**

Dark sun. Rhodes, R. **623.4**

Darke, Rick
The American woodland garden **635.9**
The color encyclopedia of ornamental grasses **635.9**

A **darker** ribbon. Leopold, E. **616.99**

The **darkness** and the light. Hecht, A. **811**

Darkness visible. Styron, W. **616.85**

Darnley, Henry Stewart, Lord, 1545-1567
About
Weir, A. Mary, Queen of Scots, and the murder of Lord Darnley **92**

Darnton, Robert
Berlin journal, 1989-1990 **943.087**

Darvill, Timothy
The concise Oxford dictionary of archaeology **930.1**

Darwin, Charles, 1809-1882
The Darwin reader **576.8**
The origin of species **576.8**
The voyage of the Beagle **508**
About
Browne, J. Charles Darwin: a biography **92**
Desmond, A. J. Darwin **92**
Gould, S. J. Ever since Darwin **576.8**
Keynes, R. D. Fossils, finches, and Fuegians **508**
See/See also pages in the following book(s):
Horvitz, L. A. Eureka!: scientific breakthroughs that changed the world **509**
Tudge, C. The time before history **599.93**

Darwin, Erasmus, 1731-1802
About
Uglow, J. S. The lunar men **920**

Darwinism *See* Evolution

Darwin's black box. Behe, M. J. **576.8**

Darwin's dangerous idea. Dennett, D. C. **146**

Darwin's ghost. Jones, S. **576.8**

Darwin's spectre. Rose, M. R. **576.8**

Dary, David
The Santa Fe Trail **978**
Seeking pleasure in the Old West **978**

Dasch, E. Julius (Ernest Julius), 1932-
(ed) Encyclopedia of earth sciences. See Encyclopedia of earth sciences **550.3**

Dasch, Ernest Julius *See* Dasch, E. Julius (Ernest Julius), 1932-

Dasch, Pat
(ed) Space sciences. See Space sciences **500.5**

Dash, Leon, 1944-
Rosa Lee **305.8**

Dash, Mike
Batavia's graveyard **910.4**
Tulipomania **635.9**

Data processing
See also Artificial intelligence; Computer science
Encyclopedias
Encyclopedia of information systems **004**
History
Ifrah, G. The universal history of computing **004**

Data processing, Electronic
Keyboarding
See Keyboarding (Electronics)

Data storage and retrieval systems *See* Information systems

Data transmission systems
See also Computer networks; Electronic mail systems; Fax transmission

Dating (Social customs)
Carter, S. Men like women who like themselves **158**
Gray, J. Mars and Venus on a date **306.7**

Dauber, Philip M.
The three big bangs **523.1**

Daughters and fathers *See* Father-daughter relationship

Daughters and mothers *See* Mother-daughter relationship

Dave Barry does Japan. Barry, D. **817**

Dave Barry hits below the Beltway. Barry, D. **817**

Dave Barry in cyberspace. Barry, D. **817**

Dave Barry is not making this up. Barry, D. **817**

Dave Barry is not taking this sitting down!. Barry, D. **817**

Dave Barry talks back. Barry, D. **817**

Dave Barry turns 40. Barry, D. **817**

Dave Barry turns 50. Barry, D. **817**

Dave Barry's complete guide to guys. Barry, D. **817**

Dave Barry's greatest hits. Barry, D. **817**

Dave Barry's only travel guide you'll ever need. Barry, D. **817**

Davenport, Basil, 1905-1966
(ed) The Portable Roman reader. See The Portable Roman reader **870.8**

Davenport, Guy, 1927-
The geography of the imagination **814**

Davenport-Hines, R. P. T. (Richard Peter Treadwell), 1953-
The pursuit of oblivion **363.45**

Davenport-Hines, Richard Peter Treadwell *See* Davenport-Hines, R. P. T. (Richard Peter Treadwell), 1953-

David, King of Israel
About
McKenzie, S. L. King David **222**
See/See also pages in the following book(s):
Wills, G. Certain trumpets p102-12 **303.3**

David, A. Rosalie (Ann Rosalie)
Handbook to life in ancient Egypt **932**

David, Ann Rosalie *See* David, A. Rosalie (Ann Rosalie)

David, Elizabeth, 1913-1992
Is there a nutmeg in the house? **641.5**

The **David** Show. Gurney, A. R.
In Gurney, A. R. Nine early plays, 1961-1973 p69-97 **812**

Davidson, Basil, 1914-
Africa in history **960**

Davidson, Cathy N., 1949-
(ed) The Oxford book of women's writing in the United States. See The Oxford book of women's writing in the United States **810.8**
(ed) The Oxford companion to women's writing in the United States. See The Oxford companion to women's writing in the United States **810.9**

Davidson, Homer L.
TV repair for beginners **621.388**

Davidson, Keay
Carl Sagan **92**
(jt. auth) Smoot, G. Wrinkles in time **523.1**

Davidson, Linda Kay
Pilgrimage: from the Ganges to Graceland: an encyclopedia **291.3**

Davidson, Robyn, 1950-
Desert places **954**

Davies, Brian, 1951-
The thought of Thomas Aquinas **230**

Davies, John, 1938-
A history of Wales **942.9**

Davies, Kevin, 1960-
Cracking the genome **599.93**

Davies, Norman
The Isles **941**

Davies, P. C. W., 1946-
About time   530.1
The fifth miracle   576.8
God and the new physics   261.5
The last three minutes   523.1
The matter myth   530
Davies, Paul See Davies, P. C. W., 1946-
Davies, Pete, 1959-
The devil's flu   614.5
Inside the hurricane   551.55
Davies, William David, 1911-
(ed) The Cambridge history of Judaism. See The Cambridge history of Judaism   296
Davis, Burke, 1913-
Sherman's march   973.7
To Appomattox   973.7
Davis, Devra Lee
When smoke ran like water   615.9
Davis, Dick, 1945-
Belonging   821
Davis, Eddie, 1921-1986
See/See also pages in the following book(s):
Dance, S. The world of Count Basie   920
Davis, Gordon See Hunt, E. Howard (Everette Howard), 1918-
Davis, Jefferson, 1808-1889
About
Cooper, W. J. Jefferson Davis, American   92
Davis, W. C. An honorable defeat   973.7
Davis, John H., 1929-
The Guggenheims (1848-1988)   920
Jacqueline Bouvier   92
Davis, Kenneth C.
Don't know much about the Bible   220.6
Davis, Kenneth Sydney, 1912-1999
FDR, into the storm, 1937-1940   92
Davis, Laura
(jt. auth) Bass, E. The courage to heal   362.83
Davis, Lee Allyn
Environmental disasters   363.7
Man-made catastrophes   904
Davis, Linda H.
Badge of courage: the life of Stephen Crane   92
Davis, Mary B.
(ed) Native America in the twentieth century. See Native America in the twentieth century   970.004
Davis, Miles
Miles, the autobiography   92
About
Troupe, Q. Miles and me: biography of Miles Davis   92
See/See also pages in the following book(s):
Feather, L. From Satchmo to Miles   920
Davis, Paul B. (Paul Benjamin), 1934-
Charles Dickens A-Z   823.009
Davis, Paul K., 1952-
100 decisive battles   904
Davis, Peter G.
The American opera singer   920
Davis, Ronald L.
John Ford   92
Davis, Stephen, 1947-
Old gods almost dead: the 40-year odyssey of the Rolling Stones   920
Davis, Wade
One river   581.6
Davis, William C., 1946-
Battle at Bull Run   973.7
An honorable defeat   973.7
Three roads to the Alamo   976.4
Dawidoff, Nicholas
In the country of country   781.642
(ed) Baseball: a literary anthology. See Baseball: a literary anthology   810.8

Dawidowicz, Lucy S.
The war against the Jews, 1933-1945   940.53
Dawkins, Richard, 1941-
Climbing Mount Improbable   576
River out of Eden   576
The selfish gene   576
Unweaving the rainbow   501
The dawn of human culture. Klein, R. G.   599.93
Daws, Gavan
Prisoners of the Japanese   940.54
Dawson, Geraldine
(jt. auth) Ozonoff, S. A parent's guide to asperger syndrome and high-functioning autism   618.92
Dawson, Ian, 1951-
(ed) Who's who in British history. See Who's who in British history   920.003
Dawson, Sophie
The art and craft of papermaking   676
Day, Clarence, 1874-1935
Life with father   818
Day, Cyrus Lawrence, 1900-1968
The art of knotting & splicing   623.88
Day, Dorothy, 1897-1980
See/See also pages in the following book(s):
Wills, G. Certain trumpets p250-62   303.3
Day, Paul
(jt. auth) Bacon, T. The ultimate guitar book   787.87
Day, Susan
(jt. auth) McMahan, E. The writer's handbook   808
Day, Timothy
A century of recorded music   780
Day, Trevor, 1955-
Oceans   551.46
Day
See also Night
The day Emily married. Foote, H.
In Foote, H. Getting Frankie married—and afterwards, and other plays   812
Day of Atonement See Yom Kippur
Day of deceit. Stinnett, R. B.   940.54
The day the world exploded, August 27, 1883. See Winchester, S. Krakatoa: the day the world exploded, August 27, 1883   551.2
Days ahead. Wilson, L.
In Wilson, L. 21 short plays p72-76   812
Days of defiance. Klein, M.   973.7
Days of infamy. Coffey, M.   355
Days of wonder. Schulman, G.   811
Dazzler: the life and times of Moss Hart. Bach, S.   92
The DC comics guide to writing comics. O'Neil, D.   808
De Balzac, Honoré See Balzac, Honoré de, 1799-1850
De Beauvoir, Simone See Beauvoir, Simone de, 1908-1986
De Chergé, Christian See Chergé, Christian de
De Coucy, Enguerrand See Coucy, Enguerrand de, 1340-1397
De Duve, Christian See Duve, Christian de, 1917-
De Fermat, Pierre See Fermat, Pierre de, 1601-1665
De Forest, John William, 1826-1906
See/See also pages in the following book(s):
Wilson, E. Patriotic gore p635-742   810.9
De Freitas, Michael See Michael X, 1933-1974
De Gaulle, Charles See Gaulle, Charles de, 1890-1970
De Ghelderode, Michel See Ghelderode, Michel de, 1898-1962
De Jong-Stout, Alisa A. See Jong-Stout, Alisa A. de
De Kooning, Willem, 1904-1997
Willem de Kooning: tracing the figure   741
De La Beckwith, Byron
About
DeLaughter, B. Never too late   345

De La Beckwith, Byron—About—*Continued*
Vollers, M. Ghosts of Mississippi   **364.1**
De la Cruz, Juana Inés *See* Juana Inés de la Cruz, 1651-1695
De la Haye, Amy
(jt. auth) Laver, J. Costume and fashion   **391**
De la Torre, Mónica *See* Torre, Mónica de la, 1969-
De Laeter, J. R. *See* Laeter, J. R. de (John R. de)
De Lange, N. R. M. (Nicholas Robert Michael), 1944-
(ed) The Illustrated history of the Jewish people. See The Illustrated history of the Jewish people   **909**
De Lange, Nicholas Robert Michael *See* De Lange, N. R. M. (Nicholas Robert Michael), 1944-
De Lesseps, Ferdinand Marie *See* Lesseps, Ferdinand Marie de, vicomte, 1805-1894
De Marly, Diana
Dress in North America v1   **391**
De Montaigne, Michel *See* Montaigne, Michel de, 1533-1592
The **de-moralization** of society. Himmelfarb, G.   **303.3**
De Pauw, Linda Grant
Battle cries and lullabies   **355**
De Pree, Christopher Gordon, 1966-
(ed) Van Nostrand's concise encyclopedia of science. See Van Nostrand's concise encyclopedia of science   **503**
De Quincey, Thomas, 1785-1859
The confessions of an English opium-eater   **824**
De Saint-Aubin, Horace *See* Balzac, Honoré de, 1799-1850
De Sola, Ralph, 1908-
(ed) Stahl, D. Abbreviations dictionary   **421.03**
De Soto, Hernando *See* Soto, Hernando de
De Soto, Hernando *See* Soto, Hernando de, ca. 1500-1542
De Tocqueville, Alexis *See* Tocqueville, Alexis de
De Vecchi, Pierluigi
Raphael   **759.5**
De Villiers, Marq
Sahara: a natural history   **508**
Water: the fate of our most precious resource   **333.91**
The **de-voicing** of society. Locke, J. L.   **302.3**
De Vonyar, Jill
Degas and the dance   **759.4**
De Vries, Mary Ann
The professional secretary's book of lists & tips   **651.3**
De Waal, Frans *See* Waal, Frans de, 1948-
Deacon, Terrence William
The symbolic species   **153.6**
Dead
Roach, M. Stiff   **611**
Dead by sunset. Rule, A.   **364.1**
Dead certainties. Schama, S.   **907**
Dead men do tell tales. Maples, W. R.   **614**
The **Dead** Sea scriptures. Dead Sea scrolls   **229**
Dead Sea scrolls
Charlesworth, J. H. Jesus and the Dead Sea scrolls   **232**
The complete Dead Sea scrolls in English   **296.1**
The Dead Sea scriptures   **229**
The Dead Sea scrolls   **296.1**
The Dead Sea scrolls uncovered   **296.1**
The Encyclopedia of the Dead Sea scrolls   **296.1**
Golb, N. Who wrote the Dead Sea scrolls?   **296.1**
Schiffman, L. H. Reclaiming the Dead Sea scrolls   **296.1**
Shanks, H. The mystery and meaning of the Dead Sea scrolls   **296.1**
Understanding the Dead Sea scrolls   **296.1**
The **Dead** Sea scrolls uncovered. Dead Sea scrolls   **296.1**
Deadly feasts. Rhodes, R.   **614.5**

The **deadly** truth. Grob, G. N.   **616**
Deaf
Herrmann, D. Helen Keller   **92**
Keller, H. The story of my life   **92**
Lash, J. P. Helen and teacher   **92**
Sacks, O. W. Seeing voices   **362.4**
      Means of communication
     See also Sign language
Deafness
Myers, D. G. A quiet world   **617.8**
      Encyclopedias
Turkington, C. The encyclopedia of deafness and hearing disorders   **617.8**
Deak, JoAnn
Girls will be girls   **649**
Dealing with difficult people in the library. Willis, M. R.   **025.5**
Dealing with genes. Berg, P.   **576.5**
Dean, Cornelia
Against the tide   **333.91**
Dean, James, 1931-1955
      About
Alexander, P. Boulevard of broken dreams: the life, times, and legend of James Dean   **92**
Holley, V. James Dean   **92**
Dear, I. C. B. *See* Dear, Ian, 1935-
Dear, Ian, 1935-
(ed) The Oxford companion to World War II. See The Oxford companion to World War II   **940.53**
Dear God, have you ever gone hungry? Ba'u, Y.   **940.53**
Dear Professor Einstein. Einstein, A.   **92**
Dearborn, Mary V.
Mailer   **92**
Dearling, Robert, 1933-
(ed) The Illustrated encyclopedia of musical instruments. See The Illustrated encyclopedia of musical instruments   **784.19**
Death
     See also Longevity; Terminal care; Terminally ill
Attig, T. The heart of grief   **155.9**
Attig, T. How we grieve   **155.9**
Benecke, M. The dream of eternal life   **612.6**
Emswiler, M. A. Guiding your child through grief   **155.9**
Finkbeiner, A. K. After the death of a child   **155.9**
Kübler-Ross, E. Life lessons   **170**
Kübler-Ross, E. Living with death and dying   **155.9**
Kübler-Ross, E. On children and death   **155.9**
Kübler-Ross, E. On death and dying   **155.9**
Levy, A. The orphaned adult   **155.9**
Lynch, T. The undertaking   **814**
Miller, S. Finding hope when a child dies   **291**
Nuland, S. B. How we die   **616.07**
Sife, W. The loss of a pet   **155.9**
Sogyal, Rinpoche. The Tibetan book of living and dying   **294.3**
Terkel, S. Will the circle be unbroken?   **128**
Tibetan book of the dead. The Tibetan book of the dead   **294.3**
Weenolsen, P. The art of dying   **155.9**
Young, G. W. The high cost of dying   **393**
     See/See also pages in the following book(s):
Peck, M. S. Denial of the soul   **179.7**
      Encyclopedias
Encyclopedia of death and dying   **306.9**
Macmillan encyclopedia of death and dying   **306.9**
      Quotations
The Oxford book of death   **808.88**
Death [play] Allen, W.
   In Allen, W. Without feathers   **817**
Death at an early age. Kozol, J.   **306.43**
Death at the priory. Ruddick, J.   **364.1**

Death be not proud. Gunther, J.   **92**
Death by chocolate cakes. Desaulniers, M.   **641.8**
Death in the afternoon. Hemingway, E.   **791.8**
Death march. Knox, D.   **940.54**
Death notices *See* Obituaries
Death of a salesman. Miller, A.   **812**
The **death** of common sense. Howard, P.   **348**
The **death** of outrage: Bill Clinton and the assault on American ideals. Bennett, W. J.   **973.929**
The **death** of Yugoslavia. See Silber, L. Yugoslavia   **949.7**
Death penalty *See* Capital punishment
Deathwatch. Genet, J.
    In Genet, J. The maids [and] Deathwatch   **842**
DeBakey, Michael E., 1908-
    The new living heart   **616.1**
    The New living heart diet. See The New living heart diet   **616.1**
The **Debate** on the Constitution   **342**
Debbie Travis' painted house. Travis, D.   **698**
DeBlieu, Jan
    Wind   **551.51**
Debo, Angie, 1890-1988
    Geronimo   **92**
Deceit and denial. Markowitz, G. E.   **615.9**
Decision making
    Connelly, O. On war and leadership   **355.3**
    Heller, R. Essential manager's manual   **658.4**
The **decision** to use the atomic bomb and the architecture of an American myth. Alperovitz, G.   **940.54**
Deck & patio planner. Riha, J.   **643**
Decks (Domestic architecture) *See* Patios
Declaration of Independence *See* United States. Declaration of Independence
The **Declaration** of Independence. Becker, C.   **973.3**
The **decline** and fall of the Roman Empire. Gibbon, E.   **937**
The **decline** and fall of the Soviet Empire. Coleman, F.   **947.085**
The **decline** of the West. Spengler, O.   **901**
Decoding darkness. Tanzi, R. E.   **616.8**
DeConde, Alexander
    (ed) Encyclopedia of American foreign policy. See Encyclopedia of American foreign policy   **327.73**
Decorating basics   **747**
Decoration, Interior *See* Interior design
Decoration and ornament
    Leigh, T. The complete book of decorative painting   **745.7**
    Logan, M. D. Mat, mount and frame it yourself   **749**
    Sloan, A. Modern paint effects   **745.7**
Decorative arts
    See also Decoration and ornament
    Art nouveau   **709.03**
    Designed for delight   **745**
    Gifts to the tsars, 1500-1700   **745**
    A Grand design   **708**
    Harwood, B. Architecture and interior design through the 18th century   **729**
    Loring, J. Tiffany's 20th century   **745**
DeCurtis, Anthony
    (ed) The Rolling Stone illustrated history of rock & roll. See The Rolling Stone illustrated history of rock & roll   **781.66**
Dedekind, Richard, 1831-1916
    See/See also pages in the following book(s):
    Bell, E. T. Men of mathematics p510-25   **920**
Deegan, Robert M. Cook- *See* Cook-Deegan, Robert M.
Deeks, Florence Amelia
    About
    McKillop, A. B. The spinster & the prophet   **941.08**
Deen, Edith
    All of the women of the Bible   **220.9**

Deep diving vehicles *See* Submersibles
Deep in a dream: the long night of Chet Baker. Gavin, J.   **92**
Deep play. Ackerman, D.   **155.6**
Dees, Morris S., Jr.
    Gathering storm   **322.4**
The **defeat** of the Spanish Armada. See Mattingly, G. The Armada   **942.05**
Defense Dept. (U.S.) *See* United States. Dept. of Defense
Defense policy *See* Military policy
A **defiant** life: Thurgood Marshall and the persistence of racism in America. Ball, H.   **92**
Defoe, Daniel, 1661?-1731
    Robinson Crusoe; criticism
    In Severin, T. In search of Robinson Crusoe   **996**
    In Souhami, D. Selkirk's Island   **996**
Defying Hitler. Haffner, S.   **92**
Degas, Edgar, 1834-1917
    About
    De Vonyar, J. Degas and the dance   **759.4**
Degas, Hilaire Germain Edgar *See* Degas, Edgar, 1834-1917
Degas and the dance. De Vonyar, J.   **759.4**
DeGrandpre, Richard J.
    Ritalin nation   **618.92**
Degrees of latitude and longitude *See* Latitude
Deirdre of the sorrows. Synge, J. M.
    In Synge, J. M. The complete plays   **822**
Deities *See* Gods and goddesses
Dejevsky, Nikolai J.
    (jt. auth) Milner-Gulland, R. R. Cultural atlas of Russia and the former Soviet Union   **947**
Delahunty, Andrew
    (ed) The Oxford dictionary of allusions. See The Oxford dictionary of allusions   **803**
Delambre, J. B. J., 1749-1822
    About
    Alder, K. The measure of all things   **526**
Delany, Annie Elizabeth *See* Delany, Bessie
Delany, Bessie
    (jt. auth) Delany, S. The Delany sisters' book of everyday wisdom   **818**
    (jt. auth) Delany, S. Having our say   **92**
Delany, Sadie
    The Delany sisters' book of everyday wisdom   **818**
    Having our say   **92**
Delany, Sarah Louise *See* Delany, Sadie
Delany family
    About
    Delany, S. Having our say   **92**
The **Delany** sisters' book of everyday wisdom. Delany, S.   **818**
DeLaughter, Bobby
    Never too late   **345**
DelFattore, Joan, 1946-
    What Johnny shouldn't read   **379**
Delft (Netherlands)
    See/See also pages in the following book(s):
    Bailey, A. Vermeer   **92**
Delgado, James P., 1958-
    (ed) Encyclopedia of underwater and maritime archaeology. See Encyclopedia of underwater and maritime archaeology   **930.1**
Deliberate prose. Ginsberg, A.   **814**
Deliver us from evil. Shawcross, W.   **909.82**
Deloria, Philip Joseph
    A Companion to American Indian history. See A Companion to American Indian history   **970.004**
Deloria, Vine
    Custer died for your sins   **970.004**
    Evolution, creationism, and other modern myths   **291.1**

Deloria, Vine—*Continued*
(comp) Documents of American Indian diplomacy. See
Documents of American Indian diplomacy
970.004
The **Delphic** boat. Danchin, A.   572.8
Delta Force (Army) *See* United States. Army. Delta
Force
DeMallie, Raymond J., 1946-
(comp) Documents of American Indian diplomacy. See
Documents of American Indian diplomacy
970.004
Dement, William C., 1928-
The promise of sleep   612.8
Demetz, Peter, 1922-
The air show at Brescia, 1909   629.13
Prague in black and gold   943.7
D'Emilio, John
Lost prophet: the life and times of Bayard Rustin
92
Democracy
Broder, D. S. Democracy derailed   328.73
Lasch, C. The revolt of the elites   306
Tocqueville, A. de. Democracy in America   973.5
See/See also pages in the following book(s):
Toffler, A. Future shock p416-30   303.4
Democracy and education. Dewey, J.   370.1
Democracy derailed. Broder, D. S.   328.73
Democracy in America. Tocqueville, A. de   973.5
The **democratic** experience. See Boorstin, D. J. The
Americans: The democratic experience   973
Democritus
See/See also pages in the following book(s):
Jaspers, K. The great philosophers   109
Demographic yearbook. United Nations. Statistical Office
304.6
The **demon** in the freezer. Preston, R.   616.9
Demoniac possession
Cuneo, M. W. American exorcism   265
Demonology
Messadié, G. A history of the devil   291
Demons and angels: a life of Jacob Epstein. Rose, J.
92
Demonstrations
See also Riots
Anderson, T. H. The movement and the sixties
303.4
Demos, John, 1937-
The unredeemed captive   973.2
Demosthenes, 384-322 B.C.
See/See also pages in the following book(s):
Hamilton, E. The echo of Greece p105-14   880.9
Dempsey, Amy
Art in the modern era   709.04
Dempsey, Jack, 1895-1983
About
Kahn, R. A flame of pure fire: Jack Dempsey and the
roaring '20s   92
Denckla, Tanya
The organic gardener's home reference   635
Denes, Magda, 1934-1996
Castles burning   940.53
Denial of the soul. Peck, M. S.   179.7
Dennett, Daniel Clement
Darwin's dangerous idea   146
Dennis, Carina
The human genome   599.93
Denominations, Religious *See* Sects
Dent, Jim
The Junction boys   796.332
The undefeated   796.332
Dent, Thomas C. *See* Dent, Tom, 1932-1998
Dent, Tom, 1932-1998
Southern journey   975
Dent atlas of American history. See Gilbert, M. The
Routledge atlas of American history   911

The **Dent** atlas of the Holocaust. See Gilbert, M. The
Routledge atlas of the Holocaust   940.53
Dental care and oral health sourcebook   617.6
Dentistry
Dental care and oral health sourcebook   617.6
History
Wynbrandt, J. The excruciating history of dentistry
617.6
Vocational guidance
Wischnitzer, S. Barron's guide to medical & dental
schools   610.69
Denton, Sally
The money and the power   979.3
Denying history. Shermer, M.   940.53
Denying the Holocaust. Lipstadt, D. E.   940.53
DePaulo, J. Raymond
Understanding depression   616.85
Dependencies *See* Colonies
Depression (Psychology)
See also Manic-depressive illness
Ainsworth, P. Understanding depression   616.85
Beardslee, W. R. Out of the darkened room
616.85
Burns, D. D. Feeling good   158
DePaulo, J. R. Understanding depression   616.85
Glenmullen, J. Prozac backlash   616.85
Mondimore, F. M. Adolescent depression   616.85
Papolos, D. F. The bipolar child   618.92
Slater, L. Love works like this   306.8
Solomon, A. The noonday demon   616.85
Styron, W. Darkness visible   616.85
See/See also pages in the following book(s):
Amen, D. Change your brain, change your life
616.89
Pollack, W. S. Real boys p303-37   305.23
Encyclopedias
Roesch, R. The encyclopedia of depression
616.85
Depression after childbirth. Dalton, K.   616.85
Depressions
See/See also pages in the following book(s):
Heilbroner, R. L. The worldly philosophers   330.1
1929
See Great Depression, 1929-1939
Depressions, Economic *See* Depressions
Deprogramming *See* Brainwashing
Derfler, Leslie
The Dreyfus affair   944.081
Dermatosclerosis *See* Scleroderma (Disease)
Dershowitz, Alan M.
The Genesis of justice   222
Shouting fire   323
Supreme injustice   324
The vanishing American Jew   305.8
Why terrorism works   303.6
Des Prez, Josquin *See* Josquin, des Pres, d. 1521
DeSalle, Rob
(ed) Epidemic! the world of infectious diseases. See
Epidemic! the world of infectious diseases
614.4
(ed) The Genomic revolution. See The Genomic revolution
599.93
Desaulniers, Marcel
Celebrate with chocolate   641.6
Death by chocolate cakes   641.8
Descartes, René, 1596-1650
The philosophical writings of Descartes   194
About
Watson, R. A. Cogito ergo sum: the life of René Descartes
92
See/See also pages in the following book(s):
Bell, E. T. Men of mathematics p35-55   920
Jaspers, K. The great philosophers   109
Mlodinow, L. Euclid's window   516

Descartes, René, 1596-1650—About—*Continued*
Russell, B. A history of Western philosophy p557-68
    109

Descartes: selected philosophical writings. See Descartes, R. The philosophical writings of Descartes
    194

Descartes to Derrida. Sedgwick, P.   **190**

Desegregation in education See School integration

Desert animals
Mares, M. A. A desert calling   **599**

Desert between the mountains. Durham, M. S.   **979**

A **desert** calling. Mares, M. A.   **599**

Desert ecology
Alcock, J. In a desert garden   **595.7**

Desert places. Davidson, R.   **954**

Desert plants
    See also Cactus
Duffield, M. R. Plants for dry climates   **635.9**

Desert queen [biography of Gertrude Bell] Wallach, J.
    92

Desert Storm Operation See Persian Gulf War, 1991

Desert victory. Friedman, N.   **956.7**

Desertion and nonsupport
    See also Child support

Design
Rybczynski, W. The look of architecture   **721**
The Work of Charles and Ray Eames   **745.4**

Design, Decorative See Decoration and ornament

Design, Industrial See Industrial design

Design for gardens. Hudak, J.   **712**

Designed for delight   **745**

Designing, building, and testing your own speaker system with projects. Weems, D. B.   **621.382**

Designing knitwear. Newton, D.   **746.43**

Designing with light. Gillette, J. M.   **792**

Designing with perennials. Harper, P.   **712**

Desire of the everlasting hills. Cahill, T.   **232**

Desmond, Adrian J., 1947-
Darwin   **92**

Desperation entertaining. Mills, B.   **642**

Desprès, Josquin See Josquin, des Pres, d. 1521

Desserts
    See also Cake
American Heart Association low-fat & luscious desserts   **641.8**
Desaulniers, M. Celebrate with chocolate   **641.6**
Heatter, M. Maida Heatter's book of great desserts
    641.8
Moosewood Restaurant book of desserts   **641.8**

D'Este, Carlo, 1936-
Patton   **92**

Destivelle, Catherine, 1960-
    See/See also pages in the following book(s):
Slung, M. B. Living with cannibals and other women's adventures   **910.4**

Destroying the world to save it. Lifton, R. J.   **299**

Detecting women. Heising, W. L.   **016.8**

Determinism and indeterminism See Free will and determinism

Detz, Joan
How to write and give a speech   **808.5**

Deutsch, Babette, 1895-1982
Poetry handbook: a dictionary of terms   **808.1**

Deutsch, David
The fabric of reality   **530**

Deutsch, Eliot
(ed) A Companion to world philosophies. See A Companion to world philosophies   **109**

Deutsch, Francine, 1948-
Halving it all   **649**

DeVeaux, Scott Knowles
The birth of bebop   **781.65**

Developing countries
    Economic conditions
Stiglitz, J. E. Globalization and its discontents
    337
    Women
    See Women—Developing countries

Developmental psychology
Eliot, L. What's going on in there?   **612.8**

Devereux, Robert, 1566-1601 See Essex, Robert Devereux, 2nd Earl of, 1566-1601

Devices and desires. Tone, A.   **363.9**

Devil
    See also Demonology
Messadié, G. A history of the devil   **291**
Pagels, E. H. The origin of Satan   **235**

The **devil** in the shape of a woman. Karlsen, C. F.
    133.4

The **devil** in the white city. Larson, E.   **364.1**

Devil-worship See Satanism

The **Devil's** dictionary. Bierce, A.
    In Bierce, A. The collected writings   **818**

The **devil's** flu. Davies, P.   **614.5**

Devine, Carol
Human rights   **323**

Devine, T. M. (Thomas Martin)
The Scottish nation 1700-2000   **941.1**

Devine, Thomas Martin See Devine, T. M. (Thomas Martin)

Devlin, Keith J.
Goodbye, Descartes   **128**
The math gene   **510**
The millennium problems   **510**

Devonshire, Georgiana Spencer Cavendish, Duchess of, 1757-1806
    About
Foreman, A. Georgiana, Duchess of Devonshire
    92

Devotional exercises
    See also Meditation

DeWalt, G. Weston
(jt. auth) Boukreev, A. The climb   **796.52**

Dewdney, A. K.
200% of nothing   **510**
A mathematical mystery tour   **510**

Dewey, John, 1859-1952
The child and the curriculum
    In Dewey, J. The school and society, and The Child and the curriculum   **372**
Democracy and education   **370.1**
The philosophy of John Dewey   **191**
The school and society
    In Dewey, J. The school and society, and The child and the curriculum   **372**
The school and society, and The child and the curriculum   **372**
Theory of the moral life   **170**
    About
Menand, L. The Metaphysical Club   **973.9**
    See/See also pages in the following book(s):
Durant, W. J. The story of philosophy p389-95
    109

Dewey, Melvil, 1851-1931
Abridged Dewey decimal classification and relative index   **025.4**
Dewey decimal classification and relative index
    025.4

Dewey, Thomas E. (Thomas Edmund), 1902-1971
    About
Karabell, Z. The last campaign   **324**

Dewey Decimal Classification
Dewey, M. Abridged Dewey decimal classification and relative index   **025.4**
Dewey, M. Dewey decimal classification and relative index   **025.4**

D'Hérelle, Félix See Hérelle, Félix d', 1873-1949

Di Piero, W. S.
Skirts and slacks   811
Di Prisco, Joseph
Field guide to the American teenager   305.23
Di Rienzo, Cola *See* Rienzo, Cola di, ca. 1313-1354
Diabetes
American Diabetes Association complete guide to diabetes   616.4
Beaser, R. S. The Joslin guide to diabetes   616.4
Diabetes sourcebook   616.4
Mayo Clinic on managing diabetes   616.4
Poirier, L. M. Women & diabetes   616.4
Saudek, C. D. The Johns Hopkins guide to diabetes   616.4

Diet therapy
Giedt, F. T. The Joslin Diabetes great chefs cook healthy cookbook   641.5
Polin, B. S. The Joslin Diabetes gourmet cookbook   641.5
Smith, C. Cooking with the diabetic chef   641.5
Diabetes sourcebook   616.4
Diagnosis
Groopman, J. E. Second opinions   610
The Johns Hopkins consumer guide to medical tests   616.07
Pagana, K. D. Mosby's diagnostic and laboratory test reference   616.07
Segen, J. C. The patient's guide to medical tests   616.07
Diagnosis, cancer. Harpham, W. S.   616.99
Diagram Group
Lambert, D. The field guide to geology   551
Dialectics *See* Logic
Dialogue for three. Pinter, H.
In Pinter, H. Complete works v3   822
A **dialogue** on oratory. Tacitus, C.
In Tacitus, C. The complete works of Tacitus p735-69   878
The **dialogues** of Plato. Plato   888
Diamant, Anita, 1951-
Living a Jewish life   296.7
Diamant, Dora, d. 1952
About
Diamant, K. Kafka's last love   92
Diamant, Kathi
Kafka's last love   92
Diamond, Jared M.
Guns, germs, and steel   303.4
The third chimpanzee   599.93
Diamonds
Campbell, G. Blood diamonds   966.4
Hart, M. Diamond: a journey to the heart of an obsession   553.8
The Nature of diamonds   553.8
Diaries
Bibliography
Adamson, L. G. Notable women in American history   920.003
Diaries v1. Isherwood, C.   92
Diaries of a young poet. Rilke, R. M.   92
The **diaries** of George Washington. Washington, G.   92
The **diaries** of Kenneth Tynan. Tynan, K.   92
The **diary** of a young girl: the definitive edition. Frank, A.   92
The **diary** of Anaïs Nin. Nin, A.   92
The **diary** of Anne Frank. Goodrich, F.   812
The **diary** of Anne Frank: the critical edition. Frank, A.   92
The **diary** of Frida Kahlo. Kahlo, F.   92
The **diary** of Samuel Pepys. Pepys, S.   92
Diaz, David
See/See also pages in the following book(s):
The Newbery & Caldecott medal books, 1986-2000 p220-26   028.5

Díaz de Vivar, Rodrigo *See* Cid, ca. 1043-1099
Díaz del Castillo, Bernal, 1496-1584
The discovery and conquest of Mexico, 1517-1521   972
Dibra, Bashkim
Dogspeak   636.7
Dickens, Charles, 1812-1870
Bleak House; criticism
In Gay, P. Savage reprisals   809.3
In Nabokov, V. V. Lectures on literature p63-124   808.3
About
Davis, P. B. Charles Dickens A-Z   823.009
Kaplan, F. Dickens   92
Oxford reader's companion to Dickens   823.009
Smiley, J. Charles Dickens   92
See/See also pages in the following book(s):
Bloom, H. The Western canon   809
Dickey, James
The James Dickey reader   818
Dickinson, A. T.
Adamson, L. G. American historical fiction   016.813
Dickinson, Emily, 1830-1886
The complete poems of Emily Dickinson   811
New poems of Emily Dickinson   811
About
Habegger, A. My wars are laid away in books: the life of Emily Dickinson   92
See/See also pages in the following book(s):
Bloom, H. The Western canon   809
Kazin, A. An American procession p161-80   810.9
Dickinson, Terence
The backyard astronomer's guide   522
From the big bang to Planet X   520
Dickson, Paul
Sputnik: the shock of the century   629.46
(comp) Toasts. See Toasts   808.88
Dictionaries *See* Encyclopedias and dictionaries
Dictionaries, Biographical *See* Biography—Dictionaries
Dictionaries, Classical *See* Classical dictionaries
Dictionaries, Picture *See* Picture dictionaries
A **dictionary** of African mythology. Scheub, H.   299
A **dictionary** of American and British euphemisms. See Holder, R. W. How not to say what you mean   423
Dictionary of American biography   920.003
Dictionary of American children's fiction, 1995-1999. Helbig, A.   028.5
Dictionary of American family names   929.4
Dictionary of American history   973.03
A **Dictionary** of American proverbs   398.9
Dictionary of American regional English   427
Dictionary of American slang   427
The **Dictionary** of anthropology   306
Dictionary of architecture & construction   720.3
A **dictionary** of Asian mythology. Leeming, D. A.   291.103
A **dictionary** of Buddhism. Keown, D.   294.3
Dictionary of Celtic mythology. MacKillop, J.   299
The **dictionary** of classical mythology. Grimal, P.   292
Dictionary of computer and Internet terms. Downing, D.   004
Dictionary of computer terms. See Downing, D. Dictionary of computer and Internet terms   004
Dictionary of confusable words   423
Dictionary of contemporary American artists. Cummings, P.   920.003
The **dictionary** of cultural literacy. See Hirsch, E. D. The new dictionary of cultural literacy   031
A **dictionary** of euphemisms. See Holder, R. W. How not to say what you mean   423
Dictionary of first names. Room, A.   929.4

A **dictionary** of folklore. Pickering, D.   398.2
Dictionary of foreign phrases and abbreviations. Guinagh, K.   422.03
Dictionary of Hispanic biography   920.003
The **dictionary** of imaginary places. Manguel, A.   809.3
Dictionary of Italian literature   850.3
A **dictionary** of language. Crystal, D.   410
Dictionary of languages. Dalby, A.   410
A **dictionary** of literary and thematic terms. Quinn, E.   803
A **dictionary** of literary terms and literary theory. Cuddon, J. A.   803
Dictionary of military terms   355
A **dictionary** of modern American usage. See Garner, B. A. Garner's modern American usage   423
A **dictionary** of names, nicknames, and surnames of persons, places, and things. Latham, E.   929.4
The **Dictionary** of national biography   920.003
Dictionary of Native American mythology. Gill, S. D.   299
Dictionary of phrase and fable, Brewer's   803
Dictionary of poetic terms. Myers, J. E.   808.1
Dictionary of poetry quotations   808.88
A **dictionary** of psychology. Colman, A. M.   150.3
A **dictionary** of quotations from Shakespeare. Shakespeare, W.   822.3
A **Dictionary** of quotations in mathematics   510
Dictionary of scientific biography   920.003
A **dictionary** of slang and unconventional English. Partridge, E.   427
The **dictionary** of space technology. See Angelo, J. A. The Facts on File dictionary of space technology   629.4
Dictionary of space technology. See Williamson, M. The Cambridge dictionary of space technology   629.4
Dictionary of symbolism. Biedermann, H.   302.2
Dictionary of symbols. Liungman, C. G.   302.2
Dictionary of symbols. Tresidder, J.   302.2
A **dictionary** of the ancient Greek world. See Sacks, D. Encyclopedia of the ancient Greek world   938.003
Dictionary of the Holocaust. Epstein, E. J.   940.53
Dictionary of the Middle Ages   940.1
A **dictionary** of the Middle East. Hiro, D.   956
Dictionary of the Napoleonic wars. Pope, S.   940.2
Dictionary of the social sciences   300.3
Dictionary of wars. Kohn, G. C.   355
Dictionary of women artists   920.003
Dictionary of world biography   920.003
A **dictionary** of world mythology. Cotterell, A.   291.103
Did Adam and Eve have navels? Gardner, M.   500
Diderot, Denis, 1713-1784
   See/See also pages in the following book(s):
Gay, P. The Enlightenment: an interpretation   190
Didion, Joan
   After Henry   814
   Fixed ideas: America since 9.11   320.5
   Where I was from   979.4
   The white album   814
   See/See also pages in the following book(s):
   Women writers at work p405-24   808
Didrikson, Babe *See* Zaharias, Babe Didrikson, 1911-1956
Diego Rivera. Hamill, P.   92
Diehl, Digby
   (jt. auth) Cole, N. Angel on my shoulder   92
Dierich, Mary
   Overcoming incontinence   616.6
Dierker, Larry, 1946-
   This ain't brain surgery   92

Diet
   See also Eating customs; Gluten-free diet
   Shintani, T. The good carbohydrate revolution   613.2
Diet and nutrition sourcebook . . .   613.2
Diet in disease
   Hagman, B. The gluten-free gourmet   641.5
Diet therapy
   See also Cancer—Diet therapy; Diabetes—Diet therapy; Heart diseases—Diet therapy
   Janowitz, H. D. Good food for bad stomachs   616.3
   Marks, D. R. The headache prevention cookbook   616.8
   Pescatore, F. The allergy and asthma cure   616.97
Dietary supplements
   Kuhn, C. Pumped   617.1
   Talbott, S. A guide to understanding dietary supplements   615
Dietrich, Marlene, 1901-1992
   About
   Riva, M. Marlene Dietrich   92
Diets, Reducing *See* Weight loss
Dietz, Howard, 1896-1983
   See/See also pages in the following book(s):
   Green, S. The world of musical comedy   920
Dietz, Maggie
   (ed) Americans' favorite poems. See Americans' favorite poems   808.81
   (ed) Poems to read. See Poems to read   808.81
Different hours. Dunn, S.   811
Difficult conversations. Stone, D.   158
Digital biology. Bentley, P. J.   570.1
Digital cameras
   Johnson, D. How to do everything with your digital camera   778.3
Digital photographer's handbook. Ang, T.   775
Digital photography *See* Photography—Digital techniques
Digital subscriber lines
   Bourne, J. DSL: a Wiley tech brief   621.382
Digital videodiscs
   Mayo, M. VideoHound's DVD guide   791.43
   Wiener, T. The off-Hollywood film guide   791.43
Dignen, Sheila
   (ed) The Oxford dictionary of allusions. See The Oxford dictionary of allusions   803
Dilbert (Comic strip)
   Adams, S. The Dilbert principle   650.1
The **Dilbert** principle. Adams, S.   650.1
Dilip Hiro *See* Hiro, Dilip
Dillard, Annie
   An American childhood   92
   The Annie Dillard reader   818
   For the time being   814
   Holy the firm
     In Dillard, A. The Annie Dillard reader   818
   Mornings like this   811
   Teaching a stone to talk   818
   The writing life   92
   (ed) Modern American memoirs. See Modern American memoirs   810.8
Dillard, James
   The chronic pain solution   616
Dillehay, Tom D.
   The settlement of the Americas   970.01
Diller, Lawrence H.
   Running on Ritalin   618.92
Dillon, Katherine V.
   (jt. auth) Goldstein, D. M. D-Day Normandy   940.54
   (jt. auth) Goldstein, D. M. The Vietnam war: the story and photographs   959.704
   (jt. auth) Goldstein, D. M. The way it was   940.54

Dillon, Katherine V.—*Continued*
(jt. auth) Prange, G. W. At dawn we slept
940.54
(jt. auth) Prange, G. W. Miracle at Midway
940.54
DiMaggio, Dom, 1917-
See/See also pages in the following book(s):
Halberstam, D. The teammates 920
DiMaggio, Joe
About
Cramer, R. B. Joe DiMaggio 92
Dimension, Fourth See Fourth dimension
Dimitrius, Jo-Ellan
Reading people 155.2
Diner, Steven J., 1944-
A very different age 973.8
The **diner's** dictionary. See Ayto, J. An A-Z of food and drink 641.03
Dinesen, Isak, 1885-1962
Letters from Africa, 1914-1931 92
Out of Africa 967.62
also in Dinesen, I. Out of Africa and Shadows on the grass 967.62
Out of Africa and Shadows on the grass 967.62
Shadows on the grass
In Dinesen, I. Out of Africa and Shadows on the grass 967.62
About
Thurman, J. Isak Dinesen 92
Dingle, Barbara
(jt. auth) Travis, D. Debbie Travis' painted house
698
Dingus, Lowell
(jt. auth) Chiappe, L. M. Walking on eggs 567.9
The **Dinner** Club. Henry, S. 338.7
Dinosaur encyclopedia. Lambert, D. 567.9
Dinosaur in a haystack. Gould, S. J. 508
Dinosaurs
Alvarez, W. T. rex and the Crater of Doom
551.7
Chiappe, L. M. Walking on eggs 567.9
Fiffer, S. Tyrannosaurus Sue 567.9
Gillette, D. D. Seismosaurus 567.9
Haines, T. Walking with dinosaurs 567.9
Lambert, D. The ultimate dinosaur book 567.9
Larson, P. L. Rex appeal 567.9
Nothdurft, W. E. The lost dinosaurs of Egypt
567.9
Powell, J. L. Night comes to the Cretaceous
576.8
Rea, T. Bone wars 560
The Scientific American book of dinosaurs 567.9
Encyclopedias
Encyclopedia of dinosaurs 567.9
Glut, D. F. Dinosaurs, the encyclopedia 567.9
Lambert, D. Dinosaur encyclopedia 567.9
Dinosaurs, the encyclopedia. Glut, D. F. 567.9
Diplomacy
Kissinger, H. Diplomacy 327.73
Diplomats
Dictionaries
Notable U.S. ambassadors since 1775 920.003
Dippie, Brian W.
The Frederic Remington Art Museum collection
92
Direction (Motion pictures) See Motion pictures—Production and direction
Direction (Theater) See Theater—Production and direction
Direction sense
See also Navigation
Jonsson, E. Inner navigation 153.7
Directories
See also subjects and names of countries, cities, etc., with the subdivision *Directories*

Directories in print 060.25
Directories in print 060.25
The **Directory** for exceptional children 371.9
Directory of directories. See Directories in print
060.25
Directory of family associations. Bentley, E. P.
929
Directory of financial aids for women. Schlachter, G. A.
378.3
Directory of historical organizations in the United States and Canada 973.06
Directory of historical societies and agencies in the United States and Canada. See Directory of historical organizations in the United States and Canada
973.06
The **Directory** of mail order catalogs 016.381
Directory of medical specialists. See The Official ABMS directory of board certified medical specialists
610.69
Directory of national trade and professional associations of the United States. See National trade and professional associations of the United States 061.025
Directory of online databases. See Gale directory of databases 025.04
Directory of physicians in the United States 610.69
Directory of portable databases. See Gale directory of databases 025.04
Directory of special libraries and information centers
026
Dirigible balloons See Airships
Dirr, Michael
Dirr's Hardy trees and shrubs 635.9
Dirr's trees and shrubs for warm climates 635.9
Dirr's Hardy trees and shrubs. Dirr, M. 635.9
Dirr's trees and shrubs for warm climates. Dirr, M.
635.9
Dirty hands. Sartre, J. P.
In Sartre, J. P. No exit, and three other plays
842
DiSabato-Aust, Tracy
The well-tended perennial garden 635.9
Disabled See Handicapped
Disadvantaged children See Socially handicapped children
Disaster!. Kurzman, D. 979.4
Disaster relief
See also Food relief
Disasters
See also Accidents; Natural disasters
Davis, L. A. Environmental disasters 363.7
Davis, L. A. Man-made catastrophes 904
Evan, W. M. Minding the machines 620.8
Garner, J. We interrupt this broadcast 070.1
Junger, S. Fire 909.82
Discipline of children See Child rearing
Discovered lands, invented pasts 759.13
The **discoverers.** Boorstin, D. J. 909
Discoveries (in geography) See Exploration
Discovering annuals. Rice, G. 635.9
The **discovery** and conquest of Mexico, 1517-1521. Díaz del Castillo, B. 972
The **discovery** of being. May, R. 150.19
The **discovery** of the Titanic. Ballard, R. D. 910.4
Discrimination
See also Hate crimes; Race discrimination; Sex discrimination
Discrimination in education
See also Segregation in education
Kozol, J. Death at an early age 306.43
Discrimination in employment
See also Affirmative action programs
Discussion See Negotiation
Disease germs See Bacteria; Germ theory of disease

Diseases
   See also Anthrax; Sick; names of specific diseases and groups of diseases; and subjects with the subdivision *Diseases*
   Boaz, N. T. Evolving health   **616.07**
   Grob, G. N. The deadly truth   **616**
   See/See also pages in the following book(s):
   The Cambridge world history of food   **641.3**
Diseases of children *See* Children—Diseases
Displaced persons *See* Refugees
Disraeli, Benjamin, Earl of Beaconsfield, 1804-1881
   See/See also pages in the following book(s):
   Strachey, L. Queen Victoria p327-66   **92**
Dissection
   Roach, M. Stiff   **611**
Dissent
   Buruma, I. Bad elements   **951.05**
Dissertations
   Turabian, K. L. A manual for writers of term papers, theses, and dissertations   **808**
   Turabian, K. L. Student's guide for writing college papers   **808**
A **distant** mirror. Tuchman, B. W.   **944**
Distant neighbors. Riding, A.   **972.08**
The **distinctive** home. Eck, J.   **728**
Distinguished African Americans in aviation and space science. Gubert, B. K.   **920.003**
Disturbing the solar system. Rubin, A. E.   **521**
The **disuniting** of America. Schlesinger, A. M.   **973**
Ditkoff, Beth Ann
   The thyroid guide   **616.4**
Diva. Campo, R.   **811**
La **diva** nicotina. See Gately, I. Tobacco   **394.1**
Diven, Gail
   (jt. auth) Breiter, B. The complete idiot's guide to knitting and crocheting   **746.43**
Diversified corporations *See* Conglomerate corporations
Diversity, Biological *See* Biological diversity
The **diversity** of life. Wilson, E. O.   **577**
Divination
   I ching. The classic of changes   **299**
The **divine** comedy. Dante Alighieri   **851**
   also in Dante Alighieri. The portable Dante   **851**
The **divine** comedy of Dante Alighieri. Dante Alighieri   **851**
The **divine** milieu. Teilhard de Chardin, P.   **230**
Divino, Cynthia L.
   (jt. auth) Freedman, M. R. Living well with asthma   **616.2**
Divorce
   See also Children of divorced parents; Remarriage
   Gardner, R. A. The parents book about divorce   **306.89**
   Wallerstein, J. S. Second chances   **306.89**
   See/See also pages in the following book(s):
   Pollack, W. S. Real boys p364-88   **305.23**
   Law and legislation
   Sitarz, D. Divorce yourself   **346.01**
   Woodhouse, V. Divorce and money   **346.01**
Divorce and money. Woodhouse, V.   **346.01**
Divorce mediation
   See also Child support
Divorce yourself. Sitarz, D.   **346.01**
Dixie, Quinton Hosford
   (jt. auth) Williams, J. This far by faith   **200**
Dixie rising. Applebome, P.   **973.929**
Dixon, Andrew Graham- *See* Graham-Dixon, Andrew
Djerassi, Carl
   This man's pill   **613.9**
Djupe, Paul A.
   Encyclopedia of American religion and politics   **322**
DK ultimate visual dictionary. See Ultimate visual dictionary   **423**

DLB-269 (Barge)
   See/See also pages in the following book(s):
   Krieger, M. J. All the men in the sea   **910.4**
DNA
   Watson, J. D. DNA: the secret of life   **576.5**
   Watson, J. D. The double helix   **572.8**
   See/See also pages in the following book(s):
   Friedman, M. Medicine's 10 greatest discoveries   **610.9**
   Maddox, B. Rosalind Franklin: the dark lady of DNA   **92**
DNA fingerprinting
   Lee, H. C. Blood evidence   **614**
Do-it-yourself housebuilding. Nash, G.   **690**
Doan, Marlyn, 1936-
   The Sierra Club family outdoors guide   **796.5**
Dobard, Raymond
   (jt. auth) Tobin, J. Hidden in plain view   **973.7**
Dobkin, David S.
   (jt. auth) Ehrlich, P. R. The birder's handbook   **598**
Dobozin, Bruce
   (jt. auth) Young, S. Allergies   **616.97**
Dobroszycki, Lucjan
   (ed) The Chronicle of the Łódź ghetto, 1941-1944. See The Chronicle of the Łódź ghetto, 1941-1944   **943.8**
Dobson, Michael
   (ed) The Oxford companion to Shakespeare. See The Oxford companion to Shakespeare   **822.3**
Dobyns, Stephen, 1941-
   Pallbearers envying the one who rides   **811**
Doctor, Ronald M.
   The encyclopedia of phobias, fears, and anxieties   **616.85**
Doctor Atkins' new diet revolution. See Atkins, R. C. Dr. Atkins' new diet revolution   **613.2**
Doctor Faustus. Marlowe, C.   **822**
The **doctor** in spite of himself. Molière
   In Molière. The misanthrope, and other plays   **842**
Doctor Jazz. Carruth, H.   **811**
Doctor Susan Love's breast book. See Love, S. M. Dr Susan Love's breast book   **618.1**
Doctors *See* Physicians
The **Doctors** book of home remedies   **616.02**
The **Doctor's** book of home remedies for dogs and cats   **636.7**
The **doctors** book of home remedies for seniors. Dollemore, D.   **613**
Doctrinal theology
   Davies, B. The thought of Thomas Aquinas   **230**
Documentary photography
   National Geographic photographs   **779**
   New York September 11   **974.7**
   Photographs then and now   **779**
   Sontag, S. Regarding the pain of others   **303.6**
   Through the lens   **779**
Documents of American Indian diplomacy   **970.004**
DOD *See* United States. Dept. of Defense
Dodge, Hazel
   (jt. auth) Connolly, P. The ancient city   **937**
Dodge, Norton T., 1927-
   About
   McPhee, J. A. The ransom of Russian art   **709.47**
Dodgers (Baseball team) *See* Brooklyn Dodgers (Baseball team)
Dodgson, Charles Lutwidge *See* Carroll, Lewis, 1832-1898
Dodman, Nicholas H.
   Dogs behaving badly   **636.7**
Dodson, Bert
   (jt. auth) Hoagland, M. B. The way life works   **570**

Dodson, James
(jt. auth) Palmer, A. A golfer's life   92
Doerr, Bobby, 1918-
See/See also pages in the following book(s):
Halberstam, D. The teammates   920
Doerr, Karin, 1951-
(jt. auth) Michael, R. Nazi-Deutsch/Nazi-German
          943.086
Does America need a foreign policy? Kissinger, H.
          327.73
Does it run in the family? Teichler-Zallen, D.   616
Does my child have a speech problem? Martin, K. L.
          618.92
Does stress damage the brain? Bremner, J. D.
          616.85
The **dog** department. Thurber, J.   818
Dog owner's home veterinary handbook. Giffin, J. M.
          636.7
Dog owner's manual. Fogle, B.   636.7
Dog racing
     See also Iditarod Trail Sled Dog Race, Alaska
The **dog** with the chip in his neck. Codrescu, A.
          814
Dogs
     American Kennel Club. The complete dog book
          636.7
     Budiansky, S. The truth about dogs   636.7
     Coppinger, R. Dogs   636.7
     Coren, S. Why we love the dogs we do   636.7
     Dibra, B. Dogspeak   636.7
     The Doctor's book of home remedies for dogs and cats
          636.7
     Dodman, N. H. Dogs behaving badly   636.7
     Dogs: the ultimate care guide   636.7
     Fogle, B. ASPCA complete dog care manual
          636.7
     Fogle, B. Dog owner's manual   636.7
     Herriot, J. James Herriot's dog stories   636.7
     Lane, M. The Humane Society of the United States
          complete guide to dog care   636.7
     McGinnis, T. The well dog book   636.7
     Morris, D. Dogs: the ultimate dictionary of over 1,000
          dog breeds   636.7
     Morris, W. My dog Skip   92
     Palika, L. K.I.S.S. guide to raising a puppy   636.7
     Petspeak   636.089
     Ross, J. Adoptable dog   636.7
     Taylor, D. The ultimate dog book   636.7
     Thomas, E. M. The social lives of dogs   636.7
     Thurber, J. The dog department   818
     Wilcox, B. Atlas of dog breeds of the world
          636.7
          Diseases
     Giffin, J. M. Dog owner's home veterinary handbook
          636.7
     McGinnis, T. The well dog book   636.7
          Encyclopedias
     Coile, D. C. Encyclopedia of dog breeds   636.7
     Fogle, B. The new encyclopedia of the dog   636.7
          Training
     Fogle, B. New complete dog training manual
          636.7
     Monks of New Skete. How to be your dog's best
          friend   636.7
Dogs behaving badly. Dodman, N. H.   636.7
Dogs that know when their owners are coming home.
     Sheldrake, R.   133.8
Dogs: the ultimate care guide   636.7
Dogspeak. Dibra, B.   636.7
Doherty, P. C.
     Isabella and the strange death of Edward II   92
Doing our own thing. McWhorter, J. H.   306.44
Dojny, Brooke
     The New England cookbook   641.5

Dolan, Brian
     Ladies of the Grand Tour   910.4
Dollemore, Doug
     The doctors book of home remedies for seniors
          613
A **doll's** house. Ibsen, H.
     In Ibsen, H. The complete major prose plays p119-
          96   839.8
     In Ibsen, H. Ibsen: four major plays   839.8
Dolnick, Edward, 1952-
     Down the great unknown   979.1
Dolphins
     The Audubon Society field guide to North American
          fishes, whales, and dolphins   597
     Montgomery, S. Journey of the pink dolphins
          599.5
     Whales, dolphins, and porpoises   599.5
Domestic animals
     See also Pets
     Herriot, J. James Herriot's animal stories   636.089
Domestic architecture
     See also House construction; Prefabricated houses
     The Elements of style   721
     Lind, C. The Wright style   728
     McAlester, V. A field guide to American houses
          728
     Susanka, S. Creating the not so big house   728
     Wiencek, H. National Geographic guide to America's
          great houses   728.8
          Designs and plans
     Altman, A. Elderhouse: planning your best home ever
          728
     Bakker, R. Elderdesign   728
     Eck, J. The distinctive home   728
     Friedman, A. The adaptable house   728
     Jacobson, M. Patterns of home   728
     Small house designs   728
     Susanka, S. Not so big solutions for your home
          728
Domestic economic assistance
     See also Community development
Domestic finance *See* Personal finance
Domestic relations
     See also Family; Visitation rights (Domestic rela-
          tions)
     The American Bar Association guide to family law
          346.01
Domestic violence
     See also Child abuse; Wife abuse
     Domestic violence & child abuse sourcebook
          362.82
     Dutton, D. G. The batterer   362.82
Domestic violence & child abuse sourcebook
          362.82
Dominions, British *See* Commonwealth countries
Domitian, Emperor of Rome, 51-96
     See/See also pages in the following book(s):
     Suetonius Tranquillus, C. The twelve Caesars   878
Don Juan. Byron, G. G. B., 6th Baron   821
Don Juan. Molière
     In Molière. Tartuffe, and other plays   842
Doña Rosita, the spinster. García Lorca, F.
     In Garcia Lorca, F. Five plays p131-90   862
Donald, David Herbert, 1920-
     Lincoln   92
Donegan, Francis
     Paint your home   698
Dong, Stella
     Shanghai, 1842-1949   951
Donia, Robert J.
     Bosnia and Hercegovina   949.7
Doniach, N. S.
     (ed) The Oxford English-Arabic dictionary of current
          usage. See The Oxford English-Arabic dictionary of
          current usage   492

Doniger, Wendy
(ed) Merriam-Webster's encyclopedia of world religions. See Merriam-Webster's encyclopedia of world religions **200.3**
Donn, Linda
The Roosevelt cousins **920**
Donnan, Kristin
(jt. auth) Larson, P. L. Rex appeal **567.9**
Donne, John, 1572-1631
The complete poetry and selected prose of John Donne **828**

See/See also pages in the following book(s):
Brooks, C. The well wrought urn **821.009**
Woolf, V. The second common reader p17-31 **820.9**

Donofrio, Beverly
Looking for Mary, or, The Blessed Mother and me **282**
Donovan, Denis M.
What did I just say!?! **649**
Don't go to the cosmetics counter without me. Begoun, P. **646.7**
Don't know much about the Bible. Davis, K. C. **220.6**
Don't let's go to the dogs tonight. Fuller, A. **92**
Doo-dah!: Stephen Foster and the rise of American popular culture. Emerson, K. **92**
Doolittle, Hilda See H. D. (Hilda Doolittle), 1886-1961
Doolittle, James Harold, 1896-1993
I could never be so lucky again **92**
About
Nelson, C. The first heroes **940.54**
Doomed in Afghanistan. Corwin, P. **958.1**
Door wide open. Kerouac, J. **92**
Doors (Musical group)
Hopkins, J. No one here gets out alive **92**
Dorland's illustrated medical dictionary **610.3**
Dorling Kindersley ultimate visual dictionary. See Ultimate visual dictionary **423**
Doron, Mia Wechsler
(jt. auth) Linden, D. W. Preemies **618.92**
Dorril, Stephen
MI6 **327.12**
Dorris, Michael
The broken cord **362.292**
See/See also pages in the following book(s):
Coltelli, L. Winged words: American Indian writers speak **897**
Dos Passos, John
See/See also pages in the following book(s):
Kazin, A. An American procession p374-87 **810.9**
Dosick, Wayne D., 1947-
Golden rules **649**
Dostoevskii, Fedor Mikhaĭlovich See Dostoyevsky, Fyodor, 1821-1881
Dostoyevsky, Fyodor, 1821-1881
About
Frank, J. Dostoevsky **92**
See/See also pages in the following book(s):
Existentialism from Dostoevsky to Sartre p52-82 **142**
Nabokov, V. V. Lectures on Russian literature **891.7**
Ozick, C. Quarrel & quandary **814**
Dot.con. Cassidy, J. **381**
The **double** bond: Primo Levi, a biography. Angier, C. **92**
Double down. Barthelme, F. **92**
The **Double-edged** helix **599.93**
Double fold. Baker, N. **025.2**
The **double** helix. Watson, J. D. **572.8**
Double victory. Takaki, R. T. **940.53**
Doubleday (Henry) Research Association See Henry Doubleday Research Association
The **Doubleday** prayer collection **242**

The **Doubleday** Roget's thesaurus in dictionary form **423**
Doubt See Belief and doubt
Douglas, Aaron, 1898-1979
See/See also pages in the following book(s):
Harlem Renaissance: art of black America **709.73**
Douglas, Ann, 1963-
The mother of all baby books **649**
Douglas, John E.
The cases that haunt us **364.1**
Douglas, Kirk, 1916-
My stroke of luck **92**
Douglas, Marjory Stoneman
The Everglades: river of grass **577.6**
Douglas, William O. (William Orville), 1898-1980
About
Murphy, B. A. Wild Bill: the legend and life of William O. Douglas **92**
Douglass, Frederick, 1817?-1895
Autobiographies **92**
Frederick Douglass **326**
Life and times of Frederick Douglass
In Douglass, F. Autobiographies **92**
My bondage and my freedom **92**
also in Douglass, F. Autobiographies **92**
Narrative of the life of Frederick Douglass, an American slave **92**
also in Douglass, F. Autobiographies **92**
See/See also pages in the following book(s):
Abdul-Jabbar, K. Black profiles in courage p73-91 **920**
Russell, D. Black genius and the American experience **920**
Dove, Rita
On the bus with Rosa Parks **811**
Selected poems **811**
Dover, Jeffrey S.
(jt. auth) Turkington, C. The encyclopedia of skin and skin disorders **616.5**
Dower, John W.
Embracing defeat **952.04**
Dowling, John E.
Creating mind **612.8**
Down syndrome
Selikowitz, M. Down syndrome **618.92**
Down the great unknown. Dolnick, E. **979.1**
Down the highway: the life of Bob Dylan. Sounes, H. **92**
Downer, Lesley
Women of the pleasure quarters **952**
Downes, John
Barron's finance & investment handbook **332.6**
Downey, Scott
(jt. auth) Bennett, J. The complete snowboarder **796.9**
Downfall. Frank, R. B. **940.54**
Downie, David
Cooking the Roman way **641.5**
Downie, Leonard, 1942-
The news about the news **071**
Downing, David C.
The most reluctant convert: C. S. Lewis's journey to faith **92**
Downing, Douglas
Dictionary of computer and Internet terms **004**
Downsize this!. Moore, M. **817**
Dowrick, Stephanie
Forgiveness and other acts of love **248.4**
Doyle, Sir Arthur Conan, 1859-1930
About
Stashower, D. Teller of tales: the life of Arthur Conan Doyle **92**
Doyle, Conan See Doyle, Sir Arthur Conan, 1859-1930
Dozier, Rush W., Jr.
Fear itself **152.4**

Dr. Atkins' age-defying diet revolution. Atkins, R. C.
613

Dr. Atkins' new diet revolution. Atkins, R. C.
613.2

Dr. Earl Mindell's unsafe at any meal. Mindell, E.
613.2

Dr. Eckener's dream machine. Botting, D.   629.133

Dr. Melissa Palmer's guide to hepatitis & liver disease. Palmer, M.   616.3

Dr. Richard Marr's fertility book. Marrs, R. P.
616.6

Dr. Seuss *See* Seuss, Dr.

Dr. Seuss & Mr. Geisel. Morgan, J.   92

Dr. Spock on parenting. Spock, B.   649

Dr. Spock's the first two years. Spock, B.   649

Dr. Spock's the school years. Spock, B.   649

Dr Susan Love's breast book. Love, S. M.   618.1

Dr. Susan Love's hormone book. See Love, S. M. Dr. Susan Love's menopause and hormone book
618.1

Dr. Susan Love's menopause and hormone book. Love, S. M.   618.1

Drabble, Margaret, 1939-
(ed) The Oxford companion to English literature. See The Oxford companion to English literature
820.3

Dracos, Ted
Ungodly: the passions, torments, and murder of atheist Madalyn Murray O'Hair   92

Drager, Kerry
Scenic photography 101   770.2

The **dragon** in the land of snows. Tsering Shakya
951

Dragons
Encyclopedias
Rose, C. Giants, monsters, and dragons   398.03

The **dragons** of Eden. Sagan, C.   153

Drake, Sir Francis, 1540?-1596
About
Bawlf, R. S. The secret voyage of Sir Francis Drake, 1577-1580   910.4

Cummins, J. G. Francis Drake   92

Drakulić, Slavenka
Café Europa   947

Drama
See also American drama; Comedy; English drama; Motion picture plays; Mysteries and miracle plays; One act plays; Tragedy

The Best stage scenes of [year]   808.82

Brook, P. The empty space   792

Collections
The Best American short plays   812.008

The Best plays of [date]   808.82

Nine plays of the modern theater   808.82

Our dramatic heritage v4-6   808.82

Dictionaries
Critical survey of drama   809.2

History and criticism
Bentley, E. The life of the drama   809.2

Brockett, O. G. History of the theatre   792.09

Masterplots II, drama series   809.2

Indexes
Ottemiller's index to plays in collections   808.82

Play index   808.82

Stories, plots, etc.
Masterplots II, drama series   809.2

Technique
Straczynski, J. M. The complete book of scriptwriting
808.2

Dramatists
Playwrights at work   812.009

Terkel, S. The spectator   791

Dramatists, American
Dictionaries
Contemporary dramatists   920.003

Dramatists, English
Dictionaries
Contemporary dramatists   920.003

Dranov, Paula
(jt. auth) West, S. The hysterectomy hoax   618.1

Drape, Joe
The race for the Triple Crown   798.4

Draper, James P., 1959-
(ed) Black literature criticism. See Black literature criticism   809

Draper, Theodore, 1912-
A struggle for power   973.3

Drawing
See also Artistic anatomy; Figure drawing; Pastel drawing

Harrison, H. Master strokes, Pastels   741.2

Hockney, D. Secret knowledge   751

Drawing down the moon. Adler, M.   133.4

Drawing the line. Wise, S. M.   179

Drawn with the sword. McPherson, J. M.   973.7

Dray, Philip
At the hands of persons unknown   364.1

Dreadnought. Massie, R. K.   940.3

The **dream** encyclopedia. Lewis, J. R.   154.6

Dream makers, dream breakers: the world of Justice Thurgood Marshall. Rowan, C. T.   92

The **dream** of eternal life. Benecke, M.   612.6

The **dream** of reason. Gottlieb, A.   180

The **dream** of the unified field. Graham, J.   811

A **dream** play. Strindberg, A.
In Our dramatic heritage v5   808.82

In Strindberg, A. Strindberg: five plays p205-64
839.7

The **dream** songs. Berryman, J.   811

Dreamers of dreams. Simon, J. I.   809.1

Dreaming with his eyes open: a life of Diego Rivera. Marnham, P.   92

Dreamland. Sachar, H. M.   940

Dreams
See also Sleep
Alvarez, A. Night   154.6

Freud, S. Interpretation of dreams   154.6

Jung, C. G. Man and his symbols   150.19

Parker, J. Parkers' complete book of dreams
154.6

See/See also pages in the following book(s):
Freud, S. The basic writings of Sigmund Freud
150.19

Encyclopedias
Lewis, J. R. The dream encyclopedia   154.6

Dreamscaping. Clausen, R. R.   712

Dreiser, Theodore, 1871-1945
About
A Theodore Dreiser encyclopedia   813.009

See/See also pages in the following book(s):
Kazin, A. An American procession p235-45   810.9

Dress *See* Clothing and dress

Dress codes of three girlhoods—my mother's, my father's, and mine. Howey, N.   306.8

Dress in North America v1. De Marly, D.   391

Dresser, Norine
Multicultural manners   395

The **dressing** station. Kaplan, J.   92

Dressler, Joshua
(ed) Encyclopedia of crime & justice. See Encyclopedia of crime & justice   364.03

Dressmaking
See also Needlework
Betzina, S. Fabric savvy   646.2

Betzina, S. Power sewing step-by-step   646.4

The Complete book of sewing   646.4

Hunnisett, J. Period costume for stage & screen
391

Dressmaking—*Continued*
Patterns
Armstrong, H. J. Patternmaking for fashion design
646.4
Drew, Elizabeth
Citizen McCain [biography of John McCain] 92
The corruption of American politics 364.1
Drexler, Madeline, 1954-
Secret agents 614.4
Dreyfus, Alfred, 1859-1935
About
Bredin, J.-D. The affair 944.081
Derfler, L. The Dreyfus affair 944.081
See/See also pages in the following book(s):
Tuchman, B. W. The proud tower p171-226
909.82
The **Dreyfus** affair. Derfler, L. 944.081
Dreyfuss, Henry, 1904-1979
Symbol sourcebook 302.2
Dried flowers *See* Flowers—Drying
Drinking problem *See* Alcoholism
Driscoll, Jeanne Watson
(jt. auth) Sichel, D. Women's moods 616.89
Driven to distraction. Hallowell, E. M. 616.85
Driving force. Livingston, J. D. 538
Driving Mr. Albert. Paterniti, M. 917.3
Driving over lemons. Stewart, C. 946
The **drowned** and the saved. Levi, P. 940.53
Drucker, Peter Ferdinand, 1909-
Management challenges for the 21st century 658
Managing in a time of great change 658
Managing the non-profit organization 658
Drug abuse
See also Hallucinogens
Beattie, M. Beyond codependency 616.86
Beattie, M. Codependents' guide to the twelve steps
616.86
Chopra, D. Overcoming addictions 616.86
Courtwright, D. T. Forces of habit 362.29
Davenport-Hines, R. P. T. The pursuit of oblivion
363.45
De Quincey, T. The confessions of an English opium-
eater 824
Drug abuse sourcebook 362.29
Drugs and controlled substances 616.86
Henderson, E. C. Understanding addiction 362.29
Kuhn, C. Buzzed 615
Streatfeild, D. Cocaine 362.29
Substance abuse sourcebook 616.86
West, J. W. The Betty Ford Center book of answers
616.86
Encyclopedias
Chepesiuk, R. The war on drugs 363.45
Miller, R. L. The encyclopedia of addictive drugs
615
Drug abuse sourcebook 362.29
Drug industry
Sargent, W. Crab wars 333.95
Talbott, S. A guide to understanding dietary supple-
ments 615
Drug plants *See* Medical botany
Drug trade, Illicit *See* Drug traffic
Drug traffic
Davenport-Hines, R. P. T. The pursuit of oblivion
363.45
Streatfeild, D. Cocaine 362.29
Encyclopedias
Chepesiuk, R. The war on drugs 363.45
Drugs
See also Hallucinogens; Materia medica; Narcotics;
Psychotropic drugs
Consumer drug reference 615
Drugs and controlled substances 616.86
Kuhn, C. Buzzed 615

Long, J. W. The essential guide to prescription drugs
615
The Merck index 615
Encyclopedias
Miller, R. L. The encyclopedia of addictive drugs
615
Drugs, Nonprescription *See* Nonprescription drugs
Drugs, Psychotropic *See* Psychotropic drugs
Drugs and controlled substances 616.86
Drugs and crime
See also Drug traffic
Drugs and sports *See* Athletes—Drug use
Druick, Douglas W.
Van Gogh and Gauguin 92
The **drunken** boat. Rimbaud, A.
In Rimbaud, A. A season in hell & The drunken
boat p92-103 841
Druyan, Ann, 1949-
(jt. auth) Sagan, C. Comet 523.6
(jt. auth) Sagan, C. Shadows of forgotten ancestors
570.1
Dry, Sarah
Curie 92
Dry goods *See* Fabrics
Dryden, John, 1631-1700
All for love 822
also in Restoration plays 822.008
See/See also pages in the following book(s):
Durant, W. J. The age of Louis XIV p321-28
940.2
DSL *See* Digital subscriber lines
DSL: a Wiley tech brief. Bourne, J. 621.382
D'Souza, Dinesh, 1961-
Ronald Reagan 92
**Du Bois, W. E. B. (William Edward Burghardt),
1868-1963**
Dusk of dawn
In Du Bois, W. E. B. Writings 818
The Oxford W. E. B. Du Bois reader 305.8
The souls of black folk 305.8
also in Du Bois, W. E. B. The Oxford W. E. B. Du
Bois reader p97-240 305.8
also in Du Bois, W. E. B. Writings 818
The suppression of the African slave-trade
In Du Bois, W. E. B. Writings 818
Writings 818
About
Gates, H. L. The future of the race 305.8
Lewis, D. L. W.E.B. DuBois 92
Du Bois, William Edward Burghardt *See* Du Bois, W.
E. B. (William Edward Burghardt), 1868-1963
Du Pré, Jacqueline, 1945-1987
About
Wilson, E. Jacqueline du Pré 92
Dual-career families
Deutsch, F. Halving it all 649
Duany, Andres
Suburban nation 307.7
Dubner, Stephen J.
Turbulent souls 92
Dubner family
About
Dubner, S. J. Turbulent souls 92
Dubofsky, Melvyn, 1934-
Labor in America 331.8
Duby, Georges
(ed) A History of private life. See A History of private
life 909
Duchamp, Marcel, 1887-1968
About
Tomkins, C. Duchamp 92
Duckett, Eleanor Shipley
Alfred the Great 92
Dudevant, Amantine Lucile Aurore Dupin *See* Sand,
George, 1804-1876

Duffield, Mary Rose
Plants for dry climates   635.9
Duffy, Eamon
Saints & sinners   282
Dugan, Alan, 1923-2003
Poems seven   811
Dugan, Robert E.
(jt. auth) Hernon, P. U.S. government on the Web
    025.04
Dugard, Martin
Into Africa   92
Dugatkin, Lee Alan, 1962-
Cheating monkeys and citizen bees   591.56
Duiker, William J., 1932-
Ho Chi Minh   92
Duino elegies. Rilke, R. M.   831
Duke, Patty
A brilliant madness   616.89
Duke University
Toor, R. Admissions confidential   378.1
Dull Knife, Cheyenne Chief, ca. 1828-1879 or 1883
See/See also pages in the following book(s):
Brown, D. A. The American West p240-46   978
Dulles, Allen Welsh, 1893-1969
About
Grose, P. Gentleman spy: the life of Allen Dulles
    92
Dulles, Foster Rhea, 1900-1970
(jt. auth) Dubofsky, M. Labor in America   331.8
The **dumb** waiter. Pinter, H.
In Pinter, H. Complete works v1   822
Dunaway, David King
How can I keep from singing: Pete Seeger   92
Dunbar, R. I. M. (Robin Ian MacDonald), 1947-
Grooming, gossip, and the evolution of language
    599.93
Dunbar, Robin Ian MacDonald *See* Dunbar, R. I. M.
(Robin Ian MacDonald), 1947-
Duncan, David Ewing
Calendar   529
Hernando de Soto   92
Duncan, Dayton
Lewis & Clark   978
(jt. auth) Ward, G. C. The West   978
Duncan, Isadora, 1878-1927
About
Kurth, P. Isadora   92
See/See also pages in the following book(s):
Life stories   920
Duncan, Robert Edward, 1919-1988
Ground work II   811
Dunea, George
(ed) The Oxford illustrated companion to medicine.
See The Oxford illustrated companion to medicine
    610.3
Dunham, William, 1947-
The mathematical universe   510
Dunn, Elsie *See* Scott, Evelyn, 1893-1963
Dunn, Erica H.
Birds at your feeder   598
Dunn, Ross E.
(jt. auth) Nash, G. B. History on trial   907
Dunn, Stephen, 1939-
Different hours   811
Local visitations   811
Loosestrife   811
Dunn, Susan, 1945-
Sister revolutions   973.3
(jt. auth) Burns, J. M. The three Roosevelts
    973.91
Dunnan, Nancy
(jt. auth) Tuckerman, N. The Amy Vanderbilt complete
book of etiquette   395
Dunne, Dominick
Justice   345

Dunne, John Gregory, 1932-
Monster   791.43
Dunnigan, James F.
The Pacific War encyclopedia   940.54
Victory at sea   940.54
Dunning, John, 1942-
On the air   791.44
Duplacey, James
The official rules of hockey   796.962
DuPont, Kathryn Cullen- *See* Cullen-DuPont, Kathryn
DuPriest, Laura
Natural beauty   646.7
Dupuy, Trevor N., 1916-1995
(comp) Dictionary of military terms. See Dictionary of
military terms   355
Durant, Ariel, 1898-1981
(jt. auth) Durant, W. J. The age of Louis XIV
    940.2
Durant, William James, 1885-1981
The age of Louis XIV   940.2
The story of philosophy   109
Durham, Eddie, 1906-1987
See/See also pages in the following book(s):
Dance, S. The world of Count Basie   920
Durham, Michael S., 1935-
Desert between the mountains   979
Durkheim, Émile, 1858-1917
Suicide, a study in sociology   179.7
Durrell, Gerald M., 1925-1995
About
Botting, D. Gerald Durrell   92
Dürrenmatt, Friedrich
Plays and essays   838
Romulus the great
In Dürrenmatt, F. Plays and essays p1-69   838
The visit   832
also in Dürrenmatt, F. Plays and essays p71-152
    838
also in Nine plays of the modern theater p199-292
    808.82
Duse, Eleonora, 1858-1924
About
Sheehy, H. Eleonora Duse   92
Dusk of dawn. Du Bois, W. E. B.
In Du Bois, W. E. B. Writings   818
Dust
Holmes, H. The secret life of dust   551.51
Dust tracks on a road. Hurston, Z. N.   92
also in Hurston, Z. N. Folklore, memoirs, and other
writings   818
Dutch-English, English-Dutch dictionary   439.3
Dutch language
Dictionaries
Dutch-English, English-Dutch dictionary   439.3
Osselton, N. E. The new Routledge Dutch dictionary
    439.3
Dutch painting
Liedtke, W. A. Vermeer and the Delft school
    759.9492
Dutchman. Baraka, I. A.
In Baraka, I. A. Dutchman, and The slave p1-38
    812
In Baraka, I. A. The LeRoi Jones/Amiri Baraka read-
er   818
Dutchman, and The slave. Baraka, I. A.   812
Dutton, Donald G., 1943-
The batterer   362.82
Dutton's nautical navigation   623.89
Dutton's navigation & piloting. See Dutton's nautical
navigation   623.89
Duty. Greene, B.   940.54
Duty first. Ruggero, E.   355
Duval, R. Shannon
(ed) Encyclopedia of ethics. See Encyclopedia of ethics
[Facts on File]   170

Duve, Christian de, 1917-
Life evolving   **576.8**
Vital dust   **570.1**
Duvoisin, Roger C., 1927-
Parkinson's disease   **616.8**
Duyff, Roberta Larson
American Dietetic Association complete food and nutrition guide   **613.2**
DVD (Digital videodiscs) *See* Digital videodiscs
Dwarfism
Richardson, J. H. In the little world   **599.9**
The **dwarfs**. Pinter, H.
In Pinter, H. Complete works v2   **822**
Dwork, Deborah
Holocaust: a history   **940.53**
Dwyer, Jim, 1957-
Actual innocence   **347**
Dwyer, William L., 1929-2002
In the hands of the people   **347**
Dyer, Alan
(jt. auth) Dickinson, T. The backyard astronomer's guide   **522**
Dyer, Davis
(ed) The Reader's companion to the American presidency. See The Reader's companion to the American presidency   **973**
Dyes and dyeing
Ball, P. Bright earth   **701**
Blumenthal, B. Hands on dyeing   **746.1**
Brown, R. The weaving, spinning, and dyeing book   **746.1**
Garfield, S. Mauve   **667**
Wells, K. Fabric dyeing & printing   **746.6**
Dying patients *See* Terminally ill
Dylan, Bob, 1941-
About
Shelton, R. No direction home: the life and music of Bob Dylan   **92**
Sounes, H. Down the highway: the life of Bob Dylan   **92**
Spitz, B. Dylan   **92**
Dymant, Dora *See* Diamant, Dora, d. 1952
Dynamics of faith. Tillich, P.   **234**
Dyson, Freeman J., 1923-
The sun, the genome, & the Internet   **303.4**
Dyson, George, 1953-
Project Orion   **629.47**
Dyson, Michael Eric
Holler if you hear me: searching for Tupac Shakur   **92**
I may not get there with you: the true Martin Luther King, Jr   **92**
Race rules   **305.8**

E

E=mc². Bodanis, D.   **530.1**
E-mail systems *See* Electronic mail systems
E.S.P. *See* Extrasensory perception
Each in his own way. Pirandello, L.
In Pirandello, L. Naked masks p277-361   **852**
Each in his season. Snodgrass, W. D.   **811**
Eads, James Buchanan, 1820-1887
See/See also pages in the following book(s):
Barry, J. M. Rising tide   **977**
Petroski, H. Engineers of dreams   **624**
Eady, Cornelius, 1954-
Brutal imagination   **811**
Eagle against the sun. Spector, R.   **940.54**
Eagles
See also Bald eagle
Eagle's plume. Beans, B. E.   **598**

Eakins, Thomas, 1844-1916
About
Thomas Eakins [exhibition catalog]   **759.13**
Eames, Charles
About
The Work of Charles and Ray Eames   **745.4**
Eames, Ray
About
The Work of Charles and Ray Eames   **745.4**
Ear
Diseases
Turkington, C. The encyclopedia of deafness and hearing disorders   **617.8**
Earhart, Amelia, 1898-1937
About
Butler, S. East to the dawn   **92**
Rich, D. L. Amelia Earhart   **92**
Ware, S. Still missing: Amelia Earhart and the search for modern feminism   **92**
See/See also pages in the following book(s):
Slung, M. B. Living with cannibals and other women's adventures   **910.4**
Earle, Alice Morse, 1851-1911
Child life in colonial days   **973.2**
Earle, Mary Alice Morse *See* Earle, Alice Morse, 1851-1911
The **earliest** relationship. Brazelton, T. B.   **155.4**
Early Christian & Byzantine art. Lowden, J.   **709.02**
Early church history *See* Church history—30-600, Early church
The **Early** Middle Ages to 1300
In New Oxford history of music v2   **780.9**
Earp, Wyatt, 1848-1929
About
Barra, A. Inventing Wyatt Earp   **92**
Tefertiller, C. Wyatt Earp   **92**
Earth
See also Gaia hypothesis
Asimov, I. Isaac Asimov's guide to earth & space   **520**
Earth almanac   **550**
Earth almanac   **550**
Earth in the balance. Gore, A., Jr.   **304.2**
Earth ponds A to Z. Matson, T.   **627**
Earth sciences
See also Geology
Earth almanac   **550**
Gates, A. E. A to Z of earth scientists   **920.003**
Morton, R. L. Music of the earth   **550**
Dictionaries
The Facts on File dictionary of earth science   **550.3**
The Oxford companion to the earth   **550.3**
Encyclopedias
Encyclopedia of earth and physical sciences   **500.2**
Encyclopedia of earth sciences   **550.3**
Environmental encyclopedia   **363.7**
The **earth** shall weep. Wilson, J.   **970.004**
Earthenware *See* Pottery
Earthly measures. Hirsch, E.   **811**
Earthquakes
Encyclopedias
Ritchie, D. Encyclopedia of earthquakes and volcanoes   **551.2**
California
Kurzman, D. Disaster!   **979.4**
The **earth's** biosphere. Smil, V.   **577**
East *See* Asia
East (Far East) *See* East Asia
East (Near East) *See* Middle East
East Asia
Fallows, J. M. Looking at the sun   **950**

East Asia—*Continued*
Religion
See/See also pages in the following book(s):
Teilhard de Chardin, P. Toward the future p134-47
    194

East European literature
Bio-bibliography
Segel, H. B. The Columbia guide to the literatures of
Eastern Europe since 1945   **809**
East Germany *See* Germany (East)
East India Company
Keay, J. The honourable company   **954.03**
Eastern Europe
Encyclopedia of Eastern Europe   **947**
History
Kaufman, J. A hole in the heart of the world
    947
Politics and government
Drakulić, S. Café Europa   **947**
Rosenberg, T. The haunted land   **947**
Stokes, G. The walls came tumbling down   **947**
Social conditions
Drakulić, S. Café Europa   **947**
Eastern question (Far East)
See also Russo-Japanese War, 1904-1905
Eastman, Mary Huse, 1870-1963
Index to fairy tales. See Index to fairy tales
    398.2
Easton, Robert, 1940-
(jt. auth) Nabokov, P. Native American architecture
    728
Eastwood, Clint
About
Schickel, R. Clint Eastwood   **92**
Easy and quick cookery *See* Quick and easy cooking
Easy riders, raging bulls. Biskind, P.   **791.43**
Easy to love, difficult to discipline. Bailey, R. A.
    649
Eat, drink and be healthy. Willett, W.   **613.2**
Eat the rich. O'Rourke, P. J.   **817**
Eating customs
Allen, S. L. In the devil's garden   **641**
Encyclopedia of food and culture   **394.1**
Haber, B. From hardtack to home fries   **394.1**
Mayle, P. French lessons   **394.1**
Wright, C. A. A Mediterranean feast   **641**
Eating disorders
See also Anorexia nervosa; Bulimia
Claude-Pierre, P. The secret language of eating disor-
ders   **616.85**
Normandi, C. E. It's not about food   **616.85**
Eating the honey of words. Bly, R.   **811**
Eating well for optimum health. Weil, A.   **613.2**
Eberhart, George M.
Mysterious creatures   **001.9**
Ebert, Roger
Roger Ebert's movie yearbook   **791.43**
(ed) Roger Ebert's book of film. See Roger Ebert's
book of film   **791.43**
Eble, Kenneth Eugene
F. Scott Fitzgerald   **813.009**
Ebner, Mark C.
(jt. auth) Knowles, H. Ain't it cool?   **791.43**
Ebola virus
Preston, R. The hot zone   **614.5**
See/See also pages in the following book(s):
Frist, W. H. When every moment counts   **613.6**
Garrett, L. The coming plague p100-54, 192-221
    614.4
Oldstone, M. B. A. Viruses, plagues, and history
    614.4
Eboshi-ori. Miyamasu
In Waley, A. The Nō plays of Japan   **895.6**
Ecclesiastical rites and ceremonies *See* Rites and cere-
monies

Ecclesiazusae. Aristophanes
In Aristophanes. The complete plays of Aristophanes
p417-62   **882**
Echevarría, Roberto González *See* González
Echevarría, Roberto
The **echo** of Greece. Hamilton, E.   **880.9**
Echoes among the stars. Walsh, P. J.   **629.4**
Echoes down the corridor. Miller, A.   **814**
Echoes of a native land. Schmemann, S.   **947**
Echoes of an autobiography. Maḥfūẓ, N.   **92**
Eck, Jeremiah
The distinctive home   **728**
Eckener, Hugo, 1868-1954
About
Botting, D. Dr. Eckener's dream machine   **629.133**
Eckert, Allan W., 1931-
A sorrow in our heart: the life of Tecumseh   **92**
Eco, Umberto
How to travel with a salmon & other essays   **854**
Ecological movement *See* Environmental movement
Ecology
See also Biological diversity; Environmental pro-
tection; Gaia hypothesis; types of ecology
Barlow, C. C. Green space, green time   **291.1**
Bright, C. Life out of bounds   **577**
Buchmann, S. The forgotten pollinators   **577**
Wilson, E. O. The diversity of life   **577**
See/See also pages in the following book(s):
Lewontin, R. C. The triple helix   **572.8**
Encyclopedias
Environmental encyclopedia   **363.7**
Life on earth   **333.95**
Ecology, Human *See* Human ecology
Economic botany
Coffey, T. The history and folklore of North American
wildflowers   **582.13**
Pollan, M. The botany of desire   **581.6**
Economic conditions
See also racial and ethnic groups, classes of per-
sons, and names of countries, cities, areas, etc., with
the subdivision Economic conditions
Kennedy, P. M. The rise and fall of the great powers
    909.08
Economic depressions *See* Depressions
Economic development
See also Economic conditions
Economic policy
United States
Berry, W. Citizenship papers   **338.1**
Economic relations, Foreign *See* International economic
relations
Economics
See also Consumption (Economics)
Fukuyama, F. Trust   **330.9**
Galbraith, J. K. The affluent society   **330**
Heilbroner, R. L. The worldly philosophers   **330.1**
Keynes, J. M. The general theory of employment, in-
terest and money   **330.1**
Marx, K. Capital   **330.1**
Smith, A. The wealth of nations   **330.1**
Sowell, T. Basic economics   **330**
Wheelan, C. J. Naked economics   **330**
Humor
O'Rourke, P. J. Eat the rich   **817**
Periodicals—Indexes
Business periodicals index   **650**
The **economics** and politics of race. Sowell, T.
    305.8
The **Economist** desk companion   **530.8**
Economists
Heilbroner, R. L. The worldly philosophers   **330.1**
Eddy, Mary Baker, 1821-1910
Science and health, with key to the Scriptures
    289.5

Eddy, Mary Baker, 1821-1910—*Continued*
About
Fraser, C. God's perfect child   **289.5**
Gill, G. Mary Baker Eddy   **92**
    See/See also pages in the following book(s):
Wills, G. Certain trumpets p173-82   **303.3**
Edelman, Hope
Motherless daughters   **155.9**
Edelman, Marian Wright
Lanterns   **92**
The measure of our success   **170**
Edey, Maitland Armstrong, 1910-1992
(jt. auth) Johanson, D. C. Lucy: the beginnings of humankind   **599.93**
Edgar, Blake
(jt. auth) Johanson, D. C. From Lucy to language   **599.93**
(jt. auth) Klein, R. G. The dawn of human culture   **599.93**
Edgar Allan Poe, A-Z. Sova, D. B.   **818**
Edge, John T.
A gracious plenty   **641.5**
The **edge** of the sea. Carson, R.   **577.7**
Edgerton, William Benbow, 1914-
(ed) Columbia dictionary of modern European literature. See Columbia dictionary of modern European literature   **803**
Edible plants
Angier, B. Field guide to edible wild plants   **581.6**
Chilies to chocolate   **641.3**
Gibbons, E. Stalking the wild asparagus   **581.6**
Thoreau, H. D. Wild fruits   **581.6**
Vaughan, J. G. The new Oxford book of food plants   **633**
    See/See also pages in the following book(s):
The Cambridge world history of food   **641.3**
Edison, Harry, 1915-1999
    See/See also pages in the following book(s):
Dance, S. The world of Count Basie   **920**
Edison, Sweets *See* Edison, Harry, 1915-1999
Edison, Thomas A. (Thomas Alva), 1847-1931
About
Israel, P. Edison   **92**
Edison's Eve. Wood, G.   **629.8**
Edith and Woodrow: the Wilson White House. Levin, P. L.   **92**
Edith Wharton abroad. Wharton, E.   **818**
Edmonds, David, 1964-
Wittgenstein's poker   **192**
(comp) The Oxford reverse dictionary. See The Oxford reverse dictionary   **423**
Edmonds, Margot
(jt. auth) Clark, E. E. Sacagawea of the Lewis and Clark expedition   **92**
Edney, A. T. B.
ASPCA complete cat care manual   **636.8**
Edney, Andrew *See* Edney, A. T. B.
Edouard Manet. Brombert, B. A.   **92**
Edouard Vuillard   **759.4**
Edson, Margaret
Wit   **812**
Education
    See also Colleges and universities; Elementary education; Special education; Teaching
    See/See also pages in the following book(s):
Pollack, W. S. Real boys p230-71   **305.23**
Tillich, P. Theology of culture   **230**
Toffler, A. Future shock p352-78   **303.4**
Aims and objectives
Kohn, A. The schools our children deserve   **371.2**
Bibliography
Education index   **370.5**

Curricula
    See also Colleges and universities—Curricula
    See/See also pages in the following book(s):
Goleman, D. Emotional intelligence p261-87   **152.4**
Encyclopedias
Encyclopedia of education   **370**
Periodicals—Indexes
Education index   **370.5**
Philosophy
Dewey, J. Democracy and education   **370.1**
Greece
    See/See also pages in the following book(s):
Hamilton, E. The echo of Greece p49-103   **880.9**
Robinson, C. E. Everyday life in ancient Greece   **938**
United States
Gross, M. L. The conspiracy of ignorance   **371**
Hirsch, E. D. The schools we need and why we don't have them   **370**
Kohn, A. The schools our children deserve   **371.2**
Postman, N. The end of education   **370**
United States—Directories
American universities and colleges   **378.73**
Barron's profiles of American colleges   **378.73**
The College blue book   **378.73**
College Entrance Examination Board. The college handbook   **378.73**
The Handbook of private schools   **370.25**
Patterson's American education   **370.25**
Peterson's competitive colleges   **378.73**
Peterson's guide to four-year colleges   **378.73**
Peterson's guide to two-year colleges   **378.73**
Peterson's private secondary schools   **373.2**
Private independent schools   **370.25**
United States—Encyclopedias
Unger, H. G. Encyclopedia of American education   **370**
Education, Discrimination in *See* Discrimination in education
Education, Elementary *See* Elementary education
Education, Higher *See* Higher education
Education, Intercultural *See* Multicultural education
Education, Segregation in *See* Segregation in education
Education index   **370.5**
The **education** of a woman: the life of Gloria Steinem. Heilbrun, C. G.   **92**
The **education** of Henry Adams. Adams, H.   **92**
Educational counseling
    See also Vocational guidance
Educational psychology
    See also Child psychology; Psychology of learning
Levine, M. D. A mind at a time   **370.15**
Montessori, M. The absorbent mind   **155.4**
Educational tests and measurements
    See also Ability—Testing; Intelligence tests
Edward II, King of England, 1284-1327
    See/See also pages in the following book(s):
Doherty, P. C. Isabella and the strange death of Edward II   **92**
Edward VI, King of England, 1537-1553
    See/See also pages in the following book(s):
Weir, A. The children of Henry VIII   **920**
Edward VII, King of Great Britain, 1841-1910
    See/See also pages in the following book(s):
Massie, R. K. Dreadnought   **940.3**
Edward Hopper and the American imagination   **759.13**
Edward Hopper: the watercolors. Mecklenburg, V. M.   **759.13**
Edward Steichen: the early years. Smith, J.   **779**
Edwards, Anne, 1927-
The Reagans: portrait of a marriage   **92**
Edwards, Elwyn Hartley
The new encyclopedia of the horse   **636.1**

Edwards, Elwyn Hartley—*Continued*
Ultimate horse   636.1
Edwards, Jonathan, 1703-1758
About
Marsden, G. M. Jonathan Edwards   92
Edwards, Paul, 1923-
(ed) The Encyclopedia of philosophy. See The Encyclopedia of philosophy   103
Edwards, Paul M., 1933-
The Korean War   951.9
Eerdmans dictionary of the Bible   220.3
Eerdmans' handbook to the world's religions   291
The **effect** of gamma rays on man-in-the-moon marigolds. Zindel, P.   812
Effort at speech. Meredith, W.   811
Egerton, John, 1935-
Speak now against the day   323.1
The **egg** and I. MacDonald, B.   818
Egielski, Richard
See/See also pages in the following book(s):
The Newbery & Caldecott medal books, 1986-2000 p47-52   028.5
Egolf, Karen
(ed) The Advertising age encyclopedia of advertising. See The Advertising age encyclopedia of advertising   659.1

Egypt
Antiquities
Aldred, C. Akhenaten: King of Egypt   932
Brier, B. Egyptian mummies   932
Egyptian art in the age of the pyramids   709.32
Egyptian treasures from the Egyptian Museum in Cairo   709.32
Hawass, Z. Valley of the golden mummies   932
Lepre, J. P. The Egyptian pyramids   932
The Quest for immortality   709.32
Robins, G. The art of ancient Egypt   709.32
Smith, W. S. The art and architecture of ancient Egypt   709.32
Verner, M. The pyramids   932
See/See also pages in the following book(s):
Ceram, C. W. Gods, graves, and scholars p75-207   930.1
Antiquities—Dictionaries
Bunson, M. R. Encyclopedia of ancient Egypt   932
Antiquities—Encyclopedias
The Oxford encyclopedia of ancient Egypt   932
Civilization
Assmann, J. The mind of Egypt   932
David, A. R. Handbook to life in ancient Egypt   932
Egypt: ancient culture, modern land   962
See/See also pages in the following book(s):
Said, E. W. Reflections on exile and other essays p153-64   814
Civilization—Dictionaries
Bunson, M. R. Encyclopedia of ancient Egypt   932
Civilization—Encyclopedias
The Oxford encyclopedia of ancient Egypt   932
History
Assmann, J. The mind of Egypt   932
Brier, B. The murder of Tutankhamen   932
Egypt: ancient culture, modern land   962
Tyldesley, J. A. Nefertiti   932
See/See also pages in the following book(s):
Potok, C. Wanderings p37-67   909
Politics and government
Murphy, C. Passion for Islam   297
Religion
Wilkinson, R. H. The complete gods and goddesses of ancient Egypt   299
Social conditions
Murphy, C. Passion for Islam   297

Social life and customs
Ghosh, A. In an antique land   962
Egypt: ancient culture, modern land   962
Egypt, Greece, and Rome. Freeman, C.   909
Egyptian art
Egyptian art in the age of the pyramids   709.32
Egyptian treasures from the Egyptian Museum in Cairo   709.32
Germond, P. An Egyptian bestiary   709.32
The Quest for immortality   709.32
Robins, G. The art of ancient Egypt   709.32
Smith, W. S. The art and architecture of ancient Egypt   709.32
Egyptian art in the age of the pyramids   709.32
An **Egyptian** bestiary. Germond, P.   709.32
Egyptian language
Roth, A. M. Hieroglyphs without mystery   493
Egyptian mummies. Brier, B.   932
Egyptian Museum
Egyptian treasures from the Egyptian Museum in Cairo   709.32
Egyptian mythology
Wilkinson, R. H. The complete gods and goddesses of ancient Egypt   299
The **Egyptian** pyramids. Lepre, J. P.   932
Egyptian treasures from the Egyptian Museum in Cairo   709.32
Ehrenhaft, George
How to prepare for the ACT, American College Testing Assessment Program. See How to prepare for the ACT, American College Testing Assessment Program   378.1
Ehrenreich, Barbara
Nickel and dimed   305.5
Ehrlich, Eugene H.
(ed) Choose the right word. See Choose the right word   423
Ehrlich, Gretel
John Muir   92
A match to the heart   92
This cold heaven   998
Ehrlich, Paul R.
The birder's handbook   598
Eicher, David J., 1961-
The longest night   973.7
Eickhoff, Randy Lee
(jt. auth) Homer The odyssey   883
Eidinow, John
(jt. auth) Edmonds, D. Wittgenstein's poker   192
Eight American poets   811.008
Eight little piggies. Gould, S. J.   576.8
Eight men and a duck. See Thorpe, I. J. 8 men and a duck   910.4
Eight weeks to optimum health. Weil, A.   613
Eighteenth century *See* World history—18th century
Einstein, Albert, 1879-1955
Dear Professor Einstein   92
The evolution of physics   530
Ideas and opinions   818
The meaning of relativity   530.1
About
Aczel, A. D. God's equation   523.1
Bjerknes, C. J. Albert Einstein   92
Bodanis, D. E=mc²   530.1
Davies, P. C. W. About time   530.1
Fölsing, A. Albert Einstein   92
Fritzsch, H. An equation that changed the world   530.1
Galison, P. L. Einstein's clocks and Poincaré's maps   529
Paterniti, M. Driving Mr. Albert   917.3
See/See also pages in the following book(s):
Brennan, R. P. Heisenberg probably slept here   920
Flowers, C. Instability rules   509

Einstein, Albert, 1879-1955—About—*Continued*
Gardner, H. Creating minds p87-135 **153.3**
Guillen, M. Five equations that changed the world
530.1
Horvitz, L. A. Eureka!: scientific breakthroughs that
changed the world **509**
Jaspers, K. The great philosophers **109**
Mlodinow, L. Euclid's window **516**
Sagan, C. Broca's brain p18-31 **500**
Einstein, Alfred, 1880-1952
Mozart **92**
Einstein's clocks and Poincaré's maps. Galison, P. L.
529
Eire, Carlos M. N.
Waiting for snow in Havana **92**
Eisaguirre, Lynne, 1951-
Sexual harassment **342**
Eiseley, Loren C., 1907-1977
The immense journey **576.8**
The night country **818**
The star thrower **818**
The unexpected universe **500**
Eisenberg, Arlene
What to expect the toddler years **649**
(jt. auth) Murkoff, H. E. What to expect the first year
649
(jt. auth) Murkoff, H. E. What to expect when you're
expecting **618.2**
Eisenberg, Howard
(jt. auth) McDermott, M. A funny thing happened on
the way to Cooperstown **92**
Eisenberg, Ruth
(jt. auth) Rubenstein, W. B. The rights of people who
are HIV positive **344**
Eisenhower, Dwight D. (Dwight David), 1890-1969
About
Ambrose, S. E. Eisenhower **92**
Ambrose, S. E. The victors **940.54**
Wicker, T. Dwight D. Eisenhower **92**
Eisenhower, Ida Stover, 1862-1942
See/See also pages in the following book(s):
Angelo, B. First mothers **920**
Eisenhower, Joanne Thompson
(jt. auth) Eisenhower, J. S. D. Yanks: the epic story of
the American Army in World War I **940.4**
Eisenhower, John S. D., 1922-
Yanks: the epic story of the American Army in World
War I **940.4**
Eisenhower, Mamie Doud, 1896-1979
About
Eisenhower, S. Mrs. Ike: memories and reflections on
the life of Mamie Eisenhower **92**
Eisenhower, Susan
Mrs. Ike: memories and reflections on the life of
Mamie Eisenhower **92**
Eisenman, Robert H.
(ed) Dead Sea scrolls. The Dead Sea scrolls uncovered
296.1
Eisler, Benita
Byron—child of passion, fool of fame **92**
El Cid *See* Cid, ca. 1043-1099
El-hi textbooks and serials in print **016.3713**
Elbert, Samuel H. (Samuel Hoyt), 1907-1997
(jt. auth) Pukui, M. K. Hawaiian dictionary **499**
Elbroch, Mark
Mammal tracks & sign **599**
Elder, John, 1947-
(ed) Nature writing. See Nature writing **508**
Elder care *See* Elderly—Care
Elderdesign. Bakker, R. **728**
Elderfield, John
Frankenthaler **92**
Elderhouse: planning your best home ever. Altman, A.
728

Elderly
See also Aging; Old age
Coles, R. Old and on their own **305.26**
Care
Consumer reports complete guide to health services for
seniors **362.6**
Diseases
See also Elderly—Health and hygiene
The Johns Hopkins medical guide to health after 50
613
Encyclopedias
Encyclopedia of aging **305.26**
The Encyclopedia of aging: a comprehensive resource
in gerontology and geriatrics **305.26**
Health and hygiene
See also Elderly—Diseases
The Johns Hopkins medical guide to health after 50
613
Housing
Altman, A. Elderhouse: planning your best home ever
728
Bakker, R. Elderdesign **728**
Law and legislation
The American Bar Association legal guide for older
Americans **346.01**
Life skills guides
See also Retirement
Elderly parents *See* Aging parents
Eldredge, Niles
Fossils **560**
The miner's canary **560**
(ed) Life on earth. See Life on earth **333.95**
Eleanor, of Aquitaine, Queen, consort of Henry II,
King of England, 1122?-1204
About
Weir, A. Eleanor of Aquitaine **92**
The **Eleanor** Roosevelt encyclopedia **92**
Elections
See/See also pages in the following book(s):
Morris, D. The new prince p169-240 **324.7**
Finance
See Campaign funds
Florida
Posner, R. A. Breaking the deadlock **324**
United States
CQ's politics in America **328.73**
United States—Encyclopedias
Moore, J. L. Elections A to Z **324.6**
United States—Statistics
America votes **324.6**
Guide to U.S. elections **324.6**
Elections A to Z. Moore, J. L. **324.6**
Electra. Euripides
In Euripides. Ten plays p207-39 **882**
Electra. Sophocles
In Sophocles. The complete plays of Sophocles p37-
74 **882**
Electric light. Heaney, S. **821**
Electric wiring
Cauldwell, R. Safe home wiring projects **621.319**
Electrical engineering
Handbooks, manuals, etc.
American electricians' handbook **621.3**
McGraw-Hill's National Electrical Code handbook
621.3
National Electrical Code handbook **621.3**
Standard handbook for electrical engineers **621.3**
Electricity
Gibilisco, S. Teach yourself electricity and electronics
621.3
Grob, B. Basic electronics **621.381**
Electronic apparatus and appliances
Maintenance and repair
Goodman, R. L. How electronic things work—and
what to do when they don't **621.381**

Electronic commerce
  Cassidy, J. Dot.con   381
Electronic data processing *See* Data processing
        Keyboarding
  See Keyboarding (Electronics)
Electronic mail systems
        Directories
  National E-mail and FAX directory   384.1
Electronic publishing
  The Columbia guide to digital publishing   070.5
Electronics
  See also Microelectronics
  Gibilisco, S. Teach yourself electricity and electronics
                         621.3
  Grob, B. Basic electronics   621.381
        Dictionaries
  The Illustrated dictionary of electronics   621.381
     Handbooks, manuals, etc.
  Electronics engineers' handbook   621.381
Electronics engineers' handbook   621.381
Electrons
  Feynman, R. P. QED   539.7
Elegant but easy cookbook, The new. Burros, M. F.
                         641.5
The **elegant** universe. Greene, B. R.   539.7
Elegy for Iris. Bayley, J.   92
The **element** of lavishness: letters of Sylvia Townsend
  Warner and William Maxwell, 1938-1978. Warner,
  S. T.   92
Elementary education
  Dewey, J. The school and society, and The child and
  the curriculum   372
Elementary particles (Physics) *See* Particles (Nuclear
  physics)
Elementary school libraries
  See also Children's libraries
The **Elements** of style   721
The **elements** of style. Strunk, W.   808
Elephants
  Alexander, S. The astonishing elephant   599.67
  Ellis, G. Wild orphans   599.67
  Payne, K. Silent thunder   599.67
  Scigliano, E. Love, war, and circuses   599.67
Eliade, Mircea, 1907-1986
  From Gautama Buddha to the triumph of Christianity
  In Eliade, M. A history of religious ideas v2
                         291
  From Muhammad to the Age of Reform
  In Eliade, M. A history of religious ideas v3
                         291
  From the Stone Age to the Eleusinian mysteries
  In Eliade, M. A history of religious ideas v1
                         291
  A history of religious ideas   291
  (ed) The Encyclopedia of religion. See The Encyclope-
  dia of religion   200.3
Elias, Maurice J.
  Emotionally intelligent parenting   649
Elias, Scott A.
  Rocky Mountains   508
Elias, Stephen
  How to file for chapter 7 bankruptcy. See How to file
  for chapter 7 bankruptcy   346.07
  Patent, copyright & trademark   346.04
  Trademark   346.04
Eliav-Feldon, Miriam, 1946-
  (ed) A Historical atlas of the Jewish people. See A
  Historical atlas of the Jewish people   909
Elijah Muhammad, 1897-1975
        About
  Evanzz, K. The messenger: the rise and fall of Elijah
  Muhammad   92
  Gardell, M. In the name of Elijah Muhammad
                         297

Eliot, George, 1819-1880
        About
  Hughes, K. George Eliot   92
  See/See also pages in the following book(s):
  Bloom, H. The Western canon   809
  Woolf, V. Women and writing p150-60   820.9
Eliot, Lise
  What's going on in there?   612.8
Eliot, T. S. (Thomas Stearns), 1888-1965
  Cocktail party
  In Eliot, T. S. The complete poems and plays, 1909-
  1950 p295-388   818
  Collected poems (1909-1935)
  In Eliot, T. S. The complete poems and plays, 1909-
  1950   818
  Collected poems, 1909-1962   811
  The complete poems and plays, 1909-1950   818
  Family reunion
  In Eliot, T. S. The complete poems and plays, 1909-
  1950 p223-94   818
  Four quartets
  In Eliot, T. S. The complete poems and plays, 1909-
  1950 p117-45   818
  Inventions of the March Hare   811
  Murder in the cathedral
  In Eliot, T. S. The complete poems and plays, 1909-
  1950 p173-221   818
  Old Possum's book of practical cats
  In Eliot, T. S. The complete poems and plays, 1909-
  1950 p149-71   818
        About
  Gordon, L. T.S. Eliot   92
  See/See also pages in the following book(s):
  Gardner, H. Creating minds p227-64   153.3
  Heaney, S. Finders keepers p28-41   821
  Kazin, A. An American procession p13-21, 310-20
                         810.9
  Kermode, F. An appetite for poetry   801
  Miłosz, C. To begin where I am p388-98   891.8
  Pritchard, W. H. Lives of the modern poets p171-201
                         821.009
  Vendler, H. H. Coming of age as a poet   820.9
Eliot, Thomas Stearns *See* Eliot, T. S. (Thomas
  Stearns), 1888-1965
Elite (Social sciences)
  Graham, L. O. Our kind of people   305.8
  Lasch, C. The revolt of the elites   306
Elizabeth I, Queen of England, 1533-1603
        About
  Hibbert, C. The virgin queen: Elizabeth I   92
  Milton, G. Big Chief Elizabeth   975.5
  Strachey, L. Elizabeth and Essex   92
  Watkins, S. The public and private worlds of Elizabeth
  I   942.05
  Weir, A. The life of Elizabeth I   92
  See/See also pages in the following book(s):
  Fraser, A. The warrior queens   920
  Weir, A. The children of Henry VIII   920
Elizabeth II, Queen of Great Britain, 1926-
        About
  Pimlott, B. The Queen: a biography of Elizabeth II
                         92
  Shawcross, W. Queen and country: the fifty-year reign
  of Elizabeth II   92
Elizabeth and Essex. Strachey, L.   92
Elledge, Scott
  E.B. White   92
Ellington, Duke, 1899-1974
  Music is my mistress   92
        About
  Nicholson, S. Reminiscing in tempo: a portrait of Duke
  Ellington   92
  See/See also pages in the following book(s):
  Ellison, R. Going to the territory p217-26   818
  Feather, L. From Satchmo to Miles   920

Ellington, Duke, 1899-1974—About—*Continued*
Hajdu, D. Lush life: a biography of Billy Strayhorn
92
Russell, D. Black genius and the American experience
920

Ellington, Elisabeth
A year of reading 028

Elliot, Jason, 1965-
An unexpected light 958.1

Elliott, Elizabeth Shippen Green *See* Green, Elizabeth Shippen, 1871-1954

Elliott, Emory, 1942-
(ed) Columbia literary history of the United States. See Columbia literary history of the United States
810.9

Ellis, Barbara W.
Taylor's guide to annuals 635.9
Taylor's guide to bulbs 635.9
Taylor's guide to perennials 635.9
(ed) Burpee complete gardener. See Burpee complete gardener 635
(ed) Rodale's all-new encyclopedia of organic gardening. See Rodale's all-new encyclopedia of organic gardening 635

Ellis, David, 1939-
D.H. Lawrence, dying game, 1922-1930 92

Ellis, Don, 1934-1978
See/See also pages in the following book(s):
Feather, L. From Satchmo to Miles 920

Ellis, Gerry
Wild orphans 599.67

Ellis, Joseph J.
American sphinx: the character of Thomas Jefferson
92
Founding brothers 973.4

Ellis, Juanita
(jt. auth) Speed, T. The personal Internet security guidebook 005.8

Ellis, Richard, 1938-
Encyclopedia of the sea 551.46
Great white shark 597
Imagining Atlantis 001.9
The search for the giant squid 594

Ellis, William S.
Glass 666

Ellis Island and the peopling of America. Yans-McLaughlin, V. 325.73

Ellis Island Immigration Station
Yans-McLaughlin, V. Ellis Island and the peopling of America 325.73

Ellis Island to Ebbet's Field. Levine, P. 796

Ellison, Ralph
Going to the territory 818
Shadow and act 814
See/See also pages in the following book(s):
Russell, D. Black genius and the American experience
920

Ellmann, Richard, 1918-1987
James Joyce 92
Oscar Wilde 92
(ed) The New Oxford book of American verse. See The New Oxford book of American verse
811.008
(ed) The Norton anthology of modern and contemporary poetry. See The Norton anthology of modern and contemporary poetry 821.008

Ellsberg, Daniel, 1931-
Secrets: a memoir of Vietnam and the Pentagon papers
959.704

Elocution *See* Public speaking

Elon, Amos
The pity of it all 943

Elshtain, Jean Bethke, 1941-
Jane Addams and the dream of American democracy
92

El´tsin, Boris Nikolaevich *See* Yeltsin, Boris

Elvin, Mark
(jt. auth) Blunden, C. Cultural atlas of China 951

Ely, Melvin Patrick
The adventures of Amos 'n' Andy 791.44

Elytēs, Odysseus, 1911-1996
The collected poems of Odysseus Elytis 889

Emancipation Proclamation (1863)
See/See also pages in the following book(s):
McPherson, J. M. Drawn with the sword 973.7

Emanoil, Mary
(ed) Encyclopedia of endangered species. See Encyclopedia of endangered species 578.68

The **embarrassment** of riches. Schama, S. 949.2

Ember, Carol R.
(ed) Encyclopedia of urban cultures. See Encyclopedia of urban cultures 307.7

Ember, Melvin
(ed) Encyclopedia of urban cultures. See Encyclopedia of urban cultures 307.7

Emblems *See* Signs and symbols

Embracing defeat. Dower, J. W. 952.04

Embryology
Nilsson, L. A child is born 612.6

Emerson, Everett, 1925-2002
Mark Twain 92

Emerson, Ken
Doo-dah!: Stephen Foster and the rise of American popular culture 92

Emerson, Ralph Waldo, 1803-1882
Collected poems & translations 811
English traits
In Emerson, R. W. The portable Emerson p395-518
818
Essays & lectures 818
Essays: first and second series
In Emerson, R. W. The portable Emerson p111-290
818
Nature
In Emerson, R. W. The portable Emerson p7-50
818
The portable Emerson 818
About
Richardson, R. D. Emerson 92
See/See also pages in the following book(s):
Kazin, A. An American procession p25-62 810.9
Matthiessen, F. O. American renaissance p3-75
810.9

Emery, Fred
Watergate 973.924

Emigrants *See* Immigrants

Emigration *See* Immigration and emigration

Emily Post wedding etiquette. Post, P. 395

Emily Post's complete book of wedding etiquette. See Post, P. Emily Post wedding etiquette 395

Emily Post's etiquette. Post, P. 395

Emma's war. Scroggins, D. 962.4

Emotional intelligence. Goleman, D. 152.4

Emotional resilience. Viscott, D. S. 158

Emotional stress *See* Stress (Psychology)

Emotionally disturbed children
Brazelton, T. B. To listen to a child 155.4
Safer, J. The normal one 158
See/See also pages in the following book(s):
Goleman, D. Emotional intelligence p231-60
152.4

Emotionally intelligent parenting. Elias, M. J. 649

Emotions
See also Anxiety; Crying
Damasio, A. R. The feeling of what happens 153
Damasio, A. R. Looking for Spinoza 152.4
Goleman, D. Emotional intelligence 152.4
Pert, C. Molecules of emotion 612.8
Shapiro, L. E. How to raise a child with a high EQ
649

Emotions—*Continued*
See/See also pages in the following book(s):
Pinker, S. How the mind works p363-424   **153**

Encyclopedias
Encyclopedia of human emotions   **152.4**

Empedocles
See/See also pages in the following book(s):
Jaspers, K. The great philosophers   **109**

Emperor of Japan: Meiji and His world, 1852-1912.
Keene, D.   **92**

Emperors
Rome
Grant, M. Collapse and recovery of the Roman Empire
    937
Suetonius Tranquillus, C. The twelve Caesars   **878**
The **emperor's** handbook. See Marcus Aurelius, Emperor
of Rome. Meditations   **188**
The **emperors** of chocolate. Brenner, J. G.   **338.7**
Empire express. Bain, D. H.   **385**
Empire of light. Perkowitz, S.   **535**
Empire statesman: the rise and redemption of Al Smith.
Slayton, R. A.   **92**
Empires of time. Aveni, A. F.   **529**
Empires on the Pacific. Thompson, R. S.   **940.54**
The **employee** rights handbook. Sack, S. M.   **344**
Employees
See also Personnel management
Civil rights
Joel, L. G. Every employee's guide to the law
    344
O'Neil, R. M. The rights of public employees
    342
Outten, W. N. The rights of employees and union
members   **344**
Sack, S. M. The employee rights handbook   **344**
Dismissal
Richardson, B. G. Career comeback   **650.14**
Employer-employee relations *See* Industrial relations
Employment applications *See* Applications for positions
Employment guidance *See* Vocational guidance
Employment management *See* Personnel management
Employment of children *See* Child labor
Employment of teenagers *See* Teenagers—Employment
Employment of women *See* Women—Employment
Employment of youth *See* Youth—Employment
Empson, Sir William, 1906-1984
See/See also pages in the following book(s):
Kermode, F. An appetite for poetry   **801**
The **empty** space. Brook, P.   **792**
Emswiler, James P.
(jt. auth) Emswiler, M. A. Guiding your child through
grief   **155.9**
Emswiler, Mary Ann
Guiding your child through grief   **155.9**
Enamel and enameling
King, J. B. Enamelling   **738**
Enamelling. King, J. B.   **738**
Enami, Sayemon
The bird-catcher in hell
In Waley, A. The Nō plays of Japan   **895.6**
The cormorant-fisher
In Waley, A. The Nō plays of Japan   **895.6**
The **enchanted** world of sleep. Lavie, P.   **612.8**
Encore Provence. Mayle, P.   **944.083**
Encounter groups *See* Group relations training
Encounter on the narrow ridge: a life of Martin Buber.
Friedman, M. S.   **92**
Encyclopaedia Britannica almanac   **031.02**
Encyclopaedia of British pottery and porcelain marks.
Godden, G. A.   **738**
Encyclopaedia of superstitions. Radford, E.   **398.03**
The **Encyclopedia** Americana   **031**
Encyclopedia Britannica, The New   **031**
Encyclopedia of 20th century American humor. Nilsen,
A. P.   **817**

The **encyclopedia** of addictive drugs. Miller, R. L.
    615
Encyclopedia of aesthetics   **111**
Encyclopedia of Africa, south of the Sahara   **967**
Encyclopedia of African-American civil rights
    305.8
Encyclopedia of African-American culture and history
    305.8
Encyclopedia of African American religions   **200.9**
The **Encyclopedia** of African and African-American reli-
gions   **299**
Encyclopedia of African peoples   **960**
Encyclopedia of aging [Macmillan Ref. USA]
    305.26
The **Encyclopedia** of aging: a comprehensive resource in
gerontology and geriatrics [Springer Pub.]
    305.26
Encyclopedia of AIDS   **362.1**
Encyclopedia of allergies. Lipkowitz, M.   **616.97**
Encyclopedia of Alzheimer's disease. Moore, E. A.
    616.8
The **encyclopedia** of Alzheimer's disease. Turkington, C.
    616.8
Encyclopedia of American associations. See Encyclope-
dia of associations   **061.025**
Encyclopedia of American cultural and intellectual his-
tory   **973.03**
Encyclopedia of American education. Unger, H. G.
    370
Encyclopedia of American foreign policy   **327.73**
Encyclopedia of American history   **973.03**
Encyclopedia of American Indian costume. Paterek, J.
    391
Encyclopedia of American law   **349**
Encyclopedia of American literature   **810.3**
Encyclopedia of American military history   **355**
Encyclopedia of American poetry, the nineteenth century
    811.009
Encyclopedia of American poetry, the twentieth century
    811.009
The **Encyclopedia** of American political history
    973.03
Encyclopedia of American prisons   **365**
Encyclopedia of American religion and politics. Djupe,
P. A.   **322**
The **encyclopedia** of American religions. Melton, J. G.
    200.9
The **encyclopedia** of American religious history. Queen,
E. L.   **200.9**
Encyclopedia of American scandal. See The New ency-
clopedia of American scandal   **973.02**
Encyclopedia of American social history   **973.03**
Encyclopedia of American studies   **973.03**
Encyclopedia of American war heroes   **920.003**
Encyclopedia of ancient Egypt. Bunson, M. R.   **932**
Encyclopedia of animal rights and animal welfare
    179
Encyclopedia of applied ethics   **170**
Encyclopedia of Arabic literature   **892**
Encyclopedia of archaeology: History and discoveries
    930.1
Encyclopedia of archaeology: The great archaeologists
    920
Encyclopedia of architectural and engineering feats.
Langmead, D.   **721**
Encyclopedia of artists   **920.003**
Encyclopedia of associations   **061.025**
Encyclopedia of astronomy and astrophysics   **520.3**
Encyclopedia of atmospheric sciences   **551.5**
Encyclopedia of battles in North America, 1517 to 1916.
Purcell, L. E.   **970**
Encyclopedia of biodiversity   **333.95**
The **Encyclopedia** of blindness and vision impairment
    362.4

Encyclopedia of British writers, 19th and 20th centuries 820.9

Encyclopedia of busine$$ and finance 650

Encyclopedia of business information sources 650

The Encyclopedia of careers and vocational guidance 331.7

Encyclopedia of China. Perkins, D. 951

The Encyclopedia of Christianity 230.003

Encyclopedia of Christmas. See Gulevich, T. Encyclopedia of Christmas and New Year's celebrations 394.26

Encyclopedia of Christmas and New Year's celebrations. Gulevich, T. 394.26

Encyclopedia of classical philosophy 180

Encyclopedia of climate and weather 551.6

Encyclopedia of computer science 004

Encyclopedia of computer science and technology. Henderson, H. 004

Encyclopedia of conflicts since World War II 909.82

Encyclopedia of constitutional amendments, proposed amendments, and amending issues, 1789-2002. Vile, J. R. 342

Encyclopedia of construction methods & materials. Spence, W. P. 690

Encyclopedia of contemporary Japanese culture 952.04

The Encyclopedia of country music 781.642

Encyclopedia of crime & justice 364.03

Encyclopedia of crime and punishment 364.03

Encyclopedia of Cuba 972.91

The encyclopedia of cults, sects, and new religions 200.3

The encyclopedia of deafness and hearing disorders. Turkington, C. 617.8

Encyclopedia of death and dying 306.9

The encyclopedia of depression. Roesch, R. 616.85

Encyclopedia of dinosaurs 567.9

Encyclopedia of dog breeds. Coile, D. C. 636.7

Encyclopedia of early Christianity 230.003

Encyclopedia of earth and physical sciences 500.2

Encyclopedia of earth sciences 550.3

Encyclopedia of earthquakes and volcanoes. Ritchie, D. 551.2

Encyclopedia of Eastern Europe 947

Encyclopedia of education 370

Encyclopedia of endangered species 578.68

Encyclopedia of environmental science. Mongillo, J. F. 363.7

Encyclopedia of ethics [Facts on File] 170

Encyclopedia of ethics [Routledge] 170

Encyclopedia of ethics in science and technology. Barber, N. 174

Encyclopedia of European social history from 1350 to 2000 940

Encyclopedia of evolution 576.8

The Encyclopedia of fantasy 809.3

The encyclopedia of fertility and infertility. Turkington, C. 616.6

The encyclopedia of figure skating. Malone, J. W. 796.91

Encyclopedia of folk, country & western music. See Stambler, I. Country music: the encyclopedia 781.642

Encyclopedia of folk heroes. Seal, G. 398.03

Encyclopedia of food and culture 394.1

Encyclopedia of forensic science. Conklin, B. G. 363.2

Encyclopedia of frontier literature. Snodgrass, M. E. 810.3

Encyclopedia of fundamentalism 200.9

Encyclopedia of gardens 635

Encyclopedia of German literature 830.3

The encyclopedia of ghosts and spirits. Guiley, R. E. 133.1

Encyclopedia of global change 363.7

Encyclopedia of gun control and gun rights. Utter, G. H. 363.3

Encyclopedia of herbal medicine. Chevallier, A. 615

Encyclopedia of herbs and their uses. See Bown, D. New encyclopedia of herbs & their uses 581.6

Encyclopedia of Holocaust literature 809

Encyclopedia of human emotions 152.4

Encyclopedia of hurricanes, typhoons and cyclones. Longshore, D. 551.55

The encyclopedia of infectious diseases. Turkington, C. 616.9

Encyclopedia of information systems 004

The Encyclopedia of insects. See The Firefly encyclopedia of insects and spiders 595.7

Encyclopedia of Jewish life before and during the Holocaust 940.53

The Encyclopedia of Judaism. See The New encyclopedia of Judaism [New York University Press] 296.03

The Encyclopedia of Judaism [Continuum] 296.03

Encyclopedia of Latin American & Caribbean art 709.8

The encyclopedia of learning disabilities. Turkington, C. 371.9

Encyclopedia of lesbian and gay histories and cultures 306.7

Encyclopedia of literature in Canada 810.3

Encyclopedia of marriage and the family. See International encyclopedia of marriage and family 306.8

The encyclopedia of medicinal plants. See Chevallier, A. Encyclopedia of herbal medicine 615

The encyclopedia of memory and memory disorders. Turkington, C. 153.1

Encyclopedia of mental health 616.89

Encyclopedia of modern American extremists and extremist groups. Atkins, S. E. 322.4

Encyclopedia of modern Asia. Levinson, D. 950

The encyclopedia of mosaic techniques. Biggs, E. 738.5

The encyclopedia of movie special effects. Netzley, P. D. 778.5

Encyclopedia of multiculturalism 305.8

The encyclopedia of mummies. Brier, B. 393

The encyclopedia of Native American religions. Hirschfelder, A. B. 299

Encyclopedia of Native American tribes. Waldman, C. 970.004

Encyclopedia of natural medicine. Murray, M. T. 615.5

An encyclopedia of naval history. Bruce, A. 359

The Encyclopedia of new media 302.23

The Encyclopedia of New York City 974.7

Encyclopedia of North American Indians 970.004

The encyclopedia of North American sports history. Hickok, R. 796

The encyclopedia of North American trees. Benvie, S. 582.16

The encyclopedia of novels into film. Tibbetts, J. C. 791.43

The encyclopedia of nutrition and good health. Ronzio, R. A. 613.2

Encyclopedia of nutritional supplements. Murray, M. T. 613.2

Encyclopedia of occultism & parapsychology 133

Encyclopedia of organized crime in the United States. Kelly, R. J. 364.1

Encyclopedia of paleontology 560

The Encyclopedia of philosophy 103

The encyclopedia of phobias, fears, and anxieties. Doctor, R. M. 616.85

The encyclopedia of planting combinations. Lord, T. 635.9

Encyclopedia of poetry and poetics. See The New Princeton encyclopedia of poetry and poetics
809.1
Encyclopedia of prophecy. Ashe, G. 133.3
Encyclopedia of psychology 150.3
Encyclopedia of psychology. See The Corsini encyclopedia of psychology and behavioral science 150.3
Encyclopedia of public health 362.1
Encyclopedia of rainforests. Jukofsky, D. 578.7
The Encyclopedia of religion 200.3
Encyclopedia of rural America 973.03
The encyclopedia of saints. Guiley, R. E. 920.003
The encyclopedia of schizophrenia and other psychotic disorders. Noll, R. 616.89
Encyclopedia of science and religion 291.103
The Encyclopedia of science and technology 503
The encyclopedia of serial killers. Newton, M.
364.03
The encyclopedia of sewing machine techniques. Bednar, N. 646.2
The encyclopedia of skin and skin disorders. Turkington, C. 616.5
The encyclopedia of sleep and sleep disorders. Thorpy, M. J. 612.8
Encyclopedia of small business 658
The encyclopedia of snakes. Mattison, C. 597.9
Encyclopedia of social issues 306
Encyclopedia of sociology 301
Encyclopedia of space exploration. Angelo, J. A.
629.4
Encyclopedia of stage lighting. Briggs, J. 792
Encyclopedia of strange and unexplained physical phenomena. Clark, J. 001.9
The encyclopedia of suicide. Evans, G. 362.28
Encyclopedia of survival techniques. Stilwell, A.
796.5
Encyclopedia of television 791.45
Encyclopedia of terrorism. Combs, C. C. 303.6
Encyclopedia of terrorism. Kushner, H. W. 303.6
Encyclopedia of the American Civil War 973.7
Encyclopedia of the American Constitution 342
Encyclopedia of the ancient Greek world. Sacks, D.
938.003
Encyclopedia of the ancient world 930
The encyclopedia of the cat. See Fogle, B. The new encyclopedia of the cat 636.8
The Encyclopedia of the Dead Sea scrolls 296.1
The encyclopedia of the dog. See Fogle, B. The new encyclopedia of the dog 636.7
Encyclopedia of the Enlightenment 940.2
Encyclopedia of the Enlightenment. Wilson, E. J.
940.2
Encyclopedia of the Great Depression and the New Deal
973.917
Encyclopedia of the Harlem Renaissance. Aberjhani
810.9
Encyclopedia of the Holocaust [Facts on File]
940.53
Encyclopedia of the Holocaust [Macmillan] 940.53
The encyclopedia of the horse. See Edwards, E. H. The new encyclopedia of the horse 636.1
Encyclopedia of the industrial revolution in America. Olson, J. S. 973.03
The Encyclopedia of the Irish in America 305.8
Encyclopedia of the Jewish religion. See The Oxford dictionary of the Jewish religion 296.03
The encyclopedia of the JFK assassination. Benson, M.
973.922
Encyclopedia of the Korean War 951.9
The Encyclopedia of the Middle Ages 909.07
The encyclopedia of the musical theatre. Gänzl, K.
792.6
Encyclopedia of the novel 809.3
Encyclopedia of the Persian Gulf War. Schwartz, R. A.
956.7

Encyclopedia of the Renaissance 940.2
Encyclopedia of the Roman Empire. Bunson, M.
937
Encyclopedia of the scientific revolution 509
Encyclopedia of the sea. Ellis, R. 551.46
Encyclopedia of the strange, mystical & unexplained. Guiley, R. E. 133
Encyclopedia of the U.S. Census 304.6
Encyclopedia of the United Nations. Moore, J. A.
341.23
Encyclopedia of the United Nations and international agreements. Osmańczyk, E. J. 341.23
Encyclopedia of the United States in the nineteenth century 973.5
Encyclopedia of the Vietnam War 959.704
Encyclopedia of the world's zoos 590.73
Encyclopedia of underwater and maritime archaeology
930.1
Encyclopedia of urban cultures 307.7
Encyclopedia of urban legends. Brunvand, J. H.
398.2
The encyclopedia of witches and witchcraft. Guiley, R. E. 133.4
Encyclopedia of women and sports. Sherrow, V.
796
Encyclopedia of women and world religion 200
Encyclopedia of women in American history 305.4
Encyclopedia of women in the ancient world. Salisbury, J. E. 305.4
Encyclopedia of women's health issues. Gay, K.
613
Encyclopedia of women's history in America. Cullen-DuPont, K. 305.4
The Encyclopedia of wood 674
Encyclopedia of world biography 920.003
Encyclopedia of world history 903
Encyclopedia of world literature in the 20th century
803

Encyclopedias and dictionaries
See also Picture dictionaries; names of languages with the subdivision Dictionaries and subjects with the subdivision Dictionaries or Encyclopedias
Britannica concise encyclopedia 031
The Columbia encyclopedia 031
The Encyclopedia Americana 031
The Essential desk reference 031.02
Famous first facts, international edition 031.02
Kane, J. N. Famous first facts 031.02
Merriam-Webster's collegiate encyclopedia 031
The New Encyclopaedia Britannica 031
The New York Public Library desk reference
031.02
The World Book encyclopedia 031
Encyclopedic handbook of cults in America. Melton, J. G. 291.9
The end of education. Postman, N. 370
The end of physics. Lindley, D. 539.7
The end of privacy. Whitaker, R. 303.4
End of the earth. Matthiessen, P. 508
The end of the peace process. Said, E. W. 956
End of the world
Gleiser, M. The prophet and the astronomer
523.1
Weber, E. J. Apocalypses 291
The end of time. Barbour, J. B. 530.1
Endangered species
See also Rare animals; Wildlife conservation
Ackerman, D. The rarest of the rare 578.68
Beacham's guide to the endangered species of North America 578.68
Chadwick, D. H. The company we keep 591.68
Crawford, M. Habitats and ecosystems 578.68
Encyclopedia of endangered species 578.68
Endangered wildlife and plants of the world
578.68

Endangered species—*Continued*

Matthiessen, P. The birds of heaven   **598**

Matthiessen, P. Tigers in the snow   **599.75**

McNamee, T. The return of the wolf to Yellowstone   **599.77**

Quammen, D. Monster of God   **591.6**

Stuart, C. Africa's vanishing wildlife   **591.9**

Wilson, E. O. The future of life   **333.95**

Endangered wildlife and plants of the world   **578.68**

Endangered wildlife of the world. See Endangered wildlife and plants of the world   **578.68**

Endgame. Rohde, D.   **949.7**

Endowments

Directories

The Foundation directory   **061.025**

Ends and Odds. Beckett, S.   **842**

The **ends** of the earth. Kaplan, R. D.   **910.4**

Endurance, Physical See Physical fitness

Endurance (Ship)

Alexander, C. The Endurance   **998**

Enelow, Wendy S.

Cover letter magic   **650.14**

An **enemy** of the people. Ibsen, H.

In Ibsen, H. The complete major prose plays p277-386   **839.8**

In Ibsen, H. Ibsen: four major plays   **839.8**

Energy See Force and energy

Energy conservation

See/See also pages in the following book(s):

Feynman, R. P. Six easy pieces   **530**

Energy resources

See also Hydrogen as fuel

Engber, Andrea

The complete single mother   **306.8**

Engelberg, Stephen, 1958-

(jt. auth) Miller, J. Germs   **358**

Engelbert, Phillis

(ed) Science, technology, and society: the impact of science in the 20th century. See Science, technology, and society: the impact of science in the 20th century   **509**

Engelbreit, Mary

Mary Engelbreit's children's companion   **645**

Engels, Friedrich, 1820-1895

(jt. auth) Marx, K. Capital   **330.1**

(jt. auth) Marx, K. The Communist manifesto of Karl Marx and Friedrich Engels   **335.4**

See/See also pages in the following book(s):

Heilbroner, R. L. The worldly philosophers   **330.1**

Engineering

See also Chemical engineering; Electrical engineering; Hydraulic engineering; Water supply engineering

Evan, W. M. Minding the machines   **620.8**

Molotch, H. L. Where stuff comes from   **620**

Petroski, H. Invention by design   **620**

Petroski, H. Remaking the world   **620**

Encyclopedias

Van Nostrand's concise encyclopedia of science   **503**

Van Nostrand's scientific encyclopedia   **503**

History

Berlow, L. H. The reference guide to famous engineering landmarks of the world   **620**

Langmead, D. Encyclopedia of architectural and engineering feats   **721**

Tobin, J. Great projects   **620**

Engineering, Genetic See Genetic engineering

Engineering materials See Materials

Engineers

Dictionaries

Notable scientists from 1900 to the present   **920.003**

Engineers of dreams. Petroski, H.   **624**

England

History

See Great Britain—History

Social life and customs

Pool, D. What Jane Austen ate and Charles Dickens knew   **820.9**

English as a global language. Crystal, D.   **420**

English drama

Bio-bibliography

Contemporary dramatists   **920.003**

Collections

Restoration plays   **822.008**

Dictionaries

Critical survey of drama   **809.2**

English dramatists See Dramatists, English

English East India Company See East India Company

English fiction

History and criticism

The Columbia history of the British novel   **823.009**

Head, D. The Cambridge introduction to modern British fiction, 1950-2000   **823.009**

English history, 1914-1945. Taylor, A. J. P.   **942.08**

English language

Crystal, D. The Cambridge encyclopedia of the English language   **420**

Hayakawa, S. I. Language in thought and action   **412**

Mencken, H. L. The American language   **427**

Acronyms

See Acronyms

Americanisms

See Americanisms

Composition and exercises

Hodges' Harbrace handbook   **808**

Dialects

Herman, L. American dialects   **427**

Dictionaries

The American Heritage college dictionary   **423**

The American Heritage dictionary of the English language   **423**

Chalker, S. The Oxford dictionary of English grammar   **428**

Dictionary of American regional English   **427**

Hendrickson, R. The Facts on File dictionary of American regionalisms   **427**

Hirsch, E. D. The new dictionary of cultural literacy   **031**

Merriam-Webster's collegiate dictionary   **423**

Metcalf, A. A. How we talk   **427**

The New Oxford American dictionary   **423**

The Oxford American dictionary and language guide   **423**

The Oxford American dictionary of current English   **423**

The Oxford companion to the English language   **420**

The Oxford dictionary for writers and editors   **428**

The Oxford English dictionary   **423**

The Oxford reverse dictionary   **423**

Random House Webster's college dictionary   **423**

Random House Webster's unabridged dictionary   **423**

Shorter Oxford English dictionary on historical principles   **423**

Ultimate visual dictionary   **423**

Webster's third new international dictionary of the English language, unabridged   **423**

Wilson, K. G. The Columbia guide to standard American English   **428**

Etymology

Barnhart, D. K. America in so many words   **422**

Fowler, H. W. The new Fowler's modern English usage   **428**

English language—Etymology—*Continued*
Korach, M. Common phrases and where they come from   **422**

Etymology—Dictionaries
The Barnhart dictionary of etymology   **422.03**
The Concise Oxford dictionary of English etymology   **422.03**
Hendrickson, R. The Facts on File encyclopedia of word and phrase origins   **422.03**
Morris, W. Morris dictionary of word and phrase origins   **422.03**
The Oxford dictionary of word histories   **422.03**

Foreign words and phrases
Manser, M. H. The Facts on File dictionary of foreign words and phrases   **422.03**
Rosten, L. The new joys of Yiddish   **439**

Foreign words and phrases—Dictionaries
Guinagh, K. Dictionary of foreign phrases and abbreviations   **422.03**
The Oxford dictionary of foreign words and phrases   **422.03**

Grammar
Chalker, S. The Oxford dictionary of English grammar   **428**
Hodges' Harbrace handbook   **808**
Huddleston, R. D. The Cambridge grammar of the English language   **425**
McMahan, E. The writer's handbook   **808**
O'Conner, P. T. Woe is I   **428**

History
See also English language—Etymology
Barnhart, D. K. America in so many words   **422**
Bryson, B. Made in America   **420**
Bryson, B. The mother tongue: English & how it got that way   **420**
McCrum, R. The story of English   **420**

Idioms
Ammer, C. The American Heritage dictionary of idioms   **427**
The Cassell dictionary of English idioms   **423**
Fowler, H. W. The new Fowler's modern English usage   **428**

Jargon
Lutz, W. The new doublespeak   **427**

Pronunciation—Dictionaries
Pronouncing dictionary of proper names   **423**

Rhyme
Espy, W. R. Words to rhyme with   **423**
Lees, G. The modern rhyming dictionary   **423**
Young, S. The new comprehensive American rhyming dictionary   **423**

Slang
Dalzell, T. Flappers 2 rappers   **427**
Dictionary of American slang   **427**
Green, J. The Cassell dictionary of slang   **427**
Partridge, E. A dictionary of slang and unconventional English   **427**
Random House historical dictionary of American slang   **427**
Spears, R. A. NTC's dictionary of American slang and colloquial expressions   **427**

Social aspects
Crystal, D. English as a global language   **420**
Lepore, J. A is for American   **306.44**
McWhorter, J. H. Doing our own thing   **306.44**

Spelling
Vos Savant, M. M. The art of spelling   **421**

Synonyms and antonyms
Bartlett's Roget's thesaurus   **423**
Choose the right word   **423**
Dictionary of confusable words   **423**
The Doubleday Roget's thesaurus in dictionary form   **423**
Kipfer, B. A. Roget's 21st century thesaurus in dictionary form   **423**

Lutz, W. The Cambridge thesaurus of American English   **423**
Merriam-Webster's collegiate thesaurus   **423**
Microsoft Encarta college thesaurus   **423**
The Oxford American thesaurus of current English   **423**
The Oxford reverse dictionary   **423**
Roget's international thesaurus   **423**

Terms and phrases
Ammer, C. The American Heritage dictionary of idioms   **427**
Baldick, C. The concise Oxford dictionary of literary terms   **803**
The Cassell dictionary of English idioms   **423**
Hendrickson, R. The Facts on File encyclopedia of word and phrase origins   **422.03**
Korach, M. Common phrases and where they come from   **422**
Metaphors dictionary   **423**
Metcalf, A. A. Predicting new words   **420**
Morris, W. Morris dictionary of word and phrase origins   **422.03**

Usage
The Associated Press stylebook and briefing on media law   **808**
Buckley, W. F. Buckley, the right word   **422**
The Chicago manual of style   **808**
Dictionary of confusable words   **423**
Fowler, H. W. The new Fowler's modern English usage   **428**
Garner, B. A. Garner's modern American usage   **423**
Lovinger, P. W. The Penguin dictionary of English usage and style   **428**
McWhorter, J. H. Doing our own thing   **306.44**
The New York Public Library writer's guide to style and usage   **808**
O'Conner, P. T. Woe is I   **428**
The Oxford dictionary for writers and editors   **428**
Wilson, K. G. The Columbia guide to standard American English   **428**

Vocabulary
See Vocabulary
English letters
The Oxford book of letters   **826**
English literature
Bio-bibliography
British authors of the nineteenth century   **920.003**
The Cambridge guide to literature in English   **820.3**
Encyclopedia of British writers, 19th and 20th centuries   **820.9**
The Oxford companion to English literature   **820.3**
Collections
The Norton anthology of English literature   **820.8**
The Oxford anthology of English literature   **820.8**
Dictionaries
The Cambridge guide to literature in English   **820.3**
The Oxford companion to English literature   **820.3**
History and criticism
Backgrounds to English literature   **820.9**
Encyclopedia of British writers, 19th and 20th centuries   **820.9**
The Oxford illustrated history of English literature   **820.9**
Pool, D. What Jane Austen ate and Charles Dickens knew   **820.9**
Ricks, C. Reviewery   **820.9**
Sanders, A. The short Oxford history of English literature   **820.9**
Woolf, V. The second common reader   **820.9**
See/See also pages in the following book(s):
Durant, W. J. The age of Louis XIV p207-43, 312-62   **940.2**

English literature—*Continued*
    Women authors—Collections
The Norton anthology of literature by women
      820.8
    Women authors—Dictionaries
The Cambridge guide to women's writing in English
      820.9
    Women authors—History and criticism
Gilbert, S. M. No man's land v3   **820.9**
Heilbrun, C. G. Hamlet's mother and other women
      820.9
Pierpont, C. R. Passionate minds   **810.9**
Woolf, V. Women and writing   **820.9**
English poetry
Poetry speaks   **808.81**
    Bio-bibliography
Contemporary poets   **920.003**
    Collections
The Best loved poems of the American people
      821.008
Christmas poems   **821.008**
The Columbia anthology of British poetry
      821.008
Good poems   **811.008**
Inventions of farewell   **821.008**
The Making of a poem   **821.008**
The New Oxford book of eighteenth century verse
      821.008
The New Oxford book of Victorian verse
      821.008
The Norton anthology of modern and contemporary
  poetry   **821.008**
The Norton book of light verse   **821.008**
The Oxford book of comic verse   **821.008**
The Oxford book of English verse   **821.008**
The Oxford book of garden verse   **821.008**
The Oxford book of sonnets   **821.008**
The Penguin book of the sonnet   **821.008**
Poems that live forever   **821.008**
Verses of the poets Laureate   **821.008**
    History and criticism
Brooks, C. The well wrought urn   **821.009**
The Columbia history of British poetry   **821.009**
Heaney, S. The redress of poetry   **821.009**
Pritchard, W. H. Lives of the modern poets
      821.009
Schmidt, M. Lives of the poets   **821.009**
Vendler, H. H. Coming of age as a poet   **820.9**
    Indexes
The Columbia Granger's Index to poetry in collected
  and selected works   **808.81**
    Women authors—Bio-bibliography
Contemporary women poets   **920.003**
    Women authors—Collections
British women poets of the Romantic era   **821.008**
    Women authors—Dictionaries
Contemporary women poets   **920.003**
English poets *See* Poets, English
The **English** Revolution, 1688-1689. Trevelyan, G. M.
      942.06
English-Spanish dictionary. See Gran diccionario
  español-inglés. English-Spanish dictionary   **463**
English traits. Emerson, R. W.
  In Emerson, R. W. The portable Emerson p395-518
      818
English wit and humor
The Oxford book of humorous prose   **827**
The **Englishman's** daughter. Macintyre, B.   **940.4**
Enigma: the battle for the code. Sebag-Montefiore, H.
      940.54
Enigmas *See* Curiosities and wonders
The **enjoyment** of music. Machlis, J.   **781.1**
Enlightened journey. Thondup, T.   **294.3**
Enlightenment
Gay, P. The Enlightenment: an interpretation   **190**

    Encyclopedias
Encyclopedia of the Enlightenment   **940.2**
Wilson, E. J. Encyclopedia of the Enlightenment
      940.2
Enright, D. J. (Dennis Joseph), 1920-2002
  (ed) The Oxford book of death. See The Oxford book
  of death   **808.88**
Enright, Dennis Joseph *See* Enright, D. J. (Dennis Jo-
  seph), 1920-2002
Enron Corp.
Bryce, R. Pipe dreams   **333.79**
Cruver, B. Anatomy of greed   **333.79**
Entanglement. Aczel, A. D.   **530.1**
Entertainers
Hirschfeld, A. Hirschfeld on line   **741.5**
Jay, R. Jay's journal of anomalies   **791**
Sonneborn, L. A to Z of American women in the per-
  forming arts   **920.003**
Terkel, S. The spectator   **791**
Entertaining
Burros, M. F. The new elegant but easy cookbook
      641.5
Kafka, B. Party food   **641.5**
Lagasse, E. Every day's a party   **642**
Mills, B. Desperation entertaining   **642**
Ohrbach, B. M. Tabletops   **642**
Pépin, J. Jacques Pépin celebrates   **641.5**
Sorosky, M. Fast & festive meals for the Jewish holi-
  days   **641.5**
Stewart, M. Great parties   **642**
Stewart, M. The Martha Stewart cookbook   **641.5**
Stewart, M. Martha Stewart's menus for entertaining
      642
Stewart, M. Special occasions   **641.5**
Entrance requirements for colleges and universities
  See Colleges and universities—Entrance requirements
Entrepreneurship
Business: the ultimate resource   **658**
Esser, T. The venture cafe   **620**
Klein, M. The change makers   **920**
Webb, P. The small business handbook   **658**
Entwined lives. Segal, N. L.   **155.4**
The **environment** A-Z. Hosansky, D.   **363.7**
Environment and pesticides *See* Pesticides—Environ-
  mental aspects
Environmental disasters. Davis, L. A.   **363.7**
Environmental encyclopedia   **363.7**
Environmental health
Callahan, J. R. Biological hazards   **615.9**
Davis, D. L. When smoke ran like water   **615.9**
Gonzalez, J. Fallout   **363.7**
Markowitz, G. E. Deceit and denial   **615.9**
Environmental influence on humans
  See also Environmental health
Diamond, J. M. Guns, germs, and steel   **303.4**
Environmental movement
Breton, M. J. Women pioneers for the environment
      920.003
Environmental policy
    Encyclopedias
Hosansky, D. The environment A-Z   **363.7**
    United States
Chadwick, D. H. The company we keep   **591.68**
Environmental pollution *See* Pollution
Environmental protection
  See also Conservation of natural resources
Commoner, B. Making peace with the planet
      304.2
Crawford, M. Habitats and ecosystems   **578.68**
Gore, A., Jr. Earth in the balance   **304.2**
Environmental sciences
Famous first facts about the environment   **363.7**
    Dictionaries
Wyman, B. C. The Facts on File dictionary of environ-
  mental science   **363.7**

Environmental sciences—*Continued*
Encyclopedias
Encyclopedia of global change   363.7
Environmental encyclopedia   363.7
Hosansky, D. The environment A-Z   363.7
Mongillo, J. F. Encyclopedia of environmental science
                                             363.7
Environmentalists
Breton, M. J. Women pioneers for the environment
                                             920.003
The **envy** of the world. Cose, E.   305.8
Epameinondas *See* Epaminondas, ca. 418-362 B.C.
Epaminondas, ca. 418-362 B.C.
About
Hanson, V. D. The soul of battle   355
The **epic** history of biology. Serafini, A.   570
The **epic** of Gilgamesh. See Gilgamesh. Gilgamesh
                                             892
Epictetus, ca. 55-ca. 135
See/See also pages in the following book(s):
Hamilton, E. The echo of Greece p157-68   880.9
Epicurus
See/See also pages in the following book(s):
Jaspers, K. The great philosophers   109
Epidemic! the world of infectious diseases 614.4
Epidemics
Epidemic! the world of infectious diseases   614.4
Garrett, L. The coming plague   614.4
Karlen, A. Man and microbes   614.4
Oldstone, M. B. A. Viruses, plagues, and history
                                             614.4
Ryan, F. Virus-X   614.4
Wills, C. Yellow fever, black goddess   614.4
Epidemiology
Davies, P. The devil's flu   614.5
Drexler, M. Secret agents   614.4
Kolata, G. Flu   614.5
Epigrams
See also Proverbs; Quotations; Toasts
Martial. Epigrams   878
Episcopal Church
The book of common prayer   264
Epistemology *See* Theory of knowledge
Epistles. Horace
In Horace. Satires, Epistles and Ars poetica
                                             878
Epodes. Horace
In Horace. The Odes and Epodes   874
Epstein, Alan, 1949-
As the Romans do   945
Epstein, Daniel Mark
Nat King Cole   92
Sister Aimee: the life of Aimee Semple McPherson
                                             92
Epstein, Edward Jay, 1935-
Dossier: the secret history of Armand Hammer
                                             92
Epstein, Eric Joseph, 1959-
Dictionary of the Holocaust   940.53
Epstein, Sir Jacob, 1880-1959
About
Rose, J. Demons and angels: a life of Jacob Epstein
                                             92
Epstein, Jason
Book business   070.5
Epstein, Joseph, 1937-
A line out for a walk   814
Snobbery: the American version   305.5
(ed) The Norton book of personal essays. See The
Norton book of personal essays   808.84
Epstein, Lee, 1958-
The Supreme Court compendium. See The Supreme
Court compendium   347
Equality
Sowell, T. The quest for cosmic justice   303.3

An **equation** that changed the world. Fritzsch, H.
                                             530.1
Equatorie of the planets. Chaucer, G.
In Chaucer, G. The complete poetry and prose of
Geoffrey Chaucer   821
Equestrianism *See* Horsemanship
Equus. Shaffer, P.   822
The **era** of reconstruction, 1865-1877. Stampp, K. M.
                                             973.8
Erasmus, Desiderius, 1466?-1536
The praise of folly   877
See/See also pages in the following book(s):
Russell, B. A history of Western philosophy p512-22
                                             109
Erdoes, Richard
(ed) American Indian myths and legends. See
American Indian myths and legends   398.2
(jt. auth) Crow Dog, L. Crow Dog   970.004
Erdrich, Louise
See/See also pages in the following book(s):
Coltelli, L. Winged words: American Indian writers
speak   897
Ergonomics *See* Human engineering
Erickson, Carolly, 1943-
Great Catherine   92
Her little majesty: the life of Queen Victoria   92
Erickson, Jon, 1948-
An introduction to fossils and minerals   560
Quakes, eruptions, and other geologic cataclysms
                                             550
Erikson, Erik H. (Erik Homburger), 1902-1994
Young man Luther   92
About
Friedman, L. J. Identity's architect: a biography of Erik
H. Erikson   92
Erlewine, Stephen Thomas
(ed) All music guide. See All music guide
                                             781.64
(ed) All music guide to country. See All music guide
to country   781.642
(ed) All music guide to jazz. See All music guide to
jazz   781.65
Ernest Hemingway, A to Z. Oliver, C. M.   813.009
Ernie Pyle's war. Tobin, J.   92
Ernst, Carl H.
Snakes in question   597.9
Ernst, Carl W., 1950-
The Shambhala guide to sufism   297
Errors
Boller, P. F. They never said it   808.88
Coffey, M. Days of infamy   355
Plait, P. C. Bad astronomy   520
Ervin, Hazel Arnett
(ed) African American literary criticism, 1773 to 2000.
See African American literary criticism, 1773 to
2000   810.9
Escapes
Howarth, D. A. We die alone   940.54
Eschatology
Polkinghorne, J. The God of hope and the end of the
world   236
Escott, Colin
Hank Williams   92
Eskimos *See* Inuit
ESP *See* Extrasensory perception
Espenshade, Edward Bowman, 1910-
(ed) Goode's world atlas. See Goode's world atlas
                                             912
Espionage
See also Spies
Stober, D. A convenient spy   327.12
Vise, D. A. The bureau and the mole   327.12
Wise, D. Spy: the inside story of how the FBI's Robert
Hanssen betrayed America   327.12
Espionage, American *See* American espionage

Espionage, Russian *See* Russian espionage
Esposito, John L.
  Islam   297
  Unholy war   322.4
  What everyone needs to know about Islam   297
  (ed) The Oxford dictionary of Islam. See The Oxford dictionary of Islam   297
  (ed) The Oxford history of Islam. See The Oxford history of Islam   297
Espy, Willard R.
  Words to rhyme with   423
Essay and general literature index   080
An **essay** concerning human understanding. Locke, J.   121
Essays
  The Art of the personal essay   808.84
  The Norton book of personal essays   808.84
  Indexes
  Essay and general literature index   080
Essays & lectures. Emerson, R. W.   818
Essays and reviews. Poe, E. A.   818
Essays: first and second series. Emerson, R. W.
  In Emerson, R. W. The portable Emerson p111-290   818
Essays of E. B. White. White, E. B.   814
Essays of Virginia Woolf. Woolf, V.   824
Essence total makeover   646.7
The **essential** Blake. Blake, W.   821
The **essential** cuisines of Mexico. Kennedy, D.   641.5
The **essential** Darwin. See Darwin, C. The Darwin reader   576.8
The **Essential** desk reference   031.02
The **essential** guide to making handmade books. Fox, G.   686.3
The **essential** guide to prescription drugs. Long, J. W.   615
Essential Judaism. Robinson, G.   296
The **essential** Jung. Jung, C. G.   150.19
The **essential** Lewis and Clark. Lewis, M.   978
Essential manager's manual. Heller, R.   658.4
Essential riding. Price, S. D.   798.2
Essential Sufism   297
The **essential** vegetarian cookbook. Shaw, D.   641.5
Essential Zen   294.3
Essentials of classic Italian cooking. Hazan, M.   641.5
Esser, Teresa
  The venture cafe   620
Essex, Robert Devereux, 2nd Earl of, 1566-1601
  About
  Strachey, L. Elizabeth and Essex   92
Essex (Whale-ship)
  Philbrick, N. In the heart of the sea   910.4
Estate planning
  The American Bar Association guide to wills and estates   346.05
  Clifford, D. Make your own living trust   346.05
  Clifford, D. Plan your estate   346.05
  Shotwell, B. Pass it on   346.05
  Strauss, S. D. Wills and trusts   346.05
Esteban *See* Estevan, d. 1539
Estés, Clarissa Pinkola
  Women who run with the wolves   155.6
Estes, Sally
  (jt. auth) Carter, B. Best books for young adults   028.1
Estevan, d. 1539
  See/See also pages in the following book(s):
  Abdul-Jabbar, K. Black profiles in courage p5-13   920
Estevanico *See* Estevan, d. 1539
Esthetics *See* Aesthetics

Estrada, Rita Clay
  (ed) Writing romances. See Writing romances   808.3
Estrogen
  Seaman, B. The greatest experiment ever performed on women   615
  Warga, C. L. Menopause and the mind   618.1
Etcoff, Nancy L., 1955-
  Survival of the prettiest   391
The **eternal** darkness. Ballard, R. D.   551.46
The **eternal** frontier. Flannery, T. F.   508
The **eternal** now. Tillich, P.   252
Etherege, Sir George, 1635?-1691
  The man of mode
  In Restoration plays   822.008
Ethica Nichomachea. See Aristotle. Ethics   170
Ethics
  See also Business ethics; Christian ethics
  Aristotle. Ethics   170
  Carter, S. L. Integrity   170
  Cohen, R. The good, the bad & the difference   170
  Coles, R. Lives of moral leadership   170
  Comte-Sponville, A. A small treatise on the great virtues   179
  Dewey, J. Theory of the moral life   170
  Edelman, M. W. The measure of our success   170
  Glover, J. Humanity   909.82
  Piaget, J. The moral judgment of the child   155.4
  Schlessinger, L. C. How could you do that?!   170
  Wolfe, A. Moral freedom   170
  Woodruff, P. Reverence   170
  See/See also pages in the following book(s):
  Marcus Aurelius, Emperor of Rome. Meditations   188
  Encyclopedias
  Encyclopedia of applied ethics   170
  Encyclopedia of ethics [Facts on File]   170
  Encyclopedia of ethics [Routledge]   170
Ethics, Jewish *See* Jewish ethics
Ethics, Medical *See* Medical ethics
Ethics, Political *See* Political ethics
Ethics, Sexual *See* Sexual ethics
Ethics. Aristotle
  also in Aristotle. The basic works of Aristotle p927-1112   888
  also in Aristotle. Introduction to Aristotle p337-581   888
The **Ethics** of organ transplants   174
Ethnic America. Sowell, T.   305.8
Ethnic groups
  See also Minorities
  Sowell, T. Ethnic America   305.8
  Sowell, T. Migrations and cultures   304.8
  Voices of multicultural America   815.008
  Encyclopedias
  Gale encyclopedia of multicultural America   305.8
  Harvard encyclopedia of American ethnic groups   305.8
Ethnic relations
  See also Culture conflict; Germany—Ethnic relations; Multicultural education; Multiculturalism; Race relations; United States—Ethnic relations
  Sowell, T. Migrations and cultures   304.8
Ethnobotany
  Davis, W. One river   581.6
Ethnology
  See/See also pages in the following book(s):
  Diamond, J. M. Guns, germs, and steel   303.4
  Dictionaries
  The Dictionary of anthropology   306
  Encyclopedias
  Worldmark encyclopedia of cultures and daily life   306

Ethnology—*Continued*
New Guinea
Flannery, T. F. Throwim way leg   995.3
Polynesia
Heyerdahl, T. Kon-Tiki: across the Pacific by raft   910.4

Ethnopsychology
Lévi-Strauss, C. The savage mind   155.8

Etiquette
Baldrige, L. Letitia Baldrige's more than manners!   649

Baldrige, L. Letitia Baldrige's new manners for new times   395
Bride's book of etiquette   395
Dresser, N. Multicultural manners   395
How to be a perfect stranger   291.3
Martin, J. Miss Manners' basic training: the right thing to say   395
Martin, J. Miss Manners' guide to domestic tranquility   395
Martin, J. Miss Manners on weddings   395
Post, P. Emily Post wedding etiquette   395
Post, P. Emily Post's etiquette   395
Tuckerman, N. The Amy Vanderbilt complete book of etiquette   395

Etzioni, Amitai
The limits of privacy   323.44
The spirit of community   307

Euclid
See/See also pages in the following book(s):
Mlodinow, L. Euclid's window   516

Euclides *See* Euclid

Euclid's window. Mlodinow, L.   516

Eudoxus, of Cnidus, ca. 400-ca. 350 B.C.
See/See also pages in the following book(s):
Bell, E. T. Men of mathematics p19-34   920

Eugenics
Glass, J. M. Life unworthy of life   940.53

Eukiah. Wilson, L.
In Wilson, L. 21 short plays p263-68   812

Euler, Leonhard, 1707-1783
See/See also pages in the following book(s):
Bell, E. T. Men of mathematics p139-52   920

Eulogies
The Book of eulogies   808.8
Remembrances and celebrations   808.8

The Eumenides. Aeschylus
In Aeschylus. The Oresteia   882

The eunuch. Terence
In Terence. Terence, the comedies   872

Euphemism
Dictionaries
Holder, R. W. How not to say what you mean   423

Eureka!: scientific breakthroughs that changed the world. Horvitz, L. A.   509

Euripides, ca. 485-ca. 406 B.C.
Alcestis
In Euripides. Ten plays p3-80   882
Andromache
In Euripides. Ten plays p101-29   882
The Bacchants
In Euripides. Ten plays p281-312   882
Electra
In Euripides. Ten plays p207-39   882
Hippolytus
In Euripides. Ten plays p67-98   882
Ion
In Euripides. Ten plays p133-72   882
Iphigenia among the Taurians
In Euripides. Ten plays p243-78   882
Iphigenia at Aulis
In Euripides. Ten plays p315-54   882
Medea
In Euripides. Ten plays p31-63   882

Ten plays   882
The Trojan women
In Euripides. Ten plays p175-204   882
See/See also pages in the following book(s):
Hamilton, E. The Greek way p271-83   880.9

The **Europa** world year book   310.5
The **Europa** year book. See The Europa world year book   310.5

Europe
Church history
Bainton, R. H. Here I stand: a life of Martin Luther   92
Oberman, H. A. Luther: man between God and the Devil   92
Civilization
Barzun, J. From dawn to decadence   940.2
Durant, W. J. The age of Louis XIV   940.2
Ortega y Gasset, J. The revolt of the masses   909
Folklore
See Folklore—Europe
Foreign relations—United States
Kagan, R. Of paradise and power   327.73
History—476-1492
Furlong, M. Visions & longings   248.2
Herlihy, D. The black death and the transformation of the west   940.1
The Oxford history of medieval Europe   940.1
Reston, J., Jr. The last apocalypse   940.1
History—1492-1789
Durant, W. J. The age of Louis XIV   940.2
History—1789-1815
Urban, M. The man who broke Napoleon's codes   940.2
History—1789-1815—Dictionaries
Pope, S. Dictionary of the Napoleonic wars   940.2
History—1789-1900
Hobsbawm, E. J. The age of revolution, 1789-1848   940.2
History—20th century
Mazower, M. Dark continent: Europe's twentieth century   940.55
History—1918-1945
Brendon, P. The dark valley: a panorama of the 1930s   909.82
Sachar, H. M. Dreamland   940
Intellectual life
Barzun, J. From dawn to decadence   940.2
Gay, P. The Enlightenment: an interpretation   190
Wilson, E. J. Encyclopedia of the Enlightenment   940.2
Politics and government
Garton Ash, T. History of the present   940.55
Social conditions
Tuchman, B. W. The proud tower   909.82
Social conditions—Encyclopedias
Encyclopedia of European social history from 1350 to 2000   940

Europe, Central *See* Central Europe
Europe, Eastern *See* Eastern Europe
European authors *See* Authors, European
European authors, 1000-1900   920.003
European Community
See also European Union
European Union
Kagan, R. Of paradise and power   327.73
European War, 1914-1918 *See* World War, 1914-1918
Euthanasia
Filene, P. G. In the arms of others   179.7
McKhann, C. F. A time to die   179.7
Peck, M. S. Denial of the soul   179.7
Evacuation and relocation of Japanese Americans, 1942-1945 *See* Japanese Americans—Evacuation and relocation, 1942-1945
Evan, William M.
Minding the machines   620.8

Evangelistic healing *See* Spiritual healing
Evans, Arthur V.
  An inordinate fondness for beetles   595.7
Evans, Colin
  The casebook of forensic detection   614
Evans, Eli N.
  Judah P. Benjamin, the Jewish Confederate   92
Evans, Glen
  The encyclopedia of suicide   362.28
Evans, Harold
  The American century   973.9
Evans, Mari, 1923-
  (ed) Black women writers (1950-1980). See Black
    women writers (1950-1980)   810.9
Evans, Richard J.
  Lying about Hitler   940.53
Evans, Stewart
  (comp) The Ultimate Jack the Ripper companion. See
    The Ultimate Jack the Ripper companion   364.1
Evans, Walker, 1903-1975
  (jt. auth) Agee, J. Let us now praise famous men
                                              976.1
  About
  Rathbone, B. Walker Evans   92
Evans-Wentz, W. Y. (Walter Yeeling), 1878-1965
  (ed) Tibetan book of the dead. The Tibetan book of
    the dead   294.3
Evans-Wentz, Walter Yeeling *See* Evans-Wentz, W. Y.
  (Walter Yeeling), 1878-1965
Evanzz, Karl
  The messenger: the rise and fall of Elijah Muhammad
                                              92
Eveleth Mines (Firm)
  Bingham, C. Class action   342
Even in quiet places. Stafford, W. E.   811
Even the stars look lonesome. Angelou, M. 814
Ever green: the Boston Celtics. Shaughnessy, D.
                                              796.323
Ever since Darwin. Gould, S. J.   576.8
Everest, George, 1790-1866
  About
  Keay, J. The great arc   526
Everest: mountain without mercy. Coburn, B.
                                              796.52
Everglades (Fla.)
  Douglas, M. S. The Everglades: river of grass
                                              577.6
Everitt, Anthony
  Cicero   92
Everitt, Brian
  The Cambridge dictionary of statistics   519.5
Evers, Medgar Wiley, 1925-1963
  About
  Vollers, M. Ghosts of Mississippi   364.1
Every day's a party. Lagasse, E.   642
Every drop for sale. Rothfeder, J.   333.91
Every employee's guide to the law. Joel, L. G.
                                              344
Every handgun is aimed at you. Sugarmann, J.
                                              363.3
Every landlord's legal guide. Portman, J. 346.04
Every sewer's guide to the perfect fit. Morris, M.
                                              646.4
Every shut eye ain't asleep   811.008
Every tenant's legal guide. Portman, J.   346.04
Every woman's quick & easy car care. Kachur, B.
                                              629.28
Everybody was so young: Gerald and Sara Murphy, a
  lost generation love story. Vaill, A.   92
Everybody's guide to small claims court. Warner, R. E.
                                              347
Everyday life in ancient Greece. Robinson, C. E.
                                              938
Everyday life in early America. Hawke, D. F.
                                              973.2

Everyday living skills *See* Life skills
Everyman (Morality)
  Everyman
    In Everyman, and medieval miracle plays
                                              822.008
    In The Oxford anthology of English literature v1
                                              820.8
Everyman, and medieval miracle plays   822.008
Everyman's Talmud. Cohen, A.   296.1
Everyone's guide to cancer therapy   616.99
Everything to gain. Carter, J.   92
Everything was possible. Chapin, T. S.   792.6
Everything you need to know about Lyme disease and
  other tick-borne disorders. Vanderhoof-Forschner, K.
                                              616.9
Evil *See* Good and evil
Evil spirits *See* Demonology
Evolution
  Avise, J. C. Genetics in the wild   591.3
  Behe, M. J. Darwin's black box   576.8
  Bloom, H. The Lucifer principle   128
  Boaz, N. T. Evolving health   616.07
  Boulter, M. C. Extinction: evolution and the end of
    man   576.8
  The Cambridge encyclopedia of human evolution
                                              599.93
  Darwin, C. The Darwin reader   576.8
  Darwin, C. The origin of species   576.8
  Dawkins, R. Climbing Mount Improbable   576
  Dawkins, R. River out of Eden   576
  Dawkins, R. The selfish gene   576
  Deloria, V. Evolution, creationism, and other modern
    myths   291.1
  Dennett, D. C. Darwin's dangerous idea   146
  Diamond, J. M. The third chimpanzee   599.93
  Duve, C. de. Life evolving   576.8
  Duve, C. de. Vital dust   570.1
  Eiseley, L. C. The immense journey   576.8
  Eldredge, N. Fossils   560
  Fortey, R. A. Life   576.8
  Fortey, R. A. Trilobite!   560
  Goodwin, B. C. How the leopard changed its spots
                                              576
  Gould, S. J. Bully for brontosaurus   508
  Gould, S. J. Eight little piggies   576.8
  Gould, S. J. Ever since Darwin   576.8
  Gould, S. J. Hen's teeth and horse's toes   576.8
  Gould, S. J. I have landed   578
  Gould, S. J. Leonardo's mountain of clams and the
    Diet of Worms   508
  Gould, S. J. The lying stones of Marrakesh 508
  Gould, S. J. The panda's thumb   576.8
  Gould, S. J. The structure of evolutionary theory
                                              576.8
  Gould, S. J. Wonderful life: the Burgess Shale and the
    nature of history   560
  Hooper, J. Of moths and men   576.8
  Jolly, A. Lucy's legacy   599.93
  Jones, S. Darwin's ghost   576.8
  Lavers, C. Why elephants have big ears   590
  Leakey, R. E. The sixth extinction   304.2
  Loewenstein, W. R. The touchstone of life   571.6
  Margulis, L. Symbiotic planet   576.8
  Marks, J. What it means to be 98% chimpanzee
                                              599.93
  Mayr, E. What evolution is   576.8
  Miller, K. R. Finding Darwin's God   231.7
  Palumbi, S. R. The evolution explosion   576.8
  Pennock, R. T. Tower of Babel   576.8
  Pinker, S. How the mind works   153
  Rose, M. R. Darwin's spectre   576.8
  Sagan, C. Shadows of forgotten ancestors   570.1
  Small, M. F. What's love got to do with it?
                                              576.8
  Tattersall, I. Extinct humans   599.93

Evolution—*Continued*
Tattersall, I. The fossil trail   **599.93**
Tattersall, I. The monkey in the mirror   **599.93**
Teilhard de Chardin, P. The phenomenon of man
    113
Tudge, C. The time before history   **599.93**
Walker, A. The wisdom of the bones   **599.93**
Weiner, J. The beak of the finch   **598**
    See/See also pages in the following book(s):
Deacon, T. W. The symbolic species   **153.6**
Lewontin, R. C. The triple helix   **572.8**
     Encyclopedias
Encyclopedia of evolution   **576.8**
Life on earth   **333.95**
Evolution, creationism, and other modern myths.
    Deloria, V.   **291.1**
The **evolution** explosion. Palumbi, S. R.   **576.8**
The **evolution** of physics. Einstein, A.   **530**
The **evolution** of useful things. Petroski, H.   **609**
Evolving health. Boaz, N. T.   **616.07**
Ewans, Martin
    Afghanistan   **958.1**
Ewen, David, 1907-1985
    American songwriters   **920.003**
    Musicians since 1900. See Musicians since 1900
    920.003
Ex libris. Fadiman, A.   **814**
Ex-service men *See* Veterans
Examinations
    See also High school equivalency examination
The **Examined** life   **190**
Excavating Jesus. Crossan, J. D.   **225.9**
Excavations (Archeology)
     Israel
Crossan, J. D. Excavating Jesus   **225.9**
Exceptional children
    See also Handicapped children
     Education—Directories
The Directory for exceptional children   **371.9**
The **excruciating** history of dentistry. Wynbrandt, J.
    617.6
Execution: the discipline of getting things done.
    Bossidy, L. A.   **658.4**
Executions *See* Capital punishment
Executive ability
    See also Leadership
    Bossidy, L. A. Execution: the discipline of getting
    things done   **658.4**
    Goleman, D. Primal leadership   **658.4**
    Peters, T. J. The circle of innovation   **658.4**
Executive departments
     United States—Directories
Washington information directory   **320.025**
Executive power
    Moynihan, D. P. Secrecy   **352**
    Simon, J. F. What kind of nation   **342**
    See/See also pages in the following book(s):
    Tuchman, B. W. Practicing history p294-303   **907**
Executives
    Henry, S. The Dinner Club   **338.7**
     Directories
Standard and Poor's register of corporations, directors,
    and executives   **338.7**
Executors and administrators
    Plotnick, C. How to settle an estate   **346.05**
The **executors** manual. See Plotnick, C. How to settle an
    estate   **346.05**
Exercise
    See also Physical fitness; T'ai chi ch'üan
    Active living every day   **613.7**
    Bailey, C. Smart exercise   **613.7**
    Callahan, L. The fitness factor   **613.7**
    Fitness and exercise sourcebook   **613.7**
    Fitness over fifty   **613**

Rosenstein, A. Water exercises for Parkinson's
    616.8
Exercise: a guide from the National Institute on Aging.
    See Fitness over fifty   **613**
Exercises, Reducing *See* Weight loss
Exiles *See* Refugees
Existentialism
    Barrett, W. Irrational man   **142**
    Existentialism from Dostoevsky to Sartre   **142**
    May, R. The discovery of being   **150.19**
    Sartre, J. P. Being and nothingness   **142**
    Sartre, J. P. Existentialism and human emotions
    142
    Tillich, P. The courage to be   **179**
    See/See also pages in the following book(s):
    Tillich, P. Theology of culture   **230**
Existentialism and human emotions. Sartre, J. P.
    142
Existentialism from Dostoevsky to Sartre   **142**
Exiting nirvana. Park, C. C.   **616.89**
Exley, Frederick
     About
Yardley, J. Misfit: the strange life of Frederick Exley
    92
Exorcism
    Cuneo, M. W. American exorcism   **265**
Expanding the envelope. Gorn, M. H.   **629.13**
Expanding universe *See* Universe
Experience. Amis, M.   **92**
Experiment central   **507.8**
Experimentation on animals *See* Animal experimenta-
    tion
Explaining Hitler. Rosenbaum, R.   **92**
Exploration
    Boorstin, D. J. The discoverers   **909**
     Atlases
Oxford atlas of exploration   **911**
Explorers
    Points unknown   **910**
    Slung, M. B. Living with cannibals and other women's
    adventures   **910.4**
     Dictionaries
Explorers and discoverers of the world   **920.003**
World explorers and discoverers   **920.003**
Explorers and discoverers of the world   **920.003**
Exploring consciousness. Carter, R.   **153**
Exploring Lewis and Clark. Slaughter, T. P.   **978**
Exploring wine. Kolpan, S.   **641.2**
Extermination of pests *See* Pest control
Extinct animals
    See also Mass extinction of species; Rare animals
    Cokinos, C. Hope is the thing with feathers   **598**
    Eldredge, N. The miner's canary   **560**
    Weidensaul, S. The ghost with trembling wings
    591.68
Extinct humans. Tattersall, I.   **599.93**
Extinction. Raup, D. M.   **560**
Extinction: evolution and the end of man. Boulter, M.
    C.   **576.8**
Extinction of species, Mass *See* Mass extinction of spe-
    cies
Extramarital relationships *See* Adultery
Extrasensory perception
    Sheldrake, R. Dogs that know when their owners are
    coming home   **133.8**
Extreme stars. Kaler, J. B.   **523.8**
Eye
     Diseases
Cassel, G. H. The eye book   **617.7**
Eye of the albatross. Safina, C.   **598**
Eye of the whale. Russell, D.   **599.5**
Eyes of the nation. Virga, V.   **973**
Eyes on the prize: America's civil rights years, 1954-
    1965. Williams, J.   **323.1**
The **Eyes** on the prize civil rights reader   **323.1**

Eyewitness to America 973
Eyewitness travel guides 910.2
Eyman, Scott, 1951-
Print the legend: the life and times of John Ford
92
Eyre, Harmon J., 1941-
(ed) Informed decisions. See Informed decisions
616.99
Ezekiel, Raphael S., 1931-
The racist mind 322.4

F

F.D.R. and his enemies. Fried, A. 92
F. Scott Fitzgerald A to Z. Tate, M. J. 813.009
Faber, Marion
(jt. auth) Lehmann, S. Rudolf Serkin 92
The **Faber** dictionary of euphemisms. See Holder, R. W.
How not to say what you mean 423
Fabric dyeing & printing. Wells, K. 746.6
The **fabric** of reality. Deutsch, D. 530
Fabric savvy. Betzina, S. 646.2
Fabricant, Florence
(ed) The New cooks' catalogue. See The New cooks'
catalogue 683
Fabrics
Betzina, S. Fabric savvy 646.2
Dictionaries
Fairchild's dictionary of textiles 677
Face
Care
Gross, K. J. Woman's face 646.7
Surgery
Hallman, T. Sam: the boy behind the mask 362.1
Facing east from Indian country. Richter, D. K.
970.004
Facing the extreme. Todorov, T. 940.53
Facing the wind. Salamon, J. 364.1
Facsimile transmission See Fax transmission
Factories
Von Drehle, D. Triangle: the fire that changed America
974.7
Facts, Miscellaneous See Curiosities and wonders
The **facts**. Roth, P. 92
Facts about American immigration. Brownstone, D. M.
325.73
Facts about Canada, its provinces and territories. Weihs,
J. R. 971
Facts about retiring in the United States 305.26
Facts about the American wars 355
Facts about the presidents. Kane, J. N. 920
Facts about the states 973
Facts about the world's languages: an encyclopedia of
the world's major languages, past and present
400
Facts on file 909.82
The **Facts** on File companion to the American short sto-
ry 813.009
The **Facts** on File dictionary of 20th-century allusions.
See Cole, S. The Facts on File dictionary of cultural
and historical allusions 031.02
The **Facts** on File dictionary of American regionalisms.
Hendrickson, R. 427
The **Facts** on File dictionary of atomic and nuclear phys-
ics 539.7
The **Facts** on File dictionary of biochemistry 572
The **Facts** on File dictionary of biotechnology and genet-
ic engineering. Steinberg, M. L. 660.6
The **Facts** on File dictionary of botany 580
The **Facts** on File dictionary of cell and molecular biolo-
gy 571.6
The **Facts** on File dictionary of computer science
004

The **Facts** on File dictionary of cultural and historical al-
lusions. Cole, S. 031.02
The **Facts** on File dictionary of earth science 550.3
The **Facts** on File dictionary of environmental science.
Wyman, B. C. 363.7
The **Facts** on File dictionary of foreign words and
phrases. Manser, M. H. 422.03
The **Facts** on File dictionary of proverbs. Manser, M. H.
398.9
The **Facts** on File dictionary of space technology. Ange-
lo, J. A. 629.4
The **Facts** on File encyclopedia of science 503
The **Facts** on File encyclopedia of science, technology,
and society. Volti, R. 503
The **Facts** on File encyclopedia of word and phrase ori-
gins. Hendrickson, R. 422.03
The **Facts** on File geometry handbook. Gorini, C. A.
516
The **Facts** on File space and astronomy handbook. Ange-
lo, J. A. 520
The **Facts** on File weather and climate handbook.
Allaby, M. 551.6
Facts on file yearbook. See Facts on file 909.82
Fadiman, Anne, 1953-
Ex libris 814
Fadiman, Clifton, 1904-1999
The new lifetime reading plan 028
(ed) World poetry. See World poetry 808.81
Fadiman, James, 1939-
(ed) Essential Sufism. See Essential Sufism 297
The **faerie** queene. Spenser, E. 821
also in Spenser, E. The works of Edmund Spenser
v1-6 828
Fagan, Brian M.
(ed) The Oxford companion to archaeology. See The
Oxford companion to archaeology 930.1
Fagan, Eleanora *See* Holiday, Billie, 1915-1959
Fagin, Dan
Toxic deception 615.9
Fahey, Anne Marie
About
Rule, A. —and never let her go 364.1
Fahlbusch, Erwin
(ed) The Encyclopedia of Christianity. See The Ency-
clopedia of Christianity 230.003
Failed crusade. Cohen, S. F. 327.73
Failure is impossible. Anthony, S. B. 92
Failure is not an option. Kranz, E. F. 629.45
Fair ball. Costas, B. 796.357
Fairbank, John King, 1907-1991
China 951
China: tradition & transformation 951
The great Chinese revolution: 1800-1985 951
Fairchild, B. H. (Bertram H.), 1942-
Early occult memory systems of the Lower Midwest
811
Fairchild, Bertram H. *See* Fairchild, B. H. (Bertram
H.), 1942-
The **Fairchild** dictionary of fashion. Calasibetta, C. M.
391
Fairchild's dictionary of textiles 677
Fairclough, Adam
Better day coming 323.1
Fairy tales
See also Fantasy fiction
Favorite folktales from around the world 398.2
Grimm, J. The complete fairy tales of the Brothers
Grimm 398.2
History and criticism
The Oxford companion to fairy tales 398.2
Indexes
Index to fairy tales 398.2
Faith
John Paul II, Pope. Crossing the threshold of hope
282

Faith—*Continued*
Terkel, S. Will the circle be unbroken? **128**
Tillich, P. Dynamics of faith **234**
Turner, J. Without God, without creed **211**
Faith and treason. Fraser, A. **942.06**
Faith healing *See* Spiritual healing
Faith of my fathers. McCain, J. S. **92**
Falkner, David
Great time coming: the life of Jackie Robinson, from baseball to Birmingham **92**
Fall, N'Goné
(ed) An Anthology of African art: the twentieth century. See An Anthology of African art: the twentieth century **709.6**
The **fall** of Berlin. Read, A. **940.54**
The **fall** of Berlin 1945. Beevor, A. **940.54**
The **fall** of Napoleon. Hamilton-Williams, D. **944.05**
Falla, P. S. (Paul Stephen), 1913-
(ed) The Concise Oxford Russian dictionary. See The Concise Oxford Russian dictionary **491.7**
(ed) The Oxford Russian dictionary. See The Oxford Russian dictionary **491.7**
Falla, Paul Stephen *See* Falla, P. S. (Paul Stephen), 1913-
Fallacies *See* Errors
Falling hard. Jones, C. **796.8**
Falling leaves. Mah, A. Y. **92**
Falling leaves return to their roots. See Mah, A. Y. Falling leaves **92**
Fallout. Gonzalez, J. **363.7**
Fallows, James M.
Looking at the sun **950**
Falola, Toyin
Key events in African history **960**
Falsehood *See* Truthfulness and falsehood
Faludi, Susan
Stiffed **305.31**
Familiar quotations. Bartlett, J. **808.88**
Family
See also types of family members
Gore, A., Jr. Joined at the heart **306.8**
Hewlett, S. A. The war against parents **649**
Hite, S. The Hite report on the family **306.8**
Lewis, O. The children of Sánchez **972.08**
Miller, A. Paths of life **306.8**
Tannen, D. I only say this because I love you **306.8**
Westheimer, R. The value of family **306.8**
Wilson, J. Q. The marriage problem **306.8**
See/See also pages in the following book(s):
Toffler, A. Future shock p211-30 **303.4**
Encyclopedias
International encyclopedia of marriage and family **306.8**
Parenthood in America **306.8**
Family. Frazier, I. **977.1**
Family business. Ginsberg, A. **92**
Family caregivers *See* Caregivers
The **family** continues. Wilson, L.
In Wilson, L. 21 short plays p137-52 **812**
Family finance *See* Personal finance
The **family** guide to preventing and treating 100 infectious illnesses. Stoffman, P. **616**
Family histories *See* Genealogy
Family life
A History of private life **909**
Ozment, S. E. Flesh and spirit **943**
Safer, J. The normal one **158**
See/See also pages in the following book(s):
Zanichkowsky, S. Fourteen **92**
Family man. Trillin, C. **817**
The **family** nutrition book. Sears, W. **613.2**
Family planning *See* Birth control
Family planning sourcebook **363.9**

Family reunion. Eliot, T. S.
In Eliot, T. S. The complete poems and plays, 1909-1950 p223-94 **818**
Family size
See also Birth control; Only child
Family violence *See* Domestic violence
Family voices. Pinter, H.
In Pinter, H. Complete works v4 **822**
Famous first facts. Kane, J. N. **031.02**
Famous first facts about American politics. Anzovin, S. **973**
Famous first facts about sports. Franck, I. M. **796**
Famous first facts about the environment **363.7**
Famous first facts, international edition **031.02**
Famous lines. Andrews, R. **808.88**
Famous people *See* Celebrities
Fancy dress *See* Costume
Fang, Li-chih *See* Fang Lizhi
Fang Lizhi
Bringing down the Great Wall **951.05**
The **Fannie** Farmer baking book. Cunningham, M. **641.8**
The **Fannie** Farmer cookbook. Farmer, F. M. **641.5**
Fannin, Caroline M.
(jt. auth) Gubert, B. K. Distinguished African Americans in aviation and space science **920.003**
Fanning, Janis
(jt. auth) Jones, M. Handcrafted ceramic tiles **738**
Fanny and Adelaide: the lives of the remarkable Kemble sisters. Blainey, A. **92**
Fanny Kemble's civil wars. Clinton, C. **92**
Fanon, Frantz, 1925-1961
About
Macey, D. Frantz Fanon **92**
Fantastic fables. Bierce, A.
In Bierce, A. The collected writings **818**
Fantastic fiction *See* Fantasy fiction
Fantasy
Jones, G. Killing monsters **302.23**
Fantasy and horror **016.8**
Fantasy fiction
See also Fairy tales; Science fiction
Bibliography
Burgess, M. Reference guide to science fiction, fantasy, and horror **016.8**
Fantasy and horror **016.8**
Reginald, R. Science fiction and fantasy literature, 1975-1991 **016.8**
Bio-bibliography
St. James guide to fantasy writers **809.3**
Supernatural fiction writers **809.3**
Dictionaries
Manguel, A. The dictionary of imaginary places **809.3**
Encyclopedias
The Encyclopedia of fantasy **809.3**
History and criticism
Fantasy and horror **016.8**
Magill's guide to science fiction and fantasy literature **809.3**
St. James guide to fantasy writers **809.3**
Supernatural fiction writers **809.3**
Wullschläger, J. Inventing wonderland **820.9**
Far away. Churchill, C. **822**
Far East *See* East Asia
Far from home. Schlissel, L. **978**
Fara, Patricia
Newton: the making of genius **92**
Faraday, Michael, 1791-1867
See/See also pages in the following book(s):
Guillen, M. Five equations that changed the world **530.1**
Malone, J. W. It doesn't take a rocket scientist **920**

Faragher, John Mack, 1945-
Daniel Boone   92
Farber, David R.
(ed) The Columbia guide to America in the 1960s. See
The Columbia guide to America in the 1960s
     973.92
Farberow, Norman L.
(jt. auth) Evans, G. The encyclopedia of suicide
     362.28
Farewell. Foote, H.   92
Fargnoli, A. Nicholas
James Joyce A to Z   823.009
William Faulkner A to Z   813.009
Fargues, Philippe
The atlas of the Arab world   909
Fariello, Griffin
Red scare   973.92
Farm animals See Domestic animals
Farm life
MacDonald, B. The egg and I   818
Farm produce
Charles, D. Lords of the harvest   664
Cummins, R. Genetically engineered food   363.1
Genetically modified foods   363.1
Pringle, P. Food, inc   363.1
Winston, M. L. Travels in the genetically modified
zone   664
Marketing
Madison, D. Local flavors   641.5
Farm tenancy
Agee, J. Let us now praise famous men   976.1
Farmer, David Hugh
The Oxford dictionary of saints   920.003
Farmer, Fannie Merritt, 1857-1915
The Fannie Farmer cookbook   641.5
Cunningham, M. The Fannie Farmer baking book
     641.8
Farming See Agriculture
Farming, Organic See Organic farming
Farnsworth, Philo T., 1906-1971
About
Stashower, D. The boy genius and the mogul
     791.45
See/See also pages in the following book(s):
Horvitz, L. A. Eureka!: scientific breakthroughs that
changed the world   509
Farquhar, George, 1677?-1707
The beaux' stratagem
In Restoration plays   822.008
Farr, J. Michael
(ed) Guide for occupational exploration. See Guide for
occupational exploration   331.7
O*NET dictionary of occupational titles. See O*NET
dictionary of occupational titles   331.7
Farrakhan, Louis
About
Gardell, M. In the name of Elijah Muhammad
     297
Levinsohn, F. H. Looking for Farrakhan   92
See/See also pages in the following book(s):
Dyson, M. E. Race rules   305.8
Gates, H. L. Thirteen ways of looking at a black man
     920
Farrand, John, 1937-1994
(jt. auth) Bull, J. L. The National Audubon Society
field guide to North American birds, Eastern region
     598
Farrell, John A.
Tip O'Neill and the Democratic century   92
Farrell, Mary
Learning computer programming   005
Farrell, Suzanne, 1945-
See/See also pages in the following book(s):
Prose, F. The lives of the muses   920

Farsoun, Samih K.
Palestine and the Palestinians   956.94
Farwell, Byron
Over there   940.4
Fascism
Bosworth, R. J. B. Mussolini   92
France
See/See also pages in the following book(s):
Kaplan, A. Y. The collaborator: the trial & execution
of Robert Brasillach   92
Germany
See National socialism
Fashion
See also Clothing and dress; Costume
History
Contemporary fashion   391
In an influential fashion   391
Laver, J. Costume and fashion   391
Peacock, J. The chronicle of Western fashion   391
Peacock, J. Men's fashion   391
Fashion design
Contemporary fashion   391
In an influential fashion   391
Dictionaries
Calasibetta, C. M. The Fairchild dictionary of fashion
     391
Fashion in costume, 1200-2000. Nunn, J.   391
Fashion industry See Clothing industry
Fassett, Kaffe
Glorious patchwork   746.46
Fast, Julius, 1918-
Body language   153.6
Fast & festive meals for the Jewish holidays. Sorosky,
M.   641.5
Fast food nation. Schlosser, E.   394.1
Fast foods See Convenience foods
Fast girls. White, E.   305.23
Fast movers. Sherwood, J. D.   959.704
Faster. Gleick, J.   529
Faster than the speed of light. Magueijo, J.   535
Fasts and feasts See Religious holidays
Judaism
See Jewish holidays
Fat. Pool, R.   616.3
Fat-free diet See Low-fat diet
Fat land. Critser, G.   613.2
Fat talk. Nichter, M.   613.2
Fatal harvest   630
The **fatal** shore. Hughes, R.   994
Fatal vision. McGinniss, J.   364.1
Fatally ill patients See Terminally ill
Fate and fatalism
May, R. Freedom and destiny   158
Fates worse than death. Vonnegut, K.   818
The **father.** Strindberg, A.
In Strindberg, A. Strindberg: five plays p19-62
     839.7
The **father:** a life of Henry James, Sr. Habegger, A.
     92
Father and child See Father-child relationship
Father-child relationship
Marzollo, J. Fathers & babies   649
Father-daughter relationship
See/See also pages in the following book(s):
Gurian, M. The wonder of girls   305.23
Father-son relationship
Ambrose, S. E. Comrades   302.3
Dorris, M. The broken cord   362.292
See/See also pages in the following book(s):
Pollack, W. S. Real boys p113-44   305.23
Fatherhood. Cosby, B.   306.8
Fathers
Cosby, B. Fatherhood   306.8
Fathers, Single parent See Single parent family
Fathers & babies. Marzollo, J.   649

Fathers and sons *See* Father-son relationship

Faulkner, William, 1897-1962
About
Brooks, C. William Faulkner: the Yoknapatawpha country ... **813.009**
Fargnoli, A. N. William Faulkner A to Z ... **813.009**
See/See also pages in the following book(s):
Kazin, A. An American procession p345-56 ... **810.9**

Faurie, Bernadette
The horse riding & care handbook ... **636.1**

Fauset, Jessie Redmon, 1882-1961
See/See also pages in the following book(s):
American women fiction writers ... **813.009**
Gilbert, S. M. No man's land v3 p121-65 ... **820.9**
Wall, C. A. Women of the Harlem Renaissance
... **810.9**

Faust, Drew Gilpin
Mothers of invention ... **973.7**

Faust. Goethe, J. W. von ... **832**

Faust, part 1. Goethe, J. W. von
In Our dramatic heritage v4 ... **808.82**

The **Faustian** bargain. Petropoulos, J. ... **709**

Favorite folktales from around the world ... **398.2**

Favreau, Marc, 1953-
(ed) Remembering slavery. See Remembering slavery
... **326**

Fawkes, Guy, 1570-1606
About
Fraser, A. Faith and treason ... **942.06**

Fax *See* Fax transmission

Fax transmission
Directories
FaxUSA ... **384.1**
National E-mail and FAX directory ... **384.1**
FaxUSA ... **384.1**

FBI *See* United States. Federal Bureau of Investigation

The **FBI**. Kessler, R. ... **363.2**

The **FBI**: a comprehensive reference guide ... **363.2**

FDR, into the storm, 1937-1940. Davis, K. S. ... **92**

Fear
See also Anxiety; Phobias
Doctor, R. M. The encyclopedia of phobias, fears, and anxieties ... **616.85**
Dozier, R. W., Jr. Fear itself ... **152.4**
Garber, S. W. Monsters under the bed and other childhood fears ... **649**
Jeffers, S. J. Feel the fear and do it anyway
... **152.4**

Fear and loathing in America. Thompson, H. S. ... **92**

Fear itself. Dozier, R. W., Jr. ... **152.4**

Fear of physics. Krauss, L. M. ... **530**

Feast of Lights *See* Hanukkah

Feast of Tabernacles *See* Sukkoth

Feasting the heart. Price, R. ... **814**

Feather, Leonard
The biographical encyclopedia of jazz ... **920.003**
From Satchmo to Miles ... **920**

Feature writing for newspapers and magazines. Friedlander, E. J. ... **070.4**

The **Fed**. Mayer, M. ... **332.1**

Federal Bureau of Investigation (U.S.) *See* United States. Federal Bureau of Investigation

Federal civil service jobs ... **351.076**

Federal courts *See* Courts—United States

Federal government
See/See also pages in the following book(s):
Boorstin, D. J. The Americans: The national experience p393-406 ... **973**
Directories
Government phone book USA ... **320.025**

Federal Party (U.S.)
Miller, J. C. The Federalist era, 1789-1801 ... **973.4**

Federal Reserve banks
Meltzer, A. H. A history of the Federal Reserve v1
... **332.1**

Federal Reserve System (U.S.). Board of Governors
Greider, W. Secrets of the temple ... **332.1**
Mayer, M. The Fed ... **332.1**
Meltzer, A. H. A history of the Federal Reserve v1
... **332.1**
Woodward, B. Maestro: Greenspan's Fed and the American boom ... **332.1**
See/See also pages in the following book(s):
Martin, J. Greenspan ... **92**

The **Federalist** ... **342**

The **Federalist** era, 1789-1801. Miller, J. C. ... **973.4**

Feel the fear and do it anyway. Jeffers, S. J. ... **152.4**

Feeling good. Burns, D. D. ... **158**

The **feeling** of what happens. Damasio, A. R. ... **153**

Feig, Paul
Kick me ... **305.23**

Feigen, Richard, 1930-
Tales from the art crypt ... **708**

Feigenbaum, Richard A.
The 529 College Savings Plan ... **378.3**

Feiler, Bruce S.
Abraham ... **222**
Walking the Bible ... **915.6**

Feinman, Jay M.
Law 101 ... **340**

Feinsilber, Mike
(jt. auth) Webber, E. Merriam-Webster's dictionary of allusions ... **803**

Feinstein, Elaine, 1930-
Ted Hughes ... **92**

Feinstein, John
A good walk spoiled ... **796.352**
The majors: in pursuit of golf's Holy Grail
... **796.352**
A march to madness ... **796.323**
Open: inside the ropes at Bethpage Black
... **796.352**

Feldman, Burton
The Nobel Prize ... **001.4**

Feldman, David, 1950-
When do fish sleep? and other imponderables of everyday life ... **031.02**
Why do clocks run clockwise? and other imponderables ... **031.02**

Feldman, Paula R.
(ed) British women poets of the Romantic era. See British women poets of the Romantic era
... **821.008**

Feldon, Miriam Eliav- *See* Eliav-Feldon, Miriam, 1946-

Felipe II, King of Spain, 1527-1598 *See* Philip II, King of Spain, 1527-1598

Felleman, Hazel
(ed) The Best loved poems of the American people. See The Best loved poems of the American people
... **821.008**
(comp) Poems that live forever. See Poems that live forever ... **821.008**

Fellman, Michael
Citizen Sherman: a life of William Tecumseh Sherman
... **92**
The making of Robert E. Lee ... **92**

Fellowships *See* Scholarships

Fell's United States coin book. See Official know-it-all guide: coins ... **737.4**

Felton-Collins, Victoria *See* Collins, Victoria F. (Victoria Felton), 1942-

Female climacteric *See* Menopause

Female role *See* Sex role

The **feminine** face of God. Anderson, S. R. ... **291**

Feminine ingenuity. Macdonald, A. L. ... **609**

The **feminine** mystique. Friedan, B. ... **305.4**

Feminine psychology *See* Women—Psychology

Femininity of God
Anderson, S. R. The feminine face of God ... **291**

Feminism
See also Women's movement
Anthony, S. B. Failure is impossible   **92**
Brownmiller, S. In our time   **305.4**
Buhle, M. J. Feminism and its discontents   **150.19**
Cullen-DuPont, K. Encyclopedia of women's history in America   **305.4**
Freedman, E. B. No turning back   **305.4**
Friedan, B. The feminine mystique   **305.4**
Goldsmith, B. Other powers: the age of suffrage, spiritualism, and the scandalous Victoria Woodhull   **92**
Greer, G. The madwoman's underclothes   **305.4**
Greer, G. The whole woman   **305.4**
Heilbrun, C. G. Hamlet's mother and other women   **820.9**
Murphy, C. The Word according to Eve   **220.8**
Rich, A. Blood, bread, and poetry   **814**
Roberts, C. We are our mothers' daughters   **305.4**
Rosen, R. The world split open   **305.4**
Sommers, C. H. Who stole feminism?   **305.4**
Steinem, G. Moving beyond words   **305.4**
Steinem, G. Outrageous acts and everyday rebellions   **305.4**
Steinem, G. Revolution from within   **155.2**
Ware, S. Still missing: Amelia Earhart and the search for modern feminism   **92**
See/See also pages in the following book(s):
Friedan, B. Life so far   **92**
Rich, A. Arts of the possible   **818**
Ward, G. C. Not for ourselves alone: the story of Elizabeth Cady Stanton and Susan B. Anthony   **92**
Feminism and its discontents. Buhle, M. J.   **150.19**
Fena, Lori
(jt. auth) Jennings, C. The hundredth window   **005.8**
Fenby, Jonathan
France on the brink   **944.083**
Fences. Wilson, A.   **812**
Fencing
Cohen, R. By the sword   **796.8**
Fenn, Elizabeth A. (Elizabeth Anne), 1959-
Pox Americana   **614.5**
Fenton, Ann D.
(comp) Peterson, C. S. Index to children's songs   **782.42**
Fenton, James, 1949-
A Garden from a hundred packets of seed   **635.9**
Leonardo's nephew   **709**
Fenton, William Nelson, 1908-
The Great Law and the Longhouse   **970.004**
Ferber, Edna, 1887-1968
See/See also pages in the following book(s):
American women fiction writers   **813.009**
Ferber, Linda S.
Masters of color and light   **759.13**
Ferguson, Everett, 1933-
(ed) Encyclopedia of early Christianity. See Encyclopedia of early Christianity   **230.003**
Ferguson, Gary Lynn
Song finder   **782.42**
Ferguson, Kitty
Measuring the universe   **523.1**
Prisons of light   **523.8**
Tycho & Kepler   **92**
Fergusson, Rosalind
(ed) The Cassell dictionary of English idioms. See The Cassell dictionary of English idioms   **423**
(ed) Manser, M. H. The Facts on File dictionary of proverbs   **398.9**
Ferling, John E.
The first of men: a life of George Washington   **92**
Setting the world ablaze   **973.3**

Ferlinghetti, Lawrence
These are my rivers   **811**
(ed) City lights pocket poets anthology. See City lights pocket poets anthology   **808.81**
Fermat, Pierre de, 1601-1665
See/See also pages in the following book(s):
Bell, E. T. Men of mathematics p56-72   **920**
Flowers, C. Instability rules   **509**
Fermat's enigma. Singh, S.   **512**
Fermat's last theorem. Aczel, A. D.   **512**
Fermat's last theorem. See Singh, S. Fermat's enigma   **512**
Fernández-Armesto, Felipe
Near a thousand tables   **641.3**
Fernández Revuelta, Alina
Castro's daughter   **92**
See/See also pages in the following book(s):
Gimbel, W. Havana dreams   **972.91**
Fernando Pessoa & Co. Pessoa, F.   **869**
Ferngren, Gary B.
(ed) The History of science and religion in the western tradition. See The History of science and religion in the western tradition   **291.1**
Ferns
Sacks, O. W. Oaxaca journal   **587**
Ferrari, Andrea
Sharks   **597**
Ferrari, Antonella
(jt. auth) Ferrari, A. Sharks   **597**
Ferrell, Pamela
Let's talk hair   **646.7**
Ferri, Vincenzo
Tortoises and turtles   **597.9**
Ferris, Gary W.
Presidential places   **917.3**
Ferris, Timothy
Seeing in the dark   **520**
The whole shebang   **523.1**
Ferro, Marc
Nicholas II   **92**
Ferry, Georgina
(jt. auth) Sulston, J. The common thread   **572.8**
Fertility
See also Infertility
Fertility control See Birth control
Fertilization of plants
Buchmann, S. The forgotten pollinators   **577**
Fest, Joachim C., 1926-
Plotting Hitler's death   **943.086**
Speer: the final verdict   **92**
Festivals
The Folklore of world holidays   **394.26**
Holidays and anniversaries of the world   **394.26**
Holidays, festivals and celebrations of the world dictionary   **394.26**
MacDonald, M. R. Celebrate the world   **398.2**
Thompson, S. E. Holiday symbols and customs   **394.26**

            Bibliography
World holiday, festival, and calendar books   **016.39426**

            United States
The American book of days   **394.26**
The Folklore of the American holidays   **394.26**
Mercuri, B. Food festival, U.S.A.   **641.5**
The **festivities**. Chekhov, A. P.
In Chekhov, A. P. The plays of Anton Chekhov p191-205   **891.7**
Fetal death See Miscarriage
A **fever** in Salem. Carlson, L. M.   **133.4**
The **fever** trail. Honigsbaum, M.   **616.9**
Feydeau, Georges, 1862-1921
The bug in her ear
In Our dramatic heritage v6   **808.82**

Feynman, Richard Phillips
The meaning of it all   **500**
The pleasure of finding things out   **500**
QED   **539.7**
Six easy pieces   **530**
About
Gleick, J. Genius: the life and science of Richard
   Feynman   **92**
Goodstein, D. L. Feynman's lost lecture   **521**
See/See also pages in the following book(s):
Brennan, R. P. Heisenberg probably slept here
   920
Greenstein, G. Portraits of discovery p121-50   **920**
Feynman's lost lecture. Goodstein, D. L.   **521**
Fiber & bead jewelry. Banes, H.   **745.59**
Fibromyalgia
Selfridge, N. Freedom from fibromyalgia   **616.7**
Starlanyl, D. Fibromyalgia & chronic myofascial pain
   syndrome   **616.7**
Wallace, D. J. Fibromyalgia: an essential guide for pa-
   tients and their families   **616.7**
Encyclopedias
Patarca, R. The concise encyclopedia of fibromyalgia
   and myofascial pain   **616.7**
Fibromyalgia & chronic myofascial pain syndrome.
   Starlanyl, D.   **616.7**
Fiction
   See also American fiction; English fiction; Fairy
   tales; Fantasy fiction; Historical fiction; Horror fic-
   tion; Love stories; Mystery fiction; Science fiction;
   Short stories
Bibliography
Fiction catalog   **016.8**
Herald, D. T. Genreflecting   **016.8**
Jacob, M. To be continued   **016.8**
Lesher, L. P. The best novels of the nineties
   016.8
Pearl, N. Now read this II   **016.8**
Saricks, J. G. The readers' advisory guide to genre fic-
   tion   **025.5**
Saricks, J. G. Readers' advisory service in the public
   library   **025.5**
What do I read next?   **016.8**
Bio-bibliography
Beacham's encyclopedia of popular fiction   **809.3**
Critical survey of long fiction   **809.3**
Encyclopedias
Encyclopedia of the novel   **809.3**
History and criticism
Critical survey of long fiction   **809.3**
Herald, D. T. Genreflecting   **016.8**
Nabokov, V. V. Lectures on literature   **808.3**
Indexes
Fiction catalog   **016.8**
Technique
Conrad, B. The complete guide to writing fiction
   808.3
Gardner, J. The art of fiction   **808.3**
Gardner, J. On becoming a novelist   **808.3**
Lukeman, N. The plot thickens   **808.3**
Maass, D. Writing the breakout novel   **808.3**
Stein, S. How to grow a novel   **808.3**
Swain, D. V. Creating characters   **808.3**
Swain, D. V. Techniques of the selling writer
   808.3
Fiction catalog   **016.8**
Fictitious places *See* Geographical myths
Fidelman, Geoffrey Mark
First lady of song: Ella Fitzgerald for the record
   92
Fiedler, Johanna
Molto agitato   **792.5**
Fiedler, Leslie A.
Fiedler on the roof   **814**
Tyranny of the normal   **814**

Fiedler on the roof. Fiedler, L. A.   **814**
Field, Elinor Whitney, 1889-1980
(ed) Newbery Medal books, 1922-1955. See Newbery
   Medal books, 1922-1955   **028.5**
Field, Ophelia
Sarah Churchill, Duchess of Marlborough   **92**
A **field** guide to American houses. McAlester, V.
   728
A **field** guide to animal tracks. Murie, O. J.   **599**
A **field** guide to boys and girls. Gilbert, S.   **305.23**
Field guide to edible wild plants. Angier, B.   **581.6**
A **field** guide to freshwater fishes: North America north
   of Mexico. Page, L. M.   **597**
The **field** guide to geology. Lambert, D.   **551**
A **field** guide to germs. Biddle, W.   **616**
A **field** guide to hawks of North America. Clark, W. S.
   598
A **field** guide to hummingbirds of North America. Wil-
   liamson, S. L.   **598**
A **field** guide to mushrooms, North America. McKnight,
   K. H.   **579.6**
A **field** guide to reptiles & amphibians. Conant, R.
   597.9
A **field** guide to rocks and minerals. Pough, F. H.
   549
Field guide to stains. Friedman, V. M.   **648**
Field guide to the American teenager. Di Prisco, J.
   305.23
A **field** guide to the birds. See Peterson, R. T. A field
   guide to the birds of eastern and central North
   America   **598**
A **field** guide to the birds of Britain and Europe.
   Peterson, R. T.   **598**
A **field** guide to the birds of eastern and central North
   America. Peterson, R. T.   **598**
Field guide to the birds of North America   **598**
A **field** guide to the invisible. Biddle, W.   **500**
A **field** guide to the mammals. Burt, W. H.   **599**
A **field** guide to western birds. Peterson, R. T.   **598**
Field guide to wildflowers, eastern region. See Thieret,
   J. W. National Audubon Society field guide to North
   American wildflowers: eastern region   **582.13**
Field photography *See* Outdoor photography
The **field**: the quest for the secret force of the universe.
   McTaggart, L.   **615.5**
Fields, Alan
Your new house   **643**
Fields, Denise
(jt. auth) Fields, A. Your new house   **643**
Fields, Dorothy, 1905-1974
See/See also pages in the following book(s):
Green, S. The world of musical comedy   **920**
Fields of battle. Keegan, J.   **973**
Fields of Greens. Somerville, A.   **641.5**
Fiffer, Steve
Tyrannosaurus Sue   **567.9**
The **Fifth** Column [play] Hemingway, E.
   In Hemingway, E. The Fifth Column, and four sto-
   ries of the Spanish Civil War p3-85   **818**
The **Fifth** Column, and four stories of the Spanish Civil
   War. Hemingway, E.   **818**
The **fifth** miracle. Davies, P. C. W.   **576.8**
Fifth of July. Wilson, L.
   In Wilson, L. The Talley trilogy p1-74   **812**
Fifth of July. See Wilson, L. 5th of July   **812**
The **fifties**. Halberstam, D.   **973.92**
The **fifties**. Wilson, E.   **818**
Fifty simple things you can do to improve your personal
   finances. See Glink, I. R. 50 simple things you can
   do to improve your personal finances   **332.024**
Fifty-two McGs. See Thomas, R. M., Jr. 52 McGs
   920
Fifty wonderful ways to be a single-parent family. See
   Ginsberg, B. G. 50 wonderful ways to be a single-
   parent family   **649**

The **fifty-year** wound. Leebaert, D.   **973.92**
Figes, Orlando
  Natasha's dance   **947**
  A people's tragedy   **947.084**
Fighting Irish (Football team) *See* Notre Dame Fighting Irish (Football team)
Fighting ships, Jane's   **623.8**
Figure drawing
  Hart, C. Human anatomy made amazingly easy   **743**
The **figured** wheel. Pinsky, R.   **811**
Figurehead & other poems. Hollander, J.   **811**
Filar, Marian, 1917-
  From Buchenwald to Carnegie Hall   **92**
The **file**. Garton Ash, T.   **327.12**
Filene, Peter G.
  In the arms of others   **179.7**
Film adaptations
        Encyclopedias
  Tibbetts, J. C. The encyclopedia of novels into film   **791.43**
Film: an international history of the medium. See Sklar, R. A world history of film   **791.43**
Film direction *See* Motion pictures—Production and direction
Film industry (Motion pictures) *See* Motion picture industry
Film production *See* Motion pictures—Production and direction
Film quotations. Nowlan, R. A.   **791.43**
Filmer, Sir Robert, ca. 1588-1653
  Patriarcha; criticism
  In Locke, J. Two treatises of government   **320.1**
Filmmaking *See* Motion pictures—Production and direction
Films *See* Motion pictures
The **final** days. Woodward, B.   **973.924**
Final exit. Humphry, D.   **179.7**
Finamore, Roy
  (ed) Stewart, M. The Martha Stewart cookbook   **641.5**
Finan, Christopher M., 1953-
  Alfred E. Smith, the happy warrior   **92**
Finance
  See also International finance
        Encyclopedias
  Encyclopedia of busine$$ and finance   **650**
Financial aid, Student *See* Student aid
Financial aid for the disabled and their families. Schlachter, G. A.   **378.3**
Financial planning, Personal *See* Personal finance
Finch, Robert, 1943-
  (ed) Nature writing. See Nature writing   **508**
Finches
  Weiner, J. The beak of the finch   **598**
Finders keepers. Heaney, S.   **821**
Finding a form. Gass, W. H.   **814**
Finding Darwin's God. Miller, K. R.   **231.7**
Finding hope when a child dies. Miller, S.   **291**
Fine, John V. A. (John Van Antwerp), Jr.
  (jt. auth) Donia, R. J. Bosnia and Hercegovina   **949.7**
Fine arts *See* Arts
Fineberg, Jonathan David
  Art since 1940   **709.04**
Finest hour. Clayton, T.   **940.54**
Fingerprints
  Cole, S. A. Suspect identities   **363.2**
Finkbeiner, Ann K., 1943-
  After the death of a child   **155.9**
Finkelman, Paul, 1949-
  Landmark decisions of the United States Supreme Court   **347**

(ed) The Encyclopedia of American political history. See The Encyclopedia of American political history   **973.03**
(ed) Encyclopedia of the United States in the nineteenth century. See Encyclopedia of the United States in the nineteenth century   **973.5**
(ed) The Library of Congress Civil War desk reference. See The Library of Congress Civil War desk reference   **973.7**
(ed) Macmillan encyclopedia of world slavery. See Macmillan encyclopedia of world slavery   **326**
Finkelstein, Louis, 1895-1991
  (ed) The Cambridge history of Judaism. See The Cambridge history of Judaism   **296**
Finley, M. I. (Moses I.), 1912-1986
  The world of Odysseus   **883**
Finley, Moses I. *See* Finley, M. I. (Moses I.), 1912-1986
Finn, Robert
  Organ transplants   **617.9**
Fire. Junger, S.   **909.82**
Fire fighters
  Halberstam, D. Firehouse   **363.34**
  Smith, D. Report from ground zero   **363.34**
Fire fighting
  Golway, T. So others might live   **628.9**
  Gottschalk, J. Firefighting   **628.9**
  Taylor, M. A. Jumping fire   **634.9**
Fire in the lake. FitzGerald, F.   **959.704**
Fire in the mind. Johnson, G.   **215**
Fire lover. Wambaugh, J.   **364.1**
The **fire** of his genius: Robert Fulton and the American dream. Sale, K.   **92**
Fire prevention
  See also types of institutions, buildings, industries, and vehicles with the subdivision *Fires and fire prevention*
  National Fire Protection Association. Fire protection handbook   **628.9**
The **fire** within the eye. Park, D.   **535**
Firearms
  Gun digest   **623.4**
        Catalogs
  Shooter's bible   **623.4**
        Law and legislation
  See Gun control
  Guns in American society   **363.3**
  Utter, G. H. Encyclopedia of gun control and gun rights   **363.3**
Firefly encyclopedia of birds   **598**
The **Firefly** encyclopedia of insects and spiders   **595.7**
Firefly encyclopedia of reptiles and amphibians   **597.9**
The **Firefly** visual dictionary. Corbeil, J.-C.   **423**
Firehouse. Halberstam, D.   **363.34**
Fires
  See also Arson
  Gottschalk, J. Firefighting   **628.9**
  O'Donnell, E. T. Ship ablaze   **910.4**
  Von Drehle, D. Triangle: the fire that changed America   **974.7**
        Hartford (Conn.)
  O'Nan, S. The circus fire   **974.6**
First aid
  First aid for children fast   **618.92**
  First aid for children fast   **618.92**
The **first** American: the life and times of Benjamin Franklin. Brands, H. W.   **92**
The **first** Americans. Adovasio, J. M.   **970.01**
First flight. Heppenheimer, T. A.   **629.13**
First great triumph. Zimmermann, W.   **973**
The **first** heroes. Nelson, C.   **940.54**
First in his class: a biography of Bill Clinton. Maraniss, D.   **92**
First ladies. Anthony, C. S.   **920**

First ladies. Caroli, B. B. **920**
First ladies. Schneider, D. **920.003**
First ladies. Truman, M. **920**
First lady of song: Ella Fitzgerald for the record. Fidelman, G. M. **92**
First mothers. Angelo, B. **920**
The **first** of men: a life of George Washington. Ferling, J. E. **92**
First person: an astonishingly frank self-portrait. Putin, V. **92**
A **first** rate tragedy. Preston, D. **998**
The **first** salute. Tuchman, B. W. **973.3**
The **first** sex. Fisher, H. E. **305.4**
First son: George W. Bush and the Bush family dynasty. Minutaglio, B. **92**
First they killed my father. Ung, L. **959.6**
First things first. Covey, S. R. **158**
The **first** three years of life. See White, B. L. The new first three years of life **155.4**
The **First** World War. Gilbert, M. **940.3**
The **First** World War. Keegan, J. **940.3**
First you build a cloud. Cole, K. C. **530**
Fischer, Bobby, 1943-
  Bobby Fischer teaches chess **794.1**
Fischer, David Hackett
  Paul Revere's ride **973.3**
Fischer, Klaus P., 1942-
  Nazi Germany **943.086**
Fish & shellfish. Peterson, J. **641.6**
Fish as food
  See also Cooking—Fish; Seafood
A **fish** caught in time. Weinberg, S. **597**
Fish culture
  See also Aquariums
Fisher, Anne B.
  If my career's on the fast track, where do I get a road map? **650.14**
Fisher, David, 1929-
  (jt. auth) Read, A. The fall of Berlin **940.54**
  (jt. auth) Read, A. The proudest day **954.03**
Fisher, David, 1946-
  (jt. auth) Fisher, E. Been there, done that **92**
Fisher, Dorothy Canfield, 1879-1958
  See/See also pages in the following book(s):
  American women fiction writers **813.009**
Fisher, Eddie
  Been there, done that **92**
Fisher, Edwin B., 1946-
  American Lung Association 7 steps to a smoke-free life **616.86**
Fisher, Helen E.
  The first sex **305.4**
Fisher, John Arbuthnot Fisher, 1st Baron, 1841-1920
  See/See also pages in the following book(s):
  Massie, R. K. Dreadnought p401-67 **940.3**
Fisher, Kathleen
  Taylor's guide to shrubs **635.9**
Fisher, Mary, 1948-
  Sleep with the angels **362.1**
Fisheries *See* Commercial fishing
Fishes
  See also Aquariums; Codfish; Coelacanth; Salmon; Shad; Tropical fish; Trout
  Mills, D. Aquarium fish **639.34**
  Mojetta, A. Simon & Schuster's guide to saltwater fish and fishing **799.1**
    North America
  The Audubon Society field guide to North American fishes, whales, and dolphins **597**
  Page, L. M. A field guide to freshwater fishes: North America north of Mexico **597**
Fishing
  Frazier, I. The fish's eye **799.1**
  Greenlaw, L. The hungry ocean **639.2**
  Hersey, J. Blues **799.1**

  Mojetta, A. Simon & Schuster's guide to saltwater fish and fishing **799.1**
  Walton, I. The compleat angler **799.1**
Fishman, Stephen
  The copyright handbook **346.04**
The **fish's** eye. Frazier, I. **799.1**
Fiske, Edward B.
  The Fiske guide to colleges **378.73**
  The Fiske guide to getting into the right college **378**
The **Fiske** guide to colleges. Fiske, E. B. **378.73**
The **Fiske** guide to getting into the right college. Fiske, E. B. **378**
Fist, stick, knife, gun. Canada, G. **305.23**
A **fistful** of lentils. Abadi, J. F. **641.5**
Fitch, Noel Riley
  Appetite for life **92**
Fitness and exercise sourcebook **613.7**
The **fitness** factor. Callahan, L. **613.7**
Fitness over fifty **613**
Fitzgerald, Ella
    About
  Fidelman, G. M. First lady of song: Ella Fitzgerald for the record **92**
    See/See also pages in the following book(s):
  Feather, L. From Satchmo to Miles **920**
Fitzgerald, F. Scott (Francis Scott), 1896-1940
  A life in letters **92**
    About
  Bruccoli, M. J. Fitzgerald and Hemingway **92**
  Cline, S. Zelda Fitzgerald **92**
  Eble, K. E. F. Scott Fitzgerald **813.009**
  Tate, M. J. F. Scott Fitzgerald A to Z **813.009**
    See/See also pages in the following book(s):
  Kazin, A. An American procession p387-97 **810.9**
  Vidal, G. United States—essays, 1952-1992 p286-305 **814**
FitzGerald, Frances, 1940-
  Fire in the lake **959.704**
  Way out there in the blue **973.927**
Fitzgerald, Francis Scott *See* Fitzgerald, F. Scott (Francis Scott), 1896-1940
Fitzgerald, Zelda, 1900-1948
    About
  Cline, S. Zelda Fitzgerald **92**
  Fitzgerald and Hemingway. Bruccoli, M. J. **92**
Fitzhugh, George, 1806-1881
  See/See also pages in the following book(s):
  Wilson, E. Patriotic gore p341-64 **810.9**
Fitzhugh, William W., 1943-
  (ed) Vikings: the North Atlantic saga. See Vikings: the North Atlantic saga **970.01**
The **five** ages of the universe. Adams, F. C. **523.1**
The **five** biggest ideas in science. Wynn, C. M. **500**
The **five** books of Moses. Bible. O.T. Pentateuch **222**
Five days in London, May 1940. Lukacs, J. **940.53**
Five decades. Neruda, P. **861**
Five equations that changed the world. Guillen, M. **530.1**
The **five** Gospels. Bible. N.T. Gospels **226**
Five hundred nations. See Josephy, A. M. 500 nations **970.004**
Five kingdoms. Margulis, L. **570**
Five past midnight in Bhopal. Lapierre, D. **363.1**
Five plays. García Lorca, F. **862**
Five plays. Hughes, L. **812**
Five sisters. Fox, J. **920**
Five-twenty-nine College Savings Plan. See Feigenbaum, R. A. The 529 College Savings Plan **378.3**
Fixed ideas: America since 9.11. Didion, J. **320.5**
Fixin' to git. Wright, J. D. **796.72**
Fixing *See* Repairing

The **flag,** the poet & the song. Molotsky, I.   973.5
Flags
United States
Molotsky, I. The flag, the poet & the song   973.5
Sedeen, M. Star-spangled banner   929.9
Shearer, B. F. State names, seals, flags, and symbols
929.9
Flags of our fathers. Bradley, J.   940.54
Flam, Jack D.
Matisse and Picasso   759.4
The **flamboya** tree. Kelly, C. O.   940.53
A **flame** of pure fire: Jack Dempsey and the roaring
'20s. Kahn, R.   92
The **flame** trees of Thika. Huxley, E.   92
Flamel, Nicolas, d. 1418
See/See also pages in the following book(s):
Connell, E. S. The Aztec treasure house p412-32
814
The **flamingo's** smile. Gould, S. J.   508
Flanders, Stephen A.
Capital punishment. See Henderson, H. Capital punish-
ment   364.66
The **flaneur.** White, E.   944
Flannery, Tim F. (Tim Fridjof), 1956-
The eternal frontier   508
Throwim way leg   995.3
Flappers 2 rappers. Dalzell, T.   427
Flash!. Schilling, G.   522
Flashing before my eyes. Schaap, D.   92
Flaste, Richard
(jt. auth) Brody, J. E. Jane Brody's good seafood book
641.6

Flatow, Ira
They all laughed   609
Flattery
Stengel, R. You're too kind   177
Flaubert, Gustave, 1821-1880
Madame Bovary; criticism
In Gay, P. Savage reprisals   809.3
In Nabokov, V. V. Lectures on literature p125-77
808.3
See/See also pages in the following book(s):
Barnes, J. Something to declare   824
Gass, W. H. Tests of time p219-62   814
Fleischman, Albert Sidney *See* Fleischman, Sid, 1920-
Fleischman, Paul
See/See also pages in the following book(s):
The Newbery & Caldecott medal books, 1986-2000
p90-103   028.5
Fleischman, Sid, 1920-
See/See also pages in the following book(s):
The Newbery & Caldecott medal books, 1986-2000
p53-62   028.5
Fleitz, David L., 1955-
Shoeless   92
Flem-Ath, Rand
(jt. auth) Wilson, C. The Atlantis blueprint   001.9
Fleming, Alexander, 1881-1955
See/See also pages in the following book(s):
Friedman, M. Medicine's 10 greatest discoveries
610.9
Horvitz, L. A. Eureka!: scientific breakthroughs that
changed the world   509
Fleming, Fergus, 1959-
Ninety degrees North   998
Fleming, Gerald
Hitler and the final solution   943.086
Fleming, John, 1919-2001
(ed) The Penguin dictionary of architecture and land-
scape architecture. See The Penguin dictionary of ar-
chitecture and landscape architecture   720.3
Fleming, Robert
The African American writer's handbook   808
Flemish painting
From Van Eyck to Bruegel   759.9493

Flesch, Rudolf Franz, 1911-1986
Why Johnny can't read—and what you can do about
it   372.4
Flesh and machines. Brooks, R. A.   629.8
Flesh and spirit. Ozment, S. E.   943
Flesh of my flesh   174
Fletcher, Sir Banister Flight, 1866-1953
Sir Banister Fletcher's A history of architecture
720.9
Fletcher, Colin, 1922-
The man who walked through time   917.91
River   917.91
Fletcher, R. A. (Richard A.)
The quest for El Cid   92
Fletcher, Richard A. *See* Fletcher, R. A. (Richard A.)
Les **fleurs** du mal. Baudelaire, C.   841
Flexner, James Thomas, 1908-2003
George Washington   92
The **flies.** Sartre, J. P.
In Sartre, J. P. No exit, and three other plays
842
Flight
History
Tobin, J. To conquer the air   629.13
Flight among the tombs. Hecht, A.   811
The **floating** brothel. Rees, S.   365
Flodin, Mickey
(jt. auth) Butterworth, R. R. Signing made easy
419
Floods
Larson, E. Isaac's storm   976.4
Ryan, W. B. F. Noah's flood   930
Mississippi River
Barry, J. M. Rising tide   977
Flook, Maria
Invisible Eden   364.1
Flooring instant answers. Bukowski, S. J.   690
Floors
Bollinger, D. Hardwood floors   694
Bukowski, S. J. Flooring instant answers   690
Flora, Joseph M.
(ed) The Companion to southern literature. See The
Companion to southern literature   810.3
Florence (Italy)
History
Hibbert, C. The House of Medici   920
Levey, Sir M. Florence   945
Lewis, R. W. B. The city of Florence   945
The **Florence** King reader. King, F.   818
Florey, Howard, Baron Florey, 1898-1968
See/See also pages in the following book(s):
Friedman, M. Medicine's 10 greatest discoveries
610.9
Florida
Description
See/See also pages in the following book(s):
White, E. B. Essays of E. B. White   814
Flower arrangement
Heffernan, C. Flowers A to Z   635.9
Hillier, M. Flowers   745.92
Jong-Stout, A. A. de. A master guide to the art of flo-
ral design   745.92
Miller, C. Harvesting, preserving, and arranging dried
flowers   745.92
Pryke, P. Flowers, flowers!   745.92
Flower gardening
Ellis, B. W. Taylor's guide to annuals   635.9
Ellis, B. W. Taylor's guide to bulbs   635.9
Ellis, B. W. Taylor's guide to perennials   635.9
Heffernan, C. Flowers A to Z   635.9
Flowers, Charles
Instability rules   509
Flowers
See also Perennials; Roses; Wild flowers
Heffernan, C. Flowers A to Z   635.9

Flowers—*Continued*
Wells, D. 100 flowers and how they got their names
582.13
Drying
Miller, C. Harvesting, preserving, and arranging dried flowers 745.92
Flowers. Hillier, M. 745.92
Flowers, flowers!. Pryke, P. 745.92
Flowers in the dustbin. Miller, J. 781.66
The **flowers** of evil. Baudelaire, C. 841
Floyd, Samuel A.
The power of black music 780.89
Flu *See* Influenza
Flu. Kolata, G. 614.5
Fluid mechanics
See also Hydraulic engineering
Flush. Woolf, V. 828
The **flyers**. Adams, N. 92
Flying *See* Flight
The **flying** book. Blatner, D. 387.7
Flying saucers *See* Unidentified flying objects
Flying Tigers (China) *See* China. Air Force. American Volunteer Group
Flying Tigers. Ford, D. 940.54
Flynn, Raymond
John Paul II 92
Flynn, Roger R., 1939-
(ed) Computer sciences. See Computer sciences
004
FM: the rise and fall of free-form rock radio. Neer, R.
791.44
Fodor's travel guides 910.2
Foerstel, Herbert N.
Banned in the U.S.A 025.2
Fogelman, Eva
Conscience & courage 940.53
Fogle, Bruce
ASPCA complete dog care manual 636.7
Dog owner's manual 636.7
New complete dog training manual 636.7
The new encyclopedia of the cat 636.8
The new encyclopedia of the dog 636.7
The **folding** cliffs. Merwin, W. S. 811
Folk art
See also Decorative arts
Folk lore *See* Folklore
Folk music
See also Klezmer music
Encyclopedias
The Garland encyclopedia of world music 780.9
United States
See also Country music
American musical traditions 781.62
American roots music 781.62
Folk songs
United States
See also Spirituals (Songs)
Sandburg, C. The American songbag 782.42
Folklore
See also Animals—Folklore; Dragons; Legends; topics as themes in folklore and names of ethnic or national groups with the subdivision *Folklore*
Brunvand, J. H. Encyclopedia of urban legends
398.2
Favorite folktales from around the world 398.2
The Folklore of world holidays 394.26
MacDonald, M. R. Celebrate the world 398.2
Saler, B. UFO crash at Roswell 001.9
Seal, G. Encyclopedia of folk heroes 398.03
Dictionaries
Pickering, D. A dictionary of folklore 398.2
Radford, E. Encyclopaedia of superstitions 398.03
Encyclopedias
Storytelling encyclopedia 398.03

Indexes
Index to fairy tales 398.2
Europe
Bulfinch, T. Bulfinch's mythology 291.1
Southern States
Petro, P. Sitting up with the dead 398.2
United States
American folklore 398.03
Brunvand, J. H. The choking Doberman and other "new" urban legends 398.2
Brunvand, J. H. Too good to be true 398.2
Brunvand, J. H. The vanishing hitchhiker 398.2
The Folklore of the American holidays 394.26
Folklore, memoirs, and other writings. Hurston, Z. N.
818
The **Folklore** of the American holidays 394.26
The **Folklore** of world holidays 394.26
Follain, John
(jt. auth) Zoya Zoya's story 958.1
Follett, Ken, 1949-
On wings of eagles 955
Fölsing, Albrecht, 1940-
Albert Einstein 92
Folsom, W. Davis
Understanding American business jargon 650
Foner, Eric
Reconstruction 973.8
The story of American freedom 323.44
Tom Paine and Revolutionary America 973.3
(ed) The Reader's companion to American history. See The Reader's companion to American history
973.03
Foner, Moe, 1915-2002
Not for bread alone 92
Fonseca, Anthony J.
Hooked on horror 016.8
Fontana, Lavinia, 1552-1614
About
Murphy, C. P. Lavinia Fontana 92
Food
See also Convenience foods; Seafood
Allen, S. L. In the devil's garden 641
Ayto, J. An A-Z of food and drink 641.03
Bourdain, A. A cook's tour 641
David, E. Is there a nutmeg in the house? 641.5
Goldstein, M. C. Controversies in food and nutrition
641.3
Harrison, J. The raw and the cooked 641.3
McHughen, A. Pandora's picnic basket 641.3
Rinzler, C. A. The new complete book of food
641.3
Weil, A. Eating well for optimum health 613.2
Wright, C. A. A Mediterranean feast 641
Biotechnology
Charles, D. Lords of the harvest 664
Cummins, R. Genetically engineered food 363.1
Genetically modified foods 363.1
Lurquin, P. F. High tech harvest 631.5
Nestle, M. Safe food 363.1
Pringle, P. Food, inc 363.1
Winston, M. L. Travels in the genetically modified zone 664
Composition
Kraus, B. Calories and carbohydrates 613.2
Mindell, E. Dr. Earl Mindell's unsafe at any meal
613.2
Dictionaries
International dictionary of food & cooking 641.03
The Oxford companion to food 641.03
Encyclopedias
Encyclopedia of food and culture 394.1
Larousse gastronomique 641.03
History
The Cambridge world history of food 641.3

Food—History—*Continued*
Fernández-Armesto, F. Near a thousand tables
    641.3

Preservation
See also Canning and preserving
Shephard, S. Pickled, potted, and canned   **641.4**
Food, Natural *See* Natural foods
Food additives
    See/See also pages in the following book(s):
Mindell, E. Dr. Earl Mindell's unsafe at any meal
    613.2

Dictionaries
Winter, R. A consumer's dictionary of food additives
    664

Food adulteration and inspection
Nestle, M. Safe food   **363.1**
Food allergies. Walsh, W. E.   **616.97**
Food allergy
Pescatore, F. The allergy and asthma cure   **616.97**
Food assistance programs *See* Food relief
Food festival, U.S.A. Mercuri, B.   **641.5**
Food habits *See* Eating customs
Food, inc. Pringle, P.   **363.1**
Food industry
Schlosser, E. Fast food nation   **394.1**
The **food** of Portugal. Anderson, J.   **641.5**
Food preparation *See* Cooking
Food relief
McGovern, G. S. The third freedom   **363.8**
Food service
    See also Restaurants
Food supply
    See also Agriculture
    See/See also pages in the following book(s):
Diamond, J. M. Guns, germs, and steel p83-191
    303.4
Foodlover's atlas of the world. Shulman, M. R.
    641.3
The **foods** of Israel today. Nathan, J.   **641.5**
Foods that harm, foods that heal   **613.2**
Fools. Simon, N.
    In Simon, N. The collected plays of Neil Simon v3
    p307-78   **812**
Football
    See also Soccer
Bissinger, H. G. Friday night lights   **796.332**
Dent, J. The Junction boys   **796.332**
Dent, J. The undefeated   **796.332**
Green, T. The dark side of the game   **796.332**
My greatest day in football   **796.332**

Statistics
Pro football register   **796.332**
Football register. See Pro football register   **796.332**
Foote, Horton
Beginnings   **92**
The chase
    In Foote, H. Collected plays v2 p61-111   **812**
A coffin in Egypt
    In Foote, H. Getting Frankie married—and after-
    wards, and other plays   **812**
Collected plays v2   **812**
The day Emily married
    In Foote, H. Getting Frankie married—and after-
    wards, and other plays   **812**
Farewell   **92**
Getting Frankie married
    In Foote, H. Getting Frankie married—and after-
    wards, and other plays   **812**
Getting Frankie married—and afterwards, and other
    plays   **812**
Laura Dennis
    In Foote, H. Getting Frankie married—and after-
    wards, and other plays   **812**
The roads to home
    In Foote, H. Collected plays v2 p171-216   **812**

Tomorrow
    In Foote, H. Getting Frankie married—and after-
    wards, and other plays   **812**
The traveling lady
    In Foote, H. Collected plays v2 p113-70   **812**
The trip to Bountiful
    In Foote, H. Collected plays v2 p1-60   **812**
Vernon Early
    In Foote, H. Getting Frankie married—and after-
    wards, and other plays   **812**
The young man from Atlanta   **812**
Foote, Shelby
The Civil War   **973.7**
Footfalls. Beckett, S.
    In Beckett, S. Ends and Odds p39-49   **842**
For cause and comrades. McPherson, J. M.   **973.7**
For colored girls who have considered suicide/when the
    rainbow is enuf. Shange, N.   **812**
For keeps. Kael, P.   **791.43**
For the glory of God. Stark, R.   **291.1**
For the love of Mike. Royko, M.   **818**
For the time being. Dillard, A.   **814**
For women only!. Null, G.   **613**
Forage plants
Brill, S. The wild vegetarian cookbook   **641.5**
Forbush, Edward Howe, 1858-1929
Birds of Massachusetts and other New England states;
    criticism
    In White, E. B. Essays of E. B. White   **814**
Force and energy
Bodanis, D. E=mc²   **530.1**
The **force** of character. Hillman, J.   **155.67**
A **force** upon the plain. Stern, K. S.   **322.4**
Forced indoctrination *See* Brainwashing
Forced labor *See* Slavery
Forces of habit. Courtwright, D. T.   **362.29**
Ford, Daniel
Flying Tigers   **940.54**
Ford, Dorothy Gardner, 1892-1967
    See/See also pages in the following book(s):
Angelo, B. First mothers   **920**
Ford, Ford Madox, 1873-1939
    See/See also pages in the following book(s):
Gass, W. H. Finding a form p77-103   **814**
Ford, Gerald R., 1913-
    See/See also pages in the following book(s):
Woodward, B. Shadow   **973.92**
Ford, Henry, 1863-1947

About
Baldwin, N. Henry Ford and the Jews   **92**
Brinkley, D. Wheels for the world   **338.7**
    See/See also pages in the following book(s):
Klein, M. The change makers   **920**
Ford, John, 1894-1973

About
Davis, R. L. John Ford   **92**
Eyman, S. Print the legend: the life and times of John
    Ford   **92**
Gallagher, T. John Ford   **791.43**
Ford, Paul F.
Companion to Narnia   **823.009**
Ford Motor Co.
Brinkley, D. Wheels for the world   **338.7**
Forecasting
    See also Weather forecasting
The 21st century   **909.83**
Dyson, F. J. The sun, the genome, & the Internet
    303.4
Jenkins, P. The next Christendom   **270**
Stille, A. The future of the past   **303.4**
    See/See also pages in the following book(s):
Moravec, H. P. Robot   **629.8**
Foreign automobiles

Maintenance and repair
Chilton's import car repair manual   **629.28**

Foreign economic relations *See* International economic relations

Foreign population *See* Immigrants

Foreign relations *See* International relations

Foreigners *See* Immigrants

Foreman, Amanda, 1968-
Georgiana, Duchess of Devonshire   **92**

Forensic anthropology
Maples, W. R. Dead men do tell tales   **614**
Pringle, H. A. The mummy congress   **393**
See/See also pages in the following book(s):
Massie, R. K. The Romanovs   **947.08**

Forensic medicine *See* Medical jurisprudence

Forensic sciences
Evans, C. The casebook of forensic detection   **614**
Lee, H. C. Blood evidence   **614**
Ramsland, K. M. The criminal mind   **808.3**
Encyclopedias
Conklin, B. G. Encyclopedia of forensic science   **363.2**

Forest ecology
See also Rain forest ecology
Heinrich, B. The trees in my forest   **577.3**

Forest fires
Taylor, M. A. Jumping fire   **634.9**

A **forest** of time. Nabokov, P.   **970.004**

Forest plants
Darke, R. The American woodland garden   **635.9**

Forest reserves
See also National parks and reserves

Forests and forestry
See also Trees

Forever, Erma. Bombeck, E.   **817**

Forgery
See also Literary forgeries
Worrall, S. The poet and the murderer   **364.1**

Forgery of works of art *See* Art—Forgeries

The **forgetting:** Alzheimer's, portrait of an epidemic. Shenk, D.   **616.8**

Forgive your parents, heal yourself. Grosskopf, B.   **155.9**

Forgiveness
Grosskopf, B. Forgive your parents, heal yourself   **155.9**
Wiesenthal, S. The sunflower   **179.7**

Forgiveness and other acts of love. Dowrick, S.   **248.4**

The **forgotten** pollinators. Buchmann, S.   **577**

Form and actuality. Spengler, O.
In Spengler, O. The decline of the West v1   **901**

Former Soviet republics
See also Soviet Union
Milner-Gulland, R. R. Cultural atlas of Russia and the former Soviet Union   **947**

Formica, Ronald J.
(ed) Famous first facts about the environment. See Famous first facts about the environment   **363.7**

Formosa *See* Taiwan

Fornay, Alfred
The African American woman's guide to successful makeup and skincare   **646.7**

Fornovo, Battle of, 1495
See/See also pages in the following book(s):
Barzini, L. G. The Italians p276-98   **945**

Forrest, Nathan Bedford, 1821-1877
About
Hurst, J. Nathan Bedford Forrest   **92**

Forschner, Karen Vanderhoof- *See* Vanderhoof-Forschner, Karen

Forster, E. M. (Edward Morgan), 1879-1970
See/See also pages in the following book(s):
Holroyd, M. Works on paper   **809**

Forster, Edward Morgan *See* Forster, E. M. (Edward Morgan), 1879-1970

Forsthoff, Cynthia, 1951-
(jt. auth) Link, J. The breast cancer survival manual   **616.99**

Forten, James, 1766-1842
About
Winch, J. A gentleman of color: the life of James Forten   **92**

Fortey, Richard A.
Fossils   **560**
Life   **576.8**
Trilobite!   **560**

Forthcoming books   **015.73**

The **forties.** Wilson, E.   **818**

Fortin, François
Sports: the complete visual reference. See Sports: the complete visual reference   **796**

Fortunate son. Puller, L. B.   **92**

Fortunato, Alfred
(jt. auth) Rabiner, S. Thinking like your editor   **808**

Forty-four, Dublin made me. See Sheridan, P. 44, Dublin made me   **92**

Forty-seven roses. See Sheridan, P. 47 roses   **92**

Forward, Susan
Toxic parents: overcoming their hurtful legacy and reclaiming your life   **362.82**

Fossey, Dian
Gorillas in the mist   **599.8**
About
Mowat, F. Woman in the mists: the story of Dian Fossey and the mountain gorillas of Africa   **92**
See/See also pages in the following book(s):
Slung, M. B. Living with cannibals and other women's adventures   **910.4**

Fossier, Robert
(ed) The Cambridge illustrated history of the Middle Ages. See The Cambridge illustrated history of the Middle Ages   **909.07**

Fossil hominids
Johanson, D. C. From Lucy to language   **599.93**
Swisher, C. C. Java man   **599.93**
Tattersall, I. Extinct humans   **599.93**
Walker, A. The wisdom of the bones   **599.93**
Wolpoff, M. H. Race and human evolution   **599.97**

Fossil mammals
Johanson, D. C. Lucy: the beginnings of humankind   **599.93**

Fossil reptiles
See also Dinosaurs

The **fossil** trail. Tattersall, I.   **599.93**

Fossils
See also Archaeopteryx; Fossil mammals
Arduini, P. Simon & Schuster's guide to fossils   **560**
Chiappe, L. M. Walking on eggs   **567.9**
Eldredge, N. Fossils   **560**
Eldredge, N. The miner's canary   **560**
Erickson, J. An introduction to fossils and minerals   **560**
Fortey, R. A. Fossils   **560**
Fortey, R. A. Trilobite!   **560**
Gould, S. J. Wonderful life: the Burgess Shale and the nature of history   **560**
Larson, P. L. Rex appeal   **567.9**
Nothdurft, W. E. The lost dinosaurs of Egypt   **567.9**
Poinar, G. O. The quest for life in amber   **560**
Rea, T. Bone wars   **560**
Schopf, J. W. Cradle of life   **576.8**
Tattersall, I. The fossil trail   **599.93**
Thompson, I. The Audubon Society field guide to North American fossils   **560**
Travels with the fossil hunters   **560**
Wallace, D. R. The bonehunters' revenge   **560**

Fossils—*Continued*

Encyclopedias

Encyclopedia of paleontology   560

Fossils, finches, and Fuegians. Keynes, R. D.   508

Foster, David R.

Thoreau's country   818

Foster, Frances Smith

(ed) The Oxford companion to African American literature. See The Oxford companion to African American literature   810.9

Foster, Lynn V.

A brief history of Mexico   972

Foster, Nelson

(ed) Chilies to chocolate. See Chilies to chocolate   641.3

Foster, R. F. (Robert Fitzroy), 1949-

W.B. Yeats   92

(ed) The Oxford illustrated history of Ireland. See The Oxford illustrated history of Ireland   941.5

Foster, Rick, 1954-

How we choose to be happy   158

Foster, Robert Fitzroy *See* Foster, R. F. (Robert Fitzroy), 1949-

Foster, Roy *See* Foster, R. F. (Robert Fitzroy), 1949-

Foster, Stephen Collins, 1826-1864

About

Emerson, K. Doo-dah!: Stephen Foster and the rise of American popular culture   92

Foster home care

Bernstein, N. The lost children of Wilder   362.7

See/See also pages in the following book(s):

Bartholet, E. Nobody's children   362.7

Foster Hospital for Small Animals (Medford, Mass.)

Tufts University. School of Veterinary Medicine. Animal ER   636.089

Foucault, Michel, 1926-1984

About

Macey, D. The lives of Michel Foucault   92

See/See also pages in the following book(s):

Said, E. W. Reflections on exile and other essays p187-97, 239-45   814

Foulkes, Christopher

(ed) Larousse encyclopedia of wine. See Larousse encyclopedia of wine   641.2

The **Foundation** directory   061.025

Foundations (Endowments) *See* Endowments

Founding brothers. Ellis, J. J.   973.4

Founding father: rediscovering George Washington. Brookhiser, R.   92

The **founding** fish. McPhee, J. A.   597

The **fountain** of age. Friedan, B.   305.26

The **four** books on architecture. Palladio, A.   720

Four corners. Brown, K. A.   978

The **four** corners. Salak, K.   910.4

Four hours in My Lai. Bilton, M.   959.704

The **four** pillars of investing. Bernstein, W.   332.6

Four plays. See Inge, W. 4 plays   812

Four quartets. Eliot, T. S.

In Eliot, T. S. The complete poems and plays, 1909-1950 p117-45   818

Four saints in three acts. Stein, G.

In Stein, G. Selected writings p577-612   818

Four wings and a prayer. Halpern, S. M.   595.7

Fourier, Jean-Baptiste-Joseph, baron, 1768-1830

See/See also pages in the following book(s):

Bell, E. T. Men of mathematics p183-205   920

Fourteen. Zanichkowsky, S.   92

Fourteenth century *See* World history—14th century

Fourth dimension

Gott, J. R. Time travel in Einstein's universe   530.1

Fourth World *See* Developing countries

Fouts, Roger

Next of kin   156

Fowler, Brenda

Iceman   937

Fowler, Damon Lee

Damon Lee Fowler's new southern kitchen   641.5

Fried chicken   641.6

Fowler, H. W.

The new Fowler's modern English usage   428

Fowler, Loretta, 1944-

The Columbia guide to American Indians of the Great Plains   970.004

Fox, Barry, 1956-

(jt. auth) Reaven, G. M. Syndrome X   616.1

Fox, Everett

(tr) Bible. O.T. Pentateuch. The five books of Moses   222

Fox, Gabrielle, 1955-

The essential guide to making handmade books   686.3

Fox, James, 1945-

Five sisters   920

Fox, Michael W., 1937-

Beyond evolution   174

Inhumane society   179

Fox, Paula

Borrowed finery   92

Fox. Rich, A.   811

Fox-Genovese, Elizabeth, 1941-

Within the plantation household   305.4

Fox, Michael J.

Lucky man   92

Foxe, John, 1516-1587

Foxe's Book of martyrs   272

Foxe's Book of martyrs. Foxe, J.   272

Foxfire [1]-11   975.8

Fradkin, Philip L.

The seven states of California   979.4

Frady, Marshall

Martin Luther King, Jr.   92

Frager, Robert, 1940-

(ed) Essential Sufism. See Essential Sufism   297

Fraistat, Neil, 1952-

(ed) Shelley, P. B. Shelley's poetry and prose   821

France, Peter, 1935-

(ed) The New Oxford companion to literature in French. See The New Oxford companion to literature in French   840.3

(ed) The Oxford guide to literature in English translation. See The Oxford guide to literature in English translation   820.9

France

Civilization

Fenby, J. France on the brink   944.083

Fascism

See Fascism—France

History

Merriman, J. M. The stones of Balazuc   944

See/See also pages in the following book(s):

Durant, W. J. The age of Louis XIV p3-86, 685-721   940.2

History—1328-1589, House of Valois

Pernoud, R. Joan of Arc   92

Tuchman, B. W. A distant mirror   944

History—1589-1789, Bourbons

Fraser, A. Marie Antoinette   92

Lever, E. Madame de Pompadour   92

Lever, E. Marie Antoinette   92

Levi, A. Cardinal Richelieu and the making of France   92

History—1789-1799, Revolution

Burke, E. Reflections on the Revolution in France   944.04

Dunn, S. Sister revolutions   973.3

Lefebvre, G. The French Revolution   944.04

Paine, T. The rights of man   320

France—History—1789-1799, Revolution—*Continued*
Schama, S. Citizens: a chronicle of the French Revolution   **944.04**
    History—1799-1815
Hamilton-Williams, D. The fall of Napoleon
        944.05
    History—1940-1945, German occupation
May, E. R. Strange victory   **940.54**
Nossiter, A. The Algeria Hotel   **940.54**
  See/See also pages in the following book(s):
Kaplan, A. Y. The collaborator: the trial & execution of Robert Brasillach   **92**
Stein, G. Selected writings p613-37   **818**
    History—1945-1958
  See/See also pages in the following book(s):
Stein, G. Selected writings p639-93   **818**
    Politics and government
Karnow, S. Paris in the fifties   **944**
    Politics and government—1815-1914
Bredin, J.-D. The affair   **944.081**
Derfler, L. The Dreyfus affair   **944.081**
    Social life and customs
Mayle, P. French lessons   **394.1**
France on the brink. Fenby, J.   **944.083**
Franchises (Retail trade)
Bond's franchise guide   **381**
Francis, of Assisi, Saint, 1182-1226
The little flowers of St. Francis   **242**
    About
Martin, V. Salvation: scenes from the life of St. Francis   **92**
Franciscans
  See/See also pages in the following book(s):
Russell, B. A history of Western philosophy p463-75   **109**
Franck, Irene M.
Famous first facts about sports   **796**
The Wilson chronology of women's achievements
        305.4
(jt. auth) Brownstone, D. M. Facts about American immigration   **325.73**
Franco Serri, Conchita
(jt. auth) Meier, M. S. Notable Latino Americans
        920.003
Frank, Anne, 1929-1945
Anne Frank's Tales from the secret annex   **839.3**
Diary of a young girl; dramatization. See Goodrich, F. The diary of Anne Frank   **812**
The diary of a young girl: the definitive edition
        92
The diary of Anne Frank: the critical edition   **92**
    About
Lindwer, W. The last seven months of Anne Frank
        940.53
Müller, M. Anne Frank   **92**
  See/See also pages in the following book(s):
Ozick, C. Quarrel & quandary   **814**
Frank, Catherine
(comp) Quotations for all occasions. See Quotations for all occasions   **808.88**
Frank, Joseph, 1918-
Dostoevsky   **92**
Frank, Katherine
Indira: the life of Indira Nehru Gandhi   **92**
Frank, Leonard Roy
(ed) Random House Webster's quotationary. See Random House Webster's quotationary   **808.88**
Frank, Richard B.
Downfall   **940.54**
Frank family
    About
Gies, M. Anne Frank remembered   **940.53**
The **Frank** Lloyd Wright companion. Storrer, W. A.
        720.973

Frankel, Ellen, 1951-
The classic tales   **296.1**
Frankel, Haskel, 1926-1999
(jt. auth) Hagen, U. Respect for acting   **792**
Frankel, Max, 1930-
The times of my life and my life with the Times
        92
Frankenthaler, Helen, 1928-
    About
Elderfield, J. Frankenthaler   **92**
Frankfort, Henri, 1897-1954
The art and architecture of the ancient Orient
        709.39
Franklin, Benjamin, 1706-1790
The autobiography of Benjamin Franklin   **92**
  also in Franklin, B. Writings   **818**
Writings   **818**
    About
Brands, H. W. The first American: the life and times of Benjamin Franklin   **92**
Cohen, I. B. Science and the founding fathers
        973.3
Jennings, F. Benjamin Franklin, politician   **92**
Morgan, E. S. Benjamin Franklin   **92**
  See/See also pages in the following book(s):
Ellis, J. J. Founding brothers   **973.4**
Williams, W. C. In the American grain p144-57
        814
Franklin, H. Bruce (Howard Bruce), 1934-
M.I.A.; or, Mythmaking in America   **959.704**
Franklin, Howard Bruce *See* Franklin, H. Bruce (Howard Bruce), 1934-
Franklin, Sir John, 1786-1847
    About
Cookman, S. Ice blink   **998**
Franklin, John Hope, 1915-
From slavery to freedom   **305.8**
Reconstruction after the Civil War   **973.8**
Franklin, Rosalind, 1920-1958
    About
Maddox, B. Rosalind Franklin: the dark lady of DNA
        92
Franklin D. Roosevelt and the New Deal, 1932-1940.
Leuchtenburg, W. E.   **973.917**
Franks, Frederick M., Jr.
(jt. auth) Clancy, T. Into the storm   **956.7**
Frantz, Pollyanne
(comp) The Children's song index, 1978-1993. See The Children's song index, 1978-1993   **782.42**
Franz Kafka's The metamorphosis   **833.009**
Fraser, Antonia, 1932-
Faith and treason   **942.06**
Marie Antoinette   **92**
Mary Queen of Scots   **92**
The warrior queens   **920**
The wives of Henry VIII   **920**
Fraser, Caroline
God's perfect child   **289.5**
Fraser, David, 1920-
Knight's cross: a life of Field Marshal Erwin Rommel
        92
Fraser, Flora
The unruly queen: the life of Queen Caroline   **92**
Fraser, Kennedy
Ornament and silence   **814**
Fraud
Boese, A. The museum of hoaxes   **001.9**
Hooper, J. Of moths and men   **576.8**
Park, R. L. Voodoo science   **500**
Sabbagh, K. A Rum affair   **580**
Frauds, Literary *See* Literary forgeries
Frawley, William, 1953-
(ed) International encyclopedia of linguistics. See International encyclopedia of linguistics   **410**

Frazer, Sir James George, 1854-1941
The new golden bough   291.1
Frazier, Ian
Coyote v. Acme   817
Family   977.1
The fish's eye   799.1
Great Plains   978
On the rez   970.004
Frazier, Joe
About
Kram, M. The ghosts of Manila   796.8
Frazier, Nancy
The Penguin concise dictionary of art history   703
Frazier family
About
Frazier, I. Family   977.1
Freaks, geeks and asperger syndrome. Jackson, L.
    618.92
The **Frederic** Remington Art Museum collection. Dippie,
B. W.   92
Frederick II, King of Prussia, 1712-1786
About
MacDonogh, G. Frederick the Great   92
Frederick, the Great See Frederick II, King of Prussia,
1712-1786
Fredriksen, John C.
American military leaders   920.003
America's military adversaries   920.003
Warbirds   623.7
Fredriksen, Paula
Jesus of Nazareth, King of the Jews   232.9
Fredston, Jill A.
Rowing to latitude   797.1
Free speech in its forgotten years. Rabban, D. M.
    342
Free to choose. Friedman, M.   330.1
Free trade
Friedman, T. L. The Lexus and the olive tree
    337
Free will and determinism
Arendt, H. The life of the mind   153
May, R. Freedom and destiny   158
Freed, Curt
Healing the brain   616.8
Freedman, David Noel, 1922-
(ed) The Anchor Bible dictionary. See The Anchor Bi-
ble dictionary   220.3
(ed) Eerdmans dictionary of the Bible. See Eerdmans
dictionary of the Bible   220.3
Freedman, Estelle B., 1947-
No turning back   305.4
Freedman, Lawrence
Kennedy's wars   973.922
Freedman, Michael R.
Living well with asthma   616.2
Freedman, Russell
See/See also pages in the following book(s):
The Newbery & Caldecott medal books, 1986-2000
p71-84   028.5
Freedman, Samuel G.
Jew vs. Jew   296
Freedom
Foner, E. The story of American freedom   323.44
Pipes, R. Property and freedom   323.4
Freedom. Hakim, J.   973
Freedom and destiny. May, R.   158
Freedom from fear. Kennedy, D. M.   973.91
Freedom from fear, and other writings. Aung San Suu
Kyi   959.1
Freedom from fibromyalgia. Selfridge, N.   616.7
Freedom in exile. Dalai Lama XIV   92
Freedom of choice movement See Pro-choice movement

Freedom of information
See also Censorship
Jones, B. M. Libraries, access, and intellectual freedom
    025.2
Freedom of speech
Rabban, D. M. Free speech in its forgotten years
    342
See/See also pages in the following book(s):
Vonnegut, K. Palm Sunday p1-17   818
Freedom to die. Humphry, D.   179.7
Freedom's daughters. Olson, L.   323.1
Freeing the natural voice. Linklater, K.   808.5
Freelancers See Self-employed
Freeman, Charles, 1947-
Egypt, Greece, and Rome   909
Freeman, Douglas Southall, 1886-1953
Lee   92
Lee's lieutenants   973.7
Freeman, Joanne B.
Affairs of honor   973.4
Freeman, John W.
The Metropolitan Opera stories of the great operas
    792.5
Freeman, Joshua Benjamin
Working-class New York   305.5
Freeman, Mark, 1927-
Gardening in your greenhouse   635.9
Freeman, Scott, 1958-
Otis!: the Otis Redding story   92
Freemasons
Ridley, J. G. The Freemasons   366
Freese, Barbara
Coal: a human history   553.2
Freimiller, Jane
(jt. auth) Ellington, E. A year of reading   028
Freitas, Michael de See Michael X, 1933-1974
French art
Kostenevich, A. G. French art treasures at the Hermit-
age   709.44
Schapiro, M. Impressionism   709.44
French art treasures at the Hermitage. Kostenevich, A.
G.   709.44
French cooking
Child, J. From Julia Child's kitchen   641.5
Child, J. Julia and Jacques cooking at home
    641.5
Child, J. Mastering the art of French cooking
    641.5
Larousse gastronomique   641.03
Peterson, J. Glorious French food   641.5
Roberts, M. Parisian home cooking   641.5
French language
Dictionaries
Cassell's French dictionary   443
Larousse French-English, English-French dictionary
    443
The Oxford-Hachette French dictionary   443
French lessons. Mayle, P.   394.1
French literature
Bio-bibliography
The New Oxford companion to literature in French
    840.3
Dictionaries
The New Oxford companion to literature in French
    840.3
History and criticism
See/See also pages in the following book(s):
Durant, W. J. The age of Louis XIV p104-63
    940.2
French national characteristics
Fenby, J. France on the brink   944.083
Karnow, S. Paris in the fifties   944
French painting
Rosenblum, R. Paintings in the Musée d'Orsay
    708

French philosophy
Descartes, R. The philosophical writings of Descartes
194
See/See also pages in the following book(s):
Durant, W. J. The age of Louis XIV p598-619
940.2
The **French** Revolution. Lefebvre, G. **944.04**
Fresco painting *See* Mural painting and decoration
Fresh & fabulous painted furniture **745.7**
Fresh air fiend. Theroux, P. **818**
Fresh water. Pielou, E. C. **553.7**
The **Freud/Jung** letters. Freud, S. **92**
Freud, Sigmund, 1856-1939
The basic writings of Sigmund Freud **150.19**
The Freud/Jung letters **92**
The Freud reader **150.19**
History of the psychoanalytic movement
In Freud, S. The basic writings of Sigmund Freud
150.19
Interpretation of dreams **154.6**
also in Freud, S. The basic writings of Sigmund
Freud **150.19**
Psychopathology of everyday life
In Freud, S. The basic writings of Sigmund Freud
150.19
Three contributions to the theory of sex
In Freud, S. The basic writings of Sigmund Freud
150.19
Totem and taboo **306**
also in Freud, S. The basic writings of Sigmund
Freud **150.19**
Wit and its relation to the unconscious
In Freud, S. The basic writings of Sigmund Freud
150.19

About
Bettelheim, B. Freud and man's soul **150.19**
Breger, L. Freud **92**
Freud: conflict and culture **150.19**
Gay, P. Freud **92**
Gay, P. A Godless Jew **150.19**
Mitchell, S. A. Freud and beyond **150.19**
Thurschwell, P. Sigmund Freud **150.19**
See/See also pages in the following book(s):
Alvarez, A. Night p119-41 **154.6**
Bloom, H. The Western canon **809**
Flowers, C. Instability rules **509**
Gardner, H. Creating minds p49-86 **153.3**
Freud and beyond. Mitchell, S. A. **150.19**
Freud and man's soul. Bettelheim, B. **150.19**
Freud: conflict and culture **150.19**
Freund, Joan Barzilay
(jt. auth) Keno, L. Hidden treasures **749.2**
Frey, Julia, 1943-
Toulouse-Lautrec **92**
Frida: a biography of Frida Kahlo. Herrera, H. **92**
Frida Kahlo. Zamora, M. **92**
Frida Kahlo [critical essays] **759.972**
Friday, Nancy
My mother/my self **155.6**
Friday night lights. Bissinger, H. G. **796.332**
Fried, Albert
F.D.R. and his enemies **92**
Fried chicken. Fowler, D. L. **641.6**
Friedan, Betty
The feminine mystique **305.4**
The fountain of age **305.26**
Life so far **92**
Friedland, Gerald W.
(jt. auth) Friedman, M. Medicine's 10 greatest discoveries **610.9**
Friedland, Susan R.
Shabbat shalom **641.5**
Friedlander, Brian S.
(jt. auth) Elias, M. J. Emotionally intelligent parenting **649**

Friedlander, Edward Jay
Feature writing for newspapers and magazines
070.4
Friedländer, Saul, 1932-
Nazi Germany and the Jews v1 **940.53**
Friedman, Avi
The adaptable house **728**
Friedman, David M., 1949-
A mind of its own **573.6**
Friedman, Howard S.
Encyclopedia of mental health. See Encyclopedia of
mental health **616.89**
Friedman, Lawrence Jacob, 1940-
Identity's architect: a biography of Erik H. Erikson
92
Friedman, Lawrence Meir, 1930-
American law in the 20th century **349**
Friedman, Maurice S., 1921-
Encounter on the narrow ridge: a life of Martin Buber
92
Friedman, Meyer, 1910-2001
Medicine's 10 greatest discoveries **610.9**
Friedman, Milton, 1912-
Free to choose **330.1**
Friedman, Norman, 1946-
Desert victory **956.7**
Friedman, Richard Elliott
Who wrote the Bible? **222**
Friedman, Rose D.
(jt. auth) Friedman, M. Free to choose **330.1**
Friedman, Thomas L.
From Beirut to Jerusalem **956**
The Lexus and the olive tree **337**
Longitudes and attitudes **973.931**
Friedman, Virginia M.
Field guide to stains **648**
Friedwald, Will, 1961-
Jazz singing **781.65**
Sinatra! the song is you **92**
Stardust melodies **782.42**
Friend, David, 1955-
(ed) Vanity Fair's Hollywood. See Vanity Fair's Hollywood **791.43**
Friends, Society of *See* Society of Friends
Friendship
Ambrose, S. E. Comrades **302.3**
Goodman, E. I know just what you mean **158**
Kephart, B. Into the tangle of friendship **158**
See/See also pages in the following book(s):
Pollack, W. S. Real boys p181-205 **305.23**
Friml, Rudolf, 1879-1972
See/See also pages in the following book(s):
Green, S. The world of musical comedy **920**
Frist, William H.
When every moment counts **613.6**
Frith, Uta, 1941-
Autism: explaining the enigma **618.92**
Fritzsch, Harald, 1943-
An equation that changed the world **530.1**
Frobisher, Sir Martin, 1539-1594
See/See also pages in the following book(s):
Connell, E. S. The Aztec treasure house p319-45
814
Froe, Felecia
(jt. auth) Dierich, M. Overcoming incontinence
616.6
Frogs
Souder, W. A plague of frogs **597.8**
Frogs. Aristophanes
In Aristophanes. The complete plays of Aristophanes
p367-415 **882**
From 0 to 1: an authoritative history of modern computing **004**
From a high place. Spender, M. **92**
From Beirut to Jerusalem. Friedman, T. L. **956**

From Buchenwald to Carnegie Hall. Filar, M.   92
From caveman to chemist. Salzberg, H. W.   540
From certainty to uncertainty. Peat, F. D.   530
From chocolate to morphine. Weil, A.   616.86
From dawn to decadence. Barzun, J.   940.2
From fin de siécle to negritude. See Poems for the millennium   808.81
From Gautama Buddha to the triumph of Christianity. Eliade, M.
  In Eliade, M. A history of religious ideas v2   291
From hardtack to home fries. Haber, B.   394.1
From Julia Child's kitchen. Child, J.   641.5
From Lucy to language. Johanson, D. C.   599.93
From morn to midnight. Kaiser, G.
  In Our dramatic heritage v5   808.82
From Muhammad to the Age of Reform. Eliade, M.
  In Eliade, M. A history of religious ideas v3   291
From my people   398.2
From noon to starry night: a life of Walt Whitman. Callow, P.   92
From postwar to millennium. See Poems for the millennium   808.81
From Satchmo to Miles. Feather, L.   920
From slavery to freedom. Franklin, J. H.   305.8
From spirituals to symphonies. Walker-Hill, H.   920
From the big bang to Planet X. Dickinson, T.   520
From the folks who brought you the weekend. Murolo, P.   331
From the secret files of J. Edgar Hoover   363.2
From the shadows. Gates, R. M.   327.73
From the Stone Age to the Eleusinian mysteries. Eliade, M.
  In Eliade, M. A history of religious ideas v1   291
From Van Eyck to Bruegel   759.9493
From zero to infinity. Reid, C.   512
Frome, Keith W., 1960-
  (ed) The Columbia book of Civil War poetry. See The Columbia book of Civil War poetry   811.008
Fromm, Erich, 1900-1980
  The art of loving   152.4
  On being human   150.19
  To have or to be?   302
Front row at the White House. Thomas, H.   92
Frontier and pioneer life
  Osborn, W. M. The wild frontier   973
  Sandburg, C. Abraham Lincoln: The prairie years and The war years   92
  See/See also pages in the following book(s):
  Faragher, J. M. Daniel Boone   92
  Encyclopedias
  Slatta, R. W. The cowboy encyclopedia   978.03
  Kansas
  Stratton, J. L. Pioneer women   978.1
  Texas
  Robinson, C. M. The men who wear the star   976.4
  West (U.S.)
  Durham, M. S. Desert between the mountains   979
  Luchetti, C. Children of the West   978
  Morgan, T. A shovel of stars   978
  Parkman, F. The Oregon Trail   978
  Raban, J. Bad land   978
  Schlissel, L. Far from home   978
  Slotkin, R. Gunfighter nation   973.9
  See/See also pages in the following book(s):
  Brown, D. A. The American West p27-58, 140-87, 347-55   978
  The Oxford history of the American West p115-52   978

West (U.S.)—Encyclopedias
  The New encyclopedia of the American West   978.03
Frontier and pioneer life in literature
  Snodgrass, M. E. Encyclopedia of frontier literature   810.3
Frontiers of space exploration. Launius, R. D.   629.45
Frost, Mark
  The greatest game ever played   796.352
Frost, Robert, 1874-1963
  Collected poems, prose, & plays   818
  The guardeen
  In Frost, R. Collected poems, prose, & plays p589-625   818
  In an art factory
  In Frost, R. Collected poems, prose, & plays p576-88   818
  A way out
  In Frost, R. Collected poems, prose, & plays p565-75   818
  About
  Parini, J. Robert Frost   92
  See/See also pages in the following book(s):
  Jarrell, R. No other book   809
  Pritchard, W. H. Lives of the modern poets p109-40   821.009
Frozen stars See Black holes (Astronomy)
Frucht, Richard
  (ed) Encyclopedia of Eastern Europe. See Encyclopedia of Eastern Europe   947
Fruit
  See also Apples
  Thoreau, H. D. Wild fruits   581.6
Frum, David, 1960-
  How we got here   973.92
Fry, Ronald W.
  Your first resume   650.14
Frye, Northrop
  Northrop Frye on Shakespeare   822.3
Fuchs, Klaus Emil Julius, 1911-1988
  See/See also pages in the following book(s):
  Rhodes, R. Dark sun   623.4
Fuegi, John
  Brecht and company   92
Fuentes, Carlos, 1928-
  The buried mirror   946
  Myself with others   864
  A new time for Mexico   972.08
Fugard, Athol
  "Master Harold"—and the boys   822
  Sorrows and rejoicings   822
  Valley song   822
Fugier, Elisabeth Hardouin- *See* Hardouin-Fugier, Elisabeth
Fujiwara, Murasaki *See* Murasaki Shikibu, b. 978?
Fukuyama, Francis
  Our posthuman future   174
  Trust   330.9
Fulbrook, Mary, 1951-
  A concise history of Germany   943
Fulfillment, Self *See* Self-realization
Fulk, Mark K., 1968-
  Understanding May Sarton   818
Fuller, Alexandra, 1969-
  Don't let's go to the dogs tonight   92
Fuller, John, 1937-
  (ed) The Oxford book of sonnets. See The Oxford book of sonnets   821.008
Fuller, Margaret, 1810-1850
  About
  Von Mehren, J. Minerva and the muse: a life of Margaret Fuller   92

Fuller, Meta Vaux Warrick, 1877-1968
See/See also pages in the following book(s):
Harlem Renaissance: art of black America   709.73
Russell, D. Black genius and the American experience
    920

Fulton, Robert, 1765-1815
    About
Sale, K. The fire of his genius: Robert Fulton and the American dream   92
The **Fun** of it   814
Fundamental life skills *See* Life skills
Fundamentalism *See* Christian fundamentalism; Islamic fundamentalism
Fundamentalism and evolution *See* Creationism
Fundamentalist movements *See* Religious fundamentalism
Funds, Scholarship *See* Scholarships
Funeral directors *See* Undertakers and undertaking
Funeral rites and ceremonies
Mitford, J. The American way of death revisited
    393
Wieseltier, L. Kaddish   296.4
Young, G. W. The high cost of dying   393
Fungi
    See also Mushrooms
Hudler, G. W. Magical mushrooms, mischievous molds
    579.5
Money, N. P. Mr. Bloomfield's orchard   579.5
Funk & Wagnalls Modern guide to synonyms & related words. See Choose the right word   423
Funnies *See* Comic books, strips, etc.
A **funny** thing happened on the way to Cooperstown. McDermott, M.   92
Funny, you don't look like a grandmother. Wyse, L.
    817

Füredi, Frank
Paranoid parenting   649
Furgurson, Ernest B., 1929-
Ashes of glory   975.5
Chancellorsville, 1863   973.7
Not war but murder   973.7
Furia, Philip, 1943-
Irving Berlin   92
Furlong, Monica
Visions & longings   248.2
Furniture
    See also Garden ornaments and furniture
Fresh & fabulous painted furniture   745.7
Keno, L. Hidden treasures   749.2
Morley, J. The history of furniture   749.2
    Repairing
Grotz, G. The furniture doctor   684.1
Lloyd, J. Furniture restoration   749
    See/See also pages in the following book(s):
New fix-it-yourself manual   643
The **furniture** doctor. Grotz, G.   684.1
Furniture finishing
Grotz, G. The furniture doctor   684.1
Lloyd, J. Furniture restoration   749
Travis, D. Debbie Travis' painted house   698
Furniture restoration. Lloyd, J.   749
Furniture: the western tradition. See Morley, J. The history of furniture   749.2
Fursenko, A. V. (Aleksandr Vasil′evich)
"One hell of a gamble"   973.922
Fursenko, Aleksandr Vasil′evich *See* Fursenko, A. V. (Aleksandr Vasil′evich)
Further along the road less traveled. Peck, M. S.
    158
Fussell, Betty Harper
Home bistro   641.5
Fussell, Paul, 1924-
Wartime: understanding and behavior in the Second World War   940.54

(ed) The Norton book of modern war. See The Norton book of modern war   808.8
Futebol: the Brazilian way of life. Bellos, A.
    796.334
The **future** is in eggs. Ionesco, E.
  In Ionesco, E. Rhinoceros, and other plays   842
Future life
    See also Heaven; Hell
The **future** of ideas. Lessig, L.   346.04
The **future** of life. Wilson, E. O.   333.95
The **future** of success. Reich, R. B.   306
The **future** of the past. Stille, A.   303.4
The **future** of the race. Gates, H. L.   305.8
Future shock *See* Culture conflict
Future shock. Toffler, A.   303.4
Futurology *See* Forecasting

G

G.I.'s *See* Soldiers—United States
Gabler, Neal
Winchell   92
Gachet, Paul, 1828-1909
    About
Saltzman, C. Portrait of Dr. Gachet   759.9492
Gaddis, John Lewis
The landscape of history   901
Gaffers, grips, and best boys. Taub, E.   791.43
Gage, Nicholas
Eleni [biography of Eleni Gatzoyiannis]   92
Greek fire   92
Gager, John G.
The origins of anti-Semitism   296.3
Gaia hypothesis
Lovelock, J. The ages of Gaia   570.1
Margulis, L. Symbiotic planet   576.8
Gaines, Patrice
Moments of grace   170
Gaiter, Dorothy J.
The Wall Street journal guide to wine   641.2
Gaius Caesar *See* Caligula, Emperor of Rome, 12-41
Galapagos Islands
Kricher, J. C. Galapagos   508
    Natural history
    See Natural history—Galapagos Islands
Galaxy (Milky Way) *See* Milky Way
Galba, Servius Sulpicius, Emperor of Rome, 3 B.C.-69
    See/See also pages in the following book(s):
Suetonius Tranquillus, C. The twelve Caesars   878
Galbraith, John Kenneth, 1908-
The affluent society   330
The Great Crash, 1929   338.5
Name-dropping   973.9
Galdikas, Biruté
Orangutan odyssey   599.8
Reflections of Eden   599.8
    See/See also pages in the following book(s):
Slung, M. B. Living with cannibals and other women's adventures   910.4
Gale, Zona, 1874-1938
Miss Lulu Bett
  In Plays by American women, 1900-1930
    812.008
    See/See also pages in the following book(s):
American women fiction writers   813.009
Gale directory of databases   025.04
Gale directory of learning worldwide   378
Gale directory of publications. See Gale directory of publications and broadcast media   070.025
Gale directory of publications and broadcast media
    070.025
Gale encyclopedia of everyday law   349
Gale encyclopedia of medicine   610.3

The **Gale** encyclopedia of mental disorders   **616.89**
Gale encyclopedia of multicultural America   **305.8**
The **Gale** encyclopedia of Native American tribes
   970.004
The **Gale** encyclopedia of psychology   **150.3**
Gale encyclopedia of science   **503**
Galens, David
   (ed) Literary movements for students. See Literary
   movements for students   **809**
Galilei, Galileo, 1564-1642
   About
   Sobel, D. Galileo's daughter   **92**
Galilei, Maria Celeste See Maria Celeste, 1600-1634
Galilei, Virginia See Maria Celeste, 1600-1634
Galileo See Galilei, Galileo, 1564-1642
Galileo. Brecht, B.
   In Our dramatic heritage v5   **808.82**
Galileo's daughter. Sobel, D.   **92**
Galimberti Jarman, Beatriz
   (ed) The Oxford Spanish dictionary. See The Oxford
   Spanish dictionary   **463**
Galison, Peter Louis
   Einstein's clocks and Poincaré's maps   **529**
Gall, Gilbert J.
   (jt. auth) Zieger, R. H. American workers, American
   unions   **331.8**
Gallagher, Eugene V.
   (jt. auth) Tabor, J. D. Why Waco?   **291.9**
Gallagher, Gary W.
   The Confederate War   **973.7**
   (ed) The Library of Congress Civil War desk refer-
   ence. See The Library of Congress Civil War desk
   reference   **973.7**
Gallagher, Maggie
   (jt. auth) Waite, L. J. The case for marriage
   306.8
Gallagher, Richard B.
   (jt. auth) Dennis, C. The human genome   **599.93**
Gallagher, Rita
   (ed) Writing romances. See Writing romances
   808.3
Gallagher, Tag
   John Ford   **791.43**
Gallagher, Winifred
   Spiritual genius   **920**
Gallati, Barbara Dayer
   (jt. auth) Ferber, L. S. Masters of color and light
   759.13
Gallaudet, T. H. (Thomas Hopkins), 1787-1851
   See/See also pages in the following book(s):
   Lepore, J. A is for American   **306.44**
Gallaudet, Thomas Hopkins See Gallaudet, T. H.
   (Thomas Hopkins), 1787-1851
Gallaudet survival guide to signing. Lane, L. G.
   419
Gallaudet University
   See/See also pages in the following book(s):
   Sacks, O. W. Seeing voices p125-59   **362.4**
Gallay, Alan
   The Indian slave trade   **326**
Galleries, Art See Art museums
The **Gallic** War. Caesar, J.   **878**
Gallo, Robert C.
   Virus hunting   **616.97**
Galloway, Joseph L., 1941-
   (jt. auth) Moore, H. G. We were soldiers once—and
   young   **959.704**
Galois, Évariste, 1811-1832
   See/See also pages in the following book(s):
   Bell, E. T. Men of mathematics p362-77   **920**
Galveston (Tex.)
   History
   Larson, E. Isaac's storm   **976.4**

Gambling
   Ainslie, T. Ainslie's complete guide to thoroughbred
   racing   **798.401**
   Scarne, J. Scarne's new complete guide to gambling
   795
   See/See also pages in the following book(s):
   Denton, S. The money and the power   **979.3**
   Orkin, M. What are the odds?   **519.2**
Game and game birds
   See also Cooking—Game
   Jones, R. F. The hunter in my heart   **799.2**
The **game** I love. Snead, S.   **796.352**
Game protection
   See also Birds—Protection
Game theory
   See also Decision making
Game time: a baseball companion. Angell, R.
   796.357
Games
   See also Card games; Sports; names of individual
   games
   Ainslie, T. Ainslie's complete Hoyle   **795**
   Cohen, L. J. Playful parenting   **649**
Games companies play. Mornell, P.   **650.14**
Gamma ray bursts
   Katz, J. I. The biggest bangs   **522**
   Schilling, G. Flash!   **522**
Gammell, Stephen, 1943-
   See/See also pages in the following book(s):
   The Newbery & Caldecott medal books, 1986-2000
   p85-89   **028.5**
Gamow, George, 1904-1968
   See/See also pages in the following book(s):
   Greenstein, G. Portraits of discovery p52-67   **920**
Gander, Forrest, 1956-
   Torn awake   **811**
Gandhi, Indira, 1917-1984
   About
   Frank, K. Indira: the life of Indira Nehru Gandhi
   92
Gandhi, Mahatma, 1869-1948
   Gandhi on non-violence   **322.4**
   About
   Chadha, Y. Gandhi   **92**
   Wolpert, S. A. Gandhi's passion   **92**
   See/See also pages in the following book(s):
   Gardner, H. Creating minds p311-53   **153.3**
Gandhi, Mohandas Karamchand See Gandhi, Mahat-
   ma, 1869-1948
Gandhi on non-violence. Gandhi, M.   **322.4**
Gandhi's passion. Wolpert, S. A.   **92**
Gangsters See Mafia
Gannon, JoAnn Pugh- See Pugh-Gannon, JoAnn
Ganon, Jill Alison, 1952-
   (jt. auth) Agnew, C. L. Twins!   **649**
Gansler, Laura Leedy, 1958-
   (jt. auth) Bingham, C. Class action   **342**
Gänzl, Kurt
   The encyclopedia of the musical theatre   **792.6**
   The musical   **792.6**
Gaposchkin, Cecilia Helena Payne, 1900-1979
   See/See also pages in the following book(s):
   Greenstein, G. Portraits of discovery p7-30   **920**
Garbarino, James
   Parents under siege   **649**
Garber, Marianne Daniels, 1948-
   (jt. auth) Garber, S. W. Monsters under the bed and
   other childhood fears   **649**
Garber, Stephen W., 1946-
   Monsters under the bed and other childhood fears
   649
Garbus, Martin, 1934-
   Courting disaster   **347**

Garcia, Jerry
About
Greenfield, R. Dark Star: an oral biography of Jerry Garcia **92**
Jackson, B. Garcia **92**
See/See also pages in the following book(s):
Brightman, C. Sweet chaos: the Grateful Dead's American adventure **920**
Garcia, Richard A., 1941-
(jt. auth) Meier, M. S. Notable Latino Americans **920.003**
García de Paredes, Angel
Cassell's Spanish-English, English-Spanish dictionary. See Cassell's Spanish-English, English-Spanish dictionary **463**
García Lorca, Federico, 1898-1936
The billy-club puppets
In Garcia Lorca, F. Five plays p13-55 **862**
Blood wedding
In García Lorca, F. Three tragedies **862**
In Our dramatic heritage v6 **808.82**
The butterfly's evil spell
In Garcia Lorca, F. Five plays p191-236 **862**
Doña Rosita, the spinster
In Garcia Lorca, F. Five plays p131-90 **862**
Five plays **862**
The house of Bernarda Alba
In García Lorca, F. Three tragedies **862**
The love of Don Perlimplin and Belisa in the garden
In Garcia Lorca, F. Five plays p105-30 **862**
Selected poems **861**
The shoemaker's prodigious wife
In Garcia Lorca, F. Five plays p57-104 **862**
Three tragedies **862**
Yerma
In García Lorca, F. Three tragedies **862**
About
Gibson, I. Federico García Lorca: a life **92**
García Márquez, Gabriel, 1928-
Living to tell the tale **92**
The story of a shipwrecked sailor **910.4**
García-Pelayo y Gross, Ramón
(ed) Gran diccionario español-inglés. English-Spanish dictionary. See Gran diccionario español-inglés. English-Spanish dictionary **463**
Gardell, Mattias
In the name of Elijah Muhammad **297**
Gardella, Robert
The Harvard Business School guide to finding your next job **650.14**
Garden cuisine. Wenner, P. F. **613.2**
Garden design
See also Landscape gardening
Anderton, S. Urban sanctuaries **635.9**
Brookes, J. Garden masterclass **712**
Clausen, R. R. Dreamscaping **712**
Harper, P. Designing with perennials **712**
Hudak, J. Design for gardens **712**
Newbury, T. 20 best garden designs **712**
Seale, A. New life for old gardens **635.9**
Van Sweden, J. A. Architecture in the garden **712**
A **Garden** from a hundred packets of seed. Fenton, J. **635.9**
Garden masterclass. Brookes, J. **712**
Garden ornaments and furniture
The Complete book of garden projects **712**
A **garden** party. Behan, B.
In Behan, B. The complete plays **822**
Garden problem solver. See Greenwood, P. AHS garden problem solver **635**
Gardening
See also Flower gardening; Garden design; Indoor gardening; Landscape gardening; Vegetable gardening

1,001 ingenious gardening ideas **635**
The American Horticultural Society gardening manual **635**
The Brooklyn Botanic Garden gardener's desk reference **635.9**
Burpee complete gardener **635**
The Complete book of garden projects **712**
Darke, R. The American woodland garden **635.9**
Duffield, M. R. Plants for dry climates **635.9**
Fenton, J. A Garden from a hundred packets of seed **635.9**
Freeman, M. Gardening in your greenhouse **635.9**
Gardening basics **635**
Greenwood, P. AHS garden problem solver **635**
Kress, S. W. The bird garden **598**
Lloyd, C. Color for adventurous gardeners **635.9**
Lord, T. The encyclopedia of planting combinations **635.9**
Smith, C. W. G. The big book of gardening secrets **635**
Springer, L. Passionate gardening **635**
Step-by-step yard & garden basics **635**
Taylor's master guide to gardening **635.9**
See/See also pages in the following book(s):
Adams, G. M. Birdscaping your garden **598**
Dictionaries
Hortus third **635**
Pollock, M. The Royal Horticultural Society shorter dictionary of gardening **635**
Encyclopedias
American Horticultural Society encyclopedia of gardening **635**
Wyman, D. Wyman's gardening encyclopedia **635**
Poetry
The Oxford book of garden verse **821.008**
Gardening, Organic *See* Organic gardening
Gardening at a glance. See Denckla, T. The organic gardener's home reference **635**
Gardening basics **635**
Gardening in your greenhouse. Freeman, M. **635.9**
Gardening with grasses. King, M. **635.9**
Gardens
Ackerman, D. Cultivating delight **508**
Gertley, J. The art of the kitchen garden **712**
Griswold, M. K. The golden age of American gardens **712**
Roberts, J. Royal landscape **942**
Design
See Garden design
Poetry
The Oxford book of garden verse **821.008**
Gardner, David
The Motley Fool's what to do with your money now **332.6**
Gardner, Herb, 1934-2003
Herb Gardner: the collected plays and the screenplay Who is Harry Kellerman and why is he saying those terrible things about me? **812**
Plays included are: A thousand clowns; The goodbye people; Thieves; I'm not Rappaport; Conversations with my father
Gardner, Howard
Creating minds **153.3**
Gardner, John, 1933-1982
The art of fiction **808.3**
On becoming a novelist **808.3**
On moral fiction **801**
The poetry of Chaucer **821**
Gardner, Martin, 1914-
Did Adam and Eve have navels? **500**
The night is large **814**
On the wild side **500**
Gardner, Richard A., 1931-2003
The parents book about divorce **306.89**

Gardner, Robert, 1929-
(jt. auth) Conklin, B. G. Encyclopedia of forensic science 363.2
Gardner, Tom
(jt. auth) Gardner, D. The Motley Fool's what to do with your money now 332.6
Gardner's art through the ages 709
Garfield, Simon
Mauve 667
Gargan, Edward A.
A river's tale 915.9
Garland, Henry B. (Henry Burnand)
The Oxford companion to German literature 830.3
Garland, Judy
About
Clarke, G. Get happy: the life of Judy Garland 92
Garland, Mary
(jt. auth) Garland, H. B. The Oxford companion to German literature 830.3
The **Garland** encyclopedia of world music 780.9
Garlic
Griffith, L. Garlic, garlic, garlic 641.6
Garlic, garlic, garlic. Griffith, L. 641.6
Garment industry See Clothing industry
Garments See Clothing and dress
Garnaut, Christine
(jt. auth) Langmead, D. Encyclopedia of architectural and engineering feats 721
Garner, Bryan A.
Garner's modern American usage 423
Garner, Joe
We interrupt this broadcast 070.1
Garner's modern American usage. Garner, B. A. 423
Garraty, John Arthur, 1920-
(ed) American national biography. See American national biography 920.003
(ed) The Reader's companion to American history. See The Reader's companion to American history 973.03
Garrett, John
John Garrett's black-and-white photography masterclass 771
Garrett, Laurie
Betrayal of trust 362.1
The coming plague 614.4
Garrick, James G.
Anybody's sports medicine book 617.1
Garrison, Tim Alan, 1961-
The legal ideology of removal 970.004
Garry, Jane
(ed) Facts about the world's languages: an encyclopedia of the world's major languages, past and present. See Facts about the world's languages: an encyclopedia of the world's major languages, past and present 400
Garten, Ina
Barefoot Contessa family style 641.5
Garton Ash, Timothy
The file 327.12
History of the present 940.55
Gascoyne-Cecil, Robert Arthur Talbot See Salisbury, Robert Arthur Talbot Gascoyne-Cecil, 3rd Marquis of, 1830-1903
Gaskell, Elizabeth Cleghorn, 1810-1865
The life of Charlotte Brontë 92
Gass, William H., 1924-
Finding a form 814
Tests of time 814
Gasset, José Ortega y See Ortega y Gasset, José, 1883-1955

Gaster, Theodor Herzl, 1906-1992
(ed) Dead Sea scrolls. The Dead Sea scriptures 229
(ed) Frazer, Sir J. G. The new golden bough 291.1
The **gate.** Bizot, F. 959.6
The **gatekeepers.** Steinberg, J. 378.1
Gately, Iain
Tobacco 394.1
Gates, Alexander E.
A to Z of earth scientists 920.003
(jt. auth) Ritchie, D. Encyclopedia of earthquakes and volcanoes 551.2
Gates, Bill, 1955-
See/See also pages in the following book(s):
Klein, M. The change makers 920
Gates, Henry Louis
The African-American century 920
Colored people 92
The future of the race 305.8
Thirteen ways of looking at a black man 920
Wonders of the African world 960
(ed) Africana. See Africana 909
(ed) The Norton anthology of African American literature. See The Norton anthology of African American literature 810.8
(ed) Richard Wright. See Richard Wright [critical essays] 813.009
Gates, Robert M.
From the shadows 327.73
Gates, William H., III See Gates, Bill, 1955-
A **gathering** of wonders. Wallace, J. 508
The **gathering** storm. Churchill, Sir W. 940.53
Gathering storm. Dees, M. S., Jr. 322.4
Gatti, Claudio, 1955-
(jt. auth) Cohen, R. In the eye of the storm: the life of General H. Norman Schwarzkopf 92
Gatzoyiannis, Eleni
About
Gage, N. Eleni 92
Gauguin, Paul, 1848-1903
About
Druick, D. W. Van Gogh and Gauguin 92
Silverman, D. Van Gogh and Gauguin 759.4
Thomson, B. Gauguin 92
Gaulle, Charles de, 1890-1970
About
Williams, C. The last great Frenchman 92
See/See also pages in the following book(s):
Kissinger, H. Diplomacy p594-619 327.73
Gauss, Carl Friedrich, 1777-1855
See/See also pages in the following book(s):
Bell, E. T. Men of mathematics p218-69 920
Mlodinow, L. Euclid's window 516
Gaustad, Edwin Scott
New historical atlas of religion in America 200.9
Gautama Buddha
About
Armstrong, K. Buddha 294.3
See/See also pages in the following book(s):
Jaspers, K. The great philosophers 109
Gavin, James, 1964-
Deep in a dream: the long night of Chet Baker 92
Gawain and the Grene Knight (Middle English poem)
Gawain and the Grene Knight
In The Oxford anthology of English literature v1 820.8
Gawande, Atul
Complications: a young surgeon's notes on an imperfect science 617
Gay, John, 1685-1732
The beggar's opera 822
also in The Oxford anthology of English literature v1 820.8

Gay, Kathlyn, 1930-
Encyclopedia of women's health issues   **613**
Gay, Peter, 1923-
The Enlightenment: an interpretation   **190**
Freud   **92**
A Godless Jew   **150.19**
My German question   **92**
The rise of modern paganism
   In Gay, P. The Enlightenment: an interpretation v1   **190**
Savage reprisals   **809.3**
The science of freedom
   In Gay, P. The Enlightenment: an interpretation v2   **190**
(ed) Freud, S. The Freud reader   **150.19**
Gay, Ruth
The Jews of Germany   **943**
Gay lifestyle *See* Homosexuality
Gay men
Kaiser, C. The gay metropolis   **305.9**
Marcus, E. Is it a choice?   **305.9**
St. James Press gay & lesbian almanac   **305.9**
   See/See also pages in the following book(s):
Bordo, S. The male body p153-67   **305.31**
The **gay** metropolis. Kaiser, C.   **305.9**
Gay women *See* Lesbians
Gayton, Narcissus Duffy
(jt. auth) Boyer, R. M. Apache mothers and daughters   **970.004**
Gaze, Delia
(ed) Dictionary of women artists. See Dictionary of women artists   **920.003**
Gazetteers
   See also Geographic names
The Columbia gazetteer of the world   **910.3**
GCHQ *See* Great Britain. Government Communications Headquarters
Gearin-Tosh, Michael
Living proof   **92**
Geary, Don
Welding   **671.5**
GED *See* High school equivalency examination
Geffen, Rela M.
(ed) Celebration & renewal. See Celebration & renewal   **296.4**
Gegax, Tom
Winning in the game of life   **158**
Gehrig, Henry Louis *See* Gehrig, Lou, 1903-1941
Gehrig, Lou, 1903-1941
About
Robinson, R. Iron horse: Lou Gehrig in his time   **92**
Geiringer, Irene
(jt. auth) Geiringer, K. Haydn: a creative life in music   **92**
Geiringer, Karl, 1899-1989
Haydn: a creative life in music   **92**
Geis, Gilbert
Crimes of the century   **345**
Geisel, Theodor Seuss *See* Seuss, Dr.
Geishas
Downer, L. Women of the pleasure quarters   **952**
Geissler, Catherine
(jt. auth) Vaughan, J. G. The new Oxford book of food plants   **633**
Geisst, Charles R.
The last partnerships   **332.6**
Geist, Bill
Little League confidential   **796.357**
Geist, William *See* Geist, Bill
Gelfant, Blanche H., 1922-
(ed) The Columbia companion to the twentieth-century American short story. See The Columbia companion to the twentieth-century American short story   **813.009**

Gell-Mann, Murray, 1929-
The quark and the jaguar   **530.1**
About
Johnson, G. Strange beauty: Murray Gell-Mann and the revolution in twentieth-century physics   **92**
   See/See also pages in the following book(s):
Brennan, R. P. Heisenberg probably slept here   **920**
Geller, Margaret J., 1947-
   See/See also pages in the following book(s):
Greenstein, G. Portraits of discovery p187-218   **920**
Gellhorn, Martha
About
Moorehead, C. Gellhorn: a twentieth-century life   **92**
Gelman, Robert B.
Protecting yourself online   **342**
Gemini: an extended autobiographical statement on my first twenty-five years of being a black poet. Giovanni, N.   **92**
Gems
   See also Precious stones
Gems. Webster, R.   **553.8**
Gems & crystals from the American Museum of Natural History. Sofianides, A. S.   **549**
Gender identity *See* Sex role
Gene mapping
   See also Genomes
Andreasen, N. C. Brave new brain   **616.89**
Bodmer, W. F. The book of man   **572.8**
Cook-Deegan, R. M. The gene wars   **572.8**
Dennis, C. The human genome   **599.93**
Wickelgren, I. The gene masters   **599.93**
The **gene** masters. Wickelgren, I.   **599.93**
Gene splicing *See* Genetic engineering
The **gene** wars. Cook-Deegan, R. M.   **572.8**
Genealogical research on the Web. Kovacs, D. K.   **929**
The **genealogist's** address book. Bentley, E. P.   **929**
The **genealogist's** companion and sourcebook. Croom, E. A.   **929**
Genealogy
Baxter, A. In search of your European roots   **929**
Bentley, E. P. Directory of family associations   **929**
Bentley, E. P. The genealogist's address book   **929**
Carmack, S. D. Organizing your family history search   **929**
Croom, E. A. The genealogist's companion and sourcebook   **929**
Greenwood, V. D. The researcher's guide to American genealogy   **929**
Kemp, T. J. Virtual roots 2.0   **929**
Kovacs, D. K. Genealogical research on the Web   **929**
Moore, D. E. The librarian's genealogy notebook   **929**
Neagles, J. C. The Library of Congress   **929**
Bibliography
Printed sources   **929**
Internet resources
Roberts, R. Genealogy via the Internet   **929**
Genealogy via the Internet. Roberts, R.   **929**
General Assembly (United Nations) *See* United Nations. General Assembly
General science index   **505**
General Slocum (Steamboat)
   See/See also pages in the following book(s):
O'Donnell, E. T. Ship ablaze   **910.4**
The **general** theory of employment, interest and money. Keynes, J. M.   **330.1**
A **general** theory of love. Lewis, T.   **152.4**

Generals
Warner, E. J. Generals in blue   920
Warner, E. J. Generals in gray   920
    Dictionaries
Ancell, R. M. The biographical dictionary of World
    War II generals and flag officers   920.003
Magill's guide to military history   355
Generals in blue. Warner, E. J.   920
Generals in gray. Warner, E. J.   920
The **generals'** war. Gordon, M. R.   956.7
Generation gap See Conflict of generations
Genes, girls, and Gamow. Watson, J. D.   92
Genesis, Book of See Bible. O.T. Genesis
Genesis. Zimmerman, R.   629.45
Genesis: a living conversation. Moyers, B.   222
The **Genesis** of justice. Dershowitz, A. M.   222
Genet, Jean, 1910-1986
    The balcony
       In Nine plays of the modern theater p293-394
       808.82
    The blacks: a clown show   842
    Deathwatch
       In Genet, J. The maids [and] Deathwatch   842
    The maids [and] Deathwatch   842
Genetic code
    Lewontin, R. C. The triple helix   572.8
Genetic engineering
    See also Biotechnology; Cloning
    Charles, D. Lords of the harvest   664
    The Double-edged helix   599.93
    Fox, M. W. Beyond evolution   174
    Fukuyama, F. Our posthuman future   174
    Hubbell, S. Shrinking the cat   660.6
    Lurquin, P. F. High tech harvest   631.5
    Rifkin, J. The biotech century   303.4
    Stock, G. Redesigning humans   176
    Wickelgren, I. The gene masters   599.93
    See/See also pages in the following book(s):
    Dyson, F. J. The sun, the genome, & the Internet
       303.4
    Dictionaries
    Steinberg, M. L. The Facts on File dictionary of bio-
    technology and genetic engineering   660.6
Genetic fingerprints See DNA fingerprinting
Genetic maps and human imaginations. Rothman, B. K.
    599.93
Genetically engineered food. Cummins, R.   363.1
Genetically modified foods   363.1
Genetics
    See also Behavior genetics; Breeding; Gene map-
    ping; Genomes; Medical genetics
    Avise, J. C. Genetics in the wild   591.3
    Berg, P. Dealing with genes   576.5
    Dawkins, R. Climbing Mount Improbable   576
    Dawkins, R. River out of Eden   576
    Dawkins, R. The selfish gene   576
    The Double-edged helix   599.93
    Keller, E. F. The century of the gene   576.5
    Marks, J. What it means to be 98% chimpanzee
       599.93
    Ridley, M. Genome   599.93
    Rothman, B. K. Genetic maps and human imaginations
       599.93
    Sagan, C. The dragons of Eden   153
    Stock, G. Redesigning humans   176
    Sykes, B. The seven daughters of Eve   599.93
    Tudge, C. The impact of the gene   576.5
    Watson, J. D. DNA: the secret of life   576.5
    See/See also pages in the following book(s):
    Beckwith, J. R. Making genes, making waves   92
    Goodwin, B. C. How the leopard changed its spots
       576
    Encyclopedias
    Genetics   576
Genetics   576

Genetics and environment See Nature and nurture
Genetics in the wild. Avise, J. C.   591.3
Genghis Khan, 1162-1227
    About
    Ratchnevsky, P. Genghis Khan: his life and legacy
       92
Genius
    Bloom, H. Genius   153.9
Genocide
    Cocker, M. Rivers of blood, rivers of gold   909
    Gourevitch, P. We wish to inform you that tomorrow
    we will be killed with our families   967.571
    Power, S. "A problem from hell"   304.6
    See/See also pages in the following book(s):
    Shawcross, W. Deliver us from evil   909.82
Genome mapping See Gene mapping
Genomes
    Danchin, A. The Delphic boat   572.8
    Davies, K. Cracking the genome   599.93
    Dennis, C. The human genome   599.93
    The Genomic revolution   599.93
    Ridley, M. Genome   599.93
    Rothman, B. K. Genetic maps and human imaginations
       599.93
    Wickelgren, I. The gene masters   599.93
The **Genomic** revolution   599.93
Genovese, Elizabeth Fox- See Fox-Genovese, Elizabeth, 1941-
Genreflecting. Herald, D. T.   016.8
The **gentleman** from New York: Daniel Patrick
    Moynihan: a biography. Hodgson, G.   92
A **gentleman** of color: the life of James Forten. Winch,
    J.   92
Gentleman spy: the life of Allen Dulles. Grose, P.
    92
Gentry, Curt, 1931-
    J. Edgar Hoover   92
    (jt. auth) Bugliosi, V. Helter skelter   364.1
Geoghegan, Thomas
    In America's court   345
Geographic names
    See also Gazetteers
    United States
    Beatty, M. A. County name origins of the United
    States   917.3
    Kane, J. N. Nicknames and sobriquets of U.S. cities,
    states, and counties   917.3
    Shankle, G. E. American nicknames   929.4
    Shearer, B. F. State names, seals, flags, and symbols
       929.9
    Twentieth century American nicknames   929.4
Geographical distribution of people See Human geog-
    raphy
Geographical myths
    See also Atlantis
    Dictionaries
    Manguel, A. The dictionary of imaginary places
       809.3
Geography
    See also Voyages and travels
    Alder, K. The measure of all things   526
    The National Geographic desk reference   910
    Dictionaries
    Merriam-Webster's geographical dictionary   910.3
    Worldmark encyclopedia of the nations   910.3
    Periodicals—Indexes
    National geographic index, 1888-1988   910
The **geography** of the imagination. Davenport, G.
    814
Geology
    See also Catastrophes (Geology)
    Erickson, J. An introduction to fossils and minerals
       560
    Lambert, D. The field guide to geology   551
    Oldroyd, D. R. Thinking about the earth   551

Geology—*Continued*
United States
McPhee, J. A. Annals of the former world   **557**
Geology, Stratigraphic *See* Stratigraphic geology
Geometric patterns *See* Patterns (Mathematics)
Geometry
Gorini, C. A. The Facts on File geometry handbook
   516
Livio, M. The golden ratio   **516.2**
Mlodinow, L. Euclid's window   **516**
Georgano, G. N. (George Nicolas)
The Beaulieu encyclopedia of the automobile. See The
Beaulieu encyclopedia of the automobile
   629.222
Georgano, George Nicolas *See* Georgano, G. N.
(George Nicolas)
Georgano, Nick *See* Georgano, G. N. (George Nicolas)
George, Henry, 1839-1897
See/See also pages in the following book(s):
Heilbroner, R. L. The worldly philosophers   **330.1**
George, John H.
(jt. auth) Boller, P. F. They never said it   **808.88**
George, Nelson
Blackface: reflections on African-Americans and the
movies   **791.43**
Hip hop America   **781.64**
George and Laura [Bush] Andersen, C. P.   **92**
George Soros on globalization. Soros, G.   **337**
George-Warren, Holly
(ed) American roots music. See American roots music
   781.62
(ed) The Rolling Stone illustrated history of rock &
roll. See The Rolling Stone illustrated history of rock
& roll   **781.66**
The **Georgetown** ladies' social club. Heymann, C. D.
   305.4
Georgia
History
See/See also pages in the following book(s):
Boorstin, D. J. The Americans: The colonial experi-
ence   **973.2**
Politics and government
Carter, J. Turning point   **975.8**
Social life and customs
Carter, J. An hour before daylight   **92**
Georgia O'Keeffe: a life. Robinson, R.   **92**
Georgiana, Duchess of Devonshire. Foreman, A.
   92
Georgiou, Elena
(ed) The World in us. See The World in us
   811.008
Gerasimo, Luisa
(comp) McGraw-Hill's big red book of resumes. See
McGraw-Hill's big red book of resumes   **650.14**
Gerassi, John
Jean-Paul Sartre v1   **92**
Gerberg, Mort
(ed) Joy in Mudville. See Joy in Mudville
   796.357
Gerdts, William H.
California impressionism   **759.13**
Gerhard Richter: forty years of painting. Storr, R.
   759.3
Gerhards, Paul
How to sell what you make   **658.8**
Geriatrics *See* Elderly—Diseases; Elderly—Health and
hygiene
Germ theory of disease
Bakalar, N. Where the germs are   **616**
Biddle, W. A field guide to germs   **616**
Germ warfare *See* Biological warfare
German cooking
Anderson, J. The new German cookbook   **641.5**
German Democratic Republic *See* Germany (East)

German drama
History and criticism
See/See also pages in the following book(s):
Dürrenmatt, F. Plays and essays p233-62   **838**
German-English bilingual books *See* Bilingual books—
English-German
German language
Dictionaries
Cassell's German dictionary   **433**
Collins German-English, English-German dictionary
   433
Michael, R. Nazi-Deutsch/Nazi-German   **943.086**
The Oxford-Duden German dictionary   **433**
German literature
Bio-bibliography
Encyclopedia of German literature   **830.3**
Garland, H. B. The Oxford companion to German liter-
ature   **830.3**
Segel, H. B. The Columbia guide to the literatures of
Eastern Europe since 1945   **809**
Dictionaries
Garland, H. B. The Oxford companion to German liter-
ature   **830.3**
Encyclopedias
Encyclopedia of German literature   **830.3**
History and criticism
The Cambridge history of German literature
   830.9
German reunification question (1949-1990)
Grass, G. Two states—one nation?   **943.087**
Germano, William P., 1950-
Getting it published   **070.5**
The **Germans**. Craig, G. A.   **943**
Germany
See also Nuremberg (Germany)
Civilization
Craig, G. A. The Germans   **943**
Elon, A. The pity of it all   **943**
Ethnic relations
Smith, H. W. The butcher's tale   **943.08**
Foreign relations—Switzerland
Ziegler, J. The Swiss, the gold, and the dead
   940.53
Foreign relations—United States
Beschloss, M. R. The conquerors: Roosevelt, Truman,
and the destruction of Hitler's Germany, 1941-1945
   940.53
History
Craig, G. A. The Germans   **943**
Craig, G. A. Germany, 1866-1945   **943.08**
Fulbrook, M. A concise history of Germany   **943**
Schulze, H. Germany   **943**
See/See also pages in the following book(s):
Durant, W. J. The age of Louis XIV p411-21
   940.2
History—0-1517
See/See also pages in the following book(s):
Tacitus, C. The complete works of Tacitus p709-32
   878
History—1740-1815
See also Seven Years' War, 1756-1763
History—1866-1918
Massie, R. K. Dreadnought   **940.3**
History—1918-1933
Haffner, S. Defying Hitler   **92**
MacMillan, M. Paris 1919   **940.3**
History—1933-1945
Burleigh, M. The Third Reich   **943.086**
Fest, J. C. Plotting Hitler's death   **943.086**
Fischer, K. P. Nazi Germany   **943.086**
Friedländer, S. Nazi Germany and the Jews v1
   940.53
Goldhagen, D. Hitler's willing executioners
   940.53
Hay, J. A history of the Third Reich   **943.086**

Germany—History—1933-1945—*Continued*
Johnson, E. A. Nazi terror   **940.53**
Klemperer, V. I will bear witness   **92**
Michael, R. Nazi-Deutsch/Nazi-German   **943.086**
Read, A. The fall of Berlin   **940.54**
Rempel, G. Hitler's children   **943.086**
Rhodes, R. Masters of death   **940.53**
Shirer, W. L. The rise and fall of the Third Reich   **943.086**
Speer, A. Inside the Third Reich   **943.086**
  History—1945-1990
  See also German reunification question (1949-1990)
Brenner, M. After the Holocaust   **943.087**
    Politics and government
Grass, G. Two states—one nation?   **943.087**
    Politics and government—1918-1933
Hitler, A. Mein Kampf   **92**
Kershaw, I. Hitler   **92**
Turner, H. A. Hitler's thirty days to power   **943.086**
    Politics and government—1933-1945
Ayçoberry, P. The social history of the Third Reich   **943.086**
Breitman, R. The architect of genocide: Himmler and the final solution   **92**
Breitman, R. Official secrets   **940.54**
Bullock, A. Hitler and Stalin   **92**
Dwork, D. Holocaust: a history   **940.53**
Kershaw, I. Hitler   **92**
Pool, J. Hitler and his secret partners   **943.086**
Rosenbaum, R. Explaining Hitler   **92**
Sereny, G. Albert Speer   **92**
Toland, J. Adolf Hitler   **92**
Van der Vat, D. The good Nazi: the life and lies of Albert Speer   **92**
  See/See also pages in the following book(s):
Fest, J. C. Speer: the final verdict   **92**
Gay, P. My German question   **92**
    Science
  See Science—Germany
    Social conditions
Ayçoberry, P. The social history of the Third Reich   **943.086**
    Social life and customs
Ozment, S. E. Flesh and spirit   **943**
Germany. Geheime Staatspolizei *See* Germany. Gestapo
Germany. Gestapo
Johnson, E. A. Nazi terror   **940.53**
Germany (East)
    Politics and government
Darnton, R. Berlin journal, 1989-1990   **943.087**
Germany (East). Ministerium für Staatssicherheit
Garton Ash, T. The file   **327.12**
Germany, 1866-1945. Craig, G. A.   **943.08**
Germany and its tribes. Tacitus, C.
  In Tacitus, C. The complete works of Tacitus p709-32   **878**
Germond, Philippe
An Egyptian bestiary   **709.32**
Germs *See* Bacteria
Germs. Miller, J.   **358**
Geronimo, Apache Chief, 1829-1909
    About
Debo, A. Geronimo   **92**
Roberts, D. Once they moved like the wind   **970.004**
  See/See also pages in the following book(s):
Brown, D. A. The American West p356-63   **978**
Brown, D. A. Bury my heart at Wounded Knee   **970.004**
Gerontology
  See also Aging; Old age
    Encyclopedias
Encyclopedia of aging   **305.26**

The Encyclopedia of aging: a comprehensive resource in gerontology and geriatrics   **305.26**
Gerrard, Jon
(jt. auth) Park, Y. H. Black belt tae kwon do   **796.8**
Gershwin, George, 1898-1937
    About
Gilbert, S. E. The music of Gershwin   **92**
  See/See also pages in the following book(s):
Green, S. The world of musical comedy   **920**
Gershwin, Ira, 1896-1983
  See/See also pages in the following book(s):
Green, S. The world of musical comedy   **920**
Gerson, Allan
The price of terror   **363.1**
Gerstner, Louis V., Jr.
Who says elephants can't dance?   **338.7**
Gertley, Jan
The art of the kitchen garden   **712**
Gertley, Michael
(jt. auth) Gertley, J. The art of the kitchen garden   **712**
Gessner, David, 1961-
Return of the osprey   **598**
Gestapo *See* Germany. Gestapo
Get happy: the life of Judy Garland. Clarke, G.   **92**
Getting Frankie married. Foote, H.
  In Foote, H. Getting Frankie married—and afterwards, and other plays   **812**
Getting Frankie married—and afterwards, and other plays. Foote, H.   **812**
Getting it published. Germano, W. P.   **070.5**
Getting past no. Ury, W.   **158**
Getty, J. Paul, 1892-1976
    About
The J. Paul Getty Museum and its collections   **708**
Gettysburg (Pa.), Battle of, 1863
Perry, M. Conceived in liberty   **973.7**
Trudeau, N. A. Gettysburg: a testing of courage   **973.7**
Wert, J. D. Gettysburg, day three   **973.7**
Gettysburg, day three. Wert, J. D.   **973.7**
Ghelderode, Michel de, 1898-1962
Red magic
  In Our dramatic heritage v6   **808.82**
Ghettoes, Inner city *See* Inner cities
Ghosh, Amitav
In an antique land   **962**
Ghost dance
  See/See also pages in the following book(s):
Brown, D. A. Bury my heart at Wounded Knee   **970.004**
Ghost soldiers. Sides, H.   **940.54**
The **ghost** sonata. Strindberg, A.
  In Strindberg, A. Strindberg: five plays p265-97   **839.7**
Ghost trio. Beckett, S.
  In Beckett, S. Ends and Odds p51-65   **842**
The **ghost** with trembling wings. Weidensaul, S.   **591.68**
Ghosts
Norman, M. Haunted America   **133.1**
Ramsland, K. M. Ghost   **133.1**
    Encyclopedias
Guiley, R. E. The encyclopedia of ghosts and spirits   **133.1**
Ghosts. Ibsen, H.
  In Ibsen, H. The complete major prose plays p197-276   **839.8**
  In Ibsen, H. Ibsen: four major plays   **839.8**
The **ghosts** of Manila. Kram, M.   **796.8**
Ghosts of Mississippi. Vollers, M.   **364.1**
Ghosts of the Titanic. Pellegrino, C. R.   **910.4**
Ghosts of Tsavo. Caputo, P.   **599.75**

Giamatti, A. Bartlett, 1938-1989
A great and glorious game 796.357
Giants
Encyclopedias
Rose, C. Giants, monsters, and dragons 398.03
Giants, monsters, and dragons. Rose, C. 398.03
Gibaldi, Joseph, 1942-
MLA handbook for writers of research papers
808
MLA style manual and guide to scholarly publishing
808
Gibb, Sir Hamilton Alexander Rosskeen, 1895-1971
(ed) Concise encyclopedia of Islam. See Concise ency-
clopedia of Islam 297
Gibbens, Byrd, 1936-
(jt. auth) Schlissel, L. Far from home 978
Gibbon, Edward, 1737-1794
The decline and fall of the Roman Empire 937
Gibbon, Guy E., 1939-
Archaeology of prehistoric native America. See Ar-
chaeology of prehistoric native America 970.01
Gibbons, Euell
Stalking the wild asparagus 581.6
Gibbons, Reginald, 1947-
It's time: poems 811
Gibilisco, Stan
Teach yourself electricity and electronics 621.3
Gibran, Kahlil, 1883-1931
The Prophet 811
Gibson, Ian, 1939-
Federico García Lorca: a life 92
The shameful life of Salvador Dalí 92
Gibson, Walter Brown, 1897-1985
Hoyle's modern encyclopedia of card games
795.4
Gibson, William, 1914-
The miracle worker 812
Giddins, Gary
Bing Crosby: a pocketful of dreams: the early years,
1903-1940 92
Visions of jazz 781.65
Gideon, Clarence Earl
About
Lewis, A. Gideon's trumpet 347
Gideon's trumpet. Lewis, A. 347
Giedt, Frances Towner
The Joslin Diabetes great chefs cook healthy cookbook
641.5
(jt. auth) Polin, B. S. The Joslin Diabetes gourmet
cookbook 641.5
Gielgud, Sir John, 1904-2000
An actor and his time 92
About
Croall, J. Gielgud 92
Gies, Frances
Life in a medieval village 940.1
(jt. auth) Gies, J. Life in a medieval city 940.1
Gies, Joseph
Life in a medieval city 940.1
(jt. auth) Gies, F. Life in a medieval village
940.1
Gies, Miep, 1909-
Anne Frank remembered 940.53
See/See also pages in the following book(s):
Fogelman, E. Conscience & courage 940.53
Giffin, James M.
Dog owner's home veterinary handbook 636.7
Gifford Pinchot and the making of modern
environmentalism. Miller, C. 92
The **gift** of therapy. Yalom, I. D. 616.89
The **Gift** of tongues 811.008
Gifted children
Winner, E. Gifted children 155.45
The **gifts** of the Jews. Cahill, T. 909
Gifts to the tsars, 1500-1700 745

Gilbert, Bill, 1931-
(jt. auth) King, L. How to talk to anyone, anytime,
anywhere 302.3
Gilbert, Martin, 1936-
The boys 940.53
The First World War 940.3
History of the twentieth century 909.82
The Holocaust 940.53
Holocaust journey 940.53
Jerusalem in the twentieth century 956.94
The Jews in the twentieth century 909
Never again 940.53
The Routledge atlas of American history 911
The Routledge atlas of the Holocaust 940.53
The Second World War 940.53
Gilbert, Sandra M.
No man's land v3 820.9
(ed) Inventions of farewell. See Inventions of farewell
821.008
(comp) The Norton anthology of literature by women.
See The Norton anthology of literature by women
820.8
Gilbert, Steven E.
The music of Gershwin 92
Gilbert, Susan
A field guide to boys and girls 305.23
Gilbreth, Frank B., 1911-2001
Cheaper by the dozen 92
Gilbreth, Frank Bunker, 1868-1924
About
Gilbreth, F. B. Cheaper by the dozen 92
Gilbreth family
About
Gilbreth, F. B. Cheaper by the dozen 92
Gilgamesh
Gilgamesh 892
Gill, Anton
Art lover: a biography of Peggy Guggenheim 92
Gill, Gillian
Mary Baker Eddy 92
Gill, Sam D., 1943-
Dictionary of Native American mythology 299
Gillan, Jennifer
(ed) Unsettling America. See Unsettling America
811.008
Gillan, Maria
(ed) Unsettling America. See Unsettling America
811.008
Gilles de la Tourette's syndrome *See* Tourette syn-
drome
Gillespie, Dizzy, 1917-1993
See/See also pages in the following book(s):
DeVeaux, S. K. The birth of bebop 781.65
Feather, L. From Satchmo to Miles 920
Lees, G. You can't steal a gift 920
Gillespie, John Birks *See* Gillespie, Dizzy, 1917-1993
Gillespie, John Thomas, 1928-
The Newbery companion 028.5
Gillespie, Michael Patrick
(jt. auth) Fargnoli, A. N. James Joyce A to Z
823.009
Gillette, David D.
Seismosaurus 567.9
Gillette, J. Michael
Designing with light 792
Theatrical design and production 792
Gilliatt, Mary
The complete book of home design 747
Gilligan, Carol, 1936-
The birth of pleasure 152.4
Gillis, Chester, 1951-
Roman Catholicism in America 282
Gillispie, Charles Coulston
(ed) Dictionary of scientific biography. See Dictionary
of scientific biography 920.003

Gilman, Charlotte Perkins, 1860-1935
See/See also pages in the following book(s):
American women fiction writers   **813.009**
Gilman, Lois
The adoption resource book   **362.7**
Gilman, Sander L.
Making the body beautiful   **617.9**
Gilmour, David, 1952-
Curzon: imperial statesman   **92**
The long recessional: the imperial life of Rudyard Kipling   **92**
Gimbel, Wendy
Havana dreams   **972.91**
Ginann *See* Baiocchi, Regina A. Harris, 1956-
The **gingerbread** lady. Simon, N.
In Simon, N. The collected plays of Neil Simon v2 p149-227   **812**
Ginsberg, Allen, 1926-1997
Collected poems, 1947-1980   **811**
Deliberate prose   **814**
Family business   **92**
Selected poems, 1947-1995   **811**
Spontaneous mind   **92**
See/See also pages in the following book(s):
Miles, B. The Beat Hotel   **810.9**
Ginsberg, Barry G., 1936-
50 wonderful ways to be a single-parent family   **649**
Ginsberg, Louis, 1895-1976
(jt. auth) Ginsberg, A. Family business   **92**
Gioia, Dana
Can poetry matter?   **809.1**
Gioia, Ted
The history of jazz   **781.65**
Giordano, John
The sewing machine guide   **646.2**
Giovanni, Nikki
Blues   **811**
Gemini: an extended autobiographical statement on my first twenty-five years of being a black poet   **92**
Love poems   **811**
The selected poems of Nikki Giovanni (1968-1995)   **811**
See/See also pages in the following book(s):
Black women writers (1950-1980)   **810.9**
Gipsies *See* Gypsies
Girard, Denis
Cassell's French dictionary. See Cassell's French dictionary   **443**
Girard, Patrick, 1950-
(jt. auth) Peres, S. The imaginary voyage   **956.94**
Giraudoux, Jean, 1882-1944
Ondine
In Our dramatic heritage v6   **808.82**
The **girl** from Andros. Terence
In Terence. Terence, the comedies   **872**
Girl meets God. Winner, L. F.   **92**
Girl singer. Clooney, R.   **92**
Girls
Deak, J. Girls will be girls   **649**
Gurian, M. The wonder of girls   **305.23**
Lamb, S. The secret lives of girls   **305.23**
Simmons, R. Odd girl out   **305.23**
Employment
See Child labor
Health and hygiene
Nichter, M. Fat talk   **613.2**
Roan, S. Our daughters' health   **613**
Sexual behavior
White, E. Fast girls   **305.23**
Wolf, N. Promiscuities   **306.7**
Girls, Teenage *See* Teenagers
Girls on the run. Ashbery, J.   **811**
Girls will be girls. Deak, J.   **649**

Girzone, Joseph F.
Never alone   **248**
A portrait of Jesus   **232.9**
GIs *See* Soldiers—United States
The **GI's** war. Hoyt, E. P.   **940.54**
Gītā *See* Mahābhārata. Bhagavadgītā
Gitler, Ira
(jt. auth) Feather, L. The biographical encyclopedia of jazz   **920.003**
Gitlin, Todd
The sixties   **973.92**
Gitlitz, David M. (David Martin)
(jt. auth) Davidson, L. K. Pilgrimage: from the Ganges to Graceland: an encyclopedia   **291.3**
Giuliani, Rudolph W.
Leadership   **658**
About
Kirtzman, A. Rudy Giuliani   **92**
Givens, Terryl
By the hand of Mormon   **289.3**
Gjertsen, Derek
(jt. auth) Allaby, M. Makers of science   **920.003**
Gladstone, W. E. (William Ewart), 1809-1898
About
Jenkins, R., Baron. Gladstone   **92**
See/See also pages in the following book(s):
Strachey, L. Queen Victoria p327-66   **92**
Gladstone, William Ewart *See* Gladstone, W. E. (William Ewart), 1809-1898
Glancey, Jonathan
The story of architecture   **720.9**
Glands
See also Prostate
Glare, P. G. W.
(ed) Oxford Latin dictionary. See Oxford Latin dictionary   **473**
Glare. Ammons, A. R.   **811**
Glasberg, Beth A.
(jt. auth) Harris, S. L. Siblings of children with autism   **649**
Glasgow, Ellen Anderson Gholson, 1873-1945
See/See also pages in the following book(s):
American women fiction writers   **813.009**
Glaspell, Susan, 1876-1948
Trifles
In Plays by American women, 1900-1930   **812.008**
Glass, James M.
Life unworthy of life   **940.53**
Glass
Ellis, W. S. Glass   **666**
Macfarlane, A. Glass: a world history   **666**
The **glass** of water. Scribe, E.
In Our dramatic heritage v4   **808.82**
Glass painting and staining
Zaccaria, D. Stained glass crafting   **748.5**
Glasser, Ronald J.
365 days   **959.704**
Glasser, William, 1925-
Choice theory   **150**
Glassman, Sallie Ann
Vodou visions   **299**
Glavan, James
(jt. auth) Corson, R. Stage makeup   **792**
Glazer, Evan, 1971-
Real-life math   **510**
Glazer, Nathan
American Judaism   **296**
Beyond the melting pot   **305.8**
Glazes
Burleson, M. The ceramic glaze handbook   **738.1**
Glazier, Michael
(ed) The Encyclopedia of the Irish in America. See The Encyclopedia of the Irish in America   **305.8**

Glazier, Stephen D.
(ed) The Encyclopedia of African and African-American religions. See The Encyclopedia of African and African-American religions 299
Gledhill, Kristen M.
(ed) Fitness and exercise sourcebook. See Fitness and exercise sourcebook 613.7
Gleick, James
Faster 529
Genius: the life and science of Richard Feynman 92
Isaac Newton 92
Gleiser, Marcelo
The prophet and the astronomer 523.1
Glenmullen, Joseph, 1950-
Prozac backlash 616.85
Glenn, Cheryl
Hodges' Harbrace handbook. See Hodges' Harbrace handbook 808
Glenn, John, 1921-
John Glenn 92
See/See also pages in the following book(s):
Space exploration 629
Glenn, Rhonda
(jt. auth) Whitworth, K. Golf for women 796.352
Glenny, Misha
The Balkans 949.6
Glines, Carroll V., 1920-
(jt. auth) Doolittle, J. H. I could never be so lucky again 92
Glink, Ilyce R., 1964-
50 simple things you can do to improve your personal finances 332.024
The **global** soul. Iyer, P. 910.4
The **global** village. McLuhan, M. 302.23
Global warming See Greenhouse effect
Global woman 331.4
Globalization
Barlow, M. Blue gold: the fight to stop the corporate theft of the world's water 333.91
Rifkin, J. The hydrogen economy 333.8
Soros, G. George Soros on globalization 337
Stiglitz, J. E. Globalization and its discontents 337
Globalization and its discontents. Stiglitz, J. E. 337
The **glorious** foods of Greece. Kochilas, D. 641.5
Glorious French food. Peterson, J. 641.5
Glorious patchwork. Fassett, K. 746.46
Glory (Motion picture)
See/See also pages in the following book(s):
McPherson, J. M. Drawn with the sword 973.7
Glory denied. Philpott, T. 92
The **glory** of their times. Ritter, L. S. 920
Glossaries See Encyclopedias and dictionaries
A **glossary** of literary terms. Abrams, M. H. 803
A **glossary** of modern sailing terms. See Rousmaniere, J. The illustrated dictionary of boating terms 797.1
Glover, Bob
The runner's handbook 796.42
Glover, Jonathan, 1941-
Humanity 909.82
Glover, Shelly-lynn Florence
(jt. auth) Glover, B. The runner's handbook 796.42
The **gloves**. Anasi, R. 796.8
Glück, Louise, 1943-
Meadowlands 811
The seven ages 811
Glut, Donald F.
Dinosaurs, the encyclopedia 567.9
Gluten-free diet
Hagman, B. The gluten-free gourmet 641.5
The **gluten-free** gourmet. Hagman, B. 641.5

Glynn, Ian, 1928-
An anatomy of thought 612.8
The **gnostic** Gospels. Pagels, E. H. 299
Gnosticism
Pagels, E. H. The gnostic Gospels 299
The **"Go ask Alice"** book of answers 613
Go back for murder. Christie, A.
In Christie, A. The mousetrap and other plays 822
Go for the goal. Hamm, M. 796.334
God
See also Femininity of God; Monotheism
Adler, M. J. How to think about God 212
Armstrong, K. A history of God 291
Buber, M. I and thou 181
Merton, T. No man is an island 248
Miles, J. God: a biography 231
Noble, D. F. The religion of technology 261.5
Price, R. Letter to a man in the fire 231
Stark, R. One true God 291.1
See/See also pages in the following book(s):
Sagan, C. Broca's brain p128-36, 281-87 500
Christianity
See also Providence and government of God
Judaism
Kushner, H. S. Who needs God 296.7
God [play] Allen, W.
In Allen, W. Without feathers 817
God and the astronomers. Jastrow, R. 523.1
God and the new physics. Davies, P. C. W. 261.5
God has ninety-nine names. Miller, J. 956
The **God** of hope and the end of the world. Polkinghorne, J. 236
The **God** particle. Lederman, L. M. 539.7
Godard, Jean Luc, 1930-
See/See also pages in the following book(s):
Sontag, S. Styles of radical will p147-89 814
Godden, Geoffrey A.
Encyclopaedia of British pottery and porcelain marks 738
Goddesses See Gods and goddesses
Gödel, Kurt
See/See also pages in the following book(s):
Flowers, C. Instability rules 509
Godfather of the Kremlin. Klebnikov, P. 92
Godin, Seth
The big red fez 005.7
A **Godless** Jew. Gay, P. 150.19
Gods and goddesses
See also Religions; names of individual gods and goddesses
Wilkinson, R. H. The complete gods and goddesses of ancient Egypt 299
See/See also pages in the following book(s):
Hamilton, E. Mythology p21-76 292
Gods and heroes in art. Impelluso, L. 700
The **gods** and symbols of ancient Mexico and the Maya. Miller, M. E. 299
God's bestseller: William Tyndale, Thomas More, and the writing of the English Bible [biography of William Tyndale] Moynahan, B. 92
God's Chinese son. Spence, J. D. 951
God's equation. Aczel, A. D. 523.1
God's favorite. Simon, N.
In Simon, N. The collected plays of Neil Simon v2 p475-545 812
God's funeral. Wilson, A. N. 200.9
Gods, graves, and scholars. Ceram, C. W. 930.1
God's name in vain. Carter, S. L. 322
Gods of war, gods of peace. Bourne, R. 200.9
God's perfect child. Fraser, C. 289.5
God's secretaries: the making of the King James Bible. Nicolson, A. 220.5
Godtalk: travels in spiritual America. Gooch, B. 200.9

Goethe, Johann Wolfgang von, 1749-1832
Faust   832
Faust, part 1
  In Our dramatic heritage v4   808.82
  See/See also pages in the following book(s):
Bloom, H. The Western canon   809
Gogh, Vincent van, 1853-1890
Dr. Gachet; criticism
  In Saltzman, C. Portrait of Dr. Gachet
    759.9492
About
Druick, D. W. Van Gogh and Gauguin   92
Silverman, D. Van Gogh and Gauguin   759.4
Gogol´, Nikolaĭ Vasil´evich, 1809-1852
  See/See also pages in the following book(s):
Nabokov, V. V. Lectures on Russian literature
    891.7
Going to the territory. Ellison, R.   818
Golant, Susan K.
  (jt. auth) Carter, R. Helping someone with mental illness   616.89
  (jt. auth) Carter, R. Helping yourself help others
    649.8
  (jt. auth) Dutton, D. G. The batterer   362.82
Golb, Norman
Who wrote the Dead Sea scrolls?   296.1
Gold, Alison Leslie
  (jt. auth) Gies, M. Anne Frank remembered
    940.53
Gold, David L.
  (ed) Random House Latin-American Spanish dictionary. See Random House Latin-American Spanish dictionary   463
Gold, Joy P.
  (jt. auth) Springer, V. G. Sharks in question   597
Gold
Bernstein, P. L. The power of gold   398
Gold in the water. Mullen, P. H., Jr.   797.2
Gold rush *See* Colorado—Gold discoveries
Goldbarth, Albert
Combinations of the Universe   811
Goldberg, Philip, 1944-
  (jt. auth) Bloomfield, H. H. Making peace with your past   158
Goldberg, Robert Alan, 1949-
Barry Goldwater   92
Goldberg, Vicki
American photography   770
The **golden** age of American gardens. Griswold, M. K.
    712
Golden Fleece (Greek mythology) *See* Argonauts (Greek mythology)
The **golden** fleece. Gurney, A. R.
  In Gurney, A. R. Nine early plays, 1961-1973 p47-68   812
The **golden** ratio. Livio, M.   516.2
Golden rules. Dosick, W. D.   649
Goldfarb, Toni L., 1945-
  (jt. auth) Fisher, E. B. American Lung Association 7 steps to a smoke-free life   616.86
Goldhagen, Daniel
Hitler's willing executioners   940.53
A moral reckoning   940.53
Goldman, Ari L., 1949-
Being Jewish   296.4
Goldman, Bob, 1955-
Brain fitness   153.1
Goldman, Merle
  (jt. auth) Fairbank, J. K. China   951
Goldmann, David R.
  (ed) American College of Physicians complete home medical guide. See American College of Physicians complete home medical guide   616.02

Goldsmith, Barbara
Other powers: the age of suffrage, spiritualism, and the scandalous Victoria Woodhull   92
Goldsmith, George
About
Goldsmith, M. The inextinguishable symphony
    940.53
Goldsmith, Martin
The inextinguishable symphony   940.53
Goldsmith, Oliver, 1728-1774
She stoops to conquer   822
Goldsmith, Rosemarie, 1917-1984
About
Goldsmith, M. The inextinguishable symphony
    940.53
Goldstein, Donald M.
D-Day Normandy   940.54
The Vietnam war: the story and photographs
    959.704
The way it was   940.54
  (jt. auth) Prange, G. W. At dawn we slept
    940.54
  (jt. auth) Prange, G. W. Miracle at Midway
    940.54
Goldstein, Mark A., 1947-
  (jt. auth) Goldstein, M. C. Controversies in food and nutrition   641.3
Goldstein, Martin, 1947-
The nature of animal healing   636.089
Goldstein, Myrna Chandler, 1948-
Controversies in food and nutrition   641.3
Goldstein, Natalie
Earth almanac. See Earth almanac   550
Goldstein, Norm
  (ed) The Associated Press stylebook and briefing on media law. See The Associated Press stylebook and briefing on media law   808
Goldstein, Sam
  (jt. auth) Brooks, R. B. Raising resilient children
    649
Goldwater, Barry M., 1909-1998
About
Goldberg, R. A. Barry Goldwater   92
  See/See also pages in the following book(s):
Vidal, G. United States—essays, 1952-1992 p827-40
    814
Goldwhite, Harold
  (jt. auth) Cobb, C. Creations of fire   540
Goleman, Daniel
Emotional intelligence   152.4
Primal leadership   658.4
Golenbock, Peter, 1946-
Amazin'   796.357
Golf
Andrisani, J. The Tiger Woods way   796.352
Feinstein, J. A good walk spoiled   796.352
Feinstein, J. The majors: in pursuit of golf's Holy Grail   796.352
Feinstein, J. Open: inside the ropes at Bethpage Black
    796.352
Frost, M. The greatest game ever played   796.352
Martino, R. The PGA manual of golf   796.352
Nicklaus, J. Golf my way   796.352
Player, G. The complete golfer's handbook
    796.352
Rubenstein, L. A season in Dornoch   796.352
Sampson, C. Masters   796.352
Snead, S. The game I love   796.352
Snead, S. Golf begins at forty   796.352
Whitworth, K. Golf for women   796.352
  See/See also pages in the following book(s):
Nicklaus, J. Jack Nicklaus   92
Golf begins at forty. Snead, S.   796.352
Golf for women. Whitworth, K.   796.352
Golf my way. Nicklaus, J.   796.352

A **golfer's** life. Palmer, A.   92

Golinkoff, Roberta M.
How babies talk   401

Gollaher, David, 1949-
Circumcision   392

Gollob, Herman
Me and Shakespeare   822.3

Golub, Leon
Nearest star   523.7

Golway, Terry, 1955-
So others might live   628.9

Gombrich, E. H. (Ernst Hans), 1909-2001
The preference for the primitive   709
The story of art   709

Gombrich, Ernst Hans See Gombrich, E. H. (Ernst Hans), 1909-2001

Gombrowicz, Witold
Ferdydurke; criticism
In Sontag, S. Where the stress falls   814

Gomes, Peter John, 1942-
The good book   220.1

Gomm, Sarah Carr- See Carr-Gomm, Sarah

González, Elián
           About
Bardach, A. L. Cuba confidential   972.91

Gonzalez, Juan
Fallout   363.7

Gonzalez, Steve, 1959-
Before you hire a contractor   690

González Echevarría, Roberto
(ed) The Cambridge history of Latin American literature. See The Cambridge history of Latin American literature   860.9

Gooch, Brad, 1952-
Godtalk: travels in spiritual America   200.9

Good and evil
Bloom, H. The Lucifer principle   128
Kushner, H. S. How good do we have to be?   296.7
Todorov, T. Facing the extreme   940.53
Watson, L. Dark nature   111

The **good** book. Gomes, P. J.   220.1
The **good** cake book. See Dalsass, D. The new good cake book   641.8
The **good** carbohydrate revolution. Shintani, T.   613.2
The **good** doctor. Simon, N.
In Simon, N. The collected plays of Neil Simon v2 p393-471   812
Good food for bad stomachs. Janowitz, H. D.   616.3
Good grooming See Personal grooming
Good hair. Bonner, L. B.   646.7
The **Good** Housekeeping step-by-step cookbook   641.5
Good morning, America. Sandburg, C.
In Sandburg, C. Complete poems of Carl Sandburg p315-435   811
The **good** Nazi: the life and lies of Albert Speer. Van der Vat, D.   92
Good news Bible. Bible   220.5
Good poems   811.008
The **good,** the bad & the difference. Cohen, R.   170
Good to great. Collins, J. C.   658
A **good** walk spoiled. Feinstein, J.   796.352

Goodall, Jane
Beyond innocence   92

Goodall, Jane, 1934-
Africa in my blood   92
In the shadow of man   599.8
Reason for hope   92
The ten trusts   333.95
Through a window   599.8

Goodbody, Mary
(jt. auth) Barrenechea, T. The Basque table   641.5

Goodbye, darkness. Manchester, W.   940.54
Goodbye, Descartes. Devlin, K. J.   128
The **goodbye** people. Gardner, H.
In Gardner, H. Herb Gardner: the collected plays and the screenplay Who is Harry Kellerman and why is he saying those terrible things about me?   812

Goode's school atlas. See Goode's world atlas   912
Goode's world atlas   912

Goodman, Bob See Goodman, Robert L.

Goodman, Ellen
I know just what you mean   158

Goodman, Jordan Elliot
(jt. auth) Downes, J. Barron's finance & investment handbook   332.6

Goodman, Linda, 1925-1995
Linda Goodman's star signs   133
Linda Goodman's sun signs   133.5

Goodman, Robert L.
How electronic things work—and what to do when they don't   621.381

Goodrich, Frances, 1891-1984
The diary of Anne Frank   812

Goodrich, Norma Lorre
King Arthur   942.01

Goodsell, Joan
(ed) Sears list of subject headings. See Sears list of subject headings   025.4

Goodstein, David L., 1939-
Feynman's lost lecture   521

Goodstein, Judith R.
(jt. auth) Goodstein, D. L. Feynman's lost lecture   521

Goodwin, Brian C.
How the leopard changed its spots   576

Goodwin, Doris Kearns
No ordinary time [biography of Franklin D. Roosevelt]   92
Wait till next year   92

Goodwin, Jan
Price of honor   305.4

Goodwin, Jason, 1964-
Lords of the horizons   956.1

Goodyear, Charles, 1800-1860
           About
Korman, R. The Goodyear story   92
Slack, C. Noble obsession   92
The **Goodyear** story. Korman, R.   92

Goodyear Tire & Rubber Company
Korman, R. The Goodyear story   92
Slack, C. Noble obsession   92

Gookin, Dan
PCs for dummies   004

Gopnik, Alison
The scientist in the crib   155.4

Gorbachev, Mikhail
On my country and the world   947.085
See/See also pages in the following book(s):
Kissinger, H. Diplomacy p785-99   327.73

Gordimer, Nadine, 1923-
Conversations with Nadine Gordimer   92
See/See also pages in the following book(s):
Women writers at work p243-84   808

Gordis, Daniel
If a place can make you cry   956.94

Gordon, Caroline, 1895-1981
See/See also pages in the following book(s):
American women fiction writers   813.009

Gordon, G. L. See Kane, Gordon, 1937-

Gordon, James Samuel, 1941-
Comprehensive cancer care   616.99

Gordon, John Steele
A thread across the ocean   384.1

Gordon, Linda
(ed) America's working women. See America's working women   **331.4**
Gordon, Lois G.
The world of Samuel Beckett, 1906-1946   **92**
Gordon, Lyndall
Charlotte Brontë   **92**
T.S. Eliot   **92**
Virginia Woolf, a writer's life   **92**
Gordon, Mary, 1949-
Joan of Arc   **92**
Seeing through places   **814**
Gordon, Matthew
Islam   **297**
Gordon, Michael R.
The generals' war   **956.7**
Gordon, Robert, 1961-
Can't be satisfied: the life and times of Muddy Waters   **92**
Gordon, W. Terrence, 1942-
Marshall McLuhan   **92**
Gordon-Reed, Annette
Thomas Jefferson and Sally Hemings   **92**
Gore, Albert, Jr.
Earth in the balance   **304.2**
Joined at the heart   **306.8**
About
Dershowitz, A. M. Supreme injustice   **324**
Posner, R. A. Breaking the deadlock   **324**
Zelnick, B. Gore: a political life   **92**
Gore, Mary Elizabeth See Gore, Tipper, 1948-
Gore, Tipper, 1948-
(jt. auth) Gore, A., Jr. Joined at the heart   **306.8**
Goreham, Gary, 1953-
Encyclopedia of rural America. See Encyclopedia of rural America   **973.03**
Goren, Charles Henry, 1901-1991
Goren's new bridge complete   **795.4**
Goren's new bridge complete. Goren, C. H.   **795.4**
Gorey, Edward, 1925-2000
About
Ross, C. The world of Edward Gorey   **92**
Gorgas, William Crawford, 1854-1920
See/See also pages in the following book(s):
McCullough, D. G. The path between the seas   **972.87**
Gorge-purge syndrome See Bulimia
Gorillas
Fossey, D. Gorillas in the mist   **599.8**
Mowat, F. Woman in the mists: the story of Dian Fossey and the mountain gorillas of Africa   **92**
Gorillas in the mist. Fossey, D.   **599.8**
Gorini, Catherine A.
The Facts on File geometry handbook   **516**
Gorky, Arshile, 1904-1948
About
Matossian, N. Black angel: the life of Arshile Gorky   **92**
Spender, M. From a high place   **92**
Gorky, Maksim, 1868-1936
The lower depths
In Our dramatic heritage v4   **808.82**
See/See also pages in the following book(s):
Nabokov, V. V. Lectures on Russian literature   **891.7**
Gorman, Michael, 1941-
The concise AACR2, 1998 revision   **025.3**
Gorn, Elliott J., 1951-
Encyclopedia of American social history. See Encyclopedia of American social history   **973.03**
Mother Jones   **92**
Gorn, Michael H.
Expanding the envelope   **629.13**
Gorst, Martin, 1960-
Measuring eternity   **115**

Gospel music
See also Spirituals (Songs)
Ward-Royster, W. How I got over   **920**
Gospel of Thomas
Pagels, E. H. Beyond belief   **229**
Gospels (Books of the New Testament) See Bible. N.T. Gospels
Gossip
Dunbar, R. I. M. Grooming, gossip, and the evolution of language   **599.93**
White, E. Fast girls   **305.23**
Gostin, Lawrence O.
(jt. auth) Rubenstein, W. B. The rights of people who are HIV positive   **344**
Gotham. Burrows, E. G.   **974.7**
Gott, J. Richard, 1947-
Time travel in Einstein's universe   **530.1**
Gottesman, Ronald
(ed) Violence in America. See Violence in America   **303.6**
Gottlieb, Anthony
The dream of reason   **180**
Gotto, Antonio M., Jr.
(jt. auth) DeBakey, M. E. The new living heart   **616.1**
Gottschalk, Jack
Firefighting   **628.9**
Gottschalk, Louis Moreau, 1829-1869
See/See also pages in the following book(s):
Schonberg, H. C. The great pianists   **920**
Gould, Glenn, 1932-1982
About
Ostwald, P. F. Glenn Gould   **92**
See/See also pages in the following book(s):
Schonberg, H. C. The great pianists   **920**
Gould, K. Lance
Heal your heart   **616.1**
Gould, Stephen Jay, 1941-2002
Bully for brontosaurus   **508**
Dinosaur in a haystack   **508**
Eight little piggies   **576.8**
Ever since Darwin   **576.8**
The flamingo's smile   **508**
The hedgehog, the fox, and the magister's pox   **303.4**
Hen's teeth and horse's toes   **576.8**
I have landed   **578**
Leonardo's mountain of clams and the Diet of Worms   **508**
The lying stones of Marrakesh   **508**
The mismeasure of man   **153.9**
The panda's thumb   **576.8**
Questioning the millennium   **901**
Rocks of ages   **291.1**
The structure of evolutionary theory   **576.8**
Triumph and tragedy in Mudville   **796.357**
An urchin in the storm   **570**
Wonderful life: the Burgess Shale and the nature of history   **560**
See/See also pages in the following book(s):
Dennett, D. C. Darwin's dangerous idea   **146**
Gourevitch, Philip
A cold case   **364.1**
We wish to inform you that tomorrow we will be killed with our families   **967.571**
Gourse, Leslie
Straight, no chaser   **92**
Government See Political science
Government, Resistance to See Resistance to government
Government Communications Headquarters (Great Britain) See Great Britain. Government Communications Headquarters
Government departments See Executive departments

The **Government** directory of addresses and telephone numbers. See Government phone book USA
320.025

Government information
Government online **025.04**
Hernon, P. U.S. government on the Web **025.04**
Government ministries *See* Executive departments
Government online **025.04**
Government phone book USA **320.025**
Government Printing Office (U.S.) *See* United States. Government Printing Office
Government publications
United States—Bibliography
Monthly catalog of United States Government publications **015.73**
Goya, Francisco, 1746-1828
About
Blackburn, J. Old man Goya **92**
Hofmann, W. Goya: to every story there belongs another **759.6**
Hughes, R. Goya **92**
Goya y Lucientes, Francisco José de *See* Goya, Francisco, 1746-1828
GPO *See* United States. Government Printing Office
A **gracious** plenty. Edge, J. T. **641.5**
Grady, Denise
The New York Times guide to alternative health. See The New York Times guide to alternative health **615.5**

Graedon, Joe
The people's pharmacy guide to home and herbal remedies **615**
Graedon, Teresa, 1947-
(jt. auth) Graedon, J. The people's pharmacy guide to home and herbal remedies **615**
Graf, Bernhard
Bridges that changed the world **624**
Graf Zeppelin (Airship)
Botting, D. Dr. Eckener's dream machine **629.133**
Graff, Henry F. (Henry Franklin), 1921-
Grover Cleveland **92**
Graham, Billy, 1918-
Just as I am **92**
See/See also pages in the following book(s):
Martin, W. C. With God on our side **261.8**
Graham, Jorie, 1951-
The dream of the unified field **811**
Never **811**
Graham, Katharine
Katharine Graham's Washington. See Katharine Graham's Washington **975.3**
Personal history **92**
See/See also pages in the following book(s):
Heymann, C. D. The Georgetown ladies' social club **305.4**

Graham, Lawrence Otis
Our kind of people **305.8**
Graham, Martha
See/See also pages in the following book(s):
Gardner, H. Creating minds p265-309 **153.3**
Ware, S. Letter to the world **920**
Wills, G. Certain trumpets p197-206 **303.3**
Graham, Stedman
You can make it happen **650.1**
Graham-Dixon, Andrew
Renaissance **709.02**
Grahame, Kenneth, 1859-1932
See/See also pages in the following book(s):
Wullschläger, J. Inventing wonderland **820.9**
Grammar
See also English language—Grammar
Pinker, S. Words and rules **401**
Gramont, Sanche de *See* Morgan, Ted, 1932-
Gran diccionario español-inglés. English-Spanish dictionary **463**

The **grand** alliance. Churchill, Sir W. **940.53**
Grand Canyon (Ariz.)
Dolnick, E. Down the great unknown **979.1**
Fletcher, C. The man who walked through time **917.91**
A **grand** delusion. Mann, R. **959.704**
A **Grand** design **708**
Granger's index to poetry. See The Columbia Granger's index to poetry in anthologies **808.81**
Grant, B. Rosemary
About
Weiner, J. The beak of the finch **598**
Grant, Cary, 1904-1986
About
McCann, G. Cary Grant **92**
Grant, John, 1949-
(ed) The Encyclopedia of fantasy. See The Encyclopedia of fantasy **809.3**
Grant, Michael, 1914-
Collapse and recovery of the Roman Empire **937**
Greek and Latin authors, 800 B.C.-A.D. 1000 **920.003**
A guide to the ancient world **938.003**
Grant, Peter R., 1936-
About
Weiner, J. The beak of the finch **598**
Grant, R. G. (Reg G.)
Flight: 100 years of aviation **629.13**
Grant, Reg G. *See* Grant, R. G. (Reg G.)
Grant, Ulysses S. (Ulysses Simpson), 1822-1885
Memoirs and selected letters **92**
About
Catton, B. Grant moves south **92**
Catton, B. Grant takes command **92**
Simpson, B. D. Ulysses S. Grant **92**
Smith, J. E. Grant **92**
See/See also pages in the following book(s):
McPherson, J. M. Drawn with the sword **973.7**
Wilson, E. Patriotic gore p131-73 **810.9**
Grant moves south. Catton, B. **92**
Granz, Norman, 1918-2001
See/See also pages in the following book(s):
Feather, L. From Satchmo to Miles **920**
Grapes
See also Wine and wine making
Grass, Günter, 1927-
Novemberland **831**
Two states—one nation? **943.087**
Grasses
King, M. Gardening with grasses **635.9**
Michener, D. Taylor's guide to ground covers **635.9**
Encyclopedias
Darke, R. The color encyclopedia of ornamental grasses **635.9**
Grassland ecology
Manning, R. Grassland **577.4**
Grateful Dead (Musical group)
Brightman, C. Sweet chaos: the Grateful Dead's American adventure **920**
Greenfield, R. Dark Star: an oral biography of Jerry Garcia **92**
McNally, D. A long strange trip **920**
See/See also pages in the following book(s):
Jackson, B. Garcia **92**
Grauer, Neil A.
Remember laughter: a life of James Thurber **92**
Graves, Robert, 1895-1985
Greek myths **292**
(tr) Suetonius Tranquillus, C. The twelve Caesars **878**
See/See also pages in the following book(s):
Jarrell, R. No other book **809**
Gravitation
Rubin, A. E. Disturbing the solar system **521**

Gravitation—*Continued*
See/See also pages in the following book(s):
Feynman, R. P. Six easy pieces   **530**
Gray, Francine du Plessix
At home with the Marquis de Sade   **92**
Simone Weil   **92**
Gray, John
Mars and Venus on a date   **306.7**
Mars and Venus starting over   **306.7**
Gray, Thomas, 1716-1771
Elegy written in a country churchyard; criticism
In Brooks, C. The well wrought urn   **821.009**
The **great** 401(k) hoax. Wolman, W.   **332.024**
The **great** age of Greek literature. See Hamilton, E. The
Greek way   **880.9**
Great American court cases   **347**
Great American trials   **347**
Great American wreaths. Stewart, M.   **745.92**
A **great** and glorious game. Giamatti, A. B.
          796.357
The **great** arc. Keay, J.   **526**
Great Basin
History
Durham, M. S. Desert between the mountains
          979
Great battles of the Civil War. Macdonald, J.
          973.7
Great books of the Western world
Adler, M. J. How to think about the great ideas
          080
Great Britain
See also England
Biography—Dictionaries
The Dictionary of national biography   **920.003**
Who was who   **920.003**
Who's who   **920.003**
Who's who in British history   **920.003**
Civilization
Backgrounds to English literature   **820.9**
Brewer, J. The pleasures of the imagination
          941.07
Bryson, B. Notes from a small island   **914.1**
Buruma, I. Anglomania   **941**
See/See also pages in the following book(s):
Emerson, R. W. The portable Emerson p395-518
          818
Colonies
The Cambridge illustrated history of the British Empire
          941.08
James, L. The rise and fall of the British Empire
          909
The Oxford history of the British Empire   **909**
Read, A. The proudest day   **954.03**
Colonies—America
Lepore, J. The name of war   **973.2**
Milton, G. Big Chief Elizabeth   **975.5**
See/See also pages in the following book(s):
Tuchman, B. W. The march of folly   **909.08**
Commerce
Keay, J. The honourable company   **954.03**
Description
Bryson, B. Notes from a small island   **914.1**
Johnson, P. Castles of England, Scotland and Wales
          941
Theroux, P. The kingdom by the sea   **914.1**
Foreign relations—United States
Stafford, D. Roosevelt and Churchill   **940.54**
History
Black, J. A history of the British Isles   **941**
Davies, N. The Isles   **941**
The Oxford history of Britain   **941**
Schama, S. A history of Britain   **941**
See/See also pages in the following book(s):
Durant, W. J. The age of Louis XIV p183-206, 244-311   **940.2**

Pipes, R. Property and freedom p121-58   **323.4**
History—0-1066
Duckett, E. S. Alfred the Great   **92**
Goodrich, N. L. King Arthur   **942.01**
King Arthur in legend and history   **942.01**
Lacey, R. The year 1000   **942.01**
History—1154-1399, Plantagenets
Doherty, P. C. Isabella and the strange death of Edward II   **92**
West, R. Chaucer, 1340-1400   **92**
See/See also pages in the following book(s):
Tuchman, B. W. A distant mirror p284-301   **944**
History—1455-1485, War of the Roses
Weir, A. The Wars of the Roses   **942.04**
History—1485-1603, Tudors
See also Spanish Armada, 1588
Fraser, A. Mary Queen of Scots   **92**
Fraser, A. The wives of Henry VIII   **920**
Hibbert, C. The virgin queen: Elizabeth I   **92**
Nicholl, C. The reckoning: the murder of Christopher
Marlowe   **92**
Starkey, D. Six wives: the queens of Henry VIII
          920
Strachey, L. Elizabeth and Essex   **92**
Weir, A. The children of Henry VIII   **920**
Weir, A. Henry VIII   **92**
Weir, A. The life of Elizabeth I   **92**
Weir, A. The six wives of Henry VIII   **920**
See/See also pages in the following book(s):
Beer, A. R. My just desire   **92**
Mattingly, G. The Armada   **942.05**
History—1485-1603, Tudors—Drama
Bolt, R. A man for all seasons   **822**
History—1603-1714, Stuarts
Fraser, A. Faith and treason   **942.06**
Macleod, J. Dynasty: the Stuarts, 1560-1807
          941.06
Pepys, S. The diary of Samuel Pepys   **92**
Tomalin, C. Samuel Pepys   **92**
Trevelyan, G. M. The English Revolution, 1688-1689
          942.06
See/See also pages in the following book(s):
Page, N. Lord Minimus   **92**
History—19th century
See also Industrial revolution
Hibbert, C. Queen Victoria   **92**
Hibbert, C. Wellington   **92**
Strachey, L. Queen Victoria   **92**
Vallone, L. Becoming Victoria   **92**
History—20th century
Massie, R. K. Dreadnought   **940.3**
Taylor, A. J. P. English history, 1914-1945
          942.08
History—1952-
Pimlott, B. The Queen: a biography of Elizabeth II
          92
Shawcross, W. Queen and country: the fifty-year reign
of Elizabeth II   **92**
History—Dictionaries
The Cambridge historical encyclopedia of Great Britain
and Ireland   **941**
History—Encyclopedias
The Columbia companion to British history   **941**
Medieval England   **942**
The Oxford companion to British history   **941**
History, Military
See Great Britain—Military history
Intellectual life
Brewer, J. The pleasures of the imagination
          941.07
Kings and rulers
Cannon, J. The Oxford illustrated history of the British
monarchy   **941**

Great Britain—*Continued*
Military history
Urban, M. The man who broke Napoleon's codes
    940.2
Ziegler, P. Soldiers: fighting men's lives, 1901-2001
    355
Moral conditions
Himmelfarb, G. The de-moralization of society
    303.3
Politics and government
Cannon, J. The Oxford illustrated history of the British monarchy   **941**
Lukacs, J. Five days in London, May 1940
    940.53
Politics and government—19th century
See/See also pages in the following book(s):
Jenkins, R., Baron. Gladstone   **92**
Politics and government—20th century
Jenkins, R., Baron. Churchill   **92**
Manchester, W. The last lion: Winston Spencer Churchill   **92**
Social life and customs
Brewer, J. The pleasures of the imagination
    941.07
Pepys, S. The diary of Samuel Pepys   **92**
Tillyard, S. K. Aristocrats   **920**
Tomalin, C. Samuel Pepys   **92**
Soldiers
See Soldiers—Great Britain
Great Britain. Army. Jewish Brigade
Blum, H. The brigade   **940.54**
Great Britain. Army. Special Operations Executive
See Great Britain. Special Operations Executive
Great Britain. Government Communications Headquarters
Smith, M. Station X   **940.54**
Great Britain. MI6
Dorril, S. MI6   **327.12**
Great Britain. Secret Intelligence Service *See* Great Britain. MI6
Great Britain. Special Operations Executive
Marks, L. Between silk and cyanide   **940.54**
Great Catherine. Erickson, C.   **92**
The **great** Chinese revolution: 1800-1985. Fairbank, J. K.   **951**
Great Christian thinkers. Küng, H.   **230**
The **great** composers and their works. Slonimsky, N.
    780.9
The **Great** Crash, 1929. Galbraith, J. K.   **338.5**
Great Depression, 1929-1939
Galbraith, J. K. The Great Crash, 1929   **338.5**
Terkel, S. Hard times   **973.91**
Watkins, T. H. The hungry years   **973.91**
Encyclopedias
Encyclopedia of the Great Depression and the New Deal   **973.917**
Great events from history II, Science and technology
    509
The **great** father. Prucha, F. P.   **970.004**
Great foreign language writers. See Reference guide to world literature   **809**
Great garden formulas   **635**
The **Great** Law and the Longhouse. Fenton, W. N.
    970.004
The **Great** Nebula in Orion. Wilson, L.
  In Wilson, L. 21 short plays p118-36   **812**
Great parties. Stewart, M.   **642**
The **great** philosophers. Jaspers, K.   **109**
The **great** pianists. Schonberg, H. C.   **920**
Great pies & tarts. Walter, C.   **641.8**
Great Plains
Description
Frazier, I. Great Plains   **978**
History
West, E. The contested plains   **978**

Great projects. Tobin, J.   **620**
The **great** railway bazaar: by train through Asia. Theroux, P.   **915**
The **great** republic. Churchill, Sir W.   **973**
The **great** rock discography. Strong, M. C.   **781.66**
Great sex after 40. Williamson, M. L.   **306.7**
The **great** shame. Keneally, T.   **304.8**
The **great** shark hunt. Thompson, H. S.   **818**
The **great** tax wars. Weisman, S. R.   **336.2**
Great thinkers of the Western world   **190**
Great time coming: the life of Jackie Robinson, from baseball to Birmingham. Falkner, D.   **92**
Great treasury of Western thought   **080**
Great vegetarian cooking under pressure. Sass, L. J.
    641.5
Great Wallenda Circus
Wilkins, C. The circus at the edge of the earth
    791.3
Great white shark. Ellis, R.   **597**
Great women masters of art. Vigué, J.   **920.003**
Great women mystery writers   **809.3**
Great world trials   **347**
The **greatest** benefit to mankind. Porter, R.   **610.9**
The **greatest** experiment ever performed on women. Seaman, B.   **615**
The **greatest** game ever played. Frost, M.   **796.352**
The **greatest** generation. Brokaw, T.   **940.54**
The **greatest** war. Astor, G.   **940.54**
Greece
Antiquities
Levi, P. Atlas of the Greek world   **938**
Biography
Plutarch. Plutarch: the lives of the noble Grecians and Romans   **920**
Biography—Dictionaries
Who was who in the Greek world, 776 BC-30 BC
    920.003
Civilization
Adkins, L. Handbook to life in ancient Greece
    938
Burckhardt, J. The Greeks and Greek civilization
    938
The Classical Greek reader   **880.8**
Connolly, P. The ancient city   **937**
Finley, M. I. The world of Odysseus   **883**
Hamilton, E. The echo of Greece   **880.9**
Hamilton, E. The Greek way   **880.9**
Levi, P. Atlas of the Greek world   **938**
Robinson, C. E. Everyday life in ancient Greece
    938
See/See also pages in the following book(s):
Gay, P. The Enlightenment: an interpretation   **190**
Russell, B. A history of Western philosophy p3-24, 218-28   **109**
Description
Keeley, E. Inventing paradise   **818**
History
Clogg, R. A concise history of Greece   **949.5**
Martin, T. R. Ancient Greece   **938**
Who was who in the Greek world, 776 BC-30 BC
    920.003
See/See also pages in the following book(s):
Potok, C. Wanderings p155-201   **909**
History—431-404 B.C., Peloponnesian War
Thucydides. The history of the Peloponnesian War
    938
History—20th century
Gage, N. Eleni [biography of Eleni Gatzoyiannis]
    92
History—Dictionaries
Sacks, D. Encyclopedia of the ancient Greek world
    938.003
Maps
Levi, P. Atlas of the Greek world   **938**

Greece—*Continued*
Religion
See/See also pages in the following book(s):
Hamilton, E. The Greek way p284-302   880.9
Robinson, C. E. Everyday life in ancient Greece
                                         938

Social life and customs
Robinson, C. E. Everyday life in ancient Greece
                                         938
Greek, C. Ray
Sacred cows and golden geese   179
Greek, Jean Swingle
(jt. auth) Greek, C. R. Sacred cows and golden geese
                                         179
Greek and Latin authors, 800 B.C.-A.D. 1000. Grant, M.
                                         920.003
Greek art
Boardman, J. Greek art   709.38
Greek authors *See* Authors, Greek
Greek cooking
Kochilas, D. The glorious foods of Greece 641.5
A **Greek-English** lexicon. Liddell, H. G. 483
Greek fire. Gage, N.   92
Greek language
Dictionaries
Liddell, H. G. A Greek-English lexicon   483
Greek literature
See also Classical literature
Collections
The Classical Greek reader   880.8
The Norton book of classical literature   880.8
History and criticism
Hamilton, E. The echo of Greece   880.9
Hamilton, E. The Greek way   880.9
Greek mythology *See* Classical mythology
Greek myths. Graves, R.   292
The **Greek** way. Hamilton, E.   880.9
The **Greeks** and Greek civilization. Burckhardt, J.
                                         938

Greeley, Andrew M., 1928-
The Catholic myth   282
Greeley, Ronald
The compact NASA atlas of the solar system
                                         523.2
Green, Elizabeth Shippen, 1871-1954
About
Carter, A. A. The Red Rose girls   759.13
Green, Jonathon
The Cassell dictionary of slang   427
Green, Michael D., 1941-
(jt. auth) Perdue, T. The Columbia guide to American
Indians of the Southeast   970.004
Green, Stanley, 1923-1990
The world of musical comedy   920
Green, Tim
The dark side of the game   796.332
Green, William Scott
The Encyclopedia of Judaism. See The Encyclopedia
of Judaism [Continuum]   296.03
Green Bay Packers (Football team)
See/See also pages in the following book(s):
Maraniss, D. When pride still mattered: a life of Vince
Lombardi   92
Green Berets *See* United States. Army. Special Forces
Green space, green time. Barlow, C. C. 291.1
Greenberg, Arthur
The art of chemistry   540
Greenberg, Irving, 1933-
The Jewish way   296.4
Greene, Bob, 1947-
Duty   940.54
Greene, Brian R., 1963-
The elegant universe   539.7
Greene, Gloria Kaufer, 1950-
The new Jewish holiday cookbook   641.5

Greene, Harry W.
Snakes   597.9
Greene, Joshua M.
(ed) Witness. See Witness   940.53
Greene, Robert *See* Greene, Bob, 1947-
Greenfield, Robert
Dark Star: an oral biography of Jerry Garcia   92
Greenfield, Susan
The private life of the brain   612.8
Greenfieldt, John
(ed) Fiction catalog. See Fiction catalog   016.8
Greenhalgh, Paul, 1955-
Art nouveau. See Art nouveau   709.03
Greenhouse. Christianson, G. E.   363.7
Greenhouse effect
Christianson, G. E. Greenhouse   363.7
See/See also pages in the following book(s):
Stevens, W. K. The change in the weather   551.5
Greenhouses
Freeman, M. Gardening in your greenhouse   635.9
Greenland
Ehrlich, G. This cold heaven   998
Mikkelsen, E. Two against the ice   998
Greenlaw, Linda, 1960-
The hungry ocean   639.2
The lobster chronicles   639
Greenoff, Jane
The cross stitcher's bible   746.44
Greenough, Horatio, 1805-1852
See/See also pages in the following book(s):
Matthiessen, F. O. American renaissance p140-52
                                         810.9
Greenough, Sarah, 1951-
Stieglitz, A. Alfred Stieglitz: the key set   779
The **Greens** cook book. Madison, D.   641.5
Greenspan, Alan
About
Martin, J. Greenspan   92
Mayer, M. The Fed   332.1
Woodward, B. Maestro: Greenspan's Fed and the
American boom   332.1
Greenspan, Dorie
Baking with Julia   641.8
Greenspan, Stanley I.
The child with special needs   362.1
(jt. auth) Brazelton, T. B. The irreducible needs of
children   155.4
Greenstein, George, 1940-
Portraits of discovery   920
Greenway, Nancy Randolph, 1946-
(jt. auth) Shotwell, B. Pass it on   346.05
Greenwich Village (New York, N.Y.)
Intellectual life
Broyard, A. Kafka was the rage   92
Wetzsteon, R. Republic of dreams   974.7
Greenwood, Pippa
AHS garden problem solver   635
Greenwood, Val D.
The researcher's guide to American genealogy
                                         929
The **Greenwood** encyclopedia of international relations.
Nolan, C. J.   327
The **Greenwood** encyclopedia of women's issues world-
wide   305.4
Greenwood-Robinson, Maggie
Hair savers for women   616.5
Greer, Germaine, 1939-
The change   618.1
The madwoman's underclothes   305.4
The whole woman   305.4
See/See also pages in the following book(s):
Fraser, K. Ornament and silence   814
Greetings, carbon-based bipeds!. Clarke, A. C.   500
Gregory, Ross
Cold War America, 1946 to 1990   973.92

Greider, William
Secrets of the temple   332.1
The soul of capitalism   330.1
Grenada
     Politics and government
See/See also pages in the following book(s):
Naipaul, V. S. The writer and the world p461-84
         824
Grendler, Paul F.
(ed) Encyclopedia of the Renaissance. See Encyclopedia of the Renaissance   940.2
Grenon, Jean-Benoit Ormal- *See* Ormal-Grenon, Jean-Benoit
Gresham, John, 1703-1751
(jt. auth) Clancy, T. Special forces   356
Grey, Lady Jane, 1537-1554
See/See also pages in the following book(s):
Weir, A. The children of Henry VIII   920
Gribbin, John R.
Almost everyone's guide to science   500
The birth of time   523.1
In search of Schrödinger's cat   530.1
Q is for quantum   539.7
Schrödinger's kittens and the search for reality   530.1
The search for superstrings, symmetry, and the theory of everything   539.7
Stardust   523
(jt. auth) Davies, P. C. W. The matter myth   530
(jt. auth) White, M. Stephen Hawking   92
Gribbin, Mary
(jt. auth) Gribbin, J. R. Almost everyone's guide to science   500
(jt. auth) Gribbin, J. R. Stardust   523
Grierson, Francis, 1848-1927
See/See also pages in the following book(s):
Wilson, E. Patriotic gore p72-88   810.9
Grieve, Christopher Murray *See* MacDiarmid, Hugh, 1892-1978
Griffin, Donald Redfield, 1915-
Animal minds   591.5
Griffin, Farah Jasmine
If you can't be free, be a mystery: in search of Billie Holiday   92
Griffin, Jasper
(ed) The Oxford history of the Roman world. See The Oxford history of the Roman world   937
Griffin, John Howard, 1920-1980
Black like me   305.8
Griffin, Joseph Howard, b. 1888
     About
Pearson, H. Under the knife   92
Griffin, Robert, 1951-
(ed) The Folklore of world holidays. See The Folklore of world holidays   394.26
Griffith, Fred
(jt. auth) Griffith, L. Garlic, garlic, garlic   641.6
Griffith, Linda
Garlic, garlic, garlic   641.6
Griffiths, Mark
(jt. auth) Pollock, M. The Royal Horticultural Society shorter dictionary of gardening   635
Griffiths, Ralph A. (Ralph Alan)
(jt. auth) Cannon, J. The Oxford illustrated history of the British monarchy   941
Grill cooking *See* Barbecue cooking
Grimal, Pierre, 1912-
The dictionary of classical mythology   292
Grimes, William
My fine feathered friend   636.5
Grimké family
     About
Perry, M. Lift up thy voice   920

Grimm, Jacob, 1785-1863
The complete fairy tales of the Brothers Grimm
         398.2
Grimm, Michele
(jt. auth) Grimm, T. The basic book of photography
         770.2
Grimm, Tom
The basic book of photography   770.2
Grimm, Wilhelm, 1786-1859
(jt. auth) Grimm, J. The complete fairy tales of the Brothers Grimm   398.2
Grinspoon, David Harry
Venus revealed   523.4
Griswold, Mac K.
The golden age of American gardens   712
Grizzard, Frank E., Jr.
George Washington: a biographical companion   92
Grizzard, Lewis
It wasn't always easy, but I sure had fun   817
The grizzly almanac. Busch, R.   599.78
Grizzly bear
Busch, R. The grizzly almanac   599.78
Treadwell, T. Among grizzlies   599.78
Grmek, Mirko D., 1924-2000
History of AIDS   616.97
Grob, Bernard
Basic electronics   621.381
Grob, Gerald N., 1931-
The deadly truth   616
Grobman, Alex
(jt. auth) Shermer, M. Denying history   940.53
Groom, Winston, 1944-
A storm in Flanders   940.4
Grooming, Personal *See* Personal grooming
Grooming, gossip, and the evolution of language. Dunbar, R. I. M.   599.93
Groopman, Jerome E.
Second opinions   610
Gropius, Walter, 1883-1969
The new architecture and the Bauhaus   724
Grose, Peter, 1934-
Gentleman spy: the life of Allen Dulles   92
Operation Rollback   327.12
Gross, John J.
(ed) The Oxford book of aphorisms. See The Oxford book of aphorisms   808.88
(ed) The Oxford book of comic verse. See The Oxford book of comic verse   821.008
Gross, Kim Johnson
Woman's face   646.7
Gross, Martin L. (Martin Louis), 1925-
The conspiracy of ignorance   371
Gross, Ramón García-Pelayo y *See* García-Pelayo y Gross, Ramón
Grosskopf, Barry, 1945-
Forgive your parents, heal yourself   155.9
Grossman, David
The yellow wind   956.95
Grossman, Mark
Encyclopedia of the Persian Gulf War   956.7
Grotz, George
The furniture doctor   684.1
Groucho: the life and times of Julius Henry Marx. Kanfer, S.   92
Ground work II. Duncan, R. E.   811
Group relations training
Lasch-Quinn, E. Race experts   305.8
Group values *See* Social values
Grout, Donald Jay, 1902-1987
A history of Western music   780.9
Groves, Leslie R., 1896-1970
     About
Norris, R. S. Racing for the bomb: General Leslie R. Groves, the Manhattan Project's indispensable man
         92

Growing herbs and vegetables. Silber, M.   635
Growing up. Baker, R.   92
Growing up Asian American   810.8
Growth disorders
   See also Birth defects; Dwarfism
The **growth** of the American Republic. Morison, S. E.   973
The **growth** of the American Republic; abridgement. See Morison, S. E. A concise history of the American Republic   973
Growth retardation *See* Dwarfism
Grun, Bernard, 1901-1972
   The timetables of history   902
Grundman, Clare, 1913-
   (jt. auth) Pulliam, T. The New York times crossword puzzle dictionary   793.73
Grundy, Valerie
   (ed) The Oxford-Hachette French dictionary. See The Oxford-Hachette French dictionary   443
Grunstein, Michael, 1946-
   (jt. auth) Clark, W. R. Are we hardwired?   155.7
Gruver, Ed, 1960-
   Koufax   92
Grzimek's animal life encyclopedia   590
Guadalupi, Gianni
   (jt. auth) Manguel, A. The dictionary of imaginary places   809.3
The **guardeen**. Frost, R.
   In Frost, R. Collected poems, prose, & plays p589-625   818
Guare, John
   Six degrees of separation   812
   See/See also pages in the following book(s):
   Playwrights at work   812.009
The **guare** fellow. Behan, B.
   In Behan, B. The complete plays   822
Guarneri String Quartet
   Steinhardt, A. Indivisible by four   920
Guatemala
   Wilkinson, D. Silence on the mountain   972.81
Gubar, Susan, 1944-
   (jt. auth) Gilbert, S. M. No man's land v3   820.9
   (comp) The Norton anthology of literature by women. See The Norton anthology of literature by women   820.8
Gubert, Betty Kaplan, 1934-
   Distinguished African Americans in aviation and space science   920.003
Guess, George *See* Sequoyah, 1770?-1843
Guests *See* Entertaining
Guevara, Che *See* Guevara, Ernesto, 1928-1967
Guevara, Ernesto, 1928-1967
           About
   Anderson, J. L. Che Guevara   92
   Taibo, P. I. Guevara, also known as Che   92
Guggenheim, Marguerite *See* Guggenheim, Peggy, 1898-1979
Guggenheim, Peggy, 1898-1979
           About
   Gill, A. Art lover: a biography of Peggy Guggenheim   92
Guggenheim family
           About
   Davis, J. H. The Guggenheims (1848-1988)   920
Guicciardini, Francesco, 1483-1540
   See/See also pages in the following book(s):
   Barzini, L. G. The Italians p157-75   945
Guidance, Vocational *See* Vocational guidance
A **Guide** book of United States coins   737.4
Guide for occupational exploration   331.7
Guide to American foreign relations since 1700. See American foreign relations since 1600   016.327
The **Guide** to American law. See West's encyclopedia of American law   340.03
Guide to America's federal jobs   351.076

A **guide** to amphibians and reptiles. Tyning, T. F.   597.9
Guide to Congress   328.73
Guide to four-year colleges, Peterson's   378.73
Guide to independent study through correspondence instruction. See The Independent study catalog   374
Guide to law schools, Barron's   378.73
Guide to literary agents   070.5
Guide to reference books   011
Guide to summer camps and summer schools   796.54
A **guide** to the ancient world. Grant, M.   938.003
Guide to the best 1,000 movies ever made, The New York times. Canby, V.   791.43
A **guide** to the end of the world. McGuire, B.   001.9
Guide to the presidency   352.23
Guide to U.S. elections   324.6
A **guide** to understanding dietary supplements. Talbott, S.   615
Guidice, Anthony
   The seven essentials of woodworking   684
Guiding your child through grief. Emswiler, M. A.   155.9
Guiley, Rosemary Ellen
   The encyclopedia of ghosts and spirits   133.1
   The encyclopedia of saints   920.003
   Encyclopedia of the strange, mystical & unexplained   133
   The encyclopedia of witches and witchcraft   133.4
Guillen, Michael
   Five equations that changed the world   530.1
Guillermoprieto, Alma, 1949-
   Looking for history   972
Guilt
   Kushner, H. S. How good do we have to be?   296.7
Guinagh, Kevin, 1897-
   Dictionary of foreign phrases and abbreviations   422.03
Guinier, Lani
   The miner's canary   323.1
Guinness, Alec
   My name escapes me   92
   A positively final appearance   92
Guinness book of records   032.02
Guinness book of world records. See Guinness book of records   032.02
Guinness world records. See Guinness book of records   032.02
Guitars
   Bacon, T. The ultimate guitar book   787.87
   Chapman, R. The complete guitarist   787.87
Gulag. Applebaum, A.   365
The **Gulag** Archipelago, 1918-1956. Solzhenitsyn, A.   365
Gulevich, Tanya
   Encyclopedia of Christmas and New Year's celebrations   394.26
   (ed) World holiday, festival, and calendar books. See World holiday, festival, and calendar books   016.39426
Gulf War, 1980-1988 *See* Iran-Iraq War, 1980-1988
Gulf War, 1991 *See* Persian Gulf War, 1991
Gulland, R. R. Milner- *See* Milner-Gulland, R. R.
Gun control
   Guns in American society   363.3
   Henderson, H. Gun control   363.3
   Sugarmann, J. Every handgun is aimed at you   363.3
   Utter, G. H. Encyclopedia of gun control and gun rights   363.3
Gun digest   623.4
Gunfighter nation. Slotkin, R.   973.9

Gunn, James E., 1923-
Isaac Asimov   813.009
Gunn, Thom
Boss Cupid   821
Gunnell, John
(ed) Standard guide to American muscle cars. See Standard guide to American muscle cars   629.222
Gunpowder plot, 1605
Fraser, A. Faith and treason   942.06
Guns, germs, and steel. Diamond, J. M.   303.4
Guns in American society   363.3
The **guns** of August. Tuchman, B. W.   940.3
Gunsmoke over the Atlantic. Coombe, J. D.   973.7
Gunther, John, 1901-1970
Death be not proud   92
Gunther, John, 1929-1947
           About
Gunther, J. Death be not proud   92
Gup, Ted, 1950-
Book of honor   327.12
Guralnick, Peter
Careless love: the unmaking of Elvis Presley   92
Last train to Memphis: the rise of Elvis Presley   92
Gurewitsch, A. David, 1902-1974
           About
Gurewitsch, E. Kindred souls: the friendship of Eleanor Roosevelt and David Gurewitsch   92
Gurewitsch, Edna
Kindred souls: the friendship of Eleanor Roosevelt and David Gurewitsch   92
Gurian, Michael
The wonder of girls   305.23
Gurion, David Ben- See Ben-Gurion, David, 1886-1973
Gurney, A. R. (Albert Ramsdell), 1930-
Nine early plays, 1961-1973   812
Contents: The comeback; The rape of Bunny Stuntz; The golden fleece; The David Show; The problem; Public affairs; The old one-two; Scenes from American life
Gurney, Albert Ramsdell See Gurney, A. R. (Albert Ramsdell), 1930-
Gurock, Jeffrey S., 1949-
(ed) American Jewish history. See American Jewish history   305.8
Gussow, Mel
Edward Albee   92
Guth, Alan H.
The inflationary universe   523.1
Guthrie, James W.
(ed) Encyclopedia of education. See Encyclopedia of education   370
Gutierrez, Eduardo, 1978-1999
           About
Breslin, J. The short sweet dream of Eduardo Gutierrez   92
Gutman, Bill
Parcells   92
Gutman, Israel
(ed) Encyclopedia of the Holocaust. See Encyclopedia of the Holocaust [Macmillan]   940.53
Gutman, Robert W.
Mozart   92
Gutman, Yisrael See Gutman, Israel
Guttenplan, D. D.
The Holocaust on trial   940.53
Guttmann, Allen
The Olympics, a history of the modern games   796.48
Women's sports   796
Guy, Richard K.
(jt. auth) Conway, J. H. The book of numbers   512

Guyana
       Politics and government
See/See also pages in the following book(s):
Naipaul, V. S. The writer and the world p485-502   824
Gwynn, Tony
See/See also pages in the following book(s):
Will, G. F. Men at work: the craft of baseball p161-230   796.357
Gymnastics
Ryan, J. Little girls in pretty boxes   796.44
Gynecology See Women—Diseases; Women—Health and hygiene
Gypsies
Lewy, G. The Nazi persecution of the gypsies   940.53

H

H & R Block income tax guide   336.2
H bomb See Hydrogen bomb
H. D. (Hilda Doolittle), 1886-1961
Collected poems, 1912-1944   811
See/See also pages in the following book(s):
Gilbert, S. M. No man's land v3 p166-207   820.9
H20: a biography of water. See Ball, P. Life's matrix   553.7
Haase, Ynez D.
(jt. auth) Beck, W. A. Historical atlas of the American West   911
Habegger, Alfred
The father: a life of Henry James, Sr   92
My wars are laid away in books: the life of Emily Dickinson   92
Haber, Barbara
From hardtack to home fries   394.1
Haber, Carol Chase
(jt. auth) Ames, L. B. Your eight-year-old   649
(jt. auth) Ames, L. B. Your one-year-old   649
(jt. auth) Ames, L. B. Your seven-year-old   649
The **habit** of being. O'Connor, F.   92
Habitats and ecosystems. Crawford, M.   578.68
Hachi no ki. Zeami
In Waley, A. The Nō plays of Japan   895.6
Hack, Garrett
Classic hand tools   621.9
Hacker, Marilyn, 1942-
Selected poems   811
Squares and courtyards   811
Hacker cracker: a journey from the mean streets of Brooklyn to the frontiers of cyberspace. Nuwere, E.   92
Hackett, Albert, 1900-1995
(jt. auth) Goodrich, F. The diary of Anne Frank   812
Hackett, David A.
(ed) The Buchenwald report. See The Buchenwald report   940.53
Hackett, Pat
(ed) Warhol, A. The Andy Warhol diaries   92
Hadadi, Letha
Healthy beauty   646.7
Hadady, Letha See Hadadi, Letha
Hades See Hell
Haffner, Sebastian
Defying Hitler   92
Hagen, Uta, 1919-
Respect for acting   792
Haggerty, George E.
(ed) Encyclopedia of lesbian and gay histories and cultures. See Encyclopedia of lesbian and gay histories and cultures   306.7
Hagman, Bette
The gluten-free gourmet   641.5

Hagoromo. Zeami
In Waley, A. The Nō plays of Japan   895.6
Hagstrom, Robert G., 1956-
The Warren Buffett way   332.6
Hahl-Koch, Jelena
Kandinsky   92
Hahn, Kristin
In search of grace   200.9
Haigh, Christopher
(ed) The Cambridge historical encyclopedia of Great
Britain and Ireland. See The Cambridge historical
encyclopedia of Great Britain and Ireland   941
Haiku
Higginson, W. J. The haiku handbook   808.1
The **haiku** handbook. Higginson, W. J.   808.1
Hail to the chief. Dallek, R.   973
Haines, Tim
Walking with dinosaurs   567.9
Hainsworth, Peter
(ed) The Oxford companion to Italian literature. See
The Oxford companion to Italian literature
    850.3
Hair, William Ivy
The Kingfish and his realm: the life and times of Huey
P. Long   92
Hair
Bonner, L. B. Good hair   646.7
Bonner, L. B. Plaited glory   646.7
Ferrell, P. Let's talk hair   646.7
Handel, G. Cutting your family's hair   646.7
Massey, L. Curly girl   646.7
Worthington, C. The complete book of hairstyling
    646.7
Diseases
Greenwood-Robinson, M. Hair savers for women
    616.5
Thompson, W. J. A. Alopecia areata   616.5
Hair savers for women. Greenwood-Robinson, M.
    616.5
Hairston family
About
Wiencek, H. The Hairstons   975
Haiti
Shacochis, B. The immaculate invasion   972.94
Social life and customs
Danticat, E. After the dance   394.25
Hajdu, David
Lush life: a biography of Billy Strayhorn   92
Hakim, Joy
Freedom   973
Haku Rakuten. Zeami
In Waley, A. The Nō plays of Japan   895.6
Halaby, Lisa *See* Nur el Hussein, Queen, consort of
Hussein, King of Jordan
Halberstam, David, 1934-
The best and the brightest   973.922
The children   323.1
The fifties   973.92
Firehouse   363.34
Playing for keeps: Michael Jordan and the world he
made   92
Summer of '49   796.357
The teammates   920
War in a time of peace   327.73
(ed) The Best American sports writing of the century.
See The Best American sports writing of the century
    796
See/See also pages in the following book(s):
Prochnau, W. W. Once upon a distant war
    959.704
Hale, Nancy, 1908-1988
See/See also pages in the following book(s):
American women fiction writers   813.009
Haley, Alex
Roots   920

Malcolm X. The autobiography of Malcolm X   92
Haley family
About
Haley, A. Roots   920
Halfway home: my life 'til now. Tynan, R.   92
Halifax, Edward Frederick Lindley Wood, 1st Earl of,
1881-1959
About
Lukacs, J. Five days in London, May 1940
    940.53
Hall, Brian, 1959-
The impossible country   949.7
Hall, Charles J.
A chronicle of American music, 1700-1995
    780.973
Chronology of Western classical music   780.9
Hall, Donald, 1928-
Old and new poems   811
The old life   811
The painted bed   811
Hall, James, III
See/See also pages in the following book(s):
Herrington, S. A. Traitors among us p251-371
    327.12
Hall, Kermit
(ed) The Oxford companion to American law. See The
Oxford companion to American law   349
(ed) The Oxford companion to the Supreme Court of
the United States. See The Oxford companion to the
Supreme Court of the United States   347
(ed) The Oxford guide to United States Supreme Court
decisions. See The Oxford guide to United States
Supreme Court decisions   342
Hall, Michael G. (Michael Garibaldi)
The last American Puritan: the life of Increase Mather,
1639-1723   92
Hall, Stephen S.
A commotion in the blood   616.07
Hall, Timothy L.
American religious leaders   920.003
Supreme Court justices   920.003
Hallett, Mark, 1947-
(jt. auth) Gillette, D. D. Seismosaurus   567.9
Halley's comet
Sagan, C. Comet   523.6
Halliday, Tim, 1945-
(ed) Firefly encyclopedia of reptiles and amphibians.
See Firefly encyclopedia of reptiles and amphibians
    597.9
Halliwell's film and video guide. See Halliwell's film
guide   791.43
Halliwell's film guide   791.43
Hallman, Tom
Sam: the boy behind the mask   362.1
Hallmarks
Wyler, S. B. The book of old silver: English,
American, foreign   739.2
Hallowell, Edward M.
Connect   158
Driven to distraction   616.85
Worry   616.85
Hallucinogenic drugs *See* Hallucinogens
Hallucinogenic plants *See* Hallucinogens
Hallucinogens
Davis, W. One river   581.6
Halperin, Michael, 1940-
(jt. auth) Pagell, R. A. International business informa-
tion   650
Halpern, Sue M.
Four wings and a prayer   595.7
Halpert, Sam, 1920-
Raymond Carver   92
Halpin, Brendan
It takes a worried man   362.1

Halsey, Ann Howard
(jt. auth) Carr, R. H. Land of a thousand hills
967.571
Halstead, Ted
The radical center   320.5
Halsted, William Stewart, 1852-1922
See/See also pages in the following book(s):
Leopold, E. A darker ribbon   616.99
Halving it all. Deutsch, F.   649
Ham, Catherine
25 gorgeous sweaters for the brand new knitter
746.43
Ham radio stations *See* Amateur radio stations
Hamblyn, Richard, 1965-
The invention of clouds   551.57
Hamer, Dean H.
Living with our genes   155.2
Hamer, Frank, 1929-
The potter's dictionary of materials and techniques
738.1
Hamer, Janet
(jt. auth) Hamer, F. The potter's dictionary of materials
and techniques   738.1
Hamill, Pete
Diego Rivera   92
Piecework   814
Why Sinatra matters   92
Hamill, Sam
The Gift of tongues. See The Gift of tongues
811.008
Hamilton, Alexander, 1757-1804
Writings   973.4
About
Brookhiser, R. Alexander Hamilton, American   92
See/See also pages in the following book(s):
Ellis, J. J. Founding brothers   973.4
Miller, J. C. The Federalist era, 1789-1801 p33-69, 84-
98   973.4
Hamilton, Ann
About
Simon, J. Ann Hamilton   92
Hamilton, Edith, 1867-1963
The echo of Greece   880.9
The Greek way   880.9
Mythology   292
The Roman way   870.9
Hamilton, George Heard
The art and architecture of Russia   709.47
Hamilton, James, 1948-
Turner   92
Hamilton, Sir William Rowan, 1805-1865
See/See also pages in the following book(s):
Bell, E. T. Men of mathematics p340-61   920
Hamilton-Williams, David
The fall of Napoleon   944.05
Hamlet's dresser. Smith, B.   92
Hamlet's mother and other women. Heilbrun, C. G.
820.9
Hamm, Charles
Irving Berlin   92
Hamm, Mia, 1972-
Go for the goal   796.334
Hamm, Thomas D., 1957-
The Quakers in America   289.6
Hammarskjöld, Dag, 1905-1961
Markings   839.7
Hammel, Bob
(jt. auth) Knight, B. Knight: my story   92
Hammer, Armand, 1898-1990
About
Epstein, E. J. Dossier: the secret history of Armand
Hammer   92
Hammerstein, Oscar, 1895-1960
About
Mordden, E. Rodgers & Hammerstein   792.6

See/See also pages in the following book(s):
Green, S. The world of musical comedy   920
Hammitt, Katherine Morland
(jt. auth) Rumpf, T. P. The Sjogren's syndrome surviv-
al guide   616.97
Hammond, Bruce
(jt. auth) Fiske, E. B. The Fiske guide to getting into
the right college   378
Hammond, Wayne G.
J.R.R. Tolkien, artist & illustrator   92
Hammond atlas of world history   911
Hammond world atlas   912
Hampsten, Elizabeth, 1932-
(jt. auth) Schlissel, L. Far from home   978
Hancock, Graham
Underworld: the mysterious origins of civilization
551.7
Hancock, LynNell
Hands to work   361.6
Hancock, Paul L.
(ed) The Oxford companion to the earth. See The Ox-
ford companion to the earth   550.3
Hancock, Thomas, 1786-1865
About
Slack, C. Noble obsession   92
Hand
Wilson, F. R. The hand   612
Surgery
Arem, A. In our hands   617
Handbook of chemistry and physics. See CRC handbook
of chemistry and physics   540
Handbook of chemistry, Lange's. See Lange's handbook
of chemistry   540
Handbook of denominations in the United States. Mead,
F. S.   280
The **handbook** of knots. Pawson, D.   623.88
Handbook of model rocketry. Stine, G. H.   629.47
Handbook of Norse mythology. Lindow, J.   293
Handbook of North American Indians   970.004
The **Handbook** of private schools   370.25
Handbook of United States coins   737.4
Handbook to life in ancient Egypt. David, A. R.
932
Handbook to life in ancient Greece. Adkins, L.
938
A **handbook** to literature. Harmon, W.   803
Handcrafted ceramic tiles. Jones, M.   738
Handedness *See* Left- and right-handedness
Handel, George Frideric, 1685-1759
About
Hogwood, C. Handel   92
See/See also pages in the following book(s):
Grout, D. J. A history of Western music   780.9
Handel, Gloria
Cutting your family's hair   646.7
Handicapped
See also Physically handicapped
Civil rights
Perritt, H. H., Jr. Americans with Disabilities Act
handbook   344
Law and legislation
Perritt, H. H., Jr. Americans with Disabilities Act
handbook   344
Handicapped children
See also Socially handicapped children
Greenspan, S. I. The child with special needs
362.1
Kersjes, M. A smile as big as the moon   371.9
Handicraft
Engelbreit, M. Mary Engelbreit's children's companion
645
Foxfire [1]-11   975.8
Gerhards, P. How to sell what you make   658.8
Kilby, J. E. By hand   745
Lyons, C. Between friends   745.5

Handicraft—*Continued*

    Marshall, M. H. Shell chic   **745.55**

    Stewart, M. Great American wreaths   **745.92**

    Stewart, M. Handmade Christmas   **745.59**

Handlin, Oscar, 1915-

    The uprooted   **325.73**

Handmade Christmas. Stewart, M.   **745.59**

Hands on dyeing. Blumenthal, B.   **746.1**

Hands to work. Hancock, L.   **361.6**

Handspring, Hiram *See* Laughlin, James, 1914-1997

Handwriting

    See also Calligraphy

The **Handy** science answer book   **500**

The **handy** weather answer book. Lyons, W. A.

    551.6

Haney, Eric L.

    Inside Delta Force   **356**

Hanks, Patrick

    Dictionary of American family names. See Dictionary of American family names   **929.4**

Hanlan, James P.

    Historical encyclopedia of American labor. See Historical encyclopedia of American labor   **331.8**

Hansberry, Lorraine, 1930-1965

    A raisin in the sun   **812**

    To be young, gifted and black   **92**

    See/See also pages in the following book(s):

    Rich, A. Blood, bread, and poetry p11-22   **814**

Hansen, Carol Rae

    (jt. auth) Devine, C. Human rights   **323**

Hansen, Eric

    Orchid fever   **635.9**

Hanson, Elizabeth, 1962-

    Animal attractions   **590.73**

Hanson, Robert D.

    Century 21 accounting: first-year course. See Century 21 accounting: first-year course   **657**

Hanson, Victor Davis

    Carnage and culture   **904**

    The soul of battle   **355**

Hanssen, Robert Philip

    About

    Vise, D. A. The bureau and the mole   **327.12**

    Wise, D. Spy: the inside story of how the FBI's Robert Hanssen betrayed America   **327.12**

Hanukkah

    See/See also pages in the following book(s):

    Strassfeld, M. The Jewish holidays p161-78   **296.4**

The **happiest** baby on the block. Karp, H.   **649**

Happily ever after: a guide to reading interests in romance fiction. See Ramsdell, K. Romance fiction   **016.8**

Happiness

    Browne, J. The nine fantasies that will ruin your life and the eight realities that will save you   **158**

    Foster, R. How we choose to be happy   **158**

    Kingwell, M. In pursuit of happiness   **170**

    Prager, D. Happiness is a serious problem   **158**

    See/See also pages in the following book(s):

    Teilhard de Chardin, P. Toward the future p107-29   **194**

Happiness is a serious problem. Prager, D.   **158**

The **happy** isles of Oceania. Theroux, P.   **919**

Haralson, Eric L.

    (ed) Encyclopedia of American poetry, the twentieth century. See Encyclopedia of American poetry, the twentieth century   **811.009**

Harari, Oren

    The leadership secrets of Colin Powell   **303.3**

Harassment, Sexual *See* Sexual harassment

Harbach, Otto, 1873-1963

    See/See also pages in the following book(s):

    Green, S. The world of musical comedy   **920**

Harbrace college handbook. See Hodges' Harbrace handbook   **808**

Harbrace handbook of English. See Hodges' Harbrace handbook   **808**

Harclerode, Peter, 1947-

    The lost masters   **709**

Hard times. Terkel, S.   **973.91**

Harden, Blaine

    A river lost   **979.7**

Hardouin-Fugier, Elisabeth

    (jt. auth) Baratay, E. Zoo: a history of zoological gardens in the West   **590.73**

Hardwick, Elizabeth

    Herman Melville   **92**

Hardwood floors. Bollinger, D.   **694**

Hardy, Grahame H.

    See/See also pages in the following book(s):

    Kanigel, R. The man who knew infinity: a life of the genius, Ramanujan   **92**

Hardy, Thomas, 1840-1928

    About

    The Oxford reader's companion to Hardy   **823.009**

    See/See also pages in the following book(s):

    Pritchard, W. H. Lives of the modern poets p15-47   **821.009**

    Woolf, V. The second common reader p222-33   **820.9**

Hardy trees and shrubs, Dirr's. Dirr, M.   **635.9**

Hare, R. M. (Richard Mervyn)

    Plato   **184**

Hare, Richard Mervyn *See* Hare, R. M. (Richard Mervyn)

Harewood, George Henry Hubert Lascelles, 7th Earl of, 1923-

    The New Kobbé's opera book. See The New Kobbé's opera book   **792.5**

Hargittai, István

    The road to Stockholm   **509**

Hargreaves, Alice Pleasance Liddell, 1852-1934

    See/See also pages in the following book(s):

    Prose, F. The lives of the muses   **920**

Harjo, Joy, 1951-

    A map to the next world   **811**

    See/See also pages in the following book(s):

    Coltelli, L. Winged words: American Indian writers speak   **897**

Harlan, Louis R.

    Booker T. Washington: the making of a black leader, 1856-1901   **92**

    Booker T. Washington: the wizard of Tuskegee, 1901-1915   **92**

Harlem Renaissance

    Aberjhani. Encyclopedia of the Harlem Renaissance   **810.9**

    The Portable Harlem Renaissance reader   **810.8**

    Wall, C. A. Women of the Harlem Renaissance   **810.9**

Harlem Renaissance and beyond: literary biographies of 100 black women writers, 1900-1945. Roses, L. E.   **810.9**

Harlem Renaissance: art of black America   **709.73**

Harleston family

    About

    Ball, E. The sweet hell inside   **920**

Harley, Sharon

    The timetables of African-American history   **305.8**

Harline, Craig E.

    Miracles at the Jesus Oak   **231.7**

Harlow, George E.

    (ed) The Nature of diamonds. See The Nature of diamonds   **553.8**

    (ed) Simon and Schuster's guide to rocks and minerals. See Simon and Schuster's guide to rocks and minerals   **549**

    (jt. auth) Sofianides, A. S. Gems & crystals from the American Museum of Natural History   **549**

Harlow, Harry F., 1905-1981
About
Blum, D. Love at Goon Park   150.19
Harman, Claire
Fanny Burney   92
Harmful to minors. Levine, J.   306.7
Harmon, Alexandra, 1945-
Indians in the making   970.004
Harmon, Charles T., 1960-
(jt. auth) Symons, A. K. Protecting the right to read
                                              025.2
Harmon, William, 1938-
A handbook to literature   803
Harmony
Piston, W. Harmony   781.2
Harold, Franklin M.
The way of the cell   571.6
Harold, Madd, 1973-
An actor's guide to performing Shakespeare   792
Harper, Michael S.
(ed) Every shut eye ain't asleep. See Every shut eye
ain't asleep   811.008
(ed) The Vintage book of African American poetry.
See The Vintage book of African American poetry
                                              811.008
Harper, Pamela
Designing with perennials   712
The **HarperCollins** Bible commentary   220.7
The **HarperCollins** Bible dictionary   220.3
The **HarperCollins** concise atlas of the Bible   220.9
The **HarperCollins** encyclopedia of Catholicism
                                              282
HarperCollins Reader's encyclopedia of American liter-
ature   810.3
The **HarperCollins** study Bible. Bible   220.5
Harper's anthology of 20th century Native American
poetry   811.008
Harper's Bible commentary. See The HarperCollins Bi-
ble commentary   220.7
Harper's Bible dictionary. See The HarperCollins Bible
dictionary   220.3
Harper's encyclopedia of mystical & paranormal experi-
ence. See Guiley, R. E. Encyclopedia of the strange,
mystical & unexplained   133
Harpham, Wendy Schlessel
Diagnosis, cancer   616.99
Harries, Meirion, 1951-
The last days of innocence   940.4
Harries, Susie
(jt. auth) Harries, M. The last days of innocence
                                              940.4
Harriman, Averell, 1891-1986
See/See also pages in the following book(s):
Galbraith, J. K. Name-dropping   973.9
Harriman, Pamela
See/See also pages in the following book(s):
Heymann, C. D. The Georgetown ladies' social club
                                              305.4
Harrington, Michael, 1928-1989
About
Isserman, M. The other American: the life of Michael
Harrington   92
Harrington, Philip S.
Star ware   522
Harris, Alice Kessler- See Kessler-Harris, Alice
Harris, Brice
(ed) Restoration plays. See Restoration plays
                                              822.008
Harris, Cyril M., 1917-
(ed) Dictionary of architecture & construction. See
Dictionary of architecture & construction   720.3
Harris, David, 1929-
The art of calligraphy   745.6
Harris, Jessica B.
The Africa cookbook   641.5

The welcome table   641.5
Harris, Jill Werman
(ed) Remembrances and celebrations. See Remembrances and celebrations   808.8
Harris, Joseph, 1951-
(jt. auth) Turkington, C. The encyclopedia of learning
disabilities   371.9
(jt. auth) Turkington, C. The encyclopedia of memory
and memory disorders   153.1
Harris, Madeline
(ed) The Gale encyclopedia of mental disorders. See
The Gale encyclopedia of mental disorders
                                              616.89
Harris, Mary See Jones, Mother, 1830-1930
Harris, Melissa
(ed) Photography past forward: Aperture at 50. See
Photography past forward: Aperture at 50   770.9
Harris, Ruth, 1958-
Lourdes   232.91
Harris, Sandra L.
Siblings of children with autism   649
Harris, Thomas Anthony, 1913?-1995
I'm OK, you're OK   158
Harris, Trudier
(ed) The Oxford companion to African American liter-
ature. See The Oxford companion to African
American literature   810.9
Harrison, Daphne Duval, 1932-
Black pearls   920
Harrison, George H.
(jt. auth) Harrison, K. America's favorite backyard
birds   598
Harrison, Hazel
Master strokes, Pastels   741.2
Harrison, J. W. Heslop- See Heslop-Harrison, J. W.
Harrison, Jim, 1937-
Off to the side   92
The raw and the cooked   641.3
The shape of the journey   811
Harrison, John, 1693-1776
About
Sobel, D. Longitude   526
Harrison, Kit
America's favorite backyard birds   598
Harrison, Ross G., 1870-1959
See/See also pages in the following book(s):
Friedman, M. Medicine's 10 greatest discoveries
                                              610.9
Hart, Basil Henry Liddell See Liddell Hart, Sir Basil
Henry, 1895-1970
Hart, Christopher
Cartooning for the beginner   741.5
Human anatomy made amazingly easy   743
Hart, James David, 1911-1990
(ed) The Oxford companion to American literature. See
The Oxford companion to American literature
                                              810.3
Hart, Lorenz, 1895-1943
See/See also pages in the following book(s):
Green, S. The world of musical comedy   920
Hart, Lowell, 1959-
The snowboard book   796.9
Hart, Matthew, 1945-
Diamond: a journey to the heart of an obsession
                                              553.8
Hart, Moss, 1904-1961
About
Bach, S. Dazzler: the life and times of Moss Hart
                                              92
Harter, Penny
(jt. auth) Higginson, W. J. The haiku handbook
                                              808.1
Hartford Circus Fire, Hartford, Conn., 1944 See
Fires—Hartford (Conn.)

The **Harvard** biographical dictionary of music
920.003
The **Harvard** book of contemporary American poetry
811.008
The **Harvard** Business School guide to finding your next job. Gardella, R.
650.14
The **Harvard** concise dictionary of music and musicians
780.3
The **Harvard** dictionary of music
780.3
Harvard encyclopedia of American ethnic groups
305.8
The **Harvard** Medical School family health guide
610
The **Harvard** Medical School guide to men's health. Simon, H. B.
613
Harvesting, preserving, and arranging dried flowers. Miller, C.
745.92
Harvey, David Alan, 1944-
Cuba
972.91
Harvey, Henry Paul See Harvey, Sir Paul, 1869-1948
Harvey, James
Movie love in the 50's
791.43
Harvey, Sir Paul, 1869-1948
The Oxford companion to classical literature. See The Oxford companion to classical literature
880.3
Harvey, Thomas S., 1912-
About
Paterniti, M. Driving Mr. Albert
917.3
Harvey, William, 1578-1657
See/See also pages in the following book(s):
Friedman, M. Medicine's 10 greatest discoveries
610.9
Harwood, Buie
Architecture and interior design through the 18th century
729
Hasidic legends
Frankel, E. The classic tales
296.1
Wiesel, E. Souls on fire
296.8
Hasidism
Wiesel, E. Souls on fire
296.8
Haskell, Barbara, 1946-
The American century
709.73
Hass, Robert, 1941-
Sun under wood
811
(ed) Into the garden. See Into the garden
808.8
Hasse, John Edward, 1948-
(ed) Jazz: the first century. See Jazz: the first century
781.65
Hastings, Max
Overlord: D-Day and the battle for Normandy
940.54
Hate crimes
King, J. Hate crime: the story of a dragging in Jasper, Texas
364.1
Hatha yoga See Yoga
Hathaway, Sandee Eisenberg
(jt. auth) Eisenberg, A. What to expect the toddler years
649
(jt. auth) Murkoff, H. E. What to expect the first year
649
(jt. auth) Murkoff, H. E. What to expect when you're expecting
618.2
Hats
Albrizio, A. Classic millinery techniques
646.5
Hatsuyuki. Komparu, Z.
In Waley, A. The Nō plays of Japan
895.6
Hauge, Michael
Writing screenplays that sell
808.2
Haunted America. Norman, M.
133.1
The **haunted** land. Rosenberg, T.
947
The **haunted** wood. Weinstein, A.
327.12
Hauptmann, Bruno Richard
See/See also pages in the following book(s):
Geis, G. Crimes of the century
345

Hauser, Barbara
(ed) Women's legal guide. See Women's legal guide
346.01
Hauser, Marc D.
Wild minds
591.5
Hauser, Robert A.
Parkinson's disease: questions and answers
616.8
Hausman, Gerald
(ed) Kebra Nagast. The Kebra Nagast
299
Havana (Cuba)
See/See also pages in the following book(s):
Eire, C. M. N. Waiting for snow in Havana
92
Havana dreams. Gimbel, W.
972.91
Havemann, Joel
A life shaken
362.1
Having faith. Steingraber, S.
618.2
Having our say. Delany, S.
92
Havlice, Patricia Pate
Index to artistic biography
920.003
Popular song index
782.42
Hawaiian dictionary. Pukui, M. K.
499
Hawaiian language
Dictionaries
Pukui, M. K. Hawaiian dictionary
499
Hawass, Zahi
Valley of the golden mummies
932
Hawke, David Freeman
Everyday life in early America
973.2
Hawking, S. W. (Stephen W.)
Black holes and baby universes and other essays
523.1
A brief history of time
523.1
The nature of space and time
530.1
The universe in a nutshell
530.1
(ed) On the shoulders of giants. See On the shoulders of giants
520
About
White, M. Stephen Hawking
92
Hawking, Stephen W. See Hawking, S. W. (Stephen W.)
Hawks
Clark, W. S. A field guide to hawks of North America
598
Hawley's condensed chemical dictionary
540.3
Hawn, William H., Jr.
(jt. auth) Berry, C. W. Computer and Internet dictionary for ages 9 to 99
004
Hawthorne, Nathaniel, 1804-1864
The portable Hawthorne
818
About
Martin, T. Nathaniel Hawthorne
813.009
Miller, E. H. Salem is my dwelling place: a life of Nathaniel Hawthorne
92
See/See also pages in the following book(s):
Kazin, A. An American procession p81-94
810.9
Matthiessen, F. O. American renaissance p179-368
810.9
Hay, Jeff
A history of the Third Reich
943.086
Hay, John Milton, 1838-1905
See/See also pages in the following book(s):
Zimmermann, W. First great triumph
973
Hay fever. Coward, N.
In Coward, N. Three plays
822
Hayakawa, Alan R.
(jt. auth) Hayakawa, S. I. Language in thought and action
412
Hayakawa, S. I.
Language in thought and action
412
(ed) Choose the right word. See Choose the right word
423
Haycraft, Howard, 1905-1991
(ed) American authors, 1600-1900. See American authors, 1600-1900
920.003

Haycraft, Howard, 1905-1991—*Continued*
(ed) British authors of the nineteenth century. See British authors of the nineteenth century   **920.003**
Hayden, Deborah
Pox: genius, madness, and the mysteries of syphilis   **616.95**
Hayden, Palmer C., 1893-1973
See/See also pages in the following book(s):
Harlem Renaissance: art of black America   **709.73**
Hayden, Robert Earl, 1913-1980
Collected poems   **811**
Hayden, Torey L.
Beautiful child   **371.9**
Haydn, Joseph, 1732-1809
About
Geiringer, K. Haydn: a creative life in music   **92**
Rosen, C. The classical style   **780.9**
See/See also pages in the following book(s):
Grout, D. J. A history of Western music   **780.9**
Hayman, Ronald, 1932-
A life of Jung   **92**
Haynes, John Earl
Venona   **327.12**
Haynsworth, Leslie
Amelia Earhart's daughters   **629.13**
Hayward, Gordon
Stone in the garden   **712**
Hazan, Marcella
Essentials of classic Italian cooking   **641.5**
Marcella cucina   **641.5**
Hazardous occupations
See also Industrial accidents
Hazen, Edith P.
(ed) The Columbia Granger's dictionary of poetry quotations. See The Columbia Granger's dictionary of poetry quotations   **808.88**
Hazen, Robert M., 1948-
Science matters: achieving scientific literacy   **500**
Hazlitt, William, 1778-1830
See/See also pages in the following book(s):
Woolf, V. The second common reader p156-66   **820.9**
Hazmat. McClatchy, J. D.   **811**
Hazony, Yoram
The Jewish state   **956.94**
HDRA encyclopedia of organic gardening. See Rodale's illustrated encyclopedia of organic gardening   **635.9**
Head, Dominic
The Cambridge introduction to modern British fiction, 1950-2000   **823.009**
The **head** game. Kahn, R.   **796.357**
Headache
Marks, D. R. The headache prevention cookbook   **616.8**
The **headache** prevention cookbook. Marks, D. R.   **616.8**
Heads of state
See also Kings and rulers; Presidents
Jackson-Laufer, G. M. Women rulers throughout the ages   **920**
Dictionaries
Fredriksen, J. C. America's military adversaries   **920.003**
Heal your heart. Gould, K. L.   **616.1**
Healing, Mental *See* Mental healing
Healing and the mind. Moyers, B.   **616**
The **healing** power of faith. Koenig, H. G.   **291.1**
Healing the brain. Freed, C.   **616.8**
Healing the mind. Stone, M. H.   **616.89**
Health
See also Physical fitness
Active living every day   **613.7**
Atkins, R. C. Dr. Atkins' age-defying diet revolution   **613**

Buhner, S. H. Vital man   **613**
The Harvard Medical School family health guide   **610**
Health matters!   **613**
Looking after your body   **613**
Marti, J. The alternative health & medicine encyclopedia   **615.5**
Ornish, D. Love & survival   **616.1**
Peck, B. The baby boomer body book   **613**
Schneider, E. L. Ageless: take control of your age and stay youthful for life   **612.6**
Weil, A. Eating well for optimum health   **613.2**
Bibliography
Consumer health information source book   **016.613**
Environmental aspects
See Environmental health
Information services
Consumer health information source book   **016.613**
Religious aspects
Koenig, H. G. The healing power of faith   **291.1**
Health, Public *See* Public health
Health care *See* Medical care
Health care policy and politics A to Z. Rovner, J.   **362.1**
Health foods *See* Natural foods
Health matters!   **613**
Health self-care
American College of Physicians complete home medical guide   **616.02**
American Medical Association family medical guide   **616.02**
The Doctors book of home remedies   **616.02**
Dollemore, D. The doctors book of home remedies for seniors   **613**
Johns Hopkins symptoms and remedies   **616.02**
Parkinson's disease   **616.8**
Simon, H. B. The Harvard Medical School guide to men's health   **613**
Weil, A. Eight weeks to optimum health   **613**
Healthy beauty. Hadadi, L.   **646.7**
The **healthy** kitchen. Weil, A.   **641.5**
Healthy quick cook, Martha Stewart's. Stewart, M.   **641.5**
Healthy women, healthy lives   **613**
Heaney, Seamus
Electric light   **821**
Finders keepers   **821**
Opened ground   **821**
The redress of poetry   **821.009**
The spirit level   **821**
(tr) Beowulf. Beowulf   **829**
About
Vendler, H. H. Seamus Heaney   **821**
Hearing aids
Myers, D. G. A quiet world   **617.8**
Hearing impaired
See also Deaf
Hearn, Maxwell K.
Splendors of Imperial China   **709.51**
Hearst, William Randolph, 1863-1951
About
Nasaw, D. The chief: the life of William Randolph Hearst   **92**
Heart
See also Blood—Circulation
Heart attack *See* Heart diseases
Heart attack!   **616.1**
Heart diseases
DeBakey, M. E. The new living heart   **616.1**
Gould, K. L. Heal your heart   **616.1**
Heart attack!   **616.1**
Klaidman, S. Saving the heart   **616.1**
Kra, S. J. What every woman must know about heart disease   **616.1**
Ornish, D. Love & survival   **616.1**

Heart diseases—*Continued*
Pashkow, F. J. The women's heart book   **616.1**
Reaven, G. M. Syndrome X   **616.1**
      Diet therapy
The New living heart diet   **616.1**
      Prevention
McGowan, M. P. Heart fitness for life   **616.1**
Heart fitness for life. McGowan, M. P.   **616.1**
The **heart** of grief. Attig, T.   **155.9**
Hearth, Amy Hill, 1958-
(jt. auth) Delany, S. Having our say   **92**
Hearts grown brutal. Cohen, R.   **949.7**
Heat Moon, William Least
Blue highways   **917.3**
River horse   **917.3**
Heatter, Maida
Maida Heatter's book of great desserts   **641.8**
Maida Heatter's brand-new book of great cookies   **641.8**
Heaven
The Book of heaven   **291**
McDannell, C. Heaven   **236**
Heavier than heaven: a biography of Kurt Cobain. Cross, C. R.   **92**
Hebblethwaite, Peter
Paul VI   **92**
Heberle, Dave
(jt. auth) Scutella, R. M. How to plan, contract, and build your own home   **690**
Hebrew language
   See also Yiddish language
      Dictionaries
Baltsan, H. Webster's New World Hebrew dictionary   **492.4**
The Oxford English-Hebrew dictionary   **492.4**
Zilkha, A. Modern English-Hebrew dictionary   **492.4**
Hebrew music *See* Jews—Music
Hebrew poetry
      Collections
Music of a distant drum   **808.81**
Hebrides (Scotland)
      Description
Boswell, J. The journal of a tour to the Hebrides with Samuel Johnson   **914.11**
      Social life and customs
Nicolson, A. Sea room: an island life in the Hebrides   **941.1**
Hecht, Anthony, 1923-
The darkness and the light   **811**
Flight among the tombs   **811**
Hedda Gabler. Ibsen, H.
   In Ibsen, H. The complete major prose plays p689-778   **839.8**
   In Ibsen, H. Ibsen: four major plays   **839.8**
   In Our dramatic heritage v4   **808.82**
The **hedgehog**, the fox, and the magister's pox. Gould, S. J.   **303.4**
Hedges, Chris
War is a force that gives us meaning   **355**
Hedrick, Joan D., 1944-
Harriet Beecher Stowe   **92**
Heen, Sheila
(jt. auth) Stone, D. Difficult conversations   **158**
Heffernan, Cecelia
Flowers A to Z   **635.9**
Heffernan, Maureen
Burpee complete gardener. See Burpee complete gardener   **635**
Hegel, Georg Wilhelm Friedrich, 1770-1831
The philosophy of Hegel   **193**
   See/See also pages in the following book(s):
Camus, A. The rebel p133-48   **303.6**
Durant, W. J. The story of philosophy p221-26   **109**

Jaspers, K. The great philosophers   **109**
Russell, B. A history of Western philosophy p730-46   **109**
Heidegger, Martin, 1889-1976
Basic writings   **193**
Being and time   **111**
On time and being   **111**
   See/See also pages in the following book(s):
Existentialism from Dostoevsky to Sartre p233-79   **142**
Heidhues, Mary F. Somers *See* Somers Heidhues, Mary F.
The **Heidi** chronicles. Wasserstein, W.
   In Wasserstein, W. The Heidi chronicles, and other plays   **812**
The **Heidi** chronicles, and other plays. Wasserstein, W.   **812**
Heidler, David Stephen, 1955-
(ed) Encyclopedia of the American Civil War. See Encyclopedia of the American Civil War   **973.7**
Heidler, Jeanne T.
(ed) Encyclopedia of the American Civil War. See Encyclopedia of the American Civil War   **973.7**
Heifetz, Aaron
(jt. auth) Hamm, M. Go for the goal   **796.334**
Heilbron, J. L.
(ed) The Oxford companion to the history of modern science. See The Oxford companion to the history of modern science   **509**
Heilbroner, Robert L.
The worldly philosophers   **330.1**
Heilbrun, Carolyn G., 1926-2003
The education of a woman: the life of Gloria Steinem   **92**
Hamlet's mother and other women   **820.9**
Heilbut, Anthony
Thomas Mann   **92**
Heilig, Gabriel
(ed) Civil service handbook. See Civil service handbook   **351.076**
Heinemann book of African women's poetry   **896**
Heinrich, Bernd, 1940-
Mind of the raven   **598**
The trees in my forest   **577.3**
Heisenberg, Werner, 1901-1976
   See/See also pages in the following book(s):
Brennan, R. P. Heisenberg probably slept here   **920**
Heisenberg probably slept here. Brennan, R. P.   **920**
Heising, Willetta L.
Detecting women   **016.8**
Helbig, Alethea
Dictionary of American children's fiction, 1995-1999   **028.5**
Helen and teacher. Lash, J. P.   **92**
Helicopters
McKinney, M. Chariots of the damned   **356**
Hell
Turner, A. K. The history of hell   **291**
Heller, Barbara R. (Barbara Rita), 1933-
(jt. auth) Kogelman, S. The only math book you'll ever need   **513**
Heller, Jules
(ed) North American women artists of the twentieth century. See North American women artists of the twentieth century   **920.003**
Heller, Nancy G.
(ed) North American women artists of the twentieth century. See North American women artists of the twentieth century   **920.003**
Heller, Robert, 1932-
Essential manager's manual   **658.4**
Hellman, Lillian, 1906-1984
Pentimento   **92**

Hellman, Lillian, 1906-1984—*Continued*
See/See also pages in the following book(s):
Playwrights at work   **812.009**
Helms, Richard
A look over my shoulder   **92**
Heloise
All-new hints from Heloise   **640**
See/See also pages in the following book(s):
Life stories   **920**
Helper, Hinton Rowan, 1829-1909
See/See also pages in the following book(s):
Wilson, E. Patriotic gore p364-79   **810.9**
Helping children with autism learn. Siegel, B.   **371.9**
Helping someone with mental illness. Carter, R.   **616.89**
Helping yourself help others. Carter, R.   **649.8**
Helter skelter. Bugliosi, V.   **364.1**
Helyar, John, 1951-
(jt. auth) Burrough, B. Barbarians at the gate: the fall of RJR Nabisco   **338.8**
Hemings, Sally, 1773-1835
About
Gordon-Reed, A. Thomas Jefferson and Sally Hemings   **92**
Hemingway, Ernest, 1899-1961
The dangerous summer   **791.8**
Death in the afternoon   **791.8**
The Fifth Column [play]
In Hemingway, E. The Fifth Column, and four stories of the Spanish Civil War p3-85   **818**
The Fifth Column, and four stories of the Spanish Civil War   **818**
About
Baker, C. Hemingway: the writer as artist   **813.009**
Bruccoli, M. J. Fitzgerald and Hemingway   **92**
Kert, B. The Hemingway women   **92**
Lynn, K. S. Hemingway   **92**
Mellow, J. R. Hemingway: a life without consequences   **92**
Oliver, C. M. Ernest Hemingway, A to Z   **813.009**
Reynolds, M. S. Hemingway   **92**
See/See also pages in the following book(s):
Kazin, A. An American procession p357-73   **810.9**
Life stories   **920**
Hemingway, Lorian, 1951-
A world turned over   **363.34**
The **Hemingway** women. Kert, B.   **92**
Hemley, Robin, 1958-
Invented Eden   **959.9**
Hemmendinger, David
(ed) Encyclopedia of computer science. See Encyclopedia of computer science   **004**
Hemming, John, 1935-
The conquest of the Incas   **985**
Hempelman, R.
(jt. auth) Osselton, N. E. The new Routledge Dutch dictionary   **439.3**
Hemphill, Ian
The spice and herb bible   **641.3**
Henderson, Bill, 1941-
(ed) The Publish-it-yourself handbook. See The Publish-it-yourself handbook   **070.5**
(ed) The Pushcart prize . . . : best of the small presses. See The Pushcart prize . . . : best of the small presses   **810.8**
Henderson, Elizabeth Connell
Understanding addiction   **362.29**
Henderson, Harry, 1951-
Capital punishment   **364.66**
Encyclopedia of computer science and technology   **004**
Gun control   **363.3**

Privacy in the information age   **323.44**
Henderson, Helene, 1963-
(ed) Domestic violence & child abuse sourcebook. See Domestic violence & child abuse sourcebook   **362.82**
(ed) Holidays, festivals and celebrations of the world dictionary. See Holidays, festivals and celebrations of the world dictionary   **394.26**
(ed) Twentieth-century literary movements dictionary. See Twentieth-century literary movements dictionary   **809**
Henderson, Robert W., 1945-
(jt. auth) Murphy, J. C. Tales of giant snakes   **597.9**
Henderson, William Charles See Henderson, Bill, 1941-
Hendrickson, Paul
The living and the dead   **959.704**
Sons of Mississippi   **305.8**
Hendrickson, Robert, 1933-
The Facts on File dictionary of American regionalisms   **427**
The Facts on File encyclopedia of word and phrase origins   **422.03**
Hendrickson, Susan
See/See also pages in the following book(s):
Malone, J. W. It doesn't take a rocket scientist   **920**
Hendrix, Jimi
About
Murray, C. S. Crosstown traffic: Jimi Hendrix and the post-war rock'n'roll revolution   **92**
Henig, Robin Marantz
The monk in the garden: how Gregor Mendel and his pea plants solved the mystery of inheritance   **92**
Henke, James
(ed) The Rolling Stone illustrated history of rock & roll. See The Rolling Stone illustrated history of rock & roll   **781.66**
Henkes, Robert
The art of black American women   **709.73**
Latin American women artists of the United States   **704**
Hennessey, Maureen Hart
Norman Rockwell   **759.13**
Henry VIII, King of England, 1491-1547
About
Fraser, A. The wives of Henry VIII   **920**
Starkey, D. Six wives: the queens of Henry VIII   **920**
Weir, A. Henry VIII   **92**
Weir, A. The six wives of Henry VIII   **920**
See/See also pages in the following book(s):
Weir, A. The children of Henry VIII   **920**
Henry, Shannon
The Dinner Club   **338.7**
Henry David Thoreau [critical essays]   **818**
Henry David Thoreau's Walden   **818**
Henry Doubleday Research Association
Rodale's illustrated encyclopedia of organic gardening. See Rodale's illustrated encyclopedia of organic gardening   **635.9**
Henry Ford and the Jews. Baldwin, N.   **92**
Henry IV. Pirandello, L.
In Pirandello, L. Naked masks p139-208   **852**
Henry Miller on writing. Miller, H.   **818**
Hen's teeth and horse's toes. Gould, S. J.   **576.8**
Henschke, Claudia I.
Lung cancer   **616.99**
Hensperger, Beth
The best quick breads   **641.8**
The bread lover's bread machine cookbook   **641.8**
Hentoff, Nat
Listen to the stories   **781.65**
Hepatitis See Liver—Diseases

Hepburn, Audrey, 1929-1993
About
Walker, A. Audrey | 92
Hepburn, Katharine, 1907-2003
Me | 92
About
Berg, A. S. Kate remembered | 92
Leaming, B. Katharine Hepburn | 92
See/See also pages in the following book(s):
Ware, S. Letter to the world | 920
Heppenheimer, T. A., 1947-
Countdown | 629.4
First flight | 629.13
Her dream of dreams: the rise and triumph of Madam
C.J. Walker. Lowry, B. | 92
Her husband's mother. Terence
In Terence. Terence, the comedies | 872
Her little majesty: the life of Queen Victoria. Erickson,
C. | 92
Heracles (Legendary character) *See* Hercules (Legendary character)
Herald, Diana Tixier
Genreflecting | 016.8
Herb gardening
Bown, D. New encyclopedia of herbs & their uses | 581.6
Cuthbertson, Y. Beginners' guide to herb gardening | 635
Silber, M. Growing herbs and vegetables | 635
Taylor's guide to vegetables & herbs | 635.9
Herb Gardner: the collected plays and the screenplay
Who is Harry Kellerman and why is he saying those
terrible things about me? Gardner, H. | 812
Herb Society of America
Bown, D. New encyclopedia of herbs & their uses | 581.6
Herbal medicine *See* Medical botany
Herbeck, Dan
(jt. auth) Michel, L. American terrorist: Timothy
McVeigh and the Oklahoma City bombing | 92
Herbert, Rosemary
(ed) The Oxford companion to crime and mystery writing. See The Oxford companion to crime and mystery writing | 809.3
Herbert, Victor
See/See also pages in the following book(s):
Green, S. The world of musical comedy | 920
Herbert, Zbigniew
See/See also pages in the following book(s):
Heaney, S. Finders keepers p167-83 | 821
Miłosz, C. To begin where I am p352-70 | 891.8
Herbs
Bown, D. New encyclopedia of herbs & their uses | 581.6
Hemphill, I. The spice and herb bible | 641.3
Rinzler, C. A. The new complete book of herbs,
spices, and condiments | 641.3
Rodale's illustrated encyclopedia of herbs | 635
Seymour, M. A brief history of thyme and other herbs | 635
Therapeutic use
Graedon, J. The people's pharmacy guide to home and
herbal remedies | 615
Karch, S. B. The consumer's guide to herbal medicine | 615
Herbst, Philip
Talking terrorism | 303.6
Hercegovina *See* Bosnia and Hercegovina
Hercules (Legendary character)
See/See also pages in the following book(s):
Hamilton, E. Mythology p224-43 | 292
Poetry
Carson, A. Autobiography of red | 811
Here be dragons. Koerner, D. | 576.8
Here but not here. Ross, L. | 92

Here I stand. Robeson, P. | 305.8
Here I stand: a life of Martin Luther. Bainton, R. H. | 92
Hereditary succession *See* Inheritance and succession
Heredity
See also Gene mapping
Darwin, C. The origin of species | 576.8
Heredity and environment *See* Nature and nurture
Hérelle, Félix d', 1873-1949
See/See also pages in the following book(s):
Malone, J. W. It doesn't take a rocket scientist | 920
The **heritage** of America. See Witness to America | 973
A **heritage** of wings. Knott, R. C. | 359.9
Herken, Gregg, 1947-
Brotherhood of the bomb | 920
Herlihy, David, 1930-1991
The black death and the transformation of the west | 940.1
Herman, Arthur, 1956-
How the Scots invented the modern world | 941.1
The idea of decline in Western history | 909.08
Joseph McCarthy | 92
Herman, Jeff, 1958-
Jeff Herman's guide to book publishers, editors, & literary agents | 070.5
Herman, Lewis
American dialects | 427
Herman, Linda
(ed) When Parkinson's strikes early. See When Parkinson's strikes early | 616.8
Herman, Marguerite Shalett
(jt. auth) Herman, L. American dialects | 427
Hermetic art and philosophy *See* Alchemy
Hermit crabs *See* Crabs
Hermitage (Saint Petersburg, Russia)
Kostenevich, A. G. French art treasures at the Hermitage | 709.44
Hermite, Charles, 1822-1901
See/See also pages in the following book(s):
Bell, E. T. Men of mathematics p448-65 | 920
Hermits
Colegate, I. A pelican in the wilderness | 291.4
Hermsen, Josée
The horse encyclopedia | 636.1
Hernon, Peter, 1944-
U.S. government on the Web | 025.04
Herodotus
See/See also pages in the following book(s):
Hamilton, E. The Greek way p159-82 | 880.9
Heroes and heroines
Encyclopedia of American war heroes | 920.003
Seal, G. Encyclopedia of folk heroes | 398.03
See/See also pages in the following book(s):
Boorstin, D. J. The Americans: The national experience p327-62 | 973
Heroines *See* Heroes and heroines
Heroism *See* Courage
Herrera, Hayden
Frida: a biography of Frida Kahlo | 92
Herrick, Robert, 1591-1674
See/See also pages in the following book(s):
Brooks, C. The well wrought urn | 821.009
Herring, Mary A.
(ed) Blackwell complementary and alternative medicine. See Blackwell complementary and alternative medicine | 615.5
Herrington, Stuart A., 1941-
Traitors among us | 327.12
Herriot, James
All creatures great and small | 92
James Herriot's animal stories | 636.089
James Herriot's cat stories | 636.8
James Herriot's dog stories | 636.7

Herriot, James—*Continued*
James Herriot's Yorkshire   **914.2**
About
Wight, J. The real James Herriot   **92**
Herrmann, Dorothy
Helen Keller   **92**
Hersey, John, 1914-1993
Blues   **799.1**
Hiroshima   **940.54**
Hershey, Milton Snavely, 1857-1945
About
Brenner, J. G. The emperors of chocolate   **338.7**
Hershey Foods Corp.
Brenner, J. G. The emperors of chocolate   **338.7**
Hershiser, Orel
See/See also pages in the following book(s):
Will, G. F. Men at work: the craft of baseball p77-159   **796.357**
Hertog, Susan
Anne Morrow Lindbergh   **92**
Hertz, Zygmunt
See/See also pages in the following book(s):
Miłosz, C. To begin where I am p169-84   **891.8**
Herzegovina *See* Bosnia and Hercegovina
Herzl, Theodor, 1860-1904
About
Peres, S. The imaginary voyage   **956.94**
Herzog, Chaim, 1918-1997
The Arab-Israeli wars   **956**
Heschel, Abraham Joshua, 1907-1972
The prophets   **224**
Heskett, John
Toothpicks and logos   **745.2**
Heslop-Harrison, J. W.
About
Sabbagh, K. A Rum affair   **580**
Hesse, Karen
See/See also pages in the following book(s):
The Newbery & Caldecott medal books, 1986-2000 p295-305   **028.5**
Hessel, Ingo
Inuit art   **704**
Hessenbruch, Arne
(ed) Reader's guide to the history of science. *See* Reader's guide to the history of science   **509**
Hessler, Peter, 1969-
River town   **951**
Hewetson, Ann
The stolen child   **616.89**
Hewitt, Don, 1922-
Tell me a story   **92**
Hewitt, Terry
The complete book of cacti & succulents   **635.9**
Hewlett, J. Monroe (James Monroe), 1868-1941
See/See also pages in the following book(s):
White, S. Stories of freedom in Black New York   **974.7**
Hewlett, James Monroe *See* Hewlett, J. Monroe (James Monroe), 1868-1941
Hewlett, Sylvia Ann, 1946-
The war against parents   **649**
Heyerdahl, Thor
Kon-Tiki: across the Pacific by raft   **910.4**
Heymann, C. David (Clemens David), 1945-
The Georgetown ladies' social club   **305.4**
Heymann, Clemens David *See* Heymann, C. David (Clemens David), 1945-
Hibbert, Arthur Raymond *See* Hibbert, Christopher, 1924-
Hibbert, Christopher, 1924-
The House of Medici   **920**
Nelson   **92**
Queen Victoria   **92**
Redcoats and rebels   **973.3**
The virgin queen: Elizabeth I   **92**

Wellington   **92**
Hickam, Homer H., 1943-
The Coalwood way   **92**
Rocket boys   **92**
Hickey, Michael, 1929-
The Korean War   **951.9**
Hickock, Richard, 1931-1965
About
Capote, T. In cold blood   **364.1**
Hickok, Ralph
The encyclopedia of North American sports history   **796**
Hicks, George, 1936-
The comfort women   **940.54**
Hicks, Greg, 1953-
(jt. auth) Foster, R. How we choose to be happy   **158**
The **hidden** face of God. Schroeder, G. L.   **215**
Hidden history. Boorstin, D. J.   **973**
Hidden in plain view. Tobin, J.   **973.7**
The **hidden** Jesus. Spoto, D.   **232.9**
Hidden minds. Tallis, F.   **154.2**
Hidden power. Marton, K.   **920**
Hidden symbols in art. Carr-Gomm, S.   **704.9**
Hidden treasures. Keno, L.   **749.2**
Hidden value. O'Reilly, C. A., III   **658**
The **hidden** Wordsworth. Johnston, K. R.   **92**
Hidy Ochiai's complete book of self-defense. Ochiai, H.   **796.8**
Hieroglyphics
See also Picture writing; Rosetta stone inscription
Roth, A. M. Hieroglyphs without mystery   **493**
See/See also pages in the following book(s):
Ceram, C. W. Gods, graves, and scholars p99-116   **930.1**
Connell, E. S. The Aztec treasure house p123-66   **814**
Hieroglyphs without mystery. Roth, A. M.   **493**
Higdon, Hal
Marathon: the ultimate training guide   **796.42**
Higgins, Kathleen Marie
(jt. auth) Solomon, R. C. A passion for wisdom   **109**
(jt. auth) Solomon, R. C. What Nietzsche really said   **193**
Higginson, William J., 1938-
The haiku handbook   **808.1**
High and mighty. Bradsher, K.   **629.2**
High-carbohydrate diet
Shintani, T. The good carbohydrate revolution   **613.2**
The **high** cost of dying. Young, G. W.   **393**
High school equivalency examination
How to prepare for the GED high school equivalency examination   **373.1**
Master the GED   **373.1**
High school libraries
See also Young adults' libraries
Catalogs
Senior high school library catalog   **011.6**
High season. Kanigel, R.   **944**
High tech *See* Technology
High tech harvest. Lurquin, P. F.   **631.5**
High technology industry
Esser, T. The venture cafe   **620**
Higher education
See also Colleges and universities
Bloom, A. D. The closing of the American mind   **973.92**
Levine, L. W. The opening of the American mind   **001.1**
Women in higher education   **378**
See/See also pages in the following book(s):
Boorstin, D. J. The Americans: The democratic experience   **973**

Highfield, Roger
The science of Harry Potter   500
Highways *See* Roads
Higonnet, Anne, 1959-
Berthe Morisot   92
Hijacking of airplanes
Longman, J. Among the heroes   974.8
Hiking
   See also Walking
Solnit, R. Wanderlust   796.51
Hileman, Victoria Armour- *See* Armour-Hileman, Victoria, 1958-
Hill, A. J.
Under pressure   910.4
Hill, Geoffrey
The orchards of Syon   821
The triumph of love   821
Hill, Helen Walker- *See* Walker-Hill, Helen
Hill, Joan C. V.
(jt. auth) Beaser, R. S. The Joslin guide to diabetes   616.4
Hill, Lewis, 1924-
Bulbs   635.9
Hill, Nancy
(jt. auth) Hill, L. Bulbs   635.9
Hill, Philip G. (Philip George), 1934-
(ed) Our dramatic heritage. See Our dramatic heritage v4-6   808.82
Hill, Samuel S.
(jt. auth) Mead, F. S. Handbook of denominations in the United States   280
Hillary's choice [biography of Hillary Rodham Clinton] Sheehy, G.   92
Hillenbrand, Laura
Seabiscuit   798.4
Hillerman, Tony
Seldom disappointed   92
Hillier, Malcolm
Container gardening through the year   635.9
Flowers   745.92
The **Hillier** gardener's guide to trees & shrubs   635.9
Hillman, Brenda
Cascadia   811
Hillman, James
The force of character   155.67
Hillstrom, Kevin
(ed) Contemporary women artists. See Contemporary women artists   920.003
(ed) Encyclopedia of small business. See Encyclopedia of small business   658
Hillstrom, Laurie
(ed) Contemporary women artists. See Contemporary women artists   920.003
(ed) Encyclopedia of small business. See Encyclopedia of small business   658
Hilton, Walter, 1340-1396
   About
Armstrong, K. Visions of God   248.2
Him, Chanrithy, 1965-
When broken glass floats   92
Himalaya Mountains
Keay, J. The great arc   526
   Description
Matthiessen, P. The snow leopard   915.4
   Natural history
   See Natural history—Himalaya Mountains
Himelstein, Shmuel, 1940-
The New encyclopedia of Judaism. See The New encyclopedia of Judaism [New York University Press]   296.03
Himes, Chester, 1909-1984
   About
Sallis, J. Chester Himes   92

Himmelfarb, Gertrude
The de-moralization of society   303.3
Himmler, Heinrich, 1900-1945
   About
Breitman, R. The architect of genocide: Himmler and the final solution   92
Hindi language
   Dictionaries
The Oxford Hindi-English dictionary   491
Hindle, Tim
(jt. auth) Heller, R. Essential manager's manual   658.4
Hinds, P. Mignon
(ed) Essence total makeover. See Essence total makeover   646.7
Hinduism
Basham, A. L. The origins and development of classical Hinduism   294.5
Klostermaier, K. K. Hinduism   294.5
Hine, Andrea
(jt. auth) Marti, J. The alternative health & medicine encyclopedia   615.5
Hine, Lewis Wickes, 1874-1940
   See/See also pages in the following book(s):
Bustard, B. I. Picturing the century   779
Hine, Robert
(ed) The Facts on File dictionary of cell and molecular biology. See The Facts on File dictionary of cell and molecular biology   571.6
Hine, Thomas, 1947-
The rise and fall of the American teenager   305.23
Hines, R. P. T. Davenport- *See* Davenport-Hines, R. P. T. (Richard Peter Treadwell), 1953-
Hiney, Tom, 1970-
Raymond Chandler   92
The **hinge** of fate. Churchill, Sir W.   940.53
Hinton, Milt, 1910-2000
   See/See also pages in the following book(s):
Lees, G. You can't steal a gift   920
Hip hop America. George, N.   781.64
Hipple, Theodore W.
(ed) Writers for young adults. See Writers for young adults   920.003
Hippolytus. Euripides
   In Euripides. Ten plays p67-98   882
Hiro, Dilip
A dictionary of the Middle East   956
The longest war   955
Hirohito, Emperor of Japan, 1901-1989
   About
Bix, H. P. Hirohito and the making of modern Japan   92
   See/See also pages in the following book(s):
Seagrave, S. The Yamato dynasty   952
Hirohito and the making of modern Japan. Bix, H. P.   92
Hiroshima (Japan)
   Bombardment, 1945
Alperovitz, G. The decision to use the atomic bomb and the architecture of an American myth   940.54
Greene, B. Duty   940.54
Hersey, J. Hiroshima   940.54
Lifton, R. J. Hiroshima in America   940.54
Smith, J. B. The last mission   940.54
Takaki, R. T. Hiroshima   940.54
Hiroshima in America. Lifton, R. J.   940.54
Hirsch, E. D. (Eric Donald), 1928-
The new dictionary of cultural literacy   031
The schools we need and why we don't have them   370
Hirsch, Edward
Earthly measures   811
How to read a poem   808.1

Hirsch, Edward—*Continued*
Lay back the darkness   **811**
On love   **811**
Hirsch, Eric Donald *See* Hirsch, E. D. (Eric Donald),
    1928-
Hirsch, Foster
Kurt Weill on stage   **92**
Hirsch, James S.
Hurricane: the miraculous journey of Rubin Carter
    92
Riot and remembrance   **976.6**
Hirschfeld, Al, 1903-2003
Hirschfeld on line   **741.5**
       About
Bell, C. Hirschfeld's New York   **741.5**
Leopold, D. Hirschfeld's Hollywood   **741.5**
Hirschfeld on line. Hirschfeld, A.   **741.5**
Hirschfelder, Arlene B.
The encyclopedia of Native American religions
    299
Native American   **970.004**
Hirschfeld's Hollywood. Leopold, D.   **741.5**
Hirschfeld's New York. Bell, C.   **741.5**
Hirschman, Leigh Ann
(jt. auth) Dillard, J. The chronic pain solution
    616
Hirsh-Pasek, Kathy
(jt. auth) Golinkoff, R. M. How babies talk   **401**
Hirshberg, Charles
(jt. auth) Zwonitzer, M. Will you miss me when I'm
gone?   **920**
Hirshfeld, Alan
Parallax   **523.8**
Hirshson, Stanley P., 1928-
General Patton: a soldier's life   **92**
Hirtle, Sheila
(jt. auth) De Villiers, M. Sahara: a natural history
    508
Hischak, Thomas
The American musical film song encyclopedia
    782.42
American theatre: a chronicle of comedy and drama,
1969-2000   **792**
The Tin Pan Alley song encyclopedia   **782.42**
The **Hispanic** American almanac   **305.8**
Hispanic American art
Henkes, R. Latin American women artists of the Unit-
ed States   **704**
St. James guide to Hispanic artists   **920.003**
Hispanic Americans
The Hispanic American almanac   **305.8**
Morales, E. Living in Spanglish   **305.8**
Olmos, E. J. Americanos   **305.8**
Rodriguez, R. Brown: the last discovery of America
    305.8
       Dictionaries
Dictionary of Hispanic biography   **920.003**
Meier, M. S. Notable Latino Americans   **920.003**
Hispanic Americans and libraries *See* Libraries and
Hispanic Americans
Hispanic literature criticism   **860.9**
Hiss, Alger
       About
Hiss, T. The view from Alger's window   **92**
See/See also pages in the following book(s):
Geis, G. Crimes of the century   **345**
Haynes, J. E. Venona   **327.12**
Hiss, Tony
The view from Alger's window   **92**
Historic buildings
See also Literary landmarks
Historic landmarks of black America. Cantor, G.
    917.3
Historic sites
Amery, C. Vanishing histories   **363.6**

Cantor, G. Historic landmarks of black America
    917.3
Curtis, N. C. Black heritage sites   **917.3**
Ferris, G. W. Presidential places   **917.3**
Loewen, J. W. Lies across America   **973**
National Geographic guide to America's historic places
    917.3
Parks directory of the United States   **917.3**
Wilson, C. The atlas of holy places & sacred sites
    291.3
Wood, M. In the footsteps of Alexander the Great
    938
The **Historical** and cultural atlas of African Americans.
See Asante, M. K. The African-American atlas
    305.8
Historical atlas of Central Europe. Magocsi, P. R.
    911
Historical atlas of East Central Europe. See Magocsi, P.
R. Historical atlas of Central Europe   **911**
The **historical** atlas of New York City. Homberger, E.
    974.7
Historical atlas of religion in America. See Gaustad, E.
S. New historical atlas of religion in America
    200.9
Historical atlas of the American West. Beck, W. A.
    911
A **Historical** atlas of the Jewish people   **909**
Historical atlas of the United States   **911**
Historical atlases
Atlas of world history   **911**
Beck, W. A. Historical atlas of the American West
    911
Hammond atlas of world history   **911**
Historical chronology
Grun, B. The timetables of history   **902**
Holidays and anniversaries of the world   **394.26**
The Timetables of American history   **902**
The Wilson calendar of world history   **902**
Historical dictionary of Buddhism. Prebish, C. S.
    294.3
Historical dictionary of terrorism. Anderson, S.
    303.6
Historical dictionary of the Persian Gulf War, 1990-
1991. Newell, C. R.   **956.7**
Historical encyclopedia of American labor   **331.8**
Historical fiction
       Bibliography
Adamson, L. G. American historical fiction
    016.813
Adamson, L. G. World historical fiction   **016.8**
The **historical** figure of Jesus. Sanders, E. P.   **232.9**
Historical geology *See* Stratigraphic geology
Historical tables, 58 BC-AD 1985. See The Wilson cal-
endar of world history   **902**
Historiography
See also Africa—Historiography; United States—
Historiography
Assmann, J. The mind of Egypt   **932**
Hobsbawm, E. J. On history   **901**
McKillop, A. B. The spinster & the prophet
    941.08
Schama, S. Dead certainties   **907**
Tuchman, B. W. Practicing history   **907**
History
See also Ancient history; Conspiracies; Military
history; Naval history; World history
Wright, R. NonZero   **303.4**
       Miscellanea
Aron, P. Unsolved mysteries of history   **902**
Shenkman, R. Legends, lies & cherished myths of
world history   **902**
       Outlines, syllabi, etc.
Encyclopedia of world history   **903**
       Philosophy
Berlin, Sir I. The sense of reality   **901**

History—Philosophy—*Continued*
Bloom, H. The Lucifer principle   **128**
Gaddis, J. L. The landscape of history   **901**
Spengler, O. The decline of the West   **901**
Toynbee, A. A study of history   **909**
       Study and teaching
Lefkowitz, M. R. Not out of Africa   **960**
Nash, G. B. History on trial   **907**
History, Ancient *See* Ancient history
History, Modern *See* Modern history
The **history**. Tacitus, C.
    In Tacitus, C. The complete works of Tacitus p419-
    673   **878**
The **history** and folklore of North American wildflowers.
    Coffey, T.   **582.13**
History of AIDS. Grmek, M. D.   **616.97**
History of art. Janson, H. W.   **709**
A **History** of art in Africa   **709.6**
History of astronomy   **520.3**
The **history** of Australia. Clarke, F. G.   **994**
A **history** of Britain. Schama, S.   **941**
A **history** of Christianity. Chadwick, O.   **270**
A **History** of civilization   **909**
A **history** of civilizations. Braudel, F.   **909**
A **history** of costume in the West. See Boucher, F.
    20,000 years of fashion   **391**
A **history** of Far Eastern art. Lee, S. E.   **709.5**
The **history** of furniture. Morley, J.   **749.2**
A **history** of God. Armstrong, K.   **291**
The **history** of hell. Turner, A. K.   **291**
A **history** of invention. Williams, T. I.   **609**
A **history** of Iraq. Tripp, C.   **956.7**
A **history** of Israel. Sachar, H. M.   **956.94**
The **history** of Japan. Perez, L. G.   **952**
The **history** of jazz. Gioia, T.   **781.65**
A **history** of mathematics. Boyer, C. B.   **510**
The **history** of Mexico. Kirkwood, B.   **972**
History of modern science and mathematics   **509**
A **history** of molecular biology. Morange, M.   **572.8**
A **history** of narrative film. Cook, D. A.   **791.43**
The **history** of pirates. Konstam, A.   **910.4**
History of Plymouth Plantation. See Bradford, W. Of
    Plymouth Plantation, 1620-1647   **974.4**
The **history** of Polish literature. Miłosz, C.   **891.8**
A **History** of private life   **909**
A **history** of psychiatry. Shorter, E.   **616.89**
A **history** of religious ideas. Eliade, M.   **291**
A **history** of Russia. Riasanovsky, N. V.   **947**
A **history** of Russian literature. Terras, V.   **891.7**
The **History** of science and religion in the western tradi-
    tion   **291.1**
The **History** of science in the United States   **509**
The **history** of shipwrecks. Konstam, A.   **910.4**
A **history** of South Africa. Thompson, L. M.   **968**
The **history** of television, 1942 to 2000. Abramson, A.
    621.388
A **history** of the Arab peoples. Hourani, A. H.   **909**
A **history** of the British Isles. Black, J.   **941**
History of the conquest of Mexico. Prescott, W. H.
    972
History of the conquest of Peru. Prescott, W. H.
    985
A **history** of the devil. Messadié, G.   **291**
A **history** of the Federal Reserve v1. Meltzer, A. H.
    332.1
History of the Internet   **004.6**
A **history** of the Jews. Johnson, P.   **909**
A **history** of the Jews in America. Sachar, H. M.
    305.8
History of the mass media in the United States
    302.23
A **history** of the Ostrogoths. Burns, T. S.   **909.07**
The **history** of the Peloponnesian War. Thucydides
    938
History of the present. Garton Ash, T.   **940.55**

History of the psychoanalytic movement. Freud, S.
    In Freud, S. The basic writings of Sigmund Freud
    150.19
History of the theatre. Brockett, O. G.   **792.09**
A **history** of the Third Reich. Hay, J.   **943.086**
History of the twentieth century. Gilbert, M.
    909.82
History of the U.S. Navy. Love, R. W.   **359**
A **history** of the wife. Yalom, M.   **306.8**
A **history** of twentieth-century Russia. Service, R.
    947.086
History of United States naval operations in World War
    II. Morison, S. E.   **940.54**
A **history** of Venice. Norwich, J. J.   **945**
A **history** of Wales. Davies, J.   **942.9**
A **history** of Western music. Grout, D. J.   **780.9**
A **history** of Western philosophy. Russell, B.   **109**
A **History** of women in the United States: state-by-state
    reference   **305.4**
A **history** of Zionism. Laqueur, W.   **956.94**
History on trial. Nash, G. B.   **907**
The **History** today companion to British history. See The
    Columbia companion to British history   **941**
Hitchcock, Alfred, 1899-1980
       About
Auiler, D. Vertigo   **791.43**
Spoto, D. The dark side of genius   **92**
Hitchcock, H. Wiley (Hugh Wiley), 1923-
(ed) The New Grove dictionary of American music.
    See The New Grove dictionary of American music
    780.973
Hitchcock, Hugh Wiley *See* Hitchcock, H. Wiley (Hugh
    Wiley), 1923-
Hitchens, Christopher
Vanity Fair's Hollywood. See Vanity Fair's Hollywood
    791.43
Why Orwell matters   **828**
Hite, Shere
The Hite report on the family   **306.8**
The **Hite** report on the family. Hite, S.   **306.8**
Hitler, Adolf, 1889-1945
Mein Kampf   **92**
       About
Bullock, A. Hitler and Stalin   **92**
Fest, J. C. Plotting Hitler's death   **943.086**
Fischer, K. P. Nazi Germany   **943.086**
Fleming, G. Hitler and the final solution   **943.086**
Kershaw, I. Hitler   **92**
Pool, J. Hitler and his secret partners   **943.086**
Rosenbaum, R. Explaining Hitler   **92**
Speer, A. Inside the Third Reich   **943.086**
Toland, J. Adolf Hitler   **92**
Turner, H. A. Hitler's thirty days to power
    943.086

See/See also pages in the following book(s):
Breitman, R. The architect of genocide: Himmler and
    the final solution   **92**
Cornwell, J. Hitler's pope: the secret history of Pius
    XII   **92**
Craig, G. A. The Germans p61-80   **943**
Fulbrook, M. A concise history of Germany p173-203
    943
Kissinger, H. Diplomacy p288-318; 350-68
    327.73
Rees, L. War of the century   **940.54**
Shirer, W. L. The rise and fall of the Third Reich
    943.086
Hitler and his secret partners. Pool, J.   **943.086**
Hitler and Stalin. Bullock, A.   **92**
Hitler and the final solution. Fleming, G.   **943.086**
Hitler's children. Rempel, G.   **943.086**
Hitler's pope: the secret history of Pius XII. Cornwell,
    J.   **92**
Hitler's thirty days to power. Turner, H. A.
    943.086

Hitler's U-boat war. Blair, C. 940.54
Hitter: the life and turmoils of Ted Williams. Linn, E. 92
HIV disease *See* AIDS (Disease)
Hively, Will
(jt. auth) Ballard, R. D. The eternal darkness 551.46
Hiyoshi, Sa-ami Yasukiyo *See* Hiyoshi, Yasukiyo
Hiyoshi, Yasukiyo
Benkei on the bridge
In Waley, A. The Nō plays of Japan 895.6
Hizer, David V.
(jt. auth) Rosenberg, A. D. The resume handbook 650.14
Ho, Chí Minh, 1890-1969
About
Duiker, W. J. Ho Chi Minh 92
Hoad, T. F.
(ed) The Concise Oxford dictionary of English etymology. See The Concise Oxford dictionary of English etymology 422.03
Hoadley, R. Bruce, 1933-
Understanding wood 684
Hoagland, Edward
Tigers & ice 814
Hoagland, Mahlon B., 1921-
The way life works 570
Hoare, Philip
Noël Coward 92
Hoban, Tana
See/See also pages in the following book(s):
Marcus, L. S. Ways of telling 741.6
Hobbes, Thomas, 1588-1679
Leviathan 320.1
See/See also pages in the following book(s):
Durant, W. J. The age of Louis XIV p548-64 940.2
Russell, B. A history of Western philosophy p546-57 109
Hobo: a young man's thoughts on trains and tramping in America. Cotton, E. J. 92
Hobsbawm, E. J. (Eric J.), 1917-
The age of revolution, 1789-1848 940.2
On history 901
Hobsbawm, Eric J. *See* Hobsbawm, E. J. (Eric J.), 1917-
Hobson, J. Allan
Out of its mind 616.89
Hobson, John Atkinson, 1858-1940
See/See also pages in the following book(s):
Heilbroner, R. L. The worldly philosophers 330.1
Hochman, Gloria
(jt. auth) Duke, P. A brilliant madness 616.89
Hochschild, Adam, 1942-
King Leopold's ghost 967.5
The unquiet ghost 947.084
Hockey
Duplacey, J. The official rules of hockey 796.962
Hockney, David
Secret knowledge 751
Hodder, Alan D.
Thoreau's ecstatic witness 818
Hodder, Honna Janes- *See* Janes-Hodder, Honna, 1966-
Hodge, Francis
Play directing 792
Hodges' Harbrace handbook 808
Hodgson, Godfrey
The gentleman from New York: Daniel Patrick Moynihan: a biography 92
Hodgson, Larry
Perennials for every purpose 635.9
Hoerschelmann, Antonia
(ed) Munch, E. Edvard Munch: theme and variation 760
Hoffa, James Riddle *See* Hoffa, Jimmy

Hoffa, Jimmy
About
Russell, T. Out of the jungle: Jimmy Hoffa and the remaking of the American working class 92
Hoffer, Peter Charles
The Salem witchcraft trials 345
(jt. auth) Hull, N. E. H. Roe v. Wade 344
Hoffman, Abbie
The best of Abbie Hoffman 303.4
Hoffman, Donald D.
Visual intelligence 152.14
Hoffman, Ian
(jt. auth) Stober, D. A convenient spy 327.12
Hoffman, M. Lee
(ed) Day, C. L. The art of knotting & splicing 623.88
Hoffman, Matthew
(ed) The Doctor's book of home remedies for dogs and cats. See The Doctor's book of home remedies for dogs and cats 636.7
(ed) Dogs: the ultimate care guide. See Dogs: the ultimate care guide 636.7
Hoffman, Miles
The NPR classical music companion 780.3
Hoffmann, Gretchen McCord
Copyright in cyberspace 346.04
Hofmann, Josef, 1876-1957
See/See also pages in the following book(s):
Schonberg, H. C. The great pianists 920
Hofmann, Mark
About
Worrall, S. The poet and the murderer 364.1
Hofmann, Werner, 1928-
Goya: to every story there belongs another 759.6
Hofrichter, Robert
(ed) Amphibians: the world of frogs, toads, salamanders and newts. See Amphibians: the world of frogs, toads, salamanders and newts 597.8
Hofstadter, Richard, 1916-1970
The age of reform from Bryan to F.D.R. 973.91
The American political tradition, and the men who made it 973
Hogan, Linda
The woman who watches over the world 92
See/See also pages in the following book(s):
Coltelli, L. Winged words: American Indian writers speak 897
Hogarth, William, 1697-1764
About
Uglow, J. S. Hogarth 92
Hogwood, Christopher
Handel 92
The **Hōka** priests. Komparu, Z.
In Waley, A. The Nō plays of Japan 895.6
Holden, Alan
Crystals and crystal growing 548
Holden, Amanda
(ed) The New Penguin opera guide. See The New Penguin opera guide 792.5
Holden, Andrew, 1964-
Jehovah's Witnesses 289.9
Holden, Anthony, 1947-
William Shakespeare 822.3
Holder, R. W.
How not to say what you mean 423
A **hole** in the heart of the world. Kaufman, J. 947
The **hole** in the universe. Cole, K. C. 530
Holiday, Billie, 1915-1959
About
Clarke, D. Wishing on the moon: the life and times of Billie Holiday 92
Griffin, F. J. If you can't be free, be a mystery: in search of Billie Holiday 92
Nicholson, S. Billie Holiday 92

Holiday, Billie, 1915-1959—About—*Continued*
O'Meally, R. G. Lady Day: the many faces of Billie
Holiday   **92**
See/See also pages in the following book(s):
Feather, L. From Satchmo to Miles   **920**
Holiday symbols. See Thompson, S. E. Holiday symbols
and customs   **394.26**
Holiday symbols and customs. Thompson, S. E.
   394.26
Holidays
     See also Christmas; New Year; Religious holidays
The American book of days   **394.26**
Chase's calendar of events   **394.26**
The Folklore of the American holidays   **394.26**
The Folklore of world holidays   **394.26**
Holidays and anniversaries of the world   **394.26**
Holidays, festivals and celebrations of the world dictio-
nary   **394.26**
Thompson, S. E. Holiday symbols and customs
   394.26
              Bibliography
World holiday, festival, and calendar books
   016.39426
Holidays, Jewish *See* Jewish holidays
Holidays and anniversaries of the world   **394.26**
Holidays, festivals and celebrations of the world dictio-
nary   **394.26**
Holistic medicine
Chopra, D. Ageless body, timeless mind   **612.6**
Lown, B. The lost art of healing   **610**
Holland *See* Netherlands
Hollander, John
Figurehead & other poems   **811**
Selected poetry   **811**
(ed) American poetry: the nineteenth century. See
American poetry: the nineteenth century
   811.008
(ed) Christmas poems. See Christmas poems
   821.008
(ed) The Literature of Renaissance England. See The
Literature of Renaissance England   **820.8**
Hollander, Robert, 1933-
Dante   **92**
Hölldobler, Bert, 1936-
The ants   **595.7**
Journey to the ants   **595.7**
Holler if you hear me: searching for Tupac Shakur.
Dyson, M. E.   **92**
Holley, Val
James Dean   **92**
Holliday, Laurel, 1946-
(comp) Children in the Holocaust and World War II.
See Children in the Holocaust and World War II
   940.53
Hollom, P. A. D. (Philip Arthur Dominic)
(jt. auth) Peterson, R. T. A field guide to the birds of
Britain and Europe   **598**
Hollom, Philip Arthur Dominic *See* Hollom, P. A. D.
(Philip Arthur Dominic)
The hollow. Christie, A.
In Christie, A. The mousetrap and other plays
   822
Hollywood cartoons. Barrier, J. M.   **791.43**
Holmes, George, 1927-
The Oxford history of medieval Europe. See The Ox-
ford history of medieval Europe   **940.1**
(ed) The Oxford history of Italy. See The Oxford his-
tory of Italy   **945**
Holmes, H. H. *See* Mudgett, Herman W., 1861-1896
Holmes, Hannah, 1963-
The secret life of dust   **551.51**
Holmes, Oliver Wendell, 1841-1935
              About
Menand, L. The Metaphysical Club   **973.9**

See/See also pages in the following book(s):
Commager, H. S. The American mind   **973**
Wilson, E. Patriotic gore p743-96   **810.9**
Holmes, Richard, 1945-
Coleridge: darker reflections, 1804-1834   **92**
Holmes, Richard, 1946-
(ed) The Oxford companion to military history. See
The Oxford companion to military history   **355**
Holmes, Roger
(ed) Taylor's master guide to gardening. See Taylor's
master guide to gardening   **635.9**
Holocaust, 1933-1945
     See also Holocaust survivors; World War, 1939-
1945—Jews
Berenbaum, M. The world must know   **940.53**
Breitman, R. Official secrets   **940.54**
Chesnoff, R. Z. Pack of thieves   **940.53**
The Chronicle of the Łódź ghetto, 1941-1944
   943.8
Cohen, R. The avengers   **940.53**
Dawidowicz, L. S. The war against the Jews, 1933-
1945   **940.53**
Dwork, D. Holocaust: a history   **940.53**
Encyclopedia of the Holocaust   **940.53**
Fleming, G. Hitler and the final solution   **943.086**
Fogelman, E. Conscience & courage   **940.53**
Frank, A. The diary of a young girl: the definitive edi-
tion   **92**
Frank, A. The diary of Anne Frank: the critical edition
   92
Friedländer, S. Nazi Germany and the Jews vl
   940.53
Gies, M. Anne Frank remembered   **940.53**
Gilbert, M. The Holocaust   **940.53**
Gilbert, M. Holocaust journey   **940.53**
Gilbert, M. Never again   **940.53**
Gilbert, M. The Routledge atlas of the Holocaust
   940.53
Glass, J. M. Life unworthy of life   **940.53**
Goldhagen, D. Hitler's willing executioners
   940.53
Goldhagen, D. A moral reckoning   **940.53**
Goldsmith, M. The inextinguishable symphony
   940.53
The Holocaust and history   **940.53**
Kruk, H. The last days of the Jerusalem of Lithuania
   940.53
Langer, L. L. Admitting the Holocaust   **940.53**
Lifton, R. J. The Nazi doctors   **940.53**
Linenthal, E. T. Preserving memory   **940.53**
Müller, M. Anne Frank   **92**
Novick, P. The Holocaust in American life
   940.53
Rhodes, R. Masters of death   **940.53**
Ryback, T. W. The last survivor   **940.53**
Shermer, M. Denying history   **940.53**
Spiegelman, A. Maus   **940.53**
Todorov, T. Facing the extreme   **940.53**
Wiesel, E. And the sea is never full   **92**
The World reacts to the Holocaust   **940.53**
Wouk, H. The will to live on   **296**
Wyman, D. S. The abandonment of the Jews
   940.53
Yahil, L. The Holocaust   **940.53**
Ziegler, J. The Swiss, the gold, and the dead
   940.53
Zuccotti, S. Under his very windows   **940.53**
              Biography
Encyclopedia of Holocaust literature   **809**
              Dictionaries
Epstein, E. J. Dictionary of the Holocaust   **940.53**
              Encyclopedias
Encyclopedia of Jewish life before and during the
Holocaust   **940.53**
Encyclopedia of the Holocaust   **940.53**

Holocaust, 1933-1945—Encyclopedias—*Continued*
The Holocaust encyclopedia   **940.53**
Historiography
Clendinnen, I. Reading the Holocaust   **940.53**
Evans, R. J. Lying about Hitler   **940.53**
Guttenplan, D. D. The Holocaust on trial   **940.53**
Johnson, E. A. Nazi terror   **940.53**
Lipstadt, D. E. Denying the Holocaust   **940.53**
Personal narratives
Art from the ashes   **940.53**
Ba'u, Y. Dear God, have you ever gone hungry?
   940.53
The Buchenwald report   **940.53**
Children in the Holocaust and World War II
   940.53
Denes, M. Castles burning   **940.53**
Encyclopedia of Holocaust literature   **809**
Filar, M. From Buchenwald to Carnegie Hall   **92**
Gilbert, M. The boys   **940.53**
Levi, P. The drowned and the saved   **940.53**
Levi, P. Survival in Auschwitz; and, The reawakening
   940.53
Lindwer, W. The last seven months of Anne Frank
   940.53
Wiesel, E. All rivers run to the sea   **92**
Wiesenthal, S. The sunflower   **179.7**
Witness   **940.53**
Poetry
Holocaust poetry   **808.81**
Holocaust, 1933-1945, in literature
Art from the ashes   **940.53**
Encyclopedia of Holocaust literature   **809**
Holocaust literature: an encyclopedia of writers and
their work   **809**
Langer, L. L. Admitting the Holocaust   **940.53**
Nothing makes you free   **808.8**
The **Holocaust**. Gilbert, M.   **940.53**
The **Holocaust**. Yahil, L.   **940.53**
The **Holocaust** and history   **940.53**
The **Holocaust** encyclopedia   **940.53**
The **Holocaust** in American life. Novick, P.   **940.53**
Holocaust journey. Gilbert, M.   **940.53**
Holocaust literature: an encyclopedia of writers and their
work   **809**
Holocaust Museum (U.S.) *See* United States Holocaust
Memorial Museum
The **Holocaust** on trial. Guttenplan, D. D.   **940.53**
Holocaust poetry   **808.81**
Holocaust survivors
Brenner, M. After the Holocaust   **943.087**
Gilbert, M. The boys   **940.53**
Kaufman, J. A hole in the heart of the world
   947
Nothing makes you free   **808.8**
Holoman, D. Kern, 1947-
Berlioz   **92**
Holroyd, Michael
Basil Street blues   **92**
Works on paper   **809**
Holt, Linda Hughey
(jt. auth) Sears, W. The pregnancy book   **618.2**
Holton, James R.
(ed) Encyclopedia of atmospheric sciences. See Ency-
clopedia of atmospheric sciences   **551.5**
Holton, Wendy M.
(jt. auth) Dalton, K. Depression after childbirth
   616.85
The **Holy** Bible [King James Bible. Oxford Univ. Press]
Bible   **220.5**
The **Holy** Bible: new revised standard version. Bible
   220.5
Holy Bible: the new King James Version. Bible
   220.5
Holy days *See* Religious holidays
Holy Office *See* Inquisition

Holy See *See* Papacy
Holy the firm. Dillard, A.
In Dillard, A. The Annie Dillard reader   **818**
Holy war, Inc. Bergen, P. L.   **958.1**
Homberger, Eric
The historical atlas of New York City   **974.7**
Hombs, Mary Ellen
American homelessness   **362.5**
Home accidents
Warner, M. L. The complete guide to Alzheimer's-
proofing your home   **362.1**
Home and exile. Achebe, C.   **828**
Home-based business
Arden, L. Work-at-home sourcebook   **338.7**
Bredin, A. The virtual office survival handbook
   658
Home bistro. Fussell, B. H.   **641.5**
Home care services
See also Caregivers
Carter, R. Helping yourself help others   **649.8**
Home comforts. Mendelson, C.   **640**
Home decoration *See* Interior design
Home Depot, Inc.
Home improvement 1-2-3. See Home improvement 1-
2-3   **643**
Home economics
See also House cleaning
Bower, L. M. Creating a healthy household   **643**
Heloise. All-new hints from Heloise   **640**
Mendelson, C. Home comforts   **640**
Home economics. Berry, W.   **814**
Home free!. Wilson, L.
In Wilson, L. 21 short plays p1-21   **812**
Home heating and air conditioning systems. Kittle, J. L.
   697
Home improvement 1-2-3   **643**
Home instruction *See* Home schooling
Home lands. Tye, L.   **909**
Home life *See* Family life
Home loans *See* Mortgages
Home nursing
McFarlane, R. The complete bedside companion
   649.8
Home schooling
Rupp, R. The complete home learning sourcebook
   371.04
Home town. Kidder, T.   **974.4**
Home VCR repair illustrated. Wilkins, R. C.
   621.388
Home video systems
Maintenance and repair
Capelo, G. R. VCR troubleshooting & repair
   621.388
Wilkins, R. C. Home VCR repair illustrated
   621.388
Homebuilding pitfalls. Thomas, L.   **690**
The **homecoming**. Pinter, H.   **822**
also in Pinter, H. Complete works v3   **822**
Homeless persons
See also Refugees
Hombs, M. E. American homelessness   **362.5**
Kozol, J. Rachel and her children   **362.5**
Homer
The Iliad   **883**
The odyssey   **883**
See/See also pages in the following book(s):
Finley, M. I. The world of Odysseus   **883**
Homer, William Innes
Stieglitz and the Photo-Secession, 1902   **779**
Homer, Winslow, 1836-1910
About
Cikovsky, N., Jr. Winslow Homer   **759.13**
Ferber, L. S. Masters of color and light   **759.13**

Homicide
See also Trials (Homicide)
Brown, E. The condemnation of Little B   **364.1**
Bugliosi, V. Helter skelter   **364.1**
Capote, T. In cold blood   **364.1**
Carrère, E. The adversary   **364.1**
Cornwell, P. D. Portrait of a killer   **364.1**
Douglas, J. E. The cases that haunt us   **364.1**
Flook, M. Invisible Eden   **364.1**
Gourevitch, P. A cold case   **364.1**
Jones, A. Women who kill   **364.1**
King, J. Hate crime: the story of a dragging in Jasper, Texas   **364.1**
Larson, E. The devil in the white city   **364.1**
McGinniss, J. Fatal vision   **364.1**
Neff, J. The wrong man   **345**
Olsen, J. I: the creation of a serial killer   **364.1**
Ruddick, J. Death at the priory   **364.1**
Rule, A. —and never let her go   **364.1**
Salamon, J. Facing the wind   **364.1**
Schiller, L. Perfect murder, perfect town   **364.1**
Smith, H. W. The butcher's tale   **943.08**
Stewart, J. B. Blind eye   **364.1**
Sullivan, R. Labyrinth   **364.1**
The Ultimate Jack the Ripper companion   **364.1**
Worrall, S. The poet and the murderer   **364.1**
Dictionaries
Newton, M. The encyclopedia of serial killers   **364.03**

Encyclopedias
Nash, J. R. World encyclopedia of 20th century murder   **364.03**
Homosexuality
See also Lesbianism
Bagemihl, B. Biological exuberance   **591.56**
Encyclopedia of lesbian and gay histories and cultures   **306.7**
Marcus, E. Is it a choice?   **305.9**
Mondimore, F. M. A natural history of homosexuality   **306.7**
See/See also pages in the following book(s):
Pollack, W. S. Real boys p206-29   **305.23**
Homosexuality in literature
The World in us   **811.008**
Homosexuality in motion pictures
Mann, W. J. Behind the screen   **791.43**
Homosexuals, Female *See* Lesbians
Homosexuals, Male *See* Gay men
Honan, Park
Shakespeare   **822.3**
Honderich, Ted
(ed) The Oxford companion to philosophy. See The Oxford companion to philosophy   **103**
Honesty
See also Truthfulness and falsehood
Honey and salt. Sandburg, C.
In Sandburg, C. Complete poems of Carl Sandburg p706-71   **811**
Honey, hush!   **817.008**
Hong, Maria
(ed) Growing up Asian American. See Growing up Asian American   **810.8**
Hong Kong (China)
Kemenade, W. van. China, Hong Kong, Taiwan, Inc.   **951**
Hong Xiuquan *See* Hung, Hsiu-ch'üan, 1814-1864
Honigsbaum, Mark
The fever trail   **616.9**
An **honorable** defeat. Davis, W. C.   **973.7**
Honour, Hugh
(ed) The Penguin dictionary of architecture and landscape architecture. See The Penguin dictionary of architecture and landscape architecture   **720.3**
The **honourable** company. Keay, J.   **954.03**

Hood, William, 1920-
(jt. auth) Helms, R. A look over my shoulder   **92**
Hooded Americanism: the history of the Ku Klux Klan. Chalmers, D. M.   **322.4**
Hook, Brian
(ed) The Cambridge encyclopedia of China. See The Cambridge encyclopedia of China   **951**
Hooked on horror. Fonseca, A. J.   **016.8**
Hooker, Joseph, 1814-1879
See/See also pages in the following book(s):
Sears, S. W. Chancellorsville   **973.7**
Hooking up. Wolfe, T.   **818**
Hooks, Bell
Remembered rapture   **808**
Salvation   **306.7**
Wounds of passion   **92**
Hoop roots. Wideman, J. E.   **92**
Hooper, Brad
The short story readers' advisory   **809.3**
Hooper, Judith
Of moths and men   **576.8**
Hooton, Joy, 1935-
(jt. auth) Wilde, W. H. The Oxford companion to Australian literature   **820.3**
Hoover, Herbert, 1874-1964
See/See also pages in the following book(s):
Hofstadter, R. The American political tradition, and the men who made it p279-310   **973**
Hoover, J. Edgar (John Edgar), 1895-1972
About
From the secret files of J. Edgar Hoover   **363.2**
Gentry, C. J. Edgar Hoover   **92**
Hoover, John Edgar *See* Hoover, J. Edgar (John Edgar), 1895-1972
Hoover, Paul, 1946-
(ed) Postmodern American poetry. See Postmodern American poetry   **811.008**
Hope, Bob, 1903-2003
About
Quirk, L. J. Bob Hope: the road well-traveled   **92**
Hope in a jar. Peiss, K. L.   **391**
Hope is the thing with feathers. Cokinos, C.   **598**
Hopfe, Lewis M., d. 1992
Religions of the world   **291**
Hopkins, Gerard Manley, 1844-1889
The poems of Gerard Manley Hopkins   **821**
Hopkins, Jerry
No one here gets out alive [biography of Jim Morrison]   **92**
Hopkins, Patricia
(jt. auth) Anderson, S. R. The feminine face of God   **291**
Hopkins, Pauline Elizabeth, 1859-1930
See/See also pages in the following book(s):
American women fiction writers   **813.009**
Hopper, Edward, 1882-1967
Edward Hopper: the art and the artist   **759.13**
About
Edward Hopper and the American imagination   **759.13**
Mecklenburg, V. M. Edward Hopper: the watercolors   **759.13**
Horace
Ars poetica
In Horace. Satires, Epistles and Ars poetica   **878**
Epistles
In Horace. Satires, Epistles and Ars poetica   **878**
Epodes
In Horace. The Odes and Epodes   **874**
The Odes and Epodes   **874**
Satires, Epistles and Ars poetica   **878**
See/See also pages in the following book(s):
Hamilton, E. The Roman way   **870.9**

Horatius Flaccus, Quintus *See* Horace
Horbury, William
(ed) The Cambridge history of Judaism. See The Cambridge history of Judaism   **296**
Hormones
Love, S. M. Dr. Susan Love's menopause and hormone book   **618.1**
Horn, Maurice, 1931-
The World encyclopedia of comics. See The World encyclopedia of comics   **741.5**
Hornbacher, Marya, 1974-
Wasted: a memoir of anorexia and bulimia   **616.85**
Hornblower, Simon
(ed) The Oxford classical dictionary. See The Oxford classical dictionary   **938.003**
Horney, Karen, 1885-1952
New ways in psychoanalysis   **150.19**
Hornung, Erik
(ed) The Quest for immortality. See The Quest for immortality   **709.32**
Horovitz, David Phillip
A little too close to God   **956.94**
(ed) Shalom, friend: the life and legacy of Yitzhak Rabin. See Shalom, friend: the life and legacy of Yitzhak Rabin   **92**
Horowitz, David, 1939-
(jt. auth) Collier, P. The Roosevelts   **920**
Horror fiction
Bibliography
Burgess, M. Reference guide to science fiction, fantasy, and horror   **016.8**
Fantasy and horror   **016.8**
Fonseca, A. J. Hooked on horror   **016.8**
Reginald, R. Science fiction and fantasy literature, 1975-1991   **016.8**
Bio-bibliography
Supernatural fiction writers   **809.3**
History and criticism
Fantasy and horror   **016.8**
King, S. Stephen King's danse macabre   **818**
Supernatural fiction writers   **809.3**
Horror films
Fonseca, A. J. Hooked on horror   **016.8**
Muir, J. K. Horror films of the 1970s   **791.43**
Horror films of the 1970s. Muir, J. K.   **791.43**
The **horse** encyclopedia. Hermsen, J.   **636.1**
Horse of a different color. Squires, J. D.   **798.4**
Horse racing
Ainslie, T. Ainslie's complete guide to thoroughbred racing   **798.401**
Drape, J. The race for the Triple Crown   **798.4**
Hillenbrand, L. Seabiscuit   **798.4**
Mitchell, E. Three strides before the wire   **798.4**
Squires, J. D. Horse of a different color   **798.4**
The **horse** riding & care handbook. Faurie, B.   **636.1**
Horseback riding *See* Horsemanship
Horsemanship
See also Rodeos
Faurie, B. The horse riding & care handbook   **636.1**
Price, S. D. Essential riding   **798.2**
Horses
Edwards, E. H. The new encyclopedia of the horse   **636.1**
Edwards, E. H. Ultimate horse   **636.1**
Faurie, B. The horse riding & care handbook   **636.1**
Hermsen, J. The horse encyclopedia   **636.1**
Morris, D. Horsewatching   **636.1**
Storey's horse-lover's encyclopedia   **636.1**
Horsewatching. Morris, D.   **636.1**
Hortus third   **635**

Horvitz, Leslie Alan
Eureka!: scientific breakthroughs that changed the world   **509**
(jt. auth) DePaulo, J. R. Understanding depression   **616.85**
Horwitz, Anthony Lander *See* Horwitz, Tony, 1958-
Horwitz, Tony, 1958-
Baghdad without a map, and other misadventures in Arabia   **915.6**
Blue latitudes   **910.4**
Confederates in the attic   **973.7**
Horwood, Jane
(ed) The Oxford Spanish dictionary. See The Oxford Spanish dictionary   **463**
Hosansky, David
The environment A-Z   **363.7**
Hoskin, Michael A.
(ed) The Cambridge illustrated history of astronomy. See The Cambridge illustrated history of astronomy   **520**
Hosking, Geoffrey A., 1942-
Russia and the Russians   **947**
Russia: people and empire, 1552-1917   **947**
Hospitality *See* Entertaining
Hospitals
See also Psychiatric hospitals
United States
Consumers' guide to hospitals   **362.1**
The **hostage**. Behan, B.
In Behan, B. The complete plays   **822**
Hostage to fortune. Kennedy, J. P.   **92**
Hostages
Whitcomb, C. Cold zero   **363.2**
Hostelling North America   **647.9**
Hostetler, John A., 1918-
Amish society   **289.7**
(ed) Amish roots. See Amish roots   **289.7**
The **hot** zone. Preston, R.   **614.5**
Hotels and motels
Sakach, D. Bed & breakfast encyclopedia   **647.9**
Sakach, D. Bed & breakfasts, country inns   **647.9**
Hothouses *See* Greenhouses
Hotlines (Telephone counseling)
Ackerman, D. A slender thread   **362.28**
Houdini, Harry, 1874-1926
About
Brandon, R. The life and many deaths of Harry Houdini   **92**
Hough, Richard Alexander, 1922-1999
Captain James Cook   **92**
Houghton family
See/See also pages in the following book(s):
Leaming, B. Katharine Hepburn   **92**
Houphouët-Boigny, Félix
See/See also pages in the following book(s):
Naipaul, V. S. The writer and the world p229-98   **824**
An **hour** before daylight. Carter, J.   **92**
Hourani, Albert Habib
A history of the Arab peoples   **909**
House. Kidder, T.   **690**
House cleaning
How to clean practically anything   **648**
House construction
See also Prefabricated houses
The Art of natural building   **690**
Buchholz, B. B. Successful homebuilding and remodeling   **690**
Gonzalez, S. Before you hire a contractor   **690**
Inwood, R. Creative country construction   **690**
Kidder, T. House   **690**
Nash, G. Do-it-yourself housebuilding   **690**
Preves, R. New house/more house   **690**
Scutella, R. M. How to plan, contract, and build your own home   **690**

House construction—*Continued*
Thomas, L. Homebuilding pitfalls   **690**
Woodson, R. D. Build your dream home for less   **690**

House furnishing *See* Interior design
The **house** of Bernarda Alba. García Lorca, F.
In García Lorca, F. Three tragedies   **862**
House of fame. Chaucer, G.
In Chaucer, G. The complete poetry and prose of Geoffrey Chaucer   **821**
House of invention. Lindsay, D.   **609**
House of Medici
     About
Hibbert, C. The House of Medici   **920**
The Medici, Michelangelo, & the art of late Renaissance Florence   **709.45**
House of Romanov
     About
Massie, R. K. The Romanovs   **947.08**
     Art collections
Gifts to the tsars, 1500-1700   **745**
House of Stuart
     About
Macleod, J. Dynasty: the Stuarts, 1560-1807   **941.06**
The **house** on Dream Street. Sachs, D.   **959.7**
House painting
Donegan, F. Paint your home   **698**
Travis, D. Debbie Travis' painted house   **698**
House plants
     See also Container gardening; Indoor gardening
Courtier, J. Indoor plants   **635.9**
Regel, P. The houseplant survival guide   **635.9**
A **house** unlocked. Lively, P.   **92**
Household equipment and supplies
     See also Kitchen utensils
     Maintenance and repair
New fix-it-yourself manual   **643**
Wing, C. The big book of small household repairs   **643**
The **houseplant** survival guide. Regel, P.   **635.9**
Houses
     See also Domestic architecture; Log cabins and houses; Prefabricated houses
Papolos, J. The virgin homeowner   **643**
     Buying and selling
The American Bar Association guide to home ownership   **346.04**
Fields, A. Your new house   **643**
Watkins, A. M. Manufactured houses   **693**
     Heating and ventilation
Kittle, J. L. Home heating and air conditioning systems   **697**
     Inspection
Becker, N. The complete book of home inspection   **643**
     Maintenance and repair
Beckstrom, R. J. Ortho's home repair problem solver   **643**
Better Homes and Gardens new complete guide to home repair & improvement   **643**
Home improvement 1-2-3   **643**
Marken, B. How to fix (just about) everything   **640**
New complete do-it-yourself manual   **643**
Sussman, J. Dare to repair   **643**
Wing, C. The big book of small household repairs   **643**
     Remodeling
Buchholz, B. B. Successful homebuilding and remodeling   **690**
Complete basements, attics & bonus rooms   **643**
Home improvement 1-2-3   **643**
Litchfield, M. W. Renovation   **643**

Vila, B. Bob Vila's complete guide to remodeling your home   **643**
Wenz, P. S. Adding to a house   **690**
Houses and monuments of Pompeii   **709.38**
Housing
     Environmental aspects
Bower, L. M. Creating a healthy household   **643**
Housing loans *See* Mortgages
Housman, A. E. (Alfred Edward), 1859-1936
The collected poems of A. E. Housman   **821**
     Drama
Stoppard, T. The invention of love   **822**
Housman, Alfred Edward *See* Housman, A. E. (Alfred Edward), 1859-1936
Houston, Samuel, 1793-1863
     See/See also pages in the following book(s):
Kennedy, J. F. Profiles in courage   **920**
Houston Astros (Baseball team)
Dierker, L. This ain't brain surgery   **92**
Houts, Peter S.
(ed) Caregiving: a step-by-step resource for caring for the person with cancer at home. See Caregiving: a step-by-step resource for caring for the person with cancer at home   **649.8**
Hoving, Thomas, 1931-
False impressions   **702.8**
Making the mummies dance   **92**
How babies talk. Golinkoff, R. M.   **401**
How brains think. Calvin, W. H.   **153.9**
How can I keep from singing: Pete Seeger. Dunaway, D. K.   **92**
How computers work. White, R.   **004**
How could you do that?!. Schlessinger, L. C.   **170**
How de body? Voeten, T.   **966.4**
How electronic things work—and what to do when they don't. Goodman, R. L.   **621.381**
How good do we have to be? Kushner, H. S.   **296.7**
How I believe. Teilhard de Chardin, P.
In Teilhard de Chardin, P. Christianity and evolution p96-132   **231.7**
How I got over. Ward-Royster, W.   **920**
How I grew. McCarthy, M.   **92**
How not to say what you mean. Holder, R. W.   **423**
How products are made   **670**
How reading changed my life. Quindlen, A.   **028**
How the Irish saved civilization. Cahill, T.   **941.5**
How the leopard changed its spots. Goodwin, B. C.   **576**
How the mind works. Pinker, S.   **153**
How the Scots invented the modern world. Herman, A.   **941.1**
How things work. Bloomfield, L.   **530**
How to argue and win every time. Spence, G.   **153.8**
How to bake. Malgieri, N.   **641.8**
How to be a perfect stranger   **291.3**
How to be a star at work. Kelley, R. E.   **658**
How to be your dog's best friend. Monks of New Skete   **636.7**
How to carve wood. Bütz, R.   **731.4**
How to clean and care for practically anything. See How to clean practically anything   **648**
How to clean practically anything   **648**
How to cook everything. Bittman, M.   **641.5**
How to cook meat. Schlesinger, C.   **641.6**
How to cook without a book. Anderson, P.   **641.5**
How to crochet. Turner, P.   **746.43**
How to do everything with your digital camera. Johnson, D.   **778.3**
How to file for bankruptcy. See How to file for chapter 7 bankruptcy   **346.07**
How to file for chapter 7 bankruptcy   **346.07**
How to fix (just about) everything. Marken, B.   **640**

How to get a green card. Lewis, L. N.   342

How to get happily published. Appelbaum, J.   **070.5**

How to grow a novel. Stein, S.   **808.3**

How to have a big wedding on a small budget. Warner, D.   **395**

How to lose friends and alienate people. Young, T.   **92**

How to obtain your U.S. immigration visa. See Anosike, B. O. Immigration manual   **342**

How to plan, contract, and build your own home. Scutella, R. M.   **690**

How to prepare for SAT I   **378.1**

How to prepare for the ACT, American College Testing Assessment Program   **378.1**

How to prepare for the Armed Forces test—ASVAB   **355**

How to prepare for the comprehensive postal exam. See Barkus, P. Comprehensive postal exam   **383**

How to prepare for the GED high school equivalency examination   **373.1**

How to publish and promote online. Rose, M. J.   **070.5**

How to raise a child with a high EQ. Shapiro, L. E.   **649**

How to read a book. Adler, M. J.   **028**

How to read a french fry. Parsons, R.   **641.5**

How to read a poem. Hirsch, E.   **808.1**

How to read and why. Bloom, H.   **028**

How to run a small business   **658.1**

How to sell what you make. Gerhards, P.   **658.8**

How to settle an estate. Plotnick, C.   **346.05**

How to speak, how to listen. Adler, M. J.   **302.2**

How-to-stop-smoking programs See Smoking cessation programs

How to talk to anyone, anytime, anywhere. King, L.   **302.3**

How to think about God. Adler, M. J.   **212**

How to think about the great ideas. Adler, M. J.   **080**

How to travel with a salmon & other essays. Eco, U.   **854**

How to win friends and influence people. Carnegie, D.   **158**

How to win your personal injury claim. Matthews, J. L.   **346.03**

How to write a children's book and get it published. Seuling, B.   **808.06**

How to write and give a speech. Detz, J.   **808.5**

How we choose to be happy. Foster, R.   **158**

How we die. Nuland, S. B.   **616.07**

How we got here. Frum, D.   **973.92**

How we grieve. Attig, T.   **155.9**

How we invented the airplane. Wright, O.   **629.13**

How we talk. Metcalf, A. A.   **427**

Howard, Hugh
(jt. auth) Vila, B. Bob Vila's complete guide to remodeling your home   **643**

Howard, Jean
Jean Howard's Hollywood   **791.43**

Howard, Luke, 1772-1864
About
Hamblyn, R. The invention of clouds   **551.57**

Howard, Michael Eliot, 1922-
(ed) The Oxford history of the twentieth century. See The Oxford history of the twentieth century   **909.82**

Howard, Philip
The death of common sense   **348**

Howarth, David Armine, 1912-
We die alone   **940.54**

Howarth, Glennys
(ed) Encyclopedia of death and dying. See Encyclopedia of death and dying   **306.9**

Howatson, M. C. (Margaret C.)
(ed) The Oxford companion to classical literature. See The Oxford companion to classical literature   **880.3**

Howatson, Margaret C. See Howatson, M. C. (Margaret C.)

Howe, Peter
Shooting under fire   **070.4**

Howell, Vernon See Koresh, David

Howells, William Dean, 1837-1920
See/See also pages in the following book(s):
Vidal, G. United States—essays, 1952-1992 p193-214   **814**

Howes, Barbara, 1914-1996
Collected poems, 1945-1990   **811**

Howey, Noelle
Dress codes of three girlhoods—my mother's, my father's, and mine   **306.8**

Hoxie, Frederick E., 1947-
(ed) American nations. See American nations   **970.004**
(ed) Encyclopedia of North American Indians. See Encyclopedia of North American Indians   **970.004**

Hoy, Angela Adair- See Adair-Hoy, Angela

Hoyle's modern encyclopedia of card games. Gibson, W. B.   **795.4**

Hoyt, Edwin Palmer
The GI's war   **940.54**

Hoyt, Erich, 1950-
(ed) Insect lives. See Insect lives   **595.7**

Hrabowski, Freeman A., 1950-
Overcoming the odds. See Overcoming the odds   **649**

Hsü, Chung-yüeh See Hsü, Immanuel Chung-yüeh, 1923-

Hsü, Immanuel Chung-yüeh, 1923-
The rise of modern China   **951**

Hsüan-tsang, ca. 596-664
About
Bernstein, R. Ultimate journey   **294.3**

Huao Indians See Waorani Indians

Huaorani Indians See Waorani Indians

Hubbard, Jan
(ed) The Official NBA encyclopedia. See The Official NBA encyclopedia   **796.323**

Hubbell, Sue
A book of bees—and how to keep them   **638**
Shrinking the cat   **660.6**
Waiting for Aphrodite   **592**

Hubble, Edwin Powell, 1889-1953
See/See also pages in the following book(s):
Flowers, C. Instability rules   **509**

Hubble Space Telescope
Chaisson, E. The Hubble wars   **522**
Voit, M. Hubble space telescope   **520**

The **Hubble** wars. Chaisson, E.   **522**

Huchra, John
See/See also pages in the following book(s):
Greenstein, G. Portraits of discovery p187-218   **920**

Hudak, Joseph
Design for gardens   **712**

Huddleston, Rodney D.
The Cambridge grammar of the English language   **425**

Hudler, George W.
Magical mushrooms, mischievous molds   **579.5**

Hudson, Gary
About
Weil, E. They all laughed at Christopher Columbus   **621.43**

Hudson, Henry, d. 1611
See/See also pages in the following book(s):
Connell, E. S. The Aztec treasure house p319-45   **814**

Hudson, Jeffrey, 1619-1681
About
Page, N. Lord Minimus   92
Hudson, John C.
(ed) Goode's world atlas. See Goode's world atlas
    912
Hudson, Winthrop S.
(jt. auth) Corrigan, J. Religion in America   200.9
Hueffer, Ford Madox See Ford, Ford Madox, 1873-1939
Huey, John
(jt. auth) Walton, S. Sam Walton, made in America
    92
Huff, Darrell
The complete how to figure it   640
Hugging the shore. Updike, J.   818
Huggins, Kathleen
The nursing mother's companion   649
Hughes, Charles W.
(comp) American hymns old and new. See American hymns old and new   782.27
Hughes, Edward James See Hughes, Ted, 1930-1998
Hughes, Howard C.
Sensory exotica   573.8
Hughes, Kathryn, 1959-
George Eliot   92
Hughes, Langston, 1902-1967
The collected poems of Langston Hughes   811
Five plays   812
I wonder as I wander   92
Little Ham
    In Hughes, L. Five plays p43-112   812
Mulatto
    In Hughes, L. Five plays p1-35   812
Remember me to Harlem: the letters of Langston Hughes and Carl Van Vechten, 1925-1964   92
Selected poems of Langston Hughes   811
Simply heavenly
    In Hughes, L. Five plays p113-81   812
Soul gone home
    In Hughes, L. Five plays p37-42   812
Tambourines to glory
    In Hughes, L. Five plays p183-258   812
About
Langston Hughes   818
Miller, R. B. The art and imagination of Langston Hughes   818
Hughes, Robert
American visions   709.73
Barcelona   946
The fatal shore   994
Goya   92
The shock of the new   709.04
Hughes, Ted, 1930-1998
Birthday letters   821
Selected poems, 1957-1994   821
(tr) Ovid. Tales from Ovid   873
About
Feinstein, E. Ted Hughes   92
Hugo, Richard F.
Making certain it goes on   811
Hull, N. E. H., 1949-
Roe v. Wade   344
Hull, Raymond, 1919-1985
(jt. auth) Peter, L. J. The Peter Principle   817
Hultkrantz, Åke
The religions of the American Indians   299
Human anatomy
Anatomica's body atlas   611
The Human body   612
Netter, F. H. Atlas of human anatomy   611
See/See also pages in the following book(s):
Friedman, M. Medicine's 10 greatest discoveries
    610.9

Human anatomy made amazingly easy. Hart, C.
    743
Human behavior
See also Behaviorism
Dunbar, R. I. M. Grooming, gossip, and the evolution of language   599.93
Edelman, M. W. The measure of our success   170
Fromm, E. To have or to be?   302
Piaget, J. The moral judgment of the child   155.4
Viscott, D. S. Emotional resilience   158
Waal, F. de. The ape and the sushi master   156
Human beings
Bloom, H. The Lucifer principle   128
Marks, J. What it means to be 98% chimpanzee
    599.93
Olson, S. Mapping human history   599.9
Rothman, B. K. Genetic maps and human imaginations
    599.93
Teilhard de Chardin, P. The phenomenon of man
    113
Watson, L. Dark nature   111
Wilson, E. O. In search of nature   113
Human beings (Theology)
See/See also pages in the following book(s):
Teilhard de Chardin, P. Toward the future p13-39
    194
The **Human** body   612
Human capital
O'Reilly, C. A., III. Hidden value   658
The **human** Christ. Allen, C.   232.9
Human cloning and human dignity   174
Human diseases and conditions   616
Human ecology
Gore, A., Jr. Earth in the balance   304.2
Kane, J. Savages   986.6
Matthiessen, P. Indian country   970.004
Williams, T. T. Red: passion and patience in the desert
    333.7
Wilson, E. O. In search of nature   113
Human engineering
Vogel, S. Cats' paws and catapults   571.4
Human experimentation in medicine
Moreno, J. D. Undue risk   174
Roach, M. Stiff   611
Human fertility
See also Infertility
Human figure in art See Artistic anatomy
The **human** genome. Dennis, C.   599.93
Human Genome Project
Bodmer, W. F. The book of man   572.8
Cook-Deegan, R. M. The gene wars   572.8
Davies, K. Cracking the genome   599.93
Dennis, C. The human genome   599.93
The Genomic revolution   599.93
Sulston, J. The common thread   572.8
Wade, N. Life script   616
Wickelgren, I. The gene masters   599.93
Human geography
Simpson, J. W. Yearning for the land   304.2
Human influence on nature
Boulter, M. C. Extinction: evolution and the end of man   576.8
Commoner, B. Making peace with the planet
    304.2
Davis, L. A. Environmental disasters   363.7
Goodall, J. The ten trusts   333.95
Leakey, R. E. The sixth extinction   304.2
Manning, R. Grassland   577.4
Palumbi, S. R. The evolution explosion   576.8
Winston, M. L. Nature wars   577.2
Encyclopedias
Encyclopedia of global change   363.7
Human origins
See also Evolution; Fossil hominids; Prehistoric peoples

Human origins—*Continued*
The Cambridge encyclopedia of human evolution
    599.93
Darwin, C. The origin of species   **576.8**
Diamond, J. M. The third chimpanzee   **599.93**
Dunbar, R. I. M. Grooming, gossip, and the evolution
    of language   **599.93**
Eiseley, L. C. The immense journey   **576.8**
Johanson, D. C. From Lucy to language   **599.93**
Johanson, D. C. Lucy: the beginnings of humankind
    599.93
Klein, R. G. The dawn of human culture   **599.93**
Leakey, R. E. The origin of humankind   **599.93**
Leakey, R. E. Origins reconsidered   **599.93**
Stringer, C. B. African exodus   **599.93**
Swisher, C. C. Java man   **599.93**
Sykes, B. The seven daughters of Eve   **599.93**
Tattersall, I. Extinct humans   **599.93**
Tattersall, I. The fossil trail   **599.93**
Tattersall, I. The monkey in the mirror   **599.93**
Tudge, C. The time before history   **599.93**
Walker, A. The wisdom of the bones   **599.93**
Wolpoff, M. H. Race and human evolution
    599.97
Human relations *See* Interpersonal relations
Human resources *See* Human capital
Human rights
Buruma, I. Bad elements   **951.05**
Devine, C. Human rights   **323**
Fang Lizhi. Bringing down the Great Wall
    951.05
Schulz, W. F., Jr. In our own best interest   **323**
Wei Jingsheng. The courage to stand alone
    951.05
Wu, H. Troublemaker   **951.05**
    Encyclopedias
Maddex, R. L. International encyclopedia of human
    rights   **323**
Humane Society of the United States
Lane, M. The Humane Society of the United States
    complete guide to dog care   **636.7**
Humanism
Fromm, E. On being human   **150.19**
Rogers, C. R. A way of being   **150.19**
Humanistic medicine *See* Holistic medicine
Humanities
    Periodicals—Indexes
Humanities index   **050**
Humanities and science *See* Science and the humanities
Humanities index   **050**
Humanity. Glover, J.   **909.82**
Hume, David, 1711-1776
    See/See also pages in the following book(s):
Gay, P. The Enlightenment: an interpretation   **190**
Russell, B. A history of Western philosophy p659-74
    109
Hume, Ivor Noël *See* Noël Hume, Ivor, 1927-
Hummingbirds
Williamson, S. L. A field guide to hummingbirds of
    North America   **598**
Humor *See* Wit and humor
Humorous poetry
The Norton book of light verse   **821.008**
The Oxford book of comic verse   **821.008**
**Humphreys, Andrew A. (Andrew Atkinson), 1810-
1883**
    See/See also pages in the following book(s):
Barry, J. M. Rising tide   **977**
Humphry, Derek, 1930-
Final exit   **179.7**
Freedom to die   **179.7**
The **hundredth** window. Jennings, C.   **005.8**
Hung, Hsiu-ch'üan, 1814-1864
    About
Spence, J. D. God's Chinese son   **951**

Hungarian refugees
Michener, J. A. The bridge at Andau   **943.9**
Hungary
    History—1956, Revolution
Michener, J. A. The bridge at Andau   **943.9**
Hunger
McGovern, G. S. The third freedom   **363.8**
Hunger of memory. Rodriguez, R.   **92**
The **hungry** ocean. Greenlaw, L.   **639.2**
The **hungry** years. Watkins, T. H.   **973.91**
Hunnisett, Jean
Period costume for stage & screen   **391**
Hunt, E. Howard (Everette Howard), 1918-
    See/See also pages in the following book(s):
Vidal, G. United States—essays, 1952-1992 p857-83
    814
Hunt, Everette Howard *See* Hunt, E. Howard (Everette
    Howard), 1918-
Hunt, John Dixon
(ed) The Oxford book of garden verse. See The Ox-
    ford book of garden verse   **821.008**
Hunter, Alberta, ca. 1895-1984
    See/See also pages in the following book(s):
Harrison, D. D. Black pearls   **920**
Hunter, Karen
(jt. auth) Queen Latifah Ladies first   **158**
The **hunter** in my heart. Jones, R. F.   **799.2**
Hunting
    See also Game and game birds
Jones, R. F. The hunter in my heart   **799.2**
The **hunting** of the President. Conason, J.   **973.929**
Huntington, Samuel P.
The clash of civilizations and the remaking of world
    order   **909.82**
Hurricane: the miraculous journey of Rubin Carter.
    Hirsch, J. S.   **92**
Hurricanes
    See also Typhoons
Davies, P. Inside the hurricane   **551.55**
Larson, E. Isaac's storm   **976.4**
Longshore, D. Encyclopedia of hurricanes, typhoons
    and cyclones   **551.55**
Hurst, Jack
Nathan Bedford Forrest   **92**
Hurston, Zora Neale, 1891-1960
Dust tracks on a road   **92**
    also in Hurston, Z. N. Folklore, memoirs, and other
    writings   **818**
Folklore, memoirs, and other writings   **818**
Mules and men
    In Hurston, Z. N. Folklore, memoirs, and other writ-
    ings   **818**
Tell my horse
    In Hurston, Z. N. Folklore, memoirs, and other writ-
    ings   **818**
Zora Neale Hurston: a life in letters   **92**
    About
Boyd, V. Wrapped in rainbows   **92**
    See/See also pages in the following book(s):
American women fiction writers   **813.009**
Gilbert, S. M. No man's land v3 p121-65   **820.9**
Pierpont, C. R. Passionate minds   **810.9**
Wall, C. A. Women of the Harlem Renaissance
    810.9
Hurt, R. Douglas
Problems of plenty   **630**
Husain, Saddam *See* Hussein, Ṣaddām
Ḥusayn, Ṣaddām *See* Hussein, Ṣaddām
Hussein, King of Jordan, 1935-1999
    See/See also pages in the following book(s):
Nur el Hussein, Queen, consort of Hussein, King of
    Jordan. Leap of faith   **92**
Hussein, Ṣaddām
    About
Mackey, S. The reckoning   **956.7**

Hussey, Mark, 1956-
  Virginia Woolf A-Z   **828**
Huston, James E.
  Menopause   **618.1**
The **Hutchinson** history of the world. See Roberts, J. M.
  The new history of the world   **909**
Hutterian Brethren
  Kraybill, D. B. On the backroad to heaven   **289.7**
Hutterite Brethren See Hutterian Brethren
Hutton, J. Thomas
  Preventing falls   **618.97**
Hutton, Ronald
  The triumph of the moon   **133.4**
Huxley, Aldous, 1894-1963
  Brave new world, and Brave new world revisited
      828
  Brave new world revisited   **303.3**
    also in Huxley, A. Brave new world and Brave new
    world revisited   **828**
  The perennial philosophy   **210**
             About
  Murray, N. R. Aldous Huxley   **92**
Huxley, Elspeth, 1907-1997
  The flame trees of Thika   **92**
Hydraulic engineering
  Outwater, A. B. Water   **551.48**
  Ward, D. R. Water wars   **333.91**
Hydrogen
  Rigden, J. S. Hydrogen   **546**
Hydrogen as fuel
  Rifkin, J. The hydrogen economy   **333.8**
Hydrogen bomb
  Rhodes, R. Dark sun   **623.4**
The **hydrogen** economy. Rifkin, J.   **333.8**
Hydroponics
  Swindells, P. The water garden encyclopedia
      635.9
Hygiene
  See also Health
Hylton, William H.
  (ed) Rodale's illustrated encyclopedia of herbs. See
  Rodale's illustrated encyclopedia of herbs   **635**
Hyman, Isabelle
  (jt. auth) Trachtenberg, M. Architecture, from prehisto-
  ry to postmodernity   **720.9**
Hyman, Paula, 1946-
  (ed) Jewish women in America. See Jewish women in
  America   **920.003**
Hymes, Diane L. Tessaglia- *See* Tessaglia-Hymes,
  Diane L.
Hymns
  See also Spirituals (Songs)
  American hymns old and new   **782.27**
Hyper-parenting. Rosenfeld, A. A.   **649**
Hyperactive children
  See also Attention deficit disorder
Hyperspace. Kaku, M.   **530.1**
Hysterectomy
  West, S. The hysterectomy hoax   **618.1**
The **hysterectomy** hoax. West, S.   **618.1**

I

I and thou. Buber, M.   **181**
I ching
  The classic of changes   **299**
I could never be so lucky again. Doolittle, J. H.   **92**
I have a name. Ignatow, D.   **811**
I have landed. Gould, S. J.   **578**
I have seen the world begin. Jensen, C.   **915**
I know just what you mean. Goodman, E.   **158**
I know why the caged bird sings. Angelou, M.   **92**
I may be wrong but I doubt it. Barkley, C.   **92**

I may not get there with you: the true Martin Luther
  King, Jr. Dyson, M. E.   **92**
I only say this because I love you. Tannen, D.
      306.8
I ought to be in pictures. Simon, N.
  In Simon, N. The collected plays of Neil Simon v3
  p217-305   **812**
I praise my destroyer. Ackerman, D.   **811**
I. Q. tests *See* Intelligence tests
I shall not be moved. Angelou, M.   **811**
I: the creation of a serial killer. Olsen, J.   **364.1**
I thought my father was God and other true tales from
  the National Story Project   **810.8**
I, Tina. Turner, T.   **92**
I want to thank my brain for remembering me. Breslin,
  J.   **92**
I will bear witness. Klemperer, V.   **92**
I wonder as I wander. Hughes, L.   **92**
Iberia. Michener, J. A.   **914.6**
IBM *See* International Business Machines Corp.
Ibn Battuta, 1304-1377
             About
  Mackintosh-Smith, T. Travels with a tangerine
      910.4
Ibrahima, Abd al-Rahman, 1762-1829
  See/See also pages in the following book(s):
  Lepore, J. A is for American   **306.44**
Ibsen, Henrik, 1828-1906
  The complete major prose plays   **839.8**
  A doll's house
    In Ibsen, H. The complete major prose plays p119-
    96   **839.8**
    In Ibsen, H. Ibsen: four major plays   **839.8**
  An enemy of the people
    In Ibsen, H. The complete major prose plays p277-
    386   **839.8**
    In Ibsen, H. Ibsen: four major plays   **839.8**
  Ghosts
    In Ibsen, H. The complete major prose plays p197-
    276   **839.8**
    In Ibsen, H. Ibsen: four major plays   **839.8**
  Hedda Gabler
    In Ibsen, H. The complete major prose plays p689-
    778   **839.8**
    In Ibsen, H. Ibsen: four major plays   **839.8**
    In Our dramatic heritage v4   **808.82**
  Ibsen: four plays [v2]   **839.8**
  Ibsen: four plays [v3]   **839.8**
  Ibsen: four major plays   **839.8**
  John Gabriel Borkman
    In Ibsen, H. The complete major prose plays p937-
    1024   **839.8**
    In Ibsen, H. Ibsen: four plays, v3   **839.8**
  The lady from the sea
    In Ibsen, H. The complete major prose plays p587-
    688   **839.8**
    In Ibsen, H. Ibsen: four plays, v3   **839.8**
  Little Eyolf
    In Ibsen, H. The complete major prose plays p861-
    936   **839.8**
    In Ibsen, H. Ibsen: four plays, v3   **839.8**
  The master builder
    In Ibsen, H. The complete major prose plays p779-
    860   **839.8**
    In Ibsen, H. Ibsen: four plays, v2   **839.8**
  Peer Gynt
    In Our dramatic heritage v4   **808.82**
  Pillars of society
    In Ibsen, H. The complete major prose plays p9-118
        839.8
    In Ibsen, H. Ibsen: four plays, v2   **839.8**
  Rosmersholm
    In Ibsen, H. The complete major prose plays p491-
    585   **839.8**
    In Ibsen, H. Ibsen: four plays, v2   **839.8**

Ibsen, Henrik, 1828-1906—*Continued*
When we dead awaken
  In Ibsen, H. The complete major prose plays p1025-
  92 **839.8**
  In Ibsen, H. Ibsen: four plays, v3 **839.8**
The wild duck
  In Ibsen, H. The complete major prose plays p387-
  490 **839.8**
  In Ibsen, H. Ibsen: four plays, v2 **839.8**
  See/See also pages in the following book(s):
  Bloom, H. The Western canon **809**
Ibsen: four plays [v2] Ibsen, H. **839.8**
Ibsen: four plays [v3] Ibsen, H. **839.8**
Ice blink. Cookman, S. **998**
Ice hockey *See* Hockey
Ice skating
  Brennan, C. Inside edge **796.91**
  Malone, J. W. The encyclopedia of figure skating
  796.91
  Ryan, J. Little girls in pretty boxes **796.44**
Icelandic literature
  See also Old Norse literature
Iceman. Fowler, B. **937**
Iconography *See* Christian art; Religious art
Icons of photography **779**
I'd hate myself in the morning. Lardner, R. **92**
The idea of decline in Western history. Herman, A.
  909.08
Ideal states *See* Utopias
Idealism
  See/See also pages in the following book(s):
  Morris, D. The new prince p23-66 **324.7**
Ideas and opinions. Einstein, A. **818**
Identification
  See also DNA fingerprinting; Forensic anthropolo-
  gy
Identity (Psychology)
  Maalouf, A. In the name of identity **302.4**
Identity's architect: a biography of Erik H. Erikson.
  Friedman, L. J. **92**
Idioms *See* English language—Idioms
Iditarod Trail Sled Dog Race, Alaska
  Paulsen, G. Winterdance **798.8**
If a place can make you cry. Gordis, D. **956.94**
If God spare my life. See Moynahan, B. God's bestsell-
  er: William Tyndale, Thomas More, and the writing
  of the English Bible [biography of William Tyndale]
  92
If my career's on the fast track, where do I get a road
  map? Fisher, A. B. **650.14**
If not, winter. Sappho **884**
If you can't be free, be a mystery: in search of Billie
  Holiday. Griffin, F. J. **92**
Ifrah, Georges
  The universal history of computing **004**
Ignatieff, Michael
  Virtual war **949.7**
Ignatow, David, 1914-1997
  I have a name **811**
  Shadowing the ground **811**
Ikhnaton *See* Akhenaton, King of Egypt, fl. ca. 1388-
  1358 B.C.
Ikke, ikke, nye, nye, nye. Wilson, L.
  In Wilson, L. 21 short plays p95-104 **812**
Ikutu. Komparu, Z.
  In Waley, A. The Nō plays of Japan **895.6**
Ilg, Frances Lillian, 1902-1981
  (jt. auth) Ames, L. B. Your five-year-old **649**
  (jt. auth) Ames, L. B. Your four-year-old **649**
  (jt. auth) Ames, L. B. Your one-year-old **649**
  (jt. auth) Ames, L. B. Your six-year-old **649**
  (jt. auth) Ames, L. B. Your three-year-old **649**
  (jt. auth) Ames, L. B. Your two-year-old **649**
The Iliad. Homer **883**

Illingworth, Valerie
  The Facts on File dictionary of computer science. See
  The Facts on File dictionary of computer science
  004
Illness *See* Diseases
Illumination of books and manuscripts
  Lovett, P. Calligraphy and illumination **745.6**
Illuminations, and other prose poems. Rimbaud, A.
  841
The **illustrated** dictionary of boating terms.
  Rousmaniere, J. **797.1**
The **Illustrated** dictionary of electronics **621.381**
The **illustrated** encyclopaedia of costume and fashion
  from 1066 to the present. Cassin-Scott, J. **391**
The **Illustrated** encyclopedia of body-mind disciplines
  615.5
The **Illustrated** encyclopedia of musical instruments
  784.19
Illustrated encyclopedia of perennials, Rodale's. Phillips,
  E. **635.9**
The **Illustrated** guide to world religions **291**
An **illustrated** history of the First World War. Keegan,
  J. **940.3**
The **Illustrated** history of the Jewish people **909**
The **illustrated** Jesus through the centuries. Pelikan, J. J.
  232.9
The **illustrated** veterinary guide for dogs, cats, birds &
  exotic pets. See Pinney, C. C. The complete home
  veterinary guide **636.089**
Illustration of books
  See also Picture books for children
Illustrations, Humorous *See* Cartoons and caricatures
Illustrators
  Marcus, L. S. Ways of telling **741.6**
  The Newbery & Caldecott medal books, 1986-2000
  028.5
  Newbery and Caldecott Medal books, 1966-1975
  028.5
  Newbery and Caldecott Medal books, 1976-1985
  028.5
ILMP. See International literary market place: ILMP
  070.5025
I'm a stranger here myself. Bryson, B. **973.92**
I'm not Rappaport. Gardner, H.
  In Gardner, H. Herb Gardner: the collected plays and
  the screenplay Who is Harry Kellerman and why
  is he saying those terrible things about me?
  812
I'm OK, you're OK. Harris, T. A. **158**
The **imaginary** invalid. Molière
  In Molière. The misanthrope, and other plays
  842
Imaginary places *See* Geographical myths
The **imaginary** voyage. Peres, S. **956.94**
Imagining Atlantis. Ellis, R. **001.9**
Imagining numbers. Mazur, B. **512**
IMF *See* International Monetary Fund
Imitation of Christ
  The imitation of Christ **242**
The **immaculate** invasion. Shacochis, B. **972.94**
The **immense** journey. Eiseley, L. C. **576.8**
Immigrants
United States
  Brownstone, D. M. Facts about American immigration
  325.73
Immigration and emigration
  See also Immigrants; Refugees; names of countries
  with the subdivision *Immigration and emigration*;
  and names of nationality groups
  Pagden, A. Peoples and empires **909**
  Sowell, T. Migrations and cultures **304.8**
Immigration manual. Anosike, B. O. **342**
Immortality
  Benecke, M. The dream of eternal life **612.6**

Immune system

Hall, S. S. A commotion in the blood   **616.07**

Diseases

Rumpf, T. P. The Sjogren's syndrome survival guide   **616.97**

Immunization *See* Vaccination

Immunological system *See* Immune system

The **impact** of the gene. Tudge, C.   **576.5**

Impelluso, Lucia

Gods and heroes in art   **700**

Imperfect control. Viorst, J.   **158**

Imperfect thirst. Kinnell, G.   **811**

Imperial Trans-Antarctic Expedition (1914-1917)

Alexander, C. The Endurance   **998**

Imperialism

Arendt, H. Origins of totalitarianism   **321.9**

The Cambridge illustrated history of the British Empire   **941.08**

Cocker, M. Rivers of blood, rivers of gold   **909**

The Oxford history of the British Empire   **909**

See/See also pages in the following book(s):

Heilbroner, R. L. The worldly philosophers   **330.1**

The **importance** of being Earnest. Wilde, O.   **822**

also in Our dramatic heritage v5   **808.82**

also in The Oxford anthology of English literature v2   **820.8**

The **impossible** country. Hall, B.   **949.7**

Impostors and imposture

Boese, A. The museum of hoaxes   **001.9**

Hemley, R. Invented Eden   **959.9**

Jay, R. Jay's journal of anomalies   **791**

Impotence

See/See also pages in the following book(s):

Sheehy, G. Understanding men's passages   **305.31**

Impressionism (Art)

Gerdts, W. H. California impressionism   **759.13**

Schapiro, M. Impressionism   **709.44**

Imwold, Denise

(ed) Anatomica's body atlas. See Anatomica's body atlas   **611**

In a desert garden. Alcock, J.   **595.7**

In a sunburned country. Bryson, B.   **994**

In America's court. Geoghegan, T.   **345**

In an antique land. Ghosh, A.   **962**

In an art factory. Frost, R.

In Frost, R. Collected poems, prose, & plays p576-88   **818**

In an influential fashion   **391**

In cold blood. Capote, T.   **364.1**

In harm's way. Stanton, D.   **940.54**

In our hands. Arem, A.   **617**

In our image. Karnow, S.   **959.9**

In our own best interest. Schulz, W. F., Jr.   **323**

In our own words   **815.008**

In our time. Brownmiller, S.   **305.4**

In Patagonia. Chatwin, B.   **918.2**

In pursuit of happiness. Kingwell, M.   **170**

In retrospect. McNamara, R. S.   **959.704**

In search of grace. Hahn, K.   **200.9**

In search of nature. Wilson, E. O.   **113**

In search of our mothers' gardens. Walker, A.   **818**

In search of Robinson Crusoe. Severin, T.   **996**

In search of Schrödinger's cat. Gribbin, J. R.   **530.1**

In search of Susy. See Gribbin, J. R. The search for superstrings, symmetry, and the theory of everything   **539.7**

In search of the old ones. Roberts, D.   **970.004**

In search of the Trojan War. Wood, M.   **939**

In search of your European roots. Baxter, A.   **929**

In search of Zarathustra. Kriwaczek, P.   **295**

In Siberia. Thubron, C.   **957**

In the absence of sun. Lee, H.   **920**

In the American grain. Williams, W. C.   **814**

In the arms of others. Filene, P. G.   **179.7**

In the beginning. Armstrong, K.   **222**

In the beginning. McGrath, A. E.   **220.5**

In the belly of the beast. Abbott, J. H.   **365**

In the country of country. Dawidoff, N.   **781.642**

In the crevice of time. Jacobsen, J.   **811**

In the devil's garden. Allen, S. L.   **641**

In the devil's snare. Norton, M. B.   **133.4**

In the eye of the storm: the life of General H. Norman Schwarzkopf. Cohen, R.   **92**

In the footsteps of Alexander the Great. Wood, M.   **938**

In the hands of a chef. Adams, J.   **641.5**

In the hands of the people. Dwyer, W. L.   **347**

In the heart of the sea. Philbrick, N.   **910.4**

In the little world. Richardson, J. H.   **599.9**

In the midst of life. Bierce, A.

In Bierce, A. The collected writings   **818**

In the name of Elijah Muhammad. Gardell, M.   **297**

In the name of identity. Maalouf, A.   **302.4**

In the next galaxy. Stone, R.   **811**

In the past lane. Kammen, M. G.   **973**

In the shadow of man. Goodall, J.   **599.8**

In the shadow of the glen. Synge, J. M.

In Synge, J. M. The complete plays   **822**

In the theater of consciousness. Baars, B. J.   **153**

In the wake of the plague. Cantor, N. F.   **614.5**

In these girls, hope is a muscle. Blais, M.   **796.323**

Incas

Bingham, H. Lost city of the Incas   **985**

Hemming, J. The conquest of the Incas   **985**

Moseley, M. E. The Incas and their ancestors   **985**

Prescott, W. H. History of the conquest of Peru   **985**

See/See also pages in the following book(s):

Connell, E. S. The Aztec treasure house p393-411   **814**

Incentive (Psychology) *See* Motivation (Psychology)

Income tax

H & R Block income tax guide   **336.2**

J.K. Lasser's your income tax   **336.2**

Weisman, S. R. The great tax wars   **336.2**

Incunabula *See* Rare books

Independent schools *See* Private schools

The **Independent** study catalog   **374**

Index of majors and graduate degrees. College Entrance Examination Board   **378.73**

Index to artistic biography. Havlice, P. P.   **920.003**

Index to children's poetry   **808.81**

Index to children's songs. Peterson, C. S.   **782.42**

Index to fairy tales   **398.2**

Index to poetry for children and young people   **808.81**

India

Description

Davidson, R. Desert places   **954**

History

See Mogul Empire

Keay, J. The honourable company   **954.03**

Keay, J. India: a history   **954**

Read, A. The proudest day   **954.03**

Tharoor, S. India   **954**

Wolpert, S. A. A new history of India   **954**

See/See also pages in the following book(s):

Naipaul, V. S. The writer and the world p1-70   **824**

History—1526-1765

McLeod, J. The history of India   **954**

Poetry

Paz, O. A tale of two gardens   **861**

Politics and government

Chadha, Y. Gandhi   **92**

Frank, K. Indira: the life of Indira Nehru Gandhi   **92**

Gandhi, M. Gandhi on non-violence   **322.4**

Read, A. The proudest day   **954.03**

India—Politics and government—*Continued*
Wolpert, S. A. Gandhi's passion   **92**
Social life and customs
Bumiller, E. May you be the mother of a hundred sons
   954.05
Surveys
Keay, J. The great arc   **526**
Indian country. Matthiessen, P.   **970.004**
Indian literature (American) *See* American literature—
Native American authors
Indian literature (East Indian) *See* Indic literature
Indian literature (North American Indian) *See* Native
American literature
The **Indian** slave trade. Gallay, A.   **326**
Indian war sites. Rajtar, S.   **970.004**
Indianapolis (Cruiser)
Stanton, D. In harm's way   **940.54**
Indians in the making. Harmon, A.   **970.004**
Indians of North America *See* Native Americans
Indic literature
Collections
Mirrorwork   **820.8**
Indigenous peoples *See* Ethnology
Indigestion
Janowitz, H. D. Good food for bad stomachs
   616.3
Indira: the life of Indira Nehru Gandhi. Frank, K.
   92
Individual retirement accounts
See also 401(k) plan
Indivisible by four. Steinhardt, A.   **920**
Indoctrination, Forced *See* Brainwashing
Indonesia
Description
See/See also pages in the following book(s):
Naipaul, V. S. Among the believers p297-430
   297
Indoor gardening
See also Container gardening; House plants
Courtier, J. Indoor plants   **635.9**
Indoor plants. Courtier, J.   **635.9**
Industrial accidents
Davis, L. A. Environmental disasters   **363.7**
Industrial arts
See also Technology
Industrial design
Heskett, J. Toothpicks and logos   **745.2**
Industrial materials *See* Materials
Industrial plants *See* Factories
Industrial relations
See/See also pages in the following book(s):
Goleman, D. Emotional intelligence p148-63
   152.4
Industrial revolution
Encyclopedias
Olson, J. S. Encyclopedia of the industrial revolution
in America   **973.03**
Industrial waste
Markowitz, G. E. Deceit and denial   **615.9**
Industries
See also High technology industry
History
Hobsbawm, E. J. The age of revolution, 1789-1848
   940.2
Periodicals—Indexes
Business periodicals index   **650**
Inequality *See* Equality
Inés de la Cruz, Juana *See* Juana Inés de la Cruz,
1651-1695
The **inextinguishable** symphony. Goldsmith, M.
   940.53
Infantile paralysis *See* Poliomyelitis
Infants
Cooke, C. The best baby shower book   **793.2**

Birth defects
See Birth defects
Care
American Academy of Pediatrics guide to your child's
sleep   **618.92**
The Baby book   **649**
Douglas, A. The mother of all baby books   **649**
Karp, H. The happiest baby on the block   **649**
Kitzinger, S. The complete book of pregnancy and
childbirth   **618.2**
Leach, P. Your baby & child   **649**
Lees, C. C. Pregnancy and birth   **618.2**
Marzollo, J. Fathers & babies   **649**
Mayo Clinic complete book of pregnancy & baby's
first year   **618.2**
Murkoff, H. E. What to expect the first year   **649**
Small, M. F. Our babies, ourselves   **649**
Stoppard, M. Complete baby and child care   **649**
Development
The Baby book   **649**
Small, M. F. Our babies, ourselves   **649**
White, B. L. The new first three years of life
   155.4
Nutrition
Sears, W. The family nutrition book   **613.2**
Infants, Premature *See* Premature infants
Infection and infectious diseases *See* Communicable
diseases
Infeld, Leopold, 1898-1968
(jt. auth) Einstein, A. The evolution of physics
   530
Infertility
Bruce, D. F. Making a baby   **618.2**
Marrs, R. P. Dr. Richard Marr's fertility book
   616.6
Turkington, C. The encyclopedia of fertility and infer-
tility   **616.6**
Infidelity, Marital *See* Adultery
Inflammatory bowel diseases
Zonderman, J. Understanding Crohn disease and ulcer-
ative colitis   **616.3**
The **inflationary** universe. Guth, A. H.   **523.1**
Influenza
Davies, P. The devil's flu   **614.5**
Kolata, G. Flu   **614.5**
See/See also pages in the following book(s):
Oldstone, M. B. A. Viruses, plagues, and history
   614.4
Information networks
See also Computer networks; Internet
Information please almanac. See The Time almanac
   031.02
Information services
See also Business—Information services; Electron-
ic publishing; Health—Information services; Hotlines
(Telephone counseling); Medicine—Information ser-
vices
Information society
See also Information technology
Lessig, L. The future of ideas   **346.04**
Reich, R. B. The future of success   **306**
Whitaker, R. The end of privacy   **303.4**
Information storage and retrieval systems *See* Infor-
mation systems
Information systems
See also Multimedia
Directories
Gale directory of databases   **025.04**
Information technology
Encyclopedias
Encyclopedia of information systems   **004**
Vocational guidance
Moreira, P. Ace the IT job interview!   **650.14**
Informed decisions   **616.99**

Inge, William, 1913-1973
4 plays   812
Bus stop
    In Inge, W. 4 plays p149-219   812
Come back, Little Sheba
    In Inge, W. 4 plays p1-69   812
The dark at the top of the stairs
    In Inge, W. 4 plays p221-304   812
Picnic
    In Inge, W. 4 plays p71-148   812
Ingenious pursuits. Jardine, L.   509
Ingram, Jay
The barmaid's brain and other strange tales from science   500
Inheritance and succession
Clifford, D. Make your own living trust   346.05
Inheriting the revolution. Appleby, J. O.   973
Inhumane society. Fox, M. W.   179
Initiative and referendum *See* Referendum
Injuries *See* Accidents; First aid
Inland navigation
Heat Moon, W. L. River horse   917.3
Inner cities
Kozol, J. Amazing grace   362.7
Inner navigation. Jonsson, E.   153.7
Inns *See* Hotels and motels
Innuit *See* Inuit
Innumeracy. Paulos, J. A.   510
Inoculation *See* Vaccination
An **inordinate** fondness for beetles. Evans, A. V.   595.7
An **inquiry** into the nature and causes of the wealth of nations. See Smith, A. The wealth of nations   330.1
Inquisition
Kamen, H. The Spanish Inquisition   272
Insane *See* Mentally ill
Hospitals
    See Psychiatric hospitals
Insanity
Jurisprudence
    See Insanity defense
Insanity defense
Kirwin, B. The mad, the bad, and the innocent   614
Inscriptions, Cuneiform *See* Cuneiform inscriptions
Insect lives   595.7
The **insect** play. Čapek, K.
    In Čapek, K. R.U.R. and The insect play   891.8
Insect societies. Wilson, E. O.   595.7
Insects
    See also Ants; Butterflies; Moths
Alcock, J. In a desert garden   595.7
The Firefly encyclopedia of insects and spiders   595.7
Insect lives   595.7
Milne, L. J. The Audubon Society field guide to North American insects and spiders   595.7
Waldbauer, G. Millions of monarchs, bunches of beetles   595.7
Wilson, E. O. Insect societies   595.7
    See/See also pages in the following book(s):
Waldbauer, G. Insects through the seasons   595.7
Insects through the seasons. Waldbauer, G.   595.7
Inside Delta Force. Haney, E. L.   356
Inside edge. Brennan, C.   796.91
Inside Rikers. Wynn, J.   365
Inside Sahara. See Palin, M. Sahara   966
Inside the animal mind. Page, G.   591.5
Inside the CIA. Kessler, R.   327.12
Inside the hurricane. Davies, P.   551.55
Inside the Third Reich. Speer, A.   943.086
Inside the Vatican. Reese, T. J.   282
Inside women's college basketball. Kent, R. G.   796.323

Insider's guide to book editors, publishers, and literary agents. See Herman, J. Jeff Herman's guide to book publishers, editors, & literary agents   070.5
Insight guides   910.2
Insomnia
    See/See also pages in the following book(s):
Lukeman, A. Sleep well, sleep deep   616.8
Inspiration *See* Creation (Literary, artistic, etc.)
Instability rules. Flowers, C.   509
Installations (Art)
Simon, J. Ann Hamilton   92
Instinct
Menninger, K. A. Love against hate   150.19
Institutions, Charitable and philanthropic *See* Charities
Instruction *See* Teaching
Instructional materials centers
    See also School libraries
Instrumental music
    See/See also pages in the following book(s):
Grout, D. J. A history of Western music   780.9
Instruments of science   502.8
Insurance
    See also Life insurance
Insurance, Accident *See* Accident insurance
Insurance, Life *See* Life insurance
Insurance, State and compulsory *See* Social security
Insurgency
Voeten, T. How de body?   966.4
Integration in education *See* School integration
Integrity. Carter, S. L.   170
Intellect
Arendt, H. The life of the mind   153
Baars, B. J. In the theater of consciousness   153
Calvin, W. H. How brains think   153.9
Goleman, D. Emotional intelligence   152.4
Jolly, A. Lucy's legacy   599.93
Sagan, C. The dragons of Eden   153
Sternberg, R. J. Successful intelligence   153.9
    See/See also pages in the following book(s):
Deacon, T. W. The symbolic species p145-64   153.6
Glynn, I. An anatomy of thought   612.8
Pinker, S. How the mind works p60-69; 183-98   153
Intellectual freedom
    See also Freedom of information
Intellectual freedom manual   323.44
Symons, A. K. Protecting the right to read   025.2
Intellectual freedom manual   323.44
Intellectual life
Seymour-Smith, M. The 100 most influential books ever written   028
Watson, P. The modern mind   909.82
Intellectuals
United States
Posner, R. A. Public intellectuals   305.5
Intelligence *See* Intellect
Intelligence, Artificial *See* Artificial intelligence
Intelligence of animals *See* Animal intelligence
Intelligence service
    See also Espionage
Germany (East)
Garton Ash, T. The file   327.12
Great Britain
Dorril, S. MI6   327.12
United States
Herrington, S. A. Traitors among us   327.12
Kessler, R. Inside the CIA   327.12
Miller, J. The cell: inside the 9/11 plot and why the FBI and CIA failed to stop it   973.931
Prados, J. Presidents' secret wars   327.12
Stinnett, R. B. Day of deceit   940.54
Theoharis, A. G. Chasing spies   327.12

Intelligence tests
Gould, S. J. The mismeasure of man   **153.9**
Sternberg, R. J. Successful intelligence   **153.9**
Intelligentsia *See* Intellectuals
Intercommunication systems
Weems, D. B. Designing, building, and testing your own speaker system with projects   **621.382**
Intercultural education *See* Multicultural education
Interdisciplinary encyclopedia of marine sciences   **551**
Interest (Economics)
Keynes, J. M. The general theory of employment, interest and money   **330.1**
Interior decoration *See* Interior design
Interior design
Bakker, R. Elderdesign   **728**
Decorating basics   **747**
Engelbreit, M. Mary Engelbreit's children's companion   **645**
Gilliatt, M. The complete book of home design   **747**
Harwood, B. Architecture and interior design through the 18th century   **729**
Home improvement 1-2-3   **643**
Jones, M. Handcrafted ceramic tiles   **738**
Jordan, W. A. The kidspace idea book   **747**
Michael, M. The new apartment book   **747**
The New decorating book   **747**
Saunders, G. Wallpaper in interior decoration   **747**
Slesin, S. Japanese style   **747.2**
Stewart, M. Martha Stewart's new old house   **728**
Susanka, S. Creating the not so big house   **728**
Susanka, S. Not so big solutions for your home   **728**
Travis, D. Debbie Travis' painted house   **698**
Intermarriage
See also Interracial marriage
Internal security
United States
Fariello, G. Red scare   **973.92**
From the secret files of J. Edgar Hoover   **363.2**
International agencies
Rieff, D. A bed for the night   **361.2**
International arbitration
Mitchell, G. J. Making peace   **941.6**
International Bank for Reconstruction and Development *See* World Bank
International Brotherhood of Teamsters, Chauffeurs, Warehousemen and Helpers of America
See/See also pages in the following book(s):
Russell, T. Out of the jungle: Jimmy Hoffa and the remaking of the American working class   **92**
International business information. Pagell, R. A.   **650**
International Business Machines Corp.
Gerstner, L. V., Jr. Who says elephants can't dance?   **338.7**
International Conference on Relocation and Redress (1983: Salt Lake City, Utah)
Japanese Americans, from relocation to redress. See Japanese Americans, from relocation to redress   **940.53**
International cooperation
Nye, J. S., Jr. The paradox of American power   **327.73**
International dictionary of ballet   **792.8**
International dictionary of food & cooking   **641.03**
International dictionary of modern dance   **792.8**
International dictionary of the English language, Webster's third new   **423**
International directories in print. See Directories in print   **060.25**

International economic relations
See also International finance
Friedman, T. L. The Lexus and the olive tree   **337**
Fukuyama, F. Trust   **330.9**
Soros, G. George Soros on globalization   **337**
Stiglitz, J. E. Globalization and its discontents   **337**
International encyclopedia of astronomy. See Astronomy encyclopedia   **520**
International encyclopedia of dance   **792.8**
International encyclopedia of linguistics   **410**
International encyclopedia of marriage and family   **306.8**
International encyclopedia of women scientists. Oakes, E. H.   **920.003**
International finance
Soros, G. George Soros on globalization   **337**
Stiglitz, J. E. Globalization and its discontents   **337**
International law
Moynihan, D. P. On the law of nations   **327.73**
International literary market place: ILMP   **070.5025**
International Monetary Fund
Stiglitz, J. E. Globalization and its discontents   **337**
See/See also pages in the following book(s):
Soros, G. George Soros on globalization   **337**
International motion picture almanac   **791.43**
International politics *See* World politics
International relations
See also World politics
Bobbitt, P. The shield of Achilles   **327**
Kaplan, R. D. Warrior politics   **320**
Moore, J. A. Encyclopedia of the United Nations   **341.23**
Spence, G. How to argue and win every time   **153.8**
Encyclopedias
Nolan, C. J. The Greenwood encyclopedia of international relations   **327**
Osmańczyk, E. J. Encyclopedia of the United Nations and international agreements   **341.23**
The **International** who's who   **920.003**
Internet
Crystal, D. Language and the Internet   **400**
Henry, S. The Dinner Club   **338.7**
History of the Internet   **004.6**
Hoffmann, G. M. Copyright in cyberspace   **346.04**
Lessig, L. The future of ideas   **346.04**
Levine, J. R. The Internet for dummies   **004.6**
Naughton, J. A brief history of the future   **621.382**
Spector, R. Amazon.com   **338.7**
Speed, T. The personal Internet security guidebook   **005.8**
See/See also pages in the following book(s):
Cassidy, J. Dot.con   **381**
Dyson, F. J. The sun, the genome, & the Internet   **303.4**
Dictionaries
Berry, C. W. Computer and Internet dictionary for ages 9 to 99   **004**
Downing, D. Dictionary of computer and Internet terms   **004**
Security measures
Jennings, C. The hundredth window   **005.8**
Social aspects
Lewis, M. Next: the future just happened   **303.4**
Internet commerce *See* Electronic commerce
The **Internet** for dummies. Levine, J. R.   **004.6**
Internet searching
Sauers, M. Using the Internet as a reference tool   **025.04**
Internment camps *See* Concentration camps

Interpersonal relations
Bing, S. Throwing the elephant   650.1
Buscaglia, L. F. Loving each other   158
Carter, S. Men like women who like themselves
    158
Fisher, A. B. If my career's on the fast track, where
    do I get a road map?   650.14
Gilligan, C. The birth of pleasure   152.4
Gray, J. Mars and Venus starting over   306.7
Hallowell, E. M. Connect   158
Hooks, B. Salvation   306.7
Jampolsky, G. G. Love is the answer: creating positive
    relationships   152.4
Lerner, H. G. The dance of intimacy   155.6
Stone, D. Difficult conversations   158
See/See also pages in the following book(s):
Toffler, A. Future shock p86-111   303.4
Interpretation of dreams. Freud, S.   154.6
also in Freud, S. The basic writings of Sigmund
    Freud   150.19
The **Interpreter's** Bible. See The New Interpreter's Bi-
ble   220.7
The **Interpreter's** dictionary of the Bible   220.3
Interpreting and translating See Translating and inter-
preting
Interracial adoption
Kennedy, R. Interracial intimacies   346.01
Interracial intimacies. Kennedy, R.   346.01
Interracial marriage
    Law and legislation
Kennedy, R. Interracial intimacies   346.01
Interracial relations See Race relations
Interview. Pinter, H.
In Pinter, H. Complete works v3   822
The **interview** kit. Beatty, R. H.   650.14
Interviewing
Beatty, R. H. The interview kit   650.14
Moreira, P. Ace the IT job interview!   650.14
Yate, M. J. Knock 'em dead   650.14
Intestines
    Diseases
See also Inflammatory bowel diseases
An **intimate** look at the night sky. Raymo, C.   520
Intimate Merton. Merton, T.   92
Intner, Sheila S., 1935-
Standard cataloging for school and public libraries
    025.3
Into Africa. Dugard, M.   92
Into the garden   808.8
Into the looking-glass wood. Manguel, A.   814
Into the storm. Clancy, T.   956.7
Into the tangle of friendship. Kephart, B.   158
Into thin air. Krakauer, J.   796.52
Into Tibet. Laird, T.   327.12
Intolerance See Toleration
Intoxicants See Narcotics
Introduction to Aristotle. Aristotle   888
An **introduction** to fossils and minerals. Erickson, J.
    560
Introduction to logic. Copi, I. M.   160
Introduction to reference work. Katz, W. A.   025.5
An **introduction** to the New Testament. Brown, R. E.
    225
Inuit
Waterman, J. Arctic crossing   998
See/See also pages in the following book(s):
Ehrlich, G. This cold heaven   998
    Art
Hessel, I. Inuit art   704
Invalids See Sick
Invasion of privacy See Right of privacy
Invented Eden. Hemley, R.   959.9
Inventing modern America. Brown, D. E.   609
Inventing paradise. Keeley, E.   818
Inventing the 19th century. Van Dulken, S.   609

Inventing the 20th century. Van Dulken, S.   609
Inventing wonderland. Wullschläger, J.   820.9
Inventing Wyatt Earp. Barra, A.   92
Invention by design. Petroski, H.   620
The **invention** of clouds. Hamblyn, R.   551.57
The **invention** of love. Stoppard, T.   822
The **invention** that changed the world. Buderi, R.
    621.3848
Inventions
Brain, M. Marshall Brain's more how stuff works
    600
Brown, D. E. Inventing modern America   609
Flatow, I. They all laughed   609
Keoke, E. D. Encyclopedia of American Indian contri-
    butions to the world   970.004
Lindsay, D. House of invention   609
Macaulay, D. The new way things work   600
Macdonald, A. L. Feminine ingenuity   609
Petroski, H. The evolution of useful things   609
Petroski, H. Invention by design   620
Van Dulken, S. Inventing the 19th century   609
Van Dulken, S. Inventing the 20th century   609
    History
Karwatka, D. Technology's past   609
Williams, T. I. A history of invention   609
Inventions of farewell   821.008
Inventions of the March Hare. Eliot, T. S.   811
Inventors
Brown, D. E. Inventing modern America   609
Carey, C. W. American inventors, entrepreneurs, and
    business visionaries   920
Karwatka, D. Technology's past   609
Uglow, J. S. The lunar men   920
Inventors, African American See African American in-
ventors
Invertebrate zoology. Barnes, R. D.   592
Invertebrates
Barnes, R. D. Invertebrate zoology   592
Hubbell, S. Waiting for Aphrodite   592
Investments
Bernstein, W. The four pillars of investing   332.6
Carlson, C. B. The smart investor's survival guide
    332.6
Downes, J. Barron's finance & investment handbook
    332.6
Gardner, D. The Motley Fool's what to do with your
    money now   332.6
Hagstrom, R. G. The Warren Buffett way   332.6
Henry, S. The Dinner Club   338.7
Lynch, P. One up on Wall Street   332.6
Quinn, J. B. Making the most of your money
    332.024
Schwab-Pomerantz, C. It pays to talk   332.024
Stern, K. To hell and back   332.6
Tobias, A. P. The only investment guide you'll ever
    need   332.024
Invisible allies. Solzhenitsyn, A.   92
Invisible Eden. Flook, M.   364.1
The **invisible** enemy. Crawford, D. H.   616
The **invisible** wall. Blumenthal, W. M.   943
Inwood, Robert
Creative country construction   690
Ion. Euripides
In Euripides. Ten plays p133-72   882
Ionesco, Eugène
The future is in eggs
In Ionesco, E. Rhinoceros, and other plays   842
The leader
In Ionesco, E. Rhinoceros, and other plays   842
Rhinoceros
In Ionesco, E. Rhinoceros, and other plays   842
In Nine plays of the modern theater p471-572
    808.82
Rhinoceros, and other plays   842

Ionesco, Eugène—*Continued*
See/See also pages in the following book(s):
Playwrights at work   812.009
Iphigenia among the Taurians. Euripides
In Euripides. Ten plays p243-78   882
Iphigenia at Aulis. Euripides
In Euripides. Ten plays p315-54   882
IQ tests *See* Intelligence tests
IRA *See* Irish Republican Army
Iran
Molavi, A. Persian pilgrimages   955
Description
See/See also pages in the following book(s):
Naipaul, V. S. Among the believers p3-82   297
Foreign relations—United States
See also Iran hostage crisis, 1979-1981
History—1979-
See also Iran-Iraq War, 1980-1988
Politics and government
Mackey, S. The Iranians   955
Wright, R. The last great revolution   955
Iran-Contra Affair, 1985-1990
The Iran Contra scandal   973.927
The Iran-Contra scandal   973.927
Iran hostage crisis, 1979-1981
Follett, K. On wings of eagles   955
Iran-Iraq War, 1980-1988
Hiro, D. The longest war   955
The **Iranians**. Mackey, S.   955
Iraq
History
Tripp, C. A history of Iraq   956.7
History—1991, Persian Gulf War
See Persian Gulf War, 1991
Politics and government
Mackey, S. The reckoning   956.7
Iraq-Iran War, 1980-1988 *See* Iran-Iraq War, 1980-1988
Iraq-Kuwait Crisis, 1990-1991 *See* Persian Gulf War, 1991
Iraqi-Iranian war, 1980-1988 *See* Iran-Iraq War, 1980-1988
Ireland, Norma Olin, 1907-
(comp) Index to fairy tales. *See* Index to fairy tales
398.2
Ireland
See/See also pages in the following book(s):
O'Faolain, N. Almost there   92
Civilization
Cahill, T. How the Irish saved civilization 941.5
Keneally, T. The great shame   304.8
History
Black, J. A history of the British Isles   941
Davies, N. The Isles   941
Moorhouse, G. Sun dancing   941.5
The Oxford illustrated history of Ireland   941.5
History—Encyclopedias
The Oxford companion to Irish history   941.5
Immigration and emigration
Keneally, T. The great shame   304.8
Social conditions
Ardagh, J. Ireland and the Irish   941.5
Ireland and the Irish. Ardagh, J.   941.5
Iris and her friends. Bayley, J.   92
Irish
History
Keneally, T. The great shame   304.8
Irish Americans
See/See also pages in the following book(s):
Glazer, N. Beyond the melting pot p217-87   305.8
Encyclopedias
The Encyclopedia of the Irish in America   305.8
Irish literature
Bio-bibliography
The Oxford companion to Irish literature   820.9

Dictionaries
The Oxford companion to Irish literature   820.9
Irish national characteristics
Ardagh, J. Ireland and the Irish   941.5
Irish poetry
Collections
The New Oxford book of Irish verse   821.008
History and criticism
Heaney, S. The redress of poetry   821.009
Irish Republican Army
Toolis, K. Rebel hearts   941.6
Iron, Ralph *See* Schreiner, Olive, 1855-1920
Iron & silk. Salzman, M.   915.1
Iron horse: Lou Gehrig in his time. Robinson, R.
92
Iron John. Bly, R.   305.31
The **iron** wall. Shlaim, A.   956.94
Irons, Peter H., 1940-
Jim Crow's children   344
A people's history of the Supreme Court   347
Irons in the fire. McPhee, J. A.   814
Iroquois Indians
See/See also pages in the following book(s):
Josephy, A. M. Now that the buffalo's gone p130-50
970.004
History
Fenton, W. N. The Great Law and the Longhouse
970.004
Irrational man. Barrett, W.   142
The **irreducible** needs of children. Brazelton, T. B.
155.4
Irregular serials & annuals. *See* Ulrich's periodicals directory
011
Irrigation
West (U.S.)
Reisner, M. P. Cadillac desert   333.91
Irving, David John Cawdell, 1938-
About
Evans, R. J. Lying about Hitler   940.53
Guttenplan, D. D. The Holocaust on trial   940.53
Irving, Shae
(ed) Nolo's encyclopedia of everyday law. *See* Nolo's encyclopedia of everyday law
340
Irwin, Bobbie
Spin off magazine presents the Spinner's companion
746.1
Irwin, John P., 1926-
Another river, another town   940.54
Irwin, P. K. *See* Page, P. K. (Patricia Kathleen), 1916-
Irwin, Patricia Kathleen Page *See* Page, P. K. (Patricia Kathleen), 1916-
Irwin, Robert, 1946-
(ed) Night and horses and the desert. *See* Night and horses and the desert
892
Is it a choice? Marcus, E.   305.9
Is the Bible true? Sheler, J. L.   220.1
Is there a nutmeg in the house? David, E. 641.5
Isaac Asimov's guide to earth & space. Asimov, I.
520
Isaacs, Arnold R.
Vietnam shadows   959.704
Isaacs, Ronald H.
Sacred seasons   296.4
Isaac's storm. Larson, E.   976.4
Isabella I, Queen of Spain, 1451-1504
See/See also pages in the following book(s):
Fraser, A. The warrior queens   920
Isabella, Queen, consort of Edward II, King of England, 1292-1358
About
Doherty, P. C. Isabella and the strange death of Edward II
92
Isabella, of France *See* Isabella, Queen, consort of Edward II, King of England, 1292-1358

Isabella and the strange death of Edward II. Doherty, P. C.   **92**

Isabelle, de France *See* Isabella, Queen, consort of Edward II, King of England, 1292-1358

Isherwood, Christopher, 1904-1986
Diaries v1   **92**

Ishi

About
Kroeber, T. Ishi in two worlds   **92**

Ishi in two worlds. Kroeber, T.   **92**

Islam
See also Islamic fundamentalism; Sufism
Armstrong, K. Islam   **297**
Ben Jelloun, T. Islam explained   **297**
Esposito, J. L. Islam   **297**
Esposito, J. L. What everyone needs to know about Islam   **297**
Gordon, M. Islam   **297**
Lippman, T. W. Understanding Islam   **297**
The Many faces of Islam   **297**
The Muslim almanac   **297**
Naipaul, V. S. Among the believers   **297**
Naipaul, V. S. Beyond belief   **297**
Nasr, S. H. Islam: religion, history, and civilization   **297**
The Oxford history of Islam   **297**
Smith, J. I. Islam in America   **297**
Wolfe, M. One thousand roads to Mecca   **297**
See/See also pages in the following book(s):
Armstrong, K. A history of God   **291**
Potok, C. Wanderings p243-77   **909**

Dictionaries
Concise encyclopedia of Islam   **297**
The Oxford dictionary of Islam   **297**

Islam and politics
Benjamin, D. The age of sacred terror   **303.6**
Esposito, J. L. Unholy war   **322.4**
Kepel, G. Jihad   **297**
Miller, J. God has ninety-nine names   **956**
Murphy, C. Passion for Islam   **297**
Pipes, D. Militant Islam reaches America   **320.5**

Islam explained. Ben Jelloun, T.   **297**

Islam in America. Smith, J. I.   **297**

Islam: religion, history, and civilization. Nasr, S. H.   **297**

Islamic art
Stierlin, H. Islamic art and architecture   **709.1**

Islamic art and architecture. Stierlin, H.   **709.1**

Islamic civilization
Ansary, M. T. West of Kabul, East of New York   **958.1**
Nasr, S. H. Islam: religion, history, and civilization   **297**

Islamic countries
See also Arab countries
Brooks, G. Nine parts of desire   **305.4**
Goodwin, J. Price of honor   **305.4**
The Muslim almanac   **297**

Description
Naipaul, V. S. Beyond belief   **297**

History
The Cambridge illustrated history of the Islamic world   **909**

Politics and government
The Many faces of Islam   **297**

Islamic fundamentalism
Pipes, D. Militant Islam reaches America   **320.5**
Rashid, A. Taliban: militant Islam, oil, and fundamentalism in Central Asia   **958.1**
See/See also pages in the following book(s):
Armstrong, K. The battle for God   **291**

Islam's Black slaves. Segal, R.   **326**

The **island** of the colorblind. Sacks, O. W.   **617.7**

Islands, Imaginary *See* Geographical myths

Islands of the Pacific
Michener, J. A. Return to paradise   **990**
Sacks, O. W. The island of the colorblind   **617.7**
Souhami, D. Selkirk's Island   **996**

Isle au Haut (Maine)
Greenlaw, L. The lobster chronicles   **639**

The **Isles**. Davies, N.   **941**

Isn't it romantic. Wasserstein, W.
In Wasserstein, W. The Heidi chronicles, and other plays   **812**

Isocrates
See/See also pages in the following book(s):
Hamilton, E. The echo of Greece p63-79   **880.9**

Israel, Paul
Edison   **92**

Israel, Wendy S.
(jt. auth) Michael, M. The new apartment book   **747**

Israel
See also Jerusalem
See/See also pages in the following book(s):
Conroy, J. Unspeakable acts, ordinary people   **323.4**
Tuchman, B. W. Practicing history p123-45, 173-87   **907**

Foreign relations
Shlaim, A. The iron wall   **956.94**

History
Gilbert, M. Jerusalem in the twentieth century   **956.94**
Peres, S. The imaginary voyage   **956.94**
Sachar, H. M. A history of Israel   **956.94**
See/See also pages in the following book(s):
Armstrong, K. The battle for God   **291**

Immigration and emigration
Szulc, T. The secret alliance   **325**

Politics and government
Friedman, T. L. From Beirut to Jerusalem   **956**
Hazony, Y. The Jewish state   **956.94**
Horovitz, D. P. A little too close to God   **956.94**
Kurzman, D. Soldier of peace: the life of Yitzhak Rabin   **92**

Social conditions
Gordis, D. If a place can make you cry   **956.94**
Horovitz, D. P. A little too close to God   **956.94**
Shipler, D. K. Arab and Jew   **956.94**

Israel-Arab conflicts
Blumenfeld, L. R. Revenge   **956.94**
Farsoun, S. K. Palestine and the Palestinians   **956.94**
Morris, B. Righteous victims   **956**
Said, E. W. The end of the peace process   **956**
Shipler, D. K. Arab and Jew   **956.94**
Shlaim, A. The iron wall   **956.94**

Israel-Arab War, 1948-1949
Collins, L. O Jerusalem!   **956.94**

Israel-Arab War, 1967
Oren, M. Six days of war   **956.04**

The **Israel** Museum, Jerusalem   **708**

Israeli-Arab relations *See* Jewish-Arab relations

Israeli cooking
Nathan, J. The foods of Israel today   **641.5**

Israeli national characteristics
Horovitz, D. P. A little too close to God   **956.94**

Isserman, Maurice
The other American: the life of Michael Harrington   **92**

It doesn't take a hero: General H. Norman Schwarzkopf. Schwarzkopf, H. N.   **92**

It doesn't take a rocket scientist. Malone, J. W.   **920**

It is so! (If you think so). Pirandello, L.
In Pirandello, L. Naked masks p61-138   **852**

It pays to talk. Schwab-Pomerantz, C.   **332.024**

It takes a worried man. Halpin, B.   **362.1**

It wasn't always easy, but I sure had fun. Grizzard, L.
817

Italian Americans
See/See also pages in the following book(s):
Glazer, N. Beyond the melting pot p181-216
305.8

Italian art
The Medici, Michelangelo, & the art of late Renaissance Florence **709.45**
Wittkower, R. Art and architecture in Italy, 1600-1750
709.45

Italian cooking
Bastianich, L. Lidia's Italian-American kitchen
641.5
Bastianich, L. Lidia's Italian table **641.5**
Bishop, J. The complete Italian vegetarian cookbook
641.5
Bugialli, G. Bugialli's Italy **641.5**
Downie, D. Cooking the Roman way **641.5**
Hazan, M. Essentials of classic Italian cooking
641.5
Hazan, M. Marcella cucina **641.5**
Negrin, M. Rustico: regional Italian country cooking
641.5
Willinger, F. H. Red, white, and greens **641.6**
See/See also pages in the following book(s):
Mayes, F. Under the Tuscan sun 945
An **Italian** education. Parks, T. 945

Italian-English bilingual books *See* Bilingual books—English-Italian

Italian literature
Bio-bibliography
The Oxford companion to Italian literature 850.3
Dictionaries
Dictionary of Italian literature 850.3
The Oxford companion to Italian literature 850.3
History and criticism
The Cambridge history of Italian literature 850.9

Italian national characteristics
Barzini, L. G. The Italians 945
The **Italians**. Barzini, L. G. 945

Italy
Antiquities
Fowler, B. Iceman 937
Civilization
Barzini, L. G. The Italians 945
History
The Oxford history of Italy 945
See/See also pages in the following book(s):
Durant, W. J. The age of Louis XIV p428-45
940.2
History—0-1559
King, R. Michelangelo & the Pope's ceiling
759.5
History—1914-1945
Lamb, R. War in Italy, 1943-1945 940.54
Politics and government
Bosworth, R. J. B. Mussolini 92
Robb, P. Midnight in Sicily 945
See/See also pages in the following book(s):
Barzini, L. G. The Italians p234-51 945
Social conditions
See/See also pages in the following book(s):
Barzini, L. G. The Italians p176-233 945
Social life and customs
Parks, T. An Italian education 945
It's not about food. Normandi, C. E. **616.85**
It's not about the bike. Armstrong, L. 92
It's time: poems. Gibbons, R. 811
Ivanov. Chekhov, A. P.
In Chekhov, A. P. The plays of Anton Chekhov p51-108 **891.7**
Iverson, Peter
We are still here **970.004**

Ives, Charles Edward, 1874-1954
About
Swafford, J. Charles Ives 92
Ives, Martine, 1975-
Caring for a child with autism **618.92**
Ivins, Molly
Molly Ivins can't say that, can she? 817
Nothing but good times ahead 817
Ivory Coast
Politics and government
See/See also pages in the following book(s):
Naipaul, V. S. The writer and the world p229-98
824
Iwo Jima, Battle of, 1945
Bradley, J. Flags of our fathers **940.54**
Iyengar, B. K. S., 1918-
Yoga **613.7**
Iyer, Pico
The global soul **910.4**
The lady and the monk **952.04**
Tropical classical 814
Izac, Edouard V. M., 1891-1990
See/See also pages in the following book(s):
Mikaelian, A. Medal of honor 920
Izenberg, Neil
(ed) Human diseases and conditions. See Human diseases and conditions 616

J

J.D. Salinger [critical essays] **813.009**
J.K. Lasser Tax Institute
How to run a small business. See How to run a small business **658.1**
J.K. Lasser's your income tax **336.2**
The **J.** Paul Getty Museum and its collections 708
J.R.R. Tolkien, artist & illustrator. Hammond, W. G.
92
Jabbar, Kareem Abdul- *See* Abdul-Jabbar, Kareem, 1947-
Jack, Belinda Elizabeth
George Sand 92
Jack the Ripper
About
Cornwell, P. D. Portrait of a killer **364.1**
The Ultimate Jack the Ripper companion **364.1**
Jackie after Jack [biography of Jacqueline Kennedy Onassis] Andersen, C. P. 92
Jackson, Andrew, 1767-1845
About
Booraem, H. Young Hickory: the making of Andrew Jackson 92
Remini, R. V. Andrew Jackson & his Indian wars
973.5
Wallace, A. F. C. The long bitter trail **970.004**
See/See also pages in the following book(s):
Hofstadter, R. The American political tradition, and the men who made it p44-66 973
Jackson, Blair
Garcia 92
Jackson, Carlton
Hattie: the life of Hattie McDaniel 92
Jackson, Ellen
(jt. auth) Jackson, T. The new perfect resume
650.14
Jackson, Jesse L., 1941-
See/See also pages in the following book(s):
Baraka, I. A. The LeRoi Jones/Amiri Baraka reader
818
Dyson, M. E. Race rules **305.8**
Jackson, Joe, 1887 or 8-1951
About
Fleitz, D. L. Shoeless 92

Jackson, Kenneth T.
(ed) The Encyclopedia of New York City. See The Encyclopedia of New York City   **974.7**
(ed) The Scribner encyclopedia of American lives. See The Scribner encyclopedia of American lives   **920.003**

Jackson, Luke
Freaks, geeks and asperger syndrome   **618.92**

Jackson, Major, 1968-
Leaving Saturn   **811**

Jackson, Shirley, 1919-1965
See/See also pages in the following book(s):
American women fiction writers   **813.009**

Jackson, Tom
The new perfect resume   **650.14**

Jackson (Miss.)
Hemingway, L. A world turned over   **363.34**

Jackson-Laufer, Guida M. (Guida Myrl)
Women rulers throughout the ages   **920**

Jackstraws. Simic, C.   **811**

Jacob, Merle
To be continued   **016.8**

Jacobi, C. G. J. (Carl Gustav Jakob), 1804-1851
See/See also pages in the following book(s):
Bell, E. T. Men of mathematics p327-39   **920**

Jacobi, Carl Gustav Jakob *See* Jacobi, C. G. J. (Carl Gustav Jakob), 1804-1851

Jacobik, Gray
Brave disguises   **811**

Jacobs, Lou
The big picture   **770**

Jacobs, Paul DuBois
(jt. auth) Seeger, P. Pete Seeger's storytelling book   **372.6**

Jacobsen, Josephine
In the crevice of time   **811**

Jacobsen, Rolf, 1907-1994
The roads have come to an end now   **839.8**

Jacobson, Julius
The classical music experience   **781.6**

Jacobson, Max, 1941-
Patterns of home   **728**

Jacobson's organ and the remarkable nature of smell. Watson, L.   **612.8**

Jacques Pépin celebrates. Pépin, J.   **641.5**

Jacques Pépin's simple and healthy cooking. Pépin, J.   **641.5**

Jadeite
Levy, A. The stone of heaven   **553.8**

Jaderstrom, Susan
Complete office handbook   **651.8**

Jaffrey, Madhur
Madhur Jaffrey's world vegetarian   **641.5**

Jagan, Cheddi, 1918-1997
See/See also pages in the following book(s):
Naipaul, V. S. The writer and the world p485-502   **824**

Jago, Lucy
The northern lights [biography of Kristian Birkeland]   **92**

Jaguar of sweet laughter. Ackerman, D.   **811**

Jahanshahi, Marjan
Parkinson's disease. See Parkinson's disease   **616.8**

Jakosky, Bruce M.
The search for life on other planets   **576.8**

Jamaica
Religion
Chevannes, B. Rastafari: roots and ideology   **299**

James I, King of Great Britain, 1566-1625
About
Nicolson, A. God's secretaries: the making of the King James Bible   **220.5**

James VI, King of Scotland *See* James I, King of Great Britain, 1566-1625

James, Chris
The complete serger handbook   **646.2**

James, Etta, 1938-
Rage to survive: the Etta James story   **92**

James, Henry, 1811-1882
About
Habegger, A. The father: a life of Henry James, Sr   **92**

James, Henry, 1843-1916
Literary criticism   **809**
The portable Henry James   **818**
See/See also pages in the following book(s):
Kazin, A. An American procession p211-34   **810.9**
Ozick, C. Quarrel & quandary   **814**
Vidal, G. United States—essays, 1952-1992 p167-86   **814**

James, Jesse, 1847-1882
About
Stiles, T. J. Jesse James   **92**

James, Lawrence
The rise and fall of the British Empire   **909**

James, P. D.
Time to be in earnest   **92**

James, William, 1842-1910
The varieties of religious experience   **210**
About
Menand, L. The Metaphysical Club   **973.9**
See/See also pages in the following book(s):
Commager, H. S. The American mind   **973**
Dewey, J. The philosophy of John Dewey   **191**
Durant, W. J. The story of philosophy p381-89   **109**

James Beard's American cookery. Beard, J.   **641.5**

The **James** Dickey reader. Dickey, J.   **818**

James family
About
Habegger, A. The father: a life of Henry James, Sr   **92**

James Herriot's animal stories. Herriot, J.   **636.089**
James Herriot's cat stories. Herriot, J.   **636.8**
James Herriot's dog stories. Herriot, J.   **636.7**
James Herriot's Yorkshire. Herriot, J.   **914.2**
James Joyce A to Z. Fargnoli, A. N.   **823.009**
James Joyce's Ulysses   **823.009**

Jamestown (Va.)
History
Noël Hume, I. The Virginia adventure   **975.5**

Jamison, Bill
(jt. auth) Jamison, C. A. American home cooking   **641.5**
(jt. auth) Jamison, C. A. A real American breakfast   **641.5**

Jamison, Cheryl Alters
American home cooking   **641.5**
A real American breakfast   **641.5**

Jammu and Kashmir (India)
See/See also pages in the following book(s):
Koul, S. The tiger ladies   **92**

Jampolsky, Gerald G., 1925-
Love is the answer: creating positive relationships   **152.4**

Jane Addams and the dream of American democracy. Elshtain, J. B.   **92**
A **Jane** Austen encyclopedia. Poplawski, P.   **823.009**
Jane Brody's allergy fighter. Brody, J. E.   **616.2**
Jane Brody's good seafood book. Brody, J. E.   **641.6**

Jane Seymour, Queen, consort of Henry VIII, King of England, 1509?-1537
See/See also pages in the following book(s):
Fraser, A. The wives of Henry VIII p225-83   **920**
Starkey, D. Six wives: the queens of Henry VIII   **920**

Janer, Albert Christ- *See* Christ-Janer, Albert
Jane's all the world's aircraft   **629.133**

Jane's fighting ships   623.8

Janes-Hodder, Honna, 1966-
Childhood cancer   618.92

Janowitz, Henry D.
Good food for bad stomachs   616.3

Jansen, Marius B.
The making of modern Japan   952

Janson, H. W. (Horst Woldemar), 1913-1982
History of art   709

Janson, Horst Woldemar *See* Janson, H. W. (Horst Woldemar), 1913-1982

Japan
The Cambridge encyclopedia of Japan   952
Reischauer, E. O. The Japanese today   952
     Civilization
Benedict, R. The chrysanthemum and the sword   952
Encyclopedia of contemporary Japanese culture   952.04
Smith, P. L. Japan   952
     Foreign relations—United States
LaFeber, W. The clash   327.73
     History
Beasley, W. G. The rise of modern Japan   952
Jansen, M. B. The making of modern Japan   952
McClain, J. L. Japan, a modern history   952
Perez, L. G. The history of Japan   952
Reischauer, E. O. Japan: the story of a nation   952
Reischauer, E. O. Japan, tradition & transformation   952
Smith, P. L. Japan   952
     History—1868-1945
Frank, R. B. Downfall   940.54
Keene, D. Emperor of Japan: Meiji and His world, 1852-1912   92
     History—1945-1952, Allied occupation
Dower, J. W. Embracing defeat   952.04
     Kings and rulers
Seagrave, S. The Yamato dynasty   952
     Politics and government
Bix, H. P. Hirohito and the making of modern Japan   92
Seagrave, S. The Yamato dynasty   952
     Social life and customs
Benedict, R. The chrysanthemum and the sword   952
Downer, L. Women of the pleasure quarters   952

Japan, a modern history. McClain, J. L.   952

Japan: the story of a nation. Reischauer, E. O.   952

Japan, tradition & transformation. Reischauer, E. O.   952

The **Japanese.** See Reischauer, E. O. The Japanese today   952

Japanese American internment during World War II. Ng, W. L.   940.53

Japanese Americans
     Evacuation and relocation, 1942-1945
Daniels, R. Prisoners without trial   940.53
Japanese Americans, from relocation to redress   940.53
Ng, W. L. Japanese American internment during World War II   940.53
See/See also pages in the following book(s):
Rehnquist, W. H. All the laws but one p184-211   342

Japanese Americans, from relocation to redress   940.53

Japanese authors *See* Authors, Japanese

Japanese cooking
Shimbo, H. The Japanese kitchen   641.5

Japanese decoration and ornament
Slesin, S. Japanese style   747.2

Japanese drama
See also Nō plays
The **Japanese** kitchen. Shimbo, H.   641.5

Japanese language
     Dictionaries
Basic Japanese-English dictionary   495.6
The Oxford-Duden pictorial English-Japanese dictionary   495.6

Japanese literature
     Collections
Modern Japanese literature   895.6
     History and criticism
Keene, D. The pleasures of Japanese literature   895.6
Keene, D. Seeds in the heart   895.6
Modern Japanese writers   920.003

Japanese national characteristics
Benedict, R. The chrysanthemum and the sword   952
Reischauer, E. O. The Japanese today   952

Japanese poetry
     Collections
One hundred poems from the Japanese   895.6

Japanese-Russian War, 1904-1905 *See* Russo-Japanese War, 1904-1905

Japanese style. Slesin, S.   747.2

The **Japanese** today. Reischauer, E. O.   952

Jardine, Lisa, 1944-
Ingenious pursuits   509

Jargon, Computer *See* Computer science—Dictionaries

Jarhead: a Marine's chronicle of the Gulf War and other battles. Swofford, A.   956.7

Jarman, Beatriz Galimberti *See* Galimberti Jarman, Beatriz

Jarrell, Randall, 1914-1965
The complete poems   811
The lost world
   In Jarrell, R. The complete poems   811
No other book   809
Selected poems
   In Jarrell, R. The complete poems   811
The woman at the Washington Zoo
   In Jarrell, R. The complete poems   811
   See/See also pages in the following book(s):
Lowell, R. Collected prose p87-98   818

Jarry, Alfred, 1873-1907
King Ubu
   In Our dramatic heritage v6   808.82

Jason, Philip K., 1941-
Masterplots II, poetry series. See Masterplots II, poetry series   809.1

Jaspers, Karl, 1883-1969
The great philosophers   109
   See/See also pages in the following book(s):
Existentialism from Dostoevsky to Sartre p158-232   142

Jastrow, Robert, 1925-
God and the astronomers   523.1

Java man. Swisher, C. C.   599.93

Jawaharlal Nehru *See* Nehru, Jawaharlal, 1889-1964

Jay, Antony
(ed) The Oxford dictionary of political quotations. See The Oxford dictionary of political quotations   808.88

Jay, Ricky
Jay's journal of anomalies   791

Jay's journal of anomalies. Jay, R.   791

Jayyusi, Salma Khadra
(ed) Anthology of modern Palestinian literature. See Anthology of modern Palestinian literature   892

Jazz. Ward, G. C.   781.65

Jazz: a critic's guide to the 100 most important recordings. Ratliff, B.   781.65

Jazz modernism. Appel, A.   781.65

Jazz music
See also Blues music
Appel, A. Jazz modernism 781.65
DeVeaux, S. K. The birth of bebop 781.65
Friedwald, W. Jazz singing 781.65
Giddins, G. Visions of jazz 781.65
Hentoff, N. Listen to the stories 781.65
Jazz: the first century 781.65
Milkowski, B. Swing it! 781.65
The New Grove dictionary of jazz 781.65
The Oxford companion to jazz 781.65
Shipton, A. A new history of jazz 781.65
Ward, G. C. Jazz 781.65
See/See also pages in the following book(s):
Gioia, T. The history of jazz 781.65
Discography
All music guide to jazz 781.65
Ratliff, B. Jazz: a critic's guide to the 100 most important recordings 781.65
Jazz musicians
Dance, S. The world of Count Basie 920
Feather, L. The biographical encyclopedia of jazz 920.003
Feather, L. From Satchmo to Miles 920
Giddins, G. Visions of jazz 781.65
Lees, G. You can't steal a gift 920
A **jazz** odyssey: the life of Oscar Peterson. Peterson, O. 92
Jazz singing. Friedwald, W. 781.65
Jazz: the first century 781.65
Jean Howard's Hollywood. Howard, J. 791.43
Jean-Jacques: the early life and work of Jean-Jacques Rousseau, 1712-1754. Cranston, M. 92
Jeanne d'Arc, Saint *See* Joan, of Arc, Saint, 1412-1431
Jeff Herman's guide to book publishers, editors, & literary agents. Herman, J. 070.5
Jeffers, John Robinson *See* Jeffers, Robinson, 1887-1962
Jeffers, Robinson, 1887-1962
The collected poetry of Robinson Jeffers 811
See/See also pages in the following book(s):
Gioia, D. Can poetry matter? 809.1
Jeffers, Susan J.
Feel the fear and do it anyway 152.4
Jefferson, Thomas, 1743-1826
The autobiography of Thomas Jefferson
In Jefferson, T. The life and selected writings of Thomas Jefferson p3-104 818
In Jefferson, T. Writings 818
The life and selected writings of Thomas Jefferson 818
Notes on the State of Virginia
In Jefferson, T. The life and selected writings of Thomas Jefferson p177-267 818
In Jefferson, T. Writings 818
A summary view of the rights of British America
In Jefferson, T. Writings 818
Writings 818
About
Adams, W. H. The Paris years of Thomas Jefferson 92
Becker, C. The Declaration of Independence 973.3
Cohen, I. B. Science and the founding fathers 973.3
Ellis, J. J. American sphinx: the character of Thomas Jefferson 92
Ferling, J. E. Setting the world ablaze 973.3
Gordon-Reed, A. Thomas Jefferson and Sally Hemings 92
Randall, W. S. Thomas Jefferson 92
Simon, J. F. What kind of nation 342
Wilkins, R. W. Jefferson's pillow 973
See/See also pages in the following book(s):
Ellis, J. J. Founding brothers 973.4

Hofstadter, R. The American political tradition, and the men who made it p18-43 973
Malone, J. W. It doesn't take a rocket scientist 920
Miller, J. C. The Federalist era, 1789-1801 p70-98 973.4
Jefferson Davis, American. Cooper, W. J. 92
Jefferson's pillow. Wilkins, R. W. 973
Jehovah's Witnesses
Holden, A. Jehovah's Witnesses 289.9
Jellis, Susan
(ed) Microsoft Encarta college thesaurus. See Microsoft Encarta college thesaurus 423
Jelloun, Tahar ben *See* Ben Jelloun, Tahar, 1944-
Jenkins, Jeffrey Eric
(ed) The Best plays of [date] See The Best plays of [date] 808.82
Jenkins, Mark, 1962-
(jt. auth) Micheli, L. J. The sports medicine bible for young athletes 617.1
Jenkins, Peter, 1951-
Looking for Alaska 979.8
A walk across America 917.3
Jenkins, Philip, 1952-
Mystics and messiahs 200.9
The next Christendom 270
Jenkins, Robert L., 1945-
(ed) The Malcolm X encyclopedia. See The Malcolm X encyclopedia 92
Jenkins, Roy, Baron, 1920-2003
Churchill 92
Gladstone 92
Jenkins, Sally
(jt. auth) Armstrong, L. It's not about the bike 92
Jenner, Edward, 1749-1823
See/See also pages in the following book(s):
Friedman, M. Medicine's 10 greatest discoveries 610.9
Jennings, Charles
The hundredth window 005.8
Jennings, Francis, 1918-
Benjamin Franklin, politician 92
Jennings, Lucy Mae, 1917-
(jt. auth) Burton, S. Procedures for the automated office 651.3
Jennison, Christopher
(jt. auth) Robinson, R. Yankee Stadium 796.357
Jensen, Carsten
I have seen the world begin 915
Jensen, Richard J.
(jt. auth) Smith, J. D. World War II on the Web 025.04
Jenson, Lois
About
Bingham, C. Class action 342
Jersey rain. Pinsky, R. 811
Jerusalem
Gilbert, M. Jerusalem in the twentieth century 956.94
History
Armstrong, K. Jerusalem 956.94
History—1948, Siege
Collins, L. O Jerusalem! 956.94
Poetry
Amichai, Y. Poems of Jerusalem; and, Love poems 892
The **Jerusalem** Bible. See Bible. The new Jerusalem Bible 220.5
Jerusalem in the twentieth century. Gilbert, M. 956.94
Jesperson, Keith Hunter
About
Olsen, J. I: the creation of a serial killer 364.1

Jessop, Violet, 1887-1971
Titanic survivor   **910.4**
Jesuits
Lacouture, J. Jesuits   **271**
Jesus and the Dead Sea scrolls. Charlesworth, J. H.   **232**

Jesus Christ
About
Bible. N.T. Gospels. The three Gospels   **226**
Cahill, T. Desire of the everlasting hills   **232**
Charlesworth, J. H. Jesus and the Dead Sea scrolls   **232**
Fredriksen, P. Jesus of Nazareth, King of the Jews   **232.9**
Miles, J. Christ: a crisis in the life of God   **232**
Vermès, G. The changing faces of Jesus   **232**
See/See also pages in the following book(s):
Jaspers, K. The great philosophers   **109**
Biography
Allen, C. The human Christ   **232.9**
Chilton, B. Rabbi Jesus   **232.9**
Crossan, J. D. Jesus   **232.9**
Girzone, J. F. A portrait of Jesus   **232.9**
Johnson, L. T. The real Jesus   **232.9**
Sanders, E. P. The historical figure of Jesus   **232.9**
Spoto, D. The hidden Jesus   **232.9**
Wilson, A. N. Jesus   **232.9**
Divinity
Rubenstein, R. E. When Jesus became God   **273**
Historicity
Allen, C. The human Christ   **232.9**
Bible. N.T. Gospels. The five Gospels   **226**
Crossan, J. D. Jesus   **232.9**
Johnson, L. T. The real Jesus   **232.9**
Meier, J. P. A marginal Jew   **232.9**
Pelikan, J. J. The illustrated Jesus through the centuries   **232.9**
Sheler, J. L. Is the Bible true?   **220.1**
Wilson, A. N. Jesus   **232.9**
Resurrection
Crossan, J. D. Who killed Jesus?   **232.9**
Jesus of Nazareth, King of the Jews. Fredriksen, P.   **232.9**

Jesus Seminar
Bible. N.T. Gospels. The five Gospels   **226**
Johnson, L. T. The real Jesus   **232.9**
Jesus through the centuries. See Pelikan, J. J. The illustrated Jesus through the centuries   **232.9**
Jew vs. Jew. Freedman, S. G.   **296**
Jewell, Elizabeth
(ed) The New Oxford American dictionary. See The New Oxford American dictionary   **423**
Jewelry
Banes, H. Fiber & bead jewelry   **745.59**
Codina, C. The complete book of jewelry making   **739.27**
McSwiney, S. The creative jeweler   **739.27**
Wells, C. W. The art & elegance of beadweaving   **745.58**
Jewels *See* Precious stones
Jewish American literature   **810.8**
Jewish-Arab relations
See also Israel-Arab conflicts
Blumenfeld, L. R. Revenge   **956.94**
Friedman, T. L. From Beirut to Jerusalem   **956**
Gordis, D. If a place can make you cry   **956.94**
Grossman, D. The yellow wind   **956.95**
Herzog, C. The Arab-Israeli wars   **956**
Morris, B. Righteous victims   **956**
Said, E. W. The end of the peace process   **956**
Shipler, D. K. Arab and Jew   **956.94**
Shlaim, A. The iron wall   **956.94**
Jewish civilization
Cultures of the Jews   **909**

See/See also pages in the following book(s):
Weinstein, M. Yiddish   **439**
Jewish cooking
Abadi, J. F. A fistful of lentils   **641.5**
Friedland, S. R. Shabbat shalom   **641.5**
Greene, G. K. The new Jewish holiday cookbook   **641.5**
Marks, G. The world of Jewish cooking   **641.5**
Nathan, J. Jewish cooking in America   **641.5**
Nathan, J. The Jewish holiday baker   **641.8**
The New York Times Passover cookbook   **641.5**
Sorosky, M. Fast & festive meals for the Jewish holidays   **641.5**
Jewish cooking in America. Nathan, J.   **641.5**
Jewish ethics
Telushkin, J. Biblical literacy   **221.6**
Telushkin, J. Jewish wisdom   **296**
The **Jewish** holiday baker. Nathan, J.   **641.8**
The **Jewish** holiday cookbook. See Greene, G. K. The new Jewish holiday cookbook   **641.5**
Jewish holidays
See also Hanukkah; Passover; Purim; Rosh ha-Shanah; Sukkoth; Yom Kippur
Greenberg, I. The Jewish way   **296.4**
Greene, G. K. The new Jewish holiday cookbook   **641.5**
Isaacs, R. H. Sacred seasons   **296.4**
Nathan, J. The Jewish holiday baker   **641.8**
Sorosky, M. Fast & festive meals for the Jewish holidays   **641.5**
Strassfeld, M. The Jewish holidays   **296.4**
See/See also pages in the following book(s):
Goldman, A. L. Being Jewish   **296.4**
Jewish holocaust (1933-1945) *See* Holocaust, 1933-1945
Jewish holocaust (1933-1945) in literature *See* Holocaust, 1933-1945, in literature
Jewish legends
Frankel, E. The classic tales   **296.1**
Isaacs, R. H. Sacred seasons   **296.4**
Jewish literature (American) *See* American literature—Jewish authors
Jewish meditation. Kaplan, A.   **296.7**
Jewish music *See* Jews—Music
Jewish New Year *See* Rosh ha-Shanah
The **Jewish** people in America   **305.8**
Jewish philosophy
Buber, M. I and thou   **181**
See/See also pages in the following book(s):
Friedman, M. S. Encounter on the narrow ridge: a life of Martin Buber   **92**
Jewish refugees
Szulc, T. The secret alliance   **325**
The **Jewish** state. Hazony, Y.   **956.94**
The **Jewish** way. Greenberg, I.   **296.4**
Jewish wisdom. Telushkin, J.   **296**
Jewish women
Dictionaries
Jewish women in America   **920.003**
Jewish women in America   **920.003**
Jews
Festivals
See Jewish holidays
Folklore
Isaacs, R. H. Sacred seasons   **296.4**
History
Cahill, T. The gifts of the Jews   **909**
Cultures of the Jews   **909**
Gilbert, M. The Jews in the twentieth century   **909**
The Illustrated history of the Jewish people   **909**
Johnson, P. A history of the Jews   **909**
Potok, C. Wanderings   **909**
See/See also pages in the following book(s):
Durant, W. J. The age of Louis XIV p454-78   **940.2**

Jews—*Continued*

History—Maps
A Historical atlas of the Jewish people   909
Identity
Tye, L. Home lands   909
Legends
See Jewish legends
Music
See also Klezmer music
Strom, Y. The book of Klezmer   781.62
Periodicals
American Jewish year book   296
Persecutions
See also Holocaust, 1933-1945; World War, 1939-1945—Jews—Rescue
Ba'u, Y. Dear God, have you ever gone hungry?   940.53
Chesnoff, R. Z. Pack of thieves   940.53
Friedländer, S. Nazi Germany and the Jews vl   940.53
Gay, P. My German question   92
Rites and ceremonies
See Judaism—Customs and practices
Social life and customs
Diamant, A. Living a Jewish life   296.7
Eastern Europe
Kaufman, J. A hole in the heart of the world   947
Egypt
Ghosh, A. In an antique land   962
Europe
Dawidowicz, L. S. The war against the Jews, 1933-1945   940.53
Encyclopedia of Jewish life before and during the Holocaust   940.53
Gilbert, M. Holocaust journey   940.53
Sachar, H. M. Dreamland   940
Yahil, L. The Holocaust   940.53
Germany
Blumenthal, W. M. The invisible wall   943
Brenner, M. After the Holocaust   943.087
Dwork, D. Holocaust: a history   940.53
Elon, A. The pity of it all   943
Friedländer, S. Nazi Germany and the Jews vl   940.53
Gay, P. My German question   92
Gay, R. The Jews of Germany   943
Goldsmith, M. The inextinguishable symphony   940.53
Johnson, E. A. Nazi terror   940.53
Great Britain
Gilbert, M. The boys   940.53
Italy
Zuccotti, S. Under his very windows   940.53
Lithuania
Kruk, H. The last days of the Jerusalem of Lithuania   940.53
Netherlands
Frank, A. The diary of a young girl: the definitive edition   92
Frank, A. The diary of Anne Frank: the critical edition   92
Müller, M. Anne Frank   92
Netherlands—Drama
Goodrich, F. The diary of Anne Frank   812
New York (N.Y.)
See/See also pages in the following book(s):
Glazer, N. Beyond the melting pot p137-80   305.8
Poland
The Chronicle of the Łódź ghetto, 1941-1944   943.8
Singer, I. B. More stories from my father's court   92

Spain
See/See also pages in the following book(s):
Kamen, H. The Spanish Inquisition   272
United States
American Jewish history   305.8
American Jewish year book   296
Dershowitz, A. M. The vanishing American Jew   305.8
Freedman, S. G. Jew vs. Jew   296
Glazer, N. American Judaism   296
The Jewish people in America   305.8
Levine, P. Ellis Island to Ebbet's Field   796
Novick, P. The Holocaust in American life   940.53
Sachar, H. M. A history of the Jews in America   305.8
See/See also pages in the following book(s):
Baldwin, N. Henry Ford and the Jews   92
Jews in literature
Fiedler, L. A. Fiedler on the roof   814
The Jews in the twentieth century. Gilbert, M.   909
The Jews of Germany. Gay, R.   943
Jewsbury, Geraldine, 1812-1880
See/See also pages in the following book(s):
Woolf, V. The second common reader p167-81   820.9
Jihad. Kepel, G.   297
Jim Crow's children. Irons, P. H.   344
Jimmy Carter, American moralist. Morris, K. E.   92
Jitney. Wilson, A.   812
Joan, of Arc, Saint, 1412-1431
About
Gordon, M. Joan of Arc   92
Pernoud, R. Joan of Arc   92
Job applications *See* Applications for positions
Job finder's guide. Krantz, L.   331.7
Job hunting
The Adams cover letter almanac & disk   650.14
Beatty, R. H. 175 high-impact cover letters   650.14
Gardella, R. The Harvard Business School guide to finding your next job   650.14
Krantz, L. Job finder's guide   331.7
Mornell, P. Games companies play   650.14
Richardson, B. G. Career comeback   650.14
Wendleton, K. Building a great résumé   650.14
Yate, M. J. Knock 'em dead   650.14
Internet resources
Bolles, R. N. Job-hunting on the Internet   025.04
Job-hunting on the Internet. Bolles, R. N.   025.04
Job placement guidance *See* Vocational guidance
Job résumés *See* Résumés (Employment)
Job security
See also Employees—Dismissal
Job stress
Reinhold, B. B. Toxic work   650.1
Jobs *See* Occupations
Jobs rated almanac. Krantz, L.   331.7
Joe Turner's come and gone. Wilson, A.   812
Joel, Lewin G.
Every employee's guide to the law   344
Johanson, Donald C.
From Lucy to language   599.93
Lucy: the beginnings of humankind   599.93
John XXIII, Pope, 1881-1963
See/See also pages in the following book(s):
Wills, G. Certain trumpets p132-44   303.3
John, Augustus, 1878-1961
See/See also pages in the following book(s):
Holroyd, M. Works on paper   809
John, Catherine Rachel
(jt. auth) Attwater, D. The Penguin dictionary of saints   920.003

John, Gwen, 1876-1939
About
Roe, S. Gwen John 92
John, Gospel of *See* Bible. N.T. John
John Brookes' natural landscapes. Brookes, J.
635.9
John Gabriel Borkman. Ibsen, H.
In Ibsen, H. The complete major prose plays p937-
1024 **839.8**
In Ibsen, H. Ibsen: four plays, v3 **839.8**
John Garrett's black-and-white photography masterclass.
Garrett, J. 771
John Paul II, Pope, 1920-
Crossing the threshold of hope 282
About
Buttiglione, R. Karol Wojtyła 92
Cornwell, J. Breaking faith 282
Flynn, R. John Paul II 92
Kwitny, J. Man of the century: the life and times of
Pope John Paul II 92
Weigel, G. Witness to hope: the biography of Pope
John Paul II 92
See/See also pages in the following book(s):
Reese, T. J. Inside the Vatican 282
John Steinbeck [critical essays] 813.009
The **Johns** Hopkins consumer guide to medical tests
616.07
The **Johns** Hopkins guide to diabetes. Saudek, C. D.
616.4
The **Johns** Hopkins medical guide to health after 50
613
Johns Hopkins symptoms and remedies 616.02
Johnsen, Ole
Minerals of the world 549
Johnson, Charles Richard, 1948-
Africans in America: America's journey through slav-
ery 326
Johnson, Claudia Alta Taylor *See* Johnson, Lady Bird,
1912-
Johnson, Dave, 1964-
How to do everything with your digital camera
778.3
Johnson, Dwight
See/See also pages in the following book(s):
Mikaelian, A. Medal of honor 920
Johnson, Eric A. (Eric Arthur), 1948-
Nazi terror 940.53
Johnson, George, 1952-
Fire in the mind 215
A shortcut through time 004
Strange beauty: Murray Gell-Mann and the revolution
in twentieth-century physics 92
Johnson, Georgia Douglas Camp, 1886-1966
Plumes
In Plays by American women, 1900-1930
812.008
Johnson, Gus, 1913-2000
See/See also pages in the following book(s):
Dance, S. The world of Count Basie 920
Johnson, Haynes Bonner, 1931-
The best of times 973.929
Sleepwalking through history 973.927
Johnson, James Weldon, 1871-1938
Complete poems 811
(ed) The Books of the American Negro spirituals. See
The Books of the American Negro spirituals
782.42
Johnson, John Rosamond, 1873-1954
(ed) The Books of the American Negro spirituals. See
The Books of the American Negro spirituals
782.42
Johnson, Joyce, 1935-
About
Kerouac, J. Door wide open 92

Johnson, Kurt, 1946-
Nabokov's Blues 92
Johnson, Lady Bird, 1912-
Wildflowers across America 582.13
Johnson, Luke Timothy
The real Jesus 232.9
Johnson, Lyndon B. (Lyndon Baines), 1908-1973
About
Caro, R. A. The years of Lyndon Johnson 92
Dallek, R. Lone star rising: Lyndon Johnson and his
times, 1908-1960 92
Kaiser, D. E. American tragedy 959.704
Reaching for glory 973.923
Taking charge 973.923
See/See also pages in the following book(s):
Galbraith, J. K. Name-dropping 973.9
Halberstam, D. The best and the brightest
973.922
Johnson, Michael, 1937-
Macmillan encyclopedia of Native American tribes
970.004
Johnson, Paul, 1928-
Castles of England, Scotland and Wales 941
A history of the Jews 909
Napoleon 92
The Renaissance 940.2
Johnson, Rebekah Baines, 1881-1958
See/See also pages in the following book(s):
Angelo, B. First mothers 920
Johnson, Robert V.
(ed) Mayo Clinic complete book of pregnancy &
baby's first year. See Mayo Clinic complete book of
pregnancy & baby's first year 618.2
Johnson, Samuel, 1709-1784
About
Boswell, J. The journal of a tour to the Hebrides with
Samuel Johnson 914.11
Boswell, J. The life of Samuel Johnson 92
See/See also pages in the following book(s):
Bloom, H. The Western canon 809
Johnson, Tim, 1947-
Spirit capture. See Spirit capture 779
Johnson, Todd M.
(ed) World Christian encyclopedia. See World Chris-
tian encyclopedia 230.003
Johnson, Virginia E.
(jt. auth) Masters, W. H. Masters and Johnson on sex
and human loving 155.3
Johnson, Walter
Soul by soul 326
Johnson, William H., 1901-1970
See/See also pages in the following book(s):
Harlem Renaissance: art of black America 709.73
Johnson-Powell, Gloria *See* Powell, Gloria J.
Johnston, Kenneth R.
The hidden Wordsworth 92
Joined at the heart. Gore, A., Jr. 306.8
Joint Steering Committee for Revision of AACR
Anglo-American cataloguing rules. See Anglo-
American cataloguing rules 025.3
Jolly, Alison
Lucy's legacy 599.93
Jones, Mother, 1830-1930
About
Gorn, E. J. Mother Jones 92
Jones, Alison
(ed) Chambers dictionary of quotations. See Chambers
dictionary of quotations 808.88
Jones, Ann, 1937-
Women who kill 364.1
Jones, Barbara M.
Libraries, access, and intellectual freedom 025.2

Jones, Bill T.
See/See also pages in the following book(s):
Gates, H. L. Thirteen ways of looking at a black man
920
Jones, Chris, 1973-
Falling hard 796.8
Jones, Derek
(ed) Censorship: a world encyclopedia. See Censorship: a world encyclopedia 363.3
Jones, G. William
Black cinema treasures 791.43
Jones, Gayl, 1949-
See/See also pages in the following book(s):
Black women writers (1950-1980) 810.9
Jones, Gerard
Killing monsters 302.23
Jones, Henry Stuart, 1867-1939
(ed) Liddell, H. G. A Greek-English lexicon 483
Jones, Jacqueline, 1948-
Labor of love, labor of sorrow 305.4
Jones, Jo, 1911-1985
See/See also pages in the following book(s):
Dance, S. The world of Count Basie 920
Jones, John Paul, 1747-1792
About
Morison, S. E. John Paul Jones 92
See/See also pages in the following book(s):
Williams, W. C. In the American grain p158-73
814
Jones, Judith
(jt. auth) Cameron, A. The L.L. Bean game and fish cookbook 641.6
Jones, Landon Y., 1943-
(ed) Lewis, M. The essential Lewis and Clark
978
Jones, LeRoi *See* Baraka, Imamu Amiri, 1934-
Jones, Mary Harris *See* Jones, Mother, 1830-1930
Jones, Mike
Handcrafted ceramic tiles 738
Jones, Quincy
Q: the autobiography of Quincy Jones 92
Jones, Robert F., 1934-
The hunter in my heart 799.2
Jones, Steve, 1944-
Darwin's ghost 576.8
(ed) The Cambridge encyclopedia of human evolution. See The Cambridge encyclopedia of human evolution 599.93
Jones, Steve, 1961-
(ed) The Encyclopedia of new media. See The Encyclopedia of new media 302.23
Jones, Warren D.
(jt. auth) Duffield, M. R. Plants for dry climates
635.9
Jong-Stout, Alisa A. de
A master guide to the art of floral design 745.92
Jonson, Ben, 1573?-1637
The complete poems 821
Jonsson, Erik, 1922-
Inner navigation 153.7
Joplin, Scott, 1868-1917
About
Berlin, E. A. King of ragtime: Scott Joplin and his era 92
Curtis, S. Dancing to a black man's tune: a life of Scott Joplin 92
Jordan, Cora, 1941-
(jt. auth) Clifford, D. Plan your estate 346.05
Jordan, Michael
About
Halberstam, D. Playing for keeps: Michael Jordan and the world he made 92
Jordan, Ruth McBride- *See* McBride-Jordan, Ruth, 1921-

Jordan, Wendy Adler, 1946-
The kidspace idea book 747
Jorgensen, Peter F.
(ed) Encyclopedia of human emotions. See Encyclopedia of human emotions 152.4
Joris, Pierre
(ed) Poems for the millennium. See Poems for the millennium 808.81
Joseph, Nez Percé Chief, 1840-1904
See/See also pages in the following book(s):
Brown, D. A. The American West p255-64 978
Brown, D. A. Bury my heart at Wounded Knee
970.004
Joseph, Charles M.
Stravinsky inside out 92
Joseph McCarthy. Herman, A. 92
Joseph Pulitzer II and the Post-dispatch. Pfaff, D. W.
92
Joseph Smith and the beginnings of Mormonism. Bushman, R. L. 289.3
Josephy, Alvin M., 1915-
500 nations 970.004
The Nez Perce Indians and the opening of the Northwest 970.004
Now that the buffalo's gone 970.004
(ed) America in 1492. See America in 1492
970.01
The **Joslin** Diabetes gourmet cookbook. Polin, B. S.
641.5
The **Joslin** Diabetes great chefs cook healthy cookbook. Giedt, F. T. 641.5
The **Joslin** guide to diabetes. Beaser, R. S. 616.4
Josquin, des Pres, d. 1521
See/See also pages in the following book(s):
Grout, D. J. A history of Western music 780.9
Jost, Kenneth
(ed) The Supreme Court A to Z. See The Supreme Court A to Z 347
The **journal** of a tour to the Hebrides with Samuel Johnson. Boswell, J. 914.11
Journal of researches into the geology and natural history of the various countries visited by H.M.S. Beagle. See Darwin, C. The voyage of the Beagle
508
Journalism
See also Broadcast journalism; Gossip; Photojournalism
Downie, L. The news about the news 071
Friedlander, E. J. Feature writing for newspapers and magazines 070.4
Reporting civil rights 323.1
Ross, L. Reporting back 070.4
Written into history 071
Journalists
See also Women journalists
Journals *See* Periodicals
Journals (Diaries) *See* Diaries
The **journals** of Anaïs Nin. See Nin, A. The diary of Anaïs Nin 92
Journals of Ayn Rand. Rand, A. 92
Journals of Sylvia Plath, 1950-1962. See Plath, S. The unabridged journals of Sylvia Plath, 1950-1962
92
Journey: new and selected poems, 1969-1999. Norris, K.
811
Journey of the pink dolphins. Montgomery, S.
599.5
Journey to Portugal. Saramago, J. 946.9
Journey to the ants. Hölldobler, B. 595.7
Journeys *See* Voyages and travels
Journeys through ADDulthood. Solden, S. 616.85
Journeys through adulthood. See Solden, S. Journeys through ADDulthood 616.85
Joy in Mudville 796.357
Joy of cooking. Rombauer, I. von S. 641.5

The **joy** of π. Blatner, D.   **516.2**
The **joy** of pickling. Ziedrich, L.   **641.4**
The **joy** of sex. Comfort, A.   **613.9**
The **joy** of signing. Riekehof, L. L.   **419**
Joyce, David
   Topiary and the art of training plants   **635.9**
Joyce, James, 1882-1941
   Ulysses; criticism
    In James Joyce's Ulysses   **823.009**
    In Nabokov, V. V. Lectures on literature p285-370
     808.3
      About
   Ellmann, R. James Joyce   **92**
   Fargnoli, A. N. James Joyce A to Z   **823.009**
   McCourt, J. James Joyce   **92**
   O'Brien, E. James Joyce   **92**
    See/See also pages in the following book(s):
   Bloom, H. The Western canon   **809**
Joyner-Kersee, Jackie
   A kind of grace   **92**
The **joys** of Yiddish. See Rosten, L. The new joys of Yiddish   **439**
Juan, Don
      About
   Castaneda, C. The teachings of Don Juan   **299**
Juana Inés de la Cruz, 1651-1695
   A Sor Juana anthology   **861**
Judah, Tim, 1962-
   Kosovo   **949.7**
Judaism
    See also God—Judaism; Hasidism
   Carroll, J. Constantine's sword   **261.2**
   Cohen, A. Everyman's Talmud   **296.1**
   Dershowitz, A. M. The vanishing American Jew
     305.8
   Freedman, S. G. Jew vs. Jew   **296**
   Glazer, N. American Judaism   **296**
   Kushner, H. S. To life!   **296**
   Robinson, G. Essential Judaism   **296**
   Telushkin, J. Jewish wisdom   **296**
   Wouk, H. This is my God: the Jewish way of life
     296
   Wouk, H. The will to live on   **296**
    See/See also pages in the following book(s):
   Armstrong, K. The battle for God   **291**
   Armstrong, K. A history of God   **291**
      Customs and practices
   Celebration & renewal   **296.4**
   Goldman, A. L. Being Jewish   **296.4**
   Greenberg, I. The Jewish way   **296.4**
   Kaplan, A. Jewish meditation   **296.7**
   Levy, N. To begin again   **296.7**
   Strassfeld, M. The Jewish holidays   **296.4**
   Wieseltier, L. Kaddish   **296.4**
      Dictionaries
The New encyclopedia of Judaism   **296.03**
The Oxford dictionary of the Jewish religion
     296.03
      Encyclopedias
The Encyclopedia of Judaism   **296.03**
Reader's guide to Judaism   **296.03**
      History
   Cahill, T. The gifts of the Jews   **909**
The Cambridge history of Judaism   **296**
   Golb, N. Who wrote the Dead Sea scrolls?   **296.1**
   Schiffman, L. H. Reclaiming the Dead Sea scrolls
     296.1
      Philosophy
    See Jewish philosophy
Judges
   O'Connor, S. D. The majesty of the law   **347**
   The Supreme Court compendium   **347**
      Dictionaries
   Hall, T. L. Supreme Court justices   **920.003**

The Supreme Court justices: a biographical dictionary
     920.003
Judson, Alexander Corbin, b. 1883
   The life of Edmund Spenser
    In Spenser, E. The works of Edmund Spenser v11
     828
Juergensmeyer, Mark
   Terror in the mind of God   **291.1**
Jukofsky, Diane
   Encyclopedia of rainforests   **578.7**
Julia and Jacques cooking at home. Child, J.   **641.5**
Julian, of Norwich, b. 1343
      About
   Armstrong, K. Visions of God   **248.2**
Juliana, b. 1343 *See* Julian, of Norwich, b. 1343
Julia's kitchen wisdom. Child, J.   **641.5**
July, William W., II
   Understanding the tin man   **158**
Jumping fire. Taylor, M. A.   **634.9**
The **Junction** boys. Dent, J.   **796.332**
Jung, C. G. (Carl Gustav), 1875-1961
   The basic writings of C. G. Jung   **150.19**
   The essential Jung   **150.19**
   Man and his symbols   **150.19**
   Memories, dreams, reflections   **92**
   The portable Jung   **150.19**
      About
   Freud, S. The Freud/Jung letters   **92**
   Hayman, R. A life of Jung   **92**
Jung, Carl Gustav *See* Jung, C. G. (Carl Gustav), 1875-1961
Junger, Sebastian
   Fire   **909.82**
   The perfect storm   **910.4**
Junior high school libraries *See* High school libraries
Juno and the paycock. O'Casey, S.
    In Our dramatic heritage v5   **808.82**
Jupiter (Planet)
   Beebe, R. F. Jupiter   **523.4**
Jupp, James
   (ed) The Australian people. See The Australian people
     994
Jury
   Dwyer, W. L. In the hands of the people   **347**
Just as I am. Graham, B.   **92**
The **just** assassins. Camus, A.
    In Camus, A. Caligula & three other plays p233-302
     842
Just lucky I guess. Channing, C.   **92**
Just six numbers. Rees, M. J.   **523.1**
Justice, Donald Rodney, 1925-
   New & selected poems   **811**
    See/See also pages in the following book(s):
   Gioia, D. Can poetry matter?   **809.1**
Justice
   Dershowitz, A. M. The Genesis of justice   **222**
   Sowell, T. The quest for cosmic justice   **303.3**
Justice. Dunne, D.   **345**
Juvenal
   Satires   **877**
Juvenalis, Decimus Junius *See* Juvenal

          K

K-I-S-S beauty. Pedersen, S.   **646.7**
K.I.S.S. guide to raising a puppy. Palika, L.   **636.7**
Kabaphēs, Kōnstantinos Petrou *See* Cavafy, Constantine P., 1863-1933
Kachur, Bridget
   Every woman's quick & easy car care   **629.28**
Kaddish
   Wieseltier, L. Kaddish   **296.4**
Kael, Pauline, 1919-2001
   For keeps   **791.43**

Kafka, Barbara
Party food   **641.5**
Roasting   **641.7**
Kafka, Franz, 1883-1924
The metamorphosis; criticism
In Franz Kafka's The metamorphosis   **833.009**
In Nabokov, V. V. Lectures on literature p251-83   **808.3**

About
Diamant, K. Kafka's last love   **92**
See/See also pages in the following book(s):
Bloom, H. The Western canon   **809**
Demetz, P. The air show at Brescia, 1909   **629.13**
Existentialism from Dostoevsky to Sartre p142-51   **142**
Langer, L. L. Admitting the Holocaust p109-24   **940.53**
Kafka was the rage. Broyard, A.   **92**
Kagan, Robert
Of paradise and power   **327.73**
Kagan, Sasha
Sasha Kagan's country inspiration   **746.43**
Kagekiyo. Zeami
In Waley, A. The Nō plays of Japan   **895.6**
Kahlo, Frida, 1907-1954
The diary of Frida Kahlo   **92**
About
Frida Kahlo   **759.972**
Herrera, H. Frida: a biography of Frida Kahlo   **92**
Zamora, M. Frida Kahlo   **92**
Kahn, Ada P.
Stress A-Z   **616.9**
(jt. auth) Doctor, R. M. The encyclopedia of phobias, fears, and anxieties   **616.85**
Kahn, Ashley
A love supreme   **781.65**
Kahn, Robert Louis, 1918-
(jt. auth) Rowe, J. W. Successful aging   **612.6**
Kahn, Roger, 1927-
The boys of summer   **796.357**
A flame of pure fire: Jack Dempsey and the roaring '20s   **92**
The head game   **796.357**
Kaiser, Charles
The gay metropolis   **305.9**
Kaiser, David E., 1947-
American tragedy   **959.704**
Kaiser, Georg, 1878-1945
From morn to midnight
In Our dramatic heritage v5   **808.82**
Kaiser, Robert Greeley, 1943-
(jt. auth) Downie, L. The news about the news   **071**
Kaku, Michio
Hyperspace   **530.1**
Kale, Tessa
(ed) The Columbia Granger's index to poetry in anthologies. See The Columbia Granger's index to poetry in anthologies   **808.81**
Kaler, James B.
Extreme stars   **523.8**
Kaliski, Burton S.
(ed) Encyclopedia of busine$$ and finance. See Encyclopedia of busine$$ and finance   **650**
Kamen, Henry
Philip of Spain   **92**
The Spanish Inquisition   **272**
Kamm, Henry
Cambodia: report from a stricken land   **959.6**
Kamman, Madeleine
The new making of a cook   **641.5**
Kammen, Michael G.
In the past lane   **973**
Kampen O'Riley, Michael
Art beyond the west   **709**

Kampuchea *See* Cambodia
Kandel, Robert S.
Water from heaven   **553.7**
Kandinsky, Wassily, 1866-1944
About
Hahl-Koch, J. Kandinsky   **92**
Messer, T. M. Vasily Kandinsky   **759.4**
Kane, Gordon, 1937-
The particle garden   **539.7**
Kane, Joe
Savages   **986.6**
Kane, Joseph Nathan, 1899-2002
Facts about the presidents   **920**
Famous first facts   **031.02**
Nicknames and sobriquets of U.S. cities, states, and counties   **917.3**
(ed) Facts about the states. See Facts about the states   **973**
Kane, William, 1947-
(ed) Health matters! See Health matters!   **613**
Kanfer, Stefan
Groucho: the life and times of Julius Henry Marx   **92**
Serious business   **741.5**
Kanigel, Robert
High season   **944**
The man who knew infinity: a life of the genius, Ramanujan   **92**
Kannami *See* Kwanze, Kiyotsugu, 1355-1406
Kansas
History
Stratton, J. L. Pioneer women   **978.1**
Kant, Immanuel, 1724-1804
Basic writings of Kant   **193**
Critique of pure reason   **193**
See/See also pages in the following book(s):
Berlin, Sir I. The sense of reality p232-48   **901**
Dewey, J. The philosophy of John Dewey   **191**
Durant, W. J. The story of philosophy p192-220   **109**
Jaspers, K. The great philosophers   **109**
Russell, B. A history of Western philosophy p701-18   **109**
Kantan
In Waley, A. The Nō plays of Japan   **895.6**
Kaplan, Alice Yaeger
The collaborator: the trial & execution of Robert Brasillach   **92**
Kaplan, Aryeh
Jewish meditation   **296.7**
Kaplan, Carla
(ed) Hurston, Z. N. Zora Neale Hurston: a life in letters   **92**
Kaplan, Cynthia
Why I'm like this   **92**
Kaplan, Ellen
(jt. auth) Kaplan, R. The art of the infinite   **515**
Kaplan, Fred, 1937-
Dickens   **92**
Gore Vidal   **92**
Kaplan, James, 1951-
(jt. auth) McEnroe, J. You cannot be serious   **92**
Kaplan, Jonathan, 1954-
The dressing station   **92**
Kaplan, Justin
(jt. auth) Bernays, A. Back then   **92**
Kaplan, Larry
(jt. auth) Tallchief, M. Maria Tallchief   **92**
Kaplan, Lawrence J. (Lawrence Jay), 1915-
Retiring right   **305.26**
Kaplan, Robert
The art of the infinite   **515**
The nothing that is   **511**
Kaplan, Robert D.
Balkan ghosts   **949.6**

Kaplan, Robert D.—*Continued*
The ends of the earth   **910.4**
Warrior politics   **320**
Kapuściński, Ryszard
The shadow of the sun   **960**
Karabell, Zachary
The last campaign   **324**
Karajan, Herbert von
About
Osborne, R. Herbert von Karajan   **92**
Karasik, Judy
The ride together   **618.92**
Karasik, Paul, 1947-
(jt. auth) Karasik, J. The ride together   **618.92**
Karate
See also Tae kwon do
Ochiai, H. Hidy Ochiai's complete book of self-defense   **796.8**
Tegnér, B. Karate: beginner to black belt   **796.8**
Karch, Steven B.
The consumer's guide to herbal medicine   **615**
Karlen, Arno
Biography of a germ   **579.3**
Man and microbes   **614.4**
Karlsen, Carol F., 1940-
The devil in the shape of a woman   **133.4**
Karmason, Marilyn G.
Majolica: a complete and illustrated survey   **738**
Karnow, Stanley
In our image   **959.9**
Paris in the fifties   **944**
Vietnam   **959.704**
Karp, Harvey
The happiest baby on the block   **649**
Karpeles, Leopold
See/See also pages in the following book(s):
Mikaelian, A. Medal of honor   **920**
Karst, Kenneth L.
(ed) Encyclopedia of the American Constitution. See Encyclopedia of the American Constitution   **342**
Karwatka, Dennis
Technology's past   **609**
Kasdorf, William E.
(ed) The Columbia guide to digital publishing. See The Columbia guide to digital publishing   **070.5**
Kashmir (India) *See* Jammu and Kashmir (India)
Kashner, Sam
The bad & the beautiful   **791.43**
A talent for genius: the life and times of Oscar Levant   **92**
Kashuk, Sonia
Real beauty   **646.7**
Kasinec, Denise, 1967-
(ed) The Schomburg Center guide to black literature from the eighteenth century to the present. See The Schomburg Center guide to black literature from the eighteenth century to the present   **809**
Kasper, Shirl, 1948-
Annie Oakley   **92**
Kasson, Joy S.
Buffalo Bill's Wild West   **791.8**
Kastenbaum, Robert
(ed) Macmillan encyclopedia of death and dying. See Macmillan encyclopedia of death and dying   **306.9**
Kate remembered [a biography of Katharine Hepburn] Berg, A. S.   **92**
Katharine Graham's Washington   **975.3**
Katz, Bill *See* Katz, William A., 1924-
Katz, Friedrich
The life and times of Pancho Villa   **92**
Katz, Jane
Swimming for total fitness   **797.2**
Katz, Jonathan I.
The biggest bangs   **522**

Katz, Linda Sternberg
(ed) Magazines for libraries. See Magazines for libraries   **011**
Katz, Michael B.
The price of citizenship   **361.6**
Katz, Solomon H.
(ed) Encyclopedia of food and culture. See Encyclopedia of food and culture   **394.1**
Katz, William A., 1924-
Introduction to reference work   **025.5**
(ed) Magazines for libraries. See Magazines for libraries   **011**
Kaufeld, John
AOL for dummies   **025.04**
Kaufer Greene, Gloria *See* Greene, Gloria Kaufer, 1950-
Kaufman, Jonathan
A hole in the heart of the world   **947**
Kaufman, Kenn
Birds of North America   **598**
Kaufmann, Walter, 1921-1980
(ed) Existentialism from Dostoevsky to Sartre. See Existentialism from Dostoevsky to Sartre   **142**
Kavanagh, Patrick, 1904-1967
See/See also pages in the following book(s):
Heaney, S. Finders keepers p146-57   **821**
Kavaya, Karol
Community quilts   **746.46**
Kawin, Bruce F., 1945-
(jt. auth) Mast, G. A short history of the movies   **791.43**
Kazdin, Alan E.
(ed) Encyclopedia of psychology. See Encyclopedia of psychology   **150.3**
Kazin, Alfred, 1915-1998
An American procession   **810.9**
Keane, Fergal
Season of blood   **967.571**
Keaton, Buster, 1895-1966
About
Keaton, E. Buster Keaton remembered   **791.43**
Meade, M. Buster Keaton: cut to the chase   **92**
Keaton, Eleanor, 1918-1998
Buster Keaton remembered   **791.43**
Keaton, Joseph Francis *See* Keaton, Buster, 1895-1966
Keats, John, 1795-1821
The complete poems of John Keats   **821**
Ode on a Grecian urn; criticism
In Brooks, C. The well wrought urn   **821.009**
Poems   **821**
About
Motion, A. Keats   **92**
See/See also pages in the following book(s):
Vendler, H. H. Coming of age as a poet   **820.9**
Keay, John
The great arc   **526**
The honourable company   **954.03**
India: a history   **954**
Kebra Nagast
The Kebra Nagast   **299**
Kee, Howard Clark
The Cambridge companion to the Bible. See The Cambridge companion to the Bible   **220.9**
Keefe, Joan
(ed) The Penguin book of women poets. See The Penguin book of women poets   **808.81**
Keegan, John, 1934-
Fields of battle   **973**
The First World War   **940.3**
An illustrated history of the First World War   **940.3**
The Second World War   **940.53**
(ed) The Book of war. See The Book of war   **355**

Keeley, Edmund
Inventing paradise   818
Keene, Donald, 1922-
Emperor of Japan: Meiji and His world, 1852-1912
    92
The pleasures of Japanese literature   895.6
Seeds in the heart   895.6
Keene, Nancy
(jt. auth) Janes-Hodder, H. Childhood cancer
    618.92
Keeping faith: memoirs of a president. Carter, J.
    92
Keeping kids safe. Shore, K.   649
Kees, Weldon
    See/See also pages in the following book(s):
Gioia, D. Can poetry matter?   809.1
Keeton, Cheryl, 1949-1986
      About
Rule, A. Dead by sunset   364.1
Keil, Sally Van Wagenen
Those wonderful women in their flying machines
    940.54
Keiler, Allan
Marian Anderson   92
Keillor, Garrison
We are still married   817
(comp) Good poems. See Good poems   811.008
Keintpoos *See* Kintpuash, Modoc Chief, 1837?-1873
Kekulé, Friedrich August, 1829-1896
    See/See also pages in the following book(s):
Horvitz, L. A. Eureka!: scientific breakthroughs that
changed the world   509
Keller, Evelyn Fox, 1936-
The century of the gene   576.5
Making sense of life   570.1
Keller, Helen, 1880-1968
The story of my life   92
      About
Herrmann, D. Helen Keller   92
Lash, J. P. Helen and teacher   92
      Drama
Gibson, W. The miracle worker   812
Kelley, Robert Earl
How to be a star at work   658
Kelley, Thomas G., 1939-
    See/See also pages in the following book(s):
Mikaelian, A. Medal of honor   920
Kelley, Virginia, 1923-1994
    See/See also pages in the following book(s):
Angelo, B. First mothers   920
Kellogg, Ann T., 1968-
In an influential fashion. See In an influential fashion
    391
Kelly, Clara Olink
The flamboya tree   940.53
Kelly, Denis, 1939-
(jt. auth) Aidells, B. The complete meat cookbook
    641.6
Kelly, Franklin
(jt. auth) Cikovsky, N., Jr. Winslow Homer
    759.13
Kelly, Geffrey B.
(ed) Bonhoeffer, D. A testament to freedom   230
Kelly, J. N. D. (John Norman Davidson)
The Oxford dictionary of popes   920.003
Kelly, Jerry, 1953-
Bushville   796.357
Kelly, John
(ed) The Hillier gardener's guide to trees & shrubs.
See The Hillier gardener's guide to trees & shrubs
    635.9
Kelly, John Norman Davidson *See* Kelly, J. N. D.
(John Norman Davidson)

Kelly, Michael, 1954-
(ed) Encyclopedia of aesthetics. See Encyclopedia of
aesthetics   111
Kelly, Michael, 1957-2003
Martyrs' Day   956.7
Kelly, Robert J.
Encyclopedia of organized crime in the United States
    364.1
Kely, Entmount *See* Keeley, Edmund
Kemble, Adelaide, 1814?-1879
      About
Blainey, A. Fanny and Adelaide: the lives of the re-
markable Kemble sisters   92
Kemble, Fanny, 1809-1893
      About
Blainey, A. Fanny and Adelaide: the lives of the re-
markable Kemble sisters   92
Clinton, C. Fanny Kemble's civil wars   92
Kemenade, Willem van
China, Hong Kong, Taiwan, Inc.   951
Kemp, Martin, 1942-
The Oxford history of western art. See The Oxford
history of western art   709
Kemp, Thomas Jay
Virtual roots 2.0   929
Kempner, Vitka
      About
Cohen, R. The avengers   940.53
Kendall, Richard
(jt. auth) De Vonyar, J. Degas and the dance
    759.4
Keneally, Thomas
American scoundrel: the life of the notorious Civil
War General Dan Sickles   92
The great shame   304.8
Kennan, George Frost, 1904-
Sketches from a life   92
      About
Grose, P. Operation Rollback   327.12
Kennedy, David M., 1941-
Freedom from fear   973.91
Kennedy, Dennis, 1940-
(ed) The Oxford encyclopedia of theatre & perfor-
mance. See The Oxford encyclopedia of theatre &
performance   792.03
Kennedy, Diana
The essential cuisines of Mexico   641.5
My Mexico   641.5
Kennedy, John F. (John Fitzgerald), 1917-1963
Profiles in courage   920
      About
Dallek, R. An unfinished life: John F. Kennedy, 1917-
1963   92
Freedman, L. Kennedy's wars   973.922
Kaiser, D. E. American tragedy   959.704
The Kennedy tapes   973.922
Kenney, C. John F. Kennedy   92
Leamer, L. The Kennedy men   920
Mahoney, R. D. Sons and brothers: the days of Jack
and Bobby Kennedy   92
Matthews, C. Kennedy & Nixon   973.922
Reeves, R. President Kennedy   92
White, T. H. The making of the president, 1960
    324.6
    See/See also pages in the following book(s):
Galbraith, J. K. Name-dropping   973.9
Halberstam, D. The best and the brightest
    973.922
Benson, M. The encyclopedia of the JFK assassination
    973.922
      Assassination
Mallon, T. Mrs. Paine's garage and the murder of John
F. Kennedy   364.1
Posner, G. L. Case closed   973.922

Kennedy, Joseph F.
(ed) The Art of natural building. See The Art of natural building   **690**
Kennedy, Joseph P., 1888-1969
Hostage to fortune   **92**
            About
Leamer, L. The Kennedy men   **920**
Mahoney, R. D. Sons and brothers: the days of Jack and Bobby Kennedy   **92**
Kennedy, Michael, 1926-
The Oxford dictionary of music   **780.3**
Kennedy, Pagan, 1962-
Black Livingstone [biography of William Henry Sheppard]   **92**
Kennedy, Paul M., 1945-
The rise and fall of the great powers   **909.08**
Kennedy, Randall
Interracial intimacies   **346.01**
Nigger   **305.8**
Kennedy, Robert F., 1925-1968
Make gentle the life of this world   **973.922**
Thirteen days   **973.922**
            About
Mahoney, R. D. Sons and brothers: the days of Jack and Bobby Kennedy   **92**
Schlesinger, A. M. Robert Kennedy and his times   **92**
Thomas, E. Robert Kennedy   **92**
Kennedy, Rose Fitzgerald, 1890-1995
See/See also pages in the following book(s):
Angelo, B. First mothers   **920**
Kennedy, Scott, 1952-
(ed) Reference sources for small and medium-sized libraries. See Reference sources for small and medium-sized libraries   **011**
Kennedy, Terry
Roofing instant answers   **695**
Kennedy & Nixon. Matthews, C.   **973.922**
Kennedy family
            About
Leamer, L. The Kennedy men   **920**
Leamer, L. The Kennedy women   **920**
The **Kennedy** men. Leamer, L.   **920**
The **Kennedy** tapes   **973.922**
The **Kennedy** women. Leamer, L.   **920**
Kennedy's wars. Freedman, L.   **973.922**
Kennelly, Brendan, 1936-
The little book of Judas   **821**
Kenner, Hugh
The Pound era   **811**
Kennett, Lee B.
Sherman   **92**
Kennewick Man
Chatters, J. Ancient encounters   **970.004**
Kenney, Charles
John F. Kennedy   **92**
Kenny, Anthony John Patrick
(ed) The Oxford history of Western philosophy. See The Oxford history of Western philosophy   **190**
Kenny, John B., d. 1988
The complete book of pottery making   **738.1**
Keno, Leigh
Hidden treasures   **749.2**
Keno, Leslie
(jt. auth) Keno, L. Hidden treasures   **749.2**
Kent, Richard G.
Inside women's college basketball   **796.323**
Kentucky Derby
Squires, J. D. Horse of a different color   **798.4**
Kenya
Dinesen, I. Out of Africa   **967.62**
Dinesen, I. Out of Africa and Shadows on the grass   **967.62**
            Description
Adamson, J. Born free   **599.75**

            Social life and customs
Huxley, E. The flame trees of Thika   **92**
Keoke, Emory Dean
Encyclopedia of American Indian contributions to the world   **970.004**
Keown, Damien, 1951-
A dictionary of Buddhism   **294.3**
Kepel, Gilles
Jihad   **297**
Kephart, Beth
Into the tangle of friendship   **158**
Kepler, Johannes, 1571-1630
            About
Ferguson, K. Tycho & Kepler   **92**
Kepler's conjecture. Szpiro, G. G.   **510**
Keppler, Johannes *See* Kepler, Johannes, 1571-1630
Kerchelich, Karen
(jt. auth) Stahl, D. Abbreviations dictionary   **421.03**
Kermode, Anita
(ed) The Oxford book of letters. See The Oxford book of letters   **826**
Kermode, Frank, 1919-
An appetite for poetry   **801**
Shakespeare's language   **822.3**
(ed) Modern British literature; ed. by F. Kermode and J. Hollander. See Modern British literature; ed. by F. Kermode and J. Hollander   **820.8**
(ed) The Oxford book of letters. See The Oxford book of letters   **826**
Kern, Jerome, 1885-1945
See/See also pages in the following book(s):
Green, S. The world of musical comedy   **920**
Kernfeld, Barry, 1950-
The New Grove dictionary of jazz. See The New Grove dictionary of jazz   **781.65**
Kerouac, Jack, 1922-1969
Atop an Underwood   **818**
Book of blues   **811**
Door wide open   **92**
Pomes all sizes   **811**
The portable Jack Kerouac   **818**
Scattered poems   **811**
Selected letters, 1940-1956   **92**
Selected letters, 1957-1969   **92**
Some of the dharma   **294.3**
Kerrey, Robert
When I was a young man   **92**
Kersee, Jackie Joyner- *See* Joyner-Kersee, Jackie
Kershaw, Ian
Hitler   **92**
Kersjes, Mike
A smile as big as the moon   **371.9**
Kert, Bernice
The Hemingway women   **92**
Kertzer, David I., 1948-
The Popes against the Jews   **261.2**
Kessler, David
(jt. auth) Kübler-Ross, E. Life lessons   **170**
Kessler, Ronald
The FBI   **363.2**
Inside the CIA   **327.12**
Kessler-Harris, Alice
Out to work   **331.4**
Ketchum, Richard M., 1922-
Saratoga   **973.3**
Kett, Joseph F.
(jt. auth) Hirsch, E. D. The new dictionary of cultural literacy   **031**
Kettlewell, Henry Bernard David, 1907-1979
            About
Hooper, J. Of moths and men   **576.8**
Kevorkian, Jack
See/See also pages in the following book(s):
Humphry, D. Freedom to die   **179.7**

Key events in African history. Falola, T.   960
Keyboarding (Electronics)
Century 21 keyboarding & information processing
    652.3
Keynes, John Maynard, 1883-1946
The general theory of employment, interest and money
    330.1
About
Skidelsky, R. J. A. John Maynard Keynes v3   92
See/See also pages in the following book(s):
Heilbroner, R. L. The worldly philosophers   330.1
Keynes, R. D.
Fossils, finches, and Fuegians   508
Keyte, Hugh
(ed) The New Oxford book of carols. See The New
Oxford book of carols   782.28
Keyzer, Amy Marcaccio
(ed) Family planning sourcebook. See Family planning
sourcebook   363.9
Khruschev, Nikita See Khrushchev, Nikita Sergeevich,
1894-1971
Khrushchev, Nikita Sergeevich, 1894-1971
About
Nikita Khrushchev   92
See/See also pages in the following book(s):
Kissinger, H. Diplomacy p568-93   327.73
Kick me. Feig, P.   305.23
Kid Antrim See Billy, the Kid
Kidder, Tracy
Home town   974.4
House   690
Kidneys
Diseases
See also Urinary incontinence
The kidspace idea book. Jordan, W. A.   747
Kierkegaard, Søren, 1813-1855
Of the difference between a genius and an apostle
In Kierkegaard, S. The present age, and Of the dif-
ference between a genius and an apostle p89-108
    230
The present age, and Of the difference between a ge-
nius and an apostle   230
See/See also pages in the following book(s):
Existentialism from Dostoevsky to Sartre p83-120
    142
Jaspers, K. The great philosophers   109
Kiernan, Ben
The Pol Pot regime   959.6
Kiernan, Frances
Seeing Mary plain: a life of Mary McCarthy   92
Kilby, Janice Eaton, 1955-
By hand   745
Kilduff, Peter
Richthofen   92
Killing Custer. Welch, J.   973.8
Killing monsters. Jones, G.   302.23
Killing the dream. Posner, G. L.   364.1
Killing the white man's Indian. Bordewich, F. M.
    970.004
Kimball, Robert, 1939-
(ed) Porter, C. The complete lyrics of Cole Porter
    782.42
Kimbrell, Andrew
(ed) Fatal harvest. See Fatal harvest   630
Kimes, Beverly Rae
Standard catalog of American cars, 1805-1942
    629.222
Kimmelman, Michael
Portraits   701
Kimmens, Andrew C.
(ed) World authors, 1900-1950. See World authors,
1900-1950   920.003
Kincaid, Jamaica
A small place   972.97
Talk stories   818

A kind of grace. Joyner-Kersee, J.   92
Kinder, Gary
Ship of gold in the deep blue sea   910.4
The kindness of strangers: the life of Tennessee Wil-
liams. Spoto, D.   92
Kindred souls: the friendship of Eleanor Roosevelt and
David Gurewitsch. Gurewitsch, E.   92
Kindred spirits. Schoen, A. M.   636.089
Kindsvatter, Peter S.
American soldiers   355
King, B. B.
Blues all around me   92
King, Dean
Patrick O'Brian   92
King, Florence
The Florence King reader   818
King, Joan Bolton
Enamelling   738
King, Joyce
Hate crime: the story of a dragging in Jasper, Texas
    364.1
King, Larry, 1933-
How to talk to anyone, anytime, anywhere   302.3
King, Martin Luther, 1929-1968
The autobiography of Martin Luther King, Jr   92
The papers of Martin Luther King, Jr.   323.1
Strength to love   252
A testament of hope   323.1
Why we can't wait   323.1
About
Bennett, L. What manner of man: a biography of Mar-
tin Luther King, Jr.   92
Branch, T. Parting the waters: America in the King
years, 1954-63   973.921
Branch, T. Pillar of fire   973.922
Dyson, M. E. I may not get there with you: the true
Martin Luther King, Jr   92
Frady, M. Martin Luther King, Jr.   92
Posner, G. L. Killing the dream   364.1
See/See also pages in the following book(s):
Wills, G. Certain trumpets p211-24   303.3
King, Michael, 1952-
Gardening with grasses   635.9
King, Neil
The romantics
In Backgrounds to English literature v2   820.9
King, Rodney
About
Cannon, L. Official negligence   979.4
King, Ross, 1962-
Brunelleschi's dome   726
Michelangelo & the Pope's ceiling   759.5
King, Stephen, 1947-
On writing   808.3
Stephen King's danse macabre   818
King Arthur. Goodrich, N. L.   942.01
King Arthur in legend and history   942.01
King David. McKenzie, S. L.   222
King Leopold's ghost. Hochschild, A.   967.5
King of ragtime: Scott Joplin and his era. Berlin, E. A.
    92
King of the world: Muhammad Ali and the rise of an
American hero. Remnick, D.   92
King Philip's War, 1675-1676
Lepore, J. The name of war   973.2
Schultz, E. B. King Philip's War   973.2
King Ubu. Jarry, A.
In Our dramatic heritage v6   808.82
The kingdom by the sea. Theroux, P.   914.1
The kingdom of infinite number. Bunch, B. H.   513
The Kingfish and his realm: the life and times of Huey
P. Long. Hair, W. I.   92

Kingman, Lee, 1919-
(ed) Newbery and Caldecott Medal books, 1966-1975.
See Newbery and Caldecott Medal books, 1966-1975
028.5
(ed) Newbery and Caldecott Medal books, 1976-1985.
See Newbery and Caldecott Medal books, 1976-1985
028.5

Kings and rulers
See also Emperors; Queens
Fraser, A. The warrior queens **920**
Kingsbury, Paul
(ed) The Encyclopedia of country music. See The Encyclopedia of country music **781.642**
Kingsolver, Barbara
Small wonder **814**
Kingston, Maxine Hong
China men **920**
Kingwell, Mark, 1963-
In pursuit of happiness **170**
Kinkead-Weekes, Mark
D.H. Lawrence, triumph to exile, 1912-1922 **92**
Kinnell, Galway, 1927-
Imperfect thirst **811**
Kinsella, Thomas, 1928-
The New Oxford book of Irish verse. See The New Oxford book of Irish verse **821.008**
The **Kinsey** Institute new report on sex. Reinisch, J.
306.7

Kinte family
About
Haley, A. Roots **920**
Kintpuash, Modoc Chief, 1837?-1873
See/See also pages in the following book(s):
Brown, D. A. Bury my heart at Wounded Knee
970.004

Kinzer, Stephen
Crescent and star **956.1**
Kiowa Indians
See/See also pages in the following book(s):
Brown, D. A. The American West p110-23 **978**
Kipel, Edward
(ed) How to clean practically anything. See How to clean practically anything **648**
Kipfer, Barbara Ann
Roget's 21st century thesaurus in dictionary form
423
(ed) Roget's international thesaurus. See Roget's international thesaurus **423**
Kiple, Kenneth F., 1939-
(ed) The Cambridge world history of food. See The Cambridge world history of food **641.3**
Kipling, Rudyard, 1865-1936
Complete verse **821**
About
Gilmour, D. The long recessional: the imperial life of Rudyard Kipling **92**
Ricketts, H. Rudyard Kipling **92**
See/See also pages in the following book(s):
Jarrell, R. No other book **809**
Orwell, G. The Orwell reader p271-83 **828**
Kiplinger's practical guide to your money. Miller, T.
332.024
Kirby, Barbara L.
(jt. auth) Bashe, P. R. The oasis guide to asperger syndrome **618.92**
Kirchner, Bill
(ed) The Oxford companion to jazz. See The Oxford companion to jazz **781.65**
Kirk, John T.
American furniture **749.2**
Kirkpatrick, Sidney
Edgar Cayce **92**
Kirkwood, Burton
The history of Mexico **972**

Kirkwood, Tom
Time of our lives **612.6**
Kirtzman, Andrew
Rudy Giuliani **92**
Kirwin, Barbara
The mad, the bad, and the innocent **614**
Kiš, Danilo
See/See also pages in the following book(s):
Gass, W. H. Finding a form p105-15 **814**
Kiser, John W.
The monks of Tibhirine **271**
KISS guide to astrology. Parker, J. **133.5**
KISS guide to beauty. See Pedersen, S. K-I-S-S beauty
646.7
A **kiss** in space. Salter, M. J. **811**
Kissinger, Henry, 1923-
Diplomacy **327.73**
Does America need a foreign policy? **327.73**
Years of renewal **92**
About
Berman, L. No peace, no honor **959.704**
See/See also pages in the following book(s):
Mann, J. About face **327.73**
Kitano, Harry
(ed) Japanese Americans, from relocation to redress. See Japanese Americans, from relocation to redress
940.53
The **kitchen** idea book. Bouknight, J. K. **643**
The **kitchen** survival guide. Brody, L. **641.5**
Kitchen utensils
Catalogs
The New cooks' catalogue **683**
Kitchener, Andrew
The natural history of the wild cats **599.75**
Kitchens
Bouknight, J. K. The kitchen idea book **643**
Kitchens: plan, remodel, build **643**
Lee, V. Kitchens: a design sourcebook **643**
Thomas, S. This Old House kitchens **643**
Kitchens: a design sourcebook. Lee, V. **643**
Kitchens: plan, remodel, build **643**
Kittle, James L., 1913-
Home heating and air conditioning systems **697**
Kittredge, William
(ed) The Portable Western reader. See The Portable Western reader **810.8**
Kitzinger, Sheila, 1929-
The complete book of pregnancy and childbirth
618.2
Kiyotsugu *See* Kwanze, Kiyotsugu, 1355-1406
Kizer, Carolyn
Cool, calm & collected **811**
KKK *See* Ku Klux Klan
Klaidman, Stephen
Saving the heart **616.1**
Klatz, Ronald, 1955-
(jt. auth) Goldman, B. Brain fitness **153.1**
Klauser, Henriette Anne
Write it down, make it happen **158**
Klausewitz, Karl von *See* Clausewitz, Carl von, 1780-1831
Klebnikov, Paul
Godfather of the Kremlin **92**
Klehr, Harvey
(jt. auth) Haynes, J. E. Venona **327.12**
Klein, Alan H., 1946-
(jt. auth) Agnew, C. L. Twins! **649**
Klein, Joe, 1946-
The natural: the misunderstood presidency of Bill Clinton **973.929**
Klein, Kathleen Gregory, 1946-
(ed) Great women mystery writers. See Great women mystery writers **809.3**
Klein, Maury, 1939-
The change makers **920**

Klein, Maury, 1939——*Continued*
Days of defiance   973.7
Klein, Richard G.
The dawn of human culture   599.93
Klemperer, Victor, 1881-1960
I will bear witness   92
Klezmer, Deborah
(ed) Women in world history. See Women in world
history   920.003
Klezmer music
Strom, Y. The book of Klezmer   781.62
Klimt, Gustav, 1862-1918
Gustav Klimt: landscapes   759.36
About
Nebehay, C. M. Gustav Klimt   759.36
Klostermaier, Klaus K., 1933-
Hinduism   294.5
Kluger, Richard
Ashes to ashes   394.1
Klungness, Leah
(jt. auth) Engber, A. The complete single mother
                                                306.8
Knappman, Edward W.
(ed) Great American trials. See Great American trials
                                                347
(ed) Great world trials. See Great world trials
                                                347
(ed) The Wilson calendar of world history. See The
Wilson calendar of world history   902
Knight, Bobby
Knight: my story   92
Knight, Marion *See* Knight, Suge
Knight, Suge
About
Sullivan, R. Labyrinth   364.1
Knights. Aristophanes
In Aristophanes. The complete plays of Aristophanes
p53-100   882
Knight's cross: a life of Field Marshal Erwin Rommel.
Fraser, D.   92
Knights Templars (Monastic and military order) *See*
Templars
Knipe, Judy
(jt. auth) Nelson, M. E. Strong women eat well
                                                613.2
KnitLit: sweaters and their stories and other writing
about knitting   746.43
The **knitter's** handy book of patterns. Budd, A.
                                                746.43
Knitting
Breiter, B. The complete idiot's guide to knitting and
crocheting   746.43
Budd, A. The knitter's handy book of patterns
                                                746.43
Buss, K. Big book of knitting   746.43
Ham, C. 25 gorgeous sweaters for the brand new knit-
ter   746.43
Kagan, S. Sasha Kagan's country inspiration
                                                746.43
KnitLit: sweaters and their stories and other writing
about knitting   746.43
Newton, D. Designing knitwear   746.43
Vogue knitting   746.43
Vogue knitting American collection   746.43
Knock 'em dead. Yate, M. J.   650.14
Knots and splices
Day, C. L. The art of knotting & splicing   623.88
Pawson, D. The handbook of knots   623.88
Knott, Richard C.
A heritage of wings   359.9
Knowledge, Theory of *See* Theory of knowledge
The **knowledge** web. Burke, J.   609

Knowles, Elizabeth M.
(ed) The Concise Oxford dictionary of quotations. See
The Concise Oxford dictionary of quotations
                                                808.88
(ed) The Oxford dictionary of phrase and fable. See
The Oxford dictionary of phrase and fable   803
(ed) The Oxford dictionary of quotations. See The Ox-
ford dictionary of quotations   808.88
Knowles, Harry
Ain't it cool?   791.43
Knowles, Owen
(ed) The Oxford reader's companion to Conrad. See
The Oxford reader's companion to Conrad
                                                823.009
Knox, Bernard MacGregor Walker
(ed) The Norton book of classical literature. See The
Norton book of classical literature   880.8
Knox, Donald, 1936-
Death march   940.54
The Korean War   951.9
Knutson, Ann
(jt. auth) Hennessey, M. H. Norman Rockwell
                                                759.13
Koba the dread. Amis, M.   947.084
Kobbé, Gustav, 1857-1918
The New Kobbé's opera book. See The New Kobbé's
opera book   792.5
Koch, Jelena Hahl- *See* Hahl-Koch, Jelena
Koch, Kenneth, 1925-2002
Making your own days   809.1
New addresses   811
A possible world   811
Sun out   811
Kochilas, Diane
The glorious foods of Greece   641.5
Koehler, Frank, 1929-
About
Gourevitch, P. A cold case   364.1
Koenig, Harold George
The healing power of faith   291.1
Koerner, David
Here be dragons   576.8
Koestenbaum, Wayne
Andy Warhol   92
Koestler, Angela J.
Understanding chronic pain   616
Kogelman, Stanley
The only math book you'll ever need   513
Kohlenberger, John R.
(jt. auth) Strong, J. The strongest Strong's exhaustive
concordance of the Bible   220.5
Kohn, Alfie
Punished by rewards   153.8
The schools our children deserve   371.2
Kohn, George C.
Dictionary of wars   355
(ed) The New encyclopedia of American scandal. See
The New encyclopedia of American scandal
                                                973.02
Kohn, Ingrid
A silent sorrow   618.3
Koja, Stephan
(ed) Klimt, G. Gustav Klimt: landscapes   759.36
Kolata, Gina
Clone   174
Flu   614.5
Kolb, Rocky
Blind watchers of the sky   523.1
Kolodny, Robert C.
(jt. auth) Masters, W. H. Masters and Johnson on sex
and human loving   155.3
Kolpan, Steven
Exploring wine   641.2

Koltsovo (Russia)
History
Schmemann, S. Echoes of a native land 947
Komaroff, Anthony L.
(ed) The Harvard Medical School family health guide.
See The Harvard Medical School family health guide
610
Komparo, Zembō Motoyasu See Komparu, Zempō
Komparu, Zempō
Hatsuyuki
In Waley, A. The Nō plays of Japan 895.6
Ikutu
In Waley, A. The Nō plays of Japan 895.6
Komparu, Zenchiku, 1405-1468?
The Hōka priests
In Waley, A. The Nō plays of Japan 895.6
Kumasaka
In Waley, A. The Nō plays of Japan 895.6
Princess Hollyhock
In Waley, A. The Nō plays of Japan 895.6
Tanikō
In Waley, A. The Nō plays of Japan 895.6
Komunyakaa, Yusef
Talking dirty to the gods 811
Thieves of paradise 811
Kon-Tiki: across the Pacific by raft. Heyerdahl, T.
910.4
Kon-Tiki Expedition (1947)
Heyerdahl, T. Kon-Tiki: across the Pacific by raft
910.4
Kondracke, Milly
About
Kondracke, M. Saving Milly 362.1
Kondracke, Morton
Saving Milly 362.1
Konigsberg, Ira
The complete film dictionary 791.4303
Konigsburg, E. L.
See/See also pages in the following book(s):
The Newbery & Caldecott medal books, 1986-2000
p266-78 028.5
Konstam, Angus
The history of pirates 910.4
The history of shipwrecks 910.4
Kooser, Ted
See/See also pages in the following book(s):
Gioia, D. Can poetry matter? 809.1
Koplow, David A., 1951-
Smallpox: the fight to eradicate a global scourge
616.9
Koppel, Ted, 1940-
Off camera 92
Korach, Myron
Common phrases and where they come from 422
Koran
The Koran 297.1
Korczak-Marla, Rozka, 1921-1988
About
Cohen, R. The avengers 940.53
Korea
See also Korea (North)
Connor, M. E. The Koreas 951.9
History
Breen, M. The Koreans 951.9
Cumings, B. Korea's place in the sun 951.9
Oberdorfer, D. The two Koreas 951.9
Korea (Democratic People's Republic) See Korea
(North)
Korea (North)
Lee, H. In the absence of sun 920
Korean Americans
Lee, H. In the absence of sun 920
Korean national characteristics
Breen, M. The Koreans 951.9

Korean War, 1950-1953
Catchpole, B. The Korean War, 1950-53 951.9
Encyclopedia of the Korean War 951.9
Hickey, M. The Korean War 951.9
Knox, D. The Korean War 951.9
Weintraub, S. MacArthur's war 951.9
Dictionaries
Edwards, P. M. The Korean War 951.9
Personal narratives
Brady, J. The coldest war: a memoir of Korea
951.9
Tomedi, R. No bugles, no drums 951.9
The **Koreans**. Breen, M. 951.9
Korea's place in the sun. Cumings, B. 951.9
Koresh, David
About
Tabor, J. D. Why Waco? 291.9
Korman, Richard
The Goodyear story 92
Kornbluh, Peter
(ed) The Iran-Contra scandal. See The Iran-Contra
scandal 973.927
Kornicki, Peter F. (Peter Francis)
(ed) The Cambridge encyclopedia of Japan. See The
Cambridge encyclopedia of Japan 952
Korper, Steffano
(jt. auth) Speed, T. The personal Internet security
guidebook 005.8
Kort, Carol
A to Z of American women in the visual arts
920.003
Kort, Michael
The Columbia guide to the Cold War 973.9
Kosinski, Jerzy N., 1933-1991
Passing by 814
Kosovo (Serbia)
History
Clark, W. K. Waging modern war 949.7
Ignatieff, M. Virtual war 949.7
Judah, T. Kosovo 949.7
McAllester, M. Beyond the Mountains of the Damned
949.7
Kostenevich, A. G. (Al'bert Grigor'evich)
French art treasures at the Hermitage 709.44
Kostenevich, Al'bert Grigor'evich See Kostenevich, A.
G. (Al'bert Grigor'evich)
Kotulak, Donna
American Medical Association complete guide to chil-
dren's health. See American Medical Association
complete guide to children's health 618.92
Koufax, Sandy, 1935-
About
Gruver, E. Koufax 92
Leavy, J. Sandy Koufax 92
Koul, Sudha
The tiger ladies 92
Kovacs, Diane K.
Genealogical research on the Web 929
Kovalevskaîâ, S. V. (Sof'îâ Vasil'evna), 1850-1891
See/See also pages in the following book(s):
Bell, E. T. Men of mathematics p406-32 920
Kovalevskaîâ, Sof'îâ Vasil'evna See Kovalevskaîâ, S.
V. (Sof'îâ Vasil'evna), 1850-1891
Kovel, Ralph M.
Kovels' antiques and collectibles price list 745.1
Kovel's dictionary of marks: pottery and porcelain
738
Kovels' know your antiques 745.1
Kovels' know your collectibles 745.1
Kovels' new dictionary of marks 738
Kovel, Terry H.
(jt. auth) Kovel, R. M. Kovels' antiques and collect-
ibles price list 745.1
(jt. auth) Kovel, R. M. Kovel's dictionary of marks:
pottery and porcelain 738

Kovel, Terry H.—*Continued*
(jt. auth) Kovel, R. M. Kovels' know your antiques
    745.1
(jt. auth) Kovel, R. M. Kovel's know your collectibles
    745.1
(jt. auth) Kovel, R. M. Kovels' new dictionary of
   marks   **738**
Kovels' antiques and collectibles price list. Kovel, R. M.
    745.1
Kovel's dictionary of marks: pottery and porcelain.
   Kovel, R. M.   **738**
Kovels' know your antiques. Kovel, R. M.   **745.1**
Kovel's know your collectibles. Kovel, R. M.   **745.1**
Kovner, Abba, 1918-1987
  Sloan Kettering   **892**
        About
  Cohen, R. The avengers   **940.53**
Kowalchik, Claire
  (ed) Rodale's illustrated encyclopedia of herbs. See
   Rodale's illustrated encyclopedia of herbs   **635**
Kozol, Jonathan
  Amazing grace   **362.7**
  Death at an early age   **306.43**
  Ordinary resurrections   **305.23**
  Rachel and her children   **362.5**
  Savage inequalities   **371.9**
Kra, Siegfried J.
  What every woman must know about heart disease
    616.1
Kraemer, Ross Shepard, 1948-
  (ed) Women in scripture. See Women in scripture
    220.9
Kragh, Helge, 1944-
  Quantum generations   **530**
Krakatoa: the day the world exploded, August 27, 1883.
  Winchester, S.   **551.2**
Krakauer, Jon
  Into thin air   **796.52**
Kram, Mark
  The ghosts of Manila   **796.8**
Kramer, Peter D.
  Listening to Prozac   **616.85**
  Should you leave?   **616.89**
Kramers, J. H., 1891-1951
  (ed) Concise encyclopedia of Islam. See Concise ency-
   clopedia of Islam   **297**
Krames, Jeffrey A.
  The Rumsfeld way   **658.4**
Krantz, Les
  Job finder's guide   **331.7**
  Jobs rated almanac   **331.7**
Kranz, Eugene F., 1933-
  Failure is not an option   **629.45**
Kranz, Gene See Kranz, Eugene F., 1933-
Krapp, Kristine M.
  (ed) Drugs and controlled substances. See Drugs and
   controlled substances   **616.86**
  (ed) Notable black American scientists. See Notable
   black American scientists   **920.003**
Krasilovsky, M. William
  This business of music   **780**
Krass, Peter
  Carnegie   **92**
Kraus, Barbara
  Calories and carbohydrates   **613.2**
Krause, Chester L.
  Standard catalog of world coins   **737.4**
Krauss, Lawrence Maxwell
  Atom   **523.1**
  Fear of physics   **530**
Krauss, Rosalind E., 1940-
  The Picasso papers   **759.4**
Kraybill, Donald B.
  On the backroad to heaven   **289.7**
  The riddle of Amish culture   **289.7**

Krebs, Barbara Blake- See Blake-Krebs, Barbara
Krebs, Nancy Funnemark
  (ed) The Nursing mother's problem solver. See The
   Nursing mother's problem solver   **649**
Kreider, Kathryn, 1950-
  (jt. auth) Blumenthal, B. Hands on dyeing   **746.1**
Kremer, S. Lillian, 1939-
  Holocaust literature: an encyclopedia of writers and
   their work. See Holocaust literature: an encyclopedia
   of writers and their work   **809**
Kress, Stephen W.
  The bird garden   **598**
Kricher, John C.
  Galapagos   **508**
Krieger, Michael J.
  All the men in the sea   **910.4**
Kriegsman, Kay Harris
  (jt. auth) Palmer, S. Spinal cord injury   **617**
Kristeller, Paul Oskar, 1905-1999
  (ed) The Renaissance philosophy of man. See The Re-
   naissance philosophy of man   **189**
Kritzer, Herbert M., 1947-
  (ed) Legal systems of the world. See Legal systems of
   the world   **340.03**
Kriwaczek, Paul
  In search of Zarathustra   **295**
Kroc, Ray
  See/See also pages in the following book(s):
  Klein, M. The change makers   **920**
Kroeber, Theodora, 1897-1979
  Ishi in two worlds   **92**
Kronecker, Leopold, 1823-1891
  See/See also pages in the following book(s):
  Bell, E. T. Men of mathematics p466-83   **920**
Kronski, Tadeusz, 1907-1958
  See/See also pages in the following book(s):
  Miłosz, C. To begin where I am p142-68   **891.8**
Krstovic, Jelena O.
  Hispanic literature criticism. See Hispanic literature
   criticism   **860.9**
Krueger, Christine L.
  (ed) Encyclopedia of British writers, 19th and 20th
   centuries. See Encyclopedia of British writers, 19th
   and 20th centuries   **820.9**
Kruk, Herman, 1897-1944
  The last days of the Jerusalem of Lithuania
    940.53
Kruk, Leonard B.
  (jt. auth) Jaderstrom, S. Complete office handbook
    651.8
Krushchev, Nikita See Khrushchev, Nikita Sergeevich,
  1894-1971
Kryza, Frank, 1950-
  The power of light   **333.79**
Ku Klux Klan
  Chalmers, D. M. Hooded Americanism: the history of
   the Ku Klux Klan   **322.4**
  Ezekiel, R. S. The racist mind   **322.4**
  See/See also pages in the following book(s):
  Bushart, H. L. Soldiers of God   **322.4**
Kübler-Ross, Elisabeth
  Life lessons   **170**
  Living with death and dying   **155.9**
  On children and death   **155.9**
  On death and dying   **155.9**
  The wheel of life   **92**
Kubrick, Stanley
        About
  Ciment, M. Kubrick   **791.43**
  LoBrutto, V. Stanley Kubrick   **92**
  Walker, A. Stanley Kubrick, director   **92**
Kugel, James L.
  The Bible as it was   **222**

Kuhl, Patricia K.
(jt. auth) Gopnik, A. The scientist in the crib
155.4

Kuhlman, Erika A., 1961-
A to Z of women in world history   920.003

Kuhn, Cynthia
Buzzed   615
Pumped   617.1

Kuhn, Daniel
Alzheimer's early stages   616.8

Kuhn, Laura Diane
Baker's biographical dictionary of twentieth-century classical musicians. See Baker's biographical dictionary of twentieth-century classical musicians
920.003
Music since 1900   780.9
(ed) Baker's dictionary of opera. See Baker's dictionary of opera   792.5

Kulik, Peter H.
(ed) Van Nostrand's scientific encyclopedia. See Van Nostrand's scientific encyclopedia   503

Kumar, Shiva
(ed) Witness. See Witness   940.53

Kumasaka. Komparu, Z.
In Waley, A. The Nō plays of Japan   895.6

Kumin, Maxine, 1925-
Always beginning   92
Connecting the dots   811
The long marriage   811
Selected poems, 1960-1990   811

Kummer, Ernst Edward, 1810-1893
See/See also pages in the following book(s):
Bell, E. T. Men of mathematics p510-25   920

Küng, Hans, 1928-
The Catholic Church   282
Great Christian thinkers   230

Kunhardt, Peter W.
(jt. auth) Kunhardt, P. B. The American president
920

Kunhardt, Philip B., 1928-
The American president   920

Kunhardt, Philip B., 1951-
(jt. auth) Kunhardt, P. B. The American president
920

Kunitz, Stanley, 1905-
The collected poems   811
Passing through   811
(ed) American authors, 1600-1900. See American authors, 1600-1900   920.003
(ed) British authors of the nineteenth century. See British authors of the nineteenth century   920.003
(ed) European authors, 1000-1900. See European authors, 1000-1900   920.003

Kunstler, James Howard
The city in mind   307.7

Kunz, Jan, 1942-
Painting beautiful watercolors from photographs
751.42

Kunzig, Robert
The restless sea   551.46

Kuper, Adam
(ed) The Social science encyclopedia. See The Social science encyclopedia   300.3

Kuper, Jessica
(ed) The Social science encyclopedia. See The Social science encyclopedia   300.3

Kuralt, Charles, 1934-1997
Charles Kuralt's America   973.92
Charles Kuralt's American moments   973.92
On the road with Charles Kuralt   973.92

Kurian, George Thomas
Encyclopedia of American studies. See Encyclopedia of American studies   973.03
Timetables of world literature   809

(ed) World Christian encyclopedia. See World Christian encyclopedia   230.003

Kurlansky, Mark
The Basque history of the world   946
Cod   639.2
Salt: a world history   553.6

Kurosawa, Akira, 1910-1998
Something like an autobiography   92

Kurs, Katherine, 1956-
(ed) Searching for your soul. See Searching for your soul   291.4

Kursmark, Louise
(jt. auth) Enelow, W. S. Cover letter magic
650.14

Kurson, Ken
(jt. auth) Giuliani, R. W. Leadership   658

Kurt Weill on stage. Hirsch, F.   92

Kurth, Peter
Isadora [Duncan]   92
Tsar: the lost world of Nicholas and Alexandra
947.08

Kurzke, Hermann
Thomas Mann   92

Kurzman, Dan
Disaster!   979.4
Soldier of peace: the life of Yitzhak Rabin   92

Kurzweil, Raymond
The age of spiritual machines   006.3

Kushner, Harold S., 1935-
How good do we have to be?   296.7
To life!   296
When bad things happen to good people   296.3
Who needs God   296.7

Kushner, Harvey W.
Encyclopedia of terrorism   303.6

Kushner, Howard I.
A cursing brain?   616.8

Kuskin, Karla
See/See also pages in the following book(s):
Marcus, L. S. Ways of telling   741.6

Kutler, Stanley I.
Dictionary of American history. See Dictionary of American history   973.03
(ed) Abuse of power. See Abuse of power
973.924

Kuwait
     History—1991, Persian Gulf War
   See Persian Gulf War, 1991

Kwanze, Kiyotsugu, 1355-1406
Sotoba Komachi
In Waley, A. The Nō plays of Japan   895.6

Kwitny, Jonathan
Man of the century: the life and times of Pope John Paul II   92

Kyger, Joanne
As ever   811

Kyoto (Japan)
     Description
Iyer, P. The lady and the monk   952.04

L

L. Frank Baum, creator of Oz. Rogers, K. M.   92
The **L.L.** Bean game and fish cookbook. Cameron, A.
641.6

La Leche League International
The Womanly art of breastfeeding. See The Womanly art of breastfeeding   649

Labor
     See also Proletariat; Teenagers—Employment; Work; Working class

Labor—*Continued*
Accidents
See Industrial accidents
Law and legislation
The American Bar Association guide to workplace law 344
Joel, L. G. Every employee's guide to the law 344
Sack, S. M. The employee rights handbook 344
United States
Dubofsky, M. Labor in America 331.8
Ehrenreich, B. Nickel and dimed 305.5
Lichtenstein, N. State of the Union: a century of American labor 331
Murolo, P. From the folks who brought you the weekend 331
Shulman, B. The betrayal of work 331.2
Stepan-Norris, J. Left out 331.8
Terkel, S. Working 331.2
Zieger, R. H. American workers, American unions 331.8
United States—Dictionaries
Murray, R. E. The lexicon of labor 331
United States—Encyclopedias
Historical encyclopedia of American labor 331.8
Labor and laboring classes *See* Working class
Labor Dept. (U.S.) *See* United States. Dept. of Labor
Labor in America. Dubofsky, M. 331.8
Labor movement
Murolo, P. From the folks who brought you the weekend 331
See/See also pages in the following book(s):
Foner, E. The story of American freedom 323.44
Encyclopedias
Historical encyclopedia of American labor 331.8
St. James encyclopedia of labor history worldwide 331.8
Labor of love, labor of sorrow. Jones, J. 305.4
Labor relations *See* Industrial relations
Labor Statistics Bureau (U.S.) *See* United States. Bureau of Labor Statistics
Labor supply
See also Teenagers—Employment
Labor unions
Dubofsky, M. Labor in America 331.8
Freeman, J. B. Working-class New York 305.5
Lichtenstein, N. State of the Union: a century of American labor 331
Zieger, R. H. American workers, American unions 331.8
United States
Outten, W. N. The rights of employees and union members 344
Stepan-Norris, J. Left out 331.8
Laboratory animal experimentation *See* Animal experimentation
Labyrinth. Sullivan, R. 364.1
Labyrinth of desire. Sullivan, R. 818
The **labyrinth** of solitude. Paz, O.
In Paz, O. The labyrinth of solitude [and other essays] p7-212 864
The **labyrinth** of solitude [and other essays] Paz, O. 864
Labyrinths. Borges, J. L. 868
Lacalamita, Tom
The ultimate pressure cooker cookbook 641.5
Lacey, Robert
The year 1000 942.01
Lackmann, Ronald W.
The encyclopedia of American television, broadcast programming Post World War II to 2000 791.45
Lacouture, Jean
Jesuits 271
Lactose-free diet *See* Milk-free diet

Ladies first. Queen Latifah 158
Ladies of the Grand Tour. Dolan, B. 910.4
Ladies' voices. Stein, G.
In Stein, G. Selected writings p555-56 818
The **lady** and the monk. Iyer, P. 952.04
Lady Day: the many faces of Billie Holiday. O'Meally, R. G. 92
A **lady,** first. Baldrige, L. 92
The **lady** from the sea. Ibsen, H.
In Ibsen, H. The complete major prose plays p587-688 839.8
In Ibsen, H. Ibsen: four plays, v3 839.8
The **lady** mechanic's total car care for the clueless. Volpe, R. 629.28
Laeter, J. R. de (John R. de)
(jt. auth) Bevan, A. W. R. Meteorites: a journey through space and time 523.5
Laeter, John R. de *See* Laeter, J. R. de (John R. de)
Lafayette, Bernard, 1940-
See/See also pages in the following book(s):
Halberstam, D. The children 323.1
LaFeber, Walter
The clash 327.73
Lafferty, Elaine
(jt. auth) Van Susteren, G. My turn at the bully pulpit 349
Lagasse, Emeril
Every day's a party 642
Lagassé, Paul
(ed) The Columbia encyclopedia. See The Columbia encyclopedia 031
Lagrange, Joseph Louis, comte de, 1736-1813
See/See also pages in the following book(s):
Bell, E. T. Men of mathematics p153-71 920
LaGuardia, Cheryl M.
(ed) Magazines for libraries. See Magazines for libraries 011
Lahita, Robert G. (Robert George), 1945-
Lupus 616.7
Laird, Thomas
Into Tibet 327.12
Lakshmi Bai, Rani of Jhansi, d. 1858
See/See also pages in the following book(s):
Fraser, A. The warrior queens 920
Lamar, Howard Roberts
(ed) The New encyclopedia of the American West. See The New encyclopedia of the American West 978.03
Lamar, Lucius Quintus Cincinnatus, 1825-1893
See/See also pages in the following book(s):
Kennedy, J. F. Profiles in courage 920
Lamb, Brian
(comp) Booknotes: life stories. See Booknotes: life stories 920
Lamb, Charles, 1775-1834
Tales from Shakespeare 822.3
Lamb, David
The Arabs 909
Lamb, Mary, 1764-1847
(jt. auth) Lamb, C. Tales from Shakespeare 822.3
Lamb, Richard
War in Italy, 1943-1945 940.54
Lamb, Sharon
The secret lives of girls 305.23
Lamb, William *See* Melbourne, William Lamb, 2nd Viscount, 1779-1848
Lambert, David, 1932-
Dinosaur encyclopedia 567.9
The field guide to geology 551
The ultimate dinosaur book 567.9
Lambton, William, 1756-1823
About
Keay, J. The great arc 526

Lamm, Lawrence W., 1896-1995
(ed) The World's great speeches. See The World's
  great speeches   **808.85**
L'Amour, Louis, 1908-1988
The Sackett companion   **813.009**
Lancaster, Burt, 1913-1994
About
Buford, K. Burt Lancaster   **92**
Lancaster, Lynne C.
When generations collide   **658.3**
The **lance** and the shield: the life and times of Sitting
  Bull. Utley, R. M.   **92**
Land of a thousand hills. Carr, R. H.   **967.571**
Land of the firebird. Massie, S.   **947**
Land of the tiger. Thapar, V.   **508**
Land of unlikeness. Lowell, R.
In Lowell, R. Collected poems   **811**
Land reform
See also Agriculture—Government policy
Land settlement
United States
Stoll, S. Larding the lean Earth   **631.4**
Land surveying See Surveying
Land use
See also Public lands
The **land** where the blues began. Lomax, A.
    781.643
Landau, Sidney I.
(ed) The Doubleday Roget's thesaurus in dictionary
  form. See The Doubleday Roget's thesaurus in dic-
  tionary form   **423**
Landforms
See also Coasts
Landlord and tenant
Portman, J. Every landlord's legal guide   **346.04**
Portman, J. Every tenant's legal guide   **346.04**
Strauss, S. D. Landlord and tenant   **346.04**
Landmark decisions of the United States Supreme
  Court. Finkelman, P.   **347**
Landmark Supreme Court cases. Lively, D. E.   **342**
Landmarks, Literary See Literary landmarks
Landmarks in mechanical engineering   **621**
Landmarks in western science. Whitfield, P.   **509**
Landon, Grelun
(jt. auth) Stambler, I. Country music: the encyclopedia
    781.642
Landon, Margaret, 1903-1993
Anna and the King of Siam [biography of Anna Harri-
  ette Leonowens]   **92**
Landscape. Pinter, H.
In Pinter, H. Complete works v3   **822**
Landscape architecture
See also Garden ornaments and furniture
Step-by-step yard & garden basics   **635**
Van Sweden, J. A. Architecture in the garden
    712
Dictionaries
The Penguin dictionary of architecture and landscape
  architecture   **720.3**
Landscape gardening
See also Garden design
Adam, J. Landscape planning   **635**
Anderton, S. Urban sanctuaries   **635.9**
Brookes, J. Garden masterclass   **712**
Brookes, J. John Brookes' natural landscapes
    635.9
Buchanan, R. Taylor's master guide to landscaping
    712
Cox, J. Landscape with roses   **635.9**
Dirr, M. Dirr's Hardy trees and shrubs   **635.9**
Dirr, M. Dirr's trees and shrubs for warm climates
    635.9
Harper, P. Designing with perennials   **712**
Hayward, G. Stone in the garden   **712**

Joyce, D. Topiary and the art of training plants
    635.9
King, M. Gardening with grasses   **635.9**
Robinson, P. The American Horticultural Society com-
  plete guide to water gardening   **635.9**
Seale, A. New life for old gardens   **635.9**
Taylor's master guide to gardening   **635.9**
The **landscape** of history. Gaddis, J. L.   **901**
Landscape painting
Klimt, G. Gustav Klimt: landscapes   **759.36**
Wilton, A. American sublime   **759.13**
Landscape planning. Adam, J.   **635**
Landscape turned red. Sears, S. W.   **973.7**
Landscape with chainsaw. Lasdun, J.   **821**
Landscape with roses. Cox, J.   **635.9**
Lane, Anthony
Nobody's perfect   **791.43**
Lane, Leonard G.
Gallaudet survival guide to signing   **419**
Lane, Marion
The Humane Society of the United States complete
  guide to dog care   **636.7**
Lane, Nancy E.
The osteoporosis book   **616.7**
Lang, Anthony E.
(jt. auth) Weiner, W. J. Parkinson's disease   **616.8**
Lang, Bernhard, 1946-
(jt. auth) McDannell, C. Heaven   **236**
Lang, Paul Henry, 1901-1991
Music in Western civilization   **780.9**
Langdon, Helen
Caravaggio   **92**
Langdon, Philip
(jt. auth) Thomas, S. This Old House kitchens
    643
Lange, Dianne
(ed) Informed decisions. See Informed decisions
    616.99
Lange, Dorothea, 1895-1965
See/See also pages in the following book(s):
Bustard, B. I. Picturing the century   **779**
Langer, Howard J.
(ed) American Indian quotations. See American Indian
  quotations   **808.88**
(ed) World War II. See World War II   **940.53**
Langer, Lawrence L.
Admitting the Holocaust   **940.53**
(ed) Art from the ashes. See Art from the ashes
    940.53
Lange's handbook of chemistry   **540**
Langewiesche, William
American ground, unbuilding the World Trade Center
    974.7
Sahara unveiled   **966**
Langguth, A. J., 1933-
Our Vietnam   **959.704**
Langhorne family
About
Fox, J. Five sisters   **920**
The **Langhorne** sisters. See Fox, J. Five sisters
    920
Langland, William, 1330?-1400?
Piers Plowman   **821**
Langley, Jim
Bicycling magazine's complete guide to bicycle main-
  tenance and repair for road and mountain bikes
    629.28
Langmead, Donald
Encyclopedia of architectural and engineering feats
    721
Langmuir, Erika
Yale dictionary of art and artists   **703**
Langston Hughes [critical essays]   **818**

Language and languages
See also Grammar; Semantics; Sign language; Sociolinguistics; names of languages or groups of cognate languages
Abram, D. The spell of the sensuous — 128
Crystal, D. Language and the Internet — 400
Deacon, T. W. The symbolic species — 153.6
Dunbar, R. I. M. Grooming, gossip, and the evolution of language — 599.93
Nunberg, G. The way we talk now — 400
Pinker, S. The language instinct — 400
Pinker, S. Words and rules — 401
Science times book of language and linguistics — 400
The World's major languages — 400
Dictionaries
Crystal, D. A dictionary of language — 410
Dalby, A. Dictionary of languages — 410
Encyclopedias
Crystal, D. The Cambridge encyclopedia of language — 400
Facts about the world's languages: an encyclopedia of the world's major languages, past and present — 400
Psychology
Golinkoff, R. M. How babies talk — 401
Language and society *See* Sociolinguistics
Language and the Internet. Crystal, D. — 400
Language in thought and action. Hayakawa, S. I. — 412
The **language** instinct. Pinker, S. — 400
The **language** of passion. Vargas Llosa, M. — 864
Languages
Vocabulary
See Vocabulary
Lanier, Sidney, 1842-1881
See/See also pages in the following book(s):
Wilson, E. Patriotic gore p450-66, 519-28 — 810.9
Lankford, John
(ed) History of astronomy. See History of astronomy — 520.3
Lannon, Richard
(jt. auth) Lewis, T. A general theory of love — 152.4
Lansky, Bruce
The very best baby name book in the whole wide world — 929.4
Lantermann, Werner, 1956-
The new parrot handbook — 636.6
Lanza, Louis
Totally dairy-free cooking — 641.5
Lao-tse *See* Lao-tzu, 6th cent. B.C.
Lao-tzu, 6th cent. B.C.
Tao te ching — 299
See/See also pages in the following book(s):
Jaspers, K. The great philosophers — 109
Lapierre, Dominique
The City of Joy — 954
Five past midnight in Bhopal — 363.1
(jt. auth) Collins, L. O Jerusalem! — 956.94
Laplace, Pierre Simon, 1749-1827
See/See also pages in the following book(s):
Bell, E. T. Men of mathematics p172-82 — 920
Lapland
Beach, H. A year in Lapland — 948.97
Laqueur, Walter, 1921-
A history of Zionism — 956.94
The Holocaust encyclopedia. See The Holocaust encyclopedia — 940.53
No end to war — 303.6
Larding the lean Earth. Stoll, S. — 631.4
Lardner, Ring, 1915-2000
I'd hate myself in the morning — 92
Large print books
Ackerman, D. Cultivating delight — 508

Andersen, C. P. Jackie after Jack — 92
Angelou, M. Even the stars look lonesome — 814
Ashcraft, T. O. Red sky in mourning — 910.4
Atkins, R. C. Dr. Atkins' new diet revolution — 613.2
Auchincloss, L. Woodrow Wilson — 92
Barry, D. Dave Barry hits below the Beltway — 817
Bathurst, B. The lighthouse Stevensons — 623.89
Benchley, P. Shark trouble — 597
Berendt, J. Midnight in the garden of good and evil — 975.8
Berg, A. S. Kate remembered (a biography of Katharine Hepburn) — 92
Bergen, P. L. Holy war, Inc. — 958.1
Bible. Holy Bible: the new King James Version — 220.5
Bosworth, P. Marlon Brando — 92
Bowden, M. Black Hawk down — 967.73
Brady, J. The coldest war: a memoir of Korea — 951.9
Bragg, R. Ava's man — 92
Brokaw, T. An album of memories — 940.54
Brokaw, T. The greatest generation — 940.54
Brokaw, T. A long way from home — 92
Brookhiser, R. Alexander Hamilton, American — 92
Brookhiser, R. America's first dynasty — 920
Bruni, F. Ambling into history: the unlikely odyssey of George W. Bush — 92
Bryson, B. I'm a stranger here myself — 973.92
Bryson, B. In a sunburned country — 994
Bryson, B. A short history of nearly everything — 500
Buford, K. Burt Lancaster — 92
Capuzzo, M. Close to shore — 597
Carter, J. Living faith — 92
Carter, J. The virtues of aging — 305.26
Cassel, G. H. The eye book — 617.7
Channing, C. Just lucky I guess — 92
Child, J. Julia's kitchen wisdom — 641.5
Churchill, Sir W. The great republic — 973
Clarke, G. Get happy: the life of Judy Garland — 92
Clinton, H. R. Living history — 92
Clooney, R. Girl singer — 92
Conant, J. Tuxedo Park — 92
Conroy, P. My losing season — 92
Dallek, R. An unfinished life: John F. Kennedy, 1917-1963 — 92
Dash, M. Tulipomania — 635.9
Dickson, P. Sputnik: the shock of the century — 629.46
Dillard, A. For the time being — 814
Dolnick, E. Down the great unknown — 979.1
Douglas, K. My stroke of luck — 92
Drew, E. Citizen McCain — 92
Feiler, B. S. Abraham — 222
Foreman, A. Georgiana, Duchess of Devonshire — 92
Fox, Michael J. Lucky man — 92
Frady, M. Martin Luther King, Jr. — 92
Fraser, A. Marie Antoinette — 92
Gerstner, L. V., Jr. Who says elephants can't dance? — 338.7
Gibaldi, J. MLA handbook for writers of research papers — 808
Glenn, J. John Glenn — 92
Gordon, M. Seeing through places — 814
Graham, B. Just as I am — 92
Gray, J. Mars and Venus starting over — 306.7
Greene, B. Duty — 940.54
Hepburn, K. Me — 92
Herriot, J. James Herriot's animal stories — 636.089
Hewitt, D. Tell me a story — 92
Hickam, H. H. The Coalwood way — 92

Large print books—*Continued*

Hillerman, T. Seldom disappointed 92
Horwitz, T. Blue latitudes 910.4
Hurston, Z. N. Dust tracks on a road 92
John Paul II, Pope. Crossing the threshold of hope 282
Johnson, P. Napoleon 92
Kagan, R. Of paradise and power 327.73
Kennedy, R. F. Thirteen days 973.922
King, M. L. Strength to love 252
Kissinger, H. Does America need a foreign policy? 327.73
Klein, J. The natural: the misunderstood presidency of Bill Clinton 973.929
Knight, B. Knight: my story 92
Kolata, G. Flu 614.5
Kondracke, M. Saving Milly 362.1
Kranz, E. F. Failure is not an option 629.45
Kuralt, C. Charles Kuralt's America 973.92
Kuralt, C. Charles Kuralt's American moments 973.92
Kurlansky, M. Salt: a world history 553.6
Leaming, B. Mrs. Kennedy 92
Lewis, R. W. B. Dante 92
Lord, W. A night to remember 910.4
Lynn, L. Still woman enough 92
Mace, N. L. The 36-hour day 618.97
Martin, S. Pure drivel 817
Masson, J. M. The nine emotional lives of cats 636.8
Mayle, P. Encore Provence 944.083
Mayle, P. French lessons 394.1
McCain, J. S. Faith of my fathers 92
McCourt, F. 'Tis 92
McCullough, D. G. John Adams 92
McMurtry, L. Crazy Horse 92
McMurtry, L. Roads 917.3
McMurtry, L. Walter Benjamin at the Dairy Queen 92
Menzer, J. The wildest ride 796.72
Milford, N. Savage beauty: the life of Edna St. Vincent Millay 92
Miller, J. The cell: inside the 9/11 plot and why the FBI and CIA failed to stop it 973.931
Morgan, E. S. Benjamin Franklin 92
Mortimer, J. C. The summer of a dormouse 92
Myers, D. G. A quiet world 617.8
The Official Scrabble players dictionary 793.73
O'Reilly, B. The no-spin zone 973.92
Osgood, C. See you on the radio 818
Palmer, A. A golfer's life 92
Paterniti, M. Driving Mr. Albert 917.3
Pépin, J. The apprentice: my life in the kitchen 92
Peterson, R. T. A field guide to the birds of eastern and central North America 598
Poitier, S. The measure of a man 92
Pollan, M. The botany of desire 581.6
Powell, C. L. My American journey 92
Preston, R. The demon in the freezer 616.9
Quirk, L. J. Bob Hope: the road well-traveled 92
Rashid, A. Taliban: militant Islam, oil, and fundamentalism in Central Asia 958.1
Rather, D. The American dream 973.92
Rees, S. The floating brothel 365
Reeve, C. Still me 92
Reichl, R. Comfort me with apples 92
Remini, R. V. Joseph Smith 92
Roach, M. Stiff 611
Sacks, O. W. Uncle Tungsten 92
Saudek, C. D. The Johns Hopkins guide to diabetes 616.4
Schaap, D. Flashing before my eyes 92
Schlosser, E. Fast food nation 394.1

Schroeder, P. 24 years of House work—and the place is still a mess 92
Sedaris, D. Me talk pretty one day 818
Sheehy, G. Hillary's choice 92
Sheridan, P. 44, Dublin made me 92
Shields, C. Jane Austen 92
Sides, H. Ghost soldiers 940.54
Smiley, J. Charles Dickens 92
Smith, L. Natural blonde 92
Souhami, D. Selkirk's Island 996
Strong, J. The strongest Strong's exhaustive concordance of the Bible 220.5
Thomas, E. M. The social lives of dogs 636.7
Tobin, J. To conquer the air 629.13
Tuchman, B. W. The first salute 973.3
Tufts University. School of Veterinary Medicine. Animal ER 636.089
Von Drehle, D. Triangle: the fire that changed America 974.7
Weil, A. The healthy kitchen 641.5
Weiner, W. J. Parkinson's disease 616.8
Whitcomb, C. Cold zero 363.2
White, E. The flaneur 944
Wilkins, R. W. Jefferson's pillow 973
Wills, G. Lincoln at Gettysburg 973.7
Winchester, S. Krakatoa: the day the world exploded, August 27, 1883 551.2
Winik, J. April 1865 973.7
Woodward, B. Bush at war 973.931

Bibliography

The Complete directory of large print books and serials 015.73

Large type books in print. See The Complete directory of large print books and serials 015.73

Larkin, David, 1936-
(jt. auth) Sprigg, J. Shaker—life, work, and art 289

Larkin, Philip
Collected poems 821
See/See also pages in the following book(s):
Amis, M. The war against cliché 824
Heaney, S. Finders keepers p158-66, 343-60 821
Heaney, S. The redress of poetry 821.009

Larousse concise dictionary, Spanish-English, English-Spanish. See Larousse diccionario compact: español inglés, inglés español 463

Larousse diccionario compact: español inglés, inglés español 463

Larousse encyclopedia of wine 641.2

Larousse English-Spanish Spanish-English dictionary 463

Larousse French-English, English-French dictionary 443

Larousse gastronomique 641.03

Larsen, Nella
See/See also pages in the following book(s):
American women fiction writers 813.009
Gilbert, S. M. No man's land v3 p121-65 820.9
Wall, C. A. Women of the Harlem Renaissance 810.9

Larson, Edward J.
(ed) The History of science and religion in the western tradition. See The History of science and religion in the western tradition 291.1

Larson, Erik
The devil in the white city 364.1
Isaac's storm 976.4

Larson, Peter
About
Fiffer, S. Tyrannosaurus Sue 567.9

Larson, Peter L.
Rex appeal 567.9

LaRussa, Tony
See/See also pages in the following book(s):
Will, G. F. Men at work: the craft of baseball p7-75
796.357

Las Vegas (Nev.)
Denton, S. The money and the power   979.3

Lascelles, George Henry Hubert *See* Harewood, George Henry Hubert Lascelles, 7th Earl of, 1923-

Lasch, Christopher
The revolt of the elites   306

Lasch-Quinn, Elisabeth
Race experts   305.8

Lasdun, James
Landscape with chainsaw   821

Lash, Joseph P., 1909-1987
Helen and teacher   92

Laskin, David, 1953-
Braving the elements   551.6

Lass, Abraham Harold, 1907-2001
(jt. auth) Cole, S. The Facts on File dictionary of cultural and historical allusions   031.02

Lassell, Michael, 1947-
(ed) The World in us. See The World in us
811.008

Lasser (J.K.) Tax Institute *See* J.K. Lasser Tax Institute

Lasser's your income tax. See J.K. Lasser's your income tax   336.2

Last, John M., 1926-
(ed) The Oxford illustrated companion to medicine. See The Oxford illustrated companion to medicine
610.3

The **last** American Puritan: the life of Increase Mather, 1639-1723. Hall, M. G.   92
The **last** apocalypse. Reston, J., Jr.   940.1
The **last** best hope of earth: Abraham Lincoln and the promise of America. Neely, M. E., Jr.   92
The **last** campaign. Karabell, Z.   324
The **last** days of innocence. Harries, M.   940.4
The **last** days of the Jerusalem of Lithuania. Kruk, H.
940.53
The **last** empire. Vidal, G.   814
The **last** face you'll ever see. Solotaroff, I.   364.66
The **last** great Frenchman. Williams, C.   92
The **last** great revolution. Wright, R.   955
The **last** lion: Winston Spencer Churchill. Manchester, W.   92
Last man down. Picciotto, R.   974.7
The **last** mission. Smith, J. B.   940.54
The **last** partnerships. Geisst, C. R.   332.6
The **last** seven months of Anne Frank. Lindwer, W.
940.53
The **last** survivor. Ryback, T. W.   940.53
The **last** three minutes. Davies, P. C. W.   523.1
Last to go. Pinter, H.
In Pinter, H. Complete works v2   822
Last train to Memphis: the rise of Elvis Presley. Guralnick, P.   92
Late and posthumous poems, 1968-1974. Neruda, P.
861

Latham, Alison
(ed) The Oxford companion to music. See The Oxford companion to music   780.3

Latham, Edward
A dictionary of names, nicknames, and surnames of persons, places, and things   929.4

Latimer, Lewis Howard, 1848-1928
See/See also pages in the following book(s):
Abdul-Jabbar, K. Black profiles in courage p178-96
920
Russell, D. Black genius and the American experience
920

Latin America
See also South America
The South American handbook   980

Biography—Dictionaries
Dictionary of Hispanic biography   920.003
Civilization
Fuentes, C. The buried mirror   946
History
The Cambridge history of Latin America   980
Chasteen, J. C. Born in blood and fire   980
Williamson, E. The Penguin history of Latin America
980

Latin American art
Barnitz, J. Twentieth-century art of Latin America
709
Brazil body & soul   709.8
Encyclopedia of Latin American & Caribbean art
709.8
Scott, J. F. Latin American art   709.8
Latin American art. Scott, J. F.   709.8
Latin American authors *See* Authors, Latin American
Latin American literature
Bio-bibliography
Concise encyclopedia of Latin American literature
860.3
Encyclopedias
Concise encyclopedia of Latin American literature
860.3
History and criticism
The Cambridge history of Latin American literature
860.9
Hispanic literature criticism   860.9
Latin American writers   920.003
Moss, J. Latin American literature and its times
860.9
Latin American literature and its times. Moss, J.
860.9
Latin American poetry
Collections
Twentieth century Latin American poetry   861
Latin American women artists of the United States. Henkes, R.   704
Latin American writers   920.003
Latin authors *See* Authors, Latin
Latin for the illiterati. Stone, J. R.   473
Latin language
Dictionaries
Oxford Latin dictionary   473
Stone, J. R. Latin for the illiterati   473
Stone, J. R. More Latin for the illiterati   473
Latin literature
See also Classical literature
Collections
The Norton book of classical literature   880.8
The Portable Roman reader   870.8
History and criticism
Hamilton, E. The Roman way   870.9
See/See also pages in the following book(s):
Gay, P. The Enlightenment: an interpretation   190
Latin poetry
The Roman poets   871.008
Latinos (U.S.) *See* Hispanic Americans
Latitude
Carter, B. Latitude   526
Latrobe, Kathy Howard
The children's literature dictionary   028.5
Latter-day Saints *See* Church of Jesus Christ of Latter-day Saints
Lauer, Josh
(ed) Science and its times. See Science and its times
509
Laufer, Guida M. Jackson- *See* Jackson-Laufer, Guida M. (Guida Myrl)
Laughlin, Greg
(jt. auth) Adams, F. C. The five ages of the universe
523.1
Laughlin, James, 1914-1997
The secret room   811

Laughlin, Kay
(comp) The Children's song index, 1978-1993. See
The Children's song index, 1978-1993 **782.42**
Launius, Roger D.
Frontiers of space exploration **629.45**
Laura Dennis. Foote, H.
In Foote, H. Getting Frankie married—and after-
wards, and other plays **812**
Laura Ingalls Wilder country. Anderson, W. T. **92**
Lauren, Ralph
About
McDowell, C. Ralph Lauren **92**
Laurie, Hilary
(ed) Verses of the poets Laureate. See Verses of the
poets Laureate **821.008**
Lautrec, Henri de Toulouse- *See* Toulouse-Lautrec,
Henri de, 1864-1901
Laux, Dorianne
(jt. auth) Addonizio, K. The poet's companion
808.1
Lavelle, Marianne
(jt. auth) Fagin, D. Toxic deception **615.9**
Lavender, Kenneth
Book repair **025.7**
Laver, James, 1899-1975
Costume and fashion **391**
Lavers, Chris
Why elephants have big ears **590**
Lavie, P. (Peretz), 1949-
The enchanted world of sleep **612.8**
Lavie, Peretz *See* Lavie, P. (Peretz), 1949-
Law
See also Constitutional law; Criminal law; Interna-
tional law; Litigation
Dictionaries
Black, H. C. Black's law dictionary **340.03**
Encyclopedias
Legal systems of the world **340.03**
United States
The American Bar Association guide to family law
346.01
Feinman, J. M. Law 101 **340**
Friedman, L. M. American law in the 20th century
349
Gale encyclopedia of everyday law **349**
Great American court cases **347**
Howard, P. The death of common sense **348**
Lewis, A. Gideon's trumpet **347**
National survey of state laws **349**
Nolo's encyclopedia of everyday law **340**
The Oxford companion to American law **349**
Van Susteren, G. My turn at the bully pulpit **349**
See/See also pages in the following book(s):
Boorstin, D. J. The Americans: The colonial experi-
ence **973.2**
United States—Dictionaries
1001 legal words you need to know **349**
United States—Encyclopedias
Encyclopedia of American law **349**
West's encyclopedia of American law **340.03**
Law 101. Feinman, J. M. **340**
Law in literature
Bibliography
Breen, J. L. Novel verdicts **016.8**
Law reform
Howard, P. The death of common sense **348**
Law schools, Barron's guide to **378.73**
Lawns
Step-by-step yard & garden basics **635**
Lawrence, D. H. (David Herbert), 1885-1930
About
Ellis, D. D.H. Lawrence, dying game, 1922-1930
92
Kinkead-Weekes, M. D.H. Lawrence, triumph to exile,
1912-1922 **92**

Thornton, W. D.H. Lawrence **823.009**
Worthen, J. D.H. Lawrence, the early years, 1885-1912
92
Lawrence, David Herbert *See* Lawrence, D. H. (David
Herbert), 1885-1930
Lawrence, Ernest Orlando, 1901-1958
About
Herken, G. Brotherhood of the bomb **920**
Lawrence, Mark Atwood, 1965-
(ed) The Vietnam War. See The Vietnam War
959.704
Lawrence, Ronald Melvin, 1926-
Preventing arthritis **616.7**
Lawrence, T. E. (Thomas Edward), 1888-1935
Seven pillars of wisdom **940.4**
About
Asher, M. Lawrence, the uncrowned king of Arabia
92
Lawrence, Thomas Edward *See* Lawrence, T. E.
(Thomas Edward), 1888-1935
Lawrence, the uncrowned king of Arabia. Asher, M.
92
Lawson, James M., 1928-
See/See also pages in the following book(s):
Halberstam, D. The children **323.1**
Lawsuits *See* Litigation
Lawyers
See also Judges
Lay back the darkness. Hirsch, E. **811**
Layden, Joseph, 1959-
(jt. auth) Kersjes, M. A smile as big as the moon
371.9
A **layperson's** guide to criminal law. Mack, R. L.
345
Lazear, Jonathon
The man who mistook his job for a life **155.2**
LC *See* Library of Congress
Le Sieg, Theo *See* Seuss, Dr.
Leach, Penelope
Your baby & child **649**
Leadbelly, 1885-1949
About
Wolfe, C. K. The life and legend of Leadbelly
92
Leader, Zachary
(ed) Amis, K. The letters of Kingsley Amis **92**
The leader. Ionesco, E.
In Ionesco, E. Rhinoceros, and other plays **842**
Leaders of the American Civil War **920.003**
Leadership
See also Elite (Social sciences)
Batstone, D. B. Saving the corporate soul & (who
knows?) maybe your own **658.4**
Cohen, E. A. Supreme command **355**
Coles, R. Lives of moral leadership **170**
Collins, J. C. Good to great **658**
Connelly, O. On war and leadership **355.3**
Fisher, H. E. The first sex **305.4**
Goleman, D. Primal leadership **658.4**
Harari, O. The leadership secrets of Colin Powell
303.3
Kaplan, R. D. Warrior politics **320**
Krames, J. A. The Rumsfeld way **658.4**
Ruggero, E. Duty first **355**
Wills, G. Certain trumpets **303.3**
Leadership. Giuliani, R. W. **658**
The leadership secrets of Colin Powell. Harari, O.
303.3
The leaf and the cloud. Oliver, M. **811**
Leakey, Richard E., 1944-
The origin of humankind **599.93**
Origins reconsidered **599.93**
The sixth extinction **304.2**
Léal, Brigitte
The ultimate Picasso **92**

Leaman, Oliver
(ed) Encyclopedia of death and dying. See Encyclopedia of death and dying   **306.9**
Leamer, Laurence
  The Kennedy men   **920**
  The Kennedy women   **920**
Leaming, Barbara
  Katharine Hepburn   **92**
  Marilyn Monroe   **92**
  Mrs. Kennedy [biography of Jacqueline Kennedy Onassis]   **92**
Leap of faith. Nur el Hussein, Queen, consort of Hussein, King of Jordan   **92**
Lear, Edward, 1812-1888
  See/See also pages in the following book(s):
  Wullschläger, J. Inventing wonderland   **820.9**
Lear, Linda J., 1940-
  Rachel Carson   **92**
Learn calligraphy. Shepherd, M.   **745.6**
Learn to sail. Conner, D.   **797.1**
The **learned** women. Molière
  In Molière. The misanthrope, and other plays
     842
Learning, Psychology of See Psychology of learning
Learning and scholarship
  See also Education
  Cahill, T. How the Irish saved civilization   **941.5**
  Quick studies   **001.1**
  See/See also pages in the following book(s):
  Durant, W. J. The age of Louis XIV p481-94
     940.2
  Emerson, R. W. The portable Emerson p51-71
     818
Learning computer programming. Farrell, M.   **005**
Learning disabilities
  See also Attention deficit disorder
  Levine, M. D. A mind at a time   **370.15**
  Peterson's colleges with programs for students with learning disabilities or attention deficit disorders
     378.73
      Encyclopedias
  Turkington, C. The encyclopedia of learning disabilities   **371.9**
Learning to fall. Simmons, P.   **291.4**
Least Heat Moon, William See Heat Moon, William Least
Leaves of grass. Whitman, W.
  In Whitman, W. Complete poetry and collected prose
     818
Leaving Saturn. Jackson, M.   **811**
Leavitt, Henrietta Swan, 1868-1921
  See/See also pages in the following book(s):
  Malone, J. W. It doesn't take a rocket scientist
     920
Leavy, Jane
  Sandy Koufax   **92**
Lebanon
      History
  Friedman, T. L. From Beirut to Jerusalem   **956**
LeBlanc, Sydney
  The architecture traveler   **720.973**
Leboyer, Frédérick
  Birth without violence   **618.4**
Leckie, Robert
  None died in vain   **973.7**
  Okinawa   **940.54**
Lectures on literature. Nabokov, V. V.   **808.3**
Lectures on Russian literature. Nabokov, V. V.
     891.7
Ledbetter, Huddie See Leadbelly, 1885-1949
Lederman, Leon M.
  The God particle   **539.7**
Ledger, Charles, 1818-1905
  See/See also pages in the following book(s):
  Honigsbaum, M. The fever trail   **616.9**

LeDoux, Joseph E.
  Synaptic self   **612.8**
Lee, Bruce
  Marching orders   **940.54**
Lee, Helie
  In the absence of sun   **920**
Lee, Henry C.
  Blood evidence   **614**
Lee, Hermione
  Virginia Woolf   **92**
  Willa Cather   **92**
Lee, John, 1931-
  (jt. auth) Friedlander, E. J. Feature writing for newspapers and magazines   **070.4**
Lee, Linda, 1948-
  Sewing edges and corners   **646.2**
Lee, Robert E. (Robert Edward), 1807-1870
      About
  Fellman, M. The making of Robert E. Lee   **92**
  Freeman, D. S. Lee   **92**
  Nolan, A. T. Lee considered   **92**
  Thomas, E. M. Robert E. Lee   **92**
Lee, Sherman E.
  A history of Far Eastern art   **709.5**
Lee, Vinny
  Kitchens: a design sourcebook   **643**
Lee, Wen Ho
      About
  Stober, D. A convenient spy   **327.12**
  Trulock, N. Code name Kindred Spirit   **327.12**
Lee-Browne, Patrick
  The modernist period, 1900-1945
    In Backgrounds to English literature v4   **820.9**
  The Renaissance
    In Backgrounds to English literature v1   **820.9**
Lee considered. Nolan, A. T.   **92**
Lee family
      About
  Lee, H. In the absence of sun   **920**
Leebaert, Derek
  The fifty-year wound   **973.92**
Leeming, David Adams, 1937-
  A dictionary of Asian mythology   **291.103**
  The world of myth   **291.1**
  (ed) Storytelling encyclopedia. See Storytelling encyclopedia   **398.03**
Lees, Carlton B., d. 1989
  (jt. auth) Johnson, L. B. Wildflowers across America
     582.13
Lees, Christoph C.
  Pregnancy and birth   **618.2**
Lees, Gene
  The modern rhyming dictionary   **423**
  You can't steal a gift   **920**
Lee's lieutenants. Freeman, D. S.   **973.7**
Leeuwenhoek, Antoni van, 1632-1723
  See/See also pages in the following book(s):
  Friedman, M. Medicine's 10 greatest discoveries
     610.9
Lefebvre, Georges, 1874-1959
  The French Revolution   **944.04**
Leffell, David J.
  Total skin   **616.5**
Lefkowitz, Mary R., 1935-
  Not out of Africa   **960**
Left (Political science) See Right and left (Political science)
Left- and right-handedness
  Coren, S. The left-hander syndrome   **152.3**
The **left-hander** syndrome. Coren, S.   **152.3**
Left out. Stepan-Norris, J.   **331.8**
Legacies: a Chinese mosaic. Lord, B. B.   **951.05**
The **legal** ideology of removal. Garrison, T. A.
     970.004
Legal reform See Law reform

Legal systems of the world 340.03
A legend in the making. Tofel, R. J. 796.357
Legend of good women. Chaucer, G.
  In Chaucer, G. The complete poetry and prose of
  Geoffrey Chaucer 821
Legends
  See also Folklore; Mythology
  Brunvand, J. H. Encyclopedia of urban legends
  398.2
              Indexes
  Index to fairy tales 398.2
            United States
  Brunvand, J. H. The choking Doberman and other
  "new" urban legends 398.2
  Brunvand, J. H. Too good to be true 398.2
  Brunvand, J. H. The vanishing hitchhiker 398.2
Legends, Hasidic See Hasidic legends
Legends, Jewish See Jewish legends
Legends, lies & cherished myths of world history.
  Shenkman, R. 902
Legends, lies, and cherished myths of American history.
  Shenkman, R. 973.02
Legends of Charlemagne. Bulfinch, T.
  In Bulfinch, T. Bulfinch's mythology 291.1
Legends of the American desert. Shoumatoff, A.
  978
Leggett, John, 1917-
  A daring young man: a biography of William Saroyan
  92
Legislation
  Congress and the Nation 328.73
Lehman, Jeffrey, 1969-
  (ed) Gale encyclopedia of multicultural America. See
  Gale encyclopedia of multicultural America
  305.8
Lehmann, Stephen
  Rudolf Serkin 92
Leibniz, Gottfried Wilhelm, Freiherr von, 1646-1716
  See/See also pages in the following book(s):
  Bell, E. T. Men of mathematics p117-30 920
  Durant, W. J. The age of Louis XIV p658-81
  940.2
  Jaspers, K. The great philosophers 109
  Russell, B. A history of Western philosophy p581-96
  109
Leibovitz, Annie
  Women 779
Leider, Emily Wortis
  Becoming Mae West 92
  Dark lover: the life and death of Rudolph Valentino
  92
Leier, Manfred
  (ed) World atlas of the oceans. See World atlas of the
  oceans 912
Leigh, Mitch, 1928-
  Wasserman, D. Man of La Mancha 812
Leigh, Tera, 1964-
  The complete book of decorative painting 745.7
Leikin, Jerrold B., 1954-
  (ed) American Medical Association complete medical
  encyclopedia. See American Medical Association
  complete medical encyclopedia 610.3
Leimberg, Stephan R.
  (jt. auth) Plotnick, C. How to settle an estate
  346.05
Leininger, Phillip, 1928-
  (ed) HarperCollins Reader's encyclopedia of American
  literature. See HarperCollins Reader's encyclopedia
  of American literature 810.3
Leiter, Richard A.
  (ed) National survey of state laws. See National survey
  of state laws 349
LeMaster, J. R., 1934-
  (ed) The Mark Twain encyclopedia. See The Mark
  Twain encyclopedia 818

LeMay, Curtis E., 1906-1990
  See/See also pages in the following book(s):
  Rhodes, R. Dark sun 623.4
Lemay, J. A. Leo (Joseph A. Leo), 1935-
  (ed) Franklin, B. Writings 818
Lemay, Joseph A. Leo See Lemay, J. A. Leo (Joseph A.
  Leo), 1935-
Lemlin, Jeanne
  Main-course vegetarian pleasures 641.5
Lemonick, Michael D.
  Other worlds 576.8
Lenin, Vladimir Il'ich, 1870-1924
              About
  Pipes, R. Russia under the Bolshevik regime
  947.084
  Service, R. Lenin—a biography 92
  Volkogonov, D. A. Lenin 92
Leningrad (Russia) See Saint Petersburg (Russia)
Lenin's tomb. Remnick, D. 947.085
Leonard, Elizabeth D.
  All the daring of the soldier 973.7
Leonard, Jonathan A.
  (jt. auth) Hobson, J. A. Out of its mind 616.89
Leonard, Robin
  Credit repair 332.7
Leonard Maltin's movie and video guide. Maltin, L.
  791.43
Leonardo, da Vinci, 1452-1519
  Ginevra de' Benci; criticism
    In Virtue & beauty 757
  Last Supper; criticism
    In Steinberg, L. Leonardo's incessant Last Supper
    759.5
  Leonardo da Vinci, master draftsman 741
  Mona Lisa; criticism
    In Sassoon, D. Becoming Mona Lisa 759.5
              About
  Bramly, S. Leonardo 92
  Brown, D. A. Leonardo da Vinci 759.5
  Marani, P. C. Leonardo da Vinci—the complete paint-
  ings 759.5
  Nuland, S. B. Leonardo da Vinci 92
  White, M. Leonardo 92
Leonardo's incessant Last Supper. Steinberg, L.
  759.5
Leonardo's mountain of clams and the Diet of Worms.
  Gould, S. J. 508
Leonowens, Anna Harriette, 1834-1914
              About
  Landon, M. Anna and the King of Siam 92
Leopold, Aldo, 1886-1948
              About
  Lorbiecki, M. Aldo Leopold 92
Leopold, David
  Hirschfeld's Hollywood 741.5
Leopold, Ellen, 1944-
  A darker ribbon 616.99
Leopold, Nathan Freundenthal, 1904 or 5-1971
  See/See also pages in the following book(s):
  Geis, G. Crimes of the century 345
Lepore, Jill, 1966-
  A is for American 306.44
  The name of war 973.2
Lepre, J. P.
  The Egyptian pyramids 932
Lerman, Philip
  (jt. auth) Walsh, J. Public enemies 364.1
Lerner, Alan Jay, 1918-1986
  My fair lady 812
  See/See also pages in the following book(s):
  Green, S. The world of musical comedy 920
Lerner, Barron H.
  The breast cancer wars 616.99
Lerner, Harriet Goldhor
  The dance of deception 155.3

Lerner, Harriet Goldhor—*Continued*
The dance of intimacy   **155.6**
Lerner, Henry M.
Miscarriage: a doctor's guide to the facts   **618.3**
Lerner, Jacqueline V.
(ed) Adolescence in America. See Adolescence in
America   **305.23**
Lerner, Richard M.
(ed) Adolescence in America. See Adolescence in
America   **305.23**
The **LeRoi** Jones/Amiri Baraka reader. Baraka, I. A.
    818

Lesbianism
Encyclopedia of lesbian and gay histories and cultures
    306.7
See/See also pages in the following book(s):
Rich, A. Blood, bread, and poetry p23-75   **814**
Lesbians
Marcus, E. Is it a choice?   **305.9**
St. James Press gay & lesbian almanac   **305.9**
Lesher, Linda Parent, 1947-
The best novels of the nineties   **016.8**
Less developed countries *See* Developing countries
Less than one. Brodsky, J.   **814**
Lesseps, Ferdinand Marie de, vicomte, 1805-1894
See/See also pages in the following book(s):
McCullough, D. G. The path between the seas
    972.87
Lesser, Wendy
Nothing remains the same   **028**
Lessig, Lawrence
The future of ideas   **346.04**
Lessing, Doris May, 1919-
African laughter   **968.91**
Under my skin   **92**
See/See also pages in the following book(s):
Pierpont, C. R. Passionate minds   **810.9**
Lessing, Gotthold Ephraim, 1729-1781
See/See also pages in the following book(s):
Gay, P. The Enlightenment: an interpretation   **190**
Jaspers, K. The great philosophers   **109**
The **lessons** of terror. Carr, C.   **303.6**
Lester, Patrick D.
The biographical directory of Native American painters
    920.003
Lester leaps in: the life and times of Lester "Pres"
Young. Daniels, D. H.   **92**
Let history judge. Medvedev, R. A.   **947.084**
Let us now praise famous men. Agee, J.   **976.1**
Letitia Baldrige's complete guide to the new manners
for the 90's. See Baldrige, L. Letitia Baldrige's new
manners for new times   **395**
Letitia Baldrige's more than manners!. Baldrige, L.
    649
Letitia Baldrige's new complete guide to executive man-
ners. Baldrige, L.   **395**
Letitia Baldrige's new manners for new times. Baldrige,
L.   **395**
Let's talk hair. Ferrell, P.   **646.7**
Letter to a man in the fire. Price, R.   **231**
Letter to the world. Ware, S.   **920**
Letter writing
See also Business letters
Letters
See also American letters; English letters
Letters from Africa, 1914-1931. Dinesen, I.   **92**
Letters of a nation   **816**
Letters of Ayn Rand. Rand, A.   **92**
The **letters** of Kingsley Amis. Amis, K.   **92**
Letters of the century   **816**
Letters to a young novelist. Vargas Llosa, M.
    808.3
Letters to Malcolm: chiefly on prayer. Lewis, C. S.
    248
Lettice & lovage. Shaffer, P.   **822**

Leuchtenburg, William Edward, 1922-
Franklin D. Roosevelt and the New Deal, 1932-1940
    973.917
(jt. auth) Morison, S. E. A concise history of the
American Republic   **973**
(jt. auth) Morison, S. E. The growth of the American
Republic   **973**
Levant, Oscar, 1906-1972
About
Kashner, S. A talent for genius: the life and times of
Oscar Levant   **92**
LeVay, Simon
(jt. auth) Freed, C. Healing the brain   **616.8**
(jt. auth) Koerner, D. Here be dragons   **576.8**
Levenson, J. C. (Jacob Claver), 1922-
(ed) Crane, S. Prose and poetry   **818**
Levenson, Jacob Claver *See* Levenson, J. C. (Jacob
Claver), 1922-
Leventhal, Alice Walker *See* Walker, Alice, 1944-
Lever, Evelyne
Madame de Pompadour   **92**
Marie Antoinette   **92**
Leverich, Lyle
Tom: the unknown Tennessee Williams   **92**
Levertov, Denise, 1923-1997
Collected earlier poems, 1940-1960   **811**
New & selected essays   **814**
Poems, 1960-1967   **811**
Poems, 1968-1972   **811**
This great unknowing   **811**
Levey, Sir Michael, 1927-
Florence   **945**
Levi, Anthony
Cardinal Richelieu and the making of France   **92**
Levi, Peter, 1931-
Atlas of the Greek world   **938**
Levi, Primo, 1919-1987
The drowned and the saved   **940.53**
The periodic table   **92**
The reawakening
In Levi, P. Survival in Auschwitz; and The reawak-
ening   **940.53**
Survival in Auschwitz; and, The reawakening
    940.53
About
Angier, C. The double bond: Primo Levi, a biography
    92
Anissimov, M. Primo Levi   **92**
Lévi-Strauss, Claude
The savage mind   **155.8**
Leviathan. Hobbes, T.   **320.1**
Levin, Gail, 1948-
(jt. auth) Hopper, E. Edward Hopper: the art and the
artist   **759.13**
Levin, Phillis, 1954-
(ed) The Penguin book of the sonnet. See The Penguin
book of the sonnet   **821.008**
Levin, Phyllis Lee
Edith and Woodrow: the Wilson White House   **92**
Levin, Simon A.
(ed) Encyclopedia of biodiversity. See Encyclopedia of
biodiversity   **333.95**
Levin, Susan
(jt. auth) Tracy, G. Crochet your way   **746.43**
Levine, John R.
The Internet for dummies   **004.6**
Levine, Judith
Harmful to minors   **306.7**
Levine, Lawrence W.
The opening of the American mind   **001.1**
Levine, Lois
(jt. auth) Burros, M. F. The new elegant but easy
cookbook   **641.5**
Levine, Marvin J., 1930-
Children for hire   **331.3**

Levine, Melvin D.
A mind at a time 370.15
Levine, Peter
Ellis Island to Ebbet's Field 796
Levine, Philip, 1928-
The mercy 811
New selected poems 811
The simple truth 811
What work is 811
Levine, Suzanne Jill
Manuel Puig and spider woman 92
Levinsohn, Florence Hamlish, 1926-
Looking for Farrakhan 92
Levinson, Daniel J., 1920-1994
The seasons of a man's life 155.6
The seasons of a woman's life 155.6
Levinson, David, 1947-
Encyclopedia of modern Asia 950
(ed) Encyclopedia of crime and punishment. See Encyclopedia of crime and punishment 364.03
(ed) Encyclopedia of human emotions. See Encyclopedia of human emotions 152.4
Levinson, Judy D.
(jt. auth) Levinson, D. J. The seasons of a woman's life 155.6
Levitt, Michael
(jt. auth) Conner, D. Learn to sail 797.1
Levy, Adrian, 1965-
The stone of heaven 553.8
Levy, Alexander
The orphaned adult 155.9
Levy, David H., 1948-
Comets 523.6
See/See also pages in the following book(s):
Malone, J. W. It doesn't take a rocket scientist 920
Levy, Edmond, 1929-1998
Making a winning short 791.43
Levy, Leonard Williams, 1923-
(ed) Encyclopedia of the American Constitution. See Encyclopedia of the American Constitution 342
Levy, Matthys
Why buildings fall down 690
Levy, Naomi
To begin again 296.7
Lewin, Roger
(jt. auth) Leakey, R. E. Origins reconsidered 599.93
(jt. auth) Leakey, R. E. The sixth extinction 304.2
(jt. auth) Swisher, C. C. Java man 599.93
Lewis, Anthony, 1927-
Gideon's trumpet 347
(ed) Written into history. See Written into history 071
Lewis, Bernard
The Middle East 956
What went wrong? 956
(ed) Music of a distant drum. See Music of a distant drum 808.81
Lewis, C. S. (Clive Staples), 1898-1963
Beyond personality
In Lewis, C. S. Mere Christianity 230
Broadcast talks
In Lewis, C. S. Mere Christianity 230
Christian behavior
In Lewis, C. S. Mere Christianity 230
Chronicles of Narnia; criticism
In Ford, P. F. Companion to Narnia 823.009
Letters to Malcolm: chiefly on prayer 248
Mere Christianity 230
Miracles 231.7
Narrative poems 821
The Screwtape letters 248
The world's last night, and other essays 230

About
Downing, D. C. The most reluctant convert: C. S. Lewis's journey to faith 92
Wilson, A. N. C.S. Lewis 92
Lewis, Clive Staples *See* Lewis, C. S. (Clive Staples), 1898-1963
Lewis, David Levering
W.E.B. DuBois 92
(ed) The Portable Harlem Renaissance reader. See The Portable Harlem Renaissance reader 810.8
Lewis, Elma, 1921-
See/See also pages in the following book(s):
Russell, D. Black genius and the American experience 920
Lewis, James R., 1949-
The astrology book 133.5
Cults in America 291.9
The dream encyclopedia 154.6
Satanism today 133.4
UFOs and popular culture 001.9
(ed) The encyclopedia of cults, sects, and new religions. See The encyclopedia of cults, sects, and new religions 200.3
Lewis, John, 1940-
See/See also pages in the following book(s):
Halberstam, D. The children 323.1
Lewis, Loida Nicolas
How to get a green card 342
Lewis, Meriwether, 1774-1809
The essential Lewis and Clark 978
The Lewis and Clark journals. See The Lewis and Clark journals 978
About
Ambrose, S. E. Undaunted courage 978
The Lewis and Clark journals 978
Slaughter, T. P. Exploring Lewis and Clark 978
Lewis, Michael
Liar's poker: rising through the wreckage on Wall Street 332.6
Moneyball 796.357
The new new thing 92
Next: the future just happened 303.4
Lewis, Michael, 1983 or 4-
About
Brown, E. The condemnation of Little B 364.1
Lewis, Oscar, 1914-1970
The children of Sánchez 972.08
Lewis, R. W. B. (Richard Warrington Baldwin), 1917-2002
The city of Florence 945
Dante 92
Lewis, Richard Warrington Baldwin *See* Lewis, R. W. B. (Richard Warrington Baldwin), 1917-2002
Lewis, Roger, 1960-
The real life of Laurence Olivier 92
Lewis, Sinclair, 1885-1951
About
Lingeman, R. R. Sinclair Lewis 92
Sinclair Lewis 813.009
Lewis, Thomas
A general theory of love 152.4
Lewis & Clark. Ambrose, S. E. 978
Lewis & Clark. Duncan, D. 978
The **Lewis & Clark Trail.** Schmidt, T. 978
Lewis and Clark Expedition (1804-1806)
Ambrose, S. E. Lewis & Clark 978
Ambrose, S. E. Undaunted courage 978
Clark, E. E. Sacagawea of the Lewis and Clark expedition 92
Duncan, D. Lewis & Clark 978
Lewis, M. The essential Lewis and Clark 978
The Lewis and Clark journals 978
Schmidt, T. The Lewis & Clark Trail 978
Slaughter, T. P. Exploring Lewis and Clark 978
The **Lewis** and Clark journals 978

Lewontin, Richard C., 1929-
The triple helix   **572.8**
Lewy, Guenter, 1923-
The Nazi persecution of the gypsies   **940.53**
The **lexicon** of labor. Murray, R. E.   **331**
Lexington (Mass.), Battle of, 1775
Fischer, D. H. Paul Revere's ride   **973.3**
The **Lexus** and the olive tree. Friedman, T. L.   **337**
Liability (Law)
Matthews, J. L. How to win your personal injury claim
    346.03
Liar's poker: rising through the wreckage on Wall
Street. Lewis, M.   **332.6**
The **liar's** tale. Campbell, J.   **177**
The **libation** bearers. Aeschylus
In Aeschylus. The Oresteia   **882**
Libel and slander
See also Gossip
The Associated Press stylebook and briefing on media
law   **808**
Liberalism
Bork, R. H. Slouching towards Gomorrah   **306**
Liberty *See* Freedom
Liberty Hyde Bailey Hortorium *See* Cornell University.
Bailey Hortorium
Liberty of speech *See* Freedom of speech
Libov, Charlotte
(jt. auth) Pashkow, F. J. The women's heart book
    616.1
Librarians
      Recruiting
Low, K. Recruiting library staff   **023**
The **librarian's** genealogy notebook. Moore, D. E.
    929
Libraries
See also Academic libraries; Public libraries
Barclay, D. A. Managing public-access computers
    025
Basbanes, N. A. Patience & fortitude   **002**
The Bowker annual library and book trade almanac
    020.5
      Censorship
Foerstel, H. N. Banned in the U.S.A   **025.2**
Intellectual freedom manual   **323.44**
Jones, B. M. Libraries, access, and intellectual freedom
    025.2
Symons, A. K. Protecting the right to read   **025.2**
      Collection development
Slote, S. J. Weeding library collections   **025.2**
      Directories
American library directory   **027**
      Periodicals
Library Journal   **020.5**
      Public relations
Wolfe, L. A. Library public relations, promotions, and
communications   **021.7**
      Special collections
Baker, N. Double fold   **025.2**
Libraries, Children's *See* Children's libraries
Libraries, School *See* School libraries
Libraries, Special *See* Special libraries
Libraries, Young adults' *See* Young adults' libraries
Libraries, access, and intellectual freedom. Jones, B. M.
    025.2
Libraries and Hispanic Americans
Moller, S. C. Library service to Spanish speaking pa-
trons   **027.6**
Libraries and students
Steele, A. T. Bare bones children's services
    027.62
Vaillancourt, R. J. Bare bones young adult services
    027.62
Library Association
See also Joint Steering Committee for Revision of
AACR

Library classification
Intner, S. S. Standard cataloging for school and public
libraries   **025.3**
Library Journal   **020.5**
Library literature. See Library literature & information
science index   **020**
Library literature & information science index   **020**
Library materials *See* Library resources
Library of Congress
See also Joint Steering Committee for Revision of
AACR;
Coles, R. When they were young   **779**
Conaway, J. America's library   **027.5**
Neagles, J. C. The Library of Congress   **929**
Virga, V. Eyes of the nation   **973**
**Library of Congress. Cataloging Policy and Support
Office**
Library of Congress subject headings   **025.4**
**Library of Congress. Office for Descriptive Catalog-
ing Policy**
See also Library of Congress. Cataloging Policy and
Support Office
**Library of Congress. Office for Subject Cataloging
Policy**
See also Library of Congress. Cataloging Policy and
Support Office
The **Library** of Congress Civil War desk reference
    973.7
Library of Congress subject headings. Library of Con-
gress. Cataloging Policy and Support Office
    025.4
Library public relations, promotions, and communica-
tions. Wolfe, L. A.   **021.7**
Library reference services *See* Reference services (Li-
braries)
Library resources
      Conservation and restoration
Baker, N. Double fold   **025.2**
Library science
      Bibliography
Library literature & information science index
    020
      Periodicals
Library Journal   **020.5**
      Periodicals—Indexes
Library literature & information science index
    020
Library service to Spanish speaking patrons. Moller, S.
C.   **027.6**
Library services to children *See* Children's libraries
Library services to Hispanic Americans *See* Libraries
and Hispanic Americans
Library services to young adults *See* Young adults' li-
braries
Librettists
Green, S. The world of musical comedy   **920**
Libya
      Politics and government
See/See also pages in the following book(s):
Maas, P. Manhunt   **364.1**
Lichtenstein, Nelson
State of the Union: a century of American labor
    331
Liddell, Alice *See* Hargreaves, Alice Pleasance Liddell,
1852-1934
Liddell, Henry George, 1811-1898
A Greek-English lexicon   **483**
Liddell Hart, Sir Basil Henry, 1895-1970
The real war, 1914-1918   **940.4**
Lidia's Italian-American kitchen. Bastianich, L.
    641.5
Lidia's Italian table. Bastianich, L.   **641.5**
Lieberman, A. (Abraham), 1938-
100 questions & answers about Parkinson [sic] disease
    616.8

Lieberman, A. (Abraham), 1938——_Continued_
Shaking-up Parkinson disease   **616.8**
Lieberman, Abraham _See_ Lieberman, A. (Abraham), 1938-
Lieberman, Trudy
Consumer reports complete guide to health services for seniors. See Consumer reports complete guide to health services for seniors   **362.6**
Liedtke, Walter A.
Vermeer and the Delft school   **759.9492**
Lies across America. Loewen, J. W.   **973**
Lieven, Anatol
Chechnya   **947.086**
Life
    See also Death
Benecke, M. The dream of eternal life   **612.6**
Deutsch, D. The fabric of reality   **530**
    See/See also pages in the following book(s):
Marcus Aurelius, Emperor of Rome. Meditations   **188**

Origin
Adams, F. C. Origins of existence   **576.8**
Davies, P. C. W. The fifth miracle   **576.8**
Duve, C. de. Life evolving   **576.8**
Duve, C. de. Vital dust   **570.1**
Fortey, R. A. Life   **576.8**
Koerner, D. Here be dragons   **576.8**
Macdougall, J. D. A short history of planet earth   **551.7**
Margulis, L. What is life?   **570.1**
Sagan, C. Shadows of forgotten ancestors   **570.1**
Schopf, J. W. Cradle of life   **576.8**

Life (Biology)
    See also Gaia hypothesis
Capra, F. The web of life   **570.1**
Duve, C. de. Life evolving   **576.8**
Duve, C. de. Vital dust   **570.1**
Gribbin, J. R. Stardust   **523**
Harold, F. M. The way of the cell   **571.6**
Hoagland, M. B. The way life works   **570**
Keller, E. F. Making sense of life   **570.1**
Lovelock, J. The ages of Gaia   **570.1**
Margulis, L. What is life?   **570.1**
Life & death. Creeley, R.   **811**
Life and death in Shanghai. Cheng, N.   **92**
The **life** and legacy of Annie Oakley. Riley, G.   **92**
The **life** and legend of Leadbelly. Wolfe, C. K.   **92**
The **life** and many deaths of Harry Houdini. Brandon, R.   **92**
The **life** and selected writings of Thomas Jefferson. Jefferson, T.   **818**
Life and times of Frederick Douglass. Douglass, F.
    _In_ Douglass, F. Autobiographies   **92**
The **life** and times of Pancho Villa. Katz, F.   **92**
Life: century of change   **779**
Life evolving. Duve, C. de   **576.8**
Life expectancy _See_ Longevity
Life in a medieval city. Gies, J.   **940.1**
Life in a medieval village. Gies, F.   **940.1**
A **life** in letters. Fitzgerald, F. S.   **92**
A **life** in the twentieth century. Schlesinger, A. M.   **92**

Life insurance
Life insurance fact book   **368.3**
Life insurance fact book   **368.3**
Life itself. Rensberger, B.   **571.6**
Life lessons. Kübler-Ross, E.   **170**
The **life** of Billy Yank. Wiley, B. I.   **973.7**
The **life** of birds. Attenborough, D.   **598**
The **life** of Charlotte Brontë. Gaskell, E. C.   **92**
The **life** of Cnaeus Julius Agricola. Tacitus, C.
    _In_ Tacitus, C. The complete works of Tacitus p677-706   **878**

The **life** of Edmund Spenser. Judson, A. C.
    _In_ Spenser, E. The works of Edmund Spenser v11   **828**
The **life** of Elizabeth I. Weir, A.   **92**
The **life** of Isaac Newton. Westfall, R. S.   **92**
A **life** of James Boswell. Martin, P.   **92**
The **life** of Johnny Reb. Wiley, B. I.   **973.7**
The **life** of Johnson. See Boswell, J. The life of Samuel Johnson   **92**
A **life** of Jung. Hayman, R.   **92**
The **life** of Langston Hughes. Rampersad, A.   **92**
The **life** of Mendelssohn. Mercer-Taylor, P. J.   **92**
The **life** of Samuel Johnson. Boswell, J.   **92**
The **life** of the drama. Bentley, E.   **809.2**
The **life** of the mind. Arendt, H.   **153**
The **life** of W.B. Yeats. Brown, T.   **92**
Life on earth   **333.95**
Life on other planets
Chown, M. The universe next door   **523.1**
Jakosky, B. M. The search for life on other planets   **576.8**
Koerner, D. Here be dragons   **576.8**
Lemonick, M. D. Other worlds   **576.8**
Rubin, A. E. Disturbing the solar system   **521**
Ward, P. D. Rare earth   **576.8**
Life out of bounds. Bright, C.   **577**
Life sciences
    Dictionaries
McGraw-Hill dictionary of bioscience   **570.3**
Life script. Wade, N.   **616**
A **life** shaken. Havemann, J.   **362.1**
Life skills
Fisher, A. B. If my career's on the fast track, where do I get a road map?   **650.14**
Life so far. Friedan, B.   **92**
Life stories   **920**
Life strategies. McGraw, P. C.   **158**
Life unworthy of life. Glass, J. M.   **940.53**
Life with father. Day, C.   **818**
Life: World War 2   **940.53**
Lifelines. Booth, P.   **811**
Life's matrix. Ball, P.   **553.7**
A **life's** work. Cusk, R.   **306.8**
Lifesaving
    See also First aid
Lift up thy voice. Perry, M.   **920**
Lifton, Robert Jay, 1926-
Destroying the world to save it   **299**
Hiroshima in America   **940.54**
The Nazi doctors   **940.53**
Light, Alan
(ed) The Vibe history of hip hop. See The Vibe history of hip hop   **782.42**
Light, Jonathan Fraser, 1957-
The cultural encyclopedia of baseball   **796.357**
Light, Michael
100 suns, 1945-1962   **623.4**
Light
Feynman, R. P. QED   **539.7**
Magueijo, J. Faster than the speed of light   **535**
Park, D. The fire within the eye   **535**
Perkowitz, S. Empire of light   **535**
Zajonc, A. Catching the light   **535**
    See/See also pages in the following book(s):
Gribbin, J. R. Schrödinger's kittens and the search for reality   **530.1**
Lighter, J. E. (Jonathan E.)
(ed) Random House historical dictionary of American slang. See Random House historical dictionary of American slang   **427**
Lighter, Jonathan E. _See_ Lighter, J. E. (Jonathan E.)
The **lighthouse** Stevensons. Bathurst, B.   **623.89**
Lighthouses
Bathurst, B. The lighthouse Stevensons   **623.89**

Lightman, Alan P., 1948-
Ancient light   523.1
Lightman, Marjorie
(jt. auth) Yans-McLaughlin, V. Ellis Island and the peopling of America   325.73
Lightner, Sam, 1985-
About
Hallman, T. Sam: the boy behind the mask   362.1
Lightning
Ehrlich, G. A match to the heart   92
Lightning man: the accursed life of Samuel F.B. Morse. Silverman, K.   92
Lights, Feast of See Hanukkah
Like men of war. Trudeau, N. A.   973.7
Limbo: blue-collar roots, white-collar dreams. Lubrano, A.   305.5
The **limits** of privacy. Etzioni, A.   323.44
Lin, Maya Ying
Boundaries   92
Lincoff, Gary
The Audubon Society field guide to North American mushrooms   579.6
Lincoln, Abraham, 1809-1865
Speeches and writings   973.7
About
Donald, D. H. Lincoln   92
McPherson, J. M. Abraham Lincoln and the second American Revolution   973.7
Miller, W. L. Lincoln's virtues   92
Morris, J. Lincoln, a foreigner's quest   92
Neely, M. E., Jr. The last best hope of earth: Abraham Lincoln and the promise of America   92
Paludan, P. S. The presidency of Abraham Lincoln   973.7
Sandburg, C. Abraham Lincoln: The prairie years and The war years   92
Walsh, J. E. Moonlight   345
White, R. C. Lincoln's greatest speech   973.7
Wills, G. Lincoln at Gettysburg   973.7
See/See also pages in the following book(s):
Cohen, E. A. Supreme command   355
Hofstadter, R. The American political tradition, and the men who made it p92-134   973
McPherson, J. M. Drawn with the sword   973.7
Vidal, G. United States—essays, 1952-1992 p664-707   814
Wilson, E. Patriotic gore p99-130   810.9
Lincoln, C. Eric (Charles Eric), 1924-2000
The black church in the African American experience   277.3
Lincoln, Charles Eric See Lincoln, C. Eric (Charles Eric), 1924-2000
Lincoln, Mary Todd, 1818-1882
About
Baker, J. H. Mary Todd Lincoln   92
Lincoln, Roger J.
The Cambridge illustrated dictionary of natural history   508
Lincoln, a foreigner's quest. Morris, J.   92
Lincoln at Gettysburg. Wills, G.   973.7
Lincoln-Douglas debates, 1858
See/See also pages in the following book(s):
Lincoln, A. Speeches and writings   973.7
Lincoln's greatest speech. White, R. C.   973.7
Lincoln's virtues. Miller, W. L.   92
Lind, Carla
The Wright style   728
Lind, Michael, 1962-
Vietnam, the necessary war   959.704
(jt. auth) Halstead, T. The radical center   320.5
Linda Goodman's star signs. Goodman, L.   133
Linda Goodman's sun signs. Goodman, L.   133.5

Lindberg, Christine A., 1954-
(ed) The Oxford American thesaurus of current English. See The Oxford American thesaurus of current English   423
Lindbergh, Anne Morrow, 1906-2001
About
Hertog, S. Anne Morrow Lindbergh   92
Lindbergh, R. No more words: a journal of my mother, Anne Morrow Lindbergh   92
Lindbergh, R. Under a wing   92
Lindbergh, Charles, Jr.
See/See also pages in the following book(s):
Geis, G. Crimes of the century   345
Lindbergh, Charles, 1902-1974
The spirit of St. Louis   629.13
About
Berg, A. S. Lindbergh   92
Lindbergh, R. Under a wing   92
Lindbergh, Reeve
No more words: a journal of my mother, Anne Morrow Lindbergh   92
Under a wing   92
Lindbergh Baby See Lindbergh, Charles, Jr.
Linden, Dana Wechsler
Preemies   618.92
Linden, Eugene
The octopus and the orangutan   591.5
Lindenthal, Gustav, 1850-1935
See/See also pages in the following book(s):
Petroski, H. Engineers of dreams   624
Linderman, Gerald F.
The world within war   940.54
Lindley, David
The end of physics   539.7
Lindow, John
Handbook of Norse mythology   293
Lindsay, Ann K., 1948-
Watercolor   751.42
Lindsay, David, 1957-
House of invention   609
Lindsey, Karen, 1944-
(jt. auth) Love, S. M. Dr Susan Love's breast book   618.1
(jt. auth) Love, S. M. Dr. Susan Love's menopause and hormone book   618.1
Lindwer, Willy
The last seven months of Anne Frank   940.53
A **line** out for a walk. Epstein, J.   814
Linenthal, Edward Tabor, 1947-
Preserving memory   940.53
Lingeman, Richard R.
Sinclair Lewis   92
Linguistics
Devlin, K. J. Goodbye, Descartes   128
Science times book of language and linguistics   400
Encyclopedias
International encyclopedia of linguistics   410
Link, John
The breast cancer survival manual   616.99
Take charge of your breast cancer   616.99
Linklater, Andro
Measuring America   973
Linklater, Kristin, 1936-
Freeing the natural voice   808.5
Linn, Edward, 1922-2000
Hitter: the life and turmoils of Ted Williams   92
Linnaeus, Carl See Linné, Carl von, 1707-1778
Linnaeus, the compleat naturalist. Blunt, W.   92
Linné, Carl von, 1707-1778
About
Blunt, W. Linnaeus, the compleat naturalist   92
Linus Pauling in his own words. Pauling, L. C.   92
Liolà. Pirandello, L.
In Pirandello, L. Naked masks p1-60   852

The **Lion** prayer collection. See The Doubleday prayer collection **242**

Lions

Adamson, J. Born free **599.75**

Caputo, P. Ghosts of Tsavo **599.75**

Thomas, E. M. The tribe of tiger **599.75**

The **lion's** grave. Anderson, J. L. **958.1**

Lipkowitz, Myron

Encyclopedia of allergies **616.97**

Lipman, Lisa R.

(jt. auth) Outten, W. N. The rights of employees and union members **344**

Lippard, Lucy R.

Overlay **709**

Lippman, Thomas W.

Understanding Islam **297**

Lipsky, Martin S., 1950-

(ed) American Medical Association complete medical encyclopedia. See American Medical Association complete medical encyclopedia **610.3**

Lipson, Eden Ross

The New York Times parent's guide to the best books for children **011.6**

Lipstadt, Deborah E.

Denying the Holocaust **940.53**

About

Evans, R. J. Lying about Hitler **940.53**

Guttenplan, D. D. The Holocaust on trial **940.53**

Lipton, Judith Eve

(jt. auth) Barash, D. P. The myth of monogamy **306.7**

Lispector, Clarice, 1925-1977

Selected cronicas **869**

Listen to the stories. Hentoff, N. **781.65**

Listening to Prozac. Kramer, P. D. **616.85**

Listening to whales. Morton, A. **599.5**

Liszt, Ferenc See Liszt, Franz, 1811-1886

Liszt, Franz, 1811-1886

See/See also pages in the following book(s):

Schonberg, H. C. The great pianists **920**

Litchfield, Michael W.

Renovation **643**

Literary criticism See Criticism

Literary criticism. James, H. **809**

Literary forgeries

Boller, P. F. They never said it **808.88**

Literary landmarks

Cyclopedia of literary places **809**

United States

Anderson, W. T. Laura Ingalls Wilder country **92**

Literary market place: LMP **070.5025**

Literary movements for students **809**

Literary prizes

See also Caldecott Medal; Coretta Scott King Award; Newbery Medal

Literature

See also African Americans in literature; Animals in literature; Blacks in literature; Characters and characteristics in literature; Children's literature; Classical literature; Homosexuality in literature; Jews in literature; Law in literature; Music and literature; Mythology in literature; Native American literature; New York (N.Y.) in literature; Politics in literature; Sagas; Spies in literature; Trials in literature; War in literature; Women in literature; Young adult literature; names of national literatures, e.g. *English literature*

Bio-bibliography

Contemporary authors **920.003**

Contemporary world writers **920.003**

Encyclopedia of world literature in the 20th century **803**

European authors, 1000-1900 **920.003**

The Reader's adviser **011**

Reference guide to world literature **809**

The Schomburg Center guide to black literature from the eighteenth century to the present **809**

World authors, 1950-1970 **920.003**

World authors, 1970-1975 **920.003**

World authors, 1975-1980 **920.003**

World authors, 1980-1985 **920.003**

World authors, 1985-1990 **920.003**

World authors, 1990-1995 **920.003**

World authors, 1995-2000 **920.003**

Biography

World authors, 1900-1950 **920.003**

Chronology

Kurian, G. T. Timetables of world literature **809**

Collections

The Norton book of modern war **808.8**

Nothing makes you free **808.8**

The Portable Renaissance reader **808.8**

Dictionaries

Abrams, M. H. A glossary of literary terms **803**

Baldick, C. The concise Oxford dictionary of literary terms **803**

Benet's reader's encyclopedia **803**

Brewer's dictionary of modern phrase & fable **803**

Brewer's dictionary of phrase and fable **803**

Carey, G. A multicultural dictionary of literary terms **803**

Columbia dictionary of modern European literature **803**

Cuddon, J. A. A dictionary of literary terms and literary theory **803**

Cyclopedia of literary characters **803**

Harmon, W. A handbook to literature **803**

Merriam-Webster's encyclopedia of literature **803**

The Oxford dictionary of phrase and fable **803**

Quinn, E. A dictionary of literary and thematic terms **803**

Encyclopedias

Cyclopedia of literary places **809**

Encyclopedia of the novel **809.3**

Encyclopedia of world literature in the 20th century **803**

Film and video adaptations

See Film adaptations

History and criticism

See also Authors

Black literature criticism **809**

Bloom, H. Genius **153.9**

Bloom, H. How to read and why **028**

Bloom, H. The Western canon **809**

Calvino, I. Why read the classics? **809**

Contemporary literary criticism **809**

James, H. Literary criticism **809**

Jarrell, R. No other book **809**

Kermode, F. An appetite for poetry **801**

Literary movements for students **809**

Literature and its times **809**

Masterpieces of world literature **809**

The Oxford guide to literature in English translation **820.9**

Ozick, C. Quarrel & quandary **814**

Reference guide to world literature **809**

Roth, P. Shop talk **809**

Said, E. W. Reflections on exile and other essays **814**

Twentieth-century literary criticism **809**

Twentieth-century literary movements dictionary **809**

Women writers at work **808**

Indexes

Essay and general literature index **080**

Philosophy

Gardner, J. On moral fiction **801**

Study and teaching

Coles, R. The call of stories **808**

Literature, Medieval *See* Medieval literature
Literature and communism *See* Communism and literature
Literature and its times   809
Literature and music *See* Music and literature
The **Literature** of Renaissance England
   In The Oxford anthology of English literature v1
       820.8
Litigation
   Bergman, P. Represent yourself in court   347
Litin, Scott C.
   (ed) Mayo Clinic family health book. See Mayo Clinic
   family health book   613
Little, Allan
   (jt. auth) Silber, L. Yugoslavia   949.7
Little, Elbert Luther, 1907-
   The Audubon Society field guide to North American
   trees   582.16
Little, Malcolm *See* Malcolm X, 1925-1965
Little B *See* Lewis, Michael, 1983 or 4-
Little Bighorn, Battle of the, 1876
   Connell, E. S. Son of the Morning Star   973.8
   Sandoz, M. The Battle of the Little Bighorn
       973.8
   Welch, J. Killing Custer   973.8
   See/See also pages in the following book(s):
   Brown, D. A. The American West p220-28   978
The **little** book of Judas. Kennelly, B.   821
Little Crow, Sioux Chief, d. 1863
   See/See also pages in the following book(s):
   Brown, D. A. Bury my heart at Wounded Knee
       970.004
Little Eyolf. Ibsen, H.
   In Ibsen, H. The complete major prose plays p861-
   936   839.8
   In Ibsen, H. Ibsen: four plays, v3   839.8
The **little** flowers of St. Francis. Francis, of Assisi, Saint
       242
Little girls in pretty boxes. Ryan, J.   796.44
Little Ham. Hughes, L.
   In Hughes, L. Five plays p43-112   812
Little League Baseball, Inc.
   Geist, B. Little League confidential   796.357
Little League confidential. Geist, B.   796.357
Little me. Simon, N.
   In Simon, N. The collected plays of Neil Simon v2
   p13-145   812
A **little** too close to God. Horovitz, D. P.   956.94
Liturgies
   See also Catholic Church—Liturgy
Liungman, Carl G., 1938-
   Dictionary of symbols   302.2
Lively, Donald E., 1947-
   Landmark Supreme Court cases   342
Lively, Penelope, 1933-
   A house unlocked   92
Liver
   Diseases
   Achord, J. L. Understanding hepatitis   616.3
   Palmer, M. Dr. Melissa Palmer's guide to hepatitis &
   liver disease   616.3
The **lives** of a cell. Thomas, L.   570.1
The **lives** of animals. Coetzee, J. M.   179
The **lives** of Beryl Markham. Trzebinski, E.   92
The **lives** of Michel Foucault. Macey, D.   92
Lives of moral leadership. Coles, R.   170
The **lives** of the great composers. Schonberg, H. C.
       920
Lives of the modern poets. Pritchard, W. H.
       821.009
The **lives** of the muses. Prose, F.   920
The **lives** of the noble Grecians and Romans. See Plutarch. Plutarch: the lives of the noble Grecians and Romans   920
Lives of the poets. Schmidt, M.   821.009

Lives of the popes. McBrien, R. P.   920
Lives of the saints. McBrien, R. P.   920.003
Lives of the saints, Butler's. Butler, A.   920.003
Livestock *See* Livestock industry
Livestock industry
   Lovenheim, P. Portrait of a burger as a young calf
       636.2
Livet, Jacques
   (jt. auth) Germond, P. An Egyptian bestiary
       709.32
Living a Jewish life. Diamant, A.   296.7
The **living** and the dead. Hendrickson, P.   959.704
Living Buddha, living Christ. Nhat Hanh, Thich
       294.3
Living by the word. Walker, A.   818
Living earth theory *See* Gaia hypothesis
Living faith. Carter, J.   92
Living fossil. Thomson, K. S.   597
The **living** heart. See DeBakey, M. E. The new living heart   616.1
The **living** heart diet. See The New living heart diet
       616.1
Living history. Clinton, H. R.   92
Living in Spanglish. Morales, E.   305.8
Living on the wind. Weidensaul, S.   598
Living proof. Gearin-Tosh, M.   92
Living to tell the tale. García Márquez, G.   92
Living well with asthma. Freedman, M. R.   616.2
Living with cannibals and other women's adventures. Slung, M. B.   910.4
Living with death and dying. Kübler-Ross, E.   155.9
Living with our genes. Hamer, D. H.   155.2
Living with spina bifida. Sandler, A.   618.92
Livingston, James D., 1930-
   Driving force   538
Livingston, Jane, 1944-
   The paintings of Joan Mitchell   759.13
Livingstone, David, 1813-1873
      About
   Dugard, M. Into Africa   92
Livingstone, Margaret S.
   Vision and art   750.1
Livio, Mario, 1945-
   The golden ratio   516.2
LJ/Library Journal. See Library Journal   020.5
Llosa, Mario Vargas *See* Vargas Llosa, Mario, 1936-
Lloyd, Christopher, 1921-
   Color for adventurous gardeners   635.9
Lloyd, John, 1956-
   Furniture restoration   749
Lloyd Webber, Andrew, 1948-
      About
   Citron, S. Sondheim and Lloyd-Webber   92
LMP. See Literary market place: LMP   070.5025
Lo, Eileen Yin-fei
   The Chinese kitchen   641.5
Loan funds, Student *See* Student loan funds
Loans
   See also Mortgages
Lobachevskiĭ, N. I. (Nikolaĭ Ivanovich), 1792-1856
   See/See also pages in the following book(s):
   Bell, E. T. Men of mathematics p294-306   920
Lobachevskiĭ, Nikolaĭ Ivanovich *See* Lobachevskiĭ, N. I. (Nikolaĭ Ivanovich), 1792-1856
LoBrutto, Vincent
   Stanley Kubrick   92
The **lobster** chronicles. Greenlaw, L.   639
Lobster fisheries
   Greenlaw, L. The lobster chronicles   639
Local flavors. Madison, D.   641.5
Local government
   See also County government; Municipal government
Local visitations. Dunn, S.   811

Lock, Stephen
(ed) The Oxford illustrated companion to medicine. See The Oxford illustrated companion to medicine
610.3

Locke, John, 1632-1704
An essay concerning human understanding 121
Two treatises of government 320.1
See/See also pages in the following book(s):
Durant, W. J. The age of Louis XIV p575-90
940.2
Russell, B. A history of Western philosophy p604-47
109

Locke, John L.
The de-voicing of society 302.3
Locked in the cabinet. Reich, R. B. 973.929
Lockwood, Lewis
Beethoven: the music and the life 92
Loder, Kurt
(jt. auth) Turner, T. I, Tina 92
Lodge, Henry Cabot, 1850-1924
See/See also pages in the following book(s):
Zimmermann, W. First great triumph 973
Łódź (Poland)
Social conditions
The Chronicle of the Łódź ghetto, 1941-1944
943.8

Loeb, Richard A., 1905 or 6-1936
See/See also pages in the following book(s):
Geis, G. Crimes of the century 345
Loebl, Suzanne
America's art museums 708
Loewe, Frederick, 1904-1988
See/See also pages in the following book(s):
Green, S. The world of musical comedy 920
Loewen, James W.
Lies across America 973
Loewenstein, Werner R.
The touchstone of life 571.6
Log cabins and houses
Burch, M. Complete guide to building log homes
694
Logan, M. David
Mat, mount and frame it yourself 749
LoGerfo, Paul, 1939-2003
(jt. auth) Ditkoff, B. A. The thyroid guide 616.4
Logging See Lumber and lumbering
Logic
See also Reasoning
Copi, I. M. Introduction to logic 160
Devlin, K. J. Goodbye, Descartes 128
Lomax, Alan, 1915-2002
The land where the blues began 781.643
Lombardi, Vince
About
Maraniss, D. When pride still mattered: a life of Vince
Lombardi 92
Lomelí, Francisco A.
(ed) Chicano literature. See Chicano literature
810.9

London (England)
History
Ackroyd, P. London: the biography 942.1
Porter, R. London, a social history 942.1
Social conditions
Porter, R. London, a social history 942.1
London, a social history. Porter, R. 942.1
Lone star rising: Lyndon Johnson and his times, 1908-1960. Dallek, R. 92
Lonely Planet guides 910.2
Long, Cheryl
Rodale organic gardening solutions 635
Long, Crawford W., 1815-1878
See/See also pages in the following book(s):
Friedman, M. Medicine's 10 greatest discoveries
610.9

Long, Huey Pierce, 1893-1935
About
Hair, W. I. The Kingfish and his realm: the life and times of Huey P. Long 92
Long, James W.
The essential guide to prescription drugs 615
The **long** bitter trail. Wallace, A. F. C. 970.004
Long day's journey into night. O'Neill, E. 812
Long distance running See Marathon running
Long life See Longevity
The **long** marriage. Kumin, M. 811
The **long** recessional: the imperial life of Rudyard Kipling. Gilmour, D. 92
A **long** strange trip. McNally, D. 920
Long walk to freedom: the autobiography of Nelson Mandela. Mandela, N. 92
A **long** way from home. Brokaw, T. 92
Longe, Jacqueline L.
(ed) Gale encyclopedia of medicine. See Gale encyclopedia of medicine 610.3
The **longest** night. Eicher, D. J. 973.7
The **longest** war. Hiro, D. 955
Longevity
See also Aging; Old age
Benecke, M. The dream of eternal life 612.6
Chopra, D. Ageless body, timeless mind 612.6
Rowe, J. W. Successful aging 612.6
Schneider, E. L. Ageless: take control of your age and stay youthful for life 612.6
Longfellow, Henry Wadsworth, 1807-1882
Poems and other writings 811
Longitude
Sobel, D. Longitude 526
Longitudes and attitudes. Friedman, T. L. 973.931
Longman, Jere
Among the heroes 974.8
Longman dictionary and handbook of poetry. See Myers, J. E. Dictionary of poetic terms 808.1
Longshore, David
Encyclopedia of hurricanes, typhoons and cyclones
551.55
Longworth, Alice Roosevelt, 1884-1980
About
Donn, L. The Roosevelt cousins 920
See/See also pages in the following book(s):
Caroli, B. B. The Roosevelt women 920
Lonier, Terri
Working solo 658
Lonsdale, Roger H.
(ed) The New Oxford book of eighteenth century verse. See The New Oxford book of eighteenth century verse 821.008
Look back in anger. Osborne, J. 822
The **look** of architecture. Rybczynski, W. 721
A **look** over my shoulder. Helms, R. 92
Looking after your body 613
Looking at the sun. Fallows, J. M. 950
Looking for a ship. McPhee, J. A. 910.4
Looking for Alaska. Jenkins, P. 979.8
Looking for Farrakhan. Levinsohn, F. H. 92
Looking for history. Guillermoprieto, A. 972
Looking for Mary, or, The Blessed Mother and me. Donofrio, B. 282
Looking for Spinoza. Damasio, A. R. 152.4
Loomis, Alfred Lee, 1887-1975
About
Conant, J. Tuxedo Park 92
Loonin, Deanne, 1963-
(jt. auth) Leonard, R. Credit repair 332.7
Loosestrife. Dunn, S. 811
Lopate, Phillip, 1943-
Portrait of my body 814
(ed) The Art of the personal essay. See The Art of the personal essay 808.84

Lopate, Phillip, 1943——*Continued*
(ed) Writing New York. See Writing New York
810.8

Lopez, Barry Holstun, 1945-
Arctic dreams 998
Of wolves and men 599.77

Lorant, Laurie Robertson- *See* Robertson-Lorant, Laurie, 1940-

Lorbiecki, Marybeth
Aldo Leopold 92

Lorca, Federico García *See* García Lorca, Federico, 1898-1936

Lord, Bette Bao
Legacies: a Chinese mosaic 951.05

Lord, Tony
The encyclopedia of planting combinations 635.9

Lord, Walter, 1917-2002
A night to remember 910.4

Lord Minimus [biography of Jeffrey Hudson] Page, N.
92

Lorde, Audre
The collected poems of Audre Lorde 811
See/See also pages in the following book(s):
Black women writers (1950-1980) 810.9

Lord's Day *See* Sabbath

Lords of the harvest. Charles, D. 664

Lords of the horizons. Goodwin, J. 956.1

Loret, John
(ed) Experiment central. See Experiment central
507.8

Loring, John, 1939-
Louis Comfort Tiffany at Tiffany & Co 92
Tiffany's 20th century 745

Lornell, Kip, 1953-
(jt. auth) Wolfe, C. K. The life and legend of Leadbelly 92

Los Alamos National Laboratory
Stober, D. A convenient spy 327.12
See/See also pages in the following book(s):
Johnson, G. Fire in the mind 215
Security measures
Trulock, N. Code name Kindred Spirit 327.12

Los Alamos Scientific Laboratory
See also Los Alamos National Laboratory

Los Angeles (Calif.)
Race relations
Cannon, L. Official negligence 979.4

Los Angeles (Calif.). Police Dept.
Cannon, L. Official negligence 979.4

Losing the race. McWhorter, J. H. 305.8

Loss (Psychology)
Attig, T. The heart of grief 155.9
Attig, T. How we grieve 155.9
Edelman, H. Motherless daughters 155.9
Finkbeiner, A. K. After the death of a child
155.9
Levy, A. The orphaned adult 155.9
Weenolsen, P. The art of dying 155.9

The loss of a pet. Sife, W. 155.9

The lost art of healing. Lown, B. 610

The lost children of Wilder. Bernstein, N. 362.7

Lost city of the Incas. Bingham, H. 985

Lost crusader: the secret wars of CIA director William Colby. Prados, J. 92

The lost dinosaurs of Egypt. Nothdurft, W. E.
567.9

Lost discoveries. Teresi, D. 509

The lost fleet. Clifford, B. 910.4

Lost in America. Nuland, S. B. 92

Lost in place. Salzman, M. 92

Lost in the cosmos. Percy, W. 818

The lost masters. Harclerode, P. 709

The lost memoirs of Edgar Cayce. See Cayce, E. My life as a seer 92

Lost prophet: the life and times of Bayard Rustin. D'Emilio, J. 92

Lost puritan: a life of Robert Lowell. Mariani, P. L.
92

Lost woods. Carson, R. 570

The lost world. Jarrell, R.
In Jarrell, R. The complete poems 811

Lott, Dale F.
American bison 599.64

Lottman, Herbert R.
Man Ray's Montparnasse 92

Loudon, Irvine
(ed) Western medicine: an illustrated history. See Western medicine: an illustrated history 610.9

Louis XIV, King of France, 1638-1715
About
Zega, A. Palaces of the Sun King 728

Louis, Father *See* Merton, Thomas, 1915-1968

Louis, Wm. Roger
(ed) The Oxford history of the British Empire. See The Oxford history of the British Empire 909
(ed) The Oxford history of the twentieth century. See The Oxford history of the twentieth century
909.82

Louis Armstrong, in his own words. Armstrong, L.
92

Louis Comfort Tiffany at Tiffany & Co. Loring, J.
92

Louise, Queen, consort of Frederick William III, King of Prussia, 1776-1810
See/See also pages in the following book(s):
Fraser, A. The warrior queens 920

Louisiana
Politics and government
Hair, W. I. The Kingfish and his realm: the life and times of Huey P. Long 92

Louisiana Purchase
The Louisiana Purchase 973.4
The **Louisiana** Purchase 973.4

Lourdes (France)
Harris, R. Lourdes 232.91

Lourie, Richard, 1940-
Sakharov 92

Loury, Glenn C.
The anatomy of racial inequality 305.8

Louvish, Simon
Monkey business 920

Love, Preston
See/See also pages in the following book(s):
Dance, S. The world of Count Basie 920

Love, Robert William, 1944-
History of the U.S. Navy 359

Love, Susan M.
Dr Susan Love's breast book 618.1
Dr. Susan Love's menopause and hormone book
618.1

Love
Ackerman, D. A natural history of love 152.4
Blum, D. Love at Goon Park 150.19
Buscaglia, L. F. Loving each other 158
Fromm, E. The art of loving 152.4
Gilligan, C. The birth of pleasure 152.4
Gray, J. Mars and Venus starting over 306.7
Hooks, B. Salvation 306.7
Jampolsky, G. G. Love is the answer: creating positive relationships 152.4
Lewis, T. A general theory of love 152.4
Menninger, K. A. Love against hate 150.19
Peck, M. S. The road less traveled 158
Richardson, B. L. What mama couldn't tell us about love 158

Love & survival. Ornish, D. 616.1

Love against hate. Menninger, K. A. 150.19

Love and living. Merton, T. 248

Love and marriage. Cosby, B. 306.8

Love at Goon Park. Blum, D.   **150.19**
Love is the answer: creating positive relationships. Jampolsky, G. G.   **152.4**
The **love** of Don Perlimplin and Belisa in the garden. García Lorca, F.
    In Garcia Lorca, F. Five plays p105-30   **862**
Love poems. Giovanni, N.   **811**
Love poetry
    Amichai, Y. Poems of Jerusalem; and, Love poems
       892
    A Book of love poetry   **808.81**
Love stories
Bibliography
    Bouricius, A. The romance readers' advisory
       016.8
    Ramsdell, K. Romance fiction   **016.8**
History and criticism
    Bouricius, A. The romance readers' advisory
       016.8
    Ramsdell, K. Romance fiction   **016.8**
Technique
    Writing romances   **808.3**
A **love** supreme. Kahn, A.   **781.65**
Love thy neighbor. Maass, P.   **949.7**
Love, war, and circuses. Scigliano, E.   **599.67**
Love works like this. Slater, L.   **306.8**
Lovell, Mary S.
    A rage to live: a biography of Richard and Isabel Burton   **92**
    The sisters: the saga of the Mitford family   **920**
Lovelock, James
    The ages of Gaia   **570.1**
Lovenheim, Peter
    Portrait of a burger as a young calf   **636.2**
The **lover**. Pinter, H.
    In Pinter, H. Complete works v2   **822**
Lovett, Patricia
    Calligraphy and illumination   **745.6**
Loving each other. Buscaglia, L. F.   **158**
Loving Picasso: the private journal of Fernande Olivier. Olivier, F.   **92**
Lovinger, Paul W.
    The Penguin dictionary of English usage and style
       428
Low, Kathleen
    Recruiting library staff   **023**
Low-carbohydrate diet
    Atkins, R. C. Dr. Atkins' new diet revolution
       613.2
Low-cholesterol diet
    See also Low-fat diet
    American Heart Association cookbook   **641.5**
    American Heart Association low-fat, low-cholesterol cookbook   **641.5**
    American Heart Association meals in minutes
       641.5
    American Heart Association quick-and-easy cookbook
       641.5
    Pépin, J. Jacques Pépin's simple and healthy cooking
       641.5
Low-fat diet
    American Heart Association low-fat & luscious desserts   **641.8**
    American Heart Association low-fat, low-cholesterol cookbook   **641.5**
    American Heart Association quick-and-easy cookbook
       641.5
    Stewart, M. Martha Stewart's healthy quick cook
       641.5
    Wenner, P. F. Garden cuisine   **613.2**
Low sodium diet *See* Salt-free diet
Low temperatures
Research
    Shachtman, T. Absolute zero and the conquest of cold
       536

Lowden, John
    Early Christian & Byzantine art   **709.02**
Lowe, Doug
    Networking for dummies   **004.6**
Lowell, Robert, 1917-1977
    Collected poems   **811**
    Collected prose   **818**
    Land of unlikeness
    In Lowell, R. Collected poems   **811**
About
    Mariani, P. L. Lost puritan: a life of Robert Lowell
       92
    See/See also pages in the following book(s):
    Heaney, S. Finders keepers p220-37   **821**
The **lower** depths. Gorky, M.
    In Our dramatic heritage v4   **808.82**
Lowery, Charles D., 1937-
    (ed) Encyclopedia of African-American civil rights. See Encyclopedia of African-American civil rights
       305.8
Lown, Bernard
    The lost art of healing   **610**
Lowry, Beverly
    Her dream of dreams: the rise and triumph of Madam C.J. Walker   **92**
Lowry, Lois
    See/See also pages in the following book(s):
    The Newbery & Caldecott medal books, 1986-2000 p114-26, 207-19   **028.5**
Lozano, Luis-Martin
    Frida Kahlo. See Frida Kahlo [critical essays]
       759.972
Lubar, Robert S.
    Dali: the Salvador Dali Museum collection   **759.6**
Lubrano, Alfred
    Limbo: blue-collar roots, white-collar dreams
       305.5
Luce, Clare Boothe, 1903-1987
About
    Morris, S. J. Rage for fame: the ascent of Clare Boothe Luce   **92**
Luce, Henry Robinson, 1898-1967
    See/See also pages in the following book(s):
    Life stories   **920**
Lucey, Donna M., 1951-
    (jt. auth) Wiencek, H. National Geographic guide to America's great houses   **728.8**
Luchetti, Cathy, 1945-
    Children of the West   **978**
Lucid, Shannon
    See/See also pages in the following book(s):
    Slung, M. B. Living with cannibals and other women's adventures   **910.4**
Lucie-Smith, Edward, 1933-
    Art today   **709.04**
    Visual arts in the twentieth century   **709.04**
Lucientes, Francisco José de Goya y *See* Goya, Francisco, 1746-1828
The **Lucifer** principle. Bloom, H.   **128**
Lucky. Sebold, A.   **362.883**
Lucky him: the life of Kingsley Amis. Bradford, R.
       92
Lucy, Liza Prior
    (jt. auth) Fassett, K. Glorious patchwork   **746.46**
Lucy: the beginnings of humankind. Johanson, D. C.
       599.93
Lucy's legacy. Jolly, A.   **599.93**
Ludden, LaVerne, 1949-
    (ed) Guide for occupational exploration. See Guide for occupational exploration   **331.7**
    O*NET dictionary of occupational titles. See O*NET dictionary of occupational titles   **331.7**
Ludlow fair. Wilson, L.
    In Wilson, L. 21 short plays p38-53   **812**

Ludlum, David M., 1910-1997
The Audubon Society field guide to North American
weather   **551.6**
Luise *See* Louise, Queen, consort of Frederick William
III, King of Prussia, 1776-1810
Lukács, Georg *See* Lukács, György, 1885-1971
Lukács, György, 1885-1971
See/See also pages in the following book(s):
Said, E. W. Reflections on exile and other essays p61-
69, 436-52   **814**
Lukacs, John, 1924-
Five days in London, May 1940   **940.53**
Lukas, J. Anthony, 1933-1997
Common ground   **305.8**
Lukas, Tony *See* Lukas, J. Anthony, 1933-1997
Lukeman, Alex, 1941-
Sleep well, sleep deep   **616.8**
Lukeman, Noah
The plot thickens   **808.3**
Lumber and lumbering
Peters, R. Woodworker's guide to wood   **684**
Lumet, Sidney
Making movies   **791.43**
Lunar expeditions *See* Space flight to the moon
Lunar Society of Birmingham (England)
Uglow, J. S. The lunar men   **920**
The **lunch-box** chronicles. Winik, M.   **306.8**
Lunden, Joan
Wake-up calls   **155.2**
Lung cancer
Henschke, C. I. Lung cancer   **616.99**
Scott, W. J. Lung cancer   **616.99**
Lung disorders sourcebook   **616.2**
Lungs
Diseases
Adams, F. V. The breathing disorders sourcebook
                                               616.2
Lung disorders sourcebook   **616.2**
Lupica, Mike
Summer of '98   **796.357**
Lupus. Lahita, R. G.   **616.7**
Lupus erythematosus, Systemic *See* Systemic lupus er-
ythematosus
Lurquin, Paul F.
High tech harvest   **631.5**
Lush life: a biography of Billy Strayhorn. Hajdu, D.
                                               92
Lusitania (Steamship)
Preston, D. Lusitania   **940.4**
Lustig, Osnat
(jt. auth) Albrizio, A. Classic millinery techniques
                                               646.5
Luther, Martin, 1483-1546
About
Bainton, R. H. Here I stand: a life of Martin Luther
                                               92
Erikson, E. H. Young man Luther   **92**
Oberman, H. A. Luther: man between God and the
Devil   **92**
See/See also pages in the following book(s):
Küng, H. Great Christian thinkers p127-53   **230**
Lutkenhoff, Marlene
(ed) Children with spina bifida. See Children with
spina bifida   **618.92**
Lutnick, Howard
On top of the world   **332.6**
Lutz, Tom
Crying   **152.4**
Lutz, William, 1940-
The Cambridge thesaurus of American English
                                               423
The new doublespeak   **427**
Lux, Thomas, 1946-
New and selected poems, 1975-1995   **811**
Lying *See* Truthfulness and falsehood

Lying about Hitler. Evans, R. J.   **940.53**
The **lying** stones of Marrakesh. Gould, S. J. **508**
Lyme disease
See also Ticks
Karlen, A. Biography of a germ   **579.3**
Vanderhoof-Forschner, K. Everything you need to
know about Lyme disease and other tick-borne disor-
ders   **616.9**
Lynch, Peter
One up on Wall Street   **332.6**
Lynch, Thomas, 1948-
The undertaking   **814**
Lynch, Wayne
Season of the 76ers   **796.323**
Lynching
Dray, P. At the hands of persons unknown   **364.1**
Lynn, Kenneth S.
Charlie Chaplin and his times   **92**
Hemingway   **92**
Lynn, Loretta
Loretta Lynn: coal miner's daughter   **92**
Still woman enough   **92**
Lynn, Richard John
(tr) I ching. The classic of changes   **299**
Lynton, Norbert
(jt. auth) Langmuir, E. Yale dictionary of art and art-
ists   **703**
Lyons, Charlotte
Between friends   **745.5**
(jt. auth) Engelbreit, M. Mary Engelbreit's children's
companion   **645**
Lyons, Deborah
Edward Hopper and the American imagination. See
Edward Hopper and the American imagination
                                               759.13
Lyons, Gene, 1943-
(jt. auth) Conason, J. The hunting of the President
                                               973.929
Lyons, Walter A. (Walter Andrew), 1943-
The handy weather answer book   **551.6**
Lysistrata. Aristophanes
In Aristophanes. The complete plays of Aristophanes
p287-328   **882**

M

M.I.A.; or, Mythmaking in America. Franklin, H. B.
                                               959.704
M: the man who became Caravaggio. Robb, P. **92**
Ma Jian
Red dust   **915.1**
Ma Rainey's black bottom. Wilson, A.   **812**
Maalouf, Amin
In the name of identity   **302.4**
Maas, Peter, 1929-2001
Manhunt   **364.1**
Maass, Donald
Writing the breakout novel   **808.3**
Maass, Peter, 1960-
Love thy neighbor   **949.7**
Mabinogion
See/See also pages in the following book(s):
Bulfinch, T. Bulfinch's mythology   **291.1**
Mabunda, L. Mpho
(ed) Dictionary of Hispanic biography. See Dictionary
of Hispanic biography   **920.003**
(ed) Great American court cases. See Great American
court cases   **347**
MacArthur, Douglas, 1880-1964
About
Weintraub, S. MacArthur's war   **951.9**
MacArthur's war. Weintraub, S.   **951.9**
Macaulay, David, 1946-
The new way things work   **600**

Macaulay, David, 1946-—*Continued*
See/See also pages in the following book(s):
The Newbery & Caldecott medal books, 1986-2000
p127-42 **028.5**
Maccabbees, Feast of the *See* Hanukkah
MacCarthy, Fiona
Byron: life and legend **92**
MacCready, Paul B.
About
Ciotti, P. More with less **92**
MacDiarmid, Hugh, 1892-1978
See/See also pages in the following book(s):
Heaney, S. Finders keepers p319-38 **821**
Heaney, S. The redress of poetry **821.009**
Macdonald, Anne L., 1920-
Feminine ingenuity **609**
MacDonald, Betty, 1908-1958
The egg and I **818**
MacDonald, Jeffrey R.
About
McGinniss, J. Fatal vision **364.1**
Macdonald, John, 1945-
Great battles of the Civil War **973.7**
MacDonald, Malcolm, 1948-
Brahms **92**
MacDonald, Margaret Read
Celebrate the world **398.2**
MacDonogh, Giles, 1955-
Frederick the Great **92**
Macdougall, J. D., 1944-
A short history of planet earth **551.7**
Mace, Nancy L.
The 36-hour day **618.97**
MacEwen, William
(jt. auth) Escott, C. Hank Williams **92**
Macey, David, 1949-
Frantz Fanon **92**
The lives of Michel Foucault **92**
Macfarlane, Alan
Glass: a world history **666**
Machiavelli, Niccolò, 1469-1527
The prince **320**
About
Viroli, M. Niccolò's smile: a biography of Machiavelli **92**
See/See also pages in the following book(s):
Wills, G. Certain trumpets p228-46 **303.3**
Machinal. Treadwell, S.
In Plays by American women, 1900-1930 **812.008**
Machine design
See also Human engineering
Machinery
Macaulay, D. The new way things work **600**
See/See also pages in the following book(s):
Sagan, C. Broca's brain p239-49 **500**
Machlis, Joseph, 1906-1998
The enjoyment of music **781.1**
Machu Picchu (Peru)
Bingham, H. Lost city of the Incas **985**
Macintosh (Computer)
The Macintosh bible **004**
The **Macintosh** bible **004**
Macintyre, Ben, 1963-
The Englishman's daughter **940.4**
Mack, Raneta Lawson, 1963-
A layperson's guide to criminal law **345**
Mackay, James A. (James Alexander), 1936-
Allan Pinkerton **92**
Mackenzie, Dana
The big splat; or, How our moon came to be **523.3**
MacKenzie, Gordon
The watercolorist's essential notebook **751.42**

MacKethan, Lucinda Hardwick
(ed) The Companion to southern literature. See The Companion to southern literature **810.3**
Mackey, Sandra, 1937-
The Iranians **955**
The reckoning **956.7**
MacKillop, James
Dictionary of Celtic mythology **299**
Mackintosh-Smith, Tim, 1961-
Travels with a tangerine **910.4**
Mackrell, Judith
(jt. auth) Craine, D. The Oxford dictionary of dance **792.8**
MacLachlan, Patricia
See/See also pages in the following book(s):
The Newbery & Caldecott medal books, 1986-2000
p35-46 **028.5**
MacLaine, Shirley
The Camino **92**
MacLeish, Archibald, 1892-1982
Archibald MacLeish: reflections **92**
Collected poems, 1917-1982 **811**
Macleod, John, 1966-
Dynasty: the Stuarts, 1560-1807 **941.06**
MacMillan, Margaret
Paris 1919 **940.3**
Macmillan encyclopedia of death and dying **306.9**
Macmillan encyclopedia of Native American tribes.
Johnson, M. **970.004**
Macmillan encyclopedia of physics **530**
Macmillan encyclopedia of physics, Supplement. See
Building blocks of matter **539.7**
Macmillan encyclopedia of world slavery **326**
MacMullan, Jackie
(jt. auth) Bird, L. Bird watching **92**
MacNair, Jennifer
(jt. auth) Kashner, S. The bad & the beautiful **791.43**
MacNeil, Robert, 1931-
(jt. auth) McCrum, R. The story of English **420**
Macy, Anne Sullivan *See* Sullivan, Anne, 1866-1936
Mad forest. Churchill, C. **822**
Mad in America. Whitaker, R. **616.89**
The **mad,** the bad, and the innocent. Kirwin, B. **614**
Madam Secretary. Albright, M. K. **92**
Madame Prime Minister. Brundtland, G. H. **92**
Maddex, Robert L., 1942-
International encyclopedia of human rights **323**
The U.S. Constitution A to Z **342**
Maddox, Brenda
Rosalind Franklin: the dark lady of DNA **92**
Maddox, John Royden, 1925-
What remains to be discovered **500**
Made in America. Bryson, B. **420**
The **Made** thing **811.008**
Madhur Jaffrey's world vegetarian. Jaffrey, M. **641.5**
Madigan, Tim
The burning **976.6**
Madison, Deborah
The Greens cook book **641.5**
Local flavors **641.5**
Vegetarian cooking for everyone **641.5**
Madison, James, 1751-1836
About
Cohen, I. B. Science and the founding fathers **973.3**
Wilkins, R. W. Jefferson's pillow **973**
Wills, G. James Madison **92**
See/See also pages in the following book(s):
Ellis, J. J. Founding brothers **973.4**
Madlansacay, Len
(jt. auth) Lewis, L. N. How to get a green card **342**

Madness. Porter, R.   616.89
The **madness** of Lady Bright. Wilson, L.
   In Wilson, L. 21 short plays p22-37   812
The **madwoman's** underclothes. Greer, G.   305.4
Maestro: Greenspan's Fed and the American boom.
   Woodward, B.   332.1
Maeterlinck, Maurice, 1862-1949
   The blind
   In Our dramatic heritage v6   808.82
Mafia
   Bonanno, B. Bound by honor   364.1
   Milito, L. Mafia wife   364.1
   Robb, P. Midnight in Sicily   945
     Dictionaries
   Sifakis, C. The Mafia encyclopedia   364.1
The **Mafia** encyclopedia. Sifakis, C.   364.1
Mafia wife. Milito, L.   364.1
Magazines *See* Periodicals
Magazines for libraries   011
Magee, Bryan
   The story of philosophy   190
Magellan, Ferdinand, 1480?-1521
   See/See also pages in the following book(s):
   Manchester, W. A world lit only by fire   940.2
Maghreb *See* North Africa
Magic
   Highfield, R. The science of Harry Potter   500
     Encyclopedias
   Ogden, T. Wizards and sorcerers   133.4
The **magic** of crazy quilting. Michler, J. M.   746.46
The **magical** maze. Stewart, I.   510
Magical mushrooms, mischievous molds. Hudler, G. W.   579.5
Magicians
   Brandon, R. The life and many deaths of Harry Houdini   92
Magida, Arthur J.
   (ed) How to be a perfect stranger. See How to be a perfect stranger   291.3
Magill, Frank Northen, 1907-
   Critical survey of drama. See Critical survey of drama   809.2
   Short story writers. See Short story writers   809.3
   (ed) Cyclopedia of literary characters. See Cyclopedia of literary characters   803
   (ed) Dictionary of world biography. See Dictionary of world biography   920.003
   (ed) Great events from history II, Science and technology. See Great events from history II, Science and technology   509
   (ed) Masterpieces of world literature. See Masterpieces of world literature   809
   (ed) Masterpieces of world philosophy. See Masterpieces of world philosophy   100
   (ed) Masterplots II, juvenile and young adult fiction series. See Masterplots II, juvenile and young adult fiction series   028.5
Magill's cinema annual   791.43
Magill's guide to military history   355
Magill's guide to science fiction and fantasy literature   809.3
Magnets
   Livingston, J. D. Driving force   538
Magnum Photos, Inc.
   New York September 11. See New York September 11   974.7
Magocsi, Paul R.
   Historical atlas of Central Europe   911
Magritte, René, 1898-1967
   Magritte   759.9493
Magueijo, João
   Faster than the speed of light   535
Mah, Adeline Yen, 1937-
   Falling leaves   92

Mahābhārata
   Mahābhārata   891
Mahābhārata. Bhagavadgītā
   The Bhagavad Gita   891
Mahan, A. T. (Alfred Thayer), 1840-1914
   See/See also pages in the following book(s):
   Zimmermann, W. First great triumph   973
Mahan, Alfred Thayer *See* Mahan, A. T. (Alfred Thayer), 1840-1914
Mahfouz, Naguib *See* Maḥfūẓ, Najīb, 1912-
Maḥfūẓ, Najīb, 1912-
   Echoes of an autobiography   92
Mahon, Derek, 1941-
   Selected poems   821
Mahoney, Richard D.
   Sons and brothers: the days of Jack and Bobby Kennedy   92
Mahony Miller, Bertha E. *See* Miller, Bertha E. Mahony, 1882-1969
Maida Heatter's book of great desserts. Heatter, M.   641.8
Maida Heatter's brand-new book of great cookies. Heatter, M.   641.8
The **maids** [and] Deathwatch. Genet, J.   842
Maier, Karl
   This house has fallen   966.9
Maier, Pauline, 1938-
   American scripture   973.3
Mail-order business
   The Directory of mail order catalogs   016.381
Mail systems, Electronic *See* Electronic mail systems
Mailer, Norman
   The time of our time   818
     About
   Dearborn, M. V. Mailer   92
   See/See also pages in the following book(s):
   Amis, M. The war against cliché   824
   Naipaul, V. S. The writer and the world p315-33   824
Mailhot, Claire B.
   Surgery: a patient's guide from diagnosis to recovery   617
Main-course vegetarian pleasures. Lemlin, J.   641.5
Maine
     Description
   Thoreau, H. D. The Maine woods   917.41
     Natural history
   See Natural history—Maine
The **Maine** woods. Thoreau, H. D.   917.41
   also in Thoreau, H. D. A week on the Concord and Merrimack rivers; Walden; The Maine woods; Cape Cod   818
Maintenance and repair *See* Repairing
Mair, Victor H., 1943-
   (ed) The Columbia history of Chinese literature. See The Columbia history of Chinese literature   895.1
   (ed) The Shorter Columbia anthology of traditional Chinese literature. See The Shorter Columbia anthology of traditional Chinese literature   895.1
Majerus, M. E. N., 1954-
     About
   Hooper, J. Of moths and men   576.8
Majerus, Michael E. N. *See* Majerus, M. E. N., 1954-
The **majesty** of the law. O'Connor, S. D.   347
Majolica: a complete and illustrated survey. Karmason, M. G.   738
Major, David C., 1938-
   100 one-night reads   028
Major, John S., 1942-
   (jt. auth) Fadiman, C. The new lifetime reading plan   028
   (jt. auth) Major, D. C. 100 one-night reads   028
   (ed) World poetry. See World poetry   808.81

The **majors:** in pursuit of golf's Holy Grail. Feinstein, J.   **796.352**

Make-believe town. Mamet, D.   **814**

Make gentle the life of this world. Kennedy, R. F.   **973.922**

Make mine a mystery. Niebuhr, G. W.   **809.3**

Make your own living trust. Clifford, D.   **346.05**

Makers of science. Allaby, M.   **920.003**

Makes me wanna holler. McCall, N.   **92**

Makeup, Theatrical See Theatrical makeup

Makeup (Cosmetics) See Cosmetics

Making a baby. Bruce, D. F.   **618.2**

Making a winning short. Levy, E.   **791.43**

Making Callaloo   **810.8**

Making certain it goes on. Hugo, R. F.   **811**

Making genes, making waves. Beckwith, J. R.   **92**

Making movies. Lumet, S.   **791.43**

The **making** of a cook. See Kamman, M. The new making of a cook   **641.5**

The **making** of a philosopher. McGinn, C.   **92**

The **Making** of a poem   **821.008**

The **making** of modern Japan. Jansen, M. B.   **952**

The **making** of Robert E. Lee. Fellman, M.   **92**

The **making** of the atomic bomb. Rhodes, R.   **623.4**

The **making** of the president, 1960. White, T. H.   **324.6**

Making PCR. Rabinow, P.   **572.8**

Making peace. Mitchell, G. J.   **941.6**

Making peace with the planet. Commoner, B.   **304.2**

Making peace with your past. Bloomfield, H. H.   **158**

Making saints. Woodward, K. L.   **282**

Making sense of life. Keller, E. F.   **570.1**

Making the body beautiful. Gilman, S. L.   **617.9**

Making the most of your money. Quinn, J. B.   **332.024**

Making the mummies dance. Hoving, T.   **92**

Making your own days. Koch, K.   **809.1**

Malamud, Bernard, 1914-1986
   See/See also pages in the following book(s):
   Langer, L. L. Admitting the Holocaust p145-55   **940.53**

Malaria
   Honigsbaum, M. The fever trail   **616.9**
   Rocco, F. The miraculous fever tree   **616.9**

Malaysia
Description
   See/See also pages in the following book(s):
   Naipaul, V. S. Among the believers p225-94   **297**

Malcolm, Janet
   Reading Chekhov   **891.7**

Malcolm, Trisha, 1960-
   Vogue knitting American collection. See Vogue knitting American collection   **746.43**

Malcolm X, 1925-1965
   The autobiography of Malcolm X   **92**
About
   Carson, C. Malcolm X: the FBI file   **92**
   The Malcolm X encyclopedia   **92**
   Perry, B. Malcolm   **92**
   See/See also pages in the following book(s):
   West, C. Race matters p95-105   **305.8**

The **Malcolm** X encyclopedia   **92**

The **male** body. Bordo, S.   **305.31**

Male role See Sex role

Málek, Jaromír
   (ed) Egypt: ancient culture, modern land. See Egypt: ancient culture, modern land   **962**

Maleskey, Gale
   Nature's medicines   **615.5**

Malgieri, Nick
   How to bake   **641.8**
   Perfect cakes   **641.8**

Malinowski, Sharon
   (ed) The Gale encyclopedia of Native American tribes. See The Gale encyclopedia of Native American tribes   **970.004**
   (ed) Notable native Americans. See Notable native Americans   **920.003**

Maliszewski-Pickart, Margaret, 1963-
   Architecture and ornament   **721**

Mallarmé, Stéphane, 1842-1898
   Collected poems   **841**
   See/See also pages in the following book(s):
   Simon, J. I. Dreamers of dreams   **809.1**

Mallett, Daryl F. (Daryl Furumi), 1969-
   (ed) Reginald, R. Science fiction and fantasy literature, 1975-1991   **016.8**

Mallon, Mary See Typhoid Mary, d. 1938

Mallon, Thomas, 1951-
   Mrs. Paine's garage and the murder of John F. Kennedy   **364.1**

Malone, John Williams
   The encyclopedia of figure skating   **796.91**
   It doesn't take a rocket scientist   **920**

Maloney, David J.
   Maloney's antiques & collectibles resource directory   **745.1**

Maloney's antiques & collectibles resource directory. Maloney, D. J.   **745.1**

Malory, Sir Thomas, 15th cent.
   Le morte d'Arthur   **398.2**

Malthus, T. R. (Thomas Robert), 1766-1834
   See/See also pages in the following book(s):
   Heilbroner, R. L. The worldly philosophers   **330.1**

Malthus, Thomas Robert See Malthus, T. R. (Thomas Robert), 1766-1834

Maltin, Leonard
   Leonard Maltin's movie and video guide   **791.43**

Mamet, David
   American buffalo
   In Nine plays of the modern theater p791-896   **808.82**
   Make-believe town   **814**
   On directing film   **791.43**
   True and false   **792**
   See/See also pages in the following book(s):
   Playwrights at work   **812.009**

Mamiya, Lawrence H.
   (jt. auth) Lincoln, C. E. The black church in the African American experience   **277.3**

Mammal tracks & sign. Elbroch, M.   **599**

Mammals
   See also Fossil mammals; groups of mammals; and names of mammals
   Burt, W. H. A field guide to the mammals   **599**
   Mares, M. A. A desert calling   **599**
   Nowak, R. M. Walker's mammals of the world   **599**
   The Smithsonian book of North American mammals   **599**
   Tudge, C. The time before history   **599.93**
   Whitaker, J. O., Jr. National Audubon Society field guide to North American mammals   **599**
   See/See also pages in the following book(s):
   Elbroch, M. Mammal tracks & sign   **599**

Mammals, Marine See Marine mammals

Man See Human beings

Influence of environment
   See Environmental influence on humans
Influence on nature
   See Human influence on nature
Origin
   See Human origins

Man, Fossil See Fossil hominids

Man, Prehistoric See Prehistoric peoples

Man and his symbols. Jung, C. G.   **150.19**

Man and microbes. Karlen, A.   **614.4**

A **man** called Intrepid. Stevenson, W.   **940.54**

A **man** for all seasons. Bolt, R.   **822**

Man-made catastrophes. Davis, L. A.   **904**

Man of La Mancha. Wasserman, D.   **812**

The **man** of mode. Etherege, Sir G.

   In Restoration plays   **822.008**

Man of the century: the life and times of Pope John Paul II. Kwitny, J.   **92**

A **man** on the moon. Chaikin, A.   **629.45**

Man Ray *See* Ray, Man, 1890-1976

Man Ray's Montparnasse. Lottman, H. R.   **92**

The **man** who broke Napoleon's codes. Urban, M.   **940.2**

The **man** who counted. Tahan, M.   **793.7**

The **man** who flew the Memphis Belle. Morgan, R.   **92**

The **man** who knew infinity: a life of the genius, Ramanujan. Kanigel, R.   **92**

The **man** who mistook his job for a life. Lazear, J.   **155.2**

The **man** who mistook his wife for a hat and other clinical tales. Sacks, O. W.   **616.8**

The **man** who walked through time. Fletcher, C.   **917.91**

Management

   Bossidy, L. A. Execution: the discipline of getting things done   **658.4**

   Business: the ultimate resource   **658**

   Camp, J. Start with no   **658.4**

   Collins, J. C. Good to great   **658**

   Drucker, P. F. Management challenges for the 21st century   **658**

   Drucker, P. F. Managing in a time of great change   **658**

   Drucker, P. F. Managing the non-profit organization   **658**

   Giuliani, R. W. Leadership   **658**

   Goleman, D. Primal leadership   **658.4**

   Heller, R. Essential manager's manual   **658.4**

   McCormack, M. H. What they don't teach you at Harvard Business School   **650.1**

   O'Reilly, C. A., III. Hidden value   **658**

   Peters, T. J. The circle of innovation   **658.4**

   Anecdotes

   Peter, L. J. The Peter Principle   **817**

Management challenges for the 21st century. Drucker, P. F.   **658**

Managing in a time of great change. Drucker, P. F.   **658**

Managing public-access computers. Barclay, D. A.   **025**

Managing stroke   **616.8**

Managing the non-profit organization. Drucker, P. F.   **658**

Manahan, Anna Anderson *See* Anderson, Anna, d. 1984

Mancall, Peter C.

   (ed) American encounters. See American encounters   **970.004**

   (ed) American nations. See American nations   **970.004**

Manchester, William

   Goodbye, darkness   **940.54**

   The last lion: Winston Spencer Churchill   **92**

   A world lit only by fire   **940.2**

Manchild in the promised land. Brown, C.   **92**

Mandela, Nelson

   Long walk to freedom: the autobiography of Nelson Mandela   **92**

   Mandela   **92**

   About

   Sampson, A. Nelson Mandela   **92**

Mandelbrot, Benoit B.

   See/See also pages in the following book(s):

   Horvitz, L. A. Eureka!: scientific breakthroughs that changed the world   **509**

Mandeville, Sir John

   About

   Milton, G. The riddle and the knight   **910.4**

Manet, Édouard, 1832-1883

   About

   Brombert, B. A. Edouard Manet   **92**

Mangelsen, Thomas D.

   Polar dance   **599.78**

Manguel, Alberto

   The dictionary of imaginary places   **809.3**

   Into the looking-glass wood   **814**

   Reading pictures   **750**

Manhattan Project

   Norris, R. S. Racing for the bomb: General Leslie R. Groves, the Manhattan Project's indispensable man   **92**

Manhunt. Maas, P.   **364.1**

Manic-depressive illness

   See also Depression (Psychology)

   Duke, P. A brilliant madness   **616.89**

   Papolos, D. F. The bipolar child   **618.92**

   See/See also pages in the following book(s):

   DePaulo, J. R. Understanding depression   **616.85**

Manion, Mark

   (jt. auth) Evan, W. M. Minding the machines   **620.8**

Mankiewicz, Richard

   The story of mathematics   **510**

Mankiller, Wilma

   Mankiller: a chief and her people   **92**

Mann, James *See* Mann, Jim, 1946-

Mann, Jim, 1946-

   About face   **327.73**

Mann, Murray Gell- *See* Gell-Mann, Murray, 1929-

Mann, Robert, 1958-

   A grand delusion   **959.704**

Mann, Thomas, 1875-1955

   Buddenbrooks; criticism

   In Gay, P. Savage reprisals   **809.3**

   About

   Heilbut, A. Thomas Mann   **92**

   Kurzke, H. Thomas Mann   **92**

Mann, William J.

   Behind the screen   **791.43**

Manners *See* Etiquette

Manners and customs

   See also Country life; names of ethnic groups, countries, cities, etc. with the subdivision *Social life and customs*

   Dresser, N. Multicultural manners   **395**

   A History of private life   **909**

   Encyclopedias

   Worldmark encyclopedia of cultures and daily life   **306**

Manning, Richard, 1951-

   Grassland   **577.4**

A **man's** journey to simple abundance. Ban Breathnach, S.   **158**

A **man's** world. Crothers, R.

   In Plays by American women, 1900-1930   **812.008**

Manser, Martin H.

   The Facts on File dictionary of foreign words and phrases   **422.03**

   The Facts on File dictionary of proverbs   **398.9**

Manslaughter *See* Homicide

Manson, Charles, 1934-

   About

   Bugliosi, V. Helter skelter   **364.1**

A **manual** for writers of dissertations. See Turabian, K. L. A manual for writers of term papers, theses, and dissertations **808**

A **manual** for writers of term papers, theses, and dissertations. Turabian, K. L. **808**

Manual of American dialects, for radio, stage, screen, and television. See Herman, L. American dialects **427**

Manual of mineral science **549**

Manual of mineralogy. See Manual of mineral science **549**

Manual of style. See United States. Government Printing Office. Style manual **808**

Manual of Zen Buddhism. Suzuki, D. T. **294.3**

Manual workers See Working class

Manuel Puig and spider woman. Levine, S. J. **92**

Manufactured houses. Watkins, A. M. **693**

The **Many** faces of Islam **297**

Many mansions. Cox, H. G. **261.2**

Many thousands gone. Berlin, I. **326**

Mao, Tse-tung See Mao Zedong, 1893-1976

Mao Zedong, 1893-1976
About
Short, P. Mao **92**
Spence, J. D. Mao Zedong **92**

The **map** that changed the world. Winchester, S. **92**

A **map** to the next world. Harjo, J. **811**

Maples, William R., 1937-1997
Dead men do tell tales **614**

Mapping human history. Olson, S. **599.9**

Mapping Mars. Morton, O. **523.4**

Mapping time. Richards, E. G. **529**

Maps
See also Atlases; Road maps

Marani, Pietro C.
Leonardo da Vinci—the complete paintings **759.5**

Maraniss, David
First in his class: a biography of Bill Clinton **92**
When pride still mattered: a life of Vince Lombardi **92**

Marat, Jean Paul, 1743-1793
Drama
Weiss, P. The persecution and assassination of Jean-Paul Marat as performed by the inmates of the Asylum of Charenton under the direction of the Marquis de Sade **832**

Marathon running
Higdon, H. Marathon: the ultimate training guide **796.42**

Marathon: the ultimate training guide. Higdon, H. **796.42**

Marcella cucina. Hazan, M. **641.5**

The **march** of folly. Tuchman, B. W. **909.08**

A **march** to madness. Feinstein, J. **796.323**

Marches (Demonstrations) See Demonstrations

Marching orders. Lee, B. **940.54**

Marcus, Eric
Is it a choice? **305.9**
Why suicide? **179.7**

Marcus, Leonard S., 1950-
Ways of telling **741.6**

Marcus Aurelius, Emperor of Rome, 121-180
Meditations **188**
See/See also pages in the following book(s):
Hamilton, E. The echo of Greece p168-77 **880.9**

Marcus Aurelius Antoninus See Marcus Aurelius, Emperor of Rome, 121-180

Mardi Gras See Carnival

Marek, Kurt W. See Ceram, C. W., 1915-1972

Mares, Michael A.
A desert calling **599**

Margaret, Duchess of Newcastle See Newcastle, Margaret Cavendish, Duchess of, 1624?-1674

A **marginal** Jew. Meier, J. P. **232.9**

Margolis, Simeon
(ed) The Johns Hopkins consumer guide to medical tests. See The Johns Hopkins consumer guide to medical tests **616.07**
(ed) The Johns Hopkins medical guide to health after 50. See The Johns Hopkins medical guide to health after 50 **613**
(ed) Johns Hopkins symptoms and remedies. See Johns Hopkins symptoms and remedies **616.02**

Margulies, Stuart
(jt. auth) Fischer, B. Bobby Fischer teaches chess **794.1**

Margulis, Lynn, 1938-
Five kingdoms **570**
Symbiotic planet **576.8**
What is life? **570.1**

Mari, Christopher
Space exploration. See Space exploration **629**

Maria Celeste, 1600-1634
About
Sobel, D. Galileo's daughter **92**

Mariani, Paul L.
The broken tower: a life of Hart Crane **92**
Lost puritan: a life of Robert Lowell **92**

Marie Antoinette, Queen, consort of Louis XVI, King of France, 1755-1793
About
Fraser, A. Marie Antoinette **92**
Lever, E. Marie Antoinette **92**

Marien, Mary Warner
Photography: a cultural history **770.9**

Marigold, Lys
(jt. auth) Popcorn, F. Clicking **650.1**

Marijuana
See/See also pages in the following book(s):
Pollan, M. The botany of desire **581.6**

Marin, Cheech, 1946-
Chicano visions **709.73**

Marinacci, Barbara, 1933-
(jt. auth) Pauling, L. C. Linus Pauling in his own words **92**

Marine animals
See also Marine mammals
Benchley, P. Shark trouble **597**

Marine biology
Carson, R. The edge of the sea **577.7**
Carson, R. Under the sea wind **577.7**
World atlas of the oceans **912**

Marine Corps (U.S.) See United States. Marine Corps

Marine ecology
Mojetta, A. Simon & Schuster's guide to saltwater fish and fishing **799.1**
See/See also pages in the following book(s):
Carson, R. Lost woods **570**
Encyclopedias
Ellis, R. Encyclopedia of the sea **551.46**

Marine mammals
See also Dolphins; Porpoises; Whales
National Audubon Society guide to marine mammals of the world **599.5**

Marine pollution
Woodard, C. Ocean's end **363.7**

Marine resources
Woodard, C. Ocean's end **363.7**

Marine sciences
Encyclopedias
Interdisciplinary encyclopedia of marine sciences **551**

Marinelli, Janet
(ed) The Brooklyn Botanic Garden gardener's desk reference. See The Brooklyn Botanic Garden gardener's desk reference **635.9**

Marines (U.S.) See United States. Marine Corps

Marion, Frances, d. 1973
About
Beauchamp, C. Without lying down   92
Marital counseling *See* Marriage counseling
Marital infidelity *See* Adultery
Marius, Richard C.
(ed) The Columbia book of Civil War poetry. See The Columbia book of Civil War poetry   **811.008**
Mark Rothko. Breslin, J. E. B.   92
Mark Twain A to Z. Rasmussen, R. K.   818
The **Mark** Twain encyclopedia   818
Marken, Bill
How to fix (just about) everything   640
Marketing
Underhill, P. Why we buy   **658.8**
Marketing of farm produce *See* Farm produce—Marketing
Markham, Beryl, 1902-1986
About
Trzebinski, E. The lives of Beryl Markham   92
Markham, Sir Clements R. (Clements Robert), 1830-1916
See/See also pages in the following book(s):
Honigsbaum, M. The fever trail   **616.9**
Markings. Hammarskjöld, D.   **839.7**
Markoe, Arnie
(ed) The Scribner encyclopedia of American lives. See The Scribner encyclopedia of American lives   **920.003**
Markoe, Karen
(ed) The Scribner encyclopedia of American lives. See The Scribner encyclopedia of American lives   **920.003**
Markowitz, Gerald E.
Deceit and denial   **615.9**
Markowitz, Harvey
(ed) American Indians. See American Indians   **970.004**
Marks, Claude, 1915-1991
(ed) World artists, 1950-1980. See World artists, 1950-1980   **920.003**
(ed) World artists, 1980-1990. See World artists, 1980-1990   **920.003**
Marks, David R.
The headache prevention cookbook   **616.8**
Marks, Gil
The world of Jewish cooking   **641.5**
Marks, Jonathan
What it means to be 98% chimpanzee   **599.93**
Marks, Laura
(jt. auth) Marks, D. R. The headache prevention cookbook   **616.8**
Marks, Leo
Between silk and cyanide   **940.54**
Marks' standard handbook for mechanical engineers   **621**
Marla, Rozka Korczak- *See* Korczak-Marla, Rozka, 1921-1988
Marlborough, Sarah Jennings Churchill, Duchess of, 1660-1744
About
Field, O. Sarah Churchill, Duchess of Marlborough   92
Marling, Karal Ann
As seen on TV   **973.92**
Merry Christmas!   **394.26**
Norman Rockwell   **759.13**
Marlowe, Christopher, 1564-1593
Doctor Faustus   **822**
Hero and Leander; criticism
In Heaney, S. The redress of poetry   **821.009**
About
Nicholl, C. The reckoning: the murder of Christopher Marlowe   92

See/See also pages in the following book(s):
Heaney, S. Finders keepers p286-99   **821**
Heaney, S. The redress of poetry   **821.009**
Marnham, Patrick
Dreaming with his eyes open: a life of Diego Rivera   92
Márquez, Gabriel García *See* García Márquez, Gabriel, 1928-
Marr, Lisa
Sexually transmitted diseases   **616.95**
Marriage
See also Divorce; Domestic relations; Family; Married people; Remarriage; Weddings
Barash, D. P. The myth of monogamy   **306.7**
Cosby, B. Love and marriage   **306.8**
Roiphe, A. R. Married   **306.8**
Waite, L. J. The case for marriage   **306.8**
Wilson, J. Q. The marriage problem   **306.8**
Yalom, M. A history of the wife   **306.8**
See/See also pages in the following book(s):
Goleman, D. Emotional intelligence p129-47   **152.4**
Encyclopedias
International encyclopedia of marriage and family   **306.8**
Marriage, Interracial *See* Interracial marriage
Marriage counseling
Kramer, P. D. Should you leave?   **616.89**
Marriage customs and rites
Bride's book of etiquette   **395**
Martin, J. Miss Manners on weddings   **395**
Post, P. Emily Post wedding etiquette   **395**
A **marriage** made in heaven—; or, Too tired for an affair. Bombeck, E.   **817**
The **marriage** problem. Wilson, J. Q.   **306.8**
Married. Roiphe, A. R.   **306.8**
Married people
Waite, L. J. The case for marriage   **306.8**
Marriott, Edward, 1966-
Plague: a story of science, rivalry, and the scourge that won't go away   **614.5**
Marrs, Richard P.
Dr. Richard Marr's fertility book   **616.6**
Marrs, Suzanne
One writer's imagination   **813.009**
Mars, Forrest, Sr.
About
Brenner, J. G. The emperors of chocolate   **338.7**
Mars, Inc.
Brenner, J. G. The emperors of chocolate   **338.7**
Mars (Planet)
Morton, O. Mapping Mars   **523.4**
Sheehan, W. Mars   **523.4**
Sheehan, W. The planet Mars   **523.4**
See/See also pages in the following book(s):
Davies, P. C. W. The fifth miracle   **576.8**
Space exploration   **629**
Mars and Venus on a date. Gray, J.   **306.7**
Mars and Venus starting over. Gray, J.   **306.7**
Marsalis, Wynton
See/See also pages in the following book(s):
Russell, D. Black genius and the American experience   **920**
Marsden, C. David
Parkinson's disease. See Parkinson's disease   **616.8**
Marsden, George M., 1939-
Jonathan Edwards   92
Marsh, Earle
(jt. auth) Brooks, T. The complete directory to prime time network and cable TV shows, 1946-present   **791.45**
Marsh, James H.
(ed) The Canadian encyclopedia. See The Canadian encyclopedia   **971**

Marsh, Othniel Charles, 1831-1899
About
Wallace, D. R. The bonehunters' revenge 560
Marshall, Andrew
The trouser people 959.1
Marshall, Edward, 1598-1675
See/See also pages in the following book(s):
Marcus, L. S. Ways of telling 741.6
Marshall, George C. (George Catlett), 1880-1959
See/See also pages in the following book(s):
Halberstam, D. The best and the brightest
  973.922
Marshall, I. N.
Who's afraid of Schrödinger's cat? 500
Marshall, John, 1755-1835
About
Simon, J. F. What kind of nation 342
Smith, J. E. John Marshall 92
Marshall, Lydie
A passion for potatoes 641.6
Marshall, Marlene Hurley
Shell chic 745.55
Marshall, Paule, 1929-
See/See also pages in the following book(s):
Black women writers (1950-1980) 810.9
Marshall, Thurgood
Thurgood Marshall 92
About
Ball, H. A defiant life: Thurgood Marshall and the persistence of racism in America 92
Rowan, C. T. Dream makers, dream breakers: the world of Justice Thurgood Marshall 92
Williams, J. Thurgood Marshall 92
Marshall Brain's more how stuff works. Brain, M.
  600
Marszalek, John F., 1939-
(ed) Encyclopedia of African-American civil rights. See Encyclopedia of African-American civil rights
  305.8
Martha Inc. Byron, C. 92
The **Martha** Stewart cookbook. Stewart, M. 641.5
The **Martha** Stewart Living cookbook 641.5
Martha Stewart's healthy quick cook. Stewart, M.
  641.5
Martha Stewart's hors d'oeuvres handbook. Stewart, M.
  641.8
Martha Stewart's menus for entertaining. Stewart, M.
  642
Martha Stewart's new old house. Stewart, M. 728
Marti, James
The alternative health & medicine encyclopedia
  615.5
Martial
Epigrams 878
Martial arts
See also Self-defense; Tae kwon do
Salzman, M. Iron & silk 915.1
Martin, Claire, 1957-
(ed) The Nursing mother's problem solver. See The Nursing mother's problem solver 649
Martin, Colin, 1939-
The Spanish Armada 942.05
Martin, Deborah L.
(ed) 1,001 ingenious gardening ideas. See 1,001 ingenious gardening ideas 635
(ed) Great garden formulas. See Great garden formulas
  635
Martin, Gerry
(jt. auth) Macfarlane, A. Glass: a world history
  666
Martin, Giles
(ed) Dewey, M. Dewey decimal classification and relative index 025.4
Martin, Gregory, 1971-
Mountain City 979.3

Martin, Judith, 1938-
Miss Manners' basic training: the right thing to say
  395
Miss Manners' guide to domestic tranquility 395
Miss Manners on weddings 395
Martin, Justin
Greenspan 92
Martin, Katherine L., 1960-
Does my child have a speech problem? 618.92
Martin, Linda Wagner- *See* Wagner-Martin, Linda
Martin, Peter, 1940-
A life of James Boswell 92
Martin, R. D. (Robert D.), 1942-
(ed) The Cambridge encyclopedia of human evolution. See The Cambridge encyclopedia of human evolution 599.93
Martin, Robert D. *See* Martin, R. D. (Robert D.), 1942-
Martin, Steve, 1945?-
Pure drivel 817
Martin, Terence
Nathaniel Hawthorne 813.009
Martin, Thomas R., 1947-
Ancient Greece 938
Martin, Toni Tipton- *See* Tipton-Martin, Toni
Martin, Valerie
Salvation: scenes from the life of St. Francis 92
Martin, Victoria C. Woodhull *See* Woodhull, Victoria C., 1838-1927
Martin, Waldo E., 1951-
(ed) Civil rights in the United States. See Civil rights in the United States 323.1
Martin, William C. (William Curtis), 1937-
With God on our side 261.8
Martínez, Julio A.
(ed) Chicano literature. See Chicano literature
  810.9
Martínez Alemán, Ana M.
(ed) Women in higher education. See Women in higher education 378
Martino, Rick
The PGA manual of golf 796.352
Marton, Kati
Hidden power 920
Marty, Martin E., 1928-
Pilgrims in their own land 277.3
Martyrs
Foxe, J. Foxe's Book of martyrs 272
Martyrs' Day. Kelly, M. 956.7
Martz, Louis Lohr
(ed) H. D. Collected poems, 1912-1944 811
Marvel. Daniels, L. 741.5
Marvel comics (New York, N.Y.)
Daniels, L. Marvel 741.5
Marvell, Andrew, 1621-1678
The complete poems 821
Marx, Groucho, 1891-1977
About
Kanfer, S. Groucho: the life and times of Julius Henry Marx 92
Marx, Julius H. *See* Marx, Groucho, 1891-1977
Marx, Karl, 1818-1883
Capital 330.1
The Communist manifesto of Karl Marx and Friedrich Engels 335.4
About
Wheen, F. Karl Marx 92
See/See also pages in the following book(s):
Camus, A. The rebel p188-226 303.6
Heilbroner, R. L. The worldly philosophers 330.1
Jaspers, K. The great philosophers 109
Marx Brothers
See also Marx, Groucho, 1891-1977
About
Louvish, S. Monkey business 920

Marxism
  See also Communism; Socialism
Mary I, Queen of England, 1516-1558
  See/See also pages in the following book(s):
  Weir, A. The children of Henry VIII   **920**
Mary, Blessed Virgin, Saint
      About
  Donofrio, B. Looking for Mary, or, The Blessed Mother and me   **282**
  Harris, R. Lourdes   **232.91**
  Pelikan, J. J. Mary through the centuries   **232.91**
Mary, Queen of Scots, 1542-1587
      About
  Fraser, A. Mary Queen of Scots   **92**
  Weir, A. Mary, Queen of Scots, and the murder of Lord Darnley   **92**
Mary Engelbreit's children's companion. Engelbreit, M.   **645**
Mary Pickford rediscovered. Brownlow, K.   **791.43**
Mary through the centuries. Pelikan, J. J.   **232.91**
Mary Tudor *See* Mary I, Queen of England, 1516-1558
Marzollo, Jean
  Fathers & babies   **649**
The **masks** of God. Campbell, J.   **291.1**
Maslin, Janet
  (jt. auth) Canby, V. The New York times guide to the best 1,000 movies ever made   **791.43**
Maslow, Abraham Harold
  Toward a psychology of being   **155.2**
Mason, Bill, 1929-
  Path of the paddle   **797.1**
Mason, George, 1725-1792
      About
  Wilkins, R. W. Jefferson's pillow   **973**
Mason, Paul
  (ed) Mason, B. Path of the paddle   **797.1**
Masons (Secret order) *See* Freemasons
Mass communication *See* Communication; Telecommunication
Mass extinction of species
  Boulter, M. C. Extinction: evolution and the end of man   **576.8**
  Leakey, R. E. The sixth extinction   **304.2**
  Powell, J. L. Night comes to the Cretaceous   **576.8**
  Raup, D. M. Extinction   **560**
Mass media
  Bok, S. Mayhem   **302.23**
  History of the mass media in the United States   **302.23**
  Jones, G. Killing monsters   **302.23**
  McLuhan, M. The global village   **302.23**
  Postman, N. Amusing ourselves to death   **302.23**
Massachusetts
      History—1600-1775, Colonial period
  Bradford, W. Of Plymouth Plantation, 1620-1647   **974.4**
  Demos, J. The unredeemed captive   **973.2**
Massey, Lorraine
  Curly girl   **646.7**
Massie, Robert K., 1929-
  Dreadnought   **940.3**
  Nicholas and Alexandra   **92**
  The Romanovs   **947.08**
Massie, Suzanne
  Land of the firebird   **947**
Masson, J. Moussaieff (Jeffrey Moussaieff), 1941-
  The nine emotional lives of cats   **636.8**
  When elephants weep   **591.5**
Masson, Jeffrey Moussaieff *See* Masson, J. Moussaieff (Jeffrey Moussaieff), 1941-
Mast, Gerald, 1940-1988
  A short history of the movies   **791.43**

The **master** builder. Ibsen, H.
  In Ibsen, H. The complete major prose plays p779-860   **839.8**
  In Ibsen, H. Ibsen: four plays, v2   **839.8**
A **master** guide to the art of floral design. Jong-Stout, A. A. de   **745.92**
"**Master** Harold"—and the boys. Fugard, A.   **822**
Master of the Senate. Caro, R. A.
  In Caro, R. A. The years of Lyndon Johnson v3   **92**
Master strokes, Pastels. Harrison, H.   **741.2**
Master the CLEP   **378.1**
Master the GED   **373.1**
Mastering the art of French cooking. Child, J.   **641.5**
Masterpieces of world literature   **809**
Masterpieces of world philosophy   **100**
Masterplots II, juvenile and young adult fiction series   **028.5**
Masterplots II, drama series   **809.2**
Masterplots II, poetry series   **809.1**
Masters, Virginia Johnson *See* Johnson, Virginia E.
Masters, William H.
  Masters and Johnson on sex and human loving   **155.3**
Masters. Sampson, C.   **796.352**
Masters and Johnson on sex and human loving. Masters, W. H.   **155.3**
Masters of color and light. Ferber, L. S.   **759.13**
Masters of death. Rhodes, R.   **940.53**
Masur, Louis P.
  (ed) "The Real war will never get in the books". See "The Real war will never get in the books"   **810.8**
Mat, mount and frame it yourself. Logan, M. D.   **749**
A **match** to the heart. Ehrlich, G.   **92**
Maté, Gabor
  Scattered   **616.85**
Materia medica
  See also Drugs
  Chevallier, A. Encyclopedia of herbal medicine   **615**
  Karch, S. B. The consumer's guide to herbal medicine   **615**
  The Merck index   **615**
  Physician's desk reference   **615**
  Plotkin, M. Medicine quest   **615**
Materials
      Encyclopedias
  Brady, G. S. Materials handbook   **620.1**
Materials handbook. Brady, G. S.   **620.1**
The **math** gene. Devlin, K. J.   **510**
Mathematical mysteries. Clawson, C. C.   **512**
A **mathematical** mystery tour. Dewdney, A. K.   **510**
Mathematical recreations
  Stewart, I. The magical maze   **510**
  Tahan, M. The man who counted   **793.7**
The **mathematical** universe. Dunham, W.   **510**
A **mathematician** reads the newspaper. Paulos, J. A.   **510**
Mathematicians
  See also Women mathematicians
  Bell, E. T. Men of mathematics   **920**
  Dunham, W. The mathematical universe   **510**
      Dictionaries
  Notable mathematicians   **920.003**
Mathematics
  See also Patterns (Mathematics); Pi
  Acheson, D. J. 1089 and all that   **510**
  Boyer, C. B. A history of mathematics   **510**
  Cole, K. C. The universe and the teacup   **510**
  Devlin, K. J. The math gene   **510**
  Devlin, K. J. The millennium problems   **510**

Mathematics—*Continued*
Dewdney, A. K. 200% of nothing   **510**
Dewdney, A. K. A mathematical mystery tour   **510**
Dunham, W. The mathematical universe   **510**
Glazer, E. Real-life math   **510**
Guillen, M. Five equations that changed the world   **530.1**
Huff, D. The complete how to figure it   **640**
Kaplan, R. The art of the infinite   **515**
Kogelman, S. The only math book you'll ever need   **513**
Mankiewicz, R. The story of mathematics   **510**
Paulos, J. A. Beyond numeracy   **510**
Paulos, J. A. Innumeracy   **510**
Paulos, J. A. A mathematician reads the newspaper   **510**
Sperling, A. P. Mathematics made simple   **510**
Stewart, I. The magical maze   **510**
Szpiro, G. G. Kepler's conjecture   **510**
Tobias, S. Overcoming math anxiety   **510**
Encyclopedias
Bunch, B. H. The Penguin desk encyclopedia of science and mathematics   **503**
History
History of modern science and mathematics   **509**
Quotations
A Dictionary of quotations in mathematics   **510**
Tables
CRC standard mathematical tables and formulae   **510**
Mathematics made simple. Sperling, A. P.   **510**
Mather, Increase, 1639-1723
About
Hall, M. G. The last American Puritan: the life of Increase Mather, 1639-1723   **92**
Mathew Brady and the image of history. Panzer, M.   **92**
Mathews, Nancy Mowll
Mary Cassatt   **92**
Matilda, Empress, consort of Henry V, Holy Roman Emperor, 1102-1167
See/See also pages in the following book(s):
Fraser, A. The warrior queens   **920**
Matilda, of Tuscany, 1046-1115
See/See also pages in the following book(s):
Fraser, A. The warrior queens   **920**
Matilde, di Canossa, contessa *See* Matilda, of Tuscany, 1046-1115
Matisse, Henri
About
Flam, J. D. Matisse and Picasso   **759.4**
Matisse, Picasso   **759.4**
Spurling, H. The unknown Matisse v1   **92**
See/See also pages in the following book(s):
Fraser, K. Ornament and silence   **814**
Matisse and Picasso. Flam, J. D.   **759.4**
Matisse, Picasso   **759.4**
Matlins, Stuart M.
(ed) How to be a perfect stranger. See How to be a perfect stranger   **291.3**
Matossian, Nouritza
Black angel: the life of Arshile Gorky   **92**
Matsakis, Aphrodite
Vietnam wives   **616.85**
Matson, Tim, 1943-
Earth ponds A to Z   **627**
Matsumoto, Chizuo *See* Asahara, Shoko
The **matter** myth. Davies, P. C. W.   **530**
A **matter** of degrees. Segrè, G.   **536**
Matthews, Chris, 1945-
Kennedy & Nixon   **973.922**
Matthews, Christopher J. *See* Matthews, Chris, 1945-

Matthews, Dawn
(ed) AIDS sourcebook. See AIDS sourcebook   **362.1**
(ed) Diabetes sourcebook. See Diabetes sourcebook   **616.4**
(ed) Lung disorders sourcebook. See Lung disorders sourcebook   **616.2**
Matthews, Joseph L.
How to win your personal injury claim   **346.03**
Matthews, William, 1942-1997
After all   **811**
Selected poems and translations, 1969-1991   **811**
Matthews, Winton E.
(ed) Dewey, M. Dewey decimal classification and relative index   **025.4**
Matthiessen, F. O. (Francis Otto), 1902-1950
American renaissance   **810.9**
Matthiessen, Francis Otto *See* Matthiessen, F. O. (Francis Otto), 1902-1950
Matthiessen, Peter
African silences   **916**
The birds of heaven   **598**
End of the earth   **508**
Indian country   **970.004**
The Peter Matthiessen reader   **818**
The snow leopard   **915.4**
Tigers in the snow   **599.75**
Mattingly, Garrett, 1900-1962
The Armada   **942.05**
Mattison, Christopher
The encyclopedia of snakes   **597.9**
Snakes of the world   **597.9**
Mattson, Mark T.
(jt. auth) Asante, M. K. The African-American atlas   **305.8**
Matuz, Roger
(ed) Contemporary Southern writers. See Contemporary Southern writers   **920.003**
Maud *See* Matilda, Empress, consort of Henry V, Holy Roman Emperor, 1102-1167
Maugham, Somerset *See* Maugham, W. Somerset (William Somerset), 1874-1965
Maugham, W. Somerset (William Somerset), 1874-1965
See/See also pages in the following book(s):
Vidal, G. United States—essays, 1952-1992 p228-50   **814**
Maugham, William Somerset *See* Maugham, W. Somerset (William Somerset), 1874-1965
Maule, Jeremy
The Oxford book of classical verse in translation. See The Oxford book of classical verse in translation   **881.008**
Mauriès, Patrick, 1952-
Cabinets of curiosities   **069**
Maus. Spiegelman, A.   **940.53**
Mauve. Garfield, S.   **667**
Max, Peter, 1937-
About
Riley, C. A. The art of Peter Max   **760**
Maxims *See* Proverbs
Maxwell, Fredric Alan
Bad boy Ballmer   **92**
Maxwell, William, 1908-2000
(jt. auth) Warner, S. T. The element of lavishness: letters of Sylvia Townsend Warner and William Maxwell, 1938-1978   **92**
Maxwell-Stuart, P. G.
Chronicle of the popes   **282**
Maxwell's demon. Von Baeyer, H. C.   **536**
Maxymuk, John
(ed) Government online. See Government online   **025.04**
May, Alex
Multimedia: digital photography   **778.3**

May, Bridget
  (jt. auth) Harwood, B. Architecture and interior design through the 18th century **729**

May, Charles E. (Charles Edward), 1941-
  Short story writers. See Short story writers **809.3**
  (ed) Critical survey of short fiction. See Critical survey of short fiction **809.3**

May, Ernest R.
  Strange victory **940.54**
  (ed) The Kennedy tapes. See The Kennedy tapes **973.922**

May, Rollo
  The courage to create **153.3**
  The discovery of being **150.19**
  Freedom and destiny **158**

May it please the court: the First Amendment **342**

May you be the mother of a hundred sons. Bumiller, E. **954.05**

Mayas
  Coe, M. D. The Maya **972**
  See/See also pages in the following book(s):
  Ceram, C. W. Gods, graves, and scholars p348-416 **930.1**

  Religion
  Miller, M. E. The gods and symbols of ancient Mexico and the Maya **299**
  Popol vuh. Popol vuh **299**

Mayer, Martin, 1928-
  The Fed **332.1**

Mayer, Ralph, 1895-1979
  The artist's handbook of materials and techniques **751.2**

Mayes, Frances
  Bella Tuscany **945**
  Under the Tuscan sun **945**

Mayes, Linda C.
  The Yale Child Study Center guide to understanding your child **649**

Mayes, Maureen D.
  The scleroderma book **616.5**

Mayflies. Wilbur, R. **811**

Mayhem. Bok, S. **302.23**

Mayle, Peter
  Acquired tastes **305.5**
  Encore Provence **944.083**
  French lessons **394.1**

Mayo, Mike, 1948-
  VideoHound's DVD guide **791.43**

Mayo Clinic complete book of pregnancy & baby's first year **618.2**
Mayo Clinic family health book **613**
Mayo Clinic on Alzheimer's disease **616.8**
Mayo Clinic on managing diabetes **616.4**

Mayr, Ernst, 1904-
  This is biology **570**
  What evolution is **576.8**

Mays, James Luther
  (ed) The HarperCollins Bible commentary. See The HarperCollins Bible commentary **220.7**

Mazower, Mark
  The Balkans: a short history **949.6**
  Dark continent: Europe's twentieth century **940.55**

Mazur, Barry, 1937-
  Imagining numbers **512**

Mazzarella, Mark
  (jt. auth) Dimitrius, J.-E. Reading people **155.2**

MCA Inc.
  See/See also pages in the following book(s):
  Bruck, C. When Hollywood had a king **92**

McAfee, Charles F.
  See/See also pages in the following book(s):
  Russell, D. Black genius and the American experience **920**

McAlester, A. Lee (Arcie Lee), 1933-
  (jt. auth) McAlester, V. A field guide to American houses **728**

McAlester, Arcie Lee *See* McAlester, A. Lee (Arcie Lee), 1933-

McAlester, Virginia, 1943-
  A field guide to American houses **728**

McAllester, Matthew, 1969-
  Beyond the Mountains of the Damned **949.7**

McArthur, Tom
  (ed) The Oxford companion to the English language. See The Oxford companion to the English language **420**

McBride, James
  The color of water [biography of Ruth McBride-Jordan] **92**

McBride-Jordan, Ruth, 1921-
  About
  McBride, J. The color of water **92**

McBrien, Richard P.
  Lives of the popes **920**
  Lives of the saints **920.003**
  (ed) The HarperCollins encyclopedia of Catholicism. See The HarperCollins encyclopedia of Catholicism **282**

McBrien, William
  Cole Porter **92**

McCabe, John, 1920-
  Cagney **92**

McCain, John S., 1911-1981
  About
  McCain, J. S. Faith of my fathers **92**

McCain, John S., 1936-
  Faith of my fathers **92**
  About
  Drew, E. Citizen McCain **92**

McCain, John Sidney, 1884-1945
  About
  McCain, J. S. Faith of my fathers **92**

McCall, Marcia
  (jt. auth) Lieberman, A. 100 questions & answers about Parkinson [sic] disease **616.8**

McCall, Nathan
  Makes me wanna holler **92**

McCandlish, Stanton
  (jt. auth) Gelman, R. B. Protecting yourself online **342**

McCann, Graham, 1961-
  Cary Grant **92**

McCann, Sally, 1952-
  (jt. auth) Morris, M. Every sewer's guide to the perfect fit **646.4**

McCartan, Gràinne
  (jt. auth) Lees, C. C. Pregnancy and birth **618.2**

McCarthy, Joseph, 1908-1957
  About
  Herman, A. Joseph McCarthy **92**

McCarthy, Mary, 1912-1989
  How I grew **92**
  About
  Brightman, C. Writing dangerously: Mary McCarthy and her world **92**
  Kiernan, F. Seeing Mary plain: a life of Mary McCarthy **92**
  See/See also pages in the following book(s):
  American women fiction writers **813.009**
  Women writers at work p208-42 **808**

McCarthy, Mary Abigail, d. 1990
  See/See also pages in the following book(s):
  Pierpont, C. R. Passionate minds **810.9**

McCarthy, Peggy
  (jt. auth) Henschke, C. I. Lung cancer **616.99**

McCarthy, Susan
  (jt. auth) Masson, J. M. When elephants weep **591.5**

McCarty, Henry *See* Billy, the Kid

McCarver, Tim
Tim McCarver's Baseball for brain surgeons and other fans **796.357**

McClain, James L., 1944-
Japan, a modern history **952**

McClatchy, J. D., 1945-
Hazmat **811**
(ed) Christmas poems. See Christmas poems **821.008**
(ed) The Vintage book of contemporary world poetry. See The Vintage book of contemporary world poetry **808.81**

McClellan, George Brinton, 1826-1885
About
Sears, S. W. George B. McClellan **92**

McCloskey, Robert, 1914-2003
See/See also pages in the following book(s):
Marcus, L. S. Ways of telling **741.6**

McCloud, Bill, 1948-
What should we tell our children about Vietnam? **959.704**

McCloud, Scott
Reinventing comics **741.5**

McComb, Gordon
Robot builder's sourcebook **629.8**

McConnell, Malcolm
(jt. auth) Smith, J. B. The last mission **940.54**

McCormack, Mark H.
What they don't teach you at Harvard Business School **650.1**

McCormick, Malcolm
(jt. auth) Reynolds, N. No fixed points **792.8**

McCorvey, Norma
About
Hull, N. E. H. Roe v. Wade **344**

McCosker, John E.
(jt. auth) Ellis, R. Great white shark **597**

McCourt, Frank
Angela's ashes **92**
'Tis **92**

McCourt, John, 1965-
James Joyce **92**

McCourt, Malachy, 1931-
A monk swimming **92**
Singing my him song **92**

McCrum, Robert
The story of English **420**

McCullers, Carson, 1917-1967
The member of the wedding **812**
About
Savigneau, J. Carson McCullers **92**
See/See also pages in the following book(s):
American women fiction writers **813.009**

McCullough, Bob
(ed) My greatest day in football. See My greatest day in football **796.332**

McCullough, David G., 1933-
John Adams **92**
Mornings on horseback [biography of Theodore Roosevelt] **92**
The path between the seas **972.87**
Truman **92**

McCully, Emily Arnold
See/See also pages in the following book(s):
The Newbery & Caldecott medal books, 1986-2000 p179-87 **028.5**

McCumber, David
Playing off the rail **794.7**

McCune, Emma
About
Scroggins, D. Emma's war **962.4**

McDaniel, Hattie, 1895-1952
About
Jackson, C. Hattie: the life of Hattie McDaniel **92**

McDannell, Colleen
Heaven **236**

McDarrah, Fred W., 1926-
(jt. auth) McDarrah, G. S. The photography encyclopedia **770.2**

McDarrah, Gloria S.
The photography encyclopedia **770.2**

McDarrah, Timothy S.
(jt. auth) McDarrah, G. S. The photography encyclopedia **770.2**

McDermott, Maurice Joseph *See* McDermott, Mickey, 1928-2003

McDermott, Mickey, 1928-2003
A funny thing happened on the way to Cooperstown **92**

McDonald, Laughlin
The rights of racial minorities **342**

McDonough, Jimmy
Shakey: Neil Young's biography **92**

McDougall, Len
The outdoors almanac **796.5**

McDowell, Colin
Ralph Lauren **92**

McEnroe, John
You cannot be serious **92**

McFarlane, Rodger
The complete bedside companion **649.8**

McFarlane, Stewart
The complete book of t'ai chi **613.7**

McGary, Jane
(ed) Bulbs of North America. See Bulbs of North America **635.9**

McGearhart, Susea
(jt. auth) Ashcraft, T. O. Red sky in mourning **910.4**

McGhee, Fredrick L., 1861-1912
About
Nelson, P. D. Fredrick L. McGhee **92**

McGinn, Colin, 1950-
The making of a philosopher **92**

McGinnis, Terri
The well cat book **636.8**
The well dog book **636.7**

McGinniss, Joe
Fatal vision **364.1**

McGonigal, David
Antarctica and the Arctic **998**

McGovern, George S. (George Stanley), 1922-
The third freedom **363.8**
About
Ambrose, S. E. The wild blue **940.54**

McGowan, Mary P., 1959-
Heart fitness for life **616.1**

McGowan Chopra, Jo
(jt. auth) McGowan, M. P. Heart fitness for life **616.1**

McGowen, Cheryl
(jt. auth) Brown, R. The weaving, spinning, and dyeing book **746.1**

McGrath, Alister E., 1953-
In the beginning **220.5**

McGraw, Phillip C., 1950-
Life strategies **158**

McGraw-Hill concise encyclopedia of science & technology **503**

McGraw-Hill dictionary of bioscience **570.3**

McGraw-Hill dictionary of scientific and technical terms **503**

McGraw-Hill encyclopedia of science & technology **503**

McGraw-Hill encyclopedia of world biography. See Encyclopedia of world biography **920.003**

McGraw-Hill illustrated telecom dictionary. Clayton, J. **621.382**

McGraw-Hill's big red book of resumes **650.14**

McGraw-Hill's National Electrical Code handbook **621.3**

McGreal, Ian Philip, 1919-
(ed) Great thinkers of the Western world. See Great thinkers of the Western world **190**

McGregor, R. S. (Ronald Stuart)
(ed) The Oxford Hindi-English dictionary. See The Oxford Hindi-English dictionary **491**

McGregor, Ronald Stuart See McGregor, R. S. (Ronald Stuart)

McGuire, Bill, 1954-
A guide to the end of the world **001.9**

McHughen, Alan, 1954-
Pandora's picnic basket **641.3**

McIntyre, Deborah
(jt. auth) Donovan, D. M. What did I just say!?! **649**

McKay, Nellie Y.
(ed) The Norton anthology of African American literature. See The Norton anthology of African American literature **810.8**

McKee, Annie, 1955-
(jt. auth) Goleman, D. Primal leadership **658.4**

McKenna, Rosemary
(ed) The Classical Greek reader. See The Classical Greek reader **880.8**

McKenna, Stephen J.
(ed) The World's great speeches. See The World's great speeches **808.85**

McKenzie, Steven L., 1953-
King David **222**

McKhann, Charles F., 1930-
A time to die **179.7**

McKie, Robin
(jt. auth) Bodmer, W. F. The book of man **572.8**
(jt. auth) Stringer, C. B. African exodus **599.93**

McKillop, A. B., 1946-
The spinster & the prophet **941.08**

McKinney, Anne, 1948-
(ed) Resumes and cover letters that have worked. See Resumes and cover letters that have worked **650.14**

McKinney, Barbara
(jt. auth) Ross, J. Adoptable dog **636.7**

McKinney, Mike
Chariots of the damned **356**

McKnight, Kent H.
A field guide to mushrooms, North America **579.6**

McKnight, Vera B.
(jt. auth) McKnight, K. H. A field guide to mushrooms, North America **579.6**

McLanahan, David J.
(jt. auth) McLanahan, S. A. Surgery and its alternatives **617**

McLanahan, Sandra A.
Surgery and its alternatives **617**

McLaughlin, Mary Martin, 1919-
(ed) The Portable medieval reader. See The Portable medieval reader **808.8**
(ed) The Portable Renaissance reader. See The Portable Renaissance reader **808.8**

McLaughlin, Virginia Yans- See Yans-McLaughlin, Virginia, 1943-

McLeod, John
The history of India **954**

McLoughlin, William Gerald
After the Trail of Tears **970.004**

McLuhan, Marshall, 1911-1980
The global village **302.23**

About
Gordon, W. T. Marshall McLuhan **92**

McLynn, F. J.
Napoleon **92**

McLynn, Frank See McLynn, F. J.

McMahan, Elizabeth
The writer's handbook **808**

McManus, James
Positively Fifth Street **795.4**

McManus, Patrick F.
Into the twilight, endlessly grousing **817**

McMaster, Juliet
(ed) The Cambridge companion to Jane Austen. See The Cambridge companion to Jane Austen **823.009**

McMillan, John, 1951-
Reinventing the bazaar **330.1**

McMurtry, Larry
Crazy Horse **92**
Roads **917.3**
Walter Benjamin at the Dairy Queen **92**

McNally, Dennis
A long strange trip **920**

McNamara, Robert S., 1916-
In retrospect **959.704**

About
Hendrickson, P. The living and the dead **959.704**
See/See also pages in the following book(s):
Halberstam, D. The best and the brightest **973.922**

McNamee, Thomas, 1947-
The return of the wolf to Yellowstone **599.77**

McNeil, Alex, 1948-
Total television **791.45**

McPartland, James M.
(jt. auth) Ozonoff, S. A parent's guide to asperger syndrome and high-functioning autism **618.92**

McPhee, John A.
Annals of the former world **557**
Coming into the country **979.8**
The founding fish **597**
Irons in the fire **814**
Looking for a ship **910.4**
The ransom of Russian art **709.47**
The second John McPhee reader **818**

McPherson, Aimee Semple, 1890-1944
About
Epstein, D. M. Sister Aimee: the life of Aimee Semple McPherson **92**

McPherson, James M.
Abraham Lincoln and the second American Revolution **973.7**
Battle cry of freedom **973.7**
Drawn with the sword **973.7**
For cause and comrades **973.7**
(ed) To the best of my ability. See To the best of my ability **920**

McQueen, Steve, 1930-1980
About
Terrill, M. Steve McQueen **92**

McReynolds, Edwin C.
The Seminoles **970.004**

McShane, Marilyn D., 1956-
(ed) Encyclopedia of American prisons. See Encyclopedia of American prisons **365**

McShann, Jay
See/See also pages in the following book(s):
Dance, S. The world of Count Basie **920**

McSwiney, Sharon
The creative jeweler **739.27**

McTaggart, Lynne
The field: the quest for the secret force of the universe **615.5**

McVeigh, Timothy J.
About
Michel, L. American terrorist: Timothy McVeigh and
the Oklahoma City bombing   92
See/See also pages in the following book(s):
Dees, M. S., Jr. Gathering storm   322.4
McVicar, Wes
Clown act omnibus   791.3
McWhorter, Diane
Carry me home   976.1
McWhorter, John H.
Doing our own thing   306.44
Losing the race   305.8
Me. Hepburn, K.   92
Me and Shakespeare. Gollob, H.   822.3
Me talk pretty one day. Sedaris, D.   818
Meacham, Jon
(ed) Voices in our blood. See Voices in our blood
                                             323.1
Mead, Frank Spencer, 1898-1982
Handbook of denominations in the United States
                                             280
Mead, Margaret, 1901-1978
Blackberry winter   92
Coming of age in Samoa   306
See/See also pages in the following book(s):
Ware, S. Letter to the world   920
Mead, Walter Russell
Special providence   327.73
Meade, Marion, 1934-
Buster Keaton: cut to the chase   92
Dorothy Parker   92
The unruly life of Woody Allen   92
Meadowlands. Glück, L.   811
Meal planning See Menus; Nutrition
Meaney, Carron A., 1950-
(ed) Encyclopedia of animal rights and animal welfare.
See Encyclopedia of animal rights and animal wel-
fare   179
The **meaning** of it all. Feynman, R. P.   500
The **meaning** of relativity. Einstein, A. 530.1
The **meaning** of Star Trek. Richards, T.   791.45
Means illustrated construction dictionary 690
Means of ascent. Caro, R. A.
In Caro, R. A. The years of Lyndon Johnson v2
                                             92
Measles
See/See also pages in the following book(s):
Oldstone, M. B. A. Viruses, plagues, and history
                                             614.4
The **measure** of a man. Poitier, S.   92
The **measure** of all things. Alder, K.   526
The **measure** of our success. Edelman, M. W. 170
Measure twice, cut once. Abram, N.   684
Measurement
Ferguson, K. Measuring the universe   523.1
Measures See Weights and measures
Measuring America. Linklater, A.   973
Measuring eternity. Gorst, M.   115
Measuring the universe. Ferguson, K.   523.1
Meat
See also Cooking—Meat
Mecca (Saudi Arabia)
Wolfe, M. One thousand roads to Mecca   297
Mech, L. David
The way of the wolf   599.77
Méchain, Pierre-François-André, 1744-1804
About
Alder, K. The measure of all things   526
Mechanical engineering
Landmarks in mechanical engineering   621
Handbooks, manuals, etc.
Marks' standard handbook for mechanical engineers
                                             621

Mechanical engineers' handbook. See Marks' standard
handbook for mechanical engineers   621
Mechanics
Vogel, S. Cats' paws and catapults   571.4
Mecklenburg, Virginia M. (Virginia McCord), 1946-
Edward Hopper: the watercolors   759.13
Medal of honor. Mikaelian, A.   920
Medea. Euripides
In Euripides. Ten plays p31-63   882
Medea. Seneca, L. A., the Younger
In The Portable Roman reader p487-527   870.8
Media See Mass media
Medical abbreviations & eponyms. Sloane, S. B.
                                             610.3
Medical botany
Chevallier, A. Encyclopedia of herbal medicine
                                             615
Coffey, T. The history and folklore of North American
wildflowers   582.13
Davis, W. One river   581.6
Rodale's illustrated encyclopedia of herbs   635
Sumner, J. The natural history of medicinal plants
                                             581.6
Medical care
See also Health self-care; Home care services
Consumer reports complete guide to health services for
seniors   362.6
Garrett, L. Betrayal of trust   362.1
Rovner, J. Health care policy and politics A to Z
                                             362.1
Medical diagnosis See Diagnosis
Medical ethics
See also Human experimentation in medicine;
Right to die
The Ethics of organ transplants   174
Moreno, J. D. Undue risk   174
Munson, R. Raising the dead   174
See/See also pages in the following book(s):
Peck, M. S. Denial of the soul   179.7
Medical genetics
The Double-edged helix   599.93
Flesh of my flesh   174
Teichler-Zallen, D. Does it run in the family?
                                             616
Wade, N. Life script   616
Medical jurisprudence
Evans, C. The casebook of forensic detection 614
Medical practice
Blackwell complementary and alternative medicine
                                             615.5
Medical sociology See Social medicine
Medici family See House of Medici
Medici, House of See House of Medici
The **Medici,** Michelangelo, & the art of late Renaissance
Florence   709.45
Medicinal plants See Medical botany
Medicine
See also Alternative medicine; Biochemistry; Ho-
listic medicine; Nursing; Psychosomatic medicine;
Sports medicine; Surgery; types of medicine; and
names of diseases and groups of diseases
American College of Physicians complete home medi-
cal guide   616.02
American Medical Association family medical guide
                                             616.02
The Doctors book of home remedies   616.02
Dollemore, D. The doctors book of home remedies for
seniors   613
Groopman, J. E. Second opinions   610
The Harvard Medical School family health guide
                                             610
Human diseases and conditions   616
Johns Hopkins symptoms and remedies   616.02
Mayo Clinic family health book   613
The Merck manual of medical information   616.02

Medicine—*Continued*

Moyers, B. Healing and the mind   616
  See/See also pages in the following book(s):
Goleman, D. Emotional intelligence p164-85
            152.4

Bibliography
Consumer health information source book   016.613

Dictionaries
Dorland's illustrated medical dictionary   610.3
Mosby's medical, nursing, & allied health dictionary
            610.3
The Oxford illustrated companion to medicine
            610.3
Sloane, S. B. Medical abbreviations & eponyms
            610.3
Stedman's medical dictionary   610.3
Taber's cyclopedic medical dictionary   610.3

Encyclopedias
American Medical Association complete medical encyclopedia   610.3
Gale encyclopedia of medicine   610.3

Handbooks, manuals, etc.
Current medical diagnosis and treatment   610.3
Merck manual of diagnosis and therapy   610.3

History
The Cambridge illustrated history of medicine
            610.9
Friedman, M. Medicine's 10 greatest discoveries
            610.9
Greenberg, A. The art of chemistry   540
Porter, R. Blood and guts   610.9
Porter, R. The greatest benefit to mankind   610.9
Western medicine: an illustrated history   610.9

Information services
Consumer health information source book   016.613

Law and legislation
See also Medical jurisprudence

Philosophy
Pollack, R. The missing moment   610

Practice
See Medical practice

Research
Gallo, R. C. Virus hunting   616.97
Peters, C. J. Virus hunter   614.5
  See/See also pages in the following book(s):
Pert, C. Molecules of emotion   612.8

Social aspects
See Social medicine

Vocational guidance
Wischnitzer, S. Barron's guide to medical & dental schools   610.69

United States—History
Cassedy, J. H. Medicine in America: a short history
            610.9
Grob, G. N. The deadly truth   616

Medicine, Pediatric *See* Children—Diseases
Medicine, Veterinary *See* Veterinary medicine
Medicine in America: a short history. Cassedy, J. H.
            610.9
Medicine quest. Plotkin, M.   615
Medicine's 10 greatest discoveries. Friedman, M.
            610.9

Medieval architecture
Prache, A. Cathedrals of Europe   726
Snyder, J. Medieval art   709.02

Medieval art
Lowden, J. Early Christian & Byzantine art
            709.02
Snyder, J. Medieval art   709.02
Medieval children. Orme, N.   305.23
Medieval church history *See* Church history—600-1500, Middle Ages

Medieval civilization
Burns, T. S. A history of the Ostrogoths   909.07
Cahill, T. How the Irish saved civilization   941.5

Gies, F. Life in a medieval village   940.1
Gies, J. Life in a medieval city   940.1
Herlihy, D. The black death and the transformation of the west py   940.1
Tuchman, B. W. A distant mirror   944

Encyclopedias
Medieval England   942
Medieval England   942
Medieval English literature
  In The Oxford anthology of English literature v1
            820.8

Medieval literature
Collections
The Portable medieval reader   808.8
Medieval philosophy
The Renaissance philosophy of man   189
Rubenstein, R. E. Aristotle's children   189
Medina, John, 1956-
The clock of ages   612.6
Meditation
Breath sweeps mind   294.3
Kaplan, A. Jewish meditation   296.7
Meditations. Marcus Aurelius, Emperor of Rome
            188

Mediterranean civilization
Freeman, C. Egypt, Greece, and Rome   909
Mediterranean cooking
Lacalamita, T. The ultimate pressure cooker cookbook
            641.5
A **Mediterranean** feast. Wright, C. A.   641
Mediterranean region
Antiquities
Perrottet, T. Route 66 A.D.   910.4
Description
Perrottet, T. Route 66 A.D.   910.4
Theroux, P. The Pillars of Hercules   910.4
Gazetteers
Grant, M. A guide to the ancient world   938.003
Social life and customs
Wright, C. A. A Mediterranean feast   641
Medved, Diane
  (jt. auth) Medved, M. Saving childhood   305.23
Medved, Michael
Saving childhood   305.23
Medvedev, Roy Aleksandrovich, 1925-
Let history judge   947.084
Medwick, Cathleen
Teresa of Avila   92
Meeks, Wayne A.
  (ed) Bible. The HarperCollins study Bible   220.5
Mehta, Ved, 1934-
All for love   92
Meier, John P.
A marginal Jew   232.9
Meier, Matt S.
Notable Latino Americans   920.003
Meier, Richard, 1934-
Building the Getty   708
Meiji, Emperor of Japan, 1852-1912
About
Keene, D. Emperor of Japan: Meiji and His world, 1852-1912   92
  See/See also pages in the following book(s):
Seagrave, S. The Yamato dynasty   952
Mein Kampf. Hitler, A.   92
Meisami, Julie Scott, 1937-
  (ed) Encyclopedia of Arabic literature. *See* Encyclopedia of Arabic literature   892
Mekong River
Description
Gargan, E. A. A river's tale   915.9
Melbourne, William Lamb, 2nd Viscount, 1779-1848
  See/See also pages in the following book(s):
Strachey, L. Queen Victoria p71-133   92

Mellow, James R.
Hemingway: a life without consequences   92
Melton, J. Gordon
American religions   200.9
The encyclopedia of American religions   200.9
Encyclopedic handbook of cults in America   291.9
The vampire book   398
(ed) Encyclopedia of African American religions. See
Encyclopedia of African American religions
200.9
(ed) Encyclopedia of occultism & parapsychology. See
Encyclopedia of occultism & parapsychology
133
(ed) Religions of the world. See Religions of the world
291
Meltzer, Allan H.
A history of the Federal Reserve v1   332.1
Meltzoff, Andrew N.
(jt. auth) Gopnik, A. The scientist in the crib
155.4
Melville, Herman, 1819-1891
Moby Dick; criticism
In Said, E. W. Reflections on exile and other essays
p356-71   814
The poems of Herman Melville   811
About
Hardwick, E. Herman Melville   92
Parker, H. Herman Melville   92
Robertson-Lorant, L. Melville   92
See/See also pages in the following book(s):
Kazin, A. An American procession p131-60   810.9
Matthiessen, F. O. American renaissance p371-514
810.9
The **member** of the wedding. McCullers, C.   812
Memoirs See Autobiography
Memoirs. Rockefeller, D.   92
Memoirs. Teller, E.   92
Memoirs and selected letters. Grant, U. S. 92
Memories, dreams, reflections. Jung, C. G. 92
Memory
Goldman, B. Brain fitness   153.1
Schacter, D. L. Searching for memory   153.1
Schacter, D. L. The seven sins of memory   153.1
Victoroff, J. I. Saving your brain   612.8
Encyclopedias
Turkington, C. The encyclopedia of memory and mem-
ory disorders   153.1
Memphis Belle (Airplane)
See/See also pages in the following book(s):
Morgan, R. The man who flew the Memphis Belle
92
Men
Ban Breathnach, S. A man's journey to simple abun-
dance   158
Bordo, S. The male body   305.31
Faludi, S. Stiffed   305.31
Health and hygiene
Buhner, S. H. Vital man   613
Men's health concerns sourcebook   613
Reed, J. The black man's guide to good health
613
Simon, H. B. The Harvard Medical School guide to
men's health   613
Psychology
Ambrose, S. E. Comrades   302.3
Bly, R. Iron John   305.31
Dutton, D. G. The batterer   362.82
July, W. W., II. Understanding the tin man   158
Lazear, J. The man who mistook his job for a life
155.2
Levinson, D. J. The seasons of a man's life
155.6
Sheehy, G. Understanding men's passages   305.31
Sexual behavior
Thornhill, R. A natural history of rape   364.1

Men at work: the craft of baseball. Will, G. F.
796.357
Men in the off hours. Carson, A.   811
Men like women who like themselves. Carter, S.
158
Men of mathematics. Bell, E. T.   920
The **men** who wear the star. Robinson, C. M.
976.4
Menand, Louis
The Metaphysical Club   973.9
Menander, of Athens, ca. 342-ca. 292 B.C.
See/See also pages in the following book(s):
Hamilton, E. The echo of Greece p139-54   880.9
Mencken, H. L. (Henry Louis), 1880-1956
The American language   427
My life as author and editor   92
A second Mencken chrestomathy   818
(ed) A New dictionary of quotations on historical prin-
ciples from ancient and modern sources. See A New
dictionary of quotations on historical principles from
ancient and modern sources   808.88
About
Teachout, T. The skeptic: the life of H.L. Mencken
92
See/See also pages in the following book(s):
Vidal, G. United States—essays, 1952-1992 p750-67
814
Mencken, Henry Louis See Mencken, H. L. (Henry
Louis), 1880-1956
Mendel, Gregor, 1822-1884
About
Henig, R. M. The monk in the garden: how Gregor
Mendel and his pea plants solved the mystery of in-
heritance   92
See/See also pages in the following book(s):
Flowers, C. Instability rules   509
Malone, J. W. It doesn't take a rocket scientist
920
Tudge, C. The impact of the gene   576.5
Mendel, Johann Gregor See Mendel, Gregor, 1822-
1884
Mendeleev, Dmitri I.
About
Strathern, P. Mendeleyev's dream   540.9
See/See also pages in the following book(s):
Horvitz, L. A. Eureka!: scientific breakthroughs that
changed the world   509
Mendeleyev's dream. Strathern, P.   540.9
Mendelson, Cheryl
Home comforts   640
Mendelssohn, Felix, 1809-1847
About
Mercer-Taylor, P. J. The life of Mendelssohn   92
Mendelssohn-Bartholdy, Jacob Ludwig Felix See Men-
delssohn, Felix, 1809-1847
Mengele, Josef
See/See also pages in the following book(s):
Lifton, R. J. The Nazi doctors p337-83   940.53
Menninger, Jeanetta Lyle
(jt. auth) Menninger, K. A. Love against hate
150.19
Menninger, Karl A. (Karl Augustus), 1893-1990
Love against hate   150.19
Mennonites
See also Amish
Kraybill, D. B. On the backroad to heaven   289.7
Menopause
Greer, G. The change   618.1
Huston, J. E. Menopause   618.1
Love, S. M. Dr. Susan Love's menopause and hor-
mone book   618.1
Moore, M. The only menopause guide you'll need
618.1
Seaman, B. The greatest experiment ever performed on
women   615

Menopause—*Continued*
Seibel, M. M. The soy solution for menopause
    618.1
Sheehy, G. The silent passage: menopause   **618.1**
Warga, C. L. Menopause and the mind   **618.1**
Menopause and the mind. Warga, C. L.   **618.1**
Men's clothing
Peacock, J. Men's fashion   **391**
Men's fashion. Peacock, J.   **391**
Men's health concerns sourcebook   **613**
Mental healing
Wise, A. Awakening the mind   **615.8**
Mental health
Restak, R. M. Mozart's brain and the fighter pilot
    612.8
Dictionaries
Encyclopedia of mental health   **616.89**
Mental illness
    See also Personality disorders
Amen, D. Change your brain, change your life
    616.89
Andreasen, N. C. Brave new brain   **616.89**
Carter, R. Helping someone with mental illness
    616.89
Neugeboren, J. Transforming madness   **616.89**
Porter, R. Madness   **616.89**
Slater, L. Prozac diary   **616.89**
Whitaker, R. Mad in America   **616.89**
Dictionaries
Encyclopedia of mental health   **616.89**
Encyclopedias
The Gale encyclopedia of mental disorders
    616.89
Jurisprudence
    See Insanity defense
Mental suggestion
    See also Brainwashing
Mental tests *See* Intelligence tests
Mentally ill
Neugeboren, J. Transforming madness   **616.89**
Institutional care
    See also Psychiatric hospitals
Mentally ill children *See* Emotionally disturbed children
Menus
Allen, S. L. In the devil's garden   **641**
Lagasse, E. Every day's a party   **642**
Sorosky, M. Fast & festive meals for the Jewish holidays
    641.5
Stewart, M. Great parties   **642**
Stewart, M. Martha Stewart's menus for entertaining
    642
Menzel, Peter
Robo sapiens: evolution of a new species   **629.8**
Menzer, Joe
The wildest ride   **796.72**
Mercer-Taylor, Peter Jameson
The life of Mendelssohn   **92**
Merchandising *See* Marketing
The **Merck** index   **615**
Merck manual of diagnosis and therapy   **610.3**
The **Merck** manual of medical information   **616.02**
The **Merck** veterinary manual   **636.089**
Mercuri, Becky
Food festival, U.S.A.   **641.5**
The **mercy**. Levine, P.   **811**
Mercy killing *See* Euthanasia
Mere Christianity. Lewis, C. S.   **230**
Meredith, William, 1919-
Effort at speech   **811**
Mergen, Bernard
Snow in America   **551.57**
Merleau-Ponty, Jean Jacques Maurice *See* Merleau-Ponty, Maurice, 1908-1961

Merleau-Ponty, Maurice, 1908-1961
    See/See also pages in the following book(s):
Said, E. W. Reflections on exile and other essays p1-14
    814
Merrell, James Hart, 1953-
(ed) American encounters. See American encounters
    970.004
(ed) American nations. See American nations
    970.004
Merriam-Webster's biographical dictionary   **920.003**
Merriam-Webster's collegiate dictionary   **423**
Merriam-Webster's collegiate encyclopedia   **031**
Merriam-Webster's collegiate thesaurus   **423**
Merriam-Webster's crossword puzzle dictionary
    793.73
Merriam-Webster's dictionary of allusions. Webber, E.
    803
Merriam-Webster's dictionary of American writers
    920.003
Merriam-Webster's encyclopedia of literature   **803**
Merriam-Webster's encyclopedia of world religions
    200.3
Merriam-Webster's geographical dictionary   **910.3**
Merrill, A. Roger
(jt. auth) Covey, S. R. First things first   **158**
Merrill, James
The changing light at Sandover   **811**
The collected poems of James Merrill   **811**
Merrill, Rebecca R.
(jt. auth) Covey, S. R. First things first   **158**
Merriman, Brian, 1757-1808
The midnight court; criticism
  In Heaney, S. The redress of poetry   **821.009**
    See/See also pages in the following book(s):
Heaney, S. The redress of poetry   **821.009**
Merriman, John M.
The stones of Balazuc   **944**
Merritt, George
(jt. auth) Escott, C. Hank Williams   **92**
Merry Christmas!. Marling, K. A.   **394.26**
Merton, Louis Thomas *See* Merton, Thomas, 1915-1968
Merton, Thomas, 1915-1968
The Asian journal of Thomas Merton   **248**
Intimate Merton   **92**
Love and living   **248**
New seeds of contemplation   **248**
No man is an island   **248**
The seven storey mountain   **92**
(ed) Gandhi, M. Gandhi on non-violence   **322.4**
Merwin, W. S. (William Stanley), 1927-
The folding cliffs   **811**
The pupil   **811**
The vixen   **811**
(tr) Dante Alighieri. Purgatorio   **851**
Merwin, William Stanley *See* Merwin, W. S. (William Stanley), 1927-
Merz, Caroline
Post-war literature 1945 to the present
  In Backgrounds to English literature v5   **820.9**
Mesopotamia *See* Iraq
Messadié, Gérald
A history of the devil   **291**
Messenger, Charles, 1941-
(ed) Reader's guide to military history. See Reader's guide to military history   **355**
The **messenger:** the rise and fall of Elijah Muhammad. Evanzz, K.   **92**
Messer, Thomas M., 1920-
Vasily Kandinsky   **759.4**
Messori, Vittorio, 1941-
(ed) John Paul II, Pope. Crossing the threshold of hope
    282
Metals, Transmutation of *See* Alchemy
Metamorphoses. Ovid   **873**
Metaphors dictionary   **423**

The **Metaphysical** Club. Menand, L.   973.9
Metaphysics
  Menand, L. The Metaphysical Club   973.9
Metaphysics. Aristotle
  In Aristotle. The basic works of Aristotle p689-926
                                               888
Metcalf, Allan A.
  How we talk   427
  Predicting new words   420
  (jt. auth) Barnhart, D. K. America in so many words
                                               422
Meteorites
  Norton, O. R. The Cambridge encyclopedia of meteor-
    ites   523.5
  Norton, O. R. Rocks from space   523.5
  See/See also pages in the following book(s):
  Bevan, A. W. R. Meteorites: a journey through space
    and time   523.5
Meteorites: a journey through space and time. Bevan, A.
  W. R.   523.5
Meteorology
  See also Climate; Weather; Weather forecasting
  Hamblyn, R. The invention of clouds   551.57
  Monmonier, M. S. Air apparent   551.6
  Reynolds, R. Cambridge guide to the weather
                                               551.5
  Rittner, D. A to Z of scientists in weather and climate
                                               920.003
          Encyclopedias
  Encyclopedia of atmospheric sciences   551.5
Methodist Church
  Tomkins, S. John Wesley   92
Methylphenidate hydrochloride *See* Ritalin
Metric system
  Alder, K. The measure of all things   526
Metropolitan government
  See also Municipal government
Metropolitan Museum of Art (New York, N.Y.)
  Avery, K. J. American drawings and watercolors in the
    Metropolitan Museum of Art v1   759.13
  Campbell, T. Tapestry in the Renaissance   746
  Cikovsky, N., Jr. Winslow Homer   759.13
  Egyptian art in the age of the pyramids. See Egyptian
    art in the age of the pyramids   709.32
  Leonardo, da Vinci. Leonardo da Vinci, master drafts-
    man   741
  Hoving, T. Making the mummies dance   92
Metropolitan Opera (New York, N.Y.)
  Fiedler, J. Molto agitato   792.5
Mets (Baseball team) *See* New York Mets (Baseball
  team)
Metzger, Bruce Manning
  (ed) The Oxford companion to the Bible. See The Ox-
    ford companion to the Bible   220.3
  (ed) The Oxford guide to ideas & issues of the Bible.
    See The Oxford guide to ideas & issues of the Bible
                                               220.3
Metzger, Philip W., 1931-
  The artist's illustrated encyclopedia   703
Mexican American cooking
  Tausend, M. Cocina de la familia   641.5
Mexican American literature *See* American literature—
  Mexican American authors
Mexican Americans
  Marin, C. Chicano visions   709.73
Mexican cooking
  Bayless, R. Rick Bayless's Mexican kitchen
                                               641.5
  Kennedy, D. The essential cuisines of Mexico
                                               641.5
  Kennedy, D. My Mexico   641.5
Mexican Indians *See* Native Americans—Mexico
Mexican national characteristics
  Paz, O. The labyrinth of solitude   864
  Riding, A. Distant neighbors   972.08

Mexican poetry
          Collections
  Reversible monuments   861
Mexicans
          United States
  See also Mexican Americans
Mexico
          Antiquities
  Smith, M. E. The Aztecs   972
          Civilization
  Paz, O. The labyrinth of solitude   864
          Description
  Sacks, O. W. Oaxaca journal   587
          History
  Díaz del Castillo, B. The discovery and conquest of
    Mexico, 1517-1521   972
  Foster, L. V. A brief history of Mexico   972
  Katz, F. The life and times of Pancho Villa 92
  Kirkwood, B. The history of Mexico   972
  Meyer, M. C. The course of Mexican history   972
  The Oxford history of Mexico   972
  Prescott, W. H. History of the conquest of Mexico
                                               972
  Womack, J. Zapata and the Mexican Revolution
                                               972.08
          Politics and government
  Fuentes, C. A new time for Mexico   972.08
  Guillermoprieto, A. Looking for history   972
          Social life and customs
  Kennedy, D. My Mexico   641.5
  Riding, A. Distant neighbors   972.08
Mexico City (Mexico)
          Social conditions
  Lewis, O. The children of Sánchez   972.08
Meyer, Michael C.
  The course of Mexican history   972
  (ed) The Oxford history of Mexico. See The Oxford
    history of Mexico   972
Meyerink, Kory L., 1954-
  (ed) Printed sources. See Printed sources   929
Meyers, Carol L.
  (ed) Women in scripture. See Women in scripture
                                               220.9
Meyers, Jeffrey, 1939-
  Orwell   92
MI6 (Great Britain) *See* Great Britain. MI6
MI6. Dorril, S.   327.12
Michael, Michele
  The new apartment book   747
Michael, Robert
  Nazi-Deutsch/Nazi-German   943.086
Michael X, 1933-1974
  See/See also pages in the following book(s):
  Naipaul, V. S. The writer and the world p141-204
                                               824
Michaelis, David
  N.C. Wyeth   92
Michel, Lou
  American terrorist: Timothy McVeigh and the Oklaho-
    ma City bombing   92
Michelangelo & the Pope's ceiling. King, R.   759.5
Michelangelo Buonarroti, 1475-1564
          About
  King, R. Michelangelo & the Pope's ceiling
                                               759.5
  The Medici, Michelangelo, & the art of late Renais-
    sance Florence   709.45
Micheli, Lyle J., 1940-
  The sports medicine bible for young athletes
                                               617.1
Michelin guides   910.2
Michener, David
  Taylor's guide to ground covers   635.9
Michener, James A., 1907-1997
  The bridge at Andau   943.9

Michener, James A., 1907-1997—*Continued*
Iberia 914.6
Return to paradise 990
Michler, J. Marsha
The magic of crazy quilting 746.46
Microbes *See* Bacteria
Microbes and people: an A-Z of microorganisms in our lives. Sankaran, N. 579
Microbiology
See also Biotechnology
Bakalar, N. Where the germs are 616
Biddle, W. A field guide to germs 616
Dictionaries
Sankaran, N. Microbes and people: an A-Z of microorganisms in our lives 579
Microchip: an idea, its genesis, and the revolution it created. Zygmont, J. 338.7
Microcomputers
Gookin, D. PCs for dummies 004
White, R. How computers work 004
Maintenance and repair
Mueller, S. Upgrading and repairing PCs 621.39
Upgrading
Mueller, S. Upgrading and repairing PCs 621.39
Microelectronics
Zygmont, J. Microchip: an idea, its genesis, and the revolution it created 338.7
Micromegas. Voltaire
In Voltaire. The portable Voltaire 848
Microorganisms
See also Bacteria
Karlen, A. Biography of a germ 579.3
Microsoft Corporation
Maxwell, F. A. Bad boy Ballmer 92
Microsoft Encarta college thesaurus 423
Mid-career changes *See* Career changes
Middle age
See also Aging
Cohen, G. D. The creative age 305.24
Levinson, D. J. The seasons of a man's life 155.6
Levinson, D. J. The seasons of a woman's life 155.6
Peck, B. The baby boomer body book 613
Sheehy, G. New passages 305.24
Sheehy, G. Understanding men's passages 305.31
Middle Ages
See also Church history—600-1500, Middle Ages; Europe—History—476-1492; Medieval civilization; World history—14th century
Adams, H. Mont-Saint-Michel and Chartres 726
Orme, N. Medieval children 305.23
Dictionaries
Dictionary of the Middle Ages 940.1
Encyclopedias
The Encyclopedia of the Middle Ages 909.07
History
Gies, F. Life in a medieval village 940.1
Gies, J. Life in a medieval city 940.1
The New Cambridge medieval history 940.1
Middle and junior high school library catalog 011.6
Middle East
See also Arab countries
Antiquities
Frankfort, H. The art and architecture of the ancient Orient 709.39
Civilization
Civilizations of the ancient Near East 939
Description
Feiler, B. S. Walking the Bible 915.6
Horwitz, T. Baghdad without a map, and other misadventures in Arabia 915.6
Kaplan, R. D. The ends of the earth 910.4
Mackintosh-Smith, T. Travels with a tangerine 910.4

Dictionaries
Hiro, D. A dictionary of the Middle East 956
History
The Continuum political encyclopedia of the Middle East 956
Lewis, B. The Middle East 956
Lewis, B. What went wrong? 956
Politics and government
The Continuum political encyclopedia of the Middle East 956
Friedman, T. L. From Beirut to Jerusalem 956
The Middle East 956
Miller, J. God has ninety-nine names 956
The **Middle** East [CQ Press] 956
Middle East War, 1991 *See* Persian Gulf War, 1991
Middle Eastern cooking
Roden, C. The new book of Middle Eastern food 641.5
The **middle** of everywhere. Pipher, M. B. 325.73
Middlebrook, Diane Wood
Anne Sexton 92
Suits me: the double life of Billy Tipton 92
Middleton, John, 1921-
(ed) Africa: an encyclopedia for students. See Africa: an encyclopedia for students 960
(ed) Encyclopedia of Africa, south of the Sahara. See Encyclopedia of Africa, south of the Sahara 967
Middletown (N.J.)
Sheehy, G. Middletown, America 974.9
Middletown, America. Sheehy, G. 974.9
Midnight in Sicily. Robb, P. 945
Midnight in the garden of good and evil. Berendt, J. 975.8
Midnight salvage. Rich, A. 811
Midway, Battle of, 1942
Ballard, R. D. Return to Midway 940.54
Prange, G. W. Miracle at Midway 940.54
Midwifery *See* Midwives
Midwives
Vincent, P. Baby catcher 618.2
Mieder, Wolfgang
(ed) A Dictionary of American proverbs. See A Dictionary of American proverbs 398.9
Migration *See* Immigration and emigration
Migrations and cultures. Sowell, T. 304.8
Mikaelian, Allen
Medal of honor 920
Mikkelsen, Ejnar, 1880-1971
Two against the ice 998
Mikula, Mark F.
(ed) Great American court cases. See Great American court cases 347
Miles, Barry, 1943-
The Beat Hotel 810.9
Miles, Elizabeth
(jt. auth) Schneider, E. L. Ageless: take control of your age and stay youthful for life 612.6
Miles, Jack, 1942-
Christ: a crisis in the life of God 232
God: a biography 231
Miles and me: biography of Miles Davis. Troupe, Q. 92
Milestones of science. Suplee, C. 509
Milford, Nancy, 1938-
Savage beauty: the life of Edna St. Vincent Millay 92
Militant Islam reaches America. Pipes, D. 320.5
Military aeronautics
See also World War, 1914-1918—Aerial operations; World War, 1939-1945—Aerial operations
Boyne, W. J. Beyond the wild blue 358.4
Knott, R. C. A heritage of wings 359.9
McKinney, M. Chariots of the damned 356

Military airplanes
    Fredriksen, J. C. Warbirds   **623.7**
Military art and science
    See also Military aeronautics; Naval art and science
    Clausewitz, C. von. On war   **355**
    Cohen, E. A. Supreme command   **355**
    O'Connell, R. L. Soul of the sword   **623.4**
    Volkman, E. Science goes to war   **623**
    Weapons & warfare   **623.4**
        Dictionaries
    Dictionary of military terms   **355**
Military forces *See* Navies
Military history
    See also Naval history
    The Book of war   **355**
    Coffey, M. Days of infamy   **355**
    Connelly, O. On war and leadership   **355.3**
    Davis, P. K. 100 decisive battles   **904**
    De Pauw, L. G. Battle cries and lullabies   **355**
    Hanson, V. D. Carnage and culture   **904**
    Hanson, V. D. The soul of battle   **355**
    The Oxford companion to military history   **355**
    Reader's guide to military history   **355**
    Shawcross, W. Deliver us from evil   **909.82**
        Dictionaries
    Kohn, G. C. Dictionary of wars   **355**
    Magill's guide to military history   **355**
        Encyclopedias
    Encyclopedia of conflicts since World War II
        909.82
Military personnel
    See also Admirals; Soldiers
Military policy
    See also National security
        United States
    See also Strategic Defense Initiative
    Freedman, L. Kennedy's wars   **973.922**
    Woodward, B. Bush at war   **973.931**
Military tanks
    Wright, P. Tank: the progress of a monstrous war machine   **358**
Military weapons
    Maas, P. Manhunt   **364.1**
    Weapons & warfare   **623.4**
Militia movements
    Dees, M. S., Jr. Gathering storm   **322.4**
    Stern, K. S. A force upon the plain   **322.4**
Milito, Lynda
    Mafia wife   **364.1**
Milk-free diet
    Lanza, L. Totally dairy-free cooking   **641.5**
Milkowski, Bill, 1954-
    Swing it!   **781.65**
Milky Way
    Croswell, K. The alchemy of the heavens   **523.1**
Mill, John Stuart, 1806-1873
    Autobiography   **92**
Millar, David
    The Cambridge dictionary of scientists. See The Cambridge dictionary of scientists   **920.003**
Millay, Edna St. Vincent, 1892-1950
    Collected poems   **811**
        About
    Milford, N. Savage beauty: the life of Edna St. Vincent Millay   **92**
    See/See also pages in the following book(s):
    Gilbert, S. M. No man's land v3 p57-120   **820.9**
Millenarianism *See* Millennium
Millennium
    The 21st century   **909.83**
    Gould, S. J. Questioning the millennium   **901**
    Weber, E. J. Apocalypses   **291**
    The **millennium** problems. Devlin, K. J.   **510**

Miller, Alice
    Paths of life   **306.8**
Miller, Arthur, 1915-
    Broken glass   **812**
    The crucible   **812**
    Death of a salesman   **812**
    Echoes down the corridor   **814**
    A view from the bridge   **812**
    See/See also pages in the following book(s):
    Playwrights at work   **812.009**
Miller, Bertha E. Mahony, 1882-1969
    (ed) Newbery Medal books, 1922-1955. See Newbery Medal books, 1922-1955   **028.5**
Miller, Cathy
    Harvesting, preserving, and arranging dried flowers
        745.92
Miller, Char
    Gifford Pinchot and the making of modern environmentalism   **92**
Miller, Christine Marie, 1950-
    (jt. auth) Ancell, R. M. The biographical dictionary of World War II generals and flag officers
        920.003
Miller, Donald L., 1944-
    City of the century   **977.3**
Miller, Edwin Haviland
    Salem is my dwelling place: a life of Nathaniel Hawthorne   **92**
Miller, Emmett
        About
    Tosches, N. Where dead voices gather   **92**
Miller, Flora Whitney
        About
    Biddle, F. M. The Whitney women and the museum they made   **708**
Miller, Henry, 1891-1980
    Henry Miller on writing   **818**
        About
    Keeley, E. Inventing paradise   **818**
Miller, James *See* Miller, Jim, 1947-
Miller, Jim, 1947-
    Flowers in the dustbin   **781.66**
Miller, Joanne
    (jt. auth) Jaderstrom, S. Complete office handbook
        651.8
Miller, John
    The cell: inside the 9/11 plot and why the FBI and CIA failed to stop it   **973.931**
Miller, John Chester, 1907-1991
    The Federalist era, 1789-1801   **973.4**
Miller, Joseph
    (ed) Sears list of subject headings. See Sears list of subject headings   **025.4**
Miller, Joseph Calder
    (ed) Macmillan encyclopedia of world slavery. See Macmillan encyclopedia of world slavery   **326**
Miller, Judith, 1948-
    Germs   **358**
    God has ninety-nine names   **956**
Miller, Judith, 1951-
    Care and repair of everyday treasures   **745.1**
Miller, Kenneth R. (Kenneth Raymond), 1948-
    Finding Darwin's God   **231.7**
Miller, Lee, 1907-1977
    See/See also pages in the following book(s):
    Prose, F. The lives of the muses   **920**
Miller, Mary Ellen
    The gods and symbols of ancient Mexico and the Maya   **299**
Miller, Nathan, 1927-
    War at sea   **940.54**
Miller, R. Baxter
    The art and imagination of Langston Hughes   **818**
Miller, Richard Lawrence
    The encyclopedia of addictive drugs   **615**

Miller, Steven F.
(ed) Remembering slavery. See Remembering slavery
326

Miller, Sukie
Finding hope when a child dies 291

Miller, Susan
Planets and possibilities 133.5

Miller, Ted
Kiplinger's practical guide to your money
332.024

Miller, Tice L.
(ed) Cambridge guide to American theatre. See Cambridge guide to American theatre 792.03

Miller, William Lee
Arguing about slavery 973.5
Lincoln's virtues 92

Millett, Allan Reed
(jt. auth) Murray, W. A war to be won 940.53

Millinery See Hats

Millions of monarchs, bunches of beetles. Waldbauer, G.
595.7

Mills, Beverly
Desperation entertaining 642

Mills, Dick
Aquarium fish 639.34

Mills, Stephen Tukel
(jt. auth) Fouts, R. Next of kin 156

Milman, Hannah
(jt. auth) Stewart, M. Great American wreaths
745.92

Milne, A. A. (Alan Alexander), 1882-1956
See/See also pages in the following book(s):
Wullschläger, J. Inventing wonderland 820.9

Milne, Alan Alexander See Milne, A. A. (Alan Alexander), 1882-1956

Milne, Lorus Johnson, 1912-
The Audubon Society field guide to North American insects and spiders 595.7

Milne, Margery Joan Greene, 1914-
(jt. auth) Milne, L. J. The Audubon Society field guide to North American insects and spiders 595.7

Milner, Clyde A., 1948-
(ed) The Oxford history of the American West. See The Oxford history of the American West 978

Milner-Gulland, R. R.
Cultural atlas of Russia and the former Soviet Union
947

Miłosz, Czesław
The collected poems, 1931-1987 891.8
The history of Polish literature 891.8
Milosz's ABCs 891.8
New and collected poems 1931-2001 891.8
A roadside dog 891.8
To begin where I am 891.8
(ed) A Book of lumininous things. See A Book of lumininous things 808.81

Milosz's ABCs. Miłosz, C. 891.8

Milton, Giles, 1966-
Big Chief Elizabeth 975.5
The riddle and the knight 910.4

Milton, John, 1608-1674
Paradise lost
In Milton, J. The Riverside Milton 821
The Riverside Milton 821
Samson Agonistes
In The Oxford anthology of English literature v1
820.8
See/See also pages in the following book(s):
Bloom, H. The Western canon 809
Brooks, C. The well wrought urn 821.009
Durant, W. J. The age of Louis XIV p207-43
940.2
Kermode, F. An appetite for poetry 801
Vendler, H. H. Coming of age as a poet 820.9

Milton, Joyce
Tramp: the life of Charlie Chaplin 92

Min, Anchee, 1957-
Red azalea 92

Mind See Intellect

Mind and body
Abram, D. The spell of the sensuous 128
Chopra, D. Ageless body, timeless mind 612.6
Chopra, D. Overcoming addictions 616.86
Devlin, K. J. Goodbye, Descartes 128
McTaggart, L. The field: the quest for the secret force of the universe 615.5
Moyers, B. Healing and the mind 616
Pert, C. Molecules of emotion 612.8
A **mind** at a time. Levine, M. D. 370.15

Mind control See Brainwashing

Mind cure See Mental healing

The **mind** of Egypt. Assmann, J. 932
A **mind** of its own. Friedman, D. M. 573.6
Mind of the raven. Heinrich, B. 598
The **mind** of the South. Cash, W. J. 975

Mindell, Earl, 1940-
Dr. Earl Mindell's unsafe at any meal 613.2

Minderović, Zoran
Notable mathematicians. See Notable mathematicians
920.003

Mindfield. Corso, G. 811
Minding animals. Bekoff, M. 591.5
Minding the machines. Evan, W. M. 620.8

Miner, Margaret
(jt. auth) Young, S. Allergies 616.97

Minerals
Chesterman, C. W. The Audubon Society field guide to North American rocks and minerals 549
Erickson, J. An introduction to fossils and minerals
560
Johnsen, O. Minerals of the world 549
Manual of mineral science 549
Pellant, C. Rocks and minerals 549
Pough, F. H. A field guide to rocks and minerals
549
Simon and Schuster's guide to rocks and minerals
549
Sofianides, A. S. Gems & crystals from the American Museum of Natural History 549
Minerals of the world. Johnsen, O. 549
The **miner's** canary. Eldredge, N. 560
The **miner's** canary. Guinier, L. 323.1

Mines and mineral resources
See also Coal mines and mining

Mingus, Charles, 1922-1979
About
Mingus, S. Tonight at noon 92
Santoro, G. Myself when I am real: the life and music of Charles Mingus 92

Mingus, Sue
Tonight at noon 92

Minimum wage
Ehrenreich, B. Nickel and dimed 305.5
Shulman, B. The betrayal of work 331.2

Minkin, Mary Jane
The Yale guide to women's reproductive health
618.1

Minor, William C., d. 1920
About
Winchester, S. The professor and the madman
423

Minorities
See also Ethnic relations
Daniels, R. Coming to America 325.73
Glazer, N. Beyond the melting pot 305.8
Guinier, L. The miner's canary 323.1
Sowell, T. Ethnic America 305.8
Encyclopedias
Encyclopedia of multiculturalism 305.8

Minorities—Encyclopedias—*Continued*
Gale encyclopedia of multicultural America   **305.8**
Harvard encyclopedia of American ethnic groups
305.8
The **minority** quarterback, and other lives in sports.
Berkow, I.   **796**
Minutaglio, Bill
First son: George W. Bush and the Bush family
dynasty   **92**
Miracle at Midway. Prange, G. W.   **940.54**
The **miracle** worker. Gibson, W.   **812**
Miracles
Harline, C. E. Miracles at the Jesus Oak   **231.7**
Lewis, C. S. Miracles   **231.7**
Woodward, K. L. The book of miracles   **291.1**
Miracles at the Jesus Oak. Harline, C. E.   **231.7**
The **miraculous** fever tree. Rocco, F.   **616.9**
Mirro, Joseph, Jr.
(ed) Childhood cancer. See Childhood cancer
618.92
Mirrorwork   **820.8**
Mirth of a nation   **817**
The **misanthrope**. Molière
In Molière. The misanthrope, and other plays
842
The **misanthrope**, and other plays. Molière   **842**
Miscarriage
Kohn, I. A silent sorrow   **618.3**
Lerner, H. M. Miscarriage: a doctor's guide to the
facts   **618.3**
Miscarriage: a doctor's guide to the facts. Lerner, H. M.
618.3
Miscegenation *See* Racially mixed people
Miscellaneous facts *See* Curiosities and wonders
The **mischievous** machinations of Scapin. Molière
In Molière. The misanthrope, and other plays
842
Misconceptions. Wolf, N.   **618.2**
Misconduct in office
See also Political corruption
The **miser**. Molière
In Molière. The misanthrope, and other plays
842
Misfit: the strange life of Frederick Exley. Yardley, J.
92
Mishler, Clifford
(jt. auth) Krause, C. L. Standard catalog of world coins
737.4
The **mismeasure** of man. Gould, S. J.   **153.9**
Miss Julie. Strindberg, A.
In Strindberg, A. Strindberg: five plays p63-112
839.7
Miss Lulu Bett. Gale, Z.
In Plays by American women, 1900-1930
812.008
Miss Manners' basic training: the right thing to say.
Martin, J.   **395**
Miss Manners' guide to domestic tranquility. Martin, J.
395
Miss Manners on painfully proper weddings. See Martin,
J. Miss Manners on weddings   **395**
Miss Manners on weddings. Martin, J.   **395**
The **missing** moment. Pollack, R.   **610**
Missionaries of Charity
Spink, K. Mother Teresa   **92**
Missions
India
Spink, K. Mother Teresa   **92**
Missions, Christian *See* Christian missions
Mississippi
Pictorial works
Welty, E. One time, one place   **976.2**
Race relations
Hendrickson, P. Sons of Mississippi   **305.8**
Rubin, R. Confederacy of silence   **976.2**

Mississippi River
Floods
See Floods—Mississippi River
Mississippi River valley
History
Barry, J. M. Rising tide   **977**
Mississippi State Penitentiary
Oshinsky, D. M. "Worse than slavery"   **365**
Mississippi valley *See* Mississippi River valley
Mistakes *See* Errors
The **misunderstanding**. Camus, A.
In Camus, A. Caligula & three other plays p75-134
842
Mitchell, Chris
(jt. auth) Miller, J. The cell: inside the 9/11 plot and
why the FBI and CIA failed to stop it   **973.931**
Mitchell, Deborah R.
The Botox miracle   **615.8**
Mitchell, Elizabeth, 1966-
Three strides before the wire   **798.4**
Mitchell, George J., 1933-
Making peace   **941.6**
Mitchell, Greg, 1947-
(jt. auth) Lifton, R. J. Hiroshima in America
940.54
Mitchell, Joan
About
Livingston, J. The paintings of Joan Mitchell
759.13
Mitchell, Joan S.
(ed) Dewey, M. Abridged Dewey decimal classification
and relative index   **025.4**
(ed) Dewey, M. Dewey decimal classification and rela-
tive index   **025.4**
Mitchell, John G.
National Geographic, the wildlife photographs   **779**
Mitchell, Margaret, 1900-1949
See/See also pages in the following book(s):
American women fiction writers   **813.009**
Pierpont, C. R. Passionate minds   **810.9**
Mitchell, Stephen, 1943-
(ed) Into the garden. See Into the garden   **808.8**
Mitchell, Stephen A., 1946-2000
Freud and beyond   **150.19**
Mitford, Jessica, 1917-1996
The American way of death revisited   **393**
About
Lovell, M. S. The sisters: the saga of the Mitford fami-
ly   **920**
Mitford, Nancy, 1904-1973
About
Lovell, M. S. The sisters: the saga of the Mitford fami-
ly   **920**
Mitford, Unity, 1914-1948
About
Lovell, M. S. The sisters: the saga of the Mitford fami-
ly   **920**
Mitford family
About
Lovell, M. S. The sisters: the saga of the Mitford fami-
ly   **920**
The **Mitford** girls. See Lovell, M. S. The sisters: the
saga of the Mitford family   **920**
Mittendorf, Bradley C., 1967-
(ed) The Oxford book of the American South. See The
Oxford book of the American South   **810.8**
Mitton, Jacqueline
Cambridge dictionary of astronomy   **520.3**
Mixed marriage *See* Interracial marriage
Mixed race people *See* Racially mixed people
Miyamasu
Eboshi-ori
In Waley, A. The Nō plays of Japan   **895.6**

Miyamura, Hiroshi H., 1925-
    See/See also pages in the following book(s):
    Mikaelian, A. Medal of honor   **920**
Mizdal, Richard
    Black & white photography for 35mm   **770**
MLA handbook for writers of research papers. Gibaldi,
    J.   **808**
Mlodinow, Leonard
    Euclid's window   **516**
Mobil travel guides   **917.3**
Mobs *See* Riots
Mobutu Sese Seko, 1930-1997
    See/See also pages in the following book(s):
    Naipaul, V. S. The writer and the world p205-28
    824
Mochedlover, Helene G., 1932-
    (ed) Ottemiller's index to plays in collections. See
    Ottemiller's index to plays in collections   **808.82**
Moctezuma *See* Montezuma II, Emperor of Mexico, ca.
    1480-1520
The **Modern** age, 1890-1960
    In New Oxford history of music v10   **780.9**
Modern American literature   **810.9**
Modern American memoirs   **810.8**
Modern architecture
    1900-1999 (20th century)
    See Architecture—20th century
Modern art
    Fineberg, J. D. Art since 1940   **709.04**
    Hughes, R. The shock of the new   **709.04**
    1800-1899 (19th century)
    See Art—19th century
    1900-1999 (20th century)
    See Art—20th century
    1900-1999 (20th century)—Dictionaries
    Chilvers, I. A dictionary of twentieth-century art
    709.04
    Encyclopedias
    Dempsey, A. Art in the modern era   **709.04**
The **modern** backpacker's handbook. See Randall, G.
    The Outward Bound backpacker's handbook
    796.51
Modern British literature; ed. by F. Kermode and J. Hol-
    lander
    In The Oxford anthology of English literature v2
    820.8
Modern civilization
    Bernier, O. The world in 1800   **909.81**
    Bloom, H. The Lucifer principle   **128**
    Watson, P. The modern mind   **909.82**
    1950-
    Huntington, S. P. The clash of civilizations and the
    remaking of world order   **909.82**
    Toffler, A. Future shock   **303.4**
    Toffler, A. Powershift   **303.4**
    Toffler, A. The third wave   **303.4**
Modern dance
    Reynolds, N. No fixed points   **792.8**
    Dictionaries
    International dictionary of modern dance   **792.8**
Modern English-Hebrew dictionary. Zilkha, A.
    492.4
Modern English-Yiddish, Yiddish-English dictionary.
    Weinreich, U.   **439**
Modern history
    Kennedy, P. M. The rise and fall of the great powers
    909.08
    The New Cambridge modern history   **909.08**
    Tuchman, B. W. The march of folly   **909.08**
    Tuchman, B. W. Practicing history   **907**
The **modern** Inquisition. Collins, P.   **282**
Modern Japanese literature   **895.6**
Modern Japanese writers   **920.003**
The **modern** mind. Watson, P.   **909.82**
Modern paint effects. Sloan, A.   **745.7**

Modern philosophy
    Gay, P. The Enlightenment: an interpretation   **190**
    Sedgwick, P. Descartes to Derrida   **190**
    Watson, P. The modern mind   **909.82**
    See/See also pages in the following book(s):
    McGinn, C. The making of a philosopher   **92**
Modern physics and ancient faith. Barr, S. M.
    291.1
Modern poetry from Africa. See The Penguin book of
    modern African poetry   **896**
The **modern** rhyming dictionary. Lees, G.   **423**
The **modern** vegetarian kitchen. Berley, P.   **641.5**
Modernism (Aesthetics)
    Steiner, W. Venus in exile   **700**
Modernism (Literature) *See* Modernism (Aesthetics)
The **modernist** period, 1900-1945. Lee-Browne, P.
    In Backgrounds to English literature v4   **820.9**
Modigliani, Amedeo, 1884-1920
    About
    Wayne, K. Modigliani & the artists of Montparnasse
    92
Modigliani & the artists of Montparnasse. Wayne, K.
    92
Moe, Christian Hollis, 1929-
    (ed) Masterplots II, drama series. See Masterplots II,
    drama series   **809.2**
Moffitt, Perry-Lynn
    (jt. auth) Kohn, I. A silent sorrow   **618.3**
Mogul Empire
    McLeod, J. The history of India   **954**
Mohammedanism *See* Islam
Mohammedans *See* Muslims
Mohawk Indians
    Demos, J. The unredeemed captive   **973.2**
Mohegan Indians
    See/See also pages in the following book(s):
    Josephy, A. M. Now that the buffalo's gone p61-71
    970.004
Mohican Indians *See* Mohegan Indians
Mojetta, Angelo
    Simon & Schuster's guide to saltwater fish and fishing
    799.1
Moka-ta-va-tah *See* Black Kettle, Cheyenne Chief,
    1803?-1868
Molavi, Afshin
    Persian pilgrimages   **955**
Molecular biology
    Lewontin, R. C. The triple helix   **572.8**
    Morange, M. A history of molecular biology
    572.8
    Rensberger, B. Life itself   **571.6**
    Dictionaries
    The Facts on File dictionary of cell and molecular bi-
    ology   **571.6**
Molecules
    Ball, P. Stories of the invisible   **541.2**
Molecules of emotion. Pert, C.   **612.8**
Molesworth, Charles, 1941-
    Marianne Moore   **92**
Molière, 1622-1673
    The critique of the school for wives
    In Molière. Tartuffe, and other plays   **842**
    The doctor in spite of himself
    In Molière. The misanthrope, and other plays
    842
    Don Juan
    In Molière. Tartuffe, and other plays   **842**
    The imaginary invalid
    In Molière. The misanthrope, and other plays
    842
    The learned women
    In Molière. The misanthrope, and other plays
    842

Molière, 1622-1673—*Continued*
The misanthrope
In Molière. The misanthrope, and other plays
842
The misanthrope, and other plays 842
The mischievous machinations of Scapin
In Molière. The misanthrope, and other plays
842
The miser
In Molière. The misanthrope, and other plays
842
The ridiculous précieuses
In Molière. Tartuffe, and other plays 842
The school for husbands
In Molière. Tartuffe, and other plays 842
The school for wives
In Molière. Tartuffe, and other plays 842
Tartuffe
In Molière. Tartuffe, and other plays 842
Tartuffe, and other plays 842
The Versailles impromptu
In Molière. Tartuffe, and other plays 842
The would-be gentleman
In Molière. The misanthrope, and other plays
842
See/See also pages in the following book(s):
Bloom, H. The Western canon 809
Durant, W. J. The age of Louis XIV p104-28
940.2

Molin, Paulette Fairbanks
(jt. auth) Hirschfelder, A. B. The encyclopedia of Native American religions 299
Moller, Sharon Chickering
Library service to Spanish speaking patrons 027.6
Mollusks
See also Squids
Molly Ivins can't say that, can she? Ivins, M. 817
Molokhovets, Elena
Classic Russian cooking 641.5
Molotch, Harvey Luskin
Where stuff comes from 620
Molotsky, Irvin
The flag, the poet & the song 973.5
Molto agitato. Fiedler, J. 792.5
Momaday, N. Scott
See/See also pages in the following book(s):
Coltelli, L. Winged words: American Indian writers speak 897
Momatiuk, Yva
See/See also pages in the following book(s):
Slung, M. B. Living with cannibals and other women's adventures 910.4
A **moment's** liberty: the shorter diary. Woolf, V.
92
Moments of being. Woolf, V. 92
Moments of grace. Gaines, P. 170
Mon (Southeast Asian people)
Armour-Hileman, V. Singing to the dead 261
Monarch butterflies
Halpern, S. M. Four wings and a prayer 595.7
Monarchs *See* Kings and rulers
Monarchy
See also Queens
Monasticism *See* Monasticism and religious orders
Monasticism and religious orders
Moorhouse, G. Sun dancing 941.5
Norris, K. The cloister walk 255
Mondimore, Francis Mark, 1953-
Adolescent depression 616.85
A natural history of homosexuality 306.7
Monet, Claude, 1840-1926
About
Tucker, P. H. Monet in the 20th century 759.4
Monet in the 20th century. Tucker, P. H. 759.4

Monetary policy
United States
Greider, W. Secrets of the temple 332.1
Mayer, M. The Fed 332.1
Woodward, B. Maestro: Greenspan's Fed and the American boom 332.1
Monette, Paul
Borrowed time 362.1
Money, Nicholas P.
Mr. Bloomfield's orchard 579.5
Money
Keynes, J. M. The general theory of employment, interest and money 330.1
The **money** and the power. Denton, S. 979.3
Moneyball. Lewis, M. 796.357
Monge, Gaspard, 1746-1818
See/See also pages in the following book(s):
Bell, E. T. Men of mathematics p183-205 920
Mongillo, John F.
Encyclopedia of environmental science 363.7
Mongkut, King of Siam, 1804-1868
About
Landon, M. Anna and the King of Siam [biography of Anna Harriette Leonowens] 92
Mongolia
Crane, G. Bones of the master 294.3
Monk, Ray
Bertrand Russell 92
Monk, Thelonious, 1917-1982
About
Gourse, L. Straight, no chaser 92
The **monk** and the hangman's daughter. Bierce, A.
In Bierce, A. The collected writings 818
The **monk** in the garden: how Gregor Mendel and his pea plants solved the mystery of inheritance. Henig, R. M. 92
A **monk** swimming. McCourt, M. 92
Monkey business. Louvish, S. 920
The **monkey** in the mirror. Tattersall, I. 599.93
The **monkey** wars. Blum, D. 179
Monkeys
See also Baboons
Monkman, Betty C.
The White House 975.3
Monks of New Skete
How to be your dog's best friend 636.7
The **monks** of Tibhirine. Kiser, J. W. 271
Monmonier, Mark S. (Mark Stephen), 1943-
Air apparent 551.6
Monologue. Pinter, H.
In Pinter, H. Complete works v4 822
Monologues
The Actor's book of movie monologues 791.43
The Best men's stage monologues of [date]
808.82
The Best women's stage monologues of [date]
808.82
The Ultimate audition book 808.82
Monotheism
Stark, R. For the glory of God 291.1
Stark, R. One true God 291.1
Monroe, Bill, 1911-1996
About
Smith, R. D. Can't you hear me callin': the life of Bill Monroe, father of bluegrass 92
Monroe, Marilyn, 1926-1962
About
Leaming, B. Marilyn Monroe 92
Monsanto Agricultural Co.
See/See also pages in the following book(s):
Charles, D. Lords of the harvest 664
Monster. Dunne, J. G. 791.43
Monster of God. Quammen, D. 591.6
Monsters
Eberhart, G. M. Mysterious creatures 001.9

Monsters—*Continued*
Encyclopedias
Rose, C. Giants, monsters, and dragons   **398.03**

Monsters under the bed and other childhood fears.
Garber, S. W.   **649**

Mont-Saint-Michel (France). Abbey
Adams, H. Mont-Saint-Michel and Chartres   **726**

Mont-Saint-Michel and Chartres. Adams, H.   **726**

Montagné, Prosper, 1865-1948
Larousse gastronomique. See Larousse gastronomique
   641.03

Montagu, Jennifer
(jt. auth) Wittkower, R. Art and architecture in Italy,
1600-1750   **709.45**

Montaigne, Michel de, 1533-1592
See/See also pages in the following book(s):
Bloom, H. The Western canon   **809**

Montale, Eugenio, 1896-1981
Collected poems, 1920-1954   **851**

Montefiore, Hugh Sebag- *See* Sebag-Montefiore, Hugh

Montefiore, Sebag
Prince of princes: the life of Potemkin   **92**

Montefiore, Simon Sebag- *See* Montefiore, Sebag

Monterrey, Manuel
(jt. auth) Olmos, E. J. Americanos   **305.8**

Montessori, Maria, 1870-1952
The absorbent mind   **155.4**
The Montessori method   **371.3**

Montessori method of education
Britton, L. Montessori play & learn   **371.3**
Montessori, M. The Montessori method   **371.3**

Montessori play & learn. Britton, L.   **371.3**

Montezuma II, Emperor of Mexico, ca. 1480-1520
See/See also pages in the following book(s):
Williams, W. C. In the American grain p27-38
   814

Montgomery, Sy
Journey of the pink dolphins   **599.5**
Search for the golden moon bear   **599.78**

A **month** in the country. Turgenev, I. S.   **891.7**

Monthly catalog of United States Government publications   **015.73**

Montini, Giovanni Battista *See* Paul VI, Pope, 1897-1978

Monuments
Amery, C. Vanishing histories   **363.6**
Loewen, J. W. Lies across America   **973**

A **mood** apart. Whybrow, P. C.   **616.89**

Moon
Mackenzie, D. The big splat; or, How our moon came
to be   **523.3**

Moon, Voyages to *See* Space flight to the moon

Moonlight. Walsh, J. E.   **345**

The **moonshot** tape. Wilson, L.
In Wilson, L. 21 short plays p251-62   **812**

Moore, Albert Joseph, 1841-1893
About
Asleson, R. Albert Moore   **759.2**

Moore, Charles B., Jr.
(jt. auth) Saler, B. UFO crash at Roswell   **001.9**

Moore, Dahrl Elizabeth
The librarian's genealogy notebook   **929**

Moore, Deborah Dash, 1946-
(ed) Jewish women in America. See Jewish women in
America   **920.003**

Moore, Dorothy Rudd, 1940-
See/See also pages in the following book(s):
Walker-Hill, H. From spirituals to symphonies
   920

Moore, Edward *See* Muir, Edwin, 1887-1959

Moore, Elaine A., 1948-
Encyclopedia of Alzheimer's disease   **616.8**

Moore, Gene, 1910-1998
(ed) The Oxford reader's companion to Conrad. See
The Oxford reader's companion to Conrad
   823.009

Moore, Gerald, 1924-
(ed) The Penguin book of modern African poetry. See
The Penguin book of modern African poetry
   896

Moore, Harold G., 1922-
We were soldiers once—and young   **959.704**

Moore, James R., 1947-
(jt. auth) Desmond, A. J. Darwin   **92**

Moore, John Allphin, 1940-
Encyclopedia of the United Nations   **341.23**

Moore, John Leo, 1927-
Elections A to Z   **324.6**

Moore, Lisa, 1973-
(jt. auth) Moore, E. A. Encyclopedia of Alzheimer's
disease   **616.8**

Moore, Marianne, 1887-1972
The complete poems of Marianne Moore   **811**
The selected letters of Marianne Moore   **92**
About
Molesworth, C. Marianne Moore   **92**
See/See also pages in the following book(s):
Gilbert, S. M. No man's land v3 p57-120   **820.9**
Jarrell, R. No other book   **809**
Women writers at work p3-31   **808**

Moore, Michael
Downsize this!   **817**

Moore, Michele
The only menopause guide you'll need   **618.1**

Moore, Patrick
Atlas of the universe   **523**
(ed) Astronomy encyclopedia. See Astronomy encyclopedia   **520**

Moore, R. Laurence (Robert Laurence), 1940-
Selling God   **200.9**

Moore, Robert Laurence *See* Moore, R. Laurence (Robert Laurence), 1940-

Moore, Sonia, d. 1995
The Stanislavski system   **792**

Moore, Undine Smith, 1904-1989
See/See also pages in the following book(s):
Walker-Hill, H. From spirituals to symphonies
   920

Moorehead, Caroline
Gellhorn: a twentieth-century life   **92**

Moorhouse, Geoffrey, 1931-
Sun dancing   **941.5**

Moosewood Restaurant book of desserts   **641.8**

Moragas, Elvira D.
(ed) Larousse English-Spanish Spanish-English dictionary. See Larousse English-Spanish Spanish-English
dictionary   **463**

Moral education
Coles, R. The call of stories   **808**
Coles, R. The moral intelligence of children
   155.4
Dosick, W. D. Golden rules   **649**

Moral freedom. Wolfe, A.   **170**

The **moral** intelligence of children. Coles, R.   **155.4**

The **moral** judgment of the child. Piaget, J.   **155.4**

Moral philosophy *See* Ethics

A **moral** reckoning. Goldhagen, D.   **940.53**

Moral theology, Christian *See* Christian ethics

Morales, Ed
Living in Spanglish   **305.8**

Morange, Michel
A history of molecular biology   **572.8**

Morash, Marian
The victory garden cookbook   **641.6**

Moravec, Hans P.
Robot   **629.8**

Mordden, Ethan, 1947-
Rodgers & Hammerstein 792.6
More, Sir Thomas, Saint, 1478-1535
Utopia 321
About
Moynahan, B. God's bestseller: William Tyndale,
Thomas More, and the writing of the English Bible
92
See/See also pages in the following book(s):
Russell, B. A history of Western philosophy p512-22
109
Drama
Bolt, R. A man for all seasons 822
More classic Italian cooking. See Hazan, M. Essentials
of classic Italian cooking 641.5
More Latin for the illiterati. Stone, J. R. 473
More matter. Updike, J. 814
More stories from my father's court. Singer, I. B.
92
More with less. Ciotti, P. 92
Moreira, Paula
Ace the IT job interview! 650.14
Moreno, Jonathan D.
Undue risk 174
Morgan, Edmund Sears
Benjamin Franklin 92
The birth of the Republic, 1763-89 973.3
Morgan, Frederick, 1922-
The one abiding 811
Morgan, J. Pierpont (John Pierpont), 1837-1913
About
Strouse, J. Morgan 92
Morgan, John Pierpont *See* Morgan, J. Pierpont (John
Pierpont), 1837-1913
Morgan, Judith
Dr. Seuss & Mr. Geisel 92
Morgan, Kenneth O.
(ed) The Oxford history of Britain. See The Oxford
history of Britain 941
Morgan, Neil Bowen, 1924-
(jt. auth) Morgan, J. Dr. Seuss & Mr. Geisel 92
Morgan, Peter W., 1951-
The appearance of impropriety 306
Morgan, Robert, 1918-2004
The man who flew the Memphis Belle 92
Morgan, Ted, 1932-
A shovel of stars 978
Wilderness at dawn 970
Morgenthau, Henry, 1856-1946
See/See also pages in the following book(s):
Tuchman, B. W. Practicing history p208-18 907
Morin, Alexander J., 1920-
(ed) Classical music: the listener's companion. See
Classical music: the listener's companion 781.6
Morison, Samuel Eliot, 1887-1976
Admiral of the ocean sea: a life of Christopher Colum-
bus 92
A concise history of the American Republic 973
The growth of the American Republic 973
History of United States naval operations in World
War II 940.54
John Paul Jones 92
The Oxford history of the American people 973
Morisot, Berthe, 1841-1895
About
Higonnet, A. Berthe Morisot 92
Morley, John, 1933-2001
The history of furniture 749.2
Mormon America. Ostling, R. N. 289.3
Mormon Church *See* Church of Jesus Christ of Latter-
day Saints
Mormons
Book of Mormon. The Book of Mormon 289.3
Brodie, F. M. No man knows my history: the life of
Joseph Smith, the Mormon prophet 92

Durham, M. S. Desert between the mountains
979
Remini, R. V. Joseph Smith 92
Mornell, Pierre
Games companies play 650.14
Morning in the burned house. Atwood, M. 811
Mornings like this. Dillard, A. 811
Mornings on horseback [biography of Theodore
Roosevelt] McCullough, D. G. 92
Moro, Javier, 1955-
(jt. auth) Lapierre, D. Five past midnight in Bhopal
363.1
Morris, Benny, 1948-
Righteous victims 956
Morris, Bruce B.
Prime time network serials 791.45
Morris, Christopher G.
(ed) Academic Press dictionary of science and technol-
ogy. See Academic Press dictionary of science and
technology 503
Morris, Desmond
Cat watching 636.8
Dogs: the ultimate dictionary of over 1,000 dog breeds
636.7
Horsewatching 636.1
Morris, Dick
The new prince 324.7
Morris, Edmund
The rise of Theodore Roosevelt 92
Theodore Rex 92
Morris, James, 1926-
See also Morris, Jan, 1926-
Morris, Jan, 1926-
Lincoln, a foreigner's quest 92
Trieste and the meaning of nowhere 945
A writer's house in Wales 942.9
Morris, Kenneth Earl, 1955-
Jimmy Carter, American moralist 92
Morris, Mary, 1913-
(jt. auth) Morris, W. Morris dictionary of word and
phrase origins 422.03
Morris, Mary, 1940-
Every sewer's guide to the perfect fit 646.4
Morris, Richard, 1939-
The big questions 501
Morris, Roger
(jt. auth) Denton, S. The money and the power
979.3
Morris, Roy
Ambrose Bierce 92
The better angel: Walt Whitman in the Civil War
92
Morris, Sylvia Jukes
Rage for fame: the ascent of Clare Boothe Luce
92
Morris, William, 1913-1994
Morris dictionary of word and phrase origins
422.03
Morris, Willie
My dog Skip 92
Morris dictionary of word and phrase origins. Morris,
W. 422.03
Morrison, Andrew L.
The antidepressant sourcebook 616.85
Morrison, Jim, 1943-1971
About
Hopkins, J. No one here gets out alive 92
Riordan, J. Break on through: the life and death of Jim
Morrison 92
Morrison, Phylis, 1927-
(jt. auth) Holden, A. Crystals and crystal growing
548
Morrison, Toni, 1931-
See/See also pages in the following book(s):
Black women writers (1950-1980) 810.9

Morrison, Toni, 1931——_Continued_
Russell, D. Black genius and the American experience
920
Women writers at work p338-75 **808**
Morrow, Charlene, 1948-
(ed) Notable women in mathematics. See Notable
women in mathematics **920.003**
Morse, Samuel Finley Breese, 1791-1872
About
Silverman, K. Lightning man: the accursed life of
Samuel F.B. Morse **92**
See/See also pages in the following book(s):
Lepore, J. A is for American **306.44**
Le **morte** d'Arthur. Malory, Sir T. **398.2**
Mortgages
Fields, A. Your new house **643**
Morticians _See_ Undertakers and undertaking
Mortimer, John Clifford, 1923-
The summer of a dormouse **92**
Morton, Alexandra, 1957-
Listening to whales **599.5**
Morton, David J., 1969-
(jt. auth) Feigenbaum, R. A. The 529 College Savings
Plan **378.3**
Morton, Laura, 1964-
(jt. auth) Lanza, L. Totally dairy-free cooking
641.5
Morton, Oliver
Mapping Mars **523.4**
Morton, R. L. (Ronald Lee)
Music of the earth **550**
Morton, Ronald Lee _See_ Morton, R. L. (Ronald Lee)
Mosaics
Biggs, E. The encyclopedia of mosaic techniques
738.5
Mosby, John Singleton, 1833-1916
See/See also pages in the following book(s):
Wilson, E. Patriotic gore p307-29 **810.9**
Mosby, Rebekah Presson
Poetry speaks. See Poetry speaks **808.81**
Mosby's diagnostic and laboratory test reference. Pagana,
K. D. **616.07**
Mosby's medical & nursing dictionary. See Mosby's
medical, nursing, & allied health dictionary
610.3
Mosby's medical, nursing, & allied health dictionary
610.3
Mosby's Rangers. Wert, J. D. **973.7**
Moschovitis, Christos J. P.
History of the Internet. See History of the Internet
004.6
Mosconi, Willie, 1913-1993
Willie Mosconi's winning pocket billiards for begin-
ners and advanced players, with a section on trick
shots **794.7**
Moseley, Michael Edward
The Incas and their ancestors **985**
Mosenfelder, Donn
(jt. auth) Fischer, B. Bobby Fischer teaches chess
794.1
Moser, Charles A.
(ed) The Cambridge history of Russian literature. See
The Cambridge history of Russian literature
891.7
Moses, Bob
See/See also pages in the following book(s):
Russell, D. Black genius and the American experience
920
Moses, Robert, 1888-1981
About
Caro, R. A. The power broker: Robert Moses and the
fall of New York **92**
Moses, Robert P. _See_ Moses, Bob
Mosier, John, 1944-
The myth of the Great War **940.4**

Moskin, J. Robert
Mr. Truman's war **940.54**
Moslem countries _See_ Islamic countries
Moslemism _See_ Islam
Moslems _See_ Muslims
Mosquitoes
Spielman, A. Mosquito **595.7**
Moss, Alfred A., 1943-
(jt. auth) Franklin, J. H. From slavery to freedom
305.8
Moss, Howard, 1922-1987
See/See also pages in the following book(s):
Gioia, D. Can poetry matter? **809.1**
Moss, Joyce, 1951-
Latin American literature and its times **860.9**
(ed) Literature and its times. See Literature and its
times **809**
The **most** reluctant convert: C. S. Lewis's journey to
faith. Downing, D. C. **92**
Motels _See_ Hotels and motels
Mother and child _See_ Mother-child relationship
Mother-child relationship
Engber, A. The complete single mother **306.8**
Mother-daughter relationship
Edelman, H. Motherless daughters **155.9**
See/See also pages in the following book(s):
Gurian, M. The wonder of girls **305.23**
Mother Jones _See_ Jones, Mother, 1830-1930
Mother Jones. Gorn, E. J. **92**
The **mother** of all baby books. Douglas, A. **649**
Mother-son relationship
See/See also pages in the following book(s):
Pollack, W. S. Real boys p81-112 **305.23**
Mother Teresa _See_ Teresa, Mother, 1910-1997
Mother Teresa's Mission of Charity _See_ Missionaries
of Charity
The **mother** tongue: English & how it got that way.
Bryson, B. **420**
Motherless daughters. Edelman, H. **155.9**
Mothers
Cheever, S. As good as I could be **306.8**
Crittenden, A. The price of motherhood **306.8**
Cusk, R. A life's work **306.8**
Friday, N. My mother/my self **155.6**
Pryor, G. Nursing mother, working mother **649**
Steingraber, S. Having faith **618.2**
Wolf, N. Misconceptions **618.2**
Mothers, Single parent _See_ Single parent family
Mothers and daughters _See_ Mother-daughter relation-
ship
Mothers and sons _See_ Mother-son relationship
Mothers of invention. Faust, D. G. **973.7**
Mothers' pensions _See_ Child welfare
Moths
Hooper, J. Of moths and men **576.8**
Waldbauer, G. Insects through the seasons **595.7**
Motion, Andrew, 1952-
Keats **92**
Motion picture actors _See_ Actors
Motion picture adaptations _See_ Film adaptations
Motion picture almanac. See International motion picture
almanac **791.43**
Motion picture cartoons _See_ Animated films
Motion picture direction _See_ Motion pictures—Produc-
tion and direction
Motion picture industry
Kurosawa, A. Something like an autobiography
92
Mann, W. J. Behind the screen **791.43**
Pictorial works
Howard, J. Jean Howard's Hollywood **791.43**
Motion picture music
Encyclopedias
Hischak, T. The American musical film song encyclo-
pedia **782.42**

Motion picture photography *See* Cinematography
Motion picture plays
          Technique
  Hauge, M. Writing screenplays that sell   **808.2**
  Straczynski, J. M. The complete book of scriptwriting
                                808.2
Motion picture producers and directors
  Biskind, P. Easy riders, raging bulls   **791.43**
          Dictionaries
  Photographers and filmmakers   **920.003**
Motion picture production *See* Motion pictures—Production and direction
Motion pictures
    See also African Americans in motion pictures;
    Film adaptations; Horror films; Musicals
  The Actor's book of movie monologues   **791.43**
  Biskind, P. Easy riders, raging bulls   **791.43**
  Chadwick, B. The reel Civil War   **791.43**
  Ebert, R. Roger Ebert's movie yearbook   **791.43**
  Halliwell's film guide   **791.43**
  Harvey, J. Movie love in the 50's   **791.43**
  International motion picture almanac   **791.43**
  Jones, G. W. Black cinema treasures   **791.43**
  Kashner, S. The bad & the beautiful   **791.43**
  Knowles, H. Ain't it cool?   **791.43**
  Magill's cinema annual   **791.43**
  Maltin, L. Leonard Maltin's movie and video guide
                                791.43
  Mayo, M. VideoHound's DVD guide   **791.43**
  Muller, E. Dark city   **791.43**
  Roger Ebert's book of film   **791.43**
  Sklar, R. A world history of film   **791.43**
  Vanity Fair's Hollywood   **791.43**
  Wiener, T. The off-Hollywood film guide   **791.43**
  See/See also pages in the following book(s):
  Sontag, S. Styles of radical will p99-122   **814**
      Cartoons and caricatures
  Leopold, D. Hirschfeld's Hollywood   **741.5**
          Dictionaries
  Konigsberg, I. The complete film dictionary
                             791.4303
  Slide, A. The new historical dictionary of the
    American film industry   **791.4303**
        History and criticism
  Cook, D. A. A history of narrative film   **791.43**
  Mast, G. A short history of the movies   **791.43**
  The Oxford history of world cinema   **791.43**
        Production and direction
  Dunne, J. G. Monster   **791.43**
  Levy, E. Making a winning short   **791.43**
  Lumet, S. Making movies   **791.43**
  Mamet, D. On directing film   **791.43**
  Taub, E. Gaffers, grips, and best boys   **791.43**
          Quotations
  Nowlan, R. A. Film quotations   **791.43**
          Reviews
  Canby, V. The New York times guide to the best
    1,000 movies ever made   **791.43**
  Kael, P. For keeps   **791.43**
  Lane, A. Nobody's perfect   **791.43**
Motion studies. See Solnit, R. River of shadows
                                778.5
Motivation (Psychology)
  Kohn, A. Punished by rewards   **153.8**
  Maslow, A. H. Toward a psychology of being
                                155.2
The **Motley** Fool's what to do with your money now.
  Gardner, D.   **332.6**
Motohiyo, Zeami *See* Zeami, 1363-1443
Motorcycle owner's manual. Wilson, H.   **629.28**
Motorcycles
  Bennett, J. S. The complete motorcycle book
                                629.28
      Maintenance and repair
  Wilson, H. Motorcycle owner's manual   **629.28**

Motoyasu, Komparu Zempo *See* Komparu, Zempō
Motoyasu, Zembō *See* Komparu, Zempō
Mount Everest Expedition (1996)
  Boukreev, A. The climb   **796.52**
  Coburn, B. Everest: mountain without mercy
                                796.52
  Krakauer, J. Into thin air   **796.52**
  Norgay, J. T. Touching my father's soul   **796.52**
Mount Saint Helens (Wash.)
  Carson, R. Mount St. Helens: the eruption and recovery of a volcano   **551.2**
  See/See also pages in the following book(s):
  Thompson, D. Volcano cowboys   **551.2**
Mountain City (Nev.)
  Martin, G. Mountain City   **979.3**
The **mountain** of the women. Clancy, L.   **92**
Mountaineering
  Boukreev, A. The climb   **796.52**
  Coburn, B. Everest: mountain without mercy
                                796.52
  Krakauer, J. Into thin air   **796.52**
  Norgay, J. T. Touching my father's soul   **796.52**
Mountains
    See also Adirondack Mountains (N.Y.); Andes; Himalaya Mountains
Mountains and rivers without end. Snyder, G.   **811**
The **mountains** of California. Muir, J.
  In Muir, J. Nature writings   **92**
Mountfort, Guy, 1905-2003
  (jt. auth) Peterson, R. T. A field guide to the birds of
    Britain and Europe   **598**
The **mousetrap.** Christie, A.
  In Christie, A. The mousetrap and other plays
                                822
The **mousetrap** and other plays. Christie, A.   **822**
Mouth
          Diseases
  Dental care and oral health sourcebook   **617.6**
The **movement** and the sixties. Anderson, T. H.
                                303.4
Movie love in the 50's. Harvey, J.   **791.43**
Moving beyond words. Steinem, G.   **305.4**
Moving out. Behan, B.
  In Behan, B. The complete plays   **822**
Moving pictures *See* Motion pictures
Mowat, Farley
  Born naked   **92**
  Never cry wolf   **599.77**
  Woman in the mists: the story of Dian Fossey and the
    mountain gorillas of Africa   **92**
Moy sand and gravel. Muldoon, P.   **821**
Moyers, Bill
  Genesis: a living conversation   **222**
  Healing and the mind   **616**
  (jt. auth) Campbell, J. The power of myth   **291.1**
Moynahan, Brian
  God's bestseller: William Tyndale, Thomas More, and
    the writing of the English Bible [biography of William Tyndale]   **92**
  The Russian century   **947.08**
Moynihan, Daniel Patrick, 1927-2003
  On the law of nations   **327.73**
  Secrecy   **352**
  (jt. auth) Glazer, N. Beyond the melting pot
                                305.8
          About
  Hodgson, G. The gentleman from New York: Daniel
    Patrick Moynihan: a biography   **92**
Mozart, Johann Chrysostom Wolfgang Amadeus *See*
  Mozart, Wolfgang Amadeus, 1756-1791
Mozart, Wolfgang Amadeus, 1756-1791
          About
  Einstein, A. Mozart   **92**
  Gutman, R. W. Mozart   **92**

Mozart, Wolfgang Amadeus, 1756-1791—About—Continued
Osborne, C. The complete operas of Mozart
792.5
Rosen, C. The classical style   780.9
Solomon, M. Mozart   92
    See/See also pages in the following book(s):
Grout, D. J. A history of Western music   780.9
Schonberg, H. C. The great pianists   920
Drama
Shaffer, P. Peter Shaffer's Amadeus   822
The **Mozart** effect. Campbell, D. G.   615.8
Mozart's brain and the fighter pilot. Restak, R. M.
612.8
Mr. Bloomfield's orchard. Money, N. P.   579.5
Mr. Truman's war. Moskin, J. R.   940.54
Mrożek, Sławomir, 1930-
Tango
    In Nine plays of the modern theater p573-671
808.82
Mrs. Ike: memories and reflections on the life of Mamie
Eisenhower. Eisenhower, S.   92
Mrs. Kennedy [biography of Jacqueline Kennedy
Onassis] Leaming, B.   92
Mrs. Paine's garage and the murder of John F. Kennedy.
Mallon, T.   364.1
Muckleshoot Indians
    See/See also pages in the following book(s):
Josephy, A. M. Now that the buffalo's gone p177-95
970.004
Muddiman, John
    (ed) Oxford Bible commentary. See Oxford Bible commentary   220.7
Mudgett, Herman W., 1861-1896
About
Larson, E. The devil in the white city   364.1
Mueller, Scott
Upgrading and repairing PCs   621.39
Muhammad, Elijah *See* Elijah Muhammad, 1897-1975
Muhammad ibn 'Abd Allāh ibn Baṭūṭah *See* Ibn
Battuta, 1304-1377
Muhammadanism *See* Islam
Muhammadans *See* Muslims
Muir, Edwin, 1887-1959
    See/See also pages in the following book(s):
Heaney, S. Finders keepers p269-80   821
Muir, Frank, 1920-1998
    (ed) The Oxford book of humorous prose. See The
Oxford book of humorous prose   827
Muir, John, 1838-1914
The mountains of California
    In Muir, J. Nature writings   92
My first summer in the Sierra
    In Muir, J. Nature writings   92
Nature writings   92
The story of my boyhood and youth   92
    also in Muir, J. Nature writings   92
The Yosemite   979.4
About
Ehrlich, G. John Muir   92
Wilkins, T. John Muir   92
Muir, John Kenneth, 1969-
Horror films of the 1970s   791.43
Mulatto. Hughes, L.
    In Hughes, L. Five plays p1-35   812
Muldoon, Paul
Moy sand and gravel   821
Poems, 1968-1998   821
Mules and men. Hurston, Z. N.
    In Hurston, Z. N. Folklore, memoirs, and other writings   818
Mullane, Deirdre
    (ed) Crossing the danger water. See Crossing the danger water   810.8

Mullen, Harryette Romell
Sleeping with the dictionary   811
Mullen, P. H., Jr.
Gold in the water   797.2
Muller, Eddie
Dark city   791.43
Müller, Melissa
Anne Frank   92
Muller, Richard A., 1944-
    (jt. auth) Dauber, P. M. The three big bangs
523.1
A **multicultural** dictionary of literary terms. Carey, G.
803
The **multicultural** dictionary of proverbs. Cordry, H. V.
398.9
Multicultural education
Schlesinger, A. M. The disuniting of America
973
Multicultural manners. Dresser, N.   395
Multicultural people *See* Racially mixed people
Multicultural poetry. See Unsettling America
811.008
Multiculturalism
Lasch-Quinn, E. Race experts   305.8
Schlesinger, A. M. The disuniting of America
973
    See/See also pages in the following book(s):
Levine, L. W. The opening of the American mind
001.1
Postman, N. The end of education   370
Encyclopedias
Encyclopedia of multiculturalism   305.8
Multimedia
Encyclopedias
The Encyclopedia of new media   302.23
Multimedia: digital photography. May, A.   778.3
Multimedia materials *See* Audiovisual materials
Multiple personality
Schreiber, F. R. Sybil   616.85
Mumford, Lewis, 1895-1990
The city in history   307.7
The culture of cities   307.7
The story of utopias   321
Mummies
Brier, B. Egyptian mummies   932
Fowler, B. Iceman   937
Hawass, Z. Valley of the golden mummies   932
Pringle, H. A. The mummy congress   393
Encyclopedias
Brier, B. The encyclopedia of mummies   393
The **mummy** congress. Pringle, H. A.   393
Munch, Edvard, 1863-1944
Edvard Munch: theme and variation   760
About
Tøjner, P. E. Munch: in his own words   92
Munch: in his own words. Tøjner, P. E.   92
Mundis, Hester
    (jt. auth) Mindell, E. Dr. Earl Mindell's unsafe at any
meal   613.2
Municipal government
Directories
Government phone book USA   320.025
Municipal planning *See* City planning
Munitions *See* Military weapons
Munro, Nell, 1979-
    (jt. auth) Ives, M. Caring for a child with autism
618.92
Munro, Penelope Margaret *See* Munro, Nell, 1979-
Munro, Ross H.
    (jt. auth) Bernstein, R. The coming conflict with China
327.73
Munson, Ronald, 1939-
Raising the dead   174
Murakami, Haruki, 1949-
Underground   364.1

Mural painting and decoration
See also Mosaics
King, R. Michelangelo & the Pope's ceiling
759.5
Seligman, P. Painting murals 751.7
Murasaki Shikibu, b. 978?
Tale of Genji; criticism
In The Tale of Genji 751
Murase, Miyeko, 1924-
The Tale of Genji. See The Tale of Genji 751
Murder *See* Homicide
Murder in the cathedral. Eliot, T. S.
In Eliot, T. S. The complete poems and plays, 1909-
1950 p173-221 818
The **murder** of Tutankhamen. Brier, B. 932
Murder trials *See* Trials (Homicide)
Murdin, Paul
(ed) Encyclopedia of astronomy and astrophysics. See
Encyclopedia of astronomy and astrophysics
520.3

Murdoch, Iris
About
Bayley, J. Elegy for Iris 92
Bayley, J. Iris and her friends 92
Conradi, P. Iris Murdoch 92
See/See also pages in the following book(s):
Amis, M. The war against cliché 824
Murie, Olaus Johan, 1889-1963
A field guide to animal tracks 599
Murkoff, Heidi Eisenberg
What to expect the first year 649
What to expect when you're expecting 618.2
(jt. auth) Eisenberg, A. What to expect the toddler
years 649
Murolo, Priscilla, 1949-
From the folks who brought you the weekend
331
Murphy, Bruce, 1962-
(ed) Benet's reader's encyclopedia. See Benet's read-
er's encyclopedia 803
Murphy, Bruce Allen
Wild Bill: the legend and life of William O. Douglas
92
Murphy, Caroline P.
Lavinia Fontana 92
Murphy, Caryle
Passion for Islam 297
Murphy, Cullen
The Word according to Eve 220.8
Murphy, Curtis
See/See also pages in the following book(s):
Halberstam, D. The children 323.1
Murphy, Gerald, 1888-1964
About
Vaill, A. Everybody was so young: Gerald and Sara
Murphy, a lost generation love story 92
Murphy, John C., 1947-
Tales of giant snakes 597.9
Murphy, Larry
(ed) Encyclopedia of African American religions. See
Encyclopedia of African American religions
200.9
Murphy, Sara, 1883-1975
About
Vaill, A. Everybody was so young: Gerald and Sara
Murphy, a lost generation love story 92
Murphy-O'Connor, J. (Jerome), 1935-
Paul 92
Murphy-O'Connor, Jerome *See* Murphy-O'Connor, J.
(Jerome), 1935-
Murray, Albert
The blue devils of Nada 700
(jt. auth) Basie, C. Good morning blues: the autobiog-
raphy of Count Basie 92

See/See also pages in the following book(s):
Gates, H. L. Thirteen ways of looking at a black man
920
Russell, D. Black genius and the American experience
920
Murray, Charles Shaar
Crosstown traffic: Jimi Hendrix and the post-war
rock'n'roll revolution 92
Murray, Sir James Augustus Henry, 1837-1915
About
Winchester, S. The professor and the madman
423
Murray, James B., Jr.
Wireless nation 384.5
Murray, Jocelyn, 1929-2001
(ed) Cultural atlas of Africa. See Cultural atlas of Afri-
ca 960
Murray, Les A., 1938-
Conscious and verbal 821
Murray, Michael T.
Encyclopedia of natural medicine 615.5
Encyclopedia of nutritional supplements 613.2
Murray, Nicholas Russell
Aldous Huxley 92
Murray, Oswyn
(ed) The Oxford history of the Roman world. See The
Oxford history of the Roman world 937
Murray, R. Emmett
The lexicon of labor 331
Murray, Tim, 1955-
(ed) Encyclopedia of archaeology: History and discov-
eries. See Encyclopedia of archaeology: History and
discoveries 930.1
(ed) Encyclopedia of archaeology: The great archaeolo-
gists. See Encyclopedia of archaeology: The great ar-
chaeologists 920
Murray, Williamson
A war to be won 940.53
Murrow, Edward R.
About
Sperber, A. M. Murrow, his life and times 92
Musculoskeletal system
Diseases
Thompson, C. E. Raising a child with a neuromuscular
disorder 618.92
The **muse** is always half-dressed in New Orleans and
other essays. Codrescu, A. 814
Museum of Broadcast Communications Encyclopedia of
television. See Encyclopedia of television
791.45
Museum of Fine Arts (Boston, Mass.)
Cikovsky, N., Jr. Winslow Homer 759.13
The **museum** of hoaxes. Boese, A. 001.9
Museum of Natural History (New York, N.Y.) *See*
American Museum of Natural History
Museums
See also Art museums; appropriate subjects with
the subdivision *Museums;* and names of galleries and
museums
Asma, S. T. Stuffed animals & pickled heads
508
Directories
Museums of the world 069.025
The Official museum directory 069.025
History
See/See also pages in the following book(s):
Mauriès, P. Cabinets of curiosities 069
Museums directory of the United States and Canada. See
The Official museum directory 069.025
Museums of the world 069.025
The **mushroom** hunter's field guide. Smith, A. H.
579.6

Mushrooms
See also Cooking—Mushrooms; Fungi
Czarnecki, J. A cook's book of mushrooms 641.6

Mushrooms—*Continued*
Lincoff, G. The Audubon Society field guide to North American mushrooms **579.6**
McKnight, K. H. A field guide to mushrooms, North America **579.6**
Smith, A. H. The mushroom hunter's field guide **579.6**
Turner, N. J. Common poisonous plants and mushrooms of North America **581.6**

Music
Classical music: the listener's companion **781.6**
Classical music: the rough guide **781.6**
Analysis, appreciation
See Music appreciation
Bio-bibliography
Baker's biographical dictionary of musicians **920.003**
Baker's biographical dictionary of twentieth-century classical musicians **920.003**
The Harvard biographical dictionary of music **920.003**
The Harvard concise dictionary of music and musicians **780.3**
Chronology
Hall, C. J. Chronology of Western classical music **780.9**
Dictionaries
The Harvard concise dictionary of music and musicians **780.3**
The Harvard dictionary of music **780.3**
Hoffman, M. The NPR classical music companion **780.3**
Kennedy, M. The Oxford dictionary of music **780.3**
The New Grove dictionary of music and musicians **780.3**
The Oxford companion to music **780.3**
Slonimsky, N. Baker's dictionary of music **780.3**
Discography
Classical music: the listener's companion **781.6**
Economic aspects
Brabec, J. Music, money, and success **780**
Krasilovsky, M. W. This business of music **780**
History and criticism
Copland, A. Music and imagination **781.1**
Day, T. A century of recorded music **780**
Grout, D. J. A history of Western music **780.9**
Hall, C. J. Chronology of Western classical music **780.9**
Kuhn, L. D. Music since 1900 **780.9**
Lang, P. H. Music in Western civilization **780.9**
Machlis, J. The enjoyment of music **781.1**
New Oxford history of music **780.9**
Norton anthology of western music **780.9**
Rosen, C. The classical style **780.9**
Rosen, C. The romantic generation **780.9**
Slonimsky, N. The great composers and their works **780.9**
Psychological aspects
Campbell, D. G. The Mozart effect **615.8**
Music, African American *See* African American music
Music, American *See* American music
Music, Gospel *See* Gospel music
Music, Jewish *See* Jews—Music
Music, Motion picture *See* Motion picture music
Music, Vocal *See* Vocal music
Music and art *See* Art and music
Music and imagination. Copland, A. **781.1**
Music and literature
Appel, A. Jazz modernism **781.65**
Music appreciation
See also Music—History and criticism
Classical music: the rough guide **781.6**
Copland, A. Music and imagination **781.1**
Jacobson, J. The classical music experience **781.6**

Machlis, J. The enjoyment of music **781.1**
Plotkin, F. Classical music 101 **781.6**
Pogue, D. Classical music for dummies **781.6**
Slonimsky, N. The great composers and their works **780.9**
Steinberg, M. The symphony **784.2**
Music Corporation of America *See* MCA Inc.
Music for chameleons. Capote, T. **818**
Music in Western civilization. Lang, P. H. **780.9**
Music industry
Brabec, J. Music, money, and success **780**
Krasilovsky, M. W. This business of music **780**
Music is my mistress. Ellington, D. **92**
Music, money, and success. Brabec, J. **780**
Music of a distant drum **808.81**
The **music** of Gershwin. Gilbert, S. E. **92**
Music of the earth. Morton, R. L. **550**
Music since 1900. Kuhn, L. D. **780.9**
Music therapy
Campbell, D. G. The Mozart effect **615.8**
Musical instruments
The Illustrated encyclopedia of musical instruments **784.19**
Musicals
Bordman, G. M. American musical theatre **792.6**
Gänzl, K. The musical **792.6**
Green, S. The world of musical comedy **920**
Mordden, E. Rodgers & Hammerstein **792.6**
See/See also pages in the following book(s):
Citron, S. Sondheim and Lloyd-Webber **92**
Chronology
Norton, R. C. A chronology of American musical theater **792.6**
Encyclopedias
Gänzl, K. The encyclopedia of the musical theatre **792.6**
Production and direction
Boland, R. Musicals! **792.6**
Musicians
See also Composers; Women musicians
Dictionaries
Baker's biographical dictionary of musicians **920.003**
Kennedy, M. The Oxford dictionary of music **780.3**
Musicians since 1900 **920.003**
The Oxford companion to music **780.3**
World musicians **920.003**
Musicians, African American *See* African American musicians
Musicians since 1900 **920.003**
The **Muslim** almanac **297**
Muslim countries *See* Islamic countries
Muslim women
Brooks, G. Nine parts of desire **305.4**
Goodwin, J. Price of honor **305.4**
Muslimism *See* Islam
Muslims
United States
Pipes, D. Militant Islam reaches America **320.5**
Muslims, Black *See* Black Muslims
Mussolini, Benito, 1883-1945
About
Bosworth, R. J. B. Mussolini **92**
See/See also pages in the following book(s):
Barzini, L. G. The Italians p133-56 **945**
Mutsuhito *See* Meiji, Emperor of Japan, 1852-1912
Muybridge, Eadweard, 1830-1904
About
Solnit, R. River of shadows **778.5**
My American century. Terkel, S. **920**
My American journey. Powell, C. L. **92**
My bondage and my freedom. Douglass, F. **92**
also in Douglass, F. Autobiographies **92**
My dog Skip. Morris, W. **92**

My double life: the memoirs of Sarah Bernhardt. Bernhardt, S. 92
My fair lady. Lerner, A. J. 812
My father's people. Rubin, L. D. 920
My fine feathered friend. Grimes, W. 636.5
My first 79 years. Stern, I. 92
My first summer in the Sierra. Muir, J.
  In Muir, J. Nature writings 92
My German question. Gay, P. 92
My greatest day in football 796.332
My just desire. Beer, A. R. 92
My Lai Massacre, Vietnam, 1968
  Bilton, M. Four hours in My Lai 959.704
My life as a seer. Cayce, E. 92
My life as author and editor. Mencken, H. L. 92
My life in the pits. Rich, R. 796.72
My losing season. Conroy, P. 92
My love affair with America. Podhoretz, N. 320.5
My Mexico. Kennedy, D. 641.5
My mother/my self. Friday, N. 155.6
My name escapes me. Guinness, A. 92
My stroke of luck. Douglas, K. 92
My Tibet. Dalai Lama XIV 951
My turn at the bully pulpit. Van Susteren, G. 349
My war. Rooney, A. A. 92
My wars are laid away in books: the life of Emily Dickinson. Habegger, A. 92
Myanmar
  Marshall, A. The trouser people 959.1
    Description
  Levy, A. The stone of heaven 553.8
    Politics and government
  Aung San Suu Kyi. Freedom from fear, and other writings 959.1
Mycology *See* Fungi
Myers, Allen C., 1945-
  (ed) Eerdmans dictionary of the Bible. See Eerdmans dictionary of the Bible 220.3
Myers, Ann
  (jt. auth) Koestler, A. J. Understanding chronic pain 616
Myers, David G.
  A quiet world 617.8
Myers, Jack Elliott, 1941-
  Dictionary of poetic terms 808.1
Myerson, Joel
  (ed) Transcendentalism. See Transcendentalism 810.8
Myself when I am real: the life and music of Charles Mingus. Santoro, G. 92
Myself with others. Fuentes, C. 864
Mysteries and miracle plays
  Everyman, and medieval miracle plays 822.008
Mysteries of the mind. Restak, R. M. 612.8
Mysterious creatures. Eberhart, G. M. 001.9
Mystery and detective stories *See* Mystery fiction
The **mystery** and meaning of the Dead Sea scrolls. Shanks, H. 296.1
Mystery and suspense writers 809.3
Mystery fiction
    Bibliography
  Bleiler, R. Reference guide to mystery and detective fiction 016.8
  Heising, W. L. Detecting women 016.8
  Niebuhr, G. W. Make mine a mystery 809.3
    Bio-bibliography
  Great women mystery writers 809.3
  Mystery and suspense writers 809.3
    Dictionaries
  Mystery and suspense writers 809.3
  The Oxford companion to crime and mystery writing 809.3
    History and criticism
  Niebuhr, G. W. Make mine a mystery 809.3
  Symons, J. Bloody murder 809.3

    Technique
  Ramsland, K. M. The criminal mind 808.3
  Roberts, G. You can write a mystery 808.3
The **mystery** of capital. Soto, H. de 330.1
Mysticism
  Armstrong, K. Visions of God 248.2
  Furlong, M. Visions & longings 248.2
    See/See also pages in the following book(s):
  James, W. The varieties of religious experience 210
  Teilhard de Chardin, P. Toward the future p40-57 194
Mysticism for beginners. Zagajewski, A. 891.8
Mystics and messiahs. Jenkins, P. 200.9
The **myth** of monogamy. Barash, D. P. 306.7
The **myth** of Sisyphus, and other essays. Camus, A. 844
The **myth** of the first three years. Bruer, J. T. 155.4
The **myth** of the Great War. Mosier, J. 940.4
Myth of the welfare queen. Zucchino, D. 362.5
Mythical animals
  See also Animals—Folklore; Dragons
  Eberhart, G. M. Mysterious creatures 001.9
    Encyclopedias
  Sax, B. The mythical zoo 398.03
The **mythical** zoo. Sax, B. 398.03
Mythology
  See also Geographical myths; Gods and goddesses; Mythical animals; mythology of particular national or ethnic groups or of particular geographic areas
  Bulfinch, T. Bulfinch's mythology 291.1
  Campbell, J. The masks of God 291.1
  Campbell, J. The power of myth 291.1
  Campbell, J. Transformations of myth through time 291.1
  Frazer, Sir J. G. The new golden bough 291.1
  Leeming, D. A. The world of myth 291.1
    Dictionaries
  Cotterell, A. A dictionary of world mythology 291.103
  Pickering, D. A dictionary of folklore 398.2
    Indexes
  Index to fairy tales 398.2
Mythology, African *See* African mythology
Mythology, Asian *See* Asian mythology
Mythology, Celtic *See* Celtic mythology
Mythology, Classical *See* Classical mythology
Mythology, Egyptian *See* Egyptian mythology
Mythology, Greek *See* Classical mythology
Mythology, Norse *See* Norse mythology
Mythology, Roman *See* Classical mythology
Mythology. Hamilton, E. 292
Mythology in art *See* Art and mythology
Mythology in literature
  Campbell, J. The masks of God 291.1

N

NAACP *See* National Association for the Advancement of Colored People
Nabhan, Gary Paul
  (jt. auth) Buchmann, S. The forgotten pollinators 577
Nabokov, Peter
  A forest of time 970.004
  Native American architecture 728
  (ed) Native American testimony. See Native American testimony 970.004
Nabokov, Vladimir Vladimirovich, 1899-1977
  Lectures on literature 808.3
  Lectures on Russian literature 891.7
  Lolita; criticism
    In Amis, M. The war against cliché 824

Nabokov, Vladimir Vladimirovich, 1899-1977—Lolita; criticism—*Continued*
Speak, memory 92
About
Boyd, B. Vladimir Nabokov 92
Johnson, K. Nabokov's Blues 92
NACA *See* United States. National Advisory Committee for Aeronautics
Nachman, Patricia Ann
You and your only child 649
Nadeau, Robert
See also Zanger, Mark H.
Naden, Corinne J.
(jt. auth) Gillespie, J. T. The Newbery companion 028.5
Naftali, Timothy J.
(jt. auth) Fursenko, A. V. "One hell of a gamble" 973.922
Nāgārjuna
See/See also pages in the following book(s):
Jaspers, K. The great philosophers 109
Nagel, Joane
American Indian ethnic renewal 970.004
Nagel, Paul C.
The Adams women 920
John Quincy Adams 92
Nagyszalanczy, Sandor
Power tools 621.9
Naipaul, V. S. (Vidiadhar Surajprasad), 1932-
Among the believers 297
Between father and son 92
Beyond belief 297
Reading & writing 92
The writer and the world 824
Naipaul, Vidiadhar Surajprasad *See* Naipaul, V. S. (Vidiadhar Surajprasad), 1932-
Naish, Darren
(jt. auth) Lambert, D. Dinosaur encyclopedia 567.9
Najibullah, Mohammed
About
Corwin, P. Doomed in Afghanistan 958.1
Naked economics. Wheelan, C. J. 330
Naked masks. Pirandello, L. 852
Name-dropping. Galbraith, J. K. 973.9
The **name** of war. Lepore, J. 973.2
Names
See also Geographic names
Mencken, H. L. The American language 427
Dictionaries
Latham, E. A dictionary of names, nicknames, and surnames of persons, places, and things 929.4
Pronunciation
Pronouncing dictionary of proper names 423
Names, Personal *See* Personal names
Names & numbers. See Literary market place: LMP 070.5025
Nanji, Azim
(ed) The Muslim almanac. See The Muslim almanac 297
Nanjing (Jiangsu Province, China) massacre, 1937
Chang, I. The rape of Nanking 951.04
Nanking massacre, Nan-ching, China, 1937 *See* Nanjing (Jiangsu Province, China) massacre, 1937
Napalm & silly putty. Carlin, G. 817
Napoleon I, Emperor of the French, 1769-1821
About
Hamilton-Williams, D. The fall of Napoleon 944.05
Johnson, P. Napoleon 92
McLynn, F. J. Napoleon 92
Schom, A. Napoleon Bonaparte 92
Schom, A. One hundred days 944.05

See/See also pages in the following book(s):
Emerson, R. W. The portable Emerson p325-45 818
Kissinger, H. Diplomacy p103-36 327.73
Wills, G. Certain trumpets p85-98 303.3
Napoleonic Wars *See* Europe—History—1789-1815; France—History—1799-1815
Narayan, R. K., 1906-2001
The Ramayana 891
Narcotic traffic *See* Drug traffic
Narcotics
See also Cocaine; Marijuana; Opium
Davenport-Hines, R. P. T. The pursuit of oblivion 363.45
Encyclopedias
Chepesiuk, R. The war on drugs 363.45
Narins, Brigham
(ed) Notable scientists from 1900 to the present. See Notable scientists from 1900 to the present 920.003
(ed) World of computer science. See World of computer science 004
Narraganset Indians
See/See also pages in the following book(s):
Josephy, A. M. Now that the buffalo's gone p48-72 970.004
Narrations *See* Monologues
Narrative of the life of Frederick Douglass, an American slave. Douglass, F. 92
also in Douglass, F. Autobiographies 92
Narrative poems. Lewis, C. S. 821
Narrowing the nation's power: the Supreme Court sides with the states. Noonan, J. T., Jr. 342
NASA *See* United States. National Aeronautics and Space Administration
Nasaw, David
The chief: the life of William Randolph Hearst 92
NASCAR *See* National Association for Stock Car Auto Racing
Nasdijj
The blood runs like a river through my dreams 92
The boy and the dog are sleeping 92
Nash, Diane, 1938-
See/See also pages in the following book(s):
Halberstam, D. The children 323.1
Nash, Gary B.
History on trial 907
(ed) Encyclopedia of American history. See Encyclopedia of American history 973.03
Nash, George, 1949-
Do-it-yourself housebuilding 690
Nash, Jay Robert
Bloodletters and badmen 920
World encyclopedia of 20th century murder 364.03
Nasr, Seyyed Hossein
Islam: religion, history, and civilization 297
Nasser, Gamal Abdel, 1918-1970
See/See also pages in the following book(s):
Vidal, G. United States—essays, 1952-1992 p1213-32 814
Natasha's dance. Figes, O. 947
Nathan, Joan
The foods of Israel today 641.5
Jewish cooking in America 641.5
The Jewish holiday baker 641.8
Nation of Islam *See* Black Muslims
National Advisory Committee for Aeronautics (U.S.)
See United States. National Advisory Committee for Aeronautics
National Aeronautics and Space Administration (U.S.)
See United States. National Aeronautics and Space Administration

National Air and Space Museum (U.S.)
Chaikin, A. Air and space   **629.13**
National anthems of the world   **782.42**
National Archives and Records Administration (U.S.)
    See United States. National Archives and Records Administration
National Association for Stock Car Auto Racing
Menzer, J. The wildest ride   **796.72**
Rich, R. My life in the pits   **796.72**
Wright, J. D. Fixin' to git   **796.72**
National Association for the Advancement of Colored People
    See/See also pages in the following book(s):
Rowan, C. T. Dream makers, dream breakers: the world of Justice Thurgood Marshall   **92**
National Audubon Society
The Audubon Society field guide to North American fishes, whales, and dolphins. See The Audubon Society field guide to North American fishes, whales, and dolphins   **597**
Bull, J. L. The National Audubon Society field guide to North American birds, Eastern region   **598**
Chartrand, M. R. The Audubon Society field guide to the night sky   **523**
Chesterman, C. W. The Audubon Society field guide to North American rocks and minerals   **549**
Kress, S. W. The bird garden   **598**
Lincoff, G. The Audubon Society field guide to North American mushrooms   **579.6**
Little, E. L. The Audubon Society field guide to North American trees   **582.16**
Ludlum, D. M. The Audubon Society field guide to North American weather   **551.6**
Milne, L. J. The Audubon Society field guide to North American insects and spiders   **595.7**
Pyle, R. M. The Audubon Society field guide to North American butterflies   **595.7**
Sibley, D. The Sibley guide to bird life & behavior   **598**
Sibley, D. The Sibley guide to birds   **598**
Smith, C. L. National Audubon Society field guide to tropical marine fishes of the Caribbean, the Gulf of Mexico, Florida, the Bahamas, and Bermuda   **597**
Thompson, I. The Audubon Society field guide to North American fossils   **560**
Udvardy, M. D. F. National Audubon Society field guide to North American birds, Western region   **598**
Whitaker, J. O., Jr. National Audubon Society field guide to North American mammals   **599**
The **National** Audubon Society field guide to North American birds, Eastern region. Bull, J. L.   **598**
National Audubon Society field guide to North American birds, Western region. Udvardy, M. D. F.   **598**
National Audubon Society field guide to North American mammals. Whitaker, J. O., Jr.   **599**
National Audubon Society field guide to North American wildflowers: eastern region. Thieret, J. W.   **582.13**
National Audubon Society field guide to North American wildflowers, western region. Spellenberg, R.   **582.13**
National Audubon Society field guide to tropical marine fishes of the Caribbean, the Gulf of Mexico, Florida, the Bahamas, and Bermuda. Smith, C. L.   **597**
National Audubon Society guide to marine mammals of the world   **599.5**
National Basketball Association
Bradley, B. Values of the game   **796.323**
National characteristics
    See also Ethnopsychology
National characteristics, American *See* American national characteristics

National characteristics, Brazilian *See* Brazilian national characteristics
National characteristics, British *See* British national characteristics
National characteristics, French *See* French national characteristics
National characteristics, Irish *See* Irish national characteristics
National characteristics, Israeli *See* Israeli national characteristics
National characteristics, Italian *See* Italian national characteristics
National characteristics, Japanese *See* Japanese national characteristics
National characteristics, Korean *See* Korean national characteristics
National characteristics, Mexican *See* Mexican national characteristics
National characteristics, Russian *See* Russian national characteristics
National characteristics, Scottish *See* Scottish national characteristics
National E-mail and FAX directory   **384.1**
National Electrical Code handbook   **621.3**
National Electrical Code handbook, McGraw-Hill's   **621.3**
National Endowment for the Arts
    See/See also pages in the following book(s):
Alexander, J. Command performance   **92**
The **national** experience. See Boorstin, D. J. The Americans: The national experience   **973**
National FAX directory. See National E-mail and FAX directory   **384.1**
National Fire Protection Association
Fire protection handbook   **628.9**
National five digit zip code and post office directory   **383**
National Football League
Green, T. The dark side of the game   **796.332**
National Gallery of Art (U.S.)
Cikovsky, N., Jr. Winslow Homer   **759.13**
Stieglitz, A. Alfred Stieglitz: the key set   **779**
National geographic (Periodical) Carter, A. A. The art of National Geographic   **741.6**
Through the lens. See Through the lens   **779**
    Indexes
National geographic index, 1888-1988   **910**
National Geographic atlas of the world   **912**
The **National** Geographic desk reference   **910**
National Geographic expeditions atlas   **910.4**
National Geographic eyewitness to the 20th century   **909.82**
National Geographic guide to America's historic places   **917.3**
National Geographic guide to the national parks of the United States   **917.3**
National Geographic guide to the state parks of the United States   **917.3**
National geographic index, 1888-1988   **910**
National Geographic photographs   **779**
National Geographic Society (U.S.)
Ambrose, S. E. Lewis & Clark   **978**
Ballard, R. D. Return to Midway   **940.54**
Caputo, P. Ghosts of Tsavo   **599.75**
Carter, A. A. The art of National Geographic   **741.6**
Chadwick, D. H. The company we keep   **591.68**
Field guide to the birds of North America. See Field guide to the birds of North America   **598**
Harvey, D. A. Cuba   **972.91**
Mitchell, J. G. National Geographic, the wildlife photographs   **779**
Mitchell, J. G. National Geographic, the wildlife photographs   **779**

National Geographic Society (U.S.)—*Continued*
The National Geographic desk reference. See The National Geographic desk reference **910**
National Geographic expeditions atlas. See National Geographic expeditions atlas **910.4**
National Geographic guide to America's historic places. See National Geographic guide to America's historic places **917.3**
National geographic index, 1888-1988. See National geographic index, 1888-1988 **910**
Photographs then and now. See Photographs then and now **779**
Sacks, O. W. Oaxaca journal **587**
Schmidt, T. The Lewis & Clark Trail **978**
Sedeen, M. Star-spangled banner **929.9**
Slung, M. B. Living with cannibals and other women's adventures **910.4**
Suplee, C. Milestones of science **509**
Through the lens. See Through the lens **779**
Trefil, J. S. Other worlds **523.2**
Wiencek, H. National Geographic guide to America's great houses **728.8**
National Geographic, the wildlife photographs. Mitchell, J. G. **779**
National Hockey League
Duplacey, J. The official rules of hockey **796.962**
National interest *See* Public interest
National Museum of the American Indian (U.S.)
Spirit capture **779**
National parks and reserves
United States
The Complete guide to America's national parks **917.3**
National Geographic guide to the national parks of the United States **917.3**
National party conventions, 1831-1992. See National party conventions, 1831-2000 **324.5**
National party conventions, 1831-2000 **324.5**
National planning *See* Social policy
National Public Radio (U.S.)
Hoffman, M. The NPR classical music companion **780.3**
National security
United States
Moynihan, D. P. Secrecy **352**
Rehnquist, W. H. All the laws but one **342**
National socialism
See also Neo-Nazis
Ayçoberry, P. The social history of the Third Reich **943.086**
Breitman, R. The architect of genocide: Himmler and the final solution **92**
Fischer, K. P. Nazi Germany **943.086**
Goldhagen, D. Hitler's willing executioners **940.53**
Hay, J. A history of the Third Reich **943.086**
Hitler, A. Mein Kampf **92**
Johnson, E. A. Nazi terror **940.53**
Lewy, G. The Nazi persecution of the gypsies **940.53**
Michael, R. Nazi-Deutsch/Nazi-German **943.086**
Petropoulos, J. The Faustian bargain **709**
Rempel, G. Hitler's children **943.086**
Rosenbaum, R. Explaining Hitler **92**
Sereny, G. Albert Speer **92**
Toland, J. Adolf Hitler **92**
Turner, H. A. Hitler's thirty days to power **943.086**
Van der Vat, D. The good Nazi: the life and lies of Albert Speer **92**
Walker, M. Nazi science **509**
See/See also pages in the following book(s):
Fest, J. C. Speer: the final verdict **92**
Fulbrook, M. A concise history of Germany p173-203 **943**

Gay, P. My German question **92**
National songs
National anthems of the world **782.42**
National survey of state laws **349**
National trade and professional associations of the United States **061.025**
National zip code and post office directory. See National five digit zip code and post office directory **383**
Nationalism
Didion, J. Fixed ideas: America since 9.11 **320.5**
See/See also pages in the following book(s):
Berlin, Sir I. The sense of reality p232-66 **901**
The Causes of the Civil War **973.7**
Said, E. W. Reflections on exile and other essays p372-435 **814**
Nationalist China *See* Taiwan
Native America in the twentieth century **970.004**
Native American architecture. Nabokov, P. **728**
Native American art
Lester, P. D. The biographical directory of Native American painters **920.003**
St. James guide to native North American artists **920.003**
See/See also pages in the following book(s):
Schobinger, J. The ancient Americans **970.01**
Native American artists
Dictionaries
St. James guide to native North American artists **920.003**
Directories
Lester, P. D. The biographical directory of Native American painters **920.003**
Native American costume
Paterek, J. Encyclopedia of American Indian costume **391**
A **Native** American encyclopedia. Pritzker, B. **970.004**
Native American literature
American Indian literature **897**
The Portable North American Indian reader **897**
Native American testimony **970.004**
Native American weapons. Taylor, C. F. **970.004**
Native American women
Sifters: Native American women's lives **920**
Native Americans
See also names of Native American peoples and linguistic families
Bordewich, F. M. Killing the white man's Indian **970.004**
Bragdon, K. J. The Columbia guide to American Indians of the Northeast **970.004**
Deloria, V. Custer died for your sins **970.004**
Dorris, M. The broken cord **362.292**
Encyclopedia of North American Indians **970.004**
Handbook of North American Indians **970.004**
Hirschfelder, A. B. Native American **970.004**
Iverson, P. We are still here **970.004**
Josephy, A. M. Now that the buffalo's gone **970.004**
Milton, G. Big Chief Elizabeth **975.5**
Nabokov, P. A forest of time **970.004**
Nagel, J. American Indian ethnic renewal **970.004**
The Native North American almanac **970.004**
Parkman, F. The Oregon Trail **978**
Richter, D. K. Facing east from Indian country **970.004**
Taylor, C. F. Native American weapons **970.004**
Waldman, C. Atlas of the North American Indian **970.004**
Weatherford, J. M. Native roots **970.004**
Wilson, J. The earth shall weep **970.004**
See/See also pages in the following book(s):
Hogan, L. The woman who watches over the world **92**

Native Americans—*Continued*
Antiquities
America in 1492   970.01
Archaeology of the Appalachian highlands
                                                  970.004
Chatters, J. Ancient encounters   970.004
Prehistoric culture change on the Colorado plateau
                                                  970.004
Schobinger, J. The ancient Americans   970.01
Antiquities—Encyclopedias
Archaeology of prehistoric native America   970.01
Art
Berlo, J. C. Native North American art   709.01
Biography—Dictionaries
Notable native Americans   920.003
Waldman, C. Biographical dictionary of American In-
dian history to 1900   920.003
Claims
Garrison, T. A. The legal ideology of removal
                                                  970.004
Matthiessen, P. Indian country   970.004
Dwellings
Nabokov, P. Native American architecture   728
Encyclopedias
American Indians   970.004
The Gale encyclopedia of Native American tribes
                                                  970.004
Johnson, M. Macmillan encyclopedia of Native
American tribes   970.004
Keoke, E. D. Encyclopedia of American Indian contri-
butions to the world   970.004
Native America in the twentieth century   970.004
Pritzker, B. A Native American encyclopedia
                                                  970.004
Waldman, C. Encyclopedia of Native American tribes
                                                  970.004
Folklore
American Indian myths and legends   398.2
Government relations
Documents of American Indian diplomacy
                                                  970.004
Josephy, A. M. Now that the buffalo's gone
                                                  970.004
Native American testimony   970.004
Osborn, W. M. The wild frontier   973
Prucha, F. P. The great father   970.004
Remini, R. V. Andrew Jackson & his Indian wars
                                                  973.5
Schultz, E. B. King Philip's War   973.2
Wallace, A. F. C. The long bitter trail   970.004
History
America in 1492   970.01
American encounters   970.004
American nations   970.004
Calloway, C. G. The American Revolution in Indian
country   973.3
A Companion to American Indian history
                                                  970.004
Josephy, A. M. 500 nations   970.004
Wickett, M. R. Contested territory   976.6
History—Sources
Native American testimony   970.004
Origin
Adovasio, J. M. The first Americans   970.01
Pictorial works
Discovered lands, invented pasts   759.13
Spirit capture   779
Quotations
American Indian quotations   808.88
Religion
American Indian myths and legends   398.2
Hultkrantz, Å. The religions of the American Indians
                                                  299
Popol vuh. Popol vuh   299

Religion—Dictionaries
Gill, S. D. Dictionary of Native American mythology
                                                  299
Religion—Encyclopedias
Hirschfelder, A. B. The encyclopedia of Native
American religions   299
Reservations
See also Pine Ridge Indian Reservation (S.D.)
Wars
Brown, D. A. Bury my heart at Wounded Knee
                                                  970.004
Lepore, J. The name of war   973.2
Osborn, W. M. The wild frontier   973
Rajtar, S. Indian war sites   970.004
Remini, R. V. Andrew Jackson & his Indian wars
                                                  973.5
Roberts, D. Once they moved like the wind
                                                  970.004
Utley, R. M. Custer: cavalier in buckskin   973.8
Welch, J. Killing Custer   973.8
Central America
See also Mayas
Great Plains
Fowler, L. The Columbia guide to American Indians of
the Great Plains   970.004
West, E. The contested plains   978
Mexico
See also Aztecs; Mayas; Yaqui Indians
Mexico—Encyclopedias
American Indians   970.004
Northwest Coast of North America
Harmon, A. Indians in the making   970.004
South America
See also Incas; Waorani Indians
Southern States
Gallay, A. The Indian slave trade   326
Perdue, T. The Columbia guide to American Indians of
the Southeast   970.004
West (U.S.)
Brown, D. A. Bury my heart at Wounded Knee
                                                  970.004
Native Americans. See Pritzker, B. A Native American
encyclopedia   970.004
The **Native** North American almanac   970.004
Native North American art. Berlo, J. C.   709.01
Native North American literature   810.9
Native roots. Weatherford, J. M.   970.004
The **native** tribes of North America. See Johnson, M.
Macmillan encyclopedia of Native American tribes
                                                  970.004
Natural beauty. DuPriest, L.   646.7
Natural blonde. Smith, L.   92
Natural childbirth
See also Midwives
Leboyer, F. Birth without violence   618.4
Natural disasters
See also Storms
Erickson, J. Quakes, eruptions, and other geologic cat-
aclysms   550
McGuire, B. A guide to the end of the world
                                                  001.9
Natural foods
Mindell, E. Dr. Earl Mindell's unsafe at any meal
                                                  613.2
Weil, A. The healthy kitchen   641.5
Natural gardening See Organic gardening
Natural history
Ackerman, D. Cultivating delight   508
Asma, S. T. Stuffed animals & pickled heads
                                                  508
Darwin, C. The voyage of the Beagle   508
Dillard, A. Teaching a stone to talk   818
Eiseley, L. C. The unexpected universe   500
Gould, S. J. Bully for brontosaurus   508
Gould, S. J. Dinosaur in a haystack   508

Natural history—*Continued*
Gould, S. J. Eight little piggies   **576.8**
Gould, S. J. The flamingo's smile   **508**
Gould, S. J. I have landed   **578**
Gould, S. J. Leonardo's mountain of clams and the
    Diet of Worms   **508**
Gould, S. J. The lying stones of Marrakesh   **508**
Keynes, R. D. Fossils, finches, and Fuegians   **508**
Nature writing   **508**
Quammen, D. The boilerplate rhino   **508**
Wallace, J. A gathering of wonders   **508**
                Dictionaries
Lincoln, R. J. The Cambridge illustrated dictionary of
    natural history   **508**
                Encyclopedias
Nature encyclopedia   **508**
                Africa
De Villiers, M. Sahara: a natural history   **508**
Matthiessen, P. African silences   **916**
                Arctic regions
Lopez, B. H. Arctic dreams   **998**
                Galapagos Islands
Kricher, J. C. Galapagos   **508**
                Himalaya Mountains
Matthiessen, P. The snow leopard   **915.4**
                Maine
    See/See also pages in the following book(s):
Heinrich, B. The trees in my forest   **577.3**
                North America
Flannery, T. F. The eternal frontier   **508**
                Rocky Mountains
Elias, S. A. Rocky Mountains   **508**
                South Asia
Thapar, V. Land of the tiger   **508**
                Utah
Williams, T. T. Red: passion and patience in the desert
     333.7
A **natural** history of homosexuality. Mondimore, F. M.
     306.7
A **natural** history of love. Ackerman, D.   **152.4**
The **natural** history of medicinal plants. Sumner, J.
     581.6
A **natural** history of rape. Thornhill, R.   **364.1**
The **natural** history of the rich. Conniff, R.   **305.5**
A **natural** history of the senses. Ackerman, D.
     152.1
The **natural** history of the wild cats. Kitchener, A.
     599.75
Natural landscapes, John Brookes'. Brookes, J.
     635.9
Natural law *See* Ethics
Natural resources
    See also Conservation of natural resources; Marine
    resources
Natural selection
    See also Biological invasions; Evolution
Darwin, C. The Darwin reader   **576.8**
Darwin, C. The origin of species   **576.8**
Dawkins, R. Climbing Mount Improbable   **576**
Dennett, D. C. Darwin's dangerous idea   **146**
Etcoff, N. L. Survival of the prettiest   **391**
Gould, S. J. Ever since Darwin   **576.8**
Gould, S. J. The panda's thumb   **576.8**
Hooper, J. Of moths and men   **576.8**
Jones, S. Darwin's ghost   **576.8**
Rose, M. R. Darwin's spectre   **576.8**
    See/See also pages in the following book(s):
Pinker, S. How the mind works p155-74   **153**
The **natural**: the misunderstood presidency of Bill Clin-
    ton. Klein, J.   **973.929**
Naturalists
Ehrlich, G. John Muir   **92**
Nature
American nature writing   **810.8**
Barlow, C. C. Green space, green time   **291.1**

The Best American science and nature writing
     500
Carson, R. Lost woods   **570**
Quammen, D. The boilerplate rhino   **508**
Nature, Effect of man on *See* Human influence on na-
    ture
Nature, Philosophy of *See* Philosophy of nature
Nature. Emerson, R. W.
    In Emerson, R. W. The portable Emerson p7-50
     818
Nature. Swenson, M.   **811**
Nature and nurture
Pinker, S. The blank slate   **155.2**
Nature conservation
    See also Wildlife conservation
Baskin, Y. A plague of rats and rubbervines   **577**
Beacham's guide to the endangered species of North
    America   **578.68**
Commoner, B. Making peace with the planet
     304.2
Wilson, E. O. The diversity of life   **577**
Wilson, E. O. The future of life   **333.95**
Nature cures. Whorton, J. C.   **615.5**
Nature encyclopedia   **508**
The **nature** of animal healing. Goldstein, M.
     636.089
The **Nature** of diamonds   **553.8**
The **nature** of prejudice. Allport, G.   **152.4**
The **nature** of space and time. Hawking, S. W.
     530.1
Nature photography
    See also Outdoor photography
Nature wars. Winston, M. L.   **577.2**
Nature writing   **508**
Nature writings. Muir, J.   **92**
Nature's medicines. Maleskey, G.   **615.5**
Naturopathy
Maleskey, G. Nature's medicines   **615.5**
                Encyclopedias
Murray, M. T. Encyclopedia of natural medicine
     615.5
Naughton, John, 1946-
A brief history of the future   **621.382**
Nautical almanacs
The Astronomical almanac   **528**
Navaho Indians *See* Navajo Indians
Navajo Indians
    See/See also pages in the following book(s):
Brown, D. A. Bury my heart at Wounded Knee
     970.004
Nasdijj. The boy and the dog are sleeping   **92**
                Social conditions
    See/See also pages in the following book(s):
Nasdijj. The blood runs like a river through my dreams
     92
Naval administration *See* Naval art and science
Naval art and science
                Dictionaries
Dictionary of military terms   **355**
                Encyclopedias
Naval warfare   **359**
Naval history
    See also Military history; names of countries with
    the subhead *Navy* or the subdivision *Naval history*
Bruce, A. An encyclopedia of naval history   **359**
Clifford, B. The lost fleet   **910.4**
                Encyclopedias
Naval warfare   **359**
Naval warfare   **359**
Navarra, Tova
    (jt. auth) Lipkowitz, M. Encyclopedia of allergies
     616.97
Navies
    See also names of countries with the subhead
    Navy

Navies—*Continued*
Jane's fighting ships 623.8
Navigation
See also Inland navigation
Dutton's nautical navigation 623.89
Psychological aspects
Jonsson, E. Inner navigation 153.7
Naylor, Phyllis Reynolds, 1933-
See/See also pages in the following book(s):
The Newbery & Caldecott medal books, 1986-2000
p167-78 028.5
Nazi-Deutsch/Nazi-German. Michael, R. 943.086
The **Nazi** doctors. Lifton, R. J. 940.53
Nazi-German. See Michael, R. Nazi-Deutsch/Nazi-
German 943.086
Nazi Germany. Fischer, K. P. 943.086
Nazi Germany and the Jews vl. Friedländer, S.
940.53
The **Nazi** persecution of the gypsies. Lewy, G.
940.53
Nazi science. Walker, M. 509
Nazi terror. Johnson, E. A. 940.53
Nazism See National socialism
NBA See National Basketball Association
NEA See National Endowment for the Arts
Neagles, James C.
The Library of Congress 929
Neagles, Mark C.
(jt. auth) Neagles, J. C. The Library of Congress
929
Neal-Schuman netguide series
Hoffmann, G. M. Copyright in cyberspace 346.04
Near a thousand tables. Fernández-Armesto, F.
641.3
Near East See Middle East
Nearer, my God. Buckley, W. F. 92
Nearest star. Golub, L. 523.7
Nebehay, Christian Michael, 1909-
Gustav Klimt 759.36
Nebeker, Frederik
(ed) From 0 to 1: an authoritative history of modern
computing. See From 0 to 1: an authoritative history
of modern computing 004
A **necessary** evil. Wills, G. 973
Needlework
See also Tapestry
Michler, J. M. The magic of crazy quilting
746.46
Reader's Digest complete guide to needlework
746.4
Neel, Alice, 1900-1984
Alice Neel 759.13
Neely, Mark E., Jr.
The last best hope of earth: Abraham Lincoln and the
promise of America 92
Neer, Richard
FM: the rise and fall of free-form rock radio
791.44
**Nefertiti, Queen, consort of Akhenaton, King of
Egypt, 14th cent. B.C.**
About
Tyldesley, J. A. Nefertiti 932
Neff, James
The wrong man 345
Neft, David S.
The sports encyclopedia: baseball 796.357
Negative blue. Wright, C. 811
Negotiation
Camp, J. Start with no 658.4
Ury, W. Getting past no 158
Negrin, Micol
Rustico: regional Italian country cooking 641.5
The **Negro** almanac. See The African American almanac
305.8

Nehru, Jawaharlal, 1889-1964
See/See also pages in the following book(s):
Galbraith, J. K. Name-dropping 973.9
Neighborhood development See Community develop-
ment
Neihardt, John Gneisenau, 1881-1973
(jt. auth) Black Elk Black Elk speaks 92
Neill, Peter, 1941-
(ed) American sea writing. See American sea writing
810.8
Nelson, Craig
The first heroes 940.54
Nelson, Glenn C.
Ceramics 738.1
Nelson, Horatio Nelson, Viscount, 1758-1805
About
Hibbert, C. Nelson 92
Nelson, Michael, 1949-
(ed) Guide to the presidency. See Guide to the presi-
dency 352.23
(ed) The Presidency A to Z. See The Presidency A to
Z 352.23
Nelson, Miriam E.
Strong women eat well 613.2
Strong women, strong bones 616.7
Nelson, Paul David, 1941-
Fredrick L. McGhee 92
Nemeroff, Charles B.
(ed) The Corsini encyclopedia of psychology and be-
havioral science. See The Corsini encyclopedia of
psychology and behavioral science 150.3
Nemiroff, Robert, d. 1991
Hansberry, L. To be young, gifted and black 92
Neo-fascism See Fascism
Neo-Nazis
See/See also pages in the following book(s):
Dees, M. S., Jr. Gathering storm 322.4
Neopaganism
Hutton, R. The triumph of the moon 133.4
Néret, Gilles
Renoir: painter of happiness 1841-1919 759.4
Nero, Emperor of Rome, 37-68
See/See also pages in the following book(s):
Suetonius Tranquillus, C. The twelve Caesars 878
Neruda, Pablo, 1904-1973
Five decades 861
Late and posthumous poems, 1968-1974 861
Selected odes of Pablo Neruda 861
Stones of the sky 861
See/See also pages in the following book(s):
Bloom, H. The Western canon 809
Nervous system
See also Spinal cord
Diseases
See also Tourette syndrome
Sacks, O. W. An anthropologist on Mars 616.8
Sacks, O. W. The man who mistook his wife for a hat
and other clinical tales 616.8
Nestle, Marion
Safe food 363.1
Netherlands
Civilization
Schama, S. The embarrassment of riches 949.2
History
Dash, M. Tulipomania 635.9
See/See also pages in the following book(s):
Durant, W. J. The age of Louis XIV p164-80
940.2
History—1940-1945, German occupation
Frank, A. The diary of a young girl: the definitive edi-
tion 92
Frank, A. The diary of Anne Frank: the critical edition
92
Gies, M. Anne Frank remembered 940.53

Netherlands—History—1940-1945, German occupation—*Continued*
Lindwer, W. The last seven months of Anne Frank
940.53
Müller, M. Anne Frank 92
History—1940-1945, German occupation—Drama
Goodrich, F. The diary of Anne Frank 812
Netherton, John
Badger, D. Snakes 597.9
Netter, Frank H., 1906-1991
Atlas of human anatomy 611
Networking for dummies. Lowe, D. 004.6
Networks, Computer *See* Computer networks
Netzley, Patricia D.
The encyclopedia of movie special effects 778.5
Neufeld, Peter J.
(jt. auth) Dwyer, J. Actual innocence 347
Neugeboren, Jay, 1938-
Transforming madness 616.89
Neurology *See* Nervous system
Neuroses
See also Anxiety; Obsessive-compulsive neurosis
Neusner, Jacob, 1932-
The Encyclopedia of Judaism. See The Encyclopedia of Judaism [Continuum] 296.03
Never. Graham, J. 811
Never again. Gilbert, M. 940.53
Never alone. Girzone, J. F. 248
Never cry wolf. Mowat, F. 599.77
Never too late. DeLaughter, B. 345
New, Gregory R.
(ed) Dewey, M. Dewey decimal classification and relative index 025.4
New, William H.
(ed) Encyclopedia of literature in Canada. See Encyclopedia of literature in Canada 810.3
New & selected essays. Levertov, D. 814
New & selected poems. Justice, D. R. 811
New addresses. Koch, K. 811
The **New** African poetry 896
New Age movement
Goodman, L. Linda Goodman's star signs 133
The **new** American Bible. Bible 220.5
The **new** American Heart Association cookbook. See American Heart Association cookbook 641.5
The **New** American poets 811.008
New American standard Bible. Bible 220.5
New and collected poems. Wilbur, R. 811
New and collected poems 1931-2001. Miłosz, C. 891.8
New and selected poems. Oliver, M. 811
New and selected poems. Soto, G. 811
New and selected poems, 1975-1995. Lux, T. 811
The **new** apartment book. Michael, M. 747
The **new** architecture and the Bauhaus. Gropius, W. 724
The **new** book of Middle Eastern food. Roden, C. 641.5
The **New** Bread Loaf anthology of contemporary American poetry 811.008
The **New** Cambridge medieval history 940.1
The **New** Cambridge modern history 909.08
The **New** Cassell's German dictionary. See Cassell's German dictionary 433
New Catholic encyclopedia 282
New Catholic encyclopedia: jubilee volume, the Wojtyla years 282
New collected poems. Oppen, G. 811
The **new** complete book of food. Rinzler, C. A. 641.3
The **new** complete book of herbs, spices, and condiments. Rinzler, C. A. 641.3
New complete do-it-yourself manual 643
New complete dog training manual. Fogle, B. 636.7
New complete guide to sewing 646.2

The **new** comprehensive American rhyming dictionary. Young, S. 423
The **New** cooks' catalogue 683
New Deal, 1933-1939
Leuchtenburg, W. E. Franklin D. Roosevelt and the New Deal, 1932-1940 973.917
Schlesinger, A. M. The coming of the New Deal, 1933-1935 973.917
Schlesinger, A. M. The politics of upheaval, 1935-1936 973.917
Encyclopedias
Encyclopedia of the Great Depression and the New Deal 973.917
The **New** decorating book 747
New dictionary of American slang. See Dictionary of American slang 427
The **new** dictionary of cultural literacy. Hirsch, E. D. 031
A **New** dictionary of quotations on historical principles from ancient and modern sources 808.88
The **new** doublespeak. Lutz, W. 427
The **new** elegant but easy cookbook. Burros, M. F. 641.5
The **New** Encyclopaedia Britannica 031
The **New** encyclopedia of American scandal 973.02
New encyclopedia of herbs & their uses. Bown, D. 581.6
The **New** encyclopedia of Judaism [New York University Press] 296.03
The **new** encyclopedia of science 503
The **New** encyclopedia of the American West 978.03
The **new** encyclopedia of the cat. Fogle, B. 636.8
The **new** encyclopedia of the dog. Fogle, B. 636.7
The **new** encyclopedia of the horse. Edwards, E. H. 636.1

New England
History
Thorson, R. M. Stone by stone 693
History—1600-1775, Colonial period
Karlsen, C. F. The devil in the shape of a woman 133.4
Schultz, E. B. King Philip's War 973.2
Intellectual life
Transcendentalism 810.8
The **New** England cookbook. Dojny, B. 641.5
The **new** English Bible. See Bible. The revised English Bible 220.5
The **new** first three years of life. White, B. L. 155.4
New fix-it-yourself manual 643
The **new** Fowler's modern English usage. Fowler, H. W. 428
The **new** garden. See Brookes, J. John Brookes' natural landscapes 635.9
The **new** German cookbook. Anderson, J. 641.5
The **new** golden bough. Frazer, Sir J. G. 291.1
The **new** good cake book. Dalsass, D. 641.8
The **New** Grove dictionary of American music 780.973
The **New** Grove dictionary of jazz 781.65
The **New** Grove dictionary of music and musicians 780.3
The **New** Grove dictionary of opera 792.5
The **New** Grove dictionary of women composers. See The Norton/Grove dictionary of women composers 920.003

New Guinea
Description
Flannery, T. F. Throwim way leg 995.3
New historical atlas of religion in America. Gaustad, E. S. 200.9
The **new** historical dictionary of the American film industry. Slide, A. 791.4303
A **new** history of India. Wolpert, S. A. 954

A **new** history of jazz. Shipton, A. **781.65**
New house/more house. Preves, R. **690**
New international dictionary of the English language, Webster's third **423**
The **New** Interpreter's Bible **220.7**
New Jersey
    See also Middletown (N.J.)
The **new** Jerusalem Bible. Bible **220.5**
The **new** Jewish holiday cookbook. Greene, G. K. **641.5**
The **new** joy of sex. See Comfort, A. The joy of sex **613.9**
The **new** joys of Yiddish. Rosten, L. **439**
The **New** Kobbé's opera book **792.5**
New life for old gardens. Seale, A. **635.9**
The **new** lifetime reading plan. Fadiman, C. **028**
The **new** living heart. DeBakey, M. E. **616.1**
The **New** living heart diet **616.1**
The **new** making of a cook. Kamman, M. **641.5**
New Mexico
    Description
    Johnson, G. Fire in the mind **215**
The **new** new thing. Lewis, M. **92**
New Orleans (La.)
    Race relations
    Johnson, W. Soul by soul **326**
New Orleans (La.), Battle of, 1815
    Remini, R. V. The Battle of New Orleans **973.5**
The **New** Oxford American dictionary **423**
The **New** Oxford book of American verse **811.008**
The **New** Oxford book of carols **782.28**
The **New** Oxford book of eighteenth century verse **821.008**
The **new** Oxford book of food plants. Vaughan, J. G. **633**
The **New** Oxford book of Irish verse **821.008**
The **New** Oxford book of Victorian verse **821.008**
The **New** Oxford companion to literature in French **840.3**
New Oxford history of music **780.9**
The **new** parrot handbook. Lantermann, W. **636.6**
New passages. Sheehy, G. **305.24**
A **new** path to the waterfall. Carver, R. **811**
The **New** Penguin opera guide **792.5**
The **new** perfect resume. Jackson, T. **650.14**
New poems. Rilke, R. M. **831**
New poems of Emily Dickinson. Dickinson, E. **811**
The **new** prince. Morris, D. **324.7**
The **New** Princeton encyclopedia of poetry and poetics **809.1**
New recipes from quilt country. Adams, M. **641.5**
The **new** Routledge Dutch dictionary. Osselton, N. E. **439.3**
New seeds of contemplation. Merton, T. **248**
New selected poems. Levine, P. **811**
The **New** shorter Oxford English dictionary on historical principles. See Shorter Oxford English dictionary on historical principles **423**
New Skete Monks *See* Monks of New Skete
New soccer techniques, tactics & teamwork. Bauer, G. **796.334**
New Testament *See* Bible. N.T.
New Thought
    See/See also pages in the following book(s):
    James, W. The varieties of religious experience **210**
A **new** time for Mexico. Fuentes, C. **972.08**
The **New** Times selective guide to colleges. See Fiske, E. B. The Fiske guide to colleges **378.73**
The **new** way things work. Macaulay, D. **600**
New ways in psychoanalysis. Horney, K. **150.19**
New words
    Metcalf, A. A. Predicting new words **420**

New Year
    Gulevich, T. Encyclopedia of Christmas and New Year's celebrations **394.26**
New York (N.Y.)
    Von Drehle, D. Triangle: the fire that changed America **974.7**
    Description
    See/See also pages in the following book(s):
    White, E. B. Essays of E. B. White **814**
    Encyclopedias
    The Encyclopedia of New York City **974.7**
    History
    Burrows, E. G. Gotham **974.7**
    Homberger, E. The historical atlas of New York City **974.7**
    Kaiser, C. The gay metropolis **305.9**
    O'Donnell, E. T. Ship ablaze **910.4**
    Intellectual life
    White, S. Stories of freedom in Black New York **974.7**
    See/See also pages in the following book(s):
    Bernays, A. Back then **92**
    Politics and government
    Kirtzman, A. Rudy Giuliani **92**
    Population
    Glazer, N. Beyond the melting pot **305.8**
    Race relations
    White, S. Stories of freedom in Black New York **974.7**
    Social conditions
    Canada, G. Fist, stick, knife, gun **305.23**
    Freeman, J. B. Working-class New York **305.5**
    Social life and customs
    Wetzsteon, R. Republic of dreams **974.7**
New York (N.Y.). Fire Dept.
    Golway, T. So others might live **628.9**
    Halberstam, D. Firehouse **363.34**
    Picciotto, R. Last man down **974.7**
    Smith, D. Report from ground zero **363.34**
New York (N.Y.). Metropolitan Opera *See* Metropolitan Opera (New York, N.Y.)
New York (N.Y.). World Trade Center *See* World Trade Center (New York, N.Y.)
New York (N.Y.) in art
    Bell, C. Hirschfeld's New York **741.5**
New York (N.Y.) in literature
    Writing New York **810.8**
New York (State)
    Wilson, E. Upstate **818**
    Politics and government
    See/See also pages in the following book(s):
    Slayton, R. A. Empire statesman: the rise and redemption of Al Smith **92**
New York Mets (Baseball team)
    Golenbock, P. Amazin' **796.357**
The **New** York Public Library African American desk reference **305.8**
The **New** York Public Library American history desk reference **973.02**
The **New** York Public Library business desk reference **651**
The **New** York Public Library desk reference **031.02**
The **New** York Public Library writer's guide to style and usage **808**
New York September 11 **974.7**
New York times
    Frankel, M. The times of my life and my life with the Times **92**
The **New** York Times almanac **031.02**
The **New** York Times book of Broadway **792**
The **New** York Times cook book. Claiborne, C. **641.5**
The **New** York times crossword puzzle dictionary. Pulliam, T. **793.73**

The **New** York Times essential library: Jazz. See Ratliff, B. Jazz: a critic's guide to the 100 most important recordings **781.65**

The **New** York Times guide to alternative health **615.5**

The **New** York times guide to the best 1,000 movies ever made. Canby, V. **791.43**

The **New** York Times Index **071**

The **New** York times manual of style and usage. Siegal, A. **808**

The **New** York Times parent's guide to the best books for children. Lipson, E. R. **011.6**

The **New** York Times Passover cookbook **641.5**

The **New** York Times second book of science questions and answers. Ray, C. C. **500**

New York Yankees (Baseball team)
Halberstam, D. Summer of '49 **796.357**
Tofel, R. J. A legend in the making **796.357**

New Yorker (Periodical)
The Fun of it **814**
Yagoda, B. About town **051**
See/See also pages in the following book(s):
Fraser, K. Ornament and silence **814**
Ross, L. Here but not here **92**

The **New** young American poets **811.008**

The **Newbery** & Caldecott medal books, 1986-2000 **028.5**

Newbery and Caldecott Medal books, 1966-1975 **028.5**

Newbery and Caldecott Medal books, 1976-1985 **028.5**

The **Newbery** companion. Gillespie, J. T. **028.5**

Newbery Medal
Gillespie, J. T. The Newbery companion **028.5**
The Newbery & Caldecott medal books, 1986-2000 **028.5**
Newbery and Caldecott Medal books, 1966-1975 **028.5**
Newbery and Caldecott Medal books, 1976-1985 **028.5**
Newbery Medal books, 1922-1955 **028.5**

Newbery Medal books, 1922-1955 **028.5**

Newbould, Brian
Schubert, the music and the man **92**

Newbury, Tim
20 best garden designs **712**

Newcastle, Margaret Cavendish, Duchess of, 1624?-1674
See/See also pages in the following book(s):
Woolf, V. Women and writing p79-88 **820.9**

Newcomb, Horace
(ed) Encyclopedia of television. See Encyclopedia of television **791.45**

Newcomb, Simon, 1835-1909
About
Carter, B. Latitude **526**

Newell, Clayton R., 1942-
Historical dictionary of the Persian Gulf War, 1990-1991 **956.7**

Newhouse, Elizabeth L.
(jt. auth) Harvey, D. A. Cuba **972.91**

Newlin, Keith, 1956-
(ed) A Theodore Dreiser encyclopedia. See A Theodore Dreiser encyclopedia **813.009**

Newman, Cathy
Women photographers at National Geographic **770.9**

Newman, Joseph Dwight
See/See also pages in the following book(s):
Dance, S. The world of Count Basie **920**

Newman, Richard, 1930-
(comp) African American quotations. See African American quotations **808.88**

The **news** about the news. Downie, L. **071**

News broadcasting See Broadcast journalism

News photography See Photojournalism

Newspapers
See also Journalism; Periodicals
Directories
Gale directory of publications and broadcast media **070.025**

Newton, Deborah
Designing knitwear **746.43**

Newton, Francis, 1917- See Hobsbawm, E. J. (Eric J.), 1917-

Newton, Sir Isaac, 1642-1727
About
Berlinski, D. Newton's gift: how Sir Isaac Newton unlocked the system of the world **92**
The Cambridge companion to Newton **530**
Fara, P. Newton: the making of genius **92**
Fritzsch, H. An equation that changed the world **530.1**
Gleick, J. Isaac Newton **92**
Westfall, R. S. The life of Isaac Newton **92**
See/See also pages in the following book(s):
Bell, E. T. Men of mathematics p90-116 **920**
Brennan, R. P. Heisenberg probably slept here **920**
Durant, W. J. The age of Louis XIV p531-47 **940.2**
Gay, P. The Enlightenment: an interpretation **190**
Guillen, M. Five equations that changed the world **530.1**
Horvitz, L. A. Eureka!: scientific breakthroughs that changed the world **509**

Newton, Keith
(ed) The Columbia Granger's Index to poetry in collected and selected works. See The Columbia Granger's Index to poetry in collected and selected works **808.81**

Newton, Michael, 1951-
The encyclopedia of serial killers **364.03**

The **next** Christendom. Jenkins, P. **270**

Next of kin. Fouts, R. **156**

Next: the future just happened. Lewis, M. **303.4**

Nexus: small worlds and the groundbreaking science of networks. Buchanan, M. **530**

Nez Percé Indians
Josephy, A. M. The Nez Perce Indians and the opening of the Northwest **970.004**
See/See also pages in the following book(s):
Brown, D. A. The American West p255-64 **978**
Brown, D. A. Bury my heart at Wounded Knee **970.004**

The **Nez** Perce Indians and the opening of the Northwest. Josephy, A. M. **970.004**

NFL See National Football League

Ng, Wendy L.
Japanese American internment during World War II **940.53**

Nguyen, Dinh Hoa, 1924-
NTC's Vietnamese-English dictionary **495.9**

Nguyen Dinh Hoa See Nguyen, Dinh Hoa, 1924-

Nguyen Tat Thành See Ho, Chí Minh, 1890-1969

Nhat Hanh, Thich
Living Buddha, living Christ **294.3**

NHL See National Hockey League

Niagara. Berton, P. **971.3**

Niagara Falls (N.Y. and Ont.)
Berton, P. Niagara **971.3**

Niccolini, Fausto, 1812?-1886
Houses and monuments of Pompeii. See Houses and monuments of Pompeii **709.38**

Niccolini, Felice, b. 1816?
Houses and monuments of Pompeii. See Houses and monuments of Pompeii **709.38**

Niccolò's smile: a biography of Machiavelli. Viroli, M. **92**

Nice, David
Prokofiev: from Russia to the West, 1891-1935
92

Nice (France)
Kanigel, R. High season   944
Nicholas II, Emperor of Russia, 1868-1918
About
Ferro, M. Nicholas II   92
Kurth, P. Tsar: the lost world of Nicholas and Alexandra   947.08
Massie, R. K. Nicholas and Alexandra   92
Massie, R. K. The Romanovs   947.08
Nicholas, of Cusa, Cardinal, 1401-1464
See/See also pages in the following book(s):
Jaspers, K. The great philosophers   109
Nicholas and Alexandra. Massie, R. K.   92
Nicholl, Charles
The reckoning: the murder of Christopher Marlowe
92

Nicholson, Stuart
Billie Holiday   92
Reminiscing in tempo: a portrait of Duke Ellington
92

Nichomachean ethics. See Aristotle. Ethics   170
Nichter, Mimi
Fat talk   613.2
Nickel and dimed. Ehrenreich, B.   305.5
Nicklaus, Jack
Golf my way   796.352
Jack Nicklaus   92
Nicknames
Kane, J. N. Nicknames and sobriquets of U.S. cities, states, and counties   917.3
Latham, E. A dictionary of names, nicknames, and surnames of persons, places, and things   929.4
Shankle, G. E. American nicknames   929.4
Twentieth century American nicknames   929.4
Nicknames and sobriquets of U.S. cities, states, and counties. Kane, J. N.   917.3
Nicknames of cities and states of the U.S. See Kane, J. N. Nicknames and sobriquets of U.S. cities, states, and counties   917.3
Nicolaus Cusanus *See* Nicholas, of Cusa, Cardinal, 1401-1464
Nicolson, Adam, 1957-
God's secretaries: the making of the King James Bible
220.5
Sea room: an island life in the Hebrides   941.1
Nicomachean ethics. See Aristotle. Ethics   170
Niebuhr, Gary Warren
Make mine a mystery   809.3
Niebuhr, H. Richard (Helmut Richard), 1894-1962
Christ and culture   261
Niebuhr, Helmut Richard See Niebuhr, H. Richard (Helmut Richard), 1894-1962
Niedecker, Lorine, 1903-1970
Collected works   811
Nielsen, Eric
(jt. auth) Patterson, J. L. Blackjack, a winner's handbook   795.4
Nietzsche, Friedrich Wilhelm, 1844-1900
The antichrist
In Nietzsche, F. W. The portable Nietzsche   193
Basic writings of Nietzsche   193
Nietzsche contra Wagner
In Nietzsche, F. W. The portable Nietzsche   193
The portable Nietzsche   193
Thus spake Zarathustra   193
also in Nietzsche, F. W. The portable Nietzsche
193
Twilight of the idols
In Nietzsche, F. W. The portable Nietzsche   193
The will to power   193
About
Safranski, R. Nietzsche   92

Solomon, R. C. What Nietzsche really said   193
See/See also pages in the following book(s):
Camus, A. The rebel p62-80   303.6
Durant, W. J. The story of philosophy p301-35
109
Existentialism from Dostoevsky to Sartre p121-33
142
Gass, W. H. Finding a form p119-45   814
Jaspers, K. The great philosophers   109
Russell, B. A history of Western philosophy p760-73
109
Nietzsche contra Wagner. Nietzsche, F. W.
In Nietzsche, F. W. The portable Nietzsche   193
Nigeria
Politics and government
Maier, K. This house has fallen   966.9
Soyinka, W. The open sore of a continent   966.9
Nigger. Kennedy, R.   305.8
Night
Alvarez, A. Night   154.6
Night. Pinter, H.
In Pinter, H. Complete works v3   822
The **night** Abraham called to the stars. Bly, R.   811
Night and horses and the desert   892
Night comes to the Cretaceous. Powell, J. L.   576.8
The **night** country. Eiseley, L. C.   818
The **night** is large. Gardner, M.   814
A **night** out. Pinter, H.
In Pinter, H. Complete works v1   822
Night picnic. Simic, C.   811
Night school. Pinter, H.
In Pinter, H. Complete works v2   822
A **night** to remember. Lord, W.   910.4
Nightingale, Florence, 1820-1910
About
Small, H. Florence Nightingale   92
Nihilism
Camus, A. The rebel   303.6
Nike is a goddess   796
Nikita Khrushchev   92
Nilsen, Alleen Pace
Encyclopedia of 20th century American humor
817
Nilsson, Lennart, 1922-
A child is born   612.6
Nims, John Frederick, 1913-1999
The powers of heaven and earth   811
Nin, Anaïs, 1903-1977
The diary of Anaïs Nin   92
See/See also pages in the following book(s):
American women fiction writers   813.009
Pierpont, C. R. Passionate minds   810.9
Nine early plays, 1961-1973. Gurney, A. R.   812
The **nine** emotional lives of cats. Masson, J. M.
636.8
The **nine** fantasies that will ruin your life and the eight realities that will save you. Browne, J.   158
Nine horses. Collins, B.   811
Nine parts of desire. Brooks, G.   305.4
Nine plays of the modern theater   808.82
Nineteen thirty-nine. See Carley, M. J. 1939
940.53
Ninety degrees North. Fleming, F.   998
Ninety-five poems. See Cummings, E. E. 95 poems
811
Nirvana (Musical group)
See/See also pages in the following book(s):
Cross, C. R. Heavier than heaven: a biography of Kurt Cobain   92
Nisqualli Indians
See/See also pages in the following book(s):
Josephy, A. M. Now that the buffalo's gone p180-211
970.004

Nixon, Hannah Milhous, 1885-1967
See/See also pages in the following book(s):
Angelo, B. First mothers 920
Nixon, Richard M. (Richard Milhous), 1913-1994
About
Abuse of power 973.924
Berman, L. No peace, no honor 959.704
Emery, F. Watergate 973.924
Matthews, C. Kennedy & Nixon 973.922
Reeves, R. President Nixon 92
Summers, A. The arrogance of power: the secret world of Richard Nixon 92
White, T. H. The making of the president, 1960 324.6
Woodward, B. The final days 973.924
See/See also pages in the following book(s):
Kissinger, H. Diplomacy p703-61 327.73
Mann, J. About face 327.73
Woodward, B. Shadow 973.92
No bugles, no drums. Tomedi, R. 951.9
No direction home: the life and music of Bob Dylan. Shelton, R. 92
No end save victory 940.54
No end to war. Laqueur, W. 303.6
No exit. Sartre, J. P.
In Sartre, J. P. No exit, and three other plays 842
No exit, and three other plays. Sartre, J. P. 842
No fixed points. Reynolds, N. 792.8
No future without forgiveness. Tutu, D. 968.06
No man is an island. Merton, T. 248
No man knows my history: the life of Joseph Smith, the Mormon prophet. Brodie, F. M. 92
No man's land. Pinter, H.
In Pinter, H. Complete works v4 822
No man's land v3. Gilbert, S. M. 820.9
No mercy: a journey to the heart of the Congo. O'Hanlon, R. 967
No more words: a journal of my mother, Anne Morrow Lindbergh. Lindbergh, R. 92
No nature. Snyder, G. 811
No ordinary time [biography of Franklin D. Roosevelt] Goodwin, D. K. 92
No other book. Jarrell, R. 809
No peace, no honor. Berman, L. 959.704
Nō plays
Waley, A. The Nō plays of Japan 895.6
The **Nō** plays of Japan. Waley, A. 895.6
No small courage 305.4
The **no-spin** zone. O'Reilly, B. 973.92
No turning back. Freedman, E. B. 305.4
No way to pick a president. Witcover, J. 324
Noah, Mordecai Manuel, 1785-1851
See/See also pages in the following book(s):
White, S. Stories of freedom in Black New York 974.7
Noah's flood. Ryan, W. B. F. 930
The **Nobel** Peace Prize and the laureates. Abrams, I. 920.003
Nobel Prize winners 920.003
Nobel Prizes
Abrams, I. The Nobel Peace Prize and the laureates 920.003
Feldman, B. The Nobel Prize 001.4
Hargittai, I. The road to Stockholm 509
Nobel Prize winners 920.003
Noble, David F.
The religion of technology 261.5
Noble obsession. Slack, C. 92
The **noble** savage: Jean-Jacques Rousseau, 1754-1762. Cranston, M. 92
Nobody's children. Bartholet, E. 362.7
Nobody's perfect. Lane, A. 791.43
Noël Hume, Ivor, 1927-
The Virginia adventure 975.5

Nofi, Albert A.
(jt. auth) Dunnigan, J. F. The Pacific War encyclopedia 940.54
(jt. auth) Dunnigan, J. F. Victory at sea 940.54
Nokes, David
Jane Austen 92
Nolan, Alan T.
Lee considered 92
Nolan, Cathal J.
The Greenwood encyclopedia of international relations 327
Notable U.S. ambassadors since 1775. See Notable U.S. ambassadors since 1775 920.003
Noll, Richard
The encyclopedia of schizophrenia and other psychotic disorders 616.89
Nolo's encyclopedia of everyday law 340
Nolo's everyday law book. See Nolo's encyclopedia of everyday law 340
Nolo's simple will book. Clifford, D. 346.05
Nomachi, Kazuyoshi, 1946-
Tibet 951
Nomads
Davidson, R. Desert places 954
Non-violence in peace and war; excerpts. See Gandhi, M. Gandhi on non-violence 322.4
Nonbook materials *See* Audiovisual materials
Nonconformity *See* Dissent
None died in vain. Leckie, R. 973.7
Nonprescription drugs
Physicians desk reference for nonprescription drugs 615
Nonrequired reading. Szymborska, W. 028.1
Nonverbal communication
Dimitrius, J.-E. Reading people 155.2
Fast, J. Body language 153.6
NonZero. Wright, R. 303.4
Noonan, John Thomas, Jr.
Narrowing the nation's power: the Supreme Court sides with the states 342
The **noonday** demon. Solomon, A. 616.85
Noor al-Hussein *See* Nur el Hussein, Queen, consort of Hussein, King of Jordan
Norgay, Jamling Tenzing
Touching my father's soul 796.52
Norgay, Tenzing *See* Tenzing Norgay, 1914-1986
Norlin, Elaina
Usability testing for library websites 025.04
The **normal** one. Safer, J. 158
Norman, Elizabeth M.
We band of angels 940.54
Norman, Marsha
Collected plays v1 812
Contents: Getting out; Third and Oak; Circus Valentine; The holdup; Traveler in the dark; Sarah and Abraham; Loving Daniel Boone; Three speeches
Norman, Michael, 1947-
Haunted America 133.1
Normandi, Carol Emery
It's not about food 616.85
Normandy (France), Attack on, 1944
Ambrose, S. E. D-Day, June 6, 1944 940.54
Goldstein, D. M. D-Day Normandy 940.54
Hastings, M. Overlord: D-Day and the battle for Normandy 940.54
Norris, George William, 1861-1944
See/See also pages in the following book(s):
Kennedy, J. F. Profiles in courage 920
Norris, Judith Stepan- *See* Stepan-Norris, Judith, 1957-
Norris, Kathleen, 1947-
The cloister walk 255
Journey: new and selected poems, 1969-1999 811
Norris, Robert S.
Racing for the bomb: General Leslie R. Groves, the Manhattan Project's indispensable man 92

Norse literature *See* Old Norse literature
Norse mythology
   Hamilton, E. Mythology   292
   Lindow, J. Handbook of Norse mythology   293
Norsemen *See* Vikings
North, Dan
   (jt. auth) Foner, M. Not for bread alone   92
North, John David
   Stonehenge   936
North Africa
      Description
   Mackintosh-Smith, T. Travels with a tangerine
           910.4
North America
      Antiquities—Encyclopedias
   Archaeology of prehistoric native America   970.01
North America
      Gazetteers
   The Columbia gazetteer of North America   917
      History
   Morgan, T. Wilderness at dawn   970
      Military history
   Keegan, J. Fields of battle   973
      Natural history
     See Natural history—North America
      Social life and customs
   American folklore   398.03
North American Indians *See* Native Americans
North American women artists of the twentieth century
           920.003
North Korea *See* Korea (North)
North Pole
     See also Arctic regions
   Fleming, F. Ninety degrees North   998
Northampton (Mass.)
   Kidder, T. Home town   974.4
Northern Ireland
     See/See also pages in the following book(s):
   Conroy, J. Unspeakable acts, ordinary people
           323.4
      History
   Coogan, T. P. The troubles   941.6
   Toolis, K. Rebel hearts   941.6
      Politics and government
   Mitchell, G. J. Making peace   941.6
Northern lights *See* Auroras
The **northern** lights [biography of Kristian Birkeland]
   Jago, L.   92
Northmen *See* Vikings
Northrop Frye on Shakespeare. Frye, N.   822.3
Northwest, Pacific *See* Pacific Northwest
Northwest Coast of North America
   Bawlf, R. S. The secret voyage of Sir Francis Drake,
     1577-1580   910.4
      Description
   Raban, J. Passage to Juneau   979.8
Northwest Passage
   Cookman, S. Ice blink   998
   Waterman, J. Arctic crossing   998
   Williams, G. Voyages of delusion   910.4
     See/See also pages in the following book(s):
   Connell, E. S. The Aztec treasure house p319-45
           814
The **Norton/Grove** dictionary of women composers
           920.003
Norton, B. H. (Bruce H.)
   (ed) Encyclopedia of American war heroes. See Ency-
     clopedia of American war heroes   920.003
Norton, Bruce H. *See* Norton, B. H. (Bruce H.)
Norton, Mary Beth
   In the devil's snare   133.4
Norton, O. Richard
   The Cambridge encyclopedia of meteorites   523.5
   Rocks from space   523.5

Norton, Richard C., 1953-
   A chronology of American musical theater   792.6
The **Norton** anthology of African American literature
           810.8
The **Norton** anthology of American literature   810.8
The **Norton** anthology of English literature   820.8
The **Norton** anthology of literature by women
           820.8
The **Norton** anthology of modern and contemporary po-
   etry   821.008
The **Norton** anthology of modern poetry. See The Nor-
   ton anthology of modern and contemporary poetry
           821.008
Norton anthology of western music   780.9
The **Norton** book of American autobiography   920
The **Norton** book of classical literature   880.8
The **Norton** book of light verse   821.008
The **Norton** book of modern war   808.8
Norton book of nature writing. See Nature writing
           508
The **Norton** book of personal essays   808.84
The **Norton** Shakespeare. Shakespeare, W.   822.3
Norway
      History
   Howarth, D. A. We die alone   940.54
      Politics and government
   Brundtland, G. H. Madame Prime Minister   92
Norwegian-English bilingual books *See* Bilingual
   books—English-Norwegian
Norwich, John Julius, 1929-
   Byzantium   949.5
   A history of Venice   945
   Shakespeare's kings   822.3
   A short history of Byzantium   949.5
Nose
   Watson, L. Jacobson's organ and the remarkable nature
     of smell   612.8
Nossiter, Adam
   The Algeria Hotel   940.54
Not for bread alone. Foner, M.   92
Not for ourselves alone: the story of Elizabeth Cady
   Stanton and Susan B. Anthony. Ward, G. C.
           92
Not I. Beckett, S.
   In Beckett, S. Ends and Odds p11-23   842
Not out of Africa. Lefkowitz, M. R.   960
Not so big solutions for your home. Susanka, S.
           728
Not under forty. Cather, W.
   In Cather, W. Stories, poems, and other writings
           818
Not war but murder. Furgurson, E. B.   973.7
Notable American women: the modern period
           920.003
Notable black American men   920.003
Notable black American scientists   920.003
Notable black American women [bk I-III]   920.003
Notable Latino Americans. Meier, M. S.   920.003
Notable mathematicians   920.003
Notable native Americans   920.003
Notable scientists from 1900 to the present   920.003
Notable U.S. ambassadors since 1775   920.003
Notable women in American history. Adamson, L. G.
           920.003
Notable women in mathematics   920.003
Notable women in the physical sciences   920.003
Notable women in world history. Adamson, L. G.
           920.003
Notes from a small island. Bryson, B.   914.1
Notes on the State of Virginia. Jefferson, T.
   In Jefferson, T. The life and selected writings of
     Thomas Jefferson p177-267   818
   In Jefferson, T. Writings   818
Nothdurft, William E.
   The lost dinosaurs of Egypt   567.9

Nothing but good times ahead. Ivins, M. 817
Nothing but the blues 781.643
Nothing like it in the world. Ambrose, S. E. 385
Nothing makes you free 808.8
Nothing remains the same. Lesser, W. 028
The nothing that is. Kaplan, R. 511
Notorious B.I.G. (Musician)
About
Sullivan, R. Labyrinth 364.1
Notorious: the life of Ingrid Bergman. Spoto, D.
92
Notre-Dame (Cathedral: Chartres, France)
Adams, H. Mont-Saint-Michel and Chartres 726
Notre Dame Fighting Irish (Football team)
See/See also pages in the following book(s):
Robinson, R. Rockne of Notre Dame 92
Novacek, Michael J.
Time traveler 92
Novak, Philip
(jt. auth) Smith, H. Buddhism: a concise introduction
294.3
Novarro, Ramon, 1899-1968
About
Soares, A. Beyond paradise: the life of Ramon
Novarro 92
Novel verdicts. Breen, J. L. 016.8
Novelists, American
See/See also pages in the following book(s):
Wilson, E. Patriotic gore p529-634 810.9
Novemberland. Grass, G. 831
Novick, Peter
The Holocaust in American life 940.53
Now read this II. Pearl, N. 016.8
Now that the buffalo's gone. Josephy, A. M.
970.004
Nowak, Ronald M.
Walker's mammals of the world 599
Nowell-Smith, Geoffrey
(ed) The Oxford history of world cinema. See The Ox-
ford history of world cinema 791.43
Nowlan, Gwendolyn Wright, 1945-
(jt. auth) Nowlan, R. A. Film quotations 791.43
Nowlan, Robert A.
Born this day 808.88
Film quotations 791.43
(ed) A Dictionary of quotations in mathematics. See A
Dictionary of quotations in mathematics 510
NPR *See* National Public Radio (U.S.)
The NPR classical music companion. Hoffman, M.
780.3
NTC's dictionary of American slang and colloquial ex-
pressions. Spears, R. A. 427
NTC's multilingual dictionary of American sign lan-
guage. Proctor, C. O. 419
NTC's Vietnamese-English dictionary. Nguyen, D. H.
495.9
Nuclear particles *See* Particles (Nuclear physics)
Nuclear physics
See also Particles (Nuclear physics)
Asimov, I. Atom 539.7
Greene, B. R. The elegant universe 539.7
Gribbin, J. R. The search for superstrings, symmetry,
and the theory of everything 539.7
Herken, G. Brotherhood of the bomb 920
Kane, G. The particle garden 539.7
Lindley, D. The end of physics 539.7
See/See also pages in the following book(s):
Johnson, G. Strange beauty: Murray Gell-Mann and
the revolution in twentieth-century physics 92
Dictionaries
The Facts on File dictionary of atomic and nuclear
physics 539.7
Nuclear rockets
Dyson, G. Project Orion 629.47

Nuclear weapons
See also Atomic bomb; Hydrogen bomb
Pictorial works
Light, M. 100 suns, 1945-1962 623.4
Nucleons *See* Particles (Nuclear physics)
Nude in art
See also Artistic anatomy
Nudelman, Meyer
About
Nuland, S. B. Lost in America 92
Nuland, Sherwin B.
How we die 616.07
Leonardo da Vinci 92
Lost in America 92
Null, Gary
AIDS: a second opinion 616.97
For women only! 613
Number concept
Bunch, B. H. The kingdom of infinite number
513
Devlin, K. J. The math gene 510
Number patterns *See* Patterns (Mathematics)
Number systems *See* Numbers
Number theory
Aczel, A. D. Fermat's last theorem 512
Clawson, C. C. Mathematical mysteries 512
Conway, J. H. The book of numbers 512
Reid, C. From zero to infinity 512
Singh, S. Fermat's enigma 512
Numbers
See also Pi
Bunch, B. H. The kingdom of infinite number
513
Mazur, B. Imagining numbers 512
Numerals
See also Numbers
Numeration *See* Numbers
Numismatics
See also Coins
Nunberg, Geoffrey, 1945-
The way we talk now 400
Nunn, Joan
Fashion in costume, 1200-2000 391
**Nur el Hussein, Queen, consort of Hussein, King of
Jordan**
Leap of faith 92
Nuremberg (Germany)
Social life and customs
Ozment, S. E. Flesh and spirit 943
Nursery rhymes
Dictionaries
The Oxford dictionary of nursery rhymes 398.8
Nurses
Norman, E. M. We band of angels 940.54
Nursing
See also Home nursing
Pagana, K. D. Mosby's diagnostic and laboratory test
reference 616.07
Dictionaries
Mosby's medical, nursing, & allied health dictionary
610.3
Nursing (Infant feeding) *See* Breast feeding
Nursing mother, working mother. Pryor, G. 649
The **nursing** mother's companion. Huggins, K. 649
The **Nursing** mother's problem solver 649
Nussbaum, David
(jt. auth) Child, J. Julia and Jacques cooking at home
641.5
(jt. auth) Child, J. Julia's kitchen wisdom 641.5
Nussbaum, Martha Craven, 1947-
(ed) Clones and clones. See Clones and clones
174
Nutrition
See also Children—Nutrition; Diet; Dietary supple-
ments; Eating customs

Nutrition—*Continued*
Atkins, R. C. Dr. Atkins' age-defying diet revolution
613
Beling, S. Powerfoods 613.2
Diet and nutrition sourcebook . . . 613.2
Duyff, R. L. American Dietetic Association complete
food and nutrition guide 613.2
Foods that harm, foods that heal 613.2
Goldstein, M. C. Controversies in food and nutrition
641.3
Mindell, E. Dr. Earl Mindell's unsafe at any meal
613.2
Murray, M. T. Encyclopedia of nutritional supplements
613.2
Nelson, M. E. Strong women eat well 613.2
Pépin, J. Jacques Pépin's simple and healthy cooking
641.5
Rinzler, C. A. The new complete book of food
641.3
Weil, A. Eating well for optimum health 613.2
Willett, W. Eat, drink and be healthy 613.2
See/See also pages in the following book(s):
The Cambridge world history of food 641.3
Encyclopedias
Ronzio, R. A. The encyclopedia of nutrition and good
health 613.2
Nuwere, Ejovi
Hacker cracker: a journey from the mean streets of
Brooklyn to the frontiers of cyberspace 92
Nybakken, James Willard
(ed) Interdisciplinary encyclopedia of marine sciences.
See Interdisciplinary encyclopedia of marine sciences
551
Nye, Joseph S., Jr.
The paradox of American power 327.73

O

O Jerusalem!. Collins, L. 956.94
Oakes, Elizabeth H., 1951-
A to Z of chemists 920.003
International encyclopedia of women scientists
920.003
Oakley, Annie, 1860-1926
About
Kasper, S. Annie Oakley 92
Riley, G. The life and legacy of Annie Oakley
92
Oakley, Violet, 1874-1961
About
Carter, A. A. The Red Rose girls 759.13
The **oasis** guide to asperger syndrome. Bashe, P. R.
618.92
Oates, Joyce Carol, 1938-
(ed) The Best American essays of the century. See The
Best American essays of the century 814
See/See also pages in the following book(s):
Women writers at work p425-51 808
Oates, Stephen B., 1936-
The approaching fury 973.5
The whirlwind of war 973.7
A woman of valor: Clara Barton and the Civil War
92
Oates, William C., 1835-1910
About
Perry, M. Conceived in liberty 973.7
The **Oath**. Baiev, K. 947.5
Oaxaca journal. Sacks, O. W. 587
Ober, Doris
(jt. auth) Miller, S. Finding hope when a child dies
291
Oberdorfer, Don
The two Koreas 951.9

Oberman, Heiko Augustinus, 1930-2001
Luther: man between God and the Devil 92
Obesity
Critser, G. Fat land 613.2
Nichter, M. Fat talk 613.2
Pool, R. Fat 616.3
Control ·
See Weight loss
Obituaries
Thomas, R. M., Jr. 52 McGs 920
Objects of desire. Rowell, M. 758
O'Brian, Patrick
About
King, D. Patrick O'Brian 92
O'Brien, David M.
Storm center 347
O'Brien, Edna
James Joyce 92
O'Brien, Patricia
(jt. auth) Goodman, E. I know just what you mean
158
O'Brien, Patrick Karl
(ed) Atlas of world history. See Atlas of world history
911
Obscenity (Law)
See also Pornography
Obsessive-compulsive disorders. Penzel, F. 616.85
Obsessive-compulsive neurosis
Normandi, C. E. It's not about food 616.85
Osborn, I. Tormenting thoughts and secret rituals
616.85
Penzel, F. Obsessive-compulsive disorders 616.85
O'Casey, Sean, 1880-1964
Juno and the paycock
In Our dramatic heritage v5 808.82
Occhiogrosso, Peter
(jt. auth) Zappa, F. The real Frank Zappa book
92
Occidental mythology. Campbell, J.
In Campbell, J. The masks of God v3 291.1
Occult sciences *See* Occultism
Occultism
See also Alchemy; Astrology; Demonology; Divi-
nation; Palmistry; Prophecies; Satanism
Eberhart, G. M. Mysterious creatures 001.9
Goodman, L. Linda Goodman's star signs 133
Dictionaries
Encyclopedia of occultism & parapsychology 133
Encyclopedias
Guiley, R. E. Encyclopedia of the strange, mystical &
unexplained 133
Ogden, T. Wizards and sorcerers 133.4
Occupational guidance *See* Vocational guidance
Occupational outlook handbook. United States. Bureau
of Labor Statistics 331.7
Occupations
America's fastest growing jobs 331.7
The Encyclopedia of careers and vocational guidance
331.7
Guide for occupational exploration 331.7
Krantz, L. Jobs rated almanac 331.7
O*NET dictionary of occupational titles 331.7
United States. Bureau of Labor Statistics. Occupational
outlook handbook 331.7
VGM's careers encyclopedia 331.7
Ocean
See also Pacific Ocean; Seashore
Carson, R. The sea around us 551.46
Kunzig, R. The restless sea 551.46
Maps
World atlas of the oceans 912
Ocean resources *See* Marine resources
Ocean sciences *See* Marine sciences

Oceania
Description
Theroux, P. The happy isles of Oceania   **919**
Oceanographic submersibles *See* Submersibles
Oceanography
Broad, W. The universe below   **551.46**
Day, T. Oceans   **551.46**
Interdisciplinary encyclopedia of marine sciences   **551**
Encyclopedias
Ellis, R. Encyclopedia of the sea   **551.46**
Oceans. Day, T.   **551.46**
Ocean's end. Woodard, C.   **363.7**
Ochiai, Hidy
Hidy Ochiai's complete book of self-defense   **796.8**
Ochoa, George
The Wilson chronology of science and technology   **502**
The Wilson chronology of the arts   **700**
O'Clair, Robert, 1923-1989
(ed) The Norton anthology of modern and contemporary poetry. See The Norton anthology of modern and contemporary poetry   **821.008**
O'Connell, Robert L.
Soul of the sword   **623.4**
O'Conner, Patricia T.
Woe is I   **428**
O'Connor, Ann
(ed) Congress A to Z. See Congress A to Z   **328.73**
O'Connor, Carol A., 1946-
(ed) The Oxford history of the American West. See The Oxford history of the American West   **978**
O'Connor, Flannery
The habit of being   **92**
See/See also pages in the following book(s):
American women fiction writers   **813.009**
O'Connor, J. Murphy- *See* Murphy-O'Connor, J. (Jerome), 1935-
O'Connor, Mary Flannery *See* O'Connor, Flannery
O'Connor, Sandra Day
The majesty of the law   **347**
Octavian *See* Augustus, Emperor of Rome, 63 B.C.-14 A.D.
The **octopus** and the orangutan. Linden, E.   **591.5**
Odd couple (female version). Simon, N.
In Simon, N. The collected plays of Neil Simon v3 p379-475   **812**
Odd girl out. Simmons, R.   **305.23**
Oddities *See* Curiosities and wonders
The **Odes** and Epodes. Horace   **874**
The **odes** of Pindar. Pindar   **884**
Odlum, Jacqueline Cochran *See* Cochran, Jacqueline, 1910?-1980
O'Donnell, Edward T., 1963-
Ship ablaze   **910.4**
Odum, Eugene Pleasants, 1913-2002
About
Craige, B. J. Eugene Odum: ecosystem ecologist & environmentalist   **92**
Odysseus (Greek mythology)
See/See also pages in the following book(s):
Hamilton, E. Mythology p291-318   **292**
The **odyssey**. Homer   **883**
OED *See* Oxford English dictionary
Oedipus at Colonus. Sophocles
In Sophocles. The complete plays of Sophocles p219-61   **882**
Oedipus the King. Sophocles   **882**
also in Sophocles. The complete plays of Sophocles p75-114   **882**
Of moths and men. Hooper, J.   **576.8**
Of paradise and power. Kagan, R.   **327.73**

Of Plymouth Plantation, 1620-1647. Bradford, W.   **974.4**
Of the difference between a genius and an apostle. Kierkegaard, S.
In Kierkegaard, S. The present age, and Of the difference between a genius and an apostle p89-108   **230**
Of the imitation of Christ. See Imitation of Christ. The imitation of Christ   **242**
Of wolves and men. Lopez, B. H.   **599.77**
O'Faolain, Nuala
Almost there   **92**
Are you somebody   **92**
Off camera. Koppel, T.   **92**
The **off-Hollywood** film guide. Wiener, T.   **791.43**
Off to the side. Harrison, J.   **92**
Offenses against the person
See also Homicide; Rape
Office management
See also Personnel management
Office practice
See also Keyboarding (Electronics)
Handbooks, manuals, etc.
Burton, S. Procedures for the automated office   **651.3**
De Vries, M. A. The professional secretary's book of lists & tips   **651.3**
Jaderstrom, S. Complete office handbook   **651.8**
The New York Public Library business desk reference   **651**
Stroman, J. Administrative assistant's & secretary's handbook   **651.3**
Office workers
See also Office practice
Kelley, R. E. How to be a star at work   **658**
The **Official** ABMS directory of board certified medical specialists   **610.69**
Official baseball register. See Baseball register   **796.357**
The **Official** Catholic directory   **282**
Official Congressional directory. United States. Congress   **328.73**
Official know-it-all guide: coins   **737.4**
The **Official** museum directory   **069.025**
The **Official** NBA encyclopedia   **796.323**
Official negligence. Cannon, L.   **979.4**
The **Official** Scrabble players dictionary   **793.73**
Official secrets. Breitman, R.   **940.54**
The **Official** World Wildlife Fund guide to the endangered species of North America. See Beacham's guide to the endangered species of North America   **578.68**
Ogden, Tom
Wizards and sorcerers   **133.4**
Ogilvie, Marilyn Bailey
(ed) The Biographical dictionary of scientists. See The Biographical dictionary of scientists   **920.003**
Oglala Indians
Black Elk. Black Elk speaks   **92**
Frazier, I. On the rez   **970.004**
Steltenkamp, M. F. Black Elk, holy man of the Oglala   **92**
O'Gorman, James F.
ABC of architecture   **720**
O'Hair, Madalyn Murray, 1919-1995
About
Dracos, T. Ungodly: the passions, torments, and murder of atheist Madalyn Murray O'Hair   **92**
O'Hanlon, Redmond
No mercy: a journey to the heart of the Congo   **967**
O'Hara, Frank, 1926-1966
The collected poems of Frank O'Hara   **811**

O'Hara, John, 1905-1970
About
Wolff, G. The art of burning bridges: a life of John O'Hara   92
Ohio
Social life and customs
Frazier, I. Family   977.1
Ohrbach, Barbara Milo
Tabletops   642
Oil painting See Painting
Ojaide, Tanure, 1948-
(ed) The New African poetry. See The New African poetry   896
O'Keeffe, Georgia, 1887-1986
About
Robinson, R. Georgia O'Keeffe: a life   92
O'Kelly, Helen Watanabe- See Watanabe-O'Kelly, Helen
Okinawa. Leckie, R.   940.54
Oklahoma
History
Wickett, M. R. Contested territory   976.6
Oklahoma City (Okla.) bombing, 1995
Michel, L. American terrorist: Timothy McVeigh and the Oklahoma City bombing   92
Oklahoma Sooners (Football team)
Dent, J. The undefeated   796.332
Old age
See also Aging; Longevity
Friedan, B. The fountain of age   305.26
Old and new poems. Hall, D.   811
Old and on their own. Coles, R.   305.26
The **old** life. Hall, D.   811
Old man Goya. Blackburn, J.   92
Old Norse literature
See also Sagas
The Sagas of Icelanders   839
The **old** one-two. Gurney, A. R.
In Gurney, A. R. Nine early plays, 1961-1973 p171-200   812
The **old** Patagonian express. Theroux, P.   918
Old Possum's book of practical cats. Eliot, T. S.
In Eliot, T. S. The complete poems and plays, 1909-1950 p149-71   818
Old Testament See Bible. O.T.
Old time radios!. Carr, J. J.   621.384
Old times. Pinter, H.
In Pinter, H. Complete works v4   822
Oldroyd, D. R. (David Roger)
Thinking about the earth   551
Oldroyd, David Roger See Oldroyd, D. R. (David Roger)
Olds, Sharon
Blood, tin, straw   811
The unswept room   811
The wellspring   811
Oldstone, Michael B. A.
Viruses, plagues, and history   614.4
Olenski, Jim
(jt. auth) Mayo, M. VideoHound's DVD guide   791.43
Oliver, Charles M.
Ernest Hemingway, A to Z   813.009
Oliver, Mary, 1935-
The leaf and the cloud   811
New and selected poems   811
A poetry handbook   808.1
West wind   811
White pine   811
Winter hours   818
Olivier, Fernande, 1881-1966
Loving Picasso: the private journal of Fernande Olivier   92

Olivier, Laurence, 1907-1989
About
Lewis, R. The real life of Laurence Olivier   92
Olmos, Edward James
Americanos   305.8
Olmsted, Frederick Law, 1822-1903
About
Rybczynski, W. A clearing in the distance: Frederick Law Olmsted and America in the nineteenth century   92
Olsen, Jack
I: the creation of a serial killer   364.1
Olsen, Kirstin
All things Shakespeare   822.3
Olshaker, Mark, 1951-
(jt. auth) Douglas, J. E. The cases that haunt us   364.1
(jt. auth) Peters, C. J. Virus hunter   614.5
Olson, Charles, 1910-1970
The collected poems of Charles Olson   811
Olson, James Stuart, 1946-
Bathsheba's breast   616.99
Encyclopedia of the industrial revolution in America   973.03
Olson, Laura R., 1967-
(jt. auth) Djupe, P. A. Encyclopedia of American religion and politics   322
Olson, Lynne
Freedom's daughters   323.1
Olson, Steve, 1956-
Mapping human history   599.9
Olympic games
See also Olympic games, 2000 (Sydney, Australia)
Guttmann, A. The Olympics, a history of the modern games   796.48
Wallechinsky, D. The complete book of the Winter Olympics   796.98
Olympic games, 2000 (Sydney, Australia)
Mullen, P. H., Jr. Gold in the water   797.2
The **Olympics,** a history of the modern games. Guttmann, A.   796.48
Omar Khayyam
Rubáiyát of Omar Khayyám   891
O'Meally, Robert G., 1948-
Lady Day: the many faces of Billie Holiday   92
O'Meara, Stephen James, 1956-
(jt. auth) Sheehan, W. Mars   523.4
Omeros. Walcott, D.   811
On becoming a novelist. Gardner, J.   808.3
On becoming a person. Rogers, C. R.   616.89
On being human. Fromm, E.   150.19
On borrowed words. Stavans, I.   92
On children and death. Kübler-Ross, E.   155.9
On death and dying. Kübler-Ross, E.   155.9
On directing film. Mamet, D.   791.43
On generation and corruption. Aristotle
In Aristotle. The basic works of Aristotle p470-531   888
On grief and reason. Brodsky, J.   814
On history. Hobsbawm, E. J.   901
On love. Hirsch, E.   811
On moral fiction. Gardner, J.   801
On my country and the world. Gorbachev, M.   947.085
On revolution. Arendt, H.   303.6
On Sunset Boulevard: the life and times of Billy Wilder. Sikov, E.   92
On the backroad to heaven. Kraybill, D. B.   289.7
On the bus with Rosa Parks. Dove, R.   811
On the law of nations. Moynihan, D. P.   327.73
On the rez. Frazier, I.   970.004
On the road with Charles Kuralt. Kuralt, C.   973.92
On the shoulders of giants   520

On the soul. Aristotle
  In Aristotle. The basic works of Aristotle p535-603
      888
  In Aristotle. Introduction to Aristotle p153-245
      888
On the water. Stone, N.   **917.3**
On the wild side. Gardner, M.   **500**
On the wing. Sayre, N.   **92**
On time and being. Heidegger, M.   **111**
On top of the world. Lutnick, H.   **332.6**
On war. Clausewitz, C. von   **355**
On war and leadership. Connelly, O.   **355.3**
On wings of eagles. Follett, K.   **955**
On writing. King, S.   **808.3**
On writing well. Zinsser, W. K.   **808**
O'Nan, Stewart, 1961-
  The circus fire   **974.6**
Onassis, Aristotle Socrates, 1906-1975
  About
  Gage, N. Greek fire   **92**
Onassis, Jacqueline Kennedy
  About
  Andersen, C. P. Jackie after Jack   **92**
  Bowles, H. Jacqueline Kennedy   **92**
  Davis, J. H. Jacqueline Bouvier   **92**
  Leaming, B. Mrs. Kennedy   **92**
  See/See also pages in the following book(s):
  Galbraith, J. K. Name-dropping   **973.9**
Once more around the park. Angell, R.   **796.357**
Once they moved like the wind. Roberts, D.
      970.004
Once upon a distant war. Prochnau, W. W.
      959.704
Ondine. Giraudoux, J.
  In Our dramatic heritage v6   **808.82**
Ondra, Nancy J.
  Taylor's guide to roses   **635.9**
The one abiding. Morgan, F.   **811**
One act plays
  The Best American short plays   **812.008**
"One hell of a gamble". Fursenko, A. V.   **973.922**
One hundred days. Schom, A.   **944.05**
One hundred decisive battles. See Davis, P. K. 100 decisive battles   **904**
One hundred flowers and how they got their names. See Wells, D. 100 flowers and how they got their names
      582.13
One hundred one-night reads. See Major, D. C. 100 one-night reads   **028**
One hundred poems from the Chinese   **895.1**
One hundred poems from the Japanese   **895.6**
One hundred questions & answers about Parkinson [sic] disease. See Lieberman, A. 100 questions & answers about Parkinson [sic] disease   **616.8**
One hundred seventy-five high-impact cover letters. See Beatty, R. H. 175 high-impact cover letters
      650.14
One hundred suns, 1945-1962. See Light, M. 100 suns, 1945-1962   **623.4**
One man's meat. White, E. B.   **818**
One more time. Royko, M.   **818**
One nation under gods. Abanes, R.   **289.3**
One parent family *See* Single parent family
One river. Davis, W.   **581.6**
One stick song. Alexie, S.   **811**
One thousand and eighty-nine and all that. See Acheson, D. J. 1089 and all that   **510**
One thousand and one ingenious gardening ideas. See 1,001 ingenious gardening ideas   **635**
One thousand roads to Mecca. Wolfe, M.   **297**
One time, one place. Welty, E.   **976.2**
One true God. Stark, R.   **291.1**
One up on Wall Street. Lynch, P.   **332.6**
One world divisible. Reynolds, D.   **909.82**
One writer's beginnings. Welty, E.   **92**

One writer's imagination. Marrs, S.   **813.009**
O'Neil, Dennis, 1939-
  The DC comics guide to writing comics   **808**
O'Neil, Denny *See* O'Neil, Dennis, 1939-
O'Neil, Robert M.
  The rights of public employees   **342**
O'Neill, Eugene, 1888-1953
  Long day's journey into night   **812**
  About
  Black, S. A. Eugene O'Neill   **92**
O'Neill, James, 1909-1973
  About
  O'Neill, J. Blood-dark track   **920**
O'Neill, Joseph, 1964-
  Blood-dark track   **920**
O'Neill, Oona *See* Chaplin, Oona
O'Neill, Thomas P. *See* O'Neill, Tip, 1912-1994
O'Neill, Tip, 1912-1994
  About
  Farrell, J. A. Tip O'Neill and the Democratic century
      92
O'Neill, William L.
  (ed) The Scribner encyclopedia of American lives, The 1960s. See The Scribner encyclopedia of American lives, The 1960s   **920.003**
O'Neill family
  About
  O'Neill, J. Blood-dark track   **920**
O*NET dictionary of occupational titles   **331.7**
Online commerce *See* Electronic commerce
Online publishing *See* Electronic publishing
Online reference services *See* Reference services (Libraries)
Only child
  Nachman, P. A. You and your only child   **649**
The only investment guide you'll ever need. Tobias, A. P.   **332.024**
The only math book you'll ever need. Kogelman, S.
      513
The only menopause guide you'll need. Moore, M.
      618.1
Only yesterday. Allen, F. L.   **973.91**
Ono, Yōko
  See/See also pages in the following book(s):
  Prose, F. The lives of the muses   **920**
Ontology
  Buber, M. I and thou   **181**
  Fromm, E. To have or to be?   **302**
  Heidegger, M. Being and time   **111**
  Heidegger, M. On time and being   **111**
  Tillich, P. The courage to be   **179**
Open all night. Bukowski, C.   **811**
Open closed open. Amichai, Y.   **892**
Open: inside the ropes at Bethpage Black. Feinstein, J.
      796.352
The open sore of a continent. Soyinka, W.   **966.9**
Opened ground. Heaney, S.   **821**
The opening of the American mind. Levine, L. W.
      001.1
Opera
  Boyden, M. The Rough Guide to opera   **792.5**
  Plotkin, F. Opera 101   **792.5**
  Pogue, D. Opera for dummies   **792.5**
  See/See also pages in the following book(s):
  Grout, D. J. A history of Western music   **780.9**
  Dictionaries
  Baker's dictionary of opera   **792.5**
  The New Grove dictionary of opera   **792.5**
  The New Penguin opera guide   **792.5**
  Stories, plots, etc.
  Freeman, J. W. The Metropolitan Opera stories of the great operas   **792.5**
  The New Kobbé's opera book   **792.5**
  Osborne, C. The complete operas of Mozart
      792.5

Opera—Stories, plots, etc.—*Continued*
Osborne, C. The complete operas of Puccini
    792.5
Osborne, C. The complete operas of Richard Wagner
    792.5
    See/See also pages in the following book(s):
The Puccini companion   92
Opera 101. Plotkin, F.   792.5
Opera and church music, 1630-1750
   In New Oxford history of music v5   780.9
Opera for dummies. Pogue, D.   792.5
Opera: the Rough Guide. See Boyden, M. The Rough
   Guide to opera   792.5
Operación Peter Pan *See* Operation Peter Pan
Operation Desert Storm *See* Persian Gulf War, 1991
Operation Iceberg. Astor, G.   940.54
Operation Overlord
Hastings, M. Overlord: D-Day and the battle for Nor-
   mandy   940.54
Operation Pedro Pan *See* Operation Peter Pan
Operation Peter Pan
   See/See also pages in the following book(s):
Eire, C. M. N. Waiting for snow in Havana   92
Operation Rollback. Grose, P.   327.12
Operations, Surgical *See* Surgery
Operetta
   See also Musicals
Opiates *See* Narcotics
Opie, Iona Archibald
   (ed) The Oxford dictionary of nursery rhymes. See The
   Oxford dictionary of nursery rhymes   398.8
   See/See also pages in the following book(s):
Marcus, L. S. Ways of telling   741.6
Opie, Peter, 1918-1982
   (ed) The Oxford dictionary of nursery rhymes. See The
   Oxford dictionary of nursery rhymes   398.8
Opinion, Public *See* Public opinion
Opium
Booth, M. Opium   615
Oppen, George, 1908-1984
New collected poems   811
Oppenheimer, Betty, 1957-
Candlemaker's companion   745.59
Oppenheimer, J. Robert, 1904-1967
    About
Herken, G. Brotherhood of the bomb   920
   See/See also pages in the following book(s):
Rhodes, R. Dark sun   623.4
Oppenheimer, Robert *See* Oppenheimer, J. Robert,
   1904-1967
Optical storage devices
   See also CD-ROMs
Optics
Park, D. The fire within the eye   535
The **optimistic** child. Seligman, M. E. P.   155.4
Opus posthumous. Stevens, W.   818
Oral contraceptives
Djerassi, C. This man's pill   613.9
Oral health sourcebook. See Dental care and oral health
   sourcebook   617.6
Orangutan
Galdikas, B. Orangutan odyssey   599.8
Galdikas, B. Reflections of Eden   599.8
Orangutan odyssey. Galdikas, B.   599.8
Orations *See* Speeches
The **orchards** of Syon. Hill, G.   821
Orchestral music
   See also Symphony
Orchid fever. Hansen, E.   635.9
Orchids
Hansen, E. Orchid fever   635.9
Ordaining women. Chaves, M.   262
Ordinary resurrections. Kozol, J.   305.23
Ordination of women
Chaves, M. Ordaining women   262

Ordnance
   See also Military weapons
Oregon country *See* Pacific Northwest
Oregon Trail
Parkman, F. The Oregon Trail   978
O'Reilly, Bill
The no-spin zone   973.92
O'Reilly, Charles A., III
Hidden value   658
Oren, Michael
Six days of war   956.04
Orenstein, Ronald I. (Ronald Isaac), 1946-
Turtles, tortoises and terrapins   597.9
The **Oresteia**. Aeschylus   882
Organ transplantation *See* Transplantation of organs,
   tissues, etc.
Organ transplants. Finn, R.   617.9
Organic farming
   See/See also pages in the following book(s):
Fatal harvest   630
The **organic** gardener's home reference. Denckla, T.
    635
Organic gardening
1,001 ingenious gardening ideas   635
Denckla, T. The organic gardener's home reference
    635
Great garden formulas   635
Long, C. Rodale organic gardening solutions   635
Rodale's all-new encyclopedia of organic gardening
    635
Rodale's illustrated encyclopedia of organic gardening
    635.9
Smith, C. W. G. The big book of gardening secrets
    635
Smith, E. C. The vegetable gardener's bible   635
Organically grown foods *See* Natural foods
Organization and management *See* Management
Organized crime
   See also Mafia
Denton, S. The money and the power   979.3
Kelly, R. J. Encyclopedia of organized crime in the
   United States   364.1
    Dictionaries
Sifakis, C. The Mafia encyclopedia   364.1
Organized labor *See* Labor unions
Organizing your family history search. Carmack, S. D.
    929
Organon. Aristotle
   In Aristotle. The basic works of Aristotle p1-212
    888
Orient *See* Asia; East Asia
Oriental cooking
Ross, R. L. S. Beyond bok choy   641.6
   See/See also pages in the following book(s):
Tsai, M. Blue Ginger   641.5
Oriental mythology. Campbell, J.
   In Campbell, J. The masks of God v2   291.1
Oriental philosophy
   See/See also pages in the following book(s):
A Companion to world philosophies   109
Orienteering
   See also Direction sense
Origami bridges. Ackerman, D.   811
Origen
   See/See also pages in the following book(s):
Küng, H. Great Christian thinkers p41-67   230
The **origin** of humankind. Leakey, R. E.   599.93
Origin of life *See* Life—Origin
Origin of man *See* Human origins
The **origin** of Satan. Pagels, E. H.   235
Origin of species *See* Evolution
The **origin** of species. Darwin, C.   576.8
The **origin** of the universe. Barrow, J. D.   523.1
Origins. See Lightman, A. P. Ancient light   523.1

The **origins** and development of classical Hinduism.
Basham, A. L.   294.5
The **origins** of anti-Semitism. Gager, J. G.   296.3
Origins of existence. Adams, F. C.   576.8
Origins of totalitarianism. Arendt, H.   321.9
Origins reconsidered. Leakey, R. E.   599.93
O'Riley, Michael Kampen *See* Kampen O'Riley,
Michael
Orkin, Michael
What are the odds?   519.2
Ormal-Grenon, Jean-Benoit
(ed) The Oxford-Hachette French dictionary. See The
Oxford-Hachette French dictionary   443
Orme, Nicholas
Medieval children   305.23
Ornament *See* Decoration and ornament
Ornament and silence. Fraser, K.   814
Ornamental plants
American Horticultural Society encyclopedia of plants
and flowers   635.9
Darke, R. The color encyclopedia of ornamental grass-
es   635.9
Dirr, M. Dirr's trees and shrubs for warm climates
635.9
Hudak, J. Design for gardens   712
Joyce, D. Topiary and the art of training plants
635.9
Michener, D. Taylor's guide to ground covers
635.9
Robinson, P. The American Horticultural Society com-
plete guide to water gardening   635.9
Encyclopedias
The American Horticultural Society A-Z encyclopedia
of garden plants   635.9
Wyman, D. Wyman's gardening encyclopedia   635
Ornelas, Kriemhild Coneè
(ed) The Cambridge world history of food. See The
Cambridge world history of food   641.3
Ornish, Dean
Love & survival   616.1
O'Rourke, P. J.
Eat the rich   817
Parliament of whores   817
The **orphaned** adult. Levy, A.   155.9
Orphée. Cocteau, J.
In Our dramatic heritage v6   808.82
Orr, Gregory
The caged owl   811
Orr, John
About
Wambaugh, J. Fire lover   364.1
Ortega y Gasset, José, 1883-1955
The revolt of the masses   909
What is philosophy?   196
Ortho's home repair problem solver. Beckstrom, R. J.
643
Ortiz, Alfonso, 1939-1997
(ed) American Indian myths and legends. See
American Indian myths and legends   398.2
Ortiz, Simon J., 1941-
See/See also pages in the following book(s):
Coltelli, L. Winged words: American Indian writers
speak   897
Orwell, George, 1903-1950
The Orwell reader   828
About
Hitchens, C. Why Orwell matters   828
Meyers, J. Orwell   92
The **Orwell** reader. Orwell, G.   828
Osborn, Ian
Tormenting thoughts and secret rituals   616.85
Osborn, William M.
The wild frontier   973
Osborne, Charles, 1927-
The complete operas of Mozart   792.5

The complete operas of Puccini   792.5
The complete operas of Richard Wagner   792.5
Osborne, John, 1929-1994
Look back in anger   822
Osborne, Lawrence
American normal   616.89
Osborne, Richard
Herbert von Karajan   92
Osborne, Robert A.
75 years of the Oscar   791.43
Osgood, Charles
See you on the radio   818
Oshinsky, David M., 1944-
"Worse than slavery"   365
Osmańczyk, Edmund Jan, 1913-1989
Encyclopedia of the United Nations and international
agreements   341.23
Osorgin family
About
Schmemann, S. Echoes of a native land   947
Ospreys
Gessner, D. Return of the osprey   598
Osselton, N. E.
The new Routledge Dutch dictionary   439.3
Ossoli, Margaret Fuller, marchesa d' *See* Fuller, Mar-
garet, 1810-1850
Osteopathic medicine
Vocational guidance
Wischnitzer, S. Barron's guide to medical & dental
schools   610.69
Osteoporosis
Lane, N. E. The osteoporosis book   616.7
Nelson, M. E. Strong women, strong bones   616.7
The **osteoporosis** book. Lane, N. E.   616.7
Ostling, Joan K.
(jt. auth) Ostling, R. N. Mormon America   289.3
Ostling, Richard N.
Mormon America   289.3
Ostwald, Peter F.
Glenn Gould   92
Oswald, Lee Harvey
About
Mallon, T. Mrs. Paine's garage and the murder of John
F. Kennedy   364.1
Posner, G. L. Case closed   973.922
Oswald, Marina
About
Mallon, T. Mrs. Paine's garage and the murder of John
F. Kennedy   364.1
The **other** American: the life of Michael Harrington.
Isserman, M.   92
The **other** Mexico. Paz, O.
In Paz, O. The labyrinth of solitude [and other es-
says] p213-325   864
Other powers: the age of suffrage, spiritualism, and the
scandalous Victoria Woodhull. Goldsmith, B.
92
Other worlds. Lemonick, M. D.   576.8
Other worlds. Trefil, J. S.   523.2
Otho, Marcus Salvius, Emperor of Rome, 32-69
See/See also pages in the following book(s):
Suetonius Tranquillus, C. The twelve Caesars   878
Otis!: the Otis Redding story. Freeman, S.   92
O'Toole, Christopher
(ed) The Firefly encyclopedia of insects and spiders.
See The Firefly encyclopedia of insects and spiders
595.7
Ottemiller's index to plays in collections   808.82
The **Ottomans**. Wheatcroft, A.   956
Otway, Thomas, 1652-1685
Venice preserved
In Restoration plays   822.008
Oudolf, Piet
(jt. auth) King, M. Gardening with grasses   635.9

Ouimet, Francis, 1893-1967
About
Frost, M. The greatest game ever played   796.352
Oumu Shinrikyō *See* Aum Shinrikyō
Our babies, ourselves. Small, M. F.   649
Our bodies, ourselves. See Our bodies, ourselves for the new century   613
Our bodies, ourselves for the new century   613
Our cosmic habitat. Rees, M. J.   523.1
Our daughters' health. Roan, S.   613
Our dramatic heritage v4-6   808.82
Our kind of people. Graham, L. O.   305.8
Our posthuman future. Fukuyama, F.   174
Our town. Wilder, T.   812
Our Vietnam. Langguth, A. J.   959.704
Ousby, Ian
The road to Verdun   940.4
(ed) The Cambridge guide to literature in English. See The Cambridge guide to literature in English   820.3
Out of Africa. Dinesen, I.   967.62
also in Dinesen, I. Out of Africa and Shadows on the grass   967.62
Out of its mind. Hobson, J. A.   616.89
Out of my life and thought. Schweitzer, A.   92
Out of place. Said, E. W.   92
Out of the blue. Bernstein, R.   973.931
Out of the darkened room. Beardslee, W. R.   616.85
Out to work. Kessler-Harris, A.   331.4
Outdoor cooking
See also Barbecue cooking
Outdoor life
McDougall, L. The outdoors almanac   796.5
Outdoor photography
Drager, K. Scenic photography 101   770.2
Outdoor recreation
Doan, M. The Sierra Club family outdoors guide   796.5
Outdoor survival *See* Wilderness survival
The **outdoors** almanac. McDougall, L.   796.5
Outer space
Weil, E. They all laughed at Christopher Columbus   621.43
Exploration
Burrows, W. E. This new ocean   629.4
Croswell, K. Planet quest   523
Launius, R. D. Frontiers of space exploration   629.45
Sagan, C. Pale blue dot   520
Space exploration   629
Zimmerman, R. The chronological encyclopedia of discoveries in space   629.4
Exploration—Encyclopedias
Angelo, J. A. Encyclopedia of space exploration   629.4
The **outline** of history. Wells, H. G.   909
Outrageous acts and everyday rebellions. Steinem, G.   305.4
Outten, Wayne N.
The rights of employees and union members   344
The **Outward** Bound backpacker's handbook. Randall, G.   796.51
Outwater, Alice B.
Water   551.48
Over-the-counter drugs *See* Nonprescription drugs
Over there. Farwell, B.   940.4
Overcoming addictions. Chopra, D.   616.86
Overcoming incontinence. Dierich, M.   616.6
Overcoming math anxiety. Tobias, S.   510
Overcoming the odds   649
Overland journeys to the Pacific
See also West (U.S.)—Exploration
Overlay. Lippard, L. R.   709

Overlord: D-Day and the battle for Normandy. Hastings, M.   940.54
The **overnight** résumé. Asher, D.   650.14
Overtime. Whalen, P.   811
Overy, R. J. (Richard James), 1947-
The Battle of Britain   940.54
The road to war   940.53
Why the Allies won   940.53
Overy, Richard James *See* Overy, R. J. (Richard James), 1947-
Ovid, 43 B.C.-17 or 18
Metamorphoses   873
Tales from Ovid   873
Owen, Stephen, 1946-
(ed) An Anthology of Chinese literature: beginnings to 1911. See An Anthology of Chinese literature: beginnings to 1911   895.1
Owens, Dana *See* Queen Latifah
Owens, Josie Wade *See* Wade, Josie
The **owner** of the house. Simpson, L. A. M.   811
Oxenbury, Helen, 1938-
See/See also pages in the following book(s):
Marcus, L. S. Ways of telling   741.6
The **Oxford** American dictionary and language guide   423
The **Oxford** American dictionary of current English   423
The **Oxford** American thesaurus of current English   423
The **Oxford** anthology of English literature   820.8
Oxford atlas of exploration   911
Oxford atlas of the world   912
Oxford Bible commentary   220.7
Oxford book of American verse, The New   811.008
The **Oxford** book of aphorisms   808.88
Oxford book of carols, The New   782.28
The **Oxford** book of classical verse in translation   881.008
The **Oxford** book of comic verse   821.008
The **Oxford** book of death   808.88
The **Oxford** book of eighteenth century verse. See The New Oxford book of eighteenth century verse   821.008
The **Oxford** book of English verse   821.008
The **Oxford** book of food plants. See Vaughan, J. G. The new Oxford book of food plants   633
The **Oxford** book of garden verse   821.008
The **Oxford** book of humorous prose   827
The **Oxford** book of letters   826
The **Oxford** book of prayer   291.4
The **Oxford** book of sonnets   821.008
The **Oxford** book of the American South   810.8
Oxford book of Victorian verse, The New   821.008
The **Oxford** book of war poetry   808.81
The **Oxford** book of women's writing in the United States   810.8
The **Oxford** classical dictionary   938.003
The **Oxford** companion to African American literature   810.9
The **Oxford** companion to American history. See The Oxford companion to United States history   973.03
The **Oxford** companion to American law   349
The **Oxford** companion to American literature   810.3
The **Oxford** companion to American military history   355
The **Oxford** companion to American theatre. Bordman, G. M.   792.03
The **Oxford** companion to archaeology   930.1
The **Oxford** companion to Australian literature. Wilde, W. H.   820.3
The **Oxford** companion to British history   941
The **Oxford** companion to Canadian literature   810.3
Oxford companion to Christian thought   230.003

The **Oxford** companion to classical literature   880.3
The **Oxford** companion to crime and mystery writing
809.3
The **Oxford** companion to English literature   820.3
The **Oxford** companion to fairy tales   398.2
The **Oxford** companion to food   641.03
The **Oxford** companion to French literature. See The New Oxford companion to literature in French
840.3
The **Oxford** companion to Irish history   941.5
The **Oxford** companion to Irish literature   820.9
The **Oxford** companion to Italian literature   850.3
The **Oxford** companion to jazz   781.65
The **Oxford** companion to Mark Twain   818
The **Oxford** companion to military history   355
The **Oxford** companion to music   780.3
The **Oxford** companion to philosophy   103
The **Oxford** companion to Shakespeare   822.3
The **Oxford** companion to the Bible   220.3
The **Oxford** companion to the earth   550.3
The **Oxford** companion to the English language
420
The **Oxford** companion to the history of modern science
509
The **Oxford** companion to the Supreme Court of the United States   347
The **Oxford** companion to United States history
973.03
The **Oxford** companion to western art   703
The **Oxford** companion to women's writing in the United States   810.9
The **Oxford** companion to World War II   940.53
The **Oxford** dictionary for writers and editors   428
The **Oxford** dictionary of allusions   803
The **Oxford** dictionary of art   703
The **Oxford** dictionary of dance. Craine, D.   792.8
The **Oxford** dictionary of English grammar. Chalker, S.
428
The **Oxford** dictionary of foreign words and phrases
422.03
The **Oxford** dictionary of humorous quotations
808.88
The **Oxford** dictionary of Islam   297
The **Oxford** dictionary of music. Kennedy, M.
780.3
The **Oxford** dictionary of nursery rhymes   398.8
The **Oxford** dictionary of philosophy. Blackburn, S.
103
The **Oxford** dictionary of phrase and fable   803
The **Oxford** dictionary of political quotations
808.88
The **Oxford** dictionary of popes. Kelly, J. N. D.
920.003
The **Oxford** dictionary of quotations   808.88
The **Oxford** dictionary of saints. Farmer, D. H.
920.003
The **Oxford** dictionary of slang   427
The **Oxford** dictionary of the Christian Church
230.003
The **Oxford** dictionary of the Jewish religion
296.03
The **Oxford** dictionary of word histories   422.03
The **Oxford** dictionary of world religions   200.3
The **Oxford-Duden** German dictionary   433
The **Oxford-Duden** pictorial English-Japanese dictionary
495.6
The **Oxford** encyclopedia of ancient Egypt   932
The **Oxford** encyclopedia of theatre & performance
792.03
The **Oxford** English-Arabic dictionary of current usage
492
Oxford English dictionary
Winchester, S. The professor and the madman
423
The **Oxford** English dictionary   423

The **Oxford** English-Hebrew dictionary   492.4
The **Oxford** guide to classical mythology in the arts, 1300-1990s. Reid, J. D.   700
The **Oxford** guide to ideas & issues of the Bible
220.3
The **Oxford** guide to literature in English translation
820.9
The **Oxford** guide to the United States Government
320.03
The **Oxford** guide to United States Supreme Court decisions   342
The **Oxford-Hachette** French dictionary   443
The **Oxford** Hindi-English dictionary   491
The **Oxford** history of Britain   941
The **Oxford** history of Islam   297
The **Oxford** history of Italy   945
The **Oxford** history of medieval Europe   940.1
The **Oxford** history of Mexico   972
The **Oxford** history of the American people. Morison, S. E.   973
The **Oxford** history of the American West   978
The **Oxford** history of the biblical world   220.9
The **Oxford** history of the British Empire   909
The **Oxford** history of the Roman world   937
The **Oxford** history of the twentieth century   909.82
The **Oxford** history of western art   709
The **Oxford** history of Western philosophy   190
The **Oxford** history of world cinema   791.43
The **Oxford** illustrated companion to medicine
610.3
The **Oxford** illustrated history of Britain. See The Oxford history of Britain   941
The **Oxford** illustrated history of English literature
820.9
The **Oxford** illustrated history of Ireland   941.5
The **Oxford** illustrated history of the Bible   220
The **Oxford** illustrated history of the British monarchy. Cannon, J.   941
The **Oxford** illustrated history of the Crusades
909.07
The **Oxford** illustrated history of the First World War. See World War I   940.3
The **Oxford** illustrated history of the Vikings   948
The **Oxford** illustrated history of theatre   792.09
The **Oxford** illustrated history of Western medicine. See Western medicine: an illustrated history   610.9
The **Oxford** illustrated history of Western philosophy. See The Oxford history of Western philosophy
190
Oxford Latin dictionary   473
The **Oxford** medical companion. See The Oxford illustrated companion to medicine   610.3
The **Oxford** reader's companion to Conrad   823.009
Oxford reader's companion to Dickens   823.009
The **Oxford** reader's companion to Hardy   823.009
Oxford reader's companion to Trollope   823.009
The **Oxford** reverse dictionary   423
The **Oxford** Russian dictionary   491.7
The **Oxford** Spanish dictionary   463
The **Oxford** starter Chinese dictionary   495.1
The **Oxford** W. E. B. Du Bois reader. Du Bois, W. E. B.   305.8
Ozer, Mark N.
(ed) Managing stroke. See Managing stroke   616.8
Ozick, Cynthia
A Cynthia Ozick reader   818
Quarrel & quandary   814
Ozment, Steven E.
Flesh and spirit   943
Ozonoff, Sally
A parent's guide to asperger syndrome and high-functioning autism   618.92

P

P.O.W.'s *See* Prisoners of war
Pacelli, Eugenio *See* Pius XII, Pope, 1876-1958
Pacific Islands *See* Islands of the Pacific
Pacific Northwest
Josephy, A. M. The Nez Perce Indians and the opening
of the Northwest   **970.004**
    Description
Raban, J. Passage to Juneau   **979.8**
Pacific Ocean
Heyerdahl, T. Kon-Tiki: across the Pacific by raft
    910.4
Thorpe, I. J. 8 men and a duck   **910.4**
The **Pacific** War. Costello, J.   **940.54**
The **Pacific** War encyclopedia. Dunnigan, J. F.
    940.54
Pack, Robert, 1929-
(ed) The Bread Loaf anthology of contemporary
American essays. See The Bread Loaf anthology of
contemporary American essays   **814**
Pack of thieves. Chesnoff, R. Z.   **940.53**
Packard, Jerrold M.
American nightmare   **305.8**
Packers (Football team) *See* Green Bay Packers (Foot-
ball team)
Paddock, Lisa Olson
Encyclopedia of American literature. See Encyclopedia
of American literature   **810.3**
(jt. auth) Rollyson, C. E. Susan Sontag   **92**
Paderewski, Ignace Jan, 1860-1941
See/See also pages in the following book(s):
Schonberg, H. C. The great pianists   **920**
Padgett, Ron
(ed) World poets. See World poets   **920.003**
Padian, Kevin
(ed) Encyclopedia of dinosaurs. See Encyclopedia of
dinosaurs   **567.9**
Pagan holiday. See Perrottet, T. Route 66 A.D.
    910.4
Pagana, Kathleen Deska, 1952-
Mosby's diagnostic and laboratory test reference
    616.07
Pagana, Timothy James, 1949-
(jt. auth) Pagana, K. D. Mosby's diagnostic and labora-
tory test reference   **616.07**
Paganism
See also Neopaganism
See/See also pages in the following book(s):
Adler, M. Drawing down the moon   **133.4**
Pagden, Anthony
Peoples and empires   **909**
Page, George
Inside the animal mind   **591.5**
Page, Jake
(jt. auth) Adovasio, J. M. The first Americans
    970.01
Page, James K. *See* Page, Jake
Page, Joseph A.
The Brazilians   **981**
Page, Lawrence M.
A field guide to freshwater fishes: North America
north of Mexico   **597**
Page, Nick
Lord Minimus [biography of Jeffrey Hudson]   **92**
Page, Norman
(ed) The Oxford reader's companion to Hardy. See
The Oxford reader's companion to Hardy
    823.009
Page, P. K. (Patricia Kathleen), 1916-
The hidden room   **811**
Page, Patricia Kathleen *See* Page, P. K. (Patricia Kath-
leen), 1916-

Page, Thomas Nelson, 1853-1922
See/See also pages in the following book(s):
Wilson, E. Patriotic gore p604-16   **810.9**
Page, Willie F., 1929-
The encyclopedia of African history and culture
    960
Pagel, Mark D.
(ed) Encyclopedia of evolution. See Encyclopedia of
evolution   **576.8**
Pagell, Ruth A.
International business information   **650**
Pagels, Elaine H., 1943-
Adam, Eve, and the serpent   **241**
Beyond belief   **229**
The gnostic Gospels   **299**
The origin of Satan   **235**
Pain
See also Suffering
The Cancer pain sourcebook   **616.99**
Dillard, J. The chronic pain solution   **616**
Koestler, A. J. Understanding chronic pain   **616**
Vertosick, F. T. Why we hurt   **616**
Paine, Jeffery, 1944-
(ed) The Poetry of our world. See The Poetry of our
world   **808.81**
Paine, Ruth
    About
Mallon, T. Mrs. Paine's garage and the murder of John
F. Kennedy   **364.1**
Paine, Thomas, 1737-1809
Common sense   **320**
The rights of man   **320**
    About
Foner, E. Tom Paine and Revolutionary America
    973.3
Paint
See also Pigments
Paint your home. Donegan, F.   **698**
The **painted** bed. Hall, D.   **811**
Painted glass *See* Glass painting and staining
Painter, Nell Irvin
Sojourner Truth   **92**
Painters
See also Artists
Painting
See also Glass painting and staining; Landscape
painting; Still-life painting; Watercolor painting
Beckett, W. Sister Wendy's 1000 masterpieces
    759
Beckett, W. The story of painting   **759**
Livingstone, M. S. Vision and art   **750.1**
Pyle, D. What every artist needs to know about paints
& colors   **752**
Understanding paintings   **759**
    19th century
Rosenblum, R. Paintings in the Musée d'Orsay
    708
    Technique
Hockney, D. Secret knowledge   **751**
Leigh, T. The complete book of decorative painting
    745.7
Mayer, R. The artist's handbook of materials and tech-
niques   **751.2**
Sloan, A. Modern paint effects   **745.7**
Weber, M. C. Brushwork essentials   **751.4**
Painting, American *See* American painting
Painting, Decorative *See* Decoration and ornament
Painting, Dutch *See* Dutch painting
Painting, Flemish *See* Flemish painting
Painting, French *See* French painting
Painting American. Cohen-Solal, A.   **759.13**
Painting murals. Seligman, P.   **751.7**
Paintings in the Musée d'Orsay. Rosenblum, R.
    708

The **paintings** of Joan Mitchell. Livingston, J.
    759.13

Paisner, Daniel
  (jt. auth) Picciotto, R. Last man down   **974.7**

Paiute Indians
  See/See also pages in the following book(s):
  Josephy, A. M. Now that the buffalo's gone p155-73
    970.004

Pakenham, Thomas, 1933-
  Remarkable trees of the world   **582.16**
  The scramble for Africa, 1876-1912   **960**

Pakistan
        Description
  See/See also pages in the following book(s):
  Naipaul, V. S. Among the believers p85-222   **297**

Palaces
  Zega, A. Palaces of the Sun King   **728**

Palaces of the Sun King. Zega, A.   **728**

Pale blue dot. Sagan, C.   **520**

Paleontology *See* Fossils

Palestine
        History
  Gilbert, M. Jerusalem in the twentieth century
    956.94
  See/See also pages in the following book(s):
  Potok, C. Wanderings p223-40   **909**
      Immigration and emigration
  Szulc, T. The secret alliance   **325**

Palestine and the Palestinians. Farsoun, S. K.
    956.94

Palestine problem, 1917- *See* Israel-Arab conflicts; Jewish-Arab relations

Palestinian Arabs
  Farsoun, S. K. Palestine and the Palestinians
    956.94
  Grossman, D. The yellow wind   **956.95**
  Shipler, D. K. Arab and Jew   **956.94**
  See/See also pages in the following book(s):
  Said, E. W. Reflections on exile and other essays
  p527-68   **814**

Palika, Liz, 1954-
  K.I.S.S. guide to raising a puppy   **636.7**

Palin, Michael
  Sahara   **966**

Palisca, Claude V., 1921-2001
  (jt. auth) Grout, D. J. A history of Western music
    780.9
  (ed) Norton anthology of western music. See Norton anthology of western music   **780.9**

Palladio, Andrea, 1508-1580
  The four books on architecture   **720**
        About
  Rybczynski, W. The perfect house: a journey with the Renaissance architect Andrea Palladio   **724**

Pallbearers envying the one who rides. Dobyns, S.
    811

Palm Sunday. Vonnegut, K.   **818**

Palmer, Arnold, 1929-
  A golfer's life   **92**

Palmer, Craig T.
  (jt. auth) Thornhill, R. A natural history of rape
    364.1

Palmer, Jeffrey B.
  (jt. auth) Palmer, S. Spinal cord injury   **617**

Palmer, Melissa
  Dr. Melissa Palmer's guide to hepatitis & liver disease
    616.3

Palmer, Sara
  Spinal cord injury   **617**

Palmerston, Henry John Temple, Viscount, 1784-1865
  See/See also pages in the following book(s):
  Strachey, L. Queen Victoria p204-52   **92**

Palmisano, Joseph M.
  (ed) World of sociology. See World of sociology
    301

Palmistry
  Reid, L. The art of hand reading   **133.6**

Palovak, Jewel
  (jt. auth) Treadwell, T. Among grizzlies   **599.78**

Paludan, Phillip S., 1938-
  The presidency of Abraham Lincoln   **973.7**

Palumbi, Stephen R.
  The evolution explosion   **576.8**

Pan Am Flight 103 Bombing Incident, 1988
  Gerson, A. The price of terror   **363.1**

Pan American Flight 103 disaster, 1988 *See* Pan Am Flight 103 Bombing Incident, 1988

Panama
        Description
  Royte, E. The Tapir's morning bath   **577.3**

Panama Canal
  McCullough, D. G. The path between the seas
    972.87

The **panda's** thumb. Gould, S. J.   **576.8**

Pandora's picnic basket. McHughen, A.   **641.3**

Panek, Richard
  Seeing and believing   **522**

Panic disorders
  Root, B. A., Jr. Understanding panic and other anxiety disorders   **616.85**

Pantheism
  See/See also pages in the following book(s):
  Teilhard de Chardin, P. Christianity and evolution p56-75   **231.7**

Panzer, Mary
  Mathew Brady and the image of history   **92**

Papacy
  See also Popes
  Duffy, E. Saints & sinners   **282**
  Maxwell-Stuart, P. G. Chronicle of the popes   **282**
  McBrien, R. P. Lives of the popes   **920**
  Reese, T. J. Inside the Vatican   **282**
  Wills, G. Papal sin   **262**
  Wills, G. Why I am a Catholic   **282**

Papal sin. Wills, G.   **262**

Paper
  Baker, N. Double fold   **025.2**

Paper crafts
  Ragsdale, L. Creative cardboard   **745.54**

Paper manufacture *See* Papermaking

Paperboy. Petroski, H.   **92**

Paperhanging
  See also Wallpaper

Papermaking
  Dawson, S. The art and craft of papermaking   **676**

The **papers** of Martin Luther King, Jr. King, M. L.
    323.1

Papolos, Demitri F.
  The bipolar child   **618.92**

Papolos, Janice
  The virgin homeowner   **643**
  (jt. auth) Papolos, D. F. The bipolar child   **618.92**

Papua New Guinea
        Description
  Salak, K. The four corners   **910.4**

Paradise and power. See Kagan, R. Of paradise and power   **327.73**

Paradise lost. Milton, J.
  In Milton, J. The Riverside Milton   **821**

The **paradox** of American power. Nye, J. S., Jr.
    327.73

Parallax. Hirshfeld, A.   **523.8**

Paramilitary militia movements *See* Militia movements

Paranoid parenting. Füredi, F.   **649**

Parapsychology
  See also Extrasensory perception; Occultism
  Eberhart, G. M. Mysterious creatures   **001.9**
  Goodman, L. Linda Goodman's star signs   **133**
  Shermer, M. Why people believe weird things
    001.9

Parapsychology—*Continued*
Dictionaries
Encyclopedia of occultism & parapsychology   133
Encyclopedias
Guiley, R. E. The encyclopedia of ghosts and spirits
 133.1
Guiley, R. E. Encyclopedia of the strange, mystical &
 unexplained   133
Parasite rex. Zimmer, C.   591.7
Parasites
 See also Symbiosis; Ticks
 Zimmer, C. Parasite rex   591.7
Parcells, Bill
About
Gutman, B. Parcells   92
Paredes, Angel García de *See* García de Paredes, Angel
Parent and child *See* Parent-child relationship
Parent-child relationship
 See also Children of divorced parents; Conflict of
 generations; Father-child relationship; Mother-child
 relationship
Beal, A. C. The black parenting book   649
Brazelton, T. B. The earliest relationship   155.4
Brazelton, T. B. To listen to a child   155.4
Brooks, R. B. Raising resilient children   649
Di Prisco, J. Field guide to the American teenager
 305.23
Donovan, D. M. What did I just say!?!   649
Friday, N. My mother/my self   155.6
Füredi, F. Paranoid parenting   649
Garbarino, J. Parents under siege   649
Gardner, R. A. The parents book about divorce
 306.89
Grosskopf, B. Forgive your parents, heal yourself
 155.9
Hite, S. The Hite report on the family   306.8
Howey, N. Dress codes of three girlhoods—my moth-
 er's, my father's, and mine   306.8
Karp, H. The happiest baby on the block   649
Mayes, L. C. The Yale Child Study Center guide to
 understanding your child   649
Pipher, M. B. Another country   306.8
Richman, S. Raising a child with autism   618.92
Small, M. F. Our babies, ourselves   649
Your adolescent   155.5
Parenthood in America   306.8
Parenting
 See also Child rearing
Bailey, R. A. Easy to love, difficult to discipline
 649
Britton, L. Montessori play & learn   371.3
Bullard, S. Teaching tolerance   649
Cheever, S. As good as I could be   306.8
Cohen, L. J. Playful parenting   649
Cusk, R. A life's work   306.8
Deutsch, F. Halving it all   649
Douglas, A. The mother of all baby books   649
Elias, M. J. Emotionally intelligent parenting   649
Engber, A. The complete single mother   306.8
Füredi, F. Paranoid parenting   649
Ginsberg, B. G. 50 wonderful ways to be a single-
 parent family   649
Hewlett, S. A. The war against parents   649
Nachman, P. A. You and your only child   649
Ozonoff, S. A parent's guide to asperger syndrome and
 high-functioning autism   618.92
Roan, S. Our daughters' health   613
Rosenfeld, A. A. Hyper-parenting   649
Sears, W. Parenting the fussy baby and high-need child
 649
Shapiro, L. E. How to raise a child with a high EQ
 649
Shore, K. Keeping kids safe   649
Spock, B. Dr. Spock on parenting   649
Taffel, R. The second family   306.8

White, B. L. Raising a happy, unspoiled child
 649
Winik, M. The lunch-box chronicles   306.8
 See/See also pages in the following book(s):
Goleman, D. Emotional intelligence p189-99
 152.4
Encyclopedias
Parenthood in America   306.8
Parenting the fussy baby and high-need child. Sears, W.
 649
Parents, Aging *See* Aging parents
Parents, Single *See* Single parent family
The **parents** book about divorce. Gardner, R. A.
 306.89
A **parent's** guide to asperger syndrome and high-
 functioning autism. Ozonoff, S.   618.92
Parents under siege. Garbarino, J.   649
Parfitt, George A. E.
(ed) Jonson, B. The complete poems   821
Parini, Jay
Robert Frost   92
(ed) The Bread Loaf anthology of contemporary
 American essays. See The Bread Loaf anthology of
 contemporary American essays   814
(ed) The Columbia anthology of American poetry. See
 The Columbia anthology of American poetry
 811.008
(ed) The Columbia history of American poetry. See
 The Columbia history of American poetry
 811.009
(ed) The Norton book of American autobiography. See
 The Norton book of American autobiography
 920
Paris (France)
Description
White, E. The flaneur   944
Intellectual life
Adams, W. H. The Paris years of Thomas Jefferson
 92
Miles, B. The Beat Hotel   810.9
Stein, G. The autobiography of Alice B. Toklas
 92
 See/See also pages in the following book(s):
Lottman, H. R. Man Ray's Montparnasse   92
Social life and customs
Karnow, S. Paris in the fifties   944
Paris 1919. MacMillan, M.   940.3
Paris in the fifties. Karnow, S.   944
Paris Peace Conference (1919-1920)
MacMillan, M. Paris 1919   940.3
Paris review
Women writers at work. See Women writers at work
 808
The **Paris** years of Thomas Jefferson. Adams, W. H.
 92
Parish, Henry II, Mrs. *See* Parish, Sister, 1910-1994
Parish, Sister, 1910-1994
About
Bartlett, A. P. Sister: the life of legendary American
 interior decorator Mrs. Henry Parish II   92
Parisi, Joseph, 1944-
(ed) The Poetry anthology, 1912-2002. See The Poetry
 anthology, 1912-2002   811.008
Parisian home cooking. Roberts, M.   641.5
Park, Clara Claiborne
Exiting nirvana   616.89
Park, David
The fire within the eye   535
Park, Jessy, 1958-
About
Park, C. C. Exiting nirvana   616.89
Park, Robert L.
Voodoo science   500
Park, Yeon Hwan
Black belt tae kwon do   796.8

Parker, Barry R.
Quantum legacy   **530.1**
Parker, Charlie, 1920-1955
See/See also pages in the following book(s):
DeVeaux, S. K. The birth of bebop   **781.65**
Feather, L. From Satchmo to Miles   **920**
Parker, Derek
(jt. auth) Parker, J. KISS guide to astrology
    133.5
(jt. auth) Parker, J. Parkers' complete book of dreams
    154.6
Parker, Dorothy, 1893-1967
The poetry and short stories of Dorothy Parker
    818
The portable Dorothy Parker   **818**
About
Meade, M. Dorothy Parker   **92**
See/See also pages in the following book(s):
American women fiction writers   **813.009**
Women writers at work p101-16   **808**
Parker, Ely Samuel, 1828-1895
See/See also pages in the following book(s):
Brown, D. A. Bury my heart at Wounded Knee
    970.004
Parker, Geoffrey, 1943-
(jt. auth) Martin, C. The Spanish Armada   **942.05**
Parker, Hershel
Herman Melville   **92**
Parker, Janet
(ed) Anatomica's body atlas. See Anatomica's body at-
las   **611**
Parker, Julia, 1932-
KISS guide to astrology   **133.5**
Parkers' complete book of dreams   **154.6**
Parker, Sybil P.
(ed) McGraw-Hill concise encyclopedia of science &
technology. See McGraw-Hill concise encyclopedia
of science & technology   **503**
Parker, Yana
The damn good resume guide   **650.14**
Parkers' complete book of dreams. Parker, J.   **154.6**
Parkinson, Peter, 1942-
The artist blacksmith   **682**
Parkinson's disease
Cram, D. L. Answers to frequently asked questions in
Parkinson's disease   **616.8**
Duvoisin, R. C. Parkinson's disease   **616.8**
Freed, C. Healing the brain   **616.8**
Hauser, R. A. Parkinson's disease: questions and an-
swers   **616.8**
Hutton, J. T. Preventing falls   **618.97**
Kondracke, M. Saving Milly   **362.1**
Lieberman, A. 100 questions & answers about Parkin-
son [sic] disease   **616.8**
Lieberman, A. Shaking-up Parkinson disease
    616.8
Parkinson's disease   **616.8**
Parkinson's disease and quality of life   **616.8**
Rosenstein, A. Water exercises for Parkinson's
    616.8
Sacks, O. W. The island of the colorblind   **617.7**
Schwarz, S. P. Parkinson's disease: 300 tips for mak-
ing life easier   **616.8**
Weiner, W. J. Parkinson's disease   **616.8**
When Parkinson's strikes early   **616.8**
Personal narratives
Havemann, J. A life shaken   **362.1**
See/See also pages in the following book(s):
Fox, Michael J. Lucky man   **92**
Parkinson's disease   **616.8**
Parkinson's disease and quality of life   **616.8**
Parkman, Francis, 1823-1893
The Oregon Trail   **978**
See/See also pages in the following book(s):
Schama, S. Dead certainties   **907**

Parkman, George, 1790-1849
See/See also pages in the following book(s):
Schama, S. Dead certainties   **907**
Parks, Gordon
See/See also pages in the following book(s):
Russell, D. Black genius and the American experience
    920
Parks, Rosa, 1913-
Quiet strength   **92**
About
Brinkley, D. Rosa Parks   **92**
See/See also pages in the following book(s):
Abdul-Jabbar, K. Black profiles in courage p206-17
    920
Parks, Suzan-Lori
Topdog/underdog   **812**
Parks, Tim
An Italian education   **945**
Parks
See also National parks and reserves
United States
National Geographic guide to the state parks of the
United States   **917.3**
Parks directory of the United States   **917.3**
See/See also pages in the following book(s):
Crawford, M. Habitats and ecosystems   **578.68**
Parks directory of the United States   **917.3**
Parkyn, Neil, 1943-
The Seventy wonders of the modern world. See The
Seventy wonders of the modern world   **720.9**
Parliament of fowls. Chaucer, G.
In Chaucer, G. The complete poetry and prose of
Geoffrey Chaucer   **821**
Parliament of whores. O'Rourke, P. J.   **817**
Parliamentary practice
Robert, H. M. Robert's rules of order   **060.4**
Sturgis, A. The standard code of parliamentary proce-
dure   **060.4**
Webster's New World Robert's rules of order
    060.4
Parmet, Herbert S.
George Bush   **92**
Paroli, Emma Trenti
(jt. auth) Linden, D. W. Preemies   **618.92**
Parr, Katherine *See* Catharine Parr, Queen, consort of
Henry VIII, King of England, 1512-1548
Parrots
Lantermann, W. The new parrot handbook   **636.6**
Parrott, Andrew
(ed) The New Oxford book of carols. See The New
Oxford book of carols   **782.28**
Parson, Ann B.
(jt. auth) Tanzi, R. E. Decoding darkness   **616.8**
Parsons, Russ
How to read a french fry   **641.5**
The **particle** explosion. See Close, F. E. The particle od-
yssey   **539.7**
The **particle** garden. Kane, G.   **539.7**
The **particle** odyssey. Close, F. E.   **539.7**
Particles (Nuclear physics)
See also Electrons
Building blocks of matter   **539.7**
Close, F. E. The particle odyssey   **539.7**
Gell-Mann, M. The quark and the jaguar   **530.1**
Kane, G. The particle garden   **539.7**
Lederman, L. M. The God particle   **539.7**
See/See also pages in the following book(s):
Greene, B. R. The elegant universe   **539.7**
Gribbin, J. R. The search for superstrings, symmetry,
and the theory of everything   **539.7**
Dictionaries
Gribbin, J. R. Q is for quantum   **539.7**
Parting the waters: America in the King years, 1954-63.
Branch, T.   **973.921**

Partnow, Elaine, 1941-
The Quotable woman. See The Quotable woman
    808.88

Partridge, Eric, 1894-1979
A dictionary of slang and unconventional English
    427

Party food. Kafka, B.   641.5

Parva naturalia. Aristotle
In Aristotle. The basic works of Aristotle p607-30
    888

Pasachoff, Jay M.
(jt. auth) Golub, L. Nearest star   523.7

Pascal, Blaise, 1623-1662
See/See also pages in the following book(s):
Bell, E. T. Men of mathematics p73-89   920
Jaspers, K. The great philosophers   109

Paschen, Elise
Poetry speaks. See Poetry speaks   808.81

Pasek, Kathy Hirsh- *See* Hirsh-Pasek, Kathy

Pashkow, Fredric J., 1945-
The women's heart book   616.1

Pass it on. Shotwell, B.   346.05

Pass the butterworms. Cahill, T.   910.4

Passage to Juneau. Raban, J.   979.8

Passing by. Kosinski, J. N.   814

Passing through. Kunitz, S.   811

Passion for Islam. Murphy, C.   297

A **passion** for potatoes. Marshall, L.   641.6

A **passion** for wisdom. Solomon, R. C.   109

Passionate gardening. Springer, L.   635

Passionate minds. Pierpont, C. R.   810.9

Passive resistance
Gandhi, M. Gandhi on non-violence   322.4

Passover
The New York Times Passover cookbook   641.5
See/See also pages in the following book(s):
Strassfeld, M. The Jewish holidays p5-45   296.4

Past and present. Carlyle, T.   824

Pasta products
See also Cooking—Pasta products

Pastel drawing
Blake, M. You can paint pastels   741.2

Pasternak, Boris Leonidovich, 1890-1960
See/See also pages in the following book(s):
Miłosz, C. To begin where I am p404-20   891.8

Pastoral peoples *See* Nomads

Pastoral psychology
Peale, N. V. The power of positive living   248
Peale, N. V. The power of positive thinking
    253.5

Patagonia (Argentina and Chile)
    Description
Chatwin, B. In Patagonia   918.2

Patarca, Roberto
The concise encyclopedia of fibromyalgia and
myofascial pain   616.7

Patchwork quilts *See* Quilts

Patent, Greg, 1939-
Baking in America   641.8

Patent, copyright & trademark. Elias, S.   346.04

Patent medicines *See* Nonprescription drugs

Patents
See also Trademarks
Elias, S. Patent, copyright & trademark   346.04
Petroski, H. The evolution of useful things   609

Paterek, Josephine
Encyclopedia of American Indian costume   391

Paterniti, Michael
Driving Mr. Albert   917.3

Paterson. Williams, W. C.   811

The **path** between the seas. McCullough, D. G.
    972.87

Path of the paddle. Mason, B.   797.1

The **path** to power. Caro, R. A.
In Caro, R. A. The years of Lyndon Johnson v1
    92

Paths of life. Miller, A.   306.8

Patience & fortitude. Basbanes, N. A.   002

The **patient's** guide to medical tests. Segen, J. C.
    616.07

Patios
Riha, J. Deck & patio planner   643
Schuttner, S. Building and designing decks   690

Patriarch: George Washington and the new American
nation. Smith, R. N.   92

Patrick, John J.
(ed) The Oxford guide to the United States Government. See The Oxford guide to the United States
Government   320.03

Patrimony. Roth, P.   92

Patriotic gore. Wilson, E.   810.9

Patternmaking for fashion design. Armstrong, H. J.
    646.4

Patterns (Mathematics)
Buchanan, M. Nexus: small worlds and the groundbreaking science of networks   530

Patterns of home. Jacobson, M.   728

Patterson, Charles, 1935-
(jt. auth) Filar, M. From Buchenwald to Carnegie Hall
    92

Patterson, David, 1948-
(ed) Encyclopedia of Holocaust literature. See Encyclopedia of Holocaust literature   809

Patterson, Floyd
See/See also pages in the following book(s):
Life stories   920

Patterson, Jerry L.
Blackjack, a winner's handbook   795.4

Patterson's American education   370.25

Patton, Bruce
(jt. auth) Stone, D. Difficult conversations   158

Patton, George S. (George Smith), 1885-1945
War as I knew it   940.54
    About
D'Este, C. Patton   92
Hanson, V. D. The soul of battle   355
Hirshson, S. P. General Patton: a soldier's life   92

Patton, Phil
(jt. auth) Yeager, J. Voyager   910.4

Patton, Sharon F.
African-American art   704

Paul VI, Pope, 1897-1978
    About
Hebblethwaite, P. Paul VI   92

Paul, the Apostle, Saint
    About
Gager, J. G. The origins of anti-Semitism   296.3
Murphy-O'Connor, J. Paul   92
Wilson, A. N. Paul: the mind of the Apostle   92
See/See also pages in the following book(s):
Küng, H. Great Christian thinkers p15-40   230

Paul, Gregory S.
(ed) The Scientific American book of dinosaurs. See
The Scientific American book of dinosaurs
    567.9

Paul Celan: poems. See Celan, P. Poems of Paul Celan
    831

Paul Revere's ride. Fischer, D. H.   973.3

Paula. Allende, I.   92

Pauling, Linus C., 1901-1994
Linus Pauling in his own words   92

Paulos, John Allen
Beyond numeracy   510
Innumeracy   510
A mathematician reads the newspaper   510

Paulsen, Gary
Winterdance   798.8

Pavelka, Ed
(ed) Bicycling magazine's 900 all-time best tips. See
Bicycling magazine's 900 all-time best tips
796.6
(ed) Bicycling magazine's basic maintenance and re-
pair. See Bicycling magazine's basic maintenance
and repair **629.28**
Pawson, Des
The handbook of knots **623.88**
Paxton, John, 1923-
(ed) The Wilson calendar of world history. See The
Wilson calendar of world history **902**
Pay television, Cable See Cable television
Paying less for college. See Peterson's college money
handbook **378.3**
Payne, Katharine, 1937-
Silent thunder **599.67**
Paz, Octavio, 1914-1998
The collected poems of Octavio Paz, 1957-1987
861
The labyrinth of solitude
In Paz, O. The labyrinth of solitude [and other es-
says] p7-212 **864**
The labyrinth of solitude [and other essays] **864**
The other Mexico
In Paz, O. The labyrinth of solitude [and other es-
says] p213-325 **864**
Selected poems **861**
A tale of two gardens **861**
PCs for dummies. Gookin, D. **004**
Peace
Bobbitt, P. The shield of Achilles **327**
Peace. Aristophanes
In Aristophanes. The complete plays of Aristophanes
p185-227 **882**
Peacock, John, 1943-
20th-century fashion **391**
The chronicle of Western fashion **391**
Men's fashion **391**
Peacock, Molly, 1947-
Cornucopia **811**
Peacock, Thomas Love, 1785-1866
See/See also pages in the following book(s):
Vidal, G. United States—essays, 1952-1992 p147-62
814
Peale, Norman Vincent
The power of positive living **248**
The power of positive thinking **253.5**
Pearl, Daniel, 1963-2002
At home in the world **070.4**
Pearl, Nancy
Now read this II **016.8**
Pearl Harbor (Oahu, Hawaii), Attack on, 1941
Prange, G. W. At dawn we slept **940.54**
Stinnett, R. B. Day of deceit **940.54**
Pictorial works
Goldstein, D. M. The way it was **940.54**
Pears, Pauline
(ed) Rodale's illustrated encyclopedia of organic gar-
dening. See Rodale's illustrated encyclopedia of or-
ganic gardening **635.9**
Pearson, Hugh
Under the knife [biography of Joseph Griffin] **92**
Pearson, Joanne
(ed) Belief beyond boundaries. See Belief beyond
boundaries **291.9**
Peary, Danny, 1949-
(jt. auth) McCarver, T. Tim McCarver's Baseball for
brain surgeons and other fans **796.357**
Peat, F. David, 1938-
From certainty to uncertainty **530**
Peattie, Antony
The New Kobbé's opera book. See The New Kobbé's
opera book **792.5**

Peck, Abraham J.
(ed) The Holocaust and history. See The Holocaust and
history **940.53**
Peck, Alan J. Avery- See Avery-Peck, Alan J. (Alan
Jeffery), 1953-
Peck, Brian
The baby boomer body book **613**
Peck, M. Scott (Morgan Scott)
Denial of the soul **179.7**
Further along the road less traveled **158**
The road less traveled **158**
The road less traveled and beyond **158**
Peck, Morgan Scott See Peck, M. Scott (Morgan Scott)
Peckaitis, Christine M.
(ed) Sperling, A. P. Mathematics made simple
510
Pedagogy See Teaching
Pedersen, Stephanie
K-I-S-S beauty **646.7**
Pederson, Jay P.
(ed) St. James guide to science fiction writers. See St.
James guide to science fiction writers **809.3**
(ed) Twentieth-century literary movements dictionary.
See Twentieth-century literary movements dictionary
809
Pediatric cancer sourcebook **618.92**
Pediatrics See Children—Diseases; Children—Health
and hygiene
Peebles, Curtis
Asteroids **523.4**
Peer Gynt. Ibsen, H.
In Our dramatic heritage v4 **808.82**
Pei, I. M., 1917-
About
Wiseman, C. I.M. Pei: a profile in American architec-
ture **92**
Peikoff, Leonard
(jt. auth) Rand, A. The voice of reason; essays in ob-
jectivist thought **191**
Peirce, Charles S. (Charles Sanders), 1839-1914
About
Menand, L. The Metaphysical Club **973.9**
Peiss, Kathy Lee
Hope in a jar **391**
Pelayo y Gross, Ramón García- See García-Pelayo y
Gross, Ramón
A **pelican** in the wilderness. Colegate, I. **291.4**
Pelikan, Jaroslav Jan, 1923-
The illustrated Jesus through the centuries **232.9**
Mary through the centuries **232.91**
Pellant, Chris
Rocks and minerals **549**
Pellegrino, Charles R.
Ghosts of the Titanic **910.4**
Pelletier, Kenneth R.
The best alternative medicine **615.5**
The **Peloponnesian** War. See Thucydides. The history of
the Peloponnesian War **938**
Peltz, Johanan
About
Blum, H. The brigade **940.54**
Penal codes See Criminal law
Penal colonies
Hughes, R. The fatal shore **994**
Rees, S. The floating brothel **365**
Pence, Gregory E.
(ed) Flesh of my flesh. See Flesh of my flesh
174
Pencils
Petroski, H. The pencil **674**
Pendergast, Sara
(ed) Reference guide to world literature. See Reference
guide to world literature **809**
(ed) St. James encyclopedia of popular culture. See St.
James encyclopedia of popular culture **973.9**

Pendergast, Tom, 1964-
(ed) Reference guide to world literature. See Reference guide to world literature **809**
(ed) St. James encyclopedia of popular culture. See St. James encyclopedia of popular culture **973.9**
The **Penguin** book of love poetry. See A Book of love poetry **808.81**
The **Penguin** book of modern African poetry **896**
The **Penguin** book of the sonnet **821.008**
The **Penguin** book of women poets **808.81**
The **Penguin** book of women's humor **817.008**
The **Penguin** companion to food. See The Oxford companion to food **641.03**
The **Penguin** concise dictionary of art history. Frazier, N. **703**
The **Penguin** desk encyclopedia of science and mathematics. Bunch, B. H. **503**
The **Penguin** dictionary of architecture and landscape architecture **720.3**
The **Penguin** dictionary of astronomy. See Mitton, J. Cambridge dictionary of astronomy **520.3**
The **Penguin** dictionary of English usage and style. Lovinger, P. W. **428**
The **Penguin** dictionary of language. See Crystal, D. A dictionary of language **410**
The **Penguin** dictionary of literary terms. See Cuddon, J. A. A dictionary of literary terms and literary theory **803**
The **Penguin** dictionary of saints. Attwater, D. **920.003**
The **Penguin** history of Latin America. Williamson, E. **980**
Penicillin
See/See also pages in the following book(s):
Friedman, M. Medicine's 10 greatest discoveries **610.9**
Peninsular Campaign, 1862
Sears, S. W. To the gates of Richmond **973.7**
Penis
Friedman, D. M. A mind of its own **573.6**
Penn family
See/See also pages in the following book(s):
Jennings, F. Benjamin Franklin, politician **92**
Pennock, Robert T.
Tower of Babel **576.8**
Penrose, Lee Miller *See* Miller, Lee, 1907-1977
Penrose, Roger
(jt. auth) Hawking, S. W. The nature of space and time **530.1**
See/See also pages in the following book(s):
Dennett, D. C. Darwin's dangerous idea **146**
Penrose, Sir Roland, 1900-1984
Picasso: his life and work **92**
Pentagon (U.S.) *See* United States. Dept. of Defense
Pentagon Papers
Ellsberg, D. Secrets: a memoir of Vietnam and the Pentagon papers **959.704**
Pentagon terrorist attack, 2001 *See* September 11 terrorist attacks, 2001
Pentateuch *See* Bible. O.T. Pentateuch
Pentimento. Hellman, L. **92**
Penzel, Fred
Obsessive-compulsive disorders **616.85**
Penzler, Otto, 1942-
(ed) Best American crime writing. See Best American crime writing **364.1**
People have more fun than anybody. Thurber, J. **818**
The **people,** yes. Sandburg, C.
In Sandburg, C. Complete poems of Carl Sandburg p439-617 **811**
Peoples and empires. Pagden, A. **909**
A **people's** history of the American Revolution. Raphael, R. **973.3**

A **people's** history of the Supreme Court. Irons, P. H. **347**
The **people's** pharmacy guide to home and herbal remedies. Graedon, J. **615**
People's Republic of China *See* China
A **people's** tragedy. Figes, O. **947.084**
The **peopling** of British North America. Bailyn, B. **973.2**
Pépin, Claudine
(jt. auth) Pépin, J. Jacques Pépin celebrates **641.5**
Pépin, Jacques
The apprentice: my life in the kitchen **92**
Jacques Pépin celebrates **641.5**
Jacques Pépin's simple and healthy cooking **641.5**
(jt. auth) Child, J. Julia and Jacques cooking at home **641.5**
Pepys, Samuel, 1633-1703
The diary of Samuel Pepys **92**
About
Tomalin, C. Samuel Pepys **92**
Pequot Indians
See/See also pages in the following book(s):
Josephy, A. M. Now that the buffalo's gone p33-73 **970.004**
Perception
Abram, D. The spell of the sensuous **128**
Hoffman, D. D. Visual intelligence **152.14**
Livingstone, M. S. Vision and art **750.1**
Percy, Walker, 1916-1990
Lost in the cosmos **818**
Signposts in a strange land **818**
Perdue, Theda, 1949-
The Columbia guide to American Indians of the Southeast **970.004**
(ed) Sifters: Native American women's lives. See Sifters: Native American women's lives **920**
Perennial all-stars. Cox, J. **635.9**
The **perennial** philosophy. Huxley, A. **210**
Perennials
Armitage, A. M. Armitage's manual of annuals, biennials, and half-hardy perennials **635.9**
Cox, J. Perennial all-stars **635.9**
DiSabato-Aust, T. The well-tended perennial garden **635.9**
Ellis, B. W. Taylor's guide to perennials **635.9**
Harper, P. Designing with perennials **712**
Hodgson, L. Perennials for every purpose **635.9**
Phillips, E. Rodale's illustrated encyclopedia of perennials **635.9**
Perennials for every purpose. Hodgson, L. **635.9**
Peres, Shimon, 1923-
The imaginary voyage **956.94**
Pérez, Louis A., 1943-
Cuba **972.91**
Perez, Louis G.
The history of Japan **952**
Pérez-Brignoli, Héctor
A brief history of Central America **972.8**
Perfect cakes. Malgieri, N. **641.8**
Perfect murder, perfect town. Schiller, L. **364.1**
The **perfect** resume. See Jackson, T. The new perfect resume **650.14**
The **perfect** storm. Junger, S. **910.4**
Performing arts
See also Dance
Encyclopedias
The Oxford encyclopedia of theatre & performance **792.03**
Period costume for stage & screen. Hunnisett, J. **391**
The **periodic** kingdom. Atkins, P. W. **541.2**
Periodic law
Atkins, P. W. The periodic kingdom **541.2**
The **periodic** table. Levi, P. **92**

Periodicals
Bibliography
El-hi textbooks and serials in print   **016.3713**
Magazines for libraries   **011**
The Standard periodical directory   **011**
Ulrich's periodicals directory   **011**
Directories
Gale directory of publications and broadcast media
    070.025
The Standard periodical directory   **011**
Ulrich's periodicals directory   **011**
Indexes
Readers' guide to periodical literature   **051**
Periodicals directory. See Ulrich's periodicals directory
    011
Perkin, William Henry, 1838-1907
About
Garfield, S. Mauve   **667**
Perkins, Agnes
(jt. auth) Helbig, A. Dictionary of American children's
    fiction, 1995-1999   **028.5**
Perkins, Barbara, 1933-
(ed) HarperCollins Reader's encyclopedia of American
    literature. See HarperCollins Reader's encyclopedia
    of American literature   **810.3**
Perkins, Dorothy
Encyclopedia of China   **951**
Perkins, George B., 1930-
(ed) HarperCollins Reader's encyclopedia of American
    literature. See HarperCollins Reader's encyclopedia
    of American literature   **810.3**
Perkowitz, S., 1939-
Empire of light   **535**
Perl, Martin L., 1927-
See/See also pages in the following book(s):
Greenstein, G. Portraits of discovery p151-86   **920**
Perl, Teri
(ed) Notable women in mathematics. See Notable
    women in mathematics   **920.003**
Permian High School (Odessa, Tex.)
Bissinger, H. G. Friday night lights   **796.332**
Pernoud, Régine, 1909-
Joan of Arc   **92**
Perón, Eva, 1919-1952
See/See also pages in the following book(s):
Naipaul, V. S. The writer and the world p346-437
    824
Perot, H. Ross *See* Perot, Ross, 1930-
Perot, Ross, 1930-
See/See also pages in the following book(s):
Wills, G. Certain trumpets p117-28   **303.3**
Perrin, Noel
A child's delight   **028.5**
Perrins, Christopher M.
(ed) Firefly encyclopedia of birds. See Firefly encyclo-
    pedia of birds   **598**
Perritt, Henry H., Jr.
Americans with Disabilities Act handbook   **344**
Perrottet, Tony
Route 66 A.D.   **910.4**
Perry, Bruce
Malcolm   **92**
Perry, Julia, 1924-1979
See/See also pages in the following book(s):
Walker-Hill, H. From spirituals to symphonies
    920
Perry, Mark, 1950-
Conceived in liberty   **973.7**
Lift up thy voice   **920**
Persecution
Foxe, J. Foxe's Book of martyrs   **272**
See/See also pages in the following book(s):
Conroy, J. Unspeakable acts, ordinary people
    323.4

The **persecution** and assassination of Jean-Paul Marat as
performed by the inmates of the Asylum of
Charenton under the direction of the Marquis de
Sade. Weiss, P.   **832**
Perseus (Greek mythology)
See/See also pages in the following book(s):
Hamilton, E. Mythology p197-208   **292**
Persia *See* Iran
Persian Gulf War, 1980-1988 *See* Iran-Iraq War, 1980-
1988
Persian Gulf War, 1991
Atkinson, R. Crusade   **956.7**
Clancy, T. Into the storm   **956.7**
Friedman, N. Desert victory   **956.7**
Gordon, M. R. The generals' war   **956.7**
Grossman, M. Encyclopedia of the Persian Gulf War
    956.7
Newell, C. R. Historical dictionary of the Persian Gulf
    War, 1990-1991   **956.7**
Schwartz, R. A. Encyclopedia of the Persian Gulf War
    956.7
Schwarzkopf, H. N. It doesn't take a hero: General H.
    Norman Schwarzkopf   **92**
Woodward, B. The commanders   **973.928**
Personal narratives
Kelly, M. Martyrs' Day   **956.7**
Swofford, A. Jarhead: a Marine's chronicle of the Gulf
    War and other battles   **956.7**
Persian pilgrimages. Molavi, A.   **955**
Persian poetry
Collections
Music of a distant drum   **808.81**
Persico, Joseph E.
Roosevelt's secret war   **940.54**
(jt. auth) Powell, C. L. My American journey   **92**
Person, Diane Goetz
(ed) The Continuum encyclopedia of children's litera-
    ture. See The Continuum encyclopedia of children's
    literature   **028.5**
Personal appearance
Berg, R. Beauty: the new basics   **646.7**
Brown, B. Bobbi Brown beauty evolution   **646.7**
DuPriest, L. Natural beauty   **646.7**
Essence total makeover   **646.7**
Etcoff, N. L. Survival of the prettiest   **391**
Fornay, A. The African American woman's guide to
    successful makeup and skincare   **646.7**
Hadadi, L. Healthy beauty   **646.7**
Kashuk, S. Real beauty   **646.7**
Pedersen, S. K-I-S-S beauty   **646.7**
Peiss, K. L. Hope in a jar   **391**
Wolf, N. The beauty myth   **305.4**
See/See also pages in the following book(s):
Bordo, S. The male body p168-228   **305.31**
Personal conduct *See* Conduct of life
Personal finance
See also Consumer credit
Downes, J. Barron's finance & investment handbook
    332.6
Feigenbaum, R. A. The 529 College Savings Plan
    378.3
Gardner, D. The Motley Fool's what to do with your
    money now   **332.6**
Glink, I. R. 50 simple things you can do to improve
    your personal finances   **332.024**
Huff, D. The complete how to figure it   **640**
Miller, T. Kiplinger's practical guide to your money
    332.024
Quinn, J. B. Making the most of your money
    332.024
Schwab-Pomerantz, C. It pays to talk   **332.024**
Tobias, A. P. The only investment guide you'll ever
    need   **332.024**
Wolman, W. The great 401(k) hoax   **332.024**

Personal grooming
Gross, K. J. Woman's face   **646.7**
Personal history. Graham, K.   **92**
The **personal** Internet security guidebook. Speed, T.   **005.8**
Personal life skills See Life skills
Personal loans
    See also Mortgages
Personal names
Lansky, B. The very best baby name book in the whole wide world   **929.4**
       Dictionaries
Latham, E. A dictionary of names, nicknames, and surnames of persons, places, and things   **929.4**
Room, A. Dictionary of first names   **929.4**
       United States
Dictionary of American family names   **929.4**
Shankle, G. E. American nicknames   **929.4**
Twentieth century American nicknames   **929.4**
Personal time management See Time management
Personality
Allport, G. Becoming   **155.2**
Dimitrius, J.-E. Reading people   **155.2**
Hamer, D. H. Living with our genes   **155.2**
LeDoux, J. E. Synaptic self   **612.8**
Maslow, A. H. Toward a psychology of being   **155.2**
Whybrow, P. C. A mood apart   **616.89**
Personality disorders
    See also Multiple personality
Kramer, P. D. Listening to Prozac   **616.85**
Whybrow, P. C. A mood apart   **616.89**
Personnel management
    See also Employees—Dismissal
Lancaster, L. C. When generations collide   **658.3**
Perspectives of world-history. Spengler, O.
    In Spengler, O. The decline of the West v2   **901**
Pert, Candace, 1946-
Molecules of emotion   **612.8**
Pertile, Lino
(ed) The Cambridge history of Italian literature. See The Cambridge history of Italian literature   **850.9**
Peru
       Antiquities
Bingham, H. Lost city of the Incas   **985**
Moseley, M. E. The Incas and their ancestors   **985**
       History
Hemming, J. The conquest of the Incas   **985**
Prescott, W. H. History of the conquest of Peru   **985**
Pesach See Passover
Pescatore, Fred, 1961-
The allergy and asthma cure   **616.97**
Peshkov, Aleksei Maksimovich See Gorky, Maksim, 1868-1936
Pesky, Johnny, 1919-
    See/See also pages in the following book(s):
Halberstam, D. The teammates   **920**
Pessoa, Fernando, 1888-1935
Fernando Pessoa & Co   **869**
    See/See also pages in the following book(s):
Bloom, H. The Western canon   **809**
Pest control
Winston, M. L. Nature wars   **577.2**
Pesticides
    See/See also pages in the following book(s):
Palumbi, S. R. The evolution explosion   **576.8**
       Environmental aspects
Winston, M. L. Nature wars   **577.2**
Pesticides industry
       Accidents
Lapierre, D. Five past midnight in Bhopal   **363.1**

Pests
    See also Parasites
Pete Seeger's storytelling book. Seeger, P.   **372.6**
Peter I, the Great, Emperor of Russia, 1672-1725
    See/See also pages in the following book(s):
Durant, W. J. The age of Louis XIV p391-410   **940.2**
Peter, Laurence J.
The Peter Principle   **817**
The **Peter** Matthiessen reader. Matthiessen, P.   **818**
The **Peter** Principle. Peter, L. J.   **817**
Peter Shaffer's Amadeus. Shaffer, P.   **822**
Peterman Schwarz, Shelley See Schwarz, Shelley Peterman, 1946-
Peters, C. J., 1940-
Virus hunter   **614.5**
Peters, Colette
Colette's cakes   **641.8**
Peters, Joseph J., 1951-
(ed) Simon and Schuster's guide to rocks and minerals. See Simon and Schuster's guide to rocks and minerals   **549**
Peters, Rick
Woodworker's guide to wood   **684**
Peters, Sally
Bernard Shaw   **92**
Peters, Thomas J.
The circle of innovation   **658.4**
Petersen, Ronald C., 1946-
(ed) Mayo Clinic on Alzheimer's disease. See Mayo Clinic on Alzheimer's disease   **616.8**
Peterson, Carolyn Sue, 1938-
Index to children's songs   **782.42**
Peterson, Franklynn
(jt. auth) Selfridge, N. Freedom from fibromyalgia   **616.7**
Peterson, James
Fish & shellfish   **641.6**
Glorious French food   **641.5**
Vegetables   **641.6**
Peterson, Oscar, 1925-
A jazz odyssey: the life of Oscar Peterson   **92**
    See/See also pages in the following book(s):
Feather, L. From Satchmo to Miles   **920**
Peterson, Roger Tory, 1908-1996
A field guide to the birds of Britain and Europe   **598**
A field guide to the birds of eastern and central North America   **598**
A field guide to western birds   **598**
Peterson, Virginia Marie, 1925-
(jt. auth) Peterson, R. T. A field guide to the birds of eastern and central North America   **598**
Peterson's annual guide to undergraduate study. See Peterson's guide to four-year colleges   **378.73**
Peterson's annual guide to undergraduate study. See Peterson's guide to two-year colleges   **378.73**
Peterson's college money handbook   **378.3**
Peterson's colleges with programs for students with learning disabilities or attention deficit disorders   **378.73**
Peterson's competitive colleges   **378.73**
Peterson's guide to colleges with programs for learning-disabled students. See Peterson's colleges with programs for students with learning disabilities or attention deficit disorders   **378.73**
Peterson's guide to four-year colleges   **378.73**
Peterson's guide to two-year colleges   **378.73**
Peterson's private secondary schools   **373.2**
Petit, Philippe, 1949-
To reach the clouds   **92**
Petrarca, Francesco, 1304-1374
    See/See also pages in the following book(s):
The Renaissance philosophy of man p23-33   **189**
Petrarch See Petrarca, Francesco, 1304-1374

Petre, Peter
  (jt. auth) Schwarzkopf, H. N. It doesn't take a hero:
    General H. Norman Schwarzkopf   92
Petro, Pamela, 1960-
  Sitting up with the dead   398.2
Petroglyphs *See* Rock drawings, paintings, and engravings
Petroleum industry
  Yergin, D. The prize   338.2
Petroleum trade *See* Petroleum industry
Petropoulos, Jonathan
  The Faustian bargain   709
Petroski, Henry
  Engineers of dreams   624
  The evolution of useful things   609
  Invention by design   620
  Paperboy   92
  The pencil   674
  Remaking the world   620
Petry, Ann Lane
  See/See also pages in the following book(s):
  American women fiction writers   813.009
Pets
    See also Domestic animals; names of animals, e.g.
    Cats; Dogs; etc.
  Goldstein, M. The nature of animal healing
    636.089
  Schoen, A. M. Kindred spirits   636.089
  Sheldrake, R. Dogs that know when their owners are
    coming home   133.8
  Sife, W. The loss of a pet   155.9
      Diseases
  Pinney, C. C. The complete home veterinary guide
    636.089
Petspeak   636.089
Pevsner, Sir Nikolaus, 1902-1983
  (ed) The Penguin dictionary of architecture and landscape architecture. See The Penguin dictionary of architecture and landscape architecture   720.3
Peynaud, Emile
  The taste of wine   641.2
Pfaff, Daniel W.
  Joseph Pulitzer II and the Post-dispatch   92
Pfalzgraf, Taryn Benbow- *See* Benbow-Pfalzgraf, Taryn
Pfeffer, Jeffrey
  (jt. auth) O'Reilly, C. A., III Hidden value   658
Pfeiffer, Ida, 1797-1858
  See/See also pages in the following book(s):
  Slung, M. B. Living with cannibals and other women's
    adventures   910.4
The PGA manual of golf. Martino, R.   796.352
PGA Tour Inc.
  Feinstein, J. A good walk spoiled   796.352
Phaedo. Plato
  In Plato. The dialogues of Plato p66-160   888
  In Plato. The portable Plato p191-278   888
Phallus *See* Penis
Pharies, David A.
  (ed) The University of Chicago Spanish dictionary. See
    The University of Chicago Spanish dictionary
    463
Pharmaceutical industry *See* Drug industry
Pharmacology
    See also Drugs
Phelps, Shirelle
  (ed) Gale encyclopedia of everyday law. See Gale encyclopedia of everyday law   349
Phenomenology
  Heidegger, M. Being and time   111
  Heidegger, M. On time and being   111
The phenomenon of man. Teilhard de Chardin, P.
    113
Philadelphia 76ers (Basketball team)
  Lynch, W. Season of the 76ers   796.323
Philanthropy *See* Charities; Endowments

Philbrick, Nathaniel
  In the heart of the sea   910.4
Philip II, King of Spain, 1527-1598
      About
  Kamen, H. Philip of Spain   92
Philip Morris, Inc.
  Kluger, R. Ashes to ashes   394.1
Philippines
      History
  Karnow, S. In our image   959.9
Philip's atlas of world history. See Atlas of world history   911
Phillips, Carl, 1959-
  Rock Harbor   811
Phillips, Ellen
  Rodale's illustrated encyclopedia of perennials
    635.9
Phillips, Ellen Haygood, 1947-
  Shocked, appalled, and dismayed!   651.7
Phillips, Kevin P.
  Arrogant capital   973.92
  Wealth and democracy   305.5
Phillips, Robert H., 1948-
  (jt. auth) Lahita, R. G. Lupus   616.7
Phillips, Roger, 1932-
  Annuals and biennials   635.9
Phillips, Ruth B.
  (jt. auth) Berlo, J. C. Native North American art
    709.01
Phillips, Wendell, 1811-1884
  See/See also pages in the following book(s):
  Hofstadter, R. The American political tradition, and the
    men who made it p135-61   973
Philoctetes. Sophocles
  In Sophocles. The complete plays of Sophocles
    p181-218   882
Philology *See* Language and languages; Linguistics
Philosophers
  Durant, W. J. The story of philosophy   109
  Jaspers, K. The great philosophers   109
  Russell, B. A history of Western philosophy   109
Philosophers' stone *See* Alchemy
The philosophical writings of Descartes. Descartes, R.
    194
Philosophy
    See also Christian philosophy
  Arendt, H. The life of the mind   153
  Blackburn, S. Think: a compelling introduction to philosophy   100
  A Companion to world philosophies   109
  The Examined life   190
  Great thinkers of the Western world   190
  Kant, I. Basic writings of Kant   193
  Magee, B. The story of philosophy   190
  Masterpieces of world philosophy   100
  Ortega y Gasset, J. What is philosophy?   196
  Russell, B. The problems of philosophy   100
  Sagan, C. Broca's brain   500
  Wilson, E. O. Consilience   121
      Dictionaries
  Blackburn, S. The Oxford dictionary of philosophy
    103
  The Cambridge dictionary of philosophy   103
  The Oxford companion to philosophy   103
  Rohmann, C. A world of ideas   103
      Encyclopedias
  Concise Routledge encyclopedia of philosophy
    103
  The Encyclopedia of philosophy   103
  Encyclopedia of the Enlightenment   940.2
  Wilson, E. J. Encyclopedia of the Enlightenment
    940.2
      History
  The Columbia history of Western philosophy   190
  Durant, W. J. The story of philosophy   109

Philosophy—History—*Continued*
Gottlieb, A. The dream of reason   **180**
Jaspers, K. The great philosophers   **109**
The Oxford history of Western philosophy   **190**
Russell, B. A history of Western philosophy   **109**
Solomon, R. C. A passion for wisdom   **109**
Philosophy, American *See* American philosophy
Philosophy, Ancient *See* Ancient philosophy
Philosophy, British *See* British philosophy
Philosophy, Chinese *See* Chinese philosophy
Philosophy, French *See* French philosophy
Philosophy, Medieval *See* Medieval philosophy
Philosophy, Modern *See* Modern philosophy
Philosophy, Moral *See* Ethics
Philosophy, Oriental *See* Oriental philosophy
Philosophy and religion
Huxley, A. The perennial philosophy   **210**
See/See also pages in the following book(s):
Fromm, E. To have or to be? p48-65   **302**
The **philosophy** of Hegel. Hegel, G. W. F.   **193**
The **philosophy** of John Dewey. Dewey, J.   **191**
Philosophy of nature
Abram, D. The spell of the sensuous   **128**
Wilson, E. O. In search of nature   **113**
Philosophy of religion *See* Religion—Philosophy
Philpott, Tom
Glory denied   **92**
Phobias
Doctor, R. M. The encyclopedia of phobias, fears, and anxieties   **616.85**
Phonetics
Study and teaching
Flesch, R. F. Why Johnny can't read—and what you can do about it   **372.4**
Phonograph records *See* Sound recordings
Phormio. Terence
In The Portable Roman reader p75-131   **870.8**
In Terence. Terence, the comedies   **872**
Photo-Secession (Group)
Homer, W. I. Stieglitz and the Photo-Secession, 1902   **779**
Photographers
See also African American photographers; Women photographers
Dictionaries
Photographers and filmmakers   **920.003**
Photographers and filmmakers   **920.003**
Photographic guide to minerals of the world. See Johnsen, O. Minerals of the world   **549**
Photographs then and now   **779**
Photography
See also Cinematography; Commercial photography; Outdoor photography; Photojournalism; War photography
Garrett, J. John Garrett's black-and-white photography masterclass   **771**
Mizdal, R. Black & white photography for 35mm   **770**
Digital techniques
Ang, T. Advanced digital photography   **775**
Ang, T. Digital photographer's handbook   **775**
Ang, T. Silver pixels   **778.3**
Johnson, D. How to do everything with your digital camera   **778.3**
May, A. Multimedia: digital photography   **778.3**
Encyclopedias
McDarrah, G. S. The photography encyclopedia   **770.2**
Exhibitions
Bustard, B. I. Picturing the century   **779**
Handbooks, manuals, etc.
Grimm, T. The basic book of photography   **770.2**
History
Goldberg, V. American photography   **770**

Marien, M. W. Photography: a cultural history   **770.9**
Photography past forward: Aperture at 50   **770.9**
Solnit, R. River of shadows   **778.5**
Willis, D. Reflections in Black   **770**
Portraits
See Portrait photography
Processing
Ang, T. Advanced digital photography   **775**
Photography, Artistic *See* Artistic photography
Photography, Commercial *See* Commercial photography
Photography, Documentary *See* Documentary photography
Photography, Journalistic *See* Photojournalism
Photography: a cultural history. Marien, M. W.   **770.9**
The **photography** encyclopedia. McDarrah, G. S.   **770.2**
Photography past forward: Aperture at 50   **770.9**
Photojournalism
Bustard, B. I. Picturing the century   **779**
Howe, P. Shooting under fire   **070.4**
Life: century of change   **779**
National Geographic photographs   **779**
Photographs then and now   **779**
Photos that changed the world   **779**
Sontag, S. Regarding the pain of others   **303.6**
Photos that changed the world   **779**
Physica. Aristotle
In Aristotle. The basic works of Aristotle p213-394   **888**
Physical anthropology
See also Human origins
Olson, S. Mapping human history   **599.9**
Schwartz, J. H. What the bones tell us   **599.93**
Physical appearance *See* Personal appearance
Physical education
See also T'ai chi ch'iian
Medical aspects
See Sports medicine
Physical fitness
Active living every day   **613.7**
Bailey, C. Smart exercise   **613.7**
Callahan, L. The fitness factor   **613.7**
Fitness and exercise sourcebook   **613.7**
Fitness over fifty   **613**
Katz, J. Swimming for total fitness   **797.2**
Spilner, M. Prevention's complete book of walking   **613.7**
Physical sciences
Encyclopedias
Encyclopedia of earth and physical sciences   **500.2**
Physically handicapped
See also Blind; Deaf
Reeve, C. Still me   **92**
Schlachter, G. A. Financial aid for the disabled and their families   **378.3**
Physicians
Lown, B. The lost art of healing   **610**
Directories
America's top doctors   **610.69**
Directory of physicians in the United States   **610.69**
The Official ABMS directory of board certified medical specialists   **610.69**
Physician's desk reference   **615**
Physicians desk reference for nonprescription drugs   **615**
Physicists
Brennan, R. P. Heisenberg probably slept here   **920**
Physics
See also Astrophysics; Nuclear physics; Relativity (Physics)

Physics—*Continued*
Barr, S. M. Modern physics and ancient faith
    291.1
Bloomfield, L. How things work   530
The Book of the cosmos   523.1
Chown, M. The universe next door   523.1
Cole, K. C. First you build a cloud   530
Cole, K. C. The hole in the universe   530
Davies, P. C. W. God and the new physics   261.5
Davies, P. C. W. The matter myth   530
Feynman, R. P. Six easy pieces   530
Guillen, M. Five equations that changed the world
    530.1
Krauss, L. M. Fear of physics   530
Lindley, D. The end of physics   539.7
Magueijo, J. Faster than the speed of light   535
On the shoulders of giants   520
Peat, F. D. From certainty to uncertainty   530
Siegfried, T. Strange matters   523.1
Suplee, C. Physics in the 20th century   530
Teller, E. Conversations on the dark secrets of physics
    530
Thorne, K. S. Black holes and time warps   530.1
      Encyclopedias
Macmillan encyclopedia of physics   530
      History
Einstein, A. The evolution of physics   530
Kragh, H. Quantum generations   530
      Philosophy
Deutsch, D. The fabric of reality   530
      Tables
CRC handbook of chemistry and physics   540
Physics in the 20th century. Suplee, C.   530
Physiological chemistry *See* Biochemistry
Physiology
    See also Immune system; Psychophysiology
Anatomica's body atlas   611
Angier, N. Woman   612.6
The Human body   612
      Encyclopedias
World of anatomy and physiology   612
Physiology, Comparative *See* Comparative physiology
Pi
Blatner, D. The joy of π 516.2
Piaget, Jean, 1896-1980
The moral judgment of the child   155.4
Pianists
Rosen, C. Piano notes   786.2
Schonberg, H. C. The great pianists   920
    See/See also pages in the following book(s):
Siepmann, J. The piano   786.2
The **piano** lesson. Wilson, A.   812
Piano music
Rosen, C. Piano notes   786.2
Piano notes. Rosen, C.   786.2
Pianos
Siepmann, J. The piano   786.2
Piburn, Sidney
(comp) The Dalai Lama. See The Dalai Lama
    294.3
Picasso, Pablo, 1881-1973
      About
Cowling, E. Picasso: style and meaning   759.4
Flam, J. D. Matisse and Picasso   759.4
Krauss, R. E. The Picasso papers   759.4
Léal, B. The ultimate Picasso   92
Matisse, Picasso   759.4
Olivier, F. Loving Picasso: the private journal of
    Fernande Olivier   92
Penrose, Sir R. Picasso: his life and work   92
Staller, N. A sum of destructions   759.4
    See/See also pages in the following book(s):
Gardner, H. Creating minds p137-85   153.3
The **Picasso** papers. Krauss, R. E.   759.4

Picciotto, Richard
Last man down   974.7
Pick, Hella
Simon Wiesenthal   92
Pickart, Margaret Maliszewski- *See* Maliszewski-
    Pickart, Margaret, 1963-
Pickering, David, 1958-
Cassell dictionary of proverbs   398.9
A dictionary of folklore   398.2
Pickford, Mary, 1893-1979
      About
Brownlow, K. Mary Pickford rediscovered   791.43
Whitfield, E. Pickford   92
Pickled, potted, and canned. Shephard, S.   641.4
Picnic. Inge, W.
    In Inge, W. 4 plays p71-148   812
Picture books for children
Marcus, L. S. Ways of telling   741.6
Shulevitz, U. Writing with pictures   808.06
Picture dictionaries
Corbeil, J.-C. The Firefly visual dictionary   423
The Oxford-Duden pictorial English-Japanese dictio-
    nary   495.6
Ultimate visual dictionary   423
Picture frames and framing
Logan, M. D. Mat, mount and frame it yourself
    749
Picture writing
    See also Hieroglyphics
Liungman, C. G. Dictionary of symbols   302.2
Picturing the century. Bustard, B. I.   779
The **pie** and pastry bible. Beranbaum, R. L.   641.8
Piecework. Hamill, P.   814
Piel, Gerard, 1915-
The age of science   509
Pielou, E. C., 1924-
Fresh water   553.7
Pierpont, Claudia Roth
Passionate minds   810.9
Pierre, Peggy Claude- *See* Claude-Pierre, Peggy
Piers Plowman. Langland, W.   821
Pietrusza, David, 1949-
(jt. auth) Williams, T. Ted Williams   92
Pigments
Mayer, R. The artist's handbook of materials and tech-
    niques   751.2
Pigs
Rath, S. The complete pig   636.4
Pilate, Pontius, 1st cent.
      About
Wroe, A. Pontius Pilate   226
Pilate: the biography of an invented man. See Wroe, A.
    Pontius Pilate   226
Pilbeam, David R.
(ed) The Cambridge encyclopedia of human evolution.
    See The Cambridge encyclopedia of human evolu-
    tion   599.93
Pilgrimage: from the Ganges to Graceland: an encyclo-
    pedia. Davidson, L. K.   291.3
Pilgrims (New England colonists)
Bradford, W. Of Plymouth Plantation, 1620-1647
    974.4
Pilgrims and pilgrimages
Davidson, L. K. Pilgrimage: from the Ganges to
    Graceland: an encyclopedia   291.3
Milton, G. The riddle and the knight   910.4
Wolfe, M. One thousand roads to Mecca   297
Pilgrims in their own land. Marty, M. E.   277.3
Pill, Birth control *See* Oral contraceptives
Pillar, Paul R., 1947-
Terrorism and U.S. foreign policy   327.73
Pillar of fire. Branch, T.   973.922
The **Pillars** of Hercules. Theroux, P.   910.4

Pillars of society. Ibsen, H.
  In Ibsen, H. The complete major prose plays p9-118
                839.8
  In Ibsen, H. Ibsen: four plays, v2   **839.8**
Pillsbury best cookies cookbook   **641.8**
Pilots, Airplane *See* Air pilots
Pilots and pilotage *See* Navigation
Pimlott, Ben, 1945-
  The Queen: a biography of Elizabeth II   **92**
Pinchot, Gifford, 1865-1946
           About
  Miller, C. Gifford Pinchot and the making of modern
    environmentalism   **92**
Pinchuk, Arie
           About
  Blum, H. The brigade   **940.54**
Pindar
  The odes of Pindar   **884**
  See/See also pages in the following book(s):
  Hamilton, E. The Greek way p85-103   **880.9**
Pine Ridge Indian Reservation (S.D.)
  Frazier, I. On the rez   **970.004**
Pinker, Steven, 1954-
  The blank slate   **155.2**
  How the mind works   **153**
  The language instinct   **400**
  Words and rules   **401**
Pinkerton, Allan, 1819-1884
           About
  Mackay, J. A. Allan Pinkerton   **92**
Pinkerton's National Detective Agency
  Mackay, J. A. Allan Pinkerton   **92**
Pinkney, Jerry, 1939-
  See/See also pages in the following book(s):
  Marcus, L. S. Ways of telling   **741.6**
Pinney, Chris C.
  The complete home veterinary guide   **636.089**
Pinsky, Robert
  The figured wheel   **811**
  Jersey rain   **811**
  The sounds of poetry   **808.5**
  (ed) Americans' favorite poems. See Americans' favor-
    ite poems   **808.81**
  (ed) Poems to read. See Poems to read **808.81**
Pinter, Harold, 1930-
  Applicant
    In Pinter, H. Complete works v3   **822**
  The basement
    In Pinter, H. Complete works v3   **822**
  Betrayal   **822**
    also in Pinter, H. Complete works v4 **822**
  The birthday party
    In Nine plays of the modern theater p395-470
                808.82
    In Pinter, H. Complete works v1   **822**
  The black and white [revue sketch]
    In Pinter, H. Complete works v2   **822**
  The caretaker
    In Pinter, H. Complete works v2   **822**
  The collection
    In Pinter, H. Complete works v2   **822**
  Complete works   **822**
  Dialogue for three
    In Pinter, H. Complete works v3   **822**
  The dumb waiter
    In Pinter, H. Complete works v1   **822**
  The dwarfs
    In Pinter, H. Complete works v2   **822**
  Family voices
    In Pinter, H. Complete works v4   **822**
  The homecoming   **822**
    also in Pinter, H. Complete works v3 **822**
  Interview
    In Pinter, H. Complete works v3   **822**

  Landscape
    In Pinter, H. Complete works v3   **822**
  Last to go
    In Pinter, H. Complete works v2   **822**
  The lover
    In Pinter, H. Complete works v2   **822**
  Monologue
    In Pinter, H. Complete works v4   **822**
  Night
    In Pinter, H. Complete works v3   **822**
  A night out
    In Pinter, H. Complete works v1   **822**
  Night school
    In Pinter, H. Complete works v2   **822**
  No man's land
    In Pinter, H. Complete works v4   **822**
  Old times
    In Pinter, H. Complete works v4   **822**
  Request stop
    In Pinter, H. Complete works v2   **822**
  The room
    In Pinter, H. Complete works v1   **822**
  Silence
    In Pinter, H. Complete works v3   **822**
  A slight ache
    In Pinter, H. Complete works v1   **822**
  Special offer
    In Pinter, H. Complete works v2   **822**
  Tea party
    In Pinter, H. Complete works v3   **822**
  That's all
    In Pinter, H. Complete works v3   **822**
  That's your trouble
    In Pinter, H. Complete works v3   **822**
  Trouble in the works
    In Pinter, H. Complete works v2   **822**
  See/See also pages in the following book(s):
  Playwrights at work   **812.009**
Pioneer life *See* Frontier and pioneer life
Pioneer women. Stratton, J. L.   **978.1**
Piot, Christine
  (jt. auth) Léal, B. The ultimate Picasso   **92**
Pious, Richard M., 1944-
  (ed) The Oxford guide to the United States Govern-
    ment. See The Oxford guide to the United States
    Government   **320.03**
Piozzi, Hester Lynch, 1741-1821
  See/See also pages in the following book(s):
  Prose, F. The lives of the muses   **920**
Pipe dreams. Bryce, R.   **333.79**
Pipes, Daniel, 1949-
  Militant Islam reaches America   **320.5**
Pipes, Richard
  Communism: a history   **335.4**
  A concise history of the Russian Revolution
                947.08
  Property and freedom   **323.4**
  Russia under the Bolshevik regime **947.084**
  The Russian Revolution   **947.08**
Pipher, Mary Bray
  Another country   **306.8**
  The middle of everywhere   **325.73**
Pirandello, Luigi, 1867-1936
  Each in his own way
    In Pirandello, L. Naked masks p277-361 **852**
  Henry IV
    In Pirandello, L. Naked masks p139-208 **852**
  It is so! (If you think so)
    In Pirandello, L. Naked masks p61-138 **852**
  Liolà
    In Pirandello, L. Naked masks p1-60 **852**
  Naked masks   **852**
  Six characters in search of an author
    In Our dramatic heritage v6   **808.82**
    In Pirandello, L. Naked masks p211-76 **852**

Pirates
  Clifford, B. The lost fleet   910.4
  Cordingly, D. Under the black flag   910.4
  Konstam, A. The history of pirates   910.4
Pirozzolo, Francis J.
  (jt. auth) Snead, S. The game I love   796.352
Pirsig, Robert M., 1928-
  Zen and the art of motorcycle maintenance   92
Piston, Walter, 1894-1976
  Harmony   781.2
Pitman, Walter C.
  (jt. auth) Ryan, W. B. F. Noah's flood   930
Pittaway, Brendan
  (jt. auth) Harclerode, P. The lost masters 709
The **pity** of it all. Elon, A.   943
Pius XII, Pope, 1876-1958
                  About
  Cornwell, J. Hitler's pope: the secret history of Pius
    XII   92
  Goldhagen, D. A moral reckoning   940.53
  Zuccotti, S. Under his very windows   940.53
Pivin, Jean Loup
  (ed) An Anthology of African art: the twentieth
    century. See An Anthology of African art: the twen-
    tieth century   709.6
Pizarro, Francisco, ca. 1475-1541
  See/See also pages in the following book(s):
  Connell, E. S. The Aztec treasure house p393-411
                                             814
  Prescott, W. H. History of the conquest of Peru
                                             985
Pizza
  Puck, W. Wolfgang Puck's pizza, pasta and more!
                                             641.8
Pizzorno, Joseph E.
  (jt. auth) Murray, M. T. Encyclopedia of natural medi-
    cine   615.5
Place names See Geographic names
Places, Imaginary See Geographical myths
Places rated almanac. Savageau, D.   307.7
Places rated retirement guide. See Savageau, D. Retire-
    ment places rated   307.7
Plagiarism
  McKillop, A. B. The spinster & the prophet
                                             941.08
Plague
  Cantor, N. F. In the wake of the plague   614.5
  Herlihy, D. The black death and the transformation of
    the west   940.1
  Marriott, E. Plague: a story of science, rivalry, and the
    scourge that won't go away   614.5
  See/See also pages in the following book(s):
  Frist, W. H. When every moment counts   613.6
  Tuchman, B. W. A distant mirror p92-125   944
A **plague** of frogs. Souder, W.   597.8
A **plague** of rats and rubbervines. Baskin, Y. 577
The **plague** race. See Marriott, E. Plague: a story of sci-
    ence, rivalry, and the scourge that won't go away
                                             614.5
Plagues: their origins, history, and future. See Wills, C.
    Yellow fever, black goddess   614.4
Plait, Philip C.
  Bad astronomy   520
Plaited glory. Bonner, L. B.   646.7
Plan your estate. Clifford, D.   346.05
Planck, Max, 1858-1947
  See/See also pages in the following book(s):
  Brennan, R. P. Heisenberg probably slept here
                                             920
The **planet** Mars. Sheehan, W.   523.4
Planet quest. Croswell, K.   523
Planets
    See also names of planets
  Bakich, M. E. The Cambridge planetary handbook
                                             523.4

  Croswell, K. Planet quest   523
  Ridpath, I. Stars and planets   520
Planets and possibilities. Miller, S.   133.5
Planned parenthood See Birth control
Planning, National See Economic policy
Planning, Regional See Regional planning
Plant chemistry See Botanical chemistry
Plant names, Popular See Popular plant names
Plantation life
  Ball, E. Slaves in the family   975.7
  Fox-Genovese, E. Within the plantation household
                                             305.4
Plants
    See also Climbing plants; Desert plants; Ferns;
    Flowers; Forage plants; Forest plants; House plants
           Collection and preservation
    See also Flowers—Drying
                  Fertilization
    See Fertilization of plants
                Soilless culture
    See Hydroponics
                  Training
  Pruning & training   635.9
Plants, Edible See Edible plants
Plants, Hallucinogenic See Hallucinogens
Plants, Industrial See Factories
Plants, Ornamental See Ornamental plants
Plants, Poisonous See Poisonous plants
Plants for dry climates. Duffield, M. R. 635.9
Plas, Rob van der, 1938-
  Bicycle repair step by step   629.28
Plastic surgery
  Copeland, M. Change your looks, change your life
                                             617.9
  Gilman, S. L. Making the body beautiful   617.9
  Reconstructive and cosmetic surgery sourcebook
                                             617.9
Plate
  Wyler, S. B. The book of old silver: English,
    American, foreign   739.2
Plater-Zyberk, Elizabeth, 1950-
  (jt. auth) Duany, A. Suburban nation   307.7
Plath, Sylvia
  The collected poems   811
  The unabridged journals of Sylvia Plath, 1950-1962
                                             92
                  About
  Wagner-Martin, L. Sylvia Plath   92
  See/See also pages in the following book(s):
  American women fiction writers   813.009
  Gilbert, S. M. No man's land v3 p266-318   820.9
  Heaney, S. Finders keepers p238-52   821
  Vendler, H. H. Coming of age as a poet   820.9
Plato
  Apology
    In Plato. The dialogues of Plato p4-40 888
  Complete works   184
  Crito
    In Plato. The dialogues of Plato p44-62 888
  The dialogues of Plato   888
  Phaedo
    In Plato. The dialogues of Plato p66-160 888
    In Plato. The portable Plato p191-278   888
  The portable Plato   888
  Protagoras
    In Plato. The portable Plato p45-117   888
  The republic   888
    also in Plato. The portable Plato p281-696 888
  Republic [abridgement]
    In Plato. The dialogues of Plato p238-386 888
  The Republic; criticism
    In Mumford, L. The story of utopias p29-51
                                             321
  Symposium
    In Plato. The dialogues of Plato p164-234 888

Plato—The Republic; criticism—*Continued*
  In Plato. The portable Plato p121-87   **888**
             About
  Hare, R. M. Plato   **184**
  See/See also pages in the following book(s):
  Durant, W. J. The story of philosophy p5-40   **109**
  Emerson, R. W. The portable Emerson p295-324
        818
  Hamilton, E. The echo of Greece p79-93   **880.9**
  Jaspers, K. The great philosophers   **109**
  Russell, B. A history of Western philosophy p104-59
        109
Plautus, Titus Maccius
  Amphitryon
  In The Portable Roman reader p22-74   **870.8**
Play
  Cohen, L. J. Playful parenting   **649**
        Psychological aspects
  Ackerman, D. Deep play   **155.6**
Play directing. Hodge, F.   **792**
Play direction (Theater) *See* Theater—Production and direction
The **play** goes on. Simon, N.   **92**
Play index   **808.82**
Play production *See* Theater—Production and direction
Play writing *See* Drama—Technique; Motion picture plays—Technique
The **playboy** of the Western world. Synge, J. M.
  In Synge, J. M. The complete plays   **822**
Player, Gary
  The complete golfer's handbook   **796.352**
Playful parenting. Cohen, L. J.   **649**
Playgrounds
  See also Parks
Playing for keeps: Michael Jordan and the world he made. Halberstam, D.   **92**
Playing off the rail. McCumber, D.   **794.7**
Plays *See* Drama—Collections; One act plays
Plays and essays. Dürrenmatt, F.   **838**
Plays by American women, 1900-1930   **812.008**
The **plays** of Anton Chekhov. Chekhov, A. P.
      891.7
Playwrights *See* Dramatists
Playwrights at work   **812.009**
The **pleasure** of finding things out. Feynman, R. P.
    500
The **pleasures** of Japanese literature. Keene, D.
    895.6
The **pleasures** of the imagination. Brewer, J.
    941.07
Pleshakov, Konstantin
  The Tsar's last armada   **952.03**
Plimpton, George
  The best of Plimpton   **818**
  Truman Capote   **92**
  (ed) Playwrights at work. See Playwrights at work
      812.009
  (ed) Women writers at work. See Women writers at work   **808**
Plomp, Michiel
  (jt. auth) Liedtke, W. A. Vermeer and the Delft school
    759.9492
The **plot** thickens. Lukeman, N.   **808.3**
Plotinus
  See/See also pages in the following book(s):
  Jaspers, K. The great philosophers   **109**
  Russell, B. A history of Western philosophy p284-97
      109
Plotkin, Fred
  Classical music 101   **781.6**
  Opera 101   **792.5**
Plotkin, Mark
  Medicine quest   **615**
Plotnick, Charles
  How to settle an estate   **346.05**

Plotting Hitler's death. Fest, J. C.   **943.086**
Plowman, Timothy Charles, 1944-1989
          About
  Davis, W. One river   **581.6**
Plumes. Johnson, G. D. C.
  In Plays by American women, 1900-1930
      812.008
Pluralism (Social sciences) *See* Multiculturalism
Plutarch, ca. 46-ca. 120
  Plutarch: the lives of the noble Grecians and Romans
      920
Plutarch, of Athens, ca. 350-430
  See/See also pages in the following book(s):
  Hamilton, E. The echo of Greece p179-209   **880.9**
Plutarch: the lives of the noble Grecians and Romans. Plutarch   **920**
Plutus. Aristophanes
  In Aristophanes. The complete plays of Aristophanes p463-501   **882**
Podell, Janet
  (jt. auth) Anzovin, S. Famous first facts about American politics   **973**
  (ed) Facts about the states. See Facts about the states   **973**
  (ed) Famous first facts, international edition. See Famous first facts, international edition   **031.02**
  (jt. auth) Kane, J. N. Famous first facts   **031.02**
Podhoretz, Norman
  My love affair with America   **320.5**
Poe, Edgar Allan, 1809-1849
  The collected tales and poems of Edgar Allan Poe
      818
  Complete poems   **811**
  Essays and reviews   **818**
  Poems and poetics   **811**
  Poetry and tales   **818**
          About
  Silverman, K. Edgar A. Poe   **92**
  Sova, D. B. Edgar Allan Poe, A-Z   **818**
  The Tales of Poe   **813.009**
  Walsh, J. E. Midnight dreary: the mysterious death of Edgar Allan Poe   **92**
  See/See also pages in the following book(s):
  Williams, W. C. In the American grain p216-33
      814
The **poem** of the Cid. Cid   **861**
Poems. Baudelaire, C.   **841**
Poems. Keats, J.   **821**
Poems. Shakespeare, W.   **821**
Poems, 1960-1967. Levertov, D.   **811**
Poems, 1968-1972. Levertov, D.   **811**
Poems, 1968-1998. Muldoon, P.   **821**
Poems and other writings. Longfellow, H. W.   **811**
Poems and poetics. Poe, E. A.   **811**
Poems for the millennium   **808.81**
Poems, new and collected, 1957-1997. Szymborska, W.   **891.8**
The **poems** of François Villon. Villon, F.   **841**
The **poems** of Gerard Manley Hopkins. Hopkins, G. M.
      821
The **poems** of Herman Melville. Melville, H.   **811**
The **poems** of J.V. Cunningham. Cunningham, J. V.
      811
Poems of Jerusalem; and, Love poems. Amichai, Y.
      892
Poems of Paul Celan. Celan, P.   **831**
The **poems** of Phillis Wheatley. Wheatley, P.   **811**
Poems seven. Dugan, A.   **811**
Poems that live forever   **821.008**
Poems to read   **808.81**
The **poet** and the murderer. Worrall, S.   **364.1**
Poetics
  Addonizio, K. The poet's companion   **808.1**
  Aristotle. Poetics   **808.1**
  Hirsch, E. How to read a poem   **808.1**

Poetics—*Continued*
Kumin, M. Always beginning   92
Oliver, M. A poetry handbook   808.1
     Dictionaries
Deutsch, B. Poetry handbook: a dictionary of terms
     808.1
Myers, J. E. Dictionary of poetic terms   808.1
The New Princeton encyclopedia of poetry and poetics
     809.1

Poetics. Aristotle
    also in Aristotle. The basic works of Aristotle
    p1455-87   888
    also in Aristotle. Introduction to Aristotle p668-713
     888

Poetry
    See also African poetry; American poetry; Arabic
    poetry; Chinese poetry; Christmas—Poetry; Classical
    poetry; English poetry; Hebrew poetry; Irish poetry;
    Japanese poetry; Latin American poetry; Mexican
    poetry; Persian poetry; Turkish poetry; types of poet-
    ry; subjects with the subdivision *Poetry*
Kumin, M. Always beginning   92
Pinsky, R. The sounds of poetry   808.5
    See/See also pages in the following book(s):
Rich, A. Arts of the possible   818
     Bio-bibliography
World poets   920.003
     Collections
Americans' favorite poems   808.81
A Book of luminous things   808.81
City lights pocket poets anthology   808.81
The Gift of tongues   811.008
Holocaust poetry   808.81
Into the garden   808.8
Koch, K. Making your own days   809.1
The Oxford book of war poetry   808.81
The Penguin book of women poets   808.81
Poems for the millennium   808.81
Poems to read   808.81
The Poetry of our world   808.81
The Vintage book of contemporary world poetry
     808.81
World poetry   808.81
     Dictionaries
The New Princeton encyclopedia of poetry and poetics
     809.1
     History and criticism
Borges, J. L. This craft of verse   809.1
Gioia, D. Can poetry matter?   809.1
Heaney, S. Finders keepers   821
Hirsch, E. How to read a poem   808.1
Kermode, F. An appetite for poetry   801
Koch, K. Making your own days   809.1
Masterplots II, poetry series   809.1
The New Princeton encyclopedia of poetry and poetics
     809.1
Simon, J. I. Dreamers of dreams   809.1
     Indexes
The Columbia Granger's index to poetry in anthologies
     808.81
The Columbia Granger's Index to poetry in collected
    and selected works   808.81
Index to children's poetry   808.81
Index to poetry for children and young people
     808.81
     Marketing
Oliver, M. A poetry handbook   808.1
     Terminology
Deutsch, B. Poetry handbook: a dictionary of terms
     808.1

Poetry and prose of William Blake. See Blake, W. The
    complete poetry and prose of William Blake
     828
The **poetry** and short stories of Dorothy Parker. Parker,
    D.   818

Poetry and tales. Poe, E. A.   818
The **Poetry** anthology, 1912-2002   811.008
A **poetry** handbook. Oliver, M.   808.1
Poetry handbook: a dictionary of terms. Deutsch, B.
     808.1
The **Poetry** of black America   811.008
The **poetry** of Chaucer. Gardner, J.   821
The **Poetry** of our world   808.81
Poetry speaks   808.81
Poets
    See also Women poets
     Dictionaries
World poets   920.003
Poets, American
     Biography
Schmidt, M. Lives of the poets   821.009
     Dictionaries
Contemporary poets   920.003
Encyclopedia of American poetry, the nineteenth
    century   811.009
Encyclopedia of American poetry, the twentieth
    century   811.009
Poets, English
     Biography
Schmidt, M. Lives of the poets   821.009
     Dictionaries
Contemporary poets   920.003
The **poet's** companion. Addonizio, K.   808.1
Poet's market   808.1
Poets of World War II   811
Pogue, David
Classical music for dummies   781.6
Opera for dummies   792.5
Pohl, Frederik, 1919-
Chasing science   500
Poinar, George O.
The quest for life in amber   560
Poinar, Roberta
(jt. auth) Poinar, G. O. The quest for life in amber
     560
Poincaré, Henri, 1854-1912
     About
Galison, P. L. Einstein's clocks and Poincaré's maps
     529
    See/See also pages in the following book(s):
Bell, E. T. Men of mathematics p526-54   920
Points unknown   910
Poirier, Laurinda M., 1960-
Women & diabetes   616.4
Poisonous animals
    See also Rattlesnakes
Poisonous plants
Turner, N. J. Common poisonous plants and mush-
    rooms of North America   581.6
Poisons and antidotes. See Turkington, C. The poisons
    and antidotes sourcebook   615.9
The **poisons** and antidotes sourcebook. Turkington, C.
     615.9
Poisons and poisoning
Barker, R. And the waters turned to blood   615.9
Callahan, J. R. Biological hazards   615.9
Turkington, C. The poisons and antidotes sourcebook
     615.9
Poisson, Jeanne Antoinette *See* Pompadour, Jeanne An-
    toinette Poisson, marquise de, 1721-1764
Poitier, Sidney
The measure of a man   92
Poker
McManus, J. Positively Fifth Street   795.4
Poker nation. Bellin, A.   795.4
The **Pol** Pot regime. Kiernan, B.   959.6
Poland
     Politics and government
Wałęsa, L. The struggle and the triumph   92

Polar bear
Mangelsen, T. D. Polar dance   **599.78**
Polar dance. Mangelsen, T. D.   **599.78**
Polar expeditions *See* Antarctica—Exploration; Arctic regions—Exploration
Polar regions
See also Antarctica; Arctic regions; North Pole; South Pole
Police
    Complaints against
See Police brutality; Police corruption
    Corrupt practices
See Police corruption
    New York (N.Y.)
See/See also pages in the following book(s):
Alvarez, A. Night p227-51   **154.6**
Police brutality
Hendrickson, P. Sons of Mississippi   **305.8**
See/See also pages in the following book(s):
Conroy, J. Unspeakable acts, ordinary people
     323.4
Police corruption
Sullivan, R. Labyrinth   **364.1**
Polin, Bonnie Sanders, 1941-
The Joslin Diabetes gourmet cookbook   **641.5**
(jt. auth) Giedt, F. T. The Joslin Diabetes great chefs cook healthy cookbook   **641.5**
The **polio** paradox. Bruno, R. L.   **616.8**
Poliomyelitis
Bruno, R. L. The polio paradox   **616.8**
See/See also pages in the following book(s):
Oldstone, M. B. A. Viruses, plagues, and history
     614.4
Polish literature
    History and criticism
Miłosz, C. The history of Polish literature   **891.8**
Polish poetry
    History and criticism
See/See also pages in the following book(s):
Miłosz, C. To begin where I am p337-51   **891.8**
Political campaigns *See* Politics
Political conventions
National party conventions, 1831-2000   **324.5**
Political corruption
Denton, S. The money and the power   **979.3**
Drew, E. The corruption of American politics
     364.1
Phillips, K. P. Arrogant capital   **973.92**
Phillips, K. P. Wealth and democracy   **305.5**
Reisner, M. P. Cadillac desert   **333.91**
Robb, P. Midnight in Sicily   **945**
Political crimes and offenses
See also Political corruption
The **political** encyclopedia of the Middle East. See The Continuum political encyclopedia of the Middle East
     956
Political ethics
Kaplan, R. D. Warrior politics   **320**
Machiavelli, N. The prince   **320**
Morgan, P. W. The appearance of impropriety
     306
Political extremism *See* Radicalism
Political handbook of the world   **324.025**
Political parties
National party conventions, 1831-2000   **324.5**
Political handbook of the world   **324.025**
    Finance
See Campaign funds
Political prisoners
Solzhenitsyn, A. The Gulag Archipelago, 1918-1956
     365
Wei Jingsheng. The courage to stand alone
     951.05
Wu, H. Bitter winds   **951.05**
Wu, H. Troublemaker   **951.05**

Political science
See also Right and left (Political science)
Aristotle. Politics   **320**
Cohen, I. B. Science and the founding fathers
     973.3
The Europa world year book   **310.5**
Hobbes, T. Leviathan   **320.1**
Locke, J. Two treatises of government   **320.1**
Machiavelli, N. The prince   **320**
Paine, T. The rights of man   **320**
Plato. The republic   **888**
Rousseau, J.-J. The social contract   **320.1**
The Statesman's year-book   **310.5**
    Handbooks, manuals, etc.
Political handbook of the world   **324.025**
    Quotations
The Oxford dictionary of political quotations
     808.88
Politicians
    United States
Galbraith, J. K. Name-dropping   **973.9**
Kennedy, J. F. Profiles in courage   **920**
    United States—Dictionaries
American political leaders, 1789-2000   **920.003**
Who's who in American politics   **920.003**
Politics
See also Political science
Morris, D. The new prince   **324.7**
Will, G. F. Restoration   **328.73**
Politics, Practical *See* Politics
Politics. Aristotle   **320**
also in Aristotle. The basic works of Aristotle p1127-1316   **888**
Politics and business *See* Business and politics
Politics and Christianity *See* Christianity and politics
Politics and Islam *See* Islam and politics
Politics and religion *See* Religion and politics
Politics and students *See* Students—Political activity
Politics in literature
Said, E. W. Reflections on exile and other essays
     814
The **politics** of upheaval, 1935-1936. Schlesinger, A. M.
     973.917
Polkinghorne, J. C. *See* Polkinghorne, John, 1930-
Polkinghorne, John, 1930-
The God of hope and the end of the world   **236**
Pollack, Howard
Aaron Copland   **92**
Pollack, Robert, 1940-
The missing moment   **610**
Pollack, William S.
Real boys   **305.23**
Real boys' voices   **305.23**
Pollan, Michael
The botany of desire   **581.6**
Pollination *See* Fertilization of plants
Pollock, Michael, 1938-
The Royal Horticultural Society shorter dictionary of gardening   **635**
Pollution
See also Environmental protection; Industrial waste; Marine pollution; Water pollution
Commoner, B. Making peace with the planet
     304.2
Davis, D. L. When smoke ran like water   **615.9**
Davis, L. A. Environmental disasters   **363.7**
Gonzalez, J. Fallout   **363.7**
Markowitz, G. E. Deceit and denial   **615.9**
Polo, Marco, 1254-1323?
The travels of Marco Polo   **915**
Polymers
Rabinow, P. Making PCR   **572.8**
Pomerantz, Carrie Schwab- *See* Schwab-Pomerantz, Carrie
Pomes all sizes. Kerouac, J.   **811**

Pomier, Natalie
(ed) The Oxford-Hachette French dictionary. See The
Oxford-Hachette French dictionary   **443**
**Pompadour, Jeanne Antoinette Poisson, marquise de,
1721-1764**
About
Lever, E. Madame de Pompadour   **92**
Pompeii (Extinct city)
Houses and monuments of Pompeii   **709.38**
Pomponazzi, Pietro, 1462-1525
See/See also pages in the following book(s):
The Renaissance philosophy of man p57-79   **189**
Poncelet, Jean Victor, 1788-1867
See/See also pages in the following book(s):
Bell, E. T. Men of mathematics p206-17   **920**
Ponds
Matson, T. Earth ponds A to Z   **627**
Ponsot, Marie
Springing   **811**
Pontecorvo, Gillo
See/See also pages in the following book(s):
Said, E. W. Reflections on exile and other essays
p282-92   **814**
Pontius Pilate *See* Pilate, Pontius, 1st cent.
Ponty, Jean Jacques Maurice Merleau- *See* Merleau-
Ponty, Maurice, 1908-1961
Ponty, Maurice Merleau- *See* Merleau-Ponty, Maurice,
1908-1961
Ponzetti, James J.
(ed) Encyclopedia of human emotions. See Encyclope-
dia of human emotions   **152.4**
(ed) International encyclopedia of marriage and family.
See International encyclopedia of marriage and fami-
ly   **306.8**
Pool, Daniel
What Jane Austen ate and Charles Dickens knew
    820.9
Pool, James, 1948-
Hitler and his secret partners   **943.086**
Pool, Robert, 1955-
Fat   **616.3**
Pool (Game)
Byrne, R. Byrne's new standard book of pool and bil-
liards   **794.7**
McCumber, D. Playing off the rail   **794.7**
Mosconi, W. Willie Mosconi's winning pocket billiards
for beginners and advanced players, with a section
on trick shots   **794.7**
The **pool** sacrifice. Zeami
In Waley, A. The Nō plays of Japan   **895.6**
Poole, Adrian
The Oxford book of classical verse in translation. See
The Oxford book of classical verse in translation
    881.008
Poor
Mexico City (Mexico)
Lewis, O. The children of Sánchez   **972.08**
New York (N.Y.)
Hancock, L. Hands to work   **361.6**
Kozol, J. Amazing grace   **362.7**
United States
Zucchino, D. Myth of the welfare queen   **362.5**
Popcorn, Faith
Clicking   **650.1**
Pope, Alexander, 1688-1744
The rape of the lock; criticism
In Brooks, C. The well wrought urn   **821.009**
Selected poetry   **821**
Pope, Hugh
Turkey unveiled   **956.1**
Pope, Nicole
(jt. auth) Pope, H. Turkey unveiled   **956.1**
Pope, Stephen
Dictionary of the Napoleonic wars   **940.2**

Popes
See also Papacy
See/See also pages in the following book(s):
Tuchman, B. W. The march of folly   **909.08**
Biography
McBrien, R. P. Lives of the popes   **920**
Dictionaries
Kelly, J. N. D. The Oxford dictionary of popes
    920.003
The **Popes** against the Jews. Kertzer, D. I.   **261.2**
Popkin, Richard Henry, 1923-
The Columbia history of Western philosophy. See The
Columbia history of Western philosophy   **190**
Poplawski, Paul
A Jane Austen encyclopedia   **823.009**
Popol vuh
Popol vuh   **299**
Popper, Sir Karl Raimund, 1902-1994
About
Edmonds, D. Wittgenstein's poker   **192**
Popular culture
Iyer, P. The global soul   **910.4**
Lewis, J. R. UFOs and popular culture   **001.9**
Taffel, R. The second family   **306.8**
United States
George, N. Hip hop America   **781.64**
Halberstam, D. The fifties   **973.92**
Kammen, M. G. In the past lane   **973**
Marling, K. A. As seen on TV   **973.92**
Schwartz, R. A. Cold War culture   **973.92**
Slotkin, R. Gunfighter nation   **973.9**
Wynter, L. E. American skin   **305.8**
United States—Encyclopedias
St. James encyclopedia of popular culture   **973.9**
Popular music
See also Blues music; Country music; Gospel mu-
sic; Rap music; Rock music
American roots music   **781.62**
Friedwald, W. Stardust melodies   **782.42**
McWhorter, J. H. Doing our own thing   **306.44**
Veloso, C. Tropical truth   **781.64**
Dictionaries
Baker's biographical dictionary of popular musicians
since 1990   **920.003**
Discography
All music guide   **781.64**
Bronson, F. The Billboard book of number 1 hits
    781.64
Whitburn, J. The Billboard book of top 40 hits
    781.64
Encyclopedias
Hischak, T. The Tin Pan Alley song encyclopedia
    782.42
Indexes
Havlice, P. P. Popular song index   **782.42**
Writing and publishing
Krasilovsky, M. W. This business of music   **780**
Songwriter's market   **782.42**
Popular plant names
Wells, D. 100 flowers and how they got their names
    582.13
Popular song index. Havlice, P. P.   **782.42**
Population
Statistics
United Nations. Statistical Office. Demographic year-
book   **304.6**
Porcelain
Marks
Godden, G. A. Encyclopaedia of British pottery and
porcelain marks   **738**
Kovel, R. M. Kovel's dictionary of marks: pottery and
porcelain   **738**
Kovel, R. M. Kovels' new dictionary of marks
    738

Pornography
See/See also pages in the following book(s):
Sontag, S. Styles of radical will p35-73   **814**
Porpoises
Whales, dolphins, and porpoises   **599.5**
The **Portable** beat reader   **810.8**
The **portable** Chaucer. Chaucer, G.   **821**
The **portable** Chekhov. Chekhov, A. P.   **891.7**
The **portable** Coleridge. Coleridge, S. T.   **828**
The **portable** Conrad. Conrad, J.   **828**
The **portable** Dante. Dante Alighieri   **851**
The **portable** Dorothy Parker. Parker, D.   **818**
The **portable** Emerson. Emerson, R. W.   **818**
The **Portable** Harlem Renaissance reader   **810.8**
The **portable** Hawthorne. Hawthorne, N.   **818**
The **portable** Henry James. James, H.   **818**
The **portable** Jack Kerouac. Kerouac, J.   **818**
The **portable** Jung. Jung, C. G.   **150.19**
The **portable** Mark Twain. Twain, M.   **818**
The **Portable** medieval reader   **808.8**
The **portable** Nietzsche. Nietzsche, F. W.   **193**
The **Portable** North American Indian reader   **897**
The **portable** Plato. Plato   **888**
The **Portable** Renaissance reader   **808.8**
The **Portable** Roman reader   **870.8**
The **portable** Thoreau. Thoreau, H. D.   **818**
The **portable** Voltaire. Voltaire   **848**
The **Portable** Western reader   **810.8**
Porter, Cole, 1891-1964
The complete lyrics of Cole Porter   **782.42**
About
McBrien, W. Cole Porter   **92**
See/See also pages in the following book(s):
Green, S. The world of musical comedy   **920**
Porter, Gene Stratton- *See* Stratton-Porter, Gene, 1863-1924
Porter, Katherine Anne, 1890-1980
See/See also pages in the following book(s):
American women fiction writers   **813.009**
Women writers at work p32-60   **808**
Porter, Roy, 1946-2002
Blood and guts   **610.9**
The greatest benefit to mankind   **610.9**
London, a social history   **942.1**
Madness   **616.89**
(ed) The Biographical dictionary of scientists. See The Biographical dictionary of scientists   **920.003**
(ed) The Cambridge illustrated history of medicine. See The Cambridge illustrated history of medicine   **610.9**
Porterfield, Kay Marie
(jt. auth) Keoke, E. D. Encyclopedia of American Indian contributions to the world   **970.004**
Portman, Janet
Every landlord's legal guide   **346.04**
Every tenant's legal guide   **346.04**
Portrait of a burger as a young calf. Lovenheim, P.   **636.2**
Portrait of a killer. Cornwell, P. D.   **364.1**
Portrait of Dr. Gachet. Saltzman, C.   **759.9492**
A **portrait** of Jesus. Girzone, J. F.   **232.9**
Portrait of Mabel Dodge at the Villa Curonia. Stein, G.
In Stein, G. Selected writings p523-30   **818**
Portrait of my body. Lopate, P.   **814**
Portrait photography
Scavullo, F. Scavullo: photographs, 50 years   **779**
Portraits. Kimmelman, M.   **701**
Portraits of discovery. Greenstein, G.   **920**
Portugal
Vincent, M. Cultural atlas of Spain and Portugal   **946**
Description
Saramago, J. Journey to Portugal   **946.9**
Portuguese cooking
Anderson, J. The food of Portugal   **641.5**

Positively Fifth Street. McManus, J.   **795.4**
A **positively** final appearance. Guinness, A.   **92**
Posner, Gerald L.
Case closed   **973.922**
Killing the dream   **364.1**
Posner, Richard A., 1939-
Breaking the deadlock   **324**
Public intellectuals   **305.5**
A **possible** world. Koch, K.   **811**
Post, Emily, 1873-1960
Post, P. Emily Post wedding etiquette   **395**
Post, P. Emily Post's etiquette   **395**
Post, Peggy, 1945-
Emily Post wedding etiquette   **395**
Emily Post's etiquette   **395**
Post, Wiley, 1898-1935
See/See also pages in the following book(s):
Yagoda, B. Will Rogers p322-30   **92**
Post Office jobs. Damp, D. V.   **383**
Post-traumatic stress disorder
Bremner, J. D. Does stress damage the brain?   **616.85**
Matsakis, A. Vietnam wives   **616.85**
Post-war literature 1945 to the present. Merz, C.
In Backgrounds to English literature v5   **820.9**
Postal delivery code *See* Zip code
Postal service
Examinations
Barkus, P. Comprehensive postal exam   **383**
Damp, D. V. Post Office jobs   **383**
Vocational guidance
Damp, D. V. Post Office jobs   **383**
A **poster** of the cosmos. Wilson, L.
In Wilson, L. 21 short plays p242-50   **812**
Posterior analytics. Aristotle
In Aristotle. Introduction to Aristotle p8-111   **888**
Postgate, Raymond William, 1896-1971
(ed) Wells, H. G. The outline of history   **909**
Postman, Alexandra S., 1968
(jt. auth) Copeland, M. Change your looks, change your life   **617.9**
Postman, Neil
Amusing ourselves to death   **302.23**
The end of education   **370**
Technopoly   **303.4**
Postmodern American poetry   **811.008**
Postpartum depression
Dalton, K. Depression after childbirth   **616.85**
Potatoes
See also Cooking—Potatoes
See/See also pages in the following book(s):
Pollan, M. The botany of desire   **581.6**
Potemkin, Grigoriĭ Aleksandrovich, kníâz, 1739-1791
About
Montefiore, S. Prince of princes: the life of Potemkin   **92**
Potok, Chaim, 1929-2002
Wanderings   **909**
(jt. auth) Stern, I. My first 79 years   **92**
Potter, John
(ed) The Cambridge companion to singing. See The Cambridge companion to singing   **782**
The **potter's** dictionary of materials and techniques. Hamer, F.   **738.1**
Potterton, Reg
(jt. auth) Milito, L. Mafia wife   **364.1**
Pottery
See also Porcelain
Burleson, M. The ceramic glaze handbook   **738.1**
Coakes, M. Creative pottery   **738**
Kenny, J. B. The complete book of pottery making   **738.1**
Nelson, G. C. Ceramics   **738.1**

Pottery—*Continued*
Dictionaries
Hamer, F. The potter's dictionary of materials and techniques **738.1**
Marks
Godden, G. A. Encyclopaedia of British pottery and porcelain marks **738**
Kovel, R. M. Kovel's dictionary of marks: pottery and porcelain **738**
Kovel, R. M. Kovels' new dictionary of marks **738**

Pough, Frederick H. (Frederick Harvey), 1906-
A field guide to rocks and minerals **549**
Poultry
See also Cooking—Poultry
Pound, Ezra, 1885-1972
The cantos of Ezra Pound **811**
Collected early poems of Ezra Pound **811**
Selected poems **811**
About
Kenner, H. The Pound era **811**
Tytell, J. Ezra Pound **92**
See/See also pages in the following book(s):
Gass, W. H. Finding a form p160-76 **814**
Kazin, A. An American procession p321-33 **810.9**
Pritchard, W. H. Lives of the modern poets p141-70 **821.009**
Pound, Roscoe, 1870-1964
See/See also pages in the following book(s):
Commager, H. S. The American mind **973**
The **Pound** era. Kenner, H. **811**
Poverty
See also Poor
Ehrenreich, B. Nickel and dimed **305.5**
Powell, Colin L.
My American journey **92**
About
Harari, O. The leadership secrets of Colin Powell **303.3**
See/See also pages in the following book(s):
Dyson, M. E. Race rules **305.8**
Gates, H. L. Thirteen ways of looking at a black man **920**
Powell, Dawn
See/See also pages in the following book(s):
Vidal, G. United States—essays, 1952-1992 p306-34 **814**
Powell, Gloria J.
See/See also pages in the following book(s):
Halberstam, D. The children **323.1**
Powell, James Lawrence, 1936-
Night comes to the Cretaceous **576.8**
Powell, John, 1954-
(ed) Magill's guide to military history. See Magill's guide to military history **355**
(ed) Weapons & warfare. See Weapons & warfare **623.4**
Powell, John A. (John Anthony)
(jt. auth) McDonald, L. The rights of racial minorities **342**
Powell, John Wesley, 1834-1902
About
Dolnick, E. Down the great unknown **979.1**
Powell, Rodney
See/See also pages in the following book(s):
Halberstam, D. The children **323.1**
Powell, Shirley, 1948-
(ed) Prehistoric culture change on the Colorado plateau. See Prehistoric culture change on the Colorado plateau **970.004**
Power, Samantha
"A problem from hell" **304.6**

Power (Social sciences)
See also Elite (Social sciences)
Nye, J. S., Jr. The paradox of American power **327.73**
Smith, H. The power game **973.92**
Toffler, A. Powershift **303.4**
Wills, G. Certain trumpets **303.3**
Power and glory. See Nicolson, A. God's secretaries: the making of the King James Bible **220.5**
The **power** broker: Robert Moses and the fall of New York. Caro, R. A. **92**
The **power** game. Smith, H. **973.92**
The **power** of black music. Floyd, S. A. **780.89**
The **power** of gold. Bernstein, P. L. **398**
The **power** of light. Kryza, F. **333.79**
The **power** of myth. Campbell, J. **291.1**
The **power** of positive living. Peale, N. V. **248**
The **power** of positive thinking. Peale, N. V. **253.5**
Power sewing step-by-step. Betzina, S. **646.4**
Power tools
Nagyszalanczy, S. Power tools **621.9**
Warner, P. The router book **684**
Powerfoods. Beling, S. **613.2**
Powers, Bruce R.
(jt. auth) McLuhan, M. The global village **302.23**
Powers, Michael D.
(ed) Children with autism. See Children with autism **618.92**
Powers, Ron
(jt. auth) Bradley, J. Flags of our fathers **940.54**
(jt. auth) Morgan, R. The man who flew the Memphis Belle **92**
The **powers** of heaven and earth. Nims, J. F. **811**
Powershift. Toffler, A. **303.4**
POWs See Prisoners of war
Pox Americana. Fenn, E. A. **614.5**
Pox: genius, madness, and the mysteries of syphilis. Hayden, D. **616.95**
Poynter, Dan
The self-publishing manual **070.5**
Prache, Anne
Cathedrals of Europe **726**
The **Practical** guide to aging **305.26**
The **practice** of the wild. Snyder, G. **814**
Practicing history. Tuchman, B. W. **907**
Prados, John
Lost crusader: the secret wars of CIA director William Colby **92**
Presidents' secret wars **327.12**
Prager, Dennis, 1948-
Happiness is a serious problem **158**
Prager, Emily
Wuhu diary **951**
Prague (Czech Republic)
History
Demetz, P. Prague in black and gold **943.7**
Prague in black and gold. Demetz, P. **943.7**
The **prairie** years [condensation] Sandburg, C.
In Sandburg, C. Abraham Lincoln: The prairie years and The war years **92**
The **praise** of folly. Erasmus, D. **877**
Prange, Gordon William, 1910-1980
At dawn we slept **940.54**
Miracle at Midway **940.54**
Prayer
Lewis, C. S. Letters to Malcolm: chiefly on prayer **248**
Prayers
The African prayer book **242**
The Doubleday prayer collection **242**
The Oxford book of prayer **291.4**
Prebish, Charles S.
Historical dictionary of Buddhism **294.3**

Precious stones
  Sofianides, A. S. Gems & crystals from the American
    Museum of Natural History   **549**
  Webster, R. Gems   **553.8**
Precipitation (Meteorology) *See* Snow
Predatory animals
  Quammen, D. Monster of God   **591.6**
Predicting new words. Metcalf, A. A.   **420**
Predictions *See* Forecasting
Preemies. Linden, D. W.   **618.92**
Prefabricated buildings
  See also Prefabricated houses
Prefabricated houses
  Friedman, A. The adaptable house   **728**
  Watkins, A. M. Manufactured houses   **693**
The **preference** for the primitive. Gombrich, E. H.
    709
Pregnancy
  See also Miscarriage
  Bruce, D. F. Making a baby   **618.2**
  Kitzinger, S. The complete book of pregnancy and
    childbirth   **618.2**
  Lees, C. C. Pregnancy and birth   **618.2**
  Mayo Clinic complete book of pregnancy & baby's
    first year   **618.2**
  Murkoff, H. E. What to expect when you're expecting
    618.2
  Nilsson, L. A child is born   **612.6**
  Sears, W. The pregnancy book   **618.2**
  Slater, L. Love works like this   **306.8**
  Steingraber, S. Having faith   **618.2**
  Wolf, N. Misconceptions   **618.2**
Pregnancy, Termination of *See* Abortion
Pregnancy and birth. Lees, C. C.   **618.2**
The **pregnancy** book. Sears, W.   **618.2**
Prehistoric animals
  See also Archaeopteryx; Dinosaurs; Extinct ani-
  mals
Prehistoric art
  See also Rock drawings, paintings, and engravings
  Bahn, P. G. The Cambridge illustrated history of pre-
  historic art   **709.01**
  Lippard, L. R. Overlay   **709**
Prehistoric culture change on the Colorado plateau
    970.004
Prehistoric man *See* Fossil hominids
Prehistoric peoples
  Fowler, B. Iceman   **937**
  Hancock, G. Underworld: the mysterious origins of
    civilization   **551.7**
  North, J. D. Stonehenge   **936**
Prejudices
  See also Antisemitism
  Allport, G. The nature of prejudice   **152.4**
  Bullard, S. Teaching tolerance   **649**
  Griffin, J. H. Black like me   **305.8**
  Young-Bruehl, E. The anatomy of prejudices
    303.3
Premarital counseling *See* Marriage counseling
Premature infants
  Linden, D. W. Preemies   **618.92**
Preminger, Alex
  (ed) The New Princeton encyclopedia of poetry and
  poetics. See The New Princeton encyclopedia of po-
  etry and poetics   **809.1**
Prepare your own last will and testament—without a
  lawyer. See Sitarz, D. Prepare your own will
    346.05
Prepare your own will. Sitarz, D.   **346.05**
Prescott, William Hickling, 1796-1859
  History of the conquest of Mexico   **972**
  History of the conquest of Peru   **985**
Prescriptions for living. Siegel, B. S.   **158**
The **present** age, and Of the difference between a genius
  and an apostle. Kierkegaard, S.   **230**

Preservation of antiquities *See* Antiquities—Collection
  and preservation
Preservation of wildlife *See* Wildlife conservation
Preserving memory. Linenthal, E. T.   **940.53**
The **Presidency** A to Z   **352.23**
The **presidency** of Abraham Lincoln. Paludan, P. S.
    973.7
President Kennedy. Reeves, R.   **92**
President Nixon. Reeves, R.   **92**
Presidential elections, 1789-2000   **324.6**
Presidential inaugurations. Boller, P. F.   **973**
Presidential places. Ferris, G. W.   **917.3**
Presidential wives. Boller, P. F.   **920**
Presidents
  See also Vice-presidents
      United States
  The American Heritage illustrated history of the presi-
    dents   **920**
  Dallek, R. Hail to the chief   **973**
  Ellis, J. J. Founding brothers   **973.4**
  Guide to the presidency   **352.23**
  Kane, J. N. Facts about the presidents   **920**
  Kunhardt, P. B. The American president   **920**
  Marton, K. Hidden power   **920**
  The Reader's companion to the American presidency
    973
  Stephanopoulos, G. All too human   **973.929**
  To the best of my ability   **920**
  Wetterau, B. Congressional Quarterly's desk reference
    on the Presidency   **973**
  The White House   **975.3**
  Woodward, B. Shadow   **973.92**
  See/See also pages in the following book(s):
  Thomas, H. Front row at the White House   **92**
      United States—Election
  American presidential campaigns and elections
    324
  Karabell, Z. The last campaign   **324**
  Presidential elections, 1789-2000   **324.6**
  White, T. H. The making of the president, 1960
    324.6
  Witcover, J. No way to pick a president   **324**
      United States—Election—2000
  Dershowitz, A. M. Supreme injustice   **324**
  Posner, R. A. Breaking the deadlock   **324**
      United States—Encyclopedias
  The Presidency A to Z   **352.23**
      United States—Family
  Anthony, C. S. America's first families   **920**
      United States—Homes
  Ferris, G. W. Presidential places   **917.3**
      United States—Inaugural addresses
  White, R. C. Lincoln's greatest speech   **973.7**
      United States—Inauguration
  Boller, P. F. Presidential inaugurations   **973**
      United States—Mothers
  Angelo, B. First mothers   **920**
      United States—Spouses
  See Presidents' spouses—United States
President's Council on Bioethics (U.S.) *See* United
  States. President's Council on Bioethics
Presidents' secret wars. Prados, J.   **327.12**
Presidents' spouses
      United States
  Anthony, C. S. First ladies   **920**
  Boller, P. F. Presidential wives   **920**
  Caroli, B. B. First ladies   **920**
  Marton, K. Hidden power   **920**
  Schneider, D. First ladies   **920.003**
  Truman, M. First ladies   **920**
Presley, Elvis, 1935-1977
      About
  Guralnick, P. Careless love: the unmaking of Elvis
  Presley   **92**

Presley, Elvis, 1935-1977—About—*Continued*
Guralnick, P. Last train to Memphis: the rise of Elvis
Presley **92**
Press
See also Broadcast journalism; Newspapers
Pressure cooker cookbook, The ultimate. Lacalamita, T.
641.5
Prester John
See/See also pages in the following book(s):
Connell, E. S. The Aztec treasure house p278-93
814
Preston, Diana
The Boxer Rebellion **951**
A first rate tragedy **998**
Lusitania **940.4**
Preston, Richard
The demon in the freezer **616.9**
The hot zone **614.5**
Preventing arthritis. Lawrence, R. M. **616.7**
Preventing falls. Hutton, J. T. **618.97**
Prevention Magazine Health Books
The Doctor's book of home remedies for dogs and
cats. See The Doctor's book of home remedies for
dogs and cats **636.7**
Prevention's complete book of walking. Spilner, M.
613.7
Prevention's ultimate guide to women's health and well-
ness **613**
Preves, Richard
New house/more house **690**
Prezzano, Susan C.
(ed) Archaeology of the Appalachian highlands. See
Archaeology of the Appalachian highlands
970.004
Price, Anne, 1946-
(ed) Middle and junior high school library catalog. See
Middle and junior high school library catalog
011.6
Price, Martin, 1920-
(ed) The Restoration and the eighteenth century. See
The Restoration and the eighteenth century
820.8
Price, Reynolds, 1933-
Clear pictures **92**
The collected poems **811**
Feasting the heart **814**
Letter to a man in the fire **231**
A whole new life **92**
Price, Steven D., 1940-
Essential riding **798.2**
The price of citizenship. Katz, M. B. **361.6**
Price of honor. Goodwin, J. **305.4**
The price of motherhood. Crittenden, A. **306.8**
The price of terror. Gerson, A. **363.1**
Priestley, Joseph, 1733-1804
About
Uglow, J. S. The lunar men **920**
See/See also pages in the following book(s):
Horvitz, L. A. Eureka!: scientific breakthroughs that
changed the world **509**
Malone, J. W. It doesn't take a rocket scientist
920
Primal leadership. Goleman, D. **658.4**
Primates
See/See also pages in the following book(s):
Waal, F. de. The ape and the sushi master **156**
A primate's memoir. Sapolsky, R. M. **599.8**
Prime time network serials. Morris, B. B. **791.45**
Primetime blues. Bogle, D. **791.45**
Primitive mythology. Campbell, J.
In Campbell, J. The masks of God v1 **291.1**
Primitive societies
See also Nomads

Primitive world: an anti-nuclear jazz musical. Baraka, I.
A.
In Baraka, I. A. The LeRoi Jones/Amiri Baraka read-
er **818**
The prince. Machiavelli, N. **320**
Prince of princes: the life of Potemkin. Montefiore, S.
92
Princess Hollyhock. Komparu, Z.
In Waley, A. The Nō plays of Japan **895.6**
Pringle, David
(ed) St. James guide to fantasy writers. See St. James
guide to fantasy writers **809.3**
Pringle, Heather Anne, 1952-
The mummy congress **393**
Pringle, Peter
Food, inc **363.1**
Print the legend: the life and times of John Ford.
Eyman, S. **92**
Printed sources **929**
Printing
Style manuals
United States. Government Printing Office. Style man-
ual **808**
Printing, Textile *See* Textile printing
Prinz, Martin, 1931-2000
(ed) Simon and Schuster's guide to rocks and minerals.
See Simon and Schuster's guide to rocks and miner-
als **549**
Prion diseases
Rhodes, R. Deadly feasts **614.5**
Prisant, Carol
Antiques roadshow primer **745.1**
Prison labor *See* Convict labor
The prisoner of Second Avenue. Simon, N.
In Simon, N. The collected plays of Neil Simon v2
p231-99 **812**
Prisoner without a name, cell without a number.
Timerman, J. **92**
Prisoners
See also Political prisoners
Abbott, J. H. In the belly of the beast **365**
Rees, S. The floating brothel **365**
Wynn, J. Inside Rikers **365**
Prisoners of the Japanese. Daws, G. **940.54**
Prisoners of war
Daws, G. Prisoners of the Japanese **940.54**
Howarth, D. A. We die alone **940.54**
Norman, E. M. We band of angels **940.54**
United States
Knox, D. Death march **940.54**
See/See also pages in the following book(s):
Philpott, T. Glory denied **92**
Prisoners of war, American *See* Prisoners of war—
United States
The prisoner's wife. Bandele, A. **92**
Prisoners without trial. Daniels, R. **940.53**
Prisons
See also Penal colonies
United States
Abbott, J. H. In the belly of the beast **365**
Oshinsky, D. M. "Worse than slavery" **365**
Rafter, N. H. Prisons in America **365**
United States—Encyclopedias
Encyclopedia of American prisons **365**
Prisons in America. Rafter, N. H. **365**
Prisons of light. Ferguson, K. **523.8**
Pritchard, James B., 1909-1997
(ed) The HarperCollins concise atlas of the Bible. See
The HarperCollins concise atlas of the Bible
220.9
Pritchard, William H.
Lives of the modern poets **821.009**
Updike **813.009**
Pritzker, Barry
A Native American encyclopedia **970.004**

Privacy, Right of *See* Right of privacy
Privacy in the information age. Henderson, H.
          323.44
Private independent schools   370.25
The **private** life of the brain. Greenfield, S.   612.8
Private lives. Coward, N.
    In Coward, N. Three plays   822
Private schools
          Directories
    The Handbook of private schools   370.25
    Peterson's private secondary schools   373.2
    Private independent schools   370.25
The **prize**. Yergin, D.   338.2
The **prize** winner of Defiance, Ohio [biography of Evelyn Ryan] Ryan, T.   92
Prizes (Rewards) *See* Awards
Pro-choice movement
    Solinger, R. Beggars and choosers   363.46
Pro football register   796.332
Probabilities
    Orkin, M. What are the odds?   519.2
The **problem**. Gurney, A. R.
    In Gurney, A. R. Nine early plays, 1961-1973 p99-113   812
Problem children *See* Emotionally disturbed children
Problem drinking *See* Alcoholism
"A **problem** from hell". Power, S.   304.6
Problem solving
    See also Decision making
Problems of plenty. Hurt, R. D.   630
Procedures for the automated office. Burton, S.
          651.3
Process and reality. Whitehead, A. N.   113
Prochnau, William W., 1937-
    Once upon a distant war   959.704
Prochnicky, Jerry
    (jt. auth) Riordan, J. Break on through: the life and death of Jim Morrison   92
Proctor, Claude O.
    NTC's multilingual dictionary of American sign language   419
Proctor, Rob
    (jt. auth) Springer, L. Passionate gardening   635
Products, Commercial *See* Commercial products
Professional associations *See* Trade and professional associations
Professional Secretaries International complete office handbook. See Jaderstrom, S. Complete office handbook   651.8
The **professional** secretary's book of lists & tips. De Vries, M. A.   651.3
Professions
    See also Occupations
The **professor** and the madman. Winchester, S.   423
Profiles in courage. Kennedy, J. F.   920
Profiles of American colleges, Barron's   378.73
Programming (Computers) *See* Computer programming
Programs, Computer *See* Computer software
Programs, Television *See* Television programs
Progressivism (United States politics)
    Diner, S. J. A very different age   973.8
Prohibition
    Behr, E. Prohibition   363.4
Project Apollo *See* Apollo project
Project Orion. Dyson, G.   629.47
Prokofiev, Sergey, 1891-1953
          About
    Nice, D. Prokofiev: from Russia to the West, 1891-1935   92
Proletariat
    Ortega y Gasset, J. The revolt of the masses   909
Proliferation of arms *See* Arms race
Promiscuities. Wolf, N.   306.7
Promiscuity
    White, E. Fast girls   305.23

The **promise** of sleep. Dement, W. C.   612.8
Pronouncing dictionary of proper names   423
Pronouncing Shakespeare's words. Coye, D. F.
          822.3
Proof. Auburn, D.   812
Propaganda
    Huxley, A. Brave new world revisited   303.3
          Encyclopedias
    Cull, N. J. Propaganda and mass persuasion
          303.3
Propaganda and mass persuasion. Cull, N. J.   303.3
Property
    See also Real estate
    Pipes, R. Property and freedom   323.4
          Law and legislation
    Woodhouse, V. Divorce and money   346.01
Property and freedom. Pipes, R.   323.4
Prophecies
    Ashe, G. Encyclopedia of prophecy   133.3
The **Prophet**. Gibran, K.   811
The **prophet** and the astronomer. Gleiser, M.   523.1
Prophets
    Heschel, A. J. The prophets   224
Prophets (Books of the Old Testament) *See* Bible. O.T. Prophets
The **proposal**. Chekhov, A. P.
    In Chekhov, A. P. The plays of Anton Chekhov p35-49   891.7
Prose, Francine, 1947-
    The lives of the muses   920
    Sicilian odyssey   945
Prose and poetry. Crane, S.   818
Prostate
          Diseases
    Walsh, P. C. The prostate   616.6
Protagoras. Plato
    In Plato. The portable Plato p45-117   888
Protecting the right to read. Symons, A. K.   025.2
Protecting yourself online. Gelman, R. B.   342
Protection of birds *See* Birds—Protection
Protection of environment *See* Environmental protection
Protection of wildlife *See* Wildlife conservation
Protestant Reformation *See* Reformation
Protests, demonstrations, etc. *See* Demonstrations
Prothero, Stephen R.
    (jt. auth) Queen, E. L. The encyclopedia of American religious history   200.9
The **proud** tower. Tuchman, B. W.   909.82
The **proudest** day. Read, A.   954.03
Proust, Marcel, 1871-1922
    Swann's way; criticism
    In Nabokov, V. V. Lectures on literature p207-49
          808.3
          About
    Carter, W. C. Marcel Proust   92
    Shattuck, R. Proust's way   843.009
    Tadié, J.-Y. Marcel Proust   92
    See/See also pages in the following book(s):
    Bloom, H. The Western canon   809
Proust's way. Shattuck, R.   843.009
Provence (France)
          Social life and customs
    Mayle, P. Encore Provence   944.083
Proverbs
    The Concise Oxford dictionary of proverbs   398.9
    Cordry, H. V. The multicultural dictionary of proverbs
          398.9
    A Dictionary of American proverbs   398.9
    Manser, M. H. The Facts on File dictionary of proverbs   398.9
    Pickering, D. Cassell dictionary of proverbs   398.9
Providence and government of God
    Kushner, H. S. When bad things happen to good people   296.3

Prown, Jules David, 1930-
  Discovered lands, invented pasts. See Discovered
    lands, invented pasts   **759.13**
Prozac backlash. Glenmullen, J.   **616.85**
Prozac diary. Slater, L.   **616.89**
Prucha, Edward J.
  (ed) Breast cancer sourcebook. See Breast cancer
    sourcebook   **616.99**
  (ed) Pediatric cancer sourcebook. See Pediatric cancer
    sourcebook   **618.92**
Prucha, Francis Paul
  The great father   **970.004**
Prudhomme, Paul
  Chef Paul Prudhomme's Louisiana kitchen   **641.5**
  Chef Paul Prudhomme's Louisiana tastes   **641.5**
Prufer, Kevin
  (ed) The New young American poets. See The New
    young American poets   **811.008**
Pruitt, David B.
  (ed) Your adolescent. See Your adolescent   **155.5**
Pruning
  Pruning & training   **635.9**
Pruning & training   **635.9**
Pryke, Paula
  Flowers, flowers!   **745.92**
Pryor, Gale
  Nursing mother, working mother   **649**
Pryor, Richard
  See/See also pages in the following book(s):
  Life stories   **920**
Psoriasis
  Cram, D. L. Coping with psoriasis   **616.5**
Psychiatric hospitals
  Whitaker, R. Mad in America   **616.89**
Psychiatry
  Bremner, J. D. Does stress damage the brain?
      616.85
  Hobson, J. A. Out of its mind   **616.89**
  Kramer, P. D. Listening to Prozac   **616.85**
  Porter, R. Madness   **616.89**
  Shorter, E. A history of psychiatry   **616.89**
  Stone, M. H. Healing the mind   **616.89**
      Encyclopedias
  Encyclopedia of mental health   **616.89**
  The Gale encyclopedia of mental disorders
      616.89
Psychic healing *See* Mental healing
Psychical research *See* Parapsychology
Psychoactive drugs *See* Psychotropic drugs
Psychoanalysis
  Alvarez, A. Night   **154.6**
  Bettelheim, B. Freud and man's soul   **150.19**
  Buhle, M. J. Feminism and its discontents   **150.19**
  Freud, S. The basic writings of Sigmund Freud
      150.19
  Freud, S. The Freud reader   **150.19**
  Freud, S. Interpretation of dreams   **154.6**
  Freud, S. Totem and taboo   **306**
  Freud: conflict and culture   **150.19**
  Fromm, E. On being human   **150.19**
  Gay, P. A Godless Jew   **150.19**
  Horney, K. New ways in psychoanalysis   **150.19**
  Jung, C. G. The basic writings of C. G. Jung
      150.19
  Jung, C. G. The essential Jung   **150.19**
  Jung, C. G. The portable Jung   **150.19**
  Menninger, K. A. Love against hate   **150.19**
  Mitchell, S. A. Freud and beyond   **150.19**
  Thurschwell, P. Sigmund Freud   **150.19**
  See/See also pages in the following book(s):
  Tillich, P. Theology of culture   **230**
Psychogenetics *See* Behavior genetics

Psychology
  See also Adjustment (Psychology); Adolescent
  psychology; Aggressiveness (Psychology); Applied
  psychology; Attitude (Psychology); Behaviorism;
  Child psychology; Developmental psychology; Edu-
  cational psychology; Ethnopsychology; Human be-
  havior; Social psychology
  Allport, G. Becoming   **155.2**
  Colman, A. M. A dictionary of psychology   **150.3**
  Glasser, W. Choice theory   **150**
  James, W. The varieties of religious experience
      210
  Jung, C. G. Man and his symbols   **150.19**
  Pinker, S. How the mind works   **153**
  Pollack, R. The missing moment   **610**
  Psychology   **150**
  Rogers, C. R. A way of being   **150.19**
  Viorst, J. Imperfect control   **158**
  Weber, R. J. The created self   **155.2**
      Encyclopedias
  The Corsini encyclopedia of psychology and behavioral
    science   **150.3**
  Encyclopedia of psychology   **150.3**
  The Gale encyclopedia of psychology   **150.3**
Psychology, Comparative *See* Comparative psychology
Psychology, Criminal *See* Criminal psychology
Psychology, Ethnic *See* Ethnopsychology
Psychology, Pastoral *See* Pastoral psychology
Psychology, Physiological *See* Psychophysiology
Psychology, Racial *See* Ethnopsychology
Psychology   **150**
Psychology of learning
  Barzun, J. Begin here   **371.1**
  Bruer, J. T. The myth of the first three years
      155.4
  Gopnik, A. The scientist in the crib   **155.4**
Psychopathology of everyday life. Freud, S.
  In Freud, S. The basic writings of Sigmund Freud
      150.19
Psychopharmaceuticals *See* Psychotropic drugs
Psychophysiology
  Moyers, B. Healing and the mind   **616**
Psychosomatic medicine
  Pert, C. Molecules of emotion   **612.8**
Psychotherapy
  See also Transactional analysis
  Burns, D. D. Feeling good   **158**
  Kramer, P. D. Listening to Prozac   **616.85**
  Kramer, P. D. Should you leave?   **616.89**
  May, R. The discovery of being   **150.19**
  Rogers, C. R. On becoming a person   **616.89**
  Yalom, I. D. The gift of therapy   **616.89**
Psychotropic drugs
  See also Antidepressants; Cocaine; Hallucinogens
  Courtwright, D. T. Forces of habit   **362.29**
  Kramer, P. D. Listening to Prozac   **616.85**
  Slater, L. Prozac diary   **616.89**
  Weil, A. From chocolate to morphine   **616.86**
PTSD *See* Post-traumatic stress disorder
Pubantz, Jerry, 1947-
  (jt. auth) Moore, J. A. Encyclopedia of the United Na-
    tions   **341.23**
Public affairs. Gurney, A. R.
  In Gurney, A. R. Nine early plays, 1961-1973 p115-
    70   **812**
The **public** and private worlds of Elizabeth I. Watkins,
  S.   **942.05**
Public documents *See* Government publications
Public enemies. Walsh, J.   **364.1**
Public figures *See* Celebrities
Public health
  See also Epidemiology; Social medicine
  Garrett, L. Betrayal of trust   **362.1**
  Rovner, J. Health care policy and politics A to Z
      362.1

Public health—*Continued*
See/See also pages in the following book(s):
Bourdain, A. Typhoid Mary   92
Encyclopedias
Encyclopedia of public health   362.1
Public intellectuals. Posner, R. A.   305.5
Public interest
Etzioni, A. The limits of privacy   323.44
Public lands
See also National parks and reserves
United States
Linklater, A. Measuring America   973
Public libraries
Moller, S. C. Library service to Spanish speaking patrons   027.6
Steele, A. T. Bare bones children's services   027.62
Vaillancourt, R. J. Bare bones young adult services   027.62
Willis, M. R. Dealing with difficult people in the library   025.5
Public opinion
See also subjects with the subdivision *Public opinion;* and names of countries with the subdivision *Foreign opinion* for materials dealing with foreign public opinion about the country
Wolfe, A. Moral freedom   170
Public relations
See also Customer relations
Libraries
See Libraries—Public relations
Public schools
Kozol, J. Savage inequalities   371.9
Boston (Mass.)
Kozol, J. Death at an early age   306.43
United States
Gross, M. L. The conspiracy of ignorance   371
Public speaking
Detz, J. How to write and give a speech   808.5
Public welfare
See also Charities; Food relief; Social medicine
Friedman, M. Free to choose   330.1
Hancock, L. Hands to work   361.6
Katz, M. B. The price of citizenship   361.6
Zucchino, D. Myth of the welfare queen   362.5
The **Publish-it-yourself** handbook   070.5
Publishers and publishing
See also Authors and publishers; Book industry; Electronic publishing
Appelbaum, J. How to get happily published   070.5
The Associated Press stylebook and briefing on media law   808
Epstein, J. Book business   070.5
Germano, W. P. Getting it published   070.5
Herman, J. Jeff Herman's guide to book publishers, editors, & literary agents   070.5
Poynter, D. The self-publishing manual   070.5
The Publish-it-yourself handbook   070.5
Rose, M. J. How to publish and promote online   070.5
The Writer's handbook   808
The Writer's market   808
Directories
American book trade directory   070.5025
International literary market place: ILMP   070.5025
Literary market place: LMP   070.5025
Publishers, distributors & wholesalers of the United States   070.5025
Handbooks, manuals, etc.
The Chicago manual of style   808
United States. Government Printing Office. Style manual   808

Publishers, distributors & wholesalers of the United States   070.5025
Publishing, Electronic *See* Electronic publishing
Publius Terentius Afer *See* Terence
Puccini, Giacomo, 1858-1924
About
Osborne, C. The complete operas of Puccini   792.5
The Puccini companion   92
Puccini, Simonetta
(ed) The Puccini companion. See The Puccini companion   92
The **Puccini** companion   92
Puck, Wolfgang
Wolfgang Puck's pizza, pasta and more!   641.8
Pueblo Indians
See/See also pages in the following book(s):
Josephy, A. M. Now that the buffalo's gone p91-123   970.004
Antiquities
Roberts, D. In search of the old ones   970.004
Puerto Ricans
New York (N.Y.)
See/See also pages in the following book(s):
Glazer, N. Beyond the melting pot p86-136   305.8
Pugh-Gannon, JoAnn
(jt. auth) Bednar, N. The encyclopedia of sewing machine techniques   646.2
Puig, Manuel
About
Levine, S. J. Manuel Puig and spider woman   92
Pukui, Mary Kawena, 1895-1986
Hawaiian dictionary   499
Pulitzer, Joseph, 1847-1911
See/See also pages in the following book(s):
Pfaff, D. W. Joseph Pulitzer II and the Post-dispatch   92
Pulitzer, Joseph, 1885-1955
About
Pfaff, D. W. Joseph Pulitzer II and the Post-dispatch   92
Pulitzer Prizes
Written into history   071
See/See also pages in the following book(s):
Gass, W. H. Finding a form p3-13   814
Puller, Lewis B., 1945-1994
Fortunate son   92
Pulliam, June Michele
(jt. auth) Fonseca, A. J. Hooked on horror   016.8
Pulliam, Tom
The New York times crossword puzzle dictionary   793.73
Pullum, Geoffrey K.
(jt. auth) Huddleston, R. D. The Cambridge grammar of the English language   425
Pumped. Kuhn, C.   617.1
Punished by rewards. Kohn, A.   153.8
The **pupil.** Merwin, W. S.   811
Pupo-Walker, Enrique
(ed) The Cambridge history of Latin American literature. See The Cambridge history of Latin American literature   860.9
Purcell, L. Edward
Encyclopedia of battles in North America, 1517 to 1916   970
(jt. auth) Burg, D. F. Almanac of World War I   940.3
Purcell, Sarah J.
(jt. auth) Purcell, L. E. Encyclopedia of battles in North America, 1517 to 1916   970
Pure drivel. Martin, S.   817
Purgatorio. Dante Alighieri   851
Purgatory. Yeats, W. B.
In Our dramatic heritage v5   808.82

Purim
See/See also pages in the following book(s):
Strassfeld, M. The Jewish holidays p187-98   **296.4**
Puritans
Hall, M. G. The last American Puritan: the life of In-
crease Mather, 1639-1723   **92**
See/See also pages in the following book(s):
Boorstin, D. J. The Americans: The colonial experi-
ence   **973.2**
The **pursuit** of oblivion. Davenport-Hines, R. P. T.
363.45
The **Pushcart** prize . . . : best of the small presses
810.8
Putin, Vladimir
First person: an astonishingly frank self-portrait
92
Puyallup Indians
See/See also pages in the following book(s):
Josephy, A. M. Now that the buffalo's gone p177-211
970.004
Puzzles
See also Crossword puzzles
Pyenson, Lewis
Servants of nature   **509**
Pyenson, Susan Sheets- *See* Sheets-Pyenson, Susan,
1949-1998
Pyle, David
What every artist needs to know about paints & colors
752
Pyle, Ernie, 1900-1945
About
Tobin, J. Ernie Pyle's war   **92**
Pyle, J. A.
(ed) Encyclopedia of atmospheric sciences. See Ency-
clopedia of atmospheric sciences   **551.5**
Pyle, Robert Michael
The Audubon Society field guide to North American
butterflies   **595.7**
Pyramids
Lepre, J. P. The Egyptian pyramids   **932**
Verner, M. The pyramids   **932**
Pythons
Murphy, J. C. Tales of giant snakes   **597.9**

Q

Q is for quantum. Gribbin, J. R.   **539.7**
Q: the autobiography of Quincy Jones. Jones, Q.
92
QED. Feynman, R. P.   **539.7**
Quakers *See* Society of Friends
The **Quakers** in America. Hamm, T. D.   **289.6**
Quakes, eruptions, and other geologic cataclysms.
Erickson, J.   **550**
Quality of life
Hallowell, E. M. Connect   **158**
Parkinson's disease and quality of life   **616.8**
Reich, R. B. The future of success   **306**
Savageau, D. Places rated almanac   **307.7**
Quammen, David, 1948-
The boilerplate rhino   **508**
Monster of God   **591.6**
Quantum Computer Services, Inc.
See also America Online Inc.
Quantum generations. Kragh, H.   **530**
Quantum legacy. Parker, B. R.   **530.1**
Quantum theory
Aczel, A. D. Entanglement   **530.1**
Barbour, J. B. The end of time   **530.1**
Einstein, A. The evolution of physics   **530**
Feynman, R. P. QED   **539.7**
Gribbin, J. R. In search of Schrödinger's cat
530.1

Gribbin, J. R. Schrödinger's kittens and the search for
reality   **530.1**
Hawking, S. W. The nature of space and time
530.1
Hawking, S. W. The universe in a nutshell   **530.1**
Johnson, G. A shortcut through time   **004**
Parker, B. R. Quantum legacy   **530.1**
See/See also pages in the following book(s):
Feynman, R. P. Six easy pieces   **530**
The **quark** and the jaguar. Gell-Mann, M.   **530.1**
Quarrel & quandary. Ozick, C.   **814**
Queen, Edward L.
The encyclopedia of American religious history
200.9
The **Queen:** a biography of Elizabeth II. Pimlott, B.
92
Queen and country: the fifty-year reign of Elizabeth II.
Shawcross, W.   **92**
Queen Latifah
Ladies first   **158**
Queen Victoria. Strachey, L.   **92**
Queenan, Joe
True believers   **796**
Queens
See also names of queens and countries with the
subdivision *Kings and rulers*
Jackson-Laufer, G. M. Women rulers throughout the
ages   **920**
The **quest** for cosmic justice. Sowell, T.   **303.3**
The **quest** for El Cid. Fletcher, R. A.   **92**
The **Quest** for immortality   **709.32**
The **quest** for life in amber. Poinar, G. O.   **560**
A **question** of choice. Weddington, S. R.   **363.46**
Questioning the millennium. Gould, S. J.   **901**
Questions and answers
Feldman, D. When do fish sleep? and other imponder-
ables of everyday life   **031.02**
Feldman, D. Why do clocks run clockwise? and other
imponderables   **031.02**
Quick & legal will book. Clifford, D.   **346.05**
Quick and easy cooking
Dalsass, D. The new good cake book   **641.8**
Quick-meal cookery *See* Quick and easy cooking
Quick studies   **001.1**
Quiet strength. Parks, R.   **92**
A **quiet** world. Myers, D. G.   **617.8**
Quilting
Barnes, C. Color   **746.46**
Fassett, K. Glorious patchwork   **746.46**
Kavaya, K. Community quilts   **746.46**
Michler, J. M. The magic of crazy quilting
746.46
Quilts
Kavaya, K. Community quilts   **746.46**
Tobin, J. Hidden in plain view   **973.7**
Quindlen, Anna
How reading changed my life   **028**
Quinine
Rocco, F. The miraculous fever tree   **616.9**
Quinlan, Karen Ann
See/See also pages in the following book(s):
Filene, P. G. In the arms of others   **179.7**
Humphry, D. Freedom to die   **179.7**
Quinn, Edward, 1932-
A dictionary of literary and thematic terms   **803**
Quinn, Elisabeth Lasch- *See* Lasch-Quinn, Elisabeth
Quinn, Jane Bryant
Making the most of your money   **332.024**
Quinn, Sally
See/See also pages in the following book(s):
Heymann, C. D. The Georgetown ladies' social club
305.4
Quinn, Susan
Marie Curie   **92**

Quirk, Lawrence J.
  Bob Hope: the road well-traveled   **92**
Quirk, Robert E.
  Fidel Castro   **92**
Quit-smoking programs *See* Smoking cessation pro-
  grams
The **Quotable** woman   **808.88**
Quotationary, Random House Webster's   **808.88**
Quotations
    See also Proverbs
  Andrews, R. The Columbia dictionary of quotations
                                            808.88
  Andrews, R. Famous lines   **808.88**
  Bartlett, J. Familiar quotations   **808.88**
  Biggs, M. Women's words   **808.88**
  Boller, P. F. They never said it   **808.88**
  Chambers dictionary of quotations   **808.88**
  The Columbia Granger's dictionary of poetry quota-
    tions   **808.88**
  The Concise Oxford dictionary of quotations
                                            808.88
  A Dictionary of quotations in mathematics **510**
  Great treasury of Western thought   **080**
  Guinagh, K. Dictionary of foreign phrases and abbrevi-
    ations   **422.03**
  Kennedy, R. F. Make gentle the life of this world
                                            973.922
  A New dictionary of quotations on historical principles
    from ancient and modern sources   **808.88**
  Nowlan, R. A. Born this day   **808.88**
  The Oxford book of aphorisms   **808.88**
  The Oxford dictionary of humorous quotations
                                            808.88
  The Quotable woman   **808.88**
  Quotations for all occasions   **808.88**
  Random House Webster's quotationary   **808.88**
  Schweitzer, A. The words of Albert Schweitzer
                                            210
  Shakespeare, W. The Columbia dictionary of quota-
    tions from Shakespeare   **822.3**
  Shakespeare, W. A dictionary of quotations from
    Shakespeare   **822.3**
  World War II   **940.53**
Quotations for all occasions   **808.88**
Quran *See* Koran

R

R. J. Reynolds Industries, Inc.
    See also RJR Nabisco Inc.
R.U.R. and The insect play. Čapek, K.   **891.8**
R.U.R. (Rossum's Universal Robots). Čapek, K.
    In Čapek, K. R.U.R. and The insect play   **891.8**
Raban, Jonathan
  Bad land   **978**
  Passage to Juneau   **979.8**
Rabaris (Indic people)
  Davidson, R. Desert places   **954**
Rabban, David M., 1949-
  Free speech in its forgotten years   **342**
Rabbi Jesus. Chilton, B.   **232.9**
Rabin, Robert J.
  (jt. auth) Outten, W. N. The rights of employees and
    union members   **344**
Rabin, Yitzhak, 1922-1995
              About
  Kurzman, D. Soldier of peace: the life of Yitzhak Ra-
    bin   **92**
  Shalom, friend: the life and legacy of Yitzhak Rabin
                                            92
Rabindranath Tagore *See* Tagore, Sir Rabindranath,
  1861-1941
Rabiner, Susan
  Thinking like your editor   **808**

Rabinow, Paul
  Making PCR   **572.8**
Rabins, Peter V.
  (jt. auth) Mace, N. L. The 36-hour day   **618.97**
Race
  Wolpoff, M. H. Race and human evolution
                                            599.97
The **race.** Schefter, J. L.   **629.45**
Race. Terkel, S.   **305.8**
Race and human evolution. Wolpoff, M. H. **599.97**
Race awareness
    See also African Americans—Race identity
Race discrimination
  Bryant, H. Shut out   **796.357**
  Cose, E. Color-blind   **305.8**
  McDonald, L. The rights of racial minorities **342**
              Law and legislation
  Carter, S. L. Reflections of an affirmative action baby
                                            342
Race experts. Lasch-Quinn, E.   **305.8**
The **race** for the Triple Crown. Drape, J. **798.4**
Race matters. West, C.   **305.8**
Race psychology *See* Ethnopsychology
Race relations
    See also Culture conflict; Ethnic relations;
    Multiculturalism; names of countries, cities, etc.,
    with the subdivision *Race relations*
  Sowell, T. The economics and politics of race
                                            305.8
Race relations and the church *See* Church and race re-
  lations
Race rules. Dyson, M. E.   **305.8**
Races of people *See* Ethnology
Rachel and her children. Kozol, J.   **362.5**
Rachmaninoff, Sergei, 1873-1943
    See/See also pages in the following book(s):
  Schonberg, H. C. The great pianists   **920**
Racial balance in schools *See* School integration
Racial intermarriage *See* Interracial marriage
Racially mixed people
  Morales, E. Living in Spanglish   **305.8**
  Rodriguez, R. Brown: the last discovery of America
                                            305.8
Racine, Jean, 1639-1699
    See/See also pages in the following book(s):
  Durant, W. J. The age of Louis XIV p132-44
                                            940.2
Racing for the bomb: General Leslie R. Groves,
  the Manhattan Project's indispensable man. Norris, R. S.
                                            92
Racism
    See also Race discrimination; White supremacy
    movements
  Bushart, H. L. Soldiers of God   **322.4**
  Ezekiel, R. S. The racist mind   **322.4**
  Kennedy, R. Nigger   **305.8**
  When race becomes real   **305.8**
The **racist** mind. Ezekiel, R. S.   **322.4**
Radar
  Buderi, R. The invention that changed the world
                                            621.3848
Radetsky, Peter
  (jt. auth) Garrick, J. G. Anybody's sports medicine
    book   **617.1**
Radford, Edwin, 1891-1973
  Encyclopaedia of superstitions   **398.03**
Radford, Mona Augusta
  (jt. auth) Radford, E. Encyclopaedia of superstitions
                                            398.03
The **radical** center. Halstead, T.   **320.5**
Radicalism
    See also Militia movements
  Alinsky, S. Rules for radicals   **322.4**
  Anderson, T. H. The movement and the sixties
                                            303.4

Radicalism—*Continued*
Atkins, S. E. Encyclopedia of modern American extremists and extremist groups **322.4**
Dees, M. S., Jr. Gathering storm **322.4**
Hoffman, A. The best of Abbie Hoffman **303.4**
Ronson, J. Them: adventures with extremists
 322.4
Stern, K. S. A force upon the plain **322.4**
The **radicalism** of the American Revolution. Wood, G. S. **973.3**
Radio
Handbooks, manuals, etc.
The ARRL handbook for radio amateurs
 621.3841
Repairing
Carr, J. J. Old time radios! **621.384**
Radio authorship
Straczynski, J. M. The complete book of scriptwriting
 808.2
Radio broadcasting
Broadcasting & cable yearbook **384.54**
Neer, R. FM: the rise and fall of free-form rock radio
 791.44
Sies, L. F. Encyclopedia of American radio, 1920-1960
 791.44
Radio I. Beckett, S.
In Beckett, S. Ends and Odds p103-12 **842**
Radio II. Beckett, S.
In Beckett, S. Ends and Odds p113-28 **842**
Radio industry *See* Radio broadcasting
Radio journalism *See* Broadcast journalism
Radio programs
Dunning, J. On the air **791.44**
Sies, L. F. Encyclopedia of American radio, 1920-1960
 791.44
Radio stations, Amateur *See* Amateur radio stations
Radzinsky, Edvard
Stalin **92**
Rafter, Nicole Hahn, 1939-
Prisons in America **365**
Rage for fame: the ascent of Clare Boothe Luce. Morris, S. J. **92**
A **rage** to live: a biography of Richard and Isabel Burton. Lovell, M. S. **92**
Rage to survive: the Etta James story. James, E.
 92
Ragsdale, Linda
Creative cardboard **745.54**
Raikas *See* Rabaris (Indic people)
Railroads
See/See also pages in the following book(s):
Cotton, E. J. Hobo: a young man's thoughts on trains and tramping in America **92**
Asia
Theroux, P. The great railway bazaar: by train through Asia **915**
China
Theroux, P. Riding the iron rooster **915.1**
Latin America
Theroux, P. The old Patagonian express **918**
United States
Ambrose, S. E. Nothing like it in the world **385**
Bain, D. H. Empire express **385**
Rain forest ecology
Royte, E. The Tapir's morning bath **577.3**
Rain forests
Encyclopedias
Jukofsky, D. Encyclopedia of rainforests **578.7**
Rainbird, Sean
(ed) Beckmann, M. Max Beckmann **769**
The **rainbow** people of God. Tutu, D. **968.06**
Raines, Theron
Rising to the light: a portrait of Bruno Bettelheim
 92
A **raisin** in the sun. Hansberry, L. **812**

Raising a child with a neuromuscular disorder. Thompson, C. E. **618.92**
Raising a child with autism. Richman, S. **618.92**
Raising a happy, unspoiled child. White, B. L. **649**
Raising resilient children. Brooks, R. B. **649**
Raising the dead. Munson, R. **174**
Rajtar, Steve, 1951-
Indian war sites **970.004**
Ralegh, Elizabeth Throckmorton *See* Raleigh, Elizabeth Throckmorton, Lady, d. 1647
Raleigh, Elizabeth Throckmorton, Lady, d. 1647
About
Beer, A. R. My just desire **92**
Ralston, Anthony
(ed) Encyclopedia of computer science. See Encyclopedia of computer science **004**
Ramanujan Aiyangar, Srinivasa, 1887-1920
About
Kanigel, R. The man who knew infinity: a life of the genius, Ramanujan **92**
The **Ramayana**. Narayan, R. K. **891**
Ramazani, Jahan, 1960-
(ed) The Norton anthology of modern and contemporary poetry. See The Norton anthology of modern and contemporary poetry **821.008**
Ramey, Gene
See/See also pages in the following book(s):
Dance, S. The world of Count Basie **920**
Rampersad, Arnold
The life of Langston Hughes **92**
Ramsdell, Kristin, 1940-
Romance fiction **016.8**
Ramsey, John Bennett
About
Schiller, L. Perfect murder, perfect town **364.1**
Ramsey, JonBenet, d. 1996
About
Schiller, L. Perfect murder, perfect town **364.1**
Ramsey, Patricia
About
Schiller, L. Perfect murder, perfect town **364.1**
Ramsland, Katherine M., 1953-
The criminal mind **808.3**
Ghost **133.1**
Rand, Ayn, 1905-1982
Journals of Ayn Rand **92**
Letters of Ayn Rand **92**
The voice of reason; essays in objectivist thought
 191
See/See also pages in the following book(s):
American women fiction writers **813.009**
Pierpont, C. R. Passionate minds **810.9**
Rand McNally commercial atlas & marketing guide
 912
Rand McNally Goode's world atlas. See Goode's world atlas **912**
Rand McNally road atlas **912**
Randall, Glenn, 1957-
The Outward Bound backpacker's handbook
 796.51
Randall, Joe
A taste of heritage **641.5**
Randall, John Herman, 1899-
(ed) The Renaissance philosophy of man. See The Renaissance philosophy of man **189**
Randall, Willard Sterne
George Washington **92**
Thomas Jefferson **92**
Randel, Don Michael
The Harvard biographical dictionary of music. See The Harvard biographical dictionary of music
 920.003
(ed) The Harvard concise dictionary of music and musicians. See The Harvard concise dictionary of music and musicians **780.3**

Randel, Don Michael—*Continued*
(ed) The Harvard dictionary of music. See The Harvard dictionary of music   **780.3**
Randolph, Ruth Elizabeth
(jt. auth) Roses, L. E. Harlem Renaissance and beyond: literary biographies of 100 black women writers, 1900-1945   **810.9**
Random House American sign language dictionary. See Costello, E. Random House Webster's American sign language dictionary   **419**
The **Random** House crossword puzzle dictionary. See Random House Webster's crossword puzzle dictionary   **793.73**
Random House dictionary of the English language. See Random House Webster's unabridged dictionary   **423**
Random House historical dictionary of American slang   **427**
Random House Latin-American Spanish dictionary   **463**
Random House unabridged dictionary. See Random House Webster's unabridged dictionary   **423**
Random House Webster's American sign language dictionary. Costello, E.   **419**
Random House Webster's college dictionary   **423**
Random House Webster's crossword puzzle dictionary   **793.73**
Random House Webster's quotationary   **808.88**
Random House Webster's unabridged dictionary   **423**

Ransom, John Crowe, 1888-1974
See/See also pages in the following book(s):
Lowell, R. Collected prose p17-28   **818**
Rao, Paul R.
(ed) Managing stroke. See Managing stroke   **616.8**
Rap music
George, N. Hip hop America   **781.64**
Rose, T. Black noise   **781.64**
The Vibe history of hip hop   **782.42**
Rape
Sebold, A. Lucky   **362.883**
Thornhill, R. A natural history of rape   **364.1**
The **rape** of Bunny Stuntz. Gurney, A. R.
In Gurney, A. R. Nine early plays, 1961-1973 p27-45   **812**
The **rape** of Nanking. Chang, I.   **951.04**
Raphael, 1483-1520
About
De Vecchi, P. Raphael   **759.5**
Raphael, Ray
A people's history of the American Revolution   **973.3**
Rare animals
See also Endangered species; Extinct animals
Ackerman, D. The rarest of the rare   **578.68**
Stuart, C. Africa's vanishing wildlife   **591.9**
Weidensaul, S. The ghost with trembling wings   **591.68**
Rare books
American book prices current   **018**
Bookman's price index   **018**
Rare earth. Ward, P. D.   **576.8**
Rare plants
See also Endangered species
The **rarest** of the rare. Ackerman, D.   **578.68**
Ras Tafari movement *See* Rastafari movement
Rashid, Ahmed
Taliban: militant Islam, oil, and fundamentalism in Central Asia   **958.1**
Râsles, Sébastien, 1657-1724
See/See also pages in the following book(s):
Williams, W. C. In the American grain p105-29   **814**
Rasmussen, R. Kent
Mark Twain A to Z   **818**

(ed) The African American encyclopedia. See The African American encyclopedia   **305.8**
(ed) Cyclopedia of literary places. See Cyclopedia of literary places   **809**
Rasputin, Grigoriĭ Efimovich, 1871-1916
See/See also pages in the following book(s):
Massie, R. K. Nicholas and Alexandra p180-203   **92**
Rastafari movement
Chevannes, B. Rastafari: roots and ideology   **299**
Kebra Nagast. The Kebra Nagast   **299**
Rastafari: roots and ideology. Chevannes, B.   **299**
Ratchnevsky, Paul
Genghis Khan: his life and legacy   **92**
Ratey, John J., 1948-
A user's guide to the brain   **612.8**
(jt. auth) Hallowell, E. M. Driven to distraction   **616.85**
Rath, Sara
The complete pig   **636.4**
Rathbone, Belinda
Walker Evans   **92**
Rather, Dan
The American dream   **973.92**
Rathmann, Peggy
See/See also pages in the following book(s):
The Newbery & Caldecott medal books, 1986-2000 p239-44   **028.5**
Rationalism
See also Enlightenment
Ratliff, Ben
Jazz: a critic's guide to the 100 most important recordings   **781.65**
Rattlesnakes
Rubio, M. Rattlesnake   **597.9**
Raup, David M.
Extinction   **560**
Ravago, Miguel
(jt. auth) Tausend, M. Cocina de la familia   **641.5**
Ravens
Heinrich, B. Mind of the raven   **598**
The **raw** and the cooked. Harrison, J.   **641.3**
RAWA *See* Revolutionary Association of the Women of Afghanistan
Rawlings, Marjorie Kinnan, 1896-1953
See/See also pages in the following book(s):
American women fiction writers   **813.009**
Ray, C. Claiborne
The New York Times second book of science questions and answers   **500**
Ray, James Earl, 1928-1998
About
Posner, G. L. Killing the dream   **364.1**
Ray, Man, 1890-1976
About
Lottman, H. R. Man Ray's Montparnasse   **92**
Raymo, Chet
An intimate look at the night sky   **520**
Razac, Olivier
Barbed wire   **323.4**
Rea, Tom, 1950-
Bone wars   **560**
Reaching for glory   **973.923**
Reaching up for manhood. Canada, G.   **305.23**
Reaction (Political science) *See* Right and left (Political science)
Read, Anthony
The fall of Berlin   **940.54**
The proudest day   **954.03**
Read, Piers Paul, 1941-
Alive   **910.4**
The Templars   **271**
The **read-aloud** handbook. Trelease, J.   **028.5**
Reader, John, 1937-
Africa: a biography of the continent   **960**

The **Reader's** adviser   **011**

The **readers'** advisory guide to genre fiction. Saricks, J. G.   **025.5**

Readers' advisory service in the public library. Saricks, J. G.   **025.5**

The **Reader's** companion to American history   **973.03**

The **Reader's** companion to the American presidency   **973**

A **Reader's** companion to the short story in English   **809.3**

Reader's Digest Association, Inc.
  Courtier, J. Indoor plants   **635.9**
  Foods that harm, foods that heal. See Foods that harm, foods that heal   **613.2**
  New complete do-it-yourself manual. See New complete do-it-yourself manual   **643**
  New fix-it-yourself manual. See New fix-it-yourself manual   **643**
  Weather. See Weather   **551.5**

Reader's Digest complete do-it-yourself manual. See New complete do-it-yourself manual   **643**

Reader's Digest complete guide to needlework   **746.4**

Reader's Digest complete guide to sewing. See New complete guide to sewing   **646.2**

Reader's digest complete guide to the Bible   **220.7**

Reader's Digest fix-it-yourself manual. See New fix-it-yourself manual   **643**

Reader's encyclopedia, Benét's   **803**

Reader's encyclopedia of American literature, HarperCollins   **810.3**

The **Reader's** encyclopedia of the American West. See The New encyclopedia of the American West   **978.03**

Reader's guide to Judaism   **296.03**

Reader's guide to military history   **355**

Readers' guide to periodical literature   **051**

Reader's guide to the history of science   **509**

Reading
  Adler, M. J. How to read a book   **028**
  Flesch, R. F. Why Johnny can't read—and what you can do about it   **372.4**
Phonetic method
  See also Phonetics

Reading & writing. Naipaul, V. S.   **92**

Reading Chekhov. Malcolm, J.   **891.7**

Reading interests of children See Children—Books and reading

Reading people. Dimitrius, J.-E.   **155.2**

Reading pictures. Manguel, A.   **750**

Reading the Holocaust. Clendinnen, I.   **940.53**

Reagan, Leslie J.
  When abortion was a crime   **363.46**

Reagan, Nancy, 1923-
About
  Edwards, A. The Reagans: portrait of a marriage   **92**

Reagan, Nelle Wilson
  See/See also pages in the following book(s):
  Angelo, B. First mothers   **920**

Reagan, Ronald, 1911-2004
  Reagan, in his own hand   **973.927**
About
  D'Souza, D. Ronald Reagan   **92**
  Edwards, A. The Reagans: portrait of a marriage   **92**
  FitzGerald, F. Way out there in the blue   **973.927**
  Johnson, H. B. Sleepwalking through history   **973.927**
  See/See also pages in the following book(s):
  Kissinger, H. Diplomacy p762-802   **327.73**
  Mann, J. About face   **327.73**
  Woodward, B. Shadow   **973.92**

Reagan, in his own hand. Reagan, R.   **973.927**

The **Reagans:** portrait of a marriage. Edwards, A.   **92**

Reagan's War. Schweizer, P.   **327.73**

A **real** American breakfast. Jamison, C. A.   **641.5**

Real beauty. Kashuk, S.   **646.7**

Real boys. Pollack, W. S.   **305.23**

Real boys' voices. Pollack, W. S.   **305.23**

Real estate
  See also Mortgages
  The American Bar Association guide to home ownership   **346.04**

Real estate business
  See also Houses—Buying and selling

The **real** Frank Zappa book. Zappa, F.   **92**

The **real** James Herriot. Wight, J.   **92**

The **real** Jesus. Johnson, L. T.   **232.9**

Real-life math. Glazer, E.   **510**

The **real** life of Laurence Olivier. Lewis, R.   **92**

The **real** war, 1914-1918. Liddell Hart, Sir B. H.   **940.4**

"The **Real** war will never get in the books"   **810.8**

Reality
  Davies, P. C. W. The matter myth   **530**
  Deutsch, D. The fabric of reality   **530**
  Gribbin, J. R. In search of Schrödinger's cat   **530.1**
  Gribbin, J. R. Schrödinger's kittens and the search for reality   **530.1**

Reason
  Kant, I. Critique of pure reason   **193**

Reason for hope. Goodall, J.   **92**

Reasoning
  See also Logic
  Spence, G. How to argue and win every time   **153.8**
  See/See also pages in the following book(s):
  Pinker, S. How the mind works p299-362   **153**

Reaven, Gerald M.
  Syndrome X   **616.1**

The **reawakening.** Levi, P.
  In Levi, P. Survival in Auschwitz; and The reawakening   **940.53**

The **rebel.** Camus, A.   **303.6**

Rebel hearts. Toolis, K.   **941.6**

Reber, Grote, 1911-2002
  See/See also pages in the following book(s):
  Malone, J. W. It doesn't take a rocket scientist   **920**

Rebora, Piero
  (comp) Cassell's Italian dictionary. See Cassell's Italian dictionary   **453**

Recchia, Zebu See Cotton, Eddy Joe

Recipes See Cooking

Recitations See Monologues

The **reckoning.** Mackey, S.   **956.7**

The **reckoning:** the murder of Christopher Marlowe. Nicholl, C.   **92**

Reclaiming the Dead Sea scrolls. Schiffman, L. H.   **296.1**

Recluses See Hermits

Recommended reference books for small and medium-sized libraries and media centers   **011**

Reconnaissance, Aerial See Aerial reconnaissance

Reconstruction (1865-1876)
  Foner, E. Reconstruction   **973.8**
  Franklin, J. H. Reconstruction after the Civil War   **973.8**
  Stampp, K. M. The era of reconstruction, 1865-1877   **973.8**

Reconstruction (1939-1951)
  Beschloss, M. R. The conquerors: Roosevelt, Truman, and the destruction of Hitler's Germany, 1941-1945   **940.53**

Reconstruction after the Civil War. Franklin, J. H.   **973.8**

Reconstructive and cosmetic surgery sourcebook
617.9
Recordings, Sound *See* Sound recordings
Recreation
See also Amusements
Recruiting library staff. Low, K.   **023**
Red azalea. Min, A.   **92**
Red Baron *See* Richthofen, Manfred von, Freiherr, 1892-1918
Red Cloud, Sioux Chief, 1822-1909
See/See also pages in the following book(s):
Brown, D. A. The American West p78-98   **978**
Brown, D. A. Bury my heart at Wounded Knee
970.004
Red-hot and righteous. Winston, D. H.   **287.9**
Red magic. Ghelderode, M. de
In Our dramatic heritage v6   **808.82**
Red: passion and patience in the desert. Williams, T. T.
333.7
The **Red** Rose girls. Carter, A. A.   **759.13**
Red scare. Fariello, G.   **973.92**
Red sky in mourning. Ashcraft, T. O.   **910.4**
Red Smith on baseball. Smith, R.   **796.357**
Red Sox (Baseball team) *See* Boston Red Sox (Baseball team)
Red, white, and greens. Willinger, F. H.   **641.6**
Redcoats and rebels. Hibbert, C.   **973.3**
Redding, Otis, 1941-1967
About
Freeman, S. Otis!: the Otis Redding story   **92**
Redesigning humans. Stock, G.   **176**
Redford, Donald B.
(ed) The Oxford encyclopedia of ancient Egypt. See The Oxford encyclopedia of ancient Egypt   **932**
Rediscovering Gandhi. See Chadha, Y. Gandhi   **92**
The **redress** of poetry. Heaney, S.   **821.009**
Reducing *See* Weight loss
Reed, Annette Gordon- *See* Gordon-Reed, Annette
Reed, Carol
Router joinery workshop   **684**
Reed, Gregory J.
(jt. auth) Parks, R. Quiet strength   **92**
Reed, James, 1944-
The black man's guide to good health   **613**
Reed, John, 1887-1920
Ten days that shook the world   **947.084**
Reed, Jonathan L.
(jt. auth) Crossan, J. D. Excavating Jesus   **225.9**
Reed, W. L.
(ed) National anthems of the world. See National anthems of the world   **782.42**
Rees, Alan M.
(ed) Consumer health information source book. See Consumer health information source book
016.613
Rees, Laurence, 1957-
War of the century   **940.54**
Rees, Martin J., 1942-
Just six numbers   **523.1**
Our cosmic habitat   **523.1**
Rees, Siân, 1965-
The floating brothel   **365**
Reese, Thomas J.
Inside the Vatican   **282**
Reeve, Christopher
Still me   **92**
Reeves, Bass
See/See also pages in the following book(s):
Abdul-Jabbar, K. Black profiles in courage p126-39
920
Reeves, Randall R.
National Audubon Society guide to marine mammals of the world. See National Audubon Society guide to marine mammals of the world   **599.5**

Reeves, Richard
President Kennedy   **92**
President Nixon   **92**
Reference books
Bibliography
American reference books annual   **011**
Guide to reference books   **011**
Katz, W. A. Introduction to reference work   **025.5**
The Reader's adviser   **011**
Recommended reference books for small and medium-sized libraries and media centers   **011**
Reference sources for small and medium-sized libraries
011
Reviews
Recommended reference books for small and medium-sized libraries and media centers   **011**
Reference Books Bulletin. See Booklist   **028.1**
Reference books for small and medium-sized libraries. See Reference sources for small and medium-sized libraries   **011**
The **reference** guide to famous engineering landmarks of the world. Berlow, L. H.   **620**
Reference guide to mystery and detective fiction. Bleiler, R.   **016.8**
Reference guide to Russian literature   **891.7**
Reference guide to science fiction, fantasy, and horror. Burgess, M.   **016.8**
Reference guide to world literature   **809**
Reference services (Libraries)
Katz, W. A. Introduction to reference work   **025.5**
Saricks, J. G. The readers' advisory guide to genre fiction   **025.5**
Saricks, J. G. Readers' advisory service in the public library   **025.5**
Sauers, M. Using the Internet as a reference tool
025.04
Reference shelf
The 21st century   **909.83**
Representative American speeches   **815.008**
See/See also pages in the following book(s):
Space exploration   **629**
Reference sources for small and medium-sized libraries
011
Referendum
Broder, D. S. Democracy derailed   **328.73**
Reflections. See MacLeish, A. Archibald MacLeish: reflections   **92**
Reflections and shadows. Steinberg, S.   **92**
Reflections in Black. Willis, D.   **770**
Reflections of an affirmative action baby. Carter, S. L.
342
Reflections of Eden. Galdikas, B.   **599.8**
Reflections on a ravaged century. Conquest, R.
909.82
Reflections on exile and other essays. Said, E. W.
814
Reflections on the Revolution in France. Burke, E.
944.04
Reformation
Bainton, R. H. Here I stand: a life of Martin Luther
92
Oberman, H. A. Luther: man between God and the Devil   **92**
Stark, R. For the glory of God   **291.1**
See/See also pages in the following book(s):
Tuchman, B. W. The march of folly   **909.08**
Refrigeration
See also Low temperatures
Refugees
Armour-Hileman, V. Singing to the dead   **261**
Pipher, M. B. The middle of everywhere   **325.73**
Refugees, Cuban *See* Cuban refugees
Refugees, Hungarian *See* Hungarian refugees
Refugees, Jewish *See* Jewish refugees
Refuges, Wildlife *See* Wildlife refuges

Regarding the pain of others. Sontag, S.   303.6
Regel, Pat, 1947-
  The houseplant survival guide   635.9
Reggae music
  Bradley, L. This is reggae music   781.646
Reginald, R., 1948-
  Science fiction and fantasy literature, 1975-1991
                                                     016.8
Regional planning
  Mumford, L. The culture of cities   307.7
The **rehearsal**. Buckingham, G. V., 2nd Duke of
  In Restoration plays   822.008
Rehnquist, William H.
  All the laws but one   342
Reich, Robert B.
  The future of success   306
  Locked in the cabinet   973.929
Reichhardt, Tony
  (ed) Space shuttle. See Space shuttle   629.45
Reichl, Ruth
  Comfort me with apples   92
Reichmann, Rosie, 1917-
  Ageless yoga   613.7
Reid, Constance
  From zero to infinity   512
Reid, Jane Davidson, 1918-
  The Oxford guide to classical mythology in the arts,
    1300-1990s   700
Reid, Lori
  The art of hand reading   133.6
Reilly, Edwin D.
  (ed) Encyclopedia of computer science. See Encyclope-
    dia of computer science   004
Reiman, Donald H.
  (ed) Shelley, P. B. Shelley's poetry and prose
                                                     821
Reinhold, Barbara Bailey
  Toxic work   650.1
Reinisch, June
  The Kinsey Institute new report on sex   306.7
Reinventing comics. McCloud, S.   741.5
Reinventing the bazaar. McMillan, J.   330.1
Reis, Ricardo *See* Pessoa, Fernando, 1888-1935
Reischauer, Edwin O. (Edwin Oldfather), 1910-1990
  Japan: the story of a nation   952
  Japan, tradition & transformation   952
  The Japanese today   952
  (jt. auth) Fairbank, J. K. China: tradition & transforma-
    tion   951
Reisner, Marc P.
  Cadillac desert   333.91
Rejwan, Nissim
  (ed) The Many faces of Islam. See The Many faces of
    Islam   297
The **relapse**. Vanbrugh, Sir J.
  In Restoration plays   822.008
Relations among ethnic groups *See* Ethnic relations
Relativity (Physics)
  Aczel, A. D. God's equation   523.1
  Barbour, J. B. The end of time   530.1
  Bjerknes, C. J. Albert Einstein   92
  Davies, P. C. W. About time   530.1
  Einstein, A. The evolution of physics   530
  Einstein, A. The meaning of relativity   530.1
  Fritzsch, H. An equation that changed the world
                                                     530.1
  Galison, P. L. Einstein's clocks and Poincaré's maps
                                                     529
  Kaku, M. Hyperspace   530.1
  Thorne, K. S. Black holes and time warps   530.1
  Wolfson, R. Simply Einstein   530.1
Religion
  See also Monotheism; Religious fundamentalism;
    Theology
  Bowker, J. World religions   200

Eerdmans' handbook to the world's religions   291
Eliade, M. A history of religious ideas   291
Turner, J. Without God, without creed   211
  See/See also pages in the following book(s):
Emerson, R. W. The portable Emerson p72-91
                                                     818
Sagan, C. Broca's brain p281-91, 308-11   500
Vonnegut, K. Palm Sunday p192-218   818
            Dictionaries
The Oxford dictionary of world religions   200.3
Rohmann, C. A world of ideas   103
            Encyclopedias
The Encyclopedia of religion   200.3
            Philosophy
Huxley, A. The perennial philosophy   210
James, W. The varieties of religious experience
                                                     210
            Social aspects
  See/See also pages in the following book(s):
Fromm, E. To have or to be? p133-67   302
Religion and art *See* Art and religion
Religion and philosophy *See* Philosophy and religion
Religion and politics
    See also Christianity and politics; Islam and poli-
      tics
Carter, S. L. God's name in vain   322
Djupe, P. A. Encyclopedia of American religion and
  politics   322
Juergensmeyer, M. Terror in the mind of God
                                                     291.1
Martin, W. C. With God on our side   261.8
Religion and science
  Barbour, I. G. When science meets religion   291.1
  Barlow, C. C. Green space, green time   291.1
  Barr, S. M. Modern physics and ancient faith
                                                     291.1
  Coles, R. The secular mind   291.1
  Davies, P. C. W. God and the new physics   261.5
  Deloria, V. Evolution, creationism, and other modern
    myths   291.1
  Feynman, R. P. The meaning of it all   500
  Gleiser, M. The prophet and the astronomer
                                                     523.1
  Gould, S. J. Rocks of ages   291.1
  The History of science and religion in the western tra-
    dition   291.1
  Jastrow, R. God and the astronomers   523.1
  Johnson, G. Fire in the mind   215
  Miller, K. R. Finding Darwin's God   231.7
  Noble, D. F. The religion of technology   261.5
  Pennock, R. T. Tower of Babel   576.8
  Schroeder, G. L. The hidden face of God   215
  Smith, H. Why religion matters   215
  Stark, R. For the glory of God   291.1
  Wilson, A. N. God's funeral   200.9
            Encyclopedias
Encyclopedia of science and religion   291.103
Religion and state *See* Church and state
Religion in America. Corrigan, J.   200.9
Religion in American life. Butler, J.   200.9
Religion in twentieth century America. Balmer, R. H.
                                                     200.9
The **religion** of technology. Noble, D. F.   261.5
Religions
    See also Gods and goddesses; Occultism; Sects
Bowker, J. World religions   200
The Cambridge illustrated history of religions
                                                     200.9
Eerdmans' handbook to the world's religions   291
Eliade, M. A history of religious ideas   291
Frazer, Sir J. G. The new golden bough   291.1
Hopfe, L. M. Religions of the world   291
The Illustrated guide to world religions   291
Miller, S. Finding hope when a child dies   291

Religions—*Continued*
Dictionaries
The Oxford dictionary of world religions   **200.3**
Encyclopedias
Merriam-Webster's encyclopedia of world religions
   200.3
Religions of the world   **291**
The **religions** of the American Indians. Hultkrantz, Å.
   299
Religions of the world   **291**
Religions of the world. Hopfe, L. M.   **291**
Religious art
   See also Christian art
Campbell, J. The power of myth   **291.1**
Religious belief *See* Faith
Religious biography
Hall, T. L. American religious leaders   **920.003**
Religious leaders of the world   **920.003**
Religious ceremonies *See* Rites and ceremonies
Religious cults *See* Cults
Religious fundamentalism
   See also Islamic fundamentalism
Armstrong, K. The battle for God   **291**
Encyclopedia of fundamentalism   **200.9**
Martin, W. C. With God on our side   **261.8**
Religious holidays
   See also Jewish holidays
Religious holidays and calendars   **291.3**
Religious holidays and calendars   **291.3**
Religious institutions
Directories
Yearbook of American and Canadian churches
   277
Religious leaders of the world   **920.003**
Religious life
   See/See also pages in the following book(s):
James, W. The varieties of religious experience
   210
Religious orders *See* Monasticism and religious orders
The **religious** right. Utter, G. H.   **277.3**
Relocation of Japanese Americans, 1942-1945 *See* Japanese Americans—Evacuation and relocation, 1942-1945
A **reluctant** tragic hero. Chekhov, A. P.
   In Chekhov, A. P. The plays of Anton Chekhov
p165-73   **891.7**
Remaking the world. Petroski, H.   **620**
Remarkable trees of the world. Pakenham, T.
   582.16
Remarriage
Gray, J. Mars and Venus starting over   **306.7**
Rembrandt Harmenszoon van Rijn, 1606-1669
About
Schama, S. Rembrandt's eyes   **92**
Rembrandt's eyes. Schama, S.   **92**
Remember laughter: a life of James Thurber. Grauer, N. A.   **92**
Remembered rapture. Hooks, B.   **808**
Remembering Jim Crow   **305.8**
Remembering slavery   **326**
Remembrances and celebrations   **808.8**
Remington, Frederic, 1861-1909
About
Dippie, B. W. The Frederic Remington Art Museum collection   **92**
Remini, Robert Vincent, 1921-
Andrew Jackson & his Indian wars   **973.5**
The Battle of New Orleans   **973.5**
Daniel Webster   **92**
John Quincy Adams   **92**
Joseph Smith   **92**
Reminiscing in tempo: a portrait of Duke Ellington. Nicholson, S.   **92**

Remnick, David
King of the world: Muhammad Ali and the rise of an American hero   **92**
Lenin's tomb   **947.085**
Resurrection   **947.086**
(ed) Life stories. See Life stories   **920**
Remote sensing
   See also Radar
Rempel, Gerhard
Hitler's children   **943.086**
Renaissance
Graham-Dixon, A. Renaissance   **709.02**
Herlihy, D. The black death and the transformation of the west   **940.1**
Johnson, P. The Renaissance   **940.2**
Manchester, W. A world lit only by fire   **940.2**
The Portable Renaissance reader   **808.8**
Dictionaries
Campbell, G. The Oxford dictionary of the Renaissance   **940.2**
Encyclopedias
Encyclopedia of the Renaissance   **940.2**
The **Renaissance**. Lee-Browne, P.
   In Backgrounds to English literature v1   **820.9**
Renaissance architecture *See* Architecture—15th and 16th centuries
Renaissance art *See* Art—15th and 16th centuries
A **Renaissance** in Harlem   **810.8**
The **Renaissance** philosophy of man   **189**
Renn, Kristen A.
(ed) Women in higher education. See Women in higher education   **378**
Rennie, Richard
(ed) The Facts on File dictionary of atomic and nuclear physics. See The Facts on File dictionary of atomic and nuclear physics   **539.7**
Renoir, Auguste, 1841-1919
About
Bailey, C. B. Renoir's portraits   **759.4**
Néret, G. Renoir: painter of happiness 1841-1919
   759.4
Renoir, J. Renoir: my father   **92**
Renoir, Jean, 1894-1979
Renoir: my father   **92**
Renoir: painter of happiness 1841-1919. Néret, G.
   759.4
Renoir's portraits. Bailey, C. B.   **759.4**
Renovation. Litchfield, M. W.   **643**
Rensberger, Boyce
Life itself   **571.6**
Renstrom, Peter G., 1943-
Constitutional rights sourcebook   **342**
Repair. Williams, C. K.   **811**
Repairing
Marken, B. How to fix (just about) everything
   640
New fix-it-yourself manual   **643**
Repairs *See* Repairing
Report from ground zero. Smith, D.   **363.34**
Report writing
Gibaldi, J. MLA handbook for writers of research papers   **808**
Turabian, K. L. A manual for writers of term papers, theses, and dissertations   **808**
Turabian, K. L. Student's guide for writing college papers   **808**
Reporters and reporting
   See also Journalism
Reporting Vietnam   **959.704**
Reporting World War II   **940.53**
Ross, L. Reporting back   **070.4**
A **reporter's** life. Cronkite, W.   **92**
Reporting back. Ross, L.   **070.4**
Reporting civil rights   **323.1**
Reporting Vietnam   **959.704**

Reporting World War II   940.53
Represent yourself in court. Bergman, P.   347
Representative American speeches   815.008
Representative government and representation
   Phillips, K. P. Wealth and democracy   305.5
Reproduction
   See also Genetics; Reproductive technology
Reproductive technology
   Clones and clones   174
   Flesh of my flesh   174
   Stock, G. Redesigning humans   176
Reptiles
   See also Snakes
   Conant, R. A field guide to reptiles & amphibians   597.9
   Firefly encyclopedia of reptiles and amphibians   597.9
   Stebbins, R. C. A field guide to Western reptiles and amphibians   597.9
   Tyning, T. F. A guide to amphibians and reptiles   597.9
The **republic**. Plato   888
   also in Plato. The portable Plato p281-696   888
Republic [abridgement] Plato
   In Plato. The dialogues of Plato p238-386   888
Republic of China, 1949- *See* Taiwan
Republic of dreams. Wetzsteon, R.   974.7
Request stop. Pinter, H.
   In Pinter, H. Complete works v2   822
Required reading   301
Rescue of Jews, 1939-1945 *See* World War, 1939-1945—Jews—Rescue
Rescue work
   Hill, A. J. Under pressure   910.4
   Krieger, M. J. All the men in the sea   910.4
Research
   See also Animal experimentation
Research paper writing *See* Report writing
The **researcher's** guide to American genealogy. Greenwood, V. D.   929
Residential construction *See* House construction
Resistance, rebellion, and death. Camus, A.   844
Resistance to government
   See also Passive resistance; Revolutions
   Benard, C. Veiled courage   958.1
   Stern, K. S. A force upon the plain   322.4
   Wills, G. A necessary evil   973
   See/See also pages in the following book(s):
   Dees, M. S., Jr. Gathering storm   322.4
Respect for acting. Hagen, U.   792
The **respectful** prostitute. Sartre, J. P.
   In Sartre, J. P. No exit, and three other plays   842
Respiration
   See also Respiratory system
Respiratory system
     Diseases
   Adams, F. V. The breathing disorders sourcebook   616.2
Respite care *See* Home care services
Restak, Richard M., 1942-
   Mozart's brain and the fighter pilot   612.8
   Mysteries of the mind   612.8
Restaurants
   Schlosser, E. Fast food nation   394.1
The **restless** sea. Kunzig, R.   551.46
Reston, James, Jr.
   The last apocalypse   940.1
Reston, James, 1909-1995
     About
   Stacks, J. F. Scotty: James B. Reston and the rise and fall of American journalism   92
Restoration. Will, G. F.   328.73

The **Restoration** and the eighteenth century
   In The Oxford anthology of English literature v1   820.8
Restoration plays   822.008
Restoring hope. West, C.   305.8
The **resume** handbook. Rosenberg, A. D.   650.14
Résumés (Employment)
   The Adams resume almanac   650.14
   Asher, D. The overnight résumé   650.14
   Enelow, W. S. Cover letter magic   650.14
   Fry, R. W. Your first resume   650.14
   Jackson, T. The new perfect resume   650.14
   McGraw-Hill's big red book of resumes   650.14
   Parker, Y. The damn good resume guide   650.14
   Resumes and cover letters that have worked   650.14
   Rosenberg, A. D. The resume handbook   650.14
   Wendleton, K. Building a great résumé   650.14
   Yate, M. J. Cover letters that knock 'em dead   650.14
   Yate, M. J. Resumes that knock 'em dead   650.14
Resumes and cover letters that have worked   650.14
Resumes that knock 'em dead. Yate, M. J.   650.14
Resurrection. Remnick, D.   947.086
Retail franchises *See* Franchises (Retail trade)
Retirement
   Facts about retiring in the United States   305.26
   Wolman, W. The great 401(k) hoax   332.024
Retirement communities
   Savageau, D. Retirement places rated   307.7
Retirement income
   See also 401(k) plan
Retirement places rated. Savageau, D.   307.7
Retiring right. Kaplan, L. J.   305.26
Return of the osprey. Gessner, D.   598
The **return** of the wolf to Yellowstone. McNamee, T.   599.77
Return to Midway. Ballard, R. D.   940.54
Return to paradise. Michener, J. A.   990
Reusable space vehicles *See* Space shuttles
Revenge. Blumenfeld, L. R.   956.94
Revere, Paul, 1735-1818
     About
   Fischer, D. H. Paul Revere's ride   973.3
Reverence. Woodruff, P.   170
Reverse acronyms, initialisms & abbreviations. See Acronyms, initialisms, & abbreviations dictionary   421.03
Reversible monuments   861
Reviewery. Ricks, C.   820.9
Revill, David, 1965-
   The roaring silence: John Cage, a life   92
The **revised** English Bible. Bible   220.5
Revivals
     Music
   See Gospel music
The **revolt** of the elites. Lasch, C.   306
The **revolt** of the masses. Ortega y Gasset, J.   909
Revolution, Industrial *See* Industrial revolution
Revolution from within. Steinem, G.   155.2
Revolutionary Association of the Women of Afghanistan
   Benard, C. Veiled courage   958.1
Revolutions
   Arendt, H. On revolution   303.6
   Camus, A. The rebel   303.6
Revuelta, Alina Fernández *See* Fernández Revuelta, Alina
Revuelta, Natica
   See/See also pages in the following book(s):
   Gimbel, W. Havana dreams   972.91
Revuelta, Naty, 1925-
     About
   Gimbel, W. Havana dreams   972.91
Rewards (Prizes, etc.) *See* Awards

Rewrites. Simon, N.   **92**

Rex appeal. Larson, P. L.   **567.9**

Rexroth, Kenneth, 1905-1982
The collected longer poems   **811**
Selected poems   **811**
(ed) One hundred poems from the Chinese. See One
hundred poems from the Chinese   **895.1**
(ed) One hundred poems from the Japanese. See One
hundred poems from the Japanese   **895.6**

Reyer, Ida See Pfeiffer, Ida, 1797-1858

Reynolds, David, 1952-
One world divisible   **909.82**

Reynolds, David West
Apollo: the epic journey to the moon   **629.45**

Reynolds, Glenn H.
(jt. auth) Morgan, P. W. The appearance of impropriety   **306**

Reynolds, Sir Joshua, 1723-1792
About
Wendorf, R. Sir Joshua Reynolds   **759.2**

Reynolds, Karina
(jt. auth) Lees, C. C. Pregnancy and birth   **618.2**

Reynolds, Michael S., 1937-2000
Hemingway   **92**

Reynolds, Moira Davison
American women scientists   **920**

Reynolds, Nancy, 1938-
No fixed points   **792.8**

Reynolds, Ross
Cambridge guide to the weather   **551.5**

Reynolds, Terry S.
(ed) Technology & American history. See Technology
& American history   **609**

Rhetoric
McMahan, E. The writer's handbook   **808**
Strunk, W. The elements of style   **808**
Zinsser, W. K. On writing well   **808**
Study and teaching
Zinsser, W. K. Writing to learn   **808**

Rhinoceros. Ionesco, E.
In Ionesco, E. Rhinoceros, and other plays   **842**
In Nine plays of the modern theater p471-572   **808.82**

Rhinoceros, and other plays. Ionesco, E.   **842**

Rhodes, Richard, 1937-
Dark sun   **623.4**
Deadly feasts   **614.5**
The making of the atomic bomb   **623.4**
Masters of death   **940.53**
Why they kill   **364.3**

Rhodesia, Southern See Zimbabwe

Rhyme
See also English language—Rhyme

Riasanovsky, Nicholas Valentine, 1923-
A history of Russia   **947**

Ricardo, David, 1772-1823
See/See also pages in the following book(s):
Heilbroner, R. L. The worldly philosophers   **330.1**

Rice, Graham
Discovering annuals   **635.9**

Rich, Adrienne
Arts of the possible   **818**
Blood, bread, and poetry   **814**
Collected early poems, 1950-1970   **811**
Fox   **811**
Midnight salvage   **811**

Rich, Buddy, 1917-1987
About
Tormé, M. Traps, the drum wonder: the life of Buddy
Rich   **92**

Rich, Doris L.
Amelia Earhart   **92**

Rich, Mari
World authors, 1995-2000. See World authors, 1995-
2000   **920.003**

(ed) World authors, 1995-2000. See World authors,
1995-2000   **920.003**

Rich, Ronda
My life in the pits   **796.72**

The **Richard** Rodgers reader   **92**

Richard Wright [critical essays]   **813.009**

Richard Wright's Native son   **813.009**

Richards, E. G. (Edward Graham)
Mapping time   **529**

Richards, Edward Graham See Richards, E. G. (Edward Graham)

Richards, James R., 1960-
ASPCA complete guide to cats   **636.8**

Richards, Phillip
Best literature by and about Blacks   **016.8**

Richards, Thomas, 1956-
The meaning of Star Trek   **791.45**

Richard's cork leg. Behan, B.
In Behan, B. The complete plays   **822**

Richardson, Bradley G.
Career comeback   **650.14**

Richardson, Brenda Lane, 1948-
What mama couldn't tell us about love   **158**

Richardson, John, 1924-
Sacred monsters   **920**
The sorcerer's apprentice   **92**

Richardson, John H., 1954-
In the little world   **599.9**

Richardson, Robert D., 1934-
Emerson   **92**

**Richelieu, Armand Jean du Plessis, Cardinal, duc de,
1585-1642**
About
Levi, A. Cardinal Richelieu and the making of France   **92**

Richelson, Jeffrey
The wizards of Langley   **327.12**

Richetti, John J.
(ed) The Columbia history of the British novel. See
The Columbia history of the British novel   **823.009**

Richman, Shira, 1972-
Raising a child with autism   **618.92**

Richmond (Va.)
History
Furgurson, E. B. Ashes of glory   **975.5**

Richter, Daniel K.
Facing east from Indian country   **970.004**

Richter, Gerhard
About
Storr, R. Gerhard Richter: forty years of painting   **759.3**

Richter, Sviatoslav, 1915-1997
See/See also pages in the following book(s):
Schonberg, H. C. The great pianists   **920**

Richthofen, Manfred von, Freiherr, 1892-1918
About
Kilduff, P. Richthofen   **92**

Rick Bayless's Mexican kitchen. Bayless, R.   **641.5**

Ricketts, Harry
Rudyard Kipling   **92**

Rickford, Russell John
Betty Shabazz: a remarkable story of survival and faith
before and after Malcolm X   **92**

Ricks, Christopher
Reviewery   **820.9**
(ed) The New Oxford book of Victorian verse. See
The New Oxford book of Victorian verse   **821.008**

The **riddle** and the knight. Milton, G.   **910.4**

The **riddle** of Amish culture. Kraybill, D. B.   **289.7**

The **riddle** of the compass. Aczel, A. D.   **912**

The **ride** together. Karasik, J.   **618.92**

Riders to the sea. Synge, J. M.
In Our dramatic heritage v5   **808.82**

In Synge, J. M. The complete plays 822
The **ridiculous** précieuses. Molière
 In Molière. Tartuffe, and other plays 842
Riding, Alan
 Distant neighbors 972.08
Riding *See* Horsemanship
Riding the iron rooster. Theroux, P. 915.1
Ridley, Jasper Godwin
 The Freemasons 366
Ridley, Matt
 Genome 599.93
Ridpath, Ian
 Stars and planets 520
Rieff, David
 A bed for the night 361.2
 Slaughterhouse 949.7
Riekehof, Lottie L.
 The joy of signing 419
Riemann, Bernhard *See* Riemann, Georg Friedrich Bernhard, 1826-1866
Riemann, Georg Friedrich Bernhard, 1826-1866
 See/See also pages in the following book(s):
 Bell, E. T. Men of mathematics p484-509 920
Riendeau, Roger E., 1950-
 A brief history of Canada 971
Rienzo, Cola di, ca. 1313-1354
 See/See also pages in the following book(s):
 Barzini, L. G. The Italians p117-32 945
Riera, Michael
 (jt. auth) Di Prisco, J. Field guide to the American teenager 305.23
Rifkin, Jeremy
 The biotech century 303.4
 The hydrogen economy 333.8
Rigden, John S.
 Hydrogen 546
 (ed) Building blocks of matter. See Building blocks of matter 539.7
 (ed) Macmillan encyclopedia of physics. See Macmillan encyclopedia of physics 530
Riggs, Thomas, 1963-
 (ed) St. James guide to Hispanic artists. See St. James guide to Hispanic artists 920.003
Right and left (Political science)
 Atkins, S. E. Encyclopedia of modern American extremists and extremist groups 322.4
Right- and left-handedness *See* Left- and right-handedness
Right of privacy
 Etzioni, A. The limits of privacy 323.44
 Gelman, R. B. Protecting yourself online 342
 Henderson, H. Privacy in the information age 323.44
 Whitaker, R. The end of privacy 303.4
The **right** stuff. Wolfe, T. 629.45
Right to choose movement *See* Pro-choice movement
Right to die
 See also Euthanasia
 Filene, P. G. In the arms of others 179.7
 Humphry, D. Final exit 179.7
 Humphry, D. Freedom to die 179.7
 Peck, M. S. Denial of the soul 179.7
Right to know *See* Freedom of information
Righteous victims. Morris, B. 956
Rights, Civil *See* Civil rights
Rights, Human *See* Human rights
Rights of animals *See* Animal rights
The **rights** of employees. See Outten, W. N. The rights of employees and union members 344
The **rights** of employees and union members. Outten, W. N. 344
The **rights** of government employees. See O'Neil, R. M. The rights of public employees 342
The **rights** of man. Paine, T. 320

The **rights** of people who are HIV positive. Rubenstein, W. B. 344
The **rights** of public employees. O'Neil, R. M. 342
The **rights** of racial minorities. McDonald, L. 342
The **rights** of union members. See Outten, W. N. The rights of employees and union members 344
The **Rights** of women 346.01
Riha, John
 Deck & patio planner 643
Rikers Island Prison (New York, N.Y.)
 Wynn, J. Inside Rikers 365
Riley, Charles A.
 The art of Peter Max 760
Riley, Glenda, 1938-
 The life and legacy of Annie Oakley 92
Riley, Gregory J. (Gregory John), 1947-
 The river of God 270
Riley-Smith, Jonathan
 (ed) The Oxford illustrated history of the Crusades. See The Oxford illustrated history of the Crusades 909.07
Rilke, Rainer Maria, 1875-1926
 Diaries of a young poet 92
 Duino elegies 831
 In Simon, J. I. Dreamers of dreams 809.1
 New poems 831
 Rilke on love and other difficulties 838
 Sonnets to Orpheus 831
 Uncollected poems 831
 See/See also pages in the following book(s):
 Gass, W. H. Tests of time p295-319 814
Rilke on love and other difficulties. Rilke, R. M. 838
Rimbaud, Arthur, 1854-1891
 Arthur Rimbaud: complete works 848
 Complete works, selected letters 848
 The drunken boat
  In Rimbaud, A. A season in hell & The drunken boat p92-103 841
 Illuminations, and other prose poems 841
 A season in hell & The drunken boat 841
 See/See also pages in the following book(s):
 Simon, J. I. Dreamers of dreams 809.1
Rimbaud, Jean Nicolas Arthur *See* Rimbaud, Arthur, 1854-1891
The **rime** of the ancient mariner. Coleridge, S. T.
 In Coleridge, S. T. The portable Coleridge 828
Rinehart, Mary Roberts, 1876-1958
 See/See also pages in the following book(s):
 American women fiction writers 813.009
Ring of fire: the Johnny Cash reader 92
Ringling Bros.-Barnum & Bailey Combined Shows, Inc.
 O'Nan, S. The circus fire 974.6
Rinzler, Carol Ann
 The new complete book of food 641.3
 The new complete book of herbs, spices, and condiments 641.3
Riordan, James
 Break on through: the life and death of Jim Morrison 92
Ríos, Alberto
 The smallest muscle in the human body 811
Riot and remembrance. Hirsch, J. S. 976.6
Riots
 Cannon, L. Official negligence 979.4
 Hirsch, J. S. Riot and remembrance 976.6
 Madigan, T. The burning 976.6
Ripken, Cal, Jr.
 See/See also pages in the following book(s):
 Will, G. F. Men at work: the craft of baseball p231-91 796.357
The **rise** and fall of the American teenager. Hine, T. 305.23

The **rise** and fall of the British Empire. James, L.
909
The **rise** and fall of the great powers. Kennedy, P. M.
909.08
The **rise** and fall of the House of Medici. See Hibbert, C. The House of Medici
The **rise** and fall of the third chimpanzee. See Diamond, J. M. The third chimpanzee 599.93
The **rise** and fall of the Third Reich. Shirer, W. L.
943.086
The **rise,** corruption, and coming fall of the House of Saud. Aburish, S. K. 953.8
The **rise** of modern China. Hsü, I. C.-Y. 951
The **rise** of modern Japan. Beasley, W. G. 952
The **rise** of modern paganism. Gay, P.
In Gay, P. The Enlightenment: an interpretation v1
190
The **rise** of Theodore Roosevelt. Morris, E. 92
Rising tide. Barry, J. M. 977
Rising Venus. Cherry, K. 811
Ritalin
DeGrandpre, R. J. Ritalin nation 618.92
Diller, L. H. Running on Ritalin 920
Stein, D. B. Ritalin is not the answer 618.92
Ritalin is not the answer. Stein, D. B. 618.92
Ritalin nation. DeGrandpre, R. J. 618.92
Ritchie, David, 1952-
Encyclopedia of earthquakes and volcanoes 551.2
Shipwrecks 910.4
Ritchie, Donald A.
(ed) The Oxford guide to the United States Government. See The Oxford guide to the United States Government 320.03
Rites and ceremonies
See also Catholic Church—Liturgy; Circumcision
How to be a perfect stranger 291.3
Ritter, Charles F., 1937-
(ed) Leaders of the American Civil War. See Leaders of the American Civil War 920.003
Ritter, Lawrence S.
The glory of their times 920
Ritter, R. M.
(ed) The Oxford dictionary for writers and editors. See The Oxford dictionary for writers and editors
428
Ritter, Robert M. *See* Ritter, R. M.
Rittner, Don
A to Z of scientists in weather and climate
920.003
Ritual *See* Rites and ceremonies
Ritz, David
(jt. auth) James, E. Rage to survive: the Etta James story 92
(jt. auth) King, B. B. Blues all around me 92
Riva, Maria
Marlene Dietrich 92
Rivard, Ken, 1947-
(jt. auth) Adams, J. In the hands of a chef 641.5
River. Fletcher, C. 917.91
The **river** at the center of the world. Winchester, S.
951
River horse. Heat Moon, W. L. 917.3
A **river** lost. Harden, B. 979.7
The **river** of God. Riley, G. J. 270
River of shadows. Solnit, R. 778.5
River out of Eden. Dawkins, R. 576
River town. Hessler, P. 951
Rivera, Diego, 1886-1957
About
Hamill, P. Diego Rivera 92
Marnham, P. Dreaming with his eyes open: a life of Diego Rivera 92
Rivera, Frida Kahlo *See* Kahlo, Frida, 1907-1954

Rivers
See also Colorado River (Colo.-Mexico); Columbia River; Mekong River
Rivers of blood, rivers of gold. Cocker, M. 909
A **river's** tale. Gargan, E. A. 915.9
The **Riverside** Milton. Milton, J. 821
Rix, Martyn
(jt. auth) Phillips, R. Annuals and biennials 635.9
RJR Nabisco Inc.
Burrough, B. Barbarians at the gate: the fall of RJR Nabisco 338.8
Roach, Mary
Stiff 611
The **road** less traveled. Peck, M. S. 158
The **road** less traveled and beyond. Peck, M. S.
158
Road maps
Rand McNally road atlas 912
The **road** to Stockholm. Hargittai, I. 509
The **road** to Verdun. Ousby, I. 940.4
The **road** to war. Overy, R. J. 940.53
Roads
McMurtry, L. Roads 917.3
The **roads** have come to an end now. Jacobsen, R.
839.8
The **roads** to home. Foote, H.
In Foote, H. Collected plays v2 p171-216 812
A **roadside** dog. Miłosz, C. 891.8
Roan, Sharon
Our daughters' health 613
Roanoke Island (N.C.)
History
Noël Hume, I. The Virginia adventure 975.5
The **roaring** silence: John Cage, a life. Revill, D.
92
Roark, Laurelee
(jt. auth) Normandi, C. E. It's not about food
616.85
Roasting. Kafka, B. 641.7
Robb, Graham
Balzac 92
Robb, Peter
M: the man who became Caravaggio 92
Midnight in Sicily 945
Robbins, Chandler S., 1918-
Birds of North America 598
Robert, Henry Martyn, 1837-1923
Robert's rules of order 060.4
Robert, Sarah Corbin
(ed) Robert, H. M. Robert's rules of order 060.4
Robert Browning's poetry. Browning, R. 821
Robert Kennedy and his times. Schlesinger, A. M.
92
Roberts, Cokie
We are our mothers' daughters 305.4
Roberts, David, 1943-
In search of the old ones 970.004
Once they moved like the wind 970.004
(ed) Points unknown. See Points unknown 910
Roberts, Elizabeth Madox, 1881-1941
See/See also pages in the following book(s):
American women fiction writers 813.009
Roberts, Gillian
You can write a mystery 808.3
Roberts, J. M. (John Morris), 1928-2003
The new history of the world 909
Twentieth century 909.82
Roberts, Jane, 1949-
Royal landscape 942
Roberts, John Morris *See* Roberts, J. M. (John Morris), 1928-2003
Roberts, Michael, 1949-
Parisian home cooking 641.5

Roberts, Molly Manning
(ed) Blackwell complementary and alternative medicine. See Blackwell complementary and alternative medicine   **615.5**
Roberts, Ralph, 1945-
Genealogy via the Internet   **929**
Robert's rules of order. Robert, H. M.   **060.4**
Robert's rules of order, Webster's New World   **060.4**
Robertson-Lorant, Laurie, 1940-
Melville   **92**
Robeson, Paul, Jr.
The undiscovered Paul Robeson   **92**
Robeson, Paul, 1898-1976
Here I stand   **305.8**
About
Robeson, P., Jr. The undiscovered Paul Robeson   **92**

See/See also pages in the following book(s):
Russell, D. Black genius and the American experience   **920**
Robey, David
(ed) The Oxford companion to Italian literature. See The Oxford companion to Italian literature   **850.3**
Robins, Gay
The art of ancient Egypt   **709.32**
Robinson, Charles M., 1949-
The men who wear the star   **976.4**
Robinson, Cyril Edward, b. 1884
Everyday life in ancient Greece   **938**
Robinson, Edwin Arlington, 1869-1935
See/See also pages in the following book(s):
Pritchard, W. H. Lives of the modern poets p83-107   **821.009**
Robinson, Francis
(ed) The Cambridge illustrated history of the Islamic world. See The Cambridge illustrated history of the Islamic world   **909**
Robinson, George
Essential Judaism   **296**
Robinson, Jackie, 1919-1972
About
Falkner, D. Great time coming: the life of Jackie Robinson, from baseball to Birmingham   **92**
Tygiel, J. Baseball's great experiment   **796.357**
Robinson, Maggie Greenwood- *See* Greenwood-Robinson, Maggie
Robinson, Peter, 1938-
The American Horticultural Society complete guide to water gardening   **635.9**
Robinson, Ray, 1920-
American original: a life of Will Rogers   **92**
Iron horse: Lou Gehrig in his time   **92**
Rockne of Notre Dame   **92**
Yankee Stadium   **796.357**
Robinson, Richard, 1956-
(ed) Genetics. See Genetics   **576**
Robinson, Roxana
Georgia O'Keeffe: a life   **92**
Robo sapiens: evolution of a new species. Menzel, P.   **629.8**
Robot builder's sourcebook. McComb, G.   **629.8**
Robot building for beginners. Cook, D.   **629.8**
Robot evolution. Rosheim, M. E.   **629.8**
Robotics *See* Robots
Robots
Brooks, R. A. Flesh and machines   **629.8**
McComb, G. Robot builder's sourcebook   **629.8**
Menzel, P. Robo sapiens: evolution of a new species   **629.8**
Moravec, H. P. Robot   **629.8**
Rosheim, M. E. Robot evolution   **629.8**
Wood, G. Edison's Eve   **629.8**

Design and construction
Cook, D. Robot building for beginners   **629.8**
Rocco, Fiammetta
The miraculous fever tree   **616.9**
Rock and roll music *See* Rock music
Rock drawings, paintings, and engravings
See/See also pages in the following book(s):
Schobinger, J. The ancient Americans   **970.01**
Rock Harbor. Phillips, C.   **811**
Rock music
Miller, J. Flowers in the dustbin   **781.66**
The Rolling Stone illustrated history of rock & roll   **781.66**
Discography
Strong, M. C. The great rock discography   **781.66**
Rock paintings *See* Rock drawings, paintings, and engravings
Rockefeller, David, 1915-
Memoirs   **92**
Rockefeller, John D. (John Davison), 1839-1937
About
Chernow, R. Titan: the life of John D. Rockefeller, Sr.   **92**

See/See also pages in the following book(s):
Klein, M. The change makers   **920**
Rocket boys. Hickam, H. H.   **92**
Rocketry
Weil, E. They all laughed at Christopher Columbus   **621.43**
Rockets, Atomic powered *See* Nuclear rockets
Rockets (Aeronautics)
See also Nuclear rockets
Models
Stine, G. H. Handbook of model rocketry   **629.47**
Rockne, Knute, 1888-1931
About
Robinson, R. Rockne of Notre Dame   **92**
Rockne of Notre Dame. Robinson, R.   **92**
Rocks
Chesterman, C. W. The Audubon Society field guide to North American rocks and minerals   **549**
Pellant, C. Rocks and minerals   **549**
Pough, F. H. A field guide to rocks and minerals   **549**
Simon and Schuster's guide to rocks and minerals   **549**
Rocks and minerals. Pellant, C.   **549**
Rocks from space. Norton, O. R.   **523.5**
Rocks of ages. Gould, S. J.   **291.1**
Rockwell, Norman, 1894-1978
About
Claridge, L. P. Norman Rockwell   **92**
Hennessey, M. H. Norman Rockwell   **759.13**
Marling, K. A. Norman Rockwell   **759.13**
Rocky Mountains. Elias, S. A.   **508**
Rodale organic gardening solutions. Long, C.   **635**
Rodale's all-new encyclopedia of organic gardening   **635**
Rodale's encyclopedia of organic gardening. See Rodale's all-new encyclopedia of organic gardening   **635**
Rodale's illustrated encyclopedia of herbs   **635**
Rodale's illustrated encyclopedia of organic gardening   **635.9**
Rodale's illustrated encyclopedia of perennials. Phillips, E.   **635.9**
Roden, Claudia
The new book of Middle Eastern food   **641.5**
Rodenbeck, Max, 1962-
Cairo   **962**
Rodenburg, Patsy
Speaking Shakespeare   **792**
Rodeos
See/See also pages in the following book(s):
Brown, D. A. The American West p377-89   **978**

Rodgers, Carolyn M., 1945-
See/See also pages in the following book(s):
Black women writers (1950-1980)   **810.9**
Rodgers, Richard, 1902-1979
About
Mordden, E. Rodgers & Hammerstein   **792.6**
The Richard Rodgers reader   **92**
Secrest, M. Somewhere for me: a biography of Richard
Rodgers   **92**
See/See also pages in the following book(s):
Green, S. The world of musical comedy   **920**
Rodgers & Hammerstein. Mordden, E.   **792.6**
Rodriguez, Junius P.
(ed) The Louisiana Purchase. See The Louisiana Purchase   **973.4**
Rodriguez, Richard, 1944-
Brown: the last discovery of America   **305.8**
Hunger of memory   **92**
Roe, Jane *See* McCorvey, Norma
Roe, Sue, 1956-
Gwen John   **92**
Roe v. Wade
Hull, N. E. H. Roe v. Wade   **344**
Weddington, S. R. A question of choice   **363.46**
Roentgen, Wilhelm Conrad *See* Röntgen, Wilhelm
Conrad, 1845-1923
Roesch, Roberta
The encyclopedia of depression   **616.85**
Roesdahl, Else
The Vikings   **948**
Roethke, Theodore, 1908-1963
The collected poems of Theodore Roethke   **811**
Roger Ebert's book of film   **791.43**
Roger Ebert's movie home companion. See Ebert, R.
Roger Ebert's movie yearbook   **791.43**
Roger Ebert's movie yearbook. Ebert, R.   **791.43**
Roger Ebert's video companion. See Ebert, R. Roger
Ebert's movie yearbook   **791.43**
Rogers, Carl R. (Carl Ransom), 1902-1987
On becoming a person   **616.89**
A way of being   **150.19**
Rogers, Katharine M.
L. Frank Baum, creator of Oz   **92**
Rogers, Pat
(ed) The Oxford illustrated history of English literature. See The Oxford illustrated history of English
literature   **820.9**
Rogers, Will, 1879-1935
About
Robinson, R. American original: a life of Will Rogers   **92**
Yagoda, B. Will Rogers   **92**
Rogerson, John
(ed) The Oxford illustrated history of the Bible. See
The Oxford illustrated history of the Bible   **220**
Roget's 21st century thesaurus in dictionary form.
Kipfer, B. A.   **423**
Roget's international thesaurus   **423**
Roget's thesaurus in dictionary form, The Doubleday   **423**
Roghaar, Linda
KnitLit: sweaters and their stories and other writing
about knitting. See KnitLit: sweaters and their stories
and other writing about knitting   **746.43**
Rohde, David
Endgame   **949.7**
Rohmann, Chris
A world of ideas   **103**
(jt. auth) Reid, J. D. The Oxford guide to classical mythology in the arts, 1300-1990s   **700**
Roiphe, Anne Richardson, 1935-
1185 Park Avenue   **92**
Married   **306.8**
Roland, Chanson de *See* Chanson de Roland

Roland (Legendary character)
Poetry
Chanson de Roland. The song of Roland   **841**
Rolle, Richard, of Hampole, 1290?-1349
About
Armstrong, K. Visions of God   **248.2**
The **Rolling** Stone illustrated history of rock & roll   **781.66**
Rolling Stones
Davis, S. Old gods almost dead: the 40-year odyssey
of the Rolling Stones   **920**
Rollyson, Carl E. (Carl Edmund)
Critical survey of drama. See Critical survey of drama   **809.2**
Encyclopedia of American literature. See Encyclopedia
of American literature   **810.3**
Susan Sontag   **92**
Roman Catholic Church *See* Catholic Church
Roman Catholicism in America. Gillis, C.   **282**
Roman de la Rose
Romaunt of the rose
In Chaucer, G. The complete poetry and prose of
Geoffrey Chaucer   **821**
Roman de Roncevaux *See* Chanson de Roland
Roman emperors *See* Emperors—Rome
Roman Empire *See* Rome
Roman mythology *See* Classical mythology
The **Roman** poets   **871.008**
The **Roman** way. Hamilton, E.   **870.9**
Romance fiction. Ramsdell, K.   **016.8**
Romance novels *See* Love stories
Romance of the Rose *See* Roman de la Rose
The **romance** of Tristan and Isolt. Tristan   **841**
The **romance** readers' advisory. Bouricius, A.   **016.8**
Romand, Jean-Claude, 1954-
About
Carrère, E. The adversary   **364.1**
Romanov, Nikolaï *See* Nicholas II, Emperor of Russia,
1868-1918
Romanov, House of *See* House of Romanov
The **Romanovs**. Massie, R. K.   **947.08**
The **romantic** generation. Rosen, C.   **780.9**
Romantic poetry and prose
In The Oxford anthology of English literature v2   **820.8**
Romanticism
Berlin, Sir I. The roots of romanticism   **141**
Romanticism, 1830-1890
In New Oxford history of music v9   **780.9**
The **romantics**. King, N.
In Backgrounds to English literature v2   **820.9**
Rombauer, Irma von Starkloff, 1877-1962
Joy of cooking   **641.5**
Romberg, Sigmund, 1887-1951
See/See also pages in the following book(s):
Green, S. The world of musical comedy   **920**
Rome, Harold, 1908-1993
See/See also pages in the following book(s):
Green, S. The world of musical comedy   **920**
Rome
Biography
Plutarch. Plutarch: the lives of the noble Grecians and
Romans   **920**
Civilization
Connolly, P. The ancient city   **937**
Hamilton, E. The Roman way   **870.9**
See/See also pages in the following book(s):
Russell, B. A history of Western philosophy p270-83   **109**
History
Caesar, J. The Gallic War   **878**
Everitt, A. Cicero   **92**
Gibbon, E. The decline and fall of the Roman Empire   **937**

Rome—History—*Continued*

Grant, M. Collapse and recovery of the Roman Empire
937

The Oxford history of the Roman world 937

Suetonius Tranquillus, C. The twelve Caesars 878

Tacitus, C. The complete works of Tacitus 878

See/See also pages in the following book(s):

Potok, C. Wanderings p203-21 909

History—Encyclopedias

Bunson, M. Encyclopedia of the Roman Empire
937

Poetry

The Roman poets 871.008

Rome (Italy)

Social life and customs

Downie, D. Cooking the Roman way 641.5

Epstein, A. As the Romans do 945

Rommel, Erwin, 1891-1944

About

Fraser, D. Knight's cross: a life of Field Marshal
Erwin Rommel 92

Romulus the great. Dürrenmatt, F.

In Dürrenmatt, F. Plays and essays p1-69 838

Roncalli, Angelo Giuseppe *See* John XXIII, Pope, 1881-1963

Ronson, Jon, 1967-

Them: adventures with extremists 322.4

Röntgen, Wilhelm Conrad, 1845-1923

See/See also pages in the following book(s):

Friedman, M. Medicine's 10 greatest discoveries
610.9

Ronzio, Robert A.

The encyclopedia of nutrition and good health
613.2

Roof, Wade Clark

(ed) Contemporary American religion. See Contemporary American religion 200.9

Roofing instant answers. Kennedy, T. 695

Roofing: the best of Fine homebuilding 643

Roofs

Kennedy, T. Roofing instant answers 695

Maintenance and repair

Roofing: the best of Fine homebuilding 643

Room, Adrian

Dictionary of first names 929.4

(comp) Brewer's dictionary of modern phrase & fable.
See Brewer's dictionary of modern phrase & fable
803

(ed) Brewer's dictionary of phrase and fable. See
Brewer's dictionary of phrase and fable 803

(ed) Dictionary of confusable words. See Dictionary of
confusable words 423

The **room**. Pinter, H.

In Pinter, H. Complete works v1 822

The **roominghouse** madrigals. Bukowski, C. 811

Rooney, Andrew A.

My war 92

Sincerely, Andy Rooney 818

Rooney, Andy *See* Rooney, Andrew A.

Roosevelt, Corinne

See/See also pages in the following book(s):

Caroli, B. B. The Roosevelt women 920

Roosevelt, Edith Kermit Carow, 1861-1948

See/See also pages in the following book(s):

Caroli, B. B. The Roosevelt women 920

Roosevelt, Eleanor, 1884-1962

About

Burns, J. M. The three Roosevelts 973.91

Cook, B. W. Eleanor Roosevelt 92

Donn, L. The Roosevelt cousins 920

The Eleanor Roosevelt encyclopedia 92

Goodwin, D. K. No ordinary time 92

Gurewitsch, E. Kindred souls: the friendship of Eleanor Roosevelt and David Gurewitsch 92

See/See also pages in the following book(s):

Caroli, B. B. The Roosevelt women 920

Galbraith, J. K. Name-dropping 973.9

Ware, S. Letter to the world 920

Wills, G. Certain trumpets p53-66 303.3

Roosevelt, Franklin D. (Franklin Delano), 1882-1945

About

Beschloss, M. R. The conquerors: Roosevelt, Truman, and the destruction of Hitler's Germany, 1941-1945
940.53

Black, C. M. Franklin Delano Roosevelt: champion of
freedom 92

Burns, J. M. The three Roosevelts 973.91

Davis, K. S. FDR, into the storm, 1937-1940 92

Donn, L. The Roosevelt cousins 920

Fried, A. F.D.R. and his enemies 92

Goodwin, D. K. No ordinary time 92

Leuchtenburg, W. E. Franklin D. Roosevelt and the
New Deal, 1932-1940 973.917

Persico, J. E. Roosevelt's secret war 940.54

Schlesinger, A. M. The coming of the New Deal,
1933-1935 973.917

Schlesinger, A. M. The crisis of the old order, 1919-
1933 973.91

Schlesinger, A. M. The politics of upheaval, 1935-
1936 973.917

Stafford, D. Roosevelt and Churchill 940.54

Stinnett, R. B. Day of deceit 940.54

See/See also pages in the following book(s):

Caroli, B. B. The Roosevelt women 920

Galbraith, J. K. Name-dropping 973.9

Hofstadter, R. The American political tradition, and the
men who made it p311-47 973

Kissinger, H. Diplomacy p369-422 327.73

Wills, G. Certain trumpets p23-34 303.3

Roosevelt, Sara Delano

See/See also pages in the following book(s):

Angelo, B. First mothers 920

Roosevelt, Theodore, 1858-1919

About

Burns, J. M. The three Roosevelts 973.91

Cooper, J. M. The warrior and the priest: Woodrow
Wilson and Theodore Roosevelt 92

Dalton, K. Theodore Roosevelt 92

Donn, L. The Roosevelt cousins 920

McCullough, D. G. Mornings on horseback 92

Morris, E. The rise of Theodore Roosevelt 92

Morris, E. Theodore Rex 92

See/See also pages in the following book(s):

Caroli, B. B. The Roosevelt women 920

Hofstadter, R. The American political tradition, and the
men who made it p203-33 973

Kissinger, H. Diplomacy p29-55 327.73

McCullough, D. G. The path between the seas
972.87

Zimmermann, W. First great triumph 973

Roosevelt and Churchill. Stafford, D. 940.54

The **Roosevelt** cousins. Donn, L. 920

Roosevelt family

About

Caroli, B. B. The Roosevelt women 920

Collier, P. The Roosevelts 920

Donn, L. The Roosevelt cousins 920

McCullough, D. G. Mornings on horseback 92

The **Roosevelt** women. Caroli, B. B. 920

The **Roosevelts**. Collier, P. 920

Roosevelt's secret war. Persico, J. E. 940.54

Root, Benjamin A., Jr.

Understanding panic and other anxiety disorders
616.85

Root, Elihu, 1845-1937

See/See also pages in the following book(s):

Zimmermann, W. First great triumph 973

Roots. Haley, A. 920

The **roots** of romanticism. Berlin, Sir I. 141

Rope
See/See also pages in the following book(s):
Pawson, D. The handbook of knots   **623.88**
Rosa Lee. Dash, L.   **305.8**
Rosalind Franklin: the dark lady of DNA. Maddox, B.
          92
Rose, Carol, 1943-
Giants, monsters, and dragons   **398.03**
Rose, June, 1926-
Demons and angels: a life of Jacob Epstein   **92**
Rose, M. J.
How to publish and promote online   **070.5**
Rose, Michael R. (Michael Robertson), 1955-
Darwin's spectre   **576.8**
Rose, Tricia
Black noise   **781.64**
Rose, Wendy
See/See also pages in the following book(s):
Coltelli, L. Winged words: American Indian writers
speak   **897**
Roseanne *See* Barr, Roseanne
Rosebud: the story of Orson Welles. Thomson, D.
          92
Rosen, Charles, 1927-
The classical style   **780.9**
Piano notes   **786.2**
The romantic generation   **780.9**
Rosen, Michael J., 1954-
(ed) Mirth of a nation. See Mirth of a nation
          817
Rosen, Philip, 1928-
(jt. auth) Epstein, E. J. Dictionary of the Holocaust
          940.53
Rosen, Ruth
The world split open   **305.4**
Rosen, Stanley, 1929-
(ed) The Examined life. See The Examined life
          190
Rosen, Winifred, 1943-
(jt. auth) Weil, A. From chocolate to morphine
          616.86
Rosenbaum, Ron
Explaining Hitler   **92**
Rosenberg, Arthur D.
The resume handbook   **650.14**
Rosenberg, David
(tr) Bible. O.T. Pentateuch. The book of J   **222**
Rosenberg, Ethel, 1915-1953
See/See also pages in the following book(s):
Rhodes, R. Dark sun   **623.4**
Rosenberg, Julius, 1918-1953
See/See also pages in the following book(s):
Rhodes, R. Dark sun   **623.4**
Rosenberg, Samuel J.
(jt. auth) Freedman, M. R. Living well with asthma
          616.2
Rosenberg, Tina
The haunted land   **947**
Rosenblum, Robert
Paintings in the Musée d'Orsay   **708**
Rosencrantz and Guildenstern are dead. Stoppard, T.
          822
also in Nine plays of the modern theater p673-790
          808.82
Rosenfeld, Alvin A.
Hyper-parenting   **649**
Rosenstein, Ann, 1958-
Water exercises for Parkinson's   **616.8**
Rosenthal, Joe, 1911-
About
Bradley, J. Flags of our fathers   **940.54**
Rosenthal, Joel Thomas, 1934-
(ed) Medieval England. See Medieval England
          942

Rosenzveig, Charles H.
The World reacts to the Holocaust. See The World re-
acts to the Holocaust   **940.53**
Roses, Lorraine Elena, 1943-
Harlem Renaissance and beyond: literary biographies
of 100 black women writers, 1900-1945   **810.9**
Roses
Cox, J. Landscape with roses   **635.9**
Ondra, N. J. Taylor's guide to roses   **635.9**
Rosetta stone inscription
See/See also pages in the following book(s):
Ceram, C. W. Gods, graves, and scholars p88-98
          930.1
Rosh ha-Shanah
See/See also pages in the following book(s):
Strassfeld, M. The Jewish holidays p95-109   **296.4**
Rosheim, Mark E.
Robot evolution   **629.8**
Rosmersholm. Ibsen, H.
In Ibsen, H. The complete major prose plays p491-
585   **839.8**
In Ibsen, H. Ibsen: four plays, v2   **839.8**
Rosner, David, 1947-
(jt. auth) Markowitz, G. E. Deceit and denial
          615.9
Rosner, Lisa
(ed) The Chronology of science. See The Chronology
of science   **509**
Ross, Alicia
(jt. auth) Mills, B. Desperation entertaining   **642**
Ross, Clifford, 1952-
The world of Edward Gorey   **92**
Ross, Edmund Gibson, 1826-1907
See/See also pages in the following book(s):
Kennedy, J. F. Profiles in courage   **920**
Ross, Elisabeth Kübler- *See* Kübler-Ross, Elisabeth
Ross, James Bruce, 1902-
(ed) The Portable medieval reader. See The Portable
medieval reader   **808.8**
(ed) The Portable Renaissance reader. See The Portable
Renaissance reader   **808.8**
Ross, John
Adoptable dog   **636.7**
Ross, John, Cherokee Chief, 1790-1866
See/See also pages in the following book(s):
McLoughlin, W. G. After the Trail of Tears
          970.004
Ross, Kenton E.
Century 21 accounting: first-year course. See Century
21 accounting: first-year course   **657**
Ross, Leonard Q. *See* Rosten, Leo, 1908-1997
Ross, Lillian, 1927-
Here but not here   **92**
Reporting back   **070.4**
(ed) The Fun of it. See The Fun of it   **814**
Ross, Nancy Wilson, 1905?-1986
Buddhism, a way of life and thought   **294.3**
Ross, Rosa Lo San
Beyond bok choy   **641.6**
Ross, Susan Deller
The Rights of women. See The Rights of women
          346.01
Rossetti, Christina Georgina, 1830-1894
The complete poems of Christina Rossetti   **821**
Rossetti, Elizabeth Eleanor Siddal *See* Siddal, Eliza-
beth, 1829-1862
Rossignol, Rosalyn
Chaucer A to Z   **821**
Rostand, Edmond, 1868-1918
Cyrano de Bergerac   **822**
also in Our dramatic heritage v4   **808.82**
Rosten, Leo, 1908-1997
The new joys of Yiddish   **439**

Rotary Rocket Company
Weil, E. They all laughed at Christopher Columbus
621.43
Rotella, Mark, 1967-
Stolen figs and other adventures in Calabria **945**
Roth, Ann Macy, 1954-
Hieroglyphs without mystery **493**
Roth, Herman, 1901-1989
About
Roth, P. Patrimony **92**
Roth, John K.
(ed) Encyclopedia of social issues. See Encyclopedia
of social issues **306**
Roth, Michael S., 1957-
(ed) Freud: conflict and culture. See Freud: conflict
and culture **150.19**
Roth, Philip
The facts **92**
Patrimony **92**
Shop talk **809**
See/See also pages in the following book(s):
Amis, M. The war against cliché **824**
Roth, Sally
The backyard bird feeder's bible **598**
Rothchild, John
(jt. auth) Lynch, P. One up on Wall Street **332.6**
Rothenberg, Jerome, 1931-
(ed) Poems for the millennium. See Poems for the mil-
lennium **808.81**
Rothenberg, Marc, 1949-
(ed) The History of science in the United States. See
The History of science in the United States
509
Rothfeder, Jeffrey
Every drop for sale **333.91**
Rothko, Mark, 1903-1970
About
Breslin, J. E. B. Mark Rothko **92**
Rothman, Barbara Katz
Genetic maps and human imaginations **599.93**
Rothschild, Miriam
See/See also pages in the following book(s):
Fraser, K. Ornament and silence **814**
The **Rough** Guide to classical music. See Classical mu-
sic: the rough guide **781.6**
The **Rough** Guide to opera. Boyden, M. **792.5**
The **Rough** guides **910.2**
Rousmaniere, John
The illustrated dictionary of boating terms **797.1**
Rousseau, Jean-Jacques, 1712-1778
Confessions **92**
The social contract **320.1**
About
Cranston, M. Jean-Jacques: the early life and work of
Jean-Jacques Rousseau, 1712-1754 **92**
Cranston, M. The noble savage: Jean-Jacques Rous-
seau, 1754-1762 **92**
Cranston, M. The solitary self: Jean-Jacques Rousseau
in exile and adversity **92**
See/See also pages in the following book(s):
Gay, P. The Enlightenment: an interpretation **190**
Russell, B. A history of Western philosophy p684-701
109
Route 66 A.D. Perrottet, T. **910.4**
Route 66: the mother road. Wallis, M. **917.8**
The **router** book. Warner, P. **684**
Router joinery workshop. Reed, C. **684**
The **Routledge** atlas of American history. Gilbert, M.
911
The **Routledge** atlas of the Holocaust. Gilbert, M.
940.53
Routledge encyclopedia of philosophy, Concise **103**
Rovner, Julie
Health care policy and politics A to Z **362.1**

Rowan, Carl Thomas, 1925-2000
Dream makers, dream breakers: the world of Justice
Thurgood Marshall **92**
Rowe, John W. (John Wallis), 1944-
Successful aging **612.6**
Rowell, Charles H.
(ed) Making Callaloo. See Making Callaloo **810.8**
Rowell, Galen A., 1940-2002
(il) Dalai Lama XIV. My Tibet **951**
(il) Muir, J. The Yosemite **979.4**
Rowell, Margit
Objects of desire **758**
Rowing to latitude. Fredston, J. A. **797.1**
Rowley, Hazel
Richard Wright **92**
Rowling, J. K.
Characters—Harry Potter
Highfield, R. The science of Harry Potter **500**
Roy Blount's book of Southern humor **817.008**
Royal, Marshall, 1912-1995
See/See also pages in the following book(s):
Dance, S. The world of Count Basie **920**
The **Royal** Horticultural Society gardeners' encyclopedia
of plants and flowers. See American Horticultural
Society encyclopedia of plants and flowers
635.9
The **Royal** Horticultural Society gardening manual. See
The American Horticultural Society gardening manu-
al **635**
The **Royal** Horticultural Society shorter dictionary of
gardening. Pollock, M. **635**
Royal Hospital (London, England)
Ziegler, P. Soldiers: fighting men's lives, 1901-2001
355
Royal landscape. Roberts, J. **942**
Royalty *See* Kings and rulers; Queens
Royko, Mike, 1932-1997
For the love of Mike **818**
One more time **818**
Royster, Willa Ward- *See* Ward-Royster, Willa, 1922-
Royte, Elizabeth
The Tapir's morning bath **577.3**
Rozensztroch, Daniel
(jt. auth) Slesin, S. Japanese style **747.2**
Rozett, Robert
(ed) Encyclopedia of the Holocaust. See Encyclopedia
of the Holocaust [Facts on File] **940.53**
Ruanda *See* Rwanda
Rubáiyát of Omar Khayyám. Omar Khayyam **891**
Rubber
Korman, R. The Goodyear story **92**
See/See also pages in the following book(s):
Slack, C. Noble obsession **92**
Rubens family
About
Rubin, L. D. My father's people **920**
Rubenstein, Lorne
A season in Dornoch **796.352**
Rubenstein, Richard E.
Aristotle's children **189**
When Jesus became God **273**
Rubenstein, William B.
The rights of people who are HIV positive **344**
Rubin, Alan E.
Disturbing the solar system **521**
Rubin, Jay, 1941-
(ed) Modern Japanese writers. See Modern Japanese
writers **920.003**
Rubin, Louis Decimus, 1923-
My father's people **920**
Rubin, Richard
Confederacy of silence **976.2**
Rubin, Richard R.
(jt. auth) Saudek, C. D. The Johns Hopkins guide to
diabetes **616.4**

Rubino, Carl R. Galvez
(ed) Facts about the world's languages: an encyclopedia of the world's major languages, past and present. See Facts about the world's languages: an encyclopedia of the world's major languages, past and present
400

Rubinstein, Anton, 1829-1894
See/See also pages in the following book(s):
Schonberg, H. C. The great pianists **920**
Rubio, Manny
Rattlesnake **597.9**
Rudacille, Deborah
The scalpel and the butterfly **179**
Ruddick, James
Death at the priory **364.1**
Rudof, Joanne Weiner
(ed) Witness. See Witness **940.53**
Ruff, Sue
(ed) The Smithsonian book of North American mammals. See The Smithsonian book of North American mammals **599**
Rüger, Axel
(jt. auth) Liedtke, W. A. Vermeer and the Delft school **759.9492**
Ruggero, Ed
Duty first **355**
Ruins *See* Excavations (Archeology)
Rule, Ann
—and never let her go **364.1**
Dead by sunset **364.1**
Rulers *See* Emperors; Heads of state; Kings and rulers; Queens
Rules for radicals. Alinsky, S. **322.4**
Rules of order *See* Parliamentary practice
A **Rum** affair. Sabbagh, K. **580**
A **rumor** of war. Caputo, P. **959.704**
Rumpf, Teri P.
The Sjogren's syndrome survival guide **616.97**
Rumsfeld, Donald H.
About
Krames, J. A. The Rumsfeld way **658.4**
The **Rumsfeld** way. Krames, J. A. **658.4**
The **runner's** handbook. Glover, B. **796.42**
Runner's world complete book of running **796.42**
Runner's world complete book of women's running. Scott, D. **796.42**
Running
See also Marathon running
Glover, B. The runner's handbook **796.42**
Runner's world complete book of running **796.42**
Scott, D. Runner's world complete book of women's running **796.42**
Running on Ritalin. Diller, L. H. **618.92**
Running with scissors. Burroughs, A. **92**
Rupp, Rebecca
The complete home learning sourcebook **371.04**
Rural life *See* Country life; Farm life
Rural sociology
See also United States—Rural conditions
Ruse, Michael
(ed) Genetically modified foods. See Genetically modified foods **363.1**
Rushdie, Salman
Step across this line **824**
Rushing, Jimmy, 1903-1972
See/See also pages in the following book(s):
Dance, S. The world of Count Basie **920**
Rusk, Dean, 1909-1994
See/See also pages in the following book(s):
Halberstam, D. The best and the brightest **973.922**
Russell, Bertrand, 1872-1970
A history of Western philosophy **109**
The problems of philosophy **100**
About
Monk, R. Bertrand Russell **92**
See/See also pages in the following book(s):
Durant, W. J. The story of philosophy p357-64 **109**
Russell, Dick
Black genius and the American experience **920**
Eye of the whale **599.5**
Russell, Roy, 1954-
(ed) The Oxford Spanish dictionary. See The Oxford Spanish dictionary **463**
Russell, Thaddeus
Out of the jungle: Jimmy Hoffa and the remaking of the American working class **92**
Russell Baker's book of American humor **817.008**
Russia
See also Russia (Federation); Soviet Union
Civilization
Figes, O. Natasha's dance **947**
Massie, S. Land of the firebird **947**
Milner-Gulland, R. R. Cultural atlas of Russia and the former Soviet Union **947**
Foreign relations—United States
Talbott, S. The Russia hand **327.73**
History
Erickson, C. Great Catherine **92**
Ferro, M. Nicholas II **92**
Hosking, G. A. Russia and the Russians **947**
Hosking, G. A. Russia: people and empire, 1552-1917 **947**
Kurth, P. Tsar: the lost world of Nicholas and Alexandra **947.08**
Massie, R. K. Nicholas and Alexandra **92**
Pipes, R. A concise history of the Russian Revolution **947.08**
Pipes, R. The Russian Revolution **947.08**
Riasanovsky, N. V. A history of Russia **947**
Warnes, D. Chronicle of the Russian tsars **947**
See/See also pages in the following book(s):
Montefiore, S. Prince of princes: the life of Potemkin **92**
Pipes, R. Property and freedom p159-208 **323.4**
History—Pictorial works
Moynahan, B. The Russian century **947.08**
Kings and rulers
Massie, R. K. The Romanovs **947.08**
Warnes, D. Chronicle of the Russian tsars **947**
Russia (Federation)
See also Russia; Soviet Union
Economic conditions
Cohen, S. F. Failed crusade **327.73**
Klebnikov, P. Godfather of the Kremlin **92**
History
Service, R. A history of twentieth-century Russia **947.086**
Politics and government
Gorbachev, M. On my country and the world **947.085**
Remnick, D. Resurrection **947.086**
Russia and the Russians. Hosking, G. A. **947**
The **Russia** hand. Talbott, S. **327.73**
Russia: people and empire, 1552-1917. Hosking, G. A. **947**
Russia under the Bolshevik regime. Pipes, R. **947.084**
Russian art
Hamilton, G. H. The art and architecture of Russia **709.47**
Massie, S. Land of the firebird **947**
McPhee, J. A. The ransom of Russian art **709.47**
The **Russian** century. Moynahan, B. **947.08**
Russian cooking
Molokhovets, E. Classic Russian cooking **641.5**
Russian Empire *See* Russia

Russian espionage
Haynes, J. E. Venona | 327.12
Herrington, S. A. Traitors among us | 327.12
Weinstein, A. The haunted wood | 327.12
Wise, D. Cassidy's run | 327.12
Russian language
Dictionaries
The Concise Oxford Russian dictionary | 491.7
The Oxford Russian dictionary | 491.7
Russian literature
Bio-bibliography
Reference guide to Russian literature | 891.7
Dictionaries
Reference guide to Russian literature | 891.7
History and criticism
The Cambridge history of Russian literature | 891.7
Nabokov, V. V. Lectures on Russian literature | 891.7
Terras, V. A history of Russian literature | 891.7
See/See also pages in the following book(s):
Berlin, Sir I. The sense of reality p194-231 | 901
Russian national characteristics
Hosking, G. A. Russia: people and empire, 1552-1917 | 947
Russian revolution *See* Soviet Union—History—1917-1921, Revolution
The **Russian** Revolution. Pipes, R. | 947.08
Russo-Japanese War, 1904-1905
Pleshakov, K. The Tsar's last armada | 952.03
Rustico: regional Italian country cooking. Negrin, M. | 641.5

Rustin, Bayard, 1910-1987
About
Anderson, J. Bayard Rustin | 92
D'Emilio, J. Lost prophet: the life and times of Bayard Rustin | 92
Rutan, Dick
(jt. auth) Yeager, J. Voyager | 910.4
Ruth, Babe, 1895-1948
About
Creamer, R. W. Babe | 92
Ruth, George Herman *See* Ruth, Babe, 1895-1948
Rutherford, Ernest, 1871-1937
See/See also pages in the following book(s):
Brennan, R. P. Heisenberg probably slept here | 920
Rutkow, Ira M.
American surgery | 617
Rwanda
Description
Carr, R. H. Land of a thousand hills | 967.571
Politics and government
Gourevitch, P. We wish to inform you that tomorrow we will be killed with our families | 967.571
Keane, F. Season of blood | 967.571
Ryan, Evelyn, d. 1998
About
Ryan, T. The prize winner of Defiance, Ohio | 92
Ryan, Frank, 1944-
Virus-X | 614.4
Ryan, Joan
Little girls in pretty boxes | 796.44
Ryan, Mike, 1960-
(jt. auth) McKinney, M. Chariots of the damned | 356
Ryan, Terry
The prize winner of Defiance, Ohio [biography of Evelyn Ryan] | 92
Ryan, William B. F.
Noah's flood | 930
Ryan family
About
Ryan, T. The prize winner of Defiance, Ohio [biography of Evelyn Ryan] | 92

Ryback, Timothy W.
The last survivor | 940.53
Rybczynski, Witold
A clearing in the distance: Frederick Law Olmsted and America in the nineteenth century | 92
The look of architecture | 721
The perfect house: a journey with the Renaissance architect Andrea Palladio | 724
Rybicki, Arkadiuz
(jt. auth) Wałęsa, L. The struggle and the triumph | 92
Rylant, Cynthia
See/See also pages in the following book(s):
The Newbery & Caldecott medal books, 1986-2000 p188-97 | 028.5
Ryssel, Paul van *See* Gachet, Paul, 1828-1909

S

S-5 (Submarine)
Hill, A. J. Under pressure | 910.4
S.A.T. *See* Scholastic Aptitude Test
Saavedra, Miguel de Cervantes *See* Cervantes Saavedra, Miguel de, 1547-1616
Sabbagh, Karl
A Rum affair | 580
Sabbath
Friedland, S. R. Shabbat shalom | 641.5
Sacagawea, b. 1786
About
Clark, E. E. Sacagawea of the Lewis and Clark expedition | 92
Slaughter, T. P. Exploring Lewis and Clark | 978
Sacagawea of the Lewis and Clark expedition. Clark, E. E. | 92
Sacajawea *See* Sacagawea, b. 1786
Sachar, Howard Morley, 1928-
Dreamland | 940
A history of Israel | 956.94
A history of the Jews in America | 305.8
Sachar, Louis, 1954-
See/See also pages in the following book(s):
The Newbery & Caldecott medal books, 1986-2000 p317-31 | 028.5
Sachs, Dana
The house on Dream Street | 959.7
Sack, Steven Mitchell, 1954-
The employee rights handbook | 344
The **Sackett** companion. L'Amour, L. | 813.009
Sacks, David
Encyclopedia of the ancient Greek world | 938.003
Sacks, Oliver W.
An anthropologist on Mars | 616.8
The island of the colorblind | 617.7
The man who mistook his wife for a hat and other clinical tales | 616.8
Oaxaca journal | 587
Seeing voices | 362.4
Uncle Tungsten | 92
Sacred art *See* Christian art
Sacred cows and golden geese. Greek, C. R. | 179
Sacred monsters. Richardson, J. | 920
Sacred music *See* Church music
Sacred seasons. Isaacs, R. H. | 296.4
Saddām Hussein *See* Hussein, Ṣaddām
Sade, marquis de, 1740-1814
About
Gray, F. du P. At home with the Marquis de Sade | 92
See/See also pages in the following book(s):
Camus, A. The rebel p36-47 | 303.6

Sade, marquis de, 1740-1814—*Continued*
Drama
Weiss, P. The persecution and assassination of Jean-Paul Marat as performed by the inmates of the Asylum of Charenton under the direction of the Marquis de Sade   832

Sade, Renée Pélagie de Montreuil, marquise de, d. 1810
About
Gray, F. du P. At home with the Marquis de Sade   92

Sader, Marion
(ed) Storytelling encyclopedia. See Storytelling encyclopedia   398.03

Sadie, Julie Anne
The Norton/Grove dictionary of women composers. See The Norton/Grove dictionary of women composers   920.003

Sadie, Stanley
(ed) The New Grove dictionary of American music. See The New Grove dictionary of American music   780.973
(ed) The New Grove dictionary of opera. See The New Grove dictionary of opera   792.5

Safe food. Nestle, M.   363.1
Safe home wiring projects. Cauldwell, R.   621.319

Safer, Jeanne
The normal one   158

Safety devices
    See also Accidents—Prevention
Safety measures *See* Accidents—Prevention

Safina, Carl
Eye of the albatross   598

Safranski, Rüdiger
Nietzsche   92

Sagan, Carl, 1934-1996
Billions and billions   500
Broca's brain   500
Comet   523.6
Cosmos   520
The dragons of Eden   153
Pale blue dot   520
Shadows of forgotten ancestors   570.1
About
Davidson, K. Carl Sagan   92

Sagan, Dorion, 1959-
(jt. auth) Margulis, L. What is life?   570.1

Sagas
The Sagas of Icelanders   839
The **Sagas** of Icelanders   839

Sage, Jacob
(jt. auth) Duvoisin, R. C. Parkinson's disease   616.8

Sage, Lorna
Bad blood   92
(ed) The Cambridge guide to women's writing in English. See The Cambridge guide to women's writing in English   820.9

Sahara. Palin, M.   966
Sahara: a natural history. De Villiers, M.   508
Sahara Desert
De Villiers, M. Sahara: a natural history   508
Langewiesche, W. Sahara unveiled   966
Palin, M. Sahara   966
Sahara unveiled. Langewiesche, W.   966

Said, Edward W.
The end of the peace process   956
Out of place   92
Reflections on exile and other essays   814

Sailing
Conner, D. Learn to sail   797.1
Sailing alone around the room. Collins, B.   811
Sailors' life *See* Seafaring life
Saint-Aubin, Horace de *See* Balzac, Honoré de, 1799-1850

Saint Helens, Mount (Wash.) *See* Mount Saint Helens (Wash.)
Saint James encyclopedia of popular culture. See St. James encyclopedia of popular culture   973.9
Saint Joan. Shaw, B.
In Our dramatic heritage v5   808.82
In The Oxford anthology of English literature v2   820.8

Saint-Just, 1767-1794
    See/See also pages in the following book(s):
Camus, A. The rebel p117-32   303.6
Saint Petersburg (Russia)
History
Volkov, S. St. Petersburg   947
Saints
    See also Christian saints; Martyrs
Saints & sinners. Duffy, E.   282
Saints and sinners   282

Sakach, Deborah
Bed & breakfast encyclopedia   647.9
Bed & breakfasts, country inns   647.9
Sakharov, Andreï Dmitrievich, 1921-1989
About
Lourie, R. Sakharov   92
Sakyamuni *See* Gautama Buddha
Salak, Kira, 1971-
The four corners   910.4
Salamon, Julie
Facing the wind   364.1
Sale, Kirkpatrick
The fire of his genius: Robert Fulton and the American dream   92
Salem (Mass.)
Drama
Miller, A. The crucible   812
History
Carlson, L. M. A fever in Salem   133.4
Hoffer, P. C. The Salem witchcraft trials   345
Norton, M. B. In the devil's snare   133.4
Salem is my dwelling place: a life of Nathaniel Hawthorne. Miller, E. H.   92
The **Salem** witchcraft trials. Hoffer, P. C.   345
Saler, Benson
UFO crash at Roswell   001.9
Salesmanship *See* Selling
Salieri, Antonio, 1750-1825
Drama
Shaffer, P. Peter Shaffer's Amadeus   822
Salinger, J. D. (Jerome David), 1919-
About
J.D. Salinger [critical essays]   813.009
Salinger, Jerome David *See* Salinger, J. D. (Jerome David), 1919-
Salisbury, Joyce E.
Encyclopedia of women in the ancient world   305.4
Salisbury, Neal
A Companion to American Indian history. See A Companion to American Indian history   970.004
Salisbury, Robert Arthur Talbot Gascoyne-Cecil, 3rd Marquis of, 1830-1903
    See/See also pages in the following book(s):
Massie, R. K. Dreadnought p189-212   940.3
Sallah, Tijan M., 1958-
(ed) The New African poetry. See The New African poetry   896
Salley, Columbus
The black 100   920
Sallis, James, 1944-
Chester Himes   92
Salmon
Behnke, R. J. Trout and salmon of North America   597
The **salmon** of doubt. Adams, D.   828

Salomé, Lou Andreas- *See* Andreas-Salomé, Lou, 1861-1937

Salomon Brothers Inc.
Lewis, M. Liar's poker: rising through the wreckage on Wall Street   **332.6**

Salt
Kurlansky, M. Salt: a world history   **553.6**

Salt-free diet
The American Heart Association low-salt cookbook   **641.5**

Salter, Mark
(jt. auth) McCain, J. S. Faith of my fathers   **92**

Salter, Mary Jo, 1954-
A kiss in space   **811**

Saltzman, Cynthia
Portrait of Dr. Gachet   **759.9492**

Salvadori, Mario George, 1907-1997
(jt. auth) Levy, M. Why buildings fall down   **690**

Salvation. Hooks, B.   **306.7**

Salvation Army
Winston, D. H. Red-hot and righteous   **287.9**

Salvation: scenes from the life of St. Francis. Martin, V.   **92**

Salvesen, Britt
(jt. auth) Druick, D. W. Van Gogh and Gauguin   **92**

Salzberg, Hugh W.
From caveman to chemist   **540**

Salzman, Jack
(ed) The Cambridge handbook of American literature. See The Cambridge handbook of American literature   **810.3**

(ed) Encyclopedia of African-American culture and history. See Encyclopedia of African-American culture and history   **305.8**

Salzman, Mark
Iron & silk   **915.1**
Lost in place   **92**

Sam: the boy behind the mask. Hallman, T.   **362.1**

Sam Walton, made in America. Walton, S.   **92**

The **same** river twice. Walker, A.   **92**

Samoan Islands
      Social life and customs
Mead, M. Coming of age in Samoa   **306**

Sampson, Anthony, 1926-
Nelson Mandela   **92**

Sampson, Curt
Masters   **796.352**

Samson Agonistes. Milton, J.
In The Oxford anthology of English literature v1   **820.8**

Samuel, Rhian
The Norton/Grove dictionary of women composers. See The Norton/Grove dictionary of women composers   **920.003**

San Francisco (Calif.)
      History
Kurzman, D. Disaster!   **979.4**

Sanchez, Sonia, 1934-
See/See also pages in the following book(s):
Black women writers (1950-1980)   **810.9**

Sanctuaries, Wildlife *See* Wildlife refuges

Sanctuary movement
See also Refugees

Sand, George, 1804-1876
      About
Jack, B. E. George Sand   **92**

Sand Creek, Battle of, 1864
See/See also pages in the following book(s):
Brown, D. A. Bury my heart at Wounded Knee   **970.004**

Sandburg, Carl, 1878-1967
Abraham Lincoln: The prairie years and The war years   **92**
The American songbag   **782.42**

Chicago poems
In Sandburg, C. Complete poems of Carl Sandburg p3-76   **811**
The complete poems of Carl Sandburg   **811**
Cornhuskers
In Sandburg, C. Complete poems of Carl Sandburg p79-147   **811**
Good morning, America
In Sandburg, C. Complete poems of Carl Sandburg p315-435   **811**
Honey and salt
In Sandburg, C. Complete poems of Carl Sandburg p706-71   **811**
The people, yes
In Sandburg, C. Complete poems of Carl Sandburg p439-617   **811**
The prairie years [condensation]
In Sandburg, C. Abraham Lincoln: The prairie years and The war years   **92**
Slabs of the sunburnt West
In Sandburg, C. Complete poems of Carl Sandburg p271-314   **811**
Smoke and steel
In Sandburg, C. Complete poems of Carl Sandburg p149-268   **811**
The war years [condensation]
In Sandburg, C. Abraham Lincoln: The prairie years and The war years   **92**

Sanders, Andrew
The short Oxford history of English literature   **820.9**

Sanders, E. P.
The historical figure of Jesus   **232.9**

Sandford, Gina
Aquarium: owner's manual   **639.34**

Sandler, Adrian
Living with spina bifida   **618.92**

Sandler, Stanley, 1937-
Segregated skies   **940.54**

Sandoz, Mari, 1896-1966
The Battle of the Little Bighorn   **973.8**
See/See also pages in the following book(s):
American women fiction writers   **813.009**

Sandra Betzina sews for your home. Betzina, S.   **646.2**

Sandstorms: days and nights in Arabia. Theroux, P.   **953**

Sandweiss, Martha A.
(ed) The Oxford history of the American West. See The Oxford history of the American West   **978**

Sankaran, Neeraja
Microbes and people: an A-Z of microorganisms in our lives   **579**

Santa Fe Institute (N.M.)
See/See also pages in the following book(s):
Johnson, G. Fire in the mind   **215**

Santa Fe Trail
Dary, D. The Santa Fe Trail   **978**

Santa Maria del Fiore (Cathedral: Florence, Italy)
King, R. Brunelleschi's dome   **726**

Santayana, George, 1863-1952
See/See also pages in the following book(s):
Durant, W. J. The story of philosophy p366-81   **109**

Santelli, Robert
(ed) American roots music. See American roots music   **781.62**

Santoro, Gene
Myself when I am real: the life and music of Charles Mingus   **92**

Sanzio, Raffaello *See* Raphael, 1483-1520

Sapolsky, Robert M.
A primate's memoir   **599.8**

Sappho
If not, winter   **884**

Sarajevo (Bosnia and Hercegovina)
Cohen, R. Hearts grown brutal   949.7
See/See also pages in the following book(s):
Sontag, S. Where the stress falls   814
Saramago, José
Journey to Portugal   946.9
Saratoga. Ketchum, R. M.   973.3
Saratoga Campaign, 1777
Ketchum, R. M. Saratoga   973.3
Sardegna, Jill
(ed) The Encyclopedia of blindness and vision impairment. See The Encyclopedia of blindness and vision impairment   362.4
Sargent, Francis W. (Francis William) *See* Sargent, William, 1946-
Sargent, John Singer, 1856-1925
About
Ferber, L. S. Masters of color and light   759.13
Sargent, William, 1946-
Crab wars   333.95
Saricks, Joyce G.
The readers' advisory guide to genre fiction   025.5
Readers' advisory service in the public library   025.5
Sarnoff, David, 1891-1971
About
Stashower, D. The boy genius and the mogul   791.45
Saroyan, William, 1908-1981
About
Leggett, J. A daring young man: a biography of William Saroyan   92
Sarton, May, 1912-1995
Coming into eighty   811
About
Fulk, M. K. Understanding May Sarton   818
See/See also pages in the following book(s):
Heilbrun, C. G. Hamlet's mother and other women p146-69   820.9
Sartor resartus. Carlyle, T.   824
Sartore, Joel
(jt. auth) Chadwick, D. H. The company we keep   591.68
Sartre, Jean Paul, 1905-1980
Being and nothingness   142
Dirty hands
In Sartre, J. P. No exit, and three other plays   842
Existentialism and human emotions   142
The flies
In Sartre, J. P. No exit, and three other plays   842
No exit
In Sartre, J. P. No exit, and three other plays   842
No exit, and three other plays   842
The respectful prostitute
In Sartre, J. P. No exit, and three other plays   842
Truth and existence   121
The words   92
About
Gerassi, J. Jean-Paul Sartre v1   92
See/See also pages in the following book(s):
Bair, D. Simone de Beauvoir   92
Existentialism from Dostoevsky to Sartre p280-374   142
Sasha Kagan's country inspiration. Kagan, S.   746.43
Sass, Lorna J.
Great vegetarian cooking under pressure   641.5
Sasson, Jack M.
(ed) Civilizations of the ancient Near East. See Civilizations of the ancient Near East   939

Sassoon, Donald
Becoming Mona Lisa   759.5
SAT *See* Scholastic Aptitude Test
Satan *See* Devil
Satanism
Lewis, J. R. Satanism today   133.4
Satanism today. Lewis, J. R.   133.4
Satellites, Artificial *See* Artificial satellites
Satinover, Jeffrey, 1947-
Cracking the Bible code   222
Satire
Lewis, C. S. The Screwtape letters   248
Satires. Juvenal   877
Satires, Epistles and Ars poetica. Horace   878
Satter, David
Age of delirium   947.085
Saudek, Christopher D.
The Johns Hopkins guide to diabetes   616.4
Saudi Arabia
History
Aburish, S. K. The rise, corruption, and coming fall of the House of Saud   953.8
Sauers, Michael
Using the Internet as a reference tool   025.04
Saunders, Gill
Wallpaper in interior decoration   747
Savage, Candace, 1949-
Aurora   538
Savage, Dan
Skipping towards Gomorrah   306
Savage beauty: the life of Edna St. Vincent Millay. Milford, N.   92
Savage inequalities. Kozol, J.   371.9
The **savage** mind. Lévi-Strauss, C.   155.8
Savage reprisals. Gay, P.   809.3
Savageau, David
Places rated almanac   307.7
Retirement places rated   307.7
Savages. Kane, J.   986.6
Savannah (Ga.)
Social life and customs
Berendt, J. Midnight in the garden of good and evil   975.8
Savant, Marilyn Mach Vos *See* Vos Savant, Marilyn Mach
Savigneau, Josyane
Carson McCullers   92
Saving and investment
Feigenbaum, R. A. The 529 College Savings Plan   378.3
Saving childhood. Medved, M.   305.23
Saving Milly. Kondracke, M.   362.1
Saving the corporate soul & (who knows?) maybe your own. Batstone, D. B.   658.4
Saving the heart. Klaidman, S.   616.1
Saving your brain. Victoroff, J. I.   612.8
Sawyer, Miriam
(jt. auth) Gubert, B. K. Distinguished African Americans in aviation and space science   920.003
Sawyer, P. H., 1928-
(ed) The Oxford illustrated history of the Vikings. See The Oxford illustrated history of the Vikings   948
Sawyer, Peter *See* Sawyer, P. H., 1928-
Sax, Boria
The mythical zoo   398.03
Saxon, A. H.
P.T. Barnum: the legend and the man   92
Say, Allen, 1937-
See/See also pages in the following book(s):
The Newbery & Caldecott medal books, 1986-2000 p198-206   028.5
Say de Kooning. Wilson, L.
In Wilson, L. 21 short plays p194-218   812
Sayemon, Enami no *See* Enami, Sayemon

Sayre, Nora
On the wing **92**
The **scalpel** and the butterfly. Rudacille, D. **179**
Scandinavian literature
See also Old Norse literature; Sagas
Scandinavians
See also Vikings
Scarne, John, 1903-1985
Scarne's encyclopedia of card games **795.4**
Scarne's new complete guide to gambling **795**
Scarne's complete guide to gambling. See Scarne, J.
Scarne's new complete guide to gambling **795**
Scarne's new complete guide to gambling. Scarne, J.
795
Scattered. Maté, G. **616.85**
Scattered poems. Kerouac, J. **811**
Scavullo, Francesco, 1929-
Scavullo: photographs, 50 years **779**
Scenarios *See* Motion picture plays
Scenes from American life. Gurney, A. R.
In Gurney, A. R. Nine early plays, 1961-1973 p201-52 **812**
Scenic art and construction. Troubridge, E. **792**
Scenic photography 101. Drager, K. **770.2**
Schaaf, Fred
40 nights to knowing the sky **520**
Schaap, Dick, 1934-2001
Flashing before my eyes **92**
(ed) Joy in Mudville. See Joy in Mudville
796.357
Schacter, Daniel L.
Searching for memory **153.1**
The seven sins of memory **153.1**
Schama, Simon
Citizens: a chronicle of the French Revolution
944.04
Dead certainties **907**
The embarrassment of riches **949.2**
A history of Britain **941**
Rembrandt's eyes **92**
Schapiro, Meyer, 1904-1996
Impressionism **709.44**
Schappert, Phil, 1956-
A world for butterflies **595.7**
Schebera, Jürgen
Kurt Weill **92**
Schechter, Abraham A.
Basic book repair methods **025.7**
Scheck, Barry
(jt. auth) Dwyer, J. Actual innocence **347**
Schefter, James L.
The race **629.45**
Schell, Jonathan, 1943-
Writing in time **973.928**
Schell, Orville
Virtual Tibet **951**
Schelling, Friedrich Wilhelm Joseph von, 1775-1854
See/See also pages in the following book(s):
Jaspers, K. The great philosophers **109**
Schellinger, Paul E., 1962-
(ed) Encyclopedia of the novel. See Encyclopedia of the novel **809.3**
Scheub, Harold
A dictionary of African mythology **299**
Schewel, Amy
(ed) The Actor's book of movie monologues. See The Actor's book of movie monologues **791.43**
Schickel, Richard
Clint Eastwood **92**
Schiff, Hilda
(ed) Holocaust poetry. See Holocaust poetry
808.81
Schiffman, Lawrence H.
Reclaiming the Dead Sea scrolls **296.1**

(ed) The Encyclopedia of the Dead Sea scrolls. See The Encyclopedia of the Dead Sea scrolls
296.1
Schiller, Friedrich, 1759-1805
Wilhelm Tell
In Our dramatic heritage v4 **808.82**
Schiller, Lawrence
Perfect murder, perfect town **364.1**
Schilling, Govert
Flash! **522**
Schindler, Oskar, 1908-1974
See/See also pages in the following book(s):
Fogelman, E. Conscience & courage **940.53**
Schizophrenia
Whitaker, R. Mad in America **616.89**
Encyclopedias
Noll, R. The encyclopedia of schizophrenia and other psychotic disorders **616.89**
Schlachter, Gail A.
Directory of financial aids for women **378.3**
Financial aid for the disabled and their families
378.3
Schlaffer, Edit, 1950-
(jt. auth) Benard, C. Veiled courage **958.1**
Schlager, Neil, 1966-
St. James encyclopedia of labor history worldwide. See St. James encyclopedia of labor history worldwide
331.8
(ed) How products are made. See How products are made **670**
(jt. auth) Richards, P. Best literature by and about Blacks **016.8**
(ed) Science and its times. See Science and its times **509**
(ed) St. James Press gay & lesbian almanac. See St. James Press gay & lesbian almanac **305.9**
Schlee, Valentina *See* Valentina, 1904-1989
Schleiermacher, Friedrich, 1768-1834
See/See also pages in the following book(s):
Küng, H. Great Christian thinkers p155-84 **230**
Schlereth, Thomas J.
Victorian America **973.8**
Schlesinger, Arthur M., 1917-
The coming of the New Deal, 1933-1935 **973.917**
The crisis of the old order, 1919-1933 **973.91**
The cycles of American history **973**
The disuniting of America **973**
A life in the twentieth century **92**
The politics of upheaval, 1935-1936 **973.917**
Robert Kennedy and his times **92**
Schlesinger, Chris
How to cook meat **641.6**
The thrill of the grill **641.7**
Schlessinger, Laura C.
How could you do that?! **170**
Schliemann, Heinrich, 1822-1890
See/See also pages in the following book(s):
Finley, M. I. The world of Odysseus **883**
Schlissel, Lillian
Far from home **978**
Schloss, Arthur David *See* Waley, Arthur, 1889-1966
Schlosser, Eric
Fast food nation **394.1**
Schmemann, Serge
Echoes of a native land **947**
Schmidt, Michael, 1947-
Lives of the poets **821.009**
Schmidt, Thomas, 1959-
The Lewis & Clark Trail **978**
Schnabel, Artur, 1882-1951
See/See also pages in the following book(s):
Schonberg, H. C. The great pianists **920**
Schneider, Carl J.
(jt. auth) Schneider, D. First ladies **920.003**
(jt. auth) Schneider, D. Slavery in America **326**

Schneider, David, 1951-
(ed) Essential Zen. See Essential Zen   294.3
Schneider, Dorothy
First ladies   920.003
Slavery in America   326
Schneider, Edward L.
Ageless: take control of your age and stay youthful for life   612.6
Schneider, Elizabeth, 1943-
Vegetables from amaranth to zucchini   641.6
Schneider, Paul
The Adirondacks   974.7
Schneider, Stephen Henry
(ed) Encyclopedia of climate and weather. See Encyclopedia of climate and weather   551.6
Schobinger, Juan
The ancient Americans   970.01
Schoen, Allen M.
Kindred spirits   636.089
Schoenberg, Arnold, 1874-1951
About
Shawn, A. Arnold Schoenberg's journey   92
Schoenberger, Nancy
Dangerous muse: the life of Lady Caroline Blackwood   92
(jt. auth) Kashner, S. A talent for genius: the life and times of Oscar Levant   92
Schoenherr, John, 1935-
See/See also pages in the following book(s):
The Newbery & Caldecott medal books, 1986-2000 p63-70   028.5
Schoepflin, Rennie B.
Christian Science on trial   289.5
Scholarship See Learning and scholarship
Scholarships
See also Student loan funds
Peterson's college money handbook   378.3
Schlachter, G. A. Directory of financial aids for women   378.3
Schlachter, G. A. Financial aid for the disabled and their families   378.3
Scholarships, fellowships and loans   378.3
Scholarships, fellowships and loans   378.3
Scholastic Aptitude Test
How to prepare for SAT I   378.1
Scholze-Stubenrecht, Werner
(ed) The Oxford-Duden German dictionary. See The Oxford-Duden German dictionary   433
Schom, Alan
Napoleon Bonaparte   92
One hundred days   944.05
The **Schomburg** Center guide to black literature from the eighteenth century to the present   809
Schönberg, Arnold See Schoenberg, Arnold, 1874-1951
Schonberg, Harold C.
The great pianists   920
The lives of the great composers   920
The **school** and society. Dewey, J.
In Dewey, J. The school and society, and The child and the curriculum   372
The **school** and society, and The child and the curriculum. Dewey, J.   372
School busing See Busing (School integration)
The **school** for husbands. Molière
In Molière. Tartuffe, and other plays   842
The **school** for wives. Molière
In Molière. Tartuffe, and other plays   842
School integration
See also Busing (School integration)
Lukas, J. A. Common ground   305.8
School libraries
See also Children's libraries; High school libraries
Catalogs
Children's catalog   011.6

Middle and junior high school library catalog   011.6
School libraries (High school) See High school libraries
Schooler, Lynn
The blue bear   599.78
Schools
See also Colleges and universities; Education; Public schools; Summer schools
The **schools** our children deserve. Kohn, A.   371.2
The **schools** we need and why we don't have them. Hirsch, E. D.   370
Schopenhauer, Arthur, 1788-1860
See/See also pages in the following book(s):
Durant, W. J. The story of philosophy p227-64   109
Schopf, J. William, 1941-
Cradle of life   576.8
Schoppa, R. Keith, 1943-
The Columbia guide to modern Chinese history   951.05
Schor, Edward L.
(ed) Caring for your school-age child. See Caring for your school-age child   649
Schorr, Daniel, 1916-
Staying tuned   92
Schreiber, Flora Rheta
Sybil   616.85
Schreiner, Olive, 1855-1920
See/See also pages in the following book(s):
Pierpont, C. R. Passionate minds   810.9
Schröder, Klaus Albrecht
(ed) Munch, E. Edvard Munch: theme and variation   760
Schrödinger, Erwin, 1887-1961
About
Gribbin, J. R. Schrödinger's kittens and the search for reality   530.1
Schrödinger's kittens and the search for reality. Gribbin, J. R.   530.1
Schroeder, Gerald L.
The hidden face of God   215
The science of God   261.5
Schroeder, Patricia
24 years of House work—and the place is still a mess   92
Schubert, Franz, 1797-1828
About
Newbould, B. Schubert, the music and the man   92
Schubert, the music and the man. Newbould, B.   92
Schulberg, Budd
Sparring with Hemingway and other legends of the fight game   796.8
Schulman, Bruce J.
The seventies   973.92
Schulman, Grace
Days of wonder   811
Schultes, Richard Evans, 1915-2001
About
Davis, W. One river   581.6
Schultz, David A., 1958-
(ed) Encyclopedia of American law. See Encyclopedia of American law   349
Schultz, Eric B., 1957-
King Philip's War   973.2
Schultz, Ted
(ed) Insect lives. See Insect lives   595.7
Schulz, William F., Jr.
In our own best interest   323
Schulze, Hagen
Germany   943
Schumacher, Michael, 1950-
Crossroads: the life and music of Eric Clapton   92

Schuttner, Scott
Building and designing decks　690
Schuyler, James
Collected poems　811
Schwab, Charles
(jt. auth) Schwab-Pomerantz, C. It pays to talk
332.024
Schwab-Pomerantz, Carrie
It pays to talk　332.024
Schwartz, Arthur, 1900-1984
　See/See also pages in the following book(s):
Green, S. The world of musical comedy　920
Schwartz, Gil
　See also Bing, Stanley
Schwartz, Jeffrey H.
What the bones tell us　599.93
Schwartz, Karlene V., 1936-
(jt. auth) Margulis, L. Five kingdoms　570
Schwartz, Morris
　　　　　About
Albom, M. Tuesdays with Morrie　92
Schwartz, Peter, 1949-
(jt. auth) Rand, A. The voice of reason; essays in objectivist thought　191
Schwartz, Richard Alan, 1951-
Cold War culture　973.92
Encyclopedia of the Persian Gulf War　956.7
Schwarz, Shelley Peterman, 1946-
Parkinson's disease: 300 tips for making life easier
616.8
Schwarzkopf, H. Norman
It doesn't take a hero: General H. Norman Schwarzkopf　92
　　　　　About
Cohen, R. In the eye of the storm: the life of General
H. Norman Schwarzkopf　92
Schweitzer, Albert, 1875-1965
Out of my life and thought　92
The words of Albert Schweitzer　210
Schweizer, Peter, 1964-
Reagan's War　327.73
Science
　See also Chaos (Science); Computer science
The Best American science and nature writing
500
The Best American science writing　500
Biddle, W. A field guide to the invisible　500
Bronowski, J. Science and human values　500
Bryson, B. A short history of nearly everything
500
Clark, J. Encyclopedia of strange and unexplained
physical phenomena　001.9
Clarke, A. C. Greetings, carbon-based bipeds!
500
Eiseley, L. C. The unexpected universe　500
Feynman, R. P. The meaning of it all　500
Feynman, R. P. The pleasure of finding things out
500
Gardner, M. Did Adam and Eve have navels?
500
Gardner, M. On the wild side　500
Great thinkers of the Western world　190
Gribbin, J. R. Almost everyone's guide to science
500
The Handy science answer book　500
Hazen, R. M. Science matters: achieving scientific literacy　500
Highfield, R. The science of Harry Potter　500
Ingram, J. The barmaid's brain and other strange tales
from science　500
Maddox, J. R. What remains to be discovered
500
Marshall, I. N. Who's afraid of Schrödinger's cat?
500
Park, R. L. Voodoo science　500

Pohl, F. Chasing science　500
Ray, C. C. The New York Times second book of science questions and answers　500
Sagan, C. Billions and billions　500
Sagan, C. Broca's brain　500
Science and technology desk reference　500
The Scientific American science desk reference
500
Shermer, M. Why people believe weird things
001.9
Wynn, C. M. The five biggest ideas in science
500
　　　　　Dictionaries
Academic Press dictionary of science and technology
503
The Facts on File encyclopedia of science　503
McGraw-Hill dictionary of scientific and technical
terms　503
　　　　　Encyclopedias
Bunch, B. H. The Penguin desk encyclopedia of science and mathematics　503
The Encyclopedia of science and technology　503
Gale encyclopedia of science　503
McGraw-Hill concise encyclopedia of science & technology　503
McGraw-Hill encyclopedia of science & technology
503
The new encyclopedia of science　503
Van Nostrand's concise encyclopedia of science
503
Van Nostrand's scientific encyclopedia　503
Volti, R. The Facts on File encyclopedia of science,
technology, and society　503
　　　　　Ethical aspects
Barber, N. Encyclopedia of ethics in science and technology　174
　　　　　Experiments
　See also particular branches of science with the
subdivision Experiments
Experiment central　507.8
Sheldrake, R. Seven experiments that could change the
world　507.8
　　　　　History
Adler, R. E. Science firsts: from the creation of science to the science of creation　509
Allaby, M. Makers of science　920.003
Barrow, J. D. The book of nothing　111
Boorstin, D. J. The discoverers　909
Bruno, L. C. Science & technology firsts　609
Burke, J. Circles: 50 round trips through history, technology, science, culture　609
The Chronology of science　509
Crump, T. A brief history of science　509
Flowers, C. Instability rules　509
Great events from history II, Science and technology
509
History of modern science and mathematics　509
Horvitz, L. A. Eureka!: scientific breakthroughs that
changed the world　509
Jardine, L. Ingenious pursuits　509
Ochoa, G. The Wilson chronology of science and technology　502
The Oxford companion to the history of modern science　509
Piel, G. The age of science　509
Pyenson, L. Servants of nature　509
Rigden, J. S. Hydrogen　546
Science: a history of discovery in the twentieth century
509
Science and its times　509
Science, technology, and society: the impact of science
in the 20th century　509
Silver, B. L. The ascent of science　509
Suplee, C. Milestones of science　509
Teresi, D. Lost discoveries　509

Science—History—*Continued*
Whitfield, P. Landmarks in western science   **509**
See/See also pages in the following book(s):
Durant, W. J. The age of Louis XIV p495-547
   940.2
Russell, B. A history of Western philosophy p525-40
   109

History—Encyclopedias
Encyclopedia of the scientific revolution   **509**
The History of science in the United States   **509**
Reader's guide to the history of science   **509**
Moral and religious aspects
See Science—Ethical aspects
Periodicals—Indexes
General science index   **505**
Philosophy
Dawkins, R. Unweaving the rainbow   **501**
Gell-Mann, M. The quark and the jaguar   **530.1**
Hawking, S. W. Black holes and baby universes and other essays   **523.1**
Holmes, H. The secret life of dust   **551.51**
Lederman, L. M. The God particle   **539.7**
Morris, R. The big questions   **501**
Silver, B. L. The ascent of science   **509**
Whitehead, A. N. Process and reality   **113**
Wilson, E. O. Consilience   **121**
Germany
Walker, M. Nazi science   **509**
United States—History
Cohen, I. B. Science and the founding fathers
   973.3
Science & technology firsts. Bruno, L. C.   **609**
Science: a history of discovery in the twentieth century
   509
Science and civilization
Science, technology, and society: the impact of science in the 20th century   **509**
Science and health, with key to the Scriptures. Eddy, M. B.   **289.5**
Science and human values. Bronowski, J.   **500**
Science and its times   **509**
Science and religion *See* Religion and science
Science and technology desk reference   **500**
Science and the Bible *See* Bible and science
Science and the founding fathers. Cohen, I. B.
   973.3
Science and the humanities
Gould, S. J. The hedgehog, the fox, and the magister's pox   **303.4**
Science fiction
See also Fantasy fiction
Bibliography
Burgess, M. Reference guide to science fiction, fantasy, and horror   **016.8**
Reginald, R. Science fiction and fantasy literature, 1975-1991   **016.8**
Bio-bibliography
St. James guide to science fiction writers   **809.3**
History and criticism
Gunn, J. E. Isaac Asimov   **813.009**
Magill's guide to science fiction and fantasy literature
   809.3
St. James guide to science fiction writers   **809.3**
Science firsts: from the creation of science to the science of creation. Adler, R. E.   **509**
Science goes to war. Volkman, E.   **623**
Science matters: achieving scientific literacy. Hazen, R. M.   **500**
The science of freedom. Gay, P.
In Gay, P. The Enlightenment: an interpretation v2
   190
The science of God. Schroeder, G. L.   **261.5**
The science of Harry Potter. Highfield, R.   **500**
The science of UFOs. Alschuler, W. R.   **001.9**

Science, technology, and society: the impact of science in the 20th century   **509**
Science times book of language and linguistics   **400**
Scientific American (Periodical)
The Amateur astronomer. See The Amateur astronomer
   520
The Scientific American book of dinosaurs   **567.9**
The Scientific American book of the brain   **612.8**
The Scientific American science desk reference   **500**
Scientific apparatus and instruments
Crump, T. A brief history of science   **509**
Encyclopedias
Instruments of science   **502.8**
Scientific expeditions
See also Exploration
Scientific experiments *See* Science—Experiments
The scientist in the crib. Gopnik, A.   **155.4**
Scientists
See also Environmentalists; Women scientists
Adler, R. E. Science firsts: from the creation of science to the science of creation   **509**
Allaby, M. Makers of science   **920.003**
The Chronology of science   **509**
Friedman, M. Medicine's 10 greatest discoveries
   610.9
Greenstein, G. Portraits of discovery   **920**
Hargittai, I. The road to Stockholm   **509**
Malone, J. W. It doesn't take a rocket scientist
   920
Rittner, D. A to Z of scientists in weather and climate
   920.003
Travels with the fossil hunters   **560**
Uglow, J. S. The lunar men   **920**
Webster, R. B. African American firsts in science and technology   **509**
Dictionaries
American men & women of science   **920.003**
The Biographical dictionary of scientists   **920.003**
The Cambridge dictionary of scientists   **920.003**
Gates, A. E. A to Z of earth scientists   **920.003**
Notable black American scientists   **920.003**
Notable scientists from 1900 to the present
   920.003
Scigliano, Eric, 1953-
Love, war, and circuses   **599.67**
Scleroderma (Disease)
Mayes, M. D. The scleroderma book   **616.5**
The scleroderma book. Mayes, M. D.   **616.5**
Scotland
Civilization
Herman, A. How the Scots invented the modern world
   941.1
Description
Boswell, J. The journal of a tour to the Hebrides with Samuel Johnson   **914.11**
Rubenstein, L. A season in Dornoch   **796.352**
History
Devine, T. M. The Scottish nation 1700-2000
   941.1
History—16th century
Fraser, A. Mary Queen of Scots   **92**
Weir, A. Mary, Queen of Scots, and the murder of Lord Darnley   **92**
Scott, Beth, 1922-1994
(jt. auth) Norman, M. Haunted America   **133.1**
Scott, Dagny
Runner's world complete book of women's running
   796.42
Scott, Evelyn, 1893-1963
See/See also pages in the following book(s):
American women fiction writers   **813.009**
Scott, Jack Cassin- *See* Cassin-Scott, Jack
Scott, Sir James George, 1851-1935
About
Marshall, A. The trouser people   **959.1**

Scott, John F., 1936-
  Latin American art   **709.8**
Scott, Michael
  Maria Meneghini Callas   **92**
Scott, Paul, 1920-1978
  See/See also pages in the following book(s):
  Fraser, K. Ornament and silence   **814**
Scott, Robert, 1811-1887
  (jt. auth) Liddell, H. G. A Greek-English lexicon
     483
Scott, Robert Falcon, 1868-1912
      About
  Preston, D. A first rate tragedy   **998**
  Solomon, S. The coldest March   **998**
  See/See also pages in the following book(s):
  Connell, E. S. The Aztec treasure house p96-122
     814
Scott, Walter J., 1954-
  Lung cancer   **616.99**
Scott-Clark, Cathy
  (jt. auth) Levy, A. The stone of heaven   **553.8**
The **Scottish** nation 1700-2000. Devine, T. M.
     941.1
Scottish national characteristics
  Herman, A. How the Scots invented the modern world
     941.1
Scottsboro case
  See/See also pages in the following book(s):
  Geis, G. Crimes of the century   **345**
Scotty: James B. Reston and the rise and fall of
  American journalism. Stacks, J. F.   **92**
Scovell, George, 1774-1861
      About
  Urban, M. The man who broke Napoleon's codes
     940.2
Scovell, Jane
  Oona [Chaplin]   **92**
Scrabble (Game)
      Dictionaries
  The Official Scrabble players dictionary   **793.73**
The **scramble** for Africa, 1876-1912. Pakenham, T.
     960
Scrambled eggs & whiskey. Carruth, H.   **811**
Screen plays *See* Motion picture plays
The **Screwtape** letters. Lewis, C. S.   **248**
Scribe, Augustin Eugène *See* Scribe, Eugène, 1791-1861
Scribe, Eugène, 1791-1861
  The glass of water
  In Our dramatic heritage v4   **808.82**
The **Scribner** encyclopedia of American lives
     920.003
The **Scribner** encyclopedia of American lives, The 1960s
     920.003
Scroggins, Deborah
  Emma's war   **962.4**
Scull, Christina
  (jt. auth) Hammond, W. G. J.R.R. Tolkien, artist & il-
  lustrator   **92**
Scutella, Richard M.
  How to plan, contract, and build your own home
     690
SDI (Ballistic missile defense system) *See* Strategic Defense Initiative
Sea animals *See* Marine animals
The **sea** around us. Carson, R.   **551.46**
Sea food *See* Seafood
Sea life *See* Seafaring life
Sea mosses *See* Algae
Sea room: an island life in the Hebrides. Nicolson, A.
     941.1
The **sea** shall embrace them. Shaw, D. W.   **910.4**
Sea shells *See* Shells
Seabiscuit (Race horse)
  Hillenbrand, L. Seabiscuit   **798.4**

Seafaring life
  Dana, R. H. Two years before the mast   **910.4**
  McPhee, J. A. Looking for a ship   **910.4**
Seafaring life in literature
  American sea writing   **810.8**
Seafood
  See also Cooking—Seafood
  Brody, J. E. Jane Brody's good seafood book
     641.6
Seagrave, Peggy
  (jt. auth) Seagrave, S. The Yamato dynasty   **952**
Seagrave, Sterling
  The Soong dynasty   **951**
  The Yamato dynasty   **952**
The **seagull.** Chekhov, A. P.
  In Chekhov, A. P. The plays of Anton Chekhov
  p109-64   **891.7**
Seal, Graham, 1950-
  Encyclopedia of folk heroes   **398.03**
Seale, Allan
  New life for old gardens   **635.9**
Seale, William
  (ed) The White House. See The White House
     975.3
SEALs *See* United States. Navy. Sea Air Land Team
Seals (Numismatics)
  Shearer, B. F. State names, seals, flags, and symbols
     929.9
Seaman, Barbara
  The greatest experiment ever performed on women
     615
  (jt. auth) Null, G. For women only!   **613**
Seami *See* Zeami, 1363-1443
Seami, Yasukiuo *See* Hiyoshi, Yasukiyo
Search and rescue operations *See* Rescue work
The **search** for life on other planets. Jakosky, B. M.
     576.8
The **search** for modern China. Spence, J. D.   **951**
The **search** for signs of intelligent life in the universe.
  Wagner, J.   **812**
The **search** for superstrings, symmetry, and the theory of
  everything. Gribbin, J. R.   **539.7**
The **search** for the giant squid. Ellis, R.   **594**
Search for the golden moon bear. Montgomery, S.
     599.78
Searching for memory. Schacter, D. L.   **153.1**
Searching for your soul   **291.4**
Searching the internet *See* Internet searching
Sears, Martha
  (jt. auth) Sears, W. Parenting the fussy baby and high-
  need child   **649**
  (jt. auth) Sears, W. The pregnancy book   **618.2**
Sears, Stephen W.
  Chancellorsville   **973.7**
  George B. McClellan   **92**
  Landscape turned red   **973.7**
  To the gates of Richmond   **973.7**
Sears, William
  The Baby book. See The Baby book   **649**
  The family nutrition book   **613.2**
  Parenting the fussy baby and high-need child   **649**
  The pregnancy book   **618.2**
Sears list of subject headings   **025.4**
Seashore
  See also Coasts
  Carson, R. The edge of the sea   **577.7**
Seashore ecology
  Dean, C. Against the tide   **333.91**
A **season** in Dornoch. Rubenstein, L.   **796.352**
A **season** in hell & The drunken boat. Rimbaud, A.
     841
Season of blood. Keane, F.   **967.571**
Season of the 76ers. Lynch, W.   **796.323**
The **seasons** of a man's life. Levinson, D. J.   **155.6**

The **seasons** of a woman's life. Levinson, D. J.   **155.6**

Seaweeds *See* Algae

Sebag-Montefiore, Hugh
Enigma: the battle for the code   **940.54**

Sebag-Montefiore, Simon *See* Montefiore, Sebag

Sebold, Alice
Lucky   **362.883**

Second Advent
See/See also pages in the following book(s):
Lewis, C. S. The world's last night, and other essays p93-113   **230**

Second chances. Wallerstein, J. S.   **306.89**

The **second** common reader. Woolf, V.   **820.9**

The **second** creation. Wilmut, I.   **174**

The **second** family. Taffel, R.   **306.8**

The **second** John McPhee reader. McPhee, J. A.   **818**

A **second** Mencken chrestomathy. Mencken, H. L.   **818**

Second opinions. Groopman, J. E.   **610**

The **second** sex. Beauvoir, S. de   **305.4**

The **Second** World War. Gilbert, M.   **940.53**

The **Second** World War. Keegan, J.   **940.53**

Secondary school libraries *See* High school libraries

Secrecy. Moynihan, D. P.   **352**

Secrest, Meryle
Frank Lloyd Wright   **92**
Somewhere for me: a biography of Richard Rodgers   **92**
Stephen Sondheim   **92**

Secret agents. Drexler, M.   **614.4**

The **secret** alliance. Szulc, T.   **325**

Secret Intelligence Service (Great Britain) *See* Great Britain. MI6

Secret knowledge. Hockney, D.   **751**

The **secret** language of eating disorders. Claude-Pierre, P.   **616.85**

The **secret** life of dust. Holmes, H.   **551.51**

The **secret** lives of girls. Lamb, S.   **305.23**

The **secret** room. Laughlin, J.   **811**

Secret service
See also Espionage; Intelligence service; Spies
The **secret** voyage of Sir Francis Drake, 1577-1580. Bawlf, R. S.   **910.4**

The **secret** war against Hanoi. Shultz, R. H.   **959.704**

Secret writing *See* Cryptography

Secretaries
Handbooks, manuals, etc.
Burton, S. Procedures for the automated office   **651.3**
De Vries, M. A. The professional secretary's book of lists & tips   **651.3**
Stroman, J. Administrative assistant's & secretary's handbook   **651.3**

Secrets: a memoir of Vietnam and the Pentagon papers. Ellsberg, D.   **959.704**

Secrets of the flesh: a life of Colette. Thurman, J.   **92**

Secrets of the night sky. Berman, B.   **520**

Secrets of the temple. Greider, W.   **332.1**

Sects
See also names of churches and sects
Lewis, J. R. Cults in America   **291.9**
Mead, F. S. Handbook of denominations in the United States   **280**
Melton, J. G. The encyclopedia of American religions   **200.9**
Melton, J. G. Encyclopedic handbook of cults in America   **291.9**
Encyclopedias
The encyclopedia of cults, sects, and new religions   **200.3**

The **secular** mind. Coles, R.   **291.1**

Secularism
See also Atheism
Coles, R. The secular mind   **291.1**

Sedaris, David
Me talk pretty one day   **818**

Sedeen, Margaret
Star-spangled banner   **929.9**

Sedgwick, Peter
Descartes to Derrida   **190**

The **seduction** of Hillary Rodham. Brock, D.   **92**

See you on the radio. Osgood, C.   **818**

Seeds in the heart. Keene, D.   **895.6**

Seeds of contemplation. See Merton, T. New seeds of contemplation   **248**

Seeger, Pete
Pete Seeger's storytelling book   **372.6**
About
Dunaway, D. K. How can I keep from singing: Pete Seeger   **92**

Seeing and believing. Panek, R.   **522**

Seeing in the dark. Ferris, T.   **520**

Seeing Mary plain: a life of Mary McCarthy. Kiernan, F.   **92**

Seeing through places. Gordon, M.   **814**

Seeing voices. Sacks, O. W.   **362.4**

The **seekers**. Boorstin, D. J.   **909**

Seeking pleasure in the Old West. Dary, D.   **978**

Seferis, George, 1900-1971
Collected poems   **889**

Segal, Nancy L., 1951-
Entwined lives   **155.4**

Segal, Ronald, 1932-
Islam's Black slaves   **326**

Segel, Harold B., 1930-
The Columbia guide to the literatures of Eastern Europe since 1945   **809**

Segen, J. C.
The patient's guide to medical tests   **616.07**

Seglin, Jeffrey L., 1956-
The AMA handbook of business letters   **651.7**

Segrè, Gino
A matter of degrees   **536**

Segregated skies. Sandler, S.   **940.54**

Segregation in education
Kozol, J. Savage inequalities   **371.9**
Law and legislation
Irons, P. H. Jim Crow's children   **344**

Seibel, Machelle M.
The soy solution for menopause   **618.1**

Seife, Charles
Zero   **511**

Sein language. Seinfeld, J.   **817**

Seinfeld, Jerry
Sein language   **817**

Seismology *See* Earthquakes

Seismosaurus. Gillette, D. D.   **567.9**

Seko, Mobutu Sese *See* Mobutu Sese Seko, 1930-1997

Sela, Avraham
(ed) The Continuum political encyclopedia of the Middle East. See The Continuum political encyclopedia of the Middle East   **956**

Seldom disappointed. Hillerman, T.   **92**

Selected cronicas. Lispector, C.   **869**

Selected early poems. Simic, C.   **811**

Selected essays. Berger, J.   **824**

Selected letters, 1940-1956. Kerouac, J.   **92**

Selected letters, 1957-1969. Kerouac, J.   **92**

Selected non-fictions. Borges, J. L.   **864**

Selected odes of Pablo Neruda. Neruda, P.   **861**

Selected poems. Ashbery, J.   **811**

Selected poems. Borges, J. L.   **861**

Selected poems. Brooks, G.   **811**

Selected poems. Creeley, R.   **811**

Selected poems. Dove, R.   **811**

Selected poems. García Lorca, F.   **861**

Selected poems. Hacker, M.   811

Selected poems. Jarrell, R.
In Jarrell, R. The complete poems   811

Selected poems. Mahon, D.   821

Selected poems. Paz, O.   861

Selected poems. Pound, E.   811

Selected poems. Rexroth, K.   811

Selected poems. Shapiro, K. J.   811

Selected poems. Tate, J.   811

Selected poems. Van Duyn, M.   811

Selected poems. Verlaine, P.   841

Selected poems. Whitman, W.   811

Selected poems, 1934-1952. Thomas, D.   821

Selected poems, 1947-1995. Ginsberg, A.   811

Selected poems, 1957-1994. Hughes, T.   821

Selected poems, 1960-1990. Kumin, M.   811

Selected poems, 1963-1983. See Simic, C. Selected early poems   811

Selected poems and prose of Paul Celan. Celan, P.   831

Selected poems and translations, 1969-1991. Matthews, W.   811

Selected poems of Langston Hughes. Hughes, L.   811

Selected poems [of] Marina Tsvetayeva. T͡Svetaeva, M. I.   891.7

The **selected** poems of Nikki Giovanni (1968-1995). Giovanni, N.   811

The **selected** poems of Yvor Winters. Winters, Y.   811

Selected poetry. Hollander, J.   811

Selected poetry. Pope, A.   821

Selected poetry of William Wordsworth. Wordsworth, W.   821

The **selected** poetry of Yehuda Amichai. Amichai, Y.   892

Selected writings. Stein, G.   818

Selected writings. Thomas, Aquinas, Saint   189

Selected writings. Valéry, P.   848

Selection, Artificial *See* Breeding

Selective guide to colleges. See Fiske, E. B. The Fiske guide to colleges   378.73

Self
LeDoux, J. E. Synaptic self   612.8
Weber, R. J. The created self   155.2
Whybrow, P. C. A mood apart   616.89
See/See also pages in the following book(s):
Jung, C. G. Man and his symbols p158-229   150.19

Self-actualization *See* Self-realization

Self-care, Health *See* Health self-care

Self-confidence
Carter, S. Men like women who like themselves   158

Self-defense
See also Martial arts
Ochiai, H. Hidy Ochiai's complete book of self-defense   796.8

Self-employed
See also Home-based business; Small business
Lonier, T. Working solo   658

Self-esteem
Queen Latifah. Ladies first   158
Steinem, G. Revolution from within   155.2

Self-fulfillment *See* Self-realization

Self image *See* Personal appearance

Self-love (Psychology) *See* Self-esteem

The **self-publishing** manual. Poynter, D.   070.5

Self-realization
See also Success
Bloomfield, H. H. Making peace with your past   158
Gegax, T. Winning in the game of life   158
Greer, G. The change   618.1
Hillman, J. The force of character   155.67

Lunden, J. Wake-up calls   155.2

Peck, M. S. Further along the road less traveled   158

Peck, M. S. The road less traveled and beyond   158

Siegel, B. S. Prescriptions for living   158

Self-respect *See* Self-esteem

The **self-tormentor**. Terence
In Terence. Terence, the comedies   872

The **selfish** gene. Dawkins, R.   576

Selfridge, Nancy
Freedom from fibromyalgia   616.7

Seligman, Martin E. P.
The optimistic child   155.4

Seligman, Patricia, 1950-
Painting murals   751.7

Selikowitz, Mark
Down syndrome   618.92

Selkirk, Alexander, 1676-1721
About
Severin, T. In search of Robinson Crusoe   996
Souhami, D. Selkirk's Island   996

Selkirk's Island. Souhami, D.   996

Selling
Gerhards, P. How to sell what you make   658.8

Selling God. Moore, R. L.   200.9

Selves. Booth, P.   811

Semantics
Hayakawa, S. I. Language in thought and action   412

Seminole Indians
McReynolds, E. C. The Seminoles   970.004

Semiotics
See also Semantics

Senate (U.S.) *See* United States. Congress. Senate

Sendak, Maurice
See/See also pages in the following book(s):
Marcus, L. S. Ways of telling   741.6

Seneca, Lucius Annaeus, the Younger, 4 B.C.-65 A.D.
Medea
In The Portable Roman reader p487-527   870.8

Seneca Indians
See/See also pages in the following book(s):
Josephy, A. M. Now that the buffalo's gone p133-50   970.004

Senior citizens *See* Elderly

Senior high school library catalog   011.6

Sense of direction *See* Direction sense

The **sense** of reality. Berlin, Sir I.   901

Senses and sensation
See also Pain
Ackerman, D. A natural history of the senses   152.1
Hughes, H. C. Sensory exotica   573.8

Sensitivity training *See* Group relations training

Sensory exotica. Hughes, H. C.   573.8

Sentance, Bryan
Art of the basket   746.41

Sepheriadēs, Geōrgios *See* Seferis, George, 1900-1971

September 11 terrorist attacks, 2001
See also World Trade Center terrorist attack, 2001
Bernstein, R. Out of the blue   973.931
Didion, J. Fixed ideas: America since 9.11   320.5
Friedman, T. L. Longitudes and attitudes   973.931
Langewiesche, W. American ground, unbuilding the World Trade Center   974.7
Longman, J. Among the heroes   974.8
Lutnick, H. On top of the world   332.6
Miller, J. The cell: inside the 9/11 plot and why the FBI and CIA failed to stop it   973.931
Picciotto, R. Last man down   974.7
Sheehy, G. Middletown, America   974.9
Woodward, B. Bush at war   973.931

Sequoyah, 1770?-1843
See/See also pages in the following book(s):
Lepore, J. A is for American   **306.44**
Serafin, Steven
(ed) Encyclopedia of world literature in the 20th century. See Encyclopedia of world literature in the 20th century   **803**
Serafini, Anthony
The epic history of biology   **570**
Sereny, Gitta
Albert Speer   **92**
Serial publications
See also Newspapers
Serious business. Kanfer, S.   **741.5**
Serkin, Rudolf, 1903-1991
About
Lehmann, S. Rudolf Serkin   **92**
Sermon on the mount
Bonhoeffer, D. The cost of discipleship   **226**
Sermons
American sermons   **252**
King, M. L. Strength to love   **252**
Tillich, P. The eternal now   **252**
Tutu, D. The rainbow people of God   **968.06**
Seroussi, Karyn
Unraveling the mystery of autism and pervasive developmental disorder   **618.92**
The **serpents** of paradise. Abbey, E.   **818**
Serri, Conchita Franco See Franco Serri, Conchita
Servants of nature. Pyenson, L.   **509**
Service, Robert
A history of twentieth-century Russia   **947.086**
Lenin—a biography   **92**
Servitude *See* Slavery
Sessine, Suzanne, 1976-
(ed) Beacham's guide to the endangered species of North America. See Beacham's guide to the endangered species of North America   **578.68**
Setting the world ablaze. Ferling, J. E.   **973.3**
The **settlement** of the Americas. Dillehay, T. D.   **970.01**
Seuling, Barbara
How to write a children's book and get it published   **808.06**
Seurat, Georges Pierre, 1859-1891
About
Courthion, P. Georges Seurat   **759.4**
Drama
Sondheim, S. Sunday in the park with George   **812**
Seuss, Dr.
About
Morgan, J. Dr. Seuss & Mr. Geisel   **92**
The **seven** ages. Glück, L.   **811**
The **seven** daughters of Eve. Sykes, B.   **599.93**
The **seven** essentials of woodworking. Guidice, A.   **684**
Seven experiments that could change the world. Sheldrake, R.   **507.8**
Seven guitars. Wilson, A.   **812**
Seven pillars of wisdom. Lawrence, T. E.   **940.4**
The **seven** sins of memory. Schacter, D. L.   **153.1**
The **seven** states of California. Fradkin, P. L.   **979.4**
The **seven** storey mountain. Merton, T.   **92**
Seven Years' War, 1756-1763
Anderson, F. The crucible of war   **973.2**
The **seventies**. Schulman, B. J.   **973.92**
The **seventy** architectural wonders of our world. See The Seventy wonders of the modern world   **720.9**
Seventy-five years of the Oscar. See Osborne, R. A. 75 years of the Oscar   **791.43**
The **Seventy** wonders of the modern world   **720.9**
Severin, Timothy
In search of Robinson Crusoe   **996**

Sevy, Grace, 1936-
(ed) The American experience in Vietnam. See The American experience in Vietnam   **959.704**
Sewell, Darrel, 1939-
(ed) Thomas Eakins. See Thomas Eakins [exhibition catalog]   **759.13**
Sewing
See also Needlework
Bednar, N. The encyclopedia of sewing machine techniques   **646.2**
Betzina, S. Power sewing step-by-step   **646.4**
Betzina, S. Sandra Betzina sews for your home   **646.2**
The Complete book of sewing   **646.4**
Giordano, J. The sewing machine guide   **646.2**
James, C. The complete serger handbook   **646.2**
Lee, L. Sewing edges and corners   **646.2**
Morris, M. Every sewer's guide to the perfect fit   **646.4**
New complete guide to sewing   **646.2**
Sewing edges and corners. Lee, L.   **646.2**
The **sewing** machine guide. Giordano, J.   **646.2**
Sewing machines
Giordano, J. The sewing machine guide   **646.2**
James, C. The complete serger handbook   **646.2**
Sex *See* Sexual behavior
Sex (Biology)
Blum, D. Sex on the brain   **612.6**
Masters, W. H. Masters and Johnson on sex and human loving   **155.3**
Mondimore, F. M. A natural history of homosexuality   **306.7**
Small, M. F. What's love got to do with it?   **576.8**
Sex change *See* Transsexualism
Sex crimes
See also Child sexual abuse
Sex differences (Psychology)
Blum, D. Sex on the brain   **612.6**
Fisher, H. E. The first sex   **305.4**
Gilbert, S. A field guide to boys and girls   **305.23**
Gurian, M. The wonder of girls   **305.23**
Mead, M. Coming of age in Samoa   **306**
Tannen, D. You just don't understand   **302.2**
Taylor, S. E. The tending instinct   **304.5**
Sex discrimination
Eisaguirre, L. Sexual harassment   **342**
Roberts, C. We are our mothers' daughters   **305.4**
Sex education
The "Go ask Alice" book of answers   **613**
Levine, J. Harmful to minors   **306.7**
Williamson, M. L. Great sex after 40   **306.7**
Sex on the brain. Blum, D.   **612.6**
Sex over 50. Block, J. D.   **613.9**
Sex role
Angier, N. Woman   **612.6**
Deutsch, F. Halving it all   **649**
Greer, G. The whole woman   **305.4**
Wolf, N. The beauty myth   **305.4**
Sexism
See also Sex discrimination
Sextet (yes). Wilson, L.
In Wilson, L. 21 short plays p87-94   **812**
Sexton, Anne
The complete poems   **811**
About
Middlebrook, D. W. Anne Sexton   **92**
See/See also pages in the following book(s):
Women writers at work p307-75   **808**
Sexual behavior
See also Sexual behavior in animals
Ackerman, D. A natural history of love   **152.4**
Bader, M. J. Arousal, the secret logic of sexual fantasies   **306.7**
Barash, D. P. The myth of monogamy   **306.7**

Sexual behavior—*Continued*
Block, J. D. Sex over 50 **613.9**
Comfort, A. The joy of sex **613.9**
Etcoff, N. L. Survival of the prettiest **391**
Hite, S. The Hite report on the family **306.8**
Masters, W. H. Masters and Johnson on sex and human loving **155.3**
Menninger, K. A. Love against hate **150.19**
Pagels, E. H. Adam, Eve, and the serpent **241**
Reinisch, J. The Kinsey Institute new report on sex **306.7**
Small, M. F. What's love got to do with it? **576.8**
See/See also pages in the following book(s):
Levine, J. Harmful to minors **306.7**
Sheehy, G. Understanding men's passages **305.31**
Sexual behavior in animals
Zuk, M. Sexual selections **591.56**
Sexual disorders
See also Impotence
Sexual ethics
See/See also pages in the following book(s):
Teilhard de Chardin, P. Toward the future p60-87 **194**
Sexual harassment
See/See also pages in the following book(s):
Bordo, S. The male body p265-80 **305.31**
Law and legislation
Bingham, C. Class action **342**
Eisaguirre, L. Sexual harassment **342**
Sexual hygiene
Williamson, M. L. Great sex after 40 **306.7**
Sexual selections. Zuk, M. **591.56**
Sexuality *See* Sexual behavior
Sexually transmitted diseases
See also Sexual hygiene
Marr, L. Sexually transmitted diseases **616.95**
Seymour, Jane *See* Jane Seymour, Queen, consort of Henry VIII, King of England, 1509?-1537
Seymour, Miranda
A brief history of thyme and other herbs **635**
Mary Shelley **92**
Seymour-Smith, Martin
The 100 most influential books ever written **028**
(ed) World authors, 1900-1950. See World authors, 1900-1950 **920.003**
Shabazz, Betty
About
Rickford, R. J. Betty Shabazz: a remarkable story of survival and faith before and after Malcolm X **92**
Shabbat shalom. Friedland, S. R. **641.5**
Shachtman, Tom, 1942-
Absolute zero and the conquest of cold **536**
Shackelford, George T. M., 1955-
(jt. auth) Tucker, P. H. Monet in the 20th century **759.4**
Shackleton, Sir Ernest Henry, 1874-1922
About
Alexander, C. The Endurance **998**
Shacochis, Bob
The immaculate invasion **972.94**
Shad
McPhee, J. A. The founding fish **597**
Shade, William G.
(ed) American presidential campaigns and elections. See American presidential campaigns and elections **324**
Shadow. Woodward, B. **973.92**
Shadow and act. Ellison, R. **814**
Shadow of heaven. Voigt, E. B. **811**
The **shadow** of the sun. Kapuściński, R. **960**
Shadowing the ground. Ignatow, D. **811**
Shadows of forgotten ancestors. Sagan, C. **570.1**

Shadows on the grass. Dinesen, I.
In Dinesen, I. Out of Africa and Shadows on the grass **967.62**
Shaffer, Peter
Equus **822**
Lettice & lovage **822**
Peter Shaffer's Amadeus **822**
Shagrin, Steve
(ed) Facts about retiring in the United States. See Facts about retiring in the United States **305.26**
The **Shaker** experience in America. Stein, S. J. **289**
Shakers
Sprigg, J. Shaker—life, work, and art **289**
Stein, S. J. The Shaker experience in America **289**
Shakespeare, Nicholas, 1957-
Bruce Chatwin **92**
Shakespeare, William, 1564-1616
The Columbia dictionary of quotations from Shakespeare **822.3**
The complete works of William Shakespeare **822.3**
A dictionary of quotations from Shakespeare **822.3**
The Norton Shakespeare **822.3**
Poems **821**
Sonnets **821**
In Vendler, H. H. The art of Shakespeare's sonnets **822.3**
About
Boyce, C. Shakespeare A to Z **822.3**
Gollob, H. Me and Shakespeare **822.3**
Holden, A. William Shakespeare **822.3**
Olsen, K. All things Shakespeare **822.3**
The Oxford companion to Shakespeare **822.3**
Wells, S. W. Shakespeare: for all time **822.3**
See/See also pages in the following book(s):
Bloom, H. The Western canon **809**
Shakespeare, W. The Columbia dictionary of quotations from Shakespeare **822.3**
Adaptations
Chute, M. G. Stories from Shakespeare **822.3**
Lamb, C. Tales from Shakespeare **822.3**
Biography
Honan, P. Shakespeare **822.3**
Criticism
Bloom, H. Shakespeare: the invention of the human **822.3**
Frye, N. Northrop Frye on Shakespeare **822.3**
Dictionaries
Coye, D. F. Pronouncing Shakespeare's words **822.3**
Dramatic production
Harold, M. An actor's guide to performing Shakespeare **792**
Rodenburg, P. Speaking Shakespeare **792**
Histories
Norwich, J. J. Shakespeare's kings **822.3**
Infuence
See/See also pages in the following book(s):
Smith, B. Hamlet's dresser **92**
Language
Kermode, F. Shakespeare's language **822.3**
Parodies, imitations, etc.
Stoppard, T. Rosencrantz and Guildenstern are dead **822**
Quotations
Shakespeare, W. A dictionary of quotations from Shakespeare **822.3**
Shakespeare A to Z. Boyce, C. **822.3**
Shakespeare: for all time. Wells, S. W. **822.3**
Shakespeare's kings. Norwich, J. J. **822.3**
Shakespeare's language. Kermode, F. **822.3**

Shakey: Neil Young's biography. McDonough, J.
92
Shaking-up Parkinson disease. Lieberman, A. **616.8**
Shakur, Tupac

About

Dyson, M. E. Holler if you hear me: searching for Tupac Shakur 92
Sullivan, R. Labyrinth **364.1**
Shakya, Tsering *See* Tsering Shakya
Shalom, friend: the life and legacy of Yitzhak Rabin
92
The **Shambhala** guide to sufism. Ernst,˙C. W. **297**
The **shameful** life of Salvador Dalí. Gibson, I. **92**
Shange, Ntozake
For colored girls who have considered suicide/when the rainbow is enuf **812**
Shanghai (China)
Dong, S. Shanghai, 1842-1949 **951**
Shankle, George Earlie
American nicknames **929.4**
Shanks, Hershel
The mystery and meaning of the Dead Sea scrolls
296.1
(ed) Understanding the Dead Sea scrolls. See Understanding the Dead Sea scrolls **296.1**
Shannon, Joyce Brennfleck
(ed) Transplantation sourcebook. See Transplantation sourcebook **617.9**
The **shape** of a pocket. Berger, J. **701**
The **shape** of the journey. Harrison, J. **811**
Shaping a nation. Wiseman, C. **720.973**
Shapiro, Harvey, 1924-
(ed) Poets of World War II. See Poets of World War II **811**
Shapiro, James S., 1955-
(ed) The Columbia anthology of British poetry. See The Columbia anthology of British poetry
821.008
Shapiro, Jerry
(jt. auth) Thompson, W. J. A. Alopecia areata
616.5
Shapiro, Karl Jay, 1913-2000
Selected poems **811**
Shapiro, Lawrence E.
How to raise a child with a high EQ **649**
The **shark** almanac. Allen, T. B. **597**
Shark trouble. Benchley, P. **597**
Sharks
Allen, T. B. The shark almanac **597**
Benchley, P. Shark trouble **597**
Capuzzo, M. Close to shore **597**
Ellis, R. Great white shark **597**
Ferrari, A. Sharks **597**
Springer, V. G. Sharks in question **597**
Steel, R. Sharks of the world **597**
Sharks in question. Springer, V. G. **597**
Sharks of the world. Steel, R. **597**
Shatkin, Laurence
(ed) Guide for occupational exploration. See Guide for occupational exploration **331.7**
Shattuck, Gardiner H.
(jt. auth) Queen, E. L. The encyclopedia of American religious history **200.9**
Shattuck, Roger
Proust's way **843.009**
Shatzky, Joel
(ed) Contemporary Jewish-American novelists. See Contemporary Jewish-American novelists
813.009
Shaughnessy, Dan
Ever green: the Boston Celtics **796.323**
Shaw, Bernard, 1856-1950
Arms and the man
In Our dramatic heritage v5 **808.82**

Saint Joan
In Our dramatic heritage v5 **808.82**
In The Oxford anthology of English literature v2
820.8

About

Peters, S. Bernard Shaw **92**
See/See also pages in the following book(s):
Holroyd, M. Works on paper **809**
Shaw, David W., 1961-
The sea shall embrace them **910.4**
Shaw, Diana, 1958-
The essential vegetarian cookbook **641.5**
Shaw, Earl
See/See also pages in the following book(s):
Russell, D. Black genius and the American experience
920
Shaw, George Bernard *See* Shaw, Bernard, 1856-1950
Shawcross, William
Deliver us from evil **909.82**
Queen and country: the fifty-year reign of Elizabeth II
92
Shawn, Allen
Arnold Schoenberg's journey **92**
Shawn, William

About

Ross, L. Here but not here **92**
See/See also pages in the following book(s):
Fraser, K. Ornament and silence **814**
Shawnee Indians
Eckert, A. W. A sorrow in our heart: the life of Tecumseh **92**
She stoops to conquer. Goldsmith, O. **822**
Shearer, Barbara Smith
(ed) Notable women in the physical sciences. See Notable women in the physical sciences **920.003**
(jt. auth) Shearer, B. F. State names, seals, flags, and symbols **929.9**
Shearer, Benjamin F.
State names, seals, flags, and symbols **929.9**
(ed) Notable women in the physical sciences. See Notable women in the physical sciences **920.003**
Sheck, Laurie
Black series **811**
Sheehan, Neil
A bright shining lie: John Paul Vann and America in Vietnam **959.704**
See/See also pages in the following book(s):
Prochnau, W. W. Once upon a distant war
959.704
Sheehan, William, 1954-
Mars **523.4**
The planet Mars **523.4**
Sheehy, Gail
Hillary's choice [biography of Hillary Rodham Clinton] **92**
Middletown, America **974.9**
New passages **305.24**
The silent passage: menopause **618.1**
Understanding men's passages **305.31**
Sheehy, Helen, 1948-
Eleonora Duse **92**
Sheets-Pyenson, Susan, 1949-1998
(jt. auth) Pyenson, L. Servants of nature **509**
Sheldrake, Rupert
Dogs that know when their owners are coming home
133.8
Seven experiments that could change the world
507.8
Sheler, Jeffery L.
Is the Bible true? **220.1**
Shell chic. Marshall, M. H. **745.55**
Shelley, Fred M., 1952-
Atlas of American politics, 1960-2000. See Atlas of American politics, 1960-2000
973.92

Shelley, Mary Wollstonecraft, 1797-1851
About
Seymour, M. Mary Shelley   92
Sunstein, E. W. Mary Shelley   92
Shelley, Percy Bysshe, 1792-1822
The complete poems of Percy Bysshe Shelley
    821
Shelley's poetry and prose   821
Shelley's poetry and prose. Shelley, P. B.   821
Shellfish
See also Crabs
Shells
Marshall, M. H. Shell chic   745.55
Shelton, Nelda
(jt. auth) Burton, S. Procedures for the automated office   651.3
Shelton, Robert, 1926-1995
No direction home: the life and music of Bob Dylan
    92
Shemel, Sidney, 1913-1992
(jt. auth) Krasilovsky, M. W. This business of music
    780
Shenk, David, 1966-
The forgetting: Alzheimer's, portrait of an epidemic
    616.8
Shenkman, Richard
Legends, lies & cherished myths of world history
    902
Legends, lies, and cherished myths of American history   973.02
Shepard, Sam, 1943-
See/See also pages in the following book(s):
Playwrights at work   812.009
Shephard, Sue
Pickled, potted, and canned   641.4
Shepherd, Jack
(jt. auth) Glover, B. The runner's handbook
    796.42
Shepherd, Jesse *See* Grierson, Francis, 1848-1927
Shepherd, Margaret
Learn calligraphy   745.6
Sheppard, Sam, d. 1970
About
Neff, J. The wrong man   345
Sheppard, William Henry, 1865-1927
About
Kennedy, P. Black Livingstone   92
Sheridan, Peter, 1952-
44, Dublin made me   92
47 roses   92
Sherman, Curt
(jt. auth) Harwood, B. Architecture and interior design through the 18th century   729
Sherman, Joan R.
(ed) African-American poetry of the nineteenth century. See African-American poetry of the nineteenth century   811.008
Sherman, William L.
(jt. auth) Meyer, M. C. The course of Mexican history
    972
Sherman, William T. (William Tecumseh), 1820-1891
About
Davis, B. Sherman's march   973.7
Fellman, M. Citizen Sherman: a life of William Tecumseh Sherman   92
Hanson, V. D. The soul of battle   355
Kennett, L. B. Sherman   92
See/See also pages in the following book(s):
Wilson, E. Patriotic gore p174-218   810.9
Sherman's march. Davis, B.   973.7
Shermer, Michael
Denying history   940.53
Why people believe weird things   001.9
Sherr, Lynn
(ed) Anthony, S. B. Failure is impossible   92

Sherrin, Ned
The Oxford dictionary of humorous quotations. See The Oxford dictionary of humorous quotations
    808.88
Sherrow, Victoria
Encyclopedia of women and sports   796
Sherwood, John Darrell, 1966-
Fast movers   959.704
Shestov, Lev, 1866-1938
See/See also pages in the following book(s):
Miłosz, C. To begin where I am p260-80   891.8
The **shield** of Achilles. Bobbitt, P.   327
Shields, Carol
Jane Austen   92
Shifman, Barry
(ed) Gifts to the tsars, 1500-1700. See Gifts to the tsars, 1500-1700   745
Shikibu, Murasaki *See* Murasaki Shikibu, b. 978?
Shiloh (Tenn.), Battle of, 1862
Daniel, L. J. Shiloh   973.7
Shilts, Randy
And the band played on   362.1
Shim, Jae K.
(jt. auth) Siegel, J. G. Accounting handbook   657
Shimbo, Hiroko
The Japanese kitchen   641.5
Shintani, Terry
The good carbohydrate revolution   613.2
Ship ablaze. O'Donnell, E. T.   910.4
Ship of gold in the deep blue sea. Kinder, G.
    910.4
Shipler, David K.
Arab and Jew   956.94
Shipman, Pat
Taking wing   568
(jt. auth) Walker, A. The wisdom of the bones
    599.93
Shipton, Alyn
A new history of jazz   781.65
Shipwrecks
Ashcraft, T. O. Red sky in mourning   910.4
Ballard, R. D. The discovery of the Titanic   910.4
Ballard, R. D. Return to Midway   940.54
Butler, D. A. Unsinkable: the full story of the RMS Titanic   910.4
Clifford, B. The lost fleet   910.4
Dash, M. Batavia's graveyard   910.4
Jessop, V. Titanic survivor   910.4
Junger, S. The perfect storm   910.4
Kinder, G. Ship of gold in the deep blue sea
    910.4
Konstam, A. The history of shipwrecks   910.4
Krieger, M. J. All the men in the sea   910.4
Lord, W. A night to remember   910.4
Pellegrino, C. R. Ghosts of the Titanic   910.4
Philbrick, N. In the heart of the sea   910.4
Shaw, D. W. The sea shall embrace them   910.4
Stanton, D. In harm's way   940.54
Encyclopedias
Encyclopedia of underwater and maritime archaeology
    930.1
Ritchie, D. Shipwrecks   910.4
Shirer, William L. (William Lawrence)
The rise and fall of the Third Reich   943.086
Shlaim, Avi
The iron wall   956.94
The **shock** of the new. Hughes, R.   709.04
Shocked, appalled, and dismayed!. Phillips, E. H.
    651.7
Shoeless. Fleitz, D. L.   92
Shoeless Joe Jackson *See* Jackson, Joe, 1887 or 8-1951
Shoemaker, Candice A.
(ed) Encyclopedia of gardens. See Encyclopedia of gardens   635

The **shoemaker's** prodigious wife. García Lorca, F.
In Garcia Lorca, F. Five plays p57-104   862
Shoolery, Judith
  (jt. auth) Teller, E. Memoirs   92
Shooter's bible   623.4
Shooting
  Gun digest   623.4
Shooting under fire. Howe, P.   070.4
Shop talk. Roth, P.   809
Shore, Kenneth
  Keeping kids safe   649
Short, Philip
  Mao   92
A **short** history of Byzantium. Norwich, J. J.   949.5
A **short** history of nearly everything. Bryson, B.
    500
A **short** history of planet earth. Macdougall, J. D.
    551.7
A **short** history of the movies. Mast, G.   791.43
A **short** history of World War I. Stokesbury, J. L.
    940.3
The **short** Oxford history of English literature. Sanders,
  A.   820.9
Short plays *See* One act plays
Short stories
  Hawthorne, N. The portable Hawthorne   818
      Bio-bibliography
  The Columbia companion to the twentieth-century
    American short story   813.009
  Critical survey of short fiction   809.3
      History and criticism
  The Columbia companion to the twentieth-century
    American short story   813.009
  Critical survey of short fiction   809.3
  The Facts on File companion to the American short
    story   813.009
  Hooper, B. The short story readers' advisory
    809.3
  A Reader's companion to the short story in English
    809.3
  Short story criticism   809.3
  Short story writers   809.3
    History and criticism—Bibliography
  Walker, W. S. Twentieth century short story explica-
    tion: new series   016.8093
        Indexes
  Short story index   808.83
Short story criticism   809.3
Short story index   808.83
The **short** story readers' advisory. Hooper, B.   809.3
Short story writers   809.3
The **short** sweet dream of Eduardo Gutierrez. Breslin, J.
    92
A **shortcut** through time. Johnson, G.   004
Shortelle, Dennis
  (jt. auth) Conklin, B. G. Encyclopedia of forensic sci-
    ence   363.2
Shorter, Edward
  A history of psychiatry   616.89
The **Shorter** Columbia anthology of traditional Chinese
  literature   895.1
Shorter encyclopedia of Islam. *See* Concise encyclope-
  dia of Islam   297
Shorter Oxford English dictionary on historical princi-
  ples   423
Shortwave radio
  See also Amateur radio stations
Shostakovich, Dmitriĭ Dmitrievich, 1906-1975
  See/See also pages in the following book(s):
  Volkov, S. St. Petersburg   947
Shotwell, Barbara, 1946-
  Pass it on   346.05
Should you leave? Kramer, P. D.   616.89
Shoumatoff, Alex
  Legends of the American desert   978

Shoup, David M., 1904-1983
  See/See also pages in the following book(s):
  Mikaelian, A. Medal of honor   920
Shouting fire. Dershowitz, A. M.   323
A **shovel** of stars. Morgan, T.   978
Show business *See* Performing arts
Showers (Parties)
  Cooke, C. The best baby shower book   793.2
Shrines
  Wilson, C. The atlas of holy places & sacred sites
    291.3
Shrinking the cat. Hubbell, S.   660.6
Shroud of the gnome. Tate, J.   811
The **shrub** identification book. Symonds, G. W. D.
    582.1
Shrubs
  The Complete encyclopedia of trees and shrubs
    635.9
  Dirr, M. Dirr's Hardy trees and shrubs   635.9
  Dirr, M. Dirr's trees and shrubs for warm climates
    635.9
  Fisher, K. Taylor's guide to shrubs   635.9
  The Hillier gardener's guide to trees & shrubs
    635.9
  Symonds, G. W. D. The shrub identification book
    582.1
Shuler, John
  (jt. auth) Hernon, P. U.S. government on the Web
    025.04
Shulevitz, Uri, 1935-
  Writing with pictures   808.06
Shulman, Beth
  The betrayal of work   331.2
Shulman, Holly Cowan
  (ed) The Eleanor Roosevelt encyclopedia. *See* The El-
    eanor Roosevelt encyclopedia   92
Shulman, Lisa M.
  (jt. auth) Weiner, W. J. Parkinson's disease   616.8
Shulman, Martha Rose
  Foodlover's atlas of the world   641.3
Shultz, Richard H., 1947-
  The secret war against Hanoi   959.704
Shump, Cynthia S.
  (jt. auth) Saudek, C. D. The Johns Hopkins guide to
    diabetes   616.4
Shurgin, Ann H., 1952-
  (ed) The Folklore of world holidays. *See* The Folklore
    of world holidays   394.26
Shurtleff, Akiko *See* Aoyagi, Akiko, 1950-
Shurtleff, William, 1941-
  The book of tofu   641.6
Shuster, Todd
  (jt. auth) Pollack, W. S. Real boys' voices
    305.23
Shut out. Bryant, H.   796.357
Shuttles, Space *See* Space shuttles
Siberia (Russia)
        Description
  Thubron, C. In Siberia   957
Sibley, David
  The Sibley field guide to birds of eastern North Ameri-
    ca   598
  The Sibley field guide to birds of western North Amer-
    ica   598
  The Sibley guide to bird life & behavior   598
  The Sibley guide to birds   598
  Sibley's birding basics   598
The **Sibley** field guide to birds of eastern North America.
  Sibley, D.   598
The **Sibley** field guide to birds of western North Ameri-
  ca. Sibley, D.   598
The **Sibley** guide to bird life & behavior. Sibley, D.
    598
The **Sibley** guide to birds. Sibley, D.   598
Sibley's birding basics. Sibley, D.   598

Siblings
  See also Twins
  Harris, S. L. Siblings of children with autism   **649**
  Karasik, J. The ride together   **618.92**
  Safer, J. The normal one   **158**
Siblings of children with autism. Harris, S. L.   **649**
Sichel, Deborah
  Women's moods   **616.89**
Sicherman, Barbara
  (ed) Notable American women: the modern period. See
    Notable American women: the modern period
    920.003
Sicilian odyssey. Prose, F.   **945**
Sicily (Italy)
  Description
  Prose, F. Sicilian odyssey   **945**
  History
  See/See also pages in the following book(s):
  Simeti, M. T. Travels with a medieval queen   **92**
Sick
  See also Terminally ill
  Lown, B. The lost art of healing   **610**
Sickle cell anemia
  Bloom, M. Understanding sickle cell disease
    616.1
Sickles, Daniel E., 1825-1914
  About
  Keneally, T. American scoundrel: the life of the notori-
    ous Civil War General Dan Sickles   **92**
Sickman, Laurence, 1906-1988
  The art and architecture of China   **709.51**
Sickness *See* Diseases
Siddal, Elizabeth, 1829-1862
  See/See also pages in the following book(s):
  Prose, F. The lives of the muses   **920**
Siddhārtha *See* Gautama Buddha
Side effects. Allen, W.   **817**
Sides, Hampton, 1962-
  Ghost soldiers   **940.54**
Sides, W. Hampton *See* Sides, Hampton, 1962-
Siegal, Allan, 1940-
  The New York times manual of style and usage
    808
Siegal, Mordecai
  (ed) The Cornell book of cats. See The Cornell book
    of cats   **636.8**
Siegel, Ben, 1925-
  (ed) Bellow, S. Conversations with Saul Bellow
    92
Siegel, Bernie S.
  Prescriptions for living   **158**
Siegel, Bryna
  Helping children with autism learn   **371.9**
Siegel, Joel G.
  Accounting handbook   **657**
Siegfried, Tom
  Strange matters   **523.1**
Sienkewicz, Thomas J.
  (ed) Encyclopedia of the ancient world. See Encyclo-
    pedia of the ancient world   **930**
Siepmann, Jeremy
  The piano   **786.2**
The **Sierra** Club family outdoors guide. Doan, M.
    796.5
Sierra Leone
  Campbell, G. Blood diamonds   **966.4**
  History—Civil War, 1991-
  Voeten, T. How de body?   **966.4**
Sies, Luther F.
  Encyclopedia of American radio, 1920-1960
    791.44
Sifakis, Carl
  The Mafia encyclopedia   **364.1**
Sife, Wallace
  The loss of a pet   **155.9**

Sifters: Native American women's lives   **920**
Sight *See* Vision
Sign language
  Butterworth, R. R. Signing made easy   **419**
  Chambers, D. P. Communicating in sign   **419**
  Costello, E. Random House Webster's American sign
    language dictionary   **419**
  Lane, L. G. Gallaudet survival guide to signing
    419
  Proctor, C. O. NTC's multilingual dictionary of
    American sign language   **419**
  Riekehof, L. L. The joy of signing   **419**
  Sacks, O. W. Seeing voices   **362.4**
  Sternberg, M. L. A. American Sign Language
    419
  Tennant, R. A. The American Sign Language
    handshape dictionary   **419**
Signing made easy. Butterworth, R. R.   **419**
Signposts in a strange land. Percy, W.   **818**
Signs and symbols
  See also Sign language
  Biedermann, H. Dictionary of symbolism   **302.2**
  Dreyfuss, H. Symbol sourcebook   **302.2**
  Liungman, C. G. Dictionary of symbols   **302.2**
  Stahl, D. Abbreviations dictionary   **421.03**
  Tresidder, J. Dictionary of symbols   **302.2**
Signs of the zodiac. Snodgrass, M. E.   **133.5**
Sigur, Hannah
  (jt. auth) Jong-Stout, A. A. de A master guide to the
    art of floral design   **745.92**
Sikhs
  Singh, P. The Sikhs   **954**
Sikov, Ed
  On Sunset Boulevard: the life and times of Billy Wil-
    der   **92**
Silber, Laura
  Yugoslavia   **949.7**
Silber, Mark
  Growing herbs and vegetables   **635**
Silber, Terry, 1940-
  (jt. auth) Silber, M. Growing herbs and vegetables
    635
Silence
  See/See also pages in the following book(s):
  Sontag, S. Styles of radical will p3-34   **814**
Silence. Pinter, H.
  In Pinter, H. Complete works v3   **822**
Silence on the mountain. Wilkinson, D.   **972.81**
Silent night. Weintraub, S.   **940.4**
The **silent** passage: menopause. Sheehy, G.   **618.1**
A **silent** sorrow. Kohn, I.   **618.3**
Silent thunder. Payne, K.   **599.67**
Silk
  See/See also pages in the following book(s):
  Hubbell, S. Shrinking the cat   **660.6**
Silko, Leslie, 1948-
  Storyteller   **818**
  See/See also pages in the following book(s):
  Coltelli, L. Winged words: American Indian writers
    speak   **897**
Silver, Brian L.
  The ascent of science   **509**
Silver pixels. Ang, T.   **778.3**
Silverman, Debora, 1954-
  Van Gogh and Gauguin   **759.4**
Silverman, Kathy Kirtland
  (jt. auth) Marrs, R. P. Dr. Richard Marr's fertility book
    616.6
Silverman, Kenneth
  Edgar A. Poe   **92**
  Lightning man: the accursed life of Samuel F.B. Morse
    92
Silverstein, Murray
  (jt. auth) Jacobson, M. Patterns of home   **728**

Silverwork
Wyler, S. B. The book of old silver: English, American, foreign **739.2**
Sim, Kevin
(jt. auth) Bilton, M. Four hours in My Lai **959.704**
Simeti, Mary Taylor
Travels with a medieval queen [biography of Empress Constance] **92**
Simic, Charles, 1938-
Jackstraws **811**
Night picnic **811**
Selected early poems **811**
The voice at 3:00 a.m **811**
Walking the black cat **811**
Simmons, Philip
Learning to fall **291.4**
Simmons, Rachel, 1966-
Odd girl out **305.23**
Simon, Harvey B. (Harvey Bruce), 1942-
The Harvard Medical School guide to men's health **613**
Simon, James F.
What kind of nation **342**
Simon, Joan
Ann Hamilton **92**
Simon, John Ivan
Dreamers of dreams **809.1**
Simon, Neil
Biloxi blues
In Simon, N. The collected plays of Neil Simon v3 p595-691 **812**
Brighton Beach memoirs
In Simon, N. The collected plays of Neil Simon v3 p479-593 **812**
Broadway bound
In Simon, N. The collected plays of Neil Simon v3 p693-803 **812**
California suite
In Simon, N. The collected plays of Neil Simon v2 p549-632 **812**
Chapter two
In Simon, N. The collected plays of Neil Simon v2 p635-737 **812**
The collected plays of Neil Simon v2-3 **812**
Fools
In Simon, N. The collected plays of Neil Simon v3 p307-78 **812**
The gingerbread lady
In Simon, N. The collected plays of Neil Simon v2 p149-227 **812**
God's favorite
In Simon, N. The collected plays of Neil Simon v2 p475-545 **812**
The good doctor
In Simon, N. The collected plays of Neil Simon v2 p393-471 **812**
I ought to be in pictures
In Simon, N. The collected plays of Neil Simon v3 p217-305 **812**
Little me
In Simon, N. The collected plays of Neil Simon v2 p13-145 **812**
Odd couple (female version)
In Simon, N. The collected plays of Neil Simon v3 p379-475 **812**
The play goes on **92**
The prisoner of Second Avenue
In Simon, N. The collected plays of Neil Simon v2 p231-99 **812**
Rewrites **92**
The Sunshine Boys
In Simon, N. The collected plays of Neil Simon v2 p303-89 **812**
Sweet Charity
In Simon, N. The collected plays of Neil Simon v3 p1-113 **812**
They're playing our song
In Simon, N. The collected plays of Neil Simon v3 p115-215 **812**
See/See also pages in the following book(s):
Playwrights at work **812.009**
Simon, Steven
(jt. auth) Benjamin, D. The age of sacred terror **303.6**
Simon & Schuster's guide to fossils. Arduini, P. **560**
Simon & Schuster's guide to saltwater fish and fishing. Mojetta, A. **799.1**
Simon and Schuster's guide to rocks and minerals **549**
Simon and Schuster's guide to trees **582.16**
Simons, Robin
(jt. auth) Greenspan, S. I. The child with special needs **362.1**
The simple truth. Levine, P. **811**
Simply Einstein. Wolfson, R. **530.1**
Simply heavenly. Hughes, L.
In Hughes, L. Five plays p113-81 **812**
Simpson, Brooks D.
Ulysses S. Grant **92**
Simpson, J. A.
(ed) The Oxford English dictionary. See The Oxford English dictionary **423**
Simpson, John W., 1952-
Yearning for the land **304.2**
Simpson, Louis Aston Marantz, 1923-
The owner of the house **811**
Simpson, O. J.
See/See also pages in the following book(s):
Dutton, D. G. The batterer **362.82**
Gates, H. L. Thirteen ways of looking at a black man **920**
Geis, G. Crimes of the century **345**
Simpson, William Kelly
(jt. auth) Smith, W. S. The art and architecture of ancient Egypt **709.32**
Sin
See/See also pages in the following book(s):
Teilhard de Chardin, P. Christianity and evolution p36-55, 187-98 **231.7**
Sinatra, Frank, 1915-1998
About
Friedwald, W. Sinatra! the song is you **92**
Hamill, P. Why Sinatra matters **92**
Zehme, B. The way you wear your hat **92**
Sinatra! the song is you. Friedwald, W. **92**
Since yesterday. Allen, F. L. **973.91**
Sincerely, Andy Rooney. Rooney, A. A. **818**
Sinclair, C. G. (Charles Gordon), 1929-
(comp) International dictionary of food & cooking. See International dictionary of food & cooking **641.03**
Sinclair, Charles Gordon *See* Sinclair, C. G. (Charles Gordon), 1929-
Sinclair, Miranda *See* Seymour, Miranda
Sinclair Lewis [critical essays] **813.009**
Singer, Isaac Bashevis, 1904-1991
More stories from my father's court **92**
Singer, Maxine
(jt. auth) Berg, P. Dealing with genes **576.5**
Singer, Ronald
(ed) Encyclopedia of paleontology. See Encyclopedia of paleontology **560**
Singers
See also African American singers
Clancy, L. The mountain of the women **92**
Davis, P. G. The American opera singer **920**
Friedwald, W. Jazz singing **781.65**

Singh, Patwant, 1925-
    The Sikhs   954
Singh, Simon
    The code book   652
    Fermat's enigma   512
Singing
    The Cambridge companion to singing   782
The **singing**. Williams, C. K.   811
Singing from the soul. Carreras, J.   92
Singing my him song. McCourt, M.   92
Singing to the dead. Armour-Hileman, V.   261
Single child *See* Only child
Single parent family
    See also Children of divorced parents
    Engber, A. The complete single mother   306.8
    Ginsberg, B. G. 50 wonderful ways to be a single-parent family   649
    Winik, M. The lunch-box chronicles   306.8
Single people
    Waite, L. J. The case for marriage   306.8
Single women
    See also Widows
Singley, Bernestine, 1949-
    (ed) When race becomes real. See When race becomes real   305.8
Sino-Japanese Conflict, 1937-1945
    Chang, I. The rape of Nanking   951.04
    Hicks, G. The comfort women   940.54
    See/See also pages in the following book(s):
    Tuchman, B. W. Stilwell and the American experience in China, 1911-45 p164-200   327.73
Sinton, Nan
    (jt. auth) Michener, D. Taylor's guide to ground covers   635.9
Siouan Indians
    See also Dakota Indians; Oglala Indians
Sioux Indians *See* Dakota Indians
Sir Banister Fletcher's A history of architecture. Fletcher, Sir B. F.   720.9
Sir Gawain and the Green Knight (Middle English poem) *See* Gawain and the Grene Knight (Middle English poem)
Sisman, Adam
    Boswell's presumptuous task   828
Sister Aimee: the life of Aimee Semple McPherson. Epstein, D. M.   92
Sister revolutions. Dunn, S.   973.3
Sister: the life of legendary American interior decorator Mrs. Henry Parish II. Bartlett, A. P.   92
Sister Wendy's 1000 masterpieces. Beckett, W.   759
Sister Wendy's American collection. Beckett, W.   709
Sisters and brothers *See* Siblings
The **sisters** Rosensweig. Wasserstein, W.   812
The **sisters:** the saga of the Mitford family. Lovell, M. S.   920
Sistine Chapel *See* Vatican. Cappella Sistina
Sitarz, Daniel, 1948-
    Divorce yourself   346.01
    Prepare your own will   346.05
Sitting Bull, Dakota Chief, 1831-1890
    About
    Utley, R. M. The lance and the shield: the life and times of Sitting Bull   92
    See/See also pages in the following book(s):
    Brown, D. A. The American West p215-27   978
Sitting up with the dead. Petro, P.   398.2
Sitwell, Dame Edith, 1887-1964
    See/See also pages in the following book(s):
    Holroyd, M. Works on paper   809
Sivananda Yoga Vedanta Center (London, England)
    Yoga, mind & body. See Yoga, mind & body   294.5
Six American poets   811.008

Six characters in search of an author. Pirandello, L.
    In Our dramatic heritage v6   808.82
    In Pirandello, L. Naked masks p211-76   852
Six Day War, 1967 *See* Israel-Arab War, 1967
Six days of war. Oren, M.   956.04
Six degrees of separation. Guare, J.   812
Six easy pieces. Feynman, R. P.   530
The **six** wives of Henry VIII. Weir, A.   920
The **six** wives of Henry VIII. See Fraser, A. The wives of Henry VIII   920
Six wives: the queens of Henry VIII. Starkey, D.   920
The **sixth** extinction. Leakey, R. E.   304.2
The **sixties**. Gitlin, T.   973.92
The **size** of thoughts. Baker, N.   814
The **Sjogren's** syndrome survival guide. Rumpf, T. P.   616.97
Skaggs, Peggy
    Kate Chopin   813.009
Skating *See* Ice skating
Skellig Michael (Monastery: Ireland)
    Moorhouse, G. Sun dancing   941.5
Skemp, Vicki
    (jt. auth) Kavaya, K. Community quilts   746.46
The **skeptic:** the life of H.L. Mencken. Teachout, T.   92
Skepticism
    See also Belief and doubt
Skerrett, P. J. (Patrick J.), 1953-
    (jt. auth) Willett, W. Eat, drink and be healthy   613.2
Skerrett, Patrick J. *See* Skerrett, P. J. (Patrick J.), 1953-
Sketches from a life. Kennan, G. F.   92
The **sketches** of Louisa May Alcott. Alcott, L. M.   818
Skidelsky, Robert Jacob Alexander, 1939-
    John Maynard Keynes v3   92
Skidmore, Thomas E.
    Brazil   981
Skills, Life *See* Life skills
Skin
    Care
    Begoun, P. Don't go to the cosmetics counter without me   646.7
    DuPriest, L. Natural beauty   646.7
    Fornay, A. The African American woman's guide to successful makeup and skincare   646.7
    Leffell, D. J. Total skin   616.5
    Mitchell, D. R. The Botox miracle   615.8
    Diseases
    Skin disorders sourcebook   616.5
    Turkington, C. The encyclopedia of skin and skin disorders   616.5
Skin disorders sourcebook   616.5
Skinheads *See* White supremacy movements
Skinner, B. F. (Burrhus Frederic), 1904-1990
    About behaviorism   150.19
    About
    Bjork, D. W. B.F. Skinner   92
Skinner, Brian J., 1928-
    (ed) The Oxford companion to the earth. See The Oxford companion to the earth   550.3
Skinner, Burrhus Frederic *See* Skinner, B. F. (Burrhus Frederic), 1904-1990
Skinner, Keith
    (comp) The Ultimate Jack the Ripper companion. See The Ultimate Jack the Ripper companion   364.1
Skipping towards Gomorrah. Savage, D.   306
Skirts and slacks. Di Piero, W. S.   811
Sklar, Robert
    A world history of film   791.43
Skolnik, Fred
    The New encyclopedia of Judaism. See The New encyclopedia of Judaism [New York University Press]   296.03

Skyjacking *See* Hijacking of airplanes
Slabs of the sunburnt West. Sandburg, C.
   In Sandburg, C. Complete poems of Carl Sandburg
   p271-314   **811**
Slack, Charles
   Noble obsession   **92**
Slander (Law) *See* Libel and slander
Slann, Martin W.
   (jt. auth) Combs, C. C. Encyclopedia of terrorism
   303.6
Slater, Lauren
   Love works like this   **306.8**
   Prozac diary   **616.89**
Slatta, Richard W., 1947-
   The cowboy encyclopedia   **978.03**
Slaughter, Thomas P.
   Exploring Lewis and Clark   **978**
Slaughterhouse. Rieff, D.   **949.7**
The **slave**. Baraka, I. A.
   In Baraka, I. A. Dutchman, and The slave p39-88
   821
Slave trade
   Gallay, A. The Indian slave trade   **326**
   Johnson, W. Soul by soul   **326**
   Segal, R. Islam's Black slaves   **326**
Slavery
   Segal, R. Islam's Black slaves   **326**
   Stark, R. For the glory of God   **291.1**
   Encyclopedias
   Macmillan encyclopedia of world slavery   **326**
   United States
   See also Abolitionists
   Ball, E. Slaves in the family   **975.7**
   Berlin, I. Many thousands gone   **326**
   Fox-Genovese, E. Within the plantation household
   305.4
   Franklin, J. H. From slavery to freedom   **305.8**
   Johnson, C. R. Africans in America: America's journey
   through slavery   **326**
   Johnson, W. Soul by soul   **326**
   Miller, W. L. Arguing about slavery   **973.5**
   Remembering slavery   **326**
   Schneider, D. Slavery in America   **326**
   Wiencek, H. The Hairstons   **975**
   See/See also pages in the following book(s):
   The Causes of the Civil War   **973.7**
   Foner, E. The story of American freedom p29-45
   323.44
Slavery in America. Schneider, D.   **326**
Slaves in the family. Ball, E.   **975.7**
Slayton, Robert A.
   Empire statesman: the rise and redemption of Al Smith
   92
Sled dog racing
   See also Iditarod Trail Sled Dog Race, Alaska
Sleep
   Alvarez, A. Night   **154.6**
   American Academy of Pediatrics guide to your child's
   sleep   **618.92**
   Dement, W. C. The promise of sleep   **612.8**
   Goldman, B. Brain fitness   **153.1**
   Lavie, P. The enchanted world of sleep   **612.8**
   Lukeman, A. Sleep well, sleep deep   **616.8**
   Sleep disorders sourcebook . . .   **616.8**
   See/See also pages in the following book(s):
   Brazelton, T. B. To listen to a child p107-22
   155.4
   Encyclopedias
   Thorpy, M. J. The encyclopedia of sleep and sleep dis-
   orders   **612.8**
Sleep disorders sourcebook . . .   **616.8**
Sleep well, sleep deep. Lukeman, A.   **616.8**
Sleep with the angels. Fisher, M.   **362.1**
Sleeping with the dictionary. Mullen, H. R.   **811**
Sleeplessness *See* Insomnia

Sleepwalking through history. Johnson, H. B.
   973.927
A **slender** thread. Ackerman, D.   **362.28**
Slesin, Suzanne, 1944-
   Japanese style   **747.2**
Slesinger, Tess, 1905-1945
   See/See also pages in the following book(s):
   American women fiction writers   **813.009**
Slezak, Linda Garratt
   (jt. auth) Mailhot, C. B. Surgery: a patient's guide
   from diagnosis to recovery   **617**
Slide, Anthony
   The new historical dictionary of the American film in-
   dustry   **791.4303**
A **slight** ache. Pinter, H.
   In Pinter, H. Complete works v1   **822**
Sloan, Alfred Pritchard, Jr.
   See/See also pages in the following book(s):
   Klein, M. The change makers   **920**
Sloan, Annie
   Modern paint effects   **745.7**
Sloan, Stephen, 1936-
   (jt. auth) Anderson, S. Historical dictionary of terror-
   ism   **303.6**
Sloan Kettering. Kovner, A.   **892**
Sloane, Eugene A.
   Sloane's complete book of bicycling   **629.227**
Sloane, Sheila B.
   Medical abbreviations & eponyms   **610.3**
Sloane's complete book of bicycling. Sloane, E. A.
   629.227
Slonimsky, Nicolas, 1894-1995
   Baker's biographical dictionary of twentieth-century
   classical musicians. See Baker's biographical dictio-
   nary of twentieth-century classical musicians
   920.003
   Baker's dictionary of music   **780.3**
   The great composers and their works   **780.9**
   Kuhn, L. D. Music since 1900   **780.9**
Slote, Stanley J.
   Weeding library collections   **025.2**
Slotkin, Richard, 1942-
   Gunfighter nation   **973.9**
Slouching towards Gomorrah. Bork, R. H.   **306**
Slung, Michele B., 1947-
   Living with cannibals and other women's adventures
   910.4
Small, Hugh, 1943-
   Florence Nightingale   **92**
Small, Meredith F.
   Our babies, ourselves   **649**
   What's love got to do with it?   **576.8**
Small business
   See also Entrepreneurship; Home-based business
   The American Bar Association legal guide for small
   business   **343**
   Burstiner, I. The small business handbook   **658.1**
   Encyclopedia of small business   **658**
   How to run a small business   **658.1**
   Lonier, T. Working solo   **658**
   Small business sourcebook   **658.1**
   Sullivan, R. The small business start-up guide
   658.1
   Webb, P. The small business handbook   **658**
The small business handbook. Burstiner, I.   **658.1**
The small business handbook. Webb, P.   **658**
Small business sourcebook   **658.1**
The small business start-up guide. Sullivan, R.
   658.1
Small claims court
   Warner, R. E. Everybody's guide to small claims court
   347
Small house designs   **728**
A **small** place. Kincaid, J.   **972.97**

A **small** treatise on the great virtues. Comte-Sponville, A. **179**

Small wonder. Kingsolver, B. **814**

The **smallest** muscle in the human body. Ríos, A. **811**

Smallpox
Fenn, E. A. Pox Americana **614.5**
Koplow, D. A. Smallpox: the fight to eradicate a global scourge **616.9**
Preston, R. The demon in the freezer **616.9**
See/See also pages in the following book(s):
Frist, W. H. When every moment counts **613.6**
Oldstone, M. B. A. Viruses, plagues, and history **614.4**

Smart exercise. Bailey, C. **613.7**

The **smart** investor's survival guide. Carlson, C. B. **332.6**

Smell
Watson, L. Jacobson's organ and the remarkable nature of smell **612.8**

Smil, Vaclav
The earth's biosphere **577**

A **smile** as big as the moon. Kersjes, M. **371.9**

Smiley, F. E.
(ed) Prehistoric culture change on the Colorado plateau. See Prehistoric culture change on the Colorado plateau **970.004**

Smiley, Jane, 1949-
Charles Dickens **92**

Smith, Adam, 1723-1790
The wealth of nations **330.1**
See/See also pages in the following book(s):
Heilbroner, R. L. The worldly philosophers **330.1**

Smith, Alexander Hanchett, 1904-1988
The mushroom hunter's field guide **579.6**

Smith, Alfred Emanuel, 1873-1944
About
Finan, C. M. Alfred E. Smith, the happy warrior **92**
Slayton, R. A. Empire statesman: the rise and redemption of Al Smith **92**

Smith, Bob, 1941-
Hamlet's dresser **92**

Smith, Brian H.
(jt. auth) Kolpan, S. Exploring wine **641.2**

Smith, C. Lavett, 1927-
National Audubon Society field guide to tropical marine fishes of the Caribbean, the Gulf of Mexico, Florida, the Bahamas, and Bermuda **597**

Smith, Charles Sprague, 1853-1910
(comp) American hymns old and new. See American hymns old and new **782.27**

Smith, Charles W. G.
The big book of gardening secrets **635**

Smith, Chris, 1966-
Cooking with the diabetic chef **641.5**

Smith, Darren L.
(ed) Counties USA. See Counties USA **352.13**
(ed) Parks directory of the United States. See Parks directory of the United States **917.3**

Smith, David L., 1954-
(ed) Encyclopedia of African-American culture and history. See Encyclopedia of African-American culture and history **305.8**

Smith, Dennis, 1940-
Report from ground zero **363.34**

Smith, Edward C., 1941-
The vegetable gardener's bible **635**

Smith, Edward Lucie- *See* Lucie-Smith, Edward, 1933-

Smith, Florence Margaret *See* Smith, Stevie, 1902-1971

Smith, Geoffrey Nowell- *See* Nowell-Smith, Geoffrey

Smith, George E., 1938-
(ed) The Cambridge companion to Newton. See The Cambridge companion to Newton **530**

Smith, Hedrick
The power game **973.92**

Smith, Helmut Walser, 1962-
The butcher's tale **943.08**

Smith, Henrietta M.
(ed) The Coretta Scott King Awards book, 1970-1999. See The Coretta Scott King Awards book, 1970-1999 **028.5**

Smith, Huston
Buddhism: a concise introduction **294.3**
Why religion matters **215**

Smith, Irene Britton, 1907-1999
See/See also pages in the following book(s):
Walker-Hill, H. From spirituals to symphonies **920**

Smith, J. Douglas, 1965-
World War II on the Web **025.04**

Smith, Jane Idleman, 1937-
Islam in America **297**

Smith, Jean
(ed) Breath sweeps mind. See Breath sweeps mind **294.3**

Smith, Jean Edward
Grant **92**
John Marshall **92**

Smith, Jessie Carney, 1930-
(ed) Black firsts: 4,000 ground-breaking and pioneering historical events. See Black firsts: 4,000 ground-breaking and pioneering historical events **305.8**
(ed) Notable black American women [bk I-III] See Notable black American women [bk I-III] **920.003**

Smith, Jessie Willcox, 1863-1935
About
Carter, A. A. The Red Rose girls **759.13**

Smith, Jim B.
The last mission **940.54**

Smith, Joel
Edward Steichen: the early years **779**

Smith, Jonathan Riley- *See* Riley-Smith, Jonathan

Smith, Joseph, 1805-1844
About
Brodie, F. M. No man knows my history: the life of Joseph Smith, the Mormon prophet **92**
Bushman, R. L. Joseph Smith and the beginnings of Mormonism **289.3**
Remini, R. V. Joseph Smith **92**

Smith, Josh
(jt. auth) Nothdurft, W. E. The lost dinosaurs of Egypt **567.9**

Smith, Liz
Natural blonde **92**

Smith, Marisa
(ed) The Actor's book of movie monologues. See The Actor's book of movie monologues **791.43**

Smith, Martin Seymour- *See* Seymour-Smith, Martin

Smith, Maynard H., 1911-1984
See/See also pages in the following book(s):
Mikaelian, A. Medal of honor **920**

Smith, Michael, 1952-
Station X **940.54**

Smith, Michael Ernest, 1953-
The Aztecs **972**

Smith, Michael G., 1968-
(ed) The Art of natural building. See The Art of natural building **690**

Smith, Myron J.
The airline encyclopedia, 1909-2000 **387.7**

Smith, Patricia, 1955-
(jt. auth) Johnson, C. R. Africans in America: America's journey through slavery **326**

Smith, Patrick L.
Japan **952**

Smith, Perry, 1928-1965
About
Capote, T. In cold blood **364.1**

Smith, Raymond A.
(ed) Encyclopedia of AIDS. See Encyclopedia of AIDS
362.1
Smith, Red, 1905-1982
Red Smith on baseball   796.357
Smith, Richard D., 1949-
Can't you hear me callin': the life of Bill Monroe, father of bluegrass   92
Smith, Richard Norton, 1953-
Patriarch: George Washington and the new American nation   92
Smith, Rosamond, 1938-
See also Oates, Joyce Carol, 1938-
Smith, Stevie, 1902-1971
Collected poems   821
Smith, Tim Mackintosh- See Mackintosh-Smith, Tim, 1961-
Smith, Walter Wellesley See Smith, Red, 1905-1982
Smith, William, 1769-1839
     About
Winchester, S. The map that changed the world
     92
Smith, William Jay, 1918-
The world below the window   811
Smith, William Stevenson, 1907-1969
The art and architecture of ancient Egypt   709.32
The **Smithsonian** book of North American mammals
     599
Smithsonian Institution. National Air and Space Museum See National Air and Space Museum (U.S.)
Smithsonian Institution. National Museum of the American Indian See National Museum of the American Indian (U.S.)
Smoke and steel. Sandburg, C.
In Sandburg, C. Complete poems of Carl Sandburg p149-268   811
Smoke-ending programs See Smoking cessation programs
Smoking
See also Marijuana; Tobacco habit
Kluger, R. Ashes to ashes   394.1
Smoking cessation programs
Fisher, E. B. American Lung Association 7 steps to a smoke-free life   616.86
Smoot, George
Wrinkles in time   523.1
Smuggling of drugs See Drug traffic
Snake hips. Soffee, A. T.   793.3
Snakes
See also Anacondas; Pythons; Rattlesnakes
Badger, D. Snakes   597.9
Ernst, C. H. Snakes in question   597.9
Greene, H. W. Snakes   597.9
Mattison, C. The encyclopedia of snakes   597.9
Mattison, C. Snakes of the world   597.9
Snakes in question. Ernst, C. H.   597.9
Snakes of the world. Mattison, C.   597.9
Snead, Sam
The game I love   796.352
Golf begins at forty   796.352
Snobbery: the American version. Epstein, J.   305.5
Snobbishness See Snobs and snobbishness
Snobs and snobbishness
Epstein, J. Snobbery: the American version   305.5
Snodgrass, Mary Ellen
Encyclopedia of frontier literature   810.3
Signs of the zodiac   133.5
(jt. auth) Carey, G. A multicultural dictionary of literary terms   803
Snodgrass, W. D. (William De Witt), 1926-
Each in his season   811
Snodgrass, William De Witt See Snodgrass, W. D. (William De Witt), 1926-
Snow
Mergen, B. Snow in America   551.57

Snow in America. Mergen, B.   551.57
The **snow** leopard. Matthiessen, P.   915.4
The **snowboard** book. Hart, L.   796.9
Snowboarding
Bennett, J. The complete snowboarder   796.9
Hart, L. The snowboard book   796.9
Snyder, Don J.
The cliff walk   92
Snyder, Gary
Mountains and rivers without end   811
No nature   811
The practice of the wild   814
Snyder, James
Medieval art   709.02
So others might live. Golway, T.   628.9
Soares, André
Beyond paradise: the life of Ramon Novarro   92
Soares, Bernard See Pessoa, Fernando, 1888-1935
Sobczak, A. J.
(ed) Cyclopedia of literary characters. See Cyclopedia of literary characters   803
(ed) Magill's guide to science fiction and fantasy literature. See Magill's guide to science fiction and fantasy literature   809.3
Sobel, Dava
Galileo's daughter   92
Longitude   526
Soccer
Araton, H. Alive and kicking   796.334
Bauer, G. New soccer techniques, tactics & teamwork   796.334
Bellos, A. Futebol: the Brazilian way of life   796.334
Hamm, M. Go for the goal   796.334
Social action
Etzioni, A. The spirit of community   307
Social anthropology See Ethnology
Social behavior See Human behavior
Social change
Diamond, J. M. Guns, germs, and steel   303.4
Dyson, F. J. The sun, the genome, & the Internet   303.4
Stille, A. The future of the past   303.4
Toffler, A. Future shock   303.4
Toffler, A. Powershift   303.4
Toffler, A. The third wave   303.4
Wright, R. NonZero   303.4
See/See also pages in the following book(s):
Fromm, E. To have or to be? p168-202   302
Social classes
See also Aristocracy; Elite (Social sciences); Working class
Lubrano, A. Limbo: blue-collar roots, white-collar dreams   305.5
Veblen, T. The theory of the leisure class   305.5
The **social** contract. Rousseau, J.-J.   320.1
Social customs See Manners and customs
Social democracy See Socialism
Social equality See Equality
Social ethics
See also Bioethics
The **social** history of the Third Reich. Ayçoberry, P.
     943.086
Social learning See Socialization
Social life and customs See Manners and customs
The **social** lives of dogs. Thomas, E. M.   636.7
Social medicine
     History
Porter, R. The greatest benefit to mankind   610.9
Social policy
     United States
Bok, D. C. The trouble with government   306
Katz, M. B. The price of citizenship   361.6

Social psychology
See also Applied psychology
Allport, G. The nature of prejudice   **152.4**
Fromm, E. On being human   **150.19**
The **Social** science encyclopedia   **300.3**
Social sciences
Dictionaries
Dictionary of the social sciences   **300.3**
Rohmann, C. A world of ideas   **103**
Encyclopedias
The Social science encyclopedia   **300.3**
Periodicals—Indexes
Social sciences index   **300.5**
Social sciences & humanities index. See Social sciences
index   **300.5**
Social sciences index   **300.5**
Social security
Social Security handbook   **368.4**
Social Security Administration See United States. So-
cial Security Administration
Social Security handbook   **368.4**
Social values
Bork, R. H. Slouching towards Gomorrah   **306**
Himmelfarb, G. The de-moralization of society
                                             303.3
Westheimer, R. The value of family   **306.8**
Socialism
See/See also pages in the following book(s):
Berlin, Sir I. The sense of reality p77-167 **901**
Tuchman, B. W. The proud tower p407-62
                                             909.82
Socialization
Sheehy, G. New passages   **305.24**
Socially handicapped children
Coles, R. Children of crisis   **305.23**
Kozol, J. Amazing grace   **362.7**
Kozol, J. Savage inequalities   **371.9**
Societies
Directories
Encyclopedia of associations   **061.025**
The World of learning   **060.25**
Society and language See Sociolinguistics
Society of Friends
Hamm, T. D. The Quakers in America   **289.6**
See/See also pages in the following book(s):
Boorstin, D. J. The Americans: The colonial experi-
ence   **973.2**
Society of Jesus See Jesuits
Sociobiology
Taylor, S. E. The tending instinct   **304.5**
See/See also pages in the following book(s):
Wilson, E. O. In search of nature   **113**
Sociolinguistics
Lepore, J. A is for American   **306.44**
Sociology
Bibliography
Required reading   **301**
Encyclopedias
Encyclopedia of sociology   **301**
World of sociology   **301**
Sociology, Christian See Christian sociology
Socrates
About
Stone, I. F. The trial of Socrates   **183**
See/See also pages in the following book(s):
Jaspers, K. The great philosophers   **109**
Russell, B. A history of Western philosophy p82-93
                                             109
Wills, G. Certain trumpets p160-70   **303.3**
Sodium chloride See Salt
SOE See Great Britain. Special Operations Executive
Soffee, Anne Thomas
Snake hips   **793.3**

Sofianides, Anna S.
Gems & crystals from the American Museum of Natu-
ral History   **549**
Software, Computer See Computer software
Sogyal, Rinpoche
The Tibetan book of living and dying   **294.3**
Soil conservation
Stoll, S. Larding the lean Earth   **631.4**
Soil microbiology
Wolfe, D. W. Tales from the underground   **578**
Sojourner Truth See Truth, Sojourner, d. 1883
Sokol, Julia
(jt. auth) Carter, S. Men like women who like them-
selves   **158**
Solal, Annie Cohen- See Cohen-Solal, Annie
Solar energy
Kryza, F. The power of light   **333.79**
See/See also pages in the following book(s):
Dyson, F. J. The sun, the genome, & the Internet
                                             303.4
Solar radiation
See also Greenhouse effect
Solar system
Greeley, R. The compact NASA atlas of the solar sys-
tem   **523.2**
Kolb, R. Blind watchers of the sky   **523.1**
Trefil, J. S. Other worlds   **523.2**
See/See also pages in the following book(s):
Goodstein, D. L. Feynman's lost lecture p145-70
                                             521
Solden, Sari
Journeys through ADDulthood   **616.85**
Soldier of peace: the life of Yitzhak Rabin. Kurzman, D.
                                             92
Soldiers
See also Women soldiers
Great Britain
Ziegler, P. Soldiers: fighting men's lives, 1901-2001
                                             355
United States
Hoyt, E. P. The GI's war   **940.54**
Kindsvatter, P. S. American soldiers   **355**
Linderman, G. F. The world within war   **940.54**
McPherson, J. M. For cause and comrades   **973.7**
Mikaelian, A. Medal of honor   **920**
United States—Biography
Fredriksen, J. C. American military leaders
                                             920.003
Soldiers: fighting men's lives, 1901-2001. Ziegler, P.
                                             355
Soldiers of freedom. Wright, K.   **355**
Soldiers of God. Bushart, H. L.   **322.4**
Solé, Carlos A.
(ed) Latin American writers. See Latin American writ-
ers   **920.003**
Solidarity (Labor union)
Wałęsa, L. The struggle and the triumph   **92**
Solinger, Rickie, 1947-
Beggars and choosers   **363.46**
(ed) Abortion wars. See Abortion wars   **363.46**
The **solitary** self: Jean-Jacques Rousseau in exile and ad-
versity. Cranston, M.   **92**
Solitude
Buchholz, E. S. The call of solitude   **155.9**
Colegate, I. A pelican in the wilderness   **291.4**
Solnit, Rebecca
River of shadows   **778.5**
Wanderlust   **796.51**
Solomon, Andrew, 1963-
The noonday demon   **616.85**
Solomon, Maynard, 1930-
Beethoven   **92**
Mozart   **92**
Solomon, Robert C.
A passion for wisdom   **109**

Solomon, Robert C.—*Continued*
What Nietzsche really said 193
Solomon, Susan, 1956-
The coldest March 998
Solotaroff, Ivan
The last face you'll ever see 364.66
Solzhenitsyn, Aleksandr, 1918-
The Gulag Archipelago, 1918-1956 365
Invisible allies 92
Somalia
Bowden, M. Black Hawk down 967.73
Some of the dharma. Kerouac, J. 294.3
Somers, Jane *See* Lessing, Doris May, 1919-
Somers Heidhues, Mary F.
Southeast Asia: a concise history 959
Somerville, Annie
Fields of Greens 641.5
Something like an autobiography. Kurosawa, A. 92
Something to declare. Alvarez, J. 814
Something to declare. Barnes, J. 824
Somewhere for me: a biography of Richard Rodgers. Secrest, M. 92
Sommer, Elyse
(ed) Metaphors dictionary. See Metaphors dictionary 423
Sommers, Christina Hoff
Who stole feminism? 305.4
Son of the Morning Star. Connell, E. S. 973.8
Sondheim, Stephen
Follies; criticism
In Chapin, T. S. Everything was possible 792.6
Sunday in the park with George 812
About
Citron, S. Sondheim and Lloyd-Webber 92
Secrest, M. Stephen Sondheim 92
Sondheim and Lloyd-Webber. Citron, S. 92
Song finder. Ferguson, G. L. 782.42
A **song** flung up to heaven. Angelou, M. 92
Song of Roland *See* Chanson de Roland
The **song** of Roland. Chanson de Roland 841
Song of the Blessed One *See* Mahābhārata. Bhagavadgītā
The **songlines.** Chatwin, B. 919.4
Songs
See also Carols; National songs; Popular music; Spirituals (Songs)
Friedwald, W. Stardust melodies 782.42
Encyclopedias
Hischak, T. The American musical film song encyclopedia 782.42
Indexes
The Children's song index, 1978-1993 782.42
Ferguson, G. L. Song finder 782.42
Havlice, P. P. Popular song index 782.42
Peterson, C. S. Index to children's songs 782.42
Songs, American *See* American songs
Songs from this Earth on turtle's back 811.008
Songs of innocence and of experience. Blake, W. 821
Songwriters *See* Composers
Songwriter's market 782.42
Sonneborn, Liz
A to Z of American women in the performing arts 920.003
(jt. auth) Kort, C. A to Z of American women in the visual arts 920.003
Sonnets. Shakespeare, W. 821
Sonnets from the Portuguese. Browning, E. B. 821
Sonnets to Orpheus. Rilke, R. M. 831
Sons and brothers: the days of Jack and Bobby Kennedy. Mahoney, R. D. 92
Sons and fathers *See* Father-son relationship
Sons and mothers *See* Mother-son relationship
Sons of Mississippi. Hendrickson, P. 305.8

Sontag, Susan, 1933-
Regarding the pain of others 303.6
Styles of radical will 814
Where the stress falls 814
(jt. auth) Leibovitz, A. Women 779
About
Rollyson, C. E. Susan Sontag 92
See/See also pages in the following book(s):
Women writers at work p376-404 808
Sooners (Football team) *See* Oklahoma Sooners (Football team)
The **Soong** dynasty. Seagrave, S. 951
Soong family *See* Sung family
Soper, Alexander Coburn, 1904-1993
(jt. auth) Sickman, L. The art and architecture of China 709.51
Sophocles
Ajax
In Sophocles. The complete plays of Sophocles p1-35 882
Antigone 882
also in Sophocles. The complete plays of Sophocles p115-47 882
The complete plays of Sophocles 882
Electra
In Sophocles. The complete plays of Sophocles p37-74 882
Oedipus at Colonus
In Sophocles. The complete plays of Sophocles p219-61 882
Oedipus the King 882
also in Sophocles. The complete plays of Sophocles p75-114 882
Philoctetes
In Sophocles. The complete plays of Sophocles p181-218 882
Trachinian women
In Sophocles. The complete plays of Sophocles p149-79 882
See/See also pages in the following book(s):
Hamilton, E. The Greek way p258-70 880.9
Soporifics *See* Narcotics
A **Sor** Juana anthology. Juana Inés de la Cruz 861
The **sorcerer's** apprentice. Richardson, J. 92
Sorcery *See* Magic
Sorel, Nancy Caldwell
The women who wrote the war 940.53
Soros, George
George Soros on globalization 337
Sorosky, Marlene
Fast & festive meals for the Jewish holidays 641.5
A **sorrow** in our heart: the life of Tecumseh. Eckert, A. W. 92
Sorrows and rejoicings. Fugard, A. 822
Soto, Gary
New and selected poems 811
Soto, Hernando de
The mystery of capital 330.1
Soto, Hernando de, ca. 1500-1542
About
Duncan, D. E. Hernando de Soto 92
See/See also pages in the following book(s):
Williams, W. C. In the American grain p45-58 814
Sotoba Komachi. Kwanze, K.
In Waley, A. The Nō plays of Japan 895.6
Soubirous, Bernadette *See* Bernadette, Saint, 1844-1879
Souder, William, 1949-
A plague of frogs 597.8
Souhami, Diana
Selkirk's Island 996
Soul by soul. Johnson, W. 326
Soul food. White, J. 641.5

Soul gone home. Hughes, L.
  In Hughes, L. Five plays p37-42 812
The **soul** of battle. Hanson, V. D. 355
The **soul** of capitalism. Greider, W. 330.1
Soul of the sword. O'Connell, R. L. 623.4
Soul on ice. Cleaver, E. 305.8
The **souls** of black folk. Du Bois, W. E. B. 305.8
  also in Du Bois, W. E. B. The Oxford W. E. B. Du
    Bois reader p97-240 305.8
  also in Du Bois, W. E. B. Writings 818
Souls on fire. Wiesel, E. 296.8
Sound
Recording and Reproducing—History
Day, T. A century of recorded music 780
Sound recordings
History
Day, T. A century of recorded music 780
Reviews
All music guide 781.64
All music guide to jazz 781.65
Classical music: the listener's companion 781.6
Classical music: the rough guide 781.6
Ratliff, B. Jazz: a critic's guide to the 100 most impor-
  tant recordings 781.65
The **sounds** of poetry. Pinsky, R. 808.5
Sounes, Howard, 1965-
Down the highway: the life of Bob Dylan 92
Soups
Vollstedt, M. The big book of soups & stews
                                            641.8
The **source** book of franchise opportunities. See Bond's
  franchise guide 381
Sources of strength. Carter, J. 248.4
Sousa, Julio de Melo e *See* Tahan, Malba, 1895-
South, Will
  (jt. auth) Gerdts, W. H. California impressionism
                                            759.13
South (U.S.) *See* Southern States
South Africa
History
Thompson, L. M. A history of South Africa 968
Politics and government
Mandela, N. Long walk to freedom: the autobiography
  of Nelson Mandela 92
Mandela, N. Mandela 92
Sampson, A. Nelson Mandela 92
Waldmeir, P. Anatomy of a miracle 968.06
Race relations
Tutu, D. No future without forgiveness 968.06
Tutu, D. The rainbow people of God 968.06
Waldmeir, P. Anatomy of a miracle 968.06
Race relations—Drama
Fugard, A. "Master Harold"—and the boys 822
**South Africa. Commission for Truth and Reconcilia-
tion**
Tutu, D. No future without forgiveness 968.06
South America
The South American handbook 980
Description
Darwin, C. The voyage of the Beagle 508
The **South** American handbook 980
South Carolina
Ball, E. Slaves in the family 975.7
South Pacific Region *See* Oceania
South Pole
  See also Antarctica
Preston, D. A first rate tragedy 998
Solomon, S. The coldest March 998
  See/See also pages in the following book(s):
Connell, E. S. The Aztec treasure house p96-122
                                            814
South Sea Islands *See* Oceania
South Seas *See* Oceania

Southeast Asia
Description
Gargan, E. A. A river's tale 915.9
History
Somers Heidhues, M. F. Southeast Asia: a concise his-
  tory 959
Southern cooking
Edge, J. T. A gracious plenty 641.5
Fowler, D. L. Damon Lee Fowler's new southern
  kitchen 641.5
Southern journey. Dent, T. 975
Southern literature *See* American literature—Southern
States
Southern Rhodesia *See* Zimbabwe
Southern States
Civilization
Applebome, P. Dixie rising 973.929
Cash, W. J. The mind of the South 975
Description
Petro, P. Sitting up with the dead 398.2
Economic conditions
  See/See also pages in the following book(s):
The Causes of the Civil War 973.7
Folklore
  See Folklore—Southern States
Humor
Roy Blount's book of Southern humor 817.008
Intellectual life
The Companion to southern literature 810.3
Politics and government
Applebome, P. Dixie rising 973.929
Race relations
Dent, T. Southern journey 975
Dray, P. At the hands of persons unknown 364.1
Egerton, J. Speak now against the day 323.1
Fairclough, A. Better day coming 323.1
King, J. Hate crime: the story of a dragging in Jasper,
  Texas 364.1
Packard, J. M. American nightmare 305.8
Remembering Jim Crow 305.8
Social life and customs
Edge, J. T. A gracious plenty 641.5
Southwest, New *See* Southwestern States
Southwest Pacific Region *See* Oceania
Southwestern States
Brown, K. A. Four corners 978
Antiquities
Roberts, D. In search of the old ones 970.004
History
Shoumatoff, A. Legends of the American desert
                                            978
Souza, Ernest *See* Scott, Evelyn, 1893-1963
Sova, Dawn B.
Agatha Christie A to Z 823.009
Edgar Allan Poe, A-Z 818
Sovereigns *See* Emperors; Kings and rulers; Queens
Soviet Union
  See also Former Soviet republics; Russia; Russia
  (Federation)
Foreign relations—United States
Fursenko, A. V. "One hell of a gamble" 973.922
Gates, R. M. From the shadows 327.73
Grose, P. Operation Rollback 327.12
Kennedy, R. F. Thirteen days 973.922
Schweizer, P. Reagan's War 327.73
History
Coleman, F. The decline and fall of the Soviet Empire
                                            947.085
Hochschild, A. The unquiet ghost 947.084
Hosking, G. A. Russia and the Russians 947
Pipes, R. Russia under the Bolshevik regime
                                            947.084
Riasanovsky, N. V. A history of Russia 947
Satter, D. Age of delirium 947.085

Soviet Union—History—*Continued*
Service, R. A history of twentieth-century Russia
    947.086
      History—1917-1921, Revolution
Figes, O. A people's tragedy   947.084
Reed, J. Ten days that shook the world   947.084
      Politics and government
Amis, M. Koba the dread   947.084
Applebaum, A. Gulag   365
Bullock, A. Hitler and Stalin   92
Conquest, R. Stalin   92
Gorbachev, M. On my country and the world
    947.085
Medvedev, R. A. Let history judge   947.084
Nikita Khrushchev   92
Remnick, D. Lenin's tomb   947.085
Solzhenitsyn, A. The Gulag Archipelago, 1918-1956
    365

Sowell, Thomas, 1930-
Basic economics   330
The economics and politics of race   305.8
Ethnic America   305.8
Migrations and cultures   304.8
The quest for cosmic justice   303.3
The **soy** solution for menopause. Seibel, M. M.
    618.1

Soybean
Seibel, M. M. The soy solution for menopause
    618.1

Soyinka, Akinwande Oluwole *See* Soyinka, Wole
Soyinka, Wole
The open sore of a continent   966.9
Space, Outer *See* Outer space
Space and time
    See also Fourth dimension
Barbour, J. B. The end of time   530.1
Bodanis, D. E=mc²   530.1
Davies, P. C. W. About time   530.1
Gott, J. R. Time travel in Einstein's universe
    530.1
Hawking, S. W. The nature of space and time
    530.1
Kaku, M. Hyperspace   530.1
Space Camp (Huntsville, Ala.) *See* U.S. Space Camp
    (Huntsville, Ala.)
Space exploration   629
Space flight
Heppenheimer, T. A. Countdown   629.4
Kranz, E. F. Failure is not an option   629.45
Space shuttle   629.45
Weil, E. They all laughed at Christopher Columbus
    621.43

Space flight to the moon
Chaikin, A. A man on the moon   629.45
Reynolds, D. W. Apollo: the epic journey to the moon
    629.45
Schefter, J. L. The race   629.45
Zimmerman, R. Genesis   629.45
Space sciences
Angelo, J. A. The Facts on File space and astronomy
    handbook   520
Space sciences   500.5
Space sciences   500.5
Space shuttle   629.45
Space shuttles
Space shuttle   629.45
Space stations
    See/See also pages in the following book(s):
Space exploration   629
Space Telescope *See* Hubble Space Telescope
Space vehicles
    See also Artificial satellites; Space shuttles
      Propulsion systems
    See also Nuclear rockets

Space warfare
    See also Strategic Defense Initiative
Space weapons
    See also Strategic Defense Initiative
Spain
Vincent, M. Cultural atlas of Spain and Portugal
    946
      Biography—Dictionaries
Dictionary of Hispanic biography   920.003
      Civilization
Fuentes, C. The buried mirror   946
      Description
Hemingway, E. The dangerous summer   791.8
Michener, J. A. Iberia   914.6
Stewart, C. Driving over lemons   946
    See/See also pages in the following book(s):
MacLaine, S. The Camino   92
      History
    See also Spanish Armada, 1588
Fletcher, R. A. The quest for El Cid   92
Kamen, H. Philip of Spain   92
Kamcn, H. The Spanish Inquisition   272
Spain: a history   946
      History—1898, War of 1898
    See Spanish-American War, 1898
      History—1936-1939, Civil War—Drama
Hemingway, E. The Fifth Column, and four stories of
    the Spanish Civil War   818
      History—1936-1939, Civil War—Fiction
Hemingway, E. The Fifth Column, and four stories of
    the Spanish Civil War   818
      Social life and customs
Stewart, C. Driving over lemons   946
Spain: a history   946
Spanish America *See* Latin America
Spanish-American War, 1898
Zimmermann, W. First great triumph   973
Spanish Armada, 1588
Martin, C. The Spanish Armada   942.05
Mattingly, G. The Armada   942.05
Spanish-English bilingual books *See* Bilingual books—
    English-Spanish
The **Spanish** Inquisition. Kamen, H.   272
Spanish language
      Dictionaries
The American Heritage Spanish dictionary   463
The Concise American Heritage Spanish dictionary
    463
Gran diccionario español-inglés. English-Spanish dic-
    tionary   463
Larousse diccionario compact: español inglés, inglés
    español   463
Larousse English-Spanish Spanish-English dictionary
    463
The Oxford Spanish dictionary   463
The University of Chicago Spanish dictionary   463
Spanish literature
      History and criticism
Hispanic literature criticism   860.9
Sparring with Hemingway and other legends of the fight
    game. Schulberg, B.   796.8
Sparrow, Joshua D.
(jt. auth) Brazelton, T. B. Touchpoints three to six
    649
Sparta (Extinct city)
    See/See also pages in the following book(s):
Russell, B. A history of Western philosophy p94-104
    109
Spawforth, Antony
(ed) The Oxford classical dictionary. See The Oxford
    classical dictionary   938.003
Speak, memory. Nabokov, V. V.   92
Speak now against the day. Egerton, J.   323.1

Speake, Jennifer
  (ed) The Oxford dictionary of foreign words and
    phrases. See The Oxford dictionary of foreign words
    and phrases   422.03
Speaking See Public speaking
Speaking for themselves. See Churchill, Sir W. Winston
    and Clementine   92
Speaking Shakespeare. Rodenburg, P.   792
Spears, Richard A.
  NTC's dictionary of American slang and colloquial ex-
    pressions   427
Special collections in libraries See Libraries—Special
    collections
Special education
  Hayden, T. L. Beautiful child   371.9
  Kersjes, M. A smile as big as the moon   371.9
  Siegel, B. Helping children with autism learn
                                                371.9
Special Forces (U.S. Army) See United States. Army.
    Special Forces
Special forces. Clancy, T.   356
Special libraries
                      Directories
  Directory of special libraries and information centers
                                                   026
Special occasions. Stewart, M.   641.5
Special offer. Pinter, H.
  In Pinter, H. Complete works v2   822
Special Operations Command (U.S.) See United States.
    Special Operations Command
Special Operations Executive (Great Britain) See
    Great Britain. Special Operations Executive
Special providence. Mead, W. R.   327.73
Speck, Jeff B.
  (jt. auth) Duany, A. Suburban nation   307.7
Speck, Scott
  (jt. auth) Pogue, D. Classical music for dummies
                                                 781.6
  (jt. auth) Pogue, D. Opera for dummies   792.5
The **spectator**. Terkel, S.   791
Spector, Robert
  Amazon.com   338.7
Spector, Ronald
  Eagle against the sun   940.54
Spector, Shmuel
  (ed) Encyclopedia of Jewish life before and during the
    Holocaust. See Encyclopedia of Jewish life before
    and during the Holocaust   940.53
  (ed) Encyclopedia of the Holocaust. See Encyclopedia
    of the Holocaust [Facts on File]   940.53
Speculation
  Lynch, P. One up on Wall Street   332.6
Speech disorders
  Martin, K. L. Does my child have a speech problem?
                                                618.92
Speech index. Sutton, R. B.   808.85
Speeches
  See also Toasts
  The World's great speeches   808.85
                       Indexes
  Sutton, R. B. Speech index   808.85
Speeches, addresses, etc., American See American
    speeches
Speeches and writings. Lincoln, A.   973.7
Speed, Tim
  The personal Internet security guidebook   005.8
Speer, Albert, 1905-1981
  Inside the Third Reich   943.086
                        About
  Fest, J. C. Speer: the final verdict   92
  Sereny, G. Albert Speer   92
  Van der Vat, D. The good Nazi: the life and lies of
    Albert Speer   92
  See/See also pages in the following book(s):
  Galbraith, J. K. Name-dropping   973.9

Speleology See Caves
The **spell** of the sensuous. Abram, D.   128
Spellenberg, Richard
  National Audubon Society field guide to North
    American wildflowers, western region   582.13
Spells See Magic
Spence, Gerry
  How to argue and win every time   153.8
Spence, Jonathan D.
  The Chan's great continent   951
  God's Chinese son   951
  Mao Zedong   92
  The search for modern China   951
  Treason by the book   951
Spence, Pam
  (ed) The Universe revealed. See The Universe revealed
                                                   523
Spence, William P. (William Perkins), 1925-
  Encyclopedia of construction methods & materials
                                                   690
Spencer, Colin
  Vegetarianism   613.2
Spencer, Herbert, 1820-1903
  See/See also pages in the following book(s):
  Durant, W. J. The story of philosophy p265-300
                                                   109
Spender, Matthew
  From a high place   92
Spengler, Oswald, 1880-1936
  The decline of the West   901
  Form and actuality
  In Spengler, O. The decline of the West v1
                                                   901
  Perspectives of world-history
  In Spengler, O. The decline of the West v2
                                                   901
  See/See also pages in the following book(s):
  Herman, A. The idea of decline in Western history
                                                 909.08
Spenser, Edmund, 1552?-1599
  The faerie queene   821
  also in Spenser, E. The works of Edmund Spenser
    v1-6   828
  The works of Edmund Spenser   828
Sperber, Ann M., 1935-1994
  Murrow, his life and times   92
Sperling, Abraham Paul, 1912-
  Mathematics made simple   510
The **spice** and herb bible. Hemphill, I.   641.3
Spices
  Hemphill, I. The spice and herb bible   641.3
  Rinzler, C. A. The new complete book of herbs,
    spices, and condiments   641.3
Spiders
  The Firefly encyclopedia of insects and spiders
                                                 595.7
  Milne, L. J. The Audubon Society field guide to North
    American insects and spiders   595.7
Spiegelman, Art
  Maus   940.53
Spiegelman, Vladek
                        About
  Spiegelman, A. Maus   940.53
Spielman, A. (Andrew), 1930-
  Mosquito   595.7
Spielman, Andrew See Spielman, A. (Andrew), 1930-
Spies
  Gup, T. Book of honor   327.12
  Trulock, N. Code name Kindred Spirit   327.12
  Weinstein, A. The haunted wood   327.12
                      Dictionaries
  Fredriksen, J. C. America's military adversaries
                                                920.003
Spies in literature
  Mystery and suspense writers   809.3

Spilner, Maggie
  Prevention's complete book of walking   **613.7**
Spin off magazine presents the Spinner's companion. Irwin, B.   **746.1**
Spina bifida
  Children with spina bifida   **618.92**
  Sandler, A. Living with spina bifida   **618.92**
Spinal cord
  Palmer, S. Spinal cord injury   **617**
Spinal cord injury. Palmer, S.   **617**
Spinelli, Jerry, 1941-
  See/See also pages in the following book(s):
  The Newbery & Caldecott medal books, 1986-2000 p143-53   **028.5**
Spink, Kathryn
  Mother Teresa   **92**
The **Spinner's** companion, Spin off magazine presents. Irwin, B.   **746.1**
Spinning
  Brown, R. The weaving, spinning, and dyeing book   **746.1**
  Irwin, B. Spin off magazine presents the Spinner's companion   **746.1**
Spinoza, Benedictus de, 1632-1677
    About
  Damasio, A. R. Looking for Spinoza   **152.4**
  See/See also pages in the following book(s):
  Durant, W. J. The age of Louis XIV p620-57   **940.2**
  Durant, W. J. The story of philosophy p113-51   **109**
  Jaspers, K. The great philosophers   **109**
  Russell, B. A history of Western philosophy p569-80   **109**
The **spinster** & the prophet. McKillop, A. B.   **941.08**
Spirit capture   **779**
The **spirit** level. Heaney, S.   **821**
The **spirit** of community. Etzioni, A.   **307**
Spirit of St. Louis (Airplane)
  Lindbergh, C. The spirit of St. Louis   **629.13**
Spiritism *See* Spiritualism
Spirits *See* Demonology; Ghosts
Spiritual genius. Gallagher, W.   **920**
Spiritual healing
  Wise, A. Awakening the mind   **615.8**
  See/See also pages in the following book(s):
  James, W. The varieties of religious experience   **210**
Spiritual life
  Campbell, J. The power of myth   **291.1**
  Dowrick, S. Forgiveness and other acts of love   **248.4**
  Gallagher, W. Spiritual genius   **920**
  Girzone, J. F. Never alone   **248**
  Hammarskjöld, D. Markings   **839.7**
  Merton, T. The Asian journal of Thomas Merton   **248**
  Merton, T. Love and living   **248**
  Merton, T. New seeds of contemplation   **248**
  Merton, T. No man is an island   **248**
  Norris, K. The cloister walk   **255**
  Searching for your soul   **291.4**
  Siegel, B. S. Prescriptions for living   **158**
  Simmons, P. Learning to fall   **291.4**
  Wise women: over two thousand years of spiritual writing by women   **200**
  See/See also pages in the following book(s):
  Peck, M. S. Further along the road less traveled p153-231   **158**
The **spiritual** life of children. Coles, R.   **291.4**

Spiritualism
  See/See also pages in the following book(s):
  Goldsmith, B. Other powers: the age of suffrage, spiritualism, and the scandalous Victoria Woodhull   **92**
Spirituals (Songs)
  See also Gospel music
  The Books of the American Negro spirituals   **782.42**
Spitz, Bob
  Dylan   **92**
Spivey, Victoria, 1906-1976
  See/See also pages in the following book(s):
  Harrison, D. D. Black pearls   **920**
Spizman, Robyn Freedman
  (jt. auth) Garber, S. W. Monsters under the bed and other childhood fears   **649**
Splicing *See* Knots and splices
Split personality *See* Multiple personality
Spock, Benjamin, 1903-1998
  Dr. Spock on parenting   **649**
  Dr. Spock's the first two years   **649**
  Dr. Spock's the school years   **649**
The **Spoils** of war   **709**
The **Spoken** word revolution   **811.008**
Spontaneous mind. Ginsberg, A.   **92**
Sponville, André Comte- *See* Comte-Sponville, André
Sport utility vehicles
  Bradsher, K. High and mighty   **629.2**
Sports
  See also Games
  Berkow, I. The minority quarterback, and other lives in sports   **796**
  The Best American sports writing   **796**
  The Best American sports writing of the century   **796**
  Franck, I. M. Famous first facts about sports   **796**
  Guttmann, A. Women's sports   **796**
  Levine, P. Ellis Island to Ebbet's Field   **796**
  Nike is a goddess   **796**
  Queenan, J. True believers   **796**
  Sports: the complete visual reference   **796**
  See/See also pages in the following book(s):
  Pollack, W. S. Real boys p272-300   **305.23**
    Encyclopedias
  Hickok, R. The encyclopedia of North American sports history   **796**
  Sherrow, V. Encyclopedia of women and sports   **796**
    Medical aspects
  See Sports medicine
Sports cars
  Adler, D. The art of the sports car   **629.222**
The **sports** encyclopedia: baseball. Neft, D. S.   **796.357**
Sports medicine
  Garrick, J. G. Anybody's sports medicine book   **617.1**
  Micheli, L. J. The sports medicine bible for young athletes   **617.1**
The **sports** medicine bible for young athletes. Micheli, L. J.   **617.1**
Sports: the complete visual reference   **796**
Spoto, Donald, 1941-
  The dark side of genius   **92**
  The hidden Jesus   **232.9**
  The kindness of strangers: the life of Tennessee Williams   **92**
  Notorious: the life of Ingrid Bergman   **92**
Spotted Tail, Brulé Sioux Chief, 1823-1881
  See/See also pages in the following book(s):
  Brown, D. A. Bury my heart at Wounded Knee   **970.004**
Sprigg, June
  Shaker—life, work, and art   **289**

Springer, Lauren
Passionate gardening   635
Springer, Victor Gruschka, 1928-
Sharks in question   597
Springing. Ponsot, M.   811
Spruce, Richard, 1817-1893
See/See also pages in the following book(s):
Honigsbaum, M. The fever trail   616.9
Sprug, Joseph W., 1922-
(comp) Index to fairy tales. See Index to fairy tales
   398.2
Spungen, Susan
(jt. auth) Stewart, M. Martha Stewart's hors d'oeuvres
handbook   641.8
Spurling, Hilary
The unknown Matisse v1   92
Sputnik: the shock of the century. Dickson, P.
   629.46
Spy: the inside story of how the FBI's Robert Hanssen
betrayed America. Wise, D.   327.12
Spying *See* Espionage
Squares and courtyards. Hacker, M.   811
Squids
Ellis, R. The search for the giant squid   594
Squires, James D.
Horse of a different color   798.4
Sramek, John J.
(jt. auth) Cutler, N. R. Understanding Alzheimer's dis-
ease   616.8
Srebrenica (Bosnia and Hercegovina)
Rohde, D. Endgame   949.7
SSA *See* United States. Social Security Administration
St. Albans, Francis Bacon, Viscount *See* Bacon, Fran-
cis, 1561-1626
St. James encyclopedia of labor history worldwide
   331.8
St. James encyclopedia of popular culture   973.9
St. James guide to Black artists   920.003
St. James guide to fantasy writers   809.3
St. James guide to Hispanic artists   920.003
St. James guide to native North American artists
   920.003
St. James guide to science fiction writers   809.3
St. James Press gay & lesbian almanac   305.9
St. Just, 1767-1794 *See* Saint-Just, 1767-1794
St. Louis post-dispatch (Newspaper)
Pfaff, D. W. Joseph Pulitzer II and the Post-dispatch
   92
St. Petersburg (Russia) *See* Saint Petersburg (Russia)
St. Petersburg. Volkov, S.   947
Stacke, Joan B.
(jt. auth) Karmason, M. G. Majolica: a complete and
illustrated survey   738
Stacks, John F.
Scotty: James B. Reston and the rise and fall of
American journalism   92
Stade, George
(ed) Encyclopedia of British writers, 19th and 20th
centuries. See Encyclopedia of British writers, 19th
and 20th centuries   820.9
Stafford, David, 1942-
Roosevelt and Churchill   940.54
Stafford, Jean, 1915-1979
See/See also pages in the following book(s):
American women fiction writers   813.009
Stafford, William Edgar, 1914-1993
Even in quiet places   811
The way it is   811
Stage lighting
Gillette, J. M. Designing with light   792
       Encyclopedias
Briggs, J. Encyclopedia of stage lighting   792
Stage makeup. Corson, R.   792
Stahl, Dean
Abbreviations dictionary   421.03

Stained glass *See* Glass painting and staining
Stained glass crafting. Zaccaria, D.   748.5
Stalin, Joseph, 1879-1953
       About
Amis, M. Koba the dread   947.084
Bullock, A. Hitler and Stalin   92
Conquest, R. Stalin   92
Hochschild, A. The unquiet ghost   947.084
Medvedev, R. A. Let history judge   947.084
Radzinsky, E. Stalin   92
See/See also pages in the following book(s):
Kissinger, H. Diplomacy p332-68; 394-422
   327.73
Rees, L. War of the century   940.54
Stalingrad, Battle of, 1942-1943
Beevor, A. Stalingrad   940.54
Stalking the wild asparagus. Gibbons, E.   581.6
Staller, Natasha
A sum of destructions   759.4
Stallworthy, Jon
(ed) A Book of love poetry. See A Book of love poet-
ry   808.81
(ed) The Oxford book of war poetry. See The Oxford
book of war poetry   808.81
Stambler, Irwin
Country music: the encyclopedia   781.642
Stamina, Physical *See* Physical fitness
Stampp, Kenneth M. (Kenneth Milton)
The era of reconstruction, 1865-1877   973.8
(ed) The Causes of the Civil War. See The Causes of
the Civil War   973.7
Standard and Poor's register of corporations, directors,
and executives   338.7
Standard catalog of American cars, 1805-1942. Kimes,
B. R.   629.222
Standard catalog of world coins. Krause, C. L.
   737.4
Standard cataloging for school and public libraries. Int-
ner, S. S.   025.3
The **standard** code of parliamentary procedure. Sturgis,
A.   060.4
Standard directory of advertisers   659.1
Standard directory of advertising agencies   659.1
Standard guide to American muscle cars   629.222
Standard handbook for electrical engineers   621.3
Standard handbook for mechanical engineers. See
Marks' standard handbook for mechanical engineers
   621
The **Standard** periodical directory   011
Standing Bear, Ponca Chief, 1829?-1908
See/See also pages in the following book(s):
Brown, D. A. Bury my heart at Wounded Knee
   970.004
The **Stanislavski** system. Moore, S.   792
Stanislavsky, Konstantin, 1863-1938
An actor prepares   792
Building a character   792
Creating a role   792
       About
Moore, S. The Stanislavski system   792
The **Stanislavsky** method. See Moore, S. The Stanislav-
ski system   792
Stanley, Debra L.
(jt. auth) Rafter, N. H. Prisons in America   365
Stanley, Henry M. (Henry Morton), 1841-1904
       About
Dugard, M. Into Africa   92
Stanley Kubrick, director. Walker, A.   92
Stanton, Doug
In harm's way   940.54
Stanton, Elizabeth Cady, 1815-1902
       About
Ward, G. C. Not for ourselves alone: the story of Eliz-
abeth Cady Stanton and Susan B. Anthony   92

Star, Alexander, 1967-
(ed) Quick studies. See Quick studies   **001.1**
Star spangled banner (Song)
Molotsky, I. The flag, the poet & the song   **973.5**
Star-spangled banner. Sedeen, M.   **929.9**
The **star** thrower. Eiseley, L. C.   **818**
Star trek: the next generation (Television program)
Richards, T. The meaning of Star Trek   **791.45**
Star ware. Harrington, P. S.   **522**
Star Wars (Ballistic missile defense system) *See* Strategic Defense Initiative
Stardust. Gribbin, J. R.   **523**
Stardust melodies. Friedwald, W.   **782.42**
Stardust melody: the life and music of Hoagy Carmichael. Sudhalter, R.   **92**
Stark, Rodney
For the glory of God   **291.1**
One true God   **291.1**
Starkey, David
Six wives: the queens of Henry VIII   **920**
Starkey, Paul, 1947-
(ed) Encyclopedia of Arabic literature. See Encyclopedia of Arabic literature   **892**
Starlanyl, Devin
Fibromyalgia & chronic myofascial pain syndrome   **616.7**
Stars
See also Black holes (Astronomy); Constellations; Supernovas
Hirshfeld, A. Parallax   **523.8**
Kaler, J. B. Extreme stars   **523.8**
Ridpath, I. Stars and planets   **520**
Atlases
Tirion, W. The Cambridge star atlas   **523.8**
Stars and planets. Ridpath, I.   **520**
Start with no. Camp, J.   **658.4**
Starting small in the wilderness. See Doan, M. The Sierra Club family outdoors guide   **796.5**
Stashower, Daniel
The boy genius and the mogul   **791.45**
Teller of tales: the life of Arthur Conan Doyle   **92**
State, Heads of *See* Heads of state
State, The
Bobbitt, P. The shield of Achilles   **327**
Hobbes, T. Leviathan   **320.1**
Locke, J. Two treatises of government   **320.1**
State and agriculture *See* Agriculture—Government policy
State governments
The Book of the states   **352.13**
Facts about the states   **973**
Noonan, J. T., Jr. Narrowing the nation's power: the Supreme Court sides with the states   **342**
Directories
Government phone book USA   **320.025**
State ministries *See* Executive departments
State names, seals, flags, and symbols. Shearer, B. F.   **929.9**
State of siege. Camus, A.
In Camus, A. Caligula & three other plays p135-232   **842**
State of the Union: a century of American labor. Lichtenstein, N.   **331**
State rights
Garrison, T. A. The legal ideology of removal   **970.004**
See/See also pages in the following book(s):
The Causes of the Civil War   **973.7**
States' rights *See* State rights
The **Statesman's** year-book   **310.5**
Statesmen
See also Heads of state; Politicians
Station X. Smith, M.   **940.54**

Statistical abstract of the United States. United States. Bureau of the Census   **317.3**
Statistical abstract of the world   **310.5**
A **Statistical** portrait of the United States   **317.3**
Statistical yearbook. United Nations. Statistical Office   **310.5**
Statistics
Encyclopaedia Britannica almanac   **031.02**
The Europa world year book   **310.5**
The New York Times almanac   **031.02**
The Statesman's year-book   **310.5**
Statistical abstract of the world   **310.5**
The Time almanac   **031.02**
United Nations. Statistical Office. Statistical yearbook   **310.5**
United States. Bureau of the Census. Statistical abstract of the United States   **317.3**
The World almanac and book of facts   **031.02**
Dictionaries
Everitt, B. The Cambridge dictionary of statistics   **519.5**
Stavans, Ilan
On borrowed words   **92**
Staying tuned. Schorr, D.   **92**
Stead, Christina, 1902-1983
The man who loved children; criticism
In Jarrell, R. No other book   **809**
Steal away. Wright, C. D.   **811**
Stealing Jesus. Bawer, B.   **277.3**
Steam navigation
See also Navigation
Stearns, Peter N.
(ed) Encyclopedia of European social history from 1350 to 2000. See Encyclopedia of European social history from 1350 to 2000   **940**
Stebbins, Robert C. (Robert Cyril), 1915-
A field guide to Western reptiles and amphibians   **597.9**
Stedman's medical dictionary   **610.3**
Steel, Rodney
Sharks of the world   **597**
Steele, Anitra T.
Bare bones children's services   **027.62**
Steen, R. Grant
(ed) Childhood cancer. See Childhood cancer   **618.92**
Steffens, Lincoln, 1866-1936
The autobiography of Lincoln Steffens   **92**
Stegner, Wallace Earle, 1909-1993
About
Benson, J. J. Wallace Stegner   **92**
Steichen, Edward, 1879-1973
Steichen's legacy   **779**
About
Smith, J. Edward Steichen: the early years   **779**
Steichen, Joanna T.
(jt. auth) Steichen, E. Steichen's legacy   **779**
Steichen's legacy. Steichen, E.   **779**
Steig, William, 1907-2003
See/See also pages in the following book(s):
Marcus, L. S. Ways of telling   **741.6**
Stein, David B.
Ritalin is not the answer   **618.92**
Stein, Gertrude, 1874-1946
The autobiography of Alice B. Toklas   **92**
also in Stein, G. Selected writings p1-237   **818**
also in Stein, G. Writings, 1903-1932   **818**
Composition as explanation
In Stein, G. Selected writings p511-23   **818**
Four saints in three acts
In Stein, G. Selected writings p577-612   **818**
Ladies' voices
In Stein, G. Selected writings p555-56   **818**
Portrait of Mabel Dodge at the Villa Curonia
In Stein, G. Selected writings p523-30   **818**

Stein, Gertrude, 1874-1946—*Continued*
Selected writings — 818
Tender buttons: objects, food, rooms
  In Stein, G. Selected writings p459-509 — 818
What happened
  In Stein, G. Selected writings p557-60 — 818
Writings, 1903-1932 — 818
Writings, 1932-1946 — 818
  See/See also pages in the following book(s):
American women fiction writers — 813.009
Pierpont, C. R. Passionate minds — 810.9
Stein, Howard
(ed) The Best American short plays. See The Best American short plays — 812.008
Stein, Sol
How to grow a novel — 808.3
Stein on writing — 808
Stein, Stephen J., 1940-
The Shaker experience in America — 289
Stein on writing. Stein, S. — 808
Steinbeck, John, 1902-1968
Conversations with John Steinbeck — 92
The grapes of wrath; criticism
  In Steinbeck, J. Working days — 818
Travels with Charley — 973
Working days — 818
      About
John Steinbeck — 813.009
  See/See also pages in the following book(s):
Naipaul, V. S. The writer and the world p334-45 — 824

Steinberg, Alan, 1945-
(jt. auth) Abdul-Jabbar, K. Black profiles in courage — 920
Steinberg, Jacques
The gatekeepers — 378.1
Steinberg, Leo, 1920-
Leonardo's incessant Last Supper — 759.5
Steinberg, Mark L.
The Facts on File dictionary of biotechnology and genetic engineering — 660.6
Steinberg, Michael
The symphony — 784.2
Steinberg, S. H. (Sigfrid Henry), 1899-1969 The Wilson calendar of world history. See The Wilson calendar of world history — 902
Steinberg, Saul, 1914-1999
Reflections and shadows — 92
Steinberg, Sigfrid Henry *See* Steinberg, S. H. (Sigfrid Henry), 1899-1969
Steinem, Gloria
Moving beyond words — 305.4
Outrageous acts and everyday rebellions — 305.4
Revolution from within — 155.2
      About
Heilbrun, C. G. The education of a woman: the life of Gloria Steinem — 92
Steiner, Wendy, 1949-
Venus in exile — 700
Steingraber, Sandra
Having faith — 618.2
Steinhardt, Arnold, 1937-
Indivisible by four — 920
Steinman, David Barnard, 1886-1960
  See/See also pages in the following book(s):
Petroski, H. Engineers of dreams — 624
Stekler, Paul
(jt. auth) Welch, J. Killing Custer — 973.8
Stella Adler: the art of acting. Adler, S. — 792
Stella Lykes (Freighter)
McPhee, J. A. Looking for a ship — 910.4
Steltenkamp, Michael F.
Black Elk, holy man of the Oglala — 92
Stemple, Jane H. Yolen *See* Yolen, Jane

Stencil work
Fresh & fabulous painted furniture — 745.7
Stendhal, Renate
(jt. auth) Chernin, K. Cecilia Bartoli — 92
Stengel, Casey
      About
Creamer, R. W. Stengel — 92
Stengel, Richard
You're too kind — 177
Step across this line. Rushdie, S. — 824
Step-by-step yard & garden basics — 635
Stepan, Peter
Icons of photography. See Icons of photography — 779
Photos that changed the world. See Photos that changed the world — 779
Stepan-Norris, Judith, 1957-
Left out — 331.8
Stephanopoulos, George
All too human — 973.929
Stephens, Alexander Hamilton, 1812-1883
  See/See also pages in the following book(s):
Wilson, E. Patriotic gore p380-437 — 810.9
Stephenson, Sir William Samuel, 1896-1989
      About
Stevenson, W. A man called Intrepid — 940.54
Steptoe, Sonja
(jt. auth) Joyner-Kersee, J. A kind of grace — 92
Stern, Gerald
This time — 811
Stern, Isaac
My first 79 years — 92
Stern, Ken, 1965-
To hell and back — 332.6
Stern, Kenneth S. (Kenneth Saul), 1953-
A force upon the plain — 322.4
Sternberg, Martin L. A.
American Sign Language — 419
Sternberg, Robert J.
Successful intelligence — 153.9
Steroids
    See also Athletes—Drug use
Stesichorus, ca. 640-ca. 550 B.C.
      About
Carson, A. Autobiography of red — 811
Steuernagel, Robert
The cellular connection — 621.385
Stevens, John F. (John Frank), 1853-1943
  See/See also pages in the following book(s):
McCullough, D. G. The path between the seas — 972.87
Stevens, Maryanne, 1948-
(jt. auth) Tucker, P. H. Monet in the 20th century — 759.4
Stevens, Wallace, 1879-1955
Collected poetry and prose — 818
Opus posthumous — 818
  See/See also pages in the following book(s):
Gioia, D. Can poetry matter? — 809.1
Jarrell, R. No other book — 809
Kermode, F. An appetite for poetry — 801
Pritchard, W. H. Lives of the modern poets p203-33 — 821.009
Stevens, William K., 1935-
The change in the weather — 551.5
Stevenson, Adlai E. (Adlai Ewing), 1900-1965
      About
Baker, J. H. The Stevensons — 920
  See/See also pages in the following book(s):
Galbraith, J. K. Name-dropping — 973.9
Stevenson, L. Harold, 1940-
(jt. auth) Wyman, B. C. The Facts on File dictionary of environmental science — 363.7

Stevenson, Robert Louis, 1850-1894
Dr. Jekyll and Mr. Hyde; criticism
In Nabokov, V. V. Lectures on literature p179-205
    808.3

See/See also pages in the following book(s):
Alvarez, A. Night p193-203 **154.6**
Stevenson, William, 1924 or 5-
A man called Intrepid **940.54**
Stevenson family
About
Baker, J. H. The Stevensons **920**
Bathurst, B. The lighthouse Stevensons **623.89**
Stewart, Chris
Driving over lemons **946**
Stewart, Henry *See* Darnley, Henry Stewart, Lord, 1545-1567
Stewart, House of *See* House of Stuart
Stewart, Ian, 1945-
The magical maze **510**
Stewart, James
About
Thomas, T. A wonderful life: the films and career of James Stewart **791.43**
Stewart, James B.
Blind eye **364.1**
Stewart, Jimmy *See* Stewart, James
Stewart, Marcia
(jt. auth) Portman, J. Every landlord's legal guide
    346.04
(jt. auth) Portman, J. Every tenant's legal guide
    346.04

Stewart, Martha
Great American wreaths **745.92**
Great parties **642**
Handmade Christmas **745.59**
The Martha Stewart cookbook **641.5**
Martha Stewart's healthy quick cook **641.5**
Martha Stewart's hors d'oeuvres handbook **641.8**
Martha Stewart's menus for entertaining **642**
Martha Stewart's new old house **728**
Special occasions **641.5**
About
Byron, C. Martha Inc. **92**
Stewart, Susan
Columbarium **811**
Stews
Vollstedt, M. The big book of soups & stews
    641.8
Stiegeler, S. E.
(ed) The Facts on File dictionary of earth science. See The Facts on File dictionary of earth science.
    550.3
Stieglitz, Alfred, 1864-1946
Alfred Stieglitz: the key set **779**
About
Homer, W. I. Stieglitz and the Photo-Secession, 1902
    779
Stieglitz and the Photo-Secession, 1902. Homer, W. I.
    779
Stierlin, Henri
Islamic art and architecture **709.1**
Stiff. Roach, M. **611**
Stiffed. Faludi, S. **305.31**
Stiglitz, Joseph E.
Globalization and its discontents **337**
Stiles, T. J.
Jesse James **92**
Still-life painting
Rowell, M. Objects of desire **758**
Still me. Reeve, C. **92**
Still missing: Amelia Earhart and the search for modern feminism. Ware, S. **92**
Still woman enough. Lynn, L. **92**
Stille, Alexander
The future of the past **303.4**

Stillman, David
(jt. auth) Lancaster, L. C. When generations collide
    658.3
A **stillness** at Appomattox. Catton, B. **973.7**
Stilwell, Alexander
Encyclopedia of survival techniques **796.5**
Stilwell, Joseph Warren, 1883-1946
About
Tuchman, B. W. Stilwell and the American experience in China, 1911-45 **327.73**
Stilwell and the American experience in China, 1911-45. Tuchman, B. W. **327.73**
Stim, Richard
(jt. auth) Elias, S. Patent, copyright & trademark
    346.04
Stimulants
See also Hallucinogens
Stine, G. Harry (George Harry), 1928-1997
Handbook of model rocketry **629.47**
Stine, George Harry *See* Stine, G. Harry (George Harry), 1928-1997
Stinnett, Robert B.
Day of deceit **940.54**
Stober, Dan
A convenient spy **327.12**
Stock, Gregory
Redesigning humans **176**
Stock, Penny
(ed) The Oxford dictionary of allusions. See The Oxford dictionary of allusions **803**
Stock exchanges
See also Wall Street (New York, N.Y.)
See/See also pages in the following book(s):
Mayer, M. The Fed **332.1**
Stocks
Cassidy, J. Dot.con **381**
Cramer, J. J. Confessions of a street addict **332.6**
Henry, S. The Dinner Club **338.7**
Lynch, P. One up on Wall Street **332.6**
Stern, K. To hell and back **332.6**
Stoffman, Phyllis, 1948-
The family guide to preventing and treating 100 infectious illnesses **616**
Stoics
See/See also pages in the following book(s):
Hamilton, E. The echo of Greece p155-77 **880.9**
Marcus Aurelius, Emperor of Rome. Meditations
    188
Russell, B. A history of Western philosophy p252-70
    109
Stokes, Donald W.
The bird feeder book **598**
The butterfly book **595.7**
Stokes field guide to birds: Eastern region **598**
Stokes field guide to birds: Western region **598**
Stokes, Gale
The walls came tumbling down **947**
Stokes, Lillian Q.
(jt. auth) Stokes, D. W. The bird feeder book
    598
(jt. auth) Stokes, D. W. The butterfly book **595.7**
(jt. auth) Stokes, D. W. Stokes field guide to birds: Eastern region **598**
(jt. auth) Stokes, D. W. Stokes field guide to birds: Western region **598**
Stokes field guide to birds: Eastern region. Stokes, D. W. **598**
Stokes field guide to birds: Western region. Stokes, D. W. **598**
Stokesbury, James L.
A short history of World War I **940.3**
Stokstad, Marilyn, 1929-
Art history **709**
The **stolen** child. Hewetson, A. **616.89**

Stolen figs and other adventures in Calabria. Rotella, M. **945**

Stoll, Steven
Larding the lean Earth **631.4**
Stolley, Richard B.
(ed) Life: century of change. See Life: century of change **779**
(ed) Life: World War 2. See Life: World War 2 **940.53**
Stone, Douglas
Difficult conversations **158**
Stone, I. F. (Isidor Feinstein), 1907-1989
The trial of Socrates **183**
Stone, Isidor Feinstein See Stone, I. F. (Isidor Feinstein), 1907-1989
Stone, Jeff, 1953-
(jt. auth) Gross, K. J. Woman's face **646.7**
Stone, Jon R., 1959-
Latin for the illiterati **473**
More Latin for the illiterati **473**
Stone, Michael
(jt. auth) Miller, J. The cell: inside the 9/11 plot and why the FBI and CIA failed to stop it **973.931**
Stone, Michael H., 1933-
Healing the mind **616.89**
Stone, Nathaniel
On the water **917.3**
Stone, Ruth, 1915-
In the next galaxy **811**
Stone by stone. Thorson, R. M. **693**
Stone in the garden. Hayward, G. **712**
The stone of heaven. Levy, A. **553.8**
Stonehenge (England)
North, J. D. Stonehenge **936**
The stones of Balazuc. Merriman, J. M. **944**
Stones of the sky. Neruda, P. **861**
Stoneware See Pottery
Stoop. Wilson, L.
In Wilson, L. 21 short plays p83-86 **812**
Stoppard, Miriam
Complete baby and child care **649**
Stoppard, Tom
Arcadia **822**
The invention of love **822**
Rosencrantz and Guildenstern are dead **822**
also in Nine plays of the modern theater p673-790 **808.82**
Travesties **822**
See/See also pages in the following book(s):
Playwrights at work **812.009**
Storey, John W. (John Woodrow), 1939-
(jt. auth) Utter, G. H. The religious right **277.3**
Storey's horse-lover's encyclopedia **636.1**
Stories from Shakespeare. Chute, M. G. **822.3**
Stories of freedom in Black New York. White, S. **974.7**
Stories of the invisible. Ball, P. **541.2**
Stories, poems, and other writings. Cather, W. **818**
Storm center. O'Brien, D. M. **347**
A storm in Flanders. Groom, W. **940.4**
Storms
See also Hurricanes; Tornadoes
Junger, S. The perfect storm **910.4**
Storr, Robert
Gerhard Richter: forty years of painting **759.3**
Storrer, William Allin
The Frank Lloyd Wright companion **720.973**
The story of a shipwrecked sailor. García Márquez, G. **910.4**
The story of American freedom. Foner, E. **323.44**
The story of architecture. Glancey, J. **720.9**
The story of art. Gombrich, E. H. **709**
The story of English. McCrum, R. **420**
The story of mathematics. Mankiewicz, R. **510**

The story of my boyhood and youth. Muir, J. **92**
also in Muir, J. Nature writings **92**
The story of my life. Keller, H. **92**
The story of painting. Beckett, W. **759**
The story of philosophy. Durant, W. J. **109**
The story of philosophy. Magee, B. **190**
The story of utopias. Mumford, L. **321**
Storyteller. Silko, L. **818**
Storytelling
Cullum, C. N. The storytime sourcebook **027.62**
MacDonald, M. R. Celebrate the world **398.2**
Seeger, P. Pete Seeger's storytelling book **372.6**
Encyclopedias
Storytelling encyclopedia **398.03**
Storytelling encyclopedia **398.03**
The storytime sourcebook. Cullum, C. N. **027.62**
Stotz, Carl E., 1910-1992
See/See also pages in the following book(s):
Wills, G. Certain trumpets p186-92 **303.3**
Stout, Alisa A. de Jong- See Jong-Stout, Alisa A. de
Stow, Josie
The African kitchen **641.5**
Stowe, Calvin Ellis, 1802-1886
See/See also pages in the following book(s):
Wilson, E. Patriotic gore p59-72 **810.9**
Stowe, Harriet Beecher, 1811-1896
Uncle Tom's cabin; criticism
In McPherson, J. M. Drawn with the sword **973.7**
About
Hedrick, J. D. Harriet Beecher Stowe **92**
See/See also pages in the following book(s):
Wilson, E. Patriotic gore p3-58 **810.9**
Strachan, Hew
(ed) World War I. See World War I **940.3**
Strachey, Lytton, 1880-1932
Elizabeth and Essex **92**
Queen Victoria **92**
Straczynski, J. Michael, 1954-
The complete book of scriptwriting **808.2**
Stradling, R. A.
(jt. auth) Vincent, M. Cultural atlas of Spain and Portugal **946**
Straight, no chaser. Gourse, L. **92**
Strain (Psychology) See Stress (Psychology)
Strand, Mark, 1934-
Blizzard of one **811**
Chicken, shadow, moon and more **811**
(ed) The Making of a poem. See The Making of a poem **821.008**
Strange beauty: Murray Gell-Mann and the revolution in twentieth-century physics. Johnson, G. **92**
The strange career of Jim Crow. Woodward, C. V. **305.8**
Strange matters. Siegfried, T. **523.1**
Strange victory. May, E. R. **940.54**
The stranger from paradise: a biography of William Blake. Bentley, G. E. **92**
Strangers from a different shore. Takaki, R. T. **305.8**
Strassfeld, Michael
The Jewish holidays **296.4**
Strategic Defense Initiative
FitzGerald, F. Way out there in the blue **973.927**
Strategy
Overy, R. J. Why the Allies won **940.53**
Strathern, Paul, 1940-
Mendeleyev's dream **540.9**
Stratigraphic geology
Hancock, G. Underworld: the mysterious origins of civilization **551.7**
Macdougall, J. D. A short history of planet earth **551.7**
Winchester, S. The map that changed the world **92**

Stratton, Joanna L.
Pioneer women   978.1
Stratton-Porter, Gene, 1863-1924
See/See also pages in the following book(s):
American women fiction writers   813.009
Straub, Deborah Gillan
(ed) Voices of multicultural America. See Voices of
multicultural America   815.008
Strauss, Claude Lévi- *See* Lévi-Strauss, Claude
Strauss, Joseph Baermann, 1870-1938
See/See also pages in the following book(s):
Petroski, H. Engineers of dreams   624
Strauss, Richard, 1864-1949
See/See also pages in the following book(s):
Tuchman, B. W. The proud tower p291-302, 308-20
    909.82
Strauss, Steven D., 1958-
Landlord and tenant   346.04
Wills and trusts   346.05
Stravinsky, Igor, 1882-1971
About
Joseph, C. M. Stravinsky inside out   92
Walsh, S. Stravinsky   92
See/See also pages in the following book(s):
Gardner, H. Creating minds p187-226   153.3
Stravinsky inside out. Joseph, C. M.   92
Strayer, Joseph Reese, 1904-1987
(ed) Dictionary of the Middle Ages. See Dictionary of
the Middle Ages   940.1
Strayhorn, Billy, 1915-1967
About
Hajdu, D. Lush life: a biography of Billy Strayhorn
    92
Streatfeild, Dominic
Cocaine   362.29
Street, Emmet *See* Behan, Brendan, 1923-1964
Street people *See* Homeless persons
Streets
New York (N.Y.)
See also Wall Street (New York, N.Y.)
Streissguth, Michael
(ed) Ring of fire: the Johnny Cash reader. See Ring of
fire: the Johnny Cash reader   92
Strength to love. King, M. L.   252
Stress (Physiology)
Bremner, J. D. Does stress damage the brain?
    616.85
Goldman, B. Brain fitness   153.1
Kahn, A. P. Stress A-Z   616.9
Stress (Psychology)
See also Anxiety; Post-traumatic stress disorder
Bremner, J. D. Does stress damage the brain?
    616.85
Kahn, A. P. Stress A-Z   616.9
Taylor, S. E. The tending instinct   304.5
Stress A-Z. Kahn, A. P.   616.9
Strickland, Bonnie R., 1936-
(ed) The Gale encyclopedia of psychology. See The
Gale encyclopedia of psychology   150.3
Strindberg, August, 1849-1912
The dance of death
In Strindberg, A. Strindberg: five plays p113-204
    839.7
A dream play
In Our dramatic heritage v5   808.82
In Strindberg, A. Strindberg: five plays p205-64
    839.7
The father
In Strindberg, A. Strindberg: five plays p19-62
    839.7
The ghost sonata
In Strindberg, A. Strindberg: five plays p265-97
    839.7

Miss Julie
In Strindberg, A. Strindberg: five plays p63-112
    839.7
Strindberg: five plays   839.7
Strindberg: five plays. Strindberg, A.   839.7
Stringer, Christopher B.
African exodus   599.93
Stroke
Managing stroke   616.8
Strom, Terry Kristen
(jt. auth) Reaven, G. M. Syndrome X   616.1
Strom, Yale
The book of Klezmer   781.62
Strom Thurmond & the politics of southern change.
Cohodas, N.   92
Stroman, James
Administrative assistant's & secretary's handbook
    651.3
Stromer, Ernst
About
Nothdurft, W. E. The lost dinosaurs of Egypt
    567.9
Strong, James, 1822-1894
The strongest Strong's exhaustive concordance of the
Bible   220.5
Strong, M. C. (Martin Charles), 1960-
The great rock discography   781.66
Strong, Martin Charles *See* Strong, M. C. (Martin
Charles), 1960-
Strong women eat well. Nelson, M. E.   613.2
Strong women, strong bones. Nelson, M. E.   616.7
The **strongest** Strong's exhaustive concordance of the
Bible. Strong, J.   220.5
Strong's exhaustive concordance of the Bible. See
Strong, J. The strongest Strong's exhaustive concor-
dance of the Bible   220.5
Stroom, Gerrold van der
(ed) Frank, A. The diary of Anne Frank: the critical
edition   92
Strouse, Jean
Morgan   92
Structural failures
Levy, M. Why buildings fall down   690
The **structure** of evolutionary theory. Gould, S. J.
    576.8
The **struggle** and the triumph. Wałęsa, L.   92
A **struggle** for power. Draper, T.   973.3
Strunk, William, 1869-1946
The elements of style   808
Struth, Thomas, 1954-
Thomas Struth, 1977-2002   779
Stuart, Chris
Africa's vanishing wildlife   591.9
Stuart, Henry *See* Darnley, Henry Stewart, Lord, 1545-
1567
Stuart, House of *See* House of Stuart
Stuart, P. G. Maxwell- *See* Maxwell-Stuart, P. G.
Stuart, Tilde
(jt. auth) Stuart, C. Africa's vanishing wildlife
    591.9
Stubenrecht, Werner Scholze- *See* Scholze-Stubenrecht,
Werner
Student aid
See also Scholarships; Student loan funds
Scholarships, fellowships and loans   378.3
Student busing *See* Busing (School integration)
Student loan funds
College Entrance Examination Board. The college
costs & financial aid handbook   378.3
Peterson's college money handbook   378.3
Scholarships, fellowships and loans   378.3
Students
Political activity
Gitlin, T. The sixties   973.92
Students and libraries *See* Libraries and students

Student's guide for writing college papers. Turabian, K.
L.   **808**
Studwell, Joe
The China dream   **951**
A **study** of history [abridged] Toynbee, A.   **909**
Stuffed animals & pickled heads. Asma, S. T. **508**
Stump, Al, 1916-1995
Cobb   **92**
Sturdy, John
(ed) The Cambridge history of Judaism. See The Cam-
bridge history of Judaism   **296**
Sturgis, Alexander
Understanding paintings. See Understanding paintings
                                                759
Sturgis, Alice
The standard code of parliamentary procedure
                                                060.4
Style manual. United States. Government Printing Office
                                                808
Styles, Carol See Carvajal, Carol Styles
Styles of radical will. Sontag, S.   **814**
Styron, William, 1925-
Darkness visible   **616.85**
See/See also pages in the following book(s):
Langer, L. L. Admitting the Holocaust p75-87
                                                940.53
Sub-Saharan Africa
            Encyclopedias
Encyclopedia of Africa, south of the Sahara   **967**
Subconsciousness
Tallis, F. Hidden minds   **154.2**
Subject headings
Library of Congress. Cataloging Policy and Support
Office. Library of Congress subject headings
                                                025.4
Sears list of subject headings   **025.4**
Submarine cables
Gordon, J. S. A thread across the ocean   **384.1**
Submarine exploration See Underwater exploration
Submarines
Hill, A. J. Under pressure   **910.4**
Tall, J. J. Submarines & deep-sea vehicles   **623.8**
Submarines & deep-sea vehicles. Tall, J. J. **623.8**
Submersibles
Tall, J. J. Submarines & deep-sea vehicles   **623.8**
Substance abuse See Drug abuse
Substance abuse sourcebook   **616.86**
Suburban nation. Duany, A.   **307.7**
Subversive activities
From the secret files of J. Edgar Hoover   **363.2**
Shultz, R. H. The secret war against Hanoi
                                                959.704
Success
See also Self-realization
Carnegie, D. How to win friends and influence people
                                                158
Gegax, T. Winning in the game of life   **158**
Graham, S. You can make it happen   **650.1**
Kelley, R. E. How to be a star at work   **658**
McCormack, M. H. What they don't teach you at Har-
vard Business School   **650.1**
McGraw, P. C. Life strategies   **158**
Peale, N. V. The power of positive living   **248**
Peale, N. V. The power of positive thinking
                                                253.5
Peters, T. J. The circle of innovation   **658.4**
Popcorn, F. Clicking   **650.1**
Successful aging. Rowe, J. W.   **612.6**
Successful homebuilding and remodeling. Buchholz, B.
B.   **690**
Successful intelligence. Sternberg, R. J.   **153.9**
Succoth (Feast of Tabernacles) See Sukkoth
Succulent plants
Cave, Y. Succulents for the contemporary garden
                                                635.9

Hewitt, T. The complete book of cacti & succulents
                                                635.9
Succulents for the contemporary garden. Cave, Y.
                                                635.9
Suchlicki, Jaime
Cuba   **972.91**
Sudan
            History—Civil War, 1983-
Scroggins, D. Emma's war   **962.4**
Sudhalter, Richard, 1938-
Stardust melody: the life and music of Hoagy
Carmichael   **92**
Suetonius Tranquillus, C., ca. 69-ca. 122
The twelve Caesars   **878**
Suffering
Brehony, K. A. After the darkest hour   **155.9**
Kushner, H. S. When bad things happen to good peo-
ple   **296.3**
Price, R. Letter to a man in the fire   **231**
Simmons, P. Learning to fall   **291.4**
Suffrage
See also Women—Suffrage
Sufism
Ernst, C. W. The Shambhala guide to sufism   **297**
Essential Sufism   **297**
Sugarmann, Josh, 1960-
Every handgun is aimed at you   **363.3**
Sugerman, Daniel
(jt. auth) Hopkins, J. No one here gets out alive [biog-
raphy of Jim Morrison]   **92**
Suicide
Ackerman, D. A slender thread   **362.28**
Durkheim, É. Suicide, a study in sociology   **179.7**
Humphry, D. Final exit   **179.7**
Marcus, E. Why suicide?   **179.7**
Peck, M. S. Denial of the soul   **179.7**
            Dictionaries
Evans, G. The encyclopedia of suicide   **362.28**
Suing (Law) See Litigation
Suits me: the double life of Billy Tipton. Middlebrook,
D. W.   **92**
Sukkoth
See/See also pages in the following book(s):
Strassfeld, M. The Jewish holidays p125-47   **296.4**
Sullivan, Anne, 1866-1936
            About
Lash, J. P. Helen and teacher   **92**
            Drama
Gibson, W. The miracle worker   **812**
Sullivan, Edward J.
(ed) Brazil body & soul. See Brazil body & soul
                                                709.8
Sullivan, Evelin E., 1947-
The concise book of lying   **177**
Sullivan, Irene F.
(jt. auth) Gill, S. D. Dictionary of Native American
mythology   **299**
Sullivan, Lynne P.
(ed) Archaeology of the Appalachian highlands. See
Archaeology of the Appalachian highlands
                                                970.004
Sullivan, Patricia
(ed) Civil rights in the United States. See Civil rights
in the United States   **323.1**
Sullivan, Randall
Labyrinth   **364.1**
Sullivan, Robert, 1940-
The small business start-up guide   **658.1**
Sullivan, Rosemary
Labyrinth of desire   **818**
Sulston, John, 1942-
The common thread   **572.8**
Sulzberger, C. L. (Cyrus Leo), 1912-1993
(jt. auth) Ambrose, S. E. The American Heritage new
history of World War II   **940.53**

Sulzberger, Cyrus Leo *See* Sulzberger, C. L. (Cyrus Leo), 1912-1993
A **sum** of destructions. Staller, N.   **759.4**
Sumerians
    See/See also pages in the following book(s):
    Potok, C. Wanderings p5-19   **909**
A **summary** view of the rights of British America. Jefferson, T.
    In Jefferson, T. Writings   **818**
Summer camp guide. See Guide to summer camps and summer schools   **796.54**
Summer camps *See* Camps
Summer employment
    See also Teenagers—Employment
Summer of '49. Halberstam, D.   **796.357**
Summer of '98. Lupica, M.   **796.357**
The **summer** of a dormouse. Mortimer, J. C.   **92**
Summer schools
    Directories
    Guide to summer camps and summer schools   **796.54**
Summers, Anthony
    The arrogance of power: the secret world of Richard Nixon   **92**
Summers, Harry G.
    Vietnam War almanac   **959.704**
Sumner, Judith
    The natural history of medicinal plants   **581.6**
Sun
    Golub, L. Nearest star   **523.7**
Sun dancing. Moorhouse, G.   **941.5**
Sun out. Koch, K.   **811**
The **sun,** the genome, & the Internet. Dyson, F. J.   **303.4**
Sun under wood. Hass, R.   **811**
Sunday in the park with George. Sondheim, S.   **812**
The **sunflower**. Wiesenthal, S.   **179.7**
Sung family
    About
    Seagrave, S. The Soong dynasty   **951**
The **Sunshine** Boys. Simon, N.
    In Simon, N. The collected plays of Neil Simon v2 p303-89   **812**
Sunstein, Cass R.
    (ed) Clones and clones. See Clones and clones   **174**
Sunstein, Emily W.
    Mary Shelley   **92**
Supernatural
    See also Spiritualism
    Encyclopedias
    Guiley, R. E. Encyclopedia of the strange, mystical & unexplained   **133**
Supernatural fiction writers   **809.3**
Supernovas
    Dauber, P. M. The three big bangs   **523.1**
    Gribbin, J. R. Stardust   **523**
Superstition
    Frazer, Sir J. G. The new golden bough   **291.1**
    Dictionaries
    Radford, E. Encyclopaedia of superstitions   **398.03**
Supervision of employees *See* Personnel management
Suplee, Curt
    Milestones of science   **509**
    Physics in the 20th century   **530**
Support of children *See* Child support
A **supposedly** fun thing I'll never do again. Wallace, D. F.   **814**
The **suppression** of the African slave-trade. Du Bois, W. E. B.
    In Du Bois, W. E. B. Writings   **818**
Supreme command. Cohen, E. A.   **355**
Supreme Court (U.S.) *See* United States. Supreme Court
The **Supreme** Court A to Z   **347**
The **Supreme** Court compendium   **347**

The **Supreme** Court justices: a biographical dictionary   **920.003**
Supreme injustice. Dershowitz, A. M.   **324**
Surgery
    See also names of diseases and names of organs and regions of the body with the subdivision *Surgery*, e.g. Heart—Surgery
    Current surgical diagnosis & treatment   **617**
    Gawande, A. Complications: a young surgeon's notes on an imperfect science   **617**
    Mailhot, C. B. Surgery: a patient's guide from diagnosis to recovery   **617**
    McLanahan, S. A. Surgery and its alternatives   **617**
    Rutkow, I. M. American surgery   **617**
Surgery, Plastic *See* Plastic surgery
Surgery and its alternatives. McLanahan, S. A.   **617**
Surreal lives. Brandon, R.   **709.04**
Surrealism
    Brandon, R. Surreal lives   **709.04**
Surveying
    Linklater, A. Measuring America   **973**
Survival after airplane accidents, shipwrecks, etc.
    Ashcraft, T. O. Red sky in mourning   **910.4**
    García Márquez, G. The story of a shipwrecked sailor   **910.4**
    Read, P. P. Alive   **910.4**
    Severin, T. In search of Robinson Crusoe   **996**
    Souhami, D. Selkirk's Island   **996**
Survival in Auschwitz; and, The reawakening. Levi, P.   **940.53**
Survival of the fittest *See* Natural selection
Survival of the prettiest. Etcoff, N. L.   **391**
Susanka, Sarah
    Creating the not so big house   **728**
    Not so big solutions for your home   **728**
Suspect identities. Cole, S. A.   **363.2**
Sussman, Allen E.
    (jt. auth) Turkington, C. The encyclopedia of deafness and hearing disorders   **617.8**
Sussman, Julie
    Dare to repair   **643**
Sutton, Amy L.
    (ed) Dental care and oral health sourcebook. See Dental care and oral health sourcebook   **617.6**
Sutton, Christine
    (jt. auth) Close, F. E. The particle odyssey   **539.7**
Sutton, Roberta Briggs
    Speech index   **808.85**
Suu Kyi *See* Aung San Suu Kyi
SUVs *See* Sport utility vehicles
Suzuki, Daisetz Teitaro, 1870-1966
    Manual of Zen Buddhism   **294.3**
Swafford, Jan
    Charles Ives   **92**
    Johannes Brahms   **92**
Swain, Dwight V.
    Creating characters   **808.3**
    Techniques of the selling writer   **808.3**
Swan, Robbyn
    (jt. auth) Summers, A. The arrogance of power: the secret world of Richard Nixon   **92**
Swan song. Chekhov, A. P.
    In Chekhov, A. P. The plays of Anton Chekhov p9-17   **891.7**
Swango, Michael
    About
    Stewart, J. B. Blind eye   **364.1**
Swanson, James A.
    (jt. auth) Strong, J. The strongest Strong's exhaustive concordance of the Bible   **220.5**
Swanson, Jenifer
    (ed) Sleep disorders sourcebook . . . See Sleep disorders sourcebook . . .   **616.8**

Swanson, Robert M.
 Century 21 accounting: first-year course. *See* Century 21 accounting: first-year course   **657**
Swartzwelder, Scott
 (jt. auth) Kuhn, C. Buzzed   **615**
 (jt. auth) Kuhn, C. Pumped   **617.1**
Sweet chaos: the Grateful Dead's American adventure. Brightman, C.   **920**
Sweet Charity. Simon, N.
 In Simon, N. The collected plays of Neil Simon v3 p1-113   **812**
The **sweet** hell inside. Ball, E.   **920**
Swenson, May, 1919-1989
 Nature   **811**
Swift, Jonathan, 1667-1745
 A tale of a tub, and other work   **827**
 See/See also pages in the following book(s):
 Durant, W. J. The age of Louis XIV p346-62   **940.2**
 Orwell, G. The Orwell reader p283-300   **828**
Swift, Margaret *See* Drabble, Margaret, 1939-
Swimming
 Katz, J. Swimming for total fitness   **797.2**
 Mullen, P. H., Jr. Gold in the water   **797.2**
Swimming for total fitness. Katz, J.   **797.2**
Swindells, Philip
 The water garden encyclopedia   **635.9**
Swing it!. Milkowski, B.   **781.65**
Swisher, Carl C.
 Java man   **599.93**
The **Swiss,** the gold, and the dead. Ziegler, J.   **940.53**
Switchboard hotlines *See* Hotlines (Telephone counseling)
Switzerland
         Foreign relations—Germany
 Ziegler, J. The Swiss, the gold, and the dead   **940.53**
Swofford, Anthony
 Jarhead: a Marine's chronicle of the Gulf War and other battles   **956.7**
Sybil. Schreiber, F. R.   **616.85**
Sykes, Bryan
 The seven daughters of Eve   **599.93**
Sykes, J. B. (John Bradbury)
 (ed) The Oxford-Duden German dictionary. *See* The Oxford-Duden German dictionary   **433**
Sykes, John Bradbury *See* Sykes, J. B. (John Bradbury)
Sylvester, James Joseph, 1814-1897
 See/See also pages in the following book(s):
 Bell, E. T. Men of mathematics p378-405   **920**
Symbiosis
 Margulis, L. Symbiotic planet   **576.8**
Symbiotic planet. Margulis, L.   **576.8**
Symbol sourcebook. Dreyfuss, H.   **302.2**
The **symbolic** species. Deacon, T. W.   **153.6**
Symbolism
 Jung, C. G. Man and his symbols   **150.19**
 Lippard, L. R. Overlay   **709**
Symbolism in art
 Carr-Gomm, S. Hidden symbols in art   **704.9**
Symbolism of numbers
    See also Numbers
Symbols *See* Signs and symbols
Symmes, Robert *See* Duncan, Robert Edward, 1919-1988
Symonds, George W. D.
 The shrub identification book   **582.1**
Symons, Ann K.
 Protecting the right to read   **025.2**
Symons, Julian, 1912-1994
 Bloody murder   **809.3**
Symphony
 Steinberg, M. The symphony   **784.2**

Symposium. Plato
 In Plato. The dialogues of Plato p164-234   **888**
 In Plato. The portable Plato p121-87   **888**
Symptoms and remedies   **616.02**
Synaptic self. LeDoux, J. E.   **612.8**
Syndrome X. Reaven, G. M.   **616.1**
Synge, J. M. (John Millington), 1871-1909
 The complete plays   **822**
 Deirdre of the sorrows
 In Synge, J. M. The complete plays   **822**
 In the shadow of the glen
 In Synge, J. M. The complete plays   **822**
 The playboy of the Western world
 In Synge, J. M. The complete plays   **822**
 Riders to the sea
 In Our dramatic heritage v5   **808.82**
 In Synge, J. M. The complete plays   **822**
 The tinker's wedding
 In Synge, J. M. The complete plays   **822**
 The well of the saints
 In Synge, J. M. The complete plays   **822**
Synge, John Millington *See* Synge, J. M. (John Millington), 1871-1909
Synoptic Gospels *See* Bible. N.T. Gospels
Syphilis
 Hayden, D. Pox: genius, madness, and the mysteries of syphilis   **616.95**
Syrian cooking
 Abadi, J. F. A fistful of lentils   **641.5**
System analysis
 Bentley, P. J. Digital biology   **570.1**
 Buchanan, M. Nexus: small worlds and the groundbreaking science of networks   **530**
System theory
    See also Chaos (Science); System analysis
 Capra, F. The web of life   **570.1**
 See/See also pages in the following book(s):
 Goodwin, B. C. How the leopard changed its spots   **576**
Systemic lupus erythematosus
 Lahita, R. G. Lupus   **616.7**
Systems, Theory of *See* System theory
Szarmach, Paul E.
 (ed) Medieval England. *See* Medieval England   **942**
Szczawinski, Adam F.
 (jt. auth) Turner, N. J. Common poisonous plants and mushrooms of North America   **581.6**
Szpiro, George G., 1950-
 Kepler's conjecture   **510**
Szulc, Tad, 1926-2001
 Fidel [Castro]   **92**
 The secret alliance   **325**
Szymborska, Wisława, 1923-
 Nonrequired reading   **028.1**
 Poems, new and collected, 1957-1997   **891.8**
 View with a grain of sand   **891.8**

T

T groups *See* Group relations training
T. rex and the Crater of Doom. Alvarez, W.   **551.7**
Taback, Simms, 1932-
 See/See also pages in the following book(s):
 The Newbery & Caldecott medal books, 1986-2000 p332-42   **028.5**
Tabernacles, Feast of *See* Sukkoth
Taber's cyclopedic medical dictionary   **610.3**
Table setting and decoration
 Ohrbach, B. M. Tabletops   **642**
Tabletops. Ohrbach, B. M.   **642**
Taboo
 Freud, S. Totem and taboo   **306**

Tabor, James D., 1946-
Why Waco?   **291.9**
Tacitus, Cornelius
The annals
  In Tacitus, C. The complete works of Tacitus p3-416
     878
The complete works of Tacitus   **878**
A dialogue on oratory
  In Tacitus, C. The complete works of Tacitus p735-
  69   **878**
Germany and its tribes
  In Tacitus, C. The complete works of Tacitus p709-
  32   **878**
The history
  In Tacitus, C. The complete works of Tacitus p419-
  673   **878**
The life of Cnaeus Julius Agricola
  In Tacitus, C. The complete works of Tacitus p677-
  706   **878**
Tadié, Jean-Yves, 1936-
Marcel Proust   **92**
Tadpoles *See* Frogs
Tae kwon do
Park, Y. H. Black belt tae kwon do   **796.8**
Taffel, Ron
The second family   **306.8**
Taft, Robert A., 1889-1953
  See/See also pages in the following book(s):
Kennedy, J. F. Profiles in courage   **920**
Tagliaferri, Mary
(ed) Breast cancer. See Breast cancer   **616.99**
Tagore, Sir Rabindranath, 1861-1941
  See/See also pages in the following book(s):
Berlin, Sir I. The sense of reality p249-66   **901**
Tahan, Malba, 1895-
The man who counted   **793.7**
T'ai chi ch'üan
McFarlane, S. The complete book of t'ai chi
    613.7
Taibo, Paco Ignacio
Guevara, also known as Che   **92**
Taine, John *See* Bell, Eric Temple, 1883-1960
Taiping Rebellion, China, 1850-1864 *See* China—His-
tory—1850-1864, Taiping Rebellion
Taishō, Emperor of Japan, 1879-1926
  See/See also pages in the following book(s):
Seagrave, S. The Yamato dynasty   **952**
Taiwan
Kemenade, W. van. China, Hong Kong, Taiwan, Inc.
    951
Takaki, Ronald T., 1939-
Double victory   **940.53**
Hiroshima   **940.54**
Strangers from a different shore   **305.8**
Take charge of your breast cancer. Link, J.   **616.99**
Taking charge   **973.923**
Taking charge of ADHD. Barkley, R. A.   **618.92**
Taking charge of asthma. Wray, B. B.   **616.2**
Taking wing. Shipman, P.   **568**
Talab, Rosemary Sturdevant
Commonsense copyright   **346.04**
Talbott, Shawn
A guide to understanding dietary supplements   **615**
Talbott, Strobe
The Russia hand   **327.73**
A **tale** of a tub, and other work. Swift, J.   **827**
The **Tale** of Genji   **751**
A **tale** of two gardens. Paz, O.   **861**
A **tale** told. Wilson, L.
  In Wilson, L. The Talley trilogy p191-262   **812**
A **talent** for genius: the life and times of Oscar Levant.
Kashner, S.   **92**
Tales from Shakespeare. Lamb, C.   **822.3**
Tales from the secret annex, Anne Frank's. Frank, A.
    839.3

Tales from the underground. Wolfe, D. W.   **578**
Tales of giant snakes. Murphy, J. C.   **597.9**
The **Tales** of Poe   **813.009**
Taliban (Afghanistan)
Rashid, A. Taliban: militant Islam, oil, and fundamen-
talism in Central Asia   **958.1**
Talk stories. Kincaid, J.   **818**
Talk to the deaf. See Riekehof, L. L. The joy of signing
    419
Talking dirty to the gods. Komunyakaa, Y.   **811**
Talking terrorism. Herbst, P.   **303.6**
Tall, J. J.
Submarines & deep-sea vehicles   **623.8**
Tall, Jeffrey *See* Tall, J. J.
Tallchief, Maria
Maria Tallchief   **92**
Talley, Wilson
(jt. auth) Teller, E. Conversations on the dark secrets
of physics   **530**
Talley & Son. Wilson, L.
  In Wilson, L. The Talley trilogy p123-90   **812**
The **Talley** trilogy. Wilson, L.   **812**
Talley's folly. Wilson, L.
  In Wilson, L. The Talley trilogy p75-122   **812**
Tallis, Frank
Hidden minds   **154.2**
Talmud
Cohen, A. Everyman's Talmud   **296.1**
Tamborlane, William V.
(ed) The Yale guide to children's nutrition. See The
Yale guide to children's nutrition   **613.2**
Tambourines to glory. Hughes, L.
  In Hughes, L. Five plays p183-258   **812**
Tanacredi, John T.
(ed) Experiment central. See Experiment central
    507.8
Tanahashi, Kazuaki, 1933-
(ed) Essential Zen. See Essential Zen   **294.3**
Tanakh. Bible. O.T.   **221.5**
Tango. Mrożek, S.
  In Nine plays of the modern theater p573-671
    808.82
Tanikō. Komparu, Z.
  In Waley, A. The Nō plays of Japan   **895.6**
Tank: the progress of a monstrous war machine. Wright,
P.   **358**
Tanks (Military science) *See* Military tanks
Tannen, Deborah
I only say this because I love you   **306.8**
You just don't understand   **302.2**
Tanzi, Rudolph E.
Decoding darkness   **616.8**
Tao te ching. Lao-tzu   **299**
Taoism
Blofeld, J. E. C. Taoism: the road to immortality
    299
Tape recordings, Audio *See* Sound recordings
Tape recordings, Video *See* Videotapes
Tapestry
Campbell, T. Tapestry in the Renaissance   **746**
Tapestry in the Renaissance. Campbell, T.   **746**
The **Tapir's** morning bath. Royte, E.   **577.3**
Tapscott, Stephen, 1948-
(ed) Twentieth century Latin American poetry. See
Twentieth century Latin American poetry   **861**
Tardiff, Joseph C.
(ed) Dictionary of Hispanic biography. See Dictionary
of Hispanic biography   **920.003**
Targeting autism. Cohen, S.   **618.92**
Tarr, David R., 1937-
(ed) Congress A to Z. See Congress A to Z
    328.73
Tartuffe. Molière
  In Molière. Tartuffe, and other plays   **842**
Tartuffe, and other plays. Molière   **842**

Tasaday (Philippine people)
  Hemley, R. Invented Eden — 959.9
A **taste** of heritage. Randall, J. — 641.5
The **taste** of wine. Peynaud, E. — 641.2
Tate, Buddy, 1913-2001
  See/See also pages in the following book(s):
  Dance, S. The world of Count Basie — 920
Tate, James, 1943-
  Selected poems — 811
  Shroud of the gnome — 811
  Worshipful Company of Fletchers — 811
Tate, Mary Jo
  F. Scott Fitzgerald A to Z — 813.009
Tattersall, Ian
  Extinct humans — 599.93
  The fossil trail — 599.93
  The monkey in the mirror — 599.93
Tatum, Beverly Daniel, 1954-
  "Why are all the Black kids sitting together in the cafeteria?" and other conversations about race — 305.8
Taub, Eric
  Gaffers, grips, and best boys — 791.43
Taub, Michael, 1946-
  (ed) Contemporary Jewish-American novelists. See Contemporary Jewish-American novelists — 813.009
Taubman, William
  Khrushchev — 92
Tausend, Marilyn
  Cocina de la familia — 641.5
Tavormina, M. Teresa (Mary Teresa), 1951-
  (ed) Medieval England. See Medieval England — 942
Tavormina, Mary Teresa *See* Tavormina, M. Teresa (Mary Teresa), 1951-
Tavris, Carol
  Anger — 152.4
Taxation
  See also Income tax
  Weisman, S. R. The great tax wars — 336.2
Taylor, A. J. P. (Alan John Percivale), 1906-1990
  English history, 1914-1945 — 942.08
Taylor, Alan John Percivale *See* Taylor, A. J. P. (Alan John Percivale), 1906-1990
Taylor, Colin F.
  Native American weapons — 970.004
Taylor, David, 1934-
  The ultimate dog book — 636.7
Taylor, Dawson
  (jt. auth) Anthony, E. Winning bowling — 794.6
Taylor, Elizabeth
  (jt. auth) Cohen, A. American pharaoh: Mayor Richard J. Daley: his battle for Chicago and the nation — 92
Taylor, Maxwell D., 1901-1987
  See/See also pages in the following book(s):
  Halberstam, D. The best and the brightest — 973.922
Taylor, Michael Ray, 1959-
  Caves — 796.52
Taylor, Murry A.
  Jumping fire — 634.9
Taylor, Nick, 1945-
  (jt. auth) Glenn, J. John Glenn — 92
Taylor, Peter Jameson Mercer- *See* Mercer-Taylor, Peter Jameson
Taylor, Sandra C.
  (ed) Japanese Americans, from relocation to redress. See Japanese Americans, from relocation to redress — 940.53
Taylor, Shelley E.
  The tending instinct — 304.5

Taylor, Todd W.
  (jt. auth) Walker, J. R. The Columbia guide to online style — 808
Taylor, Yuval
  (jt. auth) Douglass, F. Frederick Douglass — 326
Taylor's guide to annuals. Ellis, B. W. — 635.9
Taylor's guide to bulbs. Ellis, B. W. — 635.9
Taylor's guide to ground covers. Michener, D. — 635.9
Taylor's guide to ground covers, vines & grasses. See Michener, D. Taylor's guide to ground covers — 635.9
Taylor's guide to perennials. Ellis, B. W. — 635.9
Taylor's guide to roses. Ondra, N. J. — 635.9
Taylor's guide to shrubs. Fisher, K. — 635.9
Taylor's guide to vegetables & herbs — 635.9
Taylor's master guide to gardening — 635.9
Taylor's master guide to landscaping. Buchanan, R. — 712
Tea party. Pinter, H.
  In Pinter, H. Complete works v3 — 822
Teach yourself electricity and electronics. Gibilisco, S. — 621.3
Teaching
  Barzun, J. Begin here — 371.1
Teaching a stone to talk. Dillard, A. — 818
Teaching at home *See* Home schooling
Teaching tolerance. Bullard, S. — 649
The **teachings** of Don Juan. Castaneda, C. — 299
Teachout, Terry
  The skeptic: the life of H.L. Mencken — 92
The **teammates**. Halberstam, D. — 920
Teamsters Union *See* International Brotherhood of Teamsters, Chauffeurs, Warehousemen and Helpers of America
The **tech** writer's survival guide. Van Wicklen, J. — 808
The **tech** writing game. See Van Wicklen, J. The tech writer's survival guide — 808
Technical writing
  Van Wicklen, J. The tech writer's survival guide — 808
Techniques of the selling writer. Swain, D. V. — 808.3
Technology
  See also Engineering
  Brain, M. Marshall Brain's more how stuff works — 600
  Clarke, A. C. Greetings, carbon-based bipeds! — 500
  The Handy science answer book — 500
  Macaulay, D. The new way things work — 600
  Science and technology desk reference — 500
  See/See also pages in the following book(s):
  Space exploration — 629
    Dictionaries
  Academic Press dictionary of science and technology — 503
  McGraw-Hill dictionary of scientific and technical terms — 503
    Encyclopedias
  The Encyclopedia of science and technology — 503
  McGraw-Hill concise encyclopedia of science & technology — 503
  McGraw-Hill encyclopedia of science & technology — 503
  Volti, R. The Facts on File encyclopedia of science, technology, and society — 503
    History
  Bruno, L. C. Science & technology firsts — 609
  Burke, J. Circles: 50 round trips through history, technology, science, culture — 609
  Burke, J. The knowledge web — 609
  Great events from history II, Science and technology — 509

Technology—History—*Continued*
Karwatka, D. Technology's past **609**
Ochoa, G. The Wilson chronology of science and technology **502**
Science: a history of discovery in the twentieth century **509**
Science, technology, and society: the impact of science in the 20th century **509**
Technology & American history **609**
Williams, T. I. A history of invention **609**
Technology, Information *See* Information technology
Technology & American history **609**
Technology and civilization
Diamond, J. M. Guns, germs, and steel **303.4**
Dyson, F. J. The sun, the genome, & the Internet **303.4**
McLuhan, M. The global village **302.23**
Noble, D. F. The religion of technology **261.5**
Postman, N. Technopoly **303.4**
Science, technology, and society: the impact of science in the 20th century **509**
Toffler, A. Future shock **303.4**
Toffler, A. The third wave **303.4**
See/See also pages in the following book(s):
Postman, N. The end of education **370**
Technology and culture (Periodical)
Technology & American history. See Technology & American history **609**
Technology's past. Karwatka, D. **609**
Technopoly. Postman, N. **303.4**
Tecumseh, Shawnee Chief, 1768-1813
About
Eckert, A. W. A sorrow in our heart: the life of Tecumseh **92**
Tedlock, Dennis, 1939-
(tr) Popol vuh. Popol vuh **299**
Teeley, Peter
The complete cancer survival guide **616.99**
Teen age *See* Adolescence
Teenagers
Deak, J. Girls will be girls **649**
Di Prisco, J. Field guide to the American teenager **305.23**
Hine, T. The rise and fall of the American teenager **305.23**
Taffel, R. The second family **306.8**
White, E. Fast girls **305.23**
Employment
Levine, M. J. Children for hire **331.3**
Psychology
See Adolescent psychology
Teenagers' library services *See* Young adults' libraries
Tefertiller, Casey, 1952-
Wyatt Earp **92**
Tegnér, Bruce, 1928-1985
Karate: beginner to black belt **796.8**
Teichler-Zallen, Doris
Does it run in the family? **616**
Teilhard de Chardin, Pierre
Christianity and evolution **231.7**
The divine milieu **230**
How I believe
In Teilhard de Chardin, P. Christianity and evolution p96-132 **231.7**
The phenomenon of man **113**
Toward the future **194**
Telecommunication
See also Computer networks; Electronic mail systems
History of the Internet **004.6**
Naughton, J. A brief history of the future **621.382**
Dictionaries
Clayton, J. McGraw-Hill illustrated telecom dictionary **621.382**

Telecommuting
Bredin, A. The virtual office survival handbook **658**
Telegraph
See also Cipher and telegraph codes
Gordon, J. S. A thread across the ocean **384.1**
See/See also pages in the following book(s):
Silverman, K. Lightning man: the accursed life of Samuel F.B. Morse **92**
Telephone counseling *See* Hotlines (Telephone counseling)
Teleprocessing networks *See* Computer networks
Telescopes
See also Hubble Space Telescope
Harrington, P. S. Star ware **522**
Panek, R. Seeing and believing **522**
Television
See also African Americans on television; Home video systems
History
Abramson, A. The history of television, 1942 to 2000 **621.388**
Stashower, D. The boy genius and the mogul **791.45**
Repairing
Davidson, H. L. TV repair for beginners **621.388**
Television, Cable *See* Cable television
Television actors *See* Actors
Television authorship
Straczynski, J. M. The complete book of scriptwriting **808.2**
Television broadcasting
Encyclopedia of television **791.45**
Marling, K. A. As seen on TV **973.92**
Postman, N. Amusing ourselves to death **302.23**
Encyclopedias
Lackmann, R. W. The encyclopedia of American television, broadcast programming Post World War II to 2000 **791.45**
Television broadcasting of news
Garner, J. We interrupt this broadcast **070.1**
Television industry *See* Television broadcasting
Television journalism *See* Broadcast journalism
Television programs
Brooks, T. The complete directory to prime time network and cable TV shows, 1946-present **791.45**
McNeil, A. Total television **791.45**
Morris, B. B. Prime time network serials **791.45**
Terrace, V. Television sitcom factbook **791.45**
Television sitcom factbook. Terrace, V. **791.45**
Tell me a story. Hewitt, D. **92**
Tell my horse. Hurston, Z. N.
In Hurston, Z. N. Folklore, memoirs, and other writings **818**
Teller, Edward, 1908-2003
Conversations on the dark secrets of physics **530**
Memoirs **92**
About
Herken, G. Brotherhood of the bomb **920**
See/See also pages in the following book(s):
Rhodes, R. Dark sun **623.4**
Teller, Wendy
(jt. auth) Teller, E. Conversations on the dark secrets of physics **530**
Teller of tales: the life of Arthur Conan Doyle. Stashower, D. **92**
Telushkin, Joseph, 1948-
Biblical literacy **221.6**
Jewish wisdom **296**
Temkin, Ann
(jt. auth) Neel, A. Alice Neel **759.13**
Temperament
Hamer, D. H. Living with our genes **155.2**

Temperament—*Continued*
See/See also pages in the following book(s):
Goleman, D. Emotional intelligence p215-28
                                     152.4
Temperance
  See also Prohibition
Temperature
  See also Low temperatures
  Segrè, G. A matter of degrees   536
Templars
  Read, P. P. The Templars   271
Temple, Henry John *See* Palmerston, Henry John Temple, Viscount, 1784-1865
Ten days that shook the world. Reed, J.   **947.084**
Ten little Indians. Christie, A.
  In Christie, A. The mousetrap and other plays
                                 822
Ten plays. Euripides   882
The **ten** trusts. Goodall, J.   333.95
Tenant and landlord *See* Landlord and tenant
Tenant farming *See* Farm tenancy
Tender buttons: objects, food, rooms. Stein, G.
  In Stein, G. Selected writings p459-509   818
The **tending** instinct. Taylor, S. E.   **304.5**
Tenenbaum, Frances
  (ed) Taylor's master guide to gardening. See Taylor's master guide to gardening   635.9
Tenet, Stephanie
  (jt. auth) Sussman, J. Dare to repair   643
Tennant, Richard A.
  The American Sign Language handshape dictionary
                                 419
Tennis
  Total tennis: the ultimate tennis encyclopedia
                           796.342
  Wertheim, L. J. Venus envy   **796.342**
Tennyson, Alfred Tennyson, Baron, 1809-1892
  Tears, idle tears; criticism
  In Brooks, C. The well wrought urn   **821.009**
Tension (Physiology) *See* Stress (Physiology)
Tension (Psychology) *See* Stress (Psychology)
Tenzing Norgay, 1914-1986
                    About
  Norgay, J. T. Touching my father's soul   **796.52**
Terence
  The brothers
  In Terence. Terence, the comedies   872
  The eunuch
  In Terence. Terence, the comedies   872
  The girl from Andros
  In Terence. Terence, the comedies   872
  Her husband's mother
  In Terence. Terence, the comedies   872
  Phormio
  In The Portable Roman reader p75-131   **870.8**
  In Terence. Terence, the comedies   872
  The self-tormentor
  In Terence. Terence, the comedies   872
  Terence, the comedies   872
Terence, the comedies. Terence   872
Teresa, Mother, 1910-1997
                      About
  Spink, K. Mother Teresa   92
Teresa, of Avila, Saint, 1515-1582
                      About
  Medwick, C. Teresa of Avila   92
Teresa de Jesús, Saint *See* Teresa, of Avila, Saint, 1515-1582
Teresi, Dick
  Lost discoveries   509
  (jt. auth) Lederman, L. M. The God particle
                                539.7
Terkel, Louis *See* Terkel, Studs, 1912-
Terkel, Studs, 1912-
  American dreams   **973.9**

Hard times   **973.91**
My American century   **920**
Race   **305.8**
The spectator   **791**
Will the circle be unbroken?   **128**
Working   **331.2**
Term paper writing *See* Report writing
Terminal care
  Kübler-Ross, E. Living with death and dying
                                155.9
  Kübler-Ross, E. On death and dying   **155.9**
  McFarlane, R. The complete bedside companion
                                649.8
Terminally ill
  Weenolsen, P. The art of dying   **155.9**
Terrace, Vincent, 1948-
  Television sitcom factbook   **791.45**
Terras, Victor
  A history of Russian literature   **891.7**
Terrell, Peter
  Collins German-English, English-German dictionary. See Collins German-English, English-German dictionary   433
The **terrible** stories. Clifton, L.   811
Terrill, Marshall
  Steve McQueen   92
Terror in the mind of God. Juergensmeyer, M.
                                291.1
Terrorism
  See also World Trade Center terrorist attack, 2001
  Benjamin, D. The age of sacred terror   **303.6**
  Bergen, P. L. Holy war, Inc.   **958.1**
  Bernstein, R. Out of the blue   **973.931**
  Carr, C. The lessons of terror   **303.6**
  Confronting fear   **303.6**
  Dershowitz, A. M. Why terrorism works   **303.6**
  Esposito, J. L. Unholy war   **322.4**
  Friedman, T. L. Longitudes and attitudes   **973.931**
  Frist, W. H. When every moment counts   **613.6**
  Gerson, A. The price of terror   **363.1**
  Juergensmeyer, M. Terror in the mind of God
                                291.1
  Junger, S. Fire   **909.82**
  Kiser, J. W. The monks of Tibhirine   **271**
  Laqueur, W. No end to war   **303.6**
  Miller, J. The cell: inside the 9/11 plot and why the FBI and CIA failed to stop it   **973.931**
  Murakami, H. Underground   **364.1**
  Nestle, M. Safe food   **363.1**
  Pillar, P. R. Terrorism and U.S. foreign policy
                              327.73
  Pipes, D. Militant Islam reaches America   **320.5**
  Wilkinson, D. Silence on the mountain   **972.81**
                    Dictionaries
  Anderson, S. Historical dictionary of terrorism
                                303.6
  Herbst, P. Talking terrorism   **303.6**
                    Encyclopedias
  Combs, C. C. Encyclopedia of terrorism   **303.6**
  Kushner, H. W. Encyclopedia of terrorism   **303.6**
Terrorism and U.S. foreign policy. Pillar, P. R.
                                327.73
Terry, Clark, 1920-
  See/See also pages in the following book(s):
  Lees, G. You can't steal a gift   **920**
Terry, Michael, 1948-
  (ed) Reader's guide to Judaism. See Reader's guide to Judaism   **296.03**
Terry, R. C.
  (ed) Oxford reader's companion to Trollope. See Oxford reader's companion to Trollope   **823.009**
Terry, Wallace, 1938-2003
  (ed) Bloods: an oral history of the Vietnam War by black veterans. See Bloods: an oral history of the Vietnam War by black veterans   **959.704**

Teruzzi, Giorgio
(jt. auth) Arduini, P. Simon & Schuster's guide to fossils **560**
Tesar, Jenny E.
(jt. auth) Bunch, B. H. The Penguin desk encyclopedia of science and mathematics **503**
Tessaglia-Hymes, Diane L.
(jt. auth) Dunn, E. H. Birds at your feeder **598**
A **testament** of hope. King, M. L. **323.1**
A **testament** to freedom. Bonhoeffer, D. **230**
Tests of time. Gass, W. H. **814**
Teutonic peoples
Burns, T. S. A history of the Ostrogoths **909.07**
Texas
History
Davis, W. C. Three roads to the Alamo **976.4**
Robinson, C. M. The men who wear the star
976.4
Texas Rangers
Robinson, C. M. The men who wear the star
976.4
Textbooks
Bibliography
El-hi textbooks and serials in print **016.3713**
Textile industry
Dictionaries
Fairchild's dictionary of textiles **677**
History
Ulrich, L. The age of homespun **974**
Textile printing
Wells, K. Fabric dyeing & printing **746.6**
Textiles *See* Fabrics
Thailand
History
Wyatt, D. K. Thailand: a short history **959.3**
Social life and customs
Landon, M. Anna and the King of Siam [biography of Anna Harriette Leonowens] **92**
Thalberg, Sigismond, 1812-1871
See/See also pages in the following book(s):
Schonberg, H. C. The great pianists **920**
Thapar, Valmik
Land of the tiger **508**
Tharoor, Shashi, 1956-
India **954**
That time. Beckett, S.
In Beckett, S. Ends and Odds p25-37 **842**
Thatcher, Samuel S.
(jt. auth) Bruce, D. F. Making a baby **618.2**
That's all. Pinter, H.
In Pinter, H. Complete works v3 **822**
That's your trouble. Pinter, H.
In Pinter, H. Complete works v3 **822**
Thayer, Helen
See/See also pages in the following book(s):
Slung, M. B. Living with cannibals and other women's adventures **910.4**
Theater
See also Acting; Musicals
Brook, P. The empty space **792**
Dictionaries
The Cambridge guide to theatre **792.03**
Encyclopedias
The Oxford encyclopedia of theatre & performance
792.03
History
Brockett, O. G. History of the theatre **792.09**
The Oxford illustrated history of theatre **792.09**
Internet resources
Catron, L. E. Theatre sources dot com **025.04**
Production and direction
See also Motion pictures—Production and direction
Hodge, F. Play directing **792**

Germany
See/See also pages in the following book(s):
Dürrenmatt, F. Plays and essays p233-62 **838**
Japan
See also Nō plays
See/See also pages in the following book(s):
Keene, D. The pleasures of Japanese literature p99-121
895.6
New York (N.Y.)
Bloom, K. Broadway **974.7**
The New York Times book of Broadway **792**
United States
The Best plays of [date] **808.82**
Bordman, G. M. American theatre: a chronicle of comedy and drama, 1869-1914 **792**
Bordman, G. M. American theatre: a chronicle of comedy and drama, 1914-1930 **792**
Bordman, G. M. American theatre: a chronicle of comedy and drama, 1930-1969 **792**
Hischak, T. American theatre: a chronicle of comedy and drama, 1969-2000 **792**
United States—*Dictionaries*
Bordman, G. M. The Oxford companion to American theatre **792.03**
Cambridge guide to American theatre **792.03**
Theaters
Stage setting and scenery
Gillette, J. M. Theatrical design and production
792
Troubridge, E. Scenic art and construction **792**
Theatre I. Beckett, S.
In Beckett, S. Ends and Odds p69-80 **842**
Theatre II. Beckett, S.
In Beckett, S. Ends and Odds p81-101 **842**
Theatre sources dot com. Catron, L. E. **025.04**
Theatrical costume *See* Costume
Theatrical design and production. Gillette, J. M.
792
Theatrical makeup
Corson, R. Stage makeup **792**
Their finest hour. Churchill, Sir W. **940.53**
Theism
See also Atheism
Them: adventures with extremists. Ronson, J. **322.4**
A **Theodore** Dreiser encyclopedia **813.009**
Theodore Rex. Morris, E. **92**
Theoharis, Athan G.
Chasing spies **327.12**
(ed) The FBI: a comprehensive reference guide. See The FBI: a comprehensive reference guide
363.2
(ed) From the secret files of J. Edgar Hoover. See From the secret files of J. Edgar Hoover **363.2**
Theology
See also Doctrinal theology; Faith; Human beings (Theology); Secularism
Bonhoeffer, D. A testament to freedom **230**
Great thinkers of the Western world **190**
Kierkegaard, S. The present age, and Of the difference between a genius and an apostle **230**
Küng, H. Great Christian thinkers **230**
Teilhard de Chardin, P. Christianity and evolution
231.7
Dictionaries
Oxford companion to Christian thought **230.003**
Theology, Doctrinal *See* Doctrinal theology
Theology of culture. Tillich, P. **230**
Theory of knowledge
Baars, B. J. In the theater of consciousness **153**
Kant, I. Critique of pure reason **193**
Locke, J. An essay concerning human understanding
121
Sartre, J. P. Truth and existence **121**
Wilson, E. O. Consilience **121**
Theory of systems *See* System theory

The **theory** of the leisure class. Veblen, T.　305.5
Theory of the moral life. Dewey, J.　170
Therapy, Psychological *See* Psychotherapy
Therese Raquin. Zola, É.
　In Our dramatic heritage v4　808.82
Thermodynamics
　Von Baeyer, H. C. Maxwell's demon　536
　See/See also pages in the following book(s):
　Shachtman, T. Absolute zero and the conquest of cold　536
Thernstrom, Stephan
　(ed) Harvard encyclopedia of American ethnic groups.
　See Harvard encyclopedia of American ethnic groups　305.8
Theroux, Paul
　Dark star safari　916
　Fresh air fiend　818
　The great railway bazaar: by train through Asia　915
　The happy isles of Oceania　919
　The kingdom by the sea　914.1
　The old Patagonian express　918
　The Pillars of Hercules　910.4
　Riding the iron rooster　915.1
　To the ends of the earth　910.4
Theroux, Peter
　Sandstorms: days and nights in Arabia　953
Theroux, Phyllis
　(ed) The Book of eulogies. See The Book of eulogies　808.8
Thesaurus in dictionary form, The Doubleday Roget's　423
Thesaurus of American English, The Cambridge. Lutz, W.　423
These are my rivers. Ferlinghetti, L.　811
Theseus (Greek mythology)
　See/See also pages in the following book(s):
　Hamilton, E. Mythology p209-23　292
Thesmophoriazusae. Aristophanes
　In Aristophanes. The complete plays of Aristophanes p329-66　882
They all laughed. Flatow, I.　609
They all laughed at Christopher Columbus. Weil, E.　621.43
They fought like demons. Blanton, D.　973.7
They never said it. Boller, P. F.　808.88
They're playing our song. Simon, N.
　In Simon, N. The collected plays of Neil Simon v3 p115-215　812
Thich Nhat Hanh *See* Nhat Hanh, Thich
Thieret, John W.
　National Audubon Society field guide to North American wildflowers: eastern region　582.13
Thieves. Gardner, H.
　In Gardner, H. Herb Gardner: the collected plays and the screenplay Who is Harry Kellerman and why is he saying those terrible things about me?　812
Thieves' carnival. Anouilh, J.
　In Our dramatic heritage v6　808.82
Thieves of paradise. Komunyakaa, Y.　811
Think: a compelling introduction to philosophy. Blackburn, S.　100
Thinking *See* Thought and thinking
Thinking. Arendt, H.
　In Arendt, H. The life of the mind　153
Thinking about the earth. Oldroyd, D. R.　551
Thinking like your editor. Rabiner, S.　808
The **third** chimpanzee. Diamond, J. M.　599.93
The **third** freedom. McGovern, G. S.　363.8
The **Third** Reich. Burleigh, M.　943.086
The **third** wave. Toffler, A.　303.4
Third World *See* Developing countries
Thirteen days. Kennedy, R. F.　973.922

Thirteen ways of looking at a black man. Gates, H. L.　920
The **thirty-six** hour day. See Mace, N. L. The 36-hour day　618.97
This ain't brain surgery. Dierker, L.　92
This boy's life: a memoir. Wolff, T.　92
This business of music. Krasilovsky, M. W.　780
This cold heaven. Ehrlich, G.　998
This craft of verse. Borges, J. L.　809.1
This far by faith. Williams, J.　200
This great unknowing. Levertov, D.　811
This house has fallen. Maier, K.　966.9
This is biology. Mayr, E.　570
This is my God: the Jewish way of life. Wouk, H.　296
This is reggae music. Bradley, L.　781.646
This is the rill speaking. Wilson, L.
　In Wilson, L. 21 short plays p54-71　812
This man's pill. Djerassi, C.　613.9
This new ocean. Burrows, W. E.　629.4
This Old House kitchens. Thomas, S.　643
This time. Stern, G.　811
Thomas, Aquinas, Saint, 1225?-1274
　Selected writings　189
　　　About
　Davies, B. The thought of Thomas Aquinas　230
　See/See also pages in the following book(s):
　Küng, H. Great Christian thinkers p99-126　230
　Russell, B. A history of Western philosophy p452-63　109
Thomas, Anthony William *See* Thomas, Tony, 1927-1997
Thomas, Clarence
　See/See also pages in the following book(s):
　West, C. Race matters p23-32　305.8
Thomas, Dylan, 1914-1953
　A child's Christmas in Wales　828
　Selected poems, 1934-1952　821
　Under milk wood　822
　See/See also pages in the following book(s):
　Heaney, S. The redress of poetry　821.009
Thomas, Elizabeth Marshall, 1931-
　The social lives of dogs　636.7
　The tribe of tiger　599.75
Thomas, Emory M., 1939-
　Robert E. Lee　92
Thomas, Evan
　Robert Kennedy　92
Thomas, Helen
　Front row at the White House　92
Thomas, Lawrence
　Homebuilding pitfalls　690
Thomas, Lewis, 1913-1993
　The lives of a cell　570.1
Thomas, Robert McG., Jr.
　52 McGs　920
Thomas, Steve, 1942-
　This Old House kitchens　643
Thomas, Tony, 1927-1997
　A wonderful life: the films and career of James Stewart　791.43
Thomas Eakins [exhibition catalog]　759.13
Thomas Jefferson and Sally Hemings. Gordon-Reed, A.　92
Thomas Struth, 1977-2002. Struth, T.　779
Thompson, Andrea
　(jt. auth) Nachman, P. A. You and your only child　649
Thompson, Charlotte E.
　Raising a child with a neuromuscular disorder　618.92
Thompson, Cliff
　World musicians. See World musicians　920.003
　(ed) World authors, 1990-1995. See World authors, 1990-1995　920.003

Thompson, Cliff—*Continued*
(ed) World authors, 1995-2000. See World authors, 1995-2000   **920.003**
Thompson, Della
The Oxford Russian dictionary. See The Oxford Russian dictionary   **491.7**
Thompson, Dick
Volcano cowboys   **551.2**
Thompson, Dorothy
  See/See also pages in the following book(s):
Ware, S. Letter to the world   **920**
Thompson, Hunter S.
Fear and loathing in America   **92**
The great shark hunt   **818**
Thompson, Ida
The Audubon Society field guide to North American fossils   **560**
Thompson, Jim
     About
Philpott, T. Glory denied   **92**
Thompson, Leonard Monteath
A history of South Africa   **968**
Thompson, Robert Smith
Empires on the Pacific   **940.54**
Thompson, Sue Ellen, 1948-
Holiday symbols and customs   **394.26**
(ed) Holidays, festivals and celebrations of the world dictionary. See Holidays, festivals and celebrations of the world dictionary   **394.26**
Thompson, Wendy J. A.
Alopecia areata   **616.5**
Thomson, Belinda
Gauguin   **92**
Thomson, David, 1941-
Rosebud: the story of Orson Welles   **92**
Thomson, Keith Stewart
Living fossil   **597**
Thondup, Tulku
Enlightened journey   **294.3**
Thoreau, Henry David, 1817-1862
Cape Cod   **917.44**
  also in Thoreau, H. D. A week on the Concord and Merrimack rivers; Walden; The Maine woods; Cape Cod   **818**
Collected essays and poems   **818**
The Maine woods   **917.41**
  also in Thoreau, H. D. A week on the Concord and Merrimack rivers; Walden; The Maine woods; Cape Cod   **818**
The portable Thoreau   **818**
Walden
  In Thoreau, H. D. The portable Thoreau   **818**
  In Thoreau, H. D. A week on the Concord and Merrimack rivers; Walden; The Maine woods; Cape Cod   **818**
Walden and other writings of Henry David Thoreau   **818**
A week on the Concord and Merrimack rivers
  In Thoreau, H. D. A week on the Concord and Merrimack rivers; Walden; The Maine woods; Cape Cod   **818**
A week on the Concord and Merrimack rivers [excerpts]
  In Thoreau, H. D. The portable Thoreau   **818**
A week on the Concord and Merrimack rivers; Walden, or, Life in the woods; The Maine woods; Cape Cod   **818**
Wild fruits   **581.6**
     About
Foster, D. R. Thoreau's country   **818**
Henry David Thoreau   **818**
Henry David Thoreau's Walden   **818**
Hodder, A. D. Thoreau's ecstatic witness   **818**

  See/See also pages in the following book(s):
Emerson, R. W. The portable Emerson p573-95   **818**
Kazin, A. An American procession p63-80   **810.9**
Matthiessen, F. O. American renaissance p76-99, 153-75   **810.9**
Thoreau's country. Foster, D. R.   **818**
Thoreau's ecstatic witness. Hodder, A. D.   **818**
Thorne, Kip S.
Black holes and time warps   **530.1**
Thornhill, Randy
A natural history of rape   **364.1**
Thornton, Weldon
D.H. Lawrence   **823.009**
Thornton, William, 1759-1828
  See/See also pages in the following book(s):
Lepore, J. A is for American   **306.44**
Thorpe, I. J.
8 men and a duck   **910.4**
Thorpe, Nick *See* Thorpe, I. J.
Thorpy, Michael J., 1948-
The encyclopedia of sleep and sleep disorders   **612.8**
Thorson, Robert M., 1951-
Stone by stone   **693**
Those wonderful women in their flying machines. Keil, S. V. W.   **940.54**
Thought and thinking
  See also Logic; Perception; Reasoning
Calvin, W. H. How brains think   **153.9**
Hayakawa, S. I. Language in thought and action   **412**
Locke, J. An essay concerning human understanding   **121**
Silver, B. L. The ascent of science   **509**
Thought control *See* Brainwashing
The **thought** of Thomas Aquinas. Davies, B.   **230**
A **thousand** clowns. Gardner, H.
  In Gardner, H. Herb Gardner: the collected plays and the screenplay Who is Harry Kellerman and why is he saying those terrible things about me?   **812**
Thrale, Hester *See* Piozzi, Hester Lynch, 1741-1821
Thrall, William Flint, b. 1880
Handbook to literature. See Harmon, W. A handbook to literature   **803**
A **thread** across the ocean. Gordon, J. S.   **384.1**
Threatened species *See* Endangered species
The **three** big bangs. Dauber, P. M.   **523.1**
Three contributions to the theory of sex. Freud, S.
  In Freud, S. The basic writings of Sigmund Freud   **150.19**
The **three** Gospels. Bible. N.T. Gospels   **226**
Three hundred sixty-five days. See Glasser, R. J. 365 days   **959.704**
Three plays. Coward, N.   **822**
Three roads to the Alamo. Davis, W. C.   **976.4**
The **three** Roosevelts. Burns, J. M.   **973.91**
Three sisters. Chekhov, A. P.
  In Chekhov, A. P. The plays of Anton Chekhov p257-322   **891.7**
Three strides before the wire. Mitchell, E.   **798.4**
Three tragedies. García Lorca, F.   **862**
The **threepenny** opera. Brecht, B.
  In Our dramatic heritage v5   **808.82**
Thrift *See* Saving and investment
The **thrill** of the grill. Schlesinger, C.   **641.7**
Throckmorton, Bess *See* Raleigh, Elizabeth Throckmorton, Lady, d. 1647
Throckmorton, Elizabeth *See* Raleigh, Elizabeth Throckmorton, Lady, d. 1647
Through a window. Goodall, J.   **599.8**
Through the lens   **779**
Throwim way leg. Flannery, T. F.   **995.3**
Throwing the elephant. Bing, S.   **650.1**

Thubron, Colin, 1939-
In Siberia   957
Thucydides
The history of the Peloponnesian War   938
See/See also pages in the following book(s):
Hamilton, E. The Greek way p183-203   880.9
Thurber, James, 1894-1961
The dog department   818
People have more fun than anybody   818
About
Grauer, N. A. Remember laughter: a life of James
Thurber   92
Thurman, Judith, 1946-
Isak Dinesen   92
Secrets of the flesh: a life of Colette   92
Thurmond, James Strom *See* Thurmond, Strom, 1902-
2003
Thurmond, Strom, 1902-2003
About
Cohodas, N. Strom Thurmond & the politics of south-
ern change   92
Thurschwell, Pamela, 1966-
Sigmund Freud   150.19
Thurston, Herbert
(ed) Butler, A. Butler's Lives of the saints
   920.003
Thus spake Zarathustra. Nietzsche, F. W.   193
also in Nietzsche, F. W. The portable Nietzsche
   193
Thyen, O. (Olaf)
(ed) The Oxford-Duden German dictionary. See The
Oxford-Duden German dictionary   433
Thyen, Olaf *See* Thyen, O. (Olaf)
Thymus vulgaris. Wilson, L.
In Wilson, L. 21 short plays p169-88   812
Thyroid gland
Diseases
Ditkoff, B. A. The thyroid guide   616.4
The **thyroid** guide. Ditkoff, B. A.   616.4
Tibbets, Paul W.
About
Greene, B. Duty   940.54
Tibbetts, John C., 1946-
The encyclopedia of novels into film   791.43
Tiberius, Emperor of Rome, 42 B.C.-37 A.D.
See/See also pages in the following book(s):
Suetonius Tranquillus, C. The twelve Caesars   878
Tibet (China)
Laird, T. Into Tibet   327.12
Schell, O. Virtual Tibet   951
Tsering Shakya. The dragon in the land of snows
   951
See/See also pages in the following book(s):
Dalai Lama XIV. Freedom in exile   92
Pictorial works
Dalai Lama XIV. My Tibet   951
Nomachi, K. Tibet   951
Tibet (China) in motion pictures
Schell, O. Virtual Tibet   951
The **Tibetan** book of living and dying. Sogyal, Rinpoche
   294.3
Tibetan book of the dead
The Tibetan book of the dead   294.3
Ticks
See also Lyme disease
Vanderhoof-Forschner, K. Everything you need to
know about Lyme disease and other tick-borne disor-
ders   616.9
Tiffany, Louis Comfort, 1848-1933
About
Loring, J. Louis Comfort Tiffany at Tiffany & Co
   92
Tiffany & Co.
Loring, J. Louis Comfort Tiffany at Tiffany & Co
   92

Loring, J. Tiffany's 20th century   745
Tiffany's 20th century. Loring, J.   745
Tiffin, Matthew *See* Harold, Madd, 1973-
The **tiger** ladies. Koul, S.   92
The **Tiger** Woods way. Andrisani, J.   796.352
Tigers
Matthiessen, P. Tigers in the snow   599.75
Thapar, V. Land of the tiger   508
Thomas, E. M. The tribe of tiger   599.75
Tigers & ice. Hoagland, E.   814
Tigers in the snow. Matthiessen, P.   599.75
Tigges, Julie A.
(ed) Women's legal guide. See Women's legal guide
   346.01
Tiles
Jones, M. Handcrafted ceramic tiles   738
Till, Emmett
See/See also pages in the following book(s):
Abdul-Jabbar, K. Black profiles in courage p199-206
   920
Tillich, Paul, 1886-1965
The courage to be   179
Dynamics of faith   234
The eternal now   252
Theology of culture   230
Tillyard, Stella K.
Aristocrats   920
A **timbered** choir. Berry, W.   811
Time
See also Night
Aveni, A. F. Empires of time   529
Barnett, J. E. Time's pendulum   529
Duncan, D. E. Calendar   529
Galison, P. L. Einstein's clocks and Poincaré's maps
   529
Gleick, J. Faster   529
Gorst, M. Measuring eternity   115
Richards, E. G. Mapping time   529
Von Baeyer, H. C. Maxwell's demon   536
The **Time** almanac   031.02
Time and space *See* Space and time
The **time** before history. Tudge, C.   599.93
Time, love, memory. Weiner, J.   591.5
Time management
Covey, S. R. First things first   158
Heller, R. Essential manager's manual   658.4
Time of our lives. Kirkwood, T.   612.6
The **time** of our time. Mailer, N.   818
Time saving cookery *See* Quick and easy cooking
Time to be in earnest. James, P. D.   92
A **time** to die. McKhann, C. F.   179.7
Time travel in Einstein's universe. Gott, J. R.
   530.1
Time traveler. Novacek, M. J.   92
The **timeline** book of the arts. See Ochoa, G. The Wil-
son chronology of the arts   700
Timerman, Jacobo, 1923-1999
Prisoner without a name, cell without a number
   92
Times (New York, N.Y.) *See* New York times
The **Times** atlas of the world   912
The **Times** atlas of world history. See Hammond atlas of
world history   911
The **times** of my life and my life with the Times.
Frankel, M.   92
Time's pendulum. Barnett, J. E.   529
The **Times** were a changin'   973.923
The **timetables** of African-American history. Harley, S.
   305.8
The **Timetables** of American history   902
The **timetables** of history. Grun, B.   902
Timetables of world literature. Kurian, G. T.   809

Timucua Indians
  See/See also pages in the following book(s):
  Josephy, A. M. Now that the buffalo's gone p5-25
          970.004
The **Tin** Pan Alley song encyclopedia. Hischak, T.
          782.42
Tinkering with Eden. Todd, K.   **591.6**
The **tinker's** wedding. Synge, J. M.
  In Synge, J. M. The complete plays   **822**
Tintori, Karen
  Trapped: the 1909 Cherry Mine disaster   **977.3**
Tip O'Neill and the Democratic century. Farrell, J. A.
          92
Tipton, Billy, 1914-1989
        About
  Middlebrook, D. W. Suits me: the double life of Billy
  Tipton   **92**
Tipton-Martin, Toni
  (jt. auth) Randall, J. A taste of heritage   **641.5**
Tiradritti, Francesco
  (ed) Egyptian treasures from the Egyptian Museum in
  Cairo. See Egyptian treasures from the Egyptian Mu-
  seum in Cairo   **709.32**
Tirion, Wil
  The Cambridge star atlas   **523.8**
Tirnady, Frank
  (jt. auth) Lee, H. C. Blood evidence   **614**
Tirpitz, Alfred von, 1849-1930
  See/See also pages in the following book(s):
  Massie, R. K. Dreadnought p164-85   **940.3**
'Tis. McCourt, F.   **92**
Titan: the life of John D. Rockefeller, Sr. Chernow, R.
          92
Titanic (Steamship)
  Ballard, R. D. The discovery of the Titanic   **910.4**
  Butler, D. A. Unsinkable: the full story of the RMS
  Titanic   **910.4**
  Jessop, V. Titanic survivor   **910.4**
  Lord, W. A night to remember   **910.4**
  Pellegrino, C. R. Ghosts of the Titanic   **910.4**
Tito, Josip Broz, 1892-1980
        About
  West, R. Tito   **92**
Titon, Jeff Todd, 1943-
  (ed) American musical traditions. See American musi-
  cal traditions   **781.62**
Titus, Emperor of Rome, 40-81
  See/See also pages in the following book(s):
  Suetonius Tranquillus, C. The twelve Caesars   **878**
To Appomattox. Davis, B.   **973.7**
To be continued. Jacob, M.   **016.8**
To be young, gifted and black. Hansberry, L.   **92**
To begin again. Levy, N.   **296.7**
To begin where I am. Miłosz, C.   **891.8**
To conquer the air. Tobin, J.   **629.13**
To have or to be? Fromm, E.   **302**
To hell and back. Stern, K.   **332.6**
To life!. Kushner, H. S.   **296**
To listen to a child. Brazelton, T. B.   **155.4**
To reach the clouds. Petit, P.   **92**
To the actor. Chekhov, M.   **792**
To the best of my ability   **920**
To the ends of the earth. Theroux, P.   **910.4**
To the gates of Richmond. Sears, S. W.   **973.7**
Toasts
  Toasts   **808.88**
  Toasts   **808.88**
Tobacco
  Gately, I. Tobacco   **394.1**
Tobacco habit
  See also Smoking cessation programs
  Fisher, E. B. American Lung Association 7 steps to a
  smoke-free life   **616.86**
  Kluger, R. Ashes to ashes   **394.1**

Tobacco industry
  Kluger, R. Ashes to ashes   **394.1**
Tobago *See* Trinidad and Tobago
Tobias, Andrew P.
  The only investment guide you'll ever need
          332.024
Tobias, Sheila
  Overcoming math anxiety   **510**
Tobias, Steven E.
  (jt. auth) Elias, M. J. Emotionally intelligent parenting
          649
Tobin, Greg
  (ed) Saints and sinners. See Saints and sinners
          282
Tobin, Jacqueline, 1950-
  Hidden in plain view   **973.7**
Tobin, James, 1956-
  Ernie Pyle's war   **92**
  Great projects   **620**
  To conquer the air   **629.13**
Tocqueville, Alexis de
  Democracy in America   **973.5**
Todd, Kim, 1970-
  Tinkering with Eden   **591.6**
Todd, Olivier
  Albert Camus   **92**
Todorov, Tzvetan, 1939-
  Facing the extreme   **940.53**
Toerge, John E.
  (ed) Managing stroke. See Managing stroke   **616.8**
Tofel, Richard J., 1957-
  A legend in the making   **796.357**
Toffler, Alvin
  Future shock   **303.4**
  Powershift   **303.4**
  The third wave   **303.4**
Tofu
  See also Cooking—Tofu
Tøjner, Poul Erik
  Munch: in his own words   **92**
Toklas, Alice B.
        About
  Stein, G. The autobiography of Alice B. Toklas
          92
The **Tokyo** gas attack and the Japanese psyche. See
  Murakami, H. Underground   **364.1**
Toland, John
  Adolf Hitler   **92**
Toleration
  Bullard, S. Teaching tolerance   **649**
Tolkien, J. R. R. (John Ronald Reuel), 1892-1973
        About
  Hammond, W. G. J.R.R. Tolkien, artist & illustrator
          92
Tolkien, John Ronald Reuel *See* Tolkien, J. R. R. (John
  Ronald Reuel), 1892-1973
Tolstoy, Leo, graf, 1828-1910
  See/See also pages in the following book(s):
  Bloom, H. The Western canon   **809**
  Nabokov, V. V. Lectures on Russian literature
          891.7
Toltecs
  See also Aztecs
Tom: the unknown Tennessee Williams. Leverich, L.
          92
Tomalin, Claire
  Jane Austen   **92**
  Samuel Pepys   **92**
Tomedi, Rudy, 1951-
  No bugles, no drums   **951.9**
Tomkins, Calvin, 1925-
  Duchamp   **92**
Tomkins, Stephen
  John Wesley   **92**

Tomorrow. Foote, H.
    In Foote, H. Getting Frankie married—and afterwards, and other plays   **812**
Tone, Andrea, 1964-
    Devices and desires   **363.9**
Tonight at noon. Mingus, S.   **92**
Too good to be true. Brunvand, J. H.   **398.2**
Too soon to tell. Trillin, C.   **818**
Toobin, Jeffrey R.
    A vast conspiracy   **973.929**
Toolis, Kevin
    Rebel hearts   **941.6**
Tools
    See also Power tools
    Hack, G. Classic hand tools   **621.9**
Toomer, Jean, 1894-1967
    The collected poems of Jean Toomer   **811**
Toomey, David M.
    (jt. auth) Haynsworth, L. Amelia Earhart's daughters   **629.13**
Toor, Rachel
    Admissions confidential   **378.1**
Toothpicks and logos. Heskett, J.   **745.2**
Topdog/underdog. Parks, S.-L.   **812**
Topiary and the art of training plants. Joyce, D.   **635.9**
The **Torah:** the five books of Moses. Bible. O.T. Pentateuch   **222**
Tormé, Mel, 1925-1999
    Traps, the drum wonder: the life of Buddy Rich   **92**
Tormenting thoughts and secret rituals. Osborn, I.   **616.85**
Torn awake. Gander, F.   **811**
Tornadoes
    Hemingway, L. A world turned over   **363.34**
Torre, Mónica de la, 1969-
    (ed) Reversible monuments. See Reversible monuments   **861**
Torres, Gerald
    (jt. auth) Guinier, L. The miner's canary   **323.1**
Tortoises *See* Turtles
Tortoises and turtles. Ferri, V.   **597.9**
Tortora, Phyllis G.
    (jt. auth) Calasibetta, C. M. The Fairchild dictionary of fashion   **391**
Torture
    Conroy, J. Unspeakable acts, ordinary people   **323.4**
Tosches, Nick
    Where dead voices gather [biography of Emmett Miller]   **92**
Tosh, Michael Gearin- *See* Gearin-Tosh, Michael
The **total** cat. Wilbourn, C.   **636.8**
Total skin. Leffell, D. J.   **616.5**
Total television. McNeil, A.   **791.45**
Total tennis: the ultimate tennis encyclopedia   **796.342**
Totalitarianism
    Arendt, H. Origins of totalitarianism   **321.9**
    Huxley, A. Brave new world revisited   **303.3**
    Todorov, T. Facing the extreme   **940.53**
Totally dairy-free cooking. Lanza, L.   **641.5**
Totem and taboo. Freud, S.   **306**
    also in Freud, S. The basic writings of Sigmund Freud   **150.19**
Totems and totemism
    Freud, S. Totem and taboo   **306**
Touching my father's soul. Norgay, J. T.   **796.52**
Touchpoints. Brazelton, T. B.   **649**
Touchpoints three to six. Brazelton, T. B.   **649**
The **touchstone** of life. Loewenstein, W. R.   **571.6**
Tougias, Mike, 1955-
    (jt. auth) Schultz, E. B. King Philip's War   **973.2**

Toulouse-Lautrec, Henri de, 1864-1901
About
    Frey, J. Toulouse-Lautrec   **92**
A **tour** of the calculus. Berlinski, D.   **515**
Tourette syndrome
    Kushner, H. I. A cursing brain?   **616.8**
Tourgée, Albion Winegar, 1838-1905
    See/See also pages in the following book(s):
    Wilson, E. Patriotic gore p529-48   **810.9**
Toward a new Catholic Church. Carroll, J.   **282**
Toward a psychology of being. Maslow, A. H.   **155.2**
Toward the future. Teilhard de Chardin, P.   **194**
Towards zero. Christie, A.
    In Christie, A. The mousetrap and other plays   **822**
Tower of Babel *See* Babel, Tower of
Tower of Babel. Pennock, R. T.   **576.8**
Town planning *See* City planning
Townes, Charles H., 1915-
    See/See also pages in the following book(s):
    Horvitz, L. A. Eureka!: scientific breakthroughs that changed the world   **509**
Towns *See* Cities and towns
Townsend, Richard F.
    The Aztecs   **972**
Toxic deception. Fagin, D.   **615.9**
Toxic parents: overcoming their hurtful legacy and reclaiming your life. Forward, S.   **362.82**
Toxic plants *See* Poisonous plants
Toxic substances *See* Poisons and poisoning
Toxic work. Reinhold, B. B.   **650.1**
Toye, William
    (ed) The Oxford companion to Canadian literature. See The Oxford companion to Canadian literature   **810.3**
Toynbee, Arnold, 1852-1883
    A study of history [abridged]   **909**
    See/See also pages in the following book(s):
    Herman, A. The idea of decline in Western history   **909.08**
Trachinian women. Sophocles
    In Sophocles. The complete plays of Sophocles p149-79   **882**
Trachtenberg, Marvin
    Architecture, from prehistory to postmodernity   **720.9**
Track athletics
    See also Running
Tracy, Gloria
    Crochet your way   **746.43**
Trade and professional associations
    Encyclopedia of associations   **061.025**
    National trade and professional associations of the United States   **061.025**
Trade unions *See* Labor unions
Trademarks
    Elias, S. Patent, copyright & trademark   **346.04**
    Elias, S. Trademark   **346.04**
Trades *See* Occupations
Traditions *See* Manners and customs
Trafficking in drugs *See* Drug traffic
Tragedy
    See/See also pages in the following book(s):
    Hamilton, E. The Greek way p227-38   **880.9**
The **tragedy** of Cambodian history. Chandler, D. P.   **959.6**
Training of children *See* Child rearing
Trainor, Bernard E., 1928-
    (jt. auth) Gordon, M. R. The generals' war   **956.7**
Trainor, Kevin
    (ed) Buddhism: the illustrated guide. See Buddhism: the illustrated guide   **294.3**
Trains, Railroad *See* Railroads
Trains of thought. Brombert, V. H.   **92**

Traisman, Edward S.
(ed) American Medical Association complete guide to children's health. See American Medical Association complete guide to children's health **618.92**
Traitors among us. Herrington, S. A. **327.12**
Tramp: the life of Charlie Chaplin. Milton, J. **92**
Tranquillus, C. Suetonius See Suetonius Tranquillus, C., ca. 69-ca. 122
Transactional analysis
Harris, T. A. I'm OK, you're OK **158**
A **transatlantic** love affair: letters to Nelson Algren. Beauvoir, S. de **92**
Transcendentalism

Collections
Transcendentalism **810.8**
Transcendentalism **810.8**
Transcircularities. Troupe, Q. **811**
Transfigurations. Wright, J. **811**
Transformations of myth through time. Campbell, J. **291.1**
Transforming madness. Neugeboren, J. **616.89**
Translating and interpreting
The Oxford guide to literature in English translation **820.9**
Transmutation of metals See Alchemy
Transplantation of organs, tissues, etc.
The Ethics of organ transplants **174**
Finn, R. Organ transplants **617.9**
Freed, C. Healing the brain **616.8**
Munson, R. Raising the dead **174**
Transplantation sourcebook **617.9**
Transplantation sourcebook **617.9**
Transsexualism
Howey, N. Dress codes of three girlhoods—my mother's, my father's, and mine **306.8**
Trapp, J. B. (Joseph Burney), 1925-
(ed) Medieval English literature. See Medieval English literature **820.8**
Trapp, Joseph Burney See Trapp, J. B. (Joseph Burney), 1925-
Trapped: the 1909 Cherry Mine disaster. Tintori, K. **977.3**
Trapping
See also Game and game birds
Trappists
Kiser, J. W. The monks of Tibhirine **271**
Traps, the drum wonder: the life of Buddy Rich. Tormé, M. **92**
Travel
Barry, D. Dave Barry's only travel guide you'll ever need **817**
The Best American travel writing **910.4**
The **traveling** lady. Foote, H.
In Foote, H. Collected plays v2 p113-70 **812**
Traveling the world. See Theroux, P. To the ends of the earth **910.4**
Travels See Voyages and travels
Travels in the genetically modified zone. Winston, M. L. **664**
The **travels** of Marco Polo. Polo, M. **915**
Travels with a medieval queen [biography of Empress Constance] Simeti, M. T. **92**
Travels with a tangerine. Mackintosh-Smith, T. **910.4**
Travels with Alice. Trillin, C. **817**
Travels with Charley. Steinbeck, J. **973**
Travels with the fossil hunters **560**
Travers, P. L. (Pamela L.), 1899-1996
See/See also pages in the following book(s):
Women writers at work p117-37 **808**
Travers, Pamela L. See Travers, P. L. (Pamela L.), 1899-1996
Travesties. Stoppard, T. **822**
Travis, Debbie
Debbie Travis' painted house **698**

Travis, William Barret, 1809-1836
About
Davis, W. C. Three roads to the Alamo
Treadwell, Sophie, 1890-1970
Machinal
In Plays by American women, 1900-19.
Treadwell, Timothy
Among grizzlies
Treason by the book. Spence, J. D.
Treasure, G. R. R. (Geoffrey Russell Richard
(ed) Who's who in British history. See Who's British history
Treasure, Geoffrey Russell Richard See Treasu R. R. (Geoffrey Russell Richard)
Treasures from the Art Institute of Chicago
Treaties
Documents of American Indian diplomacy **970.0**
Treatise on the astrolabe. Chaucer, G.
In Chaucer, G. The complete poetry and prose o Geoffrey Chaucer **821**
Trees
The Complete encyclopedia of trees and shrubs **635.9**
Dirr, M. Dirr's Hardy trees and shrubs **635.9**
Dirr, M. Dirr's trees and shrubs for warm climates **635.9**
Heinrich, B. The trees in my forest **577.3**
The Hillier gardener's guide to trees & shrubs **635.9**
Pakenham, T. Remarkable trees of the world **582.16**
Simon and Schuster's guide to trees **582.16**
North America
Benvie, S. The encyclopedia of North American trees **582.16**
Little, E. L. The Audubon Society field guide to North American trees **582.16**
The **trees** in my forest. Heinrich, B. **577.3**
Trefil, James S., 1938-
Other worlds **523.2**
(ed) The Encyclopedia of science and technology. See The Encyclopedia of science and technology **503**
(jt. auth) Hazen, R. M. Science matters: achieving scientific literacy **500**
(jt. auth) Hirsch, E. D. The new dictionary of cultural literacy **031**
Tregear, Mary
Chinese art **709.51**
Trelease, Jim
The read-aloud handbook **028.5**
Tremblay, Kenneth R.
(ed) Small house designs. See Small house designs **728**
Tresidder, Jack, 1931-
Dictionary of symbols **302.2**
Trevelyan, George Macaulay, 1876-1962
The English Revolution, 1688-1689 **942.06**
Trewby, Mary
(ed) Antarctica: an encyclopedia from Abbott Ice Shelf to zooplankton. See Antarctica: an encyclopedia from Abbott Ice Shelf to zooplankton **998**
The **trial** of Socrates. Stone, I. F. **183**
Trials
DeLaughter, B. Never too late **345**
Dunne, D. Justice **345**
Evans, R. J. Lying about Hitler **940.53**
Geis, G. Crimes of the century **345**
Great American court cases **347**
Great American trials **347**
Great world trials **347**
Guttenplan, D. D. The Holocaust on trial **940.53**
Hoffer, P. C. The Salem witchcraft trials **345**

rials—*Continued*
Neff, J. The wrong man 345
Walsh, J. E. Moonlight 345
Trials (Homicide)
Rule, A. —and never let her go **364.1**
Rule, A. Dead by sunset **364.1**
Trials (Murder) *See* Trials (Homicide)
Trials in literature
Bibliography
Breen, J. L. Novel verdicts **016.8**
Triangle Shirtwaist Company, Inc.
Von Drehle, D. Triangle: the fire that changed America **974.7**
Triangle: the fire that changed America. Von Drehle, D. **974.7**
Tribe, Laurence H.
Abortion: the clash of absolutes **363.46**
The **tribe** of tiger. Thomas, E. M. **599.75**
Tricks & techniques of the selling writer. See Swain, D. V. Techniques of the selling writer **808.3**
Trieste (Italy)
Description
Morris, J. Trieste and the meaning of nowhere **945**
Trieste and the meaning of nowhere. Morris, J. **945**
Trifles. Glaspell, S.
In Plays by American women, 1900-1930 **812.008**
Trillin, Calvin
Family man **817**
Too soon to tell **818**
Travels with Alice **817**
Trilling, Lionel, 1905-1975
(ed) Victorian prose and poetry. See Victorian prose and poetry **820.8**
Trilobite!. Fortey, R. A. **560**
Trinidad and Tobago
Politics and government
See/See also pages in the following book(s):
Naipaul, V. S. The writer and the world p141-204 **824**
The **trip** to Bountiful. Foote, H.
In Foote, H. Collected plays v2 p1-60 **812**
Tripathy, Debu
(ed) Breast cancer. See Breast cancer **616.99**
The **triple** helix. Lewontin, R. C. **572.8**
Tripp, Charles
A history of Iraq **956.7**
Tristan
The romance of Tristan and Isolt **841**
Triumph and tragedy. Churchill, Sir W. **940.53**
Triumph and tragedy in Mudville. Gould, S. J. **796.357**
The **triumph** of love. Hill, G. **821**
The **triumph** of the moon. Hutton, R. **133.4**
Trivia *See* Curiosities and wonders
Trogdon, William *See* Heat Moon, William Least
Troilus and Cressida. Chaucer, G.
In Chaucer, G. The complete poetry and prose of Geoffrey Chaucer **821**
In Chaucer, G. The portable Chaucer **821**
Trojan War
Wood, M. In search of the Trojan War **939**
See/See also pages in the following book(s):
Hamilton, E. Mythology p197-342 **292**
Tuchman, B. W. The march of folly **909.08**
Poetry
Homer. The Iliad **883**
The **Trojan** women. Euripides
In Euripides. Ten plays p175-204 **882**
Trollope, Anthony, 1815-1882
About
Oxford reader's companion to Trollope **823.009**
Tropical classical. Iyer, P. **814**

Tropical fish
Smith, C. L. National Audubon Society field guide to tropical marine fishes of the Caribbean, the Gulf of Mexico, Florida, the Bahamas, and Bermuda **597**
Tropical rain forests *See* Rain forests
Tropical truth. Veloso, C. **781.64**
Trotsky, Leon, 1879-1940
About
Volkogonov, D. A. Trotsky **92**
Trouble in the works. Pinter, H.
In Pinter, H. Complete works v2 **822**
The **trouble** with government. Bok, D. C. **306**
Troublemaker. Wu, H. **951.05**
The **troubles.** Coogan, T. P. **941.6**
Troubridge, Emma
Scenic art and construction **792**
Troupe, Quincy
Miles and me: biography of Miles Davis **92**
Transcircularities **811**
(jt. auth) Davis, M. Miles, the autobiography **92**
The **trouser** people. Marshall, A. **959.1**
Trout
Behnke, R. J. Trout and salmon of North America **597**
Trout and salmon of North America. Behnke, R. J. **597**
Troy (Extinct city)
Finley, M. I. The world of Odysseus **883**
Wood, M. In search of the Trojan War **939**
Troyat, Henri, 1911-
Catherine the Great **92**
Trudeau, Lawrence J.
(ed) Asian American literature. See Asian American literature **810.9**
Trudeau, Noah Andre, 1949-
Gettysburg: a testing of courage **973.7**
Like men of war **973.7**
True and false. Mamet, D. **792**
True believers. Queenan, J. **796**
True north. Conway, J. K. **92**
Trulock, Notra
Code name Kindred Spirit **327.12**
Truman, Harry S., 1884-1972
About
Beschloss, M. R. The conquerors: Roosevelt, Truman, and the destruction of Hitler's Germany, 1941-1945 **940.53**
Karabell, Z. The last campaign **324**
McCullough, D. G. Truman **92**
Moskin, J. R. Mr. Truman's war **940.54**
See/See also pages in the following book(s):
Galbraith, J. K. Name-dropping **973.9**
Truman, Margaret, 1924-
First ladies **920**
Truman, Martha Ellen Young, 1852-1947
See/See also pages in the following book(s):
Angelo, B. First mothers **920**
Trust. Fukuyama, F. **330.9**
Truth, Sojourner, d. 1883
About
Painter, N. I. Sojourner Truth **92**
Truth
Cole, K. C. The universe and the teacup **510**
The **truth** about dogs. Budiansky, S. **636.7**
Truth and existence. Sartre, J. P. **121**
Truth and Reconciliation Commission (South Africa)
See South Africa. Commission for Truth and Reconciliation
Truthfulness and falsehood
Campbell, J. The liar's tale **177**
Lerner, H. G. The dance of deception **155.3**
Sullivan, E. E. The concise book of lying **177**

Tryman, Mfanya Donald
(ed) The Malcolm X encyclopedia. See The Malcolm X encyclopedia   92
Trzebinski, Errol, 1936-
The lives of Beryl Markham   92
Tsai, Ming, 1964-
Blue Ginger   641.5
Tsar: the lost world of Nicholas and Alexandra. Kurth, P.   947.08
The **Tsar's** last armada. Pleshakov, K.   952.03
Tsavo National Park (Kenya)
Caputo, P. Ghosts of Tsavo   599.75
Tseng, Ch'ing, 1568-1650
About
Spence, J. D. Treason by the book   951
Tsering Shakya
The dragon in the land of snows   951
Tsunemasa. Zeami
In Waley, A. The Nō plays of Japan   895.6
Tsung-tsai, 1925-
About
Crane, G. Bones of the master   294.3
Tsvetaeva, Marina Ivanovna, 1892-1941
Selected poems [of] Marina Tsvetayeva   891.7
See/See also pages in the following book(s):
Brodsky, J. Less than one p176-267   814
Pierpont, C. R. Passionate minds   810.9
Tubman, Harriet, 1815?-1913
See/See also pages in the following book(s):
Abdul-Jabbar, K. Black profiles in courage p103-11   920
Wills, G. Certain trumpets p39-48   303.3
Tuchman, Barbara Wertheim
A distant mirror   944
The first salute   973.3
The guns of August   940.3
The march of folly   909.08
Practicing history   907
The proud tower   909.82
Stilwell and the American experience in China, 1911-45   327.73
The Zimmermann telegram   940.3
Tucker, Andrew
(jt. auth) Laver, J. Costume and fashion   391
Tucker, Bruce
(jt. auth) Brown, J. James Brown, the godfather of soul   92
Tucker, Paul Hayes, 1950-
Monet in the 20th century   759.4
Tucker, Spencer C., 1937-
(ed) Encyclopedia of American military history. See Encyclopedia of American military history   355
(ed) Encyclopedia of the Korean War. See Encyclopedia of the Korean War   951.9
(ed) Encyclopedia of the Vietnam War. See Encyclopedia of the Vietnam War   959.704
(ed) Naval warfare. See Naval warfare   359
Tuckerman, Nancy, 1928-
The Amy Vanderbilt complete book of etiquette   395
Tudge, Colin
The impact of the gene   576.5
The time before history   599.93
The variety of life   578
(jt. auth) Wilmut, I. The second creation   174
Tuesdays with Morrie [biography of Morris Schwartz] Albom, M.   92
Tufts University. School of Veterinary Medicine
Animal ER   636.089
Tulipomania. Dash, M.   635.9
Tulips
Dash, M. Tulipomania   635.9
See/See also pages in the following book(s):
Pollan, M. The botany of desire   581.6

Tulsa (Okla.)
Race relations
Hirsch, J. S. Riot and remembrance   976.6
Madigan, T. The burning   976.6
Tune in yesterday. See Dunning, J. On the air   791.44
Tupac Shakur *See* Shakur, Tupac
Turabian, Kate L., 1893-1987
A manual for writers of term papers, theses, and dissertations   808
Student's guide for writing college papers   808
Turbulent souls. Dubner, S. J.   92
Turgenev, Ivan Sergeevich, 1818-1883
A month in the country   891.7
See/See also pages in the following book(s):
Nabokov, V. V. Lectures on Russian literature   891.7
Turing, Alan Mathison, 1912-1954
See/See also pages in the following book(s):
Flowers, C. Instability rules   509
Turkey
Antiquities
Wood, M. In search of the Trojan War   939
Description
Mackintosh-Smith, T. Travels with a tangerine   910.4
History
Goodwin, J. Lords of the horizons   956.1
Wheatcroft, A. The Ottomans   956
Politics and government
Kinzer, S. Crescent and star   956.1
Pope, H. Turkey unveiled   956.1
Turkey unveiled. Pope, H.   956.1
Turkington, Carol
The encyclopedia of Alzheimer's disease   616.8
The encyclopedia of deafness and hearing disorders   617.8
The encyclopedia of fertility and infertility   616.6
The encyclopedia of infectious diseases   616.9
The encyclopedia of learning disabilities   371.9
The encyclopedia of memory and memory disorders   153.1
The encyclopedia of skin and skin disorders   616.5
The encyclopedia of the brain and brain disorders   612.8
The poisons and antidotes sourcebook   615.9
Turkish cooking
Algar, A. E. Classical Turkish cooking   641.5
Turkish poetry
Collections
Music of a distant drum   808.81
Turner, Alice K.
The history of hell   291
Turner, Frederick W., 1937-
(ed) The Portable North American Indian reader. See The Portable North American Indian reader   897
Turner, Henry Ashby
Hitler's thirty days to power   943.086
Turner, J. M. W. (Joseph Mallord William), 1775-1851
About
Hamilton, J. Turner   92
Turner, James, 1946-
Without God, without creed   211
Turner, Jane Shoaf
Encyclopedia of Latin American & Caribbean art. See Encyclopedia of Latin American & Caribbean art   709.8
Turner, Joseph Mallord William *See* Turner, J. M. W. (Joseph Mallord William), 1775-1851
Turner, Nancy J.
Common poisonous plants and mushrooms of North America   581.6

Turner, Pauline
How to crochet 746.43
Turner, Tina
I, Tina 92
Turning point. Carter, J. 975.8
The **turtle** and the stars. Upgren, A. R. 520
Turtles
Ferri, V. Tortoises and turtles 597.9
Orenstein, R. I. Turtles, tortoises and terrapins
597.9
Turtles & tortoises. See Ferri, V. Tortoises and turtles
597.9
Turtles, tortoises and terrapins. Orenstein, R. I.
597.9
Tuscany (Italy)
Social life and customs
Mayes, F. Bella Tuscany 945
Mayes, F. Under the Tuscan sun 945
Tuskegee airmen See African American pilots
Tuskegee Institute
Harlan, L. R. Booker T. Washington: the wizard of
Tuskegee, 1901-1915 92
Washington, B. T. Up from slavery 92
Tutankhamen, King of Egypt
About
Brier, B. The murder of Tutankhamen 932
See/See also pages in the following book(s):
Ceram, C. W. Gods, graves, and scholars p176-207
930.1
Tutu, Desmond
No future without forgiveness 968.06
The rainbow people of God 968.06
(comp) The African prayer book. See The African
prayer book 242
Tuxedo Park [biography of Alfred Lee Loomis] Conant,
J. 92
TV movies. See Maltin, L. Leonard Maltin's movie and
video guide 791.43
TV repair for beginners. Davidson, H. L. 621.388
Twain, Mark, 1835-1910
The autobiography of Mark Twain 92
The portable Mark Twain 818
The wit and wisdom of Mark Twain 818
About
Cooper, R. L. Around the world with Mark Twain
818
Emerson, E. Mark Twain 92
The Mark Twain encyclopedia 818
The Oxford companion to Mark Twain 818
Rasmussen, R. K. Mark Twain A to Z 818
See/See also pages in the following book(s):
Kazin, A. An American procession p181-210
810.9
The **twelve** Caesars. Suetonius Tranquillus, C. 878
Twentieth century. Roberts, J. M. 909.82
Twentieth century American nicknames 929.4
Twentieth-century art of Latin America. Barnitz, J.
709
Twentieth century authors. See World authors, 1900-
1950 920.003
Twentieth-century fashion. See Peacock, J. 20th-century
fashion 391
Twentieth century Latin American poetry 861
Twentieth-century literary criticism 809
Twentieth-century literary movements dictionary
809
Twentieth-century science-fiction writers. See St. James
guide to science fiction writers 809.3
Twentieth century short story explication: new series.
Walker, W. S. 016.8093
Twenty best garden designs. See Newbury, T. 20 best
garden designs 712
Twenty-five gorgeous sweaters for the brand new knitter.
See Ham, C. 25 gorgeous sweaters for the brand
new knitter 746.43
Twenty-one short plays. See Wilson, L. 21 short plays
812
Twenty thousand years of fashion. See Boucher, F.
20,000 years of fashion 391
Twilight of the idols. Nietzsche, F. W.
In Nietzsche, F. W. The portable Nietzsche 193
Twins
Agnew, C. L. Twins! 649
Segal, N. L. Entwined lives 155.4
Wright, L. Twins 155.4
Two against the ice. Mikkelsen, E. 998
Two-career family See Dual-career families
Two hundred percent of nothing. Dewdney, A. K.
510
The **two** Koreas. Oberdorfer, D. 951.9
Two states—one nation? Grass, G. 943.087
Two treatises of government. Locke, J. 320.1
Two years before the mast. Dana, R. H. 910.4
Tycho & Kepler. Ferguson, K. 92
Tye, Larry
Home lands 909
Tygiel, Jules
Baseball's great experiment 796.357
Tyldesley, Joyce A.
Nefertiti 932
Tynan, Kenneth, 1927-1980
The diaries of Kenneth Tynan 92
Tynan, Ronan, 1960-
Halfway home: my life 'til now 92
Tyndale, William, d. 1536
About
Moynahan, B. God's bestseller: William Tyndale,
Thomas More, and the writing of the English Bible
92
Tyning, Thomas F.
A guide to amphibians and reptiles 597.9
Typewriting
See also Keyboarding (Electronics)
Typhoid fever
See/See also pages in the following book(s):
Bourdain, A. Typhoid Mary 92
Typhoid Mary, d. 1938
About
Bourdain, A. Typhoid Mary 92
Typhoons
See also Hurricanes
Longshore, D. Encyclopedia of hurricanes, typhoons
and cyclones 551.55
Typography See Printing
Tyrannosaurus Sue. Fiffer, S. 567.9
Tyranny of the normal. Fiedler, L. A. 814
Tyson, Neil De Grasse
Universe down to Earth 523.1
Tytell, John
Ezra Pound 92

U

U.F.O.'s See Unidentified flying objects
The **U.S.** Constitution A to Z. Maddex, R. L. 342
U.S. government on the Web. Hernon, P. 025.04
U.S. Holocaust Memorial Museum See United States
Holocaust Memorial Museum
U.S.S.R. See Soviet Union
U.S. Space Camp (Huntsville, Ala.)
Kersjes, M. A smile as big as the moon 371.9
U.S. Special Operations Command See United States.
Special Operations Command
Udvardy, Miklos D. F., 1919-1998
National Audubon Society field guide to North
American birds, Western region 598
UFO crash at Roswell. Saler, B. 001.9
UFOs See Unidentified flying objects

UFOs and popular culture. Lewis, J. R.   001.9
Uglow, Jennifer S.
 Hogarth   92
 The lunar men   920
Ujifusa, Grant
 (jt. auth) Barone, M. The almanac of American politics
                                              328.73
Ulcerative colitis See Inflammatory bowel diseases
Ulrich, Laurel
 The age of homespun   974
Ulrich's international periodicals directory. See Ulrich's
 periodicals directory   011
Ulrich's periodicals directory   011
The **Ultimate** audition book   808.82
The **ultimate** dinosaur book. Lambert, D.   567.9
The **ultimate** dog book. Taylor, D.   636.7
The **ultimate** garden designer. See Newbury, T. 20 best
 garden designs   712
The **ultimate** guitar book. Bacon, T.   787.87
Ultimate horse. Edwards, E. H.   636.1
The **ultimate** horse book. See Edwards, E. H. Ultimate
 horse   636.1
The **Ultimate** Jack the Ripper companion   364.1
Ultimate journey. Bernstein, R.   294.3
The **ultimate** Picasso. Léal, B.   92
The **ultimate** pressure cooker cookbook. Lacalamita, T.
                                              641.5
Ultimate visual dictionary   423
UN See United Nations
Unabridged dictionary, Random House Webster's
                                              423
The **unabridged** journals of Sylvia Plath, 1950-1962.
 Plath, S.   92
Unbegaun, B. O.
 (ed) The Concise Oxford Russian dictionary. See The
 Concise Oxford Russian dictionary   491.7
 (ed) The Oxford Russian dictionary. See The Oxford
 Russian dictionary   491.7
Uncle Tungsten. Sacks, O. W.   92
Uncle Vanya. Chekhov, A. P.
 In Chekhov, A. P. The plays of Anton Chekhov
 p207-55   891.7
Uncollected poems. Rilke, R. M.   831
Uncommon women and others. Wasserstein, W.
 In Wasserstein, W. The Heidi chronicles, and other
 plays   812
Uncrowned king: the life of Prince Albert. Weintraub, S.
                                              92
Undaunted courage. Ambrose, S. E.   978
The **undefeated**. Dent, J.   796.332
Under a wing. Lindbergh, R.   92
Under his very windows. Zuccotti, S.   940.53
Under milk wood. Thomas, D.   822
Under my skin. Lessing, D. M.   92
Under pressure. Hill, A. J.   910.4
Under the black flag. Cordingly, D.   910.4
Under the knife [biography of Joseph Griffin] Pearson,
 H.   92
Under the sea wind. Carson, R.   577.7
Under the Tuscan sun. Mayes, F.   945
Underdeveloped areas See Developing countries
Underground. Murakami, H.   364.1
Underground railroad
 Tobin, J. Hidden in plain view   973.7
Underhill, Paco
 Why we buy   658.8
Underhill, Roy
 The woodwright's apprentice   684
Underprivileged children See Socially handicapped children
Understanding addiction. Henderson, E. C. 362.29
Understanding Alzheimer's disease. Cutler, N. R.
                                              616.8
Understanding American business jargon. Folsom, W.
 D.   650

Understanding cancer. Coleman, C. N.   616.99
Understanding chronic pain. Koestler, A. J. 616
Understanding colon cancer. Adrouny, A. R.
                                              616.99
Understanding Crohn disease and ulcerative colitis.
 Zonderman, J.   616.3
Understanding depression. Ainsworth, P.   616.85
Understanding depression. DePaulo, J. R.   616.85
Understanding hepatitis. Achord, J. L.   616.3
Understanding Islam. Lippman, T. W.   297
Understanding May Sarton. Fulk, M. K.   818
Understanding men's passages. Sheehy, G.   305.31
Understanding paintings   759
Understanding panic and other anxiety disorders. Root,
 B. A., Jr.   616.85
Understanding sickle cell disease. Bloom, M.
                                              616.1
Understanding the Dead Sea scrolls   296.1
Understanding the tin man. July, W. W., II 158
Understanding wood. Hoadley, R. B.   684
Undertakers and undertaking
 Lynch, T. The undertaking   814
 Mitford, J. The American way of death revisited
                                              393
The **undertaking**. Lynch, T.   814
Underwater exploration
 Ballard, R. D. The discovery of the Titanic   910.4
 Ballard, R. D. The eternal darkness   551.46
 Broad, W. The universe below   551.46
 Pellegrino, C. R. Ghosts of the Titanic   910.4
                  Encyclopedias
 Encyclopedia of underwater and maritime archaeology
                                              930.1
Underwater exploration devices See Submersibles
Underworld: the mysterious origins of civilization. Hancock, G.   551.7
The **undiscovered** Paul Robeson. Robeson, P., Jr.
                                              92
Undue risk. Moreno, J. D.   174
An **unexpected** light. Elliot, J.   958.1
The **unexpected** universe. Eiseley, L. C.   500
An **unfinished** life: John F. Kennedy, 1917-1963. Dallek,
 R.   92
The **unforgiving** minute: a life of Rudyard Kipling. See
 Ricketts, H. Rudyard Kipling   92
Ung, Loung, 1970-
 First they killed my father   959.6
Unger, Debi
 (ed) The Times were a changin'. See The Times were
 a changin'   973.923
Unger, Harlow G., 1931-
 Encyclopedia of American education   370
Unger, Irwin
 (ed) The Times were a changin'. See The Times were
 a changin'   973.923
Unger, Leonard
 (ed) American writers. See American writers
                                              920.003
Ungodly: the passions, torments, and murder of atheist
 Madalyn Murray O'Hair. Dracos, T.   92
Unholy war. Esposito, J. L.   322.4
Unidentified flying objects
 Alschuler, W. R. The science of UFOs   001.9
 Lewis, J. R. UFOs and popular culture   001.9
 Saler, B. UFO crash at Roswell   001.9
Union of South Africa See South Africa
Union of Soviet Socialist Republics See Soviet Union
Union Pacific Railroad Company
 Ambrose, S. E. Nothing like it in the world   385
   See/See also pages in the following book(s):
 Bain, D. H. Empire express   385
Unions, Labor See Labor unions
United Nations
 Moore, J. A. Encyclopedia of the United Nations
                                              341.23

United Nations—*Continued*

Osmańczyk, E. J. Encyclopedia of the United Nations and international agreements **341.23**

See/See also pages in the following book(s):

Shawcross, W. Deliver us from evil **909.82**

Worldmark encyclopedia of the nations **910.3**

Hickey, M. The Korean War **951.9**

Afghanistan

Corwin, P. Doomed in Afghanistan **958.1**

United Nations. Dept. of International Economic and Social Affairs. Statistical Office *See* United Nations. Statistical Office

United Nations. General Assembly

Devine, C. Human rights **323**

United Nations. Statistical Office

Demographic yearbook **304.6**

Statistical yearbook **310.5**

United States

Foreign relations—Dictionaries

Notable U.S. ambassadors since 1775 **920.003**

United States

Archives

See Archives—United States

Armed forces

Astor, G. The greatest war **940.54**

Wright, K. Soldiers of freedom **355**

Armed Forces—Biography—Dictionaries

Ancell, R. M. The biographical dictionary of World War II generals and flag officers **920.003**

Armed forces—Examinations

How to prepare for the Armed Forces test—ASVAB **355**

Biography

Carey, C. W. American inventors, entrepreneurs, and business visionaries **920**

Ellis, J. J. Founding brothers **973.4**

Life stories **920**

The Norton book of American autobiography **920**

Terkel, S. My American century **920**

Biography—Dictionaries

Adamson, L. G. Notable women in American history **920.003**

American national biography **920.003**

American political leaders, 1789-2000 **920.003**

Biographical directory of the American Congress, 1774-1996 **328.73**

Concise dictionary of American biography **920.003**

Dictionary of American biography **920.003**

Notable American women: the modern period **920.003**

Notable black American men **920.003**

Notable black American women [bk I-III] **920.003**

The Scribner encyclopedia of American lives **920.003**

The Scribner encyclopedia of American lives, The 1960s **920.003**

Who was who in America **920.003**

Who's who in America **920.003**

Who's who of American women **920.003**

Census

Encyclopedia of the U.S. Census **304.6**

Church history

See also United States—Religion

Bawer, B. Stealing Jesus **277.3**

Chaves, M. Ordaining women **262**

Cuneo, M. W. American exorcism **265**

Gaustad, E. S. New historical atlas of religion in America **200.9**

Gillis, C. Roman Catholicism in America **282**

Lincoln, C. E. The black church in the African American experience **277.3**

Marty, M. E. Pilgrims in their own land **277.3**

Civil service

See Civil service—United States

Civilization

American decades **973.9**

American eras **973**

Boorstin, D. J. The Americans: The colonial experience **973.2**

Boorstin, D. J. The Americans: The democratic experience **973**

Boorstin, D. J. The Americans: The national experience **973**

Boorstin, D. J. Hidden history **973**

Commager, H. S. The American mind **973**

History of the mass media in the United States **302.23**

Hoffman, A. The best of Abbie Hoffman **303.4**

Isaacs, A. R. Vietnam shadows **959.704**

Kammen, M. G. In the past lane **973**

Letters of the century **816**

Postman, N. Amusing ourselves to death **302.23**

Schlesinger, A. M. The disuniting of America **973**

Schwartz, R. A. Cold War culture **973.92**

Steinbeck, J. Travels with Charley **973**

Terkel, S. American dreams **973.9**

Civilization—1970-

Frum, D. How we got here **973.92**

Schulman, B. J. The seventies **973.92**

Civilization—Dictionaries

Hirsch, E. D. The new dictionary of cultural literacy **031**

Civilization—Encyclopedias

Encyclopedia of American cultural and intellectual history **973.03**

Encyclopedia of American studies **973.03**

St. James encyclopedia of popular culture **973.9**

Climate

Laskin, D. Braving the elements **551.6**

Weather almanac **551.6**

Williams, J. The weather book **551.6**

Constitutional history

See Constitutional history—United States

Constitutional law

See Constitutional law—United States

Courts

See Courts—United States

Defenses

See also Strategic Defense Initiative

Description

Bowden, C. Blues for cannibals **973.92**

Bryson, B. I'm a stranger here myself **973.92**

Cantor, G. Historic landmarks of black America **917.3**

Cronkite, W. Around America **917.3**

Ferris, G. W. Presidential places **917.3**

Heat Moon, W. L. Blue highways **917.3**

Heat Moon, W. L. River horse **917.3**

Jenkins, P. A walk across America **917.3**

Kuralt, C. Charles Kuralt's America **973.92**

Kuralt, C. Charles Kuralt's American moments **973.92**

Kuralt, C. On the road with Charles Kuralt **973.92**

McMurtry, L. Roads **917.3**

Mobil travel guides **917.3**

National Geographic guide to America's historic places **917.3**

Paterniti, M. Driving Mr. Albert **917.3**

Steinbeck, J. Travels with Charley **973**

Stone, N. On the water **917.3**

Economic conditions

Allen, F. L. Since yesterday **973.91**

Boorstin, D. J. The Americans: The democratic experience **973**

Friedman, M. Free to choose **330.1**

United States—Economic conditions—*Continued*
Shulman, B. The betrayal of work   **331.2**
  Economic conditions—1775-1783, Revolution
Foner, E. Tom Paine and Revolutionary America
                973.3
    Economic conditions—20th century
Galbraith, J. K. The affluent society   **330**
    Economic conditions—1919-1933
Allen, F. L. Only yesterday   **973.91**
Galbraith, J. K. The Great Crash, 1929   **338.5**
Terkel, S. Hard times   **973.91**
Watkins, T. H. The hungry years   **973.91**
    Economic conditions—1933-1945
Terkel, S. Hard times   **973.91**
Watkins, T. H. The hungry years   **973.91**
  See/See also pages in the following book(s):
Foner, E. The story of American freedom p195-218
                323.44
      Economic policy
  See Economic policy—United States
        Emigration
  See United States—Immigration and emigration
       Employees
  See United States—Officials and employees
      Ethnic relations
Morales, E. Living in Spanglish   **305.8**
    Executive departments
  See Executive departments—United States
       Exploration
  See also West (U.S.)—Exploration
   Foreign economic relations
Friedman, T. L. The Lexus and the olive tree
                337
     Foreign opinion
Esposito, J. L. Unholy war   **322.4**
    Foreign population
  See Aliens—United States; Immigrants—United
States
     Foreign relations
Alperovitz, G. The decision to use the atomic bomb
  and the architecture of an American myth
                940.54
Brands, H. W. What America owes the world
                327.73
Chace, J. Acheson   **92**
Freedman, L. Kennedy's wars   **973.922**
Friedman, T. L. Longitudes and attitudes   **973.931**
Halberstam, D. War in a time of peace   **327.73**
Kennan, G. F. Sketches from a life   **92**
Kissinger, H. Diplomacy   **327.73**
Kissinger, H. Does America need a foreign policy?
                327.73
Kissinger, H. Years of renewal   **92**
Kort, M. The Columbia guide to the Cold War
                973.9
Leebaert, D. The fifty-year wound   **973.92**
Lind, M. Vietnam, the necessary war   **959.704**
Mead, W. R. Special providence   **327.73**
Moynihan, D. P. On the law of nations   **327.73**
Nye, J. S., Jr. The paradox of American power
                327.73
Pillar, P. R. Terrorism and U.S. foreign policy
                327.73
Power, S. "A problem from hell"   **304.6**
Schlesinger, A. M. The cycles of American history
                973
Will, G. F. With a happy eye but . . . America and
  the world, 1997-2002   **973.929**
Woodward, B. The commanders   **973.928**
   Foreign relations—Bibliography
American foreign relations since 1600   **016.327**
   Foreign relations—Encyclopedias
Encyclopedia of American foreign policy   **327.73**

    Foreign relations—China
Bernstein, R. The coming conflict with China
                327.73
Laird, T. Into Tibet   **327.12**
Mann, J. About face   **327.73**
Tuchman, B. W. Stilwell and the American experience
  in China, 1911-45   **327.73**
  See/See also pages in the following book(s):
Tuchman, B. W. Practicing history p188-207   **907**
    Foreign relations—Cuba
Bardach, A. L. Cuba confidential   **972.91**
    Foreign relations—Europe
Kagan, R. Of paradise and power   **327.73**
    Foreign relations—Germany
Beschloss, M. R. The conquerors: Roosevelt, Truman,
  and the destruction of Hitler's Germany, 1941-1945
                940.53
   Foreign relations—Great Britain
Stafford, D. Roosevelt and Churchill   **940.54**
    Foreign relations—Iran
  See also Iran hostage crisis, 1979-1981
    Foreign relations—Japan
LaFeber, W. The clash   **327.73**
    Foreign relations—Russia
Cohen, S. F. Failed crusade   **327.73**
Talbott, S. The Russia hand   **327.73**
    Foreign relations—Soviet Union
Fursenko, A. V. "One hell of a gamble"   **973.922**
Gates, R. M. From the shadows   **327.73**
Grose, P. Operation Rollback   **327.12**
Kennedy, R. F. Thirteen days   **973.922**
Schweizer, P. Reagan's War   **327.73**
    Foreign relations—Vietnam
Halberstam, D. The best and the brightest
                973.922
     Geographic names
  See Geographic names—United States
       Geography
Linklater, A. Measuring America   **973**
    Geography—Encyclopedias
Encyclopedia of rural America   **973.03**
      Government
  See United States—Politics and government
    Government employees
  See United States—Officials and employees
    Government publications
  See Government publications—United States
   Historical geography—Maps
Gilbert, M. The Routledge atlas of American history
                911
Historical atlas of the United States   **911**
     Historiography
Kammen, M. G. In the past lane   **973**
Schlesinger, A. M. The disuniting of America
                973
       History
  See also West (U.S.)—History
American eras   **973**
Anzovin, S. Famous first facts about American politics
                973
Churchill, Sir W. The great republic   **973**
Ferling, J. E. The first of men: a life of George Wash-
  ington   **92**
Flexner, J. T. George Washington   **92**
Foner, E. The story of American freedom   **323.44**
Hakim, J. Freedom   **973**
Morison, S. E. A concise history of the American Re-
  public   **973**
Morison, S. E. The growth of the American Republic
                973
Morison, S. E. The Oxford history of the American
  people   **973**
Randall, W. S. George Washington   **92**
Schlesinger, A. M. The cycles of American history
                973

United States—History—*Continued*
Smith, R. N. Patriarch: George Washington and the
new American nation 92
Wilkins, R. W. Jefferson's pillow 973
History—1600-1775, Colonial period
Anderson, F. The crucible of war 973.2
Bailyn, B. The peopling of British North America
973.2
Berlin, I. Many thousands gone 326
Boorstin, D. J. The Americans: The colonial experi-
ence 973.2
Hawke, D. F. Everyday life in early America
973.2
Morgan, T. Wilderness at dawn 970
See/See also pages in the following book(s):
Tuchman, B. W. The march of folly 909.08
History—1675-1676, King Philip's War
See King Philip's War, 1675-1676
History—1775-1783, Revolution
The American Revolution 973.3
Bobrick, B. Angel in the whirlwind 973.3
Calloway, C. G. The American Revolution in Indian
country 973.3
Draper, T. A struggle for power 973.3
Dunn, S. Sister revolutions 973.3
Fenn, E. A. Pox Americana 614.5
Ferling, J. E. Setting the world ablaze 973.3
Hibbert, C. Redcoats and rebels 973.3
Morgan, E. S. The birth of the Republic, 1763-89
973.3
Raphael, R. A people's history of the American Revo-
lution 973.3
Tuchman, B. W. The first salute 973.3
Wood, G. S. The radicalism of the American Revolu-
tion 973.3
See/See also pages in the following book(s):
Ferling, J. E. The first of men: a life of George Wash-
ington p111-321 92
History—1783-1809
See also Louisiana Purchase
Ellis, J. J. Founding brothers 973.4
The Louisiana Purchase 973.4
Miller, J. C. The Federalist era, 1789-1801 973.4
Morgan, E. S. The birth of the Republic, 1763-89
973.3
History—1783-1865
Appleby, J. O. Inheriting the revolution 973
History—19th century—Encyclopedias
Encyclopedia of the United States in the nineteenth
century 973.5
History—1812-1815, War of 1812
See War of 1812
History—1815-1861
Oates, S. B. The approaching fury 973.5
History—1861-1865, Civil War
See also Confederate States of America
Blanton, D. They fought like demons 973.7
Cooper, W. J. Jefferson Davis, American 92
Davis, B. To Appomattox 973.7
Fellman, M. The making of Robert E. Lee 92
Foote, S. The Civil War 973.7
Freeman, D. S. Lee 92
Gallagher, G. W. The Confederate War 973.7
Grant, U. S. Memoirs and selected letters 92
Horwitz, T. Confederates in the attic 973.7
Hurst, J. Nathan Bedford Forrest 92
Kennett, L. B. Sherman 92
Klein, M. Days of defiance 973.7
Leckie, R. None died in vain 973.7
Leonard, E. D. All the daring of the soldier
973.7
The Library of Congress Civil War desk reference
973.7
McPherson, J. M. Abraham Lincoln and the second
American Revolution 973.7

McPherson, J. M. Battle cry of freedom 973.7
McPherson, J. M. Drawn with the sword 973.7
McPherson, J. M. For cause and comrades 973.7
Morris, R. The better angel: Walt Whitman in the Civil
War 92
Nolan, A. T. Lee considered 92
Oates, S. B. The whirlwind of war 973.7
Oates, S. B. A woman of valor: Clara Barton and the
Civil War 92
Perry, M. Conceived in liberty 973.7
"The Real war will never get in the books"
810.8
Sandburg, C. Abraham Lincoln: The prairie years and
The war years 92
Sears, S. W. George B. McClellan 92
Simpson, B. D. Ulysses S. Grant 92
Smith, J. E. Grant 92
Trudeau, N. A. Like men of war 973.7
Ward, G. C. The Civil War 973.7
Wert, J. D. Mosby's Rangers 973.7
Wiley, B. I. The life of Billy Yank 973.7
Wiley, B. I. The life of Johnny Reb 973.7
Wilson, E. Patriotic gore 810.9
Winik, J. April 1865 973.7
See/See also pages in the following book(s):
Fellman, M. Citizen Sherman: a life of William Te-
cumseh Sherman 92
Rehnquist, W. H. All the laws but one p3-169
342
Thomas, E. M. Robert E. Lee 92
History—1861-1865, Civil War—Biography
Freeman, D. S. Lee's lieutenants 973.7
Warner, E. J. Generals in blue 920
Warner, E. J. Generals in gray 920
See/See also pages in the following book(s):
Wilson, E. Patriotic gore p219-466; 529-796
810.9
Leaders of the American Civil War 920.003
History—1861-1865, Civil War—Campaigns
See also Peninsular Campaign, 1862; names of bat-
tles, e.g. Gettysburg (Pa.), Battle of, 1863
Catton, B. Grant moves south 92
Catton, B. Grant takes command 92
Catton, B. A stillness at Appomattox 973.7
Davis, B. Sherman's march 973.7
Eicher, D. J. The longest night 973.7
Freeman, D. S. Lee's lieutenants 973.7
Furgurson, E. B. Ashes of glory 975.5
Macdonald, J. Great battles of the Civil War
973.7
History—1861-1865, Civil War—Causes
The Causes of the Civil War 973.7
Oates, S. B. The approaching fury 973.5
History—1861-1865, Civil War—Dictionaries
Boatner, M. M. The Civil War dictionary 973.7
History—1861-1865, Civil War—Encyclopedias
Encyclopedia of the American Civil War 973.7
**History—1861-1865, Civil War—Motion pictures and
the war**
Chadwick, B. The reel Civil War 791.43
History—1861-1865, Civil War—Naval operations
Coombe, J. D. Gunsmoke over the Atlantic 973.7
History—1861-1865, Civil War—Pictorial works
See/See also pages in the following book(s):
Panzer, M. Mathew Brady and the image of history
92
History—1861-1865, Civil War—Poetry
The Columbia book of Civil War poetry 811.008
See/See also pages in the following book(s):
Wilson, E. Patriotic gore p466-507 810.9
History—1861-1865, Civil War—Reconstruction
See Reconstruction (1865-1876)
History—1861-1865, Civil War—Sources
The Causes of the Civil War 973.7

United States—History—1815-1861—History—1861-1865, Civil War—*Continued*
   History—1861-1865, Civil War—Women
Faust, D. G. Mothers of invention   **973.7**
   History—1865-1898
Foner, E. Reconstruction   **973.8**
Franklin, J. H. Reconstruction after the Civil War   **973.8**
   History—1898, War of 1898
See Spanish-American War, 1898
   History—1898-1919
Zimmermann, W. First great triumph   **973**
   History—20th century
American decades   **973.9**
Diner, S. J. A very different age   **973.8**
Evans, H. The American century   **973.9**
   History—20th century—Pictorial works
Life: century of change   **779**
   History—1914-1918, World War
See World War, 1914-1918—United States
   History—1919-1933
Allen, F. L. Only yesterday   **973.91**
Allen, F. L. Since yesterday   **973.91**
Kennedy, D. M. Freedom from fear   **973.91**
Schlesinger, A. M. The crisis of the old order, 1919-1933   **973.91**
   History—1933-1945
Allen, F. L. Since yesterday   **973.91**
Goodwin, D. K. No ordinary time [biography of Franklin D. Roosevelt]   **92**
Kennedy, D. M. Freedom from fear   **973.91**
Leuchtenburg, W. E. Franklin D. Roosevelt and the New Deal, 1932-1940   **973.917**
Schlesinger, A. M. The coming of the New Deal, 1933-1935   **973.917**
Schlesinger, A. M. The politics of upheaval, 1935-1936   **973.917**
Weinstein, A. The haunted wood   **327.12**
See/See also pages in the following book(s):
Brokaw, T. An album of memories   **940.54**
   History—1933-1945—Encyclopedias
Encyclopedia of the Great Depression and the New Deal   **973.917**
   History—1939-1945, World War
See World War, 1939-1945—United States
   History—1945-
Gregory, R. Cold War America, 1946 to 1990   **973.92**
Kort, M. The Columbia guide to the Cold War   **973.9**
   History—1953-1961
Branch, T. Parting the waters: America in the King years, 1954-63   **973.921**
   History—1961-1974
Branch, T. Pillar of fire   **973.922**
The Columbia guide to America in the 1960s   **973.92**
Gitlin, T. The sixties   **973.92**
The Times were a changin'   **973.923**
Witcover, J. The year the dream died   **973.92**
   History—1974-1989
Johnson, H. B. Sleepwalking through history   **973.927**
   History—1989-
Johnson, H. B. The best of times   **973.929**
   History—1991, Persian Gulf War
See Persian Gulf War, 1991
   History—Bibliography
Printed sources   **929**
   History—Dictionaries
Dictionary of American history   **973.03**
Kane, J. N. Famous first facts   **031.02**
The New York Public Library American history desk reference   **973.02**

The Oxford companion to United States history   **973.03**
   History—Encyclopedias
Encyclopedia of American history   **973.03**
Olson, J. S. Encyclopedia of the industrial revolution in America   **973.03**
The Reader's companion to American history   **973.03**
   History—Fiction—Bibliography
Adamson, L. G. American historical fiction   **016.813**
   History—Historiography
See United States—Historiography
   History—Miscellanea
The New encyclopedia of American scandal   **973.02**
Shenkman, R. Legends, lies, and cherished myths of American history   **973.02**
   History—Pictorial works
Virga, V. Eyes of the nation   **973**
Witness to America   **973**
   History—Societies—Directories
Directory of historical organizations in the United States and Canada   **973.06**
   History—Sources
Eyewitness to America   **973**
Witness to America   **973**
   History, Local
See United States—Local history
   History, Military
See United States—Military history
   History, Naval
See United States—Naval history
   Immigration and emigration
See also Aliens—United States; Immigrants—United States
Anosike, B. O. Immigration manual   **342**
Brownstone, D. M. Facts about American immigration   **325.73**
Daniels, R. Coming to America   **325.73**
Handlin, O. The uprooted   **325.73**
Lewis, L. N. How to get a green card   **342**
Yans-McLaughlin, V. Ellis Island and the peopling of America   **325.73**
   Intellectual life
Bloom, A. D. The closing of the American mind   **973.92**
Boorstin, D. J. The Americans: The colonial experience   **973.2**
Boorstin, D. J. The Americans: The national experience   **973**
Commager, H. S. The American mind   **973**
Levine, L. W. The opening of the American mind   **001.1**
Menand, L. The Metaphysical Club   **973.9**
Quick studies   **001.1**
   Intellectual life—Encyclopedias
Encyclopedia of American cultural and intellectual history   **973.03**
   Internal security
See Internal security—United States
   Law
See Law—United States
   Local history
Beatty, M. A. County name origins of the United States   **917.3**
Cantor, G. Historic landmarks of black America   **917.3**
Cronkite, W. Around America   **917.3**
Facts about the states   **973**
Neagles, J. C. The Library of Congress   **929**
   Maps
See also United States—Historical geography—Maps
Rand McNally road atlas   **912**

United States—*Continued*
Military history
Buckley, G. L. American patriots 355
Encyclopedia of American war heroes 920.003
Facts about the American wars 355
Fredriksen, J. C. American military leaders
920.003
Kindsvatter, P. S. American soldiers 355
Mikaelian, A. Medal of honor 920
Purcell, L. E. Encyclopedia of battles in North America, 1517 to 1916 970
Military history—Dictionaries
Fredriksen, J. C. America's military adversaries
920.003
The Oxford companion to American military history
355
Military history—Encyclopedias
Encyclopedia of American military history 355
Military policy
See Military policy—United States
Monetary policy
See Monetary policy—United States
Moral conditions
Bowden, C. Blues for cannibals 973.92
Edelman, M. W. The measure of our success 170
Etzioni, A. The spirit of community 307
Himmelfarb, G. The de-moralization of society
303.3
Morgan, P. W. The appearance of impropriety
306
Savage, D. Skipping towards Gomorrah 306
Wolfe, A. Moral freedom 170
See/See also pages in the following book(s):
Sontag, S. Styles of radical will p193-204 814
National characteristics
See American national characteristics
National parks and reserves
See National parks and reserves—United States
National security
See National security—United States
Naval history
Love, R. W. History of the U.S. Navy 359
Morison, S. E. John Paul Jones 92
Officials and employees
O'Neil, R. M. The rights of public employees
342
Politics and government
American presidential campaigns and elections
324
Anzovin, S. Famous first facts about American politics
973
Barone, M. The almanac of American politics
328.73
Broder, D. S. Democracy derailed 328.73
CQ almanac plus 328.73
Dallek, R. Hail to the chief 973
Finan, C. M. Alfred E. Smith, the happy warrior
92
Guinier, L. The miner's canary 323.1
Hofstadter, R. The American political tradition, and the men who made it 973
Morris, D. The new prince 324.7
Phillips, K. P. Wealth and democracy 305.5
The Reader's companion to the American presidency
973
Schlesinger, A. M. The cycles of American history
973
Tocqueville, A. de. Democracy in America 973.5
Utter, G. H. The religious right 277.3
Will, G. F. Restoration 328.73
Wills, G. A necessary evil 973
See/See also pages in the following book(s):
White, E. B. Essays of E. B. White 814

Politics and government—1775-1783, Revolution
Becker, C. The Declaration of Independence
973.3
Foner, E. Tom Paine and Revolutionary America
973.3
Hamilton, A. Writings 973.4
Maier, P. American scripture 973.3
McCullough, D. G. John Adams 92
Paine, T. Common sense 320
Washington, G. Writings 973.4
Wood, G. S. The radicalism of the American Revolution 973.3
Politics and government—1783-1809
Berkin, C. A brilliant solution 342
Brookhiser, R. Alexander Hamilton, American 92
The Debate on the Constitution 342
Ellis, J. J. Founding brothers 973.4
Hamilton, A. Writings 973.4
Simon, J. F. What kind of nation 342
Washington, G. Writings 973.4
Politics and government—1783-1865
Freeman, J. B. Affairs of honor 973.4
Remini, R. V. John Quincy Adams 92
Politics and government—1815-1861
Lincoln, A. Speeches and writings 973.7
Miller, W. L. Arguing about slavery 973.5
Remini, R. V. Andrew Jackson & his Indian wars
973.5
Remini, R. V. Daniel Webster 92
Politics and government—1861-1865
Lincoln, A. Speeches and writings 973.7
Paludan, P. S. The presidency of Abraham Lincoln
973.7
Politics and government—1865-1898
Stampp, K. M. The era of reconstruction, 1865-1877
973.8
Politics and government—1898-1919
Cooper, J. M. The warrior and the priest: Woodrow Wilson and Theodore Roosevelt 92
Levin, P. L. Edith and Woodrow: the Wilson White House 92
Politics and government—20th century
Burns, J. M. The three Roosevelts 973.91
Caro, R. A. The years of Lyndon Johnson 92
Congress and the Nation 328.73
Dallek, R. Lone star rising: Lyndon Johnson and his times, 1908-1960 92
Dickson, P. Sputnik: the shock of the century
629.46
Evans, H. The American century 973.9
Farrell, J. A. Tip O'Neill and the Democratic century
92
Galbraith, J. K. Name-dropping 973.9
Halberstam, D. The fifties 973.92
Hofstadter, R. The age of reform from Bryan to F.D.R.
973.91
Mann, R. A grand delusion 959.704
Matthews, C. Kennedy & Nixon 973.922
Phillips, K. P. Arrogant capital 973.92
Podhoretz, N. My love affair with America 320.5
Schlesinger, A. M. Robert Kennedy and his times
92
Summers, A. The arrogance of power: the secret world of Richard Nixon 92
Witcover, J. No way to pick a president 324
See/See also pages in the following book(s):
Thomas, E. Robert Kennedy 92
Politics and government—1933-1945
Davis, K. S. FDR, into the storm, 1937-1940 92
The Eleanor Roosevelt encyclopedia 92
Fried, A. F.D.R. and his enemies 92
Politics and government—1945-
Leebaert, D. The fifty-year wound 973.92
Theoharis, A. G. Chasing spies 327.12

United States—Politics and government—1945—*Continued*

See/See also pages in the following book(s):

Thomas, H. Front row at the White House   92

Politics and government—1953-1961

White, T. H. The making of the president, 1960

   324.6

Wicker, T. Dwight D. Eisenhower   92

Politics and government—1961-1974

Abuse of power   973.924

Berman, L. No peace, no honor   959.704

Halberstam, D. The best and the brightest

   973.922

Kaiser, D. E. American tragedy   959.704

Kennedy, R. F. Thirteen days   973.922

Kenney, C. John F. Kennedy   92

Mahoney, R. D. Sons and brothers: the days of Jack and Bobby Kennedy   92

Reaching for glory   973.923

Reeves, R. President Kennedy   92

Reeves, R. President Nixon   92

Shultz, R. H. The secret war against Hanoi

   959.704

Taking charge   973.923

Woodward, B. The final days   973.924

Politics and government—1974-1989

D'Souza, D. Ronald Reagan   92

FitzGerald, F. Way out there in the blue   973.927

Johnson, H. B. Sleepwalking through history

   973.927

Smith, H. The power game   973.92

Woodward, B. Shadow   973.92

Politics and government—1989-

Bennett, W. J. The death of outrage: Bill Clinton and the assault on American ideals   973.929

Bok, D. C. The trouble with government   306

Conason, J. The hunting of the President   973.929

Drew, E. The corruption of American politics

   364.1

Friedman, T. L. Longitudes and attitudes   973.931

Halberstam, D. War in a time of peace   327.73

Halstead, T. The radical center   320.5

Johnson, H. B. The best of times   973.929

Klein, J. The natural: the misunderstood presidency of Bill Clinton   973.929

O'Reilly, B. The no-spin zone   973.92

Reagan, R. Reagan, in his own hand   973.927

Reich, R. B. Locked in the cabinet   973.929

Schell, J. Writing in time   973.928

Stephanopoulos, G. All too human   973.929

Toobin, J. R. A vast conspiracy   973.929

Will, G. F. With a happy eye but . . . America and the world, 1997-2002   973.929

Will, G. F. The woven figure   973.929

Woodward, B. Shadow   973.92

Politics and government—2001-

Didion, J. Fixed ideas: America since 9.11   320.5

Politics and government—Encyclopedias

Djupe, P. A. Encyclopedia of American religion and politics   322

The Encyclopedia of American political history

   973.03

The Oxford guide to the United States Government

   320.03

Politics and government—Handbooks, manuals, etc.

United States government manual   352.2

Politics and government—Maps

Atlas of American politics, 1960-2000   973.92

Popular culture

See Popular culture—United States

Presidents

See Presidents—United States

Prisons

See Prisons—United States

Public lands

See Public lands—United States

Race relations

Ball, E. Slaves in the family   975.7

Buckley, G. L. American patriots   355

Bushart, H. L. Soldiers of God   322.4

Butterfield, F. All God's children   364.1

Cose, E. Color-blind   305.8

Cose, E. The envy of the world   305.8

Du Bois, W. E. B. The Oxford W. E. B. Du Bois reader   305.8

Dyson, M. E. Race rules   305.8

The Eyes on the prize civil rights reader   323.1

Ezekiel, R. S. The racist mind   322.4

Fairclough, A. Better day coming   323.1

Gates, H. L. The future of the race   305.8

Graham, L. O. Our kind of people   305.8

Guinier, L. The miner's canary   323.1

Halberstam, D. The children   323.1

Kennedy, R. Nigger   305.8

King, M. L. The papers of Martin Luther King, Jr.

   323.1

King, M. L. A testament of hope   323.1

Lasch-Quinn, E. Race experts   305.8

Loury, G. C. The anatomy of racial inequality

   305.8

Oshinsky, D. M. "Worse than slavery"   365

Reporting civil rights   323.1

Rodriguez, R. Brown: the last discovery of America

   305.8

Takaki, R. T. Double victory   940.53

Tatum, B. D. "Why are all the Black kids sitting together in the cafeteria?" and other conversations about race   305.8

Terkel, S. Race   305.8

Tygiel, J. Baseball's great experiment   796.357

Voices in our blood   323.1

West, C. Race matters   305.8

When race becomes real   305.8

Wickett, M. R. Contested territory   976.6

Wiencek, H. The Hairstons   975

Wilkins, R. W. Jefferson's pillow   973

Williams, J. Eyes on the prize: America's civil rights years, 1954-1965   323.1

Wynter, L. E. American skin   305.8

See/See also pages in the following book(s):

Delany, S. Having our say   92

Lees, G. You can't steal a gift   920

Religion

See also United States—Church history

Balmer, R. H. Religion in twentieth century America

   200.9

Bourne, R. Gods of war, gods of peace   200.9

Butler, J. Religion in American life   200.9

Corrigan, J. Religion in America   200.9

Gaustad, E. S. New historical atlas of religion in America   200.9

Gooch, B. Godtalk: travels in spiritual America

   200.9

Hahn, K. In search of grace   200.9

Jenkins, P. Mystics and messiahs   200.9

Lewis, J. R. Cults in America   291.9

Marty, M. E. Pilgrims in their own land   277.3

Mead, F. S. Handbook of denominations in the United States   280

Melton, J. G. American religions   200.9

Melton, J. G. The encyclopedia of American religions

   200.9

United States—Religion—*Continued*
Melton, J. G. Encyclopedic handbook of cults in
America | **291.9**
Moore, R. L. Selling God | **200.9**
Wuthnow, R. After heaven | **200.9**
See/See also pages in the following book(s):
Hall, T. L. American religious leaders | **920.003**
Tillich, P. Theology of culture | **230**
Religion—Encyclopedias
Contemporary American religion | **200.9**
Djupe, P. A. Encyclopedia of American religion and
politics | **322**
Encyclopedia of African American religions | **200.9**
The encyclopedia of cults, sects, and new religions | **200.3**
Queen, E. L. The encyclopedia of American religious
history | **200.9**
Rural conditions—Encyclopedias
Encyclopedia of rural America | **973.03**
Social conditions
Allen, F. L. Only yesterday | **973.91**
Allen, F. L. Since yesterday | **973.91**
Anderson, T. H. The movement and the sixties | **303.4**
Appleby, J. O. Inheriting the revolution | **973**
Boorstin, D. J. The Americans: The democratic experi-
ence | **973**
Bork, R. H. Slouching towards Gomorrah | **306**
Bowden, C. Blues for cannibals | **973.92**
Cohen, L. A consumer's republic | **339.4**
The Columbia guide to America in the 1960s | **973.92**
Cose, E. The envy of the world | **305.8**
Foner, E. Tom Paine and Revolutionary America | **973.3**
Gitlin, T. The sixties | **973.92**
Gregory, R. Cold War America, 1946 to 1990 | **973.92**
Himmelfarb, G. The de-moralization of society | **303.3**
Lasch, C. The revolt of the elites | **306**
Leebaert, D. The fifty-year wound | **973.92**
O'Reilly, B. The no-spin zone | **973.92**
Rather, D. The American dream | **973.92**
Sheehy, G. New passages | **305.24**
A Statistical portrait of the United States | **317.3**
Terkel, S. American dreams | **973.9**
Terkel, S. Hard times | **973.91**
Terkel, S. Working | **331.2**
Tocqueville, A. de. Democracy in America | **973.5**
Tuchman, B. W. The proud tower | **909.82**
West, C. Restoring hope | **305.8**
Wilson, J. Q. The marriage problem | **306.8**
See/See also pages in the following book(s):
Sontag, S. Styles of radical will p193-204 | **814**
Social conditions—Encyclopedias
Encyclopedia of American social history | **973.03**
Encyclopedia of social issues | **306**
Social life and customs
Bryson, B. I'm a stranger here myself | **973.92**
Halberstam, D. The fifties | **973.92**
Hawke, D. F. Everyday life in early America | **973.2**
Kuralt, C. Charles Kuralt's America | **973.92**
Kuralt, C. Charles Kuralt's American moments | **973.92**
Kuralt, C. On the road with Charles Kuralt | **973.92**
Marling, K. A. As seen on TV | **973.92**
Marling, K. A. Merry Christmas! | **394.26**
Rather, D. The American dream | **973.92**
Schlereth, T. J. Victorian America | **973.8**
Ulrich, L. The age of homespun | **974**
Wood, G. S. The radicalism of the American Revolu-
tion | **973.3**

Social life and customs—1600-1775, Colonial period
De Marly, D. Dress in North America v1 | **391**
Earle, A. M. Child life in colonial days | **973.2**
Social life and customs—Encyclopedias
Encyclopedia of American social history | **973.03**
Social policy
See Social policy—United States
Soldiers
See Soldiers—United States
State governments
See State governments
Statistics
Counties USA | **352.13**
County and city data book | **317.3**
CQ's state fact finder | **317.3**
Encyclopaedia Britannica almanac | **031.02**
The New York Times almanac | **031.02**
A Statistical portrait of the United States | **317.3**
The Time almanac | **031.02**
United States. Bureau of the Census. Statistical abstract
of the United States | **317.3**
The World almanac and book of facts | **031.02**
Territorial expansion
Linklater, A. Measuring America | **973**
Travel
See United States—Description
Vice-presidents
See Vice-presidents—United States
United States. Air Force
Boyne, W. J. Beyond the wild blue | **358.4**
United States. Army
Ambrose, S. E. The victors | **940.54**
Eisenhower, J. S. D. Yanks: the epic story of the
American Army in World War I | **940.4**
See/See also pages in the following book(s):
Leonard, E. D. All the daring of the soldier | **973.7**
Military life
Wiley, B. I. The life of Billy Yank | **973.7**
United States. Army. Delta Force
Haney, E. L. Inside Delta Force | **356**
United States. Army. Infantry
Kindsvatter, P. S. American soldiers | **355**
**United States. Army. Parachute Infantry Regiment,
506th. Company E**
Ambrose, S. E. Band of brothers | **940.54**
United States. Army. Ranger Battalion, 6th
Sides, H. Ghost soldiers | **940.54**
United States. Army. Special Forces
McKinney, M. Chariots of the damned | **356**
United States. Army. Task Force Ranger
See/See also pages in the following book(s):
Bowden, M. Black Hawk down | **967.73**
United States. Army Air Forces
Nelson, C. The first heroes | **940.54**
Sandler, S. Segregated skies | **940.54**
See/See also pages in the following book(s):
Doolittle, J. H. I could never be so lucky again | **92**
United States. Bureau of Labor Statistics
Occupational outlook handbook | **331.7**
United States. Bureau of the Census
Statistical abstract of the United States | **317.3**
United States. Central Intelligence Agency
Grose, P. Gentleman spy: the life of Allen Dulles | **92**
Gup, T. Book of honor | **327.12**
Helms, R. A look over my shoulder | **92**
Kessler, R. Inside the CIA | **327.12**
Maas, P. Manhunt | **364.1**
Prados, J. Lost crusader: the secret wars of CIA direc-
tor William Colby | **92**
Prados, J. Presidents' secret wars | **327.12**

United States. Central Intelligence Agency—*Continued*
See/See also pages in the following book(s):
Miller, J. The cell: inside the 9/11 plot and why the
FBI and CIA failed to stop it   **973.931**
**United States. Central Intelligence Agency. Director-
ate of Science and Technology**
Richelson, J. The wizards of Langley   **327.12**
United States. Congress
Barone, M. The almanac of American politics
                                          328.73
Biographical directory of the American Congress,
1774-1996   **328.73**
Congress A to Z   **328.73**
Congress and the Nation   **328.73**
CQ almanac plus   **328.73**
CQ's politics in America   **328.73**
Guide to Congress   **328.73**
Miller, W. L. Arguing about slavery   **973.5**
Official Congressional directory   **328.73**
United States. Congress. Official Congressional direc-
tory   **328.73**
Will, G. F. Restoration   **328.73**
United States. Congress. Senate
Glenn, J. John Glenn   **92**
United States. Constitution
The Constitution of the United States of America
                                          342
The Federalist   **342**
United States. Constitutional Convention (1787)
Berkin, C. A brilliant solution   **342**
United States. Declaration of Independence
Becker, C. The Declaration of Independence
                                          973.3
Maier, P. American scripture   **973.3**
**United States. Dept. of Commerce. Bureau of the
Census** *See* United States. Bureau of the Census
United States. Dept. of Defense
Woodward, B. The commanders   **973.928**
**United States. Dept. of Justice. Federal Bureau of In-
vestigation** *See* United States. Federal Bureau of In-
vestigation
United States. Dept. of Labor
Reich, R. B. Locked in the cabinet   **973.929**
**United States. Dept. of Labor. Bureau of Labor Sta-
tistics** *See* United States. Bureau of Labor Statistics
United States. Federal Bureau of Investigation
The FBI: a comprehensive reference guide **363.2**
From the secret files of J. Edgar Hoover **363.2**
Gentry, C. J. Edgar Hoover   **92**
Kessler, R. The FBI   **363.2**
Theoharis, A. G. Chasing spies   **327.12**
Vise, D. A. The bureau and the mole   **327.12**
Whitcomb, C. Cold zero   **363.2**
Wise, D. Cassidy's run   **327.12**
Wise, D. Spy: the inside story of how the FBI's Robert
Hanssen betrayed America   **327.12**
See/See also pages in the following book(s):
Carson, C. Malcolm X: the FBI file   **92**
Miller, J. The cell: inside the 9/11 plot and why the
FBI and CIA failed to stop it   **973.931**
United States. Federal Reserve Board *See* Federal Re-
serve System (U.S.). Board of Governors
**United States. Federal Security Agency. Social Securi-
ty Administration** *See* United States. Social Security
Administration
United States. Government Printing Office
Style manual   **808**
United States. Library of Congress *See* Library of
Congress
United States. Marine Corps
Bradley, J. Flags of our fathers   **940.54**
Kindsvatter, P. S. American soldiers   **355**
Swofford, A. Jarhead: a Marine's chronicle of the Gulf
War and other battles   **956.7**

**United States. Military Assistance Command, Viet-
nam. Studies and Observations Group**
Shultz, R. H. The secret war against Hanoi
                                          959.704
**United States. National Advisory Committee for Aero-
nautics**
Gorn, M. H. Expanding the envelope   **629.13**
**United States. National Aeronautics and Space Ad-
ministration**
Gorn, M. H. Expanding the envelope   **629.13**
Kranz, E. F. Failure is not an option   **629.45**
Space exploration   **629**
United States. National Air and Space Museum *See*
National Air and Space Museum (U.S.)
**United States. National Archives and Records Admin-
istration**
Bustard, B. I. Picturing the century   **779**
United States. National Endowment for the Arts *See*
National Endowment for the Arts
United States. National Gallery of Art *See* National
Gallery of Art (U.S.)
United States. Navy
Knott, R. C. A heritage of wings   **359.9**
Love, R. W. History of the U.S. Navy   **359**
United States. Navy. Sea Air Land Team
Couch, D. The warrior elite   **359.9**
United States. Navy. SEALs *See* United States. Navy.
Sea Air Land Team
United States. President's Council on Bioethics
Human cloning and human dignity. See Human
cloning and human dignity   **174**
United States. Social Security Administration
Social Security handbook. See Social Security hand-
book   **368.4**
United States. Special Operations Command
Clancy, T. Special forces   **356**
United States. Superintendent of Documents
See also United States. Government Printing Office
United States. Supreme Court
Finkelman, P. Landmark decisions of the United States
Supreme Court   **347**
Garbus, M. Courting disaster   **347**
Hall, T. L. Supreme Court justices   **920.003**
Irons, P. H. A people's history of the Supreme Court
                                          347
Lewis, A. Gideon's trumpet   **347**
Lively, D. E. Landmark Supreme Court cases
                                          342
Noonan, J. T., Jr. Narrowing the nation's power: the
Supreme Court sides with the states   **342**
O'Brien, D. M. Storm center   **347**
O'Connor, S. D. The majesty of the law   **347**
The Oxford companion to the Supreme Court of the
United States   **347**
The Oxford guide to United States Supreme Court de-
cisions   **342**
Rowan, C. T. Dream makers, dream breakers: the
world of Justice Thurgood Marshall   **92**
Simon, J. F. What kind of nation   **342**
The Supreme Court A to Z   **347**
The Supreme Court compendium   **347**
The Supreme Court justices: a biographical dictionary
                                          920.003
Williams, J. Thurgood Marshall   **92**
See/See also pages in the following book(s):
Ball, H. A defiant life: Thurgood Marshall and the per-
sistence of racism in America   **92**
Smith, J. E. John Marshall   **92**
United States. Women Airforce Service Pilots *See*
Women Airforce Service Pilots (U.S.)
**United States. Work Projects Administration. Writ-
ers' Program** *See* Writers' Program
United States Chess Federation
U.S. Chess Federation's official rules of chess
                                          794.1

United States—essays, 1952-1992. Vidal, G.   **814**
United States government manual   **352.2**
United States Holocaust Memorial Museum
  Berenbaum, M. The world must know   **940.53**
  The Holocaust and history. See The Holocaust and history   **940.53**
  Linenthal, E. T. Preserving memory   **940.53**
The **United** States in the First World War   **940.3**
United States Military Academy
  Ruggero, E. Duty first   **355**
United States National Archives and Records Service
  See also United States. National Archives and Records Administration
United States Pharmacopeia drug information for the consumer. See Consumer drug reference   **615**
The **universal** history of computing. Ifrah, G.   **004**
Universe
  See also Cosmology; Philosophy of nature
  Croswell, K. The alchemy of the heavens   **523.1**
  Goodstein, D. L. Feynman's lost lecture   **521**
  Gribbin, J. R. Stardust   **523**
  Krauss, L. M. Atom   **523.1**
  Lederman, L. M. The God particle   **539.7**
  Teilhard de Chardin, P. The phenomenon of man   **113**
  The Universe revealed   **523**
  Voit, M. Hubble space telescope   **520**
  Whitehead, A. N. Process and reality   **113**
The **universe** and the teacup. Cole, K. C.   **510**
The **universe** at midnight. Croswell, K.   **523.1**
The **universe** below. Broad, W.   **551.46**
Universe down to Earth. Tyson, N. D. G.   **523.1**
The **universe** in a nutshell. Hawking, S. W.   **530.1**
The **universe** next door. Chown, M.   **523.1**
The **Universe** revealed   **523**
The **universe**, the gods, and men. Vernant, J. P.   **292**
Universities See Colleges and universities
University libraries See Academic libraries
The **University** of Chicago Spanish dictionary   **463**
The **unknown** Matisse v1. Spurling, H.   **92**
Unmarried fathers
  See also Single parent family
Unmarried mothers
  See also Single parent family
The **unquiet** ghost. Hochschild, A.   **947.084**
Unraveling the mystery of autism and pervasive developmental disorder. Seroussi, K.   **618.92**
The **unredeemed** captive. Demos, J.   **973.2**
The **unruly** life of Woody Allen. Meade, M.   **92**
The **unruly** queen: the life of Queen Caroline. Fraser, F.   **92**
Unsafe at any meal. See Mindell, E. Dr. Earl Mindell's unsafe at any meal   **613.2**
Unsettling America   **811.008**
Unsinkable: the full story of the RMS Titanic. Butler, D. A.   **910.4**
Unsolved mysteries of history. Aron, P.   **902**
Unspeakable acts, ordinary people. Conroy, J.   **323.4**
The **unswept** room. Olds, S.   **811**
Unweaving the rainbow. Dawkins, R.   **501**
Up close and personal (Motion picture)
  Dunne, J. G. Monster   **791.43**
Up from slavery. Washington, B. T.   **92**
Updike, John
  Americana and other poems   **811**
  Collected poems, 1953-1993   **811**
  Hugging the shore   **818**
  More matter   **814**
  (ed) Shapiro, K. J. Selected poems   **811**
  About
  Pritchard, W. H. Updike   **813.009**
  See/See also pages in the following book(s):
  Amis, M. The war against cliché   **824**

Upgrading and repairing PCs. Mueller, S.   **621.39**
Upgren, Arthur R.
  The turtle and the stars   **520**
The **uprooted**. Handlin, O.   **325.73**
Upstate. Wilson, E.   **818**
Urban, Mark, 1961-
  The man who broke Napoleon's codes   **940.2**
Urban areas See Cities and towns
Urban development See Urbanization
Urban life See City and town life
Urban planning See City planning
Urban renewal
  Duany, A. Suburban nation   **307.7**
Urban sanctuaries. Anderton, S.   **635.9**
Urban sociology
  See also Urbanization
  Kunstler, J. H. The city in mind   **307.7**
  Encyclopedias
  Encyclopedia of urban cultures   **307.7**
Urbanization
  Duany, A. Suburban nation   **307.7**
An **urchin** in the storm. Gould, S. J.   **570**
Urdang, Laurence
  Twentieth century American nicknames. See Twentieth century American nicknames   **929.4**
  (ed) The Timetables of American history. See The Timetables of American history   **902**
Urinary incontinence
  Dierich, M. Overcoming incontinence   **616.6**
Urofsky, Melvin I.
  (jt. auth) Finkelman, P. Landmark decisions of the United States Supreme Court   **347**
  (ed) The Supreme Court justices: a biographical dictionary. See The Supreme Court justices: a biographical dictionary   **920.003**
Urquhart, Rachel
  (jt. auth) Gross, K. J. Woman's face   **646.7**
Ury, William
  Getting past no   **158**
USA today (Newspaper) Williams, J. The weather book   **551.6**
Usability testing for library websites. Norlin, E.   **025.04**
USAF See United States. Air Force
The **use** and abuse of art. Barzun, J.   **701**
Use of time See Time management
A **user's** guide to the brain. Ratey, J. J.   **612.8**
Using the Internet as a reference tool. Sauers, M.   **025.04**
USMA See United States Military Academy
Utah
  Description
  Williams, T. T. Red: passion and patience in the desert   **333.7**
  Natural history
  See Natural history—Utah
Ute Indians
  See/See also pages in the following book(s):
  Brown, D. A. Bury my heart at Wounded Knee   **970.004**
Utensils, Kitchen See Kitchen utensils
Utilitarianism
  See also Secularism
Utley, Robert Marshall, 1929-
  Billy the Kid   **92**
  Custer: cavalier in buckskin   **973.8**
  The lance and the shield: the life and times of Sitting Bull   **92**
Utopias
  More, Sir T., Saint. Utopia   **321**
  Mumford, L. The story of utopias   **321**
  Plato. The republic   **888**
  See/See also pages in the following book(s):
  Heilbroner, R. L. The worldly philosophers   **330.1**

Utter, Glenn H.
Encyclopedia of gun control and gun rights   363.3
The religious right   277.3

V

V.D. *See* Sexually transmitted diseases
Vacation homes
Colt, G. H. The big house   920
Vaccination
See/See also pages in the following book(s):
Friedman, M. Medicine's 10 greatest discoveries   610.9
Vaill, Amanda
Everybody was so young: Gerald and Sara Murphy, a lost generation love story   92
Vaillancourt, Renée J.
Bare bones young adult services   027.62
Vaillant, George E.
Aging well   305.26
Valade, Roger M., III
(ed) The Schomburg Center guide to black literature from the eighteenth century to the present. See The Schomburg Center guide to black literature from the eighteenth century to the present   809
Valentina, 1904-1989
See/See also pages in the following book(s):
Fraser, K. Ornament and silence   814
Valentine, Amie
(jt. auth) Kashuk, S. Real beauty   646.7
Valentine, Debbie
(jt. auth) Betzina, S. Sandra Betzina sews for your home   646.2
Valentino, Rudolph, 1895-1926
About
Leider, E. W. Dark lover: the life and death of Rudolph Valentino   92
Valéry, Paul, 1871-1945
Selected writings   848
Valestuk, Lorraine, 1963-
(jt. auth) Moss, J. Latin American literature and its times   860.9
Valley of the golden mummies. Hawass, Z.   932
Valley song. Fugard, A.   822
Vallier, Tracy L., 1936-
(ed) Interdisciplinary encyclopedia of marine sciences. See Interdisciplinary encyclopedia of marine sciences   551
Vallone, Lynne
Becoming Victoria   92
The **value** of family. Westheimer, R.   306.8
Values
See also Social values
Wolfe, A. Moral freedom   170
Values of the game. Bradley, B.   796.323
The **vampire** book. Melton, J. G.   398
The **vampire** encyclopedia. Bunson, M.   398
Vampires
Melton, J. G. The vampire book   398
Encyclopedias
Bunson, M. The vampire encyclopedia   398
Van Allsburg, Chris
See/See also pages in the following book(s):
The Newbery & Caldecott medal books, 1986-2000 p25-34   028.5
Van der Meer, Jan *See* Vermeer, Johannes, 1632-1675
Van der Plas, Rob *See* Plas, Rob van der, 1938-
Van der Stroom, Gerrold *See* Stroom, Gerrold van der
Van der Vat, Dan
The good Nazi: the life and lies of Albert Speer   92
Van Doren, Charles Lincoln, 1926-
(jt. auth) Adler, M. J. How to read a book   028

(ed) Great treasury of Western thought. See Great treasury of Western thought   080
Van Doren, Mark, 1894-1972
(ed) Wordsworth, W. Selected poetry of William Wordsworth   821
Van Dulken, Stephen, 1952-
Inventing the 19th century   609
Inventing the 20th century   609
Van Duyn, Mona
Selected poems   811
Van Gogh, Vincent *See* Gogh, Vincent van, 1853-1890
Van Gogh and Gauguin. Druick, D. W.   92
Van Gogh and Gauguin. Silverman, D.   759.4
Van Nostrand's concise encyclopedia of science   503
Van Nostrand's scientific encyclopedia   503
Van Pelt, Robert Jan
(jt. auth) Dwork, D. Holocaust: a history   940.53
Van Susteren, Greta, 1954-
My turn at the bully pulpit   349
Van Sweden, James A.
Architecture in the garden   712
Van Vechten, Carl, 1880-1964
(jt. auth) Hughes, L. Remember me to Harlem: the letters of Langston Hughes and Carl Van Vechten, 1925-1964   92
Van Wicklen, Janet
The tech writer's survival guide   808
Vanbrugh, Sir John, 1664-1726
The relapse
In Restoration plays   822.008
Vance, Jeffrey, 1970-
(jt. auth) Keaton, E. Buster Keaton remembered   791.43
VanDeMark, Brian, 1960-
(jt. auth) McNamara, R. S. In retrospect   959.704
Vanderbilt, Amy
Tuckerman, N. The Amy Vanderbilt complete book of etiquette   395
Vanderbilt, Cornelius, 1873-1942
See/See also pages in the following book(s):
Klein, M. The change makers   920
Vanderbilt, Gertrude Whitney *See* Whitney, Gertrude Vanderbilt
Vanderhoof-Forschner, Karen
Everything you need to know about Lyme disease and other tick-borne disorders   616.9
VanderKam, James C.
(ed) The Encyclopedia of the Dead Sea scrolls. See The Encyclopedia of the Dead Sea scrolls   296.1
The **vanishing** American Jew. Dershowitz, A. M.   305.8
Vanishing histories. Amery, C.   363.6
The **vanishing** hitchhiker. Brunvand, J. H.   398.2
Vanishing species *See* Endangered species
Vanity Fair's Hollywood   791.43
Vann, John Paul
About
Sheehan, N. A bright shining lie: John Paul Vann and America in Vietnam   959.704
Vardon, Harry, 1870-1937
About
Frost, M. The greatest game ever played   796.352
Vargas Llosa, Mario, 1936-
The language of passion   864
Letters to a young novelist   808.3
The **varieties** of religious experience. James, W.   210
The **variety** of life. Tudge, C.   578
Vassiliev, Alexander
(jt. auth) Weinstein, A. The haunted wood   327.12
A **vast** conspiracy. Toobin, J. R.   973.929

Vatican. Cappella Sistina
  King, R. Michelangelo & the Pope's ceiling
      759.5
Vatican City
  Reese, T. J. Inside the Vatican   **282**
Vaughan, Christopher
  (jt. auth) Dement, W. C. The promise of sleep
      612.8
Vaughan, J. G. (John Griffith)
  The new Oxford book of food plants   **633**
Vaughan, John Griffith *See* Vaughan, J. G. (John Griffith)
Vaughan, William, 1943-
  Encyclopedia of artists. See Encyclopedia of artists
      920.003
Vázquez de Coronado, Francisco, 1510-1549
  See/See also pages in the following book(s):
  Connell, E. S. The Aztec treasure house p373-92
      814
VCR troubleshooting & repair. Capelo, G. R.
      621.388
VD *See* Sexually transmitted diseases
Veblen, Thorstein, 1857-1929
  The theory of the leisure class   **305.5**
  See/See also pages in the following book(s):
  Commager, H. S. The American mind   **973**
  Heilbroner, R. L. The worldly philosophers   **330.1**
Vecsey, George
  (jt. auth) Lynn, L. Loretta Lynn: coal miner's daughter
      92
  (jt. auth) Wu, H. Troublemaker   **951.05**
The **vegetable** gardener's bible. Smith, E. C.   **635**
Vegetable gardening
  Gertley, J. The art of the kitchen garden   **712**
  Morash, M. The victory garden cookbook   **641.6**
  Silber, M. Growing herbs and vegetables   **635**
  Smith, E. C. The vegetable gardener's bible   **635**
  Taylor's guide to vegetables & herbs   **635.9**
Vegetables
  See also Cooking—Vegetables; names of vegetables
  Beling, S. Powerfoods   **613.2**
  Schneider, E. Vegetables from amaranth to zucchini
      641.6
Vegetables. Peterson, J.   **641.6**
Vegetables from amaranth to zucchini. Schneider, E.
      641.6
The **vegetarian** bible. Brown, S.   **641.5**
Vegetarian cooking
  Berley, P. The modern vegetarian kitchen   **641.5**
  Bishop, J. The complete Italian vegetarian cookbook
      641.5
  Brill, S. The wild vegetarian cookbook   **641.5**
  Brown, S. The vegetarian bible   **641.5**
  Cox, P. You don't need meat   **613.2**
  Jaffrey, M. Madhur Jaffrey's world vegetarian
      641.5
  Lemlin, J. Main-course vegetarian pleasures   **641.5**
  Madison, D. The Greens cook book   **641.5**
  Madison, D. Vegetarian cooking for everyone
      641.5
  Sass, L. J. Great vegetarian cooking under pressure
      641.5
  Shaw, D. The essential vegetarian cookbook
      641.5
  Somerville, A. Fields of Greens   **641.5**
  Wenner, P. F. Garden cuisine   **613.2**
Vegetarian cooking for everyone. Madison, D.
      641.5
Vegetarian Times vegetarian beginner's guide
      613.2
Vegetarianism
  Cox, P. You don't need meat   **613.2**
  Spencer, C. Vegetarianism   **613.2**

Vegetarian Times vegetarian beginner's guide
      613.2
Veiled courage. Benard, C.   **958.1**
Velasco, Luis Alejandro, d. 2000
  About
  García Márquez, G. The story of a shipwrecked sailor
      910.4
Velázquez, Diego, 1599-1660
  About
  Brown, J. Velázquez, painter and courtier   **92**
Velie, Alan R., 1937-
  (ed) American Indian literature. See American Indian literature   **897**
Velikovsky, Immanuel, 1895-1979
  See/See also pages in the following book(s):
  Sagan, C. Broca's brain p84-127, 320-27   **500**
Veloso, Caetano, 1942-
  Tropical truth   **781.64**
Vender, Ronald
  (jt. auth) Zonderman, J. Understanding Crohn disease and ulcerative colitis   **616.3**
Vendler, Helen Hennessy
  The art of Shakespeare's sonnets   **822.3**
  Coming of age as a poet   **820.9**
  Seamus Heaney   **821**
  (ed) The Harvard book of contemporary American poetry. See The Harvard book of contemporary American poetry   **811.008**
Venereal diseases *See* Sexually transmitted diseases
Venice (Italy)
  History
  Norwich, J. J. A history of Venice   **945**
  Wills, G. Venice: lion city   **945**
Venice preserved. Otway, T.
  In Restoration plays   **822.008**
Venona. Haynes, J. E.   **327.12**
Venter, Craig *See* Venter, J. Craig
Venter, J. Craig
  See/See also pages in the following book(s):
  Davies, K. Cracking the genome   **599.93**
The **venture** cafe. Esser, T.   **620**
Venus (Planet)
  Grinspoon, D. H. Venus revealed   **523.4**
Venus envy. Wertheim, L. J.   **796.342**
Venus in exile. Steiner, W.   **700**
Venus revealed. Grinspoon, D. H.   **523.4**
Venzon, Anne Cipriano, 1951-
  (ed) The United States in the First World War. See The United States in the First World War
      940.3
Verdi, Giuseppe, 1813-1901
  About
  Berger, W. Verdi with a vengeance   **92**
Verdi with a vengeance. Berger, W.   **92**
Verdict. Christie, A.
  In Christie, A. The mousetrap and other plays
      822
Vergil *See* Virgil
Verlaine, Paul, 1844-1896
  Selected poems   **841**
Vermeer, Johannes, 1632-1675
  About
  Bailey, A. Vermeer   **92**
  Liedtke, W. A. Vermeer and the Delft school
      759.9492
  See/See also pages in the following book(s):
  Fraser, K. Ornament and silence   **814**
Vermeer and the Delft school. Liedtke, W. A.
      759.9492
Vermeer van Delft, Jan *See* Vermeer, Johannes, 1632-1675
Vermès, Géza, 1924-
  The changing faces of Jesus   **232**
  (ed) Dead Sea scrolls. The complete Dead Sea scrolls in English   **296.1**

Vernant, Jean Pierre
The universe, the gods, and men   292
Verner, Miroslav
The pyramids   932
Vernon Early. Foote, H.
In Foote, H. Getting Frankie married—and afterwards, and other plays   812
The **Versailles** impromptu. Molière
In Molière. Tartuffe, and other plays   842
Verses of the poets Laureate   821.008
Vertigo (Motion picture)
Auiler, D. Vertigo   791.43
Vertosick, Frank T.
Why we hurt   616
The **very** best baby name book in the whole wide world. Lansky, B.   929.4
A **very** different age. Diner, S. J.   973.8
Vesalius, Andreas, 1514-1564
See/See also pages in the following book(s):
Friedman, M. Medicine's 10 greatest discoveries   610.9
Vespasian, Emperor of Rome, 9-79
See/See also pages in the following book(s):
Suetonius Tranquillus, C. The twelve Caesars   878
Vespasianus, Titus Flavius Sabinus *See* Titus, Emperor of Rome, 40-81
Veterans
Matsakis, A. Vietnam wives   616.85
Veterinary medicine
Goldstein, M. The nature of animal healing   636.089
Herriot, J. All creatures great and small   92
Herriot, J. James Herriot's animal stories   636.089
Pinney, C. C. The complete home veterinary guide   636.089
Schoen, A. M. Kindred spirits   636.089
Tufts University. School of Veterinary Medicine. Animal ER   636.089
Dictionaries
Black's veterinary dictionary   636.089
Handbooks, manuals, etc.
The Merck veterinary manual   636.089
VGM's careers encyclopedia   331.7
The **Vibe** history of hip hop   782.42
Vice-presidents
United States
Waldrup, C. C. The vice presidents   920.003
Victoria, Queen of Great Britain, 1819-1901
About
Erickson, C. Her little majesty: the life of Queen Victoria   92
Hibbert, C. Queen Victoria   92
Strachey, L. Queen Victoria   92
Vallone, L. Becoming Victoria   92
Victoria and Albert Museum
Exhibitions
A Grand design   708
Victorian America. Schlereth, T. J.   973.8
Victorian prose and poetry
In The Oxford anthology of English literature v2   820.8
The **Victorians**. Cruttenden, Aidan
In Backgrounds to English literature v3   820.9
Victoroff, Jeffrey Ivan
Saving your brain   612.8
The **victors**. Ambrose, S. E.   940.54
Victory at sea. Dunnigan, J. F.   940.54
The **victory** garden cookbook. Morash, M.   641.6
Victory on Mrs. Dandywine's island. Wilson, L.
In Wilson, L. 21 short plays p105-17   812
Vidal, Gore, 1925-
The last empire   814
United States—essays, 1952-1992   814
About
Kaplan, F. Gore Vidal   92

Videodiscs, Digital *See* Digital videodiscs
Videotape recorders and recording
Maintenance and repair
See Home video systems—Maintenance and repair
Videotapes
Ebert, R. Roger Ebert's movie yearbook   791.43
Maltin, L. Leonard Maltin's movie and video guide   791.43
Wiener, T. The off-Hollywood film guide   791.43
Vietnam
Description
Sachs, D. The house on Dream Street   959.7
See/See also pages in the following book(s):
Jensen, C. I have seen the world begin   915
Foreign relations—United States
Halberstam, D. The best and the brightest   973.922
History
Karnow, S. Vietnam   959.704
Politics and government
FitzGerald, F. Fire in the lake   959.704
Mann, R. A grand delusion   959.704
See/See also pages in the following book(s):
Langguth, A. J. Our Vietnam   959.704
Vietnam. Burrows, L.   959.704
Vietnam shadows. Isaacs, A. R.   959.704
Vietnam, the necessary war. Lind, M.   959.704
Vietnam Veterans Memorial (Washington, D.C.)
See/See also pages in the following book(s):
Lin, M. Y. Boundaries   92
Vietnam War, 1961-1975
See also Mỹ Lai Massacre, Vietnam, 1968
The American experience in Vietnam   959.704
Anderson, D. L. The Columbia guide to the Vietnam War   959.704
Berman, L. No peace, no honor   959.704
Ellsberg, D. Secrets: a memoir of Vietnam and the Pentagon papers   959.704
FitzGerald, F. Fire in the lake   959.704
Goldstein, D. M. The Vietnam war: the story and photographs   959.704
Hendrickson, P. The living and the dead   959.704
Isaacs, A. R. Vietnam shadows   959.704
Kaiser, D. E. American tragedy   959.704
Karnow, S. Vietnam   959.704
Langguth, A. J. Our Vietnam   959.704
Lind, M. Vietnam, the necessary war   959.704
Mann, R. A grand delusion   959.704
Matsakis, A. Vietnam wives   616.85
McCloud, B. What should we tell our children about Vietnam?   959.704
McNamara, R. S. In retrospect   959.704
Philpott, T. Glory denied   92
Reporting Vietnam   959.704
Sheehan, N. A bright shining lie: John Paul Vann and America in Vietnam   959.704
Summers, H. G. Vietnam War almanac   959.704
The Vietnam War   959.704
See/See also pages in the following book(s):
Freedman, L. Kennedy's wars   973.922
Kissinger, H. Diplomacy p620-702   327.73
Sontag, S. Styles of radical will p205-74   814
Tuchman, B. W. The march of folly   909.08
Tuchman, B. W. Practicing history p256-66   907
Aerial operations
Sherwood, J. D. Fast movers   959.704
Encyclopedias
Encyclopedia of the Vietnam War   959.704
Journalists
Prochnau, W. W. Once upon a distant war   959.704
Medical care
Glasser, R. J. 365 days   959.704

Vietnam War, 1961-1975—*Continued*
Missing in action
Franklin, H. B. M.I.A.; or, Mythmaking in America
    959.704
Personal narratives
Bloods: an oral history of the Vietnam War by black
  veterans   **959.704**
Caputo, P. A rumor of war   **959.704**
Glasser, R. J. 365 days   **959.704**
Moore, H. G. We were soldiers once—and young
    959.704
Puller, L. B. Fortunate son   **92**
Pictorial works
Burrows, L. Vietnam   **959.704**
Secret service
Shultz, R. H. The secret war against Hanoi
    959.704
The **Vietnam** War   **959.704**
Vietnam War almanac. Summers, H. G.   **959.704**
The **Vietnam** war: the story and photographs. Goldstein,
  D. M.   **959.704**
Vietnam wives. Matsakis, A.   **616.85**
Vietnamese-English dictionary, NTC's. Nguyen, D. H.
    495.9
Vietnamese-English vocabulary. See Nguyen, D. H.
  NTC's Vietnamese-English dictionary   **495.9**
Vietnamese language
Dictionaries
Nguyen, D. H. NTC's Vietnamese-English dictionary
    495.9
The **view** from Alger's window. Hiss, T.   **92**
A **view** from the bridge. Miller, A.   **812**
A **view** of Delft: Vermeer than and now. See Bailey, A.
  Vermeer   **92**
View with a grain of sand. Szymborska, W.   **891.8**
The **vigil**. Williams, C. K.   **811**
Vigué, Jordi
  Great women masters of art   **920.003**
The **Viking** opera guide. See The New Penguin opera
  guide   **792.5**
Vikings
  The Oxford illustrated history of the Vikings   **948**
  Roesdahl, E. The Vikings   **948**
  Vikings: the North Atlantic saga   **970.01**
  See/See also pages in the following book(s):
  Connell, E. S. The Aztec treasure house p58-82
    814
Vikings: the North Atlantic saga   **970.01**
Vila, Bob
  Bob Vila's complete guide to remodeling your home
    643
Vile, John R.
  Encyclopedia of constitutional amendments, proposed
  amendments, and amending issues, 1789-2002
    342
Villa, Pancho, 1878-1923
About
Katz, F. The life and times of Pancho Villa   **92**
Villarosa, Linda
  (jt. auth) Beal, A. C. The black parenting book
    649
Villiers, George *See* Buckingham, George Villiers, 2nd
  Duke of, 1628-1687
Villon, François, b. 1431
  The poems of François Villon   **841**
Vilnius (Lithuania)
  See/See also pages in the following book(s):
  Miłosz, C. To begin where I am p27-51   **891.8**
Vincent, Glyn
  The unknown night: the madness and genius of R. A.
  Blakelock, an American painter   **92**
Vincent, Mary
  Cultural atlas of Spain and Portugal   **946**
Vincent, Peggy, 1942-
  Baby catcher   **618.2**

Vinci, Leonardo da *See* Leonardo, da Vinci, 1452-1519
The **Vintage** book of African American poetry
    811.008
The **Vintage** book of contemporary world poetry
    808.81
The **Vintage** book of Indian writing, 1947-1997. See
  Mirrorwork   **820.8**
Violence
  See also Domestic violence
  Bok, S. Mayhem   **302.23**
  Butterfield, F. All God's children   **364.1**
  Canada, G. Fist, stick, knife, gun   **305.23**
  Jones, G. Killing monsters   **302.23**
  Maalouf, A. In the name of identity   **302.4**
  Rhodes, R. Why they kill   **364.3**
  Sontag, S. Regarding the pain of others   **303.6**
  See/See also pages in the following book(s):
  Pollack, W. S. Real boys p338-63   **305.23**
Encyclopedias
  Violence in America   **303.6**
Violence and compassion. Dalai Lama XIV   **294.3**
Violence in America   **303.6**
Violence on television
  See/See also pages in the following book(s):
  Bok, S. Mayhem   **302.23**
Viorst, Judith
  Imperfect control   **158**
Virga, Vincent
  Eyes of the nation   **973**
Virgil
  The Aeneid of Virgil   **873**
  See/See also pages in the following book(s):
  Hamilton, E. The Roman way   **870.9**
The **virgin** homeowner. Papolos, J.   **643**
Virgin Mary *See* Mary, Blessed Virgin, Saint
The **virgin** queen: Elizabeth I. Hibbert, C.   **92**
Virginia
History
  Milton, G. Big Chief Elizabeth   **975.5**
  Washington, G. Writings   **973.4**
The **Virginia** adventure. Noël Hume, I.   **975.5**
Virginia Woolf A-Z. Hussey, M.   **828**
The **Virginia** Woolf reader. Woolf, V.   **828**
Viroli, Maurizio
  Niccolò's smile: a biography of Machiavelli   **92**
The **virtual** office survival handbook. Bredin, A.
    658
Virtual roots 2.0. Kemp, T. J.   **929**
Virtual war. Ignatieff, M.   **949.7**
Virtue & beauty   **757**
The **virtues** of aging. Carter, J.   **305.26**
Virus hunter. Peters, C. J.   **614.5**
Virus hunting. Gallo, R. C.   **616.97**
Virus-X. Ryan, F.   **614.4**
Viruses
  See also Ebola virus
  Crawford, D. H. The invisible enemy   **616**
  Oldstone, M. B. A. Viruses, plagues, and history
    614.4
  Ryan, F. Virus-X   **614.4**
  See/See also pages in the following book(s):
  Garrett, L. The coming plague   **614.4**
  Peters, C. J. Virus hunter   **614.5**
Viruses, plagues, and history. Oldstone, M. B. A.
    614.4
Viscott, David S., 1938-1996
  Emotional resilience   **158**
Vise, David A.
  The bureau and the mole   **327.12**
Vision
  Hoffman, D. D. Visual intelligence   **152.14**
  Livingstone, M. S. Vision and art   **750.1**
Vision and art. Livingstone, M. S.   **750.1**

Vision disorders
See also Color blindness
Dictionaries
The Encyclopedia of blindness and vision impairment
362.4
Visions & longings. Furlong, M. 248.2
Visions of God. Armstrong, K. 248.2
Visions of jazz. Giddins, G. 781.65
The **visit**. Dürrenmatt, F. 832
also in Dürrenmatt, F. Plays and essays p71-152
838
also in Nine plays of the modern theater p199-292
808.82
Visitation rights (Domestic relations)
Boland, M. L. Your right to child custody, visitation, and support 346.01
Visonà, Monica Blackmun, 1953-
A History of art in Africa. See A History of art in Africa 709.6
Visual arts in the twentieth century. Lucie-Smith, E. 709.04
A **visual** dictionary of architecture. Ching, F. 720.3
Visual intelligence. Hoffman, D. D. 152.14
Vita nuova. Dante Alighieri 851
also in Dante Alighieri. The portable Dante 851
Vital dust. Duve, C. de 570.1
Vital man. Buhner, S. H. 613
Vitamins
See also Dietary supplements
Graedon, J. The people's pharmacy guide to home and herbal remedies 615
Murray, M. T. Encyclopedia of nutritional supplements 613.2
Vitellius, Aulus, Emperor of Rome, 15-69
See/See also pages in the following book(s):
Suetonius Tranquillus, C. The twelve Caesars 878
Vivar, Rodrigo Díaz de *See* Cid, ca. 1043-1099
The **vixen**. Merwin, W. S. 811
Vizenor, Gerald Robert, 1934-
See/See also pages in the following book(s):
Coltelli, L. Winged words: American Indian writers speak 897
Vocabulary
Buckley, W. F. Buckley, the right word 422
Vocal music
The Cambridge companion to singing 782
See/See also pages in the following book(s):
Grout, D. J. A history of Western music 780.9
Vocational guidance
America's fastest growing jobs 331.7
Boldt, L. G. Zen and the art of making a living 331.7
Bolles, R. N. What color is your parachute? 331.7
The Encyclopedia of careers and vocational guidance 331.7
Fisher, A. B. If my career's on the fast track, where do I get a road map? 650.14
Guide for occupational exploration 331.7
Krantz, L. Jobs rated almanac 331.7
Reinhold, B. B. Toxic work 650.1
Richardson, B. G. Career comeback 650.14
United States. Bureau of Labor Statistics. Occupational outlook handbook 331.7
VGM's careers encyclopedia 331.7
Vocations *See* Occupations
Vodou visions. Glassman, S. A. 299
Voeten, Teun
How de body? 966.4
Vogel, Steven, 1940-
Cats' paws and catapults 571.4
Vogelsang, Arthur
(ed) The Body electric. See The Body electric 811.008

Vogue knitting 746.43
Vogue knitting American collection 746.43
Voice
Linklater, K. Freeing the natural voice 808.5
The **voice** at 3:00 a.m. Simic, C. 811
The **voice** of reason; essays in objectivist thought. Rand, A. 191
Voices in our blood 323.1
Voices of multicultural America 815.008
Voigt, Ellen Bryant, 1943-
Shadow of heaven 811
Voit, Mark
Hubble space telescope 520
Volcano cowboys. Thompson, D. 551.2
Volcanoes
Thompson, D. Volcano cowboys 551.2
Winchester, S. Krakatoa: the day the world exploded, August 27, 1883 551.2
Encyclopedias
Ritchie, D. Encyclopedia of earthquakes and volcanoes 551.2
Volkman, Ernest
Science goes to war 623
Volkogonov, Dmitriĭ Antonovich
Lenin 92
Trotsky 92
Volkov, Solomon
St. Petersburg 947
Vollers, Maryanne
Ghosts of Mississippi 364.1
Vollstedt, Maryana
The big book of soups & stews 641.8
Volpe, Ren
The lady mechanic's total car care for the clueless 629.28
Voltaire, 1694-1778
Micromegas
In Voltaire. The portable Voltaire 848
The portable Voltaire 848
Zadig
In Voltaire. The portable Voltaire 848
See/See also pages in the following book(s):
Durant, W. J. The story of philosophy p152-91 109
Gay, P. The Enlightenment: an interpretation 190
Voltaire's coconuts; or, Anglomania in Europe. See Buruma, I. Anglomania 941
Volti, Rudi
The Facts on File encyclopedia of science, technology, and society 503
Von Baeyer, Hans Christian
Maxwell's demon 536
Von Bamford, Lawrence *See* Bamford, Lawrence von, 1937-
Von Bülow, Hans *See* Bülow, Hans von, 1830-1894
Von Clausewitz, Carl *See* Clausewitz, Carl von, 1780-1831
Von Drehle, Dave
Triangle: the fire that changed America 974.7
Von Goethe, Johann Wolfgang *See* Goethe, Johann Wolfgang von, 1749-1832
Von Karajan, Herbert *See* Karajan, Herbert von
Von Linné, Carl *See* Linné, Carl von, 1707-1778
Von Mehren, Joan, 1923-
Minerva and the muse: a life of Margaret Fuller 92
Von Richthofen, Manfred *See* Richthofen, Manfred von, Freiherr, 1892-1918
Von Tirpitz, Alfred *See* Tirpitz, Alfred von, 1849-1930
Vonnegut, Kurt, 1922-
The chemistry professor [play]
In Vonnegut, K. Palm Sunday p260-90 818
Fates worse than death 818
Palm Sunday 818
Voodoo science. Park, R. L. 500

Voodooism
  Glassman, S. A. Vodou visions   299
Vos Savant, Marilyn Mach
  The art of spelling   421
Voting *See* Elections
Voudouism *See* Voodooism
The **voyage** of the Beagle. Darwin, C.   508
Voyager (Airplane)
  Yeager, J. Voyager   910.4
Voyages and travels
  See also Travel
  Cahill, T. Pass the butterworms   910.4
  Cordingly, D. Women sailors and sailors' women   910.4
  Dana, R. H. Two years before the mast   910.4
  Dolan, B. Ladies of the Grand Tour   910.4
  Horwitz, T. Blue latitudes   910.4
  Iyer, P. The global soul   910.4
  Mackintosh-Smith, T. Travels with a tangerine   910.4
  Milton, G. The riddle and the knight   910.4
  National Geographic expeditions atlas   910.4
  Points unknown   910
  Polo, M. The travels of Marco Polo   915
  Slung, M. B. Living with cannibals and other women's adventures   910.4
  Solnit, R. Wanderlust   796.51
  Theroux, P. To the ends of the earth   910.4
  Thorpe, I. J. 8 men and a duck   910.4
Voyages around the world
  Cooper, R. L. Around the world with Mark Twain   818
Voyages of delusion. Williams, G.   910.4
Vriends, Matthew M., 1937-
  (ed) Lantermann, W. The new parrot handbook   636.6
Vuillard, Édouard, 1868-1940
      About
  Edouard Vuillard   759.4

W

Waal, Frans de, 1948-
  The ape and the sushi master   156
  Bonobo   599.8
Wacker, Grant, 1945-
  (jt. auth) Butler, J. Religion in American life   200.9
Waco (Tex.) cult siege, 1993
  Tabor, J. D. Why Waco?   291.9
Waddle, Linda L.
  (jt. auth) Carter, B. Best books for young adults   028.1
Wade, Brenda
  (jt. auth) Richardson, B. L. What mama couldn't tell us about love   158
Wade, Don
  (jt. auth) Martino, R. The PGA manual of golf   796.352
Wade, Henry, 1914-2001
      About
  Hull, N. E. H. Roe v. Wade   344
Wade, Josie
  (jt. auth) Segen, J. C. The patient's guide to medical tests   616.07
Wade, Nicholas
  Life script   616
  (ed) Science times book of language and linguistics. See Science times book of language and linguistics   400
Wadyka, Sally
  (jt. auth) Brown, B. Bobbi Brown beauty evolution   646.7

Wages
      Minimum wage
  See Minimum wage
Waging modern war. Clark, W. K.   949.7
Wagner, Jane, 1935-
  The search for signs of intelligent life in the universe   812
Wagner, Linda Welshimer *See* Wagner-Martin, Linda
Wagner, Margaret E.
  (ed) The Library of Congress Civil War desk reference. See The Library of Congress Civil War desk reference   973.7
Wagner, Melissa
  (jt. auth) Friedman, V. M. Field guide to stains   648
Wagner, Richard, 1813-1883
      About
  Osborne, C. The complete operas of Richard Wagner   792.5
  See/See also pages in the following book(s):
  Sontag, S. Where the stress falls   814
Wagner-Martin, Linda
  Sylvia Plath   92
  (ed) The Oxford book of women's writing in the United States. See The Oxford book of women's writing in the United States   810.8
  (ed) The Oxford companion to women's writing in the United States. See The Oxford companion to women's writing in the United States   810.9
Wahhabis
  Lawrence, T. E. Seven pillars of wisdom   940.4
Waisman, James
  (jt. auth) Link, J. The breast cancer survival manual   616.99
Wait till next year. Goodwin, D. K.   92
Waite, Linda J.
  The case for marriage   306.8
Waiting for Aphrodite. Hubbell, S.   592
Waiting for Godot. Beckett, S.   842
  also in Nine plays of the modern theater p115-97   808.82
Waiting for snow in Havana. Eire, C. M. N.   92
Wake-up calls. Lunden, J.   155.2
The **Wakefield** Second Shepherd's play
  In The Oxford anthology of English literature v1   820.8
Wakelyn, Jon L.
  (ed) Leaders of the American Civil War. See Leaders of the American Civil War   920.003
Wakeman, Carolyn
  (jt. auth) Wu, H. Bitter winds   951.05
Wakeman, John, 1928-
  (ed) World authors, 1950-1970. See World authors, 1950-1970   920.003
  (ed) World authors, 1970-1975. See World authors, 1970-1975   920.003
Wal-Mart Stores, Inc.
  Walton, S. Sam Walton, made in America   92
Walcott, Derek
  Collected poems, 1948-1984   811
  Omeros   811
Waldbauer, Gilbert
  Insects through the seasons   595.7
  Millions of monarchs, bunches of beetles   595.7
Walden. Thoreau, H. D.
  In Thoreau, H. D. The portable Thoreau   818
  In Thoreau, H. D. A week on the Concord and Merrimack rivers; Walden; The Maine woods; Cape Cod   818
Walden and other writings of Henry David Thoreau. Thoreau, H. D.   818
Waldman, Carl
  Atlas of the North American Indian   970.004
  Biographical dictionary of American Indian history to 1900   920.003

Waldman, Carl—*Continued*
Encyclopedia of Native American tribes   970.004
Waldmeir, Patti
Anatomy of a miracle   968.06
Waldron, Ann
Eudora [Welty]   92
Waldrup, Carole Chandler, 1925-
The vice presidents   920.003
Wales
Morris, J. A writer's house in Wales   942.9
    History
Davies, J. A history of Wales   942.9
Wałęsa, Lech, 1943-
The struggle and the triumph   92
Waley, Arthur, 1889-1966
The Nō plays of Japan   895.6
A **walk** across America. Jenkins, P.   917.3
A **walk** in the woods. Bryson, B.   917.4
Walker, Aidan
(ed) The Encyclopedia of wood. See The Encyclopedia of wood   674
Walker, Alan
The wisdom of the bones   599.93
Walker, Alexander
Audrey [Hepburn]   92
Stanley Kubrick, director   92
Walker, Alice, 1944-
Anything we love can be saved   818
In search of our mothers' gardens   818
Living by the word   818
The same river twice   92
See/See also pages in the following book(s):
Black women writers (1950-1980)   810.9
Walker, C. J., Madame, 1867-1919
    About
Lowry, B. Her dream of dreams: the rise and triumph of Madam C.J. Walker   92
Walker, Enrique Pupo- *See* Pupo-Walker, Enrique
Walker, Janice R.
The Columbia guide to online style   808
Walker, Margaret, 1915-1998
See/See also pages in the following book(s):
Black women writers (1950-1980)   810.9
Walker, Mark
Nazi science   509
Walker, Martin, 1947-
The Cold War   909.82
Walker, Mary Edwards, 1832-1919
See/See also pages in the following book(s):
Mikaelian, A. Medal of honor   920
Walker, Sarah Breedlove *See* Walker, C. J., Madame, 1867-1919
Walker, Warren S., 1921-
Twentieth century short story explication: new series   016.8093
Walker-Hill, Helen
From spirituals to symphonies   920
Walker's mammals of the world. Nowak, R. M.   599
Walking
Solnit, R. Wanderlust   796.51
Spilner, M. Prevention's complete book of walking   613.7
Walking on eggs. Chiappe, L. M.   567.9
Walking the Bible. Feiler, B. S.   915.6
Walking the black cat. Simic, C.   811
Walking with dinosaurs. Haines, T.   567.9
Walkowicz, Chris
(jt. auth) Wilcox, B. Atlas of dog breeds of the world   636.7
Wall, Cheryl A.
Women of the Harlem Renaissance   810.9
Wall, Joseph Frazier
Andrew Carnegie   92
Wall painting *See* Mural painting and decoration

Wall Street (New York, N.Y.)
Cramer, J. J. Confessions of a street addict   332.6
Geisst, C. R. The last partnerships   332.6
Lewis, M. Liar's poker: rising through the wreckage on Wall Street   332.6
Stern, K. To hell and back   332.6
The **Wall** Street journal guide to wine. Gaiter, D. J.   641.2
Wallace, Anthony F. C., 1923-
The long bitter trail   970.004
Wallace, Chris *See* Notorious B.I.G. (Musician)
Wallace, Daniel J. (Daniel Jeffrey), 1949-
Fibromyalgia: an essential guide for patients and their families   616.7
Wallace, David Foster
A supposedly fun thing I'll never do again   814
Wallace, David Rains, 1945-
The bonehunters' revenge   560
Wallace, Janice Brock
(jt. auth) Wallace, D. J. Fibromyalgia: an essential guide for patients and their families   616.7
Wallace, Joseph, 1957-
A gathering of wonders   508
Wallace, Michael, 1942-
(jt. auth) Burrows, E. G. Gotham   974.7
Wallace, Sippie, 1898-1986
See/See also pages in the following book(s):
Harrison, D. D. Black pearls   920
Wallach, Janet, 1942-
Desert queen [biography of Gertrude Bell]   92
Wallechinsky, David, 1948-
The complete book of the Winter Olympics   796.98
Wallenberg, Raoul
See/See also pages in the following book(s):
Fogelman, E. Conscience & courage   940.53
Wallenstein, Peter
(ed) The Encyclopedia of American political history. See The Encyclopedia of American political history   973.03
Wallerstein, Judith S.
Second chances   306.89
Wallis, Michael, 1945-
Route 66: the mother road   917.8
(jt. auth) Mankiller, W. Mankiller: a chief and her people   92
Wallpaper
Saunders, G. Wallpaper in interior decoration   747
Wallpaper in interior decoration. Saunders, G.   747
Walls
Thorson, R. M. Stone by stone   693
The **walls** came tumbling down. Stokes, G.   947
Walser, Robert, 1878-1956
See/See also pages in the following book(s):
Gass, W. H. Finding a form p65-76   814
Walsh, John
Public enemies   364.1
Walsh, John Evangelist, 1927-
Midnight dreary: the mysterious death of Edgar Allan Poe   92
Moonlight   345
Walsh, Patrick C., 1938-
The prostate   616.6
Walsh, Patrick J.
Echoes among the stars   629.4
Walsh, Stephen, 1942-
Stravinsky   92
Walsh, William E.
Food allergies   616.97
Walter, Carole
Great pies & tarts   641.8
Walter Benjamin at the Dairy Queen. McMurtry, L.   92

Walton, Anthony
(ed) Every shut eye ain't asleep. See Every shut eye ain't asleep **811.008**
(ed) The Vintage book of African American poetry. See The Vintage book of African American poetry **811.008**
Walton, Guy
(ed) Gifts to the tsars, 1500-1700. See Gifts to the tsars, 1500-1700 **745**
Walton, Isaac See Walton, Izaak, 1593-1683
Walton, Izaak, 1593-1683
The compleat angler **799.1**
Walton, Sam
Sam Walton, made in America **92**
See/See also pages in the following book(s):
Klein, M. The change makers **920**
Waltz, Mitzi
Autistic spectrum disorders **618.92**
Wambaugh, Joseph
Fire lover **364.1**
Wanamaker, John, 1838-1922
See/See also pages in the following book(s):
Klein, M. The change makers **920**
Wandering. Wilson, L.
In Wilson, L. 21 short plays p77-82 **812**
Wanderings. Potok, C. **909**
Wanderlust. Solnit, R. **796.51**
Wanek, Catherine
(ed) The Art of natural building. See The Art of natural building **690**
Waorani Indians
Kane, J. Savages **986.6**
War
Bobbitt, P. The shield of Achilles **327**
Clausewitz, C. von. On war **355**
Hedges, C. War is a force that gives us meaning **355**
Junger, S. Fire **909.82**
Pictorial works
Howe, P. Shooting under fire **070.4**
The **war** against cliché. Amis, M. **824**
The **war** against parents. Hewlett, S. A. **649**
The **war** against the Jews, 1933-1945. Dawidowicz, L. S. **940.53**
War as I knew it. Patton, G. S. **940.54**
War at sea. Miller, N. **940.54**
War in a time of peace. Halberstam, D. **327.73**
War in Italy, 1943-1945. Lamb, R. **940.54**
War in literature
The Norton book of modern war **808.8**
War is a force that gives us meaning. Hedges, C. **355**
War Lance, Le
About
Frazier, I. On the rez **970.004**
War of 1812
Molotsky, I. The flag, the poet & the song **973.5**
War of the century. Rees, L. **940.54**
The **war** on drugs. Chepesiuk, R. **363.45**
War photography
Sontag, S. Regarding the pain of others **303.6**
War poetry
The Oxford book of war poetry **808.81**
A **war** to be won. Murray, W. **940.53**
The **war** years [condensation] Sandburg, C.
In Sandburg, C. Abraham Lincoln: The prairie years and The war years **92**
Warbirds. Fredriksen, J. C. **623.7**
Warburg family
About
Chernow, R. The Warburgs **920**
The **Warburgs**. Chernow, R. **920**
Ward, Diane Raines
Water wars **333.91**

Ward, Elisabeth I.
(ed) Vikings: the North Atlantic saga. See Vikings: the North Atlantic saga **970.01**
Ward, Gary L.
(ed) Encyclopedia of African American religions. See Encyclopedia of African American religions **200.9**
Ward, Geoffrey C.
Baseball: an illustrated history **796.357**
The Civil War **973.7**
Jazz **781.65**
Not for ourselves alone: the story of Elizabeth Cady Stanton and Susan B. Anthony **92**
The West **978**
Ward, Keith, 1938-
Christianity **230**
Ward, Lester Frank, 1841-1913
See/See also pages in the following book(s):
Commager, H. S. The American mind **973**
Ward, Peter Douglas, 1949-
Rare earth **576.8**
Ward (Clara) Singers See Clara Ward Singers
Ward-Royster, Willa, 1922-
How I got over **920**
Ware, Susan, 1950-
Letter to the world **920**
Still missing: Amelia Earhart and the search for modern feminism **92**
Warga, Claire L.
Menopause and the mind **618.1**
Warhol, Andy, 1928?-1987
The Andy Warhol diaries **92**
About
Koestenbaum, W. Andy Warhol **92**
Warner, Deborah Jean
(ed) Instruments of science. See Instruments of science **502.8**
Warner, Diane, 1937-
How to have a big wedding on a small budget **395**
Warner, Ezra J.
Generals in blue **920**
Generals in gray **920**
Warner, Mark L., 1948-
The complete guide to Alzheimer's-proofing your home **362.1**
Warner, Pat
The router book **684**
Warner, Ralph E.
Everybody's guide to small claims court **347**
(jt. auth) Portman, J. Every landlord's legal guide **346.04**
Warner, Sylvia Townsend, 1893-1978
The element of lavishness: letters of Sylvia Townsend Warner and William Maxwell, 1938-1978 **92**
Warnes, David
Chronicle of the Russian tsars **947**
Warpaths: travels of a military historian in North America. See Keegan, J. Fields of battle **973**
Warren, Earle, 1914-1994
See/See also pages in the following book(s):
Dance, S. The world of Count Basie **920**
Warren, Holly George- See George-Warren, Holly
Warren, Robert Penn, 1905-1989
The collected poems of Robert Penn Warren **811**
The **Warren** Buffett way. Hagstrom, R. G. **332.6**
Warrick, Meta Vaux See Fuller, Meta Vaux Warrick, 1877-1968
The **warrior** and the priest: Woodrow Wilson and Theodore Roosevelt. Cooper, J. M. **92**
The **warrior** elite. Couch, D. **359.9**
Warrior politics. Kaplan, R. D. **320**
The **warrior** queens. Fraser, A. **920**
Wars of the Roses, 1455-1485 See Great Britain—History—1455-1485, War of the Roses

The **Wars** of the Roses. Weir, A.   **942.04**
Warshaw, Linda Zierdt- *See* Zierdt-Warshaw, Linda
Warships
Jane's fighting ships   **623.8**
Wartime: understanding and behavior in the Second
   World War. Fussell, P.   **940.54**
Washburn, Katharine
   (ed) World poetry. See World poetry   **808.81**
Washington, Booker T., 1856-1915
Up from slavery   **92**
About
Harlan, L. R. Booker T. Washington: the making of a
   black leader, 1856-1901   **92**
Harlan, L. R. Booker T. Washington: the wizard of
   Tuskegee, 1901-1915   **92**
Washington, George, 1732-1799
The diaries of George Washington   **92**
Writings   **973.4**
About
Brookhiser, R. Founding father: rediscovering George
   Washington   **92**
Ferling, J. E. The first of men: a life of George Wash-
   ington   **92**
Ferling, J. E. Setting the world ablaze   **973.3**
Flexner, J. T. George Washington   **92**
Grizzard, F. E., Jr. George Washington: a biographical
   companion   **92**
Randall, W. S. George Washington   **92**
Smith, R. N. Patriarch: George Washington and the
   new American nation   **92**
Wilkins, R. W. Jefferson's pillow   **973**
See/See also pages in the following book(s):
Allen, T. B. The Washington Monument   **975.3**
Ellis, J. J. Founding brothers   **973.4**
Wills, G. Certain trumpets p148-56   **303.3**
Washington, Peter
   (ed) The Roman poets. See The Roman poets
   871.008
Washington (D.C.)
Katharine Graham's Washington   **975.3**
Directories
Washington information directory   **320.025**
Social conditions
Dash, L. Rosa Lee   **305.8**
Social life and customs
Boller, P. F. Presidential inaugurations   **973**
Heymann, C. D. The Georgetown ladies' social club
   305.4
Washington (State)
History
Harmon, A. Indians in the making   **970.004**
Washington information directory   **320.025**
Washington Monument (Washington, D.C.)
Allen, T. B. The Washington Monument   **975.3**
Washington post
Bernstein, C. All the president's men   **973.924**
Graham, K. Personal history   **92**
Wasps. Aristophanes
   In Aristophanes. The complete plays of Aristophanes
   p143-83   **882**
Wasserman, Dale, 1917-
Man of La Mancha   **812**
Wasserman, Lew R., 1913-2002
About
Bruck, C. When Hollywood had a king   **92**
Wasserstein, Wendy
An American daughter   **812**
The Heidi chronicles
   In Wasserstein, W. The Heidi chronicles, and other
   plays   **812**
The Heidi chronicles, and other plays   **812**
Isn't it romantic
   In Wasserstein, W. The Heidi chronicles, and other
   plays   **812**
The sisters Rosensweig   **812**

Uncommon women and others
   In Wasserstein, W. The Heidi chronicles, and other
   plays   **812**
See/See also pages in the following book(s):
Playwrights at work   **812.009**
Wasson, Ernie
   (ed) The Complete encyclopedia of trees and shrubs.
   See The Complete encyclopedia of trees and shrubs
   635.9
Wasson, Tyler
   (ed) Nobel Prize winners. See Nobel Prize winners
   920.003
Waste disposal *See* Industrial waste
Wasted: a memoir of anorexia and bulimia. Hornbacher,
   M.   **616.85**
Watanabe-O'Kelly, Helen
   (ed) The Cambridge history of German literature. See
   The Cambridge history of German literature
   830.9
Water
Ball, P. Life's matrix   **553.7**
Kandel, R. S. Water from heaven   **553.7**
Outwater, A. B. Water   **551.48**
Pielou, E. C. Fresh water   **553.7**
   See/See also pages in the following book(s):
Shoumatoff, A. Legends of the American desert
   978
Encyclopedias
Water: science and issues   **553.7**
Water animals *See* Marine animals
Water birds
   See also Albatrosses; Cranes (Birds)
Water color painting *See* Watercolor painting
Water exercises for Parkinson's. Rosenstein, A.
   616.8
Water from heaven. Kandel, R. S.   **553.7**
The **water** garden encyclopedia. Swindells, P.   **635.9**
Water pollution
De Villiers, M. Water: the fate of our most precious
   resource   **333.91**
Outwater, A. B. Water   **551.48**
Water power
   See also Hydraulic engineering
Water resources development
Barlow, M. Blue gold: the fight to stop the corporate
   theft of the world's water   **333.91**
De Villiers, M. Water: the fate of our most precious
   resource   **333.91**
Reisner, M. P. Cadillac desert   **333.91**
Water rights
Ward, D. R. Water wars   **333.91**
Water: science and issues   **553.7**
Water supply
Barlow, M. Blue gold: the fight to stop the corporate
   theft of the world's water   **333.91**
De Villiers, M. Water: the fate of our most precious
   resource   **333.91**
Outwater, A. B. Water   **551.48**
Rothfeder, J. Every drop for sale   **333.91**
Ward, D. R. Water wars   **333.91**
Water supply engineering
Matson, T. Earth ponds A to Z   **627**
Water: the fate of our most precious resource. De Vil-
   liers, M.   **333.91**
Water wars. Ward, D. R.   **333.91**
Watercolor. Lindsay, A. K.   **751.42**
Watercolor painting
Avery, K. J. American drawings and watercolors in the
   Metropolitan Museum of Art v1   **759.13**
Ferber, L. S. Masters of color and light   **759.13**
Technique
Crawshaw, A. You can paint watercolors   **751.42**
Kunz, J. Painting beautiful watercolors from photo-
   graphs   **751.42**
Lindsay, A. K. Watercolor   **751.42**

Watercolor painting—Technique—*Continued*
MacKenzie, G. The watercolorist's essential notebook
    751.42
The **watercolorist's** essential notebook. MacKenzie, G.
    751.42
The **watercourse**: poems. Zarin, C.   **811**
Watergate. Emery, F.   **973.924**
Watergate Affair, 1972-1974
  Abuse of power   **973.924**
  Bernstein, C. All the president's men   **973.924**
  Emery, F. Watergate   **973.924**
  Woodward, B. The final days   **973.924**
  Woodward, B. Shadow   **973.92**
Waterloo, Battle of, 1815
  Schom, A. One hundred days   **944.05**
Waterman, Jonathan
  Arctic crossing   **998**
Waters, Alice
  Chez Panisse vegetables   **641.6**
Waters, Muddy, 1915-1983
      About
  Gordon, R. Can't be satisfied: the life and times of
    Muddy Waters   **92**
Watkins, A. M. (Arthur Martin), 1924-
  Manufactured houses   **693**
Watkins, Arthur Martin *See* Watkins, A. M. (Arthur
Martin), 1924-
Watkins, Gloria Jean *See* Hooks, Bell
Watkins, Mary, 1939-
  See/See also pages in the following book(s):
  Walker-Hill, H. From spirituals to symphonies
    920
Watkins, Susan
  The public and private worlds of Elizabeth I
    942.05
Watkins, T. H. (Tom H.), 1936-2000
  The hungry years   **973.91**
Watkins, Tom H. *See* Watkins, T. H. (Tom H.), 1936-
2000
Watson, Burton, 1925-
  (ed) The Columbia book of Chinese poetry. See The
  Columbia book of Chinese poetry   **895.1**
Watson, James D., 1928-
  DNA: the secret of life   **576.5**
  The double helix   **572.8**
  Genes, girls, and Gamow   **92**
  See/See also pages in the following book(s):
  Flowers, C. Instability rules   **509**
  Friedman, M. Medicine's 10 greatest discoveries
    610.9
  Horvitz, L. A. Eureka!: scientific breakthroughs that
  changed the world   **509**
Watson, John Broadus, 1878-1958
  Behaviorism   **150.19**
Watson, Lyall
  Dark nature   **111**
  Jacobson's organ and the remarkable nature of smell
    612.8
Watson, Peter, 1943-
  The modern mind   **909.82**
Watson, Richard A., 1931-
  Cogito ergo sum: the life of René Descartes   **92**
Watson, Victor
  (ed) The Cambridge guide to children's books in En-
  glish. See The Cambridge guide to children's books
  in English   **028.5**
Watstein, Sarah B.
  The encyclopedia of HIV and AIDS   **616.97**
Watt, James, 1736-1819
      About
  Uglow, J. S. The lunar men   **920**
Watters, James
  (jt. auth) Howard, J. Jean Howard's Hollywood
    791.43

Watts, Alan, 1915-1973
  The way of Zen   **294.3**
Waugh, Evelyn, 1903-1966
  See/See also pages in the following book(s):
  Holroyd, M. Works on paper   **809**
Wauson, Jennifer
  (jt. auth) Stroman, J. Administrative assistant's & sec-
  retary's handbook   **651.3**
The **way** it is. Stafford, W. E.   **811**
The **way** it was. Goldstein, D. M.   **940.54**
The **way** life works. Hoagland, M. B.   **570**
A **way** of being. Rogers, C. R.   **150.19**
The **way** of the cell. Harold, F. M.   **571.6**
The **way** of the wolf. Mech, L. D.   **599.77**
The **way** of the world. Congreve, W.
  In The Oxford anthology of English literature v1
    820.8
  In Restoration plays   **822.008**
The **way** of Zen. Watts, A.   **294.3**
A **way** out. Frost, R.
  In Frost, R. Collected poems, prose, & plays p565-
  75   **818**
Way out there in the blue. FitzGerald, F.   **973.927**
The **way** things work. See Macaulay, D. The new way
  things work   **600**
The **way** to cook. Child, J.   **641.5**
The **way** to freedom. Dalai Lama XIV   **294.3**
The **way** to write for children. Aiken, J.   **808.06**
The **way** we talk now. Nunberg, G.   **400**
The **way** you wear your hat. Zehme, B.   **92**
Wayne, Kenneth
  Modigliani & the artists of Montparnasse   **92**
Ways of telling. Marcus, L. S.   **741.6**
We are our mothers' daughters. Roberts, C.   **305.4**
We are still here. Iverson, P.   **970.004**
We are still married. Keillor, G.   **817**
We band of angels. Norman, E. M.   **940.54**
We die alone. Howarth, D. A.   **940.54**
We interrupt this broadcast. Garner, J.   **070.1**
We were soldiers once—and young. Moore, H. G.
    959.704
We wish to inform you that tomorrow we will be killed
  with our families. Gourevitch, P.   **967.571**
Wealth
  See also Success
  Conniff, R. The natural history of the rich   **305.5**
  Mayle, P. Acquired tastes   **305.5**
  Phillips, K. P. Wealth and democracy   **305.5**
Wealth and democracy. Phillips, K. P.   **305.5**
The **wealth** of nations. Smith, A.   **330.1**
Weapons
  O'Connell, R. L. Soul of the sword   **623.4**
  Taylor, C. F. Native American weapons   **970.004**
  Volkman, E. Science goes to war   **623**
Weapons & warfare   **623.4**
Weapons and weaponry *See* Military weapons
Weather
  See also Meteorology
  Allaby, M. The Facts on File weather and climate
  handbook   **551.6**
  Encyclopedia of climate and weather   **551.6**
  Lyons, W. A. The handy weather answer book
    551.6
  Reynolds, R. Cambridge guide to the weather
    551.5
  Stevens, W. K. The change in the weather   **551.5**
  Weather   **551.5**
  Weather almanac   **551.6**
  Williams, J. The weather book   **551.6**
Weather   **551.5**
Weather almanac   **551.6**
The **weather** book. Williams, J.   **551.6**
Weather forecasting
  Ludlum, D. M. The Audubon Society field guide to
  North American weather   **551.6**

Weather forecasting—*Continued*
Monmonier, M. S. Air apparent   **551.6**
Reynolds, R. Cambridge guide to the weather
    551.5
Weatherford, J. McIver
Native roots   **970.004**
Weatherford, Jack *See* Weatherford, J. McIver
Weatherford, M. Lisa
(ed) Reconstructive and cosmetic surgery sourcebook.
See Reconstructive and cosmetic surgery sourcebook
    617.9
Weaver, Kathleen, 1945-
(ed) The Penguin book of women poets. See The Penguin book of women poets   **808.81**
Weaver, William, 1923-
(ed) The Puccini companion. See The Puccini companion   **92**
Weaver, William Woys
(ed) Encyclopedia of food and culture. See Encyclopedia of food and culture   **394.1**
Weaving
Brown, R. The weaving, spinning, and dyeing book
    746.1
The **weaving**, spinning, and dyeing book. Brown, R.
    746.1
The **web** of life. Capra, F.   **570.1**
Web sites
Bolles, R. N. Job-hunting on the Internet   **025.04**
Godin, S. The big red fez   **005.7**
Government online   **025.04**
Hernon, P. U.S. government on the Web   **025.04**
Norlin, E. Usability testing for library websites
    025.04
Smith, J. D. World War II on the Web   **025.04**
Webb, Philip, 1964-
The small business handbook   **658**
Webb, Sandra
(jt. auth) Webb, P. The small business handbook
    658
Webber, Andrew Lloyd *See* Lloyd Webber, Andrew, 1948-
Webber, Elizabeth, 1946-
Merriam-Webster's dictionary of allusions   **803**
Weber, Eugen Joseph, 1925-
Apocalypses   **291**
Weber, Mark Christopher, 1949-
Brushwork essentials   **751.4**
Weber, Max, 1864-1920
See/See also pages in the following book(s):
Jaspers, K. The great philosophers   **109**
Weber, Nancy S.
(jt. auth) Smith, A. H. The mushroom hunter's field guide   **579.6**
Weber, R. David, 1941-
(jt. auth) Schlachter, G. A. Financial aid for the disabled and their families   **378.3**
Weber, Robert J.
The created self   **155.2**
Webster, Daniel, 1782-1852
About
Remini, R. V. Daniel Webster   **92**
See/See also pages in the following book(s):
Kennedy, J. F. Profiles in courage   **920**
Webster, Noah, 1758-1843
See/See also pages in the following book(s):
Lepore, J. A is for American   **306.44**
Webster, Raymond B.
African American firsts in science and technology
    509
Webster, Robert
Gems   **553.8**
Webster's collegiate thesaurus. See Merriam-Webster's collegiate thesaurus   **423**
Webster's geographical dictionary. See Merriam-Webster's geographical dictionary   **910.3**

Webster's new biographical dictionary. See Merriam-Webster's biographical dictionary   **920.003**
Webster's New World Hebrew dictionary. Baltsan, H.
    492.4
Webster's New World Robert's rules of order
    060.4
Webster's third new international dictionary of the English language, unabridged   **423**
The **wedding**. Chekhov, A. P.
In Chekhov, A. P. The plays of Anton Chekhov p175-89   **891.7**
Weddings
See also Marriage customs and rites
Bride's book of etiquette   **395**
Into the garden   **808.8**
Martin, J. Miss Manners on weddings   **395**
Post, P. Emily Post wedding etiquette   **395**
Warner, D. How to have a big wedding on a small budget   **395**
Weddington, Sarah Ragle, 1945-
A question of choice   **363.46**
Wedgwood, Josiah, 1730-1795
About
Uglow, J. S. The lunar men   **920**
Weeding library collections. Slote, S. J.   **025.2**
A **week** on the Concord and Merrimack rivers. Thoreau, H. D.
In Thoreau, H. D. A week on the Concord and Merrimack rivers; Walden; The Maine woods; Cape Cod   **818**
A **week** on the Concord and Merrimack rivers [excerpts] Thoreau, H. D.
In Thoreau, H. D. The portable Thoreau   **818**
Weekes, Mark Kinkead- *See* Kinkead-Weekes, Mark
Weems, David B.
Designing, building, and testing your own speaker system with projects   **621.382**
Weenolsen, Patricia
The art of dying   **155.9**
Weeping *See* Crying
Wegener, Alfred Lothar, 1880-1930
See/See also pages in the following book(s):
Flowers, C. Instability rules   **509**
Horvitz, L. A. Eureka!: scientific breakthroughs that changed the world   **509**
Wei Jingsheng
The courage to stand alone   **951.05**
Weidensaul, Scott
The ghost with trembling wings   **591.68**
Living on the wind   **598**
Weierstrass, Karl, 1815-1897
See/See also pages in the following book(s):
Bell, E. T. Men of mathematics p406-32   **920**
Weigel, George
Witness to hope: the biography of Pope John Paul II
    92
Weight control *See* Weight loss
Weight loss
Atkins, R. C. Dr. Atkins' new diet revolution
    613.2
Nichter, M. Fat talk   **613.2**
Weights and measures
See also Metric system
The Economist desk companion   **530.8**
Weihs, Jean Riddle
Facts about Canada, its provinces and territories
    971
(jt. auth) Intner, S. S. Standard cataloging for school and public libraries   **025.3**
Weil, Andrew
Eating well for optimum health   **613.2**
Eight weeks to optimum health   **613**
From chocolate to morphine   **616.86**
The healthy kitchen   **641.5**

Weil, Elizabeth
They all laughed at Christopher Columbus   621.43
Weil, Simone, 1909-1943
About
Gray, F. du P. Simone Weil   92
See/See also pages in the following book(s):
Miłosz, C. To begin where I am p246-59   891.8
Weill, Kurt, 1900-1950
About
Hirsch, F. Kurt Weill on stage   92
Schebera, J. Kurt Weill   92
See/See also pages in the following book(s):
Green, S. The world of musical comedy   920
Weinberg, Adam D.
Edward Hopper and the American imagination. See Edward Hopper and the American imagination   759.13
Weinberg, Gerhard L.
A world at arms   940.53
Weinberg, Samantha, 1966-
A fish caught in time   597
Weiner, E. S. C. (Edmund S. C.)
(jt. auth) Chalker, S. The Oxford dictionary of English grammar   428
Weiner, Edmund S. C. *See* Weiner, E. S. C. (Edmund S. C.)
Weiner, Eva S.
(ed) The Oxford English dictionary. See The Oxford English dictionary   423
Weiner, Jonathan
The beak of the finch   598
Time, love, memory   591.5
Weiner, William J.
Parkinson's disease   616.8
Weinreich, Uriel
Modern English-Yiddish, Yiddish-English dictionary   439
Weinstein, Allen
The haunted wood   327.12
Weinstein, Miriam
Yiddish   439
Weintraub, Stanley, 1929-
MacArthur's war   951.9
Silent night   940.4
Uncrowned king: the life of Prince Albert   92
Weir, Alison
The children of Henry VIII   920
Eleanor of Aquitaine   92
Henry VIII   92
The life of Elizabeth I   92
Mary, Queen of Scots, and the murder of Lord Darnley   92
The six wives of Henry VIII   920
The Wars of the Roses   942.04
Weir, Robert E., 1952-
Historical encyclopedia of American labor. See Historical encyclopedia of American labor   331.8
Weishar, Peter
Blue Sky   778.5
Weisman, Steven R.
The great tax wars   336.2
Weiss, Michael A.
(jt. auth) Kolpan, S. Exploring wine   641.2
Weiss, Peter, 1916-1982
The persecution and assassination of Jean-Paul Marat as performed by the inmates of the Asylum of Charenton under the direction of the Marquis de Sade   832
Weiswasser, Janet Z.
(ed) The Yale guide to children's nutrition. See The Yale guide to children's nutrition   613.2
Welch, David, 1950-
(jt. auth) Cull, N. J. Propaganda and mass persuasion   303.3

Welch, James, 1940-2003
Killing Custer   973.8
See/See also pages in the following book(s):
Coltelli, L. Winged words: American Indian writers speak   897
Welch, Robert, 1947-
(ed) The Oxford companion to Irish literature. See The Oxford companion to Irish literature   820.9
The **welcome** table. Harris, J. B.   641.5
Welding
Geary, D. Welding   671.5
The **well** cat book. McGinnis, T.   636.8
The **well** dog book. McGinnis, T.   636.7
The **well** of the saints. Synge, J. M.
In Synge, J. M. The complete plays   822
The **well-tended** perennial garden. DiSabato-Aust, T.   635.9
The **well** wrought urn. Brooks, C.   821.009
Weller, Eleanor
(jt. auth) Griswold, M. K. The golden age of American gardens   712
Welles, Orson, 1915-1985
About
Thomson, D. Rosebud: the story of Orson Welles   92
Wellesley, Arthur *See* Wellington, Arthur Wellesley, Duke of, 1769-1852
Wellesley, Charles *See* Brontë, Charlotte, 1816-1855
Wellington, Arthur Wellesley, Duke of, 1769-1852
About
Hibbert, C. Wellington   92
Wells, Carol Wilcox
The art & elegance of beadweaving   745.58
Wells, Diana
100 flowers and how they got their names   582.13
Wells, Dicky, 1910-1985
See/See also pages in the following book(s):
Dance, S. The world of Count Basie   920
Wells, H. G. (Herbert George), 1866-1946
The outline of history   909
About
McKillop, A. B. The spinster & the prophet   941.08
Wells, Herbert George *See* Wells, H. G. (Herbert George), 1866-1946
Wells, Kate, 1959-
Fabric dyeing & printing   746.6
Wells, Rosemary, 1943-
See/See also pages in the following book(s):
Marcus, L. S. Ways of telling   741.6
Wells, Stanley W., 1930-
Shakespeare: for all time   822.3
The **wellspring**. Olds, S.   811
Welsh, James Michael
(jt. auth) Tibbetts, J. C. The encyclopedia of novels into film   791.43
Welty, Eudora, 1909-2001
One time, one place   976.2
One writer's beginnings   92
About
Marrs, S. One writer's imagination   813.009
Waldron, A. Eudora   92
See/See also pages in the following book(s):
American women fiction writers   813.009
Pierpont, C. R. Passionate minds   810.9
Women writers at work p157-80   808
Wenborn, Neil
(ed) The Columbia companion to British history. See The Columbia companion to British history   941
Wendleton, Kate
Building a great résumé   650.14
Wendorf, Richard
Sir Joshua Reynolds   759.2

Wenger, J. Michael
(jt. auth) Goldstein, D. M. D-Day Normandy
    940.54
(jt. auth) Goldstein, D. M. The Vietnam war: the story
and photographs   **959.704**
(jt. auth) Goldstein, D. M. The way it was
    940.54
Wenner, Paul F.
Garden cuisine   **613.2**
Wentz, W. Y. Evans- See Evans-Wentz, W. Y. (Walter
Yeeling), 1878-1965
Wenz, Philip S.
Adding to a house   **690**
Werblowsky, R. J. Zwi (Raphael Jehudah Zwi), 1924-
(ed) The Oxford dictionary of the Jewish religion. See
The Oxford dictionary of the Jewish religion
    296.03
Werblowsky, Raphael Jehudah Zwi See Werblowsky,
R. J. Zwi (Raphael Jehudah Zwi), 1924-
Werlock, Abby H. P.
The Facts on File companion to the American short
story. See The Facts on File companion to the
American short story   **813.009**
Wernick, Sarah
(jt. auth) Henschke, C. I. Lung cancer   **616.99**
(jt. auth) Nelson, M. E. Strong women, strong bones
    616.7
Wert, Jeffry D.
Custer   **92**
Gettysburg, day three   **973.7**
Mosby's Rangers   **973.7**
Wertheim, L. Jon
Venus envy   **796.342**
Wescott, Glenway, 1901-1987
The pilgrim hawk; criticism
In Sontag, S. Where the stress falls   **814**
Wesley, John, 1703-1791
About
Tomkins, S. John Wesley   **92**
Wesleyan University (Middletown, Conn.)
Admission
Steinberg, J. The gatekeepers   **378.1**
West, Cornel
Race matters   **305.8**
Restoring hope   **305.8**
(ed) Encyclopedia of African-American culture and
history. See Encyclopedia of African-American cul-
ture and history   **305.8**
(jt. auth) Gates, H. L. The African-American century
    920
(jt. auth) Gates, H. L. The future of the race
    305.8
(jt. auth) Hewlett, S. A. The war against parents
    649
See/See also pages in the following book(s):
Russell, D. Black genius and the American experience
    920
West, Elliott, 1945-
The contested plains   **978**
West, James W.
The Betty Ford Center book of answers   **616.86**
West, Mae, 1892-1980
About
Leider, E. W. Becoming Mae West   **92**
See/See also pages in the following book(s):
Pierpont, C. R. Passionate minds   **810.9**
West, Dame Rebecca, 1892-1983
See/See also pages in the following book(s):
Women writers at work p61-100   **808**
West, Richard, 1930-
Chaucer, 1340-1400   **92**
Tito   **92**
West, Sandra L.
(jt. auth) Aberjhani Encyclopedia of the Harlem Re-
naissance   **810.9**

West, Stanley
The hysterectomy hoax   **618.1**
West (U.S.)
Children
See Children—West (U.S.)
Description
Ambrose, S. E. Lewis & Clark   **978**
Frazier, I. Great Plains   **978**
Parkman, F. The Oregon Trail   **978**
Schmidt, T. The Lewis & Clark Trail   **978**
Wallis, M. Route 66: the mother road   **917.8**
Encyclopedias
The New encyclopedia of the American West
    978.03
Slatta, R. W. The cowboy encyclopedia   **978.03**
Exploration
Ambrose, S. E. Lewis & Clark   **978**
Ambrose, S. E. Undaunted courage   **978**
Duncan, D. Lewis & Clark   **978**
Lewis, M. The essential Lewis and Clark   **978**
The Lewis and Clark journals   **978**
Slaughter, T. P. Exploring Lewis and Clark   **978**
Historical geography—Maps
Beck, W. A. Historical atlas of the American West
    911
History
Bain, D. H. Empire express   **385**
Brown, D. A. The American West   **978**
Brown, D. A. Bury my heart at Wounded Knee
    970.004
Morgan, T. A shovel of stars   **978**
The Oxford history of the American West   **978**
Raban, J. Bad land   **978**
Utley, R. M. Custer: cavalier in buckskin   **973.8**
Ward, G. C. The West   **978**
Zeman, S. C. Chronology of the American West
    978
See/See also pages in the following book(s):
Ambrose, S. E. Nothing like it in the world   **385**
Social life and customs
Dary, D. Seeking pleasure in the Old West   **978**
Luchetti, C. Children of the West   **978**
Schlissel, L. Far from home   **978**
West (U.S.) in art
Dippie, B. W. The Frederic Remington Art Museum
collection   **92**
Discovered lands, invented pasts   **759.13**
West Africa
See also Sierra Leone
Description
Kaplan, R. D. The ends of the earth   **910.4**
Palin, M. Sahara   **966**
West Bank
Grossman, D. The yellow wind   **956.95**
West of Kabul, East of New York. Ansary, M. T.
    958.1
West Point (Military academy) See United States Mili-
tary Academy
West wind. Oliver, M.   **811**
Western and country music See Country music
The **Western** canon. Bloom, H.   **809**
Western civilization
Barzun, J. From dawn to decadence   **940.2**
Herman, A. The idea of decline in Western history
    909.08
See/See also pages in the following book(s):
Teilhard de Chardin, P. Toward the future p40-57
    194
Western Europe See Europe
Western medicine: an illustrated history   **610.9**
Western States See West (U.S.)
Westfall, Richard S.
The life of Isaac Newton   **92**
Westheimer, Ruth
The value of family   **306.8**

Westmacott, Mary, 1890-1976
See also Christie, Agatha, 1890-1976
Westmoreland, Susan
(ed) The Good Housekeeping step-by-step cookbook.
See The Good Housekeeping step-by-step cookbook
641.5
Westmoreland, William C.
See/See also pages in the following book(s):
Halberstam, D. The best and the brightest
973.922
Weston, Charis Wilson *See* Wilson, Charis, 1914-
West's encyclopedia of American law **340.03**
Westward movement *See* West (U.S.)—History
Wetterau, Bruce
Congressional Quarterly's desk reference on the Presidency **973**
Wetzsteon, Ross
Republic of dreams **974.7**
Whalen, Philip, 1923-2002
Overtime **811**
Whales, Chris
(jt. auth) Player, G. The complete golfer's handbook **796.352**
Whales
The Audubon Society field guide to North American fishes, whales, and dolphins **597**
Morton, A. Listening to whales **599.5**
Russell, D. Eye of the whale **599.5**
Whales, dolphins, and porpoises **599.5**
Whales, dolphins, and porpoises **599.5**
Wharton, Edith, 1862-1937
Edith Wharton abroad **818**
See/See also pages in the following book(s):
American women fiction writers **813.009**
Fraser, K. Ornament and silence **814**
What America owes the world. Brands, H. W. **327.73**
What are people for? Berry, W. **814**
What are the odds? Orkin, M. **519.2**
What color is your parachute? Bolles, R. N. **331.7**
What did I just say!?!. Donovan, D. M. **649**
What do I read next? **016.8**
What every artist needs to know about paints & colors. Pyle, D. **752**
What every woman must know about heart disease. Kra, S. J. **616.1**
What everyone needs to know about Islam. Esposito, J. L. **297**
What evolution is. Mayr, E. **576.8**
What happened. Stein, G.
In Stein, G. Selected writings p557-60 **818**
What is life? Margulis, L. **570.1**
What is philosophy? Ortega y Gasset, J. **196**
What it means to be 98% chimpanzee. Marks, J. **599.93**
What Jane Austen ate and Charles Dickens knew. Pool, D. **820.9**
What Johnny shouldn't read. DelFattore, J. **379**
What kind of nation. Simon, J. F. **342**
What mama couldn't tell us about love. Richardson, B. L. **158**
What manner of man: a biography of Martin Luther King, Jr. Bennett, L. **92**
What matters most is how well you walk through the fire. Bukowski, C. **811**
What Nietzsche really said. Solomon, R. C. **193**
What remains to be discovered. Maddox, J. R. **500**
What should we tell our children about Vietnam? McCloud, B. **959.704**
What the bones tell us. Schwartz, J. H. **599.93**
What they don't teach you at Harvard Business School. McCormack, M. H. **650.1**
What to expect the first year. Murkoff, H. E. **649**
What to expect the toddler years. Eisenberg, A. **649**

What to expect when you're expecting. Murkoff, H. E. **618.2**
What was the relationship of the Lone Ranger to the means of production. Baraka, I. A.
In Baraka, I. A. The LeRoi Jones/Amiri Baraka reader **818**
What went wrong? Lewis, B. **956**
What work is. Levine, P. **811**
What's going on in there? Eliot, L. **612.8**
What's love got to do with it? Small, M. F. **576.8**
Wheatcroft, Andrew
The Ottomans **956**
(jt. auth) Overy, R. J. The road to war **940.53**
Wheatley, Phillis, 1753-1784
The poems of Phillis Wheatley **811**
The **wheel** of life. Kübler-Ross, E. **92**
Wheelan, Charles J.
Naked economics **330**
Wheeler, Brian K., 1955-
(jt. auth) Clark, W. S. A field guide to hawks of North America **598**
Wheeler, Marcus
(ed) The Concise Oxford Russian dictionary. See The Concise Oxford Russian dictionary **491.7**
(ed) The Oxford Russian dictionary. See The Oxford Russian dictionary **491.7**
Wheels for the world. Brinkley, D. **338.7**
Wheen, Francis
Karl Marx **92**
When abortion was a crime. Reagan, L. J. **363.46**
When bad things happen to good people. Kushner, H. S. **296.3**
When broken glass floats. Him, C. **92**
When do fish sleep? and other imponderables of everyday life. Feldman, D. **031.02**
When elephants weep. Masson, J. M. **591.5**
When every moment counts. Frist, W. H. **613.6**
When generations collide. Lancaster, L. C. **658.3**
When Hollywood had a king. Bruck, C. **92**
When I was a young man. Kerrey, R. **92**
When Jesus became God. Rubenstein, R. E. **273**
When memory speaks. Conway, J. K. **808**
When Parkinson's strikes early **616.8**
When pride still mattered: a life of Vince Lombardi. Maraniss, D. **92**
When race becomes real **305.8**
When science meets religion. Barbour, I. G. **291.1**
When smoke ran like water. Davis, D. L. **615.9**
When they were young. Coles, R. **779**
When we dead awaken. Ibsen, H.
In Ibsen, H. The complete major prose plays p1025-92 **839.8**
In Ibsen, H. Ibsen: four plays, v3 **839.8**
Where dead voices gather [biography of Emmett Miller] Tosches, N. **92**
Where I was from. Didion, J. **979.4**
Where stuff comes from. Molotch, H. L. **620**
Where the germs are. Bakalar, N. **616**
Where the stress falls. Sontag, S. **814**
Wheye, Darryl
(jt. auth) Ehrlich, P. R. The birder's handbook **598**
Whiffen, Marcus
American architecture since 1780 **720.973**
The **whirlwind** of war. Oates, S. B. **973.7**
Whitaker, John O., Jr.
National Audubon Society field guide to North American mammals **599**
Whitaker, Reginald, 1943-
The end of privacy **303.4**
Whitaker, Robert
Mad in America **616.89**
Whitburn, Joel
The Billboard book of top 40 hits **781.64**

Whitcomb, Christopher, 1959-
Cold zero   363.2
White, Burton L., 1929-
The new first three years of life   155.4
Raising a happy, unspoiled child   649
White, E. B. (Elwyn Brooks), 1899-1985
Essays of E. B. White   814
One man's meat   818
Writings from the New Yorker   814
(jt. auth) Strunk, W. The elements of style   808
About
Elledge, S. E.B. White   92
White, Edmund, 1940-
The flaneur   944
White, Elwyn Brooks See White, E. B. (Elwyn Brooks), 1899-1985
White, Emily, 1966-
Fast girls   305.23
White, Evelyn C., 1954-
(ed) The Black women's health book. See The Black women's health book   613
White, Joyce, 1942-
Soul food   641.5
White, Katharine Sergeant Angell, 1892-1977
See/See also pages in the following book(s):
Life stories   920
White, Maureen
(jt. auth) Latrobe, K. H. The children's literature dictionary   028.5
White, Michael, 1959-
Leonardo   92
Stephen Hawking   92
White, Patricia Holden
(jt. auth) Fogle, B. New complete dog training manual   636.7
White, Phyllis Dorothy James See James, P. D.
White, Richard, 1965-
(ed) King Arthur in legend and history. See King Arthur in legend and history   942.01
White, Ron
How computers work   004
White, Ronald C. (Ronald Cedric), 1939-
Lincoln's greatest speech   973.7
White, Shane
Stories of freedom in Black New York   974.7
White, Theodore H., 1915-1986
The making of the president, 1960   324.6
The **white** album. Didion, J.   814
White Aryan Resistance
Ezekiel, R. S. The racist mind   322.4
White House (Washington, D.C.)
Anthony, C. S. America's first families   920
Monkman, B. C. The White House   975.3
The White House   975.3
The **White** House   975.3
White pine. Oliver, M.   811
White Sox (Baseball team) See Chicago White Sox (Baseball team)
White supremacy movements
Bushart, H. L. Soldiers of God   322.4
Ezekiel, R. S. The racist mind   322.4
See/See also pages in the following book(s):
Dees, M. S., Jr. Gathering storm   322.4
Whitehead, Alfred North, 1861-1947
Process and reality   113
Whitfield, Eileen, 1951-
Pickford   92
Whitfield, Peter
Landmarks in western science   509
Whitman, Walt, 1819-1892
Complete poetry and collected prose   818
Leaves of grass   811
In Whitman, W. Complete poetry and collected prose   818
Selected poems   811

About
Callow, P. From noon to starry night: a life of Walt Whitman   92
Morris, R. The better angel: Walt Whitman in the Civil War   92
See/See also pages in the following book(s):
Bloom, H. The Western canon   809
Jarrell, R. No other book   809
Kazin, A. An American procession p103-27   810.9
Matthiessen, F. O. American renaissance p517-625   810.9
Whitney, Elinor See Field, Elinor Whitney, 1889-1980
Whitney, Gertrude Vanderbilt
About
Biddle, F. M. The Whitney women and the museum they made   708
The **Whitney** women and the museum they made. Biddle, F. M.   708
Whittling See Wood carving
Whitworth, Kathy, 1939-
Golf for women   796.352
Who killed Jesus? Crossan, J. D.   232.9
Who needs God. Kushner, H. S.   296.7
Who says elephants can't dance? Gerstner, L. V., Jr.   338.7
Who stole feminism? Sommers, C. H.   305.4
Who was who   920.003
Who was who in Amcrica   920.003
Who was who in Native American history. See Waldman, C. Biographical dictionary of American Indian history to 1900   920.003
Who was who in the Greek world, 776 BC-30 BC   920.003
Who wrote the Bible? Friedman, R. E.   222
Who wrote the Dead Sea scrolls? Golb, N.   296.1
A **whole** new life. Price, R.   92
The **whole** shebang. Ferris, T.   523.1
The **whole** woman. Greer, G.   305.4
Wholistic medicine See Holistic medicine
Whooping cranes See Cranes (Birds)
Whorton, James C., 1942-
Nature cures   615.5
Who's afraid of Schrödinger's cat? Marshall, I. N.   500
Who's afraid of Virginia Woolf? Albee, E.   812
Who's who   920.003
Who's who among African Americans   920.003
Who's who among black Americans. See Who's who among African Americans   920.003
Who's who in America   920.003
Who's who in American art   920.003
Who's who in American politics   920.003
Who's who in art   920.003
Who's who in British history   920.003
Who's who in finance and industry   920.003
Who's who in the Bible. Calvocoressi, P.   220.9
Who's who of American women   920.003
"**Why** are all the Black kids sitting together in the cafeteria?" and other conversations about race. Tatum, B. D.   305.8
Why buildings fall down. Levy, M.   690
Why do clocks run clockwise? and other imponderables. Feldman, D.   031.02
Why elephants have big ears. Lavers, C.   590
Why geese don't get obese (and we do). Widmaier, E. P.   571
Why I am a Catholic. Wills, G.   282
Why I'm like this. Kaplan, C.   92
Why Johnny can't read—and what you can do about it. Flesch, R. F.   372.4
Why Orwell matters. Hitchens, C.   828
Why people believe weird things. Shermer, M.   001.9
Why read the classics? Calvino, I.   809
Why religion matters. Smith, H.   215

Why Sinatra matters. Hamill, P.   92
Why suicide? Marcus, E.   179.7
Why terrorism works. Dershowitz, A. M.   303.6
Why the Allies won. Overy, R. J.   940.53
Why they kill. Rhodes, R.   364.3
Why Waco? Tabor, J. D.   291.9
Why we buy. Underhill, P.   658.8
Why we can't wait. King, M. L.   323.1
Why we hurt. Vertosick, F. T.   616
Why we love the dogs we do. Coren, S.   636.7
Whybrow, P. J., 1942-
  (ed) Travels with the fossil hunters. See Travels with the fossil hunters   560
Whybrow, Peter C.
  A mood apart   616.89
Whybrow, Peter J. See Whybrow, P. J., 1942-
Wickelgren, Ingrid
  The gene masters   599.93
Wicker, Tom
  Dwight D. Eisenhower   92
Wickett, Murray R., 1965-
  Contested territory   976.6
Wide as the waters. Bobrick, B.   220.5
Wideman, John Edgar
  Hoop roots   92
Widmaier, Eric P.
  Why geese don't get obese (and we do)   571
Widows
  Caine, L. Being a widow   306.8
Wieder, Serena
  (jt. auth) Greenspan, S. I. The child with special needs   362.1
Wiegers, Michael, 1964-
  (ed) Reversible monuments. See Reversible monuments   861
Wiencek, Henry
  The Hairstons   975
  National Geographic guide to America's great houses   728.8
Wiener, Thomas
  The off-Hollywood film guide   791.43
Wiener Secession
  See/See also pages in the following book(s):
  Nebehay, C. M. Gustav Klimt   759.36
Wiesel, Elie, 1928-
  All rivers run to the sea   92
  And the sea is never full   92
  Souls on fire   296.8
Wieseltier, Leon
  Kaddish   296.4
Wiesenthal, Simon
  The sunflower   179.7
         About
  Pick, H. Simon Wiesenthal   92
Wiesner, David
  See/See also pages in the following book(s):
  The Newbery & Caldecott medal books, 1986-2000 p154-66   028.5
Wife abuse
  Dutton, D. G. The batterer   362.82
Wiggins, Arthur W.
  (jt. auth) Wynn, C. M. The five biggest ideas in science   500
Wigginton, B. Eliot
  (ed) Foxfire [1]-11. See Foxfire [1]-11   975.8
Wigginton, Eliot See Wigginton, B. Eliot
Wight, James Alfred See Herriot, James
Wight, Jim
  The real James Herriot   92
Wigoder, Geoffrey, 1922-1999
  (ed) Encyclopedia of Jewish life before and during the Holocaust. See Encyclopedia of Jewish life before and during the Holocaust   940.53

  (ed) The New encyclopedia of Judaism. See The New encyclopedia of Judaism [New York University Press]   296.03
  (ed) The Oxford dictionary of the Jewish religion. See The Oxford dictionary of the Jewish religion   296.03
Wilbourn, Carole, 1940-
  The total cat   636.8
Wilbur, Richard, 1921-
  Mayflies   811
  New and collected poems   811
  (ed) Poe, E. A. Poems and poetics   811
Wilcox, Bonnie
  Atlas of dog breeds of the world   636.7
Wild Bill: the legend and life of William O. Douglas. Murphy, B. A.   92
The wild blue. Ambrose, S. E.   940.54
Wild cats
    See also Cats; Lions; Tigers
  Kitchener, A. The natural history of the wild cats   599.75
The wild duck. Ibsen, H.
  In Ibsen, H. The complete major prose plays p387-490   839.8
  In Ibsen, H. Ibsen: four plays, v2   839.8
Wild flowers
  Coffey, T. The history and folklore of North American wildflowers   582.13
  Johnson, L. B. Wildflowers across America   582.13
  Spellenberg, R. National Audubon Society field guide to North American wildflowers, western region   582.13
  Thieret, J. W. National Audubon Society field guide to North American wildflowers: eastern region   582.13
Wild fowl See Game and game birds
The wild frontier. Osborn, W. M.   973
Wild fruits. Thoreau, H. D.   581.6
Wild minds. Hauser, M. D.   591.5
Wild orphans. Ellis, G.   599.67
Wild swans. Chang, J.   951.05
The wild vegetarian cookbook. Brill, S.   641.5
Wilde, Oscar, 1854-1900
  The ballad of Reading Gaol; criticism
  In Heaney, S. The redress of poetry   821.009
  The importance of being Earnest   822
  also in Our dramatic heritage v5   808.82
  also in The Oxford anthology of English literature v2   820.8
         About
  Belford, B. Oscar Wilde   92
  Ellmann, R. Oscar Wilde   92
    See/See also pages in the following book(s):
  Heaney, S. The redress of poetry   821.009
  Simon, J. I. Dreamers of dreams   809.1
Wilde, Ralph
  (jt. auth) Devine, C. Human rights   323
Wilde, W. H. (William Henry), 1923-
  The Oxford companion to Australian literature   820.3
Wilde, William Henry See Wilde, W. H. (William Henry), 1923-
Wilder, Billy, 1906-2002
         About
  Sikov, E. On Sunset Boulevard: the life and times of Billy Wilder   92
Wilder, Laura Ingalls, 1867-1957
         About
  Anderson, W. T. Laura Ingalls Wilder country   92
Wilder, Shirley
         About
  Bernstein, N. The lost children of Wilder   362.7
Wilder, Thornton, 1897-1975
  Our town   812

Wilder, Thornton, 1897-1975—*Continued*
See/See also pages in the following book(s):
Playwrights at work   **812.009**
Wilderness areas
See/See also pages in the following book(s):
Crawford, M. Habitats and ecosystems   **578.68**
Wilderness at dawn. Morgan, T.   **970**
Wilderness survival
Stilwell, A. Encyclopedia of survival techniques
    796.5
The **wildest** ride. Menzer, J.   **796.72**
Wildflowers across America. Johnson, L. B.   **582.13**
Wildlife conservation
See also Birds—Protection
Carson, R. Lost woods   **570**
Chadwick, D. H. The company we keep   **591.68**
Goodall, J. The ten trusts   **333.95**
Wildlife refuges
Ellis, G. Wild orphans   **599.67**
Wiles, Andrew
About
Aczel, A. D. Fermat's last theorem   **512**
Singh, S. Fermat's enigma   **512**
Wiley, Bell Irvin, 1906-
The life of Billy Yank   **973.7**
The life of Johnny Reb   **973.7**
Wilford, John Noble
(ed) Cosmic dispatches. See Cosmic dispatches
    520
Wilhelm II, German Emperor *See* William II, German
Emperor, 1859-1941
Wilhelm Tell. Schiller, F.
In Our dramatic heritage v4   **808.82**
Wilkins, Charles (Charles Everett)
The circus at the edge of the earth   **791.3**
Wilkins, Isabelle A.
(jt. auth) Kohn, I. A silent sorrow   **618.3**
Wilkins, Maurice Hugh Frederick, 1916-
See/See also pages in the following book(s):
Friedman, M. Medicine's 10 greatest discoveries
    610.9
Wilkins, Richard C.
Home VCR repair illustrated   **621.388**
Wilkins, Roger W., 1932-
Jefferson's pillow   **973**
Wilkins, Thurman
John Muir   **92**
Wilkins, Vicki
(jt. auth) Wilkins, R. C. Home VCR repair illustrated
    621.388
Wilkinson, Daniel, 1970-
Silence on the mountain   **972.81**
Wilkinson, Richard H.
The complete gods and goddesses of ancient Egypt
    299
Will, George F.
Bunts: Curt Flood, Camden Yards, Pete Rose, and oth-
er reflections on baseball   **796.357**
Men at work: the craft of baseball   **796.357**
Restoration   **328.73**
With a happy eye but . . . America and the world,
1997-2002   **973.929**
The woven figure   **973.929**
Will *See* Free will and determinism
Will the circle be unbroken? Terkel, S.   **128**
The **will** to live on. Wouk, H.   **296**
The **will** to power. Nietzsche, F. W.   **193**
Will you miss me when I'm gone? Zwonitzer, M.
    920
Willett, Felicia
(jt. auth) Lagasse, E. Every day's a party   **642**
Willett, Walter
Eat, drink and be healthy   **613.2**

William II, German Emperor, 1859-1941
See/See also pages in the following book(s):
Massie, R. K. Dreadnought   **940.3**
William Faulkner A to Z. Fargnoli, A. N.   **813.009**
William Faulkner: the Yoknapatawpha country. Brooks,
C.   **813.009**
William Wordsworth. Wordsworth, W.   **821**
Williams, C. K. (Charles Kenneth), 1936-
Repair   **811**
The singing   **811**
The vigil   **811**
Williams, Charles, 1933-
The last great Frenchman   **92**
Williams, Charles Kenneth *See* Williams, C. K.
(Charles Kenneth), 1936-
Williams, David Hamilton- *See* Hamilton-Williams, Da-
vid
Williams, Ernest
(jt. auth) Stokes, D. W. The butterfly book   **595.7**
Williams, Eunice, 1696-1786
About
Demos, J. The unredeemed captive   **973.2**
Williams, Franklin P.
(ed) Encyclopedia of American prisons. See Encyclo-
pedia of American prisons   **365**
Williams, Glyn, 1932-
Voyages of delusion   **910.4**
Williams, Hank, 1923-1953
About
Escott, C. Hank Williams   **92**
Williams, Jack, 1936-
The weather book   **551.6**
Williams, John, 1664-1729
About
Demos, J. The unredeemed captive   **973.2**
Williams, Juan
Eyes on the prize: America's civil rights years, 1954-
1965   **323.1**
This far by faith   **200**
Thurgood Marshall   **92**
Williams, Peter W.
Encyclopedia of American cultural and intellectual his-
tory. See Encyclopedia of American cultural and in-
tellectual history   **973.03**
Encyclopedia of American social history. See Encyclo-
pedia of American social history   **973.03**
Williams, Ted, 1918-2002
Ted Williams   **92**
About
Linn, E. Hitter: the life and turmoils of Ted Williams
    92
See/See also pages in the following book(s):
Halberstam, D. The teammates   **920**
Williams, Tennessee, 1911-1983
About
Leverich, L. Tom: the unknown Tennessee Williams
    92
Spoto, D. The kindness of strangers: the life of Ten-
nessee Williams   **92**
See/See also pages in the following book(s):
Playwrights at work   **812.009**
Vidal, G. United States—essays, 1952-1992 p437-49,
1131-48   **814**
Williams, Terry Tempest
Red: passion and patience in the desert   **333.7**
Williams, Thomas Lanier *See* Williams, Tennessee,
1911-1983
Williams, Trevor Illtyd
A history of invention   **609**
(ed) Science: a history of discovery in the twentieth
century. See Science: a history of discovery in the
twentieth century   **509**
Williams, William Carlos, 1883-1963
The collected poems of William Carlos Williams
    811

Williams, William Carlos, 1883-1963—*Continued*
In the American grain — 814
Paterson — 811
See/See also pages in the following book(s):
Jarrell, R. No other book — 809
Lowell, R. Collected prose p29-44 — 818
Pritchard, W. H. Lives of the modern poets p263-94 — 821.009

Williams family
About
Demos, J. The unredeemed captive — 973.2
Williamson, Edwin
The Penguin history of Latin America — 980
Williamson, Mark
The Cambridge dictionary of space technology — 629.4
Williamson, Marvel L.
Great sex after 40 — 306.7
Williamson, Sheri L.
A field guide to hummingbirds of North America — 598
Willie Mosconi's winning pocket billiards for beginners and advanced players, with a section on trick shots. Mosconi, W. — 794.7
Willing. Arendt, H.
In Arendt, H. The life of the mind — 153
Willing pocket billiards. See Mosconi, W. Willie Mosconi's winning pocket billiards for beginners and advanced players, with a section on trick shots — 794.7
Willinger, Faith Heller
Red, white, and greens — 641.6
Willis, Deborah, 1952-
Reflections in Black — 770
Willis, Mark R.
Dealing with difficult people in the library — 025.5
Willoughby, John
(jt. auth) Schlesinger, C. How to cook meat — 641.6
(jt. auth) Schlesinger, C. The thrill of the grill — 641.7
Wills, Christopher
Yellow fever, black goddess — 614.4
Wills, Garry, 1934-
Certain trumpets — 303.3
James Madison — 92
Lincoln at Gettysburg — 973.7
A necessary evil — 973
Papal sin — 262
Saint Augustine — 92
Venice: lion city — 945
Why I am a Catholic — 282
Wills
The American Bar Association guide to wills and estates — 346.05
Clifford, D. Nolo's simple will book — 346.05
Clifford, D. Quick & legal will book — 346.05
Sitarz, D. Prepare your own will — 346.05
Strauss, S. D. Wills and trusts — 346.05
Wills and trusts. Strauss, S. D. — 346.05
Wilmeth, Don B.
(ed) Cambridge guide to American theatre. See Cambridge guide to American theatre — 792.03
Wilmut, Ian
The second creation — 174
Wilson, A. N. (Andrew Norman), 1950-
C.S. Lewis — 92
God's funeral — 200.9
Jesus — 232.9
Paul: the mind of the Apostle — 92
Wilson, Andrew Norman See Wilson, A. N. (Andrew Norman), 1950-
Wilson, August
Fences — 812
Jitney — 812
Joe Turner's come and gone — 812
Ma Rainey's black bottom — 812
The piano lesson — 812
Seven guitars — 812
See/See also pages in the following book(s):
Playwrights at work — 812.009
Wilson, Charis, 1914-
See/See also pages in the following book(s):
Prose, F. The lives of the muses — 920
Wilson, Colin, 1931-
The Atlantis blueprint — 001.9
The atlas of holy places & sacred sites — 291.3
Wilson, Don E.
(ed) The Smithsonian book of North American mammals. See The Smithsonian book of North American mammals — 599
Wilson, Edith, 1896-1981
See/See also pages in the following book(s):
Harrison, D. D. Black pearls — 920
Wilson, Edith Bolling Galt, 1872-1961
About
Levin, P. L. Edith and Woodrow: the Wilson White House — 92
Wilson, Edmund, 1895-1972
The fifties — 818
The forties — 818
Patriotic gore — 810.9
Upstate — 818
Wilson, Edward O., 1929-
Consilience — 121
The diversity of life — 577
The future of life — 333.95
In search of nature — 113
Insect societies — 595.7
(jt. auth) Hölldobler, B. The ants — 595.7
(jt. auth) Hölldobler, B. Journey to the ants — 595.7
Wilson, Edwin P.
About
Maas, P. Manhunt — 364.1
Wilson, Elizabeth
Jacqueline du Pré — 92
Wilson, Ellen Judy
Encyclopedia of the Enlightenment — 940.2
Wilson, Frank R.
The hand — 612
Wilson, George, 1920-
(ed) Literature and its times. See Literature and its times — 809
Wilson, Hugo
Motorcycle owner's manual — 629.28
Wilson, James, 1949-
The earth shall weep — 970.004
Wilson, James D. (James Darrell), 1946-
(ed) The Mark Twain encyclopedia. See The Mark Twain encyclopedia — 818
Wilson, James Q.
The marriage problem — 306.8
Wilson, John Anthony Burgess See Burgess, Anthony, 1917-1993
Wilson, K. (Kevin), 1958-
(jt. auth) Stroman, J. Administrative assistant's & secretary's handbook — 651.3
Wilson, Kenneth G. (Kenneth George), 1923-
The Columbia guide to standard American English — 428
Wilson, Kevin See Wilson, K. (Kevin), 1958-
Wilson, Lanford, 1937-
5th of July — 812
21 short plays — 812
Contents: Home free!; The madness of Lady Bright; Ludlow fair; This is the rill speaking; Days ahead; Wandering; Stoop; Sextet (yes); Ikke, Ikke, nye, nye, nye; Victory on Mrs. Dandywine's island; The Great Nebula in Orion; The family continues; Brontosaurus; Thymus vulgaris; Breakfast at the track; Say de Kooning; A betrothal; Abstinence; A poster of the cosmos; The moonshot tape; Eukiah

Wilson, Lanford, 1937——_Continued_
Fifth of July
  _In_ Wilson, L. The Talley trilogy p1-74   **812**
A tale told
  _In_ Wilson, L. The Talley trilogy p191-262   **812**
Talley & Son
  _In_ Wilson, L. The Talley trilogy p123-90   **812**
The Talley trilogy   **812**
Talley's folly
  _In_ Wilson, L. The Talley trilogy p75-122   **812**
Wilson, Wilkie
  (jt. auth) Kuhn, C. Buzzed   **615**
  (jt. auth) Kuhn, C. Pumped   **617.1**
Wilson, Woodrow, 1856-1924
About
Auchincloss, L. Woodrow Wilson   **92**
Cooper, J. M. The warrior and the priest: Woodrow
  Wilson and Theodore Roosevelt   **92**
Levin, P. L. Edith and Woodrow: the Wilson White
  House   **92**
MacMillan, M. Paris 1919   **940.3**
  See/See also pages in the following book(s):
Hofstadter, R. The American political tradition, and the
  men who made it p234-78   **973**
Kissinger, H. Diplomacy p29-55   **327.73**
Tuchman, B. W. Practicing history p146-57   **907**
The **Wilson** calendar of world history   **902**
The **Wilson** chronology of science and technology.
  Ochoa, G.   **502**
The **Wilson** chronology of the arts. Ochoa, G.   **700**
The **Wilson** chronology of women's achievements.
  Franck, I. M.   **305.4**
Wilson family
About
Wilson, E. Upstate   **818**
Wilton, Andrew
American sublime   **759.13**
Winch, Julie
A gentleman of color: the life of James Forten
   92
Winchell, Walter, 1897-1972
About
Gabler, N. Winchell   **92**
Winchester, Simon
Krakatoa: the day the world exploded, August 27,
  1883   **551.2**
The map that changed the world   **92**
The professor and the madman   **423**
The river at the center of the world   **951**
Window gardening
  See also Container gardening; House plants
Windows, Stained glass _See_ Glass painting and staining
Winds
DeBlieu, J. Wind   **551.51**
Windsor Castle
Roberts, J. Royal landscape   **942**
Wine and wine making
Gaiter, D. J. The Wall Street journal guide to wine
   641.2
Kolpan, S. Exploring wine   **641.2**
Larousse encyclopedia of wine   **641.2**
Peynaud, E. The taste of wine   **641.2**
Wing, Charlie, 1939-
The big book of small household repairs   **643**
Wing, Lorna
The autistic spectrum   **618.92**
Wingate, Isabel Barnum, 1901-1987
(ed) Fairchild's dictionary of textiles. See Fairchild's
  dictionary of textiles   **677**
Winged words: American Indian writers speak. Coltelli,
  L.   **897**
Wings of morning. Childers, T.   **940.54**
Winik, Jay, 1957-
April 1865   **973.7**

Winik, Marion
The lunch-box chronicles   **306.8**
Winks, Robin W., 1930-2003
(ed) Mystery and suspense writers. See Mystery and
  suspense writers   **809.3**
Winner, Ellen
Gifted children   **155.45**
Winner, Lauren F.
Girl meets God   **92**
Winning bowling. Anthony, E.   **794.6**
Winning in the game of life. Gegax, T.   **158**
Winslow, Barbara, 1941-
(jt. auth) Jacobson, M. Patterns of home   **728**
Winston, Diane H., 1951-
Red-hot and righteous   **287.9**
Winston, Mark L.
Nature wars   **577.2**
Travels in the genetically modified zone   **664**
Winter, Ruth, 1930-
A consumer's dictionary of cosmetic ingredients
   668
A consumer's dictionary of food additives   **664**
Winter hours. Oliver, M.   **818**
Winter sports
  See also Olympic games
Winterdance. Paulsen, G.   **798.8**
Winters, Arthur Yvor _See_ Winters, Yvor, 1900-1968
Winters, CM!
(jt. auth) Norlin, E. Usability testing for library
  websites   **025.04**
Winters, Yvor, 1900-1968
The selected poems of Yvor Winters   **811**
Wire _See_ Barbed wire
Wireless nation. Murray, J. B., Jr.   **384.5**
Wiring, Electric _See_ Electric wiring
Wirths, Eduard, 1909-1945
  See/See also pages in the following book(s):
Lifton, R. J. The Nazi doctors p384-414   **940.53**
Wischnitzer, Saul
Barron's guide to medical & dental schools
   610.69
The **wisdom** of Confucius. Confucius   **181**
The **wisdom** of the bones. Walker, A.   **599.93**
Wise, Anna
Awakening the mind   **615.8**
Wise, David, 1930-
Cassidy's run   **327.12**
Spy: the inside story of how the FBI's Robert Hanssen
  betrayed America   **327.12**
Wise, Michael Owen
(tr) Dead Sea scrolls. The Dead Sea scrolls   **296.1**
(ed) Dead Sea scrolls. The Dead Sea scrolls uncovered
   296.1
Wise, Nicole
(jt. auth) Rosenfeld, A. A. Hyper-parenting   **649**
Wise, Steven M.
Drawing the line   **179**
Wise women: over two thousand years of spiritual writ-
  ing by women   **200**
Wiseman, Carter
I.M. Pei: a profile in American architecture   **92**
Shaping a nation   **720.973**
Wishing on the moon: the life and times of Billie Holi-
  day. Clarke, D.   **92**
Wisniewski, David
  See/See also pages in the following book(s):
The Newbery & Caldecott medal books, 1986-2000
  p256-65   **028.5**
Wit. Edson, M.   **812**
Wit and humor
  See also American wit and humor; Comedy; En-
  glish wit and humor; Humorous poetry
O'Rourke, P. J. Eat the rich   **817**
The Oxford dictionary of humorous quotations
   808.88

Wit and humor—*Continued*
The Penguin book of women's humor   **817.008**
Toasts   **808.88**
Wit and its relation to the unconscious. Freud, S.
In Freud, S. The basic writings of Sigmund Freud
    150.19
The **wit** and wisdom of Mark Twain. Twain, M.
    818
Witalec, Janet, 1965-
(ed) Native North American literature. See Native
North American literature   **810.9**
Witchcraft
See also Magic
Adler, M. Drawing down the moon   **133.4**
Carlson, L. M. A fever in Salem   **133.4**
Hutton, R. The triumph of the moon   **133.4**
Karlsen, C. F. The devil in the shape of a woman
    133.4
Norton, M. B. In the devil's snare   **133.4**
Stark, R. For the glory of God   **291.1**
Drama
Miller, A. The crucible   **812**
Encyclopedias
Guiley, R. E. The encyclopedia of witches and witch-
craft   **133.4**
Witcover, Jules
No way to pick a president   **324**
The year the dream died   **973.92**
With a happy eye but . . . America and the world,
1997-2002. Will, G. F.   **973.929**
With God on our side. Martin, W. C.   **261.8**
Within the plantation household. Fox-Genovese, E.
    305.4
Without end. Zagajewski, A.   **891.8**
Without feathers. Allen, W.   **817**
Without God, without creed. Turner, J.   **211**
Without lying down. Beauchamp, C.   **92**
Witness   **940.53**
Witness. Chambers, W.   **92**
Witness for the prosecution. Christie, A.
In Christie, A. The mousetrap and other plays
    822
Witness to America   **973**
Witness to hope: the biography of Pope John Paul II.
Weigel, G.   **92**
Witten, Edward
See/See also pages in the following book(s):
Mlodinow, L. Euclid's window   **516**
Wittgenstein, Ludwig, 1889-1951
About
Edmonds, D. Wittgenstein's poker   **192**
See/See also pages in the following book(s):
Gass, W. H. Finding a form p146-59   **814**
Wittgenstein's poker. Edmonds, D.   **192**
Wittkower, Rudolf, 1901-1971
Art and architecture in Italy, 1600-1750   **709.45**
The **wives** of Henry VIII. Fraser, A.   **920**
Wizards and sorcerers. Ogden, T.   **133.4**
The **wizards** of Langley. Richelson, J.   **327.12**
WNEW (Radio station: New York, N.Y.)
Neer, R. FM: the rise and fall of free-form rock radio
    791.44
Wodehouse, P. G. (Pelham Grenville), 1881-1975
See/See also pages in the following book(s):
Orwell, G. The Orwell reader p315-28   **828**
Wodehouse, Pelham Grenville *See* Wodehouse, P. G.
(Pelham Grenville), 1881-1975
Woe is I. O'Conner, P. T.   **428**
Wojtyła, Karol *See* John Paul II, Pope, 1920-
Wolf, Burt
(ed) The New cooks' catalogue. See The New cooks'
catalogue   **683**

Wolf, Molly, 1949-
KnitLit: sweaters and their stories and other writing
about knitting. See KnitLit: sweaters and their stories
and other writing about knitting   **746.43**
Wolf, Naomi
The beauty myth   **305.4**
Misconceptions   **618.2**
Promiscuities   **306.7**
The **wolf** almanac. Busch, R.   **599.77**
Wolfe, Alan
Moral freedom   **170**
Wolfe, Charles K.
The life and legend of Leadbelly   **92**
Wolfe, David W.
Tales from the underground   **578**
Wolfe, James, 1727-1759
See/See also pages in the following book(s):
Schama, S. Dead certainties   **907**
Wolfe, Lisa Ann
Library public relations, promotions, and communica-
tions   **021.7**
Wolfe, Michael, 1945-
One thousand roads to Mecca   **297**
Wolfe, Tom
Hooking up   **818**
The right stuff   **629.45**
Wolff, Alexander
Big game, small world   **796.323**
Wolff, Christoph
Johann Sebastian Bach   **92**
Wolff, Geoffrey, 1937-
The art of burning bridges: a life of John O'Hara
    92
Wolff, Kurt
Country music: the rough guide   **781.642**
Wolff, Tobias, 1945-
This boy's life: a memoir   **92**
Wolfgang Puck's pizza, pasta and more!. Puck, W.
    641.8
Wolfson, Richard, 1947-
Simply Einstein   **530.1**
Wolman, William
The great 401(k) hoax   **332.024**
Wolpert, Stanley A., 1927-
Gandhi's passion   **92**
A new history of India   **954**
Wolpoff, Milford H., 1942-
Race and human evolution   **599.97**
Wolves
Busch, R. The wolf almanac   **599.77**
Lopez, B. H. Of wolves and men   **599.77**
McNamee, T. The return of the wolf to Yellowstone
    599.77
Mech, L. D. The way of the wolf   **599.77**
Mowat, F. Never cry wolf   **599.77**
Womack, John
Zapata and the Mexican Revolution   **972.08**
Woman. Angier, N.   **612.6**
The **woman** at the Washington Zoo. Jarrell, R.
In Jarrell, R. The complete poems   **811**
Woman in the mists: the story of Dian Fossey and the
mountain gorillas of Africa. Mowat, F.   **92**
A **woman** of valor: Clara Barton and the Civil War.
Oates, S. B.   **92**
The **woman** who watches over the world. Hogan, L.
    92
The **Womanly** art of breastfeeding   **649**
Woman's face. Gross, K. J.   **646.7**
Women
See also Widows; women of particular racial or
ethnic groups, e.g. *African American women;* and
women in various occupations and professions
Beauvoir, S. de. The second sex   **305.4**
Cordingly, D. Women sailors and sailors' women
    910.4

Women—*Continued*
Wolf, N. The beauty myth   305.4
Biography
Breton, M. J. Women pioneers for the environment
    920.003
Fraser, A. The warrior queens   920
Prose, F. The lives of the muses   920
Salisbury, J. E. Encyclopedia of women in the ancient
world   305.4
Slung, M. B. Living with cannibals and other women's
adventures   910.4
Ware, S. Letter to the world   920
Women in world history   920.003
Biography—Dictionaries
Adamson, L. G. Notable women in American history
    920.003
Adamson, L. G. Notable women in world history
    920.003
Kuhlman, E. A. A to Z of women in world history
    920.003
Civil rights
See Women's rights
Diseases
Gay, K. Encyclopedia of women's health issues
    613
Healthy women, healthy lives   613
Kra, S. J. What every woman must know about heart
disease   616.1
Pashkow, F. J. The women's heart book   616.1
Poirier, L. M. Women & diabetes   616.4
Prevention's ultimate guide to women's health and
wellness   613
Education
Schlachter, G. A. Directory of financial aids for wom-
en   378.3
Women in higher education   378
See/See also pages in the following book(s):
Rich, A. Blood, bread, and poetry p188-97   814
Employment
Global woman   331.4
Employment—History
America's working women   331.4
Kessler-Harris, A. Out to work   331.4
Folklore
Estés, C. P. Women who run with the wolves
    155.6
Health and hygiene
Allison, K. C. American Medical Association complete
guide to women's health   613
Brown, B. Bobbi Brown beauty evolution   646.7
Callahan, L. The fitness factor   613.7
Gay, K. Encyclopedia of women's health issues
    613
Greenwood-Robinson, M. Hair savers for women
    616.5
Hadadi, L. Healthy beauty   646.7
Healthy women, healthy lives   613
Kashuk, S. Real beauty   646.7
Love, S. M. Dr. Susan Love's menopause and hor-
mone book   618.1
Minkin, M. J. The Yale guide to women's reproductive
health   618.1
Nelson, M. E. Strong women eat well   613.2
Null, G. For women only!   613
Our bodies, ourselves for the new century   613
Poirier, L. M. Women & diabetes   616.4
Prevention's ultimate guide to women's health and
wellness   613
Seibel, M. M. The soy solution for menopause
    618.1
Sichel, D. Women's moods   616.89
History
De Pauw, L. G. Battle cries and lullabies   355
Greer, G. The whole woman   305.4
Yalom, M. A history of the wife   306.8

History—Chronology
Franck, I. M. The Wilson chronology of women's
achievements   305.4
History—Encyclopedias
Salisbury, J. E. Encyclopedia of women in the ancient
world   305.4
Women in world history   920.003
Law and legislation
The Rights of women   346.01
Women's legal guide   346.01
Ordination
See Ordination of women
Portraits
Leibovitz, A. Women   779
Virtue & beauty   757
Psychology
Angier, N. Woman   612.6
Bass, E. The courage to heal   362.83
Buhle, M. J. Feminism and its discontents   150.19
Estés, C. P. Women who run with the wolves
    155.6
Fisher, H. E. The first sex   305.4
Friday, N. My mother/my self   155.6
Goodman, E. I know just what you mean   158
Greer, G. The change   618.1
Lerner, H. G. The dance of deception   155.3
Lerner, H. G. The dance of intimacy   155.6
Levinson, D. J. The seasons of a woman's life
    155.6
Our bodies, ourselves for the new century   613
Queen Latifah. Ladies first   158
Richardson, B. L. What mama couldn't tell us about
love   158
Sichel, D. Women's moods   616.89
Sullivan, R. Labyrinth of desire   818
Quotations
Biggs, M. Women's words   808.88
The Quotable woman   808.88
Religious life
Anderson, S. R. The feminine face of God   291
Furlong, M. Visions & longings   248.2
Wise women: over two thousand years of spiritual
writing by women   200
Religious life—Encyclopedias
Encyclopedia of women and world religion   200
Sexual behavior
Carter, S. Men like women who like themselves
    158
Wolf, N. Promiscuities   306.7
Social conditions
Freedman, E. B. No turning back   305.4
Global woman   331.4
Greer, G. The madwoman's underclothes   305.4
Greer, G. The whole woman   305.4
See/See also pages in the following book(s):
Foner, E. The story of American freedom   323.44
Social conditions—Encyclopedias
The Greenwood encyclopedia of women's issues
worldwide   305.4
Suffrage
Goldsmith, B. Other powers: the age of suffrage, spiri-
tualism, and the scandalous Victoria Woodhull
    92
Afghanistan
Benard, C. Veiled courage   958.1
Zoya. Zoya's story   958.1
China
Chang, J. Wild swans   951.05
Developing countries
Global woman   331.4
Europe
See/See also pages in the following book(s):
Tuchman, B. W. A distant mirror p204-19   944
Great Britain—History
Dolan, B. Ladies of the Grand Tour   910.4

Women—*Continued*
India
Bumiller, E. May you be the mother of a hundred sons
954.05
Kansas
Stratton, J. L. Pioneer women   978.1
Southern States
Faust, D. G. Mothers of invention   973.7
Fox-Genovese, E. Within the plantation household
305.4
United States
The Beacon book of essays by contemporary American women   814
Crittenden, A. The price of motherhood   306.8
Friedan, B. The feminine mystique   305.4
Friedan, B. The fountain of age   305.26
Reagan, L. J. When abortion was a crime   363.46
United States—Biography
Notable American women: the modern period
920.003
Sonneborn, L. A to Z of American women in the performing arts   920.003
Who's who of American women   920.003
United States—History
Cullen-DuPont, K. Encyclopedia of women's history in America   305.4
A History of women in the United States: state-by-state reference   305.4
No small courage   305.4
Roberts, C. We are our mothers' daughters   305.4
United States—History—Encyclopedias
Encyclopedia of women in American history
305.4

Women, Jewish *See* Jewish women
Women. Leibovitz, A.   779
Women & diabetes. Poirier, L. M.   616.4
Women air pilots
Haynsworth, L. Amelia Earhart's daughters
629.13
Women Airforce Service Pilots (U.S.)
Keil, S. V. W. Those wonderful women in their flying machines   940.54
Women and music in America since 1900   780.9
Women and writing. Woolf, V.   820.9
Women artists
Borzello, F. A world of our own   704
Henkes, R. The art of black American women
709.73
Henkes, R. Latin American women artists of the United States   704
Dictionaries
Contemporary women artists   920.003
Dictionary of women artists   920.003
Kort, C. A to Z of American women in the visual arts
920.003
North American women artists of the twentieth century
920.003
Vigué, J. Great women masters of art   920.003
Women astronauts
Haynsworth, L. Amelia Earhart's daughters
629.13
Women athletes
Araton, H. Alive and kicking   796.334
Guttmann, A. Women's sports   796
Nike is a goddess   796
Ryan, J. Little girls in pretty boxes   796.44
Encyclopedias
Sherrow, V. Encyclopedia of women and sports
796
Women authors
See also American literature—Women authors; American poetry—Women authors; English poetry—Women authors
Great women mystery writers   809.3
The Penguin book of women's humor   817.008

Roses, L. E. Harlem Renaissance and beyond: literary biographies of 100 black women writers, 1900-1945
810.9
Women writers at work   808
Bio-bibliography
Heising, W. L. Detecting women   016.8
Biography
Pierpont, C. R. Passionate minds   810.9
Women clergy
See also Ordination of women
Women composers
Dictionaries
The Norton/Grove dictionary of women composers
920.003
Women criminals
Rees, S. The floating brothel   365
Women in art
De Kooning, W. Willem de Kooning: tracing the figure   741
Steiner, W. Venus in exile   700
Virtue & beauty   757
Women in Christianity
Chaves, M. Ordaining women   262
Women in higher education   378
Women in literature
Heilbrun, C. G. Hamlet's mother and other women
820.9
Sullivan, R. Labyrinth of desire   818
Women in politics
Heymann, C. D. The Georgetown ladies' social club
305.4
Women in scripture   220.9
Women in the armed forces
See also Women soldiers
Women in the Bible
Deen, E. All of the women of the Bible   220.9
Murphy, C. The Word according to Eve   220.8
Women in scripture   220.9
Women in world history   920.003
Women inventors
Macdonald, A. L. Feminine ingenuity   609
Women journalists
Sorel, N. C. The women who wrote the war
940.53
Women mathematicians
Dictionaries
Notable women in mathematics   920.003
Women musicians
Women and music in America since 1900   780.9
Women of the Harlem Renaissance. Wall, C. A.
810.9
Women of the pleasure quarters. Downer, L.   952
Women photographers
Newman, C. Women photographers at National Geographic   770.9
Women pioneers for the environment. Breton, M. J.
920.003
Women poets
Heinemann book of African women's poetry   896
The Penguin book of women poets   808.81
Women rulers throughout the ages. Jackson-Laufer, G. M.   920
Women sailors and sailors' women. Cordingly, D.
910.4
Women scientists
Goodall, J. Beyond innocence   92
Reynolds, M. D. American women scientists   920
Dictionaries
Bailey, M. J. American women in science: 1950 to the present   920.003
Notable women in the physical sciences   920.003
Oakes, E. H. International encyclopedia of women scientists   920.003
Women singers *See* Singers

Women soldiers
Blanton, D. They fought like demons 973.7
De Pauw, L. G. Battle cries and lullabies 355
Fraser, A. The warrior queens 920
Leonard, E. D. All the daring of the soldier
973.7

Biography—Dictionaries
Amazons to fighter pilots 355
Women who kill. Jones, A. 364.1
Women who ruled. See Jackson-Laufer, G. M. Women
rulers throughout the ages 920
Women who run with the wolves. Estés, C. P.
155.6
The **women** who wrote the war. Sorel, N. C.
940.53
Women writers at work 808
Women's Air Service Pilots (U.S.) See Women Airforce
Service Pilots (U.S.)
The **women's** heart book. Pashkow, F. J. 616.1
Women's legal guide 346.01
Women's moods. Sichel, D. 616.89
Women's movement
Brownmiller, S. In our time 305.4
Rosen, R. The world split open 305.4
Women's rights
See also Pro-choice movement
Greer, G. The whole woman 305.4
The Rights of women 346.01
Solinger, R. Beggars and choosers 363.46
Women's sports. Guttmann, A. 796
Women's words. Biggs, M. 808.88
The **wonder** of girls. Gurian, M. 305.23
Wonderful life: the Burgess Shale and the nature of his-
tory. Gould, S. J. 560
A **wonderful** life: the films and career of James Stewart.
Thomas, T. 791.43
Wonders See Curiosities and wonders
Wonders of the African world. Gates, H. L. 960
Wood, Edward Frederick Lindley See Halifax, Edward
Frederick Lindley Wood, 1st Earl of, 1881-1959
Wood, Gaby
Edison's Eve 629.8
Wood, Ghislaine
(ed) Art deco 1910-1939. See Art deco 1910-1939
709.04
Wood, Gordon S.
The radicalism of the American Revolution 973.3
Wood, Graham
(jt. auth) Furia, P. Irving Berlin 92
Wood, Michael, 1948-
In search of the Trojan War 939
In the footsteps of Alexander the Great 938
Wood
The Encyclopedia of wood 674
Hoadley, R. B. Understanding wood 684
Peters, R. Woodworker's guide to wood 684
Wood carving
Burton, M. Architectural carving 736
Bütz, R. How to carve wood 731.4
Woodard, Colin, 1968-
Ocean's end 363.7
Woodfill, Samuel, 1883-1951
See/See also pages in the following book(s):
Mikaelian, A. Medal of honor 920
Woodhouse, Violet, 1948-
Divorce and money 346.01
Woodhull, Victoria C., 1838-1927
About
Goldsmith, B. Other powers: the age of suffrage, spiri-
tualism, and the scandalous Victoria Woodhull
92
Woodress, James Leslie
Willa Cather 92

Woodring, Carl, 1919-
(ed) The Columbia anthology of British poetry. See
The Columbia anthology of British poetry
821.008
(ed) The Columbia history of British poetry. See The
Columbia history of British poetry 821.009
Woodruff, Paul, 1943-
Reverence 170
Woods, Eldrick See Woods, Tiger
Woods, Tiger
About
Andrisani, J. The Tiger Woods way 796.352
Woodson, R. Dodge (Roger Dodge), 1955-
Build your dream home for less 690
Woodson, Roger Dodge See Woodson, R. Dodge (Roger
Dodge), 1955-
Woodstra, Chris
(ed) All music guide. See All music guide
781.64
(ed) All music guide to country. See All music guide
to country 781.642
(ed) All music guide to jazz. See All music guide to
jazz 781.65
Woodward, Bill
(jt. auth) Albright, M. K. Madam Secretary 92
Woodward, Bob, 1943-
Bush at war 973.931
The commanders 973.928
The final days 973.924
Maestro: Greenspan's Fed and the American boom
332.1
Shadow 973.92
(jt. auth) Bernstein, C. All the president's men
973.924
Woodward, C. Vann (Comer Vann), 1908-1999
The strange career of Jim Crow 305.8
Woodward, Comer Vann See Woodward, C. Vann
(Comer Vann), 1908-1999
Woodward, Kenneth L.
The book of miracles 291.1
Making saints 282
Woodward, Mark R., 1952-
(ed) Hopfe, L. M. Religions of the world 291
Woodwork
See also Carpentry; Furniture
Abram, N. Measure twice, cut once 684
Bird, L. The complete illustrated guide to shaping
wood 684
The Complete book of woodworking 684
Guidice, A. The seven essentials of woodworking
684
Hoadley, R. B. Understanding wood 684
Reed, C. Router joinery workshop 684
Underhill, R. The woodwright's apprentice 684
Warner, P. The router book 684
Woodworker's guide to wood. Peters, R. 684
Woodworking machinery
Reed, C. Router joinery workshop 684
Woodworth, Lynn
(jt. auth) McGonigal, D. Antarctica and the Arctic
998
The **woodwright's** apprentice. Underhill, R. 684
Woody Allen on Woody Allen. Allen, W. 791.43
Woolf, Virginia, 1882-1941
Essays of Virginia Woolf 824
Flush 828
A moment's liberty: the shorter diary 92
Moments of being 92
The second common reader 820.9
The Virginia Woolf reader 828
Women and writing 820.9
About
Gordon, L. Virginia Woolf, a writer's life 92
Hussey, M. Virginia Woolf A-Z 828
Lee, H. Virginia Woolf 92

Woolf, Virginia, 1882-1941—About—*Continued*
See/See also pages in the following book(s):
Bloom, H. The Western canon   809
Fraser, K. Ornament and silence   814
Gilbert, S. M. No man's land v3 p3-56   820.9
Heilbrun, C. G. Hamlet's mother and other women
  p58-97, 134-39   820.9
The **Word** according to Eve. Murphy, C.   220.8
Word games
  See also Crossword puzzles; Scrabble (Game)
Word processing
  Century 21 keyboarding & information processing
                                            652.3
Word processor keyboarding *See* Keyboarding (Elec-
  tronics)
Words *See* Vocabulary
Words, New *See* New words
The **words**. Sartre, J. P.   92
Words and rules. Pinker, S.   401
The **words** of Albert Schweitzer. Schweitzer, A.
                                            210
Words to rhyme with. Espy, W. R.   423
Wordsworth, William, 1770-1850
  Ode: intimations of immortality from recollections of
  early childhood; criticism
    In Brooks, C. The well wrought urn   821.009
  Selected poetry of William Wordsworth   821
  William Wordsworth   821
                    About
  Johnston, K. R. The hidden Wordsworth   92
  See/See also pages in the following book(s):
  Bloom, H. The Western canon   809
Work
  Fisher, A. B. If my career's on the fast track, where
    do I get a road map?   650.14
  Reich, R. B. The future of success   306
  Shulman, B. The betrayal of work   331.2
  Terkel, S. Working   331.2
              Psychological aspects
  Reinhold, B. B. Toxic work   650.1
Work-at-home sourcebook. Arden, L.   338.7
The **Work** of Charles and Ray Eames   745.4
Workaholism
  Lazear, J. The man who mistook his job for a life
                                            155.2
Working, Compulsive *See* Workaholism
Working. Terkel, S.   331.2
Working at home *See* Home-based business
Working class
  Dubofsky, M. Labor in America   331.8
  Freeman, J. B. Working-class New York   305.5
  Lubrano, A. Limbo: blue-collar roots, white-collar
    dreams   305.5
  Murolo, P. From the folks who brought you the week-
    end   331
Working couples *See* Dual-career families
Working days. Steinbeck, J.   818
Working solo. Lonier, T.   658
Working with words in business and legal writing.
  Agress, L.   808
Working women *See* Women—Employment
Workman, Fanny Bullock, 1859-1925
  See/See also pages in the following book(s):
  Slung, M. B. Living with cannibals and other women's
    adventures   910.4
The **works** of Edmund Spenser. Spenser, E. 828
Works on paper. Holroyd, M.   809
World, End of the *See* End of the world
The **World** almanac and book of facts   031.02
World artists, 1950-1980   920.003
World artists, 1980-1990   920.003
A **world** at arms. Weinberg, G. L.   940.53
World atlas, Goode's   912
World atlas of the oceans   912
World authors, 1900-1950   920.003

World authors, 1950-1970   920.003
World authors, 1970-1975   920.003
World authors, 1975-1980   920.003
World authors, 1980-1985   920.003
World authors, 1985-1990   920.003
World authors, 1990-1995   920.003
World authors, 1995-2000   920.003
World Bank
  See/See also pages in the following book(s):
  Soros, G. George Soros on globalization 337
The **world** below the window. Smith, W. J. 811
The **World** Book encyclopedia   031
The **World** Book multimedia encyclopedia. See The
  World Book encyclopedia   031
World Book's science year in review. See The World
  Book encyclopedia   031
World Book's year in review. See The World Book en-
  cyclopedia   031
World Christian encyclopedia   230.003
World economics *See* Economic conditions; Economic
  policy
World encyclopedia of 20th century murder. Nash, J. R.
                                            364.03
The **World** encyclopedia of comics   741.5
World explorers and discoverers   920.003
A **world** for butterflies. Schappert, P. 595.7
World historical fiction. Adamson, L. G. 016.8
World history
  Pagden, A. Peoples and empires   909
  Roberts, J. M. The new history of the world 909
              14th century
  Tuchman, B. W. A distant mirror   944
              18th century
    See also Enlightenment
  Craske, M. Art in Europe, 1700-1830   709.03
              19th century
  Tuchman, B. W. The proud tower   909.82
              20th century
  The Columbia history of the 20th century 909.82
  Conquest, R. Reflections on a ravaged century
                                            909.82
  Gilbert, M. History of the twentieth century
                                            909.82
  Glover, J. Humanity   909.82
  National Geographic eyewitness to the 20th century
                                            909.82
  The Oxford history of the twentieth century
                                            909.82
  Roberts, J. M. Twentieth century   909.82
  Tuchman, B. W. The proud tower   909.82
              20th century—Periodicals
  Facts on file   909.82
              20th century—Pictorial works
  Life: World War 2   940.53
                    1945-
  Reynolds, D. One world divisible   909.82
                  Dictionaries
  Worldmark encyclopedia of the nations   910.3
                  Encyclopedias
  Encyclopedia of world history   903
A **world** history of film. Sklar, R.   791.43
World holiday, festival, and calendar books
                                            016.39426
The **world** in 1800. Bernier, O.   909.81
The **World** in us   811.008
A **world** lit only by fire. Manchester, W. 940.2
World musicians   920.003
The **world** must know. Berenbaum, M.   940.53
World of anatomy and physiology   612
World of computer science   004
The **world** of Count Basie. Dance, S.   920
The **world** of Edward Gorey. Ross, C.   92
A **world** of ideas. Rohmann, C.   103
The **world** of Jewish cooking. Marks, G. 641.5
The **World** of learning   060.25

The **world** of musical comedy. Green, S.   920
The **world** of myth. Leeming, D. A.   291.1
The **world** of Odysseus. Finley, M. I.   883
A **world** of our own. Borzello, F.   704
The **world** of Samuel Beckett, 1906-1946. Gordon, L. G.   92
World of sociology   301
World poetry   808.81
World poets   920.003
World politics
    Brendon, P. The dark valley: a panorama of the 1930s   909.82
    Yergin, D. The prize   338.2
    1945——Encyclopedias
    Encyclopedia of conflicts since World War II   909.82
    1945-1991
    Walker, M. The Cold War   909.82
    1965-
    Gorbachev, M. On my country and the world   947.085
    Huntington, S. P. The clash of civilizations and the remaking of world order   909.82
    Shawcross, W. Deliver us from evil   909.82
    1991-
    Junger, S. Fire   909.82
    Laqueur, W. No end to war   303.6
    Will, G. F. With a happy eye but . . . America and the world, 1997-2002   973.929
    Encyclopedias
    Worldmark encyclopedia of the nations   910.3
The **World** reacts to the Holocaust   940.53
World religions. Bowker, J.   200
The **world** split open. Rosen, R.   305.4
World Trade Center (New York, N.Y.)
    Langewiesche, W. American ground, unbuilding the World Trade Center   974.7
    Lutnick, H. On top of the world   332.6
    Picciotto, R. Last man down   974.7
World Trade Center terrorist attack, 2001
    See also September 11 terrorist attacks, 2001
    Gonzalez, J. Fallout   363.7
    Halberstam, D. Firehouse   363.34
    New York September 11   974.7
    Smith, D. Report from ground zero   363.34
World Trade Organization
    See/See also pages in the following book(s):
    Soros, G. George Soros on globalization   337
A **world** turned over. Hemingway, L.   363.34
World War, 1914-1918
    Burg, D. F. Almanac of World War I   940.3
    Gilbert, M. The First World War   940.3
    Keegan, J. The First World War   940.3
    Keegan, J. An illustrated history of the First World War   940.3
    Liddell Hart, Sir B. H. The real war, 1914-1918   940.4
    Stokesbury, J. L. A short history of World War I   940.3
    Tuchman, B. W. The guns of August   940.3
    The United States in the First World War   940.3
    World War I   940.3
    See/See also pages in the following book(s):
    Kissinger, H. Diplomacy   327.73
    Rehnquist, W. H. All the laws but one p170-83   342
    Aerial operations
    Kilduff, P. Richthofen   92
    Armistices
    Weintraub, S. Silent night   940.4
    Campaigns
    Eisenhower, J. S. D. Yanks: the epic story of the American Army in World War I   940.4
    Groom, W. A storm in Flanders   940.4
    Mosier, J. The myth of the Great War   940.4

    Ousby, I. The road to Verdun   940.4
    Causes
    Massie, R. K. Dreadnought   940.3
    Tuchman, B. W. The Zimmermann telegram   940.3
    Naval operations
    Preston, D. Lusitania   940.4
    Peace
    Dallas, G. 1918: war and peace   940.4
    MacMillan, M. Paris 1919   940.3
    France
    Macintyre, B. The Englishman's daughter   940.4
    Great Britain
    See/See also pages in the following book(s):
    Taylor, A. J. P. English history, 1914-1945 p1-119   942.08
    Middle East
    Lawrence, T. E. Seven pillars of wisdom   940.4
    United States
    Farwell, B. Over there   940.4
    Harries, M. The last days of innocence   940.4
    See/See also pages in the following book(s):
    Tuchman, B. W. Practicing history p158-72   907
World War, 1939-1945
    Ambrose, S. E. The American Heritage new history of World War II   940.53
    Buderi, R. The invention that changed the world   621.3848
    Churchill, Sir W. Closing the ring   940.53
    Churchill, Sir W. The gathering storm   940.53
    Churchill, Sir W. The grand alliance   940.53
    Churchill, Sir W. The hinge of fate   940.53
    Churchill, Sir W. Their finest hour   940.53
    Churchill, Sir W. Triumph and tragedy   940.53
    Gilbert, M. The Second World War   940.53
    Greene, B. Duty   940.54
    Keegan, J. The Second World War   940.53
    Murray, W. A war to be won   940.53
    Overy, R. J. Why the Allies won   940.53
    Reporting World War II   940.53
    Weinberg, G. L. A world at arms   940.53
    See/See also pages in the following book(s):
    Rehnquist, W. H. All the laws but one p184-217   342
    Tobin, J. Ernie Pyle's war   92
    Aerial operations
    Ambrose, S. E. The wild blue   940.54
    Boyne, W. J. Clash of wings   940.54
    Childers, T. Wings of morning   940.54
    Clayton, T. Finest hour   940.54
    Ford, D. Flying Tigers   940.54
    Frank, R. B. Downfall   940.54
    Keil, S. V. W. Those wonderful women in their flying machines   940.54
    Nelson, C. The first heroes   940.54
    Sandler, S. Segregated skies   940.54
    Smith, J. B. The last mission   940.54
    See/See also pages in the following book(s):
    Morgan, R. The man who flew the Memphis Belle   92
    African Americans
    Sandler, S. Segregated skies   940.54
    Atrocities
    Breitman, R. Official secrets   940.54
    Lewy, G. The Nazi persecution of the gypsies   940.53
    Lifton, R. J. The Nazi doctors   940.53
    See/See also pages in the following book(s):
    Hicks, G. The comfort women   940.54
    Battles, sieges, etc.
    See World War, 1939-1945—Aerial operations; World War, 1939-1945—Campaigns; World War, 1939-1945—Naval operations

World War, 1939-1945—*Continued*
Biography—Dictionaries
Ancell, R. M. The biographical dictionary of World War II generals and flag officers   **920.003**
Campaigns
See also names of battles, campaigns, sieges, etc.
Ambrose, S. E. The victors   **940.54**
Hoyt, E. P. The GI's war   **940.54**
Linderman, G. F. The world within war   **940.54**
No end save victory   **940.54**
Patton, G. S. War as I knew it   **940.54**
Campaigns—France
Ambrose, S. E. Citizen soldiers   **940.54**
Ambrose, S. E. D-Day, June 6, 1944   **940.54**
Goldstein, D. M. D-Day Normandy   **940.54**
Campaigns—Germany
Irwin, J. P. Another river, another town   **940.54**
Campaigns—North Africa
Atkinson, R. An army at dawn   **940.54**
Campaigns—Okinawa Island
Astor, G. Operation Iceberg   **940.54**
Leckie, R. Okinawa   **940.54**
Campaigns—Pacific Ocean
Dunnigan, J. F. Victory at sea   **940.54**
Spector, R. Eagle against the sun   **940.54**
Campaigns—Philippines
Astor, G. Crisis in the Pacific   **940.54**
Knox, D. Death march   **940.54**
Sides, H. Ghost soldiers   **940.54**
Campaigns—Soviet Union
See also Stalingrad, Battle of, 1942-1943
Causes
See also National socialism
Carley, M. J. 1939   **940.53**
Overy, R. J. The road to war   **940.53**
Children
Children in the Holocaust and World War II   **940.53**
See/See also pages in the following book(s):
Kissinger, H. Diplomacy   **327.73**
Destruction and pillage
Harclerode, P. The lost masters   **709**
Petropoulos, J. The Faustian bargain   **709**
Pool, J. Hitler and his secret partners   **943.086**
The Spoils of war   **709**
Ziegler, J. The Swiss, the gold, and the dead   **940.53**
Diplomatic history
Carley, M. J. 1939   **940.53**
Lukacs, J. Five days in London, May 1940   **940.53**
Stafford, D. Roosevelt and Churchill   **940.54**
Encyclopedias
Dunnigan, J. F. The Pacific War encyclopedia   **940.54**
The Oxford companion to World War II   **940.53**
Hospitals
See World War, 1939-1945—Medical care
Internet resources
Smith, J. D. World War II on the Web   **025.04**
Jews
See also Holocaust, 1933-1945
Frank, A. The diary of a young girl: the definitive edition   **92**
Frank, A. The diary of Anne Frank: the critical edition   **92**
Müller, M. Anne Frank   **92**
Jews—Drama
Goodrich, F. The diary of Anne Frank   **812**
Jews—Rescue
Fogelman, E. Conscience & courage   **940.53**
Journalists
Sorel, N. C. The women who wrote the war   **940.53**

Medical care
Norman, E. M. We band of angels   **940.54**
Naval operations
Ballard, R. D. Return to Midway   **940.54**
Boyne, W. J. Clash of Titans   **940.54**
Dunnigan, J. F. Victory at sea   **940.54**
Miller, N. War at sea   **940.54**
Morison, S. E. History of United States naval operations in World War II   **940.54**
Stanton, D. In harm's way   **940.54**
Naval operations—Submarine
Blair, C. Hitler's U-boat war   **940.54**
Occupied territories
See also Japan—History—1945-1952, Allied occupation
Personal narratives
Astor, G. A blood-dimmed tide   **940.54**
Astor, G. Crisis in the Pacific   **940.54**
Astor, G. The greatest war   **940.54**
Astor, G. Operation Iceberg   **940.54**
Blum, H. The brigade   **940.54**
Brokaw, T. An album of memories   **940.54**
Brokaw, T. The greatest generation   **940.54**
Irwin, J. P. Another river, another town   **940.54**
Kelly, C. O. The flamboya tree   **940.53**
Levi, P. Survival in Auschwitz; and, The reawakening   **940.53**
Manchester, W. Goodbye, darkness   **940.54**
Marks, L. Between silk and cyanide   **940.54**
See/See also pages in the following book(s):
Brombert, V. H. Trains of thought   **92**
Morgan, R. The man who flew the Memphis Belle   **92**
Rooney, A. A. My war   **92**
Pictorial works
Life: World War 2   **940.53**
Poetry
Poets of World War II   **811**
Prisoners and prisons
Daws, G. Prisoners of the Japanese   **940.54**
Howarth, D. A. We die alone   **940.54**
Kelly, C. O. The flamboya tree   **940.53**
Knox, D. Death march   **940.54**
Norman, E. M. We band of angels   **940.54**
Sides, H. Ghost soldiers   **940.54**
See/See also pages in the following book(s):
O'Neill, J. Blood-dark track   **920**
Propaganda
Fussell, P. Wartime: understanding and behavior in the Second World War   **940.54**
Quotations
World War II   **940.53**
Reconstruction
See Reconstruction (1939-1951)
Reparations
Japanese Americans, from relocation to redress   **940.53**
Ziegler, J. The Swiss, the gold, and the dead   **940.53**
Resistance movements
See World War, 1939-1945—Underground movements
Secret service
Budiansky, S. Battle of wits   **940.54**
Lee, B. Marching orders   **940.54**
Marks, L. Between silk and cyanide   **940.54**
Persico, J. E. Roosevelt's secret war   **940.54**
Sebag-Montefiore, H. Enigma: the battle for the code   **940.54**
Smith, M. Station X   **940.54**
Stafford, D. Roosevelt and Churchill   **940.54**
Stevenson, W. A man called Intrepid   **940.54**
Submarine operations
See World War, 1939-1945—Naval operations—Submarine

World War, 1939-1945—*Continued*
Underground movements
Cohen, R. The avengers 940.53
Kruk, H. The last days of the Jerusalem of Lithuania 940.53

Women
Hicks, G. The comfort women 940.54
Keil, S. V. W. Those wonderful women in their flying machines 940.54

Asia
Thompson, R. S. Empires on the Pacific 940.54

Atlantic Ocean
Blair, C. Hitler's U-boat war 940.54

China
Tuchman, B. W. Stilwell and the American experience in China, 1911-45 327.73

Europe
Ambrose, S. E. Band of brothers 940.54

France
May, E. R. Strange victory 940.54
Nossiter, A. The Algeria Hotel 940.54
See/See also pages in the following book(s):
Kaplan, A. Y. The collaborator: the trial & execution of Robert Brasillach 92

Germany
Beevor, A. The fall of Berlin 1945 940.54
Beschloss, M. R. The conquerors: Roosevelt, Truman, and the destruction of Hitler's Germany, 1941-1945 940.54
Read, A. The fall of Berlin 940.54
Speer, A. Inside the Third Reich 943.086
See/See also pages in the following book(s):
Shirer, W. L. The rise and fall of the Third Reich 943.086

Great Britain
Churchill, Sir W. Closing the ring 940.53
Churchill, Sir W. The gathering storm 940.53
Churchill, Sir W. The grand alliance 940.53
Churchill, Sir W. The hinge of fate 940.53
Churchill, Sir W. Their finest hour 940.53
Churchill, Sir W. Triumph and tragedy 940.53
Clayton, T. Finest hour 940.54
Fussell, P. Wartime: understanding and behavior in the Second World War 940.54
Lukacs, J. Five days in London, May 1940 940.53
Smith, M. Station X 940.54
See/See also pages in the following book(s):
Taylor, A. J. P. English history, 1914-1945 p439-600 942.08

Italy
Lamb, R. War in Italy, 1943-1945 940.54

Japan
Frank, R. B. Downfall 940.54
Hersey, J. Hiroshima 940.54
Lee, B. Marching orders 940.54
Nelson, C. The first heroes 940.54
Spector, R. Eagle against the sun 940.54

North Africa
Atkinson, R. An army at dawn 940.54

Pacific Ocean
Costello, J. The Pacific War 940.54
Daws, G. Prisoners of the Japanese 940.54
Manchester, W. Goodbye, darkness 940.54

Soviet Union
Rees, L. War of the century 940.54

United States
Alperovitz, G. The decision to use the atomic bomb and the architecture of an American myth 940.54
Daniels, R. Prisoners without trial 940.53
Fussell, P. Wartime: understanding and behavior in the Second World War 940.54
Goodwin, D. K. No ordinary time [biography of Franklin D. Roosevelt] 92

Moskin, J. R. Mr. Truman's war 940.54
Spector, R. Eagle against the sun 940.54
Takaki, R. T. Double victory 940.53
Takaki, R. T. Hiroshima 940.54
Wyman, D. S. The abandonment of the Jews 940.53

World War I 940.3
World War II 940.53
World War II on the Web. Smith, J. D. 025.04
World Wide Web
Kemp, T. J. Virtual roots 2.0 929
World wide web sites *See* Web sites
The **world** within war. Linderman, G. F. 940.54
The **worldly** philosophers. Heilbroner, R. L. 330.1
Worldmark encyclopedia of cultures and daily life 306
Worldmark encyclopedia of the nations 910.3
World's Columbian Exposition (1893: Chicago, Ill.)
Larson, E. The devil in the white city 364.1
The **World's** great speeches 808.85
The **world's** last night, and other essays. Lewis, C. S. 230
The **World's** major languages 400
Worrall, Simon
The poet and the murderer 364.1
Worry
See also Anxiety
Hallowell, E. M. Worry 616.85
"Worse than slavery". Oshinsky, D. M. 365
Worshipful Company of Fletchers. Tate, J. 811
Worthen, John
D.H. Lawrence, the early years, 1885-1912 92
Worthington, Charles
The complete book of hairstyling 646.7
Worthington, Christa, 1955-2002
About
Flook, M. Invisible Eden 364.1
Worthington, Janet Farrar
(jt. auth) Walsh, P. C. The prostate 616.6
Wouk, Herman, 1915-
This is my God: the Jewish way of life 296
The will to live on 296
The **would-be** gentleman. Molière
In Molière. The misanthrope, and other plays 842
Wouldn't take nothing for my journey now. Angelou, M. 814
Wounded, First aid to *See* First aid
Wounds and injuries
See also Burns and scalds
Wounds of passion. Hooks, B. 92
The **woven** figure. Will, G. F. 973.929
Woyzeck. Büchner, G.
In Our dramatic heritage v4 808.82
Wrapped in rainbows. Boyd, V. 92
Wray, Betty B.
Taking charge of asthma 616.2
Wright, Bradford W., 1968-
Comic book nation 741.5
Wright, C. D.
Steal away 811
Wright, Carol V.
(jt. auth) Minkin, M. J. The Yale guide to women's reproductive health 618.1
Wright, Charles, 1935-
Appalachia 811
Negative blue 811
Wright, Clifford A., 1951-
A Mediterranean feast 641
Wright, Frank Lloyd, 1867-1959
Frank Lloyd Wright collected writings 720
About
Lind, C. The Wright style 728
Secrest, M. Frank Lloyd Wright 92

Wright, Frank Lloyd, 1867-1959—About—*Continued*
Storrer, W. A. The Frank Lloyd Wright companion
720.973
Wright, James Arlington, 1927-1980
Above the river 811
Wright, James D., 1947-
Fixin' to git 796.72
Wright, Jay
Transfigurations 811
Wright, Jim *See* Wright, James D., 1947-
Wright, Kai
Soldiers of freedom 355
Wright, Lawrence
Twins 155.4
Wright, Orville, 1871-1948
How we invented the airplane 629.13
About
Adams, N. The flyers 92
Heppenheimer, T. A. First flight 629.13
Tobin, J. To conquer the air 629.13
Wright, Patricia, 1944-
(jt. auth) Beckett, W. The story of painting 759
Wright, Patrick, 1951-
Tank: the progress of a monstrous war machine
358
Wright, Richard, 1908-1960
Black boy 92
Conversations with Richard Wright 92
Native son; criticism
In Richard Wright's Native son 813.009
About
Richard Wright 813.009
Rowley, H. Richard Wright 92
See/See also pages in the following book(s):
Ellison, R. Going to the territory p198-216 818
Wright, Robert
NonZero 303.4
Wright, Robin
The last great revolution 955
Wright, Wilbur, 1867-1912
About
Adams, N. The flyers 92
Heppenheimer, T. A. First flight 629.13
Tobin, J. To conquer the air 629.13
Wright, O. How we invented the airplane 629.13
The **Wright** style. Lind, C. 728
Wrinkles in time. Smoot, G. 523.1
Write it down, make it happen. Klauser, H. A. 158
The **writer** and the world. Naipaul, V. S. 824
Writers *See* Authors
The **Writer's** digest guide to good writing 808
Writers for young adults 920.003
Writer's guide to book editors, publishers, and literary
agents. See Herman, J. Jeff Herman's guide to book
publishers, editors, & literary agents 070.5
The **Writer's** handbook 808
The **writer's** handbook. McMahan, E. 808
A **writer's** house in Wales. Morris, J. 942.9
The **Writer's** market 808
Writers' Program
American guide series. See American guide series
917.3
Writing
See also Calligraphy; Picture writing
Writing (Authorship) *See* Authorship; Journalism
Writing dangerously: Mary McCarthy and her world.
Brightman, C. 92
Writing in time. Schell, J. 973.928
The **writing** life. Dillard, A. 92
Writing New York 810.8
Writing romances 808.3
Writing screenplays that sell. Hauge, M. 808.2
Writing the breakout novel. Maass, D. 808.3
Writing to learn. Zinsser, W. K. 808
Writing with pictures. Shulevitz, U. 808.06

Writings. Du Bois, W. E. B. 818
Writings. Franklin, B. 818
Writings. Hamilton, A. 973.4
Writings. Jefferson, T. 818
Writings. Washington, G. 973.4
Writings, 1903-1932. Stein, G. 818
Writings, 1932-1946. Stein, G. 818
Writings from the New Yorker. White, E. B. 814
Written into history 071
Wroe, Ann
Pontius Pilate 226
The **wrong** man. Neff, J. 345
WTO *See* World Trade Organization
Wu, Harry
Bitter winds 951.05
Troublemaker 951.05
Wu, Hongda Harry *See* Wu, Harry
Wuhu diary. Prager, E. 951
Wukasch, Don C.
(jt. auth) Myers, J. E. Dictionary of poetic terms
808.1
Wullschläger, Jackie
Hans Christian Andersen 92
Inventing wonderland 820.9
Würz, Hedy
(jt. auth) Anderson, J. The new German cookbook
641.5
Wuthnow, Robert
After heaven 200.9
Wyatt, David K.
Thailand: a short history 959.3
Wycherley, William, 1640-1716
The country wife
In Restoration plays 822.008
Wyeth, Andrew, 1917-
Andrew Wyeth, autobiography 92
Wyeth, N. C. (Newell Convers), 1882-1945
About
Michaelis, D. N.C. Wyeth 92
Wyeth, Newell Convers *See* Wyeth, N. C. (Newell
Convers), 1882-1945
Wyler, Seymour B., d. 1990
The book of old silver: English, American, foreign
739.2
Wyman, Bruce C.
The Facts on File dictionary of environmental science
363.7
Wyman, David S.
The abandonment of the Jews 940.53
(ed) The World reacts to the Holocaust. See The
World reacts to the Holocaust 940.53
Wyman, Donald, 1903-1993
Wyman's gardening encyclopedia 635
Wyman's gardening encyclopedia. Wyman, D. 635
Wynar, Bohdan S., 1926-
(ed) Recommended reference books for small and me-
dium-sized libraries and media centers. See Recom-
mended reference books for small and medium-sized
libraries and media centers 011
Wynbrandt, James
The excruciating history of dentistry 617.6
Wynn, Charles M.
The five biggest ideas in science 500
Wynn, Jennifer
Inside Rikers 365
Wynter, Leon E.
American skin 305.8
Wyse, Liz
(jt. auth) Lambert, D. Dinosaur encyclopedia
567.9
Wyse, Lois
Funny, you don't look like a grandmother 817

X

X-rays
See/See also pages in the following book(s):
Friedman, M. Medicine's 10 greatest discoveries
610.9
Xenophanes, of Colophon, 6th cent. B.C.
See/See also pages in the following book(s):
Jaspers, K. The great philosophers 109
Xenophon, ca. 431-ca. 352 B.C.
See/See also pages in the following book(s):
Hamilton, E. The Greek way p204-26 880.9
Xuanzang *See* Hsüan-tsang, ca. 596-664

Y

Yaakov, Juliette
(ed) Fiction catalog. See Fiction catalog 016.8
(ed) Middle and junior high school library catalog. See
Middle and junior high school library catalog
011.6
(ed) Senior high school library catalog. See Senior
high school library catalog 011.6
Yachts and yachting
See also Sailing
Yager, Jan
(jt. auth) Thorpy, M. J. The encyclopedia of sleep and
sleep disorders 612.8
Yagoda, Ben
About town 051
Will Rogers 92
(jt. auth) Westheimer, R. The value of family
306.8
Yahil, Leni
The Holocaust 940.53
The **Yale** Child Study Center guide to understanding
your child. Mayes, L. C. 649
Yale dictionary of art and artists. Langmuir, E. 703
The **Yale** guide to children's nutrition 613.2
The **Yale** guide to women's reproductive health. Minkin,
M. J. 618.1
The **Yale** younger poets anthology 811.008
Yalom, Irvin D., 1931-
The gift of therapy 616.89
Yalom, Marilyn
A history of the wife 306.8
YALSA *See* Young Adult Library Services Association
The **Yamato** dynasty. Seagrave, S. 952
Yana Indians
Kroeber, T. Ishi in two worlds 92
Yangtze River valley (China)
Winchester, S. The river at the center of the world
951

Description
Hessler, P. River town 951
Yankee Stadium (New York, N.Y.)
Robinson, R. Yankee Stadium 796.357
Yankees (Baseball team) *See* New York Yankees (Base-
ball team)
Yanks: the epic story of the American Army in World
War I. Eisenhower, J. S. D. 940.4
Yans-McLaughlin, Virginia, 1943-
Ellis Island and the peopling of America 325.73
Yaqui Indians

Religion
Castaneda, C. The teachings of Don Juan 299
Yardley, Jonathan
Misfit: the strange life of Frederick Exley 92
(ed) Mencken, H. L. My life as author and editor
92
Yarmolinsky, Babette Deutsch *See* Deutsch, Babette,
1895-1982

Yate, Martin John
Cover letters that knock 'em dead 650.14
Knock 'em dead 650.14
Resumes that knock 'em dead 650.14
Ybarra, Lea
(jt. auth) Olmos, E. J. Americanos 305.8
Yeager, Jeana
Voyager 910.4
The **year** 1000. Lacey, R. 942.01
A **year** in Lapland. Beach, H. 948.97
A **year** of reading. Ellington, E. 028
The **year** the dream died. Witcover, J. 973.92
Yearbook of American and Canadian churches 277
Yearning for the land. Simpson, J. W. 304.2
The **years** of Lyndon Johnson. Caro, R. A. 92
Years of renewal. Kissinger, H. 92
Yeats, W. B. (William Butler), 1865-1939
Among school children; criticism
In Brooks, C. The well wrought urn 821.009
Purgatory
In Our dramatic heritage v5 808.82
About
Brown, T. The life of W.B. Yeats 92
Foster, R. F. W.B. Yeats 92
See/See also pages in the following book(s):
Heaney, S. Finders keepers p103-21, 253-61, 343-60
821
Heaney, S. The redress of poetry 821.009
Pritchard, W. H. Lives of the modern poets p49-82
821.009
Yeats, William Butler *See* Yeats, W. B. (William But-
ler), 1865-1939
Yeh, Michelle Mi-Hsi
(ed) Anthology of modern Chinese poetry. See Anthol-
ogy of modern Chinese poetry 895.1
Yellow fever
See/See also pages in the following book(s):
Oldstone, M. B. A. Viruses, plagues, and history
614.4
Yellow fever, black goddess. Wills, C. 614.4
The **yellow** wind. Grossman, D. 956.95
Yellowstone National Park
McNamee, T. The return of the wolf to Yellowstone
599.77
Yeltsin, Boris
About
Talbott, S. The Russia hand 327.73
Yeoman, R. S.
A Guide book of United States coins. See A Guide
book of United States coins 737.4
Handbook of United States coins. See Handbook of
United States coins 737.4
Yergin, Daniel
The prize 338.2
Yerma. García Lorca, F.
In García Lorca, F. Three tragedies 862
Yiddish. Weinstein, M. 439
Yiddish language
Rosten, L. The new joys of Yiddish 439
Weinstein, M. Yiddish 439
Dictionaries
Weinreich, U. Modern English-Yiddish, Yiddish-
English dictionary 439
Yoerg, Sonja, 1959-
Clever as a fox 591.5
Yoga
Iyengar, B. K. S. Yoga 613.7
Reichmann, R. Ageless yoga 613.7
Yoga, mind & body 294.5
Yoga, mind & body 294.5
Yolen, Jane
(ed) Favorite folktales from around the world. See Fa-
vorite folktales from around the world 398.2

Yom Kippur
See/See also pages in the following book(s):
Strassfeld, M. The Jewish holidays p111-23 **296.4**
York, ca. 1775-ca. 1815
About
Slaughter, T. P. Exploring Lewis and Clark **978**
Yorkshire (England)
Description
Herriot, J. James Herriot's Yorkshire **914.2**
Yosemite National Park (Calif.)
Muir, J. The Yosemite **979.4**
Yoshihito See Taishō, Emperor of Japan, 1879-1926
You and your only child. Nachman, P. A. **649**
You can make it happen. Graham, S. **650.1**
You can paint pastels. Blake, M. **741.2**
You can paint watercolors. Crawshaw, A. **751.42**
You can write a mystery. Roberts, G. **808.3**
You cannot be serious. McEnroe, J. **92**
You can't steal a gift. Lees, G. **920**
You don't need meat. Cox, P. **613.2**
You just don't understand. Tannen, D. **302.2**
Youmans, Vincent, 1898-1946
See/See also pages in the following book(s):
Green, S. The world of musical comedy **920**
Young, Andrew, 1932-
See/See also pages in the following book(s):
Wills, G. Certain trumpets p70-78 **303.3**
Young, Ed
See/See also pages in the following book(s):
The Newbery & Caldecott medal books, 1986-2000 p104-13 **028.5**
Young, Glenn
(ed) The Best American short plays. See The Best American short plays **812.008**
Young, Gregory W.
The high cost of dying **393**
Young, Lester
About
Daniels, D. H. Lester leaps in: the life and times of Lester "Pres" Young **92**
See/See also pages in the following book(s):
Dance, S. The world of Count Basie **920**
Feather, L. From Satchmo to Miles **920**
Young, Margaret Levine
(jt. auth) Levine, J. R. The Internet for dummies **004.6**
Young, Neil
About
McDonough, J. Shakey: Neil Young's biography **92**
Young, Robyn V.
Notable mathematicians. See Notable mathematicians **920.003**
Young, Serinity
(ed) Encyclopedia of women and world religion. See Encyclopedia of women and world religion **200**
Young, Stephen
(ed) The Poetry anthology, 1912-2002. See The Poetry anthology, 1912-2002 **811.008**
Young, Stuart, 1938-
Allergies **616.97**
Young, Sue
The new comprehensive American rhyming dictionary **423**
Young, Toby, 1963-
How to lose friends and alienate people **92**
Young Adult Library Services Association
Carter, B. Best books for young adults **028.1**
Young adult literature
Writers for young adults **920.003**
Bibliography
Best books for young adult readers **011.6**
Carter, B. Best books for young adults **028.1**
Senior high school library catalog **011.6**

Stories, plots, etc.
Masterplots II, juvenile and young adult fiction series **028.5**
Young adults' libraries
See also High school libraries
Vaillancourt, R. J. Bare bones young adult services **027.62**
Young-Bruehl, Elisabeth
The anatomy of prejudices **303.3**
Young Hickory: the making of Andrew Jackson. Booraem, H. **92**
The **young** man from Atlanta. Foote, H. **812**
Young man Luther. Erikson, E. H. **92**
Young people's libraries See Young adults' libraries
The **youngest** minds. Barnet, A. B. **155.4**
Yount, Lisa
A to Z of biologists **920.003**
Your adolescent **155.5**
Your baby & child. Leach, P. **649**
Your eight-year-old. Ames, L. B. **649**
Your first resume. Fry, R. W. **650.14**
Your five-year-old. Ames, L. B. **649**
Your four-year-old. Ames, L. B. **649**
Your name here. Ashbery, J. **811**
Your new house. Fields, A. **643**
Your one-year-old. Ames, L. B. **649**
Your right to child custody, visitation, and support. Boland, M. L. **346.01**
Your seven-year-old. Ames, L. B. **649**
Your six-year-old. Ames, L. B. **649**
Your three-year-old. Ames, L. B. **649**
Your two-year-old. Ames, L. B. **649**
You're too kind. Stengel, R. **177**
Youth
See also Teenagers
Employment
See also Teenagers—Employment
Levine, M. J. Children for hire **331.3**
Health and hygiene
The "Go ask Alice" book of answers **613**
United States
Canada, G. Reaching up for manhood **305.23**
Youth. Coetzee, J. M. **92**
Youth hostels
Directories
Hostelling North America **647.9**
Yuan Boping
(ed) The Oxford starter Chinese dictionary. See The Oxford starter Chinese dictionary **495.1**
Yudell, Michael
(ed) The Genomic revolution. See The Genomic revolution **599.93**
Yugoslav War, 1991-1995
Clark, W. K. Waging modern war **949.7**
Cohen, R. Hearts grown brutal **949.7**
Maass, P. Love thy neighbor **949.7**
Rieff, D. Slaughterhouse **949.7**
Rohde, D. Endgame **949.7**
Silber, L. Yugoslavia **949.7**
Yugoslavia
See also Bosnia and Hercegovina
History
Cohen, R. Hearts grown brutal **949.7**
Donia, R. J. Bosnia and Hercegovina **949.7**
Hall, B. The impossible country **949.7**
History—Civil War, 1991-1995
See Yugoslav War, 1991-1995
Politics and government
Silber, L. Yugoslavia **949.7**
West, R. Tito **92**

Z

Zaccaria, Donatella
Stained glass crafting   748.5
Zacharia, Christina E.
(jt. auth) Farsoun, S. K. Palestine and the Palestinians   956.94
Zadig. Voltaire
In Voltaire. The portable Voltaire   848
Zagajewski, Adam, 1945-
Another beauty; criticism
In Sontag, S. Where the stress falls   814
Mysticism for beginners   891.8
Without end   891.8
Zaharias, Babe Didrikson, 1911-1956
See/See also pages in the following book(s):
Ware, S. Letter to the world   920
Zaidenstadt, Martin
About
Ryback, T. W. The last survivor   940.53
Zaire
Politics and government
See/See also pages in the following book(s):
Naipaul, V. S. The writer and the world p205-28   824
Zajonc, Arthur
Catching the light   535
Zaleski, Philip
(ed) The Book of heaven. See The Book of heaven   291
Zallen, Doris Teichler- *See* Teichler-Zallen, Doris
Zamora, Martha, 1940-
Frida Kahlo   92
Zanger, Mark H.
The American history cookbook   641.5
Zanichkowsky, Stephen
Fourteen   92
Zapata, Emiliano, 1879-1919
About
Womack, J. Zapata and the Mexican Revolution   972.08
Zapata and the Mexican Revolution. Womack, J.   972.08
Zappa, Frank
The real Frank Zappa book   92
Zarathustra *See* Zoroaster, fl. 6th cent. B.C.
Zarin, Cynthia
The watercourse: poems   811
Zauzich, Karl-Theodor
Roth, A. M. Hieroglyphs without mystery   493
Zeami, 1363-1443
Atsumori
In Waley, A. The Nō plays of Japan   895.6
The damask drum
In Waley, A. The Nō plays of Japan   895.6
Hachi no ki
In Waley, A. The Nō plays of Japan   895.6
Hagoromo
In Waley, A. The Nō plays of Japan   895.6
Haku Rakuten
In Waley, A. The Nō plays of Japan   895.6
Kagekiyo
In Waley, A. The Nō plays of Japan   895.6
The pool sacrifice
In Waley, A. The Nō plays of Japan   895.6
Tsunemasa
In Waley, A. The Nō plays of Japan   895.6
Zega, Andrew
Palaces of the Sun King   728
Zegers, Peter
(jt. auth) Druick, D. W. Van Gogh and Gauguin   92
Zehme, Bill
The way you wear your hat   92

Zeitlin, Maurice, 1935-
(jt. auth) Stepan-Norris, J. Left out   331.8
Zelikow, Philip, 1954-
(ed) The Kennedy tapes. See The Kennedy tapes   973.922
Zelinsky, Paul O.
See/See also pages in the following book(s):
The Newbery & Caldecott medal books, 1986-2000 p279-94   028.5
Zelnick, Bob
Gore: a political life   92
Zeman, Scott C.
Chronology of the American West   978
Zembō, Motoyasu *See* Komparu, Zempō
Zen and the art of making a living. Boldt, L. G.   331.7
Zen and the art of motorcycle maintenance. Pirsig, R. M.   92
Zen Buddhism
Bing, S. Throwing the elephant   650.1
Essential Zen   294.3
Matthiessen, P. The snow leopard   915.4
Suzuki, D. T. Manual of Zen Buddhism   294.3
Watts, A. The way of Zen   294.3
Zeng Qing *See* Tseng, Ch'ing, 1568-1650
Zeno, of Elea, b. ca. 490 B.C.
See/See also pages in the following book(s):
Bell, E. T. Men of mathematics p19-34   920
Hamilton, E. The echo of Greece p157-68   880.9
Zenobia, Queen of Palmyra
See/See also pages in the following book(s):
Fraser, A. The warrior queens   920
Zeppelins *See* Airships
Zero (The number)
Barrow, J. D. The book of nothing   111
Kaplan, R. The nothing that is   511
Seife, C. Zero   511
Zeyl, Donald J., 1944-
(ed) Encyclopedia of classical philosophy. See Encyclopedia of classical philosophy   180
Ziedrich, Linda
The joy of pickling   641.4
Zieger, Robert H.
American workers, American unions   331.8
Ziegfeld, Florenz, 1869-1932
See/See also pages in the following book(s):
Yagoda, B. Will Rogers p135-56   92
Ziegler, Charles A.
(jt. auth) Saler, B. UFO crash at Roswell   001.9
Ziegler, Jean, 1934-
The Swiss, the gold, and the dead   940.53
Ziegler, Philip
Soldiers: fighting men's lives, 1901-2001   355
Zierdt-Warshaw, Linda
(jt. auth) Mongillo, J. F. Encyclopedia of environmental science   363.7
Zilkha, Avraham
Modern English-Hebrew dictionary   492.4
Zim, Herbert S.
(jt. auth) Robbins, C. S. Birds of North America   598
Zimbabwe
Lessing, D. M. African laughter   968.91
See also pages in the following book(s):
Fuller, A. Don't let's go to the dogs tonight   92
Zimmer, Carl
Parasite rex   591.7
Zimmer, Judith
(jt. auth) Cooke, J. P. The cardiovascular cure   616.1
Zimmerman, Bonnie
(ed) Encyclopedia of lesbian and gay histories and cultures. See Encyclopedia of lesbian and gay histories and cultures   306.7

Zimmerman, Robert
The chronological encyclopedia of discoveries in space
    629.4
Genesis   629.45
Zimmerman, Robert Allen *See* Dylan, Bob, 1941-
Zimmermann, Warren, 1934-2004
First great triumph   973
The **Zimmermann** telegram. Tuchman, B. W.
    940.3
Zindel, Paul
The effect of gamma rays on man-in-the-moon marigolds   812
Zinsser, William Knowlton
On writing well   808
Writing to learn   808
Zionism
Hazony, Y. The Jewish state   956.94
Laqueur, W. A history of Zionism   956.94
Peres, S. The imaginary voyage   956.94
Sachar, H. M. A history of Israel   956.94
See/See also pages in the following book(s):
Friedman, M. S. Encounter on the narrow ridge: a life of Martin Buber   92
Zip code
National five digit zip code and post office directory   383
Zipes, Jack David
(ed) The Oxford companion to fairy tales. See The Oxford companion to fairy tales   398.2
Zodiac
Goodman, L. Linda Goodman's sun signs   133.5
Snodgrass, M. E. Signs of the zodiac   133.5
Zohar, Danah, 1945-
(jt. auth) Marshall, I. N. Who's afraid of Schrödinger's cat?   500
Zola, Émile, 1840-1902
Therese Raquin
In Our dramatic heritage v4   808.82
Zolotow, Charlotte, 1915-
See/See also pages in the following book(s):
Marcus, L. S. Ways of telling   741.6

Zonderman, Jon
Understanding Crohn disease and ulcerative colitis
    616.3
Zoology
Grzimek's animal life encyclopedia   590
Zoos
Baratay, E. Zoo: a history of zoological gardens in the West   590.73
Encyclopedia of the world's zoos   590.73
Hanson, E. Animal attractions   590.73
Zoroaster, fl. 6th cent. B.C.
    About
Kriwaczek, P. In search of Zarathustra   295
Zoroastrianism
Kriwaczek, P. In search of Zarathustra   295
Zoya
Zoya's story   958.1
Zucchino, David
Myth of the welfare queen   362.5
Zuccotti, Susan, 1940-
Under his very windows   940.53
Zucker, Martin
(jt. auth) Lawrence, R. M. Preventing arthritis
    616.7
Zug, George R., 1938-
(jt. auth) Ernst, C. H. Snakes in question   597.9
Zuk, Judith
(ed) The American Horticultural Society A-Z encyclopedia of garden plants. See The American Horticultural Society A-Z encyclopedia of garden plants
    635.9
Zuk, M. (Marlene), 1956-
Sexual selections   591.56
Zuk, Marlene *See* Zuk, M. (Marlene), 1956-
Zwick, George, 1910-
Davidson, H. L. TV repair for beginners   621.388
Zwonitzer, Mark
Will you miss me when I'm gone?   920
Zyberk, Elizabeth Plater- *See* Plater-Zyberk, Elizabeth, 1950-
Zygmont, Jeffrey
Microchip: an idea, its genesis, and the revolution it created   338.7